THE UNIVERSAL REFERENCE SYSTEM

Comparative Government and Cultures

Volume X of the

POLITICAL SCIENCE, GOVERNMENT, AND PUBLIC POLICY SERIES

Included in this series:

Volume	I	*International Affairs (Second Edition)*
Volume	II	*Legislative Process, Representation, and Decision Making*
Volume	III	*Bibliography of Bibliographies in Political Science, Government, and Public Policy*
Volume	IV	*Administrative Management: Public and Private Bureaucracy*
Volume	V	*Current Events and Problems of Modern Society*
Volume	VI	*Public Opinion, Mass Behavior, and Political Psychology*
Volume	VII	*Law, Jurisprudence, and Judicial Process*
Volume	VIII	*Economic Regulation, Business, and Government*
Volume	IX	*Public Policy and the Management of Science*
Volume	X	*Comparative Government and Cultures*

POLITICAL SCIENCE, GOVERNMENT, & PUBLIC POLICY SERIES

Volume X

Comparative Government and Cultures

An annotated and intensively indexed compilation of significant books, pamphlets, and articles, selected and processed by The UNIVERSAL REFERENCE SYSTEM—a computerized information retrieval service in the social and behavioral sciences.

Prepared under the direction of

ALFRED DE GRAZIA, GENERAL EDITOR
Professor of Social Theory in Government, New York University, and Founder, *The American Behavioral Scientist*

CARL E. MARTINSON, MANAGING EDITOR

and

JOHN B. SIMEONE, CONSULTANT

Published by
PRINCETON RESEARCH PUBLISHING COMPANY
Princeton, New Jersey

For information, address:

UNIVERSAL REFERENCE SYSTEM
32 Nassau Street, Princeton, N.J. 08540

. . . and see the subscription information contained
on the last page of this volume.

Standard Book No. 87635-010-4
Library of Congress Catalog Card No. 68-57826

Printed and Bound in the U.S.A. by
Kingsport Press, Inc., Kingsport, Tenn.

Contents

Advisory Committee* for the UNIVERSAL REFERENCE SYSTEM

*Not all members advise in all areas.

Introduction to the CODEX of Comparative Government and Cultures

Documents come within the purview of UNIVERSAL REFERENCE SYSTEM's listings on *Comparative Government and Cultures* when they describe situations and principles of human behavior existing in two or more national institutional and cultural settings. Less stress is placed upon the inclusion of items that deal with a simple national or cultural entity; in such cases, one critical point of selection is that the book, article, or report treat of the practices and customs of a given place in the light of similar (or different) behavior elsewhere. Both "developed" and "developing" nations are in the scope of these listings. Political anthropology, that is, studies of political culture, are embraced under the same terms as studies of political institutions, and their methodologies are equally depicted.

By "political" material is meant governmental affairs and events that are directly relevant to or being directly affected by government. It also means the gaining, holding, and shaping of power in all institutions.

It may be asked where one should seek in the URS Series on *Political Science, Government, and Public Policy* to locate documents on a given country—say the United States or China or the U.S.S.R. There are two ways that the URS recommends. In some cases the wisest course is to employ both of them. The simpler and more direct approach is through the Index, searching on the URS Descriptor for the name of each country, except for the United States, which would have had a prohibitively high number of entries in the Index.

A more circuitous, but nonetheless productive, route is based on our previous observation that the modern definition of the field of comparative government does not include works dealing solely with the politics of a given country or institution. The same is true of the field of International Relations, unless a section of the work discusses the foreign operations of such country or institution.

One would then search for titles on a given country *in relation to something*, and that something may be found in one or several of the CODEXes. For instance, if a student is interested in documents treating the role of scientists in the U.S.S.R., U.S.A., or China, he should go to CODEX IX, where he would find the combination of subjects he needs under USSR and PHIL/SCI (Soviet Union and Philosophy of Science) or USSR and one or more of the "Creating and Sciencing" category of the Grazian Index (I, 4, A). The same would be done for the U.S.A., China or another country.

To take another example, if one wished to locate studies of public opinion in the U.S.S.R., he should search CODEX VI (*Public Opinion, Mass Behavior, and Political Psychology*) under the USSR, or do the same for other countries. Nevertheless, in these and other cases, one may well locate materials in this volume of the same type, for a work on public opinion or on the behavior of scientists that is comparative may well contain chapters on the relevant country as well as other countries, treated both comparatively and analytically.

In addition to comparative studies and country studies, this volume includes certain methodologically oriented titles, a number of which do not even attempt comparison of governments and cultures, because they may be useful to the scholar in the field of comparative government. A considerable selection of political philosophies is also carried here, as a result of their hypothesis-generating potential.

The present CODEX contains 3,460 references and about 38,000 Index entries. These totals make it by far the largest collection of titles ever published in the field of comparative government, as well as the most deeply indexed of catalogs. Many thousands of older items have had to be left to the mercies of historical bibliographers. Some classic works are included here; but the great bulk concentrates in the years 1960 to 1966. Special volumes on 1967 and 1968 will soon be published, bringing the total listings of the field to well over 5,000.

In this CODEX, as in others, certain descriptors of the Grazian Index are dropped, either from the entry column alone or from both the entry column and internal material of the index descriptions. These are descriptors that are irrelevant to this CODEX (e.g., SOC, Sociology), or overlap with the other CODEXes directly (WAR, DIPLOM—Diplomacy), or are largely used for technical completeness or organization of the system (e.g., TOT/POP, Total Population).

It is our hope, in offering this CODEX to students of the field of Comparative Government, that they will suggest new Descriptors or index entries that they believe would add useful dimensions to bibliographic search, and will also contribute comment, rectifications of errors, and suggestions of works that were omitted for one reason or another but that should be included.

How To Use This CODEX

(Hypothetical Example is Used)

1. Frame your need as specifically as possible. (Example: "I want articles written in 1968 that deal with the activities of labor leaders and small business owners in city politics in America.")
2. Scan the Dictionary of Descriptors in this Volume, page xv and following, for URS terms that match your subject. (Example: for cities you find MUNIC and LOC/G; for labor, LABOR; for small companies, SML/CO.) Find the number of titles each Descriptor carries. For rapidity select terms having few entries; for comprehensiveness, select terms having many entries.
3. Having identified terms that match your subject, enter the Index at one of them, say SML/CO, which heads a list of works on small business. For rapid identification of highly relevant titles, search the narrow right-hand column, which contains the Critical Descriptors; these index the primary facets of a work. Even if you read every title under a Descriptor, the critical column will help you identify works of high probable value. Titles are arranged by year of publication and within each year by format: books (B), long articles (L), short articles (S), and chapters (C). The designation "N" covers serials and titles lacking dates or published over several years. The Index entry carries author, title, secondary Descriptors (which index secondary facets of the work), page of the Catalog containing full citation and annotation, and Catalog accession number. Secondary Descriptors are always arranged in the order of the Topical and Methodological Index.
4. Listings of the document would be found in fourteen

SAMPLE CATALOG LISTING

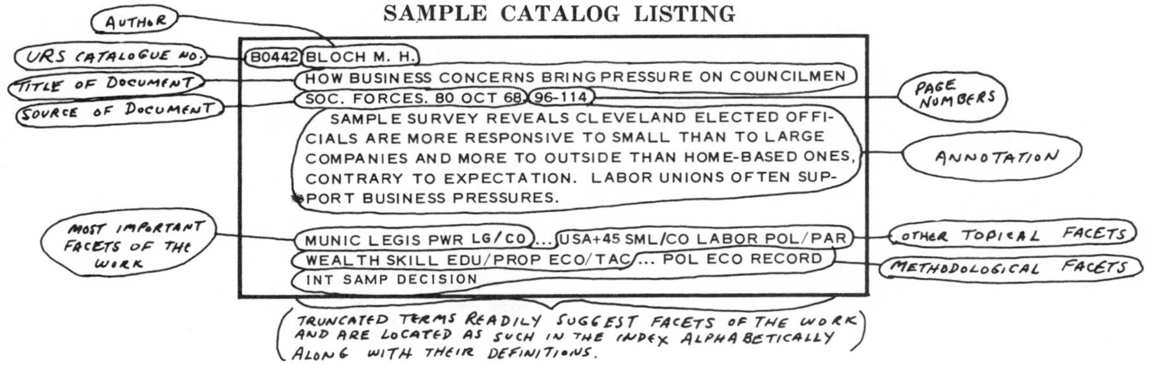

places in the Index, that is, under each of its numerous significant facets. One of them could be located in a search of "the small company in politics" as follows:

SAMPLE INDEX LISTING

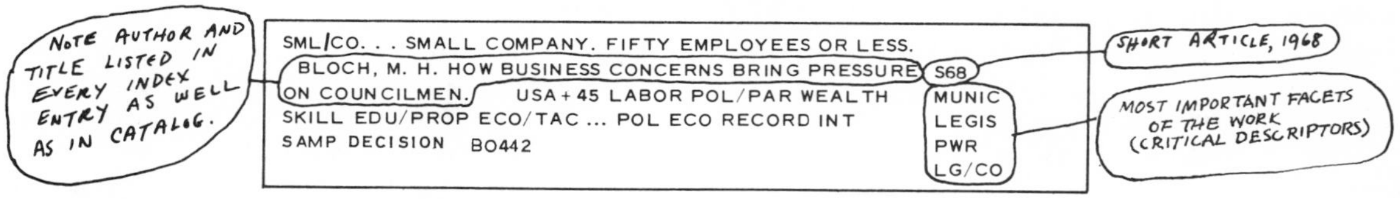

5. Jot down the page numbers and the accession numbers of items that interest you and look them up in the Catalog. There you will find the full citation and a brief annotation of each work.
6. You may locate information on methods authors employ, as well as topics they discuss. Survey the methodological Descriptors in the Grazian Index, pp. xiii-xiv, and locate the relevant Descriptors in the Index of Documents. (Example: if you wished to discover whether any studies of urban business politics had employed recorded interviews, you would look up the term INT [interviews]).
7. Read the Topical and Methodological classification of terms (Grazian Index System) once or twice to grasp the ways in which ideas and groups of related ideas are compressed. The truncated Descriptors, though obvious, are defined in the dictionary of the Index.
8. Although the Catalog is arranged alphabetically by author (except for Volumes II and III), accession numbers have been retained. The major exception to alphabetical arrangement is the group of journals and unsigned articles that begin the Catalog.
9. The Catalogs of Volumes I, IV, V, VI, VII, VIII, IX, and X do not carry Descriptors.
10. The Directory of Publishers pertains to all ten CODEXes.

Concerning the UNIVERSAL REFERENCE SYSTEM in General

The UNIVERSAL REFERENCE SYSTEM is a computerized documentation and information retrieval system employing citations of material above a modest level of quality, appearing in all social and behavioral sciences, annotated. It is indexed by author and employs a set of Standard Descriptors that are arranged according to a master system of topics and methodological techniques, plus various Unique Descriptors.

The flow chart on page x, entitled "The Universal Reference System," shows the numerous steps taken to process documents which come from the intellectual community until they cycle back into the same community as delivered instruments of improved scholarship.

Background of the Work

The many fields of social sciences have suffered for a long time from inadequate searching systems and information storage. The rate of development of periodical and book literature is well known to be far beyond the capacities of the existing book-form document retrieval services. Thousands of new books appear each year, dealing with society and man. Thousands of journals pour forth articles. Hundreds of periodicals are founded each year.

Countries outside of the United States have gone into the social sciences, so that the need for making available foreign publications in intelligible form is ever greater. If there is a light year's distance between present capabilities and the best available service in the social sciences, there is an even greater distance to be traversed in bringing into use the material being published in languages other than English.

A vicious economic cycle is at work in the matter of information retrieval, too: Scholars and students give up research because there are no tools to search with, and therefore their demand for searching tools decreases because they have learned to get along without the materials. Thus, the standards of all the social sciences are lowered because of an anticipated lack of success in handling the problem of information retrieval. The economic risk, therefore, of an information retrieval service has to be taken into account: Many professionals are like the Bengal peasant who cannot aid in his own economic development because he cannot conceive of the nature of the problem and has learned to live as a victim outside of it.

A study in the June, 1964, issue of *The American Behavioral Scientist* magazine showed what the need is today, even before the full capabilities of new systems are appreciated. One-half of a sample of social and behavioral scientists reported that, due to inadequate bibliographic aids, they had discovered significant information on some research too late to use it, and that this information would have significantly affected the scope and nature of their research. In a number of cases, the problem of the researcher was reported to be inadequate access to pre-existing materials, and in other cases was said to be insufficient means of addressing oneself to current material.

So the current ways of information retrieval, or lack thereof, are deficient with respect both to retrospective searching and to current material, not to mention the alarming problem of access to prospective material, in the form of current research project activities and current news of scientific development in relevant categories.

The international scholarly associations centered mainly in Paris have endeavored, with help of UNESCO and other sources of aid, to bring out bibliographies and abstracting services. These services are not fully used, because of their format, their incompleteness, their lack of selectivity, their formulation in traditional and conventional terms of the social sciences (slighting the so-called inter-disciplinary subject matters in methodology), and the simple indexing that they employ. Continuous efforts are being made to solve such problems. Lately, such solutions have been sought via computerized systems. The American Council of Learned Societies, for example, has funded projects at New York University to which the computer is integral.

The Universal Reference System is endeavoring to take an immediately practical view of the literature-access problem, while designing the system so that it will remain open to advances and permit a number of alterations. One must contemplate projects leading to automatic reading and indexing; retrieval of information in the form of propositions, historical dates, and other factual materials; encyclopedic information-providing services; movement into other scientific fields joining social and natural science materials; automatized printing and reproduction of a large variety of materials in quantities ranging from individual to thousands of copies, and provision for televised or other rapid-fire communication services from information retrieval centers.

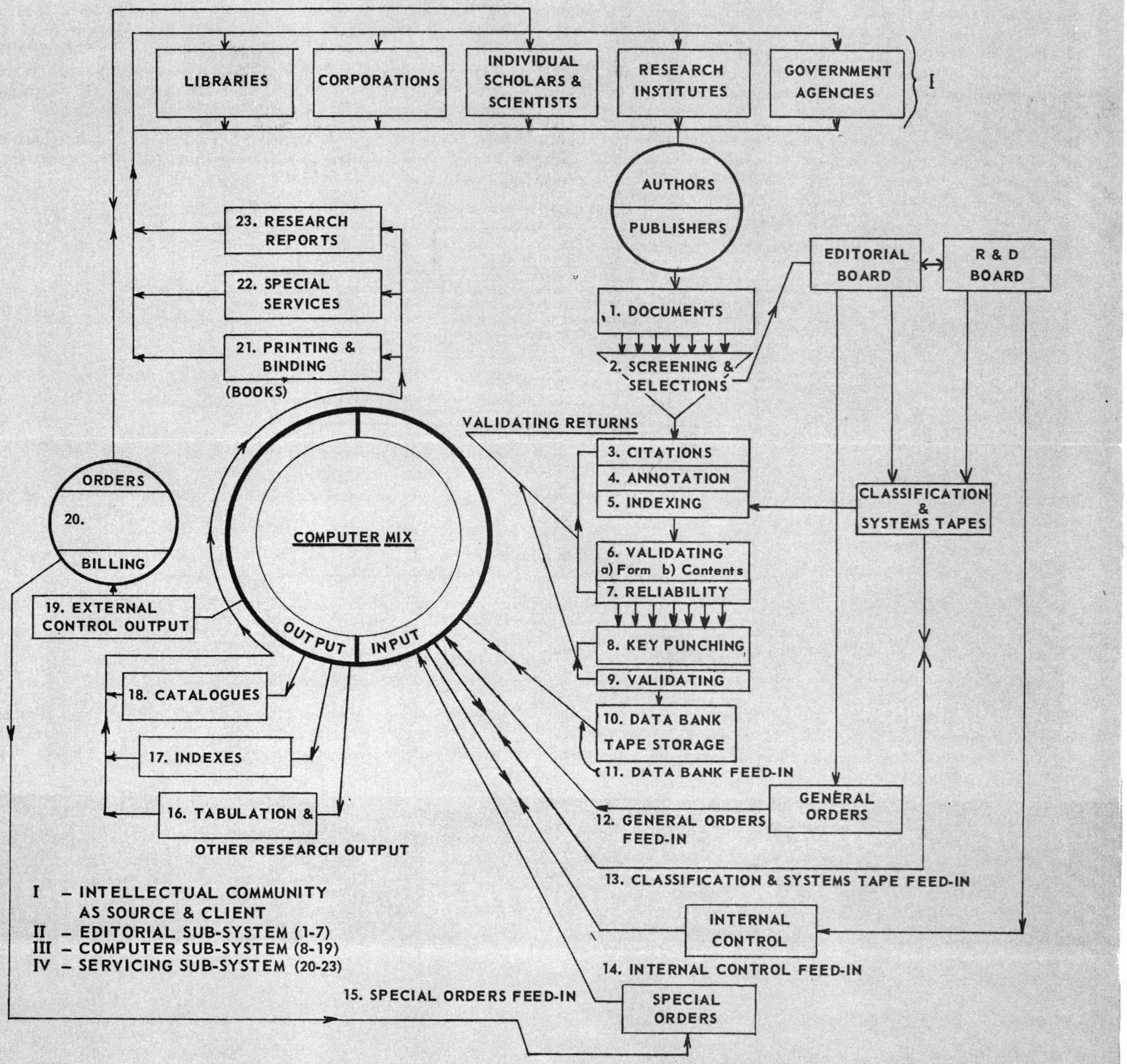

UNIVERSAL REFERENCE SYSTEM

A diagrammatic representation of the numerous steps taken to process documents which come from the intellectual community until they cycle back to the same community as pinpointed sources of information.

The Grazian Classification and Indexing System

The theory behind the URS Classification System is operational. It asks the question: *"Who* says, *'Who does what with whom, where and when, by what means, why'* and *how does he know so?"* This question leads to the general categories and subcategories of the system, which is presented in its logical form on pages **xii-xiv**, along with the truncated terms used in the computerized Index of Documents. The advantage of reading the logical classification is that one will learn in a few minutes the general meaning of the truncated terms and can usually go directly and rapidly to the proper terms in the Index.

The Grazian classification cuts across various disciplines of social science to call attention to the methodological aspects of works which would appear to be important to scholars in the behavioral, instrumental, positivistic tradition of philosophy and science.

The constant recourse to method also serves as a screening device for eliminating numerous documents that are purely evaluative, journalistic, nonempirical, or of an intuitive type. The Grazian index contains some 351 Standard Descriptor categories at the present time. To them are added Unique Descriptors as they occur. Some additional categories logically subtending from the existing ones will be added as time goes on. These will be expanded as part of the original coding as the need is shown. (Several categories may be altered, too, on the same grounds.) From two to four of the Standard and Unique Descriptors are selected as most important facets of the work and are indicated as Critical Descriptors. These are printed apart in the Index of Documents.

The possibilities of utilizing cross-categories are immediate. Cross-categories can be used (both by the searcher and by the creator of the index) to provide a more specialized bibliography. This Cross-Faceting can permit adjusting to changes in the interests of scientists. An almost infinite number of cross-categories is possible, of course. The user of the system will find it set up beyond any existing system to facilitate this. In the future, and upon request, complicated cross-category or multi-faceted searches will be performed by the Universal Reference System's machinery. The ultimate instrumental goal is Controlled Faceting—contractible or expansible according to need and logic.

In practice, the Standard Descriptors, the Unique Descriptors, the Critical Descriptors, the Multiple Faceting, and the Cross-Faceting are interlaced in the operations of documentary analysis and control. Thus, to allow for gaps in the system, to go along with conventional practice, to employ more specialized terms, and to carry important proper nouns, the indexing rules permit the documentary analyst to add Unique Descriptors to the Standard Descriptors already taken from the master list. There are 63 of these in the *Codex of Legislative Process, Representation, and Decision-Making.* The total number of descriptors finally averaged 13 per item.

Some persons have inquired whether it might be useful to print out the whole descriptor rather than a truncated term. Several reasons arbitrate against this procedure, at least for the present. In most cases there is really no single term for which the printed-out truncated descriptor is the symbol. Most Standard Descriptors stand for several synonymous words and related ideas. Printing out the full descriptor *word* would be deluding in many cases, leading searchers to believe a word has only its face meaning.

Moreover, if all truncated descriptors were spelled out, the search time (after the first few searches) would be extended greatly since the eye would have to cover much more lettering and space. Furthermore, the size of the CODEX would be at least tripled, for the space provided for permuting would have to be open enough to carry the longest, not the average, words. There are other technical difficulties.

The repetition of numerous descriptors following each entry in the Index of Documents serves the purpose of targeting the search precisely. The richness of descriptors also postpones the moment of returning to the catalogue and thus enlarges the marginal utility of the first resort to the catalogue.

The intensive indexing of each document, which ranges from 10 to 20 entries, serves a purpose. Intensive indexing permits a document to exhibit all of its important facets to the searcher. The ratio of index carriage to title carriage is here termed the "carriage ratio." The carriage ratio of the URS is much higher than that of most bibliographies. The magnitude of the difference shows the meaning of high intensity indexing. Under other systems, unlike the URS CODEX, a topic is understated in the index. And, less obviously, topics other than the one carried as a flag in the title are sunk into oblivion; thus "Relations Between France and Indochina," which may be a valuable work on questions of economic development, would probably not be indexed on that question at all.

To sum up, the URS, when used as in this CODEX, thoroughly exposes the facets of a listed document. It makes the document thoroughly *retrievable.*

Also under consideration are suggestions to eliminate (or suppress) more of the descriptors. What is the optimal number? It is difficult to say, *a priori.* Experience and experiment will tell, over time. Meanwhile, the Critical Descriptors offer a researcher the "fast search," if he pleases. The more numerous group of descriptors in the final column offers a more complete faceting.

The search time of a researcher should be an important concern of a bibliographer. Search time begins to run, of course, with the knowledge of and access to a work that probably covers a searcher's need. It runs, too, with the ingenuity of the searcher's phrasing of his need. Then it runs with the presence of the works needed in the list searched; a missing document can be translated into lost time. An index saves time, too, when the term searched is the term under which a document is indexed; the need to compromise between detailed vocabularies and generalized ones is evident: it can reasonably be argued that more time is lost in research in social science in getting on the same semantic beam than in solving substantive problems of the "real world." Finally, the structure of an index should lessen search time while permitting a rich search.

Research and experimentation are in order, and it is hoped that a by-product of the initial publications of the Universal Reference System will be an increased stimulation of research into research procedures with respect to the URS' problems and to those of other reference systems.

Topical and Methodological Index (Grazian Index System)

The truncated descriptors (left of each column) and their expanded definitions (right of each column) that follow were employed in systematically computerizing the topics and methods of the Social and Behavioral Sciences. Truncated descriptors that are underscored in the listing that follows have not been carried in the left-hand index entry column of this CODEX; several others (denoted by a double underscore) have been entirely eliminated from this CODEX. Fuller definitions are included in the Index of Documents. So are proper names, place names, organization names, and incidents.

I. TOPICS

1. TIME—SPACE—CULTURE INDEX: Cultural-temporal location of subject.

Centuries covered (e.g., -4; 14-19; 20)

PREHIST	Prehistoric.
MEDIT-7	Mediterranean and Near East, pre-Islamic.
PRE/AMER	Pre-European Americas.
CHRIST-17C	Christendom to 1700.
AFR	Sub-Sahara Africa.
ASIA	China, Japan, Korea.
S/ASIA	India, Southeast Asia, Oceania, except European settlements.
ISLAM	Islamic world.
MOD/EUR	Europe, 1700 to 1918, including European settlements.
USA-45	USA, 1700 to 1945.
WOR-45	Worldwide to 1945.
L/A+17C	Latin America since 1700.
EUR+WWI	Europe, 1918 to present, including colonies, but excluding Communist countries.
COM	Communist countries.
USA+45	USA since 1945.
WOR+45	Worldwide since 1945.
FUT	Future.
SPACE	Outer space.
UNIV	Free of historical position.
SEA	Locale of activity is aquatic.
AIR	Locale of activity is aerial.

(Nations are readily identifiable.)

2. INSTITUTIONAL INDEX: (or subject treated).

A. General

SOCIETY	Society as a whole.
CULTURE	Cultural patterns.
STRUCT	Social structure.
CONSTN	Constitution. Basic group structure.
LAW	Sanctioned practices, enforced ethics in a community.
ELITES	A power-holding group.
INTELL	Intelligentsia.
SOC/INTEG	Social Integration.
STRATA	Social strata.
CLIENT	Clients.

B. Economic type

ECO/UNDEV	Developing countries.
ECO/DEV	Developed countries.

C. Economic function

AGRI	Agriculture, including hunting.
R+D	Research and development organization.
FINAN	Financial services.
INDUS	All or most industry.
COM/IND	Communications industry.
CONSTRUC	Construction and building.
DIST/IND	Distributive system: Includes transportation, warehousing.
EXTR/IND	Extractive industry.
MARKET	Marketing system.
PROC/MFG	Processing or manufacturing.
SERV/IND	Service industry.

D. Organizations

SML/CO	Small company: 50 employees or less.
LG/CO	Company of more than 50 employees.
LABOR	Labor unions.
PROF/ORG	Professional organizations, including guilds.
PUB/INST	Habitational institutions: hospitals, prisons, sanitariums, etc.
POL/PAR	Political party.
SCHOOL	School (except University).
ACADEM	Higher learning.
PERF/ART	Performing arts groupings.
SECT	Church, sect, religious group.
FAM	Family.
KIN	Kinship groups.
NEIGH	Neighborhood.
LOC/G	Local governments.
MUNIC	Cities, villages, towns.
PROVS	State or province.
NAT/G	National governments.
FACE/GP	Acquaintance group: face-to-face association.
VOL/ASSN	Voluntary association.
INT/ORG	International organizations.

3. ORGANIC OR INTERNAL STRUCTURE INDEX: Subgroupings or substructures treated.

CONSULT	Consultants.
FORCES	Armed forces and police.
DELIB/GP	Conferences, committees, boards, cabinets.
LEGIS	Legislatures.
CT/SYS	Court systems.
EX/STRUC	Formal executive establishment.
TOP/EX	Individuals holding executive positions.
CHIEF	Chief officer of a government.
WORKER	Workers and work conditions.

4. PROCESSES AND PRACTICES: Procedures or tactics used by subject or discussed as subject.

A. Creating and Sciencing

CREATE	Creative and innovative processes.
ACT/RES	Combined research and social action.
COMPUTER	Computer techniques.
INSPECT	Inspecting quality, output, legality.
OP/RES	Operations research.
PLAN	Planning.
PROB/SOLV	Problem-solving and decision-making.
TEC/DEV	Development and change of technology.

B. Economizing

ACCT	Accounting, bookkeeping.
BAL/PWR	Balance of power.
BARGAIN	Bargaining, trade.
BUDGET	Budgeting, fiscal planning.
CAP/ISM	Enterprise, entrepreneurship.
DIPLOM	Diplomacy.
ECO/TAC	Economic measures or tactics.
FOR/AID	Foreign aid.
INT/TRADE	International trade.
RATION	Rationing, official control of goods or costs.
RENT	Renting.
TARIFFS	Tariffs.
TAX	Taxation.

C. Awarding

GIVE	Giving, philanthropy.
LICENSE	Legal permit.
PAY	Paying.
RECEIVE	Receiving of welfare.
REPAR	Reparations.
TRIBUTE	Payments to dominant by minor power, racketeering.
WORSHIP	Worship, ritual.

D. Symbolizing

DOMIN	Domination.
EDU/PROP	Education or propaganda.
LEGIT	Legitimacy.
PRESS	Printed media.
RUMOR	Rumor, gossip.
TV	Television.
WRITING	Writing.

E. Evaluating

CONFER	Group consultation.
DEBATE	Organized collective arguments.

ETIQUET	Etiquette, fashion, manners.
PRICE	Pricing.
SENIOR	Seniority.

F. Determining

ADJUD	Judicial behavior and personality.
ADMIN	Behavior of non-top executive personnel (except armed forces).
AGREE	Agreements, treaties, compacts.
AUTOMAT	Automation.
COLONIAL	Colonialism.
CONTROL	Specific ability of power to determine achievement.
EXEC	Executive, regularized management.
FEEDBACK	Feedback phenomena.
GAMBLE	Speculative activity.
LEAD	Leading.
LOBBY	Lobbying.
NEUTRAL	Neutralism, neutrality.
PARL/PROC	Parliamentary procedures (legislative).
PARTIC	Participation: civic apathy or activity.
REGION	Regionalism.
RISK	Risk, uncertainty, certainty.
ROUTINE	Procedural and work systems.
SANCTION	Sanctions of law and social law.
TASK	A specific operation within a work setting.
TIME	Timing, time-factor.

G. Forcing

ARMS/CONT	Arms control and disarmament.
COERCE	Force and violence.
CRIME	Criminal behavior.
CROWD	Mass behavior.
DEATH	Death-related behavior.
DETER	Military deterrence.
GUERRILLA	Guerrilla warfare.
MURDER	Murder, assassination.
NUC/PWR	All uses of nuclear energy.
REV	Revolution.
SUICIDE	Suicide.
WAR	War.
WEAPON	Conventional military weapons.

H. Choosing

APPORT	Apportionment of assemblies.
CHOOSE	Choice, election.
REPRESENT	Representation.
SUFF	Suffrage.

I. Consuming

DREAM	Dreaming.
LEISURE	Unobligated time expenditures.
SLEEP	Sleep-related behavior.
EATING	Eating, cuisine.

5. RELATIONS INDEX: Relationship of individuals and/or group under discussion.

CIVMIL/REL	Civil-military relation.
GOV/REL	Relations between local or state governments and governmental agencies.
GP/REL	Relations among groups, except nations.
INT/REL	Relations among sovereign states.
INGP/REL	Relations within groups.
PERS/REL	Relations between persons; interpersonal communication.
RACE/REL	Race relations.

6. CONDITIONS AND MEASURES (of activities being discussed).

ADJUST	Social adjustment, socialization.
BAL/PAY	Balance of payments.
CENTRAL	Centralization.
CONSEN	Consensus.
COST	Costs.
DEMAND	In economic sense, a demand.
DISCRIM	Social differentiation in support of inequalities.
EFFICIENCY	Effectiveness, measures.
EQUILIB	Equilibrium (technical).
FEDERAL	Federalism.
HAPPINESS	Satisfaction and unhappiness.
ILLEGIT	Bastardy.
INCOME	Income distribution, shares, earnings.
ISOLAT	Isolation and community.
LITERACY	Ability to read and write.
MAJORITY	Behavior of major parts of grouping.
MARRIAGE	Legal wedlock.
NAT/LISM	Nationalism.
OPTIMAL	Optimality in its economic usages.
OWN	Ownership.
PEACE	Freedom from conflict or termination of hostilities.
PRIVIL	Privilege, parliamentary.
PRODUC	Productivity.
PROFIT	Profit in economic sense.
RATIONAL	Instrumental rationality.
STRANGE	Estrangement or outsiders.
TOTALISM	Totalitarianism.
UTIL	Utility as in economics.
UTOPIA	Envisioned general social conditions.

7. PERSONALITY INDEX: Behavior of actors to their actions.

HABITAT	Ecology.
HEREDITY	Genetic influences on personality.
DRIVE	Drive, morale, or antithesis.
PERCEPT	Perception.
PERSON	Personality and human nature.
ROLE	Role, reference group feelings, cross-pressures.
AGE	Age factors in general.
AGE/C	Infants and children.
AGE/Y	Youth, adolescence.
AGE/A	Adults.
AGE/O	Old.
SEX	Sexual behavior.
SUPEGO	Conscience, superego, and responsibility.
RIGID/FLEX	Rigidity/flexibility; exclusive/inclusive.
ATTIT	Attitudes, opinions, ideology.
DISPL	Displacement and projection.
AUTHORIT	Authoritarianism, as personal behavior.
BIO/SOC	Bio-social processes: drugs, psychosomatic phenomena, etc.
ANOMIE	Alienation, anomie, generalized personal anxiety.

8. VALUES INDEX: Basically desired (or nondesired) conditions held or believed in by subjects.

HEALTH	Well-being, bodily and psychic integrity (sickness).
KNOWL	Enlightenment (ignorance).
LOVE	Affection, friendship (hatred).
MORAL	Rectitude, morality (immorality), goodness.
PWR	Power, participation in decision-making (impotence).
RESPECT	Respect, social class attitudes (contempt, disrespect).
SKILL	Skill, practical competence (incompetence).
WEALTH	Wealth, access to goods and services (poverty).
ALL/VALS	All, or six or more of above.
ORD/FREE	Security, order, restraint (change, experience, freedom).
SOVEREIGN	Sovereignty; home-rule.

9. IDEOLOGICAL TOPIC: Ideology discussed in work.

CATHISM	Roman Catholicism.
CONSERVE	Traditionalism.
FASCISM	Fascism.
LAISSEZ	Laissez-faire-ism (old liberal).
MARXISM	Marxism.
MYSTISM	Mysticism.
NEW/LIB	New Liberalism (welfare state).
OBJECTIVE	Value-free thought.
PACIFISM	Pacifism.
PLURISM	Socio-political order of autonomous groups.
POPULISM	Majoritarianism.
RELATISM	Relativism.
SOCISM	Socialism.
TECHRACY	Socio-political order dominated by technicians.
ALL/IDEOS	Three or more of above.

II. METHODOLOGY (What techniques are dealt with by the author and what techniques the document employs or describes).

10. ETHICAL STANDARDS APPLIED BY AUTHOR

ETHIC	Personal ethics (private and professional).
LAW/ETHIC	Ethics of laws and court processes.

POLICY	Treats ethics of public policies.

11. IDEOLOGY OF AUTHOR (where clear).

ANARCH	Anarchism.
CATH	Roman Catholic.
CONVNTL	Conventional: unsystematic acceptance of values in common currency.
FASCIST	Totalitarian with nonworker, upper class, or leader cult.
MAJORIT	Majoritarian, consensual.
MARXIST	Marxist Communist in viewpoint.
MYSTIC	Otherworldly, mystical.
OLD/LIB	Old liberal, laissez-faire.
PACIFIST	Pacifist.
PLURIST	Pluralist.
REALPOL	Realpolitik, Machiavellism.
RELATIV	Relativist.
SOCIALIST	Socialist (except Communist).
TECHNIC	Technocratic.
TRADIT	Traditional or aristocratic.
WELF/ST	Welfare state advocate.

12. FIELD INDEX: Fields, discipline, or methodological approach of document.

ART/METH	Fine Arts, Graphics, Performing Arts, Aesthetics.
CRIMLGY	Criminology.
DECISION	Decision-making and gaming (game theory).
ECO	Economics and economic enterprise.
ECOMETRIC	Econometrics, mathematical economics.
EPIST	Epistemology, sociology of knowledge.
GEOG	Demography and geography.
HEAL	Health sciences.
HIST	History (including current events).
HUM	Methods of the "Humanities." Literary analysis.
INT/LAW	International law. Uses legal approach.
JURID	Uses legal approach. Concerns largely the laws.
MGT	Administrative management.
PHIL/SCI	Scientific method and Philosophy of Science.
POL	Deals with political and power process.
PSY	Psychology.
SOC	Sociology.
SOC/WK	Social services.

13. CONCEPTS: Document is noteworthy for systematic and/or basic treatment of:

CONCPT	Subject-matter abstract concepts.
METH/CNCPT	Methodological concepts.
MYTH	Treats assumptions unconsciously accepted, fictions.
NEW/IDEA	Word inventions, new concepts and ideas.

14. LOGIC, MATHEMATICS, AND LANGUAGE

LOG	Logic: syntax, semantics, pragmatics.
MATH	Mathematics.
STAT	Statistics.
AVERAGE	Mean, average behaviors.
PROBABIL	Probability, chance.
MODAL	Modal types, fashions.
CORREL	Correlations (statistical).
REGRESS	Regression analysis.
QUANT	Nature and limits of quantification.
CLASSIF	Classification, typology, set theory.
INDICATOR	Numerical indicator, index weights.
LING	Linguistics.
STYLE	The styles and terminology of scientific communications.

15. DIRECT OBSERVATION

OBS	Trained or participant observation.
SELF/OBS	Self-observation, psycho-drama.
OBS/ENVIR	Social milieu of and resistances to observation.
CONT/OBS	Controlled direct observation.
RECORD	Recording direct observations. (But not content analysis, q.v.)

16. INTERVIEWS

INT	Interviews, short or long, in general.
STAND/INT	Standardized interviews.
DEEP/INT	Depth interviews.
UNPLAN/INT	Impromptu interview.
RESIST/INT	Social resistance to interviewing.
REC/INT	Recording, systematizing, and analyzing of interviews.

17. QUESTIONNAIRES

QU	Questionnaires in general, short or long.
DEEP/QU	Depth questionnaires, including projective or probing.
QU/SEMANT	Semantic and social problems of questionnaires.
SYS/QU	Systematizing and analyzing questionnaires.

18. TESTS AND SCALES

TESTS	Theory and uses of tests and scales.
APT/TEST	Aptitude tests.
KNO/TEST	Tests for factual knowledge, beliefs, or abilities.
PERS/TEST	Personality tests.
PROJ/TEST	Projective tests.

19. UNIVERSES AND SAMPLING

CENSUS	Census.
SAMP	Sample survey in general.
SAMP/SIZ	Sizes and techniques of sampling.
NET/THEORY	Systematic group-member connections analysis.

20. ANALYSIS OF TEMPORAL SEQUENCES

BIOG	Biography, personality development, and psychoanalysis.
HIST/WRIT	Historiography.
TIME/SEQ	Chronology and genetic series of men, institutions, processes, etc.
TREND	Projection of trends, individual and social.
PREDICT	Prediction of future events.

21. COMMUNICATION CONTENT ANALYSIS

CON/ANAL	Quantitative content analysis.
DOC/ANAL	Conventional analysis of records or documents.

22. INFORMATION STORAGE AND RETRIEVAL

OLD/STOR	Conventional libraries, books, records, tape, film.
THING/STOR	Artifacts and material evidence.
COMPUT/IR	Mechanical and electronic information retrieval.

23. GRAPHICS AND AUDIO-VISUAL TECHNIQUES: Used in the research and/or in the presentation.

AUD/VIS	Film and sound, photographs.
CHARTS	Graphs, charts, diagrams, maps.
EXHIBIT	Exhibits.
PROG/TEAC	Programmed instruction.

24. COMPARATIVE ANALYSIS INDEX

METH/COMP	Of methods, approaches, styles.
IDEA/COMP	Of ideas, methods, ideologies.
PERS/COMP	Of persons.
GP/COMP	Of groups.
GOV/COMP	Of governments.
NAT/COMP	Of nations.

25. EXPERIMENTATION

LAB/EXP	Laboratory or strictly controlled groups.
SOC/EXP	"Social" experimentation.
HYPO/EXP	Hypothetical, intellectual constructs.

26. MODELS: Intellectual representations of objects or processes.

SIMUL	Scientific models.
ORG/CHARTS	Blueprints and organization charts.
STERTYP	Stereotypes, ideologies, utopias.
GAME	Game or Decision Theory models.

27. GENERAL THEORY

GEN/LAWS	Systems based on substantive relations, such as idealism, economic determinism.
GEN/METH	Systems based on methodology, such as cycles, pragmatism, sociometry.

28. SPECIAL FORMATS

ANTHOL	Anthology, symposium, collection.
BIBLIOG	Bibliography over fifty items, or of rare utility.
BIBLIOG/A	Contains bibliography over fifty items or of rare utility, annotated.
DICTIONARY	Dictionary.
INDEX	List of names or subjects.
METH	Document heavily emphasizes methodology (Part II) rather than topics (Part I).
T	Textbook.

Dictionary of Descriptors in this Volume

(Incorporating List of Frequency of Descriptors in Index)

This Dictionary contains all Descriptors employed in this volume, and thus enables you to identify in a few minutes every Descriptor that may pertain to your subject. The frequency list calls your attention to the number of works carried under each Descriptor and assists you in determining the term at which you may most advantageously begin your search in the Index. A modest system of cross-references may be found in the Dictionary that appears in the Index.

DESCRIPTOR		*FREQUENCY*	*PAGE*
ABORIGINES	Aborigines (Australia)	7	175
ACADEM	University, graduate school	93	175
ACADEM/SCI	Academy of Sciences (U.S.S.R.)	1	177
ACTON/LORD	Lord Acton	1	178
ADEN	Aden	1	178
ADENAUER/K	Konrad Adenauer	7	178
ADJUD	Judicial and adjudicative processes and behavior	142	178
ADJUST	Social adjustment, socialization	97	182
ADMIN	Behavior of non-top executive personnel in organizational structure	509	184
AEC	Atomic Energy Commission	1	198
AFGHANISTN	Afghanistan	4	198
AFL/CIO	American Federation of Labor, Congress of Industrial Organizations	1	198
AFR	Africa	402	198
AFRICA/E	East Africa	9	209
AFRICA/SW	South-West Africa	8	209
AFRICA/W	West Africa	13	209
AGE	Age factors	12	210
AGE/A	Adults	5	210
AGE/C	Infants and children	10	210
AGE/O	Old people	4	211
AGE/Y	Youth and adolescence	19	211
AGREE	Agreements, treaties, compacts	47	211
AGRI	Agriculture, including hunting	275	213
AIR	Locale of activity is aerial	2	220
ALBANIA	Albania	5	220
ALGERIA	Algeria	24	220
ALL/IDEOS	Concerns three or more of the terms listed in the ideological topic index, p. xiii	57	221
ALL/VALS	Concerns six or more of the terms listed in the values index, p. xiii	158	222
AMMAN/MAX	Max Amman	1	227
ANARCH	Anarchist	10	227
ANOMIE	Anomie, alienation, generalized personal anxiety	26	228
ANTHOL	Anthology, symposium	196	228
ANTI/SEMIT	Anti-semitism	1	234
APPORT	Apportionment of assemblies	9	234
APRA	Alianza Popular Revolucionaria Americana, a Peruvian Political Party	1	234
AQUINAS/T	Saint Thomas Aquinas	2	234
ARABS	Arab world and culture	13	234
ARGENTINA	Argentina	15	235
ARISTOTLE	Aristotle	1	235
ARMENIA	Armenia	1	235
ARMS/CONT	Arms control, disarmament	38	235
ART/METH	Fine and performing arts	57	236
ASIA	China, Japan, Korea, Bhutan, Afghanistan, Taiwan	221	238
ASQUITH/HH	Herbert Henry Asquith	1	244
ATHENS	Athens, Greece	1	244
AUD/VIS	Film and sound, photographs	30	244
AUST/HUNG	Austria-Hungary	2	245
AUSTRALIA	Australia	37	245
AUSTRIA	Austria	13	246
AUTHORIT	Authoritarianism, personal	42	246
AUTOMAT	Automation	5	247
BA/MBUTI	Ba Mbuti—the Forest People (Congo)	1	248
BABYLONIA	Babylonia	1	248
BACON/F	Francis Bacon	1	248
BACON/R	Roger Bacon	1	248
BAKUNIN	Mikhail Bakunin	1	248
BAL/PAY	Balance of payments	29	248
BAL/PWR	Balance of power	129	249
BALKANS	Balkans	3	252
BANTU	Bantu nation and culture	2	253
BANTUSTANS	Bantustans, Republic of South Africa	2	253
BARGAIN	Bargaining, trade	23	253
BATAK	Batak Tribe, Philippines	1	254
BEHAVIORSM	Behaviorism	1	254
BELGIUM	Belgium	9	254
BENTHAM/J	Jeremy Bentham	4	255
BERLIN	Berlin	4	255
BERLIN/BLO	Berlin Blockade	3	255
BESSARABIA	Bessarabia	1	255
BIAFRA	Biafra	2	255
BIBLE	Bible	3	255
BIBLIOG	Bibliography over 50 items	573	255
BIBLIOG/A	Annotated bibliography over 50 items	272	270
BIO/SOC	Bio-social processes: drugs, psychosomatic phenomena, etc.	29	277
BIOG	Biography, personality development, psychoanalysis	124	278
BIRTH/CON	Birth control	2	282
BISMARCK/O	Otto von Bismarck	7	282
BOER/WAR	Boer War	2	282
BOLIVIA	Bolivia	3	282
BOLSHEVISM	Bolshevism, Bolshevists, Bolsheviks	12	282
BONTOC	Bontoc (Philippine tribe)	1	283
BORNEO	Borneo	2	283
BOURGUIBA	Habib Bourguiba	1	283
BOXER/REBL	Boxer Rebellion	1	283
BRAZIL	Brazil	36	284
BREHON	Brehon Law (ancient Celtic)	1	284
BUDDHISM	Buddhism	4	285
BUDGET	Budgeting, fiscal planning	73	285
BUENOS/AIR	Buenos Aires, Argentina	1	287
BULGARIA	Bulgaria	11	287
BUR/BUDGET	Bureau of the Budget	1	288
BURAGR/ECO	Bureau of Agricultural Economics	1	288
BUREAUCRCY	Bureaucracy	14	288
BURGANDA	Burganda	1	288
BURKE/EDM	Edmund Burke	7	288
BURMA	Burma	25	289
BURUNDI	Burundi	1	289
BYZANTINE	Byzantine Empire	2	290
CABINET	Cabinet	1	290
CALCUTTA	Calcutta, India	1	290
CALIFORNIA	California	1	290
CALVIN/J	John Calvin	1	290
CAMBODIA	Cambodia	8	290
CAMELOT	Project Camelot (Chile)	1	290
CAMEROON	Cameroon	3	290
CANADA	Canada	74	290
CANAL/ZONE	Panama Canal Zone	1	292
CANON/LAW	Canon law	4	293
CAP/ISM	Capitalism, entrepreneurship	125	293
CAPE/HOPE	Cape of Good Hope	1	296
CARIBBEAN	Caribbean	2	296
CASEBOOK	Casebook, (e.g., legal, sociological)	3	296
CASTRO/F	Fidel Castro	3	297
CATH	Roman Catholic	14	297

0001 AMERICAN POLITICAL SCIENCE REVIEW.
WASHINGTON: AMER POL SCI ASSOC.
QUARTERLY JOURNAL SINCE 1906 WHICH DEALS WITH GOVERNMENT, POLITICS, LAW, AND INTERNATIONAL RELATIONS. CONTAINS EXTENSIVE BOOK REVIEW SECTION AND BIBLIOGRAPHIES OF BOOKS, SERIALS, GOVERNMENT DOCUMENTS, PAMPHLETS, AND DOCTORAL DISSERTATIONS. CLASSIFIED IN FIVE CATEGORIES: POLITICAL THEORY, AMERICAN POLITICS, COMPARATIVE PUBLIC ADMINISTRATION, COMPARATIVE GOVERNMENT, AND INTERNATIONAL POLITICS.

0002 BULLETIN ANALYTIQUE DE DOCUMENTATION POLITIQUE, ECONOMIQUE, ET SOCIALE CONTEMPORAINE.
PARIS: PR UNIV DE FRANCE.
MONTHLY PUBLICATION SINCE 1946 LISTING PRINCIPAL ARTICLES FROM OVER 1,000 FRENCH AND FOREIGN PERIODICALS ON POLITICAL, SOCIAL, AND ECONOMIC ISSUES. TITLES TRANSLATED INTO FRENCH AND ANNOTATED. ANNUAL INDEX OF TITLES AND LIST OF PERIODICALS USED. ENTRIES DIVIDED INTO NATIONAL PROBLEMS OR INTERNATIONAL RELATIONS AND COMPARATIVE STUDIES. FIRST SECTION ARRANGED BY COUNTRY, SECOND BY FIELD OF STUDY.

0003 CANADIAN GOVERNMENT PUBLICATIONS (1955-)
OTTAWA: QUEEN'S PRINTER.
ANNUAL CATALOGUE INCORPORATING "DAILY CHECKLIST" AND "MONTHLY CATALOGUE OF GOVERNMENT PUBLICATIONS." ENTRIES SUBDIVIDED UNDER GENERAL TOPICS, PARLIAMENTARY PUBLICATIONS AND DEPARTMENTAL PUBLICATIONS. FIRST PART OF BOOK IN ENGLISH, SECOND IN FRENCH. INCLUDES SECTION OF INTERNATIONAL PUBLICATIONS.

0004 INTERNATIONAL BIBLIOGRAPHIE DER DEUTSCHEN ZEITSCHRIFTEN-LITERATUR.
OSNABRUCK: VERL FELIX DIETRICH.
INTERNATIONAL BIBLIOGRAPHY OF GERMAN PERIODICAL LITERATURE APPEARING SEMIANNUALLY SINCE 1897. COMPREHENSIVE INDEX OF OVER 5,000 GERMAN PERIODICALS, YEARBOOKS, TRANSACTIONS, ETC. SUBJECT AND AUTHOR INDEXES.

0005 JOURNAL OF ASIAN STUDIES.
ANN ARBOR: ASSOC ASIAN STUD.
QUARTERLY JOURNAL WITH BOOK REVIEWS AND AN ANNUAL "BIBLIOGRAPHY OF ASIAN STUDIES" SINCE 1936. LISTS BOOKS AND PERIODICAL ARTICLES IN WESTERN LANGUAGES. ENTRIES ARRANGED BY COUNTRY AND SUBDIVIDED BY SUBJECT. EACH SUBJECT IS DIVIDED INTO BOOKS AND PERIODICALS. ALSO CONTAINS AN ALPHABETICAL LISTING BY AUTHOR.

0006 JOURNAL OF MODERN HISTORY.
CHICAGO: U OF CHICAGO PRESS.
QUARTERLY, FIRST PUBLISHED IN 1929, REVIEWS BOOKS WHICH DEAL WITH POLITICAL AND DIPLOMATIC HISTORY ON A WORLDWIDE BASIS. ANNUAL AUTHOR INDEX.

0007 MIDDLE EAST JOURNAL.
WASHINGTON: MIDDLE EAST INST.
QUARTERLY PERIODICAL DEVOTED TO MIDDLE EAST SOCIAL SCIENCES AND HUMANITIES. HAS A BOOK REVIEW SECTION AND A BIBLIOGRAPHICAL LISTING. LISTINGS ARE IN ORIGINAL LANGUAGE - ENGLISH, FRENCH, GERMAN. ALSO CONTAINS SHORTER BOOK NOTICES, LIST OF RECENT BOOKS, LIST OF FORTHCOMING BOOKS, ANNUAL LIST OF PERIODICALS SURVEYED, AND ANNUAL LIST OF RESEARCH PROJECTS. FIRST PUBLISHED 1947.

0008 NEUE POLITISCHE LITERATUR.
STUTTGART: RING-VERLAG.
MONTHLY JOURNAL WITH BIMONTHLY BIBLIOGRAPHY. FIRST PUBLISHED 1956. LISTS ARTICLES FROM SELECTED GERMAN, FRENCH, AND ENGLISH-LANGUAGE POLITICAL SCIENCE PERIODICALS. ENTRIES ENTERED BY SUBJECT AND INCLUDE POLITICAL THEORY, INTERNATIONAL POLITICS, ECONOMY AND SOCIETY, GERMANY, INTERNATIONAL COMMUNISM, EAST EUROPE, RUSSIA, ASIA AND AFRICA, NORTH AND SOUTH AMERICA.

0009 PEKING REVIEW.
PEKING: PEKING REVIEW.
WEEKLY PERIODICAL EXPRESSING CHINESE COMMUNIST VIEWS. WEEKLY SUMMARY OF EVENTS, NATIONAL AND INTERNATIONAL, FOLLOWED BY ENGLISH TRANSLATIONS OF GOVERNMENT DOCUMENTS, NEWSPAPER EDITORIALS, AND PERIODICAL ARTICLES. FIRST ISSUE MARCH, 1958. INDEXED BY SUBJECT IN LAST ISSUE OF YEAR.

0010 AFRICAN RESEARCH BULLETIN.
EXETER: AFRICAN RESEARCH LTD.
MONTHLY PUBLICATION FIRST PRINTED IN 1964 WHICH SYNTHESIZES PRESS ARTICLES AND NEWS BULLETINS ON CURRENT EVENTS IN AFRICA. HAS MATERIAL ON INTERNATIONAL POLITICAL DEVELOPMENTS, INTERNAL POLITICAL DEVELOPMENTS OF INDEPENDENT AND NONINDEPENDENT TERRITORIES, POLITICAL DEVELOPMENTS WITH NATIONS OVERSEAS, SOCIAL AND CULTURAL DEVELOPMENTS.

0011 AUSTRALIAN PUBLIC AFFAIRS INFORMATION SERVICE.
SYDNEY: AUSTRALIAN PUBLIC AFF.INFO.SCE.
ISSUED MONTHLY BY NATIONAL LIBRARY OF AUSTRALIA. GUIDE TO MATERIAL ON AUSTRALIAN POLITICAL, ECONOMIC, SOCIAL, AND CULTURAL AFFAIRS. INDEXES BOOKS AND ARTICLES, BOTH DOMESTIC AND FOREIGN, DURING CURRENT OR TWO PRECEDING YEARS. INCLUDES SELECTED LIST OF AUSTRALIAN PERIODICALS. ARRANGEMENT IS ALPHABETICAL BY SUBJECT. FIRST PUBLISHED JULY, 1945.

0012 BIBLIOGRAPHIE DE LA PHILOSOPHIE.
PARIS: INST INTL COLLAB DE PHIL.
FIRST PUBLISHED IN 1937, ONLY JOURNAL OF ITS KIND IN THE WORLD DEVOTED EXCLUSIVELY TO PROVIDING UP-TO-DATE INFORMATION AND ABSTRACTS OF BOOKS PUBLISHED IN PHILOSOPHY AND RELATED FIELDS. SINCE 1954, THE ENGLISH-FRENCH JOURNAL HAS BEEN ISSUED AS A QUARTERLY BULLETIN. BOOKS CLASSIFIED BY SUBJECT; CONSECUTIVELY NUMBERED OVER EACH ANNUM; INDEXES APPEAR IN FOURTH ISSUE OF EACH YEAR.

0013 DAILY SUMMARY OF THE JAPANESE PRESS.
WASHINGTON: US GOVERNMENT.
PUBLISHED SINCE 1964 BY US EMBASSY IN TOKYO, CONTAINS TRANSLATIONS OF ARTICLES FROM MAJOR JAPANESE NEWSPAPERS.

0014 CHINA QUARTERLY.
LONDON: INFO BULLETIN LTD.
FIRST PUBLISHED IN 1935, JOURNAL IS DEVOTED TO CHINESE DOMESTIC EVENTS AND FOREIGN RELATIONS. WITH FEW EXCEPTIONS, SCHOLARLY WORK CONCENTRATES ON 20TH-CENTURY QUARTERLY SECTION OF BOOK REVIEWS OF SIGNIFICANT CURRENT STUDIES. CONTAINS ALSO A QUARTERLY CHRONICLE AND DOCUMENTATION AND AN INDEX OF DOCUMENTS.

0015 CIVIL SERVICE JOURNAL.
WASHINGTON: US GOVERNMENT.
QUARTERLY FIRST PUBLISHED BY THE US CIVIL SERVICE COMMISSION IN 1960. EACH ISSUE CONTAINS FIVE TO EIGHT OF INTEREST TO THE CIVIL SERVICE WORKING PUBLIC, AND SECTIONS ON LEGAL DECISIONS AND LEGISLATION. EACH ISSUE INCLUDES A ONE OR TWO PAGE ANNOTATED BIBLIOGRAPHY OF PRIMARILY GOVERNMENT-PUBLISHED MATERIALS ON EMPLOYEE TRAINING, PERSONNEL MANAGEMENT, AND RELATED TOPICS.

0016 HANDBOOK OF LATIN AMERICAN STUDIES.
GAINESVILLE: U OF FLA PR.
ANNOTATED ANNUAL GUIDE LISTING ABOUT 4,000 BOOKS AND ARTICLES ON ALL SUBJECTS. ITEMS ARRANGED BY SUBJECT AND BY COUNTRY. FIRST PUBLISHED 1935.

0017 INDIA: A REFERENCE ANNUAL.
NEW DELHI: INDIAN MIN OF INFO.
FIRST PUBLISHED IN 1953 BY PUBLICATIONS DIVISION OF THE MINISTRY OF INFORMATION AND BROADCASTING, WITH OBJECT OF PROVIDING AUTHENTIC INFORMATION ON VARIOUS ASPECTS ON NATIONAL LIFE WITHIN COUNTRY AND ABROAD. SELECT BIBLIOGRAPHY INCLUDES ADDITIONAL INFORMATION FROM GOVERNMENT REPORTS AND PUBLICATIONS, REFERENCE WORKS, AND OTHER BOOKS.

0018 LONDON TIMES OFFICIAL INDEX.
LONDON: LONDON TIMES, INC.
QUARTERLY, DETAILED SUBJECT INDEX TO NEWSPAPER ARTICLES. CUMULATED ANNUALLY. FIRST PUBLISHED 1906.

0019 PUBLISHERS' CIRCULAR, THE OFFICIAL ORGAN OF THE PUBLISHERS' ASSOCIATION OF GREAT BRITAIN AND IRELAND.
SURREY: PUBL CIRCULAR LTD.
WEEKLY LISTING OF BRITISH PUBLICATIONS INCLUDING PAMPHLETS AND GOVERNMENT PUBLICATIONS. CHANGED IN 1959 TO "BRITISH BOOKS" AND ISSUED MONTHLY. FIRST PUBLISHED 1873.

0020 PUBLISHERS' TRADE LIST ANNUAL.
NEW YORK: RR BOWKER.
ANNUAL COMPILATION OF CATALOGS OF MOST US PUBLISHERS AND SOME CANADIAN. FIRST PUBLISHED 1873.

0021 REVUE FRANCAISE DE SCIENCE POLITIQUE.
PARIS: PR UNIV DE FRANCE.
FRENCH QUARTERLY FIRST PUBLISHED IN 1951, CONTAINS SECTION DEVOTED TO CRITICAL REVIEWS OF RECENT IMPORTANT PUBLICATIONS IN POLITICAL SCIENCE AND SECTION LISTING RECENT PUBLICATIONS RECEIVED BY JOURNAL. CONTAINS ALSO LISTING OF BRITISH COMMONWEALTH POLITICAL SCIENCE REFERENCE WORKS AND JOURNALS.

0022 SEMINAR: THE MONTHLY SYMPOSIUM.
NEW DELHI: SEMINAR.
JOURNAL, PUBLISHED ON MONTHLY BASIS, DEVOTED TO DISCUSSIONS OF SINGLE MAJOR ISSUES DEBATED BY WRITERS OF A VARIETY OF POLITICAL PERSUASIONS. CONFINED TO PROBLEMS CRUCIAL TO INDIAN SOVEREIGNTY AND NATIONAL DEVELOPMENT. SAMPLE ISSUES: NUCLEAR WEAPONS; ROLE OF PARLIAMENT; IMPLICATIONS OF NATIONAL POLICY; LANGUAGE CONTROVERSY; ETC. EACH ISSUE CONTAINS SECTION OF SELECTED RELEVANT READINGS. APPEARED 1959.

0023 THE STATESMAN'S YEARBOOK; STATISTICAL AND HISTORICAL ANNUAL OF THE STATES OF THE WORLD.
NEW YORK: ST MARTIN'S PRESS, 1864.
CONCISE AND RELIABLE MANUAL OF DESCRIPTIVE AND STATISTICAL INFORMATION ABOUT THE GOVERNMENTS OF THE WORLD. EACH VOLUME REVISED AFTER OFFICIAL RETURNS. INFORMATION CONCERNING RULERS, CONSTITUTIONS, GOVERNMENTS, AREA, POPULATION,

ETC., GIVEN FOR EACH COUNTRY. ENTRIES ARRANGED GEOGRAPHICALLY, WITH COMPREHENSIVE INDEX, APPENDIA, AND MAPS. PARTIALLY ANNOTATED LIST OF REFERENCE BOOKS FOR EACH COUNTRY ANNUAL.

0024 SUBJECT GUIDE TO BOOKS IN PRINT: AN INDEX TO THE PUBLISHERS' TRADE LIST ANNUAL.
NEW YORK: RR BOWKER.
ARRANGED ALPHABETICALLY BY SUBJECT. BASICALLY FOLLOWS THE SUBJECT HEADINGS SET UP BY THE LIBRARY OF CONGRESS, WITH EXTENSIVE CROSS REFERENCES. ANNUAL PUBLICATION.

0025 SUMMARIES OF SELECTED JAPANESE MAGAZINES.
WASHINGTON: US GOVERNMENT.
ISSUED BY US EMBASSY, WEEKLY TRANSLATIONS AND SUMMARIES OF ARTICLES FROM LEADING JAPANESE MAGAZINES ON ALL SUBJECTS. FIRST PUBLISHED IN 1964.

0026 THE MIDDLE EAST AND NORTH AFRICA.
LONDON: EUROPA PUBLICATIONS.
SURVEY AND DIRECTORY OF 29 MIDDLE EASTERN AND NORTH AFRICAN COUNTRIES WITH GEOGRAPHICAL, HISTORICAL, AND ECONOMIC SURVEYS; CONCISE INFORMATION ABOUT POLITICAL, INDUSTRIAL, FINANCIAL, CULTURAL, AND EDUCATIONAL ORGANIZATIONS; AND A BIOGRAPHICAL SECTION OF PROMINENT PERSONALITIES OF THE REGION. BIENNIAL PUBLICATION FIRST ISSUED IN 1948.

0027 NEUE POLITISCHE LITERATUR; BERICHTE UBER DAS INTERNATIONALE SCHRIFTTUM ZUR POLITIK.
FRANKFURT: EUROPAISCHE VERLAGS, 1956.
MONTHLY GERMAN PERIODICAL TREATING ALL ASPECTS OF NATIONAL AND INTERNATIONAL POLITICS. CONTAINS EXTENSIVE BOOK REVIEW SECTION OF LATEST BOOKS PUBLISHED IN WESTERN WORLD.

0028 THE MIDDLE EAST.
LONDON: EUROPA PUBLICATIONS.
ENCYCLOPEDIA OF MIDDLE EAST. SURVEYS POLITICAL, INDUSTRIAL, SCIENTIFIC, FINANCIAL, CULTURAL, AND ECONOMIC ORGANIZATIONS. INCLUDES BIBLIOGRAPHIES. PUBLISHED ANNUALLY.

0029 AVTOREFERATY DISSERTATSII.
MOSCOW: AVTOREFERATY DISSERTATSY.
AUTHORS' ABSTRACTS OF RUSSIAN DISSERTATIONS AND THESES, ARRANGED BY SUBJECT, AT END OF EACH ISSUE OF "KNIZHNAIA LETOPIS, ORGAN GOSUDARSTVENNOI BIBLIOTEKI SSSR." WEEKLY SINCE 1907.

0030 THE GOVERNMENT OF SOUTH AFRICA (VOL. II)
CAPETOWN: CENTRAL NEWS AGENCY, 1908, 423 PP.
COMPARATIVE ANALYSIS OF GOVERNMENT AGENCIES IN SOUTH AFRICAN COLONIES. INCLUDES MINING LAWS, COMPARISON OF COURTS, CENSUS, RAILWAY ORGANIZATION AND FINANCES, POST OFFICE ACCOUNTS AND ORGANIZATION, HARBOR FINANCES, DISTRIBUTION OF GOVERNMENT FUNCTIONS, REVENUE SOURCES, EXPENDITURE COMPARISONS, CIVIL SERVICE DIAGRAMS, CONSTITUTIONAL PROVISIONS FOR HOUSES AND GOVERNOR, AND VOTING QUALIFICATION.

0031 CATALOGUE OF BOOKS, MANSUCRIPTS, ETC. IN THE CARIBBEANA SECTION OF THE N.M. WILLIAMS MEMORIAL ETHNOLOGICAL COLLECTION.
BOSTON: BOSTON COLLEGE LIB, 1932, 133 PP.
THIS BIBLIOGRAPHICAL LISTING OF MATERIALS SPECIALIZES IN JAMAICANA BUT INCLUDES OTHER CARIBBEAN COUNTRIES. MATERIALS ARE ARRANGED BY AREA.

0032 THE GUIDE TO CATHOLIC LITERATURE, 1888-1940.
DETROIT: WALTER ROMING & CO., 1940, 1239 PP.
SUBJECT-TITLE INDEX OF PUBLICATIONS IN ALL LANGUAGES ON ALL SUBJECTS BY CATHOLICS OR OF INTEREST TO CATHOLICS PUBLISHED 1888-1940. SINCE 1940 IT APPEARS ANNUALLY AS AN INTERNATIONAL, ANNOTATED BIBLIOGRAPHY WITH ENTRIES INDEXED BY AUTHOR-TITLE-SUBJECT, MORE THAN A QUARTER OF A MILLION BIOGRAPHICAL, DESCRIPTIVE, AND CRITICAL NOTES. INCLUDES INDEX OF MAGAZINES CITED IN THE GUIDE.

0033 INDIA QUARTERLY, A JOURNAL OF INTERNATIONAL AFFAIRS.
BOMBAY: ASIA PUBL HOUSE, 1945.
QUARTERLY, BEGUN IN 1945, WITH BOOK REVIEW SECTION AND A BIBLIOGRAPHICAL LISTING OF CURRENT INDIAN PUBLICATIONS IN SOCIAL SCIENCES. ANNUAL INDEX OF BOOKS, AUTHORS, AND ARTICLES. JOURNAL CONCERNED WITH INTERNATIONAL RELATIONS, ECONOMICS, AND WORLD POLITICS AND GOVERNMENT.

0034 GUIDE TO THE RECORDS IN THE NATIONAL ARCHIVES.
WASHINGTON: GOVT PR OFFICE, 1948, 68 PP.
RECORDS ARRANGED BY DEPARTMENTS AND BUREAUS OF US FEDERAL GOVERNMENT. TREATS LATIN AND CENTRAL AMERICA.

0036 CATALOGO GENERAL DE LA LIBRERIA ESPANOLA E HISPANOAMERICANA 1901-1930; AUTORES (5 VOLS., 1932-1951)
MADRID: CAMARAS OFFIC DEL LIBRO, 1951.
BIBLIOGRAPHY OF SPANISH-LANGUAGE BOOKS FROM SPAIN AND LATIN AMERICA. ENTRIES CLASSIFIED ALPHABETICALLY BY AUTHOR.

0037 LIST OF PUBLICATIONS (PERIODICAL OR AD HOC) ISSUED BY VARIOUS MINISTRIES OF THE GOVERNMENT OF INDIA (3RD ED.)
NEW DELHI: LOK SABHA SECRETARIAT, 1958, 282 PP.
LISTING OF PUBLICATIONS OF ALL MINISTRIES UNDER MINISTRY ISSUING MATERIAL. EVERY EFFORT IS MADE TO KEEP VOLUME UP-TO-DATE BY ISSUING ADDENDA AND CORRIGENDA TO VOLUME FROM TIME TO TIME. MATERIAL IS LISTED IN TABLE FORM WITHOUT INDEXES.

0038 "THE EMERGING COMMON MARKETS IN LATIN AMERICA."
FED. RES. BANK N.Y. MON. REV., 42 (SEPT. 60), 154-60.
DISCUSSES ECONOMIC INTEGRATION PROGRAM IN LATIN AMERICA. ANALYZES AGREEMENT TO ELIMINATE BARRIERS. APPRAISES STEPS TAKEN TO COORDINATE INDUSTRIAL DEVELOPMENT. CONSIDERS SIGNIFICANCE OF MONTEVIDEO TREATY IN DEVELOPMENT OF LATIN AMERICAN COMMON MARKET. PREDICTS INCREASE IN INVESTMENTS IN LATIN AMERICA.

0039 "AMERICAN BEHAVIORAL SCIENTIST."
AMER. BEHAVIORAL SCIENTIST, 5 (APR. 62), 1-39.
ENTIRE ISSUE DEVOTED TO SOCIAL RESEARCH AND AFRICAN STUDIES. SPECIAL ARTICLES DEVOTED TO POLITICAL RESEARCH IN NEW AFRICAN NATIONS; LEGAL STUDIES IN AFRICA; CENTERS OF AFRICAN RESEARCH; SOVIET RESEARCH ON AFRICA; AND UN SOURCE MATERIALS ON AFRICA.

0040 THREE PRELIMINARY BIBLIOGRAPHIES OF WORKS RELATED TO THE SOCIAL SCIENCES IN LATIN AMERICA.
SAN JOSE: PROG INTERAM INFO POP, 1962, 144 PP.
(TRES BIBLIOGRAFIAS PRELIMINARIAS DE OBRAS RELACIONADAS CON LAS CIENCIAS SOCIALES EN AMERICA LATINA) BIBLIOGRAPHIES OF BOOKS, PERIODICAL ARTICLES, AND PAMPHLETS. EMPHASIS IS ON BRAZIL AND MEXICO, BUT ALL COUNTRIES OF LATIN AMERICA ARE INCLUDED. PRIMARILY DEALS WITH SOCIOLOGY, ANTHROPOLOGY, AND AGRICULTURE.

0041 BRITISH AID.
LONDON: MIN OF OVERSEAS DEVEL, 1963, 260 PP.
OVERSEAS DEVELOPMENT INSTITUTE SURVEY OF BRITISH AID TO DEVELOPING COUNTRIES. COVERS BOTH GOVERNMENT AID AND PRIVATE CONTRIBUTIONS. CONTAINS SECTIONS ON FIELDS OF FINANCE, EDUCATION, AND TECHNICAL ASSISTANCE. HISTORICAL BACKGROUND ALSO OUTLINED.

0042 "FURTHER READING."
SEMINAR, (NOV. 64), 48-50.
BIBLIOGRAPHY ON NEHRU.

0043 AFRO ASIAN SOLIDARITY AGAINST IMPERIALISM.
PEKING: FOREIGN LANG PR, 1964, 439 PP.
DOCUMENTS, SPEECHES, AND PRESS INTERVIEWS FROM VISITS OF COMMUNIST CHINESE LEADERS TO 13 AFRICAN AND ASIAN COUNTRIES. INCLUDES PRINCIPALLY SPEECHES BY CHOU EN-LAI IN THE ARAB WORLD, EMERGING AFRICAN NATIONS, AND SOUTHEAST ASIA PERTAINING TO OVERTHROW OF "WESTERN IMPERIALISM" AND PROMOTION OF STATE SOVEREIGNTY.

0044 "FURTHER READING."
SEMINAR, (JUNE 64), 63-65.
BIBLIOGRAPHY ON KASHMIR AND "THE SUB-CONTINENTAL IMPLICATIONS OF A CRITICAL QUESTION."

0045 "FURTHER READING."
SEMINAR, (JULY 65), 39-41.
BIBLIOGRAPHY ON PRIMARY AND SECONDARY EDUCATION IN INDIA.

0046 "FURTHER READING."
SEMINAR, (MAY 65), 41-42.
BIBLIOGRAPHY "ON THE MANY FACETS OF... GOA'S CRISIS OF TRANSITION."

0047 "RESEARCH WORK 1965-1966."
HIST. STUDIES OF AUSTRAL. N.Z., 12 (OCT. 66), 464-473.
AN UNANNOTATED BIBLIOGRAPHY OF THESES BEGUN AND/OR COMPLETED IN THE PERIOD 1965-66. MATERIAL IN ENGLISH-LANGUAGE. 180 ENTRIES. MATERIAL IN BIBLIOGRAPHY CONSISTS OF MA AND PHD THESES DIVIDED INTO TWO CATEGORIES RESEARCH WORK 1966 THESES COMMENCED AND RESEARCH WORK 1966, THESES COMPLETED 1965-66.

0048 "FURTHER READING."
SEMINAR, (APR. 64), 50-53.
BIBLIOGRAPHY "ON THE FUNDAMENTALS ON INDIA'S FOREIGN POLICY IN A CHANGED INTERNATIONAL SITUATION."

0049 "FURTHER READING."
SEMINAR, (MAR. 66), 42-44.
BIBLIOGRAPHY ON URBAN DEVELOPMENT IN INDIA.

0050 "PROTEST AGAINST SOVIET INDUSTRIALIZATION ILLS IN LITHUANIA* A MEMORANDUM."
BALTIC REV., (JAN. 67), 22-31.
A MEMORANDUM FROM LITHUANIAN SCIENTISTS AND MEN OF LETTERS TO THE HEADS OF THE LITHUANIAN COMMUNIST PARTY AND LITHUANIAN GOVERNMENT. PROTESTS AGAINST MOSCOW-DIRECTED INDUSTRIALIZATION OF LITHUANIA, WHICH FAILS TO TAKE ANY ACCOUNT OF LITHUANIAN ECOLOGY, RESOURCES, OR NEEDS AND WHICH HAS ALREADY RESULTED IN THE POLLUTION AND DESTRUCTION OF MANY LITHUANIAN RESOURCES, ESPECIALLY SEACOASTS, FOREST.

0051 "A PROPOS DES INCITATIONS FINANCIERES AUX GROUPEMENTS DES COMMUNES: ESSAI D'INTERPRETATION."
REV. DROIT PUBLIC ET SCI. POL., (MAR.-APR. 67), 245-287.
ANALYZES NEW LEGISLATION IN FRANCE WHICH TENDED TO FINANCIALLY ENCOURAGE THE REGROUPING OF TRADITIONAL LOCAL POLITICAL SUBDIVISIONS. INTERPRETS THE MOTIVES, FORCES, AND RESULTS OF THIS LEGISLATION.

0052 JUNZ A.J.
PRESENT TRENDS IN AMERICAN NATIONAL GOVERNMENT.
LONDON: HANSARD SOCIETY, 1960, 232 PP.
STUDIES BY AMERICAN SCHOLARS ON DEVELOPMENTS IN AMERICAN GOVERNMENT IN THE FIFTIES. ESSAYS OF AMERICAN POLITICAL THOUGHT, ELECTION AND PARTY TRENDS, THE SUPREME COURT, CIVIL LIBERTIES, CONGRESS AND THE PRESIDENCY INCLUDED.

0053 "PROLOG"
DIGEST OF THE SOVIET UKRANIAN PRESS.
NEW YORK: PROLOG RES & PUB ASSN.
MONTHLY DIGEST IN ENGLISH SUMMARIZING SOVIET UKRANIAN NEWS RELEASES. FIRST PUBLISHED IN 1957, DIGEST CONTAINS EITHER FULL TEXT OF ORIGINAL OR EXCERPTS FROM ORIGINAL. PROVIDES BRIEF NOTES AT END OF EACH ISSUE AND PREFATORY COMMENTS WHEN NECESSARY. ANNUAL INDEX OF MAJOR UKRANIAN NEWSPAPERS AND PERIODICALS IS COMPILED EACH JANUARY. MATERIAL TOPICALLY ORGANIZED.

0054 ABDEL-MALEK A.
"THE CRISIS IN NASSER'S EGYPT."
NEW LEFT REV., 45 (SEPT. 67), 67-83.
EGYPT'S DEFEAT BY ISRAEL CONSTITUTED A MAJOR CRISIS IN NATIONAL DEVELOPMENT, RESULTS OF WHICH ARE NOT YET CLEAR. TO UNDERSTAND EVENTS, AUTHOR STUDIES ROLE OF THE ARMY IN EGYPTIAN POLITICS SINCE ITS SEIZURE OF POWER IN 1952. ARMY HAS ELIMINATED THE POLITICAL CLASS, WITHOUT WHICH A MODERN STATE CANNOT BE BUILT. PRESENT NEED IS TO MAKE THE MASSES POLITICALLY ACTIVE.

0055 ABEL T.
"THE ELEMENT OF DECISION IN THE PATTERN OF WAR."
AMER. SOCIOL. REV., 6 (1941), 853-859.
THE DECISION TO GO TO WAR IS NOT A SUDDEN ONE BUT MAY OFTEN BE DECIDED YEARS BEFORE OPEN CONFLICT ACTUALLY BEGINS. CRISIS MERELY INAUGURATES THE PHYSICAL CONFRONTATION ALREADY KNOWN TO BE PENDING. BELIEVES SUCH FOREKNOWLEDGE COULD BE USED TO PREVENT WARS AS WELL.

0056 ABERNATHY G.L.
PAKISTAN: A SELECTED, ANNOTATED BIBLIOGRAPHY (2ND ED., PAMPHLET)
NEW YORK: AMER INST PACIFIC REL, 1960, 39 PP.
CRITICALLY ANNOTATED BIBLIOGRAPHY OF ENGLISH-LANGUAGE MATERIALS DESIGNED FOR NONSPECIALIST. INCLUDES SUPPLEMENT LISTING MAJOR BOOKS AND ARTICLES PUBLISHED BETWEEN FEBRUARY 1957 AND 1960. COVERS MANY GOVERNMENT PUBLICATIONS. MATERIAL IS CLASSIFIED ACCORDING TO TYPE OF PUBLICATION.

0057 ABOSCH H.
THE MENACE OF THE MIRACLE: GERMANY FROM HITLER TO ADENAUER.
LONDON: COLLET'S HOLDINGS, 1962, 277 PP.
ARGUES THAT "GERMAN PROBLEM" STILL IS NOT SOLVED, THAT ALLIES HAVE SUBSTITUTED "DESIRES FOR REALITIES," AND THAT GERMANY MOST LIKELY WILL LEAD US INTO THIRD WORLD WAR. CONDEMNS REARMAMENT OF GERMANY. OFFERS RECENT DEVELOPMENTS IN GERMAN DOMESTIC AND FOREIGN POLITICS AS CONCLUSIVE PROOF.

0058 ABRAHAM W.E.
THE MIND OF AFRICA.
CHICAGO: U. CHI. PR., 1962, 206 PP., $4.00.
SETS UP A PARADIGM OF AFRICAN SOCIETY AND MAKES A DETAILED ACCOUNT OF THE AKAN, THE LARGEST AND MOST IMPORTANT OF GHANA'S LINGUISTIC GROUPS. THE LOSS AND RE-ESTABLISHMENT OF INDEPENDENCE 'ARE STUDIED IN LIGHT OF THE PROBLEMS WHICH THEY POSE FOR AFRICA, AND AFRICA'S DEVELOPING METHODS OF COPING WITH THEM.'

0059 ACAD RUMANIAN SCIENTIFIC DOCUMENTATION CTR.
RUMANIAN SCIENTIFIC ABSTRACTS: SOCIAL SCIENCES.
BUCHAREST: ACAD RUM SCI DOC CTR.
MONTHLY PERIODICAL FIRST PUBLISHED IN JANUARY, 1965, CONTAINING ABSTRACTS ON ECONOMICS, JURISPRUDENCE, PHILOSOPHY, PSYCHOLOGY, LOGIC, HISTORY, LINGUISTICS, AND HISTORY OF LITERATURE AND ART. ALL WORKS IN RUMANIAN, BUT TITLES AND ABSTRACTS GIVEN IN ENGLISH. WORKS ARE CURRENT WITH DATE OF ABSTRACT PUBLICATION. SUBJECT INDEX IN LAST ISSUE (DECEMBER) OF YEAR.

0060 ACHTERBERG E.
BERLINER HOCHFINANZ - KAISER, FURSTEN, MILLIONARE UM 1900.
FRANKFURT: FRITZ KNAPP VERLAG, 1965, 240 PP.
DISCUSSES "HIGH FINANCE" OF BANKING AND INDUSTRIAL TYCOONS IN BERLIN AT TURN OF LAST CENTURY. EXAMINES THEIR POLITICAL, SOCIAL, AND CULTURAL ACTIVITIES.

0061 ACOSTA SAIGNES M.
ESTUDIOS DE ETNOLOGIA ANTIGUA DE VENEZUELA (2ND ED.)
CARACAS: U CENTRAL DE VENEZUELA, 1961, 247 PP.
ETHNOLOGICAL STUDY OF EARLY NATIVE INHABITANTS OF VENEZUELA. DISCUSSES VARIOUS TRIBES AND THEIR INFLUENCES ON OTHER MIGRANT GROUPS IN CARIBBEAN AREA. INCLUDES ARCHEOLOGICAL DISCOVERIES OF PRE-HISPANIC CULTURES. CONTAINS BIBLIOGRAPHY.

0062 ADAM T.R.
GOVERNMENT AND POLITICS IN AFRICA SOUTH OF THE SAHARA.
NEW YORK: RANDOM, 1965, 173 PP.
'FORMS OF GOVERNMENT ADOPTED HAVE MAINTAINED THE GENERAL PATTERN EVOLVED UNDER COLONIAL DOMINATION. AFRICAN COMMUNITIES HAVE CONTENTED THEMSELVES IN THE INITIAL STAGES OF FREEDOM WITH THE OPERATION OF BASICALLY WESTERN SYSTEMS BY AND THROUGH AFRICAN PERSONNEL. MULTIRACIAL COMMUNITIES HAVE TO RECONCILE POLITICAL AUTHORITY OF MAJORITIES WITH SOCIAL SITUATIONS RESULTING FROM DEEP ETHNIC CLEAVAGES.'

0063 ADAMS J.
A DEFENSE OF THE CONSTITUTIONS OF GOVERNMENT OF THE UNITED STATES OF AMERICA.
ORIGINAL PUBLISHER NOT AVAILABLE, 1787, 390 PP.
DEMOCRACY CAN BE PRESERVED ONLY THROUGH A PROPER BALANCE OF POWERS. ENGLISH GOVERNMENT HAS LASTED FOR THIS REASON, WHILE GERMAN AND OTHER MONARCHICAL GOVERNMENTS FAILED THROUGH CONFUSION AS TO WHO HELD AUTHORITY. STRESSES IMPORTANCE OF US GOVERNMENT BEGINNING WELL. ALL NATIONS MUST HAVE POLITICAL PARTIES BUT CONTROL MUST BE THROUGH EITHER A MONARCHY AND STANDING ARMY, OR A BALANCE IN CONSTITUTION.

0064 ADAMS J.C., BARILE P.
THE GOVERNMENT OF REPUBLICAN ITALY (2ND ED.)
BOSTON: HOUGHTON MIFFLIN, 1966, 251 PP.
STUDIES ITALIAN FASCISM AND ITS EFFECT UPON PRESENT GOVERNMENTAL POLICIES. DISCUSSES MANY ASPECTS OF STRUCTURE OF GOVERNMENT TODAY. DEALS WITH THE CONSTITUTION, PARLIAMENT, PRESIDENT AND MINISTERS, ADMINISTRATION, LOCAL GOVERNMENT, JUDICAL SYSTEM, PARTY SYSTEM, ECONOMY, AND LABOR MOVEMENT. DISCUSSES IN DETAIL ITALY'S PROBLEMS IN ATTAINING LIBERAL DEMOCRACY.

0065 ADAMS R.
"POLITICS AND SOCIAL ANTHROPOLOGY IN SPANISH AMERICA."
HUM. ORGAN., 23 (SPRING 64), 1-4.
ANALYSIS OF RESEARCH POSSIBILITIES IN LATIN AMERICA LINKED WITH NATIONAL, REGIONAL AND INTERNATIONAL CONCERN. SINCE MOST ANTHROPOLOGICAL RESEARCH IS SPONSERED BY PARTICULAR GOVERNMENTS, AN APPRECIATION OF ITS INTERESTS IS NECESSARY.

0066 ADAMS R.N.
"ETHICS AND THE SOCIAL ANTHROPOLOGIST IN LATIN AMERICA."
AMER. BEHAVIORAL SCIENTIST, 10 (JUNE 67), 16-21.
DISCUSSES CONFLICTS OF INTEREST AND RESPONSIBILITIES AS WELL AS WIDELY DIVERGENT KINDS OF PEOPLE INVOLVED IN POLICY-MAKING IN DEVELOPING NATIONS. RELATES THESE DIFFERENCES AND CONFLICTS TO THE DIFFERING NATURE OF DEVELOPMENT IN NORTH AND LATIN AMERICA. HOPES THAT ANTHROPOLOGICAL SCHOLARS OF US AND LATIN AMERICA CAN FORM A SCHOLARLY COMMUNITY TO SOLVE PROBLEMS OF HEMISPHERE.

0067 ADAMS T.W.
"THE FIRST REPUBLIC OF CYPRUS: A REVIEW OF AN UNWORKABLE CONSTITUTION."
WESTERN POLIT. QUART., 19 (SEPT. 66), 475-490.
DISCUSSES FORMATION, STRUCTURE, AND FAILURE OF FIRST CONSTITUTION OF CYPRUS. ANALYZES MAJOR ELEMENTS OF CONSTITUTION, SHOWING FLAWS IN PROVISIONS FOR INDIVIDUAL RIGHTS. DESCRIBES AMENDMENT PROCEDURES AND EVALUATES FUTURE OF CONSTITUTIONAL SYSTEM IN CYPRUS.

0068 ADENAUER K.
MEMOIRS 1945-53.
CHICAGO: HENRY REGNERY CO, 1965, 478 PP., LC#65-26906.
TRANSLATION OF ADENAUER'S MEMOIRS FROM END OF WWII TO US VISIT IN 1953. EXAMINES RELATIONS WITH ALLIES AND OCCUPATION, ESTABLISHMENT OF FEDERAL REPUBLIC, FOREIGN POLICY, REARMAMENT, MEMBERSHIP IN NATO, AND FULL SOVEREIGNTY.

0069 ADENAUER K.
MEINE ERINNERUNGEN, 1945-53 (VOL. I), 1953-55 (VOL. II)
STUTTGART: DEUTSCHE VERLAGSANST, 1965, 1145 PP.
MEMOIRS OF KONRAD ADENAUER, BEGINNING WITH COLLAPSE OF GERMANY IN 1945, COVERING POSTWAR DEVELOPMENT OF GERMANY, PRIMARILY FROM PERSPECTIVES OF POLITICS AND INTERNATIONAL RELATIONS.

0070 ADMINISTRATIVE STAFF COLLEGE
THE ACCOUNTABILITY OF GOVERNMENT DEPARTMENTS (PAMPHLET) (REV. ED.)
HENLEY-ON-THAMES: ADMIN STAFF C, 1966, 49 PP.
DISCUSSES CONCEPT OF ACCOUNTABILITY OR PROCEDURE OF MINISTER'S BEING CALLED UPON BY PARLIAMENT TO JUSTIFY HIS ACTIONS OR ADVICE. INCLUDES PERSONS ACCOUNTABLE AND PROCESS AS IT HAS DEVELOPED IN DIFFERENT DEPARTMENTS.

0071 ADNITT F.W.
"THE RISE OF ENGLISH RADICALISM -- PART 2."
CONTEMPORARY REV., 210 (MAY 67), 258-272.
A RAPID SURVEY OF ENGLISH RADICALISM FROM THE FRENCH REVOLUTION TO 1901, INCLUDING SKETCHES OF THE CAREERS AND IDEAS OF LEADING RADICALS LIKE PAINE, BENTHAM, MILL, HOBHOUSE, AND THE CHARTISTS.

0072 ADOKO A.
"THE CONSTITUTION OF UGANDA."
TRANSITION, 7 (OCT. 67), 10-12.
ANALYZES AND REJECTS MOST CRITICISM OF UGANDAN CONSTITUTION, POINTING OUT MERITS OF IT. AUTHOR BELIEVES THAT NEW CONSTITUTION WILL INSPIRE NATIONAL UNITY. DISCUSSES ABOLITION OF KINGSHIP, METHODS FOR PRESIDENTIAL REMOVAL, EXECUTIVE CONTROL OVER THE ARMY, AND THE JUDICIAL PROCESS.

0073 ADRIAN C.R.
GOVERNING OVER FIFTY STATES AND THEIR COMMUNITIES.
NEW YORK: MCGRAW HILL, 1963, 130 PP., LC#63-13132.
DISCUSSION OF STATE AND LOCAL GOVERNMENT, RELATIONS TO FEDERAL GOVERNMENT AND COMPARISON OF SYSTEMS INCLUDING FUNCTIONS AND STRUCTURE OF COURTS, POLITICS, LEGISLATURES, AND EXECUTIVES.

0074 ADU A.L.
THE CIVIL SERVICE IN NEW AFRICAN STATES.
NEW YORK: FREDERICK PRAEGER, 1965, 242 PP., LC#65-12315.
DESCRIBES PROBLEMS AND PRINCIPLES RELATING TO GROWTH AND DEVELOPMENT OF CIVIL SERVICES IN FORMER BRITISH COLONIAL TERRITORIES. DRAWS ON EXPERIENCES IN GHANA AND OTHER STATES OF WEST AND EAST AFRICA. DESCRIBES STRUCTURE, FUNCTION, AND POLICY OF ADMINISTRATIVE MACHINERY.

0075 AFRICAN BIBLIOGRAPHIC CENTER
A CURRENT BIBLIOGRAPHY ON AFRICAN AFFAIRS.
WASHINGTON: AFRICAN BIBLIOG CTR.
BIMONTHLY EVALUATION AND REVIEWS OF CURRENT PUBLICATIONS FROM FOREIGN AND DOMESTIC PUBLISHING HOUSES. ALSO INCLUDES JOURNAL ARTICLES. ITEMS ARRANGED BY GENERAL SUBJECT AND BY GEOGRAPHICAL SUBJECT SECTION. AUTHOR INDEX. INCLUDES TOPICS SUCH AS AFRICAN STUDIES, BIBLIOGRAPHY, CIVILIZATION, COMMERCE, FOREIGN ECONOMIC ASSISTANCE, POLITICS AND GOVERNMENT, AND TECHNICAL ASSISTANCE.

0076 AFRIFA A.A.
THE GHANA COUP.
NEW YORK: HUMANITIES PRESS, 1966, 144 PP., LC#66-30177.
ANALYSIS OF FEBRUARY 24TH, 1966 COUP IN GHANA AGAINST KWAME NKRUMAH BY MEMBER OF INSURGENT FORCE. PRESENTS PERSONAL BACKGROUND AND DESCRIPTION OF GHANAIAN LIFE PRIOR AND DURING NKRUMAH ERA. EXPLAINS REASON FOR AND PROCEDURE INVOLVED IN SUCCESSFUL COUP AND PLANS OF NEW LEADERS FOR FUTURE.

0077 AGGARWALA R.C.
CONSTITUTIONAL HISTORY OF INDIA AND NATIONAL MOVEMENT INCLUDING COMPARATIVE STUDY OF MODERN INDIA CONSTITUTION.
NEW DELHI: S CHAND AND CO, 1964, 154 PP.
DEALS WITH CONSTITUTIONAL DEVELOPMENT OF INDIA, NATIONAL MOVEMENTS, AND MODERN INDIA CONSTITUTION. TRACES BRITISH RULE FROM REGULATING ACT, 1773, TO INDIAN INDEPENDENCE ACT. DISCUSSES NATIONAL SOCIAL, RELIGIOUS, TERRORIST, AND REVOLUTIONARY MOVEMENTS. NOTES STRUCTURE AND ADMINISTRATION OF CONSTITUTION, COMPARES WITH OTHER SYSTEMS, AND BRIEFLY DESCRIBES EVOLUTION OF CERTAIN GOVERNMENT AGENCIES.

0078 AGGARWALA R.N.
FINANCIAL COMMITTEES OF THE INDIAN PARLIAMENT: A STUDY IN PARLIAMENTARY CONTROL OVER PUBLIC EXPENDITURE.
NEW DELHI: S CHAND AND CO, 1966, 490 PP.
DESCRIBES INDIAN SYSTEM OF PARLIAMENTARY CONTROL OVER PUBLIC EXPENDITURE THROUGH SPECIAL COMMITTEES FROM 1950 TO 1964. DISCUSSES RESULTS OF THEIR CONTROL AND COMPARES THEM TO RESULTS OF ENGLISH PARLIAMENTARY COMMITTEES.

0079 AGGER R.E., GOLDRICH D., SWANSON B.E.
THE RULERS AND THE RULED: POLITICAL POWER AND IMPOTENCE IN AMERICAN COMMUNITIES.
NEW YORK: JOHN WILEY, 1964, 789 PP.
A STUDY OF THE DECISION-MAKING PROCESS AT THE LOCAL LEVEL. DESCRIBES, ANALYZES, AND COMPARES THE POWER STRUCTURE OF FOUR FICTITIOUS AMERICAN COMMUNITIES, FARMDALE, ORETOWN, PETROPOLIS, AND METROVILLE. COMBINES EMPIRICAL STUDIES WITH GENERAL THEORY BUILDING AND EVOLVES VARIOUS NEW CONCEPTS SUCH AS DEVELOPED DEMOCRACY.

0080 AHMED Z.
DUSK AND DAWN IN VILLAGE INDIA.
NEW YORK: FREDERICK PRAEGER, 1966, 144 PP., LC#66-11565.
STORY OF LIFE IN RURAL INDIAN VILLAGE DIRECTLY BEFORE AND AFTER INDEPENDENCE FROM BRITAIN. DISCUSSES NOTICEABLE SOCIAL CHANGES.

0081 AHN L.A.
FUNFZIG JAHRE ZWISCHEN INFLATION UND DEFLATION.
TUBINGEN: J C B MOHR, 1963, 247 PP.
DISCUSSES INFLATIONARY AND DEFLATIONARY TENDENCIES IN GERMANY SINCE WWI. EXAMINES CRISIS IN 1929, CONFLICT OVER DOLLAR, AND GOLD CRISES IN RECENT YEARS.

0082 AIKEN C.
"THE BRITISH BUREAUCRACY AND THE ORIGINS OF PARLIAMENTARY DEMOCRACY"
AM. POL. SCI. REV., 33 (FEB. 39), 26-46.
A STUDY "OF THE FACTORS THAT ARE AT WORK IN THE DETERMINATION OF BRITISH LEGISLATIVE POLICY." THE WORK OF A MINISTER AS AN INDIVIDUAL IS CONSIDERED, AS WELL AS THE FUNCTIONING OF CABINET MINISTERS IN THEIR QUASI-CORPORATE CAPACITY AND THE ORGANIZATION AND FUNCTIONS OF THE CIVIL SERVICE. SERVICE.

0083 AIR FORCE ACADEMY ASSEMBLY
CULTURAL AFFAIRS AND FOREIGN RELATIONS.
COLORADO SPRINGS: USAF ACADEMY, 1966, 98 PP.
REPORT OF AIR FORCE ACADEMY SPONSORED STUDENT CONFERENCE ON CENTRALITY OF CULTURAL DIMENSION IN FOREIGN RELATIONS. CONCLUDE THAT CULTURAL RELATIONS AS TYPIFIED BY CULTURAL EXCHANGE PROGRAMS MERIT INCREASED PRIORITY.

0084 AIR UNIVERSITY LIBRARY
LATIN AMERICA, SELECTED REFERENCES.
MONTGOMERY: AIR U, 1965, 43 PP.
ITEMS ARRANGED BY TYPE OF PUBLICATION: BOOKS, PERIODICALS, DOCUMENTS - UNDER SUBJECT HEADINGS. TREATS SOURCES ON OAS, COMMUNISM IN LATIN AMERICA, ECONOMICS, ROLE OF THE MILITARY, POLITICS, GOVERNMENT, AND EDUCATION.

0085 AIYAR S.P.
FEDERALISM AND SOCIAL CHANGE.
LONDON: ASIA PUBL HOUSE, 1961, 199 PP.
ANALYZES GOVERNMENTS AND FEDERALISM, THEIR ECONOMIC, SOCIAL, AND POLITICAL EFFECTS IN CANADA, AUSTRALIA, AND US. STUDIES EVOLUTION OF FEDERAL PRINCIPLE AND COMPARES THEORY WITH PRACTICE.

0086 AIYAR S.P., SRINIVASAN R.
STUDIES IN INDIAN DEMOCRACY.
NEW DELHI: ALLIED PUBLISHERS, 1965, 779 PP.
COLLECTION OF DESCRIPTIVE AND ANALYTICAL ESSAYS ON POLITICAL, SOCIOLOGICAL, ECONOMIC, AND CULTURAL ASPECTS OF INDIAN DEMOCRACY. INTRODUCTION PROVIDES BRIEF HISTORY OF INDIA SINCE INDEPENDENCE. CHAPTERS CLASSIFY TOPICS INTO HISTORICAL, INSTITUTIONAL AND SOCIOLOGICAL CATEGORIES, WITH ESSAYS ON PUBLIC OPINION, PRESSURE GROUPS, AND POLITICAL PARTIES.

0087 AIYAR S.P. ED.
PERSPECTIVES ON THE WELFARE STATE.
BOMBAY: MANAKTALAS, 1966, 378 PP.
COLLECTION OF ESSAYS PRESENTING VARYING VIEWPOINTS ON WELFARE STATE. PART ONE INCLUDES HISTORICAL DEVELOPMENT IN ENGLAND AND US AND APPROACHES TO ITS DEFINITION. PART TWO APPLIES THEORY TO INDIA'S SITUATION.

0088 AKE C.
"POLITICAL INTEGRATION AND POLITICAL STABILITY."
WORLD POLITICS, 19 (APR. 67), 486-499.
A RESEARCH NOTE ON THE PROBLEM OF POLITICAL INTEGRATION. HYPOTHESIS IS THAT THE POLITICAL SYSTEM MAXIMIZES ITS CHANCES FOR ACHIEVING A HIGH DEGREE OF INTEGRATION AND REMAINING STABLE IF IT IS AUTHORITARIAN, CONSENSUAL, IDENFIC, AND PATERNAL. DISCUSSES THESE CHARACTERISTICS AND TESTS THE HYPOTHESIS.

0089 AKIGA
AKIGA'S STORY: THE TIV TRIBE AS SEEN BY ONE OF ITS MEMBERS.
LONDON: OXFORD U PR, 1939, 436 PP.
NIGERIAN NATIVE'S RECORD OF STORIES AND CUSTOMS OF HIS TRIBE. INCLUDES LEGENDS AND TALES WHICH MIGHT HAVE BEEN LOST WITH DEATH OF PRESENT ELDERS OF TRIBE.

0090 AKZIN B.
STATE AND NATION.
LONDON: HUTCHINSON U LIBRARY, 1964, 214 PP.
INQUIRES INTO RELATIONSHIP OF TWO MAJOR SOCIAL PHENOMENA: THE POLITICAL PHENOMENON OF THE STATE, AND THE ETHNIC PHENOMENON OF THE NATION; STUDIES PARTS PLAYED BY EACH FACTOR IN AREAS OF HUMAN AFFAIRS, SUCH AS NATIONALISM, PLURALISM, SECESSION, AND INTEGRATION.

0091 ALBA V.
THE MEXICANS; THE MAKING OF A NATION.
NEW YORK: FREDERICK PRAEGER, 1967, 250 PP.
EXAMINES UNIFICATION OF DIVERSE ATTITUDES, PEOPLES, AND AREAS INTO NATION OF MEXICO. ESTIMATES THAT ONLY VERY SMALL PERCENTAGE OF PEOPLE ARE POLITICALLY AWARE. MAINTAINS THAT MEXICO IS DEVELOPING ECONOMICALLY AND POLITICALLY, IS SOCIALLY CONSERVATIVE, AND IS CULTURALLY DISORIENTED. THIS DISORIENTATION RESULTS FROM TRANSITIONAL PHASE IN NATIONHOOD THAT WILL BE OVERCOME.

0092 ALBI F.
TRATADO DE LOS MODOS DE GESTION DE LAS CORPORACIONES LOCALES
MADRID: AGUILAR, 1960, 771 PP.
EXAMINES MUNICIPAL PUBLIC ADMINISTRATION IN SPAIN IN ITS LEGAL AND FUNCTIONAL ASPECTS. DISCUSSES RESPONSIBILITIES OF MUNICIPAL GOVERNMENT AS OPPOSED TO NATIONAL GOVERNMENT, EXPLAINING FINANCIAL AND POLITICAL OBLIGATION OF URBAN GOVERNMENT TO MEET NEEDS OF LOCAL POPULATION. COVERS PROCESS OF INCORPORATION AND MANAGEMENT.

0093 ALBINSKI H.S.
"POLITICS AND BICULTURISM IN CANADA: THE FLAG DEBATE."
AUSTRAL. J. OF POL. AND HIST., 13 (AUG. 67), 169-188.
CONCERNS 1965 DEBATE OVER CANADIAN FLAG. THE PARLIAMENTARY BATTLE THAT OCCURRED IS DISCUSSED WITHIN THE CONTEXT OF CANADIAN SOCIETY AND THE EFFECT THAT CANADA'S BINATIONAL CHARACTER HAS ON POLITICS. EMPHASIZES THAT A DELICATELY BALANCED SYSTEM OF RESPONSIBLE GOVERNMENT CANNOT EFFECTIVELY FUNCTION WITHOUT A HIGH LEVEL OF PUBLIC COHESION AND CONSENSUS.

0094 ALBINSKI H.S. ED., PETTIT L.K. ED.
EUROPEAN POLITICAL PROCESSES: ESSAYS AND READINGS.
NEW YORK: ALLYN AND BACON, 1967, 448 PP., LC#67-28270.
RELATES GENERAL POLTICAL PHENOMENA TO PARTICULAR POLITICAL SYSTEMS. EACH SECTION TREATS A FEATURE OR FUNCTION OF THE POLITICAL PROCESS--CULTURE AND IDEOLOGY, GROUP EXPRESSION OF INTERESTS, PARTY SYSTEMS, STRUCTURAL COMPONENTS OF POLICY-MAKING, ETC. EMPHASIS ON PROCESS; THE CONTINUITY AND DYNAMIC NATURE OF POLITICS.

0095 ALBRECHT-CARRIE R.
ITALY FROM NAPOLEON TO MUSSOLINI.
NEW YORK: COLUMBIA U PRESS, 1950, 314 PP.
SURVEYS THE DEVELOPMENT OF ITALY FROM THE BEGINNING OF THE NINETEENTH CENTURY, LEADING TO THE CLIMAX OF FASCISM. ANALYZES HOW AND WHY FASCISM OCCURRED. DISCUSSES THE BACKGROUND OF MODERN ITALY, ITALY AS A NATIONAL STATE, THE TRANSITION OF WAR, AND THE FASCIST EPISODE.

0096 ALBRECHT-CARRIE R.
FRANCE, EUROPE AND THE TWO WORLD WARS.
GENEVA: LIBRAIRIE DROZ, 1960, 339 PP.
COVERS FRENCH AND EUROPEAN POLITICAL DEVELOPMENTS, FROM 1914 TO 1936. CONSIDERS THE RELATIONSHIP BETWEEN THE FRENCH DOMESTIC SITUATION AND THE FOREIGN POLICY OF FRANCE. EMPHASIZES THE EFFECTS OF WWI AND BETWEEN-WAR FRENCH POLICIES, AND HOW THE FRENCH PEOPLE WOULD NOT FACE THE UNPLEASANT REALITIES OF DEMOCRATIC POWER.

0097 ALBRECHT M.C.
"THE RELATIONSHIP OF LITERATURE AND SOCIETY."
AMER. J. OF SOCIOLOGY, 59 (MAR. 54), 425-436.
EVALUATES LITERATURE AS REFLECTION OF NORMS AND VALUES IN SOCIETY, REVEALING ETHICS, CLASS STRUGGLE, AND CERTAIN TYPES OF SOCIAL FACT. THROUGH CIRCULAR PROCESS LITERATURE SOMETIMES REINFORCES TRENDS IT DISCUSSES, ACCORDING TO EXAMPLES CITED. ALSO CONSIDERS LITERATURE AS MEDIUM FOR CROSS-CULTURAL UNDERSTANDING.

0098 ALDERFER H., STEVENS L.M..
A BIBLIOGRAPHY OF AFRICAN GOVERNMENT: 1950-1964.
LINCOLN: LINCOLN U, 1964, 119 PP.
OVER 1,500 ENTRIES COMPRISED OF BOOKS AND MAGAZINE ARTICLES ON RECENT GOVERNMENT IN AFRICAN STATES AND ORGANIZED TERRITORIES. ARRANGED ACCORDING TO GEOGRAPHIC REGIONS AND INDIVIDUAL COUNTRIES. ENTRIES ARE IN FRENCH AND ENGLISH. ENTRIES PUBLISHED FROM 1950-1964.

0099 ALEXANDER A.
"CANADA'S PARLIAMENTARY SECRETARIES: THEIR POLITICAL AND CONSTITUTIONAL POSITION."
PARLIMENTARY AFFAIRS, 20 (SUMMER 67), 248-257.
DISCUSSES DIFFERENCES IN FORMAL AND INFORMAL ASPECTS OF PARLIAMENTARY SECRETARIES. GIVES REASONS FOR THEIR INCREASING NUMBERS. EXPLAINS WHY MULTIPLE-TIER GOVERNING STRUCTURE HAS NOT BEEN ADOPTED. CONTRASTS CANADIAN AND BRITISH SYSTEMS OF GOVERNMENT.

0100 ALEXANDER L.
"WAR CRIMES, THEIR SOCIAL-PSYCHOLOGICAL ASPECTS."
AMER. J. PSYCHIAT., 105 (SEPT. 48), 170-77.
DISCUSSES THE WAR CRIME OF THE SUBMISSION OF MEMBERS OF THE MEDICAL PROFESSION IN NAZI GERMANY TO 'GROUP PRESSURE ALTHOUGH NO OVERT COERCION WAS BROUGHT TO BEAR'.

0101 ALEXANDER L.M.
WORLD POLITICAL PATTERNS.
SKOKIE: RAND MCNALLY & CO, 1957, 516 PP., LC#57-8445.
ANALYSIS OF COMPLEX PATTERNS OF POLITICAL ORGANIZATION THROUGHOUT WORLD ON CONTINENTAL, NATIONAL, AND LOCAL LEVELS. ATTEMPTS TO DETERMINE INFLUENCE OF NATIONALISM, IMPERIALISM, AND OTHER SOCIO-POLITICAL FORCES ON PATTERN OF POLITICAL CONTROL OF VARIOUS GEOGRAPHIC REGIONS. PROVIDES INTRODUCTION TO GEOGRAPHIC BASIS OF INTERNATIONAL AFFAIRS. PRIMARILY INTENDED FOR STUDENTS.

0102 ALEXANDER R.J.
ORGANIZED LABOR IN LATIN AMERICA.
NEW YORK: FREE PRESS OF GLENCOE, 1965, 274 PP., LC#65-23024.
SYMPATHETIC ACCOUNT OF DEVELOPMENT AND NATIONAL ROLE OF LATIN AMERICAN ORGANIZED LABOR. GENERAL STUDIES OF ECONOMIC AND SOCIAL BACKGROUND OF LABOR MOVEMENT, POLITICALIZATION OF MOVEMENT, AND COLLECTIVE BARGAINING AND ITS SUBSTITUTES. ANALYSES OF LABOR MOVEMENT IN 13 INDIVIDUAL COUNTRIES. SHORT BIBLIOGRAPHICAL NOTE.

0103 ALFIERI D.
DICTATORS FACE TO FACE.
NEW YORK: NEW YORK U PR, 1955, 307 PP., LC#56-5399.
PERSONAL ACCOUNT BY ITALIAN AMBASSADOR TO HITLER OF MAJOR EVENTS AND ISSUES MARKING WARTIME RELATIONSHIPS BETWEEN GERMANY AND ITALY. DESCRIBES EVENTS DURING SEVERAL MAJOR MILITARY AND DIPLOMATIC DEVELOPMENTS AND FOCUSES ON ATTITUDES AND BEHAVIOR OF HITLER, MUSSOLINI, AND HIGH-RANKING STATESMEN AND MILITARY LEADERS.

0104 ALGER C.F.
"INTERNATIONALIZING COLLEGES AND UNIVERSITIES."
INTERNATIONAL STUDIES, 11 (JUNE 67), 126-134.
SUGGESTS THAT STUDY OF INTERNATIONAL RELATIONS REQUIRES MULTIDISCIPLINARY APPROACH TO ELIMINATE PRESENT PROLIFERATION OF SEVERAL DEPARTMENTS INVOLVED IN SAME SUBJECT AREA FROM DIFFERENT APPROACHES. ADVOCATES LESS EMPHASIS ON COMPARATIVE STUDIES. PROPOSES SYSTEM FOR COORDINATING FUNCTION OF UNIVERSITIES TO FACILITATE MULTIDISCIPLINARY STUDIES.

0105 ALLEN J.S.
WORLD MONOPOLY AND PEACE.
NEW YORK: INTERNATIONAL PUBLRS, 1946, 288 PP.
ANALYSIS OF MONOPOLISTIC CAPITALISM AND IMPERIALISM FOCUSING ON POST-WWII INTERNATIONAL ECONOMIC CONDITIONS. CONSIDERS CAUSE-EFFECT RELATIONSHIP BETWEEN MONOPOLISTIC CAPITALISM AND WAR. DISCUSSES SHIFT OF POWER RELATIONS AMONG CAPITALISTIC NATIONS AS RESULT OF WWII. COUNTRIES DISCUSSED INCLUDE GERMANY, GREAT BRITAIN, US, AND USSR.

0106 ALLEN W.S.
THE NAZI SEIZURE OF POWER.
CHICAGO: QUADRANGLE BOOKS, INC, 1965, 345 PP., LC#65-10378.
STUDIES HISTORY OF SMALL TOWN IN GERMANY WITH REGARD TO ITS NAZIFICATION. CLAIMING LOCAL MEASURES AS THE KEY TO ESTABLISHING TOTALITARIANISM IN GERMANY, ATTEMPTS TO ANALYZE PROCESSES AND METHODS INSTRUMENTAL IN HITLER'S TAKEOVER, USING THALBURG IN HANOVER AS EXAMPLE. DISCUSSES DIFFERENCES IN THIS AND OTHER TOWNS, EXAMINING SIMILARITIES AND DIFFERENCES, 1930-1933.

0107 ALLIGHAN G.
VERWOERD - THE END.
LONDON: T V BOARDMAN & CO, 1961, 228 PP.
STUDY OF UNION OF SOUTH AFRICA AS SEEN IN ACTIONS OF PRIME MINISTER HENDRIK VERWOERD. DEALS WITH AFRIKANER NATURE OF WHITE POPULATION AND ITS ATTITUDE TOWARD BRITAIN AND BLACK AFRICAN. DESCRIBES APARTHEID SYSTEM AND TIGHT CONTROL OF GOVERNMENT ON ITS SOCIETY.

0108 ALLWORTH E. ED.
CENTRAL ASIA: A CENTURY OF RUSSIAN RULE.
NEW YORK: COLUMBIA U PRESS, 1967, 552 PP., LC#66-16288.
ANTHOLOGY DISCUSSES VARIOUS ASPECTS OF CENTRAL ASIAN SOCIETY AND CULTURE, 1865-1965. INCLUDES ARTICLES ON PEOPLES, LANGUAGES, MIGRATIONS, POPULATION, GEOLOGY, THE CZARS' CONQUERING OF NEW TERRITORIES, ORGANIZING AND COLONIZING OF NEW TERRITORIES, RISE OF NATIONALISM, THE 1917 REVOLUTION, AGRICULTURAL DEVELOPMENT, INDUSTRIALIZATION, AND ASIAN ART AND LITERATURE.

0109 ALMAGRO BASCH M.
ORIGEN Y FORMACION DEL PUEBLO HISPANO.
BARCELONA: VERGARA EDITORIAL, 1958, 165 PP.
ANTHROPOLOGICAL AND SOCIOLOGICAL ANALYSIS OF DEVELOPMENT OF MAN AND SOCIETY ON IBERIAN PENINSULA. COVERS PREHISTORIC SOCIETY AND CHANGES IN CULTURE FROM INFLUENCE OF INVADING ROMANS, GERMANIC TRIBES, AND ISLAM. DISCUSSES RACIAL COMPOSITION AND CONTRIBUTIONS OF VARIOUS ETHNIC GROUPS TO PRESENT HISPANIC CULTURE.

0110 ALMOND G.A.
"THE CHRISTIAN PARTIES OF WESTEN EUROPE."
WORLD POLIT., 1 (OCT. 48), 30-58.
CHARACTERIZES WESTERN EUROPEAN CATHOLIC AND CHRISTIAN DEMOCRATIC PARTIES SINCE WORLD WAR TWO, SHOWING POLITICAL AND SOCIAL COMPOSITION, THEIR INTERNATIONAL TIES, AND THEIR RELATIONSHIP TO CHURCH HIERARCHIES AND OTHER POLITICAL MOVEMENTS. CONCLUDES PARTIES MAY FORM 'THIRD FORCE' TO COUNTER COMMUNISM AND EXTREME CONSERVATISM.

0111 ALMOND G.A.
"COMPARATIVE POLITICAL SYSTEMS" (BMR)"
J. OF POLITICS, 18 (AUG. 56), 391-409.
SUGGESTS HOW APPLICATION OF CERTAIN SOCIOLOGICAL AND

ANTHROPOLOGICAL CONCEPTS MAY FACILITATE SYSTEMATIC COMPARISON AMONG MAJOR TYPES OF POLITICAL SYSTEMS. DEALS PARTICULARLY WITH PROBLEM OF CLASSIFYING POLITICAL SYSTEMS OF TODAY.

0112 ALMOND G.A. ED., COLEMAN J.S. ED.
THE POLITICS OF THE DEVELOPING AREAS.
PRINCETON: U. PR., 1960, 591 PP.
PRESENTS A THEORETICAL FRAMEWORK FOR COMPARATIVE ANALYSIS OF POLITICAL SYSTEMS. APPLIES THIS APPROACH TO DEVELOPING AREAS: SOUTHEAST ASIA, SOUTH ASIA, SUB-SAHARAN AFRICA, NEAR EAST AND LATIN AMERICA. CONCENTRATES ON POLITICAL RATHER THAN GOVERNMENTAL FUNCTION AND STRUCTURE IN THESE ANALYSES.

0113 ALMOND G.A., VERBA S.
THE CIVIC CULTURE: POLITICAL ATTITUDES AND DEMOCRACY IN FIVE NATIONS.
PRINCETON: PRINCETON U PRESS, 1963, 562 PP., LC#63-12666.
POLITICO-CULTURAL STUDY OF CIVIC VIRTUE AND ITS EFFECTIVE USE IN DEMOCRACIES. ANALYZES KINDS OF COMMUNITY LIFE, SOCIAL ORGANIZATION, AND CHILD-REARING THAT FOSTER DEVELOPMENT OF SOCIAL PATTERNS. CONTRASTS STABLE CULTURES OF US AND BRITAIN WITH GERMANY'S, HANDICAPPED BY UNDERLYING POLITICAL ATTITUDES; MEXICO'S, WITH LESSER ASPIRATIONS; AND ITALY'S, LOWEST IN POTENTIAL. USES CROSS-SECTION INTERVIEWS.

0114 ALPANDER G.G.
"ENTREPRENEURS AND PRIVATE ENTERPRISE IN TURKEY."
BUSINESS TOPICS, 15 (SPRING 67), 59-68.
DISCUSSES DEVELOPMENT OF PRIVATE ENTERPRISE IN TURKEY, WHERE PRIVATE CORPORATE ENTERPRISE HAS HAD LITTLE RECEPTIVITY; EXAMINES REASONS WHY. FOCUSES ON FIRMS THAT DO EXIST AND TREATS GROWTH PATTERNS, GEOGRAPHICAL DISTRIBUTION, PUBLIC POLICY, WHOLESALING, AND RETAILING. ANALYZES SOCIOLOGICAL AND BEHAVIORAL CHARACTERISTICS OF ENTREPRENEURS.

0115 ALSTON P.L.
STATE EDUCATION AND SOCIAL CHANGE IN THE RUSSIAN EMPIRE 1871-1914 (PAPER)
BERKELEY: UNIVERSITY OF CALIF, 1961, 486 PP.
EXAMINES STATE SECONDARY EDUCATION FOR MALES IN A TIME OF INTENSE AND SYSTEMATIC CONTACT, CONFLICT, AND COOPERATION BETWEEN TSARIST STATE AND RUSSIAN SOCIETY: THE 50 YEARS PRIOR TO WWI. SHOWS HOW URBAN ELEMENTS OF SOCIETY WERE INCREASINGLY ATTRACTED TO SCHOOLS AS THE AGENCY FOR ORDERLY AND POPULAR PURSUIT OF PROFESSIONAL OPPORTUNITY, SOCIAL ADVANCEMENT, AND POLITICAL EMANCIPATION.

0116 ALTBACH P.
"STUDENT POLITICS."
TRANSITION, 6 (JAN. 67), 25-27.
SURVEYS WORLD-WIDE STUDENT MOVEMENTS AND MAKES COMPARIONS BETWEEN THOSE IN DEVELOPED AND UNDERDEVELOPED COUNTRIES.

0117 ALTON T.P., KORBONSKI A. ET AL.
POLISH NATIONAL INCOME AND PRODUCT IN 1954, 1955, AND 1956.
NEW YORK: COLUMBIA U PRESS, 1965, 252 PP., LC#65-13617.
ESTIMATES ACTUAL POLISH MARKET PRICES, GNP/YEAR, AND ITS BASIS AND ALLOCATION WITH RESPECT TO CONSUMPTION, INVESTMENT, NATIONAL DEFENSE, AND GOVERNMENT ADMINISTRATION. BECAUSE OF GOVERNMENT PRICE MANIPULATION, OFFICIAL PRICES FAIL TO REFLECT PRODUCTION COSTS. HENCE, REVALUES ALL COMPONENTS OF NATIONAL INCOME IN TERMS OF REAL FACTOR COST.

0118 ALVIM J.C.
A REVOLUCAO SEM RUMO.
RIO DE JANEIRO: EDICOES DO VAL, 1964, 92 PP.
ANALYZES BRAZILIAN NEED FOR REVOLUTION TO GAIN PROGRESS IN UNDEVELOPED NATION. EXAMINES REASONS BEHIND 1964 REVOLT AND NEED TO REFORM BRAZIL TO ACHIEVE SOCIAL AND ECONOMIC BALANCE NATIONALLY AND INTERNATIONALLY. DISCUSSES FAULTS OF NEW GOVERNMENT IN OVERLY LIMITING DEMOCRACY IN ATTEMPT TO RESTORE ORDER.

0119 AMER ENTERPRISE INST PUB POL
SIGNIFICANT ISSUES IN ECONOMIC AID TO DEVELOPING COUNTRIES.
MENLO PARK: STANFORD U RES INST, 1960, 75 PP., LC#60-1291.
DETAILED ANALYSIS OF PROGRAMS, TRENDS, AND ISSUES THAT HAVE BEEN CENTRALLY INVOLVED IN US POLICIES ON ECONOMIC AID TO PROMOTE PROGRESS IN UNDERDEVELOPED COUNTRIES. FOCUSES ON SEVERAL SPECIFIC SITUATIONS OCCURRING DURING POST-WWII ERA; CONSIDERS FOREIGN AID ACTIVITIES OF ALLIES OF US AND OF INTERNATIONAL AGENCIES.

0120 AMERASINGHE C.F.
"SOME LEGAL PROBLEMS OF STATE TRADING IN SOUTHEAST ASIA."
VANDERBILT LAW REV., 20 (MAR. 67), 257-277.
DISCUSSES LEGAL PROBLEMS OF STATE TRADING IN SOUTHEAST ASIA. CONCERNED WITH ASPECTS OF THE INTERNATIONAL LEGAL PROBLEMS WHICH ARISE WHERE ONE PARTY IN THE TRADING TRANSACTION IS THE STATE OR A STATE ENTITY.

0121 AMERICAN COUNCIL LEARNED SOC
GOVERNMENT UNDER LAW AND THE INDIVIDUAL.
NEW YORK: AMER COUN LEARNED SOC, 1957, 73 PP., LC#57-12733.
DISCUSSIONS ON INDIVIDUAL FREEDOM IN WESTERN SOCIETY AND ITS ECONOMIC, POLITICAL, AND PHILOSOPHICAL IMPLICATIONS. COMPARES PRINCIPLES AND INSTITUTIONS OF GOVERNMENT UNDER LAW IN WEST TO PARALLEL PRINCIPLES AND INSTITUTIONS IN RUSSIAN, CHINESE, AND ISLAMIC SOCIETIES.

0122 AMERICAN FRIENDS SERVICE COMM
IN PLACE OF WAR.
NEW YORK: GROSSMAN PUBL, 1967, 115 PP., LC#67-21234.
DEVOTED TO STRATEGY OF NONVIOLENT DEFENSE. BEGINS WITH SHORT HISTORY OF THE POLICY AND OUTLINES EFFECTIVENESS AND DIFFERENT KINDS OF NONVIOLENCE, ORGANIZATION OF THE GOVERNMENT, PREPARATION OF THE NATION, AND FORMS PROTEST SHOULD TAKE IN EVENT OF INVASION.

0123 AMERICAN SOCIETY AFR CULTURE
PAN-AFRICANISM RECONSIDERED.
BERKELEY: U OF CALIF PR, 1962, 376 PP., LC#62-11491.
ANTHOLOGY OF MAIN SPEECHES, PAPERS, AND COMMENTS GIVEN AT THIRD ANNUAL CONFERENCE OF THE AMERICAN SOCIETY OF AFRICAN CULTURE HELD IN 1960. DISCUSSION DIVIDED INTO GENERAL TOPICS: PAN-AFRICANISM; POLITICS, ECONOMICS; EDUCATION; SOCIAL THOUGHT; ART; AFRICAN CULTURE AND NEGRITUDE.

0124 AMOS S.
THE SCIENCE OF POLITICS.
NEW YORK: APPLETON, 1883, 490 PP.
STRESSES IMPORTANCE OF SCIENTIFIC BASIS FOR POLITICAL STUDY AND OPPOSES SPECULATIVE, INTUITIVE METHODS PRACTICED BY POLITICIANS AND STUDENTS OF POLITICS. DISCUSSES ADVANTAGES OF USING SCIENTIFIC SYSTEM OF METHODS AND PRINCIPLES IN STUDY OF POLITICAL ECONOMY, LAW AND LEGISLATION, AND SOCIOLOGY. TOPICS DISCUSSED COVER WIDE RANGE OF POLITICAL AREAS INCLUDING LOCAL, NATIONAL, AND INTERNATIONAL PROBLEMS.

0125 ANDERSON C.W.
POLITICS AND ECONOMIC CHANGE IN LATIN AMERICA.
PRINCETON: VAN NOSTRAND, 1967, 388 PP.
ANALYSIS OF ECONOMIC CHANGE IN LATIN AMERICA THROUGH ITS RELATIONSHIP WITH POLITICAL ELEMENTS. ATTEMPTS TO SEE A SYSTEMATIC IMPACT OF POLITICAL FORCES ON DEVELOPMENT POLICY AND THUS CREATE OVER-ALL THEORETICAL STATEMENT ON DEVELOPMENTAL POLICY-MAKING IN LATIN AMERICA. DEMONSTRATES THAT "PRUDENCE MODEL" HAS BEEN APPROACH SINCE 1945 AND SUGGESTS, IN CONCLUSION, A CONSISTENT APPROACH TO DEVELOPMENT POLICY.

0126 ANDERSON C.W., VON DER MEHDEN F.R., YOUNG C.
ISSUES OF POLITICAL DEVELOPMENT.
ENGLEWOOD CLIFFS: PRENTICE HALL, 1967, 248 PP., LC#67-20651.
DISCUSS THREE MAJOR ASPIRATIONS OF EMERGING NATIONS--NATIONALISM, STABILITY, AND DEVELOPMENT. POSTULATE THAT AS FUNDAMENTAL PROBLEMS OF POLITICAL DEVELOPMENT, THEY DEAL WITH PURPOSE OF POLITICAL LIFE ITSELF. EACH AUTHOR SPECIALIZES IN DIFFERENT WORLD AREA AND BOOK ATTEMPTS TO ACHIEVE CROSS-FERTILIZATION OF APPROACH. SEE TREND TOWARD SOCIALIZATION AND STATE PLANNING IN EMERGING COUNTRIES.

0127 ANDERSON E.N., ANDERSON P.R.
POLITICAL INSTITUTIONS AND SOCIAL CHANGE IN CONTINENTAL EUROPE IN THE NINETEENTH CENTURY.
BERKELEY: U OF CALIF PR, 1967, 500 PP.
CONCENTRATES ON 19TH-CENTURY INSTITUTIONS WITH PARTICULAR EMPHASIS ON CENTRAL AND LOCAL GOVERNMENTS, POLITICAL PARTIES AND BUREAUCRACIES. COMPARES CONSTITUTIONS, STATUTES, OBSERVERS' REPORTS, AND OTHER DOCUMENTS. DISCUSSES VARIOUS STAGES OF CONFLICT BETWEEN THE OLD SOCIETY AND THE NEW AND RAPIDLY DEVELOPING INDUSTRIAL SOCIETY THAT WAS CREATING RADICAL CHANGE.

0128 ANDERSON J.
THE ORGANIZATION OF ECONOMIC STUDIES IN RELATION TO THE PROBLEMS OF GOVERNMENT (PAMPHLET)
LONDON: OXFORD U PR, 1947, 25 PP.
EXAMINES PROGRESS MADE IN APPLICATION OF ECONOMIC THEORY TO PRACTICAL PROBLEMS DURING LAST 30 YEARS IN ENGLAND. PROPOSES THERE BE INCLUDED IN MACHINERY OF GOVERNMENT A CENTRAL ECONOMIC ORGANIZATION IN WHICH ALL DEPARTMENTS CONCERNED WITH ECONOMIC PROBLEMS COULD COLLABORATE EFFECTIVELY.

0129 ANDERSON L.G.
"ADMINISTERING A GOVERNMENT SOCIAL SERVICE"
NEW ZEALAND J. OF PUBLIC ADMIN., 29 (MAR. 67), 32-46.
COMMENTS ON ADMINISTRATION OF CHILD WELFARE DIVISION OF NEW ZEALAND SOCIAL SERVICE. ONE TASK OF ADMINISTRATION IS TO CURB SOCIAL-REFORM IMPULSES OF WORKERS AND DIRECT THEM TO WORK WITH INDIVIDUALS. OTHERS ARE TO EXPLOIT SKILLS OF HIS STAFF, DIRECT ANCILLARY SERVICE, PROVIDE LIAISON BETWEEN HIS SERVICE AND THE GOVERNMENT, AND TO FOSTER STAFF MORALE.

0130 ANDERSON O.
"ECONOMIC WARFARE IN THE CRIMEAN WAR."
ECON. HIST. REV., 14 (NO.2, 61), 34-47.
A STUDY OF BRITISH AND RUSSIAN TACTICS IN CRIMEAN WAR. POINTS OUT NUMEROUS FORERUNNERS OF WW 2 ECONOMIC TACTICS. SIMILAR DOUBTS ON EFFICACY OF MANY TACTICS WERE RAISED IN

BOTH WARS.

0131 ANDERSON O.
A LIBERAL STATE AT WAR.
NEW YORK: ST MARTIN'S PRESS, 1967, 306 PP., LC#67-11670.
EXAMINES THE PROBLEMS OF PHILOSOPHY, POLITICS, AND REASON WHICH AROSE WHEN BRITAIN BECAME EMBROILED IN CRIMEAN WAR. CITES IMPORTANCE OF WAR ON BRITISH SOCIETY AND CULTURE. EXPLORES GOVERNMENT OPERATION, PUBLIC DISCUSSION, CLASS CONSCIOUSNESS, RADICAL IDEAS, LEGISLATIVE PROCESS, ECONOMIC POLICY IN TERMS OF A LIBERAL STATE'S CRISIS.

0132 ANDERSON P.R.
THE BACKGROUND OF ANTI-ENGLISH FEELING IN GERMANY, 1890-1902
WASHINGTON: AMERICAN U PR, 1939, 382 PP.
STUDY OF PUBLIC OPINION IN LATE 19TH- AND EARLY 20TH-CENTURY GERMANY, ITS INFLUENCE ON EXECUTIVE OFFICIALS, AND ITS DETERMINATION OF POLICY. CONTENDS THAT GERMAN ANTAGONISM TOWARD ENGLAND WAS INHERENT IN THE NATURE OF IDEOLOGIES AND INSTITUTIONS OF THE TWO COUNTRIES, IN THEIR POLITICAL AND SOCIAL SYSTEMS, AND IN THEIR IMPERIALISMS. ILLUSTRATES OPERATION OF GERMAN PROPAGANDA MACHINE.

0133 ANDERSON S.V.
CANADIAN OMBUDSMAN PROPOSALS.
BERKELEY: U CAL, INST GOVT STUD, 1966, 168 PP.
REVIEW OF PROPOSALS SINCE 1960 FOR CREATION OF PARLIAMENTARY GRIEVANCE COMMISSIONERS MODELED ON SCANDINAVIAN OMBUDSMAN. PROPOSALS HAVE BEEN PUT FORWARD BY MINORITY PARTIES, THEN PLACED IN LIMBO BY MAJORITY. PRESENTS CHRONOLOGY OF EVENTS AND DEBATE, ANALYZES PROPOSALS, AND APPRAISES CANADA'S NEED FOR AN OMBUDSMAN.

0134 ANDERSON S.V.
THE NORDIC COUNCIL: A STUDY OF SCANDINAVIAN REGIONALISM.
SEATTLE: U OF WASHINGTON PR, 1967, 194 PP., LC#67-21202.
DESCRIBES SCANDINAVIAN REGIONALISM BY STUDYING NORDIC COUNCIL, CONSULTATIVE ASSEMBLY OF MEMBERS OF FIVE PARLIAMENTS. DISCUSSES NATIONAL ATTITUDES TOWARD REGIONALISM AND TRACES HISTORY OF INTERPARLIAMENTARY COOPERATION. EXAMINES ORGANS OF COUNCIL AND ITS LEGISLATIVE PROCEDURE. CHRONICLES NEGOTIATIONS FOR COMMON NORDIC MARKET.

0135 ANDERSON T.
RUSSIAN POLITICAL THOUGHT; AN INTRODUCTION.
ITHACA: CORNELL U PRESS, 1967, 444 PP., LC#67-12902.
STRESSES CONTINUITY AND EVOLUTION OF RUSSIAN POLITICAL ATTITUDES TOWARD AUTOCRACY, ISOLATIONISM, AND DOGMA FROM NINTH CENTURY TO REGIME OF BREZHNEV AND KOSYGIN. SEES GREEK-MONGOL-RUSSIAN TRADITION OF POLITICAL THOUGHT AS DISTINCT FROM WESTERN TRADITION. CONTAINS BIBLIOGRAPHY OF 550 BOOKS AND ARTICLES IN MODERN EUROPEAN LANGUAGES, ARRANGED UNDER TOPIC HEADINGS ALPHABETICALLY BY AUTHOR.

0136 ANDERSON W. ED.
LOCAL GOVERNMENT IN EUROPE.
NEW YORK: APPLETON, 1939, 453 PP.
DESCRIBES LOCAL GOVERNMENT OF FRANCE, ENGLAND, GERMANY, ITALY, AND THE SOVIET UNION. ANALYZES CENTRAL-LOCAL RELATIONS. INCLUDES PRINCIPAL LOCAL LAW OF COUNTRIES DISCUSSED.

0137 ANDREN N.
GOVERNMENT AND POLITICS IN THE NORDIC COUNTRIES: DENMARK, FINLAND, ICELAND, NORWAY, SWEDEN.
STOCKHOLM: ALMQUIST & WIKSELL, 1964, 240 PP.
EXAMINES NORDIC HERITAGE AND WESTERN TRADITION, AND THE IMPACT OF ECONOMIC AND SOCIAL CHANGE. STUDIES EACH COUNTRY IN TERMS OF ITS CONSTITUTIONAL DEVELOPMENT, POPULAR REPRESENTATION, EXECUTIVE AND ADMINISTRATIVE SYSTEM, AND PARLIAMENTARY ORGANIZATION. CONCLUDES BY DISCUSSING NATIONAL AND NORDIC TRAITS, LOCAL SELF-GOVERNMENT, COOPERATION AND INTEGRATION OF THESE NATIONS, AND POLITICAL PARTY STRENGTH.

0138 ANDREWS D.H. ED., HILLMON T.J. ED.
LATIN AMERICA: A BIBLIOGRAPHY OF PAPERBACK BOOKS.
WASHINGTON: LIBRARY OF CONGRESS, 1964, 38 PP., LC#64-60047.
LISTS PAPERBACKS AVAILABLE IN 1963 ON LATIN AMERICA. EXCLUDES DICTIONARIES, TEXTBOOKS, JUVENILE LITERATURE, AND FOR THE MOST PART SPECIALIZED PAMPHLETS OR MONOGRAPHS PUBLISHED BY UNIVERSITIES AND AGENCIES. ENTRIES ARE ARRANGED ALPHABETICALLY BY AUTHOR; 240 ENTRIES. INCLUDES INDEX AND LIST OF PUBLISHERS.

0139 ANDREWS W.G.
EUROPEAN POLITICAL INSTITUTIONS.
PRINCETON: VAN NOSTRAND, 1962, 387 PP.
DISCUSSES GOVERNMENTAL SYSTEMS (POLITICAL PARTIES, ELECTION PROCESSES, LEGISLATURES, EXECUTIVE ESTABLISHMENTS) OF UK, FRANCE, GERMANY, AND USSR.

0140 ANDREWS W.G.
FRENCH POLITICS AND ALGERIA: THE PROCESS OF POLICY FORMATION 1954-1962.
NEW YORK: APPLETON, 1962, 217 PP., LC#62-15310.
COMPARATIVE CASE STUDY OF TWO FRENCH REGIMES DEALING WITH SAME PROBLEM. DIFFERENCES AND SIMILARITIES IN OPERATIONS OF FRENCH ADMINISTRATIONS VIS-A-VIS ALGERIA.

0141 ANSPRENGER F.
POLITIK IM SCHWARZEN AFRIKA.
BONN: DEUTSCHE AFRIKA GESELLSCHAFT, 1961, 516 PP.
STUDY OF RISE OF POLITICAL INDEPENDENCE IN AFRICA, WITH SUBJECT OF FRENCH COLONIAL RULE, REFORM, AND REVOLUTIONARY MOVEMENTS IN LIGHT OF RISING AFRICAN NATIONALISM DISCUSSED IN GREAT DETAIL. APPENDED BIBLIOGRAPHY CONTAINING DOCUMENTS, MAPS, CHARTS, TIMETABLES, ETC.

0142 ANSPRENGER F.
"NATIONALISM, COMMUNISM, AND THE UNCOMMITTED NATIONS: AMERICAN PROFILES."
SURVEY, 43 (AUG. 62), 79-90.
PRESENTS HISTORIES OF AFRICAN NATIONALIST LEADERS WHO BROKE WITH COMMUNISM BECAUSE IT COULD NOT FULFILL THEIR ASPIRATIONS. POINTS OUT THAT PRIMARY AFRICAN GOAL IS ECONOMIC INDEPENDENCE AND THAT AFRICANS ARE INDIFFERENT TO EUROPEAN POLITICAL IDEOLOGY, INCLUDING COMMUNISM.

0143 ANTHEM T.
"CYPRUS* WHAT NOW?"
CONTEMPORARY REV., 210 (MAY 67), 235-240.
FURTHER CRISIS OVER CYPRUS HAS BEEN FORESTALLED ONLY BY MORE SERIOUS CRISES ELSEWHERE. THIS, AS WELL AS GREAT POWER UNWILLINGNESS TO TAKE DIFFICULT DECISIONS, HAS ALSO HELD BACK ANY POSSIBLE SETTLEMENT. UNION WITH GREECE IS THE ONLY REALISTIC SOLUTION, GIVEN THE VAST MAJORITY OF THE POPULATION, WHICH IS GREEK, AND THE DISPROPORTIONATE AMOUNT OF TURKISH POWER ON THE ISLAND DOES NOT ALTER THIS.

0144 ANTHON C.G.
"THE END OF THE ADENAUER ERA."
CURR. HIST., 44 (APRIL 63), 193-201.
FOCUSES ON STABILITY OF WEST GERMAN POLITICAL SYSTEM AND ACHIEVEMENTS OF KONRAD ADENAUER. GREATEST MIRACLE IS THAT OVERWHELMING MAJORITY OF GERMANS TODAY IDENTIFY THEMSELVES WITH DEMOCRATIC INSTITUTIONS AND POLICIES OF REPUBLIC.

0145 APPADORAI A.
THE SUBSTANCE OF POLITICS (6TH ED.)
MADRAS: OXFORD U PRESS, 1952, 524 PP.
TREATS ESSENTIAL PRINCIPLES OF POLITICAL THEORY AND ORGANIZATION. PART ONE DISCUSSES THEORY; PART TWO TREATS SPECIFIC POLITIES FROM THE GREEK CITY-STATES TO MAJOR MODERN EUROPEAN STATES AND INDIA, AND CONSIDERS VARIOUS ASPECTS OF POLITIES SUCH AS LEGISLATURES, JUDICIARY, AND EXECUTIVE. INTENDED AS TEXTBOOK. BIBLIOGRAPHIES AT END OF EACH CHAPTER.

0146 APPERT K.
"BERECHTIGE VORBEHALTE DER SCHWEIZERISCHEN ZUR INTEGRATION."
SCHWEIZ. MONATSH., 43 (NO.1, 63), 52-63.
EXAMINES SWISS INTEGRATION INTO EUROPEAN COMMON MARKET AND OPPOSITION TO ENGLISH CANDIDATURE. RELATES ECONOMIC INTERESTS OF NEUTRAL STATES TO POLITICAL ATTITUDES OF SIX NATIONS. GIVES INSIGHT INTO DOMESTIC PROBLEMS. OUTLINES POSITION OF SWISS PRICES.

0147 APPLEBY P.H.
PUBLIC ADMINISTRATION IN INDIA: REPORT OF A SURVEY.
NEW DELHI: MANAGER OF PUBLICATIONS, 1953, 65 PP.
FORD FOUNDATION STUDY WITH RECOMMENDATIONS FOR IMPROVEMENT OF THE SYSTEM OF PUBLIC ADMINISTRATION IN INDIA. CRITICIZES BUREAUCRATIC OPERATIONS IN VARIOUS DEPARTMENTS AND POINTS OUT POSSIBLE IMPROVEMENT. THOROUGH SURVEY OF INDIAN PUBLIC ADMINISTRATION.

0148 APPLEMAN P.
THE SILENT EXPLOSION.
BOSTON: BEACON PRESS, 1965, 161 PP., LC#65-13530.
COMMUNICATES FACTS ABOUT AND SIGNIFICANCE OF POPULATION EXPLOSION. REFUTES VARIOUS PROPOSITIONS WHICH DOWNGRADE POPULATION EXPLOSION'S SIGNIFICANCE. TREATS IDEOLOGICAL OPPOSITION TO POPULATION CONTROL BY COMMUNISTS AND CATHOLICS. RECOMMENDS LARGE-SCALE GOVERNMENT-SPONSORED RESEARCH AND ACTION FOR POPULATION CONTROL.

0149 APTER D.E.
THE GOLD COAST IN TRANSITION.
PRINCETON: U. PR., 1955, 355 PP.
CASE STUDY OF POLITICAL INSTITUTIONAL TRANSFER OF GOLD COAST FROM TRIBAL DEPENDANCY TO PARLIAMENTARY DEMOCRACY. EXAMINES HISTORICAL BACKGROUND, INCLUDING ETHNIC ORIGINS, TRADITIONAL SYSTEM OF LIFE AND INTRODUCTION OF WESTERN RULE. PRESENT AND FUTURE OF GOLD COAST DEMOCRACY EXAMINED.

0150 APTER D.E.
"THE GOLD COAST IN TRANSITION."
PRINCETON: PRINCETON U PRESS, 1955.
A CASE STUDY OF POLITICAL INSTITUTIONAL TRANSFER, PLANNED AS THE FIRST OF TWO FIELD STUDIES IN BRITISH COLONIAL AFRICA ON THE DEVELOPMENT OF CONCILIAR ORGANS OF RULE AND SELF-GOVERNMENT. PROCEEDS FROM CONVICTION THAT DEVELOPMENT OF PARLIAMENTARY GOVERNMENT IN UNDERDEVELOPED AREAS REFINES TRADI-

TIONAL CONCEPTUAL PREMISES OF POLITICAL ASPECTS OF SOCIAL CHANGE. BIBLIOGRAPHY OF BOOKS, DOCUMENTS, OFFICIAL PAPERS.

0151 APTER D.E.
"A COMPARATIVE METHOD FOR THE STUDY OF POLITICS" (BMR)"
AMER. J. OF SOCIOLOGY, 64 (NOV. 58), 221-237.
ATTEMPTS TO BUILD GENERALIZED MODEL OF THREE DIMENSIONS - SOCIAL STRATIFICATION, POLITICAL GROUPS, AND GOVERNMENT - THAT CAN BE USED FOR EXTENSIVE COMPARISON IN SOCIOLOGICAL STUDIES OF POLITICS. HIGHLY TECHNICAL.

0152 APTER D.E.
"THE ROLE OF TRADITIONALISM IN THE POLITICAL MODERNIZATION OF GHANA AND UGANDA" (BMR)"
WORLD POLITICS, 12 (OCT. 60), 45-68.
EXAMINES THE TRADITIONAL SYSTEMS OF GHANA AND UGANDA WITH RESPECT TO THE PROBLEMS THEY POSE FOR POLITICAL MODERNIZATION. CONTENDS THAT CENTRAL PROBLEM OF BUILDING NATIONAL POLITICAL INSTITUTIONS IS TO CREATE GOVERNMENTAL FORMS THAT BRIDGE OLDER PAROCHIALISMS. COMPARES RECENT EVENTS IN GHANA AND UGANDA TO SHOW HOW THEY HAVE BEEN SHAPED BY THEIR TWO DIFFERENT KINDS OF TRADITIONALISM.

0153 APTER D.E.
THE POLITICAL KINGDOM IN UGANDA.
PRINCETON: PRINCETON U PRESS, 1961, 298 PP., LC#61-6284.
AN ANALYSIS OF THE FACTORS THAT FORM THE POLITICAL CULTURE OF UGANDA. THE AUTHOR MAINTAINS TRADITION IS SUCH THAT UGANDA'S NATIONALISM IS ETHNICALLY PAROCHIAL AND FORESEES NO SWEEPING CHANGES SUCH AS CHARACTERIZED GHANA'S DEVELOPMENT.

0154 APTER D.E.
THE POLITICS OF MODERNIZATION.
CHICAGO: U OF CHICAGO PRESS, 1965, 481 PP., LC#65-24421.
ATTEMPT TO DEVELOP A THEORY OF POLITICAL MODERNIZATION UTILIZING EMPIRICAL DATA DRAWN FROM THE EXPERIENCES OF THE AFRICAN AND LATIN AMERICAN NATIONS. APPROACH IS COMPARATIVE, WITH COMPARISONS MADE BETWEEN THE EMERGING SOCIETIES AND TO THE WESTERN DEVELOPED SOCIETIES HELD AS A STANDARD. PROPOSES THAT MODERNIZING STATES MAY NECESSARILY PASS THROUGH A PRE-DEMOCRATIC POLITICAL STATE IN SEARCH FOR PROGRESS.

0155 AQUINAS T.
ON THE GOVERNANCE OF RULERS (1265-66)
TORONTO: ST MICHAEL'S COLLEGE, 1935, 143 PP.
WRITTEN FOR KING OF CYPRUS TO EXPOUND TEACHING OF SCRIPTURE AND PHILOSOPHY ON ORIGIN OF GOVERNMENT AND ON DUTIES OF RULERS. DISCUSSES IN FIRST BOOK NECESSITY OF GOVERNMENT; MERITS AND DEMERITS OF DIFFERENT KINDS OF GOVERNMENT; REASONS FOR WHICH RULERS GOVERN; AND NATURE AND DUTIES OF SOVEREIGN. SECOND BOOK DEALS WITH SPECIFIC ASPECTS OF FOUNDING A CITY OR STATE.

0156 ARASARATNAM S.
CEYLON.
ENGLEWOOD CLIFFS: PRENTICE HALL, 1964, 182 PP., LC#64-20750.
STUDIES PROBLEMS OF CEYLON SINCE INDEPENDENCE AND AS A MEMBER OF BRITISH COMMONWEALTH. DISCUSSES HISTORY, INFLUENCE OF BUDDHISM ON INSTITUTIONS AND CULTURE, AND RACIAL AND RELIGIOUS STRUCTURE OF SOCIETY. EXAMINES COLONIAL RULE AND INFLUENCES OF PORTUGUESE, DUTCH, AND BRITISH.

0157 ARASTEH R.
"THE ROLE OF INTELLECTUALS IN ADMINISTRATIVE DEVELOPMENT AND SOCIAL CHANGE IN MODERN IRAN."
INT. REV. EDUC., 9 (63), 326-39.
EXAMINES ROLE OF INTELLECTUALS AGAINST BACKGROUND OF PERSIAN SOCIAL STRUCTURE. THE WESTERN-TRAINED ELITE EXHIBIT DISHARMONIES OF A PSYCHOLOGICAL, MORAL, SOCIAL AND POLITICAL NATURE. DISHARMONIES ARE ROOTED IN PROLONGED EXPOSURE TO EUROPEAN CONCEPTS WHICH CONFLICT WITH BASIC ASSUMPTIONS OF PERSIAN LIFE AND EXPERIENCE.

0158 ARAZI A.
LE SYSTEME ELECTORAL ISRAELIEN.
GENEVA: LIBRAIRIE DROZ, 1963, 211 PP.
MANUAL OF ISRAELI LEGISLATIVE EVOLUTION AND ELECTORAL SYSTEM. CHRONOLOGICAL AND STATISTICAL DESCRIPTION OF THE ISRAELI LEGISLATURE SINCE INDEPENDENCE IN 1948.

0159 ARCHER P.
FREEDOM AT STAKE.
LONDON: THE BODLEY HEAD, 1966, 111 PP.
DISCUSSES GOVERNMENT REPRESSION OF HUMAN RIGHTS IN ENGLAND. USES CASE STUDIES TO ILLUSTRATE NECESSITY OF LAWS TO PROTECT CITIZENS FROM ADMINISTRATIVE INJUSTICE. TREATS VIEWS AND POLICIES ON HUMAN RIGHTS IN SEVERAL COUNTRIES OUTSIDE ENGLAND.

0160 ARENDT H.
"IDEOLOGY AND TERROR: A NOVEL FORM OF GOVERNMENT."
REV. SOCIAL ECONOMICS, 15 (JULY 53), 303-327.
ATTEMPTS TO DETERMINE WHETHER TOTALITARIANISM IS A TEMPORARY REACTION TO A CRISIS SITUATION OR IS A "THING WITH A REAL NATURE." DISCUSSES ROLE OF DOMINATION, TERROR, AND LAW IN MARXIST, NAZI, AND DEMOCRATIC IDEOLOGIES. STATES THAT WHAT PREPARES MEN FOR TOTALITARIAN DOMINATION IS LONELINESS, SEEN EVER MORE FREQUENTLY IN MODERN SOCIETY.

0161 ARENDT H.
"SOCIETY AND CULTURE."
DAEDALUS, 89 (60), 278-287.
CONTENDS THAT MASS SOCIETY AND MASS CULTURE ARE INTERRELATED. INHERENT DANGER IS THAT MASS SOCIETY TENDS TO DEPRIVE THE WORLD OF ITS CULTURE. CULTURE CAN ONLY BE SAFEGUARDED BY A REALIZATION OF ITS VALUE ON THE PART OF SOCIETY.

0162 ARENSBERG C.M., KIMBALL S.T.
CULTURE AND COMMUNITY.
NEW YORK: HARCOURT BRACE, 1965, 349 PP., LC#65-72658.
ANTHROPOLOGICAL AND SOCIOLOGICAL RESEARCH ON CONNECTION BETWEEN CULTURE AND SOCIETY. THE COMMUNITY IS VIEWED AS A MASTER SOCIAL SYSTEM, THE MODEL BY WHICH A CULTURE SHOULD BE STUDIES. EXAMINES THE MEANING OF COMMUNITY, AMERICAN COMMUNITIES, CULTURAL FACTORS OF COMMUNITY LIFE, AND PROCESS.

0163 ARIKPO O.
THE DEVELOPMENT OF MODERN NIGERIA.
BALTIMORE: PENGUIN BOOKS, 1967, 176 PP.
ATTEMPTS TO EXPLAIN NIGERIAN DEVELOPMENT BY EXAMINING POLITICAL, ECONOMIC, AND CULTURAL FORCES WHICH HAVE DETERMINED NATURE AND DIRECTION OF HER CONSTITUTIONAL CHANGE. SEES MOST PRESSING PROBLEMS TO BE POVERTY, CORRUPTION, TRIBALISM, AND FACTIONALISM.

0165 ARNE S.
LE PRESIDENT DU CONSEIL DES MINISTRES SOUS LA IV REPUBLIQUE.
PARIS: PICHON ET DURAND-AUZIAS, 1962, 464 PP.
ROLE AND INFLUENCE OF THE FRENCH PRIME MINISTER DURING THE FOURTH REPUBLIC IN RELATION TO THE EXECUTIVE, THE LEGISLATURE, AND THE POLITICAL SYSTEM IN GENERAL. STATISTICAL AND GRAPHICAL EVOLUTION OF THE DECISION-MAKING PROCESS UNDER THE DIFFERENT CABINETS.

0166 ARNOLD M.
"DEMOCRACY" IN MIXED ESSAYS (2ND ED.)"
LONDON: SMITH, ELDER & CO, 1880.
DEFENDS THE DEVELOPMENT OF ENGLISH DEMOCRACY AGAINST CRITICISMS OF ARISTOCRACY, DESCRIBING DEMOCRACY AS FULLEST EXPRESSION OF SOCIETY IN ITS TIME. FEELS THAT STATE IS THE NATION IN ITS CORPORATE AND COLLECTIVE CHARACTER AND THAT ALL IN A DEMOCRACY SHOULD WORK FOR DEMOCRATIC IDEAL. PROPOSES THAT DEMOCRACY IS THE IRRESISTIBLE FORCE OF THE MODERN SPIRIT.

0167 ARNOLD M.
"EQUALITY" IN MIXED ESSAYS."
LONDON: SMITH, ELDER & CO, 1880.
CONCERNED WITH SOCIAL EQUALITY RATHER THAN EQUALITY BEFORE THE LAW. CONSIDERS EQUALITY AS THE NECESSARY PRECONDITION TO A NEW DEGREE OF CIVILIZATION IN WHICH GREATER COMMUNICATION AMONG ALL SOCIAL LEVELS WOULD DEVELOP A HIGHER, NEWER IDEALISM. EXAMINES IDEAS OF LEADING EUROPEAN THINKERS, SOCIAL STRUCTURE, AND ENGLISH ARISTOCRACY. FREQUENT REFERENCES TO FRANCE ARE MADE.

0168 ARON R. ET AL.
L'UNIFICATION ECONOMIQUE DE L'EUROPE.
NEUCHATEL: LA BACONNIERE, 1957, 162 PP.
COLLECTION OF ESSAYS WRITTEN BY OFFICIALS OF NATIONS WITHIN THE COMMON MARKET AND TWO SCHOLARS REPRESENTING GREAT BRITAIN AND SWITZERLAND. INDIVIDUAL AUTHORS PROBE ATTITUDES AND PROBLEMS OF THEIR COUNTRIES WITH REGARD TO EUROPEAN UNIFICATION. THOUGH UNITY ACHIEVED WOULD BE ECONOMIC, WRITERS RECOGNIZE POLITICAL ASPECTS OF PROBLEM.

0169 ARON R.
THE OPIUM OF THE INTELLECTUALS (TRANS. BY TERENCE KILMARTIN)
GARDEN CITY: DOUBLEDAY, 1957, 324 PP.
ANALYSIS OF LEFT-WING IDEOLOGIES AND THEIR ACCEPTANCE BY INTELLECTUALS, ESPECIALLY IN FRANCE. COMMUNIST DOCTRINE AND CONCEPTS OF REVOLUTION AND THE PROLETARIAT ARE ATTACKED AS POLITICAL MYTHS; ALIGNMENT OF MEMBERS OF INTELLIGENTSIA WITH MARXISM IS SEEN AS A DENIAL OF SOCIAL REALITY IN EFFORT TO FIND POLITICAL PARADISE AND UNIVERSAL JUSTICE.

0170 ARON R.
SOCIOLOGIE DES SOCIETES INDUSTRIELLES: ESQUISSE D'UNE THEORIE DES REGIMES POLITIQUES.
PARIS: CENTRE DOCUMENTATION CNRS, 1958, 242 PP.
STUDY OF POLITICAL REGIMES IN MODERN INDUSTRIAL SOCIETIES, CONCENTRATING ON CONSTITUTIONAL AND TOTALITARIAN GOVERNMENTS. COMPARES THE TWO, THEIR WEAKNESSES AND STRENGTHS, USING TOCQUEVILLE AND MARX AS POINTS OF REFERENCE. AUTHOR CONCLUDES THAT CHOICE BETWEEN TWO TYPES OF GOVERNMENTS IS NOT CLEAR-CUT, AND THAT MANY OF IDEOLOGICAL CONFLICTS ARE CONFLICTS OF MYTHS RATHER THAN FACTS.

0171 ASHBEE H.S.

A BIBLIOGRAPHY OF TUNISIA FROM THE EARLIEST TIMES TO THE END OF 1888.
LONDON: DULAU & CO., 1889, 144 PP.
BIBLIOGRAPHY OF ABOUT 2,000 ITEMS ON TUNISIA THROUGH 1888. INCLUDES ALL TYPES OF WORKS INCLUDING BOOKS, ARTICLES, CONSULAR REPORTS, IN ALL MAJOR EUROPEAN LANGUAGES. VIRTUALLY ALL ASPECTS OF SUBJECT ARE COVERED IN WORKS INCLUDED. ARRANGED ALPHABETICALLY BY AUTHOR, WITH INDEX OF NAMES AND SUBJECTS. PARTLY ANNOTATED.

0172 ASHFORD D.E.
"BUREAUCRATS AND CITIZENS."
ANN. ACAD. POL. SOC. SCI., 358 (MAR. 65), 89-100.
DISCUSSION OF THE ROLE OF, AND EFFECTS ON, THE BUREAUCRACY OF THE PROCESS OF MODERNIZATION OF TUNISIA, MOROCCO, AND PAKISTAN.

0173 ASHFORD D.E.
NATIONAL DEVELOPMENT AND LOCAL REFORM: POLITICAL PARTICIPATION IN MOROCCO, TUNISIA, AND PAKISTAN.
PRINCETON: PRINCETON U PRESS, 1967, 439 PP.
ANALYSIS OF GROWTH AND DEVELOPMENT AS RELATED TO PEOPLES AND TO GOVERNMENTS. STUDIES NATIONAL POLITICS AND LOCALIZED AUTHORITY, LOCAL DEVELOPMENT, AND ATTITUDINAL CHANGE. CONCLUDES IN-DEPTH EXAMINATION OF MOROCCO, TUNISIA, AND PAKISTAN WITH VIEW THAT NEW FORMS OF PARTICIPATION AND NATION-BUILDING PROGRAMS ARE PRIMARILY A PROBLEM OF THE ATTITUDE OF THE INDIVIDUAL CITIZEN.

0174 ASHLEY M.P.
GREAT BRITAIN TO 1688: A MODERN HISTORY.
ANN ARBOR: U OF MICH PR, 1961, 441 PP., LC#61-8033.
ACCOUNT OF POLITICAL HISTORY OF ENGLAND FROM ROMAN OCCUPATION THROUGH GLORIOUS REVOLUTION. EMPHASIZES INFLUENCES AND POLICIES OF INDIVIDUAL MONARCHS. CONCLUDES WITH SELECTED LIST OF READINGS.

0175 ASHRAF A.
THE CITY GOVERNMENT OF CALCUTTA: A STUDY OF INERTIA.
NEW YORK: ASIA PUBL HOUSE, 1966, 126 PP.
EXAMINES NEED FOR REORGANIZATION OF URBAN GOVERNMENT TO SUIT REQUIREMENTS OF GOVERNMENT PROGRAM OF PLANNED DEVELOPMENT. APPRAISES CALCUTTA'S CITY GOVERNMENT, RELATING IT TO ENVIRONMENT. MAINTAINS GREATEST NEED OF MUNICIPAL ORGANIZATION IS DYNAMIC EXECUTIVE LEADERSHIP.

0176 ASIA FOUNDATION
LIBRARY NOTES.
SAN FRANCISCO: ASIA FOUNDATION.
BIMONTHLY PUBLICATION SINCE 1951 LISTING MATERIALS PRIMARILY ON ASIA. INCLUDES BOOKS, UN DOCUMENTS AND REPORTS, SERIAL PUBLICATION, PAMPHLETS, FOREIGN AND DOMESTIC GOVERNMENT DOCUMENTS, AND ELUSIVE MATERIALS, CATEGORIZED BY COUNTRY AND SUBJECT. ALSO CONTAINS ABSTRACTS OF PERIODICAL ARTICLES. ANNUAL INDEX. MATERIALS IN ENGLISH.

0177 ATTIA G.E.D.
LES FORCES ARMEES DES NATIONS UNIES EN COREE ET AU MOYEN-ORIENT.
GENEVA: LIBRAIRIE DROZ, 1963, 467 PP.
FULLY DOCUMENTED LEGAL STUDY OF UN EFFORTS TO "MAINTAIN THE PEACE" THROUGH THE SENDING OF INTERNATIONAL FORCES INTO THE CONFLICT AREA. THE ROLES OF THE MAJOR POWERS, THE SECURITY COUNCIL, THE GENERAL ASSEMBLY AND PARTICIPANTS (BOTH MEMBER AND NON-MEMBER STATES OF THE UN) ARE ANALYZED IN THE KOREAN AND SUEZ CRISES.

0178 ATTIA G.E.D.
"LES FORCES ARMEES DES NATIONS UNIES EN COREE ET AU MOYEN-ORIENT."
GENEVA: LIBRAIRIE DROZ, 1963.
LEGAL STUDY OF UN EFFORTS TO "MAINTAIN THE PEACE" BY SENDING INTERNATIONAL FORCES INTO THE CONFLICT AREA. THE BIBLIOGRAPHY OF OVER 600 ITEMS INCLUDES UN AND INDIVIDUAL STATE DOCUMENTS AND BOOKS AND ARTICLES, IN FRENCH AND ENGLISH, FROM 1921 TO 1958. DOCUMENTS ARRANGED BY SOURCE AND DATE, OTHER ITEMS ALPHABETICALLY BY AUTHOR.

0179 ATTLEE C.R.
EMPIRE INTO COMMONWEALTH.
LONDON: OXFORD U PR, 1961, 53 PP.
DISCUSSES CHANGES IN CONCEPTION AND STRUCTURE OF BRITISH EMPIRE SINCE 1900. REFLECTS UPON DEVELOPMENTS IN SELF-GOVERNMENT WITHIN EMPIRE. LARGELY BASED ON PERSONAL IMPRESSIONS.

0180 AUSTIN D.A. ED.
"POLITICAL CONFLICT IN AFRICA."
GOVERNMENT AND OPPOSITION, 2 (JULY-OCT.67), 487-620.
STUDIES SINGLE-PARTY STATE IN TANZANIA, MOROCCO, AND SENEGAL. FINDS THAT SINGLE-PARTY IS INEFFECTIVE, UNSTABLE SYSTEM. EXAMINES FUNCTIONAL INDEPENDENCE OF POLITICAL SYSTEM OF NIGERIA AND EXAMPLES OF POLITICAL CONFLICT. STRESSES NOVELTY OF AFRICAN SITUATION, BRIEF HISTORY OF POLITICAL INSTITUTIONS, AND INSECURITY. NOTES DISSIMILARITIES AMONG AFRICAN POLITICAL SYSTEMS.

0181 AUSTRALIAN NATIONAL RES COUN
AUSTRALIAN SOCIAL SCIENCE ABSTRACTS.
MELBOURNE: AUSTRAL NAT RESEARCH.
A PUBLICATION OF ABSTRACTS IN THE SOCIAL SCIENCES INTENDED TO PROVIDE A SURVEY OF MATERIAL PUBLISHED IN OR RELATED TO AUSTRALIA, NEW ZEALAND, AND TERRITORIES, DEALING WITH THE VARIOUS SOCIAL SCIENCES. PUBLISHED BIANNUALLY SINCE MARCH, 1946. "ABSTRACTS" OFFERS A PRECIS OF EACH WORK COVERED AND CLASSIFIES MATERIAL ACCORDING TO DIVISIONS WITHIN THE SOCIAL SCIENCE DISCIPLINES.

0182 AUSTRUY J.
STRUCTURE ECONOMIQUE ET CIVILISATION: L'EGYPTE ET LE DESTIN ECONOMIQUE DE L'ISLAM.
PARIS: SOC ED D'ENSEIGNEMENT SUP, 1960, 366 PP.
BELIEVES THAT IDEA OF "CIVILIZATION," RATHER THAN "NATION" GOVERNS ECONOMICS OF A PARTICULAR STATE. DISCUSSES STRUCTURE AND HISTORY, SOCIOLOGY, AND ECONOMICS; USES EGYPT TO ILLUSTRATE HIS THEORY. BELIEVES ISLAM HAS AN ECONOMIC VOCATION WHICH EGYPT FEELS AND WHICH IMPEDES ADOPTION OF WESTERN SYSTEM. EGYPT WILL PROBABLY DEVELOP OWN ORIGINAL TECHNIQUES SUITABLE TO HER DEVELOPMENT.

0183 AVASTHI A. ED., VARMA S.N. ED.
ASPECTS OF ADMINISTRATION.
NEW DELHI: ALLIED PUBLISHERS, 1964, 450 PP.
ESSAYS ON PUBLIC ADMINISTRATION AND POLITICES IN INDIA. DISCUSSES PUBLIC SERVICE, FINANCIAL COMMITTEES, WELFARE ADMINISTRATION, FREEDOM OF EXPRESSION AND PARLIAMENTARY PRIVILEGES, TEACHING OF POLITICAL SCIENCE IN UNIVERSITIES, ETC. INCLUDES ESSAYS ON SCIENTIFIC RESEARCH AND ADMINISTRATION IN US AND UK.

0184 AVRAMOVIC D.
POSTWAR GROWTH IN INTERNATIONAL INDEBTEDNESS.
BALTIMORE: JOHNS HOPKINS PRESS, 1958, 228 PP., LC#58-14424.
EXAMINES INTERNATIONAL LONG-TERM CAPITAL MOVEMENTS, CHANGES IN PATTERN OF EXPORTS, AND PROBLEM OF ADJUSTMENT TO CHANGES IN BALANCE OF PAYMENTS. TABLES ON ECONOMIC GROWTH, VOLUME OF EXPORT, GROWTH IN REAL INCOME, CAPITAL FORMATION, GROWTH RATES IN IMPORTS, ETC. OF SELECTED COUNTRIES.

0185 AYAL E.B.
"VALUE SYSTEM AND ECONOMIC DEVELOPMENT IN JAPAN AND THAILAND."
J. SOC. ISSUES, 19 (JAN. 63), 35-57.
BY A COMPARATIVE STUDY OF JAPAN AND THAILAND, ESTABLISHES CAUSAL RELATIONSHIP BETWEEN VALUE SYSTEM AND MODES OF BEHAVIOR, ASSIGNING PROPER PLACE TO THE SYSTEM IN THE THEORY OF SOCIAL CHANGE BROUGHT ABOUT BY ECONOMIC DEVELOPMENT. CONCLUDES THAT VALUE SYSTEM IS A MAJOR COMPONENT OF THE DEVELOPMENT POTENTIAL OF A COUNTRY.

0186 AYEARST M.
THE BRITISH WEST INDIES: THE SEARCH FOR SELF-GOVERNMENT.
LONDON: ALLEN & UNWIN, 1960, 258 PP., LC#60-6636.
SURVEYS DEVELOPMENT OF GOVERNMENT IN WEST INDIES. TREATS PERIODS OF OLD REPRESENTATIVE AND CROWN COLONY SYSTEMS. DISCUSSES CONSTITUTIONAL AND POLITICAL DEVELOPMENTS IN THE ISLANDS AND MAINLAND COLONIES, AND BRITISH COLONIAL POLICIES AND THEIR IMPLEMENTATION. DESCRIBES PRESENT LEGISLATIVE AND EXECUTIVE BODIES, LOCAL GOVERNMENT, POLITICAL PARTIES. ASSESSES FUTURE OF FEDERATION.

0187 AYLMER G.
THE KING'S SERVANTS.
NEW YORK: COLUMBIA U PRESS, 1961, 488 PP.
DESCRIBES ADMINISTRATIVE PROCEDURES, OFFICES, AND STRUCTURES UNDER CHARLES I, 1625-42. RELATES TYPE OF BUREAUCRACY TO OVERTHROW BY CROMWELL, NOTING TYPES OF CHANGES AND INNOVATIONS.

0188 AZEVEDO T.
SOCIAL CHANGE IN BRAZIL.
GAINESVILLE: U OF FLA PR, 1963, 83 PP., LC#63-62968.
ANALYSIS OF INTENSE SOCIAL AND TECHNOLOGICAL CHANGES IN BRAZIL AS AFFECTED BY 20TH-CENTURY ACHIEVEMENTS IN TECHNOLOGY, COMMUNICATIONS, AND ATOMIC POWER. DISCUSSES BRAZILIAN SOCIAL TRADITIONS, FORMATION OF NATIONAL ETHOS, AND FAMILY AND SOCIAL STRUCTURES.

0190 BACON F.
"OF EMPIRE" (1612) IN F. BACON, ESSAYS."
NEW YORK: EP DUTTON, 1962.
DISCUSSES PROBLEMS OF RULERSHIP AND OF MAINTAINING POWER OF KINGS. SUGGESTS THAT VIGILANCE IS MOST IMPORTANT QUALITY. COMMENDS LIBERAL APPROACH TO RULING. URGES EFFORTS FOR PROSPERITY BECAUSE IT LEADS MORE TO ACCEPTANCE AND COMPLACENCE, WHEREAS POVERTY ENGENDERS REBELLION AND VIOLENCE. SUGGESTS METHODS OF USING NOBLES TO AID IN RULING, AND NON-INTERVENTION AS MOST DESIRABLE TYPE OF DIPLOMACY.

0191 BACON F.
"OF SEDITIONS AND TROUBLES" (1625) IN F. BACON, ESSAYS."
NEW YORK: EP DUTTON, 1962.
PROPOSES ECONOMIC TACTICS FOR PREVENTION AND REMEDY OF

SEDITION. CLAIMS THAT WEALTH AND IMPLEMENTATION OF TRADE WILL BE STRONG DETERRENTS TO REBELLION. FAMILIAR WITH WORK OF MACHIAVELLI, HE SUGGESTS MANY TACTICS SIMILAR TO HIS IDEAS, TO BE USED WHEN IT IS NOT POSSIBLE TO CONTROL PEOPLE ECONOMICALLY. INCLUDES USE OF PROPAGANDA AND IDENTIFICATION WITH RESPECTED FIGURES, AND PERMITTING LIMITED EXPRESSION.

0192 BADGLEY R.F., WOLFE S.
DOCTORS' STRIKE; MEDICAL CARE AND CONFLICT IN SASKATCHEWAN.
NEW YORK: ATHERTON PRESS, 1967, 250 PP.
EXAMINES PLANNING AND IMPLEMENTATION OF NORTH AMERICA'S FIRST COMPREHENSIVE MEDICAL CARE PROGRAM, SETTING OF CONFLICT, AND ATTITUDES OF DOCTORS, GOVERNMENT, AND CITIZENS. TREATS MEDICAL CARE AS SOCIAL ISSUE AND ITS RELATION TO SOCIAL WELFARE. ANALYZES MEDICAL PROFESSION UNDER PRESSURE AND STUDIES MEDICAL CARE IN CONFLICT SITUATION FROM SOCIOLOGICAL VIEWPOINT.

0193 BADI J.
THE GOVERNMENT OF THE STATE OF ISRAEL: A CRITICAL ACCOUNT OF ITS PARLIAMENT, EXECUTIVE, AND JUDICIARY.
NEW YORK: TWAYNE, 1963, 307 PP., LC#63-17404.
STUDIES DEVELOPMENT OF ISRAEL'S GOVERNMENTAL STRUCTURE, DELINEATING NATURE AND FUNCTION OF BODIES OF GOVERNMENT AND POLITICAL PARTIES. ANALYZES VARIOUS ASSEMBLIES AND CABINETS THAT HAVE DIRECTED POLICY SINCE INDEPENDENCE. STATES THAT ISRAEL'S FUTURE DEPENDS ON HER ABILITY TO SOLVE THREE PROBLEMS: ACHIEVEMENT OF ECONOMIC INDEPENDENCE, INTEGRATION OF IMMIGRANTS, AND PEACE WITH ARABS.

0194 BAER W.
"THE INFLATION CONTROVERSY IN LATIN AMERICA: SURVEY."
LATIN AMER. RESEARCH REV., 2 (SPRING 67), 3-19.
WEIGHS MONETARIST AND STRUCTURALIST POSITION AND POLICY. SHOWS THAT THOUGH BOTH CAN CLAIM LIMITED EMPIRICAL VERIFICATION, NEITHER CAN SATISFACTORILY COPE WITH INFLATION THROUGHOUT LATIN AMERICA. DISCUSSES VARIOUS STABILIZATION MEASURES IN BRAZIL. EMPHASIZES NEED FOR MORE RESEARCH. CONCLUDES ONLY THAT ANY FIXED POSITION HAS OUTLIVED ITS USEFULNESS. CAREFULLY RESEARCHED AND DETAILED OVERVIEW.

0195 BAFFREY S.A.
THE RED MYTH: A HISTORY OF COMMUNISM FROM MARX TO KHRUSHCHEV
STANFORD: STANFORD U PRESS, 1962, 120 PP.
ADAPTATIONS OF SCRIPTS FROM TV DOCUMENTARY SERIES OUTLINING HISTORY OF COMMUNISM. ATTEMPTS TO PORTRAY LOGICAL PROGRESSION OF STORY OF COMMUNISM IN DRAMATIZED FORM INTENDED FOR EDUCATION OF AVERAGE CITIZEN.

0196 BAGBY P.
CULTURE AND HISTORY.
LONDON: LONGMANS, GREEN & CO, 1958, 244 PP.
FORMULATES BY PRECISE DEFINITION AND LOGICAL ARGUMENT THE CONCEPTUAL BACKGROUND FOR A GENERAL THEORY OF CULTURAL FORMS AND CULTURE-CHANGE IN ORDER TO SHOW THAT MANY PROBLEMS OF HISTORICAL CAUSATION CAN BE FORMULATED AND RESOLVED IN THESE TERMS. DISCUSSES LINGUISTIC PROBLEMS THAT ARISE; LOGICAL METHOD IS THAT OF BRITISH EMPIRICISM AS DERIVED FROM LOCKE AND HUME.

0197 BAGEHOT W.
THE ENGLISH CONSTITUTION AND OTHER POLITICAL ESSAYS.
LONDON: CHAPMAN AND HALL, 1924, 468 PP.
DISCUSSION OF FUNDAMENTAL PRINCIPLES AND STRUCTURES OF BRITISH GOVERNMENT AND ITS PRACTICAL OPERATION. PRESENTS ANALYSES OF CABINET, MONARCHY, HOUSES OF LORDS AND COMMONS, CHANGES OF MINISTRY, CHECKS AND BALANCES, AND EXECUTIVE PECULIARITIES AND THEIR HISTORICAL DETERMINANTS.

0198 BAGEHOT W.
THE ENGLISH CONSTITUTION.
NEW YORK: WATTS, 1964, 359 PP.
THOROUGH EXAMINATION OF ENGLISH CONSTITUTION AND SYSTEM OF PARLIAMENTARY GOVERNMENT, ORIGINALLY PUBLISHED IN 1867. DISTINGUISHES BETWEEN DIGNIFIED AND EFFICIENT PARTS OF CONSTITUTION, AND DISCUSSES CABINET, MONARCHY, HOUSE OF LORDS, HOUSE OF COMMONS, AND ELABORATE SYSTEMS OF CHECKS AND BALANCES AMONG THEM. PRESENTS HISTORY OF ENGLISH SYSTEM AND CHANGES IN FROM OF PARLIAMENTARY GOVERNMENT.

0199 BAIKALOV A., RAGANOV V.
"EMERGENCY LEGISLATION IN WEST GERMANY."
INTL. AFFAIRS (USSR), 4 (APR.67) 73-76.
ARGUES THAT "EMERGENCY LAWS" WERE FORMULATED BY FORMER NAZIS AND ENCOURAGE TAKEOVER OF TOTALITARIAN REGIME. TRADE UNIONS AND EXTRA-PARLIAMENTARY OPPOSITION FIGHT THE LAWS DESPITE OFFICIAL UNITY OF SPD WITH THE CDU/CSU LED BY KIESINGER GOVERNMENT. ANALYSIS OF EFFECTS OF LAW.

0200 BAILEY S.D. ED.
THE BRITISH PARTY SYSTEM.
LONDON: LONGMANS, GREEN & CO, 1952, 211 PP.
DESCRIBES EVOLUTION OF BRITISH PARTY SYSTEM, DISCUSSES BASIC PHILOSOPHY AND POLITICAL PRINCIPLES OF THREE MAIN PARTIES, AND EXAMINES SOME OF PROBLEMS TO WHICH SYSTEM GIVES RISE.

0201 BAILEY S.K., SIMON H.A. ET AL.
RESEARCH FRONTIERS IN POLITICS AND GOVERNMENT.
WASHINGTON: BROOKINGS INST, 1955, 240 PP.
REVIEWS NEW RESEARCH IN POLITICAL SCIENCE AND NEW TECHNIQUES FOR FURTHER STUDY. EXAMINES RESEARCH AREAS OPEN TO LEGISLATORS AND ADMINISTRATORS, NEW ADVANCES IN ORGANIZATION THEORY, AND USE OF CONCEPTS OF HIERARCHY AND BARGAINING. DISCUSSES USE OF GAME THEORY IN POLITICAL BEHAVIOR ANALYSES AND RESEARCH ON NOMINATIONS AND ELECTIONS, IMPACT OF REVOLUTIONS, AND COMPARATIVE POLITICS.

0202 BAIN C.A.
VIETNAM: THE ROOTS OF CONFLICT.
ENGLEWOOD CLIFFS: PRENTICE HALL, 1967, 184 PP., LC#67-18701.
VIEWS PRESENT SITUATION IN VIETNAM IN PERSPECTIVE OF HISTORY. TRACES EVOLUTION OF NATION FROM ANCIENT ORIGINS THROUGH ERAS OF CHINESE CONQUEST, NATIONAL INDEPENDENCE, FRENCH COLONIZATION, TO 20TH-CENTURY UPHEAVAL. ASSESSES INFLUENCE OF COMPLICATED CULTURAL HERITAGE - CONFUCIANISM, CHINESE INSTITUTIONS, ETC, - ON MODERN COURSE OF EVENTS. SYMPATHETICALLY VIEWS "TRUE PLIGHT OF THE VIETNAMESE..."

0203 BALANDIER G.
"SOCIOLOGIE DE LA COLONISATION ET RELATIONS ENTRE SOCIETES GLOBALES."
CAH. INT. SOCIOL., 17 (JUL - DEC 54), 17-31.
BIBLIOGRAPHICAL EVOLUTION AND ANALYSIS OF STUDIES ON THE SOCIOLOGY OF COLONIZATION WITH SPECIAL ATTENTION TO THE PRINCIPLES OF GLOBAL HIERARCHICAL SOCIETIES AND TO THE CONFLICT BETWEEN UNIFICATION AND HOMOGENEITY. INCLUDES STUDY OF SOCIAL CLASSES IN UNDER-DEVELOPED AREAS.

0204 BALFOUR A.J.
ESSAYS SPECULATIVE AND POLITICAL.
NEW YORK: GEORGE H. DORAN, 1921, 241 PP.
INCLUDED IN SPECULATIVE ESSAYS IS "DECADENCE," AN ANALYSIS OF THE CAUSES OF THE STAGNATION AND DECAY OF SOCIETIES AND AN ATTEMPT TO DISCOVER WAYS MODERN SOCIETY CAN ESCAPE FATE OF OTHER RACES. BELIEVES IN IMPORTANCE OF SCIENTIFIC RESEARCH AND THAT, SO FAR, THERE ARE NO REGRESSIVE SYMPTOMS IN WESTERN CIVILIZATION. "ESSAYS POLITICAL" EXPRESS AUTHOR'S CHANGING VIEW OF GERMANY BEFORE AND DURING WWI.

0205 BALOGH T.
THE ECONOMIC IMPACT OF MONETARY AND COMMERCIAL INSTITUTIONS OF A EUROPEAN ORIGIN IN AFRICA.
CAIRO: NAT BANK OF EGYPT, 1964, 71 PP.
IN CONSIDERING THE ECONOMIC PROBLEMS OF EGYPT, AUTHOR SUBMITS VALUABLE ADVICE TO THE DEVELOPING COUNTRIES OF AFRICA FOR ACHIEVING A BALANCED AND RAPID GROWTH.

0206 BALYS J. ED.
LITHUANIA AND LITHUANIANS: A SELECTED BIBLIOGRAPHY.
NEW YORK: FREDERICK PRAEGER, 1961, 190 PP., LC#61-14196.
MAINLY CONTAINS BOOKS AND ARTICLES IN WEST EUROPEAN LANGUAGES. SOME MAJOR WORKS IN LITHUANIAN ARE INCLUDED. LIBRARY OF CONGRESS WAS THE MAIN SOURCE FOR BIBLIOGRAPHY. WHERE THE BOOK IS NOT AVAILABLE AT LIBRARY OF CONGRESS, SYMBOLS FOR OTHER LIBRARIES IN US THAT HAVE THE WORK ARE INDICATED. ONLY LITHUANIAN AND SLAVIC LANGUAGE TITLES ARE TRANSLATED. COVERS SOCIAL SCIENCES.

0207 BANERJEE D.N.
OUR FUNDAMENTAL RIGHTS: THEIR NATURE AND EXTENT (AS JUDICIALLY DETERMINED)
CALCUTTA: WORLD PRESS LTD, 1960, 483 PP.
DESCRIPTION OF INDIAN BASIC FREEDOMS, INCLUDING PREAMBLE TO CONSTITUTION OF INDIA AND EMPHASIS UPON RIGHTS OF EQUALITY, FREEDOM, AND PROPERTY.

0208 BANERJI A.K.
INDIA'S BALANCE OF PAYMENTS.
NEW YORK: ASIA PUBL HOUSE, 1963, 255 PP.
DISCUSSES FOREIGN TRADE, NON-COMMERCIAL TRANSACTIONS (FOREIGN MISSIONARY AND CONSUL EXPENDITURES, GOVERNMENT TRANSACTIONS, ETC.), FOREIGN INVESTMENTS, AND BALANCE OF PAYMENTS IN INDIA BETWEEN 1920 AND PRESENT.

0209 BANFIELD E.C.
"THE POLITICAL IMPLICATIONS OF METROPOLITAN GROWTH" (BMR)"
DAEDALUS, 90 (WINTER 60), 61-78.
EXAMINES EFFECTS OF RAPID POPULATION GROWTH ON POLITICAL STRUCTURE AND OUTLINES TASKS OF METROPOLITAN GOVERNMENT IN TWO CONTRASTING SYSTEMS, US AND UK. DISCUSSES RELATION OF CITIZEN TO GOVERNMENT, ADMINISTRATIVE STRUCTURES OF LOCAL GOVERNMENTS, AND PROBLEMS OF CHANGE. FEELS TASKS GOVERNMENT MUST PERFORM IN SUPPLYING GOODS AND SERVICES HAVE NO NECESSARY RELATION TO POLITICAL MATTERS.

0210 BANFIELD J.
"FEDERATION IN EAST-AFRICA."
INT. J., 18 (SPRING 63), 181-194.
EXAMINES EAST-AFRICAN EXPERIENCE WITH FEDERATION FROM THE EARLY PERIOD OF COLONIAL RULE TO THE PRESENT WITH REFERENCE TO RECENT UPSURGE OF INTEREST BY KENYA, TANGANYIKA AND UGANDA IN FEDERATION AS A REGIONAL ALTERNATIVE TO NATIONAL

DEVELOPMENT. SURVEYS ACCOMPLISHMENT AND AREAS OF CONFLICT THAT REMAIN. GREATEST OBSTACLE TO EAST-AFRICAN UNITY IS ABSENCE OF 'PRINCIPLES OF COHESION'.

0211 BANKS A.S., GREGG P.M.
"GROUPING POLITICAL SYSTEMS* Q-FACTOR ANALYSIS OF A CROSS-POLITY SURVEY."
AMER. BEHAVIORAL SCIENTIST, 9 (NOV. 65), 3-6.
USES "Q-TECHNIQUE" OF FACTOR ANALYSIS CORRELATING "THE CULTURAL INVENTORIES OF A GROUP OF TRIBES; CULTURE TRAITS ARE COUNTED." 68 POLITICAL VARIABLES FROM BANKS AND TEXTOR'S "A CROSS-POLITY SURVEY" ARE GROUPED INTO 5 FACTORS FOR ROTATION WHICH GIVE CORRESPONDING MATRIX RANKING WORLD'S STATES AS POLYARCHIC, ELITIST, CENTRIST, PERSONALIST, AND TRADITIONAL.

0212 BANKWITZ P.C.
MAXINE WEYGAND AND CIVIL-MILITARY RELATIONS IN MODERN FRANCE
CAMBRIDGE: HARVARD U PR, 1967, 545 PP., LC#67-22860.
EXAMINES GRADUAL DETERIORATION OF RELATIONS BETWEEN FRENCH CIVILIAN GOVERNMENT AND MILITARY LEADERS DURING THE PERIOD BETWEEN THE TWO WORLD WARS, WHICH LED IN 1940 TO ARMY DEFIANCE OF THE GOVERNMENT. CARRIED OUT LARGELY THROUGH ANALYSIS OF THOUGHT AND ACTION OF GENERAL MAXINE WEYGAND. EXTENSIVE BIBLIOGRAPHY.

0213 BARAN P.A.
THE POLITICAL ECONOMY OF GROWTH.
NEW YORK: PROMETHEUS PRESS, 1957, 308 PP., LC#57-7953.
FOCUSES ON CONCEPTS OF ECONOMIC SURPLUS AND MONOPOLY CAPITALISM IN ANALYZING THE DIFFICULTY DEVELOPED CAPITALIST COUNTRIES HAVE IN RATIONALLY UTILIZING THEIR ECONOMIC RESOURCES. ALSO DISCUSSES THE PROBLEMS OF ECONOMIC GROWTH PECULIAR TO UNDERDEVELOPED SOCIETIES, REGARDLESS OF LOCATION OR CULTURE.

0214 BARBU Z.
PROBLEMS OF HISTORICAL PSYCHOLOGY.
LONDON: ROUTLEDGE & KEGAN PAUL, 1960, 222 PP.
APPLICATION OF HISTORICAL CONCEPTS AND METHODS TO THE STUDY OF THE HUMAN MIND. THE FIRST PART OF THE BOOK EXAMINES GENERAL HISTORICAL AND PSYCHOLOGICAL TECHNIQUES AND THE USES OF INTERDISCIPLINARY APPROACHES IN THE STUDY OF SOCIAL AND CULTURAL DEVELOPMENT. THESE APPROACHES ARE THEN APPLIED TO THE EMERGENCE OF PERSONALITY IN THE GREEK WORLD AND TO THE ORIGINS OF ENGLISH CHARACTER.

0215 BARDOUX J.
L'ANGLETERRE RADICALE; ESSAI DE LA PSYCHOLOGIE SOCIALE (1906-1913)
PARIS: LIBRAIRIE FELIX ALCAN, 1913, 559 PP.
OFFERS DETAILED ANALYSIS OF FEELINGS, ATTITUDES, AND SOCIAL FORCES BEHIND THE "RADICAL" UK ELECTIONS OF 1906. EXAMINES THE LABOUR PARTY, SOCIAL RADICALISM, THE BUDGET AND CONSTITUTION CRISES; TRACES THE COLONIAL ISSUE, THE GERMAN QUESTION, AND THE PACIFIST MOVEMENT; ANALYZES THE RAMIFICATIONS OF BRITAIN'S ECONOMIC POLICIES, STRIKES, THE NAVY PANIC, AND THE HOME RULE BILL.

0216 BARIETY J.
"LA POLITIQUE EXTERIEURE ALLEMANDE DANS L'HIVER 1939-1940."
REV. HIST., 1 (JAN - MAR 64), 141-52.
TRACES EVOLUTION OF GERMAN FOREIGN POLICY FROM SEPT. 1939 TO MARCH 1940 EMPHASIZING RELATIONS WITH USSR, THE BALTIC AND SCANDINAVIAN COUNTRIES AS A RESULT OF THE RUSSO-FINNISH WAR, AND THE BALKANS AND THE NEAR EAST AS A RESULT OF ITALY'S DESIGNS.

0217 BARKER E.
POLITICAL THOUGHT IN ENGLAND: FROM HERBERT SPENCER TO THE PRESENT DAY.
NEW YORK: HOLT RINEHART WINSTON, 1928, 256 PP.
PRESENTS HISTORY OF ENGLISH POLITICAL THOUGHT. DISCUSSES T.H. GREEN, BRADLEY, AND BOSANQUET IN IDEALIST SCHOOL. ALSO HERBERT SPENCER AND SCIENTIFIC SCHOOL. ANALYZES THE "LAWYERS" OF MID- AND LATE-19TH CENTURY, AND ECONOMICS AND POLITICS OF BENTHAM, PEARSON, AND MAITLAND.

0218 BARKER E.
REFLECTIONS ON GOVERNMENT.
LONDON: OXFORD U PR, 1942, 424 PP.
EXAMINES GENERAL IDEAS AND FORCES OF EUROPEAN GOVERNMENT. DISCUSSES INTERNAL AND EXTERNAL PROBLEMS OF DEMOCRACY, AS WELL AS AMENDMENTS AND ALTERNATIVES. BELIEVES DEMOCRACY WILL SURVIVE TOTALITARIAN THREATS, BUT THAT IT MUST BE JUSTIFIED BY ITS WORKS. MUST HAVE CAPABLE LEADERSHIP, NOT TOO TIED TO POLITICAL PARTIES; MUST BROADEN CIVIC KNOWLEDGE; AND MUST EDUCATE CITIZENS IN DEMOCRATIC PRINCIPLES.

0219 BARKER E.
THE DEVELOPMENT OF PUBLIC SERVICES IN WESTERN EUROPE: 1660-1930.
LONDON: OXFORD U PR, 1944, 93 PP.
HISTORY OF THE DEVELOPMENT OF PUBLIC ADMINISTRATION IN ENGLAND, FRANCE, AND PRUSSIA, WITH COMPARISONS OF STRUCTURES AND FUNCTIONS. CONCENTRATES ON MILITARY CONSCRIPTION, TAXATION, SOCIAL WELFARE, AND EDUCATION.

0220 BARNES H.E.
SOCIETY IN TRANSITION: PROBLEMS OF A CHANGING ERA.
ENGLEWOOD CLIFFS: PRENTICE HALL, 1939, 999 PP.
CONSIDERS MODERN ERA AS TIME OF MAJOR CULTURAL TRANSFORMATION. CONTENDS THAT MODERN ERA IS UNLIKE ANY PREVIOUS TRANSITIONAL TIMES OWING TO RAPIDITY AND COMPLEXITY OF CONTEMPORARY TECHNOLOGICAL CHANGES. FOCUSES ON SOCIAL PROBLEMS RESULTING FROM DISCREPANCY BETWEEN MECHANICAL PROGRESS AND SOCIAL DEVELOPMENT. APPROACH IS BASICALLY HISTORICAL.

0221 BARNES H.E.
SOCIAL INSTITUTIONS IN AN ERA OF WORLD UPHEAVAL.
ENGLEWOOD CLIFFS: PRENTICE HALL, 1942, 925 PP.
ANALYSIS OF ANACHRONISTIC NATURE OF CONTEMPORARY SOCIAL THOUGHT AND INSTITUTIONAL PATTERNS WITH EMPHASIS ON COMPLEX, RAPIDLY ADVANCING MATERIAL CULTURE. FOCUSES ON MODERN AMERICAN SOCIETY.

0222 BARNETT A.D.
COMMUNIST CHINA IN PERSPECTIVE.
NEW YORK: FREDERICK PRAEGER, 1962, 88 PP., LC#62-16640.
BROAD ANALYSIS OF THE CHINESE REVOLUTION FOCUSED ON THREE ISSUES: THE PAST OUT OF WHICH COMMUNISM EMERGED; THE NATURE OF CURRENT CHINESE REVOLUTIONARY PROCESS; AND THE FUTURE PROSPECTS OF CHINA UNDER ITS COMMUNIST REGIME.

0223 BARNETT A.D. ED.
COMMUNIST STRATEGIES IN ASIA: A COMPARATIVE ANALYSIS OF GOVERNMENTS AND PARTIES.
NEW YORK: PRAEGER, 1963, 293 PP., $2.50.
A PIONEERING WORK IN THE STUDY OF COMMUNIST REGIMES AND PARTIES IN ASIA--A CLOSE INQUIRY INTO THEIR DIFFERENCES AND SIMILARITIES, THEIR RELATIONS WITH EACH OTHER, AND THE EFFECTS ON THEM OF SINO-SOVIET DISPUTE. SEVERAL SPECIALISTS IN BOTH ASIAN AND COMMUNIST AFFAIRS FOCUS ON THE SITUATION IN MONGOLIA, NORTH VIET-NAM, NORTH KOREA, JAPAN, INDIA, AND INDONESIA.

0224 BARNETT A.D.
CADRES, BUREAUCRACY, AND POLITICAL POWER IN COMMUNIST CHINA.
NEW YORK: COLUMBIA U PRESS, 1967, 563 PP., LC#67-15895.
ANALYTICAL STUDY OF POLITICAL AND GOVERNMENTAL STRUCTURE OF COMMUNIST CHINA, COVERING CENTRAL AND LOCAL GOVERNMENTS. BASED PRIMARILY ON INTERVIEWS WITH CHINESE EX-CADRE EMIGRES TO HONG KONG, 1964-65. ANALYZES PATTERNS OF ORGANIZATION, PARTY-GOVERNMENT RELATIONS, CHARACTERISTICS OF LEADERSHIP-ELITE, TECHNIQUES OF PERSONNEL MANAGEMENT, COMMUNICATION WITHIN BUREAUCRACY, CENTRAL-LOCAL GOVERNMENT RELATIONS.

0225 BARNETT D.L., NJAMA K.
MAU MAU FROM WITHIN.
LONDON: MACGIBBON AND KEE, LTD, 1966, 512 PP.
ANALYSIS OF KENYAN INDEPENDENCE MOVEMENT THAT RELIES HEAVILY ON THE LIFE-HISTORY APPROACH FOR INFORMATION AND DATA. ALSO AN AUTOBIOGRAPHY OF KARAI NJAMA, A MAJOR FIGURE IN THE MOVEMENT.

0226 BARRES M.
THE UNDYING SPIRIT OF FRANCE (TRANS. BY M. CORWIN)
NEW HAVEN: YALE U PR, 1917, 57 PP.
PATRIOTIC PAMPHLET ENCOURAGES REGAINING OF ALSACE-LORRAINE FOR ITS OWN SAKE AND FOR FRANCE'S. ARGUES AGAINST IDEA OF FRENCH AS PLEASURE-SEEKING NATION, POINTING OUT RESPONSE TO 1914 CALL TO ARMS. POINTS OUT INDIVIDUAL CASES OF HEROISM, ESPECIALLY IN VERY YOUNG SOLDIERS, CLAIMING THIS BEHAVIOR IS TYPICAL OF FRENCH SOLDIERS AND IS PART OF FRENCH NATIONAL CHARACTER.

0227 BARRES M.
THE FAITH OF FRANCE (TRANS. BY ELISABETH MARBURY)
BOSTON: HOUGHTON MIFFLIN, 1918, 294 PP.
CONTAINS LETTERS AND DIARY EXCERPTS OF FRENCHMEN FROM DIFFERENT BACKGROUNDS AND FAITHS DURING WWI. AUTHOR BELIEVES THAT "HOLY UNION" OF POLITICAL DIFFERENCES MUST BE MAINTAINED DURING WAR. EMPHASIZES NECESSITY OF MAINTAINING TRADITION, WHICH IS RECOGNITION OF PERMANENT VALUES OF A COMMUNITY AND OF A COMMON CULTURE. VALUES SHOULD BE SOUGHT IN THE PAST.

0228 BARRES M.
"THE WAR AND THE SPIRIT OF YOUTH" (PAMPHLET)
BOSTON: LITTLE BROWN, 1917, 58 PP.
MYSTICAL ANALYSIS OF FRENCH HEROISM IN WWI CLAIMS IT TO BE RESULT OF NATIONAL CULTURE, RACIAL HERITAGE, AND PERSONAL EXCELLENCE OF FRENCH SOLDIERS. DISCUSSES NORMATIVE SYSTEM WHICH ENCOURAGES ACTS OF HEROISM AND RELIGIOUS BELIEFS WHICH COMPEL AND ENABLE SOLDIERS. LAUDS WILLINGNESS OF MEN TO SEEK THEIR COUNTRY'S DESTINY, RATHER THAN THEIR OWN.

0229 BARRETT J.
THAT BETTER COUNTRY: RELIGIOUS ASPECT OF LIFE IN EASTERN AUSTRALIA, 1835-1850.
MELBOURNE: MELBOURNE UNIV PRESS, 1966, 126 PP., LC#66-12956.

ANALYSIS OF ERA OF CHANGE FROM PENAL COLONY TO RESPONSIBLE GOVERNMENT. GOLD WAS DISCOVERED, CLERGY MOVED IN WITH ONLY MEANS OF ORGANIZATION, AND, MORE IMPORTANT, WITH MEANS OF EDUCATION. STUDIES RELATION OF CHURCH, MAKE-SHIFT STATE, AND METHOD OF CONTROL USED BY CLERGY.

0230 BARRON R.
PARTIES AND POLITICS IN MODERN FRANCE.
WASHINGTON: PUBLIC AFFAIRS PRESS, 1959, 213 PP., LC#58-13405
SURVEY OF THE FRENCH PARTY SYSTEM IN GENERAL SINCE WWII. INCLUDES DOCTRINE, PROGRAM, ORGANIZATION, CLIENTELE, AND CAMPAIGN TECHNIQUES OF EACH FRENCH POLITICAL PARTY.

0231 BARRY E.E.
NATIONALISATION IN BRITISH POLITICS: THE HISTORICAL BACKGROUND.
STANFORD: STANFORD U PRESS, 1965, 397 PP.
STUDIES HISTORICAL BACKGROUND TO NATIONALIZATION IN BRITAIN, THE SOCIALIST MOVEMENT ITSELF, AND LABOR POLITICS IN RECENT YEARS. COVERS ASPECTS OF NATIONALIZATION OF VARIOUS ACTIVITIES (INDUSTRY, RAILWAY, LAND, MINES), AND TRACES, CHRONOLOGICALLY, 20TH-CENTURY POLITICAL VIEWS AND ACTIONS IN RESPONSE TO NATIONALIZATION.

0232 BARZEL R.
DIE DEUTSCHEN PARTEIEN.
GELDERN, GERMANY: L.N. SCHAFFRATH, 1953,540 PP.
DISCUSSION OF POLITICAL IDEOLOGY AND THE RISE OF POLITICAL PARTIES IN GERMANY. INCLUDES STUDY OF VARIOUS PROGRAMMATIC DIFFERENCES WHICH EXIST BETWEEN SUCH PARTIES AS THE "FREE DEMOCRATS," "CHRISTIAN DEMOCRATS," AND THE "SOCIAL DEMOCRATS."

0233 BASDEN G.T.
NIGER IBOS.
NEW YORK: BARNES AND NOBLE, 1966, 456 PP.
NON-TECHNICAL DESCRIPTION OF PRIMITIVE LIFE, CUSTOMS, AND ANIMISTIC BELIEFS OF IBO PEOPLE OF NIGERIA.

0234 BASKIN D.B.
"NATIONALITY DOCTRINE AND ANTI-SEMITISM IN THE USSR."
SOCIAL SCIENCE, 42 (APR. 67), 99-103.
AUTHOR CONTENDS THAT THE HISTORY OF THE JEWS CONTRADICTS THE CLAIM OF MARXISM TO SCIENTIFIC VALIDITY. FROM THE MARXIAN VIEW, JEWS ARE NEITHER A CLASS NOR A NATIONALITY, AND SO CHALLENGE THE MARXIAN CONCEPT OF HISTORICAL PROGRESS. THIS GENERATES A CONTRADICTORY POLICY TOWARD JEWISH CULTURE IN THE USSR. ON ONE HAND IT STIFLES EXPRESSION; ON THE OTHER, IT CONDEMNS THIS STIFLING AS COUNTERREVOLUTIONARY.

0235 BASOV V.
"THE DEVELOPMENT OF PUBLIC EDUCATION AND THE BUDGET."
SOVIET EDUCATION, 9 (FEB. 67), 23-30.
DISCUSSES SOVIET FINANCING OF EDUCATION. STATES THAT FUNDS FOR MAINTENANCE OF CHILDREN'S PRESCHOOL INSTITUTIONS COME FROM STATE RESOURCES AND PARENTS' PAYMENTS, WHEREAS ALL OTHER EDUCATION IS PAID BY STATE. PRESENTS STATISTICS ON ENROLLMENT, EXPENDITURES, AND COMPARES FIGURES WITH PRE-REVOLUTIONARY DATA. DESCRIBES METHODS BEING DEVELOPED BY GOVERNMENT FOR DETERMING BUDGETS OF INSTITUTIONS.

0236 BATOR V.
"ONE WAR* TWO VIETNAMS."
MILITARY REV., 47 (JUNE 67), 82-88.
STRESSES THAT THE "ESSENCE OF GENEVA" WAS TO SPLIT VIETNAM AND THAT PACIFISTS WHO USE THE GENEVA AGREEMENT ON FACE VALUE ARE DECEIVING THEMSELVES AS TO THE DIPLOMATIC UNDERTONES OF THE TREATY. DESCRIBES SOCIAL AND POLITICAL FORCES THAT MOTIVATED THE CONFERENCE, REASONS FOR PARTITION, TNE "REAL INTENTIONS" OF THE SIGNATORIES. CONCLUDES THAT VIETNAM MUST REMAIN DIVIDED INDEFINITELY.

0237 BATTAGLIA F.
LINEAMENTI DI STORIA DELLE DOCTRINE POLITICHE CON APPENDICI BIBLIOGRAFICHE.
ROME: SOCIETA EDITRICE DEL FORO ITALIANO, 1936, 218 PP.
CRITICAL SURVEY OF DEVELOPMENT OF POLITICAL STUDIES, FROM SPECULATIVE, SCIENTIFIC, AND HISTORICAL POINTS OF VIEW, IN PERIOD 1901-36. CONTAINS EXTENSIVE BIBLIOGRAPHICAL NOTES. SCOPE CONFINED TO ITALIAN POLITICAL STUDIES ALTHOUGH REFERENCES ARE IN MAJOR EUROPEAN LANGUAGES. INCORPORATED IN FIRST PART OF WORK IS MORE GENERAL SURVEY OF TRENDS IN ITALIAN POLITICAL THOUGHT UP TO 20TH CENTURY.

0238 BAUCHET P.
ECONOMIC PLANNING.
LONDON: HEINEMANN, 1964, 299 PP., LC#64-16665.
DESCRIBES THE FRENCH EXPERIENCE IN ECONOMIC PLANNING AS A MAJOR TRANSFORMATION OF CAPITALIST STRUCTURE. CONSIDERS PLANNING AND DEMOCRACY, BUSINESS FIRMS, AND SOCIAL CLASSES, AS WELL AS THE STRATEGY OF PLANNING FOR AN OPTIMUM.

0239 BAUER R.A., GLEICHER D.B.
"WORD-OF-MOUTH COMMUNICATION IN THE SOVIET UNION."
PUB. OPIN. QUART., 17 (FALL 53), 297-308.
ANALYZES POLITICAL IMPLICATIONS OF THE EXISTENCE OF AN UNOFFICIAL ORAL COMMUNICATIONS NETWORK IN USSR. FOR THE INTELLIGENTSIA THIS SERVES AS SUPPLEMENT TO OFFICIALLY SANCTIONED SOURCES OF INFORMATION WHEAREAS IT ACTS AS SUBSTITUTE FOR THE PEASANT. PARTICIPATION IN THIS UNOFFICIAL COMPLEXITY IS A SIGN OF ANTI-SOVIET FEELING ON PART OF THE PEASANT BUT NOT THE INTELLIGENTSIA.

0240 BAULIN J.
THE ARAB ROLE IN AFRICA.
BALTIMORE: PENGUIN BOOKS, 1962, 144 PP.
STUDY OF CONTEMPORARY NORTH AFRICA AND ITS RELATION TO REST OF CONTINENT. INCLUDES ISLAM IN AFRICA, EGYPTIAN ARABISM AND AFRICANISM, ALGERIAN NATIONALISM, TUNISIA UNDER BOURGUIBA, AND MOROCCAN MONARCHY.

0241 BAUMANN G.
GRUNDLAGEN UND PRAXIS DER INTERNATIONALEN PROPAGANDA.
ESSEN: ESSENER VERLAGSANSTALT, 1941, 280 PP.
CRITICAL INQUIRY INTO BASES AND METHODS OF INTERNATIONAL PROPAGANDA. EMPHASIS ON POLITICAL CAUSES OF THE HATRED FOR GERMANY, ESPECIALLY IN ENGLAND AND FRANCE. ENGLISH PROPAGANDA METHODS DURING WWI DISCUSSED IN DETAIL.

0242 BAYER H. ED.
WIRTSCHAFTSPROGNOSE UND WIRTSCHAFTSGESTALTUNG.
BERLIN: DUNCKER & HUMBLOT, 1960, 318 PP.
COLLECTION OF ESSAYS ON ECONOMIC PLANNING, COOPERATIVE TRADING SYSTEM, FINANCIAL POLICY, PROGNOSIS AND PLANNING IN ECONOMY OF UNDERDEVELOPED NATIONS, AND ECONOMIC POLICY IN NETHERLANDS. INCLUDES DISCUSSION OF ESSAYS PRESENTED.

0243 BAYITCH S.A.
LATIN AMERICA: A BIBLIOGRAPHICAL GUIDE.
CORAL GABLES: U OF MIAMI PR, 1961.
UNANNOTATED LISTING OF BOOKS AND ARTICLES IN ENGLISH. MAJOR EMPHASIS ON LAW.

0244 BAYNE E.A.
FOUR WAYS OF POLITICS: STATE AND NATION IN ITALY, SOMALIA, ISRAEL, AND IRAN.
NEW YORK: AMER UNIV FIELD STAFF, 1965, 320 PP., LC#65-14723.
SCRUTINIZES THE CRISES OF INTEGRATION IN THE FOUR COUNTRIES, AND THE DYNAMICS OF POLITICAL PARTICIPATION. BASED IN PART ON PERSONAL DISCUSSIONS BY THE AUTHOR WITH THREE OF THE HEADS OF STATE. INQUIRES INTO HOW NATIONAL LEADERS STRIVE TO RALLY THE SUPPORT NEEDED IN MOVING A COUNTRY INTO THE MODERN WORLD. RE: ISRAEL, CONCLUDES THAT ITS STORY IS THAT OF A MODERN INSTITUTION'S OPERATING SUCCESSFULLY.

0245 BAYNES N.H.
INTELLECTUAL LIBERTY AND TOTALITARIAN CLAIMS.
LONDON: OXFORD U PR, 1942, 79 PP.
DISCUSSES CONFLICT BETWEEN NATIONAL SOCIALISM AND TRADITION OF UNFETTERED INQUIRY. EMPHASIZES GRADUAL CHANGE OF CLIMATE AT GERMAN UNIVERSITIES FROM AN INDEPENDENT PURSUIT OF KNOWLEDGE TO MILITANT PARTISANSHIP. INCLUDES DISCUSSION OF DISINTEGRATION OF INTELLECTUAL INDEPENDENCE IN FASCIST ITALY.

0246 BEARCE G.D.
BRITISH ATTITUDES TOWARDS INDIA 1784-1858.
LONDON: OXFORD U PR, 1961, 315 PP.
STUDIES WHAT BRITISH THOUGHT ABOUT INDIA, INCLUDING CONSERVATIVES, IMPERIAL SENTIMENT, LIBERAL AND HUMANITARIAN ATTITUDES, ROMANTIC INDIA, AND INDIA IN BRITISH LITERATURE AND PHILOSOPHY.

0247 BEARD C.A.
"THE TEUTONIC ORIGINS OF REPRESENTATIVE GOVERNMENT"
AM. POL. SCI. REV., 26 (FEB. 32), 28-44.
QUESTIONS THE THEORY OF THE TEUTONIC ORIGINS OF REPRESENTATIVE INSTITUTIONS. IT DOES NOT ORIGINATE FROM INNATE LOVE OF LIBERTY OF TEUTONS IN ENGLAND. SEEMS TO HAVE ORIGINATED FROM THE ROMAN INQUISITION, A DEVICE FOR COLLECTING REVENUES FROM UNWILLING SUBJECTS. BEGAN AS INSTRUMENT OF POWER OF MONARCH IN TAXING, ENFORCING LAWS, AND COLLECTING FINES.

0248 BEARD C.A., LEWIS J.D.
"REPRESENTATIVE GOVERNMENT IN EVOLUTION"
AM. POL. SCI. REV., (APR. 32), 223-240.
TRACES EVOLUTION OF IDEAS OF REPRESENTATIVE GOVERNMENT FROM GREECE AND ROME TO 20TH CENTRUY. FINDS IT ORIGINATED IN AGRICULTURAL AGE AS INSTRUMENT OF CENTRAL AUTHORITY, DICTATORIAL IN SUBSTANCE AND MONARCHICAL IN FORM, TO SECURE OBEDIENCE OF CLASSES. IT AWAKENENED IN MASSES A SENSE OF POWER WHICH WAS EVENTUALLY PUT INTO PRACTICE. DISCUSSES QUESTION OF EFFICIENCY OF REPRESENTATIVE GOVERNMENT TODAY.

0249 BEARDSLEY R.K. ED.
STUDIES ON ECONOMIC LIFE IN JAPAN (OCCASIONAL PAPERS NO. 8)
ANN ARBOR: U OF MICH PR, 1964, 124 PP.
FOUR PAPERS ON JAPANESE ECONOMIC LIFE: A COMPARISON OF AMERICAN AND JAPANESE HOUSING; STUDY OF FINANCIAL COMBINE CENTERED IN OHARA FAMILY OF OKAYAMA; ANALYSIS OF MANUSCRIPT PUBLICATIONS IN JAPAN; AND A COMPARISON OF RURAL STANDARDS

OF LIVING WITHIN JAPAN, ANALYZING FACTORS OF VILLAGE PROSPERITY.

0250 BEATTIE J.
BUNYORO, AN AFRICAN KINGDOM.
NEW YORK: HOLT RINEHART WINSTON, 1960, 86 PP., LC#60-07331.
REPORT ON FIELD-WORK DONE HERE FROM 1951-55. COVERS HISTORY, RULERSHIP, KINSHIP, SECONDARY SOCIAL GROUPS, AND RELIGION; WITH BIBLIOGRAPHY.

0251 BEATTIE J.
OTHER CULTURES.
NEW YORK: FREE PRESS OF GLENCOE, 1964, 281 PP., LC#64-16952.
DELINEATES SOCIAL ANTHROPOLOGY AS NEW FIELD, DISCUSSING ITS METHODS, AIMS, AND VALUES. ALSO DEALS DIRECTLY WITH TOPICS STUDIED IN SOCIAL ANTHROPOLOGY, RELIGION, KINSHIP, SOCIAL CONTROL, AND SOCIAL CHANGE.

0252 BECHHOEFER B.G.
"SOVIET ATTITUDE TOWARD DISARMAMENT."
CURR. HIST., 45 (OCT. 63), 193-199.
DISCUSSES EAST-WEST NEGOTIATIONS FOR DISARMAMENT AGREEMENT, WARNING THAT 'AN AGREEMENT TO CEASE TESTS STANDING ALONE AND NOT LEADING TO MORE EXTENSIVE AGREEMENTS WILL NOT DO MUCH TO LIMIT THE ARMS RACE OR LESSEN MENACE OF NUCLEAR WAR... NEXT STEP WILL PROBABLY BE A PACKAGE PROPOSAL CONTAINING SOME POLITICAL AGREEMENTS.'

0253 BECKER H.
MAN IN RECIPROCITY: INTRODUCTORY LECTURES ON CULTURE, SOCIETY, AND PERSONALITY.
NEW YORK: FREDERICK PRAEGER, 1956, 459 PP., LC#56-7746.
SERIES OF LECTURES DISCUSSES INTERRELATED ASPECTS OF SOCIAL AND PSYCHOLOGICAL ANTHROPOLOGY, THE NATURE AND STRUCTURE OF HUMAN CULTURES, AND SOCIAL PROBLEMS. INCLUDES EFFECTS OF VARIOUS SOCIAL GROUPS AND INSTITUTIONS ON DIFFERENT TYPES OF CULTURES. DISCUSSES STRUCTURE OF VARIOUS TYPES OF SOCIAL INSTITUTIONS AND DESCRIBES SOCIAL PROCESSES AND AVENUES FOR SOCIAL ACTION ON INDIVIDUAL AND GROUP LEVELS.

0254 BECKER J.
BESSARABIEN UND SEIN DEUTSCHTUM.
WURTTEMBURG: VERLAG EDUARD KRUG, 1966, 227 PP.
DISCUSSES ECONOMIC, SOCIAL, AND CULTURAL LIFE OF GERMAN SETTLERS IN BESSARABIA UNDER RUSSIAN AND RUMANIAN RULE. DISCUSSES RELIGIOUS LIFE, LOCAL CUSTOMS, INDUSTRIAL GROWTH, AND ETHNIC COMPOSITION OF ENTIRE REGION.

0255 BECKHAM R.S.
"A BASIC LIST OF BOOKS AND PERIODICALS FOR COLLEGE LIBRARIES."
BERKELEY: U OF CALIF PR, 1963.
IN D.G. MANDELBAUM'S "RESOURCES FOR THE TEACHING OF ANTHROPOLOGY." LISTS SOURCES BY SUBJECT. MAJORITY OF ENTRIES 1950-63.

0256 BEDERMAN S.H.
THE ETHNOLOGICAL CONTRIBUTIONS OF JOHN LEDYARD (PAMPHLET)
ATLANTA: GEORGIA STATE COLL, 1964, 28 PP.
DISCUSSES IMPORTANCE OF WORK OF LEDYARD AND HIS EFFECT OF FIELD OF CULTURAL ANTHROPOLOGY. HIS STUDIES OF TAHITIANS, AMERICAN INDIANS, KAMCHATKANS, AND TARTARS ARE EVALUATED.

0257 BEDFORD S.
THE FACES OF JUSTICE: A TRAVELLER'S REPORT.
NEW YORK: SIMON AND SCHUSTER, 1961, 316 PP., LC#61-9595.
ANALYSIS OF JUSTICE, HUMANITY, AND INDIVIDUAL AS SEEN IN COURTS AT ALL LEVELS IN ENGLAND, GERMANY, AUSTRIA, SWITZERLAND, AND FRANCE. CASE STUDIES OF EACH NATION BASED ON ASSUMPTION THAT "JUSTICE TO INDIVIDUAL IS HEART OF EVERY CIVILIZATION."

0258 BEER S.H.
BRITISH POLITICS IN THE COLLECTIVIST AGE.
NEW YORK: ALFRED KNOPF, 1966, 390 PP., LC#65-11116.
IDENTIFIES DISTINCTIONS OF CONTEMPORARY POLITICAL FORMATIONS AND THEIR MODES OF ACTION THROUGH COMPARISON WITH OTHER HISTORICAL PERIODS AND THEIR POLITICAL PARTIES. ANALYZES CONTEMPORARY POLITICAL PARTIES AND INTEREST GROUPS AND THE WAYS IN WHICH THEY AFFECT PUBLIC POLICY. EMPHASIZES POLITICAL CULTURE AS ONE OF MAIN VARIABLES OF A POLITICAL SYSTEM AND AS MAJOR EXPLANATION OF INDIVIDUAL POLITICAL BEHAVIOR.

0259 BEFU H.
"THE POLITICAL RELATION OF THE VILLAGE TO THE STATE."
WORLD POLITICS, 19 (1967), 601-620.
EXAMINES POLITICAL STRUCTURE OF PRIMITIVE, CLASSICAL, AND MODERN VILLAGES AND THEIR RESPECTIVE POLITICAL RELATIONSHIPS WITH A CENTRAL AUTHORITY. REFLECTS UPON THE ROLE NATIONALISM PLAYS IN UNITING A MODERN STATE, WHEREAS IN A PRIMITIVE SOCIETY KINSHIP IS MORE IMPORTANT.

0260 BEHAR D.
BIBLIOGRAFIA HISPANOAMERICANA. LIBROS ANTIGUOS Y MODERNOS REFERENTES A AMERICA Y ESPANA.
BUENOS AIRES: LIBERIA PANAMER, 1947, 371 PP.
BIBLIOGRAPHICAL CATALOGUE OF ARGENTINA, AND OTHER BOOKS REFERRING TO AMERICA AND STUDIES OF HISTORY, ARCHEOLOGY, LINGUISTICS, FOLKLORE, SCIENCE, ETC. INCLUDES BOTH ANCIENT AND 20TH-CENTURY WORKS. MATERIALS ARE LISTED ACCORDING TO SUBJECT. INCLUDES INDEXES OF SUBJECTS AND COUNTRIES. ALL ENTRIES ARE IN SPANISH.

0261 BELFRAGE C.
THE MAN AT THE DOOR WITH THE GUN.
NEW YORK: MONTHLY REVIEW PR, 1963, 253 PP., LC#63-22680.
ANALYZES LATIN AMERICAN ATTITUDES TOWARD US AND NEEDS OF PEOPLE. EXAMINES POLITICAL AND ECONOMIC SITUATION OF ALL LATIN AMERICAN NATIONS WITH SPECIAL EMPHASIS ON CUBA AND DEVELOPMENT UNDER CASTRO.

0262 BELGION M.
"THE CASE FOR REHABILITATING MARSHAL PETAIN."
QUARTERLY REV., (APR. 67), 205-212.
AUTHOR SUPPORTS MOVEMENT FOR REPARATION TO BE DONE TO THE REPUTATION OF MARSHAL PETAIN AND PRESENTS FACTS ABOUT HIM AND REASONS WHY HE MUST BE EXONERATED OF CHARGE OF BETRAYING FRANCE UNJUSTLY. FEELS PETAIN WAS A TRAGIC FIGURE AND SUBJECT OF FATE.

0263 BELL C.
THE DEBATABLE ALLIANCE.
LONDON: OXFORD U PR, 1964, 130 PP.
ANALYSIS OF RELATIONSHIP BETWEEN USA AND GREAT BRITAIN, FOCUSING ON DEVELOPMENTS FOLLOWING WWII AND CONSIDERING ANGLO-AMERICAN RELATIONS AS KEY ELEMENT IN INTERNATIONAL POWER BALANCE.

0264 BELL D.
"TEN THEORIES IN SEARCH OF REALITY: THE PREDICTION OF SOVIET BEHAVIOR IN THE SOCIAL SCIENCES" (BMR)"
WORLD POLITICS, 10 (APR. 58), 327-365.
EXAMINES TEN THEORIES EXPLAINING SOVIET SOCIETY AND ASSESSES IN DETAIL THESE VARIOUS METHODOLOGIES. ASKS WHICH THEORIES HAVE STOOD TEST OF TIME IN EXPLAINING SOVIET BEHAVIOR AND WHICH RESEARCH ONE WOULD USE IN FUTURE POLICY-MAKING. THEORIES INCLUDE THE POLITICAL, THE SOCIOLOGICAL, THE CHARACTEROLOGICAL, AND THE HISTORICAL.

0265 BELL D.
THE END OF IDEOLOGY (REV. ED.)
NEW YORK: FREE PRESS OF GLENCOE, 1962, 474 PP., LC#59-12186.
COLLECTION OF ESSAYS DEALING WITH SOCIAL CHANGES IN AMERICA DURING THE 1950'S. EMPHASIZES FALSITY OF SIMPLIFICATION AND IDEOLOGICAL PITFALLS INTO WHICH SUCH SIMPLIFICATIONS LEAD. ARGUES THAT INADEQUACIES OF MANY AMERICAN SOCIAL THEORIES ARE DUE TO UNCRITICAL APPLICATION OF AMBIENT IDEAS FROM EUROPEAN SOCIOLOGY TO THE DIFFERENT EXPERIENCES OF AMERICAN LIFE, IN PARTICULAR, THE THEORY OF MASS SOCIETY.

0266 BELL W.
"EQUALITY AND ATTITUDES OF ELITES IN JAMAICA"
SOCIAL ECO. STUDIES, 11 (DEC. 62), 409-432.
DISCUSSES TREND TOWARD EQUALITY IN JAMAICA. DESCRIBES AND ANALYZES ATTITUDES OF JAMAICAN ELITES TOWARD EQUALITY. THESE ELITES ARE FOUND TO BE FAVORABLY DISPOSED TOWARD ECONOMIC AND SOCIAL EQUALITY, ESPECIALLY THE YOUNGER MEMBERS. A QUESTIONNAIRE TOOL WAS USED IN THIS STUDY.

0267 BELL W.
JAMAICAN LEADERS: POLITICAL ATTITUDES IN A NEW NATION.
BERKELEY: U OF CALIF PR, 1964, 229 PP., LC#64-19447.
CASE STUDY IN SOCIOLOGY OF NATIONHOOD. DESCRIBES PROBLEMS FACED BY JAMAICA IN ITS TRANSITION FROM COLONIAL DEPENDENCE TO FULL POLITICAL INDEPENDENCE. FOCUSES ON EXPLORATION AND DISCOVERY OF CAUSES OF NATIONALISM, FACTORS PRODUCING NATIONALIST ATTITUDES. WORK BASED UPON SYSTEMATIC COLLECTION, ANALYSIS, AND PRESENTATION OF QUESTIONNAIRE SURVEY.

0268 BELLER I.
"ECONOMIC POLICY AND THE DEMANDS OF LABOR."
DISSENT, 14 (MAY-JUNE 67), 263-270.
WHILE GOVERNMENTAL ECONOMIC STEPS HAVE SHOWN IT POSSIBLE TO AVOID DEPRESSIONS, SUCH ACTION HAS GENERALLY WORKED THROUGH STEPS BENEFITING THE CORPORATE STRUCTURE RATHER THAN BY STEPS TO AID THE DEPRIVED AND TO SOLVE SOCIAL PROBLEMS. FULL EMPLOYMENT HAS BEEN DROPPED AS A GOAL. THE WAR IN VIETNAM HAS DRAINED RESOURCES WHICH MIGHT HAVE GONE TO POVERTY PROGRAMS.

0269 BELLOC H.
THE SERVILE STATE (1912) (3RD ED.)
LONDON: CONSTABLE & CO, 1927, 189 PP.
AN ATTACK UPON EARLY 20TH-CENTURY CAPITALISM FROM A ROMAN CATHOLIC VIEWPOINT. CENTRAL THESIS IS THAT INDUSTRIAL SOCIETIES SUCH AS BRITAIN AND PRUSSIA, WHICH DEPARTED FROM 16TH-CENTURY CHRISTIAN TRADITIONS, WILL TEND TOWARD THE RE-ESTABLISHMENT OF SLAVERY AS RESULT OF UNSTABLE BALANCE BETWEEN CLASSES CAUSED BY LEGALLY ENFORCED LABOR REGULATIONS AND FINANCIAL OPPRESSION. INCLUDES 1913 AND 1927 PREFACES.

0270 BELLOC H.

THE RESTORATION OF PROPERTY.
NEW YORK: SHEED AND WARD, 1936, 144 PP.
AN ASSAULT ON BRITISH ECONOMIC AND SOCIAL STRUCTURE. "PROPERTY" IS DEFINED AS CONTROL OVER MEANS OF PRODUCTION, WHICH THE INDIVIDUAL WAGE-EARNER HAS LOST TO MONOPOLISTIC INSTITUTIONS SANCTIONED BY GOVERNMENT. FREEDOM TO CONTROL THE OUTPUT OF HIS ENERGIES CAN BE RESTORED TO THE INDIVIDUAL ONLY THROUGH A LEGALLY ESTABLISHED GUILD SYSTEM, WHICH NEITHER CAPITALISM NOT SOCIALISM OFFERS.

0271 BELOFF M.
NEW DIMENSIONS IN FOREIGN POLICY: A STUDY IN BRITISH ADMINISTRATION.
LONDON: ALLEN UNWIN, 1961, 208 PP.
ASSESSES PROBLEMS OF INTEGRATING NATIONAL POLITICAL SYSTEMS WITH POST-WAR INTERNATIONAL ORGANIZATIONS. PRESENT ARRANGEMENT OF WESTERN EUROPEAN AND NORTH ATLANTIC COMMUNITY POSES PROBLEMS OF CREATION, ADAPTATION, AND CO-ORDINATION. CHOOSING BETWEEN ISOLATION AND PARTICIPATION IS QUANDARY FACING GOVERNMENT LEADERS.

0272 BELSHAW C.S.
"IN SEARCH OF WEALTH; STUDY OF EMERGENCE OF COMMERCIAL OPERATIONS IN MELANESIAN SOCIETY OF SOUTHEASTERN PAPUA."
MENASHA, WIS: AMER ANTHROPOLOG ASSN, 1955, 84PP 1644
SHOWS HOW COMMERCIAL OPERATIONS ARE ORGANIZED AROUND BOTH TRADITIONAL SOCIAL RELATIONSHIPS AND THE MORE MODERN EUROPEAN MODE OF OPERATING. BOTH METHODS ARE USED BY NATIVES, DEPENDING ON RESULTS DESIRED.

0273 BENDIX R. ED., LIPSET S.M. ED.
CLASS, STATUS AND POWER: A READER IN SOCIAL STRATIFICATION.
NEW YORK: FREE PRESS OF GLENCOE, 1953, 725 PP.
GUIDE TO LITERATURE ON SOCIAL STRATIFICATION. PART ONE INCLUDES SELECTED STATEMENTS REPRESENTING DIFFERENT THEORIES OF SOCIAL STRATIFICATION. PART TWO CONTAINS STUDIES OF CONTEMPORARY AMERICAN SOCIETY. PART THREE CONTAINS SELECTIONS REPRESENTATIVE OF RESEARCH ON SOCIAL STRATIFICATION IN OTHER COUNTRIES. INCLUDES THEORETICAL AND HISTORICAL MATERIAL.

0274 BENDIX R., LIPSET S.M.
"POLITICAL SOCIOLOGY."
CURRENT SOCIOLOGY, 6 (1957), 79-169.
AN ESSAY AND BIBLIOGRAPHY WITH SPECIAL REFERENCE TO DEVELOPMENT OF RESEARCH IN US AND WESTERN EUROPE IN FIELD OF POLITICAL SOCIOLOGY. ANNOTATED LIST OF 844 WORKS IN ENGLISH AND WEST EUROPEAN LANGUAGES PUBLISHED SINCE 1950. COMPREHENSIVE CRITICAL AND DESCRIPTIVE ANNOTATIONS FOR ALL SELECTIONS. TOPICALLY CLASSIFIED IN FRENCH AND ENGLISH.

0275 BENDIX R.
NATION-BUILDING AND CITIZENSHIP: STUDIES OF OUR CHANGING SOCIAL ORDER.
NEW YORK: JOHN WILEY, 1964, 314 PP., LC#64-25898.
COMPARATIVE ANALYSIS OF PUBLIC AND PRIVATE "AUTHORITY RELATIONSHIPS" IN WESTERN, RUSSIAN, JAPANESE, AND INDIAN SOCIETIES SINCE MIDDLE AGES. AUTHORITY IN SOCIETY CHANGES FROM ESTATES, TO REGIMES, TO NATIONS, WHILE PERSONAL RELATIONS MOVE FROM MASTER-SERVANT TO INDIVIDUAL. ANALYZES RELATIONS IN TERMS OF POLITICAL, SOCIAL, AND HISTORICAL SETTINGS.

0276 BENEDETTI V.
STUDIES IN DIPLOMACY.
LONDON: HEINEMAN, 1896, 226 PP.
FRENCH AMBASSADOR TO THE COURT OF BERLIN DEFENDS HIS NATION'S SCHEME TO UNITE BELGIUM AND FRANCE, ASSERTING THAT GERMANY'S PLOT TO PLACE PRINCE LEOPOLD ON THE SPANISH THRONE LED INEVITABLY TO THE WAR OF 1870. TWO ESSAYS ON THE TRIPLE ALLIANCE AND THE CONSEQUENCES OF THE 'ARMED PEACE' INCLUDED.

0277 BENEDICT B.
A SHORT ANNOTATED BIBLIOGRAPHY RELATING TO THE SOCIOLOGY OF MUSLIM PEOPLES.
MONTREAL: MCGILL U, INST ISLAM, 1955, 115 PP.
COMPILATION OF BOOKS AND PERIODICALS, CHIEFLY IN ENGLISH AND FRENCH, LOCATED IN THE MCGILL UNIVERSITY LIBRARY AND RELATING TO SOCIOLOGY OF THE MUSLIM PEOPLE. ANNOTATED AND ARRANGED BY COUNTRY. ITEMS DATE FROM TURN OF CENTURY.

0278 BENEDICT R.
PATTERNS OF CULTURE.
BOSTON: HOUGHTON, 1934, 291 PP.
DESCRIBES CULTURES OF THREE PRIMITIVE TRIBES AND ASSERTS THAT SUCH BEHAVIORAL-STUDIES PROVIDE INSIGHT INTO THE 'SOCIAL ORDER'. ASSUMES THAT CULTURE SHAPES INDIVIDUAL BEHAVIOR DUE TO ENORMOUS MALLEABILITY OF PERSON FROM BIRTH.

0279 BENEDICT R.
"RITUAL" IN ERA SELIGMAN, ENCYCLOPEDIA OF THE SOCIAL SCIENCES."
NEW YORK: MACMILLAN, 1934.
DEFINES RITUAL AS PRESCRIBED AND ELABORATED BEHAVIOR THAT OCCURS BOTH AS AN INDIVIDUAL AND A CULTURAL TRAIT. COMPARES VARIOUS TYPES OF RITUAL AND SURVEYS EXPLANATIONS FOR THEIR OCCURRENCE. EXPLAINS SIGNIFICANCE OF CROSS-CULTURAL COMPARISONS OF RITUALS.

0280 BENES E.
INTERNATIONAL SECURITY.
CHICAGO: U. CHI. PR., 1939, 153 PP.
DISCUSSES SECURITY ASPECTS OF NEGOTIATION OF TREATIES OF MUTUAL ASSISTANCE. EXAMINES POLICY CONSISTENCIES AND INCONSISTENCIES OF GREAT POWERS. STRESSES ARBITRATION, DISARMAMENT AND SECURITY. APPRAISES ROLES OF ENGLAND AND GERMANY IN POST-WORLD WAR ONE EUROPEAN DIPLOMACY.

0281 BENES E.
DEMOCRACY TODAY AND TOMORROW.
NEW YORK: MACMILLAN, 1939, 244 PP.
EXAMINES FASCISM, NATIONAL SOCIALISM, DIVERGENCE BETWEEN AUTHORITARIANISM AND DEMOCRACY AND FAILURE OF POST WAR DEMOCRACIES AND LEAGUE OF NATIONS. SPECULATES ON SOCIAL AND POLITICAL DISINTEGRATION AND POSSIBILITY OF A SECOND WORLD WAR.

0282 BENN S.I.
"THE USES OF 'SOVEREIGNTY'."
POLITICAL STUDIES, 3 (JUNE 55), 109-122.
ATTEMPTS TO ISOLATE AND EXAMINE VARIOUS USAGES OF CONCEPT OF SOVEREIGNTY TO DISCOVER IN WHAT KINDS OF STUDY EACH MAY BE USEFUL. SEEKS TO DETERMINE WHETHER USAGES POSSESS ANY COMMON ELEMENT THAT WOULD JUSTIFY USE OF ONE WORD, "SOVEREIGNTY", TO COVER THEM ALL. DISCUSSES LEGAL AND LEGISLATIVE SOVEREIGNTY, SOVEREIGNTY OF THE STATE IN ITS INTERNATIONAL ASPECT, AND SOVEREIGNTY AS COERCIVE POWER.

0283 BENOIST C.
LA POLITIQUE.
PARIS: LEON CHAILLEY EDITEUR, 1894, 266 PP.
GENERAL STUDY OF POLITICS AND STATE FOLLOWED BY EXAMINATION OF FRANCE, ITS SOCIETY, POLITICAL POWER, STRUCTURE AND FUNCTIONS OF GOVERNMENT.

0284 BENOIT E.
"WORLD DEFENSE EXPENDITURES."
J. OF PHILOSOPHY, (1966), 7-113.
A COMPILATION AND ANALYSIS OF DEFENSE EXPENDITURES FOR 36 COUNTRIES IN US DOLLARS. EXPENDITURES, COVERING 1960-1965, ARE BROKEN DOWN INTO MILITARY PERSONNEL, R&D, MAJOR PROCUREMENTS, CONSTRUCTION, AND OPERATIONS AND MAINTENANCE CATEGORIES.

0285 BENSON M.
"SOUTH AFRICA AND WORLD OPINION."
CURR. HIST., 46 (MARCH 64), 129-135.
COUNTRY WAS EXPECTED TO PLAY A LEADING ROLE IN ADVANCE OF AFRICAN CONTINENT. INSTEAD, HAS BECOME THE 'BETE NOIRE' OF REST OF AFRICA AND TO SOME EXTENT THE WORLD AT LARGE. ONLY IN SOUTH AFRICA, SINCE HITLER, HAS A STATE BEEN BASED ON RACIALISM.

0286 BENTHAM A.
HANDBOOK OF POLITICAL FALLACIES.
BALTIMORE: JOHNS HOPKINS PR., 1952, 269 PP.
PRESENTS A HANDBOOK ON THE ART OF VERBAL WARFARE IN POLITICS. INTENDED FOR THE LOGICAL DISSECTION OF LEGISLATIVE DEBATES AND A POSSIBLE WEAPON FOR PARLIAMENTARY REFORM. CONCENTRATION OF THE USE OF LOGIC IN THE SEEMINGLY AMBIGUOUS VERBAL GAME OF POLITICS.

0287 BENTHAM J.
AN INTRODUCTION TO THE PRINCIPLES OF MORALS AND LEGISLATION.
LONDON: CLARENDON PR., 1907, 378 PP.
THEORY OF PLEASURE/PAIN AND UTILITY ANALYZING EFFICACY OF JURISPRUDENCE.

0288 BENTHAM J.
A PLAN FOR AN UNIVERSAL AND PERPETUAL PEACE (1838) (PAMPHLET)
LONDON: SWEET AND MAXWELL, LTD, 1927, 44 PP.
PROPOSES REDUCTION AND FIXATION OF FORCES IN MAJOR COUNTRIES IN EUROPE, AND EMANCIPATION OF COLONIAL DEPENDENCIES OF EACH STATE. CLAIMS THAT COLONIES ARE OF LITTLE OR NO VALUE TO MOTHER COUNTRIES, BUT A CONSTANT SOURCE OF INTERNATIONAL STRIFE. URGES ESTABLISHMENT OF INTERNATIONAL COURTS TO SETTLE DISPUTES. PAYS LITTLE HEED TO ECONOMICS OF COLONIALISM; DISPUTES EXISTENCE OF REAL CONFLICTS OF INTEREST.

0289 BENTHAM J.
THE RATIONALE OF PUNISHMENT.
ORIGINAL PUBLISHER NOT AVAILABLE, 1830, 439 PP.
STATES THAT PUNISHMENT IS A NECESSARY EVIL IN RESPONSE TO CRIME. DISCUSSES ITS USE AND ABUSE BY GOVERNMENTS, ASKING FOR LEGISLATIVE CONTROL OF IT AND WARNING THAT ABUSES MAY LEAD TO LOSS OF EFFECTIVENESS. CALLS FOR REFORMS IN JURIDICAL SYSTEM OF ENGLAND, WHICH HE CALIMS IS OFTEN UNNECESSARILY AND CAPRICIOUSLY HARSH. DISCUSSES NATURE AND TYPES OF PUNISHMENT THEN IN USE.

0290 BENTHAM J.
"ON THE LIBERTY OF THE PRESS, AND PUBLIC DISCUSSION" IN J. BOWRING, ED., THE WORKS OF JEREMY BENTHAM."
ORIGINAL PUBLISHER NOT AVAILABLE, 1843.
SERIES OF FOUR LETTERS INTENDED FOR PUBLICATION IN SPAIN, PROTESTING RESTRICTIONS ON THE PRESS AND A PROPOSED LAW ABOLISHING THE RIGHT TO HOLD POLITICAL MEETINGS. MAINTAINS THAT IT IS DESPOTISM TO ABOLISH THESE INDIVIDUAL LIBERTIES FOR ANY REASON. ALSO ATTACKS THE CORTES, SPANISH LEGISLATIVE BODY, BECAUSE IT IS AN ARISTOCRATIC BODY AND REPRESENTS ITS OWN INTERESTS RATHER THAN THOSE OF THE PEOPLE.

0291 BENTHAM J.
"PRINCIPLES OF INTERNATIONAL LAW" IN J. BOWRING, ED., THE WORKS OF JEREMY BENTHAM."
ORIGINAL PUBLISHER NOT AVAILABLE, 1843.
FOUR ESSAYS CONSIDERING OBJECTS OF INTERNATIONAL LAW, JURISDICTION, WAR, AND PEACE. AUTHOR BELIEVES THAT OBJECTS OF INTERNATIONAL LAW INCLUDE DOING NO INJURY TO OTHER NATIONS AND DOING GREATEST POSSIBLE GOOD TO OTHER NATIONS, WHILE PROTECTING WELFARE OF ONE'S OWN NATION. CONSIDERS POTENTIAL AND ACTUAL JURISDICTION, AND RIGHTFUL OR MORAL JURISDICTION. DISCUSSES CAUSES OF WAR AND PLAN FOR PEACE.

0292 BENTHAM J., MONTAGUE F.C. ED.
A FRAGMENT ON GOVERNMENT (1776)
LONDON: OXFORD U PR, 1891, 241 PP.
REFUTATION OF SECOND PART OF BLACKSTONE'S INTRODUCTION TO HIS "COMMENTARIES," CONCERNING NATURE OF LAW IN GENERAL. PRIMARILY CONCERNS NATURE OF SOVEREIGNTY. BELIEVES THAT SOVEREIGNTY REPRESENTS UNLIMITED AUTHORITY OVER PEOPLE, AND THAT IT IS NOT SUBJECT TO LAW. RESISTANCE TO SOVEREIGN MAY BE MORAL WHEN IT IS A QUESTION OF UTILITY, I.E., PRESERVING HAPPINESS OF GREATEST NUMBER OF PEOPLE.

0293 BENTWICH J.S.
EDUCATION IN ISRAEL.
PHILA: JEWISH PUBL SOC AMER, 1965, 204 PP.
ACCOUNT OF FORMS OF EDUCATION IN ISRAEL AND THEIR PRESENT ORGANIZATION AND CURRICULA. DISCUSSES ISRAELI ATTEMPTS TO SOLVE PROBLEMS OF CREATING MEANINGFUL VALUES IN A HEDONISTIC WORLD, BREAKING DOWN CLASS BARRIERS, BUILDING A SYNTHESIS OF RELIGION AND SCIENCE, AND CREATING A BETTER WAY OF LIFE IN A TECHNOLOGICAL SOCIETY.

0294 BERDYAEV N.A.
THE ORIGIN OF RUSSIAN COMMUNISM.
NEW YORK: CHAS SCRIBNER'S SONS, 1937, 229 PP.
DISCUSSES WAY IN WHICH CHARACTERISTICALLY RUSSIAN INSTITUTIONS INFLUENCED GROWTH OF RUSSIAN COMMUNISM. EMPHASIZES AMBIVALENCE OF RUSSIAN ORTHODOX RELIGION, FORMATION OF INTELLIGENTSIA, NIHILISM, AND 19TH CENTURY LITERATURE AND ITS PREDICTIONS. ENDS WITH CHAPTER ON COMMUNISM AND CHRISTIANITY.

0295 BERDYAEV N.A.
SLAVERY AND FREEDOM.
NEW YORK: CHAS SCRIBNER'S SONS, 1944, 271 PP.
AUTHOR BELIEVES IN "PERSONALIST SOCIALISM," WHICH IS THE BELIEF IN PERSONALITY OVER SOCIETY. DISAPPROVES OF ELITISM IN GROUP FORM. BELIEVES IN ARISTOCRACY OF PERSONALITY, BUT NOT IN ELITISM WHEN IT TAKES FORM OF AUTHORITARIANISM, FAMILY PROPERTY, NATIONALISM, REVOLUTIONARY DEMOCRATIC SOCIALIST GOVERNMENTS, AND "BOURGEOIS ELITES." SEES ORIGINAL SIN IN HISTORY AS BEING THE ENSLAVEMENT OF THE INDIVIDUAL.

0296 BERDYAEV N.A.
CHRISTIANITY AND CLASS WAR.
NEW YORK: SHEED AND WARD, 1933, 123 PP.
CRITICIZES MARX FOR SEEING CLASS WAR ONLY IN TERMS OF ECONOMIC CONDITIONS. BELIEVES THAT CHRISTIANS MUST NOT IGNORE FACT THAT CLASS WAR EXISTS. MARXISM CANNOT BE OPPOSED BY IDEAS BUT BY BEING. BEING IS SPIRIT, NOT MATTER. SUPREME POWER IS IN THE SPIRIT, NOT IN ECONOMICS OR CLASS WAR. BELIEVES PROBLEM OF CLASSES IS A MORAL ONE, AND CHRISTIAN ATTITUDES TOWARD MAN AND SOCIETY MUST CHANGE.

0297 BERELSON B. ET AL.
"SAMPLE SURVEYS AND POPULATION CONTROL."
PUB. OPIN. QUART., 28 (64), 361-94.
FOUR STUDIES IN LATIN AMERICA, TAIWAN, AND PAKISTAN. CENTRAL PROBLEM: 'HOW TO DO TECHNICALLY SOLID STUDIES AS FOREIGN ADVISORS WITH FEW QUALIFIED NATIONALS, IN A FOREIGN LANGUAGE, WITH LARGELY ILLITERATE PEOPLE, IN AN ALIEN CULTURE, ON A PERSONALLY DELICATE MATTER...IN A WAY THAT WILL GUIDE POLICY DECISIONS'.

0298 BERELSON B. ED., JANOWITZ M. ED.
READER IN PUBLIC OPINION AND COMMUNICATION (2ND ED.)
LONDON: MACMILLAN, 1966, 788 PP., LC#65-18560.
STUDIES PUBLIC OPINION THEORY; FORMATION AND IMPACT OF PUBLIC OPINION ON PUBLIC POLICY; COMMUNICATION MEDIA, ITA THEORIES CONTENT, AUDIENCES, AND EFFECTS. EXAMINES COMMUNICATION AND DEMOCRATIC OBJECTIVES; AND RESEARCH AND COMPARATIVE ANALYSIS METHODS.

0299 BERG E.J.
"ECONOMIC BASIS OF POLITICAL CHOICE IN FRENCH WEST AFRICA."
AMER. POLIT. SCI. REV., 54 (JUNE 60), 391-405.
ANALYZES ECONOMIC FACTORS WHICH HAVE PLAYED ROLE IN RELATIONS OF WEST AFRICAN STATES WITH ONE ANOTHER AND WITH FRENCH COMMUNITY. DISCUSSES ROLE OF TARIFF AND PRICE PROTECTION IN THEIR POLITICAL CONTEXT.

0300 BERGER M. ED., ABEL T. ED., PAGE C.H. ED.
FREEDOM AND CONTROL IN MODERN SOCIETY.
PRINCETON: VAN NOSTRAND, 1954, 325 PP., LC#54-7534.
A COLLECTION OF WRITINGS BY SUCH AUTHORS AS LAZARSFELD, MERTON, LIPSET, AND CATLIN, ON PROBLEMS OF AUTHORITY, POLITICAL PROCESS IN TRADE UNIONS, ETHNIC GROUPS, AND THE INTERPLAY OF POLITICS AND ECONOMICS. INCLUDES MACIVER'S CONTRIBUTIONS TO POLITICAL THEORY, AND OTHER QUESTIONS.

0301 BERGER M.
THE ARAB WORLD TODAY.
GARDEN CITY: DOUBLEDAY, 1962, 480 PP., LC#62-7601.
DISCUSSES HISTORY, CHARACTER, SOCIAL INSTITUTIONS, AND SOCIAL CHANGE OF ARAB SOCIETY. ANALYZES PATTERNS OF LIVING IN DESERT, VILLAGE, AND URBAN COMMUNITIES. DESCRIBES FAMILY, RELIGION, AND ECONOMIC LIFE. EXAMINES SOCIAL BASIS OF POLITICAL INSTITUTIONS, IDEOLOGIES, AND MILITARY REGIMES.

0302 BERGSON A. ED.
ECONOMIC TRENDS IN THE SOVIET UNION.
CAMBRIDGE: HARVARD U PR, 1963, 392 PP., LC#63-9548.
ESSAYS PROVIDING DETAILED ANALYSIS OF MAJOR PROBLEM AREAS IN SOVIET ECONOMIC GROWTH. SEVERAL COMPARISONS WITH ECONOMIC PROGRESS IN OTHER COUNTRIES, PRINCIPALLY IN US.

0303 BERGSTRASSER L.
GESCHICHTE DER POLITISCHEN PARTEIEN.
BERLIN: J. BENSHEIMER, 1921, 148 PP.
A DISCUSSION OF THE MAJOR POLITICAL PARTIES IN GERMANY FROM THEIR IDEOLOGICAL BEGINNINGS IN THE 18TH CENTURY TO THE REVOLUTION IN 1918.

0304 BERNHARDI F.
GERMANY AND THE NEXT WAR.
NEW YORK: LONGMANS, 1914, 288 PP.
JUSTIFIES GERMAN PARTICIPATION IN WAR ON GROUNDS THAT WAR IS A BIOLOGICAL NECESSITY, MORAL OBLIGATION, AND HISTORICAL NECESSITY FOR ATTAINING DESTINY OF WORLD POWER. ASSESSES HOSTILE POWERS AND DETAILS REQUIRED TRAINING AND DEPLOYMENT OF FORCES. STRESSES EDUCATIONAL, FINANCIAL, AND POLITICAL PREPAREDNESS FOR WAR.

0305 BERKOWITZ L.
AGGRESSION: AS A SOCIAL PSYCHOLOGICAL ANALYSIS.
NEW YORK: MCGRAW HILL, 1961, 648 PP.
PRESENTS SOCIAL AND PSYCHOLOGICAL CAUSES OF AGGRESSION AND SUGGESTS METHODS FOR LESSENING THEM. CONCLUDES THAT SOCIAL RATHER THAN BIOLOGICAL CHARACTERISTICS DETERMINE AGGRESSIVENESS. DISCUSSES HOSTILITY, INSULTS, SOCIAL PREJUDICE, INTERGROUP RIVALRIES AND WARS.

0306 BERLE A.A. JR.
"THE 20TH CENTURY CAPITALIST REVOLUTION."
NEW YORK: HARCOURT BRACE, 1954.
STUDY OF THE MODERN CORPORATION FROM A QUASI-POLITICAL ANGLE. ARGUES THAT LARGE CORPORATION MANAGEMENTS HAVE REACHED A POSITION OF CONCENTRATED ECONOMIC POWER WHICH FORCES THEM TO CONSIDER AND PARTICIPATE IN POLITICAL, INTERNATIONAL, AND PHILOSOPHICAL CONSIDERATIONS. BRIEF ANNOTATED BIBLIOGRAPHY OF AMERICAN ECONOMIC WRITINGS PUBLISHED AFTER 1933.

0307 BERLIN I.
KARL MARX, HIS LIFE AND ENVIRONMENT (3RD ED.)
OXFORD: GALAXY BOOKS, 1963, 295 PP.
ACCOUNT OF LIFE AND DOCTRINES OF KARL MARX, INCLUDING HIS PART IN REVOLUTION OF 1848 AND HIS PERIOD OF EXILE IN LONDON. DESCRIBES MARX'S WORK AS A JOURNALIST, PROPAGANDIST, STRATEGIST, AND ECONOMIC THEORIST.

0308 BERLINER J.S.
"RUSSIA'S BUREAUCRATS - WHY THEY'RE REACTIONARY."
TRANSACTIONS, 5 (DEC. 67), 53-58.
ANALYZES WHY SOVIET BUREAUCRACY TENDS TO TAKE ON A LIFE OF ITS OWN AND PURSUE POLICIES THAT FURTHER ITS OWN INTERESTS, EVEN WHEN THOSE INTERESTS CONFLICT WITH WHAT THE LEADERSHIP WANTS. AUTHOR SUGGESTS ONE REASON IS THAT BUREAUCRATIC INNOVATIONS ARE NOT REWARDED. EMPHASIZES GOVERNMENT IMPOSED RESTRICTIONS ON INNOVATIVE TECHNIQUES.

0309 BERMAN H.J.
JUSTICE IN RUSSIA; AN INTERPRETATION OF SOVIET LAW.
CAMBRIDGE: HARVARD U PR, 1950, 322 PP.
EXAMINES SOVIET LEGAL SYSTEM IN TERMS OF ASSUMPTIONS OF SOVIET SOCIAL ORDER. MAINTAINS THAT SYSTEM DOES NOT DEPEND SOLELY ON TERROR BUT HAS DEFINITE LEGAL PRINCIPLES AS WELL. STUDIES SOCIALIST AND RUSSIAN LAW AND THEIR DEVELOPMENT AND RELATIONSHIP. LOOKS AT LAWS' PARENTAL FUNCTIONS AS THEY

AFFECT EDUCATION, FAMILY LIFE, DISPUTES, LABOR, AND PSYCHIATRY.

0310 BERNATZIK H.A.
THE SPIRITS OF THE YELLOW LEAVES.
LONDON: ROBERT HALE, 1951, 222 PP.
STUDY MADE IN 1930'S OF NATIVE POPULATIONS IN SOUTHEAST ASIAN MAINLAND, EXAMINING ORIGINS AND QUESTIONING ORIGINAL POPULATION OF REGION. PEOPLE ARE OF SEVERAL TRIBES, PRIMARILY HUNTERS AND FOOD GATHERERS.

0311 BERNDT R.M., BERNDT C.H.
THE WORLD OF THE FIRST AUSTRALIANS.
CHICAGO: U OF CHICAGO PRESS, 1964, 509 PP., LC#64-15806.
RESULT OF 20 YEARS OF FIELDWORK AMONG ABORIGINES IN MANY PARTS OF AUSTRALIA. CENTERS UPON WAY ABORIGINES LIVED BEFORE COMING OF EUROPEANS. COVERS EVERY ASPECT OF LIFE: SOCIAL AND FAMILY STRUCTURE; BIRTH, PUBERTY, MARRIAGE AND DEATH RITES; RELIGION, LAW AND ORDER; ART, SONG, AND STORY. CLOSES WITH CONSIDERATION OF ABORIGINES TODAY IN PERIOD OF TRANSITION.

0312 BERNDT R.M. ED., BERNDT C.H. ED.
ABORIGINAL MAN IN AUSTRALIA.
LONDON, SYDNEY: ANGUS & ROBERTSN, 1965, 491 PP.
COLLECTION OF DETAILED ESSAYS ON ANTHROPOLOGICAL STUDIES OF ABORIGINES IN AUSTRALIA INCLUDING ARCHEOLOGICAL EVIDENCES OF CIVILIZATION, DISCUSSIONS OF SOCIETY AND CULTURE, MUSIC, AND IMPACT OF CONTEMPORARY CIVILIZATION ON THEIR PATTERNS OF CULTURE. ALSO CONTAINS CHAPTER ON A.P. ELKIN AND BIBLIOGRAPHY OF HIS WORKS.

0313 BERNHARDI F.
ON THE WAR OF TODAY.
NEW YORK: DODD MEAD, 1914, 2 VOLS., 858 PP.
DISCUSSES NECESSARY BASIS FOR ALL DOCTRINES OF WAR. DEALS WITH RELATIONSHIP OF ATTACK AND DEFENSE IN MODERN WARFARE.

0314 BERNOT R.M.
EXCESS AND RESTRAINT: SOCIAL CONTROL AMONG GUINEA MOUNTAIN PEOPLE.
CHICAGO: U OF CHICAGO PRESS, 1962, 474 PP., LC#62-10996.
SOCIAL CONTROL AND SOCIAL CUSTOM AMONG PEOPLE BELONGING TO FOUR LANGUAGE GROUPS IN EASTERN HIGHLANDS OF NEW GUINEA. DEALS WITH DUAL CONCEPT OF CONFLICT AND COOPERATION, ORDER AND DISORDER, CONFORMITY AND NONCONFORMITY. SHOWS SOMETHING OF AN ONGOING SOCIETY AND CULTURE IN PROCESS OF CHANGE.

0315 BERNSTEIN H.
A BOOKSHELF ON BRAZIL.
ALBANY: U ST OF NY, ST EDUC DEPT, 1964, 23 PP.
ANNOTATED BIBLIOGRAPHY ON BRAZIL. COVERS THE SOCIAL SCIENCES AND HUMANITIES; INCLUDES SECTIONS ON PERIODICLAS AND BIBLIOGRAPHIES.

0316 BERNSTEIN H.
VENEZUELA AND COLOMBIA.
ENGLEWOOD CLIFFS: PRENTICE HALL, 1964, 152 PP., LC#64-23572.
TRACES RISE OF NATIONALISM IN VENEZUELA AND COLOMBIA AND ILLUMINATES SOURCES OF PRESENT UNREST AND REVOLUTION. EMPHASIZES STRONG HUMANISTIC TRADITION WHICH MARKS HISTORIES OF BOTH COUNTRIES BY DESCRIBING THEIR CULTURAL AND INTELLECTUAL PASTS.

0317 BERNSTEIN T.P.
"LEADERSHIP AND MASS MOBILIZATION IN THE SOVIET AND CHINESE COLLECTIVISATION CAMPAIGNS OF 1929-30, 1955-56: COMPARISON."
CHINA Q., 11 (JULY 67), 1-47.
COMPARES DIFFERENCES IN OUTCOMES OF AGRICULTURAL NATIONALIZATION WITH RESPECT TO PRODUCTIVITY AND PUBLIC REACTIONS. SOVIETS EXPERIENCED MASS OUTBREAKS OF RIOTING, PROPERTY DESTRUCTION, AND REFUSAL TO COOPERATE OWING TO ATTEMPTS TO COMBINE THIS WITH ACHIEVING RURAL POLITICAL CONTROL. CHINA'S GREATER SUCCESS IS CLAIMED TO BE RESULT OF ITS HAVING ONLY ONE GOAL.

0318 BERREMAN G.D.
"CASTE IN INDIA AND THE UNITED STATES" (BMR)"
AMER. J. OF SOCIOLOGY, 66 (1960), 120-127.
COMPARES RACE RELATIONS IN US WITH CASTE RELATIONS IN INDIA, AND FINDS THAT THE TWO SYSTEMS OPERATE IN A SIMILAR MANNER DESPITE DIFFERENCES OF CULTURE. AUTHOR FEELS THAT TERM "CASTE SYSTEM" IS NOT UNIQUE TO INDIA AND CAN BE APPLIED TO ANY SOCIETY WITH HIERARCHICAL, ENDOGAMOUS SUBDIVISIONS WHOSE MEMBERSHIP IS HEREDITARY AND PERMANENT.

0319 BERREMAN G.D.
HINDUS OF THE HIMALAYAS.
BERKELEY: U OF CALIF PR, 1963, 430 PP., LC#63-10463.
DESCRIBES CULTURE OF AGRARIAN HINDU SOCIETY, RELATING IMPORTANCE OF PERVASIVE RELIGION TO EVERYDAY LIFE. DISCUSSES WORKINGS AND DISTINCTIONS OF CASTE SYSTEM, CASTE RELATIONS, ECONOMIC EFFECTS OF HINDUISM, KINSHIP, AND IMPACT OF GOVERNMENT PROGRAMS ON COMMUNITIES.

0320 BERRINGTON H.
HOW NATIONS ARE GOVERNED.
NEW YORK: PITMAN PUBLISHING, 1964, 112 PP., LC#64-54854.
COMPARATIVE STUDY OF POLITICAL SYSTEMS IN WORLD. ANALYZES INSTITUTIONS IN ENGLAND AND POINTS OUT DIFFERENCES IN US AND FRANCE. STUDIES COMMUNIST AND UNDERDEVELOPED NON-DEMOCRATIC STATES, AND STRESSES INSTITUTIONS THEY HAVE BORROWED FROM DEMOCRATIC ONES. BRIEFLY STUDIES INTERNATIONAL GOVERNMENTAL PROCEDURE IN UN.

0321 BESSON W.
DIE GROSSEN MACHTE - STRUKTURFRAGEN DER GEGENWARTIGEN WELTPOLITIK.
FREIBURG: VERLAG ROMBACH + CO, 1966, 81 PP.
DISCUSSES POLITICS OF WORLD POWERS SINCE WWII AND SEEKS TO ESTABLISH A GENERAL PICTURE OF WORLD-POLITICAL TENDENCIES. INCLUDES ESSAY ON MEANING AND IMPORTANCE OF KENNEDY'S LEADERSHIP.

0322 BEST H.
"THE SOVIET STATE AND ITS INCEPTION."
NEW YORK: PHILOSOPHICAL LIB, 1951.
SOCIOLOGICAL APPRAISAL OF PRE-AND POST-REVOLUTIONARY HISTORY OF USSR AND STUDY OF SOCIAL PHILOSOPHY UNDERLYING THE SOVIET MOVEMENT. UNANNOTATED BIBLIOGRAPHY OF MATERIAL PUBLISHED IN ENGLISH INCLUDED. BOOKS ARRANGED CHRONOLOGICALLY FROM 1917 THROUGH 1950: SMALL SECTION OF PERIODICALS ARRANGED BY DATE OF FIRST PUBLICATION.

0323 BETEILLE A.
CASTE, CLASS, AND POWER.
BERKELEY: U OF CALIF PR, 1965, 225 PP., LC#65-25628.
STUDY OF CASTE, CLASS, AND POWER IN A SOUTH INDIAN VILLAGE. RESEARCH INDICATES THAT THE VILLAGE'S SOCIAL STRUCTURE IS A MICROCOSM OF THE REGION IN WHICH IT IS LOCATED. STUDIES CHANGING RELATIONSHIPS OF SUCH STRUCTURE.

0324 BETTISON D.G. ED., HUGHES C.A. ED., VAN DER VGUR P.W. ED.
THE PAPUA-GUINEA ELECTIONS 1964.
CANBERRA: AUSTRALIAN NAT U, 1965, 545 PP.
STUDIES FIRST ELECTIONS HELD IN TERRITORY OF PAPUA-NEW GUINEA FOR THE HOUSE OF ASSEMBLY IN 1964. HISTORICAL BACKGROUND OF ELECTION AND ANALYSIS OF RESULTS PROVIDED PLUS TWELVE MINUTELY DETAILED CONSTITUENCY STUDIES OF VOTING AREAS. LACK OF MAJOR POLITICAL PARTIES NOTED.

0325 BEVEL D.N.
"JOURNEY TO NORTH VIETNAM."
FREEDOMWAYS, 7 (SPRING 67), 118-127.
PERSONAL ACCOUNT OF US NEGRO, ACTIVE IN CIVIL RIGHTS, WHO TOURED NORTH VIETNAM AT CHRISTMAS TIME, 1966. SHE AND FOUR OTHER US WOMEN, ALL FEELING WAR IS WRONG, RELATE THEIR EXPERIENCES AS INDIVIDUALS. FEELS MURDER IS NOT SOLUTION TO HUMAN PROBLEMS.

0326 BHALERAO C.N.
PUBLIC SERVICE COMMISSIONS OF INDIA: A STUDY.
LONDON: STERLING PUBL LTD, 1966, 271 PP.
TRACES HISTORY OF INDIAN PUBLIC SERVICE COMMISSION. ANALYZES FUNCTION AND STRUCTURE OF VARIOUS AGENCIES INCLUDING APPOINTMENT, REMOVAL, AND SUSPENSION OF COMMISSION MEMBERS. NOTES PRINCIPLES AND PROCEDURES OF MEMBER RECRUITMENT, EXAMINATIONS, AND INTERVIEWS. DISCUSSES COMMISSIONS' ADVISORY FUNCTIONS IN GOVERNMENT, AND EXAMINES RELATION BETWEEN COMMISSIONS AND GOVERNMENTS.

0327 BHAMBHRI C.P.
PARLIAMENTARY CONTROL OVER STATE ENTERPRISE IN INDIA.
NEW DELHI: METROPOLITAN BOOK, 1960, 115 PP.
STUDIES METHODS OF PARLIAMENTARY CONTROL OVER PUBLIC ENTERPRISE INCLUDING MINISTERIAL, FINANCIAL, AND AUDIT CONTROL AND CONTROL THROUGH COMMITTEES. ALSO DISCUSSES GENERAL RELATIONSHIP OF GOVERNMENT AND STATE ENTERPRISES. CONCLUDES THAT INDIAN PARLIAMENT HAS NEEDED CONTROLS AT ITS DISPOSAL, BUT THEY ARE NOT BEING FULLY UTILIZED.

0328 BHATNAGAR J.K.
"THE VALUES AND ATTITUDES OF SOME INDIAN AND BRITISH STUDENTS."
RACE, 9 (JULY 67), 27-36.
ANALYZES DATA COMPILED THROUGH POSTAL QUESTIONNAIRE ON ATTITUDES OF STUDENTS EDUCATED IN ENGLAND AND HOW EDUCATION THERE AFFECTED THEIR IMPRESSIONS OF THAT COUNTRY. VARIABLES WERE PERSONALITY-CHANGE RESISTANCE, GROUP SUPERIORITY FEELING, INDIVIDUALISM, AND IMPRESSIONS AND STEREOTYPES OF BRITISH PEOPLE.

0329 BIALEK R.W.
CATHOLIC POLITICS: A HISTORY BASED ON ECUADOR.
NEW YORK: VANTAGE, 1963, 144 PP.
ANALYSIS OF RELATION OF CHURCH AND STATE IN WESTERN WORLD BASED ON ARRIVAL OF SPANISH CONQUERORS IN 1534. STUDIES VARIOUS STAGES OF DOMINATION AND LIBERATION OF CONVERTED NATIVES. BIBLIOGRAPHY OF WORKS CITED IN TEXT AND VARIOUS PAPAL DOCUMENTS IN SPANISH.

0330 BIBLIOTECA NACIONAL
CATALOGO BREVE DE LA BIBLIOTECA AMERICANA DE JT MEDINA

(2 VOLS.)
SANTIAGO: U OF CHILE, 1954, 388 PP.
CATALOGUE OF CONTENTS OF JT MEDINA LIBRARY OF CHILEAN NATIONAL LIBRARY. INCLUDES BIBLIOGRAPHY OF BOOKS, MAPS, AND DOCUMENTS AS WELL AS OTHER COLLECTIONS OF OBJECTS OF DONOR.

0331 BIDNEY D.
THEORETICAL ANTHROPOLOGY.
NEW YORK: COLUMBIA U PRESS, 1953, 506 PP.
HISTORICAL AND CRITICAL STUDY OF THEORETICAL METANTHROPOLOGICAL POSTULATES AND ASSUMPTIONS UNDERLYING DEVELOPMENT OF MODERN CULTURAL ANTHROPOLOGY. ANALYZES PHILOSOPHY GUIDING ORGANIZATION AND INTERPRETATION OF DATA IN VARIOUS FIELDS OF ANTHROPOLOGY WITH SPECIFIC ATTENTION TO VARIOUS CONCEPTS ASSOCIATED WITH CULTURAL STUDY, PSYCHOLOGY, ETHNOLOGY, AND VARIOUS PARTICULAR PROBLEMS MET BY MAN AS HE DEVELOPED.

0332 BIDNEY D.
THE CONCEPT OF FREEDOM IN ANTHROPOLOGY.
HAGUE: MOUTON & CO, 1963, 291 PP.
SYMPOSIUM OF ANTHROPOLOGISTS DISCUSSING ROLE OF INDIVIDUALISM AND FREEDOM IN PRODUCING CULTURAL CHANGE; SOME PRESS FOR RECOGNITION OF FREEDOM'S IMPORTANCE IN ANTHROPOLOGICAL STUDIES. CASE STUDIES AND THEORETICAL WORKS.

0333 BIEBUYCK D., DOUGLAS M.
CONGO TRIBES AND PARTIES.
LONDON: ROYAL ANTHROPOLOG INST, 1961, 48 PP.
EXAMINES ETHNOGRAPHIC BACKGROUND OF CONGOLESE POLITICS. STUDIES MAIN TRIBES AND THEIR PARTY AFFILIATION. SHOWS THAT SEPARATIST MOVEMENTS ARE USUALLY SUPPORTED BY LARGE TRADITIONAL TRIBES.

0334 BILL J.A.
"THE SOCIAL AND ECONOMIC FOUNDATIONS OF POWER IN CONTEMPORARY IRAN."
MID. EAST J., 17 (AUTUMN 63), 400-18.
UTILIZING THE CLASS AS THE BASIC TOOL OF ANALYSIS, FOCUSES ATTENTION UPON THE CONCRETE ASPIRATIONS OF DEFINED GROUPS AND EXAMINES RELATIONSHIP BETWEEN SOCIO-POLITICAL PROCESSES AND SOCIAL STRUCTURE.

0335 BINANI G.D., RAMA RAO T.V.
INDIA AT A GLANCE (REV. ED.)
BOMBAY: ORIENT LONGMANS, 1954, 1756 PP.
A COMPREHENSIVE REFERENCE MANUAL ON INDIA THAT PROVIDES A CLASSIFIED SYSTEM OF INFORMATION ON 25 TOPICS OF GENERAL AND SPECIALIZED INTEREST. COORDINATES INFORMATION ON THE NATIONAL GOVERNMENT, FOREIGN POLICY, NATIONAL ECONOMY, COMMUNICATIONS, INDUSTRIAL FINANCE, PRODUCTION TRENDS, THE JUDICIAL SYSTEM, ETC. INCLUDES A GENERAL INDEX AND DETAILED TABLE OF CONTENTS.

0336 BINDER L.
RELIGION AND POLITICS IN PAKISTAN.
LOS ANGELES: UNIV OF CALIF PR, 1961, 440 PP., LC#61-7537.
STUDY OF CONFLICTING THEORIES OF THE NATURE OF AN ISLAMIC STATE, MANNER IN WHICH THEORIES WERE STATED, AND PROCESS BY WHICH THEY WERE ALTERED. ATTENTION CONCENTRATED ON VIEWS OF THOSE WHO PARTICIPATED IN DRAWING UP PAKISTANI CONSTITUTION - THE "ULAMA" AND THE "JAMA'TI-I-ISLAMI." DESCRIBES ORIGINAL THEORETICAL ORIENTATION OF PARTICIPATING GROUPS AND FAILURE OF THEIR COMPROMISE.

0337 BINDER L.
IRAN: POLITICAL DEVELOPMENT IN A CHANGING SOCIETY.
BERKELEY: U OF CALIF PR, 1962, 362 PP., LC#62-14944.
ANALYTICAL, THEORETICAL, AND EMPIRICAL RECONSTRUCTION OF CHANGING POLITICAL SYSTEM IN IRAN. DEVELOPS A WORKING BASIS FOR FORMULATING POLITICAL THEORY IN TERMS OF SYSTEM AND FUNCTION. CONTENDS THAT CONCRETE POLITICAL SYSTEMS EXHIBIT A VARYING DEGREE OF UNITY OR INTEGRATION IN STRUCTURE AND FUNCTION. MAINTAINS FOCUS ON REAL STRUCTURES OF POWER RELATIONSHIPS, RATHER THAN ABSTRACTING THEIR NATURES.

0338 BINDER L.
THE IDEOLOGICAL REVOLUTION IN THE MIDDLE EAST.
NEW YORK: WILEY, 1964, 287 PP., $6.50.
PLACES NATIONALIST MOVEMENT IN GEOGRAPHICAL, CULTURAL AND HISTORICAL SETTING. NOTES EMERGENCE OF POLITICS FREE OF RELIGIOUS DOMINATION. ANALYZES IDEOLOGICAL CONTENT OF BAA'TH PARTY, OF RADICAL REFORM NATIONALISM, AND OF PAN-ARABISM.

0339 BIRKET-SMITH K.A.J.
GESCHICHTE DER KULTUR (3RD ED., TRANS. BY HANS DIETSCHY)
ZURICH: ORELL FUSSLI VERL, 1946, 593 PP.
GENERAL DISCUSSION OF THE GROWTH OF CULTURE. DEALS WITH GENERAL PRINCIPLES OF THE SCIENCE OF CULTURAL HISTORY. TREATS EARLY CULTURAL BEGINNINGS AND ATTENDANT PROFESSIONS, AND OFFERS DETAILED EXAMINATION OF MODERN CULTURAL LIFE.

0340 BIRKHEAD G.S. ED.
ADMINISTRATIVE PROBLEMS IN PAKISTAN.
SYRACUSE: SYRACUSE U PRESS, 1966, 223 PP., LC#66-25174.
DISCUSSES PROBLEMS IN PAKISTAN RELATING TO PUBLIC ADMINISTRATION, INCLUDING ADMINISTRATION OF BASIC DEMOCRACIES, BUSINESS PARTICIPATION IN ADMINISTRATION, AGRICULTURE AND ADMINISTRATION, GOVERNMENT BY CORPORATIONS, AND ADMINISTRATIVE REFORM.

0341 BIRMINGHAM D.
TRADE AND CONFLICT IN ANGOLA.
LONDON: OXFORD U PR, 1966, 178 PP.
STUDIES IMPACT OF PORTUGAL ON ANGOLA IN RELATION TO NONCOLONIAL AFRICAN STATES, AND THE COMMERCIAL AND MILITARY EFFECTS ON AFRICA AND MBUNDU KINGDOM, IMPORTANT DURING FIRST THREE CENTURIES OF EUROPEAN CONTACT WITH THE AREA.

0342 BIRMINGHAM W. ED., NEUSTADT I. ED., OMABOE E.N. ED.
A STUDY OF CONTEMPORARY GHANA VOL I: THE ECONOMY OF GHANA.
EVANSTON: NORTHWESTERN U PRESS, 1966, 472 PP.
INTRODUCTORY SURVEY OF GHANA'S ECONOMY COLLECTS ESSAYS AND ANALYTIC TREATISES ON MACROECONOMIC STRUCTURE, FACTORS OF PRODUCTION, SECTORS OF THE ECONOMY, POLICY, AND PLANNING. INCLUDES COMPREHENSIVE CHARTS, MAPS, AND TABLES OF ECONOMIC STATISTICS.

0343 BIRNBAUM K.
"SWEDEN'S NUCLEAR POLICY."
INTERNATIONAL JOURNAL, 20 (SUMMER 65) 297-311.
FEARS OF NUCLEAR PROLIFERATION, AND THE COMPLEX CONTINGENT STRATEGIES OF TECHNOLOGICALLY SOPHISTICATED, NEUTRAL SWEDEN INTERACT TO CAUSE INERTIA AND DISAGREEMENT AMONG HER POLITCAL AND MILITARY GROUPS PERTAINING TO ACQUISITION OF NUCLEAR CAPABILITY. POLICY IS TO BUY TIME AND OPTIONS.

0344 BISHOP D.G.
THE ADMINISTRATION OF BRITISH FOREIGN RELATIONS.
SYRACUSE: U. PR., 1961, 410 PP.
A COMPREHENSIVE VIEW OF RELEVANT INSTITUTIONS, THEIR ORGANIZATION AND METHODS OF PROCEDURE. HISTORIC EXAMPLES OF DEVELOPMENT ARE PRESENTED. INCLUDES CRITICISM AND PROPOSALS FOR INSTITUTIONAL REFORM.

0345 BISHOP O.B. ED.
PUBLICATIONS OF THE GOVERNMENTS OF NOVA SCOTIA, PRINCE EDWARD ISLAND, NEW BRUNSWICK 1758-1952.
OTTAWA: NATL LIB OF CANADA, 1957, 237 PP.
INCLUDES ONLY THOSE PAMPHLETS OR BOOKS WHICH HAVE BEEN PRINTED "WITH THE IMPRINT OF, OR AT THE EXPENSE OF, OR BY AUTHORITY OF ANY ONE OF THE THREE GOVERNMENTS OF THE MARITIME PROVINCE." PAPERS, BROADSIDES, HANDBILLS, PROCLAMATIONS, AND MAPS HAVE BEEN OMITTED, AS HAVE WORKS DEALING WITH THE JUDICIAL AND MUNICIPAL ASPECTS OF GOVERNMENT.

0346 BISHOP O.B. ED.
PUBLICATIONS OF THE GOVERNMENT OF THE PROVINCE OF CANADA 1841-1867.
OTTAWA: NATL LIB OF CANADA, 1963.
BIBLIOGRAPHY COMPILED FROM HOLDINGS OF THE LAWSON MEMORIAL LIBRARY AT UNIVERSITY OF WESTERN ONTARIO, THE LEGISLATIVE LIBRARY FOR ONTARIO, AND THE LIBRARY OF THE PUBLIC ARCHIVES OF CANADA. HAS AN INTRODUCTION TO THE MATERIALS.

0347 BISSAINTHE M.
DICTIONNAIRE DE BIBLIOGRAPHIE HAITIENNE.
WASHINGTON: SCARECROW PRESS, 1951, 1052 PP., LC#51-12164.
EXTENSIVE BIBLIOGRAPHY OF BOOKS AND PAMPHLETS PUBLISHED IN HAITI OR ABROAD BY HAITIANS 1804-1949. LISTS JOURNALISTS WITH A KEY TO THEIR NEWSPAPERS. INCLUDES LIST OF PERIODICALS PUBLISHED BETWEEN 1764-1949. ITEMS IN ENGLISH, SPANISH, AND FRENCH ARRANGED ALPHABETICALLY BY AUTHOR, INCLUDING SUBJECT AND TITLE INDEXES.

0348 BLACHLY F.F., OATMAN M.E.
"THE GOVERNMENT AND ADMINISTRATION OF GERMANY."
BALTIMORE: JOHNS HOPKINS PRESS, 1920.
FIRST OF SERIES OF VOLUMES PUBLISHED BY THE INSTITUTE FOR GOVERNMENT RESEARCH CONCERNING ADMINISTRATIVE SYSTEMS OF CHIEF EUROPEAN NATIONS. EMPHASIS ON ADMINISTRATIVE AND GOVERNMENTAL SYSTEMS. UNDERLYING SOCIAL AND POLITICAL PHILOSOPHY, CONSTITUTIONAL STRUCTURE, AND POLITICAL ACTION. COVERS CENTRAL GOVERNMENT AS WELL AS SUBORDINATE UNITS. EXTENSIVE, PARTIALLY ANNOTATED, BIBLIOGRAPHY.

0349 BLACK C.E. ED.
THE TRANSFORMATION OF RUSSIAN SOCIETY.
CAMBRIDGE: HARVARD U. PR., 1960, 695 PP.
ESSAYS ON DIVERSE ASPECTS OF RUSSIAN SOCIETY OVER THE PAST TWO CENTURIES. SOVIET-RUSSIAN DEVELOPMENTS GENERALLY TREATED (WHERE APPLICABLE) WITH REGARD FOR PRE-REVOLUTIONARY TRADITION.

0350 BLACK C.E.
THE DYNAMICS OF MODERNIZATION: A STUDY IN COMPARATIVE HISTORY.
NEW YORK: HARPER & ROW, 1966, 207 PP., LC#66-20757.
DISCUSSES DEFINITION AND CHARACTERISTICS OF MODERNIZATION AND PRESENTS A CHRONOLOGICAL TIMETABLE FOR THE DEVELOPMENT OF MODERNIZING SOCIETIES. PRESENTS SEVEN MAIN PATTERNS OF GROWTH AND TRACES THE EXPERIENCES OF 175 CONTEMPORARY SOCIETIES WITH PREDICTIONS AS TO THEIR FUTURE. DISCUSSES PERIODS

OF CONSOLIDATION OF MODERNIZING LEADERSHIP, ECONOMIC AND SOCIAL TRANSFORMATION, AND INTEGRATION OF SOCIETY.

0351 BLAKE J.
FAMILY STRUCTURE IN JAMAICA.
NEW YORK: FREE PRESS OF GLENCOE, 1961, 262 PP., LC#60-10893.
STUDIES SOCIAL CONTEXT OF REPRODUCTION IN JAMAICA, INCLUDING YOUTHFUL SEXUAL UNIONS, PURPOSE AND PRACTICE IN CHILDREARING, SOCIAL STRUCTURE AND SEX ATTITUDES, METHODS OF CONTRACEPTION, AND FAMILY LIMITATION AND FERTILITY.

0352 BLANC N.
"SPAIN: LEARNING THROUGH STRUGGLE"
NEW POLITICS, 5 (FALL 66), 38-43.
SEES SPAIN UNDERGOING APPRENTICESHIP IN FREEDOM FOR DAY WHEN FRANCO REGIME NO LONGER EXISTS, WITH SPANISH EXILES, CITIZENS, AND AMERICAN DIPLOMATS EXPERIENCING CHANGES IN CONSCIOUSNESS OF POLITICAL SITUATION. EXAMINES PROBLEMS EXPERIENCED IN PAST WHICH STILL MUST BE SOLVED BY SUPPORTING SOLUTIONS PROPOSED BY SPANISH YOUTH AND RIGHTISTS.

0353 BLANCHARD L.R.
MARTINIQUE: A SELECTED LIST OF REFERENCES (PAMPHLET)
WASHINGTON: LIBRARY OF CONGRESS, 1942, 57 PP.
SOME 250 MANUSCRIPTS, BIBLIOGRAPHIES, ALMANACS, MAPS, CHARTS, PERIODICALS, NEWSPAPER ARTICLES, AND BOOKS ARRANGED TOPICALLY WITH CONCLUDING SUBJECT INDEX. ITEMS ARE ALL ANNOTATED AND FROM 1890-1942 WITH EMPHASIS ON POST-1923 PUBLICATIONS. SOME ARE IN ENGLISH, BUT MANY IN FRENCH. SOME US GOVERNMENT DOCUMENTS.

0354 BLANCHARD W.
"THAILAND."
NEW HAVEN: HUMAN REL AREA FILES, 1958.
EIGHTH VOLUME IN THE COUNTRY SERIES PUBLISHED BY THE HUMAN RELATIONS AREA FILES, PROMOTING RESEARCH AND COMPARATIVE STUDY IN SOCIAL AND BEHAVIORAL SCIENCES. THIS VOLUME EXAMINES SOCIOLOGICAL, POLITICAL, ECONOMIC ASPECTS OF THAI SOCIETY IN ORDER TO DEFINE BASIC CULTURAL AND INSTITUTIONAL PATTERNS AND TO IDENTIFY VALUES AND ATTITUDES. EXTENSIVE BIBLIOGRAPHY OF SOCIAL, POLITICAL, AND ECONOMIC SOURCES.

0355 BLAU P.M.
"SOCIAL MOBILITY AND INTERPERSONAL RELATIONS" (BMR)"
AMER. SOCIOLOGICAL REV., 21 (JUNE 56), 290-295.
EXPLORES THREE IMPLICATIONS OF HYPOTHESIS THAT OCCUPATIONAL MOBILITY CREATES SPECIAL DILEMMAS FOR INTERPERSONAL RELATIONS. INCLUDES DISCUSSIONS ON ACCULTURATION, SOCIAL INSECURITY, AND OVERCONFORMITY.

0356 BLISS P.
OF SOVEREIGNTY.
BOSTON: LITTLE BROWN, 1885, 180 PP.
DISCUSSION OF FEDERALISM IN HISTORY, POLITICAL PHILOSOPHY OF STATES RIGHTS, POWERS OF STATES TO SECEDE, AND ETHICAL IMPERATIVE OF GOVERNMENTS RELATING SPECIFICALLY TO THE US AFTER CIVIL WAR.

0357 BLITZ L.F.
THE POLITICS AND ADMINISTRATION OF NIGERIAN GOVERNMENT.
NEW YORK: FREDERICK PRAEGER, 1965, 281 PP., LC#65-25824.
INTRODUCTORY DISCUSSIONS OF NIGERIAN GOVERNMENT WHICH PROVIDE DESCRIPTION OF HISTORICAL BACKGROUND OF NIGERIAN NATION AND MAJOR GOVERNMENT INSTITUTIONS. DISCUSSES VARIOUS LEVELS OF GOVERNMENT, POLITICAL PARTIES, COURT SYSTEMS, AND FOREIGN RELATIONS. INTENDED AS INTRODUCTORY WORK FOR NIGERIAN STUDENTS.

0358 BLONDEL J.
VOTERS, PARTIES, AND LEADERS.
BALTIMORE: PENGUIN BOOKS, 1963, 271 PP.
TREATMENT OF RELATION BETWEEN BRITISH CONTEMPORARY SOCIETY AND POLITICS. DISCUSSES THE EFFECT OF ELITES AND STRATA ON ALL FORMS OF GOVERNMENT AND THE RELATION OF PARTY TO SOCIAL GROUP.

0359 BLOOMFIELD L.P.
WESTERN EUROPE AND THE UN - TRENDS AND PROSPECTS.
CAMBRIDGE: MIT CTR INTL STUDIES, 1959, 110 PP.
APPRAISAL OF ATTITUDES OF WESTERN EUROPE TOWARD UN, LISTED COUNTRY BY COUNTRY, INCLUDING UN AS IT RELATES TO EACH ONE'S NATIONAL INTERESTS, DOMESTIC POLITICS, AND SPECIAL HISTORY WITH UN.

0360 BLUM L.
PEACE AND DISARMAMENT (TRANS. BY A. WERTH)
LONDON: JONATHAN CAPE, 1932, 202 PP.
BELIEVES THAT NO INTERNATIONAL PEACE ORGANIZATION CAN BE EFFECTIVE IN AN ARMED EUROPE. DISARMAMENT IS A CAUSE, NOT AN EFFECT, OF SECURITY, AND IS ONE OF ITS ESSENTIAL ELEMENTS. BELIEVES NATIONS REFUSE TO DISARM BECAUSE THEY STILL FEAR EACH OTHER. SOCIALISM WILL LEAD TO PEACE THROUGH "MORAL DISARMAMENT." BY PUTTING PRESSURE ON GOVERNMENT, WORKING CLASS CAN HELP DESTROY OLD INSTINCTS AND CONTROL GOVERNMENT.

0361 BLUM L.
FOR ALL MANKIND (TRANS. BY W. PICKLES)
LONDON: VICTOR GOLLANCZ, 1946, 143 PP.
WRITTEN DURING VICHY REGIME IN FRANCE, DEFENDS DEMOCRATIC PRINCIPLES. SAYS FRANCE WAS DEFEATED IN WWII BECAUSE OF IRRESOLUTION OF BOURGEOISIE, NOT BECAUSE OF WEAKNESSES OF DEMOCRATIC GOVERNMENT. BOURGEOISIE IS CONSIDERED THE RULING CLASS. SEES NAZISM AS ENDING BOURGEOIS RULE, BUT ALSO TURNING BACK PROGRESS OF CIVILIZATION. PROPOSES SOCIALIST DEMOCRACY.

0362 BLUNTSCHLI J.K.
THE THEORY OF THE STATE.
LONDON: CLARENDON PRESS, 1885, 518 PP.
THOROUGH ANALYSIS COVERS FOLLOWING SUBJECTS: CONCEPT OF STATE IN ANCIENT, MEDIEVAL, AND MODERN TIMES; THE STATE AND THE NATURE OF MANKIND; THE STATE AND EXTERNAL NATURE; AND THE RISE AND FALL OF STATES. ALSO STUDIES PURPOSE AND FORMS OF THE STATE, INCLUDING THOUGHTS ON SOVEREIGNTY.

0363 BODENHEIMER E.
TREATISE ON JUSTICE.
NEW YORK: PHILOSOPHICAL LIB, 1967, 314 PP., LC#67-11987.
VIEWS JUSTICE AS MATERIAL VALUE WHICH SHAPES OR AFFECTS QUALITY OF LIFE. ASSUMES PROBLEMS OF JUSTICE ARE CONNECTED WITH CERTAIN BASIC EXISTENTIAL HUMAN NEEDS ASCERTAINED BY HUMAN PHILOSOPHICAL ENDEAVOR. REJECTS VIEW OF JUSTICE AS FRATIONAL IDEAL BEYOND OBJECTIVE METHODS OF RESEARCH. CONSIDERS CONCEPTS AND GOALS OF JUSTICE AND DIVISIONS: POLITICAL, SOCIAL, PENAL, ECONOMIC, INTERNATIONAL.

0364 BODIN J., MCRAE K.D. ED.
THE SIX BOOKES OF A COMMONWEALE (1576) (FACSIMILE REPRINT OF 1606 ENGLISH TRANSLATION)
CAMBRIDGE: HARVARD U PR, 1962, 794 PP.
SIX VOLUMES DEALING WITH SOVEREIGN POWER. COMMONWEAL IS A POLITICAL COMMUNITY IN GENERAL RATHER THAN A SPECIFIC FORM OF GOVERNMENT. SOVEREIGN MUST BE PERPETUAL AND ABSOLUTE BECAUSE IT IS THE COHESIVE FORCE IN THE POLITICAL COMMUNITY. PREFERS MONARCHICAL GOVERNMENT, BUT NOT A GOVERNMENT WHERE SOVEREIGNTY IS DIVIDED BETWEEN MONARCH, ARISTOCRACY, AND COMMONERS. ABSOLUTE MONARCH MUST RESPECT LIBERTY.

0365 BOGARDUS E.S.
"THE DEVELOPMENT OF SOCIAL THOUGHT."
LONDON: LONGMANS, GREEN & CO, 1960.
TEXTBOOK DESIGNED AS INTRODUCTION TO FIELD OF SOCIAL THOUGHT FOR COLLEGE STUDENTS. COVERS DEVELOPMENTS IN SOCIAL THOUGHT FROM BABYLONIAN ERA THROUGH THE INTEGRATION OF EASTERN AND WESTERN SOCIAL THOUGHTS IN WRITINGS OF MUKERJEE. ONE CHAPTER DEVOTED TO EACH MAJOR THINKER OR SPECIAL ERA. UNANNOTATED BIBLIOGRAPHY COVERS GENERAL PRIMARY AND SECONDARY SOURCES. MATERIAL ORGANIZED BY SUBJECT.

0366 BOHANNAN P.
SOCIAL ANTHROPOLOGY.
NEW YORK: HOLT RINEHART WINSTON, 1963, 421 PP., LC#63-13322.
INTRODUCTORY STUDY THAT DISCUSSES CULTURE, PERSONALITY, AND SOCIETY, PLUS WAYS IN WHICH MEN SEE, CRITICIZE, AND ADAPT THROUGHOUT THE WORLD. CONSIDERS ART, SPEECH, BIOLOGICAL FUNCTIONS, POWER STRUCTURES, ECONOMIC NEEDS, AND RELIGION. DISTINGUISHES IN THEORY BETWEEN SOCIAL CHANGE AS FUNCTIONAL OR EVOLUTIONAL.

0367 BOHANNAN P. ED.
LAW AND WARFARE.
GARDEN CITY: NATURAL HISTORY PR, 1967, 441 PP., LC#67-10386.
EXAMINES RESOLUTION OF CONFLICT FROM ANTHROPOLOGICAL POINT OF VIEW. DISCUSSES TWO FORMS OF RESOLUTION: FIGHTING AND ADMINISTERING OF RULES. EXPLORES NATURE OF LEGAL PHENOMENA, INSTITUTIONS AND MEANS OF PEACEFUL SETTLEMENTS, AND TYPES OF WARS AND VIOLENCE. COMPARES ETHNIC GROUPS' JUDICIAL PROCESSES AND WARFARE.

0368 BOISSEVAIN J.
SAINTS AND FIREWORKS: RELIGION AND POLITICS IN RURAL MALTA.
LONDON: ATHLONE PRESS, 1965, 180 PP., LC#65-14845.
STUDIES MALTESIAN GOVERNMENT, CHURCH AND POLITICAL PARTIES, TIES OF NEIGHBORHOOD AND FAMILY, VILLAGE SOCIAL ORGANIZATION AND LEADERSHIP, AND VILLAGE RELIGIOUS ISSUES; ALSO RESULTS OF NATIONAL POLICY DISPUTES AND METHODS OF VILLAGES TO INFLUENCE DECISIONS IN HIGHLY CENTRALIZED GOVERNMENT.

0369 BOLGAR V.
"THE PUBLIC INTEREST: A JURISPRUDENTIAL AND COMPARATIVE OVERVIEW OF SYMPOSIUM ON FUNDAMENTAL CONCEPTS OF PUBLIC LAW"
JOURNAL OF PUBLIC LAW, 12 (JAN. 63), 13-52.
SURVEYS THEORIES THAT ARE SOURCES OF DELIMITATION OF PRIVATE RIGHTS FROM PUBLIC INTERESTS AND DEMONSTRATES EVOLUTION OF CONCEPT OF PUBLIC INTEREST. COMPARES ISSUES INVOLVING LEGAL REGULATION, ESPECIALLY THOSE IN FIELD OF ADMINISTRATIVE CONTRACTS, IN FRANCE, SWITZERLAND, GERMANY, AND COMMUNIST COUNTRIES.

0370 BOLTON A.R.
SOVIET MIDDLE EAST STUDIES: AN ANALYSIS AND BIBLIOGRAPHY.
LONDON: ROYAL INST OF INTL AFF, 1959.

BIBLIOGRAPHY, IN EIGHT PARTS, COMPRISES 281 ITEMS. INCLUDES REPRESENTATIVE WORKS ON CURRENT AFFAIRS, ECONOMICS, HISTORY, SOCIAL ANTHROPOLOGY, AND SOCIAL STUDIES. ONLY MODEST SEGMENTS OF RUSSIAN WORKS ON ISLAMIC TOPICS AND ARABIC LITERATURE INCLUDED. BIBLIOGRAPHY COVERS ARAB WORLD, ARABIAN PENINSULA, EGYPT, IRAQ, PALESTINE AND JORDAN, THE SUDAN, SYRIA, AND LEBANON.

0371 BOMBACH G. ED.
STABILE PREISE IN WACHSENDER WIRTSCHAFT: DAS INFLATIONSPROBLEM.
TUBINGEN: J C B MOHR, 1960, 274 PP.
ESSAYS ON PROBLEMS OF INFLATION, MONETARY THEORY AND POLICY, CAUSES OF POST-WAR INFLATION, INFLATION IN DEVELOPING COUNTRIES, AND FINANCIAL MEASURES TO PREVENT INFLATIONARY TENDENCIES.

0372 BONAR J.
THEORIES OF POPULATION FROM RALEIGH TO ARTHUR YOUNG.
LONDON: ALLEN UNWIN, 1931, 253 PP.
HISTORICAL ANALYSIS OF THEORIES OF FAMOUS DEMOGRAPHISTS: RALEIGH, WARRINGTON, GAUNT, PETTY, HALLEY, SUSSMILCH, HUME, PRICE AND YOUNG.

0373 BONNEFOUS M.
EUROPE ET TIERS MONDE.
LEYDEN: SYTHOFF, 1961, 116 PP.
CONSIDERS EUROPE'S AID TO THE UNDERDEVELOPED COUNTRIES OF AFRICA AND QUESTIONS WHETHER THESE TECHNICAL CONNECTIONS WILL MORE FAVORABLY BIND THE COUNTRIES THAN THE FORMER HISTORICAL ONES.

0374 BORBA DE MORAES R., BERRIEN W.
MANUAL BIBLIOGRAFICO DE ESTUDOS BRASILEIROS.
RIO DE JANEIRO: GRAFICA EDITORIAL SOUZA, 1949, 895 PP.
DETAILED BIBLIOGRAPHY OF BRAZILIAN RESEARCH.

0375 BORGESE G.A.
GOLIATH: THE MARCH OF FASCISM.
NEW YORK: VIKING PRESS, 1937, 483 PP.
DESCRIBES ORIGINS AND RISE OF FASCISM IN EUROPE, FOCUSING ON ITALY. TRACES ITALIAN ROOTS BACK TO DANTE, MYTHS OF ROME, AND MACHIAVELLI. DISCUSSES EARLY CAREER OF MUSSOLINI AND HIS SUBSEQUENT ROLE IN FASCIST RISE. EXAMINES FASCIST POLICIES TOWARD CHURCH, POLITICAL PARTIES, AND LAW. FEELS EXPANSION OF ITALY IS DANGEROUS AND IMPLORES WORLD TO ACT DECISIVELY.

0376 BORKENAU F.
EUROPEAN COMMUNISM.
NEW YORK: HARPER & ROW, 1951, 564 PP.
STUDIES EUROPEAN COMMUNISM, CONCENTRATING ON EARLY COMINFORM PERIOD (1934-45). SHOWS EVOLUTION OF COMMUNIST POLICY DURING POPULAR FRONT PERIOD IN FRANCE, AND OF GENERAL COMMUNIST LINE DURING WWII. ATTEMPTS TO CLARIFY STALIN'S ATTITUDE TOWARD RISE OF HITLER, AND RUSSIAN POLICY DURING LATTER PART OF SPANISH CIVIL WAR.

0377 BORKENAU F.
THE SPANISH COCKPIT.
ANN ARBOR: U OF MICH PR, 1963, 303 PP.
EYE-WITNESS ACCOUNT OF THE POLITICAL AND SOCIAL CONFLICTS OF THE SPANISH CIVIL WAR. DISCUSSES POLITICAL DEVELOPMENTS IN THE CAMP OF THE REPUBLICAN GOVERNMENT IN SPAIN, BOTH AMONG THE MASSES AND RULING STRATA. ATTENTION DEVOTED TO HISTORY OF THE SPANISH LEFT IN ITS VARIOUS FORMS - ITS CHARACTERISTICS, ANTAGONISMS, ACHIEVEMENTS, AND FAILURES. CONTRASTS SPANISH CONFLICT TO THOSE IN OTHER COUNTRIES.

0378 BORTOLI G.
"SOCIOLOGIE DU REFERENDUM DANS LA FRANCE MODERNE."
PARIS: PICHON ET DURAND-AUZIAS, 1965, 407 PP.
APPROXIMATELY 200 FRENCH BOOKS AND PERIODICALS ARRANGED ALPHABETICALLY BY AUTHOR, PUBLISHED 1900-1963.

0379 BORTOLI G.
SOCIOLOGIE DU REFERENDUM DANS LA FRANCE MODERNE.
PARIS: PICHON ET DURAND-AUZIAS, 1965, 407 PP.
SURVEY OF DIRECT POPULAR CONSULTATION DURING FOURTH AND FIFTH REPUBLICS, THE POSITIONS, RESULTS, REACTION, AND POLITICAL IMPACT.

0380 BOSANQUET B.
THE PHILOSOPHICAL THEORY OF THE STATE (3RD ED.)
LONDON: MACMILLAN, 1920, 307 PP.
PROPOSES THEORY OF THE STATE IN WHICH INDIVIDUALS MUST BEAR RESPONSIBILITY FOR STATE ACTIONS, SINCE STATE POWER IS DERIVED FROM INDIVIDUALS. DECLARES WARS ARE RESULT OF INDIVIDUALS' STRIVING TO GAIN EVER GREATER PORTIONS OF WORLD'S ECONOMIC GOODS. STATES MAY SERVE AS INSTITUTIONS LIMITING INDIVIDUAL GREED, BUT ARE GOOD OR EVIL DEPENDING ON THE DEGREE TO WHICH THEY ENCOURAGE CHRISTIAN VIRTUES.

0381 BOSHER J.F.
"GOVERNMENT AND PRIVATE INTERESTS IN NEW FRANCE."
CAN. PUBLIC ADMIN., 10 (JUNE 67), 244-257.
DESCRIBES RELATIONSHIPS BETWEEN GOVERNMENT FINANCIAL ADMINISTRATION AND PRIVATE ENTERPRISE IN FRENCH CANADA IN 17TH AND 18TH CENTURIES. CRITICIZES TRADITIONAL HISTORICAL VIEW THAT SEES FRENCH COLONIAL GOVERNMENT AS A "LEVIATHAN" HAMPERING PRIVATE INTEREST. ARGUES THAT OPPOSITE WAS TRUE; "RAMPANT PRIVATE ENTERPRISE" OFTEN PREVENTED PROPER FUNCTIONING OF GOVERNMENT.

0382 BOSSCHERE G D.E.
"A L'EST DU NOUVEAU."
ESPRIT, 35 (JAN. 68), 133-145.
ANALYZES EVOLUTION OF EAST EUROPEAN COUNTRIES, SINCE END OF STALINISM, AWAY FROM USSR AND TOWARD DEMOCRATIZATION. FINDS THAT HOSTILITY TOWARD THE USSR HAS CRYSTALLIZED, AND TERRITORIAL AND MINORITY DISPUTES ARE GREATER THAN EVER BEFORE. COUNTRIES ARE CHARACTERIZED BY DISINTEREST IN EACH OTHERS' AFFAIRS. PEOPLE ARE RESERVED, IF NOT HOSTILE, TOWARD THEIR OWN GOVERNMENTS.

0383 BOSSUET J.B.
"POLITIQUE TIREE DE L'ECRITURE SAINTE" (1679-1709) IN J.B. BOSSUET, OEVRES DE BOSSUET.
PARIS: FIRMIN DIDOT FRERES, 1870, 184 PP.
TEACHER OF DAUPHIN 1670-79, AUTHOR HOLDS THAT PROVIDENCE DIRECTS BOTH MAN AND STATE. MAN IS A "WOLF" IN NATURAL STATE, SO GOVERNMENT IS NECESSARY. INDIVIDUALS MUST RENOUNCE OWN WILL, WHICH IS ENTRUSTED TO AND REUNITED IN MONARCH. GOVERNMENT SHOULD BE ROYAL, HEREDITARY, AND PASSED ON TO ELDEST MALE. PEOPLE SHOULD FOLLOW GOVERNMENT AS A DIVINE ORDER. DISCUSSES PROPER CHARACTERISTICS OF MONARCHY.

0384 BOSTON UNIVERSITY LIBRARIES
CATALOG OF AFRICAN GOVERNMENT DOCUMENTS AND AFRICAN AREA INDEX.
BOSTON: HALL, 1964, 471 PP.
THE LIBRARY OF CONGRESS CLASSIFICATION IS USED AND AFRICAN BOOKS AND PAMPHLETS ARE CLASSIFIED AND CATALOGUED IN THE SAME MANNER AS OTHER MATERIALS. INCLUDES ALL WORKS ACQUIRED SINCE THE LIBRARY'S INCEPTION IN 1953. SPECIAL EMPHASIS IS GIVEN TO ECONOMIC, HISTORICAL, ANTHROPOLOGICAL, AND SOCIOLOGICAL MATERIALS, THOUGH ALL FIELDS OF KNOWLEDGE ARE COVERED.

0385 BOURDIEU P.
THE ALGERIANS (TRANS. BY A.C. ROSS; REV. ED.)
BOSTON: BEACON PRESS, 1961, 208 PP.
EXAMINES SOCIAL STRUCTURE, GOVERNMENT, CITY LIFE, COLONIAL SYSTEM, AND DISRUPTION THROUGH WAR OF ALGERIAN SOCIETY. DISCUSSES CUSTOMS AND ATTITUDES OF KABYLES, SHAWIA, MOZABITES, AND ARABIC-SPEAKING PEOPLES.

0386 BOURNE H.E.
THE WORLD WAR: A LIST OF THE MORE IMPORTANT BOOKS PUBLISHED BEFORE 1937 (PAMPHLET)
WASHINGTON: LIBRARY OF CONGRESS, 1937, 17 PP.
160 ITEMS ANNOTATED. INDEXED BY AUTHOR AND ARRANGED BY TOPIC. INCLUDES FRENCH, ENGLISH, GERMAN, ITALIAN, AND OTHER LANGUAGES. ALSO CONTAINS A 17-PAGE SUPPLEMENT PRINTED AND UPDATED IN APRIL, 1934, WHICH LISTS 152 MORE BOOKS RELEVANT TO THE MILITARY HISTORY OF WORLD WAR I.

0387 BOUSCAREN A.T.
"THE EUROPEAN CHRISTIAN DEMOCRATS"
WESTERN POLIT. QUART., 2 (MAR. 49), 59-73.
EXAMINES CHRISTIAN DEMOCRATS AND ITS GROWTH AFTER WWII. GIVES COMPREHENSIVE DEFINITION OF PARTY, ITS BELIEFS, GOALS, AND METHODS. COMPOSED OF YOUNG MEN WHO PLAYED LEADING ROLES IN VARIOUS RESISTANCE MOVEMENTS, CHRISTIAN DEMOCRATS BASE THEIR POLITICS AND WIDE SUPPORT ON THE COMPATIBILITY OF CHRISTIANITY AND DEMOCRACY. ALSO INCLUDES HISTORY OF GROWTH OF THE PARTY.

0388 BOUSTEDT O., RANZ H.
REGIONALE STRUKTUR- UND WIRTSCHAFTSFORSCHUNG.
BREMEN: WALTER DOON VERLAG, 1957, 218 PP.
DISCUSSES RELATION BETWEEN REGIONAL GEOGRAPHIC AND CULTURAL CONDITIONS AND ECONOMICS. EXAMINES STRUCTURE OF REGIONS AND ECONOMIC DEVELOPMENT IN VARIOUS COUNTRIES.

0389 BOWEN R.H.
GERMAN THEORIES OF THE CORPORATIVE STATE, WITH SPECIAL REFERENCES TO THE PERIOD 1870-1919.
NEW YORK: MCGRAW HILL, 1947, 245 PP.
STUDIES THREE THEORIES OF CORPORATIVE STATE: SOCIAL CATHOLICISM, MONARCHICAL SOCIALISM, AND CARTEL CORPORATISM. ATTEMPTS TO ELUCIDATE THEORIES IN RELATION TO SOCIAL POLICIES OF PERIOD 1870-1919 IN GERMANY, AND IN RELATION TO TENDENCIES IN GERMAN SOCIAL THOUGHT. DISCUSSES ROOTS OF CORPORATIST TRADITION IN PRE-INDUSTRIAL ERA.

0391 BOWLE J.
WESTERN POLITICAL THOUGHT: AN HISTORICAL INTRODUCTION FROM THE ORIGINS TO ROUSSEAU.
NEW YORK: OXFORD U PR, 1947, 472 PP.
SELECTS AND COMPRESSES THE POLITICAL THOUGHT OF A LARGE NUMBER OF IMPORTANT PHILOSOPHERS, THEOLOGIANS, AND THINKERS

FROM ARISTOTLE ON. PROVIDES A BIBLIOGRAPHY OF BOOKS DEALING WITH POLITICAL SCIENCE PRIOR TO THE 19TH CENTURY. CONCLUDES THAT "OUR PROBLEM IS TO COMBINE AN OLD TRADITION WITH A SOCIETY FREE AND FLEXIBLE, ORDERED AND SECURE."

0392 BOYCE A.N.
EUROPE AND SOUTH AFRICA.
CAPETOWN: JUTA & CO, LTD, 1936, 440 PP.
HISTORICAL STUDY OF PARALLEL DEVELOPMENTS AND RELATED EVENTS IN EUROPE AND SOUTH AFRICA FROM 1915-39. FOCUSES ON RELATIONSHIPS BETWEEN SOUTH AFRICA AND GREAT BRITAIN BUT ALSO EMPHASIZES BROADER SOCIAL AND POLITICAL DEVELOPMENTS IN EUROPE SUCH AS RISE OF NATIONALISM AND INDUSTRIALISM AND DEMANDS FOR LIBERAL REFORM.

0393 BOZEMAN A.B.
POLITICS AND CULTURE IN INTERNATIONAL HISTORY.
PRINCETON: PRINCETON U PRESS, 1960, 558 PP., LC#60-5743.
DISCUSSES ORIGINS OF CIVILIZATION AND RELATION OF CULTURE TO POLITICS; INCLUDES MAJOR CIVILIZATIONS UP TO 1500. DEALS WITH SIMILARITIES IN GOVERNMENT, IDEOLOGY, CULTURE, AND RELATION TO CONCEPT OF INTERNATIONAL HISTORY.

0394 BOZZA T.
SCRITTORI POLITICI ITALIANI DAL 1550 AL 1650.
ROME: EDIZ DI STORIA E LETTERAT, 1949, 218 PP.
CHRONOLOGICAL ARRANGEMENT OF ITALIAN POLITICAL WRITINGS FROM 1550-1650. GIVES BIBLIOGRAPHICAL DESCRIPTION OF WRITING AND ANNOTATION AND BIBLIOGRAPHY OF ITS AUTHOR. INDICATES LIBRARY WHERE WRITING MAY BE OBTAINED. CONTAINS BRIEF HISTORICAL SURVEY AND GENERAL BIBLIOGRAPHICAL SECTION.

0395 BRACHER K.D.
DIE AUFLOSUNG DER WEIMARER REPUBLIK.
STUTTGART: RING-VERLAG, 1955, 754 PP.
STUDY OF THE WEAKNESSES AND GRADUAL POLITICAL DISINTEGRATION OF WEIMAR REPUBLIC. MAJOR SUBJECTS SUCH AS RISE OF TOTALITARIAN PARTIES, THE BUREAUCRACY, AND DEVELOPMENT OF A POWER VACUUM IN "PAPEN-SCHLEICHER ERA" DISCUSSED IN GREAT DETAIL.

0396 BRACKMAN A.C.
SOUTHEAST ASIA'S SECOND FRONT: THE POWER STRUGGLE IN THE MALAY ARCHIPELAGO.
NEW YORK: FREDERICK PRAEGER, 1966, 341 PP., LC#65-24939.
A HISTORY OF COMMUNIST AGITATION AND ATTEMPTS AT REVOLUTION IN THE MALAY PENINSULA. BELIEVES THAT THE AREA IS NOT HOMOGENEOUS AND THAT THERE IS A CONFLICT IN THE AREA BETWEEN AUTHORITARIAN AND REPRESENTATIVE SYSTEMS OF GOVERNMENT. ATTEMPTS TO PRESENT THE "STRATEGY AND TRAPS OF THE PROTAGONISTS" (COMMUNISTS). ANTI-COMMUNIST IN OUTLOOK.

0397 BRADLEY A.W.
"CONSTITUTION-MAKING IN UGANDA."
TRANSITION, 7 (AUG. 67), 25-31.
ANALYZES UGANDA GOVERNMENT'S PROPOSALS FOR A NEW CONSTITUTION. DISCUSSES FEATURES OF THE PROPOSED CONSTITUTION: UGANDA IS TO BE A UNITARY REPUBLIC; THE KINGDOMS AND DISTRICTS ARE TO DISAPPEAR AS CONSTITUTIONAL UNITS OF GOVERNMENT; CABINET GOVERNMENT WILL CHANGE TO PRESIDENTIAL EXECUTIVE FORM; AND GREATER POWERS WILL BE GIVEN THE GOVERNMENT. DISCUSSES CABINET, PRESIDENT, AND NATIONAL ASSEMBLY.

0398 BRADLEY C.P.
"THE FORMATION OF MALAYSIA."
CURR. HIST., 46 (FEB. 64), 89-94.
INDONESIAN HOSTILITY AND QUESTIONABLE LOYALTY OF CHINESE MINORITIES ARE SUFFICIENTLY GRAVE CONSIDERATIONS TO MAKE AN OPTIMISTIC PROGNOSIS FOR MALAYSIA UNWARRANTED.

0399 BRADY A.
DEMOCRACY IN THE DOMINIONS (3RD ED.)
TORONTO: TORONTO UNIV PRESS, 1958, 614 PP.
COMPARES CANADA, AUSTRALIA, NEW ZEALAND, AND SOUTH AFRICA REGARDING THEIR DEMOCRATIC DEVELOPMENT, FORMS OF GOVERNMENT, PARTY SYSTEM, MAJOR POLICIES, AND THEIR DEMOCRATIC PROSPECTS.

0400 BRAIBANTI R.J.D.
"REFLECTIONS ON BUREAUCRATIC CORRUPTION."
PUBLIC ADMINISTRATION, 40 (WINTER 62), 357-372.
ALL GOVERNMENTS EXPERIENCE CORRUPTION, WHICH IS A VERY COMPLEX PHENOMENON. AS A SOCIETY MATURES, GOVERNMENT TENDS TO BE LESS CORRUPT AND HENCE BETTER FOR THE PUBLIC INTEREST.

0401 BRAIBANTI R.J.D. ED.
ASIAN BUREAUCRATIC SYSTEMS EMERGENT FROM THE BRITISH IMPERIAL TRADITION.
DURHAM: DUKE U PR, 1966, 733 PP., LC#66-27487.
COMPARES AND CONTRASTS BUREAUCRATIC SYSTEMS OF SEPARATE NATIONS OF SOUTH ASIA. EMPHASIZES TWO RECURRENT THEMES: IMPACT AND RESILIENCY OF BRITISH BUREAUCRATIC HERITAGE, AND PERVASIVENESS OF ELITIST TRADITION.

0402 BRAIBANTI R.J.D.
RESEARCH ON THE BUREAUCRACY OF PAKISTAN.
DURHAM: DUKE U PR, 1966, 565 PP., LC#66-14888.
NARRATES PROBLEMS OF PAKISTANI GOVERNMENT IN 1947-65 SO AS TO SET TO ORDER THE PUBLIC RECORD AND IDENTIFY, CLASSIFY, AND EVALUATE SOURCE MATERIALS FOR STUDY OF PAKISTANI BUREAUCRACY. DEALS WITH HISTORY AND ORGANIZATION OF BUREAUCRACY AT LOCAL AND NATIONAL LEVELS. NOTES EFFECTS OF NATIONAL ENVIRONMENT ON GOVERNMENT OPERATION. TRACES REFORM EFFORTS.

0403 BRAMSTED E.K.
GOEBBELS AND NATIONAL SOCIALIST PROPAGANDA, 1925-1945.
EAST LANSING: MICHIGAN STATE U, 1965, 488 PP., LC#64-19392.
DISCUSSES NATURE AND DEVELOPMENT OF GERMAN PROPAGANDA METHODS. EMPHASIZES GERMAN MILITARY STRENGTH, ATTITUDE TOWARD BRITAIN, AND RUSSIAN CAMPAIGN.

0404 BRANCO R.
"LAND REFORM* THE ANSWER TO LATIN AMERICA'S AGRICULTURAL DEVELOPMENT?"
J. INTER-AMER. STUDIES, 10 (APR. 67), 225-235.
ARGUES THAT SPLITTING UP HACIENDAS AND PLANTATIONS FOR RE-DISTRIBUTION HAS SERIOUS DRAWBACKS AND IS PROFITABLE ONLY IN AREAS WITH LOW CONCENTRATION OF HUMAN AND CAPITAL RESOURCES. CRASH PROGRAMS, AS IN MEXICO, BOLIVIA, AND CUBA, SHOULD BE AVOIDED. ADVOCATES INDIRECT METHODS SUCH AS LIMITING MAXIMUM SIZE OF HOLDINGS AND PROGRESSIVE LAND TAX. SUGGESTS "HIGHLY URGENT COMPLEMENTARY MEASURES."

0405 BRANDENBURG F.
"THE RELEVANCE OF MEXICAN EXPERIENCE TO LATIN AMERICAN DEVELOPMENT."
ORBIS, 9 (SPRING 65), 190-213.
AUTHOR BELIEVES THERE IS VERY LITTLE IN MEXICO'S BASIC POLITICAL AND ECONOMIC ORGANIZATION WORTHY OF DUPLICATION BY OTHER SOUTH AMERICAN NATIONS. MEXICO HAS FOUND THE KEY TO ITS OWN POLITICAL STABILITY ACCOMPANIED BY ECONOMIC GROWTH BASED ON ITS OWN INHERITANCE, NEEDS AND REALITIES. THE OTHER LA NATIONS MUST DO THE SAME.

0406 BRASS P.R.
FACTIONAL POLITICS IN AN INDIAN STATE: THE CONGRESS PARTY IN UTTAR PRADESH.
BERKELEY: U OF CALIF PR, 1965, 262 PP., LC#65-23109.
SURVEY OF POLITICAL PRACTICES AND DEVELOPMENT IN UTTAR PRADESH. TRACES TRANSITION FROM BRITISH BUREAUCRATIC RULE TO DEMOCRATIC SELF-GOVERNMENT AND EXAMINES ROLE OF POLITICAL PARTIES IN PROVIDING STABLE GOVERNMENT AND ORIENTING SOCIETY TO MODERN POLITICAL AND ECONOMIC GOALS. ANALYZES IN DETAIL CONGRESSIONAL CONTROL BY DIFFERENT FACTIONS AND EVOLUTION OF CONGRESS PARTY FROM MASS MOVEMENT TO EFFICIENT ORGANIZATION.

0407 BRECHER M.
THE NEW STATES OF ASIA.
LONDON: OXFORD U PR, 1963, 226 PP.
POLITICAL ANALYSIS OF NEW ASIAN NATIONS. TREATS COLONIALISM AND COMING OF INDEPENDENCE, SEARCH FOR POLITICAL STABILITY, STATE SYSTEM, NEUTRALISM, AND NEW STATES IN WORLD POLITICS.

0408 BRECHER M.
SUCCESSION IN INDIA.
LONDON: OXFORD U PR, 1966, 269 PP.
RESEARCH CONFINED TO ONE POLITICAL DECISION: SHASTRI SUCCESSION TO NEHRU. AFTER SHASTRI DIED, AUTHOR OBSERVED SECOND SUCCESSION. COMPARISON OF THE TWO IS MADE, NOT WITHOUT RELEVANCE TO UNDERSTANDING ALL-INDIA POLITICS AND DECISION-MAKING IN POLITICS GENERALLY.

0409 BRECHT A.
"THE NEW GERMAN CONSTITUTION."
SOCIAL RESEARCH, 16 (DEC. 49), 425-473.
AN ANALYSIS OF THE MERITS AND DEMERITS OF THE NEW GERMAN CONSTITUTION IN ITS CHARACTER AS A DEMOCRATIC CONSTITUTION IRRESPECTIVE OF CORRECTIVE ACTIONS THAT MAY BE TAKEN BY OCCUPATION AUTHORITIES. CONTENDS THAT THE FOREMOST CONSTITUTIONAL PROBLEM OF GERMANY IS THE ESTABLISHMENT AND MAINTENANCE OF A DEMOCRATIC FORM OF GOVERNMENT IN A COUNTRY WHICH CONTAINS STRONG ANTIDEMOCRATIC ELEMENTS.

0410 BREDVOLD L.I. ED., ROSS R.G. ED.
THE PHILOSOPHY OF EDMUND BURKE.
ANN ARBOR: U OF MICH PR, 1960, 276 PP., LC#60-13177.
WRITINGS ON POLITICS, POLITICAL PARTIES, THE STATE, AND CENTRAL POLITICAL QUESTIONS: PRINCIPLES OF REFORM, DUTIES OF POPULAR REPRESENTATIVES, ETC. INCLUDES BRIEF BIOGRAPHY.

0411 BRETTON H.L.
POWER AND STABILITY IN NIGERIA: THE POLITICS OF DECOLONIZATION.
NEW YORK: PRAEGER, 1962, 208 PP.
AN ATTEMPT TO APPLY SOME LASSWELLIAN CONCEPTS IN THE AFRICAN CONTEXT. ASSERTS THAT STABILITY IS DEPENDENT ON DEVELOPMENT OF NEW POST-INDEPENDENCE IDEA-SYSTEM.

0412 BREWIS T.N., ENGLISH H.E., SCOTT A.

CANADIAN ECONOMIC POLICY.
LONDON: MACMILLAN, 1961, 365 PP.
COMPREHENSIVE TREATMENT OF ROLE OF GOVERNMENT IN ECONOMY. TRACES EFFECTS OF GOVERNMENTAL POLICY ON SUPPLY, DEMAND, COMPETITION, RESOURCE ALLOCATION, CAPITAL FORMATION, AND EMPLOYMENT CONDITIONS. INDICATES RELATIONSHIPS OF FISCAL AND MONETARY POLICIES; DESCRIBES THEIR IMPACT UPON MARKET SITUATIONS.

0413 BRIDGHAM P.
"MAO'S "CULTURAL REVOLUTION"* ORIGIN AND DEVELOPMENT."
CHINA Q., (JAN.-MAR. 67), 1-35.
GIVES HISTORY OF CULTURAL REVOLUTION, ITS NATURE AS SOCIALIST EDUCATION, ITS RELATION TO THE CULT OF MAO TSE-TUNG. MANIPULATION OF THE POPULACE USING PUBLIC MASS MEDIA BY THE VARIOUS FACTIONS IS DISCUSSED. STRUGGLE FOR POWER ANALYZED. SEES CULTURAL REVOLUTION AS PART OF ECONOMIC PROGRAM DESIGNED TO CREATE MASS ENTHUSIASM.

0414 BRIDGMAN J., CLARKE D.E.
GERMAN AFRICA: A SELECT ANNOTATED BIBLIOGRAPHY.
STANFORD: HOOVER INSTITUTE, 1965, 120 PP., LC#64-7917.
SOME 900 NEWSPAPERS, PERIODICALS, OFFICIAL AND SEMI-OFFICIAL GERMAN DOCUMENTS, AND BRITISH CONFIDENTIAL PAPERS ON GERMAN EAST AFRICA, GERMAN SOUTHWEST AFRICA, TOGO, AND CAMEROON ARE ANNOTATED. WORKS FROM 1890-1965, MOSTLY IN GERMAN.

0415 BRIERLY J.L.
THE BASIS OF OBLIGATION IN INTERNATIONAL LAW, AND OTHER PAPERS.
LONDON: OXFORD U PR, 1958, 387 PP.
COLLECTION OF JL BRIERLY'S WRITINGS ON INTERNATIONAL LAW. SELECTIONS INCLUDED ILLUSTRATE THE PROGRESSIVENESS OF HIS CONCEPTION OF LAW. TREAT MATTERS OF DOMESTIC JURISDICTION, THEORY OF IMPLIED STATE COMPLICITY IN INTERNATIONAL CLAIMS, NATURE OF DISPUTES, AND LEGISLATIVE FUNCTION IN INTERNATIONAL RELATIONS.

0416 BRIGGS A.
CHARTIST STUDIES.
NEW YORK: ST MARTIN'S PRESS, 1959, 424 PP., LC#59-65123.
PRESENTS RESULTS OF RECENT STUDIES OF THE CHARTIST MOVEMENT AND DEALS WITH CHARTISTS IN ASSORTED ENGLISH CITIES. INCLUDES PROGRAMS, SUCH AS THE LAND PLAN AND THE ANTI-CORN LAW LEAGUE.

0417 BRIGGS L.C.
THE LIVING RACES OF THE SAHARA.
CAMBRIDGE: PEABODY MUSEUM, 1958, 217 PP.
COMPREHENSIVE STUDY OF PRESENT KNOWLEDGE OF ECOLOGY AND RACIAL CHARACTERISTICS OF LIVING TRIBES OF SAHARA DESERT FROM PREHISTORIC TIMES. INCLUDES GEOGRAPHICAL SETTING, AND SEDENTARY AND NOMADIC SOCIETIES.

0418 BRIGGS L.C.
TRIBES OF THE SAHARA.
CAMBRIDGE: HARVARD U PR, 1960, 295 PP., LC#60-1988.
SEEKS TO SUMMARIZE WHAT IS KNOWN OF PEOPLES OF SAHARA: THEIR HISTORY, ENVIRONMENT, AND WAYS OF LIFE, PRESENTING DIRECT PERSONAL OBSERVATIONS. DISCUSSED ARE TUAREG, TEDA, ARAB NOMADS, AND MOORS.

0419 BRIGHT J.R.
RESEARCH, DEVELOPMENT AND TECHNOLOGICAL INNOVATION.
HOMEWOOD: RICHARD IRWIN, 1964, 764 PP., LC#64-11711.
DISCUSSION OF TECHNOLOGICAL INNOVATION AND ITS PROBLEMS. TYPICAL BUSINESS PROBLEMS ANALYZED IN ATTEMPT TO ILLUMINATE METHODS OF HANDLING ISSUES CONCERNING IDENTIFICATION OF, SUPPORT FOR, AND DEFENSE AGAINST RADICAL TECHNOLOGICAL CONCEPTS. CHANGE AND INNOVATION IN POPULATION, SOCIAL TRENDS, NATURAL RESOURCE POSITIONS, ETC. ARE CONSIDERED.

0420 BRIMMELL G.H.
COMMUNISM IN SOUTHEAST ASIA (PAMPHLET)
NEW YORK: INST OF PACIFIC RELNS, 1958, 10 PP.
UNITED KINGDOM PAPER NO. 2 PRESENTED AT THIRTEENTH CONFERENCE INSTITUTE OF PACIFIC RELATIONS, LAHORE, PAKISTAN, 1958. SEES ASIAN REVOLUTION AS LAST IN SERIES OF THREE, FOLLOWING EUROPEAN AND RUSSIAN. FOCUSES UPON BURMA, LAOS, CAMBODIA, AND INDONESIA. VIETNAM, PHILIPPINES, AND MALAYA DISCUSSED IN RELATION TO ABOVE NATIONS.

0421 BRITISH BORNEO RESEARCH PROJ
BIBLIOGRAPHY OF BRITISH BORNEO (PAMPHLET)
LONDON: BRITISH BORNEO RES PROJ, 1956, 23 PP.
SHORT ANNOTATED BIBLIOGRAPHY OF ANTHROPOLOGICAL STUDIES, COMMUNICATION, DEMOGRAPHY, ECONOMICS, EDUCATION, GEOGRAPHY, HISTORY, LAW, POLITICS, AND GOVERNMENT OF BRITISH BORNEO.

0422 BROCK C.
A GUIDE TO LIBRARY RESOURCES FOR POLITICAL SCIENCE STUDENTS AT THE UNIVERSITY OF NORTH CAROLINA (PAMPHLET)
CHAPEL HILL: U OF N C LIBRARY, 1965, 69 PP.
ANNOTATED COMPILATION OF BIBLIOGRAPHICAL SOURCES. APPROXIMATELY 500 ENGLISH-LANGUAGE PUBLICATIONS, 1900-65. ENTRIES GROUPED BY TYPE OF PUBLICATION - PERIODICAL INDEXES AND ABSTRACTS, BOOK REVIEWS, US GOVERNMENT PUBLICATIONS, PUBLICATIONS OF UN AND OTHER INTERNATIONAL AGENCIES, STATE AND FOREIGN PUBLICATIONS, TRANSLATIONS ON FOREIGN SOURCES, AND STATISTICAL SOURCES.

0423 BROCKWAY A.F.
AFRICAN SOCIALISM.
CHESTER SPRINGS: DUFOUR, 1963, 126 PP., LC#63-21144.
TRACES HISTORICAL TRANSITION FROM EUROPEAN CAPITALISM TO AFRICAN SOCIALISM. DISCUSSES SOCIALISM OF NKRUMAH OF GHANA AND NASSER OF EGYPT. ATTEMPTS EVALUATION OF AFRICA'S POSSIBLE TURN TOWARD COMMUNISM.

0424 BRODERICK G.C.
POLITICAL STUDIES.
LONDON: ROUTLEDGE & KEGAN PAUL, 1879, 567 PP.
COLLECTION OF ESSAYS COMPARING ENGLISH GOVERNMENT TO ROMAN, EVALUATING ITS COLONIAL PERFORMANCE, EDUCATION, CONSTITUTIONAL HISTORY AND LIBERAL PARTY'S CONFLICTS WITH CONSERVATIVES.

0425 BRODERSEN A.
THE SOVIET WORKER: LABOR AND GOVERNMENT IN SOVIET SOCIETY.
NEW YORK: RANDOM HOUSE, INC, 1966, 278 PP., LC#66-10534.
DISCUSSES ROLE OF THE WORKING CLASS IN CONTEMPORARY SOVIET SOCIETY. SHOWS WORKER'S ROLE IN BOLSHEVIK, MARXIST, AND LENINIST THEORY AND IN BOLSHEVIK POLICY. ANALYZES THE WORKER WITHIN STALINIST INDUSTRIALIZATION AND DURING FORMATION OF THE LABOR FORCE. DESCRIBES NEW COURSE IN SOVIET LABOR POLICY SINCE KHRUSHCHEV. EXAMINES WORKER'S RELATIONS TO INTELLIGENTSIA AND POLITICS.

0426 BRODOWSKI J.H. ED.
LATIN AMERICA TODAY.
TRENTON: TRENTON STATE COL, 1963, 37 PP.
ANNOTATED COMPILATION OF ENGLISH-LANGUAGE PERIODICALS, TEXTS, AND REFERENCE BOOKS LOCATED AT THE TRENTON STATE (NEW JERSEY) COLLEGE LIBRARY.

0427 BROEKMEIJER M.W.
DEVELOPING COUNTRIES AND NATO.
LEYDEN: AW SIJTHOFF, 1963, 208 PP.
DISCUSSES PROBLEMS OF UNDERDEVELOPED COUNTRIES, NATURE OF TECHNICAL AID FROM WEST, PRIVATE INVESTMENT, AND ORGANIZATIONAL STRUCTURE OF FOREIGN AID. MAINTAINS THAT ECONOMIC DEVELOPMENT OF UNDERDEVELOPED NATIONS CAN ONLY BE KEPT FREE FROM COMMUNIST SUBVERSION THROUGH STRENGTHENING OF NATO DETERRENT POWER.

0428 BROGAN D.W.
THE DEVELOPMENT OF MODERN FRANCE (1870-1939)
LONDON: HAMISH HAMILTON, 1940, 744 PP.
PROVIDES AN ACCOUNT OF MODERN FRENCH HISTORY FROM THE FALL OF THE SECOND EMPIRE TO THE OUTBREAK OF WWII. COVERS THE HISTORY OF THE REPUBLIC, FRENCH COLONIALISM, DEVELOPMENT OF NATIONALISM, WWI, AND THE WAR INTERIM. EMPHASIZES WWI, AND ITS ORIGIN.

0429 BROGAN D.W., VERNEY D.V.
POLITICAL PATTERNS IN TODAY'S WORLD.
NEW YORK: HARCOURT BRACE, 1963, 274 PP., LC#63-11413.
BRIEF COMPARATIVE INTRODUCTION TO POLITICAL SCIENCE. COMPARES FOUR LIBERAL DEMOCRACIES IN THEIR COMMON TRADITION, POLITICAL PROCESSES, ORGANIZATION, AND ROLE IN INTERNATIONAL RELATIONS, TO THE COMMUNIST WORLD. DISCUSSES DECLINE AND FAILURE OF DEMOCRACY'S LEADERSHIP IN FRANCE AND IN TOTALITARIAN DICTATORSHIPS.

0430 BROMAGE A.W., BROMAGE M.C.
"THE VOCATIONAL SENATE IN IRELAND"
AM. POL. SCI. REV., 34 (JUNE 40), 519-538.
AUTHORS SUMMARIZE DIFFICULTIES IN DEVISING A SUITABLE SECOND HOUSE FOR IRELAND. THEY EXAMINE THE FIRST IRISH UPPER HOUSE, 1922-36. DESCRIBES THE VOCATIONAL COMPOSITION OF THE SENATE ESTABLISHED IN 1937, ITS POWERS AND SOME OF ITS ACTION IN 1938-1939.

0431 BROMKE A.
POLAND'S POLITICS: IDEALISM VS. REALISM.
CAMBRIDGE: HARVARD U PR, 1967, 316 PP., LC#66-21331.
DISCUSSES CONFLICT BETWEEN POLITICAL IDEALISM AND POLITICAL REALISM IN POLAND. STATES THAT ROOT OF CONFLICT IS ANXIETY ABOUT NEIGHBORS' INTENTIONS. SHOWS THAT FOR 200 YEARS RIVALRY BETWEEN GERMANY AND RUSSIA HAS REPRESENTED A CONSTANT THREAD OF POLISH HISTORY. POINTS OUT THAT POLISH POLITICAL MOVEMENTS HAVE ALWAYS SPLIT, NOT OVER DOMESTIC ISSUES, BUT OVER FOREIGN POLICY.

0432 BROOKES E.H.
POWER, LAW, RIGHT, AND LOVE: A STUDY IN POLITICAL VALUES.
DURHAM: DUKE U PR, 1963, 84 PP., LC#63-18576.
DISCUSSES INTERRELATIONSHIP BETWEEN POLITICAL ACTION AND RELIGIOUS FAITH. EXAMINES CONCEPT OF POWER AS LEGITIMATE INSTRUMENT OF STATE AND DISCUSSES POSSIBILITIES OF CONTROL. FREQUENT REFERENCE TO AFRICAN POLITICS.

0433 BROOKS S., ENGELENBURG F.V.
BRITAIN AND THE BOERS.
NEW YORK: N AMER REVIEW PUB CO, 1899, 48 PP.
A PRESENTATION OF VARIOUS VIEWS RELATED TO THE QUESTION OF LEGITIMACY AND INTERNATIONAL LAW IN THE BRITAIN-BOER WAR. DISCUSSES SOME OF THE HISTORICAL CIRCUMSTANCES THAT PRODUCED THE WAR.

0434 BROSE O.J.
CHURCH AND PARLIAMENT: THE RESHAPING OF THE CHURCH OF ENGLAND 1828-1860.
STANFORD: STANFORD U PRESS, 1959, 239 PP., LC#59-7423.
STUDY OF REASONS FOR SURVIVAL OF CHURCH IN ENGLAND DURING 19TH-CENTURY WAVES OF PROGRESS, SCIENCE, AND LIBERALISM. ANALYZES WHY AND HOW METAMORPHOSIS OF CHURCH TOOK PLACE AND ITS PARTICULAR NATURE. STUDIES ADMINISTRATIVE CHANGES AND THEIR RELATION BOTH TO PATTERNS OF THOUGHT PREVAILING IN GOVERNMENT, AND TO SIMILAR PATTERNS WITHIN CHURCH AND SOCIETY AT LARGE.

0435 BROUGHTON M.
PRESS AND POLITICS OF SOUTH AFRICA.
CAPETOWN: PURNELL & SONS, 1961, 306 PP.
A STUDY OF THE NEWSPAPER ESTABLISHMENT AND ITS RELATION TO THE POLITICAL PROCESS IN SOUTH AFRICA. INCLUDES A DISCUSSION OF SOUTH AFRICAN CULTURE AT LARGE AND THE EFFORTS TO ACHIEVE CULTURAL UNITY AND NATIONAL IDENTITY.

0436 BROWN A.D.
PANAMA CANAL AND PANAMA CANAL ZONE: A SELECTED LIST OF REFERENCES.
WASHINGTON: LIBRARY OF CONGRESS, 1943, 57 PP.
LISTS, INDEXES, AND ANNOTATES 430 BOOKS, ARTICLES, AND PAMPHLETS PRIMARILY IN ENGLISH AND SPANISH PERTINENT TO THE POLITICS, SOCIAL CONDITIONS, ECONOMIC SITUATION, CULTURE, AND HISTORY OF THE PANAMA CANAL ZONE AS WELL AS TOLLS AND TRAFFIC, DEFENSES, AND INTERNATIONAL ASPECTS OF THE CANAL ITSELF. ITEMS DATE FROM 1920'S AND INCLUDE BIBLIOGRAPHIES.

0437 BROWN A.D.
BRITISH POSSESSIONS IN THE CARIBBEAN AREA: A SELECTED LIST OF REFERENCES.
WASHINGTON: LIBRARY OF CONGRESS, 1943, 192 PP.
LIST COMPILED AT REQUEST OF ANGLO-AMERICAN CARIBBEAN COMMISSION. ONLY LATEST AVAILABLE ISSUES OF REPORTS AND OTHER ANNUAL PUBLICATIONS NOTED. CONTAINS 1,487 ITEMS ON BIBLIOGRAPHIES; HISTORY; ECONOMIC AND SOCIAL CONDITIONS; POLITICS AND GOVERNMENT; INTERNATIONAL ASPECTS OF DEVELOPMENT; ETC. SELECTIONS REFER ALSO TO INDIVIDUAL COUNTRIES.

0438 BROWN A.D., JONES H.D., HELLMAN F.S.
GREECE: SELECTED LIST OF REFERENCES.
WASHINGTON: LIBRARY OF CONGRESS, 1943, 101 PP.
AIMS TO PRESENT ITEMS APPEARING IN THE DECADE PRIOR TO GERMAN INVASION OF GREECE IN 1940. INCLUDES 765 BOOKS, ARTICLES, PAMPHLETS, ETC., ON GEOGRAPHY, HISTORY, POLITICS, ECONOMICS, SOCIOLOGY, AND RECENT CRISES AND CONDITIONS IN GREECE. DEALS WITH GENERAL TOPICS AS WELL AS SPECIFIC AREAS (ATHENS, MACEDONIA, SALONIKA, THE ISLANDS, ETC.). ALSO INCLUDES AN AUTHOR INDEX.

0439 BROWN B.E.
NEW DIRECTIONS IN COMPARATIVE POLITICS.
LONDON: ASIA PUBL HOUSE, 1962, 91 PP.
EXAMINES NATURE AND TRENDS IN COMPARATIVE APPROACH TO POLITICS AND APPLIES COMPARATIVE METHOD TO STUDY OF INTERACTION BETWEEN PEOPLE AND GOVERNMENT THROUGH PARTIES, ROLE OF ARMIES IN RIVALRY FOR POWER, AND SHIFTING BALANCE AMONG PUBLIC POWERS. COMPARES POLITICS OF WEST AND NON-WEST IN CONCLUSION.

0440 BROWN C.V.
GOVERNMENT AND BANKING IN WESTERN NIGERIA.
LONDON: OXFORD U PR, 1964, 141 PP.
ANALYZES IMPLEMENTATION OF WESTERN NIGERIAN GOVERNMENT'S ECONOMIC POLICY OF AIDING INDIGENOUS BANKS. RELIES HEAVILY ON INFORMATION AND QUOTATIONS FROM COKER COMMISSION OF INQUIRY. SIGNIFICANT CASE STUDY MAY INDICATE TYPE OF RELATIONSHIP EXISTING AMONG POLITICIANS, CIVIL SERVANTS, AND PUBLIC CORPORATIONS IN WESTERN NIGERIA AND OTHER DEVELOPING AREAS.

0441 BROWN D.F.
THE GROWTH OF DEMOCRATIC GOVERNMENT.
WASHINGTON: PUBLIC AFFAIRS PRESS, 1959, 117 PP., LC#59-13659
STUDY OF DEVELOPMENT OF WESTERN DEMOCRATIC SYSTEMS BY EXAMINING STRUCTURE AND FUNCTION OF DIFFERENT SYSTEMS IN EXISTENCE. DISCUSSES PRESIDENTIAL SYSTEM, PROPORTIONAL REPRESENTATION, POLITICAL PARTIES, AND RELATIONS BETWEEN CHIEF EXECUTIVE AND LAW-MAKING BODY.

0442 BROWN D.M.
THE WHITE UMBRELLA: INDIAN POLITICAL THOUGHT FROM MANU TO GANDHI.
BERKELEY: U OF CALIF PR, 1953, 205 PP.
CONCISE SURVEY OF HINDU POLITICAL IDEAS. BRIEF ANALYSIS OF INDIAN THOUGHT ACCOMPANIED BY SERIES OF SELECTIONS FROM HINDU POLITICAL CLASSICS. BIBLIOGRAPHY LIMITED TO ENGLISH-LANGUAGE WORKS.

0443 BROWN D.M.
THE NATIONALIST MOVEMENT.
BERKELEY: U OF CALIF PR, 1961, 244 PP., LC#61-11877.
ANALYZES INDIAN POLITICAL TRADITION FROM RANADE TO BHAVE. RECORDS HOW HINDU POLITICAL THEORY HELPED TO SOLVE CRISES OF CONTEMPORARY INDIA - THOSE PRECIPITATED BY INROADS OF WESTERN CULTURE AND STRUGGLE FOR INDEPENDENCE. FIGURES SELECTED FOR INCLUSION ARE CENTRAL TO NATIONALIST MOVEMENT IN INDIA AND EMBODY ITS CHIEF ASPECTS. BIBLIOGRAPHY OF ENGLISH-LANGUAGE WORKS.

0444 BROWN J.F.
THE NEW EASTERN EUROPE.
NEW YORK: FREDERICK PRAEGER, 1966, 306 PP., LC#65-24939.
COVERS IMPORTANT POLITICAL, ECONOMIC, AND CULTURAL DEVELOPMENTS WITHIN EASTERN EUROPEAN STATES EXCLUDING ALBANIA AND YUGOSLAVIA. DISCUSSES INTRABLOC RELATIONS, EAST EUROPEAN RELATIONS WITH WESTERN POWERS, AND SUMMARY OF SITUATION AT TIME OF KHRUSHCHEV'S FALL.

0445 BROWN L.C.
LATIN AMERICA, A BIBLIOGRAPHY.
KINSVILLE: TEX COL ARTS & INDUS, 1962, 80 PP.
LIST OF MATERIALS IN LIBRARY OF TEXAS A&I ON LATIN AMERICA, WITH PARTICULAR EMPHASIS ON INTERNATIONAL RELATIONS, POLITICS, AND GOVERNMENT. CONTAINS LIST OF ARTICLES ON LATIN AMERICA.

0446 BROWN L.C. ED.
STATE AND SOCIETY IN INDEPENDENT NORTH AFRICA.
WASHINGTON: MIDDLE EAST INST, 1966, 332 PP., LC#66-20316.
COMPARES ASPECTS OF FOUR NORTH AFRICAN COUNTRIES AFTER THEIR INDEPENDENCE WAS GAINED. CONSIDERS MAIN COMMON INFLUENCES TO BE GEOGRAPHY, ARAB-MUSLIM CULTURE AND COLONIAL EXPERIENCE UNDER FRENCH.

0447 BROWN L.N., GARNER J.F.
FRENCH ADMINISTRATIVE LAW.
LONDON, WASH, DC: BUTTERWORTHS, 1967, 160 PP.
COMPARE FRENCH LAW WITH ANGLO-SAXON. EXPLAIN THE LEGAL INSTITUTIONS OF FRANCE AND BRITAIN THAT EXERCISE CONTROL OVER ACTS OF THE ADMINISTRATION. DELINEATE BASIC LEGAL STRUCTURE OF BOTH NATIONS, AND DISCUSS MERITS AND DEFECTS OF THE FRENCH SYSTEM. GIVE MANY SPECIFIC CASES.

0448 BROWN N.
NUCLEAR WAR* THE IMPENDING STRATEGIC DEADLOCK.
NEW YORK: FREDERICK PRAEGER, 1964, 238 PP., LC#64-25586.
DETAILED ANALYSIS OF MILITARY TECHNOLOGY CIRCA 1963. BALANCES EAST AND WEST, OFFENSIVE AND DEFENSIVE WEAPONS AND TACTICS. SEES IMPORTANT DIPLO-STRATEGIC DEADLOCK CAUSED BY RELATIVE BALANCE OF THERMO-NUCLEAR MISSILES. REGARDS NATO AND UN AS KEYS TO STABILIZING THE ARMS RACE.

0449 BROWN R.T.
TRANSPORT AND THE ECONOMIC INTEGRATION OF SOUTH AMERICA.
WASHINGTON: BROOKINGS INST, 1966, 288 PP., LC#66-21327.
ANALYSIS OF GEOGRAPHIC, ECONOMIC, AND POLITICAL OBSTRUCTIONS TO SOUTH AMERICAN ECONOMIC DEVELOPMENT AND INTEGRATION. TRANSPORTATION SINGLED OUT MAJOR IMPEDIMENT TO NEEDED TRADE WITHIN SOUTH AMERICA AND AMELIORATING STRATEGY CALCULATED. EXTENSIVE DATA PRESENTED. ROLE OF LAFTA AND IMPORT OF MARITIME POLICY DISCUSSED.

0450 BROWN S.D.
STUDIES ON ASIA, 1962.
LINCOLN: U OF NEB PR, 1962, 87 PP., LC#60-15432.
STUDIES VARIOUS FACTORS SHAPING CONTEMPORARY ASIA: TAISHO CRISIS OF JAPAN, 1912-13; ISLAM AND MODERN WORLD; PRIVATE SECTOR IN INDIAN ECONOMY; BUDDHISM AND POLITICAL POWER IN BURMA; AND PARTY SYSTEM OF ISRAEL.

0451 BROWN W.M.
THE EXTERNAL LIQUIDITY OF AN ADVANCED COUNTRY.
PRINCETON: PRIN U, DEPT OF ECO, 1964, 70 PP., LC#64-8379.
EXAMINES PROBLEM OF AVAILABILITY OF RESOURCES FOR FINANCING TEMPORARY DEFICITS IN BALANCE OF PAYMENTS. FOCUSES ON THEORETICAL DISCUSSION OF "ADEQUACY OF LIQUIDITY." ILLUSTRATED BY REFERENCE TO STATISTICAL DATA.

0452 BROWNSON O.A.
THE AMERICAN REPUBLIC.
NEW YORK: P O'SHEY, 1865, 439 PP.
DISCUSSION OF PRINCIPLES OF GOVERNMENT, CONSTITUTION OF US, AND ETHICAL FOUNDATIONS OF FEDERALISM. REFERS TO CIVIL WAR SPECIFICALLY WITH ANALYSIS OF SECESSION AND RECONSTRUCTION.

0453 BRUMBERG A. ED.
RUSSIA UNDER KHRUSHCHEV.
NEW YORK: FREDERICK PRAEGER, 1962, 660 PP.
PROVIDES CHRONOLOGICAL AND THEMATIC COMMENTARY ON INTERNAL DEVELOPMENTS IN USSR IN KHRUSHCHEV DECADE. THIRTY-FIVE

ARTICLES DEAL WITH ECONOMIC, SOCIAL, AND ARTISTIC DEVELOPMENTS; IDEOLOGICAL SETTING; A LOOK INTO THE FUTURE.

0454 BRUNHES J.
LA GEOGRAPHIE HUMAINE: ESSAI DE CLASSIFICATION POSITIVE PRINCIPES ET EXEMPLES (2ND ED.)
PARIS: LIBRAIRIE FELIX ALCAN, 1912, 801 PP.
ILLUSTRATED STUDY OF ENVIRONMENTAL CONDITIONS INFLUENCING DEVELOPMENT OF CIVILIZATION, WITH MONOGRAPHS ON DESERT AND MOUNTAIN SOCIETIES.

0455 BRYCE J.
STUDIES IN HISTORY AND JURISPRUDENCE (2 VOLS.)
LONDON: CLARENDON PRESS, 1901, 1100 PP.
COMPARES HISTORY AND LAW OF ROME TO THOSE OF ENGLAND. EXAMINES POLITICAL CONSTITUTIONS AND PROBLEMS OF JURISPRUDENCE. SKETCHES HISTORY AND PECULIAR CONSTITUTION OF ICELANDIC REPUBLIC. DISCUSSES CONSTITUTIONS OF US, TWO DUTCH REPUBLICS IN SOUTH AFRICA, AND AUSTRALIA. STUDIES NATURE OF OBEDIENCE AND SOVEREIGNTY, LAW OF NATURE, AND METHODS OF LEGAL SCIENCE.

0456 BRYCE J.
THE HOLY ROMAN EMPIRE.
NEW YORK: MACMILLAN, 1932, 575 PP.
BEGINNING WITH THIRD CENTURY, TRACES GROWTH AND DECLINE AS INSTITUTIONAL SYSTEM AND ENDS WITH UNIFICATION OF GERMAN EMPIRE. ELABORATES THEORY OF EMPIRE WHILE DETAILING POLITICAL HISTORY OF GERMANY AND MEDIEVAL ITALY. CONCLUDES ESSENCE OF HOLY ROMAN EMPIRE AS LOVE OF PEACE, BROTHERHOOD AND SUPREMACY OF THE SPIRITUAL LIFE.

0457 BRZEZINSKI Z., HUNTINGTON S.P.
POLITICAL POWER: USA/USSR.
NEW YORK: VIKING PRESS, 1964, 461 PP., LC#64-13299.
COMPARES POLITICAL SYSTEMS, SOCIALIZATION PROCESSES, POLITICAL LEADERSHIP, POLICY-MAKING PROCESSES, ETC., OF US AND USSR. EXAMINES RESPONSES TO CRISES BY US AND USSR LEADERSHIP.

0458 BRZEZINSKI Z.K.
THE SOVIET BLOC-UNITY AND CONFLICT.
CAMBRIDGE: HARVARD U. PR., 1960, 167 PP.
ANALYSIS PROVIDES INSIGHT INTO THE INFLUENCE OF IDEOLOGY IN SHAPING POLICIES AND ACTIONS OF SOVIET LEADERS. DISCLOSES THEIR USE OF ABSTRACT IDEALS AS INSTRUMENTS OF POWER. SHOWS HOW INTERNAL CHANGES WITHIN USSR AFFECTED POLITICAL DEVELOPMENTS IN OTHER COMMUNIST STATES ALTERING RELATIONSHIPS WITHIN THE SOVIET BLOC.

0459 BRZEZINSKI Z.K.
"PATTERNS AND LIMITS OF THE SINO-SOVIET DISPUTE."
PROBL. COMMUNISM, (SEPT.-OCT. 60), 1-7.
EXPLAINS THE DEVELOPMENT OF SINO-SOVIET DIFFERENCES AND OFFERS REASONS THEY MUST REMAIN 'FROZEN' AT A CERTAIN POINT. INDICATES THE PRESENT PATTERN OF 'DIVERGENT UNITY' CAN ENDURE FOR A LONG TIME.

0460 BRZEZINSKI Z.K.
"THE ORGANIZATION OF THE COMMUNIST CAMP."
WORLD POLIT., 13 (JAN. 61), 175-209.
OUTLINES INSTITUTIONAL ASPECTS OF SOVIET CAMP REGARDING MULTILATERAL ORGANIZATIONS AND BILATERAL AGREEMENTS SUCH AS MUTUAL AID TREATIES AND CULTURAL AGREEMENTS. DYNAMIC ASPECTS OF UNITY VIEWED THROUGH FREQUENCY OF HIGH LEVEL MEETINGS, PUBLICATIONS, MILITARY PREPONDERANCE OF USSR AND UNIFORM BLOC LITERATURE.

0461 BRZEZINSKI Z.K. ED.
AFRICA AND THE COMMUNIST WORLD.
STANFORD: U. PR., 1963, 272 PP., $5.00.
A COMPREHENSIVE REVIEW OF RECENT COMMUNIST POLICIES TOWARD AFRICA BY EIGHT AUTHORITIES ON COMMUNISM. CONTEMPORARY ANALYSIS OF PROGRAMS ADOPTED BY VARIOUS COMMUNIST STATES TO ESTABLISH THEIR INFLUENCE AMONG NEWLY EMERGING AFRICAN STATES.

0462 BRZEZINSKI Z.K.
IDEOLOGY AND POWER IN SOVIET POLITICS.
NEW YORK: FREDERICK PRAEGER, 1967, 291 PP., LC#66-18893.
MAKES DISTINCTION BETWEEN IDEOLOGICAL AND POWER INFLUENCE ON SOVIET FOREIGN POLICY, AND INDICATES LACK OF DISTINCTION BECAUSE OF DEPENDENCE OF LEADERS UPON DOGMATIC IDEOLOGY FOR DETERMINATION OF USAGE OF POWER. ANALYZES CONFLICTS IN SYSTEM CONSISTING OF THIS POWER-IDEOLOGY CONGLOMERATION. APPLICATION OF THEORY TO CURRENT FOREIGN AFFAIRS PROBLEMS.

0463 BRZEZINSKI Z.K.
THE SOVIET BLOC: UNITY AND CONFLICT (2ND ED., REV., ENLARGED)
CAMBRIDGE: HARVARD U PR, 1967, 599 PP., LC#67-12531.
EXAMINES HOW SOVIET BLOC HAS CHANGED OVER THE YEARS, WHAT PROBLEMS FACED AND CONTINUE TO FACE ITS LEADERS, AND HOW LEADERS GO ABOUT SOLVING THESE IN TERMS OF THEIR GENERAL IDEOLOGICAL ORIENTATION. ALSO SHOWS HOW INTERNAL CHANGES IN USSR AFFECTED POLITICAL DEVELOPMENTS WITHIN OTHER COMMUNIST STATES AND CHANGED THE PATTERN OF RELATIONS AMONG THEM.

0464 BUCHHEIM K.
GESCHICHTE DER CHRISTLICHEN PARTEIEN IN DEUTSCHLAND.
MUNICH: KOSEL VERLAG, 1953, 467 PP.
A STUDY OF THE EVOLUTION OF THE GERMAN CHRISTIAN PARTY MOVEMENT FROM ITS EARLY BEGINNING AT THE TURN OF THE 18TH CENTURY TO ITS RE-EMERGENCE AFTER WWII. PARTICULAR EMPHASIS IS PLACED UPON THE TRADITION OF POLITICAL FREEDOM AND THE FREEDOM OF CONSCIENCE AS ITS MAIN IDEOLOGICAL PERSUASION.

0465 BUCK P.W.
CONTROL OF FOREIGN RELATIONS IN MODERN NATIONS.
NEW YORK: NORTON, 1957, 865 PP.
ANALYSIS OF INTERNAL POLICY-MAKING FACTORS OF LATIN AMERICA, USA, COMMONWEALTH COUNTRIES, FRANCE, HOLLAND, JAPAN AND RUSSIA. DEMONSTRATES THAT A NUCLEAR STALEMATE, ECONOMIC PROGRESS AND CONTINUED COOPERATION COULD LEAD TO MORE EFFECTIVE INTERNATIONAL ORGANIZATION. ADVOCATES STABLE WORLD COMPOSED OF SEVERAL POWER CENTERS.

0466 BUELL R.
THE NATIVE PROBLEM IN AFRICA.
NEW YORK: MACMILLAN, 1928, 1045 PP.
COMPREHENSIVE STUDY OF POLITICAL, SOCIAL, AND ECONOMIC SITUATION OF A NUMBER OF AFRICAN COUNTRIES AND TERRITORIES. POINTS OUT MAIN PROBLEMS OF CONTINENT, FOCUSING ON THOSE RESULTING FROM IMPACT OF INDUSTRIAL CIVILIZATION ON PRIMITIVE PEOPLE.

0467 BUISSON L.
POTESTAS UND CARITAS.
TUBINGEN: BOHLAU VERLAG, 1958, 448 PP.
EXAMINES POWER OF PAPACY AND CHURCH LAW IN LATE MIDDLE AGES. TRACES GRADUAL CONTRACTION OF CHURCH POWER AND ULTIMATE TRIUMPH OF STATE OVER TRADITIONAL AUTHORITY OF CHURCH.

0468 BUKHARIN N., PREOBRAZHENSKY E.
THE ABC OF COMMUNISM: A POPULAR EXPLANATION OF THE PROGRAM OF THE COMMUNIST PARTY OF RUSSIA.
ANN ARBOR: U OF MICH PR, 1966, 422 PP.
COMMENTARY ON PROGRAM AND COMPLETE AND SYSTEMATIC COMPENDIUM OF MARXIST-LENINIST THEORY, ENCOMPASSING ENTIRE SPECTRUM OF COMMUNIST THEORY AND PRACTICE AS IT HAS EVOLVED SINCE MARX. INCORPORATES INTO A CONSISTENT SYNTHESIS THE CLASSICAL THEORIES OF SCIENTIFIC SOCIALISM, WORLD DEVELOPMENTS SINCE THEIR ORIGIN, DISTINCTIVE BOLSHEVIK REVISIONS, AND EXPERIENCE OF RUSSIAN REVOLUTION.

0469 BULLOCK A. ED., SHOCK M. ED.
THE LIBERAL TRADITION FROM FOX TO KEYNES.
NEW YORK: NEW YORK U PR, 1957, 288 PP., LC#57-5967.
ANTHOLOGY OF EXTRACTS FROM WRITINGS OF BRITISH STATESMEN AND INTELLECTUALS ILLUSTRATING DIFFERENT FACETS OF POLITICAL DISCUSSION. COVERS PERIOD FROM AMERICAN REVOLT TO WORLD WAR I. INCLUDES MATERIAL FROM BOOKS, PAMPHLETS, SPEECHES, LETTERS, NEWSPAPERS, ETC. FIFTY-FIVE PAGE INTRODUCTION DISCUSSES NATURE AND EVOLUTION OF LIBERAL TRADITION IN ENGLAND.

0470 BULLOCK A.
HITLER: A STUDY IN TYRANNY.
NEW YORK: BANTAM, 1961, 780 PP., $0.95.
'HE WAS IN REVOLT AGAINST... THAT LIBERAL BOURGEOIS ORDER SYMBOLIZED FOR HIM IN THE VIENNA WHICH HAD ONCE REJECTED HIM. TO DESTROY THIS WAS HIS MISSION... HE DID NOT FAIL. EUROPE MAY RISE AGAIN, BUT THE OLD EUROPE OF THE YEARS BETWEEN 1789, THE YEAR OF THE FRENCH REVOLUTION, AND 1939, THE YEAR OF HITLER'S WAR, HAS GONE FOR EVER - AND ADOLPH HITLER WAS THE ARCHITECT OF ITS RUIN.'

0471 BULLOUGH B.
"ALIENATION IN THE GHETTO."
AMER. J. OF SOCIOLOGY, 72 (MAR. 67), 469-478.
INVESTIGATION OF TWO SAMPLES OF MIDDLE-CLASS NEGROES, ONE IN TRADITIONAL GHETTOS AND ONE LIVING IN MOSTLY WHITE SUBURBAN AREAS. THE INTEGRATED SUBJECTS WERE LESS ALIENATED THAN THE OTHERS, FELT MORE IN CONTROL OF THEIR LIVES AND OF EVENTS, AND WERE MORE ORIENTED TOWARD THE MAINSTREAM OF SOCIETY THAN THE GHETTO INHABITANTS. ARGUES THAT GHETTO ALIENATION IS CIRCULAR.

0472 BULMER-THOMAS I.
THE GROWTH OF THE BRITISH PARTY SYSTEM (VOL. II) 1924-1964.
LONDON: JOHN BAKER, 1965, 328 PP.
CHRONOLOGICALLY EXAMINES BRITISH PARTY SYSTEM AS CONTEST BETWEEN CONSERVATIVE AND LABOUR PARTIES FROM 1924 LABOUR GOVERNMENT TO 1964 LABOUR VICTORY. SYSTEMATICALLY COVERS POLICIES OF BOTH PARTIES WHILE IN AND OUT OF POWER. STUDIES LEADERS OF BOTH PARTIES AND THEIR INFLUENCES.

0473 BULMER-THOMAS I.
"THE PARTY SYSTEM IN GREAT BRITAIN."
LONDON: PHOENIX HOUSE LTD, 1953.

STUDY OF ORGANIZATION AND WORKING OF PARTY SYSTEM IN PRACTICE. SKETCHES HISTORY OF PARTY ORGANIZATION BEFORE 1900 BUT EMPHASIZES DEVELOPMENT OF POLITICAL ALIGNMENTS IN 20TH CENTURY. SELECTED BIBLIOGRAPHY ORGANIZED TOPICALLY WITH MATERIAL RELATED TO SPECIFIC PARTY DEVELOPMENTS.

0474 BUNDESMIN FUR VERTRIEBENE
DIE VERTREIBUNG DER DEUTSCHEN BEVOLKERUNG AUS DER TSCHECHOSLOWAKEI.
BONN: BUNDESMIN FUR VERTRIEBENE, 1957, 818 PP.
COLLECTION OF DOCUMENTS ON EVACUATION AND EXPULSION OF GERMAN PEOPLE FROM CZECHOSLOVAKIA IN 1945-46. FOCUSES ON TREATMENT AND LIVING CONDITIONS OF LARGE GROUPS AND INDIVIDUALS.

0475 BUNDESMIN FUR VERTRIEBENE
ZEITTAFEL DER VORGESCHICHTE UND DES ABLAUFS DER VERTREIBUNG SOWIE DER UNTERBRINGUNG UND EINGLIEDERUNG DER (2 VOLS.)
BONN: BUNDESMIN FUR VERTRIEBENE, 1959, 454 PP.
CHRONOLOGICAL TABLE OF EVENTS RELATING TO GERMAN REFUGEE AND EXPULSION PROBLEM BETWEEN 1938-58. INCLUDES EXTENSIVE BIBLIOGRAPHY ON REFUGEE PROBLEMS, ASSIMILATION, RIGHTS OF DOMICILE, AND RIGHTS OF SELF-DETERMINATION IN GERMAN PARLIAMENT.

0476 BUNN R.F. ED., ANDREWS W.G. ED.
POLITICS AND CIVIL LIBERTIES IN EUROPE: FOUR CASE STUDIES.
PRINCETON: VAN NOSTRAND, 1967, 222 PP.
DESCRIBES AND ANALYZES CIVIL LIBERTIES PROBLEMS. DISCUSSES RIGHT OF PEOPLE TO ASSEMBLE PEACEABLY IN POLITICAL DEMONSTRATIONS. STUDIES CANAL AFFAIR IN FRANCE, INVOLVING THE PRIVILEGE OF A POLITICAL OFFENDER IN THE GAULLIST SYSTEM TO A FAIR TRAIL. TELLS OF FREEDOM OF PRESS IN GERMANY AND LITERARY FREEDOM IN USSR.

0477 BUNTING B.P.
THE RISE OF THE SOUTH AFRICAN REICH.
GLOUCESTER: PETER SMITH, 1964.
STUDY OF PHILOSOPHICAL AND LEGAL DEVELOPMENT AND ENACTMENT OF RACISM AND APARTHEID IN SOUTH AFRICA. PARALLELS POLICE AND GOVERNMENT ACTIONS AGAINST AFRICANS IN CONTEMPORARY SOUTH AFRICA WITH THOSE OF THIRD REICH. CONTENDS THAT A MASSIVE CONFLICT IS THREATENING TO ERUPT IF WORLD OPINION IS NOT ACTIVELY EMPLOYED AS AN INTERVENTIONARY FORCE.

0478 BURDEAU G.
O PODER EXECUTIVO NA FRANCA.
RIO DE JAN: ED REVISTA ESTUD POL, 1961, 119 PP.
ANALYSIS OF THE EVOLUTION OF THE DECISION-MAKING PROCESS AND OF THE EXECUTIVE IN THE NEW FRENCH REPUBLIC. INCREASED POWER OF THE STATE AND OF THE OFFICE OF THE PRESIDENT IN THE CONSTITUTION OF 1958.

0479 BURDETTE F.L., WILLMORE J.N., WITHERSPOON J.V.
POLITICAL SCIENCE: A SELECTED BIBLIOGRAPHY OF BOOKS IN PRINT, WITH ANNOTATIONS (PAMPHLET)
COLLEGE PARK: U MD, BUR PUB ADM, 1961, 97 PP., LC#61-64130.
CONTAINS APPROXIMATELY 250 TITLES WITH EXTENSIVE THOUGH NONCRITICAL ANNOTATIONS IN ALL FIELDS OF POLITICAL SCIENCE: AMERICAN NATIONAL GOVERNMENT, COMPARATIVE GOVERNMENT, INTERNATIONAL POLITICS, POLITICAL PARTIES, PUBLIC OPINION AND ELECTORAL PROCESS, POLITICAL THEORY, PUBLIC ADMINISTRATION, PUBLIC LAW, AND LOCAL AND STATE GOVERNMENT. DESIGNED FOR REFERENCE USERS.

0480 BURGESS J.W.
"VON HOLST'S PUBLIC LAW OF THE UNITED STATES"
POLIT. SCI. QUART., 1 (DEC. 1886), 612-635.
SECTION OF SURVEY OF PUBLIC LAW OF CIVILIZED WORLD. CROSS-EXAMINES SECTION ON US TO GET BENEFIT OF FOREIGN OPINION ON US LAW. COVERS CONSTITUTION'S GENESIS AND OPERATION IN DETAIL. COMPARES IT TO CONSTITUTIONAL LAW OF OTHER NATIONS.

0481 BURGESS J.W.
"THE RECENT CONSTITUTIONAL CRISIS IN NORWAY"
POLIT. SCI. QUART., 1 (JUNE 86), 259-294.
HISTORICAL DEVELOPMENT AND TEXT OF CONSTITUTION OF 1814 AND PACT WITH SWEDEN. ANALYSIS OF ACCEPTANCE AND SUCCESS OF CONSTITUTION IN POLITICAL STRUCTURE AND POLITICAL PROBLEMS IT FACED TRYING TO BE TOO SELF-RELIANT. SUGGESTS TRAGEDY OF BREAK WITH SWEDEN AND POSSIBLE LOSS OF ALL INDEPENDENCE GAINED.

0482 BURGHART A.
"CATHOLIC SOCIAL THOUGHT IN AUSTRIA."
SOCIAL RESEARCH, 34 (SUMMER 67), 369-382.
DEPICTS SITUATION OF CATHOLIC CHURCH IN AUSTRIAN SOCIETY AND DESCRIBES IMPORTANT SOURCES AND TENDENCIES OF CATHOLIC SOCIAL COMMENTARY. NOTES CHURCH INSTITUTIONS, CONCENTRATING ON 1930'S. DISCUSSES BROAD HISTORICAL CIRCUMSTANCES AFFECTING CHURCH ATTITUDES INCLUDING HOSTILITIES TOWARD MARXISM, EFFECTS OF VARIOUS GOVERNMENTS, AND SOCIALISM. SUMMARIZES FUNDAMENTAL SOCIAL IDEAS HELD BY MAJORITY CHURCH MEMBERSHIP.

0483 BURKE E.
THOUGHTS ON THE PROSPECT OF A REGICIDE PEACE (PAMPHLET)
ORIGINAL PUBLISHER NOT AVAILABLE, 1796, 131 PP.
CONSIDERS PROSPECT OF PEACEFUL COEXISTENCE WITH WHAT HE CALLS FRANCE'S "REPUBLIC OF REGICIDE," WARNING AGAINST IT. ALTHOUGH HE FAVORED AMERICAN INDEPENDENCE, BURKE CONSIDERS FRENCH REVOLUTION UNJUST AND ATROCIOUS. ATTACKS REGICIDE GOVERNMENT AS WILLFUL, AMBITIOUS, AND UNCONTROLLED; AND CRITICIZES REVOLUTION AS DESTRUCTIVE AND LEADING TO ANARCHY. LINKS JACOBINISM, REGICIDE, ATHEISM, AND WAR.

0484 BURKE E.
THOUGHTS ON THE CAUSE OF THE PRESENT DISCONTENTS (PAMPHLET)
ORIGINAL PUBLISHER NOT AVAILABLE, 1770, 79 PP.
CRITICIZES TREND IN LATE 1700'S TO CONSIDER RADICAL REFORMS OF GOVERNMENT AS SOLUTION TO PROBLEMS OF ALL SORTS, BOTH POLITICAL AND SOCIAL. CLAIMS RECENT UNREST AND REVOLUTION IS NOT RESULT OF POVERTY OR OPPRESSION BUT OF SPREAD OF RADICAL IDEAS. ARGUES FOR ENGLISHMEN TO KEEP COMMONS AS DEPENDENT UPON CITIZENRY AS POSSIBLE, IN THIS WAY INSURING INFLUENCE OF PEOPLE UPON GOVERNMENT.

0485 BURKE E.
LETTER TO SIR HERCULES LANGRISHE (PAMPHLET)
ORIGINAL PUBLISHER NOT AVAILABLE, 1792, 88 PP.
ARGUES FOR EQUAL RIGHTS OF IRISH CATHOLICS AND AGAINST THEN-CURRENT NOTION THAT THEY SHOULD BE SECOND-CLASS CITIZENS BECAUSE ENGLAND WAS A PROTESTANT STATE. QUESTIONS POLICY OF CONSIDERING FRENCH CANADIANS FULL CITIZENS WHILE DISCRIMINATING AGAINST IRISH. SUPPORTING HIS NOTION OF EQUALITY UNDER LEGAL PROCESS, WARNS AGAINST ANTAGONIZING LOYAL CITIZENS FOR NON-POLITICAL REASONS.

0486 BURKE E.
"ON THE REFORM OF THE REPRESENTATION IN THE HOUSE OF COMMONS" (1782) IN COLLECTED WORKS (VOL. 5)"
BOSTON: LITTLE BROWN, 1839.
DEFENDS ENGLISH CONSTITUTION AGAINST MAJOR REFORM, ATTACKING BOTH NATURAL LAW THEORIES WHICH DEMAND EQUAL REPRESENTATION FOR ALL IN ALL MATTERS, AND THOSE WHO SEEK CHANGE MERELY TO FAVOR THEIR INTERESTS. ALTHOUGH NOT SIDING WITH THOSE CLAIMING IT TO BE HIGHEST POSSIBLE FORM OF CONSTITUTION, HE STILL FEELS THAT INCREMENTAL CHANGE IS BEST IN BOTH POLICY- AND LAW-MAKING.

0487 BURKE E.
REFLECTIONS ON THE REVOLUTION IN FRANCE.
ORIGINAL PUBLISHER NOT AVAILABLE, 1790, 251 PP.
ATTACKS FRENCH REVOLUTION FOR ITS NEGATIVE EFFECTS ON CIVILIZATION AND FOR ITS IMPACT ON POLITICAL THEORY. BELIEVING EACH GENERATION TO BE INDEBTED TO PAST ACHIEVEMENTS FOR ITS LIBERTY AND LEARNING, ACCUSES REVOLUTIONARIES OF BEING PROUD AND IMPRACTICAL. CALLS REVOLUTION A MISGUIDED ATTACK ON "A MILD AND LAWFUL MONARCH" AND A REVOLT FROM PROTECTION AND GRACE.

0488 BURKE F.G.
AFRICA'S QUEST FOR ORDER.
ENGLEWOOD CLIFFS: PRENTICE HALL, 1964, 177 PP., LC#64-12854.
ANALYZES MAJOR POLITICAL AND ECONOMIC EVENTS IN AFRICA IN ORDER TO EMPHASIZE RECURRING FORCES AND THEMES IN THE AFRICAN REVOLUTION: TRIBALISM, URBANISM, YOUTH, LEADERSHIP, AND RACE. EXAMINES INTERRELATIONSHIP OF RESHAPING AND EXTENDING POLITICAL, CULTURAL, AND SOCIAL BOUNDARIES; ESTABLISHMENT OF NEW NATION STATES; AND CREATION OF NEW INTERNATIONAL RELATIONS.

0489 BURKS R.V.
THE DYNAMICS OF COMMUNISM IN EASTERN EUROPE.
PRINCETON: PRINCETON U PRESS, 1961, 244 PP., LC#61-.
STUDIES EXTENT TO WHICH COMMUNISM IS PROLETARIAN MOVEMENT AND ITS EFFECT ON EASTERN EUROPE FROM 1917-53. EXAMINES SOCIAL COMPOSITION OF PARTY, AND ANALYZES FACTORS CAUSING PEOPLE TO ACCEPT COMMUNISM. DISCUSSES COMMUNISM OF SLAVO-MACEDONIANS AND YUGOSLAVS AND PRINCIPLES OF ETHNIC PURITY. STATES THAT COMMUNISM IN EASTERN EUROPE DOES NOT REPRESENT PROLETARIAT.

0490 BURLAMAQUI J.J.
PRINCIPLES OF NATURAL AND POLITIC LAW (2 VOLS.) (1747-51)
ORIGINAL PUBLISHER NOT AVAILABLE, 1830, 466 PP.
AUTHOR DOES NOT BELIEVE MEN ARE BORN KNOWING NATURAL LAW BUT RATHER THAT THEY SO INTUITIVELY GRASP THE RIGHTNESS OR WRONGNESS OF AN OBJECT THAT THIS KNOWLEDGE SEEMS TO BE INNATE. AUTHOR SAYS THIS SHOULD BE THE BASIS OF ALL GOVERNMENT. THE CHIEF IDEA BINDING STATES TOGETHER, AND BY WHICH THEIR LAWS ARE MADE, IS THE CONTRACT BETWEEN THE STATE AND THE CITIZEN, WHICH IS BASED ON NATURAL LAW.

0491 BURLING R.
HILL FARMS AND PADI FIELDS.
ENGLEWOOD CLIFFS: PRENTICE HALL, 1965, 180 PP., LC#65-13575.
DISCUSSES LIFE AND TRADITION OF PEOPLES OF SOUTHEAST ASIA. EXAMINES AGRICULTURE, TRIBAL CUSTOMS, BUDDHISM AND HINDU INFLUENCE, INFLUENCE OF EUROPE AND MIDDLE EAST, CHINESE AND INDIAN IMMIGRATION, AND PROBLEMS OF INDEPENDENCE

SINCE WWII. CENTERS ON VIETNAM, THAILAND, AND BURMA.

0492 BURNHAM J.
THE WAR WE ARE IN, THE LAST DECADE AND THE NEXT.
NEW ROCHELLE: ARLINGTON HOUSE, 1967, 351 PP., LC#67-22705.
ANALYZES US FOREIGN POLICY IN COLD WAR CONTENDING THAT IT IS A "BEWILDERING JUMBLE" STEMMING FROM CONFLICT BETWEEN US POWER AND PREVAILING LIBERAL IDEOLOGY. DISCUSSES OBJECTIVES OF WORLD COMMUNISM WITH SPECIAL ATTENTION TO USSR'S VIEW OF US. NOTES SIGNIFICANT JUNCTURES IN EAST-WEST CONFRONTATIONS INCLUDING NATO, THE VIETNAM WAR, UN AFFAIRS, COMPETITION IN NONALIGNED NATIONS, AND CUBAN MISSILE CRISIS.

0493 BURR R.N.
OUR TROUBLED HEMISPHERE: PERSPECTIVES ON UNITED STATES-LATIN AMERICAN RELATIONS.
WASHINGTON: BROOKINGS INST, 1967, 256 PP., LC#67-25562.
TRACES HISTORY OF US RELATIONS WITH LATIN AMERICA. EVALUATES US OBJECTIVES AND INSTRUMENTS FOR ACHIEVING THEM, AND COMPARES WITH OBJECTIVES AND DEVELOPMENTAL NEEDS OF LATIN AMERICAN NATIONS. DISCUSSES EFFECT OF ALLIANCE FOR PROGRESS AND POWER OF ORGANIZATION OF AMERICAN STATES.

0494 BURRIDGE K.
MAMBU: A MELANESIAN MILLENNIUM.
LONDON: METHUEN, 1960, 296 PP.
ANTHROPOLOGICAL-SOCIOLOGICAL STUDY OF NEW GUINEAN "CARGO CULT," ONE OF A NUMBER OF NATIVE CULTS IN WHICH PARTICIPANTS ENGAGE IN STRANGE AND EXOTIC RITES AND CEREMONIES, PURPOSE OF WHICH IS TO GAIN POSSESSION OF EUROPEAN MANUFACTURED GOODS. DISCUSSES BACKGROUND AND CUSTOMS OF THESE PEOPLE AND ORIGIN AND NATURE OF THEIR "MYTH-DREAM."

0495 BURY J.B., COOK S.A. ET AL.
THE CAMBRIDGE ANCIENT HISTORY (12 VOLS.)
NEW YORK: MACMILLAN.
SERIES OF TWELVE VOLUMES ON ANCIENT HISTORY PUBLISHED FROM 1923-39, EACH WITH ANNOTATED BIBLIOGRAPHY AT END. SPAN OF WORK IS FROM "EGYPT AND BABYLONIA" IN VOLUME ONE TO THE ROMAN STATE IN 324 IN VOLUME TWELVE. MANY OF THE GENERAL HISTORIES, REFERENCE WORKS, ANCIENT SOURCES IN ALL FORMS, AND MONOGRAPHS ARE IN FOREIGN LANGUAGES, ESPECIALLY MANY ANCIENT LANGUAGES. ITEMS FROM 2,000 B.C. TO 1939.

0496 BUSIA K.A.
THE CHALLENGE OF AFRICA.
NEW YORK: PRAEGER, 1962, 150 PP., $4.00.
WRITTEN BY FORMER LEADER OF THE OPPOSITION IN GHANA, NOW IN EXILE, SEES FOUR BASIC CHALLENGES TO AFRICAN DEVELOPMENT-CULTURE, COLONIAL EXPERIENCE, COMMON HUMANITY AND MORALITY, AND RESPONSIBLE EMANCIPATION. EXPLORES IN DETAIL THE TRADITIONAL PAST AND PRESENT SOCIAL AND POLITICAL SITUATION IN AFRICA.

0497 BUSINESS ECONOMISTS' GROUP
INCOME POLICIES (PAMPHLET)
OXFORD: BUSINESS ECONOMISTS GP, 1963, 49 PP.
ANALYZES BRITISH INCOME POLICIES AND COMPARES THEM TO OTHER NATIONS. GIVES VIEWPOINTS OF INDUSTRIALIST, TRADE UNIONIST, AND GOVERNMENT REPRESENTATIVE OF FAIR WAGE AND INCOME DISTRIBUTION. ECONOMETRICIAN PROPOSES MODEL FOR DISTRIBUTION ANALYSIS.

0498 BUTLER D.E., KING A.
THE BRITISH GENERAL ELECTION OF 1966.
NEW YORK: ST MARTIN'S PRESS, 1966, 338 PP., LC#66-28082.
COMPREHENSIVE EXPLANATION OF MOST ASPECTS OF ELECTION, INCLUDING CAMPAIGNING, STRATEGY, PARTY ADMINISTRATION, TIMING, PRESS, TELEVISION, OPINION POLLS. A THOROUGH ANALYSIS OF THE RESULTS IS GIVEN. TEN CONSTITUENCIES CLOSELY EXAMINED IN TERMS OF ABOVE FACTORS.

0499 BUTTINGER J.
"VIETNAM* FRAUD OF THE 'OTHER WAR'."
DISSENT, 14 (MAY-JUNE 67), 376-384.
THE "SOCIAL REVOLUTION" IN VIETNAM, PROMISED BY THE HAWAII AND GUAM CONFERENCES, IS A TOTAL FAILURE. IT HAS NOT BEEN GIVEN SERIOUS ATTENTION, AND NO STEPS AT ALL HAVE BEEN AT LAND REFORM, THE REAL KEY TO AN IMPROVEMENT FOR THE SOUTH VIETNAMESE PEOPLE. BOTH US OFFICIALS AND CITIZENS HAVE BEEN DELUDED OR ARE DELUDING THEMSELVES ABOUT THE REAL LACK OF ANY SIGNIFICANT PROGRESS. CITES DOCUMENTS.

0500 BUTWELL R.
SOUTHEAST ASIA TODAY - AND TOMORROW.
NEW YORK: FREDERICK PRAEGER, 1964, 182 PP., LC#64-22490.
ANALYZES SOUTHEAST ASIA FROM PRE-EUROPEAN PERIOD TO ATTAINMENT OF INDEPENDENCE AND STUDIES WESTERN INFLUENCE IN PRESENT SITUATION. EXAMINES NATIONS THAT WERE ABLE TO CHOOSE FUNCTIONAL FORM OF GOVERNMENT AND THOSE STILL SEEKING WORKING SYSTEM. ORGANIZATION AND OPERATION OF THESE GOVERNMENTS, THEIR PROBLEMS AND POLICIES IN RELATION TO OTHER NATIONS, AND COMMUNISM ARE COVERED.

0501 BUTZ O.
GERMANY: DILEMMA FOR AMERICAN POLICY.
GARDEN CITY: DOUBLEDAY, 1954, 69 PP., LC#54-8072.
ANALYSIS OF DEVELOPMENT OF AMERICAN FOREIGN POLICY IN GERMANY FROM 1941-54. STRESSES STRATEGIC IMPORTANCE OF GERMANY IN COLD WAR POLITICAL RELATIONS AND SPECIFICALLY IN POSTWAR AMERICAN-SOVIET RELATIONS. FOCUSES ON BASIC AIMS NAD MOTIVES BEHIND AMERICAN POLICY DECISIONS IN REGARD TO GERMANY AND ASSESSES EFFECTIVENESS OF THESE DECISIONS.

0502 BYNKERSHOEK C., TENNEY F. ED.
QUAESTIONUM JURIS PUBLICI LIBRI DUO.
OXFORD: CLARENDON PR., 1930, 284 PP.
A CARNEGIE ENDOWMENT TRANSLATION OF THIS GREAT EIGHTEENTH CENTURY CLASSIC ON THE NATURE, RULES, AND EFFECTS OF WAR AND ON VARIOUS RIGHTS OF SOVEREIGN STATES.

0503 BYRNES R.F.
BIBLIOGRAPHY OF AMERICAN PUBLICATIONS ON EAST CENTRAL EUROPE, 1945-1957 (VOL. XXII)
BLOOMINGTON: INDIANA U PR, 1957, 213 PP.
COMPILES, ANNOTATES, AND INDEXES 2,810 ITEMS PUBLISHED IN US CONCERNING EAST CENTRAL EUROPE. ARRANGED BY COUNTRY AND SUBDIVIDED TOPICALLY. DEALS WITH AREA STUDIES, HISTORY, POLITICS, LAW, AND OTHER GENERAL SUBJECTS. INCLUDES A LONG LIST OF JOURNALS SEARCHED FOR COMPILATION.

0504 CADY J.F.
THAILAND, BURMA, LAOS AND CAMBODIA.
ENGLEWOOD CLIFFS: PRENTICE HALL, 1966, 152 PP., LC#66-28105.
STUDY OF EACH COUNTRY AND ITS INTERRELATIONSHIP WITH OTHERS. DEALS WITH EARLY CIVILIZATIONS AND BOND OF BUDDHISM AS IT AFFECTED THE DEVELOPMENT OF EACH GROUP. EXAMINES RACE AND MIGRATION OF VARIOUS GROUPS. INFLUENCE OF FRENCH AND BRITISH COLONIAL RULE AND JAPANESE OCCUPATION ARE VIEWED IN RELATION TO FORMATION OF THESE AS MODERN STATES.

0505 CAIRNS J.C.
"FRANCE, DECEMBER 1965: END OF THE ELECTIVE MONARACHY"
INT. J., 21 (WINTER 65), 93-100.
ANALYZES FRENCH PRESIDENTIAL ELECTION OF 1965, DISCUSSING DOMESTIC POLITICAL FACTORS THAT LED TO DE GAULLE'S SURPRISINGLY BAD SHOWING, RETURN TO TRADITIONAL POLITICAL PATTERNS, AND PROSPECTS FOR FUTURE.

0506 CALLEO D.P.
EUROPE'S FUTURE: THE GRAND ALTERNATIVES.
NEW YORK: HORIZON PRESS, 1965, 185 PP., LC#65-26723.
EXPLAINS MAJOR WAYS OF LOOKING AT EUROPE'S FUTURE. DISCUSSES CONFLICTING CONCEPTS OF POSTWAR NATIONALISM AND FEDERALISM. DESCRIBES COMMON MARKET IDEA OF FEDERALIST EUROPE, DE GAULLE'S CONCEPT OF A NATIONALIST EUROPE, AND US IDEA OF AN ATLANTIC EUROPE. SUGGESTS THAT A STRONG UNION OF STATES, INCLUDING BRITAIN, WOULD RESULT FROM SYNTHESIS OF BEST IN EACH CONCEPT.

0507 CALLOT E.
LA SOCIETE ET SON ENVIRONNEMENT: ESSAI SUR LES PRINCIPES DES SCIENCES SOCIALES.
PARIS: LIBRAIRIE MARCEL RIVIERE, 1952, 580 PP.
THEORETICAL AND GENERAL WORK ON PRINCIPLES OF SOCIOLOGY. AUTHOR BELIEVES SCIENTIFIC AND PHILOSOPHIC METHODS SHOULD BE INCORPORATED IN SOCIOLOGICAL STUDIES. DESCRIBES SOCIAL REALITY AS A PARTICULAR AREA AND OBJECT OF SCIENCE. DISCUSSES PHILOSOPHY OF AREA. DELINEATES LIMITS OF SOCIOLOGY AND DISTINGUISHES IT FROM OTHER SCIENCES.

0508 CALVERT A.F.
SOUTHWEST AFRICA 1884-1914 (2ND ED.)
LONDON: T WERNER LAURIE LTD, 1916, 105 PP.
HISTORY OF GERMAN OCCUPATION OF SOUTHWEST AFRICA, EMPHASIZING NATURE OF LAND, INCLUDING POPULATION, NATURAL RESOURCES, GEOLOGY AND MINERALS, AND DIAMOND INDUSTRY.

0509 CALVOCORESSI P.
WORLD ORDER AND NEW STATES: PROBLEMS OF KEEPING THE PEACE.
NEW YORK: PRAEGER, 1962, 113 PP., $4.25.
DISCUSSES ROLE OF THE GREAT POWERS AS GUARDIANS OF PEACE, AND COLD WAR INTERFERENCE WITH THIS ROLE. CONSIDERS INTERNAL INSTABILITY OF NEW AFRO-ASIAN COUNTRIES. VIEWS ASSISTANCE POSSIBLE FROM DEMOCRATIC COUNTRIES. EXAMINES UN ACTION FOR PEACE AND SUGGESTS STEPS FOR INCREASED EFFECTIVENESS.

0510 CAM H.M., TURBERVILLE A.S.
BIBLIOGRAPHY OF ENGLISH CONSTITUTIONAL HISTORY (PAMPHLET)
LONDON: G BELL & SONS, 1929, 32 PP.
AN ANNOTATED BIBLIOGRAPHY OF BOOKS AND ARTICLES DEALING WITH ENGLISH CONSTITUTIONAL HISTORY. CONTENTS ORGANIZED TOPICALLY INTO 17 CATEGORIES COVERING GENERAL WORKS, CHRONOLOGICAL PERIODS, STRUCTURE OF GOVERNMENT, CONSTITUTIONAL THEORY AND LAW, AND POLITICAL PARTIES. SOURCES COVER PERIOD THROUGH 1928. ANNOTATIONS ARE CRITICAL AS WELL AS DESCRIPTIVE AND LIST CROSS REFERENCES.

0511 CAMERON R.
"SOME LESSONS OF HISTORY FOR DEVELOPING NATIONS."
AMER. ECO. REVIEW, 57 (MAY 67).
AUTHOR FEELS THAT DEVELOPING NATIONS CAN PROFIT FROM

THE HISTORICAL EXPERIENCE OF MODERN INDUSTRIAL NATIONS AND TRACES FOUR AREAS HE FEELS ARE IMPORTANT FOR CONTEMPORARY POLICY-MAKERS. THESE AREAS INCLUDE ROLES OF CAPITAL, LABOR, EDUCATION, AND THE STATE. GOVERNMENT PARTICIPATION TENDS EITHER TO BE ONE ENCOURAGING PRIVATE ENTERPRISE OR ONE CONTROLLING PRIVATE ENTERPRISE BY EDICT AND DOMINATION.

0512 CAMERON R.
BANKING IN THE EARLY STAGES OF INDUSTRIALIZATION: A STUDY IN ECONOMIC COMPARATIVE HISTORY.
NEW YORK: OXFORD U PR, 1967, 349 PP., LC#67-10342.
ILLUMINATES RELATIONSHIP BETWEEN BANKS AND INDUSTRY IN THE INITIAL INDUSTRIAL SPURTS IN WESTERN EUROPE, RUSSIA, AND ASIA. GIVES COMPARATIVE ECONOMIC DATA ON SEVERAL COUNTRIES. NEW DATA ON JAPAN OF PARTICULAR INTEREST TO WESTERN SCHOLAR.

0513 CAMERON W.J.
NEW ZEALAND.
ENGLEWOOD CLIFFS: PRENTICE HALL, 1965, 180 PP.
STUDIES CHARACTER OF NEW ZEALAND'S POPULATION. DISCUSSES NATIVE GROUPS AND EUROPEAN COLONIZATION IN REGARD TO FORMATION OF PRESENT SOCIETY. EXPLAINS POLITICAL AND ECONOMIC STRUCTURE AND RELATION OF NEW ZEALAND TO OTHER COUNTRIES.

0514 CAMPANELLA T.
A DISCOURSE TOUCHING THE SPANISH MONARCHY... (1640)
ORIGINAL PUBLISHER NOT AVAILABLE, 1640, 232 PP.
WRITTEN TO PHILLIP IV, WHILE AUTHOR WAS IN PRISON, ADVISING KING HOW TO ATTAIN UNIVERSAL MONARCHY. ATTEMPTS TO ESTABLISH PERFECT MODEL OF GOVERNMENT. DISCUSSES PRINCE'S TREATMENT OF SUBJECTS AND MANAGEMENT OF FOREIGN AFFAIRS. NOTES PARTICULAR COUNTRIES AND APPROPRIATE GOVERNMENT FOR EACH. DISCUSSES RISE AND FALL OF GOVERNMENTS, ILLUSTRATED AND DOCUMENTED FROM PROFANE AND SACRED WRITERS.

0515 CAMPBELL G.A.
THE CIVIL SERVICE IN BRITAIN (2ND ED.)
LONDON: DUCKWORTH, 1965, 255 PP.
ANALYZES GREAT BRITAIN'S CIVIL SERVICE ADMINISTRATION DURING 19TH AND 20TH CENTURIES, INCLUDING REFORM, ORGANIZATION, RECRUITMENT, AND OVERSEAS DEPARTMENTS. DISCUSSES MINISTERIAL RESPONSIBILITY, STANDARDS, AND COMMON SERVICES.

0516 CAMPBELL P.
FRENCH ELECTORAL SYSTEMS AND ELECTIONS SINCE 1789 (2ND ED.)
NEW YORK: FREDERICK PRAEGER, 1958, 155 PP.
STUDY OF FRENCH ELECTORAL SYSTEM INCLUDES ITS PLACE IN FRENCH POLITICS, PROGRESS OF SUFFRAGE, THE SECOND BALLOT, AND PROPORTIONAL REPRESENTATION. SUMMARY OF ALL ELECTIONS AND ELECTORAL REFORMS.

0517 CANADA CIVIL SERV COMM
THE ANALYSIS OF ORGANIZATION IN THE GOVERNMENT OF CANADA (PAMPHLET)
OTTAWA: ORG DIV CAN CIV SERV COM, 1964, 79 PP.
DISCUSSES ADMINISTRATIVE FUNCTIONS AND DIVISIONS OF AUTHORITY WITHIN DEPARTMENTS OF CANADIAN GOVERNMENT. EXAMINES IN DETAIL ROLE OF DEPUTY HEAD, AND ORGANIZATION OF SUPPORT SERVICES.

0518 CANAWAY A.P.
THE FAILURE OF FEDERALISM IN AUSTRALIA.
LONDON: OXFORD U PR, 1930, 201 PP.
DISCUSSES BROAD EFFECTS OF FEDERALISM IN AUSTRALIA, AND MORE IMMEDIATE EFFECTS UPON MECHANICAL EFFICIENCY OF GOVERNMENT OPERATIONS AND UPON MENTAL PROCESSES OF INDIVIDUALS. SHOWS BEARINGS OF FEDERALISM UPON SYSTEM OF RESPONSIBLE GOVERNMENT IN AUSTRALIA, AND ANALYZES FEDERALISM IN LIGHT OF ENGLISH CONSTITUTIONAL HISTORY. POINTS UP "FLIMSINESS" OF USUAL PLEAS IN DEFENCE OF FEDERALISM.

0519 CANELAS O.A.
RADIOGRAFIA DE LA ALIANZA PARA EL ATRASO.
LA PAZ: LIBRERIA ALTIPLANO, 1963, 311 PP.
DISCUSSES PRESENT LATIN AMERICA SITUATION REGARDING US POLICIES SUCH AS ALLIANCE FOR PROGRESS. EXPLAINS REASON FOR LATIN AMERICAN REVOLUTIONS TO REMOVE US POWER. COMPARES LATIN AMERICA TO AFRO-ASIAN COUNTRIES THAT BECAME INDEPENDENT FROM COLONIAL POWERS.

0520 CANNING HOUSE LIBRARY
AUTHOR AND SUBJECT CATALOGUES OF THE CANNING HOUSE LIBRARY (5 VOLS.)
BOSTON: HALL, 1966.
BIBLIOGRAPHICAL LISTING OF BOOKS IN CANNING HOUSE LIBRARY IN LONDON PERTAINING TO LATIN AMERICA. OVER 30,000 ENTRIES OF 19TH- AND 20TH-CENTURY PUBLICATIONS. FOUR VOLUMES ON SPANISH-SPEAKING LATIN AMERICAN COUNTRIES AND ONE ON BRAZIL.

0521 CANNON J.P.
AMERICAN STALINISM AND ANTI-STALINISM (PAMPHLET)
NEW YORK: PIONEER PUBL, 1947, 48 PP.
TROTSKYITE PAMPHLET ON FUTURE OF COMMUNISM IN THE US, COMING FALL OF STALINISTS, AND TAKEOVER OF TRUE SOCIALISM.

0522 CANTOR N.F., WERTHMAN M.
THE ENGLISH TRADITION* TWENTIETH-CENTURY VIEWS OF ENGLISH HISTORY (2VOLS.)
NEW YORK: MACMILLAN, 1967, 832 PP.
BOOK OF READINGS DESIGNED FOR SURVEY COURSE IN ENGLISH HISTORY. FIRST VOLUME COVERS PERIOD 1450-1714 AND INCLUDES TOPICS SUCH AS FEUDAL HERITAGE, ORIGINS OF PARLIAMENT AND COURTS, LAW, SOCIAL ORDER, AND ECONOMY.VOLUME II BEGINS WITH THE HANOVERIAN SETTLEMENT AND TRACES POLITICAL, ECONOMIC, AND SOCIAL DEVELOPMENT TO THE PRESENT.

0523 CANTRIL H. ED.
TENSIONS THAT CAUSE WAR.
URBANA: U. ILLINOIS PR., 1950, 303 PP.
COLLECTION OF ESSAYS, BY LEADING SOCIAL SCIENTISTS, HOLDING THAT THE STUDY OF THE SCIENCES OF MAN 'TASK OF ACQUIRING SELF-KNOWLEDGE AND SOCIAL INSIGHT) IS AS VITAL AS STUDY OF PHYSICAL AND BIOLOGICAL SCIENCES. ATTEMPTS TO STUDY SCIENTIFICALLY THE CAUSES OF MAN'S TENSIONS WHICH LEAD TO WAR.

0524 CANTRIL H.
THE PATTERN OF HUMAN CONCERNS.
NEW BRUNSWICK: RUTGERS U PR, 1965, 427 PP., LC#65-23234.
SYSTEMATIC PSYCHOLOGICAL STUDY BASED ON 20,000 INTERVIEWS AND SIX YEARS OF DATA ACCUMULATION OF "REVOLUTION OF EXPECTATIONS." GOAL WAS TO UNDERSTAND EFFECTS OF CIRCUMSTANCES ON OUTLOOKS WHICH PEOPLE HOLD FOR THEMSELVES AND THEIR COUNTRIES. STUDY IS INTERNATIONAL IN SCOPE.

0525 CAPELL A.
STUDIES IN SOCIO-LINGUISTICS.
HAGUE: MOUTON & CO, 1966, 167 PP.
DISCUSSES INTERRELATIONSHIP OF FACTS IN LINGUISTICS WITH FACTS IN ANTHROPOLOGY. DIVIDED INTO THREE PARTS: SOCIO-LINGUISTIC PARALLELS; LANGUAGE AND SOCIAL CHANGE; LANGUAGE WITHIN SOCIETIES.

0526 CAPLOW T.
PRINCIPLES OF ORGANIZATION.
NEW YORK: HARCOURT BRACE, 1964, 383 PP., LC#64-25626.
ARGUES THAT HUMAN ORGANIZATIONS ARE A CLASS OF NATURAL PHENOMENA, THE ATTRIBUTES OF WHICH ARE NOT TIME OR CULTURE BOUND, AND WHOSE WORKINGS ARE ORDERLY. DEMONSTRATES THAT SINGLE THEORETICAL MODEL CAN BE USED TO ANALYZE ORGANIZATIONS OF ANY TYPE OR STRUCTURE, REGARDLESS OF CULTURAL OR HISTORICAL LOCATION.

0527 CARDINALL AW
A BIBLIOGRAPHY OF THE GOLD COAST.
ACCRA: GOVT PRINTER, 1932, 384 PP., LC#32-24984.
BIBLIOGRAPHY OF EARLY PERIOD OF BRITISH ADMINISTRATION.

0528 CAREW-HUNT R.C.
BOOKS ON COMMUNISM.
NY, LONDON: AMPERSAND PR INC, 1959, 333 PP.
BRIEF AND SELECTIVE CRITICAL ANNOTATIONS ON WORLDWIDE COMMUNISM IN NUMEROUS TOPICS INCLUDING THEORY AND BACKGROUND OF RUSSIAN REVOLUTION. LAST SECTION LISTS UK, COMMONWEALTH, AND US OFFICIAL DOCUMENTS AND PUBLICATIONS.

0529 CARIAS B.
"EL CONTROL DE LAS EMPRESAS PUBLICAS POR GRUPOS DE INTERESES DE LA COMUNIDAD."
INT. REV. OF ADMIN. SCI., 33 (1967), 47-57.
DESCRIBES SYSTEM OF CONTROL OF PUBLIC ENTERPRISE IN VENEZUELA. STATES THAT RECENT LAW GIVES WORKERS REPRESENTATION IN PUBLIC ENTERPRISE, ALTHOUGH THIS HAPPENS INFREQUENTLY. COMPARES VENEZUELAN SITUATION TO FRENCH AND BRITISH. CLAIMS THAT WORKER REPRESENTATION IS NECESSARY IN SOCIALIST STATE AND CAN BE FUNCTIONAL.

0530 CARIBBEAN COMMISSION
CURRENT CARIBBEAN BIBLIOGRAPHY.
PORT OF SPAIN, TRINDAD: KENT HSE, 1951.
VOLUME I OF THIS SERIES WAS PUBLISHED IN JUNE 1951. THE BIBLIOGRAPHY IS A CUMULATIVE WORK NOW PUBLISHED ANNUALLY. DIVIDED INTO THREE SECTIONS: (1) PERIODICALS AND NEWSPAPERS, (2) GOVERNMENT SERIALS, (3) MONOGRAPHS. A GEOGRAPHICAL INDEX AND DIRECTORY OF PUBLISHERS WITH ADDRESSES ARE APPENDED TO THE BIBLIOGRAPHY.

0531 CARIBBEAN COMMISSION
A CATALOGUE OF CARIBBEAN COMMISSION PUBLICATIONS (PAMPHLET)
PORT OF SPAIN: CARIBBEAN COMN, 1957, 25 PP.
LISTS PUBLICATIONS OF CARIBBEAN COMMISSION TO 1957. ITEMS ARRANGED BY SUBJECT.

0532 CARLYLE T.
THE FRENCH REVOLUTION (2 VOLS.)
NEW YORK: EP DUTTON, 1837, 980 PP.
EXAMINES REVOLUTION FROM TRADITIONALIST'S VIEWPOINT, INTERMIXING HISTORY WITH HIS OWN EVALUATIONS. ATTACKS BOTH INTELLECTUAL FOUNDATIONS AND PRACTICAL RESULTS OF REVOLUTION. FOLLOWS EVENTS OF 1786-1795. POINTING OUT THAT SOCIAL CONTRACT THEORISTS HAD BEEN PARTIALLY RESPONSIBLE FOR REGICIDE AND REIGN OF TERROR, ASKS IF THIS IS WHAT WAS

MEANT BY "LIBERTY, FRATERNITY, AND EQUALITY."

0533 CARNEGIE ENDOWMENT
CURRENT RESEARCH IN INTERNATIONAL AFFAIRS: SELECTED BIBLIOGRAPHY OF WORK IN PROGRESS BY PRIVATE RESEARCH AGENCIES.
NEW YORK: CARNEGIE ENDOWMENT.
ANNUAL PUBLICATION FROM 1948-1952 OF CURRENT RESEARCH BY PRIVATE RESEARCH AGENCIES, AND DEPARTMENTS AND SPECIAL RESEARCH INSTITUTES OF UNIVERSITIES IN THE US, AND, TO A LIMITED EXTENT, IN UK. RESEARCH COVERS RELATIONS BETWEEN TWO OR MORE COUNTRIES; PARTICULAR PROBLEMS WITH INTERNATIONAL SIGNIFICANCE; PROBLEMS OF PARTICULARLY CRUCIAL GEOGRAPHIC AREAS. ARRANGED ALPHABETICALLY BY INSTITUTION. INDEXES.

0534 CARNELL F. ED.
THE POLITICS OF THE NEW STATES: A SELECT ANNOTATED BIBLIOGRAPHY WITH SPECIAL REFERENCE TO THE COMMONWEALTH.
LONDON: OXFORD U PR, 1961, 171 PP.
PARTIALLY ANNOTATED BIBLIOGRAPHY OF 1599 TITLES ON THE NEW STATES OF AFRICA AND ASIA IN FRENCH AND ENGLISH. ITEMS ARE ARRANGED BY TOPIC, CROSS-REFERENCED AND INDEXED BY AUTHOR AND GEOGRAPHICAL LOCATION. SECTION ON APPROACHES TO THE STUDY OF POLITICS INCLUDES WORKS ON WESTERN STATES. COVERS GENERAL HISTORICAL BACKGROUND ON COLONIALISM AND STUDIES OF PROBLEMS IN COLONIALISM.

0535 CARPENTER G.W.
THE WAY IN AFRICA.
NEW YORK: FRIENDSHIP PRESS, 1959, 165 PP., LC#59-6037.
PRIMARILY A HISTORICAL DESCRIPTION OF MAJOR FORCES THAT HAVE INFLUENCED COURSE OF AFRICAN DEVELOPMENT DURING COLONIZATION AND POST-COLONIZATION PERIODS. DEALS WITH ROLE OF CHRISTIAN CHURCHES DURING PERIODS, AND DISCUSSES IMPACT OF INDUSTRY AND URBANIZATION AND GROWTH OF NATIONALISM.

0536 CARR E.H.
PROPAGANDA IN INTERNATIONAL POLITICS (PAMPHLET)
LONDON: OXFORD U PR, 1939, 32 PP.
TREATS PROPAGANDA IN MODERN POLITICS. DISCUSSES NATURE OF PROPAGANDA, ITS USE IN WAR, INTERNATIONAL AGREEMENTS TO RESTRAIN PROPAGANDA, ITS ORGANIZATION, AND TRUTH AND MORALITY IN INTERNATIONAL PROPAGANDA.

0537 CARR E.H.
STUDIES IN REVOLUTION.
LONDON: MACMILLAN, 1950, 227 PP.
COLLECTION OF AUTHOR'S ESSAYS ON MANY HISTORICAL REVOLUTIONS AND REVOLUTIONISTS. DISCUSSES SAINT-SIMON, COMMUNIST MANIFESTO, PROUDHON, HERZEN, LASALLE, PLEKHANOV, BOLSHEVISM, LENIN, SOREL, AND STALIN; ALSO SOME 19TH-CENTURY RUSSIAN THINKERS AND GERMAN COMMUNIST "REVOLUTION THAT FAILED."

0538 CARR E.H.
"REVOLUTION FROM ABOVE."
NEW LEFT REV., 46 (NOV. 67), 17-29.
DISCUSSES WHAT AUTHOR CONSIDERS TRAGEDY OF SOVIET COLLECTIVIZATION. BELIEVES THAT STALIN'S DECISION (IN 1929) TO COLLECTIVIZE WAS HAPHAZARD AND IMPULSIVE. LENIN HAD PROPOSED GRADUAL COLLECTIVIZATION; BUT AS A RESULT OF LOW AGRICULTURAL PRODUCTION, ESPECIALLY IN GRAIN, STALIN DECIDED TO PROCEED IMMEDIATELY. MECHANIZATION HAD NOT PROGRESSED FAR ENOUGH, AND PEASANTS OFFERED MINIMAL ASSISTANCE.

0539 CARRIL B.
PROBLEMAS DE LA REVOLUCION Y LA DEMOCRACIA.
BUENOS AIRES: EMECE EDITORES, 1956, 77 PP.
ESSAYS DISCUSSING PROBLEMS OF CONTEMPORARY GOVERNMENT, INCLUDING LIMITS ON LIBERTY IN ORGANIZED SOCIETY, REVOLUTIONARY REGIMES AND LEGITIMACY, DE FACTO REGIMES AND RELIANCE ON FORCE, AND REQUIREMENTS OF DEMOCRATIC AUTHENTICITY.

0540 CARRINGTON C.E.
THE COMMONWEALTH IN AFRICA (PAMPHLET)
P1962 284 57 02840
REPORTS ON CONFERENCE HELD BY AFRICAN COMMONWEALTH NATIONS IN 1962. DEALS WITH COLD WAR AND AFRICA, PAN-AFRICANISM, COMMON MARKET AND BRITAIN'S DESIRE TO JOIN, ECONOMIC INDEPENDENCE, DEMOCRATIC INSTITUTIONS BEST SUITED FOR PLANNING AND DEVELOPMENT IN AFRICA, AND FUTURE OF COMMONWEALTH COOPERATION IN AFRICA.

0541 CARRINGTON C.E.
THE LIQUIDATION OF THE BRITISH EMPIRE.
LONDON: GEORGE HARRAP & CO, 1951, 96 PP.
TRACES DISINTEGRATION OF BRITISH EMPIRE SINCE WWII. DISCUSSES INDEPENDENCE MOVEMENTS IN INDIA, RHODESIA, KENYA, GHANA, AND NIGERIA. EXAMINES PROBLEM OF RACE RELATIONS, FRENCH COLONIAL SYSTEM, COMMONWEALTH TRADE, AND PRINCIPLES OF COOPERATION AMONG COMMONWEALTH COUNTRIES.

0542 CARROTHERS A.W.R.
LABOR ARBITRATION IN CANADA.
TORONTO: BUTTERWORTHS, 1961, 190 PP.
EVALUATES ARBITRATION AS METHOD OF SETTLING GRIEVANCES IN LABOR DISPUTES. CONSIDERS RELEVANT SECTIONS OF ALL COLLECTIVE BARGAINING STATUTES IN CANADA AND ARBITRATION STATUTES OF COMMON LAW PROVINCES, WITH ILLUSTRATIVE CASE STUDIES IN BASIC AREAS.

0543 CARTER G.M., BROWN W.O.
TRANSITION IN AFRICA; STUDIES IN POLITICAL ADAPTATION.
BOSTON: BOSTON U AFR RES PROG, 1958, 158 PP., LC#58-12220.
FOUR PAPERS PRESENTED AT AMERICAN POLITICAL SCIENCE ASSOCIATION MEETINGS UNDER HEADING OF "PROBLEMS OF POLITICAL INTEGRATION IN AFRICA." ANALYZES PROBLEMS OF POLITICAL ADAPTATION WHICH ARISE DURING AND AFTER THE TRANSFER OF POLITICAL POWER. AREA STUDIES COVER GHANA, KENYA, NIGERIA, AND CENTRAL AFRICA.

0544 CARTER G.M.
INDEPENDENCE FOR AFRICA.
NEW YORK: PRAEGER, 1960, 172 PP., $4.50.
REVIEWS INDEPENDENCE STRUGGLES: LEADERS, RIVALRIES, FRUSTRATIONS, ACHIEVEMENTS IN KENYA, TANGANYIKA, ZANZIBAR, RHODESIAS, SOUTH AFRICA, BELGIAN CONGO, FRENCH CONGO, ANGOLA, IVORY COAST, NIGERIA. DISCUSSES POST-INDEPENDENCE PROBLEMS IN GHANA AND GUINEA. ANALYSIS BASED ON FIRST HAND EXPERIENCES WITH PROMINENT AFRICANS. EMPHASIZES TRENDS.

0545 CARTER G.M. ED.
AFRICAN ONE-PARTY STATES.
ITHACA: CORNELL U. PR., 1962, 501 PP. $7.25.
SIX MONOGRAPHS ON CONTEMPORARY HISTORY OF THE ONE PARTY STATES OF TUNISIA, SENEGAL, GUINEA, IVORY COAST, LIBERIA, AND TANGANYIKA. INCLUDES INTRODUCTORY ESSAY ON POLITICAL AND HISTORICAL TENSIONS LEADING TO ONE-PARTY STATES.

0546 CARTER G.M.
THE GOVERNMENT OF THE SOVIET UNION.
NEW YORK: HARCOURT BRACE, 1962, 181 PP., LC#63-20430.
HISTORICAL ANALYSIS OF SOVIET UNION'S PEOPLE AND POLITICAL STRUCTURE SINCE 1917. COVERS GOVERNMENT STRUCTURE AND ADMINISTRATION IN DETAIL. INCLUDES PEOPLE'S RELATIONSHIP TO GOVERNMENT, PARTY, AND METHODS FOR IMPLEMENTING PARTY POLICY.

0547 CARTER G.M. ED.
FIVE AFRICAN STATES: RESPONSES TO DIVERSITY.
ITHACA: CORNELL U. PR., 1963, 643 PP., $10.00.
FIVE POLITICAL SCIENTISTS DESCRIBE THE CONGO, DAHOMEY, CAMEROUN, RHODESIA AND NYASALAND, AND SOUTH AFRICA, RESPECTIVELY, USING A COMMON OUTLINE WHOSE MAJOR HEADINGS ARE HISTORICAL BACKGROUND, CONTEMPORARY SETTING, POLITICAL PROCESS, CONTEMPORARY ISSUES, EXTERNAL RELATIONS.

0548 CARTER G.M. ED., WESTIN A.F. ED.
POLITICS IN EUROPE.
NEW YORK: HARCOURT BRACE, 1965, 205 PP., LC#65-17351.
CASE STUDIES ON GREAT BRITAIN, FRANCE, GERMANY, THE COMMON MARKET, AND THE SOVIET UNION. THE FOUR COUNTIRES DISCUSSED REPRESENT TYPES OF POLITICAL SYSTEMS; THE COMMON MARKET, THE MOST SUCCESSFUL EUROPEAN SUPRANATIONAL ORGANIZATION. EACH CASE CONCENTRATES ON A DEFFERENT ASPECT OF POLITICAL SOCIETY: THE PRESS, THE LAW, CONSTITUTIONALISM, PRESSURE GROUPS, AND EUROPEAN INTEGRATION.

0549 CARTER G.M., HERZ J.H.
GOVERNMENT AND POLITICS IN THE TWENTIETH CENTURY (REV. ED.)
NEW YORK: FREDERICK PRAEGER, 1965, 231 PP., LC#65-25402.
COMPARATIVE ANALYSIS OF BOTH DEVELOPED AND DEVELOPING COUNTRIES. INCLUDES ROLE OF MODERN GOVERNMENT, DEMOCRACY AND TOTALITARIANISM, CHANNELS OF POLITICAL ACTION, AND INTERRELATION OF NATIONAL AND INTERNATIONAL POLITICS.

0550 CARTER G.M., KARIS T., STULTZ N.M.
SOUTH AFRICA'S TRANSKEI: THE POLITICS OF DOMESTIC COLONIALISM.
EVANSTON: NORTHWESTERN U PRESS, 1967, 200 PP., LC#67-15937.
STUDIES HISTORICAL SETTING OF, AND PRESENT PRACTICES IN, THE S. AFRICAN BANTUSTANS, WHICH ARE SEMI-AUTONOMOUS AREAS GIVEN OVER TO BLACK AFRICANS. THE TRANSKEI IS LARGEST OF THESE. CONSIDERS BANTUSTANS EXPERIMENT WITH POSSIBILITY OF DIVISION OF S. AFRICA INTO WHITE AND BLACK AREAS, AND CONCLUDES THAT THIS IS UNLIKELY SOLUTION TO S. AFRICAN PROBLEMS. FINDS TRANSKEI UNDERCAPITALIZED AND INNATELY POOR.

0551 CARVALHO C.M.
GEOGRAPHIA HUMANA; POLITICA E ECONOMICA (3RD ED.)
SAO PAULO: CO EDITORA NACIONAL, 1938, 358 PP.
TEXT DEALS WITH POLITICAL AND ECONOMIC GEOGRAPHY OF WORLD AND PARTICULARLY BRAZIL. DISCUSSES RACES, LANGUAGES, MIGRATION, URBANIZATION, PLUS ECONOMIC FACTORS OF AGRICULTURE, INDUSTRY, COMMUNICATIONS, AND RESOURCES.

0552 CARY J.
THE CASE FOR AFRICAN FREEDOM AND OTHER WRITINGS ON AFRICA.
AUSTIN: U OF TEXAS PR, 1962, 241 PP., LC#62-14502.
JOYCE CAREY'S NON-FICTION WORKS INTRODUCING AFRICA TO BRITISH PEOPLE; HIS PROPOSALS FOR DEVELOPING AFRICA BY EDUCATING HER PEOPLES.

0553 CARY J.
POWER IN MEN.
SEATTLE: U OF WASHINGTON PR, 1963, 274 PP., LC#63-18741.
PHILOSOPHICAL ANALYSIS OF POLITICAL LIBERTY IN RELATION TO THE POSITIVE POWER OF ACCOMPLISHING RATIONAL INDIVIDUAL DESIRES. PROVIDES PHILOSOPHICAL BASIS FOR RESURGENCE OF LIBERALISM. CONTENDS MAN IS FUNDAMENTALLY A LOVER OF FREEDOM AND THAT ALL TYRANNIES MUST EVENTUALLY COLLAPSE BECAUSE THEY ARE AN UNNATURAL STATE.

0554 CASSINELLI C.
"TOTALITARIANISM, IDEOLOGY AND PROPAGANDA."
J. POLIT., 22 (FEB. 60), 68-95.
ASSERTS THAT TOTALITARIAN PROPAGNADA AND IDEOLOGY AIMS PRIMARILY AT CREATING MAXIMUM INSECURITY AMONG PEOPLE IT SEEKS TO CONTROL. ATTACKS ALTERNATIVE THAT PROPAGANDA AND IDEOLOGY ATTEMPT TO MOLD POPULACE IN DOCTRINAL IMAGE OF THEIR LEADERS. DENIES THAT COMMUNISTS AND NAZIS POSSESS A DOCTRINE OR SYSTEM OF BELIEFS COVERING IMPORTANT ASPECTS OF HUMAN EXISTENCE.

0555 CASSINELLI C.W.
THE POLITICS OF FREEDOM.
SEATTLE: U OF WASHINGTON PR, 1961, 214 PP., LC#61-11580.
ANALYZES MODERN DEMOCRATIC STATE, INCLUDING ITS INSTITUTIONS, PARTIES, POLICIES, CIVIL LIBERTIES, CONSENSUS, FOUNDATIONS, AND PROSPECTS, AS WELL AS POLITICAL MYTHS OF DEMOCRATIC STATE.

0556 CASSIRER E.
AN ESSAY ON MAN: AN INTRODUCTION TO A PHILOSOPHY OF HUMAN CULTURE.
NEW HAVEN: YALE U. PR., 1944, 237 PP.
VIEWS CULTURE AS ORGANIC WHOLE WITH INNER UNITY, BUT ALSO STRESSES ITS SPECIFIC SYMBOLIC FORMS: MYTH, ART, LANGUAGE, RELIGION, HISTORY AND SCIENCE. CONCLUDES THAT HUMAN CULTURE IS THE PRODUCT OF MAN'S PROGRESSIVE SELF-LIBERATION.

0557 CASSIRER E.
THE MYTH OF THE STATE.
NEW HAVEN: YALE U PR, 1946, 303 PP.
DEFINES STRUCTURE OF MYTHICAL THOUGHT AND ROLE OF MYTH IN SHAPING SOCIETY; INCLUDES RELATIONSHIP OF MYTH, LANGUAGE, AND PSYCHOLOGY. EXAMINES STRUGGLE AGAINST MYTH IN HISTORY OF POLITICAL THEORY; INCLUDES EARLY GREEK PHILOSOPHY, MEDIEVAL THOUGHT, AND MACHIAVELLI. DISCUSSES 20TH-CENTURY HERO AND RACE WORSHIP, INFLUENCE OF HEGEL, AND TECHNIQUES OF MODERN POLITICAL MYTHS.

0558 CASTBERG F.
FREEDOM OF SPEECH IN THE WEST.
NEW YORK: OCEANA PUBLISHING, 1960, 475 PP.
STUDY OF POLITICAL FREEDOM OF SPEECH IN FRANCE, WEST GERMANY, AND US. GIVES ACCOUNT OF WHERE COURTS HAVE STOOD. PROVIDES CASES TO ILLUSTRATE NATIONS' LAWS IN RESPECT TO FREEDOM OF SPEECH. INCLUDES BACKGROUND TO HISTORICAL DEVELOPMENT OF LEGAL CONCEPTS.

0559 CATHERINE R.
LE FONCTIONNAIRE FRANCAIS.
PARIS: MICHEL, EDITIONS ALBIN, 1961, 411 PP.
INTRODUCTORY STUDY OF FRENCH CIVIL SERVANTS. AUTHOR IS PRIMARILY INTERESTED IN INTELLECTUAL AND MORAL ATTITUDES OF CIVIL SERVANTS, AND THEIR RELATIONS WITH THE GOVERNMENT, THEIR COLLEAGUES, AND CITIZENS.

0560 CATTELL D.T.
"SOVIET POLICIES IN LATIN AMERICA."
CURR. HIST., 47 (NOV. 64), 286-291.
OVERALL ATTITUDE OF USSR TOWARD LATIN AMERICA HAS CHANGED - WAS FOR A LONG TIME INDIFFERENT. FORCE OUTSIDE MOSCOW'S CONTROL (CUBAN REVOLUTION) OPENED NEW PHASE OF COMMUNIST PENETRATION IN LATIN AMERICA.

0561 CATTELL D.T.
"A NEO-MARXIST THEORY OF COMPARATIVE ANALYSIS."
SLAVIC REVIEW, 26 (DEC. 67), 657-662.
THEORY OF CLASSIFICATION OF GOVERNMENTS USING COMPARATIVE ANALYSIS. DISCUSSES SIMILARITY OF CHARACTERISTICS OF COMMUNIST AND NATIONAL SOCIALISTIC FORMS OF GOVERNMENT. PRESENTS MODELS SUCH AS "TOTALITARIAN MODEL," "DEMOCRATIC MODEL," "BUREAUCRATIC MODEL," AND THE LIKE. CATEGORIZES GOVERNMENTS BY TYPE OF PROPERTY OWNERSHIP, STRENGTH OF THE ECONOMY, SOCIAL ORGANIZATIONS AND STRATA, AND AUTHORITARIANISM.

0562 CATTELL D.T.
"THE FIFTIETH ANNIVERSARY: A SOVIET WATERSHED?"
CURRENT HISTORY, 53 (OCT. 67), 224-229, 243.
DISCUSSES POST-KHRUSHCHEV REGIME IN USSR AND SUGGESTS THAT IT REPRESENTS ATTEMPT BY ELITE TO BRING END TO ONE-MAN, CHARISMATIC SYSTEM IN FAVOR OF COLLECTIVE RULE. STUDIES AULTS OF KHRUSHCHEV REGIME AND ADVOCATES NEED TO DEVELOP NEW METHODS OF POLICY-MAKING COMPATIBLE WITH DEVELOPED ECONOMY WHILE ADAPTING GOVERNMENT TO TRADITIONAL RUSSIAN VALUES.

0563 CAUTE D.
COMMUNISM AND THE FRENCH INTELLECTUALS, 1914-1960.
NEW YORK: MACMILLAN, 1964, 413 PP.
TRACES EVOLUTION OF COMMUNIST ATTITUDES TOWARDS INTELLECTUALS, OBSERVES FLUCTUATING SUPPORT OF COMMUNISM BY INTELLECTUALS, STUDIES MALRAUX, GIDE, AND SARTRE, AND ATTEMPTS TO EVALUATE EFFECT OF POLITICAL COMMITMENT ON CREATIVE WORK.

0564 CAUTE D.
THE LEFT IN EUROPE SINCE 1789.
NEW YORK: MCGRAW HILL, 1966, 254 PP., LC#64-66177.
HISTORICAL SURVEY SEEKS TO BUILD A VIABLE MODEL OF THE LEFT, IN TERMS OF WHICH THESE SPECIFIC QUESTIONS CAN BE ANSWERED: WHEN LEFT HAS EXISTED, HISTORICAL FACTORS IN ITS GROWTH, AND SOURCE OF ITS SUPPORT. CONSIDERS "POPULAR SOVEREIGNTY" KEY TO DEFINING LEFT, RATHER THAN SUCH TERMS AS OPTIMISM, EQUALITY, RATIONALISM, OR ANTI-RACISM. TREATS HISTORY, SOCIOLOGY, DOMESTIC AND INTERNATIONAL ASPECTS.

0565 CEFKIN J.L.
THE BACKGROUND OF CURRENT WORLD PROBLEMS.
NEW YORK: DAVID MCKAY, 1967, 436 PP., LC#67-15042.
DISCUSSES FIELD OF INTERNATIONAL RELATIONS, THE COLD WAR, RISE OF NATIONALISM IN UNDEVELOPED COUNTRIES, AND QUEST FOR ECONOMIC DEVELOPMENT.

0566 CENTRAL AFRICAN ARCHIVES
A GUIDE TO THE PUBLIC RECORDS OF SOUTHERN RHODESIA UNDER THE REGIME OF THE BRITISH SOUTH AFRICA COMPANY, 1890-1923.
LONDON: LONGMANS, GREEN & CO, 1956, 282 PP.
CONSISTS OF GENERAL HISTORICAL INTRODUCTION, SUMMARY AND DESCRIPTION OF RECORDS OF BRITISH SOUTH AFRICAN COMPANY'S ADMINISTRATION, ADMINISTRATIVE HISTORY OF ALL DEPARTMENTS OF SOUTHERN RHODESIAN GOVERNMENT, AND DETAILED INDEX.

0567 CENTRAL ASIAN RESEARCH CENTRE
BIBLIOGRAPHY OF RECENT SOVIET SOURCE MATERIAL ON SOVIET CENTRAL ASIA AND THE BORDERLANDS.
LONDON: CENT ASIAN RES CENTRE, 1957.
ISSUED AS BIANNUAL SUPPLEMENT TO "CENTRAL ASIAN REVIEW." CONTINUES THE BIBLIOGRAPHIES EMBODIED IN VOLUMES I-V OF THE "REVIEW." A BRIEFLY ANNOTATED BIBLIOGRAPHY RELATING TO SOVIET PERIODICALS AND BOOKS. HIGHLY TECHNICAL SOURCE MATERIAL NOT INCLUDED. TITLES AND AUTHORS ARE TRANSLITERATED INTO ROMAN LETTERS AND ANNOTATIONS OF LENGTH AND CONTENT GIVEN IN ENGLISH. WITHIN THE TOPICS, ARRANGED BY COUNTRY.

0568 CENTRAL GAZETTEERS UNIT
THE GAZETTEER OF INDIA (VOL. I)
NEW DELHI: INDIAN MIN OF INFO, 1965, 652 PP.
REVISION AND UP-DATING OF THE INDIA GAZETTEERS, COVERING SOCIETY AND CULTURAL PATTERNS IN INDIA THROUGH 1965. INTENDED TO EDUCATE THE PUBLIC ON INDIA'S SOCIAL, ECONOMIC, AND POLITICAL INEQUALITIES AND TO RECONCILE LOCAL PATRIOTISM WITH NATIONAL LOYALTY. UNDERSCORES NATIONWIDE POVERTY, ILL-HEALTH, AND LACK OF EDUCATION AND PROMOTES NATIONAL PLANNING GUIDED BY PRINCIPLES OF SECULARISM, DEMOCRACY AND SOCIALISM.

0569 CEPEDA U.A.
EN TORNO AL CONCEPTO DEL ESTADO EN LOS REYES CATHOLICOS.
MADRID: ESCUELA DE HIST MODERNA, 1956, 225 PP.
DISCUSSES IDEA OF STATE IN SPAIN IN TIME OF CATHOLIC KINGS, INCLUDING EVOLUTION OF CONCEPT FROM MIDDLE AGES, TRANSFORMATION OF SOCIAL AND NATIONAL STRUCTURE, AND TONE OF LIFE IN THAT PERIOD. EMPHASIZES CHRONICLES OF CONTEMPORARIES.

0570 CHAKRABARTI A.
NEHRU: HIS DEMOCRACY AND INDIA.
CALCUTTA: THACKER'S PRESS & DIRECTORIES LTD, 1961, 438 PP.
BACKGROUND TO, AND GROWTH OF, DEMOCRACY IN INDIA UNDER NEHRU. INDIA'S MANY PROBLEMS DISCUSSED IN DETAIL: CLASS DIVISION, POVERTY, COMMUNIST THREAT, STUDENT OPPOSITION, AND GANDHI'S ECCENTRICITIES.

0571 CHAKRAVARTI P.C.
INDIA'S CHINA POLICY.
BLOOMINGTON: INDIANA U. PR., 1962, 180 PP., $4.95.
AN ACCOUNT OF INDIA'S INITIAL INFATUATION AND SUBSERVIENCE TO RED CHINA, THE RUDE AWAKENING OVER TIBET AND THE INDIAN BORDER, AND THE NEED TO GO MUCH FURTHER IN DEVELOPING A PRO-DEMOCRATIC POLICY IN INDIA.

0572 CHANDA A.
FEDERALISM IN INDIA.
NEW YORK: HILLARY HOUSE PUBL, 1965, 347 PP.
STUDY OF UNION-STATE RELATIONS IN INDIA WHICH TRACES PROCESS OF INDIAN CONSOLIDATION AND POLITICAL UNIFICATION. CENTERS ON EVOLUTION OF DEMOCRATIC GOVERNMENT IN INDIA AND CENTRALIZATION AND CONCENTRATION OF POLITICAL AUTHORITY IN HANDS OF SELECT FEW, WHICH WAS ESSENTIAL IN CONSOLIDATION PROCESS.

0573 CHANDLER M.J.
A GUIDE TO RECORDS IN BARBADOS.
OXFORD: BLACKWELL, 1965, 204 PP.
BIBLIOGRAPHICAL COMPILATION OF PUBLICATIONS ON BARBADOS

LOCATED IN LIBRARIES AND GOVERNMENT ARCHIVES. THE WORK WAS DONE FOR THE UNIVERSITY OF THE WEST INDIES UNDER A GRANT FROM THE ROCKEFELLER FOUNDATION. EXTENDS OVER ALL CLASSES OF ARCHIVES: CENTRAL AND LOCAL GOVERNMENT, SEMI-PUBLIC INSTITUTIONS, AND ECCLESIASTICAL AND PRIVATE RECORDS. ARRANGED MAINLY ACCORDING TO LOCATION OF RECORDS IN 1961.

0574 CHANDRA S.
PARTIES AND POLITICS AT THE MUGHAL COURT: 1707-1740.
ALIGARH: ALIGARH MUSLIM UNIV., DEPT.HIST., 1957, 309 PP.
STUDY OF ROLE OF NOBILITY IN ORGANIZATION, GROWTH, ADMINISTRATIVE STRUCTURE, SOCIAL AND CULTURAL LIFE, AND DOWNFALL OF MUGHAL EMPIRE IN MEDIEVAL PERIOD OF INDIAN HISTORY. COVERS RISE AND STRUGGLE OF POLITICAL PARTIES AT MUGHAL COURT.

0575 CHANDRASEKHAR S. ED.
ASIA'S POPULATION PROBLEMS.
NEW YORK: FREDERICK PRAEGER, 1967, 311 PP., LC#66-21773.
ANALYSIS BY NATION OF POPULATION PROBLEMS AND SOLUTIONS. DISCUSSIONS OF MIGRATION, URBANIZATION, ECONOMIC AND SOCIAL EFFECTS, BIRTH CONTROL AND ABORTION MEASURES, INTERNAL DIFFERENCES BY REGION. REPORTS ON DEVELOPMENT MEASURES BEING TAKEN.

0576 CHANG, CHIH-I
THE PARTY AND THE NATIONAL QUESTION IN CHINA (TRANS. BY GEORGE MOSELEY)
CAMBRIDGE: M I T PRESS, 1966, 186 PP., LC#66-27573.
DISCUSSES PROBLEM OF NATIONAL MINORITIES IN COMMUNIST CHINA AND COMMUNIST POLICY CONCERNING STATUS OF NATIONAL GROUPS. AFTER REVOLUTION NATIONALITIES HAD TO BE UNIFIED INTO ONE WORKING CLASS, OVERCOMING HISTORICAL ANIMOSITIES. ANNOTATED BIBLIOGRAPHY OF 70 BOOKS, ARTICLES, AND GOVERNMENT DOCUMENTS IN MODERN EUROPEAN AND ORIENTAL LANGUAGES WRITTEN 1930-65 ON PHASES OF NATIONALITY PROBLEMS.

0577 CHANG H.
WITHIN THE FOUR SEAS.
NEW YORK: TWAYNE, 1958, 254 PP., LC#58-14293.
CONSIDERS PROBLEM OF WORLD PEACE BY APPLYING THOUGHTS AND OBSERVATIONS OF CONFUCIUS TO PRESENT CONDITIONS. MAINTAINS THAT WEST MAY LEARN LESSON OF "SPIRITUAL OR CULTURAL COHESION" FROM KNOWLEDGE OF TRADITION OF EAST.

0578 CHAO K.
THE RATE AND PATTERN OF INDUSTRIAL GROWTH IN COMMUNIST CHINA.
ANN ARBOR: U OF MICH PR, 1965, 188 PP., LC#65-11514.
CONSTRUCTS INDEPENDENT INDEX OF INDUSTRIAL OUTPUT PRODUCED BY COMMUNIST CHINA FROM 1949-59. PRIMARILY BASED ON OFFICIALLY PUBLISHED DATA OF INDUSTRIAL OUTPUT. BRIEF DISCUSSION OF STATISTICAL LOGIC OF CONSTRUCTING AN OUTPUT INDEX, AND THEORETICAL COMPARISON OF VARIOUS INDEXES. ANALYZES IMPLICATIONS DRAWN FROM RESULTING OUTPUT INDEXES; CHINA'S GROWTH IS COMPARED WITH OTHER NATIONS'.

0579 CHAPMAN A.R.
"THE CIVIL WAR IN NIGERIA."
MIDSTREAM, 14 (JAN. 68), 12-25.
DISCUSSES THE SECESSION OF BIAFRA FROM NIGERIA. SHOWS THAT WHILE THE NORTH WAS POLITICALLY PREDOMINANT, THE EASTERN OR BIAFRA REGION WAS WEALTHIER AND BETTER EDUCATED. THE FAILURE OF BIAFRA'S LEGAL ATTEMPTS TO HAVE THIS REFLECTED IN THE FEDERAL GOVERNMENT LED TO ITS SECESSION. CLAIMS THAT THE SECESSION IS POPULARLY SUPPORTED, NOT THE PLAN OF A FEW SELFISH POLITICIANS.

0580 CHAPMAN B.
"THE FRENCH CONSEIL D'ETAT."
PARLIAMENTARY AFFAIRS, 12 (SPRING 59), 164-173.
EXAMINES JURISDICTION, ADMINISTRATIVE OPERATIONS, AND ADVISORY POWERS OF THE "CONSEIL D'ETAT" UNDER THE FIFTH REPUBLIC. CRITICIZES THE GREAT DELAY BETWEEN COMMENCEMENT OF A CASE AND THE FINAL VERDICT; CONTENDS THAT AN INCREASE IN COUNCILLORS, ALTHOUGH AGAINST LAW, IS CHIEF SOLUTION TO THIS DILEMMA. OBSERVES THAT CONTACT WITH PUBLIC SERVICES GUARANTEES ADMINISTRATIVE ETHIC IN THE COURT.

0581 CHAPMAN B.
THE PROFESSION OF GOVERNMENT: THE PUBLIC SERVICE IN EUROPE.
LONDON: UNWIN UNIVERSITY BOOKS, 1966, 322 PP.
TEXTBOOK OF COMPARATIVE GOVERNMENT. UNANNOTATED BIBLIOGRAPHY APPENDED TO TEXT ORGANIZED ACCORDING TO THE MAIN DIVISIONS OF THE BOOK - REFERENCE WORKS, REVIEWS, BOOKS, ARTICLES TAKEN FROM ENGLISH, FRENCH, GERMAN, ITALIAN, SCANDINAVIAN, DUTCH, AND SPANISH SOURCES. WITHIN SUBJECT DIVISIONS, BIBLIOGRAPHY ORGANIZED GEOGRAPHICALLY.

0582 CHAPMAN R.M., JACKSON W.R., MITCHELL A.V.
NEW ZEALAND POLITICS IN ACTION: THE 1960 GENERAL ELECTION.
LONDON: OXFORD U PR, 1962, 296 PP.
STUDIES 1960 GENERAL ELECTION OF NEW ZEALAND FROM MANY ANGLES, IN ORDER TO PROVIDE GENERAL DESCRIPTION OF NEW ZEALAND PARTIES AND POLITICS. PARTIES, ISSUES, BACKGROUND, AND CAMPAIGNS ARE DISCUSSED, AS WELL AS TREATMENT OF AND EFFECT ON THE ELECTIONS OF THE PRESS AND BROADCASTING. ATTITUDES OF VOTERS TOWARD ISSUES AND CANDIDATES ARE ALSO SURVEYED.

0583 CHARMATZ J.P. ED., DAGGETT H.S.
COMPARATIVE STUDIES IN COMMUNITY PROPERTY LAW.
BATON ROUGE: LOUISIANA ST U PR, 1955, 190 PP., LC#55-11817.
STUDIES OF DEVELOPMENT AND PRINCIPLES OF COMMUNITY PROPERTY LAW IN ARIZONA, CALIFORNIA, IDAHO, LOUISIANA, NEVADA, NEW MEXICO, TEXAS, AND WASHINGTON. EXAMINES THE LEGAL MARITAL PROPERTY REGIME ACCORDING TO THE PROJECT OF THE FRENCH COMMISSION FOR REVISION OF THE CIVIL CODE.

0584 CHARNAY J.P.
LE SUFFRAGE POLITIQUE EN FRANCE; ELECTIONS PARLEMENTAIRES, ELECTION PRESIDENTIELLE, REFERENDUMS.
HAGUE: MOUTON & CO, 1965, 832 PP.
EXTENSIVE SURVEY OF PARLIAMENTARY AND PRESIDENTIAL ELECTIONS, THEIR LEGAL ORGANIZATION, ADMINISTRATION, MANAGEMENT, AND SOCIOLOGICAL STRUCTURE. EMPHASIZES THE CANDIDATE AND ELECTORAL PROCESS AND ITS EVOLUTION.

0585 CHATTERJI S.K.
AFRICANISM: THE AFRICAN PERSONALITY.
CALCUTTA: BENGAL PUBLISHERS, LTD, 1960, 220 PP.
A SHORT STUDY OF THE AFRICAN PEOPLE BY AN INDIAN WHO HAS SPENT MANY YEARS IN AFRICA. CONCENTRATES ON AFRICANS' DESIRE TO BE FREE. HAS PHOTOGRAPHS OF SELECTED ART WORKS.

0586 CHEN N-R.
THE ECONOMY OF MAINLAND CHINA, 1949-1963: A BIBLIOGRAPHY OF MATERIALS IN ENGLISH.
BERKELEY: SOC SCI RES COUNCIL, 1963, 297 PP.
ENGLISH-LANGUAGE BIBLIOGRAPHY INCLUDES TRANSLATIONS OF COMMUNIST CHINESE PUBLICATIONS AND BOOKS AND ARTICLES PUBLISHED IN ENGLISH IN AND OUTSIDE MAINLAND CHINA. PART I CONTAINS REFERENCES TO PRIMARY SOURCES ORIGINATING IN COMMUNIST CHINA: OFFICIAL DOCUMENTS; REPORTS AND SPEECHES; SEMI-OFFICIAL AND NONOFFICIAL PUBLICATIONS. PART II IS RESTRICTED TO SECONDARY SOURCE MATERIAL.

0587 CHEN T.H.
THE CHINESE COMMUNIST REGIME: A DOCUMENTARY STUDY (2 VOLS.)
LOS ANGELES: U OF S CALIF PR, 1965, 238 PP.
CONSISTS OF DOCUMENTS DEALING WITH THE ORGANIZATION OF THE CHINESE COMMUNIST GOVERNMENT AND THE CHINESE COMMUNIST PARTY. EMPHASIS IS ON INTERNAL FEATURES OF THE REGIME, INCLUDING ECONOMIC POLICY AND SOCIAL AND POLITICAL REFORM.

0588 CHENG C-Y.
SCIENTIFIC AND ENGINEERING MANPOWER IN COMMUNIST CHINA, 1949-1963.
WASHINGTON: NATL SCIENCE FDN, 1965, 588 PP.
PROVIDES BACKGROUND INFORMATION ON TRAINING, UTILIZATION, AND EMPLOYMENT OF SCIENTIFIC AND ENGINEERING MANPOWER IN COMMUNIST CHINA FROM 1949-63. DISCUSSES GOVERNMENTAL POLICIES AND CONTROLS AND ROLE OF USSR IN DEVELOPING CHINA'S SPECIALIZED MANPOWER. GIVES BIOGRAPHICAL DATA ON 1,200 PROMINENT SCIENTISTS AND ENGINEERS IN MAINLAND CHINA.

0589 CHILCOTE R.H.
PORTUGUESE AFRICA.
ENGLEWOOD CLIFFS: PRENTICE HALL, 1967, 149 PP., LC#67-14849.
STUDIES DEVELOPMENTS IN PORTUGUESE POSSESSIONS IN AFRICA. DISCUSSES TRADITION OF EMPIRE AND HISTORY OF COLONIAL POLICY. DELINEATES PROBLEMS FACING PORTUGAL AND HER COLONIES TODAY AND EXAMINES INSTITUTIONAL FORCES THAT ALLOW PORTUGUESE DOMINANCE OR AFRICAN INDEPENDENCE. COMPARES AFRICAN AND PORTUGUESE CONCEPTS OF NATIONALISM AND EXAMINES POLITICAL, ECONOMIC, AND SOCIAL TRENDS IN EACH TERRITORY.

0590 CHILDS J.B.
AN ACCOUNT OF GOVERNMENT DOCUMENT BIBLIOGRAPHY IN THE UNITED STATES AND ELSEWHERE (A PAPER)
WASHINGTON: LIBRARY OF CONGRESS, 1927, 39 PP., LC#27-26008.
SURVEY OF CONDITION OF BIBLIOGRAPHY OF GOVERNMENT DOCUMENTS IN US WITH REMARKS ON GREAT BRITAIN, ITALY, INDIA, FRANCE, GERMANY. ANNOTATED BIBLIOGRAPHY OF GOVERNMENT BIBLIOGRAPHIES LISTED BY COUNTRY. INCLUDES LEAGUE OF NATIONS.

0591 CHILDS J.B.
FOREIGN GOVERNMENT PUBLICATIONS (PAMPHLET)
WASHINGTON: LIBRARY OF CONGRESS, 1928, 9 PP.
SURVEY OF IMPORTANT ACCESSIONS DURING FISCAL YEAR ENDING JUNE 39, 1927. DETAILED LIST OF OFFICIAL PUBLICATIONS WHICH CONTAIN LEGISLATIVE PROCEEDINGS, STATE LAWS AND PROCLAMATIONS FROM MEXICO, OFFICIAL GAZETTES FROM BRAZIL, AND NOTEWORTHY PUBLICATIONS LISTED BY COUNTRY FROM WHICH RECEIVED.

0592 CHILDS J.B.
THE MEMORIAS OF THE REPUBLICS OF CENTRAL AMERICA AND OF THE ANTILLES.
WASHINGTON: GOVT PR OFFICE, 1932, 170 PP., LC#32-26163.

ARRANGED BY COUNTRY AND SUBDIVIDED TOPICALLY, THESE MATERIALS ARE ESSENTIALLY THE YEARLY REPORTS OF THE VARIOUS DEPARTMENTS OF THE RESPECTIVE GOVERNMENTS. TITLES TRANSLATED BUT ITEMS THEMSELVES ARE ALL IN SPANISH OR FRENCH. ORIGINATES WITH INDEPENDENCE (ABOUT 1840) AND CONTINUES TO 1932.

0593 CHILDS J.B.
COLOMBIAN GOVERNMENT PUBLICATIONS (PAMPHLET)
WASHINGTON: LIBRARY OF CONGRESS, 1941, 41 PP.
ANNOTATED LISTING BY THE ADMINISTRATIVE UNIT PUBLISHING THE ITEM. ALL ARE IN SPANISH AND NUMBER ABOUT 350. DATE FROM INDEPENDENCE TO 1941.

0594 CHILDS J.B. ED.
A GUIDE TO THE OFFICIAL PUBLICATIONS OF THE OTHER AMERICAN REPUBLICS: ARGENTINA.
WASHINGTON: LIBRARY OF CONGRESS, 1941, 124 PP.
GUIDE PREPARED TO FILL NEED FOR PRACTICAL REFERENCE WORK OF AMERICAN REPUBLICS. ATTEMPT IS MADE TO CENTER UPON CURRENT AGENCIES AND PUBLICATIONS STRESSING INFORMATIONAL POTENTIALITIES AND GIVING BRIEF DATA ABOUT EACH WHERE SPACE PERMITS. PRESENT ARGENTINA GOVERNMENT ORGANIZATION IS USED AS ARRANGEMENT OF VOLUME.

0595 CHIU S.M.
"CHINA'S MILITARY POSTURE."
CURRENT HISTORY, 53 (SEPT. 67), 155-160.
ATTEMPTS TO EVALUATE CHINA'S MILITARY POWER, CONCENTRATING ON STRENGTH OF PEOPLE'S LIBERATION ARMY (PLA) AND NUCLEAR DEVELOPMENT. DISCUSSES ROLE OF PLA IN SUPPORTING CULTURAL REVOLUTION AND POLITICAL CONTROL SYSTEM WHICH MANAGES ARMY. MAINTAINS THAT UNTIL NUCLEAR WEAPONS SYSTEM IS OPERATIONAL, PEKING'S MILITARY POSTURE WILL BE DEFENSIVE.

0596 CHODOROV F.
THE RISE AND FALL OF SOCIETY.
NEW YORK: DEVIN ADAIR, 1959, 168 PP., LC#59-8205.
STUDY OF ECONOMIC FORCES IN SOCIETY AND THEIR IMPACT ON INSTITUTIONS AND ACTIONS OF INDIVIDUALS. EXAMINES COLLECTIVE NATURE OF SOCIETY AND ITS UNITY WITH STATE.

0597 CHOU S.H.
THE CHINESE INFLATION 1937-1949.
NEW YORK: COLUMBIA U PRESS, 1963, 319 PP., LC#62-18260.
ANALYZES PROCESS OF CHINESE INFLATION, EMPHASIZING ECONOMIC AND SOCIAL EFFECTS. EVALUATES ROLE OF WARTIME AND POSTWAR INFLATION IN DOWNFALL OF NATIONALIST REGIME AND VICTORY OF COMMUNIST PARTY. DISCUSSES GOVERNMENT'S FISCAL OPERATIONS, MILITARY EXPENDITURES, AND BALANCE-OF-PAYMENTS PROBLEMS.

0598 CHRIMES S.B.
ENGLISH CONSTITUTIONAL HISTORY (3RD ED.)
LONDON: OXFORD U PR, 1965, 202 PP.
OUTLINE OF PRESENT ENGLISH CONSTITUTION AND ITS DELEGATION OF POWERS TO KING, CABINET, PARLIAMENT, JUDGES, AND SUBJECTS. TRACES DEVELOPMENT OF CONSTITUTION FROM MEDIEVAL FOUNDATIONS THROUGH 16TH AND 17TH CENTURIES, THEORY OF COMPROMISE TO 19TH CENTURY, AND SEPARATION OF POWERS AND RISE OF CABINET GOVERNMENT. BELIEVES THAT ENGLISH CONSTITUTION OFFERS BEST SOLUTIONS TO PERENNIAL PROBLEMS.

0599 CHRISTENSEN A.N. ED.
THE EVOLUTION OF LATIN AMERICAN GOVERNMENT: A BOOK OF READINGS.
NEW YORK: HOLT RINEHART WINSTON, 1951, 747 PP.
SELECTIONS DISCUSSING HISTORICAL FACTORS, CONSTITUTIONAL BASES, AND PRACTICAL ORGANIZATION OF LATIN AMERICAN GOVERNMENTS. EMPHASIZES DISPARITY BETWEEN CONSTITUTIONS AND ACTUAL FUNCTIONING OF GOVERNMENT. SECTIONS ON LATIN AMERICAN SOCIAL PROBLEMS AND INTERNATIONAL AFFAIRS.

0600 CHU-YUAN CHENG
"THE CULTURAL REVOLUTION AND CHINA'S ECONOMY."
CURRENT HISTORY, 53 (SEPT. 67), 148-154.
EVALUATES IMPACT OF PRESENT "CULTURAL REVOLUTION" ON NATIONAL ECONOMY, EXAMINING EFFECT OF FIVE YEAR PLANS AND MAOIST POLICY. REVIEWS ECONOMC PERFORMANCE OF 1966 AND PRESENTS STATISTICS ON INDUSTRIAL AND AGRICULTURAL PRODUCTION. STUDIG CAUSE OF ECONOMIC DISTUPTION DECEMBER, 1966, AND EFFECTS ON INDUSTRIAL CENTERS, TRANSPORT SYSTEM, COMMERCIAL DISTRIBUTION CHANNELS, AND RURAL AGRICULTURAL AREAS.

0601 CHUNG Y.S. ED.
KOREA: A SELECTED BIBLIOGRAPHY 1959-1963.
SEOUL: KOREA RESEARCHER & PUBL, 1965, 117 PP.
MOST OF THE ENTRIES IN THIS BIBLIOGRAPHY ARE FOUND IN THE KOREAN UNIT OF THE LIBRARY OF CONGRESS, AND ARE OF SOUTH KOREAN ORIGIN. THE WORKS, ON BOTH NORTH AND SOUTH KOREA REFLECT REVOLUTIONARY NATURE OF THE FOUR-YEAR PERIOD COVERED. A BROAD RANGE OF FIELDS IN THE SOCIAL SCIENCES AND HUMANITIES IS COVERED. HAS AN INTROUDCTION AND LIMITED ANNOTATIONS.

0602 CLAGETT H.L.
COMMUNIST CHINA: RUTHLESS ENEMY OR PAPER TIGER (PAMPHLET)
WASHINGTON: DEPT OF THE ARMY, 1962, 137 PP.
WELL ANNOTATED BASIC AND ADVANCED MATERIALS FROM 1948-62 IN ENGLISH CONCERNED PRIMARILY WITH AIMS, STRENGTHS, AND WEAKNESSES OF COMMUNIST CHINA. INCLUDES ARTICLES, BOOKS, AND DOCUMENTS OF BOTH US AND CHINESE GOVERNMENTS. MORE THAN 1000 ITEMS TOPICALLY ARRANGED.

0603 CLARKE M.V.
MEDIEVAL REPRESENTATION AND CONSENT.
LONDON: LONGMANS, GREEN & CO, 1936, 408 PP.
A STUDY OF EARLY PARLIAMENTS IN ENGLAND AND IRELAND, PAYING PARTICULAR ATTENTION TO THE"MODUS TENENDI PARLIAMENTARIUM" AS AN IMPORTANT AND NEGLECTED SOURCE OF INFORMATION ON THE ORIGIN, NATURE, AND FUNCTIONS OF PARLIAMENTS. DISCUSSES RELATION OF "MODUS" TO MEDIEVAL WORLD VIEW, AND PRESENCE OF ELEMENTS OF REPRESENTATION AND CONSENT OF THE GOVERNED. INCLUDES LATIN TEXTS.

0604 CLIFFE L.
"TANGANYIKA'S TWO YEARS OF INDEPENDENCE."
CURR. HIST., 46 (MARCH 64), 136-141.
TANGANYIKA POOR EVEN IN AFRICAN CONTEXT, THE EXTENT OF UNDERDEVELOPMENT BEING THE MOST IMPORTANT FACT TO BE GRASPED. AGAINST THIS BACKGROUND ALL POLITICAL HAPPENINGS HAVE TO BE STUDIED.

0605 CLIGNET R., FOSTER P.
"POTENTIAL ELITES IN GHANA AND THE IVORY COAST: A PRELIMINARY SURVEY."
AMER. J. SOCIOL., 70(NOV. 64), 349-62.
A COMPARATIVE STUDY OF EMERGING ELITE GROUPS IN TWO NEWLY INDEPENDENT AFRICAN STATES. DISCUSSED TRIBAL LEADERS AS A SOURCE OF NATIONAL ELITES.

0606 CLOKIE H.M.
THE ORIGIN AND NATURE OF CONSTITUTIONAL GOVERNMENT.
LONDON: GEORGE HARRAP & CO, 1936, 156 PP.
EXAMINES FOUNDATIONS OF PARLIAMENTARIANISM AND CONSTITUTIONALISM. INQUIRES INTO BEGINNINGS OF PARLIAMENTS, UPPER CHAMBERS, POLITICAL PARTIES, CABINETS, AND WRITTEN CONSTITUTIONS. INVESTIGATES "TRUE NATURE" OF CONSTITUTIONALISM. DESCRIBES SPREAD OF CONSTITUTIONAL GOVERNMENT. SERVES AS INTRODUCTION TO FURTHER WORKS COMPARING TYPES OF PARLIAMENTARY GOVERNMENTS.

0607 CLOKIE H.M., ROBINSON J.W.
ROYAL COMMISSIONS OF INQUIRY; THE SIGNIFICANCE OF INVESTIGATIONS IN BRITISH POLITICS.
STANFORD: STANFORD U PRESS, 1937, 242 PP.
EXPLORES SIGNIFICANCE AND STATUS OF ROYAL COMMISSIONS OF INQUIRY IN RELATION TO BRITISH POLITICS. TRACES DEVELOPMENT OF COMMISSIONS, DESCRIBES THEIR PROCEDURE, AND EXAMINES THEIR FUNCTION AS A COMBINATION FACT-FINDING AND POLICY-MAKING ORGANIZATION. MAINTAINS THAT COMMISSIONS ARE DECLINING IN IMPORTANCE, BEING REPLACED BY COMMITTEES AND BOARDS, AND POLITICAL PARTY CONFERENCES.

0608 CLUBB O.E. JR.
TWENTIETH CENTURY CHINA.
NEW YORK: COLUMB. U. PR., 1964, 470 PP.
TRACES DEVELOPMENTS FROM FALL OF MANCHU DYNASTY, RISE OF THE KUOMINTANG, CHIANG KAI-SHEK ERA, WAR WITH JAPAN TO THE RISE OF COMMUNISM. SPECULATES THAT MODERN CHINA WILL NOT SPLIT THE COMMUNIST WORLD UNTIL IT BECOMES STRONG ENOUGH.

0609 CLYDE P.H.
THE FAR EAST: A HISTORY OF THE IMPACT OF THE WEST ON EASTERN ASIA.
ENGLEWOOD CLIFFS: PRENTICE HALL, 1948, 868 PP.
ANALYSIS OF HISTORICAL CHANGE IN SINO-JAPANESE POLITICS, CULTURE, ECONOMICS, AND INTERNATIONAL RELATIONS RESULTING FROM CONTACT AND CONFLICT WITH THE WEST, 1860-1940.

0610 COBBAN A.
DICTATORSHIP: ITS HISTORY AND THEORY.
NEW YORK: CHAS SCRIBNER'S SONS, 1939, 344 PP.
PRESENTS DEFINITION OF DICTATORSHIP AS UNLIMITED AND ABSOLUTE SOVEREIGNTY OF ONE; THEN ITS HISTORICAL DEVELOPMENT IN CONTEXT OF RISE OF NATION-STATE FROM DIVINE-RIGHT MONARCH TO POPULAR SOVEREIGNTY; AND FINALLY ITS FRUITION IN TOTALITARIAN VIEW OF STATE. ANALYZES DICTATORSHIPS OF EARLIER PERIODS OF HISTORY.

0611 COBBAN A.
ROUSSEAU AND THE MODERN STATE.
HAMDEN, CONN: ARCHON BOOKS, 1961, 288 PP.
ATTACKS TWO PREVAILING INTERPRETATIONS THAT SAY THAT ROUSSEAU BELIEVED IN EITHER A STRONG INDIVIDUAL OR A STRONG STATE. AUTHOR'S ANALYSIS OF ROUSSEAU'S POLITICAL WRITINGS SHOWS THAT ROUSSEAU BELIEVED THAT ONLY A STRONG STATE COULD GUARANTEE INDIVIDUAL LIBERTY. CLAIMS THAT ROUSSEAU IS FIRST AND BEST COMMENTATOR ON THE ROLE OF THE INDIVIDUAL IN THE MODERN STATE.

0612 COBBAN A.
ROUSSEAU AND THE MODERN STATE (2ND ED.)

LONDON: ALLEN & UNWIN, 1964, 181 PP.
DISCUSSION OF ROUSSEAU'S PHILOSOPHY, EMPHASIZING RELATIONSHIP BETWEEN INDIVIDUAL AND THE STATE. ROUSSEAU CHAMPIONS THE INDIVIDUAL AND HIS LIBERTY. TOPICS DISCUSSED INCLUDE THE POLITICAL WORLD OF ROUSSEAU; HIS CRITICS; LIBERTY AND THE GENERAL WILL; THE NATION STATE; ROUSSEAU'S UTOPIA; AND A COMPARISON OF ROUSSEAU AND THE MODERN POLITICAL MIND.

0613 COBLENTZ S.A.
FROM ARROW TO ATOM BOMB: THE PSYCHOLOGICAL HISTORY OF WAR.
NEW YORK: BEECHHURST PRESS INC, 1953, 539 PP., LC#53-8028.
TRACES HISTORY OF WARFARE FROM OLD STONE AGE TO PRESENT EMPHASIZING ITS PSYCHOLOGICAL BASIS. CONSIDERS TRADITIONS, HABITS OF MIND, IMPULSES, AND MASS MOTIVATIONS UNDERLYING AND CAUSING COMBAT BETWEEN MEN.

0614 COEDES G.
THE MAKING OF SOUTH EAST ASIA.
BERKELEY: U OF CALIF PR, 1966, 268 PP.
POLITICAL AND MILITARY HISTORY OF INDOCHINESE CIVILIZATIONS BASED ON GEOGRAPHICAL FACTS, PREHISTORICAL AND ETHNOLOGICAL DATA, HISTORICAL EVENTS SUCH AS WARS, CONQUESTS, INTERNAL REVOLUTIONS, AND REPERCUSSIONS OF LARGE-SCALE UPHEAVALS IN NEIGHBORING COUNTRIES. PARTICULAR EMPHASIS IS PLACED ON THE CRISES OF THE 13TH CENTURY.

0615 COHEN A.
"REVOLUTION IN ARGENTINA?"
CURRENT HISTORY, 53 (NOV. 67), 283-290.
DISCUSSES QUESTION OF WHETHER ONGANIA REALLY INITIATED A REVOLUTION. AUTHOR FEELS HE DID NOT, POINTING OUT THAT ARGENTINA'S REVOLUTION WAS ALREADY IN PROGRESS BEFORE ONGANIA, GUIDO, ARAMBU, AND BEFORE PERON. DESCRIBES THIS REVOLUTION AND THE ATTEMPTS TO REPRESS IT. FEELS ONGANIA IS LARGELY RESPONSIBLE FOR NATION'S STRUCTURAL DISEQUILIBRIUM AND POLITICAL AND ECONOMIC INSTABILITY.

0616 COHEN E.W.
THE GROWTH OF THE BRITISH CIVIL SERVICE 1780-1939.
NEW YORK: W W NORTON, 1941, 221 PP.
DEVELOPMENT OF CIVIL SERVICE BUREAUCRACY, SINECURES, PENSIONS, ADMINISTRATION PROCEDURES. ATTITUDES OF LOCAL OFFICIALS AND EFFECT ON GOVERNMENT OF CENTRALIZATION. CONTAINS BIBLIOGRAPHY CITING OFFICIAL STATE PAPERS, BOOKS, AND BIOGRAPHIES. ARRANGED BY NATURE OF SOURCE AND ALPHABETICALLY. NO FOREIGN-LANGUAGE MATERIALS.

0617 COHEN R. ED.
"POWER IN COMPLEX SOCIETIES IN AFRICA."
ANTHROPOLIGICA, 4 (NO.1, 62), 1-194.
SPECIAL ISSUE WITH FIVE STUDIES FOCUSING ON SUPERIOR-SUBORDINATE RELATIONSHIPS IN COMPLEX AFRICAN SOCIETIES. THE FRAME OF REFERENCE ALLOWS FOR STUDIES OF HIERARCHICAL RELATIONS WITHIN AN INSTITUTION AND THOSE CUTTING ACROSS SEVERAL INSTITUTIONS IN ONE SOCIETY.

0618 COHEN R.
"ANTHROPOLOGY AND POLITICAL SCIENCE: COURTSHIP OR MARRIAGE?"
AMER. BEHAVIORAL SCIENTIST, 11 (NOV.-DEC. 67), 1-7.
DISCUSSES PROBLEMS OF DEALING WITH NEW NATIONS OF AFRICA: THE POLITICAL SCIENTIST DOES NOT UNDERSTAND PRIMITIVE SOCIETY; THE ANTHROPOLOGIST IGNORES NEW INSTITUTIONS. TO CLOSE HIATUS THE TWO ARE BEGINNING A RAPPROCHEMENT, BUT AUTHOR CONTENDS THAT EACH MUST ADOPT THE METHODS AND LANGUAGE OF THE OTHER FOR THERE TO BE A REAL UNION BETWEEN THEM.

0619 COHN B.S.
DEVELOPMENT AND IMPACT OF BRITISH ADMINISTRATION IN INDIA: A BIBLIOGRAPHIC ESSAY.
NEW DELHI: INDIAN INST PUB ADMIN, 1961, 88 PP.
DESCRIBES AND HIGHLIGHTS FACETS OF BRITISH ADMINISTRATION IN INDIA THROUGH REFERENCES TO BOOKS, ARTICLES, AND PAMPHLETS RELATING TO BRITISH COLONIAL POLICY AND ADMINISTRATION. ORGANIZES, ASSESSES, AND ANNOTATES WIDE RANGE OF MATERIALS DEALING WITH THE BACKGROUND, ESTABLISHMENT, DEVELOPMENT, FUNCTIONING, AND IMPACT OF BRITISH COLONIAL ADMINISTRATION.

0620 COLE A.B., TOTTEN G.O., UYEHARA C.H.
SOCIALIST PARTIES IN POSTWAR JAPAN.
NEW HAVEN: YALE U PR, 1966, 490 PP., LC#66-21511.
COMBINES HISTORICAL METHOD WITH POLITICAL DESCRIPTION AND ANALYSIS TO STUDY JAPAN'S NON-COMMUNIST SOCIAL DEMOCRATIC PARTIES FROM 1945-61. PROVIDES HISTORICAL SURVEY OF PARTY DEVELOPMENT; OUTLINES AND EVALUATES ECONOMIC POLICIES; AND CONSIDERS FOREIGN POLICIES OF SOCIALISTS. CONSIDERS PARTY ORGANIZATION AND LEADERSHIP, RELATIONS BETWEEN PARTY AND LABOR UNIONS, AND SUPPORT FROM VARIOUS SOCIAL STRATA.

0621 COLE G.D.H.
SOCIAL THEORY.
NEW YORK: FRED A STOKES PUBL, 1920, 220 PP.
DISCUSSION OF VARIOUS ASPECTS OF SOCIAL THEORY, ESSENTIAL PRINCIPLES OF SOCIAL ORGANIZATION. EMPHASIZES MORAL AND PSYCHOLOGICAL PROBLEMS UNDERLYING SOCIAL ORGANIZATION IN ITS THEORY AND PRACTICE. CONCENTRATES ON WESTERN EUROPE. BIBLIOGRAPHY OF FIFTY-SEVEN ITEMS, ARRANGED BY CHAPTER, AND BASED ON CLASSICAL POLITICAL THINKERS SUCH AS ROUSSEAU, MARX, PLATO, MILL, ETC.

0622 COLE G.D.H.
"NAZI ECONOMICS: HOW DO THEY MANAGE IT?"
POLIT. QUART., 10 (JAN. 39), 55-68.
CONSIDERS WORKING OF NAZI ECONOMY DURING PERIOD OF INTENSE ACTIVITY LEADING UP TO CRISIS OF SEPTEMBER, 1938. INVESTIGATES REASONS BEHIND SUCCESS OF ECONOMY THAT VIOLATES ALL LAWS OF ECONOMICS AND MANAGES "TO LEAVE THE DEMOCRATIC COUNTRIES TO GLORY IN THEIR OWN TRIUMPHS OF UNEMPLOYMENT." MAINTAINS THAT FORCE IS NECESSARY TO FASCIST ECONOMY AND WELFARE IS ANTITHESIS OF ITS AIMS.

0623 COLE G.D.H.
STUDIES IN CLASS STRUCTURE.
NEW YORK: HUMANITIES PRESS, 1955, 195 PP.
ANALYZES ECONOMIC ASPECTS OF CLASS STRUCTURE IN BRITAIN AND OTHER WESTERN SOCIETIES. MAINTAINS THAT CLASSES ARE NOT SHARPLY DEFINABLE GROUPS. STUDIES METHODS OF ASSIGNING PEOPLE TO A CLASS. EXAMINES INFLUENCE OF TECHNOLOGICAL CHANGE ON CLASS STRUCTURE AND DISCUSSES CONCEPT OF MIDDLE CLASS. EMPHASIZES POSITION OF SEVERAL KINDS OF ELITES IN BRITISH SOCIETY.

0624 COLE G.D.H.
THE POST WAR CONDITIONS OF BRITAIN.
NEW YORK: PRAEGER, 1957, 483 PP.
SURVEY OF BRITIAN'S ECONOMIC CONDITIONS IN 1954 IN COMPARISON WITH THOSE OF 1938. NOTES CHANGES IN POPULATION, INCOME, PRODUCTION, TRADE, HEALTH, AND TAXATION. COMMENTS ON PROGRESS OF BRITIAN AS A WELFARE STATE.

0625 COLE G.D.H.
THE MEANING OF MARXISM.
LONDON: VICTOR GOLLANCZ, 1966, 302 PP.
RE-EVALUATION OF MARX'S ESSENTIAL IDEAS AND METHODS IN RELATION TO CONTEMPORARY SOCIAL STRUCTURES AND DEVELOPMENTS. SPECIAL EMPHASIS ON EFFECT OF MARX'S THEORIES ON STRUCTURE OF SOCIAL CLASSES AS THEY HAVE BEEN ALTERED IN MODERN SOCIETY.

0626 COLE T.
"LESSONS FROM RECENT EUROPEAN EXPERIENCE."
ANN. ACAD. POL. SOC. SCI., 292 (MAR. 54), 55-75.
DISCUSSION OF POST-WAR DEVELOPMENTS IN CIVIL SERVICE IN WESTERN EUROPE. CHANGES HAVE BENEFITED DEMOCRACY, AND AT LEAST SOME SHOULD BE TRIED IN UNITED STATES.

0627 COLEMAN J.S.
NIGERIA: BACKGROUND TO NATIONALISM.
BERKELEY: U. CALIF. PR., 1958, 510 PP.
A STUDY OF CONDITIONS STIMULATING RISE AND GROWTH OF NATIONALISM IN NIGERIA. ALSO DESCRIBES CULTURAL AND HISTORICAL BACKGROUND, AND IMPACT OF WESTERN ECONOMIC AND POLITICAL FORCES.

0628 COLEMAN J.S.
"COLLECTIVE DECISIONS."
SOCIOLOGICAL INQUIRY, 34 (SPRING 64), 166-181.
SHOWS WAYS IN WHICH RATIONAL SELF-INTEREST ACTORS CAN ENGAGE IN COLLECTIVE DECISIONS WITHOUT ENGAGING IN INTERNATIONAL WAR. INDICATES SOME OF THE STRUCTURAL CONDITIONS UNDER WHICH SUCH COLLECTIVE DECISIONS CAN BE MADE WITHOUT RECOURSE TO EXTERNAL POWER, POINTING OUT THAT DIFFERENT ORGANIZATIONS AND OTHER SOCIAL STRUCTURES VARY IN DECISION-MAKING STRUCTURE.

0629 COLEMAN J.S. ED.
"EDUCATION AND POLITICAL DEVELOPMENT."
PRINCETON: PRINCETON U PRESS, 1965.
ANTHOLOGY OF ARTICLES ON RELATIONSHIP BETWEEN EDUCATION AND MODERNIZATION. CONCENTRATES ON FIELD OF EDUCATIONAL POLICY AND PRACTICE IN THE NEW STATES. BIBLIOGRAPHIC GUIDE BY KENNETH ROTHMAN ON EDUCATION AND POLITICAL SOCIALIZATION, WITH PARTICULAR REFERENCE TO ROLE OF SCHOOLS AND SCHOOLING IN NATION-BUILDING. DESIGNED TO INDICATE RANGES OF APPROACH TO TOPIC. MAINLY ENGLISH-LANGUAGE ITEMS CITED.

0630 COLEMAN-NORTON P.R.
ROMAN STATE AND CHRISTIAN CHURCH: A COLLECTION OF LEGAL DOCUMENTS TO A.D. 535 (3 VOLS.)
LONDON: SOC. PROM. CHRIST. KNOWLEDGE,1966, 1358 PP.
COLLECTION OF LEGAL DOCUMENTS AFFECTING CHRISTIAN CHURCH DURING ROMAN EMPIRE FROM BEGINNING OF CHURCH TO CODE OF JUSTINIAN I IN 534 A.D.

0631 COLLINS B.A.
"SOME NOTES ON PUBLIC SERVICE COMMISSIONS IN THE COMMONWEALTH CARIBBEAN."
SOCIAL ECO. STUDIES, 16 (MAR. 67), 1-16.
CONSIDERS THE PUBLIC SERVICE COMMISSION ESTABLISHED BY UK AS ADAPTED TO THE CARIBBEAN ENVIRONMENT, QUESTIONING ITS

ADEQUACY IN THE NEW CONTEXT OF INDEPENDENCE. CONCLUDES THAT THE MERIT PRINCIPLE OF ADVANCEMENT IN THE PSC IS ADVANTAGEOUS, BUT THE SYSTEM MUST BE MODERNIZED FOR GREATER EFFICIENCY.

0632 COLLINS B.E., GUETZKOW H.
A SOCIAL PSYCHOLOGY OF GROUP PROCESSES FOR DECISION-MAKING.
NEW YORK: JOHN WILEY, 1964, 247 PP.
FOUNDATIONAL MATERIAL ON SOCIAL PSYCHOLOGY AS RELEVANT TO GROUP DECISION-MAKING IN GOVERNMENT AND INDUSTRY, BASED ON EMPIRICAL DATA. PRESENTS INDUCTIVE THEORY OF FACE-TO-FACE GROUPS.

0633 COLLINS H., ABRAMSKY C.
KARL MARX AND THE BRITISH LABOR MOVEMENT, YEARS OF THE FIRST INTERNATIONAL.
LONDON: MACMILLAN, 1965, 356 PP.
INVESTIGATES ROLE PLAYED BY KARL MARX IN FOUNDING OF BRITAIN'S FIRST INTERNATIONAL LABOR UNION IN 1864. ASSESSES THE INTERNATIONAL IN RELATION TO INDUSTRIAL AND POLITICAL MOVEMENT OF BRITISH WORKING CLASS. NOTES IMPACT OF BRITISH TRADE UNIONS ON WORLD SOCIALISM AND DISCUSSES FOUNDING OF PARIS COMMUNE AS A STEP IN MARX'S EFFORTS TO ORGANIZE LABOR ON A WORLDWIDE SCALE.

0634 COLLINS I.
"THE GOVERNMENT AND THE NEWSPAPER PRESS IN FRANCE, 1814-1881
LONDON: OXFORD U PR, 1959.
EXAMINES CONFLICTS BETWEEN GOVERNMENTAL REGULATIONS AND JOURNALISTIC FREEDOMS IN FRANCE IN 19TH CENTURY. ANALYZES CONTENT OF EACH OF THE PRESS LAWS OF PERIOD AND DISCUSSES INTENTIONS WHICH LAY BEHIND THEIR PASSAGE. BIBLIOGRAPHY OF SOURCES AND CONTEMPORARY WORKS APPENDED TO TEXT. INCLUDES UNPUBLISHED DOCUMENTS FOUND IN THE ARCHIVES NATIONALE, PUBLISHED DOCUMENTS, JOURNALS, MEMOIRS, ETC.

0635 COLLINS R.O., TIGNOR R.L.
EGYPT AND THE SUDAN.
ENGLEWOOD CLIFFS: PRENTICE HALL, 1967, 180 PP., LC#67-14846.
SHOWS THAT AMID ALL THE CHANGES THAT CENTURIES HAVE BROUGHT TO THESE LANDS, THE NILE'S FLOODING AND RECEDING HAVE CONSTANTLY REMAINED A FACTOR IN SUDANESE ECONOMIES. TRACES THE HISTORY OF THE PEOPLES OF THE NILE, RELATING PAST DEVELOPMENTS TO THE PRESENT. AUTHORS ARE CONCERNED ABOUT OVER-POPULATION IN EGYPT AND HOSTILITY BETWEEN THE NORTHERN AND SOUTHERN SUDANESE.

0636 COLUMBIA U SCHOOL OF LAW
PUBLIC INTERNATIONAL DEVELOPMENT FINANCING IN SENEGAL.
NEW YORK: COLUMBIA U PRESS, 1963, 150 PP.
STUDIES PROGRAMS AND RELATIONS OF FOREIGN INSTITUTIONS INVOLVED IN PUBLIC FINANCING OF ECONOMIC DEVELOPMENT IN SENEGAL. INCLUDES SENEGAL'S ECONOMIC AND POLITICAL STRUCTURE, INTERNAL ECONOMIC PLANNING, SURVEY OF ALL EXTERNAL ASSISTANCE RECEIVED, CASE STUDIES OF SPECIAL AID PROGRAMS. EVALUATES PROGRAMS TO DEVELOP MORE EFFICIENT MEANS OF ORGANIZING PUBLIC AID FROM FOREIGN SOURCES.

0637 COMISION DE HISTORIA
GUIA DE LOS DOCUMENTOS MICROFOTOGRAFIADOS POR LA UNIDAD MOVIL DE LA UNESCO.
INST PANAMERICANO DE GEOGRAFIA, 1963, 317 PP.
LIST OF BOOKS, DOCUMENTS, AND MATERIALS IN THE ARCHIVES OF SEVERAL LATIN AMERICAN NATIONS THAT HAVE BEEN MICROFILMED BY UNESCO.

0638 CONFERENCE ABORIGINAL STUDIES
AUSTRALIAN ABORIGINAL STUDIES.
MELBOURNE: OXFORD U PR, 1963, 505 PP.
CRITICAL ANALYSES OF RESEARCH DONE ON ABORIGINES IN SUCH AREAS AS ARCHEOLOGY, PHYSICAL ANTHROPOLOGY, LANGUAGES, ECOLOGY, ECONOMY, SOCIAL ORGANIZATION, RELIGION, ART, MUSIC, WOMEN'S ROLE, PSYCHOLOGY, POPULATION, AND CONTEMPORARY PROBLEMS AS CONTACTS WITH CIVILIZATION INCREASE.

0639 CONOVER H.F.
MADAGASCAR: A SELECTED LIST OF REFERENCES.
WASHINGTON: LIBRARY OF CONGRESS, 1942, 22 PP.
AN ANNOTATED BIBLIOGRAPHY OF 199 BOOKS, PERIODICALS, AND MONOGRAPHS ON MADAGASCAR. INDEX ACCORDING TO TOPIC: GENERAL SURVEYS, SCIENCES, ETHNOLOGY, DESCRIPTION ECONOMICS, GOVERNMENT, AND HISTORIES. SOURCES PRIMARILY IN FRENCH AND ENGLISH, ALTHOUGH SOME GERMAN ARE INCLUDED. CONTAINS BRIEF SECTION ON WORLD WAR II THROUGH 1942.

0640 CONOVER H.F. ED.
JAPAN-ECONOMIC DEVELOPMENT AND FOREIGN POLICY, A SELECTED LIST OF REFERENCES (PAMPHLET)
WASHINGTON: LIBRARY OF CONGRESS, 1940, 34 PP.
UNANNOTATED BIBLIOGRAPHY INCLUDES JAPANESE INDUSTRIAL DEVELOPMENT, FOREIGN TRADE, AND INTERNATIONAL RELATIONS. NOTES JAPANESE ECONOMIC AND MILITARY STATUS PLUS PREWAR EXPANSION POLICIES. CONTAINS 403 LISTINGS.

0641 CONOVER H.F. ED.
FRENCH COLONIES IN AFRICA: A LIST OF REFERENCES.
WASHINGTON: LIBRARY OF CONGRESS, 1942, 89 PP.
UNANNOTATED BIBLIOGRAPHY OF PERIODICALS, REFERENCES, AND OFFICIAL PUBLICATIONS CONTAINING 1265 WORKS PUBLISHED IN FRENCH, ENGLISH, AND GERMAN. CLASSIFICATION FOR FRENCH NORTH AFRICAN COLONIES IS BY SUBJECT WITH SUBDIVISIONS FOR EACH COUNTRY. FRENCH WEST AFRICA CLASSIFIED BY PROVINCES. INDEPENDENT SECTIONS FOR THE FOUR REMAINING FRENCH COLONIES. SPECIAL EMPHASIS ON LARGE BIBLIOGRAPHIES.

0642 CONOVER H.F. ED.
THE NETHERLANDS EAST INDIES: A SELECTED LIST OF REFERENCES.
WASHINGTON: LIBRARY OF CONGRESS, 1942, 46 PP.
BIBLIOGRAPHY OF 446 ITEMS ON HISTORY AND ECONOMIC GROWTH AND CULTURE OF DUTCH EAST INDIES. ARRANGED ALPHABETICALLY UNDER SUBJECT MATTER. INCLUDES WORKS IN NATURAL HISTORY, ETHNOLOGY, THE ARTS, EDUCATION AND MISSIONS, SPECIAL INDUSTRIES, WWII, AND WORLD ECONOMIC CRISES. CLASSIFIES BIBLIOGRAPHIES, PERIODICALS, HANDBOOKS, GENERAL SURVEYS, DIRECTORIES, AND TRAVEL BOOKS. ENGLISH, FRENCH, AND GERMAN.

0643 CONOVER H.F. ED.
NEW ZEALAND: A SELECTED LIST OF REFERENCES (PAMPHLET)
WASHINGTON: LIBRARY OF CONGRESS, 1942, 68 PP.
A DESCRIPTIVELY ANNOTATED BIBLIOGRAPHY OF 622 GOVERNMENT DOCUMENTS, BOOKS, PAMPHLETS, AND PERIODICALS IN ENGLISH. TOPICALLY ARRANGED INTO ELEVEN CATEGORIES: BIBLIOGRAPHIES, GENERAL SURVEYS, TRAVEL, HISTORY, WAR EFFORTS AND DEFENSE, ECONOMICS AND POLITICS, EDUCATION AND CULTURE, NATURAL HISTORY, THE MAORI, WESTERN SAMOA, AND NEW ZEALAND DEPENDENCIES.

0644 CONOVER H.F. ED.
SOVIET RUSSIA: SELECTED LIST OF REFERENCES.
WASHINGTON: LIBRARY OF CONGRESS, 1943, 85 PP.
AN UNANNOTATED BIBLIOGRAPHY OF 811 BOOKS, PAMPHLETS, AND PERIODICALS CONCERNING THE SOVIET UNION FROM THE BEGINNING OF THE THIRD FIVE-YEAR PLAN IN 1938 TO HER WAR EFFORT. (SOME EARLIER WORKS INCLUDED AS WELL.) TOPICALLY ARRANGED, AND INDEXED ACCORDING TO AUTHOR. SOURCES ARE EITHER ENGLISH OR TRANSLATIONS FROM THE RUSSIAN INTO ENGLISH.

0645 CONOVER H.F. ED.
THE GOVERNMENTS OF THE MAJOR FOREIGN POWERS: A BIBLIOGRAPHY.
WASHINGTON: LIBRARY OF CONGRESS, 1945, 45 PP.
LISTINGS OF 428 ENGLISH WORKS AS SUPPLEMENT TO TEXTBOOK ON FOREIGN GOVERNMENTS PUBLISHED BY US MILITARY ACADEMY AT WEST POINT. CLASSIFICATIONS FOLLOW CHAPTER HEADINGS OF THAT WORK. INCLUDES ASPECTS OF POLITICAL AND MILITARY ORGANIZATION OF FRANCE, GREAT BRITAIN, ITALY, GERMANY, USSR, AND JAPAN. AUTHOR INDEX. COMPILED FOR LIBRARY OF CONGRESS.

0646 CONOVER H.F. ED.
ITALY: ECONOMICS, POLITICS AND MILITARY AFFAIRS, 1940-1945.
WASHINGTON: LIBRARY OF CONGRESS, 1945, 85 PP.
AN UNANNOTATED BIBLIOGRAPHY OF 749 BOOKS, ARTICLES, AND GOVERNMENT PAMPHLETS IN ITALIAN AND ENGLISH ON ITALIAN ECONOMY, LEGISLATION, AND MILITARY PERFORMANCE DURING WAR YEARS. SOURCES INCLUDE MATERIAL ON WHOLE ECONOMIC LIFE OF ITALY DURING MUSSOLINI'S FINAL YEARS, COLLAPSE OF FASCIST STATE, AND PERIOD OF RECONSTRUCTION. BIBLIOGRAPHY DIVIDED INTO ECONOMIC ASPECTS AND POLITICAL-MILITARY ASPECTS.

0647 CONOVER H.F. ED.
THE NAZI STATE: WAR CRIMES AND WAR CRIMINALS.
WASHINGTON: LIBRARY OF CONGRESS, 1945, 131 PP.
BIBLIOGRAPHY COMPILED FOR US CHIEF OF COUNSEL FOR THE PERSECUTION OF AXIS CRIMINALITY. MAIN EMPHASIS ON GERMAN SOURCES BUT INCLUDES SOME FRENCH AND ENGLISH. BASIC CLASSIFICATIONS: THEORY OF WAR CRIMES; THE NATIONALIST-SOCIALIST STATE; WAR ATROCITIES. THE LAST PART IS SUBDIVIDED BY SUBJECT AND COUNTRY. INCLUDES 1,084 LISTINGS AND INDEX WITH SOME CROSS-REFERENCING.

0648 CONOVER H.F. ED.
INTRODUCTION TO EUROPE: A SELECTIVE GUIDE TO BACKGROUND READING.
WASHINGTON: LIBRARY OF CONGRESS, 1950, 382 PP., LC#50-62973.
ANNOTATED BIBLIOGRAPHY DESIGNED TO PROVIDE INTRODUCTORY KNOWLEDGE TO EUROPEAN HISTORY. ARRANGEMENT OF ITEMS IS SYSTEMATIC BY COUNTRY; SUBDIVIDED INTO FOUR SECTIONS DEALING WITH SURVEYS, DESCRIPTION OF SOCIAL CONDITIONS AND GEOGRAPHIES; HISTORICAL BACKGROUND; CONTEMPORARY EVENTS; AND A PERIODICALS SECTION. INCLUDES AUTHOR INDEX. COMPILED FOR LIBRARY OF CONGRESS.

0649 CONOVER H.F. ED.
NORTH AND NORTHEAST AFRICA; A SELECTED ANNOTATED LIST OF WRITINGS.
NEW YORK: NY PUBLIC LIBRARY, 1957, 182 PP., LC#57-60062.
AN ANNOTATED BIBLIOGRAPHY OF 343 BOOKS, PERIODICALS, AND PAMPHLETS REVIEWING SOCIAL, ECONOMIC, AND POLITICAL ASPECTS OF MAJOR ISSUES IN EACH COUNTRY UNDER CONSIDERATION. CONTENT ARRANGED GEOGRAPHICALLY: ALGERIA, MOROCCO, TUNISIA, SAHARA, LIBYA, SPANISH AFRICA, EGYPT, THE SUDAN, ETHIOPIA, AND THE SOMALILANDS. SOURCES IN ENGLISH, FRENCH, ITALIAN, AND SPANISH. MAIN CONCERN IS WITH CURRENT AFFAIRS.

0650 CONOVER H.F. ED.
NIGERIAN OFFICIAL PUBLICATIONS, 1869-1959: A GUIDE.
WASHINGTON: LIBRARY OF CONGRESS, 1959, 153 PP., LC#59-60079.
LISTINGS ARRANGED INVERSELY IN TIME: 1946-1959; ESTABLISHMENT OF LEGISLATIVE COUNCIL IN 1923; PART 3, 1861-1922. LISTINGS REPRESENT COMPROMISE BETWEEN HISTORICAL NOTE AND ALPHABETICAL LISTING. LIBRARY OF CONGRESS STYLE HAS PROVIDED GENERAL MODEL FOR FORM OF ENTRY. INCLUDES 1204 LISTINGS OF ENGLISH-LANGUAGE PUBLICATIONS WITH AN INDEX AND CROSS-REFERENCING.

0651 CONOVER H.F. ED.
OFFICIAL PUBLICATIONS OF FRENCH WEST AFRICA, 1946-1958.
WASHINGTON: LIBRARY OF CONGRESS, 1960, 88 PP., LC#60-60036.
SURVEY OF FRENCH WEST AFRICA ISSUED DURING TERM OF FOURTH FRENCH REPUBLIC. COVERS PUBLICATIONS OF AOF, WORKS BY INDIVIDUAL AUTHORS WORKING UNDER ITS AUSPICES, RELATED DOCUMENTS AND OFFICIAL FRENCH PAPERS. DOCUMENTS ARRANGED BY NATION. INCLUDES 508 LISTINGS WITH INDEX AND CROSS-REFERENCING. PUBLISHED IN FRENCH AND ENGLISH. COMPILED FOR LIBRARY OF CONGRESS.

0652 CONOVER H.F. ED.
OFFICIAL PUBLICATIONS OF SOMALILAND, 1941-1959: A GUIDE.
WASHINGTON: LIBRARY OF CONGRESS, 1960, 41 PP., LC#60-60050.
COLLECTION OF TITLES OF OFFICIAL DOCUMENTS OF RULING GOVERNMENTS OF SOMALILAND SINCE 1941. QUOTES "BIBLIOGRAFIA SOMALIA" AND GB COLONIAL PUBLICATIONS. ORGANIZED ACCORDING TO ITALIAN, BRITISH AND FRENCH RULE. INDEX INCLUDED WITH CROSS-REFERENCING. 169 ITEMS PUBLISHED IN FRENCH, ITALIAN, AND ENGLISH. COMPILED FOR LIBRARY OF CONGRESS.

0653 CONOVER H.F. ED.
SERIALS FOR AFRICAN STUDIES.
WASHINGTON: LIBRARY OF CONGRESS, 1961, 163 PP., LC#61-60072.
CONTAINS 2,000 TITLES FROM WORKING CARD FILE AT AFRICANA SECTION OF LIBRARY OF CONGRESS. ANNOTATIONS CONSIST LARGELY OF BIBLIOGRAPHICAL DETAIL. INCLUDES MATERIAL IN WESTERN AND AFRICAN LANGUAGES.

0654 CONOVER H.F. ED.
AFRICA SOUTH OF THE SAHARA.
WASHINGTON: LIBRARY OF CONGRESS, 1963, 354 PP., LC#63-60087.
SELECTED ANNOTATED BIBLIOGRAPHY OF 2173 ITEMS IN ENGLISH, FRENCH, PORTUGUESE, SPANISH, AND OTHER RELEVANT LANGUAGES BASED ON WORKS AVAILABLE IN LIBRARY OF CONGRESS. TOPICAL AND GEOGRAPHICAL CLASSIFICATION. INCLUDES SURVEY OF BIBLIOGRAPHIC WORK ON AFRICA. NON-CRITICAL ANNOTATIONS.

0655 CONQUEST R.
POWER AND POLICY IN THE USSR.
LONDON: MACMILLAN, 1961, 471 PP.
ANALYSIS OF HISTORICAL DEVELOPMENTS IN USSR. ATTEMPTS TO ILLUMINATE ATTITUDES, BACKGROUND, AND PRACTICES OF SOVIET POLITICAL LEADERSHIP. SEEKS TO ESTABLISH CRITERIA OF EVIDENCE AND HYPOTHESIS BASED ON OFFICIAL EVIDENCE AND ADMITTED EVENTS. STUDY OF POLICY ISSUES AS THEY AFFECT POWER STRUGGLE.

0656 CONRING E.
KIRCHE UND STAAT NACH DER LEHRE DER NIEDERLANDISCHEN CALVINISTEN IN DER ERSTEN HALFTE DES 17. JAHRHUNDERTS.
NEUKIRCHEN: NEUK VERL ERZIEHUNGS, 1965, 197 PP.
EXAMINES THEORIES OF CHURCH LAW, POSITION OF CHURCH IN RELATION TO SECULAR AUTHORITY, AND RIGHT OF RESISTANCE TO TYRANNY IN 17TH-CENTURY NETHERLANDS. DISCUSSES IN DETAIL CHURCH GOVERNMENT AND AUTHORITY IN COMMUNITY.

0657 CONZE W.
DIE DEUTSCHE NATION.
GOTTINGEN: VAN DEN HOECK UND RUP, 1963, 167 PP.
TRACES DEVELOPMENT OF NATIONAL UNITY AND CONSTITUTIONAL STATE IN GERMANY FROM MEDIEVAL BEGINNINGS TO PRESENT. FOCUSES ON RISE OF NATIONALISM AND ITS EXTREME EXPRESSION UNDER NAZI RULE TO CONTRIBUTE TO UNDERSTANDING OF "GERMAN PROBLEM."

0658 COOK R.C.
"THE WORLD'S GREAT CITIES: EVOLUTION OR DEVOLUTION?"
POPULATION BULLETIN, 16 (SEPT. 60), 109-131.
A RESEARCH REPORT PROJECTING THE PROBLEMS THAT FACE WORLD'S MAJOR URBAN CENTERS DUE TO UNPRECEDENTED POPULATION GROWTH. TRACES THE HISTORY OF CITY LIFE FROM ITS PREHISTORIC MEDITERRANEAN ORIGINS THROUGH GRECO-ROMAN CIVILIZATION, THE RENAISSANCE, INDUSTRIAL REVOLUTION, AND 19TH-CENTURY AMERICA. EMPHASIZES NECESSITY OF EMPLOYING TECHNICAL INNOVATION TO CURB PRESENT POPULATION TREND.

0659 COONDOO R.
THE DIVISION OF POWERS IN THE INDIAN CONSTITUTION.
CALCUTTA: BOOKLAND PRIVATE, 1964, 321 PP.
ATTEMPTS TO REFUTE CHARGE OF OVER-CENTRALIZATION BROUGHT AGAINST INDIAN CONSTITUTION. DEMONSTRATES THAT ISOLATION IS NOT A VIABLE POLICY IN MODERN SOCIAL AND ECONOMIC CONDITIONS. INDIAN CONSTITUTION RIGHTLY PROVIDES NO RIGID DIVISION OF POWERS, SHOWING PRACTICAL SENSE OF MAKERS OF CONSTITUTION.

0660 COOPER P.
"THE DEVELOPMENT OF THE CONCEPT OF WAR."
J. OF PHILOSOPHY, 2 (1965), 1-17.
SAMPLES OF ENGLISH AND JAPANESE SCHOOL CHILDREN ARE COMPARED FOR THE DEVELOPMENT OF IDEAS ABOUT WAR. DEVELOPMENT OF IDEAS IS DUE TO BOTH ENVIRONMENT AND MORE UNIVERSAL ELEMENTS INVOLVED IN LEARNING ROLES, STRATEGIES, AND LOGISTICS OF GAMES AND PLAY.

0661 COORDINATING COMM DOC SOC SCI
INTERNATIONAL REPERTORY OF SOCIAL SCIENCE DOCUMENTATION CENTERS (PAMPHLET)
PARIS: UNESCO, 1952, 42 PP.
COVERS CENTERS INTENDED MAINLY FOR SPECIALISTS IN VARIOUS SOCIAL SCIENCES. ARRANGED ALPHABETICALLY BY COUNTRY WITH A SECTION ON DOCUMENTATION CENTERS OF INTERNATIONAL ORGANIZATIONS. GIVES INFORMATION ON SUBJECTS COVERED, PUBLICATIONS, DIRECTORS, SERVICES, AND ORGANIZATIONS. PREPARED BY CO-ORDINATING COMMITTEE ON DOCUMENTATION IN THE SOCIAL SCIENCES.

0662 CORBETT P.E., SMITH A.A.
CANADA AND WORLD POLITICS.
LONDON: FABER/GWYER, 1928, 244 PP.
USING CANADA AS THE FOCAL POINT, ATTEMPTS TO EXAMINE THE GENERAL POLICIES AND PROBLEMS OF THE DOMINIONS. PROBES INTO PAST CONSTITUTIONS AND CONVENTIONS DEFINING AUTHORITY WITHIN AND AMONG THE DOMINIONS, AND SHOWS RELATIONSHIP WITH OTHER NATIONS AND INTERNATIONAL ORGANIZATIONS, I.E. LEAGUE OF NATIONS. PROPOSES IDEA OF 'PERSONAL UNION' AS BEST METHOD OF PRESERVING THE BRITISH EMPIRE'S CONSTITUTIONAL UNITY.

0663 CORDIER A.W. ED.
COLUMBIA ESSAYS IN INTERNATIONAL AFFAIRS.
NEW YORK: COLUMBIA U PRESS, 1967, 324 PP., LC#66-14078.
ESSAYS DEAL WITH FRENCH NUCLEAR STRATEGY, FRENCH FOREIGN POLICY, COMMUNISM IN SOUTHEAST ASIA, SPANISH SLAVE CODE OF 1789, MAU-MAU INSURGENCY, AND LOCAL GOVERNMENT IN CHINA, 1955-58.

0664 CORDIER H.
BIBLIOTECA SINICA.
PARIS: E GUILMATO.
ANNOTATED BIBLIOGRAPHY CONTINUED FROM 1800-1922 OF WORKS ON PRE-COMMUNIST CHINA. ITEMS ARRANGED TOPICALLY AND INCLUDE A MAJORITY OF WORKS IN CHINESE LANGUAGE. WORK DIVIDED INTO ITEMS ON CHINA PROPER, FOREIGNERS IN CHINA FROM ANCIENT TIMES, FOREIGN RELATIONS, CHINESE IN FOREIGN COUNTRIES, COLONIES OF CHINA. COVERS ALL CHINESE HISTORY.

0665 CORDIER H.
BIBLIOTHECA INDOSINICA: DICTIONAIRE BIBLIOGRAPHIQUE DES OUVRAGES RELATIFS A LA PENINSULE INDOCHINOISE.
PARIS: IMPRIMERIE NATIONALE, 1912.
WORK COVERS BURMA, SIAM, LAOS, FRENCH INDOCHINA, MALAYA, ETC. TO 1912.

0666 CORDONA G.D. ED.
INDICE BIBLIOGRAFICO GUATEMALTECO 1958.
GUATEMALA CITY: INST GUAT-AMER, 1959, 46 PP.
GUATEMALAN NATIONAL BIBLIOGRAPHY FOR 1958. INCLUDES PERIODICAL ARTICLES. ITEMS IN AN ALPHABETICAL, CLASSIFIED ARRANGEMENT.

0667 CORET A.
"LE STATUT DE L'ILE CHRISTMAS DE L'OCEAN INDIEN."
ANNU. FRANC. DR. INTER., 8 (62), 208-9.
EXAMINES INTERNATIONAL AGREEMENTS BETWEEN AUSTRALIA AND NEW ZEALAND CONCERNING CHRISTMAS ISLAND. STUDIES ECONOMIC RESOURCES AND POLITICAL DIRECTION OF THE ISLAND. DESCRIBES EFFORTS TO ACHIEVE UNIFIED NATIONAL GOVERNMENT.

0668 CORET A.
"L'INDEPENDANCE DU SAMOA OCCIDENTAL."
REV. JURID. POLIT. OUTREMER, 16 (JAN.-MARCH 62), 135-172.
DISCUSSES HISTORICAL AND GEOGRAPHIC FACTORS WHICH LED TO SAMOAN NATIONAL INDEPENDENCE. OUTLINES PROBLEMS ENCOUNTERED AT CONSTITUTIONAL CONVENTION IN 1954 HELD TO CREATE POLITICAL STRUCTURE. FOCUSES ON RELATION OF JUDICIAL ORGANIZATION TO INTERNATIONAL LAW.

0669 CORFO
CHILE, A SELECTED BIBLIOGRAPHY IN ENGLISH (PAMPHLET)
NEW YORK: CHILEAN DEVEL CORP, 1964, 21 PP.
ENGLISH-LANGUAGE BIBLIOGRAPHY OF BOOKS, PERIODICALS, GOVERNMENT DOCUMENTS, PAMPHLETS. FIRST PART CONSISTS OF PUBLICATIONS SINCE 1950; SECOND PART CONTAINS MATERIAL FROM 1700-1950. PUBLISHED BY THE NEW YORK OFFICE OF CORFO (CORPORACION DE FOMENTO DE LA PRODUCCION).

0670 CORNELL U DEPT ASIAN STUDIES
SOUTHEAST ASIA PROGRAM DATA PAPER.
ITHACA: CORNELL U, DEPT ASIAN ST, 1950.

A COLLECTION OF ARTICLES AND BIBLIOGRAPHIES PUBLISHED BY THE CORNELL UNIVERSITY SOUTHEAST ASIA PROGRAM. THE DATA PAPER HAS BEEN ISSUED IN PERIODICAL FORM SEVERAL TIMES EACH YEAR SINCE 1950. SEVERAL VOLUMES IN THE SERIES ARE DEVOTED TO COMPILING A CHECKLIST OF ALL AVAILABLE PUBLICATIONS ON INDIVIDUAL AREAS IN SOUTHEAST ASIA. COVERS INTERDISCIPLINARY STUDIES IN HUMANITIES AND SOCIAL AND NATURAL SCIENCES.

0671 CORNELL UNIVERSITY LIBRARY
SOUTHEAST ASIA ACCESSIONS LIST.
ITHACA: CORNELL U, DEPT ASIAN ST.
MONTHLY LISTING OF BOOKS, SERIALS, MONOGRAPHS, CONFERENCES, GOVERNMENT DOCUMENTS. ITEMS ARE ARRANGED BY COUNTRY. INCLUDES MATERIAL IN VARIOUS LANGUAGES FOR CAMBODIA, INDONESIA, MALAYSIA, PHILIPPINES, THAILAND, AND VIETNAM. GIVES FULL BIBLIOGRAPHIC INFORMATION.

0672 CORWIN A.F.
"CONTEMPORARY MEXICAN ATTITUDES TOWARD POPULATION, POVERTY, AND PUBLIC OPINION."
GAINESVILLE: U. FLORIDA PR., 1963, 54 PP.
ASKS WHY TO DATE MEXICO HAS SHOWN LITTLE OR NO PUBLIC CONCERN ABOUT MEASURES OF POPULATION CONTROL. AN EXPLORATORY STUDY MAKING EXTENSIVE USE OF QUESTIONNAIRES AND SAMPLINGS.

0673 COSER L.A.
"SOCIAL CONFLICT AND THE THEORY OF SOCIAL CHANGE."
BRIT. J. OF SOCIOLOGY, 8 (SEPT. 57), 197-205.
ATTEMPTS TO EXAMINE SOME FUNCTIONS OF SOCIAL CONFLICT IN PROCESS OF SOCIAL CHANGE. DEALS WITH FUNCTIONS OF CONFLICT WITHIN SOCIAL SYSTEMS; ITS RELATION TO INSTITUTIONAL RIGIDITIES, TECHNICAL PROGRESS, AND PRODUCTIVITY; AND RELATION BETWEEN SOCIAL CONFLICT AND CHANGES OF SOCIAL SYSTEMS.

0674 DE LA COSTA H.
THE BACKGROUND OF NATIONALISM AND OTHER ESSAYS.
MANILA: SOLIDARIDAD PUBL HOUSE, 1965, 89 PP.
ANALYZES CONCEPT OF NATIONALISM IN MODERN WORLD, AND MORE SPECIFICALLY IN ASIA AFTER WEST INVADED ITS CULTURE DURING WARS. CONCENTRATES ON RECENT CONCERN IN PHILIPPINES WITH NATIONAL IDENTITY AND ON THEIR TIES WITH ASIA. COVERS RIZAL, NATIONAL HERO OF PHILIPPINES - HIS IDEAS, HUMANISM, AND CONCEPT OF NATIONALITY.

0675 COSTA RICA UNIVERSIDAD BIBL
LISTA DE TESIS DE GRADO DE LA UNIVERSIDAD DE COSTA RICA.
SAN JOSE: CIUDAD U, 1962, 131 PP.
BIBLIOGRAPHICAL LISTING OF THESES ACCEPTED AT THE UNIVERSITY OF COSTA RICA IN 1961. EACH ITEM INCLUDES AN ABSTRACT. ENTRIES ARRANGED BY DEPARTMENT.

0676 COUGHLIN R.
DOUBLE IDENTITY: THE CHINESE AND MODERN THAILAND.
HONG KONG: U. PR., 1960, 222 PP.
FOCUSES ON CONTEMPORARY GROUP-LIFE OF THE CHINESE, THEIR COMMUNITY STRUCTURE, PRINCIPAL INSTITUTIONS AND INTERESTS. ANALYZES DEVELOPMENTS OCCURRING IN RELIGIOUS, POLITICAL AND OTHER INSTITUTIONAL ASPECTS OF OVERSEAS CHINESE LIFE.

0677 COUNCIL BRITISH NATIONAL BIB
BRITISH NATIONAL BIBLIOGRAPHY.
LONDON: COUN BRIT NATL BIBLIOG, 1950, 700 PP.
A SUBJECT LIST OF BRITISH BOOKS PUBLISHED FROM 1950-67 BASED UPON BOOKS DEPOSITED AT THE CLASSIFIED OFFICE OF THE BRITISH MUSEUM. OVER 20,000 ENTRIES IN EACH VOLUME.

0678 COUNCIL ON WORLD TENSIONS
RESTLESS NATIONS.
NEW YORK: DODD, MEAD, 1962, 217 PP., LC#62-16328.
COLLECTION OF ARTICLES STUDYING WORLD TENSIONS AND DEVELOPMENT, INCLUDING FIELDS OF POLITICS, ECONOMICS, EDUCATION, AND DEVELOPMENT POLICY.

0679 COUNT E.W. ED., BOWLES G.T.
FACT AND THEORY IN SOCIAL SCIENCE.
SYRACUSE: SYRACUSE U PRESS, 1964, 253 PP., LC#64-16921.
ESSAYS CONCERNED WITH ROLE OF FACT IN SOCIAL SCIENCES. FIRST CONCERN IS LIFE AND WORK OF DAVID HARING; SECOND, DEFINITIONS AND LIMITATIONS OF SOCIOLOGICAL THOUGHT; THIRD, THEORIES CONCERNING STRUCTURE OF SOCIETY AND SOCIAL BEHAVIOR; FOURTH, EXAMPLES REFLECTING INTERPRETATION OF FACTS.

0680 COUPLAND R.
EAST AFRICA AND ITS INVADERS.
LONDON: OXFORD U PR, 1938, 582 PP.
ETHNOLOGY AND HISTORY OF EAST AFRICA FROM ANTIQUITY TO DEATH OF SEYYID SAID IN 1856. FOCUSES ON CULTURAL, POLITICAL, ECONOMIC, AND TERRITORIAL IMPACT OF ARABIC AND EUROPEAN INVASION OF THIS REGION. SKETCHES EUROPEAN POWER POLITICS IN THE BACKGROUND. MISSIONARY ACTIVITIES AND THE SLAVE TRADE RECEIVE SOME MENTION.

0681 COUTROT A.
THE FIGHT OVER THE 1959 PRIVATE EDUCATION LAW IN FRANCE (PAMPHLET)
INDIANAPOLIS: BOBBS-MERRILL, 1966, 48 PP.
DESCRIBES EXECUTIVE AND PARLIAMENTARY HISTORY OF 1959 FRENCH LEGISLATION PROVIDING STATE AID TO CATHOLIC SCHOOLS. ILLUMINATES FRENCH GOVERNMENT POLICY PROCESS. ANALYZES SOCIAL CLEAVAGE IN FRENCH PUBLIC OPINION.

0682 COWAN L.G.
LOCAL GOVERNMENT IN WEST AFRICA.
NEW YORK: COLUMBIA U PRESS, 1958, 292 PP., LC#58-11900.
DEALS WITH BRITISH AND FRENCH ATTEMPTS TO CREATE FORMS OF REPRESENTATIVE GOVERNMENT IN WEST AFRICAN COLONIES DURING 1950'S. FOCUSES ON PROBLEMS RAISED BY IMPOSITION OF WESTERN FORMS ON COMMUNITIES WITH QUITE DIFFERENT INDIGENOUS POLITICAL STRUCTURES, AND ON CONFLICT BETWEEN TRIBAL CHIEFS AND ELECTED COUNCILS. COMPARES FRENCH AND BRITISH APPROACHES TO AFRICAN LOCAL, REGIONAL, AND NATIONAL SELF-GOVERNMENT.

0683 COWAN L.G.
THE DILEMMAS OF AFRICAN INDEPENDENCE.
NEW YORK: WALKER, 1964, 162 PP., LC#64-23053.
ANALYZES SOCIAL, ECONOMIC, AND POLITICAL PROBLEMS CONFRONTING NEW AFRICAN STATES. PRESENTS HOPES AND ASPIRATIONS OF LEADERSHIP AND PEOPLE COMBINED WITH PROFOUND DIFFICULTIES AND SERIOUS UNRESOLVED PROBLEMS. EXAMINES NATIONAL AND WORLD-WIDE IMPLICATIONS OF REVOLUTION. SECOND HALF OF BOOK IS DEVOTED TO REFERENCES SUCH AS CHARTS, MAPS, AND GRAPHS.

0684 COWAN L.G. ED., O'CONNELL J. ED., SCANLON D.G. ED.
EDUCATION AND NATION-BUILDING IN AFRICA.
NEW YORK: FREDERICK PRAEGER, 1965, 403 PP., LC#65-12193.
DISCUSSION OF EDUCATION'S INFLUENCE ON POLITICAL PARTY SYSTEM, ECONOMIC DEVELOPMENT, AND SOCIAL CHANGE. STUDIES ROLE OF UNIVERSITY IN PREPARING LEADERS, METHODS OF EDUCATION, AND COMPARISON OF COLONIAL, INDEPENDENT EDUCATION AND NATIONALISM. BIBLIOGRAPHY COVERS 15-YEAR PERIOD OF FIELD PUBLICATIONS, BOTH MAGAZINES AND BOOKS. OVER 300 ENTRIES IN FRENCH, GERMAN, AND ENGLISH.

0685 COWAN L.G.
"THE MILITARY AND AFRICAN POLITICS."
INT. J., 21 (SUMMER 66), 289-297.
CHRONICLES POLITICAL DEVELOPMENTS IN AFRICA LEADING TO RECENT MILITARY COUPS, INCLUDING BREAKDOWN OF POLITICAL PARTY SYSTEM, ANALYSIS OF MILITARY STRUCTURE, OFFICER CORPS, AND FUTURE OF POLITICAL CHANGE WHERE COUPS HAVE TAKEN PLACE.

0686 COWLES M. ED.
PERSPECTIVES IN THE EDUCATION OF DISADVANTAGED CHILDREN.
CLEVELAND: WORLD, 1967, 314 PP., LC#67-12075.
PAPERS EXPLORING BASIC CONCEPTS FROM SOCIAL SCIENCES AND MEDICINE AS THEY RELATE TO EDUCATION OF CULTURALLY DISADVANTAGED CHILDREN. TOPICS INCLUDE: EFFECTS OF POVERTY, APPLICABLE TECHNIQUES OF EDUCATION, AND CURRICULUM CONSIDERATIONS.

0687 COX H.
ECONOMIC LIBERTY.
LONDON: LONGMANS, GREEN & CO, 1920, 263 PP.
ESSAYS DEFEND FREEDOM OF INDIVIDUAL FROM ECONOMIC CONTROL BY STATE OR OTHER BODY. FREE ENTERPRISE MUST EXIST FOR SOCIETY TO RUN SMOOTHLY; WHAT FEW GOVERNMENT CONTROLS SHOULD EXIST MUST MERELY PROTECT INDIVIDUALS FROM IMPINGING UPON EACH OTHER'S LIBERTY.

0688 COX O.C.
CASTE, CLASS, AND RACE.
GARDEN CITY: DOUBLEDAY, 1948, 624 PP.
CONTENDS THAT THERE EXISTS SERIOUS MALADJUSTMENT BETWEEN TECHNOLOGICAL POTENTIALITIES OF WESTERN SOCIETY AND POSSIBILITIES OF BRINGING THEM INTO THE SERVICE OF HUMAN WELFARE. ARGUES THAT THIS MALADJUSTMENT IS AN INHERENT TRAIT OF THE SOCIAL ORDER. BELIEVES THAT SOCIETY SHOULD DEVISE A FUNCTIONAL PLAN FOR A STABLE AND SATISFACTORY WAY OF LIFE. USES HINDU SOCIETY TO EXEMPLIFY THEORY.

0689 COX R.H.
"LOCKE ON WAR AND PEACE."
LONDON: OXFORD U PR, 1960.
ARGUES THAT CONCEPT OF "STATE OF NATURE" HAS MEANING FOR CONTEMPORARY SOCIETY. DISCUSSES CONCEPTS OF SOVEREIGN COMMONWEALTH, STATE OF NATURE AND LAW OF NATURE, LOCKE AND CHRISTIAN TRADITION, LAW OF NATURE AS THE LAW OF NATIONS, AND ITS RELATION TO ECONOMY OF POWER. CONTAINS EXTENSIVE BIBLIOGRAPHY.

0690 COX R.H. ED.
THE STATE IN INTERNATIONAL RELATIONS.
SAN FRANCISCO: CHANDLER, 1965, 262 PP., LC#65-16764.
COLLECTION OF ESSAYS ON INDEPENDENCE, THEORY OF SOVEREIGNTY, WAR AND PEACE, CONSTITUTIONAL DEMOCRACY, FASCISM, AND FORMS OF GOVERNMENTS. EXAMINES EVILS OF SOVEREIGNTY AND METHOD OF INTEGRATION OF STATE INTO LARGER COMMUNITY OF STATES.

0691 CRABB C.V. JR.
THE ELEPHANTS AND THE GRASS* A STUDY OF NONALIGNMENT.

NEW YORK: FREDERICK PRAEGER, 1965, 237 PP., LC#65-15653.
COMPARISON OF VARIOUS VERSIONS OF NONALIGNMENT. ANALYSIS OF THEIR ORGINS IN COLONIALISM AND IN RESPONSE TO COLD WAR PRESSURES. STUDIES BEHAVIOR OF NONALIGNED NATIONS IN THE UN CONCERNING ARMS CONTROL AND DISARMAMENT. COMPARES COMMUNIST BLOC AND AMERICAN RELATIONS WITH THE "NEUTRALIST MOVEMENT."

0692 CRAIG A.
ABOVE ALL LIBERTIES.
LONDON: ALLEN & UNWIN, 1942, 205 PP.
TRACES HISTORY OF CENSORSHIP IN ENGLAND FROM 1700'S ENDING IN PRESENT OBSCENE LIBEL LAW. INVESTIGATES CHURCH INFLUENCE IN MORAL DETERMINATION AND ARGUES AGAINST ANY CENSORSHIP FROM STANDPOINT OF MAN'S RIGHT TO INTELLECTUAL FREEDOM AND SONAL ORAL DETERMINATION. DESCRIBES SEVERAL CASES OF GOVERNMENT CENSORSHIP IN ENGLAND, FRANCE, AND THE US. EXAMINES PROBLEM OF PORNOGRAPHY IN FREE LITERARY STATE.

0693 CRAIG A.
"ABOVE ALL LIBERTIES."
NEW YORK: W W NORTON, 1942.
CHAPTER-BY-CHAPTER BREAKDOWN OF BOOKS AND ARTICLES. THOSE LISTED COVER WIDER GROUND THAN CHAPTERS INDICATE. AUTHOR HAS NOT REPEATED ITEMS CONTAINED IN BIBLIOGRAPHY TO HIS BOOK "THE BANNED BOOKS OF ENGLAND."

0694 CRAIG G.A.
THE POLITICS OF THE PRUSSIAN ARMY 1640-1945.
LONDON: OXFORD U PR, 1955, 536 PP.
TRACES HISTORY OF PRUSSIAN ARMY AS POLITICAL AND SOCIAL FACTOR INFLUENCING PRUSSIAN GOVERNMENT 1640-1945. NOTES PARTICIPATION OF MILITARY LEADERS IN FORMATION OF INTERNAL AND FOREIGN POLICIES AND TRACES ARMY AS A STRATEGIC FACTOR IN PRUSSIAN INTERNATIONAL RELATIONS. DISCUSSES RELATIONS OF VARIOUS PRUSSIAN HEADS OF STATE WITH ARMY AND DESCRIBES ARMY INVOLVEMENT WITH HITLER BEFORE WWII.

0695 CRAIG G.A.
FROM BISMARCK TO ADENAUER: ASPECTS OF GERMAN STATECRAFT.
BALTIMORE: JOHNS HOPKINS PRESS, 1958, 156 PP., LC#58-59683.
LECTURES ON GERMAN NATIONAL POLICY FROM 2ND-4TH REICHS. VIEW HISTORY OF GERMAN DIPLOMACY AS A DESCENT FROM BISMARCK THROUGH WILHELMINE YEARS TO ARMY DOMINATION AND WWI. SEE POST-WWI PERIOD AS INDECISIVE AND HITLERIAN ERA AS PIT FROM WHICH EMERGED ADENAUER'S BURNISHED STATECRAFT. BELIEVE ISSUES OBSCURED BY SLOGANS, IDEOLOGIES, AND RESORTS TO FORCE.

0696 CRAIG J.
ELEMENTS OF POLITICAL SCIENCE (3 VOLS.)
EDINBURGH: WILLIAM BLACKWOOD, 1814, 1186 PP.
EARLY ATTEMPT AT A GENERAL OVERVIEW OF SCIENCE OF GOVERNMENT. BOOK ONE DEALS WITH THE NATURE OF GOVERNMENT: ITS RIGHTS, RIGHTS OF THE INDIVIDUAL AND OF SOCIETY, AND THE DISTRIBUTION OF POLITICAL POWER. BOOK TWO CONCERNS DUTIES OF GOVERNMENT: ADMINISTRATION OF LAW, NATIONAL DEFENSE, ECONOMIC REGULATION, PROPER DISTRIBUTION OR WEALTH. BOOK THREE DISCUSSES REVENUE AND TAXATION.

0697 CRAMER J.F., BROWNE G.S.
CONTEMPORARY EDUCATION: A COMPARATIVE STUDY OF NATIONAL SYSTEMS (2ND ED.)
NEW YORK: HARCOURT BRACE, 1965, 598 PP., LC#65-11365.
FOUR PART COMPARATIVE STUDY OF NATIONAL ATTITUDES AND PRACTICES IN EDUCATION. SKETCHES BASIC INFLUENCES AND BACKGROUND FACTORS DETERMINING CHARACTER OF NATIONAL SYSTEMS. DESCRIBES ADMINISTRATION, CONTROL, AND FINANCING IN SEVEN MAJOR NATIONS. DESCRIBES OPERATIONS OF SCHOOLS AND UNIVERSITIES. DEALS WITH SPECIAL PROBLEMS OF SYSTEMS IN INDIA, COMMUNIST CHINA, AND JAPAN.

0698 CRANKSHAW E.
THE NEW COLD WAR: MOSCOW V. PEKIN.
BALTIMORE: PENGUIN BOOKS, 1963, 167 PP.
POPULAR ACCOUNT OF SINO-SOVIET IDEOLOGICAL CONFLICT WITH ACCOUNT OF INITIAL DIFFERENCES IN THEIR REVOLUTIONS, THE MOSCOW DECLARATION OF 1957, AND THE CRITICAL WORLD COMMUNIST PARTY CONFERENCES IN 1960.

0699 CRANMER-BYNG J.L.
"THE CHINESE ATTITUDE TOWARDS EXTERNAL RELATIONS."
INT. J., 21 (WINTER 66), 57-77.
HISTORY OF CHINESE RELATIONS WITH NON-CHINESE PEOPLES SINCE 1793, EMPHASIZING PRESENT ATTITUDES AND DIFFERENCES BETWEEN CONFUCIAN AND MAOIST DOCTRINES, CONTEMPORARY FOREIGN POLICY, AND RELATIVE CHINESE INEXPERIENCE WITH ALLIANCES.

0700 CREMEANS C.
THE ARABS AND THE WORLD: NASSER'S ARAB NATIONALIST POLICY.
NEW YORK: PRAEGER, 1963, 338 PP., $6.50.
STUDIES EVOLUTION, STRENGTHS, WEAKNESSES AND IMPLICATIONS OF NASSER'S ARAB NATIONALISM. FOCUSES ON NASSER'S AMBITIONS, AMBIVALENCE AND POLICY FORMULATION IN POLITICAL, ECONOMIC, AND SOCIAL MATTERS. OFFERS SUGGESTIONS FOR AMERICAN FOREIGN POLICY FOR NEAR EAST.

0701 CRIBBET J.E.
"SOME REFLECTIONS ON THE LAW OF LAND - A VIEW FROM SCANDINAVIA."
NORTHWESTERN U. LAW REV., 62 (JULY-AUG.67), 277-313.
DISCUSSES SCANDINAVIAN LEGAL THINKING ON QUESTIONS OF LAND LAW. EXAMINES NATURE OF PROPER RELATIONSHIP BETWEEN PRIVATE VOLITION AND PUBLIC REGULATION IN A FREE SOCIETY. CLAIMS THAT MOST SCANDINAVIANS UPHOLD FREE ACCESS TO LAND AS PREREQUISITE FOR RACIAL EQUALITY.

0702 CRITTENDEN J.
"DIMENSIONS OF MODERNIZATION IN THE AMERICAN STATES."
AM. POL. SCI. REV., 61 (FALL 67), 989-1001.
NOTES DIFFERENCES IN "MODERNIZATION" AMONG CONTEMPORARY NATION-STATES, STUDYING MODERNIZATION LEVELS IN STATES OF US. USES 33 INDICATORS OF DEVELOPMENT, SUCH AS INCOME, EDUCATION, FERTILITY, LAND USE, URBANIZATION, POPULATION DENSITY, AND SCOPE OF GOVERNMENT. LOADS THE INDICATORS, USING THEM AS BASES OF STATISTICAL COMPARISONS AMONG STATES.

0703 CROAN M.
"POLYCENTRISM: COMMUNIST INTERNATIONAL RELATIONS."
SURVEY, 42 (JUNE 62), 9-19.
PRESENTS PROBLEMS CREATED BY SOVIET CONSTANT AND 'FRUITLESS' SEARCH TO RECONCILE NATIONAL AND INTERNATIONAL COMMUNIST AIMS AND BY THEIR STRUGGLE FOR COMMUNIST WORLD LEADERSHIP WITH CHINA. COMPARES COMMUNIST UNITY UNDER STRONG STALIN'S LEADERSHIP AND DISUNITY OF PRESENT PERIOD.

0704 CROCE B.
POLITICS AND MORALS.
NEW YORK: PHILOSOPHICAL LIB, 1945, 204 PP.
ADVOCATES LIBERALISTIC VIEW OF GOVERNMENT AND POLITICS GENERALLY. CLAIMS A MORAL BASIS FOR GOVERNMENT MUST EXIST, THAT IT MAY NOT BE DIFFERENT FROM INDIVIDUAL MORALITY, AND THAT THIS IS LIBERALISM. ATTACKS REALPOLITIKISTS. SUPPORTS UTILITARIANISM WHILE DENYING JUSTIFICATION OF MEANS BY ENDS. EVALUATES MACHIAVELLI, ROUSSEAU, AND HEGEL AS PHILOSOPHERS; SAYS SOCIALISM IS BASED ON HASTY GENERALIZATION.

0705 CROCKER W.R.
ON GOVERNING COLONIES: BEING AN OUTLINE OF THE REAL ISSUES AND A COMPARISON OF THE BRITISH, FRENCH, AND BELGIAN...
NEW YORK: MACMILLAN, 1947, 152 PP.
DISCUSSION OF COLONIAL POLICY IN AFRICA BASED ON PERSONAL OBSERVATIONS OF OFFICER AND SOLDIER IN BRITISH COLONIAL SERVICE. COMPARISON OF BRITISH, FRENCH, AND BELGIAN POLICIES AND PRACTICES. FAVORS COLONIAL SYSTEM.

0706 CROCKETT D.G.
"THE MP AND HIS CONSTITUENTS."
PARLIMENTARY AFFAIRS, 20 (SUMMER 67), 281-284.
SURVEYS TYPES OF COMMUNICATION, AND THEIR VOLUME, WHICH PASS BETWEEN A MEMBER OF PARLIAMENT AND HIS CONSTITUENTS. CONSIDERS CONFLICT BETWEEN DUTIES TO CONSTITUENTS AND DUTY TO NATION AS A WHOLE.

0707 CROOK W.H.
THE GENERAL STRIKE: A STUDY OF LABOR'S TRAGIC WEAPON IN THEORY AND PRACTICE.
CHAPEL HILL: U OF N CAR PR, 1931, 649 PP.
DISCUSSES GENERAL STRIKES BEFORE WWI IN BRITAIN, BELGIUM, FRANCE, SWEDEN, HOLLAND. ANALYZES THEORY OF GENERAL STRIKE FROM CHARTISM TO WWI. STUDIES PREPARATIONS FOR GENERAL STRIKES IN EUROPE AFTER WWI, NEGOTIATIONS WHICH PRECEDED THEM, AND SPECIFIC EVENTS OF BRITISH, GERMAN, AND AMERICAN STRIKES IN 1920'S.

0708 CROSS C.
THE FASCISTS IN BRITAIN.
NEW YORK: ST MARTIN'S PRESS, 1963, 214 PP., LC#63-18765.
INQUIRY INTO MOVEMENTS IN BRITAIN THAT HAVE CALLED THEMSELVES FASCIST. CONCENTRATES ON LIFE AND ROLE OF ONE OF MOST WIDELY KNOWN MEMBERS, SIR OSWALD MOSLEY, AN ENGLISH ARISTOCRAT WHO LED THE MOVEMENT THROUGH MOST OF THIS CENTURY.

0709 CROTHERS G.D.
THE GERMAN ELECTIONS OF 1907.
NEW YORK: COLUMBIA U PRESS, 1941, 277 PP.
ANALYZES POLITICAL PARTIES AND ISSUES PRIOR TO AND DURING 1907 ELECTION CAMPAIGN. PUBLIC OPINION OF PERIOD AND PROGRAMS OF PARTIES INVOLVED ARE EXAMINED THROUGH DOCUMENTS AND STUDY OF ELECTION RESULTS. STUDY INDICATES INCREASED NATIONALISM AND DESIRE FOR COLONIAL EXPANSION AS PRELUDE TO WWI.

0710 CROUZET F.
"WARS, BLOCKADE, AND ECONOMIC CHANGE IN EUROPE, 1792-1815."
J. ECON. HIST., 24(DEC. 64), 567-88.
EXAMINES THE IMPACT OF THE SUBSTITUTION OF CONTINENTAL FOR ENGLISH AND TRANSOCEANIC MARKETS AND THE EFFECT ON SUBSEQUENT CONTINENTAL ECONOMIC DEVELOPMENT. SUGGESTS WHAT, IN GENERAL, THESE SUBSTITUTIONS DURING THE NAPOLEANIC WARS

WERE OF LIMITED SIGNIFICANCE.

0711 CROWDER M.
A SHORT HISTORY OF NIGERIA (REV. ED.).
NEW YORK: FREDERICK PRAEGER, 1966, 416 PP., LC#66-13679.
TRACES HISTORY OF NIGERIA FROM FIRST EXPLORATION BY EUROPEANS THROUGH NATIONAL INDEPENDENCE. INCLUDES GEOGRAPHY, SOCIAL GROUPS OF THE REGION, NATIVE CULTURE, SLAVE TRADE, ECONOMIC DEVELOPMENT, GOVERNMENT BY BRITAIN, RISE OF NATIONALISM, INTERNAL POLITICS, AND TRADE. PAYS PARTICULAR ATTENTION TO NATIVE WARRIOR GROUPS IN EARLY PERIODS, EARLY NATIVE RULERS, AND KEY FIGURES IN INDEPENDENCE MOVEMENT.

0712 CROWE S.
THE LANDSCAPE OF POWER.
LONDON: THE ARCHITECTURAL PRESS, 1958, 115 PP.
EXAMINES THE LANDSCAPE OF THE BRITISH ISLES AND THE CHALLENGE OF GIGANTIC CONSTRUCTIONS AND POWER LINES. STUDIES NATURAL, PRACTICAL METHODS FOR THE NEW INDUSTRIAL AGE. INCLUDES POWER, NATIONAL PARKS, NUCLEAR POWER STATIONS, HYDRO-ELECTRIC POWER, ELECTRIC AND OIL TRANSMISSION, AIRFIELDS, AND NEW INDUSTRIES IN OLD AREAS. CONCLUDES THAT MAN MUST REGAIN HIS SENSE OF VALUE AND BEAUTY, THEN ACT FOR THE FUTURE.

0713 CROZIER B., MANSSELL G.
"FRANCE AND ALGERIA."
INT. AFF., 36 (JULY 60), 310-321.
EXPLORES THE HISTORIC BACKGROUND OF THE FRANCO-ALGERIAN CONFLICT. RECENT EVENTS AND ATTITUDES OF INVOLVED PARTIES, SUCH AS FRENCH ALGERIANS, MOSLEMS, FLN, AND FRENCH ARMY, ARE PRESENTED. DISCUSSES PROSPECTS OF FUTURE RELATIONSHIP BETWEEN FRANCE AND ALGERIA.

0714 CROZIER B.
"POUVOIR ET ORGANISATION."
ARCH. EUROP. SOCIOL., (NO.5, 64), 52-64.
ANALYZES CONCEPT OF POWER REALTIONS AMONG INDIVIDUALS. DISCUSSES DEVELOPMENT OF POWER RELATIONS AMONG MODERN SOCIETIES AND ORGANIZATIONS. POINTS OUT ROLE OF CONSTRAINT.

0715 CRUICKSHANK M.
CHURCH AND STATE IN ENGLISH EDUCATION 1870 TO PRESENT.
NEW YORK: ST MARTIN'S PRESS, 1963, 196 PP.
STUDIES INTERACTION OF SECULAR AND SECTARIAN EDUCATION WITH ATTEMPTS TO CONTROL BY GOVERNMENT THROUGH LEGAL AND FINANCIAL MEANS. CONSIDERS EFFECT OF STATE RELIGION ON SECULAR SCHOOLS.

0716 CRUTCHER J.
"PAN AFRICANISM: AFRICAN ODYSSEY."
CURR. HIST., 44 (JAN. 63), 1-7.
ANALYZES IN DETAIL FORCES WORKING AGAINST AFRICAN UNITY AND FORCES PULLING AFRICAN STATES TOGETHER. QUESTIONS STRENGTH OF PAN-AFRICANISM. MOST PROFOUND PROBLEM IS RELATION BETWEEN AFRICAN TRADITION AND PAN-AFRICANISM.

0717 CUCCORESE H.J.
HISTORIA DE LA CONVERSION DEL PAPEL MONEDA EN BUENOS AIRES, 1861-1867.
ARGENTINA: U NAC DE LA PLATA, 1959, 409 PP.
ATTEMPTS TO PRESENT HISTORY OF ECONOMIC ACTIONS, 1861-67, DEALING WITH MONETARY QUESTION AND CONVERSION OF PAPER MONEY. EXAMINES IMPORTANCE OF MONETARY POLICY AT THAT TIME, AND SUPPORT AND OPPOSITION TO CONVERSION.

0718 CULLINGWORTH J.B.
TOWN AND COUNTRY PLANNING IN ENGLAND AND WALES.
TORONTO: TORONTO UNIV PRESS, 1964, 301 PP.
STUDIES TOWN AND COUNTRY PLANNING, PAST PROGRAMS AND THEIR PROBLEMS; ORGANIZATION OF PRESENT SYSTEM; QUESTIONS OF CONTROLLED LAND VALUES, AMENITY, DERELICT LAND, LEISURE PLANNING; RESTRAINT OF URBAN GROWTH; DEVELOPMENT OF NEW TOWNS; URBAN RENEWAL; REGIONAL PLANNING; AND RELATIONSHIP BETWEEN PLANNERS AND PEOPLE PLANNED FOR.

0719 CULVER D.C.
METHODOLOGY OF SOCIAL SCIENCE RESEARCH: A BIBLIOGRAPHY.
BERKELEY: U OF CALIF PR, 1936, 159 PP.
A SELECTED AND ANNOTATED GUIDE TO MATERIALS ON THE TYPES OF METHODS AND TECHNIQUES WHICH HAVE BEEN USED IN RESEARCH IN THE SOCIAL SCIENCES. LIMITED TO STUDIES, RATHER THAN EXAMPLES, OF METHOD. SELECTION MADE FROM MATERIALS PUBLISHED IN ENGLISH SINCE 1920, EXCLUDING FIELDS OF PSYCHOLOGY AND EDUCATION. CONTAINS 1,509 ENTRIES ARRANGED IN A LOGICAL MANNER, ACCORDING TO ORDER OF STEPS IN A RESEARCH PROBLEM.

0720 CUMMINS L.
"THE FORMULATION OF THE "PLATT" AMENDMENT."
THE AMERICAS, 23 (APR. 67), 370-389.
STUDIES QUESTION OF AUTHORSHIP AND INTENT OF "PLATT" AMENDMENT TO DETERMINE OBJECTIVE OF US POLICY IN LATIN AMERICA. EXAMINES VARIOUS PRIMARY AND SECONDARY SOURCES AND CONCLUDES THAT "ITS SOLE PURPOSE WAS STRATEGIC."

0721 CUNNINGHAM W.
THE GROWTH OF ENGLISH INDUSTRY AND COMMERCE.
NEW YORK: CAMBRIDGE U PRESS, 1882, 492 PP.
DISCUSSES RUDIMENTARY FORMS OF COMMERCE IN ENGLISH HISTORY: PROPERTY, COLLECTIVE INDUSTRY, AND BARTER. RELATES FEUDAL INDUSTRY TO CHRISTIAN MORALITY AND PAPAL POLICY. EXAMINES EARLY FORMS OF PRIVATE ENTERPRISE AND MERCANTILE SYSTEM. DISCUSSES MERCANTILE SYSTEM AND APPRAISES DIRECTION OF FUTURE ENGLISH COMMERCE.

0722 CUNNINGHAM W.B.
COMPULSORY CONCILIATION AND COLLECTIVE BARGAINING.
MONTREAL: MCGILL U PR, 1958, 123 PP.
EVALUATES COMPULSORY CONCILIATION IN PROVINCE OF NEW BRUNSWICK AS TO WHETHER IT EMASCULATES COLLECTIVE BARGAINING BY STUDYING CASES OF GOVERNMENT INTERVENTION, 1947-1956. DISCUSSES WHETHER ILLEGALIZING WORK STOPPAGES UNTIL CONCILIATION IS REQUESTED POSES MAJOR DIFFICULTY TO BARGAINING.

0723 CURRENT HISTORY
"DE GAULLE'S FRANCE."
CURRENT HISTORY, 54 (MAR. 68), 129-192.
GIVES VIEWS OF DE GAULLE, THE FRENCH ECONOMY, AND FRENCH POSITION IN WORLD AFFAIRS. SAYS SOME CONSIDER DE GAULLE A MEGALOMANIAC DEVOTED TO POWER SEIZURE, ENGAGED IN A "EUROPE TO THE URALS" FANTASY; OTHERS BELIEVE HIM A GENUINE STATESMAN WHO USES FINE RHETORIC SIMPLY TO DEVELOP CONCEPTS TRANSCENDING COLD WAR. SAYS EEC IS FACED WITH GAULLIST RULE OR US INFLUENCE, AND HAS CHOSEN THE FORMER.

0724 CURRENT HISTORY
"AFRICA, 1968."
CURRENT HISTORY, 54 (FEB. 68), 65-128.
STUDIES MILITARY OPERATIONS IN S. AFRICA, NIGERIA, AND GHANA, ALSO POLITICAL DEVELOPMENTS IN ETHIOPIA, CONGO, E. AND S. AFRICAS. CONSIDERS S. AFRICA LAUNCHED ON ARMING, ITS POLITICAL POLICIES LIKELY TO END IN ALL-OUT RACE WAR. BELIEVES ETHIOPIA UNDER SECURE RULE AND ON WAY TO RAPID DEVELOPMENT. STUDIES CONFLICTING NATIONALISM AND SEPARATISM IN E. AFRICA AND CONGO, AND NEWLY CIVILIAN GHANA.

0725 CURRIE D.P. ED.
FEDERALISM AND THE NEW NATIONS OF AFRICA.
CHICAGO: U OF CHICAGO PRESS, 1964, 440 PP., LC#64-23421.
STUDIES AFRICAN PROBLEMS IN DIFFERENT REGIONS AND SYSTEM OF FEDERALISM IN AFRICA AS REGARDS ECONOMIC GROWTH, UNITY, AND TAXATION. RELATIONS OF INDIVIDUALS AND MINORITY GROUPS TO GOVERNMENT AND INTERNATIONAL LEGAL ASPECTS OF FEDERAL SYSTEM ARE EXAMINED IN COMPARISON WITH US AND CANADIAN FEDERALISM.

0726 CURTIN P.D.
THE IMAGE OF AFRICA: BRITISH IDEAS AND ACTION, 1780-1850.
MADISON: U. WISC. PR ., 1964, 524 PP., $8.00.
HISTORY OF ATTITUDES AND VALUES ASSOCIATED WITH AFRICA TO THE PRESENT. SPECIAL ATTENTION TO THE RISE OF PSEUDO-SCIENTIFIC RACISM, SOCIAL THEORY, IDEAS ABOUT THE METHODS OF 'CIVILIZING' AFRICANS, AND THE PERSISTENCE OF EUROPEAN VENTURES DESPITE FANTASTIC MORTALITY RATES.

0727 CURTIN P.D. ED.
AFRICA REMEMBERED.
MADISON: U OF WISCONSIN PR, 1967, 363 PP., LC#67-11060.
A COLLECTION OF PERSONAL NARRATIVES BY AFRICANS. ILLUMINATES AFRICAN VIEWS REGARDING ATLANTIC SLAVE TRADE OF 18TH AND 19TH CENTURIES IN WEST AFRICA BETWEEN SENEGAL AND NIGERIA. EACH NARRATIVE IS PRECEDED BY AN INTRODUCTION SETTING IT IN ITS APPROPRIATE TIME PERIOD AND CULTURAL MILIEU.

0728 CURTISS J.S.
THE RUSSIAN CHURCH AND THE SOVIET STATE 1917-1950.
BOSTON: LITTLE BROWN, 1953, 387 PP., LC#53-10235.
STUDIES RELATIONSHIP BETWEEN RUSSIAN ORTHODOX CHURCH AND SOVIET STATE DURING REVOLUTIONARY PERIOD OF 1917-50 AND EVENTUAL DOWNFALL OF CHURCH'S POWER IN MAKING NATIONAL POLICY DECISIONS.

0729 CVIJIC J.
THE BALKAN PENINSULA.
PARIS: COLIN (LIB ARMAND), 1918, 528 PP.
ANALYZES GEOPOLITICAL CHARACTER OF THE PENINSULA AND ITS ECOLOGICAL MAKEUP. IN FRENCH WITH MAPS.

0730 DAENIKER G.
STRATEGIE DES KLEIN STAATS.
STUTTGART: VERL HUBER FRAUENFELD, 1966, 230 PP.
DISCUSSES THE STRATEGY OF A SMALL STATE, SWITZERLAND, IN MAINTAINING ITSELF IN THE ATOMIC AGE. ARGUES FOR NUCLEAR ARMAMENT OF SWITZERLAND, MILITARY DEFENSE, AND CONTINUED POLITICAL EXISTENCE. DESCRIBES NEW DIMENSIONS OF THREAT DERIVING FROM NUCLEAR WEAPONS. QUESTIONS EXPHASIS ON CONVENTIONAL WEAPONS IN SWITZERLAND.

0731 DAHL R.A.
MODERN POLITICAL ANALYSIS.
ENGLEWOOD CLIFFS: PRENTICE HALL, 1965, 118 PP., LC#63-11092.
DISCUSSION OF BASIC CONCEPTS AND IDEAS, ANALYTICAL TOOLS OF POLITICAL STUDIES. EXAMINES POLITICS AS A FIELD OF STUDY;

SIMILARITIES AND CONTRASTS IN POLITICAL SYSTEMS; POWER AND INFLUENCE; POLITICAL CONFLICT, COERCION, AND POPULAR GOVERNMENT; POLITICAL EVALUATION, ETC.

0732 DAHL R.A. ED.
POLITICAL OPPOSITIONS IN WESTERN DEMOCRACIES.
NEW HAVEN: YALE U PR, 1966, 458 PP.
ESSAYS ON ACTIVE POLITICAL OPPOSITION IN TWO-PARTY DEMOCRATIC SYSTEMS. ANALYZES PATTERNS WITHIN COUNTRIES; DEFINES CHARACTERISTICS, GOALS, AND STRATEGIES. MAKES COMPARISIONS AMONG COUNTRIES AND SEEKS TO DETERMINE IF THERE IS A SINGLE STANDARD PATTERN OF OPPOSITION. DISCUSSES EXTENT OF CHANGES IN PATTERNS OF OPPOSITION AS RESULT OF DECLINING STRUCTURAL OPPOSITION, SOCIAL CLEAVAGES, ETC., SINCE WWII.

0733 DAHLIN E.
FRENCH AND GERMAN PUBLIC OPINION ON DECLARED WAR AIMS 1914-1918.
STANFORD: STANFORD U PRESS, 1933, 163 PP., LC#33-14010.
DISCUSSES FRENCH AND GERMAN PUBLIC ATTITUDES IN WWI ON ANNEXATIONS, PEACE, BELGIUM AND BUFFER STATES, RUSSIAN PEACE FORMULAS, WILSON'S PROPOSALS, ETC. CONCLUDES THAT PEACE WAS NOT REACHED BECAUSE OF "IMPERIALISTIC AIMS" OF BOTH GOVERNMENTS.

0734 DAHRENDORF R.
CLASS AND CLASS CONFLICT IN INDUSTRIAL SOCIETY.
STANFORD: STANFORD U PRESS, 1959, 336 PP., LC#59-7425.
PART TWO OF THIS BOOK, "TOWARD A SOCIOLOGICAL THEORY OF CONFLICT IN INDUSTRIAL SOCIETY," DEALS WITH GROUP THEORY RELEVANT TO REPRESENTATION, THE ROLE OF LATENT AND MANIFEST INTERESTS OF GROUPSAND QUASI-GROUPS, AND THE FUNCTIONS AND MEDIATION OF SOCIAL AND GROUP CONFT ARE

0735 DALAND R.T. ED.
PERSPECTIVES OF BRAZILIAN PUBLIC ADMINISTRATION (VOL. I)
LOS ANGELES: U OF S CAL, PUB ADM, 1963, 171 PP.
PAPERS WRITTEN FOR BRAZILIAN SCHOOL OF PUBLIC ADMINISTRATION. CONCERNED PRIMARILY WITH OVER-ALL VIEW OF BRAZILIAN ADMINISTRATION IN NATIONAL GOVERNMENT, FOCUSING ON THE ADMINISTRATION DEPARTMENT OF PUBLIC SERVICE, PERSONNEL SYSTEM, AND PLANNING.

0736 DALLIN A. ED., WESTIN A.F. ED.
POLITICS IN THE SOVIET UNION: 7 CASES.
NEW YORK: HARCOURT BRACE, 1966, 282 PP., LC#66-17594.
CASE STUDIES OF POLITICAL INTERACTION IN USSR: DE-STALINIZATION AND HERITAGE OF TERROR; TWENTY-SECOND PARTY CONGRESS, 1961; KHRUSHCHEV AND PARTY-STATE CONTROL; FREEDOM AND CONTROL IN LITERATURE, 1962-63; SOCIAL CONTROL THROUGH LAW; KHRUSHCHEV AND THE MILITARY.

0737 DALLIN D.J.
SOVIET FOREIGN POLICY AFTER STALIN.
PHILADELPHIA: LIPPINCOTT, 1961, 543 PP.
ANALYZES STALIN'S POSTWAR FOREIGN POLICY AND ITS CONTINUANCE BY MALENKOV AND KHRUSCHEV. TRACES SOVIET RELATIONS WITH SATELLITES, WEST, MIDDLE EAST AND FAR EAST. OUTLINES ALL SOVIET TREATIES, ALLIANCES, CONFERENCES, AND AGREEMENTS.

0738 DALTON G. ED.
TRIBAL AND PEASANT ECONOMIES.
GARDEN CITY: NATURAL HISTORY PR, 1967, 584 PP.
GENERAL TEXT OF ECONOMIC ANTHROPOLOGY. COVERS PRODUCTION, ALLOCATION, TRADE, AND MONEY AS ASPECTS OF NON-INDUSTRIAL ECONOMICS IN STATIC, TRADITIONAL ECONOMIES OF SUBSISTENCE AND MORE COMPLEX COMMUNITIES UNDERGOING ECONOMIC DEVELOPMENT. READINGS ARE ARRANGED BY GEOGRAPHICAL AREA.

0739 DANA MONTANO S.M.
"APLICACIONES CONCRETAS DE LAS RESOLUCIONES Y RECOMENDACIONES DE LAS CONFERENCIAS INTERAMERICANAS DE ABOGADOS"
J. INTER-AMER. STUDIES, 9 (JULY 67), 339-350.
DISCUSSES INTER-AMERICAN BAR ASSOCIATION RECOMMENDATIONS FOR STRENGTHENING JUDICIAL POWER IN LATIN AMERICAN NATIONS AND APPLICABILITY OF THESE MEASURES. COVERS IMPORTANCE OF INDEPENDENT JUDICIARY TO GUARANTEE JUSTICE. EXAMINES BALANCE OF POWER OF NATIONAL AND STATE GOVERNMENTS AND MEANS TO ASSURE IT, INCLUDING SPECIFIC CASE IN ARGENTINA.

0740 DANIELS R.V.
RUSSIA.
ENGLEWOOD CLIFFS: PRENTICE HALL, 1964, 152 PP., LC#64-23568.
ANALYSIS OF CZARIST RUSSIA AS NATION, THE REVOLUTION, AND EVOLUTION OF SOVIET SYSTEM IN ECONOMIC AND POLITICAL ASPECTS. EXAMINES PRESENT SOVIET SYSTEM.

0741 DANTE ALIGHIERI
DE MONARCHIA (CA .1310)
BOSTON: HOUGHTON, 1904, 216 PP.
ARGUES AGAINST PAPAL CLAIM TO CONTROL SECULAR AUTHORITY IN WESTERN EMPIRE. AUTHOR ADMITS THAT MAN HAS TWO SEPARATE ENDS, EARTHLY AND ETERNAL, AND THAT THE EMPEROR AND POPE, RECEIVING THEIR AUTHORITY FROM GOD, ARE THE GUIDES TO THESE AIMS. SECULAR LIFE EMPHASIZED. TO SECURE UNIVERSAL PEACE AND THE 'LIFE OF REASON,' AUTHOR STRESSES SUPREMACY OF A UNIVERSAL RULER WHO WOULD BE INDEPENDENT OF THE POPE AND CHURCH.

0742 DARLING M.
APPRENTICE TO POWER INDIA 1904-1908.
LONDON: HOGARTH PR, 1966, 256 PP.
OBSERVATIONS OF MEMBER OF INDIAN CIVIL SERVICE ON HINDU LIFE AND DEVELOPMENT OF ADMINISTRATIVE SERVICES. BASED LARGELY ON PERSONAL LETTERS AND A DIARY.

0743 DAVAR F.C.
IRAN AND INDIA THROUGH THE AGES.
BOMBAY: ASIA PUBL HOUSE, 1962, 312 PP.
HISTORY OF RELATIONS AND CULTURAL INTERCHANGE BETWEEN TWO NATIONS FROM PREHISTORIC MIGRATIONS TO PRESENT DAY. AUTHOR HOPES KNOWLEDGE OF CULTURAL AFFINITIES WILL PRODUCE MORE FRIENDLY POLITICAL RELATIONS.

0744 DAVIDSON B. ED.
THE NEW WEST AFRICA: PROBLEMS OF INDEPENDENCE.
LONDON: ALLEN & UNWIN, 1953.
ANALYSIS OF BRITISH WEST AFRICA IN REGARD TO INDEPENDENCE IN MODERN TIMES. DIFFERENT AUTHORS EXPLAIN IMPORTANCE OF AREA IN WORLD AFFAIRS, ITS BACKGROUND, DEVELOPMENT OF SELF-GOVERNMENT, ECONOMIC PROBLEMS, AFRICAN TECHNICAL PROGRESS, AND IMPORTANCE OF BRITISH RESPONSIBILITY IN AREA.

0745 DAVIDSON E.
THE TRIAL OF THE GERMANS* NUREMBERG* 1946-48.
NEW YORK: MACMILLAN, 1967, 636 PP.
PRESENTS CONNECTED SERIES OF BIOGRAPHIES OF THE 22 MAJOR NAZI RULERS AND WAR CRIMINALS WHO WERE TRIED IN NUREMBERG. EXAMINES THEIR SOCIOLOGICAL BACKGROUNDS, EDUCATION, PSYCHOLOGICAL MAKE-UP, AND VARIOUS FACTORS WHY EACH OF THEM COLLABORATED WITH HITLER.

0746 DAVIE M.R.
THE EVOLUTION OF WAR.
NEW HAVEN: YALE U. PR., 1929, 391 PP., $4.00.
ACCOUNT OF THE CONDITION OF WARFARE AMONG PRIMITIVE AND SAVAGE PEOPLES, INCLUDING PART PLAYED BY CANNIBALISM, HUMAN SACRIFICE, HEAD HUNTING, BLOOD REVENGE, WOMEN, BOOTY, RELIGION AND SEX.

0747 DAVIES E.
"NATIONAL" CAPITALISM: THE GOVERNMENT'S RECORD AS PROTECTOR OF PRIVATE MONOPOLY.
LONDON: VICTOR GOLLANCZ, 1938, 320 PP.
STUDIES GOVERNMENT CONTROL OF PRIVATE ENTERPRISE IN ENGLAND. STATES THAT CLASS THAT HAS CONTROLLED GOVERNMENT SINCE 1931 HAS IDENTIFIED ITS OWN INTEREST WITH NATION'S, THUS STRENGTHENING CAPITALIST STRUCTURE AND UTILIZING STATE RESOURCES FOR THE PROPERTIED CLASSES. FEELS COMMUNITY HAS THEREBY SUFFERED. HOPES TO RID ENGLAND OF CHAMBERLAIN GOVERNMENT AND INSTALL LABOUR PARTY.

0748 DAVIES E.
NATIONAL ENTERPRISE: THE DEVELOPMENT OF THE PUBLIC CORPORATION.
LONDON: VICTOR GOLLANCZ, 1946, 173 PP.
DISCUSSES ISSUES OF NATIONALIZATION OF BRITISH INDUSTRY, AND PROBLEMS THAT HAVE ARISEN IN REGARD TO ADMINISTRATION. ANALYZES THESE PROBLEMS IN RELATION TO PUBLIC CORPORATIONS ALREADY OPERATING, AND THOSE IN COURSE OF ESTABLISHMENT. ATTEMPTS TO DETERMINE GENERAL PRINCIPLES THAT CAN BE APPLIED TO NATIONAL ENTERPRISE TO ENSURE CONTINUED SUCCESS AND PUBLIC APPRECIATION OF ITS BENEFITS.

0749 DE ARAGAO J.G.
LA JURIDICTION ADMINISTRATIVE AU BRESIL.
RIO DE JAN: DEP DE IMPR NACIONAL, 1955, 255 PP.
REVIEWS DUAL ADMINISTRATIVE JURISDICTION, 1824-89, AND SUBSEQUENT UNITY OF JURISDICTION, 1889-PRESENT. DUALITY WAS DUE TO FACT THAT "CONSEIL D'ETAT" HAD DE JURE AUTHORITY, BUT WAS A CONSULTATIVE BODY, WITH REAL AUTHORITY EXERCISED BY OTHERS. IN 1889, REVOLUTION ESTABLISHED REPUBLICAN FEDERATIVE GOVERNMENT WITH CLEAR DIVISION OF AUTHORITY.

0750 DE CENIVAL P., FUNCK-BRETANO C., BOUSSER M.
BIBLIOGRAPHIE MAROCAINE: 1923-1933.
PARIS: LIBRAIRIE LA ROSE, 1934, 607 PP.
COLLECTS AND ARRANGES BIBLIOGRAPHIES DEALING WITH MOROCCO WHICH APPEARED IN THE REVIEW "HESPERIS" BETWEEN 1923 AND 1933. INCLUDES BOOKS, ARTICLES, AND PAMPHLETS PUBLISHED IN WESTERN LANGUAGES. ORGANIZED TOPICALLY; INCLUDES ANTHROPOLOGY, ARCHEOLOGY, LANGUAGE, BIBLIOGRAPHY, CARTOGRAPHY, SCIENCE, ARTS, HISTORY, ETC.

0751 DE GAULLE C.
"FRENCH WORLD VIEW."
UNITED ASIA, 16 (MAR.-APR. 64), 107-11.
PROCLAIMS FRENCH CONTRIBUTION TO SHRINKING WORLD, MUTUAL BENEFITS OF AID TO DECOLONIZED REGIONS, REASONS FOR ESTABLISHING DIPLOMATIC RELATION WITH CHINA.

0752 DE GRAZIA A.
COMPARATIVE SURVEY OF EUROPEAN-AMERICAN POLITICAL BEHAVIOR;

A RESEARCH PROSPECTUS.
AVAILABLE THRU URS: UNPUBLISHED, 1954.
PRESENTATION OF PLAN FOR EXPLORATION AND DEVELOPMENT FOR A COMPARATIVE SCIENCE OF POLITICAL BEHAVIOR. SEPARATE BIBLIOGRAPHIC SECTION LISTS 501 TITLES FROM THE SOCIAL SCIENCES CONTRIBUTING TO POLITICAL BEHAVIOR RESEARCH. INCLUDES JOURNAL ARTICLES AND BOOKS IN ENGLISH, FRENCH, GERMAN, SPANISH, AND ITALIAN PUBLISHED 1905 THROUGH 1953. SOURCES CLASSIFIED BY SUBJECT.

0753 DE GRE G.
"FREEDOM AND SOCIAL STRUCTURE" (BMR)"
AMER. SOCIOLOGICAL REV., 11 (OCT. 46), 529-536.
DISCUSSES PROBLEM OF FREEDOM, EXAMINING ITS NATURE, AND CONSIDERING FORMS OF SOCIAL STRUCTURE WHICH ARE CONDUCIVE TO IT. DEFINES FREEDOM IN TERMS OF PROBABILITY THAT GROUPS OR INDIVIDUALS CAN FORMULATE THEIR ENDS OF CONDUCT AND INITIATE A COURSE OF ACTION WITH MINIMUM CONSTRAINT.

0754 DE HERRERA C.D. ED.
LISTA BIBLIOGRAFICA DE LOS TRABAJOS DE GRADUACION Y TESIS PRESENTADOS EN LA UNIVERSIDAD, 1939-1960.
PANAMA CITY: U OF PANAMA, 1960, 186 PP.
COMPILATION OF THESES PRESENTED AT THE UNIVERSITY OF PANAMA. ENTRIES ARRANGED BY FACULTY AND THE SCHOOLS WITHIN EACH.

0755 DE JOMINI A.H.
THE ART OF WAR.
PHILADELPHIA: LIPPINCOTT, 1862, 410 PP.
STUDIES DEFENSE POLICY, MILITARY STRATEGY AND TACTICS FOR DIFFERENT KINDS OF WAR, SUCH AS 'WARS OF EXPEDIENCY' AND 'WARS OF INTERVENTION.' MAKES FREQUENT REFERENCE TO NAPOLEON. INCLUDES BOTH PHILOSOPHY AND DISCUSSION OF TACTICS.

0756 DE JONG L.
THE GERMAN FIFTH COLUMN IN THE SECOND WORLD WAR.
CHICAGO: U OF CHICAGO PRESS, 1956, 308 PP., LC#55-05120.
EXPOSES HITLER'S ALLEGED WORLD-WIDE FIFTH COLUMN AS GREATLY EXAGGERATED MYTH CREATED BY RUMOR AND FEAR. GERMAN AGENTS WORKED IN FEWER COUNTRIES THAN WAS BELIEVED AND EFFECTIVELY IN ONLY TWO.

0757 DE JOUVENEL B.
ON POWER: ITS NATURE AND THE HISTORY OF ITS GROWTH.
NEW YORK: VIKING PRESS, 1949, 421 PP.
PLEA FOR A REPEATED STOCKTAKING EVERY TIME THERE IS A PROPOSAL TO EXTEND THE POWER OF THE STATE OR ANY OTHER POWER-MONOPOLIZING BODY. NOTES THAT AS POWER OF STATE INCREASES, SO DOES POWER TO DO DEADLY HARM. BELIEVES THAT POWER RETAINS ITS ESSENTIAL NATURE DESPITE CHANGES IN FORMS OF EXPRESSION. ALL CLAIMS TO POLITICAL INFALLIBILITY MUST BE CHECKED. THE "PEOPLE" ARE NOT ALWAYS RIGHT.

0758 DE JOUVENEL B.
THE PURE THEORY OF POLITICS.
NEW HAVEN: YALE U PR, 1963, LC#64-24053.
ATTEMPTS TO FORMULATE NON-NORMATIVE FRAMEWORK FOR CONSIDERATION OF POLITICS. POINTS UP NECESSITY FOR FRAMEWORK IN WHICH TO STRUCTURE OBSERVATIONS. ANALYZES POLITICS FROM VIEWPOINT OF INTERPERSONAL RELATIONSHIPS, IN AN ATTEMPT TO REDUCE POLITICS TO ITS MOST BASIC PARTS. WARNING THAT ANY FORM OF POLITICAL ACTION IS DANGEROUS, SEEKS TO FIND WAY OF STRUCTURING KNOWLEDGE WITHOUT MANIPULATING IT.

0759 DE KIEWIET C.W.
THE IMPERIAL FACTOR IN SOUTH AFRICA.
NEW YORK: CAMBRIDGE U PRESS, 1937, 341 PP.
STUDY OF COLONIAL HISTORY OF SOUTH AFRICA DURING 19TH CENTURY. DISCUSSES FAILURE OF BRITISH IMPERIAL POLICY AS WELL AS GENERAL CULTURAL PROBLEMS WHICH AROSE FROM CONTACT BETWEEN NATIVES AND WHITES.

0760 DE MADARIAGA S.
L'AMERIQUE LATINE ENTRE L'OURS ET L'AIGLE.
PARIS: STOCK, 1962, 225 PP.
DESCRIBES POLITICAL EVOLUTION IN LATIN AND SOUTH AMERICA, AND ANALYZES ECONOMIC AND SOCIAL PROBLEMS, FOREIGN INFLUENCES, AND AREA'S REACTION TO COLD WAR.

0761 DE MAISTRE J.
DU PAPE (1817)
ORIGINAL PUBLISHER NOT AVAILABLE, 1817, 452 PP.
CONDEMNS FRENCH REVOLUTION FOR HAVING MADE THE CATHOLIC CHURCH ITS ENEMY. MAINTAINS THAT CHRISTIAN RELIGION RESTS ON AUTHORITY OF POPE AND GOVERNMENT ON AUTHORITY OF RELIGION. DEMANS RETURN TO RECOGNITION OF CHURCH AUTHORITY. DISCUSSES PAPACY IN RELATION TO CHURCH, TEMPORAL RULERS, CIVILIZATION AND HAPPINESS OF PEOPLE, AND CHURCHES WHICH HAVE SEPARATED FROM CATHOLIC CHURCH.

0762 DE MAN H.
THE REMAKING OF A MIND.
NEW YORK: CHAS SCRIBNER'S SONS, 1919, 289 PP.
AUTHOR TRACES THE PSYCHOLOGICAL EFFECTS THAT PARTICIPATION IN WORLD WAR I HAD ON HIM. HE NOTES THAT BEFORE THE WAR HE HAD A FEELING OF IDENTITY AS A EUROPEAN SO THAT FOR HIM THE WAR WAS A CIVIL ONE. HE CAME OUT OF THE WAR FEELING THAT EUROPE MUST UNITE AS AN INTEGRATED ECONOMIC UNIT. THIS MAY BE ACHIEVED, HE SAYS, THROUGH SOCIALISM.

0763 DE NOIA J.
GUIDE TO OFFICIAL PUBLICATIONS OF OTHER AMERICAN REPUBLICS: ECUADOR (VOL. IX)
WASHINGTON: LIBRARY OF CONGRESS, 1947, 56 PP.
CHECKLIST AND ANNOTATED BIBLIOGRAPHY OF OFFICIAL STATE PUBLICATIONS ISSUED BY THE REPUBLIC OF ECUADOR SINCE 1822. INDEXED BY TITLE AND ARRANGED BY AGENCY OR DEPARTMENT OF PUBLICATION. PROVIDES A CHECKLIST FOR ALL HOLDINGS LISTED IN THE LIBRARY OF CONGRESS CATALOG. PROJECT SPONSORED BY THE STATE DEPARTMENT WITH THE COOPERATION OF THE DIRECTOR OF THE HISPANIC FOUNDATION.

0764 DE NOIA J., CHILDS J.B., MCGEORGE H.
GUIDE TO OFFICIAL PUBLICATIONS OF THE OTHER AMERICAN REPUBLICS: EL SALVADOR.
WASHINGTON: LIBRARY OF CONGRESS, 1947, 64 PP.
ANNOTATED BIBLIOGRAPHY AND GUIDE TO GOVERNMENT PUBLICATIONS IN EL SALVADOR; ARRANGED BY AGENCY OR DEPARTMENT OF ORIGIN AND INDEXED ALPHABETICALLY BY TITLE. ALSO INCLUDES PREFATORY NOTE AND AN INTRODUCTION EXPLAINING GENERAL FACETS OF STATE STRUCTURE TO FACILITATE THE USE OF GUIDE. COMPILED FOR LIBRARY OF CONGRESS.

0765 DE NOIA J.
GUIDE TO OFFICIAL PUBLICATIONS OF THE OTHER AMERICAN REPUBLICS: NICARAGUA (VOL. XIV)
WASHINGTON: LIBRARY OF CONGRESS, 1947, 33 PP.
ANNOTATED AND INDEXED BIBLIOGRAPHY AND GUIDE TO THE HOLDINGS IN THE LIBRARY OF CONGRESS OF SERIES, SERIALS, MONOGRAPHS, AND OTHER STATE PUBLICATIONS ISSUED BY NICARAGUAN REPUBLIC. ARRANGED BY DEPARTMENT OR AGENCY OF ISSUANCE. INCLUDES GENERAL PUBLICATIONS AND OFFICIAL GAZETTES. LISTS ALL MATERIAL SINCE 1821.

0766 DE NOIA J.
GUIDE TO OFFICIAL PUBLICATIONS OF THE OTHER AMERICAN REPUBLICS: PANAMA (VOL. XV)
WASHINGTON: LIBRARY OF CONGRESS, 1947, 34 PP.
INDEXED AND ANNOTATED BIBLIOGRAPHY AND GUIDE TO OFFICIAL GOVERNMENT PUBLICATIONS AND DOCUMENTS OF PANAMA ARRANGED BY AGENCY OR DEPARTMENT OF ISSUANCE. PART OF A LIBRARY OF CONGRESS PROJECT BEGUN IN 1941 UNDER THE AEGIS OF THE STATE DEPARTMENT'S INTERDEPARTMENTAL COMMITTEE ON SCIENTIFIC AND CULTURAL COOPERATION. INCLUDES SERIALS, SERIES, AND MONOGRAPHS PUBLISHED SINCE 1903.

0767 DE NOIA J.
GUIDE TO OFFICIAL PUBLICATIONS OF OTHER AMERICAN REPUBLICS: PERU (VOL. XVII)
WASHINGTON: LIBRARY OF CONGRESS, 1948, 90 PP.
ANNOTATED CHECKLIST OF ALL OFFICIAL STATE PUBLICATIONS ISSUED SINCE INDEPENDENCE IN 1826 BY THE PERUVIAN GOVERNMENT AND AVAILABLE IN THE LIBRARY OF CONGRESS. PART OF STATE DEPARTMENT PROJECT. INCLUDES A SUBJECT-TITLE INDEX. DOCUMENTS ARE ARRANGED UNDER THE DEPARTMENT OR AGENCY OF ISSUANCE.

0768 DE REPARAZ G.
GEOGRAFIA Y POLITICA.
BARCELONA: EDITORIAL MENTORA, 1929, 277 PP.
TWENTY-FIVE LESSONS OF NATURAL HISTORY, INCLUDING POLITICS AS A PRODUCT OF GEOGRAPHY, GEOGRA AND RUSSIAN REVOLUTION, GEOGRAPHIC ANALYSIS OF IBERIAN PENINSULA, GEOGRAPHY IN HISTRY OF CHILE.

0769 DE SMITH S.A.
"CONSTITUTIONAL MONARCHY IN BURGANDA."
POLIT. QUART., 26 (JAN.-MAR. 55), 4-17.
SURVEYS POLITICAL SITUATION IN BURGANDA. PRESENTS HISTORY OF THE POLITICAL RELATIONS, THE VARIOUS REFORMS MADE, AND THE 1954 AGREEMENTS FOR INDEPENDENCE. INCLUDES DETAILED ANALYSIS OF THE DISCUSSIONS OF THE PROTECTORATE GOVERNMENT AND THE KINGDOM OF BURGANDA. CONCLUDES WITH COMMENTS ON THE PROBLEMS AND CHALLENGES OF POLITICAL INTEGRATION.

0770 DE SMITH S.A.
THE NEW COMMONWEALTH AND ITS CONSTITUTIONS.
LONDON: STEVENS, 1964, 312 PP.
SURVEYS GENERAL DEVELOPMENTS OF NEWLY SELF-GOVERNING COMMONWEALTH COUNTRIES, CONCENTRATING ON THOSE WHICH HAVE ACQUIRED NEW CONSTITUTIONS SINCE 1957. OUTLINES CONSTITUTIONAL STRUCTURE OF COMMONWEALTH ASSOCIATION AND TRANSITION OF NEW NATIONS TO SELF-GOVERNMENT. TREATS SAFEGUARDS AGAINST ABUSE OF MAJORITY POWER, BILLS OF RIGHTS AND PRESIDENTIAL REGIMES.

0771 DE SPINOZA B.
TRACTATUS THEOLOGICO-POLITICUS (TRANS. BY R. WILLIS)
ORIGINAL PUBLISHER NOT AVAILABLE, 1868, 359 PP.
FIRST INQUIRY INTO HISTORY, NATURE, AND AUTHENTICITY OF HEBREW SCRIPTURES. WARNS OF NECESSITY OF DISTINGUISHING BE-

TWEEN THEIR LETTER AND SPIRIT. ASSERTS SUPREMACY OF CIVIL POWER OVER ECCLESIASTICAL AUTHORITY. BELIEVES FREEDOM OF THOUGHT AND DISCUSSION CAN BE GRANTED WITHOUT DANGER TO CHURCH AND THAT THEIR DENIAL ENDANGERS PUBLIC PEACE AND TRUE PIETY.

0772 DE TOCQUEVILLE A.
DEMOCRACY IN AMERICA (4 VOLS.) (TRANS. BY HENRY REEVE)
LONDON: SAUNDERS & OTTEY, 1835, 1493 PP.
DEPICTS INFLUENCE OF DEMOCRATIC EQUALITY ON AMERICAN GOVERNMENT. STUDIES ORIGINS AND SOCIAL CONDITIONS OF AMERICA. EXAMINES CONSTITUTION, STATE AND LOCAL GOVERNMENT, JUDICIAL POWER, POLITICAL PARTIES, FREEDOMS. DISCUSSES EFFECT OF EQUALITY ON SOCIAL STRUCTURE AND METHODS USED TO MAINTAIN EQUALITY. PRESENTS IMPACT OF DEMOCRACY ON OPINIONS, FEELINGS, AND MANNERS OF AMERICANS.

0773 DE TOCQUEVILLE A
DEMOCRACY IN AMERICA (1834-1840) (2 VOLS. IN I; TRANS. BY G. LAWRENCE)
NEW YORK: HARPER & ROW, 1966, 784 PP.
DETAILED EXAMINATION OF AMERICA IN 1800'S BY FRENCH DEMOCRAT. DISCUSSES GOVERNMENT, CULTURE, AND LAW IN AMERICAN SOCIETY, WHICH IS VIEWED AS A PORTENT OF THE FUTURE. CONSIDERS SOCIAL EQUALITY TO BE MOST OVERWHELMING FEATURE OF AMERICAN SOCIETY, AND RELATES THIS TO SYSTEM OF GOVERNMENT, TRACING ITS ROOTS IN HISTORY AND SPECIAL ENVIRONMENTAL CONDITIONS OF US. COMPARES US FAVORABLY WITH FRANCE.

0774 DE VATTEL E.
THE LAW OF NATIONS.
ORIGINAL PUBLISHER NOT AVAILABLE, 1796, 563 PP.
LAW OF NATIONS IS A SCIENCE, "CONSISTING IN A JUST AND RATIONAL APPLICATION OF THE LAW OF NATURE" TO THE AFFAIRS OF MAN AND PRINCES. STUDY BASED ON CHRISTIAN WOLFF'S WORK ON SAME SUBJECT. DISAGREES WITH WOLFF THAT ESTABLISHMENT OF LAW IS VOLUNTARY. BELIEVES MEN RESORT TO LAW ONLY TO PROTECT THEMSELVES AGAINST "DEPRAVITY OF THE MULTITUDE." THERE ARE VOLUNTARY LAWS, BUT NECESSARY ONES COME FROM LAW OF NATURE.

0775 DE VICTORIA F., SCOTT G.B. ED.
DE INDIS ET DE JURE BELLI (1557) IN F. DE VICTORIA, DE INDIS ET DE JURE BELLI REFLECTIONES.
WASHINGTON: CARNEGIE ENDOWMENT, 1917, 475 PP.
WORK BY SPANISH THEOLOGIAN CONSISTS OF LECTURES ON THE RIGHTS OF THE INDIANS AND THE RIGHTS OF WAR. BELIEVES THAT CHRISTIANS MAY SERVE IN AND MAKE WAR. A WRONG COMMITTED IS THE ONLY JUST REASON FOR MAKING WAR. DISCUSSES PUNISHMENT OF WRONG-DOER. SUBJECTS DO NOT HAVE TO PARTICIPATE IF THEY BELIEVE WAR UNJUST. DISCUSSES LAWFULNESS OF KILLING, SEIZURE, ETC. RIGHTS OF INDIANS CONCERN RIGHTS TO PROPERTY.

0776 DE VORE B.B.
LAND AND LIBERTY; A HISTORY OF THE MEXICAN REVOLUTION.
NEW YORK: PAGEANT PR, 1966, 344 PP.
HISTORY OF MEXICAN REVOLUTION. DISCUSSES DICTATORSHIP OF PORFIRIO DIAZ, ORGANIZATION OF INTELLECTUALS INTO LIBERAL PARTY, FLORES MAGON'S MAGONISMO PARTY, FRANCISCO MADERO'S LEADERSHIP OF REVOLT, CONTROL OF GOVERNMENT BY HUERTA, CARRANZA, OBREGON, CALLES, CARDENAS, ETC. MAINTAINS THAT REVOLUTION DID MUCH TO DEVELOP STABILITY OF PRESENT MEXICAN DEMOCRATIC GOVERNMENT.

0777 DE VRIES E. ED., ECHAVARRIA J.M. ED.
SOCIAL ASPECTS OF ECONOMIC DEVELOPMENT IN LATIN AMERICA.
PARIS: UNESCO, 1963, 401 PP., $5.00.
A COLLECTION OF PAPERS SUBMITTED TO EXPERT WORKING GROUP ON SOCIAL ASPECTS OF ECONOMIC DEVELOPMENT IN LATIN AMERICA IN DECEMBER 1960. VARIOUS SPECIALISTS IN ECONOMICS, SOCIOLOGY, POLITICAL SCIENCE, SOCIAL PSYCHOLOGY, AND PUBLIC ADMINISTRATION OFFER A MORE BALANCED VIEW OF ECONOMIC DEVELOPMENT PROBLEMS IN LATIN AMERICA.

0778 DEAN V.M.
THE NATURE OF THE NON-WESTERN WORLD.
NEW YORK: MENTOR, 1957, 284 PP.
COMPARES THE WEST AND THE NON-WEST (AFRICA, ASIA, THE MIDDLE EAST, USSR, THE FAR EAST, AND LATIN AMERICA) IN THEIR HISTORICAL DEVELOPMENTS AND PRESENT-DAY CONDITIONS, CONCLUDING THAT THE BASIC DIFFERENCES ARISE FROM THE WEST'S EARLIER TECHNOLOGICAL DEVELOPMENT. SUGGESTS DIFFERENCES ARE DECREASING DUE TO CURRENT NON-WESTERN TECHNOLOGICAL PROGRESS AND THAT WEST SHOULD ASSIST IN THIS PROGRESS.

0779 DEBRAY P., SABRAN B.
LE PORTUGAL ENTRE DEUX REVOLUTIONS.
PARIS: AU FIL D'ARIANE, 1963, 112 PP.
ANALYSIS AND EVOLUTION OF THE PORTUGUESE GOVERNMENTAL AND POLITICAL PROCESS; DECISION-MAKING IN PORTUGUESE POLITICS AND ROLE OF THE PRIME MINISTER.

0780 DEBUYST F.
LAS CLASES SOCIALES EN AMERICA LATINA.
MADRID: OFIC INVESTIG SOC FRERES, 1962, 217 PP.
EXAMINES PRESENT SOCIAL STRUCTURE OF COUNTRIES OF LATIN AMERICA. ANALYZES SOCIAL MOBILITY, ECONOMIC POWER, ETHNIC COMPOSITION, INCOME, AND EDUCATIONAL OPPORTUNITIES. COMPARES AND GROUPS COUNTRIES ACCORDING TO CHANCES FOR SOCIAL MOBILITY AND WORK.

0781 DECOTTIGNIES R., DE BIEVILLE M.
LES NATIONALITES AFRICAINES.
PARIS: EDITIONS A PEDONE, 1963, 419 PP.
CONCERNS LAW IN AFRICAN STATES WHICH WERE FORMER FRENCH COLONIES. ATTEMPTS TO DISTINGUISH COMMON MANIFESTATIONS OF LAW IN STATES. STUDIES SPECIFIC LAW IN 14 STATES AND REPRODUCES ACTUAL CODES.

0782 DEGLER C.N.
THE AGE OF THE ECONOMIC REVOLUTION 1876-1900.
CHICAGO: SCOTT, FORESMAN & CO, 1967, 213 PP., LC#67-14492.
STUDIES FACTORS LEADING TO INDUSTRIALIZATION IN US, RESULTING TRANSFORMATION IN AMERICAN SOCIETY, ADVENT OF FACTORIES, AND GROWTH OF LARGE CITIES. DISCUSSES CONCOMITANT POLITICAL REFORMATION AND AGRICULTURAL REVOLUTION, SECULARIZATION OF RELIGION, ANTITRUST MOVEMENT, INFLUENCE OF DARWINISM, AND POLITICAL PARTY CAMPAIGNS AND ISSUES. COMPARES US TO EUROPEAN COUNTRIES.

0783 DEHIO L.
GERMANY AND WORLD POLITICS IN THE TWENTIETH CENTURY.
NEW YORK: ALFRED KNOPF, 1959, 142 PP.
GERMAN HISTORIAN ANALYZES PART PLAYED BY GERMANY IN POLITICS OF 1900-1950 AND SUGGESTS IDEAS OF GERMANS ABOUT WHAT THAT PART SHOULD BE. RELATES RANKE AND BISMARCK TO RISE OF GERMAN IMPERIALISM AND CONSIDERS IMPACT OF THIS ON TWO WORLD WARS. CONSIDERS VERSAILLES 35 YEARS AFTER RATIFICATION AND THEORIZES ON THE PASSING OF THE EUROPEAN SYSTEM AS CENTER OF WORLD POWER.

0784 DEHIO L.
THE PRECARIOUS BALANCE: FOUR CENTURIES OF THE EUROPEAN POWER STRUGGLE.
NEW YORK: ALFRED KNOPF, 1962, 295 PP.
DISCUSSES EUROPEAN SYSTEM OF STATES FROM MIDDLE AGES TO PRESENT. EXAMINES THREATS TO UNITY PRESENTED BY SPANISH, FRENCH, AND GERMAN "BIDS FOR SUPREMACY."

0785 DEKAT A.D.A.
COLONIAL POLICY.
CHICAGO: U. CHI. PR., 1931, 674 PP.
ANALYZES HOW DUTCH AUTHORITY, BY CONTROLLING EAST INDIA COMPANY, EXPANDED IN JAVA AND SURROUNDING ISLANDS. EVALUATES DUTCH COLONIAL POLICY, REGARDING ADMINISTRATION, EDUCATION, TAXATION, AND WAYS IN WHICH IT AFFECTED CONSTRUCTION OF THE SOCIETY.

0786 DEL TORO J.
A BIBLIOGRAPHY OF THE COLLECTIVE BIOGRAPHY OF SPANISH AMERICA.
SAN JUAN: U OF PUERTO RICO, 1938, 140 PP.
AN ANNOTATED BIBLIOGRAPHY ON THE COLLECTIVE BIOGRAPHY OF SPANISH AMERICA. MATERIAL IN SPANISH-LANGUAGE AND SOME ENGLISH. PUBLICATION OF MATERIAL RANGES FROM 1777 TO 1935. HAS 488 ENTRIES.

0787 DEL VAYO J.A.
CHINA TRIUMPHS.
NEW YORK: MONTHLY REVIEW PR, 1964, 202 PP., LC#64-23144.
JOURNALISTIC ACCOUNT OF SOCIAL AND ECONOMIC PROGRESS IN CHINA SINCE 1949. DISCUSSION OF HEALTH AND EDUCATION PROGRAMS, CULTURAL LIFE, FOREIGN POLICY, AND THE PEOPLE'S COMMUNES. ARGUES THAT CHINA IS WINNING ITS REVOLUTIONARY STRUGGLE.

0788 DELBRUCK H.
GOVERNMENT AND THE WILL OF THE PEOPLE (TRANS. BY ROY S. MACELWEE)
NEW YORK: OXFORD U PR, 1923, 192 PP.
GENERAL DISCUSSION OF CONCEPT OF POPULAR SOVEREIGNTY AND ITS RELATION TO SUCH POLITICAL PRINCIPLES AS REPRESENTATION, MAJORITY AND MINORITY WILL, REFERENDUM, ETC. INCLUDES DISCUSSION OF HISTORICAL CIRCUMSTANCES WHICH LED TO ITS RISE.

0789 DELEFORTRIE-SOU N.
LES DIRIGEANTS DE L'INDUSTRIE FRANCAISE.
PARIS: COLIN (LIB ARMAND), 1961, 280 PP.
STUDY OF THE DIRECTORS OF FRENCH INDUSTRIES. ATTEMPTS TO ASSESS THEIR COMMON CHARACTERISTICS IN ORDER TO SITUATE THEM IN FRENCH SOCIETY. AUTHOR BELIEVES THAT BY ESTABLISHING CHARACTERISTICS OF LEADERS, REFORMS CAN BE MADE IN INDUSTRY.

0790 DENISON E.F.
"SOURCES OF GROWTH IN NINE WESTERN COUNTRIES."
AMER. ECO. REVIEW, 57 (MAY 67), 325-332.
AUTHOR ISOLATES SOURCES OF OBSERVED GROWTH OF REAL NATIONAL INCOME FOR PERIOD 1950-1962. HE MEASURES CONTRIBUTION OF CHANGES IN INPUT AND OUTPUT IN RELATION TO LABOR, LAND, AND CAPITAL. ATTRIBUTES EUROPEAN GROWTH TO GAINS FROM RESOURCE ALLOCATION, TECHNOLOGICAL DEVELOPMENT, AND RECOVERY

FROM WAR DISTORTIONS.

0791 DENISON E.F., POULLIER J.P.
WHY GROWTH RATES DIFFER; POSTWAR EXPERIENCE IN NINE WESTERN COUNTRIES.
WASHINGTON: BROOKINGS INST, 1967, 494 PP., LC#67-27682.
ANALYZES ECONOMIC GROWTH RECORDS OF US AND EIGHT EUROPEAN COUNTRIES DURING POST-WWII PERIOD. ESTIMATES CONTRIBUTION TO GROWTH OF KEY VARIABLES, INCLUDING EDUCATION, CAPITAL, RESOURCES, TECHNOLOGICAL DEVELOPMENT, AND INVENTORIES. COMPARES US RATE TO OTHERS AND DECIDES THAT US ECONOMY MUST BE EVALUATED ON BASIS OF OWN POSSIBILITIES, NOT AGAINST COUNTRIES WITH DIFFERENT OPPORTUNITIES.

0792 DENNERY E.
"DEMOCRACY AND THE FRENCH ARMY."
MILITARY AFFAIRS, 5 (WINTER 41), 233-240.
ASSERTS THAT SINCE THE REVOLUTION CONSCRIPTION HAS BEEN DEMOCRATIC. WHILE ONLY THOSE WITH HIGHER EDUCATION COULD HOPE TO BECOME OFFICERS, A WIDE RANGE OF POLITICAL OPINIONS AMONG OFFICERS COULD BE FOUND. SINCE THE REVOLUTION, THE ARMY HAS BEEN THE SERVANT OF CIVIL AUTHORITY AND HAS POSED NO THREATS TO DEMOCRACY.

0793 DENNING A.
FREEDOM UNDER THE LAW.
TORONTO: CARSWELL, 1949, 126 PP.
SUMMARIZES DEVELOPMENT OF ENGLISH LAW, DETAILING ITS PROVISIONS ON PERSONAL FREEDOM, FREEDOM OF MIND AND CONSCIENCE, JUSTICE BETWEEN MAN AND STATE, AND POWERS OF EXECUTIVE.

0794 DERRICK P.
"THE WHITE PAPER ON INCOMES."
QUARTERLY REV., (APR. 67), 134-143.
LABOUR PASSED LEGISLATION IMPOSING A FREEZE ON WAGES AND PERIOD OF SEVERE RESTRAINT DURING WHICH TIME GOVERNMENT HAS POWER TO DELAY WAGE INCREASES. THE GOVERNMENT IS PUBLISHING WHITE PAPER OUTLINING LONG-TERM INCOMES POLICY TO FOLLOW PERIOD OF RESTRAINT, AND AUTHOR DISCUSSES PROBLEMS AND MEASURES THAT THE POLICY MUST INCORPORATE, SUCH AS PLACATING TRADE UNIONISTS.

0795 DESHPANDE A.M.
"FEDERAL-STATE FISCAL RELATIONS IN INDIA" (REVIEW ARTICLE)"
UNITED ASIA, 19 (MAR.-APR. 67), 129-131.
REVIEW OF KV SHASTRI'S BOOK ON PROBLEMS OF "DEVOLUTION OF TAXES AND DUTIES AS LAID DOWN IN CONSTITUTION OF INDIA." BOOK STUDIES FUNCTIONS OF FINANCE COMMISSION AND RECOMMENDS MAKING IT A PERMANENT BODY. ANALYZES INDIA'S "FISCAL EFFORT" AS OPPOSED TO ITS "TAX EFFORT" AND PRESENTS FORMULAS TO USE AS CRITERIA FOR ALLOCATION OF RESOURCES.

0796 DETTER I.
"THE PROBLEM OF UNEQUAL TREATIES."
INT. AND COMP. LAW Q., 15 (OCT. 66), 1069-1089.
THE PROLIFERATION OF NEW STATES IN THE UN AND THEIR DEMANDS TO BE TREATED AS SOVEREIGN EQUALS HAS HEATED CONTROVERSIAL NATURE OF "INEQUAL TREATIES, REBUS SIC STANTIBUS, AND PACTA SUNT SERVANDA." ASSESSES INTERNATIONAL VALIDITY OF TREATIES LIKE "CHINESE CAPITULATION TREATIES," SUGGESTS UN GENERAL ASSEMBLY AS CONTROL ORGAN.

0797 DEUTSCH K.W.
"THE GROWTH OF NATIONS: SOME RECURRENT PATTERNS OF POLITICAL AND SOCIAL INTEGRATION" (BMR)"
WORLD POLITICS, 5 (JAN. 53), 168-195.
DISCUSSES RECURRENT PROBLEMS OF NATIONAL INTEGRATION AND RECURRENT PHENOMENA IN PROCESSES OF PARTIAL SOCIAL MOBILIZATION AND NATION-BUILDING. LISTS POSSIBLE SPECIFIC UNIFORMITIES FOUND IN GROWTH OF NATIONS, AND SURVEYS TRANSITION FROM GROUP AWARENESS TO NATION-STATE.

0798 DEUTSCH K.W.
AN INTERDISCIPLINARY BIBLIOGRAPHY ON NATIONALISM, 1935-1953.
CAMBRIDGE: MIT PRESS, 1956, 165 PP.
CONTAINS 3,000 ENTRIES ON THE POLITICAL, SOCIAL, CULTURAL AND PSYCHOLOGICAL ASPECTS OF NATIONALISM. ENTRIES ARE PRIMARILY IN ENGLISH WITH GERMAN AND FRENCH SELECTIONS RANGING FROM 1935-53; FROM BOOKS AND ARTICLES ARRANGED INTO 14 SECTIONS. THE FIRST 11 LIST ENTRIES BY FIELDS (RELIGION, SOCIOLOGY, ETC.), THE REMAINING BY AREA AND COUNTRY.

0799 DEUTSCH K.W.
THE NERVES OF GOVERNMENT.
NEW YORK: FREE PRESS OF GLENCOE, 1963, 316 PP., LC#63-8415.
DEVELOPS A THEORY OF POLITICS BASED UPON ANALYTIC CONCEPTS AND MODELS, BOTH NATIONAL AND INTERNATIONAL. BUILDS A CASE AND PRESENTS SUGGESTIONS FOR THE REORGANIZATION AND REINTERPRETATION OF POLITICAL THEORY. ARGUES PROFITABILITY OF VIEWING GOVERNMENT LESS AS A PROBLEM OF POWER AND MORE AS A PROBLEM OF LEADERSHIP AND DIRECTION. EMPHASIZES ROLE OF COMMUNICATION IN GOVERNMENT DECISION-MAKING.

0800 DEUTSCH K.W.
"NATIONALISM AND SOCIAL COMMUNICATION."
CAMBRIDGE: M I T PRESS, 1966.
AN INQUIRY INTO FOUNDATIONS OF NATIONALITY AND NATIONALIST IDEAS. UNANNOTATED BIBLIOGRAPHY LISTED ALPHABETICALLY. BOOKS AND PERIODICALS RELATING TO TOPIC DIVIDED INTO 12 CATEGORIES: BIBLIOGRAPHIES AND SURVEYS, GENERAL WORKS ON NATIONALISM, POLITICAL SCIENCE, THEORY OF COMMUNICATION, CULTURAL ANTHROPOLOGY, SOCIAL PSYCHOLOGY, LINGUISTICS, GENERAL HISTORY, ECONOMICS, GEOGRAPHY, ETC.

0801 DEUTSCH K.W.
FRANCE, GERMANY AND THE WESTERN ALLIANCE.
NEW YORK: CHAS SCRIBNER'S SONS, 1967, 323 PP., LC#67-10454.
PRESENTS FINDINGS OF SURVEY WHICH INTERVIEWED ELITES IN FRANCE AND GERMANY ON SUBJECT OF WESTERN ALLIANCE. COMPARES ATTITUDES IN EACH COUNTRY AND ATTEMPTS TO RELATE ELITE ATTITUDES TO GOVERNMENT POLICY.

0802 DEUTSCHE BIBLIOTH FRANKF A M
DEUTSCHE BIBLIOGRAPHIE.
FRANKFURT: DEUT BIBLIOG FRANKFE.
WEEKLY REGISTER (JAN 1965-JULY 1967) LISTING BOOKS PUBLISHED IN THE PRECEDING YEARS (1965 AND 1966). ARRANGED BY SUBJECT AND HAS SUCH CLASSIFICATIONS AS PHILOSOPHY, LAW, AND ADMINISTRATION, SOCIAL SCIENCES, POLITICS, DEFENSE, FINE ARTS, ETC. HAS A SUBJECT-AUTHOR INDEX. FOREIGN PUBLICATIONS INCLUDED.

0803 DEUTSCHE BUCHEREI
DEUTSCHE NATIONALBIBLIOGRAPHIE.
LEIPZIG: V.E.B. VERL. FUR BUCH. BIBL.
QUARTERLY PUBLICATION LISTING CURRENT BOOKS, PAMPHLETS, AND DISSERTATIONS NOT AVAILABLE THROUGH THE REGULAR BOOK-TRADE. ARRANGEMENT IS BY SUBJECT AND RANGES FROM CATEGORIES SUCH AS CLASSICS OF MARXISM/LENINISM TO SUCH DIVERSE ITEMS AS HISTORY, YOUTH MOVEMENTS, AND PHILOSOPHY. INCLUDES FOREIGN ITEMS IF IN GERMAN.

0804 DEUTSCHE BUCHEREI
JAHRESVERZEICHNIS DES DEUTSCHEN SCHRIFTUMS.
LEIPZIG: V.E.B. VERL. FUR BUCH. BIBL.
ANNUAL BIBLIOGRAPHY OF BOOKS IN GERMAN PUBLISHED DURING THE PERIOD UNDER CONSIDERATION IN GERMANY, AUSTRIA, SWITZERLAND, AND OTHER COUNTRIES. EACH VOLUME DIVIDED INTO TWO SECTIONS: WORKS ORGANIZED BY AUTHOR; WORKS INDEXED UNDER SUBJECT.

0805 DEUTSCHE BUCHEREI
DEUTSCHES BUCHERVERZEICHNIS.
LEIPZIG: V.E.B. VERL. FUR BUCH. BIBL.
ANNUAL LISTING OF PRIMARY PUBLICATIONS IN BOTH EAST AND WEST GERMANY. ENTRIES ARRANGE ALPHABETICALLY BY AUTHOR WITH A SUBJECT INDEX. FIRST PUBLISHED 1911.

0806 DEUTSCHE INST ZEITGESCHICHTE
DIE WESTDEUTSCHEN PARTEIEN: 1945-1965.
BERLIN: DIETZ VERLAG, 1966, 585 PP.
HANDBOOK ABOUT PROGRAMS, POLITICAL IDOLOGY, ORGANIZATION AND HISTORICAL GROWTH OF WEST GERMAN PARTIES SINCE WWII. INCLUDES APPENDIX OF NAMES OF PARTIES THAT HAVE APPEARED IN GENERAL ELECTIONS, AS WELL AS A LIST OF VARIOUS ADMINISTRATIONS IN THE STATES.

0807 DEUTSCHER I.
STALIN: A POLITICAL BIOGRAPHY.
LONDON: OXFORD U PR, 1966, 648 PP.
BIOGRAPHY OF STALIN, A "REVOLUTIONARY DESPOT." DEPICTS HIS CHILDHOOD, YOUTH, AND EARLY YEARS WITH THE SOCIALIST UNDERGROUND, ATTEMPTING TO EXPLAIN HOW STALIN FORMED HIS POLITICAL OUTLOOK. DESCRIBES HIS ACTIVITIES IN 1920'S AND 1930'S, SHOWING HOW HE GAINED AND USED POWER. SUGGESTS WHAT STALIN HAS COME TO EPITOMIZE IN EYES OF PRE- AND POST-KHRUSHCHEV RUSSIA.

0808 DEUTSCHER I.
"GERMANY AND MARXISM."
NEW LEFT REV., 47 (JAN.-FEB. 68), 61-70.
ANALYZES POSSIBILITIES AND DANGERS FOR DEMOCRACY IN WEST GERMANY AS RESULT OF RISING NATIONALISM AND INCREASING POPULARITY OF NPD. SEES A REAL THREAT OF REVERSAL OF GERMAN PROGRESS TOWARD STABLE DEMOCRACY. FORESEES EVENTUAL SOCIALIST VICTORY IN EUROPE AS FORESTALLING SUCH A REVERSAL.

0809 DEUTSCHMANN P.J.
"THE MASS MEDIA IN AN UNDERDEVELOPED VILLAGE."
JOURNALISM QUART., 40 (WINTER 63), 27-35.
'EVEN AT THE LOW DEVELOPMENT LEVEL OF A SMALL ANDEAN VILLAGE, THERE ARE PERSONS RECEIVING MESSAGES FROM THE MODERN MASS MEDIA.... THE PROCESS OF MEDIA AUDIENCE BUILDING MAY BE FUNDAMENTALLY THE SAME IN THIS QUITE DIFFERENT CULTURE AS IN THE UNITED STATES.'

0810 DEWEY J.
FREEDOM AND CULTURE.
NEW YORK: PUTNAMS, 1939, 176 PP.
ANALYSIS OF RELATION OF FREE CULTURE TO FREE SOCIETY. ARGUES THAT AMERICA MUST DEMONSTRATE BY ITS CONDUCT THAT IT

USES VOLUNTARY COOPERATION TO ACHIEVE INCREASED FREEDOM. CONSIDERS SOCIAL EXPERIMENTATION AS SOURCE OF PROGRESS.

0811 DEWHURST A.
"THE WAGE MOVEMENT IN CANADA."
WORLD MARXIST REV., 10 (FEB. 67), 15-20.
DISCUSSES REASONS FOR GREATER NUMBER OF STRIKES AFFECTING MORE WORKERS AND INDUSTRIES IN CANADA IN SUMMER OF 1966. POINTS TO RISE IN COST OF LIVING AND IN PROFITS AND PRODUCTIVITY. IN ADDITION TO WAGE DEMANDS, WORKERS ARE SEEKING THE RIGHT OF A WORKER TO HIS JOB, THE RIGHT OF COLLECTIVE BARGAINING, AND RIGHT TO PICKET WITHOUT GOVERNMENT INTERFERENCE BY INJUNCTION.

0813 DEXTER L.A.
"A DIALOGUE ON THE SOCIAL PSYCHOLOGY OF COLONIALISM AND ON CERTAIN PUERTO RICAN PROFESSIONAL PERSONALITY PATTERNS."
HUMAN RELATIONS, 2 (1949), 49-64.
A DIALOGUE AMONG NINE PUERTO RICAN RESIDENTS WHO ARE PROFESSIONALS IN SUCH FIELDS AS TEACHING, LAW, SOCIOLOGY, AND PSYCHOLOGY. AUTHOR ATTEMPTS TO PRESENT PROBLEMS OF COLONIALISM, CLASS STRUCTURE, AND DRIVES WITHIN PUERTO RICAN CONTEXT BY HAVING CHARACTERS PRESENT HYPOTHESES. AUTHOR FAILS TO MAKE DISTINCTIONS BETWEEN PERSONALITY TYPE AND SOCIAL TYPE, OR BETWEEN PERSONALITY STRUCTURE AND NATIONAL CHARACTER.

0814 DEXTER L.A.
"A SOCIAL THEORY OF MENTAL DEFICIENCY."
AM. J. MENTAL DEFICIENCY, 62 (MAR. 57), 920-928.
DISCUSSES THE SOCIAL VALUES AND ROLES INVOLVED IN BEING TREATED AS RETARDED, AND IN RESPONDING AS RETARDED. IN THIS BASIC TREATMENT OF SOCIOLOGY OF MENTAL ILLNESS, THEORY REVOLVES AROUND NOTION OF MENTAL DEFICIENCY AS INABILITY TO LEARN APPROPRIATE ROLE BEHAVIOR.

0815 DEXTER N.C., RAYNER E.G.
GUIDE TO CONTEMPORARY POLITICS.
NEW YORK: PERGAMON PRESS, 1966, 330 PP., LC#65-26355.
BRIEF DISCUSSION OF PRINCIPLES AND ISSUES OF POLITICAL DEMOCRACY IN ENGLAND. BASIC TENETS OF POLITICAL PARTIES AND THEIR RELATION TO THE "DAY-TO-DAY SHIFTS OF FRONT IN CONTEMPORARY POLITICS" CONSTITUTE CENTRAL THEME OF TEXT.

0816 DIA M.
REFLEXIONS SUR L'ECONOMIE DE L'AFRIQUE NOIRE (REV. ED.)
PARIS: PRESENCE AFRIQUE, 1960, 210 PP.
PROVIDES INSIGHTS INTO DECOLONIZATION AND THE REBUILDING OF A DISTINCTLY AFRICAN ECONOMY. ADVISES HOW A BALANCED, ORDERED, AND MODERN ECONOMY CAN BE FORGED ALONG SOCIALIST LINES. OUTLINES CONCEPTS, OBJECTIVES, AND MEANS FOR PLANNING AND DEVELOPING AFRICA'S CULTURAL, SOCIAL, AND ECONOMIC HERITAGE AND FOR INTEGRATING IT WITH GLOBAL ECONOMICS. CITES EVIDENCE AND GIVES DATA SUPPORTING THESE THESES.

0817 DIA M.
THE AFRICAN NATIONS AND WORLD SOLIDARITY.
NEW YORK: PRAEGER, 1961, 145 PP., $4.85.
PRIME MINISTER OF SENEGAL ANALYZES ECONOMIC PROBLEMS OF EMERGENT AFRICAN NATIONS. ADVOCATES LEOPOLD SENGHOR'S 'AFRICAN SOLIALISM', ARGUING AGAINST USE OF SOVIET MODEL. WRITTEN BEFORE DISSOLUTION OF WEST AFRICAN FEDERATION IN 1960.

0818 DIAMANT A.
"EUROPEAN MODELS OF BUREAUCRACY AND DEVELOPMENT."
INT. REV. OF ADMIN. SCI., 32 (1967), 309-320.
DISCUSSES THE BASIC PATTERN IN THE PROCESS OF EUROPEAN MODERNIZATION, THE CONDITIONS IT PRODUCES, ITS RELATION TO BUREAUCRACY, AND THE KINDS OF POLITICAL ORGANIZATIONS WHICH AID ITS DEVELOPMENT. CONTRASTS POLITICAL STATES AS "EQUILIBRIUM MODELS" PRESERVING THE STATUS QUO AND "MOBILIZATION MODELS" MARSHALING RESOURCES FOR MAXIMUM OUTPUT* SUGGESTS THAT NEW NON-EUROPEAN STATES STUDY THESE LATTER MODELS.

0819 DIAMOND S. ED.
THE TRANSFORMATION OF EAST AFRICA.
NEW YORK: BASIC BOOKS, 1966, 623 PP., LC#66-26211.
ANTHOLOGY DISCUSSES THE TRADITIONAL CULTURES AND THE PROMISE OF THE EAST AFRICANS. ATTEMPTS TO ASSIST IN THE SOLUTION OF EDUCATIONAL AND TECHNICAL PROBLEMS. DISCUSSES THE PRECOLONIAL AND COLONIAL SETTING; RACE RELATIONS, POLITICS, AND INDUSTRIALIZATION IN THE EMERGING NATIONS; AND REGIONAL PROCESSES AND PROBLEMS.

0820 SIMON DIAZ J.
MANUAL DE BIBLIOGRAFIA DE LA LITERATURA ESPANOLA.
BARCELONA: GUSTAVO GILI, 1962, 604 PP.
BIBLIOGRAPHY OF OVER 20,000 BOOKS PUBLISHED IN LATIN AMERICA AND SPAIN FROM THE MIDDLE AGES THROUGH 20TH CENTURY. ENTRIES ARE LISTED BY CENTURY OF PUBLICATION.

0821 DICHTER E.
THE STRATEGY OF DESIRE.
GARDEN CITY: DOUBLEDAY, 1960, 314 PP., LC#60-11380.
AUTHOR EXPLAINS THAT MAN IS CONSTANTLY INFLUENCED BY OTHERS TO DO CERTAIN THINGS AS PART OF SOCIETY. THUS STUDY OF MOTIVATION AND BEHAVIOR ADDS TO CLEARER UNDERSTANDING OF WHAT CAUSES MAN TO REACT AND SHOULD ENABLE HIM TO UNDERSTAND HIS OWN SITUATION MORE FULLY.

0822 DICKEY J.S. ED.
THE UNITED STATES AND CANADA.
ENGLEWOOD CLIFFS: PRENTICE HALL, 1964, 184 PP., LC#64-21215.
RELATIONSHIP BETWEEN US AND CANADA. A STUDY OF PROBLEMS ARISING OUT OF THEIR CLOSE PROXIMITY. OUTLOOK FOR THE RELATIONSHIP FROM A CANADIAN AND AN AMERICAN PERSPECTIVE. A SOCIOLOGIST'S VIEW.

0823 DICKSON P.G.M.
THE FINANCIAL REVOLUTION IN ENGLAND.
NEW YORK: ST MARTIN'S PRESS, 1967, 580 PP., LC#67-12509.
CITES AND EXPLORES IMPORTANCE OF DEVELOPMENT OF PUBLIC CREDIT SYSTEMS TO POLITICAL, SOCIAL, AND ECONOMIC HISTORY OF 18TH CENTURY ENGLAND. NATIONAL DEBT, ADMINISTRATIVE PROBLEMS, PUBLIC CREDITORS, GOVERNMENT BORROWING, SECURITY MARETS, ARE ALL ANALYZED IN DEPTH. COMPREHENSIVE WORK INCLUDING WIDE RANGE OF DISCIPLINES.

0824 DILLARD D.
ECONOMIC DEVELOPMENT OF THE NORTH ATLANTIC COMMUNITY.
ENGLEWOOD CLIFFS: PRENTICE HALL, 1967, 747 PP., LC#67-15169.
CHRONOLOGICALLY ANALYZES NORTH ATLANTIC ECONOMY FROM MIDDLE AGES TO PRESENT, RELATING AND COMPARING EUROPEAN AND AMERICAN DEVELOPMENT. EXAMINES POLITICAL AND ECONOMIC RELATIONS, INDUSTRIALIZATION, LABOR ORGANIZATIONS, WAR, BALANCE-OF-PAYMENTS, AND ACTIONS OF COUNTRIES ON BOTH SIDES OF ATLANTIC REGARDING BACKWARD AREAS.

0825 DILLING A.R.
ABORIGINE CULTURE HISTORY - A SURVEY OF PUBLICATIONS 1954-1957.
DETROIT: WAYNE STATE U PR, 1962, 217 PP., LC#61-12268.
SURVEY OF PUBLICATIONS FROM 1954-57 ON THE ABORIGINE CULTURAL HISTORY OF AUSTRALIA, PAPUA, AND WEST NEW GUINEA BY PROFESSIONAL AND NON-PROFESSIONAL ARCHEOLOGISTS, ETHNOGRAPHERS, ETHNOLOGISTS, SOCIAL AND PHYSICAL ANTHROPOLOGISTS, PALEONTOLOGISTS, LINGUISTS, FOLKLORISTS, AND HISTORIANS. ANNOTATIONS ARE EXTENSIVE AND MAPS, CATALOG OF ALL PUBLICATIONS, AND GLOSSARY ARE INCLUDED.

0826 DILLON D.R.
LATIN AMERICA, 1935-1949; A SELECTED BIBLIOGRAPHY.
NEW YORK: UNITED NATIONS, 1952.
COMPILATION OF IMPORTANT MATERIALS ON THE LAW, HISTORY, INTERNATIONAL RELATIONS, ECONOMICS, SOCIOLOGY, AND EDUCATION OF LATIN AMERICA IN GENERAL AND INDIVIDUAL NATIONS.

0827 DITTMANN
DAS POLITISCHE DEUTSCHLAND VOR HITLER.
ZURICH: EUROPA VERLAG, 1945, 43 PP.
COLLECTION OF CHARTS AND TABLES INDICATING POLITICAL STRENGTH OF MAJOR PARTIES IN GERMANY BETWEEN 1918 AND 1933. INCLUDES 35 VOTING DISTRICTS, FROM OSTPREUSSEN TO MECKLENBURG, PLUS A CHART OF THE NATION AT LARGE.

0828 DIX R.H.
COLOMBIA: THE POLITICAL DIMENSIONS OF CHANGE.
NEW HAVEN: YALE U PR, 1967, 464 PP., LC#67-24495.
CHARACTERIZES VARIOUS REGIMES WHICH HAVE EVOLVED IN COLOMBIA TO MEET CHALLENGES OF MODERNIZATION 1934-67. INVESTIGATES FACTORS WHICH HAVE LED TO A PROCESS OF "MODERNIZATION FROM ABOVE," WITH LEADERSHIP RESTING IN HANDS OF ONCE-TRADITIONAL SOCIAL ELITE. ANALYZES CURRENT NATIONAL FRONT, OTHER PARTIES, AND OVER-ALL DYNAMICS OF POLITICS IN A LATIN AMERICAN NATION.

0829 DOBB M.
SOVIET ECONOMIC DEVELOPMENT SINCE 1917.
NEW YORK: INTERNATIONAL PUBL CO, 1966, 515 PP.
BROAD AND DETAILED HISTORICAL REVIEW OF ECONOMIC DEVELOPMENT IN THE USSR. TREATS VARIOUS FIVE YEAR PLANS, INDUSTRIALIZATION, WAR DEVELOPMENTS, RECENT YEARS, PLANNING SYSTEM, TRADE UNIONS, LABOR CONDITIONS, SOCIAL INSURANCE. EXTENSIVE COVERAGE OF CURRENT SITUATION.

0830 DODD S.C.
"THE SCIENTIFIC MEASUREMENT OF FITNESS FOR SELF-GOVERNMENT."
SCI. MON., 80 (FEB. 54), 94-99.
ESTABLISHES A CRITERIA FOR MEASURING FITNESS OF DEVELOPING NATIONS FOR ACHIEVING INDEPENDENCE. USES STATISTICAL INDICES TO MEASURE FITNESS FOR SELF-GOVERNMENT. THREE CYCLES OF MEASUREMENT ARE QUALITATIVE CYCLE, QUANTITATIVE, AND THE CORRELATIVE.

0831 DODGE D.
AFRICAN POLITICS IN PERSPECTIVE.
PRINCETON: VAN NOSTRAND, 1966, 212 PP.
STUDY OF POLITICAL DEVELOPMENTS IN AFRICA SOUTH OF THE SAHARA, FROM PRE-EUROPEAN BEGINNINGS TO PRESENT. INCLUDES DISCUSSION OF COLONIAL POLICIES OF VARIOUS EUROPEAN NATIONS AND DETAILED EXAMINATION OF POLITICAL

PROBLEMS OF INDEPENDENCE.

0832 DOERN G.B.
"THE ROYAL COMMISSIONS IN THE GENERAL POLICY PROCESS AND IN FEDERAL-PROVINCIAL RELATIONS."
CAN. PUBLIC ADMIN., 10 (DEC. 67), 417-433.
STUDIES THE FUNCTIONS AND USEFULNESS OF CANADIAN ROYAL COMMISSIONS, AD HOC BODIES APPOINTED BY THE GOVERNMENT IN POWER FOR PURPOSE OF EXPERT STUDY OF SUCH PROBLEMS AS TRANSPORTATION AND AGRICULTURE. CONCLUDES THAT SENATE COMMITTEES OR RESEARCH INSTITUTES AT UNIVERSITIES COULD BETTER SERVE THE PURPOSE; THEY WOULD EXIST IN PERPETUITY AND HAVE BETTER CHANCE OF IMPLEMENTING THEIR SUGGESTIONS.

0833 DOGAN M.
"LES OFFICIERS DANS LA CARRIERE POLITIQUE DE MARECHAL MACMAHON AU GENERAL DE GAULLE."
REV. FRANCAISE SOCIOLOGIE, 2 (APR.-JUNE 61), 88-99.
ANALYSIS AND EVOLUTION OF THE ROLE OF FRENCH OFFICERS WITHIN THE DECISION-MAKING GROUPS, THE LEGISLATURE, AND THE GOVERNMENT FROM 1870 TO THE PRESENT. SOCIAL ORIGINS AND POLITICAL TENDENCIES OF THE OFFICER GROUP.

0834 DOLCI D.
A NEW WORLD IN THE MAKING.
NEW YORK: MONTHLY REVIEW PR, 1965, 327 PP., LC#65-21053.
AN ATTEMPT TO FORMULATE MEANS OF DISCOVERING CRITERIA BY WHICH MAN CAN ACT IN A WORLD IN WHICH HISTORICAL MORAL LAWS HAVE LOST THEIR ABSOLUTE QUALITY AS GUIDING FORCES. EXAMINES NON-WESTERN COUNTRIES SUCH AS RUSSIA AND SENEGAL TO SEE HOW THEY ARE RESPONDING TO THIS TASK. EMPHASIZES FUNCTION THAT GROUPS AND ORGANIZATIONS CAN FULFILL IN BRINGING UNITY TO THE WORLD.

0835 DONALDSON A.G.
SOME COMPARATIVE ASPECTS OF IRISH LAW.
DURHAM: DUKE U PR, 1957, 293 PP., LC#57-8815.
STUDIES LEGAL AND CONSTITUTIONAL HISTORY OF IRISH LAW. DISCUSSES IRELAND IN TERMS OF INTERNATIONAL LAW AND DEVELOPMENT OF BRITISH COMMONWEALTH. COMPARISONS AND CONTRASTS DRAWN WITH OTHER COMMONWEALTH COUNTRIES TO ILLUMINATE IRELAND'S CONTRIBUTIONS. COVERS BOTH NORTHERN IRELAND AND REPUBLIC OF IRELAND, AND CONTRASTS THEIR ATTITUDES.

0836 DONNISON F.S.V.
CIVIL AFFAIRS AND MILITARY GOVERNMENT NORTH-WEST EUROPE 1944-1946.
LONDON: H M STATIONERY OFFICE, 1961, 518 PP.
STUDIES MILITARY OCCUPATION OF LIBERATED TERRITORIES BY ALLIES IN NORTHWEST EUROPE AT END OF WWII. INCLUDES INVASION, LIBERATION, AND CONQUEST OF GERMANY, AND PROBLEMS OF ADMINISTRATION.

0837 DOOB L.W.
COMMUNICATION IN AFRICA: A SEARCH FOR BOUNDARIES.
NEW HAVEN: YALE U PR, 1961, 406 PP., LC#61-16914.
ANALYSIS OF FACTORS AND VARIABLES INVOLVED IN COMMUNICATION, EMPHASIZING COMMUNICATOR, BASIC AND EXTENDING MEDIA, AND RESTRICTIONS, WITH DISCUSSION OF GOAL, SITE, MOOD, REACTION, AND CHANGES.

0838 DOOLIN D.J.
COMMUNIST CHINA: THE POLITICS OF STUDENT OPPOSITION.
STANFORD: HOOVER INSTITUTE, 1964, 70 PP., LC#64-16879.
COLLECTION OF SPEECHES AND PAPERS BY COMMUNIST CHINESE STUDENTS, OFFERED DURING THE 1957 PARTY THAW, ON ALLOWING INTELLECTUAL CRITICISM OF PARTY POLICIES. ORIGINAL OF THIS EDITION SMUGGLED INTO HONG KONG. ESPECIALLY CRITICAL OF PARTY POLICY TOWARD HU FENG, OF STALIN, OF JUDICIAL SYSTEM, AND OF QUESTIONABLE USE OF CHARGE "COUNTERREVOLUTIONARY." DISCUSSES "RANK" IN CLASSLESS SOCIETY, AND PARTY LEADERSHIP.

0839 DORWART R.A.
"THE ADMINISTRATIVE REFORMS OF FREDRICK WILLIAM I OF PRUSSIA
CAMBRIDGE: HARVARD U PR, 1953.
PRESENTS A HISTORICAL DESCRIPTION OF THE EVOLUTION OF INSTITUTIONS OF PUBLIC ADMINISTRATION IN THE CENTRAL GOVERNMENT OF BRANDENBURG-PRUSSIA. CONCENTRATES ON REFORMS IN ADMINISTRATION AND ADMINISTRATIVE ORGANIZATION INTRODUCED DURING THE REIGN OF FREDERICK WILLIAM I, 1713-40. EMPHASIS ON ROLE PLAYED BY CENTRALIZED, ABSOLUTIST PUBLIC ADMINISTRATION. BIBLIOGRAPHY OF GERMAN AND FRENCH WORKS.

0840 DOS SANTOS M.
BIBLIOGRAPHIA GERAL, A DESCRIPCAO BIBLIOGRAFICA DE LIVROS TANTO DE AUTORES PORTUGUEZES COMO BRASILEIROS...
LISBON: TYPOGRAFIA MENDONCA, 1917.
DESCRIPTIVE BIBLIOGRAPHY OF BOOKS BY BRAZILIAN AND PORTUGUESE AUTHORS PRINTED FROM 15TH TO 20TH CENTURIES; CONCERNED WITH HISTORY OF BRAZIL AND PORTUGUESE POSSESSIONS.

0841 DOUGLAS W.O.
WE THE JUDGES.
GARDEN CITY: DOUBLEDAY, 1956, 475 PP., LC#56-05439.
FOLLOWS GROWTH OF AMERICAN CONSTITUTIONAL LAW FROM MARSHALL TO WARREN, 1801-1953. DISCUSSES CHANGES IN JUDICIAL POWER, COURT-SYSTEM, LEGISLATIVE PREROGATIVES, FEDERAL VS. STATE POWER, FAIR TRIAL, AND EQUAL PROTECTION. COMPARES US EVOLUTION TO INDIAN, WHICH, WHILE RECENT, WAS MUCH MORE RAPID IN TEMPO.

0842 DOUGLAS-HOME C.
"A MISTAKEN POLICY IN ADEN."
ROUND TABLE, 69 (JAN. 68), 21-27.
ATTACKS SEPARATISTS' POLICIES IN ADEN, WHICH PREVENT ITS UNIFICATION WITH YEMEN, A COUNTRY WHOSE PEOPLE ARE CLAIMED TO BE ETHNICALLY AND CULTURALLY INDISTINGUISHABLE FROM THEMSELVES. CLAIMS BRITISH POLICY TOWARD THESE AREAS HAS BEEN REMARKABLY BAD. EXPLORES HISTORY OF COLONIALISM AND SOVEREIGNTY IN THIS REGION TO SUGGEST SOLUTIONS.

0843 DOUGLASS H.P., BRUNNER E.
THE PROTESTANT CHURCH AS A SOCIAL INSTITUTION.
NEW YORK: HARPER & ROW, 1935, 368 PP.
BASED ON RESEARCH STUDIES OF THE INSTITUTE OF SOCIAL AND RELIGIOUS RESEARCH, THIS TREATISE DISCUSSES CONSTITUENTS, CHURCH, DENOMINATIONAL ORGANIZATION, ADMINISTRATION, LAY OFFICERS, AND THE MINISTRY. INCLUDES A DETAILED EXAMINATION OF FUNCTIONAL COMMUNITY REPRESENTATION AND COOPERATION BETWEEN CHURCHES.

0844 DOUMA J. ED.
BIBLIOGRAPHY ON THE INTERNATIONAL COURT INCLUDING THE PERMANENT COURT, 1918-1964.
NEW YORK: HUMANITIES PRESS, 1966, 387 PP., LC#52-4918.
ANNOTATED BIBLIOGRAPHY COVERING 1918-64, PUBLISHED AS SUPPLEMENT TO SERIES BY HAMBRO. TWO PARTS: FIRST DEALS WITH PERMANENT COURT OF INTERNATIONAL JUSTICE; SECOND CONCERNS PRESENT COURT INSTITUTED BY UN. CONTAINS 3,572 ENTRIES IN SEVERAL LANGUAGES. INCLUDES INDEXES OF SUBJECTS AND AUTHORS.

0845 DOWNIE R.S.
GOVERNMENT ACTION AND MORALITY: SOME PRINCIPLES AND CONCEPTS OF LIBERAL-DEMOCRACY.
LONDON: MACMILLAN, 1964, 149 PP.
PHILOSOPHICAL INVESTIGATION OF PRINCIPLES ON WHICH LIBERAL DEMOCRACIES ARE BASED, USING BRITISH POLITICAL INSTITUTIONS AS EXAMPLE. STUDIES THEORIES OF MORALITY AND OF GOVERNMENTAL ACTION AND RELATIONSHIP BETWEEN MORALITY AND GOVERNMENTAL ACTION.

0846 DRAGNICH A.N.
MAJOR EUROPEAN GOVERNMENTS.
HOMEWOOD: DORSEY, 1961, 454 PP., LC#61-11608.
DISCUSSES POLITICAL INSTITUTIONS AND PROCESSES OF UK, FRANCE, GERMANY, AND USSR. INCLUDES DISCUSSION OF HISTORICAL DEVELOPMENT OF INSTITUTIONS, BUT CENTERS ON MODERN CONDITIONS.

0847 DRIVER H.E.
AN INTEGRATION OF FUNCTIONAL, EVOLUTIONARY AND HISTORICAL THEORY BY MEANS OF CORRELATIONS.
BALTIMORE: WAVERLY, 1956, 35 PP.
ATTEMPTS TO CORRELATE THE DATA OBTAINED THROUGH EVOLUTIONARY, FUNCTIONAL, AND HISTORICAL METHODS IN SUPPORT OF ETHNOLOGICAL THEORY WHICH HOLDS THAT CULTURE IS A PRODUCT OF MAN'S PHYSICAL ENVIRONMENT AND BIOLOGICAL CONSTITUTION.

0848 DRIVER H.E., DRIVER W.
ETHNOGRAPHY AND ACCULTURATION OF THE CHICHIMECA-JONAZ OF NORTHEAST MEXICO.
BLOOMINGTON: INDIANA U PR, 1963, 265 PP., LC#63-62521.
MOST ADVANCED STUDY OF ANY MEXICAN NONFARMING PEOPLE TO DATE. ANALYZES HISTORY PRIOR TO ARRIVAL OF SPANISH AND INFLUENCE OF SPANISH ON ALL ASPECTS OF LIFE AND CULTURE. MAJOR CHANGE SEEN AS ECONOMIC ONE, WITH INTRODUCTION OF DIVISION OF LABOR AND FARMING. EXAMINES OTHER CHANGES AND PRESENTS THEM BY TOPICS. SIGNIFICANT DATA INCLUDED.

0849 DRUCKER P.F.
"THE EMPLOYEE SOCIETY."
AMER. J. OF SOCIOLOGY, 58 (JAN. 53), 358-363.
EXPLORES AMERICAN SOCIETY AS AN "EMPLOYEE SOCIETY" WHERE THE BOSS HIMSELF IS USUALLY AN EMPLOYEE AND DEPENDS ON STATUS (CF. MAINE'S THESIS). CALLS FOR RESEARCH INTO IMPLICATIONS OF "MANAGEMENT" AND ITS ACCOUNTABILITY, THE REALIZATION OF HOPES AND BELIEFS THROUGH EMPLOYEE SOCIETY, RIGHTS AND DUTIES IN SUCH A SOCIETY RELATED TO POWER, EFFICIENCY, AND REDISTRIBUTION.

0850 DRYDEN S.
"LOCAL GOVERNMENT IN TANZANIA PART II"
J. OF ADMINISTRATION OVERSEAS, 6 (JULY 67), 165-178.
DETAILED DESCRIPTION OF PROGRESS IN METHODS OF LOCAL GOVERNMENT IN TANZANIA. INCLUDES ROLE OF POLITICAL PARTIES, AND METHODS OF REPRESENTATION. PROVIDES ALTERNATIVE TO SYSTEM OF POWERFUL REGIONAL COMMISSIONER BY ESTABLISHING A REGIONAL DEVELOPMENT BOARD TO ENLARGE LOCAL COUNCILS' PARTICIPATION IN DECISIONS.

0851 DU BOIS W.E.B.

THE PHILADELPHIA NEGRO: A SOCIAL STUDY.
PHILA: U OF PENN PR, 1899, 520 PP.
COMPREHENSIVE STUDY OF THE NEGRO IN PHILADELPHIA IN 1896-97. DESCRIBES BACKGROUND AND HISTORY (1638-1896) OF THE COMMUNITY; ETHNIC AND PHYSICAL CHARACTERISTICS OF THE POPULATION; EDUCATION AND OCCUPATIONS; RELIGIOUS AND FAMILY LIFE; SOCIAL AND ECONOMIC PROBLEMS; AND RELATIONS WITH WHITE COMMUNITY. BASED ON EXTENSIVE FIELD WORK. INCLUDES SPECIAL SECTION ON THE NEGRO DOMESTIC.

0852 DUCLOS P.
L'EVOLUTION DES RAPPORTS POLITIQUES DEPUIS 1750 (LIBERTE, INTEGRATION, UNITE)
PARIS: PR UNIV DE FRANCE, 1950, 344 PP.
SURVEY OF POLITICAL CIVILIZATION, EMPHASIZING PRINCIPLE OF INTEGRATION, LIBERALISM, WORLD SOLIDARITY, AND THE CONFLICT BETWEEN INDIVIDUAL AND STATE. INCLUDES US AND EUROPE.

0853 DUCLOUX L.
FROM BLACKMAIL TO TREASON.
LONDON: ANDRE DEUTSCH, 1958, 240 PP.
STUDIES POLITICAL CRIME AND CORRUPTION IN FRANCE, 1920-40. REFUTES BELIEF, ALLEGEDLY CIRCULATED BY ROYALIST PROPAGANDISTS, THAT SURETE NATIONALE WAS INSTRUMENT OF POLITICAL COERCION AND FOREIGN POWERS BETWEEN WORLD WARS.

0854 DUDLEY B.J.
"THE NOMINATION OF PARLIAMENTARY CANDIDATES IN NORTHERN NIGERIA."
J. COMMONWEALTH POLIT. STUD., 2 (NOV. 63), 45-58.
AN ATTEMPT TO 'DELINEATE THE DEGREE OF POLITICAL CHANGE THAT HAS OCCURRED IN THE NORTHERN REGION OF NIGERIA, USES AS THE FOCUS OF ANALYSIS THE PARTY SYSTEM, PARTICULARLY THE PROCEDURE FOR THE NOMINATION OF CANDIDATES FOR ELECTION TO THE NORTHERN HOUSE OF ASSEMBLY.'

0855 DUE J.F.
STATE SALES TAX ADMINISTRATION.
CHICAGO: PUBLIC ADMIN SERVICE, 1963, 259 PP., LC#63-20355.
REVIEW AND ANALYSIS OF SALES TAX STRUCTURE, ADMINISTRATION, AND OPERATION IN 33 STATES. AREAS COVERED INCLUDE: DEVELOPMENT, FORM, AND YIELDS; ADMINISTRATIVE AND PERSONNEL PRACTICE; PROCESSING OF TAX RETURNS; CONTROL OF DELINQUENTS; AUDIT; MEASURES OF LIABILITY AND TAX RATES; TREATMENT OF SERVICES AND REAL PROPERTY; EXEMPTIONS; USES; INFORMATION, COSTS, AND STUDIES; AND USE BY LOCAL GOVERNMENTS.

0856 DUFFIELD M.
KING LEGION.
NEW YORK: CAPE AND SMITH, 1931, 330 PP.
A CLASSIC ON THE ORIGIN, ORGANIZATION, AND OPERATION OF THE AMERICAN LEGION, DEALING WITH SUCH ASPECTS OF GROUP INFLUENCE AS ITS LOBBYING ACTIVITIES IN WASHINGTON AND STATE CAPITALS, IMPACT ON DRAFT LAW DEBATES AND ANTI-PATRIOTIC ORGANIZATIONS, OPPOSITION TO SOME CHURCH GOUPS, MOULDING POLICIES ON YOUTH TRAINING, TEXTBOOKS AND USE OF PUBLICITY.

0857 DUFFY J. ED., MANNERS R.A. ED.
AFRICA SPEAKS.
PRINCETON: VAN NOSTRAND, 1961, 223 PP.
COLLECTION OF ESSAYS ON MODERN AFRICA, PRIMARILY BY BLACK AFRICANS BUT WITH SOME EUROPEAN FIGURES AND WHITE AFRICANS. GENERAL TOPICS INCLUDE THE BLACK AFRICAN VISION OF AFRICA'S DESTINY; THE PROBLEMS OF NEWLY INDEPENDENT STATES (GHANA, TOGO, CONGO REPUBLIC) AND OF COUNTRIES MOVING FROM COLONIAL STATUS TO INDEPENDENCE (KENYA, THE RHODESIAS); AND PORTUGUESE AND SOUTH AFRICA.

0858 DUGARD J.
"THE REVOCATION OF THE MANDATE FOR SOUTH WEST AFRICA."
AMER. J. OF INT. LAW, 62 (JAN. 68), 78-97.
EXAMINES THE LEGALITY AND LEGAL EFFECT OF UN GENERAL ASSEMBLY'S DECISION TO TERMINATE S. AFRICA'S MANDATE FOR S.W. AFRICA CONFERRED BY LEAGUE OF NATIONS. STUDIES ASSEMBLY'S RIGHT TO DECLARE APARTHEID INCOMPATIBLE WITH MANDATE PROVISIONS, RIGHT OF LEAGUE TO TERMINATE MANDATE UNILATERALLY, AND WHETHER SUCH RIGHT SUCCEEDS TO UN. DECIDES EACH IN AFFIRMATIVE, BUT ADVISES IMPLEMENTATION BY COUNCIL.

0859 DUGGAR G.S.
RENEWAL OF TOWN AND VILLAGE I: A WORLD-WIDE SURVEY OF LOCAL GOVERNMENT EXPERIENCE.
THE HAGUE: MARTINUS NIJHOFF, 1965, 95 PP.
COMPILATION AND ANALYSIS OF DATA RECEIVED IN ANSWER TO QUESTIONNAIRES SENT TO 31 COUNTRIES. FACTS DEAL WITH ECONOMIC, FINANCIAL, AND SOCIAL POLICIES OF URBAN RENEWAL, DISTRICT RENEWAL AND TOWN AND REGIONAL PLANNING, AND NATION'S GENERAL POLICY FOR RENEWAL ADMINISTRATION.

0860 DUGUIT L.
LAW IN THE MODERN STATE (TRANS. BY FRIDA AND HAROLD LASKI)
NEW YORK: B W HUEBSCH, INC, 1919, 248 PP.
RELATES HIS THEORY OF SOCIOLOGICAL INTERPRETATION OF STATE TO MODERN PUBLIC LAW, MAINTAINING THAT LAW IS SUM OF PRINCIPLES OF MORAL CODE NECESSARY TO ACHIEVEMENT OF SOCIAL PURPOSE. DISCUSSES DISINTEGRATION OF THEORY OF SOVEREIGN STATE AND RISE OF THEORY THAT STATE'S DUTY IS TO PROVIDE PUBLIC SERVICE. DESCRIBES RELATION OF STATUTES AND ADMINISTRATIVE LAWS TO THIS THEORY.

0861 DUNAYEVSKAYA R.
MARXISM AND FREEDOM: FROM 1776 UNTIL TODAY.
NEW YORK: BOOKMAN ASSOCIATES, 1958, 384 PP.
A REINTERPRETATION OF MARXIAN THEORY. EXAMINES IMPACT OF HISTORICAL ANTECEDENTS ON THE WRITING OF "CAPITAL." MARXISM IS DEFINED AS A THEORY OF LIBERATION AND THE ANTITHESIS OF CURRENT SOVIET COMMUNIST DOCTRINE. DESCRIBES HOW MARXISM IS REALLY BEING PRACTICED IN NON-COMMUNIST SOCIETIES AND MAINTAINS THAT THEORY WAS REDEFINED AND CORRUPTED BY LENIN AND STALIN TO MEET THEIR POLITICAL ENDS.

0862 DUNCAN O.D., SCHNORE L.F.
"CULTURAL, BEHAVIORAL, AND ECOLOGICAL PERSPECTIVES IN THE STUDY OF SOCIAL ORGANIZATION" (BMR)"
AMER. J. OF SOCIOLOGY, 65 (SEPT. 59), 132-146.
THREE PERSPECTIVES DIFFER AS TO THEORETICAL FRAMES OF REFERENCE, ANALYTICAL UNITS, AND QUESTIONS THEY RAISE ABOUT NATURE OF SOCIAL ORGANIZATION. ECOLOGICAL APPROACH HAS ADVANTAGE FOR EXPLAINING VARIATIONS AND CHANGE IN SUCH PATTERNS AS BUREAUCRACY AND STRATIFICATION.

0863 DUNCOMBE H.S.
COUNTY GOVERNMENT IN AMERICA.
WASHINGTN: NAT ASSN COUNTIES RES, 1966, 288 PP., LC#66-26090
STUDIES CURRENT TRENDS AND STATUS OF ORGANIZATION, FUNCTIONS, FINANCING, AND INTERGOVERNMENTAL RELATIONS OF COUNTY GOVERNMENT. DESCRIBES SERVICES AND FUNCTIONS OF COUNTIES COMPARATIVELY, AND DISCUSSES SIGNIFICANT DIFFERENCES BETWEEN THEM, STRESSING URBAN COUNTIES AND BREAKDOWN OF TRADITIONAL FUNCTIONS WITH GROWING URBANIZATION.

0864 DUNHAM H.W.
SOCIOLOGICAL THEORY AND MENTAL DISORDER.
DETROIT: WAYNE STATE U PR, 1959, 298 PP., LC#59-9323.
ATTEMPTS TO CLARIFY RELATIONSHIP BETWEEN INCIDENCE OF MENTAL ILLNESS AND SOCIAL CLASS, ECOLOGICAL SPACE, OR TIME PERIODS. STUDIES RELATIONSHIP BETWEEN PRE-MORBID PERSONALITY AND SYMPTOMS, AND MAINTAINS THAT CULTURAL FACTORS DESCRIBE SYMPTOMS AS DISTURBED AND ALSO CAUSE DISTURBANCES. PRESENTS THEORETICAL AS WELL AS EMPIRICAL BACKGROUND FOR RESEARCH.

0865 DUNHAM W.H. JR. ED., PARGELLIS S. ED.
COMPLAINT AND REFORM IN ENGLAND 1436-1714.
NEW YORK: OXFORD U PR, 1938, 725 PP.
FIFTY CONTEMPORARY WORKS ILLUSTRATING POLITICAL, SOCIAL, RELIGIOUS, EDUCATIONAL, AND CULTURAL QUESTIONS THAT EXERCISED ENGLISHMEN OVER THREE CENTURIES. DRAWN FROM PAMPHLETS AND TRACTS AS WELL AS FROM LONGER WORKS AND STATEMENTS OF CIVIL AND RELIGIOUS AUTHORITIES, SEEKS TO CONVEY HOW ENGLISHMEN THOUGHT AND FELT, FROM HAKLUYT ON IMPERIALISM TO COWPER ON PARTY POLITICS.

0866 DUNN S.D., DUNN E.
"DIRECTED CULTURE CHANGE IN THE SOVIET UNION: SOME SOVIET STUDIES."
AMER. ANTHROPOL., 64 (APRIL. 62), 328-39.
A REVIEW OF SOVIET STUDIES OF CULTURE CHANGE, MUCH OF IT GOVERNMENTALLY-ENCOURAGED. DISTINGUISHES BETWEEN CULTURE CHANGE AND CULTURAL EXPANSION AND ASSERTS THAT MUCH OF WHAT HAS TAKEN PLACE RECENTLY FALLS INTO THE SECOND CATEGORY.

0867 DUNNING W.A.
"HISTORY OF POLITICAL THEORIES FROM LUTHER TO MONTESQUIEU."
LONDON: MACMILLAN, 1905.
SECOND VOLUME OF "HISTORY OF POLITICAL THEORIES," COVERING THE 16TH CENTURY THROUGH THE MIDDLE OF THE 18TH CENTURY. TWELVE CHAPTERS REVIEW POLITICAL PHILOSOPHY OF REFFORMATION, ANTI-MONARCHISTS, BODIN, GROTIUS, PURITAN REVOLUTION, HOBBES, SPINOZA, BOSSUET, LOCKE, HUME, AND MONTESQUIEU. BIBLIOGRAPHY OF ORIGINAL SOURCES, HISTORICAL, CRITICAL, AND DESCRIPTIVE WORKS. EUROPEAN SOURCES.

0868 DUNNING W.A.
"A HISTORY OF POLITICAL THINKERS FROM ROUSSEAU TO SPENCER."
LONDON: MACMILLAN, 1920.
CONCLUDING VOLUME OF "HISTORY OF POLITICAL THEORIES," DESIGNED TO CARRY SUBJECT THROUGH 1880. TEN CHAPTERS COVER ROUSSEAU, THE RISE OF ECONOMIC SCIENCE, AMERICAN AND FRENCH REVOLUTIONS, GERMAN IDEALISTS, THEORIES OF CONSERVATISM, ENGLISH UTILITARIANS, AND THE THEORIES OF CONSTITUTIONAL GOVERNMENT, NATIONALISM, AND SOCIALISM. BIBLIOGRAPHY OF ORIGINAL SOURCES, HISTORICAL, AND CRITICAL WORKS.

0870 DURKHEIM E.
THE ELEMENTARY FORMS OF THE RELIGIOUS LIFE.
NEW YORK: FREE PRESS OF GLENCOE, 1965, 507 PP.
STUDY OF SIMPLE RELIGION, THE PRIMITIVE SOCIETY WHERE IT IS FOUND, AND ITS ORIGIN. ANALYSIS OF RELIGIOUS PHENOMENA, ELEMENTARY BELIEFS, ATTITUDE TO RITUAL, AND ORIGIN OF THESE IDEAS. INCLUDES CHURCH, GOD, ANIMISM, NATURISM, TOTEMISM, SOUL, CULT, AND RITE. CONCLUDES THAT RELIGION, PHILOSOPHY,

AND MORALS CAN ONLY BE UNDERSTOOD IN AND THROUGH THE SOCIAL MIND OF COLLECTIVE SOCIETY.

0871 DURON J.F.
REPERTORIO BIBLIOGRAFICO HONDURENO.
HONDURAS: IMPRENTA CALDERON, 1943, 68 PP.
AN AUTHOR BIBLIOGRAPHY ON HONDURAS.

0872 DUROSELLE J.B.
LES NOUVEAUX ETATS DANS LES RELATIONS INTERNATIONALES.
PARIS: LIBRAIRIE ARMAND COLIN, 1962.
SURVEYS FOREIGN RELATIONS PROBLEMS OF NEWLY INDEPENDENT COUNTRIES. EXAMINES EXTERNAL MODELS, ESPECIALLY RUSSIA AND CHINA, THESE COUNTRIES IMITATE. ANALYZES INFLUENCE OF FORMER GOVERNING POWERS. CONSIDERS ATTITUDES TOWARDS MAJOR INTERNATIONAL PROBLEMS AND ORGANIZATIONS.

0873 DUTOIT B.
LA NEUTRALITE SUISSE A L'HEURE EUROPEENNE.
PARIS: LIBR. GEN. DR. JURIS., 1962, 139 PP.
TRACES EVOLUTION OF SWISS NEUTRALITY AND DISCUSSES THE IMPACT OF THE GROWTH OF INTERNATIONAL AND REGIONAL ORGANIZATIONS ON THIS CONCEPT.

0874 DUTT V.P.
"CHINA: JEALOUS NEIGHBOR."
CURR. HIST., 44 (MAR. 63), 135-40.
TRACES CHINA'S GRIEVANCES AGAINST INDIA. DEMONSTRATES SUCCESS OF DEMOCRATIC EXPERIMENT IN INDIA WHILE REFERRING TO CHINA'S BIG LEAP AS FAILURE WHICH RULED OUT CHINA AS ECONOMIC POLESTAR ON ASIAN HORIZON.

0875 DUVERGER M.
THE POLITICAL ROLE OF WOMEN.
PARIS: UNESCO, 1955, 221 PP.
SURVEYS POLITICAL PRACTICES OF WOMEN IN NORWAY, FRANCE, WEST GERMANY, AND YUGOSLAVIA; CONCERNED PRIMARILY WITH PART PLAYED BY WOMEN IN ELECTIONS AND IN POLITICAL LEADERSHIP. ANALYZES WAY WOMEN VOTE ACCORDING TO TYPE OF ELECTION, AGE, COMMUNITY, OCCUPATION, AND MARITAL STATUS; DISCUSSES DIFFERENCES IN FEMALE AND MALE VOTING. INCLUDES WOMEN AS POLITICAL CANDIDATES AND IN POLITICAL PARTIES AND LOBBIES.

0876 DWARKADAS R.
ROLE OF HIGHER CIVIL SERVICE IN INDIA.
BOMBAY: POPULAR BOOK DEPOT, 1958, 260 PP.
TREATS PROBLEM OF DEFINING ROLE OF HIGHER CIVIL SERVICE IN EMERGING, WELFARE-STATE ECONOMY OF INDIA. INITIAL PROBLEM IS IN TRANSFORMING ESSENTIALLY REGULATORY AND POLICE MECHANISM OF COLONIAL PERIOD INTO AN INSTRUMENT FOR PLANNING AND EXECUTING ECONOMIC AND SOCIAL DEVELOPMENT. FURTHER, DYNAMICS OF POLICY-MAKING AND OF ADMINISTRATIVE-LEGISLATIVE RELATIONSHIP MUST BE FORMULATED.

0877 DYCK H.V.
WEIMAR GERMANY AND SOVIET RUSSIA 1926-1933.
NEW YORK: COLUMBIA U PRESS, 1966, 279 PP., LC#66-14594.
STUDIES INSTABILITY OF DIPLOMATIC RELATIONS BETWEEN GERMANY AND SOVIET RUSSIA FROM 1926-1933. DISCUSSES NEUTRALITY OF TREATY OF BERLIN, INFLUENCE OF ANGLO-SOVIET BREAK ON GERMAN-SOVIET RELATIONS, AND METHODS OF POLICY FORMATION BY BOTH PARTIES.

0878 EAENZA L.
COMMUNISMO E CATTOLICESIMO IN UNA PARROCHIA DI CAMPAGNA.
MILAN: FETRINELLI EDITORE, 1959, 223 PP.
PRESENTS REACTIONS OF A MODERN RURAL COMMUNITY OF AN ITALIAN PARISH TO CONFLICTING IDEOLOGIES AND DECISION-MAKING PROCESS OF THE CATHOLIC CHURCH AND THE COMMUNIST PARTY. DISCUSSES EVOLUTION AND TRANSFORMATION OF THE TRADITIONAL RURAL CENTER DOMINATED BY THE CHURCH INTO A RESTIVE AND CONFUSED GROUP ORIENTED TOWARD A NEW IDEOLOGY AND A NEW ELITE.

0879 EARLE E.M. ED., CRAIG G.A. ED., GILBERT F. ED.
MAKERS OF MODERN STRATEGY: MILITARY THOUGHT FROM MACHIAVELLI TO HITLER.
PRINCETON: U. PR., 1943, 553 PP.
POINTS OUT USE OF MODERN WARFARE TECHNIQUES IN EUROPEAN CONFLICTS. STRESSES DEVELOPMENTS INTRODUCED BY JOMINI AND CLAUSEWITZ, EFFECTS OF NEW ECONOMIC AND IDEOLOGICAL THOUGHT ON POWER POLITICS, AND INCREASED CIVILIAN INVOLVEMENT ALONG WITH CHANGE IN NAVAL STRATEGY AFTER WORLD WAR ONE. THE EFFECTIVENESS OF HITLER'S STRATEGY AS YET UNDETERMINED.

0880 EASTON D.
"POLITICAL ANTHROPOLOGY" IN BIENNIAL REVIEW OF ANTHROPOLOGY"
STANFORD: STANFORD U PRESS, 1959.
COVERS RECENT LITERATURE DEALING WITH POLITICAL ANTHROPOLOGY. DISCUSSES CENTRAL THEMES LIKE NATURE AND FUNCTION OF LAW, IMPACT OF CIVILIZED UPON PRIMITIVE SOCIETIES, TRANSFORMATIONS OF POLITICAL ELITES, APPLICATION OF DATA TO SOLUTION OF CURRENT POLITICAL ISSUES, AND INTRODUCTION OF ANTHROPOLOGICAL CONCEPTS AND METHODS INTO STUDY OF MODERN HIGHLY COMPLEX SOCIETIES.

0881 EASTON D.
A SYSTEM ANALYSIS OF POLITICAL LIFE.
NEW YORK: JOHN WILEY, 1965, LC#65-12714.
HOLDING THAT SYSTEM ANALYSIS WILL PROVIDE A USEFUL MACROTHEORY OF SOCIAL AND POLITICAL BEHAVIOR, STUDIES METHODS AND APPLICATION OF POLITICAL SCIENCE. INCLUDES FORM AND CATEGORIES OF ANALYSIS, DEMANDS AND REGULATION OF STRESS, SOURCES AND OBJECT OF SUPPORT, AND RESPONSES AND OUTPUT AS REGULATORS OF SPECIFIC SUPPORT.

0882 EASTON S.C.
THE TWILIGHT OF EUROPEAN COLONIALISM.
NEW YORK: HOLT, 1960, 571 PP.
A SYSTEMATIC ANALYSIS OF POLITICAL MEANS BY WHICH COLONIES OF WESTERN POWERS TRIUMPHED IN THEIR STRUGGLES FOR INDEPENDENCE. CONTAINS VALUABLE INFORMATION ON POLITICAL INSTITUTIONS DEVELOPED IN COLONIES AND THEIR RELATIONSHIP TO THE IMPERIAL LEGACIES LEFT BEHIND BY COLONIAL POWERS. TREATS AT LENGTH INDEPENDENT NATIONS' ABILITY TO SURVIVE AFTER DEPARTURE OF COLONIAL RULERS. PRESENTS GHANA AS LEADING EXAMPLE IN AFRICA.

0883 EBENSTEIN W.
"INTRODUCTION TO POLITICAL PHILOSOPHY."
NEW YORK: RINEHART, 1952.
COLLECTION OF INTRODUCTORY ESSAYS TO THE MAJOR PROBLEMS OF POLITICAL PHILOSOPHY, AS REFLECTED IN THE GREAT POLITICAL THINKERS FROM PLATO TO PRESENT. ESSAYS COVER GREEK AND ROMAN POLITICAL PHILOSOPHY, MEDIEVAL CHRISTIAN THEOLOGY, PHILOSOPHY OF THE ENLIGHTENMENT, LIBERALISM, COMMUNISM, AND SOCIALISM. DETAILED, ANNOTATED BIBLIOGRAPHY OF SELECTIONS RELEVANT TO EACH CHAPTER.

0884 EBENSTEIN W.
"MODERN POLITICAL THOUGHT (2ND ED.)"
NEW YORK: HOLT RINEHART WINSTON, 1960.
A COLLECTION OF SELECTIONS FROM THE WRITINGS OF GREAT POLITICAL PHILOSOPHERS. ESSAYS ARE TOPICALLY ORGANIZED ACCORDING TO THE DISCIPLINE AND ISSUES WITH WHICH THEY DEAL. EXTENSIVE SECTION OF BIBLIOGRAPHICAL COMMENTS AND CRITICISM APPENDED TO TEXT. SOURCES AND SECONDARY MATERIAL ANNOTATED AND ORGANIZED BY RELEVANCE TO CHAPTER HEADINGS. SOURCES IN ENGLISH.

0885 EBENSTEIN W.
TWO WAYS OF LIFE.
NEW YORK: HOLT RINEHART WINSTON, 1962, 406 PP.
COMPARES POLITICAL AND ECONOMIC SYSTEMS OF MARXISM AND FREE MARKETING, THEIR SOCIO-CULTURAL EFFECTS, AND SUGGESTS WAYS OF COMBATING COMMUNISM. AIMS AT USE AS HIGH SCHOOL TEXT CONTAINS READINGS BY MARX, ENGELS, LENIN, LOCKE, ROUSSEAU, JEFFERSON, AND MILL.

0886 ECKSTEIN H., APTER D.E.
COMPARATIVE POLITICS.
NEW YORK: FREE PRESS OF GLENCOE, 1963, 746 PP., LC#63-7655.
COLLECTION OF ESSAYS THAT ATTEMPTS TO ILLUSTRATE THE STATE OF COMPARISON IN THE POLITICAL FIELD. INCLUDES ONLY THOSE ESSAYS THAT DEAL WITH A PROBLEM BY INSPECTION OF A VARIETY OF POLITICAL CONTEXTS. OUTLINES PRESENT TRENDS IN COMPARATIVE POLITICS. ANALYZES CONSTITUTIONAL GOVERNMENT, ELECTORAL SYSTEMS, TOTALITARIANISM, POLITICAL CHANGE. BIBLIOGRAPHY OF SELECTED LITERATURE INTRODUCING THE FIELD.

0887 EDDY J.P.
JUSTICE OF THE PEACE.
LONDON: CASSELL & CO LTD, 1963, 195 PP.
TRACES DEVELOPMENT OF OFFICE OF JUSTICE OF PEACE 1361-1962 WITH CONSTITUTIONAL IMPLICATIONS AND DIRECT RELATION TO EVOLVING COURT SYSTEM BASED ON COMMON LAW. CONSIDERS PRESENT ROLE OF JP IN ENGLISH JURISPRUDENCE AND STUDIES SOME BASIC PROBLEMS FACED.

0888 EDELMAN M., FLEMING R.W.
THE POLITICS OF WAGE-PRICE DECISIONS.
URBANA: U OF ILLINOIS PR, 1965, 321 PP., LC#65-10077.
ANALYSIS OF ATTEMPTS TO RESTRAIN PRICE AND WAGE LEVELS SINCE WWII. APPRAISES GAMUT OF INTERESTS, ORGANIZATIONAL AND POLITICAL PRESSURES THAT EXPLAIN WAGE-PRICE DECISION-MAKING IN POSTWAR EUROPE. EXAMINATION OF GOVERNMENTAL INSTITUTIONS AND PATTERNS OF INTERVENTION, PRIVATE AND PUBLIC ACTION, IDEOLOGIES, POLITICAL PARTIES, STRIKES, ETC.

0889 EDINGER L.J.
KURT SCHUMACHER: A STUDY IN PERSONALITY AND POLITICAL BEHAVIOR.
STANFORD: STANFORD U PRESS, 1965, 390 PP., LC#65-12731.
BIOGRAPHY OF KURT SCHUMACHER, POSTWAR LEADER IN GERMAN SOCIAL DEMOCRATIC PARTY. EXPLAINS SCHUMACHER'S POLITICAL BEHAVIOR AND MAKES IT CASE STUDY FOR STUDY OF POLITICAL LEADERSHIP; PERSONALITY AND LIFE SETTING HELP DETERMINE POLITICAL ACTIONS.

0890 EDUARDO O.D.C.
THE NEGRO IN NORTHERN BRAZIL: A STUDY IN ACCULTURATION.
NEW YORK: J J AUGUSTIN, 1948, 131 PP.

ANALYSIS OF NEGROES IN BRAZILIAN STATE OF MARANHAO IN BOTH RURAL AND URBAN SETTINGS TO DETERMINE STRENGTH OF THEIR AFRICAN CULTURE AND ITS RESISTANCE TO EUROPEAN CIVILIZATION. FOUND NEGRO ADAPTED WELL AND INTEGRATED BOTH ECONOMIC SYSTEMS AND FAMILY LIVING WITH WESTERN WAYS WITHOUT ANY CONFLICT. RETAINED MAJORITY OF AFRICAN RELIGIOUS BELIEFS, UNITING WHEN POSSIBLE WITH CATHOLICISM.

0891 EDWARDS A.C.
THE OVIMBUNDU UNDER TWO SOVEREIGNTIES.
LONDON: OXFORD U PR, 1962, 169 PP.
EXAMINES SOCIAL STRUCTURE OF OVIMBUNDU PEOPLE OF ANGOLA 1874-1911, AND ANALYZES PRESENT-DAY METHODS OF SOCIAL CONTROL. EXAMINES IN DETAIL "NETWORK OF KINSHIP AND MARRIAGE TIES."

0892 EDWARDS C.D.
TRADE REGULATIONS OVERSEAS.
NEW YORK: OCEANA PUBLISHING, 1966, 752 PP., LC#64-23357.
DISCUSSES POLICIES OF COMMON MARKET COUNTRIES, IRELAND, SOUTH AFRICA, NEW ZEALAND, AND JAPAN TOWARD MONOPOLIES, RESTRICTIVE AGREEMENTS, AND RESTRICTIVE BUSINESS PRACTICES.

0893 EDWARDS L.P.
THE NATURAL HISTORY OF REVOLUTION.
CHICAGO: U. CHI. PR., 1927, 229 PP., $3.00.
ANALYSIS OF THE REVOLUTIONARY CYCLE, DESCRIBING ITS TYPICAL SEQUENCE OF DEVELOPMENT: PRELIMINARY, THEN ADVANCED SYMPTOMS, OUTBREAK OF VIOLENCE, RISE OF RADICALS, REIGN OF TERROR AND RETURN TO NORMALCY.

0894 EGBERT D.D.
"POLITICS AND ART IN COMMUNIST BULGARIA"
SLAVIC REVIEW, 26 (JUNE 67), 204-216.
ANALYZES BULGARIAN ARTISTS' SUBSERVIENCE TO SOVIET IDEOLOGICAL DOMINANCE. FINDS THAT EVEN BULGARIAN ART MAY BE AFFECTED BY WAVE OF NATIONALISM SWEEPING COMMUNIST NATIONS. THOUGH NO NONOBJECTIVE ART HAS YET BEEN PRODUCED, NEW SPIRIT IS REFLECTED IN AVANT-GARDE DISLIKE OF SOVIET "SOCIALIST REALISM" DESPITE RISK OF OFFICIAL DISFAVOR.

0895 EGBERT D.D.
"THE IDEA OF 'AVANT-GARDE' IN ART AND POLITICS."
AMER. HISTORICAL REVIEW, 73 (DEC. 67), 339-366.
ANALYZES THE LACK OF AGREEMENT AMONG DEVOTED COMMUNISTS CONCERNING THE PROPER NATURE OF AVANT-GARDISM IN ART, AND ITS RELATION TO POLITICS. TRACES THE PATHS OF RADICALLY PROGRESSIVE LEADERS OF ART AND NOTES THE FREQUENT SYMPATHY OF THESE ARTISTS FOR COMMUNISM. EMPHASIZES THE RELUCTANCE OF AVANT-GARDE COMMUNIST ARTISTS TO SACRIFICE THEIR ART FOR THE PROMOTION OF THE PARTY.

0896 EGGAN F.
SELECTED BIBLIOGRAPHY OF THE PHILIPPINES.
CHICAGO: U OF CHICAGO PRESS, 1956, 138 PP.
SELECTED BIBLIOGRAPHY OF THE PHILIPPINES, TOPICALLY ARRANGED AND ANNOTATED. PREPARED BY PHILIPPINE STUDIES PROGRAM OF THE UNIVERSITY OF CHICAGO. PRELIMINARY EDITION PUBLISHED IN NEW HAVEN, HUMAN RELATIONS AREA FILES, 1956.

0897 EHRMANN H.W.
"FRENCH BUREAUCRACY AND ORGANIZED INTERESTS" (BMR)"
ADMINISTRATIVE SCI. Q., 5 (MAR. 61), 534-555.
ON THE BASIS OF INTERVIEWS WITH FRENCH CIVIL SERVANTS, INVESTIGATES WHETHER EXTENSIVE ADMINISTRATIVE RULE-MAKING IN THE FOURTH REPUBLIC HAS LIMITED PRESSURE-GROUP INFLUENCE OR WHETHER DIRECT IMPACT OF THE GROUPS HAS IMPINGED ON ADMINISTRATIVE AUTONOMY. IT IS FOUND THAT CERTAIN ADMINISTRATIVE PATTERNS GENERALLY INCREASE THE ACCESS OF ORGANIZED INTERESTS TO AUTHORITATIVE DECISION-MAKING.

0898 EICH H.
THE UNLOVED GERMANS.
LONDON: MCDONALD & EVANS,LTD, 1963, 255 PP.
STUDIES NATIONAL CHARACTER TRAITS OF GERMANS. DISCUSSES THEIR IDEALS AND SYMBOLS, PREDOMINANT CHARACTERISTICS, AND FAVORITE ACTIVITIES. ANALYZES OTHER PEOPLES' FEELINGS TOWARD GERMANS AND "TRADITIONAL" GERMAN PREJUDICES.
FEELS THAT GERMANS HAVE RECOGNIZED THEIR GUILT OF THIS CENTURY AND ARE BEGINNING TO REALIZE THEY NEED NOT FULFILL OTHERS' PRECONCEIVED NOTIONS OF THEIR MILITANT HABITS.

0899 EINAUDI L., GOLDHAMER H.
"ANNOTATED BIBLIOGRAPHY OF LATIN AMERICAN MILITARY JOURNALS"
J. OF LATIN AM. RES. REV., 2 (SPRING 67), 95-122.
ARRANGED BY COUNTRY, THIS SELECTION CONTAINS A DESCRIPTION OF SIZE, SCOPE, AND FORMAT OF EACH MAGAZINE AS WELL AS ANY OTHER INFORMATION THAT SEEMS PERTINENT OR IMPORTANT. PREPARED UNDER RAND CORPORATION AUSPICES. ALSO INCLUDES UNANNOTATED REVIEWS AND AN APPENDIX OF REVIEWS NO LONGER AVAILABLE.

0900 EISENSTADT S.N.
"THE PROCESS OF ABSORPTION OF NEW IMMIGRANTS IN ISRAEL" (BMR)"
HUMAN RELATIONS, 5 (1952), 223-246.
DEALS MAINLY WITH IMMIGRANTS WHO ARRIVED AFTER ESTABLISHMENT OF STATE OF ISRAEL. OBSERVES BEHAVIOR IN TYPICAL SOCIAL SITUATIONS, SUCH AS WORK, SCHOOL, ETC. DEALS WITH GENERAL BACKGROUND, MOTIVES FOR IMMIGRATION, INTERESTS, LEVELS OF ASPIRATIONS, SOCIAL PARTICIPATION AND IDENTIFICATION, ETC.

0901 EISENTADT S.N.
"POLITICAL STRUGGLE IN BUREAUCRATIC SOCIETIES"
WORLD POLITICS, 9 (OCT. 56), 15-36.
BUREAUCRATIC SYSTEMS IN ANCIENT EMPIRES - THE BYZANTINE, THE CHINESE, AND THE OTTOMAN - AND IN EUROPEAN COUNTRIES IN THE AGE OF ABSOLUTISM. EACH SYSTEM SAID TO DIFFER ACCORDING TO THE SOCIOLOGICAL CONTEXT IN WHICH THE BUREAUCRACY OPERATES.

0902 EISTER A.W.
"PERSPECTIVE ON FUNCTIONS OF RELIGION IN A DEVELOPING COUNTRY: ISLAM IN PAKISTAN."
J. SCI. STUDY OF RELIGION, (1964), 27-238.
SURVEY OF 450 PAKISTANI VILLAGERS ON RELIGIOUS ATTITUDES. CONCLUDES ISLAM OFFERS NO FIXED OR IMPENETRABLE BAR TO MORE RAPID DEVELOPMENT IN THE VILLAGES.

0903 ELAHI K.N. ED., MOID A. ED., SIDDIQUI A.H. ED.
A GUIDE TO WORKS OF REFERENCE PUBLISHED IN PAKISTAN (PAMPHLET)
KARACHI: KARACHI U LIB, PAKIS BIBLIOG, 1953, 36 PP.
SOME OF THE WORKS LISTED IN THIS GUIDE ARE ANNOTATED WHILE OTHERS ARE NOT; LOCATION IN VARIOUS PAKISTANI LIBRARIES IS GIVEN. ARRANGED UNDER SUBJECT HEADINGS.

0904 ELAZAR D.J.
"CHURCHES AS MOLDERS OF AMERICAN POLITICS."
AMER. BEHAVIORAL SCIENTIST, 4 (MAY 61), 15-18.
POINTS TO FOUR SALIENT AREAS OF CHURCH IMPACT ON THE CIVIL COMMUNITY, BASED LARGELY ON ROCKFORD, ILLINOIS. THEY ARE, FIRST, THE CONGREGATIONAL SYSTEM OF GOVERNMENT; SECOND, CHURCH ROLE AS A MEANS OF SOCIAL PROTEST; THIRD, AS A WAY OF MAINTAINING ETHNIC DISTINCTIONS; AND FOURTH, THE CHURCHES AS VEHICLES FOR VARIOUS SUBCULTURES NOT BUILT ON ETHNIC FOUNDATIONS.

0905 ELDRIDGE H.T.
THE MATERIALS OF DEMOGRAPHY: A SELECTED AND ANNOTATED BIBLIOGRAPHY.
NY: INTL UNION SCI STUDY POPULAT, 1959, 222 PP.
IDENTIFIES AND DESCRIBES SIGNIFICANT PUBLISHED WORKS IN THE FIELD OF POPULATION ANALYSIS. CITATIONS LIMITED TO POST-1940 PUBLICATIONS IN ENGLISH; COMPILATIONS IN OTHER LANU GAGES ISSUED SEPARATELY. BIBLIOGRAPHY IS TOPICALLY CLASSIFIED ACCORDING TO THE COMPONENTS OF POPULATION CHANGE: BIRTH, DEATH, AND MIGRATION. CONTAINS AN AUTHOR INDEX.

0906 ELIAS T.O.
GOVERNMENT AND POLITICS IN AFRICA.
NEW YORK: ASIA PUBL HOUSE, 1963, 288 PP.
WRITTEN VERSION OF SERIES OF LECTURES DELIVERED IN INDIA ON CONTEMPORARY PROBLEMS OF GOVERNMENT AND POLITICS IN AFRICA. MATERIAL TOPICALLY AND CHRONOLOGICALLY ARRANGED. COVERS PERIOD FROM ANCIENT AFRICAN CIVILIZATIONS THROUGH MOVEMENTS FOR REFORM IN CONTEMPORARY AFRICA. ORGANIZES MATERIAL GEOGRAPHICALLY WITHIN EACH CHAPTER. BRIEF LISTS OF BRITISH AND INDIAN SOURCES AT END OF EACH TOPIC.

0907 ELKIN A.B.
"OEEC-ITS STRUCTURE AND POWERS."
EUROP. YRB., 4 (58), 96-149.
STUDIES POWER AND JURISDICTION OF OEEC VIS A VIS ITS MEMBER GOVERNMENTS. COUNCIL IS MAIN ORGAN WITH SUBORDINATE BODIES, SUCH AS STEERING BOARD FOR TRADE. ORIGINAL RULE OF UNANIMOUS VOTE HAS CHANGED TO MAJORITY RULE IN SUBORDINATE ORGANS.

0908 ELKIN A.P.
THE AUSTRALIAN ABORIGINES - HOW TO UNDERSTAND THEM (4TH ED.)
LONDON, SYDNEY: ANGUS & ROBERTSN, 1964, 393 PP.
EXAMINES SOCIAL ORGANIZATION, LAWS, BELIEFS, AND RITUALS OF AUSTRALIAN ABORIGINES. DISCUSSES FAMILY STRUCTURE, KINSHIP AND MARRIAGE CUSTOMS, BLACK MAGIC, AND CUSTOMS ASSOCIATED WITH DEATH.

0909 ELLIOT J.H.
THE REVOLT OF THE CATALANS.
NEW YORK: CAMBRIDGE U PRESS, 1963, 633 PP.
STUDIES CATALAN REVOLUTION IN SPAIN IN 1640, EMPHASIZING ROLE OF CHIEF MINISTER OLIVARES IN PROVOKING REVOLT. DISCUSSES RELATION BETWEEN THIS REVOLT AND DECLINING FORTUNES AND AUTHORITY OF SPANISH MONARCHY IN 17TH CENTURY.

0910 ELLIS A.B.
THE EWE-SPEAKING PEOPLES OF THE SLAVE COAST OF WEST AFRICA.
OOSTERHAUF: ANTHROPOLOGICAL PUB, 1966, 331 PP.
STUDY OF EWE TRIBE, WHICH IS ONE OF FOUR SEPARATE LINGUAL GROUPS SITUATED ON WEST COAST OF AFRICA. MAJOR CONSIDERATION

IS RELIGION OF EWES AND ITS EFFECT UPON THEIR SOCIETY. VARIOUS DEITIES, SUPERSTITIONS, HUMAN SACRIFICES, PRIESTHOOD, CEREMONIES, GOVERNMENT, CUSTOMS, AND FOLKLORE AMONG TOPICS DISCUSSED.

0911 ELLISON H.J.
"THE SOCIALIST REVOLUTIONARIES."
PROBLEMS OF COMMUNISM, 16 (NOV. 67), 2-14.
PRESENTS HISTORY OF SOCIALIST REVOLUTIONARY PARTY IN RUSSIA. PARTY WAS FORMED IN 1906 AND WAS MADE UP OF AGRARIAN SOCIALISTS WHO BELIEVED IN DEVELOPING SOCIALIST SYSTEM ON STRUCTURE OF SEMI-SOCIALIST LAND TENURE. PARTY WAS NEVER WELL ORGANIZED, BUT IT ENJOYED WIDE POPULAR SUPPORT. PARTY FAILED IN 1917 IN PART BECAUSE PARTY LEADER, VIKTOR CHERNOV, LACKED ORGANIZATIONAL AND PERSONAL LEADERSHIP QUALITIES.

0912 ELWIN V. ED.
A NEW DEAL FOR TRIBAL INDIA.
NEW DELHI: MINISTRY HOME AFFAIRS, 1963, 146 PP.
CONDENSED REPORT OF THE CONSTITUTION OF INDIA ON TRIBAL POPULATION DEALING WITH ECONOMIC, SOCIAL, AND HEALTH CONDITIONS TO DETERMINE WHICH MOST NEEDED EDUCATION, FINANCIAL, AND MEDICAL ASSISTANCE.

0913 EMBREE A.T. ED.
A GUIDE TO PAPERBACKS ON ASIA; SELECTED AND ANNOTATED (PAMPHLET)
NEW YORK: ASIA SOCIETY, 1964, 89 PP.
AN ANNOTATED COMPILATION OF PAPERBOUND BOOKS AND PAMPHLETS CURRENTLY IN PRINT. LISTS OVER 500 TITLES, ALL AMERICAN PUBLICATIONS. 1966 SUPPLEMENT CONTAINS 240 PAPERBACKS PUBLISHED FROM 1964 THROUGH 1966. ENTRIES DIVIDED INTO ASIA IN GENERAL, SOUTH ASIA, SOUTHEAST ASIA, AND EAST ASIA. INCLUDES POLITICAL, HISTORICAL, ECONOMIC, SOCIAL, AND CULTURAL TOPICS.

0914 EMBREE A.T. ED., MESKILL J. ED. ET AL.
ASIA: A GUIDE TO BASIC BOOKS (PAMPHLET)
NEW YORK: ASIA SOCIETY, 1966, 57 PP.
ANNOTATED COMPILATION OF 316 ENGLISH-LANGUAGE BOOKS. ENTRIES LISTED BY COUNTRY UNDER FOUR GENERAL TOPICS: ASIA IN GENERAL, SOUTH ASIA, SOUTHEAST ASIA, AND EAST ASIA. INCLUDES MODERN POLITICAL, SOCIAL, AND ECONOMIC DEVELOPMENT. PUBLICATION DATES RANGE FROM 1920 THROUGH 1966.

0915 EMBREE J.F., DOTSON L.O.
BIBLIOGRAPHY OF THE PEOPLES AND CULTURES OF MAINLAND SOUTHEAST ASIA.
NEW HAVEN: YALE U PR, 1950, 833 PP.
THOROUGH AND EXTENSIVE BIBLIOGRAPHY OF REFERENCES DEALING WITH MAINLAND SOUTHEAST ASIA AND WRITTEN IN EUROPEAN LANGUAGES. INCLUDES MAPS, LISTS OF BIBLIOGRAPHIES, AND PERIODICALS. DIVIDED INTO SECTIONS BY COUNTRY, THEN SUBDIVIDED BY TOPICS SUCH AS ANTHROPOLOGY, ARCHEOLOGY, ETHNOLOGY, HISTORY, LANGUAGE, FOLKLORE, ETC.

0916 EMDEN C.S.
THE PEOPLE AND THE CONSTITUTION (2ND ED.)
LONDON: OXFORD U PR, 1956, 339 PP.
DEVELOPMENT OF PEOPLE'S PART IN ENGLISH GOVERNMENT. CONSTITUTIONAL HISTORY OF THE PEOPLE.

0917 EMERI C.
"LES FORCES POLITIQUES AU PARLEMENT"
REV. FRANCAISE SCI. POLIT., 3 (SEPT. 63), 728-739.
POLITICAL ANALYSIS OF FRENCH LEGISLATURE AND ITS RELATIONS WITH EXECUTIVE BRANCH. ROLE OF POLITICAL PARTIES IN FRENCH LEGISLATIVE AND DELIBERATIVE PROCESS AND THEIR INFLUENCE ON THE EXECUTIVE AND DECISION-MAKING GROUPS ARE DISCUSSED.

0918 EMERSON R.
"THE EROSION OF DEMOCRACY."
J. ASIAN STUD., 20 (NOV. 60), 1-8.
DESCRIBES CHARACTERISTICS IN SOCIETY NECESSARY FOR DEVELOPMENT OF DEMOCRACY. TREATS DEMOCRATIC PRACTICES IN ASIA AND AFRICA WITH REFERENCE TO THEIR INSTITUTIONS. COMPARES SUCCESS AND FAILURE OF DEMOCRATIC SYSTEMS IN THE LIGHT OF ASIAN ENVIRONMENT WITH PARTICULAR EMPHASIS ON ECONOMIC CONDITIONS.

0919 EMERSON R.
FROM EMPIRE TO NATION: THE RISE TO SELF-ASSERTION OF ASIAN AND AFRICAN PEOPLES.
CAMBRIDGE: HARVARD U PR, 1960, 466 PP., LC#60-5883.
ARGUES THAT RISE OF NATIONALISM AMONG NON-EUROPEAN PEOPLES IS A CONSEQUENCE OF IMPERIAL SPREAD OF WESTERN EUROPEAN CIVILIZATION. FOCUSES ON OVERSEAS EXPANSION OF EUROPE, ITS AFTERMATH, AND NATURE OF NEW NATIONALISM. EXTENSIVE NOTES AND BIBLIOGRAPHY.

0920 EMERY E., AULT P.H., AGEE W.K.
INTRODUCTION TO MASS COMMUNICATIONS.
NEW YORK: DODD, MEAD, 1960, 435 PP., LC#60-9886.
DESCRIPTIONS OF MASS COMMUNICATIONS INDUSTRIES, PROFESSIONAL WORK IN JOURNALISM. DEFINES TERMS OF MASS MEDIA AND JOURNALISM AND PLACES MASS COMMUNICATIONS IN HISTORICAL PERSPECTIVE. DETAILED DESCRIPTION OF ORGANIZATION OF MASS COMMUNICATIONS INDUSTRIES, GROWTH, AND CURRENT STATUS OF EDUCATION FOR JOURNALISM. INCLUDES SELECTED ANNOTATED BIBLIOGRAPHY.

0921 EMME E.M. ED.
THE IMPACT OF AIR POWER - NATIONAL SECURITY AND WORLD POLITICS.
PRINCETON: VAN NOSTRAND, 1959, 914 PP., LC#59-8554.
COLLECTION OF ESSAYS ON NATURE AND THEORIES OF AIR WARFARE. DISCUSSES AIR WARFARE IN WWII AND LESSONS DRAWN. COMPARES SOVIET AND US AIR POLICY AND EXAMINES AIR POWER IN EUROPE AND ASIA.

0922 EMMET C., MUHLEN N.
THE VANISHING SWASTIKA.
CHICAGO: HENRY REGNERY CO, 1961, 66 PP.
EXAMINES ATTITUDE OF POST-WAR GERMANY TOWARD NAZISM, AND INVESTIGATES INTO CAREERS OF FORMER MEMBERS OF NAZI PARTY, ESPECIALLY THOSE WHICH NOW HOLD POSITIONS IN GOVERNMENT. FINDS THAT THERE IS MUCH IGNORANCE AMONG YOUTHS ABOUT NAZI PAST.

0923 EMMET D.M.
FUNCTION, PURPOSE AND POWERS.
NEW YORK: ST MARTIN'S PRESS, 1958, 300 PP.
NOT A COMPREHENSIVE WORK ON SOCIOLOGICAL THEORY, BUT APPROACHES SUCH CONCEPTS AS SOCIAL FUNCTION, "OPEN" AND "CLOSED" MORALITY, AND CHARISMATIC POWER FROM THE POINT OF VIEW OF SOCIAL ANTHROPOLOGY. AUTHOR'S DISCIPLINE IS PHILOSOPHY.

0924 ENGELS F.
THE PEASANT WAR IN GERMANY (1850)
NEW YORK: INTERNATIONAL PUBLRS, 1927, 190 PP.
EXAMINES THE ECONOMIC, SOCIAL, AND POLITICAL STRENGTH OF THE PEASANTRY IN THEIR 1525 REVOLT, IN ORDER TO ASSESS THEIR RELIABILITY IN A SOCIALIST REVOLUTION. ARGUES THAT THE PEASANT WAR WAS SIMILAR TO THE REVOLUTIONS OF 1848 EXCEPT THAT THE GOVERNMENTS ARE MORE DEPENDENT ON THE PROLETARIANS, THUS MAKING IT LIKELY THAT THEY AND THE PEASANTRY CAN WIN A SOCIALIST REVOLUTION.

0925 ENGELS F.
HERRN EUGEN DUHRING'S REVOLUTION IN SCIENCE (1878)
NEW YORK: INTERNATIONAL PUBLRS, 1939, 385 PP.
ATTACKS DUHRING'S CONCEPT OF SOCIETY AS POWER-BASED, WITH POLITICAL CONSIDERATIONS DOMINATING ECONOMIC ONES. GIVES POINT-BY-POINT REFUTATION OF THIS CONCEPT AS BASED ON PSEUDO-SCIENTIFIC MATERIALISM WHICH TOTALLY NEGLECTS ENERGY. DEFENDS MARXIAN ECONOMIC INTERPRETATION OF HISTORY AND BELIEF IN PREVALENCE OF STRUGGLE IN SOCIETY, ESPECIALLY CLASS CONFLICT.

0926 ENGELS F.
THE ORIGIN OF THE FAMILY, PRIVATE PROPERTY, AND THE STATE (TRANS. BY E. UNTERMANN)
ORIGINAL PUBLISHER NOT AVAILABLE, 1884, 217 PP.
ATTEMPTS TO RELATE DEVELOPMENT OF THE FAMILY IN SOCIETY TO NOTIONS OF PROPERTY AND FINALLY TO CLASS STRUGGLES. BEGINNING WITH PRIMITIVE "MATRILINEAL" SOCIETY, POINTS OUT RISE OF NEW ORDER IN FAMILY RELATIONS: MALE DOMINANCE AND PROPERTY OWNERSHIP. PRESENTS CRITIQUE OF MONOGAMY AS ANTI-COMMUNAL AND THEREFORE DENYING RIGHTS OF OTHERS.

0927 ENKE S., SALERA V.
INTERNATIONAL ECONOMICS.
ENGLEWOOD CLIFFS: PRENTICE HALL, 1947, 731 PP.
DISCUSSES PRINCIPLES OF INTERNATIONAL TRADE AND FINANCE. EXAMINES CLASSICAL THEORIES, TRADE CONTROL, CARTELS, COMMERCIAL TREATIES, TRADE POLICIES OF USSR, US, AND UK, MONETARY AND FINANCIAL POLICIES, ETC.

0928 ENKE S.
ECONOMICS FOR DEVELOPMENT.
ENGLEWOOD CLIFFS: PRENTICE HALL, 1963, 616 PP., LC#63-9968.
EMPHASIZES PRINCIPLES OF ECONOMICS OF DEVELOPMENT. CONCLUDES FROM STUDY AND OBSERVATION THAT US IS UNSUCCESSFUL IN FOREIGN AID PROGRAMS BECAUSE IT IGNORES TRADITION AND VARIED INTERESTS THAT LIE AT ROOT OF ECONOMIC UNDERDEVELOPMENT. ARGUES POLICY-MAKERS ARE UNAWARE OF PRINCIPLES OF ECONOMIC THEORY. BIBLIOGRAPHY INCLUDED FOR EACH CHAPTER.

0929 ENNIS T.E.
"VIETNAM: LAND WITHOUT LAUGHTER."
CURR. HIST., 46 (FEB. 64), 101-106.
PICTURES SOUTH VIETNAM AS BRIGHTENED SINCE FALL OF NGO DYNASTY. YOUNG VIETNAMESE HAVE PLOTTED FOR GENERATIONS TO END ENCROACHMENTS OF CHINESE. 'NO ARMY CAN WITHSTAND THE STRENGTH OF AN IDEA WHOSE TIME HAS COME... YOUTH OF DISTRAUGHT LAND MAY FIND A WASHINGTON, A BOLIVAR OR GANDHI TO INSPIRE AND GUIDE THEM TO FREEDOM.'

0930 ENSOR R.C.K.
COURTS AND JUDGES IN FRANCE, GERMANY, AND ENGLAND.

LONDON: OXFORD U PR, 1933, 144 PP.
A SHORT STUDY OF LEGAL ADMINISTRATION IN FRANCE AND GERMANY AND A COMPARATIVE ANALYSIS OF BRITISH PRACTICE. OUTLINES THE COMPOSITION OF THE TWO CONTINENTAL COURT SYSTEMS. COMPARES METHODS OF FILLING JUDICIAL POSTS, COURT PROCEDURES IN CRIMINAL AND CIVIL CASES, METHODS OF APPEAL, AND ULTIMATE JUDICIAL AUTHORITY IN THE THREE COUNTRIES.

0931 EPSTEIN E.H.
"NATIONAL IDENTITY AND THE LANGUAGE ISSUE IN PUERTO RICO."
COMPARATIVE EDUCATION REVIEW, 11 (JUNE 67), 133-143.
DISCUSSES ISSUE OF HOW MUCH ENGLISH TO TEACH IN PUERTO RICAN SCHOOLS. NATIONALISTS HAVE ALWAYS OPPOSED ENGLISH INSTRUCTION, FEELING IT DEPRIVED PUERTO RICANS OF THEIR NATIONAL CHARACTER. TODAY MUCH OF ENGLISH INSTRUCTION HAS MOVED FROM PUBLIC TO PRIVATE SCHOOLS; PRIVATE INSTITUTIONS ARE CRITICIZED. RESULTS OF SURVEY SHOW THAT PRIVATE SCHOOL PUPILS DO NOT IDENTIFY LESS WITH SPANISH CULTURE.

0932 EPSTEIN F.T.
EAST GERMANY: A SELECTED BIBLIOGRAPHY (PAMPHLET)
WASHINGTON: LIBRARY OF CONGRESS, 1959, 55 PP., LC#59-60084.
SOME 350 ANNOTATED US GOVERNMENT DOCUMENTS, BIBLIOGRAPHIES, STATISTICAL HANDBOOKS, WEST GERMAN DOCUMENTS, PERIODICALS, LEGISLATION, MONOGRAPHS, AND BOOKS ON EAST GERMANY PUBLISHED 1947-58. ARRANGED TOPICALLY AND BY TYPE OF SOURCE, WITH MOST IN GERMAN. SUBJECT INDEX.

0933 EPSTEIN F.T. ED., WHITTAKER C.H. ED.
THE AMERICAN BIBLIOGRAPHY OF RUSSIAN AND EAST EUROPEAN STUDIES FOR 1964.
BLOOMINGTON: INDIANA U PR, 1966, 119 PP., LC#58-63499.
BIBLIOGRAPHICAL LISTING OF BOOKS AND ARTICLES PUBLISHED IN ENGLISH IN THE US IN 1964. ALSO INCLUDES BOOKS PUBLISHED IN ENGLISH THROUGHOUT THE WORLD WITH THE EXCEPTION OF RUSSIA AND EAST EUROPE. TRANSLATIONS NOT INCLUDED. ITEMS GROUPED BY SUBJECT AND COUNTRY. CONTAINS AUTHOR INDEX. 2,260 ENTRIES.

0934 EPSTEIN L.D.
BRITAIN - UNEASY ALLY.
CHICAGO: U CHI, CTR POLICY STUDY, 1954, 279 PP.
ANALYZES BRITISH OPINION AND REACTION TO US FOREIGN POLICY, AID, AND TRADE PROGRAMS IN POSTWAR PERIOD, 1945-52. INCLUDES ATTITUDES OF CONSERVATIVE AND LABOUR PARTIES AND OF PUBLIC. DISCUSSES DIFFERENCES IN ATTITUDES OF BOTH COUNTRIES AND MEASURES TAKEN IN KOREAN CONFLICT.

0935 EPSTEIN L.D.
"COHESION OF BRITISH PARLIAMENTARY PARTIES."
AM. POL. SCI. REV., 50 (JUNE 56), 360-377.
COHESION OF BRITISH PARLIAMENTARY PARTIES NOT MAINTAINED BY PARTY DEVICES, BUT RATHER BY SOCIO-POLITICAL ENVIRONMENT. DISCIPLINE EXPLAINED BY CONSTITUTIONAL SYSTEM, NATIONALIZATION OF POLITICS, AND SHARPER IDEOLOGICAL DIVISIONS THAN IN UNITED STATES.

0936 EPSTEIN L.D.
"BRITISH MASS PARTIES IN COMPARISON WITH AMERICAN PARTIES"
POLIT. SCI. QUART., 71 (MAR. 56), 97-125.
INDICATES THE FALLACIES INVOLVED IN REGARDING AMERICAN PARTIES, AS BACKWARD IN COMPARISON WITH EUROPEAN PARTIES PARTICULARLY BRITISH. CONTENDS THAT IT IS UNREASONABLE TO DECLARE THAT THE US ECONOMY HAS FAILED TO PRODUCE POLITICAL CLASS CONSCIOUSNESS BECAUSE THAT ECONOMY IS SOMEHOW BEHIND EUROPEAN DEVELOPMENTS. ARGUES THAT MASS-MEMBERSHIP FACTOR IS SIMILARLY NOT TO BE CONFUSED FOR POLITICAL MATURITY.

0937 ERASMUS C.J.
MAN TAKES CONTROL: CULTURAL DEVELOPMENT AND AMERICAN AID.
MINNEAPOLIS: U OF MINN PR, 1961, 365 PP., LC#61-8400.
CONCERNED WITH PRE-INDUSTRIAL PEOPLES OF UNDERDEVELOPED AREAS AND THEIR RELATION TO INDUSTRIALIZED SOCIETY. FORMULATES SIMPLE SCHEME OF CULTURAL CAUSALITY, CONGENIAL TO AN APPLIED INTEREST IN CULTURE CHANGE. ADVANCES GENERAL THEORY OF CULTURE DEVELOPMENT. INCLUDES CASE STUDY OF ECONOMIC DEVELOPMENT AND CULTURAL CHANGE IN NORTHWESTERN MEXICO.

0938 ERDMAN H.L.
THE SWATANTRA PARTY AND INDIAN CONSERVATISM.
NEW YORK: CAMBRIDGE U PRESS, 1967, 356 PP., LC#67-27128.
ANALYZES RIGHT-WING PARTY FOUNDED IN 1959. BEGINS WITH BACKGROUND OF CONSERVATIVE POLITICS IN INDIA PRIOR TO 1959; CONSIDERS CONCEPT OF CONSERVATISM AND SURVEYS DOCTRINES, POLITICAL ORGANIZATION, AND SOCIAL BACKGROUND OF RIGHT-WING PARTIES FORMING COALITION SWATANTRA PARTY. STUDIES INTERNAL STRUCTURE, LEADERSHIP, IDEOLOGY, AND ELECTORAL RESPONSE TO PARTY. CLOSES WITH RESULTS OF 1967 ELECTION.

0939 ESCUELA SUPERIOR DE ADMIN PUBL
INFORME DEL SEMINARIO SOBRE SERVICIO CIVIL O CARRERA ADMINISTRATIVA.
SAN JOSE, CR: ESCUELA ADMIN PUBL, 1962, 358 PP.
REPORT OF SEMINAR ON PUBLIC ADMINISTRATION IN CENTRAL AMERICA. DISCUSSES CIVIL SERVICE STRUCTURE, RECRUITMENT, CIVIL SERVANT EVALUATION, JOB CLASSIFICATIONS, AND ETHICS AND DISCIPLINE REQUIRED IN PUBLIC ADMINISTRATION.

0940 ESMEIN A.
ELEMENTS DE DROIT CONSTITUTIONNEL.
PARIS: LIB SOC DU RECEUIL SIREY, 1896, 841 PP.
ELEMENTS OF CONSTITUTIONAL LAW. PART I EXAMINES MODERN CONCEPT OF LIBERTY, AS IT DEVELOPED UNDER THE INSTITUTIONS ESTABLISHED BY ENGLISH LAW AND THE PRINCIPLES PROCLAIMED BY THE FRENCH REVOLUTION. PART II DEALS WITH CONSTITUTIONAL LAW OF THE FRENCH REPUBLIC AND DISCUSSES THE PRECEDENTS OF THE CONSTITUTION OF 1875, EXECUTIVE POWER, LEGISLATIVE POWER, THE HIGH COURT, AND CONSTITUTIONAL REVISION.

0941 ESTEBAN J.C.
IMPERIALISMO Y DESARROLLO ECONOMICO.
BUENOS AIRES: EDITORIAL PALESTRA, 1961, 213 PP.
ANALYZES ECONOMIC DEVELOPMENT OF ARGENTINA REGARDING ROLE OF GOVERNMENT AND PRIVATE CAPITAL IN FURTHER IMPROVEMENT AND INDUSTRIALIZATION OF NATIONAL ECONOMY. DISCUSSES NEED TO REGULATE EXTENT OF FOREIGN CAPITAL INFLUENCE IN NATIONAL ECONOMY. EXAMINES INTERNATIONAL ECONOMIC OBLIGATIONS OF ARGENTINA AND STATE OF ITS BALANCE OF PAYMENTS.

0942 ESTEVEZ A., ELIA O.H.
ASPECTOS ECONOMICO-FINANCIEROS DE LA CAMPANA SANMARITANA.
BUENOS AIRES: COM NAC EJECUTIVA, 1961, 257 PP.
EXAMINES ECONOMIC SITUATION OF SOUTH AMERICA AT TIME OF ITS REVOLUTION FOR INDEPENDENCE FROM SPAIN. ANALYZES PLAN FOR POLITICAL AND ECONOMIC DEVELOPMENT UNDER REVOLUTIONARY LEADER SAN MARTIN. DISCUSSES ROLE OF GOVERNMENT IN FORMATION OF BANKING STRUCTURE AND STABILIZATION OF ECONOMY FOR NATIONAL DEVELOPMENT.

0943 ETSCHMANN R.
DIE WAHRUNGS- UND DEVISENPOLITIK DES OSTBLOCKS UND IHRE AUSWIRKUNGEN AUF DIE WIRTSCHAFTSBEZIEHUNGEN ZWISCHEN OST U WEST
BONN: UNIV OF BONN, 1959, 213 PP.
EXAMINES ECONOMIC AND FOREIGN TRADE POLICIES OF EASTERN COUNTRIES WITH EMPHASIS ON CURRENCY STANDARDS AND FOREIGN EXCHANGE. FOCUSES ON CZECHOSLOVAKIA, POLAND, HUNGARY, RUMANIA, BULGARIA, USSR, CHINA, AND EAST GERMANY.

0944 ETTINGHAUSEN R. ED.
SELECTED AND ANNOTATED BIBLIOGRAPHY OF BOOKS AND PERIODICALS IN WESTERN LANGUAGES DEALING WITH NEAR AND MIDDLE EAST.
WASHINGTON: MIDDLE EAST INST, 1952, 111 PP.
LISTS, ANNOTATES, AND INDEXES BY AUTHOR 1,719 ITEMS COVERING THE NEAR AND MIDDLE EAST FROM ANCIENT TO PRESENT TIMES. INCLUDES MAPS, CHARTS, GUIDE BOOKS, AS WELL AS BIBLIOGRAPHIES, PERIODICALS, ETC. DEALING WITH ART, ARCHITECTURE, ARCHEOLOGY, CULTURE, HISTORY, RELIGION, LITERATURE, AND LAW IN EACH COUNTRY AND AREA. STRESSES MEDIEVAL PERIOD AND AFTER.

0945 ETZIONI A.
COMPLEX ORGANIZATIONS: A SOCIOLOGICAL READER.
NEW YORK: HOLT RINEHART WINSTON, 1961, 497 PP., LC#61-7443.
ARTICLES ON "SOCIAL UNITS WHICH ARE PREDOMINANTLY ORIENTED TO THE ATTAINMENT OF SPECIFIC GOALS," DEALING WITH THEORY, CONCEPTUAL AND APPLIED, GOALS, STRUCTURES (INCLUDING THOSE OF UNIONS, CHURCHES, HOSPITALS SCHOOLS), AND ORGANIZATIONAL CHANGE, AS WELL AS THE POSITIONS OF ORGANIZATIONS WITHIN THE FRAMEWORK OF SOCIETY AND METHODOLOGICAL DISCUSSIONS.

0946 ETZIONI A.
MODERN ORGANIZATIONS.
ENGLEWOOD CLIFFS: PRENTICE HALL, 1964, 120 PP., LC#64-17073.
DEALS WITH STRUCTURE AND VARIOUS THEORIES APPLICABLE TO IT, WITH ORGANIZATIONAL CONTROL AND LEADERSHIP (INCLUDING REPRESENTATIONAL ASPECTS OF INFORMAL LEADERS), THE CONCEPT OF ADMINISTRATIVE AND PROFESSIONAL AUTHORITY, AS WELL AS THE RELATION OF MODERN ORGANIZATIONS TO VARIOUS PUBLICS AND CLIENT SYSTEMS AND NOTES RELATIVE LACK OF CONSUMER REPRESENTATION.

0947 EUCKEN W.
THIS UNSUCCESSFUL AGE.
LONDON: WM HODGE AND CO LTD, 1951, 96 PP.
ESSAY ON INDUSTRIALIZED ECONOMY AND HOW SOCIETY CAN FUNCTION HUMANELY AND EFFICIENTLY. DISCUSSES NATURE OF MIXED ECONOMY AND BALANCING OF GOVERNMENTAL PLANNING AND FREE OPERATION OF BUSINESS COMMUNITY. EXAMINES GERMAN EXPERIENCE IN 20TH CENTURY.

0948 EULAU H.
"HD LASSWELL'S DEVELOPMENTAL ANALYSIS."
WESTERN POLIT. QUART., 11 (JUNE 58), 229-42.
DESCRIPTION AND CRITIQUE OF LASSWELL'S IDEA OF DEVELOPMENTAL ANALYSIS, SYSTEMATIZED FROM VARIOUS PUBLICATIONS. CONTRASTS EQUILIBRIUM MODELS WITH DEVELOPMENTAL MODELS, AND CRITICIZES LASSWELL FOR NOT DEFINING AND SOLVING CONFLICT.

0949 EUROPA PUBLICATIONS LIMITED
THE EUROPA YEAR BOOK.

LONDON: EUROPA PUBLICATIONS.
ANNUALLY PUBLISHED SINCE 1926 IN TWO VOLUMES. PROVIDES ESSENTIAL BIOGRAPHICAL DETAILS ABOUT CURRENT WORLD PERSONALITIES, DIRECTORY OF ESSENTIAL INFORMATION ABOUT EVERY COUNTRY INCLUDING SUBJECT MATTER AND LOCATION OF NEWSPAPERS, PERIODICALS, NEWS AGENCIES, PUBLISHERS, RADIO, AND TELEVISION. ALSO GUIDE TO EDUCATIONAL, SCIENTIFIC, CULTURAL, AND POLITICAL ORGANIZATIONS THROUGHOUT THE WORLD.

0950 EUROPEAN FREE TRADE ASSN
REGIONAL DEVELOPMENT POLICIES IN EFTA.
GENEVA: EUROPEAN FREE TRADE ASSN, 1965, 78 PP.
DETAILED DISCUSSION OF PRINCIPLES, OBJECTIVES, AND EXPERIENCES IN RELATION TO PROBLEMS OF REGIONAL DEVELOPMENT IN COUNTRIES OF AUSTRIA, DENMARK, FINLAND, NORWAY, PORTUGAL, SWEDEN, SWITZERLAND, AND UK. UNDEVELOPED, INDUSTRIALIZED, AND "OVERDEVELOPED" AREAS ARE DEFINED AND ANALYZED. INSTRUMENTS OF REGIONAL POLICIES ALSO DISCUSSED.

0951 EUSDEN J.D.
PURITANS, LAWYERS, AND POLITICS IN EARLY SEVENTEENTH-CENTURY ENGLAND.
NEW HAVEN: YALE U PR, 1958, 238 PP., LC#58-5457.
DISCUSSES PURITANISM AND COMMON LAW AND FINDS THEM ADVOCATING PARALLEL IDEOLOGIES; BOTH INSISTED ON REASON FOR UNDERSTANDING AND INSTITUTIONAL INDEPENDENCE, BOTH WERE NARROW, INTOLERANT, AND EXAGGERATED; BOTH BELIEVED IN LAW ALTHOUGH ONE WAS DIVINE AND OTHER FUNDAMENTAL. INCLUDES HISTORICAL STUDY OF CONFLICTS AND RELATIONS OF TWO GROUPS.

0952 EVANS R.H.
COEXISTENCE: COMMUNISM AND ITS PRACTICE IN BOLOGNA, 1945-1965.
SOUTH BEND: U OF NOTRE DAME, 1967, 225 PP.
ANALYZES BOLOGNA AS PARADIGM OF PEACEFUL COEXISTENCE OF COMMUNISM AND CAPITALISM. STUDIES MOTIVATION AND CONTENT OF SPECIFIC LOCAL BRAND OF COMMUNISM, AND REACTION AND RESPONSE TO IT BY SURROUNDING MIDDLE-CLASS MILIEU. EXAMINES STRENGTHS AND WEAKNESSES OF COMMUNIST ADMINISTRATION. ANALYZES REASONS FOR MODUS VIVENDI AND EXPOSTULATES ON FUTURE NEEDS.

0953 EVANS-PRITCHARD E.E., FIRTH R. ET AL.
THE INSTITUTIONS OF PRIMITIVE SOCIETY.
NEW YORK: FREE PRESS OF GLENCOE, 1956, 107 PP.
SERIES OF BBC TALKS DELIVERED UNDER TITLE "THE VALUES OF PRIMITIVE SOCIETY" PRESENT TO LAYMAN FIELDS OF INVESTIGATION OF ANTHROPOLOGICAL RESEARCH - THEIR PROMINENT CHARACTERISTIC AND ACCOMPLISHMENT: RELIGION, ECONOMIC LIFE, AESTHETICS, LAW, FAMILY AND KINSHIP, AND MODES OF THOUGHT.

0954 EVANS-PRITCHARD E.E.
ESSAYS IN SOCIAL ANTHROPOLOGY.
NEW YORK: MACMILLAN, 1962, 233 PP.
EXAMPLES OF METHOD TAUGHT STUDENTS OF ANTHROPOLOGY WHEN DOING A STUDY. DISCUSSES FIELD AND MEN IN FIELD VERY GENERALLY. ANALYZES OTHER PEOPLE'S THEORIES AND OBSERVATIONS AND FINALLY STATES OWN THEORIES AND VIEWS. COVERS WAY OF LIFE OF CENTRAL AFRICAN PEOPLE, ZANDE, FROM 1926-1930.

0955 EYBERS G.W. ED.
SELECT CONSTITUTIONAL DOCUMENTS ILLUSTRATING SOUTH AFRICAN HISTORY 1795-1910.
NEW YORK: EP DUTTON, 1918, 582 PP., LC#18-17656.
COLLECTION OF DOCUMENTS OF THE FOUR TERRITORIES THAT WERE AMALGAMATED IN 1909 INTO THE UNION OF SOUTH AFRICA. ARRANGED BY TERRITORY, AND BY GENERAL AREA OF REFERENCE (CENTRAL GOVERNMENT, LOCAL GOVERNMENT, JUSTICE) FOR CAPE OF GOOD HOPE AND NATAL, CHRONOLOGICALLY FOR ORANGE FREE STATE AND SOUTH AFRICAN REPUBLIC. EXTENSIVE INTRODUCTION ON CONSTITUTIONAL HISTORY OF SOUTH AFRICA.

0956 EZELL P.H.
"THE HISPANIC AGRICULTURATION OF THE GILA RIVER PIMAS."
AMERICAN ANTHROPOLOGIST, 63 (OCT. 61), 1-171.
STUDY OF EFFECTS OF HISPONIC CULTURE UPON GILA PIMA CULTURE. ORIGINALLY DOCTORAL THESIS AT UNIVERSITY OF ARIZONA. INFORMATION GATHERED PRIMARILY THROUGH FIRST-HAND ACCOUNTS. TREATS GEOGRAPHY, ECONOMICS, AGRICULTURE, SUBSISTENCE ACTIVITIES, TECHNOLOGY, SUPERNATURALISM, INTERPERSONAL RELATIONS, DEFENSE, AND SOCIAL CONTROL.

0957 FABER K.
DIE NATIONALISTISCHE PUBLIZISTIK DEUTSCHLANDS VON 1866 BIS 1871 (2 VOLS.)
DUSSELDORF: DROSTE VERLAG, 1963, 680 PP.
A COLLECTION OF PERIODICALS, PAMPHLETS, AND BOOKS ON NATIONALISTIC PUBLICATIONS, ARRANGED CHRONOLOGICALLY AND BY AREA. ITEMS ARE ARRANGED UNDER SUCH SUBJECTS AS THE NON-PRUSSIAN STATES OF NORTHERN GERMANY, EFFECTS OF THE WAR ON PARTY LIFE, GERMAN-RUSSIAN RELATIONS, ETC. IT CONTAINS AN AUTHOR INDEX, AND COVERS MATERIAL PUBLISHED FROM 1866 THROUGH THE SPRING OF 1871.

0958 FAGEN R.R.
POLITICS AND COMMUNICATION.
BOSTON: LITTLE BROWN, 1966, 162 PP., LC#66-18746.
COMMUNICATION APPROACH TO STUDY OF COMPARATIVE POLITICS. INCLUDES EVALUATION OF MEDIA AND RELEVANT MATERIAL, DETERMINANTS OF COMMUNICATION PATTERNS, POLITICAL IMAGES AND SYSTEMS, COMMUNICATION CONTROL AND RESTRAINT.

0959 FAGG J.E.
CUBA, HAITI, AND THE DOMINICAN REPUBLIC.
ENGLEWOOD CLIFFS: PRENTICE HALL, 1965, 181 PP., LC#65-23298.
EXAMINATION OF THREE MAIN CARIBBEAN NATIONS, CUBA, HAITI, AND DOMINICAN REPUBLIC AS TO DEVELOPMENT AS COLONIES AND REPUBLICS. DISCUSSES REVOLUTION AGAINST COLONIAL RULERS AND INFLUENCE OF US IN HISTORY OF EACH COUNTRY.

0960 FAGUET E.
LE LIBERALISME.
PARIS: SOCIETE FRANCAISE IMPRIM, 1903, 337 PP.
SYSTEMATICALLY TREATS STATE'S RIGHTS AND INDIVIDUAL LIBERTIES. INCLUDES EQUALITY AND FREEDOM OF THOUGHT AND ASSOCIATION. CONSIDERS ARISTOCRACY AND NATIONAL SOVEREIGNTY AS AGAINST LIBERTY.

0961 FAHS C.B.
"POLITICAL GROUPS IN THE JAPANESE HOUSE OF PEERS."
AM. POL. SCI. REV., 34 (OCT. 40), 896-919.
TRACES HISTORICAL DEVELOPMENT OF JAPANESE HOUSE OF PEERS, AND NOTES FAILURE OF HOUSE TO DEVELOP ALONG NON-PARTISAN LINES. CITES EVOLVEMENT OF SIX DISTINCT, ANTAGONISTIC SPLINTER GROUPS.

0962 FAHS C.B.
"GOVERNMENT IN JAPAN."
NEW YORK: NYC COL, INST PAC REL, 1940.
PART OF THE DOCUMENTATION OF AN INQUIRY ORGANIZED BY THE INSTITUTE OF PACIFIC RELATIONS INTO THE PROBLEMS ARISING FROM THE CONFLICT IN THE FAR EAST. ITS PURPOSE WAS TO OFFER AN IMPARTIAL AND CONSTRUCTIVE ANALYSIS OF THE SITUATION IN FAR EAST WITH VIEW TO INDICATING MAJOR ISSUES TO BE CONSIDERED IN ADJUSTMENT OF INTERNATIONAL RELATIONS. ANALYSIS OF ECONOMIC AND POLITICAL CONDITIONS. ANNOTATED BIBLIOGRAPHY.

0963 FAINSOD M.
HOW RUSSIA IS RULED (REV. ED.)
CAMBRIDGE: HARVARD, CTR RUSS RES, 1964, 648 PP., LC#63-11418
FIRST SCHOLARLY STUDY OF SOVIET GOVERNMENT OF THE POST-STALIN ERA TO 1962 TO LOOK INTO FORCES AND FACTORS THAT PRODUCED BOLSHEVIK REVOLUTION AND LATER TRANSFORMED ITS CHARACTER, TO TRACE THE PARTY'S CHANGING ROLE, TO DESCRIBE PATTERNS AND INSTRUMENTS OF RULE, TO PORTRAY THE IMPACT OF STATE CONTROL OF FARM AND FACTORY, AND TO APPRAISE THE PROBLEMS AND PROSPECTS OF THE SOVIET POLITICAL SYSTEM.

0964 FALKENBERG J.
KIN AND TOTEM; GROUP RELATIONS OF AUSTRALIAN ABORIGINES IN THE PORT KEATS DISTRICT.
OSLO: OSLO U PRESS, 1962, 272 PP.
STUDY OF SOCIAL ORGANIZATION AND RELATIONSHIPS AMONG ABORIGINAL TRIBES. ANALYZES KINSHIP SYSTEMS AND DISTINGUISHES BETWEEN TWO STRUCTURAL FORMS OF CLAN AND HORDE. DISCUSSES DISINTEGRATION OF LOCAL CLANS, ENDOGAMOUS GENERATION LINES, MOIETIES, SECTIONS, SUBSECTIONS, AND TOTEMIC RELATIONS. INCLUDES DISTINCTION BY SEX GROUPS AND AGE-GRADES. CLOSES WITH PERSONALITY OF INDIVIDUAL.

0965 FALL B.B.
THE TWO VIETNAMS.
NEW YORK: PRAEGER, 1963, 493 PP., $7.95.
HISTORICAL ANALYSIS OF VIETNAM SINCE DIEN BIEN PHU. INCLUDES BIOGRAPHICAL STUDIES OF HO CHI MINH AND NGO DINH DIEM AND THEIR INFLUENCE ON VIETNAM. STUDIES CONTEMPORARY POLITICS.

0966 FALL B.B.
STREET WITHOUT JOY.
NEW YORK: STACKPOLE, 1964, 408 PP., LC#64-23038.
REVISED AND UPDATED VERSION OF A HISTORY OF THE INDOCHINA WAR FROM WWII THROUGH MID-1964. DISCUSSES TACTICS OF INSURGENCY WAR, SET-PIECE BATTLE, FRENCH AND AMERICAN STRATEGY AND PRACTICE, LOSS OF LAOS, AND FUTURE OF REVOLUTIONARY WAR. MAINTAINS THAT COMPARATIVE ANALYSES OF SIMILAR WARS SHOW THAT THE ESSENTIAL FACTOR IS POPULAR SUPPORT. A DETAILED ACCOUNT.

0967 FALL B.B.
"THE VIET-MINH REGIME."
ITHACA: CORNELL U, DEPT ASIAN ST, 1956.
STUDY OF VIET-MINH REGIME IN ORGANIZATIONAL AND ADMINISTRATIVE ASPECTS. INSTITUTIONAL ANALYSIS SUPPORTED BY CULTURAL RESEARCH. AUTHOR DISCUSSES PERSONALITY AND CHARACTER OF LEADERS, PARTICULARLY HO CHI MINH, IDEOLOGICAL FOUNDATIONS OF RULING PARTY, ECONOMIC DEVELOPMENT, ORGANIZATION OF ARMY. SELECTED BIBLIOGRAPHY CONFINED TO WORKS SPECIALIZING ON VIETMINH REGIME IN FRENCH, ENGLISH, AND RUSSIAN.

0968 FALL B.B. ED.
HO CHI MINH ON REVOLUTION: SELECTED WRITINGS, 1920-66.
NEW YORK: FREDERICK PRAEGER, 1967, 389 PP., LC#67-20481.

BASIC WRITINGS OF HO CHI MINH BASED ON HIS VIEWS OF THE EVILS OF COLONIALISM AND HIS EFFORTS TO ELIMINATE THEM FROM VIETNAM. DISCUSSES PLACE OF COMMUNISM IN HIS REVOLUTIONARY MOVEMENT.

0969 FANON F.
TOWARD THE AFRICAN REVOLUTION.
NEW YORK: MONTHLY REVIEW PR, 1967, 197 PP., LC#67-19256.
POLITICAL ESSAYS, ARTICLES, AND NOTES PUBLISHED 1952-61. PRESENTS COMPLEXITY OF LIFE OF THE "COLONIZED", ITS DIVERSE ASPECTS AND INTERRELATIONS, AND YET ITS SAMENESS. EXPOSES CLOSE RELATIONSHIP BETWEEN COLONIZED AND COLONIZER AND DESCRIBES WORLD OF THE FORMER AS A "RESPONSE TO ALL FORMS OF OPPRESSION." DEALS ONLY WITH FRENCH COLONIES.

0970 FANON F.
BLACK SKIN, WHITE MASKS: THE EXPERIENCES OF A BLACK MAN IN A WHITE WORLD.
NEW YORK: GROVE PRESS, 1967, 232 PP., LC#67-30411.
EXPERIENCES AND OBSERVATIONS OF A NEGRO PSYCHIATRIST IN THE ANTILLES WHO IS CONCERNED WITH THE WARPING OF THE NEGRO PSYCHE BY A "SUPERIOR" WHITE CULTURE. AUTHOR BELIEVES IT IS SENSELESS FOR CONTEMPORARY NEGROES TO DENY THEIR CULTURE. DEALS WITH THE MODERN NEGRO'S ATTITUDES IN THE WHITE WORLD. DEVOTED TO A PSYCHOPATHOLOGICAL AND PHILOSOPHICAL EXPLANATION OF THE CONDITION OF BEING A NEGRO.

0971 FARIES J.C.
THE RISE OF INTERNATIONALISM.
NEW YORK: GRAY, 1915, 207 PP.
PRESENTS PRINCIPLES OF, AND STIMULI TO INTERNATIONALISM. DISCUSSES EFFECTS OF POPULATION LEVEL, LANGUAGE, AND EDUCATIONAL FACILITIES ON SUBJECT. FINDS INTERNATIONAL FAIRS, DIPLOMATIC CONFERENCES, ETC., ARE EFFECTIVE MEANS TO PEACE.

0972 FARMER B.H.
CEYLON: A DIVIDED NATION.
LONDON: OXFORD U PR, 1963, 72 PP.
PRESENTS POLITICAL STRIFE INFLUENCED BY THE PAST, CENTURIES OF COLONIALISM, AND THE EVOLUTION OF INDEPENDENT GOVERNMENT.

0973 FARRELL R.B. ED.
APPROACHES TO COMPARATIVE AND INTERNATIONAL POLITICS.
EVANSTON: NORTHWESTERN U PRESS, 1966, 368 PP., LC#66-17012.
PAPERS FROM A NORTHWESTERN CONFERENCE OF SOCIAL SCIENTISTS WHO OFFERED LINKAGES BETWEEN STUDY OF COMPARATIVE POLITICS AND INTERNATIONAL RELATIONS. DEVELOPED FROM BELIEF THAT DISCIPLINARY BOUNDARIES HAD MADE A NO-MAN'S-LAND OF THE COMPARATIVE STUDY OF THE INTERACTION OF DOMESTIC AND FOREIGN POLITICS. IMPORTANT THEORETICAL PAPERS BY ROSENAU AND ALGER INCLUDED AMONG OTHERS.

0974 FARWELL G.
MASK OF ASIA: THE PHILIPPINES.
NEW YORK: FREDERICK PRAEGER, 1966, 227 PP., LC#66-1808.
OBSERVATIONS ON HISTORICAL EMERGENCE OF PHILIPPINE ISLANDS INTO WORLD POLITICS: GROWTH OF NATIONALISM, CULTURE, TRADITIONS OF ISLANDS, RELIGIOUS AND SOCIAL STRUCTURE, THE POSSIBILITIES OF DEMOCRACY IN ASIA. SHORT BIBLIOGRAPHY INCLUDED.

0975 FATOUROS A.A.
GOVERNMENT GUARANTEES TO FOREIGN INVESTORS.
NEW YORK: COLUMBIA U PRESS, 1962, 411 PP., LC#62-12873.
ANALYZES VARIOUS FORMS AND MODALITIES BY WHICH STATES ENTER INTO ARRANGEMENTS WITH FOREIGN INVESTORS. ALSO STUDIES ASPECTS SUCH AS EXCHANGE RESTRICTIONS, EMPLOYMENT OF FOREIGN PERSONNEL, LEGAL EFFECTS OF TREATY PROMISES, AND STATE CONTRACTS.

0976 FAUST J.J.
A REVOLUCAO DEVORA SEUS PRESIDENTES.
RIO DE JANEIRO: EDITORA SAGA, 1965, 162 PP.
EXAMINES BRAZILIAN NATIONAL POLITICS FROM 1960 TO 1964 AND DISCUSSES POLITICAL LEADERS AND PROGRAMS AS JUDGED BY AUTHOR, FRENCH CORRESPONDENT IN BRAZIL. COVERS ELECTIONS, QUADROS, REVOLUTION OF 1964, AND NEW POLITICAL PATTERNS SINCE MILITARY TOOK ACTIVE PART IN POLITICS.

0977 FAWCETT J.E.S.
THE BRITISH COMMONWEALTH IN INTERNATIONAL LAW.
LONDON: OXFORD U PR, 1963, 243 PP.
A STUDY OF THE MAKE-UP, LEGAL STATUS, TYPES OF INTERNATIONAL LAW ADHERED TO, PATTERNS OF INTERNAL LEGAL RELATIONS, AND LEGAL RELATIONSHIP TO CO-OPERATIVE INTERNATIONAL BODIES FOUND IN THE BRITISH COMMONWEALTH OF NATIONS AS OF 1962. ALL RELEVANT CASES, LEGISLATION, TREATIES, AND AGREEMENTS ARE CITED.

0978 FAY S.B.
THE ORIGINS OF THE WORLD WAR (2ND REV. ED. 2 VOLS.)
NEW YORK: MACMILLAN, 1967, 1212 PP.
VOLUME I* BEFORE SARAJEVO, VOLUME II* AFTER SARAJEVO. AN EXTENSIVE EXAMINATION OF WWI. DISCUSSES UNDERLYING CAUSES, SYSTEM OF SECRET ALLIANCES, TRIPLE ENTENTE, TRIPLE ALLIANCE, BALKAN PROBLEMS, TREATIES, ASSASSINATION OF FERDINAND, MOBILIZATIONS AND DECLARATION OF WAR.

0979 FAYERWEATHER J.
THE EXECUTIVE OVERSEAS: ADMINISTRATIVE ATTITUDES AND RELATIONSHIPS IN A FOREIGN CULTURE.
SYRACUSE: SYRACUSE U PRESS, 1959, 195 PP., LC#59-11259.
STUDIES RELATIONSHIPS BETWEEN US AND FOREIGN EXECUTIVES. SURVEYS OPINIONS ABOUT ADMINISTRATIVE RELATIONSHIPS IN MANY COUNTRIES AND OBSERVES SELECTED MANAGERIAL GROUPS IN MEXICO. DISCUSSES CULTURAL DIFFERENCES AND PROPOSES CONCEPTUAL PLAN TO ALLEVIATE DIFFICULTIES IN INTERNATIONAL BUSINESS TRANSACTIONS.

0980 FEFFERO G.
THE PRINCIPLES OF POWER (TRANS. BY T. JAECKEL)
NEW YORK: G P PUTNAM'S SONS, 1942, 319 PP.
CLAIMS RIGHT TO GOVERN CAN ONLY BE JUSTIFIED BY SUPERIORITY. STATES THAT WWII IS BEING BROUGHT ON BY BREAKDOWN OF ALL LEGITIMACY IN EUROPEAN GOVERNMENTS. CALLS FALL OF FRENCH GOVERNMENT "DEMISE OF LAST GREAT LEGITIMATE POWER" IN EUROPE AND SIGNAL OF TRIUMPH OF CHAOS. DISPUTES USE OF REVOLUTION, AT ANY TIME, TO CHANGE GOVERNMENT AND DERIDES SYSTEM OF MAJORITARIAN GOVERNMENT.

0981 FEIBLEMAN J.
THE THEORY OF HUMAN CULTURE.
NEW YORK: DUELL, SLOAN & PEARCE, 1946, 361 PP.
PRESENTS THEORY OF CONSTITUTION OF HUMAN CULTURE IN WHICH CULTURE IS DEFINED AS ORGANIZATION OF VALUES. ATTEMPTS TO ESTABLISH PRINCIPLES OF SOCIOLOGY BY EMPLOYING ONTOLOGY AS INSTRUMENT OF ANALYSIS. DISCUSSES ORGANIZATION, TYPES, AND DEVELOPMENT OF CULTURES.

0982 FEINE H.E.
REICH UND KIRCHE.
AALEN: SCIENTIA VERLAG, 1966, 322 PP.
EXAMINES RELATIONSHIP BETWEEN CHURCH AND STATE FROM END OF MIDDLE AGES TO 1806. DISCUSSES SURVIVAL OF ROMAN LAW IN CHURCH LAW, WORK OF PROMINENT HISTORIANS, AND SOURCES OF CHURCH LAW AND PRACTICES.

0983 FEIS H.
BETWEEN WAR AND PEACE: THE POTSDAM CONFERENCE.
PRINCETON: PRINCETON U PRESS, 1960, 367 PP., LC#60-12230.
DEALS WITH POTSDAM CONFERENCE AFTER WWII; ALSO COVERS PRECEDING EVENTS FROM TIME OF GERMAN SURRENDER. INCLUDES EXTENSIVE NOTES ON ACTUAL US DEALINGS WITH GERMANS AND PLANS FOR RESTORATION, LEND-LEASE, ETC. COMPLETE RESOLUTIONS OF BERLIN CONFERENCE.

0984 FEIT E.
SOUTH AFRICA, THE DYNAMICS OF THE AFRICAN NATIONAL CONGRESS.
LONDON: OXFORD U PR, 1962, 73 PP.
DISCUSSES FACTORS INHIBITING EFFECTIVE ORGANIZATION OF MASSES OF SOUTH AFRICA'S BLACK POPULATION AGAINST INCREASINGLY OPPRESSIVE AFRIKANER GOVERNMENT.

0985 FELD W.
"NATIONAL ECONOMIC INTEREST GROUPS AND POLICY FORMATION IN THE EEC."
POLIT. SCI. QUART., 81 (SEPT. 66), 392-411.
70 INTERVIEWS WITH INTEREST GROUP, POLITICAL PARTY, GOVERNMENT MINISTRY, AND EEC OFFICIALS ARE BASIS OF THIS STUDY OF THE ROUTES INTEREST GROUP DEMANDS TAKE. DISCERNS PREFERENCE FOR WORKING THROUGH OWN NATION'S GOVERNMENT AND PARTY OFFICIALS. RESULTS EVALUATED IN TERMS OF EASTON'S SYSTEM.

0986 FERNEUIL T.
LES PRINCIPES DE 1789 ET LA SCIENCE SOCIALE.
PARIS: LIB HACHETTE ET CIE, 1889, 359 PP.
EXAMINES HISTORICAL PRECURSORS, SOCIAL FORCES, AND IDEOLOGICAL TRENDS OF THE FRENCH REVOLUTION IN TERMS OF SOCIOLOGY AND POLITICAL SCIENCE. DEALS WITH CONSTITUTIONAL STRUCTURE, CONCEPTS OF INDIVIDUALISM AND COLLECTIVISM, AND THE ROLE OF THE STATE AND ITS VARIOUS FUNCTIONS. STRESSES GENERAL CONCEPTS SUCH AS NATURAL RIGHTS AND LEGITIMACY RATHER THAN EMPIRICAL DATA.

0987 FERRERO G.
PEACE AND WAR (TRANS. BY BERTHA PRITCHARD)
LONDON: MACMILLAN, 1933, 244 PP.
SERIES OF LECTURES DISCUSSES HISTORY OF WARFARE AND MAN'S OBSESSION WITH IT. GREATEST THREAT TO WESTERN CIVILIZATION IS "SUPER WAR" WAGED WITHOUT REASON. BELIEVES MAN NEEDS TO REDISCOVER HUMANISTIC AND CHRISTIAN VALUES. THERE MUST BE NO MORE WAR, BECAUSE THE MORE TERRIBLE THE WAR, THE HARDER IT IS TO ESTABLISH LASTING PEACE. THOSE WHO TOOK INITIATIVE IN ENDING MONARCHY SHOULD HELP BRING ABOUT END TO REVOLUTION.

0988 FESLER J.W.
"FRENCH FIELD ADMINISTRATION: THE BEGINNINGS."
COMP. STUD. SOC. HIST., 5 (OCT. 62), 76-111.
USES A DEVELOPMENTAL FOCUS TO EXAMINE IN DETAIL THE EARLY STAGES OF FRENCH FIELD ADMINISTRATION (LATE 12TH TO 14TH CENT.) AND ITS CONTRIBUTION TO THE DEVELOPMENT OF THE

NATION-STATE.

0989 FICHTE J.G.
ADDRESSES TO THE GERMAN NATION.
LA SALLE: OPEN COURT, 1922, 269 PP.
SPEECHES GIVEN TO GERMAN PEOPLE AFTER GERMAN DEFEAT IN FRANCO-PRUSSIAN WAR. SPEECHES GLORIFY EVERYTHING GERMAN AND ARE REGARDED AS THE BEGINNING OF GERMAN NATIONALISM. IDEAS OF CLOSED COMMERIAL STATE, PRINCIPLE OF NATIONALITY, SUPERIORITY OF GERMAN CULTURE, AND DEVELOPMENT OF EDUCATION HAD PROFOUND EFFECT ON FUTURE DEVELOPMENT OF GERMANY.

0990 FIELD G.C.
POLITICAL THEORY.
LONDON: METHUEN, 1956, 297 PP.
DISCUSSES VARIOUS ASPECTS OF POLITICAL THEORY AS CONCEPT OF SOVEREIGNTY, STATE, INDIVIDUAL LIBERTY, ETC. EXAMINES IN DETAIL MACHINERY OF DEMOCRACY AND RELATIONS BETWEEN STATES. CONCLUDES WITH ESSAY ON RELATION BETWEEN POLITICS, ECONOMICS, AND ETHICS.

0991 FIELD G.L.
THE SYNDICAL AND CORPORATIVE INSTITUTIONS OF ITALIAN FASCISM
NEW YORK: COLUMBIA U PRESS, 1938, 209 PP.
EXAMINES FASCISM IN ITALY BY CONSIDERING ITS THREE MAJOR INSTITUTIONS: DICTATORSHIP, SYNDICATE, AND CORPORATION. THE FIRST HAD THOROUGH LEGAL CONTROL, THE SECOND PROVIDED STATE CONTROL OF CAPITAL AND LABOR, AND THE THIRD HAD CONTROL OF VARIOUS ECONOMIC ACTIVITIES. WRITTEN AT PEAK OF FASCISM'S POPULARITY, WORK ATTEMPTS TO BE ANALYTIC.

0992 FIELD H.
ANCIENT AND MODERN MAN IN SOUTHWESTERN ASIA: II.
CORAL GABLES: U OF MIAMI PR, 1961, 293 PP., LC#56-12176.
DETAILED STATISTICAL ANTHROPOMETRIC STUDY OF INHABITANTS OF 11 SOUTHWEST ASIAN COUNTRIES. BULK OF STUDY CONSISTS OF CHARTS AND TABLES INDICATING COMPARATIVE PHYSICAL MEASUREMENTS OF DIFFERENT TRIBES.

0993 FIELD M.G.
SOVIET SOCIALIZED MEDICINE.
NEW YORK: FREE PRESS OF GLENCOE, 1967, 253 PP.
THIS VOLUME ILLUMINATES THE HISTORY, PROBLEMS, AND PRESENT CIRCUMSTANCES OF THE SOVIET MEDICAL ESTABLISHMENT. EMPLOYS A SYSTEMATIC SOCIOLOGICAL APPROACH IN EXAMINING SOCIALIZED MEDICINE IN RELATION TO SOVIET IDEOLOGY AND POLITICAL AND ECONOMIC SYSTEMS. DESCRIBES BACKGROUND, PRINCIPLES, ORGANIZATION, ADMINISTRATION, AND FINANCES.

0994 FIELDHOUSE D.K.
THE COLONIAL EMPIRES: A COMPARATIVE SURVEY FROM THE 18TH CENTURY.
LONDON: WEIDENFIELD & NICOLSON, 1966, 450 PP.
TWO-PART SURVEY OF GREAT COLONIAL EMPIRES OF EUROPE. FIRST COMPARES AMERICAN EXPANSIONS OF SPAIN, PORTUGAL, FRANCE, HOLLAND, AND ENGLAND PRIOR TO 1815. POST-1815 COMES NEXT. CONSIDERS DISINTEGRATION OF ONE SET OF EMPIRES DUE TO REVOLUTIONS IN EUROPE, AND REBUILDING OF NEW TYPE WHICH INCLUDED US.

0995 FIFIELD R.H.
"WOODROW WILSON AND THE FAR EAST."
NEW YORK: THOMAS Y CROWELL, 1952.
DIVIDED INTO MANUSCRIPT SOURCES: OFFICIAL AND PRIVATE PAPERS; PRINTED SOURCES; OFFICIAL DOCUMENTS OF US, FRANCE, CHINA, GERMANY, GREAT BRITAIN, JAPAN, RUSSIA; AND MEMOIRS, BIOGRAPHIES, SPECIAL STUDIES, HISTORIES, ARTICLES, AND NEWSPAPERS.

0996 FIFIELD R.H.
"THE DIPLOMACY OF SOUTHEAST ASIA: 1945-1958."
NEW YORK: HARPER & ROW, 1958.
ARGUES THAT PERIOD 1945-58 WAS FORMATIVE FOR NATIONAL DEVELOPMENT AND INTERNATIONAL RECOGNITION FOR STATES OF SOUTHEAST ASIA. FOCUSES ON ASIAN RELATIONS WITH CONSIDERATIONS OF BACKGROUND OF INDEPENDENCE, REGIONALISM, AND ROLE OF UNITED NATIONS. LARGE BIBLIOGRAPHY ORGANIZED ALPHABETICALLY BY COUNTRY.

0997 FIGANIERE J.C.
BIBLIOTHECA HISTORICA PORTUGUEZA.
LISBON: NA TIPOGRAFIA DO PANORAMA, 1850, 349 PP.
BIBLIOGRAPHY OF PORTUGUESE BOOKS AND DOCUMENTS ON PORTUGUESE POLITICAL, CIVIL, AND RELIGIOUS HISTORY. ALSO INCLUDES PORTUGUESE POSSESSIONS.

0998 FIGGIS J.N.
CHURCHES IN THE MODERN STATE (2ND ED.)
LONDON: LONGMANS, GREEN & CO, 1914, 271 PP.
FOUR LECTURES ON CHURCH-STATE RELATIONS. DISCUSSES RIGHTS OF FREE CHURCHES IN A FREE STATE AND DIVISION OF POWERS BETWEEN THEM. SHOWS DEVELOPMENT OF LAWYERS' PREJUDICE AGAINST GIVING FREEDOM TO CHURCHES, AND URGES A MORE REALISTIC AND MORE USEFUL VIEW. COMPARES PAPACY'S POWER TO THAT OF A NATIONAL STATE.

0999 FIKS M.
PUBLIC ADMINISTRATION IN ISRAEL (PAMPHLET)
NEW YORK: PERSONNEL RES ASSN, 1958, 29 PP.
ANALYSIS OF CIVIL SERVICE AND OTHER PUBLIC EMPLOYMENT IN ISRAEL, INCLUDING EDUCATIONAL SYSTEM. EXAMINES STRUCTURE AND PERSONNEL OF PUBLIC ADMINISTRATION AND BENEFITS OF PUBLIC EMPLOYMENT.

1000 FILIPINIANA BOOK GUILD
THE COLONIZATION AND CONQUEST OF THE PHILIPPINES BY SPAIN.
MANILA: FILIPINIANA BOOK GUILD, 1965, 355 PP.
DOCUMENTS DATING 1559-77, CONCERNING CONQUEST OF PHILIPPINES. RANGE FROM PHILIP II'S LETTER TO VELASCO IN 1559, TO SANDE'S RELATION OF 1577 DESCRIBING STATE OF AFFAIRS IN PHILIPPINES. DOCUMENTS WRITTEN MAINLY BY MISSIONARIES AND CONQUERORS TREAT CONQUEST OF INDIANS, INDIAN CULTURE, SPANISH CONQUERORS, COLONIZATION, ETC.

1001 FINDLATER R. ED.
"US."
TWENT. CENTURY, 173 (64), 4-117.
A SET OF ARTICLES ANALYZING WHAT THE ENGLISH PEOPLE THINK OF THEMSELVES. GERMAN AND RUSSIAN VIEWS OF THE ENGLISH ARE ALSO PRESENTED.

1002 FINER H.
REPRESENTATIVE GOVERNMENT AND A PARLIAMENT OF INDUSTRY. A STUDY OF THE GERMAN FEDERAL ECONOMIC COUNCIL.
DUBUQUE: WC BROWN, 1923, 273 PP.
DISCUSSES GENESIS OF GERMAN ECONOMIC COUNCIL, ITS COMPOSITION, STATUS, AND PROCEDURE, AND ITS OPERATION IN WAR AND REVOLUTION. CONCLUDES WITH COMPARISON BETWEEN ENGLAND AND GERMANY.

1003 FINER S.E.
THE MAN ON HORSEBACK: ROLE OF THE MILITARY IN POLITICS.
LONDON: PALL MALL, 1962, 268 PP.
ASSERTS GOVERNMENTS OF COUNTRIES WITH WEAK POLITICAL STRUCTURES HAVE HISTORICALLY BEEN SUBJECTED TO INTERFERENCE FROM THE MILITARY AND DISCUSSES MEANS BY WHICH THE MILITARY HAS TRADITIONALLY USED TO DO SO. CONCLUDES SUCH INTERFERENCE WILL NOT CEASE UNTIL THE POLITICAL ORGANIZATION OF THE STATE BECOMES SUPERIOR TO THAT OF THE MILITARY ESTABLISHMENT.

1004 FINER S.E.
ANONYMOUS EMPIRE: STUDY OF THE LOBBY IN GREAT BRITAIN.
NEW YORK: HUMANITIES PRESS, 1966, 173 PP.
ANALYZES AND EVALUATES TYPES AND DEGREES OF LOBBIES, OR INTEREST GROUPS, IN ENGLAND. SAYS THEY REALLY CONTROL PUBLIC OPINION, DETERMINE LEGISLATION, AND VIRTUALLY RULE EMPIRE. INCLUDES DISCUSSION OF LOBBY AS CONCEPT. COVERS VARIOUS LOBBYING TECHNIQUES, DEVELOPED SINCE 1958, THAT DIMINISH ROLE OF PARLIAMENT.

1005 FINLAY D.J.
"THE GHANA COUP...ONE YEAR LATER."
TRANSACTIONS, 4 (MAR. 67), 16-22.
ASKS WHETHER GHANA CAN MOVE FROM A MILITARY COUP D'ETAT TO A STABLE, DEVELOPED, DEMOCRATIC FUTURE AND CONCLUDES THAT THE SITUATION IS PROMISING. REVIEWS THE CAUSES OF THE COUP, THE REACTIONS TO IT, AND EXAMINES THE RECORD OF THE NEW GOVERNMENT.

1006 FIRST R.
SOUTH WEST AFRICA.
BALTIMORE: PENGUIN BOOKS, 1963, 259 PP.
STORY OF THE TWO SOUTH-WEST AFRICAS: ONE WHITE, THE OTHER BLACK; A PICTURE OF APARTHEID AS PRACTICED IN THE AREA CONTROLLED BY UNION OF SOUTH AFRICA. THE AUTHOR WAS PLACED UNDER HOUSE ARREST IN JOHANNESBURG FOR GATHERING INFORMATION FOR THIS BOOK. EXPOSES THE UNFAIRNESS OF BOTH APARTHEID AND SOUTH AFRICA'S "MANDATE."

1007 FIRTH R.
PRIMITIVE POLYNESIAN ECONOMY.
LONDON: ROUTLEDGE & KEGAN PAUL, 1939, 385 PP.
DISCUSSES ECONOMY OF TIKOPIA, A MODERN PRIMITIVE POLYNESIAN SOCIETY. STUDIES AGRICULTURE AND POPULATION, KNOWLEDGE AND TECHNIQUES OF ECONOMICS, AND LABOR SITUATION. ANALYZES ROLE OF RITUAL IN PRODUCTIVE ACTIVITY, ECONOMIC FUNCTIONS OF CHIEFS, AND PROPERTY AND CAPITAL IN PRODUCTION. DESCRIBES POLYNESIAN PRINCIPLES OF DISTRIBUTION AND PAYMENT, EXCHANGE, AND VALUE.

1008 FIRTH R.
HISTORY AND TRADITIONS OF TIKOPIA.
WELLINGTON, N.Z.: POLYNESIAN SOC, 1961, 203 PP.
SOCIOLOGICAL ANALYSIS OF POLYNESIAN SOCIETY, USING TRADITIONAL MATERIAL, PARTICULARLY TALES, AS PRIMARY SOURCE. REVEALS EXISTING SOCIAL SYSTEM, ESPECIALLY GROUP STRUCTURE.

1009 FIRTH R.
ELEMENTS OF SOCIAL ORGANIZATION (3RD ED.)
BOSTON: BEACON PRESS, 1961, 260 PP.
CONCERNS SOCIAL-ANTHROPOLOGICAL ORGANIZATIONS, CONCEPTS, AND VALUES, FOCUSING ON THE STRUCTURE, ART, MORALITY, AND

RELIGION OF PRIMITIVE SOCIETIES, AND MAKING COMPARISONS BETWEEN WESTERN AND PRIMITIVE CULTURES. REFLECTS SHIFT IN ANTHROPOLOGY FROM PURELY STRUCTURAL CONSIDERATIONS TO INDIVIDUAL BEHAVIORAL ASPECTS.

1010 FISCHER L.
THE SOVIETS IN WORLD AFFAIRS.
NEW YORK: ALFRED KNOPF, 1960, 616 PP.
HISTORY OF SOVIET FOREIGN RELATIONS, 1917-29, INCLUDING VERSAILLES, BOLSHEVIK ATTITUDES TOWARD POLAND, UK, JAPAN, CHINESE REVOLUTION, DISARMAMENT, AND PARTICIPATION IN INTERNATIONAL CONFERENCES.

1011 FISCHER L.
THE LIFE OF LENIN.
NEW YORK: HARPER & ROW, 1964, 703 PP., LC#64-14385.
BIOGRAPHY OF LENIN FROM BEGINNINGS OF REVOLUTION AGAINST TSARIST RUSSIA, THROUGH WWI, TO FOUNDING OF FIRST COMMUNIST STATE. STATES THAT HIS STRENGTH OF WILL, ORGANIZATIONAL ABILITY, AND COMPLETE DEDICATION TO REVOLUTION MADE HIM A GREAT LEADER.

1012 FISCHER-GALATI S.A.
RUMANIA; A BIBLIOGRAPHIC GUIDE (PAMPHLET)
WASHINGTON: LIBRARY OF CONGRESS, 1963, 75 PP., LC#63-60076.
CRITICALLY ANNOTATED BIBLIOGRAPHY OF ESSENTIAL PUBLICATIONS, PRIMARILY MONOGRAPHS AND PERIODICALS, IN BOTH RUMANIAN AND WESTERN LANGUAGES. GUIDE CONSISTS OF TWO PARTS: A CONCISE BIBLIOGRAPHIC SURVEY COVERING IN ELEVEN SECTIONS MAJOR CATEGORIES OF KNOWLEDGE EXCLUSIVE OF MEDICINE AND NATURAL SCIENCE; DETAILED LISTING, ALPHABETICALLY ARRANGED AND CONSECUTIVELY NUMBERED, OF 748 ENTRIES DISCUSSED IN SURVEY.

1013 FISHEL L.H. JR. ED., QUARLES B. ED.
THE NEGRO AMERICAN: A DOCUMENTARY HISTORY.
CHICAGO: SCOTT, FORESMAN & CO, 1967, 536 PP., LC#67-26184.
SELECTED DOCUMENTS WHICH ATTEMPT TO SHOW THAT NEGRO HAS PLAYED SIGNIFICANT ROLE IN AMERICAN HISTORY. POINTS OUT THAT TOWARD MIDDLE OF 19TH CENTURY, NEGRO BEGAN TO SHAPE HIS OWN DESTINY. SHOWS NEGRO'S STATUS IN COLONIAL, REVOLUTIONARY, AND 19TH-CENTURY SOCIETY. COVERS ATTITUDES TOWARD SLAVERY AND MOVEMENT OUT OF SLAVERY. INCLUDES RECENT DOCUMENTS ON CIVIL RIGHTS STRUGGLE.

1014 FISHER M. ED.
PROVINCES AND PROVINCIAL CAPITALS OF THE WORLD.
METUCHEN: SCARECROW PRESS, 1967, 210 PP.
LISTS 141 NATIONS WITH FOLLOWING INFORMATION: COMMON AND OFFICIAL NAME FOR NATION, NATIVE NAME, NATIONAL CAPITAL CITY, LOCATION OF COUNTRY ACCORDING TO CONTINENT, DESCRIPTION OF MAJOR AND MINOR ADMINISTRATIVE DIVISIONS, AND SPECIFIC NAMING OF MAJOR ADMINISTRATIVE DIVISION AND SEATS OF ADMINISTRATION.

1015 FISK E.K. ED.
NEW GUINEA ON THE THRESHOLD; ASPECTS OF SOCIAL, POLITICAL, AND ECONOMIC DEVELOPMENT.
LONDON: LONGMANS, GREEN & CO, 1966, 290 PP.
PAPERS ON ECONOMICS, SOCIAL PROBLEMS, AND POLITICS OF SITUATION IN PAPUA, NEW GUINEA, AT PRESENT AND DURING NEXT DECADE. COVERS HISTORICAL BACKGROUND, ECONOMIC STRUCTURE, RESOURCES, TRADE, DEMOGRAPHY, EDUCATION, LITERACY, SOCIAL CHANGE, ROLE OF WOMEN, EXPATRIATES, GROWTH OF TERRITORIAL ADMINISTRATION, AND ADVANCE TO RESPONSIBLE GOVERNMENT.

1016 FITZGERALD C.P.
CHINA, A SHORT CULTURAL HISTORY.
NEW YORK: FREDERICK PRAEGER, 1950, 619 PP.
GENERAL HISTORY OF CHINA FROM PREHISTORIC BEGINNINGS TO END OF MANCHU DYNASTY IN 1911. INCLUDES MAPS, PLATES, AND ILLUSTRATIONS.

1017 FITZGERALD C.P.
A CONCISE HISTORY OF EAST ASIA.
NEW YORK: FREDERICK PRAEGER, 1966, 306 PP., LC#66-17361.
HISTORICAL STUDY OF EAST ASIA CONCERNING CHINA, JAPAN, KOREA, AND SOUTHEAST ASIA. DEALS WITH EACH IN REGARD TO ITS EARLY CIVILIZATION, PERIOD OF WESTERN INTERVENTION, AND PRESENT SITUATION.

1018 FITZGERALD C.P.
THE BIRTH OF COMMUNIST CHINA (2ND ED.)
NEW YORK: FREDERICK PRAEGER, 1966, 288 PP., LC#65-27021.
ANALYZES CHINESE REVOLUTION; EXAMINES HISTORY OF THE MOVEMENT. STUDIES INTRODUCTION AND DEVELOPMENT OF COMMUNISM IN STRUGGLE FOR REPUBLIC. DEALS WITH NATIONALIST CONTROL OF OVERNMENT AND WWII UNITY LEADING TO LATER COMMUNIST VICTORY. VIEWS CHINA SINCE EARLY 1950'S AND CHINESE POLICY IN FAR EAST AND TOWARD WEST.

1019 FITZGIBBON R.H.
"DICTATORSHIP AND DEMOCRACY IN LATIN AMERICA."
INT. AFF., 37 (JAN. 60), 48-57.
HISTORICAL APPROACH SEEKING TO ACHIEVE BETTER UNDERSTANDING OF PROBLEM. DESCRIBES CURRENTS OF CHANGE DIRECTED TOWARD REFORM AND MODERNIZATION. CALLS FOR ECONOMIC AND POLITICAL INTEGRATION OF LATIN AMERICAN COUNTRIES.

1020 FITZGIBBON R.H., JOHNSON K.F.
"MEASUREMENT OF LATIN AMERICAN POLITICAL CHANGE."
AMER. POLIT. SCI. REV., 55 (SEPT. 61), 515-26.
METHOD OF QUANTITATIVE SCORING OF LATIN AMERICAN COUNTRIES ON INDICES OF DEMOCRACY AND POLITICS BY EXPERT JUDGE'S RATINGS, SHOWING SHIFTS FROM COUNTRY TO COUNTRY OVER A 15-YEAR PERIOD.

1021 FITZSIMMONS T., MALOF P. ET AL.
"USSR: ITS PEOPLE, ITS SOCIETY, ITS CULTURE."
NEW HAVEN: HUMAN REL AREA FILES, 1960.
ANALYSIS DEFINING DOMINANT SOCIOLOGICAL, POLITICAL, AND ECONOMIC ASPECTS OF FUNCTIONING SOCIETY, AND IDENTIFICATION OF PATTERNS OF CHARACTERISTIC BEHAVIOR. EMPHASIS ON SOCIAL ORGANIZATION, VALUES AND PATTERNS OF LIVING; INCLUDES MATERIAL ON POLITICAL AND ECONOMIC ORGANIZATION OF SOCIETY. CONTAINS EXTENSIVE SELECTED AND SOMEWHAT SPECIALIZED BIBLIOGRAPHY.

1022 FLECHTHEIM O.K.
DIE DEUTSCHEN PARTEIEN SEIT 1945.
BERLIN: CARL HEYMANNS VERL, 1955, 158 PP.
COLLECTION OF DOCUMENTS ON NATURE AND FUNCTION OF POLITICAL PARTIES IN WEST GERMANY SINCE 1945. INCLUDES EXCERPTS FROM STANDING RULES AS WELL AS DISCUSSIONS OF CONSTITUTIONAL POSITION AND SOURCES OF FINANCIAL SUPPORT.

1023 FLECHTHEIM O.K.
DOKUMENTE ZUR PARTEIPOLITISCHEN ENTWICKLUNG IN DEUTSCHLAND SEIT 1945 (2 VOLS.)
BERLIN: HERBERT WENDLER & CO, 1963, 1087 PP.
DOCUMENTARY STUDY OF THE PROGRAMS AND STANDING RULES OF POLITICAL PARTIES IN WEST GERMANY SINCE 1945. INCLUDES BRIEF INTRODUCTION SUMMARIZING SOME MAJOR PROGRAMMATIC DECLARATIONS OF THE PARTIES.

1024 FLEMING W.G.
"AUTHORITY, EFFICIENCY, AND ROLE STRESS: PROBLEMS IN THE DEVELOPMENT OF EAST AFRICAN BUREAUCRACIES."
ADMINISTRATIVE SCI. Q., 2 (DEC. 66), 386-404.
AN ANALYSIS BY COUNTRY OF BRITISH EXPERIENCES IN EAST AFRICA IN ATTEMPTING TO IMPOSE BUREAUCRATIC STRUCTURES UPON EXISTING POLITICAL SYSTEMS. STRESSES IMPOSSIBILITY OF MAXIMIZING BOTH EFFICIENCY AND AUTHORITY, AND EXPLORES CURRENT ATTEMPTS BY THESE NATIONS TO MODERNIZE THE NATIONAL POLITICAL STRUCTURE. INCLUDES BACKGROUND FOR RESEARCH INTO VARIOUS ASPECTS OF COLONIALISM, SOCIOLOGY, AND POLITICAL SYSTEMS.

1025 FLETCHER-COOKE J.
"THE EMERGING AFRICAN STATE."
COLORADO QUARTERLY, 16 (SUMMER 67), 49-63.
AFRICA HAS A DIFFICULT TASK AHEAD, GIVEN ENORMOUS PROBLEM OF IGNORANCE, POVERTY, AND DISEASE. YET THE WEST WILL DO NEITHER AFRICA NOR ITSELF A SERV+CE IF IT INSISTS ON MEASURING EVERYTHING AFRICAN AGAINST WESTERN STANDARDS.

1026 FLINT J.E.
NIGERIA AND GHANA.
ENGLEWOOD CLIFFS: PRENTICE HALL, 1966, 176 PP., LC#66-16343.
HISTORY OF GHANA AND NIGERIA EMPHASIZES PRE-EUROPEAN ORIGINS, EUROPEAN IMPACT, SLAVE TRADE, 19TH CENTURY AND COLONIAL PERIOD, WITH MAPS AND SUGGESTED READINGS.

1027 FLOREN LOZANO L.
BIBLIOGRAFIA DE LA BIBLIOGRAFIA DOMINICANA.
TRUJILLO: ROQUES ROMAN, 1948, 66 PP.
BIBLIOGRAPHY OF BIBLIOGRAPHIES ON DOMINICAN REPUBLIC. ENTRIES ARRANGED BY SUBJECT, AND SPANISH-LANGUAGE ITEMS ARE ANNOTATED. CONTAINS 230 ENTRIES, MAJORITY IN SPANISH LANGUAGE. INCLUDES INDEX OF AUTHORS, SUBJECTS, AND BIOGRAPHIES.

1028 FLORENCE P.S.
THE LOGIC OF BRITISH AND AMERICAN INDUSTRY; A REALISTIC ANALYSIS OF ECONOMIC STRUCTURE AND GOVERNMENT.
LONDON: G ROUTLEDGE & SONS, 1953, 368 PP.
COMPARATIVE STUDY OF INDUSTRIAL SYSTEMS BEGINS BY DEFINING APPROACH. DISCUSSES INDUSTRIAL STRUCTURE, RELATIONS OF INDUSTRY AND CONSUMER, RELATIONS WITHIN FIRM, GOVERNMENT OF FREE ENTERPRISE CAPITALISM, AND NATIONALIZATION; INCLUDES LABOR RELATIONS. EXAMINES TREND OF INVESTMENT AND EMPLOYMENT, DELEGATION OF AUTHORITY, MEASURES OF EFFICIENCY, PATTERNS OF LOCATION, AND TYPES OF MANAGEMENT.

1029 FLORENCE P.S.
ECONOMICS AND SOCIOLOGY OF INDUSTRY; A REALISTIC ANALYSIS OF DEVELOPMENT.
NEW YORK: WATTS, 1964, 258 PP.
CONTAINS ANALYSIS OF INDUSTRIAL DEVELOPMENT AND RELATION OF SOCIOLOGY AND ECONOMICS TO ITS STUDY. EXAMINES INDUSTRY'S ECONOMIC AND SOCIAL MOBILITY, URBANIZATION AND INDUSTRIAL LOCATION, ORGANIZATIONAL SYSTEMS, INDUSTRIAL GOVERNMENT, INDUSTRIALIZATION IN UNDERDEVELOPED COUNTRIES, SOCIAL LIMITS ON ECONOMIC DEVELOPMENT, AND SOCIAL RESEARCH.

1030 FLORES R.H.
CATALOGO DE TESIS DOCTORALES DE LAS FACULTADES DE LA UNIVERSIDAD DE EL SALVADOR.
EL SALVADOR: U DE EL SALVADOR, 1960, 620 PP.
CATALOG OF DOCTORAL THESES PRESENTED FROM 1878 TO 1960 AT UNIVERSITY OF EL SALVADOR. ENTRIES ARRANGED BY FACULTY AND CLASSIFIED BY DEWEY CLASSIFICATION SYSTEM.

1031 FLORES X.
LA TRADICION CATOLICA Y EL FUTURO POLITICO DE ESPANA (PAMPHLET)
NEW YORK: IBERICA PUB CO, 1958, 27 PP.
ARTICLES ON ROLE OF CATHOLIC CHURCH IN FUTURE POLITICAL AND SOCIAL DEVELOPMENT OF SPAIN. DEALS WITH CATHOLIC SOCIAL ACTION, CHANGES IN SPANISH VIEW OF CHURCH, CHRISTIAN DEMOCRATIC MOVEMENT IN SPAIN, AND CONTEMPORARY CHURCH-STATE RELATIONS.

1032 FLOURNOY F.
PARLIAMENT AND WAR.
LONDON: KING, 1927, 282 PP.
PROVIDES EXAMPLES OF PARLIAMENTARY INFLUENCE ON WAR DECISION: AFGHAN, BOER, PERSIAN, CHINESE, ABYSSINIAN, AND CRIMEAN WARS, WW 1 AND OCCUPATION OF EGYPT. CONCLUDES MORE PARLIAMENTARY CONTROL OVER WAR DECISION NEEDED SINCE MORE REPRESENTATIVE OF POPULACE THAN CABINET.

1033 FOGARTY M.P.
ECONOMIC CONTROL.
LONDON: ROUTLEDGE & KEGAN PAUL, 1955, 324 PP.
DISCUSSES ISSUES OF GOVERNMENTAL CONTROL OF ECONOMY, ESPECIALLY IN BRITAIN, INCLUDING PRODUCTION DECISIONS, DECISIONS ABOUT OBJECTIVES, AND PROBLEMS OF CONTROL. STUDIES DIFFERENT ECONOMIC AREAS OF CONTROL. BIBLIOGRAPHY OF 300 ENTRIES IN ENGLISH, 1932-52, BOOKS, ARTICLES, DOCUMENTS, ARRANGED BY CHAPTER, THEN TOPOGRAPHICALLY.

1034 FORBES A.H. ED.
CURRENT RESEARCH IN BRITISH STUDIES.
MARQUETTE: NORTHERN MICH U PR, 1964, 88 PP.
LIST OF 700 US AND CANADIAN SCHOLARS ENGAGED IN RESEARCH IN BRITISH AND IMPERIAL HISTORY. SCHOLARS TOGETHER WITH RESEARCH INTERESTS ARE LISTED BY MAJOR HISTORICAL PERIODS AND BY SUBJECT. INCLUDES BIOGRAPHICAL STUDIES; PARLIAMENTARY GOVERNMENT; ADMINISTRATION;CONSTITUTIONAL AND LEGAL HISTORY; CULTURAL, LITERARY, AND RELIGIOUS HISTORY; AND EXTERNAL AFFAIRS.

1035 FORD P.
CARDINAL MORAN AND THE A. L. P.
MELBOURNE: MELBOURNE UNIV PRESS, 1966, 319 PP., LC#66-17534.
ANALYZES ENCOUNTER BETWEEN CARDINAL AND SOCIALISM IN AUSTRALIA, AS IT DEVELOPED 1890-1907. CONCENTRATES ON EFFECTS ON AUSTRALIAN LABOR PARTY, AND FOUNDATIONS OF CATHOLIC SOCIAL THOUGHT AND ACTION IN MODERN AUSTRALIAN SOCIETY. FEELS MORAN'S FIGHT AGAINST SOCIALISM AS OBJECTIVE OF LABOR PARTY ILLUSTRATES NOT ONLY ERA INVOLVED, BUT IMPACT THAT AN ACTIVE CLERGYMAN CAN HAVE ON CIVIC LIFE.

1036 FORDE C.D.
AFRICAN WORLDS.
LONDON: OXFORD U PR, 1954, 243 PP.
PORTRAYS AND INTERPRETS WORLD-OUTLOOKS OF A NUMBER OF AFRICAN PEOPLES, INCLUDING DOMINANT BELIEFS AND ATTITUDES AS REVEALED IN EXPRESSIONS OF BELIEF AND IN CUSTOMS AND ETHICAL PRESCRIPTIONS IN RITUAL AND SECULAR CONTEXTS.

1037 FORDE L.D.
HABITAT, ECONOMY AND SOCIETY.
NEW YORK: EP DUTTON, 1952, 500 PP.
RELATIONSHIP OF ECOLOGY TO CULTURE IN NON-EUROPEAN COUNTRIES. DESCRIBES THREE DIFFERENT TYPES OF SOCIETY: PASTORAL, CULTIVATING, AND FOOD GATHERING, USING SPECIFIC EXAMPLES. DEMOGRAPHIC ANALYSIS AND ECOLOGICAL INFLUENCES IN SOCIAL STRUCTURE ARE INCLUDED.

1038 FORM W.H. ED., BLUM A.A. ED.
INDUSTRIAL RELATIONS AND SOCIAL CHANGE IN LATIN AMERICA.
GAINESVILLE: U OF FLA PR, 1965, 177 PP., LC#65-18667.
ATTEMPTS TO EVOLVE THEORIES OF INDUSTRIAL RELATIONS THROUGH COMPARATIVE ANALYSIS. ESSAYS UNIFIED BY COMMON THESIS THAT THE STATE OF A NATION'S INDUSTRIAL RELATIONS IS CORRELATED TO SOCIAL CHANGES WITHIN THAT COUNTRY.

1039 FORTES M. ED., EVANS-PRITCHARD E. ED.
AFRICAN POLITICAL SYSTEMS.
LONDON: OXFORD U PR, 1948, 302 PP.
SEEKS TO LAY THE GROUNDWORK FOR THE STUDY OF AFRICAN POLITICAL ORGANIZATION ON A BROAD, COMPARATIVE BASIS BY ANALYZING THE FACTS AND THEORY OF AFRICAN NATIVE SOCIAL ORGANIZATION IN SEVERAL TRIBES.

1040 FORTESCU J.
IN PRAISE OF ENGLISH LAW (1464) (TRANS. BY S.B. CHRIMES)
NEW YORK: CAMBRIDGE U PRESS, 1942, 235 PP.
PRAISES CONSTITUTIONALISM IN MONARCHICAL STATES AS JUST AND EFFICIENT MEANS OF PROVIDING ORDER AND AUTHORITY. CLAIMS THAT KINGS DO NOT HAVE RIGHT TO CHANGE LAWS MADE BY PARLIAMENT AND TRADITION SINCE THERE IS A DIFFERENCE BETWEEN REGAL AND POLITICAL GOVERNMENT SIMILAR TO MODERN DISTINCTION BETWEEN EXECUTIVE AND LEGISLATIVE BRANCHES OF GOVERNMENT. DEALS WITH BOTH CIVIL AND CRIMINAL LAWS.

1041 FORTESCUE G.K. ED.
SUBJECT INDEX OF THE MODERN WORKS ADDED TO THE LIBRARY OF THE BRITISH MUSEUM IN THE YEARS 1881-1900 (3 VOLS.)
LONDON: W CLOWES & SONS, LTD, 1903.
CONTAINS ABOUT 155,000 ENTRIES REFERRING TO BOOKS FIRST PUBLISHED OR REISSUED BETWEEN JANUARY, 1881, AND DECEMBER, 1900. UNDER EACH COUNTRY ARE FOUND WORKS ON ANTIQUITIES, ARMY, COLONIES, CONSTITUTION AND GOVERNMENT, HISTORY, LAW, NAVY, POLITICS, SOCIAL LIFE, TOPOGRAPHY, TRADE, AND FINANCE.

1042 FORTESCUE J., PLUMMER C. ED.
THE GOVERNANCE OF ENGLAND (1471-76)
LONDON: OXFORD U PR, 1926, 387 PP.
EARLIEST CONSTITUTIONAL TREATISE WRITTEN IN ENGLISH. EXAMINES GOVERNMENTAL EVILS OF HIS TIME, AND PROPOSES REMEDIES. PROPOSES REORGANIZATION OF PRIVY COUNCIL, STRENGTHENING OF CROWN, AND REDUCTION OF POWER OF NOBLES. URGES KING TO AVOID WEAKNESSES OF LANCASTRIAN RULE, ITS UNSOUND FINANCE, AND ITS LACK OF GOVERNANCE AND JUSTICE.

1043 FOSTER P.
EDUCATION AND SOCIAL CHANGE IN GHANA.
CHICAGO: U OF CHICAGO PRESS, 1965, 322 PP.
A CASE STUDY OF EDUCATIONAL DEVELOPMENT IN GHANA AS THE FIRST AND MOST COMPLEX AFRICAN NATION TO ACHIEVE RECENT INDEPENDENCE. STUDIES DOCUMENTS RELATING TO HISTORICAL BACKGROUND OF GOLD COAST, TRADITIONS OF WESTERN EDUCATION, AND CONTEMPORARY PRACTICES, ESPECIALLY IN SECONDARY SCHOOLS. EXAMINES ROLE OF SCHOOL SYSTEMS AND EDUCATIONAL DEMANDS OF ECONOMIC AND SOCIAL GROWTH.

1044 FOX A.
THE POWER OF SMALL STATES: DIPLOMACY IN WORLD WAR TWO.
CHICAGO: U. CHI. PR., 1959, 212 PP.
COUNTRIES EXAMINED ARE TURKEY, FINLAND, NORWAY, SWEDEN AND SPAIN. SPECIFIC CONDITIONS LISTED BY WHICH SMALL NATIONS CAN SUCCESSFULLY RESIST PRESSURE OF GREAT POWERS. AUTHOR CONCLUDES THAT SMALL STATES MAKE DECISIONS WHICH INCREASE THE IMBALANCE BETWEEN GREAT POWER CONSTELLATIONS WHEREAS THE LATTER MUST MODIFY PROPOSALS DUE TO COMPETITION OVER FORMER.

1045 FOX K.A., SENGUPTA J.K., THORBECKE E.
THE THEORY OF QUANTITATIVE ECONOMIC POLICY WITH APPLICATIONS TO ECONOMIC GROWTH AND STABILIZATION.
NEW YORK: SIGNET BOOKS, 1966, 514 PP.
IN TEXTBOOK FORM PRESENTS BASIC THEORY OF QUANTITATIVE ECONOMIC POLICY AND SUPPLIES MOTIVATIONAL AND EMPIRICAL CONTENT FOR THEORY. DISCUSSES PARTICULAR ECONOMETRIC OR STABILIZATION MODELS FROM PERSPECTIVE OF POLICY-MAKING. SHOWS HOW THEORY MAY BE EXTENDED INTO REGIONAL SUBDIVISIONS OF A NATIONAL ECONOMY. DISCUSSES MODELS OF ECONOMIC GROWTH AND DEVELOPMENT PLANNING.

1046 FRANCIS M.J.
"THE US PRESS AND CASTRO: A STUDY IN DECLINING RELATIONS."
JOURNALISM QUARTERLY, (SUMMER 67), 257-266.
STUDY OF TREATMENT OF CUBAN REVOLUTION FROM JANUARY OF 1959 TO APRIL OF 1961 BY 17 LEADING AMERICAN NEWSPAPERS. FOCUSES ON MISINTERPRETATION OF EVENTS BY PRESS DURING EARLY STAGES OF REVOLUTION AND GRADUAL INCREASE IN ANTI-CASTRO SENTIMENT IN NEWSPAPERS AS REVOLUTION PROGRESSED.

1047 FRANCIS R.G.
THE PREDICTIVE PROCESS.
RIO PIEDRAS: SOCIAL SCI RES CTR, 1960, 142 PP.
EXAMINES ROLE OF PREDICTION IN SCIENCE AND TRACES IDEA OF PROGRESS AS ADVANCED BY STATESMEN AND PHILOSOPHERS IN WESTERN SOCIETY, WITH PARTICULAR EMPHASIS ON ITS DEVELOPMENT IN US. DISCUSSES BRIEFLY PREDICTIVE PROCESS IN ECONOMIC SPHERE.

1048 FRANCK T.M.
EAST AFRICAN UNITY THROUGH LAW.
NEW HAVEN: YALE U PR, 1964, 184 PP., LC#64-20916.
ANALYSIS OF THE "CONSOCIATIONAL" APPROACH TO UNITY IN EAST AFRICA AS A FUNCTIONALIST PATTERN APPLICABLE TO TOTAL UNIFICATION OF AFRICA AS WELL AS REGIONAL UNION. THE METHODS OF BUILDING UNITY THROUGH THE CREATION OF "LEGAL-CONSTITUTIONAL TECHNIQUES" AND INSTITUTION BUILDING ARE REVIEWED.

1049 FRANK E. ED.
LAWMAKERS IN A CHANGING WORLD.
ENGLEWOOD CLIFFS: PRENTICE HALL, 1966, 186 PP., LC#66-28110.
ESSAYS IN COMPARATIVE GOVERNMENT WHICH FOCUS ON LEGISLATURE AND PEOPLE, RELATIONSHIPS, AND STRUCTURAL FRAMEWORK ENTERING LAWMAKING PROCESS. LEGISLATURE AS AN INSTITUTION IS PERCEIVED IN HUMAN TERMS.

1050 FRANK T.
A HISTORY OF ROME.
NEW YORK: HOLT, 1923, 613 PP.
COMPREHENSIVE SURVEY OF 'POLITICAL AND CULTURAL FORTUNES OF THE ANCIENT REPUBLIC WHICH IN SO MANY RESPECTS DID PIONEER WORK IN DEMOCRATIC GOVERNMENT.' TOPICS INCLUDE: PUNIC WARS BETWEEN ROME AND CARTHAGE, SOCIETY IN DAYS OF CATO, ROMAN CONSTITUTION, GRACCHAN REFORMS, THE FIRST TRIUMVIRATE, THE CIVIL WAR, AUGUSTUS' EMPIRE, DOMITIAN, M. AURELIUS, CONSTANTINE AND CAUSES OF ROME'S DECLINE.

1051 FRANKEL J.
THE MAKING OF FOREIGN POLICY: AN ANALYSIS OF DECISION-MAKING
LONDON: OXFORD U PR, 1963, 231 PP.
STUDY OF FOREIGN POLICY-MAKING INVOLVES INTERNATIONAL AND DOMESTIC ENVIRONMENT, RATIONALITY, DISCUSSION OF CHOICE, AND DECISIONAL STAGES, INCLUDING FOREIGN MINISTRY, SUBSIDIARY SERVICES AND AGENCIES, AND PROCESS OF POLICY FORMATION.

1052 FRANKEL S.H.
"ECONOMIC ASPECTS OF POLITICAL INDEPENDENCE IN AFRICA."
INT. AFF., 36 (OCT. 60), 440-446.
RAISES SERIOUS DOUBTS REGARDING EFFECTS OF POLITICAL INDEPENDENCE ON ECONOMY OF EMERGENT AFRICAN STATES. EXPLAINS THEORY IN ECONOMIC TERMS OF ABSOLUTE INDEPENDENCE COUPLED WITH ABSOLUTE ISOLATION. SHOWS HOW NEW AFRICA IS ESTABLISHING ECONOMIC RELATIONSHIP WITH REST OF THE WORLD, BUT FEELS PRESENT CONDITIONS IN AFRICA OFFER LITTLE INDUCEMENT FOR CAPITAL AND SKILLED ASSISTANCE FROM ABROAD.

1053 FRANZ G.
KULTURKAMPF.
MUNICH: VERL GEORG D W CALLWEY, 1955, 355 PP.
EXAMINES RELATIONS BETWEEN CHURCH AND STATE IN MIDDLE EUROPE FROM FRENCH REVOLUTION TO PRUSSIAN KULTURKAMPF. DISCUSSES NATIONAL MOVEMENTS IN AUSTRIA, SWITZERLAND, BAVARIA, PRUSSIA, AND SMALLER GERMAN STATES.

1054 FRANZ G. ED.
TEILUNG UND WIEDERVEREINIGUNG.
GOTTINGEN: MUSTERSCHMIDT VERLAG, 1963, 299 PP.
COLLECTION OF ESSAYS ON POLITICAL PROBLEMS OF DIVISION AND REUNIFICATION IN EUROPE AND ASIA. DISCUSSES DIVISION OF NETHERLANDS, IRELAND, POLAND, ITALY, GERMANY, KOREA, AND VIETNAM.

1055 FREEMAN H.A., PAULLIN O.
COERCION OF STATES IN FEDERAL UNIONS (PAMPHLET)
PHILA: PACIFIST RESEARCH BUREAU, 1943, 67 PP.
EXAMINE HISTORICAL DEVELOPMENT OF NATIONAL FEDERATIONS, WITH RESPECT TO INFLUENCES WORKING TOWARD OR FROM UNITY, GIVING SPECIAL ATTENTION TO USE OF FORCE. GIVE PACIFIST VIEW OF FEDERALISM AND MANNER OF ACHIEVING WORLD PEACE UTILIZING IT. CONSIDER COHESIVE FORCES PRESENT IN WORLD THAT COULD CONTRIBUTE TO NONVIOLENT SOLUTION TO WWII, WHICH AT TIME OF WRITING WAS IN SECOND YEAR OF US INVOLVEMENT.

1056 FREISEN J.
STAAT UND KATHOLISCHE KIRCHE IN DEN DEUTSCHEN BUNDESSTAATEN (2 VOLS.)
AMSTERDAM: VERLAG P SCHIPPERS, 1964, 910 PP.
DISCUSSES ROLE OF CATHOLIC CHURCH IN RELATION TO MARRIAGE LAWS, ADMINISTRATION OF INHERITANCE LAWS, EDUCATION, ETC., IN GERMAN STATES OF LIPPE, WALDECK-PYRMONT, ANHALT, SCHWARZBURG-RUDOLSTADT, SCHWARZBURG-SONDERSHAUSEN, REUSS-GREIZ, REUSS-SCHLEIZ, SACHSEN-ALTENBURG, SACHSEN-COBURG, AND SACHSEN-GOTHA FROM 1800 TO PRESENT.

1057 FRENCH D.S.
"DOES THE U.S. EXPLOIT THE DEVELOPING NATIONS?"
COMMONWEAL, 86 (MAY 67), 257-259.
WHILE REJECTING ANY DOCTRINAIRE APPROACH, THIS ESSAY ARGUES THAT THE US IS SYSTEMATICALLY WORKING TO PRESERVE AN INTERNATIONAL ECONOMIC ORDER WHICH IS DISADVANTAGEOUS TO THE UNDERDEVELOPED COUNTRIES. THE US HAS SHOWN ITSELF COMMITTED TO THE PRESENT SYSTEM, AS IN THE COCOA CONFERENCE, THOUGH UNDER THIS SYSTEM THE INCOME OF DEVELOPED NATIONS IS GROWING FAR MORE RAPIDLY THAN THAT OF UNDERDEVELOPED NATIONS.

1058 FREUND G.
"ADENAUER AND THE FUTURE OF GERMANY."
INT. J., 18, (AUTUMN 63), 458-468.
ASSERTS THAT ADENAUER, AS OUTSTANDING GERMAN STATESMAN OF TWENTIETH CENTURY, HAS HELPED GERMANY ACHIEVE MAJOR STATUS IN WESTERN DEFENSE POLICY. HOWEVER, OTHERS WILL DETERMINE GERMANYS FUTURE ROLE.

1059 FREY F.W.
THE TURKISH POLITICAL ELITE.
CAMBRIDGE: M I T PRESS, 1965, 483 PP., LC#65-13834.
SCHOLARLY INVESTIGATION OF SOCIAL BACKGROUNDS OF MODERN TURKISH POLITICAL ELITES AND RELATIONSHIP BETWEEN THESE BACKGROUNDS AND FUNCTIONING OF TURKISH POLITICAL SYSTEMS. FOCUSES ON DEPUTIES TO GRAND NATIONAL ASSEMBLY AND THREE MAJOR TYPES OF ELITE STATUS: INTELLECTUAL, OFFICIAL, AND LOCAL.

1060 FREYRE G.
THE PORTUGUESE AND THE TROPICS.
LISBON: INTL CONG HIST OF DISCOV, 1961, 296 PP.
DISCUSSES PORTUGUESE METHODS AND CONCEPTS OF INTEGRATING INHABITANTS OF TROPIC AREAS INTO NEW COMPLEX CULTURAL AND SOCIAL PATTERNS. EMPHASIZES VARIOUS ART FORMS RESULTING FROM PROCESS OF INTEGRATING NON-EUROPEANS INTO EUROPEAN-BASED CULTURE.

1061 FRIED R.C.
THE ITALIAN PREFECTS.
NEW HAVEN: YALE U PR, 1963, 343 PP., LC#63-13960.
STUDY ATTEMPTS TO OUTLINE MAIN STAGES OF ITALIAN FIELD DEVELOPMENT, WHICH AUTHOR SITUATES WITHIN DEVELOPING PREFECTORAL SYSTEM. PERHAPS FIRST ATTEMPT TO ANALYZE AND DESCRIBE ANY PREFECTORAL SYSTEM OTHER THAN FRENCH.

1062 FRIED R.C.
COMPARATIVE POLITICAL INSTITUTIONS.
NEW YORK: MACMILLAN, 1966, 152 PP., LC#66-17389.
VOLUME ONE IN SERIES "GOVERNMENT IN THE MODERN WORLD." ANALYZES EXECUTIVES, LEGISLATURES, COURTS, BUREAUCRACIES, ARMED FORCES, POLITICAL PARTIES, AND ELECTORATES. EACH CHAPTER CONSIDERS POTENTIAL SOURCES OF POWER AND WEAKNESS, TREATED UNDER UNIFORM SET OF 12 CATEGORIES.

1063 FRIEDLAND W.H. ED., ROSBERG C.E. ED.
AFRICAN SOCIALISM.
STANFORD: U. PR., 1964, 313 PP., $6.75.
ELEVEN ESSAYS EXAMINING THE VARIOUS PRAGMATIC ECONOMIC AND SOCIAL IDEOLOGIES WHICH ARE COVERED BY THE TERM 'AFRICAN SOCIALISM.' PART 2 STUDIES IN DETAIL THE NATIONAL PROGRAMS OF SPECIFIC COUNTRIES. FINAL PORTION CONSISTS OF BASIC DOCUMENTS, INCLUDING SOME WORK OF THE LATE GEORGE PADMORE.

1064 FRIEDMANN G.
INDUSTRIAL SOCIETY: THE EMERGENCE OF THE HUMAN PROBLEMS OF AUTOMATION.
NEW YORK: FREE PRESS OF GLENCOE, 1955, 436 PP.
HUMANISTIC ANALYSIS OF MAN'S ROLE IN A MECHANIZED TECHNOLOGICAL SOCIETY. ATTEMPTS AN INTERDISCIPLINARY OVERVIEW OF THE PROBLEM OF DEHUMANIZATION CREATED BY AUTOMATION, DRAWING FROM PHYSIOLOGY, ANTHROPOLOGY, ECONOMICS, SOCIOLOGY, AND INDUSTRIAL PSYCHOLOGY. CONCLUSIONS OF THIS STUDY IN THE FINAL VOLUME OF THE SERIES "THE MACHINE AND HUMANISM."

1065 FRIEDMANN W. ED.
THE PUBLIC CORPORATION: A COMPARATIVE SYMPOSIUM (UNIVERSITY OF TORONTO SCHOOL OF LAW COMPARATIVE LAW SERIES, VOL. I)
TORONTO: CARSWELL, 1954, 612 PP.
CONCERNS LEGAL STATUS AND ORGANIZATION OF THE PUBLIC CORPORATION. INCLUDES 14 ESSAYS ON THE PUBLIC CORPORATION IN AUSTRALIA, CANADA, FRANCE, GERMANY, ENGLAND, INDIA, ISRAEL, ITALY, NEW ZEALAND, SOUTH AFRICA, SWEDEN, US, USSR; STUDIES OF LEGAL RELATIONS OF A NATIONALIZED INDUSTRY (BRITAIN'S NATIONAL COAL BOARD) AND AN INTERNATIONAL PUBLIC CORPORATION; AND A FINAL COMPARATIVE ANALYSIS.

1066 FRIEDMANN W.
METHODS AND POLICIES OF PRINCIPAL DONOR COUNTRIES IN PUBLIC INTERNATIONAL DEVELOPMENT FINANCING: PRELIMINARY APPRAISAL.
NEW YORK: COLUMBIA U LAW SCHOOL, 1962, 49 PP.
ANALYZES FOREIGN AID MACHINERY IN US, UK, WEST GERMANY, AND FRANCE, AS WELL AS EEC, SHOWING THERE IS AGREEMENT ON PRE-EMINENCE OF NEED FOR TECHNICAL ASSISTANCE, BUT DISAGREEMENT ON CONCEPT AND PRINCIPLES OF CAPITAL AID FOR DEVELOPING COUNTRIES. POINTS OUT NATURE OF OTHER ISSUES UPON WHICH NATIONS AGREE AND DIFFER. SUGGESTS FURTHER TASKS FOR MULTILATERAL COORDINATION.

1067 FRIEDRICH C.J.
"TOTALITARIANISM."
CAMBRIDGE: HARVARD U. PR., 1954, 386 PP.
COVERS ALL ASPECTS OF TOTALITARIANISM: ITS NATURE AND THEORY. PSYCHOLOGICAL ATTITUDES EXPRESSED AND INTELLECTUAL LIFE IN SOCIETIES SUBJECT TO TOTALITARIANISM AND ORGANIZATION OF THOSE REGIMES ARE ALSO DISCUSSED.

1068 FRIEDRICH C.J., BRZEZINSKI Z.K.
TOTALITARIAN DICTATORSHIP AND AUTOCRACY.
CAMBRIDGE: HARVARD U. PR., 1954, 346 PP.
ATTEMPTS TO DEFINE TOTALITARIANISM BY EXAMINING CHARACTERISTICS OF THREE MODERN SOCIETIES: NAZI GERMANY, FASCIST ITALY AND COMMUNIST RUSSIA. EXPLORES THE FUNCTIONING OF LEADERS, THEORY, TERROR, PROPAGANDA, ORGANIZATION, AND ECONOMICS IN DYNAMICS OF TOTALITARIANISM. BRIEF DISCUSSION OF AREAS IN WORLD SOCIETY NOT UNDER AUTOCRATIC RULE.

1069 FRIEDRICH C.J.
MAN AND HIS GOVERNMENT: AN EMPIRICAL THEORY OF POLITICS.
NEW YORK: MCGRAW HILL, 1963, 737 PP., LC#63-15892.
LOOKS AT POLITICAL EXPERIENCE OF MANKIND IN ORDER TO SEE WHAT CONTRIBUTES TO POLITICAL ORDER AND THE GOOD LIFE AND WHAT DETRACTS. CONSIDERS POLITICAL PERSON AND POLITICAL ACT; DIMENSIONS OF POWER; JUSTICE; EQUALITY; FREEDOM;

GOVERNING PROCESSES; MODES OF OPERATION; AND RANGE AND LEVELS OF GOVERNMENT.

1070 FRIEDRICH C.J.
REVOLUTION: NOMOS VIII.
NEW YORK: ATHERTON PRESS, 1966, 246 PP., LC#65-28141.
ESSAYS DISCUSS REVOLUTION IN RELATION TO SEVERAL AREAS OF SOCIAL SCIENCES AND EMPHASIZE 20TH-CENTURY SOCIO-POLITICAL CONDITIONS. EMPHASIS IS NOT ON CONCRETE HISTORICAL ANALYSIS; INSTEAD ENTRIES ARE ARRANGED IN THREE GENERAL CONCEPTUAL CATEGORIES STRESSING GENERAL THEORY OF REVOLUTION, IDEOLOGY OF INTERNATIONAL POLITICAL ORDER, AND PROBLEMS RESULTING FROM MARXIST MODES OF REVOLUTION.

1071 FRITZ H.E.
THE MOVEMENT FOR INDIAN ASSIMILATION, 1860-1890.
PHILA: U OF PENN PR, 1963, 244 PP., LC#62-11272.
STUDY OF FEDERAL INDIAN POLICY DURING PERIOD OF CRISIS IN US: AMERICAN INDIAN RELATIONS FOLLOWING CIVIL WAR. GIVES PARTICULAR ATTENTION TO GRANT'S "PEACE POLICY" AND FORCES THAT ESTABLISHED IT; SHOWS IT WAS PHASE OF PROTESTANT MOVEMENT FOR ASSIMILATION OF INDIANS, WHICH CULMINATED WITH PASSAGE OF DAWES ACT. ALSO TREATS CATHOLIC REACTION TO MOVEMENT.

1072 FROMM E.
MARX'S CONCEPT OF MAN.
NEW YORK: FREDERICK UNGAR PUBL, 1964, 260 PP., LC#61-11935.
BULK OF VOLUME CONTAINS ENGLISH TRANSLATION OF MARX'S "PHILOSOPHICAL MANUSCRIPTS." FROMM'S INTRODUCTION ANALYZES MARX'S PHILOSOPHY, ARGUING THAT ITS ORIGINS CAN BE FOUND IN HUMANISTIC WESTERN PHILOSOPHICAL TRADITION OF SPINOZA, GOETHE, AND HEGEL. ARGUMENT STRUCTURED AROUND DISCUSSION OF MARX'S CONCEPTION OF MAN.

1073 FRYKLUND R.
100 MILLION LIVES: MAXIMUM SURVIVAL IN A NUCLEAR WAR.
NEW YORK: MACMILLAN, 1962, 175 PP., LC#62-12896.
A REPORTER'S ATTEMPT TO EXPLAIN CONFLICTING PROPOSALS FOR NUCLEAR-WAR STRATEGY. DESCRIBES IN DETAIL PROPOSED STRATEGY WHICH COULD BROADEN US DETERRENT AND DEFENSE ABILITY, AND HELP US TO ENDURE AN ACCIDENTAL WAR WITHOUT SENSELESS SLAUGHTER.

1074 FUCHS W.P. ED.
STAAT UND KIRCHE IM WANDEL DER JAHRHUNDERTE.
STUTTGART: KOHLHAMMER VERLAG, 1966, 219 PP.
ESSAYS ON CHURCH-STATE RELATION IN CONTINENTAL EUROPE AND ENGLAND FROM AGE OF CONSTANTINE TO PRESENT. EXAMINES RISE OF POLITICAL FREEDOM, NONCONFORMISM IN ENGLAND, CHRISTIAN CHURCH AND MODERN DEMOCRACY, ETC.

1075 FULLER G.H. ED.
TURKEY: A SELECTED LIST OF REFERENCES.
WASHINGTON: LIBRARY OF CONGRESS, 1944, 114 PP.
CONTAINS 916 LISTINGS OF BOOKS AND ARTICLES, MOST PUBLISHED 1930-44, DEALING WITH MANY ASPECTS OF MODERN AND HISTORICAL TURKEY, INCLUDING GEOGRAPHY, GEOLOGY, POLITICAL HISTORY, ECONOMIC AND SOCIAL CONDITIONS, ART AND LETTERS. INCLUDES LISTING OF MAPS AND OTHER BIBLIOGRAPHIES. MANY ENTRIES IN FRENCH AND GERMAN.

1076 FULLER J.F.C.
THE CONDUCT OF WAR, 1789-1961.
NEW BRUNSWICK: RUTGERS U PR, 1961, 352 PP., LC#61-10261.
AUTHOR BELIEVES THAT IF IMPACT ON WARFARE OF CHANGES IN CIVILIZATION HAD BEEN PROPERLY CONSIDERED, THE WORLD SITUATION WOULD BE LESS CONFUSED AND DANGEROUS. CONSIDERS EFFECT OF PRESSURES OF ECONOMIC, POLITICAL, AND SOCIAL DEVELOPMENT ON WARFARE. STUDIES EFFECTS OF FRENCH, INDUSTRIAL, AND RUSSIAN REVOLUTIONS ON WAR, AND CONSIDERS INCREASED DESTRUCTIVE CAPACITY OF MODERN WARFARE.

1077 FURNIA A.H.
THE DIPLOMACY OF APPEASEMENT: ANGLO-FRENCH RELATIONS AND THE PRELUDE TO WORLD WAR II 1931-1938.
THE UNIVERSITY PR OF WASH, DC, 1960, 454 PP., LC#60-14506.
DISCUSSES BRITISH AND FRENCH FOREIGN POLICY IN RELATION TO COLLECTIVE SECURITY AND MAINTENANCE OF STATUS QUO. TRACES IN DETAIL DIPLOMATIC MANEUVERS OF FRENCH AND ENGLISH OFFICIALS PRIOR TO WWII.

1078 FURNISS E.S.
"WEAKNESSES IN FRENCH FOREIGN POLICY-MAKING."
PRINCETON: CENT. INT. STUD., 1954, 52 PP.
ATTEMPTS TO SHOW CONSEQUENCES WITHIN POLITICAL STRUCTURE OF FOURTH FRENCH REPUBLIC THAT HAVE FOLLOWED UPON FAILURE OF FRENCH TO UNITE BEHIND INSTITUTIONAL SYSTEM AFTER WORLD WAR TWO. RELATES THIS FAILURE TO WEAK FOREIGN POLICY AND REEXAMINATION OF EUROPEAN POLICY BY US.

1079 FURNISS E.S.
FRANCE, TROUBLED ALLY.
NEW YORK: HARPER, 1960, 512 PP.
FOCUSES ON POLICIES OF AND CONTINUITY BETWEEN FOURTH AND FIFTH REPUBLICS. ASSESSES DE GAULLE'S DOMESTIC AND FOREIGN PROGRAMS. STRESSES NEED TO STUDY FRENCH FOREIGN POLICY IN RELATION TO THE GALLIC SOCIAL AND ECONOMIC SITUATION IN WHICH IT WAS CREATED.

1080 FURNIVALL J.S.
COLONIAL POLICY AND PRACTICE A COMPARATIVE STUDY OF BURMA, AND NETHERLANDS INDIA.
LONDON: CAMBRIDGE UNIV PRESS, 1948, 568 PP.
SURVEYS HISTORY OF COLONIALISM IN BURMA AND INDONESIA AND ANALYZES COMPARATIVE BENEFIT OF BRITISH AND DUTCH RULE. ARGUES THAT, FOR SAKE OF EUROPEAN POWERS AS WELL AS COLONIES, THE LATTER MUST BE INDEPENDENT. REASONS THAT INDEPENDENCE IS THE NATURAL RESULT OF THE JAPANESE INVASION.

1081 FURNIVALL J.S.
NETHERLANDS INDIA.
NEW YORK: MACMILLAN, 1939, 502 PP.
STUDIES ECONOMIC AND SOCIAL DEVELOPMENT OF NETHERLANDS INDIA WITH SPECIAL REFERENCE TO ITS NATURE AS A PLURALISTIC SOCIETY. HISTORICALLY TRACES GENERAL POLITICAL AND ECONOMIC CHANGES IN ENVIRONMENT AND RELATES THEM TO VAST DIFFERENCES IN CULTURE AND RACE OF ITS INHABITANTS. FOLLOWS RISE OF LIBERALISM AND NOTES MAJOR CHANGES IN COLONIAL POLICY.

1082 FURTADO C.
THE ECONOMIC GROWTH OF BRAZIL: A SURVEY FROM COLONIAL TO MODERN TIMES.
BERKELEY: U OF CALIF PR, 1963, 285 PP., LC#63-12818.
INTRODUCTORY TEXT TO HISTORIC PROCESS OF BRAZIL'S ECONOMIC GROWTH. DISCUSSES ECONOMIC BASES OF TERRITORIAL OCCUPATION; SLAVERY ECONOMY OF TROPICAL AGRICULTURE (16TH AND 17TH CENTURIES); SLAVERY ECONOMY OF MINING (18TH CENTURY) AND ECONOMIC TRANSITION TO PAID LABOR; ECONOMY OF TRANSITION TO AN INDUSTRIAL SYSTEM.

1083 FUSARO A.
"THE EFFECT OF PROPORTIONAL REPRESENTATION ON VOTING IN THE AUSTRALIAN SENATE."
PARLIAMENTARY AFFAIRS, 20 (FALL 67), 329-336.
SINCE ADOPTION OF PROPORTIONAL REPRESENTATION, IN L949, THE AUSTRALIAN GOVERNMENT HAS NEVER HAD A MAJORITY OF MORE THAN FOUR. THE NEW ELECTION SYSTEM ELIMINATED THE LOPSIDED AND UNREPRESENTATIVE MAJORITIES OF THE PAST. SENATE'S POSITION IN CONSTITUTIONAL SYSTEM HAS BEEN ENHANCED BY NEW SYSTEM. IT CANNOT CONTROL GOVERNMENT, AS HOUSE CAN, BUT IT CAN AFFECT GOVERNMENT PROGRAMS.

1084 FYFE H.
THE BRITISH LIBERAL PARTY.
LONDON: ALLEN & UNWIN, 1928, 272 PP.
SKETCHES DEVELOPMENT OF LIBERAL PARTY 1868-1925, DISCUSSING REASONS FOR ITS ORGANIZATION, ITS DEBT TO OTHER PARTIES, ITS INTERNAL STRUGGLES, ITS RISE TO POWER, AND ITS STATE IN 1927. ITS RELATION TO SOCIALISM, THE ANGLICAN CHURCH, AND THE CONSERVATIVE PARTY IS EXPLORED, ALONG WITH ITS SEARCH FOR SOLID LEADERSHIP.

1085 GABLE R.W.
"CULTURE AND ADMINISTRATION IN IRAN."
MIDDLE EAST J., 13 (FALL 59), 407-421.
OBSERVATIONS ON IRANIAN INDIVIDUAL CHARACTERISTICS, RELIGION, SOCIETY, ETC., THAT HAVE BEARING ON THE IRANIAN SYSTEM OF ADMINISTRATION.

1086 GAJENDRAGADKAR P.B.
LAW, LIBERTY AND SOCIAL JUSTICE.
NEW YORK: ASIA PUBL HOUSE, 1965, 159 PP.
DISCUSSES HINDU RELATION TO MODERN LAW AND NOTIONS OF FREEDOM IN INDIA. STUDIES PROSPECT OF SOCIO-ECONOMIC PLANNING'S INTERFERING WITH PERSONAL LIBERTY, AND MEANS OF HARMONIOUS ADJUSTMENT.

1087 GALBRAITH J.K.
THE NEW INDUSTRIAL STATE.
BOSTON: HOUGHTON MIFFLIN, 1967, 427 PP., LC#67-11826.
DEPICTS CHANGES IN MODERN ECONOMIC LIFE AS A CONSEQUENCE OF ADVANCING TECHNOLOGY, SPECIALIZED LABOR, AND CONTROL OF INDUSTRY BY SMALL NUMBER OF LARGE CORPORATIONS. ARGUES THAT THE PLANNED DECISION HAS REPLACED TRADITIONAL MARKET OF CAPITALIST THEORY; ALL INDUSTRIAL SOCIETY SHOWS POINTS OF CONVERGENCE AND GOVERNMENT ITSELF IS ALTERED BY ITS RELATIONSHIP WITH INDUSTRIALIZATION.

1088 GALENSON W. ED.
LABOR IN DEVELOPING COUNTRIES.
BERKELEY: U OF CALIF PR, 1962, 299 PP., LC#62-16108.
FIVE ESSAYS ON LABOR RELATIONS IN VARIOUS ENVIRONMENTAL SETTINGS. EXAMINE TRADE UNION POWER IN UNDERDEVELOPED NATIONS, THE INFLUENCE OF UNIONS IN POLITICS, COLLECTIVE BARGAINING, AND WAGE DIFFERENTIALS. ANALYZE PROBLEMS INVOLVED IN CONVERSION OF A BACKWARD PEASANTRY TO AN INDUSTRIAL WORK FORCE.

1089 GALLOWAY G.B.
CONGRESS AND PARLIAMENT: THEIR ORGANIZATION AND OPERATION IN

THE US AND THE UK: PLANNING PAMPHLET NO. 93.
WASHINGTON: NATL PLANNING ASSN, 1955, 105 PP., LC#55-4850.
COMPARES ASPECTS OF CONTEMPORARY PARLIAMENTARY PRACTICE IN THE US CONGRESS AND THE BRITISH PARLIAMENT. TREATS PLANNING THE LEGISLATIVE PROGRAM, COMMITTEE STRUCTURE AND OPERATION, LEGISLATIVE INVESTIGATIONS, LEGISLATIVE LEADERSHIP, PARTY ORGANIZATION, CONTROL OF POLICY AND ADMINISTRATION, AND SECOND CHAMBERS.

1090 GALTUNG J.
"EAST-WEST INTERACTION PATTERNS."
JOURNAL OF PEACE RESEARCH, (1966), 46-177.
GENERAL SYSTEM OF PROPOSITIONS DEVELOPED CONCERNING RELATIONS BETWEEN TWO ALLIANCES, EACH HEADED BY ONE OR MORE BIG POWERS. THEN NATO AND WARSAW PACT RELATIONS ANALYZED TO TEST HYPOTHESIS THAT INTERACTION BETWEEN 2 BLOCKS WILL BE MAINLY BETWEEN BIG POWERS, LESS FROM BIG POWERS TO SMALL POWERS, AND VERY LITTLE BETWEEN SMALL POWERS. HYPOTHESIS TESTED ON DATA FROM 15 TYPES OF INTERACTION.

1091 GALTUNG J.
"ON THE EFFECTS OF INTERNATIONAL ECONOMIC SANCTIONS, WITH EXAMPLES FROM THE CASE OF RHODESIA."
WORLD POLITICS, 19 (APR. 67), 378-416.
USES RHODESIA AS A SOURCE OF EXAMPLES AND ILLUSTRATIONS FOR AN EXPLORATORY STUDY OF INTERNATIONAL ECONOMIC SANCTIONS. PURPOSE IS TO GET SOME IMPRESSIONS ABOUT THE PSYCHOLOGICAL AND SOCIAL MECHANISMS OF ECONOMIC BOYCOTT WHEN THEY ARE OPERATING. DISCUSSES THE GENERAL THEORY OF SANCTIONS AND THE DEFENSE AGAINST THEM.

1092 GAMARNIKOW M.
"THE NEW ROLE OF PRIVATE ENTERPRISE."
EAST EUROPE, 16 (AUG. 67), 2-9.
RESURGENCE OF PRIVATE ENTERPRISE IN EASTERN EURPOE ALLOWS EMPLOYMENT OPPORTUNIES AND INDICATES A NEW PROFIT CONSCIOUSNESS. INCLUDES DISCUSSION OF PROBLEMS CONFRONTING FUTURE PRIVATE DEVELOPMENT.

1093 GAMBLE S.D.
NORTH CHINA VILLAGES: SOCIAL, POLITICAL, AND ECONOMIC ACTIVITIES BEFORE 1933.
BERKELEY: U OF CALIF PR, 1963, 352 PP., LC#63-21616.
STUDY OF VILLAGE LIFE IN HOPEI, SHANSI, HONAN, AND SHANTUNG. GENERAL SUMMARY OF FINDINGS AND RELATIONSHIP TO POLITICAL AND HISTORICAL EVENTS OF PERIOD. DESCRIPTION AND DISCUSSION OF VARIOUS PHASES OF VILLAGE LIFE AND ORGANIZATION. CONTAINS DETAILED STORIES OF 11 SAMPLE VILLAGES.

1094 GAMER R.E.
"URGENT SINGAPORE, PATIENT MALAYSIA."
INT. J., 21 (WINTER 66), 42-56.
INVESTIGATES OBSTACLES TO POLITICAL UNITY BETWEEN MALAYSIA AND SINGAPORE, INCLUDING DIFFERENCES OF ECONOMICAL TACTICS AND POLITICAL POLICIES, DOMESTIC AND FOREIGN.

1095 GANGAL S.C.
"SURVEY OF RECENT RESEARCH: INDIA AND THE COMMONWEALTH"
INT. STUDIES, 6 (JAN. 65), 333-344.
"THIS IS A SURVEY (BOOKS AND ARTICLES) OF PRIMARY AND SECONDARY SOURCES ON A DOMINANT ASPECT OF INDIA'S FOREIGN POLICY AND RELATIONS, NAMELY INDIA'S MEMBERSHIP OF, AND ROLE IN, THE COMMONWEALTH FROM 1947 UP TO DATE." WRITINGS HAVE BEEN CLASSIFIED INTO BOOKS AND ARTICLES AND ARE SURVEYED IN CHRONOLOGICAL ORDER.

1096 GANGULI B.N.
ECONOMIC INTEGRATION.
BOMBAY: ASIA PUBL HOUSE, 1961, 13 PP.
DISCUSSION OF CONCEPT AND IMPLICATIONS OF ECONOMIC INTEGRATION ON REGIONAL, NATIONAL, AND INTERNATIONAL CHANGE. FOCUSES ON ECONOMIC GROUPS UNDERGOING CHANGES IN BEHAVIOR PATTERNS DUE TO PROCESS OF ECONOMIC CHANGE.

1097 GANJI M.
INTERNATIONAL PROTECTION OF HUMAN RIGHTS.
GENEVA: LIBRAIRIE DROZ, 1962, 310 PP.
COMPARATIVE STUDY EMPHASIZES HUMANITARIAN INTERVENTION, SLAVERY, AND EUROPEAN CONVENTION ON HUMAN RIGHTS. INCLUDES UNIVERSAL RIGHTS DECLARATION, DRAFTING OF COVENANTS, AND IMPLEMENTATION MEASURES.

1098 GARCEAU O.
"INTEREST GROUP THEORY IN POLITICAL RESEARCH."
ANN. ACAD. POL. SOC. SCI., (SEPT. 58), 104-112.
GROUP THEORY IS ONE OF THE MOST SYSTEMATIC SCHEMES FOR STUDYING THE AMERICAN POLITICAL SYSTEM, AND REQUIRES VARIETY IN NEW RESEARCH RELATING TO THE ROLE OF GROUP MEMBERS, THE RESPONSIBILITY OF GROUP LEADERS, AND THE CONSEQUENCES OF PRESSURE POLITICS FOR PUBLIC POLICY.

1099 GARCIA E.
LA ADMINISTRACION ESPANOLA.
MADRID: INST DE ESTUDIOS POLIT, 1961, 239 PP.
STUDY OF CONTEMPORARY PUBLIC ADMINISTRATION IN SPAIN. EXAMINES EXISTING CONCEPTS OF ADMINISTRATIVE ORGANIZATION AND PROBLEMS OF SPANISH SYSTEM ON LOCAL AND NATIONAL LEVELS.

1100 GARCON M.
LETTRE OUVERTE A LA JUSTICE.
PARIS: EDITIONS ALBIN MICHEL, 1966, 142 PP.
FIRST OF SERIES OF "LETTERS," WRITTEN BY NOTABLE FRENCH LITERARY FIGURES, ATTACKING DIFFERENT EVILS IN SOCIETY. WRITTEN AS GROUP OF FIVE LETTERS TO "JUSTICE," ATTACKS SLOWNESS OF JUDICIAL PROCESS; GOVERNMENT FOR NOT UPHOLDING JUSTICE; SUGGESTIONS THAT JUDICIARY MAKE USE OF SCIENTIFIC PROCEDURES AND DEVICES; AND LAWYERS FOR VARIOUS PRACTICES, SUCH AS WAY IN WHICH THEY OFTEN EXACT PAYMENT.

1101 GARDINIER D.E.
CAMEROON: UNITED NATIONS CHALLENGE TO FRENCH POLICY.
LONDON: OXFORD U PR, 1963, 142 PP.
STUDY OF EFFECTS OF UN TRUSTEESHIP IN CAMEROON ON THE POLITICAL RELATIONSHIPS BETWEEN CAMEROON AND FRANCE. DISCUSSES CAMEROON'S INDEPENDENCE AS IT INFLUENCES DEVELOPMENT OF FRENCH FOREIGN POLICY AND AS IT AFFECTS CAMEROON'S RELATIONS WITH ITS AFRICAN NEIGHBORS.

1102 GAMARNIKOW M.
"INFLUENCE-BUYING IN WEST AFRICA."
EAST EUROPE, 3 (JULY 64), 2-8.
ASSERTS AID FROM SOVIET BLOC COUNTRIES TO WEST AFRICAN NATIONS HAS BEEN ONLY MODERATELY SUCCESSFUL IN SECURING COMMUNIST POLITICAL GOALS. CONCLUDES NATIONALISM, RATHER THAN COMMUNISM OR SOCIALISM, APPEARS TO BE THE CONTROLLING IDEOLOGY.

1103 GARTHOFF R.L.
SOVIET STRATEGY IN THE NUCLEAR AGE.
NEW YORK: PRAEGER, 1958, 283 PP., $4.50.
PROJECTION OF FUTURE STRATEGY BASED ON ANALYSIS OF PRESENT SOVIET STRATEGY. EMPHASIZES SOVIET STRATEGICAL AIM AT STABILITY BECAUSE OF IDEOLOGICAL DESIRE TO IMPROVE AND STRENGTHEN THEIR POSITION AS WORLD POWER. GIVES SOME ESTIMATES OF THE SOVIET MILITARY LEADERSHIP POTENTIAL IN THERMONUCLEAR WAR.

1104 GATZKE H.W.
GERMANY'S DRIVE TO THE WEST.
BALTIMORE: JOHNS HOPKINS PRESS, 1950, 316 PP.
STUDY OF GERMANY'S WESTERN WAR AIMS DURING WWI. DISCUSSES ANTECEDENTS AND TACTICS EMPLOYED FOR WESTERN EXPANSION. CONSIDERS THE DISPUTE BETWEEN THE AGRICULTURALLY MINDED EASTERN EXPANSIONISTS AND THE INDUSTRY-MINDED WESTERN EXPANSIONISTS. FOLLOWS THE COURSE OF THE WAR'S INFLUENCE ON GERMANY'S GOVERNMENT.

1105 GATZKE H.W.
STRESEMANN AND THE REARMAMENT OF GERMANY.
BALTIMORE: JOHNS HOPKINS PRESS, 1954, 132 PP., LC#54-11254.
STUDY BASED ON UNPUBLISHED PAPERS OF DR. STRESEMANN. DETAILS COURSE AND METHODS OF POST-WWI GERMAN REARMAMENT. DISCUSSES EFFECTS OF POLITICAL FACT OF REICHSWEHR ACTIVITY, POLITICAL REALITIES AND POSTWAR ATTITUDES THAT PERMITTED AND ABETTED REARMAMENT. CONCLUDES WITH DISCUSSION OF DR. STRESEMANN'S ORGANIZATIONAL GENIUS AND ITS CONTRIBUTION TO REARMAMENT.

1106 GEERTZ C.
PEDDLERS AND PRINCES: SOCIAL DEVELOPMENT AND ECONOMIC CHANGE IN TWO INDONESIAN TOWNS.
CHICAGO: U. CHI. PR., 1963, 162 PP., $5.00.
CONCERNED WITH THE SOCIOLOGICAL CHANGES ALREADY UNDERWAY IN THE 'PRE-TAKE-OFF' PERIOD. COMPARES ENTREPRENEURIAL GROUPS IN TWO INDONESIAN TOWNS. AN ATTEMPT TO ANALYZE THE IMPORTANT STAGES AND VARIABLES INVOLVED IN THE PROCESS OF TRANSITION TO MODERN ECONOMIC GROWTH.

1107 GEERTZ C. ED.
OLD SOCIETIES AND NEW STATES: THE QUEST FOR MODERNITY IN ASIA AND AFRICA.
NEW YORK: FREE PRESS OF GLENCOE, 1963, 310 PP., LC#63-8416.
STUDIES POLITICAL DEVELOPMENT IN STATES WHICH HAVE ACHIEVED INDEPENDENCE SINCE 1945. INCLUDES COMPARATIVE STUDIES OF NEW STATES; CULTURAL POLICY; POLITICAL RELIGION; THE INTEGRATIVE REVOLUTION; EQUALITY, MODERNITY AND CIVIL POLITICS; PROBLEMS OF LAW IN AFRICA; ROLE OF EDUCATION DEVELOPMENT; AND POLITICAL SOCIALIZATION AND CULTURE CHANGE.

1108 GEHLEN M.P.
"THE POLITICS OF COEXISTENCE: SOVIET METHODS AND MOTIVES."
BLOOMINGTON: INDIANA U PR, 1967.
LISTING OF 70 BOOKS--RUSSIAN- AND ENGLISH-LANGUAGE PUBLICATIONS--PERTAINING TO THE POLITICAL, MILITARY, ECONOMIC, AND IDEOLOGICAL ASPECTS OF RUSSIA'S COEXISTENCE POLICY WITH CAPITALIST, NEUTRAL, AND COMMUNIST COUNTRIES FROM THE DEATH OF STALIN THROUGH THE 23RD PARTY CONGRESS.

1109 GELLHORN W.
OMBUDSMEN AND OTHERS: CITIZENS' PROTECTORS IN NINE COUNTRIES
CAMBRIDGE: HARVARD U PR, 1967, 448 PP., LC#66-23465.

STUDIES INSTITUTION OF OMBUDSMAN, REPRESENTATIVE OF PEOPLE IN CASES OF GOVERNMENTAL INJUSTICE. INCLUDES COUNTRIES OF DENMARK, FINLAND, NEW ZEALAND, NORWAY, SWEDEN, YUGOSLAVIA, POLAND, USSR, AND JAPAN. APPLIES FINDINGS TO DEVELOPMENT OF SUCH AN INSTITUTION IN US.

1111 GENTILE G.
GENESIS AND STRUCTURE OF SOCIETY (TRANS. BY H.S. HARRIS)
URBANA: U OF ILLINOIS PR, 1960, 228 PP., LC#60-8346.
DISCUSSES STRUCTURE OF SOCIETY IN TERMS OF RELATIONS BETWEEN STATE AND ECONOMICS, RELIGION, AND SCIENCE. EXAMINES NATURE OF INDIVIDUAL IN SOCIETY AND MAKES GENERAL OBSERVATIONS ABOUT ROLE OF HISTORY AND POLITICS.

1113 GEORGE M.
THE WARPED VISION.
PITTSBURGH: U OF PITTSBURGH PR, 1965, 238 PP., LC#65-14623.
ANALYZES BRITISH APPEASEMENT FOREIGN POLICY, PERIOD 1933-1939. CONCENTRATES ON ATTITUDES OF LEADERS OF CONSERVATIVE GOVERNING GROUP, WHOM AUTHOR HOLDS PRIMARILY RESPONSIBLE FOR APPEASEMENT POLICIES.

1114 GERARD-LIBOIS J.
KATANGA SECESSION.
MADISON: U OF WISCONSIN PR, 1966, 377 PP., LC#66-22851.
ANALYZES WHERE THE IDEA FOR KATANGA'S SECESSION ORIGINATED, HOW IT WAS DEVELOPED AND PROCLAIMED, AND WHAT FACTORS CALLED A HALT TO THE SECESSION. BASES ACCOUNT ON COLLECTIONS OF PUBLIC SOURCES CURRENTLY AVAILABLE AND ON ORAL ACCOUNTS AND UNPUBLISHED DOCUMENTS; THESE PERMIT AN UNDERSTANDING OF THE SECESSION AND ITS WORKINGS, PARTICULARLY IN MATTERS INVOLVING MILITARY PERSONNEL AND ASSISTANCE.

1115 GERMANY FOREIGN MINISTRY
DOCUMENTS ON GERMAN FOREIGN POLICY 1918-1945, SERIES C (1933-1937) VOLS. I-V.
WASHINGTON: US GOVERNMENT, 1954, 3562 PP.
CHRONICLES RISE OF THIRD REICH IN GERMANY, CONSISTING ENTIRELY OF DOCUMENTS DESCRIBING IMMENSE RANGE OF GERMAN DIPLOMATIC ACTIVITY, INCLUDING LETTERS, TELEGRAMS, AND MEMORANDA, SENT AND RECEIVED BY GERMAN FOREIGN MINISTRY. PUBLISHED DURING 1954-66.

1116 GERSCHENKRON A.
THE STABILITY OF DICTATORSHIPS.
NEW HAVEN: YALE U HARVARD FDN, 1963, 36 PP.
ANALYTICAL DESCRIPTION OF DEVICES OF PROPAGANDA AND SUPPRESSION EMPLOYED BY DICTATORIAL GOVERNMENTS TO CONTROL AND WIN SUPPORT OF POPULATION. DESCRIBES CONDITIONS OF STABILITY THAT ARE ESSENTIAL IN DICTATORSHIP. MUCH OF DISCUSSION CENTERS ON 19TH- AND 20TH-CENTURY EUROPEAN DICTATORSHIPS.

1117 GESELLSCHAFT RECHTSVERGLEICH
BIBLIOGRAPHIE DES DEUTSCHEN RECHTS (BIBLIOGRAPHY OF GERMAN LAW, TRANS. BY COURTLAND PETERSON)
KARLSRVHE: VERLAG CF MULLER, 1964, 584 PP.
ANALYTIC AND THOROUGHLY CATEGORIZED BIBLIOGRAPHY OF WORKS, DOCUMENTS, STUDIES, TEXTS, ETC., INVOLVING GERMAN LAW. INCLUDES A LENGTHY INTRODUCTION BY PROFESSOR FRITZ BAUR ELUCIDATING GERMAN LAW AND LEGAL PROCEDURES SINCE 1949. BILINGUAL EDITION WITH ENGLISH AND GERMAN ANNOTATION.

1118 GEWIRTH A. ED.
POLITICAL PHILOSOPHY.
NEW YORK: MACMILLAN, 1965, 123 PP., LC#65-11878.
EXAMINES NATURE, BASIC QUESTIONS, AND MORAL CRITERIA OF POLITICAL PHILOSOPHY. COLLECTS WRITINGS OF HOBBES, LOCKE, ROUSSEAU, HEGEL, MARX, AND J.S. MILL AS THEY DISCUSS REASONS WHY MEN LIVE IN SOCIETY, OBEY GOVERNMENT, AND HAVE POLITICAL POWER. ALSO DISCUSSES QUESTIONS ON ENDS AND LIMITS OF POWER, NATURAL RIGHTS, SOVEREIGNTY, CLASS STRUGGLE, AND LIBERTY.

1119 GHAI D.P. ED.
PORTRAIT OF A MINORITY: ASIANS IN EAST AFRICA.
LONDON: OXFORD U PR, 1965, 154 PP.
DISCUSSES PROBLEMS OF ASIAN COMMUNITY IN EAST AFRICA WHICH CONSISTS MOSTLY OF INDIANS AND PAKISTANI. CONSIDERS THEIR RELATIONSHIP WITH NATIVE EAST AFRICANS AS AREA'S MOST CRUCIAL RACIAL PROBLEM. CONTAINS SIX STUDIES PROVIDING GENERAL SURVEYS OF SOCIAL, POLITICAL, ECONOMIC, AND EDUCATIONAL CONDITIONS OF ASIAN POPULATION.

1120 GHANI A.R.
PAKISTAN: A SELECT BIBLIOGRAPHY.
JAHORE: PAKIS ASSN ADVANCEMT SCI, 1951, 339 PP.
LOCATES AND DESCRIBES BOOKS, PAMPHLETS, AND ARTICLES IN PERIODICAL LITERATURE PUBLISHED IN ENGLISH AND BEARING ON PAKISTAN. CONTAINS 9,000 SELECTED UP-TO-DATE REFERENCES ON GEOGRAPHY, PEOPLES OF PAKISTAN, ECONOMY, INDUSTRIES, AGRICULTURE, ETC. DOES NOT INCLUDE ANNOTATIONS. ALL MATERIAL IS IN ENGLISH.

1121 GHOSH P.K.
THE CONSTITUTION OF INDIA: HOW IT HAS BEEN FRAMED.
CALCUTTA: WORLD PRESS LTD, 1966, 427 PP.
PRESENTS HISTORICAL BACKGROUND OF INDIAN CONSTITUTION. NARRATES CONTEMPORARY POLITICAL EVENTS, SHOWING HOW THEY INFLUENCED DELIBERATIONS OF INDIAN CONSTITUENT ASSEMBLY. DISCUSSES SEVERAL SUPREME AND HIGH COURT DECISIONS THAT AMENDED CONSTITUTION, AND ANALYZES REGIONAL FORCES MAKING AMENDMENTS NECESSARY.

1122 GIBBS S.L. ED.
PEOPLES OF AFRICA.
NEW YORK: HOLT RINEHART WINSTON, 1965, 594 PP., LC#65-10276.
DESCRIBES IN DETAIL FIFTEEN MAJOR GROUPS OF SUB-SAHARAN AFRICA. THESE GROUPS ARE REPRESENTATIVE OF AFRICAN PEOPLES BY REASON OF THEIR ECONOMY, RACE, LANGUAGE, FAMILY, OR ECOLOGICAL ZONE.

1123 GIFFORD P. ED., LOUIS W.R. ED.
BRITAIN AND GERMANY IN AFRICA.
NEW HAVEN: YALE U PR, 1967, 825 PP., LC#67-24500.
ESSAYS TREAT ANGLO-GERMAN COLONIAL RIVALRY AND FORMS OF COLONIAL ADMINISTRATION AFTER OCCUPATION OF AFRICA. DEVOTE SPECIAL ATTENTION TO WWI AND CONSIDER SIMILARITIES AND DIFFERENCES OF BRITISH AND GERMAN COLONIAL RULE. EXAMINE LEADERSHIP, ATTITUDES, RESISTANCE AND REBELLION, SOCIAL DISCORD, TAXATION, AND BRITISH POLICY OF INDIRECT RULE. CONCLUDE WITH HISTORIOGRAPHICAL ESSAY.

1124 GILBERT S.P.
"WARS OF LIBERATION AND SOVIET MILITARY AID POLICY."
ORBIS, 10 (FALL 66), 839-858.
SOVIETS TRIFURCATE WAR INTO THREE CATEGORIES OF GENERAL, LIMITED AND WARS OF NATIONAL LIBERATION. DOCTRINE CALLS FOR ALWAYS PROMOTING NATIONAL LIBERATION, JUDICIOUSLY HANDLING LIMITED WAR FOR FEAR OF ESCALATION, AND AVOIDING GENERAL WAR WITH THE US. AUTHOR ANALYZES SOVIET MILITARY AID 1954-1964 TO NON-COMMUNIST COUNTRIES AND FINDS DOCTRINE GENERALLY OPERATIONALIZED WITH INTERESTS OF WEST AND CHINA VARIABLES.

1126 GILG P.
DIE ERNEUERUNG DES DEMOKRATISCHEN DENKENS IM WILHELMINISCHEN DEUTSCHLAND.
WIESBADEN: FRANK STEINER VERLAG, 1965, 280 PP.
A GENERAL HISTORY OF DEMOCRATIC TENDENCIES IN GERMANY UNDER WILHELM II. DISCUSSES THE TRANSFORMATIONS OF POLITICAL THINKING UNDER NEW INDUSTRIAL CONDITIONS AND EXPLAINS THE RISE OF DEMOCRATIC THINKING IN TERMS OF DECLINE OF IMPORTANCE OF BISMARCK IN THE POWER STRUGGLE.

1127 GILL R.T.
ECONOMIC DEVELOPMENT: PAST AND PRESENT (2ND ED.)
ENGLEWOOD CLIFFS: PRENTICE HALL, 1967, 120 PP., LC#67-14771.
ANALYZES FACTORS OF ECONOMIC DEVELOPMENT AND COMPARES GROWTH OF ECONOMICALLY ADVANCED COUNTRIES TO PROBLEMS FACED BY UNDEVELOPED NATIONS TODAY. EXAMINES US GROWTH AND INDIAN AND CHINESE APPROACHES TO DEVELOPMENT.

1128 GILLIN J.P.
"POSSIBLE CULTURAL MALADJUSTMENT IN MODERN LATIN AMERICA."
J. INTER-AMER. STUD., 5 (APR. 63), 149-60.
A THEORETICAL DISCUSSION OF CULTURAL INCONSISTENCIES, COMPROMISES, COMPATIBILITY, AND FOREIGN CULTURAL INFLUENCES WITH APPLICATION TO LATIN AMERICA.

1129 GILLY A.
INSIDE THE CUBAN REVOLUTION.
NEW YORK: MONTHLY REVIEW PR, 1964, 88 PP.
JOURNALIST REPORTS INTERNAL SITUATION IN CUBA AND IMPORTANT FORCES IN REVOLUTION DURING 1962-63. EXAMINES CUBAN PROBLEM FROM VIEWPOINT OF PRO-REVOLUTIONIST. CONCENTRATES ON ADVANCES, DOMESTIC AND FOREIGN OBSTACLES, AND EXISTING POSSIBILITIES AND METHODS TO ACHIEVE THEM.

1130 GILMORE M.P.
ARGUMENT FROM ROMAN LAW IN POLITICAL THOUGHT, 1200-1600.
CAMBRIDGE: HARVARD U PR, 1941, 148 PP., LC#41-35035.
ESSAY ILLUSTRATING TWO GENERAL PROBLEMS: THE EXISTENCE OF AN AUTHORITATIVE TRADITION, AND RELATION OF INDIVIDUALS TO THAT TRADITION. ANALYZES EXAMPLES OF WAY IN WHICH POLITICAL THEORISTS ADAPT DISTINCTIONS TAKEN FROM JUSTINIAN COMPILATION OF ROMAN LAW AND MODIFY THEM TO OWN USES. EXAMPLES CHOSEN FROM 1200-1600, DURING EMERGENCE OF NATIONAL STATE IN EUROPE. BIBLIOGRAPHY OF SOURCES AND MODERN WORKS.

1131 GINIEWSKI P.
THE TWO FACES OF APARTHEID.
CHICAGO: HENRY REGNERY CO, 1965, 373 PP., LC#65-19164.
DISCUSSES BACKGROUND OF RELATIONSHIPS BETWEEN WHITE SOUTH AFRICANS AND BANTU (AFRICAN PEOPLE INVOLVED IN APARTHEID CONTROVERSY). DISCUSSES VARIOUS GOVERNMENT PROGRAMS UNDERTAKEN FOR BENEFIT OF BANTU. COMPARES APARTHEID TO AMERICAN GOVERNMENT'S TREATMENT OF NEGROES AND INDIANS. ATTEMPTS TO DISCUSS IDEOLOGY AND GOALS OF BOTH BANTUSTAN AND APARTHEID SIDES OF CONTROVERSY.

1132 GINSBURG M. ED.
LAW AND OPINION IN ENGLAND.

BERKELEY: U OF CALIF PR, 1959, 405 PP.
RELATION OF DEVELOPMENTS IN ENGLISH LAW TO PUBLIC OPINION DISCUSSED IN 17 LECTURES DELIVERED AT LONDON SCHOOL OF ECONOMIC AND POLITICAL SCIENCE, 1957-58. COVERS PROPERTY, LABOR, CRIME, ADMINISTRATION, AND HEALTH.

1133 GINSBURG N., ROBERTS CF J.R.
"MALAYA."
SEATTLE: U OF WASHINGTON PR, 1958.
EXAMINES THE NEW STATE OF MALAYA IN LIGHT OF SYSTEMS OF ORGANIZATION THAT HAVE CHARACTERIZED THE OLD STATE. DESCRIBES ENVIRONMENTAL, SOCIAL, ECONOMIC, POLITICAL, AND ETHNOGRAPHIC CHARACTERISTICS OF MALAYAL. ANALYZES PROBLEMS THAT FACE THE NEW NATION: THOSE DEALING WITH COMMUNICATIONS, POLITICAL ORGANIZATION, AND ECONOMIC DEVELOPMENT. UNANNOTATED BIBLIOGRAPHY OF SOURCES IN ENGLISH.

1134 GINSBURGS G.
"PEKING-LHASA-NEW DELHI."
POLIT. SCI. QUART., 75 (SEPT. 60), 338-354.
SURVEYS CHINESE-TIBETAN RELATIONS FROM PRE-COMMUNIST DAYS TO PRESENT. TRACES GROWTH OF CHINESE POWER IN TIBET FROM 1950-54 PERIOD OF MODERATION, THROUGH PERIOD OF INCREASED USE OF FORCE TO '59 UPRISING AND ITS SUPPRESSION. CONCLUDES THAT TIBET, NOW FULLY CONTROLLED BY PEKING, IS BEING USED AS BASE FOR PENETRATION SOUTHWARD.

1135 GIRALDO JARAMILLO G.
BIBLIOGRAFIA DE BIBLIOGRAFIAS COLOMBIANAS.
BOGOTA: EDITORIAL PAX, 1954, 192 PP.
INCLUDES GENERAL BIBLIOGRAPHIES, SUBJECT-CLASSIFIED BIBLIOGRAPHIES, PUBLICATIONS OF RELIGIOUS ORDERS, PERSONAL BIBLIOGRAPHIES, AND BIBLIOGRAPHIES OF COLOMBIAN LITERATURE. APPROXIMATELY 500 ENTRIES, ALL IN SPANISH. INCLUDES INDEX OF AUTHORS.

1136 GIROD R.
"LE SYSTEME DES PARTIS EN SUISSE."
REV. DROIT PUBLIC ET SCI. POL., 6 (DEC. 64), 1114-1133.
ANALYSIS OF THE SWISS LEGISLATURE AND POLITICAL PARTIES. DISCUSSES COALITION SYSTEM AT NATIONAL AND LOCAL LEVELS. EXAMINES CHRONOLOGICAL EVOLUTION OF SWISS MULTI-PARTY LEGISLATIVE PROCESS.

1137 GITLOW A.L.
ECONOMICS OF THE MOUNT HAGEN TRIBES, NEW GUINEA.
NEW YORK: J J AUGUSTIN, 1947, 110 PP.
STUDIES ECONOMY OF NATIVE CULTURE, FOCUSING ON INFLUENCE OF PHYSICAL ENVIRONMENT, INSTITUTIONS, AND VARIOUS MOTIVATIONS.

1138 GLADE W.P. JR., ANDERSON C.W.
THE POLITICAL ECONOMY OF MEXICO.
MADISON: U. WISC. PR., 1963, 242 PP., $5.00.
FIRST SECTION, 'REVOLUTION AND DEVELOPMENT: A MEXICAN REPRISE,' BY W.P. GLADE, IS AN ATTEMPT TO EXPLORE RELATIONS BETWEEN REVOLUTIONARY SOCIAL CHANGE AND SUCCESSFUL ECONOMIC GROWTH IN MEXICO. IN THE SECOND SECTION, 'BANKERS AS REVOLUTIONARIES: POLITICS AND DEVELOPMENT BANKING IN MEXICO,' C.W. ANDERSON GIVES A CASE STUDY OF MEXICO'S DEVELOPMENT BANKS, VIEWING THESE INSTITUTIONS PRIMARILY IN THEIR POLITICAL RATHER THAN THEIR ECONOMIC ROLE. BOTH ARE EXPERIMENTS IN THE USE OF INTER-DISCIPLINARY APPROACHES AS A WAY OF GETTING AT SOME BASIC PROBLEMS OF ECONOMIC DEVELOPMENT.

1139 GLADSTONE A.E.
"THE POSSIBILITY OF PREDICTING REACTIONS TO INTERNATIONAL EVENTS."
J. SOC. ISSUES, 11 (1955), 21-28.
SEES GREAT UNCERTAINTY AS TO WHICH VARIABLES ARE RELEVANT FOR PREDICTION OF WAR, AS RETARDING PROBLEM IN ANY SCIENTIFIC INVESTIGATION OF WAR. SUGGESTS DEVISING CONCEPTUAL SCHEME AS FRAMEWORK FOR INVESTIGATION AND PROCEEDS TO OFFER PRELIMINARY OUTLINE OF SCHEME OF FACTORS IN INTERNATIONAL SITUATION WHICH MAY BE RELEVANT TO OCCURANCE OF WAR.

1140 GLAZER M.
THE FEDERAL GOVERNMENT AND THE UNIVERSITY.
PRINCETON: PRIN U INDUS REL CTR, 1966, 4 PP.
CONTAINS MAGAZINE AND JOURNAL ARTICLES DEALING WITH FEDERAL GOVERNMENT SUPPORT OF SOCIAL SCIENCE RESEARCH AND IMPACT OF PROJECT CAMELOT. ALL ENTRIES ARE IN ENGLISH AND WERE PUBLISHED 1960-66. ARRANGED ACCORDING TO FOLLOWING TOPICS: GOVERNMENT-UNIVERSITY RELATIONS, GOVERNMENT SUPPORT FOR SOCIAL SCIENCE RESEARCH, AND PROJECT CAMELOT.

1141 GLAZER M.
"LAS ACTITUDES Y ACTIVIDADES POLITICAS DE LOS ESTUDIANTES DE LA UNIVERSIDAD DE CHILE."
APORTES, 5 (JULY 67), 43-79.
EXAMINES POLITICAL ATTITUDES AND ACTIVITIES OF UNIVERSITY OF CHILE STUDENTS. DISCUSSES SPECIFIC CASES OF DEPARTMENTS OF HISTORY, ENGINEERING, AND MEDICINE DEALING WITH FACTORS INFLUENCING STUDENT POLITICAL PARTICIPATION AND VIEWS ON NATIONAL AND INTERNATIONAL PROBLEMS. COVERS EXTENT OF STUDENTS' INFLUENCE ON NATIONAL POLITICS AND POLITICAL PARTIES.

1142 GLEASON J.H.
THE GENESIS OF RUSSOPHOBIA IN GREAT BRITAIN: A STUDY OF THE INTERACTION OF POLICY AND OPINION.
CAMBRIDGE: HARVARD U PR, 1950, 314 PP.
STUDIES THE DISRUPTION OF CORDIALITY AND THE GROWTH OF HOSTILITY BETWEEN RUSSIA AND BRITAIN BETWEEN 1815 AND 1841. AUTHOR BELIEVES ANGLO-RUSSIAN HOSTILITY WAS THE FRUIT OF COMPETITIVE IMPERIAL AMBITIONS, WHICH TRANSFORMED TWO POWERS HITHERTO REMOTE INTO NEIGHBORS IN THEIR COLONIAL SPHERES. EMPLOYS BOTH PRIMARY AND SECONDARY SOURCES.

1143 GLENN N.D., ALSTON J.P.
"RURAL-URBAN DIFFERENCES IN REPORTED ATTITUDES AND BEHAVIOR"
J. SOCIAL ISSUES, 47 (MAR. 67), 381-400.
WITH THE AID OF PUBLIC OPINION POLL DATA EXAMINES: 1) HOW CLOSELY DO POPULAR STEREOTYPES CORRESPOND TO REALITY OF URBAN THOUGHT AND BEHAVIOR? 2) TO WHAT EXTENT ARE FARMERS MIDDLE CLASS IN ATTITUDES AND TO WHAT EXTENT DO THEY RESEMBLE URBAN MIDDLE CLASS? 3) ARE THERE RURAL-URBAN DIFFERENCES IN ATTITUDE THAT REFLECT INHERENT DIFFERENCES IN RURAL AND URBAN SOCIAL STRUCTURE?

1144 GLOBERSON A.
"SOCIAL GROWTH IN THE DEVELOPING COUNTRIES."
COEXISTENCE, 4 (JAN. 67), 63-69.
OF PRIMARY IMPORTANCE IN ASSISTANCE TO DEVELOPING NATIONS ARE PROGRAMS FOR SOCIAL GROWTH, SINCE IN LONG RUN, SOCIAL GROWTH IS NECESSARY TO ECONOMIC GROWTH. IT IS INSUFFICIENT AND POSSIBLY DAMAGING MERELY TO OFFER ECONOMIC AID WHICH DEPENDS ON FOREIGN TECHNICIANS OR WHICH PROVIDES TOOLS BUT NOT SKILL. ASSISTANCE IN DEVELOPING WORK PRACTICES AND MODES OF APPROACH TO SOCIAL AND ECONOMIC AFFAIRS IS OF GREAT AID TOO.

1145 GLUCKMAN M.
CUSTOM AND CONFLICT IN AFRICA.
NEW YORK: FREE PRESS OF GLENCOE, 1956, 172 PP.
EXAMINES SOCIAL ORGANIZATION OF AFRICAN SOCIETIES HAVING NO GOVERNMENTAL INSTITUTIONS. CONCLUDES THAT ESTABLISHMENT OF PATTERN OF ORDER AND MORALITY IS MANY TIMES VERY SIMILAR TO PARALLEL PROCESSES IN HIGHLY DEVELOPED CULTURES. CONTENDS THAT CONFLICTS ARISE FROM CERTAIN CUSTOMARY ALLEGIANCES AND EXAMINES SOCIAL RESTRAINTS ON CONFLICT. INCLUDES NATURE OF SOCIAL AUTHORITY, THE FAMILY, WITCHCRAFT, AND "COLOUR-BAR."

1146 GLUCKMAN M.
ANALYSIS OF A SOCIAL SITUATION IN MODERN ZULULAND.
MANCHESTER: MANCHESTER UNIV PR, 1958, 77 PP.
DEALS WITH WHITE-AFRICAN RELATIONS IN NORTHERN ZULULAND OF SOUTH AFRICA, INCLUDING ITS SOCIAL ORGANIZATION, SOCIAL CHANGE SUCH AS DEVELOPMENT OF ZULU NATION, AND PROCESSES OF SOCIAL CHANGE.

1147 GLUCKMAN M.
ORDER AND REBELLION IN TRIBAL AFRICA.
NEW YORK: FREE PRESS, 1963, 273 PP., $6.00.
A COLLECTION OF ESSAYS DEALING WITH DEVELOPMENT OF THE AUTHOR'S CONCEPTS OF AFRICAN POLITICS. FREQUENT REBELLIONS WERE ASSOCIATED WITH OCCURRENCE OF 'RITUALS OF REBELLION' WHICH EMPHASIZED SECULAR DISPUTES AND THEIR UNDERLYING CONFLICTS OF SOCIAL PRINCIPLE. LEADS TO 'A GENERAL THEORY OF RITUAL, AS WELL AS TO CERTAIN GENERAL PROPOSITIONS, AS ABOUT THE POSITION OF OFFICIALS REPRESENTING CONFLICTING INTERESTS WITHIN A HIERARCHY, TYPIFIED BY THE AFRICAN CHIEF UNDER COLONIAL RULE.'

1148 GLUCKMAN M.
"CIVIL WAR AND THEORIES OF POWER IN BAROTSE-LAND: AFRICAN AND MEDIEVAL ANALOGIES."
YALE LAW J., 72(SUMMER 63), 1515- 46.
BAROTSE THEORY OF POLITICAL REPRESENTATION, LEGAL RESTRAINTS ON THE KING AND OTHER OFFICERS, AND THE LAWS OF TREASON AND OF SUCCESSION TO THE THRONE. ALSO CONSIDERS THE INTERRELATIONSHIPS BETWEEN REVOLTS AND HOW PEOPLE ADHERE TO REBELLIOUS LEADERS.

1149 GLUCKMAN M. ED.
CLOSED SYSTEMS AND OPEN MINDS: THE LIMITS OF NAIVETY IN SOCIAL ANTHROPOLOGY.
LONDON: OLIVER & BOYD, 1964, 274 PP.
COLLECTION OF ESSAYS BASED ON INTENSIVE FIELD STUDIES IN INDIAN AND AFRICAN VILLAGES. INCLUDES THEORETICAL INQUIRIES INTO THE LIMITS OF SOCIAL ANTHROPOLOGY AND THE RELATION BETWEEN ANTHROPOLOGY AND THE OTHER SOCIAL SCIENCES.

1150 GODECHOT J.
FRANCE AND THE ATLANTIC REVOLUTION OF THE EIGHTEENTH CENTURY 1770-1799.
NEW YORK: FREE PRESS, 1965, 279 PP., LC#65-16268.
DISCUSSES THE FRENCH REVOLUTION AS PART OF A SOCIAL, CULTURAL, AND PHILOSOPHICAL UPHEAVAL. ANALYZES THE CAUSES COMMON TO THE WAVE OF REVOLUTIONS IN THIS PERIOD, INCLUDING THE MASSIVE POPULATION INCREASE, THE ACCOMPANYING ECONOMIC CRISES, AND THE ENLIGHTENMENT.

1151 GODWIN W., PRIESTLEY F.E.L. ED.
ENQUIRY CONCERNING POLITICAL JUSTICE AND ITS INFLUENCE ON MORALS AND HAPPINESS (1793)
TORONTO: U OF TORONTO PRESS, 1946, 463 PP.
"HIGH CIVILIZATION" IS ONE IN WHICH MAN HAS UTMOST HAPPINESS AND PLEASURE. MOST DESIRABLE STATE OF EXISTENCE FOR MAN IS IN SOCIETY. GOVERNMENT SHOULD SUPPRESS INJUSTICE, BUT ITS EFFECT HAS BEEN TO PERPETUATE IT. GOVERNMENT SHOULD MAINTAIN GENERAL SECURITY WITH SMALLEST ENCROACHMENT ON INDIVIDUAL LIBERTY. JUSTICE IS STANDARD FOR MAN. FORBEARANCE SHOULD BE PRACTICED BY INDIVIDUALS AND GOVERNMENT.

1152 GOETHE J.W., WEITZ H.J. ED.
GOETHE UBER DIE DEUTSCHEN.
FRANKFURT: INSEL VERLAG, 1965, 71 PP.
COLLECTION OF STATEMENTS FROM GOETHE'S WRITINGS ON GERMAN CHARACTER, CULTURE, AND MODES OF LIFE.

1153 GOFF F.R. ED.
FIFTEENTH CENTURY BOOKS IN THE LIBRARY OF CONGRESS.
WASHINGTON: LIBRARY OF CONGRESS, 1950, 82 PP.
THIS REVISED CHECKLIST OF 15TH-CENTURY INCUNABULA UPDATES PREVIOUS LIBRARY OF CONGRESS RECORDS, NOTABLY THE 1940 PUBLICATION "INCUNABULA IN AMERICAN LIBRARIES, A SECOND CENSUS" BY MARGARET STILLWELL. EDITOR WARNS THAT THOUGH THIS IS THE MOST COMPLETE RECORD TO DATE, THE LIBRARIES' INCUNABULA ARE NOT COMPLETELY CATALOGUED AT THIS TIME.

1154 GOFFMAN E.
THE PRESENTATION OF SELF IN EVERYDAY LIFE.
EDINBURGH: UNIV OF EDINBURGH, 1956, 161 PP.
ANALYSIS OF INTERACTION BETWEEN INDIVIDUALS. STUDIES PERFORMANCE TO BUILD IMAGE - TO DRAMATIZE, MYSTIFY, MISREPRESENT, AND EXAGGERATE SELF. INCLUDES REGIONAL BEHAVIOR AND THE 'TEAM' IMAGE. ACTS ARE ALSO EXAMINED AS DISCREPANT ROLES, AS COMMUNICATION OUT OF CHARACTER, AND AS THE ART OF IMPRESSION MANAGEMENT. CONCLUDES THAT THE ROLE OF EXPRESSION IS CONVEYING IMPRESSIONS OF SELF.

1155 GOLAY J.F.
"THE FOUNDING OF THE FEDERAL REPUBLIC OF GERMANY."
CHICAGO: U OF CHICAGO PRESS, 1958.
DISCUSSES PROCESS IN WHICH CONSTITUTIONAL FOUNDATIONS OF THE GERMAN FEDERAL REPUBLIC ORIGINATED IN PREVIOUS GERMAN CONSTITUTIONAL AND POLITICAL DEVELOPMENT. REVIEWS PRESENT NEEDS AND INTERESTS OF WEST GERMAN PEOPLE AND INFLUENCES BROUGHT TO BEAR BY WESTERN ALLIED GOVERNMENTS. PARTIALLY ANNOTATED BIBLIOGRAPHY OF 19 GERMAN AND AMERICAN DOCUMENTS AND VARIOUS BOOKS, PERIODICALS, AND NEWSPAPERS.

1156 GOLDBERG A.
"THE MILITARY ORIGINS OF THE BRITISH NUCLEAR DETERRENT."
INT. AFF., 40 (OCT. 64), 600-618.
CHRONOLOGY OF THE DEVELOPMENT OF BRITISH AIR FORCES SINCE WW 2, DESCRIBING AND EVALUATING SPECIFIC BOMBER-PROGRAMS. ANALYSIS OF STRATEGIC AND ECONOMIC FACTORS INVOLVED IN THE ESTABLISHMENT OF CONCEPT OF NUCLEAR DETERRENCE AS CORE OF BRITISH DEFENSE POLICY.

1157 GOLDMAN M.I.
"COMPARATIVE ECONOMIC SYSTEMS: A READER."
NEW YORK: RANDOM HOUSE, INC, 1964.
A COLLECTION OF CLASSICAL AND CONTEMPORARY ARTICLES ON THE MAJOR ECONOMIC SYSTEMS OF THE 19TH AND 20TH CENTURIES: SYNDICALISM, CAPITALISM, SOCIALISM, FASCISM, AND COMMUNISM. EXTENSIVE SELECTED UNANNOTATED BIBLIOGRAPHY OF WORKS PUBLISHED IN ENGLISH BETWEEN 1919-62. SOME SOURCES EARLIER, BUT MOST FROM 1950-62. ENTRIES TOPICALLY ARRANGED ACCORDING TO THE ORGANIZATION OF THE BOOK.

1158 GOLDMAN M.I.
"A BALANCE SHEET OF SOVIET FOREIGN AID."
FOREIGN AFFAIRS, 43 (JAN. 65), 349-360.
ANALYSIS OF THE EFFECTS OF THE 3.5 BILLION DOLLARS OF FOREIGN AID PROVIDED BY THE SOVIETS OVER LAST DECADE. FOUND IMPRESSIVE TECHNICAL AND PROPAGANDA COUPS LIKE ASWAN AND BHILAI, BUT GENERALLY SOVIETS DISCOVERED SAME FRUSTRATIONS AND LACK OF COMMENSURATE POLITICO-ECONOMIC PAYOFFS AS US.

1159 GOLDSCHMIDT W.
UNDERSTANDING HUMAN SOCIETY.
LONDON: ROUTLEDGE & KEGAN PAUL, 1959, 253 PP.
DISCUSSES DEVELOPMENT OF MAN IN SOCIETY, CHARACTER AND EVOLUTION OF SOCIAL FORMS, AND TECHNOLOGICAL CHANGES THAT HAVE REQUIRED NEW SOLUTIONS TO SOCIAL EXISTENCE. CONCLUDES WITH ESSAY ON SCIENTIFIC STUDY OF SOCIETY.

1160 GOLDWIN R.A. ED., STOURZH G. ED.,
READINGS IN RUSSIAN FOREIGN POLICY.
NEW YORK: OXFORD U PR, 1959, 775 PP., LC#59-9820.
SELECTIONS ARRANGED TOPICALLY; INCLUDES PRIMARY AND SECONDARY SOURCE MATERIALS AND MAPS. AMONG TOPICS COVERED ARE: THE RUSSIAN PEOPLE, CZARISM AND RUSSIAN REVOLUTION, WORLD REVOLUTION AND NATIONAL INTEREST, THEORY OF COMMUNISM, RUSSIA AND THE EAST, IDEOLOGY AND BALANCE OF POWER, COLD WAR, HUNGARIAN AND YUGOSLAVIAN SOCIALISM, AND "WHAT GUIDES RUSSIAN FOREIGN POLICY?"

1161 GOLEMBIEWSKI R.T.
MEN, MANAGEMENT, AND MORALITY; TOWARD A NEW ORGANIZATIONAL ETHIC.
NEW YORK: MCGRAW HILL, 1965, 320 PP., LC#65-22106.
TREATS PROBLEMS OF EHTICAL CONSEQUENCE IN ORGANIZATION OF WORK AND DESCRIBES STRUCTURAL INNOVATIONS AND MANAGERIAL TECHNIQUES THAT MAY BE EFFECTIVE AND MORAL SOLUTIONS TO ORGANIZATIONAL PROBLEMS. STUDIES ORGANIZATION THAT ALLOWS INDIVIDUAL DEVELOPMENT, RELATION OF MAN TO ORGANIZATION, INDIVIDUAL RESPONSIBILITY, AUTHORITARIANISM, DECENTRALIZING, AND ORGANIZATION UNDER COMMUNISM, CAPITALISM, AND SOCIALISM.

1163 GONZALEZ M.P.
"CUBA, UNA REVOLUCION EN MARCHA."
CUADERNOS AMERICANOS, (JULY-AUG. 67), 7-24.
EXAMINES CUBAN REVOLUTION, COMPARING MANY ASPECTS WITH WAR IN VIETNAM. CRITICIZES US INVOLVEMENT AND POLICIES AS IMPERIALISTIC, AND MAINTAINS THAT US IS FOLLOWING SAME POLICIES WITH VIETNAM. CONTENDS CONDITIONS IMPROVED IN CUBA AFTER REVOLUTION. SPECULATES ON FUTURE OF CUBA AND VIETNAM.

1164 GONZALEZ NAVARRO M.
LA COLONIZACION EN MEXICO, 1877-1910.
MEXICO C: TALLERES DE IMPRESION, 1960, 160 PP.
EXAMINES PROGRAMS OF MEXICAN GOVERNMENT TO PROMOTE IMMIGRATION AND COLONIZATION OF LAND. DISCUSSES ATTEMPTS TO OFFER HOMESTEADING OPPORTUNITIES TO FOREIGNERS IN ORDER TO IMPROVE AGRICULTURE AND INCREASE POPULATION. EXPLAINS THE PROBLEMS IN PROGRAM AND THE ENDING OF OFFICIAL METHOD, WHICH ADOPTED PRIVATE ACTIVITIES BY INDIVIDUALS WILLING TO HANDLE THEIR OWN AFFAIRS DESPITE TROUBLES OF CLIMATE AND LOW PAY.

1165 GONZALEZ PALENCIA A
ESTUDIO HISTORICO SOBRE LA CENSURA GUBERNATIVA EN ESPANA 1800-1833.
MADRID: TIPOGRAFIA DE ARCHIVOS, 1934, 292 PP.
STUDY OF GOVERNMENTAL CENSORSHIP IN SPAIN FROM 1800-1833. EXAMINES LAWS OF PRESS AND HOW APPLIED TO PUBLICATIONS IN PERIOD. LISTS BOOKS CENSORED BY GOVERNMENT AND POLICIES RELATED TO IMPORT AND EXPORT OF BOOKS.

1166 GONZALEZ PEDRERO E.
ANATOMIA DE UN CONFLICTO.
MEXICO CITY: FACULTAD U VERACRUZ, 1963, 136 PP.
ANALYSIS OF WORLD AFFAIRS AND RELATIONS AMONG NATIONS IN PRESENT COLD WAR SITUATION. EXAMINES STATUS OF UNDERDEVELOPED COUNTRIES IN REGARD TO POLITICS OF LARGER MORE POWERFUL NATIONS.

1167 GOOCH G.P.
ENGLISH DEMOCRATIC IDEAS IN THE SEVENTEENTH CENTURY (2ND ED.)
NEW YORK: CAMBRIDGE U PRESS, 1927, 315 PP.
CONCERNED WITH DEMOCRATIC FEATURES OF ENGLISH MONARCHICAL GOVERNMENT. BEGINS WITH ORIGIN AND GROWTH OF DEMOCRATIC IDEAS. DISCUSSES ORIGIN OF REPUBLICANISM AND FOUNDATION OF REPUBLIC; PRESENTS VIEW OF ANTAGONISTS OF OLIGARCHY AND INCLUDES POLITICAL IDEAS OF THE ARMY, RISE OF INFLUENTIAL RELIGIOUS BODIES, AND REVOLUTION OF 1688. RELATIONS WITH US AND COMMONWEALTH AND MOVEMENT FOR LAW REFORM ARE STUDIED.

1168 GOOD E.M.
"CAPITAL PUNISHMENT AND ITS ALTERNATIVES IN ANCIENT NEAR EASTERN LAW."
STANFORD LAW REV., 19 (MAY 67), 947-977.
ANALYZES CONSISTENCIES AND INCONSISTENCIES IN REGULATIONS CONCERNING CAPITAL PUNISHMENT IN ANCIENT NEAR EASTERN LAW. DEBATES WHETHER CAPITAL OFFENSES DO POINT TO VALUES HELD BY SOCIETIES WHICH PRODUCED EXTANT LEGAL MATERIALS. OUTLINES KNOWN OFFENSES REQUIRING DEATH PENALTY. CONTENDS A SOCIETY'S VALUES MAY BE NEGATIVELY EXHIBITED IN ITS PUNISHMENTS FOR THE CRIMES IT MOST DETESTS.

1169 GOODE W.J.
WORLD REVOLUTION AND FAMILY PATTERNS.
NEW YORK: FREE PRESS OF GLENCOE, 1963, 432 PP., LC#63-13538.
DESCRIBES AND INTERPRETS CHANGES IN FAMILY PATTERNS THAT HAVE OCCURRED OVER PAST FIFTY YEARS IN JAPAN, CHINA, INDIA, THE WEST, AFRICA, AND THE ARAB COUNTRIES, IN ORDER TO RELATE THEM TO VARIOUS ALTERATIONS IN OTHER INSTITUTIONS. ARGUES THAT SOCIOLOGICAL GENERALIZATIONS APPLY TO BOTH PRIMITIVE AND CIVILIZED SOCIETIES, AND THAT SOCIOLOGICAL INSIGHTS MUST BE TESTED BY HISTORICAL DATA.

1170 GOODENOUGH W.H.
"A PROBLEM IN MALAYO-POLYNESIAN SOCIAL ORGANIZATION" (BMR)"
AMERICAN ANTHROPOLOGIST, 57 (FEB. 55), 71-83.
DISCUSSES PROBLEM OF ASCERTAINING NONUNILINEAR DESCENT GROUPS IN THE ORIGINAL MALAYO-POLYNESIAN GROUP. FINDS THAT THERE WERE TWO TYPES OF KIN GROUPS ASSOCIATED WITH LAND. ONE WAS AN UNRESTRICTED DESCENT GROUP, WHILE MEMBERSHIP IN THE OTHER WAS DETERMINED BY PARENTAL RESIDENCE. STATES THAT THE STRUCTURE OF BOTH GROUPS HELPED RESOLVE LAND DISTRIBUTION PROBLEMS.

1171 GOODMAN E.
SOVIET DESIGN FOR A WORLD STATE.
NEW YORK: COLUMB. U. PR., 1960, 512 PP.
PUBLIC STATEMENTS OF SOVIET ELITE INDICATE WELL-DEFINED EXPECTATIONS AND DESIGN FOR WORLD STATE. TRACKS DOWN ORIGINS OF DOCTRINES, SUCH AS CO-EXISTENCE OR WORLD ORDER, IN WRITINGS OF MARX, ENGELS, LENIN, STALIN, ET AL.

1172 GOODMAN G.K. ED.
IMPERIAL JAPAN AND ASIA: A REASSESSMENT (PAMPHLET)
NY: COLUMBIA U, EAST ASIAN INST, 1967, 80 PP., LC#67-28178.
ESSAYS INTERPRET ATTITUDES, INTENTIONS, GOALS, POLICIES, AND PROGRAMS OF IMPERIAL JAPAN IN ASIA. TOPICS RANGE FROM BEGINNINGS OF JAPANESE EMPIRE, IDEOLOGY OF JAPANESE IMPERIALISM, RELATIONS WITH CHINA, WWII, TO RELATIONS WITH SOUTHEAST ASIA. ANALYZE DECISION-MAKING PROCESS IN WHICH JAPAN CHOSE WAR WITH US, PAN-ASIANISM, LEADERSHIP, ECONOMY, OCCUPATION IN SOUTHEAST ASIA, AND EXPANSIONIST POLICIES.

1173 GOODNOW H.F.
THE CIVIL SERVICE OF PAKISTAN: BUREAUCRACY IN A NEW NATION.
NEW HAVEN: YALE U PR, 1964, 328 PP., LC#64-20918.
COVERS CONDITIONS PRIOR TO 1958 UNDER INDIAN CIVIL SERVICE OF ENGLAND. AFTER 1958 PERIOD OF MILITARY RULE LED TO INDEPENDENT CIVIL SERVICE. DONE AS CASE STUDY OF BUREAUCRACY IN UNDEVELOPED NATIONS. ANALYZES POLITICAL ORGANIZATION IN ALL NEW STATES. APPENDIX OF FISCAL REPORTS AND GOVERNMENT JOB TITLES. EXTENSIVE BIBLIOGRAPHY OF BOOKS AND ARTICLES ON INDIA AND BUREAUCRACY DEVELOPMENT.

1174 GOODSELL J.N.
"BALAGUER'S DOMINICAN REPUBLIC."
CURRENT HISTORY, 53 (NOV. 67), 298-302, 309.
DISCUSSES SITUATION AND POLICY OF BALAGUER'S NATION. FEELS MAJOR UNCERTAINTIES EXIST IN DOMINICAN REPUBLIC'S FUTURE. STATES THAT BALAGUER HAS MADE A GOOD START ON ECONOMIC RECOVERY BUT HE IS NOT OVER THE HUMP. FINDS THAT POLITICAL THREATS TO GOVERNMENT DO NOT HELP ECONOMIC DEVELOPMENT.

1175 GOPAL R.
INDIAN MUSLIMS: A POLITICAL HISTORY (1858-1947)
BOMBAY: ASIA PUBL HOUSE, 1959, 351 PP.
DISCUSSES MUSLIM POLITICS AND HINDU-MUSLIM POLITICAL INTERACTIONS AND TENSIONS UP TO 1947 PARTITION OF BRITISH INDIA. POINTS OUT THAT SELF-APPOINTED LEADERS WERE OFTEN UNREPRESENTATIVE OF REGIONAL ATTITUDES. SHOWS HOW THIS CONTRIBUTED TO TENSIONS BETWEEN MUSLIMS, HINDUS, AND BRITISH.

1176 GOPAL S.
BRITISH POLICY IN INDIA 1858-1905.
CAMBRIDGE: CAMBRIDGE UNIV PRESS, 1965, 423 PP.
STUDY OF FIRST PHASE OF BRITISH RULE IN INDIA UNDER THE CROWN. NOT PRIMARILY CONCERNED WITH INDIAN ATTITUDES AND REACTIONS, BUT WITH IDEAS AND ASPIRATIONS OF BRITISH PARTIES AND STATESMEN, THEIR WAYS AND METHODS OF IMPLEMENTING THEM, AND THE CONSEQUENCES, ANTICIPATED AND UNINTENDED, OF THESE EFFORTS.

1177 GORDON B.K.
THE DIMENSIONS OF CONFLICT IN SOUTHEAST ASIA.
ENGLEWOOD CLIFFS: PRENTICE HALL, 1966, 201 PP., LC#66-14699.
ANALYZES CERTAIN MAJOR INTRA-REGIONAL CONFLICTS IN ORDER TO EMPHASIZE SEPARATE AND DISTINCT CHARACTER OF INDIVIDUAL SOUTHEAST ASIAN NATIONS. EXAMINES INITIAL, TENTATIVE EFFORTS AMONG LEADERS IN SOUTHEAST ASIA TO ESTABLISH RELATIVELY FORMAL PATTERNS OF COLLABORATION AMONG THEIR STATES. DISCUSSES COLLABORATION AS A REGIONAL REFLECTION OF A GLOBAL TENDENCY AND AS COMPARATIVE BEHAVIORAL POLITICS.

1178 GORDON L.
"THE ORGANIZATION FOR EUROPEAN ECONOMIC COOPERATION."
INT. ORGAN., 10 (FEB. 56), 1-11.
CONTENDS OEEC HAS HAD INFLUENCE ON ATTITUDES AND ACTIONS OF MEMBER STATES. EXAMINES SUCCESSES IN ALLOCATION OF AID, TRADE AND PAYMENTS LIBERALIZATION, PRODUCTIVITY INCREASE, AND CURRENCY STABILIZATION. OEEC FAILED IN RECOVERY PROGRAMS, ECONOMIC INTEGRATION.

1179 GORDON M., LERNER D.
"THE SETTING FOR EUROPEAN ARMS CONTROLS* POLITICAL AND STRATEGIC CHOICES OF EUROPEAN ELITES."
J. OF CONFLICT RESOLUTION, 9 (DEC. 65), 419-433.
PANELS OF GERMAN, BRITISH AND FRENCH ELITES WERE SURVEYED IN 1954, 1955, 1956, 1959, 1961, AND 1965, (FOR WHICH ALL DATA WERE NOT READY). STUDY USES 1961 DATA TO TEST ACCEPTABILITY OF "FUTURE AMERICAN STRATEGIC MOVES." FOCUS ON EUROPE'S SEEING SOVIET THREAT, DESIRABILITY OF NEGOTIATED ARMS CONTROL AGREEMENTS, NATO TACTICS, INTRA-EUROPEAN ACTIONS AND USE OF UN TO MEET THIS THREAT.

1180 GORDON M.S.
THE ECONOMICS OF WELFARE POLICIES.
NEW YORK: COLUMBIA U PRESS, 1963, 159 PP., LC#63-14113.
DETAILED ANALYSIS OF PROBLEMS INVOLVED IN DEVELOPMENT OF WELFARE POLICIES WITH EMPHASIS ON RELATIONSHIP OF WELFARE TO ECONOMIC GROWTH. COMPARES WELFARE PROGRAMS IN US TO THOSE IN OTHER COUNTRIES AND DISCUSSES INCOME REDISTRIBUTION, UNEMPLOYMENT COMPENSATION, AND VARIOUS WELFARE INSURANCE PROGRAMS.

1181 GORER G.
AFRICA DANCES: A BOOK ABOUT WEST AFRICAN NEGROES.
LONDON: FABER AND FABER, 1935, 363 PP., LC#35-16904.
DESCRIBES CUSTOMS OF WEST AFRICAN NEGROES. STUDIES THEIR RELIGION, CULTIC PRACTICE, ATHLETIC AND DANCE PRACTICES, AGRICULTURE, AND SOCIAL STRUCTURE. TREATS GOVERNMENT SYSTEM, ADMINISTRATIVE CUSTOMS, TAXATION, MILITARY SERVICE, AND NEGRO ATTITUDES TOWARD COLONIAL GOVERNMENT. SHOWS ROLE OF MAGIC AND INFLUENCE OF CHRISTIANITY.

1182 GORER G., RICKMAN J.
THE PEOPLE OF GREAT RUSSIA: A PSYCHOLOGICAL STUDY.
LONDON: CRESSET PRESS, 1949, 235 PP.
ATTEMPTS TO ISOLATE AND ANALYZE PRINCIPAL MOTIVES THAT INFORM AND UNDERLIE TYPICAL BEHAVIOR OF THE GREAT RUSSIAN PEOPLE. EXPLORES MEANS BY WHICH THESE MOTIVES ARE ELICITED AND MAINTAINED IN THE CHILDREN OF THE SOCIETY, SO THAT SOCIETY MAINTAINS ITS IDENTITY. DEVELOPS "SWADDLING HYPOTHESIS." FINDS POLICY IS FORMED BY SMALL GROUP OF LEADERS. FINDS BASIC FEAR OF FOREIGNERS PREVALENT.

1183 GORWALA A.D.
THE ADMINISTRATIVE JUNGLE (PAMPHLET)
PATNA, INDIA: PATNA U PRESS, 1957, 47 PP.
ESSAY ON PUBLIC ADMINISTRATION BRIEFLY DEALING WITH GOVERNMENT RELATIONS, POLICY PLANNING, BUREAUCRATIC PROCESS AND MAINTAINING WORKING RELATIONS BETWEEN LOCAL AND NATIONAL GOVERNMENT.

1184 GOSNELL H.F.
"BRITISH ROYAL COMMISSIONS OF INQUIRY"
POLIT. SCI. QUART., 49 (MAR. 34), 84-118.
DISCUSSES ROYAL COMMISSIONS OF INQUIRY AS PART OF BRITISH PARLIAMENTARY SYSTEM. PRESENTS METHODS OF DERIVING THEIR COMPOSITION AND SYSTEM OF ORGANIZATION. DESCRIBES IMPORTANCE PLACED ON THEIR REPORTS ON POLICY QUESTIONS AS EXPRESSED BY PRESS RECEPTIONS. EXAMINES REPORTS' EFFECTS ON POLICY DECISIONS.

1185 GOULD J.
"THE KOMSOMOL AND THE HITLER JUGEND."
BRIT. J. SOC., 2 (DEC. 51), 305-14.
POINTS OUT EMPHASIS GIVEN EDUCATION AS INSTRUMENT OF SOCIAL CONTROL IN TOTALITARIAN SOCIETIES. COMPARES AND CONTRASTS CONTENT OF KOMSOMOL HANDBOOK AND NAZI PRIMER. FINDS AIM TO BE IEDOLOGICAL CONFORMITY AMONG YOUTH.

1186 GOULD J. ED.
PENGUIN SURVEY OF THE SOCIAL SCIENCES* 1965.
BALTIMORE: PENGUIN BOOKS, 1965, 184 PP.
NINE PAPERS ON DEVELOPMENTS IN THE SOCIAL SCIENCES INCLUDE D. BELL'S "12 MODES OF PREDICTION," AND OTHERS ON SOCIAL LEARNING, TRAINING FOR SOCIAL RESEARCH, TRENDS AND PROBLEMS IN SOVIET STUDIES, CHANGE IN SMALL-SCALE SOCIETIES, URBANIZATION, BRITISH KINSHIP AND ASCRIPTION PRACTICES, ETC.

1187 GOULD S.H. ED.
SCIENCES IN COMMUNIST CHINA.
WASHINGTON: AMER. ASSOC. ADVANCE. SCI., 1961, 884 PP. $14.00
INCLUDES 26 TECHNICAL AND SOCIOLOGICAL RESEARCH ARTICLES. CONCLUDES THAT CHINA IS NOT ON PAR WITH WESTERN SCIENCE.

1188 GOURE L.
CIVIL DEFENSE IN THE SOVIET UNION.
BERKELEY: U OF CALIF PR, 1962, 207 PP., LC#61-18875.
ARGUES THAT SOVIET CIVIL DEFENSE SYSTEM IS MUCH BETTER THAN THAT OF US. CLARIFIES SOVIET CIVIL DEFENSE ACTIVITIES AND ATTITUDES AND VIEWS BEHIND THEM. TRACES PROGRAM BEFORE AND AFTER 1954. DISCUSSES ITS SCOPE AND ORGANIZATION. APPENDIXES OUTLINE SPECIFIC PROGRAMS OF SOVIET DEFENSE.

1189 GOURNAY B.
PUBLIC ADMINISTRATION.
NEW YORK: CULTURAL CTR FRENCH EM, 1963, 207 PP.
ANNOTATED TOPICAL LISTING OF 1,000 BOOKS, COURSES, MANUALS, ANTHOLOGIES, MAGAZINE ARTICLES, THESES, REPORTS OF STUDY GROUPS, AND DOCUMENTS EMANATING FROM CENTRAL FRENCH ADMINISTRATIONS. ALL ITEMS DEAL WITH PUBLIC ADMINISTRATIONS IN METROPOLITAN FRANCE; ALL WERE PUBLISHED 1944-58 AND MOST ARE IN FRENCH. CONCLUDING AUTHOR AND PUBLISHER INDEX. TITLES AND ANNOTATIONS GIVEN IN ENGLISH.

1190 GRAHAM B.D.
THE FORMATION OF THE AUSTRALIAN COUNTRY PARTIES.
CANBERRA: AUSTRALIAN NAT U, 1966, 326 PP.
EXAMINES ELECTORAL AND PARLIAMENTARY STRATEGIES OF THE FIRST AUSTRALIAN COUNTRY PARTIES AND THEIR EFFECT ON PARTY SYSTEM. ANALYZES SOCIAL AND ECONOMIC FACTORS WHICH PRODUCED THE PARTIES AND ENABLED THEM TO SURVIVE. INCLUDES BRIEF

HISTORY OF SIMILAR AGRARIAN MOVEMENTS IN NORTH AMERICA, ILLUSTRATING PARALLELS BETWEEN EXPERIENCES OF THE TWO CONTINENTS.

1191 GRAHAM G.S.
THE POLITICS OF NAVAL SUPREMACY; STUDIES IN BRITISH MARITIME ASCENDANCY.
NEW YORK: CAMBRIDGE U PRESS, 1965, 132 PP.
EXAMINES CONSEQUENCES AND LIMITATIONS OF BRITISH NAVAL SUPREMACY WITHIN FRAMEWORK OF 19TH-CENTURY POLITICS; INCLUDES FOREIGN POLICY AND NAVAL STRATEGY. BEGINS WITH BRITAIN'S POWER ON THE ATLANTIC, THEN CONCENTRATES ON THE PACIFIC WHERE IMPERIAL ATTENTION SHIFTED IN 19TH CENTURY. CLOSES WITH MEDITERRANEAN CORRIDOR FROM GIBRALTAR TO BOMBAY AND ILLUSION OF "PAX BRITANNICA."

1192 GRAHAM I.C.C., LEIB B.S.
PUBLICATIONS OF THE SOCIAL SCIENCE DEPARTMENT, THE RAND CORPORATION, 1948-1966.
NEW YORK: THE RAND CORP, 1966, 97 PP.
UNANNOTATED LISTING OF BOOKS, PAPERS, REPORTS, MEMORANDA, AND TRANSLATIONS PUBLISHED BY OR FOR RAND CORPORATION. ONE HALF OF THE PUBLICATIONS TREAT VARIOUS FACETS OF SOVIET GOVERNMENT AND POLITICAL POLICIES. INCLUDES MATERIAL ON MOST EVERY COUNTRY AND MUCH EMPHASIS ON INTERNATIONAL RELATIONS AND PROBLEMS OF MODERN WARFARE. INDEXED BY AUTHOR.

1193 GRAHAM R.
"BRAZIL'S DILEMMA."
CURRENT HISTORY, 53 (NOV. 67), 291-297, 308.
EXPLORES SUCCESS OF CASTELO BRANCO GOVERNMENT IN BRAZIL. NOTES THAT POLITICAL SYSTEM THIS GOVERNMENT INHERITED WAS BASED ON INCONGRUOUS POLICY OF MAINTAINING TRADITIONAL POLITICAL POWER BASE WHILE SUCCESSIVELY INCORPORATING NEWER FORCES. DISCUSSES PROSPECTS FOR FUTURE. FEELS NO NEW CRISES WILL OVERTAKE BRAZIL.

1194 GRAMPP W.D.
THE MANCHESTER SCHOOL OF ECONOMICS.
STANFORD: STANFORD U PRESS, 1960, 155 PP., LC#60-9050.
STUDIES NATURE, ACTIONS, AND THEORIES OF MANCHESTER SCHOOL. SHOWS REASONS WHY SCHOOL FORCED GREAT BRITAIN TO REPEAL CORN LAWS AND THEREBY COMMIT ITSELF FINALLY TO FREE TRADE. STATES THAT SCHOOL, UNLIKE CLASSICAL ONE, WAS A GROUP OF AGITATORS, AND ITS MEMBERS SPENT LESS TIME REASONING ABOUT THEIR PURPOSES THAN IN WINNING COUNTRY OVER TO THEM.

1195 GRANT C.F.
STUDIES IN NORTH AFRICA.
NEW YORK: EP DUTTON, 1923, 304 PP.
HISTORY OF NORTH AFRICA, 850 B.C.-1830 A.D. DISCUSSES MUS LIM CONQUESTS AND THOSE OF THE ROMANS AND EUROPEANS. ALSO INCLUDES CHANGES IN CULTURES AND GOVERNMENTS AND EFFECTS OF RELIGIONS ON POLITICS.

1196 GRANT C.H.
"RURAL LOCAL GOVERNMENT IN GUYANA AND BRITISH HONDURAS."
SOCIAL ECO. STUDIES, 16 (MAR. 67), 57-77.
ASSESSES THE NEED FOR ECONOMIC DEVELOPMENT THROUGH EFFICIENT VILLAGE COUNCILS WHICH ACT WITH GREATER AUTONOMOUS RESPONSIBILITY INSTEAD OF ACTING ONLY AS EXECUTIVE AGENCIES FOR CENTRAL GOVERNMENT.

1197 GRASES P.
ESTUDIOS BIBLIOGRAFICOS.
CARACAS: IMPRENTA NACIONAL, 1961, 387 PP.
BIBLIOGRAPHY OF VENEZUELA.

1198 GRASSMUCK G.L., SALIBI K.
"A MANUAL OF LEBANESE ADMINISTRATION."
BEIRUT: CATHOLIC PR, 1955.
A GENERAL MANUAL COVERING THE GOVERNMENTAL AND ADMINISTRATIVE OPERATIONS OF LEBANON. PROVIDES BRIEF DESCRIPTIVE HISTORY OF ADMINISTRATIVE DEVELOPMENT SINCE INDEPENDENCE. DIAGRAMMATIC DESCRIPTION OF EACH MAJOR DIVISION IN PRESENT ADMINISTRATION, BASED UPON LEGISLATIVE DECREES OF 1952-53; ENDEAVORS TO SPECIFY AGENCIES, FUNCTIONS, AND DUTIES. PARTIALLY ANNOTATED BIBLIOGRAPHY OF WORKS ON TOPIC SINCE WWI.

1199 GRAUBARD S.R. ED.
"TOWARD THE YEAR 2000: WORK IN PROGRESS."
DAEDALUS, (SUMMER 67), 1-994.
PAPERS FROM AMERICAN ACADEMY OF ARTS AND SCIENCES' COMMISSION ON YEAR 2000. DESCRIBES COMMISSION AND SUGGESTS ALTERNATIVE CHOICES IN FUTURE DECISIONS OF SOCIETY. STUDIES FORECASTING, EVALUATES SOCIAL PREDICTIONS, AND EXAMINES ISSUES OF POLITICS, EDUCATION, BEHAVIOR AND PERSONALITY, CHURCHES, YOUTH, ROLES, PRIVACY, COMMUNICATION, INTERNATIONAL RELATIONS, AND PSYCHOLOGICAL PERSPECTIVES.

1200 GRAYSON H.
ECONOMIC PLANNING UNDER FREE ENTERPRISE.
WASHINGTON: PUBLIC AFFAIRS PRESS, 1954, 134 PP., LC#54-8222.
DISCUSSES PRINCIPLES AND TECHNIQUES OF ECONOMIC PLANNING AND FORECASTING IN US, CANADA, AND UK. EXAMINES FORMAL ORGANIZATIONS, EMPLOYMENT POLICIES, AND LONG-TERM PLANNING.

1201 GREAT BRIT COMM MINISTERS PWR
REPORT.
LONDON: GT BR COMM ON MIN POWERS, 1932, 138 PP.
CONSIDERS POWERS EXERCISED BY OR UNDER DIRECTION OF MINISTERS OF THE CROWN BY WAY OF DELEGATED LEGISLATION AND JUDICIAL DECISION. SUGGESTS SAFEGUARDS NECESSARY TO SECURE CONSTITUTIONAL PRINCIPLES OF PARLIAMENTARY SOVEREIGNTY AND SUPREMACY OF THE LAW.

1202 GREAT BRITAIN CENTRAL OFF INF
CONSTITUTIONAL DEVELOPMENT IN THE COMMONWEALTH.
LONDON: H M STATIONERY OFFICE, 1964, 40 PP.
SUMMARY OF LONG-RANGE DEVELOPMENT OF CONSTITUTIONAL GOVERNMENT IN THE COMMONWEALTH AND REVIEW OF CURRENT STATUS OF CONSTITUTIONAL GOVERNMENT IN MEMBER NATIONS AND IN DEPENDENCIES WHICH ARE MOVING TOWARD INDEPENDENCE.

1203 GREAVES H.R.
THE FOUNDATIONS OF POLITICAL THEORY.
LONDON: ALLEN & UNWIN, 1958, 208 PP.
DISCUSSES CENTRAL CONCEPTS AND PRINCIPLES OF POLITICAL THEORY. ATTEMPTS TO SUGGEST WHY GUIDING PRINCIPLES SHOULD BE SOUGHT. EXAMINES QUESTIONS OF OBLIGATION, POLITICAL PURPOSE, INDIVIDUAL AND MORALITY, SOCIAL GOOD, ETC.

1205 GREBLER L.
URBAN RENEWAL IN EUROPEAN COUNTRIES: ITS EMERGENCE AND POTENTIALS.
PHILA: U OF PENN PR, 1964, 132 PP., LC#63-21714.
STUDY OF EUROPEAN EFFORTS, SUCCESSES, AND FAILURES AT URBAN RENEWAL. POINTS OUT THAT RENEWAL OFTEN GOES ON INDEPENDENTLY OF NATIONAL PROGRAMS. ALSO SHOWS THAT BRITISH EFFORTS HAVE BEEN FAR MORE SUSTAINED AND EFFECTIVE THAN THOSE OF NATIONS ON CONTINENT.

1206 GREEN L.P., FAIR T.J.D.
DEVELOPMENT IN AFRICA.
JOHANNESBURG: WITWATERSRAND U. PR., 1962, 203 PP.
STUDY PROMPTED BY AND DIRECTED TO CURRENT PROBLEMS ARISING IN AFRICA AS RADICAL SOCIAL, ECONOMIC, POLITICAL CHANGES MULTIPLY. OBJECTIVE IS TO ANALYZE PROCESSES AND PRINCIPLES CREATING EVOLVING PATTERN OF DEVELOPMENT AND PROVIDE FRAMEWORK FOR ANALYSIS OF ITS DETAILS SUCH AS POPULATION DISTRIBUTION AND URBANIZATION. BRIEFLY DISCUSSES RACE RELATIONS AND CONTEMPORARY POLITICAL PROBLEMS. BIBLIOGRAPHY INCLUDED.

1207 GREEN M.M.
IBO VILLAGE AFFAIRS.
NEW YORK: FREDERICK PRAEGER, 1964, 262 PP.
SOCIAL ANTHROPOLOGICAL RECOUNT OF BOOK WRITTEN 26 YEARS PRIOR TO DATE. DEALS WITH VILLAGE ORGANIZATION: STRUCTURE, CONOMY, MILITARY, AND LEGAL ASPECTS. ALSO DISCUSSES EXOGAMY, WOMEN'S GROUPS, AND TEMPERAMENT FACTORS.

1208 GREEN T.H.
PRINCIPLES OF PUBLIC ADMINISTRATION.
LONDON: LONGMANS, GREEN & CO, 1941, 252 PP.
COMPRISING VOLUME TWO OF GREEN'S PHILOSOPHICAL WORKS, THIS IDEALISTIC TREATISE ON OBLIGATION REFLECTS GREEN'S ATTITUDE TOWARD THE NATURE OF MAN AS NEO-KANTIAN, WITH OVERTONES OF ROUSSEAU. FEELING THAT MAN HAS INHERENT DIGNITY AND WORTH, GREEN THOUGHT THAT POLITICAL SYSTEMS SHOULD SERVE ONLY TO GUARD THE FREEDOM OF THE INDIVIDUAL. HIS FOREMOST CONVICTION WAS THE FUTILITY OF LEGISLATING MORALITY.

1209 GREGG J.L.
POLITICAL PARTIES AND PARTY SYSTEMS IN GUATEMALA, 1944-1963.
GAINESVILLE: U OF FLA PR, 1965, 173 PP.
IN CONTEXT OF PREVAILING POLITICAL SYSTEMS AND ENVIRONMENT, EXAMINES ORGANIZATION, LEADERSHIP, IDEOLOGY, AND ACTIVITY OF THE VARIOUS GROUPS PURPORTING TO HAVE CONSTITUTED POLITICAL PARTIES OPERATING IN GUATEMALA, 1944-63. ASSESSES DOMINANT FEATURES OF VARIOUS GUATEMALAN POLITICAL REGIMES.

1210 GREGORY R.
"THE MINISTER'S LINE: OR, THE M4 COMES TO BERKSHIRE. PART I."
PUBLIC ADMINISTRATION, 45 (SUMMER 67), 113-128.
EXAMINES COMPLEX PROBLEMS BRITISH MINISTRY OF TRANSPORT ENCOUNTERED IN FIXING ROUTE FOR NEW HIGWAY M4. DISCUSSES CRITERIA FOR SETTLING "MOTORWAY" LINES AND DEALS WITH THE STATUTORY AND CONVENTIONAL PLANNING PROCEDURES FOLLOWED BY THE MINISTRY.

1211 GRETTON P.
MARITIME STRATEGY - A STUDY OF DEFENSE PROBLEMS.
NEW YORK: FREDERICK PRAEGER, 1965, LC#65-25485.
DISCUSSES HISTORY AND PRINCIPLES OF MARITIME STRATEGY, FACTORS AFFECTING IT (NUCLEAR WEAPONS), AND INSTRUMENTS OF MARITIME STRATEGY (SUBMARINES, AIR-CRAFT CARRIERS,ETC.). EXAMINES SIZE OF BRITISH FORCES AND THAT OF POTENTIAL ENEMIES.

1212 GRIEB K.J.
"THE UNITED STATES AND THE CENTRAL AMERICAN CONFEDERATION."
THE AMERICAS, 24 (OCT. 67), 107-121.

DISCUSSES ATTEMPTS TO FORM A UNION OF THE CENTRAL AMERICAN STATES DURING THE HARDING ADMINISTRATION. RELATES US STATE DEPARTMENT ATTITUDES AND ACTIONS CONCERNING THE PROPOSED FEDERATION AND CONSIDERS REASONS FOR US HESITATION IN PROMOTING IT. ALTHOUGH US EVENTUALLY BACKED THE UNION, A GUATEMALAN COUP DESTROYED THE FEDERATION.

1213 GRIERSON P.
BOOKS ON SOVIET RUSSIA 1917-42: A BIBLIOGRAPHY AND A GUIDE TO READING.
LONDON: METHEUN, 1943, 354 PP.
PRIMARILY LISTS BOOKS PUBLISHED IN BRITAIN. INCLUDES SOME FROM OVERSEAS WITH A FEW IN FOREIGN LANGUAGES. ARRANGED BY TOPICS IN AN INFORMAL STYLE COVERING ALL ASPECTS OF SOVIET LIFE AND MATERIAL ON SOVIET LEADERS.

1214 GRIFFIN A.P.C. ED.
A LIST OF BOOKS ON THE DANISH WEST INDIES (PAMPHLET)
WASHINGTON: LIBRARY OF CONGRESS, 1901, 18 PP.
SOME 55 ANNOTATED BOOKS IN ENGLISH, FRENCH, AND DANISH ON VARIOUS TOPICS CONCERNING DANISH WEST INDIES. PUBLISHED FROM 1764-1900 WITH THREE US GOVERNMENT DOCUMENTS INCLUDED. SOME 23 ARTICLES IN PERIODICALS ARRANGED BY DATE. THESE IN ENGLISH AND DANISH FROM 1861-1901. SOME 19 ARTICLES FROM US CONSULAR REPORTS FROM 1881-1900. SIX ARTICLES FROM DANISH GOVERNMENT PUBLICATIONS DATING 1868-1870.

1215 GRIFFIN A.P.C. ED.
A LIST OF BOOKS ON PORTO RICO.
WASHINGTON: LIBRARY OF CONGRESS, 1901, 55 PP.
ANNOTATED LIST OF 150 BOOKS AND US GOVERNMENT DOCUMENTS ALPHABETICALLY ARRANGED BY AUTHOR FOLLOWED BY ABOUT 200 UNANNOTATED PERIODICAL ARTICLES ARRANGED BY DATE. LISTING OF ABOUT 90 PORTO RICAN ADMINISTRATIVE DOCUMENTS AND REPORTS OF LOCAL ORGANIZATIONS IS AT END. ITEMS PUBLISHED FROM 1834 TO 1900 WITH MANY IN SPANISH. ALL TOPICS COVERED.

1216 GRIFFIN A.P.C. ED.
LIST OF BOOKS ON THE CABINETS OF ENGLAND AND AMERICA (PAMPHLET)
WASHINGTON: LIBRARY OF CONGRESS, 1903, 8 PP.
ANNOTATION OF ABOUT 30 ITEMS, ARRANGED ALPHABETICALLY BY AUTHOR. INCLUDES COMPARATIVE TREATISES. ENGLISH-LANGUAGE MATERIALS BY ENGLISH AND AMERICAN AUTHORS. DATE FROM MIDDLE OF 9TH CENTURY TO 1903. COVERS CONSTITUTIONAL GOVERNMENT, CABINET STRUCTURE, COMPARISONS AND CONTRASTS. UNINDEXED. COMPILED FOR LIBRARY OF CONGRESS.

1217 GRIFFIN A.P.C. ED.
SELECT LIST OF REFERENCES ON GOVERNMENT OWNERSHIP OF RAILROADS (PAMPHLET)
WASHINGTON: LIBRARY OF CONGRESS, 1903, 14 PP.
ANNOTATED, UNINDEXED. ABOUT 100 ITEMS OF ENGLISH, FRENCH, AND GERMAN SOURCES. ARTICLES FROM 1871. BOOKS FROM 1870'S. TREATS VARIOUS ASPECTS OF GOVERNMENT CONTROL OF RAILROADS, AND LEGAL, ECONOMIC, AND POLITICAL RAMIFICATIONS. COMPILED FOR LIBRARY OF CONGRESS.

1218 GRIFFIN A.P.C. ED.
LIST OF REFERENCES ON BUDGETS OF FOREIGN COUNTRIES (PAMPHLET)
WASHINGTON: LIBRARY OF CONGRESS, 1904, 9 PP.
ANNOTATED. OVER 130 ITEMS IN FRENCH, GERMAN, ENGLISH, AND ITALIAN. ARRANGED ALPHABETICALLY BY AUTHOR AND COUNTRY. NOT INDEXED. BOOKS, ARTICLES, AND REPORTS CHIEFLY FROM THE 1870'S THROUGH 1902 ON BUDGETING, GOVERNMENTAL ACCOUNTING, FINANCIAL AFFAIRS, ETC. COMPILED FOR LIBRARY OF CONGRESS.

1219 GRIFFIN A.P.C. ED.
LIST OF BOOKS ON RAILROADS IN FOREIGN COUNTRIES.
WASHINGTON: LIBRARY OF CONGRESS, 1905, 70 PP.
ANNOTATED, LISTED BY COUNTRY, INDEXED BY AUTHOR AND SUBJECT. GERMAN, FRENCH, ENGLISH, AND ITALIAN SOURCES FROM 1890'S - 1905. INCLUDES PRINTED STATISTICS, ABSTRACTS, RAILROAD PERIODICALS, REPORTS, ETC. PURPORTS "TO PROVIDE MEANS OF ASCERTAINING THE MAIN PROVISIONS OF RAILROAD ADMINISTRATION IN THE SEVERAL COUNTRIES OF EUROPE." OVER 300 ITEMS. COMPILED FOR LIBRARY OF CONGRESS.

1220 GRIFFITH E.S. ED.
RESEARCH IN POLITICAL SCIENCE: THE WORK OF PANELS OF RESEARCH COMMITTEE, APSA.
PRINCETON* UNIV. REF. SYSTEM, 1948, 238 PP., LC#49-63042.
ARTICLES, MANY BY LEADING MEN IN THE FIELD, DISCUSSING PROBLEMS OF POLITICAL SCIENCE RESEARCH. IN ADDITION TO STANDARD DIVISIONS, STUDY OF WAR, MILITARY OCCUPATION, AND POLITICAL COMMUNICATIONS ARE INCLUDED. EDITOR CLOSES WITH CHAPTERS ON METHOD AND PROSPECTS. INCLUDES LIST OF SOURCES.

1221 GRIFFITH S.B.
"COMMUNIST CHINA'S CAPACITY TO MAKE WAR."
FOR. AFF., 43 (JAN. 62), 217-236.
ASSESSES COMMUNIST CHINA'S MILITARY CAPABILITIES IN TERMS OF: ATOMIC-NUCLEAR SYSTEMS, PRESENT LEADERSHIP AND REGIME, EXISTANT AND POTENTIAL POPULATION, TECHNICAL PERSONNEL, GEOGRAPHICAL POSITION, AND LEVEL OF IDEOLOGICAL COMMITMENT TO THE PARTY. ALSO EXAMINES STRUCTURE AND RESOURCES OF PEOPLE'S LIBERATION ARMY.

1222 GRIFFITH W.
THE PUBLIC SERVICE (PAMPHLET)
LONDON: BRITISH COUNCIL, 1957, 48 PP.
SURVEY OF PUBLIC SERVICE, ITS HISTORY, STRUCTURE, AND RELATIONS WITH BRITISH GOVERNMENT. STUDY AIMED AT MAKING VOTERS AWARE AND KNOWLEDGEABLE OF METHODS OF SELECTION AND TRAINING FOR PUBLIC SERVICE. STRESSES NEED FOR HIGH QUALITY PEOPLE IN GOVERNMENT.

1223 GRIFFITH W.
THE WELSH (2ND ED.)
CARDIFF: U OF WALES PRESS, 1964.
TRACES THE GROWTH OF A SOCIAL PATTERN IN WALES. SHOWS HOW THIS SOCIAL PATTERN IS BASED UPON THE WELSH LANGUAGE. TRACES THE INFLUENCE OF THE PURITAN OUTLOOK UPON THE NATIONAL CHARACTER, MANIFESTING ITSELF IN A POLITICAL PHILOSOPHY, IN A RADICALISM WHICH HAS YET TO DECLARE ITSELF FULLY, AS WELL AS IN A CODE OF RELIGIOUS AND SOCIAL BEHAVIOR. SURVEYS WELSH LITERATURE, MUSIC, AND OTHER ARTS.

1224 GRIFFITH W.E.
THE SINO-SOVIET RIFT.
CAMBRIDGE: M.I.T. PR., 1964, 508 PP., $2.95.
CHRONOLOGICAL ACCOUNT, COMPREHENSIVELY DOCUMENTED, OF SINO-SOVIET CONTROVERSY, NOTING REACTIONS TO SOVIET-YUGOSLAV RAPPROCHEMENT, CUBAN CRISIS AND ITS AFTERMATH, PARTY CONRESSES, AND TEST BAN TREATY. COVERS PERIOD: FEB. 62-JAN. 63.

1225 GRIFFITH W.E. ED.
COMMUNISM IN EUROPE (2 VOLS.)
CAMBRIDGE: M I T PRESS, 1964, 406 PP., LC#64-21409.
STUDY IS INTENDED TO RELATE IN DEPTH THE INTERACTION BETWEEN DOMESTIC DEVELOPMENTS AND SINO-SOVIET RIFT DEVELOPMENTS WITHIN MAJOR EUROPEAN COMMUNIST STATES. MAJOR ATTENTION IS GIVEN TO INTERNAL DEVELOPMENTS WITHIN THE SEVERAL PARTIES AND STATES.

1226 GRIMAL H.
HISTOIRE DU COMMONWEALTH BRITANNIQUE.
PARIS: PR UNIV DE FRANCE, 1965, 127 PP.
EXPLAINS ORIGINS OF COMMONWEALTH, ITS EVOLUTION, AND WHAT IT IS TODAY. UNIQUE NATURE DUE TO FOLLOWING: COLONIZATION BASED ON COMMERCIAL OR RELIGIOUS PURPOSES RATHER THAN MILITARY ONES; COLONIES ALL SHARED COMMERCIAL, HUMANITARIAN, AND ANTI-COLONIAL INTERESTS. IN ALL CASES POLITICAL CONCEPTS WERE NOT SO RIGID THAT THEY COULD NOT ADAPT TO CHANGING TIMES OR PLACES.

1227 GRIMOND J.
THE LIBERAL CHALLENGE.
LONDON: HOLLIS AND CARTER, 1963, 317 PP.
ASSUMES POLITICS ARE FOUNDED ON ETHICS AND MEANT TO SERVE SOCIETY. MAINTAINS THAT BRITISH DEMOCRACY NEEDS PARLIAMENTARY AND CIVIL SERVICE REFORM TO BETTER SERVE THE PEOPLE. DISCUSSES POLITICAL REFORM IN AREAS OF ECONOMICS, EDUCATION, WELFARE AND COMMUNAL SERVICES, AND DEFENSE AND FOREIGN AFFAIRS.

1228 GRIMSHAW A.D.
"URBAN RACIAL VIOLENCE IN THE UNITED STATES: CHANGING ECOLOGICAL CONSIDERATIONS."
AMER. J. OF SOCIOLOGY, 66 (SEPT. 60), 109-119.
ANALYZES CHANGES IN PATTERNS OF RACIAL VIOLENCE FROM PRE-TO POST-WWII IN US. IN "CLASSIC" PERIOD OF RACE RIOTING, CHARACTER OF VIOLENCE REFLECTED SOCIAL AND CULTURAL CHARACTERISTICS OF PERSONS FROM SPECIFIC URBAN LOCALES. SINCE WWII, RIOT PARTICIPANTS WITH VARYING SOCIAL AND DEMOGRAPHIC ATTRIBUTES HAVE GONE TO AREAS OTHER THAN THEIR OWN, AND HAVE EXPRESSED A NEW TYPE OF MILITANCY.

1229 GRISMER R.
A NEW BIBLIOGRAPHY OF THE LITERATURES OF SPAIN AND SPANISH AMERICA.
MINNEAPOLIS: PERRINE BOOK CO, 1941, 248 PP., LC#41-24332.
LIST OF BOOKS, PERIODICALS, DISSERTATIONS, ETC., MOSTLY IN SPANISH BUT INCLUDING OTHER LANGUAGES, ARRANGED ALPHABETICALLY. TITLES INCLUDE ANTHROPOLOGY, ARCHAEOLOGY, ART, ECONOMICS, EDUCATION, GEOGRAPHY, HISTORY, LAW, PHILOSOPHY, ETC.

1230 GRODZINS M.
AMERICANS BETRAYED: POLITICS AND THE JAPANESE EXPANSION.
CHICAGO: U OF CHICAGO PRESS, 1949, 445 PP.
TREATS US DECISION TO EVACUATE JAPANESE AMERICANS FROM PACIFIC COAST DURING EARLY MONTHS OF WWII. EXAMINES ACTUAL HISTORICAL EVENTS AND IMPLICATIONS OF POLICY DECISION. DISCUSSES EFFECT OF PUBLIC OPINION ON NATIONAL POLICY, RELATIONSHIPS BETWEEN STATES AND FEDERAL GOVERNMENT, RESPECTIVE POLICY-MAKING ROLES OF ADMINISTRATION AND LEGISLATURE, AND POLITICAL STATUS OF MINORITY GROUPS.

1231 GROGAN V.

ADMINISTRATIVE TRIBUNALS IN THE PUBLIC SERVICE.
DUBLIN: INST PUBLIC ADMIN, 1962, 76 PP.
STUDIES GROUPS WHOSE FUNCTION IS TO JUDGE ISSUES ARISING IN ADMINISTRATION OF JUDICIAL CONTROL OVER TRIBUNALS AND ADMINISTRATIVE LAW. COMPARES IRISH AND ENGLISH ADMINISTRATIVE SYSTEMS.

1232 GROSS B.M. ED.
ACTION UNDER PLANNING: THE GUIDANCE OF ECONOMIC DEVELOPMENT.
NEW YORK: MCGRAW HILL, 1967, 314 PP., LC#66-29773.
DISCUSSION OF PLANNING POLICIES, THE INSTITUTIONAL AND CULTURAL CONTEXT OF IMPLEMENTATION, THE BIOPHYSICAL ENVIRONMENT, LIMITATIONS OF "PERFECT PLANNING," ETC. INCLUDES ARTICLES ON ECONOMIC ACTIVATION, PLANNING AND SOCIAL ORDER, ACTIVATING NATIONAL PLANS, DEVELOPING NATIONAL-PLANNING PERSONNEL, ETC.

1233 GROSS J.A.
"WHITEHALL AND THE COMMONWEALTH."
J. COMMONWEALTH POLIT. STUD., 2 (NOV. 64), 189-206.
HISTORICAL DEVELOPMENT OF THE RISE AND FALL OF THE COLONIAL OFFICE IN THE BRITISH EMPIRE STRUCTURE. ANALYZES AND EVALUATES FORTHCOMING ABSORPTION OF COLONIAL OFFICE BY THE COMMONWEALTH RELATIONS OFFICE IN LIGHT OF BRITAIN'S CHANGING ROLE IN THE WORLD TODAY.

1234 GROSSER A.
"FRANCE AND GERMANY IN THE ATLANTIC COMMUNITY."
INT. ORGAN., 17 (SUMMER 63), 550-574.
ATTEMPTS TO PUT INTO PROPER PERSPECTIVE THE NATURE OF THE ATLANTIC COMMUNITY BY A DISCUSSION OF THE ROLES OF THE TWO EXTREMES IN THE GROUP - FRANCE AND GERMANY.

1235 GROSSER A.
THE FEDERAL REPUBLIC OF GERMANY: A CONCISE HISTORY.
NEW YORK: FREDERICK PRAEGER, 1964, 150 PP., LC#64-16677.
HISTORY OF GERMANY SINCE WWII. TOPICS INCLUDE POLITICAL INSTITUTIONS, ELECTIONS AND PARTY POLITICS, IDEOLOGY, SOCIAL AND MORAL ORDER, AND THE FEDERAL REPUBLIC IN INTERNATIONAL LIFE.

1236 GROSSMAN G.
"SOVIET GROWTH: ROUTINE, INERTIA, AND PRESSURE."
AMER. ECON. REV., 50 (MAY 60), 62-72.
STUDY SOURCE OF INITIATIVE IN SOVIET ECONOMIC GROWTH. POLITICAL LEADERSHIP ACKNOWLEDGED PRIME MOVER. RESISTANCE OF BUREAUCRACY TO NEW TECHNIQUES AND PRODUCTS IS SERIOUS OBSTACLE IN RACE WITH CAPITALISM. CHAIN OF COMMAND TRANSMITS PRESSURE FROM ABOVE, OVERCOMING OBSTACLES BY SANCTIONS AND INCENTIVES.

1237 GROVE J.W.
GOVERNMENT AND INDUSTRY IN BRITAIN.
LONDON: LONGMANS, GREEN & CO, 1962, 514 PP.
REVIEWS, SYSTEMATICALLY AND COMPREHENSIVELY, THE SUBJECT OF RELATIONS BETWEEN GOVERNMENT AND INDUSTRY. WRITTEN FROM VIEWPOINT OF CENTRAL ADMINISTRATION, SHOWS HOW DEPARTMENTS STAND IN CENTER OF "ENVIRONMENT" MADE UP OF VARIOUS AGENCIES THROUGH WHICH DEPARTMENTS WORK. DESCRIBES GOVERNMENT AS "REGULATOR, PROMOTER, ENTREPRENEUR, AND PLANNER."

1238 GROVES H.E.
THE CONSTITUTION OF MALAYSIA.
SINGAPORE: MALAYSIA PUBL LTD, 1964, 239 PP.
DISCUSSES GENERAL CHARACTERISTICS OF MALAYSIAN CONSTITUTION AND ARRANGES ARTICLES AROUND INSTITUTIONS AND CONCEPTS WITH WHICH DOCUMENT IS CONCERNED. SHOWS HOW CONSTITUTION HAS BEEN INTERPRETED BY COURTS AND BY LEGISLATURE. AREAS COVERED ARE SELECTION OF RULER, CABINET, CONFERENCE OF RULERS, PARLIAMENT, ELECTIONS, JUDICIARY, FEDERALISM, CITIZENSHIP, LIBERTIES, AND AGENCIES.

1239 GRUNDY K.W.
"RECENT CONTRIBUTIONS TO THE STUDY OF AFRICAN POLITICAL THOUGHT."
WORLD POLITICS, 18 (JULY 66), 647-689.
AN ANNOTATED BIBLIOGRAPHY ON STUDIES OF AFRICAN POLITICAL THOUGHT. ENGLISH-LANGUAGE AND SOME FRENCH. MATERIAL RANGES FROM 1956 TO 1965; 81 ENTRIES. THE AUTHOR REVIEWS SOME OF THE PRINCIPAL PUBLICATIONS DEALING WITH AFRICAN POLITICAL ATTITUDES, IDEAS, AND IDEOLOGIES.

1240 GRUNDY K.W.
"AFRICA IN THE WORLD ARENA."
CURRENT HISTORY, 52 (MAR. 67), 129-136.
SUGGESTS NECESSITY OF COMPREHENDING INTERNAL SITUATIONS OF NEW AFRICAN NATIONS IN ORDER TO UNDERSTAND FOREIGN POLICY WHICH IS USUALLY BASED ON ANTICOLONIAL STRUGGLE. COUNTRY BY COUNTRY ANALYSIS OF ALIGNMENT WITH EAST OR WEST, AND CAUSES OF SUCH ALIGNMENT. INFLUENCE OF RED CHINA IS GROWING, BUT REACTION IS SAME AS TO USA AND USSR-NO DEPENDENCE ON COLONIZING POWER.

1241 GRUNER E.
"PRENSA, PARTIDOS POLITICOS, Y GRUPOS DE PRESION EN SUIZA."
REV. INST. CIENC. SOC., (NO.3, 64), 151-61.
ANALYZES RELATIONSHIP AMONG THE PRESS, POLITICAL PARTIES, AND PRESSURE GROUPS IN SWITZERLAND. DISCUSSES ROLE OF THE PRESS IN MAINTAINING POLITICAL STABILITY.

1242 GRZYBOWSKI K.
SOVIET LEGAL INSTITUTIONS.
ANN ARBOR: U OF MICH PR, 1962, 284 PP., LC#62-12163.
DESCRIBES SOVIET JUDICIAL PROCESS, EMPHASIZING ATTEMPT OF FRAMERS TO RESHAPE IDEAS AND ATTITUDES OF SOVIET CITIZENS THROUGH EDUCATION. ROLE OF COURTS AS AN EDUCATIONAL FORCE AND POWER THEY POSSESS TO ENFORCE THEIR DICTATES ARE DISCUSSED. COMPARISONS ARE MADE TO US SYSTEM REGARDING CRIMES, PUNISHMENT, PROCESSES, AND INSTITUTIONS.

1243 GUDIN E.
INFLACAO (2ND ED.)
RIO DE JAN: LIVRARIA AGIR EDIT, 1959, 262 PP.
EXAMINES BRAZILIAN INFLATION IN REGARD TO ECONOMIC GROWTH AND DEVELOPMENT. DISCUSSES INTERNATIONAL TRADE, COFFEE PRODUCTION, BALANCE OF PAYMENTS, AND INDUSTRIALIZATION. COVERS PLANNING BY NATIONAL GOVERNMENT TO LIMIT INFLATIONARY INCREASES.

1244 GUENA Y.
HISTORIQUE DE LA COMMUNAUTE.
PARIS: FAYARD, 1962, 192 PP.
DISCUSSES EVOLUTION OF FRENCH UNION AND THE DEVELOPMENT OF INDEPENDENCE IN THE 14 FORMER FRENCH SUB-SAHARAN COLONIES IN THE PERIOD FROM 1946 TO 1962.

1245 GUERIN D.
SUR LE FASCISME: FASCISME ET GRAND CAPITAL (VOL. II)
PARIS: FRANCOIS MASPERA, 1965, 313 PP.
ANALYSIS IN DEPTH OF NATURE OF FASCISM. DISCUSSES COMMON TRAITS OF GERMAN AND ITALIAN REGIMES. PLACES FASCISM IN HISTORICAL, ECONOMIC, AND SOCIAL CONTEXTS TO SHOW CAUSES FOR AND WEAKNESSES OF IT.

1246 GUETZKOW H.
"THE POTENTIAL OF CASE STUDY IN ANALYZING INTERNATIONAL CONFLICT."
WORLD POLIT., 14 (APRIL 62), 548-52.
AN EVALUATION OF A BOOK 'THE SAAR CONFLICT' BY JACQUES FREYMOND ABOUT POTENTIAL INTERNATIONAL CONFLICT. IT IS AN HISTORIC AND ANALYTIC STUDY OF GERMAN-FRENCH DISPUTE OVER SAAR AND OF THE METHOD USED TO RESOLVE IT.

1247 GUEVARA E.
GUERRILLA WARFARE.
NEW YORK: MONTHLY REVIEW PR., 1961, 127 PP.
SYNTHESIZES THE GUERRILLA EXPERIENCES OF THIS CUBAN REVOLUTIONARY COMMUNIST AND COVERS: GENERAL PRINCIPLES OF GUERRILLA WARFARE, THE GUERRILLA BAND AND THE ORGANIZATION OF THE GUERRILLA FRONT.

1248 GUIMARAES A.P.
INFLACAO E MONOPOLIO NO BRASIL.
RIO DE JANEIRO: ED CIVIL BRASIL, 1963, 181 PP.
STUDY OF INFLATION IN BRAZIL. EXAMINES THEORIES OF INFLATION, GOVERNMENT'S ROLE, WAGE SCALE, INTERNATIONAL INFLUENCES, AND RELATION OF INFLATION TO DEVELOPING ECONOMIES.

1249 GUINS G.C.
"SOVIET LAW AND SOVIET SOCIETY."
THE HAGUE: MARTINUS NIJHOFF, 1954.
DISCUSSION AND LENGTHY NOTES AND BIBLIOGRAPHY ON VARIOUS ASPECTS OF SOVIET LAW AND SOCIETY: ETHICAL FOUNDATIONS OF THE SOVIET STRUCTURE; MACHANISM OF THE PLANNED SOCIETY; DUTIES AND RIGHTS OF PEASANTS AND WORKERS; RULERS AND TOILERS; THE FAMILY AND THE STATE; SOVIET JUSTICE; NATIONAL MINORITIES AND THEIR AUTONOMY; PEOPLE'S DEMOCRACIES AND SOVIET PATTERN FOR A UNITED WORLD.

1250 GUIZOT F.P.G.
HISTORY OF THE ORIGIN OF REPRESENTATIVE GOVERNMENT IN EUROPE.
LONDON: HG BOHN, 1861, 520 PP.
TRACES DEVELOPMENT OF REPRESENTATION IN FRANCE, SPAIN, AND ENGLAND 350-1850. CHAPTERS DEAL WITH PRIMITIVE INSTITUTIONS, EFFECT OF MILITARY SERVICE, AND CONSTITUTIONAL DEVELOPMENT. SECOND PART OF BOOK DEALS WITH TRANSFORMATION OF ENGLAND FROM ABSOLUTE TO CONSTITUTIONAL MONARCHY AND WITH RISE OF PARLIAMENT.

1251 GUMPLOWICZ L.
RECHTSSTAAT UND SOZIALISMUS.
OSNABRUCK: OTTO ZELLER, 1964, 548 PP.
DISCUSSES TRADITIONAL CONCEPTS OF THEORY OF STATE AS PUBLIC AND PRIVATE LAW, ROLE OF JURISPRUDENCE, AND EXAMINES CONCEPT OF PEOPLE AND STATE IN KANT, SAVIGNY, GROTIUS, HOBBES, AND MANY OTHERS. DISCUSSES PRINCIPLES OF COMMUNISM AND SOCIALISM.

1252 GUNN G.E.
THE POLITICAL HISTORY OF NEWFOUNDLAND 1832-1864.
TORONTO: TORONTO UNIV PRESS, 1966, 249 PP.

DOCUMENTED HISTORY OF THREE DECADES OF POLITICAL DISORDER THAT FOLLOWED ESTABLISHMENT OF REPRESENTATIVE GOVERNMENT IN 1832. FEELS MOST HISTORIANS ARE TOO INVOLVED IN TIMES AND GIVE BIASED EXPLANATIONS FOR INSTABILITY. ANALYZES DOCUMENTS OF NEW GOVERNMENT TO STUDY STRUCTURE OF PARTIES, CAUSES FOR DISORDER, AND EFFECTS OF CONSTITUTIONAL CHANGE ON WHOLE SOCIETY.

1253 GURLAND A.R.L.
POLITICAL SCIENCE IN WESTERN GERMANY: THOUGHTS AND WRITINGS, 1950-1952 (PAMPHLET)
WASHINGTON: LIBRARY OF CONGRESS, 1952, LC#52-60058.
MORE THAN 300 ANNOTATED ITEMS PUBLISHED DURING THE THREE YEAR SPAN, 1950-52. INCLUDES ARTICLES FROM JOURNALS, BOOKS, AND ESSAYS ABOUT HALF OF WHICH ARE IN GERMAN. PRECEDED BY INTRODUCTORY ESSAY AND FOLLOWED BY AUTHOR INDEX. TOPICS INCLUDE FOREIGN POLICY, IDEOLOGY, HISTORY, AND NAZIISM.

1254 GURR T.
NEW ERROR-COMPENSATED MEASURES FOR COMPARING NATIONS* SOME CORRELATES OF CIVIL VIOLENCE.
PRINCETON: CTR OF INTL STUDIES, 1966, 126 PP.
IMPORTANT FORMULATIONS ON THE IMPROVEMENT OF METHODOLOGIES IN CROSS-NATIONAL STUDIES. PRESENTS CONCEPT OF "OPTIMUM ERROR INTERVAL FOR QUANTIFIED CROSS NATIONAL DATA," OFFERS FOUR NEW POLITICAL, SOCIO-ECONOMIC INDICATORS AS ILLUSTRATIONS. STUDY PRESENTED IN FRAMEWORK OF DEPRIVATION-CONTROL CONFLICT MODEL OF CIVIC VIOLENCE.

1255 GURVITCH G.
"MAJOR PROBLEMS OF THE SOCIOLOGY OF LAW."
J. SOCIAL PHILOSOPHY, 6 (APR. 40), 197-215.
DISCUSSES THE INTER-RELATEDNESS OF SOCIOLOGY, MORALITY, RELIGION, LAW, AND PHILOSOPHY. IS CONCERNED WITH GENERAL PHILOSOPHIC APPROACH TO THE SOCIOLOGY OF LAW RATHER THAN SOCIOLOGICAL JURISPRUDENCE. THESIS CONCERNS IMPORTANCE OF MORAL AND RELIGIOUS BASES IN STUDY OF THE SOCIOLOGY OF LAW.

1256 GURVITCH G.
TRAITE DE SOCIOLOGIE (2 VOLS.)
PARIS: PR UNIV DE FRANCE, 1958.
COLLECTION OF ESSAYS ANALYZING THE PROBLEMS AND METHODS OF POLITICAL, PSYCHOLOGICAL, AND INDUSTRIAL SOCIOLOGY. EACH SELECTION FOLLOWED BY A FAIRLY EXTENSIVE BIBLIOGRAPHY, PRIMARILY OF WORKS IN FRENCH PUBLISHED SINCE 1940.

1257 GUSFIELD J.R.
"EQUALITARIANISM AND BUREAUCRATIC RECRUITMENT."
ADMINISTRATIVE SCI. Q., 2 (MAR. 58), 521-541.
DISCUSSION OF SOCIAL BACKGROUNDS OF CIVIL SERVANTS IN US AND UK. EQUALITARIANISM HAS HAD MORE EFFECT IN THE US THAN IN UK IN STAFFING THE CIVIL SERVICE WITH NONARISTOCRATS.

1258 GUTTERIDGE W.
MILITARY INSTITUTIONS AND POWER IN THE NEW STATES.
NEW YORK: FREDERICK PRAEGER, 1964, 182 PP.
STUDY OF ROLE OF MILITARY IN NEW NATIONS; EXAMINES POWER AND INFLUENCE OF ARMED FORCES AS ELITE GROUP IN SOCIETY. DISCUSSES ORGANIZATION, ATTITUDE, AND FUNCTION OF MILITARY IN DEVELOPING NATIONS.

1259 GUZZARDI W.
"THE DECLINE OF THE STERLING CLUB."
FORTUNE, 77 (FEB. 68), 113, 208-210.
DISCUSSES THE DECLINE OF INFLUENCE OF BRITAIN OVER COMMONWEALTH MEMBERS AS EVINCED BY THE REFUSAL OF AUSTRALIA, INDIA, SOUTH AFRICA, AND KUWAIT TO DEVALUATE ALONG WITH BRITAIN. DISCUSSES THOSE EVENTS LEADING TO, AND FOLLOWING, THE DEVALUATION THAT CONTRIBUTED TOWARD OTHER NATIONS' REFUSAL TO FOLLOW SUIT.

1260 GWYN R.J.
THE SHAPE OF SCANDAL: A STUDY OF A GOVERNMENT IN CRISIS.
TORONTO: CLARK, IRWIN + CO, 1965, 248 PP.
ANALYSIS OF CAUSES OF, AND REASONS FOR, SCANDALS OF NOV.-JULY, 1964, UNDER GOVERNMENT OF LESTER PEARSON. ATTEMPTS TO EXPLAIN SITUATION AS A POLITICAL ISSUE.

1261 GYORGY A.
GEOPOLITICS: THE NEW GERMAN SCIENCE.
BERKELEY: U. CALIF. PR., 1944, 283 PP.
EXAMINES WRITINGS OF KARL HAUSHOFFER AND OTHERS FOR DEFINITIONS OF 'GEOPOLITICS'. CONCLUDES THAT IT WAS USED BY GERMAN SCIENTISTS TO DESCRIBE MAN IN TERMS OF RACE, TIME, SPACE, GEOGRAPHY, AND HISTORY. CONCEPT USED BY NAZIS TO JUSTIFY STRUGGLE FOR WORLD DOMINANCE.

1262 H T.
GRUNDZUGE DES CHINESISCHEN VOLKSCHARACTERS.
WURZBURG: ECHTER-VERLAG, 1964, 134 PP.
EXAMINES CHINESE NATIONAL CHARACTER AS EXPRESSED IN ART, POETRY, AND MUSIC. ANALYZES PROBLEM OF CONTINUITY IN CHARACTER AND HISTORICAL EXPERIENCE.

1263 HAAR C.M.
LAW AND LAND: ANGLO-AMERICAN PLANNING PRACTICE.
CAMBRIDGE: HARVARD U PR, 1964, 290 PP., LC#64-11129.
EXAMINES CITY PLANNING IN CONTEXT OF US AND BRITISH LEGAL SYSTEMS. HOPES TO INDICATE HOW INSTITUTIONS OF LAW AND PROPERTY CAN BE MOLDED INTO A MORE RATIONAL AND EFFECTIVE MEANS OF ORGANIZING LAND USE. TREATS THEORY AND FRAMEWORK OF PLANNING, FORMULATION OF PLANS, THE INDIVIDUAL'S RELATION TO MACHINERY OF PLANNING, AND FINANCIAL BASES OF PLANNING.

1264 HAAS E.B.
THE UNITING OF EUROPE.
STANFORD: U. PR., 1958, 552 PP.
DEMONSTRATES PROCESSES BY WHICH POLITICAL COMMUNITIES ARE FORMED AMONG SOVEREIGN STATES. CASE-STUDY OF EUROPEAN COAL AND STEEL COMMUNITY WHICH WAS INFLUENTIAL IN DEVELOPING HABITS OF QUASI-FEDERAL CONDUCT. INDICATES THAT POLITICAL UNITY IN A PLURALISTIC SOCIETY DOES NOT NEED MAJORITY SUPPORT OR IDENTICAL AIMS.

1265 HAAS E.B.
"CONSENSUS FORMATION IN THE COUNCIL OF EUROPE."
LONDON: STEVENS, 1960, 70 PP.
ANALYZES VOTING BEHAVIOR IN COUNCIL OF EUROPE TO DISCOVER WHETHER AND HOW NATIONAL LOYALTIES DECLINE AND REGIONAL LOYALTIES GROW AMONG THE ELITE OF PARLIAMENTARIANS. DEVELOPS NEW STATISTICAL INDEX FOR OBSERVING VOTING BEHAVIOR IN INTERNATIONAL PARLIAMENTARY ASSEMBLIES.

1266 HAAS E.B., SCHMITTER P.C.
"ECONOMICS AND DIFFERENTIAL PATTERNS OF POLITICAL INTEGRATION: PROJECTIONS ABOUT UNITY IN LATIN AMERICA."
INT. ORGAN., 18 (AUTUMN 64), 705-37.
PRESENTS THESIS THAT 'UNDER MODERN CONDITIONS THE RELATIONSHIP BETWEEN ECONOMIC AND POLITICAL UNION HAD BEST BE TREATED AS A CONTINUUM.... POLITICAL IMPLICATIONS CAN BE ASSOCIATED WITH MOST MOVEMENTS TOWARD ECONOMIC INTEGRATION EVEN WHEN THE CHIEF ACTORS THEMSELVES DO NOT ENTERTAIN SUCH NOTIONS AT THE TIME OF ADOPTING THEIR NEW CONSTUITIVE CHARTER.' CITES LAFTA AS EXAMPLE.

1267 HABERLER G.
A SURVEY OF INTERNATIONAL TRADE THEORY (PAMPHLET)
PRINCETON, NJ: PRIN U INTL FINAN, 1961, 78 PP.
PRESENTS OUTLINE OF INTERNATIONAL TRADE THEORY, INCLUDING SKETCH OF MONETARY THEORY OF BALANCE OF PAYMENTS. STUDIES CLASSICAL THEORY OF COMPARATIVE COSTS AND INTERNATIONAL VALUES FROM HUME TO MARSHALL AND MODERN DEVELOPMENTS OF PURE THEORY. EXAMINES TERMS OF TRADE AND MECHANISM OF BALANCE OF PAYMENTS, SINCE THEORIES MUST ACCOUNT FOR MONEYED ECONOMIES.

1268 HABERMAS J.
STRUKTURWANDEL DER OFFENTLICHKEIT.
BERLIN: H LUCHTERHAND VERL, 1962, 291 PP.
STUDY OF NATURE AND DEVELOPMENT OF PUBLIC OPINION IN THE MODERN NATION-STATE. POLITICAL AND SOCIAL FUNCTIONS AND THEIR GRADUAL TRANSFORMATION WITHIN THE MODERN LIBERAL STATE ARE DISCUSSED AT LENGTH.

1269 HACHMANN R., KOSSACK G. ET AL.
VOLKER ZWISCHEN GERMANEN UND KELTEN.
NEUMUNSTER: KARL WACHHOLTZ VERL, 1962, 144 PP.
DISCUSSES SETTLEMENTS OF CELTS AND GERMANS BETWEEN RHINE, MAIN, AND ELBE RIVERS AT TIME OF BIRTH OF CHRIST. EXAMINES DATA FROM HISTORICAL, ARCHEOLOGICAL, AND PHILOLOGICAL POINT OF VIEW. TABLES AND MAPS.

1270 HACKETT J.
ECONOMIC PLANNING IN FRANCE; ITS RELATION TO THE POLICIES OF THE DEVELOPED COUNTRIES OF WESTERN EUROPE (PAMPHLET)
NEW YORK: ASIA PUBL HOUSE, 1965, 55 PP.
DISCUSSES ECONOMIC PLANNING IN WESTERN EUROPE, ESPECIALLY FRANCE, IN ORDER TO APPLY SYSTEM TO PLANNING IN INDIA. EXAMINES REASONS FOR PLANNING IN MIXED ECONOMIES, CONSIDERATIONS THAT DETERMINE APPROACH, AND METHODS OF PLANNING. INVESTIGATES FRENCH SYSTEM, ITS OPERATION, AND ITS RESULTS. EXPLORES PROBLEMS OF PLANNING AND METHODS TO DEAL WITH THEM.

1271 HACKETT J., HACKETT A.M.
L'ECONOMIE BRITANNIQUE: PROBLEMES ET PERSPECTIVES.
PARIS: COLIN (LIB ARMAND), 1966, 219 PP.
ATTEMPTS TO EXPLAIN TO THE FRENCH, ECONOMIC PROBLEMS AND POLITICAL ECONOMICS OF THE BRITISH. DISCUSSES KEY PROBLEMS 1950-60. ANALYZES NEW TENDENCIES SINCE 1961 AND INDICATES SOLUTIONS TO PROBLEMS.

1272 HADDAD J.A.
REVOLUCAO CUBANA E REVOLUCAO BRASILEIRA.
RIO DE JANEIRO: ED CIVIL BRASIL, 1961, 325 PP.
ANALYZES CUBAN REVOLUTION RELATING AND COMPARING IT TO NEEDS OF BRAZIL. DISCUSSES REFORSM IN CUBA AND ORTANCE OF AGRARIAN AND URBAN REFORMS IN ALL LATIN AMERICA. EXAMINES EXPORT OF REVOLUTION AND REFORM FROM CUBA TO WHOLE AREA AND US REACTION.

1273 HADWIGER D.F., TALBOTT R.B.

PRESSURES AND PROTEST.
SAN FRANCISCO: CHANDLER, 1965, 336 PP., LC#64-8160.
DISCUSSES THE KENNEDY FARM PROGRAM AND THE WHEAT REFERENDUM OF 1963 IN THE FORM OF A CASE STUDY. FARMER COMMITTEE SYSTEMS OF THE DEPT. OF AGRICULTURE, FARMER ORGANIZATIONS AND METHODS, AND THE DYNAMICS OF A FARM REFERENDUM ARE EXAMINED.

1274 HAEFELE E.T., STEINBERG E.B.
GOVERNMENT CONTROLS ON TRANSPORT.
WASHINGTON: BROOKINGS INST, 1965, 102 PP., LC#65-28379.
STUDIES NEED FOR TRANSPORT INVESTMENT IN EMERGING NATIONS OF AFRICA AND UTILIZATION OF EXISTING FACILITIES. PROBLEM OF CONTROL IS INTENSIFIED WHERE TWO NATIONS SHARE FACILITIES AS THEY DO ON MUCH OF CONTINENT. EXAMINES INSTITUTIONS, POLICIES, AND CONTROLS THAT DETERMINE TRANSPORT PATTERNS.

1275 HAHN C.H.L., VEDDER H., FOURIE L.
THE NATIVE TRIBES OF SOUTH WEST AFRICA.
NEW YORK: BARNES AND NOBLE, 1966, 211 PP.
SUMMARY DISCUSSIONS OF DEVELOPMENT OF CULTURAL TRADITIONS OF FIVE PRINCIPAL NATIVE TRIBES OF SOUTH WEST AFRICA. DE- SCRIBE ORIGIN, TRIBAL AND GOVERNMENT STRUCTURE, RELIGIOUS RITES AND BELIEFS AND OTHER MAJOR CULTURAL ASPECTS OF TRIBES.

1276 HAIGH G.
"FIELD TRAINING IN HUMAN RELATIONS FOR THE PEACE CORPS."
J. SOCIAL PSYCHOLOGY, 68 (FEB. 66), 3-13.
FIELD WORK WITH AMERICAN INDIAN GROUPS PRIOR TO OVERSEAS EXPERIENCE HELPS PEACE CORPS TRAINEES TO ADJUST TO VALUES OF ANOTHER CULTURE GROUP AND TO UNDERSTAND THE IMPLICIT VAL- UES AND DRIVES THE TRAINEES POSSESS AS MEMBERS OF A DISTINCT CULTURE GROUP.

1277 HAILEY L.
"TOMORROW IN AFRICA."
SUSSEX: AFRICA BUREAU, 1957, 12 PP.
DISCUSSES RACIAL PROBLEM IN AFRICA. GIVES SUMMARY OF NATIVE STATUS IN ALL NATIONS SOUTH OF THE SAHARA.

1278 HAILEY L.
THE REPUBLIC OF SOUTH AFRICA AND THE HIGH COMMISSION TERRITORIES.
LONDON: OXFORD U PR, 1963, 136 PP.
DESCRIBES RELATION OF HIGH COMMISSION TERRITORIES TO SOUTH AFRICA, ESPECIALLY SINCE LATTER LEFT COMMONWEALTH IN 1961. INCLUDES EFFORTS BY UNION TO SECURE INCORPORATION, AND PRESENT ATTITUDES TOWARD INCORPORATION.

1279 HAIM S.G. ED.
ARAB NATIONALISM.
LOS ANGELES: UCLA, NEAR EAST CTR, 1962, 255 PP., LC#64-11492
ESSAYS ON ARAB NATIONALISM, PHILOSOPHY OF REVOLUTION, AND WORLD UNITY, TRANSLATED FROM ARABIC. BIBLIOGRAPHY OF WESTERN AND ARABIC PUBLICATIONS.

1280 HAJDA J., KOLAJA J.
THE COLD WAR VIEWED AS A SOCIOLOGICAL PROBLEM (PAMPHLET)
CHICAGO: CZECH FORGN INST EXILE, 1955, 28 PP.
DESCRIBES COLD WAR AND THREE SIDES COMPETING FOR LOYALTY OF THOSE BEHIND IRON CURTAIN: COMMUNIST GOVERNMENT, WEST, AND POLITICAL REFUGEES AND EMIGREES. SUGGESTS MORE EFFECTIVE COLD WAR POLICY FOR WEST, ESPECIALLY EMPHASIZING ROLE OF THIRD GROUP.

1281 HALBWACHS M.
POPULATION AND SOCIETY: INTRODUCTION TO SOCIAL MORPHOLOGY (TRANS. BY DUNCAN AND PFAUTZ)
NEW YORK: FREE PRESS OF GLENCOE, 1960, 207 PP., LC#59-12187.
DISCUSSES PHYSICAL STRUCTURE OF GROUPS AND POPULATIONS. DRAWS ON FINDINGS IN DEMOGRAPHY AND ECONOMIC HISTORY OF IN- DUSTRIAL AND AGRICULTURAL ENTERPRISES. EXAMINES POPULATION GROWTH, MIGRATIONS, MORTALITY RATES, ETC.

1282 HALDANE R.B.
BEFORE THE WAR.
NEW YORK: FUNK/WAGNALLS, 1920, 234 PP.
TRACES FOREIGN POLICY OF BRITISH GOVERNMENT IN PERIOD FROM JANUARY 1906 TO AUGUST 1914. PLACES BLAME FOR THE OUT- BREAK OF WORLD WAR ONE ON THE GERMANS.

1283 HALE O.J.
THE CAPTIVE PRESS IN THE THIRD REICH.
PRINCETON: PRINCETON U PRESS, 1964, 353 PP., LC#64-12182.
DESCRIBES STRUCTURE OF GERMAN PRESS AND HOW IT WAS TURNED INTO GIANT NAZI PUBLISHING MONOPOLY. BEGINS WITH AC- QUISITION OF FIRST PARTY NEWSPAPER AND TRACES COMPLETE TAKE-OVER THROUGH WWII. MAX AMMAN, DIRECTOR OF PARTY'S PUBLISHING HOUSE, WORKED WITH A LARGE DEGREE OF AUTONOMY IN EFFECTING TRANSFER OF PRIVATELY OWNED PAPERS INTO HIS COMBINE, BUT WITH HITLER'S GUIDANCE.

1284 HALEVY E.
IMPERIALISM AND THE RISE OF LABOR (2ND ED.)
LONDON: ERNEST BENN, LTD, 1951, 442 PP.
DISCUSSES IN DEPTH POLITICAL HISTORY OF BOER WAR AND ITS AFTERMATH - DOMINATION AND AGGRESSIVE IMPERIALISM OF LORD SALISBURY AND CHAMBERLAIN, WAR ITSELF, UNIONIST CABINET POLICIES, BIRTH OF LABOR PARTY, AND DECLINE OF UNIONISTS. TREATS PERIOD BETWEEN 1895-1914.

1285 HALEVY E.
THE ERA OF TYRANNIES (TRANS. BY R. K. WEBB)
GARDEN CITY: DOUBLEDAY, 1965, 324 PP., LC#65-20055.
SELECTION OF HALEVY'S WRITINGS FROM 1902-36, DEALING WITH THE DANGEROUS AUTHORITARIAN TREND FEARED IN THE PROGRESS OF SOCIALISM. ESSAYS BEGIN WITH ANALYSIS OF SAINT-SIMON'S THEORIES ON ALL SUCCEEDING SOCIALIST THOUGHT, PROCEED THROUGH SERIES OF STUDIES OF SPECIFIC CASES IN DEVELOPMENT OF ENGLISH SOCIALISM, AND CONCLUDE WITH PESSIMISTIC VISION OF A NEW AGE OF TYRANNY.

1286 HALEVY E.
THE ERA OF TYRANNIES (TRANS. BY R. K. WEBB)
GARDEN CITY: DOUBLEDAY, 1965, 323 PP., LC#65-20055.
ARTICLES, EXTRACTS, LECTURES, AND PROPOSITIONS RANGING FROM 1902-36, ON SOCIALISM. TRACE ORIGIN AND DESCENT OF IDEAS, SHOWING AN AWARENESS OF THEIR AUTONOMOUS AND CREATIVE ROLE. MAINTAIN THAT A NEW ERA OF TYRANNIES, IN CLASSICAL GREEK SENSE OF WORD, BEGAN WITH WAR AND REVOLUTION, 1914-18.

1287 HALL R.C.
"REPRESENTATION OF BIG BUSINESS IN THE HOUSE OF COMMONS."
PUBLIC OPINION QUART., 2 (JULY 38), 473-477.
DISCUSSES INFLUENCE OF INDUSTRIAL ORGANIZATIONS IN THE HOUSE OF COMMONS, NOTING REPRESENTATION, BY AN OFFICER OF NEARLY EVERY IMPORTANT NATIONAL BUSINESS ASSOCIATION, IN THE 1937 HOUSE OF COMMONS. ONE HUNDRED AND NINE MEMBERS OF PARLIAMENT WERE DIRECTORS OF TWO OR MORE CORPORATIONS. AUTHOR IS PRO-BIG-BUSINESS AND VIEWS INDUSTRY'S INFLUENCE IN PARLIAMENT AS ADVANTAGEOUS FOR DEMOCRACY.

1288 HALLER W.
DER SCHWEDISCHE JUSTITIEOMBUDSMAN.
ZURICH: POLYGRAPHISCHER VERLAG, 1964, 320 PP.
DISCUSSES BASIC FOUNDATIONS OF SWEDISH LAW, HISTORY OF OFFICE OF PARLIAMENTARY COMMISSIONER FOR JUDICIAL AND CIVIL- ADMINISTRATION, AND FUNCTIONS AND RESPONSIBILITIES OF COM- MISSIONER (JUSTITIEOMBUDSMAN). COMPARES HIS FUNCTION TO SIMILAR PRACTICES IN OTHER COUNTRIES.

1289 HALLGARTEN G.W.
DAMONEN ODER RETTER.
FRANKFURT: EUROPAISCHE VERLAGS, 1957, 331 PP.
TRACES HISTORY OF DICTATORSHIPS FROM EARLY BEGINNINGS IN 6TH-CENTURY GREECE TO PRESENT. EXAMINES EPOCHS OF INDUSTRIAL CAPITALISM AND PROLETARIAN MASS MOVEMENTS AND RISE OF FASCISM AND COMMUNISM.

1290 HALLOWELL J.H.
MAIN CURRENTS IN MODERN POLITICAL THOUGHT.
NEW YORK: HOLT RINEHART WINSTON, 1950, 759 PP.
INTERPRETS POLITICAL PHILOSOPHY SINCE 1600, EMPHASIZING THE THOUGHT OF MAJOR POLITICAL PHILOSOPHERS AS FOUNDATION OF MODERN POLITICAL PHILOSOPHY. ALSO CONSIDERS THEOLOGICAL PRESUPPOSITIONS OF POLITICAL THOUGHT. CONSIDERS LIBERALISM, SOCIALISM, NIHILISM, AND ATTEMPTS TO RECONCILE CHRISTIANITY WITH THE CONTEMPORARY SITUATION.

1291 HALPERIN M.H.
THE POLITICS OF SOCIAL CHANGE IN THE MIDDLE EAST AND NORTH AFRICA.
PRINCETON: U. PR., 1963, 434 PP.
ANALYZES CAUSES AND CHARACTER OF PROFOUND SOCIAL REVOLU- TION IN THE AREA. EXAMINES FORCES, GROUPS, IDEAS, AND INSTI- TUTIONS. ESTIMATES POSSIBLE POLITICAL TREND.

1292 HALPERIN M.H., PERKINS D.H.
COMMUNIST CHINA AND ARMS CONTROL.
CAMBRIDGE: HARV CTR ASIAN STUD, 1965, 191 PP.
ATTEMPTS TO IDENTIFY AND CLARIFY FACTORS AFFECTING FORMULATION OF COMMUNIST CHINA'S POLICIES TOWARD ARMS CONTROL AND DISARMAMENT ISSUES. ASSESSES IMPLICATIONS OF SUCH POLICIES, PARTICULARLY FOR US SECURITY AND ARMS CONTROL OBJECTIVES. CONSIDERS RELEVANT POLITICAL, IDEOLOGICAL, ECONOMIC, TECHNOLOGICAL, MILITARY, AND CULTURAL FACTORS, AS WELL AS HISTORICAL AND TRADITIONAL ATTITUDES OF THE CHINESE.

1293 HALPERIN S.
THE POLITICAL WORLD OF AMERICAN ZIONISM.
DETROIT: WAYNE STATE U PR, 1961, 431 PP., LC#61-10126.
A REMARKABLY COMPLETE STUDY OF THE ORIGINS, WORLD SETTING, CONFLICTS, AND EXTERNAL RELATIONS OF A MOVEMENT THAT LED TO THE STATE OF ISRAEL. RICH CHAPTERS DEAL WITH THE INTERNAL DYNAMICS OF PRESSURE GROUPS, THE ROLE OF IDEOLOGY IN SOCIAL MOVEMENTS, PROPAGANDA TACTICS, DEMOCRACY WITHIN ORGANIZATIONS, AND THE SOCIAL CONTEXT OF THEOLOGY.

1294 HALPERIN S.W.
MUSSOLINI AND ITALIAN FASCISM.
PRINCETON: VAN NOSTRAND, 1964, 191 PP.

STUDIES PROGRESS OF FASCISM 1901-43, FROM ITS ROOTS IN TURN-OF-THE-CENTURY GOVERNMENTAL FORMS, THROUGH SOCIALISM, TO ITS DOWNFALL IN WWII. DISCUSSES RELATION OF FASCISM TO NAZISM, THE CHURCH, PROPAGANDA, AND MUSSOLINI HIMSELF. ATTRIBUTES ITS SUCCESS TO HIS POWER AS A LEADER, AND ITS FAILURE TO HIS WEAKNESS AS A STATESMAN AND AN INTELLECTUAL.

1295 HALPERN A.M.
"THE EMERGENCE OF AN ASIAN COMMUNIST BLOC."
ANN. AMER. ACAD. POLIT. SOC. SCI., 349 (SEPT. 63), 117-29.
DISCUSSES MOVEMENT OF ASIAN COMMUNIST COUNTRIES TOWARDS CHINESE CAMP. ANALYZES RELATIONS OF NORTH KOREA AND NORTH VIETNAM WITH CHINA, 1959-63. ASSESSES POSSIBILITY OF ASIAN COMMUNIST BLOC IN NEAR FUTURE.

1296 HALPERN B.
"THE ORIGINS OF THE CRISIS."
MIDSTREAM, 13 (JUNE-JULY 67), 8-20.
STUDY OF THE BACKGROUND OF MAY, 1967, ISRAELI-ARAB CONFLICT, STEMMING FROM FAILURE TO CONVERT 1948-49 ARMISTICE AGREEMENTS INTO PEACE TREATIES AND DISPUTES REGARDING ITS PROVISIONS, THROUGH CONTINUING DIFFICULTIES AND FAILURES IN THE UN.

1297 HALPERN J.M.
GOVERNMENT, POLITICS, AND SOCIAL STRUCTURE IN LAOS.
NEW HAVEN: YALE U, SE ASIA STUD, 1964, 197 PP., LC#64-16987.
SURVEYS THE NATIONAL AND LOCAL GOVERNMENT OF LAOS. EXAMINES SOME OF THE FUNDAMENTAL PATTERNS OF GOVERNMENTAL STRUCTURE ON BOTH LEVELS, CORRELATING THESE WITH TRADITIONAL FAMILY STRUCTURE AND WITH OBSERVATIONS ON LAOTIAN CHARACTER. DISCUSSES RELIGION, FOREIGN INFLUENCE, CHANGING VALUE SYSTEMS, INDIVIDUAL MOBILITY, AND THE CLASH AND INTERACTION OF ROYAL, WESTERN, AND COMMUNIST SYSTEMS.

1298 HALSEY A.H.
"THE CHANGING FUNCTIONS OF UNIVERSITIES IN ADVANCED INDUSTRIAL SOCIETIES."
HARVARD EDUCATIONAL REV., 30 (SPRING 60), 118-127.
WESTERN CULTURE'S COLLEGES AND UNIVERSITIES, IN ASSUMING ADDED FUNCTIONS OF RESEARCH AND PROFESSIONAL TRAINING, HAVE BECOME MORE CLOSELY INTEGRATED WITH SOCIETY IN GENERAL AND HAVE INCREASED THEIR POTENTIAL AS SOURCES OF ECONOMIC AND SOCIAL CHANGE.

1299 HAMADY S.
TEMPERAMENT AND CHARACTER OF THE ARABS.
NEW YORK: TWAYNE, 1960, 282 PP., LC#60-09942.
STUDIES CHARACTER OF ARABS IN AN ATTEMPT TO EXPLAIN POLITICAL SYSTEMS AND BEHAVIOR. CHANGING NATURE OF INTERNATIONAL RELATIONS HAS PUT EXTREME STRESS ON THESE PEOPLE, MADE POSSIBLE BY FEATURES OF COMMON CULTURAL PERSONALITY. DISCUSSES RELATIONSHIPS, IDENTIFICATION, INTELLECT, AND OUTLOOK.

1300 HAMIL H.M. ED.
DICTATORSHIP IN SPANISH AMERICA.
NEW YORK: ALFRED KNOPF, 1965, 242 PP., LC#64-23731.
ESSAYS DISCUSSING SEVERAL DIVERSE FACTORS WHICH LED TO DEVELOPMENT OF LATIN AMERICAN FORM OF DICTATORSHIP AND WHICH DISTINGUISH IT FROM DICTATORSHIPS OF OTHER REGIONS. DISCUSS ITS ORIGINS IN IBERIA AND ITS DEVELOPMENT IN POLITICAL AND SOCIAL STRIFE OF 19TH CENTURY. CONCLUDE WITH DISCUSSION OF MID-20TH-CENTURY DICTATORSHIPS.

1301 HAMILTON W.B. ED.
THE TRANSFER OF INSTITUTIONS.
DURHAM: DUKE U PR, 1964, 312 PP., LC#64-8539.
ESSAYS ON THE TRANSMISSION OF INSTITUTIONS AND CULTURES FROM BRITAIN TO UNDERDEVELOPED AREAS OF THE WORLD. ANALYZE GENERAL ASPECTS OF THE THEORY AND PROBLEMS INVOLVED IN THE TRANSFER OF INSTITUTIONS. CONSIDER SUCH PROBLEMS MAINLY IN AREAS ALREADY SETTLED WITH ANCIENT CULTURES OF THEIR OWN, RATHER THAN AREAS OPEN TO COLONIZATION.

1302 HAMILTON W.B. ED., ROBINSON K. ED., GOODWIN C.D.W. ED.
A DECADE OF THE COMMONWEALTH, 1955-1964.
DURHAM: DUKE U PR, 1966, 567 PP., LC#65-28466.
DISCUSSES BRITISH COMMONWEALTH 1955-64, INCLUDING INDEPENDENCE OF SOME OF ITS MEMBERS, INTRA-COMMONWEALTH RELATIONS, INTERNATIONAL INTERCHANGE OF INSTITUTIONS AND CULTURE, AND INTERNATIONAL AND ECONOMIC RELATIONS.

1303 HAMILTON W.H., ADAIR D.
THE POWER TO GOVERN.
NEW YORK: W W NORTON, 1937, 249 PP.
DISCUSSES CHARACTER, PARTICULARS, AND EFFECT ON COMMERCE OF THE CONSTITUTION WITH RESPECT TO PUBLIC OPINION, ECONOMY, PROBLEMS IN 1937, AND THE DOCUMENT ITSELF. EXAMINES ASPECTS OF SPECIFIC WARTIME POWERS, TREATIES, TAXES, TARIFFS, AND OTHER MEANS OF ENFORCEMENT. USES HISTORICAL LINGUISTICS TO DETERMINE WHAT CONSTITUTION'S FRAMERS INTENDED BY THEIR PHRASING.

1304 HAMM H.
ALBANIA - CHINA'S BEACHHEAD IN EUROPE.
NEW YORK: FREDERICK PRAEGER, 1963, 176 PP., LC#63-14679.
STUDY OF ALBANIAN POLITICS AND SOCIETY EMPHASIZES RELATIONS WITH RED CHINA AND USSR, ALBANIA'S FINAL SPLIT WITH THE SOVIET UNION AND ALLEGIANCE TO RED CHINA, AND THE DOMESTIC CONDITIONS AND IDEOLOGICAL BASIS FOR THE SHIFT, INCLUDING EVENTS OF THE TWENTY-SECOND PARTY CONGRESS.

1305 HAMMER E.J.
"THE STRUGGLE FOR INDOCHINA."
STANFORD: STANFORD U PRESS, 1954.
HISTORY OF INDOCHINA FROM WWII TO 1954. DESCRIPTION AND ANALYSIS OF JAPANESE, FRENCH, AND COMMUNIST INFLUENCES ON NATIONAL DEVELOPMENT. DISCUSSION OF POLITICAL DEVELOPMENTS AS INFLUENCED BY INTERNATIONAL AFFAIRS AND INTERNAL CRISES. INCLUDES SELECTED BIBLIOGRAPHY OF GOVERNMENT DOCUMENTS, BOOKS, AND ARTICLES.

1306 HAMMOND B.
BANKS AND POLITICS IN AMERICA FROM THE REVOLUTION TO THE CIVIL WAR.
PRINCETON: PRINCETON U PRESS, 1957, 771 PP., LC#57-8667.
STUDIES THE POLITICAL AND CULTURAL FORCE OF BUSINESS ENTERPRISE AS ILLUSTRATED IN THE HISTORY OF BANKS. GIVES SOME ATTENTION TO PARALLEL POLITICAL AND ECONOMIC HISTORY IN CANADA.

1307 HAMMOND B.E.
THE POLITICAL INSTITUTIONS OF THE ANCIENT GREEKS.
LONDON: CLAY & SONS, 1895, 122 PP.
SCIENTIFIC AND COMPARATIVE STUDY OF GREEK POLITICAL INSTITUTIONS WITHIN FRAMEWORK OF EUROPEAN POLITICAL BODIES. DISCUSSES SPARTA, GREEK CITIES, THE ACHAEAN LEAGUE, AND ARISTOTLE'S CONCEPTION OF A POLITY.

1308 HAMMOND M.
"CITY-STATE AND WORLD STATE."
CAMBRIDGE: HARVARD U PR, 1951.
TRACES CONFLICT IN POLITICAL THOUGHT BETWEEN DOMINANT POLITICAL CONCEPT OF CITY-STATE, AS ESTABLISHED BY PLATO AND ARISTOTLE, AND PRESSING NEED TO FIND THEORETICAL BASIS FOR LARGER POLITICAL ORGANIZATIONS WHICH AROSE IN LATER GREEK AND ROMAN PERIODS. INTENDED FOR STUDENT OF GENERAL HISTORY OF POLITICAL THEORY. UNANNOTATED, TOPICALLY ARRANGED BIBLIOGRAPHY OF REFERENCES AND DISCUSSIONS OF MODERN RESEARCH.

1309 HAMMOND R.J.
"RACE ATTITUDES AND POLICIES IN PORTUGUESE AFRICA IN THE NINETEENTH AND TWENTIETH CENTURIES."
RACE, 9 (OCT. 67), 205-216.
BELIEVES THAT A MULTIRACIAL SOCIETY EXISTED ONLY IN COASTAL REGIONS WHERE POPULATION CONSISTED OF OFFICIALS AND DEPORTED CRIMINALS. REVIEWS BOOKS AND GOVERNMENT REPORTS THAT DECRY ATTEMPTS TO RAISE STANDARD OF NEGRO SOCIETY AND EDUCATION TO THAT OF WHITES. PRIVATE MORALS AND PUBLIC POLICY ARE NOW AT VARIANCE, AND IT WILL TAKE A PROGRAM OF EDUCATION AND INDOCTRINATION TO ELIMINATE PREJUDICE.

1310 HAMSON C.J.
EXECUTIVE DISCRETION AND JUDICIAL CONTROL; AN ASPECT OF THE FRENCH CONSEIL D'ETAT.
LONDON: STEVENS, 1954, 222 PP.
STUDIES THE FRENCH POLITICAL INSTITUTION, DISCUSSING THE PROCEDURES AND RESPONSIBILITY OF THE CONSEIL. PRESENTS THE HISTORICAL DEVELOPMENTS AND EXAMINES THE PRINCIPLES UPON WHICH THE CONSEIL D'ETAT WORKS AS THE HIGHEST COURT IN FRANCE. CONCLUDES WITH A COMPARISON OF THE ENGLISH AND THE FRENCH JUDICIAL SYSTEM AT THIS HIGH LEVEL.

1311 HANAK H.
GREAT BRITAIN AND AUSTRIA-HUNGARY DURING THE FIRST WORLD WAR: A STUDY IN THE FORMATION OF PUBLIC OPINION.
LONDON: OXFORD U PR, 1962, 312 PP.
DISCUSSES BRITISH PRESS ATTITUDES TOWARD AUSTRIA-HUNGARY AND WWI. DESCRIBES YUGOSLAV PROPAGANDA EFFORTS AND WORK OF SERBIAN RELIEF FUND. STUDIES CZECHS IN ENGLAND AND BRITISH OPPOSITION TO DISMEMBERMENT OF AUSTRIA-HUNGARY. DISCUSSES CHANGING ATTITUDES OF BRITISH PRESS TOWARD AUSTRIA-HUNGARY AT END OF WAR.

1312 HANCE W.A.
AFRICAN ECONOMIC DEVELOPMENT.
NEW YORK: HARPER & ROW, 1958, 307 PP., LC#58-7060.
SERIES OF STUDIES WHOSE COMMON THEME IS ECONOMIC DEVELOPMENT IN AFRICA SOUTH OF THE SAHARA. INCLUDES CASES IN AGRICULTURAL AND INDUSTRIAL DEVELOPMENT, ANALYSIS OF TRANSPORT PROBLEMS IN TROPICAL AFRICA, AND PAPERS CONCERNED WITH INDIVIDUAL AFRICAN AREAS - LIBERIA, CENTRAL AFRICA, MADAGASCAR. INCLUDES SELECTED BIBLIOGRAPHY.

1313 HANKE L. ED.
HANDBOOK OF LATIN AMERICAN STUDIES.
GAINESVILLE: U OF FLA PR, 1966, 424 PP., LC#36-32633.
PUBLISHED ANNUALLY SINCE 1935, THE HANDBOOK IS A GUIDE TO WORKS ON LATIN AMERICA IN THE HUMANITIES AND THE SOCIAL SCIENCES, DIFFERENT FIELDS BEING SELECTED EACH YEAR.

INTRODUCTORY ARTICLES ARE INCLUDED. ANNOTATED.

1314 HANNA A.J.
EUROPEAN RULE IN AFRICA (PAMPHLET)
LONDON: ROUTLEDGE & KEGAN PAUL, 1961, 36 PP.
HISTORY OF EUROPEAN COLONIALISM IN AFRICA IN LAST CENTURY. TRACES EXPANSION INTO CONTINENT, BY COUNTRY, PERIOD BEFORE WWII, PERIOD OF NATIONALISM AND FOUNDATION OF STATES, 1940-60.

1315 HANNA W.J., HANNA J.L.
POLITICS IN BLACK AFRICA: A SELECTIVE BIBLIOGRAPHY OF RELEVANT PERIODICAL LITERATURE.
EAST LANSING: MICHIGAN STATE U, 1964, 139 PP., LC#64-64995.
LIST OF PERIODICAL ARTICLES SPECIFICALLY DESIGNED FOR SOCIAL SCIENTIST SPECIALIZING IN AFRICAN AFFAIRS. LISTS 1,283 ITEMS IN FRENCH AND ENGLISH ON TRADITION AND CHANGE, COMMUNICATION, URBANIZATION, ECONOMY, COLONIALISM, NATIONALISM, LOCAL AND NATIONAL GOVERNMENT, LAW, INFLUENTIALS, POLITICAL PARTIES AND SELECTIONS, RACE RELATIONS, LABOR, AND INTERNATIONAL AFFAIRS.

1316 HANRIEDER W.F.
WEST GERMAN FOREIGN POLICY 1949-1963: INTERNATIONAL PRESSURE AND DOMESTIC RESPONSE.
STANFORD: STANFORD U PRESS, 1967, 275 PP., LC#67-13657.
DISCUSSES RELATIONSHIP BETWEEN WEST GERMAN FOREIGN POLICY GOALS AND CONDITIONS OF EXTERNAL OPERATIONAL ENVIRONMENT IN WHICH THEY ARE PURSUED. EXAMINES RELATIONSHIPS BETWEEN FOREIGN POLICY GOALS AND INTERNATIONAL MOTIVATIONAL ENVIRONMENT, SHOWING ROLE OF GOVERNING COALITIONS AND PRESSURE GROUPS. RELATES EXTERNAL DIMENSIONS OF POLICY OBJECTIVES TO INTERNAL DIMENSIONS.

1317 HANSARD SOCIETY PARL GOVT
WHAT ARE THE PROBLEMS OF PARLIAMENTARY GOVERNMENT IN WEST AFRICA?
LONDON: CHISWICK PRESS, 1958, 168 PP.
COLLECTION OF ESSAYS ON POLITICAL DEVELOPMENTS IN WEST AFRICA. DISCUSSES ROLE OF POLITICAL PARTIES AND PARLIAMENTARY PROCESS. ASSUMES THAT "FUNDAMENTAL PROBLEM IS TO ADAPT BRITISH PARLIAMENTARY INSTITUTIONS TO WEST AFRICA."

1318 HANSER C.J.
GUIDE TO DECISION: ROYAL COMMISSION.
TOTOWA: BEDMINSTER PR, 1965, 274 PP., LC#65-24957.
DESCRIBES FUNCTION OF ROYAL COMMISSION OF GREAT BRITAIN, THAT COUNTRY'S RANKING INVESTIGATORY AND ADVISORY BODY, IN DETERMINING GOVERNMENT POLICY AND ACTION. CITES COMMISSION INQUIRIES AND ACTIONS REGARDING POLICE, CIVIL SERVICE, DIVORCE, BRITISH COAL INDUSTRY, EDUCATION, HEALTH AS EXAMPLES. DESCRIBES MEMBERSHIP, METHODS OF OPERATION, AND PROBLEMS OF THE COMMISSION. SUGGESTS CREATION OF EQUIVALENT US BODY.

1319 HANSON A.H.
THE STRUCTURE AND CONTROL OF STATE ENTERPRISES IN TURKEY.
ANKARA: PUBLIC ADMIN INST, 1959, 24 PP.
ANALYZES SYSTEM OF STATE ENTERPRISES, DEFINES FEW MAIN PROBLEMS, AND MAKES SUGGESTIONS FOR THEIR SOLUTIONS. EMPHASIZES DEVELOPMENTS AND CHANGES IN SYSTEM TO 1959. STRESSES AREAS OF ORGANIZATION AND STATE CONTROL OR RESPONSIBILITY.

1320 HANSON A.H.
MANAGERIAL PROBLEMS IN PUBLIC ENTERPRISE.
NEW YORK: ASIA PUBL HOUSE, 1962, 148 PP.
ANALYZES PROBLEMS OF MANAGEMENT IN PUBLIC ENTERPRISE SUCH AS ORGANIZATIONAL FORMS, PARLIAMENTARY ACCOUNTABILITY, RELATIONS WITH MINISTERS, EFFICIENCY, AND PRICE AND PROFIT POLICIES. INCLUDES TYPES OF PUBLIC ENTERPRISE AND THEIR RELATIONS WITH STATE. DISCUSSES EXPERIENCES AND SOLUTIONS OF OTHER AREAS OF WORLD AS THEY APPLY TO PROBLEMS IN INDIA.

1321 HANSON A.H.
"INDIA AFTER THE ELECTIONS."
WORLD TODAY, 23 (MAY 67), 188-197.
DESCRIBES THE IMPACT OF NEHRU S DEATH ON THE CURRENT POLITICAL SCENE. SUGGESTS THAT LEADERSHIP VACUUM AND THE GRADUAL DECLINE OF CONGRESS AS A POLITICAL AND ELECTORAL FORCE HAVE CREATED THE THREAT OF DEFECTION TO COMMUNIST OR ANTI-CONGRESS PARTIES. SUGGESTS INFLUENCE OF THE SHIFT IN POLITICAL GRAVITY FROM DELHI TO THE STATE CAPITALS. WARNS OF THE IMMEDIATE DANGER OF "BALKANIZATION" AND POLITICAL CRISIS.

1322 HANSON J.W. ED., BREMBECK C.S. ED.
EDUCATION AND THE DEVELOPMENT OF NATIONS.
NEW YORK: HOLT RINEHART WINSTON, 1966, 529 PP., LC#66-10088.
ANTHOLOGY ON IMPACT OF EDUCATION IN FORMATION OF DEVELOPING NATIONS. DISCUSSES WORLD TASK, ETHICS, ECONOMIC FACTORS, PLANNING, AND INTERNATIONAL CONTRIBUTIONS OF EDUCATION.

1323 HAPGOOD D.
AFRICA: FROM INDEPENDENCE TO TOMORROW.
NEW YORK: ATHENEUM PUBLISHERS, 1965, 221 PP., LC#65-15912.
STRESSES CURRENT THEMES OF INDEPENDENT BLACK AFRICA: PROBLEMS OF ECONOMY AND GOVERNMENT; EFFECTS OF FOREIGN AID; URBANIZATION; AND EDUCATION.

1324 HAQ M.
THE STRATEGY OF ECONOMIC PLANNING.
LONDON: OXFORD U PR, 1963, 266 PP.
DETAILED CASE STUDY OF ECONOMIC PLANNING AND DEVELOPMENT IN PAKISTAN, FOCUSING LARGELY ON THREE FIVE YEAR PLANS FROM 1955 TO 1965. DISCUSSES GENERAL CONCEPTS AND RATIONALE BEHIND KEY PLANNING DECISIONS AND PROVIDES THOROUGHLY DOCUMENTED ACCOUNTS OF PROGRESS MADE DURING FIVE YEAR PLANS.

1325 HARBISON F.H., ED., MEYERS C.A., ED.
MANPOWER AND EDUCATION.
NEW YORK: MCGRAW HILL, 1965, 343 PP., LC#64-20529.
CONCERNS PROCESSES OF HUMAN RESOURCE DEVELOPMENT AND THEIR RELATIONSHIP TO ECONOMIC GROWTH IN NEW DEVELOPING NATIONS. DETAILED PICTURE OF INDIVIDUAL COUNTRIES RATHER THAN GENERAL ANALYSIS; MAKES SUMMARY OF PRINCIPLES EVIDENT IN ALL CASES. EMPHASIS ON EFFECT OF EDUCATION.

1326 HARBISON F.H., MYERS C.A.
EDUCATION, MANPOWER, AND ECONOMIC GROWTH.
NEW YORK: MCGRAW HILL, 1964, 229 PP., LC#63-20723.
ANALYSIS OF ECONOMIC, POLITICAL, AND SOCIAL DEVELOPMENT FROM PERSPECTIVE OF EDUCATION, TRAINING, AND ENERGIZING OF HUMAN RESOURCES. A POLICY-ORIENTED WORK, MORE CONCERNED WITH STUDYING APPROPRIATE POLICIES AND STRATEGIES OF HUMAN RESOURCE DEVELOPMENT THAN ESTIMATING THE RETURNS ON INVESTMENTS IN MAN. PROVIDES A GLOBAL ANALYSIS OF HUMAN RESOURCE DEVELOPMENT, QUANTITATIVELY AND QUALITATIVELY.

1327 HARBRON J.D.
"UNIFICATION IN CANADA: FAIT ACCOMPLI"
US NAVAL INSTITUTE PROCEEDINGS, 93 (AUG. 67), 76-86.
DISCUSSES RECENT SUCCESSFUL UNIFICATION OF ROYAL CANADIAN NAVY AND IMPORTANT ROLE OF DEFENSE MINISTER P.T. HELLYER. ANALYZES PROBLEMS OF MORALE AND PERSONNEL ATTITUDES THAT HE SHOULD HAVE SOLVED. RECOMMENDS THAT NATIONS ATTEMPTING SUCH MILITARY UNIFICATION RECOGNIZE IMPORTANCE OF HUMAN ELEMENT IN A RAPIDLY CHANGING SYSTEM.

1328 HARDT J.P.
THE COLD WAR ECONOMIC GAP.
NEW YORK: FREDERICK PRAEGER, 1961, 112 PP., LC#61-10509.
DISCUSSION OF US AND SOVIET ECONOMIC STRENGTH; MAINTAINS THAT GAP BETWEEN TWO COUNTRIES HAS NARROWED CONSIDERABLY. OUTLINES POLICIES INTENDED TO INCREASE US ECONOMIC POWER.

1329 HARDY M.J.L.
BLOOD FEUDS AND THE PAYMENT OF BLOOD MONEY IN THE MIDDLE EAST.
LEYDEN: BRILL, 1963, 106 PP.
STUDY OF CUSTOM OF BLOOD MONEY IN TRIBAL LAW OF NOMADIC PEOPLES IN OUTLYING PARTS OF ARABIAN PENINSULA. DISCUSSES ROOTS OF CUSTOM IN ANCIENT ARAB HISTORY AND RECENT MODIFICATION AND COMPROMISE WITH MODERN LEGAL PROCESSES OWING TO INTERVENTION OF SECULAR AUTHORITY.

1330 HARE T.
A TREATISE ON THE ELECTION OF REPRESENTATIVES, PARLIAMENTARY AND MUNICIPAL.
LONDON: LONGMANS, GREEN & CO, 1861, 338 PP.
ANALYSIS OF REPRESENTATIVE GOVERNMENT INCLUDES THESE SUBJECTS: RIGHTS OF MAJORITY AND MINORITY, HARMONY THROUGH VOLUNTARY ASSOCIATION, CREATION OF CONSTITUENCIES, ELECTORAL SYSTEM, SELECTION OF REPRESENTATIVES, AND ACTUAL PROBLEMS AND DUTIES INVOLVED IN ELECTION. THOROUGH STUDY BASED ON ENGLISH SYSTEM AFTER ACT OF 1832, WHICH MADE REPRESENTATION MORE DIRECT AND ON A WIDER BASIS.

1331 HARIOU M.
LA SOUVERAINTE NATIONALE.
ORIGINAL PUBLISHER NOT AVAILABLE, 1912, 154 PP.
QUESTIONS WHETHER NATIONAL SOVEREIGNTY, STATE SOVEREIGNTY, AND ELECTORAL SOVEREIGNTY ARE THE SAME THING. BELIEVES THAT THE STATE IS THE NATION AND VICE VERSA. CONCEPT OF STATE IS INDIVISIBLE, WHILE IDEA OF NATIONS CAN BE BROKEN INTO DIFFERENT ELEMENTS. POWERS OF GOVERNMENT ARE AUTONOMOUS AND NOT DIRECTED BY GENERAL WILL. ELECTORAL WILL SHOULD BE ORGANIZED AS A POWER OF GOVERNMENT.

1332 HARLEY G.W.
MASKS AS AGENTS OF SOCIAL CONTROL IN NORTHEAST LIBERIA.
CAMBRIDGE: HARVARD U PEABODY MUS, 1950, 70 PP.
ANTHROPOLOGIST SHOWS HOW A SOCIETY WAS GOVERNED BY CHIEFS WHO SUPPOSEDLY INVOKED SPIRIT OF ANCESTORS CONTAINED IN MASKS AS METHOD OF CONTROLLING POPULATION.

1333 HARLOW R.V.
THE HISTORY OF LEGISLATIVE METHODS IN THE PERIOD BEFORE 1825
NEW HAVEN: YALE U PR, 1917, 269 PP., LC#17-30135.
TRACES GROWTH OF COMMITTEE SYSTEMS IN LAWMAKING BODIES OF COLONIES AND STATES FROM 1750 TO 1790, AND IN HOUSE OF REPRESENTATIVES FROM BEGINNING TO 1825. DISCUSSES BOTH FORMAL ORGANIZATION, PROVIDED BY RULES, AND INFORMAL, SUPPLIED BY POLITICAL PARTIES.

1334 HARMON R.B.
POLITICAL SCIENCE: A BIBLIOGRAPHICAL GUIDE TO THE LITERATURE
METUCHEN: SCARECROW PRESS, 1965, 388 PP., LC#65-13557.
UNANNOTATED COMPILATION OF 2,500 ENGLISH-LANGUAGE BOOKS PUBLISHED 1859 THROUGH 1963. INCLUDES SEPARATE INDEXES FOR JOURNALS, GOVERNMENT DOCUMENTS, AND AUTHORS. ENTRIES DIVIDED INTO TEN GENERAL CATEGORIES AND THEN SUBDIVIDED. INCLUDES SECTION ON GENERAL REFERENCE WORKS AND BIBLIOGRAPHIES AND A SECTION ON RESEARCH AND METHODOLOGY IN POLITICAL SCIENCE. EXCELLENT AND THOROUGH COVERAGE OF POLITICAL SCIENCE.

1335 HARMON R.B.
SOURCES AND PROBLEMS OF BIBLIOGRAPHY IN POLITICAL SCIENCE (PAMPHLET)
SAN JOSE: DIBCO PRESS, 1966, 73 PP., LC#66-18521.
A REVISED AND ENLARGED EDITION OF THE AUTHOR'S "BIBLIOGRAPHY OF BIBLIOGRAPHIES IN POLITICAL SCIENCE." MOST COMPREHENSIVE LISTING OF BIBLIOGRAPHIES, CURRENT AND RETROSPECTIVE, IN POLITICAL SCIENCE. INDEXED UNDER GENERAL TOPICS. SEPARATE AUTHOR-TITLE INDEX AND SEPARATE LISTING OF BIBLIOGRAPHIC PERIODICALS. GOOD SECTION ON GENERAL BIBLIOGRAPHIES OF VALUE TO POLITICAL SCIENCE. 244 ENTRIES.

1336 HARNON E.
"CRIMINAL PROCEDURE IN ISRAEL - SOME COMPARATIVE ASPECTS."
U. PENN. LAW REV., 115 (MAY 67), 1091-1110.
DESCRIBES PRE-1965 RULES OF CRIMINAL PROCEDURE IN ISRAEL: A COMBINATION OF OTTOMAN LAW, LEGISLATION OF BRITISH MANDATE, AND AMENDMENTS INTRODUCED BY STATE OF ISRAEL. DISCUSSES NEW CRIMINAL LEGISLATION OF 1965, ITS PROVISIONS FOR ADVERSARY SYSTEM, PROSECUTION, JURY, AND FAIR TRIAL. COMPARES NEW ISRAELI SYSTEM WITH AMERICAN, SHOWING HOW ISRAEL HAS TRIED TO SHORTEN AND SIMPLIFY LEGAL PROCEEDINGS.

1337 HARPER S.N.
THE GOVERNMENT OF THE SOVIET UNION.
PRINCETON: VAN NOSTRAND, 1938, 204 PP.
DISCUSSES SOVIET INSTITUTIONS, GOVERNMENTAL STRUCTURES, AND METHODS OF GOVERNING IMMEDIATELY PRECEDING AND AFTER BOLSHEVIK RISE TO POWER. INCLUDES ECONOMIC STRUCTURES AND PLANS, PARTY POLICY, LAW-MAKING, PUBLIC ADMINISTRATION, AND PUBLIC SERVICES. ALSO TREATS ROLE OF INDIVIDUAL IN A COLLECTIVIZED STATE, INTERNATIONAL RELATIONSHIPS, GOAL OF WORLD REVOLUTION, AND 1937-38 TREASON TRIALS.

1338 HARRINGTON M.
THE OTHER AMERICA: POVERTY IN THE UNITED STATES.
LONDON: MACMILLAN, 1962, 191 PP., LC#62-8555.
A STUDY OF THE ECONOMIC UNDERWORLD OF MIGRANT FARM WORKERS, THE AGED, MINORITY GROUPS, AND OTHER ECONOMICALLY UNDERPRIVILEGED CLASSES. OFFERS PROPOSITION THAT POVERTY FORMS A CULTURE, NECESSITATING NEW COMMUNITIES, AND OFFERS VALUABLE BACKGROUND FOR FUNCTIONAL REPRESENTATION DEVELOPING IN CONNECTION WITH THE ECONOMIC OPPORTUNITY ACT OF 1964.

1339 HARRIS G.M.
COMPARATIVE LOCAL GOVERNMENT.
LONDON: HUTCHINSON U LIBRARY, 1948, 207 PP.
SURVEYS LOCAL GOVERNMENT IN EUROPE, US, AND RUSSIA. EMPHASIS IS PLACED ON AREAS OF FINANCE AND METHOD OF SELECTION OF OFFICIALS. ALSO COMPARES THE RESPECTIVE GOVERNMENT SERVICES.

1340 HARRIS M.
"THE NATURE OF CULTURAL THINGS."
NEW YORK: RANDOM HOUSE, INC, 1964.
REFERENCES INCLUDE WORKS IN PHILOSOPHY, ANTHROPOLOGY, PSYCHOLOGY, SOCIOLOGY, AND HISTORY WHICH ARE RELEVANT TO AUTHOR'S THESIS. ONLY MOST RECENT WORKS CITED, WITH SEVERAL ARTICLES AND PAMPHLETS.

1341 HARRIS M.
THE NATURE OF CULTURAL THINGS.
NEW YORK: RANDOM HOUSE, INC, 1964, 209 PP., LC#67-19713.
EXPLANATION OF ASPECTS OF CULTURE GROUNDED IN NONVERBAL BEHAVIOR OF INDIVIDUALS. GOAL IS SEPARATION OF EXPLANATION OF "CULTURAL ITEMS" FROM THEIR DEFINITION. DESCRIBES SYSTEM OF CULTURAL INQUIRY BASED ON OBSERVATION OF BEHAVIORAL STREAMS OF EVENTS: ACTIONS OF NONVERBAL THING (BODY PART) AND ENVIRONMENTAL EFFECTS OF THE ACTION. SMALL STREAMS OF EVENTS COMBINE TO FORM VARIOUS CLASSIFIABLE CULTURE INDEXES.

1342 HARRIS M.
PATTERNS OF RACE IN THE AMERICAS.
NEW YORK: WALKER, 1964, 154 PP., LC#64-23054.
DESCRIBES CULTURES OF NORTH AND SOUTH AMERICAN INDIANS. ANTHROPOLOGICAL IN CONTEXT, WORK INCLUDES DISCUSSION OF RELIGION, MISCEGENATION, SLAVERY, AND VILLAGE LIFE. EMPHASIZES HISTORY OF THE AMERICAN INDIANS SINCE THE CONQUISTADORES.

1343 HARRIS R.L., KEARNEY R.N.
"A COMPARATIVE ANALYSIS OF THE ADMINISTRATIVE SYSTEMS OF CANADA AND CEYLON."
ADMIN. SCI. QUART., 8 (DEC. 63), 339-60.
ATTEMPTS TO IDENTIFY CULTURAL VARIABLES INFLUENCING PUBLIC ADMINISTRATION IN AN INDUSTRIALLY WELL-DEVELOPED WESTERN NATION AND A DEVELOPING NEW STATE. UTILIZES AN ECOLOGICAL-ENVIRONMENTAL APPROACH, A NEW TECHNIQUE OF COMPARATIVE ANALYSIS FOR THE STUDY OF FOREIGN SYSTEMS OF PUBLIC ADMINISTRATION.

1344 HARRIS R.L.
"COMMUNISM AND ASIA: ILLUSIONS AND MISCONCEPTIONS."
INT. AFF., 39 (JAN. 63), 13-23.
DISCUSSES PREREQUISITES NEEDED FOR COMMUNIST EXPANSION THROUGHOUT ASIA. MAINTAINS THAT INTERNAL COMMUNIST PARTY NECESSARY FOR PENETRATION. REVIEWS CURRENT EVENTS IN SOUTHEAST ASIA AND FORMS ESTIMATES ON INEVITABILITY OF COMMUNISM IN THIS AREA.

1345 HARRIS R.L.
POLITICAL ORGANIZATION OF THE MBEMBE NIGERIA.
LONDON: MIN OF OVERSEAS DEVEL, 1965, 224 PP.
STUDY OF MBEMBE POLITICAL INSTITUTIONS FOCUSING PRIMARILY ON CHIEFSHIP AND ITS RELATION TO MBEMBE SOCIAL STRUCTURE. ALSO DISCUSSES CULTURAL AND POLITICAL VARIATIONS AMONG SEPARATE MBEMBE TRIBES.

1346 HARRISON B.
SOUTH-EAST ASIA: A SHORT HISTORY (3RD ED.)
NEW YORK: ST MARTIN'S PRESS, 1966, 278 PP., LC#66-13529.
WRITTEN FOR THE GENERAL READER AND STUDENT, NOT THE SPECIALIST SCHOLAR. OFFERS INTRODUCTION TO HISTORY OF SOUTHEAST ASIAN COUNTRIES TO THE PRESENT. DISCUSSES COLONIAL INFLUENCES ON RELIGION, CULTURE, ECONOMY, AND POLITICS.

1347 HARRISON S.S.
INDIA: THE MOST DANGEROUS DECADE.
PRINCETON: PRINCETON U PRESS, 1960, 350 PP., LC#60-5749.
STUDY OF INDIA IN 1960'S PROBES NATURE OF HER PECULIAR CHALLENGE AND DEFINES ISSUES CRUCIAL TO HER FUTURE: REGIONALISM IN LANGUAGE, CULTURE, AND POLITICS; NEW CASTE LOBBIES; GRAND STRATEGY OF INDIAN COMMUNISM; PARTY POLITICS. EXAMINES CHANCES FOR NATIONAL SURVIVAL, DECIDING THAT SURVIVAL IS POSSIBLE, BUT HER "DEMOCRACY" WILL SEEM TOTALITARIAN BY WESTERN DEFINITIONS.

1348 HART B.H.L.
THE MEMOIRS OF CAPTAIN LIDDELL HART (VOL. I)
LONDON: CASSELL & CO LTD, 1965, 434 PP.
AUTOBIOGRAPHY OF CAPTAIN IN BRITISH ARMY; COVERS YEARS 1914-1937. BEGINS WITH YOUTH AND EARLY CAREER AS A MILITARY CORRESPONDENT; DISCUSSES NEW CONCEPTIONS OF MECHANIZED WARFARE, INTRODUCTION OF MECHANIZED FORCES AND AIRPOWER, MILITARY DEVELOPMENTS, FRUSTRATIONS, AND BRITAIN'S STRATEGIC POLICY. INCLUDES DISCUSSION OF LLOYD GEORGE AND T. E. LAWRENCE.

1349 HARTLEY A.
A STATE OF ENGLAND.
NEW YORK: HILLARY HOUSE PUBL, 1963, 255 PP.
STUDY OF BRITISH SOCIETY SINCE WWII AND IMPACT OF REDUCTION OF WORLD POSITION ON INTELLECTUAL COMMUNITY. INDICATES SENSE OF FRUSTRATION HAS HIT PEOPLE AS RESULT OF POOR ECONOMIC CONDITIONS AND LOSS OF WORLD PRESTIGE. EXAMINES STATUS OF WELFARE STATE, INTELLECTUAL ATTITUDE, FOREIGN AFFAIRS, AND EDUCATIONAL SYSTEM AS REMEDIES FOR NATIONAL DECLINE.

1350 HARTUNG F.
ENLIGHTENED DESPOTISM (PAMPHLET)
LONDON: LONDON HISTORICAL ASSN, 1957, 32 PP.
CHARACTERIZES ENLIGHTENED DESPOTISM AS "ENLIGHTENED ABSOLUTISM" SO AS TO DISTINGUISH IT FROM TYRANNY. ABSOLUTISM DEFINED AS A MONARCHICAL GOVERNMENT NOT LIMITED BY A REPRESENTATIVE OR OTHER AUTONOMOUS BODY. ENGLIGHTENED ABSOLUTISM IS DEFINED AS A FORM OF GOVERNMENT PARTICULARLY INFLUENCED BY THE POLITICAL PHILOSOPHY OF THE ENLIGHTENMENT. CONSIDERS FREDERICK THE GREAT AND OTHERS.

1351 HARVARD WIDENER LIBRARY
INDOCHINA: A SELECTED LIST OF REFERENCES.
CAMBRIDGE: HARVARD, WIDENER LIB, 1945, 108 PP.
LISTING OF MAINLY FRENCH-LANGUAGE WORKS IN THE WIDENER LIBRARY AT HARVARD. ARRANGED BY COUNTRY AND TOPIC. SOME WORKS ARE ANNOTATED.

1352 HASSAN M.F.
"THE SECOND FOUR-YEAR PLAN OF VENEZUELA."
J. INTER-AMER. STUDIES, 10 (1967), 296-320.
EVALUATION OF VENEZUELA'S FOUR-YEAR PLAN SURVEYS ITS OBJECTIVES AND CRITICIZES THE FEASIBILITY OF ITS METHODS. NDICATES THAT FASTER GROWTH RATE, HIGHER RATE OF EMPLOYMENT, AND ECONOMIC DIVERSIFICATION COULD BE ACHIEVED THROUGH "IMPROVEMENT OF THE INVESTMENT CLIMATE" AND THAT THIS IS POSSIBLE UNDER SOUND POLICY MANAGEMENT.

1353 HATCH J.
AFRICA TODAY-AND TOMORROW: AN OUTLINE OF BASIC FACTS AND

MAJOR PROBLEMS.
NEW YORK: PRAEGER, 1962, 343 PP., $4.00.
GENERAL SURVEY OF HISTORICAL BACKGROUND OF AFRICAN TERRITORIES. COUNTRY BY COUNTRY EXAMINATION OF POLITICAL AND CONSTITUTIONAL DEVELOPMENTS - ECONOMIC AND SOCIAL PROBLEMS. CONCLUDES WITH OBSERVATIONS ON BROAD ISSUES: PAN-AFRICANISM, REACTIONS TO COLD WAR, ROLE IN UN, AND RACIAL PREJUDICES.

1354 HATCH J.C.
NEW FROM AFRICA.
LONDON: DENNIS DOBSON, 1956, 123 PP.
RECORD OF TWO-MONTH TRIP TO TEN AFRICAN COUNTRIES ON EVE OF INDEPENDENCE, WITH SUGGESTIONS FOR FUTURE OF BRITISH AFRICA.

1355 HATTERSLEY A.F.
A SHORT HISTORY OF DEMOCRACY.
NEW YORK: CAMBRIDGE U PRESS, 1930, 274 PP.
SURVEYS HISTORY OF DEMOCRATIC GOVERNMENT, EXAMINES FORMS AND PRINCIPLES OF DEMOCRACY, AND OUTLINES PROCESS THROUGH WHICH DEMOCRATIC INSTITUTIONS HAVE GONE. BEGINS WITH MEANING OF DEMOCRACY AND DISCUSSES DEMOCRACY IN ATHENS AND ROME. COVERS DEMOCRATIC THOUGHT IN MIDDLE AGES AND INFLUENCE OF REFORMATION ON DEVELOPMENT OF DEMOCRACY. CONCLUDING CHAPTERS TREAT 19TH- AND 20TH-CENTURY DEMOCRACIES.

1356 HATTICH M.
NATIONALBEWUSSTSEIN UND STAATSBEWUSSTSEIN IN DER PLURALISTISCHEN GESELLSCHAFT.
MAINZ: V HASE UND KOHLER VERL, 1966, 126 PP.
DISCUSSES NATURE OF STATE AND NATION AND POLITICAL CONSCIOUSNESS IN PLURALISTIC SOCIETY. MAINTAINS THAT FUNCTIONAL CONCEPTION OF STATE PREVENTS ITS GLORIFICATION AND FACILITATES OBJECTIVE CONSCIOUSNESS OF STATE.

1357 HAUSER M.
DIE URSACHEN DER FRANZOSISCHEN INFLATION IN DEN JAHREN 1946-1952.
WINTERTHUR: P G KELLER, 1961, 105 PP.
DISCUSSES THEORETICAL BASIS AND GENERAL DEVELOPMENT OF FRENCH INFLATION BETWEEN 1946 AND 1952. EXAMINES PRICE DEVELOPMENTS, SUPPLY OF MONEY TO PRIVATE AND PUBLIC SECTOR OF ECONOMY, AND CHANGES IN GOLD AND CREDIT STANDARDS ABROAD.

1358 HAUSER O.
PREUSSISCHE STAATSRASON UND NATIONALER GEDANKE.
NEUMUNSTER: KARL WACHHOLTZ VERL, 1960, 285 PP.
DISCUSSES ORIGINS OF PRUSSIAN ADMINISTRATION IN SCHLESWIG-HOLSTEIN, NATIONAL MOVEMENTS, AND ATTITUDE TOWARD LANGUAGE PROBLEM IN NORTHERN SCHLESWIG. EXAMINES BROADER IMPLICATIONS OF CULTURAL NATIONALISM IN SCHLESWIG-HOLSTEIN BETWEEN 1860 AND 1920.

1359 HAUSER P. ED., SCHNORE L.F. ED.
THE STUDY OF URBANIZATION.
NEW YORK: JOHN WILEY, 1965, 554 PP., LC#65-24223.
PRESENTS AN INVENTORY AND APPRAISAL OFTHE STUDY OF URBANIZATION IN SUCH FIELDS AS ECONOMICS, GEOGRAPHY, HISTORY, POLITICAL SCIENCE, SOCIOLOGY, AND ANTHROPOLOGY. POINTS OUT GAPS IN KNOWLEDGE IN BOTH ANTECEDENTS AND CONSEQUENCES OF URBANIZATION. INDICATES THE IMPORTANCE OF CROSS-CULTURAL RESEARCH, ESPECIALLY IN DEVELOPING AREAS. ESSAYS BY W. S. SAYRE AND N. POLSBY, O. LEWIS, G. SJOBERG, ET AL.

1360 HAUSER R.
AUTORITAT UND MACHT.
HEIDELBERG: VERLAG L SCHNEIDER, 1949, 431 PP.
DISCUSSES NATURE OF STATE AND AUTHORITY AS CONCEIVED BY LEADING PROTESTANT AND CATHOLIC THINKERS. EXAMINES NOTIONS OF NATURE OF MAN, BASES OF AUTHORITY OF STATE, AND COMMON ORIGIN OF STATE IN SOCIAL ETHICS OF LUTHER AND CALVIN.

1361 HAUSHOFER K.
WEHR-GEOPOLITIK.
BERLIN: JUNKER/DUNNHAUPT, 1941, 195 PP.
TREATISE ON DEFENSE AND MILITARY GEOGRAPHY RANGING FROM PRE-WORLD WAR ONE PERIOD TO EARLY WORLD WAR TWO DAYS. EXPLAINS THE VARIOUS MILITARY DEFENSES USED BY GERMANY AND OFFERS INSIGHTS INTO MILITARY GEOGRAPHY BEFORE AND AFTER FIRST WORLD WAR.

1362 HAVIGHURST R.J., MOREIRA J.R.
SOCIETY AND EDUCATION IN BRAZIL.
PITTSBURGH: U OF PITTSBURGH PR, 1965, 263 PP., LC#65-14298.
A STUDY OF EDUCATION AS A MAJOR AGENT IN IMPLEMENTING BRAZIL'S RAPID SOCIAL AND ECONOMIC DEVELOPMENT. TRACES THE COUNTRY'S EVOLUTION FROM AN EXPLOITED COLONY TO A MODERN REPUBLIC WITH CAPACITY TO BECOME THE "COLOSSUS" OF SOUTH AMERICA. EXAMINES THE INCREASING DEMANDS PLACED ON SCHOOLS AND UNIVERSITIES BY CULTURAL, POLITICAL, AND INDUSTRIAL GROWTH. STATISTICAL ANALYSES OF MAJOR ASPECTS OF GROWTH.

1363 HAWTREY R.
INCOMES AND MONEY.
NEW YORK: BARNES AND NOBLE, 1967, 260 PP.
DISCUSSES BRITISH POSTWAR ECONOMY WITH EMPHASIS ON GOVERNMENT FISCAL POLICY. DENIES IDEAS THAT MONETARY EXPANSION IS NECESSARY FOR FULL EMPLOYMENT AND THAT ADVERSE BALANCE OF PAYMENTS INDICATES TOO HIGH COSTS. DESCRIBES WAGE LEVEL FLUCTUATIONS AND PRAISES HIGH BANK RATE. TREATS OVER-EMPLOYMENT, CREDIT REGULATION, SPECIFIC AREAS OF GOVERNMENT MONETARY POLICY, AND INTERNATIONAL ECONOMIC DEVELOPMENTS.

1364 HAY P.
FEDERALISM AND SUPRANATIONAL ORGANIZATIONS: PATTERNS FOR NEW LEGAL STRUCTURES.
URBANA: U OF ILLINOIS PR, 1966, 335 PP.
EXAMINES NATURE OF SUPRANATIONAL EEC LAW AND ITS RELATION TO THE DOMESTIC LAW OF MEMBER STATES. DISCUSSES PROVISIONS OF THE TREATY ESTABLISHING THE EUROPEAN ECONOMIC COMMUNITY, AND POINTS OUT "FEDERAL" CHARACTER OF EEC AND ITS LAW. REJECTS TRADITIONAL NOTION THAT SOVEREIGNTY IS AN INALIENABLE ATTRIBUTE OF STATEHOOD, AND FINDS THAT MEMBERS OF EEC HAVE ACTUALLY TRANSFERRED THEIR SOVEREIGN POWERS.

1365 HAY S.N., CASE M.H.
SOUTHEAST ASIAN HISTORY: A BIBLIOGRAPHICAL GUIDE.
NEW YORK: FREDERICK PRAEGER, 1962, 138 PP.
CONTAINS 632 ENTRIES PRIMARILY IN ENGLISH (ALSO IN FRENCH AND DUTCH) ARRANGED BY COUNTRY. LISTINGS INCLUDE BOOKS, ARTICLES, DOCUMENTS, AND DISSERTATIONS PUBLISHED FROM 1900-1961 ON THE HISTORY OF SOUTHEAST ASIA.

1366 HAYAKAWA S.I.
LANGUAGE IN ACTION.
NEW YORK: HARCOURT, 1941, 345 PP.
PRESENTS PRINCIPLES OF SEMANTICS AS A GUIDE TO IMPROVING HUMAN INTERACTIONS. EXAMINES THE FUNCTION AND NATURE OF LANGUAGE. DESCRIBES IN DETAIL THE MECHANISMS OF LINGUISTIC COMMUNICATION AS USED, IN PARTICULAR, FOR ACHIEVING COOPERATION AND FOR POOLING KNOWLEDGE. CONCLUDES WITH DEMONSTRATIVE READING SELECTIONS.

1367 HAYCRAFT J.
BABEL IN SPAIN.
LONDON: HAMISH HAMILTON, 1958, 222 PP.
RECORD OF WRITER'S EXPERIENCES WHILE LIVING AND WORKING IN CORDOBA. OBSERVATIONS ON LIFE OF MIDDLE-CLASS SPANIARDS. RELATES EXPERIENCES IN SETTING UP A LANGUAGE SCHOOL.

1368 VON HAYEK F.A.
THE ROAD TO SERFDOM.
CHICAGO: U. CHI. PR., 1944, 249 PP.
CRITICISM OF THE SOCIALIST OR 'PLANNED ECONOMY' TENDENCIES THAT HAVE DEVELOPED AND BEEN ACCEPTED AS INEVITABLE BY WESTERN DEMOCRACIES. SEES SOCIALISM ENDING IN EITHER CIVIL WAR OR EMERGENCE OF NATIONAL DICTATORSHIPS. ADVOCATES RETURN TO NINETEENTH CENTURY LIBERALISM WITH EMPHASIS ON INDIVIDUAL FREEDOM. ADVISES ADAPTATION OF THIS PHILOSOPHY TO TWENTIETH CENTURY.

1369 VON HAYEK F.A.
THE CONSTITUTION OF LIBERTY.
CHICAGO: U OF CHICAGO PRESS, 1960, 570 PP., LC#59-11618.
DISCUSSES CONCEPT OF FREEDOM AND MEANS OF ACHIEVING IT. EXAMINES FACTORS THAT DETERMINE GROWTH OF ALL CIVILIZATIONS AND INSTITUTIONS THE WEST HAS DEVELOPED TO SECURE INDIVIDUAL LIBERTY. TESTS PRINCIPLES OF FREEDOM AGAINST INSTITUTIONS OF THE WELFARE STATE, SHOWING HOW OFTEN PURSUIT OF THE SAME GOALS BY DIFFERENT METHODS MAY EITHER ENHANCE OR DESTROY LIBERTY.

1370 HAYTER T.
"FRENCH AID TO AFRICA* ITS SCOPE AND ACHIEVEMENTS."
INTERNATIONAL AFFAIRS (U.K.), 41 (APR.65), 236-251.
THE BULK OF ALL FRENCH AID GOES TO HER FORMER COLONIES IN SUB-SAHARAN AFRICA. HAYTER TRACES DEVELOPMENT OF RELATIONAL CONCEPTS OF ASSIMILATION AND ASSOCIATION WHICH LED TO PEACEFUL POLITICAL INDEPENDENCE, WITH FRANCE THEN THROUGH AID AND FAVORED TRADE POLICIES MAINTAINING OLD ECONOMIC STANDARDS. EEC POLICIES AND FRENCH CULTURAL PRIDE ARE SEEN AS INTERACTING TO CREATE AID POLICY AIMED AT ECONOMIC INDEPENDENCE.

1371 HAZARD B.H. JR.
KOREAN STUDIES GUIDE.
BERKELEY: U OF CALIF PR, 1954, 220 PP.
CONTAINS 491 BOOKS AND ARTICLES IN ENGLISH, FRENCH, AND KOREAN FROM 1500-1953. ARRANGED BY SUBJECT. EMPHASIS ON KOREAN HISTORY; SELECTIVE; INTRODUCTION ON EACH CHAPTER.

1372 HAZARD J.N.
"SETTLING DISPUTES IN SOVIET SOCIETY: THE FORMATIVE YEARS OF LEGAL INSTITUTIONS."
NEW YORK: COLUMBIA U PRESS, 1960.
PROPOSES TO TEST WITH SOVIET DATA THE THESIS THAT MODERN MAN CAN SETTLE HIS DISPUTES WITHOUT ELABORATELY ORGANIZED TRIBUNALS, LEGAL REPRESENTATION, COMPLICATED LAWS, RULES OF PROCEDURE, AND EVIDENCE. TRACES EVOLUTION OF CRIMINAL LAW AND PROCEDURE ALONGSIDE CIVIL JURISDICTION AND PROCEDURE. INCLUDES BIBLIOGRAPHY OF BOOKS, ARTICLES, SERIAL PUBLICATIONS, COLLECTIONS OF STATUTORY MATERIAL, ETC. IN RUSSIAN.

1373 HAZARD J.N.
"THE SOVIET SYSTEM OF GOVERNMENT."
CHICAGO: U OF CHICAGO PRESS, 1960.
A TEXTBOOK OF COMPARATIVE GOVERNMENT EMPHASIZING THE RELATION OF FORMAL, LEGAL INSTITUTIONS TO CONTEXTUAL ELEMENTS OF A POLITICAL SYSTEM--IDEOLOGY, SOCIAL STRUCTURE, PRESSURE GROUPS, ETC. SOVIET INSTITUTIONS ANALYZED IN TERMS OF THEIR OPERATION, FACTORS OF INFLUENCE, DEVELOPING TRENDS, AND CONTRAST TO WESTERN SYSTEMS. ANNOTATED BIBLIOGRAPHY OF DOCUMENTS, BOOKS, AND PERIODICALS PUBLISHED SINCE WORLD WAR II.

1374 HAZLEWOOD A.
THE ECONOMICS OF DEVELOPMENT: AN ANNOTATED LIST OF BOOKS AND ARTICLES PUBLISHED 1958-1962.
LONDON: OXFORD U PR, 1964, 104 PP.
CONFINED TO ENGLISH-LANGUAGE PUBLICATIONS OF PERIOD 1958-1962. ORGANIZED BY CONTENT AND TYPE OF STUDY: THEORIES AND PROBLEMS; HISTORICAL STUDIES; AREA STUDIES; NATIONAL INCOME AND COMPONENTS; POPULATION, LABOR, AND MANAGEMENT; AGRICULTURE AND LAND; INDUSTRY; COMMERCE AND TRANSPORT; MONEY AND BANKING; GOVERNMENT; INTERNATIONAL ECONOMICS.

1375 HEADLAM-MORLEY
BIBLIOGRAPHY IN POLITICS FOR THE HONOUR SCHOOL OF PHILOSOPHY, POLITICS AND ECONOMICS (PAMPHLET)
LONDON: OXFORD U PR, 1949, 56 PP.
UNANNOTATED BIBLIOGRAPHY DESIGNED PRIMARILY FOR THOSE WORKING FOR THE HONOUR SCHOOL; THUS IT IS NEITHER EXHAUSTIVE NOR SELF-CONTAINED. ENTRIES ARRANGED INTO NINE TOPICAL CLASSIFICATIONS COVERING HISTORY AND THEORY OF POLITICAL INSTITUTIONS FROM HOBBES THROUGH 1948. LISTS BOTH 19TH AND 20TH CENTURY WORKS, WITH EMPHASIS ON MORE RECENT PUBLICATIONS.

1376 HEADY F.
PUBLIC ADMINISTRATION: A COMPARATIVE PERSPECTIVE.
ENGLEWOOD CLIFFS: PRENTICE HALL, 1966, 115 PP., LC#66-17372.
A COMPREHENSIVE EFFORT TO ASSESS THE PRESENT STATE OF THE COMPARATIVE STUDY OF PUBLIC ADMINISTRATION AND TO CHARACTERIZE ADMINISTRATIVE SYSTEMS IN A WIDE RANGE OF CONTEMPORARY NATION-STATES. COLLATES ADMINISTRATIVE SYSTEMS OF WIDE VARIATION; FOCUSES ON PUBLIC BUREAUCRACIES AS COMMON GOVERNMENTAL INSTITUTIONS AND PLACES EMPHASIS UPON RELATIONSHIPS BETWEEN BUREAUCRACIES AND POLITICAL REGIME TYPES.

1377 HEAPHEY J.
"THE ORGANIZATION OF EGYPT* INADEQUACIES OF A NONPOLITICAL MODEL FOR NATION-BUILDING."
WORLD POLITICS, 18 (JAN. 66), 177-193.
BELIEVES THE DOCTRINE OF RAPID ECONOMIC DEVELOPMENT COUPLED WITH ORGANIZATION THEORY IS INADEQUATE POLITICAL PHILOSOPHY FOR A NATION-STATE. USING EGYPT AS AN EXAMPLE. AUTHOR DESCRIBES FAILURES OF THE VARIOUS ASPECTS OF HER STRUCTURAL STRATEGY--COOPERATIVES, DECENTRALIZATION, AND NATIONALIZATION.

1378 HEASMAN D.J.
"THE GIBRALTAR AFFAIR."
INTERNATIONAL JOURNAL, 22 (SPRING 67), 265-277.
REVIEWS CONTROVERSY BETWEEN SPAIN AND GREAT BRITAIN OVER GIBRALTAR. SPANISH REFUSAL TO RECOGNIZE GIBRALTAR'S MOVE TOWARD SELF-GOVERNMENT IS BASED ON TERMS OF TREATY OF UTRECHT, WHICH CEDES GIBRALTAR TO HER WHENEVER BRITAIN DECIDES TO ALIENATE THE COLONY FROM THE UK. REVIEWS CONFLICT OF OPINION WITHIN BRITAIN * DISPUTE WITH SPAIN DESIRABLE, BUT CEDING GIBRALTAR UNPOPULAR AND UNWISE ACTION.

1379 HEATH D.B.
"BOLIVIA UNDER BARRIENTOS."
CURRENT HISTORY, 53 (NOV. 67), 275-282, 307.
EXAMINES RECENT DEVELOPMENTS IN BOLIVIA, REVEALING THE INTRICATE INTERPLAY OF VALUES, PERSONALITIES, AND EVENTS THAT COMBINE TO SHAPE ITS CURRENT SITUATION. DISCUSSES RECENT REVOLUTIONARY MOVEMENTS AND BOLIVIA'S FOREIGN RELATIONS. NOTES THAT ALTHOUGH DOMESTIC UNREST CONTINUES TO PLAGUE THE COUNTRY, BOLIVIA'S ECONOMY IS BECOMING PROGRESSIVELY STRONGER.

1380 HEBAL J.J.
"APPROACHES TO REGIONAL AND METROPOLITAN GOVERNMENTS IN THE UNITED STATES AND CANADA."
CAN. PUBLIC ADMIN., 10 (JUNE 67), 197-208.
DISCUSSES RECENT CONTRIBUTIONS US AND CANADIAN POLITICAL SCIENTISTS HAVE MADE TO THEORY OF REGIONAL GOVERNMENT. SHOWS APPLICABILITY OF THEORY TO EXISTING PROBLEMS. COMPARES RECENT DEVELOPMENTS IN REGIONAL AND METROPOLITAN GOVERNMENTS IN US AND CANADA. SUGGESTS TRENDS WHICH MAY BE EXPECTED BY THE YEAR 2000.

1382 HECKSCHER G.
"GROUP ORGANIZATION IN SWEDEN."
PUBLIC OPINION QUART., 3 (JAN. 39), 130-135.
DISCUSSES END OF LAISSEZ-FAIRE AND DEVELOPMENT OF CO-OPERATIVE ASSOCIATIONS AND INDUSTRIAL UNIONS IN SWEDEN SINCE THE 1880'S. EMPHASIZES TREND TOWARD CENTRALIZED AUTHORITY. NOTES RAPID EXPANSION OF AGRICULTURAL ASSOCIATIONS FROM 1929-1939.

1383 HEGEL G.W.F.
PHILOSOPHY OF RIGHT.
LONDON: OXFORD U PR, 1942, 382 PP.
ATTEMPTS TO PORTRAY THE STATE AS INHERENTLY RATIONAL. BELIEVES THAT IT IS THE HARDEST THING FOR MAN TO BE ALIENATED FROM REASON AND SPIRIT UNDERLYING LAWS AND FROM KNOWLEDGE OF THE RIGHTS AND DUTIES OF BOTH MAN AND THE STATE. SEES STATE AS EMBODIMENT OF ETHICS, AND ARGUES PHILOSOPHICALLY FOR GOVERNMENT OF LAWS. DISCUSSES ROLE OF CHURCH AND CITES WAR AS HAVING AN ETHICAL ASPECT.

1384 HEIMANN E.
COMMUNISM, FASCISM, OR DEMOCRACY?
NEW YORK: W W NORTON, 1938, 288 PP.
BEGINS WITH RELATION OF CAPITALISM TO DEMOCRACY AND DISCUSSES POLITICAL AND ECONOMIC INSTITUTIONS OF AN INDIVIDUALISTIC DEMOCRACY. COMPARES AND CONTRASTS CLASSICAL SOCIALISM, COMMUNISM, AND FASCISM TO DEMOCRACY. INCLUDES DISINTEGRATION OF HUMANISTIC PHILOSOPHY, PROBLEMS OF LIBERTY AND EQUALITY, ORGANIZATION AND INTEGRATION IN EACH TYPE OF POLITICAL SYSTEM, AND LOGIC MOTIVATING EACH SYSTEM.

1385 HEIMSATH C.H.
INDIAN NATIONALISM AND HINDU SOCIAL REFORM.
PRINCETON: U. PR., 1964, 379 PP., :8.50.
TRACES THE DEVELOPMENT OF THE SOCIAL REFORM MOVEMENT IN THE 19TH AND 20TH CENTURIES--FROM ROMMOHUN ROY TO GANDHI--WITH SPECIAL EMPHASIS ON THE PERIOD BEFORE THE FIRST WORLD WAR AND DISCUSSES ITS RELATIONSHIP TO MODERN NATIONALISM. AN EPILOGUE GIVES THE MAIN COURSE OF THE MOVEMENT AFTER INDEPENDENCE IN 1947.

1386 HEINBERG J.G.
"THE PERSONNEL OF FRENCH CABINETS, 1871-1930."
AM. POL. SCI. REV., 25 (MAY 31), 389-396.
STATISTICAL ANALYSIS OF TYPES OF MEN WHO HELD CABINET POSTS UNDER THIRD REPUBLIC. CATEGORIES INCLUDE EDUCATION, OCCUPATION, AND POLITICAL EXPERIENCE BEFORE CABINET APPOINTMENT. EVIDENCE INDICATES MOST WERE PROFESSIONALS WITH POLITICAL EXPERIENCE. NUMBER OF LAWYERS AND PROFESSORS WAS INCREASING, THE MILITARY DECLINING. ALSO, MORE AND MORE MINISTERS WERE BEING SELECTED FROM THE CHAMBER OF DEPUTIES.

1387 HEINSIUS W. ED.
ALLGEMEINES BUCHER-LEXICON ODER VOLLSTANDIGES ALPHABETISCHES VERZEICHNIS ALLER VON 1700 BIS ZU ENDE...(1892)
LEIPZIG: GLEDISCH BROCKHAUS, 1812.
BIBLIOGRAPHY OF GERMAN PUBLICATIONS FROM 1700-1812 IN 19 VOLUMES.

1388 HELANDER S.
DAS AUTARKIEPROBLEM IN DER WELTWIRTSCHAFT.
BERLIN: DUNCKER & HUMBLOT, 1955, 684 PP.
DISCUSSES TRADE AND CREDIT POLICIES OF MAJOR POWERS IN RELATION TO PRINCIPLE OF ECONOMIC SELF-SUFFICIENCY. EXAMINES COLONIAL POLICIES AND COMPARES POLICY OF SMALL AND LARGE NATIONS.

1389 HELMREICH E.
A FREE CHURCH IN A FREE STATE?
BOSTON: D C HEATH, 1964, 111 PP., LC#63-23317.
ESSAYS DISCUSSING RELATIONSHIPS BETWEEN CATHOLIC CHURCH AND GOVERNMENTS OF FRANCE, GERMANY, AND ITALY FROM 1864 TO 1914. DISCUSSES INFLUENCE AND IMPORTANCE OF CHURCH IN MID-19TH CENTURY, CONSEQUENCES OF ITALIAN UNIFICATION AND GERMAN KULTURKAMPF, AND ANTICLERICALISM IN FRANCE AS IT DEVELOPED AFTER FRENCH REVOLUTION.

1390 HELMREICH E.C.
"KADAR'S HUNGARY."
CURR. HIST., 48 (MAR. 65), 142-148.
EVEN THOUGH REVOLUTION OF 1956 UNSUCCESSFUL, DEMAND FOR MORE LIBERAL POLICIES EXPRESSED BY INSURGENTS OF THAT TIME HAS BEEN FULFILLED. NO INCLINATION IN BUDAPEST TO TURN FROM MOSCOW TO PEKING OR ELSEWHERE DESPITE GROWING INDEPENDENCE.

1391 HEMMERLE J. ED.
SUDETENDEUTSCHE BIBLIOGRAPHIE 1949-1953.
MARBURG: JG HERDER INSTITUTE, 1959, 323 PP.
LIST OF BOOKS, BIBLIOGRAPHICAL WORKS, ARTICLES, AND PAMPHLETS ON GEOGRAPHY, ETHNOGRAPHY, POLITICAL DEVELOPMENTS, ECONOMIC AND SOCIAL STRUCTURE, ADMINISTRATIVE AND LEGAL HISTORY, AND CULTURAL AND SPIRITUAL LIFE OF GERMAN SETTLEMENT IN SUDETENLAND. INCLUDES CZECHOSLOVAKIAN PUBLICATIONS. SOME 4,839 ENTRIES ARRANGED ALPHABETICALLY AND BY SUBJECT. LISTS WORKS PUBLISHED BETWEEN 1949 AND 1953.

1392 HEMPSTONE S.
THE NEW AFRICA.
LONDON: FABER AND FABER, 1961, 664 PP.
JOURNALIST'S OBSERVATIONS OF AFRICA SOUTH OF SAHARA, NORTH OF CONGO. LAYMAN'S VIEW OF THE LAND, PEOPLE, AND INDEPENDENCE MOVEMENTS. INCLUDES HISTORICAL BACKGROUND AND PREDICTIONS FOR FUTURE ECONOMIC, POLITICAL, AND SOCIAL DEVELOPMENT. ANNOTATED BIBLIOGRAPHY INCLUDES WORKS OF GENERAL AND DETAILED NATURE IN RECENT US, EUROPEAN, AND AFRICAN PUBLI-

CATIONS.

1393 HENDEL S. ED.
THE SOVIET CRUCIBLE.
PRINCETON: VAN NOSTRAND, 1959, 594 PP., LC#59-8657.
COLLECTION OF WRITINGS ON BACKGROUND OF USSR AND MARXIST DOCTRINE AND THEORY AS INCORPORATED BY BOLSHEVIK REVOLUTION. EXAMINES SOVIET SYSTEM IN RELATION TO THEORY UNDER LENIN, STALIN, AND POST-STALIN ERA. DEALS WITH THEIR INFLUENCE ON CHANGES IN POLICY AND DOCTRINE RELATED TO ECONOMY AND POLITICAL MATTERS.

1394 HENDERSON G.P. ED.
REFERENCE MANUAL OF DIRECTORIES (16 VOLS.)
LONDON: JONES & EVANS BOOK SHOP, 1959.
ANNOTATED LIST, INDEX, AND GUIDE TO THE DIRECTORIES OF ALL COUNTRIES. FOURTEEN VOLUMES COVER EUROPE, THE AMERICAS, ASIA, AFRICA, AND AUSTRALASIA. VOLUME 15 CONSISTS OF A MANUAL TO INTERNATIONAL DIRECTORIES, TOPICALLY AND GEOGRAPHICALLY CLASSIFIED; INDEXED BY TITLE. VOLUME 16 CONTAINS A GENERAL INDEX TO ALL CATALOGED TITLES.

1395 HENDERSON W.O.
THE GENESIS OF THE COMMON MARKET.
CHICAGO: QUADRANGLE BOOKS, INC, 1962, 201 PP., LC#62-20924.
STUDIES EVOLUTION OF EUROPEAN ECONOMIC COOPERATION FROM ANGLO-FRENCH COMMERCIAL TREATY OF 1786 TO CREATION OF EEC AFTER WWII. DISCUSSES SUCH MATTERS AS THE SLAVE TRADE, FISHERIES, AND COMMUNICATIONS.

1396 HENKYS R. ED.
DEUTSCHLAND UND DIE OSTLICHEN NACHBARN.
STUTTGART: KREUZ-VERLAG, 1966, 237 PP.
COLLECTION OF ESSAYS ON GERMAN REFUGEE PROBLEM ESPECIALLY IN RELATION TO ASSIMILATION, RIGHTS OF DOMICILE, POLISH ATTITUDE TOWARD ODER-NEISSE REGIONS, AND WEST GERMAN GOVERNMENT POSITION ON EASTERN BORDER.

1397 HENLE P. ED.
LANGUAGE, THOUGHT AND CULTURE.
ANN ARBOR: U OF MICH PR, 1958, 273 PP., LC#58-5908.
RELATION OF LANGUAGE TO GROUP THOUGHT PROCESSES AND PERCEPTIONS OF EXPERIENCE. DISCUSSES HOW JUDGMENT AND UNDERSTANDING ARE SHAPED BY PARTICULAR LANGUAGE PATTERNS.

1398 HENNIG P.
GEOPOLITIK (2ND ED.)
BERLIN: B G TEUBNER, 1931, 396 PP.
STUDY OF THE INFLUENCE OF GEOGRAPHY IN THE CREATION OF NATION-STATES. DISCUSSES THE INFLUENCE OF NATURAL BORDERS, LOCATION OF CAPITALS, PROBLEMS OF OVERPOPULATION, COLONIAL POLITICS AND EXAMINES THE RELATION OF RACE AND NATIONALITY TO PHYSICAL CONDITIONS.

1399 HERBST J.
THE GERMAN HISTORICAL SCHOOL IN AMERICAN SCHOLARSHIP; A STUDY IN THE TRANSFER OF CULTURE.
ITHACA: CORNELL U PRESS, 1965, 262 PP., LC#64-8259.
FOCUSES ON FIVE REPRESENTATIVE GERMAN-TRAINED AMERICAN SCHOLARS - H. ADAMS, J. BURGESS, R. ELY, F. PEABODY, AND A. SMALL. SHOWS THAT ALTHOUGH THEY WERE SUCCESSFUL IN ATTEMPT TO ORGANIZE AMERICAN UNIVERSITIES ALONG GERMAN LINES, THEIR ATTEMPTS TO INTRODUCE THE METHODOLOGY AND IDEOLOGY OF THE GERMAN SOCIAL SCIENCES ULTIMATELY MET WITH FAILURE THAT WAS INEVITABLE. RELATES SCHOLARSHIP TO SOCIAL REFORM.

1400 HERMANN F.G.
DER KAMPF GEGEN RELIGION UND KIRCHE IN DER SOWJETISCHEN BESATZUNGSZONE DEUTSCHLANDS.
STUTTGART: QUELL VERLAG, 1966, 138 PP.
DISCUSSES RELATIONSHIP BETWEEN CHURCH AND STATE IN SOVIET ZONE OF OCCUPATION OF GERMANY (EAST GERMANY). EXAMINES ATHEISTIC PROPAGANDA, INVASIONS OF RELIGIOUS FREEDOM, IDEAS OF LENIN, STALIN, KHRUSHCHEV, ULBRICHT, AND GROTEWOHL ON RELIGION, ETC.

1401 HERMANS F.A.
THE REPRESENTATIVE REPUBLIC.
SOUTH BEND: U OF NOTRE DAME, 1958, 578 PP.
DEFINES REPRESENTATIVE REPUBLIC AS A SYSTEM WHICH ASSIGNS A CREATIVE ROLE TO LEADERSHIP AND TO POLITICAL PARTIES. THE GUARANTOR OF THE STABILITY OF THIS SYSTEM IS A TWO-PARTY SYSTEM COUPLED WITH SINGLE-MEMBER DISTRICTS. EXAMINES "THE PROPER CHANNELS OF GOVERNMENT" IN THE UNITED STATES AND IN MANY OTHER COUNTRIES OF THE WORLD.

1402 HERNANDEZ URBINA A.
LOS PARTIDOS Y LA CRISIS DEL APRA.
LIMA, PERU: EDICIONES RIAZ, 1956, 119 PP.
ANALYZES ACTIVITIES AND RELATIONSHIP OF PERUVIAN POLITICAL PARTIES IN POSTWAR PERIOD. COMPARES PROGRAMS OF VARIOUS PARTIES, INCLUDING SOCIALIST, COMMUNIST, AND NATIVE REFORM PARTY, APRA. EXPLAINS ACTIONS OF PUBLIC IN RECENT ELECTIONS AND RELATIONSHIP OF PARTIES IN CONGRESS.

1403 HERNANDEZ-ARREGU J.
IMPERIALISMO Y CULTURA (LA POLITICA EN LA INTELIGENCIA ARGENTINA)
BUENOS AIRES: EDITORIAL AMERINDA, 1957, 333 PP.
HERNANDEZ-ARREGUI ANALYZES INFLUENCE OF IMPERIALISTIC GOVERNMENT OVER INTELLECTUAL ACTIVITIES IN ARGENTINA. STUDIES ART AND LITERATURE AS INTERDEPENDENT PRODUCTS OF POLITICAL-SOCIAL PHENOMENA. TREATS JUAN MANUEL DE ROSAS AS CENTRAL FIGURE IN SCHISM CREATED BY RIVAL FASCIST AND COMMUNIST FACTIONS OPERATING DURING PERON REGIME OF 1930-55. HISTORICAL ANTECEDENTS ARE DISCUSSED.

1404 HERRICK B.H.
URBAN MIGRATION AND ECONOMIC DEVELOPMENT IN CHILE.
CAMBRIDGE: M I T PRESS, 1965, 126 PP., LC#66-17754.
EXAMINATION OF CHILEAN ECONOMY DURING PERIOD 1940-60 AS AN EXAMPLE OF A COUNTRY IN WHICH INCIPIENT TENDENCIES TOWARD ECONOMIC DEVELOPMENT DECAYED INTO STAGNATION AND IN WHICH URBAN MIGRATION ASSUMED A FORM REFLECTING THE ECONOMIC AND DEMOGRAPHIC CONDITIONS SURROUNDING IT. COORDINATES RECORD OF CHILE'S ECONOMIC DEVELOPMENT WITH AN ACCOUNT OF ITS CONCOMITANT INTERNAL MIGRATION.

1405 HERRICK M.D.
CATALOG OF AFRICAN GOVERNMENT DOCUMENTS AND AFRICAN AREA INDEX (2ND REV. ED.)
BOSTON: HALL, 1964, 471 PP.
VOLUME REDUPLICATES CARD CATALOG OF AFRICAN GOVERNMENT DOCUMENTS USING LIBRARY OF CONGRESS CLASSIFICATION. ALL FIELDS OF KNOWLEDGE RELATED TO AFRICA ARE COVERED, WITH SPECIAL EMPHASIS ON ECONOMIC, HISTORICAL, ANTHROPOLOGICAL, AND SOCIOLOGICAL MATERIALS. COMPLETE INDEX INCLUDED.

1406 HERRMANN K.
DAS STAATSDENKEN BEI LEIBNIZ.
BONN: H BOUVIER & CO, VERLAG, 1958, 124 PP.
DISCUSSES LEIBNITZ'S CONCEPTIONS OF NATURE AND FUNCTION OF STATE, LAW, EDUCATION, AND RELATIONS BETWEEN CHURCH AND STATE. INCLUDES BRIEF DISCUSSION OF POLITICAL THOUGHT DURING LEIBNITZ'S LIFETIME.

1407 HERSKOVITS M.J.
THE ECONOMIC LIFE OF PRIMITIVE PEOPLES.
NEW YORK: ALFRED KNOPF, 1940, 495 PP., LC#40-27218.
PRESENTS SOME OF THE AVAILABLE INFORMATION ON ECONOMIC ACTIVITIES OF PRIMITIVE PEOPLES. CONSIDERS QUESTIONS OF ECONOMIC SCIENCE THAT ARE SUSCEPTIBLE TO EXAMINATION THROUGH USE OF THESE DATA. SUGGESTS LINES OF ATTACK THAT MAY PROFITABLY BE DEFINED FOR FUTURE RESEARCH IN COMPARATIVE ECONOMICS. ANALYZES METHODS OF PRODUCTION, EXCHANGE AND DISTRIBUTION, PROPERTY, AND ECONOMIC SURPLUS.

1408 HERSKOVITS M.J. ED., HARWITZ M. ED.
ECONOMIC TRANSITION IN AFRICA.
EVANSTON: NORTHWESTERN U PRESS, 1964, 444 PP.
COLLECTION OF PAPERS ANALYZING ECONOMIC GROWTH OF SUB-SAHARA AFRICA. DISCUSSES INDIGENOUS CHARACTER, DEVELOPMENT PLANNING, AND PROBLEMS.

1409 HERSKOVITS M.J.
MAN AND HIS WORK.
NEW YORK: ALFRED KNOPF, 1947, 678 PP.
DESCRIBES SCIENCE OF CULTURAL ANTHROPOLOGY AND MAN, INCLUDING NATURE, MATERIALS, STRUCTURE, AND ASPECTS OF CULTURE, PLUS CULTURAL DYNAMICS AND VARIATION.

1410 HERSKOVITS M.J.
CULTURAL ANTHROPOLOGY.
NEW YORK: ALFRED KNOPF, 1955, 569 PP., LC#55-95171.
SURVEY OF ANTHROPOLOGY FOR BEGINNING STUDENT. SECTIONS ON SETTING, ASPECTS, AND NATURE OF CULTURE, CULTURAL STRUCTURE AND DYNAMICS. BIBLIOGRAPHY OF 200 ENTRIES, 1897-953, IN ENGLISH, LISTED ALPHABETICALLY BY AUTHOR AND INCLUDING BOOKS AND ARTICLES.

1411 HESS A.G.
CHASING THE DRAGON: A REPORT ON DRUG ADDICTION IN HONG KONG.
NEW YORK: FREE PRESS OF GLENCOE, 1965, 182 PP., LC#64-22504.
DETAILED REPORT ON DRUG ADDICTION IN HONG KONG PROVIDING STATISTICS ON EXTENT OF ADDICTION, BACKGROUND OF ADDICTS, AND HISTORY OF ADDICTION IN BOTH CHINA AND HONG KONG. DISCUSSES PREVENTIVE MEASURES AND TREATMENT. HEAVILY DOCUMENTED.

1412 HEYDTE A F.
SOZIOLOGIE DER DEUTSCHEN PARTEIEN.
MUNICH: ISAR VERLAG, 1955, 365 PP.
DISCUSSES THE ROLE OF GERMAN POLITICAL PARTIES WITHIN THE CONSTITUTIONAL FRAMEWORK. PROBES INTO THE SOCIAL CHARACTER OF THE ELECTORATE AS WELL AS THE PARTY.

1413 HEYMANN F.G.
POLAND AND CZECHOSLOVAKIA.
ENGLEWOOD CLIFFS: PRENTICE HALL, 1966, 181 PP., LC#66-22803.
HISTORY OF THE PEOPLES OF POLAND AND CZECHOSLOVAKIA, WITH GREAT EMPHASIS ON EARLY HISTORY OF THE WEST SLAVS. EXAMINES DEVELOPMENT OF MORAVIAN EMPIRE, BOHEMIA, LITH-

UANIA, AND REIGNS OF CHARLES IV AND CASIMIR III. SURVEYS AGE OF CZECH REFORMATION, THE JAGIELLONS, AND POLITICAL AND CULTURAL REVOLUTION. ANALYZES CZECH STATE SINCE WWI, UNDER THE GERMANS, SOVIETS, AND ITS OWN COMMUNIST REGIME.

1414 HICKS U.K.
DEVELOPMENT FROM BELOW.
LONDON: OXFORD U PR, 1961, 549 PP.
COMPARATIVE STUDY OF DEVELOPMENT OF LOCAL GOVERNMENT STRUCTURES AND FINANCIAL AND ECONOMIC SYSTEMS IN SEVERAL UNDERDEVELOPED COUNTRIES OF BRITISH COMMONWEALTH. ORIENTATION IS SCHOLARLY AND TECHNICAL. CONSIDERS DEVELOPMENTS FROM BEGINNINGS OF COLONIAL ERA TO PRESENT.

1415 HIDAYATULLAH M.
DEMOCRACY IN INDIA AND THE JUDICIAL PROCESS.
NEW YORK: ASIA PUBL HOUSE, 1966, 89 PP.
DISCUSSES FUNDAMENTAL PRINCIPLES OF DEMOCRACY AND EVOLUTION OF DEMOCRATIC GOVERNMENT IN INDIA. APPRAISES CAPACITY OF DEMOCRACY IN INDIA TO WITHSTAND LOSS OF NEHRU. EXAMINES INDIAN JUDICIAL PROCESS AND ITS RELATION TO PRESERVATION OF DEMOCRATIC VALUES OF INDIAN PEOPLE.

1416 HILL C.R.
BANTUSTANS: THE FRAGMENTATION OF SOUTH AFRICA.
LONDON: OXFORD U PR, 1964, 112 PP.
STUDY OF THE BANTUSTANS, SELF-GOVERNING NATIVE RESERVES WHICH ARE PART OF SOUTH AFRICA'S APARTHEID POLICY FOR COMPLETE NATIVE SOCIAL AND TERRITORIAL OSTRACISM. ARTIFICIAL STATES ARE INTENDED TO CORRESPOND WITH ETHNIC GROUPS SUCH AS NATAL AND THE TRANSKEI.

1417 HILL R.L.
A BIBLIOGRAPHY OF THE ANGLO-EGYPTIAN SUDAN FROM THE EARLIEST TIMES TO 1937.
LONDON: OXFORD U PR, 1939, 213 PP.
UNANNOTATED BIBLIOGRAPHY CONCERNING ALL TERRITORIES FORMERLY UNDER PRE-MAHDIST EGYPTIAN RULE WHICH WERE ADMINISTERED FROM KHARTOUM. BIBLIOGRAPHICAL REFERENCES AS BRIEF AS POSSIBLE. WORKS DEALING WITH MORE THAN ONE SUBJECT ARE RECORDED IN TEXT UNDER BROADEST HEADING ONLY; CROSS REFERENCES FOUND IN SUBJECT INDEX. ENTRIES TOPICALLY ARRANGED. SELECTED PRIMARILY FROM 18TH-19TH-CENTURY PUBLICATIONS IN ENGLISH.

1418 HILSMAN R.
TO MOVE A NATION: THE POLITICS OF FOREIGN POLICY IN THE ADMINISTRATION OF JOHN F. KENNEDY.
GARDEN CITY: DOUBLEDAY, 1967, 602 PP., LC#67-10407.
DISCUSSES INTRICACIES OF FOREIGN POLICY-MAKING DURING KENNEDY ADMINISTRATION, DOCUMENTING NEGOTIATIONS, CRISES, AND POLITICAL COUPS DURING THE EARLY '60'S. SOME OF THE SUBJECTS TREATED INCLUDE: CUBAN CRISIS, LAOS, INDONESIA, CONGO CRISIS, RELATIONS WITH COMMUNIST CHINA, AND VIETNAM.

1419 HIMMELFARB G.
LORD ACTON: A STUDY IN CONSCIENCE AND POLITICS.
CHICAGO: U. CHI. PR., 1952, 260 PP.
SUSPICION OF POWER, HIGH IDEALS AND MODEST EXPECTATIONS IN POLITICS ARE CONTEMPLATED IN THIS BIOGRAPHY. EMPHASIS ON HISTORICAL, POLITICAL AND RELIGIOUS INFLUENCES ON ACTON. DENUNCIATIONS OF NATIONALISM, RACISM AND STATISM FOUND APPLICABLE FOR LIBERALS TODAY.

1420 HINDEN R.
EMPIRE AND AFTER.
LONDON: ESSENTIAL BOOKS, LTD, 1949, 195 PP.
STUDY OF BRITISH IMPERIAL ATTITUDES, EMPHASIZING PRESENT CENTURY AND DOMESTIC PRESSURES BEHIND POLICIES, INCLUDING DISSOLUTION OF EMPIRE. AUTHOR'S ATTITUDE ANTI-IMPERIALIST.

1421 HINDLEY D.
"FOREIGN AID TO INDONESIA AND ITS POLITICAL IMPLICATIONS."
PACIFIC AFFAIRS, 36 (SUMMER 63), 107-119.
FEELS THAT FOREIGN AID IS PRIMARILY A TOOL WITH WHICH DONOR GOVERNMENTS SEEK TO PRODUCE POLITICAL RESULTS TO BENEFIT THEMSELVES. OUTLINES SOURCES, AMOUNTS, AND UTILIZATION OF AID RECEIVED BY INDONESIAN GOVERNMENT SINCE 1949. EXAMINES SHORT-TERM AND LONGER-TERM EFFECTS OF THIS AID ON POLITICAL SITUATION WITHIN INDONESIA.

1422 HINTON W.
FANSHEN: A DOCUMENTARY OF REVOLUTION IN A CHINESE VILLAGE.
NEW YORK: MONTHLY REVIEW PR, 1966, 637 PP., LC#66-23525.
STUDIES EFFECTS OF COMMUNIST REVOLUTION ON ONE CHINESE VILLAGE. THROUGH MICROCOSM OF VILLAGE REVEALS ESSENCE OF THE GREAT ANTI-FEUDAL, ANTI-IMPERIALIST REVOLUTION THAT TRANSFORMED CHINA. INCLUDES THE COMMUNITY'S SELF-EXAMINATION OF ITS EXPERIENCES IN THE 1940'S. SHOWS METHODS USED TO SEIZE LAND FROM LANDLORDS, CONDUCT OF VILLAGE LEADERS, AND DESTRUCTION OF POWER AND PRIVILEGES OF GENTRY.

1423 HIRAI N.
"SHINTO AND INTERNATIONAL PROBLEMS."
WORLD JUSTICE, 6 (DEC. 64), 172-84.
THROUGH A STUDY OF SHINTO, HOPES TO POINT OUT WAYS OF FACING SPECIFIC WORLD PROBLEMS, E.G. PEACE MOVEMENT, INTERRELIGIOUS COOPERATION, RACIAL TENSION, UN'S POSITION. PRESENTING SHINTO'S VIEWS, GOES ON TO DISCUSS ITS DEFICIENCIES ON BOTH A NATIONAL AND INTERNATIONAL LEVEL. REGARDS POTENTIAL AS GREAT.

1424 HIRSCH F.E.
EUROPE TODAY; A BIBLIOGRAPHY (2ND ED.)
TRENTON: TRENTON STATE COL, 1957, 24 PP.
ANNOTATED BIBLIOGRAPHY OF MATERIALS IN THE TRENTON STATE TEACHERS LIBRARY IN THE AREAS OF EUROPEAN HISTORY, GEOGRAPHY, AND INTERNATIONAL AFFAIRS. EMPHASIS ON RECENT PUBLICATIONS; MAJORITY OF TITLES PUBLISHED IN MID-1950'S. ARRANGEMENT BY AREA RATHER THAN COUNTRY, EXCEPTING THE FEW TRADITIONAL POWERS. ANNOTATIONS INCLUDE AUTHORITY OF WRITER, SCOPE OF BOOK, APPROACH, AND BIAS.

1425 HISPANIC LUSO-BRAZILIAN COUN
LATIN AMERICA; AN INTRODUCTION TO MODERN BOOKS IN ENGLISH CONCERNING THE COUNTRIES OF LATIN AMERICA (2ND ED., PAMPH)
LONDON: LONDON LIB ASSOC, 1966, 41 PP.
ANNOTATED BIBLIOGRAPHY OF BOOKS, PAMPHLETS, AND PERIODICALS ON LATIN AMERICA LISTED BY TOPIC AND COUNTRY THAT ARE READILY AVAILABLE.

1426 HISPANIC SOCIETY OF AMERICA
CATALOGUE (10 VOLS.)
BOSTON: HALL, 1965.
BIBLIOGRAPHY OF BOOKS ON VARIOUS FACETS OF LATIN AMERICA DURING THE COLONIAL PERIOD. INCLUDES MATERIAL ON SPAIN AND PORTUGAL.

1427 HISTORICAL RESEARCH INSTITUTE
A SHORT BIBLIOGRAPHY OF INDO-MUSLIM HISTORY.
LAHORE, PAKISTAN: PUNJAB UNIV, 1961, 160 PP.
INTENDED TO PROVIDE GUIDANCE ON WAYS OF OBTAINING INFORMATION ON THE PERIOD 1858-1961, THE MOST IMPORTANT PERIOD IN THE HISTORY OF THE SUBCONTINENT. COVERS FIELDS SUCH AS THE NATIONAL MOVEMENT, POLITICAL PARTIES, BIBLIOGRAPHY, EDUCATION AND THE ALIGARH MOVEMENT.

1428 HITLER A.
MEIN KAMPF.
NEW YORK: STACKPOLE, 1939, 669 PP.
AUTOBIOGRAPHY INCLUDING HITLER'S IDEAS CONCERNING GERMAN SOCIALISM, HIS VIEW ON THE STATE AND WORLD ORGANIZATION, AND HIS PLANS TO ACHIEVE WORLD DOMINATION.

1429 HITLER A.
MEIN KAMPF (UNABR. ENG. VERSION) (1925)
NEW YORK: REYNAL & CO, INC, 1941, 1003 PP.
HITLER'S RELATION OF FORMATIVE EVENTS OF HIS LIFE AND THOUGHT. CHIEF OF THESE WAS THE DEFEAT OF 1918, WHICH HE THINKS WAS ENGINEERED BY JEWS AND SOCIALISTS. IF GERMANY IS KEPT FREE OF THESE FOREIGN POLLUTANTS IT WILL BE STRONG. ATTACKS THE VERSAILLES TREATY NOT BECAUSE IT IS UNJUST BUT BECAUSE IT KEEPS GERMANY WEAK. BASIS OF NATIONAL SOCIALISM IS DESTRUCTION OF TREATY AND OF FOREIGN INFLUENCES.

1430 HLA MYINT U.
THE ECONOMICS OF THE DEVELOPING COUNTRIES.
LONDON: HUTCHINSON & CO, 1965, 192 PP., LC#65-15656.
RELATES THE NATURE AND CAUSES OF THE POVERTY OF UNDERDEVELOPED COUNTRIES AND THE NEED TO DO SOMETHING ABOUT IT. USES ALTERNATIVE MODELS OF ANALYSIS TO ILLUSTRATE THE DIFFERENT TYPES OF UNDERDEVELOPED COUNTRY AT DIFFERENT STAGES OF DEVELOPMENT. MAINLY CONCERNED WITH THE THEORETICAL PROBLEMS OF LONG-TERM ECONOMIC DEVELOPMENT, AUTHOR OPPOSES ARBITRARY FOREIGN AID.

1431 HO PING-TI
THE LADDER OF SUCCESS IN IMPERIAL CHINA: ASPECTS OF SOCIAL MOBILITY, 1368-1911.
NEW YORK: COLUMB. U. PR., 1962, 385 PP., $8.00.
EFFECTS OF CONFUCIANISM ON SOCIAL STRATIFICATION, EDUCATION AND WEALTH AS DETERMINANTS OF HIGH STATUS, INSTITUTIONS PROMOTING UPWARD MOBILITY AND LACK OF THEM TO PREVENT DOWNWARD MOBILITY. STATISTICAL ELITE STUDY AT NATIONAL, PROVINCIAL, AND LOCAL LEVELS.

1432 HOBBES T., TONNIES F. ED.
THE ELEMENTS OF LAW, NATURAL AND POLITIC (1650)
LONDON: CAMBRIDGE UNIV PRESS, 1928, 195 PP.
WORK IS DIVIDED INTO TWO PARTS, "HUMAN NATURE" AND "ELEMENTS OF LAW," AND CONSIDERS POWERS AND RIGHTS OF SOVEREIGNTY. MAN'S NATURE IS MADE UP OF REASON AND PASSION. CONCORD IS IMPOSSIBLE WITHOUT GOVERNMENT. PEOPLE GIVE RIGHTS TO SOVEREIGN, AND PARTICULAR RIGHTS AND DEMANDS CEASE TO EXIST. DEFINES MASTER AND SERVANT AND DISCUSSES SUCCESSION. BELIEVES MONARCHY IS GOVERNMENT LEAST SUBJECT TO PASSION.

1433 HOBBES T.
BEHEMOTH (1668)
ORIGINAL PUBLISHER NOT AVAILABLE, 1840, 258 PP.
DESCRIBES CIVIL WARS IN ENGLAND 1640-1660 FROM MONARCHIST VIEWPOINT. SUPPORTS GOVERNMENT OF CHARLES I AND CRITICIZES AND ATTACKS CROMWELL, PRESBYTERIANS, CATHOLICS, AND

OTHER NON-ANGLICANS. CONSIDERS MORAL AND ETHICAL ASPECTS OF REBELLION AND FITS THEM INTO HIS OWN GENERAL POLITICAL PHILOSOPHY, IN WHICH REVOLUTION IS NEVER JUSTIFIABLE.

1434 HOBBES T.
LEVIATHAN.
NEW YORK: DUTTON, 1950, 130 PP.
SCIENTIFIC ATTACK ON THE 'LAWS OF NATURE' AND THEIR DEPENDENCE UPON MORALITY. ARGUES THAT SOVEREIGNTY IS INDIVISIBLE AND UNLIMITED AND THAT STATE AUTHORITY SHOULD NOT BE CIRCUMSCRIBED BY CHURCH OR CONSCIENCE. ASSERTS THAT NATURE OF MAN IS TO BE POWER-HUNGRY AND DISTRUSTFUL OF OTHERS. IN ORDER TO ENSURE PEACEFUL SECURITY, ADVOCATES ABSOLUTE GOVERNMENT.

1435 HOBBS C.C.
SOUTHEAST ASIA, 1935-45: A SELECTED LIST OF REFERENCE BOOKS (PAMPHLET)
WASHINGTON: LIBRARY OF CONGRESS, 1946, 85 PP.
ANNOTATED BIBLIOGRAPHY LISTS BOOKS AND SIGNIFICANT MONOGRAPHS IN FRENCH, ENGLISH, AND DUTCH PERTINENT TO SOUTHEAST ASIA. AREA DIVISIONS INCLUDE BURMA, SIAM, INDOCHINA, MALAYA, AND THE EAST INDIAN ARCHIPELAGO (INDONESIA). INCLUDES ECONOMICS, GEOGRAPHY, SOCIAL CONDITIONS, GOVERNMENTS, WWII AND RECONSTRUCTION, CULTURE, AND POLITICS. CONTAINS APPROXIMATELY 750 LISTINGS.

1436 HOBBS C.C.
INDOCHINA, A BIBLIOGRAPHY OF THE LAND AND PEOPLE.
WASHINGTON: LIBRARY OF CONGRESS, 1950, 365 PP., LC#51-60006.
ANNOTATED BIBLIOGRAPHY LISTS PUBLICATIONS IN WESTERN LANGUAGES, RUSSIAN, AND VIETNAMESE COVERING HISTORY, GEOGRAPHY, ECONOMICS, SOCIAL CONDITIONS, GOVERNMENT, AND CULTURE OF INDOCHINA. INCLUDES NEWSPAPERS AND PERIODICALS. CONTAINS 1,850 LISTINGS PLUS SUBJECT INDEX.

1437 HOBBS C.C.
SOUTHEAST ASIA: AN ANNOTATED BIBLIOGRAPHY OF SELECTED REFERENCES IN WESTERN LANGUAGES (REV. ED.)
WASHINGTON: LIBRARY OF CONGRESS, 1964, 180 PP., LC#63-60089.
LISTS 535 REFERENCES AND PROVIDES COMPREHEHSIVE ANNOTATION SUMMARIZING THE TEXTS. ITEMS COVER DECADE FROM 1952 AND ARE ARRANGED BY COUNTRY AND SUBJECT (HISTORY, POLITICS, ECONOMICS, SOCIAL CONDITIONS, CULTURE, GOVERNMENT). ALSO PROVIDES AN EXTENSIVE INDEX. COUNTRIES INCLUDE BURMA, THAILAND, CAMBODIA, VIETNAM, LAOS, MALAYSIA, INDONESIA, AND THE PHILIPPINES.

1438 HOBSBAWM E.J.
PRIMITIVE REBELS; STUDIES IN ARCHAIC FORMS OF SOCIAL MOVEMENT IN THE 19TH AND 20TH CENTURIES.
MANCHESTER: MANCHESTER UNIV PR, 1959, 208 PP.
ANALYZES REBELLIOUS SOCIAL MOVEMENTS AS PRIMITIVE FORM OF ORGANIZED SOCIAL PROTEST. EXAMINES THE SOCIAL BANDIT IN GENERAL TERMS, AND IN THE MAFIA, THE CITY MOB, AND THE LABOR SECTS. INCLUDES THE MILLENARIANISM OF THE LAZZARETTI, THE ANDALUSIAN ANARCHISTS, THE SICILIAN FASCI, AND PEASANT COMMUNISM, ALL OF WHICH HOPE FOR COMPLETE AND RADICAL CHANGE IN THE WORLD. ENDS WITH STUDY OF RITUAL IN PROTEST GROUPS.

1439 HOBSON J.A.
THE WAR IN SOUTH AFRICA: ITS CAUSES AND EFFECTS.
LONDON: JAMES NISBET & CO, 1900, 324 PP.
EXAMINES CONDITIONS OF BOER REPUBLICS, INCLUDING CAPE COLONY, TRANSVAAL, AND ORANGE FREE STATE. EMPHASIZES CORRUPTION, SUZERAINTY, AND THE OUTLANDERS.

1440 HOBSON J.A.
THE EVOLUTION OF MODERN CAPITALISM.
NEW YORK: CHAS SCRIBNER'S SONS, 1912, 449 PP.
TRACES DEVELOPMENT OF CAPITALISM FROM MEDIEVAL STATES TO 1900'S, EMPHASIZING EFFECTS OF MECHANIZATION UPON IT. DISCUSSES INDUSTRIALIZATION'S EFFECTS ON WELL-BEING OF VARIOUS CLASSES, DECIDING LOWER CLASSES BENEFIT LEAST. ATTEMPTS TO FIND HUMANISTIC SOLUTION TO THIS PROBLEM. CLAIMS MACHINE TENDING IS MAJOR DYSFUNCTION OF INDUSTRIALISM, SINCE WORK IS SO DULL THAT CONSUMPTION WILL NOT COMPENSATE FOR IT.

1441 HOCART A.M.
KINGSHIP.
LONDON: OXFORD U PR, 1927, 250 PP.
TRACES DIVINE KINGSHIP FROM ANCIENT AND PRIMITIVE PEOPLES TO MODERN STATES. FINDS THE INSTITUTION TO BE UNIVERSAL AND THE RITUAL OF KINGSHIP TO BE NEARLY IDENTICAL EVERYWHERE. CONCLUDES THAT KINGSHIP DERIVES FROM THE ANCIENT NEAR EAST AND THAT IT SPREAD FROM THERE ALL OVER THE WORLD.

1442 HOCKING W.E.
PRESENT STATUS OF THE PHILOSOPHY OF LAW AND OF RIGHTS.
NEW HAVEN: YALE U PR, 1926, 97 PP.
DISCUSSES PHILOSOPHY OF LAW AND RIGHTS, PARTICULARLY AS GUIDE TO LAWMAKERS. USES APPROACHES OF STAMMLER AND KOHLER TO DELINEATE QUESTION OF WHETHER LAW SERVES ONLY "RIGHT" OR ALSO CULTURE. DISCUSSES FUNCTION OF LAW IN SEEKING TO EFFECT CERTAIN CONDITIONS, LIKE EQUALITY, BY PRESUMING THEM. SEES RIGHT OF INDIVIDUAL TO SELF-DEVELOPMENT AS THE ONLY NATURAL RIGHT. SUGGESTS WAYS LAW MAY ENCOURAGE IT WITHIN SOCIETY.

1443 HODGETTS J.E.
"THE CIVIL SERVICE AND POLICY FORMATION."
CAN. J. OF ECO. AND POL. SCI., 23 (NOV. 57), 467-479.
CANADIAN STUDIES IN THE FORMING OF POLICY AS VIEWED FROM THE VANTAGE POINT OF THE CIVIL SERVANT. DISCUSSES THE NEED FOR THE CIVIL SERVANT TO LOOK IN ALL DIRECTIONS BEFORE FORMING POLICY.

1444 HODGKIN T.
NATIONALISM IN COLONIAL AFRICA.
NEW YORK: NEW YORK U PR, 1957, 216 PP., LC#57-8133.
DESCRIBES AND ACCOUNTS FOR THE POLITICAL INSTITUTIONS AND IDEAS OF AFRICAN NATIONALISM IN RELATION TO HISTORICAL DEVELOPMENT. BRIEF ACCOUNTS OF POLICIES PURSUED BY COLONIAL POWERS AS FACTORS IN EMERGING TYPES OF NATIONALISM. EXAMINES CHARACTERISTIC FEATURES OF NEW PROTO-INDUSTRIAL AFRICAN TOWNS. INCLUDES SELECTED BIBLIOGRAPHY.

1445 HODGKINSON R.G.
THE ORIGINS OF THE NATIONAL HEALTH SERVICE: THE MEDICAL SERVICES OF THE NEW POOR LAW, 1834-1871.
BERKELEY: U OF CALIF PR, 1967, 725 PP.
STUDIES GROWTH OF BRITISH STATE MEDICAL SERVICES FROM POOR LAW OF 1834 TO 20TH-CENTURY WELFARE STATE. EXAMINES INADEQUACIES OF THIS LAW WHICH DETHRONED WEALTHY RISTOCRATS BUT OFFERED LITTLE MEDICAL RELIEF FOR POOR IN NEW RBAN SLUMS. REVIEWS LATER NATIONAL HEALTH SERVICE WHICH GREW OUT OF OMISSIONS OF POOR LAW AND GAVE RISE TO A NEW POLITICS OF POVERTY. DISCUSSES PRESENT FAILURES AND WEAKNESSES.

1446 HOEVELER H.J. ED.
INTERNATIONALE BEKAMPFUNG DES VERBRECHENS.
HAMBURG: VERLAG DEUTSCHE POLIZEI, 1966, 264 PP.
TRACES DEVELOPMENT OF INTERNATIONAL CRIMINOLOGY WITH REFERENCE TO DRUG ADDICTION, MAFIA, PROSTITUTION, ETC. DISCUSSES RISE OF EUROPEAN INTERNATIONAL LEGAL ORDER WITH EMPHASIS ON EXTRADITION AGREEMENTS. EXAMINES BRIEFLY POLICE METHODS IN SWITZERLAND, AUSTRIA, ENGLAND (SCOTLAND YARD), AND US (FBI).

1447 HOFMANN W.
"THE PUBLIC INTEREST PRESSURE GROUP: THE CASE OF THE DEUTSCHE STADTETAG."
PUBLIC ADMINISTRATION, 45 (FALL 67), 245-260.
TREATS DEUTSCHE STADTETAG (DST), GERMAN ASSOCIATION OF CITIES AND TOWNS, AS INTEREST GROUP. DISCUSSES ITS ORIGINS AND DEVELOPMENT FROM 1905-66. STUDIES ITS ORGANIZATION AND GROUP STRUCTURE AND FUNCTIONS OF TIS THREE MAIN ORGANS. DESCRIBES CHANGING PLACE OF LOCAL GOVERNMENT AS GERMANY MOVED FROM CENTRALIIZING STATE TO FEDERAL REPUBLIC. EXPLORES DST'S POLITICAL ACTIVITIES AS PRESSURE GROUP.

1448 HOLDSWORTH M. ED.
SOVIET AFRICAN STUDIES 1918-1959.
LONDON: ROYAL INST OF INTL AFF, 1961, 156 PP.
ANALYZES SOVIET WRITINGS ON AFRICA PUBLISHED FROM 1920 TO 1958; IN TWO PARTS: GENERAL FUNCTIONAL STUDIES, AND REGIONAL STUDIES. CONCENTRATES ON AFRICA SOUTH OF THE SAHARA. BRIEF ANNOTATIONS INDICATE CONTENTS OF INDIVIDUAL ENTRIES OR THE PARTICULAR AUTHOR'S LINE OF APPROACH. SHORT ACCOUNT OF SOVIET INSTITUTIONS CONCERNED WITH AFRICAN STUDIES IS GIVEN.

1449 HOLDSWORTH W.S.
A HISTORY OF ENGLISH LAW; THE COMMON LAW AND ITS RIVALS (VOL. IV)
LONDON: METHUEN, 1924, 600 PP.
CONCERNED WITH DEVELOPMENT OF MODERN ENGLISH LAW AND INFLUENCES SHAPING LEGAL STRUCTURE. BEGINS WITH PUBLIC LAW OF 16TH CENTURY AND CLOSES WITH ENACTED LAW OF 16TH AND EARLY 17TH CENTURIES. INCLUDES CRIMINAL LAW AND PROCEDURE, LAND LAW AND ECCLESIASTICAL LAW, CIVIL PROCEDURE, USE OF COMMON LAW, PROCLAMATIONS AND STATUTES, COMMERCIAL AND AGRICULTURAL POLICIES, AND LAW IN EUROPEAN COURTS.

1450 HOLDSWORTH W.S.
THE HISTORIANS OF ANGLO-AMERICAN LAW.
NEW YORK: COLUMBIA U PRESS, 1928, 175 PP.
SURVEYS WORK OF SOME ENGLISH AND AMERICAN LAWYERS IN FIELD OF ANGLO-AMERICAN LEGAL HISTORY: 17TH AND 18TH CENTURY HISTORIANS, LATE 19TH CENTURY OXFORD LAWYERS, MAITLAND, AND OTHERS. SUGGESTS THAT STUDY OF LEGAL HISTORY CAN TEACH LEGISLATURES HOW TO MAKE LAWS THAT WILL COMMAND RESPECT, AND TEACH CITIZENS HOW TO RESPECT LAW.

1451 HOLDSWORTH W.S.
A HISTORY OF ENGLISH LAW; THE CENTURIES OF SETTLEMENT AND REFORM (VOL. X)
LONDON: METHUEN, 1938, 600 PP.
HISTORY OF PUBLIC LAW AND OF SOURCES AND DEVELOPMENTS WHICH SHAPED 18TH-CENTURY ENGLISH LAW. EMPHASIZES POLITICAL BACKGROUND, PARLIAMENTARY SYSTEM, BEGINNING OF CABINET FORM OF GOVERNMENT AND OF COLONIAL CONSTITUTIONAL LAW. DISCUSSES DEVELOPMENTS IN SPHERE OF LOCAL GOVERNMENT SUCH AS STATUTES

RELATING TO COMMERCE AND INDUSTRY. INCLUDES LOCAL LAW BODIES AND ROYAL PREROGATIVE, AND EXECUTIVE AND LEGISLATIVE POWER.

1452 HOLDSWORTH W.S.
A HISTORY OF ENGLISH LAW; THE CENTURIES OF SETTLEMENT AND REFORM (VOL. XI)
LONDON: METHUEN, 1938, 658 PP.
CONCERNS PUBLIC AND ENACTED LAW OF 18TH CENTURY. BEGINS WITH RELATIONS OF GREAT BRITAIN TO IRELAND, COLONIES, AND INDIA. DISCUSSES MERITS AND DEFECTS OF 18TH-CENTURY CONSTITUTION, FORMALITIES OF LEGISLATION, AND CONTRIBUTION OF 18TH-CENTURY STATUTES TO LEGAL DEVELOPMENT. INCLUDES CRIMINAL LAW, LAND LAW, CONTRACT AND TORT, AND CIVIL PROCEDURE. ENDS WITH PRIVATE BILL LEGISLATION.

1453 HOLDSWORTH W.S.
A HISTORY OF ENGLISH LAW; THE CENTURIES OF DEVELOPMENT AND REFORM (VOL. XIV)
LONDON: METHUEN, 1964, 403 PP.
CONCERNED WITH LEGAL DEVELOPMENTS IN PERIOD FROM REFORM ACT OF 1832 TO JUDICATURE ACTS OF 1873-75. BEGINS WITH DIVISIONS IN TORY AND WHIG PARTIES. DISCUSSES PUBLIC LEADERS AND RELATION OF ENGLISH LAW TO INTERNATIONAL LAW; INCLUDES PUBLIC LAW, CENTRAL GOVERNMENT AND EXECUTIVE STRUCTURE, LAW-MAKING POWERS OF BRANCHES OF GOVERNMENT, AND LOCAL GOVERNMENT. ENDS WITH REVIEW OF EMPIRE.

1454 HOLDSWORTH W.S., GOODHART A.L. ED., HANBURY H.G. ED.
A HISTORY OF ENGLISH LAW; THE CENTURIES OF SETTLEMENT AND REFORM (VOL. XVI)
LONDON: METHUEN, 1966, 196 PP.
CONCERNED WITH CHANCELLORS, MASTERS OF THE ROLLS, LORDS JUSTICES IN CHANCERY, VICE-CHANCELLORS, AND CIVILIAN JUDGES IN PERIOD OF REFORM, 1833-75. DISCUSSES CAREER, WRITINGS, AND MAJOR CASES OF PROMINENT LEGAL FIGURES. DISCUSSES JUDICIAL COMMITTEE OF THE PRIVY COUNCIL, ITS MEMBERS, DECISIONS, AND ACHIEVEMENTS. CLOSES WITH EFFECT OF MODERN CODES OF LAW AND NEED FOR COMPARATIVE LAW STUDIES.

1455 HOLLANDER P.
THE NEW MAN AND HIS ENEMIES: A STUDY OF THE STALINIST CONCEPTIONS OF GOOD AND EVIL PERSONIFIED (DOCTORAL THESIS)
PRINCETON: PRIN U, DEPT OF SOC, 1963, 327 PP.
STUDY OF SOCIALIST REALISM AND TWO INHERENT LITERARY STEREOTYPES: THE "NEW MAN" WHO STANDS FOR NEW TYPE OF HUMAN BEING SUPPOSEDLY A PRODUCT OF SOCIAL CHANGES AND POLITICAL TRAINING, AND THE "ENEMY" WHO REPRESENTS ALL THOSE HOSTILE TO REGIME. FINDS IT WAS DYSFUNCTIONAL FOR TOTALITARIAN REGIMES TO ATTEMPT TO INCULCATE ULTIMATE VALUES, FOR THESE BECOME SOURCES FOR PERSONAL AUTONOMY AND INDEPENDENCE.

1456 HOLLERAN M.P.
CHURCH AND STATE IN GUATEMALA.
NEW YORK: COLUMBIA U PRESS, 1949, 359 PP.
DESCRIBES INTIMATE RELATION BETWEEN DEVELOPMENT OF CULTURE AND GOVERNMENT, AND PRESENCE OF CATHOLIC CHURCH, BEGINNING WITH EARLY MISSIONARIES. DISCUSSES CHURCH AS STRONG SOCIALIZING AGENT AND OFFERS REASONS FOR ITS SUCCESS.

1457 HOLLERMAN L.
JAPAN'S DEPENDENCE ON THE WORLD ECONOMY.
PRINCETON: PRINCETON U PRESS, 1967, 291 PP., LC#66-26586.
STUDIES ENCOUNTER BETWEEN GOVERNMENTAL ECONOMIC PLANNING VIDUAL PREROGATIVES. IDENTIFIES STRUCTURAL DIFFICULTIES OF TIES OF JAPAN'S ECONOMY DURING LIBERALIZATION AND EVALUATES POLICIES ASSOCIATED WITH LIBERALIZATION.

1458 HOLT R.T., TURNER J.E.
THE POLITICAL BASIS OF ECONOMIC DEVELOPMENT.
PRINCETON: VAN NOSTRAND, 1966, 411 PP.
ANALYZES ECONOMIC DEVELOPMENT AS A FUNCTION OF POLITICAL AND SOCIAL CHANGE, USING HISTORICAL EXAMPLES. COMPARES POLITICAL SYSTEMS AND THEIR RESPECTIVE EFFECTS ON CULTURE AND ECONOMIC GROWTH.

1459 HONDURAS CONSEJO NAC DE ECO
PLAN NACIONAL DE DESARROLLO ECONOMICO Y SOCIAL DE HONDURAS 1965-69.
TEGUCIGALPA: SECRETAR NAC DE ECO, 1965, 1111 PP.
FOUR PART PLAN FOR ECONOMIC AND SOCIAL DEVELOPMENT OF HONDURAS FROM 1965 TO 1969 PREPARED BY HONDURAN NATIONAL COUNCIL OF ECONOMICS. COVERS GENERAL PROBLEMS OF ECONOMY AND PROGRAM METHOD, PUBLIC INVESTMENT, AGRICULTURAL DEVELOPMENT, AND INDUSTRIAL DEVELOPMENT.

1460 HONINGMAN J.J.
THE WORLD OF MAN.
NEW YORK: HARPER & ROW, 1959, 940 PP., LC#58-13969.
TRACES HUMAN EVOLUTION FROM STANDPOINT OF RELATIONSHIP OF CULTURE TO BIOLOGICAL NATURE OF MAN. TREATS METHODOLOGY OF ANTHROPOLOGICAL INQUIRY. DISCUSSES FACTORS THAT WHEN TAKEN TOGETHER REPRESENT "A CULTURE," THE BASIC INTERNAL PROCESSES AND ORGANIZATIONAL FRAMEWORK OF CULTURE, AND THE RELATIONSHIP OF MAN TO HIS CULTURE. BRIEFLY TRACES GROWTH OF WESTERN CULTURE.

1461 HOOK S.
THE PARADOXES OF FREEDOM.
BERKELEY: U OF CALIF PR, 1962, 152 PP., LC#62-16335.
DISCUSSES AND EXAMINES DEMOCRATIC VALUES SUCH AS HUMAN RIGHTS, RATIONALISM, REPRESENTATION, JUDICIAL REVIEW, CONSCIENCE, AND THE RIGHT TO REVOLUTION.

1462 HOOK S.
"THE ENLIGHTENMENT AND MARXISM."
J. HISTORY OF IDEAS, 29 (JAN.-MAR. 68), 93-108.
RELATES PERIOD AND IDEAS OF EUROPEAN ENLIGHTENMENT TO MARXISM, BASICALLY ON COMMON GROUNDS OF RATIONALISM AND THE BELIEF IN HUMAN RIGHTS. DIFFERENCES IN METHODOLOGICAL ORIENTATION ARE NOTED, AS WELL AS DIFFERENCES IN VIEW OF IMPORTANCE OF HISTORY AND POSSIBILITY OF SCIENTIFICALLY INTERPRETING HISTORY.

1463 HOOKER R.
OF THE LAWS OF ECCLESIASTICAL POLITY (1594) (ABR. BY J. S. MARSHALL)
SEWANEE, TENN: UNIV. PRESS, U. OF THE SOUTH, 1950, 150 PP.
THEORY OF CHURCH AND STATE AS AGENTS OF GOD'S REDEMPTION OF FALLEN MAN, AIDING MAN TO REGAIN FULNESS OF LIFE BOTH TEMPORALLY AND ETERNALLY. KING RULES BY DIVINE RIGHT, BUT IS PROPERLY SUBJECT TO CONSTITUTION AND TO NATURAL AND POSITIVE LAW. POSITIVE LAW, WHICH MUST ACCORD WITH REASON AND NATURAL LAW, DEPENDS ON ASSENT OF THE GOVERNED, THROUGH THEIR REPRESENTATIVES, AND CANNOT EXIST OTHERWISE.

1464 HOOVER INSTITUTION
UNITED STATES AND CANADIAN PUBLICATIONS ON AFRICA.
STANFORD: HOOVER INSTITUTE.
UNANNOTATED ANNUAL LISTING (SINCE 1962) OF BOOKS, PAMPHLETS, AND SERIAL PUBLICATIONS DEALING WITH SOCIAL SCIENCES AND HUMANITIES OF SUB-SAHARA AFRICA. PART I ARRANGES ITEMS BY SUBJECT; PART II BY TYPE OF PUBLICATION UNDER SPECIFIC REGION. CONTAINS AUTHOR INDEX.

1465 HOPE M.
"THE RELUCTANT WAY: SELF-IMMOLATION IN VIETNAM."
ANTIOCH REV., 27 (JULY 67), 149-163.
DISCUSSES VIETNAMESE ATTITUDE TOWARD SELF-IMMOLATION AND SEEKS TO DISCOVER RELATION TO CULTURAL VALUES AND UNDERLYING MOTIVATION. SEES EXPLANATION IN CLASH BETWEEN TRADITIONAL COLLECTIVE SOCIETY AND CHRISTIAN IDEALS OF INDIVIDUAL ACTION AND SALVATION.

1466 HOPKINS J.F.K. ED.
ARABIC PERIODICAL LITERATURE, 1961.
CAMBRIDGE: HEFFER & SONS, LTD, 1966, 104 PP.
ANNOTATED BIBLIOGRAPHICAL GUIDE TO 23 ARABIC PERIODICALS PUBLISHED IN 1961, BOTH WITHIN AND OUTSIDE ARABIC-SPEAKING AREAS. LIST WAS COMPILED UNDER AUSPICES OF THE MIDDLE EAST CENTRE OF CAMBRIDGE UNIVERSITY. ARTICLES ARE CLASSIFIED IN 18 TOPICAL CATEGORIES COVERING CURRENT AFFAIRS, SOCIAL SCIENCES, SCIENCE AND TECHNOLOGY, AND POLITICAL QUESTIONS. ALL ARABIC NAMES AND TITLES TRANSLITERATED.

1467 HOPKINSON T.
SOUTH AFRICA.
NEW YORK: TIME, INC, 1964, 160 PP., LC#64-23718.
FROM "LIFE'S" WORLD LIBRARY - SURVEYS SOUTH AFRICA, ITS HISTORY AND MODERN LIFE, EMPHASIZING PROBLEMS OF APARTHEID.

1468 HORECKY P.L.
"LIBRARY OF CONGRESS PUBLICATIONS IN AID OF USSR AND EAST EUROPEAN RESEARCH."
SLAVIC REVIEW, 23 (JAN. 64), 309-327.
AN ANNOTATED BIBLIOGRAPHY OF RESEARCH AIDS PUBLISHED BY THE LIBRARY OF CONGRESS TO ASSIST IN RESEARCHING USSR AND EAST EUROPEAN MATERIAL IN THE LIBRARY OF CONGRESS. CONTAINS ENTRIES IN ENGLISH, RANGING FROM 1929-1963.

1469 HORN O.B.
BRITISH PUBLIC OPINION AND THE FIRST PARTITION OF POLAND.
EDINBURGH & LONDON: OLIVER& BOYD, 1945, 98 PP.
COLLECTS AND ANALYZES BRITISH SENTIMENT 1772 TO 1775 ON THE POLISH PREDICAMENT; SHOWS CONCLUSIVELY THAT PUBLIC OPINION SUPPORTED GOVERNMENT'S POLICY OF INACTION, AND THAT MANY FACTORS MADE IT DIFFICULT FOR ENGLAND TO ACT, NOTABLY THE LACK OF ALLIES ON THE CONTINENT; SHOWS DIFFERENCE BETWEEN 18TH- AND 19TH-CENTURY VIEWS OF POLAND.

1470 HORNE A.J.
THE COMMONWEALTH TODAY.
LONDON: LONDON LIB ASSOC, 1965, 107 PP.
LISTS BOOKS PUBLISHED IN RECENT YEARS ON POLITICS AND CULTURE IN BRITISH COMMONWEALTH. ARRANGED GEOGRAPHICALLY AND BY SUBJECT. DOES NOT INCLUDE FOREIGN-LANGUAGE PUBLICATIONS; CONTAINS 720 ENTRIES.

1471 HORNE D.
THE LUCKY COUNTRY: AUSTRALIA TODAY.
BALTIMORE: PENGUIN BOOKS, 1964, 223 PP.
JOURNALISTIC LOOK AT AUSTRALIAN CULTURE, SOCIAL STRUCTURE, AND POLITICAL SYSTEM. DISCUSSES POWER STRUCTURE

OF THE SIXTIES AND PLURALITY OF POLITICAL AND SOCIAL INSTITUTIONAL RELATIONSHIPS MODELED ON GREAT BRITAIN'S. ANALYZES KEY ISSUES OF AUSTRALIAN DOMESTIC AND FOREIGN POLICY: RACE RELATIONS AND ALLIANCES WITH WEST AND EAST.

1472 HORNEY K.
THE NEUROTIC PERSONALITY OF OUR TIME.
NEW YORK: W W NORTON, 1937, 299 PP.
FOCUSES ON CULTURAL CONDITIONS OF NEUROSIS; DE-EMPHASIZES EFFECT OF CHILDHOOD AND OF BIOLOGICAL AND PHYSIOLOGICAL CONDITIONS. CONFLICTS DISCUSSED INCLUDE ANXIETY, HOSTILITY, NEED FOR LOVE AND AFFECTION, AND REJECTION. EXAMINES ROLE OF SEXUALITY, NEUROTIC COMPETITIVENESS, AND QUEST FOR POWER, PRESTIGE, AND POSSESSION. COMPETITIVENESS, GUILT FEELINGS, MASOCHISM, AND FEAR OF COMPETITION ARE ALSO STUDIED.

1473 HOROWITZ I.L.
REVOLUTION IN BRAZIL.
NEW YORK: EP DUTTON, 1964, 430 PP., LC#64-13916.
EXAMINES ECONOMIC, SOCIAL, AND POLITICAL CHANGES IN BRAZIL TODAY. AUTHOR ANALYZES 20TH-CENTURY DEVELOPMENT AND INCLUDES OBSERVATIONS OF BRAZILIAN SOCIAL SCIENTISTS AND POLITICAL LEADERS ON NEED FOR CHANGES IN ECONOMIC AND POLITICAL STRUCTURE AND BRAZIL'S POSITION IN WORLD AFFAIRS.

1474 HOSELITZ B.F.
"THE ROLE OF CITIES IN THE ECONOMIC GROWTH OF UNDERDEVELOPED COUNTRIES" IN "SOCIOLOGICAL ASPECTS OF ECONOMIC GROWTH"(BMR)
NEW YORK: FREE PRESS OF GLENCOE, 1960.
SUGGESTS VARIOUS PROBLEM AREAS THAT ARISE IN STUDYING THE PROCESS OF URBANIZATION AND IN THE STUDY OF TOWNS AND CITIES OF UNDERDEVELOPED AREAS. DISCUSSES IMPACT OF MEDIEVAL URBAN CENTERS ON WESTERN CULTURE, AND ENLARGES R. REDFIELD'S TYPOLOGY OF RURAL-URBAN RELATIONSHIPS. AUTHOR OFFERS A NUMBER OF POSSIBLE NEW APPROACHES TO STUDY OF INTERRELATION BETWEEN URBANIZATION AND INDUSTRIALIZATION.

1475 HOSELITZ B.F., WEINER M.
"ECONOMIC DEVELOPMENT AND POLITICAL STABILITY IN INDIA"
DISSENT, 8 (SPRING 61), 172-179.
THEORIZES THAT ECONOMIC DEVELOPMENT AND POLITICAL STABILITY IN INDIA ARE NOT POSITIVELY RELATED. MAINTAINS THAT DEVELOPMENT BENEFITS FROM POLITICAL ACTIVITY AND FOSTERS POLITICAL INSTABILITY. DEVELOPMENT POLICY OF INDIA WILL NOT HELP POLITICAL SITUATION; SOLUTION MUST COME FROM WITHIN POLITICS.

1476 HOSELITZ B.F. ED.
ECONOMICS AND THE IDEA OF MANKIND.
NEW YORK: COLUMB. U. PR., 1965, 277 PP., $6.95.
ESSAYS BASED ON ASSUMPTION THAT MANKIND INTERDEPENDENT. STUDY HOW MANKIND WOULD FUNCTION AS WHOLE IN PRODUCTION, DISTRIBUTION, AND CONSUMPTION OF GOODS AND WHAT WOULD CHARACTERIZE SUCH AN ECONOMY.

1477 HOSHII I.
"JAPAN'S STAKE IN ASIA."
ORIENT/WEST, 12 (1967), 89-143.
DISCUSSES RELATION OF JAPAN TO REST OF ASIA. HER AMBIGUOUS ROLE IN THE EAST HAS BEEN CAUSE FOR MUCH CONCERN. BASICALLY CAPITALISTIC, SHE CONFRONTS ONE OF THE LARGEST COMMUNIST COUNTRIES. ANALYZES POSSIBILITY OF JAPAN'S JOINING AFRO-ASIAN BLOC.

1478 HOSKINS H.L.
"ARAB SOCIALISM IN THE UAR."
CURR. HIST., 44 (JAN. 63), 8-12.
NASSER'S PROGRAM FOR THE IMPROVEMENT OF EGYPTIAN LIVING STANDARDS IS FOREDOOMED TO FAILURE WHATEVER THE SUCCESS OF INDUSTRIALIZATION AND RECOVERY OF WASTE LANDS IF POPULATION CONTINUES TO INCREASE AT PRESENT RATE. THE THREE PERCENT INCREASE MIGHT OVERRUN IMPROVEMENTS IN ECONOMY WITHIN A FEW YEARS.

1479 HOUN F.S.
"THE COMMUNIST MONOLITH VERSUS THE CHINESE TRADITION."
ORBIS, 8 (WINTER 65), 894-921.
UPON ANALYSIS OF LONG CHINESE HISTORY THE AUTHOR FINDS THAT A MONOLITHIC TOTALITARIANISM LIKE THAT PRACTICED BY THE COMMUNIST REGIME HAS NEVER EXISTED. HE SEARCHES IN MANY SOCIETAL AREAS FOR EVIDENCE OF COMPARABLE CONTROL PATTERNS. CONCLUDES THAT VIABILITY OF THE REGIME IS FUNCTION OF ITS RELATION TO SOCIETAL VALUES, ABILITY TO SOLVE PROBLEMS, AND ITS PROPAGANDA MONOPOLY.

1480 HOUN F.W.
CENTRAL GOVERNMENT OF CHINA, 1912-1928.
MADISON: U OF WISCONSIN PR, 1957, 246 PP., LC#57-9807.
AN INSTITUTIONAL STUDY OF GOVERNMENTAL SYSTEMS OPERATING IN CHINA DURING THE EARLY PERIOD OF THE REPUBLIC. UTILIZES A FUNCTIONAL APPROACH IN ORDER TO ILLUSTRATE THE CAUSES UNDERLYING THE FAILURE OF POLITICAL SYSTEMS ADOPTED SUCCESSIVELY FROM OUTBREAK OF REVOLUTION IN 1911 TO KUOMINTANG'S EXPEDITION OF 1928. UNANNOTATED BIBLIOGRAPHY OF WORKS IN CHINESE AND WESTERN LANGUAGES.

1481 HOWARD M.
"BRITAIN'S DEFENSE: COMMITMENTS AND CAPABILITIES."
FOR.AFF., 39 (OCT. 60), 81-91.
EVALUATES BRITISH FOREIGN POLICY. CONCLUDES SHE IS COURTING DISASTER BY ASSUMING RESPONSIBILITIES BEYOND HER CAPACITY TO SUSTAIN. VIEWS POLICY-MAKING AS DIALECTICAL PROCESS.

1482 HOWE R.W.
BLACK AFRICA: FROM PRE-HISTORY TO THE EVE OF THE COLONIAL ERA.
NEW YORK: WALKER, 1966, 318 PP., LC#67-14265.
HISTORICAL NARRATIVE COVERS ALL TERRITORY SOUTH OF THE SAHARA, TRADE AND CONQUEST, AND DEVELOPMENT OF AGGRESSIVE AND PROGRESSIVE STATES. ALSO EXAMINES TRIBAL SOCIETIES, THE SPREAD OF RELIGION, COLONIZATION, AND INDEPENDENCE. PROVIDES A SURVEY OF AFRICAN HISTORY AND OFFERS A SELECT BIBLIOGRAPHY OF FRENCH AND ENGLISH TITLES.

1483 HOYT E.C.
NATIONAL POLICY AND INTERNATIONAL LAW* CASE STUDIES FROM AMERICAN CANAL POLICY* MONOGRAPH NO. 1 -- 1966-1967.
DENVER: U OF DENVER, 1966, 80 PP.
ANALYSIS CONSIDERS HYPOTHESES ON THE INFLUENCE OF INTERNATIONAL LAW ON FOREIGN POLICY MAKING. ASSUMES IMPORTANCE OF ISSUES, POWER OF PARTICIPANTS, AND LEGAL BACKGROUNDS OF DECISION-MAKERS ARE IMPORTANT VARIABLES. CALLS FOR BUILDING DATA BANK FROM CASE STUDIES SUCH AS HIS OF AMERICAN EFFORTS TO BUILD PANAMA CANAL IN ACCORDANCE WITH TREATIES.

1484 HSU F.L.K.
"COHESION AND DIVISION IN THE AMERICAN WORLD" HSU F.L.K. CLAN, CASTE, AND CLUB."
PRINCETON: VAN NOSTRAND, 1963, 335 PP.
DISCUSSES THE CULTURAL NEED FOR SOCIABILITY AND FREE ASSOCIATIONS OR CLUBS IN THE USA IN A SETTING OF COMPARATIVE ANTHROPOLOGY. THE FUNDAMENTAL PRINCIPLE GOVERNING AFFILIATIONS IN CLUBS IS CONTRACT. CLUBS ARE NEEDED TO BALANCE AMERICAN SELF-RELIANCE AND EARLY INDEPENDENCE FROM FAMILIES AND AID THE INDIVIDUAL BOTH BY ALLOWING CONFORMITY AND REBELLIOUS CATHEXES.

1485 HSU U.T.
THE INVISIBLE CONFLICT.
HONG KONG: CHINA VIEWPOINTS, 1958, 204 PP.
FIRST-HAND RECORD OF CONTEST BETWEEN CHINESE NATIONALISTS AND CHINESE COMMUNIST UNDERGROUND DURING 14-YEAR PERIOD ENDING IN 1944. GIVES EYEWITNESS ACCOUNT OF COMMUNISTS' SUBVERSIVE TACTICS IN CHINA, ESPIONAGE ACTIVITIES AND ORGANIZATIONAL PROCEDURES; AND DESCRIBES STRATEGEMS BY WHICH GOVERNMENT AGENTS TRAPPED THEIR OPPONENTS.

1486 HUBERMAN L.
MAN'S WORLDLY GOODS: THE STORY OF THE WEALTH OF NATIONS.
NEW YORK: HARPER & ROW, 1936, 349 PP.
EXPLAINS, IN TERMS OF DEVELOPMENT OF ECONOMIC INSTITUTIONS, WHY CERTAIN DOCTRINES AROSE WHEN THEY DID, HOW THEY ORIGINATED IN FABRIC OF SOCIAL LIFE, HOW THEY WERE DEVELOPED, MODIFIED, AND REJECTED. DISCUSSES CLASSIC CYCLE OF FEUDALISM, CAPITALISM, AND MARXISM.

1487 HUCKER C.O.
CHINA: A CRITICAL BIBLIOGRAPHY (PAMPHLET)
TUCSON: U OF ARIZONA PR, 1962, 125 PP., LC#62-10624.
SELECTED, GRADED, AND ANNOTATED LIST OF 2285 BOOKS, ARTICLES, AND INDIVIDUAL CHAPTERS OR SECTIONS OF BOOKS THAT CONTRIBUTE SIGNIFICANTLY TO ACADEMIC STUDY OF TRADITIONAL AND MODERN CHINA. WORKS ARRANGED TOPICALLY WITH EMPHASIS ON POST-1940 ITEMS IN ENGLISH, BUTH FRENCH AND GERMAN LANGUAGE ALSO. AUTHOR INDEX.

1488 HUGHES A.J.
EAST AFRICA: THE SEARCH FOR UNITY-KENYA, TANGANYIKA, UGANDA, AND ZANZIBAR.
BALTIMORE: PENGUIN BOOKS, 1963, 277 PP.
EXAMINES BACKGROUND AND POLITICAL DEVELOPMENT OF SEPARATE TERRITORIES AND THEIR EXPERIMENT IN FEDERATION INCLUDING DIVERSE FOREIGN INFLUENCES AND MAU MAU ACTIVITIES.

1489 HUGHES C.C., TREMBLAY M.A. ET AL.
PEOPLE OF COVE AND WOODLOT; COMMUNITIES FROM THE VIEWPOINT OF SOCIAL PSYCHIATRY.
NEW YORK: BASIC BOOKS, 1960, 574 PP., LC#60-13283.
SECOND VOLUME OF STIRLING COUNTY STUDY OF PSYCHIATRIC DISORDER AND SOCIOCULTURAL ENVIRONMENT DESCRIBING RELEVANT SOCIOCULTURAL FACTORS. DISCUSSES DEMOGRAPHY OF STIRLING COUNTY AND SELECTION OF CONTRASTING SOCIOCULTURAL ENVIRONMENTS, ACADIAN, PROTESTANT-ENGLISH, DEPRESSED COMMUNITIES, AND COUNTY SEAT. APPENDIXES INCLUDE FAMILY LIFE AND CHILD-REARING SURVEYS.

1490 HUGHES E.C.
"SOCIAL CHANGE AND STATUS PROTEST: AN ESSAY ON THE MARGINAL MAN" (BMR)"
PHYLON, 10 (1949), 58-65.
DISCUSSION OF THE IDEAL AND ACTUAL POSITION OF THE NEGRO

WITHIN THE AMERICAN CLASS STRUCTURE. THE AUTHOR'S ANALYSIS OF THE CONTRADICTIONS OF THIS SITUATION RESTS HEAVILY ON ROBERT PARK'S CONCEPTION OF "MARGINALITY." PAPER POINTS OUT VARIETIES AND TYPES OF "MARGINALITY" IN EUROPEAN (PARTICULARLY ENGLISH) AND AMERICAN SOCIETY.

1491 HUGHES T.L.
"SCHOLARS AND FOREIGN POLICY* VARIETIES OF RESEARCH EXPERIENCE."
BACKGROUND, 9 (NOV. 65), 199-214.
IN THIS ARTICLE THE DIRECTOR, BUREAU OF INTELLIGENCE AND RESEARCH, DEPARTMENT OF STATE, OUTLINES THE GOVERNMENT'S PLAN FOR LICENSING SOCIAL SCIENCE RESEARCH IN THE WAKE OF THE "CAMELOT AFFAIR." HOW ALL INVOLVED, FROM THE SCHOLAR, THE HOST SUBJECT, UP TO THE PRESIDENT, WILL BE TREATED AND BENEFIT IS PRESENTED.

1492 HULL W.I.
INDIA'S POLITICAL CRISIS.
BALTIMORE: JOHNS HOPKINS PRESS, 1930, 190 PP.
PRESENTS "A DETACHED, HISTORICAL ACCOUNT OF THE EVENTS LEADING UP TO INDIA'S POLITICAL CRISIS OF 1929," AND INTERPRETS "IN AN UNBIASED, NON-PARTISAN MANNER THE ASPIRATIONS OF THE VARIOUS POLITICAL PARTIES AS TO INDIA'S FUTURE." BOOK AMPLY DOCUMENTS TWO MAIN INDIAN OPINIONS: SECESSIONIST AND THOSE WHO WISHED INDIA TO REMAIN IN EMPIRE AS A "MINISTERIAL GOVERNMENT."

1493 HUME D.
"OF TAXES" IN D. HUME, POLITICAL DISCOURSES (1752)"
ORIGINAL PUBLISHER NOT AVAILABLE, 1752.
CALLS FOR REASONABLE APPROACH TO TAXATION, CLAIMING THAT MODERATE TAXES INCREASE INDUSTRY OF THE POOR, RAISE PRODUCTION, LOWER PRICES, AND MAY EVEN IMPROVE LIVING STANDARD OF POOR. HUME WARNS OF HIGH TAXES, WHICH MIGHT FORCE POOR TO CALL FOR INCREASED WAGES, THEREBY MOVING BURDEN TO THE WEALTHY.

1494 HUME D.
"IDEA OF A PERFECT COMMONWEALTH" IN D. HUME, POLITICAL DISCOURSES (1752)"
ORIGINAL PUBLISHER NOT AVAILABLE, 1752.
DISCUSSES GOVERNMENTAL, INDUSTRIAL, AND SOCIETAL CHARACTERISTICS OF IDEAL STATES. COMPARES HIS IDEAS TO THOSE OF THOMAS MORE AND PLATO. GIVES CRITICISMS OF THEIR IDEAL GOVERNMENTS. HUME SUGGESTS A LIMITED MONARCHY, SIMILAR TO THE MODERN ENGLISH SYSTEM OF GOVERNMENT WITH RESPECT TO LIMITING POWERS OF THE KING. INCLUDES SUGGESTIONS FOR LESSENING OPPRESSION, BUT MAKES NO ATTEMPT TO BE SYSTEMATIC.

1495 HUMPHREYS R.A.
LATIN AMERICAN HISTORY: A GUIDE TO THE LITERATURE IN ENGLISH.
LONDON: OXFORD U PR, 1958, 197 PP.
SELECTIVE GUIDE COVERS LITERATURE ON ANCIENT PERIODS AND CULTURE THROUGH MODERN LATIN AMERICA. HISTORY INTERPRETED HERE AS EXCLUDING ARCHAEOLOGY, ETHNOLOGY, GEOGRAPHY, AND LITERATURE. INCLUDES LIST OF PERIODICAL PUBLICATIONS, AUTHOR INDEX, AND BIOGRAPHICAL INDEX.

1496 HUNKIN P.
ENSEIGNEMENT ET POLITIQUE EN FRANCE ET EN ANGLETERRE.
PARIS: PUBL DE L'INST PEDAG NATL, 1962, 159 PP.
COMPARATIVE STUDY OF EDUCATION AS RELATED TO POLITICS IN FRANCE AND ENGLAND FROM 1789, EMPHASIZING LEGISLATION, NATIONAL AND ACADEMIC DEVELOPMENT, AND POLITICAL IMPACT UPON SCHOOL SYSTEMS.

1497 HUNT E.F.
SOCIAL SCIENCE.
NEW YORK: MACMILLAN, 1961, 887 PP., LC#61-5387.
INTRODUCTION TO SOCIAL SCIENCES. APPROACH ATTEMPTS TO PRESENT AN INTEGRATED IMAGE OF HUMAN SOCIETY. EMPHASIS ON CULTURE AS A UNIFYING CONCEPT FOR STUDYING HUMAN RELATIONSHIPS. CHAPTERS ON ECONOMICS, POLITICAL ORGANIZATION, AND INTERNATIONAL RELATIONS.

1498 HUNT G.L.
CALVINISM AND THE POLITICAL ORDER.
PHILADELPHIA: WESTMINSTER PR, 1965, 216 PP., LC#65-23269.
ESSAYS CONCERNING RELATIONSHIPS BETWEEN CALVINISM AND POLITICS. ESSAYS DISCUSS BOTH GENERAL, THEORETICAL PROBLEMS AND SPECIFIC HISTORICAL SITUATIONS. MOST FORCUS ON POLITICAL BELIEFS OF EMINENT FIGURES, SUCH AS JOHN LOCKE, BRAHAM LINCOLN, AND WOODROW WILSON.

1499 HUNTER E.
BRAIN-WASHING IN RED CHINA.
NEW YORK: VANGUARD, 1953, 341 PP.
DESCRIBES THE CHINESE TECHNIQUES OF PSYCHOLOGICAL WARFARE EMPLOYING BRAIN-WASHING. THE PROCESS CAUSED THE INDIVIDUAL TO THINK IN A NEW FORM OF RATIONALITY. A SLOW PROCESS WITHOUT VIOLENCE WHICH CAPTURES THE MIND'S WEAKER EVALUATIONS AND DISTORTS REALITY.

1500 HUNTER G.
THE NEW SOCIETIES OF TROPICAL AFRICA.
LONDON: OXFORD U PR, 1962, 376 PP.
INTERPRETATION AND EVALUATION OF INFORMATION ON AFRICA, COVERING ALL FIELDS AND ATTEMPTING TO DRAW AN ACCURATE PICTURE OF A SERIES OF NATIONAL SOCIETIES IN A MOMENT OF ACUTE CRISIS AND TRANSITION; ALSO FORECASTS HOW THEY WILL CHANGE. COVERS MAINLY EAST, WEST, AND CENTRAL AFRICA; BASED LARGELY ON PERSONAL TRAVEL AND INTERVIEWS SPONSORED BY INSTITUTE OF RACE RELATIONS.

1501 HUNTER G.
EDUCATION FOR A DEVELOPING REGION; A STUDY IN EAST AFRICA.
LONDON: OXFORD U PR, 1963, 119 PP.
STUDY OF EDUCATIONAL OPPORTUNITIES FOR STUDENTS IN KENYA, UGANDA, AND TANGANYIKA AND IMPORTANCE OF EDUCATION TO POLICIES OF EAST AFRICAN GOVERNMENT. DISCUSSES DEVELOPMENT OF AFRICAN EDUCATION AND PRESENT FACILITIES.

1502 HUNTER R.
REVOLUTION: WHY, HOW, WHEN?
NEW YORK: HARPER & ROW, 1940, 383 PP.
SURVEYS CONDITIONS LEADING TO REVOLUTIONS 1776-1939, AND CONSIDERS IMPORTANCE OF LEADERSHIP, ECONOMIC UPHEAVAL, WAR, AND CYCLIC CHANGE IN GIVING THEM FORCE AND IMPETUS. CLAIMS THAT REVOLUTION IS AN EVIL, SOMETIMES NECESSARY BUT USUALLY LEADING TO UNREST AND INSTABILITY FOR EXTENDED PERIODS AFTER THEY OCCUR. DISCUSSES BASIC TECHNIQUES OF AGITATION.

1503 HUNTINGTON E.
CIVILIZATION AND CLIMATE (2ND ED.)
NEW HAVEN: YALE U PR, 1922, 333 PP.
TRACES CULTURAL IMPACT OF CLIMATE ON MAN'S ABILITY TO LIVE AND WORK AND ON CIVILIZATIONS IN GENERAL, AND DESCRIBES IDEAL CLIMATE AS WELL AS EFFECT OF PARTICULARLY SIGNIFICANT CLIMATIC PHENOMENA.

1504 HUNTINGTON E.
MAINSPRINGS OF CIVILIZATION.
NEW YORK: WILEY, 1945, 660 PP.
ANALYZES ROLE OF BIOLOGICAL INHERITANCE AND PHYSICAL ENVIRONMENT IN INFLUENCING COURSE OF HISTORY, INTERPRETING THE MAIN TRENDS OF HISTORY IN LIGHT OF THESE 2 FACTORS. ALSO DISCUSSES EVOLUTION OF HUMAN CULTURE AND ITS PRESENT SITUATION.

1505 HUNTINGTON S.P.
"POLITICAL MODERNIZATION* AMERICA VS EUROPE."
WORLD POLITICS, 18 (APR. 66), 376-414.
A COMPARISON, FROM 15TH CENTURY TO THE PRESENT, OF THE THREE DISTINCT PATTERNS OF POLITICAL MODERNIZATION ON THE CONTINENT, IN GREAT BRITAIN, AND IN US. HE DEMONSTRATES, THROUGH THE AMERICAN EXPERIENCE, THAT SOME INSTITUTIONS AND SOME ASPECTS OF A SOCIETY MAY BECOME HIGHLY MODERN WHILE OTHER INSTITUTIONS AND ASPECTS RETAIN MUCH OF THEIR TRADITIONAL FORM AND SUBSTANCE.

1506 HUNTINGTON S.P.
"INTRODUCTION: SOCIAL SCIENCE AND VIETNAM."
ASIAN SURVEY, 7 (AUG. 67), 503-506.
MAINTAINS THAT LACK OF KNOWLEDGE AND UNDERSTANDING OF VIETNAMESE CULTURE, INTERMS OF LACK OF RESEARCH C SCHOLARSHIP AS WELL AS IN TERMS OF BROADLY DIFFUSED POPULAR KNOWLEDGE, HAS CONTRIBUTED TO "SHRILLNESS AND SUPERFICIALITY" OF DEBATE OVER US POLICY. DISCUSSES EFFORTS OF COUNCIL ON VIETNAMESE STUDIES TO REMEDY SITUATION.

1507 HUREWITZ J.C.
"LEBANESE DEMOCRACY IN ITS INTERNATIONAL SETTING."
MID. EAST J., 17 (AUTUMN 63), 487-506.
EXPLAINS WORKINGS OF LEBANESE 'CONFESSIONAL DEMOCRACY.' TRACES POLITICAL DEVELOPMENTS AND RELATIONS OF MAJOR POWERS AND LEBANON SINCE 1840. CONCLUDES THAT INTERVENTIONS OF GREAT POWERS PRODUCED CUMULATIVELY POSITIVE CONSEQUENCES.

1508 HURST C.
GREAT BRITAIN AND THE DOMINIONS.
CHICAGO: U. CHI. PR., 1928, 511 PP.
DISCUSSES INTERNATIONAL AND DOMESTIC RELATIONS OF BRITISH EMPIRE. EMPHASIS ON EMPIRE AS POLITICAL UNIT ALTHOUGH SPECIFIC NATIONAL CHARACTERISTICS ARE EXPLORED IN DEPTH.

1509 HUTCHINS F.G.
THE ILLUSION OF PERMANENCE: BRITISH IMPERIALISM IN INDIA.
PRINCETON: PRINCETON U PRESS, 1967, 217 PP., LC#67-15828.
EXAMINES ORIGINS AND DEVELOPMENT OF BRITISH RULE IN INDIA, DISCUSSING HISTORICAL BACKGROUNDS AND DOMINANT CULTURAL ATTITUDES. TRACES EVOLUTION OF BRITISH DOMINATION, ORIGINALLY CONCEIVED AS A TEMPORARY VENTURE IN SOCIAL AND MORAL REFORM, INTO PERMAMENT INDIAN SUBJUGATION, RESULTING FROM GRADUAL GROWTH OF PREJUDICE, THEN CRYSTALLIZED BY REACTION TO THE GREAT MUTINY OF 1857.

1510 HUTTON J.
THE CONSTITUTION OF THE UNION OF SOUTH AFRICA: BIBLIOGRAPHY (PAMPHLET)
CAPETOWN: U OF CAPETOWN, 1946, 25 PP.

LISTS 142 ITEMS DEALING WITH CONSTITUTION OF SOUTH AFRICA. MATERIAL IS ARRANGED UNDER BROAD SUBJECT DIVISIONS AND UNDER EACH SUBDIVISION RELEVANT WORKS ARE ENTERED IN CHRONOLOGICAL ORDER OF PUBLICATION. ALPHABETICAL INDEX OF AUTHORS IS ADDED. MAJORITY OF PUBLICATIONS ARE IN ENGLISH.

1511 HUXLEY J., DEANE P.
"THE FUTURE OF THE COLONIES."
LONDON: PILOT PR., 1944, 64 PP.
PRESENTS HISTORICAL BACKGROUND OF COLONIAL GROWTH AND DEVELOPMENT, AND THROUGH STUDY OF PRESENT SITUATION PREDICTS FUTURE ROLE OF COLONIAL NATIONS IN WORLD SOCIETY. CITES SPECIFIC CHARACTERISTICS OF AFRICAN NATIONS AS TO CULTURIAL AND ECONOMIC DEVELOPMENT. RELATES WORLD CHANGES TO COLONIAL SITUATION.

1512 HUXLEY J.
FREEDOM AND CULTURE.
NEW YORK: COLUMBIA U PRESS, 1951, 270 PP.
SIX ARTICLES ON FREEDOM IN MODERN WORLD, INCLUDING FREEDOMS OF EDUCATION, INFORMATION, SCIENCE, AND RIGHTS OF CREATIVE ARTIST.

1513 HUXLEY M., CAPA C.
FAREWELL TO EDEN.
NEW YORK: HARPER & ROW, 1964, 243 PP., LC#64-20546.
PHOTOGRAPHIC AND TEXTUAL RECORD OF THE PASSING OF PRIMITIVE CULTURE OF AMAHUACA INDIANS OF REMOTE PERUVIAN MOUNTAINS, WHOSE STONE-AGE SOCIETY IS GIVING WAY TO DOMINANT WHITE CIVILIZATION. EXAMINES HUMAN DEGRADATION WHICH MAY ACCOMPANY CHANGE AND CONCLUDES PAINFUL PROCESS COULD BE MODIFIED IF MORE SOCIAL AND TECHNICAL ASSISTANCE WERE OFFERED BY DEDICATED MISSIONARIES.

1514 HUXLEY T.H.
METHOD AND RESULTS: ESSAYS.
NEW YORK: APPLETON, 1911, 423 PP.
PROPOSES SYSTEM OF DEMOCRATIC GOVERNMENT WHICH RECOGNIZES BASIC INEQUALITIES OF MANKIND IN ABILITIES. DISAGREES WITH ROUSSEAU'S DERIVATION OF NATURAL RIGHTS OF MAN BY SUPPORTING CONCEPT THAT RIGHTS MUST BE LINKED TO POWERS. DISPUTES IDEA OF ANY FORM OF NATURAL RIGHTS WITH PSYCHOLOGICAL ARGUMENTS. PROPOSES USE OF GOVERNMENT FOR IMPLEMENTING SOCIAL CHANGE AS WELL AS SERVING AS A LIMITING AGENCY.

1515 HYDE D.
"COMMUNISM IN LATIN AMERICA."
WORLD JUSTICE, 4 (SEPT. 62), 14-37.
DISCUSSES COMMUNIST EXPECTATIONS IN LATIN AMERICA. ARGUES THAT THEY SEE LATIN AMERICA AS RIPE FOR POLITICAL UPHEAVAL. POINTS OUT THAT CUBAN REVOLUTION IMPROVED MORALE OF COMMUNISTS THROUGHOUT LATIN AMERICA. ANALYZES REASONS LATIN AMERICA SEEN AS NEXT PLACE FOR CHANGE. BELIEVES STRONG CATHOLIC CHURCH COULD TURN THE TIDE.

1516 HYDE D.
THE PEACEFUL ASSAULT.
CHESTER SPRINGS: DUFOUR, 1963, 127 PP., LC#63-21146.
STUDIES NEW TACTICS OF USSR TO EXPORT COMMUNISM THROUGH SUBVERSION AND ECONOMIC PENETRATION. EXAMINES RATIONALE OF PEACEFUL CO-EXISTENCE AND BURYING CAPITALISM. USES EGYPT AS A CASE STUDY.

1517 HYMES D. ED.
THE USE OF COMPUTERS IN ANTHROPOLOGY.
HAGUE: MOUTON & CO, 1965, 558 PP.
SERIES OF PAPERS AND SUMMARIES OF DISCUSSION OF SYMPOSIA SPONSORED BY THE WENNER-GREN FOUNDATION FOR ANTHROPOLOGICAL RESEARCH IN 1962. TOPICS COVER: STRUCTURE AND USE OF COMPUTERS, GENERAL AND SPECIFIC MODES OF USE, SPECIAL RESEARCH AREAS. SPECIFIC APPLICATIONS TO ANTHROPOLOGY INCLUDE: LEXICOGRAPHY, MODELS OF LANGUAGES, FOLKLORE RESEARCH, AND CLASSIFICATION AND GROUPING.

1518 IANNI O.
ESTADO E CAPITALISMO.
RIO DE JANEIRO: ED CIVIL BRASIL, 1965, 270 PP.
ANALYZES ECONOMIC AND SOCIAL STRUCTURE OF BRAZIL SINCE INDUSTRIALIZATION IN 20TH CENTURY. EXAMINES ACTIONS OF PRIVATE SECTOR IN DEVELOPMENT AND TREATS ROLE OF NATIONAL GOVERNMENT IN PARTICIPATING IN AND ENCOURAGING DEVELOPMENT OF INDUSTRY.

1519 IBERO-AMERICAN INSTITUTES
IBEROAMERICANA.
STOCKHOLM: IBERO-AMER INST, 1964.
BIBLIOGRAPHIC COMPILATION OF BOOKS AND PAMPHLETS IN THE LIBRARIES OF THE IBERO-AMERICAN INSTITUTES OF STOCKHOLM AND GOTHENBURG. ITEMS ARRANGED BY AUTHOR, COUNTRY, AND SUBJECT.

1520 IBRAHIM-HILMY
THE LITERATURE OF EGYPT AND THE SOUDAN: FROM THE EARLIEST TIMES TO THE YEAR 1885 INCLUSIVE (2 VOLS.)
YADUZ,LIECHTENSTEIN: KRAUS REPRINT LTD, 1966, 87PP
PUBLISHED ORIGINALLY 1888. INCLUDES BOOKS, PERIODICALS, SCIENTIFIC PAPERS, MAPS, ANCIENT MANUSCRIPTS, ETC. MANY FOREIGN-LANGUAGE ENTRIES. ARRANGED ALPHABETICALLY BY TOPICS AND AUTHORS. CONTENTS LISTED FOR SOME TITLES.

1521 IDENBURG P.J.
"POLITICAL STRUCTURAL DEVELOPMENT IN TROPICAL AFRICA."
ORBIS, 11 (SPRING 67), 256-270.
EXAMINES DEVELOPMENT OF STATE STRUCTURES IN AFRICA IN TERMS OF DISCERNIBLE TRENDS. NOTES THAT MANY TRADITIONAL CHIEFS HAVE CONSIDERABLE POWER, SOME COMBINING BOTH TRIBAL AND STATE AUTHORITY, SOME FORMING PROFESSIONAL GROUPS. FINDS THAT FORMER BRITISH COLONIES TEND TO RETAIN COLONIAL STRUCTURE, AND THAT MANY STATES ARE CONSTITUTIONAL DEMOCRACIES IN THEORY IF NOT YET IN PRACTICE.

1522 IIZAWA S.
POLITICS AND POLITICAL PARTIES IN JAPAN.
TOKYO: FOR AFFAIRS ASSOC JAPAN, 1938, 49 PP.
REVIEWS THE HISTORY OF PARTY POLITICS FROM 1868-1938, FROM FIRST FLOURISH TO DECLINE IN 1930'S AS A RESULT OF GROWING MILITARISM. PREDICTS PARTIES WILL AGAIN RISE TO RESTORE REPRESENTATIVE GOVERNMENT TO JAPAN.

1523 IKE N.
JAPANESE POLITICS.
NEW YORK: ALFRED KNOPF, 1957, 300 PP., LC#57-5065.
INTRODUCTORY SURVEY OF JAPANESE POLITICS IN TERMS OF SETTING, DOMINANT POLITICAL FORCES, AND BASIC POLITICAL PROCESSES. ESTABLISHES A GENERAL FRAMEWORK FOR ANALYZING JAPANESE POLITICS IN ITS TOTALITY. BIBLIOGRAPHY OF WORKS CONSULTED: NEWSPAPERS, BOOKS, AND ARTICLES IN BOTH ENGLISH AND JAPANESE.

1524 IMAZ J.L.
LOS QUE MANDAN.
BUENOS AIRES: ED U BUENOS AIRES, 1964, 250 PP.
ANALYZES LEADERSHIP OF INFLUENTIAL SECTORS OF ARGENTINE SOCIETY AND GOVERNMENT SINCE 1936. DISCUSSES BACKGROUND AND ATTITUDES OF LEADERS OF ARMED FORCES, LAND OWNERS, CHURCH LEADERS, INDUSTRIALISTS, UNIONISTS, PROFESSIONAL POLITICIANS, AND NATIONAL AND PROVINCIAL OFFICIALS.

1525 INADA S. ED.
INTRODUCTION TO SCIENTIFIC WORKS IN HUMANITIES AND SOCIAL SCIENCES PUBLISHED IN JAPAN.
TOKYO: JAPAN MINISTRY EDUCATION, 1951, 223 PP.
OVER 80 ITEMS. EACH CONSISTS OF SEVERAL PAGES (USUALLY BY THE AUTHOR) ANALYZING AND SUMMARIZING THE CONTENT. INCLUDES A CATALOGUE OF EACH SCHOLAR'S PUBLISHED WORKS. ARRANGED ACCORDING TO TOPICS SUCH AS LITERATURE, PHILOSOPHY, LAW, ECONOMICS, ETC. SERVES AS BOTH AN INTRODUCTION TO JAPANESE SCHOLARSHIP AND A BIBLIOGRAPHY.

1526 INAYATULLAH
BUREAUCRACY AND DEVELOPMENT IN PAKISTAN.
PESHAWAR: PAKIS. ACAD. RURAL DEV., 1962,450 PP.
PAPERS READ AT SEMINAR OF PAKISTAN ACADEMY FOR RURAL DEVELOPMENT DEALING WITH PROBLEMS OF BUREAUCRACY IN DEVELOPING COUNTRY, STRUCTURE OF PAKISTAN'S GOVERNMENT AND BUREAUCRACY, LOCAL GOVERNMENT AND RURAL DEVELOPMENT, AND TRAINING OF BUREAUCRATS TO FURTHER SOCIO-ECONOMIC PROGRESS.

1527 INDER S.
"AFTER THE CORONATION."
NEW GUINEA, 2 (OCT. 67), 50-55.
CONSIDERS EFFECT OF NEW RULER UPON ECONOMIC AND POLITICAL ASPECTS OF TONGA. EXAMINES STRUCTURAL AND PROCEDURAL FACTORS IN ITS GOVERNMENT AND COMPARES PERSONAL CHARACTERISTICS OF PAST AND PRESENT RULERS. TRACES DEVELOPMENT OF POLITICAL STABILITY AND ECONOMIC ISOLATIONISM 1918-1965.

1528 INDIA (REPUBLIC) PARLIAMENT
CLASSIFIED LIST OF PUBLIC UNDERTAKINGS AND OTHER BODIES IN INDIA.
NEW DELHI: LOK SABHA SECRETARIAT, 1958, 116 PP.
LISTS UNDERTAKINGS OF INDIAN GOVERNMENT, INCLUDING ESTABLISHMENT OF CORPORATIONS BY ACT OF PARLIAMENT, INSTITUTES, UNIVERSITIES, COUNCILS, COMMITTEES, BOARDS, COMMISGIONS, AND JOINT STOCK COMPANIES.

1529 INDIA PUBLICATIONS BRANCH
CATALOGUE OF GOVERNMENT OF INDIA CIVIL PUBLICATIONS.
NEW DELHI: CENTRAL PUBLICNS BRANCH, 1966, 761 PP.
CATALOGUE OF REPORTS AND PUBLICATIONS ISSUED THROUGH AGENCY OF GOVT OF INDIA PUBLICATION BRANCH, FIRST ESTABLISHED IN 1924. CATALOGUE, WHICH LISTS PUBLICATIONS UNDER TITLES, SUBJECT, AND AUTHOR, IS INTENDED AS PRICE LIST BUT SERVES AS ONLY REFERENCE LIST OF PUBLICATIONS ISSUED SO FAR. SUPPLEMENTS WILL COVER PERIOD AFTER 1959 THROUGH PRESENT. ARRANGED BY SUBJECT AND INCLUDES INDEX.

1530 INDIAN COMM PREVENTION CORRUPT
REPORT, 1964.
NEW DELHI: MINISTRY HOME AFFAIRS, 1964, 299 PP.
PROCEDURES OF DEALING WITH BRIBERY AND CORRUPTION IN LOCAL GOVERNMENT. REGULATIONS, MEASURES, SPECIAL POLICE ESTAB-

LISHMENT, SOCIAL CLIMATE. RESULTS, CONCLUSIONS, AND RECOMMENDATIONS.

1531 INDIAN COUNCIL WORLD AFFAIRS
DEFENCE AND SECURITY IN THE INDIAN OCEAN AREA.
NEW DELHI: IND COUNCIL WORLD AFF, 1958, 180 PP.
STUDIES COUNTRIES BORDERING INDIAN OCEAN. COVERS GEOGRAPHY, ECONOMIC BASES OF MILITARY SECURITY, PEOPLES, GROUP AND SEPARATE PROBLEMS OF COUNTRIES, ARMAMENTS AND ARMED FORCES, INTERESTS OF OUTSIDE POWERS, AND REGIONAL PROBLEMS OF SECURITY.

1532 INDIAN INSTITUTE PUBLIC ADMIN
CASES IN INDIAN ADMINISTRATION.
NEW DELHI: INDIAN INST PUB ADMIN, 1963, 261 PP.
CASE STUDIES OF VARIED INDIAN PUBLIC PROGRAMS INTENDED TO ILLUSTRATE ADMINISTRATIVE DECISION-MAKING AND VARIOUS OTHER FACETS OF ADMINISTRATIVE PROCESS.

1533 INDIAN NATIONAL CONGRESS
SOUVENIR, 66TH SESSION.
NEW DELHI: INDIAN NAT CONG, 1961, 570 PP.
COLLECTION OF ARTICLES DEALING WITH HISTORY OF INDIAN CONGRESS, ITS POLICIES, AND METHODS OF OPERATION: AGRICULTURAL AND INDUSTRIAL DEVELOPMENT UNDER A SECOND FIVE YEAR PLAN; DISCUSSION OF GUJARAT WHERE CONGRESS WAS HELD: ITS LAND, HISTORY, CULTURE, LANGUAGE, LITERATURE, EDUCATION, ADMINISTRATION, AND ECONOMY.

1534 INGHAM K.
A HISTORY OF EAST AFRICA.
LONDON: LONGMANS, GREEN & CO, 1962, 458 PP.
HISTORY OF EAST AFRICA FROM ANCIENT TIMES TO MODERN CONSTITUTIONAL DEVELOPMENT AND EMERGENCE OF AFRICAN NATIONALISM. INCLUDES CHAPTERS ON EAST AFRICA, INTERNATIONAL DIPLOMACY, COLONIAL ADMINISTRATION, THE SECOND WORLD WAR, AND POLITICS AND ADMINISTRATION FROM 1919-1939. CHARTS, MAPS, AND SELECT BIBLIOGRAPHY IN ENGLISH AND FRENCH.

1535 INST INTL DES CIVILISATION DIF
THE CONSTITUTIONS AND ADMINISTRATIVE INSTITUTIONS OF THE NEW STATES.
BRUSSELS: INTL INST DIFF CIVILIZ, 1965, 886 PP.
EXAMINES LEGAL, ECONOMIC, POLITICAL, AND SOCIAL ASPECTS OF CONSTITUTIONS IN NEW STATES AND ADMINISTRATIVE ASPECTS OF THEM. ATTEMPTS DETERMINATION OF EFFECTIVENESS IN VARIOUS COUNTRIES.

1536 INSTITUTE COMP STUDY POL SYS
DOMINICAN REPUBLIC ELECTION FACT BOOK.
WASHINGTON: INST COMP STUDY POL, 1966, 55 PP., LC#66-23504.
DISCUSSES POLITICAL HISTORY, POLITICAL PARTIES, ELECTION ISSUES, LAWS, AND STRUCTURE OF GOVERNMENT OF DOMINICAN REPUBLIC. ANALYZES 1962 ELECTION. TABLES ON ELECTORATE, PRESIDENTIAL ELECTION RETURNS, AND DISTRIBUTION OF SEATS IN SENATE AND CHAMBER OF DEPUTIES IN 1962.

1537 INSTITUTE FOR STUDY OF USSR
YOUTH IN FERMENT.
MUNICH, GERMANY: INST. STUDY USSR, 1962, 101 PP., $0.75.
A COLLECTION OF 14 ESSAYS ON SOVIET YOUTH AND ART, MUSIC, LITERATURE, THE ARMED FORCES, POLITICS AND FAMILY LIFE. 'SOVIET YOUNG PEOPLE ARE REFUSING TO ACCEPT THE IDEALS OF THE OLDER GENERATION AND TO MOLD THEMSELVES ON THE TRADITIONS OF THE PAST.'

1538 INSTITUTE OF HISPANIC STUDIES
HISPANIC AMERICAN REPORT.
STANFORD: INST HISP AM BRAZ STUD.
MONTHLY PUBLICATION SINCE 1948 WHICH REVIEWS BOOKS ON CONTEMPORARY SOCIAL SCIENCES AND HUMANITIES IN LATIN AMERICA, SPAIN, AND PORTUGAL. EMPHASIS ON INTERNATIONAL RELATIONS, POLITICS, AND ECONOMICS. SOURCES IN ENGLISH, SPANISH, AND PORTUGUESE.

1539 INSTITUTE OF PUBLIC ADMIN
A SHORT HISTORY OF THE PUBLIC SERVICE IN IRELAND.
DUBLIN: INST PUBLIC ADMIN, 1962, 48 PP.
ATTEMPTS TO TRACE HISTORY OF IRISH CIVIL SERVICE FROM BEGINNING IN 1215 A.D., SHOWING COMPLEX AND SOMEWHAT ILLOGICAL DEPARTMENTAL DIVISIONS - THE RESULT OF YEARS OF DEVELOPMENT THROUGH BRITISH AND IRISH ADMINISTRATION.

1540 INSTITUTE POLITISCHE WISSEN
POLITISCHE LITERATUR (3 VOLS.)
FRANKFURT: INST FUR POL WISS, 1955.
A COLLECTION OF PERIODICALS (1953-54) REVIEWING PUBLICATIONS ON POLITICAL LITERATURE. THE PERIODICALS APPEAR MONTHLY AND INCLUDE REVIEWS (IN GERMAN) OF FOREIGN PUBLICATIONS FOR YEARS 1952-55.

1541 INT. BANK RECONSTR. DEVELOP.
ECONOMIC DEVELOPMENT OF KUWAIT.
BALTIMORE: JOHNS HOPKINS PR., 1965, 194 PP.
KUWAIT IS FOURTH LARGEST OIL PRODUCER IN WORLD AND SECOND ONLY TO VENEZUELA AS AN OIL EXPORTER. SUMMARIZES RESULTS OF FINDINGS AND RECOMMENDATIONS OF TWO 'ECONOMIC MISSIONS' TO COUNTRY. DOMESTIC NEEDS AND INVESTMENT OPPORTUNITIES ARE EMPHASIZED WITH REVALUATION OF TARIFFS AND IMPORT RESTRICTIONS.

1542 INTERAMERICAN CULTURAL COUN
LISTA DE LIBROS REPRESENTAVOS DE AMERICA.
WASHINGTON: PAN AMERICAN UNION, 1959, 364 PP.
ANNOTATED BIBLIOGRAPHY OF THE MOST SIGNIFICANT PUBLICATIONS IN THE SOCIAL SCIENCES. ENTRIES ARRANGED BY COUNTRY.

1543 INTERNATIONAL AFRICAN INST
ETHNOGRAPHIC SURVEY OF AFRICA: WEST CENTRAL AFRICA (VOLS. I-III, 1951-1953)
LONDON: INTERNATL AFRICAN INST, 1951, 320 PP.
STUDY OF TRIBAL GROUPINGS, DISTRIBUTION, ENVIRONMENT, SOCIETY, POLITICAL STRUCTURE, RELIGIOUS RITES, AND ART OF PEOPLE OF WEST CENTRAL AFRICA. EACH VOLUME COVERS SPECIFIC TRIBE OR AREA. SOUTHERN LUNDA AND PEOPLES OF N. RHODESIA, BELGIAN CONGO, AND ANGOLA ARE IN I. II COVERS OVIMBUNDU OF ANGOLA; III, LOZI OF NORTHWEST RHODESIA. INCLUDES BIBLIOGRAPHY FOR SPECIFIC READINGS ON EACH TRIBE.

1544 INTERNATIONAL AFRICAN INST
ETHNOGRAPHIC SURVEY OF AFRICA: SOUTHERN AFRICA (VOLS. I-III, 1952-1954)
LONDON: INTERNATL AFRICAN INST, 1952, 257 PP.
STUDY OF TRIBAL GROUPINGS, DISTRIBUTION, ENVIRONMENT, SOCIETY, POLITICAL STRUCTURE, RELIGIOUS RITES, AND ART OF PEOPLE OF SOUTH AFRICA. VOLUME I STUDIES SWAZI, II SOUTHERN SOTHO, AND III TSWANA TRIBES. BIBLIOGRAPHY IN EACH VOLUME FOR FURTHER READING ON SPECIFIC TRIBES.

1545 INTERNATIONAL AFRICAN INST
ETHNOGRAPHIC SURVEY OF AFRICA: NORTH EASTERN AFRICA (VOLUMES 1-2, 1955-56)
LONDON: INTERNATL AFRICAN INST, 1955, 356 PP.
STUDY OF TRIBAL GROUPINGS, DISTRIBUTION, ENVIRONMENT, SOCIETY, POLITICAL AND ECONOMIC STRUCTURE, AND RELIGIOUS RITES OF PEOPLES IN NORTH EASTERN AFRICA. VOLUME I COVERS PEOPLE OF HORN OF AFRICA: SOMALI, AFAR, AND SAHO. VOLUME II COVERS GALLA OF ETHIOPIA AND PEOPLES IN KAFA AND JANJERO. BIBLIOGRAPHY OF SPECIFIC READINGS ON TRIBES.

1546 INTERNATIONAL AFRICAN INST
ETHNOGRAPHIC SURVEY OF AFRICA: WESTERN AFRICA: PEOPLES OF THE NIGER-BENUE CONFLUENCE.
LONDON: INTERNATL AFRICAN INST, 1955, 160 PP.
STUDY OF NUPE, IGBIRA, AND IGALA TRIBES, PLUS ALL IDOMA-SPEAKING PEOPLES. ARCA KNOWN FOR WARS OVER FERTILE LAND NEAR RIVERS, DOWN WHICH TRIBES MIGRATED. FEEL ALL SAME LANGUAGE BACKGROUND AND UNIQUE DIALECTS RESULT OF EARLY CONTACT WITH EUROPEAN CIVILIZATIONS. NUPE ARE MOSTLY HIGHLY ORGANIZED POLITICALLY, BEING ISLAMS WHILE OTHER TRIBES VERY CLANNISH. BIBLIOGRAPHY OF SPECIFIC READINGS ON EACH TRIBE.

1547 INTERNATIONAL AFRICAN INST
SELECT ANNOTATED BIBLIOGRAPHY OF TROPICAL AFRICA.
LONDON: INTERNATL AFRICAN INST, 1956.
GENERAL BIBLIOGRAPHY OF WORKS LISTED UNDER SEVEN MAJOR SUBJECT HEADINGS: GEOGRAPHY, ETHNOGRAPHY, SOCIOLOGY, LINGUISTICS, GOVERNMENT AND ADMINISTRATION, ECONOMICS, EDUCATION, MISSIONS, AND HEALTH. ANNOTATED WITH INTRODUCTIONS TO MAJOR SECTIONS.

1548 INTERNATIONAL AFRICAN INST
ETHNOGRAPHIC SURVEY OF AFRICA; WESTERN AFRICA: PAGAN PEOPLES OF CENTRAL AREA OF NORTHERN NIGERIA (VOL. XII)
LONDON: INTERNATL AFRICAN INST, 1956, 146 PP.
STUDY OF ABOUT 50 DIVERSE COMMUNITIES AND TRIBES. ATTEMPTS TO LINK CERTAIN TRIBES FOR FIRST TIME THROUGH LANGUAGE SIMILARITIES OR DIALECTS. TRIES TO TRACE CERTAIN SOCIAL HABITS AND INSTITUTIONS AMONG TRIBES TO ESTABLISH SIMILARITY OF CULTURAL ORIGINS. POINTS OUT DIFFERENCES AS WELL.

1549 INTERNATIONAL AFRICAN INST
SOCIAL IMPLICATIONS OF INDUSTRIALIZATION AND URBANIZATION IN AFRICA SOUTH OF THE SAHARA.
NEW YORK: COLUMBIA U PRESS, 1956, 744 PP.
PRESENTS A SURVEY OF STUDIES ON SOCIAL EFFECTS OF ECONOMIC DEVELOPMENT AND URBANIZATION IN AFRICA. DISCUSSES LABOR PROBLEMS, WORKING CONDITIONS, AND SOCIAL PATTERNS OF URBAN LIFE.

1550 INTERNATIONAL AFRICAN INST
ETHNOGRAPHIC SURVEY OF AFRICA: WESTERN AFRICA: THE BENIN KINGDOM.
LONDON: INTERNATL AFRICAN INST, 1957, 212 PP.
STUDY OF EDO-SPEAKING PEOPLES OF SOUTHWESTERN NIGERIA, ISHAN TRIBES, AND URHOBO AND ISOKO OF NIGER DELTA. THIS AREA UNIQUE AS VILLAGES ARE ORGANIZED POLITICALLY BY AGE OF MALES, AND PRACTICE PRIMOGENITURE. ECONOMIES ARE ALL BASED ON OIL PALMS YET EACH SECTOR IS DISTINCT IN CULTURE, LANGUAGE, ETC. BIBLIOGRAPHY OF SPECIFIC READINGS ON EACH TRIBE WITH SOME ENTRIES IN FRENCH.

1551 INTERNATIONAL AFRICAN INST
ETHNOGRAPHIC SURVEY OF AFRICA: WESTERN AFRICA: THE WOLOF OF SENEGAMBIA.
LONDON: INTERNATL AFRICAN INST, 1957, 110 PP.
STUDIES WOLOF TRIBE AND ALSO LEBU, AND SERER TRIBES. COVERS VARIETY OF CULTURE PRESENT FROM VILLAGES TO CITIES, AND ILLITERACY TO COLLEGE GRADUATES. ARCA HAS ARISTOCRACY FROM BEST OF FRENCH AND ISLAMIC WORLDS AS WELL AS SLAVES. BIBLIOGRAPHY OF SPECIFIC READINGS ON EACH TRIBE; SOME ENTRIES FRENCH.

1552 INTERNATIONAL AFRICAN INST
ETHNOGRAPHIC SURVEY OF AFRICA: WESTERN AFRICA: PEOPLES OF THE MIDDLE NIGER REGION, NORTHERN NIGERIA.
LONDON: INTERNATL AFRICAN INST, 1960, 140 PP.
STUDY OF RIVERAIN PEOPLES YAURI, BORGU, ZURU, AND KONTAGORA. MIDDLE NIGER REGION OR NORTH-EAST HINTERLAND INCLUDES ACHIPAWA, KAMUKU, BASA, GWARI, AND KORO. FIRST STUDY WITH TRIBES GROUPED IN THIS WAY BUT FELT ALL SHARE TRADITIONAL LANGUAGE AND CULTURAL BACKGROUND. ALL ARE SHARING NEIGHBORS YET RETAIN HIGH CULTURAL DISTINCTIVENESS. BIBLIOGRAPHY OF SPECIFIC READINGS ON EACH TRIBE OR AREA.

1553 INTERNATIONAL ASSOCIATION RES
AFRICAN STUDIES IN INCOME AND WEALTH.
CHICAGO: QUADRANGLE BOOKS, INC, 1963, 433 PP., LC#63-11846.
COLLECTION OF PAPERS ON DEVELOPING AFRICAN ECONOMY, DEALING WITH NATIONAL ACCOUNTS, PLANNING, INCOME ESTIMATION, AND CALCULATION OF STATUS AND NEEDS OF NATIONAL ECONOMY IN AREA. PREPARED BY INTERNATIONAL ASSOCIATION FOR RESEARCH IN INCOME AND WEALTH.

1554 INTERNAT.CTR.AFRICAN DOC.
BULLETIN OF INFORMATION ON THESES AND STUDIES IN PROGRESS OR PROPOSED.
BRUSSELS: INT CTR AFR ECO DOCUM.
SEMI-ANNUAL BULLETIN PUBLISHED IN FRENCH AND ENGLISH SINCE 1963. EACH ISSUE CONTAINS ABOUT 175 TITLES OF UNPUBLISHED WORKS IN THE HUMAN, ECONOMIC, AND SOCIAL SCIENCES. ANNOTATIONS PROVIDE BRIEF SUMMARIES AND THE NAME AND ADDRESS OF AUTHOR. INCLUDES AN INDEX OF INSTITUTIONS, A SUBJECT AND TITLE INDEX, AND A GEOGRAPHICAL INDEX. MORE RECENT ISSUES PROVIDE A CLASSIFIED ARRANGEMENT.

1555 INTERNATIONAL COMN JURISTS
JUSTICE ENSLAVED.
GENEVA: INTL COMN OF JURISTS, 1955, 535 PP.
COLLECTION OF DOCUMENTS ON ABUSE OF JUSTICE IN COMMUNIST COUNTRIES. CITES VIOLATIONS OF FREEDOM OF SPEECH, FREE ELECTIONS, PROPERTY RIGHTS, ETC.

1556 INTERNATIONAL ECONOMIC ASSN
ECONOMICS OF INTERNATIONAL MIGRATION.
NEW YORK: ST MARTIN'S PRESS, 1958, 502 PP.
DEVELOPS ANALYTICAL TOOLS FOR INTERPRETING MIGRATION. COMPARATIVELY STUDIES EXPERIENCE OF REPRESENTATIVE COUNTRIES OF EMIGRATION AND IMMIGRATION, AND CHANGING GOVERNMENT POLICIES; SCALE AND FUTURE OF INTRA-CONTINENTAL MIGRATION IN EUROPE AND ASIA; SOCIAL PROBLEMS OF ASSIMILATION; EXTENT TO WHICH MIGRATION CAN HELP RELIEVE POPULATION PRESSURES AND CONTRIBUTE TO GROWTH OF UNDERDEVELOPED LANDS.

1557 INTERNATIONAL LABOUR OFFICE
EMPLOYMENT, UNEMPLOYMENT AND LABOUR FORCE STATISTICS (PAMPHLET)
GENEVA: INTL LABOUR OFFICE, 1948, 130 PP.
SEEKS TO ESTABLISH A COMPREHENSIVE SCHEME OF STATISTICAL DATA AND TO STATE AN IDEAL SYSTEM TOWARD WHICH DIFFERENT COUNTRIES SHOULD DEVELOP; PROVIDES COMMON GROUND OF DEFINITION, PROCEDURE, AND PRESENTATION. INCLUDES METHODS OF GATHERING DATA. COVERS TYPES OF EMPLOYMENT AND PROBLEMS, TYPES OF UNEMPLOYMENT AND PROBLEMS, AND INTERNATIONAL COMPARABILITY OF DATA. CLOSES WITH RESOLUTIONS FOR FUTURE.

1558 INTERNATIONAL LABOUR OFFICE
EMPLOYMENT AND ECONOMIC GROWTH.
GENEVA: INTL LABOUR OFFICE, 1964, 219 PP.
STUDIES UNEMPLOYMENT AND UNDEREMPLOYMENT AND MEASURES TO DEAL WITH THEM. GIVES STATISTICAL BACKGROUND IN VARIOUS COUNTRIES AND RELATES ECONOMIC DEVELOPMENT TO FULL EMPLOYMENT. ALSO CONSIDERS INTERNATIONAL TACTICS NECESSARY TO HELP UNDERDEVELOPED NATIONS TO RAISE EMPLOYMENT LEVELS.

1559 INTERNATIONAL PRESS INSTITUTE
THE PRESS IN AUTHORITARIAN COUNTRIES.
ZURICH: INTERNATIONAL PRESS INST, 1959, 201 PP.
SURVEYS POSITION OF THE PRESS UNDER AUTHORITARIAN REGIMES SINCE WWII. GIVES COUNTRY-BY-COUNTRY REPORT ON METHODS OF CENSORSHIP AND CONTROL, AND DEGREE OF SUPPRESSING OPPOSITION PAPERS. EXAMINES LIBERALIZATION TRENDS OF LATE 1950'S, FOLLOWING DEATH OF STALIN. GIVES SUMMARY OF GOVERNMENT POLICY TOWARD IT AND IMPACT OF IDEOLOGY UPON REPORTING.

1560 INTERPARLIAMENTARY UNION
PARLIAMENTS: COMPARATIVE STUDY ON STRUCTURE AND FUNCTIONING OF REPRESENTATIVE INSTITUTIONS IN FIFTY-FIVE COUNTRIES.
LONDON: CASSELL & CO LTD, 1966, 346 PP.
COMPARES STRUCTURE, ORGANIZATION, FUNCTION, AND POWERS OF PARLIAMENTS IN DIFFERENT COUNTRIES, AND HOW THESE ARE DETERMINED BY VARYING CONDITIONS AND ATTITUDES. SPECIAL DISCUSSION OF PARLIAMENTS' GROWING CONTROL OVER EXECUTIVE.

1561 INTL CONF ON POPULATION
POPULATION DYNAMICS: INTERNATIONAL ACTION AND TRAINING PROGRAMS.
BALTIMORE: JOHNS HOPKINS PRESS, 1964, 248 PP., LC#65-24792.
COLLECTION OF PAPERS ON POPULATION CONTROL; RECENT DEVELOPMENTS; PROGRAMS IN INDIA, PAKISTAN, JAPAN, KOREA, TAIWAN, CHINA, PUERTO RICO, US, CHILE, AND OTHER LATIN AMERICAN COUNTRIES; VALUE OF ATTITUDE STUDIES ON CONTRACEPTION AND PLANNING; AND NEW MULTIDISCIPLINARY TRAINING TECHNIQUE.

1562 INTL CONF ON WORLD POLITICS-5
EASTERN EUROPE IN TRANSITION.
BALTIMORE: JOHNS HOPKINS PRESS, 1966, 364 PP., LC#66-24409.
REPORT OF FIFTH INTERNATIONAL CONFERENCE ON WORLD POLITICS HELD IN THE NETHERLANDS, 1965. STUDIES COUNTRIES OF CENTRAL, EASTERN, AND SOUTHEASTERN EUROPE, AND FACTORS UNDERLYING TRANSFORMATION OF THIS AREA. DISCUSSES GROWTH OF POLYCENTRISM UNDER THE IMPACT OF SINO-SOVIET CONFLICT, POST-1957 INTERBLOC ORGANIZATIONS, AND CHANGING IDEOLOGICAL, POLITICAL, AND SOCIAL ATTITUDES.

1563 INTL UNION LOCAL AUTHORITIES
METROPOLIS.
THE HAGUE: MARTINUS NIJHOFF, 1961, 45 PP.
NEARLY 1,000 ENTRIES IN FIELD OF CITY MANAGEMENT AND PUBLIC ADMINISTRATION, IN FRENCH, ENGLISH, AND GERMAN. MATERIAL ON NORTH AMERICA IS EXCLUDED. COVERS FINANCE, EDUCATION, WELFARE, HEALTH, HOUSING, PLANNING, TRANSPORTATION, AND CRIME.

1564 IOVTCHOUK M.T., OSSIPOV G.
"ON SOME THEORETICAL PRINCIPLES AND METHODS OF SOCIOLOGICAL INVESTIGATIONS (IN RUSSIAN)."
VOP. FILOZOF., 16 (NO.12, 62), 23-34.
ANALYZES AND COMPARES ECONOMIC ADVANCE OF SOVIET UNION AND USA. DISCUSSES FUTURE PROBLEMS THAT MAY ARISE OUT OF CONFLICT BETWEEN COMMUNIST AND CAPITALIST ECONOMIC SYSTEMS. SUPPORTS THESIS OF SUPERIORITY OF MARXIST SYSTEM.

1565 IOWA STATE U CTR AGRI AND ECO
RESEARCH AND EDUCATION FOR REGIONAL AND AREA DEVELOPMENT.
AMES: IOWA ST U CTR AGRI ECO DEV, 1966, 287 PP., LC#66-12842
INDIVIDUAL ANALYSES OF SPECIFIC AREA PROBLEMS IN REGIONAL GROWTH, PRIMARILY ON ECONOMIC LEVEL, SUCH AS APPALACHIA. CONSIDERS TECHNICAL ASPECTS OF RESEARCH FOR PLANNING AND GIVES SEVERAL RESEARCH PROPOSALS. FOUND THAT RESEARCH IS EDED ON NEW LEVELS BECAUSE OLD KNOWLEDGE IS FALSE IN TODAY'S SOCIETY.

1566 IRELE A.
"A DEFENSE OF NEGRITUDE."
TRANSACTIONS, 3 (MAR. 64), 9-11.
PHILOSOPHICAL DISCUSSION OF COMMON NEGRO CULTURE AND ITS ROOTS AND ORIGINS. DEFENDS NEGRITUDE AS VALID CULTURAL CONCEPT AND ATTEMPTS TO DEMONSTRATE ITS VALUE BY COMPARISON WITH EUROPEAN CULTURE.

1567 IRIKURA J.K.
SOUTHEAST ASIA: SELECTED ANNOTATED BIBLIOGRAPHY OF JAPANESE PUBLICATIONS.
NEW HAVEN: HUMAN REL AREA FILES, 1956, 544 PP., LC#56-71519.
CONTAINS 965 EXTENSIVELY ANNOTATED ITEMS ON HISTORY, GOVERNMENT, ECONOMY, FOREIGN RELATIONS, FOREIGN TRADE, HEALTH, WELFARE AND EDUCATION, AND MINORITIES OF AREA. PARTICULAR EMPHASIS ON JAPAN-SOUTHEAST ASIAN RELATIONS. WORKS ON BURMA, INDOCHINA, INDONESIA, MALAYA, PHILIPPINES, AND THAILAND.

1568 IRION F.C.
PUBLIC OPINION AND PROPAGANDA.
NEW YORK: THOMAS Y CROWELL, 1950, 782 PP.
BEGINS WITH A HISTORICAL INTRODUCTION TO CONCEPT OF PUBLIC OPINION; PROCEEDS TO DISCUSS INSTRUMENTS RESPONSIBLE FOR SHAPING OF OPINION SUCH AS PRESS, RADIO, AND CINEMA. ALSO DISCUSSES THE INFLUENCE WHICH SUCH INSTITUTIONS AS FAMILY, CHURCH, AND STATE MAY HAVE ON PUBLIC OPINION.

1569 ISAAC J.
ECONOMICS OF MIGRATION.
NEW YORK: OXFORD U PR, 1947, 285 PP.
DEALS WITH ECONOMIC AND SOCIAL ASPECTS OF THE MIGRATION OF FREE INDIVIDUALS. DISCUSSES HOW MIGRATION BECAME A DETERMINING FACTOR IN MOULDING THE SOCIAL STRUCTURE OF THE WESTERN WORLD FROM THE NAPOLEONIC WARS TO WWI. EMPHASIZES THE EFFECTS OF MIGRATION ON CAPITAL DISPOSAL AND POPULATION DISTRIBUTION.

1570 ISAACS H.R., ROSS E.

AFRICA: NEW CRISES IN THE MAKING (PAMPHLET)
NEW YORK: FOREIGN POLICY ASSN, 1952, 56 PP.
EXAMINES CONDITIONS IMMEDIATE TO NATIVE POLITICAL INDEPENDENCE, ESPECIALLY APARTHEID EXTREMISM, WHITE SUPERIORITY, AND MUTUAL DISTRUST.

1571 ISRAEL J.
THE CHINESE STUDENT MOVEMENT, 1927-1937; A BIBLIOGRAPHICAL ESSAY BASED ON THE RESOURCES OF THE HOOVER INSTITUTION.
STANFORD: HOOVER INSTITUTE, 1959, 29 PP.
AN ANNOTATED BIBLIOGRAPHY OF WORKS IN BOTH CHINESE AND ENGLISH RELATING TO THE CHINESE STUDENT MOVEMENT FROM THE FOUNDING OF THE NANKIN GOVERNMENT TO THE OUTBREAK OF THE SINO-JAPANESE WAR. BIBLIOGRAPHIC AIDS, BOOKS, AND PERIODICALS ARRANGED CHRONOLOGICALLY AND CRITICALLY EVALUATED. TITLES COVER PUBLICATIONS FROM 1935-59, AND APPEAR IN ROMAN-SCRIPT AS WELL AS CHARACTERS.

1572 ISRAEL J.
"THE RED GUARDS IN HISTORICAL PERSPECTIVE: CONTINUITY AND CHANGE IN THE CHINESE YOUTH MOVEMENT."
CHINA Q., 30 (APR.-JUNE 67), 1-32.
ANALYZES ORIGIN AND DEVELOPMENT OF RED GUARDS. EVALUATES THEIR CONTROL AND INFLUENCE ON PARTY, EMPHASIZING CHANGES IN PARTY STRUCTURE SINCE ITS ORIGIN IN 1920'S. SEES RED GUARDS AS PASSING PHASE. PARTY OF 1960'S WAS TOO STRONG TO GIVE UP ITS CONTROL. GROUP WAS LAST ATTEMPT TO PROVE THAT "IDEOLOGY AND ZEAL COULD TRIUMPH OVER POLITICAL PRUDENCE AND ECONOMIC MOTIVES." REVOLUTION HAS DIED.

1573 ISSAWI C.
EGYPT IN REVOLUTION: AN ECONOMIC ANALYSIS.
NEW YORK: OXFORD U. PR., 1963, 343 PP.
OUTLINES EGYPTIAN HISTORY, RELIGION AND ECONOMIC EMERGENCE IN 1920 TO 1952 COUP D'GTAT OF NASSER. FOLLOWS WITH A THOROUGH DESCRIPTION OF MODERN EGYPT AS TO 'ARAB SOCIALISM', HUMAN RESOURCES AND POPULATION PROBLEMS, NATIONAL INCOME, AGRICULTURAL AND INDUSTRIAL SITUATUATION, FINANCIAL PICTURE AND POLICIES.

1574 JACKSON G.
THE SPANISH REPUBLIC AND THE CIVIL WAR, 1931-1939.
PRINCETON: U. PR., 1965, 578 PP., $12.50.
UTILIZING PRESS EXTRACTS AND INTERVIEWS WITH 120 POLITICAL AND NON-POLITICAL FIGURES, ATTEMPTS TO SHOW SIGNIFICANCE OF EVENTS TO SPANISH PEOPLE.

1575 JACKSON G.D.
COMINTERN AND PEASANT IN EAST EUROPE 1919-1930.
NEW YORK: COLUMBIA U PRESS, 1966, 339 PP., LC#66-15489.
ANALYSIS OF COMINTERN IN THEORY AND PRACTICE IN REGARD TO ITS POLICY TOWARD PEASANTRY AND PEASANT POLITICAL MOVEMENTS IN EASTERN EUROPE. EXPLAINS PROBLEMS OF PEASANT SOCIETIES IN TRANSITION AND MOVEMENTS THAT DEVELOPED IN EASTERN EUROPE. DISCUSSES IMPORTANCE OF PEASANT IN COMINTERN POLICY AND DETAILS RELATION OF COMINTERN TO BULGARIA, POLAND, YUGOSLAVIA, RUMANIA, AND CZECHOSLOVAKIA, AND TO THEIR PEASANT MOVEMENTS.

1576 JACKSON W.A.D.
RUSSO-CHINESE BORDERLANDS.
PRINCETON: VAN NOSTRAND, 1962, 126 PP.
CONCERNED WITH HISTORY AND POLITICAL GEOGRAPHY OF THE LANDS ALONG THE RUSSO-CHINESE BORDER. TRACES TENSIONS WHICH HAVE EXISTED IN THE PAST AND THE TREATIES AND AGREEMENTS WHICH HAVE EASED THEM. VIEWS GEO-POLITICAL FUTURE FOR THIS BORDER AS ONE OF STABILITY AND COOPERATION.

1577 JACOB H.
GERMAN ADMINISTRATION SINCE BISMARCK: CENTRAL AUTHORITY VERSUS LOCAL AUTONOMY.
NEW HAVEN: YALE U PR, 1963, 324 PP., LC#63-7937.
ANALYZES AND COMPARES SECOND REICH, WEIMAR REPUBLIC, THIRD REICH, AND GERMAN FEDERAL REPUBLIC IN HISTORICAL PERSPECTIVE. STUDIES INSTITUTIONS AND ADMINISTRATIVE POLICIES. EXAMINES DEVELOPMENT OF CONTROLS, LEGALISTIC PERSPECTIVES, PARTY INFILTRATION, AND LARGE-SCALE PERSONNEL CHANGES. INCLUDES GERMAN CIVIL SERVICE, QUEST FOR RESPONSIVENESS, AND ADAPTIVE CHARACTERISTICS.

1578 JACOB H. ED., VINES K.N. ED.
POLITICS IN THE AMERICAN STATES; A COMPARATIVE ANALYSIS.
BOSTON: LITTLE BROWN, 1965, 493 PP., LC#65-17333.
EXAMINES NATURE OF STATE POLITICAL SYSTEMS. TREATS HOW PRIVATE CITIZENS, INDIVIDUALLY OR IN GROUPS OR PARTIES INFLUENCE GOVERNMENT. CONSIDERS POLICY-MAKING INSTITUTIONS AND THEIR PROCESSES OF DECISION-MAKING. ANALYZES PROGRAMS AND POLICIES OF GOVERNMENTS TO STUDY RESULTS OF POLITICAL STRUGGLE. DEFINES BOUNDARIES ON STATES' ACTIONS.

1579 JACOBS N. ED.
CULTURE FOR THE MILLIONS?
PRINCETON: VAN NOSTRAND, 1959, 200 PP.
DISCUSSIONS OF MASS CULTURE AS RELATED TO ARTS AND MASS MEDIA BY SEVERAL ARTISTS, CRITICS, AND SOCIAL SCIENTISTS. ALSO CONSIDERS SOCIO-POLITICAL CHANGES WHICH HAVE CONTRIBUTED TO DEVELOPMENT OF MASS CULTURE.

1580 JACOBSSON P.
SOME MONETARY PROBLEMS, INTERNATIONAL AND NATIONAL.
NEW YORK: OXFORD U PR, 1958, 374 PP.
STUDIES ON MAJOR ECONOMIC PROBLEMS OF 1917-58, BOTH INTERNATIONAL AND NATIONAL. DISCUSSES ARMAMENTS EXPENDITURE, PLAN FOR INTERNATIONAL BANK, GOLD AND MONETARY PROBLEMS, INVESTMENT POLICIES, TRADE AND FINANCIAL RELATIONS AMONG COUNTRIES, AND EMPLOYMENT PROGRAMS IN DIFFERENT COUNTRIES.

1581 JAECKH A.
WELTSAAT; ERLEBTES UND ERSTREBTES.
STUTTGART: DEUTSCHE VERLAGSANST, 1960, 340 PP.
AUTOBIOGRAPHY OF A GERMAN POLITICAL THINKER AND ADVISER TO GERMAN POLITICAL LEADERS FROM TIME OF KAISER THROUGH WEIMAR REPUBLIC TO KONRAD ADENAUER; ORIENTALIST MEMOIRS OF HIS VARIED LIFE, EMPHASIZING HIS POLITICAL INVOLVEMENTS IN A VARIETY OF ADVISORY AND ACADEMIC CAPACITIES IN GERMANY, ENGLAND, US.

1582 JAFFEE A.J.
"POPULATION TRENDS AND CONTROLS IN UNDERDEVELOPED COUNTRIES."
LAW CONTEMP. PROBL., 25 (SUMMER 60), 508-535.
OFFERS HISTORY OF POPULATION GROWTH, AND ANALYSIS OF POPULATION DISTRIBUTION AND BIRTH-DEATH RATES. COMPARES SOCIO-ECONOMIC FACTORS RELATED TO POPULATION GROWTH AND FERTILITY IN UNDERDEVELOPED COUNTRIES WITH THOSE IN DEVELOPED ONES. SPECULATES ON POSSIBLE FUTURE GROWTH OF POPULATION AND ITS EFFECT ON ECONOMIC DEVELOPMENT, EMPLOYMENT, AND STANDARD OF LIVING.

1583 JAIN G.
"INDIA REJECTS THE POWER RACE* REALISM ABOUT NUCLEAR WEAPONS."
ROUND TABLE, (APR. 67), 135-140.
POINTS OUT RECENT INDIAN NON-INTEREST IN CHINESE NUCLEAR TESTING AS LOGICAL DEVELOPMENT. DISCUSSES INDIAN FOREIGN POLICY AS IT RELATES TO NUCLEAR WEAPONS. ALSO CONSIDERS NEHRU'S ACTIONS DURING 1950'S.

1584 JAIN R.K.
MANAGEMENT OF STATE ENTERPRISES.
BOMBAY: MANAKTALAS, 1967, 532 PP.
EXAMINES OBJECTIVELY PROBLEMS FACING THE PUBLIC SECTOR IN INDIA WITH A VIEW TO FINDING A WAY FORWARD DURING TRANSITIONAL STAGE OF SOCIAL TRANSFORMATION. SEEKS WAYS TO ESTABLISH AND STRENGTHEN POWER OF DEMOCRATIC INSTITUTIONS WITHIN SOCIETY WHERE PUBLIC SECTOR CONTROLS INDUSTRIES. ANALYZES INTERNAL AND FINANCIAL ORGANIZATION OF SUCH INDUSTRIES, AS WELL AS PERSONNEL MANAGEMENT.

1585 JAIN R.S.
THE GROWTH AND DEVELOPMENT OF GOVERNOR-GENERAL'S EXECUTIVE COUNCIL 1858-1919.
NEW DELHI: S CHAND AND CO, 1962, 236 PP.
ANALYZES DUAL POSITION OF COUNCIL IN INDIA UNDER BRITISH RULE. COUNCIL MADE POLICIES TO GOVERN INDIA, BUT WAS REALLY EXECUTIVE AGENT OF BRITISH CABINET, SOURCE OF ULTIMATE AUTHORITY. CONCENTRATES ON REVEALING REAL POSITIONS OF MEMBERS OF COUNCIL BY STUDYING THEIR DEALINGS WITH VARIOUS AUTHORITIES. FEELS THEIR LEGAL STATUS DID NOT "SQUARE" WITH THEIR REAL POSITIONS.

1586 JAIN S.C.
THE STATE AND AGRICULTURE.
ALLAHABAD, INDIA: KITAB MAHAL, 1965, 173 PP.
COMPARES AGRICULTURAL POLICIES OF CAPITALIST, MARXIST, AND MIXED ECONOMIES, AND EXAMINES THESE POLICIES AS CASE STUDY IN INDIAN EXPERIENCE, INCLUDING SURVEY OF MAIN PROBLEMS OF INDIAN AGRICULTURE AND PROCESS OF POLICY FORMATION FOR OVERCOMING THEM.

1587 JAIRAZBHOY R.A.
FOREIGN INFLUENCE IN ANCIENT INDIA.
BOMBAY: ASIA PUBL HOUSE, 1963, 195 PP.
ACCOUNT OF IMPACT UPON FORMATION OF INDIAN CULTURE BY FOREIGN CONQUERERS: MESOPOTAMIAN, PERSIAN, GREEK, ROMAN, PARTHO-SASSANIAN, AND MUSLIM. SHOWS PARTICULAR INFLUENCES UPON ART, LANGUAGE, RELIGION, AND EDUCATION.

1588 JAKOBSON M.
THE DIPLOMACY OF THE WINTER WAR.
CAMBRIDGE: HARVARD U PR, 1961, 281 PP., LC#61-5578.
DISCUSSES SOVIET-FINNISH CONFLICT OF 1939-40 AND PRAISES FINNS FOR THEIR DEFENSE OF DEMOCRACY AND FREEDOM AGAINST SOVIET ENCROACHMENT. DISCUSSES WAR IN RELATION TO TOTAL EUROPEAN SITUATION. TRACES DIPLOMATIC AND MILITARY COURSE OF CONFLICT UP TO 1940 FINNISH-SOVIET PEACE TREATY.

1589 JANICKE M.
"MONOPOLISMUS UND PLURALISMUS IM KOMMUNISTISCHEN HERRSCHAFTSSYSTEM"
ZEITSCHRIFT FUR POLITIK, 14 (JUNE 67), 150-161.
SUBJECTS CONCEPTS OF BUREAUCRATIC ABSOLUTISM AND PLURALISM TO CRITICAL ANALYSIS. DISCUSSES "TOTALITARIAN CRISIS"

OF PARTY REGIME IN USSR, CZECHOSLOVAKIA, AND YUGOSLAVIA. MAINTAINS THAT IDEOLOGICAL RIGIDITY AND UNIFORM INFLUENCE OF PARTY DOCTRINE IS DISINTEGRATING IN SOME MEASURE IN YUGOSLAVIA WHEREAS OTHER COMMUNIST COUNTRIES, INCLUDING USSR, ARE STILL MONOLITHIC IN STRUCTURE AND ATTITUDE.

1590 JANIS I.L.
"DECISIONAL CONFLICT: A THEORETICAL ANALYSIS."
J. CONFL. RESOLUT., 3 (1959), 6-27.
ANALYZES PSYCHOLOGICAL CAUSES AND CONSEQUENCES OF DECISIONAL CONFLICTS MANIFESTED DURING WW 1. AMBIGUOUS POSITION OF WORLD LEADERS IN THESE CONFLICTS IN LIGHT OF PUBLIC OPINION.

1591 JANSEN M.B. ED.
CHANGING JAPANESE ATTITUDES TOWARD MODERNIZATION.
PRINCETON: U. PR., 1965, 546 PP., $9.00.
ESSAYS DEFINE CHANGING CONCEPTION OF MODERNIZATION, SHOW SOCIAL AND INTELLECTUAL PREPAREDNESS, FOCUSING ON 19TH CENTURY ATTITUDE CHANGES. EVALUATE NEW VALUES AND RELATE THEIR IMPACT ON WRITERS, INTELLECTUALS, AND RELIGIOUS LEADERS. ALSO TREAT EFFECT OF MODERNIZATION ON CHINA AND INDIA.

1592 JARVIE I.C.
THE REVOLUTION IN ANTHROPOLOGY.
NEW YORK: HUMANITIES PRESS, 1964, 248 PP., LC#64-14658.
PRIMARILY A STUDY OF ANTHROPOLOGICAL TRADITION, SECONDLY, GIVES ATTENTION TO THE PHILOSOPHY OF SCIENCE DEVELOPED BY KARL POPPER AS APPLIED TO THE STUDY OF SOCIETY. ILLUSTRATION IS GIVEN BY WAY OF DISCUSSION OF THE MESSIANIC MOVEMENTS KNOWN AS "CARGO CULTS" OF PRIMITIVE PEOPLES SUDDENLY CONFRONTED BY MODERN TECHNOLOGY.

1593 JASNY H.
KHRUSHCHEV'S CROP POLICY.
GLASGOW: GEORGE OUTRAM CO, LTD, 1965, 243 PP.
ANALYZES KHRUSHCHEV'S AGRICULTURAL PROGRAMS THAT BROUGHT ABOUT FAILURES IN ECONOMY. CONCLUDES THAT EXCESSIVE CONCERN WITH MAIZE, PULSE, AND SUGARBEET CAUSED FAILURE. COMPARES SOVIET CROP PRACTICES WITH THOSE OF OTHER NATIONS. FEELS KHRUSHCHEV MAY HAVE BEEN JUSTIFIED, OWING TO UNIQUENESS OF NATURAL RESOURCES.

1594 JAY R.
"RELIGION AND POLITICS IN RURAL CENTRAL JAVA."
DETROIT: CELLAR BOOK SHOP, 1963, 117 PP.
A CASE STUDY OF THE DEGREE OF ISLAMIC ORIENTATION ON THE PART OF THE PEASANTRY. CONCLUDES THAT THE LOCALE IS 'RENT BY A MARKED DIVISION BETWEEN ADHERENTS OF THE ABAUGAN WORLD VIEW, THE TRADITIONAL-SYNCRETIC RELIGION OF THE JAVANESE PEASANTRY, ON THE ONE HAND, AND THOSE IDENTIFYING WITH MORE OR LESS ORTHODOX ISLAMIC SANTRI ORIENTATION, ON THE OTHER. THIS SCHISM HAS BECOME ONE OF THE BASIC DETERMINANTS OF JAVANESE SOCIAL AND POLITICAL HISTORY SINCE INDEPENDENCE.'

1595 JEFFRIES C.
TRANSFER OF POWER: PROBLEMS OF THE PASSAGE TO SELF-GOVERNMENT.
NEW YORK: FREDERICK PRAEGER, 1960, 148 PP.
DISCUSSES PROBLEMS OF INDEPENDENCE, CONDITIONS REQUIRED TO MAKE IT EFFECTIVE, AND ROLE OF BRITISH GOVERNMENT IN ACHIEVING EFFECTIVE TRANSFER OF POWER. EXAMINES EXPERIENCE OF CEYLON, MALAYA, GOLD COAST, NIGERIA, CARIBBEAN AREA, AND CENTRAL AFRICA.

1596 JELAVICH C. ED., JELAVICH B. ED.
THE BALKANS IN TRANSITION: ESSAYS ON THE DEVELOPMENT OF BALKAN LIFE AND POLITICS SINCE THE EIGHTEENTH CENTURY.
BERKELEY: U. CALIF. PR., 1963, 451 PP.
TREATS TRADITIONS, PATTERN OF DEVELOPMENT AND PROBLEMS OF TRANSITION COMMON TO SEVEN BALKAN STATES. COVERS OTTOMAN-LEGACY, GEOPOLITICS, SOVIET AND WESTERN INFLUENCES, ECONOMIC AND SOCIAL CHANGE, AND CURRENT CULTURAL ACTIVITY.

1597 JELAVICH C., JELAVICH B.
THE BALKANS.
ENGLEWOOD CLIFFS: PRENTICE HALL, 1965, 148 PP., LC#65-14999.
HISTORY OF ALBANIA, BULGARIA, GREECE, RUMANIA, AND YUGOSLAVIA. EMPHASIS ON THOSE ASPECTS OF PAST WHICH CONTRIBUTE TO UNDERSTANDING OF PRESENT. MAIN TOPIC IS BALKAN NATIONALISM AND THE DEVELOPMENT OF EACH STATE AS A POLITICAL UNIT. HISTORY BEGINS WITH MEDIEVAL PERIOD BUT CONCENTRATES ON 19TH AND 20TH CENTURIES.

1598 JELLINEK G.
LA DECLARATION DES DROITS DE L'HOMME ET DU CITOYEN (1895) (TRANSLATED FROM GERMAN BY G. FARDIS)
NEW YORK: HOLT RINEHART WINSTON, 1902, 101 PP.
STUDY OF ORIGINS OF CONCEPT OF RIGHTS OF MAN THROUGH HISTORY OF DEVELOPMENT AND MODIFICATION OF INSTITUTIONS. NOTES IMPORTANCE OF FRENCH DECLARATION OF RIGHTS OF MAN. BELIEVES AMERICAN BILL OF RIGHTS, RATHER THAN ROUSSEAU'S "SOCIAL CONTRACT," WAS BASIS FOR FRENCH DECLARATION. STUDIES AMERICAN COLONIAL STATE CHARTERS. COMPARES AND CONTRASTS DECLARATION OF RIGHTS OF MAN AND BILL OF RIGHTS.

1599 JEMOLO A.C.
CHURCH AND STATE IN ITALY 1850-1950 (TRANS. BY DAVID MOORE)
OXFORD: BLACKWELL, 1960, 344 PP.
TRACES RELATIONS OF CHURCH AND STATE IN ITALY FROM STRONG OPPOSITION TO CHURCH CONTROL IN 1850'S THROUGH FASCISM TO CONFESSIONAL PARTY, CHRISTIAN DEMOCRATS, IN 1950'S.

1600 JENCKS C.E.
"SOCIAL STATUS OF COAL MINERS IN BRITAIN SINCE NATIONALIZATION."
AMER.J. OF COMPARATIVE LAW, 26 (JULY 67),301-312.
FINDS COAL MINERS' WAGES, WORKING CONDITIONS, FRINGE BENEFITS, LABOR-MANAGEMENT REALTIONS, HOUSING, AND GENERAL WELFARE HAVE IMPROVED SINCE NATIONALIZATION. DISCUSSES MINERS' ATTITUDES TOWARD THEIR "LOW" SOCIAL POSITION, AND SHOWS HOW THESE ATTITUDES AFFECT INDUSTRIAL RELATIONS.

1601 JENKINS C.
POWER AT THE TOP: A CRITICAL SURVEY OF THE NATIONALIZED INDUSTRIES.
LONDON: MACGIBBON AND KEE, LTD, 1959, 292 PP.
INVESTIGATES NATIONALIZED INDUSTRY IN ENGLAND, ESPECIALLY SHORTCOMINGS OF SYSTEM SUCH AS EMPLOYING EXECUTIVES IN PRIVATE INDUSTRY TO HEAD PUBLIC INDUSTRIES. PUBLIC CORPORATIONS ARE BEING RUN TO HELP PRIVATE INTERESTS AND ARE NOT DIFFERENT ENOUGH FROM THE PRIVATE CORPORATIONS THEY REPLACED. ADVOCATES FURTHER ACTION BY LABOUR PARTY IN DEVELOPING TRUE PUBLIC ENTERPRISE.

1602 JENKS C.W.
"THE CHALLENGE OF UNIVERSALITY."
PROC. AMER. SOC. INT. LAW, (1959), 85-98.
A GREATER UNDERSTANDING OF THE VARIOUS LAW SYSTEMS FOUND THROUGHOUT THE WORLD WILL LEAD TO A SYSTEM OF INTERNATIONAL LAW THAT WILL BENEFIT ALL MANKIND BY ENSURING MAN'S RIGHTS AND FREEDOM.

1603 JENKS E.J.
LAW AND POLITICS IN THE MIDDLE AGES.
NEW YORK: HENRY HOLT & CO, 1897, 352 PP.
ATTEMPTS TO SELECT FROM MEDIEVAL HISTORY THOSE IDEAS AND INSTITUTIONS THAT INFLUENCED AND AFFECTED LATER CIVILIZATION. DESCRIBES SOCIAL FORCES THAT WORKED ON RUDIMENTARY NOTIONS OF LAW, FUSING ITS HISTORY WITH THAT OF SOCIETY. NOTES DEVELOPMENT OF BASIC TYPICAL SOCIETIES: CLAN, STATE, AND PARTNERSHIP. BELIEVES STATE-CLAN STRUGGLE HOLDS KEY TO INTERNAL POLITICS OF MIDDLE AGES.

1604 JENNINGS W.I.
THE COMMONWEALTH IN ASIA.
LONDON: CLARENDON PRESS, 1951, 124 PP.
ANALYSIS OF THE PROBLEMS RESULTING FROM INDEPENDENCE OF CEYLON, INDIA, AND PAKISTAN FROM UNITED KINGDOM; EXAMINES TENTATIVE SOLUTIONS. DISCUSSES DIVERSITY OF PEOPLES, COMMUNALISM, EDUCATION, CLASS DIVISIONS, RESPONSIBLE GOVERNMENT, CONSTITUTIONS OF CEYLON AND INDIA, AND RELATIONS WITH THE COMMONWEALTH.

1605 JENNINGS W.I.
THE QUEEN'S GOVERNMENT.
BALTIMORE: PENGUIN BOOKS, 1954, 158 PP.
BRIEF INTRODUCTION TO INSTITUTIONS OF BRITISH GOVERNMENT, WITH PARTICULAR EMPHASIS ON HISTORY AND DEVELOPMENT OF BRITISH CONSTITUTION. SURVEYS THE PERSONAL AND POLITICAL ROLE OF THE MONARCH; THE PARTY SYSTEM; THE NATURE, FUNCTION, AND ORGANIZATION OF PARLIAMENT; GOVERNMENTAL ADMINISTRATION; PRIME MINISTER AND CABINET; AND THE JUDICIAL SYSTEM.

1606 JENNINGS W.I.
PARTY POLITICS: THE GROWTH OF PARTIES (VOL. II)
NEW YORK: CAMBRIDGE U PRESS, 1961, 404 PP.
STUDIES GROWTH OF POLITICAL PARTIES IN ENGLAND, INCLUDING PARTY ORIGINS; LIBERAL SUPREMACY, 1830-85; LIBERAL DECLINE; LABOUR PARTY, 1918-40; AND CONSERVATIVE PARTY, 1922-45.

1607 JENNINGS W.I.
PARTY POLITICS: THE STUFF OF POLITICS (VOL.III)
NEW YORK: CAMBRIDGE U PRESS, 1962, 492 PP.
STUDIES NATURE OF PARTY POLITICS IN ENGLAND, INCLUDING POLITICAL CONFLICT, WHIG CONSTITUTION, CHURCH AND KING, LIBERTY, NATIONALISM, WELFARE STATE, AND BRITISH SOCIALISM.

1608 JENNINGS W.I.
THE COMMONWEALTH IN ASIA.
NEW YORK: OXFORD U PR, 1951, 124 PP.
EXAMINES PROBLEMS IN INDIA, CEYLON, AND PAKISTAN CREATED BY INDEPENDENCE. BEGINS WITH HISTORY OF ETHNIC ORIGINS, EMPHASIZING DIVERSITY OF PEOPLE, AND EUROPEAN INFILTRATION. DISCUSSES COMMUNALISM, EDUCATION, AND CLASS DIVISIONS AS PROBLEMS. FINAL CHAPTERS DEAL WITH INDEPENDENCE, POLITICAL FORMS, AND CONCEPT OF RESPONSIBLE GOVERNMENT; INCLUDES CONSTITUTIONS OF EACH COUNTRY AND COMMONWEALTH RELATIONS.

1609 JENNINGS W.I.

PARLIAMENT.
LONDON: CAMBRIDGE UNIV PRESS, 1939, 540 PP.
DESCRIBES AND ANALYZES WORKING OF PARLIAMENTARY PORTION OF MACHINERY OF GOVERNMENT. DISCUSSES COMPOSITION OF PARLIAMENT, MEMBERS AND THEIR INTERESTS, PARTIES AND OFFICIALS OF HOUSES. DESCRIBES FRAMEWORK OF ORATORY, ART OF MANAGEMENT, AND TECHNIQUE OF OPPOSITION. TREATS PROCESS OF LEGISLATION, FINANCIAL CONTROL, HOUSE OF LORDS, PRIVATE LEGISLATION, AND HOUSE OF COMMONS.

1610 JENNINGS W.I.
THE APPROACH TO SELF-GOVERNMENT.
CAMBRIDGE, ENGLAND: U. PR., 1956, 204 PP.
A SERIES OF BROADCAST LECTURES DISCUSSING THE CONSTITUTIONAL PROBLEMS FACED BY COLONIAL NATIONS APPROACHING INDEPENDENCE. SHOWS ADAPTATION OF BRITISH CONSTITUTIONAL TRADITION IN CEYLON, INDIA AND PAKISTAN.

1611 JENNINGS W.I.
NATIONALISM, COLONIALISM, AND NEUTRALISM (PAMPHLET)
LEEDS, ENGL.: LEEDS U. PRESS, 1957, 12 PP.
DISCUSSES ASIAN NATIONALISM AND RESULTING COMMUNALISM, COLONIALISM, AND NEUTRALISM AS THEY AFFECT POLITICAL ISSUES AND STRUCTURE IN SEVERAL ASIAN COUNTRIES. EXPLAINS EFFECTS NATIONALISM HAS ON POLITICAL AFFILIATIONS OF ASIAN STUDENTS IN BRITAIN. MAINTAINS THAT NATIONALISM AND NEUTRALISM ARE EMOTIONS AND WILL LAST, ALTHOUGH NEUTRALIST POLICY OF INDIA IS DANGEROUS ONE.

1612 JENNINGS W.I.
CABINET GOVERNMENT (3RD ED.)
LONDON: CAMBRIDGE UNIV PRESS, 1959, 586 PP.
DESCRIBES WORKING OF CABINET FORM OF GOVERNMENT IN BRITAIN. COLLECTS PRECEDENTS REGULATING CONVENTIONS OF CABINET GOVERNMENT. DISCUSSES CONSTITUTION, CHOICE OF PRIME MINISTER, ADMINISTRATIVE STRUCTURE, FUNCTION OF MINISTERS, AND INTERDEPARTMENTAL RELATIONS. STUDIES TREASURY CONTROL, STRUCTURE AND FUNCTION OF CABINET.

1613 JENNINGS W.I.
DEMOCRACY IN AFRICA.
NEW YORK: CAMBRIDGE U PRESS, 1963, 89 PP.
EXAMINES POLITICAL PROBLEMS OF EMERGING NATIONS ONCE UNDER BRITISH RULE AS THEY SET UP GOVERNMENTS. DISCUSSES RELATIONSHIP OF WESTERN CULTURE TO AFRICAN CULTURE WITH ITS NATIONALISM AND RAPIDLY CHANGING SOCIETIES. STUDIES BRITISH FORM OF DEMOCRACY AND ITS APPLICABILITY FOR AFRICA. STATES THAT PROBLEMS OF NATIONS TRYING TO BE DEMOCRACIES CAN BE SOLVED.

1614 JENSEN L.
"MILITARY CAPABILITIES AND BARGAINING BEHAVIOR."
J. OF CONFLICT RESOLUTION, 9 (JUNE 65), 155-163.
SOVIET AND AMERICAN CONCESSIONS IN DISARMAMENT NEGOTIATIONS ARE COMPARED TO CHANGING DEFENSE EXPENDITURES AND TO PUBLIC PERCEPTIONS OF IMMINENCE OF WAR IN ORDER TO TEST HYPOTHESIS THAT NATIONS MOST SERIOUSLY NEGOTIATE FROM POSITION OF STRENGTH. FINDS GROUNDS FOR REJECTION.

1615 JESSOP T.E.
A BIBLIOGRAPHY OF DAVID HUME AND OF SCOTTISH PHILOSOPHY FROM FRANCIS HUTCHESON TO LORD BALFOUR.
LONDON: A BROWN & SONS, LTD, 1938, 201 PP.
EXHAUSTIVE ANNOTATED LISTING OF HUME'S WORKS FOLLOWED BY MATERIALS IN ALL LANGUAGES COMMENTING ON HIS LIFE AND WORK. ALSO INCLUDED IS LESS EXTENSIVE LISTING OF OTHER SCOTTISH PHILOSOPHERS IN ALPHABETICAL ORDER. WORKS COVER A BIOGRAPHY AND PHILOSOPHY AND ARE ALSO ANNOTATED. WORKS INCLUDE LETTERS AND ESSAYS AS WELL AS BOOKS.

1616 JHA C.
INDIAN GOVERNMENT AND POLITICS.
PATNA: NOVELTY AND CO, 1960, 200 PP.
STUDIES PROCESSES AND MORES OF INDIAN POLITICAL SYSTEM. STATES GOALS OF SOCIAL RECONSTRUCTION. DISCUSSES FEATURES OF AND RIGHTS UNDER INDIAN CONSTITUTION, SYSTEM OF ELECTIONS, FUNCTION OF PARLIAMENT, JUDICIAL SYSTEM, STATE GOVERNMENT AND ITS RELATION TO NATIONAL GOVERNMENT, AND PUBLIC SERVICES. BELIEVES THAT POLITICAL SYSTEM CAN ADAPT TO SOCIAL RECONSTRUCTION.

1617 JOHN OF SALISBURY
THE STATESMAN'S BOOK (1159) (TRANS. BY J. DICKINSON)
NEW YORK: ALFRED KNOPF, 1927, 410 PP.
COMMONWEALTH EXISTS THROUGH DIVINE FAVOR, WITH PRINCE AS ITS HEAD. RIGHT OF PRINCE TO GOVERN IS DIVINE, AND RELATIONSHIP TO PEOPLE IS PATERNAL. "HIGHER LAW" IS SUPREME OVER ALL GOVERNMENTS. BELIEVES IN PAPAL SUPREMACY; CHURCH, LIKE GOVERNMENT, IS INSTRUMENT OF APPLYING HIGHER LAW. TYRANNICIDE IS JUSTIFIABLE BY "HIGHER LAW." MEN, IF GOOD AND FREE FROM SIN, CAN LIVE WITHOUT GOVERNMENT AND BY LAW ALONE.

1618 JOHNSON A.F.
BIBLIOGRAPHY OF GHANA: 1930-1961.
LONDON: LONGMANS, GREEN & CO, 1964, 210 PP.
ANNOTATED AND INDEXED BIBLIOGRAPHY OF ITEMS DEALING WITH GHANA; ARRANGED TOPICALLY, SEPARATELY LISTS BIBLIOGRAPHIES, PERIODICALS, REFERENCE MATERIALS, AND GOVERNMENT PUBLICATIONS. INCLUDES AN INTRODUCTION SURVEYING PAST BIBLIOGRAPHIES. ITEMS ARE VERY DIVERSIFIED: MAPS, SPEECHES, SURVEYS, REPORTS, ETC. CHIEFLY IN EUROPEAN LANGUAGES. ALSO SURVEYS LITERATURE OF THE GOLD COAST.

1619 JOHNSON H.G. ED.
ECONOMIC NATIONALISM IN OLD AND NEW STATES.
CHICAGO: U OF CHICAGO PRESS, 1967, 145 PP., LC#67-20573.
PRESENTS MODEL FOR STUDY OF ECONOMIC NATIONALISM IN NEW STATES. STUDIES 19TH-CENTURY RELATIONSHIP BETWEEN NATIONALISM AND DEVELOPMENT, INFLUENCE OF NATIONALISM ON BRITISH ECONOMIC POLICY, AND ROLE OF NATIONALISM IN COMMUNIST CHINA, MEXICO, CANADA, AND MALI. FINDS THAT ROLE AND INFLUENCES DIFFER GREATLY. SURVEYS ECONOMIC THEORIES ABOUT DEVELOPMENT AND RELATIONS OF OLD AND NEW STATES.

1620 JOHNSON H.M.
SOCIOLOGY: A SYSTEMATIC INTRODUCTION.
NEW YORK: HARCOURT BRACE, 1960, 688 PP., LC#60-10390.
PRESENTS ACCOUNT OF FOUNDATIONS OF CONTEMPORARY SOCIOLOGY, EMPHASIZING INSTITUTIONAL VARIATION. DESCRIBES STRUCTURAL AND FUNCTIONAL ANALYSES, SOCIALIZATION, KINSHIP GROUPS, ECONOMIC SYSTEM, POLITICS, RELIGION, STRATIFICATION, SOCIAL DEVIATION, AND SOCIAL CHANGE.

1621 JOHNSON J.J.
POLITICAL CHANGE IN LATIN AMERICA: THE EMERGENCE OF THE MIDDLE SECTORS.
STANFORD: STANFORD U PRESS, 1958, 272 PP.
ANALYZES CIRCUMSTANCES IN WHICH POLITICALLY AMBITIOUS URBAN GROUPS HAVE RISEN TO POWER SINCE LATE 19TH CENTURY AND HOW THEIR INFLUENCE UPON DECISION-MAKING ON A NATIONAL LEVEL HAS CONTRIBUTED TO CURRENT SOCIO-ECONOMIC ORIENTATION OF GOVERNMENTS OF ARGENTINA, BRAZIL, CHILE, MEXICO, URUGUAY. INCLUDES EXTENSIVE STATISTICAL ANALYSES FOR COMPARATIVE PURPOSES AND ANNOTATED BIBLIOGRAPHY OF OVER 900 ITEMS.

1622 JOHNSON J.J. ED.
THE ROLE OF THE MILITARY IN UNDERDEVELOPED COUNTRIES.
PRINCETON: U. PR., 1962, 423 PP., $8.50.
INTRODUCES STUDY WITH THEORETICAL PIECES BY JOHNSON, SHILS AND PYE. DEVELOPS CONCEPT WITH SPECIFIC WORKS CONTRIBUTED BY LIEUWEN/ALBA (LATIN AMERICA), PAUKER (INDONESIA), PYE (BURMA), WILSON (THAI), HALPERN (MIDDLE EAST AND ISRAEL) AND COLEMAN/BRICE (SUB-SAHARAN AFRICA). INCLUDES GENERAL OBSERVATIONS ON CERTAIN CONCEPTS OF LIFE IN UNDERDEVELOPED COUNTRIES.

1623 JOHNSON J.J. ED.
CONTINUITY AND CHANGE IN LATIN AMERICA.
STANFORD: STANFORD U PRESS, 1964, 282 PP., LC#64-17001.
EIGHT PAPERS STUDY CHANGES IN STATUS AND BEHAVIOR OF 8 SOCIAL GROUPS: PEASANTS, THE MILITARY, RURAL LABOR, URBAN LABOR, INDUSTRIALISTS, STUDENTS, WRITERS, AND ARTISTS. R.P. DORE CONTRIBUTES A SUMMARY PAPER COMPARING LATIN AMERICAN SOCIAL GROUPS WITH THEIR COUNTERPARTS IN JAPAN. CONTRIBUTORS INCLUDE C. WAGLEY, R.N. ADAMS, W.P. STRASSMANN, F.P. ELLISON, G. CHASE, L.N. MCALISTER, K.H. SILVERT, AND F. BONILLA.

1624 JOHNSON K.F.
"CAUSAL FACTORS IN LATIN AMERICAN POLITICAL INSTABILITY."
WEST. POLIT. QUART., 17 (SEPT. 64), 432-446.
APPLYING THE 'POLITICAL CULTURE' CONCEPT OF ALMOND AND VERBA, THE AUTHOR SEEKS TO FORMULATE A SYSTEMATIC THEORY OF INSTABILITY IN LATIN AMERICA AS AN INTERACTION SET WHICH CAN BE EITHER OPERATIONALIZED EMPIRICALLY OR INVOKED THEORETICALLY. TENTATIVE HYPOTHESES AMENABLE TO PRECISION TESTING WITH A RIGOROUS METHODOLOGY ARE ALSO SUGGESTED.

1625 JOHNSON N.
PARLIAMENT AND ADMINISTRATION: THE ESTIMATES COMMITTEE 1945-65.
NEW YORK: AUGUSTUS M. KELLEY, 1966, 187 PP.
ANALYZES ORGANIZATION AND FUNCTIONS OF MAJOR COMMITTEE OF HOUSE OF COMMONS. CLASSIFIES AND SUMMARIZES MATERIAL PRODUCED BY COMMITTEE TO DISPROVE THAT "VEIL OF SECRECY" COVERS ALL IMPORTANT ACTIONS OF PARLIAMENT. TAKES THREE MAJOR COMMITTEE REPORTS AS DETAILED CASE STUDIES OF WAY COMMITTEE WORKS. INCLUDES STUDY OF 1965 PROPOSALS THAT MIGHT AFFECT FUTURE OF COMMITTEE.

1626 JOHNSON P. ED., LABEDZ L. ED.
KHRUSHCHEV AND THE ARTS: POLITICS OF SOVIET CULTURE, 1962-1964.
CAMBRIDGE: M I T PRESS, 1965, 300 PP., LC#64-8311.
SURVEY OF SOVIET CULTURE EXAMINES ATTITUDES, POLICY, AND RELATIONS OF KHRUSHCHEV WITH ARTISTIC COMMUNITY. PRESENTS DOCUMENTS OF CONFERENCES AND ARTICLES BY THOSE INVOLVED IN DEBATE ON SOVIET ART AND CULTURE.

1627 JOINER C.A.
"THE UBIQUITY OF THE ADMINISTRATIVE ROLE IN COUNTERINSURGENC
ASIAN SURVEY, 7 (AUG. 67), 540-554.
MAINTAINS THAT STRENGTH OF NATIONAL LIBERATION FRONT

ACTIVITIES IN SOUTH VIETNAM IS GREATEST IN AREAS WHICH HAVE TRADITIONALLY BEEN, AND STILL ARE, INEFFICIENTLY ADMINISTERED BY NATIONAL GOVERNMENT. DISCUSSES ATTITUDES OF SOUTH VIETNAMESE ADMINISTRATORS AND OVER-ALL ADMINISTRATIVE STRUCTURE. STRESSES NEED FOR "ADAPTIVE AND PURPOSEFUL" ORGANIZATIONS TO IMPLEMENT NATIONAL POLICIES.

1628 JONAS E.
DIE VOLKSKONSERVATIVEN 1928-1933.
DUSSELDORF: DROSTE VERLAG, 1965, 198 PP.
DISCUSSES CREATION AND RISE OF NATIONAL CONSERVATIVE PARTY, ITS INNER CONFLICTS ABOUT NATIONAL UNITY AND ITS COLLAPSE UNDER HITLER. INCLUDES APPENDIX GIVING STANDING RULES AND CORRESPONDENCE OF IMPORTANT LEADERS.

1629 JONES C.K., GRANIER J.A.
A BIBLIOGRAPHY OF LATIN AMERICAN BIBLIOGRAPHIES (2ND ED.)
WASHINGTON: GOVT PR OFFICE, 1943, 311 PP.
LIST OF BIBLIOGRAPHIES, COLLECTIVE BIBLIOGRAPHIES, HISTORIES OF LITERATURE, AND GENERAL AND MISCELLANEOUS WORKS (ENCYCLOPEDIAS). ARRANGED ACCORDING TO COUNTRIES AND INCLUDES INDEX. APPROXIMATELY 3,000 ENTRIES; MAJORITY IN SPANISH, OTHERS IN ENGLISH.

1630 JONES D.H. ED.
AFRICA BIBLIOGRAPHY SERIES: EAST AFRICA.
LONDON: INTERNATL AFRICAN INST, 1966, 61 PP.
ANNOTATED BIBLIOGRAPHY OF WORKS IN LIBRARY OF INTERNATIONAL AFRICAN INSTITUTE. ETHNOGRAPHY, SOCIOLOGY, LINGUISTICS, AND GENERAL. IN FRENCH, ENGLISH, AND GERMAN. WORKS COVER 1929-60.

1631 JONES H.D.
UNESCO: A SELECTED LIST OF REFERENCES.
WASHINGTON: LIBRARY OF CONGRESS, 1948, 56 PP.
242 BOOKS, OFFICIAL DOCUMENTS, PAMPHLETS, ARTICLES ANNOTATED TO INDICATE CONTENT, CONNECTION OF AUTHOR TO UNESCO, AND OTHER PERTINENT INFORMATION. INDEXED BY AUTHOR AND LISTED BY SUBJECT. PURPORTS TO SELECT BASIC MATERIAL THAT COVERS THE BACKGROUND, HISTORY, PURPOSE, FUNCTION, AND PROGRAM OF UNESCO.

1632 JONES H.D., WINKLER R.L.
KOREA, AN ANNOTATED BIBLIOGRAPHY OF PUBLICATIONS IN WESTERN LANGUAGES.
WASHINGTON: LIBRARY OF CONGRESS, 1950, 145 PP., LC#50-62963.
ANNOTATED LISTING OF VARIOUS TYPES OF PUBLICATIONS PERTINENT TO KOREAN HISTORY AND ECONOMIC, SOCIAL, AND POLITICAL BACKGROUND. INCLUDES GEOGRAPHY, TRAVEL, GOVERNMENT, AGRICULTURE, LANGUAGE, RELIGION, ART, MUSIC, AND OTHERS. NOTES AVAILABLE MAPS, CITY PLANS, AND PERIODICALS. CONTAINS 753 LISTINGS WITH AUTHOR AND SUBJECT INDEX.

1633 JONES R.
AFRICA BIBLIOGRAPHY SERIES: SOUTH EAST CENTRAL AFRICA AND MADAGASCAR.
LONDON: INTERNATL AFRICAN INST, 1961, 53 PP.
ANNOTATED BIBLIOGRAPHY OF WORKS IN LIBRARY OF INTERNATIONAL AFRICAN INSTITUTE. FRENCH, GERMAN, AND ENGLISH WORKS IN ETHNOGRAPHY, SOCIOLOGY, LINGUISTICS, AND GENERAL. WORKS COVER 1929-59.

1634 JONES T.B., WARBURTON E.A. ET AL.
A BIBLIOGRAPHY ON SOUTH AMERICAN ECONOMIC AFFAIRS: ARTICLES IN NINETEENTH CENTURY PERIODICALS (PAMPHLET)
MINNEAPOLIS: U OF MINN PR, 1955, 146 PP., LC#55-7033.
UNANNOTATED LISTING BY NATION,SUBDIVIDED INTO SUBJECT HEADINGS. CHRONOLOGICALLY ARRANGED. ALL WESTERN EUROPEAN LANGUAGES WITH 6200 UNIQUE ITEMS. PERIODICALS USED ARE INDEXED.

1635 JORDAN W.K.
THE DEVELOPMENT OF RELIGIOUS TOLERATION IN ENGLAND.
LONDON: ALLEN, 1940, 4VOLS., 2091 PP.
TRACES SUBJECT FROM BEGINNING OF ENGLISH REFORMATION TO RESTORATION IN 1660. DEFINES PHILOSOPHICAL AND HISTORICAL ROOTS OF TOLERANCE AND INTOLERENCE TO EMPHASIZE SIGNIFICANCE OF CHANGE. REVIEWS CONTRIBUTIONS TO DEVELOPMENT OF CONCEPT BY SECULAR, RELIGIOUS AND PHILOSOPHICAL FORCES, BOTH DOMINANT AND MINORITY.

1636 JOSEPHSON E. ED., JOSEPHSON M. ED.
MAN ALONE: ALIENATION IN MODERN SOCIETY.
NEW YORK: DELL PUBL CO, 1964, 592 PP.
STUDIES ON ALIENATION VIEWED AS CONDITION TYPICAL OF MODERN INDUSTRIAL SOCIETIES, LINKED TO MAN'S ESTRANGEMENT. SHOWS SOME WAYS IN WHICH MAN HAS RESPONDED TO THIS ESTRANGEMENT. DEALS WITH TOPICS SUCH AS WORK AND LEISURE, MASS CULTURE, SCIENCE, WAR, AND INTEGRATION.

1637 JOSHI P.S.
THE TYRANNY OF COLOUR.
DURBAN,S.A.: E.P. & COMMERCIAL PRINT. CO., 1942,318 PP.
STUDIES INDIAN'S PROBLEM IN SOUTH AFRICA FROM FIRST IMMIGRATIONS OF 1860 THROUGH 1939, INCLUDING RACIAL POLICIES OF GOVERNMENT AGAINST INDIAN MINORITY, LATTER'S REACTION, AND GENERAL DISCUSSIONS OF RACE PROBLEMS IN SOUTH AFRICA.

1638 JOUVENEL B D.E.
THE ART OF CONJECTURE.
NEW YORK: BASIC BOOKS, 1967, 307 PP., LC#67-12649.
DISCUSSES THE NEW EMPHASIS BY GOVERNMENTS ON POLICY PLANNING COMMISSIONS WHICH PREDICT FUTURE SOCIAL PROBLEMS AND THEIR SOLUTION. AUTHOR FINDS GREATEST PROBLEM TO BE THAT THESE BOARDS CAN ONLY ADVISE THE GOVERNMENT AND THAT MOST SOLUTIONS ARE POLITICALLY INEXPEDIENT. THUS THE MACHINERY FOR MEETING FUTURE NEEDS IS IN PLACE BUT IS LARGELY INOPERATIVE. THIS IS A DANGER TO FUTURE STABILITY.

1639 JUCKER-FLEETWOOD E.
MONEY AND FINANCE IN AFRICA.
NEW YORK: PRAEGER, 1964, 335 PP.
STUDIES FINANCIAL PROBLEMS OF EMERGING COUNTRIES IN AFRICA. NOTES ROLE OF CENTRAL BANKS IN LAYING FOUNDATIONS FOR CURRENCY EXCHANGE, FOREIGN EXCHANGE RESERVES, SUPPORT OF GOVERNMENT PROGRAMS. FOLLOWS ESTABLISHMENT OF COMMERCIAL BANKS AND OTHER FINANCIAL INSTITUTIONS. OUTLINES MODERN AFRICAN DEVELOPMENT PLANS AND THEIR FINANCING.

1640 JUDD P. ED.
AFRICAN INDEPENDENCE: THE EXPLODING EMERGENCE OF THE NEW AFRICAN NATIONS.
NEW YORK: DELL PUBL CO, 1963, 512 PP.
ESSAYS PRESENT BACKGROUNDS, POLITICAL STRUGGLES, AND PROBLEMS OF INDEPENDENCE AMONG EMERGENT NATIONS.

1641 JULIEN C.A.
L'AFRIQUE DU NORD EN MARCHE: NATIONALISMES MUSULMANS ET SOUVERAINETE FRANCAISE (2ND ED)
PARIS: JULLIARD PUBL, 1952, 414 PP.
EXAMINES CONFLICT BETWEEN RISING NORTH AFRICAN NATIONALISM AND FRENCH COLONIAL RULE, INCLUDING PANARABISM, THE ORIGIN OF NATIONALISM, POLITICAL CRISES, AND TESTS OF FORCE.

1642 JUNOD V.
HANDBOOK OF AFRICA.
NEW YORK: N.Y.U., 1963, 472 PP., $10.00.
PROVIDES, BY TERRITORIES, DATA AND INFORMATION OF A POLITICAL, ECONOMIC, SOCIAL, DEMOGRAPHIC, GEOGRAPHIC, AND HISTORIC NATURE. FACTUAL AND DESCRIPTIVE ACCOUNT WITH STRONG EMPHASIS ON STATISTICS.

1643 JURJI E.J.
THE GREAT RELIGIONS OF THE MODERN WORLD.
PRINCETON: U. PR., 1947, 387 PP.
INDICATES THE SPIRITUAL CORE AND DEVELOPMENT OF THE MAJOR CONTEMPORARY RELIGIONS. RELATES THEM TO PRESENT CRISIS IN HUMAN VALUES AND FAITH. INCLUDES BIOGRAHIES OF MAJOR THEOLOGIANS.

1644 INTERNATIONAL COMMISSION OF JURISTS
THE CITIZEN AND THE ADMINISTRATION: THE REDRESS OF GRIEVANCES (PAMPHLET)
LONDON: STEVENS, 1961, 104 PP.
REPORT OF BRITISH SECTION OF THE INTERNATIONAL COMMISSION OF JURISTS ON METHODS OF REDRESS OPEN TO CITIZENS MALTREATED BY THOSE IN AUTHORITY. CONCLUDES THAT SYSTEM OF APPEALS IS DESIRABLE AND SUGGESTS APPOINTMENT OF "THE PARLIAMENTARY COMMISIONER," AN OFFICIAL LIKE SWEDISH OMBUDSMAN TO REPRESENT PEOPLE'S APPEALS.

1645 JUSTINIAN
THE DIGEST (DIGESTA CORPUS JURIS CIVILIS) (2 VOLS.)
(TRANS. BY C. H. MONRO)
NEW YORK: CAMBRIDGE U PRESS, 1909, 800 PP.
THE DIGEST OF JUSTINIAN'S CODIFICATION OF CIVIL LAW. DEALS WITH LAWS OF DIVORCE, ADOPTION, SLAVERY, AND SO ON. PRECEDING THE DIGEST IS THE EXPLANATION OF JUSTINIAN'S REASON FOR THE WORK, WHICH WAS THE DESIRE TO CONSOLIDATE THE EXISTING LEGAL STRUCTURE OF THE ROMAN EMPIRE.

1646 KAACK H.
DIE PARTEIEN IN DER VERFASSUNGSWIRKLICHKEIT DER BUNDESREPUBLIK.
FLANDERS, N.J.: O'HARE BOOKS, 1964, 128 PP.
INTRODUCTION TO THE HISTORY AND STRUCTURE OF THE POLITICAL PARTIES OF THE GERMAN FEDERAL REPUBLIC. DISCUSSES THE ELECTIONS ON NATIONAL AND STATE LEVEL AND SOME OF THE PROGRAMMATIC CHANGES THAT HAVE OCCURRED SINCE 1945.

1647 KAAS L.
DIE GEISTLICHE GERICHTSBARKEIT DER KATHOLISCHEN KIRCHE IN PREUSSEN (2 VOLS.)
AMSTERDAM: VERLAG P SCHIPPERS, 1965, 962 PP.
EXAMINES JURISDICTION OF CATHOLIC CHURCH IN PRUSSIA FROM REFORMATION TO PRESENT. DISCUSSES DISPUTES WITH STATE AS WELL AS STRUCTURE AND PROCESSES OF ECCLESIASTICAL COURTS.

1648 KADEN E.H., SPRINGER M.
DER POLITISCHE CHARAKTER DER FRANZOSISCHEN KULTURPROPAGANDA AM RHEIN.
BERLIN: FRANZ VAHLEN, 1923, 86 PP.

STUDY OF METHODS AND AIMS OF FRENCH PROPAGANDA IN EFFORT TO DECLARE RHINE RIVER THE NATURAL BORDER OF THE FRENCH NATION AND CULTURE.

1649 KAGZI M.C.
THE INDIAN ADMINISTRATIVE LAW.
NEW DELHI: METROPOLITAN BOOK, 1962, 250 PP.
DISCUSSES OPERATION OF ADMINISTRATIVE AGENCIES, NATURE OF ADMINISTRATIVE ACTION, PRINCIPLE OF DELEGATION AND FUNCTIONING OF ADMINISTRATIVE TRIBUNALS. EXAMINES JUDICIAL CONTROL OF ADMINISTRATIVE DECREES, PROCEEDINGS AGAINST PUBLIC AUTHORITIES, AND PUBLIC CORPORATIONS IN MODERN INDIA.

1650 KAHIN G.M. ED.
MAJOR GOVERNMENTS OF ASIA (2ND ED.)
ITHACA: CORNELL U PRESS, 1963, 719 PP., LC#63-15940.
STUDY IN COMPARATIVE GOVERNMENT DEVOTED TO CHINA, PAKISTAN, INDIA, INDONESIA, AND JAPAN. EACH GOVERNMENT IS HANDLED BY A DIFFERENT AUTHOR WHO HAS ARRANGED MATERIAL ACCORDING TO HIS OWN JUDGEMENT. ALL TREAT HISTORICAL BACKGROUND OF PRESENT POLITICAL ORGANIZATION. INCLUDES SECTION OF SELECTED READINGS.

1651 KALDOR N.
ESSAYS ON ECONOMIC POLICY (VOL. II)
LONDON: DUCKWORTH, 1964, 320 PP.
FIRST PART OF STUDY DISCUSSES ECONOMIC POLICIES FOR MAINTAINING INTERNATIONAL STABILITY WITH SPECIFIC REFERENCE TO PROBLEMS IN INTERNATIONAL TRADE AND PAYMENTS. SECOND PART DEVOTED TO DISCUSSIONS OF VARIED TOPICS IN ECONOMIC CONDITIONS OF FIVE DIFFERENT COUNTRIES.

1652 KALLEN H.M.
CULTURAL PLURALISM AND THE AMERICAN IDEA.
PHILA: U OF PENN PR, 1956, 203 PP., LC#56-11801.
DEFENDS CULTURAL PLURALISM AS PART OF AMERICAN IDEOLOGY AND A MAJOR STRENGTH. USES SOCIAL AND RELIGIOUS ARGUMENTS TO SUPPORT CLAIMS THAT AMERICANIZATION IS NOT A PROCESS OF SUBMISSION OF A PERSONALITY OR A SUBCULTURE TO THE LARGER GROUP, BUT A PROLIFERATION OF MANY CULTURES SHARING COMMON BONDS OF AMERICAN IDEAL.

1653 KANET R.E.
"RECENT SOVIET REASSESSMENT OF DEVELOPMENTS IN THE THIRD WORLD."
RUSSIAN REVIEWS, 27 (JAN. 68), 27-41.
DISCUSSES VIEWS OF SOVIET THEORETICIANS CONCERNING THE POLITICAL DEVELOPMENTS IN NONALIGNED COUNTRIES. CONSIDERS SOVIET IDEOLOGICAL MODELS FOR DEVELOPING NATIONS. DIVIDES DEVELOPING COUNTRIES INTO SIX CATEGORIES OF STATES ON BASIS OF DEGREES OF FEUDALISM, BOURGEOIS CONTROL, AND PRO- OR ANTI-IMPERIALISM.

1654 KANN R.A.
THE MULTINATIONAL EMPIRE (2 VOLS.)
NEW YORK: COLUMBIA U PRESS, 1950, 832 PP.
DISCUSSES NATIONALISM AND NATIONAL REFORM IN THE HABSBURG MONARCHY, 1848-1918. REPRESENTS THE CONFLICT BETWEEN NATIONAL INTERESTS AND THE MULTINATIONAL EMPIRE'S SURVIVAL. DISCUSSES CULTURAL AND IDEOLOGICAL BACKGROUND OF THE PERIOD. ANALYZES THE EMPIRE AND NATIONALITIES, NATIONAL GROUPS WITH AND WITHOUT INDEPENDENT NATIONAL POLITICAL HISTORY, AND EMPIRE REFORM.

1655 KANOUTE P.
"AFRICAN SOCIALISM."
TRANSACTIONS, 3 (NOV. 64).
CONTRASTS AND COMPARES EUROPEAN AND AFRICAN FORMS OF SOCIALISM. CLAIMS DIFFERENT CULTURAL HERITAGE RESULTS IN DIFFERENT POLITICAL SYSTEMS, WHICH ARE OUTWARDLY SIMILAR, BUT ACTUALLY UNIQUE.

1656 KANTOR H.
A BIBLIOGRAPHY OF UNPUBLISHED DOCTORAL DISSERTATIONS AND MASTERS' THESES DEALING WITH GOVTS, POL, INT REL OF LAT AM.
WASHINGTON, D.C.: INTER-AM.BIB. & LIB. ASSN.,1953, 85 PP.
UNANNOTATED BIBLIOGRAPHY OF UNPUBLISHED RESEARCH PAPERS CONPILED FOR THE LATIN AMERICAN AFFAIRS COMMITTEE OF THE AMERICAN POLITICAL SCIENCE ASSOCIATION. OUTLINES THE TOPICS WHICH HAVE RECEIVED MOST ATTENTION AND THOSE WHICH HAVE BEEN NEGLECTED IN AREAS OF GOVERNMENT, POLITICS, AND INTERNATIONAL RELATIONS.

1657 KANTOROWICZ E.
THE KING'S TWO BODIES; A STUDY IN MEDIEVAL POLITICAL THEOLOGY.
PRINCETON: PRINCETON U PRESS, 1957, 568 PP., LC#57-5448.
STUDIES SOURCES AND ASPECTS OF THE LEGAL FICTION, FIRST CODIFIED BY ELIZABETHAN JURISTS, OF THE KING AS BOTH "BODY NATURAL" AND "BODY POLITIC" OR "CORPORATION SOLE." IMPORTANT SOURCES INCLUDE IDEAS OF MYSTICAL BODY OF CHRIST; KING AND POPE AS GOD'S VICEGERENTS IN TEMPORAL AND SPIRITUAL REALMS; AND ROMAN LEGAL VIEWS OF THE EMPEROR AS JUSTICE. AMONG LEGAL CONCERNS ARE CONTINUITY, COMPOSITION, AND FICTION OF STATE.

1658 KAPIL R.L.
"ON THE CONFLICT POTENTIAL OF INHERITED BOUNDARIES IN AFRICA."
WORLD POLITICS, 18 (JULY 66), 656-673.
AUTHOR ARGUES THERE IS LOW CONFLICT POTENTIAL IN AFRICA OVER PRESENT BOUNDARIES. THE FEW DISPUTES OF CONSEQUENCE ARE GENERATED BY THOSE STATES WHOSE LEADERSHIP REPRESENTS TRADITION TRANSCENDING COLONIAL PERIOD (ETHIOPIA, MOROCCO) OR A CULTURALLY HOMOGENEOUS POLITY (SOMALIA). PREDICTS CHANGE BY PEACEFUL ECONOMIC INTEGRATION.

1659 KAPLAN M.A.
"COMMUNIST COUP IN CZECHOSLOVAKIA."
PRINCETON: CENT. INT. STUD., 1960, 40 PP.
CASE STUDY OF COUP FOLLOWS EVENTS LEADING UP TO IT. TESTS HYPOTHESIS THAT COUP PLANNED FROM VERY BEGINNING AS PART OF COMMUNIST STAGE-BY-STAGE TAKEOVER IN EASTERN EUROPE. GIVES ARGUMENTS FOR AND AGAINST HYPOTHESIS.

1660 KAPP W.K.
HINDU CULTURE: ECONOMIC DEVELOPMENT AND ECONOMIC PLANNING IN INDIA.
NEW YORK: ASIA PUBL., 1963, 228 PP.
ANALYZES ECONOMIC DEVELOPMENT AND PLANNING IN TERMS OF 'HINDUISM, AS A RELIGION AND AS A SOCIAL SYSTEM...IN AN EFFORT TO DETERMINE THE EXTENT TO WHICH HINDU CULTURE SERVES OR CONTRADICTS THE SOCIAL PURPOSES OF INDIA'S DEVELOPMENT EFFORT. CONCLUDES THAT CERTAIN ASPECTS OF HINDU CULTURE, TOGETHER WITH THE RELATED ADMINISTRATIVE DEFECTS, HAVE RETARDED ECONOMIC GROWTH IN INDIA IN THE PAST AND ARE LIKELY TO FRUSTRATE THE AIMS OF ECONOMIC DEVELOPMENT IN THE FUTURE.'

1661 KARIEL H.S.
IN SEARCH OF AUTHORITY: TWENTIETH-CENTURY POLITICAL THOUGHT.
NEW YORK: FREE PRESS OF GLENCOE, 1964, 258 PP., LC#64-21205.
DISCUSSION OF CURRENT STATE OF POLITICAL PHILOSOPHY THROUGH ANALYSES OF POLITICAL WRITINGS OF NIETZSCHE, FREUD, MANNHEIM, SOREL, MICHAEL OAKESHOTT, ERICH FROMM, MAYO, LENIN, WEBER, CAMUS, NIEBUHR, MARITAIN, DEWEY. ORGANIZED AROUND CONCEPTS OF CONSTITUTIONALISM, ORGANIZATION AS AN END, DOCTRINES OF QUIETISM AND ACTIVISM.

1662 KARNJAHAPRAKORN C.
MUNICIPAL GOVERNMENT IN THAILAND AS AN INSTITUTION AND PROCESS OF SELF-GOVERNMENT.
BANGKOK: THAMMASAT U. PUB. ADMIN., 1962, 249 PP.
ANALYZES DEVELOPMENT OF PHILOSOPHY AND PRACTICE OF MUNICIPAL SELF-GOVERNMENT. FINDS THAT THAILAND CAN ACCEPT FORM OF SELF-GOVERNMENT USED IN WESTERN DEMOCRACIES BUT NOT ITS PHILOSOPHY. DISCUSSES PROBLEM OF KEEPING MUNICIPAL GOVERNMENT IN THAILAND AND SUGGESTS WAYS TO GAIN ACCEPTANCE FOR IT.

1663 KAROL K.S.
CHINA, THE OTHER COMMUNISM (TRANS. BY TOM BAISTOW)
NEW YORK: HILL AND WANG, 1967, 474 PP., LC#66-27608.
TRACES HISTORY OF COMMUNIST CHINA, EXAMINING CHANGES IN PARTY ORGANIZATION, CONTROL, AND INTERNAL AND EXTERNAL OBJECTIVES. DISCUSSES POLITICAL ORGANIZATION AND IDEOLOGICAL INDOCTRINATION OF PEASANT POPULATION, ITS EFFECTS ON THE RURAL CULTURE, AND SPECIFIC PROLETARIAN RESPONSES. INCLUDES STRUCTURE AND FUNCTION OF NATIONAL GOVERNMENT AND DISCUSSES CHINESE INTERNATIONAL RELATIONS AND WORLD GOALS.

1664 KARPAT K.H.
"TURKEY'S POLITICS: THE TRANSITION TO A MULTI-PARTY SYSTEM."
PRINCETON: PRINCETON U PRESS, 1959.
ANALYSIS OF POLITICAL TRANSFORMATION IN TURKEY AS SYNTHESIS OF VARIOUS INTERACTING CULTURAL, ECONOMIC, SOCIAL, AND PERSONAL CONFLICTS. SPECIAL EMPHASIS PLACED ON SOCIO-ECONOMIC FACTORS. DEALS PRIMARILY WITH EVENTS IN YEARS 1945-50; HISTORY OF TURKISH TRANSFORMATION OUTLINED. EXTENSIVE BIBLIOGRAPHY OF BOOKS, ARTICLES, PAMPHLETS, AND PARTY PUBLICATIONS, PERIODICALS, RECORDS, REVIEWS, AND NEWSPAPERS.

1665 KASFIR N.
"THE UGANDA CONSTITUENT ASSEMBLY DEBATE."
TRANSITION, 7 (OCT.-NOV. 67), 52-59.
REVIEWS 1967 DEBATES OF UGANDAN CONGRESS ON IMPORTANT POINTS IN CONSTITUTION ADOPTED IN SEPTEMBER, 1967. THESE POINTS INCLUDED PRESIDENTIAL POWERS, PREVENTATIVE DETENTION, FEDERALISM, AND LEGAL ENFORCEMENT AND ENACTMENT OF THE NEW CONSTITUTION. MAJOR OPPOSITIONS WERE TO EXPANSION OF PRESIDENTIAL POWERS AND TO DETAINMENT OF AGITATORS.

1666 KASTARI P.
LA PRESIDENCE DE LA REPUBLIQUE EN FINLANDE.
PARIS: EDITIONS DE LA BACONNIERE, 1962, 96 PP.
ANALYZES ROLE OF PRESIDENT IN FINNISH POLITICAL SYSTEM AS A CENTER OF DECISION-MAKING. DISCUSSES STRONG INFLUENCE OF LEGISLATURE IN SPITE OF PRESIDENTIAL SYSTEM OF ELECTIONS. PROVIDES CHRONOLOGICAL DESCRIPTION OF EACH PRESIDENT'S POWER AND INFLUENCE SINCE INDEPENDENCE IN 1917.

1667 KASUNMU A.B.
NIGERIAN FAMILY LAW.

LONDON, WASH, DC: BUTTERWORTHS, 1966, 303 PP.
EXAMINES NIGERIAN FAMILY LAW IN LIGHT OF EXISTING ENGLISH LAW ON SUBJECT AND FIRST-HAND INFORMATION COLLECTED ON RESEARCH TOURS. DISCUSSES NATURE AND SOURCES OF NIGERIAN LAW, CUSTOMARY LAW SYSTEM, MARRIAGE STATUTES, LEGITIMACY, ADOPTION, PARENTAL RIGHTS AND DUTIES, AND SUCCESSION. INCLUDES TABLES OF STATUTES AND CASES.

1668 KATEB G.
UTOPIA AND ITS ENEMIES.
NEW YORK: FREE PRESS OF GLENCOE, 1963, 244 PP., LC#63-8418.
ANALYSIS OF TWO TYPES OF ANTI-UTOPIAN ATTITUDES: THOSE WHICH WERE ARTICULATED IN PAST BUT ARE STILL APPLICABLE TO-DAY; THOSE ELICITED IN DIRECT ANSWER TO MODERN UTOPIANISM, EMBODYING THE ADVANCES IN TECHNOLOGICAL, SCIENTIFIC, AND PSYCHOLOGICAL KNOWLEDGE. EVALUATES THESE POSITIONS FROM A UTOPIAN BIAS. DISCUSSES SELECTED MEANS NEEDED TO MAINTAIN UTOPIA AND THREE UTOPIAN ENDS: PEACE, ABUNDANCE, AND VIRTUE.

1669 KAUFMANN R.
MILLENARISME ET ACCULTURATION.
BRUSSELS: ED L'INST SOC L'UNIV, 1964, 132 PP.
STUDY OF IMPACT OF MESSIANIC RELIGIONS, SUCH AS SEVENTH-DAY ADVENTISTS AND JEHOVAH'S WITNESSES, IN AFRICA. AUTHOR BELIEVES POPULARITY OF MESSIANISM IS IN PART RELIGIOUS PRO-TEST AGAINST COLONIAL DOMINATION AND IS IN PART DUE TO DISLOCATION BROUGHT ABOUT BY MEETING OF WESTERN AND TRADITIONAL AFRICAN SOCIETIES. INCLUDES BIBLIOGRAPHY OF ABOUT 250 ITEMS.

1670 KAUNDA K.
ZAMBIA: INDEPENDENCE AND BEYOND: THE SPEECHES OF KENNETH KAUNDA.
LONDON: THOMAS NELSON & SONS, 1966, 265 PP.
COLLECTION OF SPEECHES BY PRESIDENT OF ZAMBIA. DISCUSSES END OF COLONIALISM AND THE TRANSITION TO INDEPENDENCE. DESCRIBES BIRTH OF COUNTRY, PROBLEMS IT HAS ENCOUNTERED, AND HOPES FOR THE FUTURE. PICTURES STRUCTURE AND ADMINISTRATION, METHODS USED TO SOLVE PROBLEMS OF RACE RELATIONS, AND STRATEGIES OF ECONOMIC DEVELOPMENT.

1671 KAUPER P.G.
"CHURCH AND STATE: COOPERATIVE SEPARATISM."
MICH. LAW REV., 60 (NOV. 61), 1-40.
A MIDDLE VIEW, EXTRACTED IN THE LEGALISTIC MANNER, AND DEFENDED COMPETENTLY, BETWEEN STRICT SEPARATISM AND CHURCH-STATE INTEGRATION. THE PERPLEXITY OF THE PROBLEM IS SEEN IN THE INTERMINGLING OF FUNCTIONS IN THE CONTEXT OF A SOCIAL COMMUNITY WHERE BOTH THE SECULAR AND RELIGIOUS SOCIETIES INVOLVE THE SAME HUMAN RESOURCES. DISCUSSES PROBLEMS OF EDUCATION AND TAXATION.

1672 KAZAMIAS A.M.
EDUCATION AND QUEST FOR MODERNITY IN TURKEY.
CHICAGO: U OF CHICAGO PRESS, 1966, 304 PP.
CHRONOLOGICAL EXAMINATION OF EDUCATION IN TURKISH SOCIETY FROM ISLAMIC TIMES TO PRESENT. DISCUSSES EDUCATIONAL SYSTEM AND CURRICULUM AND IMPACT ON POLITICAL CULTURE AND CHANGE IN REACHING MODERN REPUBLICAN GOVERNMENT.

1673 KEAY E.A., RICHARDSON S.S.
THE NATIVE AND CUSTOMARY COURTS OF NIGERIA.
LONDON: SWEET AND MAXWELL, LTD, 1966, 381 PP.
LEGAL ANTHROPOLOGICAL STUDY EXAMINES THE SPECIFIED NIGE-RIAN COURTS, DISCUSSING ORIGINS, JURISTICTION, STAFF, AND LAWS TO BE ADMINISTERED. THE SYSTEM OF CONTROL AND APPEAL, AS WELL AS POWER OF REVIEW IS STUDIED. ALSO INCLUDES THE GENERAL PROCEDURE FOR BOTH CRIMINAL AND CIVIL MATTERS THE VARIATIONS FOR REGIONS WITHIN NIGERIA ARE PRESENTED, AS ARE MOSLEM AND CHRISTIAN INFLUENCES ON THE LEGAL SYSTEM.

1674 KECSKEMETI P.
"THE 'POLICY SCIENCES': ASPIRATION AND OUTLOOK."
WORLD POLIT., 4 (JULY 52), 520-35.
SUGGESTS THAT SOCIETY NEEDS TO CONSTRUCT A COMPREHENSIVE THEORY OF BEHAVIOR BECAUSE FACTUAL AND SPECIALIZED KNOWLEDGE OF SOCIAL PHENOMENA, IF APPLIED BY POLICY MAKERS, WOULD BRING AS GREAT TRANSFORMATION TO SOCIAL AND POLITICAL FIELDS AS THE TECHNOLOGICAL APPLICATION OF NATURAL SCIENCES DID IN FIELD OF MASTERY OVER NATURAL FORCES. PRESENTS IDEAS OF LEADING AUTHORITIES IN THE FIELD OF METHODOLOGY.

1675 KEDOURIE E.
NATIONALISM (REV. ED.)
LONDON: HUTCHINSON & CO, 1961, 151 PP.
DISCUSSES THE PHILOSOPHICAL ORIGINS AND THE ACTUAL DEVEL-OPMENT OF NATIONALISM IN EUROPE FROM ITS INCEPTION IN THE 19TH CENTURY THROUGH THE 1950'S

1676 KEE R.
REFUGEE WORLD.
LONDON: OXFORD U PR, 1961, 153 PP.
DESCRIPTIVE PICTURE OF CONDITIONS OF STARVATION AND POVERTY AMONG REFUGEES, CONCENTRATING ON GERMANY AND AUSTRIA. SHOWS HORROR OF LIVING IN REFUGEE CAMPS, AND SUGGESTS WHAT IS NEEDED TO ALLEVIATE PROBLEMS: MORE MONEY, A FRESH APPROACH TO RESPONSIBILITY ON THE PART OF ALL BUREAUCRACIES CONCERNED, AND BETTER AND MORE READILY AVAILABLE HOUSING.

1677 KEE W.S.
"CENTRAL CITY EXPENDITURES AND METROPOLITAN AREAS."
NATIONAL TAX J., 18 (1965), 337-353.
ANALYSIS OF THIRTY-SIX MAJOR CITIES INDICATES THAT THE CENTRAL-CITY EXPENDITURES MAY BE MORE PER CAPITA THAN IN THE SURROUNDING METROPOLITAN AREA BUT THAT SUBURBANITES ARE CHIEF BENEFICIARIES. ARGUES FOR WIDER ADOPTION OF CITY-COUNTY GOVERNMENTS.

1678 KEESING F.M.
THE SOUTH SEAS IN THE MODERN WORLD.
NEW YORK: JOHN DAY, 1941, 393 PP.
SURVEYS ISLAND REGION OF PACIFIC IN ATTEMPT TO DEFINE PO-LITICAL, STRATEGIC, AND ECONOMIC ROLE OF OCEANIC ISLANDS IN MODERN WORLD. CONCENTRATES ON ECONOMIC STRUCTURE OF ISLAND AND FORMS OF GOVERNMENT AS MODIFIERS OF CULTURE.

1679 KEESING F.M.
CULTURE CHANGE: AN ANALYSIS AND BIBLIOGRAPHY OF ANTHRO-POLOGICAL SOURCES TO 1952.
STANFORD: STANFORD U PRESS, 1953, 242 PP., LC#53-10842.
PRESENTS IN CHRONOLOGICAL ORDER (FOR MOST PART ON A YEARLY BASIS) SIGNIFICANT WORKS WRITTEN IN FIELDS OF CUL-TURAL DYNAMICS AND APPLIED ANTHROPOLOGY. FOCUSES PRIMARILY ON WORKS BY PROFESSIONAL ANTHROPOLOGISTS ON PHENOMENA OF CHANGE. EARLIEST LISTINGS ARE FROM 1865. LANGUAGES INCLUDE ITALIAN, SCANDINAVIAN, SLAVIC, ENGLISH, FRENCH, GERMAN, AND SPANISH. INCLUDES ANALYTICAL SURVEY.

1680 KEESING F.M.
THE ETHNOHISTORY OF NORTHERN LUZON.
STANFORD: STANFORD U PRESS, 1962, 362 PP., LC#62-9563.
ANTHROPOLOGICAL STUDY OF NATIVE PEOPLES. ILLUSTRATES MAN'S ABILITY TO REFORMULATE HIS CULTURE, OFTEN RAPIDLY, TO MEET CHANGING CIRCUMSTANCES OF A NEW ENVIRONMENT. GIVES HIS-TORICAL RECORD OF CULTURAL CONTACT AND CHANGE IN SEVERAL TRIBAL GROUPS IN THE NORTHERN LUZON AREA.

1681 KEIL S.
SEXUALITAT - ERKENNTNISSE UND MASS-STABE.
STUTTGART: KREUZ-VERLAG, 1966, 252 PP.
EXAMINES SEXUAL BEHAVIOR AND NORMS IN SOCIAL STRUCTURE FROM PRE-INDUSTRIAL SOCIETY TO PRESENT. DISCUSSES BIRTH CONTROL, CHANGES IN AUTHORITY, RESPONSIBILITY, AND ETHICAL STANDARDS.

1682 KEITH G.
THE FADING COLOUR BAR.
LONDON: ROBERT HALE, 1966, 220 PP.
REVIEWS RECENT CHANGES IN GOVERNMENT OF CENTRAL AFRICA. PRIMARILY CONCERNS THE FADING OF COLOR BAR IN ZAMBIA AND NEW ATTITUDES TOWARD INTEGRATION. SEES EUROPEANS AS HAVING CHANGED CENTURY-OLD VIEWS OVERNIGHT, AND MARVELS AT 71,000 WHITES LIVING UNDER BLACK GOVERNMENT AND LIKING IT.

1683 KELF-COHEN R.
NATIONALISATION IN BRITAIN: THE END OF DOGMA.
NEW YORK: ST MARTIN'S PRESS, 1959, 310 PP.
CRITICAL DISCUSSION OF THE NATIONALIZATION OF INDUSTRIES IN GREAT BRITAIN BY A FORMER SUPPORTER OF THIS ECONOMIC TACTIC. DISCUSSES WHICH INDUSTRIES ARE NATIONALIZED AND WHAT THE FUTURE IS FOR SUCH INDUSTRIES.

1684 KELLEHER G.W.
"THE COMMON MARKET ANTITRUST LAWS: THE FIRST TEN YEARS."
ANTI-TRUST BULLETIN, 7 (WINTER 67), 1219-1253.
ANALYZES STRUCTURE AND EFFECTIVENESS OF EEC ANTITRUST REGULATIONS, DISCUSSING ECONOMIC CONSEQUENCES, JUDICIAL MACHINERY, AND INTERNATIONAL COOPERATION AND ENFORCEMENT. DISCUSSES COMMISSION'S SETUP FOR HANDLING REGULATION ON AN INTERNATIONAL BASIS, ITS POWERS, AND ITS METHODS.

1685 KELLER J.W.
GERMANY, THE WALL AND BERLIN.
NEW YORK: VANTAGE, 1964, 437 PP.
TRACES DEVELOPMENT AND FLUCTUATIONS OF 'GERMAN PUBLIC OPINION AS EXPRESSED BY GERMAN POLITICIANS AND IN GERMAN PERIODICALS CONCERNING THE FUTURE OF BERLIN AND THE FOREIGN POLICY TO BE FOLLOWED BY WEST GERMANY.'

1686 KELLEY G.A.
"THE POLITICAL BACKGROUND OF THE FRENCH A-BOMB."
ORBIS, 4 (FALL 60), 251-67.
TRACES FRENCH ATOMIC POLICY RE NATIONAL INTEREST AND FOLLOWS POLICIES OF PRE-DE GAULLE GOVERNMENTS. ADVOCATES CLAIM VALUE FOR PRESTIGE BARGAINING FOR EUROPEAN AND UNIVER-SAL LEADERSHIP. OPPONENTS EMPHASIZE USELESSNESS, ECONOMIC COST AND DIFFICULTY OF NEGOTIATIONS WITH USSR, HOLDING REALISM REQUIRES ACCEPTANCE OF THIS FACT.

1687 KENEN P.B.
BRITISH MONETARY POLICY AND THE BALANCE OF PAYMENTS 1951-57.

CAMBRIDGE: HARVARD U PR, 1960, 325 PP., LC#60-11556.
SURVEYS BRITAIN'S DOMESTIC ECONOMIC POLICIES, ESPECIALLY HER MONETARY POLICIES, IN THE LIGHT OF HER BALANCE-OF-PAYMENTS POSITION, FOCUSING ON GOVERNMENT'S ATTITUDE AND RESPONSE TO BALANCE-OF-PAYMENTS CRISIS. CONTENDS THAT ATTEMPTS TO MAINTAIN EXTERNAL BALANCE HAVE REVOLUTIONIZED BANK OF ENGLAND POLICIES, AFFECTING VOLUME PRICE OF CREDIT RATHER THAN CONDITIONS IN DISCOUNT MARKET.

1688 KENNEDY M.D.
A SHORT HISTORY OF COMMUNISM IN ASIA.
LONDON: WEIDENFIELD & NICOLSON, 1957, 556 PP.
TRACES MAIN DEVELOPMENTS IN RISE OF NATIONALISM AND COMMUNISM IN COUNTRIES OF SOUTH AND EAST ASIA. EXAMINES COMMUNIST STRATEGY IN LIGHT OF WORLD AFFAIRS AND IN RELATION TO RUSSIAN POLITICS.

1689 KENNEDY R.
BIBLIOGRAPHY OF INDONESIAN PEOPLES AND CULTURES (2ND REV. ED.)
NEW HAVEN: YALE U, SE ASIA STUD, 1962, 207 PP., LC#62-20539.
COMPREHENSIVE INTERNATIONAL BIBLIOGRAPHY OF ALL EXTANT BOOKS AND ARTICLES ON PEOPLES AND CULTURES OF INDONESIA. MAIN FOCUS OF INTEREST IS ANTHROPOLOGY AND SOCIOLOGY, INCLUDING ETHNOGRAPHY, ARCHEOLOGY, LINGUISTICS, AND STUDIES OF ACCULTURATION. ALSO INCORPORATES RELEVANT MATERIAL ON GEOGRAPHY, COLONIAL ADMINISTRATION, EDUCATION AND ECONOMICS. CLASSIFICATION BY TRIBES WITHIN ISLAND GROUPS.

1690 KENNETT L.
THE FRENCH ARMIES IN THE SEVEN YEARS' WAR.
DURHAM: DUKE U PR, 1967, 165 PP., LC#67-18529.
STUDIES L'ARMEE DU ROI AS AN INSTITUTION WITH A VIEW TO ILLUSTRATING PAST ASPECTS AND PROBLEMS OF WARFARE. SEES IN MILITARY A MICROCOSM OF 18TH-CENTURY FRENCH SOCIETY AND LOUIS XV'S GOVERNMENT, WITH SAME VICES OF COMPLACENT TRADITIONALISM AND INEQUALITY. TO EXPLAIN MEDIOCRE SUCCESS OF FRENCH ARMY, COMPARISIONS ARE MADE WITH FORCES AND GOALS OF AUSTRIA, ENGLAND, AND RUSSIA.

1691 KENYA MINISTRY ECO PLAN DEV
AFRICAN SOCIALISM AND ITS APPLICATION TO PLANNING IN KENYA (PAMPHLET)
NAIROBI: KENYA MIN ECO PLAN DEV, 1964, 56 PP.
REPORTS ON CONFERENCE OF AFRICAN COMMONWEALTH NATIONS AFRICAN FORM OF SOCIALISM IN DEVELOPMENT SINCE INDEPENDENCE OF NATION. INDICATES AREAS AND METHOD OF GOVERNMENTAL ACTIVITY IN ECONOMY.

1692 KEPHART C.
RACES OF MAN.
NEW YORK: PHILOSOPHICAL LIB, 1960, 565 PP., LC#60-13647.
FOLLOWS MIGRATIONS AND INTERACTIONS OF RACES THROUGH HISTORY. DISCUSSES EFFECT OF CONTACT AND INTERBREEDING. STUDIES ECONOMIC FORCES CAUSING MOVEMENT OF RACES, THEIR CONTACTS WITH EACH OTHER, AND GRADUAL SOLIDIFICATION OF MAJOR RACES PRESENTLY EXTANT.

1693 KER A.M.
MEXICAN GOVERNMENT PUBLICATIONS: A GUIDE TO THE MORE IMPORTANT PUBLICATIONS OF THE GOVERNMENT OF MEXICO, 1821-1936.
WASHINGTON: GOVT PR OFFICE, 1940, 333 PP., LC#40-26001.
BIBLIOGRAPHY OF IMPORTANT PUBLICATIONS OF BUREAUS AND DEPARTMENTS. DOES NOT INCLUDE PUBLICATIONS OF THE MAXIMILIAN GOVERNMENT. INCLUDES HISTORIES AND DESCRIPTIONS OF THE EXECUTIVE AND LEGISLATIVE BRANCHES OF GOVERNMENT. KEY CODE PROVIDES LOCATION INFORMATION.

1694 KEREKES T. ED.
THE ARAB MIDDLE EAST AND MUSLIM AFRICA.
NEW YORK: PRAEGER, 1961, 126 PP.
ESSAYS SETTING FORTH PRESENT ROLE OF ISLAM IN ARAB MIDDLE EAST AND MUSLIM AFRICA. DISCUSS POLITICAL, SOCIAL AND ECONOMIC DEVELOPMENTS AS WELL AS CHANGING INTELLECTUAL ATTITUDES AND INTER-GENERATIONAL CONFLICTS.

1695 KERNER R.J.
SLAVIC EUROPE: A SELECTED BIBLIOGRAPHY IN THE WESTERN EUROPEAN LANGUAGES.
CAMBRIDGE: HARVARD U PR, 1918, 402 PP.
LISTED BY SUBJECT WITH MORE IMPORTANT ITEMS EMPHASIZED. ALL WESTERN EUROPEAN LANGUAGES INCLUDED. EVERY VARIETY OF SOURCE WITH CONCLUDING AUTHOR INDEX. ITEMS NUMBER 4500.

1696 KERNER R.J.
NORTHEAST ASIA: A SELECTED BIBLIOGRAPHY (2 VOLS.)
BERKELEY: U OF CALIF PR, 1939, 1296 PP.
TOPICALLY ARRANGED WITHIN REGIONAL AND NATIONAL CATEGORIES. INCLUDES EVERY TYPE OF SOURCE AND SOURCES IN ALL LANGUAGES WITH TRANSLITERATED TITLES. CROSS-REFERENCED WITH CONCLUDING SUBJECT INDEX. ITEMS NUMBER 14,000 IN TWO VOLS.

1697 KERR C., ET A.L.
INDUSTRIALISM AND INDUSTRIAL MAN.
CAMBRIDGE: HARVARD U PR, 1960, 331 PP., LC#60-15239.
EXAMINES PROCESS OF INDUSTRIALIZATION AND ITS EFFECT ON WORKERS AND SOCIETY IN VARIOUS COUNTRIES. APPROACH IS ABSTRACT RATHER THAN FACTUAL, AND AN ATTEMPT IS MADE TO FORMULATE PARADIGMS FOR PREDICTING OUTCOME OF INDUSTRIALIZATION ON SOCIETY AND ON MANKIND.

1698 KERR M.H.
ISLAMIC REFORM: THE POLITICAL AND LEGAL THEORIES OF MUHAMMAD 'ABDUH AND RASHID RIDA.
BERKELEY: U OF CALIF PR, 1966, 249 PP., LC#65-24177.
STUDY OF CERTAIN ISLAMIC THEORIES OF RELIGIOUS BASIS OF LAW AND GOVERNMENT. INTERPRETATION OF CLASSIC JURISTIC TRADITION OF THOUGHT, WITH PARTICULAR EMPHASIS ON ELEMENTS CRUCIAL TO MODERN REFORMATION POLICIES. ANALYZES EFFORTS OF TWO LEADING MODERNISTS TO DEVELOP CONCEPTS OF NATURAL LAW, POPULAR SOVEREIGNTY, AND UTILITARIAN JURISPRUDENCE. SELECT BIBLIOGRAPHY.

1699 KERSELL J.E.
PARLIAMENTARY SUPERVISION OF DELEGATED LEGISLATION.
LONDON: STEVENS, 1960, 178 PP.
STUDY DEALING WITH LEGISLATIVE TECHNIQUES OF CONTROLLING GOVERNMENT. ASSUMES THE MOST APPROPRIATE INSTITUTION TO SUPERVISE USE OF DELEGATED LEGISLATIVE POWERS IS PARLIAMENT. IF EXECUTIVE OFFICIALS EXERCISE THESE POWERS EFFECTIVELY, SOUND TECHNIQUES OF CONTROL MUST RESULT.

1700 KEYES J.G.
A BIBLIOGRAPHY OF WESTERN LANGUAGE PUBLICATIONS CONCERNING NORTH VIETNAM IN THE CORNELL LIBRARY.
ITHACA: CORNELL U, DEPT ASIAN ST, 1966, 292 PP.
SUPPLEMENT TO 1964 BIBLIOGRAPHY INCLUDES MAINLY MATERIALS PUBLISHED DURING THE 1960'S ABOUT NORTH VIETNAM. GROUPED BY SUBJECT AND INDEXED BY AUTHOR, OVER 1500 ITEMS ANNOTATED. ARTICLES, BOOKS, PAMPHLETS, DOCUMENTS, MICROFILMS. ITEMS FROM 1945-1964, INCLUSIVE. ALSO ANNOTATES THE US JOINT PUBLICATIONS RESEARCH SERVICE MATERIAL ON NORTH VIETNAM.

1701 KEYFITZ N.
"WESTERN PERSPECTIVES AND ASIAN PROBLEMS."
HUM. ORGAN., 1 (SPRING 60), 28-31.
CONTENDS THAT DIFFERENT BACKGROUNDS PRODUCE VARYING PERSPECTIVES OF THE SAME PROBLEM. ASIAN AND EUROPEAN ATTITUDES REGARDING TECHNICAL ASSISTANCE, WORK, CORRUPTION, POPULATION GROWTH AND FAMILY ARE CONTRASTED AND ELUCIDATED.

1702 KHADDURI M.
WAR AND PEACE IN THE LAW OF ISLAM.
BALTIMORE: JOHNS HOPKINS PR., 1955, 321 PP., $5.50.
AIMS TO RECONSTRUCT THE CLASSICAL LEGAL THEORY OF ISLAM, AS WELL AS PRINCIPLES AND RULES GOVERNING ISLAM'S RELATIONS WITH NON-MUSLIM COUNTRIES. ALSO DISCUSSES THE EFFORTS IN RECENT TIMES AIMED AT ADAPTING ISLAM TO THE PRINCIPLES AND PURPOSES OF THE MODERN COMMUNITY OF NATIONS. DIVIDED INTO: FUNDAMENTAL CONCEPTS OF MUSLIM LAW, THE LAW OF WAR: THE JIHAD: THE LAW OF PEACE.

1703 KHADDURI M., LIEBESNY H.J.
LAW IN THE MIDDLE EAST.
WASHINGTON: MIDDLE EAST INST, 1955, 393 PP.
COMPARES ISLAMIC AND WESTERN LAW, WITH SPECIAL EMPHASIS ON THE DIFFERENCES IN SPIRITUAL BELIEFS WHICH UNDERLIE SIGNIFICANT DISSIMILARITIES IN PENAL AND CIVIL CODES. DISCUSSES CONSTITUTIONAL ORGANIZATION, PRE-ISLAMIC BACKGROUND, COURT SYSTEMS, LAW SCHOOLS, AND INFLUENCE OF WESTERN JUDICIAL PROCEDURE IN RECENT TIMES.

1704 KHADDURI M.
MODERN LIBYA: A STUDY IN POLITICAL DEVELOPMENT.
BALTIMORE: JOHNS HOPKINS PR., 1963, 404 PP.
OUTLINES EXISTENCE AS ITALIAN COLONY, BRITISH-OCCUPIED COUNTRY DURING WW 2, ENTITY UNDER UN AUSPICES AND FINALLY, ITS EMERGENCE AS INDEPENDENT NATION. EVOLUTION OF ITS CONSTITUTIONAL MONARCHY AND GOVERNMENT-MACHINERY ARE DESCRIBED ALONG WITH HISTORY OF REGIMES TO 1961. FACTORS OF UNITY, COHESION AND DEVELOPMENT ARE ASSESSED. TEXT OF WHEELUS AIR-BASE AGREEMENT INCLUDED.

1705 KHALIQUZZAMAN C.
PATHWAY TO PAKISTAN.
LONDON: LONGMANS, GREEN & CO, 1961, 432 PP.
MEMOIRS OF MEMBER OF PAKISTAN MUSLIM LEAGUE UNFOLDING NATURE OF MUSLIM MOVEMENTS IN INDIA. DISCUSSES POLITICAL CONFLICTS BETWEEN INDIAN NATIONAL CONGRESS AND BRITAIN AND ATTITUDE TOWARD MUSLIM RIGHTS.

1706 KHAMA T.
"POLITICAL CHANGE IN AFRICAN SOCIETY."
SUSSEX: AFRICA BUREAU, 1956, 16 PP.
STUDIES THE DEVELOPMENT OF REPRESENTATIVE GOVERNMENT FROM THE TIME OF THE FIRST WHITE COLONIZATION. CONCLUDES THERE IS A NEED FOR CLOSE COOPERATION BETWEEN TRIBAL CHIEFS AND NEWLY RISING POLITICAL STATESMEN.

1707 KHAN A.W.
INDIA WINS FREEDOM: THE OTHER SIDE.
KARACHI: PAKISTAN EDUCATION PUBL, 1961, 405 PP.

EXAMINES MAULANA AZAD'S "INDIA WINS FREEDOM" AND SEEKS TO PRESENT BIRTH, PROGRESS, AND CULMINATION OF PAKISTAN MOVEMENT. DISCUSSES LEADERSHIP OF INDIAN NATIONAL CONGRESS AND RISE OF MUSLIM STRUGGLE FOR INDEPENDENCE.

1708 KIDD K.E., ROGERS E.S., KENYON W.A.
BRIEF BIBLIOGRAPHY OF ONTARIO ANTHROPOLOGY (PAMPHLET)
TORONTO: UNIVERSITY PRESS, 1964, 20 PP.
ANTHROPOLOGY OF ONTARIO COVERS PREHISTORIC AND HISTORIC ARCHEOLOGY, ETHNOLOGY, LINGUISTICS, AND FOLKLORE. PHYSICAL ANTHROPOLOGY MUST ALSO BE INCLUDED. FIRST LISTS SEVERAL GENERAL WORKS ON ONTARIO.

1709 KIDDER F.E. ED., BUSHONG ED.
THESES ON PAN AMERICAN TOPICS.
WASHINGTON: PAN AMERICAN UNION, 1962, 124 PP.
UNANNOTATED LISTING OF DOCTORAL THESES FROM US AND CANADA RELATING TO THE AMERICAS. INDEXED BY AUTHOR, SCHOOL, AND TOPIC. TOPICS INCLUDE GENERAL HISTORY, POLITICS, INTERNATIONAL RELATIONS, ECONOMICS, SOCIAL CONDITIONS, CULTURE, GOVERNMENT, HEALTH, FINE ARTS, LAW, LANGUAGES, RELIGION, GEOGRAPHY, AND OTHERS. THESES PERTAIN PRINCIPALLY TO CENTRAL AND SOUTH AMERICA. CONTAINS 2,253 LISTINGS.

1710 KILSON M.L.
"LAND AND POLITICS IN KENYA: AN ANALYSIS OF AFRICAN POLITICS IN A PLURAL SOCIETY."
WEST. POLIT. QUART., 10 (SEPT. 57), 559-581.
ANALYZES FACTORS WHICH CONTRIBUTED TO PAST POLITICAL ACTIVITY AMONG NATIVES IN KENYA FOR INSIGHT INTO POSSIBLE COURSE SUCH ACTIVITY MAY TAKE IN FUTURE. CONCLUDES FUTURE DEPENDS MAINLY ON HOW BRITISH RESOLVE PROBLEMS INHERENT IN THE PLURAL SOCIETY OF KENYA.

1712 KINDERSLEY R.
THE FIRST RUSSIAN REVISIONISTS.
LONDON: OXFORD U PR, 1962, 260 PP.
STUDIES FAILURE OF LEGAL MARXISM AND ITS RELATION TO BOLSHEVISM IN 1890'S. DISCUSSES EARLY RUSSIAN MARXISM AND ITS VICTORY OVER RUSSIAN POPULISM. EXAMINES DIFFERENCES BETWEEN THEM AND DESCRIBES VOGUE OF LEGAL MARXISM AT TURN OF THE CENTURY. ROLE OF PETER STRUVE AS INITIATOR OF REVISIONISM IN RUSSIA IS CENTRAL THEME.

1713 KINDLEBERGER C.P.
FOREIGN TRADE AND THE NATIONAL ECONOMY.
NEW HAVEN: YALE U PR, 1962, 265 PP., LC#62-16236.
STUDY OF FOREIGN TRADE TYPE AND QUANTITY OF A NATION'S IMPORTS AND EXPORTS AND IMPACT OF SUCH TRADE ON NATIONAL ECONOMY. DISCUSSES TRANSPORTATION, RESOURCES, CAPITAL, TECHNOLOGY, AND RELATIONSHIP BETWEEN PUBLIC AND PRIVATE SECTORS IN VARIOUS NATIONS.

1714 KINDLEBERGER C.P.
"MASS MIGRATION, THEN AND NOW."
FOREIGN AFFAIRS, 43 (JULY 65), 647-658.
COMPARISON OF THE MASS MIGRATION OF EUROPEANS TO THE US IN THE 19TH AND EARLY 20TH CENTURIES WITH THE MODERN MIGRATION OF WORKERS FROM SOUTHERN EUROPE AND AFRICA TO THE FULL EMPLOYMENT MARKETS OF NORTHERN EUROPE TODAY. MAIN DIFFERENCE FOUND IN THE ROLE OF EUROPEAN GOVERNMENTS IS IN CONTRACTING AND CARING FOR WORKERS. HAS BEEN FORCE FOR LABOR LAW AND ECONOMIC EQUALIZATION IN EUROPE.

1715 KING M.L. JR.
WHERE DO WE GO FROM HERE: CHAOS OR COMMUNITY?
NEW YORK: HARPER & ROW, 1967, 209 PP.
DISCUSSES POWER AND ITS MANY FORMS IN RACIAL STRUGGLE IN AMERICA. EXAMINATION OF PRESENT SCENE BY ONE OF THE BEST KNOWN NEGRO LEADERS. INCLUDES BLACK POWER, RACISM AND THE WHITE BACKLASH, THE DILEMMA OF NEGRO AMERICANS, AND PROSPECTS FOR THE FUTURE. ASSERTS THAT MEMBERS OF "WORLD HOUSE" MUST LEARN TO LIVE TOGETHER IN NONVIOLENT COEXISTENCE, EVEN PEACE AND LOVE.

1716 KINGSBURY E.C.
"LAW AS COMPACT: ANCIENT ISRAEL'S CONTRIBUTION TO THE UNDERSTANDING OF LAW."
J. HUMAN RELATIONS, 15 (1967), 411-422.
DISCUSSES UNDERSTANDING OF LAW BY THE ANCIENT HEBREWS AS MANIFESTED BY THEIR COVENANTS WITH GOD. EMPHASIZES THE ISRAELITES' TECHNIQUES OF LAW-MAKING AND LAW INTERPRETATION AND PARALLELS AMERICAN LEGAL IDEALS WITH THOSE OF ISRAEL. EMPHASIZES THE NOTION OF LAW AS A COMPACT, OF LAW AS SUPREME. ADVOCATES CHANGING LAW THROUGH LEGAL STRUCTURES.

1717 KINGSLEY M.H.
WEST AFRICAN STUDIES.
LONDON: MACMILLAN, 1899, 640 PP.
DESCRIPTION OF RELIGION, CULTURE, COLONIAL INFLUENCES, MEDICINE, LAW, AND PROPERTY OWNERSHIP. DISCUSSION OF GENETIC DIFFERENCES AMONG AFRICANS.

1718 KINNEAR J.B.
PRINCIPLES OF CIVIL GOVERNMENT.
LONDON: SMITH, ELDER & CO, 1887, 237 PP.
DESCRIBES SCIENCE AND NATURE OF GOVERNMENT; ITS OBJECTS, REPRESENTATIVE GOVERNMENT, CONDITIONS OF NATIONAL UNITY, CONSTITUTIONS, LOCAL GOVERNMENT, AND NATIONAL OBLIGATIONS.

1719 KINTNER W.R.
ORGANIZING FOR CONFLICT: A PROPOSAL.
ORBIS, 2 (SUMMER 58), 155-74.
DISCUSSION OF ROLE OF EXECUTIVE IN THE FORMULATION AND EXECUTION OF US NATIONAL SECURITY POLICY. ANALYZES AGENCIES RESPONSIBLE FOR SUCH POLICY AND COMPARES THEM WITH SOVIET STRUCTURES, AND MAKES PROPOSALS FOR GREATER COORDINATION BETWEEN PLANS AND PROGRAMS.

1720 KIRCHHEIMER O.
GEGENWARTSPROBLEME DER ASYLGEWAHRUNG.
COLOGNE: WESTDEUTSCHER VERLAG, 1959, 65 PP.
EXAMINES POLITICAL AND LEGAL IMPLICATIONS OF GRANTING ASYLUM TO POLITICAL REFUGEES. SHOWS THAT MODERN MASS MIGRATIONS RESULTING FROM POLITICAL UPHEAVAL AND PERSECUTION HAVE MADE OLDER DOCTRINES INAPPLICABLE. MAINTAINS THAT STRICT OBSERVANCE OF PRINCIPLE OF POLITICAL ASYLUM IS NECESSARY TO PREVENT 'ARBITRARY RULE AND DESTRUCTION OF FREEDOM."

1721 KIRDAR U.
THE STRUCTURE OF UNITED NATIONS ECONOMIC AID TO UNDERDEVELOPED COUNTRIES.
THE HAGUE: MARTINUS NIJHOFF, 1966, 361 PP., LC#66-54220.
DETAILED STUDY OF VARIOUS FORMS OF FINANCIAL AND TECHNICAL ASSISTANCE TO UNDERDEVELOPED COUNTRIES, EMPHASIZING AID PROGRAMS THAT ARE MEDIATED AND ADMINISTERED BY UN AND OTHER INTERNATIONAL BODIES. STRESSES INTERNATIONAL NATURE OF ECONOMIC AID PROGRAMS IN RELATION TO BOTH ORGANIZATIONAL STRUCTURE AND POLITICAL IMPLICATIONS.

1722 KIRKENDALL R.S.
SOCIAL SCIENTISTS AND FARM POLITICS IN THE AGE OF ROOSEVELT.
COLUMBIA: U OF MO PR, 1966, 358 PP., LC#66-14032.
STUDIES A SIGNIFICANT AND CONTROVERSIAL FEATURE OF NEW DEAL: ROLE OF INTELLECTUALS IN ITS DEVELOPMENT. FOCUSES ON ENTRY OF SOCIAL SCIENTISTS INTO POLITICS. EXAMINES CHARACTER AND ROLE OF THE "SERVICE INTELLECTUAL," ONE WHO FEELS HIS SERVICES ARE NEEDED BY SOCIETY. SHOWS SOCIAL SCIENTISTS' ACTIVITIES IN ELEVATING PRODUCTION CONTROL, PLANNING FOR RURAL POOR, AND ELEVATING BUREAU OF AGRICULTURAL ECONOMICS.

1723 KIRKLAND E.C.
A BIBLIOGRAPHY OF SOUTH ASIAN FOLKLORE.
BLOOMINGTON: INDIANA U PR, 1966, 291 PP.
BIBLIOGRAPHY OF ITEMS CONCERNED WITH ALL TYPES OF FOLKLORE OF SOUTH ASIAN COUNTRIES. NOTES GEOGRAPHICAL AREA, LINGUISTIC, TRIBAL OR ETHNIC GROUP, AND TYPE OF FOLKLORE. DIVISIONS SUCH AS ART, CUSTOM, MAGIC, MUSIC, ETC. APPROXIMATELY 7,000 ITEMS FROM SEVEN COUNTRIES.

1724 KIRKPATRICK F.A.
A HISTORY OF THE ARGENTINE REPUBLIC.
NEW YORK: CAMBRIDGE U PRESS, 1931, 255 PP.
BRITISH ANALYSIS OF ARGENTINIAN POLITICAL, HISTORICAL, SOCIAL, AND ECONOMIC DEVELOPMENT; STRESSES RELATIONSHIP WITH UK. STARTS WITH SPANISH CONQUEST AND SUBSEQUENT MUNICIPAL PERIOD, 1580-1776. COVERS VICEROYALTY OF 1786-1810, BRITISH INVASIONS, INDEPENDENCE, LEADERSHIP OF SAN MARTIN, AND THE CONSTITUTION. CONCLUDING DISCUSSIONS ON PROBLEMS OF 20TH-CENTURY PROGRESS AND MOVEMENTS OF DEMOCRACY.

1725 KIRKWOOD K.
BRITAIN AND AFRICA.
LONDON: CHATTO AND WINDUS, 1965, 235 PP.
HISTORY OF RELATIONS BETWEEN BRITAIN AND SUB-SAHARA AFRICA BY PERIOD (TO 1914, TO 1939, TO 1964), AND BY REGION (EAST, WEST, AND SOUTH AFRICA). CONCLUDING CHAPTER ON RELATIONS WITH INDEPENDENT AFRICA EMPHASIZES BRITAIN'S CHANGING ROLE AND POLICIES.

1726 KIRPICEVA I.K.
HANDBUCH DER RUSSISCHEN UND SOWJETISCHEN BIBLIOGRAPHIEN (5 VOLS.)
LEIPZIG: VEB VERL FUR BUCH BIBL, 1962.
ANNOTATED BIBLIOGRAPHICAL SURVEY OF SOVIET AND RUSSIAN BIBLIOGRAPHIES FROM 18TH CENTURY THROUGH 1959. INFORMATION GIVEN IN TABLE FORM; RUSSIAN CHARACTERS TRANSLITERATED AND FREQUENTLY TRANSLATED INTO GERMAN. TOPICALLY CLASSIFIED AND INDEXED BY AUTHOR. INCLUDES COMPREHENSIVE AND SPECIALIZED BIBLIOGRAPHIES, WORKS WITH APPENDED SUPPLEMENTARY READING LISTS, AND PERIODICALS.

1727 KIS T.I.
LES PAYS DE L'EUROPE DE L'EST: LEURS RAPPORTS MUTUELS ET LE PROBLEME DE LEUR INTEGRATION DANS L'ORBITE DE L'USSR.
LOUVAIN: EDITORIAL NAUWELAERTS, 1964, 271 PP.
EXAMINES MUTUAL INTERESTS OF EAST EUROPEAN COUNTRIES AND THEIR INTEGRATION AS SOVIET SATELLITES SINCE WWII. STUDIES DISINTEGRATION OF RUSSIAN EMPIRE, NEW POLICY OF INTEGRATION WITH "POPULAR DEMOCRACIES" IN EUROPE, AND COMMUNIST IDEOLOGY CONCERNING THE STATE, INDIVIDUAL RIGHTS, POLITICS, AND

INTERNATIONAL RELATIONS. INCLUDES BIBLIOGRAPHY OF ABOUT 280 ITEMS.

1728 KISSINGER H.A.
THE NECESSITY FOR CHOICE.
NEW YORK: HARPER, 1961, 370 PP.
APPRAISAL OF MAJOR ISSUES CONFRONTING USA FOREIGN POLICY. FEELS UNITED STATES' POSITION IN WORLD HAS DETERIORATED IN PAST DECADE AND CHALLENGES POLICY MAKERS TO RESOLVE THE MANY ISSUES WHICH HAVE BEEN IGNORED SINCE 1945, PRIMARILY, DETERRENCE, LIMITED WAR PLANS, ARMS CONTROL AND THE ATLANTIC COMMUNITY.

1729 KITCHEN H. ED.
A HANDBOOK OF AFRICAN AFFAIRS.
NEW YORK: FREDERICK PRAEGER, 1964, 311 PP., LC#64-16680.
COUNTRY-BY-COUNTRY POLITICAL GUIDE TO AFRICA. INCLUDES BRIEF HISTORCAL SUMMARY, DESCRIPTION OF ARMED FORCES OF EACH COUNTRY, AND ORGANIZATION OF AFRICAN UNITY. FOUR ARTICLES ON CONTEMPORARY AFRICAN PROSE AND POETRY.

1730 KITTLER G.D.
EQUATORIAL AFRICA: THE NEW WORLD OF TOMORROW.
LONDON: THOMAS NELSON & SONS, 1959, 190 PP., LC#59-10498.
A CURSORY LOOK AT THE CENTRAL AFRICAN NATIONS: THEIR CULTURAL SIMILARITIES AND DIFFERENCES, SOCIAL SYSTEMS, ECONOMIC PROBLEMS, POLITICAL STRUCTURES; STORIES OF LIVES OF NORMAL AFRICAN PEOPLE, THEIR HABITS AND INTERESTS. ILLUSTRATED.

1731 KLEIMAN R.
ATLANTIC CRISIS; AMERICAN DIPLOMACY CONFRONTS A RESURGENT EUROPE.
NEW YORK: W W NORTON, 1963, 158 PP., LC#63-22748.
CONCERNED WITH KENNEDY'S "GRAND DESIGN" TO CREATE AN ATLANTIC PARTNERSHIP AND THE SETBACK IT RECEIVED BY DE GAULLE'S VETO IN 1963. SEEKS TO ANSWER WHY DE GAULLE THWARTED THIS CONCEPT AND WHY HE VOTOED BRITAIN'S ENTRY INTO COMMON MARKET. EXAMINES SHORTCOMINGS OF US AND OTHER EUROPEAN COUNTRIES; REVIEWS JOHNSON'S POSITION AND PRESENTS GOALS FOR A FUTURE ATLANTIC PARTNERSHIP AND ITS SUCCESS.

1732 KLEIN J.
SAMPLES FROM ENGLISH CULTURES (2 VOLS.)
NEW YORK: HUMANITIES PRESS, 1965, 660 PP.
FIRST SECTION DESCRIBES THREE ISOLATED COMMUNITIES, DIFFERING IN LOCATION, ATTITUDE, AND BACKGROUND. SECTION II DESCRIBES ADULT LIFE IN ENGLISH WORKING AND MIDDLE CLASSES. FINAL SECTION (VOL. II) DEALS WITH CHILD-REARING PRACTICES FROM INFANCY ONWARD IN DIFFERING SOCIAL CLASSES AND DISCUSSES SOCIOLOGICAL ASPECTS OF VARYING TRADITIONS, PRACTICES, AND ATTITUDES.

1733 KLUCKHOHN C.
"PATTERNING AS EXEMPLIFIED IN NAVAHO CULTURE" IN EDWARD SAPIR, LANGUAGE, CULTURE, AND PERSONALITY (BMR)"
MENASHA, WIS: SAPIR MEM FUND, 1941.
A CONTINUATION AND SYSTEMATIC ELABORATION ON EDWARD SAPIR'S CONCEPTS OF PATTERN AND CONFIGURATION. DISCUSSES STRUCTURAL REGULARITIES IN OVERT CULTURE SEEN IN THE OPTATIVE, IMPERATIVE, AND INDICATIVE MODES. EXAMINES THREE COMPLEXES OF PATTERNS ACTIVITY, WITH SPECIAL EMPHASIS ON THE NAVAHO CULTURE. ANALYZES STRUCTURAL REGULARITIES IN COVERT CULTURE AS SUB-CONFIGURATION AND INTEGRATION.

1734 KNORR K.E.
BRITISH COLONIAL THEORIES 1570-1850.
TORONTO: U. PR., 1944, 429 PP.
EXAMINES THE ADVANTAGES AND DISADVANTAGES OF ESTABLISHMENT AND MAINTENANCE OF OVERSEAS COLONIES. MAJOR ARGUMENTS AND IDEAS ARE ARRANGED TOPICALLY AS WELL AS CHRONOLOGICALLY.

1735 KNOWLES A.F.
"NOTES ON A CANADIAN MASS MEDIA POLICY."
CAN. PUBLIC ADMIN., 10 (JUNE 67), 223-233.
COMMENTS ON ASPECTS OF CANADIAN MASS COMMUNICATION PROBLEM, ESPECIALLY EDUCATIONAL USE OF TELEVISION. ADVOCATES STRICTER STANDARDS OF STATION PROGRAMMING AND PROVIDES CRITERIA TO JUDGE PERFORMANCE. DISCUSSES DANGERS IN TOO MUCH GOVERNMENT CONTROL. COMPARES NATIONAL EDUCATIONAL TELEVISION TO THAT OF US.

1736 KOENTJARANINGRAT R.
A PRELIMINARY DESCRIPTION OF THE JAVANESE KINSHIP SYSTEM.
NEW HAVEN: YALE U PR, 1957, 112 PP.
DESCRIBES KINSHIP SYSTEM IN SOUTH CENTRAL JAVA, RESTRICTING STUDY TO HIGHER SOCIAL LEVELS OF WHICH AUTHOR IS A MEMBER AND OBSERVER. EMPHASIZES KINSHIP BEHAVIOR AND INCLUDES TERMINOLOGY.

1737 KOGAN N.
THE POLITICS OF ITALIAN FOREIGN POLICY.
NEW YORK: PRAEGER, 1963, 178 PP.
BROAD INVESTIGATION OF ITALIAN POLITICAL SYSTEM, ORIENTED TOWARDS QUESTIONS OF FOREIGN POLICY. ANALYZES METHODS BY WHICH POLITICAL DECISIONS AFFECTING FOREIGN POLICY ARE MADE, KINDS OF DECISIONS MADE, AND FORCES OPERATING TO INFLUENCE THEM.

1738 KOH S.J.
STAGES OF INDUSTRIAL DEVELOPMENT IN ASIA.
PHILA: U OF PENN PR, 1966, 461 PP., LC#65-22081.
STUDY OF COMPARATIVE HISTORY OF THE COTTON INDUSTRY IN JAPAN, INDIA, CHINA, AND KOREA. DISCUSSES THREE FACTORS WHICH HAD LIMITING EFFECT ON INDUSTRIALIZATION IN THESE COUNTRIES. PRIOR ECONOMIC EXPERIENCE, SOCIAL ORGANIZATION, AND POLITICAL INSTITUTIONS. CONTAINS NUMEROUS CHARTS AND TABLES.

1739 KOHN H.
REVOLUTIONS AND DICTATORSHIPS.
CAMBRIDGE: HARVARD U PR, 1939, 420 PP.
CRITICAL IDEOLOGICAL STUDY OF DEVELOPING REVOLUTIONS AND DICTATORSHIPS OF 1920'S AND 1930'S, SEEN AS ANTITHETICAL TO LIBERAL WESTERN NATIONALISM. VIEWED AGAINST BACKGROUND OF FRENCH REVOLUTION AND NAPOLEONIC INDIVIDUALISM, NAZISM AND FASCISM BECOME DEMENTED NATIONALISM, IRONICALLY ORIGINATING IN MESSIANISM OF ANCIENT JEWS. DISCUSSES RISE OF FASCIST AND COMMUNIST STATES AND REVOLUTIONS IN TURKISH AND ARAB WORLDS.

1740 KOHN H.
THE IDEA OF NATIONALISM.
NEW YORK: MACMILLAN, 1944, 735 PP.
STUDY OF THE FORMATION OF MODERN NATIONALISM, FROM THE PERIOD OF ANCIENT GREECE AND ISRAEL TO THE OUTBREAK OF THE FRENCH REVOLUTION. WESTERN HISTORY IS INTERPRETED AND EVALUATED DURING THIS PERIOD AS SETTING THE PATTERN FROM WHICH, INITIATED BY THE FRENCH REVOLUTION, EMERGED THE AGE OF NATIONALISM. SPECIFIC HISTORICAL PERIODS SUCH AS THE RENAISSANCE ARE SEEN WITHIN FRAMEWORK OF DEVELOPING NATIONALISM.

1741 KOHN H.
PROPHETS AND PEOPLES: STUDIES IN NINETEENTH CENTURY NATIONALISM.
NEW YORK: MACMILLAN, 1952, 213 PP.
ANALYSIS OF POLITICAL CONTRIBUTIONS TO THEORY OF SOVEREIGN NATION-STATE BY J.S. MILL, MICHELET, MAZZINI, TREITSCHKE, AND DOSTOEVSKY.

1742 KOHN H. ED.
THE MIND OF MODERN RUSSIA.
NEW BRUNSWICK: RUTGERS U. PR., 1955, 298 PP.
FOCUSES ON NATIONAL TRADITIONS WHICH HAVE FORMED THE RUSSIAN CHARACTER AND RUSSIAN HISTORY. THE DEBATE ABOUT RUSSIA AND THE WEST, LEGACY OF PETER THE GREAT, PAN-SLAVISM, RADICAL RUSSIA (CHERNYSHEVSKY), HERZEN'S REVOLUTIONARY IDEAS AND LENIN'S REVOLUTION ARE TOPICS TREATED IN DEPTH.

1743 KOHN H.
NATIONALISM: ITS MEANING AND HISTORY.
NEW YORK: MACMILLAN, 1955, 171 PP., LC#55-10910.
STUDIES HISTORICAL GROWTH OF NATIONALISM, USING WRITINGS OF MAJOR POLITICAL PHILOSOPHERS FROM MACHIAVELLI TO SUN YAT-SEN. COMPARES FORMS OF NATIONALISM IN DIFFERENT COUNTRIES, AND CONSIDERS IT A MAJOR IDEOLOGY PRESENTING REAL THREAT TO WESTERN CIVILIZATION.

1744 KOHN H.
AMERICAN NATIONALISM.
NEW YORK: MACMILLAN, 1957, 272 PP., LC#57-8101.
DISCUSSES CHIEF PROBLEMS IN AMERICAN NATIONALISM FROM VIEWPOINT OF STUDENT OF COMPARATIVE NATIONALISM. COMPARES THESE PROBLEMS TO THOSE OF NATIONAL MOVEMENTS IN OTHER AREAS OF WORLD, PARTICULARLY EUROPE. TREATS ORIGINS OF AMERICAN NATIONALISM, ITS RELATIONSHIP TO MOTHER COUNTRY, ITS FEDERAL STRUCTURE, AND ITS POSITION WITHIN COMMUNITY OF NATIONS.

1745 KOHN H.
PAN-SLAVISM: ITS HISTORY AND IDEOLOGY.
NOTRE DAME: U. PR., 1960, 468 PP.
PARTICULAR EMPHASIS ON SECOND HALF OF 19TH CENTURY. THE FACTORS GENERATING AND INFLUENCING PAN-SLAVISM ARE TREATED IN DETAIL. CITES VARIOUS OBSTRUCTIVE FACTORS SUCH AS HETEROGENEITY AND WEAK SELF-IDENTIFICATION AS SLAVS AMONG THE NUMEROUS ETHNIC CATEGORIES.

1746 KOHN H.
"GERMANY IN WORLD POLITICS."
CURR. HIST., 44 (APRIL 63), 202-207.
PRO-WESTERN POLICY OF ADENAUER ERA WILL PROBABLY BE SUPPLEMENTED BY NEW EASTERN POLICY IN POST-ADENAUER PERIOD. SUCH POLICY MUST NOT CHANGE GERMANY'S FAITHFUL ADHERENCE TO NATO WHICH MADE POSSIBLE GERMAN DEVELOPMENT 'TOO PRECIOUS' TO ALLOW TO BE UNDERMINED BY DE GAULLE'S NATIONALIST AMBITIONS OR BY MISTAKEN GERMAN EASTERN POLICY.

1747 KOHN H., SOKOLSKY W.
AFRICAN NATIONALISM IN THE TWENTIETH CENTURY.
PRINCETON: VAN NOSTRAND, 1965, 192 PP.
DISCUSSES MODERN AFRICAN NATIONALISM - ITS DEVELOPMENT IN THREE SELECTED COUNTRIES. WITH COLLECTION OF SHORT ARTICLES.

1748 KOHN W.S.G.
"THE SOVEREIGNTY OF LIECHTENSTEIN."
AMER. J. OF INT. LAW, 61 (APR. 67), 547-557.
EXAMINES SOVIET OBJECTION IN 1949 TO GRANTING MEMBERSHIP TO LIECHTENSTEIN IN INTERNATIONAL COURT OF JUSTICE. MAINTAINS LIECHTENSTEIN DOES POSSESS SOVEREIGNTY SINCE IT HAS UNLIMITED POWER OVER CITIZENS AND SUBJECTS, RESTRICTED ONLY BY CONSTITUTION. DISCUSSES PRINCIPALITY'S SIZE, HISTORY, GOVERNMENT, ETC., WHICH INDICATE THAT SHE IS NOT PART OF SWITZERLAND.

1749 KOLARZ W.
RUSSIA AND HER COLONIES.
LONDON: PHILIP, 1952, 335 PP.
DEFINES RUSSIAN COLONIES AS ETHNICALLY NON-RUSSIAN AREAS OF RUSSIA. DISCUSSES WHETHER INFLUENCE OF SOVIET UNION IS BENEFICIAL OR DETRIMENTAL TO THE DEVELOPMENT AND NATIONAL ASPIRATIONS OF HER COLONIES.

1750 KOLARZ W.
THE PEOPLES OF THE SOVIET FAR EAST.
NEW YORK: FREDERICK PRAEGER, 1954, 194 PP., LC#53-8350.
STUDIES ORIGINAL PEOPLES IN SOVIET FAR EAST AND EFFECTS OF RUSSIAN COLONIALIZATION OF AREA. INCLUDES PROBLEMS OF ADJUSTING RUSSIAN POLITICAL SYSTEM TO INDIGINOUS SYSTEM, CHANGES IN GOVERNING POLICY AS REGIMES IN RUSSIA WERE OVERTHROWN, AND RELATIONS BETWEEN RUSSIANS AND NATIONALITY GROUPS OF SOVIET FAR EAST.

1751 KOLARZ W.
"THE IMPACT OF COMMUNISM ON WEST AFRICA."
INT. AFF., 38 (APRIL 62), 156-69.
DESCRIBES LEFT LEANING PARTIES OF WEST AFRICA AS 'FELLOW TRAVELERS' NOT YET CERTAIN OF THEIR INTENTIONS. MAIN COMMUNIST ATTACK IS DIRECTED AT TRAINING OF YOUNG AFRICAN LEADERS, JOURNALISTS AND THROUGH WORLD FEDERATION OF TRADE UNIONS. CAPTURE OF MASS LEFT-WING PARTIES WOULD BE DONE BY INTERNAL COMMUNIST 'PUTSCH' OR BY COMPELLING NATIONALIST PARTIES TO MERGE WITH THEM. COMMUNIST HAVE ARRICAN SOUL AGAINST THEM.

1752 KOLARZ W.
BOOKS ON COMMUNISM.
NEW YORK: OXFORD U PR, 1964, 568 PP.
ARRANGED BY SUBJECT AND BY COUNTRY, INCLUDING OFFICIAL DOCUMENTS AND PUBLICATIONS. ALL 2,500 ITEMS USEFULLY ANNOTATED AND ALL IN ENGLISH. EMPHASIS ON USSR.

1753 KOLKOWICZ R.
THE SOVIET MILITARY AND THE COMMUNIST PARTY.
PRINCETON: PRINCETON U PRESS, 1967, 429 PP.
ANALYSIS OF INTERNAL COERCION AND EXTERNAL MILITANCY AS CHARACTERIZED BY THE SOVIET AUTHORITARIAN SYSTEM. STUDIES THE DYNAMICS OF PARTY-MILITARY RELATIONS THROUGH HISTORICAL PERSPECTIVE, IN INSTITUTIONAL DIALOGUE AND CONFLICT, AND IN THE PRESENT DILEMMA. INCLUDES HISTORICAL INFLUENCES AND REACTIONS. CONCLUDES THAT THE SOVIET TREND IS TOWARD MODERATION AND CHANGE IN POLITICAL AND SOCIAL AFFAIRS.

1754 KOMIYA R. ED.
POSTWAR ECONOMIC GROWTH IN JAPAN.
BERKELEY: U OF CALIF PR, 1966, 260 PP., LC#66-22705.
STUDY OF RAPID ECONOMIC PROGRESS MADE BY THE JAPANESE SINCE 1955 INCLUDES PUBLIC FINANCE AND MONETARY POLICY, TAX POLICY, PRICE PROBLEMS, ECONOMIC GROWTH AND THE BALANCE OF PAYMENTS, EMPLOYMENT AND LABOR, AND INCOME DISTRIBUTION. ALSO ANALYZES BUSINESS FLUCTUATIONS AND THE STABILIZATION POLICY, AND DEVELOPMENT OF POSTWAR JAPANESE EXECUTIVES.

1755 KONCZACKI Z.A.
PUBLIC FINANCE AND ECONOMIC DEVELOPMENT OF NATAL 1893-1910.
DURHAM: DUKE U PR, 1967, 224 PP., LC#67-23301.
STUDIES ECONOMIC HISTORY AND PUBLIC FINANCE OF NATAL AS COLONY OF BRITAIN UNTIL 1893, AND TRACES VARIATIONS IN GOVERNMENT REVENUE AND EXPENDITURES AND PUBLIC FINANCE FROM INDEPENDENCE IN 1893 TO FEDERATION WITH UNION OF SOUTH AFRICA IN 1910. EMPHASIZES IMPACT OF PUBLIC FINANCE ON ECONOMIC DEVELOPMENT.

1756 KORNBERG A.
CANADIAN LEGISLATIVE BEHAVIOR: A STUDY OF THE 25TH PARLIAMENT.
NEW YORK: HOLT RINEHART WINSTON, 1967, 166 PP., LC#67-26163.
INVESTIGATES LEGISLATIVE BEHAVIOR WITHIN THE CONTEXTS OF ROLES AND REFERENCE GROUPS. EMPLOYS INTERVIEW DATA TO ASCERTAIN THE INFLUENCE OF SOCIETY AND THE LEGISLATIVE INSTITUTION ON THE LEGISLATOR. DISCUSSES THE IMPORTANCE OF HIS PRE-ELECTION VALUES AND ATTITUDES VERSUS THOSE HE DEVELOPS WHILE IN OFFICE. ALSO ANALYZES ESSENTIAL FEATURES OF PARLIAMENTARY SYSTEM THAT MIGHT INFLUENCE THE LEGISLATOR.

1757 KORNHAUSER W.
"THE POLITICS OF MASS SOCIETY."
NEW YORK: FREE PRESS OF GLENCOE, 1959.
EXAMINES HISTORICAL AND CONTEMPORARY SITUATIONS MARKED BY WIDESPREAD READINESS TO ABANDON CONSTITUTIONAL MODES OF POLITICAL ACTIVITY IN FAVOR OF UNCONTROLLED MASS ACTION. ANALYZES SOURCES OF SUPPORT FOR COMMUNISM, FASCISM, AND OTHER POPULAR MOVEMENTS THAT OPERATE OUTSIDE OR AGAINST INSTITUTIONAL ORDER. CENTRAL ARGUMENT DISTINGUISHES BETWEEN MASS AND PLURALIST SOCIETY. UNANNOTATED BIBLIOGRAPHY.

1758 KOSAMBI D.D.
MYTH AND REALITY.
BOMBAY: GR BHATKAL, 1962, 186 PP.
TRACES PRIMITIVE ROOTS OF INDIAN MYTHS AND RITUAL SURVIVING TO PRESENT. DISCUSSES GODDESS CULTS, CULT MIGRATIONS, LAND AND PEOPLE, TRASE ROUTES, ETC. MANY ILLUSTRATIONS.

1759 KOUSOULAS D.G.
REVOLUTION AND DEFEAT; THE STORY OF THE GREEK COMMUNIST PARTY.
LONDON: OXFORD U PR, 1965, 306 PP.
ANALYSIS OF DEVELOPMENT OF GREEK COMMUNIST PARTY FROM START IN 1918 THROUGH ITS AFFILIATION WITH COMINTERN AND ITS PARTICIPATION IN GREEK POLITICS AND LEGISLATIVE PROCESS. COVERS PARTY STRUCTURE AND POLICIES IN DIFFERENT PERIODS OF ACTIVITY, INCLUDING ITS REVOLUTIONARY MOVEMENT AND AFTERMATH OF DEFEAT.

1760 KOVNER M.
"THE SINO-SOVIET DISPUTE: COMMUNISM AT THE CROSSROADS."
CURR. HIST., 47 (SEPT. 64), 129-135.
'NOT FULLY UNDERSTOOD IN TERMS OF IDEOLOGICAL DIFFERENCES BUT SHOULD NOT BE ALLOWED TO OBSCURE OTHER CURRENTS WITHIN THE COMMUNIST WORLD OF PERHAPS MORE IMMEDIATE RELEVANCE AND OF WHICH PEKING'S QUARREL WITH MOSCOW IS ONLY A PART.'

1761 KRABBE H.
THE MODERN IDEA OF THE STATE.
NEW YORK: APPLETON, 1922, 281 PP.
ATTEMPTS TO FORMULATE NEW SYSTEM OF POLITICAL ANALYSIS WITH GREATER APPLICATION TO EUROPEAN POLITICS IN LIGHT OF DEVELOPMENTS OF WWI. RATHER THAN DESCRIPTIVE, IT SEEKS TO BE PREDICTIVE, USING MAJOR STRENGTHS AND TRENDS OF POLITICAL FORCES. MAJOR CONSIDERATIONS ARE NEW INTERNATIONAL POWER STRUCTURE, SOVEREIGNTY, INTERNAL LEGAL SYSTEMS, AND GOVERNMENTAL TYPES.

1762 KRACKE E.A. JR.
"CIVIL SERVICE IN EARLY SUNG CHINA, 960-1067."
CAMBRIDGE: HARVARD U PR, 1953.
DISCUSSION OF EARLY SUNG CIVIL SERVICE WITH PARTICULAR EMPHASIS ON THE DEVELOPMENT OF CONTROLLED SPONSORSHIP TO FOSTER ADMINISTRATIVE RESPONSIBILITY. ANNOTATED BIBLIOGRAPHY APPENDED TO TEXT.

1763 KRADER L.
SOCIAL ORGANIZATION OF THE MONGOL-TURKIC PASTORAL NOMADS.
NEW YORK: HUMANITIES PRESS, 1963, 403 PP., LC#63-63704.
EXAMINES SOCIAL STRUCTURE OF NOMADIC TRIBES OF MONGOL AND TURKIC DESCENT. DISCUSSES FAMILY STRUCTURE, KIN RELATIONS, VILLAGE LIFE, LEGAL STRUCTURE, AND MARRIAGE CUSTOMS.

1764 KRAEHE E.
METTERNICH'S GERMAN POLICY: THE CONTEST WITH NAPOLEON, 1799-1814, VOL. 1.
PRINCETON: U. PR., 1963, 351 PP., $3.50.
PRESENTS HISTORICAL-BIOGRAPHICAL STUDY OF METTERNICH'S DIPLOMATIC APPROACH TO GERMAN POLITICS. WISHING TO SEPARATE CZARIST RUSSIA AND POST NAPOLEONIC FRANCE, DESIRED A STRONG GERMAN CONFEDERATION. VIEWS METTERNICH AS A HIGHLY SKILLED DIPLOMAT AND A SUCCESSFUL EXPLOITER. CONTRASTS HIS POLICIES WITH COUNT STADION.

1765 KRECH D., CRUTCHFIELD R.S., BALLACHEY E.L.
INDIVIDUAL IN SOCIETY; A TEXTBOOK OF SOCIAL PSYCHOLOGY.
NEW YORK: MCGRAW HILL, 1962, 564 PP., LC#61-18134.
INTRODUCTION TO SOCIAL PSYCHOLOGY WITH INTERPERSONAL BEHAVIOR EVENT AS UNIT OF ANALYSIS. USES SOCIAL ANTHROPOLOGY AND SOCIOLOGY AS WELL AS COGNITIVE THEORY AND EXPERIMENTS IN STUDY. COVERS BASIC PSYCHOLOGICAL FACTORS OF MOTIVATION, COGNITION, AND INTERPERSONAL RESPONSES; SOCIAL ATTITUDES, SOCIAL AND CULTURAL HABITAT, AND GROUPS; ORGANIZATIONS, AND ROLE OF INDIVIDUAL.

1766 KRENZ F.E.
"THE REFUGEE AS A SUBJECT OF INTERNATIONAL LAW."
INT. AND COMP. LAW Q., 15 (JAN. 66), 90-116.
ADVOCATES APPROACH TO LAW OF ASYLUM TO MEET PRESENT SITUATION OF INDIVIDUALS IN INTERNATIONAL LAW. SOME KIND OF FORMAL RECOGNITION OF INDIVIDUAL RIGHT TO ASYLUM IS CALLED FOR, PLUS THE CREATION OF AN INTERNATIONAL EXECUTIVE FOR REFUGEES AND THEIR "LOCUS STANDI" BEFORE AN APPROPRIATE TRIBUNAL.

1767 KREY A.C.
THE FIRST CRUSADE.
PRINCETON: PRINCETON U PRESS, 1921, 299 PP.
DETAILED CHRONICLE OF FIRST CRUSADE TO HOLY LAND; TRANSLATES EYE-WITNESS ACCOUNTS. BEGINS WITH CONDITIONS IN EUROPE AND RESPONSE TO URBAN'S PLEA FOR A CRUSADE. RELATES JOURNEY BY STAGES - CONSTANTINOPLE, NICAEA, ANTIOCH, AND

FINAL CAPTURE OF JERUSALEM. DISCUSSES IMPORTANT BATTLES AND LEADERS; INCLUDES DISSENSION AMONG LEADERS, DISORGANIZATION OF ARMY, AND QUARRELS ABOUT HOLY GRAIL.

1768 KRIS E., SPEIER H. ET AL.
GERMAN RADIO PROPAGANDA: REPORT ON HOME BROADCASTS DURING THE WAR.
NEW YORK: OXFORD U PR, 1944, 529 PP.
CRITICAL ANALYSIS OF GERMAN HOME BROADCASTING OF PROPAGANDA DURING WWII. STUDIES CONSTITUTION OF THE AUDIENCE, CONTENT AND AIM OF MESSAGES, AND ACTUAL METHOD OF PRESENTATION IN SPECIFIC SITUATIONS. EMPHASIZES MANIPULATION OF PUBLIC ATTITUDES THROUGH A COMBINATION OF HOPE AND FEAR. SUGGESTS THAT ALLIED POSTWAR PROPAGANDA BE USED TO RECONSTRUCT GERMAN ATTITUDES.

1769 KRISTOF L.K.D.
"THE STATE-IDEA, THE NATIONAL IDEA AND THE IMAGE OF THE FATHERLAND."
ORBIS, 11 (SPRING 67), 238-255.
DISCUSSES AND ILLUSTRATES CONCEPTS IN GEOPOLITICS, PARTICULARLY THE STATE-IDEA, HERE CONSIDERED AS PRE-EMINENTLY POLITICAL, GOAL-ORIENTED, AND A CONCEPT OF THE INTELLIGENTSIA; AND THE NATIONAL IDEA, BELIEVED LESS POLITICAL, MORE HISTORICAL AND TRADITION-BOUND, AND MORE A CONCEPT OF THE MASSES. SAYS BOTH IMPLY MAN LINKED TO THE LAND, WHILE "FATHERLAND" IS MORE OF A GEOPOLITICAL "FUSING."

1770 KROEBER A.L., WATERMAN T.T.
SOURCE BOOK IN ANTHROPOLOGY.
NEW YORK: HARCOURT BRACE, 1931, 571 PP.
EXAMINES HISTORY OF ANTHROPOLOGY; EVOLUTION; HEREDITY AND RACE; PREHISTORY; SUBSISTENCE AND MATERIAL CULTURE; SOCIAL, AESTHETIC, AND RELIGIOUS CULTURE; AND DYNAMICS OF CULTURE.

1771 KROEBER A.L.
THE NATURE OF CULTURE.
CHICAGO: U CHI, CTR POLICY STUDY, 1952, 437 PP.
EXAMINES THEORIES OF CULTURE, KINSHIP AND SOCIAL STRUCTURE, AMERICAN INDIANS, PSYCHOLOGICAL QUESTIONS, AND HISTORY AND PROCESS OF CIVILIZATION.

1772 KROEBER A.L.
ANTHROPOLOGY: BIOLOGY AND RACE.
NEW YORK: HARCOURT BRACE, 1963, 209 PP., LC#63-12159.
SELECTED CHAPTERS OF KROEBER'S "ANTHROPOLOGY" DEALING SPECIFICALLY WITH RACE AND BIOLOGY. SELECTIONS DISCUSS ANTHROPOLOGY AS A SCIENCE; MAN'S PLACE IN NATURE; LIVING RACES; PROBLEMS OF RACE DIFFERENCES; AND CULTURAL PSYCHOLOGY.

1773 KROGER K.
"ZUR ENTWICKLUNG DER STAATSZWECKLEHRE IM 19 JAHRHUNDERT."
NEUE POLITISCHE LITERATUR, 12 (1967), 152-155.
REVIEWS HESPE'S WORK ON DEVELOPMENT OF IDEA OF PURPOSE OF THE STATE IN 19TH CENTURY. MAINTAINS THAT GERMAN THEORIES OF PURPOSE OF STATE CANNOT BE CONSIDERED A "SELF-CONTAINED PROCESS OF SCIENTIFIC DEVELOPMENT." SUGGESTS THAT CHANGE FROM TELEOLOGICAL CONCEPTION OF STATE TO A "CAUSAL-SCIENTIFIC" ORIENTATION IMPLIES SUBSTANTIAL DEVIATION FROM "SELF-CONTAINED PROCESS."

1774 KROLL M.
"POLITICAL LEADERSHIP AND ADMINISTRATIVE COMMUNICATIONS IN NEW NATION STATES* CASE STUDY OF TRINIDAD AND TOBAGO."
SOCIAL ECO. STUDIES, 16 (MAR. 67), 17-33.
STUDIES THE NEED FOR NEW COMMUNICATION PROCESSES IN NEW STATES; ANALYZES THE INFLUENCE OF PREVIOUS SYSTEMS. SHOWS HOW THE WITHDRAWAL OF COLONIAL ORDER IN TRINIDAD LEFT THE STATE WITHOUT TRAINED ADMINISTRATORS. EXECUTIVE AUTHORITY GRAVITATED TO A SMALL EXECUTIVE ELITE WHICH CHANNELED COMMUNICATION DOWNWARD, AS ORDERS. RECEIVERS ON LOWER SOCIAL LEVELS WERE MANIPULATED BY SYMBOLS.

1775 KROPOTKIN P.
THE CONQUEST OF BREAD.
LONDON: CHAPMAN AND HALL, 1913, 298 PP.
EXPRESSES AUTHOR'S IDEAS FOR ESTABLISHMENT OF SOCIALIST STATE, AND REVIEWS SOME PAST ATTEMPTS TO ESTABLISH SOCIALISM AND COMMUNAL LIVING. BELIEVES THAT MEANS OF PRODUCTION SHOULD BE COLLECTIVE PROPERTY. THERE MUST BE EXPROPRIATION TO INSURE WELL-BEING OF ALL. ONCE PROPERTY IS ABOLISHED, SOCIETY WILL BE ESTABLISHED IN FORM OF COMMUNISTIC ANARCHY, MADE UP OF FREE GROUPS ESTABLISHED THROUGH FREE AGREEMENTS.

1776 KROPOTKIN P.
L'ANARCHIE.
ORIGINAL PUBLISHER NOT AVAILABLE, 1896, 59 PP.
ADVOCATES SOCIETY IN WHICH GOODS WILL BE REDISTRIBUTED AND THERE WILL BE NO MORE RULING MINORITIES. SOCIETY WILL BE MADE UP OF INDIVIDUALS. IT WILL BE ABLE TO WITHSTAND CONFLICT, BECAUSE CONFLICT WITHOUT WEIGHT OF AUTHORITATIVE BODY IS CREATIVE. SOCIETY WILL HAVE NO MORE DIVISIONS BETWEEN EXPLOITED AND EXPLOITER. ANARCHY SEEKS THE COMPLETE DEVELOPMENT OF THE INDIVIDUAL AND OF VOLUNTARY ASSOCIATIONS.

1777 KRUEGER H.
ALLGEMEINE STAATSLEHRE.
STUTTGART: W. KOHLHAMMERVERL, 1964, 1028 PP.
COMPREHENSIVE STUDY OF THE STATE IN ITS VARIOUS FORMS AND RELATIONSHIPS. EXAMINES ITS ESSENCE, ITS ACTIVITY AND THE VALUES PERTAINING TO THAT ACTIVITY, AND ITS POWER IN CONNECTION WITH THE CITIZEN'S OBEDIENCE. UNDER THESE HEADINGS CONSIDERS RELATIONSHIPS BETWEEN STATE AND SOCIETY, RELIGION, THE ECONOMY, THE ELECTORATE, AND THE INDIVIDUAL CITIZEN.

1778 KRUGLAK T.E.
THE TWO FACES OF TASS.
MINNEAPOLIS: U. MINN. PR., 1962, $5.00.
A HISTORY OF USSR'S INTERNATIONAL NEWS AGENCY WHOSE FUNCTION IS TO COLLECT MATERIALS AND DISSEMINATE PROPAGANDA, AND PROVIDE INTELLIGENCE FOR THE SOVIET GOVERNMENT.

1779 KRUSE H.
DAS STAATSANGEHORIGKEITSRECHT DER ARABISCHEN STAATEN.
ALFRED METZNER VERLAG, 1955, 118 PP.
DISCUSSES ORIGIN AND NATURE OF CITIZENSHIP LAWS IN ARAB STATES FROM EARLY ISLAMIC TRADITIONS TO PRESENT. EXAMINES RELIGIOUS AND POLITICAL CONDITIONS FOR CITIZENSHIP IN EGYPT, SYRIA, LEBANON, IRAQ, JORDAN, LIBYA, SAUDI-ARABIA, AND YEMEN.

1780 KUNSTADTER P.
THE LUA (LAWA) OF NORTHERN THAILAND: ASPECTS OF SOCIAL STRUCTURE, AGRICULTURE, AND RELIGION.
PRINCETON: CTR OF INTL STUDIES, 1965, 56 PP.
ETHNOGRAPHIC STUDY BASED ON TWO YEAR STAY IN LUA; ONE VILLAGE USED AS SAMPLE. EMPHASIZES TRADITIONAL MOUNTAIN VILLAGES IGNORED BY TRADE ROUTES AND BUDDHISM.

1781 KUPER H. ED.
URBANIZATION AND MIGRATION IN WEST AFRICA.
BERKELEY: U OF CALIF PR, 1965, 227 PP., LC#65-19248.
STUDIES PERTAINING TO LOCATION AND NATURE OF WEST AFRICAN CITIES. COVERS URBAN MIGRATION AND SETTLEMENT, ITS RELATIONSHIP WITH LANGUAGE, LABOR MIGRATION AMONG THE MOSSI OF THE UPPER VOLTA, THE URBAN COMMUNITY OF OSHOGBO, SOCIAL ALIGNMENT AND IDENTITY IN A WEST AFRICAN CITY, POLITICAL IMPLICATIONS OF MIGRATION IN WEST AFRICA, AND THE ECONOMICS OF THE MIGRANT LABOR SYSTEM.

1782 KUPER L.
PASSIVE RESISTANCE IN SOUTH AFRICA.
TORONTO: CLARK, IRWIN + CO, 1956.
HISTORY OF PASSIVE RESISTANCE MOVEMENTS IN SOUTH AFRICA AFTER WWII, BEGUN BY INDIAN MINORITY, TAKEN UP BY AFRICANS AND COLOREDS, CAUSING WHITE REACTION AND COUNTERACTION.

1783 KUPER L.
AN AFRICAN BOURGEOISIE.
NEW HAVEN: YALE U PR, 1965, 452 PP., LC#64-20925.
RACE, CLASS, AND POLITICS IN SOUTH AFRICA - EMPHASIZES DILEMMAS AND PERSPECTIVE OF AFRICAN MIDDLE-CLASS, ITS MAKEUP AND ORGANIZATION, FOCUSING ON BOURGEOISIE OF DURBAN, SOUTH AFRICA.

1784 KURL S.
ESTONIA: A SELECTED BIBLIOGRAPHY.
WASHINGTON: US GOVERNMENT, 1958, 74 PP., LC#58-60040.
ITEMS ON ESTONIA IN ENGLISH, FRENCH, GERMAN, AND ITALIAN. PREFERENCE GIVEN TO MORE RECENT PUBLICATIONS. INCLUDES ITEMS ON GENERAL REFERENCE AIDS; THE LAND AND PEOPLE; HISTORY; RELIGION; LAW; POLITICS AND GOVERNMENT; ECONOMICS; SOCIAL CONDITIONS; INTELLECTUAL LIFE; LANGUAGE AND LITERATURE. SOME BRIEF ANNOTATIONS. 491 TITLES.

1785 KURZMAN D.
SUBVERSION OF THE INNOCENTS: PATTERNS OF COMMUNIST PENETRATION OF AFRICA, THE MIDDLE EAST AND AFRICA.
NEW YORK: RANDOM, 1963, 570 PP., $6.95.
AN APPRAISAL OF COMMUNIST METHODS OF INFILTRATION AND SUBVERSION IN THE AFRO-ASIAN WORLD IN THE CONTEXT OF THE HISTORICAL AND CULTURAL BACKGROUNDS OF THE VARIOUS NATIONS AND REGIONS CONSIDERED.

1786 KUZNETS S.
MODERN ECONOMIC GROWTH.
NEW HAVEN: YALE U PR, 1966, 528 PP., LC#66-21524.
CONSIDERS RELEVANCE OF "WESTERN ECONOMICS" TO ANALYSIS OF STRUCTURE AND PROCESS IN OTHER COUNTRIES. DISCUSSES CYCLES IN ECONOMY AFFECTED BY TECHNOLOGICAL AND IDEOLOGICAL INNOVATION FROM HISTORICAL VIEWPOINT, AND EFFECTS OF POLITICAL SYSTEMS. REVIEWS AGGREGATE STRUCTURE OF GROWTH OF NATIONS IN MODERN TIMES.

1787 KYLE K.
"BACKGROUND TO THE CRISIS"
SURVIVAL, 9 (AUG. 67), 246-249.
PROGRAM BY BBC ON ARAB-ISRAELI CRISIS. STATES THAT BRITAIN'S "INTELLECTUAL INCOHERENCE" CAUSED PROBLEM AND THAT ARABS ARE COMPLETELY IN RIGHT. WEST SUPPORTS ISRAEL

DESPITE THIS KNOWLEDGE OUT OF GUILT OVER JEWS. DISCUSSES ISRAEL'S RIGHT TO EXISTENCE, RUSSIAN POSITION, AND SITUATION OF BORDER RAIDS AND REPRISALS. WRITTEN BEFORE OUTBREAK OF WAR IN JUNE, 1967.

1788 KYRIAK T.E. ED.
ASIAN DEVELOPMENTS: A BIBLIOGRAPHY.
ANNAPOLIS: RES MICROFILM PUBL.
QUARTERLY PERIODICAL INDEXING ALL JOINT PUBLICATIONS RESEARCH SERVICE MATERIALS TRANSLATED IN THAT QUARTER. FOREIGN DOCUMENTS, SCHOLARLY WORKS, AND OTHER MATERIALS NOT AVAILABLE IN ENGLISH ARE INDEXED BY SUBJECT AND CROSS-REFERENCED WITH OTHER THREE AREA BIBLIOGRAPHIES IN THIS SERIES. ALL ITEMS ARE IN SOCIAL SCIENCES WITH ABOUT 110 ITEMS INCLUDED. BEGUN 1962.

1789 KYRIAK T.E. ED.
CHINA: A BIBLIOGRAPHY.
ANNAPOLIS: RES MICROFILM PUBL.
MONTHLY PERIODICAL INDEXING ALL JOINT PUBLICATIONS RESEARCH SERVICE MATERIALS TRANSLATED IN THE MONTH COVERED. FOREIGN DOCUMENTS, SCHOLARLY WORKS, AND OTHER MATERIALS NOT AVAILABLE IN ENGLISH ARE INDEXED BY SUBJECT AND CROSS-REFERENCED WITH THE OTHER THREE AREA BIBLIOGRAPHIES IN THIS SERIES. ALL ITEMS ARE IN SOCIAL SCIENCES. BEGUN 1962.

1790 LA BOETIE E.
ANTI-DICTATOR (1548) (TRANS. BY H. KUNZ)
NEW YORK: COLUMBIA U PRESS, 1942, 54 PP.
ANALYZES HOW TYRANTS GET POWER AND MAINTAIN IT, ASSUMING THAT REAL POWER LIES IN HANDS OF THE PEOPLE. CLAIMS THEY MAY FREE THEMSELVES FROM DESPOTS BY AN ACT OF WILL UNACCOMPANIED BY VIOLENCE. HOLDS PEOPLE RESPONSIBLE FOR SERVITUDE AND SLAVERY BECAUSE IT IS THEIR TOLERATION OF SERVITUDE WHICH KEEPS THEM ENSLAVED. CONTENDS THAT ORDINARILY THEY MUST BE FORCED BUT MAY SOMETIMES BE TRICKED INTO IT.

1791 LA DOCUMENTATION FRANCAISE
L'AFRIQUE A TRAVERS LES PUBLICATIONS DE LA DOCUMENTATION FRANCAISE; BIBLIOGRAPHIE 1945-1961 (PAMPHLET)
PARIS: LA DOCUMENTAT FRANCAISE, 1961, 107 PP.
BIBLIOGRAPHY OF PUBLICATIONS OF SECRETARIAT GENERAL DU GOUVERNEMENT ON AFRICA FOR PERIOD 1945-1961. MATERIAL IS ORGANIZED CHRONOLOGICALLY UNDER GEOGRAPHIC REGION. INCLUDES A CHRONOLOGY OF THE ACCESSION TO INDEPENDENCE OF AFRICAN STATES.

1793 LA PONCE J.A.
THE PROTECTION OF MINORITIES.
HONOLULU: U OF HAWAII PRESS, 1960, 236 PP.
STUDY OF MINORITIES. DISCUSSES DEFINITIONS AND TYPES OF MINORITIES; DIFFERING RIGHTS CLAIMED BY DIFFERENT MINORITIES; TREATY GUARANTEES OF MINORITY RIGHTS; GUARANTEES OF MINORITY RIGHTS IN CONSTITUTIONS; IMPACT OF MINORITY GROUPS UPON FORM OF GOVERNMENT AND UPON STRUCTURE OF LEGISLATIVE AND EXECUTIVE STRUCTURES; MINORITIES, ELECTORAL SYSTEMS, AND POLITICAL PARTIES.

1794 LA PONCE J.A.
THE GOVERNMENT OF THE FIFTH REPUBLIC: FRENCH POLITICAL PARTIES AND THE CONSTITUTION.
BERKELEY: U OF CALIF PR, 1961, 415 PP., LC#60-14656.
BEGINNINGS, DEVELOPMENT, PARTIES, AND PERSONALITIES OF FIFTH FRENCH REPUBLIC, INCLUDING CHARTS AND TABLES OF VOTING STATISTICS. CONCLUDES THAT REPUBLIC IN 1960 HAD REALIZED GOALS OF FOUNDERS (SHIFT OF POWER FROM LEGISLATURE TO EXECUTIVE), BUT FUTURE REMAINS UNCERTAIN BECAUSE OF ALGERIAN PROBLEM AND DEPENDENCE OF SYSTEM UPON PERSONALITY OF DE GAULLE RATHER THAN SOUND CONSTITUTION.

1795 LABEDZ L.
"IDEOLOGY: THE FOURTH STAGE."
PROBL. COMMUNISM, 8 (NOV. 59), 1-10.
HISTORICAL DISCUSSION OF MARXIST IDEOLOGY AND ITS ROLE IN USSR. IDEOLOGY IS ADAPTED TO CIRCUMSTANCES AND IS UTILIZED TO PROVIDE RATIONALIZATION FOR STATE AND PARTY POLICIES AND SERVES AS THE BASIS OF THE REGIME'S LEGITIMACY. SUCH PROBLEMS AS STATE POWER AND FUNCTIONS, CULTURAL EDUCATION, AND COMMODITY CIRCULATION ARE CONSIDERED.

1796 LAHAYE R.
LES ENTREPRISES PUBLIQUES AU MAROC.
PARIS: LIBRAIRIE DE MEDICIS, 1961, 340 PP.
ANALYSIS OF STATE OWNERSHIP AND PARTICIPATION IN PUBLIC SERVICES AND INDUSTRY IN MOROCCO. DESCRIBES ENTERPRISES, ANALYZES THEIR STRUCTURE, AND DISCUSSES THEIR ECONOMIC AND ADMINISTRATIVE EVOLUTION. STATE PARTNERSHIP IN PRIVATE INDUSTRY IS IMPORTANT TO ECONOMIC DEVELOPMENT, AS WELL AS STATE OWNERSHIP WHERE INDUSTRY HAS NOT DEVELOPED SUCCESSFULLY. DISCUSSES GROWTH OF ADMINISTRATIVE JURISPRUDENCE.

1797 LAHBABI M.
LE GOUVERNEMENT MAROCAIN A L'AUBE DU XXE SIECLE.
RABAT: ED TECHNIQUES NORD AFR, 1958, 217 PP.
STUDY OF MOROCCAN GOVERNMENT BEFORE BEGINNING OF FRENCH PROTECTORATE IN 1912. MAINTAINS THAT COLONIAL REFORMS SET BACK PROGRESS OF MOROCCAN DEMOCRACY AND JUDICIAL INSTITUTIONS. IT IS ONLY WITH FREEDOM THAT OLD NATIONAL INSTITUTIONS CAN AGAIN BE EFFECTIVE, HENCE IMPORTANCE OF THIS STUDY.

1798 LALL B.G.
"GAPS IN THE ABM DEBATE."
BUL. ATOMIC SCIENTISTS, 23 (APR. 67), 45-46.
POINTS OUT THAT US OFFICIALS IN DISCUSSING HOPES FOR AN AGREEMENT WITH THE USSR AGAINST BUILDING AN ANTI-BALLISTIC MISSILE SYSTEM FAIL TO POINT OUT ESTABLISHED SOVIET DISINTEREST IN SUCH A MOVE WHEN UNACCOMPANIED BY REDUCTIONS IN OFFENSIVE STRENGTH. ALSO NOTES LACK OF COUNTER-PRESSURE IN US EXECUTIVE ESTABLISHMENT TO MILITARY DESIRES.

1799 LAMB B.P.
INDIA: A WORLD IN TRANSITION.
NEW YORK: FREDERICK PRAEGER, 1963, 374 PP., LC#63-10825.
ATTEMPTS TO BRING TOGETHER VARIED FACTS AND TRENDS ILLUMINATING THE FABRIC OF INDIAN LIFE AS A WHOLE, ESPECIALLY THOSE DEVELOPMENTS WHICH HELP TO EXPLAIN CONTEMPORARY POLITICS. CONSIDERS HISTORICAL, GEOGRAPHICAL, AND CLIMATIC BACKGROUND; PROGRESSES TO SIGNIFICANT FEATURES OF RELIGION, SOCIAL RELATIONS, EDUCATION, POLITICAL ISSUES, AND GOVERNMENT STRUCTURE; CONCLUDES ON EMERGENT FOREIGN POLICY.

1800 LAMBERT D.
"LA TRANSPOSITION DU REGIME PRESIDENTIEL HORS DES ETATS-UNIS; LE CAS DE L'AMERIQUE LATINE."
REV. DROIT PUBLIC ET SCI. POL., 3 (SEPT. 63), 577-600.
ANALYZES PRESIDENTIAL SYSTEM IN CENTRAL AND SOUTH AMERICA AND EVOLUTION OF LEGISLATURES INTO INDEPENDENT BODIES. SUGGESTS REASONS FOR FAILURE OF PRESIDENTIAL SYSTEM AND VIEWS IT IN HISTORICAL AND CHRONOLOGICAL PERSPECTIVE. ALSO TREATS PRESIDENTIAL RELATIONS WITH LEGISLATIVE BODIES.

1801 LAMBERT J.
LATIN AMERICA: SOCIAL STRUCTURES AND POLITICAL INSTITUTIONS.
BERKELEY: U OF CALIF PR, 1967, 330 PP.
EXAMINES LATIN AMERICAN POLITICS AND SOCIETIES IN TERMS OF DISTINCT, INDIVIDUAL CATEGORIES RATHER THAN TREATING LATIN AMERICA AS ONE LARGE ENTITY. STUDIES THREE TYPES OF DIVISIONS: THOSE OF WESTERN EUROPE WITH FULLY DEVELOPED ECONOMIC AND SOCIAL STRUCTURES, UNDERDEVELOPED COUNTRIES WITH ARCHAIC SOCIAL STRUCTURES, AND COUNTRIES OF UNEQUAL DEVELOPMENT AND DUAL SOCIAL STRUCTURES.

1802 LAMBERT W.E., KLINEBERG O.
CHILDREN'S VIEWS OF FOREIGN PEOPLES: A CROSS-NATIONAL STUDY.
NEW YORK: APPLETON, 1967, 319 PP., LC#66-24057.
BY INTERVIEWING 3,100 CHILDREN FROM 11 NATIONS, STUDIES ORIGIN AND DEVELOPMENT OF GENERALIZATIONS ABOUT MEMBERS OF SPECIFIC NATIONAL GROUPS. COMPARES GROUPS STUDIED, FOCUSING ON CHILDREN'S CONCEPTION OF THEMSELVES, THEIR OWN NATIONAL GROUP, AND FOREIGN PEOPLES. PRESENTS THEORY ABOUT EDUCATIONAL FUNCTIONS AND ENDURING SIGNIFICANCE OF EARLY ATTITUDES TOWARD OTHER NATIONALITIES.

1803 LAMBIRI I.
SOCIAL CHANGE IN A GREEK COUNTRY TOWN.
WASHINGTON: CTR PLAN ECO RES, 1965, 165 PP.
STUDY OF CULTURAL AND SOCIAL PROBLEMS CREATED IN GREEK TOWN BY RAPID INDUSTRIALIZATION AND UNAVOIDABLE INCREASED PARTICIPARTION OF WOMEN IN INDUSTRIAL EMPLOYMENT.

1804 LANDAU J.M.
"PARLIAMENTS AND PARTIES IN EGYPT."
NEW YORK: FREDERICK PRAEGER, 1954.
TRACES DEVELOPMENT OF PARLIAMENTARY INSTITUTIONS AND POLITICAL PARTIES IN EGYPT. EXAMINES EXTENT OF EUROPEAN INFLUENCE ON INCEPTION, EVOLUTION, AND DISRUPTION. BASED ON ARABIC AND EUROPEAN SOURCES, WITH GREATEST SIGNIFICANCE GIVEN TO PRIMARY SOURCE-MATERIAL FOR THE POLITICAL-CONSTITUTIONAL HISTORY OF EGYPT SINCE 1860. BIBLIOGRAPHY OF 139 MANUSCRIPTS, ARCHIVAL, AND SOURCE MATERIALS.

1805 LANDAUER C.
EUROPEAN SOCIALISM (2 VOLS.)
BERKELEY: U OF CALIF PR, 1959, 1894 PP., LC#59-5744.
A HISTORY OF IDEAS AND MOVEMENTS OF EUROPEAN SOCIALISM FROM THE INDUSTRIAL REVOLUTION TO HITLER'S SEIZURE OF POWER. A COMPARATIVE ANALYSIS OF CROSS-CURRENTS AND DEVELOPMENTS IN INDIVIDUAL EUROPEAN COUNTRIES.

1806 LANDE C.H.
LEADERS, FACTIONS, AND PARTIES.
NEW HAVEN: YALE U, SE ASIA STUD, 1965, 148 PP., LC#65-18996.
ANALYSIS OF PHILIPPINE POLITICS AT NATIONAL, PROVINCIAL, AND LOCAL LEVELS. INSIGHTS INTO FUNCTION OF FACTIONS, ROLE OF LEADERS, AND ACTIVITY OF POLITICAL PARTIES. CONTAINS LIST OF SOUTHEAST ASIA PUBLICATIONS (YALE UNIVERSITY), UNDER FIVE CATEGORIES: BIBLIOGRAPHIES, CULTURAL REPORTS, TRANSLATIONS, MONOGRAPHS, AND SPECIAL PUBLICATIONS. RANGE 1949-1964.

1807 LANE J.P.

"FUNCTIONS OF MASS MEDIA IN BRAZIL'S 1964 CRISIS."
JOURNALISM QUARTERLY, (SUMMER 67), 297-306.
DISCUSSES USE OF MASS MEDIA AS PROPAGANDA DEVICE BY PRESIDENT GOULART AND HIS ALLIES AND BY VARIOUS FACTIONS STRUGGLING TO OUST GOULART IN 1964. CONSIDERS BOTH SOCIAL AND POLITICAL FUNCTIONS OF MEDIA IN AFFECTING MAJOR ISSUES IN UNDERDEVELOPED COUNTRIES. EMPHASIZES UNWISE OVERINDULGENCE IN PROPAGANDA VIA MASS MEDIA BY GOULART'S ALLIES WHICH HELPED CAUSE HIS OUSTER.

1808 LANGER P.F.
"JAPAN'S RELATIONS WITH CHINA."
CURR. HIST., 46 (APRIL 64), 193-198.
CONCLUDES THAT ASIA AND CHINA WILL PROBABLY LOOM LESS LARGE ON JAPANESE HORIZON, JAPAN 'LOOKING OUTWARD.' MORE OPPORTUNITIES FOR COMPETITION IN SOUTH ASIA, KOREA AND ELSEWHERE AS LONG AS WESTERN POLICY CONTINUES TO OFFER JAPAN INCENTIVES FOR ALIGNMENT WITH NON-COMMUNIST NATIONS.

1809 LANGER W.L.
THE FRANCO-RUSSIAN ALLIANCE: 1890-1894.
CAMBRIDGE: HARVARD U PR, 1929, 455 PP.
HISTORY OF FRENCH-RUSSIAN RELATIONS AT CLOSE OF 19TH CENTURY. SHOWS HOW BISMARCKIAN POLICY WAS NULLIFIED BY HIS SUCCESSORS, THEREBY MAKING THE ALLIANCE POSSIBLE. OBJECT OF BOOK IS TO PLACE THE ALLIANCE IN ITS EUROPEAN CONTEXT AND EXPLAIN IT AS THE PRODUCT OF THE GENERAL INTERNATIONAL SITUATION. STRICTLY CHRONOLOGICAL APPROACH. POSITION AND POLICY OF ENGLAND ARE DETAILED.

1810 LANGER W.L.
"FAREWELL TO EMPIRE."
FOR. AFF., 14 (OCT. 62), 115-130.
ANALYZES FACTORS ACCOUNTING FOR DEVELOPMENT OF MODERN IMPERIALISM AND STATES THAT, IN SPITE OF ITS DECLINE TODAY, IT HAS LEFT AN INDELIBLE MARK ON FORMER SUBJECT STATES.

1811 LANGERHANS H.
"NEHRU'S BITTERNESS."
FRANKFURTER H., 19 (1964), 157-171.
EXTENSIVE REVIEW OF NEHRU'S WRITINGS AND A COMMENTARY ON THE SUCCESSION OF INDIAN POLICIES OF RECENT TIMES, ENDING WITH THE DISILLUSIONMENT OVER 'ASIATIC REALITY.'

1812 LAPENNA I.
STATE AND LAW: SOVIET AND YUGOSLAV THEORY.
NEW HAVEN: YALE U PR, 1964, 135 PP.
DISCUSSES BASIC MARXIST VIEWS OF STATE AND LAW ESPECIALLY FROM SOVIET AND YUGOSLAV PERSPECTIVE OF THEORY. EXAMINES DEVELOPMENT OF THEORY OF LAW IN THESE TWO COUNTRIES.

1813 LAPIERRE J.W.
"TRADITION ET MODERNITE A MADAGASCAR."
ESPRIT, 35 (JAN. 68), 57-68.
MAIN PROBLEM INDUSTRIAL NATIONS HAVE IN HELPING UNDERDEVELOPED NATIONS IS TO OVERCOME LACK OF ETHNIC UNDERSTANDING AND TRADITIONALISM OF PEOPLE. SEES TECHNICAL DEVELOPMENT AS A STAGE BETWEEN COLONIALISM AND ECONOMIC COOPERATION. IN MADAGASCAR, EFFORTS TO AID RURAL POPULATION ARE MISUNDERSTOOD AS COLONIALIST POLICIES. PEASANTS WITHDRAW AND LOOK TO LOCAL CUSTOMS AND HEROES, NOT THEIR GOVERNMENT.

1814 LAPONCE J.A.
"THE GOVERNMENT OF THE FIFTH REPUBLIC."
BERKELEY: U OF CALIF PR, 1961.
SURVEY OF FRENCH POLITICAL PARTIES AND THE CONSTITUTION OF THE FIFTH REPUBLIC THROUGH JUNE 1960. REVIEWS PARTIES, IDEOLOGIES, AND PRESSURE GROUPS, MOST NOTABLY THE COMMUNISTS, INDEPENDENTS, SFIO, MRP, UNR, AND THE RADICAL PARTY. DISCUSSES ORGANIZATION, POWERS, AND FUNCTIONS OF THE EXECUTIVE, NATIONAL ASSEMBLY, AND SENATE. SELECTED, ANNOTATED BIBLIOGRAPHY OF POST-1914 WORKS IN FRENCH AND ENGLISH.

1815 LAPRADE W.T.
PUBLIC OPINION AND POLITICS IN EIGHTEENTH CENTURY ENGLAND.
NEW YORK: MACMILLAN, 1936, 462 PP.
STRUGGLE FOR POWER 1700-42 AND EFFECT ON POLICY, OPINIONS, LEADERSHIP, AND NATIONALISM OF LACK OF STRONG RULER ANALYZED. RELATES CHANGING POLITICAL AND RELIGIOUS BELIEFS; RISE OF PROTESTANTISM AND DECLINE OF "DIVINE RIGHT" CONCEPT TO UPHEAVAL IN GOVERNMENT.

1816 LAQUEUR W.Z.
THE FATE OF THE REVOLUTION: INTERPRETATIONS OF SOVIET HISTORY.
NEW YORK: MACMILLAN, 1967, 216 PP., LC#67-22401.
COMPARES AND ANALYZES INTERPRETATIONS OF SOVIET AND NON-SOVIET HISTORIANS ON SIGNIFICANCE OF THE RUSSIAN REVOLUTION. DESCRIBES PROBLEMS AND DILEMMAS WHICH THEY HAVE FACED; RANGES FROM CONSIDERATION OF EARLY MISUNDERSTANDINGS TO DISCUSSION OF QUESTIONS IN WHICH HISTORIANS ENGAGE TODAY. ESTABLISHES BACKGROUND OF EACH HISTORIAN'S POINT OF VIEW.

1817 LAQUEUR W.Z.
COMMUNISM AND NATIONALISM IN THE MIDDLE EAST.
NEW YORK: PRAEGER, 1957, 375 PP., $6.50.
TRACES THE DEVELOPMENT OF COMMUNISM IN AREA AND ANALYZES THE POLITICAL, ECONOMIC AND SOCIAL CONDITIONS WHICH AID IN ITS GROWTH. INCLUDES DISCUSSION OF NATIONALISM, RIGHT-WING EXTREMISM, AND THE ROLE OF THE NATIVE INTELLEGENSIA.

1818 LAQUEUR W.Z. ED.
THE MIDDLE EAST IN TRANSITION.
NEW YORK: PRAEGER, 1958, 513 PP.
THIRTY-SIX ESSAYS COVER SOCIAL AND POLITICAL CHANGE. FOCUSES ON POLITICAL IDEOLOGY, COMMUNISM, SOVIET STRATEGY IN MIDDLE EAST. STUDIES TRENDS OF INDIVIDUAL COUNTRIES AND REGION AS WHOLE.

1819 LAQUEUR W.Z.
THE SOVIET UNION AND THE MIDDLE EAST.
NEW YORK: PRAEGER, 1959, 366 PP.
FOLLOWS EVOLUTION OF SOVIET ATTITUDE SINCE 1917. ANALYZES SOVIET MOTIVES IN MIDDLE EAST. STUDIES RECENT POLICY TRENDS. CONTENDS SOVIET SEEMS TO SUPPORT NATIONAL MOVEMENTS BUT HAS LONG-RANGE AIMS FOR AREA.

1820 LAQUEUR W.Z. ED., LABEDZ L. ED.
THE FUTURE OF COMMUNIST SOCIETY.
NEW YORK: FREDERICK PRAEGER, 1962, 196 PP., LC#62-9509.
ESSAYS EXAMINE COMMUNISM IN PAST AND PRESENT TO PROJECT ITS FUTURE. BEGIN WITH THIRD CPSU PROGRAM OF 1961, STUDY ITS ECONOMIC PLANS, AND ANALYZE IDEOLOGICAL CHANGES. TREAT MARXIAN PHILOSOPHY AND PRACTICE, FUNCTION OF LAW, SOCIAL INSTITUTIONS, UTOPIAN TRADITION, AND WITHERING AWAY OF STATE. CONCLUDE WITH RUSSIA AND CHINA (TWO ROADS TO COMMUNISM), SOCIAL AND ECONOMIC POLICY, AND FUTURE GOALS.

1821 LAQUEUR W.Z. ED., LABEDZ L. ED.
POLYCENTRISM.
NEW YORK: FREDERICK PRAEGER, 1962, 259 PP., LC#62-18268.
ANALYZES DECLINE OF MONOLITHIC COMMUNISM IN RECENT YEARS, INCLUDING THE SINO-SOVIET SCHISM, REVISIONISM, AND THE IMPACT OF POLYCENTRISM ON COMMUNIST PARTIES IN EASTERN EUROPE, WESTERN EUROPE, AND THE UNDERDEVELOPED WORLD.

1822 LAQUEUR W.Z.
"BONN IS NOT WEIMAR* REFLECTIONS ON THE RADICAL RIGHT IN GERMANY."
COMMENTARY, 43 (MAR. 67), 33-42.
PREDICTS THAT NPD WILL NOT BECOME IMPORTANT. COMPARES SITUATION TO RISE OF NAZIS. ADMITS POSSIBILITY THAT NATIONALISM WILL BECOME DOMINANT. ASSURES THAT DUE TO RELATIVE MILITARY AND POLITICAL UNIMPORTANCE RESULTING FROM WAR, THE REASONS TO BE ALARMED AT THE GROWTH OF THE NPD ARE MINIMAL.

1823 LARKIN E.
"ECONOMIC GROWTH, CAPITAL INVESTMENT, AND THE ROMAN CATHOLIC CHURCH IN NINETEENTH-CENTURY IRELAND."
AMER. HISTORICAL REVIEW, 72 (APR. 67), 852-884.
A STUDY OF THE BETTERMENT OF THE CATHOLIC CHURCH'S FINANCIAL SITUATION DURING THE 19TH CENTURY, PARTICULARLY IN LIGHT OF THE GENERALLY WEAK ECONOMIC SITUATION IN IRELAND. PARTICULAR ATTENTION IS PAID TO THE ISSUE OF WHETHER THE CHURCH, THROUGH CONCENTRATION OF CAPITAL AND ENTREPRENEURIAL TALENT, DECREASED THE POSSIBILITIES FOR IRISH ECONOMIC GROWTH.

1824 LARSON A. ED.
A WARLESS WORLD.
NEW YORK: MCGRAW/HILL, 1963, 174 PP.
OUTLINES PROBLEMS AND ADVANTAGES THAT MANKIND WOULD ENCOUNTER IN A WORLD WITHOUT WAR, FOCUSING ATTENTION ON THE ECONOMIC AND PSYCHOLOGICAL ISSUES INVOLVED. CONTRIBUTORS TO BOOK INCLUDE: TOYNBEE, SOHN AND MILLIS.

1825 LARUS J. ED.
COMPARATIVE WORLD POLITICS.
BELMONT: WADSWORTH, 1965, 274 PP., LC#64-21773.
PROVIDES READINGS INTRODUCING PRE-MODERN INTERSTATE RELATIONS OF CHINESE EMPIRE, PRE-MUSLIM INDIA, AND ISLAMIC COMMUNITY, PLUS CLASSICAL WESTERN NATION-STATE. ALSO SEEKS TO PRESENT EVIDENCE OF CONTINUITY AND DISCONTINUITY BETWEEN WESTERN NATION-STATE SYSTEM AND NON-WESTERN ANTECEDENTS.

1826 LASKER B.
ASIA ON THE MOVE.
NEW YORK: HOLT, 1945, 207 PP.
STUDIES THE MOVEMENT OF POPULATIONS IN EASTERN ASIA, CITING SUCH FACTORS AS THE 'SHIFT TO THE CITY' AND DISLOCATION CAUSED BY WW 2. PROBLEMS OF OVER-POPULATION AND ECONOMIC UNDERDEVELOPMENT ARE SCRUTINIZED. BOOK WAS WRITTEN IN ANTICIPATION OF IMMEDIATE PROBLEMS THAT WOULD FACE THE WORLD AFTER WW 2.

1828 LASKI H.J.
LIBERTY IN THE MODERN STATE.
NEW YORK: HARPER & ROW, 1930, 256 PP.
CONCERNED WITH TWO BASIC CONCEPTS: LIBERTY IS AN ABSENCE OF RESTRAINT, AND IF THERE BE A BODY POLITIC WITH UNLIMITED

POLITICAL POWER, THOSE OVER WHOM IT RULES ARE ENSLAVED. A BALANCE BETWEEN LIBERTY AND AUTHORITY MUST BE MAINTAINED, AS A GOVERNMENT IS NOT ENTITLED TO SUPPRESS ANY FACET OF THE POPULACE; FREEDOM IS A PLEA FOR TOLERATION AND THE RIGHTS OF REASON.

1829 LASKI H.J.
THE STATE IN THEORY AND PRACTICE.
NEW YORK: VIKING PRESS, 1935, 366 PP.
ANALYZES EVOLUTION OF DEMOCRATIC FORMS OF CAPITALISM, HOW THE ECONOMICS OF 1800'S AFFECTED IT, AND PROBLEMS OF 20TH CENTURY. CLAIMS STATE IS ALWAYS INSTRUMENT OF DOMINANT ECONOMIC CLASS AND THAT ITS ESSENCE IS POWER TO COERCE. THEORY OF STATE CLOSELY PARALLELS MARX'S. APPLIES THIS THEORY TO 1930'S, PREDICTING DEMISE OF DEMOCRACY AS RESULT OF ACTIONS TO PROTECT CAPITALISTS' INTERESTS DURING ECONOMIC DISASTER.

1830 LASKI H.J.
REFLECTIONS ON THE REVOLUTIONS OF OUR TIME.
NEW YORK: VIKING PRESS, 1943, 417 PP.
ATTACKS CAPITALISM AS DYSFUNCTIONAL FOR THE WELFARE OF THE MASSES AND CLAIMS EARLY CRITICISMS OF SOVIET UNION ARE UNWARRANTED AND PREMATURE. LAUDS USSR AS PORTENTOUS OF NEW CIVILIZATION. PROPOSES A PLANNED DEMOCRACY AS IDEAL STATE SINCE IT WOULD BE IMMUNE TO FLUCTUATIONS OF "FREE" MARKET SYSTEM, CLAIMING GOVERNMENT INTERVENTION HAS BEEN PROVED NECESSARY BY FAILURE OF CAPITALISM TO SOLVE SOCIAL PROBLEMS.

1831 LASKI H.S.
THE AMERICAN DEMOCRACY.
NEW YORK: CRITERION, 1948, 785 PP.
ATTEMPTS TO ANALYZE THE NATURE OF AMERICAN PEOPLE AND THE WAY THEIR CHARACTER AFFECTS SYSTEM OF GOVERNMENT. CONSIDERS NATIONAL AND LOCAL GOVERNMENTAL INSTITUTIONS, INDUSTRY, WORKERS, EDUCATION, CULTURE, AND MASS MEDIA TO BE SIGNIFICANT FACTORS IN DETERMINING POLITICAL BEHAVIOR, AND DISCUSSES THEIR EFFECT IN US.

1832 LASKIN B.
CANADIAN CONSTITUTIONAL LAW: TEXT AND NOTES ON DISTRIBUTION OF LEGISLATIVE POWER (2ND ED.)
TORONTO: CARSWELL, 1960, 1061 PP.
STUDIES NATURE OF CANADIAN FEDERALISM; THE "ASPECT DOCTRINE" OF CONSTITUTIONALITY; LEGISLATIVE RESTRICTIONS ON POWER OF COURTS TO PASS ON CONSTITUTIONALITY OF LEGISLATION; AND GENERAL POWER OF CANADIAN PARLIAMENT. DISCUSSES NATIONAL AND LOCAL REGULATION OF ECONOMIC ACTIVITY; TAXING POWERS; ADMINISTRATION OF JUSTICE; AND CANADIAN CRIMINAL LAW. PROVIDES IMPORTANT CASES TO ILLUSTRATE TOPICS.

1833 LASSWELL H.D.
"PERSON, PERSONALITY, GROUP, CULTURE" (BMR)"
PSYCHIATRY, 2 (NOV. 39), 533-561.
DISCUSSES METHOD BY WHICH MEANING OF TERMS IN SCIENCE OF INTERPERSONAL RELATIONS MAY BE CLARIFIED. DISCUSSES RELATION OF PERSONALITY TRAITS TO CULTURE TRAITS AND RELATION OF THE TWO AS WHOLES. INCLUDES RESISTANCE OF INTERPERSONAL METHODOLOGY TO SYSTEMIC ANALYSIS AND PRESENTS METHOD FOR OBSERVING THE WHOLE PERSONALITY. OUTLINES GENERAL CATEGORIES OF PERSONALITY STUDY.

1834 LASSWELL H.D., LEITES N. ET AL.
LANGUAGE OF POLITICS.
NEW YORK: STEWART, 1949, 398 PP.
SUGGESTS THAT STUDY OF POLITICS CAN BE ADVANCED BY QUANTITATIVE ANALYSIS OF POLITICAL DISCOURSE. DESCRIBES LANGUAGE AS A 'POWER-FACTOR' AND DEMONSTRATES PRACTICAL REALITIES OF STYLE IN POLITICAL SPEECH. PRESENTS METHODS OF STUDYING THE LANGUAGE OF POLITICS AND APPLIES THESE PROCEDURES TO COMMUNIST EXPRESSION SINCE 1918.

1835 LASSWELL H.D.
"THE POLICY SCIENCES OF DEVELOPMENT."
WORLD POLIT., 17 (JAN. 65), 286-309.
'SELF-SUSTAINING LEVEL OF CREATIVE CONCERN WITH THE POWER VALUE AND ITS DIVERSE MODES OF INSTITUTIONAL EXPRESSION... CAN PROVIDE AN INCLUSIVE FRAME OF REFERENCE FOR THE DECISION-MAKERS AND CHOOSERS INVOLVED IN GIVING OR RECEIVING ASSISTANCE OR IN DIRECTING SELF-SUSTAINING AND INTEGRATED GROWTH.'

1836 LATIN AMERICAN STUDIES ASSN
"RESEARCH ON EDUCATION IN LATIN AMERICA."
LATIN AMER. RESEARCH REV., 3 (FALL 67), 1-76.
ARTICLES RELATED TO EDUCATIONAL RESEARCH IN LATIN AMERICA INCLUDE ONE ON STUDY OF LATIN AMERICA IN THE USSR. EXAMINE THE AMOUNT OF SUPPORT GIVEN TO EDUCATION BY GOVERNMENT, THE STATUS OF SECONDARY SCHOOLS, AND THE DEVELOPMENT OF COUNSELING IN LATIN AMERICAN SCHOOLS.

1837 LATORRE A.
UNIVERSIDAD Y SOCIEDAD.
BALTIMORE: NEWMAN PRESS, 1964.
EXAMINES CONCEPT OF UNIVERSITY AND ITS RELATION TO SOCIETY AS EXPRESSED IN HISTORY AND SPANISH EXPERIENCE. DISCUSSES UNIVERSITY EDUCATION, RESEARCH, CULTURAL INFLUENCE, REFORM, FINANCIAL RESOURCES, AND STATUS OF STUDENT AND PROFESSOR.

1838 LATOURETTE K.S.
CHINA.
ENGLEWOOD CLIFFS: PRENTICE HALL, 1964, 152 PP., LC#64-23560.
EXAMINES WHY COMMUNISTS SUCCEEDED IN TAKING OVER MAINLAND, HOW SUCCESSFULLY AIMS HAVE BEEN CARRIED OUT, HOW MUCH OLD CHINA PERSISTS, AND PROSPECTS FOR CONTINUED COMMUNIST CONTROL. GIVES HISTORICAL BACKGROUND.

1839 LAULICHT J.
"PUBLIC OPINION AND FOREIGN POLICY DECISIONS."
JOURNAL OF PEACE RESEARCH, (1965), 47-160.
SURVEY DATA OF CANADIAN VOTERS' AND LEADERS' OPINIONS ON NUCLEAR WEAPONS, CONVENTIONAL FORCES, THE UN, CO-EXISTENCE, AND FOREIGN AID ARE ANALYZED. HE CLAIMS PUBLIC OPINION DOES AFFECT GOVERNMENT POLICY, BUT "PUBLIC" IS NOT A UNITY AND ALL SEGMENTS ARE NOT EQUALLY INFLUENTIAL.

1840 LAUTERBACH A.
ECONOMIC SECURITY AND INDIVIDUAL FREEDOM: CAN WE HAVE BOTH?
ITHACA: CORNELL U PRESS, 1948, 178 PP.
DISCUSSES RELATIONSHIP OF PLANNED ECONOMIC STABILITY TO BOTH TOTALITARIANISM AND DEMOCRACY. CONTRASTS LAISSEZ-FAIRE AND TOTALITARIAN SOLUTIONS TO ECONOMIC PROBLEMS IN SOCIETY. MAINTAINS THAT ECONOMIC WELFARE IS ESSENTIAL TO FREEDOM, BUT THAT ECONOMIC SECURITY SHOULD MEAN ONLY THE GUARANTEE THAT OPPORTUNITIES WILL ALWAYS BE AVAILABLE FOR THOSE WILLING TO WORK.

1841 LAVEN P.
RENAISSANCE ITALY: 1464-1534.
NEW YORK: G P PUTNAM'S SONS, 1966, 288 PP., LC#66-25643.
HISTORY OF RENAISSANCE ITALY OBSERVED FROM VARIOUS VIEWPOINTS: MANUFACTURING INDUSTRIES, TRADE, FINANCE, EXTERNAL RELATIONS, INTERNAL AFFAIRS, POLITICAL THOUGHT AND LANGUAGE, HISTORY, SCIENCE, MEDICINE AND TECNOLOGY, RELIGION, ART AND ARCHITECTURE.

1842 LAVRIN J.
"THE TWO WORLDS."
RUSSIAN REVIEWS, 27 (JAN. 68), 3-16.
DESCRIBES THE TWO PERSONALITIES OF RUSSIA, AND THE CONTROVERSY BETWEEN THE WESTERN-MINDED LIBERALS, AND THE SLAVOPHILES. THE LATTER INSISTED THAT RUSSIA HAD NOT ONLY A MENTALITY BUT A CULTURE AND A HISTORICAL DESTINY, THE ESSENCE OF WHICH WAS DIFFERENT FROM, OR SUPERIOR TO, THAT OF EUROPE.

1843 LAVROFF D.-G.
LES LIBERTES PUBLIQUES EN UNION SOVIETIQUE (REV. ED.)
PARIS: EDITIONS A PEDONE, 1963, 265 PP.
DISCUSSION OF FREEDOM AND ITS PHILOSOPHICAL BASIS. EMPHASIZES INDIVIDUAL RIGHTS AND RELATIONS OF STATE AND PUBLIC.

1844 LAWLEY F.E.
THE GROWTH OF COLLECTIVE ECONOMY VOL. 1: NATIONAL.
LONDON: PS KING & SON, 1938, 520 PP.
ARGUES AGAINST "MENACE" OF PRIVATE PROPERTY, STATING THAT COLLECTIVIZATION IS PREREQUISITE TO DYNAMIC ECONOMY. COMPARES METHODS OF OBTAINING GOVERNMENT CONTROL OF PROPERTY IN VARIOUS COUNTRIES, USING WARTIME CONTROL AS EXEMPLAR OF EFFECTIVENESS. DEFENDS AGRARIAN REFORMS AND NATIONALIZATION OF MAJOR INDUSTRIES. ARGUMENT EXTENDED TO INTERNATIONAL SPHERE IN A SECOND VOLUME.

1845 LAWLEY F.E.
THE GROWTH OF COLLECTIVE ECONOMY VOL. 2: INTERNATIONAL.
LONDON: PS KING & SON, 1938, 501 PP.
FIRST VOLUME ARGUED THAT COLLECTIVIZATION IS NECESSARY FOR A DYNAMIC ECONOMY. SECOND VOLUME EXTENDS ARGUMENT TO INTERNATIONAL SPHERE, ARGUING THAT ECONOMIC NATIONALISM SHOULD BE SUPERSEDED BY INTERNATIONALISM. CLAIMS THAT FAULT OF FASCISM, NAZISM, COMMUNISM, AND NEW DEAL IS NATIONALISM RATHER THAN EXCESS CONTROL.

1846 LAWRENCE P.
ROAD BELONG CARGO: A STUDY OF CARGO MOVEMENT IN SOUTHERN MADANG DISTRICT, NEW GUINEA.
MANCHESTER: MANCHESTER UNIV PR, 1964, 291 PP.
STUDY OF NATIVE CULT IN WHICH WORSHIPERS PERFORM MAGICAL RITES TO PRODUCE EUROPEAN MANUFACTURED GOODS OR TO PROCURE THEM. NATIVES BELIEVE WHITE MAN HAS PREVENTED THEIR BETTERMENT, AND THAT WESTERN GOODS AND KNOWLEDGE ORIGINATE IN WORLD OF GODS AND SPIRITS.

1847 LAWRENCE P. ED., MEGGITT M.J. ED.
GODS, GHOSTS, AND MEN IN MELANESIA: SOME RELIGIONS OF AUSTRALIAN NEW GUINEA AND THE NEW HEBRIDES.
MELBOURNE: OXFORD U PR, 1965, 298 PP.
DELINEATES PRINCIPAL FEATURES OF TRADITIONAL RELIGIONS IN MELANESIA. FINDS GEOGRAPHICAL IRREGULARITY WITH MUCH DIFFUSION IN THE AREA. CONCLUDES THAT NO SYSTEM EXISTS TO ACCOUNT FOR SEPARATE RELIGIONS.

1848 LAWRIE G.
"WHAT WILL CHANGE SOUTH AFRICA?"
ROUND TABLE, 69 (JAN. 68), 41-55.
EXAMINES RECENT CHANGES IN ACTIONS OF SOUTH AFRICA REGARDING TRADE IN AFRICA, DIPLOMATIC RELATIONS WITH NEW STATES, AND RACIAL PRACTICES. ANALYZES THESE ATTITUDE MODIFICATIONS, QUESTIONING THEIR REPRESENTATION OF NEW RACIAL AND DIPLOMATIC POLICIES, MORE ACCEPTABLE TO OUTSIDE WORLD. TRACES DEVELOPMENT OF RULING ELITE, SEEKING CLUES TO THIS IN HISTORICAL TRENDS.

1849 LEBON J.H.C.
AN INTRODUCTION TO HUMAN GEOGRAPHY.
LONDON: HUTCHINSON U LIBRARY, 1952, 191 PP.
INTRODUCTORY EXPOSITION OF HUMAN GEOGRAPHY, WHICH IS DESCRIBED AS MACRO-GEOGRAPHY (DEALING WITH GENERAL RELATIONSHIPS BETWEEN MAN AND HIS ENVIRONMENT). ATTEMPTS TO INTERPRET THOUGHT OF LEADING 20TH-CENTURY GEOGRAPHERS. DISCUSSES EFFECTS OF ENVIRONMENTAL CONDITIONS ON MASS MIGRATION AND ON EARLY STAGES OF ECONOMIC AND SOCIAL DEVELOPMENT.

1850 LEBRUN J., LEFEVRE P.C.
BIBLIOGRAPHIE DE LA FERTILITE DES SOLS ET ELEMENTS DE SOCIOLOGIE RURALE EN AFRIQUE AU SUD DU SAHARA.
BRUSSELS: CEN DOC ECO ET SOC AFR, 1964, 182 PP.
ANNOTATED BIBLIOGRAPHY OF POST-1945 WORKS IN WESTERN LANGUAGES COVERING PRACTICAL AGRICULTURE AND RURAL SOCIOLOGY IN DEVELOPING COUNTRIES. CONTAINS 1,413 TITLES ARRANGED IN A TOPICALLY CLASSIFIED SYSTEM WHICH CONCENTRATES ON TECHNIQUES AND METHODS OF AGRICULTURE. INCLUDES A COMPLETE LIST OF CROSS REFERENCES, A LIST OF PERIODICALS AND COLLECTIONS CITED, AND A GEOGRAPHICAL INDEX.

1851 LECKY W.E.H.
DEMOCRACY AND LIBERTY (2 VOLS.)
LONDON: LONGMANS, GREEN & CO, 1899, 1169 PP.
DESCRIBES DECLINE IN RESPECT FOR PARLIAMENTARY GOVERNMENT AND DIFFICULTY IN RECONCILING THIS FORM OF GOVERNMENT WITH EXTREME DEMOCRACY. MODERN DEMOCRATIC PARLIAMENTS TEND TO BREAK UP INTO SMALL GROUPS, THEREBY WEAKENING EXECUTIVE, DESTROYING PARTY SYSTEM, GIVING DISPROPORTIONATE STRENGTH TO MINORITIES, AND REDUCING LEGISLATION TO CLASS BRIBERY. LESS DEMOCRATIC PARLIAMENTS REPRESENT BEST INTERESTS OF NATION.

1852 LEDERER E.
STATE OF THE MASSES.
NEW YORK: W W NORTON, 1940, 245 PP.
BELIEVES THAT THE MODERN DICTATORIAL STATE, THE STATE OF THE MASSES, IS UNIQUE IN HISTORY. ASSERTS THAT FASCISM IS AN EFFORT TO BREAK DOWN GROUPS AND TURN THEM INTO CROWDS. THROUGH GROUPS SOCIETY CAN EXPRESS ITSELF NORMALLY, WHEREAS CROWDS ARE ANTI-SOCIAL. MODERN DICTATORSHIPS, PARTICULARLY FASCIST STATES, DISRUPT HISTORY BECAUSE THEY RESORT TO MASS EMOTIONS AND TERROR.

1853 LEDERER W.
THE BALANCE ON FOREIGN TRANSACTIONS: PROBLEMS OF DEFINITION AND MEASUREMENT (PAMPHLET)
PRINCETON: PRIN U, DEPT OF ECO, 1963, 76 PP., LC#63-20994.
ATTEMPTS TO CLARIFY AND UNIFY PURPOSE FOR WHICH ANALYSIS OF DATA COMPILED ON INTERNATIONAL TRANSACTIONS IS INTENDED. TRIES TO DETERMINE FOCUS FOR ANALYSIS IN TERMS OF SPECIFIC KINDS OF TRANSACTIONS. ANALYZES DATA AND INSTITUTIONS IN US TO DECIDE WHICH TYPE OF DATA IS BEST FOR FORMULATING AND DISCUSSING PUBLIC POLICY.

1854 LEDERMAN W.R. ED.
THE COURTS AND THE CANDIAN CONSTITUTION.
LONDON: MCCLELLAND AND STEWART, 1964, 250 PP.
TRACES EFFECTS AND DEVELOPMENT OF CANADIAN SUPREME COURT INFLUENCES ON CONSTITUTIONALISM AND PROCESS OF INTERPRETATION. CONSIDERS MERITS OF HAVING REVIEW OF LEGISLATION AND EFFECT ON PARLIAMENT.

1855 LEE C.
THE POLITICS OF KOREAN NATIONALISM.
BERKELEY: U OF CALIF PR, 1963, 342 PP., LC#63-19029.
ACCOUNT OF KOREANS' STRUGGLES FOR INDEPENDENCE FROM FOREIGN REGIMES. ATTEMPTS TO DISCOVER UNIFORMITIES AND RECURRING PATTERNS OF NATIONALIST POLITICAL MOVEMENTS. EXAMINES LATER HALF OF YI DYNASTY (1392-1910), CHANGES THAT CULMINATED IN JAPANESE ANNEXATION IN 1910, JAPANESE RULE FROM 1919-45, AND ACTIVITIES OF NATIONALISTS ABROAD AND WITHIN KOREA.

1856 LEE D.
FREEDOM AND CULTURE.
ENGLEWOOD CLIFFS: PRENTICE HALL, 1959, 179 PP., LC#59-15584.
ESSAYS ON SEVERAL DIVERSE WORLD CULTURES REVEALING THEIR BASIC CONCEPTS OF PERSONAL FREEDOM, AUTONOMY, AND THE INDIVIDUAL. FOREIGN CULTURES OFTEN COMPARED WITH VARIOUS ASPECTS OF AMERICAN CULTURE. APPROACHES CULTURE AS SYMBOLIC SYSTEM WHICH TRANSFORMS PHYSICAL REALITY INTO EXPERIENCED REALITY.

1857 LEE J.M.
"PARLIAMENT IN REPUBLICAN GHANA."
PARLIAM. AFF., 16 (AUTUMN 63), 276-95.
A CRITICAL ASSESSMENT OF THE PRESENT POLITICAL SITUATION IN GHANA, COMPARING THE INDEPENDENCE PARLIAMENT OF 1957-1960 WITH THE REPUBLICAN PARLIAMENT OF 1960-1963.

1858 LEES-SMITH H.B.
SECOND CHAMBERS IN THEORY AND PRACTICE.
LONDON: ALLEN & UNWIN, 1923, 256 PP.
SURVEYS SECOND CHAMBERS OF BRITISH DOMINIONS. DESCRIBES BRITISH PARLIAMENTARY GOVERNMENT AND FUNCTIONS ASSIGNED TO SECOND CHAMBER. EXAMINES SECOND CHAMBERS IN CANADA, AUSTRALIA, NEW ZEALAND, SOUTH AFRICA, NORWAY, AND IRELAND IN TERMS OF THEIR SUCCESS IN AVOIDING BEING STRICTLY A PARTY INSTRUMENT AND NOT REPRESENTING PEOPLE. ADVOCATES CONTROL OF POWERS OF CHAMBER.

1859 LEFEVRE R.
THE NATURE OF MAN AND HIS GOVERNMENT.
CALDWELL: CAXTON PRINTERS, 1959, 87 PP., LC#59-05901.
DISCUSSES NATURE OF MAN AND APPROPRIATE GOVERNMENTAL ORGANIZATION AND POLICY, ARGUING THAT RECENT DEVELOPMENTS IN US GOVERNMENT HAVE POLLUTED IDEAL OF FOUNDING FATHERS, ESPECIALLY ALLEGED COLLECTIVE REDUCTIONS OF INDIVIDUAL LIBERTY. INCLUDES SUGGESTIONS FOR ACTION.

1860 LEGRES A.
"LES FONCTIONS D'UN PARLEMENT MODERNE."
REV. DROIT PUBLIC ET SCI. POL., 779 (JUNE 67), 43-51.
POPULAR STUDY OF MODERN FRENCH PARLIAMENTARY FUNCTIONS AND ACTIVITIES INCLUDING DEBATE.

1861 LEGUM C.
PAN-AFRICANISM: A SHORT POLITICAL GUIDE.
NEW YORK: PRAEGER, 1962, 296 PP., $5.75.
TRACES ORIGINS AND GROWTH OF PAN-AFRICANISM LISTING THE COHESIVE AND DIVISIVE FACTORS. EMPHASIZES INTER-RELATION BETWEEN CULTURE AND POLITICS. SEES ANTI-COLONIALISM, RACIALISM, NON-ALIGNMENT, EXPRESSION OF AFRICAN PERSONALITY AND FEAR OF BALKANIZATION AS ESSENTIAL ELEMENTS. DOES NOT EVALUATE OR PREDICT BUT MERELY RECORDS. 25 APPENDICES GIVE FULL TEXT OF IMPORTANT PAN-AFRICAN DOCUMENTS.

1862 LEGUM C.
"THE DANGERS OF INDEPENDENCE"
TRANSACTIONS, 2 (OCT. 62), 11-13.
COMPARES UGANDA TO PREVIOUSLY INDEPENDENT NATIONS REGARDING PROBLEMS OF ORDER ESTABLISHMENT, CREATING NATIONAL FEELING, PROMOTING GOVERNMENT LOYALTY. DISCUSSES PROBLEM OF BUGANDA AND ITS REFUSAL TO ACCEPT UGANDA'S DOMINATION.

1863 LEHMAN R.L. ED., PRICE F.W. ED.
AFRICA SOUTH OF THE SAHARA (PAMPHLET)
NEW YORK: MISSIONARY RES LIB, 1961, 70 PP.
GEOGRAPHICAL ARRANGEMENT IS USED IN LISTING BOOKS IN THIS BIBLIOGRAPHY. AREAS DEALT WITH ARE: WEST AFRICA, EQUATORIAL AFRICA, SOUTH AFRICA, CENTRAL AFRICA, EAST AFRICA, AND MADAGASKAR. HAS SECTION ON REFERENCE AND BIBLIOGRAPHICAL WORKS AND GENERAL WORKS. A VARIETY OF FIELDS ARE COVERED. SOME WORKS ARE ANNOTATED.

1864 LEHMBRUCH G.
"WAHLREFORM UND POLITISCHES SYSTEM."
NEUE POLITISCHE LITERATUR, 12 (1967), 146-151.
CRITICIZES IDEA THAT POLITICAL BEHAVIOR IS INFLUENCED BY INSTITUTIONAL FACTORS. EXAMINES POSITION THAT INSTITUTIONAL CHANGES IN NETHERLANDS ELECTORAL SYSTEM WOULD RESULT IN CONSOLIDATION OF PARTY SYSTEM. MAINTAINS EMPHASIS ON INFLUENCE OF INSTITUTIONS RESULTS IN A-HISTORICAL AND A-SOCIOLOGICAL ABSTRACTIONS WHICH DEPRIVE SUCH INQUIRIES OF EMPIRICAL CONTENT.

1865 LEIBLER I.
SOVIET JEWRY AND HUMAN RIGHTS.
VICTORIA: HUMAN RIGHTS PUBL, 1966, 78 PP.
EXAMINES DISCRIMINATORY TREATMENT OF JEWS IN USSR AND RESPONSE THERETO BY SOVIET INTELLECTUALS. DISCUSSES ATTITUDE OF AUSTRALIAN COMMUNISTS AND PROGRESSIVES TOWARD JEWISH PROBLEM IN USSR.

1866 LEIGH M.B. ED.
CHECK LIST OF HOLDINGS ON BORNEO IN THE CORNELL UNIVERSITY LIBRARIES (PAMPHLET)
ITHACA: CORNELL U, DEPT ASIAN ST, 1966, 74 PP.
EXTENSIVE BIBLIOGRAPHICAL LISTING OF MONOGRAPHS AND SERIALS COMPILED FOR CORNELL'S SOUTHEAST ASIA PROGRAM. MANY ENTRIES IN DUTCH. PUBLICATIONS TREAT VARIOUS ASPECTS OF BORNEO; INCLUDES POLITICAL MATERIAL. MONOGRAPHS ARE SUBDIVIDED INTO BORNEO IN GENERAL, INDONESIAN BORNEO, AND EAST MALAYSIA AND BRUNEI. SERIALS SUBDIVIDED INTO INDONESIAN BORNEO AND EAST MALAYSIA AND BRUNEI.

1867 LEIGHTON A.H.
MY NAME IS LEGION; FOUNDATIONS FOR A THEORY OF MAN IN RELATION TO CULTURE (VOL. I)
NEW YORK: BASIC BOOKS, 1959, 452 PP., LC#59-13486.
DISCUSSES PSYCHIATRIC DISORDERS AS THEY OCCUR IN

PARTICULAR ENVIRONMENT, TYPES OF DISORDERS. AND MAIN CAUSES. DELINEATES PROPOSITIONS RELATING CHARACTERISTICS OF DISORDERS TO THOSE OF SOCIOCULTURAL ENVIRONMENT. STUDIES RESEARCH QUESTIONS AND CONCEPTS FOR INVESTIGATION OF PROBLEM. FIRST VOLUME OF STIRLING COUNTY STUDY OF PSYCHIATRIC DISORDER AND SOCIOCULTURAL ENVIRONMENT.

1868 LEIGHTON D.C., HARDING J.S. ET AL.
THE CHARACTER OF DANGER (VOL. III)
NEW YORK: BASIC BOOKS, 1963, 545 PP., LC#63-15998.
PRESENTS RESULTS OF STIRLING COUNTY STUDY OF PSYCHIATRIC DISORDER AND SOCIOCULTURAL ENVIRONMENT. DISCUSSES METHODS AND OVER-ALL PREVALENCE FIGURES. FINDS ASSOCIATION BETWEEN SOCIOCULTURAL DISINTEGRATION AND PREVALENCE OF DISORDER.

1869 LEITES N.
A STUDY OF BOLSHEVISM.
GLENCOE: FREE PR., 1953, 639 PP.
DEFINES BOLSHEVIK OPERATIONAL CODE AS REPRESENTATIVE OF COMMUNIST SPIRIT. ANALYZES POLITBURO POLITICS, COMMUNIST ETHICS, THE PARTY, AND PROPAGANDA METHODS. DISCUSSES HISTORY OF RUSSIAN ELITES FROM LENIN TO MALENKOV.

1870 LEITES N.
A STUDY OF BOLSHEVISM.
NEW YORK: FREE PRESS OF GLENCOE, 1953, 639 PP.
EXAMINES PRINCIPLES, POLICIES, HABITS, AND EXPECTATIONS OF THE BOLSHEVIKS. CONCENTRATES ON INTENSIVE ANALYSIS OF RECORDED WORDS OF LENIN AND STALIN. SHOWS THAT STUDY OF BOLSHEVIK "OPERATIONAL CODE" IS A CLUE TO DELINEATION OF BOLSHEVIK SPIRIT. POINTS OUT AMBIGUITY, INCONSISTENCY, AND INCOMPLETENESS OF BOLSHEVIK CODE.

1871 LEITES N.
ON THE GAME OF POLITICS IN FRANCE.
STANFORD: STANFORD U PRESS, 1959, 190 PP., LC#59-7426.
STUDY OF MAJOR DOMESTIC POLITICAL STRATEGY DURING THE SECOND PHASE OF THE FOURTH REPUBLIC. EMPHASIZES FACTIONS AND INDIVIDUALS, INCLUDING EUROPEAN DEFENSE COMMUNITY, THE COMMON MARKET, AND RADICALISM.

1872 LEITZ F.
DIE PUBLIZITAT DER AKTIENGESELLSCHAFT.
FRANKFURT: F LEITZ, 1929, 291 PP.
STUDY OF PUBLIC STATEMENTS OF GERMAN CORPORATIONS CONCERNING THEIR STATUTES, FINANCIAL REPORTS, STOCK MARKET PROSPECTS, ETC. DISCUSSES THEIR LEGAL DUTIES AS WELL AS A COMPARISON WITH PRACTICES IN ENGLAND, AMERICA, FRANCE, AND BELGIUM.

1873 LEMARCHAND R.
POLITICAL AWAKENING IN THE BELGIAN CONGO.
BERKELEY: U OF CALIF PR, 1964, 357 PP., LC#64-21774.
ANALYZES NATIONALIST DEVELOPMENT IN CONGO DURING TERMINAL PHASE OF BELGIAN RULE, PRECOLONIAL ENVIRONMENT, AND ARAB DOMINATION. DISCUSSES DEVELOPMENT, ORGANIZATION, AND FUNCTIONING OF CONGOLESE PARTY SYSTEM, ITS CONSTITUTIONAL BACKGROUND, ETHNIC NATIONALISM, AND SOCIO-ECONOMIC DEVELOPMENT.

1874 LEMARCHAND R.
"SOCIAL CHANGE AND POLITICAL MODERNISATION IN BURUNDI."
J. OF MOD. AFR. STUD., 4 (DEC. 66), 401-434.
EXPLORES INTERACTION OF SOCIAL CHANGE AND POLITICAL STABILITY IN BURUNDI. RELATES CHANGES IN ELITES TO DECLINE OF MONARCHIAL POWER. STUDIES GENERAL STRATIFICATION OF UPPER ECHELONS IN BURUNDI'S POWER STRUCTURE.

1875 LEMBERG E. ED., EDDING F.
DIE VERTRIEBENEN IN WESTDEUTSCHLAND (3 VOLS.)
KIEL: FERDINAND HIRT, 1959, 1940 PP.
COLLECTION OF ESSAYS ON REFUGEE PROBLEM IN WEST GERMANY. EXAMINES DIFFICULTIES OF ASSIMILATION FROM CULTURAL, LEGAL, AND ECONOMIC PERSPECTIVES. DISCUSSES PROBLEMS OF ADMINISTRATION AND ANALYZES IN DETAIL IMPACT OF REFUGEES ON VARIOUS SECTORS OF ECONOMY SUCH AS AGRICULTURE, TRADES, ETC.

1876 LEMERT E.M.
SOCIAL PATHOLOGY.
NEW YORK: MCGRAW HILL, 1951, 459 PP., LC#51-2206.
CONTAINS A THEORETICAL STATEMENT OF THE CONCEPT OF SOCIAL PATHOLOGY SUPPORTED BY DATA FROM PATHOLOGIES SUCH AS PROSTITUTION, CRIMINALITY, AND ALCOHOLISM. APPENDIX CONTAINS SUGGESTED OUTLINE TO BE FOLLOWED IN STUDYING AND WRITING THE LIFE HISTORY OF A DEVIANT.

1877 LENG S.C.
JUSTICE IN COMMUNIST CHINA: A SURVEY OF THE JUDICIAL SYSTEM OF THE CHINESE PEOPLE'S REPUBLIC.
NEW YORK: OCEANA PUBLISHING, 1967, 196 PP., LC#67-14398.
INTRODUCTORY SURVEY OF DEVELOPMENT, ORGANIZATION, AND FUNCTIONING OF JUDICIAL SYSTEM FOCUSES ON JUDICIAL PATTERN RATHER THAN LAW; LAWS ARE TREATED ONLY WITHIN CONTEXT OF ADMINISTRATION OF JUSTICE. CONCERNED PRIMARILY WITH HISTORY OF "PEOPLE'S JUSTICE" SINCE 1920 AND WITH MACHINERY AND PROCEDURES BY WHICH JUSTICE IS ADMINISTERED. INCLUDES COURT SYSTEM, POLICE, LAWYERS, AND TRIAL SYSTEMS.

1878 LENIN V.I.
STATE AND REVOLUTION.
NEW YORK: INTERNATIONAL PUBLRS, 1943, 103 PP.
A PHILOSOPHICAL ANALYSIS OF THE RELATION OF A PROLETARIAN SOCIALIST REVOLUTION TO THE STATE. SURVEYS THE WRITINGS OF MARX AND ENGELS ON THE STATE, DWELLING ON THOSE ASPECTS OF THEIR TEACHING WHICH LENIN BELIEVES HAVE BEEN OPPORTUNISTICALLY DISTORTED. SUMMARIZES THE EXPERIENCES OF THE RUSSIAN REVOLUTIONS OF 1905 AND 1917.

1879 LENIN V.I.
LEFT WING COMMUNISM: AN INFANTILE DISORDER (1920)
NEW YORK: INTERNATIONAL PUBLRS, 1943, 101 PP.
CRITICIZES ATTEMPTS BY COMMUNIST PARTIES OUTSIDE OF USSR AND BY MENSHEVIKS AND SOCIALIST-REVOLUTIONARIES IN RUSSIA TO ESTABLISH A DICTATORSHIP OF THE MASSES WITHOUT RECOGNIZING THAT MASSES HAVE THEIR OWN STRATIFICATION. CLAIMS THAT RASHNESS AND DISREGARD FOR PARLIAMENTARIANISM DISPLAY AN AWARENESS OF HISTORICAL TRENDS WITHOUT RECOGNITION OF POLITICAL REALITY, WHICH IS THE MAJOR FLAW OF SUCH GROUPS.

1880 LENIN V.I.
SELECTED WORKS (12 VOLS.)
LONDON: LAWRENCE & WISHART, 1954, 3600 PP.
TWELVE-VOLUME WORK COVERS LENIN'S PHILOSOPHIES CONCERNING VARIOUS ASPECTS OF SOCIETY. INCLUDES WORKS ON CAPITALISM, POLITICS, AGRARIANISM, THE WORKER, THE INTELLIGENTSIA, ECONOMICS, WAR, NATIONAL GOVERNMENT, PARTY ORGANIZATION, THE REVOLUTIONS, AND SOCIAL STRUCTURE IN GENERAL.

1881 LENIN V.I.
WHAT IS TO BE DONE? (1902)
MOSCOW: FOREIGN LANG PUBL HOUSE, 1961, 183 PP.
DISCUSSES CHARACTER AND MAIN CONTENT OF POLITICAL AGITATION, AS SEEN BY LENIN IN 1901. CONSIDERS ORGANIZATIONAL TASKS OF THE PARTY, AND PLAN FOR BUILDING MILITANT, TOTALLY RUSSIAN ORGANIZATION. ATTACKS CURRENT ECONOMISTS FOR SUPPORTING OPPRESSION AND PROCLAIMS WORKING CLASS TO BE CAPABLE OF POWERFUL COLLECTIVE ACTION, PROPOSING USE OF NEWSPAPER "ISKA" AS ITS ORGAN.

1882 LENSKI G.E.
POWER AND PRIVILEGE: A THEORY OF SOCIAL STRATIFICATION.
NEW YORK: MCGRAW HILL, 1966, 467 PP., LC#65-28594.
COMPARES, CONTRASTS, AND SYNTHESIZES THEORIES OF MOSCA, SPENCER, SUMNER, PARETO, VEBLEN, SOROKIN, PARSONS, DAHRENDORF, AND MARX WITH RELATION TO SOCIAL STRATIFICATION. AUTHOR CONCENTRATES ON CAUSES OF SOCIAL STRATIFICATION RATHER THAN THE CONSEQUENCES. CONSIDERS PROPOSITIONS ABOUT THE DISTRIBUTIVE SYSTEMS OF HUNTING AND GATHERING, SIMPLE AND ADVANCED HORTICULTURAL, AGRARIAN, AND INDUSTRIAL SOCIETIES.

1883 LENZ F.
DIE BEWEGUNGEN DER GROSSEN MACHTE.
WURTTEMBERG, GERMANY: ULRICH STEINER VERLAG, 1953, 35 PP.
EXAMINES RISE OF USSR AND US TO POSITIONS OF WORLD POWER. DISCUSSES CONCEPT OF BALANCE OF POWER, WRITINGS OF FAMOUS HISTORIANS ON WORLD HISTORY AND TRENDS, AND PRINCIPLES OF NATIONAL GROWTH AND HISTORICAL EVOLUTION.

1884 LEONARD L.L.
INTERNATIONAL ORGANIZATION.
NEW YORK: MCGRAW HILL, 1951, 600 PP.
TRACES HISTORY AND CHARACTERISTICS OF INTERNATIONAL ORGANIZATIONS AND DELINEATES BEGINNINGS OF LEAGUE OF NATIONS, UN. COMPARES PROCESSES OF DECISION-MAKING AND IMPLEMENTATION WITH THOSE OF SOVEREIGN STATES. EXAMINES POLITICAL, ECONOMIC,D SOCIAL, AND COLONIAL ACTIVITIES OF THE LEAGUE AND UN. DISCUSSES ORGANIZATION AND FUNCTION OF SEPARATE UN ORGANS AND RECOUNTS PAST ACTIONS OF UN AND LEAGUE.

1885 LEONARD T.J.
THE FEDERAL SYSTEM OF INDIA.
TUCSON: ARIZONA ST U BUR GOV RES, 1963, 15 PP.
DISCUSSES DISTRIBUTION OF ADMINISTRATIVE AND POLITICAL POWER IN FEDERAL SYSTEM OF INDIA. COMPARES METHODS AND TRADITIONS WITH US PRACTICES.

1886 LEONTIEF W.
ESSAYS IN ECONOMICS.
NEW YORK: OXFORD U PR, 1966, 252 PP., LC#66-24437.
THREE-PART STUDY OF STRUCTURE AND APPLICATION OF ECONOMIC THEORY STRESSES ASPECTS OF NONMATHEMATICAL ECONOMICS. DISCUSSES GENERAL METHODS OF THEORIZING AND INVESTIGATES SPECIFIC ANALYTICAL PROBLEMS IN KEYNESIAN AND OTHER GENERAL ECONOMIC THEORY. EXAMINES IMPORTANT PROBLEMS IN SPECIFIC APPLICATIONS OF ECONOMIC THEORY IN SUCH AREAS AS AUTOMATION AND FOREIGN AID.

1887 LEPOINTE G., VANDENBOSSCHE
ELEMENTS DE BIBLIOGRAPHIE SUR L'HISTOIRE DES INSTITUTIONS ET DES FAITS SOCIAUX, 987-1875.
PARIS: EDITIONS MONT-CHRESTIEN, 1958, 232 PP.

UNANNOTATED BIBLIOGRAPHY OF 3,324 WORKS IN FRENCH PUBLISHED BETWEEN 1928-56. ALPHABETICALLY ARRANGED BY AUTHOR AND INDEXED BY SUBJECT AND AUTHOR. EMPHASIS ON GENERAL, RATHER THAN REGIONAL, WORKS.

1888 LERNER D.
THE PASSING OF TRADITIONAL SOCIETY: MODERNIZING THE MIDDLE EAST.
GLENCOE: FREE PR., 1958, 466 PP.
THE MODERNIZATION PROCESS AND INDIVIDUAL RESPONSES ARE RELATED BY USE OF LAZARSFELD'S 'LATENT-STRUCTURE ANALYSIS'. BASES STUDY ON GROUP-INTERVIEWS AMONG RESIDENTS OF TURKEY, LEBANON, EGYPT, SYRIA, JORDAN AND IRAN.

1889 LERNER D.
"WILL EUROPEAN UNION BRING ABOUT MERGED NATIONAL GOALS."
ANN. AMER. ACAD. POLIT. SOC. SCI., 348 (JULY 63), 34-45.
ANALYZES 'ELITE THOUGHT' IN GERMANY, FRANCE, ENGLAND AND FOCUSES ATTENTION ON POLICIES OF DE GAULLE. CONCLUDES THAT THERE HAS BEEN A MERGING OF NATIONAL GOALS IN THE ECONOMIC SPHERE BUT A NOTABLE DIVERGENCE OF POLITICAL AND CULTURAL AIMS AT PRESENT TIME. DE GAULLE'S NATIONALIST VISION OF EUROPE IS UNFEASIBLE AND DETRIMENTAL TO EUROPEAN UNION. SEES SOLUTION TO EUROPEAN UNITY IN SACRIFICE OF NATIONAL GOALS.

1890 LERNER R. ED., MAHDI M. ED.
MEDIEVAL POLITICAL PHILOSOPHY.
NEW YORK: FREE PRESS OF GLENCOE, 1963, 532 PP., LC#63-8419.
SOURCEBOOK OF MEDIEVAL POLITICAL PHILOSOPHY, CONSISTING OF 25 ESSAYS ARRANGED IN THREE SECTIONS: ISLAM, JUDAISM, AND CHRISTIANITY. DESIGNED AS INTRODUCTION TO SOURCES OF MODERN THEOLOGICAL-POLITICAL THOUGHT. SOME MAJOR AUTHORS INCLUDE BACON, AQUINAS, ALFARABI, AVICENNA, AND MAIMONIDES. INTRODUCTORY PASSAGES SUPPLYING BACKGROUND OF AUTHOR AND WORK PRECEDE INDIVIDUAL ESSAYS.

1891 LERNER W.
"THE HISTORICAL ORIGINS OF THE SOVIET DOCTRINE OF PEACEFUL COEXISTENCE."
LAW CONTEMP. PROBL., 29 (AUTUMN 64), 865-70.
REVIEWS SOVIET POLICIES, SHOWING THAT DOCTRINE OF PEACEFUL COEXISTENCE HAS ALTERNATED WITH THAT OF WORLD REVOLUTION. CONCLUDES THAT COEXISTENCE IS DOCTRINE OF CONVENIENCE, NOT CONVICTION.

1892 LEROY P.
L'ORGANIZATION CONSTITUTIONNELLE ET LES CRISES.
PARIS: PICHON ET DURAND-AUZIAS, 1966, 328 PP.
EXAMINES CONSTITUTIONAL ORGANIZATION DURING CRISIS, EMPHASIZING PRE-EMINENCE OF EXECUTIVE POWER, REDUCTION OF LEGISLATIVE AND JUDICIAL POWER, AND REFERENDUM. INCLUDES MAJOR DISCUSSION OF CRISIS PROVISIONS UNDER THE FIFTH REPUBLIC.

1893 LETHBRIDGE H.J.
CHINA'S URBAN COMMUNES.
HONG KONG: DRAGONFLY BOOKS, 1961, 74 PP.
ANALYZES STRUCTURE OF THESE COMMUNES WHICH PROVIDE SOCIAL ORGANIZATION FOR ONE FOURTH OF WORLD'S PEOPLE. SEES SIGNIFICANCE OF THESE COMMUNES FOR REST OF WORLD SINCE CHINA FEELS US WILL BE ORGANIZED THIS WAY "WHEN WORKERS AND PEASANTS SEIZE POWER." COVERS ORIGIN OF COMMUNAL IDEA, ITS PLACE IN CHINESE IDEOLOGY, AND REASONS FOR ITS RAPID GROWTH SINCE 1960.

1894 LETHBRIDGE H.J.
THE PEASANT AND THE COMMUNES.
HONG KONG: GREEN PAGODA PR, 1963, 202 PP.
DESCRIBES ROLE OF CHINESE PEASANT IN COMMUNAL SYSTEM. EVALUATES COMMUNIST AGRARIAN POLICY, 1921-58. DISCUSSES SOCIAL ASPECTS OF COMMUNES AND SUGGESTS REASONS FOR THEIR FAILURE TO SOLVE ASIA'S FARM PROBLEM. REVIEWS ALTERNATIVE SOLUTIONS. COMPARES RUSSIA'S AND CHINA'S EXPERIENCES.

1895 LEVCIK B.
"WAGES AND EMPLOYMENT PROBLEMS IN THE NEW SYSTEM OF PLANNED MANAGEMENT IN CZECHOSLOVAKIA."
INTERNATIONAL LABOR REVIEW, 95 (APR. 67), 299-314.
ECONOMIC REFORMS IN CZECHOSLOVAKIA HAVE RECENTLY GIVEN MUCH GREATER INDIVIDUAL RESPONSIBILITY TO WORKERS WHILE MAINTAINING THE PRINCIPLE OF CENTRAL PLANNING. AUTHOR VIEWS THIS AS PROGRESSIVE PROGRAM OFFERING WIDER WAGE DIFFERENTIALS, RAISING MORALE, AND INCREASING WORKER MOBILITY. EXPECTS THIS DIVERSIFIED APPROACH TO IMPROVE PRODUCTION AND THE ECONOMY IN GENERAL.

1896 LEVI W.
"INDIAN NEUTRALISM RECONSIDERED."
PACIF. AFF., 37 (SUMMER 64), 137-147.
RE-EXAMINES INDIA'S POLICY IN LIGHT OF THEIR BORDER DISPUTE WITH CHINA. FINDS THAT ALTHOUGH THE PEOPLE TEND TO RETAIN THEIR SAME ISOLATIONIST OPINIONS, INDIA HAS NECESSARILY CHANGED. FEELS THAT ALTHOUGH INDIA BENEFITTED FROM NEUTRALISM, IT 'COULD ONLY EXIST IF IMPORTANT OTHER NATIONS WERE NOT NEUTRALIST.' LOOKS TO A RE-EXAMINATION OF INDIAN NEUTRALISM IN THE FACE OF REALITY.

1897 LEVI W.
"THE CONCEPT OF INTEGRATION IN RESEARCH ON PEACE."
BACKGROUND, 9 (AUG. 65), 111-126.
INTEGRATION IS ACCEPTED AS A NECESSARY PROCESS FOR PACIFYING THE INTERNATIONAL SYSTEM. LEVI COMPARES INTEGRATION IN NATIONAL STATES WHICH ARE INTERNALLY PEACEFUL TO THE INTEGRATIVE ACTIVITIES IN THE INTERNATIONAL SYSTEM. FINDS THE ESSENTIAL DIFFERENCE IN THE LACK OF EMOTIONAL ATTACHMENT TO AN OVER-ALL END, LIKE BUILDING AND MAINTAINING A PEACEFUL INTERNATIONAL ORGANIZATION IN THE INTERNATIONAL SYSTEM.

1898 LEVI W.
"THE ELITIST NATURE OF NEW ASIA'S FOREIGN POLICY."
ASIAN SURVEY, 7 (NOV. 67), 762-775.
AUTHOR STATES THAT THE LEADERS OF THE NEW ASIAN COUNTRIES WERE INSPIRED BY NATIONALISM WHILE THE MASSES, ESPECIALLY IN THE RURAL AREAS, HAD NOT YET DEVELOPED A NATIONAL CONSCIOUSNESS. THE LEADERS BEGAN DEVOTING THEMSELVES TO PROMOTING NATIONALISM. THE NATIONALISM THAT RESULTED CHANGED FROM A WESTERN ORIENTATION TO IDEALS ROOTED IN NATIVE CULTURE.

1899 LEVIN L.A.
BIBLIOGRAFIIA BIBLIOGRAFII PROIZVEDENII K. MARKSA, F. ENGELSA, V.I. LENINA.
MOSCOW: GOS IZD POLIT LIT, 1961, 238 PP.
RUSSIAN BIBLIOGRAPHY OF MARX, ENGELS, AND LENIN.

1900 LEVIN M.G., POTAPOV L.P.
THE PEOPLES OF SIBERIA.
CHICAGO: U OF CHICAGO PRESS, 1956, 948 PP.
HISTORICAL AND ETHNOGRAPHIC STUDY OF OVER 30 TRIBES OF SOUTHERN AND NORTHERN SIBERIA AND SIBERIAN TRIBES OF FAR EAST. DISCUSSES LIVES, CUSTOMS, CULTURE, AND SOCIO-ECONOMIC CONDITIONS OF TRIBES.

1901 LEVIN M.G.
ETHNIC ORIGINS OF THE PEOPLES OF NORTHEASTERN ASIA.
TORONTO: U OF TORONTO PRESS, 1963, 350 PP.
ETHNOGENETIC STUDY OF RACIAL ORIGIN AND RELATION TO CULTURE, CONCENTRATING MOSTLY ON HEREDITARY ASPECTS AND INTERPLAY OF RACES IN PRODUCING HYBRIDS. STUDIES EFFECT OF CULTURE ON RACIAL PURITY.

1902 LEVINE L.
SYNDICALISM IN FRANCE (2ND ED.)
NEW YORK: COLUMBIA U PRESS, 1914, 229 PP.
CONCERNED WITH REVOLUTIONARY SYNDICALISM IN THEORY AND PRACTICE; TREATS IT AS FUSION OF REVOLUTIONARY SOCIALISM AND TRADE UNIONISM. REVIEWS LABOR MOVEMENT IN FRANCE, 1789-1871, TO COMMUNE AND ORIGIN OF GENERAL CONFEDERATION OF LABOR. EXPLICATES DOCTRINES OF THEORISTS AND DEVELOPMENTS SINCE 1902. SURVEYS CHARACTERISTICS AND CONDITIONS OF FRENCH SOCIETY MAKING FRANCE RECEPTIVE TO SYNDICALISM.

1903 LEVINE R.A.
"ANTI-EUROPEAN VIOLENCE IN AFRICA: A COMPARATIVE ANALYSIS."
J. CONFL. RESOLUT., 3 (DEC. 59), 420-429.
ANALYZES INCIDENCE OF VIOLENCE BY APPLYING THE 'CONFLICT-DRIVE' PSYCHOLOGICAL THEORY TO SEVERAL ACTUAL SITUATIONS IN AFRICA AND DERIVES HYPOTHESIS FOR PREDICTING SCOPE OF DISORDER. SUPPOSITION BASED ON CONSISTENCY OF COLONIAL REPRESSION PRACTICED BY FORMER RULING POWERS.

1904 LEVINE R.A.
"THE INTERNALIZATION OF POLITICAL VALUES IN STATELESS SOCIETIES."
HUM. ORG., 19 (SUMMER 60), 51-58.
STUDY OF TWO EAST AFRICAN SOCIETIES LED AUTHOR TO CONCLUDE THAT EVEN STATELESS SOCIETIES HAVE AUTHORITY STRUCTURES WITH REGARD TO ALLOCATION OF POWER. LOCAL DECISION-MAKING UNIT PROVIDES ADULTS WITH MODEL FOR BEHAVIOR TOWARDS INCIPIENT STRUCTURES IN WIDER SOCIETY.

1905 LEVINE R.A. ED.
"THE ANTHROPOLOGY OF CONFLICT."
J. CONFL. RESOLUT., 5 (MAR. 61), 3-108.
CROSS-CULTURAL STUDY OF INTRAFAMILY, INTRA COMMUNITY, INTERCOMMUNITY STRUCTURAL LEVELS. EVALUATION OF CULTURAL PATTERNS, SOURCES, AND FUNCTIONS OF CONFLICT BASED ON SPECIALIZED LITERATURE.

1906 LEVY J-P.
THE ECONOMIC LIFE OF THE ANCIENT WORLD.
CHICAGO: U OF CHICAGO PRESS, 1967, 147 PP., LC#67-20575.
TRACES EVOLUTION OF MAN'S ECONOMIC ACTIVITY FROM GRECO-ORIENTAL CULTURE BEFORE ALEXANDER TO THE FALL OF ROME. DESCRIBES PREMONETARY STATES, ADVENT OF MONEY, GROWTH OF COMMERCE, AND SOCIAL CONSEQUENCES OF COMMERCIAL ACTIVITY FOR EACH PERIOD COVERED: EARLY EGYPTIAN, PHOENICIAN, CLASSICAL GREEK, AND CARTHAGINIAN, ETRUSCAN, EARLY AND LATE ROMAN CULTURES.

1907 LEVY M.
THE STRUCTURE OF SOCIETY.
PRINCETON: U. PR., 1952, 584 PP., $5.00.
OFFERS PROCEDURE WHEREBY SEGMENT OF A SOCIETY MAY BE

ANALYZED AND RELATED TO THE WHOLE. EMPHASIZES NECESSITY FOR INTELLIGENT DEFINITIONS OF ALL TERMS USED IN ANY SOCIAL-SCIENCE INQUIRY.

1908 LEWIN E.
ROYAL EMPIRE SOCIETY BIBLIOGRAPHIES NO. 9: SUB-SAHARA AFRICA.
LONDON: ROYAL COMMONWEALTH SOC, 1945, 104 PP.
INTENDED TO DEAL SPECIFICALLY WITH SOUTH AFRICA, DIVIDES SOURCES INTO FOUR CATEGORIES: ADMINISTRATIVE, POLITICAL, ECONOMIC, AND SOCIOLOGICAL.

1909 LEWIN J.
POLITICS AND LAW IN SOUTH AFRICA.
NEW YORK: MONTHLY REVIEW PR, 1963, 115 PP.
EXAMINATION OF RELATION OF AFRIKANER NATIONALISM, AFRICAN NATIONALISM, AND ENGLISH ECONOMIC INTERESTS TO PRESENT FORM OF GOVERNMENT IN SOUTH AFRICA. EXPLAINS DEVELOPMENT OF SEPARATE NATIONALISM OF WHITE AFRICAN AND ATTAINMENT OF POWER DESPITE LARGER BLACK AFRICAN POPULATION AND MORE POWERFUL BRITISH ECONOMIC INFLUENCE.

1910 LEWIN P.
THE FOREIGN TRADE OF COMMUNIST CHINA* ITS IMPACT ON THE FREE WORLD.
NEW YORK: FREDERICK PRAEGER, 1964, 128 PP., LC#64-16671.
IN THE FUTURE ANY MAJOR CHANGES IN CHINA'S BEHAVIOR AS A BUYER OR SELLER IN THE INTERNATIONAL MARKETS COULD HAVE IMPORTANT CONSEQUENCES. THEREFORE, LEWIN PRESENTS A HISTORY OF CHINESE TRADING PRACTICES (PRE & POST REVOLUTION), DEVELOPMENTAL EXPERIENCES UNDER COMMUNISM, HER MODEST FOREIGN AID PROGRAM, AND THE REACTIONS OF TRADE PATTERNS TO SINO-SOVIET SPLIT. WEALTH OF DATA ON ALL OF ABOVE.

1911 LEWIS B.
"THE QUEST FOR FREEDOM--A SAD STORY OF THE MIDDLE EAST."
ENCOUNTER, 22 (MARCH 64), 29-40.
DISCUSSES THE ATTEMPT TO INTRODUCE REPRESENTATIVE AND CONSTITUTIONAL GOVERNMENT IN THE MIDDLE EAST, AND ITS GENERAL FAILURE IN ALL BUT ISRAEL, TURKEY AND LEBANON. ALSO CONSIDERS ECONOMIC AND POLITICAL RADICALISM AS A POWERFUL FORCE WHICH HAS GIVEN NEW DRIVE AND DIRECTION TO ARAB NATIONALISM.

1912 LEWIS B.W.
"BRITISH PLANNING AND NATIONALIZATION."
NEW YORK: TWENTIETH CENT FUND, 1952.
DESCRIBES ACQUISITION OF POWER BY BRITISH LABOR PARTY AND SUMMARIZES INITIAL OPERATIONS OF THE NATIONALIZED INDUSTRIES. EXPLORES SELECTED AREAS IN WHICH LABOR GOVERNMENT HAS UNDERTAKEN TO CONTROL ECONOMIC LIFE OF THE NATION: COAL, TRANSPORT, IRON, STEEL, AND ELECTRIC POWER INDUSTRIES, NATIONAL HEALTH SERVICE, HOUSING, AGRICULTURE. TOPICALLY ARRANGED, UNANNOTATED BIBLIOGRAPHY OF BOOKS, MONOGRAPHS, ETC.

1913 LEWIS E.
MEDIEVAL POLITICAL IDEAS.
NEW YORK: ALFRED KNOPF, 1954, 356 PP.
A TEXTBOOK OF MEDIEVAL POLITICAL THOUGHT COVERING THE PERIOD BETWEEN THE INVESTITURE STRUGGLE AND 15TH CENTURY. COLLECTION OF DOCUMENTS AND COMMENTARIES TOPICALLY ORGANIZED; SELECTIONS REVEAL CHARACTERISTIC FEATURES OF THE SYSTEMS OF MOST ORIGINAL PUBLICISTS AND PROVIDE VIEWPOINTS TYPICAL OF ALL MEDIEVAL THOUGHT AND IMPORTANT SCHOOLS. DETAILED DESCRIPTION OF SOURCES LOCATED IN NOTES.

1914 LEWIS E.G.
"PARLIAMENTARY CONTROL OF NATIONALIZED INDUSTRY IN FRANCE."
AM. POL. SCI. REV., 51 (SEPT. 57), 669-684.
STUDIES METHODS USED BY PARLIAMENT, AND NOTES THAT WHILE PARLIAMENT MAINTAINS LITTLE INFLUENCE ON MAJOR DECISIONS IT RETAINS POTENTIALLY ENORMOUS POWERS AND HAS DEVELOPED EFFECTIVE CONTROL OVER THE NATIONALIZED INDUSTRIES. CITES INCREASING CONTROL THROUGH USE OF COMMITTEES CREATED TO STUDY AND CHECK ABUSES.

1915 LEWIS R., CROSSLEY H.M.
"OPINION SURVEYING IN KOREA."
PUB. OPIN. QUART., 28 (SUMMER 64), 257-72.
DISCUSSES THE DIFFICULTIES, ACCOMPLISHMENTS AND PROSPECTS OF SURVEY RESEARCH IN A COUNTRY WHICH HAS ASSIGNED IT AN IMPORTANT AND INCREASING ROLE IN POLITICAL AND SOCIAL DEVELOPMENT.

1916 LEWIS W.A.
POLITICS IN WEST AFRICA.
LONDON: ALLEN & UNWIN, 1965, 90 PP.
ANALYSIS OF PRESENT-DAY POLITICS IN WEST AFRICA. STUDIES ORIGIN AND BASIS OF POLITICAL PARTIES, ISSUES OF ECONOMIC POLICY, INTERNATIONAL RELATIONS, FEDERALISM, SINGLE PARTY SYSTEM, AND FORM OF REPRESENTATION AND PROSEPCT FOR CHANGE.

1917 LEYBURN J.G.
THE HAITIAN PEOPLE (REV. ED.)
NEW HAVEN: YALE U PR, 1966, 342 PP.
DESCRIBES THE SOCIAL STRUCTURE ESTABLISHED IN HAITI AFTER GAINING INDEPENDENCE IN 1804. SETS GROWTH OF SOCIAL INSTITUTIONS IN CONTEXT OF ORIGINS IN SLAVERY AND FRENCH COLONIAL LIFE. EXAMINES THE DEVELOPMENT OF SOCIAL INSTITUTIONS DURING 19TH CENTURY, CONSIDERING THE IMPACT OF DAILY EXIGENCIES UPON LOGICAL SOCIAL STRUCTURES.

1918 LEYDER J.
BIBLIOGRAPHIE DE L'ENSEIGNEMENT SUPERIEUR ET DE LA RECHERCHE SCIENTIFIQUE EN AFRIQUE INTERTROPICALE (2 VOLS.)
BRUSSELS: CEN DOC ECO ET SOC AFR, 1960, 287 PP.
ANNOTATED BIBLIOGRAPHY OF 1,025 WORKS IN WESTERN LANGUAGES COVERING PERIOD 1940-59. MATERIAL IS CHRONOLOGICALLY ARRANGED AND PROVIDES ANALYTICAL ANNOTATIONS IN FRENCH TOGETHER WITH COMPLETE BIBLIOGRAPHICAL INFORMATION. MANY SOURCES GATHERED FROM DOCUMENTS OF OFFICIAL ORGANS AND SCIENTIFIC INSTITUTIONS. CONTAINS A COMPREHENSIVE ALPHABETICAL INDEX.

1919 LEYS C.
"MODELS, THEORIES, AND THE THEORY OF POLITICAL PARTIES"
POLITICAL STUDIES, 7 (JUNE 59), 127-146.
AN APPROACH TO A NEW THEORY OF THE INFLUENCE OF ELECTORAL SYSTEMS ON PARTY SYSTEMS THROUGH THE PRESENTATION OF FORMALLY CONSTRUCTED ANALOGUES, OR "MODELS." PRESENTS A GRAPHIC EXAMINATION OF THE DOCTRINE THAT THE SIMPLE-MAJORITY, SINGLE-BALLOT SYSTEM OF VOTING, IN SINGLE-MEMBER CONSTITUENCIES, FAVORS TWO-PARTY SYSTEMS, WHILE PROPORTIONAL SYSTEMS OF REPRESENTATION FAVOR MULTIPARTY SYSTEMS.

1920 LEYS W.
ETHICS FOR POLICY DECISIONS.
NEW YORK: PRENTICE HALL, 1952, 362 PP.
SURVEY OF MAJOR SYSTEMS OF ETHICS FROM PLATO TO DEWEY. CONTENDS THAT IF ONE ADOPTS A PHILOSOPHICAL STANCE IN WHICH ANY POLICY SOLUTION IS QUESTIONED, THEN ALTERNATIVES BECOME MORE APPARENT.

1921 LI C.M. ED.
INDUSTRIAL DEVELOPMENT IN COMMUNIST CHINA.
NEW YORK: PRAEGER, 1964, 205 PP., $5.00.
PRESENTS UP TO DATE INFORMATION AND CRITICAL ANALYSES ON CAPITAL FORMATION, WORK-INCENTIVE POLICY, ECONOMIC PLANNING, CHANGES IN THE STEEL INDUSTRY, HANDICRAFTS AND AGRICULTURE, SINO-SOVIET TRADE AND EXCHANGE RATES, AND THE DIFFICULTIES IN MEASURING CHINESE INDUSTRIAL OUTPUT.

1922 LIBRARY HUNGARIAN ACADEMY SCI
HUNGARIAN PUBLICATIONS ON ASIA AND AFRICA, 1950-1962: A SELECTED BIBLIOGRAPHY (PAMPHLET)
BUDAPEST: HUNG ACAD SCI PUBL, 1963, 106 PP.
MATERIALS ON AFRICA AND ASIA WRITTEN ONLY BY HUNGARIAN AUTHORS. ARRANGED BY CONTINENT AND SUBDIVIDED BY COUNTRY. MOST OF 800 ITEMS IN HUNGARIAN, BUT SOME IN FRENCH. HUNGARIAN TITLES TRANSLATED. MOST WORKS ARE SCHOLARLY IN NATURE WITH CONCLUDING AUTHOR INDEX.

1923 LICHFIELD N.
"THE EVALUATION OF CAPITAL INVESTMENT PROJECTS IN TOWN CENTRE REDEVELOPMENT."
PUBLIC ADMINISTRATION, 45 (SUMMER 67), 129-147.
DISCUSSES FINANCIAL COST AND RETURNS IN BRITISH TOWN CENTER DEVELOPMENT SCHEMES. REVIEWS LIMITATIONS IN CONVENTIONAL ECONOMIC ANALYSES OF THE SITUATION. PROPOSES COST-BENEFIT ANALYSIS METHOD AS A TOOL FOR RATIONAL PUBLIC DECISION-MAKING, AND OUTLINES SCHEME'S TECHNIQUE.

1924 LICHTHEIM G.
MARXISM.
NEW YORK: FREDERICK PRAEGER, 1961, 410 PP., LC#61-08694.
EXAMINES CULTURAL EVOLUTION OF MARXISM, ITS PHILOSOPHIC, ECONOMIC, AND POLITICAL FOUNDATIONS. CONSIDERS INFLUENCE ON AND BY OTHER THEORIES OF ITS PERIOD, COMPARING IT TO NATIONALISM, DEMOCRACY, ANARCHISM, AND VICTORIAN BOURGEOIS SOCIETY.

1925 LIEBER F.
CIVIL LIBERTY AND SELF GOVERNMENT: VOLUME 2.
PHILADELPHIA: J B LIPPINCOTT, 1853, 371 PP.
FIRST PART OF VOLUME CONSISTS OF NINE CHAPTERS DISCUSSING EFFECTS AND USES OF INSTITUTIONAL SELF-GOVERNMENT AND ANALYZING CONCEPTS OF IMPERATORIAL SOVEREIGNTY AND CENTRALIZATION. SECOND PART CONSISTS OF 25 APPENDIXES ANALYZING IMPORTANT DOCUMENTS AND SPECIALIZED PROBLEMS CONCERNING CIVIL LIBERTY AND SELF-GOVERNMENT.

1926 LIEBERSON S.
"THE IMPACT OF RESIDENTIAL SEGREGATION ON ETHNIC ASSIMILATION" (BMR)"
SOCIAL FORCES, 40 (OCT. 61), 52-57.
THE RESIDENTIAL SEGREGATION OF IMMIGRANTS IN 10 AMERICAN CITIES IS RE-EXAMINED FOR SPECIFIC IMMIGRANT GROUPS TO ASCERTAIN THE IMPACT OF SEGREGATION ON OTHER ASPECTS OF ETHNIC ASSIMILATION. ABILITY TO SPEAK ENGLISH, CITIZENSHIP, INTERMARRIAGE, AND OCCUPATIONAL COMPOSITION ARE VIEWED AS FUNCTIONS OF RESIDENTIAL PATTERNS AND OTHER ECOLOGICAL

FACTORS.

1927 LIEBKNECHT W.P.C.
SOCIALISM (2 PTS.; 1875, 1894) (PAMPHLET)
CHICAGO: CHARLES H KERR, 1900, 64 PP.
CLAIMS THAT IN MODERN DEMOCRACY WORKERS ARE STILL SUBJUGATED BECAUSE WEALTH REMAINS IN CAPITALIST HANDS. ADVOCATES MAKING THE NATIONAL ECONOMY AS DEMOCRATIC AS THE POLITICAL SPHERE. SECOND PART GIVES THE SOCIALIST PROGRAM, WHICH INCLUDES THE ABOLITION OF CHILD LABOR, AN EIGHT-HOUR DAY, A THREE-DAY WEEKEND, AND THE ABOLITION OF NIGHT WORK.

1928 LIENHARDT G.
SOCIAL ANTHROPOLOGY.
LONDON: OXFORD U PR, 1964, 215 PP.
DIFFERENTIATES CULTURAL ANTHROPOLOGY FROM SOCIOLOGY AND HISTORY, EMPHASIZING RELEVANCE OF PAST AND PHYSICAL REALITIES TO PRESENT CULTURE. DISCUSSES EFFECTS OF ENVIRONMENT, ECONOMICS, AND POLITICS ON SOCIETY.

1929 LIEUWEN E.
GENERALS VS PRESIDENTS: NEOMILITARISM IN LATIN AMERICA.
NEW YORK: FREDERICK PRAEGER, 1964, 160 PP., LC#64-22492.
AN EXAMINATION OF THE CHANGES MADE BY PRESIDENT KENNEDY IN THE TRADITIONAL US POLICY TOWARD THE LATIN AMERICAN MILITARY. EMPHASIZES PRESENT-DAY MILITARISM AND THE RELATION BETWEEN ARMED FORCES AND THE SOCIO-POLITICAL CRISIS IN MOST LATIN AMERICAN COUNTRIES. ARGUMENT RESTS UPON BASIC ASSUMPTION THAT LATIN AMERICA IS PRESENTLY IN THE MIDST OF AN ACUTE SOCIAL, ECONOMIC, AND POLITICAL CRISIS.

1930 LIGGETT E.
BRITISH POLITICAL ISSUES: VOLUME 1.
NEW YORK: PERGAMON PRESS, 1964, 232 PP., LC#64-8868.
FIRST VOLUME OF FOUR VOLUME SERIES. PROVIDES GENERAL SURVEY OF PARTY POLITICS AND ITS RELATIONSHIPS TO NATIONAL GOVERNMENT AND FOREIGN POLICY, BRITISH JUDICIAL SYSTEM, AND GOVERNMENT AGENCIES PUBLISHING POLITICAL REPORTS AND INFORMATION. FOCUSES ON RECENT POLITICAL ISSUES AND DEVELOPMENTS.

1931 LIGOT M.
"LA COOPERATION MILITAIRE DANS LES ACCORDS, PASSES ENTRE LA FRANCE ET LES ETATS AFRICAINS ET MALGACHE D'EXPRESSION." FRANCAISE.
REV. JURID. POLIT. OUTREMER, 17 (OCT.-DEV. 63), 517-32.
EXAMINES MILITARY AGREEMENTS OF FRANCE AND FRENCH SPEAKING AFRICAN COUNTRIES. BECAUSE OF STRATEGIC POSITION OF AFRICAN COUNTRIES, FRANCE CONTINUES POLICY OF DEFENDING FORMER COLONIES. GIVES LARGE AMOUNTS OF TECHNICAL AID.

1932 LINDSAY K.
EUROPEAN ASSEMBLIES: THE EXPERIMENTAL PERIOD 1949-1959.
NEW YORK: PRAEGER, 1960, 267 PP.
EXAMINES EXPERIMENTIAL BEGINNINGS OF EUROPEAN ASSEMBLIES. OUTLINES RELATIONS WITH NATIONAL BODIES, INHERENT PROBLEMS AND POSSIBILITIES FOR FUTURE EVOLUTION.

1933 LINEBARGER P.
PSYCHOLOGICAL WARFARE.
WASHINGTON, DC: COMBAT FORCES PR, 1948, 259 PP.
DEFINES CONCEPT OF PSYCHOLOGICAL WARFARE AND ITS INHERENT LIMITS. DESCRIBES ITS USE IN BOTH WWI AND WWII AND STUDIES ACTUAL PROCEDURES IN PLANNING AND OPERATION.

1934 LING D.L.
"TUNISIA: FROM PROTECTORATE TO REPUBLIC."
BLOOMINGTON: INDIANA U PR, 1967.
BOOK IN GENERAL TRACES DEVELOPMENT OF TUNISIA FROM A FRENCH PROTECTORATE THROUGH ITS FIGHT FOR INDEPENDENCE INTO A MODERN NATION. GOOD BIBLIOGRAPHIC LISTING OF TUNISIAN GOVERNMENT PUBLICATIONS, FRENCH, BRITISH, AND AMERICAN PUBLICATIONS, DIPLOMATIC DOCUMENTS AND CORRESPONDENCE, PERIODICALS, AND NEWSPAPERS. 200 ENTRIES.

1935 LINTON R.
THE CULTURAL BACKGROUND OF PERSONALITY.
NEW YORK: APPLETON, 1945, 157 PP.
STUDIES INTERRELATIONSHIP OF CULTURE, SOCIETY AND INDIVIDUAL. FEELS CULTURE DOMINANT FACTOR IN ESTABLISHING BASIC PERSONALITY TYPE IN SOCIETIES AND IN FORMATION OF STATUS PERSONALITIES IN EACH.

1936 LIPPMANN W.
THE METHOD OF FREEDOM.
NEW YORK: MACMILLAN, 1934, 117 PP.
ANALYSIS OF CHALLENGES TO FREE GOVERNMENT, AND PRINCIPLES ACCORDING TO WHICH IT FUNCTIONS. DISCUSSES RELATIONSHIPS BETWEEN REPRESENTATIVE DEMOCRACY AND COMPENSATED ECONOMY. DIFFERENTIATES BETWEEN 19TH-CENTURY PRINCIPLES OF FREE GOVERNMENT AND THOSE EMERGING SINCE WWI. ANALYZES EVENTS AND CHANGES CAUSING NEW PRINCIPLES TO DEVELOP AND APPLICATION OF NEW PRINCIPLES IN POLITICAL AND ECONOMIC PROBLEMS.

1937 LIPSCOMB J.F.
WHITE AFRICANS.
LONDON: FABER AND FABER, 1955, 172 PP.
STUDY OF MULTIRACIAL STATUS OF KENYA AND PROSPECTS FOR MAINTAINING IT, WITH AFRICAN, EUROPEAN, AND ASIAN ELEMENTS INTERACTING AT ECONOMIC, SOCIAL, AND POLITICAL LEVELS.

1938 LIPSET S.M.
AGRARIAN SOCIALISM.
BERKELEY: U OF CALIF PR, 1950, 315 PP.
RISE AND EFFECTS OF SOCIALISM AMONG FARMERS IN SASKATCHEWAN. SOCIAL, POLITICAL, AND ECONOMIC EFFECTS OF COOPERATIVE COMMONWEALTH FEDERATION IN CANADA.

1939 LIPSET S.M., BENDIX R.
"POLITICAL SOCIOLOGY."
CURRENT SOCIOLOGY, 6 (1957), 79-169.
ESSAY ON NATURE AND METHODOLOGY OF POLITICAL SOCIOLOGY WITH SPECIAL REFERENCE TO DEVELOPMENT OF RESEARCH IN US AND WESTERN EUROPE. INCLUDES LENGTHY BIBLIOGRAPHY OF WORKS IN FIELD.

1940 LIPSET S.M., BENDIX R.
SOCIAL MOBILITY IN INDUSTRIAL SOCIETY.
BERKELEY: U OF CALIF PR, 1959, 309 PP., LC#58-12829.
AN EXAMINATION OF THE VALIDITY OF A NUMBER OF WIDELY ACCEPTED GENERALIZATIONS RELATING TO SOCIAL MOBILITY. CONTESTS THREE STATEMENTS: THAT THERE HAS BEEN LESS SOCIAL MOBILITY IN EUROPE THAN IN THE US; THAT SOCIAL MOBILITY TENDS TO DECLINE AS INDUSTRIAL SOCIETIES MATURE; AND THAT OPPORTUNITIES FOR ENTRANCE INTO THE BUSINESS ELITE BECOME MORE RESTRICTED WITH MATURE INDUSTRIALIZATION.

1941 LISTER L.
EUROPE'S COAL AND STEEL COMMUNITY.
NEW YORK: TWENTIETH CENTURY FUND, 1960, 495 PP.
TRACES THE DEVELOPMENT OF THE ECSC DURING ITS FIRST SIX YEARS OF EXISTENCE. TREATS ECSC AS A STEP TOWARDS EUROPEAN INTEGRATION. VIEWING ITS PROBLEMS IN ECONOMIC TERMS, OFFERS SUGGESTIONS FOR IMPROVING EFFICIENCY THROUGH GREATER INTERNATIONAL SPECIALIZATION.

1942 LITT T.
FREIHEIT UND LEBENS ORDNUNG.
HEIDELBERG: QUELLE UND MEYER, 1962, 172 PP.
INQUIRY INTO CONCEPT OF FREEDOM IN ITS RELATION TO THE STATE, THE ECONOMY, AND THE SCIENCES. INCLUDES DETAILED DISCUSSION OF COMMUNIST NOTION OF FREEDOM. ATTEMPTS TO COMPARE AND RECONCILE THE WESTERN AND EASTERN CONCEPTIONS OF FREEDOM.

1943 LIVINGSTON W.S.
FEDERALISM IN THE COMMONWEALTH - A BIBLIOGRAPHICAL COMMENTARY.
LONDON: CASSELL & CO LTD, 1963, 237 PP.
LIST OF BOOKS, PAMPHLETS, PERIODICALS, AND GOVERNMENT PUBLICATIONS ON FEDERALISM IN CANADA, AUSTRALIA, WEST INDIES, INDIA, PAKISTAN, MALAYA, NIGERIA, RHODESIA, AND NYASALAND. INCLUDES FEW FOREIGN-LANGUAGE PUBLICATIONS. ARRANGED GEOGRAPHICALLY AND BY SUBJECT. LISTS RECENT PUBLICATIONS.

1944 LLOYD H.D.
THE SWISS DEMOCRACY.
LONDON: ALLEN & UNWIN, 1908, 273 PP.
DISCUSSES SUCCESS OF SWISS IN COMBINING SOCIALISM WITH DEMOCRACY, ESPECIALLY IN TREATMENT OF WORKERS, IN NATIONALIZATION OF CERTAIN INDUSTRIES, IN MAINTENANCE OF CANTONS' INDIVIDUALITY, IN CONTROL OF MONOPOLIES, AND IN INDIVIDUAL LIBERTY. SUGGESTS EXAMPLES TO BE FOLLOWED IN US.

1945 LOBINGIER C.S.
THE PEOPLE'S LAW OR POPULAR PARTICIPATION IN LAW-MAKING.
NEW YORK: MACMILLAN, 1909, 429 PP.
A STUDY OF THE EVOLUTION OF POPULAR PARTICIPATION IN LAW-MAKING FROM ANCIENT FOLKMOOT TO MODERN REFERENDUM. SPECIAL ATTENTION GIVEN TO ORIGINS AND DEVELOPMENT OF US CONSTITUTION AND POPULAR RATIFICATION IN THE VARIOUS STATES. FINAL SECTION DISCUSSES POPULAR PARTICIPATION IN LAW-MAKING OUTSIDE THE US.

1946 LOCKE J.
TWO TREATISES OF GOVERNMENT (1690)
NEW YORK: HAFNER PUBL, 1947, 311 PP.
ATTEMPT TO JUSTIFY ENGLISH REVOLUTION OF 1688, AND CHANGE IN LINE OF SUCCESSION, BY FOUNDING WILLIAM III'S TITLE ON CONSENT OF PEOPLE. STRESSES CONSENT OF PEOPLE AS BASIS FOR GOVERNMENT. MAN CONSENTS TO GOVERNMENT BECAUSE OF "INCONVENIENCE OF STATE OF NATURE." IMPLICATION OF POSITION IS THAT MEN ARE EQUAL, AND THAT STATE'S FUNCTION IS TO PROVIDE EQUAL PROTECTION OF MAN'S NATURAL RIGHTS.

1947 LOCKE J., GOUGH J.W. ED.
THE SECOND TREATISE OF GOVERNMENT: AN ESSAY CONCERNING THE TRUE ORIGINAL EXTENT AND END OF CIVIL GOVERNMENT (3RD ED.)
NEW YORK: BARNES AND NOBLE, 1966, 124 PP.
DISCUSSES STATE OF NATURE IN WHICH ALL MEN ARE FREE AND EQUAL AND HAVE RIGHT TO DEFEND LAWS OF NATURE. CONTRASTS THIS WITH CIVIL SOCIETY AND ITS COMMON JUDGE. ADMITS

INCONVENIENCE OF STATE OF NATURE AND SUGGESTS ESTABLISHMENT OF NONABSOLUTE GOVERNMENT. PURPOSE OF GOVERNMENT IS TO SAFEGUARD NATURAL RIGHTS, ESPECIALLY RIGHT OF PROPERTY. STATES LIMITS OF PROPER CIVIL GOVERNMENT.

1948 LOCKWOOD W.W.
"THE SOCIALISTIC SOCIETY: INDIA AND JAPAN."
FOREIGN AFFAIRS, 37 (OCT. 58), 117-130.
CONTRASTS INDIAN AND JAPANESE PHILOSOPHY AND PRACTICE OF INDUSTRIAL ENTERPRISE. POINTS OUT CONTRAST BETWEEN BUSINESS LEADERSHIP AND CAPITALISTIC ORIENTATION OF JAPAN, AND POLITICAL INITIATIVE AND SOCIALIST ORIENTATION OF INDIA. SHOWS DIFFERENCES IN EACH GOVERNMENT'S ACTIONS TO INFLUENCE RATE OF CAPITAL FORMATION AND INVESTMENT. COMPARES BANKING SYSTEMS IN TWO COUNTRIES.

1949 LOCKWOOD W.W., ED.
THE STATE AND ECONOMIC ENTERPRISE IN JAPAN; ESSAYS IN THE POLITICAL ECONOMY OF GROWTH.
PRINCETON: PRINCETON U PRESS, 1965, 753 PP., LC#65-15386.
EXAMINES RAPID ECONOMIC MODERNIZATION OF JAPAN SINCE 1868. SUGGESTS THAT JAPAN'S UNIQUENESS IN ECONOMIC GROWTH CAN BE ATTRIBUTED TO INTERPLAY OF INITIATIVES ENERGIZING INDUSTRIALIZATION. DISCUSSES PHASES OF GROWTH, ROLE OF AGRICULTURE, SOURCES OF ENTREPRENEURSHIP, GOALS OF PROGRESS AND POSSIBILITIES OF CONTINUENCE, RELATIONS OF ECONOMY WITH POLITICAL DEMOCRACY, AND PARALLELS WITH EUROPE.

1950 LODGE G.C.
"REVOLUTION IN LATIN AMERICA."
FOREIGN AFFAIRS, 44 (JAN. 66), 173-197.
THE NATURE OF TRUE SOCIAL REVOLUTION AND THE PROBLEMS ONE MUST DEAL WITH IN LATIN AMERICA ARE PRESENTED. THE ROLES OF THE CHURCH, WORKERS GROUPS, AND THE NEW MANAGERS AS KEY REVOLUTIONARY FORCES ARE ANALYZED. AUTHOR SEES NEED FOR AMERICAN COUNTERPART GROUPS TO WORK COOPERATIVELY WITH THE ABOVE LATIN AMERICAN FORCES.

1951 LODGE H.C. ED.
THE HISTORY OF NATIONS (25 VOLS.)
NEW YORK: COLLIERS, 1928.
COLLECTION OF ESSAYS ON WORLD HISTORY BY LEADING AUTHORITIES. INCLUDES BIBLIOGRAPHY AND INDEXES.

1952 LOEWENBERG G.
"PARLIAMENTARISM IN WESTERN GERMANY: THE FUNCTIONING OF THE BUNDESTAG" (BMR)"
AM. POL. SCI. REV., 55 (MAR. 61), 87-102.
STUDIES GERMANY'S "LIVING CONSTITUTION" IN AN ATTEMPT TO DETERMINE WHETHER PARLIAMENTARY INSTITUTIONS CAN IN REALITY FUNCTION AS A PARLIAMENTARY SYSTEM OF GOVERNMENT. AUTHOR EXAMINES THE COMPOSITION OF THE BUNDESTAG, THE DEPUTY, HIS RELATION TO HIS PARTY, AND THE RELATION OF GOVERNMENT AND PARLIAMENT TO CONCLUDE THAT PARLIAMENTARY FORMS IN GERMANY DO NOT FUNCTION AS A PARLIAMENTARY SYSTEM OF GOVERNMENT.

1953 LOEWENSTEIN K.
"THE PRESIDENCY OUTSIDE THE UNITED STATES: A STUDY IN COMPARATIVE POLITICAL INSTITUTIONS."
J. OF POLITICS, 11 (AUG. 49), 447-496.
TREATS THE PRESIDENT AS GOVERNMENT'S CHIEF EXECUTIVE IN NATIONAL ADMINISTRATION, AND THE ROLE OF THE PRESIDENT IN INTERNATIONAL POLITICS. THEN EXAMINES THE PRESIDENCY IN THE PRESIDENTIAL SYSTEM, IN THE PARLIAMENTARY REPUBLIC, IN ASSEMBLY GOVERNMENT, AND IN THE DEVELOPING AUTHORITARIAN PRESIDENTIAL SYSTEM. CONCLUDES THAT PRESIDENCY COMBINES EFFECTIVE LEADERSHIP AND DEMOCRATIC CONTROL.

1954 LOFCHIE M.F.
"OKELLO'S REVOLUTION."
TRANSITION, 7 (OCT.-NOV. 67), 36-45.
EXAMINES ZANZIBAR REVOLUTION TO DISCOVER WHETHER IT WAS PRODUCT OF A CONSPIRACY. EVALUATES ATTEMPTS TO BLAME IT ON RIGHTIST AND LEFTIST GROUPS. COMPARES FACTS REPORTED BY PRESS WITH AUTHOR'S EXPERIENCE AND SEEKS EXPLANATION OF OKELLO'S 1967 DEFEAT. TIES THIS TO LOSS OF MILITARY CONTROL.

1955 LOGERECI A.
"ALBANIA AND CHINA* THE INCONGRUOUS ALLIANCE."
CURRENT HISTORY, 52 (APR. 67), 227-231.
BRIEF HISTORY OF SOVIET-ALBANIAN RIFT. ALBANIA'S TURN TO CHINA FOR LEADERSHIP. CHINA FINDS ALBANIAN EFFORTS USEFUL FOR PROPAGANDA PURPOSES. CONTROL OF INTERNAL AFFAIRS HAS ALSO BEEN ACHIEVED BY ACTIVE TAKEOVER OF PARTY APPARATUS AS WELL AS TECHNOLOGY.

1956 LOMBARDO TOLEDANO V
EL NEONAZISMO; SUS CHARACTERISTICAS Y PELIGROS.
MEXICO C: ESCUELA NAC CIENC POL, 1960, 109 PP.
ANALYZES DEVELOPMENT AND DANGER OF NEO-NAZI RESURGENCE IN GERMANY AND OTHER COUNTRIES. DISCUSSES ORIGINS OF NAZISM AS BEING DIRECT RESULT OF GERMAN IMPERIALISM IN 20TH CENTURY. CRITICIZES WEST GERMANY AS RETURNING TO FORMER POLICY OF IMPERIALISM THROUGH HARBORING NAZIS AND ALLOWING THEM TO INFLUENCE GOVERNMENT POLICY.

1957 LONDON K. ED.
"SINO-SOVIET RELATIONS IN THE CONTEXT OF THE 'WORLD SOCIALIST SYSTEM'."
IN (LONDON K, UNITY AND CONTRADICTION, NEW YORK: PRAEGER, 1962, 409-421).
'THE COHESION OF THE COMMUNIST BLOC, WHILE BASED ON THE PRINCIPLES OF MARXISM-LENINISM, IS ACHIEVED BY INTERNATIONAL COMMUNIST ORGANIZATION... WRITER IS RELUCTANT TO BELIEVE THAT THE COMMUNISTS WOULD SACRIFICE, FOR WHATEVER CAUSE, THEIR GREATEST ASSET - UNITY OF THE SOCIALIST CAMP.'

1958 LONDON K. ED.
EASTERN EUROPE IN TRANSITION.
BALTIMORE: JOHNS HOPKINS PRESS, 1966, 364 PP., LC#66-24409.
STUDIES POLITICAL, SOCIAL, AND ECONOMIC CHANGES IN EASTERN EUROPE SINCE KHRUSHCHEV ERA. EXAMINES TRANSITION FROM SYSTEM OF RIGID CONTROL BY USSR TO ONE OF LOOSELY CONNECTED SEMI-INDEPENDENT NATIONS. COVERS NATURE OF NATIONALISM AND EFFECT OF SINO-SOVIET SPLIT.

1959 LONDON DAILY TELEGRAPH
ELECTION '66: GALLUP ANALYSIS OF THE VOTING RESULTS.
LONDON: DAILY TELEGRAPH, 1966, 154 PP.
STATISTICAL ANALYSIS OF BRITISH ELECTIONS IN 1966. INCLUDES ARTICLES SETTING OUT MAIN FEATURES OF ELECTIONS, RECORDING CONSTITUENCY RESULTS, AND ON NEW HOUSE OF COMMONS. EACH ELECTORAL DISTRICT IS ANALYZED, SHOWING ELECTORATE, TURNOUT, NUMBER OF VOTES FOR EACH CANDIDATE, MAJORITY, AND "SWING" FROM 1959 TO 1964. A "TELEGRAPH" CORRESPONDENT ANALYZES WHY LABOUR WON.

1960 LONDON LIBRARY ASSOCIATION
ATHENAEUM SUBJECT INDEX. 1915-1918.
LONDON: LONDON LIB ASSOC.
AN ANNUAL SUBJECT INDEX TO PERIODICALS PUBLISHED BETWEEN 1915 AND 1918. INCLUDES SUBJECT ENTRIES, WITH AUTHOR INDEXES COVERING THE YEARS 1915-16 AND 1917-19. CONCENTRATES ON GENERAL SOCIAL SCIENCE PERIODICALS.

1961 LONG H.A.
USURPERS - FOES OF FREE MAN.
NEW YORK: POST PRINT CO, 1957, 115 PP.
DEFENDS CONSTITUTIONALISM AGAINST WHAT AUTHOR SEES TO BE ONSLAUGHT OF ADMINISTRATIONAL JURISDICTION. WARNS OF EXCESS IN FEDERAL CENTRALIZATION OF POWER. DISCUSSES FEDERAL GOVERNMENT BEFORE AND AFTER FDR. CLAIMS SUPREME COURT HAS USURPED MUCH OF POWER OF CONGRESS THROUGH PROCESS REVERSING INTERPRETATIONS OF THE CONSTITUTION TO SUIT JUSTICES.

1962 LOOMIE A.J.
THE SPANISH ELIZABETHANS: THE ENGLISH EXILES AT THE COURT OF PHILIP II.
NEW YORK: FORDHAM U PR, 1963, 280 PP., LC#63-14407.
ANALYZES CHIEF WAYS IN WHICH SPAIN AIDED EXILES DURING ANGLO-SPANISH WAR. COVERS BASIC RELATIONSHIP BETWEEN SPAIN AND ENGLISH CATHOLICS AND PROBLEMS THAT SPAIN'S POLICY CREATED. ANALYZES FIVE LEADING REFUGEES, USING THEIR CASES TO ILLUSTRATE BASIC TRENDS AND DIFFICULTIES IN SPANISH POLICY.

1963 LOOMIS C.P., BEEGLE J.A.
RURAL SOCIOLOGY.
ENGLEWOOD CLIFFS: PRENTICE HALL, 1957, 488 PP., LC#57-05316.
INTRODUCTORY SOCIOLOGY WITH SPECIAL APPLICATION TO STUDY OF RURAL, AGRICULTURAL SOCIETIES. EMPHASIS ON DEVELOPING TERMINOLOGY AND METHODOLOGY. NON-SPECIFIC.

1964 LOOS W.A. ED.
RELIGIOUS FAITH AND WORLD CULTURE.
NEW YORK: PRENTICE HALL, 1951, 294 PP.
ESTABLISHES THAT THE ESSENCE OF CIVILIZATION IS THE MORAL DISPOSITION OF THE INDIVIDUAL. INTERPRETS THE NATURE AND MEANING OF RELIGION, ANALYZES THE BREAKDOWN OF OUR CULTURE AND SUGGESTS WAYS TO STEM THE FLOODTIDE OF DISINTEGRATION.

1965 LOPEZ M.M. ED.
CATALOGOS DE PUBLICACIONES PERIODICAS MEXICANAS.
MEXICO CITY: EDIT STYLO DURANG, 1959.
BIBLIOGRAPHY OF MEXICAN PERIODICALS EXCLUDING DAILY AND ART REPRODUCTION PUBLICATIONS. CLARIFIES CONTENT OF PERIODICAL WHERE TITLE IS NOT CLEAR. INDICATES PAGE NUMBER, PUBLISHER, ILLUSTRATIONS, COSTS, PLACE PUBLISHED, ADVERTISEMENTS, DATES OF PUBLICATION AND OTHER PERTINENT INFORMATION. LISTED ALPHABETICALLY BY STATE OR DISTRICT. BASED ON PUBLICATIONS CURRENT IN 1928.

1966 LOPEZIBOR J.
"L'EUROPE, FORME DE VIE."
TABLE RONDE, 181 (FEB. 63), 162-75.
EUROPEAN WAY OF LIFE IS PRESENTED IN LIGHT OF PARTICULAR HISTORIC ATTITUDES THAT PERMITTED BIRTH AND DEVELOPMENT OF EUROPEAN NATIONS. STUDIES ITS CULTURAL PATTERNS AND RELATES THEM TO CHRISTIAN CONSCIENCE WHICH IS SEEN AS FIRST COMMON BASIS FOR EUROPEAN UNITY.

1967 LOPEZ-AMO A.

LA MONARQUIA DE LA REFORMA SOCIAL.
MADRID: EDICIONES RIALP, 1952, 314 PP.
DIALECTIC BETWEEN HUMAN RIGHTS AND FREEDOM, AND POWER OF THE RULING MONARCH. EXAMINED ARE: LEGITIMACY OF MONARCH, LEGITIMACY OF REVOLUTION, FREEDOM AND DEMOCRACY, MEDIEVAL AND MODERN STATES. INDIVIDUAL AND ORGANIC SOCIETY, FRUSTRATION OF SOCIAL REFORM, AND ROLE OF RULING MONARCH IN SOCIAL REFORM.

1968 LORWIN L.L.
ADVISORY ECONOMIC COUNCILS.
WASHINGTON: BROOKINGS INST, 1931, 84 PP.
SKETCHES SOURCES OF THE IDEA OF ECONOMIC COUNCILS AND OUTLINES VARIOUS TYPES OF THEM. STUDIES GERMAN AND FRENCH COUNCILS, SUMMARIZING WESTERN WORLD'S MOST SIGNIFICANT EXPERIENCE WITH ONE TYPE OF COUNCIL. DESCRIBES MAIN PROBLEMS RELATING TO GROWTH OF ADVISORY ECONOMIC COUNCILS AND INDICATES THEIR POSSIBILITIES.

1969 LOUCKS W.N.
COMPARATIVE ECONOMIC SYSTEMS (5TH ED.)
NEW YORK: HARPER & ROW, 1957, 862 PP., LC#57-8333.
COMPARATIVE STUDY OF ALTERNATIVE FORMS OF ECONOMIC ORGANIZATION WITH EMPHASIS ON ECONOMIC SYSTEMS IN ACTION. DISCUSSES EXPANDING FACETS OF SOCIALISM IN BRITAIN, RECENT DEVELOPMENTS IN SOVIET ECONOMY, AND NEWLY PROMINENT POTENTIALITIES OF CAPITALISM. UNANNOTATED BIBLIOGRAPHY RELATING TO POLITICO-ECONOMIC MATERIALS APPENDED TO EACH CHAPTER.

1970 LOVEDAY P., MARTIN A.W.
PARLIAMENT FACTIONS AND PARTIES: THE FIRST THIRTY YEARS OF RESPONSIBLE GOVERNMENT IN NEW SOUTH WALES, 1856-1889.
MELBOURNE: UNIVERSITY PRESS, 1966, 207 PP., LC#66-13036.
DESCRIBES EMERGENCE AND FUNCTIONING OF "FACTION" SYSTEM: A FORM OF REPRESENTATIVE GOVERNMENT IN WHICH SMALL, WELL-KNIT FOLLOWERS PROVIDE POWER-HUNGRY LEADERS WITH A NUCLEUS (FACTION) AROUND WHICH TO BUILD PARLIAMENTARY MAJORITIES. COLLECTIVE CABINET RESPONSIBILITY EXISTS DESPITE ABSENCE OF FORMAL PARTIES. SYSTEM BREAKS DOWN AND PARTIES EVOLVE WITH CHANGED ECONOMIC AND SOCIAL ORDER (LARGE ELECTORATE).

1971 LOVELL R.I.
THE STRUGGLE FOR SOUTH AFRICA, 1875-1899.
NEW YORK: MACMILLAN, 1934, 438 PP.
ANALYSIS OF SOUTH AFRICA AS SEEN IN DIPLOMATIC RELATIONS AND WAR IN THIS AREA. DEALS WITH EUROPEAN EXPANSION AND IN DETAIL WITH ANGLO-GERMAN RELATIONS, THE TWO MOST IMPORTANT POWERS ACTIVE IN SOUTH AFRICA. DISCUSSES POLICIES OF CECIL RHODES AND CONQUEST OF SOUTHERN RHODESIA.

1972 LOW D.A.
"LION RAMPANT."
J. COMMONWEALTH POLIT STUD., 2 (NOV. 64), 235-252.
OUTLINES FACTORS LEADING TO ESTABLISHMENT AND MAINTENANCE OF BRITISH AUTHORITY OVER ASIAN AND AFRICAN PEOPLES, TRACING METHODS USED TO PERPETUATE DOMINION.

1973 LOWELL A.L.
GOVERNMENTS AND PARTIES IN CONTINENTAL EUROPE (VOL. I)
CAMBRIDGE: HARVARD U PR, 1896, 380 PP.
CONSIDERS SEPARATELY THE NATIONS OF EUROPE, THEIR GOVERNMENTS, POLITICAL PARTIES, CONSTITUTIONS, AND STRUCTURE. ALSO DISCUSSES RELATION BETWEEN LOCAL AND NATIONAL GOVERNMENT IN EACH.

1974 LOWELL A.L.
GOVERNMENTS AND PARTIES IN CONTINENTAL EUROPE, VOL. II.
BOSTON: HOUGHTON MIFFLIN, 1896, 455 PP.
DISCUSSES VARIOUS ASPECTS OF THE INTERNAL POLITICS OF GERMANY, AUSTRIA-HUNGARY, AND SWITZERLAND, INCLUDING DYNAMICS OF POLITICAL POWER WITHIN EACH NATION, HISTORY OF POLITICAL PARTIES, AND INSTITUTIONS PECULIAR TO EACH.

1975 LOWENSTEIN A.K.
BRUTAL MANDATE: A JOURNEY TO SOUTH WEST AFRICA.
NEW YORK: MACMILLAN, 1962, 257 PP., LC#62-14204.
WORKINGS OF UN IN REPUBLIC OF SOUTH AFRICA. AN APPRAISAL OF US GOVERNMENT POLICY AND AN INDICATION OF WHAT CONCERNED INDIVIDUALS COULD DO.

1976 LOWER A.R.M., SCOTT F.R. ET AL.
EVOLVING CANADIAN FEDERALISM.
DURHAM: DUKE U PR, 1958, 187 PP., LC#58-11382.
ESSAYS BY CANADIAN LECTURERS ON PROBLEMS OF FEDERALISM PECULIAR TO CANADA. FOR EXAMPLE: NO PRESCRIBED PROCEDURE FOR AMENDING CONSTITUTION; BI-RACIAL SOCIETY; EVOLUTION FROM A BRITISH COLONY TO INDEPENDENT STATE.

1977 LUKASZEWSKI J.
"WESTERN INTEGRATION AND THE PEOPLE'S DEMOCRACIES."
FOREIGN AFFAIRS, 46 (JAN. 68), 377-387.
BELIEVES THAT CENTRAL EUROPEAN COUNTRIES OUGHT TO COUNTERBALANCE THEIR TIES WITH THE USSR BY CLOSER SOCIAL, ECONOMIC, AND POLITICAL RELATIONS WITH WESTERN EUROPE. HOPES FOR A UNIFIED CENTRAL EUROPE IN ECONOMIC ALLIANCE WITH THE EUROPEAN ECONOMIC COMMUNITY. DISCUSSES USSR'S OPPOSITION TO CENTRAL EUROPEAN ALLIANCE; FEDERATIONS HAVE BEEN VETOED BY MOSCOW AS A BOURGEOIS CONSPIRACY AGAINST THE USSR.

1978 LUNDBERG G.A.
"THE CONCEPT OF LAW IN THE SOCIAL SCIENCES"(BMR)"
PHILOSOPHY OF SCIENCE, 5 (APR. 38), 189-203.
DEMONSTRATES THAT THE APPARENT DIFFICULTY OF APPLYING THE METHODS OF NATURAL SCIENCE OF SOCIOLOGICAL PHENOMENA RESULTS NOT FROM ANY INTRINSIC CHARACTERISTICS OF SOCIOLOGICAL DATA, BUT FROM THE RETENTION IN SOCIOLOGY OF POSTULATES LONG SINCE REPUDIATED IN SCIENCE. CONTENDS THAT THE TERM SCIENTIFIC LAW CAN AND SHOULD MEAN EXACTLY WHAT IT MEANS IN THE OTHER SCIENCES.

1979 LUNDBERG G.A.
CAN SCIENCE SAVE US.
NEW YORK: LONGMANS, 1961, 150 PP.
EXPLORES PRE-SCIENTIFIC THOUGHTWAYS IN TECHNOLOGICAL AGE. DEPICTS THE TRANSITION TO SCIENCE IN HUMAN RELATIONS. STUDIES PROBLEM OF EDUCATION, ARTS, LITERATURE AND THE SPIRITUAL LIFE IN A SCIENTIFIC CONTEXT. GIVES INSIGHT INTO ATTITUDES OF TOTALITARIAN REGIMES.

1980 LUNT D.C.
THE ROAD TO THE LAW.
NEW YORK: MCGRAW HILL, 1932, 279 PP.
TRACES DEVELOPMENT OF LAW 1500-1930, IN ENGLAND, CANADA, AMERICA, AND AUSTRALIA AND EFFECT OF IT THERE UPON JURISPRUDENCE IN US. PURPORTS TO DEMONSTRATE VITAL AND CHANGEABLE NATURE OF THIS TYPE OF COMMON LAW, GIVING MORE IMPORTANT CASES AND DECISIONS AS ILLUSTRATIVE OF SIGNIFICANT CHANGES.

1981 LUZ N.V.
A LUTA PELA INDUSTRIALIZACAO DO BRAZIL.
SAO PAULO: DIFUSAO EUROPEIA DO LIVRO, 1961, 216 PP.
ANALYZES INDUSTRIALIZATION OF BRAZIL FROM 1808 AS COLONY TO 1930 WHEN ECONOMIC NATIONALISM AND AGRICULTURAL DECLINE LED BRAZIL TO PUBLIC POLICY OF ENDORSING AND SUPPORTING NATIONAL INDUSTRIES.

1982 LYFORD J.P.
THE AGREEABLE AUTOCRACIES.
NEW YORK: OCEANA PUBLISHING, 1961, 221 PP., LC#60-16612.
CONTAINS 13 CONVERSATIONS WITH JOURNALISTS AND PROFESSORS ON AUTOCRATIC NATURE OF AMERICAN INSTITUTIONS AND REASONS FOR THIS AUTOCRACY. INCLUDES R. HUTCHINS ON DEMOCRACY; T. WHITE ON THE PRESS; R. NIEBUHR ON RELIGION; S. CHASE ON BUSINESS; E. HEFFER, A. RASKIN, AND P. JACOPS ON UNIONS; AND S. BAILEY ON POLITICAL PARTIES.

1983 LYNN D.B., SAWREY W.L.
"THE EFFECTS OF FATHER-ABSENCE ON NORWEGIAN BOYS AND GIRLS."
J. ABNORMAL SOC. PSYCH., 59 (SEPT. 59), 258-262.
CONCERNS EFFECTS OF FATHER-ABSENCE ON CHILDREN, FATHER-LESS FAMILIES BEING COMPARED WITH FATHER-PRESENT ONES. DATA SHOWED THAT FATHER-ABSENT BOYS TENDED TO BE IMMATURE, STRONGLY FATHER-IDENTIFIED, AND MORE MASCULINE. THESE BOYS ALSO DEMONSTRATED POORER PEER ADJUSTMENT THAN FATHER-PRESENT BOYS AND FATHER-ABSENT GIRLS. FATHER-ABSENT GIRLS WERE MORE DEPENDENT ON THE MOTHER THAN FATHER-PRESENT GIRLS.

1984 LYON B., VERHULST A.E.
MEDIEVAL FINANCE.
PROVIDENCE: BROWN U PRESS, 1967, 100 PP., LC#67-19657.
COMPARES FINANCIAL INSTITUTIONS IN FLEMISH, ENGLISH, NORMAN, AND FRENCH ROYAL SYSTEMS. EXPLAINS RELATIONSHIP TO POLITICAL, ECONOMIC, AND SOCIAL DEVELOPMENT; COVERS OPERATION, DEVELOPMENT, AND MUTUAL INTERACTION OF SYSTEMS.

1985 LYON P.
NEUTRALISM.
LONDON: LEICESTER UNIV PRESS, 1963, 215 PP.
SEES NEUTRALISM AS AN IDEOLOGY. COMPARATIVE APPROACH TO NEUTRALIST REGIMES INCLUDING SIX PROTOTYPES. NOTES AND CASE STUDIES ON FAILURE OF BELGRADE CONFERENCE. SEES NEUTRALISM AS NECESSARY "BUFFER FORCE" IN INTERNATIONAL POLITICS.

1986 LYONS F.S.L.
THE IRISH PARLIAMENTARY PARTY, 1890-1910: STUDIES IN IRISH HISTORY (VOL. 4)
LONDON: FABER AND FABER, 1950, 284 PP.
EXAMINES POLITICAL DEVELOPMENT AFTER PARNELL'S DEPOSITION EMPHASIZING STRUGGLE FOR POWER, THE LIBERAL ALLIANCE, AND NATIONAL DIRECTORY. INCLUDES PERSONNEL STUDY: EXPERIENCE, OCCUPATION, AND ATTITUDE TOWARD CONSTITUENCIES.

1987 MAC DONALD H.M. ED.
THE INTELLECTUAL IN POLITICS.
AUSTIN: U OF TEXAS PR, 1966, 122 PP., LC#66-29160.
REPRINTS CONFERENCE PAPERS DISCUSSING DEFINITION, EFFECTIVENESS, AND ROLE OF INTELLECTUAL IN POLITICS IN US, USSR, PERU, GERMANY, SWEDEN, GREAT BRITAIN, MEXICO. BASIC BELIEF THAT EMERGED WAS NECESSITY FOR INTELLECTUAL TO REMAIN TRUE TO TASK OF BEING "THE CONSCIENCE OF HUMANITY." AUTHORS ARE: M. FAINSOD, GUNNAR HECKSCHER, DENIS BROGAN, J. BRADEMAS, K.

MEHNERT, D.C. VILLEGAS, F.M. QUESADA, E.K. MCCARTHY.

1988 MAC MILLAN W.M.
THE ROAD TO SELF-RULE.
NEW YORK: FREDERICK PRAEGER, 1959, 296 PP.
BASICALLY HISTORICAL STUDY OF COLONIAL EVOLUTION OF AFRICAN PEOPLE UNDER BRITISH RULE. DESCRIBES SOCIAL AND CULTURAL BACKGROUNDS AND EXTENT TO WHICH BRITISH COLONIAL RULE HAS ALTERED OLD WAY OF LIFE. DISCUSSES PROGRESS TOWARD INDEPENDENCE BEING MADE BY AFRICANS UNDER BRITISH CONTROL.

1989 MAC MILLAN W.M.
BANTU, BOER, AND BRITON: THE MAKING OF THE SOUTH AFRICAN NATIVE PROBLEM.
LONDON: OXFORD U PR, 1963, 382 PP.
EXPANDED EDITION OF A BOOK PUBLISHED IN 1929 DEALING WITH THE RELATIONS BETWEEN WHITE SOUTH AFRICANS AND BLACK INHABITANTS. NEW EDITION STRESSES ROLE OF MISSIONARY JOHN PHILIP. AUTHOR TRIES TO SHOW "WHAT REALLY HAPPENED" IN HISTORY OF THE AREA BECAUSE HE FEELS SOUTH AFRICANS HAVE MISREAD THEIR HISTORY AND INSTITUTED APARTHEID POLICY UNDER A DELUDED SENSE OF THEIR OWN PAST.

1990 MACDONALD D.
AFRICANA; OR, THE HEART OF HEATHEN AFRICA, VOL. II: MISSION LIFE.
LONDON: SIMPKIN, MARSHALL, 1882, 371 PP.
HISTORY OF MISSIONARY EFFORT IN "DARKEST AFRICA," WRITTEN BY A MISSIONARY OF LATE 19TH CENTURY. TRACES DEVELOPMENT FROM LIVINGSTONE THROUGH BEGINNINGS OF CONTACT WITH SLAVERY. DEVOTES LARGE PORTION TO PICTURE OF MISSION'S EVERYDAY LIFE. APPENDIX OF NATIVE TALES.

1991 MACFARQUHAR R. ED.
THE HUNDRED FLOWERS.
LONDON: STEVENS, 1960, 324 PP.
COLLECTION OF STATEMENTS AND CRITICISMS MADE BY CHINESE STUDENTS, DOCTORS, BUSINESSMEN, CIVIL SERVANTS, PEASANTS, AND WORKERS ABOUT CHINESE REGIME. LARGELY PUBLISHED IN "PEOPLE'S DAILY." CRITICISMS WERE MADE AT MAO TSE-TUNG'S INSTIGATION IN 1957.

1992 MACFARQUHAR R. ED.
CHINA UNDER MAO: POLITICS TAKES COMMAND.
CAMBRIDGE: M I T PRESS, 1966, 525 PP., LC#66-25630.
ESSAYS FROM "CHINA QUARTERLY" SINCE 1960 DEAL WITH POLITICS AND ORGANIZATION, ECONOMIC DEVELOPMENT, CULTURE, SOCIETY, FOREIGN RELATIONS, AND RECENT CHINESE HISTORY, WITH ATTENTION TO ABIDING THEORIES AND PRACTICES OF CHINESE COMMUNISM.

1993 MACHIAVELLI N.
THE ART OF WAR.
LONDON: NUTT, 1905, 249 PP.
CENTERS ATTENTION ON ORIGIN AND STRUCTURE OF ARMY. POINTS TO NECESSITY OF FORMING NATIONAL ARMY BY CONSCRIPTION. CONSIDERS SYSTEM OF MERCENARY FORCES A WASTEFUL FAILURE. CRITICIZES ITALY FOR SEPARATING CIVIL AND MILITARY LIFE.

1995 MACHIAVELLI N.
THE DISCOURSES (1516)
NEW HAVEN: YALE U PR, 1950, 585 PP.
UTILIZING LIVY'S "HISTORY OF ROME" FOR EXAMPLES, ILLUSTRATES THEOREMS FOR MAINTAINING POWER IN POLITICAL STATES. CLAIMS THESE THEOREMS HAVE VALIDITY OF NATURAL LAWS. THEY INCLUDE IDEAS THAT IT IS PASSION AND DESIRE THAT MOVE MEN TO ACTION; THAT THERE IS NO MORALITY IN POLITICS; THAT END JUSTIFIES THE MEANS; THAT RELIGION SHOULD BE MANIPULATED TO SERVE RULERS; AND THAT POWER IS BASIS FOR AUTHORITY.

1996 MACIVER R.M.
COMMUNITY: A SOCIOLOGICAL STUDY; BEING AN ATTEMPT TO SET OUT THE FUNDAMENTAL LAWS OF SOCIAL LIFE.
LONDON: MACMILLAN, 1920, 438 PP.
CONCERNED WITH SCIENCE OF SOCIETY AS A UNITY. DISCUSSES MEANING OF SOCIAL FACT AND SOCIAL LAW; COVERS GENERAL RELATION OF COMMUNITY AND ASSOCIATION, AND OF COMMUNITY AND STATE. SECTION DEVOTED TO RELATIONSHIP OF SOCIOLOGY TO OTHER SOCIAL SCIENCES. EXAMINES ELEMENTS, STRUCTURE, AND INSTITUTIONS OF COMMUNITY; LAWS OF COMMUNAL DEVELOPMENT, SOCIALIZATION AND COMMUNAL ECONOMY, AND CONTROL.

1997 MACIVER R.M.
THE MODERN STATE.
LONDON: OXFORD U PR, 1926, 504 PP.
DISCUSSES RISE AND NATURE OF MODERN STATE FROM PRIMITIVE SOCIETIES TO PRESENT CONFLICT BETWEEN INDIVIDUALISM AND COLLECTIVISM. EXAMINES THEORIES OF CITIZENSHIP, SOVEREIGNTY AND RULE OF LAW, PARTY GOVERNMENT, AND CONCLUDES WITH BRIEF DISCUSSION OF POLITICAL THOUGHT AT TURN OF 20TH CENTURY.

1998 MACIVER R.M.
SOCIETY: ITS STRUCTURE AND CHANGES.
NEW YORK: ROY LONG & R R SMITH, 1931, 569 PP.
TEXT ON SYSTEM OF SOCIOLOGY. OFFERS DEFINITIONS OF PRIMARY SOCIAL CONCEPTS AND PRELIMINARY ANALYSIS OF SOCIAL RELATIONSHIPS. DESCRIBES ASPECTS OF MAIN TYPES OF SOCIAL GROUPING AND INTERRELATIONSHIPS. EXAMINES SOCIAL ORDER AS DEPENDENT ON EXTERNAL WORLD. SEEKS TO INTERPRET TRENDS IN SOCIAL CHANGE. BIBLIOGRAPHIES ACCOMPANY EACH CHAPTER.

1999 MACIVER R.M. ED.
GREAT EXPRESSIONS OF HUMAN RIGHTS.
NEW YORK: HARPER, 1950, 321 PP.
SURVEYS MAGNA CHARTA, THE AMERICAN BILL OF RIGHTS, NATURAL LAWS, THE DECLARATION OF THE RIGHTS OF MAN AND CITIZEN. STUDIES LINCOLN'S POLITICAL ACTION. DISCUSSES THE FUNERAL ORATION OF PERICLES. RELATES INDIVIDUAL FREEDOM TO SOCIAL DETERMINISM.

2000 MACKENZIE K.R.
THE ENGLISH PARLIAMENT.
HAMMONSWORTH, ENGLAND: PELICAN BOOKS, 1950, 178 PP.
HISTORICAL STUDY OF ENGLAND'S PARLIAMENT AND EXPLANATION OF HOW IT WORKS. DESIGNED TO BRING OUT SPECIAL CONTRIBUTION OF EACH PERIOD RATHER TRACE ITS DEVELOPMENT. INCLUDES CONTEMPORARY PROBLEMS AND SUGGESTS POSSIBLE LINE FOR FUTURE DEVELOPMENT.

2001 MACKENZIE R.D.
"ECOLOGY, HUMAN."
ENCYCL. SOC. SCI., NEW YORK: MACMILLAN, 1949, VOL.5, 314-15.
DEALS WITH THE SPATIAL ASPECTS OF THE SYMBIOTIC RELATIONS OF HUMAN BEINGS AND HUMAN INSTITUTIONS. OFFERS MANY IMPORTANT PROBLEMS FOR RESEARCH: DISTRIBUTION AND COMPOSITION OF POPULATION, DELIMITATION OF NATURAL TERRITORIAL GROUPING, ZONES OF COMMUNAL INFLUENCE, ETC.

2002 MACKINTOSH J.P.
"NIGERIA'S EXTERNAL AFFAIRS."
J. COMMONWEALTH POLIT. STUD., 2 (NOV. 64), 189-206.
UNDERTAKES A STUDY OF THE HISTORY OF NIGERIA'S RELATIVE ISOLATIONISM, PRESENTING THE POLITICAL ISSUES FACING NIGERIA TODAY IN ITS RELATIONS WITH AFRICA AND GREAT BRITAIN. EVALUATES NIGERIA'S SMALL BUT INCREASING INTEREST IN FOREIGN AFFAIRS.

2003 MACLEOD I.
NEVILLE CHAMBERLAIN.
NEW YORK: ATHENEUM PUBLISHERS, 1961, 319 PP.
BIOGRAPHY OF CHAMBERLAIN BY A POLITICAL HEIR WHO MAKES USE OF PRIVATE LETTERS, PAPERS, AND DIARIES. EMPHASIZES HIS ROLE AS "RADICAL SOCIAL REFORMER" WHO INITIATED PROJECTS AND LEGISLATION INFLUENTIAL TO CHARACTER OF BRITISH SOCIAL GOVERNMENT. APPENDS SEVERAL HISTORIC DOCUMENTS.

2004 MACLEOD W.C.
"THE ORIGIN AND HISTORY OF POLITICS."
NEW YORK: JOHN WILEY, 1931.
INTRODUCTION TO POLITICAL DEVELOPMENT WITH EMPHASIS ON A METHODOLOGY RESTING ON MODERN ETHNOLOGY. DISCUSSION OF HISTORIC POLITICAL INSTITUTIONS INCLUDING PRIMITIVE CIVILIZATIONS. PARTICULAR EMPHASIS ON POLITICAL DEVELOPMENT OF EUROPE AND AMERICA. CONTAINS LIST OF REFERENCES.

2005 MACLURE M. ED., ANGLIN D. ED.
AFRICA: THE POLITICAL PATTERN.
TORONTO: TORONTO UNIV PRESS, 1961, 124 PP.
ESSAYS DISCUSSING GENERAL PROBLEMS IN POLITICAL DEVELOPMENT AND CULTURAL AFFAIRS IN SUB-SAHARA AFRICA. EACH ESSAY DEVOTED TO PROBLEMS OF SEPARATE COUNTRY OR REGION.

2006 MACPHERSON C.B.
THE POLITICAL THEORY OF POSSESSIVE INDIVIDUALISM.
LONDON: OXFORD U PR, 1962, 310 PP.
PRESENTS THEORY OF POSSESSIVE INDIVIDUALISM AND ENGLISH POLITICAL THOUGHT FROM 17TH TO 19TH CENTURIES AND ITS RELATION TO POLITICAL THINKERS OF THAT TIME, INCLUDING LOCKE, LEVELLERS, HARRINGTON.

2007 MACRAE D. JR.
"ROLL CALL VOTES AND LEADERSHIP."
PUBLIC OPINION QUART., 20 (FALL 56), 534-558.
DESCRIBES METHOD FOR MEASURING PARTIES' RELATIVE CONCERN WITH ORGANIZATIONAL LOYALTY AND IDEOLOGY. CLAIMS THAT PARTY LABELS ARE LESS DEPENDENT ON ATTITUDES TOWARD ISSUES IN AMERICA THAN IN EUROPE.

2008 MACRAE D.G.
"THE BOLSHEVIK IDEOLOGY; THE INTELLECTUAL AND EMOTIONAL FACTORS IN COMMUNIST AFFILIATION" (BMR)"
CAMBRIDGE JOURNAL, 5 (DEC. 51), 164-177.
ATTEMPTS TO EXAMINE MARXISM IN ITS BOLSHEVIK FORM NOT AS A SYSTEM OR METHOD, BUT AS THE SOCIAL OPERATION OF AN IDEOLOGY. CONSIDERS THE APPEAL OF BOLSHEVISM AS A POLITICO-SOCIAL CREED: ITS INTELLECTUAL CLAIM TO SCIENTIFIC STATUS, ITS EMOTIONAL CLAIM AS A SALVATIONIST RELIGION, AND ITS IDEALISTIC CLAIM TO EQUALITY. VIEWS THESE LEVELS OF APPEAL AGAINST THE SUCCESSION OF MARXIST PROPHETS AND LEADERS.

2009 MACRIDIS R.C., BROWN B.E.
THE DE GAULLE REPUBLIC: QUEST FOR UNITY.

HOMEWOOD: DORSEY PR., 1960, 400 PP., $9.00.
DISCUSSES HOW FIFTH FRENCH REPUBLIC SOUGHT TO ACHIEVE BASIS FOR COHESIVE GOVERNMENT THROUGH THE PRESIDENTIAL ROLE, WITH ITS MULTIPLE POWERS. SEES PRESIDENT AS IRRESPONSIBLE POLITICALLY SINCE NOT ACCOUNTABLE TO PUBLIC OR LEGISLATURE BUT RATHER A SPECIAL ELECTORAL GROUP.

2010 MACRIDIS R.C.
"INTEREST GROUPS IN COMPARATIVE ANALYSIS."
J. OF POLITICS, 23 (FEB. 61), 25-45.
A SUMMARY AND CRITIQUE OF INTEREST GROUP THEORY FROM TRUMAN TO ALMOND, WITH A NEW STATEMENT: "INTEREST," LIKE ANY OTHER ACTIVITY IN A SYSTEM IS CONDITIONED BY SECULAR FORCES THAT HAVE SHAPED THE POLITICAL CULTURE OF THE COMMUNITY, AND THE BEST WAY TO A THEORY OF COMPARATIVE POLITICS IS TO LOOK AT POLITICAL CULTURE, SOCIAL CONFIGURATION, LEADERSHIP, AND GOVERNMENTAL INSTITUTIONS. GIVES REVIEW OF LITERATURE.

2011 MACRIDIS R.C. ED.
FOREIGN POLICY IN WORLD POLITICS (3RD ED.)
ENGLEWOOD CLIFFS: PRENTICE HALL, 1967, 401 PP., LC#67-12251.
COMPARES FOREIGN POLICIES OF MAJOR NATIONS, ANALYZING PARTICULAR GOVERNMENTAL STRUCTURES, NATIONAL WORLD-VIEWS, CHARACTERISTICS OF HISTORICAL AND GEOGRAPHICAL POSITION TO ELUCIDATE THEIR DIRECTION, EFFICACY, AND EFFECT ON FUTURE POLICY-MAKING.

2012 MACRO E.
BIBLIOGRAPHY OF THE ARABIAN PENINSULA (PAMPHLET)
CORAL GABLES: U OF MIAMI PR, 1958, 80 PP., LC#58-12170.
LIST OF 2,380 TITLES IN MANY EUROPEAN LANGUAGES CONCERNING ALL ASPECTS OF THE PENINSULA INCLUDING ITS PEOPLE, GEOGRAPHY AND NATURAL HISTORY, AND TRAVELERS' RECORDS. ENTRIES FROM 19TH CENTURY TO ABOUT 1950 ARRANGED BY AUTHOR. INCLUDES BOOKS, JOURNALS, GOVERNMENT REPORTS AND SOME NEWSPAPER ARTICLES.

2013 MADAN G.R.
ECONOMIC THINKING IN INDIA.
NEW DELHI: S CHAND AND CO, 1966.
SURVEYS INDIAN ECONOMIC THOUGHT FROM ANCIENT TIMES. CHAPTERS ON MOST INFLUENTIAL INDIVIDUALS, AND EMPHASIZING CURRENT ECONOMIC POLICIES OF GOVERNMENT AND POLITICAL GROUPS.

2014 MADHOK B.
POLITICAL TRENDS IN INDIA.
NEW DELHI: S CHAND AND CO, 1959, 162 PP.
STUDY OF INDIAN POLITICS, WITH REFERENCE TO THE CONFLICT BETWEEN COMMUNISM AND CAPITALISM. DISCUSSES POLITICAL PARTIES, ELECTION RESULTS, AND THE CASTE STRUCTURE. EMPHASIZES INTERNAL AND EXTERNAL DANGERS OF COMMUNISM. CONCLUDES WITH DISCUSSION OF THE FUTURE OF DEMOCRACY IN INDIA.

2015 MAGATHAN W.
"SOME BASES OF WEST GERMAN MILITARY POLICY."
J. CONFL. RESOLUT., 4 (MAR. 60), 123-37.
FOCUSES ON WEST GERMAN CONCERN ABOUT ITS SECURITY POLICY, EMPHASIZING ITS DEVELOPMENT IN TERMS OF STRUCTURE, ECONOMICS AND DEMOGRAPHY. OUTLINES BOTH MILITARY POLICY AND ARMED FORCES DEPLOYMENT.

2016 MAHAR J.M.
INDIA: A CRITICAL BIBLIOGRAPHY.
TUCSON: U OF ARIZONA PR, 1964, 119 PP., LC#64-17992.
LIST OF 2023 TITLES, MOSTLY BOOKS WITH FEW FOREIGN-LANGUAGE SOURCES. ARRANGED BY TOPIC IN DETAIL; PUBLICATIONS SINCE 1940 GIVEN GREATEST ATTENTION.

2017 MAICHEL K.
CATALOG OF SOVIET AND RUSSIAN NEWSPAPERS AT THE HOOVER INSTITUTION OF WAR, REVOLUTION AND PEACE.
STANFORD: STANFORD U PRESS, 1966, 235 PP., LC#66-26281.
PRESENTS A CHECKLIST OF RUSSIAN PERIODICALS DATING BACK TO 19TH CENTURY. LISTS 1,108 TITLES (IMPERIAL, SOVIET, AND EMIGRE) AS OF JANUARY, 1966. ARRANGED ALPHABETICALLY BY TITLE, IN TRANSLITERATED RUSSIAN. PARTIALLY ANNOTATED IN ENGLISH. HOLDINGS ITEMIZED BY DATE AND NUMBER. INCLUDES ABOUT 85 PER CENT OF HOLDINGS AT HOOVER INSTITUTION.

2018 MAIER H.
REVOLUTION UND KIRCHE.
FREIBURG: VERLAG ROMBACH + CO, 1959, 249 PP.
EXAMINES ORIGIN AND NATURE OF CHRISTIAN-DEMOCRATIC PARTIES OF EUROPE. FOCUSES ON CATHOLIC-LIBERAL AND CATHOLIC-SOCIAL MOVEMENTS IN FRANCE FROM REVOLUTION OF 1789 TO 1850.

2019 MAIER J. ED., WEATHERHEAD R.W. ED.
POLITICS OF CHANGE IN LATIN AMERICA.
NEW YORK: FREDERICK PRAEGER, 1964, 258 PP., LC#64-13382.
COLLECTION OF ESSAYS BY LATIN AMERICAN SPECIALISTS. ANALYZES CHANGES IN POLITICS AND SOCIAL STRUCTURE IN CONTEMPORARY LATIN AMERICA, NOTING BRAZIL AS ESPECIALLY DIFFERENT IN BACKGROUND AND DEVELOPMENT. EXAMINES INTERACTION OF ALL WESTERN HEMISHPERE NATIONS, ALSO CONCEPT OF ALLIANCE FOR PROGRESS.

2020 MAINE H.S.
ANCIENT LAW.
NEW YORK: HOLT, 1887, 400 PP.
STUDIES ANCIENT CODES AND THEIR ECO-POLITICAL BACKGROUND. ANALYZES THE CONCEPTS OF LAW OF NATURE AND EQUITY. CONSIDERS ANCIENT AND MODERN IDEAS ABOUT WILLS AND SUCCESSIONS AND EXPLORES THE EARLY HISTORY OF CONTRACTS, PROPERTY AND CRIME.

2021 MAINE H.S.
LECTURES ON THE EARLY HISTORY OF INSTITUTIONS.
NEW YORK: HENRY HOLT & CO, 1875, 412 PP.
A SOCIAL AND LEGAL HISTORY OF BASIC INSTITUTIONS IN EARLY CULTURES. SPECIAL ATTENTION IS GIVEN TO ANCIENT IRISH (BREHON) LAW AS APPLIED IN EARLY CELTIC SOCIETIES. DISCUSSES KINSHIP AS BASIS OF PROPERTY OWNERSHIP, ROLE OF THE CHIEF, DIVISIONS OF FAMILY, AND GROWTH AND DIFFUSION OF IDEAS. FINAL CHAPTERS DEAL WITH ROMAN LAW AND CONCEPT OF SOVEREIGNTY AS INTERPRETED BY BENTHAM, AUSTIN, AND BLACKSTONE.

2022 MAIR L.P.
NEW NATIONS.
CHICAGO: U OF CHICAGO PRESS, 1963, 235 PP.
TREATS NATIONS EMERGING FROM COLONIAL STATUS FROM STANDPOINT OF CHANGES IN SOCIETY. NOTES WESTERN INFLUENCE ON COLONIAL "SMALL SCALE SOCITIES" IN MODES OF LIVELIHOOD AND SOCIAL STRUCTURE. CENTERING ON AFRICAN COLONIES, DISCUSSES CHANGING FAMILY AND POLITICAL SYSTEMS, NEW RELIGIONS, TRENDS IN TOWN AND CITY FORMATION. OUTLINES FORMATION PROCESSES OF NEW STATES AND SOCIAL EFFECTS OF WESTERN TECHNICAL IDEAS.

2023 MAIR L.P.
AN INTRODUCTION TO SOCIAL ANTHROPOLOGY.
LONDON: OXFORD U PR, 1965, 283 PP.
DISCUSSES DEFINITION AND DEVELOPMENT OF DISCIPLINE AND CURRENT AREAS OF RESEARCH, AND PRESENTS INTRODUCTORY STUDY OF ASPECTS OF CULTURE.

2024 MAIR L.P.
"BUSOGA LOCAL GOVERNMENT"
J. COMMONWEALTH POL. ST., 5 (JULY 67), 91-107.
DISCUSSES EXPECTATIONS OF BRITISH WITH WHICH THEY MADE LAWS ABOUT CONDUCT OF LOCAL AFFAIRS AND COMPARES THEM TO AFRICAN REALITIES. USING BUSOGA AS ONE CASE, STUDIES GOALS FOR WHICH AFRICANS ADMINISTERED RULES. PROVIDES DETAILED DESCRIPTION OF SYSTEM AND FUNCTIONING OF LOCAL GOVERNMENT UNDER BRITISH.

2025 MAIR L.P.
"REPRESENTATIVE LOCAL GOVERNMENT AS A PROBLEM IN SOCIAL CHANGE."
J. AFR. ADMIN., 10 (JAN. 58), 11-24.
DISCUSSION OF PROBLEMS WHICH FACE THE DEVELOPMENT OF REPRESENTATIVE GOVERNMENT IN NEWLY INDEPENDENT, ECONOMICALLY UNDER-DEVELOPED NATIONS, ESPECIALLY THOSE IN AFRICA. AUTHOR PARTICULARLY CONCERNED WITH NATURE OF THE TRADITIONAL RULING CLASS AND THE FUNCTIONING OF EMERGENT POLITICAL ELITES.

2026 MAJUMDAR D.N., MADAN T.N.
AN INTRODUCTION TO SOCIAL ANTHROPOLOGY.
BOMBAY: ASIA PUBL HOUSE, 1963, 304 PP.
SURVEY OF SOCIAL BEHAVIOR OF MAN IN HIS TRIBAL AND INSTITUTIONAL SETTING IN INDIA. STUDIES PHYSICAL TRAITS OF MAN, HIS BASIC NEEDS, AND HIS JOINING OF GROUPS OR SOCIAL ORGANIZATION WHICH LEADS TO MARRIAGE, GOVERNMENT, LAWS, ETC. DEALS SEPARATELY WITH TRIBAL INDIA AND ITS CASTE SYSTEM.

2027 MALAN V.D.
"THE SILENT VILLAGE."
COEXISTENCE, 4 (JAN. 67), 5-61.
A DECAYING VILLAGE ON AN INDIAN RESERVATION IS HERE TAKEN AS SYMBOLIC OF THE VALUES BEING LOST OR CHANGED IN THE URBAN AND TECHNOLOGICAL REVOLUTION OF TODAY. CRUCIAL VARIABLES CITED ARE REPLACEMENT OF VALUE OF LIVING IN PRESENT BY ORIENTATION TO FUTURE PROGRESS, CHANGE FROM CONSENSUS TO AGGRESSIVE LEADERSHIP BASED ON MAJORITY RULE, AND RESPONSIBILITY FOR OTHERS BECOMING AN ASSUMED CHOICE.

2028 MALENBAUM W.
"GOVERNMENT, ENTREPRENEURSHIP, AND ECONOMIC GROWTH IN POOR LANDS."
WORLD POLITICS, 19 (OCT. 66), 52-68.
DEVELOPMENT PROJECTS IN THE LAST DECADE HAVE SPURRED SOME GROWTH, BUT TOO LITTLE TO REDUCE THE DIFFERENTIAL BETWEEN RICH AND POOR NATIONS, AND BETWEEN THE MODERN AND TRADITIONAL ELEMENTS IN THE STRUCTURE OF THE DEVELOPING NATIONS. DEVELOPMENT PLANS MUST RELATE GROWTH IN MODERN SECTORS TO CHANGE IN THE TRADITIONAL. THIS REQUIRES ENTERPRENEURSHIP WHICH ONLY GOVERNMENT CAN PROVIDE IN THE POOR NATIONS

2029 MALINOWSKI B.
"THE PRIMITIVE ECONOMICS OF THE TROBRIAND ISLANDERS" (BMR)"
ECO. J., 31 (MAR. 21), 1-16.
DISCUSSES NATURAL RESOURCES OF TROBRIANDERS AND SURVEYS MANNER IN WHICH THEY ARE USED. CONSIDERS AGRICULTURE, LAND TENURE, PRODUCTION, AND ORGANIZATION. RELATES ELEMENTS OF MAGIC, SOCIAL STRUCTURE, CULTURE, AND

INFLUENCE OF CHIEF. CONCLUDES THAT ECONOMY OF PRIMITIVE CULTURE IS VERY COMPLEX AND DIVERSIFIED.

2030 MALINOWSKI B.
CRIME AND CUSTOM IN SAVAGE SOCIETY.
NEW YORK: HARCOURT BRACE, 1926, 132 PP.
INQUIRES INTO STRUCTURE OF FORCES OF LAW AND ORDER IN SAVAGE SOCIETIES. STUDIES NORTH-WEST MELANESIA TO ESTABLISH THESIS THAT LAWS ARE ENFORCED BY PSYCHOLOGICAL AND SOCIAL INDUCEMENTS. EXAMINES ECONOMIC OBLIGATIONS, RELIGIOUS AND FAMILY LAW, RECIPROCITY AS BASIS OF SOCIAL STRUCTURE, CRIME, AND PUNISHMENT THROUGH SORCERY.

2031 MALINOWSKI B.
MAGIC, SCIENCE AND RELIGION.
GARDEN CITY: DOUBLEDAY, 1954, 274 PP.
A SOCIOLOGICAL STUDY OF PRIMITIVE MAN AND HIS BELIEFS. PRESENTS RELIGION AS A KEY FACTOR IN LIFE AND GROUP STRUCTURE, INCLUDING FEASTS, RITES, AND MAGIC CYCLES. IN ADDITION TO BASIC THEORY, A THOROUGH EXPLANATION IS GIVEN OF THE BELIEFS AND PRACTICES OF THE KIRIWINA NATIVES IN THE TROBRIAND ISLANDS.

2032 MALINOWSKI B.
SEX, CULTURE, AND MYTH.
NEW YORK: HARCOURT BRACE, 1962, 346 PP., LC#62-19590.
FINDS RELIGION ROOTED DEEPLY IN HUMAN LIFE AND EMOTION, AND UNITED IN SUBSTANCE, FORM, AND FUNCTION. ALL RELIGIOUS DEVELOPMENT PROBABLY CONSISTS IN GROWING PREDOMINANCE OF ETHICAL PRINCIPLE AND INCREASING FUSION OF SENSE OF PROVIDENCE AND FAITH IN IMMORTALITY. BASES CONCLUSION ON DETAILED ANALYSIS OF FAMILY, CULTURE, AND BELIEFS OF RELIGIONS OF THE WORLD.

2033 MALLORY J.R.
"THE MINISTER'S OFFICE STAFF* AN UNREFORMED PART OF PUBLIC SERVICE."
CAN. PUBLIC ADMIN., 10 (MAR. 67), 25-34.
STUDY OF THE CANADIAN MINISTER'S PERSONAL STAFFS - THEIR FUNCTIONS, ORGANIZATION, ETC. DISCUSSES CIVIL SERVICE BUREAUCRACY WHICH IS SUPPOSED TO BE NONPOLITICAL BUT IS IN FACT POLITICAL RATHER THAN BUREAUCRATIC, APPOINTED RATHER THAN ELECTED, AND OPERATIVE IN AREAS NOT CONSTITUTIONALLY SPECIFIED. PROBLEMS AND SPECIFIC CASES CITED.

2034 MALTHUS T.R.
PRINCIPLES OF POLITICAL ECONOMY.
ORIGINAL PUBLISHER NOT AVAILABLE, 1820, 599 PP.
BASICALLY A LAISSEZ-FAIRE THEORIST, BUT CONTENDS THAT SOME FORM OF GOVERNMENT INFLUENCE ON ECONOMY IS DESIRABLE. TAKES ISSUE WITH ADAM SMITH ON CONCEPT OF SAVING AS MEANS OF INCREASING WEALTH, STATING THAT THIS TENDS TO DECREASE PRODUCTION. DISCUSSES EFFECT OF DEMAND UPON WEALTH AND LAUDS RICARDO'S DISCUSSION OF IT. PROPOSES COMMERCE AS MEASURE OF WEALTH.

2035 MANGLAPUS R.S.
"ASIAN REVOLUTION AND AMERICAN IDEOLOGY."
FOREIGN AFFAIRS, 45 (JAN. 67), 344-352.
DISCUSSES CHANGE IN ASIAN SOCIETY FROM STABILITY TO REVOLUTION. EMPHASIZES INAPPLICABILITY OF AMERICAN IDEALS TO ASIAN SITUATION. COMPARES CHARACTERISTICS OF AMERICAN REVOLUTION: TRADITION OF DISSENT, FRONTIERS, AND RICH LAND TO ASIAN REVOLUTION. ADVOCATES SOCIAL REVOLUTION TO CLOSE CLASS GAP AND TO RELEASE PEOPLE FROM BONDS OF CENTRALIZED POWER BUT URGES THAT REVOLUTION BE UNIQUE TO EACH COUNTRY.

2036 MANIS J.G. ED., CLARK S.I. ED.
MAN AND SOCIETY.
NEW YORK: MACMILLAN, 1960, 784 PP., LC#60-5157.
INTRODUCTORY COLLEGE TEXT FOR SOCIOLOGY. ANTHOLOGY INCLUDES WORKS ON ANTHROPOLOGY, STRATIFICATION, POWER AND LEADERSHIP, AND GROUP BEHAVIOR. CONTRIBUTORS INCLUDE LIPPMAN, SPENCER, RUSSELL, FDR, SCHWEITZER, MARX, MILL, FREUD, CHURCHILL, AND MEAD.

2037 MANNHEIM E.
DIE TRAGER DER OFFENTLICHEN MEINUNG.
LEIPZIG: RUDOLF M ROHRER, 1933, 145 PP.
STUDIES MAN'S EXISTENCE AS A SOCIAL BEING. MAINTAINS THAT WITH ADVENT OF 19TH CENTURY, MAN SUDDENLY RELEASED FROM ISOLATION BECAME, AS A RESULT OF INDUSTRIALIZATION AND TECHNOLOGY, A SOCIAL BEING SUBJECT TO PRESSURES OF NEW PUBLIC EXISTENCE.

2038 MANNHEIM K.
MAN AND SOCIETY IN AN AGE OF RECONSTRUCTION.
NEW YORK: HARCOURT BRACE, 1940, 469 PP.
STUDY OF CONFLICT OF TOTALITARIANISM AND THE OLD LIBERAL ORDER OF EUROPE. THEORETICAL ANALYSIS OF CRISES OF LIBERAL DEMOCRACY IN EUROPE. ANALYSIS OF PROBLEMS RAISED FOR HUMAN FREEDOM BY REALITY OF SOCIAL AND ECONOMIC PLANNING, SOCIAL CAUSES OF CONTEMPORARY CULTURAL CRISES, RATIONAL AND IRRATIONAL ELEMENTS OF MODERN SOCIETY. EXTENSIVE BIBLIOGRAPHY BASED ON AUTHOR'S PERSONAL PREFERENCES.

2039 MANNING H.T.
THE REVOLT OF FRENCH CANADA 1800-1835.
NEW YORK: ST MARTIN'S PRESS, 1962, 426 PP.
STUDIES FRENCH-CANADIAN NATIONALISM DURING VITAL STAGE OF DEVELOPMENT, AND OF RECTION TO THE MOVEMENT IN ENGLAND. IN EARLY 19TH CENTURY ONLY THE FRENCH-SPEAKING POPULATION LAID CLAIM TO TITLE OF CANADIAN. DISCUSSES FUNDAMENTAL ISSUES AND STANCE OF GOVERNOR VS ASSEMBLY WITHIN THE COLONY. CONTAINS BIBLIOGRAPHICAL INVORMATION AND DISCRIPTIVE FOOTNOTES.

2040 MANNONI D.O.
PROSPERO AND CALIBAN: THE PSYCHOLOGY OF COLONIZATION.
NEW YORK: PRAEGER, 1956, 218 PP.
EXPLORES PSYCHOLOGICAL ATTITUDES OF MALAGASY NATIVES AS MANIFESTED IN FAMILY, RELIGION, MORES, AND TRADITIONS. ANALYZES REACTION TO EUROPEAN CULTURE AND TO INDEPENDENCE. ALSO STUDIES EUROPEAN REACTION TO MALAGASY CULTURE.

2041 MANSERGH N.
SOUTH AFRICA 1906-1961: THE PRICE OF MAGNANIMITY.
NEW YORK: FREDERICK PRAEGER, 1962, 104 PP., LC#62-9592.
SHOWS THE GOOD INTENTIONS OF THOSE PRINCIPALLY RESPONSIBLE FOR THE 1906 FREE UNION BETWEEN SOUTH AFRICAN PROVINCES, BUT CONCLUDES THAT THE PRICE OF MAGNANIMITY HAS BEEN HIGH AND HAS BEEN PAID FOR LARGELY BY ENGLISH-SPEAKING MINORITY AND NON-EUROPEAN MAJORITY IN THE UNION.

2042 MANSERGH N.
"THE PARTITION OF INDIA IN RETROSPECT."
INT. J., 21 (WINTER 66), 1-19.
DISCUSSES PROBLEMS CREATED BY CREATION OF INDEPENDENT INDIA AND PAKISTAN, AND DIFFERENT INTERPRETATIONS GIVEN TO PARTITION: SUCCESSION OR SECESSION. INCLUDES HISTORICAL BACKGROUND.

2043 MANSUR F.
PROCESS OF INDEPENDENCE.
LONDON: ROUTLEDGE & KEGAN PAUL, 1962, 192 PP.
COMPARATIVE STUDY OF POLITICS OF INDEPENDENCE IN INDIA, PAKISTAN, INDONESIA, AND GHANA. DISCUSSES EDUCATION OF INTELLECTUAL ELITE, THEIR ASSUMPTION OF POWER, AND THEIR ROLE IN CONSTITUTION-MAKING. CONCLUDES WITH ANALYSIS OF POLITICAL PARTIES.

2044 MAO TSE-TUNG
ON SOME IMPORTANT PROBLEMS OF THE PARTY'S PRESENT POLICY.
PEKING: FOREIGN LANG PR, 1961, 40 PP.
PROPOSES POLICY OF INTERNAL COEXISTENCE WITH THOSE WHO DO NOT FAVOR THE PARTY. CLAIMS THAT STUDENTS, TEACHERS, AND OTHER EDUCATED PEOPLE ARE NOT A REAL DANGER TO PARTY. STATES MOST IMPORTANT PROBLEM TO BE FORWARDING INTERESTS OF FARM LABORERS AND PEASANTS. SAYS THAT GOODS OF MIDDLE PEASANTS WHICH HAVE BEEN REDISTRIBUTED SHOULD BE RETURNED. THEY ARE TO RECEIVE VOICE IN GOVERNMENT.

2045 MAO TSE-TUNG
NEW DEMOCRACY.
SHANGHAI: CHINESE AMERICAN PUB, 1949, 83 PP.
PROPOSES APPLYING SCIENTIFIC METHOD TO PROBLEMS OF GOVERNMENT, CLAIMING THAT PRAGMATISM SHOULD BE SOLE CRITERION FOR EVALUATING VARIOUS IDEAS AND SYSTEMS. CLAIMS THAT CHINA MUST SEEK A NEW CULTURE DEVOID OF PERMENTING WESTERN INFLUENCE. THIS SHOULD BE THE SCIENTIFIC CULTURE OF SOCIALISM. WARNS AGAINST CAPITALISTIC DEMOCRACIES, SINCE THEIR HIGHEST ACHIEVEMENT IS IMPERIALISM.

2046 MARCH J.G.
"PARTY LEGISLATIVE REPRESENTATION AS A FUNCTION OF ELECTION RESULTS."
PUBLIC OPINION QUART., 21 (WINTER 57), 521-542.
REPORT ON A STUDY OF RELATIONSHIP BETWEEN VOTES AND LEGISLATIVE REPRESENTATION IN ENGLAND AND UNITED STATES. DESCRIBES PROCESS BY WHICH REPRESENTATIVENESS OF DEMOCRATIC INSTITUTIONS MAY BE EVALUATED.

2047 MARES V.E.
"EAST EUROPE'S SECOND CHANCE."
CURR. HIST., 47 (NOV. 64), 272-9.
DISCUSSES TRENDS AT WORK IN EAST EUROPE. DE-STALINIZATION HAS ASSUMED DE-SATELLIZATION. AUTHOR LABELS INDEPENDENT ACTIONS (YUGOSLAVIA IN 1948, HUNGARY IN 1956 AND RUMANIA IN 1964) AS AMAZING. ASSERTS THAT POLICIES BE CO-ORDINATED IN ORDER TO BUILD A STRONG EAST EUROPE COMMONWEALTH.

2048 MARIAS J.
"A PROGRAM FOR EUROPE."
J. INT. AFF., 16 (NO.1, 62), 7-17.
EUROPE MUST UNITE THROUGH A PROCESS OF INCORPORATION. SEEKS TO DISCOVER WHY THE UNDERTAKING OF UNITY HAS NOT BEEN STRONG. SUGGESTS SYSTEM OF INTERNAL PROGRAMS, EACH DESIGNED FOR AN INDIVIDUAL COUNTRY, BUT ALL INTER-RELATED TO ACCOMPLISH THIS AIM.

2049 MARITAIN J.
FREEDOM IN THE MODERN WORLD.

NEW YORK: CHAS SCRIBNER'S SONS, 1936, 218 PP.
SUPPORTS NOTION OF FREE WILL OVER THAT OF DETERMINISM, CALLING THIS "AUTHENTIC HUMANISM." CONSIDERS ROLE OF CHRISTIANITY IN SERVING AS A POLITICAL PHILOSOPHY, AND THE RELATION OF RELIGION AND CULTURE. FROM THE STANDPOINT OF THIS AUTHENTIC HUMANISM, LIKENS COMMUNISM AND CAPITALISM TO EACH OTHER, SINCE BOTH ARE MATERIALISTIC. CONSIDERS MEANS OF APPLYING THIS HUMANISM TO POLITICS.

2050 MARITAIN J.
SCHOLASTICISM AND POLITICS.
NEW YORK: MACMILLAN, 1939, 248 PP.
CONSIDERS APPLICATION OF SCHOLASTICISM TO FORMULATING A CONCEPT OF THE STATE, ITS PURPOSE, AND FUNCTIONS. PRESENTS CATHOLIC INTERPRETATIONS OF PERSONALITY, FREEDOM, MEANING OF LIFE, AND THE FAILURE OF MATERIALISM. DISCUSSES RELATIONSHIPS OF PHILOSOPHY AND SOCIETY, DEMOCRACY AND AUTHORITY, FREUD AND MATERIALISM, AND CHRISTIANITY AND SOCIETY. STRIVES TO ESTABLISH CHRISTIAN PARADIGM TO COPE WITH POLITICS.

2051 MARITAIN J.
THE RIGHTS OF MAN AND NATURAL LAW.
NEW YORK: CHAS SCRIBNER'S SONS, 1943, 118 PP.
ANALYZES MODERN POLITICAL INSTITUTIONS, NOTING THOSE FACTORS HE CONSIDERS TO BE OF MOST VALUE AND TO HAVE MOST UNIVERSAL JUSTIFICATION. THESE ARE: THE COMMON GOOD, POLITICAL AUTHORITY LEADING MEN TO THE COMMON GOOD, AND THE INTRINSIC MORALITY OF THE COMMON GOOD AND POLITICAL LIFE. BELIEVES IT IS POSSIBLE TO HAVE FUNCTIONAL LINK BETWEEN RELIGION AND LAW WITHOUT HAVING RELIGIOUS STATE.

2052 MARITAIN J.
L'HOMME ET L'ETAT.
PARIS: PR UNIV DE FRANCE, 1953, 204 PP.
DISCUSSES CENTRAL CONCEPTS OF POLITICAL PHILOSOPHY, SUCH AS SOVEREIGNTY, MEANS OF CONTROL, NATURAL LAW AND HUMAN LAW, PROBLEM OF AUTHORITY, AND RELATION BETWEEN CHURCH AND STATE. CONCLUDES WITH PLEA FOR NECESSITY OF POLITICAL UNIFICATION OF MANKIND.

2053 MARK M.
"MUST WE FIGHT SOCIAL REVOLUTIONS OF THE LEFT?"
BACKGROUND, 9 (AUG. 65), 163-170.
AUTHOR FEELS THAT SPLITS IN THE COMMUNIST CAMP, THE EVOLUTIONARY MODERATION OF THE SOVIET UNION, AND THE SUCCESS OF DE GAULLE'S POLICIES TOWARD ALGERIA IN COMPARISON TO FAILURE OF AMERICA'S HARD POLICY TOWARD CUBA, ALL SUGGEST THAT NAIONAL REVOLUTIONS OF THE LEFT CAN BE ACCOMMODATED.

2054 MARKHAM V.R.
SOUTH AFRICA, PAST AND PRESENT.
LONDON: SMITH, ELDER & CO, 1900, 443 PP.
FIRST SECTION RELATES HISTORICAL AND POLITICAL ANTECEDENTS OF BOER WAR. WHILE SEEKING TO PROVIDE SOME PERSPECTIVE, AUTHOR FEELS BRITISH AIMS ARE MORE JUST, AS DUTCH RULE WOULD BE "CORRUPT OLIGARCHY ON RACIAL LINES." SECOND SECTION DEALS WITH COLOR PROBLEM, NATIVE EDUCATION AND LEGISLATION, AND JUSTICE OF BOTH BLACK AND WHITE CLAIMS. PART THREE CONSISTS OF TRAVEL IMPRESSIONS.

2055 MARQUAND H.A., PHILIP A. ET AL.
ORGANIZED LABOUR IN FOUR CONTINENTS.
LONDON: LONGMANS, GREEN & CO, 1939, 518 PP.
ELEVEN ESSAYS BY DIFFERENT AUTHORS COVERING THE STATE OF ORGANIZED LABOR IN FRANCE, GERMANY, BRITAIN, ITALY, SCANDINAVIA, USSR, US, CANADA, MEXICO, AUSTRALIA, AND JAPAN. EACH TRACES THE DEVELOPMENT OF UNIONISM FROM 1919 TO 1937 AND ITS RELATION TO THE ECONOMIC, POLITICAL, AND SOCIAL CLIMATE IN EACH COUNTRY. EFFECTS OF GLOBAL AND INTERNAL EVENTS ON LABOR MOVEMENTS ARE ALSO EXAMINED.

2056 MARRARO H.R.
AMERICAN OPINION ON THE UNIFICATION OF ITALY.
NEW YORK: COLUMBIA U PRESS, 1932, 345 PP., LC#32-7356.
WRITTEN TO SHOW AMERICA'S ATTITUDE TOWARD EFFORT OF ITALIANS TO FREE THEMSELVES FROM ALIEN RULE AND TO UNIFY SEPARATE STATES. TREATS REVOLUTIONARY OUTBREAKS OF 1848, ROMAN REPUBLIC, FOREIGN DESPOTISM, MARTYRS OF ITALIAN LIBERTY IN AMERICA, VICTOR EMANUEL II, CREATION OF ITALIAN CONFEDERACY, AND EMERGENCE OF ITALIAN KINGDOM.

2057 MARRIOTT J.A.
DICTATORSHIP AND DEMOCRACY.
LONDON: OXFORD U PR, 1935, 217 PP.
SUPPORTS PLURALISM IN WORLD GOVERNMENT, STATING THAT, ALTHOUGH POPULISM IS BEST FOR ENGLAND, PERHAPS THERE ARE COUNTRIES WHERE DICTATORSHIPS ARE BETTER. ATTEMPTS TO APOLOGIZE FOR CONCESSIONS BEING MADE TO HITLER AT THAT TIME, BY DISCUSSING PREVIOUS DICTATORSHIPS THROUGHOUT EUROPE'S HISTORY AND CLAIMING THAT WHATEVER SYSTEM MAINTAINS PEACE IS OF VALUE.

2058 MARSH D.C.
THE FUTURE OF THE WELFARE STATE.
BALTIMORE: PENGUIN BOOKS, 1964, 140 PP.
EXAMINES ASSUMPTIONS ON WHICH BRITISH SOCIAL POLICIES ARE BASED, WAYS BRITAIN HAS ATTEMPTED TO ACHIEVE POST-WWII AIMS, AND APPLICABILITY OF TITLE "WELFARE STATE." ARGUES THAT WELFARE STATE MUST SERVE NEEDS OF CITIZENS AND THAT 20TH-CENTURY CONCEPT HAS BEEN RESTRAINED BY 19TH-CENTURY SYSTEM OF ADMINISTRATION. WARNS THAT LARGEST DANGER IS IN INERTIA OF MACHINE ITSELF AND ADVOCATES REMODELING.

2059 MARSILIUS/PADUA
DEFENSOR PACIS (1324)
NEW YORK: MACMILLAN, 1928, 510 PP.
ATTACKS NOTION OF PAPAL AUTHORITY IN CIVIL MATTERS, BELIEVING IT TO LEAD TO CIVIL STRIFE AND DISORDER. DECLARES THAT THERE WAS NO DIVINE REVELATION OF PAPAL SUPREMACY. DECIDES THAT DUE TO NATURE OF POLITICS AND MEN, THERE CAN BE NO ABSOLUTE AUTHORITY; RATHER, PROVISION MUST BE MADE FOR HUMAN ERROR. THIS CHALLENGES THE IDEA OF PAPAL INFALLIBILITY. REDEFINES ROLE OF CHURCH IN POLITICS.

2060 MARTELLI G.
"PORTUGAL AND THE UNITED NATIONS."
INT. AFF., 40 (JULY 64), 453-65.
PORTUGAL'S DEFIANCE OF UN WITH RESPECT TO HER COLONIES RESULTS FROM BOTH SELF-INTEREST AND CONVICTION THAT MOTHER COUNTRY HAS MISSION IN AFRICA.

2061 MARTIN B.K.
THE TRIUMPH OF LORD PALMERSTON.
NEW YORK: DIAL, 1924, 259 PP.
STUDY OF INTERACTION OF PUBLIC OPINION AND POLITICAL ACTIVITY IN ENGLAND BEFORE CRIMEAN WAR. DISCUSSES KEY EVENTS LEADING TO START OF WAR AND FOCUSES ON POPULARITY OF LORD PALMERSTON, LEADING WHIG STATESMAN, AND HIS SUCCESSFUL MANIPULATION OF PUBLIC OPINION.

2063 MARTIN L.W.
"THE MARKET FOR STRATEGIC IDEAS IN BRITAIN: THE 'SANDYS ERA'"
AM. POL. SCI. REV., 56 (MAR. 62), 23-40.
ANALYSIS OF BRITISH DEFENSE MEASURES AND COMMITMENTS. INCLUDES STUDY OF MILITARY, DIPLOMATIC,AND ECONOMIC RESOURCES AND VARIOUS DEFENSE STRATEGIES. CONSIDERS PROBLEMS FACED BY MINISTER OF DEFENCE IN SEARCH FOR ADVANCED MODES OF DEFENSE.

2064 MARTIN L.W.
DIPLOMACY IN MODERN EUROPEAN HISTORY.
NEW YORK: MACMILLAN, 1966, 138 PP., LC#66-17387.
ESSAYS DISCUSSING CENTRAL IMPORTANCE OF DIPLOMACY IN WESTERN EUROPEAN POLITICAL RELATIONS FROM TIME OF ITS ORIGIN IN 15TH-CENTURY ITALY TO ITS MODIFICATIONS AND REFINEMENTS IN COLD WAR ERA. TOPICS ARE BROAD IN SCOPE AND ORIENTATION IS SCHOLARLY AND TECHNICAL. EMPHASIS IS ON SOCIAL, HISTORICAL, AND POLITICAL FACTORS.

2065 MARTINDALE D.
SOCIAL LIFE AND CULTURAL CHANGE.
PRINCETON: VAN NOSTRAND, 1962, 528 PP.
REVIEWS VARIOUS BRANCHES OF SOCIAL BEHAVIORALISM, THEORY OF SOCIAL GROUPS AND INSTITUTIONS, THEORY OF COMMUNITY AND CIVILIZATION. MAJOR FOCUS OF STUDY IS ON FORMATION OF COMMUNITIES AND KIND OF SOCIAL THOUGHT THAT ARISES IN CONNECTION WITH COMMUNITIES. USES FIVE MAJOR CASE HISTORIES, FOUR OF WHICH ARE DRAWN FROM ANCIENT WORLD, TO TEST AUTHOR'S CONCLUSIONS ON INTELLECTUAL LIFE.

2066 MARTINDALE D.
COMMUNITY, CHARACTER AND CIVILIZATION: STUDIES IN SOCIAL BEHAVIORISM.
NEW YORK: FREE PRESS OF GLENCOE, 1963, 467 PP., LC#63-13540.
EXAMINATION OF NUMEROUS SOCIOLOGICAL STUDIES TO ILLUSTRATE VARIANCE OF THEORIES AND METHODOLOGIES. THE NATURE AND PLACE OF SOCIAL BEHAVIORISM IN SOCIOLOGICAL THEORY.

2067 MARTINET G.
MARXISM OF OUR TIME: OR THE CONTRADICTIONS OF SOCIALISM.
NEW YORK: MONTHLY REVIEW PR, 1964, 126 PP., LC#64-17415.
CRITICIZES LACK OF A MODERN MARXIST THEORY AND FORCED DEPENDENCE UPON THE ORIGINAL UNADAPTED TENETS OF MARX. CHANGES IN MODERN WORLD NECESSITATE RENOVATION.

2068 MARTINEZ J.R.
THREE CASES OF COMMUNISM: CUBA, BRAZIL, AND MEXICO.
DUBUQUE: WC BROWN, 1964, 154 PP.
UNDERSCORES FACTS OF COMMUNISM AS ITS WORK IS ILLUSTRATED IN CUBA, BRAZIL, AND MEXICO. PRESENTS BACKGROUND OF LATIN AMERICAN SCENE AND SHOWS EVOLUTION OF COMMUNIST IDEOLOGY AND PERSONALITIES IN THREE COUNTRIES. ANALYZES RISE OF CASTRO, ROLE OF LC PRESTES IN BRAZIL, AND ACTIVITIES OF COMMUNIST PARTY IN MEXICAN REVOLUTION.

2069 MARTINEZ RIOS J. ED.
BIBLIOGRAFIA ANTROPOLOGICA Y SOCIOLOGICA DEL ESTADO DE OAXACA.
MEXICO CITY: INST INVESTIG SOC, 1961, 154 PP.
BIBLIOGRAPHY OF ANTHROPOLOGY AND SOCIOLOGY OF MEXICAN STATE OF OAXACA. IN FIVE PARTS DEALING WITH APPLIED ANTHRO-

POLOGY, FOLKLORE, LINGUISTICS, PHYSICAL ANTHROPOLOGY, INDIAN CODICES, AND ARCHAEOLOGY.

2070 MARTINS A.F.
REVOLUCAO BRANCA NO CAMPO.
SAO PAULO: EDITORA BRASILIENSE, 1962, 202 PP.
EXAMINES RURAL AGRICULTURAL ECONOMY OF BRAZIL, EXPLAINING IMPORTANCE OF MODERNIZATION OF PRODUCTION BY MORE EXTENSIVE ELECTRICAL FACILITIES AND USE OF MODERN MACHINERY. COMPARES DEVELOPMENT OF US AGRICULTURE THROUGH APPLICATION OF MODERN ELECTRICAL POWER TO THE SLOW DEVELOPMENT OF BRAZILIAN RURAL AREAS.

2071 MARTZ J.D.
CENTRAL AMERICA: THE CRISIS AND THE CHALLENGE.
CHAPEL HILL: U OF N CAR PR, 1959, 356 PP.
TREATMENT OF CENTRAL AMERICAN POLITICS SINCE WWII. FACTS, PERSONS, AND CHARACTERISTICS OF CENTRAL AMERICAN POLITICAL AFFAIRS. EFFECTS OF CENTRAL AMERICAN POLITICS ON US.

2072 MARTZ J.D.
"THE PLACE OF LATIN AMERICA IN THE STUDY OF COMPARATIVE POLITICS."
J. OF POLITICS, 28 (FEB. 66), 57-80.
SURVEY OF MODERN COMPARATIVE POLITICS LITERATURE WITH AN EYE FOR HOW THE SCHOLARS INCLUDED LATIN AMERICA WITHIN THEIR THEORETICAL SYSTEMS. NOTES CONTROVERSY OVER FITTING LATIN AMERICA IN WITH OTHER "NON-WESTERN" STATES, AND SO HE TESTS DIFFERENT PROPOSITIONS AND TAXONOMIC SYSTEMS EXPLICITLY FOR RELEVANCE TO LATIN AMERICA; IT DIVERGES FROM MOST PATTERNS.

2073 MARVICK D. ED.
POLITICAL DECISION-MAKERS.
NEW YORK: FREE PRESS, 1961, 347 PP.
SERIES OF ESSAYS DISCUSSING POLITICAL LEADERS OF FRANCE, INDIA, BRITAIN, GERMANY AND AMERICA. ANALYZES THEIR SOCIAL, ECONOMIC AND EDUCATIONAL BACKGROUNDS AS WELL AS MOTIVATING INFLUENCES DETERMINING THEIR ENTRANCE INTO POLITICS. CONCLUDES WITH AN OVER-ALL SURVEY OF THE STUDY OF POLITICAL ELITES AND A REVIEW OF THE PSYCHO-ANALYTIC METHOD OF THE STUDY OF POLITICAL PERSONALITIES.

2074 MARWICK A.
"THE LABOUR PARTY AND THE WELFARE STATE IN BRITAIN, 1900-1948."
AMER. HISTORICAL REVIEW, 73 (DEC. 67), 380-403.
ANALYZES THE CONTRIBUTIONS OF THE LABOUR PARTY TO THE ESTABLISHMENT OF THE WELFARE STATE IN BRITAIN. DISCUSSES WHAT THE PARTY CONTRIBUTED TO SOCIAL LEGISLATION ENACTED BEFORE 1945, AND THE LABOR PARTY'S IDEAS AND THEORIES ON SOCIAL POLICY. THE LEGISLATION OF 1945-48 IS EXAMINED WITH REFERENCE TO LABOUR PARTY THEORIES.

2075 MARX F.M.
THE PRESIDENT AND HIS STAFF SERVICES PUBLIC ADMINISTRATION SERVICES NUMBER 98 (PAMPHLET)
CHICAGO: PUBLIC ADMIN SERVICE, 1947, 26 PP.
DEFINES OFFICE OF PRESIDENT IN TERMS OF ITS CONSTITUTIONAL STRUCTURE AND THE LEGISLATION WHICH HAS EXPANDED ITS POWERS. DISCUSSES THE VARIOUS AGENCIES DIRECTLY RESPONSIBLE TO THE PRESIDENT AND HOW THEY INCREASE HIS POWER. IS DESIGNED TO ACQUAINT THE FOREIGN READER WITH THE EXECUTIVE BRANCH.

2076 MARX H.L. JR. ED.
STATE AND LOCAL GOVERNMENT.
NEW YORK: H W WILSON, 1962, 191 PP., LC#62-15535.
STUDIES GOVERNMENT AT COMMUNITY, METROPOLITAN, COUNTY, AND STATE LEVELS, COMPACTS AND AUTHORITIES, REPRESENTATION, AND ROLE OF FEDERAL GOVERNMENT, DRAWN FROM PERIODICAL LITERATURE.

2077 MARX K.
THE CLASS STRUGGLES IN FRANCE.
NEW YORK: INTERNATIONAL PUBLRS, 1934, 159 PP.
EXPLANATION OF THE REVOLUTIONARY MOVEMENTS IN FRANCE FROM 1848 TO 1850 IN TERMS OF ECONOMIC CONDITIONS. MAINTAINS THAT WORLD TRADE CRISIS CAUSED OUTBREAKS, AND THAT RETURN OF PROSPERITY IN 1849 RESULTED IN CRUSHING OF REVOLUTION AND RETURN OF REACTIONARY GOVERNMENTS.

2078 MARX K., ENGELS F.
THE CIVIL WAR IN THE UNITED STATES.
NEW YORK: INTERNATIONAL PUBLRS, 1937, 325 PP.
COLLECTION OF WRITINGS BY MARX AND ENGELS ON CIVIL WAR IN US. ARTICLES APPEARED IN "NEW YORK DAILY TRIBUNE" AND "VIENNA PRESSE" IN 1861-62. INCLUDES CORRESPONDENCE BETWEEN MARX AND ENGELS ON EUROPE'S AND ESPECIALLY ENGLAND'S ATTITUDE TOWARD THE WAR. MAINTAINS THAT EMANCIPATION OF WORKERS DEPENDED ON PRELIMINARY DESTRUCTION OF SLAVERY.

2079 MARX K.
THE GERMAN IDEOLOGY, PARTS 1 AND 3 (1846)
LONDON: LAWRENCE & WISHART, 1938, 214 PP.
FIRST PART OF THIS MATERIALISTIC EXPOSITION OF HISTORY CONTAINS A HISTORY OF MATERIAL PRODUCTION THAT SHOWS THE GROWTH OF PRIVATE PROPERTY AND THE CAUSAL RELATIONSHIPS BETWEEN ECONOMICS, POLITICS, AND LAW. PART THREE IS A CRITIQUE OF THE "TRUE SOCIALISTS," THE MEN (GRUN, PUTTMANN, KUHLMAN, ET AL.) WHO ADAPTED FRENCH SOCIALISM TO THE GERMAN BOURGEOISIE, THUS ABANDONING THE WORKING-CLASS REVOLUTION.

2080 MARX K.
THE EIGHTEENTH BRUMAIRE OF LOUIS BONAPARTE (1852)
NEW YORK: LABOR NEWS CO, 1951, 186 PP.
DESCRIBES EVENTS OF 1848-1852, WHICH SAW LOUIS BONAPARTE BECOME KING OF FRANCE, FROM VIEWPOINT OF MATERIALISTIC HISTORY, RELATING EVENTS TO WHAT MARX SAW AS THEIR ECONOMIC CAUSES. CLAIMS BOURGEOISIE HAD TO ELECT BONAPARTE KING TO PROTECT THEIR OWN ECONOMIC INTERESTS. SEES EVENTS AS CONFLICTS OF BOURGEOIS SOCIETY, WITH STRUGGLE BETWEEN UPPER AND MIDDLE CLASSES OPPRESSING THE LOWER.

2081 MARX K., ENGELS F.
THE COMMUNIST MANIFESTO.
IN (MENDEL A. ESSENTIAL WORKS OF MARXISM, NEW YORK: BANTAM. BOOKS, 1961, CHAPTER 1, PAGES 13-44).
SETS FORTH THE DOCTRINE OF CLASS STRUGGLE BETWEEN THE RULING BOURGEOISIE AND THE PROLETARIAT, AND DESCRIBES HOW THE LATTER WILL RISE UP AND CONQUER ITS OPPRESSORS. UNTIL THE COMPLETE SUPPRESSION OF THE BOURGEOISIE, THE DICTATORSHIP OF THE PROLETARIAT WOULD PREVAIL. EVENTUALLY, IT WOULD WITHER AWAY, ALONG WITH THE STATE, A CLASSLESS SOCIETY EMERGING.

2082 MARX K.
THE POVERTY OF PHILOSOPHY (1847)
NEW YORK: INTERNATIONAL PUBLRS, 1963, 233 PP., LC#63-10632.
WRITTEN IN CONTRADICTION OF PROUDHON'S "THE PHILOSOPHY OF MISERY." CRITICIZES PROUDHON'S RESORTING TO PHILOSOPHY AS "FEEBLE HEGELIANISM." MAINTAINS THAT PROUDHON DOES NOT UNDERSTAND ECONOMIC DEVELOPMENT. BELIEVES THAT FORM OF SOCIETY IS A "PRODUCT OF MEN'S RECIPROCAL ACTION." MEN ARE NOT FREE TO CHOOSE PRODUCTIVE FORCES. PROUDHON'S THEORY OF ECONOMIC CONTRADICTIONS SERVES THE "PETTY BOURGEOIS."

2083 MARX K.
REVOLUTION AND COUNTER-REVOLUTION.
ORIGINAL PUBLISHER NOT AVAILABLE, 1896, 148 PP.
REPORTS AND INTERPRETS GERMAN REVOLUTION OF 1848 AS A CLASS STRUGGLE. LINKS UPRISING TO GERMANY'S INABILITY TO COMPETE WITH REST OF EUROPE INDUSTRIALLY, AND SUFFERING OF LOWER CLASSES WHICH RESULTED. DECLINE OF MIDDLE CLASS IS SEEN AS BASIC CAUSE OF DEFEAT OF GOVERNMENT. ATTACKS MIDDLE-CLASS RISE TO POWER AS INCREASING POVERTY AND SUPPRESSION OF THE LOWER CLASSES.

2084 MAS LATRIE L.
RELATIONS ET COMMERCE DE L'AFRIQUE SEPTENTRIONALE OU MAGREB AVEC LES NATIONS CHRETIENNES AU MOYEN AGE.
PARIS: LIBRAIRIE FIRMIN DIDOT ET CIE., 1886, 550 PP.
SURVEY OF NORTH AFRICA OR THE MAGREB DURING THE MIDDLE AGES, EMPHASIZING CONFLICTING CHRISTIAN AND ARAB CIVILIZATION, FOREIGN INVASION, AND COMMERCE. EXAMINES CUSTOMS, DYNASTIES, AND PIRACY.

2085 MASON E.S.
THE PARIS COMMUNE: AN EPISODE IN THE HISTORY OF THE SOCIALIST MOVEMENT.
NEW YORK: MACMILLAN, 1930, 386 PP.
PRESENTS AN ACCOUNT OF THE COMMUNE AND A SOCIALIST AND COMMUNIST INTERPRETATION OF THE COMMUNE. THE EVENT IS VIEWED NOT MERELY AS AN INCIDENT IN THE HISTORY OF FRANCE, BUT AS AN EPOCH-MAKING EVENT IN THE WORLDWIDE BOURGEOISIE-PROLETARIAT REVOLUTION. AUTHOR DOES NOT AGREE WITH CLASS-STRUGGLE BASIS FOR THEBCOMMUNE.

2086 MASON E.S.
ECONOMIC DEVELOPMENT IN INDIA AND PAKISTAN.
CAMBRIDGE: HARV CTR INTL AFFAIRS, 1966, 67 PP., LC#66-28532.
EXAMINES DIVERGENT TRENDS OBSERVABLE IN INDIAN AND PAKISTANI ECONOMIES, 1960-65. ANALYZES NATURE AND AMOUNT OF FOREIGN ASSISTANCE RECEIVED BY BOTH NATIONS, SHOWING HOW EACH MANAGED FOREIGN EXCHANGE. DESCRIBES METHODS OF EXPORT PROMOTION AND IMPORT REPLACEMENT. DISCUSSES AGRICULTURAL PRIORITIES AND POLICIES.

2087 MASON J.B. ED., PARISH H.C. ED.
THAILAND BIBLIOGRAPHY.
GAINESVILLE: U OF FLORIDA LIB, 1958, 245 PP.
CONTAINS MORE THAN 2,300 ENTRIES, MANY ANNOTATED, TO BOOKS, ARTICLES, AND DOCUMENTS IN NINE WESTERN LANGUAGES. WORKS ON HISTORY, GOVERNMENT, INTERNATIONAL RELATIONS, PUBLIC ADMINISTRATION, ECONOMICS, ARCHEOLOGY, GEOGRAPHY, SOCIOLOGY, EDUCATION, ART, LANGUAGE STUDY, AND THE NATURAL SCIENCES. HAS A LIST OF BIBLIOGRAPHIES.

2088 MASSEY V.
CANADIANS AND THEIR COMMONWEALTH: THE ROMANES LECTURE DELIVERED IN THE SHELDONIAN THEATRE JUNE 1, 1961 (PAMPHLET)
LONDON: OXFORD U PR, 1961, 20 PP.
ADDRESS TO AN ENGLISH AUDIENCE ASKING THAT CANADA BE JUDGED BY WHAT SHE DOES WITH HER VAST RESOURCES. DISCUSSES

CANADA'S PLURALISM, HER ROLE AS INTERPRETER BETWEEN US AND GREAT BRITAIN, AND ATTITUDE TOWARD COMMONWEALTH TODAY. BRIEFLY SURVEYS PROBLEMS OF COMMONWEALTH WITH WHICH CANADIANS ARE CONCERNED.

2089 MASUR G.
NATIONALISM IN LATIN AMERICA* DIVERSITY AND UNITY.
NEW YORK: MACMILLAN, 1966, 278 PP., LC#66-12974.
HISTORIAN DRAWS FROM THE SOCIAL SCIENCES TO PRESENT A PICTURE OF NATIONALISM IN LATIN AMERICA. VIEWS IT GENERALLY AS IT DEVELOPED FROM THE MIXING OF IBERIAN AND NATIVE CULTURES IN THE HEMISPHERE AS A WHOLE. ALSO TRACES DISPARATE NATIONALIST PHENOMENA IN THE VARIOUS COUNTRIES. CONCENTRATES ON RELATION BETWEEN NATIONALISM AND DEVELOPMENT.

2090 MATHER F.C.
PUBLIC ORDER IN THE AGE OF THE CHARTISTS.
MANCHESTER: MANCHESTER UNIV PR, 1959, 250 PP.
DISCUSSES PROBLEM OF MAINTAINING ORDER AND PREVENTING RIOTS AS DEALT WITH IN ENGLAND FROM 1822-70 INCLUDING POLICE AND MILITARY ORGANIZATIONS AND SECRET SERVICE.

2091 MATOS J. ED.
LAS ACTUALES COMMUNIDADES DE INDIGENAS: HUAROCHIRI EN 1955.
LIMA: U NAC MAYOR DE SAN MARCOS, 1958, 341 PP.
SOCIOLOGICAL STUDY OF CONTEMPORARY INDIAN COMMUNITIES IN PERU. ANALYZES BASIS OF COMMUNITY LIFE AND RELATIONSHIP OF COMMUNITY TO FAMILY, SOCIAL STRUCTURE, NATIONAL GOVERNMENT, LEGAL SYSTEM, EDUCATION, RELIGION, AND ECONOMY.

2092 MATTHEWS D.G. ED.
A CURRENT VIEW OF AFRICANA (PAMPHLET)
WASHINGTON: AFRICAN BIBLIOG CTR, 1964, 32 PP.
SELECTED AND ANNOTATED BIBLIOGRAPHY ON AFRICAN AFFAIRS.

2093 MATTHEWS D.G.
"A CURRENT BIBLIOGRAPHY ON ETHIOPIAN AFFAIRS: A SELECT BIBLIOGRAPHY FROM 1950-1964."
AFR. BIBLIOG. CTR., SPEC. SERIES, 3 (MAR. 65), 1-46.
A PARTIALLY ANNOTATED BIBLIOGRAPHY OF 594 BOOKS, ARTICLES, AND OFFICIAL DOCUMENTS PUBLISHED BETWEEN 1950-64 ON ETHOPIA. EMPHASIS PLACED ON ENGLISH-LANGUAGE PUBLICATIONS, BUT SOME SOURCES IN FRENCH, RUSSIAN, ITALIAN, AND GERMAN. BRIEF DESCRIPTIVE ANNOTATIONS SUPPLIED WHEN TITLE INSUFFICIENTLY CLEAR TO EXPLAIN CONTENTS OF A GIVEN PUBLICATION. A SYSTEMATIC GUIDE FOR RESEARCH OR GENERAL USE.

2094 MATTHEWS D.G. ED.
"A CURRENT BIBLIOGRAPHY ON SUDANESE AFFAIRS; A SELECT BIBLIOGRAPHY FROM 1960-1964."
AFR. BIBLIOG. CTR., SPEC. SERIES, 3 (JULY 65), 1-28.
COMPREHENSIVE LISTING OF 378 UNANNOTATED BOOKS, OFFICIAL DOCUMENTS, AND PERIODICAL ENTRIES, WHICH COVER SUBJECTS OF GOVERNMENT AND RELIGION. EMPHASIS ON ENGLISH-LANGUAGE PUBLICATIONS ISSUED BETWEEN 1960-65. RUSSIAN ENTRIES TRANSLITERATED; GERMAN, FRENCH, AND ITALIAN SOURCES INCLUDED.

2095 MATTHEWS D.G. ED.
"ETHIOPIAN OUTLINE: A BIBLIOGRAPHIC RESEARCH GUIDE."
AFR. BIBLIOG. CTR., SPEC. SERIES, 4 (FEB. 66), 1-17.
SUPPLEMENT TO "A CURRENT BIBLIOGRAPHY ON ETHIOPIAN AFFAIRS." PREPARED FOR INTERNATIONAL CONFERENCE OF ETHIOPIAN STUDIES HELD APRIL 2-8, 1966. CONTAINS CHRONOLOGICAL AND RESEARCH DATA LISTING NEW ETHIOPIAN CABINET AS OF APRIL 11, 1966. SUBJECT BIBLIOGRAPHY OF 93 UNANNOTATED ENTRIES PUBLISHED BETWEEN 1960-65; AUTHOR INDEX.

2096 MATTHEWS D.G. ED.
"PRELUDE-COUP D'ETAT-MILITARY GOVERNMENT: A BIBLIOGRAPHICAL AND RESEARCH GUIDE TO NIGERIAN POL AND GOVT, JAN, 1965-66."
AFR. BIBLIOG. CTR., SPEC. SERIES, 4 (MAR. 66), 1-21.
FIRST ISSUE OF "BIBLIO-RESEARCH SERIES," DESIGNED TO AUGMENT BIBLIOGRAPHICAL INFORMATION WITH CHRONOLOGICAL, BIOGRAPHICAL, AND RESEARCH DATA. CONTAINS CHRONOLOGY OF EVENTS FROM 1965-66; LISTING OF MEMBERS OF NIGERIAN FEDERAL GOVERNMENT AS OF MARCH 31, 1965; LISTING OF OTHER MINISTERS AND GOVERNORS; AND A BIBLIOGRAPHY OF GOVERNMENT MATERIALS FROM 1964-65 ARRANGED GEOGRAPHICALLY.

2097 MATTHEWS D.R.
THE SOCIAL BACKGROUND OF POLITICAL DECISION-MAKERS.
GARDEN CITY: DOUBLEDAY, 1954, 62 PP., LC#54-10200.
BRIEF ANALYSIS OF THEORETICAL WRITINGS AND FACTUAL STUDIES ABOUT SOCIAL AND PSYCHOLOGICAL BACKGROUNDS OF GOVERNMENT OFFICIALS. CONSIDERS POLITICS AND DECISION-MAKING, RECRUITMENT OF DECISION-MAKERS, DECISION-MAKERS AND SOCIAL CHANGE.

2098 MATTHEWS R.
AFRICAN POWDER KEG: REVOLT AND DISSENT IN SIX EMERGENT NATIONS.
LONDON: THE BODLEY HEAD, 1966, 223 PP.
DEALS WITH INEQUALITIES BETWEEN RULERS AND RULED, NATURES OF LEADERS OF SIX NATIONS CONSIDERED, LACK OF EDUCATION IN GOVERNMENT, AND PERSONAL AMBITION OF EACH WOULD-BE LEADER.

2099 MATTHEWS R.O.
"THE SUEZ CANAL DISPUTE* A CASE STUDY IN PEACEFUL SETTLEMENT."
INTL. ORGANIZATION, 21 (WINTER 67), 79-101.
AN EXAMINATION OF THE ROLE OF THE UN AND METHODS USED FOR SETTLING THE SUEZ CONFLICT OF 1956 PEACEFULLY. ROLES OF THE VARIOUS GOVERNMENTS AND PERSONALITIES INVOLVED ARE PRESENTED. AUTHOR HYPOTHESIZES FROM THIS CASE AS TO HOW FUTURE INTERNATIONAL CONFLICTS MAY BE RESOLVED PEACEFULLY.

2100 MATTHIAS E. ED., MORSEY R. ED.
DAS ENDE DER PARTEIEN 1933.
DUSSELDORF: DROSTE VERLAG, 1960, 816 PP.
COLLECTION OF ESSAYS ON DISINTEGRATEION OF POLITICAL PARTIES IN GERMANY BETWEEN END OF WEIMAR REPUBLIC AND RISE OF HITLER. MAINTAIN THAT FAILURE OF POLITICAL PARTIES TO TAKE REALISTIC VIEW OF IMPENDING CRISIS CONTRIBUTED SUBSTANTIALLY TO VICTORY OF NATIONAL SOCIALISM.

2101 MAUD J.
AID FOR DEVELOPING COUNTRIES.
LONDON: U OF LONDON PRESS, 1964, 23 PP.
DISCUSSES IMPORTANCE OF FOREIGN AID TO POLITICAL SECURITY AND OBLIGATION OF DEVELOPED NATIONS TO UNDEVELOPED. GIVES ANALYSIS OF BRITAIN'S SPENDING COMPARED TO REST OF FREE WORLD AND COMMUNIST BLOC.

2102 MAUGHAM R.
NORTH AFRICAN NOTEBOOK.
LONDON: CHAPMAN AND HALL, 1948, 146 PP.
RECOUNTS AUTHOR'S JOURNEY THROUGH MOORISH SPAIN AND ACROSS NORTH AFRICA. INCLUDES DISCUSSION OF SOCIAL AND POLITICAL CURRENTS OF EACH COUNTRY.

2103 MAURRAS C.
ENQUETE SUR LA MONARCHIE (1909)
PARIS: NOUVELLE LIB NATIONALE, 1925, 615 PP.
ADVOCATED THE RE-ESTABLISHMENT OF A TRADITIONAL, HEREDITARY MONARCH. BELIEVED THAT SUCH A KING, REGARDLESS OF HIS PERSONAL WORTH, WOULD BY HIS POSITION BEST REPRESENT THE INTEREST OF THE STATE. OPPOSED DEMOCRATIC STATE BECAUSE IT LACKED "CONTINUITY." IDEA OF HEREDITY AND CONTINUITY ALSO INCLUDED CONCEPTS OF SELECTION AND RACE. MONARCHY SHOULD BE AUTHORITARIAN AND DECENTRALIZED - FREED OF BUREAUCRACY.

2104 MAXIMOFF G.P. ED.
THE POLITICAL PHILOSOPHY OF BAKUNIN: SCIENTIFIC ANARCHISM.
NEW YORK: FREE PRESS OF GLENCOE, 1953, 434 PP.
BIOGRAPHICAL SKETCH OF BAKUNIN PRECEDES DETAILED EXPOSITION OF HIS PHILOSOPHY: CRITICISM OF EXISTING SOCIETY, SYSTEM OF ANARCHISM, AND MEANS HE PROPOSED TO IMPLEMENT HIS THEORIES.

2105 MAYANJA A.
"THE GOVERNMENT'S PROPOSALS ON THE NEW CONSTITUTION."
TRANSITION, 7 (AUG.-SEPT. 67), 20-25.
CRITICIZES PROPOSED CONSTITUTION FOR UGANDA AS FALLING FAR SHORT OF WHAT IT SHOULD BE. CLAIMS ENTIRELY TOO MUCH POWER IS INVESTED IN PRESIDENT. WARNS OF POSSIBLE EFFECTS OF THIS UPON FREEDOM AND PARLIAMENTARY PROCESS.

2106 MAYNE A.
DESIGNING AND ADMINISTERING A REGIONAL ECONOMIC DEVELOPMENT PLAN WITH SPECIFIC REFERENCE TO PUERTO RICO (PAMPHLET)
PARIS: ORG FOR ECO COOP AND DEV, 1961, 62 PP.
STUDIES METHODS OF DESIGNING REGIONAL ECONOMIC DEVELOPMENT PLANS STRESSING NEED TO EVALUATE POTENTIALS, TRANSLATE OBJECTIVES INTO PROGRAMS, CHOOSE ALTERNATIVE PROGRAMS, AND COORDINATE PLANS. MAINTAINS THAT ONE REASON FOR PROGRAM FAILURES IS NEGLECT OF PUBLIC ADMINISTRATION PROCEDURE AND GOVERNMENT DECISION-MAKING PROCESS. LOOKS AT SOCIAL AND ECONOMIC DEVELOPMENT SINCE 1940.

2107 MAYNE R.
THE COMMUNITY OF EUROPE.
LONDON: GOLLANCZ, 1963, 192 PP.
BRIEF HISTORY OF EVOLVING ENTITY OF THE EUROPEAN COMMUNITY, INCLUDING POLITICAL AND ECONOMIC BACKGROUND, POST-WAR DEBATES, BRITISH 'DILEMMA,' AND EUROPE'S RELATION TO REST OF WORLD. ALSO DISCUSSES VARIOUS EUROPEAN REGIONAL ORGANIZATIONS.

2108 MAYO H.B.
DEMOCRACY AND MARXISM.
NEW YORK: OXFORD U PR, 1955, 364 PP., LC#55-7539.
PRESENTS A SURVEY AND ASSESSMENT OF MARXISM, AS CONCEIVED BY LENIN AND STALIN AND AS MANIFESTED IN CONTEMPORARY USSR. ANALYZES AND ASSESSES DEMOCRACY. AUTHOR BELIEVES THAT THE DEMOCRAT OUGHT TO UNDERSTAND BOTH COMMUNISM AND DEMOCRACY. DISCUSSES DIALECTICAL MATERIALISM, THE ECONOMIC INTERPRETATION OF HISTORY, THE CLASS STRUGGLE, REVOLUTION, AND MORALITY AND RELIGION.

2109 MAYO H.B.
AN INTRODUCTION TO DEMOCRATIC THEORY.
NEW YORK: OXFORD U PR, 1960, 310 PP., LC#60-07063.

THEORETICAL CONSIDERATION OF DEMOCRACY: METHODS, ETHICS, JUSTIFICATIONS, VALUES, AND DERIVATION. SOME SPECIFIC EXAMPLES. CRITICISM AND PROBLEMS OF POPULAR GOVERNMENT GIVEN.

2110 MAZRUI A.A.
"ON THE CONCEPT 'WE ARE ALL AFRICANS'."
AMER. POLIT. SCI. REV., 57 (MARCH 63), 88-97.
A THOROUGH REVIEW OF THE VARIOUS ASPECTS OF AFRICAN SELF-CONSCIOUSNESS. A CLEAR DISTINCTION IS MADE BETWEEN NARROWER TERRITORIAL OR TRIBAL NATIONALISMS AND THE WIDE CONTINENTALISTIC BRAND.

2111 MAZRUI A.A.
THE ANGLO-AFRICAN COMMONWEALTH; POLITICAL FRICTION AND CULTURAL FUSION.
NEW YORK: PERGAMON PRESS, 1967, 163 PP., LC#66-29595.
EXAMINES THIRD COMMONWEALTH AND STRONG AFRICAN INFLUENCE ON ITS AFFAIRS. TRACES DEVELOPMENT OF AFRICAN RESISTANCE TO COLONIAL RULE AND OF EUROPEAN ECONOMIC COMMUNITY'S IMPACT ON COMMONWEALTH AFRICA. DISCUSSES COMMON ATTACHMENT OF BRITISH AND AFRICANS TO MONARCHICAL VALUES AND INFLUENCE OF ENGLISH LANGUAGE AND LITERATURE ON AFRICAN NATIONALISM, ESPECIALLY NYERERE'S TRANSLATION OF "JULIUS CAESAR."

2112 MAZZINI J.
"FROM THE COUNCIL TO GOD" (1870) IN J. MAZZINI, ESSAYS."
NEW YORK: EP DUTTON, 1936.
ATTACKS THE VATICAN COUNCIL OF 1870, WHICH PROCLAIMED THE INFALLIBILITY OF THE POPE. SAYS THAT, BY ABANDONING THE PRINCIPLES OF EARLY CHRISTIANITY, THE CATHOLIC CHURCH IS ALLOWING ITSELF TO OPPRESS ALL PEOPLE. SPECIFICALLY, IN ITALY IT STANDS IN THE WAY OF THE PEOPLE'S HAPPINESS BY BLOCKING UNIFICATION. CLAIMS THAT THE CHURCH NOW SERVES ITS OWN ENDS AND NOT THOSE OF GOD.

2113 MAZZINI J.
THE DUTIES OF MAN.
NEW YORK: DUTTON, 1955, 336 PP.
'WHATEVER MEN HAVE SAID, MATERIAL INTERESTS HAVE NEVER CAUSED, AND NEVER WILL CAUSE, A REVOLUTION. REVOLUTIONS HAVE THEIR ORIGIN IN THE MIND, IN THE VERY ROOT OF LIFE: NOT IN THE BODY, IN THE MATERIAL ORGANISM. A RELIGION OR A PHILOSOPHY, LIES AT BASE OF EVERY REVOLUTION.' CONCEIVES NATIONS 'NOT AS MONSTERS LIKE THE LEVIATHAN OF HOBBES BUT AS SUBLIMATED INDIVIDUAL HUMAN BEINGS.'

2114 MBEKI G.
SOUTH AFRICA: THE PEASANT'S REVOLT.
BALTIMORE: PENGUIN BOOKS, 1964, 156 PP.
DISCUSSES APARTHEID RULE IN SOUTH AFRICA AND SOME OF THE METHODS EMPLOYED BY WHITE MINORITY GOVERNMENT TO RETAIN AND CONSOLIDATE ITS RULE. EXAMINES VARIOUS RESISTANCE MOVEMENTS AMONG PEASANT COMMUNITIES AND CONCLUDES WITH EXAMINATION OF FUNCTIONS OF NATIONALIST GOVERNMENT.

2115 MBOYA T.
"RELATIONS BETWEEN THE PRESS AND GOVERNMENT IN AFRICA."
TRANSACTIONS, 2 (JUNE 62), 11-14.
DISCUSSES RELATION OF PRESS TO NEW GOVERNMENTS WITH RESPECT TO MOLDING PUBLIC OPINION FOR OR AGAINST GOVERNMENT POLICY. CRITICIZES HANDLING OF AFRICAN INDEPENDENCE MOVEMENT BY INTERNATIONAL PRESS.

2116 MBOYA T.
"AFRICAN SOCIALISM."
TRANSACTIONS, 3 (MAR. 63), 17-20.
DISCUSSES AFRICAN SOCIALISM AS NATURAL DEVELOPMENT RESULTING FROM CULTURE. ADVOCATES PAN AFRICANISM BECAUSE OF CULTURAL SIMILARITIES OF AN "AGRICULTURAL" PEOPLE. WARNS AGAINST TAKING MORE THAN TECHNOLOGICAL ASSISTANCE FROM OTHER COUNTRIES.

2117 MC CLELLAN G.S. ED.
INDIA.
NEW YORK: H W WILSON, 1960, 164 PP., LC#60-8238.
ESSAYS ON SOCIO-ECONOMIC AND POLITICAL PROBLEMS, DISCUSSING NEUTRALITY, TIBET, KASHMIR, AND RELATIONS WITH THE US. GANDHI AND NEHRU ARE ALSO CONSIDERED.

2118 MC DOWELL R.B.
IRISH PUBLIC OPINION, 1750-1800.
LONDON: FABER AND FABER, 1943, 306 PP.
STUDY OF ATTITUDES CONCERNING SOCIO-POLITICAL PROBLEMS EMPHASIZING REFORM, RADICALISM AND THE UNION. DISCUSSION INCLUDES THE HOUSE OF COMMONS, CONTROVERSIALISTS, THE TITHE DISPUTE, REGENCY CRISIS, AND VOLUNTEERS.

2119 MC WILLIAM M.
"THE WORLD BANK AND THE TRANSFER OF POWER IN KENYA."
J. COMMONWEALTH POLIT. STUD., 2 (MAY 64), 141-160.
EVALUATES STUDY MADE IN 1961 BY WORLD BANK COMMISSION, WHICH ANALYZED KENYA'S ECONOMIC CRISIS, PROBLEMS CONNECTED WITH TRANSFER OF POWER, GOVERNMENT'S DEVELOPMENT PROGRAM AND KENYA'S ECONOMIC POLICIES.

2120 MCALISTER L.N.
"CHANGING CONCEPTS OF THE ROLE OF THE MILITARY IN LATIN AMERICA."
ANN. ACAD. POL. SOC. SCI., (JULY 65), 85-98.
LAYS SIDE-BY-SIDE THE CONFLICTING INTERPRETATIONS WHICH HAVE BEEN GIVEN TO THE RELATIONSHIP BETWEEN POLITICAL AND SOCIAL CHANGE IN LATIN AMERICA AND THE PARTICIPATION OF THE MILITARY IN THE BODY POLITIC. DIFFERENTIATES "TRADITIONAL" ANTI-MILITARY HYPOTHESES AND "REVISIONIST" VIEWS OF MILITARY AS SYMPTOM OF POLITICAL ILLS. ADVOCATES MORE DEPTH STUDIES OF SINGLE COUNTRIES PRIOR TO HEMISPHERIC GENERALIZATIONS.

2121 MCALLISTER J.T. JR.
"THE POSSIBILITIES FOR DIPLOMACY IN SOUTHEAST ASIA."
WORLD POLITICS, 19 (JAN. 67), 258-305.
REVIEWS EIGHT BOOKS RELATING TO DIPLOMATIC HISTORY AND PRESENT SITUATION OF DIPLOMACY IN SOUTHEAST ASIA. BEGINS WITH ANGLO-FRENCH RIVALRY, COLONIALISM, AND INTERREGIONAL WARS. DISCUSSES DIFFICULTY OF SUCCESSFUL DIPLOMACY IN CONFLICT BETWEEN STRONG INTERNATIONAL POWER AND INTENSE LOCAL POER. EXAMINES RESULTS OF 1954 GENEVA AGREEMENTS, LAOTIAN CRISIS, AND VIETNAM WAR.

2122 MCAUSLAN J.P.W., GHAI Y.P.
"CONSTITUTIONAL INNOVATION AND POLITICAL STABILITY IN TANZANIA: A PRELIMINARY ASSESSMENT."
J. OF MOD. AFR. STUD., (DEC. 66), 479-515.
EVALUATES PERFORMANCE OF TANZANIAN GOVERNMENT UP TO 1966, CRITICIZING ITS INSTABILITY, EXCESSIVE POWER VESTED IN THE PRESIDENT, LACK OF PROVISION FOR SUCCESSION. FEELS THAT OUT-OUTLOOK IS FAIRLY HOPEFUL, AS LONG AS BUREAUCRACY DOES NOT BECOME TOO RIGID OR PRESIDENT TOO POWERFUL.

2123 MCBRYDE F.W.
CULTURAL AND HISTORICAL GEOGRAPHY OF SOUTHWEST GUATEMALA.
WASHINGTON: SMITHSONIAN INST, 1945, 184 PP.
ECOLOGICALLY-ORIENTED STUDY OF ISOLATED PEOPLES. DISPLAYS AND ANALYZES INTENSIVE AGRARIANISM OF TRIBES.

2124 MCCALL D.F.
AFRICA IN TIME PERSPECTIVE.
WORCESTER: EBENEZER BAYLIS, 1964.
CONSIDERS PROBLEMS IN ATTEMPTS TO DISCOVER THE HISTORY OF AFRICA WHICH IS STILL UNWRITTEN. AUTHOR DESIRES TO MOVE BEYOND WHAT IS WRITTEN TO INTERPRETING ARCHEOLOGICAL EVIDENCE, LANGUAGE, ART ANALYSIS. ANTHROPOLOGICAL EVIDENCE OF ALL TYPES ARE USED AND HISTORIAN SEEKS OWN ANSWERS. CHAPTER BY CHAPTER BIBLIOGRAPHY INCLUDED.

2125 MCCLEERY W.
"AN INTERVIEW WITH J. DOUGLAS BROWN ON THE 'WHY' OF VIETNAM"
UNIVERSITY, (SUMMER 67),11-16.
ARGUES DURING INTERVIEW THAT THE BASIC ISSUE IN VIETNAM IS NOT ECONOMIC, BUT RELIGIO-PHILOSOPHICAL. STRESSES THAT THE WESTERN HUMANIST CONCEPT OF INDIVIDUALISM OUGHT TO BE DEFENDED ANYWHERE AT ANY PRICE. TERMS SOVIET GOVERNMENT "MILITARY SOCIALISM." DISCUSSES SUCH TOPICS AS SOCIALIZATION IN THE US, ECONOMIC IMPACT OF VIETNAM WAR, US IMPERIALIST TRENDS, ETC.

2126 MCCLINTOCK R.
THE MEANING OF LIMITED WAR.
BOSTON: HOUGHTON MIFFLIN, 1967, 239 PP., LC#67-10558.
EMPHASIS OF STUDY IS ON OBJECTIVES OF 20TH-CENTURY LIMITED WARFARE. STUDIES MANNER IN WHICH CONFLICTS OF THE PAST 2 DECADES HAVE BEEN SETTLED. SPECIFIC WARS STUDIED INCLUDE GREEK CIVIL WAR, KOREAN WAR, ARAB-ISERAELI WARS OF 1946-49 AND 1956, "WARS OF NATIONAL LIBERATION" IN VIETNAM, AND CHINESE ATTACK ON HIMALAYAN FRONTIERS OF INDIA. INCLUDES EXAMINATION OF US DEFENSE POLICY.

2127 MCCLOSKY H., TURNER J.E.
THE SOVIET DICTATORSHIP.
NEW YORK: MCGRAW HILL, 1960, 657 PP.
INVESTIGATES TSARIST ANCESTRY, MARXIAN INTELLECTUAL HERITAGE AND THE OLIGARCHICAL COMMUNIST PARTY. DESCRIBES THE FUNCTION-PRINCIPLES OF ORGANIZATION, COMPOSITION AND OPERATION OF COMMUNIST PARTY. THEORY AND PRACTICE OF SOVIET GOVERNMENT IN ITS FORMAL AND INFORMAL STRUCTURES IS ASSAYED. RELATIONSHIP OF BOTH ANALYZED AND SOURCE OF DICTATORIAL POWER DEFINED. FOCUSES ON TOTALITARIAN ASPECTS OF REGIME.

2128 MCCOWN A.C.
THE CONGRESSIONAL CONFERENCE COMMITTEE.
NEW YORK: COLUMBIA U PRESS, 1927, 270 PP.
ATTEMPTS TO ANALYZE AND TRACE ORIGIN AND EVOLUTION OF CONFERENCE COMMITTEE AND ITS OPERATION AS PART OF LEGISLATIVE MACHINERY. STUDY OF TARIFF CONFERENCE OF 1883 AND COMPARISON BETWEEN CONGRESSIONAL CONFERENCE COMMITTEE SYSTEM AND METHODS OF ADJUSTING DIFFERENCES IN FRANCE.

2129 MCDOUGAL M.S.
"THE COMPARATIVE STUDY OF LAW FOR POLICY PURPOSES."
YALE LAW J., 6 (JUNE 52), 915-946.
COMPARATIVE LAW STUDY IS VITAL IN POLICY-MAKING. POINTS OUT EXISTING INADEQUACIES IN THIS AREA AND BIDS FOR A TEAM OF SPECIALISTS TO DEVELOP REMEDIES THROUGH CONCENTRATED

STUDY OF FOREIGN JUDICIAL SYSTEMS AND LAWS. EVALUATES ROLES OF STATES, ASSOCIATIONS, POLITICAL PARTIES AND PRESSURE GROUPS. SEES A BASIC DRIVE FOR POWER IN THESE GROUPS.

2130 MCHENRY D.E.
HIS MAJESTY'S OPPOSITION: STRUCTURE AND PROBLEMS OF THE BRITISH LABOUR PARTY 1931-1938.
BERKELEY: U OF CALIF PR, 1940, 320 PP.
SKETCHES BRIEFLY THE ORIGINS AND GROWTH OF THE LABOR PARTY. DEALS MAINLY WITH EXAMINATION OF LABOR ORGANIZATION AND ITS RECORD SINCE GENERAL ELECTIONS OF 1931. STUDY CONFINED TO EXAMINING PARTY RESOURCES AND TRACING TRENDS DURING THIS BRIEF PERIOD.

2131 MCHENRY D.E.
THE THIRD FORCE IN CANADA: THE COOPERATIVE COMMONWEALTH FEDERATION, 1932-1948.
BERKELEY: U OF CALIF PR, 1950, 351 PP.
STORY OF NEW CANADIAN POLITICAL PARTY, BUILT ON PATTERN OF BRITISH LABOUR PARTY. ARGUES THAT CCF IS A MIDDLE WAY BETWEEN REACTION AND REVOLUTION ANALYSIS OF PARTY ORGANIZATION, POLICY, AND PROSPECTS.

2132 MCILWAIN C.H.
THE HIGH COURT OF PARLIAMENT AND ITS SUPREMACY
B1910 1878 408.
NEW HAVEN: YALE U PR, 1910, 408 PP.
OF LAW, DEVELOPMENT OF LEGISLATION, PARLIAMENT AS A COURT RELATION OF JUDICIARY AND LEGISLATURE, AND DEVELOPMENT OF PARLIAMENT TO ROLE OF SUPREMACY. FOCUSES ON GROWTH OF ENGLISH HIGH COURT DURING THE MIDDLE AGES.

2133 MCILWAIN C.H.
CONSTITUTIONALISM AND THE CHANGING WORLD.
NEW YORK: MACMILLAN, 1939, 312 PP.
ANALYZES HISTORICAL DEVELOPMENT OF GOVERNMENTAL PROCESSES THAT ARE THE BASIS OF THE MODERN WORLD. STUDY FOCUSES ON ENGLISH SYSTEM, AND INCLUDES DISCUSSION OF SOVEREIGNTY, DUE PROCESS, FUNDAMENTAL LAW BEHIND THE US CONSTITUTION, GOVERNMENT BY LAW, AND LIBERAL AND TOTALITARIAN IDEALS. ALSO STUDIES MAGNA CARTA, HOUSE OF COMMONS, AND ENGLISH JUDGES.

2134 MCILWAIN C.H.
CONSTITUTIONALISM, ANCIENT AND MODERN.
ITHACA: CORNELL U PRESS, 1940, 162 PP.
BELIEVES THAT TO SECURE LIBERTY MEN MUST FIGHT FOR LEGAL LIMITS ON ARBITRARY POWER AND FOR GOVERNMENTAL RESPONSIBILITY TO THE GOVERNED. DISCUSSES DEFINITIONS AND CONCEPTIONS OF CONSTITUTIONALISM. CONSIDERS CONSTITUTIONALISM IN ROME, MIDDLE AGES, AND FROM MEDIEVAL TO MODERN TIMES. DISCUSSES PROBLEMS OF MODERN CONSTITUTIONALISM.

2135 MCILWAIN C.H.
CONSTITUTIONALISM: ANCIENT AND MODERN.
ITHACA: CORNELL U PRESS, 1947, 182 PP.
TRACES DEVELOPMENT OF CONSTITUTIONALISM BY NOTING ITS SALIENT FEATURES IN COUNTRIES WHERE ITS DEVELOPMENT IS MOST OBVIOUS AND MOST DIRECTLY RELATED TO CONTEMPORARY SYSTEMS. DEFINES CONSTITUTIONALISM IN MODERN USAGE. CONSIDERS ROME, EUROPE IN MIDDLE AGES, AND BOTH EUROPE AND US NOW. OUTLINES BASIC PROBLEMS OF MODERN CONSTITUTIONALISM.

2136 MCIVER R.M.
THE MODERN STATE.
LONDON: OXFORD U PR, 1926, 504 PP.
PRESENTS MODERN STATE AS A PRODUCT OF SOCIAL EVOLUTION. EXPLAINS HOW IT ACQUIRES SPECIFIC FUNCTIONS AND SPECIFIC MEANS OF SERVICE, RELINQUISHING CERTAIN CLAIMS AND VINDICATING OTHERS. SHOWS HOW, THROUGH STRUGGLES FOR POWER, IT HAS ESTABLISHED ITS FOUNDATIONS MORE BROADLY AND SECURELY. ANALYZES EVOLUTION AND NATURE OF MODERN THEORIES OF THE STATE.

2137 MCIVOR R.C.
CANADIAN MONETARY, BANKING, AND FISCAL DEVELOPMENT.
TORONTO: MACMILLAN CO OF CANADA, 1958, 263 PP.
HISTORICAL APPROACH TO DEVELOPMENTS, INSTITUTIONAL AND THEORETICAL, WITHIN CANADIAN ECONOMY SINCE 17TH CENTURY, FOCUSING ON EVOLUTION OF COMMERICAL BANKING. IN ANALYZING ECONOMY OF TODAY, AUTHOR FINDS THAT COMPLEMENTARY USE OF MONETARY AND FISCAL INSTRUMENTS IS ESSENTIAL FOR ECONOMIC STABILITY.

2138 MCKAY V. ED.
AFRICAN DIPLOMACY STUDIES IN THE DETERMINANTS OF FOREIGN POLICY.
NEW YORK: FREDERICK PRAEGER, 1966, 210 PP., LC#66-13669.
COMPARATIVE STUDY OF ECONOMIC, CULTURAL, MILITARY, AND POLITICAL DETERMINANTS OF AFRICAN DIPLOMACY. DISCUSSES THE ASPIRATIONS AND INHERENT RACISM OF AFRICA'S POLITICS IN ATTEMPT TO DETERMINE WHY ITS STATES ACT AS THEY DO AND WHAT ATTITUDE THE US SHOULD TAKE TOWARD THEM.

2139 MCKISACK M.
THE PARLIAMENTARY REPRESENTATION OF THE ENGLISH BOROUGHS DURING THE MIDDLE AGES.
LONDON: OXFORD U PR, 1932, 180 PP.
ANALYSIS OF PARLIAMENTARY INSTITUTIONS IN MEDIEVAL ENGLAND AND BOROUGH REPRESENTATION IN THE VARIOUS COUNCILS CONVENED FOR JUDICIAL, LEGISLATIVE, AND ADMINISTRATIVE PURPOSES. DISCUSSES METHODS OF ELECTION AND TAXATION AND PROBLEMS OF ATTENDANCE AND PAYMENT OF PARLIAMENTARY PERSONNEL. PRESENTS NEW INFORMATION FROM LOCAL ARCHIVES ON MEMBERSHIP AND ADMINISTRATION OF THE VARIOUS COUNCILS.

2140 MCLANE C.B.
"SOVIET DOCTRINE AND THE MILITARY COUPS IN AFRICA."
INTERNATIONAL JOURNAL, 21 (SUMMER 66), 298-310.
DIFFERENTIATES TWO PATTERNS OF SOVIET FOREIGN POLICY STRATEGIES TOWARD AFRICA= 1) REGULAR DIPLOMATIC AND FOREIGN AID RELATIONS WITH ALL INDEPENDENT STATES, 2) SPECIAL RELATIONS WITH MODEL STATES SUCH AS ALGERIA AND GHANA. MILITARY COUPS IN THE "MODEL" STATES HAVE CAUSED SOVIETS TO STRESS REGULAR DIPLOMACY RATHER THAN DOCTRINAIRE RELATIONS.

2141 MCLAUGHLIN M.R.
RELIGIOUS EDUCATION AND THE STATE: DEMOCRACY FINDS A WAY.
CAMBRIDGE: HARVARD LAW SCHOOL, 1967, 439 PP., LC#67-21368.
DESCRIBES HOW WESTERN DEMOCRACIES, OTHER THAN US, HAVE SOLVED PROBLEMS OF RELIGION'S ROLE IN PUBLIC EDUCATION AND RELATION OF STATE TO CHURCH-AFFILIATED SCHOOLS. FINDS THAT RELIGION IS GIVEN IMPORTANT ROLE IN EDUCATION AND THAT CHURCHRELATED SCHOOLS ARE SUPPORTED BY STATE. BELIEVES THAT CONTROVERSY CAN BE SOLVED BY DEMOCRATIC METHODS. AUTHOR IS CATHOLIC NUN.

2142 MCLEAN J.M.
THE PUBLIC SERVICE AND UNIVERSITY EDUCATION.
PRINCETON: PRINCETON U PRESS, 1949, 241 PP.
CONSIDERS BASIC ISSUES OF SOCIAL AND GOVERNMENTAL ORGANIZATION, SOCIAL AND ADMINISTRATIVE VALUES, AND BASIC TRENDS IN PUBLIC ADMINISTRATION. IS PRIMARILY CONCERNED WITH ROLE OF UNIVERSITY IN TRAINING ABLE AND RESPONSIBLE ADMINISTRATORS TO MEET GROWING NEED FOR QUALIFIED GOVERNMENT PERSONNEL. COMPARES AMERICAN AND BRITISH ATTEMPTS.

2143 MCLENNAN B.N.
"EVOLUTION OF CONCEPTS OF REPRESENTATION IN INDONESIA"
J OF ASIAN AND AFRICAN STUDIES, 1 (OCT. 66), 279-289.
ANALYZES DEVELOPMENT OF POLITICAL IDEOLOGY IN INDONESIA THAT PRECEDED ACTUAL PRACTICE. THEIR THEORY OF REPRESENTATION, HOWEVER, IS UNIQUE IN THAT MEN IN OFFICE DEVELOPED IT TO EXPLAIN THEIR METHOD OF ARRIVING THERE. FEELS THIS IS TRUE OF MOST AREAS WHERE THEORY PRECEDES PRACTICE AND IS ONE REASON FOR INDONESIA'S POLITICAL INSTABILITY.

2144 MCNAIR A.D.
THE LAW OF TREATIES: BRITISH PRACTICE AND OPINIONS.
NEW YORK: COLUMBIA U PRESS, 1938, 578 PP.
PRESENTS BRITISH PRACTICE IN THE CONCLUSION, TERMINATION, INTERPRETATION, SCOPE, AND MODIFICATION OF TREATIES. STATES LAWS WHICH ARE RELEVANT TO PRECEDING TOPICS. LEGAL SOURCES WITH WHICH IT DEALS ARE PRECEDENTS OF BRITISH GOVERNMENT AND DECISIONS OF BRITISH COURTS. AUTHOR EMPHASIZES THAT WORK IS NOT AN OFFICIAL GOVERNMENT ONE AND THAT IT IS NOT A TREATISE ON THE INTERNATIONAL LAW OF TREATIES.

2145 MCNEAL R.H.
THE BOLSHEVIK TRADITION: LENIN, STALIN, KHRUSHCHEV.
ENGLEWOOD CLIFFS: PRENTICE HALL, 1963, 181 PP., LC#63-7988.
TRACES BOLSHEVISM THROUGH THE CAREERS OF THREE PRINCIPAL PROTAGONISTS IN AND EVOLUTIONARY DISCUSSION OF DEVELOPMENT OF BOLSHEVIK TRADITION.

2146 MCNEIL E.B.
"PSYCHOLOGY AND AGGRESSION."
J. CONFL. RESOLUT., 3 (SEPT. 59), 195-293.
DESCRIBES CURRENT STATUS OF THEORY AND FACT IN PSYCHOLOGICAL STUDY OF AGGRESSION, EXAMINING PROGRESS MADE IN EXPLORING MANY FACETS OF ENMITY. RELATIONSHIP BETWEEN AGGRESSION AND MAN'S NEEDS AND CONFLICTS IS SURVEYED. URGES MORE INTENSIVE SCRUTINY OF SOURCES AND MODES FOR CONTROLLING MAN'S AGITATED NATURE.

2147 MCNELLY T. ED.
SOURCES IN MODERN EAST ASIAN HISTORY AND POLITICS.
NEW YORK: APPLETON, 1967, 422 PP., LC#67-18502.
PROVIDES SUPPLEMENTARY READING FOR COURSES IN HISTORY, POLITICS, AND IDEOLOGIES OF MODERN CHINA, JAPAN, KOREA, AND VIETNAM. EDITORIAL NOTES SUMMARIZE RECENT POLITICAL HISTORY OF EAST ASIA AND SUGGEST SIGNIFICANCE AND INTERRELATIONS OF SELECTIONS. DOCUMENTS COVER REFORM AND REVOLUTION IN CHINA, EMERGENCE OF JAPANESE EMPIRE WWI AND WWII IN FAR EAST, COMMUNIST RULE IN CHINA, AND WAR IN VIETNAM.

2148 MCPHEE A.
THE ECONOMIC REVOLUTION IN BRITISH WEST AFRICA.
LONDON: ROUTLEDGE & KEGAN PAUL, 1926, 322 PP.
ANALYSIS OF ECONOMIC SITUATION IN WEST AFRICA AS RELATED TO BRITISH EMPIRE. COVERS GEOGRAPHY, TRADE, TRANSPORTATION,

FINANCE, AND NATIVE POPULATION IN THEIR ECONOMIC EFFECTS ON ECONOMY OF WEST AFRICA.

2149 MCPHEE W.N.
FORMAL THEORIES OF MASS BEHAVIOR.
NEW YORK: FREE PRESS OF GLENCOE, 1963, 244 PP., LC#62-15345.
DISCUSSES MASS BEHAVIOR IN RELATION TO SURVIVAL OF CULTURE, SOCIAL INFLUENCE AND VOTING BEHAVIOR, "NATURAL EXPOSURE AND THE THEORY OF POPULARITY," ELECTION CAMPAIGN APPEALS, ETC.

2150 MCSHERRY J.E.
RUSSIA AND THE UNITED STATES UNDER EISENHOWER, KHRUSHCHEV, AND KENNEDY.
UNIVERSITY PARK: PENN STATE U PR, 1965, 227 PP.
INTERPRETIVE ANALYSIS OF OFFICIAL AND UNOFFICIAL SOVIET STATEMENTS MADE WHILE SIX INTERNATIONAL CRISES INVOLVING US ANS USSR WERE IN PROGRESS. MUCH OF ANALYSIS BASED ON STATEMENT BY KHRUSHCHEV. DESCRIBES INTRIGUES AND WORKINGS IN SOVIET POLITICS DURING THESE CRISES.

2151 MCWHINNEY E.
JUDICIAL REVIEW IN THE ENGLISH-SPEAKING WORLD (3RD ED.)
TORONTO: U OF TORONTO PRESS, 1965, 244 PP.
EXAMINES ROLE OF ENGLISH-SPEAKING COURTS FACED WITH DIVERSE WRITTEN CONSTITUTIONS. ADVOCATES GREATER AND MORE DYNAMIC PARTICIPATION IN POLICY-MAKING BY COURTS.

2152 MEAD M. ED.
CULTURAL PATTERNS AND TECHNICAL CHANGE.
NEW YORK: COLUMBIA U PRESS, 1953, 348 PP.
MANUAL PREPARED FOR WORLD FEDERATION FOR MENTAL HEALTH. SURVEY DESIGNED FOR EXPERTS HAVING TECHNICAL KNOWLEDGE IN VARIOUS FIELDS WHO ARE SENT FOR BENEFIT OF UNDERDEVELOPED COUNTRIES. EMPHASIS UPON FACILITATING HARMONIOUS CHANGE WHICH WILL PRODUCE MINIMUM OF STRAIN UPON INDIVIDUALS.

2153 MEAD M.
CONTINUITIES IN CULTURAL EVOLUTION.
NEW HAVEN: YALE U PR, 1964, 467 PP., LC#64-12654.
COMMUNICATION OF CULTURE IS PRIMARY THEME AND ITS EFFECT ON SOCIETY AS AN EVOLVING ENTITY. MEANS OF COMMUNICATION THROUGH CULTURE AND THEIR IMPORTANCE ARE CONSIDERED WITH SPECIAL REFERENCE TO THE GROUP. EXPLORES STATE OF KNOWLEDGE OF SOCIO-CULTURAL PROCESS, AND SUGGESTS CONDITIONS FOR IMPROVEMENT.

2154 MEADE J.E., WELLS S.J., LIESNER H.H.
CASE STUDIES IN EUROPEAN ECONOMIC UNION.
LONDON: OXFORD U. PR., 1962, 424 PP.
CONSIDER ECONOMIC MECHANISMS AND ARRANGEMENTS NECESSARY TO EFFECTIVE ECONOMIC UNION. BASE ANALYSIS ON STUDY OF BELGIUM-LUXEMBOURG UNION, BENELUX, AND EUROPEAN COAL AND STEEL COMMUNITY.

2155 MEAGHER R.F.
PUBLIC INTERNATIONAL DEVELOPMENT FINANCING IN SUDAN.
NEW YORK: COLUMBIA U LAW SCHOOL, 1965, 127 PP.
STUDIES PROGRAMS AND RELATIONS OF FOREIGN INSTITUTIONS INVOLVED IN PUBLIC FINANCING OF ECONOMIC DEVELOPMENT IN SUDAN. INCLUDES SUDAN'S ECONOMIC AND POLITICAL STRUCTURE, TEN YEAR PLAN, PUBLIC FINANCIAL INSTITUTIONS; NEED FOR EXTERNAL ASSISTANCE, ITS SOURCES AND AMOUNT; CASE STUDIES OF IMPORTANT AID IN TRANSPORTATION, IRRIGATION, AND INDUSTRY.

2156 MECHAM J.L.
"LATIN AMERICAN CONSTITUTIONS: NOMINAL AND REAL" (BMR)"
J. OF POLITICS, 21 (MAY 59), 258-275.
INQUIRY INTO HOW WIDELY GOVERNMENT IN OPERATION DEPARTS FROM CONSTITUTIONAL MANDATE IN LATIN AMERICA. AUTHOR DISCUSSES OPERATIVE AND NOMINAL CONSTITUTIONS AND CONCLUDES THAT THE NOMINAL CONSTITUTION IS SO OFTEN IGNORED BECAUSE IT FAILS TO TAKE INTO ACCOUNT THE LACK OF DEMOCRATIC EDUCATION OF ITS CITIZENRY.

2157 MECRENSKY E.
SCIENTIFIC MANPOWER IN EUROPE.
NEW YORK: PERGAMON PRESS, 1958, 188 PP., LC#58-14062.
COMPARATIVE STUDY OF SKILLED SCIENTIFIC MANPOWER IN PUBLIC SERVICE OF ENGLAND, US, AND EUROPEAN NATIONS. COVERS TRAINING, SALARIES, AND AIMS TO FIND WAYS OF HOLDING THEM IN GOVERNMENT JOBS. BIBLIOGRAPHY OF SPECIFIC STUDIES BY COUNTRIES. CHARTS OF PEOPLE INTERVIEWED, SCHOOLS FOR SCIENTISTS, ETC.

2158 MEEK C.K., MACMILLAN W.M., HUSSEY E.R.
EUROPE AND WEST AFRICA.
LONDON: OXFORD U PR, 1940, 143 PP.
ANALYSIS OF CULTURAL CHANGE AND ADMINISTRATION IN WEST AFRICA. PRIMARILY CONCERNED WITH AFRICAN ECONOMIC, SOCIAL, AND POLITICAL DEVELOPMENTS; TREATS RELATION TO EUROPE, ADJUSTMENT TO CHANGING CONDITIONS AS RESULT OF WESTERNIZATION, AND ROLE OF EDUCATION.

2159 MEGGITT M.J.
DESERT PEOPLE.
LONDON, SYDNEY: ANGUS & ROBERTSN, 1962, 348 PP.
DETAILED ANALYSIS OF WALBIRI SOCIETY. PROVIDES REFERENCE POINTS TO FACILITATE PLACING OF CENTRAL TRIBES IN OVER-ALL COMPARATIVE FRAMEWORK. DISCUSSES GENEALOGICAL CONNECTION IN ORIENTING ABORIGINAL SOCIAL BEHAVIOR. ANALYZES SEVERAL TRIBAL INSTITUTIONALIZED SITUATIONS, SUCH AS BIRTH AND DEATH. TREATS RESPONSE TO CONTACT WITH EUROPEANS.

2160 MEHDI M.T.
PEACE IN THE MIDDLE EAST.
NEW YORK: NEW WORLD PRESS, 1967, 108 PP., LC#67-20933.
CONTENDS THAT HITLER'S PERSECUTION OF JEWS IN WWII WHICH LED TO RISE OF ZIONISM MUST BE CALLED FUNDAMENTAL MOTIVE FOR ESTABLISHMENT OF ISRAEL IN 1948. DISCUSSES NATURE OF WORLDWIDE ANTI-SEMITISM AND OF BASIC CONFLICTS WHICH EXIST BETWEEN ISRAEL AND ARAB NATIONS. PROPOSES SOLUTION BASED ON GRADUAL DISSOLUTION OF ISRAEL BY MIGRATIONS OF JEWS TO THEIR NATIVE COUNTRIES, AUSTRALIA, OR NORTH AMERICA.

2161 MEHNERT K.
DER SOWJETMENSCH.
STUTTGART: DEUTSCHE VERLAGSANST, 1958, 497 PP.
DISCUSSES FAMILY LIFE, NATURE OF POLITICAL AND INTELLECTUAL FREEDOM, ATTITUDES TOWARD AUTHORITY, SUCCESS, AND PROPERTY, AND ROLE OF EDUCATION AND RELIGION IN MODERN RUSSIA. BASED ON EXTENSIVE TRAVELS IN USSR BETWEEN 1929-1957.

2162 MEHNERT K.
SOVIET MAN AND HIS WORLD.
NEW YORK: FREDERICK PRAEGER, 1962, 310 PP., LC#62-8964.
ANTI-SOVIET ANALYSIS OF RUSSIAN SOCIETY, CULTURE, POLITICS, AND ECONOMY. DISCUSSES SOVIET SOCIAL FRAMEWORK, FAMILY, PROSPERITY, EDUCATION, PLANNING, AND CONSEQUENCES OF THE 1917 REVOLUTION. ATTEMPTS TO SHOW WHICH PRE-REVOLUTION TRAITS HAVE DISAPPEARED AND WHAT NEW FEATURES HAVE EMERGED.

2163 MEHROTRA S.R.
INDIA AND THE COMMONWEALTH 1885-1929.
LONDON: ALLEN & UNWIN, 1965, 287 PP.
STUDIES TRANSFORMATION OF BRITISH EMPIRE INTO COMMONWEALTH. EMPHASIZES ROLE INDIANS PLAYED IN MAKING IT MULTIRACIAL. ANALYZES THREE MAJOR POLITICAL PARTIES IN INDIA AND THEIR ATTITUDES TO BRITAIN IN THIS PERIOD. REVEALS INTERNATIONAL POLITICAL SCIENCE THAT LED TO COMMONWEALTH'S PRESENT STATUS. BIBLIOGRAPHY OF FURTHER READINGS ON SUBJECT OR ON EACH COUNTRY AT TIME.

2164 MEIER R.L.
A COMMUNICATIONS THEORY OF URBAN GROWTH.
CAMBRIDGE: M I T PRESS, 1962, 184 PP., LC#62-20480.
INTERDISCIPLINARY STUDY IN THE SOCIAL AND NATURAL SCIENCES ON PROMISING POTENTIAL OF COMMUNICATIONS THEORY FOR EXPLAINING URBAN GROWTH AND ORGANIZATION. DISCUSSION BASED ON CONCEPTION OF CITY AS AN OPEN SYSTEM THAT MUST, IF VIABLE, CONSERVE NEGATIVE ENTROPY (INFORMATION). MEASURES ENTROPY BY AN ACCOUNTING SYSTEM THAT CONSIDERS STOCK OF AVAILABLE KNOWLEDGE AND MESSAGES RECEIVED.

2165 MEIER R.L.
DEVELOPMENTAL PLANNING.
NEW YORK: MCGRAW HILL, 1965, 420 PP., LC#64-25855.
ANALYSIS OF INTERNATIONAL DEVELOPMENTAL PLANNING AS SEEN IN CASE OF PUERTO RICO. COVERS ORGANIZATION OF PLANNING, INDUSTRIAL DEVELOPMENT, EDUCATIONAL DEVELOPMENT, AND INTEGRATION OF PLANNING. COMPARES PUERTO RICAN EXPERIENCE WITH THAT OF OTHER DEVELOPING NATIONS.

2166 MEINECKE F.
MACHIAVELLISM.
NEW HAVEN: YALE U PR, 1957, 438 PP.
DISCRIBES DOCTRINE OF RAISON D'ETAT AND ITS PLACE IN MODERN HISTORY. DISCUSSES AGE OF NASCENT ABSOLUTISM, AGE OF MATURE ABSOLUTISM, AND MACHIAVELLISM, IDEALISM, AND HISTORICISM IN RECENT GERMAN HISTORY.

2167 MELADY T.
THE WHITE MAN'S FUTURE IN BLACK AFRICA.
NEW YORK: MACFADDEN, 1962, 208 PP., $0.60.
CONSIDERS WHITE MAN'S FUTURE IN LIGHT OF RAPID TRANSFORMATION IN AFRICA. FORSEES DISASTER IF WHITE MAN CLINGS TO DOMINANT POSITION. PREDICTS POSITIVE OUTCOME IF POLITICAL AND ECONOMIC EQUALITY IS ADOPTED.

2168 MELADY T.
FACES OF AFRICA.
NEW YORK: MACMILLAN, 1964, 338 PP., $7.50.
COUNTRY BY COUNTRY STUDY OF HISTORY AND POLITICAL, ECONOMIC, SOCIAL, AND EDUCATIONAL PROBLEMS OF AFRICAN TERRITORIES AS WELL AS A PROJECTION OF TRENDS AND PREDICTION OF POSSIBLE FUTURE DEVELOPMENTS. MORE DESCRIPTIVE THAN ANALYTICAL.

2169 MENARD O.D.
THE ARMY AND THE FIFTH REPUBLIC.
LINCOLN: U OF NEB PR, 1967, 265 PP., LC#67-18269.

CONSIDERS WHY THE TRADITIONALLY APOLITICAL FRENCH ARMY BECAME A POLITICAL FORCE AND HOW IT ATTEMPTED TO PLAY AN ACTIVE POLITICAL ROLE BETWEEN 1958-62. DISCUSSES THE GROWTH OF THE ARMY'S POLITICAL NEUTRALITY UNTIL WWII. EXAMINES THE REPERCUSSIONS GENERATED BY THE COLONIAL WARS. ANALYZES THE SOCIAL STRUCTURE AND PROFESSIONAL AND POLITICAL ATTITUDES OF THE OFFICER CORPS.

2170 MENDEL A.P. ED.
POLITICAL MEMOIRS 1905-1917 BY PAUL MILIUKOV (TRANS. BY CARL GOLDBERG)
ANN ARBOR: U OF MICH PR, 1967, 508 PP., LC#67-25341.
PRESENTSPERSONAL ACCOUNT OF STRUGGLE OF LIBERALS TO ESTABLISH CONSTITUTIONAL, REPRESENTATIVE GOVERNMENT IN RUSSIA FROM 1905-17. DISCUSSES MILIUKOV'S ROLE IN ATTEMPT, FOREIGN AFFAIRS DURING PERIOD, PROCESS OF MODERNIZING RURAL ECONOMY, AND ESTABLISHMENT OF PROVISIONAL GOVERNMENT IN 1917. PROVIDES PORTRAITS OF OTHER LEADERS OF PERIOD.

2171 MENDELSON W.
"JUDICIAL REVIEW AND PARTY POLITICS" (BMR)"
VANDERBILT LAW REV., 12 (MAR. 59), 447-457.
CONTENDS THAT COURT INTRUSION UPON NATIONAL POLICY IS STRONGEST IN PERIODS OF PARTY WEAKNESS AND IRRESPONSIBILITY. EXAMINES CORRELATION BETWEEN JUDICIAL SUPREMACY AND PARTY INEFFICIENCY. COMPARES US, UK, AND AUSTRALIA. CONCLUDES THAT JUDICIAL PERSUASIVENESS MULTIPLIES WHEN POLITICAL OPPOSITION IS LACKING.

2172 MENDELSSOHN S.
SOUTH AFRICAN BIBLIOGRAPHY (2 VOLS.)
LONDON: KEGAN, PAUL& CO, 1910.
A COMPREHENSIVE BIBLIOGRAPHY OF LITERATURE RELATING TO SOUTH AFRICA FROM THE EARLIEST PERIOD TO 1910. ENTRIES ARE CRITICALLY AND DESCRIPTIVELY ANNOTATED, AND CATALOGUED ALPHABETICALLY BY AUTHOR. MOST WORKS PUBLISHED BETWEEN 1880-1910. AUTHOR'S INTRODUCTION PROVIDES LENGTHLY SUMMARY OF SOUTH AFRICAN HISTORY.

2173 MENDELSSOHN S. ED.
MENDELSSOHN'S SOUTH AFRICA BIBLIOGRAPHY (VOL. I)
LONDON: KEGAN, PAUL& CO, 1910, 1008 PP.
COMPREHENSIVE LIST, BY AUTHOR, OF THE MENDELSSOHN LIBRARY OF WORKS IN ENGLISH, FRENCH, GERMAN. BOOKS COVER ALL FIELDS RELATED TO SOUTH AFRICA.

2174 MENDIETA Y. NUNEZ L.
THEORIE DES GROUPEMENTS SOCIAUX SUIVI D'UNE ETUDE SUR LE DROIT SOCIAL.
PARIS: RIVIERE PUBLISHING CO, 1957, 335 PP.
TWO STUDIES PUBLISHED IN SPANISH IN 1950 AND 1953. FIRST IS PURELY A SOCIOLOGICAL STUDY, IN WHICH AUTHOR DEFINES AND CHARACTERIZES SOCIAL GROUPS. VIEWS SOCIAL BOUNDARIES AS ARTIFICIALLY CONSTRUCTED, AS CONTROLLING BEHAVIOR AND IDEAS, AND AS RELATIVELY INESCAPABLE. SECOND STUDY CLARIFIES AND MITIGATES PESSIMISM OF FIRST, SAYING JUDICIAL AND POLITICAL INTERVENTION CAN CORRECT INEQUALITIES.

2175 MENDL W.
"FRENCH ATTITUDES ON DISARMAMENT."
SURVIVAL, 9 (DEC. 67), 393-398.
FRENCH ABSENCE FROM EIGHTEEN NATION DISARMAMENT CONFERENCE FOUND TO BE RESULT OF A POLICY AIMED AT RESTORING FRANCE'S POWER STATUS AND ACHIEVING GOALS OF NATIONAL SECURITY. TRACES COURSE OF DISARMAMENT SINCE L945. CONTINUING OPPOSITION TO ARMS CONTROL IS SEEN AS A PERSISTENT THEME IN FRENCH FOREIGN POLICY.

2176 MENON K.P.S.
MANY WORLDS.
LONDON: OXFORD U PR, 1965, 324 PP.
INDIAN STATEMENTS RECALLING COLONIAL INDIA AND STRUGGLE FOR INDEPENDENCE, RISE OF COLD WAR AND STRUGGLE OF TWO WORLDS, AND EMERGENCE OF NEW NATIONS AND ITS EFFECT ON INTERNATIONAL RELATIONS AND POWER.

2177 MENZEL J.M. ED.
THE CHINESE CIVIL SERVICE: CAREER OPEN TO TALENT?
BOSTON: D C HEATH, 1963, 110 PP., LC#63-12327.
STRUCTURE AND COMPOSITION OF CHINESE CIVIL SERVICE IN ITS HISTORICAL DEVELOPMENT. EXAMINES BACKGROUND AND EDUCATIONAL REQUIREMENTS AND MOBILITY IN GOVERNMENT.

2178 MERILLAT H.C.L. ED.
LEGAL ADVISERS AND INTERNATIONAL ORGANIZATIONS.
NEW YORK: OCEANA PUBLISHING, 1966, 124 PP., LC#66-20029.
LEGAL COUNSELS TO SEVERAL INTERNATIONAL ORGANIZATIONS COMMENT ON THE INTERACTION OF NATIONAL AND INTERNATIONAL LAW WITHIN THESE BODIES, THE CREATION OF INTERNATIONAL LAW, AND THE ROLES AND BACKGROUNDS OF THE ADVISERS.

2179 MERKL P.H.
THE ORIGIN OF THE WEST GERMAN REPUBLIC.
NEW YORK: OXFORD U PR, 1963, 269 PP., LC#63-9627.
ANALYSIS OF FORMATION OF REPUBLIC OF WEST GERMANY; DRAFTING OF CONSTITUTION EXAMINED IN REGARD TO OUTSIDE INFLUENCE. POSTWAR GERMAN SOCIETY, PARLIAMENTARY COUNCIL FORMATION, POLICY-MAKING, AND POLITICAL PRESSURES ARE DISCUSSED.

2180 MERKL P.H.
"EUROPEAN ASSEMBLY PARTIES AND NATIONAL DELEGATIONS."
J. CONFL. RESOLUT., 8 (MAR. 64), 50-64.
EXAMINES FORMATION AND GROWTH OF COMMUNITY-WIDE PARTIES WITHIN VARIOUS EUROPEAN PARLIAMENTARY ASSEMBLIES WITH REGARD TO THEIR SETTING, THEIR ORGANIZATION, AND THEIR VOTING BEHAVIOR. THESE PARTIES RIVAL THE COHESION OF THE ORIGINAL UNITS OF REPRESENTATION, THE NATIONAL DELEGATIONS.

2181 MERKL P.H.
GERMANY: YESTERDAY AND TOMORROW.
NEW YORK: OXFORD U PR, 1965, 362 PP., LC#65-22799.
ANALYZES PROMINENT ISSUES OF GERMAN HISTORY. DESCRIBES POST-WAR POLITICS AND ECONOMICS AND QUESTIONS FUTURE DIRECTIONS OF GERMAN DEMOCRACY.

2182 MERRIAM A.
CONGO: BACKGROUND OF CONFLICT.
EVANSTON: NORTHWESTERN U. PR., 1961, 368 PP., $6.00.
DESCRIBES ECONOMIC, SOCIAL, AND POLITICAL SITUATION IN CONGO BEFORE INDEPENDENCE AS BACKGROUND TO SUBSEQUENT CONFLICT AND INSTABILITY. BASES CHRONOLOGICAL ACCOUNT OF EVENTS ON FIRST-HAND OBSERVATIONS. ILLUSTRATES IMPORTANCE OF CONGO TO FREE WORLD.

2183 MERRIAM C.E.
SYSTEMATIC POLITICS.
CHICAGO: U OF CHICAGO PRESS, 1945, 349 PP.
STUDIES EVOLUTION OF POLITICAL ACHIEVEMENT AND EFFORT. ANALYZES POLITICAL BEHAVIOR IN LIGHT OF FACTORS THAT SURROUND INSTITUTIONAL FORMS, IDEOLOGIES, AND POLITICAL PATTERNS. DEALS WITH FOUNDATION OF POLITICS, PURPOSES OF GOVERNMENT, TOOLS AND SKILLS OF POLITICS, ORGANS OF GOVERNMENT, INFORMAL GOVERNMENT, STABILITY AND CHANGE, INTERRELATIONSHIPS BETWEEN POLITICAL SOCIETIES, AND TRENDS.

2184 MERRITT R.L. ED., ROKKAN S. ED.
COMPARING NATIONS* THE USE OF QUANTITATIVE DATA IN CROSS-NATIONAL RESEARCH.
NEW HAVEN: YALE U PR, 1966, 584 PP., LC#66-12509.
25 PAPERS PRESENTED BY RUMMEL, ALKER, NORTH, LASSWELL, K. DEUTSCH, RUSSETT, AND OTHERS TO YALE DATA CONFERENCE AIMED AT MAKING VARIOUS RESEARCH EFFORTS USING QUANTITATIVE CROSS-NATIONAL COMPARISONS THEORETICALLY CUMULATIVE. METHODS OF MAKING AND ANALYZING DATA PRESENTED IN CONTEXT OF CURRENT RESEARCH PROBLEMS OF THESE NOTED SCHOLARS AND THEIR INSTITUTIONS. EXTENSIVE BIBLIOGRAPHY.

2185 MERRITT R.L.
"SELECTED ARTICLES AND DOCUMENTS ON COMPARATIVE GOVERNMENT AND CROSS-NATIONAL RESEARCH."
AM. POL. SCI. REV., 60 (SEPT. 66), 747-752.
AN UNANNOTATED BIBLIOGRAPHY OF COMPARATIVE GOVERNMENT AND CROSS-NATIONAL RESEARCH. ENGLISH-LANGUAGE AND SOME FRENCH, GERMAN, AND ITALIAN. MATERIAL RANGES FROM 1965-66. CONTAINS 160 ENTRIES.

2186 MERTON R.K.ED. LAZARSFELD P.F. ED.
"SOCIAL STRUCTURE AND ANOMIE" (BMR)
AMER. SOCIOLOGICAL REV., 3 (OCT. 38), 672-682.
PRESENTS SYSTEMATIC APPROACH TO STUDY OF SOCIO-CULTURAL SOURCES OF DEVIANT BEHAVIOR. CONSIDERS WAYS IN WHICH SOCIAL STRUCTURES EXERT PRESSURES ON INDIVIDUALS TO REBEL AGAINST NONCONFORMIST ACTIVITY. CONCERNED WITH NONBIOLOGICAL PRESSURES.

2187 MEYER A.G.
LENINISM.
NEW YORK: FREDERICK PRAEGER, 1962, 324 PP., LC#62-10312.
SURVEYS LENIN'S THOUGHT AND THAT OF HIS ASSOCIATES, INCLUDING PHILOSOPHY TOWARD PARTY, PARTICIPATION IN RUSSIAN REVOLUTION, LENINISM IN POWER, AND NEW IMAGE OF CAPITALIST SOCIETY IN HIS WRITING.

2188 MEYER A.J.
MIDDLE EASTERN CAPITALISM: NINE ESSAYS.
CAMBRIDGE: HARVARD U. PR., 1959, 161 PP.
SYSTEMATIC ANALYSIS OF ECONOMIC GROWTH OF IRAQ, KUWAIT, CYPRUS, ISRAEL, ET AL. CONSIDERS WHETHER ECONOMIC PROSPERITY WILL CONTINUE. SUGGESTS THAT WEST IMPROVE UNDERSTANDING OF ECONOMICS OF MIDDLE EAST WITHOUT DELAY.

2189 MEYER E.W. ED.
POLITICAL PARTIES IN WESTERN GERMANY (PAMPHLET)
WASHINGTON: LIBRARY OF CONGRESS, 1951, 52 PP.
A BIBLIOGRAPHY OF DAILY AND WEEKLY NEWSPAPERS, PERIODICALS, OFFICIAL PARTY PUBLICATIONS, AND PARTY PUBLICATIONS OF PROFESSIONAL GROUPS IN WEST GERMANY.

2190 MEYER E.W.
POLITICAL PARTIES IN WESTERN GERMANY (PAMPHLET)
WASHINGTON: LIBRARY OF CONGRESS, 1951, 49 PP.

INVESTIGATION OF POLITICAL PARTIES IN WESTERN GERMANY, 1951. GERMAN POLITICAL SCIENTIST SURVEYS AND ANALYZES CURRENT POLITICAL SPECTRUM. SPECIFIC PARTIES, PECULARITIES OF THE GERMAN SITUATION, PRESSURE GROUPS, COALITION GOVERNMENT, FREQUENT CRITICISMS OF PARTIES, AND BERLIN SITUATION.

2191 MEYER F.S. ED.
THE AFRICAN NETTLE.
NEW YORK: JOHN DAY, 1965, 253 PP., LC#65-15135.
EXAMINES POLITICAL PROBLEMS FACING EMERGING NATIONS OF AFRICA. DISCUSSES DISENGAGEMENT OF EUROPEAN POWERS AND FRUSTRATION OF DECOLONIZATION. INCLUDES FRESH ANALYSES OF POLITICS OF SOUTH AFRICA. SUGGESTS THAT AFRICAN NATIONS PER SE DO NOT EXIST; IN ACTUALITY, RACIAL NATIONALISM PERMEATES SUB-SAHARAN AFRICA.

2192 MEYER P. ET AL.
THE JEWS IN THE SOVIET SATELLITES.
SYRACUSE: U. PR., 1953, 637 PP.
STUDIES STATUS AND TREATMENT OF JEWS BEFORE, DURING AND AFTER WW 2 IN CZECHOSLOVAKIA, POLAND, RUSSIA, HUNGARY, RUMANIA AND BULGARIA. ANALYZES RISE OF ANTI-SEMITISM IN SOVIET BLOC IN REGARD TO CENTRAL EUROPEAN SOCIAL, POLITICAL AND ETHNIC CHARACTERISTICS.

2193 MEYRIAT J. ED.
LA SCIENCE POLITIQUE EN FRANCE, 1945-1958; BIBLIOGRAPHIES FRANCAISES DE SCIENCES SOCIALES (VOL. I)
PARIS: FDN NAT DES SCIENCES POL, 1960, 134 PP.
ANNOTATED BIBLIOGRAPHY OF 603 ENTRIES REPRESENTING FRENCH POLITICAL SCIENCE PUBLICATIONS SINCE 1945, WITH EMPHASIS ON PERIOD OF 1950-58. MATERIAL SEPARATED INTO NINE CATEGORIES REPRESENTING METHODOLOGICAL, HISTORICAL, THEORETICAL, INSTITUTIONAL, INTERNATIONAL, AND NATIONAL STUDIES. SPECIAL INDEXES TO SCHOLARLY PERIODICALS, AUTHORS, AND EDITORS.

2194 MEZERIK A.G.
APARTHEID IN THE REPUBLIC OF SOUTH AFRICA (PAMPHLET)
NEW YORK: INTL REVIEW SERVICE, 1964, 109 PP.
ANALYSIS OF TREATMENT OF NATIVE POPULATION, MEANS TAKEN IN RACIAL DISCRIMINATION, AND REACTION OF WHITE AND NONWHITE POPULATION TO APARTHEID. DETAILS UN ATTITUDE AND REACTION TO SOUTH AFRICAN POLICY.

2195 MICHAEL F.
"KHRUSHCHEV'S DISLOYAL OPPOSITION: STRUCTURAL CHANGE AND POWER STRUGGLE IN COMMUNIST BLOC."
ORBIS, 7 (SPRING 63), 49-76.
FORMERLY COMMUNIST POLICY WAS DIRECTED BY MOSCOW, BUT TODAY MANY CENTERS, I.E. 'POLYCENTRISM,' EXISTS. REASONS FOUND IN THE DIFFERENT HISTORIES, IDEOLOGICAL CLIMATES, AND NATIONAL INTERESTS OF COMMUNIST COUNTRIES.

2196 MICHAEL H.N. ED.
STUDIES IN SIBERIAN ETHNOGENESIS.
TORONTO: U OF TORONTO PRESS, 1962, 313 PP.
DESCRIBES CULTURAL EFFECT ON ETHNOLOGY AND ITS IMPORTANCE IN CONTACT AND INTERMIXING OF TRIBES. USES HISTORIC-LINGUISTIC METHODOLOGY AND TRACES ROOTS OF EXISTING CULTURES AND RACES, AND THEIR EFFECTS ON ARTS AND LANGUAGE AT PRESENT.

2197 MICHAELY M.
CONCENTRATION IN INTERNATIONAL TRADE.
AMSTERDAM: NORTH HOLLAND PUBL CO, 1962.
EMPIRICAL STUDY OF COMMODITY AND GEOGRAPHIC CONCENTRATION IN INTERNATIONAL TRADE IN GOODS. SEEKS TO DETERMINE MAGNITUDE OF THIS CONCENTRATION, TO DISTINGUISH MAJOR FACTORS WHICH CONTRIBUTE TO IT, AND TO EXPLORE A FEW OF ITS MOST IMPORTANT EFFECTS. DEFINES MAIN ATTRIBUTES OF COUNTRIES WHOSE TRADE TENDS TO BE HIGHLY CONCENTRATED, AND THUS SUGGESTS CAUSES FOR CONCENTRATION.

2198 MICHELS R.
POLITICAL PARTIES.
NEW YORK: FREE PRESS OF GLENCOE, 1915, 434 PP.
SOCIOLOGICAL ANALYSIS OF POLITICAL PARTIES FOCUSING ON CAUSES AND FACTORS INVOLVED IN THE EMERGENCE OF STRONG POLITICAL LEADERSHIP. EMPHASIZES SUCH FACTORS AS AFFECTS OF EXERCISE OF POWER ON LEADERS AND THEIR AUTOCRATIC TENDENCIES. DISCUSSES OLIGARCHICAL TENDENCIES INHERENT IN DEMOCRACY AND DIFFICULTIES WHICH IT IMPOSES ON REALIZATION OF DEMOCRATIC GOALS.

2199 MICHELS R.
"SOME REFLECTIONS ON THE SOCIOLOGICAL CHARACTER OF POLITICAL PARTIES" (BMR)"
AM. POL. SCI. REV., 21 (NOV. 27), 753-772.
ANALYZES ORIGIN AND BEHAVIOR OF THE POLITICAL PARTY. HISTORICALLY TRACES VARYING FORMS OF THE CHARISMATIC PARTY TO DEMONSTRATE THAT CHARISMA LENDS ITSELF TO ALL POLITICAL VIEWPOINTS. OUTLINES CHARACTERISTICS OF PARTIES WHICH HAVE FOR THEIR BASES INTERESTS OF SOCIAL OR ECONOMIC CLASSES, OR PRINCIPLES OF WELTANSCHAUUNG AND UBERWELTANSCHAUUNG. CONTENDS THAT POWER IS ONLY GOAL OF PARTY.

2200 MICKIEWICZ E.P.
SOVIET POLITICAL SCHOOLS: THE COMMUNIST PARTY ADULT INSTRUCTION SYSTEM.
NEW HAVEN: YALE U PR, 1967, 190 PP., LC#67-13445.
ASSESSES THE STRENGTHS AND WEAKNESSES OF THE SOVIET ADULT POLITICAL EDUCATION SYSTEM. IMPLICATIONS OF THE INSTITUTIONS FOR THE FACTORY WORKER, THE TEACHER, AND THE URBAN INTELLIGENTSIA ARE CONSIDERED. ATTEMPTS TO SHOW PROCESS BY WHICH THE STUDENT IS INDUCED TO PARTICIPATE IN AND IDENTIFY WITH THE POLITICAL CULTURE.

2201 MIDDLE EAST INSTITUTE
CURRENT RESEARCH ON THE MIDDLE EAST.
WASHINGTON: MIDDLE EAST INST.
SERIES OF ANNUAL SURVEYS BEGINNING IN 1955. REFERENCES TO RESEARCH IN HISTORY AND AFFILIATED FIELDS; POLITICAL SCIENCE AND GOVERNMENT; ECONOMICS; BEHAVIORAL SCIENCES; LAW; PHILOSOPHY AND RELIGION; HISTORY OF SCIENCE; ETC. INCLUDES INDEX TO RESEARCHERS AND ITEMS ON BIBLIOGRAPHIC COLLECTIONS. SPARSE ANNOTATIONS.

2202 MID-EUROPEAN LAW PROJECT
CHURCH AND STATE BEHIND THE IRON CURTAIN.
NEW YORK: FREDERICK PRAEGER, 1955, 311 PP., LC#55-8105.
ANALYSIS OF LEGAL POSITION OF CHURCH IN EACH COUNTRY BEHIND IRON CURTAIN. COVERS HISTORY OF EACH CHURCH AND VIEWS OF CHURCH LEADERS. "HOSTILITY TOWARD RELIGION IS DEEPLY ROOTED IN COMMUNIST PHILOSOPHY." BIBLIOGRAPHIES FOR FURTHER READING ON EACH COUNTRY.

2203 MILIBAND R.
PARLIAMENTARY SOCIALISM.
NEW YORK: MONTHLY REVIEW PR, 1961, 356 PP., LC#64-18206.
TRACES THE HISTORY OF THE LABOUR PARTY IN ENGLAND FROM THE BEGINNING OF THIS CENTURY WITH EMPHASIS ON ITS ROLE IN PARLIAMENTARY POLITICS.

2204 MILIBAND R. ED., SAVILLE J. ED.
THE SOCIALIST REGISTER: 1964.
NEW YORK: MONTHLY REVIEW PR, 1964, 308 PP.
SOME 18 ESSAYS ON CURRENT SOCIALIST AND COMMUNIST THEORY, POLITICS, ECONOMICS, AND BEHAVIOR. EMPHASIS IS ON EVENTS AND PROGRESS IN ENGLAND, BUT 1964 EDITION INCLUDES COMMENTARY ON NASSER, MAOISM, WEST GERMANY, ALLIANCE FOR PROGRESS, AND OTHER ITEMS OF INTERNATIONAL SIGNIFICANCE. ALSO INCLUDES REVIEWS OF PERTINENT BOOKS AND ARTICLES.

2205 MILL J.S.
UTILITARIANISM, LIBERTY, AND REPRESENTATIVE GOVERNMENT.
NEW YORK: EP DUTTON, 1910, 393 PP.
SUPPORTS UTILITARIAN BELIEF THAT FOUNDATION OF MORALS IS UTILITY OR GREATEST HAPPINESS PRINCIPLE, BUT ATTACHES MANY QUALIFICATIONS TO DEFINITION OF HAPPINESS. DISCUSSES RELATION OF HAPPINESS OF INDIVIDUAL TO OTHER PEOPLE'S. DEFINES LIBERTY AS FREEDOM OF THOUGHT AND INDIVIDUALITY. DEVELOPS SYSTEM OF REPRESENTATIVE GOVERNMENT THAT SUPPLIES NECESSARY CONTROLS AND ALLOWS MAXIMUM FREEDOM POSSIBLE.

2206 MILL J.S.
ON LIBERTY.
NEW YORK: F S CROFTS & CO, 1946, 104 PP.
TREATS VALUE AND NATURE OF HUMAN FREEDOM AND CONFLICTS THAT ARISE BETWEEN CITIZEN AND STATE AND INDIVIDUAL AND MASSES. DISCUSSES VALUE TO SOCIETY OF INDIVIDUAL FREEDOM. STATES CASE FOR LIBERTY OF THOUGHT AND DISCUSSION, OF DEVELOPMENT OF INDIVIDUALITY, AND OF UNITING. EXAMINES LEGITIMATE DEGREE OF CONTROL SOCIETY MAY EXERCISE OVER MAN.

2207 MILL J.S.
"AN ESSAY ON GOVERNMENT" (PAMPHLET)
ORIGINAL PUBLISHER NOT AVAILABLE, 1780, 31 PP.
CLAIMS PURPOSE OF GOVERNMENT IS TO SECURE GREATEST GOOD FOR GREATEST NUMBER. CRITICIZES MONARCHY AND ARISTOCRACY AS INEFFICIENT SYSTEMS BY WHICH TO ACHIEVE THIS. CONSIDERS REPRESENTATION AS ONLY POSITIVE MEANS OF INSURING THIS. LAUDS CONSTITUTIONALISM, THOUGH HE FEELS EVEN THIS IS INSUFFICIENT TO GUARANTEE FREEDOM AND PROPERTY UNLESS IT IS COUPLED WITH REPRESENTATIVE SYSTEM.

2208 MILL J.S.
"CIVILIZATION" IN DISSERTATIONS AND DISCUSSIONS."
NEW YORK: HOLT RINEHART WINSTON, 1882.
CONSIDERS CIVILIZATION AS DIRECT CONVERSE OF BARBARISM IN INQUIRY INTO WHETHER CIVILIZATION IS GOOD OR BAD; EXAMINES 19TH-CENTURY SOCIETY AND SEEKS TO DISCOVER WHAT SHOULD BE PRESERVED FROM OLD FORMS AND WHAT SHOULD BE ADOPTED IN NEW ERA. POINTS OUT PROGRESSIVE, CIVILIZED FEATURES AS WELL AS REGRESSIVE BARBARIC FEATURES. INCLUDES POLITICAL STRUCTURES AND SOCIAL ARRANGEMENTS; COMPARES IDEAS.

2209 MILL J.S.
SOCIALISM (1859)
ORIGINAL PUBLISHER NOT AVAILABLE, 1891, 214 PP.
CLASSIFYING HIMSELF AS A DEMOCRATIC SOCIALIST, MILL ADVOCATED COMMON OWNERSHIP IN THE RAW MATERIALS OF THE WORLD AND EQUAL PARTICIPATION IN ALL BENEFITS OF COMBINED LABOR.

HOWEVER, HE FELT THAT THESE THINGS WERE FAR AWAY AND SHOULD BE ACHIEVED THROUGH EVOLUTIONARY RATHER THAN REVOLUTIONARY MEANS. NOT A STATE BUT AN INDIVIDUAL FORM OF SOCIALISM IS FAVORED, AND PRIVATE OWNERSHIP IS NOT EXCLUDED.

2210 MILLAR T.B.
"THE COMMONWEALTH AND THE UN."
ROUND TABLE, 69 (JAN. 68), 35-40.
DISCUSSES SIMILARITIES IN UN AND COMMONWEALTH, CLAIMING TENDENCY HAS BEEN FOR THEM TO BE INCREASINGLY ALIKE. ATTEMPTS ANALYSIS OF BRITISH ATTITUDES TOWARD BOTH AND ASSESSMENT OF TRENDS IN POLICY REGARDING BOTH. EVALUATES ROLE OF COMMONWEALTH IN POLITICAL AND ECONOMIC SITUATION OF THE 1960'S.

2211 MILLER A.S.
PRIVATE GOVERNMENTS AND THE CONSTITUTION (PAMPHLET)
SANTA BARBARA: CTR DEMO INST, 1959, 15 PP.
BOTH PRIVATE AND PUBLIC GOVERNING POWER SHOULD BE RECOGNIZED IN CONSTITUTIONAL THEORY. AN INQUIRY INTO THE DECISION-MAKING PROCESS IS AN EFFECTIVE MEANS OF BRINGING ABOUT SUCH RECOGNITION. PROBES "FUNCTIONAL FEDERALISM" OF GROUP PROCESS, CONSENSUS, PUBLIC FUNCTIONS OF GROUPS AND THEIR REGULATION, AND THE ISSUE OF NATIONALIZING THE DECISION-MAKING PROCESS IN AREAS OF MAJOR PUBLIC CONCERN.

2212 MILLER E.
"LEGAL ASPECTS OF UN ACTION IN THE CONGO."
AMER. J. INT. LAW, 55 (JAN. 61), 1-28.
ATTEMPTS TO DEMONSTRATE THAT CONSIDERATIONS OF LAW AND PRINCIPLE CAN PLAY A ROLE IN INTERNATIONAL ACTION, IN SPITE OF POLITICAL CONFLICT AND TENSION.

2213 MILLER J.D.B.
THE NATURE OF POLITICS.
LONDON: DUCKWORTH, 1962, 295 PP.
EXAMINES POLITICS AS A FIELD OF STUDY, ATTEMPTING TO SET UP AN ANALYTICAL FRAMEWORK FOR ITS CONSIDERATION. COVERS BASES AND FUNCTIONS OF, AND INTERESTS AND INSTITUTIONS IN, POLITICS, ALONG WITH THEIR NATURE, FUNCTION, AND PROCESS. DISCUSSES ROLE OF THEORY, AND POLITICS AS AN OCCUPATION.

2214 MILLER P.
THE NEW ENGLAND MIND: THE SEVENTEENTH CENTURY.
NEW YORK: MACMILLAN, 1939, 528 PP.
DEFINES AND CLASSIFIES THE PRINCIPAL CONCEPTS OF THE PURITAN MIND IN COLONIAL NEW ENGLAND. SPECIAL ATTENTION GIVEN TO THE ORIGINS, INTERRELATIONS, AND SIGNIFICANCE OF LEADING IDEAS. PURITANISM IS DESCRIBED AS THE MOST POWERFUL AND COHERENT EXPRESSION OF EARLY AMERICAN THOUGHT. FOUR MAJOR ASPECTS ARE CONSIDERED: RELIGION AND LEARNING, COSMOLOGY, ANTHROPOLOGY, AND SOCIOLOGY.

2215 MILLER W.J., ROBERTS H.L., SHULMAN M.D.
THE MEANING OF COMMUNISM.
MORRISTOWN, NJ: SILVER BURDETT, 1963, 192 PP., LC#63-10162.
INTRODUCTION TO COMMUNIST THEORY AND PRACTICE FROM CONSERVATIVE VIEW. BEGINS WITH MARXIST THEORY; DISCUSSES LENIN AND HIS ROLE IN COMMUNIST PARTY, POLITICAL STRUCTURE, AND HARDENING OF COMMUNIST DICTATORSHIP UNDER STALIN; AND INCLUDES USSR IN WWII, LIFE IN USSR IN 1960'S, FOREIGN POLICY, INTERNATIONAL COMMUNISM, AND INTERNATIONAL RELATIONS.

2216 MILLIKAW M.F. ED., BLACKMER D.L.M. ED.
THE EMERGING NATIONS: THEIR GROWTH AND UNITED STATES POLICY.
BOSTON: LITTLE BROWN, 1961, 168 PP., LC#61-12119.
ANALYSIS OF PROCESS OF TRANSITION FROM "TRADITIONAL TO MODERN SOCIETY," POINTING OUT FACTORS THAT WILL BE DETERMINED BY US ACTIONS IN THESE NATIONS. IT IS ESSENTIAL TO FREE WORLD THAT US PERCEIVE THESE FACTORS AND INFLUENCE THESE NATIONS TO BE INDEPENDENT, DEMOCRATIC, AND PEACE-LOVING.

2217 MILNE R.S.
GOVERNMENT AND POLITICS IN MALAYSIA.
BOSTON: HOUGHTON MIFFLIN, 1967, 259 PP.
TRACES HISTORY OF NATION AND DEVELOPMENT OF ITS POLITICAL INSTITUTIONS. EXAMINES STRUCTURE AND FUNCTION OF MALAYSIA'S POLITICAL SYSTEM. DEALS WITH DEVELOPMENTS IN 1966 WHEN INDONESIA ADOPTED MORE CONCILIATORY ATTITUDE TOWARD THE FEDERATION, AND WITH PROSPECTS AND POLITICS OF SINGAPORE.

2218 MILONE P.D.
URBAN AREAS IN INDONESIA.
BERKELEY: U OF CALIF PR, 1966, 225 PP.
EXAMINES URBAN STRUCTURES AND CHANGING RELATIONSHIPS IN INDONESIA FROM EARLY COLONIAL PERIOD TO PRESENT. INCLUDES EXTENSIVE APPENDIX LISTING GROWTH RATES, COMPOSITION OF POPULATION, ETC.

2219 MILTON J.
THE READIE AND EASY WAY TO ESTABLISH A FREE COMMONWEALTH.
ORIGINAL PUBLISHER NOT AVAILABLE, 1660, 20 PP.
ATTACKS CHARACTER OF CHARLES I AS UNWORTHY OF RULER OF ENGLAND AND PROPOSES SYSTEM OF DEMOCRATIC ARISTOCRACY. PRAISES ACTIONS OF CROMWELL AND DISAGREES WITH TRADITIONAL NOTION OF DIVINE RIGHT OF KINGS. CALLS REGAL GOVERNMENT BURDENSOME, EXPENSIVE, USELESS, AND DANGEROUS, CLAIMING THAT PEOPLE OF ENGLAND BECAME CONVINCED OF THIS AFTER LONG EXPERIENCE WITH MONARCHY.

2220 MINAR D.W.
IDEAS AND POLITICS: THE AMERICAN EXPERIENCE.
HOMEWOOD: DORSEY, 1964, 435 PP., LC#64-24702.
PREMISE OF THE BOOK IS THAT POLITICAL THOUGHT SHOULD BE SEEN IN TERMS OF ITS RELATIONSHIP TO OTHER VARIABLES OF POLITICAL LIFE: BEHAVIOR, ACTION, INSTITUTIONS, POLICY, ETC. PHILOSOPHICAL IN NATURE, BOOK DISCUSSES CONTRIBUTIONS OF THE PROTESTANT REFORMATION, REVOLUTIONARY THOUGHT IN AMERICA, JACKSONIAN POLITICS, ABOLITIONISM, AND THE THREE BRANCHES OF GOVERNMENT.

2221 MINER H.M., DE VOS G.
OASIS AND CASBAH: ALGERIAN CULTURE AND PERSONALITY IN CHANGE
ANN ARBOR: U OF MICH PR, 1960, 236 PP.
COMPARES ARABS IN OASES, WHO WERE RELATIVELY UNTOUCHED BY FRENCH INFLUENCE, TO THOSE LIVING IN URBANIZED, MODERN AREAS WHO WERE INFLUENCED. CLARIFIES RELATIONSHIP BETWEEN CULTURE AND PERSONALITY TRAITS IN SITUATION OF CHANGE, AND SHOWS DIFFERENT RATES OF CHANGE AMONG TRAITS. ANALYZES COVARIATION OF SPECIFIC CULTURAL BELIEFS AND PERSONALITY TRAITS.

2222 MINIFIE J.M.
PEACEMAKER OR POWDER-MONKEY.
LONDON: MCCLELLAND AND STEWART, 1960, 181 PP.
DISCUSSES CANADA'S ROLE IN REVOLUTIONARY, UNSTABLE WORLD SITUATION AND ITS POTENTIAL TO BECOME LEADER OF "MIDDLE NATIONS." DISCUSSES IMPORTANCE OF CANADA'S MAINTENANCE OF NEUTRALITY AND SIGNIFICANT ROLE IT CAN ASSUME BY AVOIDING TOTALLY SUBORDINATE ROLE TO US IN MATTERS OF MILITARY AND FOREIGN POLICY.

2223 MINISTERE DE L'EDUC NATIONALE
CATALOGUE DES THESES DE DOCTORAT SOUTENUES DEVANT LES UNIVERSITAIRES FRANCAISES.
PARIS: MIN DE L'EDUCATION NAT.
ANNUAL PUBLICATION SINCE 1884 LISTING DOCTORAL THESES IN FRENCH UNIVERSITIES. ITEMS ARRANGED BY UNIVERSITY AND FACULTY, THEN ALPHABETICALLY BY AUTHOR.

2224 MINISTERE FINANCES ET ECO
BULLETIN BIBLIOGRAPHIQUE.
PARIS: MIN FIN ET AFFAIRS ECO.
PUBLISHED FIVE TIMES A YEAR SINCE 1948, THIS PERIODICAL CONTAINS ABSTRACTS FROM BOOKS AND ARTICLES PERTAINING TO CURRENT ECONOMIC LIFE. EMPHASIS PRIMARILY ON FRENCH COLONIES AND FORMER COLONIES. SOURCES PRIMARILY FRENCH; SOME ENGLISH. TOPICS INCLUDE POLITICAL INSTITUTIONS, ECONOMIC ORGANIZATIONS, PRODUCTION, EXCHANGES. GEOGRAPHICAL INDEX.

2225 GT BRIT MIN OVERSEAS DEV LIB
TECHNICAL CO-OPERATION -- A BIBLIOGRAPHY.
LONDON: MIN OF OVERSEAS DEVEL.
MONTHLY LISTING, FIRST PUBLISHED 1964, OF CURRENT OFFICIAL PUBLICATIONS OF THE COMMONWEALTH, DOCUMENTS, PROCESSED AND UNPUBLISHED MATERIALS, AND OTHER REPORTS AND BULLETINS FROM FOREIGN INSTITUTIONS. ENTRIES PERTAIN TO ECONOMIC, SOCIAL, LEGAL, AND STATISTICAL ASPECTS OF TECHNICAL DEVELOPMENT.

2226 MIT CENTER INTERNATL STUDIES
BIBLIOGRAPHY OF THE ECONOMIC AND POLITICAL DEVELOPMENT OF INDONESIA.
CAMBRIDGE: M I T PRESS, 1953, 169 PP.
BIBLIOGRAPHY INTENDED PRIMARILY FOR USE OF STAFF MEMBERS OF PROJECT ON ECONOMIC AND POLITICAL DEVELOPMENT OF INDONESIA AT CENTER FOR INTERNATIONAL STUDIES, MIT. CONTAINS 2353 ITEMS IN DUTCH, ENGLISH, AND INDONESIAN AVAILABLE IN THE US. INCLUDES SECTIONS ON BASIC REFERENCE AND STATISTICAL WORKS; HISTORICAL AND DESCRIPTIVE WORKS.

2227 MIT CENTER INTERNATL STUDIES
"A PLAN OF RESEARCH IN INTERNATIONAL COMMUNICATION: A REPORT."
WORLD POLIT., 6 (APRIL 54), 358-77.
STATES THAT STUDIES OF COMMUNICATION REPRESENT REASSESSMENT OF THE INTELLECTUAL TOOL OF SOCIAL SCIENTISTS. CALLS FOR A BETTER DEFINITION OF TERMS LIKE IDEOLOGY, POWER, LAW, OPINION, IN SUCH A WAY THAT THEY CAN BE OF USE IN DESCRIBING HUMAN INTERACTIONS.

2228 MIT CENTER INTERNATL STUDIES
OFFICIAL SERIAL PUBLICATIONS RELATING TO ECONOMIC DEVELOPMENT IN AFRICA SOUTH OF THE SAHARA.
CAMBRIDGE: M I T PRESS, 1961, 44 PP.
LISTS ALL ENGLISH-LANGUAGE REPORTS ON ECONOMIC DEVELOPMENT AVAILABLE IN US UP TO DECEMBER 1960; MOST ARE OFFICIAL GOVERNMENT PUBLICATIONS, THOUGH SOME MAJOR PRIVATE CORPORATIONS ARE INCLUDED; ARRANGED BY COUNTRY.

2229 MITCHELL B.R. ED.

ABSTRACT OF BRITISH HISTORICAL STATISTICS.
NEW YORK: CAMBRIDGE U PRESS, 1962, 513 PP.
ABSTRACT ATTEMPTS TO PRESENT THE MAJOR TIME SERIES FOR UK ECONOMY OVER AS LONG A HISTORICAL PERIOD AS POSSIBLE. EARLIEST FIGURE IS FOR YEAR 1199, BUT FOR MANY TOPICS CONTINUOUS MATERIAL BEGINS IN THE 18TH CENTURY AND FOR MOST IN 19TH. RESTRICTED TO ECONOMIC STATISTICS. EACH SECTION IS PRECEDED WITH AN INTRODUCTION AND CONCLUDED WITH A BIBLIOGRAPHY.

2230 MITCHELL P.
AFRICAN AFTERTHOUGHTS.
LONDON: HUTCHINSON & CO, 1954, 288 PP.
NARRATES AUTHOR'S CAREER AS GOVERNOR OF PROTECTORATE OF UGANDA AND AS DISTRICT OFFICER BEFORE THAT. EXAMINES HISTORY OF COLONIALISM, KAISER'S WAR, INDIRECT RULE, LAND TENURE, AND SITUATION FROM 1935-40. DISCUSSES EFFECTS OF WWII, ACTIONS OF MAU MAU, AND SITUATION IN 1954.

2231 MITCHELL W.C.
"THE SHAPE OF POLITICAL THEORY TO COME: FROM POLITICAL SOCIOLOGY TO POLITICAL ECONOMY."
AMER. BEHAVIORAL SCIENTIST, 11 (NOV.-DEC. 67), 8-20.
DEFINES POLITICAL SOCIOLOGY AS THE STUDY OF THE STATE, INCLUDING ITS LEGITIMACY, USE OF FORCE, AND ROLE OF INTEREST GROUPS. IN SECTION ON POLITICAL ECONOMY, ANALYZES HOW MONEY IS COLLECTED AND SPENT AND WHO BENEFITS FROM IT. STRESSES THE ROLE ECONOMICS PLAYS IN THE GOVERNMENT PROCESS, AND ADVOCATES MAKING POLITICAL ECONOMY A FIELD OF STUDY.

2232 MOCKLER-FERRYMAN A.
BRITISH WEST AFRICA.
LONDON: SWAN SONNENSCHEIN, 1900, 512 PP.
COMPREHENSIVE STUDY OF BRITISH POSSESSIONS IN WEST AFRICA WHICH ALSO TRACES HISTORY OF EUROPEAN COLONIALISM IN AFRICA, STRESSING ITS SIGNIFICANCE IN INTERNATIONAL POLITICS. EXAMINES EACH BRITISH WEST AFRICAN POSSESSION IN DETAIL, DISCUSSING PROBLEMS OF GOVERNMENT AND TRADE; EXPLORATIONS AND MILITARY CONFLICTS; AND DIFFICULTIES ARISING FROM CULTURAL DIFFERENCES OF BRITISH AND AFRICANS.

2233 MOCTEZUMA A.P.
EL CONFLICTO RELIGIOSO DE 1926 (2ND ED.)
MEXICO CITY: EDITORIAL JUS, 1960, 563 PP.
STUDY OF 1926 CHURCH-STATE CONFLICT IN MEXICO. COVERS BACKGROUND LEADING TO RELIGIOUS PERSECUTION AND REBELLION. EXAMINES LEGAL LIMITATIONS ON CHURCH ACTIVITY AND PUBLIC OPINION REGARDING POLICIES OF GOVERNMENT AND PROGRAMS OF CHURCH.

2234 MODELSKI G. ED.
SEATO-SIX STUDIES.
VANCOUVER: PUB. REL. CENTER, U. BRIT. COLUMB., 1962, 287 PP.
CONCERNED WITH FUNCTIONS OF SEATO, PLACE OF SMALL NATIONS WITHIN SEATO, ROLE OF TWO LARGE MEMBER STATES, COMMUNIST CHINA AND INDIA, AND THEIR RELATIONS TO MEMBER STATES. ALSO COVERS ROLE OF GREAT POWERS IN ASIAN TRADE RELATIONSHIPS.

2235 MOGI S.
"THE PROBLEM OF FEDERALISM: A STUDY IN THE HISTORY OF POLITICAL THEORY."
NEW YORK: MACMILLAN, 1931.
COMPREHENSIVE AND CRITICAL SURVEY OF HISTORICAL DEVELOPMENT AND PRACTICAL APPLICATION OF IDEA OF FEDERALISM AS A FORM OF STATE ORGANIZATION. COVERS PROGRESS OF IDEA THROUGH 18TH-CENTURY EUROPE AND US, FROM ITS CONCEPTION TO MODERN TIMES; HISTORY OF BRITISH FEDERAL IDEAS; AND GERMAN CONCEPTIONS OF FEDERALISM.

2236 MOHL R.V.
DIE GESCHICHTE UND LITERATUR DER STAATSWISSENSCHAFTEN (3 VOLS.)
BONN: FERDINAND ENKE VERLAG, 1855, 2053 PP.
SURVEYS HISTORY OF, AND LITERATURE ON, POLITICAL SCIENCE AND POLITICAL ECONOMY. NOT FORMALLY A BIBLIOGRAPHY, BUT AN EXTENDED TREATMENT OF MAJOR WORKS AND DEVELOPMENTS IN THE SCIENCE OF GOVERNMENT.

2237 MOLLAU G.
INTERNATIONAL COMMUNISM AND WORLD REVOLUTION: HISTORY AND METHODS.
NEW YORK: PRAEGER, 1961, 357 PP.
TRACES INTERNATIONAL COMMUNIST MOVEMENT FROM 1848 TO PRESENT. INCLUDES DISCUSSION OF THE RUSSIAN REVOLUTION, THE SOVIET UNION, THE COMINTERN, THE COMINFORM AND THE METHODS USED TO ACHIEVE SOVIET GOALS.

2238 MONAS S.
THE THIRD SECTION: POLICE AND SOCIETY IN RUSSIA UNDER NICHOLAS I.
CAMBRIDGE: HARVARD U PR, 1961, 354 PP., LC#61-6350.
RECORDS DEVELOPMENT OF THE RUSSIAN POLITICAL POLICE BY NICHOLAS I AS THE "THIRD SECTION" OF THE IMPERIAL CHANCERY. DESIGNED ON PRUSSIAN MODELS AS AN ATTEMPT TO REGULATE SOCIAL AND POLITICAL UNREST UNDER A "BEAUTIFUL AUTOCRACY" OF PATERNAL BENEVOLENCE, THE "THIRD SECTION" IS SHOWN HERE TO HAVE BEEN PLANNED AS A TEMPORARY INSTITUTION WHICH SURVIVED ITS CREATOR AND HIS IDEALISTIC VISION.

2239 MONGER G.W.
THE END OF ISOLATION.
NEW YORK: THOMAS NELSON AND SONS, 1963, 343 PP.
DISCUSSES BRITISH FOREIGN POLICY 1900-1907 AND DECLINE OF HER EMPIRE AND PAX BRITANNICA WHICH MADE ISOLATIONISM AND A LACK OF ALLIES AN IMPRACTICAL FOREIGN POLICY. CONSIDERS CRITICAL EVENTS PRIOR TO WWI: RISE OF GERMANY AND JAPAN; RUSSO-JAPANESE WAR; RUSSIAN ENTENTE, AND MOROCCAN CRISIS. EXAMINES ESPECIALLY BRITAIN'S RELATIONS WITH FRANCE AND GERMANY.

2240 MONNIER J.P.
"LA SUCCESSION D'ETATS EN MATIERE DE RESPONSABILITE INTERNATIONALE."
ANNU. FRANC. DR. INTER., 8 (1962), 65-90.
DISCUSSES QUESTION OF LEGAL OBLIGATIONS OF MANY STATES THAT HAVE ALTERED CONSTITUTIONAL STRUCTURE. SHOWS THAT RECENT JURIDICAL DECISIONS HAS LEFT PROBLEM UNRESOLVED. CONCLUDES ALTERED STATE HAS RETROACTIVE RESPONSIBILITY.

2241 MONROE A.D.
"BRITAIN AND THE EUROPEAN COMMUNITY."
CURR. HIST., 45 (NOV. 63), 271-275.
EFTA TOO SMALL, UNBALANCED, TOO LITTLE NATURAL COHESION TO OFFER A REAL ALTERNATIVE TO EEC. LIKE EFTA, COMMONWEALTH PRESENTS NO VIABLE ALTERNATIVE. BRITAIN MUST SEEK EITHER CLOSER ASSOCIATION WITH EEC OR DEVELOP GREATER FREEDOM IN WORLD AFFAIRS.

2242 MONTAGU A.
MAN'S MOST DANGEROUS MYTH: THE FALLACY OF RACE.
NEW YORK: COLUMBIA U PRESS, 1952, 362 PP., LC#52-9813.
SEEKS TO DEMONSTRATE THE FALSITIES OF THE "MYTH OF RACE." INDICATES THAT BIOLOGICAL DIFFERENCES IN RACES DO EXIST, BUT DENIES THEY ARE SIGNIFICANT ENOUGH TO JUSTIFY DISCRIMINATION. INCLUDES BIBLIOGRAPHY OF APPROXIMATELY 800 ITEMS.

2243 MONTAGUE J.B. JR.
CLASS AND NATIONALITY; ENGLISH AND AMERICAN STUDIES.
NEW HAVEN: COLLEGE AND U PR, 1963, 346 PP., LC#62-19468.
EXAMINES CONCEPTS OF SOCIAL CLASS, NATIONALITY, AND NATIONAL CHARACTER. ILLUSTRATES ANALYTICAL USE OF TERMS CLASS, STATUS, AND POWER AND PROVIDES OVERVIEW OF ENGLISH AND AMERICAN SOCIAL STRUCTURE. STUDIES TWO SOCIETIES MORE CLOSELY BY COMPARISON OF RESEARCH STUDIES.

2244 DE MONTESQUIEU C.
CONSIDERATIONS ON THE CAUSES OF THE GREATNESS OF THE ROMANS AND THEIR DECLINE (1748 TRANS. BY D. LOWENTHAL)
NEW YORK: FREE PRESS, 1965, 243 PP., LC#65-25247.
GREATNESS IS HERE EQUATED WITH SIZE AND POWER, DECLINE WITH WEAKNESS. GREATNESS ALSO HAS MORAL DIMENSIONS, I.E., ROMAN VIRTUE. IN EMPHASIS ON POWER AND CONQUEST, AUTHOR HAS MACHIAVELLIAN VIEWS. PRAISE OF ROME IS PRAISE OF A REPUBLIC WHERE PEOPLE ARE PROTECTED AGAINST TYRANNY, BUT CANNOT DIRECT STATE. INWARD MORAL STRENGTH DERIVES FROM DEDICATION TO PURSUIT OF IMPERIALISM. CHRISTIANITY IS SPURNED.

2245 MONTGOMERY H., CAMBRAY P.G.
"A DICTIONARY OF POLITICAL PHRASES AND ILLUSIONS WITH A SHORT BIBLIOGRAPHY."
NEW YORK: EP DUTTON, 1906.
BIBLIOGRAPHY INCLUDES WORKS ON POLITICAL SUBJECTS RELEVANT TO ENGLISH DOMESTIC AND FOREIGN POLICY. PARTICULARLY EMPHASIZES COLONIAL ISSUE. INDEX OF NAMES. DICTIONARY GIVES HISTORY AND EVOLUTION OF COMMONLY USED POLITICAL TERMS.

2247 MOODIE G.C.
"THE GOVERNMENT OF GREAT BRITAIN."
NEW YORK: THOMAS Y CROWELL, 1961.
INTRODUCTION TO BRITISH POLITICS AND GOVERNMENT WITH EMPHASIS ON SOCIAL-ECONOMIC CONTEXT OF POLITICAL STRUCTURE. FRAMEWORK OF STUDY IS LARGELY INSTITUTIONAL WITH SOME REFERENCE TO APPROACHES BASED ON DECISION-MAKING AND THEORIES OF GROUP INTERACTION. CONTAINS BIBLIOGRAPHICAL GUIDE.

2248 MOORE C.H.
TUNISIA SINCE INDEPENDENCE.
BERKELEY: U OF CALIF PR, 1965, 230 PP., LC#65-12926.
ILLUSTRATES THE POLITICS OF MODERNIZATION OF A ONE-PARTY SYSTEM. EXPLAINS HISTORICAL CONDITIONS THAT MAKE ONE-PARTY RULE POSSIBLE. DISCUSSES TO WHAT EXTENT THE PARTY IS A POLITICAL FORCE DISTINCT FROM ITS LEADER. ANALYZES THE INSTITUTIONAL RELATIONSHIPS BETWEEN PARTY AND THE STATE ADMINISTRATION AT THE NATIONAL AND REGIONAL LEVELS.

2249 MOORE J.R.
THE ECONOMIC IMPACT OF THE TVA.
KNOXVILLE: U OF TENN PR, 1967, 160 PP., LC#67-12217.

COLLECTION OF ESSAYS FROM SYMPOSIUM CELEBRATING TVA'S 30TH ANNIVERSARY. CONSIDERS ROLE OF ELECTRIC POWER IN ECONOMIC DEVELOPMENT, PROBLEMS OF TVA MODELED PROJECTS IN IRAN AND COLUMBIA, RELATION OF REGIONAL DEVELOPMENT TO NATIONAL PROSPERITY. CONTROVERSIES OVER SOCIALISM AND ANTI-TRUST EXPOSURES REVIEWED. WANTS CONGRESSIONAL SANCTION FOR INCREASED SCOPE OF ACTIVITY TO MEET GENERAL ECONOMIC MATURITY.

2250 MOORE W.E. ED., FELDMAN A.S. ED.
LABOR COMMITMENT AND SOCIAL CHANGE IN DEVELOPING AREAS.
NEW YORK: SOCIAL SCI RES COUNCIL, 1960, 378 PP., LC#60-53440
ANALYTICAL STUDY OF NEWLY DEVELOPING AREAS, WITH PARTICULAR EMPHASIS ON PROBLEM OF LABOR MOTIVATION IN UNFAMILIAR TASKS. EXAMINES COMMITMENT OF INDUSTRIAL LABOR BOTH IN SHORT-RUN OBJECTIVE PERFORMANCE OF MODERN ECONOMIC ACTIVITY AND LONG-RUN AND DEEP-SEATED ACCEPTANCE OF ATTITUDES AND BELIEFS APPROPRIATE TO A MODERNIZED ECONOMY.

2251 MOORE W.E.
THE IMPACT OF INDUSTRY.
ENGLEWOOD CLIFFS: PRENTICE HALL, 1965, 117 PP., LC#65-23228.
INTRODUCTION TO SERIES OF STUDIES ON "MODERNIZATION OF TRADITIONAL SOCIETIES. "ATTEMPTS TO PRESENT OVER-ALL VIEW OF INTERPLAY OF PROCESSES OF CHANGE. DISCUSSES WORLD INDUSTRIAL REVOLUTION; CREATION OF A COMMON CULTURE; CONDITIONS FOR INDUSTRIALIZATION; INDUSTRIAL ORGANIZATION; AND THE FUTURE OF INDUSTRIAL SOCIETY.

2252 MORAES F.
THE REVOLT IN TIBET.
NEW YORK: MACMILLAN, 1960, 223 PP., LC#60-6644.
DESCRIBES COMMUNIST CHINESE INVASION OF TIBET WHICH BEGAN IN 1950 AND DOCUMENTS AIMS AND BACKGROUND OF INVASION. DESCRIBES ECONOMIC EXPLOITATION AND RELIGIOUS AND SOCIAL REPRESSION OF TIBETANS BY CHINESE; ANALYZES TIBET'S ROLE IN CURRENT RELATIONS BETWEEN INDIA AND RED CHINA.

2253 MORE T.
UTOPIA (1516) (TRANS. BY R. ROBYNSON)
NEW YORK: THE HERITAGE PRESS, 1935, 165 PP.
PRESENTS IDEAL STATE BASED ON COMMUNAL PROPERTY AND SCORN OF CONSPICUOUS CONSUMPTION, NEGLECTING ALMOST TOTALLY IMPORTANT PSYCHOLOGICAL ASPECTS OF MEN. COMMUNITY IS A LIMITED MONARCHY AND OWNERSHIP IS COMMON ONLY TO ARISTOCRATS, PEASANTS STILL BEING DISENFRANCHISED. VALUES LEARNING AND CONTEMPLATION, BUT ALSO PROVIDES SOUND FACTUAL DISCUSSIONS OF ECONOMICS.

2254 MORGAN H.W. ED.
AMERICAN SOCIALISM 1900-1960.
ENGLEWOOD CLIFFS: PRENTICE HALL, 1964, 146 PP., LC#64-14978.
STUDY OF 20TH-CENTURY SOCIALISM IN US, INCLUDING ITS ACTIVITIES IN POLITICS AND RELATION TO EXISTING ORDER. EXAMINES ITS CONNECTION WITH NEGRO, IMMIGRANT, FARMER, YOUNG INTELLECTUALS, LABOR, DEPRESSION, AND CONTEMPORARY WORLD.

2255 MORGAN L.H.
ANCIENT SOCIETY (1877)
NEW YORK: MERIDIAN BOOKS, 1964, 471 PP., LC#64-21789.
THROUGH STUDY OF KIN NAMES OF AMERICAN INDIANS AND ASIATIC PEOPLES, AUTHOR DEMONSTRATES THE SOCIAL EVOLUTION OF THE FAMILY. IN ANCIENT TIMES PROMISCUITY WAS THE RULE; THIS EVOLVED INTO CONSANGUINE GROUPS OF BROTHERS AND SISTERS, THENCE INTO POLYGAMY, AND FINALLY INTO MONOGAMY. AUTHOR BUILDS HIS THESIS IN TERMS OF A CULTURAL HISTORY OF MAN, WITH EMPHASIS ON GOVERNMENT, PROPERTY, AND HOME LIFE.

2256 MORGENSTERN O.
STRATEGIE - HEUTE (2ND ED.)
STUTTGART: FISCHER VERLAG, 1962, 320 PP.
DISCUSSES PROBLEMS OF MILITARY STRATEGY RESULTING FROM US-USSR CONFRONTATION. EXAMINES TECHNOLOGICAL ADVANCES, ECONOMIC STRENGTH, PROBLEMS OF MILITARY SECURITY, PROLIFERATION OF NUCLEAR WEAPONS, AND FEASIBILITY OF LIMITED WAR. CENTERS ON COMPARISON BETWEEN US AND USSR.

2257 MORGENTHAU R.S.
POLITICAL PARTIES IN FRENCH-SPEAKING WEST AFRICA.
LONDON: OXFORD U PR, 1964, 445 PP.
BRIEFLY PRESENTS AFRICAN SOCIAL AND POLITICAL SETTING. EXAMINES FRENCH POLICY IN AFRICA AND DEVELOPMENT OF AFRICAN INSTITUTIONS, INCLUDING WEST AFRICAN REPRESENTATIVES IN FRENCH PARLIAMENT. DISCUSSES SITUATION IN SENEGAL, IVORY COAST, GUINEA, AND MALI. CONCLUDES WITH GENERAL ANALYSIS OF MOVEMENT TOWARD SOVEREIGNTY AND GROWTH OF POLITICAL PARTIES. PARTY PROBLEMS INCLUDE FINANCES, MASS SUPPORT, AND PROGRAM.

2258 MORISON D.
"AFRICAN STUDIES IN THE SOVIET UNION."
RUSS. REV., 22 (JULY 63), 301-314.
AFRICAN STUDIES IN USSR ARE CHARACTERIZED BY PRE-OCCUPATION WITH IDEOLOGICAL BASIS - ARGUMENT RATHER THAN INQUIRY-AND RELIANCE ON SECOND-HAND MATERIAL. RUSSIANS ARE TRYING TO 'SHOW THE VALUE OF THE SOVIET CONTRIBUTION TO AFRICAN STUDIES' WHILE AT THE SAME TIME TO SECURE 'EMOTIONAL SYMPATHY OF AFRICANS FOR A POLITICAL POINT OF VIEW.'

2259 MORLEY C.
GUIDE TO RESEARCH IN RUSSIAN HISTORY.
SYRACUSE: SYRACUSE U PRESS, 1951, 227 PP.
SELECTIVE ANNOTATIONS, SIGNIFICANT TITLES DESIGNATED, INDICATION OF LOCATION OF ITEMS IN AMERICA. DESIGNED TO SERVE AS HANDBOOK IN RUSSIAN HISTORY SEMINARS. INCLUDES AUTHOR AND SUBJECT INDEXES. SECTIONS ON RUSSIAN COLLECTIONS IN AMERICAN LIBRARIES; BASIC HISTORICAL AIDS; GEOGRAPHICAL AND BIBLIOGRAPHICAL DICTIONARIES; RUSSIAN BIBLIOGRAPHIES. 840 ITEMS WITH TRANSLITERATED AND TRANSLATED TITLES.

2260 MORRALL J.B.
"POLITICAL THOUGHT IN MEDIEVAL TIMES."
LONDON: HUTCHINSON & CO, 1958.
STUDY OF MEDIEVAL POLITICAL THOUGHT INTENDED FOR NON-SPECIALIST. ATTEMPTS TO DEFINE CHARACTER OF POLITICAL THOUGHT IN RELATION TO ROMAN EMPIRE, CHURCH, AND BARBARIANS. DISCUSSION OF EVOLUTION OF STATE AND PROBLEM OF AUTHORITY WITHIN CHRISTIAN COMMONWEALTH. GENERAL AND SPECIALIZED BIBLIOGRAPHY.

2261 MORRIS A.J.A.
PARLIAMENTARY DEMOCRACY IN THE NINETEENTH CENTURY.
NEW YORK: PERGAMON PRESS, 1967, 200 PP., LC#67-21276.
TRACES EVOLUTION OF BRITISH CONSTITUTION FROM TENUOUS BEGINNINGS OF PARLIAMENTARY DEMOCRACY TO EMERGENCE OF INDUSTRY AND TRADE IN 19TH CENTURY. CONSIDERS ENLARGEMENT OF FRANCHISE IN 1832 AS START OF ACTUAL DEMOCRACY STRESSES DYNAMIC NATURE OF BRITISH CONSTITUTION. DISCUSSES PARTIES, PARLIAMENT, ROYALTY, CABINET MINISTERS, CIVIL SERVICE, LOCAL GOVERNMENT, AND POLITICAL SOVEREIGNTY.

2262 MORRIS I.
NATIONALISM AND THE RIGHT WING IN JAPAN: A STUDY OF POST WAR TRENDS.
LONDON: OXFORD U. PR., 1960, 476 PP., $8.00.
ANALYSIS OF TRENDS, ORGANIZATIONS, PERSONALITIES, AND EVENTS OF POSTWAR ERA. CONCLUDES THAT, IF DEMOCRACY FAILS, A RIGHT-WING DICTATORSHIP WILL PREVAIL. A SOCIAL-PSYCHOLOGICAL ANALYSIS OF THE POTENTIAL RECEPTIVITY OF THE GENERAL PUBLIC TO RIGHT-WING LEADERSHIP.

2263 MORRIS J.
THE PRESENCE OF SPAIN.
NEW YORK: HARCOURT BRACE, 1964, 119 PP., LC#64-15682.
PICTORIAL HISTORY OF SPAIN, ITS PEOPLE, THEIR VALUES, AND WAY OF LIFE SINCE 1500. SHORT TEXT ANALYZES PICTURES OF ART, CITIES, COUNTRYSIDE, ETC., POINTING OUT TRADITIONAL BELIEFS AND PRACTICES WHILE REVEALING THEIR ORIGINS.

2264 MORRIS-JONES W.H.
"PARLIAMENT IN INDIA."
PHILA: U OF PENN PR, 1957.
STUDY DEVOTED FOR MOST PART TO CENTRAL PARLIAMENT, EMPHASIZING INSTITUTIONAL ORGANIZATION OF PARLIAMENT, ITS EVOLUTION AND CONSTRUCTIVE ACCOMPLISHMENTS. DISCUSSES PARTY ORGANIZATION, EXECUTIVE STRUCTURE, QUESTIONS OF PROCEDURE AND PRIVILEGE. INCLUDES SELECT BIBLIOGRAPHY AND APPENDIXES ON CONSTITUTION, DATES OF SESSION, VOTING FIGURES, SPECIFIC BILLS.

2265 MORRISON C.
THE POWERS THAT BE.
LONDON: SCM PRESS, 1960, 144 PP.
CRITICAL STUDY OF ROMANS 13:1-7 FOCUSING ON ATTITUDE TOWARD FREEDOM, CIVIL RESPONSIBILITY, AND DIVINE AUTHORITY EXPRESSED IN THESE VERSES. PRESENTS HISTORY AND EVALUATION OF RECENT INTERPRETATIONS AND REVIEWS MAJOR CRITICISMS BROUGHT TO BEAR AGAINST THESE INTERPRETATIONS.

2266 MORRISON H.
GOVERNMENT AND PARLIAMENT.
LONDON: OXFORD U PR, 1954, 390 PP.
DEALS WITH THE INSIDE WORKINGS OF BRITISH GOVERNMENT AND RELATED COMMITTEES. CONCENTRATES ON LESS-WELL KNOWN FEATURES OF GOVERNMENT, RECENT DEVELOPMENTS, AND PROPOSALS FOR CHANGE.

2267 MOSELY P.E. ED.
THE SOVIET UNION, 1922-1962: A FOREIGN AFFAIRS READER.
NEW YORK: FREDERICK PRAEGER, 1963, 497 PP., LC#63-10826.
STUDIES POLITICAL HISTORY EMPHASIZING THE STALIN ERA. DISCUSSES REVOLUTIONARY RUSSIA, STRATEGY, AND PEACEFUL COEXISTENCE.

2268 MOSK S.A.
INDUSTRIAL REVOLUTION IN MEXICO.
BERKELEY: U OF CALIF PR, 1954, 331 PP.
ANALYZES REVOLUTION IN MEXICAN ECONOMY SINCE 1940, BASIC ATTITUDES OF INDUSTRIAL DRIVE, AND PERSPECTIVES OF BUSINESS, GOVERNMENT, AND LABOR. DISCUSSES GOVERNMENTAL POLICIES ENCOURAGING INDUSTRIAL DEVELOPMENT. SURVEYS DEVELOPMENTS IN PRINCIPAL INDUSTRIAL FIELDS.

2269 MOSS W.
POLITICAL PARTIES IN THE IRISH FREE STATE.

NEW YORK: COLUMBIA U PRESS, 1933, 235 PP.
BACKGROUND AND DESCRIPTION OF PARTY SYSTEM, ITS ORGANIZATION, CAMPAIGNS, TACTICS, AND PARTY STATEMENTS. INCLUDES DISCUSSION OF SINN FEIN, THE NATIONAL LEGUE, AND CANDITATES' BIOGRAPHIES.

2270 MOTE M.E.
SOVIET LOCAL AND REPUBLIC ELECTIONS.
STANFORD: HOOVER INSTITUTE, 1965, 123 PP., LC#65-26268.
PAPER DESCRIBES 1963 ELECTIONS IN LENINGRAD BASED ON OFFICIAL DOCUMENTS, PRESS ACCOUNTS, AND PRIVATE INTERVIEWS. GENERAL FEATURES OF PAPER APPLY TO ALL OF USSR. PAPER COVERS STEPS IN ELECTION PROCESS ONE-BY-ONE AS THEY OCCUR. TIME INVOLVED IS SIX OR SEVEN WEEKS, FROM MID-JANUARY TO MARCH 3.

2271 MOUMOUNI A.
L'EDUCATION EN AFRIQUE.
PARIS: FRANCOIS MASPERA, 1964, 393 PP.
ATTEMPTS TO ILLUMINATE EDUCATIONAL PROBLEMS, IMPLICATIONS AND SOLUTIONS, IN AFRICA, ESPECIALLY IN FORMER FRENCH COLONIES. TRACES DEVELOPMENT OF EDUCATION FROM PRE-COLONIAL TIMES TO PRESENT. REFORMS HAVE BEEN LAUDABLE BUT INSUFFICIENT. ATTEMPTS MADE TO MOVE AWAY FROM NARROWLY FRENCH, COLONIALIST VIEWPOINT. AUTHOR BELIEVES REFORMS MUST BE BASED ON USAGE OF AFRICAN LANGUAGES.

2272 MOUSKHELY M.
"LA NAISSANCE DES ETATS EN DROIT INTERNATIONAL PUBLIC."
REV. GEN. DR. INT. PUB., 66 (NO.3, 62), 469-85.
FORMATION OF NEW STATES RAISES SEVERAL PROBLEMS. ANALYZES RELATION OF CONSEQUENCES TO DOMESTIC AND INTERNATIONAL. STUDIES DIRECTION OF DEVELOPMENT OF STIMSON DOCTRINE AND SUPRA-NATIONAL ORGANIZATIONS.

2273 MOUSSA P.
THE UNDERPRIVILEGED NATIONS.
LONDON: SIDGWICK + JACKSON, 1962, 198 PP.
ANALYSIS OF INTERNATIONAL IMPLICATIONS OF POLITICAL AND ECONOMIC GROWTH OF UNDERDEVELOPED COUNTRIES THROUGHOUT WORLD. VIEWS PROBLEMS OF UNDERDEVELOPED COUNTRIES ON COMPARATIVE BASIS WITH CONDITIONS OF INDUSTRIALIZED, PROSPEROUS COUNTRIES. STRESSES IMPORTANCE OF POLICIES OF WORLD POWERS TOWARD POORER NATIONS IN MAINTAINING INTERNATIONAL POLITICAL STABILITY.

2274 MOYER K.E.
FROM IRAN TO MORROCCO; FROM TURKEY TO THE SUDAN: A SELECTED AND ANNOTATED BIBLIOGRAPHY OF NORTH AFRICA AND NEAR EAST...
NEW YORK: MISSIONARY RES LIB, 1957, 51 PP.
BIBLIOGRAPHICAL SELECTION ON NORTH AFRICA AND NEAR AND MIDDLE EAST AREA DRAWN OUT OF CONTENTS OF MISSIONARY RESEARCH LIBRARY AT UNION THEOLOGICAL SEMINARY. VOLUME CONTAINS APPROXIMATELY 650 ENTRIES WITH BRIEF DESCRIPTIVE NOTES. MATERIAL IS CLASSIFIED GEOGRAPHICALLY AND TOPICALLY. DOES NOT CONTAIN INDEXES. REFERENCES TO ECONOMICS, POLITICS, FOREIGN RELATIONS, AND GOVERNMENT.

2275 MOZINGO D.
"CONTAINMENT IN ASIA RECONSIDERED."
WORLD POLITICS, 19 (APR. 67), 361-377.
DISCUSSES WHY A CONTAINMENT POLICY IN ASIA HAS NOT BEEN FEASIBLE. APPRAISES CHINESE INTENTIONS IN ASIA AND DISCUSSES OBSTIACLES TO CHINESE PRE-EMINENCE THERE. DISCUSSES AMERICAN PROBLEMS IN ASIA.

2276 MOZINGO D.
"CHINA AND INDONESIA."
CHICAGO TODAY, 4 (SPRING 67), 44-45.
TREATS PEKING'S INVOLVEMENT IN INDONESIA'S INTERNAL FFAIRS. QUESTIONS WHETHER CHINA PLAYED ANY ROLE IN ATTEMPTED COUP OF OCTOBER FIRST.

2277 MOZINGO D.P.
"CHINA'S RELATIONS WITH HER ASIAN NEIGHBORS."
CURR. HIST., 47 (SEPT. 64), 156-61.
RELATIONS DICTATED BY OVERRULING AIM OF SUPREMACY OF CHINESE STATE. IN ACCORDANCE, PEKING ACTIVELY SUPPORTS OR MAINTAINS STUDIED INDIFFERENCE TO FATE OF OTHER COMMUNIST PARTIES. 'CAN LOOK IN VAIN FOR ANY STRIDENT CHINESE CALL OF REVOLUTION IN REFERENCE TO ANY COUNTRY THAT HAS ALREADY MADE ITS ACCOMMODATION TO CHINA'S IMMEDIATE INTERESTS.'

2278 MU FU-SHENG
"THE WILTING OF THE HUNDRED FLOWERS: FREE THOUGHT IN CHINA TODAY."
LONDON: HEINEMANN, 1962, 343 PP.
TRACES INTELLECTUAL HISTORY OF CHINA. DESCRIBES PRESENT INTELLECTUAL ATTITUDES. BASED ON FIRST-HAND OBSERVATIONS.

2279 MUEHLMANN W.E.
"L'IDEE NATIONALE ALLEMANDE ET L'IDEE NATIONALE FRANCAISE."
REV. PSYCHOL. PEUPLES, 7 (1952), 348-362.
COMPARES AND SUGGESTS HISTORICAL ORIGIN OF THE NATIONAL ETHOS OF GERMANY WITH THAT OF FRANCE: CHARACTERISTIC OF THE GERMANS IS THEIR CONCEPT OF NATIONAL SUPERIORITY, A ROMANTIC VIEW OF NATION-HOOD, A SUSCEPTIBILITY TO RACIAL AND NATIONAL DISCRIMINATION. THE FRENCH HAVE A SPECIFIC REALISTIC CONCEPT OF NATION-HOOD, VALUE CIVILIZATION AND THEIR INFLUENCE UPON IT AND REJECT EMPHASIS ON RACIAL DISTINCTIONS.

2280 MUELLER-DEHAM A.
HUMAN RELATIONS AND POWER; SOCIO-POLITICAL ANALYSIS AND SYNTHESIS.
NEW YORK: PHILOSOPHICAL LIB, 1957, 410 PP.
MAINTAINS THAT ALL SOCIOLOGICAL CONCEPTS CAN BE STUDIED WITH SOCIAL RELATIONS AND POWER AS BASIS. PRESENTS THOROUGH VIEW OF POWER AS INFLUENCE ON MAN AND CAUSE OF SOCIAL PROCESSES. APPLIES NEW SOCIOLOGY TO POLITICAL THEORY, INSTITUTIONS, AND STATE STRUCTURE. DEALS WITH SOCIOLOGICAL THOUGHT ON ETHICAL PROBLEMS OF POWER AND POLITICS.

2281 MUHAMMAD A.C.
THE EMERGENCE OF PAKISTAN.
NEW YORK: COLUMBIA U PRESS, 1967, 418 PP., LC#67-12535.
ACCOUNT OF LAST DAYS OF BRITISH EMPIRE IN INDIA AND UPHEAVALS THAT ATTENDED PARTITION OF SUBCONTINENT INTO UNION OF INDIA AND PAKISTAN. SPECIFIC PROBLEMS OF PAKISTAN IN ESTABLISHING POLITICAL AND ECONOMIC SYSTEM. RESULTING RELATION BETWEEN SECTS, STATES, AND BRITISH COMMONWEALTH.

2282 MUKERJI S.N. ED.
ADMINISTRATION OF EDUCATION IN INDIA.
BARODA: ACHARYA BOOK DEPOT, 1962, 679 PP.
DETAILED DISCUSSIONS OF EDUCATIONAL ADMINISTRATION STRESSING ADVANCES MADE IN FIELD DURING RECENT YEARS. DEAL WITH GENERAL SUBJECT AREAS SUCH AS RELATIONS BETWEEN VARIOUS SUPERVISORY AGENCIES AND SCHOOLS, AND DIFFERENT AREAS AND BRANCHES OF EDUCATION. SEPARATE SECTIONS ON EACH UNION TERRITORY.

2283 MULLER A.L.
"SOME NON-ECONOMIC DETERMINANTS OF THE ECONOMIC STATUS OF ASIANS IN AFRICA."
S. AFR. J. OF ECONOMICS, 33 (MAR. 65), 72-79.
DISCUSSES SOCIAL, CULTURAL, AND RELIGIOUS CUSTOMS AND BELIEFS OF AFRICAN RESIDENTS OF ASIAN DESCENT. PORTRAYS THE FRICTION ARISING FROM RELATIONS BETWEEN ASIAN COMMUNITY AND OTHER RACIAL GROUPS, PARTICULARLY IN ITS BEARING ON SIZE AND COMPOSITION OF LABOR FORCE AND QUALITY OF PRODUCTIVE SERVICES RENDERED BY ASIANS. SINGLES OUT RELIGIOUS BELIEFS AND ASIAN ECONOMIC AND SOCIAL DISCRIMINATION FOR STUDY.

2284 MULLER C.F.J. ED., VAN JAARSVELD F.A. ED., VAN WIJK T. ED.
A SELECT BIBLIOGRAPHY OF SOUTH AFRICAN HISTORY; A GUIDE FOR HISTORICAL RESEARCH.
PRETORIA: U OF SOUTH AFRICA, 1966, 215 PP.
LISTS BOOKS AND SOME UNPUBLISHED THESES ON VARIOUS SOUTH AFRICAN HISTORICAL SUBJECTS. MAJORITY OF ENTRIES DUTCH PUBLICATIONS; MANY ENGLISH-LANGUAGE SOURCES AND SOME EUROPEAN INCLUDED. ALL TITLES TRANSLATED INTO ENGLISH. ITEMS ARRANGED ALPHABETICALLY BY AUTHOR UNDER SUBJECT AND PERIOD; 2,521 ENTRIES PUBLISHED IN 20TH CENTURY. AUTHOR INDEX.

2285 MULLER H.J.
FREEDOM IN THE WESTERN WORLD.
NEW YORK: HARPER & ROW, 1963, 428 PP., LC#63-8427.
SYNTHESIS OF VARIOUS MAJOR DEVELOPMENTS THAT AFFECTED WESTERN CIVILIZATION THROUGH DARK AGES TO MODERN DEMOCRACY. RELIGIOUS AND POLITICAL STRUGGLES, ADVANCES OF COLLECTIVE WEALTH AND POWER THROUGH COMMERCE AND TECHNOLOGY, CREATIVITY IN ART AND SCIENTIFIC THOUGHT, AND EVOLVEMENT OF IDEAS THAT PROMOTED BELIEF IN MAN'S DIGNITY AND FITNESS FOR FREEDOM ARE DEVELOPMENTS THAT ARE DISCUSSED.

2286 MUMFORD L.
THE CONDUCT OF LIFE.
NEW YORK: HARCOURT BRACE, 1951, 342 PP.
LAST PART OF A SERIES TITLED "TECHNICS AND CIVILIZATION," "THE CONDITION OF MAN," AND "THE CULTURE OF CITIES." NOTES EVOLUTION OF CULTURAL AND ETHICAL VALUES IN HUMAN SOCIETY AND ATTEMPTS AN INTEGRATION OF THEM IN AN "ORGANIC SYNCRETISM." CONSIDERS THE BASIS OF HUMAN DEVELOPMENT, MORAL AMBIGUITIES, AND RENEWAL. CONTAINS BIBLIOGRAPHY.

2287 MUMFORD L.
THE TRANSFORMATIONS OF MAN.
NEW YORK: HARPER & ROW, 1956, 249 PP., LC#56-6030.
TRACES DEVELOPMENT OF MAN AND NATURE OF HUMAN ACTION, MOTIVATION, THOUGHT, AND VALUES FROM EARLIEST TIMES. COMMENT IS GENERAL, RELATING ONLY TO BROAD IDEAS AND PERIODS IN HISTORY. INCLUDES GROWTH OF RELIGIOUS VALUES, MAN'S CONCEPTS OF FAMILY, GOD, THE STATE, AND THE REASONS FOR EXISTENCE. TRACES MAN'S CONCEPT OF KNOWLEDGE AND HIS PURSUIT AND USES OF IT.

2288 MUNGER E.S.
AFRICAN FIELD REPORTS 1952-1961.
CAPETOWN: C STRUIK, 1961, 808 PP.
PERSONAL REPORTS COVERING WIDE RANGE OF POLITICAL DEVELOPMENTS IN TROPICAL AFRICA AND SOUTH AFRICA, INCLUDING LEADERS, EVENTS, AND CONDITIONS.

2289 MUNGER E.S.
AFRIKANER AND AFRICAN NATIONALISM: SOUTH AFRICAN PARALLELS AND PARAMETERS.
LONDON: OXFORD U PR, 1967, 142 PP.
CONCERNED WITH HISTORY AND CONTEMPORARY POLITICS OF SOUTH AFRICA, SPECIFIC PURPOSE IS A COMPARATIVE INTERPRETATION OF THE TWO NATIONALISMS (WHITE AND BLACK) OF SOUTH AFRICA. GIVES POLITICAL EXPLANATION FOR SOCIOLOGICAL PATTERN OF CONFLICT, AS WHITE AND BLACK COME IN CONTACT IN CITIES OF SOUTH AFRICA.

2290 MUNZENBERG W.
PROPAGANDA ALS WAFFE.
PARIS: ED DU CARREFOUR, 1937, 281 PP.
DISCUSSION OF NATURE OF NATIONAL SOCIALIST PROPAGANDA IN GERMANY. CITES EXAMPLES OF ANTI-BOLSHEVIK AND ANTI-JEWISH PLUS ANTI-DEMOCRATIC PROPAGANDA EFFORTS. MAINTAINS THAT HITLER PROPAGANDA, BECAUSE OF ITS VAST EXAGGERATIONS, MUST EVENTUALLY BECOME ITS OWN EXECUTIONER.

2291 MURACCIOLE L.
"LES CONSTITUTIONS DES ETATS AFRICAINS D'EXPRESSION FRANCAISE: LA CONSTITUTION DU 16 AVRIL 1962 DE LA REPUBLIQUE DU TCHAD."
REV. JURID. POLIT. OUTREMER, 16 (APR.-JUNE 62), 265-78.
PRESENTS AND COMMENTS BRIEFLY ON NEW AND MORE COMPREHENSIVE CONSTITUTION OF CHAD. COMMENTARY EMPHASIZES POWER OF THE PRESIDENT. HIS POWERS MAY BE CENSURED AND MODIFIED BY TWO-THIRDS MAJORITY VOTE OF THE ASSEMBLY.

2292 MURACCIOLE L.
"LA BANQUE CENTRALE DES ETATS DE L'AFRIQUE DE L'OUEST."
REV. JURID. POLIT. OUTREMER, 16 (JULY-SEPT. 62), 375-424.
COMPREHENSIVE ANALYSIS OF ACTIVITIES OF CENTRAL BANK OF WESTERN AFRICAN STATES DURING 1961 AND ITS RECENT EVOLUTION. RELATES ACTIVITIES TO INTERNATIONAL ECONOMIC RELATIONS. DISCUSSES MAJOR SOURCES OF COMMERCE AND PRODUCTION. CONCLUDES WITH ANALYSIS OF MONETARY AND FINANCIAL INSTITUTIONS.

2293 MURDOCK G.P.
AFRICA: ITS PEOPLES AND THEIR CULTURE HISTORY.
NEW YORK: MCGRAW HILL, 1959, 456 PP., LC#59-8552.
DETAILED SURVEY OF TRIBES INCLUDING MORES, EXPANSION, AND IMPACT UPON CIVILIZATION. SHORT BIBLIOGRAPHY AT END OF EACH OF 55 CHAPTERS RELATING TO THAT CHAPTER, IN ENGLISH, FRENCH, AND GERMAN; LISTED ALPHABETICALLY BY AUTHOR.

2294 MURDOCK G.P.
CULTURE AND SOCIETY.
PITTSBURGH: U OF PITTSBURGH PR, 1965, 376 PP., LC#65-18206.
ESSAYS IN CULTURAL ANTHROPOLOGY. TOPICS INCLUDE RELATION OF ANTHROPOLOGY TO OTHER DISCIPLINES, NATURE OF CULTURE, DYNAMICS OF CULTURAL CHANGE, SOCIAL ORGANIZATION, RELIGION, AND CROSS-CULTURAL COMPARISON.

2295 MURET C.T.
"FRENCH ROYALIST DOCTRINES SINCE THE REVOLUTION."
NEW YORK: COLUMBIA U PRESS, 1933.
EXAMINES ROYALIST DOCTRINE AND DEPICTS EVOLUTION THROUGH 18TH-19TH CENTURIES. DISCUSSES IDEAS OF LEADING REPRESENTATIVES ON NATURE AND OBJECT OF SOCIETY, RELATION OF INDIVIDUAL TO STATE, ORIGIN AND NATURE OF SOVEREIGNTY, PURPOSE AND CHARACTER OF MONARCHY, ORGANIZATION OF STATE, RELATIONS OF CHURCH TO STATE. POINTS OUT GENERAL SIGNIFICANCE OF THINKER FOR ROYALIST THEORY. LARGE BIBLIOGRAPHY INCLUDED.

2296 MURPHEY R.
"ECONOMIC CONFLICTS IN SOUTH ASIA."
J. CONFL. RESOLUT., 4 (MAR. 60), 83-95.
DISCUSSES AREA'S ECONOMIC SITUATION INCLUDING PROSPECTS FOR INDUSTRIALIZATION, ECONOMIC INDEPENDENCE, INCREASING PER CAPITA INCOME, AND THE GENERATION AND CONTROL OF CAPITAL. CONCLUDES CONFLICTS ARISE FROM THE FRUSTRATION OF ASIAN AMBITIONS, DERIVED FROM WESTERN MODELS, WHICH DO NOT COINCIDE WITH CIRCUMSTANCES.

2297 MURPHY G.
IN THE MINDS OF MEN: THE STUDY OF HUMAN BEHAVIOR AND SOCIAL TENSIONS IN INDIA.
NEW YORK: BASIC, 1953, 292 PP.
REPORTS CONSTRUCTIVE FORCES FOSTERING NATIONAL UNITY, AND CAUSES OF SOCIAL TENSION SUCH AS HINDU-MOSLEM CONFLICTS AND CONFLICTS AMONG CASTES. DEMONSTRATES UNESCO'S FUNCTION AS AMELIORATIVE FORCE IN SOCIAL CONTEXT.

2298 MURPHY J.C.
"SOME IMPLICATIONS OF EUROPE'S COMMON MARKET.
IN (COOK P, ECONOMIC DEVELOPMENT AND INTERNATIONAL TRADE,."
DALLAS: SOUTHERN METHODIST U. PR., 1959, P. 33-49).
RAISES TWO QUESTIONS: 1)WILL GEOGRAPHIC DISTRIBUTION OF PRODUCTION AND PATTERN OF TRADE BENEFIT EUROPE AND FREE WORLD, AND 2)WILL COMMON MARKET LEAD TO LARGER SCALE ECONOMIC PRODUCTION. SUPPORTS AFFIRMATIVE ANSWER TO BOTH QUESTIONS.

2299 MURVAR V.
"MAX WEBER'S CONCEPT OF HEIROCRACY: A STUDY IN THE TYPOLOGY OF CHURCH-STATE RELATIONS"
SOCIOLOGICAL ANALYSIS, 28 (SUMMER 67), 69-84.
RECOMMENDS UTILIZATION OF WEBER'S CONCEPTUAL TOOLS IN INTERDISCIPLINARY RESEARCH ON CHURCH-STATE RELATIONS. PRESENTS SOME BASIC AND UNIVERSAL MONISTIC SOCIETAL STRUCTURES IN CONTRAST TO EARLY DUALISM OF WEST. FINDS BOTH SETS OF STRUCTURES INSTRUCTIVE FOR MAN IN HIS SEARCH FOR PLURALISTIC SOLUTIONS WHILE STILL "HAUNTED" BY MONISTIC VALUE-SYSTEMS OF THE PAST.

2300 MUSEUM FUR VOLKERKUNDE WIEN
ZENTRALAMERIKA MEXIKO VOLKER UND KULTUREN.
VIENNA: MUSEUM FUR VOLKERKUNDE, 1964, 44 PP.
DISCUSSES HISTORY, SOCIAL STRUCTURE, AND CULTURAL DEVELOPMENT OF PEOPLE OF CENTRAL AMERICA. EXAMINES FOLK ART, WEAVING, TRADITIONAL DRESS, CERAMIC ART, RELIGIONS, AND AGRICULTURE. PICTURES AND MAPS.

2301 MUSSO AMBROSI L.A. ED.
BIBLIOGRAFIA DE BIBLIOGRAFIAS URUGUAYAS.
MONTEVIDEO: AGRUPACION BIB, 1964, 102 PP.
URUGUAYAN BIBLIOGRAPHY OF BIBLIOGRAPHIES INCLUDING BOOKS, PERIODICALS, PAMPHLETS, AND NEWSPAPER ARTICLES. OVER 200 ENTRIES ARE URUGUAYAN BIBLIOGRAPHIC PERIODICALS. ABOUT 650 MATERIALS LISTED.

2302 MYERS F.M.
THE WARFARE OF DEMOCRATIC IDEALS.
YELLOW SPRINGS: ANTIOCH, 1956, 261 PP., LC#56-6504.
ATTEMPTS TO CLARIFY FUNDAMENTAL ISSUES WHICH SEPARATE VARIOUS PHILOSOPHIES ON THE MEANING OF DEMOCRACY. GOAL IS FORMULATION OF WORKABLE CRITERION BY WHICH ALTERNATIVE MEANINGS MAY BE EXAMINED. INCLUDES ANALYSES OF TRADITIONAL EMPIRICISM, NEO-THOMISM, PROTESTANT ABSOLUTISMS, AND INSTRUMENTALISM.

2303 NAHM A.C.
JAPANESE PENETRATION OF KOREA, 1894-1910.
STANFORD: STANFORD BOOKSTORE, 1959, 103 PP.
BIBLIOGRAPHY OF 100,000 PAGES FROM ARCHIVES AND DOCUMENTS SECTION OF THE JAPANESE GENERAL IN SEOUL, COVERING PERIOD FROM SINO-JAPANESE WAR OF 1894 TO JAPANESE ANNEXATION OF KOREA IN 1910. UNIQUE DOCUMENTS ARE PRESERVED ON MICROFILM AT HOOVER INSTITUTE. INCLUDES SELECTIVE DESCRIPTIVE ANNOTATIONS. EMPHASIS PLACED ON KOREAN FOREIGN RELATIONS AND JAPANESE-ASIAN POLICIES. CONTAINS CHRONOLOGY WITH ITEMS.

2304 NAHUMI M.
"THE POWERS IN THE MIDDLE EAST CONFLICT."
NEW OUTLOOK, 10 (JULY-AUG. 67), 11-19.
EXPLORES SOURCES OF SIX-DAY WAR, GENERAL AND IMMEDIATE, AND CONSIDERS ROLE OF US AND USSR IN PROVOKING, RESTRAINING, AND SUPPLYING ACTIONS, ESPECIALLY BREAKDOWN OF RELATIONS BETWEEN USSR AND UAR.

2305 NAKAMURA H.
THE WAYS OF THINKING OF EASTERN PEOPLES.
TOKYO: JAP NAT COMM FOR UNESCO, 1960, 657 PP.
ANALYZES THOUGHT PATTERNS OF FOUR ASIAN PEOPLES (INDIAN, CHINESE, JAPANESE, AND TIBETAN) AS REVEALED IN THEIR LANGUAGE, LOGIC, AND CULTURAL PRODUCTS. IN HISTORY AND SPREAD OF BUDDHISM LIE CLUES TO FUNDAMENTALLY DIFFERING MODES OF THOUGHT BETWEEN EAST AND WEST.

2306 NALBANDIAN L.
THE ARMENIAN REVOLUTIONARY MOVEMENT.
BERKELEY: U OF CALIF PR, 1963, 247 PP., LC#63-13806.
COMPREHENSIVE EXAMINATION OF ORIGINS, OBJECTIVES, ACTIVITIES, AND ACHIEVEMENTS OF ARMENIAN POLITICAL PARTIES THAT AROSE DURING LAST HALF OF 19TH CENTURY. DEVELOPMENTS ANALYZED IN RELATION TO SIMILAR NATIONAL REVOLUTIONARY FORCES AT WORK IN WESTERN EUROPE, RUSSIA, AND THE BALKANS. COVERS ARMED STRUGGLE AGAINST OTTOMAN GOVERNMENT, BEGINNING IN 1862 AND EXTENDING TO 1896.

2307 NAMBOODIRIPAD E.M.
ECONOMICS AND POLITICS OF INDIA'S SOCIALIST PATTERN.
NEW DELHI: PEOPLE'S PUBL HOUSE, 1966, 419 PP.
DISCUSSES AND ASSESSES PLANNED ECONOMY IN INDIA SINCE INDEPENDENCE. MAINTAINS THAT INDIA HAS FAILED TO BUILD A SOCIALIST SOCIETY AND THAT CAPITALIST FORMS OF EXPLOITATION ARE PERPETUATED ON EVER-INCREASING SCALE.

2308 NAMIER L.
PERSONALITIES AND POWERS.
LONDON: HAMILTON, 1955, 157 PP.
RELATES BRITISH HISTORY OF 17TH AND 18TH CENTURY TO DIPLOMACY OF 20TH. ALSO COVERS DIPLOMACY FROM 1919 ON.

2309 NAMIER L.B.
THE STRUCTURE OF POLITICS AT THE ACCESSION OF GEORGE III.
NEW YORK: ST MARTIN'S PRESS, 1965, 602 PP.
PRESENTS FUNCTIONAL ANALYSIS OF PARLIAMENT, 1761-1784, STUDYING ACTIONS OF INDIVIDUALS IN GOVERNMENT. DISCUSSES TYPES OF INDIVIDUALS ATTRACTED, STRUCTURE OF ELECTORATE,

RESULTS OF 1761 ELECTION, EFFECT OF SHROPSHIRE POLITICS UPON NATIONAL GOVERNMENT, AND EFFECT OF AMERICAN REVOLUTION UPON PARLIAMENT AND THE CAREERS OF INDIVIDUALS WITHIN IT.

2310 NARAIN D.
HINDU CHARACTER (A FEW GLIMPSES)
BOMBAY: U OF BOMBAY, 1957, 238 PP.
NATIONAL CHARACTER STUDY OF HINDU PEOPLE. REEXAMINES DISTINCTIONS BETWEEN EAST AND WEST. NOTES DIFFERENCES IN TEMPERAMENT AMONG ASIAN NATIONS. CLAIMS THAT WEAKNESSES OF HINDU CHARACTER ARE OVER-INDULGENT CHILDHOOD AND OVER-SEVERE CONSCIENCE. HOPES THAT INCREASED CONTACT WITH WEST WILL RELAX CONSCIENCE AND HELP HINDU BECOME LESS SEVERE.

2311 NARAIN J.P.
SWARAJ FOR THE PEOPLE.
RAJGHAT: AKHIL BHARAT SARVA SEVA, 1961, 32 PP.
ARGUMENTS AND PROPOSALS ON REFORMING INDIA'S POLITICAL INSTITUTIONS AND PROCESSES TO MAKE THEM "MORE DEMOCRATIC, EFFICIENT, ENDURING, AND MEANINGFUL." EMPHASIZES EDUCATION, DISTRIBUTION OF POWER, DEVELOPMENT OF "SOCIAL CONSCIOUSNESS," ELIMINATION OF ELECTORAL CONTESTS IN VILLAGE COMMUNITIES, ETC. CONCLUDES THAT PEOPLE MUST TAKE LARGER ROLE IN SHAPING NATIONAL WILL.

2312 NARASIMHAN V.K.
THE PRESS, THE PUBLIC AND THE ADMINISTRATION (PAMPHLET)
NEW DELHI: INDIAN INST PUB ADMIN, 1961, 68 PP.
ANALYZES ROLE OF PRESS IN INDIA AS VITAL SOURCE OF COMMUNICATION BETWEEN PEOPLE AND GOVERNMENT. FEELS PRESS SHOULD ACT AS "MEDIATOR" BETWEEN PUBLIC AND ADMINISTRATION, AND SUGGESTS CHANGES NECESSARY FOR THIS FUNCTION. SEES THIS ROLE AS BEST WAY PRESS CAN SERVE PEOPLE IN FUTURE.

2313 NASH M. ED., CHIN R. ED.
"PSYCHO-CULTURAL FACTORS IN ASIAN ECONOMIC GROWTH."
J. SOC. ISSUES, 19 (JAN. 63), 1-87.
ARTICLES ON CHARACTERISTICS OF ASIAN ECONOMIC GROWTH, BY VARIOUS EXPERTS. ATTEMPTS TO DEMONSTRATE THAT PSYCHOLOGY, SOCIOLOGY, AND ANTHROPOLOGY SHOULD PLAY AN IMPORTANT ROLE IN SHAPING ECONOMIC POLICY AND IN CONDUCTING ECONOMIC RESEARCH FOR ASIA.

2314 NASH M.
"SOCIAL PREREQUISITES TO ECONOMIC GROWTH IN LATIN AMERICA AND SOUTHEAST ASIA."
ECON. DEVELOP. CULT. CHANGE, 12(APR 64), 225-42.
COMPARATIVE STUDY OF MODERNIZING NATION IN LATIN AMERICA AND A NEWLY INDEPENDENT NATION OF SOUTHEAST ASIA. EMPLOYS MACRO-STRUCTURAL ANALYSIS AND MICRO-ANALYSIS TO FIT ROLE PERCEPTIONS IN THEIR INSTUTIONAL CONTEXT.

2315 NASH M.
MACHINE AGE MAYA.
CHICAGO: U OF CHICAGO PRESS, 1967, 155 PP.
DISCUSSES THE INDUSTRIALIZATION OF A GUATEMALAN COMMUNITY. DESCRIBES AN INDIAN MOUNTAIN COMMUNITY, WHICH HAS SUCCESSFULLY ADAPTED TO THE OPERATION OF LATIN AMERICA'S LARGEST TEXTILE MILL. DISCUSSES IMPACT OF THE FACTORY ON THE COMMUNITY, E.G., RAISING THE STANDARD OF LIVING AND CREATING NEW WORK HABITS. COMPARES THE RELIGIOUS PRACTICES AND BELIEFS OF FACTORY AND FARM WORKER.

2316 NASRI A.R. ED.
A BIBLIOGRAPHY OF THE SUDAN 1938-1958.
LONDON: OXFORD U PR, 1962, 171 PP.
BIBLIOGRAPHY COVERING MANY FIELDS IN THE SOCIAL, NATURAL, AND PHYSICAL SCIENCES. EXCLUDES MANUSCRIPTS, MAPS, AND DAILY NEWSPAPER MATERIAL. WITHIN EACH SUBJECT AREA, ARRANGEMENT IS ALPHABETICAL BY AUTHOR. ARABIC TITLES ARE GIVEN IN A TRANSLITERATED FORM WITH A BRIEF ENGLISH TRANSLATION.

2317 NATHAN M.
THE SOUTH AFRICAN COMMONWEALTH: CONSTITUTION, PROBLEMS, SOCIAL CONDITIONS.
JOHANNESBURG: SPECIALTY PR S AFR, 1919, 483 PP.
DESCRIBES SYSTEM OF GOVERNMENT IN SOUTH AFRICA AS OF 1919; SHOWS RELATIONSHIP TO GREAT BRITAIN AND COMMONWEALTH. AUTHOR FEELS ANCESTRY AND HISTORY OF PEOPLE ASSURES CONTINUATION OF IDEALS OF LIBERTY, CIVILIZATION, AND HONOR.

2318 NATIONAL BANK OF LIBYA
INFLATION IN LIBYA (PAMPHLET)
TRIPOLI: NATIONAL BANK OF LIBYA, 1961, 86 PP.
DEFINES INFLATION IN GENERAL, AND ANALYZES WIDELY RECOGNIZED TENDENCY IN LIBYAN ECONOMY FOR THE GENERAL PRICE LEVEL TO RISE. ATTEMPTS TO FIND OUT MOST EFFECTIVE AND PRACTICAL WAYS TO COPE WITH INFLATION WITHOUT ADVERSELY AFFECTING ECONOMIC DEVELOPMENT.

2319 NATIONAL BOOK CENTRE PAKISTAN
BOOKS ON PAKISTAN: A BIBLIOGRAPHY.
KARACHI: STERLING PRINTING & PUB, 1965, 71 PP.
EMPHASIZES CULTURAL ASPECTS; INCLUDES BOOKS ON PAKISTAN PUBLISHED OUTSIDE THE COUNTRY. SECTIONS ON HISTORY, IDEOLOGY, AND POLITICS; CONSTITUTIONAL STUDIES; ADMINISTRATION AND BASIC DEMOCRACY; SOCIOLOGY, CUSTOM AND FOLKLORE. ALL PUBLICATIONS ARE IN ENGLISH. CONTAINS INDEXES OF PUBLISHERS AND TITLES.

2320 NATIONAL BOOK LEAGUE
THE COMMONWEALTH IN BOOKS: AN ANNOTATED LIST.
LONDON: NATL BOOK LEAGUE, 1964, 126 PP.
LISTS BOOKS ON GEOGRAPHY, HISTORY, SOCIOLOGY, POLITICS, LAW, AND LOCAL GOVERNMENT; BOOKS IN FRENCH FROM CANADIAN PUBLISHERS. ANNOTATED AND ARRANGED BY SUBJECT. CONTAINS BOOKS PUBLISHED SINCE APPROXIMATELY 1950.

2321 NATIONAL OFF STATE GOVT THAI
STATISTICAL BIBLIOGRAPHY: AN ANNOTATED BIBLIOGRAPHY OF THAI GOVERNMENTAL STATISTICAL PUBLICATIONS.
BANGKOK: THAILAND CENTL OFF STAT, 1963, 173 PP.
ABOUT 115 TITLES ARE LISTED, ANNOTATED AND TRANSLATED. MOST OF THEM ARE POST-WWII.

2322 NATIONAL REFERRAL CENTER SCI
A DIRECTORY OF INFORMATION RESOURCES IN THE UNITED STATES; SOCIAL SCIENCES.
WASHINGTON: LIBRARY OF CONGRESS, 1965, 218 PP., LC#65-62583.
ANNOTATED GUIDE TO INFORMATION ACTIVITY CENTERS IN THE US. ENTRIES LISTED ALPHABETICALLY BY ORGANIZATIONAL NAME. SUBJECT INDEX IS PROVIDED IN WHICH FULL NAMES OF THE INFORMATION RESOURCES ARE LISTED UNDER SUBJECT HEADINGS. CONTAINS DATA ON LOCATION, INTERESTS, SERVICE RESTRICTIONS, AND PUBLICATIONS OF EACH AGENCY.

2323 NATIONAL SCIENCE FOUNDATION
DIRECTORY OF SELECTED RESEARCH INSTITUTES IN EASTERN EUROPE.
NEW YORK: COLUMBIA U PRESS, 1967, 445 PP., LC#66-20496.
DESCRIPTIVE GUIDE TO LOCATION AND CHARACTER OF SCIENTIFIC RESEARCH INSTITUTES IN SIX COUNTRIES: BULGARIA, CZECHOSLOVAKIA, HUNGARY, POLAND, RUMANIA AND YUGOSLAVIA. PRIME PURPOSE IS TO DESCRIBE SCOPE OF CURRENT SCIENTIFIC ACTIVITIES IN EASTERN EUROPE AND TO LIST NAMES OF PERSONNEL IN CHARGE OF THESE ACTIVITIES AND THEIR CORRESPONDENCE ADDRESSES.

2324 NATSAGDORJ A.S.
"THE ECONOMIC BASIS OF FEUDALISM IN MONGOLIA."
MODERN ASIAN STUDIES, 1 (JULY 67), 265-281.
PUTS FORWARD MARXIST INTERPRETATION OF NOMADIC FEUDALISM, GIVING FACTS TO PERMIT READER TO EVALUATE THEM, WHILE ALSO PERMITTING COMPARISON WITH OTHER AGRICULTURALLY BASED SOCIETIES IN ASIA. SHOWS FOUNDATIONS FOR THIS INTERPRETATION.

2325 NEALE A.D.
THE FLOW OF RESOURCES FROM RICH TO POOR.
CAMBRIDGE: HARV CTR INTL AFFAIRS, 1960, 83 PP.
DISCUSSES PROBLEMS ENCOUNTERED BY HEALTHY NATIONS IN MOBILIZING AND TRANSFERRING RESOURCES TO POORER NATIONS. ADVOCATES INCREASE IN SPEED AND AMOUNT OF FLOW OF RESOURCES FROM RICH TO POOR NATIONS AND ATTRIBUTES LIMITATIONS OF VOLUME OF AID TO POOR NATIONS TO POLITICAL RATHER THAN ECONOMIC FACTORS.

2326 NEALE R.S.
"WORKING CLASS WOMEN AND WOMEN'S SUFFRAGE."
LABOR HISTORY, (MAY 67), 16-34.
EXAMINES WOMEN'S DEMAND FOR FRANCHISE AND PART PLAYED BY WORKING-CLASS WOMEN IN ORIGIN OF MILITANT, SUFFRAGETTE PHASE OF DEMAND. DISCUSSES WAGE DIFFERENTIATION, TRADE UNIONISM AMONG WOMEN. EMPHASIZES INCIDENT INVOLVING ANNIE KENNEDY'S QUESTION TO SIR EDWARD GREY ABOUT LIBERAL GOVERNMENT GIVING VOTES TO WOMEN. SAYS WORKING-CLASS WOMEN'S PARTICIPATION WAS SLIGHT AND INEFFECTIVE.

2327 NEEDHAM T.
"SCIENCE AND SOCIETY IN EAST AND WEST."
SCI. SOC., 28 (64), 385-408.
DISCUSSES THE PROBLEM OF HUMANIZING BUREAUCRACY THROUGHOUT CHINESE HISTORY. 'CHINA WAS HOMEOSTATIC, CYBERNETIC IF YOU LIKE, BUT NEVER STAGNANT.' CHINESE INVENTIONS THAT SHOCKED EUROPEAN CULTURE TIME AFTER TIME WERE TAKEN IN STRIDE BY CHINA. NOTES THOSE FEATURES OF CHINESE SOCIETY WHICH ALLOW THE INTEGRATION AND ASSIMILATION OF IDEAS OF SOCIAL CHANGE.

2328 NEEDLER M.C.
"THE POLITICAL DEVELOPMENT OF MEXICO."
AMER. POLIT. SCI. REV., 55 (JUNE 61), 308-12.
CONTENDS THAT MEXICO HAS BEEN MORE DEMOCRATIC AND STABLE THAN OTHER LATIN AMERICAN COUNTRIES DUE TO SPECIAL TYPE OF POLITICAL INSTITUTION.

2329 NELSON G.R. ED.
FREEDOM AND WELFARE: SOCIAL PATTERNS IN THE NORTHERN COUNTRIES OF EUROPE.
COPENHAGEN: MUNKSGAARD, 1953, 538 PP.
SURVEYS SOCIAL PATTERNS IN SCANDINAVIA, FOCUSING ON GOVERNMENTAL PROGRAMS IN FIELDS OF SOCIAL AND ECONOMIC WELFARE. PROGRAMS COVER LABOR, FAMILY WELFARE, HOUSING, HEALTH,

AND SOCIAL SECURITY. REVIEWS HISTORY AND GEOGRAPHY OF EACH COUNTRY.

2330 NESS G.D.
BUREAUCRACY AND RURAL DEVELOPMENT IN MALAYSIA.
BERKELEY: U OF CALIF PR, 1967, 257 PP., LC#67-14115.
ATTEMPTS TO EXPLAIN MALAYSIA'S UNIQUE EXPERIENCE IN DEVELOPMENT PLANNING AND EXECUTION. CONCERNED WITH DEVELOPMENT OF ITS TOTAL PATTERN, WITH FORMATION AND OPERATION OF ORGANIZATIONS RESPONSIBLE FOR PUBLIC INVESTMENT PROGRAM. EXAMINES RELATION BETWEEN ECONOMIC DEVELOPMENT AND PUBLIC INVESTMENT.

2331 NEUBAUER D.E.
"SOME CONDITIONS OF DEMOCRACY."
AM. POL. SCI. REV., 61 (FALL 67), 1003-1009.
REFUTES THESIS THAT POLITICAL DEMOCRACY IN NATION STATES IS DIRECT FUNCTION OF SOCIO-ECONOMIC DEVELOPMENT. COMPARES SOCIO-ECONOMIC PROGRESS AND "DEGREE OF DEMOCRATICNESS," AS EXPRESSED IN ELECTORAL POLICIES. FINDS A THRESHOLD LEVEL OF SOCIO-ECONOMIC DEVELOPMENT NECESSARY FOR COMPLEX POLITICAL DEVELOPMENTS LIKE DEMOCRACY. BEYOND THIS THRESHOLD, DEGREE OF DEMOCRACY IS NOT A FUNCTION OF SOCIO-ECONOMIC STATUS.

2332 NEUBURGER O.
OFFICIAL PUBLICATIONS OF PRESENT-DAY GERMANY: GOVERNMENT, CORPORATE ORGANIZATIONS, AND NATIONAL SOCIALIST PARTY.
WASHINGTON: GOVT PR OFFICE, 1942, 130 PP., LC#41-50721.
ANNOTATED BIBLIOGRAPHY OF PUBLICATIONS ISSUED BY THE GERMAN GOVERNMENT SINCE 1933. INCLUDES AN INTRODUCTORY GUIDE TO GOVERNMENTAL STRUCTURE, LISTS OF BIBLIOGRAPHIC AIDS AND GAZETTES OF OCCUPIED TERRITORIES, NAZI PARTY PUBLICATIONS, ETC. ALSO INDICATES METHOD OF PUBLICATION AND PROVIDES AN INDEX OF ORGANIZATIONS.

2333 NEUBURGER O.
GUIDE TO OFFICIAL PUBLICATIONS OF OTHER AMERICAN REPUBLICS: HONDURAS (VOL. XIII)
WASHINGTON: LIBRARY OF CONGRESS, 1947, 31 PP.
PROVIDES AN ANNOTATED BIBLIOGRAPHY AND CHECKLIST OF OFFICIAL PUBLICATIONS, SERIES, SERIALS, AND MONOGRAPHS ISSUED SINCE 1821 BY THE REPUBLIC OF HONDURAS AND AVAILABLE IN THE LIBRARY OF CONGRESS. ORGANIZED BY AGENCY OR DEPARTMENT WHERE ISSUED AND INDEXED BY TITLE. PART OF A PROJECT SPONSORED BY THE STATE DEPARTMENT.

2334 NEUBURGER O.
GUIDE TO OFFICIAL PUBLICATIONS OF THE OTHER AMERICAN REPUBLICS: HAITI (VOL. XII)
WASHINGTON: LIBRARY OF CONGRESS, 1947, 25 PP.
LIST OF OFFICIAL PUBLICATIONS ISSUED BY THE REPUBLIC OF HAITI SINCE 1804; ARRANGED BY DEPARTMENT OR AGENCY OF ISSUANCE; INDEXED ALPHABETICALLY BY TITLE, AND ANNOTATED. SERVES AS A CHECKLIST AND GUIDE TO ALL SERIES, SERIALS, AND MONOGRAPHS ISSUED BY THE HAITIAN GOVERNMENT SINCE INDEPENDENCE AND LISTED IN LIBRARY OF CONGRESS CATALOG.

2335 NEUBURGER O.
GUIDE TO OFFICIAL PUBLICATIONS OF THE OTHER AMERICAN REPUBLICS: VENEZUELA (VOL. XIX)
WASHINGTON: LIBRARY OF CONGRESS, 1948, 59 PP.
COMPILES ALL STATE PUBLICATIONS PUBLISHED BY VENEZUELA SINCE ITS INDEPENDENCE IN 1811 AND AVAILABLE IN THE LIBRARY OF CONGRESS. PART OF A PROJECT UNDER THE AUSPICES OF THE STATE DEPARTMENT'S INTERDEPARTMENTAL COMMITTEE ON SCIENTIFIC AND CULTURAL COOPERATION. INCLUDES SERIALS, MONOGRAPHS, AND BOOKS. ARRANGED BY AGENCY OR DEPARTMENT OF ISSUANCE. PROVIDES AN INDEX TO TITLES.

2336 NEUMANN R.G.
THE GOVERNMENT OF THE GERMAN FEDERAL REPUBLIC.
NEW YORK: HARPER & ROW, 1966, 192 PP., LC#66-22517.
HISTORICAL INTRODUCTION TO GERMANY'S GOVERNMENTAL STRUCTURE, THE CONTROVERSIAL ISSUE OF REUNIFICATION AND ITS POLITICAL SIGNIFICANCE; GERMANY'S PLACE IN EUROPEAN AND ATLANTIC WORLDS. DISCUSSES REASONS FOR HER POLITICAL STABILITY AND INSTABILITY, AND POINTS OF COOPERATION AND FRICTION BETWEEN GERMANY AND HER NEIGHBORS. CONSIDERS WHICH ASPECTS OF ADENAUER REGIME WILL HAVE LASTING SIGNIFICANCE.

2337 NEUMANN S.
PERMANENT REVOLUTION: THE TOTAL STATE IN A WORLD AT WAR.
NEW YORK: HARPER & ROW, 1942, 388 PP.
CONCERNED WITH DICTATORSHIP AS A SOCIAL PHENOMENON, ITS ROOTS, CAUSES, AND EFFECTS. INTERPRETS TOTALITARIANISM IN EUROPE BEFORE WWII AND CONCENTRATES ON NAZISM. DISCUSSES MEANS, METHODS, AND PREREQUISITES OF REVOLUTION.

2338 NEUMANN S. ED.
"MODERN POLITICAL PARTIES: APPROACHES TO COMPARATIVE POLITIC
CHICAGO: U OF CHICAGO PRESS, 1956.
ANTHOLOGY OF INDEPENDENT STUDIES WHICH ATTEMPTS TO PRESENT IN CONCRETE FORM CONSISTENT PATTERNS OF AND PROBLEMS OF MAJOR POLITICAL PARTIES. CONTAINS STUDY OF PARTY DEVELOPMENTS IN UK FROM STAGE OF GOVERNING ELITE TO ORGANIZED MASS PARTIES, ANALYSIS OF COMMONWEALTH POLITICS, FRENCH POLITICAL PARTIES, PARTY ORGANIZATION IN US, BELGIUM, SCANDINAVIA, USSR, JAPAN, GERMANY, AND EASTERN EUROPE. BIBLIOGRAPHY.

2339 NEUMANN S.
"COMPARATIVE POLITICS: A HALF CENTURY APPRAISAL"
J. OF POLITICS, 19 (AUG. 57), 369-390.
DISCUSSES EVOLUTION OF COMPARATIVE POLITICS IN US, RELATING IT TO GROWTH IN OTHER SOCIAL SCIENCES. NOTES CHANGES IN WORLD POLITICS MAKING KNOWLEDGE OF OTHER NATIONS' GOVERNMENTS INCREASINGLY IMPORTANT. CLAIMS TREND IS TOWARD INCREASING USE OF MODELS AND THEORY IN ATTEMPT TO QUANTIFY POLITICAL KNOWLEDGE.

2340 NEUMANN S.
"PERMANENT REVOLUTION: TOTALITARIANISM IN THE AGE OF INTERNATIONAL CIVIL WAR (2ND ED.)"
NEW YORK: FREDERICK PRAEGER, 1965.
LIMITS ANALYSIS TO TOTALITARIAN DICTATORSHIPS IN EUROPE WITH SPECIAL EMPHASIS UPON FASCIST AUTOCRACIES. COMPARES DICTATORIAL HIERARCHY WITH DEMOCRATIC FRAMEWORK IN HISTORICAL SETTING OF EUROPE DURING ARMISTICE PERIOD. ANALYZES SOCIAL STRUCTURE OF TOTALITARIAN RULE AS COMPARED WITH DEMOCRATIC. EXTENSIVE BIBLIOGRAPHY IS INTENDED FOR EXPERT IN FIELD.

2341 NEUMARK S.D.
ECONOMIC INFLUENCES ON THE SOUTH AFRICAN FRONTIER, 1652-1836
STANFORD: STANFORD U PRESS, 1957, 195 PP., LC#56-7273.
DEALS WITH ECONOMIC FACTORS BEHIND EXPANSION MOVEMENT IN SOUTH AFRICAN HISTORY. USING COMMODITY APPROACH, ANALYZES DEMAND, PRICES, AND PRODUCTION. HYPOTHESIZES THAT REMOTE PARTS OF FRONTIER AND WHOLE ECONOMY WERE CLOSELY TIED TO MARKET OF CAPETOWN, AND THEREFORE TO MILITARY AND COMMERICAL MARITIME TRAFFIC AND TRADE. PROVIDES HISTORICAL BACKGROUND; INCLUDES AGRICULTURAL MARKET AND LABOR PROBLEMS.

2342 NEVITT A.A. ED.
THE ECONOMIC PROBLEMS OF HOUSING.
NEW YORK: ST MARTIN'S PRESS, 1966, 350 PP.
CONFERENCE PAPERS OF INTERNATIONAL ECONOMIC ASSOCIATION. INCLUDES COMMENTS ON POLITICAL ECONOMY OF HOUSING, SLUMS, GOVERNMENTAL RESPONSIBILITIES, RENT CONTROL, HOUSE-BUILDING, FINANCING, FEDERAL HOUSING POLICY IN USA, SOCIALIST HOUSING POLICY, AS WELL AS SPECIFIC REPORTS BY COUNTRY CONCENTRATING ON HOUSING QUESTION.

2343 NEW ZEALAND COMM OF ST SERVICE
THE STATE SERVICES IN NEW ZEALAND.
WELLINGTON, N.Z.: RE OWEN, 1962, 470 PP.
REPORT OF ROYAL COMMISSION OF INQUIRY INTO ORGANIZATION, STAFFING, AND METHODS OF CONTROL AND OPERATION OF DEPARTMENTS OF STATE. RECOMMENDS SEVERAL CHANGES TOWARD INCREASED EFFICIENCY, ECONOMY, AND IMPROVED SERVICE IN DISCHARGE OF PUBLIC BUSINESS.

2344 NEWARK F.H.
NOTES ON IRISH LEGAL HISTORY (2ND ED.)
BELFAST: QUEEN'S UNIV, 1964, 29 PP.
SURVEYS EVOLUTION OF IRISH LEGAL HISTORY FROM 12TH CENTURY TO PRESENT. DISCUSSES INTRODUCTION OF ENGLISH LAW, CONFLICT WITH NATIVE LAW, AND GRADUAL EXTENSION OF ENGLISH LAW IN 17TH CENTURY. EXAMINES SYSTEM OF COURTS BEFORE AND AFTER GOVERNMENT OF IRELAND ACT IN 1920.

2345 NEWBURY C.W.
BRITISH POLICY TOWARDS WEST AFRICA: SELECT DOCUMENTS 1786-1874.
LONDON: OXFORD U PR, 1965, 656 PP.
VOLUME PROVIDES MATERIALS FOR HISTORY OF EUROPEAN RELATIONS WITH WEST AFRICA FOR THE PERIOD FROM THE TERMINATION OF SLAVE TRADE UNTIL SOME TEN YEARS BEFORE INTERNATIONAL PARTITION. MOST OF MATERIAL IS COLLECTED FROM STATE PAPERS PUBLISHED FOR THE FIRST TIME IN THIS REFERENCE.

2346 NEWMAN J.H.
A LETTER ADDRESSED TO THE DUKE OF NORFOLK ON THE OCCASION OF MR. GLADSTONE'S RECENT EXPOSTULATION.
LONDON: BM PICKERING, 1875, 131 PP.
ANSWER TO ATTACK BY GLADSTONE ON CATHOLICS, CHARGING THAT THEY CANNOT BE TRUSTWORTHY SUBJECTS OF STATE. NEWMAN NOTES THAT PAPAL POWER OF SUPREME DIRECTION DOES NOT MEAN MINUTE MANAGEMENT, THAT PAPAL INFALLIBILITY IS NOT "NEW" OR STRINGENTLY INVOKED, OR THAT ALL CHRISTIANS OBEY BIBLE. GLADSTONE THUS FEARS POWER OF RELIGION, NOT OF POPE. ULTIMATE GUIDE OF CATHOLIC IS CONSCIENCE.

2347 NEWMAN R.P.
RECOGNITION OF COMMUNIST CHINA? A STUDY IN ARGUMENT.
NEW YORK: MACMILLAN, 1961, 318 PP., LC#61-15184.
DISCUSSES "SHOULD US EXTEND DIPLOMATIC RECOGNITION TO COMMUNIST CHINA?" ATTEMPTS TO DEVELOP LOGICAL ARGUMENTS FOR VIABLE ALTERNATIVES, ASSUMING THE MORAL, POLITICAL, AND LEGAL ISSUES. CONCLUDES THAT SOME SORT OF MODIFICATION IS CALLED FOR.

2348 NICHOLAS W.

"VILLAGE FACTIONS AND POLITICAL PARTIES IN RURAL WEST BENGAL."
J. COMMONWEALTH POLIT. STUD., 2 (NOV. 63), 17-32.
DESCRIBES CAREFULLY THE FUNCTIONING OF SOME INSTITUTIONS OF DEMOCRACY, PARTICULARLY POLITICAL PARTIES, IN RURAL WEST BENGAL. ALSO EXAMINES BRIEFLY FOUR FACTORS OF PRIMARY IMPORTANCE IN VILLAGE POLITICAL RELATIONS: CASTE, NEIGHBORHOOD, ECONOMICS, AND KINSHIP.

2349 NICHOLLS W.H.
SOUTHERN TRADITION AND REGIONAL PROGRESS.
CHAPEL HILL: U OF N CAR PR, 1960, 202 PP.
DISCUSSES THE CONFLICT BETWEEN SOUTHERN TRADITIONS AND PROGRESS. ANALYZES INTERRELATIONSHIPS BETWEEN THE AGRICULTURAL AND NONAGRICULTURAL SECTORS OF SOUTHERN ECONOMY. AUTHOR BELIEVES THAT SOUTH MUST CHOOSE BETWEEN TRADITION AND PROGRESS AND DEMONSTRATES THAT SOUTH'S TRADITION IS DISPENSABLE. ANALYZES POLITICAL, ECONOMIC, AND SOCIAL STRUCTURE OF THE SOUTH.

2350 NICOL D.
AFRICA - A SUBJECTIVE VIEW.
NEW YORK: HUMANITIES PRESS, 1964, 88 PP.
FIVE LECTURES GIVEN AT UNIVERSITY OF GHANA IN 1963. STRESSES PRAGMATIC ADJUSTMENT OF IDEALS TO AFRICAN MILIEU, IMPORTANCE OF UNEMOTIONAL REACTION TO WESTERN VIEWS AND CRITICISMS, AND USE OF SUCH CRITICISMS AS MAY BE HELPFUL. DISCUSSES POLITICS, PAN-AFRICANISM, LEADERS, UNIVERSITIES, CIVIL SERVICE, WRITERS ON AND OF AFRICA. SUGGESTS WHAT IS GOOD AND WHAT MUST BE DONE TO IMPROVE CONDITIONS.

2351 NICOLSON H.
"THE MEANING OF PRESTIGE."
CAMBRIDGE, ENGLAND: U. PR., 1937, 36 PP.
EVALUATES PRESENT ROLE OF GREAT BRITAIN IN RELATION TO EUROPEAN NATIONS. ALTHOUGH BRITISH POWER IS DECLINING, HER NATIONAL CHARACTERISTICS OF GENTLENESS, TOLERANCE AND REASONABLENESS ALLOW HER TO MAINTAIN A HIGH INDEX OF PRESTIGE. CONSIDERATE USE OF POWER IN THE PAST HAS PRESERVED UNITED KINGDOM'S GOOD REPUTATION.

2352 NICOLSON H.
CURZON: THE LAST PHASE, 1919-1925.
NEW YORK: HARCOURT BRACE, 1939, 416 PP.
TRACES CAREER OF LORD CURZON AS FOREIGN SECRETARY FROM 1918-24. USES PAPERS, TELEGRAMS, DISPATCHES, MINUTES, AND RECORDS OF INTERVIEWS FOR DETAILED EXAMINATION OF HIS ACTIVITIES AND PROBLEMS OF BRITISH FOREIGN POLICY.

2353 NICOLSON H.
THE CONGRESS OF VIENNA.
NEW YORK: HARCOURT, 1946, 312 PP.
DIPLOMATIC HISTORY OF THE DECADE 1812-1822 FOCUSING ATTENTION UPON THE SHIFTING COALITIONS AMONG THE POWERS WHICH DEFEATED NAPOLEON. EMPHASIZES THE DANGERS OF 'PERSONAL DIPLOMACY'.

2354 NICOLSON H.
DIPLOMACY (3RD ED.)
LONDON: OXFORD U PR, 1963, 268 PP.
DISCUSSES ORIGINS AND EVOLUTION OF DIPLOMATIC PRACTICE, RECENT CHANGES IN METHOD, ITS RELATION TO COMMERCE, AND ADMINISTRATION OF THE FOREIGN SERVICE. ALSO EXAMINES ROLE OF LEAGUE OF NATIONS AS INSTRUMENT OF DIPLOMACY. RESTRICTED TO DISCUSSION OF "MANAGEMENT OF INTERNATIONAL RELATIONS BY NEGOTIATIONS."

2355 NICOLSON H.G.
THE OLD DIPLOMACY AND THE NEW.
LONDON: DAVIES MEM INST POL STUD, 1961, 10 PP.
BRIEF DISCUSSION OF NEW "DEMOCRATIC" DIPLOMACY WHICH CONSIDERS ADJUSTMENT OF MODERN DIPLOMATIC CONCEPTS AND METHODS TO MORE "CAUTIOUS" SYSTEM THAT WAS PRACTICED PRIOR TO WWI. EMPHASIS IS ON BRITISH DIPLOMACY BUT DISCUSSION EXTENDS TO ISSUES OF INTERNATIONAL IMPORTANCE.

2356 NICULESCU B.
COLONIAL PLANNING: A COMPARATIVE STUDY.
NEW YORK: MACMILLAN, 1958, 208 PP.
CONSIDERS PROCESSES OF DEVELOPMENTAL PLANNING IN AFRICAN NATIONS. SHOWS GROWTH OF IDEA WITH COLONIAL EMPIRES AND MACHINERY OF PLANNING IN FORMER COLONIES. ANALYZES SEVERAL PLANS NOW IN USE AND APPRAISES THEIR ACHIEVEMENTS.

2357 NIEBUHR R.
MORAL MAN AND IMMORAL SOCIETY* A STUDY IN ETHICS AND POLITICS.
NEW YORK: CHAS SCRIBNER'S SONS, 1932, 284 PP.
THESIS IS: THE RELIGIOUS AND SECULAR LIBERAL MOVEMENT WAS UNCONSCIOUS OF THE BASIC DIFFERENCE BETWEEN THE MORALITY OF NDIVIDUALS AND IMMORALITY OF GROUPS, NATIONS, RACES, ETC. INDIVIDUALS, BY NATURE AND FROM EDUCATION, ARE CAPABLE OF SYMPATHETIC, JUST, OBJECTIVE BEHAVIOR. COLLECTIVES, AS HISTORY PROVES, ARE PERISTENTLY EGOISTIC, AND PREDOMINANTLY POLITICAL RATHER THAN ETHICAL.

2358 NIEBUHR R.
THE CHILDREN OF LIGHT AND THE CHILDREN OF DARKNESS: A VINDICATION OF DEMOCRACY AND CRITIQUE OF TRADITIONAL DEFENSE
NEW YORK: CHAS SCRIBNER'S SONS, 1947, 190 PP.
PRESENTS A POLITICAL PHILOSOPHY, BASED UPON RELIGIOUS AND THEOLOGICAL CONVICTIONS, OF MAN, COMMUNITY, AND PROPERTY. DISCUSSES MARXIST ILLUSIONS ABOUT NATURE OF PROPERTY, AND DEMOCRATIC TRADITIONS OF PLURALISM. ANALYZES VARIOUS IDEAS OF UNIVERSALISM AND PROPOSES A WORLD COMMUNITY TO BRING PEACE AND DEMOCRATIC INSTITUTIONS TO ALL MEN.

2359 NIEBUHR R.
"THE SOCIAL MYTHS IN THE COLD WAR."
J. INT. AFFAIRS, 21 (1967), 40-56.
SOCIAL MYTH IS SEEN AS BASIS FOR NATIONAL PRIDE AND JUSTIFICATION. DISTORTION OF INTENT, ACTIONS, IDEOLOGIES BY OVERSIMPLIFICATION OR OTHERWISE IS GIVEN AS A MAJOR CAUSE OF INTERNATIONAL STRESS. MORAL JUSTIFICATION OF ACTIONS HAS BECOME IMMEDIATE METHOD OF US, AND ALSO ADOPTED BY OTHERS. RELATION TO WAR IN VIETNAM.

2360 NIEBUHR R., MORGANTHAU H.
"THE ETHICS OF WAR AND PEACE IN THE NUCLEAR AGE."
WAR/PEACE REPORT, 7 (FEB. 67), 3-8.
DIALOGUE BETWEEN NIEBUHR AND MORGANTHAU ON ETHICS OF RELATIONS AMONG NATION-STATES. INCLUDES DISCUSSIONS OF JUSTICE VS. NATIONAL SELF-INTEREST, MEANS VS. ENDS IN WARS, POSSIBILITIES FOR UN, AND THE VIETNAM WAR. CONCLUDE THAT MORALITY AS WELL AS SELF-INTEREST IS INEVITABLE IN HUMAN DECISIONS; ENDS CANNOT JUSTIFY NUCLEAR MEANS; UN CANNOT SOON BE A POWER; US IS MISTAKEN TO STAY IN VIETNAM.

2361 NIEDERGANG M.
LA REVOLUTION DE SAINT-DOMINGUE.
PARIS: LIBRAIIE PLON, 1966, 230 PP.
ANALYZES DOMINICAN REPUBLIC REVOLUTION OF APRIL, 1965 CAUSING US AND INTER-AMERICAN TROOPS TO OCCUPY NATION. DISCUSSES EVENTS FROM DEALTH OF TRUJILLO TO INTERVENTION DEALING WITH DOMINICAN POLITICS AND US INFLUENCE IN ITS AFFAIRS. EXAMINES EXTENT OF COMMUNITST CONTROL AND POWER IN REVOLUTIONARY GROUPS.

2362 NIPPERDEY T.
DIE ORGANISATION DER DEUTSCHEN PARTEIEN VOR 1918.
DUSSELDORF: DROSTE VERLAG, 1961, 454 PP.
DISCUSSES DEVELOPMENT OF MAJOR PARTIES IN GERMANY FROM END OF "REACTIONARY PERIOD" (1875-1880) TO END OF WWI. EXAMINES STRUCTURAL CHANGES IN TERMS OF CHANGING HISTORICAL, TECHNOLOGICAL, POLITICAL, AND SOCIAL CIRCUMSTANCES.

2363 NIRRNHEIM O.
DAS ERSTE JAHR DES MINISTERIUMS BISMARCK UND DIE OEFFENTLICHE MEINUNG (HEIDELBERGER ABHANDLUNGEN, 20. HEFT)
HEIDELBERG: CARL WINTERS, 1908, 624 PP.
ON BASIS OF PUBLISHED MATERIALS PRESENTS PUBLIC OPINION AND ITS ATTITUDE TOWARD BISMARCK DURING FIRST YEAR OF HIS PRIME MINISTERSHIP. STUDIES VARIOUS DOMESTIC AND INTERNATIONAL PROBLEMS.

2364 NKRUMAH K.
AFRICA MUST UNITE.
LONDON: HEINEMAN, 1963, 229 PP., $5.95.
THE PRESIDENT OF GHANA PRESENTS THE CASE FOR PAN-AFRICAN UNITY. ON BASIS OF COMPARISON WITH OTHER MAJOR POLITICAL UNIONS SUCH AS USA, USSR, AUSTRALIA AND CANADA, PROVIDES BLUEPRINT FOR AFRICAN CONTINENTAL GOVERNMENT. BACK-GROUND DESCRIPTION OF AFRICAN HISTORY WITH PARTICULAR EMPHASIS ON DEVELOPMENT OF GHANA.

2365 NOBECOURT R.G.
LES SECRETS DE LA PROPAGANDE EN FRANCE OCCUPEE.
PARIS: LIB ARTHEME FAYARD, 1962, 530 PP.
ANALYSIS OF PROPAGANDA EMPLOYED IN OCCUPIED FRANCE DURING WWII AND METHODS USED. EXAMINES ORGANIZATION AND OPERATION OF VICHY GOVERNMENT IN RELATION TO ITS PROPAGANDA ACTIVITIES IN FRANCE. ALSO STUDIES GERMAN AND ALLIED PROPAGANDA REGARDING WAR. DETAILS APPROACH USED AFTER OPENING OF SECOND FRONT IN EAST AND THIS CHANGE ON INFORMATION AND DISTRIBUTION.

2366 NOEL G.E.
THE NEW BRITAIN AND HAROLD WILSON: INTERIM REPORT, 1966 GENERAL ELECTION.
LONDON: CAMPION PR, 1966, 103 PP.
SURVEYS HAROLD WILSON'S FIRST 500 DAYS AS PRIME MINISTER. SKETCHES CHANGES IN WILSON'S ACTIVITIES AFTER HE TOOK OFFICE. PICTURES "NEW BRITAIN" HE SPOKE OF AND TRIED TO CREATE. ATTEMPTS TO ASSESS WILSON'S ACHIEVEMENT.

2367 NOLTE E.
"ZUR PHANOMENOLOGIE DES FASCHIMUS."
VIERTELJAHRESH. ZEITGESCH., 10 (OCT. 62), 373-407.
PRESENTS PSYCHOLOGY AND DOCTRINES OF FASCIST LEADERS AND MOVEMENTS COMPARED FOR SEVERAL COUNTRIES - ITALY, GERMANY, TURKEY, ETC.

2368 NOLTE E.

THREE FACES OF FASCISM.
NEW YORK: HOLT RINEHART WINSTON, 1966, 560 PP., LC#66-10262.
A COMPREHENSIVE ACCOUNT OF FASCISM IN FRANCE, GERMANY, AND ITALY. EXAMINES ITS RISE AND FALL, METAPOLITICAL BACKGROUNDS, SOCIO-POLITICAL ASPECTS, AND ITS FOUNDATIONS IN BOURGEOIS SOCIETY. AUTHOR IS NEO-HEGELIAN IN CLAIMING HISTORY IS RESULT OF PHILOSOPHICAL PROGRESSION. ANALYZES RISE OF FASCISM THROUGH BACKGROUND, DOCTRINE, AND HISTORY.

2369 NOMAD M.
POLITICAL HERETICS: FROM PLATO TO MAO TSE-TUNG.
ANN ARBOR: U OF MICH PR, 1963, 367 PP., LC#63-9895.
BRIEF DISCUSSION OF LIVES AND THEORIES OF MANY "LEFTISTS" FROM PLATO TO MAO. EMPHASIS ON UTOPIANS, NIHILISTS, SOCIAL AND ECONOMIC MARXISTS, SOCIALISTS, SYNDICALISTS, AND ANARCHISTS.

2370 NORDEN A.
WAR AND NAZI CRIMINALS IN WEST GERMANY: STATE, ECONOMY, ADMINISTRATION, ARMY, JUSTICE, SCIENCE.
BERLIN: NATL FRONT DEM GERMANY, 1965, 402 PP.
CLAIMS THAT NAZI WAR CRIMINALS ARE TAKING OVER WEST GERMAN GOVERNMENT WHICH WILL PRECIPITATE WWIII. CASTIGATES BONN GOVERNMENT FOR CESSATION OF PROSECUTION OF WAR CRIMINALS. DESCRIBES HITLER'S SECRET POLICE AND POLITICAL MACHINE, AND HIS STAFF FOR EXTERMINATION OF JEWS. LISTS SPECIFIC INDIVIDUALS, DESCRIBING FORMER NAZI ACTIVITIES AND CURRENT POSITION IN GOVERNMENT.

2371 NORDSKOG J.E.
SOCIAL REFORM IN NORWAY.
LOS ANGELES: U OF S CALIF PR, 1935, 177 PP.
STUDY OF NATIONALISM AND SOCIAL DEMOCRACY IN NORWAY, INCLUDING EMERGENCE OF NATIONAL SOCIAL UNITY, FUNCTION OF POLITICAL PARTIES, LABOR MOVEMENT, INDUSTRIAL DISPUTES, AND LEGISLATIVE ACHIEVEMENTS FOR SOCIAL AMELIORATION.

2372 NORTH R.C.
"THE NEW EXPANSIONISM."
PROBL. COMMUNISM, 9 (JAN. 60), 23-30.
HISTORICALLY, IDEOLOGICALLY AND PSYCHOLOGICALLY CONCERNED WITH PEKING'S 'DRIVE FOR EMPIRE'. DEMONSTRATES MAO TSE TUNG'S DILEMMA WITH EXISTING SYSTEM CHARACTERIZED BY FORCEFUL COMMUNIST NATIONALISM. CHINA'S CONDEMNATION OF INDIA SCRUTINIZED.

2373 NORTH R.C.
"DIE DISKREPANZ ZWISCHEN REALITAT UND WUNSCHBILD ALS INNENPOLITISCHER FAKTOR."
OSTEUROPA, 10 (NOV.-DEC. 60), 766-69.
CONSIDERS DIFFERENCES BETWEEN REAL AND IDEAL VALUES AS INSTRUMENTAL IN CAUSING TENSION AND DISAPPOINTMENT. ARGUES THAT PRODUCTIVE FUNCTIONS OF SOCIETY ARE AFFECTED IN DIRECT RELATION TO MAGNITUDE OF DIFFERENCES. APPLIES CONCEPTUAL MODEL TO ANALYSIS OF COMMUNIST CHINA.

2374 NORTHEDGE F.S.
"BRITISH FOREIGN POLICY AND THE PARTY SYSTEM."
AMER. POLIT. SCI. REV., 54 (SEPT. 60), 635-46.
SEES DIFFERENCE BETWEEN BRITISH PARTIES' VIEWS ON FOREIGN POLICY AS RECENTLY DIMINISHING, DUE TO ACUTELY LIMITED OPTION. BELIEVES MAJOR DISPUTE TO BE ANALYSIS OF INTERNATIONAL TENSIONS AND DEGREE OF EMPHASIS ON UN. ALSO SEES CRUCIAL PROBLEM FOR FUTURE AS UNITY IN LABOR PARTY.

2375 NORTHROP F.S.C. ED., LIVINGSTON H.H. ED.
CROSS-CULTURAL UNDERSTANDING: EPISTEMOLOGY IN ANTHROPOLOGY.
NEW YORK: HARPER & ROW, 1964, 396 PP., LC#64-10591.
COLLECTION OF ESSAYS ON CULTURAL PHILOSOPHIES AND ANTHROPOLOGICAL METHODS OF INQUIRY. EXAMINE SEVERAL CULTURES AND SEEK TO DISTINGUISH BETWEEN INNATE AND CULTURALLY DETERMINED BEHAVIOR.

2376 NORTHROP F.S.C.
"ASIAN MENTALITY AND UNITED STATES FOREIGN POLICY."
ANN. AMER. ACAD. POLIT. SOC. SCI., 276 (JULY 51), 118-128.
EXPLAINS THE ATTITUDES OF ASIANS TOWARDS UNITED STATES FOREIGN POLICY ON THE BASIS OF BOTH THEIR INTUITIVE RELIGIOUS SYSTEMS WHICH FAVOR MEDITATION AND COMPROMISE,AND BOTH THEIR AND THE ISLAMIC PEOPLES' EXPERIENCES UNDER WESTERN IMPERIALISM.

2377 NORTHWESTERN UNIVERSITY LIB
JOINT ACQUISITIONS LIST OF AFRICANA.
EVANSTON: NORTHWESTERN U AFR DEP.
COMPILATION OF MATERIALS (BOOKS, ARTICLES, DOCUMENTS) RECEIVED BY LIBRARIES IN US ON ASPECTS OF AFRICAN CULTURE AND DEVELOPMENT. PUBLISHED SINCE 1961 AND APPEARS SIX TIMES EACH YEAR. CONSISTS OF TITLES PUBLISHED IN CURRENT YEAR AND FIVE PRECEDING ONES. INCLUDES FOREIGN LANGUAGE MATERIAL; ARRANGED ALPHABETICALLY. EACH ISSUE CONTAINS APPROXIMATELY 800 TITLES.

2378 NOVE A.
THE SOVIET ECONOMY.
NEW YORK: FREDERICK PRAEGER, 1961, 328 PP., LC#61-16579.
INTRODUCTION SURVEY OF SOVIET ECONOMY, INCLUDING ITS PRODUCTIVE ENTERPRISES, ADMINISTRATION, CHANGING NATURE OF ITS PROBLEMS, AND BASIC CONCEPTS OF SOVIET ECONOMICS.

2379 NUGENT J.B.
"ECONOMIC THOUGHT, INVESTMENT CRITERIA, AND DEVELOPMENT STRATEGIES IN GREECE* A POSTWAR SURVEY."
ECO. DEV. AND CULTURAL CHANGE, 15 (APR. 67), 331-335.
RECOGNIZES THE NEED FOR ECONOMIC ANALYSIS AND LONG-RANGE PLANNING IN GREECE. CITES VARVARESSO'S PLANS FOR RESIDENTIAL CONSTRUCTION AND PAPANDREOU'S USE OF CHENERY'S ANALYSIS FOR INDUSTRIALIZATION AIMS AS STEPS TOWARD THESE GOALS. CONSIDERS THE SECOND FIVE-YEAR PLAN AND MOVES TOWARD COMMON-MARKET INTERACTION OTHER HEALTHY SIGNS FOR THE LONG-NEEDED DEVELOPMENTAL ECONOMIC POLICY.

2380 NUMELIN R.
"THE BEGINNINGS OF DIPLOMACY."
NEW YORK: PHILOSOPHICAL LIB, 1950.
SOCIOLOGICAL ESSAY BASED ON ETHNOLOGICAL FIELD RESEARCHES OF TECHNIQUES OF DIPLOMACY OF NONLITERATE PEOPLES. EXTENSIVE BIBLIOGRAPHY IS COMPOSED OF HISTORICAL AND PHILOSOPHICAL LITERATURE, LITERATURE OF INTERNATIONAL LAW AND SOCIOLOGY, ETHNOLOGICAL, ETHNO-SOCIOLOGICAL, AND GEOGRAPHICAL LITERATURE IN EUROPEAN LANGUAGES.

2381 NYE J.
"TANGANYIKA'S SELF-HELP."
TRANSACTIONS, 3 (NOV. 63), 35-39.
TANGANYIKA'S PROGRAM OF USING VOLUNTARY LABOR TO INCREASE VALUE OF CAPITAL IN COUNTRY CRITICIZED AND EVALUATED. DECLINE IN NATIONALISTIC SPIRIT AND CONFLICT BETWEEN GOVERNMENT AND LABOR BLAMED FOR INEFFICIENCY; BIPARTISAN POLITICAL SYSTEM SUGGESTED AS REMEDY.

2382 NYE J.S. JR.
PAN-AFRICANISM AND EAST AFRICAN INTEGRATION.
CAMBRIDGE: HARVARD U PR, 1965, 307 PP., LC#65-22063.
ATTEMPT TO IMPROVE UNDERSTANDING OF THE PROCESS OF INTEGRATION AMONG STATES BY PRESENTING A DETAILED ANALYSIS OF THE FEDERATIONAL FAILURE IN EAST AFRICA IN 1963. THERE IS A CONCENTRATION ON THE EFFECT OF IDEOLOGY UPON INTEGRATION RELATIVE TO THE ABOVE CASE AND OTHER ATTEMPTS TO OPERATIONALIZE "PAN-AFRICANISM."

2383 NYERERE J.K.
FREEDOM AND UNITY/UHURU NA UMOJA: A SELECTION FROM WRITINGS AND SPEECHES, 1952-65.
NEW YORK: OXFORD U PR, 1967, 366 PP.
WORKS BY NYERERE, ILLUSTRATING HIS CONTRIBUTION TO POLITICAL THOUGHT AND DEVELOPMENT IN AFRICA. EMPHASIZES DEMOCRATIC CHANGE IN AFRICA FROM WITHIN AND OPPOSITION TO CHANGE FROM WITHOUT BY FORCES OVER WHICH AFRICANS HAVE NO CONTROL.

2384 O'BRIEN F.
CRISIS IN WORLD COMMUNISM* MARXISM IN SEARCH OF EFFICIENCY.
NEW YORK: FREE PRESS OF GLENCOE, 1965, 191 PP., LC#65-16439.
GRANTS THAT TECHNOLOGISTS LIKE BREZHNEV NOW RUN USSR BUT CLAIMS THEY STILL OPERATE IN AMBIENCE OF MARXISM AND THAT THEREFORE THE WAYS IN WHICH DOCTRINAL MARXISM INSPIRE AND IMPINGE ON DOMESTIC AND INTERNATIONAL POLICIES -- AIMED AT CREATING THE SOVIET STATE AS A TECHNOLOGICAL IDEAL, FRATERNAL COMMUNISM AS A MODEL INTERNATIONAL SYSTEM, AND PEACEFUL COEXISTENCE AS WORLD'S BEST POLICY-- SHOULD BE ANALYZED.

2385 O'BRIEN W.V. ED.
THE NEW NATIONS IN INTERNATIONAL LAW AND DIPLOMACY* THE YEAR BOOK OF WORLD POLITY* VOLUME III.
NEW YORK: FREDERICK PRAEGER, 1965, 323 PP., LC#65-13962.
4 ESSAYS ATTEMPT TO RECONCILE THE WESTERN CHARACTER OF MUCH OF INTERNATIONAL LAW WITH THE POSTWAR DEVELOPMENT OF A PLURALISTIC INTERNATIONAL SYSTEM WITH MANY NON-WESTERN CULTURE STATES. PAPERS TREAT: "INDEPENDENCE AND PROBLEMS OF STATE SUCCESSION, MILITARY SERVITUDE AND THE NEW NATIONS, UNITED STATES RECOGNITION POLICY TOWARD THE NEW NATIONS, THE NEW STATES AND THE UNITED NATIONS."

2386 O'BRIEN W.V.
"EVENTS AND TRENDS: PATTERNS OF AFRICAN INTERNATIONAL POLITICAL BEHAVIOR."
WORLD JUSTICE, 8 (DEC. 66), 194-210.
AN ANNOTATED BIBLIOGRAPHY OF PATTERN OF AFRICAN INTERNATIONAL POLITICAL BEHAVIOR. MATERIAL IN ENGLISH-LANGUAGE AND SOME FRENCH AND GERMAN. 34 ENTRIES. MATERIAL RANGES FROM 1957-66.

2387 O'CONNELL M.R.
IRISH POLITICS AND SOCIAL CONFLICT IN THE AGE OF THE AMERICAN REVOLUTION.
PHILA: U OF PENN PR, 1965, 444 PP., LC#64-24494.
ILLUSTRATED STUDY RELATING SOCIAL AND POLITICAL DEVELOPMENT INCLUDING CLASS CONFLICTS AND PRESSURES OF RADICALISM AND REFORM. EMPHASIZES FORMATION AND ACTIVITIES OF VOLUNTEERS.

2388 O'HEARN P.J.T.
PEACE, ORDER AND GOOD GOVERNMENT; A NEW CONSTITUTION FOR CANADA.
TORONTO: MACMILLAN CO OF CANADA, 1964, 325 PP.
PROPOSES CHANGES IN CANADIAN CONSTITUTION IN ALL AREAS; SUPPLIES REASONS FOR CHANGES AND PRESENTS POSSIBILITIES OF THESE TAKING PLACE.

2389 O'LEARY T.J.
ETHNOGRAPHIC BIBLIOGRAPHY OF SOUTH AMERICA.
NEW HAVEN: HUMAN REL AREA FILES, 1963, 386 PP., LC#63-20695.
BIBLIOGRAPHY OF APPROXIMATELY 11,000 ENGLISH, SPANISH, OR PORTUGUESE BOOKS, ARTICLES, DOCUMENTS, AND DISSERTATIONS ON ETHNOGRAPHY OF SOUTH AMERICAN TRIBES. REFERENCES RANGE FROM 1880-1961, AND ARE ARRANGED BY COUNTRY AND THEN ALPHABETICALLY BY TRIBE.

2390 O'NEILL C.E.
CHURCH AND STATE IN FRENCH COLONIAL LOUISIANA: POLICY AND POLITICS TO 1732.
NEW HAVEN: YALE U PR, 1966, 313 PP., LC#66-21529.
STUDIES ATTITUDES AND ACTIVITIES OF CIVIL AND RELIGIOUS INSTITUTIONS IN FRENCH COLONY OF LOUISIANA FROM BEGINNING OF COLONY TO RETROCESSION TO KING BY COMPANY OF INDIES; THEIR COOPERATION AND CONFLICT, AND THEIR MOTIVES.

2391 O'NEILL R.J.
THE GERMAN ARMY AND THE NAZI PARTY, 1933-1939.
NEW YORK: JAMES H HEINEMAN, 1966, 286 PP., LC#67-11678.
TRACES RISE OF INFLUENCE OF HITLER AND NAZI PARTY OVER THE ARMY. NOTES THAT HIGH COMMAND IN 1932 WAS SCHOOLED TO BE PROFESSIONAL AND NONPOLITICAL, AND WAS CONSERVATIVE AND CHRISTIAN. INDICATES ARMY HELD NO INDEPENDENT AGGRESSIVE DESIGNS PRIOR TO HITLER'S ACCESSION AS WAR MINISTER. SHOWS HOW PARTY EXPLOITED HIGH COMMAND, ISOLATED OPPONENTS LIKE FRITSCH, AND INFLUENCED REGULARS, IN SEIZING ARMY CONTROL.

2392 OAKESHOTT M.
THE SOCIAL AND POLITICAL DOCTRINES OF CONTEMPORARY EUROPE.
LONDON: CAMBRIDGE UNIV PRESS, 1939, 223 PP.
COLLECTS ORIGINAL AND AUTHENTIC TEXTS WHICH ILLUSTRATE TENETS OF MAIN SCHOOLS OF SOCIAL AND POLITICAL DOCTRINES OF EUROPE. STUDIES REPRESENTATIVE DEMOCRACY, CATHOLICISM, COMMUNISM, FASCISM AND NATIONAL SOCIALISM, PORTRAYING INTELLECTUAL SYSTEMS ADDUCED TO EXPLAIN GOVERNMENTS' CONDUCT, RATHER THAN TO SHOW HOW REGIMES OPERATE.

2393 OBUKAR C., WILLIAMS J.
THE MODERN AFRICAN.
LONDON: MCDONALD & EVANS,LTD, 1965, 146 PP.
AIMED AT PREPARING CITIZENS OF NEWLY INDEPENDENT AFRICAN STATES FOR PARTICIPATING IN EVERY ASPECT OF LIFE IN SOVEREIGN STATE. DISCUSSES FARMING, INDUSTRY, POLITICS, EDUCATION, LEISURE, AND ECONOMICS.

2394 ODEGARD P.H.
POLITICAL POWER AND SOCIAL CHANGE.
NEW BRUNSWICK: RUTGERS U PR, 1966, 111 PP., LC#62-28215.
ETHICS OF GOVERNMENT, PAST, PRESENT, AND FUTURE, COMPARED AND RELATED TO ECONOMIC, HISTORICAL, AND SOCIAL EVOLUTION. SKETCHES EFFECT OF TECHNOLOGY AND POPULATION ON POWER AND GIVES BRIEF HISTORY OF ITS ABUSE.

2395 ODINGA O.
NOT YET UHURU.
NEW YORK: HILL AND WANG, 1967, 323 PP., LC#67-26850.
AUTOBIOGRAPHY OF OGINGA ODINGA, CONTROVERSIAL LEADER OF KENYA. TELLS STORY OF HIS LIFE AND POLITICAL ACTIVITY. ATTEMPTS TO SHOW THERE HAVE BEEN CONSISTENT THREADS RUNNING THROUGH AFRICANS' STRUGGLE FOR FREEDOM AND THROUGH HIS OWN POLICIES. DISCUSSES CONTEMPORARY POLITICAL SCENE; EXPLAINS HIS BREAK WITH KENYATTA; AND SUMS UP HIS POLITICAL BELIEFS.

2396 OECD
STATISTICS OF BALANCE OF PAYMENTS 1950-61.
PARIS: ORG FOR ECO COOP AND DEV, 1961, 134 PP.
PRESENTS AND COMPARES STATISTICS FOR NATIONS IN OECD EACH YEAR REGARDING THEIR BALANCE OF PAYMENTS. INCLUDES SEPARATE LISTS FOR EACH MEMBER NATION IN ALPHABETICAL ORDER.

2397 OECD
FOOD AID: ITS ROLE IN ECONOMIC DEVELOPMENT.
PARIS: ORG FOR ECO COOP AND DEV, 1963, 85 PP.
SURVEY OF ECONOMIC IMPLICATIONS OF FOOD AID PROGRAMS INSTITUTED BY MEMBER NATIONS OF ORGANIZATION FOR ECONOMIC CO-OPERATION AND DEVELOPMENT. EMPHASIS ON CONTRIBUTION OF FOOD AID TO ECONOMIC IMPROVEMENT IN UNDERDEVELOPED COUNTRIES.

2398 OECD
DEVELOPMENT ASSISTANCE EFFORTS - POLICIES OF THE MEMBERS.
PARIS: ORG FOR ECO COOP AND DEV, 1964, 114 PP.
REPORT BY DEVELOPMENT ASSISTANCE COMMITTEE OF OECD ON VOLUME OF AID, GEOGRAPHIC DISTRIBUTION, CONDITIONS FOR ASSISTANCE, COORDINATION EFFORTS, TECHNICAL AID, AND PROPOSALS ON STRENGTHENING ASSISTANCE EFFORTS OF OECD.

2399 OECD
MEDITERRANEAN REGIONAL PROJECT: TURKEY; EDUCATION AND DEVELOPMENT.
PARIS: ORG FOR ECO COOP AND DEV, 1965, 189 PP.
REVIEWS PRESENT EDUCATIONAL STRUCTURE AND POLICY IN TURKEY; TREATS ROLE OF EDUCATION IN SOCIAL AND ECONOMIC DEVELOPMENT. DISCUSSES FACILITIES, TEACHER TRAINING AND SUPPLY, AND ADMINISTRATION. EXAMINES COST OF EDUCATIONAL DEVELOPMENT, PRESENT EXPENDITURES, AND FUTURE NEEDS. COVERS ECONOMIC TARGETS AND MANPOWER, OCCUPATIONAL CLASSIFICATIONS, DEMAND AND SUPPLY, AND PARTICIPATION.

2400 OECD
THE MEDITERRANEAN REGIONAL PROJECT: ITALY; EDUCATION AND DEVELOPMENT.
PARIS: ORG FOR ECO COOP AND DEV, 1965, 216 PP.
CONCERNED WITH RELATION OF EDUCATIONAL PLANNING TO ECONOMIC DEVELOPMENT AND SOCIAL ADVANCEMENT. OPENS WITH SURVEY OF TRENDS IN PAST AND TARGETS FOR 1975; EXAMINES OCCUPATIONAL STRUCTURE OF EMPLOYMENT AND TRAINING FACILITIES IN PAST DECADE. DISCUSSES WAYS OF ACHIEVING PROPOSED GOALS, STRUCTURE OF SYSTEM, FINANCING. ENDS WITH METHODOLOGY FOR ESTIMATING OCCUPATIONAL STRUCTURE IN 1951, 1961, AND 1975.

2401 OECD
THE MEDITERRANEAN REGIONAL PROJECT: GREECE; EDUCATION AND DEVELOPMENT.
PARIS: ORG FOR ECO COOP AND DEV, 1965, 195 PP.
BEGINS WITH ECONOMIC FRAMEWORK AND ROLE OF EDUCATION. RELATES EDUCATIONAL PLANNING TO ECONOMIC GROWTH AND SOCIAL ADVANCEMENT; DISCUSSES EXISTING SYSTEM AND GOAL FOR 1974. EXAMINES ADJUSTMENTS THAT WILL HAVE TO BE MADE, RESOURCES FOR EXPANSION, AND OUTLINE OF PLAN; INCLUDES STRUCTURE OF SYSTEM, MANPOWER NEEDS, AND EDUCATIONAL NEEDS IN AGRICULTURE. CLOSES WITH EXPENDITURES FOR EDUCATION TO 1974.

2402 OECD
THE MEDITERRANEAN REGIONAL PROJECT: SPAIN; EDUCATION AND DEVELOPMENT.
PARIS: ORG FOR ECO COOP AND DEV, 1965, 135 PP.
SURVEYS PRESENT EDUCATIONAL SYSTEM, ASSESSES LONG-TERM EDUCATIONAL NEEDS, AND FORMULATES PLANS AND FINANCIAL ESTIMATES TO MEET NEEDS. BEGINS WITH SUMMARY OF PRESENT EDUCATIONAL POLICY; DISCUSSES ORGANIZATION AND ADMINISTRATION OF EDUCATION, COST, QUALITY, OCCUPATIONAL STRUCTURE OF LABOR FORCE, AND EDUCATIONAL LEVELS. CLOSES WITH EXPENDITURES ON EDUCATION.

2403 OECD DEVELOPMENT CENTRE
CATALOGUE OF SOCIAL AND ECONOMIC DEVELOPMENT INSTITUTES AND PROGRAMMES* RESEARCH.
PARIS: ORG FOR ECO COOP AND DEV, 1966, 452 PP.
LISTING OF RESEARCH INSTITUTES AND THEIR ACTIVITIES IN FIELD OF SOCIAL AND ECONOMIC DEVELOPMENT. THIRTY NON-IRON-CURTAIN NATIONS SURVEYED. ALL DATA IN ENGLISH.

2404 OECD SEMINAR REGIONAL DEV
REGIONAL DEVELOPMENT IN ISRAEL.
PARIS: ORG FOR ECO COOP AND DEV, 1964, 46 PP.
DISCUSSES INSTITUTIONS FOR REGIONAL PLANNING IN ISRAEL, THEIR ADMINISTRATION AND IMPLEMENTATION OF PROGRAMS AT NATIONAL AND REGIONAL LEVELS. STUDIES DEVELOPMENT IN LAKHISH REGION IN PARTICULAR; OBJECTIVES AND ASPECTS OF PLAN AND CHANGES ACCOMPLISHED BY DEVELOPMENT PROGRAM.

2405 OGBURN W.F.
SOCIAL CHANGE WITH RESPECT TO CULTURE AND ORIGINAL NATURE.
NEW YORK: B W HUEBSCH, INC, 1922, 365 PP.
INQUIRY INTO SOCIAL CHANGE, ITS FUNCTIONS, FAILINGS, RESULTS, AND METHODS. DO SOCIAL CHANGES REFLECT BIOLOGICAL MODIFICATIONS? ARE THEY POSSIBLE WITHOUT THEM? DISTINGUISHES BETWEEN BIOLOGICAL, SOCIAL, AND PSYCHOLOGICAL CHANGE.

2406 OGBURN W.F. ED., DUNCAN O.D. ED.
ON CULTURE AND SOCIAL CHANGE.
CHICAGO: U OF CHICAGO PRESS, 1964, 363 PP., LC#64-23418.
SHOWS RELATION OF INNOVATION AND DEVELOPMENT TO SOCIETY. STUDIES IMPACT OF GREAT MEN AND INVENTIONS ON CULTURE, TRENDS IN SOCIETY, AND RELATION OF INVENTIONS AND THE STATE. SPECIFICALLY ANALYZES SHORT-RUN CHANGES, 1923-48, IN ECONOMICS. DISCUSSES METHODOLOGY.

2407 OGDEN F.D.
THE POLL TAX IN THE SOUTH.
UNIVERSITY: U ALABAMA PR, 1958, 301 PP., LC#58-08773.
STUDIES WHAT POLL TAX IS, HOW IT OPERATES, AND ITS VALUE AS VOTING PREREQUISITE. PRESENTS HISTORICAL SUMMARY, MEANS OF ADMINISTERING IT, ITS EFFECTS ON VOTER PARTICIPATION AND RELATION BETWEEN TAX AND CORRUPTION.

2408 OGILVIE C.
THE KING'S GOVERNMENT AND THE COMMON LAW, 1471-1641.
OXFORD: BLACKWELL, 1958, 176 PP.
DISCUSSES THE POLITICAL AND CONSTITUTIONAL HISTORY OF THE ENGLISH KING'S GOVERNMENT. STUDY INCLUDES THE ORIGINS OF COMMON LAW, DEVELOPMENT OF COMMON LAW PROCEDURE, CREATION OF

EQUITABLE JURISDICTION, CRIMINAL LAW, THE RESTORATION OF ORDER, AND THE ORGANIZATION OF CHANCERY. ALSO EXAMINES THE KING'S COUNCIL AND THE CIVIL LAW, ATTACK ON THE KING'S GOVERNMENT, AND HIS FINAL DEFEAT OF THE COMMON LAW.

2409 OGILVY-WEBB M.
THE GOVERNMENT EXPLAINS: A STUDY OF THE INFORMATION SERVICES
MYSTIC, CONN: VERRY LAWRENCE, 1965, 229 PP.
STUDIES BRITAIN'S GOVERNMENT INFORMATION SERVICES: THEIR DEVELOPMENT FROM TENTATIVE BEGINNINGS TO PRESENT DAY; WAY IN WHICH THEY ARE ORGANIZED AND FUNCTION; PROBLEMS OF STAFFING. ATTEMPTS TO ASSESS THEIR PERFORMANCE AND THE JOB THEY DO ON THE HOME FRONT.

2410 OGOT B.
"FROM CHIEF TO PRESIDENT."
TRANSACTIONS, 3 (SEPT. 63), 26-30.
EXAMINES PROBLEMS OF UNITY AND LEADERSHIP IN AFRICA FROM HISTORICAL-ANTHROPOLOGICAL VIEWPOINT. LACK OF COMMON HERITAGE AND CERTAIN RELIGIOUS SIMILARITIES DISCUSSED. PROPOSES ELEVATION OF CHIEFS TO POSITIONS OF LEADERSHIP.

2411 OJHA I.C.
"CHINA'S CAUTIOUS AMERICAN POLICY."
CURRENT HISTORY, 53 (SEPT. 67), 135-140, 175-176.
POINTS OUT THAT MAO-LIN-CHOU STRATEGY, THOUGH BASICALLY CAUTIOUS, RULES OUT NEITHER INTERVENTION IN VIETNAM NOR POSSIBLE WAR WITH US. CHINESE NUCLEAR DETERRENT IS AIMED AT GAINING MORE FREEDOM OF ACTION IN FOREIGN POLICY WITHOUT RISKING NUCLEAR DESTRUCTION. ASSUMES CHINA WILL CONTINUE ITS MINIMUM RISK POLICY WITH BOTH USSR AND US.

2412 OLDMAN J.H.
WHITE AND BLACK IN AFRICA.
LONDON: LONGMANS, GREEN & CO, 1930, 73 PP.
A CRITIQUE OF RHODES LECTURES OF GENERAL SMUTS, WHO MAINTAINED THAT ADVANCE OF AFRICA COULD BE ACHIEVED ONLY THROUGH "A HIGHER CIVILIZATION IN THE FORM OF WHITE SETTLEMENT." ARGUES THAT DEVELOPMENT OF AFRICA MUST INSTEAD BE TURNED OVER TO NATIVE LEADERSHIP AND ALL CLAIMS TO POLITICAL PRIVILEGE MUST BE RENOUNCED.

2413 OLIVER D.L.
"A LEADER IN ACTION," IN D. A. OLIVER, SOLOMON ISLAND SOCIETY."
CAMBRIDGE: HARVARD U PR, 1955.
A CULTURAL AND SOCIETAL STUDY OF THE CAREER OF A HIGH-RANKING LEADER IN A SOLOMON ISLAND VILLAGE. OUTLINES THE LEADER'S FEAST-GIVING ACTIVITIES AND HIS PLANS FOR CONSOLIDATING HIS POSITION AS THE MOST RENOWNED MAN OF AREA. INDICATES HOW ONE EXCEPTIONAL INDIVIDUAL MAKES EFFECTIVE USE OF HIS CULTURAL MEANS TO ACHIEVE NEARLY UNIVERSALLY DESIRED CULTURAL GOALS.

2414 OLIVER R., ATMORE A.
AFRICA SINCE 1800.
NEW YORK: CAMBRIDGE U PRESS, 1967, 304 PP., LC#67-11527.
COMPREHENSIVE TRACING OF AFRICAN CULTURAL, POLITICAL, AND RELIGIOUS DEVELOPMENT UNDER FOREIGN RULE AND SOVEREIGNTY. DIVIDES AFRICA INTO NORTH, NORTHEAST, NORTHWEST CENTRAL, EAST CENTRAL, WEST CENTRAL, AND SOUTH AND DISCUSSES SEPARATELY.

2415 OLLE-LAPRUNE J.
LA STABILITE DES MINISTRES SOUS LA TROISIEME REPUBLIQUE, 1879-1940.
PARIS: PICHON ET DURAND-AUZIAS, 1962, 376 PP.
ANALYTICAL HISTORY OF MINISTERIAL TURNOVER DURING FRENCH THIRD REPUBLIC, EMPHASIZING COMPARATIVE STABILITY DURING PERIODS OF CRISIS AND NORMALITY, INCLUDING MECHANISMS AND FORMS OF STABILITY.

2416 OLSON M. JR.
THE ECONOMICS OF WARTIME SHORTAGE.
DURHAM: DUKE U PR, 1963, 152 PP., LC#63-17328.
INVESTIGATES HISTORICALLY THE EFFECTS OF WAR UPON A NATION AND TO WHAT EXTENT THAT NATION CAN ADJUST PHYSICALLY AND ECONOMICALLY. SHOWS BRITAIN'S PROBLEMS IN REVOLUTIONARY AND NAPOLEONIC WARS. THEN CONSIDERS POSITION OF UK IN WWI AND COMPARES IT WITH GERMANY. FINALLY CONSIDERS BRITAIN'S LOSSES IN FOOD IMPORTS DURING WWII AND DRAWS THEORETICAL SPECULATIONS FROM RESULTS OF STUDY.

2417 OMAN C.
A HISTORY OF THE ART OF WAR: THE MIDDLE AGES FROM THE FOURTH TO THE FOURTEENTH CENTURY.
LONDON: METHUEN, 1898, 667 PP.
DEALS WITH THE CHARACTERISTIC TACTICS, STRATEGY AND MILITARY ORGANIZATION OF THE ART OF WAR FROM THE DOWNFALL OF ROMAN EMPIRE TO THE FOURTEENTH CENTURY, AND ILLUSTRATES THEM BY DETAILED ACCOUNTS OF TYPICAL CAMPAIGNS AND BATTLES.

2418 ONSLOW C. ED.
ASIAN ECONOMIC DEVELOPMENT.
NEW YORK: FREDERICK PRAEGER, 1965, 243 PP.
STUDIES OF ECONOMIC DEVELOPMENT IN SIX ASIAN COUNTRIES, INCLUDING BURMA, CEYLON, INDIA, MALAYA, PAKISTAN, AND THAILAND, LISTED BY COUNTRY, AND SUMMARIZED BY A COMPARATIVE ANALYSIS BY THE EDITOR.

2419 ONUOHA B.
THE ELEMENTS OF AFRICAN SOCIALISM.
LONDON: ANDRE DEUTSCH, 1965, 139 PP.
SUBMITS ELEMENTS OF AFRICAN NEO-SOCIALISM DESIGNED TO PRESERVE SOCIAL AND SPIRITUAL VALUES IGNORED BY EUROPEANS AND TO ESTABLISH ECONOMIC SYSTEM FITTED TO AFRICAN SOCIETY. REJECTS INJUSTICES OF LAISSEZ-FAIRE OR MARXISM. DESCRIBES SOCIALIST STRUCTURE AND INSTITUTIONS AND RELATIONSHIP WITH RELIGIOUS BODIES. DEFINES IDEOLOGICAL CONCEPTS PERTINENT TO PURSUIT OF SOCIALISM.

2420 OOSTEN F.
"SUDVIETNAM IM JAHR VOR DER ENTSCHEIDUNG."
AUSSENPOLITIK, 18 (JULY 67), 439-445.
BRIEFLY REVIEWS AND ANALYZES MILITARY SITUATION AND OPERATIONS IN SOUTH VIETNAM IN SUMMER OF 1967. FOCUSES ON MANEUVERS OF US TROOPS AND INCREASED VIETCONG ACTIVITY. EVALUATES POSSIBILITIES FOR NEGOTIATION AND POLITICAL CLIMATE AND STABILITY IN SOUTH VIETNAM PRIOR TO SEPTEMBER ELECTION.

2421 OPERATIONS AND POLICY RESEARCH
PERU ELECTION MEMORANDA (PAMPHLET)
WASHINGTON: OPER & POL RES, INC, 1964, 38 PP.
STUDY OF GOVERNMENTAL STRUCTURE AND REPRESENTATION BY EXAMINATION OF 1963 PERUVIAN ELECTIONS. DISCUSSES LAWS GOVERNING ELECTORAL QUALIFICATIONS AND PROCEDURES.

2422 OPERATIONS AND POLICY RESEARCH
URUGUAY: ELECTION FACTBOOK: NOVEMBER 27, 1966 (PAMPHLET)
WASHINGTON: INST COMP STUDY POL, 1966, 53 PP., LC#66-29840.
ATTEMPTS TO CLARIFY ISSUES IN ELECTIONS THAT WERE COMING WHEN THIS PAMPHLET WAS WRITTEN AND TO PUT THEM IN HISTORICAL PERSPECTIVE. IDENTIFIES THE NUMEROUS PARTIES AND FACTIONS, DESCRIBES THEIR PROGRAMS, AND PRESENTS BRIEF BIOGRAPHIES OF CANDIDATES AND LEADING POLITICAL FIGURES. INCLUDES RELEVANT DATA ON PAST ELECTION RESULTS, CURRENT ELECTORAL LAWS SYSTEM OF REPRESENTATION, AND STRUCTURE OF GOVERNMENT.

2423 OPERATIONS AND POLICY RESEARCH
NICARAGUA: ELECTION FACTBOOK: FEBRUARY 5, 1967 (PAMPHLET)
WASHINGTON: INST COMP STUDY POL, 1967, 39 PP., LC#67-16332.
ATTEMPTS TO CLARIFY SURFACE AND UNDERLYING ISSUES IN THE "COMING" NICARAGUAN ELECTIONS, AND TO PUT THEM IN HISTORICAL PERSPECTIVE. IDENTIFIES THE NUMEROUS PARTIES AND FACTIONS, DESCRIBES THEIR PROGRAMS AND PRESENTS BRIEF BIOGRAPHIES OF CANDIDATES AND LEADING POLITICAL FIGURES. INCLUDES RELEVANT DATA ON PAST ELECTION RESULTS, CURRENT ELECTORAL LAWS, SYSTEM OF REPRESENTATION, AND STRUCTURE OF GOVERNMENT.

2424 OPPENHEIMER F.
THE STATE.
NEW YORK: VANGUARD PRESS, 1914, 302 PP.
FROM SOCIOLOGICAL BUT NOT JURISTIC POINT OF VIEW, TRACES DEVELOPMENT OF STATE FROM PRIMITIVE TO MODERN TIMES. CONSIDERS ALL STATES TO BE CLASS STATES, WHICH HAVE ARISEN NOT FROM "SOCIAL CONTRACT" BUT BY SEIZURE OF LAND BY A GROUP THAT BECOMES RULING CLASS. SEES PRINCIPLE IN EARLY HERDSMEN'S CONQUEST OF FARMERS AND IN GROWTH OF FEUDAL, MARITIME, AND CONSTITUTIONAL STATES THAT MAY BECOME CLASSLESS.

2425 ORDONNEAU P.
"LES PROBLEMES POSES PAR L'INDEPENDANCE DES NOUVEAUX ETATS AFRICAINS ET MALGACHE SUR LE PLAN DU CONTENTIEUX." ADMINISTRATIF.
REV. JURID. POLIT. OUTREMER, 16 (OCT.-DEC. 62), 541-614.
DEPICTS DECOLONIALIZATION PROCESS IN NEW AFRICAN STATES AND IN MADAGASCAR. CLARIFIES PROBLEMS RAISED BY LIMITED COMPETENCE.

2426 ORFIELD L.B.
THE GROWTH OF SCANDINAVIAN LAW.
PHILA: U OF PENN PR, 1953, 363 PP.
DEVELOPMENT OF LAW AND LEGAL INSTITUTIONS IN DENMARK, ICELAND, NORWAY, AND SWEDEN. CHAPTERS LISTED BY COUNTRY, WITH HISTORICAL AND POLITICAL BACKGROUND.

2427 ORG FOR ECO COOP AND DEVEL
THE MEDITERRANEAN REGIONAL PROJECT: AN EXPERIMENT IN PLANNING BY SIX COUNTRIES.
PARIS: ORG FOR ECO COOP AND DEV, 1965, 39 PP.
RELATES EDUCATION TO ECONOMIC GROWTH AND SOCIAL ADVANCEMENT IN GREECE, YUGOSLAVIA, SPAIN, TURKEY, PORTUGAL, AND ITALY. ESTIMATES FUTURE EDUCATIONAL NEEDS ACCORDING TO ECONOMIC CRITERIA, SOCIAL AND CULTURAL OBJECTIVES, AND DEMOGRAPHIC TRENDS. FORMULATES PROPOSALS FOR 1961-75. ANALYZES COSTS, ADMINISTRATION, EDUCATIONAL STRUCTURE, DEMAND AND SUPPLY, MANPOWER, AND ROLE OF TEACHERS.

2428 ORGANSKI A.F.K.
THE STAGES OF POLITICAL DEVELOPMENT.
NEW YORK: ALFRED KNOPF, 1965, 231 PP., LC#65-13462.

ATTEMPT TO BUILD THE FRAMEWORK FOR A THEORY OF COMPARATIVE DEVELOPMENTAL POLITICS IN TERMS OF THE CHANGING NATURE AND FUNCTIONS OF GOVERNMENT AS NATIONS PASS THROUGH RECOGNIZABLE STAGES. THE STAGES HE POSITS ARE* "(1) THE POLITICS OF PRIMITIVE UNIFICATION, (2) THE POLITICS OF INDUSTRIALIZATION, (3) THE POLITICS OF NATIONAL WELFARE, AND (4) THE POLITICS OF ABUNDANCE."

2429 ORNES G.E.
TRUJILLO: LITTLE CAESAR OF THE CARIBBEAN.
LONDON: THOMAS NELSON & SONS, 1958, 338 PP., LC#58-9038.
STUDY OF PERSONALITY AND ROLE OF TRUJILLO. SHOWS HIS LACK OF DEFINITE, ROUNDED PERSONALITY AND POLITICAL PHILOSOPHY. POINTS OUT HIS DICTATORSHIP AS "ONE OF THE MOST BRAZEN SWINDLES EVER PERPETRATED AGAINST A NATION." DESCRIBES TRUJILLO'S FAMILY BACKGROUND, RISE TO POWER, AND "SCOUNDREL METHODS" OF RULE.

2430 ORTEGA Y GASSET J.
MAN AND CRISIS.
NEW YORK: W W NORTON, 1958, 217 PP., LC#58-9282.
PRESENT DAY VIEWED, IN TERMS OF THEORY OF CYCLES OF CRISIS IN HISTORY, AS PERIOD OF CRISIS IN WHICH AGE WHICH BEGAN WITH GALILEO WILL END. IN SUCH PERIODS OF CRISIS, MEN CHARACTERISTICALLY TURN INWARD AND LOOK BACKWARD IN HISTORY TOWARD PURER AND SIMPLER MODES OF THOUGHT AND BEING. RENAISSANCE AS WELL AS PRESENT A PERIOD OF CRISIS. MODERN CRISIS IS RESULT OF COMPLEXITY.

2431 ORTON W.A.
THE ECONOMIC ROLE OF THE STATE.
CHICAGO: U OF CHICAGO PRESS, 1950, 192 PP.
HISTORICAL STUDY OF ACTIVITIES OF GOVERNMENT IN ECONOMY OF NATION. ANALYZES POWERS OF STATE AND HOW APPLIED TO CONTROL OR REGULATE ECONOMIC DEVELOPMENT.

2432 OTERO L.M.
HONDURAS.
MADRID: ED CULTURA HISPANICA, 1963, 399 PP.
DISCUSSION OF PRESENT-DAY HONDURAS, INCLUDING SOCIAL STRUCTURE, POPULATION, ECONOMY, CULTURAL INTEGRATION, AND RELIGION. EMPHASIZES EVOLUTION OF HONDURAN NATIONAL IDENTITY.

2433 OTTENBERG S. ED., OTTENBERG P. ED.
CULTURES AND SOCIETIES OF AFRICA.
NEW YORK: RANDOM HOUSE, INC, 1960, 614 PP., LC#60-6194.
READINGS ON PEOPLE OF AFRICA AND THEIR TRIBAL GROUPING, ENVIRONMENT, POLITICAL INSTITUTIONS AND LAWS, AND BELIEFS AND VALUES. ALL STUDIES REFER TO SPECIFIC TRIBAL EXAMPLES. TREATS FUTURE OF SOCIETY THROUGH CULTURAL CONTACT AND CHANGE.

2434 OVERSEAS DEVELOPMENT INST.
EFFECTIVE AID.
LONDON: MIN OF OVERSEAS DEVEL, 1967, 129 PP.
EXAMINES AID ADMINISTRATION, TERMS AND CONDITIONS OF FOREIGN AID, AND TECHNICAL ASSISTANCE TO UNDERDEVELOPED NATIONS. DISCUSSES PRACTICES IN GERMANY, FRANCE, UK, AND US.

2435 OVERSTREET G.D., WINDMILLER M.
COMMUNISM IN INDIA.
BERKELEY: U OF CALIF PR, 1959, 603 PP., LC#58-12832.
A BROAD ANALYSIS OF INDIAN HISTORY. EMPHASIZES COMMUNIST PARTY OF INDIA WITH REGARD TO COMMUNIST AND NON-COMMUNIST INFLUENCES AFFECTING COURSE OF INDIAN COMMUNISM. STUDIES INDIAN COMMUNIST PARTY IN ITS WORLD-WIDE AS WELL AS NATIONAL CONTEXT. CONSTITUTES AN EXAMINATION OF ONE MAJOR GROUP OF POLITICAL LEADERS IN INDIA. EXTENSIVE BIBLIOGRAPHY.

2436 OWEN G.
INDUSTRY IN THE UNITED STATES.
BALTIMORE: PENGUIN BOOKS, 1966, 215 PP.
LOOK AT MANAGEMENT OF AMERICAN INDUSTRY STUDIES DECISION-MAKING PROCESS AND TRAINING OF MANAGERS TO MAKE DECISIONS. ATTRIBUTES SUCCESS OF AMERICAN BUSINESS TO HIGH ESTEEM IN WHICH BUSINESS HAS BEEN HELD, HIGH CALIBER OF BUSINESSMEN, AND GOVERNMENT'S CONTRIBUTION TO PROSPERITY. COMPARES AMERICAN MEN AND METHODS TO BRITISH COUNTERPARTS AND SUGGESTS MEANS FOR IMPROVEMENT IN BRITISH SYSTEM.

2437 PADELFORD N.J. ED., GOODRICH L. ED.
THE UNITED NATIONS IN THE BALANCE* ACCOMPLISHMENTS AND PROSPECTS.
NEW YORK: FREDERICK PRAEGER, 1965, 482 PP., LC#65-24725.
THIS COLLECTION OF ESSAYS ORIGINALLY APPEARED AS A SPECIAL ISSUE OF "INTERNATIONAL ORGANIZATION" IN 1965 COMMEMORATING THE TWENTIETH ANNIVERSARY OF THE UNITED NATIONS. THE PAPERS TRACE THE EVOLUTION OF THE UN AS AN INTERNATIONAL ORGANIZATION, ASSESS ITS RECORD IN COOPERATION AND CONFLICT, PRESENT THE UN POLICIES OF MAJOR MEMBERS AND BLOCS, AND CONTEMPLATE THE FUTURE.

2438 PADELFORD N.J.
"POLITICS AND THE FUTURE OF ECOSOC."
INT. ORGAN., 15 (AUTUMN 61), 564-80.
CONCERNED WITH PRESSURES TO INCREASE SIZE AND SCOPE OF ECOSOC. CONSIDERS AMENDMENTS ALLOWING INCREASED REPRESENTATION OF AFRO-ASIAN STATES AND EFFECT OF CHANGES. EXAMINES FINANCIAL STRAIN ON UN AND US FROM DEMANDS FOR INCREASED FUNDS FOR ECONOMIC AND TECHNICAL ASSISTANCE.

2439 PADELFORD N.J. ED., EMERSON R. ED.
AFRICA AND WORLD ORDER.
NEW YORK: FREDERICK PRAEGER, 1963, 152 PP., LC#63-10264.
ON CONTEMPORARY AFRICA, INCLUDING ITS BEHAVIOR IN UN, ITS UNIFICATION MOVEMENTS, PAN-AFRICANISM, AND IMPACT ON COMMONWEALTH.

2440 PADMORE G.
PAN-AFRICANISM OR COMMUNISM.
LONDON: DOBSON, 1956, 463 PP.
TRACES DEVELOPMENT OF NEGRO POLITICAL MOVEMENTS, SUCH AS GARVEYISM, BLACK ZIONISM, PAN-AFRICANISM, AS BACKGROUND TO CONTEMPORARY AFRICAN POLITICS. COMPARES COLONIAL SYSTEMS OF DIFFERENT COLONIAL POWERS IN AFRICA. DEALS EXTENSIVELY WITH GOLD COAST, KENYA, AND NIGERIA. FORESEES STRUGGLE IN AFRICA BETWEEN PAN-AFRICANISM AND COMMUNISM, THOUGH DENIES AFRICANS ATTRACTED BY LATTER.

2441 PAGE S.W.
LENIN AND WORLD REVOLUTION.
NEW YORK: NEW YORK U PR, 1959, 252 PP., LC#59-6250.
ANALYSIS OF LENIN'S BEHAVIOR AND THOUGHT THROUGHOUT MARXIST MOVEMENT, AND WORLDWIDE IMPACT OF HIS TEACHINGS. LENIN'S ROLE IN SHAPING USSR GLOBAL AND DOMESTIC POLICIES IS EVALUATED IN PSYCHOLOGICAL TERMS. HIS FANATICISM IS ATTRIBUTED PRIMARILY TO A COMPULSION TO DOMINATE, AND HIS TEACHINGS ARE SEEN AS RATIONALIZATIONS FOR HIS PERSONAL STRIVINGS.

2442 PAGINSKY P.
GERMAN WORKS RELATING TO AMERICA, 1493-1800; A LIST COMPILED FROM THE COLLECTIONS OF THE NEW YORK PUBLIC LIBRARY.
NEW YORK: NY PUBLIC LIBRARY, 1942, 217 PP.
ANNOTATED BIBLIOGRAPHY OF WORKS IN GERMAN. ARRANGED CHRONOLOGICALLY WITH ANNOTATIONS IN ENGLISH.

2443 PAI G.A.
"TAXATION AND PLANNING IN INDIA: A BIRDS-EYE VIEW."
UNITED ASIA, 19 (MAR.-APR. 67), 112-118.
ANALYZES POSSIBILITIES OF DIRECT OR INDIRECT TAXATION AS "EGALITARIAN" MEASURES IN INDIA. FINDS TAXES HAVE WIDENED INCOME GAP, SHOWING THAT CONGRESS GOVERNMENT FAVORS WEALTHY CLASS. PROPOSES GOVERNMENT REDUCE BURDEN OF INDIRECT TAXATION ON COMMON MAN BY ENFORCING COLLECTION OF ASSESSED DIRECT TAXES. RECOMMENDS INCREASE OF DIRECT TAXATION TO LEVEL OF INDIRECT.

2444 PAIKERT G.C.
THE GERMAN EXODUS.
THE HAGUE: MARTINUS NIJHOFF, 1962, 97 PP.
"SELECTIVE STUDY ON POST WWII EXPULSION OF GERMAN POPULATIONS AND ITS EFFECTS," PARTICULARLY ON WEST GERMANY. INCLUDES MOTIVES AND LEGAL BASIS OF EXODUS, IMMIGRANTS' RESETTLEMENT, EFFECT ON SOCIO-CULTURAL GEOGRAPHY OF WEST GERMANY, AND SOLUTIONS TO PROBLEMS OF INTEGRATION OF NATIONAL MINORITIES.

2445 PAINE T., FONER P.S. ED.
"THE AGE OF REASON IN T. PAINE, THE COMPLETE WRITINGS OF THOMAS PAINE (VOL. 1) (1794-95)"
NEW YORK: CITADEL PRESS, 1945.
ATTEMPTS TO REFUTE STORIES OF CREATION, GARDEN OF EDEN, RESURRECTION, MIRACLES, REVELATION, ETC., BASING ARGUMENTS ON SCIENCE AND REASON. BELIEVES CHRISTIANITY IS "DEROGATORY TO THE ALMIGHTY" AND REPUGNANT TO REASON. DOES NOT DENY GREATNESS OF JESUS. BELIEVES THAT BY UNAIDED REASON MAN CAN KNOW THERE IS A GOD AND THAT HE HAS CERTAIN DUTIES TOWARD HIM. WHEN OPINIONS ARE FREE, TRUTH WILL PREVAIL.

2446 PAINE T.
RIGHTS OF MAN.
NEW YORK: E.P. DUTTON & CO., INC., 1791, 191 PP.
WRITTEN IN ANSWER TO BURKE'S "REFLECTIONS," DEFENDS FRENCH REVOLUTION AS STEP TO FREE MAN FROM CORRUPT CUSTOMS AND DIVINE-RIGHT PRIVILEGE. SUPPORTS CONCEPTS OF GOVERNMENT AS SERVICE TO PEOPLE AND OF THE MUTUAL OBLIGATION OF EACH, AND ATTACKS BURKE'S THESIS THAT LAWS IMPLICITLY REQUIRE OBEDIENCE BECAUSE THEY ARE DICTATES OF GOVERNMENT. DEFENDS RIGHT OF PEOPLE TO CHANGE CORRUPT RULERS.

2447 PAK H.
"CHINA'S MILITIA AND MAO TSE-TUNG'S 'PEOPLE'S WAR'."
ORBIS, 11 (SPRING 67), 285-294.
TRACES HISTORY AND EXAMINES STRUCTURE OF CHINESE MILITIA, RELATING USE OF MILITIA TO MAO'S "PEOPLE'S WAR." OBSERVES THAT PERHAPS ONE HALF OF CHINA'S 650 MILLION PEOPLE TAKE PART IN ITS REGULAR DRILLS IN ADDITION TO THEIR WORK, USUALLY PEASANT LABOR. NOTES INTENSE ANTI-US MILITARISTIC SPIRIT, AND CONSTANT USE OF CRISES TO KEEP MORALE HIGH. SEES SOME RESISTANCE TO AND DIFFICULTIES IN CURRENT SYSTEM.

2448 PALACIOS A.L.
PETROLEO, MONOPOLIOS, Y LATIFUNDIOS.
BUENOS AIRES: GUILLERMO KRAFT, 1957, 405 PP.
EXAMINES ECONOMIC STRUCTURE OF OIL, MONOPOLY, AND LAND IN ARGENTINA. EXPLAINS NEED FOR NATIONALIZATION OF RESOURCES AND ELIMINATION OF ECONOMIC CONTROL BY FOREIGN CAPITAL. DISCUSSES NEED FOR NATIONAL GOVERNMENT TO HELP IMPROVE INDUSTRIAL OUTPUT AND TO END UNFAIR OPERATIONS.

2449 PALMER E.E. ED.
"POLITICAL MAN" IN E. PALMER, PROBLEMS IN DEMOCRATIC CITIZENSHIP.
SYRACUSE: SYR U, MAXWELL SCHOOL, 1958, 150 PP.
ATTEMPTS TO INCREASE UNDERSTANDING OF DEMOCRACY BY FOCUSING ATTENTION UPON RELATION OF INDIVIDUAL CITIZENS TO THE DEMOCRATIC PROCESS AND BY APPLYING THESE NOTIONS OF PROCESS TO SPECIFIC CASES. ALSO AIMS AT ENCOURAGING PARTICIPATION OF CITIZENS IN GROUP ACTIVITIES DIRECTED TOWARD SOLUTION OF THE SOCIAL PROBLEMS OF US SOCIETY.

2450 PALMER E.E. ED.
THE COMMUNIST CHALLENGE.
SYRACUSE: SYR U, MAXWELL SCHOOL, 1958, 125 PP.
PRESENTS BASIC STRUCTURE OF IDEAS OF WORLD COMMUNISM, AS THEY HAVE DEVELOPED SINCE THE PUBLICATION OF THE COMMUNIST MANIFESTO IN 1848. REVIEWS GENERAL PROBLEMS OF DEALING WITH UNCOMMITTED NATIONS AND BASIC CONCEPTS AND PROGRAMS OF US FOREIGN POLICY. OFFERS SUGGESTIONS FOR PREVENTING SPREAD OF COMMUNISM AND FACILITATING PEACE.

2451 PALMER N.D., PERKINS H.C.
INTERNATIONAL RELATIONS.
BOSTON: HOUGHTON MIFFLIN, 1957, 860 PP.
STUDIES PATTERN OF INTERNATIONAL RELATIONS FIRST FROM THEORETICAL VIEWPOINT. CONSIDERS BASIC INSTRUMENTS FOR PROMOTION OF NATIONAL INTEREST: DIPLOMACY, PROPAGANDA, ECONOMICS, WAR, AND IMPERIALISM. TREATS CONTROLS OF INTER-STATE RELATIONS, SUCH AS BALANCE OF POWER, INTERNATIONAL LAW, TREATIES, AND INTERNATIONAL ORGANIZATIONS. DISCUSSES MAJOR CHANGES AFTER WWII.

2452 PALMER N.D.
THE INDIAN POLITICAL SYSTEM.
BOSTON: HOUGHTON MIFFLIN, 1961, 277 PP.
COMPREHENSIVE VIEW OF EVOLVING INDIAN POLITICAL SYSTEM IN RELATION TO HER CULTURE, SOCIETY, AND HISTORY. DISCUSSES THE NATIONALIST MOVEMENT, INDIAN STATE, CENTRAL GOVERNMENT, POLITICAL PARTIES, AND FOREIGN RELATIONS AS BASIC THEMES.

2453 PALMER R.R.
TWELVE WHO RULED.
PRINCETON: U. PR., 1941, 417 PP.
HISTORICAL NARRATIVE OF CLIMAX OF FRENCH REVOLUTION (1793-4) DURING WHICH FRANCE WAS RULED BY COMMITTEE OF PUBLIC SAFETY HEADED BY ROBESPIERRE SUPPORTED BY CARNOT, COUTHON BARERE ET AL. DESCRIBES SUDDEN RISE OF NATIONALISM, REPUBLICAN ANTI-CLERICAL VIOLENCE AND ASCENDANCY OF FIRST MODERN DICTATORSHIP 'FROM THE CONFLICTS OF REVOLUTIONARY ENTHUSIASM.'

2454 PAN S., LYONS D.
VIETNAM CRISIS.
NEW YORK: TWIN CIRCLE PUBL CO, 1966, 334 PP., LC#66-23533.
HISTORY OF VIETNAM FROM ITS BEGINNINGS TO PRESENT TIME, BASED ON LONG ASSOCIATIONS WITH VIETNAMESE. FOCUSES ON PERIOD FROM WWII TO 1966. DISCUSSES PRESENT POSITIONS OF NORTH AND SOUTH VIETNAMESE GOVERNMENTS AND PEOPLE, AND US AND FRENCH POLICIES, HOPES THAT SPREAD OF COMMUNIST CHINA WILL BE CHECKED BY VIETNAM WAR.

2455 PAN AMERICAN UNION
REPERTORIO DE PUBLICACIONES PERIODICAS ACTUALES LATINO-AMERICANAS.
PARIS: UNESCO, 1958.
DIRECTORY OF LATIN AMERICAN PERIODICALS ARRANGED BY DEWEY DECIMAL SYSTEM.

2456 PAN AMERICAN UNION
PUBLICATIONS: PAU AND OFFICIAL RECORDS OF THE OAS, IN ENGLISH, SPANISH, PORTUGUESE, AND FRENCH, 1958-59.
WASHINGTON: PAN AMERICAN UNION, 1959, 32 PP.
"LISTS PUBLICATIONS AVAILABLE FOR SALE AND ISSUED BY PAN AMERICAN UNION...REPORTS AND STUDIES OF ACTIVITIES IN THE AMERICAN REPUBLICS...MONOGRAPHS...PERIODICALS...OFFICIAL RECORDS OF THE OAS." ITEMS CLASSIFIED BY SUBJECT.

2457 PANIKKAR K.M.
INDIAN STATES AND THE GOVERNMENT OF INDIA.
GLASGOW: UNIVERSITY PRESS, 1927, 169 PP.
ANALYZES AND INTERPRETS INDIA'S UNIQUE SYSTEM OF POLITY. RELATIONS BETWEEN INDIAN PRINCES AND GOVERNMENT ARE EXPLORED WITH SOME SPECULATION ON THEIR FUTURE EVOLUTION ROLE OF ENGLAND, GROWTH OF CENTRAL POWER, EKTENSION OF IMPERIAL AUTHORITY, RIGHTS OF SOVEREIGNTY, AND CONSTITUTIONAL POSITION DISCUSSED.

2458 PANIKKAR K.M.
THE AFRO-ASIAN STATES AND THEIR PROBLEMS.
NEW YORK: JOHN DAY, 1959, 104 PP.
OUTLINE OF PROBLEMS OF EMERGENT NATION, POLITICAL, ECONOMIC, AND SOCIAL. NECESSITY FOR NEW GOVERNMENT, EDUCATIONAL FAILINGS, BREAKDOWN OF EXISTING SOCIAL STRUCTURE, AND ECONOMIC DEPENDENCE ARE EXAMINED.

2459 PANIKKAR K.M.
THE STATE AND THE CITIZEN (2ND ED.)
BOMBAY: ASIA PUBL HOUSE, 1960, 166 PP.
DISCUSSES QUESTIONS OF POVERTY, TECHNOLOGICAL CHANGE, INDIAN DOCTRINES OF POLITICS, EDUCATION IN INDIA, AND GROWTH OF POPULATION. RELATES THESE ISSUES TO DUTY AND RIGHTS OF CITIZENS IN DEMOCRATIC COUNTRIES.

2460 PANIKKAR K.M. ED., PERSHAD A. ED.
THE VOICE OF FREEDOM: SELECTED SPEECHES OF PANDIT MOTILAL NEHRU.
NEW YORK: ASIA PUBL HOUSE, 1961, 563 PP.
SELF-EXPLAINED AND FULLY ANNOTATED SPEECHES BY PANDIT MOTILAL NEHRU. CONGRESSIONAL SPEECHES STRESS RESPONSIBLE SELF-GOVERNMENT AND INDEPENDENCE; UNITED PROVINCE COUNCIL SPEECHES CONCERN MONTAGU-CHELMSFORD REFORMS; LEGISLATIVE ASSEMBLY SPEECHES COVER VARIOUS LAWS AND BILLS.

2461 PANIKKAR K.M.
REVOLUTION IN AFRICA.
BOMBAY: ASIA PUBL HOUSE, 1961, 202 PP.
STUDIES EMERGENCE OF AFRICA: NATIONALISM; RISE OF NATION STATES; POLITICAL PARTIES AND LEADERS; PAN-AFRICANISM; POLITICS IN UNDER-DEVELOPED COUNTRIES; CASE STUDY OF GUINEA.

2462 PANJABI K.L. ED.
THE CIVIL SERVANT IN INDIA.
BOMBAY: BHARATIYI VIDYA BHAUAN, 1965, 356 PP.
COLLECTION OF STATEMENTS BY RETIRED MEMBERS OF CIVIL SERVICE, REVIEWING THEIR WORK IN THE SERVICE, TRAINING (FORMAL AND PERSONAL), DISCIPLINE, WORKING CONDITIONS, AS WELL AS TRIALS, COMPENSATIONS, AND CHERISHED IDEALS. MANY ARE HUMOROUS AND PERSONAL REFLECTIONS, INTIMATELY PICTURING ADMINISTRATION OF PRE-INDEPENDENCE INDIA.

2463 PAPANEK G.F.
PAKISTAN'S DEVELOPMENT: SOCIAL GOALS AND PRIVATE INCENTIVES.
CAMBRIDGE: HARVARD U PR, 1967, 400 PP., LC#67-22871.
ANALYZES THE UNEXPECTEDLY HIGH RATE OF ECONOMIC GROWTH IN PAKISTAN; FINDS THE SOURCE IN A SUCCESSFUL MIXING OF PRIVATE ENTERPRISE AND GOVERNMENT ECONOMIC INTERVENTION. COMPREHENSIVE INDUSTRIAL SURVEY OF PAKISTAN IS INCLUDED.

2464 PARANJAPE H.K.
THE FLIGHT OF TECHNICAL PERSONNEL IN PUBLIC UNDERTAKINGS.
NEW DELHI: INDIAN INST PUB ADMIN, 1964, 191 PP.
INVESTIGATES "FLIGHT OF TECHNICAL PERSONNEL" FROM ONE PUBLIC ENTERPRISE TO ANOTHER OR TO PRIVATE ENTERPRISE IN INDIA, ITS EXTENT, ACUTENESS OF PROBLEM, WHICH INDUSTRIES AND TYPES OF PERSONNEL ARE AFFECTED, PROBLEMS IT CAUSES SUCH AS NONAVAILABILITY OF PERSONNEL, CAUSES OF MIGRATION, AND SOLUTIONS TO MAINTAIN STEADY AVAILABILITY OF TECHNICAL PERSONNEL.

2465 PARETO V.
THE MIND AND SOCIETY (4 VOLS.)
NEW YORK: HARCOURT BRACE, 1935, 2050 PP.
HOLDS THAT HUMAN BEHAVIOR IS NONRATIONAL, BASED ON CERTAIN NATURAL INSTINCTS AND DRIVES INHERENT IN HUMAN BEINGS, AND THAT "THEORIES, THEOLOGIES, PROGRAMS, AND FAITHS" ARE DERIVED FROM THESE DRIVES. APPLIES THIS TO EXTENSIVE ANALYSIS OF SOCIETY, HISTORY, AND POLITICS. ALSO CONSIDERS ECONOMICS, SOVEREIGNTY, AND CLASSES, DESCRIBING AN IDEAL STATE SIMILAR TO NAZI GERMANY.

2466 PARETO V.
SOCIOLOGICAL WRITINGS (TRANS. BY DERICK MURFIN)
NEW YORK: FREDERICK PRAEGER, 1966, 335 PP.
GENERAL DISCUSSION OF PRINCIPLES OF SOCIOLOGY AND THEIR APPLICATION TO ANALYSIS OF POLITICAL AND SOCIAL SYSTEM. INCLUDES AN INTRODUCTION BY EDITOR OUTLINING THEORY AND PROVIDING A GENERAL CRITIQUE THEREOF. ALSO INCLUDES A BRIEF BIOGRAPHICAL SUMMARY.

2467 PARK A.G.
BOLSHEVISM IN TURKESTAN 1917-1927.
NEW YORK: COLUMBIA U PRESS, 1957, 428 PP., LC#57-5804.
ANALYZES AIMS, METHODS, AND ACHIEVEMENTS OF SOVIET POLICY IN CENTRAL ASIA DURING FIRST DECADE AFTER REVOLUTION. DRAWS ON FULL RANGE OF SOVIET SOURCES FOR DETAILS ON IMPACT OF BOLSHEVIK RULE OVER MOSLEMS IN TSARIST COLONY OF TURKESTAN. CONTENDS THAT SOVIET POLICY DID NOT VARY SIGNIFICANTLY FROM THAT PURSUED IN RUSSIAN EMPIRE.

2468 PARK R.L. ED., TINKER I. ED.
LEADERSHIP AND POLITICAL INSTITUTIONS IN INDIA.
PRINCETON: U. PR., 1959, 486 PP.
TRADITIONS OF INDIAN LEADERSHIP ARE DISCUSSED ALONG WITH

AN EVALUATION OF PERSONAL QUALITIES OF THREE MAJOR POLITICAL FIGURES. STUDY INCLUDES AN ANALYSIS OF PUBLIC ADMINISTRATION AND RURAL DEVELOPMENT.

2469 PARRINDER G.
AFRICAN TRADITIONAL RELIGION.
LONDON: HUTCHINSON U LIBRARY, 1954, 160 PP.
STUDY OF AFRICAN RELIGION WITH REGARD TO ITS INFLUENCE AND FORM. EXAMINES CONCEPTS OF UNIVERSE AND GOD AND HOW RITUAL IS APPLIED TO NORMAL LIFE. DISCUSSES EFFECT ON ORGANIZATION OF AFRICAN SOCIETY.

2470 PARRIS H.W.
GOVERNMENT AND THE RAILWAYS IN NINETEENTH-CENTURY BRITAIN.
LONDON: ROUTLEDGE & KEGAN PAUL, 1965, 244 PP.
DESCRIBES NEW FUNCTION OF CENTRAL GOVERNMENT IN 19TH CENTURY, THAT OF CONTROLLING RAILWAYS ON BEHALF OF PUBLIC. DISCUSSES NEW AGENCIES INSTITUTED TO DEAL WITH RAILWAYS, THEIR INFLUENCE ON POLICIES, THEIR FUNCTIONS, AND THEIR ROLE IN IMPROVING SERVICE. EXAMINES RAILWAYS' EFFECTS ON GOVERNMENTAL POLICIES, IMPACT OF LEADERS ON RAILWAY COMPANIES, AND INTERCOMPANY RELATIONS.

2471 PARSONS T.
THE STRUCTURE OF SOCIAL ACTION.
NEW YORK: MCGRAW HILL, 1937, 817 PP.
TRACES THE DEVELOPMENT OF THE POSITIVISTIC THEORY OF ACTION AND POINTS OUT THE EMERGENCE OF A REVOLUTIONARY THEORY OF ACTION FROM THE POSITIVE TRADITION. ANALYZES THE PRINCIPLE CHARACTERISTICS OF CAPITALISM AND CONCLUDES WITH SYSTEMATIC THEORY OF MAX WEBER'S DOCTRINE.

2472 PARSONS T. ED., SHILS E.A. ED.
TOWARD A GENERAL THEORY OF ACTION.
CAMBRIDGE: HARVARD U PR, 1951, 506 PP.
SOCIAL RELATIONS DEPARTMENT OF HARVARD DISCUSSES STATE OF SOCIAL ACTION THEORY. GIVES FRAME OF REFERENCE FOR THEORY AND ITS RELATIONSHIP TO SOCIOLOGY, CULTURAL ANTHROPOLOGY AND SOCIAL PSYCHOLOGY, EMPHASIZING MOTIVATION AND VALUES.

2473 PASSIN H.
"THE SOURCES OF PROTEST IN JAPAN."
AMER. POLIT. SCI. REV., 56 (JUNE 1962), 391-403.
ANALYZES EVENTS IN JAPAN DURING SPRING OF 1960, WHICH LEAD TO CANCELLATION OF EISENHOWER'S TRIP. SEES CAUSES OF THIS PROTEST AS: JAPAN'S NEED TO PROVE HERSELF TO WEST, HER CLASS CONFLICT AS STAGE OF INDUSTRIAL SOCIETY, HUMILIATION OF HER DEFEAT IN LAST WAR, AND TYPICAL MODERN DISCONTENT OF MASS SOCIETY.

2474 PASTOR R.S., BRUGADA R.S.
A STATEMENT OF THE LAWS OF PARAGUAY IN MATTERS AFFECTING BUSINESS (2ND ED.)
WASHINGTON: PAN AMERICAN UNION, 1962, 284 PP.
SUMMARY IN ENGLISH OF CONSTITUTIONAL, STATUTORY, AND REGULATORY PROVISIONS OF PARAGUAY (IN 1962) RELEVANT TO COMMERCIAL, INDUSTRIAL, AND LABOR CONCERNS AND THE PERSONS THEY INVOLVE.

2475 PATAI R.
CULTURES IN CONFLICT; AN INQUIRY INTO THE SOCIO-CULTURAL PROBLEMS OF ISRAEL AND HER NEIGHBORS (2ND REV. ED.)
NEW YORK: HERZL PRESS, 1961, 80 PP.
LOOKS AT TRADITIONAL SOCIAL STRUCTURE, VALUES, AND ATTITUDES OF ARAB STATES. PORTRAYS MODERN, WESTERN CULTURE OF ISRAEL AND VALUES OF EUROPEAN JEWS IN ISRAEL; COMPARES CULTURE OF EUROPEAN AND ORIENTAL JEWS. ANALYZES TRANSITION FROM TRADITIONAL TO MODERN SOCIETY IN ISRAEL AND ARAB STATES, AND CONSIDERS POSSIBILITY OF CULTURAL UNDERSTANDING BETWEEN ISRAEL AND HER NEIGHBORS. TREATS WADI SALIB EVENTS.

2476 PATAI R.
GOLDEN RIVER TO GOLDEN ROAD: SOCIETY, CULTURE, AND CHANGE IN THE MIDDLE EAST (2ND ED.)
PHILA: U OF PENN PR, 1967, 461 PP., LC#60-63174.
DISCUSSES MIDDLE EASTERN CULTURE IN GENERAL. ANALYZES SIGNIFICANT ASPECTS OF MIDDLE EASTERN SOCIAL ORGANIZATION, INCLUDING THE FAMILY, SEX MORES AND POSITION OF WOMEN, COUSIN MARRIAGE, AND NOBLE AND VASSAL TRIBES. COMPARES ROLE OF RELIGION WITH ITS ROLE IN WESTERN AND FAR EASTERN CULTURES. EXPLORES SOCIO-CULTURAL CHANGES NOW OCCURRING ESPECIALLY NATIONALISM AND WESTERNIZATION.

2477 PAULSEN M.G. ED.
LEGAL INSTITUTIONS TODAY AND TOMORROW.
NEW YORK: COLUMBIA U PRESS, 1959, 346 PP., LC#59-14820.
COLLECTION OF ESSAYS ON JUDICIAL AND ADMINISTRATIVE LAW-MAKING PROCESSES IN US. EXAMINES ROLE OF LEGAL PROFESSION, CONGRESS, STATE LEGISLATURES, ADMINISTRATIVE AGENCIES, AND COURTS. ALSO DISCUSSES LEGAL INSTITUTIONS IN ENGLAND.

2478 PAUW B.A.
THE SECOND GENERATION.
LONDON: OXFORD U PR, 1963, 219 PP.
EXAMINES STRUCTURE OF BANTU FAMILY IN URBANIZED EAST LONDON, SOUTH AFRICA. DESCRIBES CEREMONIAL ACTIVITIES, PRE-MARITAL RELATIONS, MARRIAGE CUSTOMS, HOUSEHOLD AND FAMILY STRUCTURE, AND LARGER SOCIAL UNIVERSE.

2479 PAYNO M.
LA REFORMA SOCIAL EN ESPANA Y MEXICO.
MEXICO CITY: U NAC INST HIST MEX, 1958, 127 PP.
ANALYZES SPANISH AND MEXICAN SOCIAL REFORM REGARDING CHURCH PROPERTY IN 19TH AND 20TH CENTURIES. EXAMINES LEGAL POSITION OF CATHOLIC CHURCH AS LARGEST LANDOWNER IN BOTH COUNTRIES AND BENEFICIAL ADVANTAGES OF FREEDOM FROM TAXES. ALSO DISCUSSES TIGHT LEGAL RESTRICTIONS ON CHURCH ACTIVITY AS REVOLUTION BROUGHT ANTI-CLERICAL LIBERALS TO POWER.

2480 PAZ O.
THE LABYRINTH OF SOLITUDE; LIFE AND THOUGHT IN MEXICO (TRANS. BY LYSANDER KEMP)
NEW YORK: GROVE PRESS, 1961, 212 PP., LC#61-11777.
POET PROBES MEXICAN CHARACTER AND CULTURE. FINDS THAT SILENCE, IRONY, AND FORMALIZATION OF SOCIAL LIFE ARE MASKS THAT PERMIT MEXICAN TO CONCEAL HIS PERSONALITY. COMMENTARY ON PLIGHT OF CONTEMPORARY LATIN AMERICAN IN MODERNIZING WORLD. TRACES DEVELOPMENT OF MEXICAN CULTURE FROM FIRST EUROPEAN CONQUEST UNTIL PRESENT. DISCUSSES PLACE OF MEXICAN INTELLIGENTSIA IN CULTURE.

2481 PEASLEE A.J.
CONSTITUTIONS OF NATIONS* THIRD REVISED EDITION (VOLUME I* AFRICA)
GENEVA: MARTINUS NIJHOFF, 1965, 1108 PP.
COMPILATION OF ALL AFRICAN NATIONS' CONSTITUTIONS. COMPLETE WITH TEXTS, SUMMARIES, ANNOTATIONS, BIBLIOGRAPHIES AND GEOGRAPHICAL INFORMATION.

2482 PECKERT J.
DIE GROSSEN UND DIE KLEINEN MAECHTE.
STUTTGART: DEUTSCHE VERLAGSANST, 1961, 193 PP.
THEORETICAL PRESENTATION OF CHANGES IN THE NATIONAL INTEREST OF VARIOUS MODERN STATES AND RELATION OF THESE CHANGES TO THREE IMPORTANT CONTEMPORARY PROBLEM AREAS: THE POLITICS OF ALLIANCES, POLITICS VIS-A-VIS DEVELOPING NATIONS, AND THE POLITICS OF EUROPE.

2483 PELCOVITS N.A.
OLD CHINA HANDS AND THE FOREIGN OFFICE.
NEW YORK: KINGS CROWN PR, 1948, 347 PP.
STUDY OF THE OPINIONS AND ATTITUDES ON ANGLO-CHINESE RELATIONS HELD BY BRITISH MERCHANTS ENGAGED IN THE CHINA TRADE, AND OF THEIR RELEVANCE TO THE FORMATION, IN THE 19TH CENTURY OF BRITISH FOREIGN POLICY TOWARD CHINA. DISCUSSES THE EVENTS THAT CAUSED THE BRITISH GOVERNMENT TO DECIDE AGAINST MAKING CHINA A "SECOND INDIA."

2484 PELLING H.
A SHORT HISTORY OF THE LABOUR PARTY (2ND ED.)
LONDON: MACMILLAN, 1965, 142 PP.
STUDIES DEVELOPMENT OF LABOUR PARTY FROM FORMATION TO 1964 LABOUR GOVERNMENT. DEALS WITH PROBLEMS OF PARLIAMENTARY LEADERSHIP, AND RELATIONS WITH LABOR UNIONS AND MEMBERS. DEEPENS UNDERSTANDING OF POLICIES AND POLITICAL SITUATION UNDER WILSON MINISTRY ON WHICH FUTURE OF PARTY DEPENDS. MAINTAINS THAT CLOSE AFFILIATION OF UNIONS AND PARTY IS ENDED.

2485 PELLING H.M.
A HISTORY OF BRITISH TRADE UNIONISM.
BALTIMORE: PENGUIN BOOKS, 1963, 287 PP.
TRACES ORIGINS OF BRITISH TRADE UNIONISM IN EARLY 1800'S COVERS ITS DEVELOPMENT THROUGH WWI AND WWII. RELATES ITS STATUS IN EARLY 1960'S AND IMPORTANCE OF ITS EFFECT UPON BRITISH GOVERNMENT.

2486 PELZER K.J.
SELECTED BIBLIOGRAPHY ON THE GEOGRAPHY OF SOUTHEAST ASIA (3 VOLS., 1949-1956)
NEW HAVEN: YALE U, SE ASIA STUD, 1949.
INTENDED AS REFERENCE AND READING LIST FOR STUDENTS OF PHYSICAL, CULTURAL, ECONOMIC, AND POLITICAL GEOGRAPHY OF SOUTHEAST ASIA. VOLUME I REFERS TO GENERAL STUDIES AND VOLUME II TO PHILIPPINES IN PARTICULAR. VOLUME III, PUBLISHED IN 1956, HAS BEEN EXPANDED TO DEVOTE GREATER ATTENTION TO ANTHROPOLOGY IN MALAYA. ORGANIZED BY CONTENT OF GENERAL DISCIPLINES.

2487 PENDLE G.
PARAGUAY: A RIVERSIDE NATION (3RD ED.)
LONDON: OXFORD U PR, 1967, 96 PP.
EXAMINES CONTEMPORARY LIFE IN PARAGUAY. FINDS THAT PARAGUAYAN HISTORY HAS BEEN SHAPED BY ITS GEOGRAPHY. NATIONAL PROBLEMS TODAY ARE ESSENTIALLY SAME AS THEY HAVE BEEN FOR FOUR CENTURIES. FINDS LITTLE EVIDENCE OF PHYSICAL CHANGE. ISOLATION HAS RETARDED ECONOMIC AND SOCIAL DEVELOPMENT, YET CONTRIBUTED TO STRONG NATIONAL CHARACTER. ANALYZES OCCUPATIONAL GROUPS, SOME LITERARY AND POLITICAL FIGURES.

2488 PENTONY D.E. ED.
RED WORLD IN TUMULT: COMMUNIST FOREIGN POLICIES.

SAN FRANCISCO: CHANDLER, 1962, 296 PP.
COLLECTION OF ESSAYS CONCERNED WITH DYNAMIC MOVEMENT OF COMMUNIST EXPANSION AND ITS SIGNIFICANT MOMENTUM IN TWENTIETH CENTURY. EXAMINES DISPUTE BETWEEN CHINA AND RUSSIA AND APPEAL OF COMMUNISM IN UNDERDEVELOPED AREAS. STUDIES COMMUNIST PATTERNS OF WORLD ORGANIZATION.

2489 PERAZA SARAUSA F.
BIBLIOGRAFIAS CUBANAS.
WASHINGTON: GOVT PR OFFICE, 1945, 58 PP.
ANNOTATED BIBLIOGRAPHY OF BIBLIOGRAPHIES ON CUBA. ENTRIES DATE FROM 1861 THROUGH 1944. OFFERS BRIEF OUTLINE OF CUBA'S BIBLIOGRAPHICAL HISTORY. FIRST SECTION IS GENERAL BIBLIOGRAPHIES, SECOND IS BIBLIOGRAPHIES ACCORDING TO SUBJECT, THIRD IS PERSONAL BIBLIOGRAPHIES. 485 ENTRIES WITH ANNOTATIONS IN SPANISH. INCLUDES INDEX.

2490 PERAZA SARAUSA F. ED.
DIRECTORIO DE REVISTAS Y PERIODICOS DE CUBA.
GAINESVILLE: U OF FLA PR, 1964, 21 PP.
A LISTING OF CUBAN MAGAZINES AND NEWSPAPERS WITH DETAILED BIBLIOGRAPHIC INFORMATION. ITEMS ARE ARRANGED BY CUBAN PROVINCE AND CITY IN ALPHABETICAL ORDER FOR 1964 LISTING DATE FOUNDED, DIRECTOR, FREQUENCY, AND PRICE. INCLUDES SECTION ON CUBAN PUBLICATIONS PRODUCED OUTSIDE OF CUBA.

2491 PEREZ ORTIZ R. ED.
ANUARIO BIBLIOGRAFICO COLOMBIANO, 1961.
BOGOTA: INST CARO Y CUERVO, 1963, 178 PP.
COLOMBIAN BIBLIOGRAPHICAL ANNUAL FOR 1961 COVERING GENERAL PUBLICATIONS FOR THAT YEAR.

2492 PERKINS D., VAN DEUSEN G.G.
THE AMERICAN DEMOCRACY: ITS RISE TO POWER.
NEW YORK: MACMILLAN, 1964, 687 PP., LC#64-14963.
TRACES HISTORICAL DEVELOPMENT FROM THE NEW WORLD TO A WORLD POWER AND INVOLVEMENT WITH EUROPEAN AND LATIN AMERICAN POLITICS.

2493 PERKINS D.H.
"ECONOMIC GROWTH IN CHINA AND THE CULTURAL REVOLUTION(1960-APRIL 1967)"
CHINA Q., 30 (APR.-JUNE 67), 33-48.
QUESTIONS DEGREE TO WHICH ECONOMIC ISSUES HAVE BEEN MAJOR SOURCE OF CONFLICT WITHIN CHINESE COMMUNIST LEADERSHIP, AND WHETHER IMPACT OF EVENTS OF EARLY 1967 ON ECONOMY HAS BEEN GREAT ENOUGH TO REDUCE CHINA'S FUTURE RATE OF GROWTH. ANALYZES ECONOMIC GROWTH AND POLICY, 1958-65, AND FINDS THAT EXPERIENCES OF THOSE YEARS CONVINCED MANY PARTY LEADERS THAT SUSTAINED GROWTH WAS POSSIBLE.

2494 PERLMANN H.
"UPHEAVAL IN TURKEY."
MID. EAST. AFF., 11 (JUNE-JULY 60), 174-9.
DISCUSSES TENSIONS AND SENSITIVE RELATIONS AMONG MIDDLE EASTERN NATIONS, FOCUSING ON TURKEY BEFORE AND AFTER MILITARY COUP D'ETAT. SHOWS ATTEMPT TO ESTABLISH DEMOCRATIC FORM OF GOVERNMENT.

2496 PETERSON W.C.
THE WELFARE STATE IN FRANCE.
LINCOLN: U OF NEB PR, 1960, 115 PP., LC#60-61504.
ANALYZES EXTENT TO WHICH FRANCE SINCE WWII HAS BECOME WELFARE STATE OR HAS ATTEMPTED TO ALTER PATTERN OF INCOME DISTRIBUTION TO GIVE MORE PEOPLE EQUAL SHARE AND MINIMUM STANDARD OF LIVING. CONCENTRATES ON SHOWING HOW SOCIAL SECURITY SYSTEM HAS BECOME INSTRUMENT FOR REDISTRIBUTION OF INCOME. SHOWS HOW PATTERNS OF DISTRIBUTION ARE ALTERED AS RESULT OF GOVERNMENTAL WELFARE EXPENDITURES.

2497 PETRAS J.
"GUERRILLA MOVEMENTS IN LATIN AMERICA - I."
NEW POLITICS, 6 (WINTER 67), 80-94.
EXPLORES PARTICULAR HISTORICAL EXPERIENCES WHICH UNDERLIE GUERRILLA MOVEMENTS IN GUATEMALA, COLOMBIA, VENEZUELA, AND PERU. EXPLAINS EFFECT OF BREAKDOWN OF GOVERNMENT'S AUTHORITY ON SUCCESS OF MOVEMENTS AND CAUSES OF BREAKDOWNS. FINDS EACH GUERRILLA REVOLUTION HAS UNIQUE ASPECTS THAT REQUIRE SPECIAL CONSIDERATION.

2498 PHADINIS U. ED., MOORTHY S.D. ED.
DOCUMENTS ON ASIAN AFFAIRS: A SELECT BIBLIOGRAPHY.
NEW DELHI: INDIAN COUNCIL, 1959, 153 PP.
LIMITED TO DOCUMENTS AVAILABLE IN THE ENGLISH LANGUAGE AND ABOUT ASIAN COUNTRIES. INDICATES WHERE TEXTS OF THE DOCUMENTS CAN BE FOUND. DEALS WITH POLITICAL, ECONOMIC, AND SOCIAL AFFAIRS.

2499 PHELPS E.S. ED.
THE GOAL OF ECONOMIC GROWTH: SOURCES, COSTS, BENEFITS.
NEW YORK: W W NORTON, 1962, 176 PP., LC#62-20921.
ESSAYS ON WISDOM OF US GROWTH POLICIES, POSSIBILITY OF ACHIEVING GOALS THROUGH USE OF EXISTING RESOURCES, AND GOVERNMENT CONTROL OF GROWTH. VIEW PAST GROWTH IN US, AND ANALYZE POSSIBILITIES FOR THE FUTURE. COMPARE SOVIET AND US ECONOMIES. DESCRIBE METHODS THROUGH WHICH GROWTH IS ACHIEVED.

2500 PHILIPPINE ISLANDS BUREAU SCI
ETHNOLOGICAL SURVEY: THE BONTOC IGOROT.
MANILA: BUR OF PUBLIC PRINTING, 1905, 266 PP.
STUDY OF BONTOC AS TYPICAL OF PRIMITIVE MOUNTAIN FARMER TRIBE OF LUZON. MAINTAINS PEOPLE ARE PEACEFUL AND INDUSTRIOUS AND WILL ADVANCE FIRST SINCE THE RELIGIOUS, POLITICAL, ECONOMIC, AND SOCIAL INSTITUTIONS ARE DEMOCRATIC. STUDY MADE BY LIVING WITH TRIBE FOR SIX MONTHS.

2501 PHILIPPINE STUDIES PROGRAM
SELECTED BIBLIOGRAPHY ON THE PHILIPPINES, TOPICALLY ARRANGED AND ANNOTATED.
NEW HAVEN: HUMAN REL AREA FILES, 1956, 138 PP.
GENERAL PHILIPPINE BIBLIOGRAPHY WITH ANNOTATED REFERENCES TO IMPORTANT HISTORICAL, ECONOMIC, ANTHROPOLOGICAL, GOVERNMENTAL, AND RELIGIOUS WORKS ON THE PHILIPPINES.

2502 PHILLIPS C.S.
THE DEVELOPMENT OF NIGERIAN FOREIGN POLICY.
EVANSTON: NORTHWESTERN U. PR., 1964, 154 PP., $5.95.
FOREIGN POLICY DEVELOPMENTS FROM 1959 TO 1963. SPECIAL REFERENCE TO 1959 ELECTION, THE PERIOD BETWEEN THE ELECTION AND INDEPENDENCE IN OCTOBER 1960, AND THE CREATION OF THE REPUBLIC IN 1963. DETAILED ATTENTION TO INTERNAL STRUGGLE ATTENDENT UPON FOREIGN POLICY FORMATION.

2503 PHILLIPS O.H.
CONSTITUTIONAL AND ADMINISTRATIVE LAW (3RD ED.)
LONDON: SWEET AND MAXWELL, LTD, 1962, 855 PP.
EXAMINES ENGLISH LAW, INCLUDING ANALYSIS OF CONSTITUTION AND PARLIAMENT, CROWN AND CENTRAL GOVERNMENT, JUDICIAL SYSTEM, AND RIGHTS AND DUTIES OF CITIZENRY, AND ADMINISTRATIVE LAW AND RELATION TO COMMONWELATH.

2504 PHILLIPSON C.
THE INTERNATIONAL LAW AND CUSTOM OF ANCIENT GREECE AND ROME.
LONDON: MACMILLAN, 1911, 830 PP.
OFFERS A COMPREHENSIVE AND SYSTEMATIC ACCOUNT OF THE SUBJECT. TRIES TO REVEAL THE EXISTENCE OF A SYSTEM OF INTERNATIONAL LAW IN THE ANCIENT WORLD. WORK IS BASED ON GREEK AND ROMAN BASIC SOCIAL INSTITUTIONS.

2505 PICKERING J.F.
"RECRUITMENT TO THE ADMINISTRATIVE CLASS, 1960-1964: PART 2"
PUBLIC ADMINISTRATION, 45 (SUMMER 67), 169-199.
INVESTIGATES PERFORMANCE OF CANDIDATES IN TWO COMPETITIONS TO THE ADMINISTRATIVE CLASS OF THE CIVIL SERVICE. EMPLOYS DUAL METHOD OF ANALYSIS, EXAMINING AVERAGE MARKS OF CANDIDATES OF DIFFERING EDUCATIONAL BACKGROUND, AND IDENTIFYING FACTORS STRONGLY ASSOCIATED WITH PERFORMANCE IN OPEN COMPETITION.

2506 PICKLES D.
THE FIFTH FRENCH REPUBLIC.
NEW YORK: FREDERICK PRAEGER, 1960, 222 PP., LC#60-8738.
ANALYZES CONSTITUTION OF 4 OCT., 1958: ITS PURPOSES AND HOW THEY WERE ACHIEVED AFTER FIRST YEAR. AUTHOR ANALYZES POLITICAL CONTEXT OF CONSTITUTION TO CLARIFY WHY IT WAS CONTROVERSIAL BEFORE VOTED ON, THEN DESCRIBES ESSENTIAL PROVISIONS AND LAWS. FULL TEXT OF CONSTITUTION INCLUDED.

2507 PIDDINGTON R.
AN INTRODUCTION TO SOCIAL ANTHROPOLOGY (VOL. II)
LONDON: OLIVER & BOYD, 1957, 376 PP.
EXAMINES GEOGRAPHICAL INFLUENCE ON CULTURE, MATERIAL THINGS AND CULTURE, METHODS OF FIELD WORK, CULTURE AND PERSONALITY, AND CULTURAL CONTACT. ALSO STUDIES MORE COMPLEX SOCIETIES.

2508 PIERCE R.A.
RUSSIAN CENTRAL ASIA, 1867-1917: A SELECTED BIBLIOGRAPHY (PAMPHLET)
BERKELEY: U OF CALIF PR, 1953, 28 PP.
SELECTED LIST OF MATERIAL DESIGNED TO AID SPECIALISTS IN RESEARCH IN FIELD. MAIN STRESS IS ON DOMESTIC DEVELOPMENTS. ITEMS ARE ARRANGED BY SUBJECT CONTENT: HISTORY, RUSSIAN CONQUEST, ADMINISTRATION, WWI IMPACT, ECONOMICS, ETHNOGRAPHY, NATIVE LAW, CULTURAL DEVELOPMENT, EDUCATION, AND GEOGRAPHY. INCLUDES 483 ENTRIES.

2509 PIERCE R.A.
RUSSIAN CENTRAL ASIA, 1867-1917.
BERKELEY: U OF CALIF PR, 1960, 359 PP., LC#59-11314.
A SURVEY OF THE EXPANSION OF RUSSIA'S ASIAN FRONTIERS AND COLONIZATION OF THE BORDERLANDS WHICH OCCURRED BETWEEN 1867-1917. TREATS TERRITORIAL CONQUEST AND ADMINISTRATION IN TERMS OF STRUCTURE, ORGANIZATION, REFORM, AND DEVELOPMENT. DISCUSSES COLONIZATION, URBAN DEVELOPMENT, ECONOMIC DEVELOPMENT, AND THE CLASH OF EASTERN AND WESTERN CULTURES. CONCLUDES WITH COLLAPSE OF TSAR AND COLONIAL INHERITANCE.

2510 PIKE F.B. ED.
THE CONFLICT BETWEEN CHURCH AND STATE IN LATIN AMERICA.

NEW YORK: KNOPF, 1964, 239 PP., $2.50.
AN EXAMINATION OF THE ROOTS OF THE LONG-ENDURING CONFLICT BETWEEN CLERICAL AND ANTICLERICAL FORCES AND ITS IMPACTS UPON LATIN SOCIETY.

2511 PIKE F.B. ED.
FREEDOM AND REFORM IN LATIN AMERICA.
SOUTH BEND: U OF NOTRE DAME, 1967, 308 PP., LC#59-10417.
EXAMINES CHANGES SHAPING TRENDS IN LATIN AMERICA: DESIRE FOR INDIVIDUAL FREEDOM, SOCIAL AND ECONOMIC REFORM, AND RISE OF ARTICULATE MIDDLE CLASS. POINTS UP NECESSITY FOR FASTER ECONOMIC PROGRESS WITHIN FRAMEWORK OF TRADITIONAL WESTERN VALUES. DEFENDS FIGHTERS FOR FREEDOM. COVERS POPULATION PROBLEM AND ROLES OF CATHOLIC CHURCH AND US IN LATIN AMERICAN FREEDOMS AND REFORMS.

2512 PINNICK A.W.
COUNTRY PLANNERS IN ACTION.
SIDCUP, KENT, ENGL.: LAMBARDE PRESS, 1964, 128 PP
DISCUSSES COUNTRY PLANNING PROGRAM IN DORSET TO ILLUSTRATE DECISION-MAKING PROCESS, CONTROL OF EXPERTS BY POLITICIANS, AND DRASTIC NEED FOR CHANGE IN FINANCIAL BASIS OF PROGRAM. INCLUDES PROPOSAL TO BUILD NEW TOWN, METHODS BY WHICH INDUSTRY CREEPS INTO AREA TO AVOID BEING RESTRICTED, AND PLANNING FOR CHILDREN, LEISURE, AND AMENITIES. ATTEMPTS TO PROVIDE INFORMATION TO PUBLIC TO CHANGE ATTITUDES.

2513 PINTO F.B.M.
ENRIQUECIMENTO ILICITO NO EXERCICIO DE CARGOS PUBLICOS.
RIO DE JANEIRO: COM EDIT FORENSE, 1960, 411 PP.
ANALYZES CORRUPTION AND GRAFT OF PUBLIC OFFICIALS IN AMERICAS, WITH EMPHASIS ON BRAZIL. COMPARES LATIN AMERICAN COUNTRIES AND US. DISCUSSES CONSTITUTIONAL AND LEGAL CONTROL AND RESTRICTION ON PUBLIC OFFICIALS AND HOW THESE ARE VIOLATED. EXAMINES REASONS AND ETHICAL NORMS AS BASIS FOR DEVELOPING SYSTEM TO COMBAT ABUSE OF PUBLIC POWER AND POSITION.

2514 PIPES R.
THE FORMATION OF THE SOVIET UNION.
CAMBRIDGE: HARVARD U. PR., 1964, 365 PP., $7.95.
HISTORICAL ACCOUNT OF THE DISINTEGRATION OF THE RUSSIAN EMPIRE, AND ON ITS RUINS, THE ERECTION OF THE MULTINATIONAL COMMUNIST STATE.

2515 PIQUEMAL M.
"LES PROBLEMES DES UNIONS D'ETATS EN AFRIQUE NOIRE."
REV. JURID. POLIT. OUTREMER, 16 (JAN.-MARCH 62), 21-58.
EXPLORES PROBLEMS FACING DEVELOPING AFRICAN COUNTRIES. MAJOR DILEMMA IS WHETHER OR NOT TO ADOPT FEDERALIST SYSTEM. SHOWS SOCIAL STRATIFICATION OF OLD COLONIAL SYSTEMS. PRESENTS POLITICAL IDEOLOGIES OF AFRICAN LEADERS. DISCUSSES POSSIBILITIES FOR ECONOMIC UNION, AND ANALYZES FRANCE'S ROLE IN THIS PROJECT.

2516 PISTRAK L.
"SOVIET VIEWS ON AFRICA."
PROBL. COMMUNISM, 11 (MAR.-APR. 62), 24-31.
UNTIL 1955, SOVIET AFRICANISTS CONDEMNED NATIONALIST LEADERS AND MOVEMENTS AS 'PETTY-BOURGEOIS.' IN '55, AMENDED STALINIST THEORY ON COLONIAL REVOLUTION BY PROLETARIAT IN FAVOR OF KHRUSHCHEV'S 'PEACEFUL COEXISTENCE.' FIND NATIONAL-DEMOCRATIC STATE AN INTERMEDIATE POLITICAL SYSTEM.

2517 PITCHER G.M. ED.
BIBLIOGRAPHY OF GHANA.
KUMASI: LIBRARY KUMASI COL. OF TECHN, 1960,177 PP.
LISTING OF PUBLICATIONS ABOUT GHANA ISSUED BETWEEN 1957-59. ENTRIES ARRANGED UNDER BROAD HEADINGS; MANY HAVE BRIEF ANNOTATIONS. THE SOCIAL SCIENCES, HUMANITIES, AND NATURAL AND PHYSICAL SCIENCES ARE COVERED.

2518 PITTMAN J., PITTMAN M.
PEACEFUL COEXISTENCE.
NEW YORK: INTERNATIONAL PUBLRS, 1964, 156 PP., LC#64-8445.
DISCUSSES PEACEFUL COEXISTENCE IN THEORY AND PRACTICE IN SOVIET UNION WITH EMPHASIS ON ITS BEARING ON FOREIGN POLICY, MILITARY DOCTRINE, AND ATTITUDE OF RUSSIAN PEOPLE TOWARD US. CONSIDERS EFFECTS ON SINO-SOVIET RIFT ON COEXISTENCE ASPIRATIONS OF RUSSIA AND US.

2519 PLANCK C.R.
THE CHANGING STATUS OF GERMAN REUNIFICATION IN WESTERN DIPLOMACY, 1955-1966.
BALTIMORE: JOHNS HOPKINS PRESS, 1967, 65 PP., LC#67-22894.
ANALYZES BACKGROUND OF CURRENT DEVELOPMENTS IN STATUS OF GERMAN REUNIFICATION. EXAMINES MAJOR JUNCTURES IN EAST-WEST DIPLOMACY AFTER GERMANY JOINED NATO FROM PERSPECTIVE OF BONN'S EFFORTS TO REUNIFY. INCLUDES DISCUSSION OF GENEVA SUMMIT CONFERENCE, BERLIN CRISIS, KENNEDY'S AND DE GAULLE'S INITIATIVES IN EUROPE.

2520 PLANK J.N. ED.
CUBA AND THE UNITED STATES: LONG RANGE PERSPECTIVES.
WASHINGTON: BROOKINGS INST, 1967, 265 PP., LC#67-21483.
ANTHOLOGY CONSIDERS VARIOUS ASPECTS OF THE CUBAN SITUATION WITHIN A LONG-RANGE FRAMEWORK. DEALS WITH THE HISTORY OF US-CUBAN RELATIONS; THE SOURCES AND THE FOREIGN AND DOMESTIC CONSEQUENCES OF CASTRO'S REVOLUTION; BUSINESS AND ECONOMIC RELATIONS; HEMISPHERIC RELATIONS; EUROPEAN REACTIONS AND ATTITUDES; CASTRO AS PRODUCT AND AGENT OF THE COLD WAR; AND MILITARY AFFAIRS.

2521 PLANK J.N.
"THE CARIBBEAN* INTERVENTION, WHEN AND HOW."
FOREIGN AFFAIRS, 44 (OCT. 65), 37-48.
STRATEGIC IMPORTANCE, NATURE OF COMMUNIST THREAT, AND SOCIETAL STRENGTHS AND WEAKNESSES OF EL SALVADOR, GUATEMALA, PANAMA, NICARAGUA, COSTA RICA, HONDURAS, HAITI, DOMINICAN REPUBLIC, AND VENEZUELA ARE SKETCHED IN TERMS OF US INTERVENTION ALTERNATIVES. ADVOCATES DELAYED RESPONSE.

2522 PLATE H.
PARTEIFINANZIERUNG UND GRUNDESETZ.
BERLIN: DUNCKER & HUMBLOT, 1966, 139 PP.
DISCUSSES DUTY OF POLITICAL PARTIES TO REPORT FINANCIAL EXPENDITURES AND MAKES RECOMMENDATIONS THAT WOULD MAKE THE CONSTITUTIONAL REQUIREMENT A REALITY. CONTAINS MATERIAL ON INCOME OF PARTIES AND DISCUSSES VARIOUS PLANS TO FINANCE PARTIES.

2523 PLATO
APOLOGY" IN PLATO, THE COLLECTED DIALOGUES. ED. BY E. HAMILTON AND H. CAIRNS (TRANS. BY H. TREDENNICK)
NEW YORK: PANTHEON BOOKS, 1961.
PRESENTS SOCRATES' SPEECH AT HIS TRIAL IN DEFENSE OF HIS WAY OF LIVING AND HIS MISSION TO STING MEN LIKE A GADFLY. ANSWERS CHARGES OF CORRUPTING YOUTH AND OF BELIEVING IN GODS OTHER THAN THOSE OF WHICH STATE APPROVES. HE ACCEPTS HIS DEATH SENTENCE CALMLY AND CONFIDENTLY; FEELS THAT HIS LIFE HAS BEEN DEVOTED TO PUBLIC SERVICE AND BETTERING MEN AND STATE, EVEN THOUGH HE IS MISUNDERSTOOD.

2524 PLAYFAIR G., SINGTON D.
THE OFFENDERS: THE CASE AGAINST LEGAL VENGEANCE.
NEW YORK: SIMON AND SCHUSTER, 1957, 305 PP., LC#57-12403.
PRESENTS SIX CRIMINAL CASES TO SUPPORT FOLLOWING THESES: ALL PUNISHMENT BY KILLING IS WRONG; ABOLITION OF DEATH PENALTY MUST BE SOUGHT AS FIRST STEP IN PROGRAM OF PENAL REFORM; THROUGH PRACTICE OF DETERRENT-RETRIBUTIVE THEORY OF PUNISHMENT, SOCIETY VIOLATES INDIVIDUAL RIGHTS AND FAILS TO PROTECT ITSELF; CLINICAL OR CURATIVE APPROACH MUST BE TAKEN TO PROBLEM OF CRIME.

2525 PLAYFAIR R.L. ED.
"A BIBLIOGRAPHY OF ALGERIA."
LONDON: JOHN MURRAY, 1889.
PARTIALLY ANNOTATED BIBLIOGRAPHY OF WRITINGS IN FRENCH AND ENGLISH ON ALGERIA FROM THE EXPEDITION OF CHARLES THE FIFTH IN 1541 TO 1887. INCLUDES GEOGRAPHY, HISTORY, COMMENTARY ON PIRACY, NATURAL RESOURCES, TRAVEL, NATURE OF THE POPULUS, AND VARIOUS TOPICS IN ECONOMIC DEVELOPMENT DURING THE 19TH CENTURY.

2526 PLAYFAIR R.L. ED.
"A BIBLIOGRAPHY OF MOROCCO."
LONDON: JOHN MURRAY, 1893.
ANNOTATED BIBLIOGRAPHY OF WORKS IN VARIOUS LANGUAGES REGARDING MOROCCO FROM EARLIEST TIMES THROUGH THE END OF 1891. INCLUDES ROMAN AND GREEK WRITINGS AND EARLY EXPLORERS' ACCOUNTS OF GEOGRAPHY, THE PEOPLE, AND THEIR CULTURE. LATER WORKS INCLUDE HISTORY OF THE COUNTRY, ECONOMICS, SOCIAL CONDITIONS, RELIGION, LEADERS, MILITARY SUBJECTS, INTERNATIONAL RELATIONS, ETC.

2527 PLAZA G.
"FOR A REGIONAL MARKET IN LATIN AMERICA."
FOR. AFF., 34 (JULY 59), 607-16.
EVALUATES NEEDS OF GROWING MIDDLE CLASS AND EXPECTATIONS OF MASSES IN LATIN AMERICAN SOCIAL REVOLUTION NOW BEGINNING. SUGGESTS THAT ONLY ECONOMIC INTEGRATION WILL ALLOW EFFICIENT USE OF ECONOMIC AND POLITICAL RESOURCES.

2528 PLISCHKE E.
"INTEGRATING BERLIN AND THE FEDERAL REPUBLIC OF GERMANY."
J. OF POLITICS, 27 (FEB. 65), 35-65.
ANALYZES IN DETAIL WEST BERLIN RELATION WITH WEST GERMANY IN LEGAL, POLITICAL, ADMINISTRATIVE, AND FINANCIAL TERMS. ASSERTS THAT INTEGRATION REQUIRES EFFECTIVE GOVERNMENT AND VIABLE ECONOMY IN ORDER TO THWART EAST GERMAN PRESSURES AND CLAIMS ON IT.

2529 PLISCHKE E.
CONDUCT OF AMERICAN DIPLOMACY (3RD REV. ED.)
PRINCETON: VAN NOSTRAND, 1967, 677 PP.
EMPHASIZES PRINCIPLES, PROCEDURES, AND GOVERNMENTAL MACHINERY INVOLVED IN CONDUCT OF FOREIGN RELATIONS OF US. ANALYSIS OF ESSENCE, DEVELOPMENT, AND FUNCTION OF DIPLOMACY. INCLUDES DISCUSSION OF CHANGING TRENDS IN BASIC TOOLS OF MODERN DIPLOMACY, COLD WAR EFFECTS, AND PROBLEMS INVOLVED IN DIPLOMATIC PRACTICE.

2530 PLUMPTRE A.F.W.
"PERSPECTIVE ON OUR AID TO OTHERS."
INTERNATIONAL JOURNAL, 22 (SUMMER 67), 484-499.
DISCUSSES RAPID GROWTH OF CANADIAN FOREIGN AID PROGRAM AND CHANGES MADE SINCE WWII.

2531 POBEDONOSTSEV K.P.
REFLECTIONS OF A RUSSIAN STATESMAN.
ANN ARBOR: U OF MICH PR, 1965, 271 PP.
TRANSLATES WRITINGS OF ULTRA-CONSERVATIVE TSARIST ON RELATION OF CHURCH AND STATE, PRESS, LAW, THE CHURCH, POWER, AND DEMOCRACY. ORIGINALLY PUBLISHED IN 1896, NEW TRANSLATION GIVES INSIGHT INTO UPPER ECHELONS OF RUSSIAN MONARCHY AND ITS VIEWPOINT.

2532 POGANY A.H., POGANY H.L.
POLITICAL SCIENCE AND INTERNATIONAL RELATIONS, BOOKS RECOMMENDED FOR AMERICAN CATHOLIC COLLEGE LIBRARIES.
METUCHEN: SCARECROW PRESS, 1967, 387 PP., LC#67-10196.
UNANNOTATED LISTING OF 5,800 BOOKS PERTINENT TO POLITICAL SCIENCE AND INTERNATIONAL RELATIONS. ORGANIZED AROUND HISTORY OF WORLD POLITICAL THEORY, POLITICAL AND CONSTITUTIONAL HISTORY OF WORLD, GOVERNMENT ADMINISTRATION, POLITICAL ECONOMY, INTERNATIONAL LAW, AND INTERNATIONAL RELATIONS. ENTRIES PRINCIPALLY TAKEN FROM 1955-66 PERIOD. AUTHOR AND SUBJECT INDEX.

2533 POHLENZ M.
GRIECHISCHE FREIHEIT.
HEIDELBERG: QUELLE UND MEYER, 1955, 212 PP.
DISCUSSES RISE OF IDEA OF FREEDOM IN GREECE FROM PRE-CLASSICAL PERIOD TO STOICS. EXAMINES IMPACT OF PERSIAN WARS ON ITS DEVELOPMENT AND SEEKS TO ESTABLISH POLITICAL AND LEGAL CONCEPTS OF FREEDOM. DISCUSSES PROBLEM OF FREEDOM OF WILL AND DECISION; CONCLUDES WITH COMPARISON OF GREEK AND CHRISTIAN CONCEPTS OF FREEDOM.

2534 POLE J.R.
POLITICAL REPRESENTATION IN ENGLAND AND THE ORIGINS OF THE AMERICAN REPUBLIC.
NEW YORK: ST MARTIN'S PRESS, 1966, 606 PP.
SHOWS PARALLEL FORCES IN ENGLAND AND AMERICA WHICH GAVE RISE TO FORMATION OF MAJORITY RULE FUNDAMENTAL TO REPRESENTATIVE DEMOCRACY OF BOTH COUNTRIES. ILLUMINATES COALITION BETWEEN POWERFUL MERCANTILE INTERESTS AND CONCENTRATED URBAN MASSES.

2535 POLK W.R.
THE UNITED STATES AND THE ARAB WORLD.
CAMBRIDGE: HARVARD U PR, 1965, 320 PP., LC#65-16688.
THE ARAB AREA AND PEOPLES ARE INTRODUCED IN THE FRAMEWORK OF THE HISTORICAL FACTORS WHICH BIND THEM TOGETHER. THE IMPACT OF THE WEST ON THEM GENERALLY IS PRESENTED AND REINFORCED WITH A DESCRIPTION OF THEIR DEVELOPMENTAL PATTERNS INDIVIDUALLY. FROM THE ABOVE A PICTURE OF THE NEW ARAB IS FORMED UPON WHICH A SKETCH OF AMERICAN ACTIONS AND INTERESTS HAS BEEN DRAWN.

2536 POLLARD A.F.
THE EVOLUTION OF PARLIAMENT.
LONDON: LONGMANS, GREEN & CO, 1926, 398 PP.
EXAMINES ENGLISH PARLIAMENT, FACT AND MYTH. INCLUDES ANALYSIS OF ITS ROLE IN WORLD HISTORY, ITS DEVELOPMENT AND GROWTH, AND ITS IMPORTANCE TO THE BRITISH REALM. IS NOTABLY THOROUGH ON FORMATION AND GROWTH OF HIGH COURT DURING MEDIEVAL PERIOD. CONCLUDES WITH PLEA FOR FLEXIBILITY OF PARLIAMENTARY GOVERNMENT.

2537 POLLOCK F.
THE GENIUS OF THE COMMON LAW.
NEW YORK: COLUMBIA U PRESS, 1912, 141 PP.
EXAMINES HISTORY OF ENGLISH COMMON LAW TO DETERMINE ITS EFFECT ON MODERN ATTITUDES. MAINTAINS THAT COMMON LAW HAD NO SPECIFIC POINT OF BEGINNING AND THAT IT UNDERGOES CONSTANT CHANGE. ARGUES AGAINST FORMALISM AND SLAVISHNESS TO PRECEDENT. WARNS AGAINST HASTY BORROWING OF FOREIGN ELEMENTS OF LAW. DISCUSSES DANGER TO COMMON LAW, REMEDIES AND REFORM, AND COMMON LAW IN RELATION TO TRADE.

2538 POLLOCK F., MAITLAND F.W.
THE HISTORY OF ENGLISH LAW BEFORE THE TIME OF EDWARD I (2 VOLS, 2ND ED.)
BOSTON: LITTLE BROWN, 1898, 1379 PP.
COMPREHENSIVE STUDY FIRST CONCENTRATES ON PERIODS OF ENGLISH LEGAL HISTORY: ANGLO-SAXON, NORMAN, ROMAN-CANONICAL, AND THE AGES OF GLENVILL AND BRACTON. LONGER SECOND PART DEALS WITH DOCTRINES AND RULES: TENURE, SORTS AND CONDITIONS OF MEN, JURISDICTION AND COMMUNITIES, OWNERSHIP AND POSSESSION, CONTRACT FAMILY LAW, INHERITANCE, CRIME AND TORT, AND PROCEDURE. NEW CHAPTER I IN SECOND EDITION.

2539 POLLOCK J.K. ED.
GERMAN DEMOCRACY AT WORK.
ANN ARBOR: U OF MICH PR, 1955, 208 PP.
STUDY OF WEST GERMAN POLITICAL PROCESS AS SEEN IN 1953 ELECTIONS. EXAMINES POLITICAL PARTY ACTIVITY AND LOCAL AND NATIONAL VOTING BEHAVIOR.

2540 POLSKY N.
HUSTLERS, BEATS, AND OTHERS.
CHICAGO: ALDINE, 1967, 218 PP., LC#67-11415.
AMERICAN DEVIANT SOCIAL BEHAVIOR GROUPS DISCUSSED. DISCUSSES DECLINE OF AMERICAN POOLROOM AS RESULT OF CHANGES IN SOCIAL STRUCTURE. INTRODUCES THEORY OF "CRIME AS MOONLIGHTING" IN DISCUSSION OF POOL HUSTLERS. CRITICIZES NEGLIGENCE OF CRIMINOLOGY TEXTBOOKS IN SEVERAL AREAS. PRESENTS EMPIRICAL STUDY OF "BEAT" DELINQUENT SUBCULTURE AND DISCUSSES SOCIOLOGY OF PORNOGRAPHY.

2541 POMEROY W.J.
HALF A CENTURY OF SOCIALISM.
NEW YORK: INTERNATIONAL PUBLRS, 1967, 126 PP., LC#67-28137.
DISCUSSES STATE OF SOVIET SOCIETY AFTER ITS FIRST 50 YEARS, DECIDING THAT GREAT STRIDES HAVE BEEN MADE IN ALL FIELDS TOWARD INTEGRATING CULTURE, TECHNOLOGY, AND PERSONALITY IN USSR. CLAIMS TREND IS TOWARD PRODUCING COLLECTIVIST MENTALITY COUPLED WITH AN EXCELLENT GRASP OF TECHNOLOGY. FROM THIS, PREDICTS REALIZATION OF COMMUNIST SOCIETY WITHIN 50 YEARS.

2542 PONOMARYOV B.
"THE OCTOBER REVOLUTION - BEGINNING OF THE EPOCH OF SOCIALISM AND COMMUNISM."
WORLD MARXIST REV., 10 (NOV. 67), 45-58.
RETROSPECTIVE LOOK AT SIGNIFICANCE OF OCTOBER REVOLUTION, AND DISCUSSION OF PRESENT AND FUTURE STATUS OF SOCIALISM. CONSIDERS SOCIALISM THE HERITAGE OF THE REVOLUTION AND THE BASIS OF PROLETARIAN INTERNATIONALISM. SEES INTERNATIONALISM AS AIMED AT MUTUAL ASSISTANCE, SOLIDARITY, AND EFFORTS FOR PEACE. OPPOSES WAR AS A MARXIST-LENINIST METHOD. REJECTS STALINIST CULT OF INDIVIDUAL IN FAVOR OF PARTY LEADERSHIP.

2543 POPLAI S.L. ED.
NATIONAL POLITICS AND 1957 ELECTIONS IN INDIA.
NEW DELHI: METROPOLITAN BOOK, 1957, 172 PP.
EXAMINES PARTY ACTIVITIES BETWEEN ELECTIONS AND POLICY STATEMENTS OF MAJOR PARTIES CONCERNING ELECTIONS. ISSUES INCLUDE ECONOMY AND NATIONALISM.

2544 POPPINO R.E.
"IMBALANCE IN BRAZIL."
CURR. HIST., 44 (FEB. 63), 100-105.
CHRONIC POLITICAL INDECISION AND CONTINUED RAMPANT INFLATION HAS SERVED TO OBSCURE FACT THAT BRAZIL HAS PRESERVED OPEN POLITICAL SYSTEM AND BASICALLY FREE ECONOMY. OBSERVES THAT, DESPITE STRONG PRESSURES FROM LEFT AND RIGHT, EXTREMES OF MILITARY COUP D'ETAT AND SOCIAL REVOLUTION AVERTED.

2545 POSNER M.V., WOOLF S.J.
ITALIAN PUBLIC ENTERPRISE.
CAMBRIDGE: HARVARD U PR, 1967, 170 PP.
STUDIES THE HISTORY, GROWTH, AND ROLE OF STATE ENTERPRISE IN ITALY IN THE LAST 15 YEARS. TYPICAL EXAMPLES OF STATE ENTERPRISES ANALYZED AS TO STRUCTURE, CONTROL, FINANCE, AND PERFORMANCE.

2546 POUND R.
ORGANIZATION OF THE COURTS (PAMPHLET)
CHICAGO: AMER JUDICATURE SOC, 1914, 28 PP.
BRIEFLY TRACES HISTORY OF COURT SYSTEMS IN US, INCLUDING ORIGINS IN EUROPE AND DISTINCTIVE CHARACTER OF AMERICAN DEVELOPMENT. POINTS UP HISTORICAL CONDITIONS AND HERITAGE THAT CREATED ORGANIZATIONAL STRUCTURE PECULIAR TO AMERICAN SYSTEM AND SHOWS ADVANTAGES OF SUCH A STRUCTURE. PROPOSES CHANGES THAT WOULD CONCENTRATE JUDICIAL RESPONSIBILITY IN A CHIEF JUSTICE AND GIVE HIM CORRESPONDING POWER.

2547 POUND R.
INTERPRETATIONS OF LEGAL HISTORY.
NEW YORK: MACMILLAN, 1923, 170 PP.
STUDIES 19TH-CENTURY HISTORICAL SCHOOL OF JURISPRUDENCE, EXAMINING ETHICAL, POLITICAL, POSITIVIST, AND ECONOMIC INTERPRETATIONS OF LEGAL HISTORY. REJECTS ORGANISMIC MODEL OF LAW AND ASSUMPTION THAT A SINGLE CAUSE IS AT WORK IN LEGAL DEVELOPMENT. NOTES MIXTURE OF THE RATIONAL AND IRRATIONAL IN LAW. VIEWING LAW AS A BUILDING ERECTED AND CONTINUALLY ALTERED BY MEN, PROPOSES ENGINEERING INTERPRETATION.

2548 POUND R.
THE FORMATIVE ERA OF AMERICAN LAW.
BOSTON: LITTLE BROWN, 1938, 188 PP.
DISCUSSES JURISTIC THEORY AS PRACTICED IN COLONIAL AND POST-REVOLUTIONARY AMERICA. EXAMINES ORIGINS AND DEVELOPMENT OF CHIEF LEGAL AGENCIES FROM INDEPENDENCE TO CIVIL WAR. ANALYZES LEGAL PORTIONS OF FEDERAL AND STATE CONSTITUTIONS AND MAJOR REFORM MOVEMENTS. DISCUSSES INFLUENCES OF CLASS SELF-INTEREST AND INDIVIDUAL JUDICIAL PSYCHOLOGY ON THE FORMATION OF THE LAW.

2549 POWELL D.
"THE EFFECTIVENESS OF SOVIET ANTI-RELIGIOUS PROPAGANDA."

PUBLIC OPINION QUART., 31 (FALL 67), 366-380.
DISCUSSES VALUE OF SOVIET PROPAGANDA, STATING IT TO BE OF LITTLE OR NO USE IN AFFECTING CHANGES IN DEISTIC GROUPS. PROPOSES THAT ITS MAJOR VALUE IS IN REINFORCING BELIEFS OF ATHEISTS AND THEREBY INSURING THEIR SUPPORT. CLAIMS THAT RELIGION IS NO LONGER MAJOR TARGET OF THE PARTY.

2550 POWELL J.D.
"MILITARY ASSISTANCE AND MILITARISM IN LATIN AMERICA."
WESTERN POLITICAL Q., 18 (JUNE 65), 382-392.
SEES DILEMMA IN US DESIRES TO BLOCK COMMUNIST SUBVERSION IN LATIN AMERICA THROUGH THE PROVISIONING OF MILITARY ASSISTANCE PROGRAMS WHICH STRENGTHEN THE INTERNAL POLITICAL POSITION OF THE MILITARY, AND ALLIANCE GOALS OF FOSTERING "REPRESENTATIVE AND RESPONSIVE GOVERNMENTS." HIS DEVELOPMENTAL CLASSIFICATION SYSTEM AND DEFENSE STATISTICS LEND CREDENCE TO HIS POLICY PROPOSALS.

2551 POWELL R.L.
"COMMUNIST CHINA'S MILITARY POTENTIAL."
CURR. HIST., 47 (SEPT. 64), 136-142.
'DESPITE THEIR RECOGNIZED POWER (SHEER NUMBERS) ARMED FORCES SUFFER FROM A NUMBER OF IMPORTANT WEAKNESSES: NO NUCLEAR CAPABILITY AND NOT SELF-SUFFICIENT IN TERMS OF PRODUCTION OF CONVENTIONAL WEAPONS.'

2552 POWELSON J.P.
LATIN AMERICA: TODAY'S ECONOMIC AND SOCIAL REVOLUTION.
NEW YORK: MCGRAW HILL, 1964, 303 PP., LC#63-20719.
DISCUSSION OF LATIN AMERICAN ECONOMICS BY LATIN AND NORTH AMERICANS. STUDIES THE ECONOMIC REVOLUTION; INDIVIDUAL AND COLLECTIVE APPROACHES TO DEVELOPMENT; AGRARIAN REFORM; MONOPOLY; PRIMARY PRODUCTS; EXPERIENCES WITH COPPER, SUGAR, OIL, AND COFFEE; INFLATION; ECONOMIC INTEGRATION; FOREIGN AID; NATIONAL ECONOMIC PLANNING; AND REVOLUTION - OLD AND NEW.

2553 PRABHAKAR P.
"SURVEY OF RESEARCH AND SOURCE MATERIALS; THE SINO-INDIAN BORDER DISPUTE."
INT. STUDIES, 7 (JULY 65), 120-127.
ENTRIES DEAL WITH LEGAL CLAIMS OF THE DISPUTE, CHINESE GOALS IN THE AREA, AND THE IMPACT OF THE DISPUTE ON WORLD POLITICS. TREATS FOREIGN POLICY OF INDIA.

2554 PRASAD B.
THE ORIGINS OF PROVINCIAL AUTONOMY.
NEW DELHI: ATMA RAM & SONS, 1960, 288 PP.
HISTORICAL DISCUSSION OF RELATIONS BETWEEN CENTRAL GOVERNMENT AND PROVINCIAL GOVERNMENTS IN INDIA FROM 1860 TO 1919. EMPHASIS IS ON EVOLUTION OF DECENTRALIZATION IN ITS EARLY PHASES AND TRANSFER OF GOVERNMENT AND POLITICAL AUTHORITY TO POPULAR CONTROL IN PROVINCIAL FIELD.

2555 PRATT I.A.
MODERN EGYPT: A LIST OF REFERENCES TO MATERIAL IN THE NEW YORK PUBLIC LIBRARY.
NEW YORK: NY PUBLIC LIBRARY, 1929, 320 PP.
EXTENSIVE LIST OF WORKS DEALING WITH ASPECTS OF MODERN EGYPT. INCLUDES SECTIONS ON ANTHROPOLOGY AND ETHNOLOGY, GEOGRAPHY, HISTORY, GOVERNMENT, LAW, FOREIGN RELATIONS, ECONOMIC HISTORY, ETC. MATERIAL IS ARRANGED TOPICALLY BUT INCLUDES AUTHOR INDEX.

2556 PRELOT M.
"LA INFLUENCIA POLITICA Y ELECTORAL DE LA PRENSA EN LA FRANCIA ACTUAL."
REV. INST. CIENC. SOC., (NO.3, 64), 121-28.
ANALYZES OPPOSITION OF FRENCH PRESS TO THE MAJORITY PARTIES. DISCUSSES REASONS FOR DECLINING INFLUENCE OF PARTY PRESS AND FOR GROWTH OF AUDIO-VISUAL MEDIA. SUGGESTS WAYS TO REVIVE THE PRESS.

2557 PRESSE UNIVERSITAIRES
ANNEE SOCIOLOGIQUE.
PARIS: PR UNIV DE FRANCE.
BEGUN IN 1896, IT IS THE OLDEST PERIODICAL IN THE FIELD OF CURRENT SOCIOLOGY BIBLIOGRAPHIES. AN ANNUAL LISTING OF BOOKS INTERNATIONAL IN SCOPE, BUT STRESSING FRENCH WORKS. ARRANGED BY SUBJECT. ALSO PUBLISHED UNDER TITLE OF "ANNALES SOCIOLOGIQUES."

2558 PRESTHUS R.V.
"BEHAVIOR AND BUREAUCRACY IN MANY CULTURES."
PUBLIC ADMIN. REV., 19 (WINTER 59), 25-35.
"COMPARATIVE ADMINISTRATION NEEDS AN EXPLICIT SYNTHESIS BETWEEN CONCEPTUAL THEORY AND EMPIRICAL FIELD RESEARCH."

2559 PREVITE-ORTON C.W. ED., BROOKE Z.N. ED.
THE CAMBRIDGE MEDIEVAL HISTORY (8 VOLS.)
CAMBRIDGE: UNIVERSITY PRESS, 1936.
GENERAL HISTORY OF MIDDLE AGES WITH GENERAL BIBLIOGRAPHY, INDEX, AND PORTFOLIO OF ILLUSTRATIONS AND MAPS IN EACH VOLUME.

2560 PRICE A.G.
THE WESTERN INVASIONS OF THE PACIFIC AND ITS CONTINENTS.
LONDON: OXFORD U PR, 1963, 236 PP.
STUDIES INVASION OF PACIFIC TERRITORIES BY WESTERN WHITES AND VAST CHANGES IN CULTURE AND PHYSICAL LANDSCAPE WHICH RESULTED. DIVIDES PACIFIC TERRITORIES INTO SIX AREAS, AND EXAMINES SIMILARITIES AND DIFFERENCES IN INVASION OF EACH. EVALUATES WESTERN COLONIALISM AND EFFECTS IT HAS HAD ON PRESENT POLITICAL STRUCTURE OF THE TERRITORIES.

2561 PRICE D.K.
"THE PARLIAMENTARY AND PRESIDENTIAL SYSTEMS" (BMR)"
PUBLIC ADMIN. REV., 3 (FALL 43), 317-334.
EXAMINATION OF CLASSIC THEORY OF PARLIAMENTARY GOVERNMENT WITH A VIEW TO ITS INAPPLICABILITY TO US LEGISLATIVE-EXECUTIVE RELATIONS. CONTESTS ASSUMPTIONS THAT LEGISLATURE ALONE REPRESENTS THE PEOPLE AND THAT ADMINISTRATIVE OFFICIALS ARE RESPONSIBLE TO THE PEOPLE ONLY THROUGH THE LEGISLATURE. THIS RELATIONSHIP HANDICAPS BOTH LEGISLATIVE AND EXECUTIVE BRANCHES IN WORKING TOGETHER.

2562 PROEHL P.O.
FOREIGN ENTERPRISE IN NIGERIA.
CHAPEL HILL: U OF N CAR PR, 1965, 250 PP., LC#65-19387.
DISCUSSES LEGAL ENVIRONMENT FOR FOREIGN INVESTMENT IN NIGERIA IN CONTEXT OF POLITICAL, ECONOMIC, AND SOCIAL DEVELOPMENT. COVERS CONDITIONS OF LABOR, TAXATION, AND NATIONALIZATION.

2563 PROUDHON J.P.
IDEE GENERALE DE LA REVOLUTION AU XIXE SIECLE (1851)
ORIGINAL PUBLISHER NOT AVAILABLE, 1868, 320 PP.
BEGINS WITH CALL TO BOURGEOISIE TO HELP BRING ABOUT A REVOLUTION THAT WILL BE A BASIC RESTRUCTURING OF THE ECONOMICS OF SOCIETY RATHER THAN A POLITICAL REVOLUTION. REVOLUTION OF 1789 WAS NOT COMPLETE, BECAUSE IT WAS CONCERNED WITH GOVERNMENT RATHER THAN SOCIETY. REVOLUTION SHOULD BE BROUGHT ABOUT THROUGH WORKERS' ASSOCIATIONS. THEIR IMPORTANCE IS IN THEIR DENIAL OF GOVERNMENTAL RULE.

2564 OAU PROVISIONS SECTION
ORGANIZATION OF AFRICAN UNITY: BASIC DOCUMENTS AND RESOLUTIONS (PAMPHLET)
ADDIS ABABA: ORG OF AFRICAN UNITY, 1964, 79 PP.
CHARTER AND RESOLUTIONS CONCERNING PURPOSE, MEMBERSHIP, STRUCTURE, AND PROCEDURES OF THIS ORGANIZATION FOR PROMOTING EMERGING STATES OF AFRICA. RESOLUTIONS INCLUDE NUCLEAR TESTING, EDUCATION, ECONOMIC MEASURES, AND RELATIONSHIP TO UN AND OTHER NATIONS.

2565 PUFENDORF S.
LAW OF NATURE AND OF NATIONS (ABRIDGED)
ORIGINAL PUBLISHER NOT AVAILABLE, 1716, 339 PP.
"MORAL ENTITIES" WERE DESIGNED BY GOD FOR THE REGULATION OF HUMAN LIFE. THEY EXIST IN THE STATE, WHICH IS THAT CONDITION IN WHICH MEN ARE SETTLED FOR EXERCISE OF ACTIONS. POWER IS "THAT BY WHICH A MAN IS QUALIFIED TO DO A THING LAWFULLY AND WITH A MORAL EFFECT." DISCUSSES MORAL KNOWLEDGE AND ACTION, STATE OF NATURE, LAW OF NATURE, DUTY OF MAN TOWARD HIMSELF AND GOD, SELF-DEFENSE, TREATIES, AND SO ON.

2566 PUNDEEF M.V.
BULGARIA; A BIBLIOGRAPHIC GUIDE.
WASHINGTON: LIBRARY OF CONGRESS, 1965, 98 PP., LC#65-60006.
A BIBLIOGRAPHIC SURVEY AND LISTING OF 1,243 WORKS ABOUT BULGARIA, PRIMARILY IN BULGARIAN, GERMAN, RUSSIAN, AND FRENCH. CLASSIFIED INTO SEVEN CATEGORIES OF POLITICAL, HISTORICAL, CULTURAL, AND ECONOMIC INTEREST. MOST BOOKS POSTDATE 1930; EMPHASIS ON CURRENCY OF MATERIAL. LIBRARY OF CONGRESS COMPILATION.

2567 PYE L.W.
"THE NON-WESTERN POLITICAL PROCESS" (BMR)"
J. OF POLITICS, 20 (AUG. 58), 468-486.
OUTLINES AND ANALYZES 17 DOMINANT AND DISTINCTIVE CHARACTERISTICS OF THE NON-WESTERN POLITICAL PROCESS. CONTENDS THAT IT IS NECESSARY FOR SPECIALISTS ON DIFFERENT AREAS TO ADVANCE GENERALIZED MODELS OF THIS COMMON POLITICAL PROCESS; ONLY THEN, BY EXAMINING WAYS IN WHICH PARTICULAR NON-WESTERN COUNTRIES DIFFER FROM THE GENERALIZED MODELS, DOES IT BECOME POSSIBLE TO ENGAGE IN COMPARATIVE ANALYSIS.

2568 PYE L.W.
SOUTHEAST ASIA'S POLITICAL SYSTEMS.
ENGLEWOOD CLIFFS: PRENTICE HALL, 1967, 97 PP., LC#67-20230.
DISCUSSES NATURE AND FUNCTION OF SOUTHEAST ASIAN POLITICAL SYSTEMS, EMPHASIZING GEOGRAPHICAL, CULTURAL, AND IDEOLOGICAL DIVERSITY. NOTES GOVERNMENTAL STRUCTURE, PARTY SYSTEMS, AND LEADERSHIP. SEES FOUNDATIONS OF SYSTEMS IN HISTORY, SOCIAL STRUCTURE, IDEOLOGIES, AND HUMAN ECOLOGIES. COMMENTS ON PERFORMANCE OF GOVERNMENTS AND NOTES PROSPECTS AND PROBLEMS FOR FUTURE. COMPARES GOVERNMENTS AND SYSTEMS.

2569 PYLEE M.V.
CONSTITUTIONAL GOVERNMENT IN INDIA (2ND REV. ED.)
BOMBAY: ASIA PUBL HOUSE, 1965, 824 PP.
DISCUSSES RISE AND NATURE OF CONSTITUTIONAL GOVERNMENT IN

INDIA. EXAMINES FUNDAMENTAL RIGHTS, OPERATION OF NATIONAL AND STATE GOVERNMENTS, AND FEDERAL SYSTEM.

2570 PYRAH G.B.
IMPERIAL POLICY AND SOUTH AFRICA 1902-1910.
LONDON: OXFORD U PR, 1955, 272 PP.
DISCUSSES BRITISH IMPERIAL POLICY IN SOUTH AFRICA AFTER BOER WAR AND GRANTING RESPONSIBLE GOVERNMENT TO EX-BOER REPUBLICS AS LINK BETWEEN GLADSTONIAN IMPERIAL POLICY AND EMERGENCE OF COMMONWEALTH IDEA IN 1917.

2571 QUAISON-SACKEY A.
AFRICA UNBOUND: REFLECTIONS OF AN AFRICAN STATESMAN.
NEW YORK: PRAEGER, 1963, 174 PP., $4.95.
GHANA'S REPRESENTATIVE TO THE U.N. DISCUSSES THE AFRICAN INDEPENDENCE MOVEMENT, THE AFRICAN PERSONALITY, UNITY, NEUTRALISM AND NON-ALIGNMENT, AND AFRICA AND THE U.N. MAIN OBJECTIVE IS TO CORRECT THE IMAGE OF AFRICA AS A DARK CONTINENT INHABITED SOLELY BY SAVAGES.

2572 QUAN K.L. ED.
INTRODUCTION TO ASIA: A SELECTIVE GUIDE TO BACKGROUND READING.
WASHINGTON: LIBRARY OF CONGRESS, 1955, 214 PP., LC#54-60018.
BIBLIOGRAPHY "INTENDED TO HELP THE PUBLIC UNDERSTAND THE PROBLEMS AND ASPIRATIONS OF ASIA, THEIR CAUSES, THEIR HISTORICAL GROWTH, THEIR CULTURAL BACKGROUND, AND THEIR RELATIONS TO THE WEST." STANDARD AND AUTHORITATIVE WORKS ON ALL COUNTRIES IN ASIA ARE INCLUDED. LIMITED MOSTLY TO ENGLISH-LANGUAGE SOURCES; ANNOTATED.

2573 QUERARD J.M.
LA FRANCE LITTERAIRE (12 VOLS.)
PARIS: LIBRAIRIE FIRMIN-DIDOT & CIE., 1827.
EXTENSIVE AND COMPREHENSIVE BIBLIOGRAPHY ARRANGED BY AUTHOR LISTING BOOKS, TRANSLATIONS, AND OTHER WORKS BY FRENCH HISTORIANS, SCIENTISTS, AND MEN OF LETTERS, AS WELL AS FOREIGN WRITERS USING FRENCH. INCLUDES BIOGRAPHIC AND BIBLIOGRAPHIC INFORMATION FOR EACH ENTRY. COVERS CHIEFLY THE 17TH, 18TH, AND EARLY 19TH CENTURIES.

2574 QUESTER G.H.
"ON THE IDENTIFICATION OF REAL AND PRETENDED COMMUNIST MILITARY DOCTRINE."
J. OF CONFLICT RESOLUTION, 10 (JUNE 66), 172-179.
BASED ON "HONEST PERCEPTIONS OF STRATEGIC REALITY" STAGES AND PATTERNS OF RATIONALLY "FALSE STATEMENTS" CAN BE PREDICTED FOR NATIONS AS THEIR RELATIVE STRATEGIC CAPABILITIES CHANGE. SOVIET AND CHINESE STATEMENTS TEND TO CORROBORATE SUCH A MODEL.

2575 QUIGG P.W. ED.
AFRICA: A FOREIGN AFFAIRS READER.
NEW YORK: FREDERICK PRAEGER, 1964, 346 PP., LC#64-12589.
PROBLEMS OF EMERGING AFRICA, PAST AND PRESENT, EFFECTS OF COLONIALISM, EMERGING NATIONALISM, AND VIEWS OF NEW AFRICAN LEADERS ARE COVERED.

2576 QURESHI I.H.
THE STRUGGLE FOR PAKISTAN.
KARACHI: U OF KARACHI PRESS, 1965, 394 PP.
SURVEYS HISTORY OF MUSLIM-HINDU RELATIONS FROM 1857 TO SEPARATION AFTER WWII AND ESTABLISHMENT OF SEPARATE MUSLIM STATE.

2577 RADCLIFFE-BROWN A.R.
"ON THE CONCEPT OF FUNCTION IN SOCIAL SCIENCE" (BMR)"
AMERICAN ANTHROPOLOGIST, 37 (JULY-SEPT. 35), 394-402.
DISCUSSES FUNCTION IN HUMAN SOCIETY. INDICATES THAT THE FUNCTION OF ANY RECURRENT ACTIVITY IS THE PART IT PLAYS IN SOCIAL LIFE AS A WHOLE AND THE CONTRIBUTION IT MAKES TO AINTAINANCE OF STRUCTURAL CONTINUITY. COMPARES THIS CONCEPT OF FUNCTION WITH THAT OF SEVERAL ETHNOLOGISTS.

2578 RADIN P.
THE METHOD AND THEORY OF ETHNOLOGY.
NEW YORK: BASIC BOOKS, 1966, 278 PP., LC#66-23376.
DISCUSSES METHODS OF ANTHROPOLOGY OF PRIMITIVES FROM VIEWPOINT OF HUMANISM AND AIMS AT SPECIFYING RULES AND LIMITATIONS FOR IT, DISCUSSING TYPES OF OBSERVATION, CULTURE PATTERNS, AND EFFECT OF OBSERVER'S CULTURE ON HIS STUDIES.

2579 RAE D.
THE POLITICAL CONSEQUENCES OF ELECTORAL LAWS.
NEW HAVEN: YALE U PR, 1967, 173 PP., LC#67-24511.
EMPLOYS MATHEMATICAL TOOLS IN DEFINING RELATIONSHIP BETWEEN ELECTORAL SYSTEM AND POLITICS. STUDIES ELECTIONS 1945-65 IN 20 DEMOCRATIC NATIONS. FINDS THAT BOTH PROPORTIONAL AND PLURALITY SYSTEMS FAVOR FEWER LARGE PARTIES OVER MORE SMALL ONES. MEASURES PARTY FRACTIONALIZATION AND CATEGORIZES VARIOUS KINDS OF ELECTORAL LAWS.

2580 RAEFF M.
ORIGINS OF THE RUSSIAN INTELLIGENTSIA: THE EIGHTEENTH-CENTURY NOBILITY.
NEW YORK: HARCOURT BRACE, 1966, 248 PP., LC#66-19152.
STUDIES ELEMENTS SHAPING LIFE OF THE 18TH-CENTURY RUSSIAN NOBLEMAN. EXAMINES THE FAMILY, EDUCATION, RELATIONS TO OTHER INDIVIDUALS, AND EXPERIENCES AS AN ACTIVE MEMBER OF RUSSIAN SOCIETY. EMPHASIZES ROLE OF INTELLECTUAL EXPERIENCES ACQUIRED WITHIN FRAMEWORK. HISTORY BASED ON OFFICIAL GOVERNMENT SOURCES; MEMOIRS, DIARIES AND LETTERS; CONTEMPORARY LITERATURE; AND BIOGRAPHIES.

2581 RAGHAVAN M.D.
INDIA IN CEYLONESE HISTORY, SOCIETY AND CULTURE.
BOMBAY: ASIA PUBL HOUSE, 1964, 190 PP.
ANALYSIS OF SOCIAL AND CULTURAL RELATIONS BETWEEN INDIA AND CEYLON. DISCUSSES STRUCTURE OF CEYLONESE SOCIETY AND INFLUENCE OF INDIA ON RELIGION, LANGUAGE, ART, LAW, AND CUSTOMS.

2582 RAHNER H.
KIRCHE UND STAAT IM FRUHEN CHRISTENTUM.
MUNICH: KOSEL VERLAG, 1961, 493 PP.
DISCUSSES CHURCH-STATE RELATIONS FROM FIRST CENTURY TO GREAT SCHISM IN NINTH CENTURY. EXAMINES FREEDOM OF FAITH, SEPARATION OF CHURCH AND STATE POWERS, AND PROTESTS AGAINST POWER OF CHURCH. MANY DOCUMENTS.

2583 RAISON T.
WHY CONSERVATIVE?
BALTIMORE: PENGUIN BOOKS, 1964, 144 PP.
DISCUSSES TORY PARTY IN ENGLAND AND POLICIES WHICH ARE OPEN TO IT IN DEALING WITH CONTEMPORARY SOCIAL PROBLEMS. COVERS WELFARE, EDUCATION, DIPLOMACY, DEFENSE, AND ECONOMY, DEFENDING CONSERVATISM AS VIABLE ALTERNATIVE AND AS THE ONE WHICH WILL RESULT IN MOST SUCCESSFUL FORM OF DEMOCRACY.

2584 RAM J.
THE SCIENCE OF LEGAL JUDGMENT: A TREATISE...
ORIGINAL PUBLISHER NOT AVAILABLE, 1835, 146 PP.
STUDY OF THE COURTS OF WESTMINSTER HALL IN THE EARLY 19TH-CENTURY AND THE AUTHORITY AND PROCESSES BY WHICH LEGAL JUDGMENTS ARE PASSED. OUTLINES THE GENERAL PRINCIPLES OF ENGLISH LAW AND THE PRECEDENT ON WHICH DECISIONS ARE BASED. DISCUSSES METHODS OF PRACTICE AND THE DUTIES OF THE JUDGE. CIVIL LAW, CUSTOM OF MERCHANTS, THE CANON LAW, AND THE LAW OF NATIONS ARE GIVEN SPECIAL ATTENTION.

2585 RAMA C.M.
"PASADO Y PRESENTE DE LA RELIGION EN AMERICA LATINA."
CUADERNOS AMERICANOS, (JULY-AUG. 67), 25-43.
ASSERTS CHRISTIANITY IN LATIN AMERICA AND IMPORTANCE OF HER RESISTANCE OF WESTERN RELIGIONS. PRESENTS STATISTICS ON NUMBER OF CATHOLICS AND PROTESTANTS IN VARIOUS LATIN AMERICAN COUNTRIES. REVIEWS HISTORY OF CATHOLIC CHURCH IN LATIN AMERICA, STRUCTURE OF RELIGIOUS SOCIETY, AND EFFECTS OF POLITICS ON POLICIES OF CHURCH.

2586 RAMAZANI R.K.
"CHURCH AND STATE IN MODERNIZING SOCIETY: THE CASE OF IRAN."
AMER. BEHAV. SCI., 7(JAN. 64), 26-28.
ANALYSIS OF THE ACCOMODATION AND CONFLICT BETWEEN THE TRADITIONAL ISLAMIC HIERARCHY AND THE IRANIAN GOVERNMENTS THAT HAVE BEEN IN POWER FROM THE 16TH CENTURY TO THE PRESENT.

2587 RAMAZANI R.K.
THE MIDDLE EAST AND THE EUROPEAN COMMON MARKET.
CHARLOTTESVILLE: U. VA. PR., 1964, 152 PP., $3.75.
STUDIES ADVERSE EFFECT OF EEC ON MAJOR MIDDLE EASTERN EXPORTS: PETROLEUM, GRAINS, FRUIT, ETC. ALSO EXPLORES POSITIVE AND NEGATIVE REACTIONS TOWARD EEC: ATTEMPTS AT COOPERATION BY NON-ARAB COUNTRIES, OPPOSITION BY ARAB COUNTRIES.

2588 RAMUNDO B.A.
PEACEFUL COEXISTENCE: INTERNATIONAL LAW IN THE BUILDING OF COMMUNISM.
BALTIMORE: JOHNS HOPKINS PRESS, 1967, 262 PP., LC#67-12421.
EXPLORES SOVIET POSITION ON BASIC QUESTIONS OF INTERNATIONAL LAW AND LEGAL PROBLEMS. EXAMINES MANNER IN WHICH SOVIETS UTILIZE INTERNATIONAL LAW TO SUPPORT POLICY OBJECTIVES AND COMPARES WITH OTHER COUNTRIES. FOCUSES ON IMPACT OF LAW OF PEACEFUL COEXISTENCE UPON CONCEPTS OF INTERNATIONAL LAW. ILLUSTRATES HOW PRINCIPLES OF PEACEFUL COEXISTENCE ARE USED TO SUPPORT SPECIFIC SOVIET POLICIES.

2589 RANDALL F.B., RANDALL L.
"COMMUNISM IN THE HIGH ANDES."
PROBL. COMMUNISM, 1 (JAN-FEB 61).
POINTS OUT FAILURE OF COMMUNISM TO MAKE HEADWAY IN PERU, BOLIVIA AND ECUADOR AFTER WW 2 IN LIGHT OF POVERTY, CLASS-STRUGGLE AND OTHER SIGNS OF READINESS FOR TAKE-OVER. TWO REASONS CITED ARE LACK OF CONCENTRATION ON COUNTRY AND ALIENATION OF INTELLECTUALS BY ANTI-PEASANT ATTITUDE OF COMMUNISTS.

2590 RANDALL F.B.
STALIN'S RUSSIA.
LONDON: MACMILLAN, 1965, 328 PP., LC#65-18559.
CONSIDERS ALL ASPECTS OF STALIN'S RULE, INCLUDING BIO-

GRAPHICAL MATERIAL, AS IT TRANSFORMED RUSSIA FROM AGRARIAN TO INDUSTRIAL STATE.

2591 RANNEY A.
THE DOCTRINE OF RESPONSIBLE PARTY GOVERNMENT.
URBANA: U OF ILLINOIS PR, 1962, 176 PP., LC#53-5225.
CONSIDERS PROBLEM OF INSURING RESPONSIBILITY IN AMERICAN PARTY GOVERNMENT. CLAIMS EXTENDED TERM OF OFFICE MEANS POLITICIANS ARE NOT DIRECTLY AND IMMEDIATELY ANSWERABLE FOR THEIR ACTION AND RAISE PROBLEMS OF CONTROL. DISCUSSES PAST POLITICAL THEORY ON REPRESENTATION AND WEIGHS MERITS OF ALTERNATIVE SYSTEMS.

2592 RAO K.V.
PARLIAMENTARY DEMOCRACY OF INDIA.
CALCUTTA: WORLD PRESS LTD, 1961, 369 PP.
CRITICAL STUDY OF INDIAN DEMOCRACY FOCUSES ON BOTH LEGAL AND POLITICAL PROVISIONS OF INDIAN CONSTITUTION. APPRAISES EXTENT TO WHICH CONSTITUTION HAS ENABLED ESTABLISHMENT OF DEMOCRATIC REPUBLIC IN INDIA. EXAMINES WORKING OF EXECUTIVE STRUCTURE, PARLIAMENT, AND COURT SYSTEMS UNDER PROVISIONS OF CONSTITUTION. ADVOCATES IMMEDIATE ATTENTION TO THOSE PROVISIONS THAT REQUIRE AMENDMENT.

2593 RAPHAEL M.
PENSIONS AND PUBLIC SERVANTS.
HAGUE: MOUTON & CO, 1964, 171 PP.
STUDY OF DEVELOPMENT OF PENSION AND ANNUITY PROGRAMS FOR BRITISH PUBLIC SERVANTS. EXAMINES ADMINISTRATIVE PROBLEMS AND STRUCTURE OF PAST AND PRESENT SYSTEM.

2594 RAPPARD W.E.
THE GOVERNMENT OF SWITZERLAND.
PRINCETON: VAN NOSTRAND, 1936, 164 PP.
GENERAL SURVEY OF ORIGINS AND NATURE OF POLITICAL TRADITIONS IN SWITZERLAND. DESCRIBES GEOGRAPHICAL, ETHNIC, LINGUISTIC, AND RELIGIOUS INFLUENCES. TRACES EVOLUTION OF SWISS GOVERNMENT FROM LOOSE CONFEDERACY OF SOVEREIGN STATES INTO FEDERAL UNION SIMILAR IN MANY ASPECTS TO US'S. SPECIAL MENTION IS MADE OF POLICY OF NEUTRALITY AND SWISS ROLE IN WWI AND IN LEAGUE OF NATIONS.

2595 RATZEL F.
ANTHROPO-GEOGRAPHIE.
STUTTGART: VON ENGELHORN, 1882, 506 PP.
STUDY OF THE INFLUENCE OF THE PHYSICAL ENVIRONMENT ON THE NATURE OF MAN AND HIS SOCIAL AND POLITICAL EXPRESSIONS. DISCUSSION OF NATIONAL BOUNDARIES, DISTRIBUTION OF HUMAN SETTLEMENTS, THE ROLE OF SEAS AND OCEANS, PLUS A DISCUSSION OF THE ANIMAL AND PLANT WORLD.

2596 RAUM O.
"THE MODERN LEADERSHIP GROUP AMONG THE SOUTH AFRICAN XHOSA."
SOCIOLOGUS, 17 (WINTER 67), 115-130.
TRACES HISTORY OF LEADERSHIP OF S. AFRICAN XHOSA FROM BEGINNINGS OF XHOSA CONTACT WITH WHITES. BEFORE 1870, THREE IMAGINATIVE INDIVIDUALS WERE SUCCESSIVE LEADERS, AND THEIR ROLES WERE NOT INSTITUTIONALIZED. AFTER 1870, AS CONTACT BECAME MORE SIGNIFICANT, AGENTS AND INTERPRETERS ASSUMED LEADERSHIP. FROM 1920, TEACHERS AND CLERGY BECAME ACCEPTED LEADERS, AND ARE TODAY, ALONG WITH DOCTORS AND LAWYERS.

2597 RAVKIN A.
THE NEW STATES OF AFRICA (HEADLINE SERIES, NO. 183((PAMPHLET)
NEW YORK: FOREIGN POLICY ASSN, 1967, 63 PP., LC#67-25598.
INTRODUCTION TO SITUATION AND PROBLEMS OF NEWLY-INDEPENDENT AFRICAN STATES, INCLUDING POLITICAL, ECONOMIC, AND SOCIAL ASPECTS. AFRICA EQUIPPED NEITHER TO ACCEPT MODERN WORLD ORDER NOR TO CHANGE IT.

2598 RAWLINSON H.G.
INDIA: A SHORT CULTURAL HISTORY.
NEW YORK: APPLETON, 1938, 452 PP.
HISTORY OF INDIAN PEOPLE, CONCENTRATING ON THEIR LITERATURE, ART, CONTACTS WITH OTHER CULTURES. COVERS PRE-HISTORY TO MODERN TIMES, WITH LITTLE EMPHASIS UPON BRITISH PERIOD. LOOKS UPON INDIA AS UNIQUE AND IMPORTANT CONTRIBUTOR TO WORLD CULTURE. INCLUDES EXTENSIVE BIBLIOGRAPHY OF PRIMARY AND SECONDARY SOURCE MATERIAL, MUCH OF IT IN SANSKRIT AND OTHER INDIAN LANGUAGES.

2599 RAY A.
INTER-GOVERNMENTAL RELATIONS IN INDIA: A STUDY OF INDIAN FEDERALISM.
NEW YORK: TAPLINGER PUBL CO, 1966, 184 PP.
COMPREHENSIVE ANALYSIS OF INDIAN FEDERAL SYSTEM. DISCUSSES CONSTITUTIONAL AND ACTUAL OPERATIONAL RELATIONS BETWEEN THE CENTRE AND THE STATES. ANALYZES HISTORICAL SETTING OF INDIAN FEDERATION, AND COMPARES INDIAN EXPERIENCE TO THAT OF WEST GERMANY, US, SWITZERLAND, CANADA, AND USSR.

2600 RAY J.
"THE EUROPEAN FREE-TRADE ASSOCIATION AND ITS IMPACT ON INDIA'S TRADE."
INT. STUDIES, 3 (JULY 61), 25-44.
TRACES EVENTS LEADING UP TO THE FORMATION OF THE EUROPEAN FREE TRADE AREA. HISTORY OF INDIA'S TRADE WITH COUNTRIES OF THE PACT IS ANALYZED WITH STRESS ON HER EXPORTS TO ENGLAND. SURVEYS EFFECTS ON INDIA'S FUTURE TRADE WITH THESE NATIONS FROM POINT OF VIEW OF TARIFF, INCREASED PRODUCTIVITY AND INCOME OF THE MEMBER NATIONS.

2601 RAZAFIMBAHINY J.
"L'ORGANISATION AFRICAINE ET MALGACHE DE COOPERATION ECONOMIQUE."
REV. JURID. POLIT., 17 (APR.-JUNE 1962), 177-201.
STUDIES STRUCTURE OF ORGANIZATION OF AFRICAN STATES AND MADAGASCAR FOR ECONOMIC COOPERATION. STUDIES ITS METHODS OF ACHIEVING ECONOMIC, TECHNICAL, SCIENTIFIC AND CULTURAL COOPERATION BETWEEN DEVELOPING AFRICAN COUNTRIES. EVALUATES CURRENT PROGRAMS AND ACHIEVEMENTS TO DATE.

2602 READ J.S.
"CENSORED."
TRANSITION, 7 (AUG.-SEPT. 67), 37-41.
UGANDAN PUBLICATION DISCUSSES CENSORSHIP IN AFRICA. IMPORTED BOOKS MAY BE BANNED ON THE BASIS OF A MINISTER'S SUBJECTIVE JUDGMENT IN MOST COUNTRIES. IN SOME, BLANKET BANS MAY BE IMPOSED ON BOTH NATIVE AND FOREIGN AUTHORS AND PUBLISHERS. DISCUSSES PHILOSOPHY OF, AND AFRICAN HISTORY OF, CENSORSHIP. LAMENTS THE EFFECT OF STRICTNESS ON LONG-DELAYED FLOWERING OF AFRICAN LITERATURE.

2603 READ M.
EDUCATION AND SOCIAL CHANGE IN TROPICAL AREAS.
LONDON: THOMAS NELSON & SONS, 1956, 130 PP.
COLLECTION OF ESSAYS UNIFIED BY COMMON APPLICATION OF METHODS OF SOCIAL ANTHROPOLOGY TO EDUCATIONAL PROBLEMS. STUDIES IMPACT OF NEW IDEAS, WAYS OF LIVING, AND METHODS OF WORKING ON PEOPLES WHO HAVE EXISTED FOR SEVERAL CENTURIES IN A TRADITIONAL CULTURAL SETTING. EMPHASIS ON MANNER IN WHICH NEW IDEAS ARE PRESENTED, AND RECEPTION GIVEN NEW IDEAS IN TERMS OF CHANGING PATTERNS OF LIVING.

2604 REAMAN G.E.
THE TRAIL OF THE BLACK WALNUT.
SCOTTDALE: HERALD PRESS, 1957, 256 PP.
STUDIES SETTLEMENT OF UPPER CANADA, ESPECIALLY ONTARIO, BY PENNSYLVANIA GERMANS WHO MIGRATED THERE SHORTLY AFTER 1776. INCLUDES DISCUSSION OF MINORITY GROUPS THAT MIGRATED TO AMERICA, AND EXAMINES CONTRIBUTIONS OF SUCH GROUPS TO AMERICAN AND CANADIAN CULTURE.

2605 REDFIELD R.
THE FOLK CULTURE OF YUCATAN.
CHICAGO: U OF CHICAGO PRESS, 1942, 416 PP.
SUMMARIZES FIELD WORK DONE ON FOLK CULTURE OF YUCATAN PENINSULA. AUTHOR DEMONSTRATES CONNECTIONS BETWEEN HIS DATA AND GENERAL SOCIOLOGICAL THEORIES. COMPARES TRIBAL VILLAGE, PEASANT VILLAGE, TOWN, AND CITY. MAINTAINS THAT IN THAT ORDER THEY ARE PROGRESSIVELY LESS ISOLATED AND HOMOGENEOUS, LESS TRADITIONAL, AND SHOW MORE SECULARIZATION AND INDIVIDUALIZATION OF BEHAVIOR.

2606 REDFIELD R.
THE PRIMITIVE WORLD AND ITS TRANSFORMATIONS.
ITHACA: CORNELL U PRESS, 1953, 185 PP.
DISCUSSES CHANGES CIVILIZATION MADE IN MANKIND. DEFINES CIVILIZATION AS "MODIFICATION AND TRANSFORMATION OF PRIMITIVE LIFE." CONCEIVES OF PASSAGE FROM PRECIVILIZED TO CIVILIZED LIFE AS A CONTINUOUS PROCESS IN WHICH MAN BREAKS DOWN AND REBUILDS HIMSELF - HIS WAYS OF THINKING, HIS SELF-MANAGEMENT, AND HIS ETHICAL JUDGMENTS.

2607 REED W.A.
ETHNOLOGICAL SURVEY PUBLICATIONS (VOL. II)
MANILA: PHILIPPINE BUR SCIENCE, 1904, 199 PP.
ETHNOLOGICAL STUDY OF NEGRITO PYGMIES OF ZAMBALES IN PHILIPPINE ISLANDS. PROVIDES ANTHROPOLOGICAL DATA, CULTURAL AND SOCIAL CHARACTERISTICS, AND DESCRIPTIONS OF RELIGIOUS RITUALS. ALSO CONTAINS MATERIAL ON DIALECT OF NABOLOI TRIBE OF BENGUET AND ON BATAK TRIBE OF PALAWAN.

2608 REES D.
THE AGE OF CONTAINMENT.
NEW YORK: ST MARTIN'S PRESS, 1967, LC#67-10650.
ANALYSIS OF RECENT POLITICAL HISTORY AS RELATING TO CONFLICT BETWEEN USA & USSR REFERRED TO AS COLD WAR. COVERS ALL MAJOR EVENTS SINCE WW2 AND EXPLAINS BRIEFLY FORMULATION OF US POLICY, UPS AND DOWNS OF INTERNATIONAL TURMOIL. SEES FUNDAMENTAL REASON AS MARXIST PHILOSOPHY OF SOVIET LEADERS O SEE COMMUNISM AS WAVE OF THE FUTURE. CHRONOLOGICAL TABLE.

2609 REICH N.
LABOR RELATIONS IN REPUBLICAN GERMANY.
NEW YORK: OXFORD U PR, 1938, 292 PP.
TREATS EMPLOYER-EMPLOYEE RELATIONSHIPS, 1918-1933, IN WEIMAR REPUBLIC. STUDIES COLLECTIVE ORGANIZATION OF INDUSTRIAL RELATIONS WITHIN FRAMEWORK OF TRADITIONAL POLITICAL DEMOCRACY. ANALYZES ECONOMIC PROVISIONS OF WEIMAR CONSTITUTION, ROLE OF LABOR IN THE REPUBLIC, ARBITRATION METHODS,

ORGANIZATION WITHIN THE SHOPS, AND ULTIMATE FAILURE OF THE REPUBLIC.

2610 REISCHAUER R.
"JAPAN'S GOVERNMENT--POLITICS."
LONDON: THOMAS NELSON & SONS, 1939.
EXAMINES FUNDAMENTALS OF JAPANESE POLITICAL THEORY AND EVOLUTION OF STATE FROM PRIMITIVE TRIBAL FORM TO STRONGLY CENTRALIZED GOVERNMENT OF 20TH CENTURY. ANALYZES POLITICAL AND CULTURAL SIGNIFICANCE OF POLICY OF "THE IMPERIAL WAY." LENGTHY DISCUSSION OF ORGANIZATION OF JAPANESE GOVERNMENT IN 1939. SHORT SELECT BIBLIOGRAPHY IN ENGLISH.

2611 REISKY-DUBNIC V.
COMMUNIST PROPAGANDA METHODS.
NEW YORK: PRAEGER, 1961, 287 PP., $6.00.
LISTS METHODS AND OBJECTIVES OF CULTURAL POLICY. TRACES INTELLIGENTSIA STRUGGLE WITHIN UNIVERSITIES. PROBLEM OF CULTURAL CO-EXISTENCE WITH WEST IS DISCUSSED. COMPREHENSIVE BIBLIOGRAPHY AND INDEX OF MARXIST LITERATURE INCLUDED.

2612 REISS I.
"LE DECLENCHEMENT DE LA PREMIERE GUERRE MONDIALE."
REV. HIST., 2 (OCT - DEC 64), 415-26.
HISTORY OF PERIOD FROM JUNE 28 TO AUGUST 4, 1914 AND THE EVENTS WHICH TOOK PLACE IN THOSE DAYS WHICH RESULTED IN THE OUTBREAK OF WAR. EMPHASIZES GUILT OF GERMANY FOR THE RESULTING CONFLICT.

2613 REISS J.
GEORGE KENNANS POLITIK DER EINDAMMUNG.
BERLIN: COLLOQUIUM VERLAG, 1957, 100 PP.
EXAMINES BASIC CONTENT OF KENNAN'S FORMULATION OF POLICY OF CONTAINMENT. DISCUSSES RISE OF POLICY AND ITS APPLICATION IN TRUMAN DOCTRINE, MARSHALL PLAN, NATO, RIO PACT, ETC. STUDIES CHARACTER OF SOVIET SYSTEM, AIMS AND TACTICS OF BOLSHEVISM, AND BRIEFLY DISCUSSES POLICY OF LIBERATION.

2614 REMAK J.
THE GENTLE CRITIC: THEODOR FONTANE AND GERMAN POLITICS, 1848-1898.
SYRACUSE: SYRACUSE U PRESS, 1964, 104 PP., LC#64-16920.
ANALYZES GERMAN SOCIETY AND POLITICAL THOUGHT IN SECOND HALF OF 19TH CENTURY ACCORDING TO FONTANE, GERMAN NOVELIST OF PERIOD. COVERS FONTANE'S LIFE AND POLITICAL DEALINGS BEFORE STUDYING PEOPLE IN THEIR ROLES IN SOCIETY - JUNKERS, VICARS, ETC. ANALYZES BISMARCK IN DETAIL AND RELATIONSHIP BETWEEN PRUSSIA AND HIS EMPIRE. UNLIKE MOST GERMAN CRITICS, FONTANE GIVES FAVORABLE VIEW OF THIS PERIOD.

2615 RENFIELD R.L.
"A POLICY FOR VIETNAM."
YALE REV., 56 (SUMMER 67), 481-505.
CRITICIZES PREMISES OF US POLICY IN VIETNAM. CALLS "CONTAINMENT" OUTDATED AND THE DOMINO THEORY NAIVE. QUESTIONS THE WISDOM OF US UNWILLINGNESS TO NEGOTIATE WITH THE NLF AND US WILLINGNESS TO UNDERWRITE THE SOUTHERN MILITARY REGIME. URGES US TO OVERCOME ITS OBSESSION WITH IDEOLOGY. ARGUES STRONGLY THAT US POLICY SHOULD DEFINITELY BE REASSESSED AND REVERSED.

2616 RENNER K.
MENSCH UND GESELLSCHAFT - GRUNDRISS EINER SOZIOLOGIE (2ND ED.)
VIENNA: VERL WIENER VOLKSBUCHH, 1965, 398 PP.
DISCUSSES PRINCIPLES OF HUMAN SOCIETY FROM SOCIOLOGICAL POINT OF VIEW. EXAMINES FAMILY STRUCTURE, LIFE PROCESSES AND CONSCIOUSNESS, RELATION OF INDIVIDUAL TO SOCIETY, LAW AND STATE, AND WAR AND POST-WAR ECONOMIC CONDITIONS.

2617 RESHETAR J.S.
PROBLEMS OF ANALYZING AND PREDICTING SOVIET BEHAVIOR.
NEW YORK: DOUBLEDAY, 1955, 69 PP.
EXAMINES THE IDEOLOGICAL AND CULTURAL APPROACHES TO SOVIET BEHAVIOR, DISCUSSES ESTIMATES OF SOVIET CAPABILITIES AND SETS DOWN THE LIMITS OF RELIABLE KNOWLEDGE ABOUT THE SOVIET UNION. INSISTS THAT STUDY OF SOVIET BEHAVIOR CANNOT BE CONFINED TO STUDY OF RUSSIAN PEOPLE, BUT MUST TAKE COGNIZANCE OF INFLUENCE OF OTHER SLAVIC PEOPLES.

2618 RESHETAR J.S. JR.
A CONCISE HISTORY OF THE COMMUNIST PARTY OF THE SOVIET UNION (REV. ED.)
NEW YORK: FREDERICK PRAEGER, 1964, 372 PP., LC#64-23544.
HISTORY OF RUSSIA'S COMMUNIST PARTY, BEFORE AND AFTER REVOLUTION; INCLUDES GROWTH FROM FACTION TO PARTY, SEIZURE OF POWER, LENINISM IN PRACTICE, STALINISM, AND STALIN'S HEIRS.

2619 REYNOLDS B.
MAGIC, DIVINATION AND WITCHCRAFT AMONG THE BAROTSE OF NORTHERN RHODESIA.
BERKELEY: U OF CALIF PR, 1963, 181 PP.
ANTHROPOLOGICAL STUDY OF PRACTICES, TOOLS, PERSONALITIES, AND EFFECTS OF MAGICAL PRACTICES AMONG A RHODESIAN TRIBE.

2620 RHODESIA-NYASA NATL ARCHIVES
A SELECT BIBLIOGRAPHY OF RECENT PUBLICATIONS CONCERNING THE FEDERATION OF RHODESIA AND NYASALAND (PAMPHLET)
SALISBURY: NAT ARCH RHODES NYAS, 1960, 13 PP.
UNANNOTATED CLASSIFIED BIBLIOGRAPHY OF POST-1950 PUBLICATIONS IN ENGLISH. COVERS OFFICIAL PERIODICAL PUBLICATIONS, GOVERNMENT PUBLICATIONS ON SPECIAL TOPICS, NEWSPAPERS, PERIODICALS, AND BOOKS. SELECTIONS CONCERN SUBJECTS OF HISTORICAL, POLITICAL, ECONOMIC, GEOLOGICAL, AND ANTHROPOLOGICAL INTEREST.

2621 RICHARDSON H.G., SAYLES G.O.
THE ADMINISTRATION OF IRELAND 1172-1377.
DUBLIN: IRISH MANUSCRIPTS COMN, 1963, 300 PP.
EXAMINATION OF IRISH ADMINISTRATION, 1172-1377, WITH DESCRIPTION OF EACH IMPORTANT OFFICE AND BRANCH OF GOVERNMENT, INCLUDING LISTS OF MINISTER, IRISH TREASURER'S ACCOUNTS, AND ILLUSTRATIVE DOCUMENTS.

2622 RICHERT F.
DIE NATIONALE WELLE.
STUTTGART: SEEWALD VERLAG, 1966, 206 PP.
TRACES EVOLUTION OF RADICAL RIGHT IN GERMAN POLITICS FROM BISMARCK TO PRESENT. EXAMINES ITS ANTI-PARLIAMENTARIANISM, CULTURAL NATIONALISM, AND WILLINGNESS TO SACRIFICE HUMAN FREEDOM IN NAME OF NATIONAL UNITY. EXAMINES ROLE AND IDEOLOGICAL ORIENTATION OF NATIONAL DEMOCRATIC PARTY IN WEST GERMAN POLITICS.

2623 RICHMAN B.M.
"CAPITALISTS & MANAGERS IN COMMUNIST CHINA."
HARVARD BUSINESS REV., 45 (JAN. 67), 57-78.
AUTHOR REPORTS ON PERSONAL VISIT TO COMMUNIST CHINA IN 1966. ARTICLE COMMENTS ON MANY AREAS OF CHINESE PRODUCTION. CONCLUDES THAT CHINESE IDEOLOGY, THOUGH MORE FLEXIBLE THAN SOVIET POLICY IN PAST, STILL OBSTRUCTS PROGRESS, AND THAT CHINESE ECONOMY MUST SUPPLY MANAGERS WITH EFFECTIVE PERSONAL INCENTIVES. ESPECIALLY INTERESTING IS THE REPORT ON THE 300,000 CAPITALIST MANAGERS PERMITTED TO SUPERVISE INDUSTRY.

2624 RIDLEY C.E., NOLTING O.F.
THE CITY-MANAGER PROFESSION.
CHICAGO: U OF CHICAGO PRESS, 1934, 143 PP.
DESCRIBES INCREASINGLY TECHNICAL NATURE OF CITY GOVERNMENT AND CONSEQUENT NEED TO HAVE TECHNICIANS ABLE TO ADMINISTER A CITY. TRACES HISTORY OF IDEA OF A CITY-MANAGER AND MAKES SUGGESTIONS HOW BEST A CITY MIGHT SELECT HIM.

2625 RIDLEY F., BLONDEL J.
PUBLIC ADMINISTRATION IN FRANCE.
LONDON: ROUTLEDGE & KEGAN PAUL, 1964, 336 PP.
DETAILED DESCRIPTION OF FRENCH ADMINISTRATIVE ORGANIZATION, FUNCTIONS, POWERS. COMPARES EFFECT ON REPRESENTATIVENESS OF ADMINISTRATION OF FRENCH TECHNOCRATIC AND BRITISH LIBERAL IDEOLOGIES.

2626 RIES J.C.
THE MANAGEMENT OF DEFENSE: ORGANIZATION AND CONTROL OF THE US ARMED SERVICES.
BALTIMORE: JOHNS HOPKINS PRESS, 1964, 212 PP., LC#64-18122.
REAPPRAISAL OF DEFENSE ORGANIZATION. FAVORS COMMITTEE METHOD OF ORGANIZATION--CONCLUDING THAT AMERICAN POLITICAL ENVIRONMENT DEMANDS PLURALISTIC DEFENSE STRUCTURE WHICH ALLOCATES RESPONSIBILITY IN KEEPING WITH AUTHORITY. URGES RATIONALIZATION OF DECISION-MAKING AND RESTORATION OF ORGANIZATIONAL EQUILIBRIUM.

2627 RIESENBERG P.N.
INALIENABILITY OF SOVEREIGNTY IN MEDIEVAL POLITICAL THOUGHT.
NEW YORK: COLUMBIA U PRESS, 1956, 204 PP., LC#56-5425.
EXAMINES INFLUENCE OF SOVEREIGN INALIENABILITY UPON DEVELOPMENT OF NATIONAL MONARCHIES DURING MIDDLE AGES, INCLUDING CONCEPT OF OFFICE AND RESPONSIBILITY, CONTINUITY, REVOCATION, AND THE "INTELLECTO."

2628 RIESMAN D.
"SOME QUESTIONS ABOUT THE STUDY OF AMERICAN CHARACTER IN THE TWENTIETH CENTURY."
ANN. ACAD. POL. SOC. SCI., 370 (MAR. 67), 36-47.
SAYS WORK ON AMERICAN CHARACTER IS FRAGMENTARY. DISCUSSES WHAT IS AMERICAN ABOUT AMERICA, NATIONAL CHARACTER FOR MEN AND WOMEN, ETHNIC AND SOCIAL CLASS DIFFERENCES, THE ROLE OF THE MASS MEDIA, POCKETS OF RESISTANCE TO CHANGE, NATIONAL CHARACTER AND INSTITUTIONS, CHANGE IN AMERICAN CHARACTER, AND NATIONAL CHARACTER IN RELATION TO POLITICS AND FOREIGN POLICY.

2629 RIESMAN D., RIESMAN E.T.
CONVERSATIONS IN JAPAN: MODERNIZATION, POLITICS, AND CULTURE.
NEW YORK: BASIC BOOKS, 1967, 371 PP., LC#67-17861.
PORTRAIT OF CONTEMPORARY JAPANESE SOCIETY. CONSISTS PRIMARILY OF CONVERSATIONS AND DIALOGUES BETWEEN THE AUTHORS AND LEADING INTELLECTUALS AND PROMINENT FIGURES IN JAPAN'S CULTURAL, ACADEMIC, POLITICAL, AND BUSINESS LIFE. ALMOST A TRAVELOGUE IN DIALOGUE, EMPHASIZES THE YOUNG, THE NEW, AND

THE MODERN IN JAPAN.

2630 RINGHOFER K.
STRUKTURPROBLEME DES RECHTES.
VIENNA: MANZSCHE VERLAGS, 1966, 101 PP.
EXAMINES PROBLEM OF NATIONAL AND STATE CITIZENSHIP IN FEDERAL REPUBLIC OF AUSTRIA. DISCUSSES VARIOUS CITIZENSHIP LAWS AND THEIR APPLICABILITY, AND THE CONCEPT OF NATIONAL INTEREST IN AWARDING OF NATIONAL CITIZENSHIP.

2631 RINTELEN F.
"L'HOMME EUROPEEN."
TABLE RONDE, 181 (FEB. 63), 123-38.
STATES THAT SPIRITUAL SOURCES OF EUROPEAN MAN ARE CLASSIC HUMANISM AND CHRISTIAN HERITAGE. SHOWS HOW FAITH IN SUPREMACY OF SPIRIT, DUALISM, AND LIBERTY CONSTITUTE HIS ESSENTIAL CHARACTER. POINTS OUT THAT TENDENCY TO SEPARATE THE PROBLEMS OF LIBERTY FROM ITS THEOLOGICAL BASIS IS THREATENING EUROPEAN UNITY FOUNDED ON COMMON HERITAGE.

2632 RIPLEY W.Z.
A SELECTED BIBLIOGRAPHY OF THE ANTHROPOLOGY AND ETHNOLOGY OF EUROPE.
NEW YORK: APPLETON, 1899, 160 PP.
NEARLY 2,000 TITLES IN ALL EUROPEAN LANGUAGES ON PRE-HISTORIC ARCHAEOLOGY, HISTORICAL ETHNOLOGY, AND PHYSICAL ANTHROPOLOGY PUBLISHED 1850-98. INDEXED BY AUTHOR, PUBLISHING DATE. ALSO INCLUDES SOME TITLES IN DEMOGRAPHY, FOLKWAYS, GEOGRAPHY, AND TRAVEL. REFERENCES CONTAINED ARE TO BOOKS AND PERIODICALS.

2633 RISTIC D.N.
YUGOSLAVIA'S REVOLUTION OF 1941.
UNIVERSITY PARK: PENN STATE U PR, 1966, 175 PP., LC#66-18191
STUDY OF YUGOSLAVIAN COUP D'ETAT OF MARCH, 1941, WRITTEN BY AN EYEWITNESS. DISCUSSES FACTORS WHICH SHAPED YUGOSLAV PUBLIC OPINION: TRADITIONAL ANTI-GERMANISM, SYMPATHY WITH HEROISM OF US AND ENGLAND, AND DESIRE TO AVOID FATE OF POLAND AND FRANCE. SHOWS HOW MANY YUGOSLAVIANS RESISTED AXIS PRESSURE TO SIGN TRIPARTITE PACT. RECORDS MAJOR PERSONALITIES AND ISSUES OF THE COUP.

2634 RIVKIN A.
"AFRICAN ECONOMIC DEVELOPMENT: ADVANCED TECHNOLOGY AND THE STAGES OF GROWTH."
J. HUM. REL., 8 (SUMMER 60), 617-645.
CONCERNED WITH BASIC PROBLEM AREAS OF AFRICAN ECONOMIC DEVELOPMENT (INCLUDING AGRICULTURE, MINING, TRANSPORTATION, AND LABOR), AND ROLE ADVANCED FREE WORLD TECHNOLOGY CAN PLAY IN ENSURING FREEDOM AND INDEPENDENCE OF AFRICAN STATES. POINTS OUT DANGERS OF EXCESSIVE RAPIDITY IN GROWTH, AND INCORPORATING TECHNOLOGY INTO CULTURAL PROCESSES OF AFRICA.

2635 RIVKIN A.
THE AFRICAN PRESENCE IN WORLD AFFAIRS.
NEW YORK: MACMILLAN, 1963, 304 PP., LC#63-13542.
DISCUSSES MAJOR IDEOLOGICAL ASPECTS OF POLITICAL REVOLUTION IN AFRICAN STATES SOUTH OF SAHARA IN 1950'S. EMPHASIZES PROBLEMS OF POLITICAL GROWTH AND ECONOMIC CHANGE AND THEIR INFLUENCE ON STATES' INTERNATIONAL ROLES. POINTS OUT IMPORTANCE OF CLOSE AMERICAN ATTENTION TO INTERNAL DYNAMICS OF STATES' ECONOMIC AND POLITICAL STRUGGLES TO ENSURE THEIR ALIGNMENT WITH FREE WORLD.

2636 RIVLIN B. ED., SZYLIOWICZ J.S. ED.
THE CONTEMPORARY MIDDLE EAST* TRADITION AND INNOVATION.
NEW YORK: RANDOM HOUSE, INC, 1965, 576 PP., LC#64-18229.
OVER 50 ARTICLES BY WESTERN AND MIDDLE EASTERN SCHOLARS FOCUSES ON POLITICAL, SOCIAL, AND CULTURAL CHANGE.

2637 RIZK C.
LE REGIME POLITIQUE LIBANAIS.
PARIS: PICHON ET DURAND-AUZIAS, 1966, 170 PP.
ANALYZED MODERN ECONOMIC, POLITICAL, AND SOCIAL STRUCTURE OF LEBANON. DISCUSSES COMBINATION OF ARAB AND WESTERN CULTURES AND OUTLOOKS IN FORMATION OF PRESENT ECONOMY AND POLITICAL ORGANIZATION. EXAMINES POLITICAL PARTIES AND ADMINISTRATIVE PATTERNS IN ACTION TODAY. ALSO COVERS RELATIONSHIP OF MOSLEM AND CHRISTIAN GROUPS IN MAINTAINING FUNCTIONING NATIONAL GOVERNMENT.

2638 ROBBINS J.J.
THE GOVERNMENT OF LABOR RELATIONS IN SWEDEN.
CHAPEL HILL: U OF N CAR PR, 1942, 361 PP.
STUDIES METHODS OF SETTLING LABOR DISPUTES BEFORE WWII IN SWEDEN AND RELATIONSHIP OF GOVERNMENT TO LABOR AND INDUSTRY DISPUTES, ADVANCING FROM SIMPLE ADVISORY BARGAINING IN CONTRACT SETTLEMENTS TO JURISPRUDENCE OF LABOR COURT. ALSO DISCUSSES PROBLEMS OF INSTITUTIONAL AUTONOMY IN DEMOCRACY WITHOUT DENYING PROTECTION OF LAW.

2639 ROBBINS L.
THE THEORY OF ECONOMIC POLICY IN ENGLISH CLASSICAL POLITICAL ECONOMY.
NEW YORK: ST MARTIN'S PRESS, 1952, 217 PP.
BRIEF SURVEY OF CLASSICAL BRITISH ECONOMIC POLICY AND ITS EFFECTS AND INTERACTIONS WITH PRESENT POLICY. COMPARISON OF IT WITH OTHER THEORIES OF ITS PERIOD AND ROLE OF POLITICAL IDEOLOGY IN INFLUENCING ECONOMIC POLICY.

2640 ROBERT H.M.
PARLIAMENTARY LAW.
NEW YORK: CENTURY CO, 1923, 588 PP.
GENERAL DISCUSSION OF METHODS OF TRANSACTING BUSINESS IN PARLIAMENTARY BODIES - CONDUCT OF ELECTIONS, DUTIES OF MEMBERS, BY-LAWS, MOTIONS, ETC. INCLUDES ANSWERS TO QUESTIONS ON PARLIAMENTARY LAW AND DEFINITIONS OF PARLIAMENTARY TERMS.

2641 ROBERTS H.L.
RUSSIA AND AMERICA.
NEW YORK: NEW AMERICAN LIB, 1956, 251 PP., LC#55-11968.
BASED UPON DISCUSSIONS OF STUDY GROUP AT COUNSEL ON FOREIGN RELATIONS, 1953-55. REPORT RESTS UPON FAITH IN DEMOCRATIC PROCESS AS MEANS OF MEETING COMPLEX PROBLEMS CONFRONTING THE US IN THIS CENTURY. DISCUSSED ARE THE COMMUNIST THREAT, VARIOUS ASPECTS OF US FOREIGN POLICY, AND AREAS OF CONFLICT: GERMANY, EASTERN EUROPE, AND SOUTHEAST ASIA.

2642 ROBERTS S.H.
HISTORY OF FRENCH COLONIAL POLICY.
LONDON: KING, 1929, 741 PP.
HISTORICALLY REVIEWS THE FIFTY YEARS OF FRENCH COLONIZATION AND DISCUSSES THE THEORIES BEHIND THE MOVEMENT. ANALYZES ITS ECONOMIC,POLICAL AND ADMINISTRATIVE PROBLEMS. INCLUDES A STUDY OF FRENCH EMPIRE SINCE 1914.

2643 ROBERTS HL
FOREIGN AFFAIRS BIBLIOGRAPHY, 1952-1962.
NEW YORK: RR BOWKER, 1964, 752 PP., LC#33-7094.
A SELECTED AND ANNOTATED CUMULATIVE BIBLIOGRAPHY OF BOOKS ON INTERNATIONAL RELATIONS BASED LARGELY UPON NOTES APPEARING QUARTERLY IN "FOREIGN AFFAIRS." RETAINS SCHEMATIC CLASSIFICATION OF EARLIER VOLUMES: GENERAL INTERNATIONAL RELATIONS, THE WORLD SINCE 1914, AND THE WORLD BY REGIONS, EMPHASIZING ANALYTICAL, CHRONOLOGICAL, AND REGIONAL TREATMENTS RESPECTIVELY. LIMITED TO WORKS PUBLISHED FROM 1953-62.

2644 ROBERTSON A.H.
THE LAW OF INTERNATIONAL INSTITUTIONS IN EUROPE.
NEW YORK: OCEANA, 1961, 140 PP.
DISCUSSES THE 'EUROPEAN IDEA' (ITS POLITICAL SIGNIFICANCE AND IDEOLOGICAL CONNOTATION) AND TRACES HISTORICAL DEVELOPMENT OF THIS CONCEPT THROUGH MAJOR TREATIES, CONFERENCES AND COOPERATIVE ORGANIZATIONS. ASSIGNS SPECIAL PLACE FOR HUMAN RIGHTS IN COUNCIL OF EUROPE PHILOSOPHY.

2645 ROBERTSON A.H.
HUMAN RIGHTS IN EUROPE.
MANCHESTER: U. PR., 1963, 280 PP.
ANALYZES EUROPEAN CONVENTION TEN YEARS AFTER ITS CONCEPTION, FOCUSING ON THE APPLICATION OF THE IDEALS SET FORTH IN THE CHARTER. STUDIES THE VARIOUS BODIES CREATED TO CARRY OUT THE DOCTRINES, AND, USING CASE STUDIES, DRAWS CONCLUSIONS AS TO THE EFFICACY OF THE ORGANIZATION AS A GUARANTOR OF HUMAN RIGHTS.

2646 ROBERTSON D.H., DENNISON S.
THE CONTROLS OF INDUSTRY.
LONDON: JAMES NISBET & CO, 1960, 158 PP.
DISCUSSES PROBLEMS OF PRODUCTION, DISTRIBUTION, AND GOVERNMENT CONTROL IN CONTEMPORARY SOCIETY. EXAMINES STRUCTURE OF ECONOMIC ORGANIZATION FOR UTILIZING RESOURCES, ATTEMPTING TO FIND OUT HOW IT WORKS TO ASCERTAIN HOW BEST IT MAY BE CONTROLLED. SPECIFIES DISTINQUISHING CHARACTERISTICS OF MODERN INDUSTRY AND ANALYZES THEM FUNCTIONALLY.

2647 ROBERTSON H.M.
SOUTH AFRICA, ECONOMIC AND POLITICAL ASPECTS.
DURHAM: DUKE U PR, 1957, 192 PP., LC#57-08817.
VIEWS EFFECT OF APARTHEID ON ECONOMIC DEVELOPMENT, POLITICAL PARTIES, DEVELOPMENT OF CONSTITUTIONALISM, AND LEGISLATION. INCLUDES BACKGROUND FOR SOCIO-ECONOMIC ANALYSIS OF RACE RELATIONS IN PARTICULAR CASE STUDIES.

2648 ROBINSON A.D.
DUTCH ORGANIZED AGRICULTURE IN INTERNATIONAL POLITICS, 1945-1960.
THE HAGUE: NIJHOFF, 1962, 192 PP.
AN ANALYSIS OF THE NATURE AND PARTICIPATION OF PRESSURE GROUPS IN SEVERAL FOREIGN ISSUES OF EUROPEAN UNITY.

2649 ROBINSON E.A.G.
ECONOMIC CONSEQUENCES OF THE SIZE OF NATIONS.
NEW YORK: ST MARTIN'S PRESS, 1960, 447 PP.
ANALYSIS OF RELATION OF SIZE OF NATIONS TO THEIR ECONOMIC PROSPERITY. DISCUSSES SIZE IN RELATION TO ECONOMIC EFFICIENCY, ADAPTABILITY, AND STABILITY AND TO PROBLEMS OF EXECUTIVE ADMINISTRATION AND TO FOREIGN AID POLICIES.

2650 ROBINSON T.W.
"A NATIONAL INTEREST ANALYSIS OF SINO-SOVIET RELATIONS."

INTL. STUDIES Q., 11 (JUNE 67), 135-175.
APPLIES HANS MORGENTHAU'S NATIONAL-INTEREST FORMULATION TO SINO-SOVIET RELATIONS TO STUDY APPLICATION OF TRADITIONAL THEORY TO COMMUNIST WORLD. DISCUSSES NATIONAL INTEREST THEORY IN DETAIL; INQUIRES INTO NATIONAL INTERESTS OF CHINA AND USSR, RELATION OF POWER AND INTEREST, AND INFLUENCE OF NUCLEAR WEAPONS ON INTERESTS. ANALYZES SINO-SOVIET ALLIANCE IN TERMS OF COUNTRIES' NATIONAL INTERESTS.

2651 ROBINSON W.C.
"URBANIZATION AND FERTILITY: THE NON-WESTERN EXPERIENCE (BMR)"
MILBANK MEMORIAL FUND QUART., 41 (JULY 63), 291-308.
EMPIRICAL INVESTIGATION OF RELATIONSHIP BETWEEN URBANIZATION AND FERTILITY IN LESSER-DEVELOPED NATIONS. OUTLINES GENERALLY ACCEPTED POSITION ON THIS QUESTION; EXAMINES THIS POSITION CRITICALLY IN LIGHT OF RECENT DATA; AND SUGGESTS CONCLUSIONS THAT REQUIRE A SUBSTANTIAL MODIFICATION OF PRESENT VIEW ON THE BASIS OF STATISTICAL DIFFERENTIALS.

2652 ROCHE J.
LA COLONISATION ALLEMANDE ET LE RIO GRANDE DO SUL.
RIO DE JANEIRO: INST ETUD AM LAT, 1959, 683 PP.
EXAMINES GERMAN IMMIGRATION TO AND COLONIZATION OF SOUTHERN BRAZIL, SPECIFICALLY STATE OF RIO GRANDE DO SUL. COVERS EARLY COLONISTS FROM 1824 TO POSTWAR GERMAN REFUGEES. ANALYZES THEIR INFLUENCE ON ECONOMIC AND POLITICAL CHANGE AND DEVELOPMENT IN SOUTH AND ON NATIONAL LEVEL.

2653 ROCHE J.P.
COURTS AND RIGHTS: THE AMERICAN JUDICIARY IN ACTION (2ND ED.)
NEW YORK: RANDOM HOUSE, INC, 1961, 143 PP., LC#66-14886.
TREATS STRUCTURE OF AMERICAN FEDERAL AND STATE JUDICIAL SYSTEM, FREQUENTLY CONTRASTING IT WITH BRITISH AND FRENCH SYSTEMS FOR EMPHASIS. DISCUSSES PLACE OF CITIZEN - HIS FREEDOMS AND RIGHTS IN LEGAL PROCESSES. PROVIDES OVERVIEW OF DEVELOPMENT OF BRITISH LAW, WITH REFERENCES.

2654 ROCHET W.
"THE OCTOBER REVOLUTION AND THE STRUGGLE OF THE FRENCH COMMUNISTS."
WORLD MARXIST REV., 10 (NOV. 67), 23-30.
CONSIDERS OCTOBER REVOLUTION SIGNIFICANT IN PROVING THAT WORKING CLASS CAN BUILD SOCIALISTIC STATE. BELIEVES RUSSIAN EXPERIENCE HAS MADE TRANSITION TO SOCIALISM EASIER FOR OTHER COUNTRIES. OBJECTS TO FRENCH BOURGEOISIE AND STATE MONOPOLIES. WANTS PEACEFUL TRANSITION TO SOCIALISM IN FRANCE BY WAY OF "GENUINE DEMOCRACY." NOTES RELATION BETWEEN FRENCH COMMUNIST AND SOCIALIST PARTIES AND NEED FOR SOLIDARITY.

2655 RODNICK D.
THE NORWEGIANS: A STUDY IN NATIONAL CULTURE.
WASHINGTON: PUBLIC AFFAIRS PRESS, 1955, 165 PP., LC#55-8570.
DESCRIBES NORWEGIAN NATIONAL CULTURE. BASED ON INTERVIEWS WITH NATIVES THROUGHOUT NORWAY IN HOMES, SCHOOLS, AND GROUP ACTIVITY AREAS IN 1950. ENCOMPASSES ATTITUDES, FAMILY, VARYING AGE GROUPS, URBAN AND RURAL LIFE, RELIGIOUS PATTERNS, AND POLITICAL TRENDS.

2656 RODRIGUEZ M.
CENTRAL AMERICA.
ENGLEWOOD CLIFFS: PRENTICE HALL, 1965, 178 PP., LC#65-14996.
INTERPRETIVE ESSAYS ON CENTRAL AMERICAN HISTORY AND ITS RELATION TO PRESENT POLITICAL AND SOCIAL REALITIES. NATIONALISM, COLONIALISM, SOCIALISM, AND DEMOCRACY AND THEIR SIGNIFICANCE IN CENTRAL AMERICA ARE DISCUSSED.

2657 ROELOFS H.M.
THE LANGUAGE OF MODERN POLITICS: AN INTRODUCTION TO THE STUDY OF GOVERNMENT.
HOMEWOOD: DORSEY, 1967, 380 PP., LC#67-21006.
INTRODUCTORY TEXT STUDIES POLITICS AS THE ACTIVITY OF POLITICIANS TALKING TO ONE ANOTHER RATHER THAN AS DECISION-MAKING PROCESS OR INSTITUTIONAL ARRANGEMENT. DEFINES NATURE OF POLITICAL TALK AND DISCUSSES NATION-STATE, WORK OF JUDGES AND ADMINISTRATORS, AND VARIATIONS IN STYLE AND DIRECTION. COMPARES DIFFERENT STATES AND CLOSES WITH TALK OF INTERNATIONAL POLITICS.

2658 ROGERS C.B.
THE SPIRIT OF REVOLUTION IN 1789: A STUDY OF PUBLIC OPINION ...AT THE BEGINNING OF THE FRENCH REVOLUTION.
PRINCETON: PRINCETON U PRESS, 1949, 363 PP.
EXAMINATION OF POPULAR OPINION AS EXPRESSED IN POLITICAL SONGS AND OTHER LITERATURE. HAS CHRONOLOGICAL STRUCTURE AND EXTENSIVE BIBLIOGRAPHY, INCLUDING NEW CATALOGUE OF POLITICAL SONGS OF 1789. SHOWS THAT MUCH OF THE SPIRIT OF FRENCH REVOLUTION PRESERVED ITSELF IN SONG.

2659 ROGGER H.
"EAST GERMANY: STABLE OR IMMOBILE."
CURR. HIST., 48 (MAR. 65), 135-141.
ULBRICHT'S REGIME, FOR REASONS OF ITS OWN, HAS HAD TO RESIST THE NEW WAVE OF DE-STALINIZATION SET OFF BY SOVIET PARTY CONGRESS OF 1961. THE NEGOTIATIONS, AGREEMENTS, AND GUARANTEES NEEDED TO BRING ABOUT GERMAN RE-UNIFICATION WOULD REQUIRE VASTLY GREATER CHANGES IN SOVIET SPHERE. NOT LIKELY TO TAKE PLACE WHILE ULBRICHT REMAINS IN CHARGE.

2660 ROGGER H. ED., WEBER E. ED.
THE EUROPEAN RIGHT.
BERKELEY: U OF CALIF PR, 1966, 589 PP., LC#65-18562.
ANTHOLOGY OF ESSAYS ON THE RIGHTEST ELEMENT IN 11 EUROPEAN NATIONS. STUDIES ARE GENERAL SYNTHETIC ANALYSES OF RIGHT-WING MOVEMENTS AND THEIR ORIGINS; THEIR RELATIONS WITH CONSERVATIVE OR MODERATE SUPPORTERS OF THE ESTABLISHED ORDER; AND THEIR LEFT-WING CRITICS. UNANNOTATED LIST OF SUGGESTED READINGS APPENDED TO EACH ESSAY, COVERING CONSERVATIVE POLITICS IN THE COUNTRY UNDER DISCUSSION.

2661 ROGIN M.
"ROUSSEAU IN AFRICA."
TRANSACTIONS, 3 (SEPT. 63), 23-25.
ROUSSEAU'S PHILOSOPHY OF GOVERNMENT AND CIVILIZATION IS COMPARED WITH MODERN AFRICAN LEADERS'. DRAWS SIMILARITIES IN ADMIRATION FOR "NOBLE SAVAGE" BUT WARNS AGAINST "GENERAL WILL" BECOMING DICTATORSHIP.

2662 ROGOFF N.
"SOCIAL STRATIFICATION IN FRANCE AND IN THE UNITED STATES" (BMR)"
AMER. J. OF SOCIOLOGY, 58 (JAN. 53), 347-357.
INDICATES SOCIAL STRATIFICATION IN US RESEMBLES THAT IN FRANCE TODAY, BUT IT DIFFERED HISTORICALLY. IN OPINION SURVEYS, FRENCHMEN PLACE THEMSELVES IN FOUR CLASSES, AMERICANS ONLY TWO: WORKING AND MIDDLE CLASS. STATES THAT IN BOTH SOCIETIES SELF-APPRAISAL OF POSITION IS CLOSELY RELATED TO OCCUPATION, AND THERE ARE HIGH RATES OF SOCIAL MOBILITY.

2663 ROHEIM G.
PSYCHOANALYSIS AND ANTHROPOLOGY.
NEW YORK: INTL UNIVERSITIES PR, 1950, 496 PP.
RELATES CULTURE, PERSONALITY, AND THE UNCONSCIOUS THROUGH PSYCHOANALYSIS OF SEVERAL PRIMITIVE PEOPLES OVER THE EARTH. DISCUSSES EFFECTS OF ENVIRONMENT ON PSYCHOLOGICAL MAKEUP.

2664 ROIG E.
MARTI, ANTIIMPERIALISTA.
HAVANA: MIN DE RELACIONES EXTER, 1961, 135 PP.
ANALYZES NATIONALISM AND ANTI-IMPERIALISM OF CUBAN PHILOSOPHER-PATRIOT, JOSE MARTI. EXPLAINS BACKGROUND OF MARTI'S ATTITUDE CONCERNING INDEPENDENCE OF CUBA AND WESTERN HEMISPHERE FROM POLITICAL OR ECONOMIC DOMINANCE BY EUROPE OR US.

2665 ROKKAN S., CAMPBELL A.
"NORWAY AND THE UNITED STATES OF AMERICA."
INT. SOCIAL SCI. J., 12 (JAN.-MAR. 60), 69-99.
ANALYSIS OF SIMILARITIES AND DIFFERENCES IN RECRUITMENT OF ACTIVE PARTICIPANTS IN ELECTORAL CONTESTS IN NORWAY AND US. BASED ON SAMPLE INTERVIEWS AND ELECTION DATA. RESEARCH DISCUSSES DIFFERENT CONDITIONS IN ELECTION POLICIES AND IN PARTICIPATION VARIANCES. ANALYSIS OF FINDINGS IS DETAILED, CONCLUSIONS DEPENDING ON SOCIOLOGICAL GROUPINGS. THIS "MACRO-MICRO" ANALYSIS IS AN IMPORTANT RESEARCH TOOL.

2666 ROMEIN J.
THE ASIAN CENTURY.
BERKELEY: U OF CALIF PR, 1965, 448 PP.
DISCUSSES HISTORY OF NATIONAL MOVEMENTS IN ASIA AND RELATION OF TRADITION TO NEWLY EMERGING SOCIAL PATTERNS. DESCRIBES HISTORICAL DEVELOPMENT OF ASIA IN THREE ASPECTS: ITS EXTENT, ITS SHORTNESS COMPARED TO ITS SIGNIFICANCE, AND ITS RESULTS.

2667 RONNING C.
"NANKING: 1950."
INTERNATIONAL JOURNAL, 22 (SUMMER 67), 441-456.
REPORT OF CANADIAN POLICY IN CHINA 1945-51, DURING AUTHOR'S SERVICE AS CANADIAN AMBASSADOR TO CHINA. BELIEVES CANADA SHOULD RECOGNIZE THE PEKING GOVERNMENT TO CONTINUE CANADA'S IMPORTANT PEACE-KEEPING ROLE.

2668 RONNING C.N.
LAW AND POLITICS IN INTER-AMERICAN DIPLOMACY.
NEW YORK: WILEY, 1963, 167 PP.
'CONFUSING LEGAL PATTERN EMERGED AS RESULT OF TWO CONFLICTING DESIRES AMONG THE STATES: THE DESIRE FOR ORDER AND PREDICTABILITY ON THE ONE HAND, THE DESIRE FOR FREEDOM OF ACTION ON THE OTHER.' EXPLORES CURRENT POLITICAL, SOCIAL AND ECONOMIC FACTORS UNDERLYING SHIFTING DOCTRINES.

2669 ROOS H.
A HISTORY OF MODERN POLAND FROM THE FOUNDATION OF THE STATE IN THE FIRST WORLD WAR TO THE PRESENT DAY.
LONDON: EYRE AND SPOTTISWOODE, 1966, 303 PP.
STUDY OF 20TH-CENTURY POLISH DIPLOMATIC AND POLITICAL HISTORY. DISCUSSES PATTERNS OF SOCIETY AND POLITICAL IDEAS. TOUCHES UPON LITERARY AND ACADEMIC CONCEPTS THAT

SHAPED POLISH ATTITUDES. SHOWS THE MANY PARTITIONS AND BOUNDARIES OF THE COUNTRY.

2670 ROOT W.
"REPORT FROM PARIS - DE GAULLE: WHICH WAY TO THE FUTURE?"
AMER. SCHOLAR, 37 (WINTER 67), 94-110.
ANALYZES PROPOSED CHANGES IN DE GAULLE'S FOREIGN POLICY. EMPHASIZES IMPORTANCE TO DE GAULLE OF AN INDEPENDENT FRENCH MIND. DISCUSSES POSSIBILITIES OF FRENCH ALIGNMENT WITH RED CHINA AND/OR USSR. DISCUSSES REASONS FOR FRENCH WITHDRAWAL FROM NATO, FRANCE AS A NUCLEAR POWER, AND FRENCH INFLUENCE IN THE COMMON MARKET, THE MIDDLE EAST, AND CANADA.

2671 ROSCIO J.G.
OBRAS.
CARACAS: LA DECIM CONF INTERAMER, 1953, 489 PP.
WRITINGS OF A PHILOSOPHICAL LEADER OF SOUTH AMERICAN LIBERATION MOVEMENTS. INCLUDES "THE TRIUMPH OF LIBERTY OVER DESPOTISM."

2672 ROSE D.L., HOC V.V.
THE VIETNAMESE CIVIL SERVICE.
E LANSING: MICH ST VIET ADVISORY, 1961, 467 PP.
MANY DOCUMENTS AND INTERVIEWS, REVIEW NATURE AND SCOPE OF SYSTEM, EMPLOYEE CLASSIFICATION AND COMPENSATION, PROCEDURE OF RECRUITMENT, PROMOTIONS, AND OTHER ADMINISTRATIVE MATTERS. INCLUDES CHARTS AND LISTS. AUTHOR EVALUATES SYSTEM AS BASICALLY INEFFICIENT DUE TO ORIENTATION TOWARD BENEFIT AND SECURITY OF WORKERS RATHER THAN UTILITY.

2673 ROSE R.
"THE POLITICAL IDEALS OF ENGLISH PARTY ACTIVISTS" (BMR)"
AM. POL. SCI. REV., 56 (JUNE 62), 360-371.
ANALYZES THE ROLE OF ENGLISH PARTY ACTIVISTS IN POLICY FORMULATION, IN ORDER TO CLARIFY THE INTERPLAY OF PARTIES, PRESSURE GROUPS, AND POLICY DEMANDS OF PARTY ACTIVISTS. CONCLUDES THAT ATTITUDES ON QUESTIONS OF POLICY ARE RANDOMLY DISTRIBUTED AMONG CONSTITUENCY, PARTIES, AND PARTY ACTIVISTS. ATTRIBUTES THIS DIVERSITY TO THE PLURALITY OF MOTIVES LEADING INDIVIDUALS TO BECOME ACTIVE.

2674 ROSE R. ED., HEIDENHEIMER A. ED.
"COMPARATIVE STUDIES IN POLITICAL FINANCE: A SYMPOSIUM."
J. POLIT., 25 (NOV. 63), 643-871.
A COLLECTION OF PAPERS BY WELL-KNOWN SPECIALISTS, EXAMINING INTENSIVELY THE PARTICULAR PATTERN OF POLITICAL FINANCE IN EIGHT DEMOCRATIC STATES. EACH ARTICLE CONCERNS A BASIC SET OF QUESTIONS ABOUT PARTY MEMBERSHIP, INCOME, EXPENDITURE, SUBSIDIES, LAWS AND CAMPAIGN COSTS. INCLUDES AUSTRALIA, BRITAIN, INDIA, ISRAEL, ITALY, JAPAN, THE PHILIPPINES, AND WEST GERMANY.

2675 ROSE S.
"ASIAN NATIONALISM* THE SECOND STAGE."
INTERNATIONAL AFFAIRS (U.K.), 43 (APR.67), 282-292.
TRACES TRANSITION IN OBJECTIVES OF ASIAN NATIONALISM FROM STRUGGLE FOR INDEPENDENCE TO ONE OF SURVIVAL. CONTENDS THIS CONCERN FOR SURVIVAL RESULTS IN MORE PRAGMATIC, LESS DOGMATIC POLICIES. POLICY ATTENDS TO REGIONAL & BORDER DISPUTES, NOT TO GLOBAL CONCERNS. SUGGESTS NO NECESSITY FOR CHOICE BETWEEN WESTERN AND COMMUNIST SYSTEMS EXISTS IN ASIA, ONLY CONCERN FOR INDEPENDENCE AND NATIONAL UNITY.

2676 ROSENAU J.N. ED.
INTERNATIONAL ASPECTS OF CIVIL STRIFE.
PRINCETON: PRINCETON U PRESS, 1964, 322 PP., LC#64-16727.
COLLECTED ESSAYS RELATE DOMESTIC CONFLICT TO INTERNATIONAL POLITICS, EMPHASIZING INTERVENTION, INTERNATIONAL SETTLEMENT, AND INTERNATIONAL COALITIONS.

2677 ROSENBERG A.
DEMOCRACY AND SOCIALISM.
BOSTON: BEACON, 1965, 364 PP., $2.45.
DEFINES AND EXPLORES DEMOCRACY BEFORE 1845, FOCUSING ON OUTSTANDING FIGURES AND MOVEMENTS. STUDIES CONTRIBUTIONS OF MARX AND ENGELS TO POLITICAL MOVEMENT, ANALYZES DEFEAT OF DEMOCRACY IN FRANCE, 1848, AND SUBSEQUENT GROWTH OF SOCIALIST MOVEMENT.

2678 ROSENBERG C.G. JR., NOTTINGHAM J.
"THE MYTH OF "MAU-MAU:" NATIONALISM IN KENYA."
NEW YORK: FREDERICK PRAEGER, 1966.
ALTERNATIVE INTERPRETATION OF MILITANT AFRICAN NATIONALISM CONCERNED WITH MODERN ORIGINS OF AFRICAN POLITICS AND PATTERN OF DEVELOPMENT WITH PARTICULAR EMPHASIS ON POLITICIZATION AND MOBILIZATION OF KIKUYU PEOPLE. ARGUES THAT "MAU-MAU" WAS INTEGRAL PART OF ONGOING, RATIONALLY CONCEIVED NATIONALIST MOVEMENT. CONCLUDES WITH EXTENSIVE NOTES AND BIBLIOGRAPHY.

2679 ROSENBLUTH G.
THE CANADIAN ECONOMY AND DISARMAMENT.
NEW YORK: ST MARTIN'S PRESS, 1967, 189 PP., LC#67-78912.
FULL-LENGTH STUDY OF ECONOMIC CONSEQUENCES OF DISARMAMENT FOR CANADA. CONCLUDES THAT ECONOMIC DISLOCATION FROM GENERAL AND COMPLETE CANADIAN DISARMAMENT WOULD BE SMALL IF ADVANCE PLANS WERE MADE. STUDIES NATURE AND EXTENT OF CANADIAN DEFENSE EXPENDITURES, AND GROUPS AND AREAS MOST AFFECTED THEREBY. USES DETAILED THEORETICAL AND STATISTICAL ANALYSES. ASKS GOVERNMENT TO EXTEND DISARMAMENT STUDIES.

2680 ROSENFARB J.
FREEDOM AND THE ADMINISTRATIVE STATE.
NEW YORK: HARPER & ROW, 1948, 274 PP.
DEALS WITH EVOLUTION OF ADMINISTRATIVE STATE, STATUS OF FREEDOM AND DEMOCRACY, POSITION OF LABOR, CONDITION OF LAW AND GOVERNMENT IN ADMINISTRATIVE STATE. THE DRIVE TO MANAGED ECONOMY IS EXAMINED AND RELATED TO CONDITION AND FREEDOM OF DEMOCRATIC LIFE UNDER THIS SYSTEM. INDICATES THAT MANAGED ECONOMY IS NECESSARY AND AT ODDS WITH CONCEPT OF DEMOCRATIC REPRESENTATIVE GOVERNMENT.

2681 ROSENTHAL A.H.
THE SOCIAL PROGRAMS OF SWEDEN.
MINNEAPOLIS: U OF MINN PR, 1967, 193 PP., LC#67-27098.
TRACES THE DEVELOPMENT OF THE SWEDISH PROGRAMS AND PROVIDES DETAILED DESCRIPTIONS OF THE SOCIAL SECURITY, HEALTH INSURANCE, PUBLIC HEALTH, AND WELFARE PROGRAMS, WITH CASE EXAMPLES. EVALUATES AND COMPARES THE PROGRAMS WITH THEIR US COUNTERPARTS. CONSIDERS EFFECT OF SYSTEM ON PERSONAL FREEDOM.

2682 ROSENZWEIG F.
HEGEL UND DER STAAT.
AALEN: SCIENTIA VERLAG, 1962, 260 PP.
CRITICAL ANALYSIS OF HEGEL'S CONCEPT OF THE STATE AND PHILOSOPHY OF LAW. TRACES DEVELOPMENT OF HEGEL'S THOUGHT FROM EARLIEST BEGINNINGS AT STUTTAGRT AND TUBINGEN, TO MATURITY AND COMPLETION AT BERLIN.

2683 ROSKAM K.L.
APARTHEID AND DISCRIMINATION.
LEYDEN: AW SIJTHOFF, 1960, 179 PP.
STUDIES RELATIONSHIPS BETWEEN WHITE AND RESPECTIVE NON-WHITE ETHNIC GROUPS IN UNION OF SOUTH AFRICA, INCLUDING HISTORICAL BACKGROUND, DISCRIMINATION AS UNDERLYING PRINCIPLE OF SOUTH AFRICAN SOCIETY, AND MAKEUP OF SOUTH AFRICAN NATION.

2684 ROSNER J.
DER FASCHISMUS.
VIENNA: SELBSTVERL JAKOB ROSNER, 1966, 255 PP.
DISCUSSES ORIGIN, NATURE, AND AIMS OF FASCISM. EXAMINES CONCEPTS OF RACISM, ANTI-SEMITISM, CLASS STRUGGLE, DEMOCRACY, AND NATIONAL COMMUNITY, WITH EMPHASIS ON EXPRESSIONS OF FASCISM IN ITALY, GERMANY, AND AUSTRIA BETWEEN 1920 AND 1945.

2685 ROSOLIO D.
TEN YEARS OF THE CIVIL SERVICE IN ISRAEL (1948-1958) (PAMPHLET)
WASHINGTON: GOVT PR OFFICE, 1959, 23 PP.
RECORDS OF ESTABLISHMENT OF MINISTRIES AND PUBLIC SERVICES IN 1948, NUMBERS AND CHARACTERISTICS OF CIVIL SERVANTS, ADMINISTRATIVE PROCEDURE, WORKING CONDITIONS, AND BENEFITS OF CIVIL SERVANTS. RECOMMENDS COMMISSION "KEEP UP THE GOOD WORK" AND MAINTAIN ITS HIGH STANDARDS OF SERVICE.

2686 ROSS A.M. ED.
INDUSTRIAL RELATIONS AND ECONOMIC DEVELOPMENT.
NEW YORK: ST MARTIN'S PRESS, 1966, 413 PP., LC#66-28213.
PAPERS PRESENTED AT RESEARCH CONFERENCE OF INTERNATIONAL INSTITUTE FOR LABOUR STUDIES. DISCUSS ROLES OF STATE AND POLITICAL PARTIES IN INDUSTRIAL RELATIONS OF DEVELOPING COUNTRIES, SOURCES AND FUNCTIONS OF UNION LEADERSHIP, DISTRIBUTION OF DECISION-MAKING POWER IN WAGE DETERMINATION, ROLES OF COLLECTIVE BARGAINING AND LEGISLATION IN INCOME POLICY, AND PARTICIPATION OF INTEREST GROUPS IN PLANNING.

2687 ROSS R., VAN DEN HAAG E.
THE FABRIC OF SOCIETY.
NEW YORK: HARCOURT BRACE, 1957, 777 PP.
ESSENTIALLY ANALYTICAL SOCIOLOGICAL TEXT WHICH DESCRIBES SOCIETY IN TERMS OF THE REGULARITIES OBSERVED BY THE SOCIAL SCIENCES. DEALS FIRST WITH "PERSONALITY," THEN WITH "GROUPS," "CULTURE," AND "SOCIETY." PART II EXPOUNDS ON SCIENTIFIC METHOD AND TEXT ATTEMPTS TO INTEGRATE AS MANY METHODS AND THEORIES AS IS PRACTICABLE.

2688 ROSSITER C.L.
CONSTITUTIONAL DICTATORSHIP; CRISIS GOVERNMENT IN THE MODERN DEMOCRACIES.
PRINCETON: PRINCETON U PRESS, 1948, 322 PP.
STUDY OF NATURE OF CONSTITUTIONAL DICTATORSHIP IN HISTORY AS EXAMINED IN PERIOD OF CRISIS IN GERMAN REPUBLIC, FRENCH REPUBLIC, GREAT BRITAIN, AND US. COVERS CHANCES OF TIGHT CONTROL FORMALLY OR INFORMALLY OBTAINED UNDER DEMOCRATIC GOVERNMENT, AND DANGERS OF ITS APPLICATION TO WHOLE SYSTEM.

2689 ROSTOW W.W.
"RUSSIA AND CHINA UNDER COMMUNISM."

WORLD POLIT., 7 (JULY 55), 513-31.
SEEKS TO SET FORTH CERTAIN MAJOR SIMILARITIES AND DIFFERENCES BETWEEN THESE COUNTRIES. EXAMINES (1) ROLE OF INTELLECTUALS (2) LEADERSHIP (3) PROBLEM OF EXTERNAL EXPANSION FOR INTERNATIONAL COMMUNISM. CONCLUDES WITH DIRECTION TOWARD A FOREIGN AMERICAN POLICY.

2690 ROTBERG R.
"THE RISE OF AFRICAN NATIONALISM: THE CASE OF EAST AND CENTRAL AFRICA."
WORLD POLIT., 15 (OCT. 62), 75-90.
AFRICAN NATIONALISM IS DIFFERENT IN THAT IT'S A COMMON PROTEST AGAINST ALIEN OR WHITE RULE. IT BEGAN AS WRANGLING OVER EXISTING CONDITIONS, MANIFESTING ITSELF RELIGIOUSLY. LATER, POLITICAL PARTIES WERE ORGANIZED. FINALLY, THE MOVEMENT (NO PROGRAMS FOR IMPROVEMENT WERE EVIDENT) BECAME ONE OF DRASTIC CHANGE I.E. SELF-RULE AND IMMEDIATE INDEPENDENCE.

2691 ROTBERG R.
"THE FEDERATION MOVEMENT IN BRITISH EAST AND CENTRAL AFRICA."
J. COMMONWEALTH POLIT. STUD., 2 (MAY 64), 141-160.
COMPARES BRITISH CENTRAL AFRICA, WHERE WHITE DOMINATION INFLUENCED AND ASSERTED ITSELF IN THE DEVELOPMENT OF THE FEDERATION OF RHODESIA AND NYASALAND, AND BRITISH EAST AFRICA WHERE AFRICAN SENTIMENT PREVAILED AND BLOCKED THE FEDERATION OF KENYA, UGANDA AND TANGANYIKA.

2692 ROTBERG R.I.
A POLITICAL HISTORY OF TROPICAL AFRICA.
NEW YORK: HARCOURT BRACE, 1965, 429 PP., LC#65-21072.
COMPREHENSIVE DEVELOPMENT OF GOVERNMENT IN SOUTHERN AFRICA. EARLY EMPIRES, INTERNATIONAL SLAVE TRADE, COLONIALISM, WESTERN INFLUENCES, AND INDEPENDENCE EXAMINED.

2693 ROTBERG R.I.
"COLONIALISM AND AFTER: THE POLITICAL LITERATURE OF CENTRAL AFRICA - A BIBLIOGRAPHIC ESSAY."
AFRICAN FORUM, 2 (WINTER 67), 66-73.
SELECTIVE SURVEY OF ABOUT 80 BOOKS AND ARTICLES IN ENGLISH ON VARIOUS ASPECTS OF POLITICS IN ZAMBIA, MALAWI, AND RHODESIA. EXCLUDES GOVERNMENT DOCUMENTS.

2694 ROTH A.R.
"CAPITAL-MARKET DEVELOPMENT IN ISRAEL AND BRAZIL: TWO EXAMPLES OF THE ROLE OF LAW IN DEVELOPMENT."
STANFORD LAW REV., 19 (JUNE 67), 1277-1306.
EXAMINES EXPERIENCES OF ISRAEL AND BRAZIL IN BUILDING VIABLE LEGAL INSTITUTIONS TO AID IN DEVELOPMENT OF DOMESTIC CAPITAL MARKET. RECOGNIZES IMPORTANCE OF LAW IN ECONOMIC DEVELOPMENT. PRESENTS EXPERIENCES WITH REGULATION OF COMPANIES AND THEIR SECURITIES, PROFESSIONAL INTERMEDIARIES, AND TRADING MARKETS. SUCH REGULATION HELPS USE OF FOREIGN AID AND IMPROVES BALANCE OF PAYMENTS.

2695 ROTHCHILD D.
"THE LIMITS OF FEDERALISM: AN EXAMINATION OF POLITICAL INSTITUTIONAL TRANSFER IN AFRICA."
J. OF MOD. AFR. STUD., 4 (NOV. 66), 275-293.
DISCUSSES FAILURE OF CLASSICAL FEDERALISM AS EMPLOYED IN EUROPE TO ACHIEVE REGIONAL AND CONTINENTAL UNITY IN AFRICA. EXAMINES MAIN FACTORS CONTRIBUTING TO FAILURE: ATTITUDE OF LEADERS, AND PREVAILING POLITICAL, ECONOMIC, AND SOCIAL CONDITIONS. SEES NEW NATIONS FACING EXTREMES OF UNITARY GOVERNMENT AND LOOSE INTER-UNIT ARRANGEMENTS, AND NEEDING TO FIND CONSTITUTIONAL SYSTEMS TO RECONCILE THESE EXTREMES.

2696 ROUGEMONT D.
"LES NOUVELLES CHANCES DE L'EUROPE."
TABLE RONDE, 18 (FEB. 63), 149-61.
EXAMINES THREE SIGNIFICANT FACTORS SHAPING SITUATION OF MODERN EUROPE: 1)EFFORTS FOR UNIFICATION OF EUROPEAN COMMUNITY 2)POLITICAL WITHDRAWAL OF EUROPE FROM FORMER COLONIES, COINCIDENT WITH ADOPTION BY THIRD WORLD OF EUROPEAN CIVILIZATION, AND 3)UNREGULARIZED SPREAD OF EUROPEAN ADMINISTRATIVE TECHNIQUES.

2697 ROUSSEAU J.J.
A LASTING PEACE.
ORIGINAL PUBLISHER NOT AVAILABLE, 1819, 128 PP.
CRITICIZES SAINT-PIERRE'S PLAN FOR EUROPEAN PEACE-KEEPING FEDERATION. SAINT-PIERRE'S ASSUMPTION THAT PRINCES WILL RECONGNIZE ADVANTAGES OF HIS PLAN IS DISPUTED BY ROUSSEAU, WHO ARGUES THAT RULERS DO NOT RECONGNIZE THEIR OWN SELF-INTEREST. OF WAR GENERALLY, ROUSSEAU SAYS ONLY SELF-DEFENSE CAN JUSTIFY SUCH OUTRAGEOUS ACTION.

2698 ROUSSEAU J.J.
"DISCOURSE ON THE ORIGIN OF INEQUALITY" (1755) IN THE SOCIAL CONTRACT AND DISCOURSES."
NEW YORK: EP DUTTON, 1950.
AN INQUIRY INTO THE NATURAL AND ARTIFICIAL ASPECTS OF THE CIVILIZED HUMAN CONDITION. ARGUES THAT BECAUSE IMBALANCE DOES NOT EXIST IN NATURE, MAN IS INNATELY GOOD AND ABHORS HIS FELLOWMEN'S SUFFERING; THEREFORE, EGOISM, WHICH PRODUCES INEQUALITY, IS THE PRODUCT OF CIVILIZATION, AND THE IDEAL SOCIETY IS THE ONE WHICH PROVIDES A JUST BALANCE BETWEEN MAN'S NATURAL INDOLENCE AND HIS CIVILIZED EGOISM.

2699 ROUSSEAU J.J.
"A DISCOURSE ON POLITICAL ECONOMY" (1755) IN THE SOCIAL CONTRACT AND DISCOURSES."
NEW YORK: EP DUTTON, 1950.
ESSAY ON JUST AND LEGITIMATE MANAGEMENT OF ECONOMY IN GOVERNMENT FOR THE COMMON GOOD OF SOCIETY. THE IDEAL STATE IS DESCRIBED AS CONSISTING OF THE GENERAL WILL OF SOCIETY, WITH THE WELL-BEING OF ALL ITS MEMBERS AS ITS PRINCIPAL AIM. TAXES, THEREFORE, SHOULD BE LEVIED ACCORDINGLY, WITH HEAVY IMPOSTS ON ALL LUXURIES AND EXEMPTIONS FOR THOSE WHO HAVE ONLY THE NECESSITIES FOR SUSTAINING LIFE.

2700 ROUSSEAU J.J.
THE SOCIAL CONTRACT.
ORIGINAL PUBLISHER NOT AVAILABLE, 1762, 148 PP.
PRESENTS IDEA OF THE STATE AS A FORM OF CONTRACT BETWEEN RULER AND CITIZEN, WITH RIGHTS AND PRIVILEGES BELONGING TO EACH. ATTACKS NOTION OF DIVINE RIGHT, CLAIMING THAT THE OBLIGATION IS NOT A METAPHYSICAL BUT A UTILITARIAN BOND. OPENS WAY FOR REVOLUTION BY STATING THAT IF RULERS DO NOT MAINTAIN ORDER AND SERVE THE COMMON GOOD, THEY ARE BREAKING THE CONTRACT. SUPPORTS IDEA OF MAN'S INHERENT MORALITY.

2701 ROWAT D.C. ED.
THE OMBUDSMAN: CITIZEN'S DEFENDER.
TORONTO: U OF TORONTO PRESS, 1965, 348 PP.
STUDIES THAT OFFICER OF PARLIAMENT WHO INVESTIGATES COMPLAINTS FROM CITIZENS AGAINST UNJUST ADMINISTRATIVE ACTION AND SEEKS A REMEDY. ANALYZES PRESENT OMBUDSMAN SYSTEMS, RELATED INSTITUTIONS, PROPOSED SCHEMES, AND DATA FROM OMBUDSMAN CASES IN SWEDEN, FINLAND, DENMARK, NORWAY, AND NEW ZEALAND. CONCLUDES THAT OMBUDSMAN SHOULD BE AN IMPORTANT ADDITION TO DEMOCRATIC GOVERNMENT.

2702 ROWE C.
VOLTAIRE AND THE STATE.
NEW YORK: COLUMBIA U PRESS, 1955, 254 PP., LC#55-09097.
DISCUSSES VOLTAIRE'S THEORY OF NATION AND OF INTERNATIONAL RELATIONS, EXAMINING HIS PERSONAL PATRIOTISM AND VALUE HE ASSIGNED LOVE OF COUNTRY.

2703 ROWE J.W.
THE ARGENTINE ELECTIONS OF 1963 (PAMPHLET)
WASHINGTON: OPER & POL RES, INC, 1965, 40 PP.
ANALYSIS OF 1963 NATIONAL AND LOCAL ELECTIONS IN ARGENTINA. DISCUSSES PROPORTIONAL REPRESENTATION, POLITICAL PARTIES, CAMPAIGNS, AND RESULTS. INCLUDES INFORMATION ON 1965 CONGRESSIONAL ELECTIONS.

2704 ROWLAND J.
A HISTORY OF SINO-INDIAN RELATIONS; HOSTILE CO-EXISTENCE.
PRINCETON: VAN NOSTRAND, 1967, 248 PP., LC#66-29857.
INSIGHTS INTO RED CHINA'S DRIVE TO ACCOMMODATE AN EXPLODING POPULATION AND PROJECT ITS POWER. FOCUSES ON HIMALAYAN BOUNDARY REGIONS WHERE TENSIONS MOUNT BETWEEN COMMUNIST CHINA AND INDIA. ORIGIN, NATURE, AND SIGNIFICANCE OF THIS TENSION IS DISCUSSED. CLUES GIVEN TO QUESTION OF PEKING'S INTENTIONS IN ASIA.

2705 ROY N.C.
THE CIVIL SERVICE IN INDIA.
CALCUTTA: FIRMA KL MUKHOPADHYAY, 1960, 355 PP.
DISCUSSES STRUCTURE OF INDIAN GOVERNMENT, RECRUITMENT OF CIVIL SERVANTS, SALARIES, PUBLIC SERVICE COMMISSIONS, AND POLITICAL CONTROL OVER ADMINISTRATIVE APPARATUS.

2706 ROYAL GEOGRAPHICAL SOCIETY
BIBLIOGRAPHY OF BARBARY STATES (4 SUPPLEMENTARY PAPERS)
LONDON: ROYAL GEOGRAPHICAL SOCIETY, 1893,LC#10-17941
FOUR-VOLUME BIBLIOGRAPHY ON TRIPOLI AND CYRENAICA, TUNISIA FROM EARLIEST TIMES TO 1889, ALGERIA FROM EXPEDITIONS OF CHARLES V IN 1541 TO 1887, AND MOROCCO FROM EARLIEST TIMES TO 1891.

2707 RUBEN P. ED.
DIE REKLAME IHRE KUNST UND WISSENSCHAFT.
BERLIN: HERMAN & PAETEL VERL, 1913, 304 PP.
GENERAL DISCUSSION OF THE ART OF ADVERTISING. INCLUDES STUDIES OF THE PSYCHOLOGY OF ADVERTISING AS WELL AS NUMEROUS EXAMINATIONS OF THE PRACTICES OF SUCH DIVERSE INDUSTRIES AS THE RAILROAD AND CIGARETTE MANUFACTURES. ALSO INCLUDED ARE DISCUSSIONS OF SWISS AND POLISH PRACTICES AND A COMPARISON OF GERMAN AND AMERICAN METHODS. CONTAINS MANY ILLUSTRATIONS.

2708 RUBINSTEIN A.Z.
"YUGOSLAVIA'S OPENING SOCIETY."
CURR. HIST., 48 (MAR. 65), 149-153.
DURING PAST 15 YEARS YUGOSLAVIA HAS EXPERIENCED TRANSFORMATION FROM STALINIST PROTOTYPE OF SOCIALISM TOWARD ESTABLISHMENT OF INSTITUTIONS AND PROCEDURES COMMITTED TO DEMOCRATIC PROCESS. INCREASINGLY NON-AUTHORITARIAN SOLUTION TO ITS COMPLEX PROBLEMS. OPERATION OF NEW CONSTITUTION

WILL BE MEASURE OF SUCCESS.

2709 RUBINSTEIN A.Z. ED., THUMM G.W. ED.
THE CHALLENGE OF POLITICS: IDEAS AND ISSUES (2ND ED.)
ENGLEWOOD CLIFFS: PRENTICE HALL, 1965, 475 PP., LC#65-12155.
COLLECTION OF WRITINGS ON POLITICS DEALING WITH RELATION OF MAN TO SOCIETY, POLITICAL EQUALITY, GOVERNMENTAL POWER, FREEDOM VERSUS AUTHORITY, GOVERNMENTAL STRUCTURE, AND RELATIONS AMONG STATES.

2710 RUCKER B.W.
"WHAT SOLUTIONS DO PEOPLE ENDORSE IN FREE PRESS-FAIR TRIAL DILEMMA?"
JOURNALISM QUARTERLY, (SUMMER 67), 240-244.
REPORT ON EXPERIMENTAL STUDY WHICH IDENTIFIES FIVE DISTINCT GROUPS OF PEOPLE HOLDING DIVERGENT OPINIONS ON FREE PRESS-FREE TRIAL ISSUES. USES AND DESCRIBES Q TECHNIQUE OF SAMPLING AND ANALYZING PUBLIC OPINION.

2711 RUDE G.
WILKES AND LIBERTY.
LONDON: OXFORD U PR, 1962, 240 PP.
STUDIES POLITICAL MOVEMENTS, PETITIONS, DEMONSTRATIONS, AND INDUSTRIAL UNREST IN LONDON AT TIME OF JOHN WILKE'S POLITICAL CAREER. EXAMINES SOCIAL CONDITIONS AND SEEKS TO DETERMINE HISTORICAL SIGNIFICANCE OF WILKITE MOVEMENT.

2712 RUDMAN H.C.
THE SCHOOL AND STATE IN THE USSR.
NEW YORK: MACMILLAN, 1967, 286 PP., LC#67-15981.
STUDY OF THE COMPLEX INTERRELATIONSHIPS BETWEEN SOVIET SCHOOLS, THE STATE, AND THE COMMUNIST PARTY. EMPHASIZES ORGANIZATION AND MANAGEMENT, DECISION-MAKING AND IMPLEMENTATION, AND ANALYZES ADMINISTRATION. INCLUDES AGENCIES OF BOTH PARTY AND GOVERNMENT THAT MOST DIRECTLY AFFECT CONTENT AND CONDUCT OF EDUCATION AND EXAMINES ROLE OF TRADE UNIONS IN ADMINISTRATION AND CONTROL OF EDUCATION.

2713 RUDOLPH L.I., RUDOLPH S.
"GENERALS AND POLITICIANS IN INDIA."
PACIF. AFF., 37 (SPRING 64), 5-19.
THE ROLE OF THE MILITARY IN INDIAN POLITICS HAS CHANGED DUE TO THE REPLACEMENT OF A CONCERN WITH PEACEFUL INITIATIVES WITH A CONCERN FOR MILITARY SECURITY.

2714 RUDY Z.
ETHNOSOZIOLOGIE SOWJETISCHER VOLKER.
MUNICH: FRANCKE VERLAG, 1962, 244 PP.
DISCUSSES RISE OF CULTS, SOCIAL AND ECONOMIC CONDITIONS, AND SPIRITUAL LIFE OF SUB-CULTURES IN USSR. STUDIES IN DETAIL SOCIAL STRUCTURE AND GROUP INTERACTION.

2715 RUEFF J.
BALANCE OF PAYMENTS.
NEW YORK: MACMILLAN, 1967, 256 PP.
PRESENTATION OF VARIOUS PROPOSALS FOR SOLVING BALANCE-OF-PAYMENTS DILEMMA AS IT AFFECTS INTERNATIONAL FINANCE AND COMMERCE AND THE STANDARD OF LIVING IN EVERY CURRENCY AREA. DISCUSSION INCLUDES US BALANCE-OF-PAYMENTS DEFICITS IN THE 1960'S, THEORY OF TRANSFERS WITH KEYNES' VIEWS, ELEMENTS FOR A DISCOUNT THEORY, ETC. THROUGHOUT TEXT AUTHOR TAKES INTO ACCOUNT POLITICAL FACTORS AS WELL AS ECONOMIC.

2716 RUITENBEER H.M.
THE DILEMMA OF ORGANIZATIONAL SOCIETY.
NEW YORK: EP DUTTON, 1963, 220 PP., LC#63-24814.
EXPLORES EFFECTS OF MASS SOCIETY UPON INDIVIDUALS. FRIEDRICH CONSIDERS LOYALTY AND AUTHORITY. REISMAN, WHYTE, MERTON, AND MEAD COVER TECHNICAL ADVANCES, EDUCATION, AND LEISURE, AND KARL JASPERS DISCUSSES BUREAUCRACY AS FORM OF TOTALITARIANISM. ALSO CONSIDERS EFFECTS ON URBANISM AND RELIGION.

2717 RUMEU DE ARMAS A. ED.
ESPANA EEN EL AFRICA ATLANTICA.
MADRID: INST ESTUD AFRICANOS, 1957.
DOCUMENTS CHRONICLING SPANISH EXPERIENCE IN WEST AFRICA FROM 1344 TO 1549, INCLUDING LETTERS, ROYAL DECREES, INTERNATIONAL AGREEMENTS, AND SECRET INSTRUCTIONS.

2718 RUMMEL R.J.
A FOREIGN CONFLICT BEHAVIOR CODE SHEET.
WORLD POLITICS, 18 (JAN. 66), 283-296.
A RESEARCH NOTE ON EMPIRICALLY DERIVED TYPOLOGY OF FOREIGN CONFLICT BEHAVIOR. PRESENTED TO ENABLE RESEARCHERS TO COLLECT DATA, AND BUILD UP COMMON DATA POOL. THE CODE HAS ALREADY BEEN TESTED AND REVISED. DIAGRAM OF CODE SHEET INCLUDED.

2719 RUSSETT B.M.
WORLD HANDBOOK OF POLITICAL AND SOCIAL INDICATORS.
NEW HAVEN: YALE U PR, 1964, 373 PP., LC#64-20933.
PRESENTS DATA SIGNIFICANT TO THE DEVELOPMENT OF THE SCIENCE OF COMPARATIVE AND INTERNATIONAL POLITICS; ILLUSTRATES A VARIETY OF MEANS FOR ANALYZING THIS DATA. COMPARES NATIONS ON VARIOUS POLITICALLY RELEVANT INDEXES AND EXAMINES INTERRELATIONSHIPS OF DIFFERENT POLITICAL, ECONOMIC, SOCIAL, AND CULTURAL DEVELOPMENTS. DATA SERIES SELECTED ACCORDING TO THE CRITERIA OF ACCURACY AND AVAILABILITY.

2720 RUSTOW D.A.
THE POLITICS OF COMPROMISE.
PRINCETON: PRINCETON U PRESS, 1955, 257 PP., LC#55-6702.
STUDY OF PARTIES AND CABINET GOVERNMENT IN SWEDEN EMPHASIZING NECESSITY AND EFFECTUALITY OF COMPROMISE POLICY IN SWEDISH POLITICS. DISCUSSES SEVERAL SUCCESSFUL PROGRAMS IN SOCIAL AND ECONOMIC PLANNING. PROVIDES CURSORY ACCOUNT OF SOCIAL WELFARE, LABOR RELATIONS, AND FOREIGN POLICY. TRACES DEVELOPMENT OF SWEDISH DEMOCRACY.

2721 RUSTOW D.A.
"THE MILITARY IN MIDDLE EASTERN SOCIETY AND POLITICS."
WASHINGTON: BROOKINGS INST., 1963, 20 PP.
TRACES PAST AND PRESENT HISTORY OF MILITARY INTERVENTION IN COUNTRIES' INTERNAL AFFAIRS AND ASSESSES THEIR FUTURE ROLES.

2722 RUSTOW D.A.
A WORLD OF NATIONS; PROBLEMS OF POLITICAL MODERNIZATION.
WASHINGTON: BROOKINGS INST, 1967, 306 PP., LC#67-26139.
EMPHASIZES POLITICAL PROBLEMS OF NEWLY DEVELOPING NATIONS, ESPECIALLY MODERNIZATION AND NATION-STATE. CONTRASTS EXPERIENCES OF NEW COUNTRIES WITH EARLIER WESTERN HISTORY. EXAMINES DESIRE FOR AUTHORITY, IDENTITY, AND EQUALITY; ANALYZES DYNAMIC FEATURES OF POLITICAL LEADERSHIP WITHIN CHARISMATIC, MILITARY, AND SINGLE-PARTY REGIMES; AND DISCUSSES RIVAL APPEALS OF DEMOCRACY AND COMMUNISM.

2723 RUTH J.M.
"THE ADMINISTRATION OF WATER RESOURCES IN GUATEMALA."
PUBLIC & INTL. AFF., 5 (SPRING 67), 249-278.
STUDIES CONTROL OF WATER IN GUATEMALA AS A MODEL OF PROBLEMS IN HANDLING NATURAL RESOURCES. CONSIDERS THE ROLE OF GOVERNMENT IN COORDINATING DEMANDS OF HYDRO-ELECTRIC PROJECTS, IRRIGATION, COMMUNITY WATER SUPPLY, RECREATION, AND FLOOD CONTROL. SUGGESTS MORE DETAILED, COORDINATED, AND COMPREHENSIVE PLANNING, EITHER ON THE CABINET LEVEL OR ON AN AUTONOMOUS PROJECT LEVEL, LIKE TVA.

2724 RYDER A.J.
THE GERMAN REVOLUTION OF 1918; A STUDY OF GERMAN SOCIALISM IN WAR AND REVOLT.
CAMBRIDGE: CAMBRIDGE UNIV PRESS, 1967, 304 PP., LC#67-10057.
STUDIES EFFECT OF WWI ON GERMAN SOCIALISM AND SPLIT OF UNITED PARTY INTO TWO OPPOSING GROUPS. EXAMINES RESULTS OF GERMAN REVOLUTION OF 1918 ON SOCIALIST PARTIES' RELATIONS. TRACES CHANGES IN SOCIALIST GROUPS AND THEIR COALITIONS DURING THIS PERIOD. DISCUSSES REGROUPING OF SOCIALISTS AFTER REVOLUTION AND DEVELOPMENT AND DISSOLUTION OF INDEPENDENT SOCIALISM

2725 RYDINGS H.A.
THE BIBLIOGRAPHIES OF WEST AFRICA (PAMPHLET)
NIGERIA: IBADAN UNIV PRESS, 1961, 36 PP.
ANNOTATED BIBLIOGRAPHICAL GUIED TO SOURCES OF BIBLIOGRAPHICAL INFORMATION CONCERNED WITH LITERATURE OF WEST AFRICA. CONTAINS 50 ENTRIES IN WESTERN LANGUAGE, MOST OF WHICH WERE PUBLISHED SINCE 1925. ARRANGED GEOGRAPHICALLY INTO GENERAL AND REGIONAL STUDIES. TABLES APPENDED TO TEXT BRIEFLY INDICATE PERIOD COVERED, NUMBER OF ENTRIES, ARRANGEMENT, SCOPE, AND LIMITATIONS OF EACH ENTRY.

2726 SAAB H.
"THE ARAB SEARCH FOR A FEDERAL UNION."
WORLD JUSTICE, 6 (DEC. 64), 147-71.
PRESENTS HISTORICAL ANALYSIS OF ARABIC QUEST FOR A PAN-ARAB FEDERATION, TRACING THE VARIOUS ATTEMPTS AND FAILURES DURING PAST QUARTER CENTURY. CITES CHANGING GOALS FROM INDEPENDECE TO INTER-DEPENDENCE. PRESENTS THE VARIOUS IDEOLOGIES OF ARAB SOCIALISM AND BAATHIST PARTY, AND POINTS OUT THE REVOLUTIONARY NATURE OF ARAB NATIONALISM. FEELS NEED TO LOOK TOWARDS A LOOSER ORGANIZATION OF A CONFEDERAL NATURE.

2727 SABINE G.H.
"THE TWO DEMOCRATIC TRADITIONS" (BMR)"
PHILOSPHICAL REVIEW, 61 (OCT. 52), 451-474.
STATES THAT THERE HAVE BEEN TWO STRANDS IN DEMOCRATIC TRADITION: ONE ANGLO-AMERICAN, THE OTHER FRENCH. THE FORMER GAVE PRIMARY IMPORTANCE TO LIBERTY, THE LATTER TO EQUALITY. ANALYZES HISTORICAL REASONS FOR THIS DIFFERENCE OF EMPHASIS. SUGGESTS THAT BOTH WERE TIED TOGETHER BY IDEALS THAT GAVE RISE TO CONCEPTS SUCH AS "CONSENT" AND "CONTRACT."

2728 SABLE M.H.
MASTER DIRECTORY FOR LATIN AMERICA.
LOS ANGELES: U CAL LAT AMER STUD, 1965, 438 PP.
CONTAINS TEN DICTIONARIES WITH NAMES AND ADDRESSES OF ORGANIZATIONS, ETC., CONNECTED WITH LATIN AMERICA BOTH IN THE REGION AND THE US. INCLUDES GOVERNMENTAL ESTABLISHMENTS AND POLITICAL PARTIES AS WELL AS OTHERS CONCERNED WITH AGRICULTURE, BUSINESS FINANCE, COMMUNICATIONS, EDUCATION AND RESEARCH, LABOR COOPERATIVES, RELIGION, AND INTERNATIONAL

COOPERATION.

2729 SAFRAN M.
EGYPT IN SEARCH OF POLITICAL COMMUNITY: AN ANALYSIS OF THE INTELLECTUAL AND POLITICAL EVOLUTION OF EGYPT, 1804-1952.
CAMBRIDGE U. PR., 1961, 298 PP.
REVIEW OF INTELLECTUAL HISTORY. TRACES CAUSES OF POLITICAL INSTABILITY AND AMBIVALENCE TOWARDS WEST AND WESTERN CULTURE. CONCLUDES THAT EGYPTIAN LEADERS HAVE FAILED TO DEVELOP VIABLE IDEOLOGY TO REPLACE BELIEF-SYSTEM OF ISLAM.

2730 SAHLINS M.D. ED., SERVICE E.R. ED.
EVOLUTION AND CULTURE.
ANN ARBOR: U OF MICH PR, 1960, 131 PP., LC#60-7930.
ARGUMENT IN FAVOR OF SEVERAL GENERAL PRINCIPLES FUNDAMENTAL TO THEORY OF CULTURAL EVOLUTION. PROVIDES EXPOSITION OF DUAL NATURE OF EVOLUTION - ITS PARTICULAR AND ITS GENERAL ASPECTS - AND DISCUSSES CONFUSIONS THAT HAVE RESULTED FROM FAILING TO DISTINGUISH BETWEEN THEM. EXAMINES THE MECHANICS AND CONSEQUENCES OF PARTICULAR CULTURAL EVOLUTION. CONTAINS BIBLIOGRAPHY OF POST-1930 ENGLISH WORKS.

2731 SAINDERICHIN P., POLI J.
HISTORIE SECRETE D'UNE ELECTION, DECEMBER 5-19, 1965.
PARIS: LIBRAIIE PLON, 1966, 252 PP.
EXAMINES HISTORY OF 1965 FRENCH PRESIDENTIAL ELECTION EMPHASIZING POLITICAL STRATEGY, CANDIDATES, AND BEHIND-THE-SCENES INTRIGUES.

2732 SAINT-PIERRE C.I.
SCHEME FOR LASTING PEACE (TRANS. BY H. BELLOT)
ORIGINAL PUBLISHER NOT AVAILABLE, 1738, 140 PP.
PROPOSES AN OBLIGATORY AND PERMANENT SYSTEM OF INTERNATIONAL ARBITRATION, ACCEPTED BY EACH COUNTRY IN EUROPE AND IMPOSED ON RECALCITRANTS; AN INTERNATIONAL TRIBUNAL, FOR ARBITRATION OF DISPUTES; AND AN INTERNATIONAL ARMED FORCE TO COMPEL ACCEPTANCE OF ITS DECISIONS. CLAIMS THIS WILL ALSO LEAD TO RISE IN COMMERCE AND PRODUCTION BY CONTRIBUTING TO PEACE AND FREE TRADE.

2733 SAKAI R.K. ED.
STUDIES ON ASIA, 1960.
LINCOLN: U OF NEB PR, 1960, 97 PP., LC#60-15432.
STUDIES VARIOUS SOCIAL FORCES OF EMERGENT ASIA AND AREA'S HISTORY: A RURAL COMMUNITY IN MALAYA, LABOR PRODUCTIVITY IN COMMUNIST CHINA, AND VOICE OF AMERICA IN ASIA.

2734 SAKAI R.K. ED.
STUDIES ON ASIA, 1961.
LINCOLN: U OF NEB PR, 1961, 85 PP., LC#60-15432.
STUDIES FORCES SHAPING CONTEMPORARY ASIA AND AREA'S HISTORY: NATIONALISM, INVESTMENT IN INDIA, JAPANESE IMPERIALISM, AND RELIGION AND POLITICS IN BURMA.

2735 SAKAI R.K.
STUDIES ON ASIA, 1963.
LINCOLN: U OF NEB PR, 1963, 196 PP., LC#60-15432.
ASIAN HISTORY AND POLITICAL FORCES SHAPING CONTEMPORARY ASIA: NATIONALISM IN MEIJI JAPAN, TAIWAN AND US POLICY, RELIGIOUS POLITICS IN ISRAEL, AND INDIAN POLITICAL TRENDS.

2736 SAKAI R.K.
STUDIES ON ASIA, 1964.
LINCOLN: U OF NEB PR, 1964, 186 PP., LC#60-15432.
ASIAN HISTORY AND POLITICAL FORCES SHAPING CONTEMPORARY ASIA, EMPHASIZING CHINA AND JAPAN. INCLUDES SINO-SOVIET-BRITISH RESPONSES TO INDIAN NATIONALISM; POSTWAR JAPAN-KOREA RELATIONS; AND POLITICAL IDEOLOGY IN MALAYSIA.

2737 SAKAI R.K.
STUDIES ON ASIA, 1965.
LINCOLN: U OF NEB PR, 1965, 209 PP., LC#60-15432.
ASIAN HISTORY AND FORCES SHAPING CONTEMPORARY ASIA: JAPAN; OPENING OF KOREA; MEIJI CONSTITUTION; AMERICAN POLICY IN SOUTHEAST ASIA; AND JAPANESE SUFFRAGE MOVEMENT.

2738 SAKAI R.K.
STUDIES ON ASIA, 1966.
LINCOLN: U OF NEB PR, 1966, 185 PP., LC#60-15432.
ASIAN HISTORY AND FORCES SHAPING CONTEMPORARY ASIA, EMPHASIZING MANY RELIGIOUS CURRENTS. DEALS WITH BUDDHIST RESURGENCE IN INDIA AND CEYLON, BUDDHISM IN JAPAN, JAPANESE COMMUNIST PARTY, AND US GUNBOAT DIPLOMACY.

2739 SALETORE B.A.
INDIA'S DIPLOMATIC RELATIONS WITH THE WEST.
BOMBAY: POPULAR BOOK DEPOT, 1958, 430 PP., LC#58-11844.
DISCUSSES ORIGIN OF SCIENCE OF DIPLOMACY AND DIPLOMATIC THEORY IN INDIA FROM EARLIEST TIMES UNTIL 185 B.C. EXAMINES RELATIONS BETWEEN INDIA AND PERSIA; GREECE, AND ROMAN EMPIRE; AND DIPLOMATIC ETIQUETTE AND PRACTICE IN ROMAN EMPIRE.

2740 SALETORE B.A.
INDIA'S DIPLOMATIC RELATIONS WITH THE EAST.
BOMBAY: POPULAR BOOK DEPOT, 1960, 524 PP.
DISCUSSES DIPLOMATIC MISSIONS EXCHANGED BETWEEN INDIA, CHINA, PERSIA, CENTRAL ASIA, TIBET, NEPAL, CEYLON, AND CAMBODIA, WITH EMPHASIS ON RELATIONS BETWEEN INDIA AND CHINA FROM 600 A.D. TO 1300.

2741 SALISBURY H.E.
BEHIND THE LINES - HANOI.
NEW YORK: HARPER & ROW, 1967, 243 PP., LC#67-21219.
EXTENSIVE ANSWERS TO MANY QUESTIONS ABOUT NORTH VIETNAM, ITS PEOPLE, LEADERS, POLICIES. CONSIDERS EFFECTS OF US ACTIONS, POSSIBILITIES FOR PEACE, PHILOSOPHICAL DIFFERENCES.

2742 SALKEVER L.R., FLYNN H.M.
SUB-SAHARA AFRICA (PAMPHLET)
GLENVIEW, ILL: SCOTT, FORESMAN, 1963, 72 PP.
EXAMINES HISTORIC PAST AND NEW PATTERNS OF AFRICAN TRADE, TECHNOLOGY, EDUCATION, AND GOVERNMENT. FOCUSES UPON CURRENT PROBLEMS OF ECONOMIC DEVELOPMENT, PATHWAYS TO ECONOMIC GROWTH, AND INTERNATIONAL RELATIONS.

2743 SALVADORI M.
"EL CAPITALISMO EN LA EUROPA DE LA POSGUERRA."
REV. INST. CIENC. SOC., (NO.3, 64), 211-30.
ANALYZES DEVELOPMENT OF THEORY AND PRACTICE OF CAPITALISM IN WESTERN EUROPE AFTER WW 2 AND ITS RELATION TO INDIVIDUALISM, RATIONALISM, AND MATERIALISM. DISCUSSES STATE CAPITALISM AND LIBERAL PRIVATE CAPITALISM IN RELATION TO ECONOMIC REBIRTH OF WESTERN EUROPE.

2744 SALVADORI M.
ITALY.
ENGLEWOOD CLIFFS: PRENTICE HALL, 1965, 184 PP., LC#65-20602.
SURVEY OF SOCIO-POLITICAL MOVEMENTS IN ITALY, TRACING THEIR ROMAN HERITAGE THROUGH MIDDLE AGES, THEIR INFLUENCE ON ITALIAN CULTURE, AND THEIR EFFECT ON CONTEMPORARY LIFE. ANNOTATED BIBLIOGRAPHY INCLUDES ENGLISH AND ITALIAN BOOKS AND PERIODICALS FROM 20TH CENTURY.

2745 SALVEMINI G.
PRELUDE TO WORLD WAR II.
GARDEN CITY: DOUBLEDAY, 1954, 519 PP., LC#53-13510.
BEGINS WITH ITALY'S RISE TO POWER AND MUSSOLINI'S CONTROL OF POWER. TRACES MUSSOLINI-HITLER RELATIONSHIP. TREATS AT LENGTH ITALO-ETHIOPIAN WAR. SHOWS MUSSOLINI TO BE INCOMPETENT AND NOT THE GREAT STATESMAN MANY HAVE BELIEVED HIM TO BE.

2746 SALYZYN V.
"FEDERAL-PROVINCIAL TAX SHARING SCHEMES."
CAN. PUBLIC ADMIN., 10 (JUNE 67), 161-166.
EXAMINES GROWING INADEQUACY OF EXISTING PROVINCIAL AND MUNICIPAL TAX STRUCTURES TO PROVIDE FOR EXPANDING NEEDS OF THESE GOVERNMENTS. EVALUATES POSSIBLE BENEFITS FROM THE SHARING OF A TAX BY TWO LEVELS OF GOVERNMENT. CLARIFIES THEORETICAL AND PRACTICAL DISTINCTIONS AMONG ALL FORMS OF TAX-SHARING ARRANGEMENTS; EXAMINES CURRENT SCHEMES AND SUGGESTS ALTERNATIVES.

2747 SANCHEZ A.L.
EL CONCEPTO DEL ESTADO EN EL PENSAMIENTO ESPANOL DEL SIGLO XVI.
MADRID: MARISAL, 1959, 192 PP.
STUDIES IDEA OF STATE IN SPANISH THOUGHT OF 16TH CENTURY, INCLUDING ORIGINS FROM MEDIEVAL JURISPRUDENCE, EXECUTIVE, LEGISLATIVE, AND JUDICIAL POWER, THE JUST WAR, AND RIGHT OF THE MAJORITY.

2748 SANCHEZ J.D.
"DESARROLLO ECONOMICO Y FUTURO DE COLOMBIA."
CENTRO, 3 (FEB. 67), 44-54.
MAINTAINS COLOMBIA PROMISES MOST RAPID ECONOMIC DEVELOPMENT OF ALL SOUTH AMERICAN NATIONS, DUE TO HER RICH NATURAL RESOURCES. EXAMINES AGRICULTURAL, MINERAL, AND INDUSTRIAL DEVELOPMENT IN PAST 10 YEARS. COLOMBIA DEPENDS TOO MUCH ON COFFEE EXPORTATION, HOWEVER, AND MUST DIVERSIFY EXPORTATIONS TO CONTINUE ECONOMIC DEVELOPMENT.

2749 SANCHEZ J.M.
REFORM AND REACTION.
CHAPEL HILL: U OF N CAR PR, 1964, 241 PP., LC#64-13560.
STUDIES CAUSES AND RESULTS OF SPAINISH CIVIL WAR AS IT IS RELATED TO THE CHURCH, CONFLICT OF PLUTOCRACY, THEOCRACY, DEMOCRACY, AND FISCISM. DESCRIBES PLACE OF CHURCH IN SPANISH OLITICAL HISTORY AS MOVING FORCE, AND ITS RELATION TO SOCIAL STRUCTURE.

2750 SANDEE J.
EUROPE'S FUTURE CONSUMPTION.
AMSTERDAM: NORTH HOLLAND PUBL CO, 1964, 363 PP.
STUDY IN PURPOSE AND APPLICATION OF CONSUMPTION ANALYSIS: 13 ESSAYS (4 IN FOREIGN LANGUAGES) PREDICTING FUTURE CONSUMPTION IN EUROPEAN COUNTRIES. MAIN CONCLUSION IS THAT CONSUMPTION FUNCTIONS ARE NEARLY THE SAME ALL OVER EUROPE.

2751 SANDERS R.
"MASS SUPPORT AND COMMUNIST INSURRECTION."
ORBIS, 9 (SPRING 65), 214-231.
COMMUNISTS CONSIDER MASS SUPPORT AS KEY ELEMENT IN WAGING REVOLUTIONARY WARS. AUTHOR STUDIES PATTERNS OF MASS BEHAVIOR IN GREEK, INDOCHINESE, PHILIPPINE, MALAYSIAN, AND SOUTH VIETNAMESE CASES OF COMMUNIST INSURGENCY. HE DESIRES TO DETERMINE THE AMOUNT OF POPULAR SUPPORT NEEDED FOR VICTORY, WHETHER SUPPORT MUST BE WIDESPREAD THROUGH COUNTRY OR ONLY IN SELECTED AREAS, AND IF SUPPORT AND CONTROL ARE DIFFERENT.

2752 SANTAYANA G.
"REASON IN SOCIETY" IN G. SANTAYANA, THE LIFE OF REASON."
NEW YORK: CHAS SCRIBNER'S SONS, 1955.
CIVILIZATION IS NECESSARY FOR LIFE OF REASON, BUT GOVERNMENT AND INDUSTRY ARE NOT NECESSARILY REASONABLE. INDUSTRY HAS PRODUCED MATERIALISM AND TOO MUCH LUXURY. REMEDY IS THROUGH BETTER DISTRIBUTION OF GOODS. GOVERNMENT IS THE POLITICAL REPRESENTATIVE OF CUSTOM AND INERTIA, BUT IT MAY BECOME RATIONAL. AUTHOR ALSO DISCUSSES WAR, FREE AND IDEAL SOCIETY, ARISTOCRATIC IDEAL, DEMOCRACY, AND PATRIOTISM.

2753 SANTHANAM K.
DEMOCRATIC PLANNING.
NEW YORK: ASIA PUBL HOUSE, 1961, 201 PP.
EXAMINES CONSTITUTIONAL AND POLITICAL DEVELOPMENTS IN INDIA; ANALYZES ECONOMIC PLANNING AND REFORM MEASURES. CONCLUDES WITH DISCUSSION OF CONGRESSIONAL POLICIES AND THEIR RELATION TO DEMOCRATIC TRADITIONS AND CONVENTIONS.

2754 SARGENT S.S. ED., SMITH M.W. ED.
CULTURE AND PERSONALITY.
NEW YORK: VIKING FUND, 1949, 219 PP., $1.50.
COLLECTION OF ESSAYS DISCUSSING THE EFFECTS OF CULTURAL FORCES UPON THE INDIVIDUAL'S PERSONALITY. DEFINES CONCEPTS OF CULTURE AND PERSONALITY, OFFERS TECHNIQUES FOR STUDYING THESE TWO CONCEPTS, EVALUATES RECENT CULTURAL STUDIES AND MAKES SUGGESTIONS FOR FUTURE ONES.

2755 SARKISYANZ E.
"NATIONALISM, CAPITALISM, AND THE UNCOMMITED NATIONS: MARXISM AND ASIAN CULTURAL TRADITIONS."
SURVEY, 43 (AUG. 62), 55-64.
DISCUSSES COMMUNIST PENETRATION IN ASIA BY MEANS OF IDENTIFICATION WITH TRADITION, CONFUCIANISM AND BUDHISM. DESCRIBES CHINESE CONQUEST OF TIBET BY USE OF PANCHEN LAMA. SUGGESTS THAT U NU STEMMED COMMUNISM IN BURMA BY IDENTIFYING SOCIALISM AND WELFARE STATE AS ECONOMIC MEANS FOR BUDHIST ESCHATOLOGICAL GOALS.

2756 SASTRI K.V.S.
FEDERAL-STATE FISCAL RELATIONS IN INDIA: A STUDY OF THE FINANCE COMMISSION AND TECHNIQUES OF FINANCIAL ADJUSTMENT.
LONDON: OXFORD U PR, 1966, 142 PP.
STUDIES INDIAN FINANCE COMMISSION, ITS ROLE IN FEDERAL-STATE STRUCTURE, ITS PRINCIPLES, AND PROCEDURES. ANALYZES PROBLEM OF RELATED TAX EFFORTS OF STATES IN FEDERATION. PROPOSES DISTRIBUTABLE POOLS OF UNION TAX-REVENUES AND DISCUSSES PROCEDURES FOR DISTRIBUTING THEM.

2757 SAUVAGET J., CAHEN C. ED.
INTRODUCTION TO THE HISTORY OF THE MIDDLE EAST (A BIBLIOGRAPHICAL GUIDE)
BERKELEY: U OF CALIF PR, 1965, 252 PP., LC#64-25271.
AN ENGLISH TRANSLATION WHICH REVISES AND ADDS TO SAUVAGET'S ORIGINAL 1943 PUBLICATION. IN THREE PARTS, THE BOOK COVERS SOURCES, DISCUSSES THE MAIN REFERENCE WORKS, AND CLASSIFIES WORKS BY PERIOD AND REGION. CONTAINS FREQUENT CROSS REFERENCES AND HAS A LENGTHY NAME INDEX.

2758 SAUVY A.
LE POUVOIR ET L'OPINION.
PARIS: LIBRAIRIE PAYOT, 1949, 188 PP.
ANALYSIS OF PUBLIC OPINION AND EXAMINATION OF FRENCH POLITICAL AND SOCIAL PSYCHOLOGY AND ITS EFFECTS ON POLICY. DISCUSSES HOW PUBLIC IS INFORMED AND ITS REACTION TO GOVERNMENTAL ACTIVITY.

2759 SAVELYEV N.
"MONOPOLY DRIVE IN INDIA."
INTERNATIONAL AFFAIRS (USSR) 4 (APR.67), 35-40.
ARGUES THAT INDIAN NEUTRALITY ENDANGERED BY INCREASED POLITICAL ACTIVITY OF INDIAN MONOPOLY BOURGEOISIE. INDIAN AND WESTERN CAPITALISM CLOSELY LINKED IN RESISTING DEMANDS FOR ECONOMIC, SOCIAL, AND DEMOCRATIC REFORM. DISCUSSION OF INTERNAL PARTY ALLIANCES AND RIGHT-WING REACTIONARY DRIVE TO POWER. NOTES POLITICAL CONSCIOUSNESS AND CLASS MATURITY OF MASSES.

2760 SAUER W.
"NATIONAL SOCIALISM: TOTALITARIANISM OR FASCISM?"
AMER. HISTORICAL REVIEW, 73 (DEC. 67), 404-424.
ANALYZES INTERPRETATIONS OF GERMAN NAZISM. BEFORE 1939 SCHOLARS ATTEMPTED TO EXPLAIN NATIONAL SOCIALISM AS FASCISM. DURING WWII THE EXPLANATION WAS IN TERMS OF A UNIQUE GERMAN PHENOMENON. DURING COLD WAR, SOCIALISM HAS BEEN INTERPRETED AS TOTALITARIANISM. SURVEYS PAST EFFORTS AT INTERPRETATION, REVIEWS CONTEMPORARY STUDIES IN THE FIELD, AND DEVELOPS SUGGESTIONS FOR FURTHER INTERPRETIVE ANALYSES.

2761 SAYEED K.
"PATHAN REGIONALISM."
S. ATLAN. QUART., 63 (64), 478-506.
HOW THE 5 MILLION PATHANS (AFGHANS) OF PAKISTAN HAVE AGITATED AND FOUGHT FOR THEIR TRIBAL INDEPENDENCE. THE CULTURE, INSTITUTIONS, AND SOCIAL DEVELOPMENT OF THE AREA ARE DESCRIBED.

2762 SCALAPINO R.A., MASUMI J.
PARTIES AND POLITICS IN CONTEMPORARY JAPAN.
BERKELEY: U OF CALIF PR, 1962, 190 PP., LC#61-14279.
ANALYSIS OF POSTWAR JAPANESE POLITICS REGARDING THEIR INTERNATIONAL AND DOMESTIC ASPECTS. DESCRIBES COMPOSITION AND ORGANIZATION OF JAPANESE POLITICAL PARTIES AND OPERATION OF POLITICAL PROCESS.

2763 SCALAPINO R.A. ED.
THE COMMUNIST REVOLUTION IN ASIA* TACTICS, GOALS, AND ACHIEVEMENTS.
ENGLEWOOD CLIFFS: PRENTICE HALL, 1965, 405 PP., LC#65-26708.
THE EDITOR PRESENTS A GENERAL AND HISTORICAL FRAMEWORK FOR A COMPARATIVE ANALYSIS OF COMMUNIST EFFORTS. INCLUDES TYPES AND STAGES NECESSARY FOR SUCCESSFUL TAKEOVERS AND DATA WHERE AVAILABLE ON THE FIT OF THE VARIOUS ASIAN PARTIES INTO THIS STRUCTURE. DETAIL IS PROVIDED BY THE INCLUSION OF PAPERS ON CHINA, MONGOLIA, KOREA, LAOS, VIETNAM, JAPAN, MALAYSIA, INDONESIA, BURMA, INDIA, NEPAL, AND CEYLON.

2764 SCALAPINO R.A. ED.
"A SURVEY OF ASIA IN 1966."
ASIAN SURVEY, 7 (JAN.-FEB. 67), 1-80, 83-150 .
ESSAYS ON EVENTS AND CONDITIONS IN ASIA IN 1966. STUDIES CULTURAL REVOLUTION IN CHINA, GROWTH OF MONGOLIAN PEOPLE'S REPUBLIC, EFFORTS BY KOREA TO IMPROVE GOVERNMENT AND SOCIAL SYSTEM, AND SOUTH VIETNAM'S POLITICS. DISCUSSES POLITICAL AND DIPLOMATIC SITUATION IN TAIWAN, PHILIPPINES, CAMBODIA, LAOS, JAPAN, INDIA, NEPAL, PAKISTAN, CEYLON, BURMA, THAILAND, MALAYSIA, AND INDONESIA.

2765 SCANLON D.G. ED.
INTERNATIONAL EDUCATION: A DOCUMENTARY HISTORY.
NY: COLUMBIA U TEACHERS COLLEGE, 1960, 196 PP., LC#60-14305.
HISTORY OF DEVELOPMENTS IN FIELD AND STUDY OF INTERNATIONAL EDUCATION. COLLECTION OF ESSAYS INCLUDES BIOGRAPHIES OF PIONEERS IN FIELD, STUDIES OF INTERNATIONAL ORGANIZATION, CROSS-CULTURAL EXCHANGES, EDUCATIONAL PRACTICES, AND INTERNATIONAL COMMUNICATION.

2766 SCARROW H.A.
THE HIGHER PUBLIC SERVICE OF THE COMMONWEALTH OF AUSTRALIA.
DURHAM: DUKE U PR, 1957, 180 PP., LC#57-13024.
CASE STUDY OF PUBLIC SERVICE BUREAUCRACY IN AUSTRALIA, FROM ITS BEGINNINGS AS MACHINERY WAS SET UP THROUGH ITS GROWTH AND DEVELOPMENT TO PRESENT ORGANIZATION. DISCUSSES COMPOSITION OF SERVICE AND ITS ROLE IN GOVERNMENTAL STRUCTURE.

2767 SCHACHTER G.
"REGIONAL DEVELOPMENT IN THE ITALIAN DUAL ECONOMY"
ECO. DEV. AND CULTURAL CHANGE, 15 (JULY 67), 398-407.
EXAMINES REGIONAL DUALISM IN ITALIAN ECONOMY AND EFFECTS ON ECONOMIC DEVELOPMENT. OBSTACLES TO DEVELOPMENT ARE DEPENDENCY OF ONE REGION ON ANOTHER, MARKET PROBLEMS, AND MASS MIGRATION. STUDIES ROLE OF GOVERNMENT IN EQUALIZING DEVELOPMENT IN EACH REGION THROUGH MIXED GOVERNMENT ENTERPRISES AND PLANNED INDUSTRIAL DEVELOPMENT OF AGRICULTURAL REGIONS.

2768 SCHADERA I.
SELECT BIBLIOGRAPHY OF SOUTH AFRICAN NATIVE LIFE AND PROBLEMS.
LONDON: OXFORD U PR, 1941, 249 PP.
BIBLIOGRAPHY OF SOUTH AFRICA DEALING WITH ANTHROPOLOGY, ECONOMIC, POLITICAL, SOCIAL, LINGUISTIC ASPECTS OF LIFE IN SOUTH AFRICA.

2769 SCHAFFER B.B.
"THE CONCEPT OF PREPARATION* SOME QUESTIONS ABOUT THE TRANSFER OF SYSTEMS OF GOVERNMENT."
WORLD POLITICS, 18 (OCT. 65), 42-67.
AUTHOR CRITICIZES THE THEORY OF ATTEMPTING TO TRANSFER WESTERN POLITICAL SYSTEMS TO DEPENDENT AREAS. HE GIVES AN EXTENSIVE HISTORY OF THE THEORY AND OPERATION OF THE UK'S EFFORT OF PREPARING HER COLONIES FOR STATEHOOD, AND CRITICIZES FACETS OF IT.

2770 SCHAPIRO J.S.
"SOCIAL REFORM AND THE REFORMATION."
NEW YORK: COLUMBIA U PRESS, 1909.
PRESENTATION OF NEGLECTED ECONOMIC ASPECTS OF LUTHERAN REVOLT. EXAMINATION OF INFLUENCE OF SOCIAL CONDITIONS ON

RELIGIOUS MOVEMENT. INCLUDES GROWTH OF MONOPOLIES,INTRODUCTION OF ROMAN LAW, PEASANTS' REVOLT, ATTITUDE OF MARTIN LUTHER TO REVOLT. IN CONCLUSION DEALS WITH SCHEMES OF REFORM -- SECULAR STATE OR DIVINE EVANGELICAL REFORM. BIBLIOGRAPHY IN GERMAN.

2771 SCHAPIRO J.S.
"LIBERALISM AND THE CHALLENGE OF FASCISM."
NEW YORK: MCGRAW HILL, 1949.
STUDY OF FORMATION OF PATTERN OF LIBERALISM IN ENGLAND AND FRANCE, WHERE ITS IDEALS AND POLICIES BECAME MODELS FOR OTHER NATIONS OF EUROPE. TREATS OF ORIGINS OF FASCISM IN THESE COUNTRIES. ARGUES THAT PROUDHON WAS HARBINGER OF FASCISM AS WAS CARLYLE. ANALYZES REIGN OF LOUIS NAPOLEON IN THIS LIGHT. EXTENSIVE BIBLIOGRAPHY ARRANGED BY CHAPTER. DISCUSSIONS OF TOQUEVILLE AND MILL.

2772 SCHAPIRO L.
THE COMMUNIST PARTY OF THE SOVIET UNION.
LONDON: EYRE, 1960, 631 PP.
FINDS THE METHOD OF GOVERNING ESTABLISHED BY LENIN AND DEVELOPED BY STALIN AS UNIQUE IN HISTORY OF POLITICAL SYSTEMS BECAUSE OF THE PARTY'S USE OF IDEOLOGY AND DISCIPLINE AS MEANS OF TOTALITARIAN CONTROLS OVER COURTS, TRADE UNIONS AND OTHER INSTITUTIONS IN USSR. DEMONSTRATES LEADER-PARTY RELATIONSHIP IN LENIN, STALIN, AND POST-STALIN ERAS TO BE BASICALLY DIFFERENT.

2773 SCHAPIRO L., UTECHIN S.V.
"SOVIET GOVERNMENT TODAY."
POLIT. QUART., 32 (APR.-JUNE 61), 124-38.
CONSIDERS HOW FAR THE CHANGES SINCE STALIN'S DEATH HAVE BEEN IN THE DIRECTION OF GREATER FREEDOM AND DEMOCRACY. BASED ON STUDY OF GOVERNMENTS OF UNION REPUBLICS, THEIR LEGAL ADMINISTRATION, LOCAL GOVERNMENTS AND THE EFFECTS OF GOVERNMENT ACTS ON THE GOVERNED.

2774 SCHATTEN F.
COMMUNISM IN AFRICA.
NEW YORK: FREDERICK PRAEGER, 1966, 352 PP., LC#65-14187.
CONSIDERS INTERACTIONS AND CHARACTERISTICS OF AFRICAN NATIONALISM, COMMUNIST ACTIVITIES, AND POSITION OF THE WEST. STATES THAT END OF WESTERN COLONIALISM WAS DUE TO EAST-WEST CONFLICT RATHER THAN ENLIGHTENED POLICY OF WEST. DISCUSSES COMMUNIST GOALS, SUCCESSES, AND FAILURES IN AFRICA. CONCLUDES THAT WEST MUST TRY TO RECOVER MORAL INITIATIVE, AND HELP AFRICA TO ATTAIN INDEPENDENT EXISTENCE.

2775 SCHATTSCHNEIDER E.E., JONES V., BAILEY S.K.
A GUIDE TO THE STUDY OF PUBLIC AFFAIRS.
NY: WILLIAM SLOAN ASSOCIATES, 1952, 135 PP.
RESEARCH AID AND PROCEDURAL GUIDE TO FIELD OF PUBLIC AFFAIRS. COVERS RESEARCH METHOD AND TECHNIQUE IN THE STUDY OF NEWSPAPERS, PRESSURE GROUPS, FEDERAL GOVERNMENT AGENCIES, CONGRESSMEN, CITY GOVERNMENT, BUDGETS, STATUTES, AND JUDICIAL DECISIONS.

2776 SCHECHTMAN J.B.
"MINORITIES IN THE MIDDLE EAST."
INDIA QUART., 17 (JULY-SEPT., 61), 242-57.
DISCUSSES NUMBERS AND FATES OF CHRISTIAN, JEWISH, AND KURDISH MINORITIES IN ARAB STATES.

2777 SCHECHTMAN J.B.
ON WINGS OF EAGLES: THE PLIGHT, EXODUS, AND HOMECOMING OF ORIENTAL JEWRY.
NEW YORK: THOMAS YOSELOFF, 1961, 429 PP., LC#61-6156.
STUDIES HISTORY AND RECENT PLIGHT OF VARIOUS JEWISH COMMUNITIES OF ORIENT. DESCRIBES PROCEDURE OF THEIR EXODUS FROM ARAB COUNTRIES, NON-ARAB MOSLEM COUNTRIES, AND MAGHREB. CONCENTRATES ON IMPACT ON COUNTRY LEFT BEHIND AND PROBLEMS OF INTEGRATING IN ISRAEL.

2778 SCHECHTMAN J.B.
POSTWAR POPULATION TRANSFERS IN EUROPE: 1945-1955.
PHILA: U OF PENN PR, 1962, 417 PP., LC#62-7200.
DISCUSSES THE REDISTRIBUTION OF ETHNIC GROUPS THAT FOLLOWED THE END OF WWII IN EUROPE. EMPHASIZES THE MIGRATION OF GERMANS FROM CZECHOSLOVAKIA, POLAND, HUNGARY, RUMANIA, AND YUGOSLAVIA. ALSO DISCUSSES IMPLICATIONS OF POLISH-SOVIET AND CZECH-SOVIET EXCHANGES OF POPULATION. DISCUSSES FUNDAMENTAL IDEOLOGICAL PROBLEMS ARISING FROM THE TRANSFER OF POPULATION IN THE LIGHT OF POSTWAR DEVELOPMENTS.

2779 SCHECHTMAN J.B.
THE REFUGEE IN THE WORLD: DISPLACEMENT AND INTEGRATION.
NEW YORK: BARNES, 1963, 424 PP., $8.50.
STUDY OF THE GLOBAL NATURE OF THE REFUGEE PROBLEM FROM 1945 TO 1963. TRACES THE ORIGINS, DEVELOPMENT, AND THE ATTEMPTED SOLUTIONS TO THE SPECIFIC REFUGEE PROBLEMS CONSIDERED.

2780 SCHECTER J.
THE NEW FACE OF BUDDHA: BUDDHISM AND POLITICAL POWER IN SOUTHEAST ASIA.
NEW YORK: COWARD-MCMANN, 1967, 300 PP., LC#67-10560.
DESCRIBES NEW BUDDHISM AS MORE THAN RELIGION AND PHILOSOPHY; IT IS NATIONALISM, IDEOLOGY, AND ULTIMATE SOURCE OF ASIAN VALUES. SHOWS THAT IN TRADITIONAL BUDDHISM, CHURCH AND STATE WERE UNITED AND THIS FORCE OF RELIGION AS JUSTIFICATION FOR RULE REMAINS. DISCUSSES PERSONALITIES IN FOREFRONT OF NEW BUDDHISM: PRINCE SIHANOUK AND VIETNAM'S THICH TRI QUANG.

2781 SCHEFFLER H.W.
"THE GENESIS AND REPRESSION OF CONFLICT: CHOISEUL ISLAND."
AMER. ANTHROPOL., 66 (AUG 64), 789-94.
ON THE THEORY OF WARFARE AND THE FUNCTION OF THE STATE AS MAINTAINING ORDER OR DIRECTING CHANGE. 'MULTIPLE FACTIONS KEEP SORTING THEMSELVES OUT DIFFERENTLY IN AN AVID AND CALCULATING AND FORCEFUL PURSUIT OF INTERESTS, AND THIS IS ALL THE 'ORDER' THERE IS....'

2782 SCHEIBER H.N.
THE WILSON ADMINISTRATION AND CIVIL LIBERTIES 1917-1921.
ITHACA: CORNELL U PRESS, 1960, 69 PP.
ANALYSIS OF CIVIL LIBERTIES IN US DURING WWI AND ATTITUDE OF FEDERAL GOVERNMENT IN CONTROLLING POPULATION IN REGARD TO NATIONAL SECURITY. EXAMINES LEGISLATION LIMITING RIGHTS AND EXECUTIVE APPLICATION OF RESTRICTIVE LAWS.

2783 SCHELER M.
SCHRIFTEN ZUR SOZIOLOGIE UND WELTANSCHAUUNGSLEHRE (GESAMMELTE WERKE, BAND 6; 2ND ED.)
MUNICH: FRANCKE VERLAG, 1963, 455 PP.
ESSAYS ON SOCIOLOGY AND WELTANSCHAUUNGEN, ORGANIZED UNDER THREE HEADINGS: MORALS, NATION AND WELTANSCHAUUNG, CHRISTIANITY AND SOCIETY. WELTANSCHAUUNG DOES NOT REFER TO PHILOSOPHICAL POSITION, BUT TO ORGANICALLY AND HISTORICALLY DEVELOPED WAY IN WHICH GREAT COHERENT GROUPS VIEW AND VALUE WORLD, SOUL, AND LIFE.

2784 SCHELLING T.C.
"NUCLEAR STRATEGY IN EUROPE."
WORLD POLIT., 14 (OCT 61), 421-32.
DISCUSSES DANGERS OF AN ACCIDENTAL WAR IN EUROPE, BETWEEN THE USSR AND THE FREE WORLD, WHICH MIGHT MUSHROOM INTO A GLOBAL CONFLICT IF NUCLEAR WEAPONS ARE INTRODUCED.

2785 SCHIEDER T. ED.
DOCUMENTS ON THE EXPULSION OF THE GERMANS FROM EASTERN-CENTRAL-EUROPE (VOL. II/III)
BONN: FED MIN REFUG& WAR VICTIM, 1961, 569 PP.
REPORTS ON THE FATE OF ETHNIC GERMANS IN HUNGARY AND RUMANIA PRIOR TO, DURING, AND AFTER WWII. DETAILS TRANSFERS AND EXPULSION OF POPULATION BY SS AND USSR. CONTAINS DOCUMENTS, LAWS, AND DECREES. ALSO CONTAINS INFORMATION ON LIVING CONDITIONS IN POST-WAR YEARS.

2786 SCHIEDER T.
THE STATE AND SOCIETY IN OUR TIMES (TRANS. BY C.A.M. SYM)
LONDON: THOMAS NELSON & SONS, 1962.
STUDIES CONCERNED WITH RELATION BETWEEN POLITICAL AND SOCIAL STRUCTURE, INCLUDING REVOLUTION IN NINETEENTH CENTURY, POLITICAL PARTY IN GERMANY, AND RENEWAL OF THE SENSE OF HISTORY.

2788 SCHLESINGER J.A.
HOW THEY BECAME GOVERNOR; A STUDY OF COMPARATIVE STATE POLITICS, 1870-1950.
E LANSING: MICH ST U, GOVT RES, 1957, 103 PP.
ANALYZES POLITICAL CAREERS OF ALL GOVERNORS ELECTED IN US FROM 1870 TO 1950, AND FINDS A PATTERN IN THEIR POLITICAL BACKGROUND. FOCUSES ON CHANGES, AND FINDS STATE LEGISLATURE IS NO LONGER SPRINGBOARD TO GOVERNOR'S OFFICE. DISCUSSES DECREASED PRESTIGE OF STATE AS AGAINST NATIONAL POLITICS. EXAMINES OFFICE CAREERS OF GOVERNORS, STATE PATTERNS OF ELECTION AND LEGISLATION, LAW ENFORCEMENT, MINOR OFFICES.

2789 SCHMIDT-VOLKMAR E.
DER KULTURKAMPF IN DEUTSCHLAND 1871-1890.
GOTTINGEN: MUSTERSCHMIDT VERLAG, 1962, 387 PP.
EXAMINES CHURCH-STATE RELATIONS IN GERMANY UNDER BISMARCK. TRACES DISPUTES OF PRUSSIA WITH CATHOLIC CHURCH AND ITS IMPACT ON PARTY LIFE, OTHER GERMAN STATES, AND EUROPE IN GENERAL.

2790 SCHMOLLER G.
THE MERCANTILE SYSTEM AND ITS HISTORICAL SIGNIFICANCE: ILLUSTRATED CHIEFLY FROM PRUSSIAN HISTORY (TRANS.)
NEW YORK: MACMILLAN, 1896, 95 PP.
ANALYSIS OF THE DEVELOPMENT OF MERCANTILISM AND ECONOMIC EVOLUTION FROM SIMPLE TRIBAL SUBSISTENCE TO COMPLEX NATIONAL AND INTERNATIONAL ECONOMIC SYSTEMS. ARGUES THAT ECONOMIC FORCES, WHILE PURSUING THEIR OWN ENDS, SHOULD SERVE THE STATE AND CONVERSELY THE STATE SHOULD PLACE ITS POWER IN THE SERVICE OF NATIONAL ECONOMY. SPECIFIC EXAMPLE OF THIS IDEAL IS GIVEN IN AN EXAMINATION OF PRUSSIA'S SILK INDUSTRY.

2791 SCHNAPPER B.
LA POLITIQUE ET LE COMMERCE FRANCAIS DANS LE GOLFE DE GUINEE DE 1838 A 1871.

HAGUE: MOUTON & CO, 1961, 286 PP.
STUDY OF FRENCH POLITICAL AND COMMERCIAL IMPERIALISM ON THE GULF OF GUINEA, EMPHASIZING FORTIFIED COMMERCIAL INSTALLATIONS, COLONIZATION, AND TRADE PRODUCTS.

2792 SCHNEIDER H.W.
"MAKING THE FASCIST STATE."
LONDON: OXFORD U PR, 1928.
INVESTIGATES CONSTRUCTION OF FASCIST THEORIES INTERMS OF VARYING PRACTICAL SITUATIONS INTO WHICH THE MOVEMENT WAS FORCED BY CIRCUMSTANCES. EMPHASIZES INTERACTION BETWEEN FACT AND PHILOSOPHIC FICTION, PRACTICAL EXIGENCIES AND SOCIAL THEORIES. EXTENSIVE BIBLIOGRPAHY DEALS WITH GENERAL POLITICAL THEORY AND HISTORY OF FASCISM RATHER THAN WITH TECHNICAL DETAILS. MAJORITY OF WORKS ARE IN ITALIAN.

2793 SCHNITGER F.M.
FORGOTTEN KINGDOMS IN SUMATRA.
LEYDEN: BRILL, 1964, 226 PP.
NONTECHNICAL DESCRIPTIONS OF SEVERAL AREAS OF WILDERNESS IN SUMATRA AND OF CUSTOMS OF NATIVE INHABITANTS OF THESE AREAS. ATTEMPTS TO PROVIDE GENERAL INFORMATION CONCERNING HISTORY AND ETHNOLOGY OF ANCIENT SUMATRAN KINGDOMS AND CIVILIZATIONS. INTENDED AS POPULAR BOOK.

2794 SCHOCKEL E.
DAS POLITISCHE PLAKAT.
MUNICH: ZENTRAL VERL DER NSDAP, 1939, 247 PP.
DISCUSSION OF PLACARDS AND POSTERS AS INSTRUMENTS OF POLITICAL PROPAGANDA. MAINTAINS THAT PLACARDS HAVE CONTRIBUTED TO "CLEANSING OF NATIONAL SOUL" AND TO RISE OF GERMAN POWER AND NEW IDEOLOGY.

2795 SCHOENBRUN D.
"VIETNAM* THE CASE FOR EXTRICATION."
COLUMBIA UNIV. FORUM, 9 (FALL 66), 4-9.
COMMENTS ON WAR IN VIETNAM. POSITION TAKEN IS THAT WAR MUST BE ENDED. ADVOCATES NEGOTIATIONS AMONG THE VIETNAMESE. PROPOSES NEUTRALIZATION SIMILAR TO AUSTRIAN STATE TREATY. IMMEDIATE CONCERN MUST BE WITH CHANGE OF ATTITUDE.

2796 SCHOEPS H.J.
KONSERVATIVE ERNEUERUNG IDEEN ZUR DEUTSCHEN POLITIK.
STUTTGART: ERNST KLETT VERLAG, 1958, 152 PP.
DISCUSSES APPLICATION OF CONSERVATIVE PRINCIPLES TO MODERN MASS SOCIETY. ATTEMPTS TO ANALYZE OPERATION OF CONSERVATIVE PRINCIPLES WITHIN FRAMEWORK OF NON-MARXIST SOCIALISM AND THE CREATION OF A LEADERSHIP ELITE ON BASIS OF PARLIAMENTARY DEMOCRACY.

2797 SCHONS D.
BOOK CENSORSHIP IN NEW SPAIN (NEW WORLD STUDIES, BOOK II)
ANN ARBOR: EDWARDS BROTHERS, 1949, 45 PP.
REGISTER OF 96 COPIES OF LETTERS AND SUMMARIES OF LETTERS DEALING WITH PUNITIVE CENSORSHIP OF 17TH-CENTURY BOOKS, FILED BY SPANISH SUPREME COUNCIL OF THE INQUISITION, SUPPLEMENTED BY CORRESPONDENCE EXCHANGED BETWEEN THE SPANISH AND MEXICAN INQUISITIONS. ASSERTS THAT INQUISITORIAL LETTERS WERE NOT MERE INDEXES OF PROHIBITED BOOKS, BUT INDICATORS OF ISSUES FACING CHURCH AND STATE IN THAT PERIOD.

2798 SCHORN H.
DER RICHTER IM DRITTEN REICH; GESCHICHTE UND DOKUMENTE.
FRANKFURT: V KLOSTERMANN, 1959, 743 PP.
INDICATES THAT IN NAZI GERMANY THERE WERE COURAGEOUS JUDGES, THAT THERE IS A JUSTICE HIGHER THAN LAW, AND THAT INJUSTICE REMAINS UNJUST EVEN WHEN IT IS PROMULGATED AS LAW. BASES STUDY OF JUDGES IN NAZI GERMANY UPON MATERIALS FROM THE MINISTRY OF JUSTICE, JUDGES, CHURCHES, THE BAR, POLITICAL PARTIES, INCLUDING NAZI ACCUSATION AGAINST JUDGES.

2799 SCHRAM S.
MAO TSE-TUNG.
NEW YORK: SIMON AND SCHUSTER, 1966, 351 PP., LC#67-12918.
A BIOGRAPHY OF MAO WITH EMPHASIS ON HIS ADAPTATION OF MARXISM TO THE SPECIFIC SETTING OF CHINESE CULTURE AND SOCIETY.

2800 SCHRAMM W.
THE PROCESS AND EFFECTS OF MASS COMMUNICATION.
URBANA: U. ILL. PR., 1954, 586 PP., $6.00.
AMONG SEVERAL POINTS CONSIDERED ARE: HOW ATTENTION IS SECURED, HOW OPINIONS AND ATTITUDES ARE CREATED AND ALTERED, AND HOW MEANING IS TRANSFERRED FROM ONE FIELD TO ANOTHER. INTERNATIONAL COMMUNICATION IS ASSESSED AS IT RELATES TO PROPAGANDA AND PSYCHOLOGICAL WARFARE.

2801 SCHULER E.A.
THE PAKISTAN ACADEMIES FOR RURAL DEVELOPMENT COMILLA AND PESHAWAR 1959-1964.
E LANSING: ASIAN STUD CTR, MSU, 1965, 116 PP.
BIBLIOGRAPHY OF MATERIALS ON PAKISTAN ACADEMIES FOR RURAL DEVELOPMENT ESTABLISHED SINCE 1959. LISTS TRAINING MATERIALS (MANUALS), REPORTS FOR GOVERNMENT OFFICIALS OF PAKISTAN, AND PROFESSIONAL LITERATURE ON DEVELOPMENT AND NATION-BUILDING PRODUCED BY ACADEMIES. ARRANGED ALPHABETICALLY AND BY ACADEMY. ENGLISH-LANGUAGE SOURCES PUBLISHED 1959-64.

2802 SCHUMAN S.I.
LEGAL POSITIVISM: ITS SCOPE AND LIMITATIONS.
DETROIT: WAYNE STATE U PR, 1963, 265 PP., LC#62-14874.
PRESENTS PHILOSOPHY OF LAW, EXAMINING THE ETHICS AND OBLIGATION OF LEGAL THEORIES AND RELATING THEM TO PURPOSIVE CONDUCT. DISCUSSES THE DICHOTOMY BETWEEN "IS" AND "OUGHT." STUDIES ULTIMATE GOALS, SCIENCE, AND NATURE OF MAN IN TERMS OF POLITICAL THEORIES. CONCLUDES WITH COMPARISON AND ANALYSIS OF THE POLITICS OF PHILOSOPHY.

2803 SCHUMM S.
"INTEREST REPRESENTATION IN FRANCE AND GERMANY."
CAHIERS DE BRUGES, 3 (1958), 139-147.
DISCUSSES METHODS OF ORGANIZING ECONOMIC PRESSURE GROUPS INTO GOVERNMENT STRUCTURE. QUESTIONS THAT SUCH UNION WILL BRING ABOUT COMPROMISES OF DIFFERENT ASPECTS OF ECONOMY FOR NATIONAL INTEREST. EXAMINES GERMAN NATIONAL ECONOMIC COUNCIL UNDER WEIMAR CONSTITUTION AND FRENCH NATIONAL ECONOMIC COUNCIL. MAINTAINS THAT ECONOMIC COUNCIL AND PARLIAMENTARY GOVERNMENT ARE INCOMPATIBLE.

2804 SCHUMPETER J.A.
CAPITALISM, SOCIALISM, AND DEMOCRACY (3RD ED.)
NEW YORK: HARPER & ROW, 1950, 431 PP.
DISCUSSES MARXIST DOCTRINE IN NONTECHNICAL MANNER. PROCEEDS TO CAPITALISM, AND TRIES TO SHOW THAT SOCIALIST FORM OF SOCIETY WILL EMERGE FROM INEVITABLE DECOMPOSITION OF CAPITALIST SOCIETY. EXAMINES PROBLEMS THAT BEAR UPON CONDITIONS IN WHICH SOCIALISM MAY BE EXPECTED TO BE AN ECONOMIC SUCCESS.

2805 SCHURMANN F.
IDEOLOGY AND ORGANIZATION IN COMMUNIST CHINA.
BERKELEY: U OF CALIF PR, 1966, 540 PP., LC#66-15324.
THEORIZES THAT IDEOLOGY AND ORGANIZATION AROSE IN RED CHINA BECAUSE A TRADITIONAL SOCIAL SYSTEM NO LONGER EXISTED TO GIVE UNITY TO SOCIETY. TRACES STRUGGLE IN MAINLAND COUNTRYSIDE AND CITIES TO CREATE AND IMPOSE STRUCTURES OF ORGANIZATION ON THE NATION. STUDIES THE PARTY, GOVERNMENT BUREAUCRACY AND MANAGEMENT, CONCEPTS OF CONTROL, AND ORGANIZATION OF CITIES AND VILLAGES.

2806 SCHUTZ W.W.
RETHINKING GERMAN POLICY; NEW APPROACHES TO REUNIFICATION.
NEW YORK: FREDERICK PRAEGER, 1967, 200 PP.
STATES THAT GERMAN REUNIFICATION WILL BE ACHIEVED ONLY THROUGH CONSENT OF USSR. URGES NEW PEACE CONFERENCE TO RESOLVE PROBLEMS LEFT OVER FROM WWII AND TO PLAN EAST-WEST SECURITY PROGRAM AND TEN-YEAR PLAN TO ESTABLISH NEGOTIATIONS WITH US AND USSR FOR REUNIFICATION. SEES UNITY VALUABLE TO UNITED EUROPE. ADVOCATES GERMAN INITIATION OF PLANS.

2807 SCHWARTZ B.
LAW AND THE EXECUTIVE IN BRITAIN: A COMPARATIVE STUDY.
NEW YORK: NEW YORK U PR, 1949, 388 PP.
STUDY OF EXECUTIVE POWER AND ADMINISTRATIVE LAW IN UK. EXECUTIVE HAS INCREASED IN SIZE AND POWER AND TENDS TO MAKE LAW AS WELL AS CARRY IT OUT; THERE IS NEED FOR ADDITIONAL CONTROL OVER BUREAUCRACY.

2808 SCHWARTZ B.
FRENCH ADMINISTRATIVE LAW AND THE COMMON-LAW WORLD.
NEW YORK: NEW YORK U PR, 1954, 367 PP., LC#54-5276.
COMPARES FRENCH LAW WITH THE ANGLO-AMERICAN SYSTEM, WITHIN THE CONTEXT OF THEIR ECONOMIC, HISTORICAL, POLITICAL, AND SOCIAL HERITAGES. PURPOSE IS TO FIND POSSIBLE AREAS OF IMPROVEMENT IN THE AMERICAN LEGAL SYSTEM. EMPHASIZES THE RELATIONS OF THE THREE BRANCHES OF GOVERNMENT - LEGISLATIVE, EXECUTIVE, AND JUDICIAL - TO EACH OTHER, AND THE INTERRELATION OF LOCAL, STATE, AND FEDERAL GOVERNMENTS. CITES MANY CASES.

2809 SCHWARTZ B.
THE ROOTS OF FREEDOM: A CONSTITUTIONAL HISTORY OF ENGLAND.
NEW YORK: HILL AND WANG, 1967, 248 PP., LC#67-14653.
EVOLUTION OF ENGLISH LAW AND INSTITUTIONS WITH FOCUS ON GROWTH OF PARLIAMENTARY GOVERNMENT. TRACES INFLUENCE OF ENGLISH CONSTITUTION ON AMERICA. IDEA OF LAW EXPRESSED AS CHECK ON GOVERNMENTAL POWER.

2810 SCHWARTZ H.
THE RED PHOENIX: RUSSIA SINCE WORLD WAR II.
NEW YORK: FREDERICK PRAEGER, 1961, 417 PP., LC#61-11062.
TRACES INTERNAL POLITICAL DEVELOPMENT, ECONOMIC GROWTH, SCIENTIFIC ADVANCES, AND FOREIGN RELATIONS OF USSR SINCE WWII. DISCUSSES US-SOVIET RELATIONS AND COMPETITION AS WELL AS RELATIONS WITH RED CHINA.

2811 SCHWARTZ M.
"THE 1964 PRESIDENTIAL ELECTIONS THROUGH SOVIET EYES."
WESTERN POLITICAL Q., 19 (DEC. 66), 663-671.
SOVIET PRESS, CONCERNED OVER GOLDWATER'S NOMINATION AS EVIDENCE OF A STRONG ANTI-SOVIET ELEMENT IN AMERICAN POL-

ITICS, STRESSED SUPERIORITY OF DEMOCRATS FOREIGN POLICY PROGRAM. CHINESE VIEWS ON ELECTION ALSO DISCUSSED AS A FACTOR IN SINO-SOVIET CONFLICT.

2812 SCHWARTZ M.A.
PUBLIC OPINION AND CANADIAN IDENTITY.
BERKELEY: U OF CALIF PR, 1967, 300 PP.
COMPILATION AND INTERPRETATION OF GALLUP POLL MATERIALS ON CANADIAN PUBLIC OPINION. DESCRIBES HOW CANADIANS VIEW THEIR NATION AND ROLE OF POLITICAL PARTIES IN SHAPING A MORE INTEGRATED NATIONAL IDENTITY. EXAMINES EXTENT OF REGIONAL AND ETHNIC DIVISION. ILLUSTRATES USEFULNESS OF SURVEY DATA IN ANALYZING LARGE-SCALE SOCIAL SYSTEMS.

2813 SCOTT D.J.R.
RUSSIAN POLITICAL INSTITUTIONS.
NEW YORK: RINEHART, 1958, 265 PP., LC#58-4632.
STUDIES INTERNAL GOVERNMENT STRUCTURE AND ORGANIZATION, POLITICAL PERIODS, THE UNION, COLLECTIVE ADMINISTRATION, REPRESENTATIVE BODIES, AND METHODS USED TO SECURE COOPERATION. BIBLIOGRAPHY OF 50 ENTRIES, 1902-65, IN ENGLISH, LISTED TOPICALLY: TEXTBOOKS, STUDIES OF SOVIET POLITICS, SPECIAL ASPECTS OF POLITICS, BACKGROUND, AND JOURNALS.

2814 SCOTT J.P.
AGGRESSION.
CHICAGO: U. CHI. PR., 1958, 148 PP., $3.75.
PROBING THE CAUSES AND CONTROL OF AGGRESSION, SCOTT EXPLORES ANIMAL RESEARCH AS IT RELATES OR CONTRASTS WITH THE FACTS OF HUMAN BEHAVIOR. PROBLEMS OF AGGRESSION AND POSSIBLE SOLUTIONS ARE PRESENTED ACTUATED BY NEW DISCOVERIES IN BIOLOGICAL AND PSYCHOLOGICAL AREAS.

2815 SCOTT J.W.
"SOURCES OF SOCIAL CHANGE IN COMMUNITY, FAMILY, AND FERTILITY IN A PUERTO RICAN TOWN."
AMER. J. OF SOCIOLOGY, 72 (MAR. 67), 520-530.
REPORT ON A STUDY OF WOMEN IN A PUERTO RICAN TOWN IN PROCESS OF INDUSTRIAL AND OTHER SOCIOECONOMIC CHANGE. RESULTS INDICATE THAT EMPLOYED AND BETTER EDUCATED WOMEN ARE ASSOCIATED WITH MORE EQUALITARIAN FAMILY ORGANIZATION, AS OPPOSED TO PATRIARCHAL, AND WITH A LOWER FERTILITY RATE.

2816 SCOTT R.E.
"MEXICAN GOVERNMENT IN TRANSITION (REV ED)"
URBANA: U OF ILLINOIS PR, 1964.
STUDY OF MEXICO'S EVOLVING SYSTEM OF POLITICS THROUGH GENERALIZING APPROACH. CONSIDERS SOCIAL, PSYCHOLOGICAL, AND PHYSICAL CONDITIONS WHICH MAKE UP MEXICAN POLITICAL CULTURE AND DISCUSSES THEM AS FACTORS IN GROUP APPROACH TO STUDY OF POLITICAL PROCESS. CONTAINS ANALYSIS OF FORMAL CONSTITUTIONAL STRUCTURE AND GOVERNMENT AGENCIES. INCLUDES EXTENSIVE BIBLIOGRAPHY IN SPANISH AND ENGLISH.

2817 SCOTT W.A.
"EMPIRICAL ASSESSMENT OF VALUES AND IDEOLOGIES."
AMER. SOCIOL. REV., 24 (JUNE 59), 299-310.
DESCRIBES THEORETICAL AND METHODOLOGICAL RESEARCH FOR ASSESSMENT OF VALUES AND IDEOLOGIES OF A CULTURE. CULTURE DEFINED AS SHARED PSYCHOLOGICAL ATTRIBUTES OF ITS MEMBERS. INFERS IDEOLOGIES FROM CROSS-CORRELATION OF THE MORAL IDEALS OF THREE GROUPS IN USA.

2818 SCOVILLE W.J.
"GOVERNMENT REGULATION AND GROWTH IN THE FRENCH PAPER INDUSTRY DURING THE EIGHTEENTH CENTURY."
AMER. ECO. REVIEW, 57 (MAY 67), 283-293.
EXAMINATION OF ECONOMIC HISTORY OF PAPER INDUSTRY. AUTHOR FINDS DIRECT CORRELATION BETWEEN THE INDUSTRY'S EXPANSION AND RELAXATION OF DIRECT GOVERNMENTAL CONTROLS. IN THIS PERIOD LARGE-SCALE CAPITALISTIC ENTERPRISE BECAME MORE COMMON. EXPLORES CHANGING ROLE OF GOVERNMENT, METHODS IT USED TO RELAX CONTROL AND ENCOURAGE INDIVIDUALS, AND AREAS WHERE GOVERNMENT CONTROL SHOULD HAVE BEEN RELAXED BUT WASN'T.

2819 SEELEY J.R.
THE EXPANSION OF ENGLAND.
LONDON: MACMILLAN, 1902, 309 PP.
BRIEF HISTORY OF ENGLAND IN THE EIGHTEENTH CENTURY-ANALYZES THE OLD COLONIAL SYSTEM, THE EFFECT OF THE NEW WORLD ON THE OLD AND THE EXPANSION OF COMMERCE. SURVEYS CONQUEST OF INDIA AND ITS INFLUENCE ON ENGLAND.

2820 SEGAL A.
"THE INTEGRATION OF DEVELOPING COUNTRIES: SOME THOUGHTS ON EAST AFRICA AND CENTRAL AMERICA."
J. COMMON MARKET STUDIES, 5 (MAR. 67), 252-283.
NOTES THE CONSISTENT DESIRE OF EMERGING COUNTRIES FOR REGIONAL ALLIANCES WITH EACH OTHER DESPITE RECORD OF FAILURE. COMPARES THE SUCCESS OF THE CENTRAL AMERICAN COMMON MARKET WITH THE GROWING DISINTEGRATION OF THE EAST AFRICAN ECONOMIC UNION. CONCLUDES THAT THE LACK OF A POLITICAL THREAT IN THE CACM GAVE IT THE SUPPORT OF DEVELOPED NATIONS. SUGGESTS THAT POLITICAL UNITY MAY COST ECONOMIC INTEGRATION.

2821 SEGAL R.
SANCTIONS AGAINST SOUTH AFRICA.
BALTIMORE: PENGUIN BOOKS, 1964, 272 PP.
TWENTY-TWO ARTICLES FROM INTERNATIONAL CONFERENCE ON ECONOMIC SANCTIONS AGAINST SOUTH AFRICA OF 1964, DESCRIBING ECONOMIC, RACIAL, POLITICAL, LEGAL, AND STRATEGIC ASPECTS OF SANCTIONS.

2822 SEIDLER G.L.
"MARXIST LEGAL THOUGHT IN POLAND."
SLAVIC REVIEW, 26 (SEPT. 67), 382-394.
SINCE WWII, POLISH LEGAL THEORY HAS FOCUSED PRIMARILY ON SOCIOLOGICAL ASPECTS OF THE LAW. RESEARCH INDICATES THAT THIS FOCUS BENEFITED INTEREST GROUPS. AS A RESULT NEW PROBLEMS ARE BEING CONSIDERED. THOSE RECEIVING SPECIAL ATTENTION ARE: EVALUATION OF POSITIVE LAW; RELATIONSHIP BETWEEN LEGAL AND SOCIALIST CONSCIOUSNESS; AND COMPREHENSIVE LEGAL RESEARCH. ARTICLE IS CONFINED TO PRESENTATION OF PROBLEMS.

2823 SELF P., STORING H.J.
THE STATE AND THE FARMER.
BERKELEY: U OF CALIF PR, 1963, 251 PP.
DISCUSSES AGRICULTURAL POLICIES AND POLITICS IN GREAT BRITAIN BETWEEN 1945-61. ANALYZES THE CLOSE AND PERVASIVE COOPERATION BETWEEN GOVERNMENT AND PRINCIPAL AGRICULTURAL ORGANIZATIONS. EXPLORES CHARACTER AND HISTORY OF PARTNERSHIP AND REVIEWS PROBLEMS AND CONFLICTS OVER THE ADMINISTRATION OF PUBLIC POLICY.

2824 SELIGMAN E.R.A.
ESSAYS IN TAXATION.
LONDON: MACMILLAN, 1895, 418 PP.
DISCUSSES TAXATION, PRIMARILY IN US: ITS DEVELOPMENT, FORMS, PROLIFERATION, AND THEORY, PREDATING INCOME TAX. CONSIDERS TYPES OF TAXES AND DEFECTS OF EACH - FISCAL, POLITICAL, ETHICAL, AND ECONOMIC. BASIC TYPES INCLUDE: SINGLE, INHERITANCE, CORPORATION, PROPERTY, AND TARIFFS. ALSO EXAMINES REFORMS IN ENGLAND, NEW ZEALAND, AND PRUSSIA.

2825 SELOSOEMARDJAN O.
SOCIAL CHANGES IN JOGJAKARTA.
ITHACA: CORNELL U PRESS, 1962, 447 PP., LC#62-14114.
VIEWS SOCIAL, ECONOMIC, POLITICAL CHANGE IN INDONESIA, RESULT OF 1958 REVOLUTION. EFFECT OF DUTCH AND JAPANESE OCCUPATIONS ON JAVANESE CULTURE AND THE ROLE OF JAVA AS A LEADER IN ECONOMIC AND SOCIAL PROGRESS IN THE AREA ARE CONSIDERED.

2826 SEMINAR REPRESENTATIVE GOVT
AFRO-ASIAN ATTITUDES: SEMINAR ON REPRESENTATIVE GOVERNMENTS-PUBLIC LIBERTIES IN STATES OF ASIA AND AFRICA, RHODES, 1958.
LUCKNOW, INDIA: PRABHAKAR SAHIT, 1961, 149 PP.
CONSIDERS PROBLEMS AND CONDITIONS OF POLITICAL TRANSFORMATION AND DEVELOPING DEMOCRACIES IN EMERGENT AFRO-ASIAN STATES, WITH REFERENCE TO SIAMESE DEMOCRACY, SOUTH VIETNAMESE GOVERNMENT, AND ARAB TRADITIONAL ORDER.

2827 SENGHOR L.S.
AFRICAN SOCIALISM (PAMPHLET)
NEW YORK: AMER SOC AFR CULTURE, 1959, 49 PP.
DESCRIBES MALI FEDERATION, PLOTS COURSE OF MALI'S ECONOMIC, POLITICAL, EDUCATIONAL, AND SOCIAL PROGRESS TOWARD INDEPENDENCE, AND EXAMINES MALI ATTITUDES TOWARD OTHER AFRICAN STATES, FRANCE, US, AND USSR. PRESENTS A CRITICAL ANALYSIS OF MARXISM IN AFRICAN NEGRO LIGHT.

2828 SENGHOR L.S.
RAPPORT SUR LA DOCTRINE ET LA PROGRAMME DU PART I.
PARIS: ED PRESENCE AFRICAINE, 1959, 90 PP.
DISCUSSES FEDERATION OF MALI, EMPHASIZING SOCIALISM AS A HUMANISTIC METHOD; INCLUDES COMMUNITY, NATIONALIZATION OF PROPERTY, AND MARXIST IDEOLOGY.

2829 SERENI A.P.
THE ITALIAN CONCEPTION OF INTERNATIONAL LAW.
NEW YORK: COLUMB. U. PR., 1943, 353 PP.
MAJOR PURPOSE IS TO SHOW THAT THE FASCISM OF THE PRE-WAR ERA WAS A DEVIATION FROM THE NORMAL COURSE OF ITALIAN JUSTICE AND FREEDOM.

2830 SERRANO MOSCOSO E.
A STATEMENT OF THE LAWS OF ECUADOR IN MATTERS AFFECTING BUSINESS (2ND ED.)
WASHINGTON: PAN AMERICAN UNION, 1955, 191 PP.
SUMMARY IN ENGLISH OF CONSTITUTIONAL, STATUTORY, AND REGULATORY PROVISIONS OF ECUADOR RELEVANT TO COMMERCIAL CONCERNS; COVERS LAWS IN FORCE IN 1955. INCLUDES LAWS ON MARRIAGE, TAXATION, AND COMMERCE.

2831 SETHE P.
SCHICKSALSSTUNDEN DER WELTGESCHICHTE (6TH ED.)
FRANKFURT: VERL HEINR SCHEFFLER, 1960, 328 PP.
GENERAL HISTORY OF FOREIGN POLICY OF GREAT POWERS FROM CHARLES V TO CHURCHILL. DISCUSSES WARS AND STRUGGLES FOR NATIONALY UNITY.

2832 SETON-WATSON H.

FROM LENIN TO KHRUSHCHEV: THE HISTORY OF WORLD COMMUNISM.
NEW YORK: PRAEGER, 1961, 432 PP., $2.25.
HISTORY AND COMPARATIVE ANALYSIS OF COMMUNIST MOVEMENTS, EMPHASIZING NATIONAL COMMUNIST MOVEMENTS. DISTINGUISHES BETWEEN MOVEMENTS BEFORE AND AFTER SEIZURE OF POWER. TRACES DEVELOPMENT OF STATE MACHINE AND SOCIAL STRUCTURE IN SOVIET UNION. CONCLUDES WITH OBSERVATIONS ON PRESENT FAVORING OR HINDERING COMMUNIST REVOLUTION.

2833 SETON-WATSON H.
THE NEW IMPERIALISM.
CHESTER SPRINGS: DUFOUR, 1963, 136 PP.
SURVEYS SOVIET IMPERIALISM, POINTING OUT ITS ORIGINS IN OLD RUSSIA. FOLLOWS ITS DEVELOPMENT FROM POST-REVOLUTIONARY PERIOD TO POST-WW 2 PERIOD. DESCRIBES SOVIET POLICIES TOWARD MINORITY GROUPS IN USSR, TOWARD SATELLITE STATES AND TOWARD NEW NATIONS.

2834 SETON-WATSON H.
THE RUSSIAN EMPIRE, 1801-1917.
LONDON: OXFORD U PR, 1967, 813 PP.
SURVEYS DEVELOPMENT OF RUSSIA FROM ALEXANDER I TO NICHOLAS II. EMPHASIZES SOCIAL AND POLITICAL HISTORY AND INCLUDES INSTITUTIONS, CLASSES, POLITICAL MOVEMENTS, AND IMPORTANT INDIVIDUALS. EXAMINES FOREIGN POLICY FROM RUSSIAN VIEW; CONSIDERS NON-RUSSIAN PEOPLES OF EMPIRE, MILITARY EVENTS, DEVELOPMENT OF AGRICULTURE AND INDUSTRY, REFORMS, IDEOLOGIES, POLITICAL PARTIES, AND BIRTH OF MARXISM.

2835 SETTON K.M. ED., WINKLER H.R. ED.
GREAT PROBLEMS IN EUROPEAN CIVILIZATION.
ENGLEWOOD CLIFFS: PRENTICE HALL, 1966, 610 PP., LC#66-11190.
EXAMINATION OF THE PROMINENT FACTORS IN THE CREATION OF THE WESTERN WORLD. INCLUDES ESSAYS ON FREEDOM AND TYRANNY IN ANCIENT WORLD, TRIUMPH OF CHRISTIANITY, BYZANTIUM AND THE WEST, AND MEDIEVAL SOCIETY. ALSO STUDIES GROWTH OF POLITICAL AUTHORITY, MEANING OF THE RENAISSANCE, PROTESTANT-CATHOLIC SPLIT, 17TH-CENTURY WORLD VIEW, AND GROWTH AND CRISIS OF SOCIAL, INDUSTRIAL, AND POLITICAL FORCES IN MODERN WORLD.

2836 SEYLER W.C.
"DOCTORAL DISSERTATIONS IN POLITICAL SCIENCE IN UNIVERSITIES OF THE UNITED STATES AND CANADA."
AM. POL. SCI. REV., 60 (SEPT. 66), 778-803.
AN UNANNOTATED BIBLIOGRAPHY OF DOCTORAL DISSERTATIONS IN POLITICAL SCIENCE. MATERIAL IS FROM LATE 1965 TO 1966. ENGLISH LANGUAGE. CONTAINS 1,150 ENTRIES.

2837 SHAFER B.C.
NATIONALISM: MYTH AND REALITY.
NEW YORK: HARCOURT BRACE, 1955, 319 PP., LC#55-5636.
EXAMINES MEANING OF NATIONALISM, HOW AND WHY IT AROSE, ILLUSIONS ABOUT ITS ORIGINS, AND RELATION TO FUNDAMENTAL SIMILARITIES AMONG MEN AND NATIONS. STUDIES BOTH IDEA AND INSTITUTION; CONCENTRATES ON US, UK, AND FRANCE; BUT MAKES COMPARISONS WITH OTHER NATIONALISMS. INCLUDES METAPHYSICAL, PHYSICAL, AND CULTURAL MYTHS; ECONOMIC AND SOCIAL BASIS; AND NATION-STATE AS MEANS AND END.

2838 SHAFFER H.G.
THE COMMUNIST WORLD: MARXIST AND NON-MARXIST VIEWS.
NEW YORK: APPLETON, 1967, 558 PP., LC#67-21993.
INTRODUCES GENERAL PHILOSOPHY OF COMMUNIST WORLD, POINTING OUT ASPECTS OF HOMOGENEITY AND HETEROGENEITY. GROUPS INDIVIDUAL COMMUNIST NATIONS BY GEORGRAPHICAL AREAS, PRESENTING NATIVE AND FOREIGN VIEWS OF MARXIST IDEOLOGY. MOST MARXIST VIEWS REFLECT OFFICIAL EXPRESSIONS FROM COMMUNIST NATIONS.

2839 SHAKABPA T.W.D.
TIBET: A POLITICAL HISTORY.
NEW HAVEN: YALE U PR, 1967, 369 PP., LC#67-13448.
CLARIFIES EVOLUTION OF THAT FORM OF RELIGIOUS GOVERNMENT UNIQUE IN TIBET. USES AS EVIDENCE 67 ORIGINAL TIBETAN SOURCES, INCLUDING RARE GOVERNMENT RECORDS NO LONGER ACCESSIBLE AND OTHER MATERIALS NOT PREVIOUSLY CITED IN ENGLISH WORKS. INCORPORATES ORAL INFORMATION AVAILABLE TO AUTHOR AS MEMBER OF A NOBLE FAMILY. NEW EVIDENCE GIVEN ON POLITICAL STATUS OF CONTEMPORARY TIBET, AND CHINESE TAKEOVER.

2840 SHANKS M. ED.
THE LESSONS OF PUBLIC ENTERPRISE.
LONDON: JONATHAN CAPE, 1963, 313 PP.
EXAMINES STATE OF PUBLIC ENTERPRISE IN ENGLAND IN 1963, EVALUATING RELATIONSHIP WITH GOVERNMENT, THE PUBLIC, CUSTOMERS, WORKERS, AND PRIVATE INDUSTRIES. DISCUSSES PROBLEM OF WHO DECIDES PUBLIC INTEREST, PROBLEMS OF PARLIAMENTARY CONTROL; COMPARES WITH CASES ON CONTINENT.

2841 SHANNON R.T.
GLADSTONE AND THE BULGARIAN AGITATION OF 1876.
LONDON: THOMAS NELSON & SONS, 1963, 308 PP.
HISTORICAL STUDY OF ENGLISH PUBLIC OPINION REGARDING TURKISH ATROCITIES AGAINST BULGARIAN NATIONALISTS IN 1876, AS EXAMINATION OF PUBLIC MORAL CONSCIENCE OF VICTORIAN ERA AND REACTION TO DISRAELI GOVERNMENT'S PRO-TURKISH POLICY.

2842 SHAPIRO H.L.
MAN, CULTURE, AND SOCIETY.
NEW YORK: OXFORD U PR, 1956, 371 PP., LC#56-5429.
COLLECTION OF ESSAYS TRACES BIOLOGICAL BEGINNINGS AND CULTURAL DEVELOPMENT OF MAN FROM PREHISTORIC TO MODERN TIMES. DISCUSSES NATURE AND GROWTH OF VARIOUS CULTURES AND PATTERNS OF CULTURAL CHANGE. DISCUSSES LANGUAGE AND WRITING, FAMILY AND SOCIAL GROUPS, ECONOMICS, AND RELIGION AS DETERMINANT FACTORS IN CULTURE.

2843 SHAPIRO J.P.
"SOVIET HISTORIOGRAPHY AND THE MOSCOW TRIALS: AFTER THIRTY YEARS."
RUSSIAN REVIEWS, 27 (JAN. 68), 68-77.
DISCUSSES THE SOVIET PROCESS OF "REHABILITATION" OF VICTIMS OF THE 1936-38 GREAT PURGE. REHABILITATION CAN BE EITHER PUBLIC, BY THE SOVIET PRESS'S PUBLICATION OF THE VICTIM'S BIOGRAPHY, OR JUDICIAL. DISCUSSES THE "REHABILITATION" OF MANY PROMINENT BOLSHEVIK LEADERS.

2844 SHAPIRO P.S.
COMMUNICATIONS OR TRANSPORT: DECISION-MAKING IN DEVELOPING COUNTRIES.
CAMBRIDGE: MIT CTR INTL STUDIES, 1967, 215 PP.
MAKES COMPARISON OF USES OF INVESTMENT IN TRANSPORT AND IN COMMUNICATIONS FOR DEVELOPING COUNTRIES. PROPOSES METHOD FOR INVESTMENT DECISION-MAKING, AND ANALYZES RELEVANT DATA. STATES THAT NATIONAL INVESTMENT STRATEGIES DEPEND ON COMMUNIST OR NON-COMMUNIST IDEOLOGY, ON THEORIES OF ECONOMIC PLANNING, ON SITUATIONAL CONDITIONS, AND ON METHODS OF ANALYSIS. PROPOSES MODEL FOR STAGING OF INVESTMENT.

2845 SHARKANSKY I.
"ECONOMIC AND POLITICAL CORRELATES OF STATE GOVERNMENT EXPENDITURE: GENERAL TENDENCIES AND DEVIANT CASES."
MIDWEST J. OF POLI. SCI., 11 (MAY 67), 173-192.
STUDIES DIFFERENCES IN STATE GOVERNMENT EXPENDITURES AND PUBLIC SERVICES TO DETERMINE CAUSES OF DIFFERENCES. USING NEW MEASURES OF POLITICAL ASPECTS OF EXPENDITURES, FINDS THAT AMOUNT SPENT RESPONDS MORE TO FEDERAL AID, TAX EFFORT, STATE-LOCAL CENTRALIZATION, AND POLITICAL RESULTS OF PREVIOUS EXPENDITURES THAN TO PER CAPITA PERSONAL INCOME OR POPULATION. BUT NO CLEAR PATTERN WAS DISCERNIBLE.

2846 SHARMA B.M.
THE REPUBLIC OF INDIA; CONSTITUTION AND GOVERNMENT.
NEW YORK: TAPLINGER PUBL CO, 1966, 655 PP.
DETAILED STUDY OF INDIAN STATE AND NATIONAL GOVERNMENT MACHINERY. EXPLAINS ARTICLES OF CONSTITUTION; PRESENTS HISTORICAL AND POLITICAL BACKGROUND OF COUNTRY; AND SHOWS HOW CONSTITUTION EVOLVED TO MEET PEOPLE'S NEEDS AND ASPIRATIONS. CRITICIZES WORKINGS OF GOVERNMENTS IN SEVERAL AREAS AND SUGGESTS MEANS FOR MORE EFFICIENCY.

2847 SHARMA M.P.
PUBLIC ADMINISTRATION IN THEORY AND PRACTICE.
ALLAHABAD, INDIA: KITAB MAHAL, 1958, 508 PP.
DISCUSSES THEORY OF PUBLIC ADMINISTRATION, ITS ORGANIZATION, VARIOUS REGULATORY AGENCIES AND COMMISSIONS, PERSONNEL ADMINISTRATION, AND ADMINISTRATIVE LAW AND RESPONSIBILITY IN CONTEXT OF INDIAN, BRITISH, AN US EXPERIENCE.

2848 SHARMA R.S.
ASPECTS OF POLITICAL IDEAS AND INSTITUTIONS IN ANCIENT INDIA
NEW DELHI: MOTILAL BANARSIDASS, 1959, 254 PP.
DISCUSSES ROLE OF PROPERTY, FAMILY, CASTE, FOLK ASSEMBLIES, LAND REVENUE SYSTEMS, RELIGION, LAW, AND POLITICS IN ANCIENT INDIAN CULTURE. ALSO EXAMINES HISTORIOGRAPHY OF INDIAN POLITY UP TO 1930 AND RISE OF FEUDALISM BETWEEN 400 AND 600 A.D.

2849 SHARMA S.A.
PARLIAMENTARY GOVERNMENT IN INDIA.
ALLAHABAD: CENTRAL BOOK DEPT, 1965, 242 PP.
SURVEYS ALL ASPECTS OF INDIAN GOVERNMENT FROM MAKING OF CONSTITUTION TO DETAILS OF PUBLIC FINANCE AND LOCAL GOVERNMENTAL SYSTEMS. INCLUDES DISCUSSION OF JUDICIAL AND ADMINISTRATIVE TRIBUNALS AND WORK OF PLANNING COMMISSIONS.

2850 SHARMA S.P.
"THE INDIA-CHINA BORDER DISPUTE: AN INDIAN PERSPECTIVE."
AMER. J. INT. LAW, 59 (JAN. 65), 16-47.
PRESENTS CLAIMS AND COUNTER-CLAIMS OF PARTIES IN DISPUTE. ASSESSES PAST JURIDICAL PRACTISES. SUPPORTS INDIA'S CLAIM ON GEOGRAPHICAL, HISTORICAL, AND LEGAL GROUNDS.

2851 SHARMA T.R.
THE WORKING OF STATE ENTERPRISES IN INDIA.
BOMBAY: VORA & CO, 1961, 232 PP.
STUDY OF GROWTH OF STATE INTEREST IN INDUSTRIES, LEADING TO EVENTUAL NATIONALIZATION. ANALYZES ADMINISTRATION OF SUCH INDUSTRIES, SHOWING EXTENT OF MINISTERIAL CONTROL, RELATIONSHIP AND RESPONSIBILITY OF STATE UNDERTAKINGS TO THE LEGISLATURE, LABOR PROBLEMS, AND PRICE POLICY. OBSERVES THAT PUBLIC UNDERSTANDING MUST SEE THAT INDIAN NATIONALIZATION IS INSPIRED BY FISCAL, SECURITY, AND SOCIAL MOTIVES.

2852 SHATTEN F.
"POLYCENTRISM: AFRICA: NATIONALISM AND COMMUNISM."
SURVEY, 42 (JUNE 62), 148-59.
POINTS OUT THAT EARLY CONFLICTS OF INTEREST BETWEEN COMMUNIST PARTIES OF COLONIAL POWERS AND INABILITY OF ORTHODOX COMMUNISM TO ADAPT IDEOLOGY TO CONDITIONS IN AFRICA DISCOURAGED MANY AFRICANS FROM COMMUNISM. SUGGESTS THAT AFRICA MAY BECOME COMMUNIST IF PERMITTED TO CHOOSE ITS OWN MODEL OF SOCIALISM.

2853 SHAW S.J.
THE FINANCIAL AND ADMINISTRATIVE ORGANIZATION AND DEVELOPMENT OF OTTOMAN EGYPT 1517-1798.
PRINCETON: PRIN U ORIENTAL STUD, 1958.
EXAMINES TOTAL ADMINISTRATIVE SYSTEM OF EGYPT FROM OTTOMAN CONQUEST TO NAPOLEON'S EXPEDITION. CONCENTRATES ON OBJECTIVES OF REGIME AND DEGREE TO WHICH THEY WERE FULFILLED. COVERS REVENUES OF EMPIRE AND METHOD OF COLLECTING MORE FULLY THAN SPENDING. BIBLIOGRAPHY OF WORKS CITED AND REFERENCES USED.

2854 SHAW T.S. ED.
"FEDERAL, STATE AND LOCAL GOVERNMENT PUBLICATIONS."
LIBRARY TRENDS, 15 (JULY 66), 3-194.
ENTIRE ISSUE OF PERIODICAL CONCERNS ITSELF WITH PROBLEMS OF HANDLING GOVERNMENT DOCUMENTS IN LIBRARIES. TREATS BIBLIOGRAPHY, ACQUISITION, CATALOGUING, AND USE OF SUCH DOCUMENTS IN VARIOUS KINDS OF LIBRARIES. REFERENCES END EACH CHAPTER.

2855 SHEIKH N.A.
SOME ASPECTS OF THE CONSTITUTION AND THE ECONOMICS OF ISLAM.
SURREY: WOKING MUSLIM MISS & LIT, 1957, 246 PP.
DISCUSSES CONSTITUTION, ECONOMIC STRUCTURE, EMPLOYMENT POLICY, AND LAND REFORM IN PAKISTAN. EMPHASIZES CHARACTER OF PEOPLE AND NATURE OF ISLAMIC FAITH IN RELATION TO GOVERNMENT POLICIES.

2856 SHELBY C. ED.
LATIN AMERICAN PERIODICALS CURRENTLY RECEIVED IN THE LIBRARY OF CONGRESS AND IN LIBRARY OF DEPARTMENT OF AGRICULTURE.
WASHINGTON: LIBRARY OF CONGRESS, 1944, 249 PP.
ANNOTATED LISTING BY TITLE OF 1,600 CURRENTLY RECEIVED PERIODICALS, EXCLUDING NEWSPAPERS, TECHNICAL JOURNALS, OR YEARBOOKS. MOST IN SPANISH OR PORTUGUESE WITH SOME ENGLISH. CRITERIA FOR INCLUSION IS PERIODICAL'S CHIEF CONCERN WITH LATIN AMERICA. INDEX BY COUNTRY OF PUBLICATION AND SUBJECT.

2857 SHELDON C.H.
"PUBLIC OPINION AND HIGH COURTS: COMMUNIST PARTY CASES IN FOUR CONSTITUTIONAL SYSTEMS."
WESTERN POLIT. QUART., 20 (JUNE 67), 341-360.
THEORIZES THAT IN ALL CONSTITUTIONAL SYSTEMS, HIGHEST COURTS WILL ALWAYS RULE CONSISTENTLY WITH PUBLIC OPINION IN CRUCIAL AREAS, E.G., IN THREATS FROM SUBVERSIVE GROUPS LIKE COMMUNIST PARTY. ANALYZES COURT RULINGS FROM 1950-61 IN US, CANADA, AUSTRALIA, AND WEST GERMANY TO PROVE THEORY, FOR COURT'S OPINIONS CHANGED WITH POLITICAL TIDE DURING THIS PERIOD.

2858 SHEPHERD W.G.
ECONOMIC PERFORMANCE UNDER PUBLIC OWNERSHIP: BRITISH FUEL AND POWER.
NEW HAVEN: YALE U PR, 1965, 161 PP., LC#65-12546.
REVIEWS SOME LESSONS THAT HAVE BEEN DRAWN FROM EXPERIENCE OF BRITISH NATIONALIZED INDUSTRY. TESTS BOTH LOGICAL CONSISTENCY THAT CRITERIA OF "LESSONS" ARE BASED ON AND CORRECTNESS OF THEIR FACTUAL CONCLUSIONS. STUDY CENTERS ON QUESTION OF EFFICIENT RESOURCE ALLOCATION IN BRITISH FUEL AND POWER INDUSTRIES.

2859 SHIELS W.E.
KING AND CHURCH: THE RISE AND FALL OF THE PATRONATO REAL.
CHICAGO: LOYOLA U PR, 1961, 399 PP., LC#61-11113.
STUDIES ORIGIN, GROWTH AND DECLINE OF SYSTEM OF PATRONATO REAL, WHICH ENABLED SPANISH MONARCH TO EXERCISE GREAT AUTHORITY IN CHURCH AFFAIRS, SPECIFICALLY IN MANAGEMENT OF SPANISH MISSIONARY SYSTEM IN NORTH AMERICA. CONTAINS TEXTS (IN SPANISH) OF BULLS, DECREES, AND INSTRUCTIONS THAT UNDERLIE DEVELOPMENT OF PATRONATO REAL.

2860 SHIGEO N.
"THE GREAT CULTURAL REVOLUTION."
JAPAN QUARTERLY, 14 (OCT.-DEC. 67), 434-442.
EXAMINES INHERENT NATURE AND PROBLEMS OF CHINA'S GREAT CULTURAL REVOLUTION. CLAIMS THAT SITUATION IS NOT FAVORABLE TO MAO-LIN FACTION. FORESEES HEAVY EMPHASIS ON AND STRONG RELATIONSHIP BETWEEN AUTUMN FOOD PRODUCTION AND FATE OF MAO. TRACES DEVELOPMENT OF FOOD PRODUCTIVITY FROM 1962 TO 1967.

2861 SHILS E.
"THE INTELLECTUALS IN THE POLITICAL DEVELOPMENT OF THE NEW STATES."
WORLD POLIT., 12 (60), 329-368.
DISCUSSES ROLE OF INTELLECTUALS IN NEW STATES OF AFRICA AND ASIA, CONCLUDING THAT IN NO STATE FORMATIONS IN ALL HISTORY HAVE INTELLECTUALS PLAYED A GREATER ROLE. FUTURE ROLE DEPENDS ON CONTINUING ABILITY TO OUTWEIGH TRADITIONAL INCIVILITY OF NEW STATES.

2862 SHILS E.A., JANOWITZ M.
"COHESION AND DISINTEGRATION IN THE WEHRMACHT IN WORLD WAR II."
PUBLIC OPINION QUART., 12 (SUMMER 48), 280-315.
PROVIDES AN EXAMPLE OF THE SOCIOLOGICAL AND PSYCHOLOGICAL ANALYSIS WHICH THE PROPAGANDIST MUST MAKE IF HE IS TO OBTAIN MAXIMAL RESPONSE TO HIS COMMUNICATIONS. AN INTENSIVE EXAMINATION OF THE SOCIAL STRUCTURE OF THE GERMAN ARMY, THE SYMBOLS TO WHICH IT RESPONDED, NAZI ATTEMPTS TO BOLSTER ITS MORALE, AND ALLIED ATTEMPTS TO BREAK IT DOWN. ANALYZES BEHAVIOR PATTERNS OF INDIVIDUAL IN PRIMARY GROUP.

2863 SHIRATO I.
JAPANESE SOURCES ON THE HISTORY OF THE CHINESE COMMUNIST MOVEMENT (PAMPHLET)
NY: COLUMBIA U, EAST ASIAN INST, 1953, 69 PP., LC#53-12343.
ANNOTATED BIBLIOGRAPHY OF SELECTED MATERIALS IN JAPANESE DEALING WITH THE HISTORY OF THE CHINESE COMMUNIST MOVEMENT. MATERIALS ARE FROM THE EAST ASIATIC LIBRARY OF COLUMBIA UNIVERSITY AND A DIVISION OF THE LIBRARY OF CONGRESS. LISTS ONLY BOOKS OR PARTS THEREOF, MONOGRAPHS, PAMPHLETS, AND SIGNIFICANT PERIODICAL ARTICLES.

2864 SHIRER W.L.
THE RISE AND FALL OF THE THIRD REICH: A HISTORY OF NAZI GERMANY.
NEW YORK: SIMON SCHUSTER, 1960, 1245 PP.
COMREHENSIVE AND COMPLETE HISTORY OF RISE TURBULENT LIFE AND ULTIMATE FALL OF HITLER'S GERMANY. DOCUMENTARY RESEARCH FINDINGS SUBSTANTIATE AUTHOR'S VIEWS ON HISTORICAL EVENTS. EXPRESSES FEARS THAT UNLESS FORCES PRODUCING SUCH CONFLICTS ARE INTERRUPTED IN TIME WORLD MIGHT FIND ITSELF ON ROAD TO TOTAL DISASTER.

2865 SHIROKOGOROFF S.M.
ETHNICAL UNIT AND MILIEU.
SHANGHAI: EDWARD EVANS & SONS, 1924, 36 PP.
AN INQUIRY INTO THE SCIENTIFIC RELATION BETWEEN MAN'S CULTURE AND HIS BIOLOGICAL FUNCTION. THE AUTHOR MAINTAINS THAT MAN'S CULTURAL WORLD IS THE "PRODUCT OF A PURELY BIOLOGICAL FUNCTION." OFFERS COLLECTION OF SCIENTIFIC PROPOSITIONS INTENDED TO EXPLAIN THE ORIGIN AND NATURE OF HUMAN CULTURE.

2866 SHRIMALI K.L.
EDUCATION IN CHANGING INDIA.
BOMBAY: ASIA PUBL HOUSE, 1965, 256 PP.
DISCUSSES ADMINISTRATION AND INTERNAL ASPECTS OF EDUCATION IN MODERN INDIA. EXAMINES QUALITY OF TEACHERS, PROBLEM OF INTEGRATION OF DIVERSE CULTURAL UNITS, FOREIGN ASPECTS SUCH AS UNESCO INVOLVEMENT, COMMONWEALTH COOPERATION, AND THE LIKE.

2867 SHUMSKY A.
THE CLASH OF CULTURES IN ISRAEL: A PROBLEM FOR EDUCATION.
NY: COLUMBIA U TEACHERS COLLEGE, 1955, 170 PP., LC#55-10872.
ANALYZES IMPACT OF ETHNIC GROUP CONTACTS AND TENSIONS ON AN ISRAELI CHILD OF JEWISH ORIENTAL BACKGROUND. EMPHASIZES MANIFESTATIONS AND CONSEQUENCES OF THIS IMPACT ON THE SCHOOL. REVIEWS MAJOR WRITINGS AND RESEARCH ON PROBLEM. SUGGESTS WAYS AND ILLUSTRATES PROGRAMS BY WHICH SCHOOLS CAN IMPROVE ETHNIC GROUP RELATIONSHIPS.

2868 SIDGWICK H.
THE ELEMENTS OF POLITICS.
LONDON: MACMILLAN, 1891, 623 PP.
A COMPREHENSIVE STUDY OF POLITICAL THEORY AND PRACTICE IN RELATION TO 19TH-CENTURY SOCIETY. THE SCOPE, CONCEPTION AND PRINCIPLES OF POLITICS ARE BASED ON WRITINGS OF J.S. MILL AND BENTHAM. MAJOR AREAS DISCUSSED INCLUDE JURISPRUDENCE, INTERNATIONAL LAW, MAINTENANCE AND STRUCTURE OF GOVERNMENT, RELATION OF JUDICIARY TO LEGISLATURE AND EXECUTIVE, LOCAL AND FEDERAL GOVERNMENTS, AND SOVEREIGNTY AND ORDER.

2869 SIEGFRIED A.
TABLEAU POLITIQUE DE LA FRANCE DE L'OUEST SOUS LA TROISIEME REPUBLIQUE.
PARIS: LIB ARTHEME FAYARD, 1913, 531 PP.
A POLITICAL STUDY OF WESTERN FRANCE DURING THE THIRD REPUBLIC. DESCRIBES THE ORGANIZATIONAL-POLITICAL CLIMATE OF DIFFERENT DEPARTMENTS. ATTEMPTS TO MAP VARIATIONS IN POLITICAL TASTES OVER TIME AND IN SEVERAL GEOGRAPHICAL REGIONS. DISCUSSES FACTORS RELEVANT TO POLITICAL OPINION, INCLUDING SOCIAL CLASS.

2870 SIEKANOWICZ P., GSOVSKI V. ED.
LEGAL SOURCES AND BIBLIOGRAPHY OF POLAND.
NEW YORK: FREDERICK PRAEGER, 1964, 311 PP., LC#64-15524.
MATERIALS ORGANIZED CHRONOLOGICALLY AND BY SUBJECT FROM PREPARTITION (1500'S) TO PRESENT. INCLUDE DOCUMENTS AND SECONDARY SOURCES. ITEMS USUALLY IN POLISH WITH INDEXES TO

CURRENT LAWS, AUTHORS, SUBJECTS, AND TITLES FOLLOWING 1,750 ITEMS.

2871 SIEYES E.J., BASTID P. ED.
LES DISCOURS DE SIEYES DANS LES DEBATS CONSTITUTIONNELS DE L'AN III (2 ET 18 THERMIDOR)
PARIS: LIB HACHETTE ET CIE, 1939, 115 PP.
SPEECHES CONCERN PROPOSED FRENCH CONSTITUTION OF 1793. ADVOCATE ESTABLISHMENT OF JURY TO HEAR COMPLAINTS AGAINST CONSTITUTION. TASKS OF GOVERNMENT ARE TO PROPOSE LAWS, TO PUT THEM INTO EFFECT, AND TO MAKE THIS POSSIBLE THROUGH ESTABLISHING EXECUTIVE POWER. PROPOSE UNICAMERAL LEGISLATURE, LARGER THAN OTHER BRANCHES OF GOVERNMENT, BUT WITHOUT POWER TO ISSUE ITS OWN DECREES.

2872 SILBERMAN B.S.
JAPAN AND KOREA; A CRITICAL BIBLIOGRAPHY.
TUCSON: U OF ARIZONA PR, 1962, 120 PP., LC#62-11821.
ANNOTATED BIBLIOGRAPHY OF 1,933 ITEMS ON JAPAN AND KOREA, SELECTED FOR THEIR AVAILABILITY AND AUTHORITATIVENESS. ARRANGED WITHIN TOPICAL CLASSIFICATIONS BY THESE TWO CRITERIA; AN AUTHORITATIVE INACCESSIBLE WORK, FOR EXAMPLE, TAKES PRECEDENCE OVER A LESS AUTHORITATIVE, BUT MORE AVAILABLE, WORK. INCLUDES PUBLICATIONS IN WESTERN LANGUAGES, PRIMARILY FROM 20TH CENTURY, WITH EMPHASIS ON CURRENT SOURCES.

2873 SILBERMAN B.S. ED., HAROOTUNIAN H.D. ED.
MODERN JAPANESE LEADERSHIP; TRANSITION AND CHANGE.
TUCSON: U OF ARIZONA PR, 1966, 433 PP., LC#66-18532.
REVISED PAPERS DELIVERED AT CONFERENCE ON NINETEENTH-CENTURY JAPANESE ELITES. EXAMINES THE TOKUGAWA VILLAGE HEADMAN, THE TRANSFORMATION OF OUTCAST LEADERS, SOCIAL VALUES AND LEADERSHIP IN LATE TOKUGAWA THOUGHT, CHRISTIAN SAMURAI, ELITE TRANSFORMATION IN THE UPPER CIVIL SERVICE, TRANSFORMATION OF MILITARY ELITE, AND GROWTH OF POLITICAL PARTIES AND LEADERSHIP IN RURAL JAPAN.

2874 SILBERMAN L.
"CHANGE AND CONFLICT IN THE HORN OF AFRICA."
FOR. AFF., 37 (JULY 59), 649-659.
IDENTIFIES POLITICAL ISSUES INVOLVED IN SCHEDULED WITHDRAWAL OF ITALY AND BRITAIN FROM SOMALIA AND BRITISH SOMALILAND IN 1960. CITES CULTURAL, HISTORICAL, POLITICAL AND ECONOMIC DIFFERENCES DIVIDING TWO AREAS. EXPRESSES HOPE OF A LOOSE UNION AND PEACEFUL SOLUTION OF FRONTIER PROBLEM.

2875 SILBERNER E.
"THE PROBLEM OF WAR IN NINETEENTH CENTURY ECONOMIC THOUGHT."
PRINCETON: U. PR., 1946, 333 PP.
ANALYZES IDEAS OF 19TH CENTURY ECONOMISTS ON RELATIONSHIP BETWEEN WAR AND ECONOMICS, THE PART WAR PLAYED IN ECONOMIC EVOLUTION, THE EFFECT OF DISARMAMENT ON THE NATIONAL ECONOMY, AND SOCIAL REFORM AS MEANS TO WORLD PEACE.

2876 SILONE I.
THE SCHOOL FOR DICTATORS.
NEW YORK: ATHENEUM PUBLISHERS, 1963, 244 PP., LC#63-17861.
USES DIALOGUE FORM AND ALLEGORICAL CHARACTERS CRITICALLY TO ANALYZE NAZI AND FASCIST IDEOLOGIES IN PRE-WWII EUROPE. ATTEMPTS TO EXPOSE FALSIFICATION OF HISTORY BY DICTATORIAL GOVERNMENTS AND TO DEFINE SOCIAL FACTORS THAT FACILITATE RISE OF TOTALITARIAN GOVERNMENTS.

2877 SILVERT K.H. ED.
EXPECTANT PEOPLES: NATIONALISM AND DEVELOPMENT.
NEW YORK: RANDOM HOUSE, INC, 1963, 489 PP., LC#63-19716.
STUDIES BY SEVERAL HISTORIANS AND SOCIAL SCIENTISTS ON DISTINCT NATIONALISM IN DEVELOPED AND LESS DEVELOPED STATES. EXAMINES BOTH TRADITIONAL AND MODERN FORMS OF NATIONALISM, AND WAYS IN WHICH CULTURE, RACE, IDEOLOGY, AND CLASS AFFECT ITS FORM. ESTABLISHES A FUNCTIONAL APPROACH WHICH, THROUGH ITS UNIVERSAL APPLICATION, EMBRACES ALL VARIETIES OF PATTERNS AND INSTITUTIONS OF NATIONALISM.

2878 SIMMS R.P.
URBANIZATION IN WEST AFRICA; A REVIEW OF CURRENT LITERATURE.
EVANSTON: NORTHWESTERN U PRESS, 1965, 109 PP., LC#65-19464.
REVIEW OF PUBLICATIONS DATED FROM 1950 TO AUGUST 1962, BASICALLY FOCUSED ON SOCIAL ASPECTS OF URBANIZATION. CLASSIFIED INTO FOUR CATEGORIES: SUBSTANTIVE, METHODOLOGICAL, EMPIRICAL AND THEORETICAL, AND BIBLIOGRPHICAL WORKS. ONE CHAPTER DEVOTED TO ANNOTATED BIBLIOGRPHY OF 234 PERIODICALS, BOOKS, AND MONOGRAPHS. SUPPLEMENTARY BIBLIOGRAPHY COVERING PERIOD 1962-64 APPENDED TO REGULAR LISTING.

2879 SIMOES DOS REIS A.
BIBLIOGRAFIA DAS BIBLIOGRAFIAS BRASILEIRAS.
RIO DE JANEIRO: INST.NACIONAL DO LIVRO, 1942,186 PP.
BIBLIOGRAPHY OF BRAZILIAN BIBLIOGRAPHIES. INCLUDES BOOKS AND PERIODICALS. ENTRIES ARE ARRANGED ALPHABETICALLY BY AUTHOR.

2880 SIMON Y.R.
NATURE AND FUNCTIONS OF AUTHORITY.
MILWAUKEE: MARQUETTE UNIV PRESS, 1940, 78 PP.
ATTEMPTS TO DETERMINE WHETHER IT IS POSSIBLE TO DISCOVER PRINCIPLES TO WHICH ONE CAN REFER IN PROPORTIONING LIBERTY AND AUTHORITY. CONCLUDES THAT PROGRESS OF LIBERTY IS IDENTIFIED CORRECTLY WITH PROGRESS OF MAN AND SOCIETY, PROVIDED LIBERTY IS TERMINAL. PROGRESS OF LIBERTY MEANS DECAY OF AUTHORITY IF AUTHORITY REPRESENTS SERVITUDE. AUTHORITY PREVAILS WHEN COMMON ACTION IS REQUIRED.

2881 SINAI I.R.
THE CHALLENGE OF MODERNISATION* THE WEST'S IMPACT ON THE NON-WESTERN WORLD.
NEW YORK: W W NORTON, 1964, 256 PP.
THE WEST CAN FIND ITS WAY OUT OF DESPAIR AND FEAR OF THE EAST BY FACING UP TO THE FAILURES OF IMPERIALISM AND BUSINESS ORIENTED POLICIES, AND RECOGNIZING THAT SOCIALISM IS EQUALLY IRRELEVANT FOR THE PRE-DEMOCRATIC, ECONOMICALLY PRIMITIVE ASIA STATES. WEST SHOULD HELP THEM FIND AN EASTERN WAY TO POLITICAL PROGRESS. VARIOUS ELITES COMPARED.

2882 SINGER K.
THE IDEA OF CONFLICT.
MELBOURNE: U. PR., 1949, 181 PP.
TRACES IDEA OF CONFLICT BY ANALYZING PAST STRIFE AND SHOWING HOW EMBODIED IN PRESENT WORLD CONFLICTS. DENOTES INTERPLAY OF FORCES AND VARIETY OF ORDINARY OCCASIONS FROM WHICH CONFLICTS ARISE.

2883 SINGER M.R.
THE EMERGING ELITE: A STUDY OF POLITICAL LEADERSHIP IN CEYLON.
CAMBRIDGE: M.I.T. PR., 1964, 203 PP.
IDENTIFIES SOCIOECONOMIC CHARACTERISTICS, ATTITUDES, AND SELF-IMAGES OF CONTEMPORARY POLITICAL, CIVIL SERVICE, TRADE-UNION, AND RURAL ELITES. EMERGING ELITES SYNTHESIZE TRADITIONAL AND WESTERN VALUES. ARE ESSENTIALLY MIDDLE-CLASS, REPRESENTING MIDDLE-CLASS INTERESTS.

2884 SINGH B.
"ITALIAN EXPERIENCE IN REGIONAL ECONOMIC DEVELOPMENT AND LESSONS FOR OTHER COUNTRIES."
ECO. DEV. AND CULTURAL CHANGE, 15 (APR. 67).
AFTER ANALYZING ITALY'S ATTEMPT TO DEVELOP ITS SOUTH TO BALANCE THE RAPID ECONOMIC EXPANSION OF ITS NORTH, AUTHOR CONCLUDES THAT EFFICIENCY IN REGIONAL ECONOMIC DEVELOPMENT WOULD BE MORE EFFECTIVE IF IT IS MORE DISCRIMINATORY, FAVORING HIGHER YIELDING ZONES IN WHICH COMPLETELY INTERRELATED PROGRAMS CAN BE DEVELOPED ON ALL LEVELS INSTEAD OF BROAD BUT LESS DIRECTED PLANNING.

2885 SINGH H.L.
PROBLEMS AND POLICIES OF THE BRITISH IN INDIA, 1885-1898.
NEW YORK: ASIA PUBL HOUSE, 1963, 284 PP.
EXAMINES INDO-BRITISH EMPIRE IN PERIOD OF ITS CLIMAX AND INCREASED INDIAN DEMANDS FOR GREATER, MORE ACTIVE SHARE IN GOVERNMENT AND ADMINISTRATION. DISCUSSES VASTNESS AND COMPLEXITY OF ADMINISTRATION PROBLEMS WHICH MADE SHARING OF GOVERNMENT POWER WITH INDIANS IMPERATIVE. CRITICIZES ENGLISH FAILURE TO ADJUST POLICIES TO CHANGING CIRCUMSTANCES. FOCUSES ON CIVIL SERVICE, LEGISLATIVE, AND MILITARY ISSUES.

2886 SINGTON D., WEIDENFELD A.
THE GOEBBELS EXPERIMENT.
LONDON: JOHN MURRAY, 1942, 260 PP.
STUDY OF NAZI PROPAGANDA MACHINERY INCLUDES ORGANIZATION, PARTY PRESS, PROPAGANDA MINISTRY, BROADCASTING, RELATION TO ARMED FORCES, CONTROL, AND RELATION TO FINE ARTS.

2887 SINOR D.
INTRODUCTION A L'ETUDE DE L'EURASIE CENTRALE.
WIESBADEN: OTTO HARRASSOWITZ, 1963, 371 PP.
GUIDE TO LITERATURE ON LANGUAGE, HISTORY, AND ETHNOLOGY OF CENTRAL ASIA. WORKS WERE SELECTED ONLY AFTER HAVING BEEN REVIEWED BY AUTHOR. MATERIAL IS ARRANGED BY ETHNIC GROUP AND BY CHRONOLOGICAL PERIOD. INCLUDES AUTHOR INDEX. CONTAINS EXTENSIVE BIBLIOGRAPHIC MATERIAL.

2888 SIPPEL D.
"INDIENS UNSICHERE ZUKUNFT."
NEUE POLITISCHE LITERATUR, 12 (1967), 200-220.
CRITICAL REVIEW OF MAJOR WORKS ON INDIAN POLITICS, SOCIETY, AND ECONOMY. POINTS TO ESTABLISHMENT OF SOUTH ASIA INSTITUTE AT HEIDELBERG UNIVERSITY WHERE INTERDISCIPLINARY APPROACHES TO ETHNOLOGY, ECONOMICS, TROPICAL HYGIENE, GEOGRAPHY, AND AGRARIAN POLITICS SEEK TO MAKE CONTRIBUTIONS TO UNDERSTANDING OF PROBLEMS OF SOUTH ASIA. SUGGESTS OPPORTUNITIES FOR RESEARCH.

2889 SIRSIKAR V.M.
POLITICAL BEHAVIOR IN INDIA.
BOMBAY: MANAKTALAS, 1965, 276 PP.
REPORT ON VOTING BEHAVIOR OF POONA, INDIA IN 1962 GENERAL ELECTIONS, INCLUDING BACKGROUND, POLITICAL PARTIES IN ACTION, CAMPAIGNING, CANDIDATES, AND VOTERS.

2890 SISSON C.H.
THE SPIRIT OF BRITISH ADMINISTRATION AND SOME EUROPEAN COMPARISONS.

LONDON: FABER AND FABER, 1959, 162 PP.
ANALYSIS OF INDIVIDUAL IN, AND ORGANIZATION OF, BRITISH PUBLIC ADMINISTRATION AND ITS RELATION TO LAW AND POLITICS. COMPARES BRITISH SYSTEM WITH THAT OF FRANCE, GERMANY, AND SWEDEN.

2891 SISSONS C.B.
CHURCH AND STATE IN CANADIAN EDUCATION: AN HISTORICAL STUDY.
TORONTO: RYERSON PRESS, 1959, 414 PP.
COMPREHENSIVE STUDY OF CANADIAN CHURCH-STATE RELATIONS THROUGHOUT HISTORY; DIVIDED INTO SECTIONS, EACH COVERING ONE PROVINCE OR AREA. AUTHOR IS WORRIED ABOUT CANADIANS' PREOCCUPATION TODAY WITH RIGHTS OF MINORITIES, AND FEELS THAT ONLY RIGHT A MINORITY CAN SAFELY BE GIVEN IS RIGHT IN FREE DISCUSSION TO PERSUADE MAJORITY OF JUSTICE OF THEIR CAUSE; THIS IS ESPECIALLY TRUE IN FIELD OF EDUCATION.

2892 SITHOLE N.
AFRICAN NATIONALISM.
LONDON: OXFORD U PR, 1959, 174 PP.
A YOUNG BLACK SOUTH AFRICAN WRITES ABOUT HIS BELIEF THAT PEOPLE OF ALL RACES SHOULD LEARN TO RESPECT ONE ANOTHER AND WORK TOGETHER IF THE INTERESTS OF BLACK AND WHITE ARE TO BE SERVED.

2893 SKALWEIT S.
FRANKREICH UND FRIEDRICH DER GROSSE.
BONN: LUDWIG ROHRSCHEID VERLAG, 1952, 201 PP.
ANALYZES PUBLIC OPINION IN FRANCE OF 18TH CENTURY TOWARD PRUSSIA AND PARTICULARLY THE REIGN OF FREDERICK THE GREAT. ATTEMPTS TO DISCOVER BASIC MOTIVES AND RELATE THEM TO SOCIAL AND POLITICAL ORIGINS. BASED ON MEMOIRS, DIARIES, CORRESPONDENCE, AND POLITICAL PAMPHLETS.

2894 SKILLING H.G.
"COMMUNISM: NATIONAL OR INTERNATIONAL."
INT. J., 15 (WINTER 59), 36-48.
QUESTION EMANATES FROM PROLIFERATION, AFTER 1945, OF PEOPLE'S DEMOCRACIES WHEN USSR SOUGHT TO IMPOSE ITS WILL THROUGH ADMINISTRATIVE AND POLICE METHODS. TITO, SINO-SOVIET DISPUTE AND DE-STALINIZATION DISCUSSED. WHILE SOVIET UNION IS NOT OMNIPOTENT IN THIS SPHERE OF INFLUENCE, THE WEST CAN DO LITTLE TO AFFECT OUTCOME. WARNED AGAINST TAKING ACTION WHICH COULD SOLIDIFY COMMUNIST BLOC.

2895 SKILLING H.G.
THE GOVERNMENTS OF COMMUNIST EAST EUROPE.
NEW YORK: THOMAS Y CROWELL, 1966, 256 PP., LC#66-14616.
COMPARATIVE STUDY OF GOVERNMENTS, BRINGING OUT HISTORY OF RISE OF EASTERN EUROPEAN REGIMES. ANALYZES CONSTITUTIONAL FORMS AND PARTY STRUCTURE, THE EXECUTIVES OF STATES, PLUS INNER COUNCILS AND CENTRAL COMMITTEES OF POWER ELITE. SHOWS HOW VARIOUS INTEREST GROUPS AFFECT DECISION-MAKING AND EXECUTION OF POLICY; DEMONSTRATES THAT TOTALITARIANISM IS IN GREAT TRANSITION IN EASTERN EUROPE.

2896 SKILLING H.G.
"THE RUMANIAN NATIONAL COURSE."
INT. J., 21 (FALL 66), 470-483.
DESCRIBES RESURGENT NATIONALISM IN RUMANIA AND RESULTING INDEPENDENT POLICY WITHIN COMMUNIST BLOC. ALSO CONSIDERS REPERCUSSIONS IN NON-COMMUNIST WORLD RESULTING FROM SUCH INDEPENDENCE.

2897 SKINNER E.P.
THE MOSSI OF UPPER VOLTA: THE POLITICAL DEVELOPMENT OF A SUDANESE PEOPLE.
STANFORD: U. PR., 1964, 236 PP., $6.50.
COMPREHENSIVE, FIELDWORK-BASED DESCRIPTION OF THE SOCIAL, ECONOMIC, LEGAL, AND RELIGIOUS FORCES THAT BUTTRESSED THE FEUDAL MOSSI POLITICAL SYSTEM FOR SEVEN CENTURIES. CONSIDERS THE EFFECTS OF MODERN POLITICAL INSTITUTIONS LEADING TO THE END OF FEUDALISM IN 1960.

2898 SKLAR R.L.
NIGERIAN POLITICAL PARTIES: POWER IN AN EMERGENT AFRICAN NATION.
PRINCETON: U. PR., 1963, 578 PP., $12.50.
A DEFINITIVE STUDY OF PARTIES DURING THE FINAL PHASE OF BRITISH RULE. THE UNIFYING THEME IS THE POLITICAL CONVERGENCE OF THE GROWTH OF NATIONALISM, THE PERSISTENCE OF CULTURAL PARTICULARISM, AND THE CRYSTALLIZATION OF EMERGENT CLASS INTERESTS. WITH CASE STUDIES OF SITUATIONS OF PARTY COMPETITION AND INTRA-PARTY CONFLICT. EXHAUSTIVE IN DETAIL.

2899 SLATER J.
A REVALUATION OF COLLECTIVE SECURITY* THE OAS IN ACTION.
COLUMBUS: OHIO STATE U PR, 1965, 56 PP., LC#65-20317.
AUTHOR COLLECTS STATEMENTS OF IR THEORETICIANS ON COLLECTIVE SECURITY. FINDS THAT IN CONCENTRATING ON A UNIVERSAL MODEL THEY HAVE EITHER POSITED A PREORDAINED MILLENNIUM OR AN UNWORKABLE BEAST. FINDS THAT COLLECTIVE SECURITY IS HOWEVER A VIABLE CONCEPT FOR REGIONAL ORGANIZATIONS. DERIVES THIS FROM ANALYSIS OF CASES IN WHICH OAS CONSIDERED COLLECTIVE ACTION.

2900 SLOAN P.
"FIFTY YEARS OF SOVIET RULE."
QUARTERLY REV., 305 (OCT. 67), 367-378.
DISCUSSES SOVIET PROGRESS SINCE 1917 REVOLUTION. NOTES BACKWARDNESS AND OPPRESSIVENESS OF TSARIST RULE. BELIEVES THAT PRESS DOES NOT GIVE ADEQUATE COVERAGE TO GREAT PROGRESS MADE IN RUSSIA. USSR HAS INDEED INTRODUCED A NEW SOCIAL SYSTEM AND CULTURE THAT ARE FIRMLY ESTABLISHED. DESCRIBES ADVANCES IN LAND AND ECONOMIC REFORM, EDUCATIONAL SYSTEM, HEALTH, HOUSING, AND PRODUCTION OF CONSUMER GOODS.

2901 SLOTKIN J.S.
FROM FIELD TO FACTORY; NEW INDUSTRIAL EMPLOYEES.
NEW YORK: FREE PRESS OF GLENCOE, 1960, 156 PP., LC#59-15921.
DEVELOPS A THEORY ON THE RECRUITMENT AND COMMITMENT OF LABOR FORCE IN UNDERDEVELOPED AREAS. APPROACHES PROBLEM AS A SOCIAL ANTHROPOLOGIST AND CONTENDS THAT, CULTURALLY SPEAKING, UNDERDEVELOPED AREAS ARE THOSE WHICH HAVE NOT ADOPTED THE BODY OF CUSTOMS CONSTITUTING INDUSTRIALISM. DISCUSSES HOW NEW INDUSTRIAL LABOR FORCE IS CONFRONTED BY NOVEL CULTURAL AND SOCIAL SITUATIONS IN PROCESS OF ADAPTATION.

2902 SLOTKIN J.S. ED.
READINGS IN EARLY ANTHROPOLOGY.
NEW YORK: WENNER GREN FDN ANTH, 1965, 530 PP., LC#65-16645.
SURVEY OF WESTERN CIVILIZATION, INCLUDING ARCHEOLOGY, PHYSICAL ANTHROPOLOGY, AND ETHNOLOGY. BRIEF COMMENTS ON MEN WITH EXCERPTS FROM WORKS IN SCIENCE, PHILOSOPHY, LITERATURE, AND MOST DISCIPLINES.

2903 SMEDLEY A.
THE GREAT ROAD: THE LIFE AND TIMES OF CHU TEH.
NEW YORK: MONTHLY REVIEW PR, 1956, 461 PP., LC#56-11272.
STORY OF THE FIRST 60 YEARS (1886-1946) OF GENERAL CHU TEH, COMMANDER IN CHIEF OF THE PEOPLE'S LIBERATION ARMY OF CHINA. COVERS THE GENERAL'S PARTICIPATION IN THE WAR AGAINST JAPAN AND IN THE CHINESE COMMUNIST REVOLUTION. MORE OF A HISTORY OF THE REVOLUTION THAN A BIOGRAPHY, THE VOLUME RELATES THE EXPERIENCES OF THE AUTHOR AS SHE ACCOMPANIED THE CHINESE REVOLUTIONARIES.

2904 SMELSER N.J. ED., LIPSET S.M. ED.
SOCIAL STRUCTURE AND MOBILITY IN ECONOMIC DEVELOPMENT.
CHICAGO: ALDINE PUBLISHING CO, 1966, 399 PP., LC#66-12458.
THEORIZES THAT PROCESSES OF CHANGE THAT CONSTITUTE SOCIAL AND ECONOMIC DEVELOPMENT ARE INTERRELATED AND THAT THESE CHANGES ARE ACCOMPANIED BY CHANGES IN SOCIAL STRUCTURE. REVIEWS THEORETICAL AND METHODOLOGICAL ISSUES, EXPLORES TRADITIONAL AND MODERN STRATIFICATION SYSTEMS, AND STUDIES EFFECTS OF ECONOMIC DEVELOPMENT, CULTURAL VALUES, SOCIAL MECHANISMS, POLITICS, AND PERSONALITY ON SOCIAL MOBILITY.

2905 SMITH A.
THE WEALTH OF NATIONS.
ORIGINAL PUBLISHER NOT AVAILABLE, 1776, 486 PP.
ASSUMES PRIMARY PSYCHOLOGICAL DRIVE IN MAN IS SELF-INTEREST AND THAT THERE IS A NATURAL ORDER IN THE UNIVERSE WHICH MAKES INDIVIDUAL STRIVINGS RESULT IN SOCIAL GOOD. CONCLUDES THAT BEST PROGRAM IS TO LEAVE ECONOMIC PROCESS ALONE. JUSTIFIES SELF-INTEREST AND BUSINESS ENTERPRISE. PRESENTS FIRST FORMULATION OF IDEA THAT SOURCE OF VALUE IN COMMODITIES IS LABOR.

2906 SMITH D.D.
"MODAL ATTITUDE CLUSTERS* A SUPPLEMENT FOR THE STUDY OF NATIONAL CHARACTER."
SOCIAL FORCES, 44 (JUNE 66), 526-533.
EMPHASIS ON PERSONALITY IS RESPONSIBLE FOR IMPASSE IN NATIONAL CHARACTER RESEARCH. THE CONCEPTION OF MODAL ATTITUDE CLUSTERS IS PRESENTED TO FULLY SUPPLEMENT MANY WEAKNESSES RESULTING FROM PERSONALITY PERSPECTIVE.

2907 SMITH E.W.
THE GOLDEN STOOL: SOME ASPECTS OF THE CONFLICT OF CULTURES IN AFRICA.
LONDON: HOLBORN PUBL HOUSE, 1927, 328 PP.
GIVES GENERAL PICTURE OF AFRICA IN 1920'S, WITH ANECDOTES, PERSONAL VIEWS OF AFRICANS, THEIR CUSTOMS, LANGUAGE, AND ATTITUDES.

2908 SMITH E.W. ED.
AFRICAN IDEAS OF GOD.
EDINBURGH: EDINBURGH HOUSE PR, 1950, 308 PP.
SYMPOSIUM ON IDEAS OF GOD AMONG DIFFERENT AFRICAN PEOPLES. ESSAYS ARE BASED ON AUTHOR'S INTIMATE PERSONAL KNOWLEDGE AND ARE NOT SUPPOSED TO REPRESENT A GENERAL SURVEY OF AFRICAN IDEAS OF GOD. SOME OF THE COUNTRIES AND AREAS COVERED INCLUDE: NORTHERN NYASALAND, NORTHERN RHODESIA, SOUTH AFRICA, THE CONGO, UGANDA, THE NUBA MOUNTAINS, AND SIERRA LEONE. HAS A BIBLIOGRAPHY.

2909 SMITH G.
A CONSTITUTIONAL AND LEGAL HISTORY OF ENGLAND.
NEW YORK: CHAS SCRIBNER'S SONS, 1955, 565 PP., LC#55-7297.

TRACES THE HISTORY OF LAW IN ENGLAND FROM EARLY ANGLO-SAXON TIMES TO THE PRESENT. SHOWS HOW EXTENSION OF NATIONAL TERRITORY CAUSED CREATION OF SEMI-INDEPENDENT LORDS WHO COULD INSIST UPON CERTAIN PRINCIPLES OF JUSTICE, WHICH CAME TO INCLUDE ALL OF LAW. EXTENSION OF THE PROPERTY BASE IN THE 17TH-19TH CENTURIES GAVE THE MIDDLE CLASS A CLAIM TO JUSTICE AND ITS ADMINISTRATION.

2910 SMITH H.E. ED.
READINGS IN ECONOMIC DEVELOPMENT AND ADMINISTRATION IN TANZANIA.
DAR SALAAM: U SALAAM PUB ADMIN, 1966, 598 PP.
CREATES HEREWITH FIRST SOURCE BOOK FOR TANZANIAN ECONOMY, INCLUDING GOVERNMENT DOCUMENTS, RESEARCH REPORTS, AND JOURNALISTIC CONTRIBUTIONS. BRIEFLY DESCRIBES HISTORY AND SPECIFIC PROBLEMS, THEN DEALS WITH MONETARY SYSTEM, FINANCE, LABOR, INDUSTRIALIZATION, PLANNING, INTERNATIONAL TRADE, AND MUCH-DESIRED INTEGRATION OF EAST AFRICA.

2911 SMITH J.E.
"THE GERMAN DEMOCRATIC REPUBLIC AND THE WEST."
INTERNATIONAL JOURNAL, 22 (SPRING 67), 210-230.
EXAMINES GDR OF RECENT YEARS, INCLUDING CONSTRUCTION OF BERLIN WALL. LAMENTS LACK OF ACCESS TO INFORMATION FLOW FROM GDR. HISTORICAL AND PHILOSOPHICAL BASIS OF COMMUNISM IN GERMANY. SEES STABILIZATION OF GOVERNMENT MOSTLY BECAUSE OF RECENT ECONOMIC UPSWING.

2912 SMITH J.E.
"RED PRUSSIANISM OF THE GERMAN DEMOCRATIC REPUBLIC."
BUL. ATOMIC SCIENTISTS, 23 (MAY 67), 24-30.
HOWEVER TRUE IT MAY HAVE BEEN BEFORE 1961, THE POPULAR US VIEW OF EAST GERMANY AS THE MOST RIGID, STALINIST, AND ECONOMICALLY UNSUCCESSFUL STATE IN THE EAST BLOC IS NO LONGER ACCURATE. THE BERLIN WALL, PARADOXICALLY, AND OTHER FACTORS, INCLUDING ULBRICHT'S OFTEN UNRECOGNIZED ABILITIES, HAVE LED TO STRIKING IMPROVEMENTS IN MOST ASPECTS OF THE GDR, THOUGH THERE IS LITTLE INTELLECTUAL LIBERALIZATION.

2913 SMITH J.E.
"THE RED PRUSSIANISM OF THE GERMAN DEMOCRATIC REPUBLIC."
POLITICAL STUDIES, 82 (SEPT. 67), 368-385.
EVALUATES CHANCES OF SUCCESS FOR GDR AND ULBRICHT, FINDING THEM QUITE FAVORABLE. REFERS TO GREAT CHANGES SINCE 1961 IN POWER STRUCTURE, USE OF TERRORISM AND PROPAGANDA, AND SLACKENING OF SUPPRESSION OF INTELLECTUAL COMMUNITY AS INDICATORS OF GROWING VITALITY.

2914 SMITH M.G.
GOVERNMENT IN ZAZZAU 1800-1950.
LONDON: OXFORD U PR, 1960, 371 PP.
STUDY OF GOVERNMENT IN ZARIA REGION OF NORTHERN NIGERIA, SHOWING ITS DEVELOPMENT IN 19TH CENTURY UNDER TRIBAL LEADERSHIP, AND ITS PRESENT-DAY, POSTCOLONIAL COMPOSITION. THEORY OF STRUCTURAL CHANGE IS DEVELOPED THROUGH ANALYSIS OF CHANGES WHICH WERE PART OF PROCESS WHICH TRANSFORMED GOVERNMENT SYSTEMS.

2915 SMITH M.G.
KINSHIP AND COMMUNITY IN CARRIACOU.
NEW HAVEN: YALE U PR, 1962, 345 PP., LC#62-08264.
DEPICTS LIFE AND CULTURE OF SMALL WEST INDIAN TRIBE, ANALYZING MAJOR FACTORS OF SOCIAL STRUCTURE INCLUDING MATING, RELIGION, LINEAGE, DIVISION OF LABOR, SOCIAL CLASS, AND FAMILY RELATIONS.

2916 SMITH P. ED.
A HISTORY OF MODERN CULTURE (2 VOLS.)
NEW YORK: HENRY HOLT & CO, 1934.
HISTORY OF DEVELOPMENT OF WESTERN CULTURE AND IDEAS FROM 1583 TO 1776 WITH INDEX AND BIBLIOGRAPHY.

2917 SMITH R.M.
CAMBODIA'S FOREIGN POLICY.
ITHACA: CORNELL U PRESS, 1965, 273 PP., LC#65-15375.
TELLS HOW CAMBODIA HAS USED A POLICY OF NONALIGNMENT TO FURTHER ITS OWN INTERESTS IN DEALING WITH EAST AND WEST. IT DESCRIBES MUCH OF THE RECENT HISTORY OF CAMBODIA'S RELATIONS WITH OTHER SOUTHEAST ASIAN COUNTRIES AND CRISES. THE BOOK WAS RESEARCHED IN CAMBODIA.

2918 SMITH T.E.
"ELECTIONS IN DEVELOPING COUNTRIES: A STUDY OF ELECTORAL PROCEDURES USED IN TOPICAL AFRICA, SOUTH-EAST ASIA..."
NEW YORK: ST MARTIN'S PRESS, 1960.
SUMMARY OF VARIOUS ELECTORAL METHODS WHICH HAVE BEEN TRIED IN INTRODUCING DEMOCRACY TO DEVELOPING COUNTRIES IN TROPICAL AFRICA, INDIA, SOUTH-EAST ASIA, AND BRITISH CARIBBEAN. CONTAINS INFORMATION ON ELECTORAL ADMINISTRATION AND GEOGRAPHY, REGISTRATION, FRANCHISE, MINORITIES AND ELECTORAL SYSTEM, ETC. BIBLIOGRAPHY ARRANGED BY COUNTRY.

2919 SMITH T.V.
THE DEMOCRATIC WAY OF LIFE.
CHICAGO: U OF CHICAGO PRESS, 1926, 211 PP.
EXPOSITION OF DEMOCRATIC IDEALS DISCUSSES DEMOCRACY AS FRATERNITY, LIBERTY, AND EQUALITY; INCLUDES FUNCTIONS OF DEMOCRACY THAT MIGHT BE CALLED RELIGIOUS. DEFINES PLACE OF WORK IN A DEMOCRATIC SOCIETY, GOALS, AND VALUES OF ESTABLISHING "GOOD LIFE." CONCLUDES WITH DEMOCRATIC LEADERSHIP. TREATISE IS MORE PHILOSOPHICAL THAN EMPIRICAL; REFERS THROUGHOUT TO POLITICAL THINKERS AND CONCEPTS.

2920 SMITH T.V.
THE PROMISE OF AMERICAN POLITICS.
CHICAGO: U OF CHICAGO PRESS, 1936, 290 PP.
FORCEFUL ROLE INDIVIDUALISM HAS PLAYED IN HISTORY OF WORLD POLITICS IS DISCUSSED, NOTING RISE OF LIBERALISM AS CONCEIVED BY LOCKE, BENTHAM, AND JEFFERSON. FREEDOM OF THOUGHT, SPEECH, AND CONSENT ARE ALSO TREATED, AND FASCISM, COMMUNISM, PARLIAMENTARIANISM COMPARED. CLOSES WITH STUDY OF AMERICANISM AND INCLUDES DEMOCRATIC ELEMENTS, JUDICIAL SUPREMACY, CLASS STRUCTURE, AND CITIZEN PARTICIPATION.

2921 SMUTS J.C.
AFRICA AND SOME WORLD PROBLEMS.
LONDON: OXFORD U PR, 1930, 184 PP.
GENERAL SMUTS' 1929 LECTURES IN ENGLAND ON SEVERAL AFRICAN TOPICS: DAVID LIVINGSTONE, CECIL RHODES, THE DISCOVERY AND SETTLEMENT OF THE CONTINENT, AND THE QUESTION OF NATIVE POLICY IN SOUTH AFRICA. SMUTS STOUTLY DEFENDS RHODES'S NEW GLEN GREY LEGISLATION WHEREBY WHITES AND BLACKS ARE GUARANTEED SEPARATE AND PARALLEL RIGHTS AND DEVELOPMENT. INCLUDES DISCUSSION OF LEAGUE AND WORLD PEACE.

2922 SMYTHE H.H.
"NEHRU AND INDIAN FOREIGN POLICY."
UNITED ASIA, 16 (SEP-OCT 64), 288-291.
PRESENTS BRIEF OUTLINE OF NEHRU'S PLACE IN WORLD AFFAIRS AS THE LEADING FORCE OF THE NON-ALIGNED NATIONS. CITES HIS CHANGING ROLE IN WORLD AFTER CHINESE BORDER DISPUTE AND GOA INCIDENT, POLICY TOWARDS PAKISTAN AND AFRICAN NATIONS, AND HIS PERSONAL EASTERN ORIENTED - WESTERN EDUCATED BACKGROUND.

2923 SNELLEN I.T.
"APARTHEID* CHECKS AND CHANGES."
INTERNATIONAL AFFAIRS (U.K.), 43, (APR.67), 293-306.
ANALYZES APARTHEID AS MEANS OF HANDLING EXTERNAL PROBLEMS OF DECOLONIZATION, RACIAL EQUALITY, NATIONALISM, & STRUGGLE BETWEEN EAST & WEST. REVIEWS SOCIO-ECONOMIC & POLITICAL ASPECTS OF APARTHEID. DISCUSSES BOTH INTERNAL AND EXTERNAL REPERCUSSIONS OF ITS IMPLEMENTATION. CONCLUDES APARTHEID IN PRESENT FORM WILL PROBABLY NOT SURVIVE SINCE IMPETUS FOR CHANGE ARISES FROM TENSION BETWEEN ITS THEORY AND PRACTICE.

2924 SNOW P.G.
"A SCALOGRAM ANALYSIS OF POLITICAL DEVELOPMENT."
AMER. BEHAVIORAL SCIENTIST, 9 (MAR. 66), 33-36.
GUTTMAN SCALOGRAM ANALYSIS IS MODIFIED FOR USE ON "FINISHED" POLITICAL CHARACTERISTICS DERIVED FROM BANKS AND TEXTOR'S "A CROSS POLITY SURVEY." APPLIED TO LATIN AMERICAN POLITICAL DEVELOPMENT RANKINGS AS TEST. CORRELATIONS ARE HIGH AND APPEAR TO CLEARLY DELINEATE CHARACTERISTICS AND PATTERNS OF DEVELOPMENT.

2925 SOARES G., HAMBLIN R.L.
"SOCIO-ECONOMIC VARIABLES AND VOTING FOR THE RADICAL LEFT: CHILE 1952."
AM. POL. SCI. REV., 61 (FALL 67), 1053-1065.
INVESTIGATES SOCIO-ECONOMIC BASES OF CHILEAN POLITICS TO FIND WHETHER OR NOT DEGREE OF INDUSTRIALIZATION AFFECTS DEGREE OF ALIENATED VOTES. STUDIES RADICAL VOTES IN 1952, 1958, 1964 CHILEAN ELECTIONS, OBSERVING FACTORS LIKE CLASS POLARIZATION, RELATIVE ECONOMIC DEPRIVATION, ANOMIE, INDUSTRIALIZATION, AND URBANIZATION. CONCLUDES THESE ARE INDEPENDENT VARIABLES, ALL INVOLVED IN A MULTIPLIER EFFECT.

2926 SOBEL L.A. ED.
SOUTH VIETNAM: US-COMMUNIST CONFRONTATION IN SOUTHEAST ASIA 1961-65.
NEW YORK: FACTS ON FILE, INC, 1966, 238 PP., LC#66-23943.
REFERENCE BOOK IN JOURNALISTIC STYLE ON SPECIFIC EVENTS IN VIETNAM FROM 1961-65. PRESENTS GEOGRAPHIC ASPECTS OF STRUGGLE, US AID TO DIEM, GROWING US INTERVENTION IN 1962, OVERTHROW OF DIEM AND CIVIL WAR OF 1963, EXPANSION OF WAR TO NORTH VIETNAM IN 1964, AIR WAR, PEACE ATTEMPTS, US BUILD-UP IN SOUTH, AND DOMESTIC PROBLEMS IN US IN 1965.

2927 SOEMARDJORN S.
"SOME SOCIAL AND CULTURAL IMPLICATIONS OF INDONESIA'S PLANNED AND UNPLANNED DEVELOPMENT."
REV. POLIT., 25(JAN. 63), 64-90.
FOCUSES UPON 'THE MOST SIGNIFICANT SOCIAL AND CULTURAL CHANGES WHICH HAVE OCCURRED IN INDONESIAN SOCIETY IN RECENT YEARS AND IN THE WAKE OF THE EIGHT-YEAR DEVELOPMENT PLAN FOR 1961 TO 1969.'

2928 SOKOL A.E.
SEAPOWER IN THE NUCLEAR AGE.
WASHINGTON: PUBLIC AFFAIRS PRESS, 1961, 268 PP., LC#59-15850
INVESTIGATES SEA POWER AS MAJOR ASPECT OF NATIONAL POWER AND MILITARY FORCE. SEA POWER CONTRIBUTES GREATLY TO INTER-

NATIONAL TRADE AND IS ONE MILITARY AREA IN WHICH US IS CONSIDERABLY MORE ADVANCED THAN USSR. SUGGESTS RECONSIDERATION OF SEA POWER POLICY IN LIGHT OF NUCLEAR AGE.

2929 SOLOVEYTCHIK G.
"BOOKS ON RUSSIA."
CONTEMPORARY REV., (MAR. 64), 113-123.
AN ANNOTATED BIBLIOGRAPHY OF BOOKS ON RUSSIA PUBLISHED IN 1964. ENGLISH-LANGUAGE. CONTAINS 10 ENTRIES. MATERIAL COVERS RUSSIAN HISTORY AND CINEMA.

2930 SOLOW R.M.
THE NATURE AND SOURCES OF UNEMPLOYMENT IN THE UNITED STATES (PAMPHLET)
UPPSALA: ALMQUIST & WIKSELL, 1964, 51 PP.
CONTAINS WICKSELL LECTURES OF 1964 CONCERNING QUESTION OF UNEMPLOYMENT. DISCUSSES THEORY OF AUTOMATION AND ABUNDANCE IN RELATION TO US ECONOMY. MAINTAINS THAT STATISTICS SHOW NO APPROACH TO SATIATION WITH CONSUMPTION, NOR ANY SPECTACULAR ACCELERATION OF PRODUCTIVITY. OUTPUT PER MANHOUR IN US MANUFACTURING HAS RISEN ONLY SLIGHTLY FASTER SINCE WWII THAN IT DID BEFORE.

2931 SOLT L.F.
"PURITANISM, CAPITALISM, DEMOCRACY, AND THE NEW SCIENCE."
AMER. HISTORICAL REVIEW, 73 (OCT. 67), 18-29.
RELATES PROTESTANT INDIVIDUALISTIC, NON-TRADITIONAL PHILOSOPHIES TO REJECTION OF CLASSICAL SCIENTIFIC AUTHORITY. LINKS DOWNFALL OF SCHOLASTICISM TO INCREASING ATTEMPTS TO CONTROL MATERIAL WORLD. PARALLELING THIS IN POLITICS WERE REJECTION OF DIVINE RIGHT AND RISE OF DEMOCRATIC THEORIES OF THE STATE.

2932 SOMMER T.
"BONN CHANGES COURSE."
FOREIGN AFFAIRS, 45 (APR. 67), 477-491.
DISCUSSES GENERAL DIRECTION OF GERMANY'S FUTURE FOREIGN POLICY UNDER KIESINGER-BRANDT COALITION. PREDICTS FOREIGN POLICY CHANGES IN THREE AREAS: IN GERMANY'S RELATIONS WITH ITS WESTERN ALLIES, WITH THE COMMUNIST NATIONS, AND WITH EAST GERMANY. APPRAISES COALITION GOVERNMENT AS REALISTIC AND PRACTICAL IN ITS DOCTRINE OF DETENTE TOWARD EAST GERMANY AND ITS CONCEPT OF COOPERATIVE PARTITION WITH HER.

2933 SONOLET L.
L'AFRIQUE OCCIDENTALE FRANCAISE.
PARIS: LIB HACHETTE ET CIE, 1912, 238 PP.
ILLUSTRATED STUDY OF COLONIAL WESTERN AFRICA INCLUDING COMMERCE, CITY LIFE, RAILROADS, SOCIAL CUSTOMS OF NATIVES, AND THEIR PRACTICAL INTEGRATION WITHIN THE WHITE POWER STRUCTURE.

2934 SOROKIN P.
CONTEMPORARY SOCIOLOGICAL THEORIES.
NEW YORK: HARPER, 1928, 785 PP.
SURVEYS PRINCIPLE SOCIOLOGICAL THEORIES IN ORDER TO ESTABLISH TO WHAT EXTENT THEY ARE SCIENTIFICALLY VALID. DESCRIBES VARIOUS INTERPRETATIONS OF THE STRUGGLE FOR EXISTENCE AND THE SOCIOLOGY OF WAR. CONCLUDES WITH ANALYSIS AND DEFINITION OF SOCIOLOGY.

2935 SOROKIN P.A.
SOCIOLOGICAL THEORIES OF TODAY.
NEW YORK: HARPER & ROW, 1966, 676 PP., LC#66-14173.
PRESENTS ANALYSES OF GENERAL SOCIOLOGICAL THEORIES 1925-65. DISCUSSES INTERCONNECTION OF SOCIO-CULTURAL PHENOMENA, NOMINALIST-ATOMISM, BIO-SOCIETAL ASPECTS, AND INTERRELATIONISM AS PREVALENT NOTION.

2936 SOUTH AFRICA COMMISSION ON FUT
INTERIM AND FINAL REPORTS ON FUTURE FORM OF GOVERNMENT IN THE SOUTH-WEST AFRICAN PROTECTORATE (PAMPHLET)
CAPETOWN: UNION OF SOUTH AFRICA, 1921, 12 PP.
REPORT ON FUTURE FORM OF GOVERNMENT IN UNION OF SOUTH AFRICA, METHOD OF REPRESENTATION OF PEOPLE, AND CHANGES IN ADMINISTRATION OF WITHDRAWAL OF MARTIAL LAW.

2937 SOUTH AFRICA STATE LIBRARY
SOUTH AFRICAN NATIONAL BIBLIOGRAPHY, SANB.
PRETORIA: S AFRICA STATE LIB.
LISTING OF PUBLICATIONS RECEIVED BY STATE LIBRARY IN PRETORIA DURING TWO-MONTH PERIODS. TEXTS IN ENGLISH AND AFRIKAANS. INCLUDES ANNUAL REPORTS OF GOVERNMENTAL DEPARTMENTS. CONTAINS LARGE SECTION ON SOCIAL SCIENCES: ECONOMICS, LAW, PUBLIC ADMINISTRATION, EDUCATION, SOCIOLOGY, SOCIOGRAPHY. BIMONTHLY PUBLICATION.

2938 SOUTH AFRICAN CONGRESS OF DEM
FACE THE FUTURE.
JOHANNESBURG: S AFR CONG DEM, 1960, 19 PP.
CALL FROM ORGANIZATION OF BLACKS AND A FEW WHITES TO STRIVE FOR ABOLITION OF APARTHEID AND FREEDOM FOR ALL RACES. MUST BE ACHIEVED BY EDUCATION, UNDERSTANDING, AND COOPERATION. INCLUDES FREEDOM CHARTER OF 1955, WHICH PUTS FORTH STATEMENTS OF EQUAL RIGHTS, FRIENDSHIP, AND PEACE.

2939 SOUTH PACIFIC COMMISSION
INDEX OF SOCIAL SCIENCE RESEARCH THESES ON THE SOUTH PACIFIC
NOUMEA: SOUTH PACIFIC COMMISSION, 1957, 79 PP.
ANNOTATED LIST OF UNIVERSITY-HELD SOCIAL SCIENCE RESEARCH THESES ON THE SOUTH PACIFIC WHICH HAVE SOME SOCIAL, POLITICAL, OR ECONOMIC BEARING ON COMMISSION'S AREA OF CONCERN. PROVIDES INFORMATION ON SIZE, SCOPE, AND INTENTION OF EACH AUTHOR'S WORK; INCLUDES QUOTATIONS OF PASSAGES STATING INTENTIONS WHEN AVAILABLE. NOT INDEXED.

2940 SOUTHALL A. ED.
SOCIAL CHANGE IN MODERN AFRICA.
LONDON: OXFORD U PR, 1961, 337 PP.
SELECTION OF STUDIES PRESENTED AT THE FIRST INTERNATIONAL AFRICAN SEMINAR IN KAMPALA, 1959. PUBLISHED FOR THE INTERNATIONAL AFRICAN INSTITUTE. DISCUSSES ITEMS RANGING FROM SOCIAL CHANGE AND DEMOGRAPHY TO THE STATUS OF WOMEN AND MARRIAGE.

2941 SPAAK P.H.
"THE SEARCH FOR CONSENSUS: A NEW EFFORT TO BUILD EUROPE."
FOR. AFF., 43 (JAN. 62), 199-209.
ANALYZES PROBLEMS OF COMMON MARKET AND ATLANTIC ALLIANCE, SEEING THEM AS CLOSELY INTERRELATED. CONSIDERS NATIONALISM AND ITS RECENT UPSURGE TO BE 'INTEGRATED', EUROPE'S BASIC PROBLEM AND STUDIES POSITION OF FRANCE AND GERMANY IN THIS LIGHT.

2942 SPEARS E.L.
TWO MEN WHO SAVED FRANCE: PETAIN AND DE GAULLE.
LONDON: EYRE AND SPOTTISWOODE, 1966, 222 PP.
DESCRIBES AUTHOR'S PERSONAL EXPERIENCES WITH GENERAL PETAIN DURING WWI, SHOWING HIS GREAT LEADERSHIP ABILITY AND IMPORTANT ROLE IN VICTORY IN WWI. INCLUDES TRANSLATION OF PETAIN'S ACCOUNTS OF MUTINIES IN FRENCH ARMY IN 1917. DISCUSSES GENERAL DE GAULLE'S PERSONALITY AND ROLE IN MAKING FRANCE THE STRONG NATION SHE IS TODAY.

2943 SPENCER F.A.
WAR AND POSTWAR GREECE: AN ANALYSIS BASED ON GREEK WRITINGS.
WASHINGTON: LIBRARY OF CONGRESS, 1952, 175 PP.
SURVEYS POLITICAL AND SOCIAL EVENTS IN POSTWAR GREECE USING GREEK SOURCES PUBLISHED 1944-52: BOOKS, NEWSPAPERS, AND PERIODICALS. DISCUSSES SOURCES DEALING WITH AXIS INVASION AND OCCUPATION, GREEK RESISTANCE FORCES, LIBERATION, THE CIVIL WAR, THE LULL (1945-1946), COMMUNIST AGRESSION, RECONSTRUCTION. ALSO LISTS BOOKS ON SOCIAL AND CULTURAL PATTERNS. GENERAL INTRODUCTION TO SOURCES. UNINDEXED.

2944 SPENCER H.
SOCIAL STATICS.
NEW YORK: SCHALKENBACH, 1954, 430 PP.
ATTEMPTS TO BUILD UP A BASIC THEORY OF THE ETHICS OF FUNDAMENTAL ECONOMICS. ANALYZES THE RIGHTS OF LIFE AND PERSONAL LIBERTY, THE RIGHT TO PROPERTY, THE RIGHT TO FREE SPEECH. SURVEYS POLITICAL DUTIES OF INDIVIDUAL TO STATE. DISCUSSES REGULATION OF COMMERCE.

2945 SPENCER P.
THE SAMBURU: A STUDY OF GERONTOCRACY IN A NOMADIC TRIBE.
BERKELEY: U OF CALIF PR, 1965, 341 PP.
ANTHROPOLOGICAL STUDY OF NOMADIC EAST AFRICAN TRIBE WHICH IS GOVERNED BY OLDER MEN. SHOWS HOW POLYGAMOUS SOCIETY AND RULE OF ELDERS AFFECTS YOUTH, ESPECIALLY MALES, AND COMPARES TRIBE WITH NEIGHBORING PEOPLES.

2946 SPENCER R.C.
"PARTY GOVERNMENT AND THE SWEDISH RISKDAG."
AM. POL. SCI. REV., 39 (JUNE 45), 437-458.
DISCUSSES THE SWEDISH POLITICAL SYSTEM AS "AN EXCELLENT LABORATORY FOR TESTING PRINCIPLES OF DEMOCRACY, OF REPRESENTATION, AND OF PARTY GOVERNMENT." ON THE CONTRARY, IT SEEMS TO REFUTE CERTAIN NOTIONS ABOUT THE "PARLIAMENTARY-MAJORITY" BASIS FOR JUDGING OF "STRONG GOVERNMENT" IN A DEMOCRACY. DISCUSSES HOW POLITICAL SCIENCE CONCEPTS ARE AFFECTED, CONSTITUTIONAL FACILITIES FOR PARTY GOVERNMENT, AND OTHERS.

2947 SPICER E.H. ED.
HUMAN PROBLEMS IN TECHNOLOGICAL CHANGE.
NEW YORK: RUSSELL SAGE FDN, 1952, 307 PP., LC#52-11862.
CASEBOOK OF STUDIES INVOLVING A SIGNIFICANT TECHNOLOGICAL ADVANCE INTRODUCED TO AN UNDERDEVELOPED GROUP. PROBLEMS, ADVANTAGES, METHODS, AND RESULTS ARE TREATED.

2948 SPINELLI A.
"EUROPEAN UNION IN THE RESISTANCE."
GOVERNMENT AND OPPOSITION, 2 (APR.-JULY 67), 321-328.
TRACES GROWTH AND SPREAD OF RESISTANCE PROGRAM, EMPHASIZING DEVELOPMENT OF CONCEPT OF FEDERALISM. DISCUSSES CONCEPTION AS FORMULATED IN VENTOTENE MANIFESTO AND DRAFT DECLARATION OF THE EUROPEAN RESISTANCES AND THE FEDERALIST PROGRAMS OF THE 1950'S.

2949 SPINKA M.
THE CHURCH IN SOVIET RUSSIA.
NEW YORK: OXFORD U PR, 1956, 179 PP., LC#56-9429.

TRACES RELATIONS OF HEADS OF CHURCH AND STATE FROM FALL OF CZAR AND OCTOBER REVOLUTION TO 1955. DIVIDES EVENTS ACCORDING TO PATRIARCH OF TIME; TIKHON, SERGEI, AND ALEXEI, AND SHOWS RESISTENANCE AGAINST GRADUAL BUT INEVITABLE SUBORDINATION OF CHURCH.

2950 SPIRO H.J.
"NEW CONSTITUTIONAL FORMS IN AFRICA."
WORLD POLIT., 13 (OCT. 60), 69-76.
SUGGESTS THAT BECAUSE THE CONSTITUTIONAL TECHNIQUES, TRADITIONS, STANDARDS, CONCEPTS OF SOVEREIGNTY AND OTHER OLD WORLD INSTITUTIONS MAY BE BOTH INAPPLICABLE AND RESTRICTIVE TO AFRICAN DEVELOPMENT, MODERN NATIONS SHOULD REFRAIN FROM IMPOSING OWN CONSTITUTIONAL INSTITUTIONS ON AFRICA. ENCOURAGES AFRICANS TO EXERCISE THEIR OWN IMAGINATION AND CREATIVITY IN ORDER TO MAKE A PERSONAL CONTRIBUTION TO MANKIND.

2951 SPIRO H.S. ED.
PATTERNS OF AFRICAN DEVLOPMENT: FIVE COMPARISONS.
ENGLEWOOD CLIFFS: PRENTICE HALL, 1967, 144 PP., LC#67-14837.
FIVE ESSAYS BY POLITICAL THEORISTS (ONE AFRICAN AND FOUR AMERICAN) ON PROBABLE DIRECTIONS OF AFRICAN POLITICAL DEVELOPMENT. CENTER ON QUESTION OF WHETHER AFRICAN DEVELOPMENT WILL BE REPETITIOUS, ESPECIALLY RELATIVE TO THE LATIN AMERICAN EXAMPLE, OR INNOVATORY.

2952 SPITTMANN I.
"EAST GERMANY: THE SWINGING PENDULUM."
PROBLEMS OF COMMUNISM, 16 (JULY-AUG. 67), 14-20.
EXAMINES RISE AND FALL OF BOTH MAJOR POLITICAL PARTIES IN EAST GERMANY SINCE CONSTRUCTION OF BERLIN WALL. DECLARES TENDENCIES IN GOVERNMENT TO BE NEO-STALINISTIC.

2953 SPOONER F.P.
SOUTH AFRICAN PREDICAMENT.
NEW YORK: FREDERICK PRAEGER, 1961, 288 PP., LC#61-11021.
DESCRIBES ECONOMICS OF APARTHEID. INCLUDES HISTORICAL BACKGROUND, RACE RELATIONSHIPS, POLITICAL SITUATION, RECENT PROSPERITY, INCOME OF RACE GROUPS, VULNERABILITY OF ECONOMY, ECONOMIC CONSEQUENCES OF APARTHEID, AND FUTURE PROSPECTS.

2954 SPRING D.
THE ENGLISH LANDED ESTATE IN THE NINETEENTH CENTURY: ITS ADMINISTRATION.
BALTIMORE: JOHNS HOPKINS PRESS, 1963, 216 PP., LC#63-10814.
ATTEMPTS TO DESCRIBE ENGLISH LANDOWNER OF 19TH CENTURY IN HIS SOCIAL, ECONOMIC, AND POLITICAL FUNCTIONS, INCLUDING ANATOMY OF ESTATE ADMINISTRATION, AND RELATION OF LANDOWNER TO STATE.

2955 SPRINGER H.W.
"FEDERATION IN THE CARIBBEAN: AN ATTEMPT THAT FAILED."
INT. ORGAN., 16 (AUG. 62), 758-75.
TRACES EVOLUTION OF PLANS FOR CARIBBEAN FEDERATION AND DISCUSSES THE FORCES WHICH WORKED FOR AND AGAINST ITS ESTABLISHMENT.

2956 SPROTT W.J.H.
SCIENCE AND SOCIAL ACTION.
NEW YORK: FREE PRESS OF GLENCOE, 1954, 164 PP.
EXAMINES SOCIOLOGY AS MEANS OF IMPROVING LIFE SITUATION. GENERALLY DISCUSSES BASIC THEORIES OF SOCIOLOGY DEALING WITH ASSIMILATION, GROUPS, KNOWLEDGE, AND PERSONALITY.

2957 SPROUT H., SPROUT M.
"ENVIRONMENTAL FACTORS IN THE STUDY OF INTERNATIONAL POLITICS."
J. CONFL. RESOLUT., 1 (DEC. 57), 309-28.
VIEWS CONCEPT OF MAN-MILIEU RELATIONSHIP AS FRUITFUL APPROACH TO ANALYSIS OF FOREIGN POLICY AND TO ESTIMATION OF STATE CAPABILITIES. CONSIDERS CONCEPT COMPLEMENT TO, NOT ALTERNATIVE TO, OTHER APPROACHES.

2958 SPULBER N.
THE STATE AND ECONOMIC DEVELOPMENT IN EASTERN EUROPE.
NEW YORK: RANDOM HOUSE, INC, 1966, 179 PP., LC#66-14883.
EXAMINES ROLE OF STATE IN ECONOMIC DEVELOPMENT OF SOVIET TYPE OF COUNTRY. STUDIES HISTORY OF STATE WITH RESPECT TO INDUSTRIALIZATION, CITING THE BALKAN COUNTRIES 1860-1960 IN THEIR CHANGE OF ECONOMIC STRUCTURE - CHANGE ACCOMPANIED BY EXPANSION OF STATE OWNERSHIP AND ECONOMIC ACTIVITY. COMPARES CAPITALISM TO STRUCTURED DEVELOPMENT WITH ITS CONCOMITANT DISCRIMINATION AND SELF-STYLED SUCCESS.

2959 SQUIBB G.D.
THE HIGH COURT OF CHIVALRY.
LONDON: OXFORD U PR, 1959, 301 PP.
DISCUSSES HISTORY OF HIGH COURT OF CHIVALRY IN ENGLAND (ONLY SURVIVING ENGLISH CIVIL LAW COURT). DISCUSSES ITS INACTIVITY SINCE EARLY 18TH CENTURY AND ITS REVIVAL IN 1954. ATTEMPTS TO CLEAR UP MISCONCEPTIONS CONCERNING COURT'S HISTORY AND JURISDICTION.

2960 SQUIRES J.D.
BRITISH PROPAGANDA AT HOME AND IN THE UNITED STATES FROM 1914 TO 1917.
CAMBRIDGE: HARVARD U PR, 1953, 113 PP.
ANALYSIS OF BRITISH PROPAGANDA DISTRIBUTED IN USA DURING WWI. REGARDS AMERICAN ENTRANCE INTO WAR AS ACHIEVEMENT OF MAJOR BRITISH PROPAGANDA GOAL. CONTENDS THAT EFFECTIVENESS OF BRITISH PROPAGANDA PROGRAM DURING WAR DEMONSTRATES NECESSITY AND POTENTIAL OF PROPAGANDA AS INSTRUMENT OF MODERN WARFARE.

2961 SRINIVAS M.N.
SOCIAL CHANGE IN MODERN INDIA.
BERKELEY: U OF CALIF PR, 1966, 194 PP., LC#66-14413.
TREATS CONCEPTS OF SANSKRITIZATION AND WESTERNIZATION IN MODERN INDIA AND THEIR IMPACT ON RELIGIOUS, CULTURAL, AND SOCIAL CHANGE. DISCUSSES EXPRESSIONS OF CASTE MOBILITY AND SECULARIZATION. CONCLUDES WITH EXAMINATION OF VIABILITY OF STUDYING ONE'S SOCIETY.

2962 SSU-YU T., KENJI M., HIROMITSU K.
JAPANESE STUDIES ON JAPAN AND THE FAR EAST: A SHORT BIOGRAPHICAL AND BIBLIOGRAPHICAL INTRODUCTION.
HONG KONG: HONG KONG UNIV PR, 1961, 485 PP.
COMPILATION 760 SCHOLARS LISTING 5,000 WORKS SELECTED BY THEM AS HAVING PARTICULAR IMPORTANCE. UNDER EACH SUBJECT AUTHORS ARRANGED ALPHABETICALLY. CONTAINS ITEMS ON FAR EASTERN LEGAL INSTITUTIONS, POLITICS AND GOVERNMENT; ECONOMICS AND ECONOMIC DEVELOPMENT; SOCIOLOGY; INTERNATIONAL REALTIONS; HISTORY; AND CULTURE. ITEMS IN JAPANESE.

2963 STAAR R.F.
"ELECTIONS IN COMMUNIST POLAND."
MIDWEST. J. POLIT. SCI., 2 (MAY 58), 57-75.
BRIEF HISTORY OF POSTWAR POLAND'S ELECTIONS AND REFERENDUMS. EMPHASIZES EARLY COMMUNIST TECHNIQUES OF INTIMIDATION, COERCION AND FRAUD TO WIN ELECTIONS. CONCLUDES WITH ANALYSIS OF MORE RECENT DEMOCRATIC MACHINERY BEING USED NOW.

2964 STAAR R.F.
"HOW STRONG IS THE SOVIET BLOC."
CURR. HIST., 45 (OCT. 63), 209-215.
SURVEYS COMMUNIST-BLOC DEVELOPMENTS IN EAST CENTRAL EUROPE AND OBSERVES THAT ARMS BUILD-UP THROUGHOUT EASTERN EUROPE INDICATES SHIFT IN EMPHASIS TOWARD PURELY MILITARY ASPECTS OF POWER. USSR EXPERIENCING DIFFICULTY IN ATTEMPT TO DEVELOP CO-ORDINATION IN EASTERN EUROPE ALTHOUGH THE IMAGE IN WEST IS ONE OF SATELLITE LEADERS STRIVING TO LIBERALIZE COUNTRIES.

2965 STAAR R.F.
"RETROGRESSION IN POLAND."
CURR. HIST., 48 (MAR. 65), 154-160.
TIGHTENING OF POLICY IN AGRICULTURE, EDUCATION, MILITARY SECURITY AND ECONOMIC PLANNING INDICATES GOMULKA PUSHING TOWARDS GREATER CONFORMITY EVEN THOUGH LIBERALIZATION BEING PERMITTED IN OTHER COMMUNIST REGIMES.

2966 STADLER K.R.
THE BIRTH OF THE AUSTRIAN REPUBLIC, 1918-1921.
LEYDEN: AW SIJTHOFF, 1966, 207 PP., LC#66-16271.
ACCOUNT OF EVENTS AND NEGOTIATIONS THAT LED TO FORMATION OF FIRST AUSTRIAN REPUBLIC AFTER WWI. DISCUSSION CENTERS ON PROBLEMS INVOLVING POLITICAL ISSUES, QUESTIONS OF TERRITORIAL SETTLEMENT, AND ECONOMIC ISSUES.

2967 STAHL W. ED.
EDUCATION FOR DEMOCRACY IN WEST GERMANY: ACHIEVEMENT - SHORTCOMINGS - PROSPECTS.
NEW YORK: FREDERICK PRAEGER, 1961, 356 PP., LC#61-14811.
BELIEVES THAT DEMOCRATIC DEVELOPMENT OF WEST GERMANY HAS PROGRESSED. EXAMINES THE BASIC ATTITUDES OF YOUTH, AND POLITICAL EDUCATION IN SCHOOLS, UNIVERSITIES, AND YOUTH GROUPS, NOTING INFLUENCE OF THE "BUNDESWEHR," ADULT EDUCATION, AND MASS MEDIA. STUDIES GERMAN CULTURE AND RESEARCH IN YOUTH EDUCATION. SAYS REBUILDING BASIC ATTITUDES IS HARD BUT WITH EDUCATION GERMANS CAN AGAIN TAKE LEADERSHIP ROLE.

2968 STALIN J.
PROBLEMS OF LENINISM.
NEW YORK: INTERNATIONAL PUBLRS, 1934, 95 PP.
ATTACKS ZINOVIEV AND SOCIAL DEMOCRATS FOR GIVING WORK OF LENIN SUCH LIMITED SCOPE, AND PRESENTS POINT-BY-POINT REFUTATION OF THEIR CRITICISMS. ZINOVIEV BELIEVED LENINISM WAS A TYPE OF MARXISM APPLICABLE ONLY TO COUNTRIES WHERE THE PEASANTRY DOMINATES. STALIN BELIEVES IT IS A THEORY AND TACTIC OF DICTATORSHIP OF THE PROLETARIAT IN GENERAL, THOUGH USSR WAS PARTICULARLY WELL SUITED TO ITS APPLICATION.

2969 STANLEY C.J.
LATE CH'ING FINANCE: HU KUANG-YUNG AS AN INNOVATOR.
CAMBRIDGE: HARVARD U PR, 1961, 117 PP.
STUDY OF FINANCIAL CAREER OF HU 1860-1880, A MERCHANT-BANKER IN CHINA. ANALYZES HIS FUNCTIONS AS PURCHASING AGENT FOR GOVERNMENT DURING TAIPING REBELLION. CONCENTRATES ON POLICY OF CONTRACTING FOREIGN LOANS TO SUPPORT ARMIES SINCE TAXATION WAS INADEQUATE. HU SERVED DURING TRANSITIONAL PERIOD OF DECENTRALIZATION OF GOVERNMENT BUDGET SYSTEM.

2970 STARCKE V.
DENMARK IN WORLD HISTORY.
PHILA: U OF PENN PR, 1962, 381 PP.
HISTORY OF DENMARK, FROM EARLY MIGRATIONS TO PRESENT; DENMARK'S CULTURAL CONTRIBUTIONS. INCLUDES 15-PAGE BIBLIOGRAPHY OF HISTORICAL WORKS, MOST IN DANISH, SOME IN ENGLISH, PUBLISHED IN 20TH CENTURY AND LATE 19TH CENTURY.

2971 STARK H.
SOCIAL AND ECONOMIC FRONTIERS IN LATIN AMERICA (2ND ED.)
DUBUQUE: WC BROWN, 1961, 427 PP., LC#61-13707.
TEXTBOOK COVERING SOCIAL, ECONOMIC, AND POLITICAL CONDITIONS IN LATIN AMERICA. DISCUSSES CONTINENT AS A WHOLE: LANDS AND PEOPLES, POLITICO-MILITARY ORGANIZATION, COMMUNISM, ANTI-YANKEEISM, ECONOMIC PROGRAMS, PRODUCTION ACTIVITIES, AND INTERNATIONAL RELATIONSHIPS. OFFERS PREDICTIONS FOR FUTURE DEVELOPMENT AND ROLE OF LATIN AMERICA.

2972 STAROBIN J.R.
"COMMUNISM IN WESTERN EUROPE."
FOREIGN AFFAIRS, 44 (OCT. 65), 62-77.
ATTEMPTS TO ACCOUNT FOR THE UTTER LACK OF UNITY OF PURPOSE AND COOPERATION FOUND IN THE COMMUNIST PARTIES OF WESTERN EUROPE. HAS COUNTRY-BY-COUNTRY ANALYSIS. PEACEFUL COEXISTENCE, DE- STALINIZATION, EUROPEAN AND AMERICAN VITALITY AND THE SINO- SOVIET SPLIT HAVE BEEN DEMORALIZING FACTORS.

2973 STARR R.E.
POLAND 1944-1962: THE SOVIETIZATION OF A CAPTIVE PEOPLE.
BATON ROUGE: LOUISIANA ST U PR, 1962, 300 PP., LC#62-15027.
ATTEMPTS TO COMPARE SOME FEATURES OF SO-CALLED POLISH PEOPLE'S DEMOCRACY WITH THEIR COUNTERPARTS IN USSR AND OTHER EAST EUROPEAN SATELLITE COUNTRIES. EXAMINES GOVERNMENTAL DYNAMICS, INCLUDING ANALYSES OF LEGISLATIVE FOUNDATIONS AND ELECTIONS. STUDIES DOMESTIC, FOREIGN, AND DEFENSE POLICIES, DOMINANT POLITICAL PARTY, AND PRESSURE GROUPS AND QUASI-POLITICAL ORGANIZATIONS.

2974 STATIST REICHSAMTE
BIBLIOGRAPHIE DER STAATS- UND WIRSCHAFTSWISSENSCHAFTEN.
DRESDEN: BIBLIOG DES STAATS, 1941, 930 PP.
A COLLECTION OF MONTHLY PERIODICALS LISTING WORKS PUBLISHED IN THE FIELDS OF ECONOMICS AND POLITICS. LISTING LARGELY BOOKS AND PERIODICALS, IT IS CATEGORIZED INTO SUCH FIELDS AS HISTORY OF SCIENCE, BUSINESS ADMINISTRATION, ECONOMIC CONDITIONS, PUBLIC FINANCE, ETC. INCLUDES FOREIGN MATERIAL AND COVERS WORKS PUBLISHED IN THE PRECEDING ONE TO TWO YEARS; GERMAN PRIMARILY.

2975 STEINBERG C.S.
THE MASS COMMUNICATORS: PUBLIC RELATIONS, PUBLIC OPINION, AND MASS MEDIA.
NEW YORK: HARPER & ROW, 1958, 470 PP., LC#58-6139.
ATTEMPTS TO EXPLAIN FORM AND PRACTICE OF PUBLIC RELATIONS AS APPLIED TO PUBLIC OPINION AND MASS COMMUNICATION. COVERS IMPORTANCE OF TYPE OF MEDIA USED, HOW ORGANIZED, AND WHAT GROUP IS OBJECT OF INFORMATION AS WELL AS COMPARISON OF PROPAGANDA AND PUBLIC RELATIONS AS USED BY PUBLIC AND PRIVATE GROUPS.

2976 STEINER K.
LOCAL GOVERNMENT IN JAPAN.
STANFORD: STANFORD U PRESS, 1965, 564 PP., LC#64-17005.
PROVIDES OVERVIEW OF ALL ASPECTS OF JAPANESE LOCAL GOVERNMENT SYSTEM AND ATTEMPTS TO DETERMINE DEGREE OF LOCAL AUTONOMY - IN LAW AND IN PRACTICE. APPRAISES POST-WAR REFORMS. USES ELECTORAL STATISTICS EXTENSIVELY.

2977 STEINMETZ H.
"THE PROBLEMS OF THE LANDRAT: A STUDY OF COUNTY GOVERNMENT IN THE US ZONE OF GERMANY."
J. OF POLITICS, 11 (MAY 49), 318-334.
DISCUSSES ROLE AND PROBLEMS OF COUNTY GOVERNMENT IN AMERICAN OCCUPIED ZONES OF GERMANY AFTER WWII. MENTIONS HOUSING, HEALTH, WELFARE, AND PRICE CONTROLS INITIATED AFTER WWII, AND PROBLEM CREATED BY HITLER'S PLANNED, WARTIME ECONOMY.

2978 STEPHEN J.F.
LIBERTY, EQUALITY, FRATERNITY.
NEW YORK: HOLT & WILLIAMS, 1873, 350 PP.
SAYS MILL'S UTILITARIAN CONCEPTS OF MAN ARE SOPHISTRY. MAN IS SUBJECT TO RELIGIOUS, MORAL, GOVERNMENTAL, AND SOCIAL RESTRICTIONS. DENIES VALIDITY OF EQUALITY AND FRATERNITY, AND DECLARES THESE CONCEPTS UNADAPTABLE TO RELIGIOUS BELIEF. EMPHASIZES VALUE OF UNITY OF RELIGIOUS BELIEF, AND DEFENDS RIGHT TO IMPOSE IT. MAN KNOWS ONLY THROUGH EXPERIENCE; THERE ARE NO PHILOSOPHICAL CERTAINTIES.

2979 STERN F.
"THE POLITICS OF CULTURAL DESPAIR."
BERKELEY: U OF CALIF PR, 1965.
STUDY IN PATHOLOGY OF CULTURAL CRITICISM THROUGH AN ANALYSIS OF WRITINGS OF LAGARDE, LANGBEHN, AND MOELLER VAN DER BRUCK. UNANNOTATED BIBLIOGRAPHY OF MOST SIGNIFICANT WORKS CITED IN NOTES AND FOOTNOTES. INCLUDES SECTION OF PRIMARY AND SECONDARY SOURCES CONCERNING THE THREE CRITICS AND SECTION OF WORKS RELATING TO MODERN EUROPEAN POLITICS AND CULTURE. PRIMARY SOURCES DATE FROM 19TH - 20TH CENTURIES.

2980 STERN F.
THE POLITICS OF CULTURAL DESPAIR.
GARDEN CITY: DOUBLEDAY, 1965, 426 PP.
A STUDY IN THE PATHOLOGY OF CULTURAL DESPAIR. ANALYZES THE THOUGHT AND INFLUENCE OF THREE LEADING CRITICS OF MODERN GERMANY LANGHBEN, LAGARDE AND MOELLER VAN DEN BRUCK. SHOWS THE DANGERS AND DILEMMAS OF A PECULIAR TYPE OF CULTURAL DESPAIR. THESE THREE MEN WERE MORE THAN THE CRITICS OF GERMANY'S CULTURAL CRISIS; THEY WERER ITS SYMPTOMS AND VICTIMS AS WELL.

2981 STERNBERG F.
THE MILITARY AND INDUSTRIAL REVOLUTION OF OUR TIME.
NEW YORK: FREDERICK PRAEGER, 1959, 359 PP., LC#59-7948.
ANALYSIS OF MAJOR CHANGES AND DEVELOPMENTS IN MILITARY AND INDUSTRIAL TECHNIQUES IN POSTWAR WORLD. EXAMINES US AND SOVIET MILITARY STRENGTH, NUCLEAR WEAPONS, AND RELATIONSHIP BETWEEN MILITARY AND INDUSTRY IN NEW INDUSTRIAL REVOLUTION.

2982 STEUBER F.A.
THE CONTRIBUTION OF SWITZERLAND TO THE ECONOMIC AND SOCIAL DEVELOPMENT OF LOW-INCOME COUNTRIES (PAMPHLET)
WINTERTHUR: P G KELLER, 1961, 62 PP.
DISCUSSES SWITZERLAND'S ROLE IN ECONOMIC AID TO LOW-INCOME COUNTRIES, INCLUDING MOTIVES FOR AID, TRADE, INVESTMENT, LOANS, CONTRIBUTIONS OF FEDERAL AND VOLUNTARY ORGANIZATIONS, EXPANSION OF PROGRAM, AND BILATERAL APPROACH TO AID.

2983 STEVENS G.G.
EGYPT YESTERDAY AND TODAY.
NEW YORK: HOLT, 1963, 234 PP.
EXPLORES 1952-1962 EGYPTIAN REVOLUTION FOCUSING ATTENTION ON CRUCIAL INCIDENTS OF 1955 AND THE SUEZ AFFAIR. SETS IN HISTORICAL PERSPECTIVE THE COUNTRY'S POLITICAL, SOCIAL AND ECONOMIC INSTITUTIONS. ANSWERS QUESTIONS: HOW GENUINE IS EGYPT'S RECENT POLICY OF NEUTRALITY, ITS ATTITUDE TOWARD ISRAEL AND WHAT DIFFICULTIES LIE BEHIND RELATIONS WITH OTHER ARAB STATES.

2984 STEWARD J.H.
THEORY OF CULTURE CHANGE; THE METHODOLOGY OF MULTILINEAR EVOLUTION.
URBANA: U OF ILLINOIS PR, 1955, 244 PP., LC#55-7372.
SETS FORTH CERTAIN CONCEPTS AND METHODS NEEDED TO DEVELOP A GENERAL METHODOLOGY FOR DETERMINING REGULARITIES IN FUNCTIONAL INTERRELATIONSHIPS OF CULTURAL PATTERNS AND IN PROCESSES OF CULTURE WHICH HAVE OCCURRED INDEPENDENTLY AMONG SOCIETIES IN DIFFERENT PARTS OF THE WORLD. PRESENTS A BROAD STATEMENT OF SCIENTIFIC OBJECTIVE AND OF CERTAIN HEURISTIC CONCEPTS AND PROCEDURES VITAL TO THIS OBJECTIVE.

2985 STEWARD J.H.
"THE CONCEPT AND METHOD OF CULTURAL ECOLOGY" IN T.H. STEWARD'S THEORY OF CULTURAL CHANGE."
URBANA: U OF ILLINOIS PR, 1955.
ATTEMPTS TO DEVELOP THE CONCEPT OF ECOLOGY IN RELATION TO HUMAN BEINGS AS A HEURISTIC DEVICE FOR UNDERSTANDING THE EFFECT OF ENVIRONMENT UPON CULTURE. DISTINGUISHES CULTURAL ECOLOGY FROM THE OTHER CONCEPTS OF ECOLOGY AND DEMONSTRATES HOW IT MUST SUPPLEMENT THE USUAL HISTORICAL APPROACH OF ANTHROPOLOGY IN ORDER TO DETERMINE THE CREATIVE PROCESSES INVOLVED IN ADAPTATION OF CULTURE TO ITS ENVIRONMENT.

2986 STIFEL L.D.
THE TEXTILE INDUSTRY - A CASE STUDY OF INDUSTRIAL DEVELOPMENT IN THE PHILIPPINES (PAPER)
ITHACA: CORNELL U, DEPT ASIAN ST, 1963, 193 PP.
REPORTS ON RAPID DEVELOPMENT OF PHILIPPINE TEXTILE INDUSTRY CAUSED BY GOVERNMENT IMPORT CONTROLS, AN ABUNDANCE OF US SURPLUS COTTON, PLUS AMPLE SUPPLY OF CAPITAL, SOME FROM US FOREIGN AID. NOTES THAT SHORTAGES OF MANAGERIAL RESOURCES AND SKILLED LABOR ARE CONCEALED BY LACK OF EMPHASIS ON EFFICIENCY AND THAT COSTS OF ENCOURAGING TEXTILE INDUSTRY ARE HIGH IN RELATION TO BENEFITS ACCRUING TO THE ECONOMY.

2987 STIRNIMANN H.
NGUNI UND GNONI; EINE KULTURGESCHICHTLICHE STUDIE (ACTA ETHNOLOGICA ET LINGUISTICA, NUMBER 6)
VIENNA: OSTERR ETHNOLOG GES, 1963, 192 PP.
COMPARATIVE STUDY OF WARRIOR, CATTLE-GROWING NGONI PEOPLE OF MALAWI AND THE NGUNI PEOPLE OF NATAL IN THE UNION OF SOUTH AFRICA, NOTING MANY RELATIONSHIPS BETWEEN THE TWO CULTURES.

2988 STOKES W.S.
"HONDURAS: AN AREA STUDY IN GOVERNMENT."
MADISON: U OF WISCONSIN PR, 1950.
STUDY OF POLITICAL ROUTINE BASED ON LENGTHY FREE OBSERVATION AND SCHOLARLY RESEARCH. DISCUSSES GEOGRAPHICAL SETTING AND EVOLUTION OF GOVERNMENT AND POLITICS; EARLY CONSTITUTIONS; LAW AND THE SYSTEM OF COLONIAL COURTS; ORGAN-

IZATION AND PROCEDURE OF MODERN COURTS; ADMINISTRATIVE UNITS AND PROCEDURE; DEVELOPMENT OF POLITICAL PARTIES; ELECTORAL SYSTEM AND REPRESENTATION. EXTENSIVE SPANISH BIBLIOGRAPHY.

2989 STOLPER W.F.
GERMANY BETWEEN EAST AND WEST: THE ECONOMICS OF COMPETITIVE COEXISTENCE.
WASHINGTON: NATL PLANNING ASSN, 1960, 80 PP., LC#60-15350.
COMPARISON OF ECONOMIC DEVELOPMENT AND POLITICAL SITUATIONS IN EAST AND WEST GERMANY SINCE WWII. ANALYZES "ECONOMIC PROSPECTS OF EAST AND WEST GERMANY IN NEXT 15 YEARS." STUDIES RELATION BETWEEN ECONOMIC MOVES AND POLITICAL ROLE OF WEST GERMANY IN THE COLD WAR STRUGGLE FOR CONTROL OF UNDEVELOPED NATIONS.

2990 STOUT H.M.
BRITISH GOVERNMENT.
NEW YORK: OXFORD U PR, 1953, 433 PP., LC#52-14156.
DESCRIPTION OF THE PRESENT-DAY STRUCTURE AND PRACTICE OF BRITISH GOVERNMENT, INTENDED FOR AMERICAN STUDENTS. EXAMINES THE GOVERNMENT IN LIGHT OF POSTWAR DEVELOPMENTS - NEW ELECTIONS, EXPANSION OF GOVERNMENTAL FUNCTIONS UNDER THE WELFARE STATE CONCEPT, NEW COMMONWEALTH RELATIONS, ETC. DISCUSSES THE CONSTITUTION AND CONSTITUTIONAL RIGHTS, STRUCTURE OF THE PRINCIPAL INSTITUTIONS, AND POLICY FORMATION.

2991 STRACHEY J.
THE END OF EMPIRE.
NEW YORK: FREDERICK PRAEGER, 1960, 351 PP., LC#60-5459.
STUDY OF UK RELATION TO WORLD AS EMPIRE DISSOLVES AND COMMONWEALTH EMERGES. COMPARES MEANING OF EMPIRE TO MOTHER NATION, I.E., UK, AND TO COLONIES. ECONOMIC, SOCIAL, AND POLITICAL PROSPECTS OPEN TO POST-IMPERIAL NATIONS. ATTEMPTS TO DEVELOP AN EVOLVING THEORY OF IMPERIALISM.

2992 STRACHEY J.
"COMMUNIST INTENTIONS."
PARTISAN REV., 29 (SPRING 62), 215-37.
TRACES EVOLUTION OF USSR FROM INTERNATIONALIST MOVEMENT TO RUSSIAN 'NATION-STATE-WITH-A-MISSION.' DISCUSSES ATTITUDE OF COMMUNISTS TOWARD WAR AND AGGRESSION IN GENERAL, PRESENTS FALLACIES OF ORIGINAL COMMUNIST PROGNOSIS, ANALYZES SINO-SOVIET CONTROVERSEY, PARTICULARLY WITH RESPECT TO NUCLEAR WAR. BELIEVES THERE IS NEW SOVIET ATTITUDE DUE TO APPARITION OF NEW WEAPONS AND DIVERGENCIES FROM ORIGINAL DOGMA.

2993 STRAFFORD P.
"FRENCH ELECTIONS."
WORLD TODAY, 23 (MAY 67), 198-206.
ANALYZES RESULTS OF RECENT FRENCH ELECTIONS IN WHICH GAULLIST FORCES GAINED A MINIMAL PARLIAMENTARY MAJORITY. SHOWS THE EVOLUTION OF A COMMUNIST AND CENTER-LEFT COALITION AND SUGGESTS ITS IMPACT ON FUTURE FRENCH POLITICS. ALSO OFFERS REASONS FOR THE RELATIVE FAILURE OF THE DEMOCRATIC CENTER PARTY, LED BY JEAN LECANUET. CONCLUDES THAT LEFTISTS MAY FORM A COMMON FRONT AGAINST GAULLIST RIGHT.

2995 STRAUSS L. ED., CROPSEY J. ED.
HISTORY OF POLITICAL PHILOSOPHY.
SKOKIE: RAND MCNALLY & CO, 1963, 790 PP., LC#63-7143.
PRESENTS POLITICAL PHILOSOPHIES OF 35 POLITICAL PHILOSOPHERS FROM PLATO TO JOHN DEWEY IN BELIEF THAT POLITICAL SCIENCE MUST BE STUDIED AGAINST PHILOSOPHICAL BACKGROUND. POSITIONS PRESENTED INCLUDE THOSE OF THOMAS AQUINAS, LUTHER, FRANCIS BACON, HOBBES, ROUSSEAU, ADAM SMITH, JAMES MILL, HEGEL, DE TOCQUEVILLE, JOHN STUART MILL, MARX, AND NIETZSCHE.

2996 STRAUSZ-HUPE R. ED., HAZARD H.W.
THE IDEA OF COLONIALISM.
NEW YORK: FREDERICK PRAEGER, 1958, 496 PP., LC#58-8669.
ANALYZES GENERAL CONCEPT AND MISUNDERSTANDINGS OF VARIOUS TYPES OF COLONIALISM AS WELL AS PROBLEMS INVOLVED. COVERS PATTERNS AND TYPES OF COLONIAL EMPIRES THAT HAVE EVOLVED FROM BRITISH EMPIRE TO ALGERIA. CONCENTRATES ON DIFFERENT PHILOSOPHIES AND POLICIES OF DIFFERENT TYPES OF GOVERNMENTS. CONSIDERS PROBLEMS OF COLONIALISM TODAY AND ROLE OF UN IN SOLVING THEM.

2997 STRAYER J.R.
"PROBLEMS OF DICTATORSHIP* THE RUSSIAN EXPERIENCE."
FOREIGN AFFAIRS, 44 (JAN. 66), 264-274.
FITS THE GOVERNMENT OF THE SOVIET UNION ON A SCALE DERIVED FROM SHORT SURVEY OF DEVELOPMENT OF THE NATION-STATE IN WESTERN EUROPE. FINDS IT AT THE STAGE IN WHICH HEREDITARY AND/OR DICTATORIAL RULERS ARE FORCED TO GRANT INDEPENDENT INFLUENCE TO IMPORTANT GROUPS. SHOWS HOW THIS IS A FACTOR IN THE SINO-SOVIET DISPUTE.

2998 STRONG C.F.
MODERN POLITICAL CONSTITUTIONS.
LONDON: SIDGWICK + JACKSON, 1958, 383 PP.
INTRODUCTORY TEXT ON CONSTITUTIONAL POLITICS. CONSIDERS MEANING OF POLITICAL CONSTITUTIONALISM, AND THE ORIGINS AND GROWTH OF THE CONSTITUTIONAL STATE. ANALYZES IN DETAIL COMPARATIVE CONSTITUTIONAL POLITICS. CONSIDERS DIRECT DEMOCRATIC CHECKS, CONSTITUTIONAL CHECKS AMONG NON-EUROPEAN PEOPLES, ECONOMIC ORGANIZATION OF THE STATE, AND THE CHARTER OF THE UN. DISCUSSES OUTLOOK FOR CONSTITUTIONALISM.

2999 STRONG C.F.
HISTORY OF MODERN POLITICAL CONSTITUTIONS.
NEW YORK: G P PUTNAM'S SONS, 1964, 389 PP., LC#63-14083.
DEFINES POLITICAL CONSTITUTIONALISM; STUDIES ITS GROWTH AND ORIGINS IN THE STATE; CLASSIFIES FORMS OF STATES AND CONSTITUTION; AND DISCUSSES CONSTITUTIONAL DIVISIONS OF GOVERNMENT. EXAMINES RISE OF NATIONALISM THROUGHOUT WORLD, WORLDWIDE ECONOMIC ORGANIZATION, AND THE UN CHARTER.

3000 STUART G.H.
FRENCH FOREIGN POLICY.
NEW YORK: CENTURY, 1921, 392 PP.
TRACES POLICY OF FRENCH FOREIGN OFFICE FROM CRISIS OF FASHODA - 1898 - TO THE CRIME OF SARAJEVO - 1914. INCLUDES DISCUSSION OF THE ENTENTE CORDIALE, THE MOROCCAN CRISIS, AND THE AGADIR AFFAIR.

3001 STUBEL H.
THE MEWU FANTZU.
NEW HAVEN: HUMAN REL AREA FILES, 1958, 66 PP.
DESCRIBES CULTURE AND SOCIETY OF TIBETAN TRIBE OBSERVED WHILE LIVING WITH THEM. BRIEFLY DISCUSSES RELIGION, SUPERSTITION, RELATIONS WITH CHINESE, AND FAMILY ORGANIZATION.

3002 STUCKI C.W. ED.
AMERICAN DOCTORAL DISSERTATIONS ON ASIA 1933-62 (A PAPER)
ITHACA: CORNELL U, DEPT ASIAN ST, 1963, 175 PP.
BIBLIOGRAPHY OF DISSERTATIONS ON ASIA. INCLUDES PHILOSOPHY AND RELIGION, CULTURE, EDUCATION, ECONOMICS, GEOGRAPHY, HISTORY, SOCIOLOGY, ANTHROPOLOGY, GOVERNMENT AND POLITICS, AND LANGUAGE FOR ALL ASIAN, SOUTH, AND SOUTHEASTERN NATIONS. APPROXIMATELY 2,300 LISTINGS INDEXED BY TOPIC AND AUTHOR.

3003 STURZO L.
THE INTERNATIONAL COMMUNITY AND THE RIGHT OF WAR (TRANS. BY BARBARA BARCLAY CARTER)
NEW YORK: RICHARD R SMITH, 1929, 293 PP.
STUDY OF THE SOCIOLOGICAL AND HISTORICAL ASPECTS OF WAR AND THE FORMATION OF INTERNATIONAL STRUCTURES TOWARD THE CONTROL AND/OR JUSTIFICATION OF WAR. ARGUES THAT THE THREE THEORIES ADVANCED TO EXPLAIN THE RIGHT OF WAR ARE INCOMPLETE AND CAN BE SUPPLANTED BY A FOURTH PROPOUNDING THAT WAR, LIKE SLAVERY AND DUELS, IS NOT A NECESSARY HUMAN CONDITION AND CAN BE ELIMINATED THROUGH CIVILIZED INTERNATIONAL LAW.

3004 SUAREZ F.
A TREATISE ON LAWS AND GOD THE LAWGIVER (1612) IN SELECTIONS FROM THREE WORKS, VOL. II.
LONDON: OXFORD U PR, 1944, 625 PP.
ANALYZES LEGAL SYSTEMS OF EUROPE, 1500-1620, FROM VIEWPOINT OF SCHOLASTICISM. CLAIMS LAW TO BE JUST CONCERN OF THEOLOGY BECAUSE BOTH CONCERN RULES OF HUMAN ACTION. DECIDES THAT LAW IS A DIVISION OF THEOLOGY. CONSIDERS LAW TO BE A POSITIVE RATHER THAN NEGATIVE SYSTEM, ENFORCING VIRTUE AS WELL AS PROSCRIBING SIN. CONCLUDES THAT ALL LAW STEMS FROM GOD AND NATURAL LAW.

3005 SUAREZ F.
"ON WAR" (1621) IN SELECTIONS FROM THREE WORKS, VOL. I."
LONDON: OXFORD U PR, 1944.
DENIES THAT WAR IS INTRINSICALLY EVIL, CLAIMING THAT ANY SOVEREIGN PRINCE HAS POWER TO INITIATE IT IF HE FEELS THAT IT IS NECESSARY TO PREVENT GREATER EVIL. EVEN AGGRESSIVE WAR IS ALLOWABLE UNDER CERTAIN CIRCUMSTANCES. STATES THAT CHRISTIAN PRINCES HAVE RECOURSE TO POPE AS A HIGHER AUTHORITY, BUT IF HE DOES NOT INTERVENE THEY MAY ACT AS FREE AGENTS. SEDITION IS JUSTIFIED AGAINST TYRANTS.

3006 SUBRAMANIAM V.
"REPRESENTATIVE BUREAUCRACY: A REASSESSMENT."
AM. POL. SCI. REV., (FALL 67), 1010-1019.
DISCUSSES TERM "REPRESENTATIVE BUREAUCRACY" AND NATURE AND DESIRABILITY OF SYSTEM IT IMPLIES. SAYS TERM REFERS TO CIVIL SERVICE IN WHICH RATIO OF UPPER, MIDDLE, LOWER CLASS EMPLOYEES IS SAME AS CLASS RATIO OF POPULATION; IN FACT, MOST CIVIL SERVICES ARE RUN BY MIDDLE CLASS, AND ARE REPRESENTATIVE ONLY IN MIDDLE-CLASS NATIONS LIKE US. DOUBTS ADVANTAGES OF REPRESENTATIVE BUREAUCRACY, WERE IT FEASIBLE.

3007 SULLIVAN J.H.
"THE PRESS AND POLITICS IN INDONESIA."
JOURNALISM QUARTERLY, 44 (SPRING 67), 99-106.
GIVES HISTORY OF JOURNALISM IN INDONESIA DURING RECENT YEARS. DISCUSSES WITHDRAWAL OF FREEDOM OF PRESS, AND WHAT PART THE PRESS PLAYED IN THAT PROCESS. PREDICTIONS ABOUT CURRENT AND FUTURE DEVELOPMENTS ARE GIVEN.

3008 SUMNER W.G.
FOLKWAYS: STUDY OF THE SOCIOLOGICAL IMPORTANCE OF USAGES, MANNERS, CUSTOMS, MORES, AND MORALS.
BOSTON: GINN AND CO, 1906, 692 PP.
DEFINES FOLKWAYS AND MORES AS HABITS AND CUSTOMS THAT

SATISFY NEEDS. STUDIES MORES INVOLVING STRUGGLE FOR EXISTENCE, LABOR, WEALTH, SOCIAL STRUCTURE, SLAVERY, TYPES OF MURDER, SEX, MARRIAGE, INCEST, PEACE, JUSTICE, KINSHIP, SACRIFICES, UNCLEANNESS, SORCERY, DRAMA, SPORTS, EDUCATION, VIRTUE, AND ASCETICISM.

3009 SUNG C.H.
"POLITICAL DIAGNOSIS OF KOREAN SOCIETY* A SURVEY OF MILITARY AND CIVILIAN VALUES."
ASIAN SURVEY, 7 (MAY 67), 329-340.
STUDIES ATTITUDES TO STABILITY FACTORS IN SOUTH KOREAN SOCIETY AS EXPRESSED BY CIVILIAN AND MILITARY GROUPS. SUCH ELEMENTS AS THE CHANCES FOR PERSONAL SUCCESS, SELF-ASSESSMENT, AND ATTITUDES TOWARD DEMOCRACY'S CHANCES IN KOREA WERE MEASURED, AND THE CONCLUSION IS THAT THOUGH SOME LATENT ELEMENTS OF INSTABILITY EXIST, KOREAN SOCIETY IS NOT SERIOUSLY THREATENED BY POLITICAL INSTABILITY.

3010 SVALASTOGA K.
PRESTIGE, CLASS, AND MOBILITY.
COPENHAGEN: SCANDINAVIAN U BOOKS, 1959, 466 PP.
REPORTS ON SAMPLE SURVEY IN DENMARK ON OCCUPATIONAL PRESTIGE, SOCIAL MOBILITY AND STRATA, AND DIFFERENTIAL CLASS BEHAVIOR. COMPARES THIS WITH ENGLAND.

3011 SVALASTOGA K.
SOCIAL DIFFERENTIATION.
NEW YORK: DAVID MCKAY, 1965, 174 PP., LC#65-17199.
DISCSEUSS SOCIAL STRATIFICATION AND SIZE OF SOCIETY, INTERNATIONAL COMPARISON OF PESTIGE MEASUREMENTS, CASTE RANK IN RAMPURA, SOCIAL MOBILTY INTERACTION AND ITEGRATION; MEASURING STATUS. MODELS OF SOCIAL DIFFERENTIATION.

3012 SVARLIEN O.
AN INTRODUCTION TO THE LAW OF NATIONS.
NEW YORK: MCGRAW HILL, 1955, 478 PP., LC#56-6173.
INTRODUCTORY TEXT IN INTERNATIONAL LAW. TREATS EACH TOPIC IN LIGHT OF ITS HISTORY, OF ITS LAW, AND IN TERMS OF TRENDS AND DEVELOPMENT. INCLUDES STUDY OF THE INTERNATIONAL COMMUNITY, THE FUNCTION OF STATES IN INTERNATIONAL LAW, TERRITORIAL PROBLEMS, DIPLOMATIC RELATIONS, HOSTILE RELATIONS BETWEEN NATIONS, AND THE INDIVIDUAL IN INTERNATIONAL LAW. BIBLIOGRAPHY OF ABOUT 200 ITEMS.

3013 SWARTZ M.J. ED., TURNER V.W. ED., TUDEN A. ED.
POLITICAL ANTHROPOLOGY.
CHICAGO: ALDINE PUBLISHING CO, 1966, 309 PP., LC#66-15210.
COLLECTION OF ESSAYS FROM VIEWPOINT THAT POLITICS IS NOT STATIC BUT A DYNAMIC PROCESS, A CONTINUUM RELATED TO PAST AND PRESENT, CONTINUALLY INFLUENCED BY PRESSURES WITHIN AND OUTSIDE A SOCIETY. EMPIRICAL STUDIES OF SOCIETIES FROM AFRICA TO ALASKA, SHOWING POLITICS AS GLOBAL PHENOMENON BASED ON CONFLICT BETWEEN COMMON GOOD AND INTERESTS OF GROUPS, AND ON RELIGIOUS, PSYCHOLOGICAL, AND SOCIOCULTURAL PRESSURES.

3014 SWAYZE H.
POLITICAL CONTROL OF LITERATURE IN THE USSR, 1946-1959.
CAMBRIDGE: HARVARD U PR, 1962, 301 PP., LC#62-9432.
ANALYZES METHODS OF CONTROLLING IMAGINATIVE WRITING IN USSR. OUTLINES BASIC ASSUMPTIONS AND AIMS OF SOVIET LITERARY POLICIES, DISCUSSES PROBLEM WITH WHICH THEY HAVE HAD TO COPE, AND DESCRIBES MAIN FEATURES OF LITERARY CONTROL STRUCTURE.

3015 SWEARER H.R., LONGAKER R.P.
CONTEMPORARY COMMUNISM: THEORY AND PRACTICE.
BELMONT: WADSWORTH, 1963, 405 PP., LC#63-18331.
PRIMARY SOURCE MATERIALS, FACTUAL DATA, AND INTERPRETIVE ESSAYS ON MAJOR ISSUES WITHIN COMMUNIST SPHERE. EARLY CHAPTERS DEAL WITH MARXIST-LENINIST THEORY; ROLE AND APPEAL OF COMMUNIST IDEOLOGY; POLITICAL, ECONOMIC, AND SOCIAL STRUCTURE OF USSR; AND CHANGING NATURE OF SOVIET SYSTEM. LAST HALF OF BOOK TREATS GOALS AND TECHNIQUES OF FOREIGN POLICY AND VARIETIES OF COMMUNISM IN WORLD.

3016 SWEARER H.R.
"AFTER KHRUSHCHEV: WHAT NEXT."
CURR. HIST., 47 (NOV. 64), 257-265.
THE PARTY WILL DETERMINE OUTCOME OF ANY LEADERSHIP STRUGGLE. SECRETARIAT WAS LAUNCHING PAD FOR STALIN AND KHRUSHCHEV. POSSIBLE HEIRS TO KHRUSHCHEV'S POST LISTED.

3017 SWEARINGEN A.R. ED.
SOVIET AND CHINESE COMMUNIST POWER IN THE WORLD TODAY.
NEW YORK: BASIC BOOKS, 1966, 127 PP., LC#66-29266.
FIVE PAPERS AIMED AT ISOLATING AND ANALYZING THE CRUCIAL CIAL AREAS OF CHANGE AND STABILITY IN THE INTERNAL SOCIETIES OF THE SOVIET UNION AND COMMUNIST CHINA, THEIR RELATIONS WITH ONE ANOTHER, AND THE PROSPECTS FOR AN AMERICAN DETENTE WITH THE SOVIET UNION AND/OR CONFRONTATION WITH CHINA.

3018 SWEET E.C.
CIVIL LIBERTIES IN AMERICA.
PRINCETON: VAN NOSTRAND, 1966, 352 PP.
STUDY OF MAJOR ISSUES OF CIVIL LIBERTIES AND RELEVANT CASES. EXAMINES LIBERTIES REGARDING DUE PROCESS, RELIGION, SPEECH, INVESTIGATION, ASSOCIATION, SEARCH AND SEIZURE, RIGHT TO COUNSEL, VOTING, AND CITIZENSHIP.

3019 SWEEZY P.M.
THE PRESENT AS HISTORY.
NEW YORK: MONTHLY REVIEW PR, 1953, 376 PP., LC#53-12728.
COLLECTION OF ESSAYS COMMENTING ON CONTEMPORARY ECONOMIC PROBLEMS, GERMAN AND AMERICAN CAPITALISM, PAST ECONOMIC THINKERS, AND PROBLEMS OF POLITICAL ECONOMY. SOCIALIST POINT OF VIEW.

3020 SWIFT M.G.
MALAY PEASANT SOCIETY IN JELEBU.
LONDON: ATHLONE PRESS, 1965, 181 PP.
STUDY OF SOCIAL ORGANIZATION OF MALAY PEASANTS IN ADMINISTRATIVE DISTRICT OF JELEBU WHICH FOCUSES ON ECONOMIC ACTIVITY AND MATRILINEAL KINSHIP SYSTEM. TREATS POLITICAL STRUCTURE, FAMILY AND DOMESTIC GROUPS, AND SOCIAL STRATIFICATION.

3021 SYKES G.M.
CRIME AND SOCIETY.
NEW YORK: RANDOM HOUSE, INC, 1956, 125 PP., LC#56-07692.
STUDIES RELATION BETWEEN CRIME AND CULTURE, AND EFFECTS OF EACH ON BREAKING OF RULES. CLASSIFIES CRIME, STUDIES BEHAVIOR OF SOCIETY TOWARDS CRIMINALS, AND RELATES AGE, SEX, RACE, AND SOCIO-ECONOMIC STATUS TO CRIME.

3022 SYME R.
COLONIAL ELITES: ROME, SPAIN, AND THE AMERICAS.
LONDON: OXFORD U PR, 1958, 66 PP.
COMBINES GENERAL THEORY OF HISTORY WITH SPECIFIC EXAMPLES. STATING THAT MODERN HISTORY DID NOT BEGIN WITH RENAISSANCE, AS MANY CLAIM, DRAWS PARALLELS IN EMPIRES OF ROME, SPAIN, AND ENGLAND AND EXAMINES THEORY THAT INTERNAL DECAY IS COMMON TO EMPIRES. DISCUSSES GIBBON AND TOYNBEE ON MATTER OF DECLINING CIVILIZATIONS.

3023 SYMONDS R.
"REFLECTIONS IN LOCALISATION."
J. COMMONWEALTH POLIT. STUD., 2 (NOV. 64), 219-234.
STUDIES THE TRANSFER OF ADMINISTRATIVE POWER IN FORMER BRITISH COLONIES BY WHICH NATIONALS REPLACED EXPATRIATES. BRITISH POLICY IS COMPARED IN EACH COLONY AS TO DEGREE OF EDUCATION, POLITICAL AWARENESS AND ADMINISTRATIVE TRAINING ACHIEVED.

3024 SYMONDS R.
THE BRITISH AND THEIR SUCCESSORS.
EVANSTON: NORTHWESTERN U PRESS, 1966, 287 PP.
STUDY IN DEVELOPMENT OF GOVERNMENTAL SERVICES IN FORMER COLONIES OF BRITAIN, INCLUDING WEST AFRICA AND EAST AFRICA, TREATING EDUCATION AND MILITARY POLICIES, CIVIL SERVICES, AND COMPARISONS WITH OTHER EMPIRES.

3025 SYRKIN M.
"THE RIGHT TO BE ORDINARY."
MIDSTREAM, 13 (JUNE-JULY 67), 3-7.
RECAPITULATION OF EVENTS IN ISRAELI-ARAB CONFLICT OF MAY 1967, REAFFIRMING NECESSITY FOR ARABS TO RECOGNIZE ISRAEL'S RIGHT TO EXIST AS A SOVEREIGN STATE. MENTIONS EFFECTS OF STANCES ASSUMED BY GREAT POWERS IN TERMS OF WORLD PRESTIGE.

3026 SZALAY L.B.
"SOVIET DOMESTIC PROPAGANDA AND LIBERALIZATION."
ORBIS, 11 (SPRING 67), 210-218.
NOTES WESTERN TENDENCY TO SEE USSR'S TURN TOWARD GROUP LEADERSHIP AND LOOSER ECONOMIC POLICY AS "LIBERALIZATION." INVESTIGATES IMPLICATIONS OF THESE MEASURES FOR SOVIET MAN, DEEMING SUCH STRUCTURAL CHANGES LESS IMPORTANT THAN WHAT THE MAN IS TAUGHT TO THINK ABOUT THEM. STUDIES HISTORY OF, AND CURRENT TRENDS IN, USSR PROPAGANDA; SEES AN ORGANIZED, FLEXIBLE, STRONGLY IDEOLOGICAL USE OF ALL MASS MEDIA.

3027 SZLADITS C.
BIBLIOGRAPHY ON FOREIGN AND COMPARATIVE LAW: BOOKS AND ARTICLES IN ENGLISH (SUPPLEMENT 1962)
NEW YORK: OCEANA PUBLISHING, 1964, 134 PP., LC#55-11076.
ANNOTATES AND LISTS 3,431 ITEMS ARRANGED TOPICALLY; BOOKS, ARTICLES, PAMPHLETS, SERIALS, DOCUMENTS, ETC., PERTINENT TO COMPARATIVE LAW, PUBLIC LAW, INTERNATIONAL LAW, COMMERCIAL LAW, CRIMINAL LAW, AND PRIVATE LAW. INCLUDES BIBLIOGRAPHIES, REFERENCES, LISTS OF INSTITUTIONS OF COMPARATIVE LAW, ETC.

3028 SZULC T.
TWILIGHT OF THE TYRANTS.
NEW YORK: HENRY HOLT & CO, 1959, 312 PP., LC#59-11747.
ACCOUNT OF DOWNFALL OF FIVE MID-20TH CENTURY LATIN AMERICAN DICTATORS RESULTING FROM DEMOCRATIC REVOLUTIONS OF 1950'S STRESSES TYRANNY AND CORRUPTION OF GOVERNMENT UNDER EACH DICTATOR AND DESCRIBES THEIR CAREERS AND PERSONAL LIVES. COUNTRIES DISCUSSED ARE BRAZIL, ARGENTINA, PERU, COLOMBIA, AND VENEZUELA.

3029 SZTARAY Z.

BIBLIOGRAPHY ON HUNGARY.
NEW YORK: KOSSUTH FDN, 1960, 100 PP., LC#60-14411.
UNANNOTATED BIBLIOGRAPHY OF WRITINGS ON HUNGARY IN NON-HUNGARIAN LANGUAGES, PRINCIPALLY ENGLISH, FRENCH, GERMAN, AND SPANISH. COVERS GEOGRAPHY, HISTORY INCLUDING HUNGARIAN REVOLUTION, POLITICAL AND SOCIAL LIFE, FOREIGN AFFAIRS, ECONOMICS, RELIGION, LANGUAGE, CULTURE, AND FINE ARTS. CONTAINS APPROXIMATELY 1,500 LISTINGS.

3030 TABORSKY E.
CONFORMITY UNDER COMMUNISM (PAMPHLET)
WASHINGTON: PUBLIC AFFAIRS PRESS, 1958, 38 PP., LC#58-10885.
STUDY OF COMMUNIST INDOCTRINATION TECHNIQUES IN EASTERN EUROPE. DISCUSSES FUNCTION OF SCHOOL SYSTEMS, MASS MEDIA, AND SOCIAL ORGANIZATIONS IN PROGRAM OF CREATION OF "COMMUNISTIC MAN." EXPLAINS INTENSIFICATION OF INDOCTRINATION PROGRAM DURING POST-STALIN ERA.

3031 TABORSKY E.
"CHANGE IN CZECHOSLOVAKIA."
CURR. HIST., 48 (MAR. 65), 168-174.
LIBERAL TRENDS PERMEATING INTELLECTUAL SCENE HAVE NOT YET FOUND WAY INTO ACTUAL POLITICAL PRACTICE WHICH REMAINS AS RIGID AND TOTALITARIAN AS EVER. GOVERNMENT FOUND DEFERRING FAITHFULLY TO SOVIET LINE IN ALL SIGNIFICANT MATTERS OF COMMUNIST POLICY AND STRATEGY.

3032 TABORSKY E.
"THE COMMUNIST PARTIES OF THE 'THIRD WORLD' IN SOVIET STRATEGY."
ORBIS, 11 (SPRING 67), 128-148.
EXAMINES NATURE OF COMMUNIST PARTIES IN UNDERDEVELOPED NATIONS OF AFRICA, ASIA, AND AMERICA. FINDS THEM FAULTY IN ORGANIZATION, SOCIAL COMPOSITION, DISCIPLINE, IDEOLOGY, AND RECRUITING; AND UNDERMINED BY SHAKY LEGAL STATUS AND SINO OR SOVIET FACTIONS. CONSIDERS RUSSIA DISTRESSED BY DIFFICULTY OF ESTABLISHING TRUE COMMUNIST VANGUARD IN UNDERDEVELOPED NATIONS, AND INCLINED TO BLUR PRINCIPLES TO REACH GOALS.

3033 TACHAKKYO K.
BIBLIOGRAPHY OF KOREAN STUDIES: A BIBLIOGRAPHICAL GUIDE TO KOREAN PUBLICATIONS ON KOREAN STUDIES APPEARING 1945-1958.
SEOUL: KOREA U ASIATIC RES CTR, 1961, 410 PP.
SOME 863 WELL-ANNOTATED BOOKS AND ARTICLES ARRANGED WITHIN TOPICAL HEADINGS. ALL ITEMS PUBLISHED FROM 1945-58 IN KOREAN, BUT AUTHORS, TITLES, AND ANNOTATIONS ARE PRESENTED IN ENGLISH. TOPIC HEADINGS INCLUDE POLITICS, ECONOMICS, LAW, KOREAN LANGUAGE AND LITERATURE, KOREAN HISTORY, AND PHILOSOPHY. TITLE, AUTHOR, AND PUBLISHER INDEXES FOLLOW.

3034 TAGGART F.J.
ROME AND CHINA.
BERKELEY: U. CALIF. PR., 1939, 283 PP.
INDICATES THAT WARS, UNDERTAKEN BY CHINA AND ROME IN NATIONAL INTEREST, LED INEVITABLY TO CONFLICTS AMONG NORTHERN EUROPEAN PEOPLES AND TO INVASION OF ROMAN EMPIRE.

3035 TAINE H.A.
THE ANCIENT REGIME.
ORIGINAL PUBLISHER NOT AVAILABLE, 1876, 421 PP.
AUTHOR EXAMINES CONTEMPORARY FRANCE IN LIGHT OF PRE-REVOLUTIONARY FRANCE. UTILIZING TAX RECORDS, DIARIES, AND GOVERNMENT DOCUMENTS, HE SHOWS THE SOCIAL, POLITICAL, AND ECONOMIC FABRIC OF THE OLD REGIME. HE POINTS OUT THE WEAK SPOTS, SUCH AS THE UNBALANCED TAX STRUCTURE AND DISAFFECTION IN THE ARMY. HIS PORTRAYALS OF PEASANT LIFE AND THE FLIRTATION WITH LIBERALISM SHOW WHY REVOLUTION WAS INEVITABLE.

3036 TAINE H.A.
THE FRENCH REVOLUTION (3 VOLS.) (TRANS. BY J. DURAND)
NEW YORK: HOLT RINEHART WINSTON, 1885.
EXTENSIVE EXAMINATION OF ORIGINS AND RESULTS OF FRENCH REVOLUTION CONSIDERS SOCIAL, ECONOMIC, AND POLITICAL FACTORS. TREATS ROLE OF POLITICAL PARTIES AND LEADERS, WEAKNESSES OF OLD GOVERNMENTS, AND ESTABLISHMENT OF REVOLUTIONARY GOVERNMENT. REVIEWS PROGRAM OF JACOBINS, CONCEPTION OF STATE, AND REVOLUTIONARY DESTRUCTIVENESS. INCLUDES INFLUENTIAL PROPAGANDISTS.

3037 TAINE H.A.
MODERN REGIME (2 VOLS.)
NEW YORK: HOLT RINEHART WINSTON, 1890, 656 PP.
AUTHOR ASSERTS THAT THE FRENCH SOCIAL STRUCTURE HAS REMAINED ALMOST INTACT DESPITE EIGHT FORMS OF GOVERNMENT SINCE THE REVOLUTION. BUT HE FINDS GREAT WEAKNESSES WITHIN THE STRUCTURE: A DECLINE IN MORALITY AND BIRTH RATE, AN INCREASED PURSUIT OF PLEASURE, AND A STERILE PREOCCUPATION WITH CAREER. THE SOURCE OF THIS WEAKNESS IS THE ENCROACHING STATE FIRST FORMED BY NAPOLEON.

3038 TAKEUCHI T.
WAR AND DIPLOMACY IN THE JAPANESE EMPIRE.
NEW YORK: DOUBLEDAY, 1935, 505 PP.
UNDERTAKES TO EXAMINE AND EVALUATE THE PROCESSES OF FORMULATING, EXECUTING, AND CONTROLLING THE JAPANESE FOREIGN POLICY SINCE THE ESTABLISHMENT OF A PARLIAMENTARY SYSTEM OF GOVERNMENT IN 1890. THE PRIMARY EMPHASIS IS PLACED UPON PROCEDURE RATHER THAN THE SUBSTANCE OF POLICY.

3039 TAMBIAH S.J.
"THE POLITICS OF LANGUAGE IN INDIA AND CEYLON."
MODERN ASIAN STUDIES, 1 (JULY 67), 215-240.
ARGUES THAT LANGUAGE PLAYS TREMENDOUS ROLE IN POLITICS IN INDIA AND CEYLON, BOTH IN PARTY AND ADMINISTRATIVE ROLES STATES THAT MAJOR PROBLEM IS THE FIGHTING OF MODERN BATTLES WITH TRADITIONALISTIC SLOGANS AND REVIVALISTIC DOGMA.

3040 TAN C.C.
THE BOXER CATASTROPHE.
NEW YORK: COLUMBIA U PRESS, 1955, 276 PP., LC#55-7834.
ANALYZES BOXER REBELLION. DISCUSSES INFLUENCE OF POLICIES OF VICEROYS AND GOVERNORS ON NATIONAL POLICY. ALSO STUDIES MANCHURIAN CRISIS CREATED BY RUSSIAN OCCUPATION AFTER BOXER REBELLION. VIEWS REBELLION AS STRUGGLE OF THE CHINESE PEOPLE AGAINST FOREIGN IMPERIALISM.

3041 TANG P.S.H.
"SINO-SOVIET TENSIONS."
CURR. HIST., 45 (OCT. 63), 223-229.
'PRESENT STATE OF TENSION BETWEEN LEADERS OF COMMUNIST CHINA AND USSR MAY STEM FROM KHRUSHCHEV'S DECISION TO SACRIFICE STRENGTHS OF SINO-SOVIET PARTNERSHIP UPON ALTAR OF TRADITIONAL WESTERN STATECRAFT. COMMUNIST-INSPIRED NON-COMMUNIST FACADE WAS OF GREAT VALUE IN ACHIEVING VICTORIES ON MAINLAND CHINA, NORTH KOREA, NORTH VIET NAM AND CUBA.'

3042 TANHAM B.K.
"COMMUNIST REVOLUTIONARY WARFARE: THE VIETMINH IN INDOCHINA."
NEW YORK: PRAEGER, 1961.
ANALYZES MODERN POLITICAL, ECONOMIC, MILITARY TACTICS LEADING TO SUCCESSFUL WARFARE. USES VIETMINH STRUGGLE AGAINST FRENCH IN INDOCHINA AS REFERENCE POINT.

3043 TANNENBAUM F.
PEACE BY REVOLUTION.
NEW YORK: COLUMBIA U PRESS, 1933, 310 PP.
DEVELOPMENT OF MEXICAN REVOLUTION, ANALYZING ITS BACKGROUND IN CULTURE, RACE RELATIONS, ECONOMIC NECESSITY, EDUCATION, AND POLITICS, AND ITS HERITAGE IN MODERN MEXICO'S GOVERNMENT, POLICIES, AND POLITICS. IMPORTANCE OF THE INDIAN IN MEXICAN HISTORY IS DISCUSSED.

3044 TANNENBAUM F.
"THE BALANCE OF POWER IN SOCIETY."
POLIT. SCI. QUART., 61 (DEC. 46), 481-505.
ARGUES THAT INSTITUTIONAL GROWTH OCCURS ONLY WITHIN A SOCIAL FRAMEWORK OF CONTROVERSY. TRUE WELL-BEING OF ANY SOCIETY LIES IN DIVERSITY, RATHER THAN IDENTITY, OF INTERESTS. CLAIMS THAT SOCIAL CONFLICT IS A CONSTITUENT OF THE PROCESS OF INSTITUTIONAL LIFE, AND ITS END WOULD SIGNIFY END OF LIFE ITSELF. ILLUSTRATES WITH EXAMPLES OF FAMILY, CHURCH, STATE, LABOR, CAPITAL, AND ENTIRE ECONOMY.

3045 TANNER R.
"WHO GOES HOME?"
TRANSACTIONS, 3 (MAR.-JUNE 63), 30-33, 32-36.
ANALYZES CAUSES AND CATEGORIES OF EUROPEANS LEAVING TANGANYIKA AFTER INDEPENDENCE. DISCUSSES GROWTH OF NONALIGNED CULTURE IN CIVIL SERVICE AND ATTEMPTS AT PRESERVING NATIONALISM AMONG GOVERNMENT EMPLOYEES.

3046 TANTER R., MIDLARSKY M.
"A THEORY OF REVOLUTION."
J. OF CONFLICT RESOLUTION, 11 (SEPT. 67), 264-280.
EMPIRICAL EXAMINATION OF CHANGES IN ECONOMIC DEVELOPMENT, LEVEL OF EDUCATION, AND SOME CAUSES OF REVOLUTION, REGARDING EXTENT OF THEIR ASSOCIATION WITH CERTAIN CHARACTERISTICS OF REVOLUTION. EXPLORES DIFFERENCES IN ASIAN AND LATIN AMERICAN REVOLUTIONS, PRIMARILY ON BASIS OF ACTUAL AMOUNT OF SOCIAL CHANGE RESULTING FROM REVOLUTION.

3047 TATU M.
"URSS: LES FLOTTEMENTS DE LA DIRECTION COLLEGIALE."
REALITES, (NOV. 67), 62-65.
ANALYZES SOVIET POLICY ERRORS. BELIEVES THAT SOVIET INVOLVEMENT IN ARAB-ISRAELI CRISIS WAS A MISTAKE, THAT ITS POLICY WAS IMPROVISED, IRRESPONSIBLE, AND FACILE. KHRUSHCHEV MADE ERRORS IN HIS CALCULATIONS, BUT SOVIET LEADERS TODAY ARE CHARACTERIZED BY A COLLECTIVE PARALYSIS IN DECISION-MAKING. BREZHNEV HAS CONSIDERED YOUNGER LEADERS WITH IDEAS OF REFORM A THREAT TO HIM.

3048 TATZ C.M.
SHADOW AND SUBSTANCE IN SOUTH AFRICA.
PIETERMARITZBURG: U NATAL PR, 1962, 238 PP.
DISCUSSES DEVELOPMENT AND IMPLEMENTATION OF GROUP SEGREGATION IN SOUTH AFRICA FROM 1903-1960. EMPHASIZES LAND POLICIES DEVELOPED BY COMMITTEES ON NATIVE AFFAIRS AND THE NATIONAL PARTY; STUDIES NATIVE REACTIONS.

3049 TAUBER K.

"ASPECTS OF NATIONALIST-COMMUNIST COLLABORATION IN POSTWAR GERMANY."
J. CENT. EUROPE. AFF., 20 (APR. 60), 51-68.
DISCUSSES JOINT EFFORT OF EXTREME RIGHT AND EXTREME LEFT TO EFFECT REUNIFICAT&ON OF GERMANY. RELATES SOVIET ATTEMPTS TO PRESENT VIEWPOINT TO PUBLIC, PARTICULARLY TO WEST GERMANS, IN POSTWAR PERIOD.

3050 TAWNEY R.H.
RELIGION AND THE RISE OF CAPITALISM.
NEW YORK: HARCOURT BRACE, 1926, 336 PP.
TRACES DEVELOPMENT OF RELIGIOUS THOUGHT ON SOCIAL AND ECONOMIC MATTERS IN PERIOD OF TRANSITION FROM FEUDALISM TO INDUSTRIALISM. DISCUSSES MEDIEVAL BACKGROUND, REFORMS ON THE CONTINENT, CHURCH OF ENGLAND, AND PURITAN MOVEMENT AS INFLUENTIAL IN AFFECTING CAPITALISM.

3051 TAWNEY R.H.
EQUALITY.
LONDON: ALLEN & UNWIN, 1964, 248 PP.
ATTACKS NOTION OF BRITISH EQUALITY, CLAIMING THAT INSTEAD OF BECOMING LESS STRATIFIED, BRITISH SOCIETY HAS BECOME EVEN MORE SO. POINTS TO INHERITED WEALTH AND EDUCATIONAL SYSTEM AS MAJOR FLAWS IN ATTEMPTS AT IMPLEMENTING EQUALITY. ADVOCATES REMOVAL OF SOCIAL AND ECONOMIC INEQUALITIES, EQUAL EDUCATION FOR ALL CHILDREN, AND EQUALIZING ACCESS TO IMPORTANT GOODS AND SERVICES.

3052 TAX S.
HERITAGE OF CONQUEST.
LONDON: GLENCOE FREE PRESS, 1952, 312 PP., LC#51-13787.
DISCUSSIONS OF CULTURAL, SOCIAL, AND ECONOMIC CONDITIONS OF UNEDUCATED RURAL INHABITANTS OF MEXICO AND CENTRAL AMERICA.

3053 TAYLOR D.M.
THE BRITISH IN AFRICA.
CHESTER SPRINGS: DUFOUR, 1962, 185 PP., LC#64-22679.
TRACES BRITISH COLONIALISM IN AFRICA FROM INCEPTION. SLAVERY, DOMINATION, "WHITE MAN'S BURDEN," ADMINISTRATION, ECONOMIC POLICIES, AND PREPARATION FOR SOVEREIGNTY EXAMINED. VIEWS LASTING EFFECT OF BRITAIN UPON POLITICAL, ECONOMIC, AND CULTURAL PRACTICES.

3054 TAYLOR E.
RICHER BY ASIA.
BOSTON: HOUGHTON, 1964, 420 PP.
'IN HEARTS AND MINDS OF MEN LIES SOLUTION OF WORLD'S DISEASE AND NOT IN PACTS AND ARMAMENTS... BUILDING BRIDGES BETWEEN EAST AND WEST ONLY HOPE OF AVOIDING FINAL WORLD WAR OR PREPARING MEN FOR WORLD GOVERNMENT.' ENJOINS WORLD-CITIZENRY TO APPRECIATE PRINCIPLES THAT GOVERN 'ORIENTALS.'

3055 TAYLOR J.V.
CHRISTIANITY AND POLITICS IN AFRICA.
BALTIMORE: PENGUIN BOOKS, 1957, 127 PP.
ESSAY ON CHRISTIANITY'S POLITICAL ROLE IN AFRICA ON BRINK OF INDEPENDENCE. INCLUDES ETHICS OF CHURCH PARTICIPATION, CHURCH-STATE RELATIONS, AND POSSIBLE ACTION BY CHURCH.

3056 TAYLOR M.G.
"THE ROLE OF THE MEDICAL PROFESSION IN THE FORMULATION AND EXECUTION OF PUBLIC POLICY" (BMR)"
CAN. J. OF ECO. AND POL. SCI., 26 (FEB. 60), 108-127.
EXAMINES RELATION OF MEDICAL PROFESSION TO CANADIAN GOVERNMENT. DISCUSSES ROLE OF PROFESSION AS SELF-GOVERNING GROUP AND ITS RESISTANCE TO OUTSIDE CONTROL. TREATS CANADIAN MEDICAL ASSOCIATION'S FUNCTION AS INTEREST OR PRESSURE GROUP IN AREAS OF MEDICAL PRACTICES AND STANDARDS AND ORGANIZING AND FINANCING OF MEDICAL SERVICES. REVEALS GROUP INVOLVEMENT IN PUBLIC ADMINISTRATION IN SEVERAL AREAS.

3057 TAYLOR P.B. JR.
"PROGRESS IN VENEZUELA."
CURRENT HISTORY, 53 (NOV. 67), 270-274, 308.
STATES THAT VENEZUELA'S GROWTH SINCE 1958 HAS BEEN VERY FAST AND VERY SUCCESSFUL. THAT IN GENERAL, APART FROM BASIC INDUSTRIAL AND AGRARIAN SECTORS, ECONOMIC DEVELOPMENT AS BEEN LARGELY UNCONTROLLED AND IN PRIVATE HANDS. DISCUSSES EFFECTS OF THIS FACT. ANALYZES REASONS FOR INCREASING POLITICAL STABILITY, AND MAKES PREDICTIONS ABOUT 1968 ELECTIONS.

3058 TEMPERLEY H.
THE FOREIGN POLICY OF CANNING: 1822-1827.
LONDON: BELL, 1925, 606 PP.
ATTEMPTS TO EVALUATE FAMOUS FOREIGN MINISTER BY RELATING HIM TO OTHER DIPLOMATIC PERSONALITIES AND EVENTS OF HIS TIME. BECAME INFLUENTIAL IN ENGLAND AND EUROPE IN 1825.

3059 TEMPERLEY H.W.V.
SENATES AND UPPER CHAMBERS; THEIR USE AND FUNCTION IN THE MODERN STATE...
LONDON: CHAPMAN AND HALL, 1910, 343 PP.
SURVEYS UPPER CHAMBERS OF ENGLISH-SPEAKING WORLD AND CONTINENT WITH COMPARATIVE EMPHASIS ON UK. DISCUSSES STRUCTURE, BASES OF POLITICAL POWER, AND FUNCTIONS, WITH SPECIAL SECTION ON REFORM IN HOUSE OF LORDS. ANALYZES BICAMERAL SYSTEMS AND PROS AND CONS OF HEREDITARY VERSUS ELECTED UPPER HOUSES. INCLUDES US STATE LEGISLATURES, PARTISANSHIP, REPRESENTATION OF RELIGIOUS BODIES, AND DISSOLUTION POWERS.

3060 TEMPLE W.
AN ESSAY UPON THE ORIGINAL AND NATURE OF GOVERNMENT (PAMPHLET)
LOS ANGELES: AUGUSTAN REPRINT, 1964, 60 PP.
ESSAY WRITTEN IN 1672, TRACING EVOLUTION OF PRIMITIVE GOVERNMENT AND ANALYZING ELEMENTS WHICH LED TO MODERN POLITICAL INSTITUTIONS, REJECTING SOCIAL CONTRACT AND ADVOCATING PARTIARCHAL THEORY OF GOVERNMENT.

3061 TENDLER J.D.
"TECHNOLOGY AND ECONOMIC DEVELOPMENT* THE CASE OF HYDRO VS THERMAL POWER."
POLIT. SCI. QUART., 80 (JUNE 65), 236-253.
A COMPARISON OF ARGENTINE AND BRAZILIAN EXPERIENCES IN THE DEVELOPMENT OF PUBLIC POWER FACILITIES OVER THE LAST TWO DECADES. ADVISES THAT THE DEVELOPMENT OF ELECTRIC CAPACITY THROUGH HYDRO POWER, WHILE ORIGINALLY MORE EXPENSIVE, IS IN LONG RUN BETTER FOR THE DEVELOPING COUNTRY BECAUSE IT PROMOTES LOCAL INDUSTRY, SKILLS AND INTEGRATION RATHER THAN HIGH TECHNOLOGY IMPORTS NECESSITATED BY THERMAL SYSTEMS.

3062 TENG S., BIGGERSTAFF K.
AN ANNOTATED BIBLIOGRAPHY OF SELECTED CHINESE REFERENCE WORKS (REV. ED.)
CAMBRIDGE: HARVARD U PR, 1950, 326 PP.
AN EXTENSIVELY ANNOTATED BIBLIOGRAPHY, PROVIDING CRITICAL AND DESCRIPTIVE ANALYSES OF BIBLIOGRAPHIES, ENCYCLOPEDIAS, DICTIONARIES, GEOGRAPHICAL WORKS, BIOGRAPHICAL WORKS, TABLES, YEARBOOKS, AND SINOLOGICAL INDEXES. HAS CROSS REFERENCES AND A COMBINED INDEX AND GLOSSARY. MATERIALS LISTED DATE FROM 3RD THROUGH 20TH CENTURIES. CHRONOLOGICALLY ARRANGED WITHIN FORMAT HEADINGS.

3063 TEPASKE J.J. ED., FISHER S.N. ED.
EXPLOSIVE FORCES IN LATIN AMERICA.
COLUMBUS: OHIO STATE U. PR., 1964, 196 PP., $4.75.
EIGHT PAPERS COVER SOVIET POLICY AND CUBA, ROLE OF INTELLECTUAL IN PROMOTING CHANGE, FORCES OF CHURCH AND MILITARY IN LATIN AMERICAN LIFE. EXAMINES IMPACT OF LAND REFORM AND PROBLEMS OF POPULATION EXPLOSION AND OF POVERTY. LASTLY, PRESENTS OBSERVATIONS ON ALLIANCE FOR PROGRESS.

3064 TEW B.
WEALTH AND INCOME.
MELBOURNE: MELBOURNE UNIV PRESS, 1965, 223 PP.
ANALYZES ECONOMIC AND FINANCIAL SYSTEMS OF BRITAIN AND AUSTRALIA. EMPHASIZES CONTEMPORARY PROBLEMS SUCH AS INFLATION, UNEMPLOYMENT, AND RELATIONS BETWEEN "MOTHER COUNTRY AND WORLD." SETS UP SYSTEM OF PAPER MONEY AND NOTES AS BASIS FOR ALL EXCHANGES AND APPLIES SYSTEM TO CURRENT FUNCTIONS BETWEEN TWO NATIONS.

3065 THAILAND NATIONAL ECO DEV
THE NATIONAL ECONOMIC DEVELOPMENT PLAN: 1961-66: SECOND PHASE 1964-66.
BANGKOK: THAINATL ECO DEV BOARD, 1964, 214 PP.
REPORT OF PROPOSED PLAN FOR ECONOMY FOR 1964-66. COVERS PROGRESS OF PHASE ONE OF PLAN AND REVISIONS NECESSARY FOR PHASE TWO. STUDIES SPECIFIC SECTOR PROGRAMS THAT WILL BE CARRIED OUT IN PERIOD, IN FIELDS OF TRANSPORTATION, WELFARE, EDUCATION ETC. GOAL IS TO RAISE PER CAPITA INCOME THREE PER CENT PER YEAR. STRESSES GOVERNMENT SPENDING IN PRIVATE SECTORS OF ECONOMY.

3066 THE AFRICA 1960 COMMITTEE
MANDATE IN TRUST; THE PROBLEM OF SOUTH WEST AFRICA.
LONDON: AFRICA 1960 COMMITTEE, 1960, 31 PP.
DISCUSSION OF MANDATE OF SOUTH AFRICA OVER SOUTH WEST AFRICA. COVERS BACKGROUND OF SOUTH WEST AFRICA AS GERMAN COLONY MADE MANDATE IN 1918 AND STATUS OF AREA IN INTERNATIONAL AFFAIRS AND DOMESTIC SITUATIONS. OPPOSES PRESENT SITUATION OF SOUTH AFRICAN CONTROL OVER TERRITORY AND SEEKS CHANGE IN STATUS.

3067 THE ECONOMIST (LONDON)
THE COMMONWEALTH AND EUROPE.
LONDON: ECONOMIST INTELLIG UNIT, 1960, 606 PP.
COLLECTION AND ANALYSIS OF FACTS RELEVANT TO PATTERNS OF TRADE IN COMMONWEALTH AND EEC. INCLUDES CHAPTERS ON PRODUCTION AND TRADE OF FOODSTUFFS, RAW MATERIALS, MANUFACTURES. ANALYZES TRADE SYSTEMS IN "OLDER DOMINIONS" OF THE COMMONWEALTH, ASIAN MEMBERS, TROPICAL AFRICA, AND WEST INDIES.

3068 THEOBALD R. ED.
THE NEW NATIONS OF WEST AFRICA.
NEW YORK: H W WILSON, 1960, 175 PP., LC#60-08240.
EXAMINES PROBLEMS OF NEW NATIONS, ECONOMIC AND POLITICAL. ANALYZES MAJOR PROBLEMS OF SPECIFIC COUNTRIES. VIEWS RELATIONSHIP WITH EX-COLONIAL POWERS AND EFFECTS OF COLONIALISM

ON ECONOMIC AND POLITICAL PRACTICES.

3069 THEROUX P.
"HATING THE ASIANS."
TRANSITION, 7 (OCT.-NOV. 67), 46-52.
EXAMINES ROLE OF ASIANS IN AFRICA AND SOURCES OF DEEP HATRED THAT NATIVES BEAR TOWARD THEM. DECRIES RACISM THAT IS RESULTING IN MASS EXODUS OF ASIANS FROM KENYA, UGANDA, AND TANZANIA. POINTS OUT CONTRIBUTIONS OF ASIANS IN POLITICAL, ECONOMIC, AND CULTURAL AREAS. CRITICIZES GROWING ANTI-ASIAN FEELINGS.

3070 THIBAUDET A.
LES IDEES POLITIQUES DE LA FRANCE.
PARIS: LIBRAIRIE STOCK DELAMAIN ET BOUTELLEAU, 1932, 264 PP.
COMPARES POLITICAL ATTITUDES ON SEPARATION OF POWER, INDUSTRIALISM, RADICALISM, JACOBINISM, AND THE THOUGHT OF JAURES.

3071 THIEN T.T.
"VIETNAM: A CASE OF SOCIAL ALIENATION."
INTERNATIONAL AFFAIRS (UK), 43 (JULY 67), 445-467.
TRACES POLITICAL HISTORY OF VIETNAM SINCE UNIFICATION IN 1802 TO ILLUSTRATE GROWTH OF ALIENATION OF AGRICULTURAL PEASANTS FROM RULING ELITES. WITH INFLUX OF US MONEY THIS GAP IS INCREASING. MAINTAINS THAT SOLUTIONS NECESSITATE IDENTIFICATION OF OFFICIALS WITH PEASANTS AND PEASANT REPRESENTATION IN GOVERNMENT. US MUST DIRECT AID AWAY FROM OFFICIALS AND VIETNAMESE MUST REFORM ARMY AND CIVIL SERVICE.

3072 THIERRY S.S.
LE VATICAN SECRET.
PARIS: CALMAN-LEVY, 1962, 233 PP.
DESCRIBES AND ANALYZES ADMINISTRATION AND DECISION-MAKING PROCESS OF VATICAN CITY. TREATS DELIBERATIVE PROCESS AND EXECUTIVE MANAGEMENT FROM HISTORICAL AND EVOLUTIONARY PERSPECTIVE.

3073 THIESENHUSEN W.C.
CHILE'S EXPERIMENTS IN AGRARIAN REFORM.
MADISON: U OF WISCONSIN PR, 1966, 230 PP., LC#66-29119.
ANALYZES LAND REFORM EXPERIMENTS IN CHILE, WHERE TRADITIONAL AGRARIAN STRUGGLE STILL DOMINATES. CONSIDERING FOUR LARGE FARMS THAT WERE COLONIZED, ISOLATES MAJOR FACTORS FOR THE SUCCESS OR FAILURE OF THE SHARECROPPER COLONISTS. STUDY IS PREDICATED ON THE IDEA THAT WHEN A MORE INCLUSIVE REFORM COMES, TECHNICIANS WILL BE AIDED BY STUDIES OF HOW SMALL-SCALE REFORM WORKS.

3074 THOM J.M.
GUIDE TO RESEARCH MATERIAL IN POLITICAL SCIENCE (PAMPHLET)
WASHINGTON: WASHINGTON U LIBS, 1952, 34 PP.
AN ANNOTATED BIBLIOGRAPHY IN POLITICAL SCIENCE MATERIAL. 233 ENTRIES. MATERIAL IN ENGLISH AND SOME FRENCH, GERMAN, ITALIAN AND RUSSIAN.

3075 THOMAN R.S., CONKLING E.C.
GEOGRAPHY OF INTERNATIONAL TRADE.
ENGLEWOOD CLIFFS: PRENTICE HALL, 1967, 186 PP., LC#67-18931.
TRENDS, PATTERNS, AND PROBLEMS OF INTERNATIONAL TRADE WITH RELATIVELY LITTLE EMPHASIS ON GEOGRAPHIC ASPECTS OF THIS TRADE. EXTENSIVE USE OF CHARTS BUT MOST ARE DESCRIPTIVE IN NATURE. EMPHASIS ON TRADE PATTERNS OF IDEOLOGICALLY OR ECONOMICALLY RELATED NATIONS AND ON LOGISTICS OF TRADING CONCERNS, COMMERCIAL CENTERS, COUNTRIES, AND INTERNATIONAL ORGANIZATIONS.

3076 THOMAS D.H.
GUIDE TO THE DIPLOMATIC ARCHIVES OF WESTERN EUROPE.
PHILA: U OF PENN PR, 1959, 389 PP., LC#57-9123.
AN UNANNOTATED BIBLIOGRAPHY OF THE DIPLOMATIC ARCHIVES OF THE COUNTRIES OF WESTERN EUROPE. MATERIAL IN THE FOLLOWING LANGUAGES: ENGLISH, GERMAN, FRENCH, DUTCH, ITALIAN, DANISH, NORWEGIAN, PORTUGUESE, SPANISH, SWEDISH, SWISS. 400 ENTRIES.

3077 THOMAS F.C. JR.
"THE PEACE CORPS IN MOROCCO."
MIDDLE EAST J., 19 (SUMMER 65), 273-283.
CRITIQUE OF FIRST PEACE CORPS MISSION TO MOROCCO BY ITS DIRECTOR. NOTES PROBLEMS OF FITTING IDEALISTIC SELF-HELP-ORIENTED PERSONNEL INTO PRE-EXISTING FORMALIZED FRENCH FOREIGN AID TECHNICAL PROGRAMS. MORE GENERAL PROBLEMS OF DEVISING SUCCESSFUL PEACE CORPS PROGRAM ALSO DISCUSSED.

3078 THOMAS P.
DOWN THESE MEAN STREETS.
NEW YORK: ALFRED KNOPF, 1967, 333 PP.
AUTOBIOGRAPHY OF A DARK-SKINNED PUERTO RICAN, IN NEW YORK AND IN THE SOUTH. PICTURES THE CULTURE OF THIS UNASSIMILATED MINORITY GROUP WITH ITS CULT OF MASCULINITY (MACHISMO). THE AUTHOR ALSO TREATS THE IDENTITY PROBLEM OF A BLACK MAN WHOSE BACKGROUND IS HISPONIC, AND RECOUNTS HIS MOVE SOUTH SEEKING TO DISCOVER WHO HE IS.

3079 THOMPSON D., MARSH N.S.
"THE UNITED KINGDOM AND THE TREATY OF ROME."
INT. COMP. LAW QUART., 11 (JAN. 62), 73-88.
ASSESSES LEGAL ARGUMENTS REGARDING THE ENTRY OF UNITED KINGDOM INTO THE COMMON MARKET UNDER THE TREATY OF ROME PROVISIONS. OUTLINES ADMINISTRATIVE AND JUDICIAL ASPECTS OF THE SYSTEM AND INDICATES WHAT ACTION PARLIAMENT MIGHT TAKE (IN VIEW OF ENGLISH COMMON LAW) WITH REGARD TO LABOR UNIONS. FORESEES A HARMONIZATION OF LAWS.

3080 THOMPSON E.T. ED.
PERSPECTIVES ON THE SOUTH: AGENDA FOR RESEARCH.
DURHAM: DUKE U PR, 1967, 231 PP., LC#67-20397.
PRINTS PAPERS FROM INTERDISCIPLINARY SYMPOSIUM OF CENTER FOR SOUTHERN STUDIES, DUKE UNIVERSITY. THEORETICAL APPROACH AIMS AT ASKING NEW AND MORE RELEVANT QUESTIONS ABOUT SOUTHERN PROBLEMS. EFFORT DIRECTED AT IDENTIFYING "NEW SOUTH," AIMING TOWARD FULLER INTEGRATION WITH MAINSTREAM OF AMERICAN LIFE. SEES NEGRO AS NO LONGER CHIEF PROBLEM BUT AS ONE IN COMPLEX OF REGIONAL, NATIONAL, AND INTERNATIONAL PROBLEMS.

3081 THOMPSON F.M.L.
ENGLISH LANDED SOCIETY IN THE NINETEENTH CENTURY.
TORONTO: TORONTO UNIV PRESS, 1963, 374 PP.
HISTORY OF DECLINE OF ARISTOCRATIC POWER IN BRITAIN IN LAST CENTURY, ECONOMIC HISTORY OF LANDED INTEREST, ITS ROLE AS SOCIAL GROUP, INCLUDING LIFE OF LANDED ARISTOCRAT, ESTATES IN RAILWAY AGE, AND ECLIPSE OF LANDED INTEREST THROUGH 1939.

3082 THOMPSON J.H. ED., REISCHAUER R.D. ED.
MODERNIZATION OF THE ARAB WORLD.
PRINCETON: VAN NOSTRAND, 1966, 249 PP.
DIVERSE OPINIONS ON AND APPROACHES TO STUDY OF MODERN ARAB WORLD. EXAMINES INTERACTIONS OF TRADITIONAL PAST, CURRENT REALITIES, AND FUTURE EXPECTATIONS. EXPLORES IMPEDING AND POSITIVE ELEMENTS OF PAST, PROBLEMS OF ECONOMIC GROWTH, INTRA-ARAB AND ARAB-ISRAELI RELATIONS, POPULATION, AND SOCIAL INSTABILITY. COMPARES PROCESS OF MODERNIZATION IN ARAB COUNTRIES AND GIVES REASONS FOR DIFFERENCES.

3083 THOMPSON J.M.
RUSSIA, BOLSHEVISM, AND THE VERSAILLES PEACE.
PRINCETON: PRINCETON U PRESS, 1966, 429 PP., LC#66-17712.
STUDIES ROLE OF RUSSIA AT PARIS PEACE CONFERENCE OF 1919. SHOWS THAT, THOUGH RUSSIA WAS NOT REPRESENTED AT CONFERENCE, THE PEACEMAKERS ATTACHED GREAT IMPORTANCE TO RUSSIAN QUESTION. EXAMINES HOW, AND FROM WHAT MOTIVES, PEACEMAKERS DEALT WITH THREAT OF BOLSHEVISM AND STRUGGLE FOR POWER IN RUSSIA. FOCUSES ON RELATIONSHIPS BETWEEN PEACE CONFERENCE AND SOVIET AND WHITE RUSSIAN GOVERNMENTS.

3084 THOMPSON J.W., PADOVER S.K.
SECRET DIPLOMACY: A RECORD OF ESPIONAGE AND DOUBLE-DEALING: 1500-1815.
LONDON: JARROLDS PUBLISHERS, LTD, 1937, 286 PP.
ATTEMPTS TO SHOW THAT UNDERCOVER OPERATIONS HAVE BEEN UNIVERSALLY EMPLOYED, AND THAT SPYING AND BRIBERY HAVE PLAYED A LARGER ROLE IN DIPLOMATIC HISTORY THAN HERETOFORE BELIEVED. BOOK BASED ON OFFICIAL DOCUMENTS, MEMOIRS, MEMORANDA OF MINISTERS, POLICE REPORTS, LETTERS, AND INFORMATION OF SPIES. EXTENSIVE BIBLIOGRAPHY ARRANGED ACCORDING TO CHAPTER SUBJECTS.

3085 THOMPSON V., ADLOFF R.
MINORITY PROBLEMS IN SOUTHEAST ASIA.
STANFORD: STANFORD U PRESS, 1955, 295 PP., LC#55-6688.
ANALYZES THE PROBLEMS THAT SOUTHEAST ASIAN MINORITIES HAVE WITH EACH OTHER AND THE PROBLEMS THAT SOUTHEAST ASIAN STATES FACE IN THEIR RELATIONS WITH ONE ANOTHER AND WITH THE WORLD AT LARGE. DISCUSSES THE CHINESE, INDIAN, AND CHRISTIAN MINORITIES. INCLUDES BUDDHIST MAJORITY'S PROBLEMS WITH CHRISTIANS IN CAMBODIA AND LAOS, AND THE IMPACT OF THESE PROBLEMS ON ASIAN-WESTERN RELATIONS.

3086 THORBURN H.G. ED.
PARTY POLITICS IN CANADA.
LONDON: PRENTICE HALL INTL, 1963, 172 PP.
COLLECTION OF ESSAYS ON STRUCTURE OF CANADIAN PARTY SYSTEM. EMPHASIZES LACK OF SHARP IDEOLOGICAL DIFFERENCES AMONG MAJOR PARTIES. DISCUSSES REGIONAL POLITICS, CRITICISMS OF POLITICAL LEADERSHIP, AND RELATIONS BETWEEN POLITICS AND BUSINESS.

3087 THORD-GRAY I.
GRINGO REBEL.
CORAL GABLES: U OF MIAMI PR, 1960, 487 PP., LC#61-7437.
PERSONAL VIEW OF MEXICAN REVOLUTION IN 20TH CENTURY BY FOREIGNER PARTICIPATING ON REBEL SIDE. DESCRIBES PERSONALITIES AND POLITICAL AND MILITARY EVENTS RELATED TO GOVERNMENT AND REVOLUTION IN MEXICO DURING UPHEAVAL.

3088 THORNBURG M.W.
PEOPLE AND POLICY IN THE MIDDLE EAST.
NEW YORK: NORTON, 1964, 250 PP., $5.00.
STUDY OF MEN'S BEHAVIOR PATTERNS AS INDIVIDUALS AND AS MEMBERS OF THE BASIC SOCIAL UNITS, THE IMPACT OF WESTERN TECHNOLOGY UPON THE MIDDLE EAST, AND THE CHANGES THAT HAVE

TAKEN PLACE IN THAT AREA IN THE PAST SEVERAL DECADES.

3089 THORNTON M.J.
NAZISM, 1918-1945.
NEW YORK: PERGAMON PRESS, 1966, 181 PP., LC#66-16456.
INTRODUCTORY ACCOUNT OF HISTORY OF NAZISM TRACING DEVELOPMENTS FROM RISE OF NAZIS AND THEIR GAINING CONTROL OF GERMAN GOVERNMENT TO THEIR DEFEAT AND CONSEQUENT DIVISION OF GERMANY. DISCUSSES RACISM AND OTHER IDEOLOGICAL TENETS OF NAZISM, LIFE AND IDEAS OF HITLER, DESTRUCTION OF WEIMAR REPUBLIC, HITLER'S PREWAR FOREIGN POLICY, AND OTHER MAJOR ISSUES. INTENDED FOR STUDENTS.

3090 THORNTON T.P. ED.
THE THIRD WORLD IN SOVIET PERSPECTIVE: STUDIES BY SOVIET WRITERS ON THE DEVELOPING AREAS.
PRINCETON: U. PR., 1964, 355 PP., $7.50.
ESSAYS TREAT ASIAN, AFRICAN, AND LATIN AMERICAN ECONOMIC DEVELOPMENT, CLASS RELATIONSHIPS, POLITICAL FORCES, AND AGRARIAN REFORM. ALSO TREAT RESEARCH PROBLEMS AND METHODS.

3091 THUCYDIDES
THE PELOPONESIAN WARS.
NEW YORK: TWAYNE, 1963, 335 PP.
DESCRIBES STRUGGLE BETWEEN ATHENS AND SPARTA FOR SUPREMACY IN GREECE. SEES WAR AS CONFLICT OF TWO IDEAS: ATHENIAN IMPERIALISM AND GREEK PASSION FOR AUTONOMY. SEES WAR ALSO AS CONFLICT BETWEEN TWO WAYS OF LIFE: ATHENIAN DEMOCRACY AND SPARTAN DISCIPLINED CONSERVATISM.

3092 TIERNEY B.
THE CRISIS OF CHURCH AND STATE 1050-1300.
ENGLEWOOD CLIFFS: PRENTICE HALL, 1964, 210 PP., LC#64-23072.
CAREFULLY SELECTED DOCUMENTS RELATING TO CONFLICT BETWEEN WESTERN CHURCH AND STATE, 1050-1300. DOCUMENTS AND EXTENSIVE COMMENTARY REVEAL DEBATE OF PRACTICAL POLITICS VS. POLITICAL THEORY. BEGINS WITH INTRODUCTION TO PERIOD (WRITINGS OF AUGUSTINE, ETC.); COVERS "INVESTITURE CONTEST," REVIVAL OF ARISTOTELIAN THOUGHT, AND RISE OF AQUINAS' THEORIES.

3093 TIKHOMIROV I.A.
"DIVISION OF POWERS OR DIVISION OF LABOR?"
SOVIET LAW & GOVERNMENT, 5 (SPRING 67), 11-19.
RE-EXAMINES SOVIET RELATIONSHIP BETWEEN BALANCE OF POWER AND DIVISION OF LABOR UNDER NEW SOCIO-ECONOMIC CONDITIONS. ALTHOUGH MARXIST THEORY CALLS FOR ABOLISHMENT OF DIVISION OF LABOR, MAINTAINS THAT IT IS STILL NECESSARY FOR EFFECTIVE POWER STRUCTURE. ESPECIALLY DISCUSSES RELATIONSHIPS AMONG GOVERNMENTAL AGENCIES AND EVOLUTION OF LAW ENFORCEMENT DEPARTMENTS.

3094 TILLION G.
ALGERIA: THE REALITIES.
NEW YORK: ALFRED KNOPF, 1958, 115 PP., LC#58-10980.
BASED ON AUTHOR'S FIELD WORK IN ALGERIA, DESCRIBES OVERPOPULATED CONDITIONS, ECONOMIC DEGRADATION, AND SOCIAL DECAY OF THE COUNTRY. DISCUSSES COMPARATIVE PROBLEMS OF OVERPOPULATION, COLONIALISM, AND CONSERVATION. PROPOSES A FRANCO-ALGERIAN UNION IN ORDER TO SOLVE ECONOMIC PROBLEMS.

3095 TILLY C., RULE J.
MEASURING POLITICAL UPHEAVAL* RESEARCH MONOGRAPH NO. 19.
PRINCETON: CTR OF INTL STUDIES, 1965, 113 PP.
INTERNAL WAR IS TODAY A FACTOR OF GREAT IMPORT IN INTERNATIONAL RELATIONS. THE AUTHORS ATTEMPT A SCHEME FOR CLASSIFYING AND QUANTIFYING THE VARIABLE OF POLITICAL UPHEAVAL, WHICH IS "MUTUAL, COLLECTIVE, VIOLENT COERCION." SCHEME BASED ON THE MEASUREMENT OF MAGNITUDE, ORGANIZATION, FOCUS, AND ISOMORPHY. THEY DISCUSS PREVIOUS ATTEMPTS AT CLASSIFYING AND MEASURING INTERNAL VIOLENCE.

3096 TILMAN R.O. ED., COLE T. ED.
THE NIGERIAN POLITICAL SCENE.
DURHAM: DUKE U PR, 1962, 340 PP., LC#62-18315.
DISCUSSES BACKGROUND AND PROBLEMS OF ECONOMIC AND POLITICAL DEVELOPMENT OF FEDERATION OF NIGERIA DURING 1950'S. SEVERAL AUTHORS REPRESENT DIVERSE SOCIAL SCIENCE FIELD. MAJOR TOPICS' DISCUSSED INCLUDE TRADITIONAL SOCIO-POLITICAL SYSTEM IN NIGERIA, NATURE OF ITS FEDERALISM, AND FUTURE OF DEMOCRACY IN NIGERIA AND AFRICA IN GENERAL.

3097 TILMAN R.O.
"MALAYSIA: THE PROBLEMS OF FEDERATION."
WESTERN POLIT. QUART., 16 (DEC. 63), 897-911.
DISCUSSES IN DETAIL THE PROBLEMS OF MALAYSIAN FEDERALISM. INCLUDES COMMUNAL CHARACTER OF TERRITORIES, THE ROLE OF ISLAM, AND LANGUAGE FACTORS AND LANGUAGE ISSUES.

3098 TILMAN R.O.
BUREAUCRATIC TRANSITION IN MALAYA.
DURHAM: DUKE U PR, 1964, 175 PP., LC#64-20418.
TRACES TRANSITIONAL PROCESS OF BUREAUCRACY IN MALAYA FROM BEGINNING OF BRITISH COLONIALISM UNTIL CREATION OF FEDERATION OF MALAYSIA IN 1963. DEMONSTRATES PROCESS OF SYNTHESIS OF BRITISH SYSTEM AND SOUTHEAST ASIAN SOCIETY TO CREATE VERY EFFICIENT, LARGELY INDIGENOUS, BUREAUCRACY.

3099 TINDALE N.B., LINDSAY H.A.
ABORIGINAL AUSTRALIANS.
MELBOURNE: JACARANDA PRESS, 1963, 143 PP.
ANTHROPOLOGIST AND AUTHOR COLLABORATE IN COMPILING SIMPLIFIED SUMMARY OF WHAT IS NOW KNOWN ABOUT AUSTRALIAN ABORIGINES. TREATS HISTORY AND MIGRATIONS, DAILY LIFE, ART, LITERATURE, FAMILY RELATIONSHIPS, TOTEMS, AND LIFE CYCLE. ILLUSTRATED.

3100 TINGSTEN H.
POLITICAL BEHAVIOR.
LONDON: PS KING & SON, 1937, 231 PP.
STUDY OF VOTING TRENDS IN NORTHERN COUNTRIES WITH SPECIAL REGARD TO ATTITUDES OF WOMEN, DIFFERENT AGE, SOCIAL, AND OCCUPATIONAL GROUPS, AND POPULAR PARTICIPATION IN ELECTIONS IN GENERAL.

3101 TINGSTEN H.
THE PROBLEM OF DEMOCRACY.
TOTOWA: BEDMINSTER PR, 1965, 210 PP., LC#65-17629.
TRACES HISTORY OF DEMOCRACY AS SEEN IN THE OBJECTIFICATION OF PRINCIPLES IN SITUATIONS WHICH TESTED THEM. PAYS SPECIAL ATTENTION TO THE BALANCE BETWEEN CONSENSUS AND CONFLICT. DISCUSSES THE POSSIBILITY OF COMBINING DEMOCRACY AND SOCIALISM, AND WHAT MAKES FOR STABILITY AND VITALITY IN A DEMOCRACY, AND THE DIFFERENCES BETWEEN DICTATORSHIPS AND DEMOCRACY. ASSERTS THAT DEMOCRACY IS UNDER ATTACK.

3102 TINKER H.
INDIA AND PAKISTAN.
NEW YORK: FREDERICK PRAEGER, 1962, 228 PP., LC#62-17298.
POLITICAL ANALYSIS OF INDIA AND PAKISTAN EMPHASIZING IMPACT OF 19TH-CENTURY IDEAS OF REPRESENTATIVE GOVERNMENT AND 20TH-CENTURY IDEAS OF RIGHT OF ALL PEOPLE TO INDEPENDENCE. INCLUDES BRIEF ACCOUNT OF THE NATURE OF TRADITIONAL SOCIETY AND TRADITIONAL SYSTEMS OF AUTHORITY AND GOVERNMENT; DISCUSSES POLITICAL MOVEMENTS AND PARTIES, THE CASTE SYSTEM, CHECKS ON GOVERNMENT, AND FUTURE TRENDS.

3103 TINKER H.
"POLITICS IN SOUTHEAST ASIA."
POLIT. STUD., 12 (OCT. 64), 385-388.
SURVEY OF SOME BIBLIOGRAPHICAL RESOURCES AND PRESENTATION OF MAJOR THESES OF TEN DIFFERENT TEXTS. CONCLUDES THAT SAMPLE ILLUSTRATES KINDS OF PROBLEMS WHICH MUST BE TACKLED BY THE STUDENT SEEKING TO UNDERSTAND THE NATURE OF GOVERNMENT IN THE NEW STATES.

3104 TINKER H.
BALLOT BOX AND BAYONET - PEOPLE AND GOVERNMENT IN EMERGENT ASIAN COUNTRIES.
LONDON: OXFORD U PR, 1964, 126 PP., LC#64-5587.
RECONSIDERS COMMON OBSERVATION THAT DEMOCRACY HAS 'FAILED' IN ASIA. DENIES THAT ALL ATTRIBUTES OF DEMOCRACY ARE ESSENTIAL OR ADEQUATE IN ASIA. PRESENTS EVIDENCE OF EMERGENCE OF ORIGINAL POLITICAL IDEAS AND MOVEMENTS, THEREBY PROVIDING AN ALTERNATIVE TO THE CONVENTIONS OF WESTERN DEMOCRACY. APPROACH IS BROADLY HISTORICAL.

3105 TIRYAKIAN E.A.
"APARTHEID AND POLITICS IN SOUTH AFRICA."
J. POLIT., 23 (NOV. 60), 682-97.
FOCUSSES ON ELECTORAL CAMPAIGN IN SOUTH AFRICA IN APRIL-MAY 1948. SUGGESTS THAT ALL MAJOR POLITICAL DEVELOPMENTS SINCE CAN BE TRACED BACK TO THAT TIME. EFFECT ON NATIONAL ECONOMY NOTED.

3106 TISDALE H.
"THE PROCESS OF URBANIZATION" (BMR)
SOCIAL FORCES, 20 (MAR. 42), 311-316.
PROPOSES THAT URBANIZATION IS PROCESS OF POPULATION CONCENTRATION CAUSED BY UTILIZATION OF TECHNOLOGICAL DEVICES. PRODUCT OF CONCENTRATION, CITIES, GIVES SOCIETY CULTURAL CHARACTER. DIFFERENT PEOPLES AND TECHNOLOGIES CAN PRODUCE DIFFERENT CULTURES BUT PROCESS OF URBANIZATION IS ALWAYS THE SAME.

3107 TITIEV M.
THE SCIENCE OF MAN.
NEW YORK: HOLT RINEHART WINSTON, 1954, 668 PP., LC#63-13943.
SURVEY OF ANTHROPOLOGY ORGANIZED AROUND BIOLOGICAL ORIGIN OF MAN AND HUMAN CULTURE, HISTORY OF CULTURAL DEVELOPMENT, AND ANALYSIS OF CULTURAL AND BIOCULTURAL BEHAVIOR. INCLUDES DEVELOPMENT OF EARLY MAN FROM THE APE; COMPARISON OF CULTURES DATING FROM LOWER PALEOLITHIC TIMES; AND IMPORTANCE OF SOCIAL GROUPS, RELIGION, HEREDITY, NONVERBAL ARTS, GAMES, AND ECOLOGY IN DETERMINING CULTURAL PATTERNS.

3108 TIVEY L.
"THE POLITICAL CONSEQUENCES OF ECONOMIC PLANNING."
PARLIAMENTARY AFFAIRS, 20 (FALL 67), 297-314.
BELIEVES THAT POLITICAL VALUES IN ECONOMIC PLANNING HAVE BEEN NEGLECTED. MAIN PROBLEM LIES WITH FACT THAT GOVERNMENT HAS NEITHER CONTROL NOR PREROGATIVE OVER THE PRIME AGENTS OF

PRODUCTION. INTEREST GROUPS PLAY TOO GREAT A ROLE IN PLANNING. BELIEVES THAT PRIMACY OF TRADITIONAL POLITICAL PROCESS MUST BE MAINTAINED, AND THAT FINAL AUTHORITY ON ECONOMIC PLANNING MATTERS MUST REST WITH GOVERNMENT.

3109 TIVEY L.J.
NATIONALISATION IN BRITISH INDUSTRY.
LONDON: JONATHAN CAPE, 1966, 219 PP.
DESCRIBES DEVELOPMENT OF IDEAS ABOUT NATIONALIZATION IN BRITAIN, CIRCUMSTANCES IN WHICH NATIONALIZATION FIRST TOOK PLACE, PARLIAMENTARY PROCESS OF LEGISLATION, AND BASIC STRUCTURE OF PUBLIC CORPORATIONS AS THEY HAVE EMERGED. PICTURES NATIONALIZATION IN PRACTICE AND INDUSTRIAL RECORD OF CORPORATIONS. EXAMINES PROBLEMS OF INTERNAL ORGANIZATION, EXTERNAL RELATIONS, AND CONTROVERSIES OVER NATIONALIZATION.

3110 TODD W.B.
A BIBLIOGRAPHY OF EDMUND BURKE.
LONDON: RUPERT HART-DAVIS, 1964, 312 PP.
AN ANNOTATED BIBLIOGRAPHY ON THE WRITINGS OF EDMUND BURKE WITH MOST ATTENTION GIVEN TO THE SEPARATE EDITIONS AND SELECTIONS OF HIS WORK. ABOUT 800 ENTRIES. MATERIAL IS IN ENGLISH LANGUAGE AND SOME FRENCH.

3111 TOMASIC D.
"POLITICAL LEADERSHIP IN CONTEMPORARY POLAND."
J. HUM. RELAT., 9 (NO.2, 61), 191-206.
ATTEMPTS TO SHOW WHICH CONDITIONS, CIRCUMSTANCES AND SOCIAL FORCES HAVE RESISTED SOVIETIZATION AND WHICH HAVE PROMOTED IT IN CONTEMPORARY POLAND. ANALYZES BACKGROUNDS OF POLISH LEADERS WITH RESPECT TO THEIR LIFE-LONG AFFILIATIONS WITH COMMUNISM. APPRAISES INFLUENCE OF CHURCH, PARTY POWER AND ORGANIZATION, GEOGRAPHIC HISTORY, AND CULTURE.

3112 TOMASIC D.A.
NATIONAL COMMUNISM AND SOVIET STRATEGY.
WASHINGTON: PUBLIC AFFAIRS PRESS, 1957, 225 PP., LC#57-6901.
CONCERNED WITH TITOISM IN TERMS OF SOVIET STRATEGY. GIVES ORIGINS AND DEVELOPMENTS OF TITOISM, AND DESCRIBES ITS FORMS AS THEY HAVE DEVELOPED IN OTHER STATES. DISCUSSES YUGOSLAVIA'S CIVIL WAR, BRITISH-RUSSIAN RIVALRY IN EASTERN EUROPE, AND COMMUNIST WORLD CONSPIRACY. EMPHASIZES THE SIGNIFICANCE OF TITO'S INDEPENDENT ROAD TO COMMUNISM.

3113 TOMPKINS S.R.
THE TRIUMPH OF BOLSHEVISM: REVOLUTION OR REACTION?
NORMAN: U OF OKLAHOMA PR, 1967, 331 PP., LC#66-22714.
ARGUES CONTINUITY OF METHODS AND SPIRIT BETWEEN TSARIST AND COMMUNIST RUSSIA. BOTH EMPLOYED REPRESSION OF FOES, GOVERNMENT BY INTRIGUE, DISTORTION OF ORDINARY MEANING OF WORDS, AND SIMULTANEOUS DESIRE FOR PEACE AND WAR. COVERS DOMESTIC AND INTERNATIONAL POLICY FROM BEFORE 1920 TO POST WWII. SEES BOLSHEVIK REVOLUTION AS CHARACTERISTIC RUSSIAN EFFORT TO PREVENT FUTURE ILLS, NOT CURE PRESENT ONES.

3114 TONNIES F.
KRITIK DER OFFENTLICHEN MEINUNG.
BERLIN: JULIUS SPRINGER, 1922, 583 PP.
SOCIOLOGICAL STUDY OF NATURE AND IMPORTANCE OF PUBLIC OPINION. DISCUSSES VARIOUS EXPRESSIONS OF PUBLIC OPINION IN THE POLITICAL, LEGAL, AND MORAL WORLD. INCLUDES STUDY OF PUBLIC OPINION IN US, ENGLAND, AND FRANCE.

3115 TONNIES F.
FUNDAMENTAL CONCEPTS OF SOCIOLOGY (1887) (TRANS. BY C. LOOMIS)
NEW YORK: AMERICAN BOOK, 1940, 293 PP.
SETS UP BASIC DICHOTOMY IN SOCIETY OF IDEAL TYPES OF GEMEINSCHAFT AND GESELLSCHAFT. FIRST TYPE OF RELATIONSHIP REFERS TO FAMILY AND PRIMARY SOCIAL GROUPS. GESELLSCHAFT IS NAME FOR RATIONAL ASSOCIATIONS SUCH AS BUSINESS AND GOVERNMENT. PROVIDES BASIS FOR COMPARISON OF LARGE GROUPS BY COMPARING THESE ASPECTS. DISCUSSES THESE AS SOURCES OF SOCIAL CONTROL AND ROOTS OF FORMAL SANCTIONS.

3116 TORMIN W.
GESCHICHTE DER DEUTSCHEN PARTEIEN SEIT 1848.
STUTTGART: KOHLHAMMER VERLAG, 1966, 304 PP.
GENERAL HISTORY OF GERMAN POLITICAL PARTIES FROM 1848 TO 1965. EXAMINES IN DETAIL FUNCTION AND POWER OF PARTIES IN WEIMAR REPUBLIC AND CAUSES OF COLLAPSE IN 1930-33. CONCLUDES WITH DISCUSSION OF MAJOR PARTIES IN WEST GERMANY SINCE WWII.

3117 TOTOK W., WEITZEL R.
HANDBUCH DER BIBLIOGRAPHISCHEN NACHSCHLAGEWERKE.
FRANKFURT: V KLOSTERMANN, 1954, 258 PP.
BIBLIOGRAPHY OF GERMAN BIBLIOGRAPHIES IN GENERAL AND SPECIFIC SUBJECTS.

3118 TOUVAL S.
SOMALI NATIONALISM: INTERNATIONAL POLITICS AND THE DRIVE FOR UNITY IN THE HORN OF AFRICA.
CAMBRIDGE: HARVARD U. PR., 1963, 215 PP., $4.95.
THE FIRST SYSTEMATIC ACCOUNT OF THE DEVELOPMENT OF SOMALI NATIONALISM AND ITS FORMS IN THE SEVERAL SOMALI INHABITED COUNTRIES, TERRITORIES OF EAST AFRICA. CONFLICTING GOALS BETWEEN THE SOMALIS AND THEIR NEIGHBORS HAVE RESULTED IN CRITICAL BUT RESOLVABLE TENSIONS.

3119 TOUVAL S.
"THE SOMALI REPUBLIC."
CURR. HIST., 46 (MARCH 64), 156-162.
PROGRESS TOWARD ECONOMIC DEVELOPMENT AND IMPROVEMENT IN LIVING CONDITIONS EXPECTED TO CONTINUE. HOWEVER CONTINUED INTERNAL INSTABILITY PROMISES UNVARYING ATTENTION OF EAST, WEST AND OTHER INTERESTED PARTIES.

3120 TOUVAL S.
"AFRICA'S FRONTIERS* REACTIONS TO A COLONIAL LEGACY."
INTERNATIONAL AFFAIRS (UK), 42 (OCT. 66), 641-654.
COMPARES AFRICA'S BORDERS AND THEIR FOUNDING TO THOSE ELSEWHERE AND CHALLENGES THE ASSUMPTION THAT THEY ARE ARTIFICIAL AND WILL LEAD TO NATIONALIST REVOLUTIONS AND WARS. DISCUSSES AFRICAN CONFERENCES TREATING BORDER SANCTITY, AND SURVEYS POST-INDEPENDENCE BORDER DISPUTES. COMPARISON MADE TO LATIN AMERICAN DEVELOPMENT. CONCLUDES THAT CONFLICT IS POSSIBLE BUT IT WILL REFLECT POLITICS, NOT GEOGRAPHY.

3121 TOUVAL S.
"THE ORGANIZATION OF AFRICAN UNITY AND AFRICAN BORDERS."
INTL. ORGANIZATION, 21 (WINTER 67), 102-127.
THIS ARTICLE TRACES THE CRYSTALLIZATION OF THE DOCTRINE PROCLAIMED BY THE ORGANIZATION OF AFRICAN UNITY IN 1964 STATING THAT EXISTING BORDERS IN AFRICA SHOULD BE ACCEPTED RATHER THAN ABOLISHING BORDERS WHICH WERE FELT TO BE LEGACIES OF THE COLONIAL POWERS. THE PROBLEM OF BORDER DISPUTES HAS BEEN A PREDOMINANT CONCERN FOR THE OAU.

3122 TOWSTER J.
POLITICAL POWER IN THE USSR: 1917-1947.
NEW YORK: OXFORD U PR, 1948, 443 PP.
A STUDY OF THE DEVELOPMENT OF THEORY AND STRUCTURE OF THE SOVIET GOVERNMENT. TRACES THE EVOLUTION OF BASIC CONCEPTS OF STATE AND LAW, CONSTITUTION, CLASS, AND NATIONALITY. DESCRIBES THE STRUCTURAL ARRANGEMENTS OF POWER AND THE ROLE OF DIVERSE SOCIAL, POLITICAL, AND IDEOLOGICAL FORCES. ANALYZES PAST AND PROSPECTIVE TRENDS IN TERMS OF AUTHORITY AND LIBERTY, POLITICAL CONTROL, AND CAPACITY FOR CHANGE.

3123 TOYNBEE A.
THE REALIGNMENT OF EUROPE.
NEW YORK: OXFORD U. PR., 1955, 619 PP.
DEALS WITH SOCIO-POLITICAL TRENDS AND DEVELOPMENTS IN POST-WAR EUROPE. TRACES STEPS TOWARD ECONOMIC REHABILITATION EXPANSION OF SOVIET CONTROL, AND THE HECTIC RESURRECTION OF POLITICAL LIFE IN GREECE, ITALY AND WESTERN EUROPE.

3124 TOYNBEE A.
"BRITAIN AND THE ARABS: THE NEED FOR A NEW START."
INT. AFF., 40 (OCT. 64), 638-646.
CONCLUDES THAT BRITAIN'S 'HOLDING ON TO' ITS REMAINING ARAB EMPIRE IS NEITHER MORAL NOR REALISTIC AND EXPRESSES HOPE THAT DISENGAGEMENT WILL OCCUR QUICKLY AND QUIETLY.

3125 TOYNBEE A.J.
CIVILIZATION ON TRIAL.
NEW YORK: OXFORD U PR, 1948, 263 PP.
APPROACHES CIVILIZATIONS AS SMALLEST INTELLIGIBLE FIELDS OF HISTORICAL STUDY. EMPHASIS ON GRAECO-ROMAN, BYZANTINE, ISLAMIC, AND WEST EUROPEAN CIVILIZATIONS. FINDS A RISE AND DECLINE PATTERN, BUT CONSIDERS IT A HEALTHY BASE FOR THE GAMBLE OF CREATIVITY. FOR ATOMIC AGE URGES COOPERATIVE WORLD GOVERNMENT ON RELIGIOUS FOUNDATIONS. FEELS CIVILIZATIONS ARE SECOND TO RELIGIONS THEY PRODUCE, IN WHICH LIE FUTURE HOPES.

3126 TRAGER F.N. ED.
MARXISM IN SOUTHEAST ASIA.
STANFORD: U. PR., 1959, 381 PP., $7.50.
DISCUSSES NATURE OF MARXISM IN RELATION TO THE INDIGENOUS IDEOLOGIES AND CURRENT DOMESTIC AND INTERNATIONAL POLITICAL PROCESSES OF BURMA, THAILAND, VIET NAM, AND INDONESIA. ALSO ANALYZES THE HISTORICAL EVENTS WHICH AFFECTED THE SPREAD OF THE IDEOLOGY IN THE AREA, AS WELL AS THE PARTICULAR CHARACTER IT HAS ASSUMED IN EACH OF THESE COUNTRIES.

3127 TRAGER F.N.
ANNOTATED BIBLIOGRAPHY OF BURMA.
NEW HAVEN: HUMAN REL AREA FILES, 1956, 230 PP.
AN ANNOTATED BIBLIOGRAPHY OF BURMA. MATERIAL IN ENGLISH LANGUAGE AND SOME FRENCH, GERMAN, AND SPANISH; 1018 ENTRIES. PUBLICATION OF MATERIAL RANGES FROM 1821-1955.

3128 TREADGOLD D.W. ED.
SOVIET AND CHINESE COMMUNISM* SIMILARITIES AND DIFFERENCES.
SEATTLE: U OF WASHINGTON PR, 1967, 452 PP., LC#66-19575.
COLLECTION OF ESSAYS DISCUSSING IDEOLOGICAL, POLITICAL, ECONOMIC, AND SOCIAL ASPECTS OF SOVIET AND CHINESE SYSTEMS. SECTIONS ON PRE-COMMUNIST ERAS, TRANSFORMATION, LAW, SOCIAL CHANGE, INTERNATIONAL AFFAIRS. EXTENSIVE COMPARATIVE ESSAYS WRITTEN BY PYE, LIPSON, LOWENTHAL, ZAGORIA, ET AL.

3129 TREITSCHKE H.
POLITICS.
NEW YORK: MACMILLAN, 1916, 1049 PP.
TREATS THE NATURE AND SOCIAL FOUNDATIONS OF THE STATE. ANALYZES SOME VARIETIES OF POLITICAL CONSTITUTIONS. CONSIDERS STATE'S INFLUENCE UPON RULERS AND RULED. POINTS OUT GOVERNMENT FUNCTIONS IN RELATION TO INTERNATIONAL INTERCOURSE.

3130 TREUE W.
DEUTSCHE PARTEIPROGRAMME 1861-1961.
GOTTINGEN: MUSTERSCHMIDT VERLAG, 1961, 404 PP.
BRIEF HISTORY OF GERMAN POLITICAL PARTIES (1861-1961), WITH DOCUMENTS ON PARTY PROGRAMS AND IDEOLOGIES FROM FOUNDATION OF PROGRESSIVE PARTY IN 1861 TO INDEPENDENT VOTER SOCIETY (UWG) IN 1960.

3131 TREVELYAN G.M.
THE TWO-PARTY SYSTEM IN ENGLISH POLITICAL HISTORY (PAMPHLET)
LONDON: OXFORD U PR, 1926, 27 PP.
LECTURE ON HISTORY OF TWO-PARTY SYSTEM IN ENGLISH POLITICS EXPLORES BOTH CONTINUITY OF PARTIES IN BRITISH HISTORY BEFORE PRESENT CENTURY, AND BASIS FOR WHIG AND TORY POWER THROUGH TWO CENTURIES.

3132 TRISKA J.F., FINLEY D.D.
"SOVIET-AMERICAN RELATIONS* A MULTIPLE SYMMETRY MODEL."
J. OF CONFLICT RESOLUTION, 9 (MAR. 65), 37-53.
DUPREEL'S STIMULUS-RESPONSE INTERACTION CONFLICT THEOREM FOUND NOT ONLY TO EXPLAIN COLD WAR ARMS RACE AND DETERRENCE, BUT ALSO OFFERED AS BASIS FOR SYMMETRY MODEL FOR DIPLOMATIC RESPONSES AND INVENTIONS BY BOTH SIDES IN COLD WAR. KEY IS COMPETITIVE-RECIPROCAL MISPERCEPTIONS OF OTHER'S POSITION PROMPTING GROSS RESPONSES IN "KIND AND DEGREE" AD INFINITUM.

3133 TSURUMI K.
ADULT SOCIALIZATION AND SOCIAL CHANGE: JAPAN BEFORE AND AFTER DEFEAT IN WORLD WAR II.
PRINCETON: PRIN U, DEPT OF POL, 1966, 561 PP.
EXPLORES POSSIBILITIES IN THEORY AND SUBSTANTIVE ANALYSIS THAT SOCIALIZATION IS NOT LIMITED TO CHILDHOOD BUT TAKES PLACE ALSO IN ADULTHOOD. EXAMINES TWO JAPANESE VALUE SYSTEMS (THAT BEFORE, AND THAT AFTER WWII) AND SOCIALIZATION IN BOTH. ANALYZES RELATIONSHIP BETWEEN SOCIAL CHANGE AND PERSONALITY CHANGE.

3134 TOTEMEYER G.
SOUTH AFRICA; SOUTHWEST AFRICA: A BIBLIOGRAPHY, 1945-1963.
FREIBURG: INST KULTURWISSENSCHAF, 1964, 284 PP.
FIRST ATTEMPT TO COMPILE SYSTEMATICALLY LITERATURE PUBISHED SINCE 1945. DESIGNED TO ILLUSTRATE PRESENT POSITION OF SOUTH AFRICA AND ENCOURAGE FURTHER STUDY IN FIELD. MATERIAL IS ORGANIZED TOPICALLY: POLITICS, SOCIAL SCIENCE, ANTHROPOLOGY, EDUCATION, NEWSPAPERS, PERIODICALS, ETC. PRINTED IN ENGLISH AND AFRIKANEER.

3135 TUCKER R.C.
"TOWARDS A COMPARATIVE POLITICS OF MOVEMENT-REGIMES" (BMR)"
AM. POL. SCI. REV., 55 (JUNE 61), 281-297.
CONSIDERS NEW APPROACH TO THEORETICAL STUDY OF SOVIET POLITICAL HISTORY AND INSTITUTIONS. SUGGESTS PROBLEM SHOULD BE STUDIED AS PHENOMENON OF METAMORPHOSIS OF MOVEMENT-REGIMES. ANALYZES POLITICS IN USSR, SHOWING CONTINUITY OF BOLSHEVIK MOVEMENT-REGIME, 1917-53. STATES THAT RISE OF STALINISM WAS METAMORPHOSIS OF ORIGINAL BOLSHEVIK MOVEMENT-REGIME INTO A NEW MOVEMENT-REGIME OF THE FUHRER TYPE.

3136 TUCKER R.C.
THE SOVIET POLITICAL MIND.
NEW YORK: PRAEGER, 1963, 238 PP.
EXPLORES PATTERNS OF THOUGHT, WAYS OF PERCEIVING THE WORLD, PSYCHOLOGICAL ATTITUDES, IDEOLOGICAL PREMISES AND WORKING THEORIES. DISTINGUISHES RELATIONSHIP BETWEEN IDEOLOGY AND POLICY UNDER SOVIET-COMMUNIST SYSTEM. POINTS OUT DISCREPANCY BETWEEN POLITICAL OUTLOOKS OF STATE AND CITIZEN 'OFFICIAL RUSSIA AND POPULAR RUSSIA).

3137 TURKEVICH J.
"SOVIET SCIENCE APPRAISED."
FOREIGN AFFAIRS, 44 (APR. 66), 489-500.
COMPARISON OF STRENGTHS AND WEAKNESSES, ACHIEVEMENTS AND FAILURES OF AMERICAN AND SOVIET SCIENTIFIC ESTABLISHMENTS. DISCUSSES GENERAL MILITARY, PROPAGANDA, AND PEACEFUL EFFECTS OF SCIENTIFIC DISCOVERIES, THEN GIVES SCIENCE-BY-SCIENCE BREAKDOWN.

3138 TURNBULL C.M.
THE FOREST PEOPLE.
NEW YORK: SIMON AND SCHUSTER, 1961, 288 PP., LC#61-12850.
IN SEVERAL EXTENDED VISITS TO ITURI FOREST IN NORTHEAST CORNER OF WHAT WAS THE BELGIAN CONGO, AUTHOR BECAME INTIMATELY ACQUAINTED WITH ITS PYGMY INHABITANTS. THE BA MBUTI, OR FOREST PEOPLE, AS THEY CALL THEMSELVES, MOVE FROM CAMP TO CAMP, SURVIVING ON JUNGLE GAME. THEIR CUSTOMS, CLOTHING, RELIGIOUS RITUALS, FAMILY LIFE, AND RELATIONS WITH NEIGHBORING NEGRO TRIBES ARE ALL DESCRIBED.

3139 TURNBULL C.M.
THE LONELY AFRICAN.
NEW YORK: SIMON AND SCHUSTER, 1962, 251 PP., LC#62-9611.
ILLUSTRATES EFFECTS OF PERSONAL PROBLEMS OF TRANSITION ON THE RURAL AFRICAN TRIBESMAN. ANALYZES PROBLEMS OF CONFLICT AND LONELINESS WHICH ARISE WHEN CHANGING MODES OF LIFE AFFECT TRADITIONAL BELIEF, FAITH, AND VALUES. CONTRASTS DIFFERENT NATURES OF URBAN AND RURAL PROBLEMS BY OFFERING SPECIFIC REFERENCES TO URBAN COMMUNITIES IN JUXTAPOSITION TO BIOGRAPHIES FROM A SMALL VILLAGE TRIBE.

3140 TURNER A.C.
FREE SPEECH AND BROADCASTING.
OXFORD: BLACKWELL, 1948, 32 PP., LC#44-7540.
ANALYZES BASIC PRINCIPLES OF FREEDOM OF COMMUNICATION AND DESCRIBES FUNCTION OF BROADCASTING ORGANIZATIONS. INCLUDES COMPARISON OF US AND BRITISH FREEDOMS.

3141 TURNER M.C. ED.
LIBROS EN VENTA EN HISPANOAMERICA Y ESPANA.
NEW YORK: RR BOWKER, 1964, 1891 PP.
EXTENSIVE LIST OF SPANISH-LANGUAGE BOOKS IN PRINT. DIVIDED INTO AUTHOR AND SUBJECT INDEXES.

3142 TURNER R.H.
"SPONSORED AND CONTEST MOBILITY IN THE SCHOOL SYSTEM."
AMER. SOCIOLOGICAL REV., 25 (DEC. 60), 855-867.
EXAMINES DIFFERENCES BETWEEN AMERICAN AND ENGLISH SYSTEMS OF SOCIAL CONTROL AND EDUCATION WHICH REFLECT DIVERGENCE BETWEEN FOLK NORMS GOVERNING MODES OF UPWARD MOBILITY. DISCUSSES DIFFERENT VALUES PLACED UPON EDUCATION, THE CONTENT OF EDUCATION, EXAMINATION SYSTEMS, AND RELATION OF SOCIAL CLASS TO CLIQUE FORMATION.

3143 TUTSCH H.E.
FACETS OF ARAB NATIONALISM.
DETROIT: WAYNE STATE U PR, 1965, 157 PP., LC#65-12128.
FOCUSES ON INTELLECTUAL, SOCIAL, POLITICAL PROBLEMS THAT CAUSE UNREST. ASSERTS THAT THERE IS MORE THAN ONE NATIONALISM AMONG ARABS AND THAT ISRAEL DID NOT CREATE MAJOR PROBLEMS. RATHER, REGIONAL INSUFFICIENCY IN WESTERN TECHNOLOGY AND CONFLICTS OF DIVERSE ARAB NATIONALISMS ARE RESPONSIBLE.

3144 TYSKEVIC S.
DIE EINHEIT DER KIRCHE UND BYZANZ (TRANS. BY F.K. LIESNER)
WURZBURG: AUGUSTINUS VERLAG, 1962, 112 PP.
EXAMINES FORCES OF DISINTEGRATION IN CHRISTIAN CHURCH FROM ERA OF PERSECUTIONS TO FINAL SEPARATE EXISTENCE OF BYZANTINE CHURCH IN 11TH CENTURY. DISCUSSES FURTHER DISINTEGRATION OF CHRISTENDOM IN EASTERN EUROPE AFTER FINAL SPLIT IN 1054 A.D.

3145 TYSON G.
NEHRU: THE YEARS OF POWER.
NEW YORK: FREDERICK PRAEGER, 1966, 206 PP.
ATTEMPTS TO ASSESS NEHRU'S YEARS OF POWER. TRACES HIS RISE TO POWER, INDIA AS A NATION, MALTHUSIAN DEMANDS, FOREIGN POLICY, INTERNATIONAL RELATIONS, LANGUAGE QUESTION, AND ESTABLISHMENT OF DEMOCRACY.

3146 CAIRO: DAR AL-KUTUB AL-MISRIYAH
A BIBLIOGRAPHICAL LIST OF TUNISIA.
CAIRO: NATIONAL LIBRARY PRESS, 1961, 42 PP.
AN UNANNOTATED AND UNCLASSIFIED LIST OF BOOKS, PERIODICALS, AND PAMPHLETS IN WESTERN LANGUAGES HOUSED IN THE NATIONAL LIBRARY AT CAIRO. PROVIDES COMPLETE BIBLIOGRAPHICAL DATA ON 19TH-AND 20TH-CENTURY PUBLICATIONS PLUS THE EGYPTIAN NATIONAL LIBRARY CALL NUMBERS. INCLUDES TITLE INDEX AND SEPARATE DIVISIONS FOR ENGLISH- AND ARABIC-LANGUAGE ENTRIES. SELECTIONS ARE OF HISTORICAL, POLITICAL, OR RELIGIOUS VALUE.

3147 CAIRO: DAR AL-KUTUB AL-MISRIYAH
A BIBLIOGRAPHICAL LIST OF ARABIAN PENINSULA.
CAIRO: EGYPTIAN LIBRARY PRESS, 1963.
AN UNANNOTATED BILINGUAL BIBLIOGRAPHY OF BOOKS AND PERIODICALS HOUSED IN THE NATIONAL LIBRARY AT CAIRO. THE ENGLISH-ARAB BIBLIOGRAPHY IS UNCLASSIFIED BUT COMPREHENSIVE. COVERS 19TH-AND 20TH-CENTURY PUBLICATIONS IN WESTERN LANGUAGES WITH EMPHASIS ON CURRENT MATERIALS. ARRANGED BY SUBJECT, TITLE, AND GEOGRAPHIC AREA.

3148 ULAM A.
THE BOLSHEVIKS.
LONDON: MACMILLAN, 1965, 595 PP., LC#65-18463.
GIVES ACCOUNT OF FORMATION OF MODERN RUSSIAN STATE, SEEKING LEADERS WHO WERE MOST RESPONSIBLE FOR ITS SUCCESS AND GIVING BIOGRAPHIES OF THESE MEN. CONCENTRATES ON 1900-1924, THOUGH GIVING BACKGROUND TO 1820, FOCUSING ON LENIN AND THE GROUP FORMED AROUND HIM, THE BOLSHEVIKS. DESCRIBES HIS RELATIONSHIP TO THEM AND THEIR EFFECT UPON HIM.

3149 ULAM A.B.
TITOISM AND THE COMINFORM.

CAMBRIDGE: HARVARD U. PR., 1952, 243 PP.
ANALYZES YUGOSLAV COMMUNIST PARTY IN COMPARISON WITH OTHER COMMUNIST GOVERNMENTS. EVALUATES SOVIET-YUGOSLAV DISPUTE. DISCUSSES COMINFORM AND 'PEOPLE'S DEMOCRACIES'.

3150 ULAM A.B.
THE NEW FACE OF SOVIET TOTALITARIANISM.
CAMBRIDGE: HARVARD U. PR., 1963, 236 PP.
STALINISM DESCRIBED, ITS EFFECTIVENESS APPRAISED AND COMPARED TO SOVIET SYSTEM AS ALTERED UNDER KHRUSHCHEV. POSSIBLE FUTURE POLICIES OF RUSSIAN LEADERSHIP EXTRAPOLATED.

3151 ULC O.
"CLASS STRUGGLE AND SOCIALIST JUSTICE: THE CASE OF CZECHOSLOVAKIA."
AM. POL. SCI. REV., 61 (SEPT. 67), 727-743.
ATTEMPTS TO ASSESS DEGREE OF POLITICAL BIAS IN POST-1948 CZECHOSLOVAKIAN COURTS. EVALUATES CONFLICT THROUGH ANALYZING CLASS STRUCTURE. CONTENDS THAT COMMUNIST PARTY HAS NOT GIVEN UP DISCRIMINATORY CONCEPT OF CLASS JUSTICE WHICH SUBORDINATES LAW TO POLITICS. FINDS THAT ABSENCE OF LEGAL "DEFINITENESS" IS NECESSARY TO TOTALITARIAN FORM OF GOVERNMENT.

3152 ULLMAN W.
PRINCIPLES OF GOVERNMENT AND POLITICS IN THE MIDDLE AGES.
NEW YORK: BARNES AND NOBLE, 1961, 217 PP.
SURVEYS FORMS OF GOVERNMENT AND THEIR MANDATES, DIVIDING THEM INTO THREE MAJOR GROUPS: CHURCH, KING, AND PEOPLE. DISCUSSES ROLE OF PAPAL AUTHORITY IN SECULAR MATTERS, RELATIONSHIP OF CHURCH AND KING, NOTION OF SOVEREIGNTY AS IT WAS THEN UNDERSTOOD, FOUNDATIONS OF REGAL POWER, AND MAIN POLITICAL THEORIES. COMPARES ENGLISH AND FRENCH GOVERNMENTAL EVOLUTION.

3153 ULLMANN W.
A HISTORY OF POLITICAL THOUGHT: THE MIDDLE AGES.
BALTIMORE: PENGUIN BOOKS, 1965, 247 PP.
ANALYSIS OF PREVAILING THEORY OF GOVERNMENT IN MIDDLE AGES VIEWED AS AN EFFLUENCE OF THE DOMINATING RELIGIOUS IDEA ITSELF AND AN OFFSHOOT AND PRACTICAL APPLICATION OF THE DEDUCTIVE METHOD OF REASONING. EXAMINES HISTORY OF POLITICAL IDEAS AS A HISTORY OF CONFLICT BETWEEN THEOCRATIC THEORY OF GOVERNMENT AND THEORY OF COMMUNITY POWER. BIBLIOGRAPHY OF RECENT WORKS IN WESTERN LANGUAGES.

3154 UMENDRAS H.
LES SOCIETES FRANCAISES: BIBLIOGRAPHIES FRANCAISES DE SCIENCE SOCIALES (VOL. III)
PARIS: FDN NAT DES SCIENCES POL, 1962, 124 PP.
ANNOTATED BIBLIOGRAPHY OF 506 WORKS IN FRENCH ON THE ECONOMIC, SOCIAL, POLITICAL, AND RELIGIOUS CHARACTERISTICS OF FRENCH RURAL SOCIETY. SOURCES TAKEN FROM POST-1913 STUDIES, WITH EMPHASIS PLACED ON RECENT WORKS. ENTRIES ARE TOPICALLY ARRANGED AND INDEXED BY AUTHOR. SPECIAL APPENDIX OF BIBLIOGRAPHIES, PERIODICALS, ARCHIVES, AND ATLASES.

3155 UNITED NATIONS
SPACE ACTIVITIES AND RESOURCES: REVIEW OF UNITED NATION'S NATIONAL AND INTERNATIONAL PROGRAMS.
NEW YORK: UNITED NATIONS, 1965, 172 PP.
OVER-ALL VIEW OF DEVELOPMENTS IN USE OF SPACE FOR PEACE AND BENEFIT OF MAN. COVERS ACTIVITIES OF SPECIAL AGENCIES AND INTERNATIONAL GROUPS AIDING UN. GIVES BREAKDOWN OF SPACE ACTIVITIES IN 37 SEPARATE NATIONS. EXPLANATIONS AND EVALUATIONS BY SECRETARY-GENERAL.

3156 UN ECONOMIC AND SOCIAL COUNCIL
ANALYTICAL BIBLIOGRAPHY OF INTERNATIONAL MIGRATION STATISTICS, SELECTED COUNTRIES, 1925-1950.
NEW YORK: UNITED NATIONS, 1955, 195 PP.
ANALYTICAL BIBLIOGRAPHY FOR 24 SELECTED COUNTRIES CONTAINING A COMPREHENSIVE CROSS-INDEX OF SUBJECT MATTER AVAILABLE TO USERS OF INTERNATIONAL MIGRATION DATA FOR YEARS AND COUNTRIES COVERED. PART I PRESENTS LIST OF PRIMARY SOURCES CONTAINING STATISTICAL DATA. PART II SHOWS YEARS FOR WHICH DATA ARE AVAILABLE IN EACH SOURCE. PART III CONTAINS SOURCES OF DETAILED CLASSIFICATIONS.

3157 UN ECONOMIC AND SOCIAL COUNCIL
WORLD POPULATION PROSPECTS AS ASSESSED IN 1963.
NEW YORK: UNITED NATIONS, 1966, 149 PP.
PROJECTS PRESENT POPULATION GROWTH TO YEAR 2000 IN WORLD, SPECIFIC REGIONS, AND AREAS. INCLUDES INFORMATION ON DATA AND METHOD OF PROJECTION.

3158 UN ECONOMIC COMN ASIA & FAR E
ECONOMIC SURVEY OF ASIA AND THE FAR EAST, 1954.
BANGKOK: UN ECAFE, 1955, 223 PP.
SURVEYS RECENT ECONOMIC DEVELOPMENTS IN INDIVIDUAL ASIAN COUNTRIES AND IN REGION AS A WHOLE. GIVES STATISTICAL DATA ON PRODUCTION, MONEY AND PRICE MOVEMENTS, VALUE OF IMPORTS AND EXPORTS, AND MONETARY AND FINANCIAL INDICATORS IN EACH COUNTRY.

3159 UN SECRETARY GENERAL
PLANNING FOR ECONOMIC DEVELOPMENT.
NEW YORK: UNITED NATIONS, 1963, 156 PP.
REPORTS ON ECONOMIC PLANNING AND TECHNIQUES USED IN SEVERAL COUNTRIES. EXAMINES ORGANIZATION AND MANAGEMENT OF PLANS, AS WELL AS NATIONAL AND INTERNATIONAL POLICIES.

3160 UNECA LIBRARY
BOOKS ON AFRICA IN THE UNECA LIBRARY.
NEW YORK: UNITED NATIONS, 1962, 318 PP.
SELECTED LIST OF MONOGRAPHS CONCERNING ECONOMIC AND SOCIAL CONDITIONS OF AFRICA AND AFRICAN COUNTRIES. MAJORITY OF TITLES ARE GOVERNMENTAL PUBLICATIONS. TITLES ARE DIVIDED FIRST BY REGION, THEN BY GROUP OF COUNTRIES SPEAKING SAME LANGUAGE. CONTAINS AUTHOR, TITLE, AND SUBJECT INDEXES. INCLUDES 2,031 ENTRIES

3161 UNECA LIBRARY
NEW ACQUISITIONS IN THE UNECA LIBRARY.
NEW YORK: UNITED NATIONS, 1962.
PERIODICAL LISTING OF RECENT BOOKS, MONOGRAPHS, SERIAL PUBLICATIONS AND PERIODICALS COVERING CURRENT SOCIAL, ECONOMIC, CULTURAL, AND TECHNICAL PROBLEMS OF WORLD WITH SPECIAL ATTENTION TO AFRICA AND DEVELOPING NATIONS. FIRST PUBLISHED 1962. ITEMS, IN ALL LANGUAGES, ARRANGED BY SUBJECT.

3162 UNESCO
DOCUMENTATION IN THE SOCIAL SCIENCES.
PARIS: UNESCO, 1952.
CONSISTS OF FOUR INTERNATIONAL BIBLIOGRAPHIES INCLUDED IN THE UNESCO SERIES OF THE GENERAL PROGRAM FOR SOCIAL SCIENCE DOCUMENTATION. PURPOSE OF THIS PROGRAM IS "TO SUPPLY EACH SOCIAL SCIENCE DISCIPLINE WITH THE BASIC BIBLIOGRAPHICAL INSTRUMENTS ESSENTIAL TO IT." THE BIBLIOGRAPHIES ATTEMPT TO RECORD ALL PUBLICATIONS CONCERNED WITH EACH DISCIPLINE: ECONOMICS, POLITICAL SCIENCE, ANTHROPOLOGY, AND SOCIOLOGY.

3163 UNESCO
WORLD COMMUNICATIONS: PRESS, RADIO, TELEVISION, FILM (4TH ED.)
PARIS: UNESCO, 1964.
AN AUTHORITATIVE REFERENCE WORK FOR MASS COMMUNICATIONS STUDIES AND MASS MEDIA ENTERPRISES. ASSESSES INTERNATIONAL MASS COMMUNICATIONS FACILITIES AND THEIR EFFECTIVE USE IN ACCELERATING ECONOMIC AND SOCIAL PROGRESS. BASED ON INFORMATION CONTAINED IN GOVERNMENTAL COMMUNICATIONS, OFFICIAL PUBLICATIONS, AND TECHNICAL JOURNALS, PROVIDES A COUNTRY-BY-COUNTRY ANALYSIS OF TECHNICAL FACILITIES.

3164 UNESCO
"APARTHEID."
UNESCO COURIER, (MAR. 67), 4-34.
THIS ENTIRE ISSUE OF THE UNESCO COURIER IS DEVOTED TO APARTHEID IN SOUTH AFRICA. IT INCLUDES EXCERPTS FROM A UNESCO REPORT ON THE EFFECTS OF APARTHEID ON EDUCATION, SCIENCE, CULTURE, AND INFORMATION IN SOUTH AFRICA. IT ALSO DEALS WITH APARTHEID EFFECTS ON CULTURE IN ARTICLES WRITTEN BY A NUMBER OF NOTED SOUTH AFRICAN LITERARY FIGURES.

3165 UNESCO
PRINCIPLES AND PROBLEMS OF NATIONAL SCIENCE POLICIES.
NEW YORK: UNITED NATIONS, 1967, 99 PP.
REPORT OF MEETING OF COORDINATORS OF SCIENCE POLICY STUDIES OF UN. TWELVE NATIONS STATED THEIR GOVERNMENTS' POLICIES, PLANS FOR SCIENTIFIC RESEARCH, AND PROBLEMS. AIM IS TO DEFINE COMMON FEATURES OF SCIENTIFIC POLICY AND DETERMINE DATA NEEDED TO PREPARE SCIENTIFIC POLICIES FOR NATIONS AT DIFFERENT DEVELOPING STAGES.

3166 UNION OF SOUTH AFRICA
REPORT CONCERNING ADMINISTRATION OF SOUTH WEST AFRICA (6 VOLS.)
PRETORIA: U OF SOUTH AFRICA, 1937, 3000 PP.
YEARLY REPORTS, 1922-37, BY GOVERNMENT OF UNION OF SOUTH AFRICA TO COUNCIL OF LEAGUE OF NATIONS CONCERNING ADMINISTRATION OF SOUTH WEST AFRICA. COVERS TOPICS OF LEGISLATION, INTERNATIONAL RELATIONS, CONSTITUTION, COURT SYSTEM, PRISONS, ARMS AND POLICE, DEMOGRAPHY, FINANCE AND TAXES, INDUSTRY, AGRICULTURE, NATIVE AFFAIRS, HEALTH, TRADE, MISSIONS, AND ECONOMY.

3168 UNIVERSAL REFERENCE SYSTEM
COMPARATIVE GOVERNMENT AND CULTURES (VOLUME X)
PRINCETON* UNIV. REF. SYSTEM, 1967, 1200 PP.
COMPUTERIZED INFORMATION RETRIEVAL SYSTEM DESCRIBING SITUATIONS AND PRINCIPLES OF HUMAN BEHAVIOR EXISTING IN TWO OR MORE NATIONAL INSTITUTIONS AND CULTURAL SETTINGS. ABOUT 3000 ITEMS FROM ALL TYPES OF PUBLICATIONS IN ENGLISH AND EUROPEAN LANGUAGES ARE ANNOTATED AND INDEXED. TO BE PUBLISHED EARLY 1968. QUARTERLY GAZETTES BEGAN AUG., 1967. SOURCES PREDOMINANTLY 20TH CENTURY.

3169 UNIVERSITY OF CALIFORNIA
STATISTICAL ABSTRACT OF LATIN AMERICA.
LOS ANGELES: U CAL LAT AMER STUD, 1955.
ANNUAL OF STATISTICS ON LATIN AMERICA NATIONS AND TERRI-

TORIES LISTED BY SUBJECT WITH SOURCES. PUBLISHED ANNUALLY SINCE 1955.

3170 UNIVERSITY OF FLORIDA LIBRARY
DOORS TO LATIN AMERICA; RECENT BOOKS AND PAMPHLETS.
GAINESVILLE: INTERAMER BIBLIOG, 1954.
QUARTERLY INTER-AMERICAN BIBLIOGRAPHY FIRST PUBLISHED 1954. DEALS WITH SOCIAL SCIENCES AND THE HUMANITIES. ANNOTATES MATERIALS PUBLISHED IN US ON LATIN AMERICA.

3171 UNRUH J.M.
"SCIENTIFIC INPUTS TO LEGISLATIVE DECISION-MAKING (SUPPLEMENT)"
WESTERN POLIT. QUART., 17 (SEPT. 64), 53-60.
AUTHOR, A CALIFORNIA STATE LEGISLATOR, CRITIS THE FACT THAT MOST SCIENTISTS AND SCHOLARS DEVOTE THEIR TECHNICAL QUALITIES AND CREATIVE CAPABILITIES TO THE FEDERAL GOVERNMENT AND DO NOT PAY HEED TO THE NEEDS OF STATE GOVERNMENT. OUTLINES THE UNFORTUNATE CONSEQUENCES, PARTICULARLY IN STATE LEGISLATURES, AND REPORTS ON STEPS CURRENTLY BEING TAKEN IN CALIFORNIA TO FOSTER MORE PRODUCTIVE COOPERATION.

3172 UNSTEAD J.F.
A WORLD SURVEY FROM THE HUMAN ASPECT.
LONDON: U OF LONDON PRESS, 1949, 452 PP.
DISCUSSES RELATIONSHIP BETWEEN NATURAL GEOGRAPHY AND CULTURAL DEVELOPMENT. SUCH ITEMS AS MIGRATIONS, AGRICULTURE, POPULATION, ETC., DISCUSSED IN DETAIL. ALSO INCLUDES GENERAL STUDY OF THE "RHYTHM OF REGIONS." APPENDED ARE NUMEROUS MAPS AND DIAGRAMS.

3173 UPTON A.F.
FINLAND IN CRISIS 1940-1941.
ITHACA: CORNELL U PRESS, 1965, 318 PP.
ORIGINAL FINNISH SOURCES AND DOCUMENTS USED TO DESCRIBE THE WINTER WAR OF 1939-1941. EMPHASIS ON EXPLANATION OF HOW THE FINNS CAME TO PARTICIPATE IN THE GERMAN ATTACK ON THE SOVIET UNION IN 1941.

3174 URE P.N.
THE ORIGIN OF TYRANNY.
LONDON: CAMBRIDGE UNIV PRESS, 1922, 374 PP.
EXAMINES EARLY HISTORY OF ATHENS, SAMOS, EGYPT, LYDIA, ARGOS, CORINTH, ROME, AND OTHERS TO DETERMINE ORIGINS OF TYRANNY. CONCLUDES THAT ORIGINS OF TYRANTS' POWER WERE COMMERCIAL. MERCENARIES, MONETARY REFORMS AND INNOVATIONS, PUBLIC WORKS, LABOR LEGISLATION, COLONIAL POLICY, AND COMMERCIAL ALLIANCES WITH FOREIGN STATES WERE ALL CHARACTERISTIC OF GOVERNMENT OF EARLY TYRANTS.

3175 URQUIDI V.L.
THE CHALLENGE OF DEVELOPMENT IN LATIN AMERICA.
NEW YORK: FREDERICK PRAEGER, 1964, 209 PP., LC#64-16692.
EXAMINES OVER-ALL CONDITION AND PROSPECTS OF THE LATIN AMERICAN ECONOMY. SINGLES OUT SPECIFIC ECONOMIC ASPECTS SUCH AS TRADE TRENDS, MONETARY PROBLEMS, PRIMARY PRODUCTS PRICES, AND FOREIGN CAPITAL.

3176 US ATOMIC ENERGY COMMISSION
ATOMIC ENERGY IN THE SOVIET UNION: TRIP REPORT OF THE US ATOMIC ENERGY DELEGATION, MAY 1933.
WASHINGTON: US GOVERNMENT, 1963, 83 PP.
DETAILED DESCRIPTION OF ELEVEN-DAY TOUR OF 14 SITES, INCLUDING TEN LARGEST SCIENTIFIC INSTALLATIONS. US DELEGATION WAS TREATED MOST CORDIALLY, WITH ALL QUESTIONS ANSWERED FREELY. USSR PROGRAM WAS FOUND ESPECIALLY AMBITIOUS IN HIGH ENERGY ACCELERATORS, CONTROLLED THERMONUCLEAR REACTIONS, AND TRANSURANIUM RESEARCH, BUT HAD LITTLE BIOLOGICAL WORK. US-USSR TECHNIQUES COMPARED. GIVES TEXT OF EXCHANGE AGREEMENT.

3177 US CONGRESS JT ATOM ENRGY COMM
PEACEFUL USES OF ATOMIC ENERGY, HEARING.
WASHINGTON: US GOVERNMENT, 1962, 148 PP.
WITNESSES' STATEMENTS DESCRIBE SPECIFIC PEACEFUL USES OF ATOMIC POWER. PRINCIPAL EMPHASIS ON ANALYSIS OF EDUCATIONAL SYSTEM IN USSR INCLUDING STANDARDS, POLICIES, AND PUBLIC ATTITUDES. COMPARES US EDUCATION TO USSR AND GIVES RECOMMENDATIONS FOR IMPROVEMENTS. COMMENTS ON LACK OF QUALIFIED SCIENTISTS, ENGINEERS, AND TEACHERS; NOTES POSSIBLE SOLUTIONS TO PROBLEM . NOTES SOVIET SCHOOL EXAMINATIONS.

3178 US CONSULATE GENERAL HONG KONG
REVIEW OF THE HONG KONG CHINESE PRESS.
WASHINGTON: US GOVERNMENT.
TRANSLATIONS OF MAJOR ARTICLES IN HONG KONG NEWSPAPERS. QUARTERLY INDEX.

3179 US CONSULATE GENERAL HONG KONG
CURRENT BACKGROUND.
WASHINGTON: US GOVERNMENT.
FIRST PUBLISHED 1950. EACH ISSUE FOCUSES ON A PARTICULAR SUBJECT AND CONTAINS TRANSLATIONS FROM VARIOUS CHINESE COMMUNIST NEWSPAPERS AND PERIODICALS PERTAINING TO THAT SUBJECT. QUARTERLY INDEX.

3180 US CONSULATE GENERAL HONG KONG
EXTRACTS FROM CHINA MAINLAND MAGAZINES.
HONG KONG: US CONSULATE GENERAL.
FULL TRANSLATIONS OF ARTICLES APPEARING IN CHINESE COMMUNIST PERIODICALS. WEEKLY PUBLICATION SINCE 1955. EACH ISSUE CONTAINS ABOUT SIX TRANSLATED PIECES. ISSUES QUARTERLY CLASSIFIED INDEX.

3181 US CONSULATE GENERAL HONG KONG
SURVEY OF CHINA MAINLAND PRESS.
WASHINGTON: US GOVERNMENT.
FIRST PUBLISHED 1950, CONTAINS TRANSLATIONS AND SUMMARIES FROM NEW CHINA NEWS AGENCY AND MAJOR COMMUNIST NEWSPAPERS AND PERIODICALS. QUARTERLY INDEX.

3182 US CONSULATE GENERAL HONG KONG
US CONSULATE GENERAL, HONG KONG, PRESS SUMMARIES.
WASHINGTON: US GOVERNMENT.
AN EXTENSIVE PROGRAM TRANSLATING CHINESE COMMUNIST NEWSPAPERS AND PERIODICALS. FOUR SEPARATE SERIES PUBLICATIONS, EACH CONTAINING A QUARTERLY CLASSIFIED INDEX.

3183 US DEPARTMENT OF DEFENSE
US SECURITY ARMS CONTROL, AND DISARMAMENT 1961-1965 (PAMPHLET)
WASHINGTON: US GOVERNMENT, 1965, 140 PP.
CONTAINS 750 PAPERS DEALING WITH THE PROBLEMS OF ARMS CONTROL AND DISARMAMENT AND PUBLISHED FROM OCTOBER, 1961, TO JANUARY, 1965. MATERIALS ON POLICIES, STRATEGIES, CONCEPTS, NEGOTIATIONS, NUCLEAR WEAPONRY, AND SPACE AS THE NEW DIMENSION OF POLITICO-MILITARY CONFLICT ARE INCLUDED.

3184 US DEPARTMENT OF STATE
BIBLIOGRAPHY (PAMPHLETS)
WASHINGTON: DEPT OF STATE.
SERIES OF 75 BIBLIOGRAPHIES BETWEEN 1949 AND 1953 CONTAINING FROM EIGHT TO 127 PAGES ON TOPICS OF ECONOMIC, POLITICAL, AND SOCIAL INTEREST. EMPHASIS ON INTERNATIONAL ORGANIZATIONS, FOREIGN AID AND DEVELOPMENT, AND SUCH SPECIAL TOPICS AS PSYCHOLOGICAL WARFARE. LITTLE ANNOTATION AND MOST WORKS ORIGINATE AFTER 1920, AND INCLUDE PRIMARILY ARTICLES, BOOKS, AND GOVERNMENT DOCUMENTS. INDEX IN PAMPHLET 75.

3185 US DEPARTMENT OF STATE
SOVIET BIBLIOGRAPHY (PAMPHLET)
WASHINGTON: DEPT OF STATE, 1949.
SERIES OF SOME 110 SEPARATE BIBLIOGRAPHIES PUBLISHED FROM 1949 TO 1953, AVERAGING ABOUT 18 PAGES EACH, AND CONTAINING MORE THAN 10,000 ITEMS. PUBLISHED BIMONTHLY AND INCLUDES ONLY ENGLISH-LANGUAGE WORKS SELECTED FROM SCHOLARLY JOURNALS, SPEECHES, GOVERNMENT DOCUMENTS, AND BOOKS. ARRANGED TOPICALLY AND ANNOTATED. ALL MATERIALS ARE CURRENT TO DATE OF BIBLIOGRAPHY. SUBJECT INDEX.

3186 US DEPARTMENT OF STATE
DOCUMENTS ON GERMAN FOREIGN POLICY, 1918-1945 (13 VOLS.)
WASHINGTON: DEPT OF STATE, 1950.
A JOINT PUBLICATION FROM THE BRITISH FOREIGN OFFICE AND THE US DEPARTMENT OF STATE OF DOCUMENTS FROM CAPTURED ARCHIVES OF THE GERMAN FOREIGN MINISTRY AND THE REICH CHANCELLORY. LIMITED TO POST-1918 PAPERS IN ORDER TO ESTABLISH GERMAN FOREIGN POLICY PRECEDING AND DURING WWII. THIRTEEN VOLUMES COVER HITLER'S ASSUMPTION OF POWER IN 1933 TO THE GERMAN DECLARATION OF WAR FOLLOWING PEARL HARBOR.

3187 US DEPARTMENT OF STATE
RESEARCH ON EASTERN EUROPE (EXCLUDING USSR)
WASHINGTON: DEPT OF STATE, 1952.
LISTING OF COMPLETED AND IN PROGRESS RESEARCH PROJECTS REPORTED BY SCHOLARS TO EXTERNAL RESEARCH STAFF. PUBLISHED ERRATICALLY FROM 1952-58. PUBLISHED LARGELY TO INDICATE COMPLETION AND AVAILABILITY OF NEW RESEARCH. RESEARCH IS LISTED BY COUNTRY WITH WHICH IT IS CONCERNED. INCLUDES SOME PROJECTS BEGUN AS EARLY AS 1941 BUT BELIEVED NOT TO HAVE BEEN PUBLISHED. PUBLISHED IN 10 PARTS.

3188 US DEPARTMENT OF STATE
RESEARCH ON AFRICA (EXTERNAL RESEARCH LIST NO 5-25)
WASHINGTON: DEPT OF STATE, 1966, 55 PP.
LIST OF SOCIAL SCIENCE RESEARCH SUBMITTED BY PRIVATE US SCHOLARS AND RESEARCH CENTERS TO DEPT. OF STATE CURRENTLY IN PROGRESS OR COMPLETED BUT UNPUBLISHED FOR THE PERIOD AUGUST 1965 THROUGH FEBRUARY 1966. MAJORITY OF ENTRIES ANNOTATED ITEMS TREAT ASIA IN GENERAL AND THEN INDIVIDUAL COUNTRIES. PUBLISHED ANNUALLY SINCE 1965.

3189 US DEPARTMENT OF STATE
RESEARCH ON THE AMERICAN REPUBLICS (EXTERNAL RESEARCH LIST NO 6-25)
WASHINGTON: DEPT OF STATE, 1966, 108 PP.
LIST OF SOCIAL SCIENCE RESEARCH SUBMITTED BY PRIVATE US SCHOLARS AND RESEARCH CENTERS TO DEPT. OF STATE ON LATIN AND SOUTH AMERICA CURRENTLY IN PROGRESS OR COMPLETED DURING AUGUST 1965 THROUGH FEBRUARY 1966 BUT UNPUBLISHED AS OF LATTER DATE. MAJORITY OF ENTRIES ANNOTATED. TREATS AREA IN GENERAL, THEN DIVIDED INTO CARIBBEAN, MIDDLE AMERICA, AND SOUTH AMERICA. PUBLISHED ANNUALLY SINCE 1965.

3190 US DEPARTMENT OF STATE
RESEARCH ON THE MIDDLE EAST (EXTERNAL RESEARCH LIST NO 4-25)
WASHINGTON: DEPT OF STATE, 1966, 28 PP.
LIST OF SOCIAL SCIENCE RESEARCH SUBMITTED BY PRIVATE US SCHOLARS AND RESEARCH CENTERS TO DEPT OF STATE ON MIDDLE EAST CURRENTLY "IN PROGRESS" OR "COMPLETED" DURING AUGUST 1965-FEBRUARY 1966 BUT UNPUBLISHED AS OF LATTER DATE. MAJORITY OF ENTRIES ANNOTATED. TREATS MIDDLE EAST AS WHOLE, THEN INDIVIDUAL COUNTRIES. PUBLISHED ANNUALLY SINCE 1965.

3191 US DEPARTMENT OF STATE
RESEARCH ON THE USSR AND EASTERN EUROPE (EXTERNAL RESEARCH LIST NO 1-25)
WASHINGTON: DEPT OF STATE, 1966, 63 PP.
LIST OF SOCIAL SCIENCE RESEARCH SUBMITTED BY PRIVATE US SCHOLARS AND RESEARCH CENTERS TO DEPT OF STATE ON COMMUNIST COUNTRIES OF EASTERN EUROPE CURRENTLY "IN PROGRESS" OR "COMPLETED" BUT UNPUBLISHED AS OF LATTER DATE FOR PERIOD AUGUST 1965 THROUGH FEBRUARY 1966. MAJORITY OF ENTRIES ANNOTATED. ANNUAL PUBLICATION SINCE 1965.

3192 US DEPARTMENT OF STATE
RESEARCH ON WESTERN EUROPE, GREAT BRITAIN, AND CANADA (EXTERNAL RESEARCH LIST NO 3-25)
WASHINGTON: DEPT OF STATE, 1966, 120 PP.
SERIAL PUBLICATION OF DEPT OF STATE RECORDING SOCIAL SCIENCE RESEARCH SUBMITTED BY SCHOLARS IN US FOR PERIOD AUGUST 1965 THROUGH FEBRUARY 1966. ENTRIES ARRANGED BY SUBJECT AND CLASSIFIED AS "IN PROGRESS" OR "COMPLETED." APPEARS ANNUALLY SINCE 1965. MAJORITY OF ENTRIES ANNOTATED.

3193 US DEPARTMENT OF THE ARMY
GUIDE TO JAPANESE MONOGRAPHS AND JAPANESE STUDIES ON MANCHURIA: 1945-1960.
WASHINGTON: DEPT OF THE ARMY, 1962, 182 PP.
SOME 210 WELL- ANNOTATED MONOGRAPHS WRITTEN AFTER WORLD WAR II AND EMPHASIZING MILITARY OPERATIONS IN THE PACIFIC AND MANCHURIA (PRIOR TO WWII). MONOGRAPHS ARE VARIOUSLY INDEXED BY OPERATIONAL LISTINGS, TOPIC, AND UNIT. ALL IN ENGLISH AND WRITTEN BY FORMER OFFICERS OF JAPANESE ARMY AND NAVY UPON DIRECTION OF US GOVERNMENT.

3194 US DEPARTMENT OF THE ARMY
COMMUNIST CHINA: A STRATEGIC SURVEY: A BIBLIOGRAPHY (PAMPHLET NO. 20-67)
WASHINGTON: DEPT OF THE ARMY, 1966, 143 PP.
BIBLIOGRAPHIC PROBE INTO THE ECONOMIC, SOCIOLOGICAL, MILITARY, AND POLITICAL MAKE-UP OF COMMUNIST CHINA. FOCUSES ON EMERGENCE AS STRATEGIC THREAT. ABSTRACTS FROM OVER 650 PERIODICAL ARTICLES, BOOKS, AND STUDIES IN ENGLISH. INCLUDES CHINA'S POLICY TO SOUTH ASIA AS A WHOLE AND TO INDIVIDUAL COUNTRIES. MAPS, CHARTS, AND DATA APPENDED.

3195 US DEPARTMENT OF THE ARMY
SOUTH ASIA: A STRATEGIC SURVEY (PAMPHLET NO. 550-3)
WASHINGTON: DEPT OF THE ARMY, 1966, 175 PP.
750 PERIODICAL ARTICLES, GOVERNMENT PUBLICATIONS, AND BOOKS PERTAINING TO MILITARY, POLITICAL, AND ECONOMIC FACETS OF SOUTH ASIAN COUNTRIES ARE ANNOTATED. ALL SOURCES CITED ARE ENGLISH-LANGUAGE PUBLICATIONS OF 1960'S THROUGH 1966. ENTRIES ARRANGED BY COUNTRY AND SUBJECT. INCLUDES SECTION OF GENERAL MATERIALS FOR RESEARCH AND REFERENCE.

3196 US HOUSE COMM BANKING-CURR
INTERNATIONAL DEVELOPMENT ASSOCIATION ACT AMENDMENT.
WASHINGTON: GOVT PR OFFICE, 1964, 104 PP.
COMMITTEE REPORT ON ACT TO AMEND INTERNATIONAL ASSOCIATION ACT IN ORDER THAT US MAY BE AUTHORIZED TO PARTICIPATE IN INCREASE OF RESOURCES OF INTERNATIONAL DEVELOPMENT ASSOCIATION. STATEMENTS BY SENATORS HARVEY, PATMAN, RUESS, AND SECRETARY OF STATE RUSK.

3197 US HOUSE COMM FOREIGN AFFAIRS
REPORT OF THE SPECIAL STUDY MISSION TO AFRICA, SOUTH AND EAST OF THE SAHARA (PAMPHLET)
WASHINGTON: GOVT PR OFFICE, 1956, 151 PP.
SURVEY OF CONGRESSIONAL VISIT TO SOUTHERN AFRICA DESCRIBING CONDITIONS IN EACH COUNTRY OR TERRITORY. EXPLAINS MEDICAL PROBLEMS IN AFRICA AND FACILITIES AVAILABLE. DEALS WITH US POLICY, AID PROGRAMS, AND COLONIAL SITUATION.

3198 US HOUSE COMM SCI ASTRONAUT
GOVERNMENT, SCIENCE, AND INTERNATIONAL POLICY (PAMPHLET)
WASHINGTON: US GOVERNMENT, 1967, 81 PP.
SIX PAPERS, BY SCIENTISTS FROM VARIOUS NATIONS, PRESENTED TO PANEL ON SCIENCE AND TECHNOLOGY OF SCIENCE AND ASTRONAUTICS COMMITTEE. MOST DEAL PRIMARILY WITH BACKGROUND OF SCIENTIFIC RESEARCH, GOVERNMENT SCIENCE POLICIES, AND SCIENCE-INDUSTRY RELATION IN SPECIFIC COUNTRIES. SI LESS CONCERNED WITH SCIENCE AND FOREIGN AFFAIRS THAN TITLE INDICATES, BUT SOME ATTENTION IS GIVEN TO THIS SUBJECT.

3199 US LIBRARY OF CONGRESS
ACCESSIONS LIST - INDIA.
WASHINGTON: LIBRARY OF CONGRESS.
MONTHLY PUBLICATION SINCE 1962 LISTING BOOKS, SERIALS, MONOGRAPHS, AND GOVERNMENT DOCUMENTS WITH INDIAN IMPRINT. SOURCES PRIMARILY IN ASIAN LANGUAGES; SOME ENGLISH. MATERIALS ARRANGED BY LANGUAGE WITH AUTHOR INDEX. ANNUAL CUMULATIVE AUTHORS AND SERIALS INDEXES. TITLES TRANSLATED INTO ENGLISH.

3200 US LIBRARY OF CONGRESS
ACCESSIONS LIST -- ISRAEL.
WASHINGTON: LIBRARY OF CONGRESS.
MONTHLY LISTING, FIRST ISSUED 1964, OF BBOKS, SERIALS, GOVERNMENT DOCUMENTS, AND MONOGRAPHS PUBLISHED IN ISRAEL. MATERIALS IN HEBREW AND ENGLISH. ARRANGED BY AUTHOR AND SUBJECT. ANNUAL AUTOHOR AND SERIALS INDEXES.

3201 US LIBRARY OF CONGRESS
SOUTHERN ASIA ACCESSIONS LIST.
WASHINGTON: LIBRARY OF CONGRESS.
PERIODICAL PUBLISHED QUARTERLY THROUGH 1956 UNDER TITLE "SOUTHERN ASIA: PUBLICATIONS IN WESTERN LANGUAGES, A QUARTERLY ACCESSION LIST." FROM 1956 TO DECEMBER, 1960, PUBLISHED MONTHLY UNDER CURRENT TITLE AT WHICH TIME DISCONTINUED. EACH POST-1956 VOLUME ARRANGED BY COUNTRY AND SUBJECT (FOR WESTERN LANGUAGES) AND SIMILAR SEPARATE LISTING FOR EASTERN-LANGUAGE PUBLICATIONS. ITEMS CURRENT TO PUBLICATION OF LISTING.

3202 US LIBRARY OF CONGRESS
EAST EUROPEAN ACCESSIONS INDEX.
WASHINGTON: LIBRARY OF CONGRESS.
MONTHLY LIST OF PUBLICATIONS RECEIVED FROM IRON CURTAIN COUNTRIES. ENTRIES ARE ARRANGED MONTHLY BY COUNTRY AND GROUPED UNDER 17 SUBJECTS LISTED IN CONTENTS. ABOUT 15,000 ENTRIES ARE RECEIVED MONTHLY IN ALL EASTERN LANGUAGES PLUS ENGLISH.

3203 US LIBRARY OF CONGRESS
BRITISH MALAYA AND BRITISH NORTH BORNEO.
WASHINGTON: LIBRARY OF CONGRESS, 1943, 103 PP.
OVER 900 ENTRIES IN ALL TOPICS CONCERNED WITH THESE COUNTRIES' ECONOMIC AND TRADE CONDITIONS, AGRICULTURE, HISTORY, EDUCATION, LANGUAGE.

3204 US LIBRARY OF CONGRESS
RUSSIA: A CHECK LIST PRELIMINARY TO A BASIC BIBLIOGRAPHY OF MATERIALS IN THE RUSSIAN LANGUAGE.
WASHINGTON: LIBRARY OF CONGRESS, 1944, 99 PP.
SERIES PUBLISHED IN 1944-46 LISTING RUSSIAN-LANGUAGE MATERIALS ON "BELLES LETTRES"; FINE ARTS; LAWS AND INSTITUTIONS PRIOR TO 1918; FOLKLORE; LINGUISTICS, AND LITERARY FORMS; CHURCH AND EDUCATION PRIOR TO 1918; HISTORY, INCLUDING AUXILIARY SCIENCES, PRIOR TO 1918; REFERENCE BOOKS; AND THE SOVIET UNION.

3205 US LIBRARY OF CONGRESS
NETHERLANDS EAST INDIES.
WASHINGTON: LIBRARY OF CONGRESS, 1945, 200 PP.
ANNOTATED LISTING OF APPROXIMATELY 1,500 BOOKS PUBLISHED AFTER 1930 AND PERIODICALS AFTER 1932 IN DUTCH AND ENGLISH PERTINENT TO THE NETHERLANDS EAST INDIES. INCLUDES GEOGRAPHY, GOVERNMENT, ECONOMICS, LANGUAGES, SOCIAL CONDITIONS, CULTURE, HISTORY, LAW, EDUCATION, AND HEALTH PROBLEMS.

3206 US LIBRARY OF CONGRESS
BRAZIL: A GUIDE TO THE OFFICIAL PUBLICATIONS OF BRAZIL.
WASHINGTON: LIBRARY OF CONGRESS, 1948, 224 PP.
BIBLIOGRAPHY OF MATERIALS IN LIBRARY OF CONGRESS PUBLISHED BY BRAZILIAN GOVERNMENT IN 19TH AND 20TH CENTURIES; ALL IN SPANISH AND PORTUGUESE, ARRANGED ACCORDING TO BRANCH OF GOVERNMENT: EXECUTIVE, LEGISLATIVE, JUDICIAL; APPROXIMATELY 2,000 ITEMS.

3207 US LIBRARY OF CONGRESS
EAST EUROPEAN ACCESSIONS LIST (VOL. I)
WASHINGTON: LIBRARY OF CONGRESS, 1951, 1500 PP., LC#51-60032
RECORD OF EASTERN EUROPEAN MONOGRAPHS AND PERIODICALS SINCE 1939 IN ENGLISH AND LANGUAGE OF ORIGINAL COUNTRY; ARRANGED BY COUNTRY AND DIVIDED INTO PERIODICALS AND MONOGRAPHS WHICH ARE FURTHER DIVIDED INTO SUBJECTS.

3208 US LIBRARY OF CONGRESS
INTRODUCTION TO AFRICA; A SELECTIVE GUIDE TO BACKGROUND READING.
WASHINGTON: UNIVERSITY PR WASH, 1952, 237 PP., LC#52-60007.
AN ANNOTATED BIBLIOGRAPHY OF CLOSE TO 700 BOOKS, ARTICLES AND REVIEWS CONCERNING AFRICA. CLASSIFICATION OF ENTRIES IS SYSTEMATIC BY REGION, WITH GENERAL SURVEYS, HISTORICAL MATERIAL, AND WRITING ON CONTEMPORARY ISSUES AND NATIVE CULTURES PRESENTED FOR EACH COUNTRY. SPECIAL SECTIONS GIVEN TO TOPICS SUCH AS RACE PROBLEMS. SOURCES IN ENGLISH, FRENCH, SPANISH, PORTUGUESE, AND ITALIAN.

3209 US LIBRARY OF CONGRESS
EGYPT AND THE ANGLO-EGYPTIAN SUDAN: A SELECTIVE GUIDE TO BACKGROUND READING (PAMPHLET)
WASHINGTON: UNIVERSITY PR WASH, 1952, 27 PP., LC#52-60008.
LIST OF BASIC WORKS WITH LENGTHY ANNOTATIONS. ARRANGED UNDER GENERAL, HISTORICAL, AND CONTEMPORARY ISSUES.

3210 US LIBRARY OF CONGRESS
RESEARCH AND INFORMATION ON AFRICA: CONTINUING SOURCES.
WASHINGTON: LIBRARY OF CONGRESS, 1954, 70 PP., LC#54-60024.
ANNOTATED LIST OF 519 PERIODICALS, SERIALS, AND OTHER REGULARLY APPEARING PUBLICATIONS DEALING WITH, OR EMANATING FROM, AFRICA. ARRANGED BY COUNTRY WHERE THE ITEM IS PUBLISHED. PERIODICALS IN ALL EUROPEAN LANGUAGES. INDEXED BY TITLE OF PUBLICATION AND BY INSTITUTION.

3211 US LIBRARY OF CONGRESS
INDEX TO LATIN AMERICAN LEGISLATION: 1950-1960 (2 VOLS.)
WASHINGTON: LIBRARY OF CONGRESS, 1960, 1474 PP.
COMPREHENSIVE AND TOPICALLY ARRANGED INDEX TO IMPORTANT AND RELEVANT LEGISLATION ENACTED BY LATIN AMERICAN GOVERNMENTS; INDEXES 30,000 ITEMS. INCLUDES "MATTERS OF GENERAL INTEREST, BASIC CODES, AND ORGANIC LAWS WITH THEIR AMENDMENTS"; EXCLUDES PRIVATE LEGISLATION, CONFERRING OF HONORS, APPOINTMENTS, DISMISSALS, ETC.

3212 US LIBRARY OF CONGRESS
A LIST OF AMERICAN DOCTORAL DISSERTATIONS ON AFRICA.
WASHINGTON: LIBRARY OF CONGRESS, 1962, 69 PP., LC#62-60088.
700 THESES, ON SUBJECTS RELATING TO AFRICA, WHICH HAVE BEEN ACCEPTED BY US AND CANADIAN UNIVERSITIES FROM LATE 19TH CENTURY TO 1961. ARRANGED ALPHABETICALLY BY AUTHOR.

3213 US LIBRARY OF CONGRESS
SOUTHEAST ASIA.
WASHINGTON: LIBRARY OF CONGRESS, 1964, 180 PP., LC#63-60089.
AN UPDATED VERSION OF 1952 LIBRARY OF CONGRESS PUBLICATION "SOUTHEAST ASIA: AN ANNOTATED BIBLIOGRAPHY OF SELECTED REFERENCE SOURCES." CONTAINS 535 ENTRIES, EACH WITH A CRITICAL APPRAISAL IN SUBSTANTIVE LANGUAGE OF THE TEXT, BIBLIOGRAPHY, MAPS, ILLUSTRATIONS, STATISTICAL TABLES, AND DOCUMENTS. COVERS HISTORY, GOVERNMENT, ECONOMICS, SOCIAL CONDITIONS, AND CULTURAL LIFE OF THE AREA.

3214 US LIBRARY OF CONGRESS
RARE BOOKS DIVISION: GUIDE TO ITS COLLECTION AND SERVICES.
WASHINGTON: LIBRARY OF CONGRESS, 1965, 51 PP., LC#64-60071.
DESCRIBES THE HOLDINGS IN ITS VARIOUS RARE BOOKS COLLECTIONS: JEFFERSON AND PETER FORCE LIBRARIES, THE VOLLBEHR COLLECTION OF INCUNABULA AND THE GUTENBERG BIBLE; COLLECTIONS OF EARLY AMERICAN IMPRINTS, WESTERN AMERICANA, CONFEDERATE STATES IMPRINTS, ETC. ALSO INDICATES PROCEDURES FOR UTILIZING THE FACILITIES OF VARIOUS COLLECTIONS AND EXHIBITS.

3215 US LIBRARY OF CONGRESS
NIGERIA: A GUIDE TO OFFICIAL PUBLICATIONS.
WASHINGTON: LIBRARY OF CONGRESS, 1966, 166 PP., LC#66-61703.
REVISION OF A SIMILAR GUIDE PUBLISHED IN 1959 WHICH COVERS PUBLICATIONS ISSUED BY NIGERIAN GOVERNMENTS FROM THE ESTABLISHMENT OF BRITISH ADMINISTRATION IN NIGERIA IN 1861 TO 1865. ALSO LISTS SELECTION OF DOCUMENTS RELEVANT TO NIGERIA AND THE BRITISH CAMEROONS ISSUED BY VARIOUS BRITISH GOVERNMENT OFFICES AND BY THE LEAGUE OF NATIONS AND UN.

3216 US SENATE SPEC COMM FOR AID
COMPILATION OF STUDIES AND SURVEYS.
WASHINGTON: GOVT PR OFFICE, 1957, 1581 PP.
PRESENTS RESULTS OF STUDIES AND SURVEYS OF US FOREIGN AID PROGRAM. DISCUSSES ROLE OF PRIVATE ORGANIZATIONS, AGRICULTURAL SURPLUS DISPOSAL, AID TECHNIQUES OF COMMUNIST BLOC, AND OPERATION OF US AID PROGRAMS IN ASIA, AFRICA, AND LATIN AMERICA.

3217 US SENATE SPEC COMM FOR AID
HEARINGS BEFORE THE SPECIAL COMMITTEE TO STUDY THE FOREIGN AID PROGRAM.
WASHINGTON: GOVT PR OFFICE, 1957, 745 PP.
STATEMENTS BY PUBLIC AND PRIVATE OFFICIALS ON US FOREIGN AID POLICIES AND OBJECTIVES. EXAMINES COSTS, NEED FOR SEPARATION OF MILITARY AND ECONOMIC AID, ATTITUDE OF US PEOPLE, SOVIET AID, ROLE OF INTERNATIONAL AGENCIES, COMPARISON OF SOVIET AND US AID TECHNIQUES, TECHNICAL ASSISTANCE PROGRAMS, RESPONSIBILITIES OF PRIVATE ENTERPRISE, ETC.

3218 UTECHIN S.V.
RUSSIAN POLITICAL THOUGHT: A CONCISE HISTORY.
NEW YORK: FREDERICK PRAEGER, 1964, 320 PP., LC#64-13492.
SURVEY OF IDEOLOGY INCLUDING MEDIEVAL, MUSCOVITE, AND PETRINE RUSSIA, WITH EMPHASIS ON OFFICIAL NATIONALITY, SLAVOPHILISM, REVOLUTIONARY ANTI-COMMUNISM, AND TERRORISM. BIBLIOGRAPHY OF APPROXIMATELY 480 ENGLISH, GERMAN, AND FRENCH BOOKS AND PERIODICALS FROM 1913 THROUGH 1963 IS ARRANGED ALPHABETICALLY BY AUTHOR UNDER CHAPTER HEADINGS.

3219 UYEHARA C.H. ED.
CHECKLIST OF ARCHIVES IN THE JAPANESE MINISTRY OF FOREIGN AFFAIRS.
WASHINGTON: LIBRARY OF CONGRESS, 1954, 262 PP., LC#53-60045.
AN ANNOTATED CHECKLIST OF 2,116 REELS OF MICROFILM CONTAINING REPRODUCTIONS OF OVER 2 MILLION PAGES OF ARCHIVES OF THE JAPANESE MINISTRY OF FOREIGN AFFAIRS, COVERING THE PERIOD 1868 TO 1945. INTRODUCTION DESCRIBES INCEPTION OF PROJECT, PROCESS OF MICROFILMING, AND METHOD EMPLOYED IN COMPILATION OF CHECKLIST. CHECKLIST CONSISTS OF TWO SECTIONS: ARCHIVES AND GENERAL ANALYTICAL INDEX. TRANSLITERATED.

3220 VALEN H., KATZ D.
POLITICAL PARTIES IN NORWAY.
OSLO: J CHR GUNDERSON, 1964, 383 PP.
EXAMINES POLITICAL PARTIES ON THE LOCAL LEVEL. ANALYZES THEIR STRUCTURE AND METHODS, AND DISCUSSES THE CHARACTER OF LOCAL LEADERS. THEN VIEWS NORWEGIAN POLITICS AT A GRASS ROOTS LEVEL. STATISTICS ARE BASED ON A 1957-58 ELECTION.

3221 VALERIANO N.D., BOHANNAN T.R.
COUNTER-GUERRILLA OPERATIONS: THE PHILLIPINE EXPERIENCE.
NEW YORK: PRAEGER, 1962, 275 PP., $5.95.
PRESENTS CASE STUDY OF CONTEMPORARY ANTI-GUERRILLA WARFARE USING PHILIPPINES AS AN EXAMPLE OF SUCCESSFUL USE OF MODERN TECHNIQUES IN SOUTHEAST ASIA.

3222 VALI F.A.
THE QUEST FOR A UNITED GERMANY.
BALTIMORE: JOHNS HOPKINS PRESS, 1967, 318 PP., LC#67-16914.
ANALYSIS OF PROBLEMS INVOLVED IN REUNIFICATION OF GERMANY. PRESENTS FACTS, PLUS VIEWS AND MOTIVATIONS OF GERMANS. DISCUSSES ISSUES FROM BOTH EAST AND WEST PERSPECTIVES.

3223 VALJAVEC F.
AUSGEWAHLTE AUFSATZE.
MUNICH: R OLDENBOURG, 1963, 418 PP.
DISCUSSES INTELLECTUAL AND CULTURAL DEVELOPMENT IN SOUTHEAST EUROPE (BALKAN COUNTRIES), WITH EMPHASIS ON INTERACTION BETWEEN DIVERGENT NATIONALITIES AND CULTURE GROUPS. EXAMINES RISE OF GERMAN NATIONAL CONSCIOUSNESS IN HUNGARY AND CONTRIBUTIONS OF GERMAN CULTURE IN BALKANS.

3224 VALLET R.
"IRAN: KEY TO THE MIDDLE EAST."
MIL. REV., 14 (NOV. 61), 54-61.
IRAN'S MEMBERSHIP IN CENTRAL TREATY ORGANIZATION, THE ALLIANCE WHICH REPLACED THE BAGHDAD PACT AFTER IRAQ'S DEFECTION, MIGHT BE IMPAIRED BECAUSE OF DEVELOPMENTS IN ECONOMIC AND POLITICAL FIELD. SITUATION EVALUATED IN LIGHT OF CONDITIONS IN NEIGHBORING COUNTRIES OF IRAQ, TURKEY, SAUDI ARABIA, KUWAIT AND LEBANON.

3225 VAN BILJON F.J.
STATE INTERFERENCE IN SOUTH AFRICA.
LONDON: PS KING & SON, 1939, 322 PP.
STUDY OF POLICIES OF SOUTH AFRICAN GOVERNMENT ON ECONOMY AND HOW PRIVATE BUSINESS FUNCTIONS UNDER COORDINATION OF SOUTH AFRICAN DOMESTIC AND INTERNATIONAL BUSINESS ACTIVITIES.

3226 VAN DEN BERG M.
"SOME METHODOLOGICAL ASPECTS OF SOUTH AFRICA'S FIRST E.D.P."
S. AFR. J. OF ECONOMICS, 33 (MAR. 65), 3-16.
DESCRIBES LOGIC OF REASONING FOLLOWED IN CALCULATING BASIC FIGURES OF OVER-ALL ECONOMIC GROWTH RATE IN ECONOMIC DEVELOPMENT PROGRAMS. DISCUSSES METHODOLOGY OF THE CALCULATIONS AND THE CONSTRUCTIVE ROLE PLAYED BY INCREMENTAL CAPITAL-OUTPUT RATIO. PROVIDES STATISTICAL TABLES EMPLOYED IN CALCULATING BASIC GROWTH RATES.

3227 VAN DEN BERGHE P.L.
SOUTH AFRICA: A STUDY IN CONFLICT.
MIDDLETON: WESLEYAN U PR, 1965, 371 PP., LC#65-14053.
DISCUSSES THE CONFLICT, PAST, PRESENT, AND FUTURE. SHOWS HOW THE BOER TRADITION OF BENEVOLENT PATERNALISTIC DESPOTISM HAS HARDENED INTO RUTHLESS RACIAL TYRANNY AND HOW RACE FACTORS AFFECT EVERY ASPECT OF NATIONAL LIFE.

3228 VAN DEN BERGHE P.L. ED.
AFRICA: SOCIAL PROBLEMS OF CHANGE AND CONFLICT.
SAN FRANCISCO: CHANDLER, 1965, 549 PP., LC#65-15417.
GENERAL READINGS ON AFRICAN CULTURE, SOCIETY, POLITICAL ASPECTS OF SOCIAL CHANGE, URBANIZATION, ECONOMIC DEVELOPMENTS, AND RACIAL CONFLICTS AS RESULT OF SOCIAL CHANGE.

3229 VAN DER KROEF J.M.
"INDONESIA: THE BATTLE OF THE 'OLD' AND THE 'NEW ORDER'."
AUSTRALIAN OUTLOOK, 21 (APR. 67), 18-43.
DESPITE STEPS BY THE SUHARTO REGIME TO ESTABLISH THE "NEW ORDER," PRO-SUKARNO AND PRO-COMMUNIST SYMPATHY IN INDONESIA MAY WELL BE SUFFICIENT TO BRING WIDESPREAD DISORDER IF SUKARNO, WHO BALANCED POWER CENTERS AGAINST EACH OTHER AND CREATED IDEOLOGICAL COMMON GROUND, IS REMOVED.

3230 VAN GULIK R.H.
SEXUAL LIFE IN ANCIENT CHINA.
LEYDEN: BRILL, 1961, 392 PP.
OUTLINE OF SEXUAL CUSTOMS IN CHINA FROM FEUDAL ERA OF 1500-771 B.C. THROUGH MING DYNASTY OF 1368-1644 A.D., WITH PURPOSE OF SERVING AS REFERENCE BOOK FOR FURTHER RESEARCH.

3231 VAN RENSBURG P.
GUILTY LAND: THE HISTORY OF APARTHEID.
NEW YORK: FREDERICK PRAEGER, 1962, 224 PP., LC#62-9588.
AN ANTI-APARTHEID SOUTH AFRICAN DISCUSSES NATION'S RACIAL POLICIES. ANALYZES MAJOR SOCIAL, ECONOMIC, AND POLITICAL FORCES THAT DOMINATE SOUTH AFRICA. SHOWS THAT AFRIKANER NATIONALISM MAY HAVE PROVIDED PATTERN FOR AFRICAN NATIONALISM. HOPES COLOR REVOLUTION WILL COME SOON AND DESTROY EVILS OF WHITE DOMINATION.

3232 VAN VALKENBURG S.
"ELEMENTS OF POLITICAL GEOGRAPHY."
ENGLEWOOD CLIFFS: PRENTICE HALL, 1944.
TREATS ELEMENTS THROUGH MODERN REGIONAL EXAMPLES. CONTAINS GENERAL DISCUSSION OF PROBLEMS OF POLITICAL GEOGRAPHY. "LEITMOTIV" OF WORK IS THEORY OF CYCLE TREND IN THE DEVELOPMENT OF NATIONS. EXAMINES PHYSICAL, ECONOMIC, AND HUMAN FACTORS IN POLITICAL-GEOGRAPHICAL EVALUATION OF STATE WITH SPECIAL REFERENCE TO FRANCE. TREATS SUBJECT OF COLONIAL EXPANSION IN CONCLUSION. INCLUDES ENGLISH BIBLIOGRAPHY.

3233 VANDENBOSCH A.
"POWER BALANCE IN INDONESIA."
CURR. HIST., 46 (FEB. 64), 95-100.
ALTHOUGH SUKARNO AVOWEDLY NEUTRAL, HIS STRONG ANTI-CAPITALIST SENTIMENTS AND SUPPORT WHICH USSR GAVE INDONESIA IN ITS STRUGGLE FOR CONTROL OF WEST IRIAN, ARE UNDOUBTEDLY FACTORS WHICH TEND TO INCLINE HIS NEUTRALISM IN FAVOR OF COMMUNIST BLOC.

3234 VARG P.A.
MISSIONARIES, CHINESE, AND DIPLOMATS: THE AMERICAN PROTESTANT MISSIONARY MOVEMENT IN CHINA, 1890-1952.
PRINCETON: PRINCETON U PRESS, 1958, 335 PP., LC#58-7134.
SEES HISTORY OF PROTESTANT MISSIONS IN CHINA AS A PROBLEM IN RELATIONSHIP BETWEEN TWO BASICALLY DIFFERENT CULTURES: WEST AND EAST. INTEREST CENTERS ON DIFFICULTIES IN ATTEMPTING TO EXPORT THE AMERICAN IDEOLOGIES OF CHRISTIANITY, DEMOCRACY, OR CAPITALISM. SHEDS LIGHT ON CONTEMPORARY PROPAGANDA PROBLEMS.

3235 VATCHER W.H. JR.
WHITE LAAGER: THE RISE OF AFRIKANER NATIONALISM.
NEW YORK: FREDERICK PRAEGER, 1965, 309 PP.
EXAMINES FORCES THAT HAVE CONTRIBUTED TO DEVELOPMENT OF AFRIKANER NATIONALISM AND AFFECTED ITS DIRECTION. FIRST PART OF WORK IS HISTORICAL, DEPENDING HEAVILY ON SECONDARY SOURCES. REMAINING MATERIAL IS DRAWN FROM DIRECT STUDIES OF SOUTH AFRICA IN 1955-56 AND 1960-61.

3236 VEBLEN T.
IMPERIAL GERMANY AND THE INDUSTRIAL REVOLUTION.
NEW YORK: VIKING PRESS, 1915, 343 PP.
DESCRIBES RAPID STRIDES IN MACHINE TECHNOLOGY MADE BY DYNASTIC GERMANY. CONTRASTS ITS EMERGENT SYSTEM WITH THAT OF ENGLAND. POINTS TO FUTURE OF DYNASTIC STATES AND WESTERN DEMOCRACIES.

3237 VEBLEN T.
AN INQUIRY INTO THE NATURE OF PEACE AND THE TERMS OF ITS PERPETUATION.
NEW YORK: MACMILLAN, 1917, 367 PP.
CONCERNS TERMS UPON WHICH PEACE CAN BE INSTITUTED AND PERPETUATED, CONDITIONS IN WORLD SITUATION WHICH WOULD MAKE PEACE POSSIBLE, AND EFFECTS OF ESTABLISHING PEACE. BELIEVES PEACE WILL BE OBTAINED IN SPITE OF THE STATE, RATHER THAN THROUGH IT. APPEALS TO PATRIOTISM HAVE BEEN USED TO DETRIMENT OF ESTABLISHING PEACE. SUGGESTS NEUTRALIZATION OF CITIZENSHIP AND ABOLITION OF FINANCIAL COMPETITION.

3238 VECCHIO G.D.
L'ETAT ET LE DROIT.
PARIS: DALLOZ, 1964, 184 PP.
DISCUSSES BASIC ELEMENTS OF STATE (TERRITORY, PEOPLE, SOVEREIGNTY), HISTORICAL EVOLUTION, EXECUTIVE, LEGISLATIVE, AND JUDICIAL FUNCTIONS, INTERNATIONAL LEGAL COMMUNITY WITH PARTICULAR REFERENCE TO UN, AND CONCLUDES WITH DISCUSSION OF AIM OF STATE. INCLUDES BRIEF ANALYSIS OF FUNCTION OF ITALIAN LEGISLATURE UNDER CONSTITUTION.

3239 VEIT O.
GRUNDRISS DER WAHRUNGSPOLITIK.
FRANKFURT: FRITZ KNAPP VERLAG, 1961, 844 PP.
EXAMINES CENTRAL CONCEPTS OF POLITICS OF CURRENCY STANDARDS. DISCUSSES FOREIGN EXCHANGE, CREDIT, GOLD AND SILVER STANDARDS, AND MONEY ECONOMY IN GERMANY SINCE 1857. ANALYZES POLICIES OF OTHER EUROPEAN COUNTRIES, USSR, AND US.

3240 VENABLE V.
HUMAN NATURE: THE MARXIAN VIEW.
NEW YORK: ALFRED KNOPF, 1945, 217 PP.
SYSTEMATIC ANALYSIS OF WHAT MARX AND ENGELS ACTUALLY THOUGHT ABOUT MAN, DETERMINANTS OF MAN'S DEVELOPMENT AND TRANSFORMATION, SPRINGS OF HUMAN MOTIVATION, AND SCIENTIFIC METHODS TO BE FOLLOWED BOTH FOR UNDERSTANDING HUMAN NATURE AND FOR CHANGING IT.

3241 VENKATESWARAN R.J.
CABINET GOVERNMENT IN INDIA.
NEW YORK: HILLARY HOUSE PUBL, 1967, 200 PP.
ANALYZES CONSTITUTIONAL POSITION AND DAY-TO-DAY OPERATION OF INDIAN CENTRAL CABINET SINCE INDEPENDENCE. ALSO STUDIES EXTENT TO WHICH CABINET SYSTEM, MODELED ON THAT OF BRITAIN, HAS TAKEN ROOT IN INDIA AND HOW FAR INDIA HAS FOLLOWED BRITISH PRECEDENTS AND CONVENTIONS. POINTS OUT STRONG AND WEAK POINTS OF CABINET SYSTEM.

3242 VERAX
"L'EUROPE ET LA FRANCE SUR LA SELLETTE."
REV. DES DEUX MONDES, (JAN. 68), 143-150.
HOLDS THAT DE GAULLE HAS IN EFFECT VETOED BRITAIN'S MEMBERSHIP IN COMMON MARKET AGAINST WISHES OF ALL THE OTHER PARTNERS. FRENCH TACTICS MAY HAVE SERIOUS REPERCUSSIONS, BUT TACTICS HAVE BEEN HIDDEN FROM FRENCH BY GOVERNMENT PROPAGANDA. BELIEVES THAT FRENCH REFUSAL TO DISCUSS BRITISH MEMBERSHIP IN EEC IS AN ANTI-EUROPEAN DECISION. FRENCH STAND MANY LEAD TO BREAK WITH OTHER FIVE MEMBERS OF EEC.

3243 VERGNAUD P.
L'IDEE DE LA NATIONALITE ET DE LA LIBRE DISPOSITION DES PEUPLES DANS SES RAPPORTS AVEC L'IDEE DE L'ETAT.
GENEVA: LIBRAIRIE DROZ, 1955, 258 PP.
STUDIES NATIONALISTIC IDEOLOGIES FROM ITALY OF 1500'S TO PRESENT. CONCENTRATES ON DOCTRINES FROM 1870-1950. INCLUDES RENAN, BARRES, MAURRAS, JAURES, HITLER, LENIN, AND STALIN. AUTHOR BELIEVES MODERN IDEOLOGY CHARACTERIZED BY IDEAS OF RACE AND CLASS.

3244 VERHAEGEN P.
BIBLIOGRAPHIE DE L'URBANISATION DE L'AFRIQUE NOIRE: SON CADRE, SES CAUSES, ET SES CONSEQUENCES ECONOMIQUES, SOCIALES...
BRUSSELS: CEN DOC ECO ET SOC AFR, 1962, 387 PP.
A 2,500-ITEM BIBLIOGRAPHY RELATING TO CAUSES OF URBANIZATION IN AFRICA, THE SOCIAL AND ECONOMIC CONSEQUENCES THEREOF, AND THE SOCIO-CULTURAL MUTATIONS CAUSED BY THIS URBANIZATION.

3245 VERMOT-GAUCHY M.
L'EDUCATION NATIONALE DANS LA FRANCE DE 1975.
MONACO: ED DU ROCHER, 1965, 335 PP.
ANALYZES CURRENT THOUGHT CONCERNING EDUCATIONAL POLICY IN FRANCE. DISCUSSES RESULTS THAT APPLICATION OF THIS POLICY WILL HAVE FROM 1960-75. DISCUSSES PAST TRADITIONS AND EXISTING POLICIES, FORECASTS FUTURE POLICIES, AND OUTLINES PROSPECTS FROM 1970-75. BELIEVES THAT GROWTH IN EDUCATIONAL INSTITUTIONS HAS BEGUN TO BRING ABOUT DESIRABLE CURRICULUM AND OTHER EDUCATIONAL REFORMS.

3246 VERNEY D.V.
PUBLIC ENTERPRISE IN SWEDEN.
LIVERPOOL: LIVERPOOL U PRESS, 1959, 132 PP.
EXPLAINS SWEDISH ECONOMIC SYSTEM, PAYING PARTICULAR ATTENTION TO PUBLIC ACCOUNTABILITY. BEGINS WITH PUBLIC ENTERPRISE WITHOUT NATIONALIZATION AND COMPARES WITH UK. DISCUSSES GROWTH OF TRADING AGENCIES AND STATE COMPANIES, FORM OF SWEDISH PUBLIC ENTERPRISE, AND PROBLEM OF ACCOUNTABILITY. INCLUDES CIVIL SERVICE FORMALISM, SOCIAL DEMOCRATIC PARTY, ALTERNATIVES, AND FUTURE REFORMS.

3247 VIANNA F.J.
EVOLUCAO DE POVO BRASILEIRO (4TH ED.)
RIO DE JANEIRO: LIV J OLYMPIO ED, 1956, 313 PP.
STUDY OF HISTORICAL, SOCIAL, AND POLITICAL DEVELOPMENT OF BRAZILIAN PEOPLE. DISCUSSES SOCIAL STRUCTURE, POLITICAL INSTITUTIONS, AND RACIAL COMPOSITION OF BRAZIL AND CHANGES SINCE COLONIAL TIMES.

3248 VIARD R.
LA FIN DE L'EMPIRE COLONIAL FRANCAIS.
PARIS: MAISONNEUVE, 1963, 163 PP.
HISTORY OF THE DEVELOPMENT OF INDEPENDENCE IN THE FORMER FRENCH COLONIAL POSSESSIONS AND THE EVOLUTION OF THE FRENCH UNION.

3249 VICO G.B.
DIRITTO UNIVERSALE (1722) (VOL. 2, PARTS 1,2, AND 3, OF G.B. VICO, OPERE)
BARI, ITALY: G LATERZA & FIGLI, 1936, 840 PP.
MAINTAINS THAT GOD IS BEGINNING NOT ONLY OF RELIGION, BUT OF JURISPRUDENCE. MAN, LIKE GOD, POSSESSES ATTRIBUTES OF KNOWLEDGE, WILL, AND POWER. IN LEGAL SPHERE THESE CORRESPOND TO PROPERTY, LIBERTY, AND WARDSHIP. THEY TOGETHER COMPOSE AUTHORITY, IN INDIVIDUAL, FAMILY, AND STATE. CIVIL AUTHORITY IS, IN TURN, POLITICAL SOVEREIGNTY DERIVING JUSTIFICATION FROM EMBODIMENT OF FINITE KNOWLEDGE STRIVING FOR INFINITE.

3250 VIEN N.C.
SEEKING THE TRUTH.
NEW YORK: VANTAGE, 1966, 195 PP.
INSIDE VIEW OF POLITICAL SITUATION IN VIETNAM AFTER FRENCH DEFEAT. TELLS HOW PEOPLE WERE PRESSURED BY FRENCH AND BY VIET CONG. DESCRIBES RESHUFFLE OF OFFICES IN DAI REGIME. COVERS ACTIVITIES AND THOUGHTS OF NGUYEN KY.

3251 VIERECK P.
CONSERVATISM REVISITED: THE REVOLT AGAINST REVOLT 1815-1949.
NEW YORK: CHAS SCRIBNER'S SONS, 1949, 187 PP.
IN THE "CRISIS-TIME" OF 1949, THE AUTHOR SUGGESTS THAT CULTURAL AND POLITICAL CONSERVATISM MAY BE BEST CREDO TO SUSTAIN FREE AND RATIONAL SOCIETY IN THE FACE OF EXPANSIONIST COMMUNISM. SEEKS TO CONSERVE HUMANE AND ETHICAL VALUES OF WEST. HETERODOX INTERPRETATION OF METTERNICH'S POLITICAL THOUGHT.

3252 VIGNES D.
"L'AUTORITE DES TRAITES INTERNATIONAUX EN DROIT INTERNE."
ETUD. DR. COMP., 23 (1962), 475-85.
EMPLOYES QUANTITATIVE ANALYSIS TO ASCERTAIN FACTORS NECESSARY TO INSURE APPLICABILITY OF AN INTERNATIONAL TREATY TO NATIONAL LAW. INCLUDES ANALYSIS OF ARTICLE 55 OF 1958 FRENCH CONSTITUTION.

3253 VIGON J.
TEORIA DEL MILITARISMO.
MADRID: EDICIONES RIALP, 1955, 324 PP.
REFLECTION ON MILITARISM IN WESTERN WORLD, INCLUDING ITS RELATION TO NATIONALISM, IMPERIALISM, PACIFISM, ANTIMILITARISM, MILITARY INTERVENTION, AS WELL AS POLITICAL IMPLICATIONS OF MILITARISM.

3254 VILAKAZI A.
ZULU TRANSFORMATIONS: A STUDY OF THE DYNAMICS OF SOCIAL CHANGE.
PIETERMARITZBURG: U NATAL PR, 1962, 168 PP.
EXAMINES SOCIAL ORDER OF ZULUS ON THE YUSWA RESERVE INCLUDING COMPARISON BETWEEN CHRISTIAN AND TRADITIONAL ATTITUDES AND NATIVE LIFE IN APARTHEID SOCIETY. BIBLIOGRAPHY OF 100 ENTRIES PUBLISHED 1870-1958. INCLUDES ENGLISH LANGUAGE BOOKS, ARTICLES, AND JOURNALS; ARRANGED ALPHABETICALLY BY AUTHOR.

3255 VINACKE H.M.
A HISTORY OF THE FAR EAST IN MODERN TIMES (6TH ED.)
NEW YORK: APPLETON, 1959, 877 PP., LC#59-7077.
A HISTORY OF CHINA, JAPAN, KOREA, AND EASTERN RUSSIA SINCE THE TIME OF THE MOVEMENT TO BRING CHINA INTO AN ENLARGED CONTACT WITH THE WORLD. FOCUSES ON THE POLITICAL, ECONOMIC, AND SOCIAL STRUCTURES OF ASIAN COUNTRIES, AND THE WESTERN IMPACT ON THESE INSTITUTIONS.

3256 VINCENT S.
"SHOULD BIAFRA SURVIVE?"
TRANSITION, 7 (OCT.-NOV. 67), 46-51.
CONSIDERS POSSIBILITY AND EFFECTS OF THE SURVIVAL OF BIAFRA AS A STATE. EXAMINES POSSIBILITIES OF IBO LEADERS' SUCCESSFULLY INTEGRATING OTHER TRIBES, FINDING THEM HIGHLY DUBIOUS. REPORTS FEELINGS OF MANY LEADERS THAT IT WOULD BE DESTRUCTIVE TO TOTAL AFRICAN UNITY. FORESEES LONG HOSTILITIES CREATED BY TACTICS OF JUNTA IN CONTROL.

3257 VITO F.
"RECENT DEVELOPMENTS IN THE THEORY OF DEMOCRATIC ADMIN" INTL POL SCI ASS'N CONFERENCE ON PUBLIC ADMINISTRATION...
INTL POLI SCO ASSOC, 1953, 56 PP.
WORKING PAPER COMPARING GOVERNMENT OWNERSHIP OR CONTROL OF INDUSTRY IN ENGLAND, FRANCE, AND ITALY.

3258 VITTACHIT
EMERGENCY '58.
LONDON: ANDRE DEUTSCH, 1959.
GIVES BACKGROUND AND CONDITIONS LEADING TO CEYLONESE RACE RIOTS 1958, RELATING THEM TO LACK OF LEADERSHIP, SOCIAL STRUCTURE, LEGAL FAILURES, AND COMMUNIST INSTIGATION.

3259 VOELKMANN K.
HERRSCHER VON MORGEN?
VIENNA: ECON VERLAG, 1964, 412 PP.
STUDIES "THIRD WORLD," WHICH MAY RULE TOMARROW'S WORLD. WHILE EUROPE HAS DECLINED IN IMPORTANCE THE DEVELOPING NATIONS HAVE MOVED FROM PERIPHERY OF WORLD POLITICS TOWARD CENTER. STUDIES NATIONS THROUGHOUT WORLD AND TRENDS THAT DETERMINE THEIR CONDUCT VIS-A-VIS THE GREAT POWERS.

3260 VOGT E.Z.
PEOPLE OF RIMROCK.
CAMBRIDGE: HARVARD U PR, 1966, 342 PP., LC#66-23469.
A COMPARATIVE STUDY OF FIVE CULTURES: THE NAVAHO INDIANS, THE ZUNI INDIANS, THE SPANISH-AMERICANS, THE MORMONS, AND TEXAS HOMESTEADERS. DISCUSSES SOCIALIZATION TECHNIQUES, GEOGRAPHICAL AND CULTURAL SETTING, INTERCULTURAL RELATIONS, KINSHIP SYSTEMS, ECOLOGY AND ECONOMY, POLITICAL STRUCTURES, AND PATTERNS OF WORSHIP.

3261 VOLPICELLI Z.
RUSSIA ON THE PACIFIC AND THE SIBERIAN RAILWAY.
LONDON: MARSTON, 1899, 373 PP.
BRIEF HISTORY OF RUSSIAN EXPANSION TO THE URAL AND SUBSEQUENT CONQUEST OF SIBERIA. ANALYZES POLITICAL CAUSES OF THE ANNEXATION OF AMUR REGION, DEPICTS TRENDS OF RUSSIAN EXPANSION.

3262 VON ARSENIEW W.
DIE GEISTIGEN SCHICKSALE DES RUSSISCHEN VOLKES.
GRAZ: VERLAG STYRIA, 1966, 303 PP.
DISCUSSES POLARIZED NATURE OF RUSSIAN CHARACTER AS EXPRESSED ON ONE HAND IN ITS DISCIPLINED INTELLECTUAL ATTITUDE AND ON OTHER ITS SENSUOUSNESS AND PASSION FOR THE CHAOTIC. EXAMINES INFLUENCE OF CHURCH ON INTELLECTUAL LIFE AND ATTITUDE OF RUSSIAN PEOPLE TOWARD CZARIST RULE. MAKES SOME OBSERVATIONS ON ORIGINS AND NATURE OF REVOLUTIONARY MOVEMENTS IN RUSSIA.

3263 VON BECKERATH E., BRINKMANN C. ET AL.
HANDWORTERBUCH DER SOCIALWISSENSCHAFTEN (II VOLS.)
STUTTGART: FISCHER VERLAG, 1956.
A HANDBOOK OF SOCIAL SCIENCE ARRANGED TOPICALLY AND ALPHABETICALLY. DISCUSSES SUCH CULTURAL ASPECTS AS UNEMPLOYMENT, FOREIGN TRADE, BANKSPACE SYSTEMS, VOTING RIGHTS AND APPENDS TO EACH A BIBLIOGRAPHY OF THE LITERATURE. INCLUDED ARE FOREIGN MATERIALS, THOUGH MAJORITY ARE IN GERMAN.

3264 VON BECKERATH E. ED., GIERSCH H. ED.
PROBLEME DER NORMATIVEN OEKONOMIK UND DER WIRTSCHAFTSPOLITISCHEN BERATUNG.
BERLIN: DUNCKER & HUMBLOT, 1963, 611 PP.
DISCUSSES BASIS AND LIMITATIONS OF "NORMATIVE ECONOMICS" AND ROLE OF ECONOMIC EXPERTS IN INSTITUTIONS AND POLICY-MAKING.

3265 VON DER MEHDEN F.R.
RELIGION AND NATIONALISM IN SOUTHEAST ASIA.
MADISON: U. WISC. PR., 1963, 25 PP., $5.00.
EXAMINES THE ROLE OF RELIGION IN THE NATIONALIST MOVEMENTS OF THREE COUNTRIES OF SOUTHEAST ASIA: BURMA, INDONESIA, AND THE PHILIPPINES. ISOLATES RELIGION AS AN IMPORTANT VARIABLE RESPONSIBLE FOR THE BULK OF NATIONALISM AND TRACES THE IMPACT OF ONE UPON THE OTHER.

3266 VON EICKSTEDT E.
TURKEN, KURDEN UND IRANER SEIT DEM ALTERTUM.
STUTTGART: FISCHER VERLAG, 1961, 123 PP.
DISCUSSES CUSTOMS AND TRADITIONS OF TURKS, KURDS, AND PERSIANS SINCE ANCIENT TIMES. EXAMINES THEIR ORIGIN AND CULTURAL ADVANCES AS WELL AS THEIR RELATIONS WITH EACH OTHER.

3267 VON FURER-HAIMEN E.
AN ANTHROPOLOGICAL BIBLIOGRAPHY OF SOUTH ASIA (VOL. I)
HAGUE: MOUTON & CO, 1958, 748 PP.
BIBLIOGRAPHY OF 5,316 ENTRIES INDEXED BY AREA, SUBJECT, AND AUTHOR PUBLISHED FROM 1800-1954. INCLUDES BOOKS, PERIODICALS, FIELD RESEARCH IN SOCIAL, CULTURAL, AND MATERIAL ANTHROPOLOGY, FOLKLORE, PREHISTORIC ARCHAEOLOGY, AND PHYSICAL ANTHROPOLOGY.

3268 VON FURER-HAIMEN E.
AN ANTHROPOLOGICAL BIBLIOGRAPHY OF SOUTH ASIA (VOL. II)
HAGUE: MOUTON & CO, 1964, 459 PP.
BIBLIOGRAPHY OF 3771 ENTRIES BY AREA, SUBJECT, AND AUTHOR FROM 1955-59. INCLUDES BOOKS, PERIODICALS, FIELD RESEARCH, AND DOCTORAL DISSERTATIONS IN SOCIAL, MATERIAL, AND CULTURAL ANTHROPOLOGY. ALSO HAS REFERENCES TO FOLKLORE AND PREHISTORIC ARCHAEOLOGY.

3269 VON GRUNEBAUM G.E.
MODERN ISLAM: THE SEARCH FOR CULTURAL IDENTITY.
NEW YORK: VINTAGE BOOKS, 1964, 406 PP.
CONCERNED WITH THE STRUCTURE OF THE ISLAMIC COMMUNITY AND ITS REACTION TO DIRECTION BY THE WEST OF ISLAM'S DEVELOPMENT IN THE LAST 100 YEARS. ANALYZES THE PECULIAR COHESIVENESS OF THE MUSLIM COMMUNITY, ITS EXPANSIVE AND ADAPTIVE POWER, THE PECULIARITIES OF MUSLIM NATIONALISM, THE POLITICAL ROLE OF THE UNIVERSITY IN THE NEAR EAST, ACCULTURATION AS A THEME IN CONTEMPORARY ARAB LITERATURE, AND CULTURAL INFLUENCES.

3270 VON HARPE W.
DIE SOWJETUNION FINNLAND UND SKANDANAVIEN, 1945-1955.
TUBINGEN: BOHLAU VERLAG, 1956, 67 PP.
TWO REPORTS ABOUT POSTWAR INTERNATIONAL RELATIONSHIPS, CONCENTRATING ON USSR'S RELATIONSHIPS WITH FINLAND AND SCANDINAVIA. TREATS FINNISH PARTICIPATION IN WWII, RUSSIAN-FINNISH MUTUAL ASSISTANCE PACT, FINLAND'S SPECIAL POSITION IN SOVIET SPHERE OF INFLUENCE, POST-STALIN RELATIONSHIPS, RETURN OF PORKKALA; POSTWAR NORTHERN EUROPE, SCANDINAVIA BETWEEN ATLANTIC PACT AND EASTERN BLOC.

3271 VON HAYEK F.A.
MONETARY NATIONALISM AND INTERNATIONAL STABILITY.
NEW YORK: LONGMANS, GREEN & CO, 1937, 94 PP.
CONCENTRATES ON THEORETICAL ISSUES RESPONSIBLE FOR RISE OF MONETARY NATIONALISM; EXAMINES POLICIES AND PRACTICES EMPLOYED BY NATIONS. DISCUSSES INTERNATIONAL STANDARD VERSUS NATIONAL CURRENCIES, MERITS OF VARIOUS POLITICAL SYSTEMS, FUNCTION AND MECHANISM OF INTERNATIONAL FLOWS OF MONEY, AND CAPITAL MOVEMENTS. CLOSES WITH GOLD AS STANDARD, EXCHANGE RATES, AND CREDIT.

3272 VON HIPPEL E.
GESCHICHTE DER STAATSPHILOSOPHIE (2 VOLS.)
MEISENHEIM: VERLAG ANTON HAIN, 1957, 791 PP.
DISCUSSES HISTORY OF POLITICAL THEORY FROM OLDEST CULTURES (INDIA, CHINA) TO END OF 19TH CENTURY (MARX, HEGEL, TOLSTOI).

3273 VON KOENIGSWALD H.
SIE SUCHEN ZUFLUCHT.
ESSLINGEN: BECHTE VERLAG, 1960, 80 PP.
DISCUSSES REFUGEE PROBLEM IN BERLIN BASED ON PERSONAL EXPERIENCES. DESCRIBES INDIVIDUAL TRAGEDIES AND MEASURES OF SUPPRESSION OF EAST GERMAN REGIME.

3274 VON LAUE T.H.
"WESTERNIZATION, REVOLUTION AND THE SEARCH FOR A BASIS OF AUTHORITY - RUSSIA IN 1917."
SOVIET STUDIES, 19 (OCT. 67), 155-180.
AUTHOR BELIEVES THAT USSR BELONGS TO THE DEVELOPING COUNTRIES IN THE SENSE THAT IT HAS, LIKE OTHER UNDERDEVELOPED COUNTRIES, IMPLEMENTED WESTERN COMPONENTS OF MODERNIZATION, AND, IN MANY CASES, WESTERN TECHNIQUES OF POWER. DISCUSSES THE LEADERSHIP OF THE BOLSHEVIK REVOLUTION.

3275 VON MERING O.
A GRAMMAR OF HUMAN VALUES.
PITTSBURGH: U. PR., 1961, 288 PP.
UNDERTAKES AN EXPLORATION OF VALUES AND PROBLEMS OF DETERMINING HOW AND WHY THEY ARE FORMED. DEALS WITH SPECIFIC EXPERIMENTS ON VALUE FORMATION AND HOW CULTURES AFFECT VALUES.

3276 VON RENESSE E.A., KRAWIETZ W., BIERKAEMPER C.
UNVOLLENDETE DEMOKRATIEN.
COLOGNE: WESTDEUTSCHER VERLAG, 1965, 429 PP.
EXAMINES FORMS OF ORGANIZATION AND STRUCTURES OF POWER IN NON-COMMUNIST DEVELOPING NATIONS IN ASIA, AFRICA, AND NEAR EAST. STUDIES LEGAL AND POLITICAL STATUS OF THESE LANDS AND THEIR SOCIAL AND ECONOMIC BACKGROUNDS. EMPIRICAL-INDUCTIVE APPROACH.

3277 VON STACKELBERG K.
ALLE KRETER LUGEN VORURTEILE UBER MENSCHEN UND VOLKER.
VIENNA: ECON VERLAG, 1965, 212 PP.
STUDY OF NATIONAL PREJUDICE; INCLUDES COUNTRIES FROM ALL CONTINENTS. METHOD OF INQUIRY LARGELY BY PUBLIC OPINION POLLS.

3278 VON STEIN L.J.
THE HISTORY OF THE SOCIAL MOVEMENT IN FRANCE, 1789-1850 (TRANS. BY K. MENGELBERG)
TOTOWA: BEDMINSTER PR, 1964, 467 PP., LC#64-13771.
TRACES FRENCH SOCIAL HISTORY FROM REVOLUTION THROUGH UPHEAVAL OF 1848. IN THREE PARTS: CONCEPT OF SOCIETY AND REVOLUTION UNTIL 1830; SOCIALISM AND COMMUNISM, 1830-48; AND MONARCHY SINCE 1848. FIRST WRITTEN IN 1850.

3279 VORSPAN A., LIPMAN E.J.
JUSTICE AND JUDAISM.
NEW YORK: UN AM HEB CONGREG, 1959, 271 PP.
COMPREHENSIVELY APPLIES JUDAISM TO ALL PHASES OF MODERN LIFE, CONSIDERING EACH IN CONTEXT OF JEWISH PHILOSOPHY. GIVES RESULTING ATTITUDES ABOUT OTHER RELIGIONS, INTERNATIONAL RELATIONS, ECONOMICS ETC. CONSIDERS CULTURAL IMPLICATIONS OF PERVASIVE RELIGIOUS ORIENTATION.

3280 VUCINICH A.
THE SOVIET ACADEMY OF SCIENCES.
STANFORD: STANFORD U PRESS, 1956, 157 PP., LC#55-11552.
EXAMINES TWO INTERRELATED PROBLEMS: THE ORGANIZATION OF SCIENTIFIC INQUIRY IN SOVIET UNION, AND THE SOCIAL ROLE OF SOVIET SCIENCE AND SCIENTISTS. TREATS THESE PROBLEMS IN TERMS OF THEIR BEARING UPON THE ACADEMY OF SCIENCES OF THE USSR.

3281 VUCINICH W.S.
"WHITHER RUMANIA."
CURR. HIST., 48 (MAR. 65), 161-167.
ABLE TO ACHIEVE LARGE DEGREE OF INDEPENDENCE FROM MOSCOW. STRESS ON CONCEPT OF NATIONAL SOVEREIGNTY WITHIN COMECON HAS PREVAILED. DE-CENTRALIZATION OF COMMUNIST MONOLITH CONTINUES UNABATED, HOWEVER THERE IS DANGER THAT LEADERS MAY TRY TO GO TOO FAR TOO FAST.

3282 WABEKE B.H. ED.
A GUIDE TO DUTCH BIBLIOGRAPHIES.
WASHINGTON: LIBRARY OF CONGRESS, 1951, 193 PP., LC#51-60014.
A PARTIALLY ANNOTATED BIBLIOGRAPHY OF 756 BOOKS, PAMPHLETS, AND PERIODICALS, ALL DUTCH PUBLICATIONS THAT SERVE A BIBLIOGRAPHICAL PURPOSE. INTENDED TO FACILITATE THE STUDY OF THE NETHERLANDS, INDONESIA, SURINAM, CURACAO, AS WELL AS FLEMISH LITERATURE AND HISTORY. TOPICALLY ARRANGED, AND INDEXED BY AUTHOR, TITLE, AND SUBJECT.

3283 WADE E.C.S., PHILLIPS G.G.
CONSTITUTIONAL LAW; AN OUTLINE OF THE LAW AND PRACTICE OF THE CONSTITUTION.
LONDON: LONGMANS, GREEN & CO, 1950, 535 PP.
EXAMINES THE ENGLISH SYSTEM OF GOVERNMENT. BROAD STUDY INCLUDES NATURE OF CONSTITUTION AND GENERAL PRINCIPLES FOR AUTHORITY, PARLIAMENT, EXECUTIVE, AND JUDICIARY; DESCRIBES GOVERNMENT ON LOCAL LEVEL. CONSIDERS ADMINISTRATIVE LAW, CITIZEN AND STATE, MILITARY FORCES, AND RELATIONS WITH THE COMMONWEALTH.

3284 WAELBROECK M.
"THE APPLICATION OF EEC LAW BY NATIONAL COURTS."
STANFORD LAW REV., 19 (JUNE 67), 1248-1276.
DESCRIBES APPLICATION OF EEC LAW BY LEGAL SYSTEMS OF MEMBER STATES AND POINTS OUT PROBLEMS OF APPLICATION. GENERAL PROBLEMS INCLUDE SOURCES AND INTERPRETATION OF EEC LAW AND CONFLICTS WITH NATIONAL LAWS. MORE SPECIFIC DIFFICULTIES ARE DIRECT APPLICABILITY OF DIRECTIVES AND OF PROVISIONS IMPOSING OBLIGATIONS ON MEMBER STATES.

3285 WAGLEY C.
AMAZON TOWN: A STUDY OF MAN IN THE TROPICS.
NEW YORK: MACMILLAN, 1953, 305 PP.
STUDY BY AUTHOR OF LIFE IN RURAL UNDEVELOPED BRAZILIAN COMMUNITY ON AMAZON RIVER. ANALYSIS OF CULTURE AND STRUCTURE OF SOCIETY BY RESIDENCE IN COMMUNITY AND INFORMATION GAINED FROM OTHERS IN THE AREA.

3286 WAGLEY C.
INTRODUCTION TO BRAZIL.
NEW YORK: COLUMBIA U PRESS, 1963, 322 PP., LC#63-17538.
GENERAL ANALYSIS OF BRAZILIAN SOCIAL, ECONOMIC, AND POLITICAL LIFE. DISCUSSES GEOGRAPHY, SOCIAL CLASSES, EDUCATIONAL SYSTEM, FAMILY AND COMMUNITY LIFE, AND RELATIONSHIP BETWEEN RELIGION AND STATE.

3287 WAINHOUSE D.W.
REMNANTS OF EMPIRE: THE UNITED NATIONS AND THE END OF COLONIALISM.
NEW YORK: HARPER ROW, 1964, 153 PP.
CONSIDERS BALANCE SHEET OF WESTERN COLONIALISM AND RELATIONSHIPS BEING DEVELOPED IN PROCESS OF LIQUIDATING LAST VESTIGES OF EMPIRE. DISCUSSES TERRITORIES RANGING FROM LARGE DEPENDENCIES TO TINY ISLANDS, IN FRAMEWORK OF PRESSING ISSUES AND METROPOLES INVOLVED.

3288 WAINWRIGHT M.D., MATTHEWS N.
A GUIDE TO WESTERN MANUSCRIPTS AND DOCUMENTS IN THE BRITISH ISLES RELATING TO SOUTH AND SOUTHEAST ASIA.
LONDON: OXFORD U PR, 1965, 532 PP.
INCLUDES ALL OBTAINABLE WORKS AFTER 1450 ON ALL SUBJECTS. WITHIN INDIVIDUAL CATEGORIES WORKS ARE ARRANGED IN CHRONOLOGICAL ORDER. MANUSCRIPTS ARE CLASSIFIED UNDER LIBRARY WHERE AVAILABLE.

3289 WALDMAN E.
THE GOOSE STEP IS VERBOTEN: THE GERMAN ARMY TODAY.
NEW YORK: FREE PRESS OF GLENCOE, 1964, 294 PP., LC#64-23077.
SEEKS TO ANALYZE AND EVALUATE THE CONCEPTUAL AND CONSTITUTIONAL BASIS OF THE WEST GERMAN ARMY, ITS EXECUTION, AND ITS EXPRESSION IN CONTEMPORARY GERMAN MILITARY REALITY. QUESTIONNAIRE TECHNIQUE WAS USED TO DISCOVER THE POLITICAL KNOWLEDGE AND ATTITUDES OF GERMAN SOLDIERS. MUCH EMPHASIS IS GIVEN TO THE STRUCTURE AND PROBLEMS OF THE MILITARY HIERARCHY.

3290 WALKER A.A. ED.
OFFICIAL PUBLICATIONS OF SIERRA LEONE AND GAMBIA.
WASHINGTON: LIBRARY OF CONGRESS, 1963, 92 PP., LC#63-60090.
BIBLIOGRAPHY OF DOCUMENTS PUBLISHED SINCE ESTABLISHMENT OF CENTRAL GOVERNMENT AND PERTINENT PUBLICATIONS OF BRITISH GOVERNMENT RELATED TO ITS COLONIAL ADMINISTRATION. ARRANGED BY COUNTRY AND SUBDIVIDED ALPHABETICALLY BY AUTHOR AND TITLE UNDER PUBLISHER. CENSUS AND DEVELOPMENT PLANNING UNDER SEPARATE TOPIC. AUTHOR AND SUBJECT INDEX INCLUDED. CONTAINS 730 ITEMS IN ENGLISH.

3291 WALKER A.A. ED.
THE RHODESIAS AND NYASALAND: A GUIDE TO OFFICIAL PUBLICATIONS.
WASHINGTON: LIBRARY OF CONGRESS, 1965, 285 PP., LC#65-60089.
COMPREHENSIVE BIBLIOGRAPHY OF 1,889 ITEMS ON PUBLISHED RECORDS OF FORMER FEDERATION OF RHODESIA AND NYASALAND, FROM 1889-1963. INCLUDES PUBLICATIONS OF BRITISH COLONIAL GOVERNMENT. ARRANGED GEOGRAPHICALLY, BY GOVERNMENTAL DEPARTMENTS AND AUTHORS. INCLUDES INDEX.

3292 WALKER F.D.
AFRICA AND HER PEOPLES.
EDINBURGH: EDINBURGH HOUSE PR, 1924, 144 PP.
INTRODUCES ALL AFRICA: GEOGRAPHY, ORGANIZATION OF SOCIETIES, RELIGIONS (ANIMISM, MAGIC, POLYTHEISM, ISLAM), TOWN AND TRIBAL LIFE (PRIMARILY STUDIES YORUBAS, ZULUS, MUSLIM TRIBES). FOCUSES ON BLACK AFRICANS. SURVEYS IMPACT OF WESTERN TECHNOLOGY. STRESSES POSSIBILITIES NOT ONLY OF AFRICA, BUT ALSO AFRICANS. COMMISSIONED BY UNITED COUNCIL FOR MISSIONARY EDUCATION.

3293 WALLAS G.
HUMAN NATURE IN POLITICS (3RD ED.)
NEW YORK: ALFRED KNOPF, 1921, 313 PP.
STUDIES EFFECT OF HUMAN NATURE ON DEVELOPMENT OF POLITICAL INSTITUTIONS. TREATS ROLE OF INSTINCT AND IMPULSE AND DISCUSSES MATERIAL AND METHOD OF POLITICAL REASONING; ANALYZES POLITICAL MORALITY AND REPRESENTATIVE GOVERNMENT. INCLUDES POLITICAL SOLIDARITY, RELATIONS BETWEEN ELECTED REPRESENTATIVES ANDD NONELECTED OFFICIALS, AND POLITICAL FORCE OF ELECTIONS; EMPHASIZES DEMOCRATIC ELEMENTS.

3294 WALLBANK T.W. ED.
DOCUMENTS ON MODERN AFRICA.
PRINCETON: VAN NOSTRAND, 1964, 191 PP.
SELECTED READINGS TO CHARACTERIZE THE DISTINCT PERIODS OF HISTORY IN SUB-SAHARAN AFRICA IN THE LAST CENTURY. EMPHASIS IS ON RECENT PERIOD OF INDEPENDENCE.

3295 WALSTON H.
AGRICULTURE UNDER COMMUNISM.
CHESTER SPRINGS: DUFOUR, 1962, 108 PP., LC#62-10661.
DESCRIBES AGRARIAN HISTORY OF COMMUNIST COUNTRIES AND METHODS USED TO SOLVE PROBLEM OF AGRICULTURAL WORKERS' RESISTANCE TO GOVERNMENT INTERFERENCE. EVALUATES SUCCESS OF COMMUNIST CHANGES. MAINTAINS INNOVATOR MUST SEE THAT CHANGE BRINGS "BETTER AND HAPPIER LIFE" TO CULTIVATORS.

3296 WALTER E.
"VERS UNE CLASSIFICATION SCIENTIFIQUE DE LA SOCIOLOGIA."
DIALECTICA, 16 (NO., 62), 354-60.
DEALS WITH EPISTEMOLOGIC PROBLEM IN EMPIRICAL SCIENCES. SUGGESTS BETTER CLASSIFICATION OF METHODS IN ORDER TO ADAPT THEM TO MODERN TECHNOLOGY AND POLICY PLANNING DEVICES.

3297 WALTERS F.P.
A HISTORY OF THE LEAGUE OF NATIONS.
LONDON: OXFORD U. PR., 1952.
TRACES THE RISE AND DECLINE OF LEAGUE IN 20-YEAR EXISTENCE. ANALYZES POLITICAL DISPUTES, INTERNAL DISSENSION, AND ECONOMIC DIFFICULTIES. EXPLORES DIFFICULTY OF PROTECTING MINORITIES AND PROBLEMS CREATED BY UPSURGE OF NATIONALISM.

3298 WALTZ K.N.
FOREIGN POLICY AND DEMOCRATIC POLITICS: THE AMERICAN AND BRITISH EXPERIENCE.
BOSTON: LITTLE BROWN, 1967, 331 PP.
EXAMINES FOREIGN POLICY AS FASHIONED BY DOMESTIC INSTITUTIONS. STUDIES BACKGROUND OF POLICY DECISIONS, POLITICAL PERFORMANCE, GOVERNMENTAL STRUCTURE, INFLUENCE OF ATTITUDES AND PARTY POLICY, AND EXECUTIVE ARRANGEMENTS. ALSO DISCUSSES POLITICS OF BRITISH MILITARY POLICY, AMERICAN POLICY AND FOREIGN AID, AND RELATIONS AMONG BRITAIN, EUROPE, AND US.

3299 WANDERSCHECK H.
WELTKRIEG UND PROPAGANDA.
BERLIN: MITTLER, 1936, 260 PP.
EXAMINATION OF ENGLISH WAR PROPAGANDA BETWEEN 1914 AND BEGINNING OF NOVEMBER REVOLUTION OF 1918 IN GERMANY. ATTEMPTS TO DISCOVER "LAWS, BASES, AND PRINCIPLES OF PROPAGANDA" SO THAT THESE DISCOVERIES MAY BECOME USEFUL FOR THE NEW TASK OF NATIONAL ENLIGHTENMENT, AND RECOGNITION OF PROPAGANDA BY THE NEW GERMANY UNDER HITLER.

3300 WANDERSCHECK H.
FRANKREICHS PROPAGANDA GEGEN DEUTSCHLAND.
BERLIN: JUNKER & DUNNHAUPT VERL, 1940, 62 PP.
DISCUSSION OF THE HISTORY OF FRENCH ANTI-GERMAN PROPAGANDA. MAINTAINS THAT AIM OF FRENCH PROPAGANDA HAS ALWAYS BEEN THE POLITICAL DISINTEGRATION OF GERMANY, WITH THE AID OF "ENGLISH-JEWISH WAR MONGERS."

3301 WANG Y.C.
CHINESE INTELLECTUALS AND THE WEST 1872-1949.
CHAPEL HILL: U OF N CAR PR, 1966, 557 PP., LC#66-10207.
INTENSIVE STUDY OF MIGRATION OF CHINESE INTELLECTUALS ABROAD TO STUDY. INVESTIGATES THEIR EFFECT ON CHINESE SOCIETY AND ADVANCEMENT, THEIR ROLES AS LEADERS OF CHINA, AND CONTRIBUTIONS TO CULTURAL READJUSTMENT OF CHINA TO COMMONISM. SECOND PART ANALYZES ACHIEVEMENTS AND FAILURES OF A FEW SELECTED RETURNED STUDENTS.

3302 WARBURG J.P.
"THE CENTRAL EUROPEAN CRISIS: A PROPOSAL FOR WESTERN INITIATIVE."
ANN. AMER. POLIT. SOC. SCI., 324 (JULY 59) 17-25.
APPEAL TO BRING ISSUE OF INTERFERENCE WITH WESTERN ACCESS TO WEST BERLIN BEFORE UN. URGES MILITARY AND POLITICAL DISENGAGEMENT IN BERLIN AND NEUTRALIZATION OF BOTH SECTORS. ESTIMATES THAT DISENGAGEMENT WILL BRING GRADUAL LIBERATION OF EASTERN EUROPE.

3303 WARD L., COMMAGER H.S. ED.
LESTER WARD AND THE WELFARE STATE.
INDIANAPOLIS: BOBBS-MERRILL, 1967, 441 PP., LC#66-22579.
A COLLECTION OF WARD'S POLITICAL WRITINGS, SELECTED WITH REFERENCE TO HIS THEORY OF A WELFARE SOCIETY. CONTAINS ESSAYS AND EXCERPTS FROM BOOKS THAT CENTER ON A DYNAMIC SOCIAL PHILOSOPHY, BASED ON THE EVOLUTIONARY PRINCIPLE OF MAN'S MASTERY OF NATURE AND CALLING FOR THE RULE OF SOCIETY BY SOCIETY AND FOR SOCIETY. INCLUDES A BIOGRAPHICAL AND CRITICAL INTRODUCTION AND PREFATORY NOTES TO THE WORKS.

3304 WARD P.W.
"SOVEREIGNTY: A STUDY OF A CONTEMPORARY POLITICAL NOTION."
LONDON: G ROUTLEDGE & SONS, 1928.
DISTINGUISHES AND SURVEYS THREE PERIODS IN THE DEVELOPMENT OF CONCEPT: ITS EMERGENCE FROM ANCIENT TRADITION AND LATE MEDIEVAL USAGE; ENUNCIATION AND APPLICATION BY ABSOLUTE MONARCHS; REINTERPRETATION SINCE 1688 AND HISTORICAL RISE OF RESPONSIBLE GOVERNMENT. SHORT BIBLIOGRAPHY REFERS TO CLASSIC STUDIES OF POLITICS OF NATIONALISM.

3305 WARD R.E. ED.
A GUIDE TO JAPANESE REFERENCE AND RESEARCH MATERIALS IN THE FIELD OF POLITICAL SCIENCE.
ANN ARBOR: U OF MICH PR, 1950, 104 PP.
SELECTED ANNOTATED BIBLIOGRAPHY. REFERS ONLY TO POLITICAL DEVELOPMENTS SINCE 1868 AND INCLUDES FEW WORKS PUBLISHED AFTER 1940. ITEMS IN FIELDS OF HISTORY, ECONOMY, METHODOLOGY, AND GENERAL BACKGROUND. GREAT MAJORITY OF WORKS IN JAPANESE WITH EXCEPTIONS IN FIELD OF METHODOLOGY. NO WORKS ON FOREIGN RELATIONS INCLUDED. ARRANGED TOPICALLY. CONTAINS LIST OF PUBLISHERS.

3306 WARD R.E., WATANABE H.
JAPANESE POLITICAL SCIENCE: A GUIDE TO JAPANESE REFERENCE AND RESEARCH MATERIALS (2ND ED.)
ANN ARBOR: U OF MICH PR, 1961, 210 PP.
A BRIEFLY ANNOTATED BIBLIOGRAPHY OF 1,759 ITEMS, LARGELY LIMITED TO JAPANESE TITLES WHICH TREAT POLITICAL SCIENCE SUBJECTS AND DEVELOPMENTS IN JAPAN SINCE THE MEIJI RESTORATION (1868). FOCUSES UPON RESULTS OF POST-1945 SCHOLARSHIP WHICH APPEAR IN BOOK RATHER THAN ARTICLE FORM. ARRANGED INTO 27 TOPICAL HEADINGS, AND INDEXED BY AUTHOR AND EDITOR. ANNOTATIONS EVALUATE UTILITY OF ITEM FOR REFERENCE PURPOSES.

3307 WARD R.E. ED., EUSTOW D.A. ED.
POLITICAL MODERNIZATION IN JAPAN AND TURKEY.
PRINCETON: U. PR., 1964, 502 PP., $8.75.
SEARCHES SYSTEMATICALLY IN THE HISTORICAL EXPERIENCES OF THESE COUNTRIES FOR ANSWERS TO TWO QUESTIONS: FIRST, HOW ACCOUNT FOR THEIR RELATIVE SUCCESS IN MODERNIZATION. SECOND, HOW ACCOUNT FOR THE DIFFERENCES IN THEIR RATES AND PATTERNS OF MODERNIZATION. EXAMINES SUCH INSTITUTIONS AS EDUCATION, THE MASS MEDIA, THE CIVIL BUREAUCRACY, THE MILITARY, AND POLITICAL LEADERSHIP AND POLITICAL PARTIES, SUGGESTS HOW SPECIFIC INSTITUTIONS MAY AFFECT PARTICULAR POLITICAL OUTCOMES.

3308 WARD W.E.
GOVERNMENT IN WEST AFRICA.
LONDON: ALLEN & UNWIN, 1965, 269 PP.
DISCUSSES COMPARATIVE SYSTEMS OF GOVERNMENT AND POLITICAL INTERACTION IN EACH. RELATES GENERAL CONCEPTS TO AFRICA IN ORDER TO JUDGE CONSTITUTIONAL AND POLITICAL SITUATION IN CHANGE FROM COLONIAL TO INDEPENDENT RULE.

3309 WARNER W.L., SROLE L.
THE SOCIAL SYSTEM OF AMERICAN ETHNIC GROUPS.
NEW HAVEN: YALE U PR, 1945, 318 PP.
DISCUSSES ETHNIC GROUPS AND SOCIAL STRATIFICATION, ETHNIC VALUE SYSTEMS, ETHNIC CHURCH STRUCTURES, AND FORMAL AND INFORMAL ETHNIC ASSOCIATIONS, PROVIDING A BACKGROUND TO AN EXAMINATION OF ETHNIC LOBBIES AND REPRESENTATIONAL PROBLEMS IN THE UNITED STATES.

3310 WARNER W.L. ED.
A BLACK CIVILIZATION - A SOCIAL STUDY OF AN AUSTRALIAN TRIBE
NEW YORK: HARPER & ROW, 1958, 516 PP., LC#58-7939.
EXAMINES FAMILY AND KINSHIP STRUCTURE, CAUSES AND METHODS OF WARFARE, TOTEMISM AND MEDICINE MAGIC, DEATH RITUALS, AND SOCIAL CHANGE OF MURNGIN TRIBE IN AUSTRALIA. CHARTS, PLATES, FIGURES, MAPS.

3311 WARNER W.L.
THE LIVING AND THE DEAD: A STUDY OF SYMBOLIC LIFE OF AMERICANS.
NEW HAVEN: YALE U PR, 1959, 528 PP., LC#59-6804.
AN INVESTIGATION INTO THE MEANINGS AND FUNCTIONS OF SOME OF THE SYMBOLS OF CONTEMPORARY AMERICA, BASED ON FIELD RESEARCH ON POLITICAL, HISTORICAL, AND RELIGIOUS SYMBOLS, PAST AND PRESENT. STARTING WITH FACTUAL ANALYSES OF SYMBOLIC USAGE AS APPLIED TO PERSONS, INSTITUTIONS, AND CULTURAL PHENOMENA, MOVES TO ABSTRACT AND THEORETICAL EXAMINATION OF SIGNIFICANCE OF SYMBOLS TO MAN'S MENTAL LIFE.

3312 WARREN S.
THE AMERICAN PRESIDENT.
ENGLEWOOD CLIFFS: PRENTICE HALL, 1967, 176 PP., LC#67-25927.
EXAMINES EVOLUTION OF US PRESIDENCY TO PRESENT STATE OF

IMPORTANCE. DEALS WITH PLACE OF PRESIDENCY IN CONSTITUTION, GIVING EXAMPLES OF HOW SOME MEN WHO OCCUPIED IT VIEWED ITS NATURE. INCLUDES OUTSIDERS' COMMENTS ON THE OFFICE, WHICH IS FURTHER EVALUATED BY MEANS OF OFFICIAL STATEMENTS AND OF POLICIES FELT TO REFLECT THE RANGE OF ROLES REQUIRED BY CIRCUMSTANCES AND PRECEDENT.

3313 WASSERMAN L.
"HANDBOOK OF POLITICAL "ISMS"
NEW YORK: ASSOCIATION PRESS, 1941.
OBJECTIVE DESCRIPTION OF MAIN ELEMENTS CHARACTERIZING THE COMPETING SOCIAL PHILOSOPHIES OF THE 1940'S. DOES NOT ATTEMPT INTERPRETIVE STUDY OR A COMPARISON OF THE IDEOLOGY WITH ITS OPERATIONAL MECHANICS. ILLUSTRATES HISTORICAL SETTING AND SOCIAL CONTEXT IN WHICH NEW IDEOLOGIES TRIUMPHED. EXTENSIVE UNANNOTATED BIBLIOGRAPHY OF WORKS PUBLISHED SINCE 1913 IN ENGLISH.

3314 WATT D.C.
BRITAIN AND THE SUEZ CANAL.
LONDON: ROYAL INST OF INTL AFF, 1956, 51 PP.
DOCUMENTARY ANALYSIS OF THE EXTENT OF BRITISH INTEREST IN THE NATURE AND EFFICIENCY OF MANAGEMENT OF THE SUEZ CANAL. INCLUDES SEVEN DOCUMENTS VITAL TO THE ISSUE: TEXT OF EGYPTIAN DECREE NATIONALIZING THE CANAL; TEXT OF 1888 CONVENTION OF FREE NAVIGATION OF THE SUEZ; ANGLO-EGYPTIAN TREATY OF 1936; SUEZ CANAL BASE AGREEMENT OF 1954; EXTRACTS FROM VARIOUS SUEZ COMPANY CONCESSIONS; AND SEVERAL TABLES.

3315 WATT D.C.
"RESTRICTIONS ON RESEARCH* THE FIFTY-YEAR RULE AND BRITISH FOREIGN POLICY."
INTERNATIONAL AFFAIRS (U.K.), 41 (JAN.65),89-95.
COMPARISON OF BRITISH AND AMERICAN PRACTICES CONCERNING ACCESS FOR SERIOUS SCHOLARS TO FOREIGN POLICY ARCHIVES AND PUBLIC PAPERS. PRESENTS INSIGHTS INTO PROBLEMS OF WRITING AND UNDERSTANDING MODERN DIPLOMATIC HISTORY.

3316 WEBB L.C.
CHURCH AND STATE IN ITALY: 1947-1957 (PAMPHLET)
CANBERRA: AUSTRALIAN NAT U, 1958, 60 PP.
DISCUSSES CHURCH-STATE RELATIONS IN ITALY FROM END OF WWII TO 1957. ANALYZES EFFECTS OF FASCIST COLLAPSE, GERMAN OCCUPATION, RESISTANCE, EPISODE OF THE SALO REPUBLIC, AND NEGOTIATION OF THE ARMISTICE. STUDIES COMMUNIST ATTITUDES, CONFLICTS OF CONSTITUTIONAL NORMS, AND INFLUENCE OF JACQUES MARITAIN ON THE CHURCH.

3317 WEBB S., WEBB B.
INDUSTRIAL DEMOCRACY.
LONDON: LONGMANS, GREEN & CO, 1920, 899 PP.
ANALYZES THE TRADE UNION IN THE UNITED KINGDOM. INTERNAL STRUCTURE OF VOLUNTARY UNIONS AS CLASS DEMOCRACIES; FUNCTIONS, METHODS, AND POLICY OF THE TRADE UNION; AND BASIC THEORY ARE THE MAJOR TOPICS DISCUSSED. PERSONAL INVESTIGATION BY AUTHORS CONTRIBUTES TO THEIR ANALYSIS. CONCLUDES THAT THE TRADE UNION HAS A POSITIVE INFLUENCE ON NATIONAL GOVERNMENT.

3318 WEBER J.
EOTVOS UND DIE UNGARISCHE NATIONALITATENFRAGE.
MUNICH: R OLDENBOURG, 1966, 154 PP.
DISCUSSES HUNGARIAN NATIONALITY PROBLEM AS CONCEIVED BY BARON EOTVOS, POET, PHILOSOPHER, SCIENTIST, AND POLITICIAN. EXAMINES RISE OF NATIONALISM AMONG VARIOUS NATIONALITY GROUPS IN HUNGARY IN 1848, AND DISCUSSES IDEA OF NATIONS IN RELATION TO FREEDOM AND EQUALITY.

3319 WEBER M.
GENERAL ECONOMIC HISTORY.
GREENBERG, NY: ADELPHI, 1927, 401 PP.
GENERAL ECONOMIC HISTORY OF THE WEST, ANALYZING ECONOMIC LIFE WITH SPECIAL REFERENCE TO THE PREPARATION FOR AND DEVELOPMENT OF MODERN CAPITALISM. NEVER COMPLETED BY AUTHOR BUT PIECED TOGETHER FROM NOTES BY HIS STUDENTS.

3320 WEBER M.
STAATSSOZIOLOGIE.
BERLIN: DUNCKER & HUMBLOT, 1956, 129 PP.
DISCUSSES CENTRAL CONCEPTS OF STATE ORGANIZATION FROM SOCIOLOGICAL POINT OF VIEW. EXAMINES QUESTION OF LEGITIMACY AND BUREAUCRATIC ADMINISTRATION. INCLUDES DISCUSSION OF PARTY ORGANIZATION AND PARLIAMENTARY RULE. DISTINGUISHES LEGAL, TRADITIONAL, AND CHARISMATIC RULE.

3321 WEBER M.
WIRTSCHAFT UND GESELLSCHAFT (2ND VOL.)
TUBINGEN: J C B MOHR, 1956, 840 PP.
DISCUSSES LAW, POLITICAL COMMUNITIES, AND CONCEPTS OF POLITICAL POWER FROM SOCIOLOGICAL POINT OF VIEW. EMPHASIZES QUESTION OF LEGITIMACY.

3322 WEBSTER C.
THE FOREIGN POLICY OF CASTLEREAGH: 1815-1822.
LONDON: BELL, 1925, 584 PP.
EXAMINATION OF POST-NAPOLEONIC BRITISH DIPLOMATIC HISTORY. CHARACTERIZES THIS ERA AS AGE OF STRONG ALLIANCES AND POPULAR UNREST.

3323 WEBSTER C.
THE FOREIGN POLICY OF PALMERSTON - 1830 TO 1841.
LONDON: BELL, 1951, 521 PP.
CONCERNS EUROPE AND THE EASTERN QUESTION. ASSERTS THAT PERIOD COVERED REPRESENTS THE HEIGHT OF BRITISH LEADERSHIP AS 'PROTECTOR OF DEMOCRACY.' CREDITS THAT SUCCESS TO ABILITIES OF LORD PALMERSTON.

3324 WEDGE B., MUROMCEW C.
"PSYCHOLOGICAL FACTORS IN SOVIET DISARMAMENT NEGOTIATION."
J. OF CONFLICT RESOLUTION, 9 (MAR. 65), 16-36.
ALL SOVIET STATEMENTS AT THE EIGHTEEN NATION DISARMAMENT CONFERENCE, MARCH 1962-APRIL 1963, WERE SURVEYED FOR "CONSISTENT POSITIONS AND PATTERNS OF NEGOTIATING BEHAVIOR." BASIC ASSUMPTIONS CONCERNING "THE NATURE OF MAN AND STATE," AND ASSUMPTIONS CONCERNING RESOLUTION OF DIFFERENCES THROUGH NEGOTIATION ARE FOUND WHICH DIFFER FROM THOSE IN WEST.

3325 WEHLER H.V.
SOZIALDEMOKRATIE UND NATIONALSTAAT.
WURZBURG: HOLZNER VERLAG, 1962, 281 PP.
DISCUSSES NATIONALITY PROBLEM AND RISE OF SOCIAL DEMOCRACY IN GERMANY FROM 1848-1914. EXAMINES CULTURAL-POLITICAL QUESTIONS PRESENTED BY PRUSSIAN POLISH PEOPLE, NORTHERN SCHLESWIG, AND ALSACE-LORRAINE. ALSO DISCUSSES POLES IN WESTERN GERMANY AND ATTITUDE TOWARD NATIONALITIES IN OTHER COUNTRIES (AUSTRIA, RUSSIA).

3326 WEIL E.
PHILOSOPHIE POLITIQUE.
PARIS: LIBR PHILOSOPHIQUE J VRIN, 1956, 261 PP.
THEORETICAL WORK ON PHILOSOPHY OF POLITICS. CONCERNED WITH ABSTRACTIONS OF POLITICS. CONSIDERS MORALITY INVOLVED, SOCIETY, STATE, AND INTERACTION OF STATE, SOCIETY, AND THE INDIVIDUAL. AUTHOR BELIEVES STATE IS ESSENTIAL FOR INDIVIDUAL TO FUNCTION, BUT REASONABLE MAN MUST SEE THAT STATE IS REASONABLE AND NOT OVERLY RESTRICTIVE.

3327 WEINER H.E.
BRITISH LABOR AND PUBLIC OWNERSHIP.
WASHINGTON: PUBLIC AFFAIRS PRESS, 1960, 111 PP., LC#59-15840
TRACES THROUGH THE BRITISH TRADE UNION CONGRESS THE EVOLUTION OF IDEA OF NATIONALIZATION AS AN OBJECTIVE OF BRITISH TRADE UNIONISM. ANALYZES ENVIRONMENT AND IDEAS THAT HAVE GOVERNED UNIONISM'S ATTITUDES TOWARD PUBLIC OWNERSHIP OF CERTAIN INDUSTRIES AND SERVICES.

3328 WEINER M.
POLITICAL CHANGE IN SOUTH ASIA.
CALCUTTA: FIRMA KL MUKHOPADHYAY, 1963, 285 PP.
ESSAYS CONCERNING POLITICAL CHANGE PRIMARILY IN INDIA. DESCRIBES CULTURAL BACKGROUND AND GOVERNMENTAL STRUCTURES. COMPARES POLITICAL CHANGE IN PAKISTAN AND CEYLON WITH INDIA. COVERS ECONOMIC DEVELOPMENT AND POLITICAL STABILITY.

3329 WEINSTEIN B.
GABON: NATION-BUILDING ON THE OGOOUE.
CAMBRIDGE: M I T PRESS, 1966, 287 PP., LC#67-13393.
ANALYTICAL STUDY OF NATION-BUILDING IN GABON. DISCUSSES REASONS WHY GABONESE WANT TO BUILD AND MAINTAIN A NATION, FORCES GIVING PEOPLE SENSE OF COMMON IDENTITY, AND ROLE OF HUMAN WILLPOWER. ATTEMPTS TO PROVE GABONESE ATTITUDES ARE RELEVANT FOR NATION-BUILDING PROCESSES EVERYWHERE. INCLUDES INSIGHTS INTO HISTORICAL, ETHNIC, AND SOCIOLOGICAL BACKGROUND OF GABON.

3330 WEINSTEIN F.B.
VIETNAM'S UNHELD ELECTIONS: THE FAILURE TO CARRY OUT THE 1956 REUNIFICATION ELECTIONS... (MONOGRAPH)
ITHACA: CORNELL U, DEPT ASIAN ST, 1966, 65 PP.
DESCRIBES EVENTS SURROUNDING HANOI'S ATTEMPTS TO BRING ABOUT REUNIFICATION OF VIETNAM THROUGH ELECTIONS PRESCRIBED BY GENEVA AGREEMENTS OF 1956. INDICATES THAT NORTH VIETNAM'S LEADERS BELIEVE US ENCOURAGED SAIGON TO REJECT GENEVA PLAN. CONCLUDES THAT ANY REALISTIC APPROACH TO NEGOTIATIONS IN THE PRESENT (1966) CONFLICT MUST RECOGNIZE HANOI'S EFFORTS TO IMPLEMENT ELECTIONS AND THE REASONS FOR FAILURE.

3331 WEISSBERG G.
"MAPS AS EVIDENCE IN INTERNATIONAL BOUNDARY DISPUTES: A REAPPRAISAL."
AMER. J. INT. LAW, 57 (OCT. 63), 781-803.
DISCUSSES NEW EMPHASIS ON MAPS AS IMPORTANT EVIDENCE IN BOUNDARY DISPUTES. GIVES 3 EXAMPLES FROM CASES IN INTERNATIONAL COURT OF JUSTICE. DISCUSSES INDIA-CHINA BOUNDARY CONFLICT.

3332 WELLS H.
"THE OAS AND THE DOMINICAN ELECTIONS."
OBIS, 7 (SPRING 63), 150-63.
EXPLORES FACTORS CONTRIBUTING POSITIVELY TO FIRST FREE ELECTION IN DOMINICAN REPUBLIC. DETAILS OAS ROLE: PROVIDED TECHNICAL ASSISTANCE FOR SETTING UP DEMOCRATIC ELECTORAL

PROCEDURES, AND OUTSIDE OBSERVERS AT CAMPAIGN END AND ON ELECTION DAY. GIVES CHRONOLOGICAL EVENTS, MAY '61-DEC. '62.

3333 WERNETTE J.P.
GOVERNMENT AND BUSINESS.
NEW YORK: MACMILLAN, 1964, 534 PP., LC#64-12864.
STUDY OF RELATIONSHIPS BETWEEN GOVERNMENT AND BUSINESS, ENABLING THE "THOUGHTFUL CITIZEN" TO BETTER UNDERSTAND PUBLIC PROBLEMS AND GOVERNMENT ACTION. COVERS SUCH TOPICS AS COMPETITION AND MONOPOLY, ECONOMIC GROWTH, PROTECTIVE LABOR LEGISLATION, CONSERVATION, INTERNATIONAL TRADE POLICIES, AND REGULATION OF PRIVATE FINANCIAL ACTIVITIES.

3334 WERTHEIM W.F.
EAST-WEST PARALLELS.
CHICAGO: QUADRANGLE BOOKS, INC, 1964, 284 PP.
A SOCIOLOGICAL STUDY OF ECONOMIC AND CULTURAL GROWTH OF SOUTHEAST ASIA, EMPHASIZING CONDITIONS AND CHANGES IN INDONESIA. CONCLUDES WITH "SOCIOLOGICAL APPROACH TO INDONESIAN HISTORY." DEPICTS NATIONALISM, RELIGIOUS REFORM MOVEMENTS, AND CORRUPTION.

3335 WEST F.J.
POLITICAL ADVANCEMENT IN THE SOUTH PACIFIC.
MELBOURNE, OXFORD U. PR., 1961, 186 PP.
DESCRIBES COLONIAL ADMINISTRATION OF FIJI, TAHITI AND SAMOA AND ANALYZES THE DEGREE AND EFFECTIVENESS OF LOCAL SELF-GOVERNMENT. CONCLUDES THAT A PARTIAL SUCCESS HAS BEEN ACHIEVED IN THIS AREA, WITH RESPONSIBILITY FOR FUTURE DEVELOPMENT RESTING WITH NATIVE LEADERS AS WELL AS WITH THE ADMINISTRATIVE POWERS.

3336 WHEARE K.C.
MODERN CONSTITUTIONS (HOME UNIVERSITY LIBRARY)
LONDON: OXFORD U PR, 1951, 216 PP.
DEFINES CONSTITUTION. DISCUSSES HOW CONSTITUTIONS MAY BE CLASSIFIED; WHAT THEY SHOULD CONTAIN, CONSTITUTIONAL AUTHORITY, CONSTITUTIONAL CHANGES; AND PROSPECTS FOR CONSTITUTIONAL GOVERNMENT. BELIEVES WAR, ABSOLUTISM, AND THOSE WHO ABUSE CONSTITUTIONAL FREEDOMS POSE SOME OF GREATEST THREATS TO CONSTITUTIONAL GOVERNMENT.

3337 WHEARE K.C.
GOVERNMENT BY COMMITTEE; AN ESSAY ON THE BRITISH CONSTITUTION.
LONDON: OXFORD U PR, 1955, 264 PP.
EXAMINES CONDUCT OF GOVERNMENT THROUGH GROUPS OF PEOPLE ACTING COLLECTIVELY IN COMMITTEES. STUDIES SIX TYPES OF COMMITTEES ACCORDING TO THEIR FUNCTIONS - COMMITTEES TO ADVISE, INQUIRE, NEGOTIATE, LEGISLATE, ADMINISTER, AND CONTROL. COMPARES COMMITTEES ON THEIR EFFECTIVENESS AND SHORTCOMINGS. ALSO COMPARES OFFICERS OF COMMITTEES. STATES THAT WELL-LED COMMITTEES ENSURE DEMOCRACY.

3338 WHEARE K.C.
LEGISLATURES.
LONDON: OXFORD U PR, 1963, 247 PP.
DISCUSSION OF PLACE AND PURPOSE OF LEGISLATURES IN MODERN COUNTRIES. EXAMINES FUNCTION OF LEGISLATURES IN MAKING OF PEACE AND WAR, THEIR POWER, INFLUENCE UPON THEM, AND CAUSES OF THEIR DECLINE.

3339 WHEARE K.C.
FEDERAL GOVERNMENT (4TH ED.)
NEW YORK: OXFORD U PR, 1964, 266 PP.
COMPARES AND CONTRASTS ORGANIZATION, INSTITUTIONS, DIVISION OF POWERS, BASIC PRINCIPLES, CONSTITUTIONS, ROLE OF GOVERNMENT IN ECONOMY, AND DEVELOPMENT OF COUNTRIES IN WORLD WITH FEDERAL SYSTEM OF GOVERNMENT. ESTABLISHES REQUIREMENTS FOR A FEDERAL SYSTEM.

3340 WHEELER G.
"RACIAL PROBLEMS IN SOVIET MUSLIM ASIA."
LONDON: OXFORD U. PR., 1960, 62 PP.
DESCRIBES IMPACT OF RUSSIANS AND THEIR CIVILIZATION ON THE MUSLIM PEOPLES IN THE SIX UNION REPUBLICS IN THE USSR. THERE ARE RACIAL PROBLEMS IN THE EASTERN REPUBLICS BUT AUTHOR ASSERTS THAT MUSLIM ATTITUDE TOWARD SOVIET REGIME IS DIFFICULT TO ASSESS.

3341 WHEELER G.
THE PEOPLES OF SOVIET CENTRAL ASIA: A BACKGROUND BOOK.
LONDON: THE BODLEY HEAD, 1966, 126 PP.
STUDIES MUSLIM PEOPLES INHABITING SOUTHERN RUSSIA, NORTH OF PERSIA AND AFGHANISTAN, FROM HISTORICAL POINT OF VIEW. EMPHASIZES EFFECTS ON CULTURE AS REGIMES CHANGED IN RUSSIA, AND PRESENT-DAY SOVIETIZATION. INCLUDES CHAPTER ON ETHNOLOGY AND ENVIRONMENT.

3342 WHEELER-BENNETT J.W.
THE NEMESIS OF POWER (2ND ED.)
NEW YORK: ST MARTIN'S PRESS, 1964, 831 PP.
HISTORY OF GERMAN ARMY, FROM DEFEAT IN WWI TO ITS REESTABLISHMENT IN WEST GERMANY, EMPHASIZES ROLE OF OFFICER CORPS AS RESPONSIBLE FOR NATURE AND CONTINUITY OF ARMY'S EMBROILMENT IN POLITICS. PRIMARILY COVERS WWII PERIOD, THE PECULIAR RELATIONSHIP BETWEEN HITLER AND THE GENERAL STAFF.

3343 WHITAKER A.P.
ARGENTINE UPHEAVAL.
NEW YORK: FREDERICK PRAEGER, 1956, 179 PP., LC#55-12018.
DISCUSSES FALL OF PERON AND RISE OF NEW REGIME IN ARGENTINA. EXAMINES SOCIAL STRUCTURE OF COUNTRY, POLITICAL PARTIES, AND FOREIGN POLICY UNDER BOTH REGIMES. CONCLUDES WITH PROBLEMS FACING US IN ITS ARGENTINE RELATIONS.

3344 WHITAKER A.P., JORDAN D.C.
NATIONALISM IN CONTEMPORARY LATIN AMERICA.
NEW YORK: FREE PRESS OF GLENCOE, 1966, 228 PP., LC#66-12891.
TRACES DEVELOPMENT OF LATIN AMERICAN "MULTIFORM NATIONALISM" FROM 1930'S TO PRESENT. EMPHASIZES BASIC POLITICAL, HISTORICAL, AND CULTURAL DIVERSITIES OF NATIONALISM IN EACH LATIN AMERICAN COUNTRY, BUT IDENTIFIES CONCERN WITH MATERIAL WELL-BEING AND SOCIAL JUSTICE AS MAJOR CHARACTERISTICS OF ENTIRE LATIN AMERICAN NATIONALIST GROWTH. DISCUSSES TEN COUNTRIES INDIVIDUALLY.

3345 WHITE C.L., RENNER G.T.
HUMAN GEOGRAPHY: AN ECOLOGICAL STUDY OF GEOGRAPHY.
NEW YORK: APPLETON, 1948, 692 PP.
AUTHORS HOLD THAT GEOGRAPHY IS PRIMARILY HUMAN ECOLOGY, OR THE STUDY OF HUMAN SOCIETY IN RELATION TO THE EARTH BACKGROUND. TEXT TREATS THE CONTENT, POINT OF VIEW, AND TOOLS OF GEOGRAPHY. DISCUSSES CLIMATIC AND MINERAL FACTORS OF THE NATURAL ENVIRONMENT. ANALYZES THE RACE, CULTURE, DISTRIBUTION, AND POPULATION DENSITY OF MAN AS MODIFIERS OF THE GEOGRAPHIC EQUATION.

3347 WHITE D.S.
SEEDS OF DISCORD.
SYRACUSE: U. PR., 1964, 471 PP.
TRACES RISE OF FREE FRANCE AND ITS RELATIONSHIP WITH WESTERN ALLIES, REVEALING CONFLICTS BETWEEN DE GAULLE AND CHURCHILL, FDR, HULL AND OTHERS, SAYING THERE IS A DISTANCE BETWEEN HIM AND OTHER MEN WHICH OTHERS HAVE TO UNDERSTAND OR FORGIVE.

3348 WHITE J.
"WEST GERMAN AID TO DEVELOPING COUNTRIES."
INTERNATIONAL AFFAIRS (U.K.) 41, (JAN.65), 74-88.
THE HISTORY AND GOALS OF WEST GERMAN AID TO THE DEVELOPING COUNTRIES IS ILLUSTRATIVE OF GENERAL PROBLEMS FACED BY ALL DONORS AND THOSE PECULIAR TO GERMANY. INTERESTINGLY, POLITICAL CONSIDERATIONS (OTHER THAN HALLSTEIN DOCTRINE) ARE OF LITTLE IMPORT COMPARED TO DESIRE TO PROMOTE GROWTH, FREE ENTERPRISE, AND TRADE. UK- GERMAN DATA COMPARED.

3349 WHITE J.W.
"MASS MOVEMENTS AND DEMOCRACY: SOKAGAKKAI IN JAPANESE POLITICS."
AM. POL. SCI. REV., 61 (SEPT. 67), 744-750.
DISCUSSES ROLE OF SOKAGAKKAI SECT IN JAPANESE POLITICS. EXAMINES GROUP'S VALUES OF ABSOLUTE FREEDOM, EQUALITY, HAPPINESS - IDEALS IT SEEKS THROUGH AGENCY OF POLITICAL SYSTEM. DISCUSSES GROUP'S IDEAL AND ACTUAL FUNCTIONS, AND ASSESS ITS PRESENT AND FUTURE EFFECTS ON JAPANESE ATTITUDES AND SYSTEMS.

3350 WHITE R.J. ED.
THE CONSERVATIVE TRADITION.
LONDON: NICHOLAS KAYE, 1950, 256 PP.
COLLECTION OF ESSAYS BY LEADING ENGLISH STATESMEN, PHILOSOPHERS, WRITERS, AND PAMPHLETEERS ON THE CONSERVATIVE TRADITION. DISCUSSES HUMAN NATURE AND POLITICS, POLITICAL RESPONSIBILITY, FUNCTIONS OF GOVERNMENT, POLITICAL AND ECONOMIC CHANGES, ETC. INCLUDES AN INTRODUCTION GIVING BASIC HISTORICAL BACKGROUND.

3351 WHITE W.L., STRICK J.C.
"THE TREASURY BOARD AND PARLIAMENT."
CAN. PUBLIC ADMIN., 10 (JUNE 67), 209-222.
DISCUSSES LITTLE-KNOWN CANADIAN TREASURY BOARD AND PRESENT SECRETARIAT ADVISING IT. EXPLAINS POLITICAL DIMENSIONS OF BOARD AND THE WAY THESE ARE RELATED TO ITS CENTRAL POSITION IN OVERSEEING GOVERNMENT FINANCIAL ACTIVITIES. SUGGESTS MEANS OF IMPROVING BOARD'S ADMINISTRATIVE PROCEDURES.

3352 WHITEFORD A.H.
TWO CITIES OF LATIN AMERICA: A COMPARATIVE DESCRIPTION OF SOCIAL CLASSES.
GARDEN CITY: DOUBLEDAY, 1964, 266 PP., $1.45.
A STUDY WHICH DETAILS THE CRITERIA FOR MEMBERSHIP IN ANY GIVEN PART OF THE SOCIAL HIERARCHY, COMPARES INTERCLASS RELATIONSHIPS, AND DESCRIBES THE SIGNIFICANTLY DIFFERENT LIMITS AND MEANS OF UPWARD MOBILITY.

3353 WHITEMAN M.M. ED.
DIGEST OF INTERNATIONAL LAW* VOLUME 5, DEPARTMENT OF STATE PUBLICATION 7873.
WASHINGTON: GOVT PR OFFICE, 1965, 1175 PP.
THIS IS CHAPTER XIII IN A STATE DEPARTMENT SERIES ON

WORLD PRACTICES AND LEGAL ACTIONS EMBRACING CURRENT INTERNATIONAL LAW. EXTENSIVE CITATION OF POLICY STATEMENTS AND LEGAL DOCUMENTS. CONCERNS "RIGHTS AND DUTIES OF STATES." OTHERS IN SERIES WHICH COMMENCED IN 1963 TREAT MANY FACETS OF INTERNATIONAL LAW FROM RECOGNITION TO TERRITORIAL SEAS.

3354 WHITING K.R.
THE SOVIET UNION TODAY: A CONCISE HANDBOOK.
NEW YORK: FREDERICK PRAEGER, 1962, 405 PP., LC#62-13749.
CONDENSATION OF SOVIET HISTORY. ITS DISCUSSION OF NATIONALITY, TRANSPORTATION, LEADERSHIP, AND INTERNATIONAL COMMUNISM IS INTRODUCTORY IN CHARACTER.

3355 WICKENS G.M., SAVORY R.M.
PERSIA IN ISLAMIC TIMES: A PRACTICAL BIBLIOGRAPHY OF ITS HISTORY, CULTURE AND LANGUAGE (PAMPHLET)
MONTREAL: MCGILL U PR, 1964, 57 PP.
INTENDED AS "BASIC DESIDERATE LIST" FOR UNDERGRADUATE AND GRADUATE WORK. WORKS ARE ARRANGED ACCORDING TO LANGUAGE GROUP. MATERIAL IS OF VALUE TO SOCIAL SCIENTIST INTERESTED IN RELIGIOUS, HISTORICAL, ECONOMIC, AND LINGUISTIC ASPECTS OF CULTURE. INCLUDES INDEX.

3356 WIENER F.B.
CIVILIANS UNDER MILITARY JUSTICE; THE BRITISH PRACTICE SINCE 1689 ESPECIALLY IN NORTH AMERICA.
CHICAGO: U OF CHICAGO PRESS, 1967, 346 PP., LC#67-25530.
DESCRIBES DEVELOPMENT OF PROCEDURE OF MILITARY TRIALS FOR CIVILIANS IN BRITISH SERVICE, BEGINNING WITH MUTINY ACT OF 1689 AND ENDING WITH ARMY AND AIR FORCE ACTS OF 1955. EMPHASIZES COURT-MARTIALS OF REVOLUTIONARIES DURING REVOLUTIONARY WAR. INCLUDES DECISIONS BY BRITISH JUDGE ADVOCATES GENERAL ON CONSTITUTIONALITY OF TRIALS. DETAILED APPENDIXES PROVIDE NAMES OF ALL CIVILIANS TRIED.

3357 WIGGIN L.M.
THE FACTION OF COUSINS: A POLITICAL ACCOUNT OF THE GRENVILLES, 1733-1763.
NEW HAVEN: YALE U PR, 1958, 351 PP., LC#58-6549.
TESTS VALIDITY OF HISTORICAL THEORY THAT POLITICAL ORGANIZATION IN 18TH-CENTURY ENGLAND WAS VESTED IN FAMILY SOCIAL STRUCTURE RATHER THAN IN POLITICAL PARTIES. STUDIES THE FIRST GENERATION OF THE GRENVILLES OF BUCKINGHAMSHIRE AND THEIR POLITICAL ADVANCEMENT. CONCLUDES THAT FAMILY "PARTIES" DID NOT EXIST ANY MORE THAN POLITICAL PARTIES DID.

3358 WILBER D.N.
ANNOTATED BIBLIOGRAPHY OF AFGHANISTAN.
NEW HAVEN: HUMAN REL AREA FILES, 1956, 259 PP., LC#62-21993.
ANNOTATED AND INDEXED BIBLIOGRAPHY OF 1,230 ITEMS ON MODERN AFGHANISTAN. INCLUDES PUBLICATIONS IN EUROPEAN LANGUAGES AND WORKS IN RUSSIAN, ARABIC, PERSIAN, AND PUSHTU PUBLISHED WITHIN AND OUTSIDE AFGHANISTAN. SECOND EDITION INCLUDES SUPPLEMENT COVERING WORKS APPEARING BETWEEN 1956 AND 1962. ITEMS OF GREATER INTEREST MARKED BY ASTERISK.

3359 WILBER L.A.
"THE GOVERNMENTAL STRUCTURE OF MISSISSIPPI: ITS STRENGTHS AND WEAKNESSES."
SOUTHERN QUART., 6 (OCT. 67), 65-94.
SURVEY OF MISSISSIPPI GOVERNMENT PRESENTED IN TERMS OF ITS CONSTITUTION, ITS LEGISLATURE AND LEGISLATIVE APPORTIONMENT PROBLEMS, ITS EXECUTIVE BRANCH, ITS COURTS, ITS MUNICIPAL AND COUNTY GOVERNMENTS, AND ITS NEW SYSTEM OF SCHOOL DISTRICTS. MAKES WIDE USE OF STATISTICS AND OF COMPARISON WITH OTHER STATES. FINDS MISSISSIPPI GOVERNMENT TYPICAL. BELIEVES INDUSTRIALIZATION WILL ACCELERATE CHANGES.

3360 WILBUR C.M.
CHINESE SOURCES ON THE HISTORY OF THE CHINESE COMMUNIST MOVEMENT (PAMPHLET)
NY: COLUMBIA U, EAST ASIAN INST, 1950, 56 PP.
ANNOTATED BIBLIOGRAPHY OF MATERIALS IN THE EAST ASIATIC LIBRARY OF COLUMBIA UNIVERSITY, LISTING WORKS IN CHINESE DEALING WITH THE CHINESE COMMUNIST MOVEMENT. PRESENTS BOOKS, PERIODICALS, AND ARTICLES IN A CHRONOLOGICAL FRAMEWORK FROM THE ORIGINS UP TO OCTOBER, 1949. ITEMS ENTERED UNDER PERIOD WITH WHICH THEY DEAL RATHER THAN BY DATE OF PUBLICATION. CROSS REFERENCES AND SUBJECT-PERSONAGE INDEX INCLUDED.

3361 WILCOX W.A.
PAKISTAN; THE CONSOLIDATION OF A NATION.
NEW YORK: COLUMBIA U PRESS, 1963, 276 PP., LC#63-9873.
STUDY OF DEVELOPMENT OF PAKISTAN UNDER PRINCELY STATES, LEADING TO INDEPENDENCE. EXAMINES PROBLEMS OF GOVERNING AND UNIFIYING PAKISTAN AS MODERN STATE AND PROGRAMS UNDERTAKEN BY NATIONAL GOVERNMENT. EXPLAINS RELATIONSHIP OF PAKISTAN TO INDIA.

3362 WILCOX W.A.
INDIA, PAKISTAN AND THE RISE OF CHINA.
NEW YORK: WALKER, 1964, 143 PP.
'ULTIMATE FATE OF ASIA HINGES ON ABILITY OF STATES OCCUPYING REGION FORMERLY CALLED HINDUSTAN TO MAINTAIN FREEDOM AND INTEGRITY, TO OVERCOME INTERNAL AND EXTERNAL FORCES THREATENING THEM.' DEATH OF NEHRU AND CHINESE INVASION OF 1962 INDICATED INDIA'S INEFFECTIVE LEADERSHIP. URGES ESTABLISHMENT OF NATIONAL SECURITY OBJECTIVES OVER NARROWER POLITICAL AND IDEOLOGICAL GOALS.

3363 WILDING N., LAUNDY P.
"AN ENCYCLOPEDIA OF PARLIAMENT."
LONDON: CASSELL & CO LTD, 1958.
COLLECTION OF INFORMATION RELATING TO PARLIAMENT AND ITS ASSOCIATED SUBJECTS. HEADINGS ARE ARRANGED IN ONE ALPHABETICAL SEQUENCE. ENTRIES CHOSEN FOR THEIR RELEVANCE TO THE CREATION AND GROWTH OF POWERS, PRIVILEGES, AND PRECEDENTS OF PARLIAMENT, OR FOR THEIR INFLUENCE ON ITS CUSTOMS AND PROCEDURES. UNANNOTATED BIBLIOGRAPHY OF POLITICAL BIOGRAPHIES AND WORKS CONCERNING THE PARLIAMENTS OF UK.

3364 WILDNER H.
DIE TECHNIK DER DIPLOMATIE.
STUTTGART: SPRINGER VERLAG, 1959, 342 PP.
DISCUSSES EVOLUTION OF DIPLOMATIC TECHNIQUES, ROLE OF FOREIGN MINISTER, TECHNIQUES OF NEGOTIATION, DIPLOMACY OUTSIDE OFFICIAL FRAMEWORK, AND DIPLOMATIC APPARATUS AS SUBJECT TO PUBLIC CRITICISM AND CONTROL.

3365 WILLIAMS B. ED.
THE SELBORNE MEMORANDUM.
LONDON: OXFORD U PR, 1925, 184 PP.
COLLECTION OF OFFICIAL DOCUMENTS, KNOWN COLLECTIVELY AS SELBORNE MEMORANDUM, REVIEWING MUTUAL RELATIONS OF BRITISH SOUTH AFRICAN COLONIES IN 1907 LEADING TO UNION. LONG INTRODUCTION. CORRESPONDENCE CONCERNS CAUSE OF SOUTH AFRICAN DISUNION, ITS EFFECTS ON RAILWAY DEVELOPMENT, FISCAL POLICY, AND ECONOMIC POSITION.

3366 WILLIAMS F.R.A.
"FUNDAMENTAL RIGHTS AND THE PROSPECT FOR DEMOCRACY IN NIGERIA."
U. PENN. LAW REV., 115 (MAY 67), 1073-1090.
DEALS WITH CONSTITUTIONAL PROBLEMS OF NIGERIA. DISCUSSES CAUSES OF DISSATISFACTION WITH CONSTITUTION THAT AROSE AT TIME OF INDEPENDENCE. ANALYZES POSSIBILITY OF DEVISING NEW CONSTITUTION CAPABLE OF ENSURING STABLE, VIRILE, AND POPULAR GOVERNMENT WHILE SAFEGUARDING INDIVIDUALS' RIGHTS.

3367 WILLIAMS L.E.
OVERSEAS CHINESE NATIONALISM: THE GENESIS OF THE PAN-CHINESE MOVEMENT IN INDONESIA, 1900-1916.
NEW YORK: FREE PRESS OF GLENCOE, 1960, 235 PP., LC#60-9582.
A STUDY OF CHINESE POPULATIONS IN INDONESIA. ATTEMPTS TO SHOW THAT DECISIONS FOR OR AGAINST COMMUNISM OR DEMOCRACY WILL BE MADE ON A NATIONALISTIC BASIS: SOUTHEAST ASIANS WILL SUPPORT IDEOLOGY WHICH APPEARS TO OFFER GREATER STRENGTH TO THEIR NATIONALIST CAUSES.

3368 WILLIAMS P.M., GOLDEY D.B.
"THE FRENCH GENERAL ELECTION OF MARCH 1967."
PARLIMENTARY AFFAIRS, 20 (SUMMER 67), 206-221.
DISCUSSES COURSE AND CHARACTER OF 1967 ELECTION IN WHICH GAULLISTS WON A VICTORY AND SUFFERED A SETBACK. DEALS IN SOME DETAIL WITH MARSEILLES CONSTITUENCY AND WITH SOCIALISTS IN NORTHERN INDUSTRIAL AREA.

3369 WILLIAMSON H.F. ED., BUTTRICK J.A.
ECONOMIC DEVELOPMENT - PRINCIPLES AND PATTERNS.
ENGLEWOOD CLIFFS: PRENTICE HALL, 1954, 576 PP., LC#54-9455.
COLLECTION OF ESSAYS ON FACTORS AND MEASURES IMPORTANT TO ECONOMIC GROWTH. EXAMINES ROLE OF NATURAL RESOURCES, DEMOGRAPHIC PATTERNS, LABOR FORCE, TECHNOLOGY, FOREIGN TRADE AND CAPITAL TRANSFERS, AND CULTURAL FACTORS. INCLUDES CASE STUDIES IN ECONOMIC DEVELOPMENT (JAPAN, KOREA, INDIA, MEXICO).

3370 WILLIAMSON J.A.
GREAT BRITAIN AND THE COMMONWEALTH.
LONDON: ADAMS & CHARLES BLACK, 1965, 214 PP.
HISTORY OF FORMATION, DEVELOPMENT, AND RELATIONS OF BRITISH EMPIRE AND COMMONWEALTH. TREATS TRANSFORMATION OF EMPIRE TO COMMONWEALTH IN DETAIL BY COVERING POLITICAL FIGURES AND WORLD EVENTS DURING PERIOD. DISCUSSES PROS AND CONS OF BRITISH POLICY TOWARD SUBJECTS.

3371 WILLNER A.R.
THE NEOTRADITIONAL ACCOMMODATION TO POLITICAL INDEPENDENCE* THE CASE OF INDONESIA * RESEARCH MONOGRAPH NO. 26.
PRINCETON: CTR OF INTL STUDIES, 1966, 71 PP.
THESIS& THAT MANY NEW STATES WHEN INDEPENDENT SUPERIMPOSE INDIGENOUS VALUES AND TRADITIONAL BEHAVIOR PATTERNS ON THE MODERN ORGANIZATIONAL STRUCTURES BEQUEATHED THEM BY CO-ONIALISM. MOREOVER, THIS OCCURS MOST FREQUENTLY IN THE BUREAUCRACIES WHICH MUST IMPLEMENT POLICY. INDONESIA'S DEVELOPMENT AS A GUIDED DEMOCRACY IS OFFERED AS A CASE STUDY.

3372 WILLOUGHBY W.C.
RACE PROBLEMS IN THE NEW AFRICA: A STUDY OF THE RELATION OF BANTU AND BRITONS IN THOSE PARTS OF BANTU AFRICA...
LONDON: OXFORD U PR, 1923, 296 PP.
ATTEMPTS TO EXPLORE "SOUL" OF BANTU PEOPLE. CONTAINS SECTIONS ON BANTU TRIBAL RELATIONS; BANTU LIFE AND THOUGHT;

RELIGION; LAWS AND POLITICS; AND EDUCATION. PART III DEALS WITH EUROPEANIZATION OF BANTU AFRICA AND TASK OF CHURCH IN THEIR EDUCATION.

3373 WILLOUGHBY W.F.
PRINCIPLES OF PUBLIC ADMINISTRATION WITH SPECIAL REFERENCE TO THE NATIONAL AND STATE GOVERNMENTS OF THE UNITED STATES.
WASHINGTON: BROOKINGS INST, 1927, 720 PP.
A STUDY OF THE ORGANIZATION AND CONDUCT OF FEDERAL AND STATE ADMINISTRATIONS, WITH EMPHASIS ON ROLES AND PRACTICES OF THE EXECUTIVE AND LEGISLATIVE BRANCHES AND THEIR RELATED AGENCIES. EXAMINES INTERNAL ORGANIZATION AND OPERATING SERVICES, PERSONNEL, MATERIEL, AND FINANCE PROCEDURES AND CONTROL.

3374 WILLOUGHBY W.W.
THE ETHICAL BASIS OF POLITICAL AUTHORITY.
NEW YORK: MACMILLAN, 1930, 460 PP.
COMPLETE STUDY OF CLASSICAL FORMS OF POLITICAL AUTHORITY AS VIEWED BY THE ETHICAL MORALIST. ANALYSIS INCLUDES BASIS FOR ETHICAL INQUIRY, PROS AND CONS OF VARIOUS GOVERNMENTAL STYLES, AND PRESENTATION OF ETHICO-JURISTIC THEORY. DRAWS NO GENERAL CONCLUSION, BUT GIVES VIEW ON ETHICAL BASIS OF EACH AUTHORITY FORM AS IT IS STUDIED.

3375 WILLS A.J.
AN INTRODUCTION TO THE HISTORY OF CENTRAL AFRICA.
LONDON: OXFORD U PR, 1967, 412 PP.
VIEWS EARLY INVASIONS OF EUROPEAN TRADERS THROUGHOUT THE CONTINENT, GROWTH OF SLAVE TRADE AND DISRUPTION OF AFRICAN LIFE, AND MISSIONS. THEN CONFINES ITSELF TO BRITISH COLONIZATION ALONG ZAMBEZI AND ESTABLISHMENT OF TERRITORIES, DESCRIBING POLICIES AND CHARACTERISTICS OF TERRITORIES UP TO END OF COLONIAL PHASE.

3376 WILLSON F.M.G.
ADMINISTRATORS IN ACTION.
TORONTO: TORONTO UNIV PRESS, 1961, 349 PP.
CASE STUDIES OF BRITISH ADMINISTRATION SYSTEM DESIGNED TO TEACH MANAGEMENT TECHNIQUES.

3377 WILMERDING L. JR.
THE ELECTORAL COLLEGE.
NEW BRUNSWICK: RUTGERS U PR, 1958, 217 PP.
TRACES HISTORICAL BACKGROUND OF ELECTORAL COLLEGE AND CONSIDERS THREE CURRENTLY PROPOSED PLANS FOR ITS REFORM: THE DISTRICT SYSTEM, NATIONAL PLEBISCITE, AND PROPORTIONAL VOTING.

3378 WILPERT C.
"A LOOK IN THE MIRROR AND OVER THE WALL."
COMMONWEAL, 86 (MAY 67), 224-225.
RESULTS OF A RECENT SURVEY SHOW ATTITUDES IN WEST GERMANY CHANGING TOWARD REUNIFICATION WITH EAST GERMANY. MOST GERMANS FAVOR A PRAGMATIC POLICY, WITH SOME PROGRESS TOWARD REUNIFICATION. THERE IS A DECLINE IN THOSE WHO ARE STRONGLY COMMITTED TO REUNIFICATION, AND FEW ARE WILLING TO SEE REUNIFICATION AT THE COST OF BASIC CHANGES IN THE FEDERAL REPUBLIC.

3379 WILSON J.Q.
"A GUIDE TO REAGAN COUNTRY* THE POLITICAL CULTURE OF SOUTHERN CALIFORNIA."
COMMENTARY, 43 (MAY 67), 37-45.
THE SURPRISING SUCCESS OF RONALD REAGAN, AND OF "REAGANISM," CAN BE TRACED PRIMARILY TO A WIDESPREAD CONCERN FOR LOSS OF VALUES. SOUTHERN CALIFORNIA IS EXAMINED AS A POLITICAL CULTURE DISPLAYING THIS CONCERN, AND IS COMPARED TO SAN FRANCISCO BAY AREA. RESIDENTS ARE SEEN AS HAVING A SET OF VALUES WHICH CONTENT THEM. THE DANGER OF "MORALITY" AS A POLITICAL ISSUE IS NOTED.

3380 WILSON P. ED.
GOVERNMENT AND POLITICS OF INDIA AND PAKISTAN: 1885-1955; A BIBLIOGRAPHY OF WORKS IN WESTERN LANGUAGES.
BERKELEY: U CAL INST ASIA STUD, 1956, 357 PP., LC#56-63303.
BIBLIOGRAPHY INCLUDES BOOKS, PAMPHLETS, AND NONSERIAL GOVERNMENT PUBLICATIONS. WORKS ARRANGED UNDER BROAD SUBJECT DIVISIONS AND CHRONOLOGICALLY BY DATE OF PUBLICATION. WORKS INDEXED BY AUTHOR, TITLE, BY SERIES, AND PUBLISHER. INCLUDES 5,294 ITEMS ON GENERAL HISTORY, POLITICS, CONSTITUTIONAL HISTORY, GOVERNMENT AND ADMINISTRATION, AND INTERNATIONAL RELATIONS.

3381 WILSON P.
SOUTH ASIA; A SELECTED BIBLIOGRAPHY ON INDIA, PAKISTAN, CEYLON (PAMPHLET)
NEW YORK: AMER INST PACIFIC REL, 1957, 43 PP.
UNANNOTATED BIBLIOGRAPHY OF INTRODUCTORY LITERATURE, INCLUDING BIBLIOGRAPHIES, REFERENCE WORKS, AND PRIMARY SOURCE MATERIAL, STRESSING RECENT WORKS CONCERNING INDIA, PAKISTAN, AND CEYLON. CLASSIFIED WITHIN GEOGRAPHICAL DIVISIONS BY CHRONOLOGICAL SUBJECT OR FORMAT OF WORK.

3382 WILSON T.
FINANCIAL ASSISTANCE WITH REGIONAL DEVELOPMENT (PAMPHLET)
FREDERICTON, N.B., CANADA: U. OF GLASGOW, 1964, 75 PP.
ANALYZES TYPES OF POLICY ACTION THAT WILL CAUSE GREATEST RATE OF ECONOMIC GROWTH IN ATLANTIC PROVINCES. CONCENTRATES ON STUDYING TAX INCENTIVES TO PROMOTE ECONOMIC AND INDUSTRIAL GROWTH. CONSIDERS COSTS OF GOVERNMENT AND METHODS OF APPLYING NEW POLICIES.

3383 WILSON T.
POLICIES FOR REGIONAL DEVELOPMENT.
LONDON: OLIVER & BOYD, 1964, 93 PP.
COMPARES OFFICIAL MEASURES FOR REGIONAL DEVELOPMENT ADOPTED BY CANADA AND ENGLAND. FOCUSES ON USE OF TAX INCENTIVES AND OTHER BUDGETARY INDUCEMENTS. DESCRIBES EFFECTS OF MOBILITY ON CENTERS OF GROWTH, FINANCIAL ASSISTANCE TO INDUSTRY, AND COST TO GOVERNMENT.

3384 WILSON U.
EDUCATION AND CHANGING WEST AFRICAN CULTURE.
NY: COLUMBIA U TEACHERS COLLEGE, 1963, 125 PP., LC#63-19047.
STUDIES IMPACT OF EDUCATION ON WEST AFRICA, INCLUDING HISTORICAL BACKGROUND, PHELPS-STOKES REPORTS, STRESSES OF URBANIZATION ON EDUCATION, BRITISH COLONIAL EDUCATION POLICY, AND THE QUALITY OF EDUCATION.

3385 WILSON W.
THE STATE: ELEMENTS OF HISTORICAL AND PRACTICAL POLITICS.
BOSTON: D C HEATH, 1918, 554 PP.
DISCUSSES OBJECTS AND FUNCTIONS OF GOVERNMENT, NATURE OF LAW; EXAMINES STRUCTURE OF GOVERNMENT OF MAJOR BELLIGERENT POWERS OF WWI, INCLUDING US.

3386 WINKS R.W. ED.
THE HISTORIOGRAPHY OF THE BRITISH EMPIRE-COMMONWEALTH.
DURHAM: DUKE U PR, 1966, 596 PP., LC#66-15555.
COLLECTION OF ESSAYS ON HISTORY AND HISTORICAL LITERATURE OF BRITISH COMMONWEALTH. EMPHASIZES RECENT LITERATURE AND INTERPRETATIONS, LARGELY SINCE WWII. SEEKS TO EXPLAIN TRENDS IN WRITING OF COMMONWEALTH HISTORY AND POINTS TO "UNCHARTED WATERS" IN BRITISH HISTORIOGRAPHY.

3387 WINT G. ED.
ASIA: A HANDBOOK.
NEW YORK: FREDERICK PRAEGER, 1965, 856 PP., LC#65-13263.
ARTICLES ABOUT RELATIONS BETWEEN THE ASIAN STATES AND THE REST OF THE WORLD, FOCUSING ON THE GROWTH IN WORLD POWER EXERCISED BY THESE COUNTRIES. GIVE BASIC COUNTRY-BY-COUNTRY INFORMATION AND SURVEYS, EMPHASIZING POLITICAL, SOCIAL, ECONOMIC, CULTURAL, AND RELIGIOUS ASPECTS OF ASIA, WITH MAPS AND EXTRACTS FROM TREATIES AND AGREEMENTS SIGNED SINCE WWII.

3388 WINT G. ED.
"ASIA: A HANDBOOK."
NEW YORK: FREDERICK PRAEGER, 1966.
COMPREHENSIVE REFERENCE WORK ON ASIA CONTAINING ESSAYS ON POLITICAL, SOCIAL, ECONOMIC, CULTURAL, AND RELIGIOUS ASPECTS OF ASIA; MAPS; EXTRACTS FROM TREATIES AND AGREEMENTS SIGNED SINCE 1945; AND BASIC INFORMATION AND SURVEYS ON EACH NATION. UNANNOTATED BIBLIOGRAPHY OF AMERICAN PUBLICATIONS RELEASED SINCE 1952, WITH EMPHASIS ON POST-1960 WORKS.

3389 WINTER E.H., STEWARD J.H. ED. ET AL.
CONTEMPORARY CHANGE IN TRADITIONAL SOCIETIES: VOLUME I - INTRODUCTION AND AFRICAN TRIBES.
URBANA: U OF ILLINOIS PR, 1967, 519 PP., LC#66-25557.
FIVE ANTHROPOLOGISTS SYSTEMATICALLY OBSERVE AND ANALYZE PROBLEMS OF MODERNIZATION AND THEIR APPLICATION TO SOCIETIES OF TANGANYIKA, KENYA, AND NIGERIA. DEFINE TRADITIONAL CULTURE AND THE PRECONTACT STATE OF EACH SOCIETY. EXAMINE MECHANISMS THAT MEDIATED FACTORS OF MODERNIZATION FROM NATIONAL AND WORLD CONTEXTS TO LOCAL SOCIETIES, AND EMPHASIZE INTERACTION OF THESE CULTURES WITH FORCES OF CHANGE.

3390 WIONCZEK M.
"LATIN AMERICA FREE TRADE ASSOCIATION."
INT. CONCIL., 551 (JAN. 65), 80 PP.
CRITIQUE OF LATIN AMERICAN NATIONALISM AS A STRUCTURE ON TRADE AND ECONOMIC DEVELOPMENT IN THAT AREA. CITES UTILITY OF LAFTA IN REGIONAL COOPERATION.

3391 WISEMAN H.V.
BRITAIN AND THE COMMONWEALTH.
NEW YORK: BARNES AND NOBLE, 1967, 157 PP., LC#67-16629.
DISCUSSES COMMONWEALTH IN WORLD CONTEXT WITH EMPHASIS ON BRITISH INFLUENCE. COMPARES SOCIAL AND POLITICAL SYSTEMS OF MEMBER NATIONS WITH BRITISH MODEL. INCLUDES FORMAL AND INFORMAL TIES WITHIN COMMONWEALTH, AND EXAMINES MEANING OF MEMBERSHIP. PROJECTS FUTURE POLITICAL AND ECONOMIC RELATIONSHIPS AMONG MEMBERS AND COMMENTS ON FUTURE ROLE IN WORLD AFFAIRS. SUGGESTS THAT TIES AMONG MEMBERS MAY BE WEAKENING.

3392 WITHERELL J.W.
OFFICIAL PUBLICATIONS OF FRENCH EQUATORIAL AFRICA, FRENCH CAMEROONS, AND TOGO, 1946-1958 (PAMPHLET)
WASHINGTON: LIBRARY OF CONGRESS, 1964, 78 PP., LC#64-60029.

AN ANNOTATED BIBLIOGRAPHY OF 405 PUBLICATIONS CONCERNED WITH AFRIQUE EQUATORIALE FRANCAISE AND THE TRUST TERRITORIES WHICH WERE ISSUED DURING THE TERM OF THE FOURTH REPUBLIC. COVERS PUBLICATIONS OF GOVERNMENT GENERAL OF FRENCH EQUATORIAL AFRICA, GOVERNMENTS OF FOUR TERRITORIES WHICH COMPRISED AEF, AND THE ADMINISTRATIONS IN THE CAMEROONS AND TOGO FROM 1946-58. SOURCES IN FRENCH AND ENGLISH.

3393 WITTFOGEL K.A.
"ORIENTAL DESPOTISM: A COMPARATIVE STUDY OF TOTAL POWER."
NEW HAVEN: YALE U PR, 1957.
SYSTEMATICALLY DESCRIBES AND ANALYZES PATTERNS OF CLASS AND PROPERTY IN SOCIETY WHOSE LEADERS HOLD POWER THROUGH THE STATE AND NOT LAND. EVALUATES CONCEPTIONS OF ELITES, AND PHENEMONA SUCH AS LANDLORDISM, CAPITALISM, GENTRY, AND GUILD. EXTENSIVE BIBLIOGRAPHY IN RELEVANT EUROPEAN AND ASIAN LANGUAGES.

3394 WODDIS J.
AFRICA, THE WAY AHEAD.
NEW YORK: INTERNATIONAL PUBLRS, 1963, 174 PP., LC#64-17900.
INDICATES PROBLEMS AFRICANS ARE FACING CONCERNING INDEPENDENCE AND SELF-GOVERNMENT, ECONOMIC DEVELOPMENT, AND PAN-AFRICANISM. ANALYZES ATTITUDES OF AFRICAN PEOPLE, ORGANIZATIONS, AND STATESMEN, MAINTAINING THEY SHOW PATH LIKELY TO BE TRAVELED IN FUTURE.

3395 WOHLSTETTER R.
"CUBA AND PEARL HARBOR* HINDSIGHT AND FORESIGHT."
FOREIGN AFFAIRS, 43 (JULY 65), 691-707.
COMPARISON OF THE PEARL HARBOR AND CUBAN MISSILE CRISES IN TERMS OF INTELLIGENCE PROBLEMS AND THE TENUOUS BASIS OF INTELLIGENCE SUCCESSES. NOT ONLY IS RELIABLE INFORMATION HARD TO GET IN TIME, BUT IT IS OFTEN DROWNED OUT BY NOISE OR DISBELIEVED BECAUSE OF POLITICAL AND TECHNOLOGICAL ASSUMPTIONS ABOUT THE ENEMY'S MOTIVES AND CAPABILITIES.

3396 WOLF C.
FOREIGN AID: THEORY AND PRACTICE IN SOUTHERN ASIA.
PRINCETON: U. PR., 1960, 442 PP., $7.50.
ATTEMPTS TO CO-ORDINATE THEORY AND PRACTICE IN THE DISPOSITION OF FOREIGN-AID THROUGH A CONSIDERATION OF ALTERNATIVE METHODS OF DERIVING AN EFFECTIVE ALLOCATION FORMULA. THROUGHOUT BOOK, ATTEMPTS ARE MADE TO QUANTIFY PROXIMATE OBJECTIVES OF FOREIGN-AID AND TO SUBJECT THE RESULTING HYPOTHESES TO EMPIRICAL VERIFICATION.

3397 WOLF C. JR.
"THE POLITICAL EFFECTS OF SOME MILITARY PROGRAMS* SOME INDICATIONS FROM LATIN AMERICA."
ORBIS, 8 (WINTER 65), 871-893.
IN LATIN AMERICAN STUDIES A VARIETY OF OFTEN CONFLICTING HYPOTHESES HAVE BEEN SUGGESTED TO EXPLAIN AND PREDICT TRENDS IN THE INFLUENCE OF MILITARY ELITES AND THE ROLE OF US MILITARY AID IN THIS PROCESS. AFTER REVIEWING THESE THEORIES, WOLF STATISTICALLY TESTS THEM BY CORRELATING FITZGIBBON'S DEMOCRATIC STATUS DATA WITH DEFENSE AND AID EXPENDITURES.

3398 WOLFE B.D.
THREE WHO MADE A REVOLUTION.
NEW YORK: DIAL, 1948, 661 PP.
HISTORICAL BIOGRAPHY OF LENIN, TROTSKY, AND STALIN AND THEIR ROLES IN RUSSIAN REVOLUTION. MAINTAINS THAT THEIR LIVES WERE SERIES OF CONTROVERSIES THAT MADE CONTENT OF RUSSIAN HISTORY FROM REVOLUTION OF 1917 TO PURGES OF 1937. DISCUSSES THEIR CONFLICT WITH TSARISM, CAPITALISM, AND EACH OTHER.

3399 WOLFE B.D.
MARXISM; ONE HUNDRED YEARS IN THE LIFE OF A DOCTRINE.
NEW YORK: DIAL, 1965, 404 PP., LC#64-75226.
STUDIES MARXIST WRITINGS AND HERITAGE. MAINTAINS THAT THERE IS GREAT AMBIGUITY IN ORIGINAL AND PRESENT MARXIST DOCTRINE. ASKS WHETHER IT SUPPORTS NATIONALISM OR INTERNATIONALISM; "DEFENSISM," DEFEATISM, OR PACIFISM; AND DEMOCRACY OF DICTATORSHIP, BECAUSE OF RADICAL CHANGES IN INTERPRETATIONS OF ORIGINAL IDEOLOGY.

3400 WOLFE D.M. ED.
LEVELLER MANIFESTOES OF THE PURITAN REVOLUTION.
NEW YORK: THOMAS NELSON AND SONS, 1944, 440 PP.
COLLECTION OF MANIFESTOES OF THE LEVELLERS, A POLITICAL PARTY THAT PLAYED AN ACTIVE ROLE IN THE ENGLISH REVOLUTION OF 1642-49. WORK INCLUDES SUPPLEMENTARY COMMENTARIES BY EDITOR. MANIFESTOES ARE IMPORTANT BECAUSE INCLUDED IN THEM ARE FUNDAMENTAL IDEAS OF LIBERTY AND GOVERNMENT, USUALLY ATTRIBUTED TO LOCKE, THAT WERE INCORPORATED IN THE DECLARATION OF INDEPENDENCE AND IN THE CONSTITUTION.

3401 WOLFE T.W.
"KHRUSHCHEV'S DISARMAMENT STRATEGY."
ORBIS, 4 (SPRING 60), 13-27.
STRATEGY HAS THE SOLE AIM OF REDUCING WESTERN STRENGTH WHILE INCREASING POWER OF USSR. KHRUSHCHEV HAS NEVER RENOUNCED TRADITIONAL SOVIET RELIANCE ON VIOLENCE AS WEAPON IN THE WORLD REVOLUTIONARY STRUGGLE. AUTHOR SEES FEAR OF SURPRISE ATTACK, ECONOMIC PRESSURES, AND A 'POWER-DEAL' AS POSSIBLE SOURCES OF 'GENUINE' SOVIET INTEREST IN DISARMING.

3402 WOLFERS A.
BRITAIN AND FRANCE BETWEEN TWO WORLD WARS.
NEW YORK: HARCOURT BRACE, 1940, 446 PP.
DISCUSSES FOREIGN POLICIES OF BRITAIN AND FRANCE DURING INTERIM PERIOD, 1918-38. RELATES TREATY OF VERSAILLES, ECONOMIC TACTICS, AND POLITICAL ISOLATION TO ONSET OF WWII. IMPLICATES US IN POLICY ERRORS OF THESE TWO COUNTRIES.

3403 WOLFF R.L.
THE BALKANS IN OUR TIME.
CAMBRIDGE: HARVARD U PR, 1956, 618 PP., LC#56-6529.
INTRODUCTORY STUDY OF BALKAN COUNTRIES - YUGOSLAVIA, RUMANIA, BULGARIA, AND ALBANIA. DESCRIBES COUNTRIES AND PEOPLE, GIVING HISTORY FROM FOURTH CENTURY TO WWII. ANALYZES BALKAN ECONOMY SINCE WWII. STUDIES WAR YEARS, COMMUNIST TAKE-OVER, SOVIET-YUGOSLAV DISPUTE, YUGOSLAVIA SINCE BREAK WITH COMINFORM, POLITICAL LIFE IN BALKANS SINCE 1948, BALKAN ECONOMIES SINCE 1948, BALKAN RELIGION, EDUCATION, CULTURE.

3404 WOLFINGER R.E.
"REPUTATION AND REALITY IN THE STUDY OF COMMUNITY POWER."
AMER. SOCIOLOGICAL REV., 25 (OCT. 60), 636-644.
AN ATTEMPT TO EXPLORE THE UTILITY OF THE REPUTATIONAL METHOD FOR THE STUDY OF LOCAL POLITICAL SYSTEMS. CONCLUDES IT IS AN ADEQUATE AND MEANINGFUL METHOD.

3405 WOLPERT S.
INDIA.
ENGLEWOOD CLIFFS: PRENTICE HALL, 1965, 178 PP., LC#65-20603.
HISTORICAL STUDY OF DEVELOPMENT OF MODERN INDIA. COVERS BACKGROUND OF HINDU SOCIETY AND ITS INTERACTION WITH ISLAM. DISCUSSES BRITISH COLONIAL RULE AND RISE OF NATIONALISM TO NEHRU PERIOD.

3406 WOOD H.B.
NEPAL BIBLIOGRAPHY.
EUGENE: AMER NEPAL EDUCATN FDN, 1959, 108 PP.
NEARLY COMPLETE LIST OF MATERIALS BEFORE 1950. COVERS ALL PUBLISHED WESTERN-LANGUAGE MATERIALS ABOUT NEPAL-- HISTORY, GEOGRAPHY, ECONOMICS, AND POLITICS-- UP TO 1959. INCLUDES SOME ILLUSTRATIVE ASIAN-LANGUAGE MATERIALS. ARRANGEMENT IS ALPHABETICAL.

3407 WOODRUFF W.
IMPACT OF WESTERN MAN.
NEW YORK: ST MARTIN'S PRESS, 1967, 375 PP., LC#66-17299.
EXAMINES CAREFULLY AND EXTENSIVELY THE EFFECT UPON THE MODERN WORLD OF EUROPEAN IDEAS AND DEVELOPMENTS, CONCENTRATING ON THE ECONOMIC SPHERE. COMMENCES WITH COLONIAL EMPIRES OF 1750, GOES THROUGH WORLD-WIDE DISPERSAL, EUROPEAN BANKING CENTERS, TECHNOLOGICAL PROGRESS, CHANGING TRADE PATTERNS. COVERS ECONOMIC DEVELOPMENTS THROUGH 2 CENTURIES.

3408 WOODS H.D. ED.
PATTERNS OF INDUSTRIAL DISPUTE SETTLEMENT IN FIVE CANADIAN INDUSTRIES.
MONTREAL: MCGILL U, IND REL SEC, 1958, 395 PP.
STUDIES GOVERNMENT INTERVENTION IN SETTLEMENT OF LABOR DISPUTES AND ROLE OF CANADIAN LABOR RELATIONS LAW IN SETTLING THEM. COMPARES MEDIATION, ARBITRATION, AND LABOR LAW IN CANADA AND US. GIVES GENERAL INTERPRETATION OF CONTEMPORARY ACCOMMODATION THEORY.

3409 WOODS H.D., OSTRY S.
LABOUR POLICY AND LABOUR ECONOMICS IN CANADA.
TORONTO: MACMILLAN CO OF CANADA, 1962, 534 PP.
EXPLORES LABOR POLICY AND ECONOMICS IN CANADA, CONSIDERING ROLE OF GOVERNMENT IN LABOR RELATIONS, LABOR-RELATIONS BOARDS, ARBITRATION AND NEGOTIATIONS, LABOR FORCE, UNEMPLOYMENT, WAGES, AND FUTURE OF LABOR IN CANADIAN ECONOMY.

3410 WOOLBERT R.G.
FOREIGN AFFAIRS BIBLIOGRAPHY, 1932-1942.
NEW YORK: HARPER & ROW, 1945, 705 PP., LC#33-7094.
A SELECTED AND ANNOTATED LIST OF 10,000 BOOKS ON INTERNATIONAL RELATIONS COVERING THE DECADE FROM MID-1932 TO MID-1942. INCLUDES BOOKS IN ALL WESTERN LANGUAGES AS WELL AS TURKISH, HEBREW, ARABIC, CHINESE, AND JAPANESE. BOOKS CLASSIFIED INTO ANALYTICAL, CHRONOLOGICAL, AND REGIONAL TREATMENTS, AND INDEXED BY AUTHOR.

3411 WORLEY P.
ASIA TODAY (REV. ED.) (PAMPHLET)
TRENTON: TRENTON STATE COL, 1960, 35 PP.
BIBLIOGRAPHICAL GUIDE TO THE MOST GENERALLY USEFUL MATERIALS IN THE TRENTON STATE COLLEGE LIBRARY FOR STUDENTS OF ASIAN AFFAIRS. BOOKS RANGE FROM TRAVEL GUIDES TO TECHNICAL ECONOMIC AND SOCIOLOGICAL AREA STUDIES, VIRTUALLY ALL OF WHICH BEAR POST-1950 PUBLICATION DATES. ENTRIES BOTH CRITICALLY AND DESCRIPTIVELY ANNOTATED, AND ARRANGED BY GEOGRAPHICAL AREA.

3412 WORMUTH F.D.

THE ORIGINS OF MODERN CONSTITUTIONALISM.
NEW YORK: HARPER & ROW, 1949, 243 PP.
ANALYZES THE CONTRIBUTIONS OF THE CROMWELLIAN CONSTITUTIONS TO MODERN GOVERNMENT. DESCRIBES THE INTRODUCTION INTO POLITICAL SCIENCE OF SEPARATION OF POWERS, BICAMERALISM, THE WRITTEN CONSTITUTION, AND JUDICIAL REVIEW. TRACES THE TRADITION OF CONSTITUTIONALISM FROM ANCIENT GREECE TO 17TH-CENTURY BRITAIN.

3413 WOYTINSKY W.S., WOYTINSKY E.S.
WORLD COMMERCE AND GOVERNMENTS: TRENDS AND OUTLOOK.
NEW YORK: TWENTIETH CENT FUND, 1955, 907 PP., LC#55-8797.
EXTENSIVE SURVEY OF WORLD TRANSPORTATION, TRADE, AND POLITICAL SYSTEMS, INCLUDING BALANCE OF PAYMENTS AND INTERNATIONAL INVESTMENT, TARIFFS, RAILROADS, AVIATION, AND PUBLIC DEBTS.

3414 WRAITH R., SIMPKINS E.
CORRUPTION IN DEVELOPING COUNTRIES.
NEW YORK: W W NORTON, 1964, 211 PP.
EXAMINES PATTERN OF CORRUPTION IN BRITISH INSTITUTIONAL SYSTEM DURING 18TH AND 19TH CENTURIES AND INFLUENCE ON AFRICAN SYSTEMS, ESPECIALLY IN NIGERIA, DURING 20TH CENTURY.

3415 WRAITH R.E.
EAST AFRICAN CITIZEN.
LONDON: OXFORD U PR, 1959, 238 PP.
GENERAL SURVEY OF CITIZENSHIP IN BRITISH EAST AFRICA. BROADLY DISCUSSES POLITICAL, SOCIAL, ECONOMIC, AND RACIAL CONDITIONS, AND BASIC PROBLEMS OF GOVERNMENT IN THE AREA. COMPARES EAST AND WEST AFRICA, EMPHASIZING IMPACT OF GHANA ON BRITISH EAST AFRICA. INCLUDES APPENDIXES AND INDEX.

3416 WRAITH R.E.
"ADMINISTRATIVE CHANGE IN THE NEW AFRICA."
AFRICAN AFFAIRS, 66 (JULY 67), 231-240.
OUTLINES TRENDS WHICH HAVE DEVELOPED SINCE INDEPENDENCE IN THE STATES OF ENGLISH-SPEAKING AFRICA IN THE FIELD OF PUBLIC ADMINISTRATION. DESCRIBES IMPORTANT CURRENT PROBLEMS; CITES STUDIES THAT HAVE BEEN MADE. INCLUDES CIVIL SERVICE, PUBLIC CORPORATIONS, LOCAL GOVERNMENT, APPLICATION OF ADMINISTRATIVE LAW. WRITTEN BEFORE MILITARY COUPS IN WEST AFRICA.

3417 WRIGGINS W.H.
"CEYLON: DILEMMAS OF A NEW NATION."
PRINCETON: PRINCETON U PRESS, 1960.
ANALYSIS OF THE COMPLEXITIES OF CEYLON'S POLITICAL SYSTEM AND AN EXAMINATION OF FUNDAMENTAL PROBLEMS THAT HAVE DOMINATED PUBLIC AFFAIRS SINCE INDEPENDENCE. SUGGESTS DEVELOPMENTS IN CEYLON MAY PROGNOSTICATE POSSIBILITIES FOR THE FUTURE OF OTHER NEWLY INDEPENDENT COUNTRIES IN ASIA. UNANNOTATED BIBLIOGRAPHY OF PUBLIC DOCUMENTS, BOOKS, PAMPHLETS, AND PERIODICALS. MOST SOURCES POST-1950 AND IN ENGLISH.

3418 WRIGHT G.
THE RESHAPING OF FRENCH DEMOCRACY.
NEW YORK: HARCOURT BRACE, 1948, 277 PP.
AN INTERPRETATION OF FRENCH POST-WAR CONSTITUTIONAL GOVERNMENT; MORE ESPECIALLY, A NARRATIVE AND ANALYTICAL ACCOUNT OF THE MAKING OF THE FRENCH CONSTITUTION OF THE FOURTH REPUBLIC. TAKES INTO ACCOUNT THE CONFLICTING POLITICAL FORCES, ECONOMIC STRESSES, COLONIAL UNREST, ETC., WHICH MADE THE ESTABLISHMENT OF A NEW CONSTITUTION MORE DIFFICULT.

3419 WRIGHT G.
RURAL REVOLUTION IN FRANCE: THE PEASANTRY IN THE TWENTIETH CENTURY.
STANFORD: U. PR., 1964, 271 PP., $6.00.
TRACES GRADUAL AWAKENING OF FRENCH PEASANTRY--AT FIRST TO A NEW SELF-CONSCIOUSNESS, AND LATER TO SYNDICALIST ORGANIZATION AND POLITICAL ACTION. DISCUSSES RIVAL EFFORTS OF THE COMMUNISTS AND CATHOLICS IN THE COUNTRYSIDE. CONCLUDES WITH AN ANALYSIS AND TENTATIVE ASSESSMENT OF THE FIFTH REPUBLIC'S NEW COURSE IN THE AREA OF RURAL REFORM.

3420 WRIGHT P.Q. ED.
PUBLIC OPINION AND WORLD POLITICS.
CHICAGO: U OF CHICAGO PRESS, 1933, 237 PP.
EXAMINES PUBLIC OPINION AND EFFECTS OF PROPAGANDA. DISCUSSES PUBLIC OPINION AS A FACTOR IN GOVERNMENT AND STRATEGIES OF OPINION-MOLDERS. STUDIES METHODS, SLOGANS, SYMBOLS, AND HISTORY OF POLITICAL PROPAGANDA. FOCUSES ON STRATEGY OF REVOLUTIONARY AND WAR PROPAGANDA.

3421 WRIGHT Q.
A STUDY OF WAR.
CHICAGO: U OF CHICAGO PRESS, 1964, 451 PP.
STUDIES PHENOMENON OF WAR, ITS HISTORY, CAUSES, AND CONTROL. ATTEMPTS TO EXPLAIN WHY MILITARY BUDGETS RISE WHEN WAR IS CONSIDERED "OBSOLETE." MAINTAINS THAT SOLUTION TO PREVENTION OF WAR IS "ADAPTIVE STABILITY WITHIN WORLD-COMMUNITY," BUT THAT TECHNICAL AND SOCIAL DEVELOPMENTS ARE ACCENTUATING CONFLICT. INCLUDES EFFECTS OF WAR ON PEOPLE, LEGAL ASPECTS, AND STRUGGLE FOR POWER.

3422 WRIGHT Q.
"THE ESCALATION OF INTERNATIONAL CONFLICTS."
J. OF CONFLICT RESOLUTION, 9 (DEC. 65), 434-449.
FORMULA FOR THE PREDICTION OF WAR ESCALATION PROBABILITIES IS DERIVED WHICH IS A MODIFICATION OF RICHARDSON'S ARMS RACE FORMULA. 46 CONFLICTS STUDIED FROM WORLD WAR I TO THE PRESENT. MAGNITUDES OF KEY FACTORS AND ESCALATION PROBABILITIES GIVEN FOR THESE CONFLICTS, WHICH ARE CLASSED BY "NO HOSTILITIES," HOSTILITIES BUT NO ESCALATION, HOSTILITIES WITH ESCALATION, AND WORLD WARS.

3423 WRIGHT W.R.
"FOREIGN-OWNED RAILWAYS IN ARGENTINA: A CASE STUDY OF ECONOMIC NATIONALISM."
BUSINESS HISTORICAL REVIEW, 41 (SPRING 67), 62-93.
STUDIES THE CHANGING NATIONALISTIC ATTITUDES TOWARD FOREIGN RAILROAD IN ARGENTINA, FROM THE INTERNATIONALISM OF ALBERDI, MITRE, AND SARMIENTO, WHO INVITED BRITISH RR DEVELOPMENT IN 19TH CENTURY, TO THE XENOPHOBIC ECONOMIC NATIONALISM BEGUN BY DE ROSAS AND CONTINUED INTERMITTENTLY UP TO PERON. CRITICIZES ARGENTINE NATIONALIZATION OF RAILROADS AS LEADING TO ECONOMIC STASIS.

3424 WRONG D.H.
AMERICAN AND CANADIAN VIEWPOINTS.
WASHINGTON: AMER COUNCIL ON EDUC, 1955, 62 PP., LC#55-12179.
PRESENTS BRIEF SUMMARY OF NATIONAL VALUE SYSTEMS OF AMERICANS AND CANADIANS. COMPARES ATTITUDES ON FAMILY, RELIGION, EDUCATION, ECONOMIC ACTIVITIES, GOVERNMENT, SOCIAL CLASSES, AND LAW. COMPARES TWO SIMILAR INDUSTRIAL NATIONS TO DISCOVER DIFFERENCES.

3425 WUEST J.J. ED., VERNON M.C. ED.
NEW SOURCE BOOK IN MAJOR EUROPEAN GOVERNMENTS.
CLEVELAND: WORLD, 1966, 700 PP., LC#66-13148.
DESIGNED PRIMARILY TO PROVIDE BASIC SOURCE MATERIALS FOR TEACHERS AND STUDENTS OF POLITICAL SCIENCE. MATERIAL RELATES TO EUROPEAN GOVERNMENTS AND CONSISTS OF ORIGINAL DOCUMENTS, FROM THE MAGNA CARTA TO THE PRESENT DAY. EMPHASIZES THE POLITICAL STRUCTURE OF BRITAIN, FRANCE, GERMANY, AND RUSSIA. THE GOVERNMENT STRUCTURES OF ITALY, VATICAN CITY, SWITZERLAND, AND TURKEY ARE ALSO DOCUMENTED.

3426 WUNDERLICH F.
LABOR UNDER GERMAN DEMOCRACY, ARBITRATION 1918-1933.
NEW YORK: NEW SCHOOL SOC RES, 1940, 100 PP.
DESCRIBES CONFLICT BETWEEN LABOR AND CAPITAL AS INFLATION SOARED AND ECONOMY RECOILED UNDER REPARATIONS PAYMENTS. MAIN BATTLEFIELD WAS ARBITRATION AND HEREIN ARE DESCRIBED METHODS AND ACHIEVEMENTS OF BOTH SIDES.

3427 WUORINEN J.H.
"SCANDINAVIA."
ENGLEWOOD CLIFFS: PRENTICE HALL, 1965.
BIBLIOGRAPHICAL ESSAY OF ENGLISH BOOKS AND PERIODICALS FROM 1929-1964. ARRANGED BY GROUP TOPICS INCLUDING GENERAL HISTORIES, OFFICIAL PUBLICATIONS, ECONOMIC AND SOCIAL DEVELOPMENTS, FOREIGN POLICY AND AFFAIRS, AND SCANDINAVIAN COOPERATION. APPROXIMATELY 200 ENTRIES.

3428 WUORINEN J.H.
SCANDINAVIA.
ENGLEWOOD CLIFFS: PRENTICE HALL, 1965, 146 PP., LC#65-20604.
SURVEY OF SOCIO-POLITICAL CLIMATE OF SCANDINAVIA, INCLUDING GEOGRAPHY, POPULAR ORIGINS AND CHARACTERISTICS, AND HISTORICAL TRENDS.

3429 WURFEL S.W.
FOREIGN ENTERPRISE IN COLOMBIA.
CHAPEL HILL: U OF N CAR PR, 1965, 563 PP.
DISCUSSES LEGAL ENVIRONMENT FOR FOREIGN INVESTMENT IN COLOMBIA IN CONTEXT OF POLITICAL, ECONOMIC, AND SOCIAL DEVELOPMENT. COVERS ASSETS AND LIABILITIES OF COLOMBIA, DEVELOPMENT PROGRAMS NOW UNDER WAY, AND LEGAL INSTITUTIONS AND THEIR IMPACT ON INVESTMENT.

3430 WYCKOFF T.
"THE ROLE OF THE MILITARY IN LATIN AMERICAN POLITICS."
WESTERN POLIT. Q., 113 (SEPT. 60), 745-763.
STUDY OF THE THREE ROLES THAT FORCE PLAYS IN LATIN AMERICAN GOVERNMENTS. EXAMINES THE UNDERLYING SOCIAL AND ECONOMIC CONDITIONS IN THESE STATES THAT DETERMINE THE ROLE OF THE MILITARY.

3431 YAKOBSON S. ED.
FIVE HUNDRED RUSSIAN WORKS FOR COLLEGE LIBRARIES (PAMPHLET)
NEW YORK: AMER COUN LEARNED SOC, 1948, 38 PP.
AN ELEMENTARY BIBLIOGRAPHY SUGGESTING A BASIC LIBRARY OF RUSSIAN WORKS DEALING WITH RUSSIA IN SUCH AREAS AS CULTURE, POLITICAL HISTORY, GEOGRAPHY, LAW, ETC. DOES NOT INCLUDE PERIODICALS, NEWSPAPERS, SPECIALIZED MONOGRAPHS, OR ORIGINAL RUSSIAN BELLETRISTIC LITERATURE. PUBLISHED AS A GUIDE FOR SMALL LIBRARIES ESTABLISHING A BASIC COLLECTION. ALL ENTRIES PRINTED IN RUSSIAN, BUT NOT IN CYRILLIC ALPHABET.

3432 YAMAMURA K.

ECONOMIC POLICY IN POSTWAR JAPAN.
BERKELEY: U OF CALIF PR, 1967, 320 PP.
EXAMINES TWO POSTWAR ECONOMIC POLICIES - DEMOCRATIZATION IMPOSED BY "ALLIED POWERS" AND SUBSEQUENT REACTION OF DE-DEMOCRATIZATION PURSUED AND FORMULATED BY THE INDEPENDENT GOVERNMENT. CONSIDERS BOTH POLICIES IN TERMS OF WHAT, WHY, AND HOW. INCLUDES EXAMINATION OF JAPANESE ECONOMIC INSTITUTIONS AND POSTWAR GROWTH.

3433 YANAGA C.
"JAPAN SINCE PERRY."
NEW YORK: MCGRAW HILL, 1949.
COMPREHENSIVE SURVEY OF HISTORY OF JAPAN'S TRANSFORMATION INTO A MODERN POWER AND A STRONG STATE CAPABLE OF COPING WITH 19TH-CENTURY NATIONALISM AND EXPANSIONISM. COVERS PERIOD OF JAPANESE WESTERNIZATION FROM 1853 THROUGH OCCUPATION AND RECONSTRUCTION. EMPHASIS ON POLITICAL AND MILITARY INSTITUTIONS AS WELL AS CULTURAL AND ECONOMIC ASPECTS OF NATIONAL DEVELOPMENT. BIBLIOGRAPHY IN WESTERN LANGUAGES.

3434 YANG KUNG-SUN
THE BOOK OF LORD SHANG.
LONDON: PROBSTHAIN, 1928, 346 PP.
INTRODUCES SHANG YANG AND HIS RELATION TO LEGAL PRINCIPLES FOCUSES ON HISTORICAL AND LITERARY CRITICISM. SHOWS SHANG TO HAVE AIDED DEVELOPMENT OF SCHOOL OF LAW.

3435 YEAGER L.B.
INTERNATIONAL MONETARY RELATIONS: THEORY, HISTORY, AND POLICY.
NEW YORK: HARPER & ROW, 1966, 504 PP., LC#66-10055.
INVESTIGATES THEORY OF HOW THE SEVERAL ALTERNATIVE SYSTEMS OF INTERNATIONAL MONETARY RELATIONS OPERATE, INCLUDING SOME ABSTRACT ANALYSIS OF POLICY MEASURES. SURVEYS POLICIES PURSUED BY WORLD GOVERNMENTS OVER PAST THREE CENTURIES, AND DISCUSSES SOME PRESENT-DAY PROPOSALS FOR INTERNATIONAL MONETARY POLICY CHANGES.

3436 YEFREMOV A.
"THE TRUE FACE OF THE WEST GERMAN NATIONAL-DEMOCRATS."
INTERNATIONAL AFFAIRS (USSR), 4 (APR.67), 69-73.
ASSOCIATES EMERGENCE OF NEO-NAZI PARTIES WITH WESTERN OCCUPATION AUTHORITIES AND GFR GOVERNMENT ANALYSIS OF NCD, ITS CONSTITUENCY AND LEADERS, THE EXTENT OF ITS INFLUENCE, ITS FOREIGN POLICY AND AMBIGUOUS DOMESTIC PROGRAMS. ARGUES THAT IMPORTANT FACTOR IN RESTRAINING REVIVAL OF NAZISM IS INFLUENCE OF SOVIET UNION.

3437 YOUNG A.N.
CHINA'S WARTIME FINANCE AND INFLATION.
CAMBRIDGE: HARVARD U PR, 1965, 421 PP., LC#65-22049.
DISCUSSES CHINA'S FINANCIAL POLICIES FROM JAPAN'S INVASION IN 1937 TO END OF WWII. EXAMINES REVENUE AND EXPENDITURE, FOREIGN FINANCIAL AID, CURRENCY MANAGEMENT, AND INFLATION.

3438 YOUNG G.
THE HILL TRIBES OF NORTHERN THAILAND.
BANGKOK: SIAM SOCIETY, 1962, 93 PP.
DESCRIBES DERIVATION, LOCATION, POPULATION, RELIGION, ECONOMY, SOCIAL CUSTOMS, AND FORM OF VILLAGE GOVERNMENT FOR 16 TRIBES. DISCUSSES GROUP RELATIONS AND LINGUISTIC SIMILARITIES.

3439 YOUNG T.C. ED.
NEAR EASTERN CULTURE AND SOCIETY.
PRINCETON: PRINCETON U PRESS, 1951, 250 PP.
COLLECTION OF PAPERS ON BACKGROUND OF ISLAMIC CULTURE AND PEOPLE. DISCUSSES INTERACTION OF ISLAMIC AND WESTERN THOUGHT AND INTERNATIONAL RELATIONS AMONG ISLAMIC NATIONS AND ATTITUDE TOWARD WEST.

3440 YU LIEN YEN CHIU
INDEX TO THE CLASSIFIED FILES ON COMMUNIST CHINA.
HONG KONG: UNION RES INST, 1962, 197 PP.
A REVISED, UPDATED EDITION OF THE UNION RESEARCH INSTITUTE INDEX TO MATERIAL ON COMMUNIST CHINA. CLASSIFIED INTO FIVE MAIN DEPARTMENTS: POLITICAL AND SOCIAL, MILITARY, FINANCIAL AND ECONOMIC, CULTURAL AND EDUCATIONAL, GENERAL. INDEX IS GUIDE TO SYSTEM USED BY STAFF OF THE UNION RESEARCH INSTITUTE. THE INSTITUTE PROVIDES MATERIAL IN ORIGINAL CHINESE ON MICROFILM OR PHOTOSTAT. TRANSLATION PROVIDED.

3441 YUAN TUNG-LI
CHINA IN WESTERN LITERATURE.
NEW HAVEN: YALE U PR, 1958, 802 PP., LC#58-59833.
BIBLIOGRAPHY OF WORKS ON CHINA PUBLISHED BETWEEN 1921 TO 1957 IN ENGLISH, FRENCH, AND GERMAN. DESCRIBES 18,000 WORKS BUT DOES NOT INCLUDE PERIODICAL ARTICLES UNLESS PUBLISHED SUBSEQUENTLY AS INDEPENDENT MONOGRAPHS. AUTHORS NAMES IN ROMAN AND CHINESE CHARACTERS. WORKS ARRANGED ACCORDING TO SUBJECT. TWO APPENDICES AND INDEX OF NAMES. PORTUGUESE WRITINGS ON MACAO INCLUDED.

3442 YUAN TUNG-LI
A GUIDE TO DOCTORAL DISSERTATIONS BY CHINESE STUDENTS IN AMERICA, 1905-1960.
WASHINGTON: SINO-AMER CULTUR SOC, 1961, 248 PP., LC#61-16700
PROVIDES A COMPLETE RECORD OF 2,789 DISSERTATIONS SUBMITTED BY CHINESE STUDENTS AND ACCEPTED BY AMERICAN UNIVERSITIES BETWEEN YEARS 1905-60. ARRANGED UNDER TWO BROAD CLASSES: HUMANITIES, SOCIAL, AND BEHAVIORAL SCIENCES; PHYSICAL, BIOLOGICAL, AND ENGINEERING SCIENCES. WITHIN EACH CLASS, ENTRIES ARRANGED ALPHABETICALLY BY AUTHOR. APPENDIX CONTAINS STATISTICAL TABLES OF DISCIPLINES AND INSTITUTIONS.

3443 YUKIO O.
THE VOICE OF JAPANESE DEMOCRACY, AN ESSAY ON CONSTITUTIONAL LOYALTY (TRANS BY J. E. BECKER)
BALTIMORE: KELLY & WALSH, LTD, 1918, 108 PP.
DISCUSSES RELATIONSHIP OF JAPANESE IMPERIAL HOUSE AND CONSTITUTIONAL GOVERNMENT BEFORE WWI. DESCRIBES NATIONAL POLITICAL PARTIES' ORGANIZATION AND THEIR RESPONSIVENESS TO WISHES OF PEOPLE. NOTES MEANS OF FINDING OUT POPULAR SENTIMENT AND SPECIFIC PROCESSES USED IN RUNNING CONSTITUTIONAL GOVERNMENT. DISCUSSES COMPETITION FOR LOYALTY BETWEEN IMPERIAL HOUSE AND CONSTITUTION.

3444 ZABLOCKI C.J. ED.
SINO-SOVIET RIVALRY.
NEW YORK: FREDERICK PRAEGER, 1966, 242 PP., LC#66-26555.
DISCUSSES IMPLICATIONS FOR US POLICY OF THE SINO-SOVIET CONFLICT. ANTHOLOGY INCLUDES ARTICLES ON THE ORIGINS OF THE RIVALRY AND ITS IMPACT ON EUROPE, ASIA, AFRICA, LATIN AMERICA, AND THE US. DISCUSSES WHETHER USSR PLANNED TO INVADE CHINA IN 1963 TO STOP CHINESE NUCLEAR TESTS, AND WHETHER US HAS MORE TO FEAR FROM USSR OR CHINA.

3445 ZAGORIA D.S.
"THE FUTURE OF SINO-SOVIET RELATIONS."
ASIAN SURV., 1 (APR. 61), 3-14.
MAO'S STRATEGY, PROMISING A FASTER ROAD TO POWER, IS MORE APPEALING THAN KHRUSHCHEV'S WHICH INVOLVES A GAMBLE THAT WILL BE WON ONLY IF USSR WINS ITS ECONOMIC RACE WITH THE WEST.

3446 ZALESKI E.
PLANNING REFORMS IN THE SOVIET UNION 1962-1966.
CHAPEL HILL: U OF N CAR PR, 1967, 203 PP., LC#67-17035.
EXAMINES SOVIET ECONOMIC PLANNING AND ADMINISTRATION SPECIFICALLY DEALING WITH CHANGES AND REFORMS IN PERIOD 1962-66. DISCUSSES STRUCTURE OF NATIONAL PLANNING AND DECISION-MAKING ON ECONOMIC POLICY AND EXTENT OF CENTRAL CONTROL AND UNIT INDEPENDENCE. COVERS DIFFERENCE IN CHANGES SINCE REMOVAL OF KHRUSHCHEV.

3447 ZARTMAN I.W.
"THE SAHARA--BRIDGE OR BARRIER."
INT. CONCIL. 541 (JAN. 63), 62 PP.
ASSAYS THE STRENGTHS AND WEAKNESSES OF PAN-AFRICANISM, THE NOW DEFUNCT COMMON ORGANIZATION OF THE SAHARAN REGIONS, THE ARAB MAGHRED (NORTH AFRICAN UNITY), 'MOROCCO IRREDENTA', AND THE CASABLANCA GROUP.

3448 ZARTMAN I.W.
GOVERNMENT AND POLITICS IN NORTHERN AFRICA.
NEW YORK: PRAEGER, 1963, 205 PP., $5.00.
ANALYZES POLITICAL AND SOCIAL EVOLUTION AS WELL AS CONTEMPORARY EVENTS IN MOROCCO, ALGERIA, TUNISIA, LIBYA, UNITED ARAB REPUBLIC, SUDAN, ETHIOPIA AND SOMALIA. CONSIDERS THESE COUNTRIES AS A COHERENT GROUPING OF AFRICAN STATES, A FULCRUM FOR ARAB NATIONALISM AND A FORCE IN THE ISLAMIC WORLD. FOCUSES ATTENTION ON DILEMMA OF DEMOCRACY IN AREA.

3449 ZARTMAN I.W.
MOROCCO: PROBLEMS OF NEW POWER.
NEW YORK: ATHERTON, 1964, 276 PP., $7.95.
A STUDY OF THE DECISION-MAKING PROCESS IN MOROCCO FROM 1956 TO 1961, WITH SPECIFIC RESEARCHABLE PROBLEMS CONSIDERED.

3450 ZARTMAN I.W.
"LES RELATIONS ENTRE LA FRANCE ET L'ALGERIA DEPUIS LES ACCORDS D'EVIAN."
REV. FRANCAISE SCI. POL., 6 (DEC. 64), 1087-1113.
TRACES FRANCO-ALGERIAN ECONOMIC, POLITICAL AND CULTURAL RELATIONS IN PERIOD FROM 1962 TO 1964.

3451 ZARTMAN I.W.
INTERNATIONAL RELATIONS IN THE NEW AFRICA
ENGLEWOOD CLIFFS: PRENTICE HALL, 1966, 175 PP., LC#66-16339.
STUDY OF THE PATTERNS AND PROCESSES OF THE INTERNATIONAL RELATIONS AMONGST THE 17 NATIONS OF NORTH AND WEST AFRICA. ASSUMES THAT NATION'S PRIMARY RELATIONS ARE WITH ITS NEIGHBORS AND THAT THEORIES DERIVED FROM OLD STATES ARE APPLICABLE TO NEW ONES. APPLIES THESE IR THEORIES TO THE GENERAL RELATIONS IN THE AREA TO TEST AND REFINE THEM.

3452 ZAUBERMAN A.
"SOVIET BLOC ECONOMIC INTEGRATION."
PROBL. COMMUNISM, 8 (JULY-AUG. 59) 23-29.
ASSERTS THAT BLOCK ECONOMIC INTEGRATION

HAS FAR-REACHING POLITICAL IMPLICATIONS. INDICATES THAT IT MAY COMMEND ITSELF TO SOVIET POLICY-MAKERS AS MEANS OF STRENGTHENING INTRA-BLOC TIES AND THEREBY CONSOLIDATING SOVIET POLITICAL HEGEMONY OVER EASTERN EUROPE.

3453 ZEINE Z.N.
THE EMERGENCE OF ARAB NATIONALISM (REV. ED.)
BEIRUT: KHAYAT'S, 1966, 205 PP.
DISCUSSES ARAB NATIONALISM AS IT ROSE FROM THE OTTOMAN AND BRITISH DOMINATIONS TO ASSERTION OF INDEPENDENCE; SHOWS HOW YOUNG TURKS PROMOTED REDISCOVERY OF ARAB IDENTITY BEFORE AND DURING WAR YEARS UP TO 1918. PRIMARILY TREATS TURKISH-ARAB RELATIONS DURING THIS TIME. PORTRAYS EFFECTS OF IMPACT OF WEST IN WAKE OF OTTOMAN RULE AND EFFECT OF ISLAM ON TURKISH-ARAB RESPONSE.

3454 ZENKOVSKY S.A.
PAN-TURKISM AND ISLAM IN RUSSIA.
CAMBRIDGE: HARVARD U PR, 1960, 345 PP., LC#60-5399.
STUDIES POLITICAL AND SOCIAL IMPLICATIONS OF ISLAM THAT SERVED TO UNITE TURKIC PEOPLES OF RUSSIA, 1905-20. RELATES THEIR BACKGROUND AND THEIR CULTURAL AND SOCIAL DIFFERENCES FROM EUROPEAN NATIONAL GROUPS WITHIN RUSSIA. REVEALS TURKIC NATIONALISM PER SE WEAKER THAN COMMON ATTACHMENT TO MOSLEM RELIGION AND CULTURE. INCLUDES STUDIES OF TATARS, KAZAKHS, UZBEKS, JADIDS, AND AZERBAIJAN AREA.

3455 ZIESEL K.
DAS VERLORENE GEWISSEN.
MUNICH: JF LEHMANNS VERLAG, 1962, 232 PP.
ATTACK ON MORAL AND SPIRITUAL DECAY OF PUBLIC OFFICIALS IN GERMANY SINCE WWII. ACCUSES POLITICIANS OF LACK OF RESPONSIBILITY AND CONCERN FOR HUMANITY AND CALLS FOR A GATHERING OF ALL DECENT MEN TO PREVENT MORAL COLLAPSE OF GERMANY.

3456 ZIMMERMAN I.
A GUIDE TO CURRENT LATIN AMERICAN PERIODICALS: HUMANITIES AND SOCIAL SCIENCES.
GAINESVILLE, FLA.: KALLMAN PUB. CO., 1961,167 PP.LC#61-15751
ANNOTATED BIBLIOGRAPHY OF PERIODICALS PUBLISHED IN LATIN AMERICA OR THE US THAT ARE DESIGNED PRIMARILY FOR CIRCULATION WITHIN SOUTH AMERICA, CENTRAL AMERICA, MEXICO, OR THE WEST INDIES. YEAR 1958 SET AS BOUNDARY OF INCLUSION. ANNOTATIONS PROVIDE ADEQUATE CRITICAL AND DESCRIPTIVE INFORMATION. EXTRA BIBLIOGRAPHICAL DATA FOUND IN TITLE LIST AND CHRONOLOGICAL LIST.

3457 ZINKIN T.
REPORTING INDIA.
TORONTO: CLARK, IRWIN + CO, 1962, 224 PP.
SURVEYS POSTWAR INDIA, EXAMINING BASE OF SOCIETY AND POLITICAL ACTIVITIES UNDER BRITISH RULE AND IN INDEPENDENCE. DISCUSSES CONFLICT AND POLICY LEADING TO PARTITION AND COMMUNIST ACTIVITY IN INDIA.

3458 ZINKIN T.
CHALLENGES IN INDIA.
NEW YORK: WALKER, 1966, 248 PP.
DISCUSSES INDIAN DOMESTIC ISSUES AND EVENTS SINCE THE DEATH OF NEHRU. ANALYZES EFFECTS OF HIS ADMINISTRATION AND CHANGES SHASTRI INTRODUCED. CONSIDERS PROBLEMS OF AGRICULTURAL SELF-SUFFICIENCY AND INDUSTRIALIZATION FROM PRE-INDEPENDENCE TO SHASTRI. RELATED PROBLEMS OF CIVIL SERVICE CORRUPTION AND INDIAN-PAKISTANI RELATIONS ARE ALSO INCLUDED.

3459 ZINN H.
VIETNAM THE LOGIC OF WITHDRAWAL.
BOSTON: BEACON PRESS, 1967, 131 PP., LC#67-14112.
A REBUKE BY THE AUTHOR TO AMERICA'S CONTINUED MILITARY PRESENCE IN VIETNAM. THE PRICE OF THAT PRESENCE, IN LIVES, IN NATIONAL HONOR, AND IN MONEY NEEDED TO BUILD THE GREAT SOCIETY AND HELP WITH THE ECONOMIC DEVELOPMENT OF SOUTHEAST ASIA, IS FOUND INDEFENSIBLE.

3460 ZIOCK H.
SIND DIE DEUTSCHEN WIRKLICH SO?
SCHWARZWALD: HORST ERDMANN VERL, 1965, 363 PP.
COLLECTION OF ESSAYS BY FOREIGNERS ON GERMAN CULTURE AND CHARACTER. DISCUSSES CONTRIBUTIONS MADE BY GERMANS IN PHILOSOPHY AND SCIENCE, BASIC PRESUPPOSITIONS OF GERMAN MIND, AND DISCONTINUITY IN GERMAN HISTORY.

3461 ZOLBERG A.R.
"MASS PARTIES AND NATIONAL INTEGRATION: THE CASE OF THE IVORY COAST" (BMR)"
J. OF POLITICS, 25 (FEB. 63), 36-48.
CASE STUDY OF THE ROLE OF MASS ORGANIZATIONS IN AFRICAN NATIONAL INTEGRATION. SUGGESTS THAT IVORY COAST POLITICAL PARTIES OFTEN REINFORCE OBSTACLES TO NATION-BUILDING WHILE ASSERTING ITS BENEFICENT GOALS. STATES THAT PARTIES ALSO TEND TO CREATE NEW OBSTACLES TO ACHIEVEMENT OF GOALS SPECIFIED BY PARTY LEADERS.

3462 ZOLBERG A.R.
CREATING POLITICAL ORDER.
SKOKIE: RAND MCNALLY & CO, 1966, 168 PP., LC#66-19458.
DISCUSSES EMERGENCE OF ONE-PARTY NATIONS IN WEST AFRICA, 1950-65, COVERING PROBLEM OF NATIONALISM VS. TRIBALISM, USE OF ONE-PARTY GOVERNMENT IN ACHIEVING UNITY, AND DIFFICULTIES OF ESTABLISHING ORDER IN NEW NATIONS. COMPARES EFFECTIVENESS OF CONSTITUTIONAL VS. INSTITUTIONAL GOVERNMENT.

3463 ZOLLSCHAN G.K. ED., HIRSCH W. ED.
EXPLORATIONS IN SOCIAL CHANGE.
BOSTON: HOUGHTON MIFFLIN, 1964, 832 PP.
ESSAYS ON GENERAL PERSPECTIVES OF SOCIAL CHANGE AND SOCIAL SYSTEM MODELS OF CHANGE. INCLUDES WORKING PAPERS IN THEORY OF INSTITUTIONALIZATION. GENERAL STUDIES DEAL WITH ASPECTS OF PSYCHO-SOCIAL MODELS OF CHANGE, HISTORICAL PERSPECTIVES, CULTURAL CHANGE AND CONTACT, SOCIAL MOBILITY, AND ECONOMIC CHANGE.

3464 ZOPPO C.E.
"NUCLEAR TECHNOLOGY, MULTIPOLARITY, AND INTERNATIONAL STABILITY."
WORLD POLITICS, 18 (JULY 66), 579-606.
ZOPPO DESCRIBES UNBALANCING EFFECT OF NUCLEAR WEAPONS ON THE INTERNATIONAL SYSTEM: ARMS-CONTROL CONCEPTS ARE CONTRADICTORY TO TRADITIONAL BALANCE OF POWER THEORY, WAR HAS LOST MUCH OF ITS PAST LEGITIMACY, AND TECHNOLOGICAL FACTORS OF WAR MAKE POLITICAL AND MILITARY MISCALCULATIONS IRREVERSIBLE AND INTOLERABLE. ABILITY OF LEADERS TO ADJUST TO TECHNICAL CHANGE IS PROPOSED FOR GREATER SYSTEM STABILITY.

3465 ZWEIG F.
THE WORKER IN AN AFFLUENT SOCIETY: FAMILY LIFE AND INDUSTRY.
NEW YORK: FREE PRESS OF GLENCOE, 1961, 268 PP.
INTENSIVE STUDY OF WORKING CLASS BEHAVIOR IN THE HOME AND FACTORY. COVERS SEVERAL AGE GROUPS AND INCLUDES STATUS OF WOMAN AS PROVIDER.

3466 RUUD J.
TABOO, A STUDY OF MALAGASY CUSTOMS AND BELIEFS.
NEW YORK: HUMANITIES PRESS, 1960, 329 PP.
STUDIES TYPES AND DEVELOPMENT OF SANCTIONS, NORM, MORES, AND TABOOS IN PRIMITIVE CULTURE, THEIR DERIVATIONS AND EFFECTS UPON CULTURE. DISCUSSES CONCEPT OF ANTITHESIS AND ITS IMPORTANCE TO MAN

INDEX OF DOCUMENTS

A

ABA....AMERICAN BAR ASSOCIATION

ABDEL-MALEK A. H0054

ABEL T. H0055,H0300

ABERNATHY G.L. H0056

ABILITY TESTS....SEE KNO/TEST

ABM/DEFSYS....ANTI-BALLISTIC MISSILE DEFENSE SYSTEMS

ABORIGINES....ABORIGINES (AUSTRALIA)

B62
DILLING A.R.,ABORIGINE CULTURE HISTORY - A SURVEY OF PUBLICATIONS 1954-1957. GUINEA...SOC CHARTS NAT/COMP BIBLIOG/A AUSTRAL ABORIGINES. PAGE 41 H0825 — S/ASIA HIST/WRIT CULTURE KIN

B62
FALKENBERG J.,KIN AND TOTEM; GROUP RELATIONS OF AUSTRALIAN ABORIGINES IN THE PORT KEATS DISTRICT. SOCIETY STRATA STRUCT GP/REL PERS/REL MARRIAGE AGE ATTIT SEX...SOC STAT CHARTS AUSTRAL ABORIGINES. PAGE 48 H0964 — KIN INGP/REL CULTURE FAM

B63
CONFERENCE ABORIGINAL STUDIES,AUSTRALIAN ABORIGINAL STUDIES. ECO/UNDEV INT/TRADE COLONIAL ADJUST HABITAT HEREDITY...GEOG PSY LING SOC/EXP ANTHOL WORSHIP 20 AUSTRAL ABORIGINES. PAGE 32 H0638 — SOC SOCIETY CULTURE STRUCT

B63
TINDALE N.B.,ABORIGINAL AUSTRALIANS. KIN CREATE ROLE...SOC MYTH TREND 20 AUSTRAL ABORIGINES MIGRATION. PAGE 155 H3099 — CULTURE DRIVE ECO/UNDEV HABITAT

B64
BERNDT R.M.,THE WORLD OF THE FIRST AUSTRALIANS. S/ASIA ECO/UNDEV WORKER PROB/SOLV EFFICIENCY ROLE ...SOC MYTH WORSHIP AUSTRAL ABORIGINES. PAGE 16 H0311 — CULTURE KIN STRUCT DRIVE

B64
ELKIN A.P.,THE AUSTRALIAN ABORIGINES - HOW TO UNDERSTAND THEM (4TH ED.). FAM NEIGH DEATH MARRIAGE ATTIT BIO/SOC HABITAT...PSY SOC MYTH WORSHIP AUSTRAL ABORIGINES. PAGE 45 H0908 — CULTURE STRUCT SOCIETY KIN

B65
BERNDT R.M.,ABORIGINAL MAN IN AUSTRALIA. LAW DOMIN ADMIN COLONIAL MARRIAGE HABITAT ORD/FREE...LING CHARTS ANTHOL BIBLIOG WORSHIP 20 AUSTRAL ABORIGINES MUSIC ELKIN/AP. PAGE 16 H0312 — SOC CULTURE SOCIETY STRUCT

ABORTION....ABORTION

ABOSCH H. H0057

ABRAHAM W.E. H0058

ABRAMSKY C. H0633

ABRIKOSSOV, DIMITRI....SEE ABRIKSSV/D

ABRIKSSV/D....DIMITRI ABRIKOSSOV

ACAD RUMANIAN SCI DOC CTR H0059

ACAD/ASST....ACADEMIC ASSISTANCE COUNCIL (U.K.)

ACADEM....UNIVERSITY, COLLEGE, GRADUATE SCHOOL, HIGHER EDUCATION

N
CHINA QUARTERLY. COM AGRI INDUS ACADEM POL/PAR INT/TRADE CONFER GOV/REL...TIME/SEQ CON/ANAL INDEX 20. PAGE 1 H0014 — BIBLIOG/A ASIA DIPLOM POLICY

N
AVTOREFERATY DISSERTATSII. USSR INTELL ACADEM NAT/G DIPLOM GOV/REL KNOWL CONCPT. PAGE 2 H0029 — BIBLIOG MARXISM MARXIST COM

N
INADA S.,INTRODUCTION TO SCIENTIFIC WORKS IN HUMANITIES AND SOCIAL SCIENCES PUBLISHED IN JAPAN. LAW CULTURE ACADEM EDU/PROP...ART/METH HUM 20 CHINJAP. PAGE 76 H1525 — BIBLIOG/A NAT/G SOC S/ASIA

N
INTERNATIONAL CENTRE AFRICAN,BULLETIN OF INFORMATION ON THESES AND STUDIES IN PROGRESS OR PROPOSED. LAW CULTURE FINAN INDUS LABOR TEC/DEV EDU/PROP...GEOG SOC NAT/COMP 20. PAGE 78 H1554 — BIBLIOG/A ACT/RES ACADEM INTELL

N
MINISTERE DE L'EDUC NATIONALE,CATALOGUE DES THESES DE DOCTORAT SOUTENNES DEVANT LES UNIVERSITAIRES FRANCAISES. FRANCE LAW DIPLOM ADMIN...HUM SOC 20. PAGE 111 H2223 — BIBLIOG ACADEM KNOWL NAT/G

B38
DUNHAM W.H. JR.,COMPLAINT AND REFORM IN ENGLAND 1436-1714. UK LAW ACADEM NAT/G POL/PAR SCHOOL PRESS COLONIAL PARL/PROC MORAL...SOC/WK ANTHOL 15/18 HAKLUYT/R COWPER/W. PAGE 43 H0865 — ATTIT SOCIETY SECT

B42
BAYNES N.H.,INTELLECTUAL LIBERTY AND TOTALITARIAN CLAIMS. EUR+WWI GERMANY ITALY INTELL POL/PAR CIVMIL/REL NAT/LISM SOCISM CONCPT. PAGE 12 H0245 — KNOWL FASCISM EDU/PROP ACADEM

B45
HARVARD WIDENER LIBRARY,INDOCHINA: A SELECTED LIST OF REFERENCES. CAMBODIA FRANCE S/ASIA VIETNAM COLONIAL...POLICY 19/20. PAGE 67 H1351 — BIBLIOG/A ACADEM DIPLOM NAT/G

B49
MCLEAN J.M.,THE PUBLIC SERVICE AND UNIVERSITY EDUCATION. UK USA-45 DELIB/GP EX/STRUC TOP/EX ADMIN ...GOV/COMP METH/COMP NAT/COMP ANTHOL 20. PAGE 107 H2142 — ACADEM NAT/G EXEC EDU/PROP

B51
HUXLEY J.,FREEDOM AND CULTURE. UNIV LAW SOCIETY R+D ACADEM SCHOOL CREATE SANCTION ATTIT KNOWL...HUM ANTHOL 20. PAGE 76 H1512 — CULTURE ORD/FREE PHIL/SCI IDEA/COMP

B52
SCHATTSCHNEIDER E.E.,A GUIDE TO THE STUDY OF PUBLIC AFFAIRS. LAW LOC/G NAT/G LEGIS BUDGET PRESS ADMIN LOBBY...JURID CHARTS 20. PAGE 139 H2775 — ACT/RES INTELL ACADEM METH/COMP

B53
KANTOR H.,A BIBLIOGRAPHY OF UNPUBLISHED DOCTORAL DISSERTATIONS AND MASTERS' THESES DEALING WITH GOVTS, POL, INT REL OF LAT AM. L/A+17C INT/ORG POL/PAR ACT/RES OP/RES CONFER ATTIT...INT/LAW PHIL/SCI 20. PAGE 83 H1656 — BIBLIOG ACADEM DIPLOM NAT/G

B54
GIRALSO JARAMLLO G.,BIBLIOGRAFIA DE BIBLIOGRAFIAS COLOMBIANAS. L/A+17C ACADEM SECT CREATE EDU/PROP ...ART/METH GEOG LING TREND 20 COLOMB. PAGE 57 H1135 — BIBLIOG/A CULTURE PHIL/SCI ECO/UNDEV

B54
US LIBRARY OF CONGRESS,RESEARCH AND INFORMATION ON AFRICA: CONTINUING SOURCES. ISLAM ECO/UNDEV AGRI INDUS R+D ACADEM NAT/G INT/TRADE...SOC 20. PAGE 161 H3210 — BIBLIOG/A AFR PRESS COM/IND

B55
KHADDURI M.,LAW IN THE MIDDLE EAST. LAW CONSTN ACADEM FAM EDU/PROP CT/SYS SANCTION CRIME...INT/LAW GOV/COMP ANTHOL 6/20 MID/EAST. PAGE 85 H1703 — ADJUD JURID ISLAM

B56
VUCINICH A.,THE SOVIET ACADEMY OF SCIENCES. USSR STRUCT ACADEM NAT/G EDU/PROP ADMIN LEAD ROLE ...BIBLIOG 20 ACADEM/SCI. PAGE 164 H3280 — PHIL/SCI CREATE INTELL PROF/ORG

B57
CENTRAL ASIAN RESEARCH CENTRE,BIBLIOGRAPHY OF RECENT SOVIET SOURCE MATERIAL ON SOVIET CENTRAL ASIA AND THE BORDERLANDS. AFGHANISTN INDIA PAKISTAN UAR USSR ECO/UNDEV AGRI EXTR/IND INDUS ACADEM ADMIN ...HEAL HUM LING CON/ANAL 20. PAGE 28 H0567 — BIBLIOG/A COM CULTURE NAT/G

B57
SOUTH PACIFIC COMMISSION,INDEX OF SOCIAL SCIENCE RESEARCH THESES ON THE SOUTH PACIFIC. S/ASIA ACADEM ADMIN COLONIAL...SOC 20. PAGE 147 H2939 — BIBLIOG/A ACT/RES SECT CULTURE

L57
LIPSET S.M.,"POLITICAL SOCIOLOGY." NAT/G POL/PAR ECO/TAC PARTIC CHOOSE PWR...BIBLIOG/A 20. PAGE 97 H1939 — SOC ALL/IDEOS ACADEM

N57
JENNINGS W.I.,NATIONALISM, COLONIALISM, AND NEUTRALISM (PAMPHLET). ASIA INDIA S/ASIA UK INTELL ACADEM POL/PAR 20. PAGE 81 H1611 — NAT/LISM COLONIAL NEUTRAL ATTIT

B58
INDIA (REPUBLIC) PARLIAMENT,CLASSIFIED LIST OF PUBLIC UNDERTAKINGS AND OTHER BODIES IN INDIA. INDIA ACADEM LG/CO CONSULT LEGIT CONFER GOV/REL 20. PAGE 76 H1528 — NAT/G LEGIS LICENSE PROF/ORG

B58
SCHOEPS H.J.,KONSERVATIVE ERNEUERUNG IDEEN ZUR DEUTSCHEN POLITIK. GERMANY ELITES SOCIETY ACADEM CHOOSE SOCISM 19/20. PAGE 140 H2796 — POL/PAR IDEA/COMP CONSERVE NAT/G

B59
CONOVER H.F.,NIGERIAN OFFICIAL PUBLICATIONS, 1869-1959: A GUIDE. NIGER CONSTN FINAN ACADEM SCHOOL FORCES PRESS ADMIN COLONIAL...HIST/WRIT 19/20. PAGE 33 H0650 — BIBLIOG NAT/G CON/ANAL

B59
ISRAEL J.,THE CHINESE STUDENT MOVEMENT, 1927-1937; A BIBLIOGRAPHICAL ESSAY BASED ON THE RESOURCES OF — BIBLIOG/A ACADEM

THE HOOVER INSTITUTION. ASIA INTELL NAT/G EDU/PROP ATTIT
20. PAGE 79 H1571

B59
SISSONS C.B.,CHURCH AND STATE IN CANADIAN SECT
EDUCATION: AN HISTORICAL STUDY. CANADA ACADEM NAT/G EDU/PROP
SCHOOL LEGIS REGION MAJORITY...MAJORIT WORSHIP PROVS
18/20 CHURCH/STA. PAGE 145 H2891 GP/REL

B60
DE HERRERA C.D.,LISTA BIBLIOGRAFICA DE LOS TRABAJOS BIBLIOG
DE GRADUACION Y TESIS PRESENTADOS EN LA L/A+17C
UNIVERSIDAD, 1939-1960. PANAMA DIPLOM LEAD...SOC NAT/G
20. PAGE 38 H0754 ACADEM

B60
EMERY E.,INTRODUCTION TO MASS COMMUNICATIONS. COM/IND
ACADEM PROF/ORG SCHOOL ACT/RES EDU/PROP ATTIT PRESS
...CONCPT BIBLIOG/A. PAGE 46 H0920 CON/ANAL
CULTURE

B60
FLORES R.H.,CATALOGO DE TESIS DOCTORALES DE LAS BIBLIOG
FACULTADES DE LA UNIVERSIDAD DE EL SALVADOR. ACADEM
EL/SALVADR LAW DIPLOM ADMIN LEAD GOV/REL...SOC L/A+17C
19/20. PAGE 52 H1030 NAT/G

B60
LEYDER J.,BIBLIOGRAPHIE DE L'ENSEIGNEMENT SUPERIEUR BIBLIOG/A
ET DE LA RECHERCHE SCIENTIFIQUE EN AFRIQUE ACT/RES
INTERTROPICALE (2 VOLS.). AFR CULTURE ECO/UNDEV ACADEM
AGRI PLAN EDU/PROP ADMIN COLONIAL...GEOG SOC/INTEG R+D
20 NEGRO. PAGE 96 H1918

S60
HALSEY A.H.,"THE CHANGING FUNCTIONS OF UNIVERSITIES ACADEM
IN ADVANCED INDUSTRIAL SOCIETIES." R+D EDU/PROP CREATE
REPRESENT ROLE ORD/FREE PWR TREND. PAGE 65 H1298 CULTURE
ADJUST

S60
TURNER R.H.,"SPONSORED AND CONTEST MOBILITY IN THE AGE/Y
SCHOOL SYSTEM." UK USA+45 ELITES STRATA ACADEM NAT/COMP
FACE/GP EDU/PROP CONTROL INGP/REL ADJUST ATTIT SCHOOL
PERSON...METH/COMP 20. PAGE 157 H3142 STRUCT

B61
HOLDSWORTH M.,SOVIET AFRICAN STUDIES 1918-1959. BIBLIOG/A
USSR ACADEM NAT/G DIPLOM REGION KNOWL 20. PAGE 72 AFR
H1448 HABITAT
NAT/COMP

B61
YUAN TUNG-LI,A GUIDE TO DOCTORAL DISSERTATIONS BY BIBLIOG
CHINESE STUDENTS IN AMERICA, 1905-1960. ASIA ACADEM
CULTURE SOCIETY ECO/UNDEV NAT/G PROB/SOLV DIPLOM ACT/RES
LEAD ATTIT...HUM SOC STAT 20. PAGE 172 H3442 OP/RES

B62
HUNKIN P.,ENSEIGNEMENT ET POLITIQUE EN FRANCE ET EN EDU/PROP
ANGLETERRE. FRANCE UK CONSTN ACADEM SECT CHIEF LEGIS
DELIB/GP PROB/SOLV CONTROL REV ORD/FREE CONSERVE IDEA/COMP
...BIBLIOG 18/20. PAGE 75 H1496 NAT/G

B62
MANSUR F.,PROCESS OF INDEPENDENCE. GHANA INDIA NAT/COMP
INDONESIA PAKISTAN CONSTN ELITES INTELL STRUCT POL/PAR
ACADEM NAT/G REV PWR 20. PAGE 102 H2043 SOVEREIGN
COLONIAL

B62
MUKERJI S.N.,ADMINISTRATION OF EDUCATION IN INDIA. SCHOOL
ACADEM LOC/G PROVS ROUTINE...POLICY STAT CHARTS 20. ADMIN
PAGE 114 H2282 NAT/G
EDU/PROP

B62
US LIBRARY OF CONGRESS,A LIST OF AMERICAN DOCTORAL BIBLIOG
DISSERTATIONS ON AFRICA. SOCIETY SECT DIPLOM AFR
EDU/PROP ADMIN...GEOG 19/20. PAGE 161 H3212 ACADEM
CULTURE

N62
US CONGRESS JT ATOM ENRGY COMM,PEACEFUL USES OF NUC/PWR
ATOMIC ENERGY, HEARING. USA+45 USSR TEC/DEV ATTIT ACADEM
RIGID/FLEX...TESTS CHARTS EXHIBIT METH/COMP 20 SCHOOL
CONGRESS. PAGE 159 H3177 NAT/COMP

B63
HARTLEY A.,A STATE OF ENGLAND. UK ELITES SOCIETY DIPLOM
ACADEM NAT/G SCHOOL INGP/REL CONSEN ORD/FREE ATTIT
NEW/LIB...POLICY 20. PAGE 67 H1349 INTELL
ECO/DEV

B64
AVASTHI A.,ASPECTS OF ADMINISTRATION. INDIA UK MGT
USA+45 FINAN ACADEM DELIB/GP LEGIS RECEIVE ADMIN
PARL/PROC PRIVIL...NAT/COMP 20. PAGE 9 H0183 SOC/WK
ORD/FREE

B64
BOSTON UNIVERSITY LIBRARIES,CATALOG OF AFRICAN BIBLIOG
GOVERNMENT DOCUMENTS AND AFRICAN AREA INDEX. AFR ACADEM
NAT/G...SOC 20. PAGE 19 H0384

B64
DOOLIN D.J.,COMMUNIST CHINA: THE POLITICS OF MARXISM
STUDENT OPPOSITION. CHINA/COM ELITES STRATA ACADEM DEBATE
NAT/G WRITING CT/SYS LEAD PARTIC COERCE TOTALISM AGE/Y
20. PAGE 42 H0838 PWR

B64
HARBISON F.H.,EDUCATION, MANPOWER, AND ECONOMIC PLAN
GROWTH. WOR+45 ECO/DEV ECO/UNDEV ACADEM LABOR TEC/DEV
SCHOOL WORKER UTIL...IDEA/COMP NAT/COMP. PAGE 66 EDU/PROP
H1326 SKILL

B64
LATORRE A.,UNIVERSIDAD Y SOCIEDAD. SPAIN EDU/PROP ACADEM
LEAD GP/REL PERS/REL ATTIT KNOWL. PAGE 92 H1837 CULTURE
ROLE
INTELL

B64
NICOL D.,AFRICA - A SUBJECTIVE VIEW. AFR INT/ORG NAT/G
PLAN ADMIN COLONIAL PARL/PROC PARTIC REGION GOV/REL LEAD
LITERACY ATTIT...BIBLIOG 20 CIVIL/SERV. PAGE 118 CULTURE
H2350 ACADEM

B64
VALEN H.,POLITICAL PARTIES IN NORWAY. NORWAY ACADEM LOC/G
PARTIC ROUTINE INGP/REL KNOWL...QU 20. PAGE 161 POL/PAR
H3220 PERSON

B64
VON GRUNEBAUM G.E.,MODERN ISLAM: THE SEARCH FOR ISLAM
CULTURAL IDENTITY. ACADEM NEIGH WRITING NAT/LISM CULTURE
...HUM CONCPT 19/20 MUSLIM MID/EAST ARABS. PAGE 163 CREATE
H3269 SECT

S64
UNRUH J.M.,"SCIENTIFIC INPUTS TO LEGISLATIVE CREATE
DECISION-MAKING (SUPPLEMENT)" USA+45 ACADEM NAT/G DECISION
PROVS GOV/REL GOV/COMP. PAGE 159 H3171 LEGIS
PARTIC

B65
BENTWICH J.S.,EDUCATION IN ISRAEL. ISRAEL CULTURE SECT
STRATA PROB/SOLV TEC/DEV ADJUST ALL/VALS 20 JEWS. EDU/PROP
PAGE 15 H0293 ACADEM
SCHOOL

B65
CHENG C.-Y.,SCIENTIFIC AND ENGINEERING MANPOWER IN WORKER
COMMUNIST CHINA, 1949-1963. CHINA/COM USSR ELITES CONSULT
ECO/DEV R+D ACADEM LABOR NAT/G EDU/PROP CONTROL MARXISM
UTIL...POLICY BIBLIOG 20. PAGE 29 H0588 BIOG

B65
COWAN L.G.,EDUCATION AND NATION-BUILDING IN AFRICA. EDU/PROP
AFR CULTURE ECO/UNDEV POL/PAR ACT/RES LEAD COLONIAL
SOVEREIGN...METH/COMP ANTHOL BIBLIOG 20. PAGE 34 ACADEM
H0684 NAT/LISM

B65
CRAMER J.F.,CONTEMPORARY EDUCATION: A COMPARATIVE EDU/PROP
STUDY OF NATIONAL SYSTEMS (2ND ED.). CHINA/COM NAT/COMP
EUR+WWI INDIA USA+45 FINAN PROB/SOLV ADMIN CONTROL SCHOOL
ATTIT...IDEA/COMP METH/COMP 20 CHINJAP. PAGE 35 ACADEM
H0697

B65
HAVIGHURST R.J.,SOCIETY AND EDUCATION IN BRAZIL. SCHOOL
BRAZIL PORTUGAL ECO/UNDEV INDUS NAT/G CREATE ACADEM
INSPECT COLONIAL ADJUST DEMAND LITERACY...CENSUS ACT/RES
TREND CHARTS 16/20. PAGE 68 H1362 CULTURE

B65
HERBST J.,THE GERMAN HISTORICAL SCHOOL IN AMERICAN CULTURE
SCHOLARSHIP; A STUDY IN THE TRANSFER OF CULTURE. NAT/COMP
GERMANY USA+45 INTELL SOCIETY ACADEM PLAN ATTIT HIST/WRIT
IDEA/COMP. PAGE 70 H1399

B65
NATIONAL REFERRAL CENTER SCI,A DIRECTORY OF INDEX
INFORMATION RESOURCES IN THE UNITED STATES; SOCIAL R+D
SCIENCES. USA+45 PROF/ORG...PSY SOC 20. PAGE 116 ACADEM
H2322 ACT/RES

B65
NORDEN A.,WAR AND NAZI CRIMINALS IN WEST GERMANY: FASCIST
STATE, ECONOMY, ADMINISTRATION, ARMY, JUSTICE, WAR
SCIENCE. GERMANY GERMANY/W MOD/EUR ECO/DEV ACADEM NAT/G
EX/STRUC FORCES DOMIN ADMIN CT/SYS...POLICY MAJORIT TOP/EX
PACIFIST 20. PAGE 119 H2370

B65
OECD,MEDITERRANEAN REGIONAL PROJECT: TURKEY; EDU/PROP
EDUCATION AND DEVELOPMENT. FUT TURKEY SOCIETY ACADEM
STRATA FINAN NAT/G PROF/ORG PLAN PROB/SOLV ADMIN SCHOOL
COST...STAT CHARTS 20 OECD. PAGE 120 H2399 ECO/UNDEV

B65
OECD,THE MEDITERRANEAN REGIONAL PROJECT: ITALY; SCHOOL
EDUCATION AND DEVELOPMENT. ITALY SOCIETY STRATA EDU/PROP
FINAN NAT/G PROF/ORG WORKER PLAN PROB/SOLV ADMIN ECO/UNDEV
...STAT CHARTS METH 20 OECD. PAGE 120 H2400 ACADEM

B65
OECD,THE MEDITERRANEAN REGIONAL PROJECT: GREECE; EDU/PROP
EDUCATION AND DEVELOPMENT. FUT GREECE SOCIETY AGRI SCHOOL
FINAN NAT/G PROF/ORG WORKER PLAN PROB/SOLV ADMIN ACADEM
DEMAND ATTIT 20 OECD. PAGE 120 H2401 ECO/UNDEV

B65
OECD,THE MEDITERRANEAN REGIONAL PROJECT: SPAIN; ECO/UNDEV
EDUCATION AND DEVELOPMENT. FUT SPAIN STRATA FINAN EDU/PROP
NAT/G WORKER PLAN PROB/SOLV ADMIN COST...POLICY ACADEM
STAT CHARTS 20 OECD. PAGE 120 H2402 SCHOOL

B65
ORG FOR ECO COOP AND DEVEL,THE MEDITERRANEAN PLAN
REGIONAL PROJECT: AN EXPERIMENT IN PLANNING BY SIX ECO/UNDEV
COUNTRIES. FUT GREECE SPAIN TURKEY YUGOSLAVIA ACADEM
SOCIETY FINAN NAT/G PROF/ORG EDU/PROP ADMIN REGION SCHOOL
COST...POLICY STAT CHARTS 20 OECD. PAGE 121 H2427

B65
SABLE M.H.,MASTER DIRECTORY FOR LATIN AMERICA. AGRI INDEX
COM/IND FINAN R+D ACADEM LABOR NAT/G POL/PAR L/A+17C

VOL/ASSN INT/TRADE EDU/PROP 20. PAGE 136 H2728 — INT/ORG DIPLOM

B65
SHRIMALI K.L.,EDUCATION IN CHANGING INDIA. INDIA CULTURE DIPLOM FOR/AID GP/REL RACE/REL ATTIT SOC/INTEG 20 UNESCO CMN/WLTH. PAGE 143 H2866 — EDU/PROP PROF/ORG ACADEM

B65
VERMOT-GAUCHY M.,L'EDUCATION NATIONALE DANS LA FRANCE DE 1975. FRANCE FUT CULTURE ELITES R+D SCHOOL PLAN EDU/PROP EFFICIENCY...POLICY PREDICT CHARTS INDEX 20. PAGE 162 H3245 — ACADEM CREATE TREND INTELL

S65
"FURTHER READING." INDIA NAT/G ADMIN 20. PAGE 2 H0045 — BIBLIOG EDU/PROP SCHOOL ACADEM

S65
HUGHES T.L.,"SCHOLARS AND FOREIGN POLICY* VARIETIES OF RESEARCH EXPERIENCE." COM/IND DIPLOM ADMIN EXEC ROUTINE...MGT OBS CONGRESS PRESIDENT CAMELOT. PAGE 75 H1491 — ACT/RES ACADEM CONTROL NAT/G

S65
TRISKA J.F.,"SOVIET-AMERICAN RELATIONS* A MULTIPLE SYMMETRY MODEL." USA+45 USSR ACADEM ACT/RES EDU/PROP COERCE PERCEPT...NET/THEORY CHARTS NAT/COMP GEN/LAWS COLD/WAR. PAGE 157 H3132 — SIMUL EQUILIB DIPLOM

S65
WATT D.C.,"RESTRICTIONS ON RESEARCH* THE FIFTY-YEAR RULE AND BRITISH FOREIGN POLICY." ACADEM PERCEPT ...HIST/WRIT NAT/COMP TIME. PAGE 166 H3315 — UK USA+45 DIPLOM

B66
BRAIBANTI R.,RESEARCH ON THE BUREAUCRACY OF PAKISTAN. PAKISTAN LAW CULTURE INTELL ACADEM LOC/G SECT PRESS CT/SYS...LING CHARTS 20 BUREAUCRCY. PAGE 20 H0402 — HABITAT NAT/G ADMIN CONSTN

B66
FARRELL R.B.,APPROACHES TO COMPARATIVE AND INTERNATIONAL POLITICS. RUSSIA SOCIETY ACADEM GOV/REL GP/REL...METH/CNCPT NET/THEORY GOV/COMP HYPO/EXP SOC/EXP GEN/METH ANTHOL. PAGE 49 H0973 — DIPLOM NAT/COMP NAT/G

B66
GLAZER M.,THE FEDERAL GOVERNMENT AND THE UNIVERSITY. CHILE PROB/SOLV DIPLOM GIVE ADMIN WAR ...POLICY SOC 20. PAGE 57 H1140 — BIBLIOG/A NAT/G PLAN ACADEM

B66
KIRKENDALL R.S.,SOCIAL SCIENTISTS AND FARM POLITICS IN THE AGE OF ROOSEVELT. ACADEM PLAN ECO/TAC GIVE ADMIN CONTROL PRODUC...SOC 20 NEW/DEAL ROOSEVLT/F BURAGR/ECO. PAGE 86 H1722 — AGRI INTELL POLICY NAT/G

B66
MERRITT R.L.,COMPARING NATIONS* THE USE OF QUANTITATIVE DATA IN CROSSNATIONAL RESEARCH. ACADEM DIPLOM GP/REL...PHIL/SCI STAT TREND GP/COMP PERS/COMP GEN/METH ANTHOL BIBLIOG INDEX. PAGE 109 H2184 — NAT/COMP MATH COMPUT/IR QUANT

B66
OECD DEVELOPMENT CENTRE,CATALOGUE OF SOCIAL AND ECONOMIC DEVELOPMENT INSTITUTES AND PROGRAMMES* RESEARCH. ACT/RES PLAN TEC/DEV EDU/PROP...SOC GP/COMP NAT/COMP. PAGE 120 H2403 — ECO/UNDEV ECO/DEV R+D ACADEM

L66
"FEDERAL, STATE AND LOCAL GOVERNMENT PUBLICATIONS." ACADEM LOC/G NAT/G PROVS SCHOOL EFFICIENCY ...PHIL/SCI ANTHOL. PAGE 143 H2854 — BIBLIOG OP/RES METH

S66
"RESEARCH WORK 1965-1966." NEW/ZEALND ELITES ACADEM LOC/G MUNIC POL/PAR PROVS DIPLOM COLONIAL...SOC 20 AUSTRAL. PAGE 2 H0047 — BIBLIOG NAT/G CULTURE S/ASIA

S66
MARTZ J.D.,"THE PLACE OF LATIN AMERICA IN THE STUDY OF COMPARATIVE POLITICS." AFR ASIA CULTURE STRUCT ECO/UNDEV ACADEM CREATE...CLASSIF NAT/COMP. PAGE 104 H2072 — L/A+17C GOV/COMP STERTYP GEN/LAWS

S66
TURKEVICH J.,"SOVIET SCIENCE APPRAISED." USA+45 R+D ACADEM FORCES DIPLOM EDU/PROP WAR EFFICIENCY PEACE SKILL OBS. PAGE 157 H3137 — USSR TEC/DEV NAT/COMP ATTIT

B67
NATIONAL SCIENCE FOUNDATION,DIRECTORY OF SELECTED RESEARCH INSTITUTES IN EASTERN EUROPE. BULGARIA CZECHOSLVK HUNGARY POLAND ROMANIA INTELL ACADEM NAT/G ACT/RES 20. PAGE 116 H2323 — INDEX R+D COM PHIL/SCI

B67
RIESMAN D.,CONVERSATIONS IN JAPAN: MODERNIZATION, POLITICS, AND CULTURE. CHINA/COM STRATA STRUCT ECO/DEV INDUS ACADEM EDU/PROP...ART/METH SOC MODAL INT IDEA/COMP SOC/INTEG 20 CHINJAP HIROSHIMA. PAGE 131 H2629 — CULTURE SOCIETY ASIA

B67
RUDMAN H.C.,THE SCHOOL AND STATE IN THE USSR. COM USSR ACADEM LABOR LOC/G PUB/INST EDU/PROP GP/REL ROLE...POLICY DECISION MGT CHARTS 20. PAGE 136 H2712 — SCHOOL ADMIN NAT/G POL/PAR

L67
GLAZER M.,"LAS ACTITUDES Y ACTIVIDADES POLITICAS DE LOS ESTUDIANTES DE LA UNIVERSIDAD DE CHILE." CHILE NAT/G POL/PAR EDU/PROP LOBBY ATTIT 20. PAGE 57 H1141 — ACADEM AGE/Y PARTIC ELITES

L67
GRAUBARD S.R.,"TOWARD THE YEAR 2000: WORK IN PROGRESS." FUT ACADEM SECT DELIB/GP DIPLOM EDU/PROP AGE/Y PERSON ROLE...PSY ANTHOL. PAGE 60 H1199 — PREDICT PROB/SOLV SOCIETY CULTURE

L67
LATIN AMERICAN STUDIES ASSN,"RESEARCH ON EDUCATION IN LATIN AMERICA." L/A+17C NAT/G HABITAT...GOV/COMP ANTHOL 20. PAGE 92 H1836 — EDU/PROP SCHOOL ACADEM R+D

S67
ALGER C.F.,"INTERNATIONALIZING COLLEGES AND UNIVERSITIES." WOR+45...NAT/COMP SIMUL. PAGE 5 H0104 — DIPLOM EDU/PROP ACADEM GP/REL

S67
BHATNAGAR J.K.,"THE VALUES AND ATTITUDES OF SOME INDIAN AND BRITISH STUDENTS." INDIA UK ECO/UNDEV LEGIT COLONIAL GP/REL SOVEREIGN...QU 20. PAGE 16 H0328 — NAT/COMP ATTIT EDU/PROP ACADEM

S67
DOERN G.B.,"THE ROYAL COMMISSIONS IN THE GENERAL POLICY PROCESS AND IN FEDERAL-PROVINCIAL RELATIONS." CANADA CONSTN ACADEM PROVS CONSULT DELIB/GP LEGIS ACT/RES PROB/SOLV CONFER CONTROL EFFICIENCY...METH/COMP 20 SENATE ROYAL/COMM. PAGE 42 H0832 — R+D EX/STRUC GOV/REL NAT/G

S67
HUNTINGTON S.P.,"INTRODUCTION: SOCIAL SCIENCE AND VIETNAM." VIETNAM CULTURE 20. PAGE 75 H1506 — ACADEM KNOWL PROF/ORG SOCIETY

S67
MCCLEERY W.,"AN INTERVIEW WITH J. DOUGLAS BROWN ON THE 'WAY' OF VIETNAM" COM VIETNAM INTELL ECO/DEV ACADEM NAT/G COERCE PERSON SUPEGO ORD/FREE 20. PAGE 106 H2125 — ATTIT WAR COLONIAL MARXISM

S67
MITCHELL W.C.,"THE SHAPE OF POLITICAL THEORY TO COME: FROM POLITICAL SOCIOLOGY TO POLITICAL ECONOMY." ACADEM NAT/G BUDGET TAX LEGIT LOBBY GOV/REL INGP/REL...SOC NEW/IDEA TREND CHARTS 20 MONEY. PAGE 112 H2231 — ECO/TAC GEN/LAWS

S67
SIPPEL D.,"INDIENS UNSICHERE ZUKUNFT." INDIA CULTURE ACADEM POL/PAR LEGIS COLONIAL CHOOSE SOVEREIGN...JURID 20. PAGE 144 H2888 — SOCIETY STRUCT ECO/UNDEV NAT/G

N67
US HOUSE COMM SCI ASTRONAUT,GOVERNMENT, SCIENCE, AND INTERNATIONAL POLICY (PAMPHLET). INDIA NETHERLAND ECO/DEV ECO/UNDEV R+D ACADEM PLAN DIPLOM FOR/AID CONFER...PREDICT 20 CHINJAP. PAGE 160 H3198 — NAT/G POLICY CREATE TEC/DEV

B79
BRODERICK G.C.,POLITICAL STUDIES. IRELAND UK ROMAN/EMP LAW ACADEM LOC/G NAT/G DIPLOM PARL/PROC SUFF GP/REL LAISSEZ...ANTHOL. PAGE 21 H0424 — CONSTN COLONIAL

ACADEM/SCI....ACADEMY OF SCIENCES (U.S.S.R.)

B56
VUCINICH A.,THE SOVIET ACADEMY OF SCIENCES. USSR STRUCT ACADEM NAT/G EDU/PROP ADMIN LEAD ROLE ...BIBLIOG 20 ACADEM/SCI. PAGE 164 H3280 — PHIL/SCI CREATE INTELL PROF/ORG

ACADEMY OF SCIENCES (U.S.S.R.)....SEE ACADEM/SCI

ACBC....ACTION COUNCIL FOR BETTER CITIES

ACCOUNTING....SEE ACCT

ACCT....ACCOUNTING, BOOKKEEPING

ACD....UNITED STATES ARMS CONTROL AND DISARMAMENT AGENCY

ACHESON/D....DEAN ACHESON

ACHTERBERG E. H0060

ACLU....AMERICAN CIVIL LIBERTIES UNION

ACOSTA SAIGNES M. H0061

ACQUAINTANCE GROUP....SEE FACE/GP

ACT/RES....RESEARCH FACILITATING SOCIAL ACTION

ACTION....ALLEGHENY COUNCIL TO IMPROVE OUR NEIGHBORHOODS

ACTON/LORD....LORD ACTON

B52
HIMMELFARB G.,LORD ACTON: A STUDY IN CONSCIENCE AND POLITICS. MOD/EUR NAT/G POL/PAR SECT LEGIS TOP/EX EDU/PROP ADMIN NAT/LISM ATTIT PERSON SUPEGO MORAL ORD/FREE...CONCPT PARLIAMENT 19 ACTON/LORD. PAGE 71 H1419
PWR BIOG

ADA....AMERICANS FOR DEMOCRATIC ACTION

ADAIR D. H1303

ADAM T.R. H0062

ADAMS J. H0063

ADAMS J.C. H0064

ADAMS R.N. H0065,H0066

ADAMS T.W. H0067

ADAMS/J....PRESIDENT JOHN ADAMS

ADAMS/JQ....PRESIDENT JOHN QUINCY ADAMS

ADAMS/SAM....SAMUEL ADAMS

ADDICTION....ADDICTION

ADEN

S68
DOUGLAS-HOME C.,"A MISTAKEN POLICY IN ADEN." YEMEN CULTURE ECO/UNDEV INDUS FORCES WORKER DIPLOM ECO/TAC CONTROL 20 ADEN. PAGE 42 H0842
SOVEREIGN COLONIAL POLICY REGION

ADENAUER K. H0068,H0069

ADENAUER/K....KONRAD ADENAUER

B58
CRAIG G.A.,FROM BISMARCK TO ADENAUER: ASPECTS OF GERMAN STATECRAFT. GERMANY INTELL FORCES ECO/TAC CONFER COERCE WAR GP/REL ORD/FREE PWR CONSERVE 19/20 BISMARCK/O ADENAUER/K. PAGE 35 H0695
DIPLOM LEAD NAT/G

B62
ABOSCH H.,THE MENACE OF THE MIRACLE: GERMANY FROM HITLER TO ADENAUER. EUR+WWI GERMANY/W CULTURE FORCES PRESS NUC/PWR WAR CHOOSE 20 HITLER/A ADENAUER/K. PAGE 3 H0057
DIPLOM PEACE POLICY

L63
FREUND G.,"ADENAUER AND THE FUTURE OF GERMANY." EUR+WWI FUT GERMANY/W FORCES LEGIT ADMIN ROUTINE ATTIT DRIVE PERSON PWR...POLICY TIME/SEQ TREND VAL/FREE 20 ADENAUER/K. PAGE 53 H1058
NAT/G BIOG DIPLOM GERMANY

S63
ANTHON C.G.,"THE END OF THE ADENAUER ERA." EUR+WWI GERMANY/W CONSTN EX/STRUC CREATE DIPLOM LEGIT ATTIT PERSON ALL/VALS...RECORD 20 ADENAUER/K. PAGE 7 H0144
NAT/G TOP/EX BAL/PWR GERMANY

S63
KOHN H.,"GERMANY IN WORLD POLITICS." EUR+WWI GERMANY GERMANY/W USSR NAT/G POL/PAR TOP/EX ATTIT ...CONCPT TREND GEN/LAWS 20 NATO ADENAUER/K. PAGE 87 H1746
ACT/RES ORD/FREE BAL/PWR

B65
ADENAUER K.,MEMOIRS 1945-53. EUR+WWI GERMANY/W ECO/DEV CHIEF FORCES ECO/TAC WAR GOV/REL PWR SOVEREIGN 20 NATO ADENAUER/K. PAGE 3 H0068
BIOG DIPLOM NAT/G PERS/REL

B66
NEUMANN R.G.,THE GOVERNMENT OF THE GERMAN FEDERAL REPUBLIC. EUR+WWI GERMANY/W LOC/G EX/STRUC LEGIS CT/SYS INGP/REL PWR...BIBLIOG 20 ADENAUER/K. PAGE 117 H2336
NAT/G POL/PAR DIPLOM CONSTN

ADJUD....JUDICIAL AND ADJUDICATIVE PROCESSES

B03
FAGUET E.,LE LIBERALISME. FRANCE PRESS ADJUD ADMIN DISCRIM CONSERVE SOCISM...TRADIT SOC LING WORSHIP PARLIAMENT. PAGE 48 H0960
ORD/FREE EDU/PROP NAT/G LAW

B07
BENTHAM J.,AN INTRODUCTION TO THE PRINCIPLES OF MORALS AND LEGISLATION. UNIV CONSTN CULTURE SOCIETY NAT/G CONSULT LEGIS JUDGE ADJUD CT/SYS...JURID CONCPT NEW/IDEA. PAGE 14 H0287
LAW GEN/LAWS

B08
THE GOVERNMENT OF SOUTH AFRICA (VOL. II). SOUTH/AFR STRATA EXTR/IND EX/STRUC TOP/EX BUDGET ADJUD ADMIN CT/SYS PRODUC...CORREL CENSUS 19 RAILROAD CIVIL/SERV POSTAL/SYS. PAGE 2 H0030
CONSTN FINAN LEGIS NAT/G

N19
POUND R.,ORGANIZATION OF THE COURTS (PAMPHLET). MOD/EUR UK USA-45 ADJUD PWR...GOV/COMP 10/20 EUROPE. PAGE 127 H2546
CT/SYS JURID STRUCT ADMIN

B21
STUART G.H.,FRENCH FOREIGN POLICY. CONSTN INT/ORG NAT/G POL/PAR EX/STRUC FORCES PLAN ECO/TAC DOMIN EDU/PROP ADJUD COERCE ATTIT DRIVE RIGID/FLEX ALL/VALS...POLICY OBS RECORD BIOG TIME/SEQ TREND. PAGE 150 H3000
MOD/EUR DIPLOM FRANCE

B24
HOLDSWORTH W.S.,A HISTORY OF ENGLISH LAW; THE COMMON LAW AND ITS RIVALS (VOL. IV). UK SEA AGRI CHIEF ADJUD CONTROL CRIME GOV/REL...INT/LAW JURID NAT/COMP 16/17 PARLIAMENT COMMON/LAW CANON/LAW ENGLSH/LAW. PAGE 72 H1449
LAW LEGIS CT/SYS CONSTN

B26
MALINOWSKI B.,CRIME AND CUSTOM IN SAVAGE SOCIETY. SOCIETY FAM SECT LEGIT SANCTION MARRIAGE MYSTISM ...PSY SOC 19/20 MELANESIA CANON/LAW. PAGE 102 H2030
LAW CULTURE CRIME ADJUD

B29
CAM H.M.,BIBLIOGRAPHY OF ENGLISH CONSTITUTIONAL HISTORY (PAMPHLET). UK LAW LOC/G NAT/G POL/PAR SECT DELIB/GP ADJUD ORD/FREE 19/20 PARLIAMENT. PAGE 25 H0510
BIBLIOG/A CONSTN ADMIN PARL/PROC

B29
STURZO L.,THE INTERNATIONAL COMMUNITY AND THE RIGHT OF WAR (TRANS. BY BARBARA BARCLAY CARTER). CULTURE CREATE PROB/SOLV DIPLOM ADJUD CONTROL PEACE PERSON ORD/FREE...INT/LAW IDEA/COMP PACIFIST 20 LEAGUE/NAT. PAGE 150 H3003
INT/ORG PLAN WAR CONCPT

B32
LUNT D.C.,THE ROAD TO THE LAW. UK USA-45 LEGIS EDU/PROP OWN ORD/FREE...DECISION TIME/SEQ NAT/COMP 16/20 AUSTRAL ENGLSH/LAW COMMON/LAW. PAGE 99 H1980
ADJUD LAW JURID CT/SYS

B32
MCKISACK M.,THE PARLIAMENTARY REPRESENTATION OF THE ENGLISH BOROUGHS DURING THE MIDDLE AGES. UK CONSTN CULTURE ELITES EX/STRUC TAX PAY ADJUD PARL/PROC APPORT FEDERAL...POLICY 13/15 PARLIAMENT. PAGE 107 H2139
NAT/G MUNIC LEGIS CHOOSE

B33
ENSOR R.C.K.,COURTS AND JUDGES IN FRANCE, GERMANY, AND ENGLAND. FRANCE GERMANY UK LAW PROB/SOLV ADMIN ROUTINE CRIME ROLE...METH/COMP 20 CIVIL/LAW. PAGE 46 H0930
CT/SYS EX/STRUC ADJUD NAT/COMP

B35
NORDSKOG J.E.,SOCIAL REFORM IN NORWAY. NORWAY INDUS NAT/G POL/PAR LEGIS ADJUD...SOC BIBLIOG SOC/INTEG 20. PAGE 119 H2371
LABOR ADJUST

B35
RAM J.,THE SCIENCE OF LEGAL JUDGMENT: A TREATISE... UK CONSTN NAT/G LEGIS CREATE PROB/SOLV AGREE CT/SYS ...INT/LAW CONCPT 19 ENGLSH/LAW CANON/LAW CIVIL/LAW CTS/WESTM. PAGE 129 H2584
LAW JURID EX/STRUC ADJUD

B37
UNION OF SOUTH AFRICA,REPORT CONCERNING ADMINISTRATION OF SOUTH WEST AFRICA (6 VOLS.). SOUTH/AFR INDUS PUB/INST FORCES LEGIS BUDGET DIPLOM EDU/PROP ADJUD CT/SYS...GEOG CHARTS 20 AFRICA/SW LEAGUE/NAT. PAGE 158 H3166
NAT/G ADMIN COLONIAL CONSTN

B38
FIELD G.L.,THE SYNDICAL AND CORPORATIVE INSTITUTIONS OF ITALIAN FASCISM. ITALY CONSTN STRATA LABOR EX/STRUC TOP/EX ADJUD ADMIN LEAD TOTALISM AUTHORIT...MGT 20 MUSSOLIN/B. PAGE 50 H0991
FASCISM INDUS NAT/G WORKER

B38
HOLDSWORTH W.S.,A HISTORY OF ENGLISH LAW; THE CENTURIES OF SETTLEMENT AND REFORM (VOL. X). INDIA UK CONSTN NAT/G CHIEF LEGIS ADMIN COLONIAL CT/SYS CHOOSE ORD/FREE PWR...JURID 18 PARLIAMENT COMMONWLTH COMMON/LAW. PAGE 72 H1451
LAW LOC/G EX/STRUC ADJUD

B38
HOLDSWORTH W.S.,A HISTORY OF ENGLISH LAW; THE CENTURIES OF SETTLEMENT AND REFORM (VOL. XI). UK CONSTN NAT/G EX/STRUC DIPLOM ADJUD CT/SYS LEAD CRIME ATTIT...INT/LAW JURID 18 CMN/WLTH PARLIAMENT ENGLSH/LAW. PAGE 73 H1452
LAW COLONIAL LEGIS PARL/PROC

B38
MCNAIR A.D.,THE LAW OF TREATIES: BRITISH PRACTICE AND OPINIONS. UK CREATE DIPLOM LEGIT WRITING ADJUD WAR...INT/LAW JURID TREATY. PAGE 107 H2144
AGREE LAW CT/SYS NAT/G

B38
POUND R.,THE FORMATIVE ERA OF AMERICAN LAW. CULTURE NAT/G PROVS LEGIS ADJUD CT/SYS PERSON SOVEREIGN
CONSTN LAW

...POLICY IDEA/COMP GEN/LAWS 18/19. PAGE 127 H2548
CREATE JURID

B39
SIEYES E.J.,LES DISCOURS DE SIEYES DANS LES DEBATS CONSTITUTIONNELS DE L'AN III (2 ET 18 THERMIDOR). FRANCE LAW NAT/G PROB/SOLV BAL/PWR GOV/REL 18 JURY. PAGE 144 H2871
CONSTN ADJUD LEGIS EX/STRUC

B40
KER A.M.,MEXICAN GOVERNMENT PUBLICATIONS: A GUIDE TO THE MORE IMPORTANT PUBLICATIONS OF THE GOVERNMENT OF MEXICO, 1821-1936. CHIEF ADJUD 19/20 MEXIC/AMER. PAGE 85 H1693
BIBLIOG NAT/G EXEC LEGIS

B40
WUNDERLICH F.,LABOR UNDER GERMAN DEMOCRACY, ARBITRATION 1918-1933. GERMANY NAT/G PAY REPAR ADJUD CT/SYS GP/REL...MAJORIT 20. PAGE 171 H3426
LABOR WORKER INDUS BARGAIN

B42
ROBBINS J.J.,THE GOVERNMENT OF LABOR RELATIONS IN SWEDEN. SWEDEN LAW CONSTN ADJUD CT/SYS GP/REL ...JURID 20. PAGE 132 H2638
NAT/G BARGAIN LABOR INDUS

B45
MERRIAM C.E.,SYSTEMATIC POLITICS. FUT POL/PAR DELIB/GP DIPLOM ADJUD ADMIN LEAD CHOOSE ATTIT...MGT PHIL/SCI TREND. PAGE 109 H2183
NAT/G METH/CNCPT CREATE

B49
DENNING A.,FREEDOM UNDER THE LAW. MOD/EUR UK LAW SOCIETY CHIEF EX/STRUC LEGIS ADJUD CT/SYS PERS/REL PERSON 17/20 ENGLSH/LAW. PAGE 40 H0793
ORD/FREE JURID NAT/G

B49
SCHONS D.,BOOK CENSORSHIP IN NEW SPAIN (NEW WORLD STUDIES, BOOK II). SPAIN LAW CULTURE INSPECT ADJUD CT/SYS SANCTION GP/REL ORD/FREE 14/17. PAGE 140 H2797
CHRIST-17C EDU/PROP CONTROL PRESS

B49
WORMUTH F.D.,THE ORIGINS OF MODERN CONSTITUTIONALISM. GREECE UK LEGIS CREATE TEC/DEV BAL/PWR DOMIN ADJUD REV WAR PWR...JURID ROMAN/REP CROMWELL/O. PAGE 170 H3412
NAT/G CONSTN LAW

B50
BERMAN H.J.,JUSTICE IN RUSSIA; AN INTERPRETATION OF SOVIET LAW. USSR LAW STRUCT LABOR FORCES AGREE GP/REL ORD/FREE SOCISM...TIME/SEQ 20. PAGE 15 H0309
JURID ADJUD MARXISM COERCE

B52
THOM J.M.,GUIDE TO RESEARCH MATERIAL IN POLITICAL SCIENCE (PAMPHLET). ELITES LOC/G MUNIC NAT/G LEGIS DIPLOM ADJUD CIVMIL/REL GOV/REL PWR MGT. PAGE 154 H3074
BIBLIOG/A KNOWL

S52
MCDOUGAL M.S.,"THE COMPARATIVE STUDY OF LAW FOR POLICY PURPOSES." FUT NAT/G POL/PAR CONSULT ADJUD PWR SOVEREIGN...METH/CNCPT IDEA/COMP SIMUL 20. PAGE 106 H2129
PLAN JURID NAT/LISM

B54
HAMSON C.J.,EXECUTIVE DISCRETION AND JUDICIAL CONTROL; AN ASPECT OF THE FRENCH CONSEIL D'ETAT. EUR+WWI FRANCE MOD/EUR UK NAT/G EX/STRUC PARTIC CONSERVE...JURID BIBLIOG/A 18/20 SUPREME/CT. PAGE 65 H1310
ELITES ADJUD NAT/COMP

B54
JENNINGS I.,THE QUEEN'S GOVERNMENT. UK POL/PAR DELIB/GP ADJUD ADMIN CT/SYS PARL/PROC REPRESENT CONSERVE 13/20 PARLIAMENT. PAGE 80 H1605
NAT/G CONSTN LEGIS CHIEF

B54
MITCHELL P.,AFRICAN AFTERTHOUGHTS. UGANDA CONSTN NAT/G ADJUD COERCE WAR 20 WWI MAU/MAU. PAGE 112 H2230
BIOG CHIEF COLONIAL DOMIN

B54
SCHWARTZ B.,FRENCH ADMINISTRATIVE LAW AND THE COMMON-LAW WORLD. FRANCE CULTURE LOC/G NAT/G PROVS DELIB/GP EX/STRUC LEGIS PROB/SOLV CT/SYS EXEC GOV/REL...IDEA/COMP ENGLSH/LAW. PAGE 140 H2808
JURID LAW METH/COMP ADJUD

B55
DE ARAGAO J.G.,LA JURIDICTION ADMINISTRATIVE AU BRESIL. BRAZIL ADJUD COLONIAL CT/SYS REV FEDERAL ORD/FREE...BIBLIOG 19/20. PAGE 37 H0749
EX/STRUC ADMIN NAT/G

B55
KHADDURI M.,WAR AND PEACE IN THE LAW OF ISLAM. CONSTN CULTURE SOCIETY STRATA NAT/G PROVS SECT FORCES TOP/EX CREATE DOMIN EDU/PROP ADJUD COERCE ATTIT RIGID/FLEX ALL/VALS...CONCPT TIME/SEQ TOT/POP VAL/FREE. PAGE 85 H1702
ISLAM JURID PEACE WAR

B55
KHADDURI M.,LAW IN THE MIDDLE EAST. LAW CONSTN ACADEM FAM EDU/PROP CT/SYS SANCTION CRIME...INT/LAW GOV/COMP ANTHOL 6/20 MID/EAST. PAGE 85 H1703
ADJUD JURID ISLAM

B55
LIPSCOMB J.F.,WHITE AFRICANS. SOCIETY STRUCT AGRI ECO/TAC ADJUD COLONIAL COERCE PERS/REL ADJUST. PAGE 97 H1937
RACE/REL HABITAT ECO/UNDEV ORD/FREE

B55
SMITH G.,A CONSTITUTIONAL AND LEGAL HISTORY OF ENGLAND. UK ELITES NAT/G LEGIS ADJUD OWN HABITAT POPULISM...JURID 20 ENGLSH/LAW. PAGE 145 H2909
CONSTN PARTIC LAW CT/SYS

B55
WHEARE K.C.,GOVERNMENT BY COMMITTEE; AN ESSAY ON THE BRITISH CONSTITUTION. UK NAT/G LEGIS INSPECT CONFER ADJUD ADMIN CONTROL TASK EFFICIENCY ROLE POPULISM 20. PAGE 167 H3337
DELIB/GP CONSTN LEAD GP/COMP

B55
WRONG D.H.,AMERICAN AND CANADIAN VIEWPOINTS. CANADA USA+45 CONSTN STRATA FAM SECT WORKER ECO/TAC EDU/PROP ADJUD MARRIAGE...IDEA/COMP 20. PAGE 171 H3424
DIPLOM ATTIT NAT/COMP CULTURE

B56
DOUGLAS W.O.,WE THE JUDGES. INDIA USA+45 USA-45 LAW NAT/G SECT LEGIS PRESS CRIME FEDERAL ORD/FREE ...POLICY GOV/COMP 19/20 WARRN/EARL MARSHALL/J SUPREME/CT. PAGE 42 H0841
ADJUD CT/SYS CONSTN GOV/REL

L56
EISENTADT S.N.,"POLITICAL STRUGGLE IN BUREAUCRATIC SOCIETIES" ASIA CULTURE ADJUD SANCTION PWR BUREAUCRCY OTTOMAN BYZANTINE. PAGE 45 H0901
ADMIN CHIEF CONTROL ROUTINE

B57
CONOVER H.F.,NORTH AND NORTHEAST AFRICA; A SELECTED ANNOTATED LIST OF WRITINGS. ALGERIA MOROCCO SUDAN UAR CULTURE INT/ORG PROB/SOLV ADJUD NAT/LISM PWR WEALTH...SOC 20 UN. PAGE 32 H0649
BIBLIOG/A DIPLOM AFR ECO/UNDEV

B57
LONG H.A.,USURPERS - FOES OF FREE MAN. LAW NAT/G CHIEF LEGIS DOMIN ADJUD REPRESENT GOV/REL ORD/FREE LAISSEZ POPULISM...POLICY 18/20 SUPREME/CT ROOSEVLT/F CONGRESS CON/INTERP. PAGE 98 H1961
CT/SYS CENTRAL FEDERAL CONSTN

S57
HAILEY,"TOMORROW IN AFRICA." CONSTN SOCIETY LOC/G NAT/G DOMIN ADJUD ADMIN GP/REL DISCRIM NAT/LISM ATTIT MORAL ORD/FREE...PSY SOC CONCPT OBS RECORD TREND GEN/LAWS CMN/WLTH 20. PAGE 64 H1277
AFR PERSON ELITES RACE/REL

B58
BRIERLY J.L.,THE BASIS OF OBLIGATION IN INTERNATIONAL LAW, AND OTHER PAPERS. WOR+45 WOR-45 LEGIS...JURID CONCPT NAT/COMP ANTHOL 20. PAGE 21 H0415
INT/LAW DIPLOM ADJUD SOVEREIGN

B58
CUNNINGHAM W.B.,COMPULSORY CONCILIATION AND COLLECTIVE BARGAINING. CANADA NAT/G LEGIS ADJUD CT/SYS GP/REL...MGT 20 NEW/BRUNS STRIKE CASEBOOK. PAGE 36 H0722
POLICY BARGAIN LABOR INDUS

B58
MATOS J.,LAS ACTUALES COMMUNIDADES DE INDIGENAS: HUAROCHIRI EN 1955. PERU FAM NAT/G SECT EDU/PROP ADJUD GP/REL INGP/REL 20 INDIAN/AM. PAGE 105 H2091
STRUCT NEIGH KIN ECO/UNDEV

B58
OGDEN F.D.,THE POLL TAX IN THE SOUTH. USA+45 USA-45 CONSTN ADJUD ADMIN PARTIC CRIME...TIME/SEQ GOV/COMP METH/COMP 18/20 SOUTH/US. PAGE 120 H2407
TAX CHOOSE RACE/REL DISCRIM

B58
SHARMA M.P.,PUBLIC ADMINISTRATION IN THEORY AND PRACTICE. INDIA UK USA+45 USA-45 EX/STRUC ADJUD ...POLICY CONCPT NAT/COMP 20. PAGE 142 H2847
MGT ADMIN DELIB/GP JURID

B58
STRONG C.F.,MODERN POLITICAL CONSTITUTIONS. LAW CHIEF DELIB/GP EX/STRUC LEGIS ADJUD CHOOSE FEDERAL POPULISM...CONCPT BIBLIOG 20 UN. PAGE 150 H2998
CONSTN IDEA/COMP NAT/G

B58
STUBEL H.,THE MEWU FANTZU. CHINA/COM INDIA EDU/PROP ADJUD CRIME GP/REL OWN...OBS 20 TIBET. PAGE 150 H3001
CULTURE STRUCT SECT FAM

B58
WOODS H.D.,PATTERNS OF INDUSTRIAL DISPUTE SETTLEMENT IN FIVE CANADIAN INDUSTRIES. CANADA USA+45 CONSULT ADJUD GP/REL...JURID GOV/COMP METH/COMP ANTHOL 20. PAGE 170 H3408
BARGAIN INDUS LABOR NAT/G

S58
STAAR R.F.,"ELECTIONS IN COMMUNIST POLAND." EUR+WWI SOCIETY INT/ORG NAT/G POL/PAR LEGIS ACT/RES ECO/TAC EDU/PROP ADJUD ADMIN ROUTINE COERCE TOTALISM ATTIT ORD/FREE PWR 20. PAGE 148 H2963
COM CHOOSE POLAND

B59
MATHER F.C.,PUBLIC ORDER IN THE AGE OF THE CHARTISTS. UK CULTURE ADJUD CONTROL. PAGE 105 H2090
ORD/FREE FORCES COERCE CIVMIL/REL

B59
PAULSEN M.G.,LEGAL INSTITUTIONS TODAY AND TOMORROW. UK USA+45 NAT/G PROF/ORG PROVS ADMIN PARL/PROC ORD/FREE NAT/COMP. PAGE 124 H2477
JURID ADJUD JUDGE LEGIS

B59
SCHORN H.,DER RICHTER IM DRITTEN REICH; GESCHICHTE
ADJUD

UND DOKUMENTE. GERMANY NAT/G LEGIT CT/SYS INGP/REL MORAL ORD/FREE RESPECT...JURID GP/COMP 20. PAGE 140 H2798 JUDGE FASCISM

B59
SQUIBB G.D.,THE HIGH COURT OF CHIVALRY. UK NAT/G FORCES ADJUD WAR 14/20 PARLIAMENT ENGLSH/LAW. PAGE 148 H2959 CT/SYS PARL/PROC JURID

B59
VITTACHIT,EMERGENCY '58. CEYLON UK STRUCT NAT/G FORCES ADJUD CRIME REV NAT/LISM 20. PAGE 163 H3258 RACE/REL DISCRIM DIPLOM SOVEREIGN

S59
MENDELSON W.,"JUDICIAL REVIEW AND PARTY POLITICS" (BMR)" UK USA+45 USA-45 NAT/G LEGIS PROB/SOLV EDU/PROP ADJUD EFFICIENCY...POLICY NAT/COMP 19/20 AUSTRAL SUPREME/CT. PAGE 109 H2171 CT/SYS POL/PAR BAL/PWR JURID

S59
SILBERMAN L.,"CHANGE AND CONFLICT IN THE HORN OF AFRICA." EUR+WWI ITALY UK CULTURE FORCES ECO/TAC ADJUD COLONIAL ATTIT ORD/FREE PWR...DECISION METH/CNCPT HIST/WRIT SOMALI 20. PAGE 144 H2874 AFR TIME/SEQ

B60
CASTBERG F.,FREEDOM OF SPEECH IN THE WEST. FRANCE GERMANY USA+45 USA-45 LAW CONSTN CHIEF PRESS DISCRIM...CONCPT 18/20. PAGE 28 H0558 ORD/FREE SANCTION ADJUD NAT/COMP

B60
PICKLES D.,THE FIFTH FRENCH REPUBLIC. ALGERIA FRANCE CHOOSE GOV/REL ATTIT CONSERVE...CHARTS 20 DEGAULLE/C. PAGE 125 H2506 CONSTN ADJUD NAT/G EFFICIENCY

C60
HAZARD J.N.,"SETTLING DISPUTES IN SOVIET SOCIETY: THE FORMATIVE YEARS OF LEGAL INSTITUTIONS." USSR NAT/G PROF/ORG PROB/SOLV CONTROL CT/SYS ROUTINE REV CENTRAL...JURID BIBLIOG 20. PAGE 68 H1372 ADJUD LAW COM POLICY

B61
BAYITCH S.A.,LATIN AMERICA: A BIBLIOGRAPHICAL GUIDE. LAW CONSTN LEGIS JUDGE ADJUD CT/SYS 20. PAGE 12 H0243 BIBLIOG L/A+17C NAT/G JURID

B61
CARNELL F.,THE POLITICS OF THE NEW STATES: A SELECT ANNOTATED BIBLIOGRAPHY WITH SPECIAL REFERENCE TO THE COMMONWEALTH. CONSTN ELITES LABOR NAT/G POL/PAR EX/STRUC DIPLOM ADJUD ADMIN...GOV/COMP 20 COMMONWLTH. PAGE 27 H0534 BIBLIOG/A AFR ASIA COLONIAL

B61
CARROTHERS A.W.R.,LABOR ARBITRATION IN CANADA. CANADA LAW NAT/G CONSULT LEGIS WORKER ADJUD ADMIN CT/SYS 20. PAGE 27 H0542 LABOR MGT GP/REL BARGAIN

B61
JUSTICE,THE CITIZEN AND THE ADMINISTRATION: THE REDRESS OF GRIEVANCES (PAMPHLET). EUR+WWI UK LAW CONSTN STRATA NAT/G CT/SYS PARTIC COERCE...NEW/IDEA IDEA/COMP 20 OMBUDSMAN. PAGE 82 H1644 INGP/REL CONSULT ADJUD REPRESENT

B61
RAO K.V.,PARLIAMENTARY DEMOCRACY OF INDIA. INDIA EX/STRUC TOP/EX COLONIAL CT/SYS PARL/PROC ORD/FREE ...POLICY CONCPT TREND 20 PARLIAMENT. PAGE 130 H2592 CONSTN ADJUD NAT/G FEDERAL

B62
CARTER G.M.,THE GOVERNMENT OF THE SOVIET UNION. USSR CULTURE LOC/G DIPLOM ECO/TAC ADJUD CT/SYS LEAD WEALTH...CHARTS T 20 COM/PARTY. PAGE 27 H0546 NAT/G MARXISM POL/PAR EX/STRUC

B62
FATOUROS A.A.,GOVERNMENT GUARANTEES TO FOREIGN INVESTORS. WOR+45 ECO/UNDEV INDUS WORKER ADJUD ...NAT/COMP BIBLIOG TREATY. PAGE 49 H0975 NAT/G FINAN INT/TRADE ECO/DEV

B62
GROGAN V.,ADMINISTRATIVE TRIBUNALS IN THE PUBLIC SERVICE. IRELAND UK NAT/G CONTROL CT/SYS...JURID GOV/COMP 20. PAGE 61 H1231 ADMIN LAW ADJUD DELIB/GP

B62
GRZYBOWSKI K.,SOVIET LEGAL INSTITUTIONS. USA+45 USSR ECO/DEV NAT/G EDU/PROP CONTROL CT/SYS CRIME OWN ATTIT PWR SOCISM...NAT/COMP 20. PAGE 62 H1242 ADJUD LAW JURID

B62
JAIN R.S.,THE GROWTH AND DEVELOPMENT OF GOVERNOR-GENERAL'S EXECUTIVE COUNCIL 1858-1919. INDIA UK CONSTN EX/STRUC LEGIS ADJUD ADMIN INGP/REL ATTIT 19/20. PAGE 79 H1585 NAT/G DELIB/GP CHIEF CONSULT

B62
KAGZI M.C.,THE INDIAN ADMINISTRATIVE LAW. INDIA LG/CO CONTROL CT/SYS...CONCPT 20. PAGE 83 H1649 JURID ADJUD DELIB/GP NAT/G

B62
PHILLIPS O.H.,CONSTITUTIONAL AND ADMINISTRATIVE LAW (3RD ED.). UK INT/ORG LOC/G CHIEF EX/STRUC LEGIS BAL/PWR ADJUD COLONIAL CT/SYS PWR...CHARTS 20. PAGE 125 H2503 JURID ADMIN CONSTN NAT/G

B62
TYSKEVIC S.,DIE EINHEIT DER KIRCHE UND BYZANZ (TRANS. BY F.K. LIESNER). ROMAN/EMP ADJUD GP/REL 1/17 CHRISTIAN BYZANTINE. PAGE 157 H3144 SECT NAT/G CATHISM ATTIT

L62
ORDONNEAU P.,"LES PROBLEMES POSES PAR L'INDEPENDANCE DES NOUVEAUX ETATS AFRICAINS ET MALGACHE SUR LE PLAN DU CONTENTIEUX." FRANCE ISLAM MADAGASCAR LAW STRATA ECO/UNDEV NAT/G LEGIS LEGIT ...JURID TIME/SEQ 20. PAGE 121 H2425 AFR ADJUD COLONIAL SOVEREIGN

S62
FESLER J.W.,"FRENCH FIELD ADMINISTRATION: THE BEGINNINGS." CHRIST-17C CULTURE SOCIETY STRATA NAT/G ECO/TAC DOMIN EDU/PROP LEGIT ADJUD COERCE ATTIT ALL/VALS...TIME/SEQ CON/ANAL GEN/METH VAL/FREE 13/15. PAGE 49 H0988 EX/STRUC FRANCE

S62
MONNIER J.P.,"LA SUCCESSION D'ETATS EN MATIERE DE RESPONSABILITE INTERNATIONALE." UNIV CONSTN INTELL SOCIETY ADJUD ROUTINE PERCEPT SUPEGO...GEN/LAWS TOT/POP 20. PAGE 112 H2240 NAT/G JURID INT/LAW

S62
THOMPSON D.,"THE UNITED KINGDOM AND THE TREATY OF ROME." EUR+WWI INT/ORG NAT/G DELIB/GP LEGIS INT/TRADE RIGID/FLEX...CONCPT EEC PARLIAMENT CMN/WLTH 20. PAGE 154 H3079 ADJUD JURID

B63
EDDY J.P.,JUSTICE OF THE PEACE. UK LAW CONSTN CULTURE 14/20 COMMON/LAW. PAGE 44 H0887 CRIME JURID CT/SYS ADJUD

B63
FAWCETT J.E.S.,THE BRITISH COMMONWEALTH IN INTERNATIONAL LAW. LAW INT/ORG NAT/G VOL/ASSN OP/RES DIPLOM ADJUD CENTRAL CONSEN...NET/THEORY CMN/WLTH TREATY. PAGE 49 H0977 INT/LAW STRUCT COLONIAL

B63
FRIEDRICH C.J.,MAN AND HIS GOVERNMENT: AN EMPIRICAL THEORY OF POLITICS. UNIV LOC/G NAT/G ADJUD REV INGP/REL DISCRIM PWR BIBLIOG. PAGE 53 H1069 PERSON ORD/FREE PARTIC CONTROL

B63
ROBERTSON A.H.,HUMAN RIGHTS IN EUROPE. CONSTN SOCIETY INT/ORG NAT/G VOL/ASSN DELIB/GP ACT/RES PLAN ADJUD REGION ROUTINE ATTIT LOVE ORD/FREE RESPECT...JURID SOC CONCPT SOC/EXP UN 20. PAGE 132 H2645 EUR+WWI PERSON

L63
BOLGAR V.,"THE PUBLIC INTEREST: A JURISPRUDENTIAL AND COMPARATIVE OVERVIEW OF SYMPOSIUM ON FUNDAMENTAL CONCEPTS OF PUBLIC LAW" COM FRANCE GERMANY SWITZERLND LAW ADJUD ADMIN AGREE LAISSEZ ...JURID GEN/LAWS 20 EUROPE/E. PAGE 18 H0369 CONCPT ORD/FREE CONTROL NAT/COMP

B64
BEATTIE J.,OTHER CULTURES. UNIV LAW FAM POL/PAR SECT ADJUD OWN ALL/VALS WEALTH...SOC NAT/COMP SOC/INTEG 20. PAGE 13 H0251 METH/CNCPT CULTURE STRUCT

B64
HALLER W.,DER SCHWEDISCHE JUSTITIEOMBUDSMAN. DENMARK FINLAND NORWAY SWEDEN LEGIS ADJUD CONTROL PERSON ORD/FREE...NAT/COMP 20 OMBUDSMAN. PAGE 64 H1288 JURID PARL/PROC ADMIN CHIEF

B64
HOLDSWORTH W.S.,A HISTORY OF ENGLISH LAW; THE CENTURIES OF DEVELOPMENT AND REFORM (VOL. XIV). UK CONSTN LOC/G NAT/G POL/PAR CHIEF EX/STRUC ADJUD COLONIAL ATTIT...INT/LAW JURID 18/19 TORY/PARTY COMMONWLTH WHIG/PARTY COMMON/LAW. PAGE 73 H1453 LAW LEGIS LEAD CT/SYS

B64
LIGGETT E.,BRITISH POLITICAL ISSUES: VOLUME 1. UK LAW CONSTN LOC/G NAT/G ADJUD 20. PAGE 97 H1930 POL/PAR GOV/REL CT/SYS DIPLOM

B64
MINAR D.W.,IDEAS AND POLITICS: THE AMERICAN EXPERIENCE. SECT CHIEF LEGIS CREATE ADJUD EXEC REV PWR...PHIL/SCI CONCPT IDEA/COMP 18/20 HAMILTON/A JEFFERSN/T DECLAR/IND JACKSON/A PRESIDENT. PAGE 111 H2220 CONSTN NAT/G FEDERAL

B64
NEWARK F.H.,NOTES ON IRISH LEGAL HISTORY (2ND ED.). IRELAND UK PARL/PROC ORD/FREE SOVEREIGN 12/20 ENGLSH/LAW. PAGE 117 H2344 CT/SYS JURID ADJUD NAT/G

B64
SIEKANOWICZ P.,LEGAL SOURCES AND BIBLIOGRAPHY OF POLAND. COM POLAND CONSTN NAT/G PARL/PROC SANCTION CRIME MARXISM 16/20. PAGE 143 H2870 BIBLIOG ADJUD LAW JURID

B64
SZLADITS C.,BIBLIOGRAPHY ON FOREIGN AND COMPARATIVE LAW: BOOKS AND ARTICLES IN ENGLISH (SUPPLEMENT 1962). FINAN INDUS JUDGE LICENSE ADMIN CT/SYS PARL/PROC OWN...INT/LAW CLASSIF METH/COMP NAT/COMP BIBLIOG/A JURID ADJUD LAW

20. PAGE 151 H3027

B65
GAJENDRAGADKAR P.B.,LAW, LIBERTY AND SOCIAL JUSTICE. INDIA CONSTN NAT/G SECT PLAN ECO/TAC PRESS POPULISM...SOC METH/COMP 20 HINDU. PAGE 54 H1086 ORD/FREE LAW ADJUD JURID

B65
GWYN R.J.,THE SHAPE OF SCANDAL: A STUDY OF A GOVERNMENT IN CRISIS. CANADA LEGIS ADJUD CT/SYS SANCTION CMN/WLTH 20 PEARSON/L. PAGE 63 H1260 ELITES NAT/G CRIME

B65
HAEFELE E.T.,GOVERNMENT CONTROLS ON TRANSPORT. AFR RHODESIA TANZANIA DIPLOM ECO/TAC TARIFFS PRICE ADJUD CONTROL REGION EFFICIENCY...POLICY 20 CONGO. PAGE 64 H1274 ECO/UNDEV DIST/IND FINAN NAT/G

B65
INST INTL DES CIVILISATION DIF,THE CONSTITUTIONS AND ADMINISTRATIVE INSTITUTIONS OF THE NEW STATES. AFR ISLAM S/ASIA NAT/G POL/PAR DELIB/GP EX/STRUC CONFER EFFICIENCY NAT/LISM...JURID SOC 20. PAGE 77 H1535 CONSTN ADMIN ADJUD ECO/UNDEV

B65
KAAS L.,DIE GEISTLICHE GERICHTSBARKEIT DER KATHOLISCHEN KIRCHE IN PREUSSEN (2 VOLS.). PRUSSIA CONSTN NAT/G PROVS SECT ADJUD ADMIN ATTIT 16/20. PAGE 82 H1647 JURID CATHISM GP/REL CT/SYS

B65
MCWHINNEY E.,JUDICIAL REVIEW IN THE ENGLISH-SPEAKING WORLD (3RD ED.). CANADA UK WOR+45 LEGIS CONTROL EXEC PARTIC...JURID 20 AUSTRAL. PAGE 108 H2151 GOV/COMP CT/SYS ADJUD CONSTN

B65
POBEDONOSTSEV K.P.,REFLECTIONS OF A RUSSIAN STATESMAN. RUSSIA LAW ELITES EDU/PROP PRESS ADJUD MARRIAGE ATTIT PWR...MAJORIT TRADIT 19 CHURCH/STA. PAGE 127 H2531 TOTALISM POLICY CONSTN NAT/G

B65
SWIFT M.G.,MALAY PEASANT SOCIETY IN JELEBU. MALAYSIA FAM INT/TRADE ADJUD OWN WEALTH...SOC WORSHIP 20. PAGE 151 H3020 STRUCT ECO/UNDEV CULTURE SOCIETY

B66
GARCON M.,LETTRE OUVERTE A LA JUSTICE. FRANCE NAT/G PROB/SOLV PAY EFFICIENCY MORAL 20. PAGE 55 H1100 ORD/FREE ADJUD CT/SYS

B66
GORDON B.K.,THE DIMENSIONS OF CONFLICT IN SOUTHEAST ASIA. S/ASIA FORCES ADJUD REGION...CHARTS 20. PAGE 59 H1177 DIPLOM NAT/COMP INT/ORG VOL/ASSN

B66
KEAY E.A.,THE NATIVE AND CUSTOMARY COURTS OF NIGERIA. NIGERIA CONSTN ELITES NAT/G TOP/EX PARTIC REGION...DECISION JURID 19/20. PAGE 84 H1673 AFR ADJUD LAW

B66
LEROY P.,L'ORGANIZATION CONSTITUTIONNELLE ET LES CRISES. FRANCE NAT/G ADJUD CONTROL PARL/PROC WAR ...POLICY BIBLIOG 20. PAGE 95 H1892 CONSTN PWR EXEC LEGIS

B66
MERILLAT H.C.L.,LEGAL ADVISERS AND INTERNATIONAL ORGANIZATIONS. LAW NAT/G CONSULT OP/RES ADJUD SANCTION TASK CONSEN ORG/CHARTS. PAGE 109 H2178 INT/ORG INT/LAW CREATE OBS

B66
O'NEILL C.E.,CHURCH AND STATE IN FRENCH COLONIAL LOUISIANA: POLICY AND POLITICS TO 1732. PROVS VOL/ASSN DELIB/GP ADJUD ADMIN GP/REL ATTIT DRIVE ...POLICY BIBLIOG 17/18 LOUISIANA CHURCH/STA. PAGE 120 H2390 COLONIAL NAT/G SECT PWR

B66
SWEET E.C.,CIVIL LIBERTIES IN AMERICA. LAW CONSTN NAT/G PRESS CT/SYS DISCRIM ATTIT WORSHIP 20 CIVIL/LIB. PAGE 151 H3018 ADJUD ORD/FREE SUFF COERCE

B66
WEINSTEIN F.B.,VIETNAM'S UNHELD ELECTIONS: THE FAILURE TO CARRY OUT THE 1956 REUNIFICATION ELECTIONS... (MONOGRAPH). VIETNAM/S VIETNAM/N LEGIT CONFER ADJUD WAR PEACE 20 TREATY GENEVA/CON UNIFICA. PAGE 166 H3330 AGREE NAT/G CHOOSE DIPLOM

L66
KRENZ F.E.,"THE REFUGEE AS A SUBJECT OF INTERNATIONAL LAW." FUT LAW NAT/G CREATE ADJUD ISOLAT STRANGE...RECORD UN. PAGE 88 H1766 INT/LAW DISCRIM NEW/IDEA

S66
TOUVAL S.,"AFRICA'S FRONTIERS* REACTIONS TO A COLONIAL LEGACY." L/A+17C CONFER ADJUD COLONIAL APPORT CONSEN NAT/LISM RESPECT...RECORD NAT/COMP. PAGE 156 H3120 AFR GEOG SOVEREIGN WAR

B67
BOHANNAN P.,LAW AND WARFARE. CULTURE CT/SYS COERCE REV PEACE...JURID SOC CONCPT ANTHOL 20. PAGE 18 H0367 METH/COMP ADJUD WAR LAW

B67
DAVIDSON E.,THE TRIAL OF THE GERMANS* NUREMBERG* 1946-48. EUR+WWI GERMANY CULTURE NAT/G LEAD PERSON HEALTH...CRIMLGY PSY SOC BIOG JEWS. PAGE 37 H0745 FASCISM ADJUD TOTALISM WAR

B67
GELLHORN W.,OMBUDSMEN AND OTHERS: CITIZENS' PROTECTORS IN NINE COUNTRIES. WOR+45 LAW CONSTN LEGIS INSPECT ADJUD ADMIN CONTROL CT/SYS CHOOSE PERS/REL...STAT CHARTS 20. PAGE 55 H1109 NAT/COMP REPRESENT INGP/REL PROB/SOLV

B67
LENG S.C.,JUSTICE IN COMMUNIST CHINA: A SURVEY OF THE JUDICIAL SYSTEM OF THE CHINESE PEOPLE'S REPUBLIC. CHINA/COM LAW CONSTN LOC/G NAT/G PROF/ORG CONSULT FORCES ADMIN CRIME ORD/FREE...BIBLIOG 20 MAO. PAGE 94 H1877 CT/SYS ADJUD JURID MARXISM

B67
RAE D.,THE POLITICAL CONSEQUENCES OF ELECTORAL LAWS. EUR+WWI ICELAND ISRAEL NEW/ZEALND UK USA+45 ADJUD APPORT GP/REL MAJORITY...MATH STAT CENSUS CHARTS BIBLIOG 20 AUSTRAL. PAGE 129 H2579 POL/PAR CHOOSE NAT/COMP REPRESENT

B67
WIENER F.B.,CIVILIANS UNDER MILITARY JUSTICE; THE BRITISH PRACTICE SINCE 1689 ESPECIALLY IN NORTH AMERICA. UK USA-45 LAW CONSTN CRIME REV...DECISION CHARTS NAT/COMP BIBLIOG 17/20. PAGE 168 H3356 CT/SYS FORCES ADJUD

L67
"A PROPOS DES INCITATIONS FINANCIERES AUX GROUPEMENTS DES COMMUNES: ESSAI D'INTERPRETATION." FRANCE NAT/G LEGIS ADMIN GOV/REL CENTRAL 20. PAGE 3 H0051 LOC/G ECO/TAC APPORT ADJUD

L67
KELLEHER G.W.,"THE COMMON MARKET ANTITRUST LAWS: THE FIRST TEN YEARS." EUR+WWI INDUS PRICE ADJUD AGREE CONTROL PROFIT...POLICY 20 EEC. PAGE 84 H1684 INT/ORG INT/TRADE MARKET NAT/G

S67
ADOKO A.,"THE CONSTITUTION OF UGANDA." AFR UGANDA LOC/G CHIEF FORCES LEGIS ADJUD EXEC CHOOSE NAT/LISM ...IDEA/COMP 20. PAGE 4 H0072 NAT/G CONSTN ORD/FREE LAW

S67
AMERASINGHE C.F.,"SOME LEGAL PROBLEMS OF STATE TRADING IN SOUTHEAST ASIA." PROB/SOLV ADJUD CONTROL CT/SYS GP/REL 20. PAGE 6 H0120 INT/TRADE NAT/G INT/LAW PRIVIL

S67
ANTHEM T.,"CYPRUS* WHAT NOW?" CYPRUS GREECE TURKEY NAT/G BUDGET MAJORITY 20 NATO. PAGE 7 H0143 DIPLOM COERCE INT/TRADE ADJUD

S67
GREGORY R.,"THE MINISTER'S LINE: OR, THE M4 COMES TO BERKSHIRE. PART I." UK CONSTN DIST/IND LEGIS TOP/EX PLAN ADJUD...GEOG 20. PAGE 60 H1210 DECISION CONSTRUC NAT/G DELIB/GP

S67
HARNON E.,"CRIMINAL PROCEDURE IN ISRAEL - SOME COMPARATIVE ASPECTS." ISRAEL USA+45 CLIENT EX/STRUC LEGIS...JURID NAT/COMP 20. PAGE 67 H1336 ADJUD CONSTN CT/SYS CRIME

S67
MATTHEWS R.O.,"THE SUEZ CANAL DISPUTE* A CASE STUDY IN PEACEFUL SETTLEMENT." FRANCE ISRAEL UAR UK NAT/G CONTROL LEAD COERCE WAR NAT/LISM ROLE ORD/FREE PWR ...INT/LAW UN 20. PAGE 105 H2099 PEACE DIPLOM ADJUD

S67
MAYANJA A.,"THE GOVERNMENT'S PROPOSALS ON THE NEW CONSTITUTION." AFR UGANDA LAW CHIEF LEGIS ADJUD REPRESENT FEDERAL PWR 20. PAGE 105 H2105 CONSTN CONFER ORD/FREE NAT/G

S67
READ J.S.,"CENSORED." UGANDA CONSTN INTELL SOCIETY NAT/G DIPLOM PRESS WRITING ADJUD ADMIN COLONIAL RISK...IDEA/COMP 20. PAGE 130 H2602 EDU/PROP AFR CREATE

S67
RUCKER B.W.,"WHAT SOLUTIONS DO PEOPLE ENDORSE IN FREE PRESS-FAIR TRIAL DILEMMA?" LAW NAT/G CT/SYS ATTIT...NET/THEORY SAMP CHARTS IDEA/COMP METH 20. PAGE 136 H2710 CONCPT PRESS ADJUD ORD/FREE

S67
SEIDLER G.L.,"MARXIST LEGAL THOUGHT IN POLAND." POLAND SOCIETY R+D LOC/G NAT/G ACT/RES ADJUD CT/SYS SUPEGO PWR...SOC TREND 20 MARX/KARL. PAGE 141 H2822 MARXISM LAW CONCPT EFFICIENCY

S67
TIKHOMIROV I.A.,"DIVISION OF POWERS OR DIVISION OF LABOR?" USSR NAT/G DELIB/GP ADJUD GP/REL MARXISM SOCISM 20. PAGE 155 H3093 BAL/PWR WORKER STRATA ADMIN

S67
ULC O.,"CLASS STRUGGLE AND SOCIALIST JUSTICE: THE CASE OF CZECHOSLOVAKIA." COM CZECHOSLVK LAW CONSTN ELITES STRUCT NAT/G CRIME GP/REL MARXISM 20. PAGE 158 H3151 TOTALISM CT/SYS ADJUD STRATA

S67
WILLIAMS F.R.A.,"FUNDAMENTAL RIGHTS AND THE PROSPECT FOR DEMOCRACY IN NIGERIA." FUT NIGERIA SOCIETY ECO/UNDEV LEGIS ADJUD CHOOSE 20. PAGE 168 H3366 CONSTN LAW ORD/FREE NAT/G

S67
WRAITH R.E.,"ADMINISTRATIVE CHANGE IN THE NEW AFRICA." AFR LG/CO ADJUD INGP/REL PWR...RECORD GP/COMP 20. PAGE 171 H3416 ADMIN NAT/G LOC/G ECO/UNDEV

S68
DUGARD J.,"THE REVOCATION OF THE MANDATE FOR SOUTH WEST AFRICA." SOUTH/AFR WOR+45 STRATA NAT/G DELIB/GP DIPLOM ADJUD SANCTION CHOOSE RACE/REL ...POLICY NAT/COMP 20 AFRICA/SW UN TRUST/TERR LEAGUE/NAT. PAGE 43 H0858 AFR INT/ORG DISCRIM COLONIAL

S68
SHAPIRO J.P.,"SOVIET HISTORIOGRAPHY AND THE MOSCOW TRIALS: AFTER THIRTY YEARS." USSR NAT/G LEGIT PRESS CONTROL LEAD ATTIT MARXISM...NEW/IDEA METH 20 TROTSKY/L STALIN/J KHRUSH/N. PAGE 142 H2843 HIST/WRIT EDU/PROP SANCTION ADJUD

B91
SIDGWICK H.,THE ELEMENTS OF POLITICS. LOC/G NAT/G LEGIS DIPLOM ADJUD CONTROL EXEC PARL/PROC REPRESENT GOV/REL SOVEREIGN ALL/IDEOS 19 MILL/JS BENTHAM/J. PAGE 143 H2868 POLICY LAW CONCPT

B96
ESMEIN A.,ELEMENTS DE DROIT CONSTITUTIONNEL. FRANCE UK CHIEF EX/STRUC LEGIS ADJUD CT/SYS PARL/PROC REV GOV/REL ORD/FREE...JURID METH/COMP 18/19. PAGE 47 H0940 LAW CONSTN NAT/G CONCPT

B98
POLLOCK F.,THE HISTORY OF ENGLISH LAW BEFORE THE TIME OF EDWARD I (2 VOLS, 2ND ED.). UK CULTURE LOC/G LEGIS LICENSE AGREE CONTROL CT/SYS SANCTION CRIME...TIME/SEQ 13 COMMON/LAW CANON/LAW. PAGE 127 H2538 LAW ADJUD JURID

B99
LECKY W.E.H.,DEMOCRACY AND LIBERTY (2 VOLS.). LAW CONSTN STRATA POL/PAR SECT WORKER DIPLOM ADJUD REPRESENT NAT/LISM CONSERVE. PAGE 93 H1851 LEGIS NAT/G POPULISM ORD/FREE

ADJUST....SOCIAL ADJUSTMENT, SOCIALIZATION. SEE ALSO INGP/REL

B33
MANNHEIM E.,DIE TRAGER DER OFFENTLICHEN MEINUNG. ADJUST ATTIT...PSY 19/20. PAGE 102 H2037 SOC CULTURE CONCPT INDUS

B35
NORDSKOG J.E.,SOCIAL REFORM IN NORWAY. NORWAY INDUS NAT/G POL/PAR LEGIS ADJUD...SOC BIBLIOG SOC/INTEG 20. PAGE 119 H2371 LABOR ADJUST

B37
HORNEY K.,THE NEUROTIC PERSONALITY OF OUR TIME. SOCIETY PERS/REL ADJUST HAPPINESS ANOMIE ATTIT DRIVE SEX LOVE PWR CONCPT. PAGE 74 H1472 PSY PERSON STRANGE CULTURE

B48
EDUARDO O.D.C.,THE NEGRO IN NORTHERN BRAZIL: A STUDY IN ACCULTURATION. BRAZIL ECO/UNDEV FAM SECT PAY REGION HABITAT CATHISM MYSTISM...GEOG OBS SOC/INTEG WORSHIP 20 NEGRO MARANHAO. PAGE 44 H0890 CULTURE ADJUST GP/REL

B50
HARLEY G.W.,MASKS AS AGENTS OF SOCIAL CONTROL IN NORTHEAST LIBERIA. AFR LIBERIA LAW CULTURE ADJUST CONSEN MORAL...GEOG SOC WORSHIP 20. PAGE 66 H1332 CONTROL ECO/UNDEV SECT CHIEF

B52
CALLOT E.,LA SOCIETE ET SON ENVIRONNEMENT: ESSAI SUR LES PRINCIPES DES SCIENCES SOCIALES. GP/REL ADJUST CONSEN ISOLAT HABITAT PERCEPT PERSON ...BIBLIOG SOC/INTEG 20. PAGE 25 H0507 SOCIETY PHIL/SCI CULTURE

B53
MEAD M.,CULTURAL PATTERNS AND TECHNICAL CHANGE. BURMA GREECE NIGERIA ECO/UNDEV AGRI INDUS SCHOOL SECT CREATE FEEDBACK HABITAT...PSY METH/COMP BIBLIOG 20 UN. PAGE 108 H2152 HEALTH TEC/DEV CULTURE ADJUST

S53
ROGOFF N.,"SOCIAL STRATIFICATION IN FRANCE AND IN THE UNITED STATES" (BMR)" FRANCE USA+45 WORKER ADJUST PERSON...SOC 20. PAGE 133 H2662 STRUCT STRATA ATTIT NAT/COMP

B54
KOLARZ W.,THE PEOPLES OF THE SOVIET FAR EAST. RUSSIA USSR STRUCT LEAD ISOLAT NAT/LISM...CHARTS 20. PAGE 88 H1750 COLONIAL RACE/REL ADJUST CULTURE

B55
FRIEDMAN G.,INDUSTRIAL SOCIETY: THE EMERGENCE OF THE HUMAN PROBLEMS OF AUTOMATION. UNIV CULTURE ECO/DEV TEC/DEV INGP/REL HAPPINESS RATIONAL UTOPIA ROLE...HUM SOC TIME/SEQ 20. PAGE 53 H1064 AUTOMAT ADJUST ALL/VALS CONCPT

B55
LIPSCOMB J.F.,WHITE AFRICANS. SOCIETY STRUCT AGRI ECO/TAC ADJUD COLONIAL COERCE PERS/REL ADJUST. PAGE 97 H1937 RACE/REL HABITAT ECO/UNDEV ORD/FREE

S55
DE SMITH S.A.,"CONSTITUTIONAL MONARCHY IN BURGANDA." AFR UGANDA UK STRUCT CHIEF REGION INGP/REL ADJUST NAT/LISM SOVEREIGN CONSERVE ...POLICY 19/20 BURGANDA. PAGE 38 H0769 NAT/G DIPLOM CONSTN COLONIAL

C55
STEWARD J.H.,"THE CONCEPT AND METHOD OF CULTURAL ECOLOGY" IN T.H. STEWARD'S THEORY OF CULTURAL CHANGE." SOCIETY INGP/REL...CONCPT CON/ANAL METH/COMP 20. PAGE 149 H2985 HABITAT CULTURE CREATE ADJUST

B56
BECKER H.,MAN IN RECIPROCITY: INTRODUCTORY LECTURES ON CULTURE, SOCIETY, AND PERSONALITY. LAW FAM SECT REGION GP/REL ADJUST ATTIT PERSON...BIBLIOG 20. PAGE 13 H0253 CULTURE STRUCT SOC PSY

B56
DEUTSCH K.W.,AN INTERDISCIPLINARY BIBLIOGRAPHY ON NATIONALISM, 1935-1953. CULTURE SOCIETY SECT ATTIT HABITAT HEREDITY PERCEPT ROLE WEALTH...METH/CNCPT LING 20. PAGE 40 H0798 BIBLIOG/A NAT/LISM COLONIAL ADJUST

B56
INTERNATIONAL AFRICAN INST,SOCIAL IMPLICATIONS OF INDUSTRIALIZATION AND URBANIZATION IN AFRICA SOUTH OF THE SAHARA. SOUTH/AFR INDUS LABOR MUNIC WORKER TEC/DEV...SOC OBS TREND ANTHOL 20. PAGE 77 H1549 AFR ECO/UNDEV ADJUST CULTURE

B56
KALLEN H.M.,CULTURAL PLURALISM AND THE AMERICAN IDEA. RACE/REL ADJUST PERSON ORD/FREE LAISSEZ ...PLURIST GEN/LAWS ANTHOL. PAGE 83 H1652 PLURISM CULTURE GP/REL SECT

B57
KOENTJARANINGRAT R.,A PRELIMINARY DESCRIPTION OF THE JAVANESE KINSHIP SYSTEM. INDONESIA STRATA FAM INGP/REL ADJUST MARRIAGE AGE/C AGE/Y AGE/A PERSON ...OBS CHARTS DICTIONARY 20 JAVA. PAGE 87 H1736 KIN STRUCT ELITES CULTURE

B58
ALMAGRO BASCH M.,ORIGEN Y FORMACION DEL PUEBLO HISPANO. PREHIST SPAIN REGION WAR RACE/REL HABITAT ORD/FREE...SOC SOC/INTEG 20. PAGE 5 H0109 CULTURE GP/REL ADJUST

B58
GLUCKMAN M.,ANALYSIS OF A SOCIAL SITUATION IN MODERN ZULULAND. AFR PERS/REL ADJUST DISCRIM EQUILIB NAT/LISM...SOC RECORD AUD/VIS 20 ZULULAND. PAGE 57 H1146 CULTURE RACE/REL STRUCT GP/REL

S59
LYNN D.B.,"THE EFFECTS OF FATHER-ABSENCE ON NORWEGIAN BOYS AND GIRLS." NORWAY CULTURE PERS/REL ADJUST DISPL LOVE...PSY CORREL STAT INT CON/ANAL CHARTS SOC/INTEG 20. PAGE 99 H1983 SOC FAM AGE/C ANOMIE

B60
BARBU Z.,PROBLEMS OF HISTORICAL PSYCHOLOGY. GREECE MEDIT-7 UK CULTURE TEC/DEV ADJUST RATIONAL ATTIT PERCEPT...METH/CNCPT NEW/IDEA TIME/SEQ GEN/METH. PAGE 11 H0214 PERSON PSY HIST/WRIT IDEA/COMP

B60
JHA C.,INDIAN GOVERNMENT AND POLITICS. INDIA SERV/IND POL/PAR PROVS LEGIS CT/SYS CHOOSE GOV/REL FEDERAL 20. PAGE 81 H1616 NAT/G PARL/PROC CONSTN ADJUST

B60
MINER H.M.,OASIS AND CASBAH: ALGERIAN CULTURE AND PERSONALITY IN CHANGE. ALGERIA FRANCE SOCIETY MUNIC COLONIAL ATTIT...INT PROJ/TEST CHARTS 20. PAGE 111 H2221 GP/COMP PERSON CULTURE ADJUST

B60
STRACHEY J.,THE END OF EMPIRE. UK WOR+45 WOR-45 DIPLOM INT/TRADE DOMIN ADJUST ORD/FREE WEALTH ...SOCIALIST GOV/COMP TIME COMMONWLTH. PAGE 150 H2991 COLONIAL ECO/DEV BAL/PWR LAISSEZ

S60
HALSEY A.H.,"THE CHANGING FUNCTIONS OF UNIVERSITIES IN ADVANCED INDUSTRIAL SOCIETIES." R+D EDU/PROP REPRESENT ROLE ORD/FREE PWR TREND. PAGE 65 H1298 ACADEM CREATE CULTURE ADJUST

S60
TURNER R.H.,"SPONSORED AND CONTEST MOBILITY IN THE SCHOOL SYSTEM." UK USA+45 ELITES STRATA ACADEM FACE/GP EDU/PROP CONTROL INGP/REL ADJUST ATTIT PERSON...METH/COMP 20. PAGE 157 H3142 AGE/Y NAT/COMP SCHOOL STRUCT

B61
BROUGHTON M.,PRESS AND POLITICS OF SOUTH AFRICA. SOUTH/AFR NAT/G COLONIAL GP/REL ADJUST 20. PAGE 22 H0435 NAT/LISM PRESS PWR CULTURE

B61
HUNT E.F.,SOCIAL SCIENCE. DIPLOM ECO/TAC ROUTINE GP/REL DEMAND DISCRIM EFFICIENCY HABITAT ALL/IDEOS ...SOC T 20. PAGE 75 H1497 CULTURE ADJUST STRATA ROLE

B61
NIPPERDEY T.,DIE ORGANISATION DER DEUTSCHEN PARTEIEN VOR 1918. GERMANY CONSTN STRUCT TEC/DEV CHOOSE ADJUST ATTIT...CONCPT TIME/SEQ 19/20. POL/PAR PARL/PROC NAT/G

PAGE 118 H2362

B61
STAHL W.,EDUCATION FOR DEMOCRACY IN WEST GERMANY: ACHIEVEMENT SHORTCOMINGS - PROSPECTS. GERMANY/W SOCIETY NAT/G FORCES PLAN PROB/SOLV PRESS ALL/VALS ...POLICY MAJORIT CONCPT ANTHOL 20. PAGE 148 H2967 — EDU/PROP POPULISM AGE/Y ADJUST

L61
EZELLPH,"THE HISPANIC AGRICULTURATION OF THE GILA RIVER PIMAS." FAM TEC/DEV PERS/REL ADJUST...GEOG MYTH CHARTS BIBLIOG WORSHIP 17/20. PAGE 48 H0956 — CULTURE SOC AGRI DRIVE

B62
BERNOT R.M.,EXCESS AND RESTRAINT: SOCIAL CONTROL AMONG GUINEA MOUNTAIN PEOPLE. CULTURE FAM KIN CT/SYS COERCE WAR PERS/REL MARRIAGE HABITAT SEX ...MYTH 20 NEW/GUINEA. PAGE 16 H0314 — SOCIETY CONTROL STRUCT ADJUST

B62
HAY S.N.,SOUTHEAST ASIAN HISTORY: A BIBLIOGRAPHICAL GUIDE. STRATA KIN NAT/G REGION GUERRILLA REV WAR ADJUST HABITAT PERCEPT ALL/IDEOS...CHARTS 5/20. PAGE 68 H1365 — BIBLIOG/A S/ASIA CULTURE

B62
MEGGITT M.J.,DESERT PEOPLE. ECO/UNDEV KIN CREATE PROB/SOLV CONTROL DRIVE ROLE...GEOG SOC MYTH CHARTS BIBLIOG 20 AUSTRAL. PAGE 108 H2159 — ADJUST CULTURE INGP/REL HABITAT

B63
CONFERENCE ABORIGINAL STUDIES,AUSTRALIAN ABORIGINAL STUDIES. ECO/UNDEV INT/TRADE COLONIAL ADJUST HABITAT HEREDITY...GEOG PSY LING SOC/EXP ANTHOL WORSHIP 20 AUSTRAL ABORIGINES. PAGE 32 H0638 — SOC SOCIETY CULTURE STRUCT

B63
GOODE W.J.,WORLD REVOLUTION AND FAMILY PATTERNS. AFR CHINA/COM INDIA UAR CREATE ADJUST ATTIT SEX ...SOC 20 CHINJAP. PAGE 58 H1169 — FAM NAT/COMP CULTURE MARRIAGE

B63
HUNTER G.,EDUCATION FOR A DEVELOPING REGION; A STUDY IN EAST AFRICA. AFR TANZANIA UGANDA NAT/G TEC/DEV INGP/REL ADJUST LITERACY ATTIT 20 AFRICA/E. PAGE 75 H1501 — EDU/PROP POLICY ECO/UNDEV EFFICIENCY

B63
JENNINGS W.I.,DEMOCRACY IN AFRICA. UK CULTURE STRUCT ECO/UNDEV DIPLOM COLONIAL GP/REL ADJUST NAT/LISM ORD/FREE...GOV/COMP 20 THIRD/WRLD. PAGE 81 H1613 — PROB/SOLV AFR CONSTN POPULISM

B63
LETHBRIDGE H.J.,THE PEASANT AND THE COMMUNES. CHINA/COM COM USSR NEIGH PROB/SOLV ADJUST EFFICIENCY...POLICY METH/COMP NAT/COMP 20. PAGE 95 H1894 — MARXISM ECO/TAC AGRI WORKER

B63
OLSON M. JR.,THE ECONOMICS OF WARTIME SHORTAGE. FRANCE GERMANY MOD/EUR UK AGRI PROB/SOLV ADMIN DEMAND WEALTH...POLICY OLD/LIB 17/20. PAGE 121 H2416 — WAR ADJUST ECO/TAC NAT/COMP

B63
SINGH H.L.,PROBLEMS AND POLICIES OF THE BRITISH IN INDIA, 1885-1898. INDIA UK NAT/G FORCES LEGIS PROB/SOLV CONTROL RACE/REL ADJUST DISCRIM NAT/LISM RIGID/FLEX...MGT 19 CIVIL/SERV. PAGE 144 H2885 — COLONIAL PWR POLICY ADMIN

S63
ZOLBERG A.R.,"MASS PARTIES AND NATIONAL INTEGRATION: THE CASE OF THE IVORY COAST" (BMR)" AFR IVORY/CST CONSTN VOL/ASSN DIPLOM LEAD GP/REL INGP/REL 20. PAGE 173 H3461 — POL/PAR ECO/UNDEV NAT/G ADJUST

C63
HSU F.L.,"COHESION AND DIVISION IN THE AMERICAN WORLD" HSU FL. CLAN, CASTE, AND CLUB." CULTURE EDU/PROP CONFER SANCTION PERSON...PSY GP/COMP. PAGE 74 H1484 — PERS/REL AGE/Y ADJUST VOL/ASSN

B64
ANDREWS D.H.,LATIN AMERICA: A BIBLIOGRAPHY OF PAPERBACK BOOKS. SECT INT/TRADE EDU/PROP WAR GOV/REL ADJUST NAT/LISM ATTIT...ART/METH LING BIOG 20. PAGE 7 H0138 — BIBLIOG L/A+17C CULTURE NAT/G

B64
COUNT E.W.,FACT AND THEORY IN SOCIAL SCIENCE. UNIV HABITAT...BIOG TREND CHARTS ANTHOL BIBLIOG. PAGE 34 H0679 — STRUCT SOC CULTURE ADJUST

B64
CULLINGWORTH J.B.,TOWN AND COUNTRY PLANNING IN ENGLAND AND WALES. UK LAW SOCIETY CONSULT ACT/RES ADMIN ROUTINE LEISURE INGP/REL ADJUST PWR...GEOG 20 OPEN/SPACE URBAN/RNWL. PAGE 36 H0718 — MUNIC PLAN NAT/G PROB/SOLV

B64
GREEN M.M.,IBO VILLAGE AFFAIRS. AFR FORCES PERS/REL ADJUST ISOLAT ATTIT HABITAT PERSON ALL/VALS...JURID RECORD SOC/INTEG 20 IBO. PAGE 60 H1207 — MUNIC CULTURE ECO/UNDEV SOC

B64
HUXLEY M.,FAREWILL TO EDEN. SOCIETY ACT/RES EDU/PROP HEALTH...SOC AUD/VIS. PAGE 76 H1513 — ECO/UNDEV SECT CULTURE ADJUST

B64
JOSEPHSON E.,MAN ALONE: ALIENATION IN MODERN SOCIETY. WOR+45 ECO/DEV WORKER WAR LEISURE RACE/REL ANOMIE ATTIT PERCEPT PERSON ALL/VALS...ANTHOL 20. PAGE 82 H1636 — STRANGE CULTURE SOCIETY ADJUST

B64
POWELSON J.P.,LATIN AMERICA: TODAY'S ECONOMIC AND SOCIAL REVOLUTION. L/A+17C INTELL SOCIETY STRUCT AGRI INDUS NAT/G DIPLOM ECO/TAC REV...POLICY 20. PAGE 128 H2552 — ECO/UNDEV WEALTH ADJUST PLAN

B65
BENTWICH J.S.,EDUCATION IN ISRAEL. ISRAEL CULTURE STRATA PROB/SOLV TEC/DEV ADJUST ALL/VALS 20 JEWS. PAGE 15 H0293 — SECT EDU/PROP ACADEM SCHOOL

B65
BRASS P.R.,FACTIONAL POLITICS IN AN INDIAN STATE: THE CONGRESS PARTY IN UTTAR PRADESH. INDIA UK CONSTN CULTURE ECO/UNDEV LOC/G DOMIN COLONIAL CROWD GP/REL ADJUST CENTRAL RIGID/FLEX SOVEREIGN 20 UTTAR/PRAD CONGRESS/P. PAGE 20 H0406 — POL/PAR PROVS LEGIS CHOOSE

B65
HARBISON F.,MANPOWER AND EDUCATION. AFR CHINA/COM IRAN L/A+17C S/ASIA TEC/DEV ADJUST OPTIMAL SKILL ...ANTHOL 20. PAGE 66 H1325 — ECO/UNDEV EDU/PROP WORKER NAT/COMP

B65
HAVIGHURST R.J.,SOCIETY AND EDUCATION IN BRAZIL. BRAZIL PORTUGAL ECO/UNDEV INDUS NAT/G CREATE INSPECT COLONIAL ADJUST DEMAND LITERACY...CENSUS TREND CHARTS 16/20. PAGE 68 H1362 — SCHOOL ACADEM ACT/RES CULTURE

B65
KOUSOULAS D.G.,REVOLUTION AND DEFEAT; THE STORY OF THE GREEK COMMUNIST PARTY. GREECE INT/ORG EX/STRUC DIPLOM FOR/AID EDU/PROP PARL/PROC ADJUST ATTIT 20 COM/PARTY. PAGE 88 H1759 — REV MARXISM POL/PAR ORD/FREE

B65
MAIR L.,AN INTRODUCTION TO SOCIAL ANTHROPOLOGY. LAW STRATA FINAN FAM KIN SECT INT/TRADE RACE/REL ADJUST PRODUC...T 20. PAGE 101 H2023 — SOC STRUCT CULTURE SOCIETY

B65
O'BRIEN F.,CRISIS IN WORLD COMMUNISM* MARXISM IN SEARCH OF EFFICIENCY. COM ECO/DEV PLAN INT/TRADE WAR ADJUST PEACE...STAT TIME/SEQ GOV/COMP NAT/COMP COLD/WAR. PAGE 119 H2384 — MARXISM USSR DRIVE EFFICIENCY

S65
LEVI W.,"THE CONCEPT OF INTEGRATION IN RESEARCH ON PEACE." NAT/G VOL/ASSN DIPLOM TASK ADJUST NAT/LISM PEACE DRIVE LOVE...PSY NET/THEORY GEN/LAWS. PAGE 95 H1897 — CONCPT IDEA/COMP INT/ORG CENTRAL

S65
MARK M.,"MUST WE FIGHT SOCIAL REVOLUTIONS OF THE LEFT?" L/A+17C USA+45 ECO/UNDEV DIPLOM ADJUST PERCEPT...IDEA/COMP NAT/COMP. PAGE 103 H2053 — NAT/LISM REV MARXISM CREATE

S65
THOMAS F.C. JR.,"THE PEACE CORPS IN MOROCCO." CULTURE MUNIC PROVS CREATE ROUTINE TASK ADJUST STRANGE...OBS PEACE/CORP. PAGE 154 H3077 — MOROCCO FRANCE FOR/AID EDU/PROP

B66
AHMED Z.,DUSK AND DAWN IN VILLAGE INDIA. INDIA S/ASIA UK CULTURE SOCIETY NAT/G DOMIN COLONIAL HABITAT SOVEREIGN...SOC DICTIONARY 20. PAGE 4 H0080 — NEIGH ECO/UNDEV AGRI ADJUST

B66
AIYAR S.P.,PERSPECTIVES ON THE WELFARE STATE. INDIA S/ASIA UK CONSTN ECO/UNDEV NAT/G INGP/REL CENTRAL NAT/LISM ATTIT...CONCPT ANTHOL BIBLIOG 20. PAGE 4 H0087 — NEW/LIB WELF/ST IDEA/COMP ADJUST

B66
CAPELL A.,STUDIES IN SOCIO-LINGUISTICS. CULTURE ADJUST...CLASSIF IDEA/COMP SOC/EXP BIBLIOG 20. PAGE 26 H0525 — LING SOC PHIL/SCI CORREL

B66
ELLIS A.B.,THE EWE-SPEAKING PEOPLES OF THE SLAVE COAST OF WEST AFRICA. AFR FORCES ADJUST...LING RECORD GP/COMP WORSHIP 20 AFRICA/W DEITY. PAGE 45 H0910 — MYTH CULTURE HABITAT

B66
FISK E.K.,NEW GUINEA ON THE THRESHOLD; ASPECTS OF SOCIAL, POLITICAL, AND ECONOMIC DEVELOPMENT. AGRI NAT/G INT/TRADE ADMIN ADJUST LITERACY ROLE...CHARTS ANTHOL 20 NEW/GUINEA. PAGE 51 H1015 — ECO/UNDEV SOCIETY

B66
HANSON J.W.,EDUCATION AND THE DEVELOPMENT OF NATIONS. DIPLOM TASK ADJUST EFFICIENCY...POLICY ANTHOL 20. PAGE 66 H1322 — ECO/UNDEV EDU/PROP NAT/G PLAN

B66
KOMIYA R.,POSTWAR ECONOMIC GROWTH IN JAPAN. ELITES NAT/G EX/STRUC TEC/DEV BUDGET DIPLOM CONTROL BAL/PAY PRODUC...BIBLIOG 20 CHINJAP. PAGE 88 H1754 — ECO/DEV POLICY PLAN ADJUST

B66
MACFARQUHAR R.,CHINA UNDER MAO: POLITICS TAKES COMMAND. CHINA/COM COM AGRI INDUS CHIEF FORCES DIPLOM INT/TRADE EDU/PROP TASK REV ADJUST...ANTHOL 20 MAO. PAGE 100 H1992
ECO/UNDEV TEC/DEV ECO/TAC ADMIN

B66
SILBERMAN B.S.,MODERN JAPANESE LEADERSHIP; TRANSITION AND CHANGE. NAT/G POL/PAR CHIEF ADMIN REPRESENT GP/REL ADJUST RIGID/FLEX...SOC METH/COMP ANTHOL 19/20 CHINJAP CHRISTIAN. PAGE 144 H2873
LEAD CULTURE ELITES MUNIC

B66
SOROKIN P.A.,SOCIOLOGICAL THEORIES OF TODAY. SOCIETY STRUCT FAM SECT GP/REL ADJUST...PHIL/SCI PSY TREND METH/COMP 20. PAGE 147 H2935
SOC CULTURE METH/CNCPT EPIST

B66
SWEARINGEN A.R.,SOVIET AND CHINESE COMMUNIST POWER IN THE WORLD TODAY. COM USA+45 ECO/UNDEV CREATE LEAD WAR ADJUST...TREND NAT/COMP ANTHOL COLD/WAR KHRUSH/N. PAGE 151 H3017
USSR ASIA DIPLOM ATTIT

B66
THOMPSON J.H.,MODERNIZATION OF THE ARAB WORLD. FUT ISRAEL STRUCT ECO/UNDEV DIPLOM INGP/REL ATTIT ...CENSUS ANTHOL 20 ARABS. PAGE 154 H3082
ADJUST ISLAM PROB/SOLV NAT/COMP

B66
WHEELER G.,THE PEOPLES OF SOVIET CENTRAL ASIA: A BACKGROUND BOOK. ISLAM USSR STRATA STRUCT FORCES REV WAR HABITAT 7/20. PAGE 167 H3341
COLONIAL DOMIN CULTURE ADJUST

S66
HAIGH G.,"FIELD TRAINING IN HUMAN RELATIONS FOR THE PEACE CORPS." CONSULT CREATE EDU/PROP ADMIN TASK GP/REL ATTIT PERSON...PSY OBS SOC/EXP PEACE/CORP. PAGE 64 H1276
CULTURE PERS/REL FOR/AID ADJUST

S66
KAPIL R.L.,"ON THE CONFLICT POTENTIAL OF INHERITED BOUNDARIES IN AFRICA." MOD/EUR MOROCCO UAR EX/STRUC DIPLOM LEGIT REGION ADJUST...RECORD NAT/COMP GEN/LAWS. PAGE 83 H1658
AFR COLONIAL PREDICT GEOG

B67
ASHFORD D.E.,NATIONAL DEVELOPMENT AND LOCAL REFORM: POLITICAL PARTICIPATION IN MOROCCO, TUNISIA, AND PAKISTAN. MOROCCO PAKISTAN CULTURE PROB/SOLV ATTIT ...POLICY SOC METH/COMP NAT/COMP BIBLIOG 20 TUNIS. PAGE 9 H0173
PARTIC ECO/UNDEV ADJUST NAT/G

B67
BADGLEY R.F.,DOCTORS' STRIKE; MEDICAL CARE AND CONFLICT IN SASKATCHEWAN. CANADA NAT/G PROF/ORG GP/REL ADJUST ATTIT...HEAL SOC 20. PAGE 10 H0192
HEALTH PLAN LABOR BARGAIN

B67
CARTER G.M.,SOUTH AFRICA'S TRANSKEI: THE POLITICS OF DOMESTIC COLONIALISM. SOUTH/AFR ECO/UNDEV AGRI NAT/G PROVS PLAN DOMIN REPRESENT ADJUST DISCRIM ...OBS BIBLIOG 20 BANTUSTANS TRANSKEI. PAGE 27 H0550
STRATA GOV/REL COLONIAL POLICY

B67
COWLES M.,PERSPECTIVES IN THE EDUCATION OF DISADVANTAGED CHILDREN. CULTURE OP/RES PLAN PERS/REL ADJUST HABITAT PERCEPT KNOWL WEALTH ...SOC/WK IDEA/COMP ANTHOL 20. PAGE 34 H0686
EDU/PROP AGE/C TEC/DEV SCHOOL

B67
DALTON G.,TRIBAL AND PEASANT ECONOMIES. SOCIETY FINAN FAM INT/TRADE RATION ADJUST WEALTH...CHARTS ANTHOL BIBLIOG T. PAGE 37 H0738
SOC ECO/UNDEV NAT/COMP

B67
HUTCHINS F.G.,THE ILLUSION OF PERMANENCE: BRITISH IMPERIALISM IN INDIA. INDIA UK CULTURE STRUCT NAT/G REV GP/REL RACE/REL ADJUST DISCRIM ATTIT MORAL PWR SOC/INTEG 18/20. PAGE 75 H1509
COLONIAL CONTROL SOVEREIGN CONSERVE

B67
KORNBERG A.,CANADIAN LEGISLATIVE BEHAVIOR: A STUDY OF THE 25TH PARLIAMENT. CANADA NAT/G POL/PAR PARL/PROC CHOOSE INGP/REL ADJUST ANOMIE RIGID/FLEX ...SOC STAND/INT CHARTS SOC/EXP 20 PARLIAMENT. PAGE 88 H1756
ATTIT LEGIS ROLE

B67
POLSKY N.,HUSTLERS, BEATS, AND OTHERS. FACE/GP PRESS CRIME ADJUST ANOMIE DRIVE WEALTH...PSY SOC 20. PAGE 127 H2540
CULTURE CRIMLGY NEW/IDEA STRUCT

B67
THOMAS P.,DOWN THESE MEAN STREETS. GP/REL RACE/REL ADJUST...SOC SELF/OBS 20. PAGE 154 H3078
DISCRIM KIN CULTURE BIOG

B67
VALI F.A.,THE QUEST FOR A UNITED GERMANY. GERMANY PROB/SOLV DIPLOM ADJUST...BIBLIOG 20. PAGE 161 H3222
NAT/G ATTIT PLAN CENTRAL

L67
GALTUNG J.,"ON THE EFFECTS OF INTERNATIONAL ECONOMIC SANCTIONS, WITH EXAMPLES FROM THE CASE OF RHODESIA." NAT/G DIPLOM EDU/PROP ADJUST EFFICIENCY ATTIT MORAL...OBS CHARTS 20. PAGE 55 H1091
SANCTION ECO/TAC INT/TRADE ECO/UNDEV

S67
AKE C.,"POLITICAL INTEGRATION AND POLITICAL STABILITY." ELITES POL/PAR LEAD ADJUST EFFICIENCY ATTIT AUTHORIT DRIVE...CONCPT 20. PAGE 4 H0088
CULTURE NAT/G CONTROL GP/REL

S67
BULLOUGH B.,"ALIENATION IN THE GHETTO." CULTURE NEIGH GP/REL INGP/REL ATTIT...PSY SOC SAMP. PAGE 23 H0471
DISCRIM ANOMIE ADJUST

S67
CATTELL D.T.,"THE FIFTIETH ANNIVERSARY: A SOVIET WATERSHED?" USSR CONSTN ECO/DEV NAT/G LEAD TOTALISM 20 KHRUSH/N. PAGE 28 H0562
MARXISM CHIEF POLICY ADJUST

S67
MANGLAPUS R.S.,"ASIAN REVOLUTION AND AMERICAN IDEOLOGY." USA+45 SOCIETY CAP/ISM DIPLOM ADJUST CENTRAL...NAT/COMP 20. PAGE 102 H2035
REV POPULISM ATTIT ASIA

S67
RONNING C.,"NANKING: 1950." ASIA CANADA CHINA/COM NAT/G PLAN ECO/TAC REV ADJUST 20. PAGE 133 H2667
DIPLOM ROLE PEACE

S67
SOARES G.,"SOCIO-ECONOMIC VARIABLES AND VOTING FOR THE RADICAL LEFT: CHILE 1952." CHILE INDUS NAT/G WORKER ADJUST STRANGE ANOMIE WEALTH...METH/CNCPT CORREL 20. PAGE 146 H2925
STRATA POL/PAR CHOOSE STAT

S67
TANTER R.,"A THEORY OF REVOLUTION." ASIA CUBA L/A+17C S/ASIA SOCIETY NAT/G ADJUST...CONCPT CHARTS. PAGE 152 H3046
REV ECO/UNDEV EDU/PROP METH/COMP

S67
WILSON J.Q.,"A GUIDE TO REAGAN COUNTRY* THE POLITICAL CULTURE OF SOUTHERN CALIFORNIA." NEIGH PROVS PARTIC CHOOSE ADJUST CONSEN PERSON CONSERVE CALIFORNIA REAGAN/RON. PAGE 169 H3379
CULTURE ATTIT MORAL

B97
JENKS E.J.,LAW AND POLITICS IN THE MIDDLE AGES. CHRIST-17C CULTURE STRUCT KIN NAT/G SECT CT/SYS GP/REL...CLASSIF CHARTS IDEA/COMP BIBLIOG 8/16. PAGE 80 H1603
LAW SOCIETY ADJUST

B99
DU BOIS W.E.B.,THE PHILADELPHIA NEGRO: A SOCIAL STUDY. CULTURE STRATA KIN CRIME SUFF ADJUST DISCRIM ISOLAT HABITAT HEREDITY ALL/VALS SOC/INTEG 17/19 NEGRO PHILADELPH. PAGE 42 H0851
INGP/REL RACE/REL SOC CENSUS

ADJUSTMENT, SOCIAL....SEE ADJUST

ADLER/A....ALFRED ADLER

ADLOFF R. H3085

ADMIN....ORGANIZATIONAL BEHAVIOR, NONEXECUTIVE

N
AUSTRALIAN NATIONAL RES COUN,AUSTRALIAN SOCIAL SCIENCE ABSTRACTS. NEW/ZEALND CULTURE SOCIETY LOC/G CT/SYS PARL/PROC...HEAL JURID PSY SOC 20 AUSTRAL. PAGE 9 H0181
BIBLIOG/A POLICY NAT/G ADMIN

N
CONOVER H.F.,MADAGASCAR: A SELECTED LIST OF REFERENCES. MADAGASCAR STRUCT ECO/UNDEV NAT/G ADMIN ...SOC 19/20. PAGE 32 H0639
BIBLIOG/A SOCIETY CULTURE COLONIAL

B
DEUTSCHE BIBLIOTH FRANKF A M,DEUTSCHE BIBLIOGRAPHIE. EUR+WWI GERMANY ECO/DEV FORCES DIPLOM LEAD...POLICY PHIL/SCI SOC 20. PAGE 40 H0802
BIBLIOG LAW ADMIN NAT/G

N
AMERICAN POLITICAL SCIENCE REVIEW. USA+45 USA-45 WOR+45 WOR-45 INT/ORG ADMIN...INT/LAW PHIL/SCI CONCPT METH 20 UN. PAGE 1 H0001
BIBLIOG/A DIPLOM NAT/G GOV/COMP

N
CIVIL SERVICE JOURNAL. PARTIC INGP/REL PERS/REL ...MGT BIBLIOG/A 20. PAGE 1 H0015
ADMIN NAT/G SERV/IND WORKER

N
HANDBOOK OF LATIN AMERICAN STUDIES. LAW CULTURE ECO/UNDEV POL/PAR ADMIN LEAD...SOC 20. PAGE 1 H0016
BIBLIOG/A L/A+17C NAT/G DIPLOM

N
PUBLISHERS' TRADE LIST ANNUAL. LAW POL/PAR ADMIN PERSON ALL/IDEOS...HUM SOC 19/20. PAGE 1 H0020
BIBLIOG NAT/G DIPLOM POLICY

N
SUBJECT GUIDE TO BOOKS IN PRINT: AN INDEX TO THE PUBLISHERS' TRADE LIST ANNUAL. UNIV LAW LOC/G
BIBLIOG ECO/DEV

DIPLOM WRITING ADMIN LEAD PERSON...MGT SOC. PAGE 2 H0024
POL/PAR NAT/G

N
SUMMARIES OF SELECTED JAPANESE MAGAZINES. LAW CULTURE ADMIN LEAD 20 CHINJAP. PAGE 2 H0025
BIBLIOG/A ATTIT NAT/G ASIA

N
NEUE POLITISCHE LITERATUR; BERICHTE UBER DAS INTERNATIONALE SCHRIFTTUM ZUR POLITIK. WOR+45 LAW CONSTN POL/PAR ADMIN LEAD GOV/REL...POLICY IDEA/COMP. PAGE 2 H0027
BIBLIOG/A DIPLOM NAT/G NAT/COMP

N
DEUTSCHE BUCHEREI,JAHRESVERZEICHNIS DES DEUTSCHEN SCHRIFTUMS. AUSTRIA EUR+WWI GERMANY SWITZERLND LAW LOC/G DIPLOM ADMIN...MGT SOC 19/20. PAGE 40 H0804
BIBLIOG WRITING NAT/G

N
DEUTSCHE BUCHEREI,DEUTSCHES BUCHERVERZEICHNIS. GERMANY LAW CULTURE POL/PAR ADMIN LEAD ATTIT PERSON ...SOC 20. PAGE 40 H0805
BIBLIOG NAT/G DIPLOM ECO/DEV

N
MINISTERE DE L'EDUC NATIONALE,CATALOGUE DES THESES DE DOCTORAT SOUTENNES DEVANT LES UNIVERSITAIRES FRANCAISES. FRANCE LAW DIPLOM ADMIN...HUM SOC 20. PAGE 111 H2223
BIBLIOG ACADEM KNOWL NAT/G

B01
GRIFFIN A.P.C.,A LIST OF BOOKS ON THE DANISH WEST INDIES (PAMPHLET). L/A+17C WEST/IND CULTURE LOC/G ...GEOG MGT 18/20. PAGE 61 H1214
BIBLIOG/A SOCIETY COLONIAL ADMIN

B01
GRIFFIN A.P.C.,A LIST OF BOOKS ON PORTO RICO. PUERT/RICO CULTURE LOC/G...GEOG MGT 19/20. PAGE 61 H1215
BIBLIOG/A SOCIETY COLONIAL ADMIN

B03
FAGUET E.,LE LIBERALISME. FRANCE PRESS ADJUD ADMIN DISCRIM CONSERVE SOCISM...TRADIT SOC LING WORSHIP PARLIAMENT. PAGE 48 H0960
ORD/FREE EDU/PROP NAT/G LAW

B03
GRIFFIN A.P.C.,LIST OF BOOKS ON THE CABINETS OF ENGLAND AND AMERICA (PAMPHLET). MOD/EUR UK USA-45 CONSTN NAT/G CONSULT EX/STRUC 19/20. PAGE 61 H1216
BIBLIOG/A GOV/COMP ADMIN DELIB/GP

B03
GRIFFIN A.P.C.,SELECT LIST OF REFERENCES ON GOVERNMENT OWNERSHIP OF RAILROADS (PAMPHLET). MOD/EUR NAT/G ADMIN...MGT GOV/COMP 19/20. PAGE 61 H1217
BIBLIOG/A SOCISM OWN DIST/IND

B05
GRIFFIN A.P.C.,LIST OF BOOKS ON RAILROADS IN FOREIGN COUNTRIES. MOD/EUR ECO/DEV NAT/G CONTROL SOCISM...JURID 19/20 RAILROAD. PAGE 61 H1219
BIBLIOG/A SERV/IND ADMIN DIST/IND

B08
THE GOVERNMENT OF SOUTH AFRICA (VOL. II). SOUTH/AFR STRATA EXTR/IND EX/STRUC TOP/EX BUDGET ADJUD ADMIN CT/SYS PRODUC...CORREL CENSUS 19 RAILROAD CIVIL/SERV POSTAL/SYS. PAGE 2 H0030
CONSTN FINAN LEGIS NAT/G

B12
POLLOCK F.,THE GENIUS OF THE COMMON LAW. CHRIST-17C UK FINAN CHIEF ACT/RES ADMIN GP/REL ATTIT SOCISM ...ANARCH JURID. PAGE 127 H2537
LAW CULTURE CREATE

B12
SONOLET L.,L'AFRIQUE OCCIDENTALE FRANCAISE. FRANCE AGRI INDUS NAT/G SECT FORCES INT/TRADE EDU/PROP RACE/REL HEALTH ORD/FREE...CHARTS 19/20 NEGRO AFRICA/W. PAGE 147 H2933
DOMIN ADMIN COLONIAL AFR

B17
HARLOW R.V.,THE HISTORY OF LEGISLATIVE METHODS IN THE PERIOD BEFORE 1825. USA-45 EX/STRUC ADMIN COLONIAL LEAD PARL/PROC ROUTINE...GP/COMP GOV/COMP HOUSE/REP. PAGE 66 H1333
LEGIS DELIB/GP PROVS POL/PAR

B19
NATHAN M.,THE SOUTH AFRICAN COMMONWEALTH: CONSTITUTION, PROBLEMS, SOCIAL CONDITIONS. SOUTH/AFR UK CULTURE INDUS EX/STRUC LEGIS BUDGET EDU/PROP ADMIN CT/SYS GP/REL RACE/REL...LING 19/20 CMN/WLTH. PAGE 116 H2317
CONSTN NAT/G POL/PAR SOCIETY

N19
ADMINISTRATIVE STAFF COLLEGE,THE ACCOUNTABILITY OF GOVERNMENT DEPARTMENTS (PAMPHLET) (REV. ED.). UK CONSTN FINAN NAT/G CONSULT ADMIN INGP/REL CONSEN PRIVIL 20 PARLIAMENT. PAGE 3 H0070
PARL/PROC ELITES SANCTION PROB/SOLV

N19
ANDERSON J.,THE ORGANIZATION OF ECONOMIC STUDIES IN RELATION TO THE PROBLEMS OF GOVERNMENT (PAMPHLET). UK FINAN INDUS DELIB/GP PLAN PROB/SOLV ADMIN 20. PAGE 6 H0128
ECO/TAC ACT/RES NAT/G CENTRAL

N19
BENTHAM J.,A PLAN FOR AN UNIVERSAL AND PERPETUAL PEACE (1838) (PAMPHLET). NAT/G FORCES BAL/PWR INT/TRADE ADMIN AGREE CT/SYS ARMS/CONT SOVEREIGN WEALTH GEN/LAWS. PAGE 14 H0288
INT/ORG INT/LAW PEACE COLONIAL

N19
CANADA CIVIL SERV COMM,THE ANALYSIS OF ORGANIZATION IN THE GOVERNMENT OF CANADA (PAMPHLET). CANADA CONSTN EX/STRUC LEGIS TOP/EX CREATE PLAN CONTROL GP/REL 20. PAGE 26 H0517
NAT/G MGT ADMIN DELIB/GP

N19
FIKS M.,PUBLIC ADMINISTRATION IN ISRAEL (PAMPHLET). ISRAEL SCHOOL EX/STRUC BUDGET PAY INGP/REL ...DECISION 20 CIVIL/SERV. PAGE 50 H0999
EDU/PROP NAT/G ADMIN WORKER

N19
GORWALA A.D.,THE ADMINISTRATIVE JUNGLE (PAMPHLET). INDIA NAT/G LEGIS ECO/TAC CONTROL GOV/REL ...METH/COMP 20. PAGE 59 H1183
ADMIN POLICY PLAN ECO/UNDEV

N19
GRIFFITH W.,THE PUBLIC SERVICE (PAMPHLET). UK LAW LOC/G NAT/G PARTIC CHOOSE DRIVE ROLE SKILL...CHARTS 20 CIVIL/SERV. PAGE 61 H1222
ADMIN EFFICIENCY EDU/PROP GOV/REL

N19
POUND R.,ORGANIZATION OF THE COURTS (PAMPHLET). MOD/EUR UK USA-45 ADJUD PWR...GOV/COMP 10/20 EUROPE. PAGE 127 H2546
CT/SYS JURID STRUCT ADMIN

N19
SOUTH AFRICA COMMISSION ON FUT,INTERIM AND FINAL REPORTS ON FUTURE FORM OF GOVERNMENT IN THE SOUTH-WEST AFRICAN PROTECTORATE (PAMPHLET). SOUTH/AFR NAT/G FORCES CONFER COLONIAL CONTROL 20 AFRICA/SW. PAGE 147 H2936
CONSTN REPRESENT ADMIN PROB/SOLV

B20
HALDANE R.B.,BEFORE THE WAR. MOD/EUR SOCIETY INT/ORG NAT/G DELIB/GP PLAN DOMIN EDU/PROP LEGIT ADMIN COERCE ATTIT DRIVE MORAL ORD/FREE PWR...SOC CONCPT SELF/OBS RECORD BIOG TIME/SEQ. PAGE 64 H1282
POLICY DIPLOM UK

C20
BLACHLY F.F.,"THE GOVERNMENT AND ADMINISTRATION OF GERMANY." GERMANY CONSTN LOC/G PROVS DELIB/GP EX/STRUC FORCES LEGIS TOP/EX CT/SYS...BIBLIOG/A 19/20. PAGE 17 H0348
NAT/G GOV/REL ADMIN PHIL/SCI

B22
KRABBE H.,THE MODERN IDEA OF THE STATE. LAW CHIEF DIPLOM DOMIN ADMIN REPRESENT CENTRAL ORD/FREE ...NEW/IDEA GOV/COMP IDEA/COMP. PAGE 88 H1761
SOVEREIGN CONSTN PHIL/SCI

B24
BAGEHOT W.,THE ENGLISH CONSTITUTION AND OTHER POLITICAL ESSAYS. UK DELIB/GP BAL/PWR ADMIN CONTROL EXEC ROUTINE CONSERVE...METH PARLIAMENT 19/20. PAGE 10 H0197
NAT/G STRUCT CONCPT

B26
FORTESCUE J.,THE GOVERNANCE OF ENGLAND (1471-76). UK LAW FINAN SECT LEGIS PROB/SOLV TAX DOMIN ADMIN GP/REL COST ORD/FREE PWR 14/15. PAGE 52 H1042
CONSERVE CONSTN CHIEF NAT/G

B27
WILLOUGHBY W.F.,PRINCIPLES OF PUBLIC ADMINISTRATION WITH SPECIAL REFERENCE TO THE NATIONAL AND STATE GOVERNMENTS OF THE UNITED STATES. FINAN PROVS CHIEF CONSULT LEGIS CREATE BUDGET EXEC ROUTINE GOV/REL CENTRAL...MGT 20 BUR/BUDGET CONGRESS PRESIDENT. PAGE 169 H3373
NAT/G EX/STRUC OP/RES ADMIN

B28
FYFE H.,THE BRITISH LIBERAL PARTY. UK SECT ADMIN LEAD CHOOSE GP/REL PWR SOCISM...MAJORIT TIME/SEQ 19/20 LIB/PARTY CONSRV/PAR. PAGE 54 H1084
POL/PAR NAT/G REPRESENT POPULISM

B29
CAM H.M.,BIBLIOGRAPHY OF ENGLISH CONSTITUTIONAL HISTORY (PAMPHLET). UK LAW LOC/G NAT/G POL/PAR SECT DELIB/GP ADJUD ORD/FREE 19/20 PARLIAMENT. PAGE 25 H0510
BIBLIOG/A CONSTN ADMIN PARL/PROC

B30
CANAWAY A.P.,THE FAILURE OF FEDERALISM IN AUSTRALIA. UK PROB/SOLV ADMIN EFFICIENCY ATTIT ...POLICY NAT/COMP 20 AUSTRAL. PAGE 26 H0518
FEDERAL NAT/G CONSTN OP/RES

B31
DEKAT A.D.A.,COLONIAL POLICY. S/ASIA CULTURE EX/STRUC ECO/TAC DOMIN ADMIN COLONIAL ROUTINE SOVEREIGN WEALTH...POLICY MGT RECORD KNO/TEST SAMP. PAGE 39 H0785
DRIVE PWR INDONESIA NETHERLAND

B32
CARDINALL AW,A BIBLIOGRAPHY OF THE GOLD COAST. AFR UK NAT/G EX/STRUC ATTIT...POLICY 19/20. PAGE 26 H0527
BIBLIOG ADMIN COLONIAL DIPLOM

B33
ENSOR R.C.K.,COURTS AND JUDGES IN FRANCE, GERMANY, AND ENGLAND. FRANCE GERMANY UK LAW PROB/SOLV ADMIN ROUTINE CRIME ROLE...METH/COMP 20 CIVIL/LAW. PAGE 46 H0930
CT/SYS EX/STRUC ADJUD NAT/COMP

C33
MURET C.T.,"FRENCH ROYALIST DOCTRINES SINCE THE REVOLUTION." FRANCE CONSTN NAT/G SECT ADMIN LEAD SOVEREIGN...POLICY BIOG IDEA/COMP BIBLIOG 18/20.
POL/PAR ATTIT INTELL

PAGE 115 H2295 CONSERVE

B34
DE CENIVAL P.,BIBLIOGRAPHIE MAROCAINE: 1923-1933. FRANCE MOROCCO SECT ADMIN LEAD GP/REL ATTIT...LING 20. PAGE 37 H0750 BIBLIOG/A ISLAM NAT/G COLONIAL

B34
RIDLEY C.E.,THE CITY-MANAGER PROFESSION. CHIEF PLAN ADMIN CONTROL ROUTINE CHOOSE...TECHNIC CHARTS GOV/COMP BIBLIOG 20. PAGE 131 H2624 MUNIC EX/STRUC LOC/G EXEC

L34
GOSNELL H.F.,"BRITISH ROYAL COMMISSIONS OF INQUIRY" UK CONSTN LEGIS PRESS ADMIN PARL/PROC...DECISION 20 PARLIAMENT. PAGE 59 H1184 DELIB/GP INSPECT POLICY NAT/G

B35
DOUGLASS H.P.,THE PROTESTANT CHURCH AS A SOCIAL INSTITUTION. CULTURE FINAN NEIGH PROF/ORG OP/RES ADMIN...POLICY SOC/WK STAT BIBLIOG. PAGE 42 H0843 SECT PARTIC INGP/REL GP/REL

B35
GORER G.,AFRICA DANCES: A BOOK ABOUT WEST AFRICAN NEGROES. STRUCT LOC/G SECT FORCES TAX ADMIN COLONIAL...ART/METH MYTH WORSHIP 20 NEGRO AFRICA/W CHRISTIAN RITUAL. PAGE 59 H1181 AFR ATTIT CULTURE SOCIETY

B37
UNION OF SOUTH AFRICA,REPORT CONCERNING ADMINISTRATION OF SOUTH WEST AFRICA (6 VOLS.). SOUTH/AFR INDUS PUB/INST FORCES LEGIS BUDGET DIPLOM EDU/PROP ADJUD CT/SYS...GEOG CHARTS 20 AFRICA/SW LEAGUE/NAT. PAGE 158 H3166 NAT/G ADMIN COLONIAL CONSTN

B38
FIELD G.L.,THE SYNDICAL AND CORPORATIVE INSTITUTIONS OF ITALIAN FASCISM. ITALY CONSTN STRATA LABOR EX/STRUC TOP/EX ADJUD ADMIN LEAD TOTALISM AUTHORIT...MGT 20 MUSSOLIN/B. PAGE 50 H0991 FASCISM INDUS NAT/G WORKER

B38
HARPER S.N.,THE GOVERNMENT OF THE SOVIET UNION. COM USSR LAW CONSTN ECO/DEV PLAN TEC/DEV DIPLOM INT/TRADE ADMIN REV NAT/LISM...POLICY 20. PAGE 67 H1337 MARXISM NAT/G LEAD POL/PAR

B38
HOLDSWORTH W.S.,A HISTORY OF ENGLISH LAW; THE CENTURIES OF SETTLEMENT AND REFORM (VOL. X). INDIA UK CONSTN NAT/G CHIEF LEGIS ADMIN COLONIAL CT/SYS CHOOSE ORD/FREE PWR...JURID 18 PARLIAMENT COMMONWLTH COMMON/LAW. PAGE 72 H1451 LAW LOC/G EX/STRUC ADJUD

B38
RAWLINSON H.G.,INDIA: A SHORT CULTURAL HISTORY. INDIA LAW STRATA FORCES INT/TRADE ADMIN COLONIAL PERSON...GEOG HUM BIBLIOG WORSHIP 20. PAGE 130 H2598 CULTURE SECT MYTH ART/METH

B38
REICH N.,LABOR RELATIONS IN REPUBLICAN GERMANY. GERMANY CONSTN ECO/DEV INDUS NAT/G ADMIN CONTROL GP/REL FASCISM POPULISM 20 WEIMAR/REP. PAGE 130 H2609 WORKER MGT LABOR BARGAIN

B39
ANDERSON W.,LOCAL GOVERNMENT IN EUROPE. FRANCE GERMANY ITALY UK USSR MUNIC PROVS ADMIN GOV/REL CENTRAL SOVEREIGN 20. PAGE 7 H0136 GOV/COMP NAT/COMP LOC/G CONSTN

B39
FURNIVALL J.S.,NETHERLANDS INDIA. INDIA NETHERLAND CULTURE INDUS NAT/G DIPLOM ADMIN WEALTH...POLICY CHARTS 17/20. PAGE 54 H1081 COLONIAL ECO/UNDEV SOVEREIGN PLURISM

B39
HITLER A.,MEIN KAMPF. EUR+WWI FUT MOD/EUR STRUCT INT/ORG LABOR NAT/G POL/PAR FORCES CREATE PLAN BAL/PWR DIPLOM ECO/TAC DOMIN EDU/PROP ADMIN COERCE ATTIT...SOCIALIST BIOG TREND NAZI. PAGE 71 H1428 PWR NEW/IDEA WAR

S39
AIKEN C.,"THE BRITISH BUREAUCRACY AND THE ORIGINS OF PARLIAMENTARY DEMOCRACY" UK TOP/EX ADMIN. PAGE 4 H0082 MGT NAT/G LEGIS

C39
REISCHAUER R.,"JAPAN'S GOVERNMENT--POLITICS." CONSTN STRATA POL/PAR FORCES LEGIS DIPLOM ADMIN EXEC CENTRAL...POLICY BIBLIOG 20 CHINJAP. PAGE 131 H2610 NAT/G S/ASIA CONCPT ROUTINE

S40
FAHS C.B.,"POLITICAL GROUPS IN THE JAPANESE HOUSE OF PEERS." ELITES NAT/G ADMIN GP/REL...TREND CHINJAP. PAGE 48 H0961 ROUTINE POL/PAR LEGIS

C40
FAHS C.B.,"GOVERNMENT IN JAPAN." FINAN FORCES LEGIS TOP/EX BUDGET INT/TRADE EDU/PROP SOVEREIGN ...CON/ANAL BIBLIOG/A 20 CHINJAP. PAGE 48 H0962 ASIA DIPLOM NAT/G ADMIN

B41
COHEN E.W.,THE GROWTH OF THE BRITISH CIVIL SERVICE 1780-1939. UK NAT/G SENIOR ROUTINE GOV/REL...MGT METH/COMP BIBLIOG 18/20. PAGE 31 H0616 OP/RES TIME/SEQ CENTRAL

ADMIN

B41
STATIST REICHSAMTE,BIBLIOGRAPHIE DER STAATS- UND WIRSCHAFTSWISSENSCHAFTEN. EUR+WWI GERMANY FINAN ADMIN. PAGE 149 H2974 BIBLIOG ECO/DEV NAT/G POLICY

B42
BARKER E.,REFLECTIONS ON GOVERNMENT. EUR+WWI SOCIETY LEGIS EDU/PROP ADMIN LEAD PARTIC CHOOSE TOTALISM AUTHORIT ORD/FREE SOCISM 20. PAGE 11 H0218 NAT/G POPULISM ACT/RES GEN/LAWS

B42
NEUBURGER O.,OFFICIAL PUBLICATIONS OF PRESENT-DAY GERMANY: GOVERNMENT, CORPORATE ORGANIZATIONS, AND NATIONAL SOCIALIST PARTY. GERMANY CONSTN COM/IND POL/PAR EDU/PROP PRESS 20 NAZI. PAGE 117 H2332 BIBLIOG/A FASCISM NAT/G ADMIN

B42
SIMOES DOS REIS A.,BIBLIOGRAFIA DAS BIBLIOGRAFIAS BRASILEIRAS. BRAZIL ADMIN COLONIAL 20. PAGE 144 H2879 BIBLIOG NAT/G DIPLOM L/A+17C

B43
LEWIN E.,ROYAL EMPIRE SOCIETY BIBLIOGRAPHIES NO. 9: SUB-SAHARA AFRICA. ECO/UNDEV TEC/DEV DIPLOM ADMIN COLONIAL LEAD 20. PAGE 96 H1908 BIBLIOG AFR NAT/G SOCIETY

S43
PRICE D.K.,"THE PARLIAMENTARY AND PRESIDENTIAL SYSTEMS" (BMR)" USA-45 NAT/G EX/STRUC PARL/PROC GOV/REL PWR 20 PRESIDENT CONGRESS PARLIAMENT. PAGE 128 H2561 LEGIS REPRESENT ADMIN GOV/COMP

B44
BARKER E.,THE DEVELOPMENT OF PUBLIC SERVICES IN WESTERN WUROPE: 1660-1930. FRANCE GERMANY UK SCHOOL CONTROL REPRESENT ROLE...WELF/ST 17/20. PAGE 11 H0219 GOV/COMP ADMIN EX/STRUC

B45
CONOVER H.F.,THE GOVERNMENTS OF THE MAJOR FOREIGN POWERS: A BIBLIOGRAPHY. FRANCE GERMANY ITALY UK USSR CONSTN LOC/G POL/PAR EX/STRUC FORCES ADMIN CT/SYS CIVMIL/REL TOTALISM...POLICY 19/20. PAGE 32 H0645 BIBLIOG NAT/G DIPLOM

B45
MERRIAM C.E.,SYSTEMATIC POLITICS. FUT POL/PAR DELIB/GP DIPLOM ADJUD ADMIN LEAD CHOOSE ATTIT...MGT PHIL/SCI TREND. PAGE 109 H2183 NAT/G METH/CNCPT CREATE

B46
DAVIES E.,NATIONAL ENTERPRISE: THE DEVELOPMENT OF THE PUBLIC CORPORATION. UK LG/CO EX/STRUC WORKER PROB/SOLV COST ATTIT SOCISM 20. PAGE 37 H0748 ADMIN NAT/G CONTROL INDUS

B47
CROCKER W.R.,ON GOVERNING COLONIES: BEING AN OUTLINE OF THE REAL ISSUES AND A COMPARISON OF THE BRITISH, FRENCH, AND BELGIAN... AFR BELGIUM FRANCE UK CULTURE SOVEREIGN...OBS 20. PAGE 35 H0705 COLONIAL POLICY GOV/COMP ADMIN

B47
DE NOIA J.,GUIDE TO OFFICIAL PUBLICATIONS OF THE OTHER AMERICAN REPUBLICS: EL SALVADOR. EL/SALVADR LAW LEGIS EDU/PROP CT/SYS 20. PAGE 38 H0764 BIBLIOG/A CONSTN NAT/G ADMIN

B47
DE NOIA J.,GUIDE TO OFFICIAL PUBLICATIONS OF THE OTHER AMERICAN REPUBLICS: NICARAGUA (VOL. XIV). NICARAGUA LAW LEGIS ADMIN CT/SYS...JURID 19/20. PAGE 38 H0765 BIBLIOG/A EDU/PROP NAT/G CONSTN

B47
DE NOIA J.,GUIDE TO OFFICIAL PUBLICATIONS OF THE OTHER AMERICAN REPUBLICS: PANAMA (VOL. XV). PANAMA LAW LEGIS EDU/PROP CT/SYS 20. PAGE 38 H0766 BIBLIOG/A CONSTN ADMIN NAT/G

B47
MARX F.M.,THE PRESIDENT AND HIS STAFF SERVICES PUBLIC ADMINISTRATION SERVICES NUMBER 98 (PAMPHLET). FINAN ADMIN CT/SYS REPRESENT PWR 20 PRESIDENT. PAGE 104 H2075 CONSTN CHIEF NAT/G EX/STRUC

B47
NEUBURGER O.,GUIDE TO OFFICIAL PUBLICATIONS OF OTHER AMERICAN REPUBLICS: HONDURAS (VOL. XIII). HONDURAS LAW LEGIS ADMIN CT/SYS...JURID 19/20. PAGE 117 H2333 BIBLIOG/A NAT/G EDU/PROP CONSTN

B48
GUIDE TO THE RECORDS IN THE NATIONAL ARCHIVES. ECO/UNDEV ADMIN COLONIAL 16/20. PAGE 2 H0034 BIBLIOG NAT/G L/A+17C DIPLOM

B48
DE NOIA J.,GUIDE TO OFFICIAL PUBLICATIONS OF OTHER AMERICAN REPUBLICS: PERU (VOL. XVII). PERU LAW LEGIS ADMIN CT/SYS...JURID 19/20. PAGE 38 H0767 BIBLIOG/A CONSTN NAT/G EDU/PROP

B48
MINISTERE FINANCES ET ECO,BULLETIN BIBLIOGRAPHIQUE. AFR EUR+WWI FRANCE CULTURE STRUCT FINAN NAT/G ACT/RES INT/TRADE ADMIN REGION PRODUC STAT. PAGE 111 H2224 BIBLIOG/A ECO/UNDEV TEC/DEV COLONIAL

B48
US LIBRARY OF CONGRESS,BRAZIL: A GUIDE TO THE OFFICIAL PUBLICATIONS OF BRAZIL. BRAZIL L/A+17C CONSULT DELIB/GP LEGIS CT/SYS 19/20. PAGE 160 H3206
BIBLIOG/A NAT/G ADMIN TOP/EX

B49
BORBA DE MORAES R.,MANUAL BIBLIOGRAFICO DE ESTUDOS BRASILEIROS. BRAZIL DIPLOM ADMIN LEAD...SOC 20. PAGE 19 H0374
BIBLIOG L/A+17C NAT/G ECO/UNDEV

B49
HEADLAM-MORLEY,BIBLIOGRAPHY IN POLITICS FOR THE HONOUR SCHOOL OF PHILOSOPHY, POLITICS AND ECONOMICS (PAMPHLET). UK CONSTN LABOR MUNIC DIPLOM ADMIN 19/20. PAGE 69 H1375
BIBLIOG NAT/G PHIL/SCI GOV/REL

B49
MCLEAN J.M.,THE PUBLIC SERVICE AND UNIVERSITY EDUCATION. UK USA-45 DELIB/GP EX/STRUC TOP/EX ADMIN ...GOV/COMP METH/COMP NAT/COMP ANTHOL 20. PAGE 107 H2142
ACADEM NAT/G EXEC EDU/PROP

B49
SCHWARTZ B.,LAW AND THE EXECUTIVE IN BRITAIN: A COMPARATIVE STUDY. UK USA+45 LAW EX/STRUC PWR ...GOV/COMP 20. PAGE 140 H2807
ADMIN EXEC CONTROL REPRESENT

L49
BRECHT A.,"THE NEW GERMAN CONSTITUTION." GERMANY/W NAT/G CHIEF EX/STRUC LEGIS PROB/SOLV ADMIN REPRESENT TOTALISM ORD/FREE PLURISM...MAJORIT CHARTS 20. PAGE 20 H0409
CONSTN DIPLOM SOVEREIGN FEDERAL

B50
FIGANIERE J.C.,BIBLIOTHECA HISTORICA PORTUGUEZA. BRAZIL PORTUGAL SECT ADMIN. PAGE 50 H0997
BIBLIOG NAT/G DIPLOM COLONIAL

B50
LIPSET S.M.,AGRARIAN SOCIALISM. CANADA POL/PAR OP/RES ECO/TAC ADMIN ATTIT...TIME/SEQ NAT/COMP SOC/EXP 20 SASKATCH. PAGE 97 H1938
SOCISM AGRI METH/COMP STRUCT

B50
LYONS F.S.L.,THE IRISH PARLIAMENTARY PARTY, 1890-1910: STUDIES IN IRISH HISTORY (VOL. 4). IRELAND DELIB/GP LEGIS PAY EDU/PROP ADMIN GP/REL ATTIT...BIBLIOG 19/20 PARLIAMENT PARNELL/CS DIRECT/NAT. PAGE 99 H1986
POL/PAR CHOOSE NAT/G POLICY

B50
MCHENRY D.E.,THE THIRD FORCE IN CANADA: THE COOPERATIVE COMMONWEALTH FEDERATION, 1932-1948. CANADA EX/STRUC LEGIS REPRESENT 20 LABOR/PAR. PAGE 107 H2131
POL/PAR ADMIN CHOOSE POLICY

B50
WADE E.C.S.,CONSTITUTIONAL LAW; AN OUTLINE OF THE LAW AND PRACTICE OF THE CONSTITUTION. UK LEGIS DOMIN ADMIN GP/REL 16/20 CMN/WLTH PARLIAMENT ENGLSH/LAW. PAGE 164 H3283
CONSTN NAT/G PARL/PROC LAW

B50
WARD R.E.,A GUIDE TO JAPANESE REFERENCE AND RESEARCH MATERIALS IN THE FIELD OF POLITICAL SCIENCE. LAW CONSTN LOC/G PRESS ADMIN...SOC CON/ANAL METH 19/20 CHINJAP. PAGE 165 H3305
BIBLIOG/A ASIA NAT/G

C50
STOKES W.S.,"HONDURAS: AN AREA STUDY IN GOVERNMENT." HONDURAS NAT/G POL/PAR COLONIAL CT/SYS ROUTINE CHOOSE REPRESENT...GEOG RECORD BIBLIOG 19/20. PAGE 149 H2988
CONSTN LAW L/A+17C ADMIN

B51
US LIBRARY OF CONGRESS,EAST EUROPEAN ACCESSIONS LIST (VOL. I). POL/PAR DIPLOM ADMIN LEAD 20. PAGE 160 H3207
BIBLIOG/A COM SOCIETY NAT/G

B51
WEBSTER C.,THE FOREIGN POLICY OF PALMERSTON - 1830 TO 1841. MOD/EUR UK LAW CONSTN INTELL SOCIETY STRUCT NAT/G FORCES TOP/EX CREATE BAL/PWR PWR 19. PAGE 166 H3323
ADMIN PERSON DIPLOM

B52
HIMMELFARB G.,LORD ACTON: A STUDY IN CONSCIENCE AND POLITICS. MOD/EUR NAT/G POL/PAR SECT LEGIS TOP/EX EDU/PROP ADMIN NAT/LISM ATTIT PERSON SUPEGO MORAL ORD/FREE...CONCPT PARLIAMENT 19 ACTON/LORD. PAGE 71 H1419
PWR BIOG

B52
SCHATTSCHNEIDER E.E.,A GUIDE TO THE STUDY OF PUBLIC AFFAIRS. LAW LOC/G NAT/G LEGIS BUDGET PRESS ADMIN LOBBY...JURID CHARTS 20. PAGE 139 H2775
ACT/RES INTELL ACADEM METH/COMP

B52
US DEPARTMENT OF STATE,RESEARCH ON EASTERN EUROPE (EXCLUDING USSR). EUR+WWI LAW ECO/DEV NAT/G PROB/SOLV DIPLOM ADMIN LEAD MARXISM...TREND 19/20. PAGE 159 H3187
BIBLIOG R+D ACT/RES COM

B53
APPLEBY P.H.,PUBLIC ADMINISTRATION IN INDIA: REPORT OF A SURVEY. INDIA LOC/G OP/RES ATTIT ORD/FREE 20. PAGE 7 H0147
ADMIN NAT/G EX/STRUC GOV/REL

B53
MEYER P.,THE JEWS IN THE SOVIET SATELLITES. CZECHOSLVK POLAND SOCIETY STRATA NAT/G BAL/PWR ECO/TAC EDU/PROP LEGIT ADMIN COERCE ATTIT DISPL PERCEPT HEALTH PWR RESPECT WEALTH...METH/CNCPT JEWS VAL/FREE NAZI 20. PAGE 110 H2192
COM SECT TOTALISM USSR

B53
PIERCE R.A.,RUSSIAN CENTRAL ASIA, 1867-1917: A SELECTED BIBLIOGRAPHY (PAMPHLET). USSR LAW CULTURE NAT/G EDU/PROP WAR...GEOG SOC 19/20. PAGE 125 H2508
BIBLIOG COLONIAL ADMIN COM

B53
STOUT H.M.,BRITISH GOVERNMENT. UK FINAN LOC/G POL/PAR DELIB/GP DIPLOM ADMIN COLONIAL CHOOSE ORD/FREE...JURID BIBLIOG 20 COMMONWLTH. PAGE 150 H2990
NAT/G PARL/PROC CONSTN NEW/LIB

C53
BULNER-THOMAS I.,"THE PARTY SYSTEM IN GREAT BRITAIN." UK CONSTN SECT PRESS CONFER GP/REL ATTIT ...POLICY TREND BIBLIOG 19/20 PARLIAMENT. PAGE 23 H0473
NAT/G POL/PAR ADMIN ROUTINE

C53
DORWART R.A.,"THE ADMINISTRATIVE REFORMS OF FREDRICK WILLIAM I OF PRUSSIA. GERMANY MOD/EUR CHIEF CONTROL PWR...BIBLIOG 16/18. PAGE 42 H0839
ADMIN NAT/G CENTRAL GOV/REL

C53
KRACKE E.A. JR.,"CIVIL SERVICE IN EARLY SUNG CHINA, 960-1067." ASIA GP/REL...BIBLIOG/A 10/11. PAGE 88 H1762
ADMIN NAT/G WORKER CONTROL

B54
BINANI G.D.,INDIA AT A GLANCE (REV. ED.). INDIA COM/IND FINAN INDUS LABOR PROVS SCHOOL PLAN DIPLOM INT/TRADE ADMIN...JURID 20. PAGE 17 H0335
INDEX CON/ANAL NAT/G ECO/UNDEV

B54
JENNINGS I.,THE QUEEN'S GOVERNMENT. UK POL/PAR DELIB/GP ADJUD ADMIN CT/SYS PARL/PROC REPRESENT CONSERVE 13/20 PARLIAMENT. PAGE 80 H1605
NAT/G CONSTN LEGIS CHIEF

B54
MOSK S.A.,INDUSTRIAL REVOLUTION IN MEXICO. MARKET LABOR CREATE CAP/ISM ADMIN ATTIT SOCISM...POLICY 20 MEXIC/AMER. PAGE 113 H2268
INDUS TEC/DEV ECO/UNDEV NAT/G

B54
TOTOK W.,HANDBUCH DER BIBLIOGRAPHISCHEN NACHSCHLAGEWERKE. GERMANY LAW CULTURE ADMIN...SOC 20. PAGE 156 H3117
BIBLIOG/A NAT/G DIPLOM POLICY

S54
COLE T.,"LESSONS FROM RECENT EUROPEAN EXPERIENCE." EUR+WWI EX/STRUC 20. PAGE 31 H0626
GOV/COMP ADMIN REPRESENT

C54
LANDAU J.M.,"PARLIAMENTS AND PARTIES IN EGYPT." UAR NAT/G SECT CONSULT LEGIS TOP/EX PROB/SOLV ADMIN COLONIAL...GEN/LAWS BIBLIOG 19/20. PAGE 90 H1804
ISLAM NAT/LISM PARL/PROC POL/PAR

B55
APTER D.E.,THE GOLD COAST IN TRANSITION. FUT CONSTN CULTURE SOCIETY ECO/UNDEV FAM KIN LOC/G NAT/G POL/PAR LEGIS TOP/EX EDU/PROP LEGIT ADMIN ATTIT PERSON PWR...CONCPT STAT INT CENSUS TOT/POP VAL/FREE. PAGE 7 H0149
AFR SOVEREIGN

B55
BAILEY S.K.,RESEARCH FRONTIERS IN POLITICS AND GOVERNMENT. CONSTN LEGIS ADMIN REV CHOOSE...CONCPT IDEA/COMP GAME ANTHOL 20. PAGE 10 H0201
R+D METH NAT/G

B55
CRAIG G.A.,THE POLITICS OF THE PRUSSIAN ARMY 1640-1945. CHRIST-17C EUR+WWI MOD/EUR PRUSSIA STRUCT DIPLOM ADMIN REV WAR...SOC BIBLIOG 17/20. PAGE 35 H0694
FORCES NAT/G ROLE CHIEF

B55
DE ARAGAO J.G.,LA JURIDICTION ADMINISTRATIVE AU BRESIL. BRAZIL ADJUD COLONIAL CT/SYS REV FEDERAL ORD/FREE...BIBLIOG 19/20. PAGE 37 H0749
EX/STRUC ADMIN NAT/G

B55
RESHETAR J.S.,PROBLEMS OF ANALYZING AND PREDICTING SOVIET BEHAVIOR. USSR CULTURE ECO/DEV AGRI DIST/IND EXTR/IND PROC/MFG NAT/G SECT TOP/EX ACT/RES ADMIN PWR WEALTH...SOC METH TOT/POP VAL/FREE 20. PAGE 131 H2617
COM ATTIT

B55
SVARLIEN O.,AN INTRODUCTION TO THE LAW OF NATIONS. SEA AIR INT/ORG NAT/G CHIEF ADMIN AGREE WAR PRIVIL ORD/FREE SOVEREIGN...BIBLIOG 16/20. PAGE 151 H3012
INT/LAW DIPLOM

B55
TAN C.C.,THE BOXER CATASTROPHE. ASIA UK USSR ELITES POL/PAR VOL/ASSN FORCES PROB/SOLV DIPLOM ADMIN COLONIAL NAT/LISM PEACE TREATY 19/20 BOXER/REBL. PAGE 152 H3040
REV NAT/G WAR

B55
WHEARE K.C.,GOVERNMENT BY COMMITTEE; AN ESSAY ON THE BRITISH CONSTITUTION. UK NAT/G LEGIS INSPECT CONFER ADJUD ADMIN CONTROL TASK EFFICIENCY ROLE POPULISM 20. PAGE 167 H3337
DELIB/GP CONSTN LEAD GP/COMP

L55
ROSTOW W.W.,"RUSSIA AND CHINA UNDER COMMUNISM." CHINA/COM USSR INTELL STRUCT INT/ORG NAT/G POL/PAR TOP/EX ACT/RES PLAN ADMIN ATTIT ALL/VALS MARXISM ...CONCPT OBS TIME/SEQ TREND GOV/COMP VAL/FREE 20. PAGE 134 H2689
COM ASIA

C55
GRASSMUCK G.L.,"A MANUAL OF LEBANESE ADMINISTRATION." LEBANON PLAN...CHARTS BIBLIOG/A 20. PAGE 60 H1198
ADMIN NAT/G ISLAM EX/STRUC

B56
CENTRAL AFRICAN ARCHIVES,A GUIDE TO THE PUBLIC RECORDS OF SOUTHERN RHODESIA UNDER THE REGIME OF THE BRITISH SOUTH AFRICA COMPANY, 1890-1923. UK STRUCT NAT/G WRITING GP/REL 19/20. PAGE 28 H0566
BIBLIOG/A COLONIAL ADMIN AFR

B56
INTERNATIONAL AFRICAN INST,SELECT ANNOTATED BIBLIOGRAPHY OF TROPICAL AFRICA. NAT/G EDU/PROP ADMIN HEALTH. PAGE 77 H1547
BIBLIOG/A AFR SOC HABITAT

B56
IRIKURA J.K.,SOUTHEAST ASIA: SELECTED ANNOTATED BIBLIOGRAPHY OF JAPANESE PUBLICATIONS. CULTURE ADMIN RACE/REL 20 CHINJAP. PAGE 78 H1567
BIBLIOG/A S/ASIA DIPLOM

B56
JENNINGS W.I.,THE APPROACH TO SELF-GOVERNMENT. CEYLON INDIA PAKISTAN S/ASIA UK SOCIETY POL/PAR DELIB/GP LEGIS ECO/TAC EDU/PROP ADMIN EXEC CHOOSE ATTIT ALL/VALS...JURID CONCPT GEN/METH TOT/POP 20. PAGE 81 H1610
NAT/G CONSTN COLONIAL

B56
MANNONI D.O.,PROSPERO AND CALIBAN: THE PSYCHOLOGY OF COLONIZATION. AFR EUR+WWI FAM KIN MUNIC SECT DOMIN ADMIN ATTIT DRIVE LOVE PWR RESPECT...PSY SOC CONCPT MYTH OBS DEEP/INT BIOG GEN/METH MALAGASY 20. PAGE 102 H2040
CULTURE COLONIAL

B56
VUCINICH A.,THE SOVIET ACADEMY OF SCIENCES. USSR STRUCT ACADEM NAT/G EDU/PROP ADMIN LEAD ROLE ...BIBLIOG 20 ACADEM/SCI. PAGE 164 H3280
PHIL/SCI CREATE INTELL PROF/ORG

B56
WEBER M.,STAATSSOZIOLOGIE. STRUCT LEGIT ADMIN PARL/PROC SUPEGO CONSERVE JURID. PAGE 166 H3320
SOC NAT/G POL/PAR LEAD

B56
WILSON P.,GOVERNMENT AND POLITICS OF INDIA AND PAKISTAN: 1885-1955; A BIBLIOGRAPHY OF WORKS IN WESTERN LANGUAGES. INDIA PAKISTAN CONSTN LOC/G POL/PAR FORCES DIPLOM ADMIN WAR CHOOSE...BIOG CON/ANAL 19/20. PAGE 169 H3380
BIBLIOG COLONIAL NAT/G S/ASIA

L56
EISENTADT S.N.,"POLITICAL STRUGGLE IN BUREAUCRATIC SOCIETIES" ASIA CULTURE ADJUD SANCTION PWR BUREAUCRCY OTTOMAN BYZANTINE. PAGE 45 H0901
ADMIN CHIEF CONTROL ROUTINE

S56
EPSTEIN L.D.,"COHESION OF BRITISH PARLIAMENTARY PARTIES." UK STRUCT ADMIN ROUTINE INGP/REL PWR ...GP/COMP PARLIAMENT. PAGE 47 H0935
NAT/G PARL/PROC POL/PAR

S56
KHAMA T.,"POLITICAL CHANGE IN AFRICAN SOCIETY." CONSTN SOCIETY LOC/G NAT/G POL/PAR EX/STRUC LEGIS LEGIT ADMIN CHOOSE REPRESENT NAT/LISM MORAL ORD/FREE PWR...CONCPT OBS TREND GEN/METH CMN/WLTH 17/20. PAGE 85 H1706
AFR ELITES

C56
FALL B.B.,"THE VIET-MINH REGIME." VIETNAM LAW ECO/UNDEV POL/PAR FORCES DOMIN WAR ATTIT MARXISM ...BIOG PREDICT BIBLIOG/A 20. PAGE 48 H0967
NAT/G ADMIN EX/STRUC LEAD

C56
NEUMANN S.,"MODERN POLITICAL PARTIES: APPROACHES TO COMPARATIVE POLITIC. FRANCE UK EX/STRUC DOMIN ADMIN LEAD REPRESENT TOTALISM ATTIT...POLICY TREND METH/COMP ANTHOL BIBLIOG/A 20 CMN/WLTH. PAGE 117 H2338
POL/PAR GOV/COMP ELITES MAJORIT

B57
BISHOP O.B.,PUBLICATIONS OF THE GOVERNMENTS OF NOVA SCOTIA, PRINCE EDWARD ISLAND, NEW BRUNSWICK 1758-1952. CANADA UK ADMIN COLONIAL LEAD...POLICY 18/20. PAGE 17 H0345
BIBLIOG NAT/G DIPLOM

B57
CENTRAL ASIAN RESEARCH CENTRE,BIBLIOGRAPHY OF RECENT SOVIET SOURCE MATERIAL ON SOVIET CENTRAL ASIA AND THE BORDERLANDS. AFGHANISTN INDIA PAKISTAN UAR USSR ECO/UNDEV AGRI EXTR/IND INDUS ACADEM ADMIN ...HEAL HUM LING CON/ANAL 20. PAGE 28 H0567
BIBLIOG/A COM CULTURE NAT/G

B57
DONALDSON A.G.,SOME COMPARATIVE ASPECTS OF IRISH LAW. IRELAND NAT/G DIPLOM ADMIN CT/SYS LEAD ATTIT SOVEREIGN...JURID BIBLIOG/A 12/20 CMN/WLTH. PAGE 42 H0835
CONSTN LAW NAT/COMP INT/LAW

B57
IKE N.,JAPANESE POLITICS. INTELL STRUCT AGRI INDUS FAM KIN LABOR PRESS CHOOSE ATTIT...DECISION BIBLIOG 19/20 CHINJAP. PAGE 76 H1523
NAT/G ADMIN POL/PAR CULTURE

B57
SCARROW H.A.,THE HIGHER PUBLIC SERVICE OF THE COMMONWEALTH OF AUSTRALIA. LAW SENIOR LOBBY ROLE 20 AUSTRAL CIVIL/SERV COMMONWLTH. PAGE 138 H2766
ADMIN NAT/G EX/STRUC GOV/COMP

B57
SOUTH PACIFIC COMMISSION,INDEX OF SOCIAL SCIENCE RESEARCH THESES ON THE SOUTH PACIFIC. S/ASIA ACADEM ADMIN COLONIAL...SOC 20. PAGE 147 H2939
BIBLIOG/A ACT/RES SECT CULTURE

L57
BENDIX R.,"POLITICAL SOCIOLOGY." CULTURE INTELL LABOR POL/PAR SECT LEGIS EDU/PROP ADMIN CHOOSE CIVMIL/REL ATTIT...IDEA/COMP 20. PAGE 14 H0274
BIBLIOG/A ACT/RES SOC

S57
HAILEY,"TOMORROW IN AFRICA." CONSTN SOCIETY LOC/G NAT/G DOMIN ADJUD ADMIN GP/REL DISCRIM NAT/LISM ATTIT MORAL ORD/FREE...PSY SOC CONCPT OBS RECORD TREND GEN/LAWS CMN/WLTH 20. PAGE 64 H1277
AFR PERSON ELITES RACE/REL

S57
HODGETTS J.E.,"THE CIVIL SERVICE AND POLICY FORMATION." CANADA NAT/G EX/STRUC ROUTINE GOV/REL 20. PAGE 72 H1443
ADMIN DECISION EFFICIENCY POLICY

B58
LIST OF PUBLICATIONS (PERIODICAL OR AD HOC) ISSUED BY VARIOUS MINISTRIES OF THE GOVERNMENT OF INDIA (3RD ED.). INDIA ECO/UNDEV PLAN...POLICY MGT 20. PAGE 2 H0037
BIBLIOG NAT/G ADMIN

B58
CARTER G.M.,TRANSITION IN AFRICA; STUDIES IN POLITICAL ADAPTATION. AFR CENTRL/AFR GHANA NIGERIA CONSTN LOC/G POL/PAR ADMIN GP/REL FEDERAL...MAJORIT BIBLIOG 20. PAGE 27 H0543
NAT/COMP PWR CONTROL NAT/G

B58
COLEMAN J.S.,NIGERIA: BACKGROUND TO NATIONALISM. AFR SOCIETY ECO/DEV KIN LOC/G POL/PAR TEC/DEV DOMIN ADMIN DRIVE PWR RESPECT...TRADIT SOC INT SAMP TIME/SEQ 20. PAGE 31 H0627
NAT/G NAT/LISM NIGERIA

B58
COWAN L.G.,LOCAL GOVERNMENT IN WEST AFRICA. AFR FRANCE UK CULTURE KIN POL/PAR CHIEF LEGIS CREATE ADMIN PARTIC GOV/REL GP/REL...METH/COMP 20. PAGE 34 H0682
LOC/G COLONIAL SOVEREIGN REPRESENT

B58
DWARKADAS R.,ROLE OF HIGHER CIVIL SERVICE IN INDIA. INDIA ECO/UNDEV LEGIS PROB/SOLV GP/REL PERS/REL ...POLICY WELF/ST DECISION ORG/CHARTS BIBLIOG 20 CIVIL/SERV INTRVN/ECO. PAGE 44 H0876
ADMIN NAT/G ROLE PLAN

B58
KINTNER W.R.,ORGANIZING FOR CONFLICT: A PROPOSAL. USSR STRUCT NAT/G LEGIS ADMIN EXEC PEACE ORD/FREE PWR...CONCPT OBS TREND NAT/COMP VAL/FREE COLD/WAR 20. PAGE 86 H1719
USA+45 PLAN DIPLOM

B58
MASON J.B.,THAILAND BIBLIOGRAPHY. S/ASIA THAILAND CULTURE EDU/PROP ADMIN...GEOG SOC LING 20. PAGE 104 H2087
BIBLIOG/A ECO/UNDEV DIPLOM NAT/G

B58
OGDEN F.D.,THE POLL TAX IN THE SOUTH. USA+45 USA-45 CONSTN ADJUD ADMIN PARTIC CRIME...TIME/SEQ GOV/COMP METH/COMP 18/20 SOUTH/US. PAGE 120 H2407
TAX CHOOSE RACE/REL DISCRIM

B58
PAN AMERICAN UNION,REPERTORIO DE PUBLICACIONES PERIODICAS ACTUALES LATINO-AMERICANAS. CULTURE ECO/UNDEV ADMIN LEAD GOV/REL 20 OAS. PAGE 123 H2455
BIBLIOG L/A+17C NAT/G DIPLOM

B58
SCOTT D.J.R.,RUSSIAN POLITICAL INSTITUTIONS. RUSSIA USSR CONSTN AGRI DELIB/GP PLAN EDU/PROP CONTROL CHOOSE EFFICIENCY ATTIT MARXISM...BIBLIOG/A 13/20. PAGE 141 H2813
NAT/G POL/PAR ADMIN DECISION

B58
SHARMA M.P.,PUBLIC ADMINISTRATION IN THEORY AND PRACTICE. INDIA UK USA+45 USA-45 EX/STRUC ADJUD ...POLICY CONCPT NAT/COMP 20. PAGE 142 H2847
MGT ADMIN DELIB/GP JURID

B58
SHAW S.J.,THE FINANCIAL AND ADMINISTRATIVE ORGANIZATION AND DEVELOPMENT OF OTTOMAN EGYPT 1517-1798. UAR LOC/G FORCES BUDGET INT/TRADE TAX EATING INCOME WEALTH...CHARTS BIBLIOG 16/18 OTTOMAN NAPOLEON/B. PAGE 143 H2853
FINAN ADMIN GOV/REL CULTURE

S58
MAIR L.P.,"REPRESENTATIVE LOCAL GOVERNMENT AS A PROBLEM IN SOCIAL CHANGE." ECO/UNDEV KIN LOC/G NAT/G SCHOOL JUDGE ADMIN ROUTINE REPRESENT RIGID/FLEX RESPECT...CONCPT STERTYP CMN/WLTH 20. PAGE 101 H2025
AFR PWR ELITES

S58
PYE L.W.,"THE NON-WESTERN POLITICAL PROCESS" (BMR)" AFR ASIA ISLAM S/ASIA DIPLOM ADMIN LEAD LOBBY ROUTINE CONSEN...DECISION 20. PAGE 128 H2567
CULTURE POL/PAR NAT/G LOC/G

S58
STAAR R.F.,"ELECTIONS IN COMMUNIST POLAND." EUR+WWI SOCIETY INT/ORG NAT/G POL/PAR LEGIS ACT/RES ECO/TAC EDU/PROP ADJUD ADMIN ROUTINE COERCE TOTALISM ATTIT ORD/FREE PWR 20. PAGE 148 H2963
COM CHOOSE POLAND

C58
GOLAY J.F.,"THE FOUNDING OF THE FEDERAL REPUBLIC OF GERMANY." GERMANY/W CONSTN EX/STRUC DIPLOM ADMIN CHOOSE...DECISION BIBLIOG 20. PAGE 58 H1155
FEDERAL NAT/G PARL/PROC POL/PAR

C58
WILDING N.,"AN ENCYCLOPEDIA OF PARLIAMENT." UK LAW CONSTN CHIEF PROB/SOLV DIPLOM DEBATE WAR INGP/REL PRIVIL...BIBLIOG DICTIONARY 13/20 CMN/WLTH PARLIAMENT. PAGE 168 H3363
PARL/PROC POL/PAR NAT/G ADMIN

B59
CONOVER H.F.,NIGERIAN OFFICIAL PUBLICATIONS, 1869-1959: A GUIDE. NIGER CONSTN FINAN ACADEM SCHOOL FORCES PRESS ADMIN COLONIAL...HIST/WRIT 19/20. PAGE 33 H0650
BIBLIOG NAT/G CON/ANAL

B59
EPSTEIN F.T.,EAST GERMANY: A SELECTED BIBLIOGRAPHY (PAMPHLET). COM GERMANY/E LAW AGRI FINAN INDUS LABOR POL/PAR EDU/PROP ADMIN AGE/Y 20. PAGE 47 H0932
BIBLIOG/A INTELL MARXISM NAT/G

B59
GINSBURG M.,LAW AND OPINION IN ENGLAND. UK CULTURE KIN LABOR LEGIS EDU/PROP ADMIN CT/SYS CRIME OWN HEALTH...ANTHOL 20 ENGLSH/LAW. PAGE 56 H1132
JURID POLICY ECO/TAC

B59
HANSON A.H.,THE STRUCTURE AND CONTROL OF STATE ENTERPRISES IN TURKEY. TURKEY LAW ADMIN GOV/REL EFFICIENCY...CHARTS 20. PAGE 66 H1319
NAT/G LG/CO OWN CONTROL

B59
INTERAMERICAN CULTURAL COUN,LISTA DE LIBROS REPRESENTAVOS DE AMERICA. CULTURE DIPLOM ADMIN 20. PAGE 77 H1542
BIBLIOG/A NAT/G L/A+17C SOC

B59
JENNINGS W.I.,CABINET GOVERNMENT (3RD ED.). UK POL/PAR CHIEF BUDGET ADMIN CHOOSE GP/REL 20. PAGE 81 H1612
DELIB/GP NAT/G CONSTN OP/RES

B59
LEMBERG E.,DIE VERTRIEBENEN IN WESTDEUTSCHLAND (3 VOLS.). GERMANY/W CULTURE STRUCT AGRI PROVS ADMIN ...JURID 20 MIGRATION. PAGE 94 H1875
GP/REL INGP/REL SOCIETY

B59
PARK R.L.,LEADERSHIP AND POLITICAL INSTITUTIONS IN INDIA. S/ASIA CULTURE ECO/UNDEV LOC/G MUNIC PROVS LEGIS PLAN ADMIN LEAD ORD/FREE WEALTH...GEOG SOC BIOG TOT/POP VAL/FREE 20. PAGE 123 H2468
NAT/G EXEC INDIA

B59
PAULSEN M.G.,LEGAL INSTITUTIONS TODAY AND TOMORROW. UK USA+45 NAT/G PROF/ORG PROVS ADMIN PARL/PROC ORD/FREE NAT/COMP. PAGE 124 H2477
JURID ADJUD JUDGE LEGIS

B59
ROSOLIO D.,TEN YEARS OF THE CIVIL SERVICE IN ISRAEL (1948-1958) (PAMPHLET). ISRAEL NAT/G RECEIVE 20. PAGE 134 H2685
ADMIN WORKER GOV/REL PAY

B59
SISSON C.H.,THE SPIRIT OF BRITISH ADMINISTRATION AND SOME EUROPEAN COMPARISONS. FRANCE GERMANY/W SWEDEN UK LAW EX/STRUC INGP/REL EFFICIENCY ORD/FREE ...DECISION 20. PAGE 144 H2890
GOV/COMP ADMIN ELITES ATTIT

B59
SITHOLE N.,AFRICAN NATIONALISM. UNIV CULTURE SECT ADMIN COLONIAL CHOOSE. PAGE 145 H2892
RACE/REL AFR NAT/LISM PERSON

S59
CHAPMAN B.,"THE FRENCH CONSEIL D'ETAT." FRANCE NAT/G CONSULT OP/RES PROB/SOLV PWR...OBS 20. PAGE 29 H0580
ADMIN LAW CT/SYS LEGIS

S59
DUNCAN O.D.,"CULTURAL, BEHAVIORAL, AND ECOLOGICAL PERSPECTIVES IN THE STUDY OF SOCIAL ORGANIZATION" (BMR)" UNIV STRATA EX/STRUC PROB/SOLV ADMIN ATTIT SOC/INTEG 20 BUREAUCRCY. PAGE 43 H0862
CULTURE METH/COMP SOCIETY HABITAT

S59
GABLE R.W.,"CULTURE AND ADMINISTRATION IN IRAN." IRAN EXEC PARTIC REPRESENT PWR. PAGE 54 H1085
ADMIN CULTURE EX/STRUC INGP/REL

S59
PRESTHUS R.V.,"BEHAVIOR AND BUREAUCRACY IN MANY CULTURES." EXEC INGP/REL 20. PAGE 128 H2558
ADMIN EX/STRUC GOV/COMP METH/CNCPT

C59
COLLINS I.,"THE GOVERNMENT AND THE NEWSPAPER PRESS IN FRANCE, 1814-1881. FRANCE LAW ADMIN CT/SYS ...CON/ANAL BIBLIOG 19. PAGE 32 H0634
PRESS ORD/FREE NAT/G EDU/PROP

B60
JUNZ A.J.,PRESENT TRENDS IN AMERICAN NATIONAL GOVERNMENT. LEGIS DIPLOM ADMIN CT/SYS ORD/FREE ...CONCPT ANTHOL 20 CONGRESS PRESIDENT SUPREME/CT. PAGE 3 H0052
POL/PAR CHOOSE CONSTN NAT/G

B60
ALBI F.,TRATADO DE LOS MODOS DE GESTION DE LAS CORPORACIONES LOCALES. SPAIN FINAN NAT/G BUDGET CONTROL EXEC ROUTINE GOV/REL ORD/FREE SOVEREIGN ...MGT 20. PAGE 5 H0092
LOC/G LAW ADMIN MUNIC

B60
ALMOND G.A.,THE POLITICS OF THE DEVELOPING AREAS. AFR ISLAM L/A+17C S/ASIA SOCIETY ECO/UNDEV NAT/G ADMIN PERCEPT KNOWL SOVEREIGN...CONCPT GEN/LAWS 20. PAGE 6 H0112
EX/STRUC ATTIT NAT/LISM

B60
BHAMBHRI C.P.,PARLIAMENTARY CONTROL OVER STATE ENTERPRISE IN INDIA. INDIA DELIB/GP ADMIN CONTROL INGP/REL EFFICIENCY 20 PARLIAMENT. PAGE 16 H0327
NAT/G OWN INDUS PARL/PROC

B60
BRZEZINSKI Z.K.,THE SOVIET BLOC-UNITY AND CONFLICT. COM USSR CONSTN DOMIN ADMIN TOTALISM PWR...SOC MYTH RECORD TREND STERTYP GEN/LAWS GEN/METH TOT/POP 20. PAGE 23 H0458
ATTIT EDU/PROP

B60
EASTON S.C.,THE TWILIGHT OF EUROPEAN COLONIALISM. AFR S/ASIA CONSTN SOCIETY STRUCT ECO/UNDEV INDUS NAT/G FORCES ECO/TAC COLONIAL CT/SYS ATTIT KNOWL ORD/FREE PWR...SOCIALIST TIME/SEQ TREND CON/ANAL 20. PAGE 44 H0882
FINAN ADMIN

B60
FLORES R.H.,CATALOGO DE TESIS DOCTORALES DE LAS FACULTADES DE LA UNIVERSIDAD DE EL SALVADOR. EL/SALVADR LAW DIPLOM ADMIN LEAD GOV/REL...SOC 19/20. PAGE 52 H1030
BIBLIOG ACADEM L/A+17C NAT/G

B60
FURNISS E.S.,FRANCE, TROUBLED ALLY. EUR+WWI FUT CULTURE SOCIETY BAL/PWR ADMIN ATTIT DRIVE PWR ...TREND TOT/POP 20 DEGAULLE/C. PAGE 54 H1079
NAT/G FRANCE

B60
HARRISON S.S.,INDIA: THE MOST DANGEROUS DECADES. INDIA CONSTN STRATA POL/PAR SECT PLAN ADMIN CHOOSE GP/REL TOTALISM MARXISM...LING 20 NEHRU/J. PAGE 67 H1347
CULTURE ECO/UNDEV PROB/SOLV REGION

B60
HAUSER O.,PREUSSISCHE STAATSRASON UND NATIONALER GEDANKE. PRUSSIA SOCIETY PRESS ADMIN...CONCPT 19/20. PAGE 68 H1358
NAT/LISM NAT/G ATTIT PROVS

B60
HAYEK F.A.,THE CONSTITUTION OF LIBERTY. UNIV LAW CONSTN WORKER TAX EDU/PROP ADMIN CT/SYS COERCE DISCRIM...IDEA/COMP 20. PAGE 68 H1369
ORD/FREE CHOOSE NAT/G CONCPT

B60
KERR C.,INDUSTRIALISM AND INDUSTRIAL MAN. CULTURE SOCIETY ECO/UNDEV NAT/G ADMIN PRODUC WEALTH ...PREDICT TREND NAT/COMP 19/20. PAGE 85 H1697
WORKER MGT ECO/DEV INDUS

B60
LEYDER J.,BIBLIOGRAPHIE DE L'ENSEIGNEMENT SUPERIEUR ET DE LA RECHERCHE SCIENTIFIQUE EN AFRIQUE INTERTROPICALE (2 VOLS.). AFR CULTURE ECO/UNDEV AGRI PLAN EDU/PROP ADMIN COLONIAL...GEOG SOC/INTEG 20 NEGRO. PAGE 96 H1918
BIBLIOG/A ACT/RES ACADEM R+D

B60
MEYRIAT J.,LA SCIENCE POLITIQUE EN FRANCE, 1945-1958; BIBLIOGRAPHIES FRANCAISES DE SCIENCES SOCIALES (VOL. I). EUR+WWI FRANCE POL/PAR DIPLOM ADMIN CHOOSE ATTIT...IDEA/COMP METH/COMP NAT/COMP 20. PAGE 110 H2193
BIBLIOG/A NAT/G CONCPT PHIL/SCI

B60
PIERCE R.A.,RUSSIAN CENTRAL ASIA, 1867-1917. ASIA RUSSIA CULTURE AGRI INDUS EDU/PROP REV NAT/LISM ...CHARTS BIBLIOG 19/20 BOLSHEVISM INTERVENT. PAGE 125 H2509
COLONIAL DOMIN ADMIN ECO/UNDEV

B60
PINTO F.B.M.,ENRIQUECIMENTO ILICITO NO EXERCICIO DE CARGOS PUBLICOS. BRAZIL L/A+17C USA+45 ELITES TRIBUTE CONTROL INGP/REL ORD/FREE PWR...NAT/COMP 20. PAGE 126 H2513
ADMIN NAT/G CRIME LAW

B60
ROBINSON E.A.G.,ECONOMIC CONSEQUENCES OF THE SIZE OF NATIONS. AGRI INDUS DELIB/GP FOR/AID ADMIN EFFICIENCY...METH/COMP 20. PAGE 132 H2649 CONCPT INT/ORG NAT/COMP

B60
ROY N.C.,THE CIVIL SERVICE IN INDIA. INDIA POL/PAR ECO/TAC INCOME...JURID MGT 20 CIVIL/SERV. PAGE 135 H2705 ADMIN NAT/G DELIB/GP CONFER

B60
SCANLON D.G.,INTERNATIONAL EDUCATION: A DOCUMENTARY HISTORY. ADMIN CONTROL ATTIT PERCEPT...BIOG ANTHOL METH 20. PAGE 138 H2765 EDU/PROP INT/ORG NAT/COMP DIPLOM

B60
SMITH M.G.,GOVERNMENT IN ZAZZAU 1800-1950. NIGERIA UK CULTURE SOCIETY LOC/G ADMIN COLONIAL ...METH/CNCPT NEW/IDEA METH 19/20. PAGE 146 H2914 REGION CONSTN KIN ECO/UNDEV

B60
SOUTH AFRICAN CONGRESS OF DEM,FACE THE FUTURE. SOUTH/AFR ELITES LEGIS ADMIN REGION COERCE PEACE ATTIT 20. PAGE 147 H2938 RACE/REL DISCRIM CONSTN NAT/G

B60
US LIBRARY OF CONGRESS,INDEX TO LATIN AMERICAN LEGISLATION: 1950-1960 (2 VOLS.). NAT/G DELIB/GP ADMIN PARL/PROC 20. PAGE 161 H3211 BIBLIOG/A LEGIS L/A+17C JURID

B60
WORLEY P.,ASIA TODAY (REV. ED.) (PAMPHLET). COM ECO/UNDEV AGRI FINAN INDUS POL/PAR FOR/AID ADMIN MARXISM 20. PAGE 170 H3411 BIBLIOG/A ASIA DIPLOM NAT/G

S60
"THE EMERGING COMMON MARKETS IN LATIN AMERICA." FUT L/A+17C STRATA DIST/IND INDUS LABOR NAT/G LEGIS ECO/TAC ADMIN RIGID/FLEX HEALTH...NEW/IDEA TIME/SEQ OAS 20. PAGE 2 H0038 FINAN ECO/UNDEV INT/TRADE

S60
APTER D.E.,"THE ROLE OF TRADITIONALISM IN THE POLITICAL MODERNIZATION OF GHANA AND UGANDA" (BMR)" AFR GHANA UGANDA CULTURE NAT/G POL/PAR NAT/LISM ...CON/ANAL 20. PAGE 8 H0152 CONSERVE ADMIN GOV/COMP PROB/SOLV

S60
BANFIELD E.C.,"THE POLITICAL IMPLICATIONS OF METROPOLITAN GROWTH" (BMR)" UK USA+45 LOC/G PROB/SOLV ADMIN GP/REL...METH/COMP NAT/COMP 20. PAGE 10 H0209 TASK MUNIC GOV/COMP CENSUS

S60
BRZEZINSKI Z.K.,"PATTERNS AND LIMITS OF THE SINO-SOVIET DISPUTE." ASIA CHINA/COM COM FUT STRATA NAT/G EX/STRUC FORCES BAL/PWR DIPLOM ECO/TAC DOMIN EDU/PROP ADMIN COERCE WAR ATTIT RIGID/FLEX ...GEN/LAWS VAL/FREE 20. PAGE 23 H0459 POL/PAR PWR REV USSR

S60
EMERSON R.,"THE EROSION OF DEMOCRACY." AFR FUT LAW CULTURE INTELL SOCIETY ECO/UNDEV FAM LOC/G NAT/G FORCES PLAN TEC/DEV ECO/TAC ADMIN CT/SYS ATTIT ORD/FREE PWR...SOCIALIST SOC CONCPT STAND/INT TIME/SEQ WORK 20. PAGE 46 H0918 S/ASIA POL/PAR

S60
FRANKEL S.H.,"ECONOMIC ASPECTS OF POLITICAL INDEPENDENCE IN AFRICA." AFR FUT SOCIETY ECO/UNDEV COM/IND FINAN LEGIS PLAN TEC/DEV CAP/ISM ECO/TAC INT/TRADE ADMIN ATTIT DRIVE RIGID/FLEX PWR WEALTH ...MGT NEW/IDEA MATH TIME/SEQ VAL/FREE 20. PAGE 53 H1052 NAT/G FOR/AID

S60
GINSBURGS G.,"PEKING-LHASA-NEW DELHI." CHINA/COM FUT INDIA S/ASIA KIN NAT/G PROVS SECT FORCES BAL/PWR ECO/TAC DOMIN EDU/PROP LEGIT ADMIN REGION GUERRILLA PWR...TREND TIBET 20. PAGE 57 H1134 ASIA COERCE DIPLOM

S60
GROSSMAN G.,"SOVIET GROWTH: ROUTINE, INERTIA, AND PRESSURE." COM STRATA NAT/G DELIB/GP PLAN TEC/DEV ECO/TAC EDU/PROP ADMIN ROUTINE DRIVE WEALTH COLD/WAR 20. PAGE 62 H1236 POL/PAR ECO/DEV USSR

S60
NORTH R.C.,"DIE DISKREPANZ ZWISCHEN REALITAT UND WUNSCHBILD ALS INNENPOLITISCHER FAKTOR." ASIA CHINA/COM COM FUT ECO/UNDEV NAT/G PLAN DOMIN ADMIN COERCE PERCEPT...SOC MYTH GEN/METH WORK TOT/POP 20. PAGE 119 H2373 SOCIETY ECO/TAC

S60
TAYLOR M.G.,"THE ROLE OF THE MEDICAL PROFESSION IN THE FORMULATION AND EXECUTION OF PUBLIC POLICY" (BMR)" CANADA NAT/G CONSULT ADMIN REPRESENT GP/REL ROLE SOVEREIGN...DECISION 20 CMA. PAGE 153 H3056 PROF/ORG HEALTH LOBBY POLICY

C60
FITZSIMMONS T.,"USSR: ITS PEOPLE, ITS SOCIETY, ITS CULTURE." USSR FAM SECT DIPLOM EDU/PROP ADMIN RACE/REL ATTIT...POLICY CHARTS BIBLIOG 20. PAGE 51 H1021 CULTURE STRUCT SOCIETY COM

C60
HAZARD J.N.,"THE SOVIET SYSTEM OF GOVERNMENT." USSR SOCIETY INDUS NAT/G POL/PAR DIPLOM CT/SYS...JURID CHARTS BIBLIOG/A 20. PAGE 69 H1373 COM NAT/COMP STRUCT ADMIN

C60
SMITH T.E.,"ELECTIONS IN DEVELOPING COUNTRIES: A STUDY OF ELECTORAL PROCEDURES USED IN TOPICAL AFRICA, SOUTH-EAST ASIA..." AFR S/ASIA UK ROUTINE GOV/REL RACE/REL...GOV/COMP BIBLIOG 20. PAGE 146 H2918 ECO/UNDEV CHOOSE REPRESENT ADMIN

N60
RHODESIA-NYASA NATL ARCHIVES,A SELECT BIBLIOGRAPHY OF RECENT PUBLICATIONS CONCERNING THE FEDERATION OF RHODESIA AND NYASALAND (PAMPHLET). MALAWI RHODESIA LAW CULTURE STRUCT ECO/UNDEV LEGIS...GEOG 20. PAGE 131 H2620 BIBLIOG ADMIN ORD/FREE NAT/G

B61
AYLMER G.,THE KING'S SERVANTS. UK ELITES CHIEF PAY CT/SYS WEALTH 17 CROMWELL/O CHARLES/I. PAGE 9 H0187 ADMIN ROUTINE EX/STRUC NAT/G

B61
BISHOP D.G.,THE ADMINISTRATION OF BRITISH FOREIGN RELATIONS. EUR+WWI MOD/EUR INT/ORG NAT/G POL/PAR DELIB/GP LEGIS TOP/EX ECO/TAC DOMIN EDU/PROP ADMIN COERCE 20. PAGE 17 H0344 ROUTINE PWR DIPLOM UK

B61
BURDEAU G.,O PODER EXECUTIVO NA FRANCA. EUR+WWI FRANCE CONSTN DELIB/GP LEGIT ADMIN ATTIT ALL/VALS CONCPT. PAGE 24 H0478 TOP/EX POL/PAR NAT/G LEGIS

B61
BURDETTE F.L.,POLITICAL SCIENCE: A SELECTED BIBLIOGRAPHY OF BOOKS IN PRINT, WITH ANNOTATIONS (PAMPHLET). LAW LOC/G NAT/G POL/PAR PROVS DIPLOM EDU/PROP ADMIN CHOOSE ATTIT 20. PAGE 24 H0479 BIBLIOG/A GOV/COMP CONCPT ROUTINE

B61
CARNELL F.,THE POLITICS OF THE NEW STATES: A SELECT ANNOTATED BIBLIOGRAPHY WITH SPECIAL REFERENCE TO THE COMMONWEALTH. CONSTN ELITES LABOR NAT/G POL/PAR EX/STRUC DIPLOM ADJUD ADMIN...GOV/COMP 20 COMMONWLTH. PAGE 27 H0534 BIBLIOG/A AFR ASIA COLONIAL

B61
CARROTHERS A.W.R.,LABOR ARBITRATION IN CANADA. CANADA LAW NAT/G CONSULT LEGIS WORKER ADJUD ADMIN CT/SYS 20. PAGE 27 H0542 LABOR MGT GP/REL BARGAIN

B61
CATHERINE R.,LE FONCTIONNAIRE FRANCAIS. FRANCE NAT/G INGP/REL ATTIT MORAL ORD/FREE...T CIVIL/SERV. PAGE 28 H0559 ADMIN GP/REL LEAD SUPEGO

B61
COHN B.S.,DEVELOPMENT AND IMPACT OF BRITISH ADMINISTRATION IN INDIA: A BIBLIOGRAPHIC ESSAY. INDIA UK ECO/UNDEV NAT/G DOMIN...POLICY MGT SOC 19/20. PAGE 31 H0619 BIBLIOG/A COLONIAL S/ASIA ADMIN

B61
ETZIONI A.,COMPLEX ORGANIZATIONS: A SOCIOLOGICAL READER. CLIENT CULTURE STRATA CREATE OP/RES ADMIN ...POLICY METH/CNCPT BUREAUCRCY. PAGE 47 H0945 VOL/ASSN STRUCT CLASSIF PROF/ORG

B61
FREYRE G.,THE PORTUGUESE AND THE TROPICS. L/A+17C PORTUGAL SOCIETY PERF/ART ADMIN TASK GP/REL ...ART/METH CONCPT SOC/INTEG 20. PAGE 53 H1060 COLONIAL METH PLAN CULTURE

B61
GARCIA E.,LA ADMINISTRACION ESPANOLA. SPAIN GOV/REL ...CONCPT METH/COMP 20. PAGE 55 H1099 ADMIN NAT/G LOC/G DECISION

B61
HICKS U.K.,DEVELOPMENT FROM BELOW. UK INDUS ADMIN COLONIAL ROUTINE GOV/REL...POLICY METH/CNCPT CHARTS 19/20 CMN/WLTH. PAGE 71 H1414 ECO/UNDEV LOC/G GOV/COMP METH/COMP

B61
LAHAYE R.,LES ENTREPRISES PUBLIQUES AU MAROC. FRANCE MOROCCO LAW DIST/IND EXTR/IND FINAN CONSULT PLAN TEC/DEV ADMIN AGREE CONTROL OWN...POLICY 20. PAGE 90 H1796 NAT/G INDUS ECO/UNDEV ECO/TAC

B61
LENIN V.I.,WHAT IS TO BE DONE? (1902). RUSSIA LABOR NAT/G POL/PAR WORKER CAP/ISM ECO/TAC ADMIN PARTIC ...MARXIST IDEA/COMP GEN/LAWS 19/20. PAGE 94 H1881 EDU/PROP PRESS MARXISM METH/COMP

B61
MARX K.,THE COMMUNIST MANIFESTO. IN (MENDEL A. ESSENTIAL WORKS OF MARXISM, NEW YORK: BANTAM. FUT MOD/EUR CULTURE ECO/DEV ECO/UNDEV AGRI FINAN INDUS MARKET PROC/MFG LABOR MUNIC POL/PAR CONSULT FORCES CREATE PLAN ADMIN ATTIT DRIVE RIGID/FLEX ORD/FREE PWR RESPECT MARX/KARL WORK. PAGE 104 H2081 COM NEW/IDEA CAP/ISM REV

B61
MAYNE A.,DESIGNING AND ADMINISTERING A REGIONAL ECONOMIC DEVELOPMENT PLAN WITH SPECIFIC REFERENCE ECO/UNDEV PLAN

TO PUERTO RICO (PAMPHLET). PUERT/RICO SOCIETY NAT/G DELIB/GP REGION...DECISION 20. PAGE 105 H2106 CREATE ADMIN

B61
MIT CENTER INTERNATIONAL STU,OFFICIAL SERIAL PUBLICATIONS RELATING TO ECONOMIC DEVELOPMENT IN AFRICA SOUTH OF THE SAHARA. AFR SOCIETY AGRI FINAN INDUS LG/CO ADMIN 20. PAGE 111 H2228 BIBLIOG ECO/UNDEV ECO/TAC NAT/G

B61
MONAS S.,THE THIRD SECTION: POLICE AND SOCIETY IN RUSSIA UNDER NICHOLAS I. MOD/EUR RUSSIA ELITES STRUCT NAT/G EX/STRUC ADMIN CONTROL PWR CONSERVE ...DECISION 19 NICHOLAS/I. PAGE 112 H2238 ORD/FREE COM FORCES COERCE

B61
NARASIMHAN V.K.,THE PRESS, THE PUBLIC AND THE ADMINISTRATION (PAMPHLET). INDIA COM/IND CONTROL REPRESENT GOV/REL EFFICIENCY...ANTHOL 20. PAGE 116 H2312 NAT/G ADMIN PRESS NEW/LIB

B61
NOVE A.,THE SOVIET ECONOMY. USSR ECO/DEV FINAN NAT/G ECO/TAC PRICE ADMIN EFFICIENCY MARXISM ...TREND BIBLIOG 20. PAGE 119 H2378 PLAN PRODUC POLICY

B61
ROSE D.L.,THE VIETNAMESE CIVIL SERVICE. VIETNAM CONSULT DELIB/GP GIVE PAY EDU/PROP COLONIAL GOV/REL UTIL...CHARTS 20. PAGE 134 H2672 ADMIN EFFICIENCY STAT NAT/G

B61
SCHNAPPER B.,LA POLITIQUE ET LE COMMERCE FRANCAIS DANS LE GOLFE DE GUINEE DE 1838 A 1871. FRANCE GUINEA UK SEA EXTR/IND NAT/G DELIB/GP LEGIS ADMIN ORD/FREE...POLICY GEOG CENSUS CHARTS BIBLIOG 19. PAGE 139 H2791 COLONIAL INT/TRADE DOMIN AFR

B61
SHARMA T.R.,THE WORKING OF STATE ENTERPRISES IN INDIA. INDIA DELIB/GP LEGIS WORKER BUDGET PRICE CONTROL GP/REL OWN ATTIT...MGT CHARTS 20. PAGE 142 H2851 NAT/G INDUS ADMIN SOCISM

B61
STANLEY C.J.,LATE CH'ING FINANCE: HU KUANG-YUNG AS AN INNOVATOR. ASIA NAT/G FORCES BUDGET TAX WAR GOV/REL COST...POLICY BIOG CHARTS BIBLIOG 19. PAGE 148 H2969 FINAN ECO/TAC CIVMIL/REL ADMIN

B61
WARD R.E.,JAPANESE POLITICAL SCIENCE: A GUIDE TO JAPANESE REFERENCE AND RESEARCH MATERIALS (2ND ED.). LAW CONSTN STRATA NAT/G POL/PAR DELIB/GP LEGIS ADMIN CHOOSE GP/REL...INT/LAW 19/20 CHINJAP. PAGE 165 H3306 BIBLIOG/A PHIL/SCI

B61
WEST F.J.,POLITICAL ADVANCEMENT IN THE SOUTH PACIFIC. CONSTN CULTURE POL/PAR LEGIS DOMIN ADMIN CHOOSE SOVEREIGN VAL/FREE 20 FIJI TAHITI SAMOA. PAGE 167 H3335 S/ASIA LOC/G COLONIAL

B61
WILLSON F.M.G.,ADMINISTRATORS IN ACTION. UK MARKET TEC/DEV PARL/PROC 20. PAGE 169 H3376 ADMIN NAT/G CONSTN

S61
EHRMANN H.W.,"FRENCH BUREAUCRACY AND ORGANIZED INTERESTS" (BMR)" FRANCE NAT/G DELIB/GP ROUTINE ...INT 20 BUREAUCRCY CIVIL/SERV. PAGE 45 H0897 ADMIN DECISION PLURISM LOBBY

S61
MILLER E.,"LEGAL ASPECTS OF UN ACTION IN THE CONGO." AFR CULTURE ADMIN PEACE DRIVE RIGID/FLEX ORD/FREE...WELF/ST JURID OBS UN CONGO 20. PAGE 111 H2212 INT/ORG LEGIT

S61
NEEDLER M.C.,"THE POLITICAL DEVELOPMENT OF MEXICO." STRUCT NAT/G ADMIN RIGID/FLEX...TIME/SEQ TREND MEXIC/AMER TOT/POP VAL/FREE 19/20. PAGE 116 H2328 L/A+17C POL/PAR

C61
MOODIE G.C.,"THE GOVERNMENT OF GREAT BRITAIN." UK LAW STRUCT LOC/G POL/PAR DIPLOM RECEIVE ADMIN COLONIAL CHOOSE...BIBLIOG 20 PARLIAMENT. PAGE 112 H2247 NAT/G SOCIETY PARL/PROC GOV/COMP

B62
BINDER L.,IRAN: POLITICAL DEVELOPMENT IN A CHANGING SOCIETY. IRAN OP/RES REV GP/REL CENTRAL RATIONAL PWR...PHIL/SCI NAT/COMP GEN/LAWS 20. PAGE 17 H0337 LEGIT NAT/G ADMIN STRUCT

B62
BROWN L.C.,LATIN AMERICA, A BIBLIOGRAPHY. EX/STRUC ADMIN LEAD ATTIT...POLICY 20. PAGE 22 H0445 BIBLIOG L/A+17C DIPLOM NAT/G

B62
COSTA RICA UNIVERSIDAD BIBL,LISTA DE TESIS DE GRADO DE LA UNIVERSIDAD DE COSTA RICA. COSTA/RICA LAW LOC/G ADMIN LEAD...SOC 20. PAGE 34 H0675 BIBLIOG/A NAT/G DIPLOM ECO/UNDEV

B62
ESCUELA SUPERIOR DE ADMIN PUBL,INFORME DEL SEMINARIO SOBRE SERVICIO CIVIL O CARRERA ADMINISTRATIVA. L/A+17C ELITES STRATA CONFER CONTROL GOV/REL INGP/REL SUPEGO 20 CENTRAL/AM CIVIL/SERV. PAGE 47 H0939 ADMIN NAT/G PROB/SOLV ATTIT

B62
FRIEDMANN W.,METHODS AND POLICIES OF PRINCIPAL DONOR COUNTRIES IN PUBLIC INTERNATIONAL DEVELOPMENT FINANCING: PRELIMINARY APPRAISAL. FRANCE GERMANY/W UK USA+45 USSR WOR+45 FINAN TEC/DEV CAP/ISM DIPLOM ECO/TAC ATTIT 20 EEC. PAGE 53 H1066 INT/ORG FOR/AID NAT/COMP ADMIN

B62
GROGAN V.,ADMINISTRATIVE TRIBUNALS IN THE PUBLIC SERVICE. IRELAND UK NAT/G CONTROL CT/SYS...JURID GOV/COMP 20. PAGE 61 H1231 ADMIN LAW ADJUD DELIB/GP

B62
GROVE J.W.,GOVERNMENT AND INDUSTRY IN BRITAIN. UK FINAN LOC/G CONSULT DELIB/GP INT/TRADE ADMIN CONTROL...BIBLIOG 20. PAGE 62 H1237 ECO/TAC INDUS NAT/G GP/REL

B62
HO PING-TI,THE LADDER OF SUCCESS IN IMPERIAL CHINA: ASPECTS OF SOCIAL MOBILITY, 1368-1911. INTELL STRATA FAM KIN MUNIC NAT/G PROVS SCHOOL DELIB/GP DOMIN EDU/PROP ADMIN ROUTINE PERSON ALL/VALS...SOC STAT BIOG HIST/WRIT TIME/SEQ VAL/FREE. PAGE 71 H1431 ASIA CULTURE

B62
INAYATULLAH,BUREAUCRACY AND DEVELOPMENT IN PAKISTAN. PAKISTAN ECO/UNDEV EDU/PROP CONFER ...ANTHOL DICTIONARY 20 BUREAUCRCY. PAGE 76 H1526 EX/STRUC ADMIN NAT/G LOC/G

B62
INGHAM K.,A HISTORY OF EAST AFRICA. NAT/G DIPLOM ADMIN WAR NAT/LISM...SOC BIOG BIBLIOG. PAGE 77 H1534 AFR CONSTN COLONIAL

B62
INSTITUTE OF PUBLIC ADMIN,A SHORT HISTORY OF THE PUBLIC SERVICE IN IRELAND. IRELAND UK DIST/IND INGP/REL FEDERAL 13/20 CIVIL/SERV. PAGE 77 H1539 ADMIN WORKER GOV/REL NAT/G

B62
JAIN R.S.,THE GROWTH AND DEVELOPMENT OF GOVERNOR-GENERAL'S EXECUTIVE COUNCIL 1858-1919. INDIA UK CONSTN EX/STRUC LEGIS ADJUD ADMIN INGP/REL ATTIT 19/20. PAGE 79 H1585 NAT/G DELIB/GP CHIEF CONSULT

B62
KARNJAHAPRAKORN C.,MUNICIPAL GOVERNMENT IN THAILAND AS AN INSTITUTION AND PROCESS OF SELF-GOVERNMENT. THAILAND CULTURE FINAN EX/STRUC LEGIS PLAN CONTROL GOV/REL EFFICIENCY ATTIT...POLICY 20. PAGE 83 H1662 LOC/G MUNIC ORD/FREE ADMIN

B62
MUKERJI S.N.,ADMINISTRATION OF EDUCATION IN INDIA. ACADEM LOC/G PROVS ROUTINE...POLICY STAT CHARTS 20. PAGE 114 H2282 SCHOOL ADMIN NAT/G EDU/PROP

B62
NEW ZEALAND COMM OF ST SERVICE,THE STATE SERVICES IN NEW ZEALAND. NEW/ZEALND CONSULT EX/STRUC ACT/RES ...BIBLIOG 20. PAGE 117 H2343 ADMIN WORKER TEC/DEV NAT/G

B62
OLLE-LAPRUNE J.,LA STABILITE DES MINISTRES SOUS LA TROISIEME REPUBLIQUE, 1879-1940. FRANCE CONSTN POL/PAR LEAD WAR INGP/REL RIGID/FLEX PWR...POLICY CHARTS 19/20. PAGE 121 H2415 LEGIS NAT/G ADMIN PERSON

B62
PHILLIPS O.H.,CONSTITUTIONAL AND ADMINISTRATIVE LAW (3RD ED.). UK INT/ORG LOC/G CHIEF EX/STRUC LEGIS BAL/PWR ADJUD COLONIAL CT/SYS PWR...CHARTS 20. PAGE 125 H2503 JURID ADMIN CONSTN NAT/G

B62
SELOSOEMARDJAN O.,SOCIAL CHANGES IN JOGJAKARTA. INDONESIA NETHERLAND ELITES STRATA STRUCT FAM POL/PAR CREATE DIPLOM INT/TRADE EDU/PROP ADMIN GOV/REL...SOC 20 JAVA CHINJAP. PAGE 141 H2825 ECO/UNDEV CULTURE REV COLONIAL

B62
TAYLOR D.,THE BRITISH IN AFRICA. UK CULTURE ECO/UNDEV INDUS DIPLOM INT/TRADE ADMIN WAR RACE/REL ORD/FREE SOVEREIGN...POLICY BIBLIOG 15/20 CMN/WLTH. PAGE 153 H3053 AFR COLONIAL DOMIN

B62
THIERRY S.S.,LE VATICAN SECRET. CHRIST-17C EUR+WWI MOD/EUR VATICAN NAT/G SECT DELIB/GP DOMIN LEGIT SOVEREIGN. PAGE 154 H3072 ADMIN EX/STRUC CATHISM DECISION

B62
UNECA LIBRARY,NEW ACQUISITIONS IN THE UNECA LIBRARY. LAW NAT/G PLAN PROB/SOLV TEC/DEV ADMIN REGION...GEOG SOC 20 UN. PAGE 158 H3161 BIBLIOG AFR ECO/UNDEV INT/ORG

B62
US LIBRARY OF CONGRESS,A LIST OF AMERICAN DOCTORAL DISSERTATIONS ON AFRICA. SOCIETY SECT DIPLOM EDU/PROP ADMIN...GEOG 19/20. PAGE 161 H3212 BIBLIOG AFR ACADEM CULTURE

S62
BRAIBANTI R.,"REFLECTIONS ON BUREAUCRATIC CORRPUTION." LAW REPRESENT 20. PAGE 20 H0400 CONTROL MORAL

ADMIN
GOV/COMP
S62

PIQUEMAL M.,"LES PROBLEMES DES UNIONS D'ETATS EN AFRIQUE NOIRE." FRANCE SOCIETY INT/ORG NAT/G DELIB/GP PLAN LEGIT ADMIN COLONIAL ROUTINE ATTIT ORD/FREE PWR...GEOG METH/CNCPT 20. PAGE 126 H2515
AFR
ECO/UNDEV
REGION
S62

SPRINGER H.W.,"FEDERATION IN THE CARIBBEAN: AN ATTEMPT THAT FAILED." L/A+17C ECO/UNDEV INT/ORG POL/PAR PROVS LEGIS CREATE PLAN LEGIT ADMIN FEDERAL ATTIT DRIVE PERSON ORD/FREE PWR...POLICY GEOG PSY CONCPT OBS CARIBBEAN CMN/WLTH 20. PAGE 148 H2955
VOL/ASSN
NAT/G
REGION
C62

BACON F.,"OF EMPIRE" (1612) IN F. BACON, ESSAYS." ELITES NAT/G PROB/SOLV DIPLOM ADMIN CONTROL WEALTH 16/17 KING. PAGE 9 H0190
PWR
CHIEF
DOMIN
GEN/LAWS
B63

ADRIAN C.R.,GOVERNING OVER FIFTY STATES AND THEIR COMMUNITIES. USA+45 CONSTN FINAN MUNIC NAT/G POL/PAR EX/STRUC LEGIS ADMIN CONTROL CT/SYS ...CHARTS 20. PAGE 4 H0073
PROVS
LOC/G
GOV/REL
GOV/COMP
B63

ARAZI A.,LE SYSTEME ELECTORAL ISRAELIEN. ISRAEL NAT/G ADMIN ALL/VALS PARLIAMENT. PAGE 8 H0158
LEGIS
CHOOSE
POL/PAR
B63

BLONDEL J.,VOTERS, PARTIES, AND LEADERS. UK ELITES LOC/G NAT/G PROVS ACT/RES DOMIN REPRESENT GP/REL INGP/REL...SOC BIBLIOG 20. PAGE 18 H0358
POL/PAR
STRATA
LEGIS
ADMIN
B63

BROGAN D.W.,POLITICAL PATTERNS IN TODAY'S WORLD. FRANCE USA+45 USSR WOR+45 CONSTN STRUCT PLAN DIPLOM ADMIN LEAD ROLE SUPEGO...PHIL/SCI 20. PAGE 21 H0429
NAT/COMP
NEW/LIB
COM
TOTALISM
B63

COMISION DE HISTORIO,GUIA DE LOS DOCUMENTOS MICROFOTOGRAFIADOS POR LA UNIDAD MOVIL DE LA UNESCO. SOCIETY ECO/UNDEV INT/ORG ADMIN...SOC 20 UNESCO. PAGE 32 H0637
BIBLIOG
NAT/G
L/A+17C
DIPLOM
B63

DALAND R.T.,PERSPECTIVES OF BRAZILIAN PUBLIC ADMINISTRATION (VOL. I). BRAZIL LAW ECO/UNDEV SCHOOL CHIEF TEC/DEV CONFER CONTROL GP/REL ATTIT ROLE PWR...ANTHOL 20. PAGE 37 H0735
ADMIN
NAT/G
PLAN
GOV/REL
B63

DE VRIES E.,SOCIAL ASPECTS OF ECONOMIC DEVELOPMENT IN LATIN AMERICA. CULTURE SOCIETY STRATA FINAN INDUS INT/ORG DELIB/GP ACT/RES ECO/TAC EDU/PROP ADMIN ATTIT SUPEGO HEALTH KNOWL ORD/FREE...SOC STAT TREND ANTHOL TOT/POP VAL/FREE. PAGE 39 H0777
L/A+17C
ECO/UNDEV
B63

DEBRAY P.,LE PORTUGAL ENTRE DEUX REVOLUTIONS. EUR+WWI PORTUGAL CONSTN LEGIT ADMIN ATTIT ALL/VALS ...DECISION CONCPT 20 SALAZAR/A. PAGE 39 H0779
NAT/G
DELIB/GP
TOP/EX
B63

DUE J.F.,STATE SALES TAX ADMINISTRATION. OP/RES BUDGET PAY ADMIN EXEC ROUTINE COST EFFICIENCY PROFIT...CHARTS METH/COMP 20. PAGE 43 H0855
PROVS
TAX
STAT
GOV/COMP
B63

FRIED R.C.,THE ITALIAN PREFECTS. ITALY STRATA ECO/DEV NAT/LISM ALL/IDEOS...TREND CHARTS METH/COMP BIBLIOG 17/20 PREFECT. PAGE 53 H1061
ADMIN
NAT/G
EFFICIENCY
B63

GLUCKMAN M.,ORDER AND REBELLION IN TRIBAL AFRICA. EUR+WWI LAW CULTURE STRATA KIN MUNIC DELIB/GP ACT/RES DOMIN EDU/PROP LEGIT ADMIN COERCE CHOOSE ATTIT PERSON ORD/FREE PWR...SOC CHARTS GEN/LAWS TOT/POP VAL/FREE. PAGE 57 H1147
AFR
SOCIETY
B63

GOURNAY B.,PUBLIC ADMINISTRATION. FRANCE LAW CONSTN AGRI FINAN LABOR SCHOOL EX/STRUC CHOOSE...MGT METH/COMP 20. PAGE 59 H1189
BIBLIOG/A
ADMIN
NAT/G
LOC/G
B63

INDIAN INSTITUTE PUBLIC ADMIN,CASES IN INDIAN ADMINISTRATION. INDIA AGRI NAT/G PROB/SOLV TEC/DEV ECO/TAC ADMIN...ANTHOL METH 20. PAGE 77 H1532
DECISION
PLAN
MGT
ECO/UNDEV
B63

JACOB H.,GERMAN ADMINISTRATION SINCE BISMARCK: CENTRAL AUTHORITY VERSUS LOCAL AUTONOMY. GERMANY GERMANY/W LAW POL/PAR CONTROL CENTRAL TOTALISM FASCISM...MAJORIT DECISION STAT CHARTS GOV/COMP 19/20 BISMARCK/O HITLER/A WEIMAR/REP. PAGE 79 H1577
ADMIN
NAT/G
LOC/G
POLICY
B63

KAPP W.K.,HINDU CULTURE: ECONOMIC DEVELOPMENT AND ECONOMIC PLANNING IN INDIA. INDIA S/ASIA CULTURE ECO/TAC EDU/PROP ADMIN ALL/VALS...POLICY MGT TIME/SEQ VAL/FREE 20. PAGE 83 H1660
SECT
ECO/UNDEV
B63

KURZMAN D.,SUBVERSION OF THE INNOCENTS: PATTERNS OF COMMUNIST PENETRATION OF AFRICA, THE MIDDLE EAST AND AFRICA. AFR ASIA ISLAM S/ASIA CULTURE NAT/G FORCES PLAN EDU/PROP ADMIN ATTIT...CONCPT INT UNPLAN/INT TIME/SEQ. PAGE 89 H1785
COM
COERCE
B63

LEONARD T.J.,THE FEDERAL SYSTEM OF INDIA. INDIA MUNIC NAT/G PROVS ADMIN SOVEREIGN...IDEA/COMP 20. PAGE 94 H1885
FEDERAL
MGT
NAT/COMP
METH/COMP
B63

MAYNE R.,THE COMMUNITY OF EUROPE. UK CONSTN NAT/G CONSULT DELIB/GP CREATE PLAN ECO/TAC LEGIT ADMIN ROUTINE ORD/FREE PWR WEALTH...CONCPT TIME/SEQ EEC EURATOM 20. PAGE 105 H2107
EUR+WWI
INT/ORG
REGION
B63

MENZEL J.M.,THE CHINESE CIVIL SERVICE: CAREER OPEN TO TALENT? ASIA ROUTINE INGP/REL DISCRIM ATTIT ROLE KNOWL ANTHOL. PAGE 109 H2177
ADMIN
NAT/G
DECISION
ELITES
B63

MILLER W.J.,THE MEANING OF COMMUNISM. USSR SOCIETY ECO/DEV EX/STRUC WORKER TEC/DEV ADMIN TOTALISM ...POLICY CONCPT CHARTS BIBLIOG T 20 COLD/WAR LENIN/VI STALIN/J. PAGE 111 H2215
MARXISM
TRADIT
DIPLOM
NAT/G
B63

OLSON M. JR.,THE ECONOMICS OF WARTIME SHORTAGE. FRANCE GERMANY MOD/EUR UK AGRI PROB/SOLV ADMIN DEMAND WEALTH...POLICY OLD/LIB 17/20. PAGE 121 H2416
WAR
ADJUST
ECO/TAC
NAT/COMP
B63

RICHARDSON H.G.,THE ADMINISTRATION OF IRELAND 1172-1377. IRELAND CONSTN EX/STRUC LEGIS JUDGE CT/SYS PARL/PROC...CHARTS BIBLIOG 12/14. PAGE 131 H2621
ADMIN
NAT/G
PWR
B63

RUITENBEER H.M.,THE DILEMMA OF ORGANIZATIONAL SOCIETY. CULTURE ECO/DEV MUNIC SECT TEC/DEV EDU/PROP NAT/LISM ORD/FREE...NAT/COMP 20 RIESMAN/D WHYTE/WF MERTON/R MEAD/MARG JASPERS/K. PAGE 136 H2716
PERSON
ROLE
ADMIN
WORKER
B63

SELF P.,THE STATE AND THE FARMER. UK ECO/DEV MARKET WORKER PRICE CONTROL GP/REL...WELF/ST 20 DEPT/AGRI. PAGE 141 H2823
AGRI
NAT/G
ADMIN
VOL/ASSN
B63

SHANKS M.,THE LESSONS OF PUBLIC ENTERPRISE. UK LEGIS WORKER ECO/TAC ADMIN PARL/PROC GOV/REL ATTIT ...POLICY MGT METH/COMP NAT/COMP ANTHOL 20 PARLIAMENT. PAGE 142 H2840
SOCISM
OWN
NAT/G
INDUS
B63

SINGH H.L.,PROBLEMS AND POLICIES OF THE BRITISH IN INDIA, 1885-1898. INDIA UK NAT/G FORCES LEGIS PROB/SOLV CONTROL RACE/REL ADJUST DISCRIM NAT/LISM RIGID/FLEX...MGT 19 CIVIL/SERV. PAGE 144 H2885
COLONIAL
PWR
POLICY
ADMIN
B63

STIFEL L.D.,THE TEXTILE INDUSTRY - A CASE STUDY OF INDUSTRIAL DEVELOPMENT IN THE PHILIPPINES (PAPER). PHILIPPINE WORKER CAP/ISM INT/TRADE TARIFFS RECEIVE PRICE ADMIN COST EFFICIENCY WEALTH...BIBLIOG 20. PAGE 149 H2986
S/ASIA
ECO/UNDEV
PROC/MFG
NAT/G
B63

SWEARER H.R.,CONTEMPORARY COMMUNISM: THEORY AND PRACTICE. COM USSR SOCIETY ECO/DEV POL/PAR FORCES PLAN ADMIN LEAD NAT/LISM...POLICY ANTHOL 20 LENIN/VI COM/PARTY. PAGE 151 H3015
MARXISM
CONCPT
DIPLOM
NAT/G
B63

TUCKER R.C.,THE SOVIET POLITICAL MIND. COM INTELL NAT/G TOP/EX EDU/PROP ADMIN COERCE TOTALISM ATTIT PWR MARXISM...PSY MYTH HYPO/EXP 20. PAGE 157 H3136
STRUCT
RIGID/FLEX
ELITES
USSR
B63

UN SECRETARY GENERAL,PLANNING FOR ECONOMIC DEVELOPMENT. ECO/UNDEV FINAN BUDGET INT/TRADE TARIFFS TAX ADMIN 20 UN. PAGE 158 H3159
PLAN
ECO/TAC
MGT
NAT/COMP
B63

US ATOMIC ENERGY COMMISSION,ATOMIC ENERGY IN THE SOVIET UNION: TRIP REPORT OF THE US ATOMIC ENERGY DELEGATION, MAY 1933. USSR R+D NAT/G CONSULT CREATE DIPLOM ADMIN ROUTINE EFFICIENCY PRODUC KNOWL SKILL ...NAT/COMP 20 AEC TRAVEL TREATY. PAGE 159 H3176
METH/COMP
OP/RES
TEC/DEV
NUC/PWR
B63

WALKER A.A.,OFFICIAL PUBLICATIONS OF SIERRA LEONE AND GAMBIA. GAMBIA SIER/LEONE UK LAW CONSTN LEGIS PLAN BUDGET DIPLOM...SOC SAMP CON/ANAL 20. PAGE 164 H3290
BIBLIOG
NAT/G
COLONIAL
ADMIN
B63

WEINER M.,POLITICAL CHANGE IN SOUTH ASIA. CEYLON INDIA PAKISTAN S/ASIA CULTURE ELITES ECO/UNDEV EX/STRUC ADMIN CONTROL CHOOSE CONSERVE...GOV/COMP ANTHOL 20. PAGE 166 H3328
NAT/G
CONSTN
TEC/DEV
L63

BOLGAR V.,"THE PUBLIC INTEREST: A JURISPRUDENTIAL AND COMPARATIVE OVERVIEW OF SYMPOSIUM ON FUNDAMENTAL CONCEPTS OF PUBLIC LAW" COM FRANCE GERMANY SWITZERLND LAW ADJUD ADMIN AGREE LAISSEZ
CONCPT
ORD/FREE
CONTROL
NAT/COMP

...JURID GEN/LAWS 20 EUROPE/E. PAGE 18 H0369

L63
FREUND G.,"ADENAUER AND THE FUTURE OF GERMANY." EUR+WWI FUT GERMANY/W FORCES LEGIT ADMIN ROUTINE ATTIT DRIVE PERSON PWR...POLICY TIME/SEQ TREND VAL/FREE 20 ADENAUER/K. PAGE 53 H1058
NAT/G BIOG DIPLOM GERMANY

S63
ARASTEH R.,"THE ROLE OF INTELLECTUALS IN ADMINISTRATIVE DEVELOPMENT AND SOCIAL CHANGE IN MODERN IRAN." ISLAM CULTURE NAT/G CONSULT ACT/RES EDU/PROP EXEC ATTIT BIO/SOC PERCEPT SUPEGO ALL/VALS ...POLICY MGT PSY SOC CONCPT 20. PAGE 8 H0157
INTELL ADMIN IRAN

S63
ROUGEMONT D.,"LES NOUVELLES CHANCES DE L'EUROPE." EUR+WWI FUT ECO/DEV INT/ORG NAT/G ACT/RES PLAN TEC/DEV EDU/PROP ADMIN COLONIAL FEDERAL ATTIT PWR SKILL...TREND 20. PAGE 135 H2696
ECO/UNDEV PERCEPT

S63
RUSTOW D.A.,"THE MILITARY IN MIDDLE EASTERN SOCIETY AND POLITICS." FUT ISLAM CONSTN SOCIETY FACE/GP NAT/G POL/PAR PROF/ORG CONSULT DOMIN ADMIN EXEC REGION COERCE NAT/LISM ATTIT DRIVE PERSON ORD/FREE PWR...POLICY CONCPT OBS STERTYP 20. PAGE 136 H2721
FORCES ELITES

S63
TANNER R.,"WHO GOES HOME?" CULTURE GP/REL SOC/INTEG 20 TANGANYIKA MIGRATION. PAGE 152 H3045
ADMIN COLONIAL NAT/G NAT/LISM

B64
ANDREN N.,GOVERNMENT AND POLITICS IN THE NORDIC COUNTRIES: DENMARK, FINLAND, ICELAND, NORWAY, SWEDEN. DENMARK FINLAND ICELAND NORWAY SWEDEN POL/PAR CHIEF LEGIS ADMIN REGION REPRESENT ATTIT CONSERVE...CHARTS BIBLIOG/A 20. PAGE 7 H0137
CONSTN NAT/G CULTURE GOV/COMP

B64
AVASTHI A.,ASPECTS OF ADMINISTRATION. INDIA UK USA+45 FINAN ACADEM DELIB/GP LEGIS RECEIVE PARL/PROC PRIVIL...NAT/COMP 20. PAGE 9 H0183
MGT ADMIN SOC/WK ORD/FREE

B64
BAUCHET P.,ECONOMIC PLANNING. FRANCE STRATA LG/CO CAP/ISM ADMIN PARL/PROC DEMAND OPTIMAL ATTIT PWR SOCISM...POLICY CHARTS 20. PAGE 12 H0238
ECO/DEV NAT/G PLAN ECO/TAC

B64
BENDIX R.,NATION-BUILDING AND CITIZENSHIP: STUDIES OF OUR CHANGING SOCIAL ORDER. WOR+45 CULTURE LOC/G GOV/REL INGP/REL ORD/FREE PWR 20. PAGE 14 H0275
PARTIC NAT/COMP ADMIN AUTHORIT

B64
BERNSTEIN H.,A BOOKSHELF ON BRAZIL. BRAZIL ADMIN COLONIAL...HUM JURID SOC 20. PAGE 16 H0315
BIBLIOG/A NAT/G L/A+17C ECO/UNDEV

B64
BROWN C.V.,GOVERNMENT AND BANKING IN WESTERN NIGERIA. AFR NIGERIA GOV/REL GP/REL...POLICY 20. PAGE 22 H0440
ADMIN ECO/UNDEV FINAN NAT/G

B64
CULLINGWORTH J.B.,TOWN AND COUNTRY PLANNING IN ENGLAND AND WALES. UK LAW SOCIETY CONSULT ACT/RES ADMIN ROUTINE LEISURE INGP/REL ADJUST PWR...GEOG 20 OPEN/SPACE URBAN/RNWL. PAGE 36 H0718
MUNIC PLAN NAT/G PROB/SOLV

B64
ETZIONI A.,MODERN ORGANIZATIONS. CLIENT STRUCT DOMIN CONTROL LEAD PERS/REL AUTHORIT...CLASSIF BUREAUCRCY. PAGE 47 H0946
MGT ADMIN PLAN CULTURE

B64
FLORENCE P.S.,ECONOMICS AND SOCIOLOGY OF INDUSTRY; A REALISTIC ANALYSIS OF DEVELOPMENT. ECO/UNDEV LG/CO NAT/G PLAN...GEOG MGT BIBLIOG 20. PAGE 51 H1029
INDUS SOC ADMIN

B64
FORBES A.H.,CURRENT RESEARCH IN BRITISH STUDIES. UK CONSTN CULTURE POL/PAR SECT DIPLOM ADMIN...JURID BIOG WORSHIP 20. PAGE 52 H1034
BIBLIOG PERSON NAT/G PARL/PROC

B64
FRANCK T.M.,EAST AFRICAN UNITY THROUGH LAW. MALAWI TANZANIA UGANDA UK ZAMBIA CONSTN INT/ORG NAT/G ADMIN ROUTINE TASK NAT/LISM ATTIT SOVEREIGN ...RECORD IDEA/COMP NAT/COMP. PAGE 52 H1048
AFR FEDERAL REGION INT/LAW

B64
GESELLSCHAFT RECHTSVERGLEICH,BIBLIOGRAPHIE DES DEUTSCHEN RECHTS (BIBLIOGRAPHY OF GERMAN LAW, TRANS. BY COURTLAND PETERSON). GERMANY FINAN INDUS LABOR SECT FORCES CT/SYS PARL/PROC CRIME...INT/LAW SOC NAT/COMP 20. PAGE 56 H1117
BIBLIOG/A JURID CONSTN ADMIN

B64
GOODNOW H.F.,THE CIVIL SERVICE OF PAKISTAN: BUREAUCRACY IN A NEW NATION. INDIA PAKISTAN S/ASIA ECO/UNDEV PROVS CHIEF PARTIC CHOOSE EFFICIENCY PWR ...BIBLIOG 20. PAGE 59 H1173
ADMIN GOV/REL LAW NAT/G

B64
GREBLER L.,URBAN RENEWAL IN EUROPEAN COUNTRIES: ITS EMERGENCE AND POTENTIALS. EUR+WWI UK ECO/DEV LOC/G NEIGH CREATE ADMIN ATTIT...TREND NAT/COMP 20 URBAN/RNWL. PAGE 60 H1205
MUNIC PLAN CONSTRUC NAT/G

B64
HALLER W.,DER SCHWEDISCHE JUSTITIEOMBUDSMAN. DENMARK FINLAND NORWAY SWEDEN LEGIS ADJUD CONTROL PERSON ORD/FREE...NAT/COMP 20 OMBUDSMAN. PAGE 64 H1288
JURID PARL/PROC ADMIN CHIEF

B64
HERSKOVITS M.J.,ECONOMIC TRANSITION IN AFRICA. FUT INT/ORG NAT/G WORKER PROB/SOLV TEC/DEV INT/TRADE EQUILIB INCOME...ANTHOL 20. PAGE 70 H1408
AFR ECO/UNDEV PLAN ADMIN

B64
IBERO-AMERICAN INSTITUTES,IBEROAMERICANA. STRUCT ADMIN SOC. PAGE 76 H1519
BIBLIOG L/A+17C NAT/G DIPLOM

B64
INDIAN COMM PREVENTION CORRUPT,REPORT, 1964. INDIA NAT/G GOV/REL ATTIT ORD/FREE...CRIMLGY METH 20. PAGE 76 H1530
CRIME ADMIN LEGIS LOC/G

B64
KAACK H.,DIE PARTEIEN IN DER VERFASSUNGSWIRKLICHKEIT DER BUNDESREPUBLIK. GERMANY/W ADMIN PARL/PROC CHOOSE...JURID 20. PAGE 82 H1646
POL/PAR PROVS NAT/G

B64
MAHAR J.M.,INDIA: A CRITICAL BIBLIOGRAPHY. INDIA PAKISTAN CULTURE ECO/UNDEV LOC/G POL/PAR SECT PROB/SOLV DIPLOM ADMIN COLONIAL PARL/PROC ATTIT 20. PAGE 101 H2016
BIBLIOG/A S/ASIA NAT/G LEAD

B64
MARSH D.C.,THE FUTURE OF THE WELFARE STATE. UK CONSTN NAT/G POL/PAR...POLICY WELF/ST 20. PAGE 103 H2058
NEW/LIB ADMIN CONCPT INSPECT

B64
MOUMOUNI A.,L'EDUCATION EN AFRIQUE. UNIV CULTURE ELITES INTELL EDU/PROP ADMIN COLONIAL...LING TREND BIBLIOG 20. PAGE 114 H2271
SCHOOL AFR PROB/SOLV

B64
MUSSO AMBROSI L.A.,BIBLIOGRAFIA DE BIBLIOGRAFIAS URUGUAYAS. URUGUAY DIPLOM ADMIN ATTIT...SOC 20. PAGE 115 H2301
BIBLIOG NAT/G L/A+17C PRESS

B64
NATIONAL BOOK LEAGUE,THE COMMONWEALTH IN BOOKS: AN ANNOTATED LIST. CANADA UK LOC/G SECT ADMIN...SOC BIOG 20 CMN/WLTH. PAGE 116 H2320
BIBLIOG/A JURID NAT/G

B64
NICOL D.,AFRICA - A SUBJECTIVE VIEW. AFR INT/ORG PLAN ADMIN COLONIAL PARL/PROC PARTIC REGION GOV/REL LITERACY ATTIT...BIBLIOG 20 CIVIL/SERV. PAGE 118 H2350
NAT/G LEAD CULTURE ACADEM

B64
OECD SEMINAR REGIONAL DEV,REGIONAL DEVELOPMENT IN ISRAEL. ISRAEL STRUCT ECO/UNDEV NAT/G REGION...GEOG 20. PAGE 120 H2404
ADMIN PROVS PLAN METH/COMP

B64
PARANJAPE H.K.,THE FLIGHT OF TECHNICAL PERSONNEL IN PUBLIC UNDERTAKINGS. INDIA PAY DEMAND HAPPINESS ORD/FREE...MGT QU 20 MIGRATION. PAGE 123 H2464
ADMIN NAT/G WORKER PLAN

B64
RAPHAEL M.,PENSIONS AND PUBLIC SERVANTS. UK NAT/G PLAN INGP/REL COST EFFICIENCY ATTIT...POLICY 17/20 CIVIL/SERV. PAGE 130 H2593
RECEIVE ADMIN INCOME AGE/O

B64
RIDLEY F.,PUBLIC ADMINISTRATION IN FRANCE. FRANCE UK EX/STRUC CONTROL PARTIC EFFICIENCY 20. PAGE 131 H2625
ADMIN REPRESENT GOV/COMP PWR

B64
RUSSET B.M.,WORLD HANDBOOK OF POLITICAL AND SOCIAL INDICATORS. WOR+45 COM/IND ADMIN WEALTH...GEOG 20. PAGE 136 H2719
DIPLOM STAT NAT/G NAT/COMP

B64
SZLADITS C.,BIBLIOGRAPHY ON FOREIGN AND COMPARATIVE LAW: BOOKS AND ARTICLES IN ENGLISH (SUPPLEMENT 1962). FINAN INDUS JUDGE LICENSE ADMIN CT/SYS PARL/PROC OWN...INT/LAW CLASSIF METH/COMP NAT/COMP 20. PAGE 151 H3027
BIBLIOG/A JURID ADJUD LAW

B64
THORNBURG M.W.,PEOPLE AND POLICY IN THE MIDDLE EAST. ISLAM ECO/UNDEV FAM KIN MUNIC NAT/G NEIGH POL/PAR SECT DELIB/GP LEGIS PLAN ECO/TAC DOMIN ADMIN ATTIT HEALTH RESPECT...SOC CONCPT METH/CNCPT OBS TIME/SEQ TOT/POP VAL/FREE. PAGE 154 H3088
TEC/DEV CULTURE

B64
TILMAN R.O.,BUREAUCRATIC TRANSITION IN MALAYA. MALAYSIA S/ASIA UK NAT/G EX/STRUC DIPLOM...CHARTS BIBLIOG 20. PAGE 155 H3098 — ADMIN COLONIAL SOVEREIGN EFFICIENCY

B64
TINKER H.,BALLOT BOX AND BAYONET - PEOPLE AND GOVERNMENT IN EMERGENT ASIAN COUNTRIES. CEYLON INDIA INDONESIA PHILIPPINE POL/PAR ADMIN COLONIAL LEAD PARL/PROC CHOOSE CONSEN ORD/FREE SOVEREIGN PLURISM...GOV/COMP THIRD/WRLD. PAGE 155 H3104 — MYTH S/ASIA NAT/COMP NAT/LISM

B64
TURNER M.C.,LIBROS EN VENTA EN HISPANOAMERICA Y ESPANA. SPAIN LAW CONSTN CULTURE ADMIN LEAD...HUM SOC 20. PAGE 157 H3141 — BIBLIOG L/A+17C NAT/G DIPLOM

B64
WAINHOUSE D.W.,REMNANTS OF EMPIRE: THE UNITED NATIONS AND THE END OF COLONIALISM. FUT PORTUGAL WOR+45 NAT/G CONSULT DOMIN LEGIT ADMIN ROUTINE ATTIT ORD/FREE...POLICY JURID RECORD INT TIME/SEQ UN CMN/WLTH 20. PAGE 164 H3287 — INT/ORG TREND COLONIAL

B64
WARD R.E.,POLITICAL MODERNIZATION IN JAPAN AND TURKEY. ASIA ISLAM S/ASIA CONSTN CULTURE STRATA COM/IND POL/PAR FORCES ACT/RES ECO/TAC DOMIN EDU/PROP LEGIT ADMIN CHOOSE ATTIT ALL/VALS...STAT TIME/SEQ VAL/FREE CHINJAP. PAGE 165 H3307 — SOCIETY TURKEY

B64
WERNETTE J.P.,GOVERNMENT AND BUSINESS. LABOR CAP/ISM ECO/TAC INT/TRADE TAX ADMIN AUTOMAT NUC/PWR CIVMIL/REL DEMAND...MGT 20 MONOPOLY. PAGE 167 H3333 — NAT/G FINAN ECO/DEV CONTROL

B64
WHEELER-BENNETT J.W.,THE NEMESIS OF POWER (2ND ED.). EUR+WWI GERMANY TOP/EX TEC/DEV ADMIN WAR PERS/REL RIGID/FLEX ROLE ORD/FREE PWR FASCISM 20 HITLER/A. PAGE 167 H3342 — FORCES NAT/G GP/REL STRUCT

B64
WITHERELL J.W.,OFFICIAL PUBLICATIONS OF FRENCH EQUATORIAL AFRICA, FRENCH CAMEROONS, AND TOGO, 1946-1958 (PAMPHLET). CAMEROON CHAD FRANCE GABON TOGO LAW ECO/UNDEV EXTR/IND INT/TRADE...GEOG HEAL 20. PAGE 169 H3392 — BIBLIOG/A AFR NAT/G ADMIN

B64
WRAITH R.,CORRUPTION IN DEVELOPING COUNTRIES. NIGERIA UK LAW ELITES STRATA INDUS LOC/G NAT/G SECT FORCES EDU/PROP ADMIN PWR WEALTH 18/20. PAGE 171 H3414 — ECO/UNDEV CRIME SANCTION ATTIT

B64
ZARTMAN I.W.,MOROCCO: PROBLEMS OF NEW POWER. ISLAM CULTURE ECO/UNDEV AGRI POL/PAR SCHOOL FORCES ADMIN ...CONCPT STAT INT CENSUS TIME/SEQ CHARTS WORK VAL/FREE 20. PAGE 172 H3449 — CHOOSE MOROCCO DELIB/GP DECISION

L64
MACKINTOSH J.P.,"NIGERIA'S EXTERNAL AFFAIRS." UK CULTURE ECO/UNDEV NAT/G VOL/ASSN EDU/PROP LEGIT ADMIN ATTIT ORD/FREE PWR 20. PAGE 100 H2002 — AFR DIPLOM NIGERIA

L64
ROTBERG R.,"THE FEDERATION MOVEMENT IN BRITISH EAST AND CENTRAL AFRICA." AFR RHODESIA UGANDA ECO/UNDEV NAT/G POL/PAR FORCES DOMIN LEGIT ADMIN COERCE ATTIT ...CONCPT TREND 20 TANGANYIKA. PAGE 135 H2691 — VOL/ASSN PWR REGION

L64
SYMONDS R.,"REFLECTIONS IN LOCALISATION." AFR S/ASIA UK STRATA INT/ORG NAT/G SCHOOL EDU/PROP LEGIT KNOWL ORD/FREE PWR RESPECT CMN/WLTH 20. PAGE 151 H3023 — ADMIN MGT COLONIAL

S64
GROSS J.A.,"WHITEHALL AND THE COMMONWEALTH." EUR+WWI MOD/EUR INT/ORG NAT/G CONSULT DELIB/GP LEGIS DOMIN ADMIN COLONIAL ROUTINE PWR CMN/WLTH 19/20. PAGE 62 H1233 — EX/STRUC ATTIT TREND

S64
HORECKY P.L.,"LIBRARY OF CONGRESS PUBLICATIONS IN AID OF USSR AND EAST EUROPEAN RESEARCH." BULGARIA CZECHOSLVK POLAND USSR YUGOSLAVIA NAT/G POL/PAR DIPLOM ADMIN GOV/REL...CLASSIF 20. PAGE 73 H1468 — BIBLIOG/A COM MARXISM

S64
JOHNSON K.F.,"CAUSAL FACTORS IN LATIN AMERICAN POLITICAL INSTABILITY." CULTURE NAT/G VOL/ASSN EX/STRUC FORCES EDU/PROP LEGIT ADMIN COERCE REV ATTIT KNOWL PWR...STYLE RECORD CHARTS WORK 20. PAGE 81 H1624 — L/A+17C PERCEPT ELITES

S64
LOW D.A.,"LION RAMPANT." EUR+WWI MOD/EUR S/ASIA ECO/UNDEV NAT/G FORCES TEC/DEV ECO/TAC LEGIT ADMIN COLONIAL COERCE ORD/FREE RESPECT 19/20. PAGE 99 H1972 — AFR DOMIN DIPLOM UK

S64
NEEDHAM T.,"SCIENCE AND SOCIETY IN EAST AND WEST." INTELL STRATA R+D LOC/G NAT/G PROVS CONSULT ACT/RES CREATE PLAN TEC/DEV EDU/PROP ADMIN ATTIT ALL/VALS ...POLICY RELATIV MGT CONCPT NEW/IDEA TIME/SEQ WORK WORK. PAGE 116 H2327 — ASIA STRUCT

C64
GOLDMAN M.I.,"COMPARATIVE ECONOMIC SYSTEMS: A READER." COM ECO/UNDEV NAT/G BUDGET CAP/ISM ADMIN TOTALISM MARXISM SOCISM...MGT ANTHOL BIBLIOG 19/20. PAGE 58 H1157 — NAT/COMP CONTROL IDEA/COMP

C64
SCOTT R.E.,"MEXICAN GOVERNMENT IN TRANSITION (REV ED)" CULTURE STRUCT POL/PAR CHIEF ADMIN LOBBY REV CHOOSE GP/REL DRIVE...BIBLIOG METH 20 MEXIC/AMER. PAGE 141 H2816 — NAT/G L/A+17C ROUTINE CONSTN

B65
ADU A.L.,THE CIVIL SERVICE IN NEW AFRICAN STATES. AFR GHANA FINAN SOVEREIGN...POLICY 20 CIVIL/SERV AFRICA/E AFRICA/W. PAGE 4 H0074 — ECO/UNDEV ADMIN COLONIAL NAT/G

B65
AIYAR S.P.,STUDIES IN INDIAN DEMOCRACY. INDIA STRATA ECO/UNDEV LABOR POL/PAR LEGIS DIPLOM LOBBY REGION CHOOSE ATTIT SOCISM...ANTHOL 20. PAGE 4 H0086 — ORD/FREE REPRESENT ADMIN NAT/G

B65
APTER D.E.,THE POLITICS OF MODERNIZATION. AFR L/A+17C CULTURE NAT/G POL/PAR ADMIN COLONIAL NAT/LISM ATTIT RIGID/FLEX PWR...SOC CONCPT. PAGE 8 H0154 — ECO/UNDEV GEN/LAWS STRATA CREATE

B65
BERNDT R.M.,ABORIGINAL MAN IN AUSTRALIA. LAW DOMIN ADMIN COLONIAL MARRIAGE HABITAT ORD/FREE...LING CHARTS ANTHOL BIBLIOG WORSHIP 20 AUSTRAL ABORIGINES MUSIC ELKIN/AP. PAGE 16 H0312 — SOC CULTURE SOCIETY STRUCT

B65
CAMPBELL G.A.,THE CIVIL SERVICE IN BRITAIN (2ND ED.). UK DELIB/GP FORCES WORKER CREATE PLAN ...POLICY AUD/VIS 19/20 CIVIL/SERV. PAGE 26 H0515 — ADMIN LEGIS NAT/G FINAN

B65
CHEN T.H.,THE CHINESE COMMUNIST REGIME: A DOCUMENTARY STUDY (2 VOLS.). CHINA/COM LAW CONSTN ELITES ECO/UNDEV LEGIS ECO/TAC ADMIN CONTROL PWR ...SOC 20. PAGE 29 H0587 — MARXISM POL/PAR NAT/G

B65
CRAMER J.F.,CONTEMPORARY EDUCATION: A COMPARATIVE STUDY OF NATIONAL SYSTEMS (2ND ED.). CHINA/COM EUR+WWI INDIA USA+45 FINAN PROB/SOLV ADMIN CONTROL ATTIT...IDEA/COMP METH/COMP 20 CHINJAP. PAGE 35 H0697 — EDU/PROP NAT/COMP SCHOOL ACADEM

B65
DUGGAR G.S.,RENEWAL OF TOWN AND VILLAGE I: A WORLD-WIDE SURVEY OF LOCAL GOVERNMENT EXPERIENCE. WOR+45 CONSTRUC INDUS CREATE BUDGET REGION GOV/REL...QU NAT/COMP 20 URBAN/RNWL. PAGE 43 H0859 — MUNIC NEIGH PLAN ADMIN

B65
GOLEMBIEWSKI R.T.,MEN, MANAGEMENT, AND MORALITY; TOWARD A NEW ORGANIZATIONAL ETHIC. CONSTN EX/STRUC CREATE ADMIN CONTROL INGP/REL PERSON SUPEGO MORAL PWR...GOV/COMP METH/COMP 20 BUREAUCRCY. PAGE 58 H1161 — LG/CO MGT PROB/SOLV

B65
GOPAL S.,BRITISH POLICY IN INDIA 1858-1905. INDIA UK ELITES CHIEF DELIB/GP ECO/TAC GP/REL DISCRIM ATTIT...IDEA/COMP NAT/COMP PERS/COMP BIBLIOG/A 19/20. PAGE 59 H1176 — COLONIAL ADMIN POL/PAR ECO/UNDEV

B65
HARMON R.B.,POLITICAL SCIENCE: A BIBLIOGRAPHICAL GUIDE TO THE LITERATURE. WOR+45 WOR-45 R+D INT/ORG LOC/G NAT/G DIPLOM ADMIN...CONCPT METH. PAGE 67 H1334 — BIBLIOG POL/PAR LAW GOV/COMP

B65
HART B.H.L.,THE MEMOIRS OF CAPTAIN LIDDELL HART (VOL. I). UK NAT/G PLAN TEC/DEV DIPLOM ADMIN WEAPON GOV/REL PERS/REL ATTIT PWR FASCISM...POLICY 20. PAGE 67 H1348 — FORCES BIOG LEAD WAR

B65
HISPANIC SOCIETY OF AMERICA,CATALOGUE (10 VOLS.). PORTUGAL PRE/AMER SPAIN NAT/G ADMIN...POLICY SOC 15/20. PAGE 71 H1426 — BIBLIOG L/A+17C COLONIAL DIPLOM

B65
INST INTL DES CIVILISATION DIF,THE CONSTITUTIONS AND ADMINISTRATIVE INSTITUTIONS OF THE NEW STATES. AFR ISLAM S/ASIA NAT/G POL/PAR DELIB/GP EX/STRUC CONFER EFFICIENCY NAT/LISM...JURID SOC 20. PAGE 77 H1535 — CONSTN ADMIN ADJUD ECO/UNDEV

B65
INT. BANK RECONSTR. DEVELOP.,ECONOMIC DEVELOPMENT OF KUWAIT. ISLAM KUWAIT AGRI FINAN MARKET EX/STRUC TEC/DEV ECO/TAC ADMIN WEALTH...OBS CON/ANAL CHARTS 20. PAGE 77 H1541 — INDUS NAT/G

B65
KAAS L.,DIE GEISTLICHE GERICHTSBARKEIT DER KATHOLISCHEN KIRCHE IN PREUSSEN (2 VOLS.). PRUSSIA CONSTN NAT/G PROVS SECT ADJUD ADMIN ATTIT 16/20. PAGE 82 H1647 — JURID CATHISM GP/REL CT/SYS

B65
MOORE C.H.,TUNISIA SINCE INDEPENDENCE. ELITES LOC/G POL/PAR ADMIN COLONIAL CONTROL EXEC GOV/REL — NAT/G EX/STRUC

TOTALISM MARXISM...INT 20 TUNIS. PAGE 112 H2248 SOCISM

B65
NATIONAL BOOK CENTRE PAKISTAN,BOOKS ON PAKISTAN: A BIBLIOGRAPHY. PAKISTAN CULTURE DIPLOM ADMIN ATTIT ...MAJORIT SOC CONCPT 20. PAGE 116 H2319 BIBLIOG CONSTN S/ASIA NAT/G

B65
NEWBURY C.W.,BRITISH POLICY TOWARDS WEST AFRICA: SELECT DOCUMENTS 1786-1874. AFR UK INT/TRADE DOMIN ADMIN COLONIAL CT/SYS COERCE ORD/FREE...BIBLIOG/A 18/19. PAGE 117 H2345 DIPLOM POLICY NAT/G WRITING

B65
NORDEN A.,WAR AND NAZI CRIMINALS IN WEST GERMANY: STATE, ECONOMY, ADMINISTRATION, ARMY, JUSTICE, SCIENCE. GERMANY GERMANY/W MOD/EUR ECO/DEV ACADEM EX/STRUC FORCES DOMIN ADMIN CT/SYS...POLICY MAJORIT PACIFIST 20. PAGE 119 H2370 FASCIST WAR NAT/G TOP/EX

B65
OECD,MEDITERRANEAN REGIONAL PROJECT: TURKEY; EDUCATION AND DEVELOPMENT. FUT TURKEY SOCIETY STRATA FINAN NAT/G PROF/ORG PLAN PROB/SOLV ADMIN COST...STAT CHARTS 20 OECD. PAGE 120 H2399 EDU/PROP ACADEM SCHOOL ECO/UNDEV

B65
OECD,THE MEDITERRANEAN REGIONAL PROJECT: ITALY; EDUCATION AND DEVELOPMENT. ITALY SOCIETY STRATA FINAN NAT/G PROF/ORG WORKER PLAN PROB/SOLV ADMIN ...STAT CHARTS METH 20 OECD. PAGE 120 H2400 SCHOOL EDU/PROP ECO/UNDEV ACADEM

B65
OECD,THE MEDITERRANEAN REGIONAL PROJECT: GREECE; EDUCATION AND DEVELOPMENT. FUT GREECE SOCIETY AGRI FINAN NAT/G PROF/ORG WORKER PLAN PROB/SOLV ADMIN DEMAND ATTIT 20 OECD. PAGE 120 H2401 EDU/PROP SCHOOL ACADEM ECO/UNDEV

B65
OECD,THE MEDITERRANEAN REGIONAL PROJECT: SPAIN; EDUCATION AND DEVELOPMENT. FUT SPAIN STRATA FINAN NAT/G WORKER PLAN PROB/SOLV ADMIN COST...POLICY STAT CHARTS 20 OECD. PAGE 120 H2402 ECO/UNDEV EDU/PROP ACADEM SCHOOL

B65
OGILVY-WEBB M.,THE GOVERNMENT EXPLAINS: A STUDY OF THE INFORMATION SERVICES. UK DELIB/GP LEGIS WORKER BUDGET DIPLOM 20. PAGE 121 H2409 EDU/PROP ATTIT NAT/G ADMIN

B65
ORG FOR ECO COOP AND DEVEL,THE MEDITERRANEAN REGIONAL PROJECT: AN EXPERIMENT IN PLANNING BY SIX COUNTRIES. FUT GREECE SPAIN TURKEY YUGOSLAVIA SOCIETY FINAN NAT/G PROF/ORG EDU/PROP ADMIN REGION COST...POLICY STAT CHARTS 20 OECD. PAGE 121 H2427 PLAN ECO/UNDEV ACADEM SCHOOL

B65
PADELFORD N.,THE UNITED NATIONS IN THE BALANCE* ACCOMPLISHMENTS AND PROSPECTS. NAT/G VOL/ASSN DIPLOM ADMIN COLONIAL CT/SYS REGION WAR ORD/FREE ...ANTHOL UN. PAGE 122 H2437 INT/ORG CONTROL

B65
PANJABI K.L.,THE CIVIL SERVANT IN INDIA. INDIA UK NAT/G CONSULT EX/STRUC REGION GP/REL RACE/REL 20. PAGE 123 H2462 ADMIN WORKER BIOG COLONIAL

B65
ROTBERG R.I.,A POLITICAL HISTORY OF TROPICAL AFRICA. EX/STRUC DIPLOM INT/TRADE DOMIN ADMIN RACE/REL NAT/LISM PWR SOVEREIGN...GEOG TIME/SEQ BIBLIOG 1/20. PAGE 135 H2692 AFR CULTURE COLONIAL

B65
ROWAT D.C.,THE OMBUDSMAN: CITIZEN'S DEFENDER. DENMARK FINLAND NEW/ZEALND NORWAY SWEDEN CONSULT PROB/SOLV FEEDBACK PARTIC GP/REL...SOC CONCPT NEW/IDEA METH/COMP ANTHOL BIBLIOG 20. PAGE 135 H2701 INSPECT CONSTN NAT/G ADMIN

B65
SHARMA S.A.,PARLIAMENTARY GOVERNMENT IN INDIA. INDIA FINAN LOC/G PROVS DELIB/GP PLAN ADMIN CT/SYS FEDERAL...JURID 20. PAGE 142 H2849 NAT/G CONSTN PARL/PROC LEGIS

B65
SLATER J.,A REVALUATION OF COLLECTIVE SECURITY* THE OAS IN ACTION. L/A+17C USA+45 NAT/G ADMIN COERCE ORD/FREE PWR...GOV/COMP IDEA/COMP GEN/LAWS OAS. PAGE 145 H2899 REGION INT/ORG FORCES

B65
STEINER K.,LOCAL GOVERNMENT IN JAPAN. CONSTN CULTURE NAT/G ADMIN CHOOSE...SOC STAT 20 CHINJAP. PAGE 149 H2976 LOC/G SOCIETY JURID ORD/FREE

B65
ULAM A.,THE BOLSHEVIKS. COM USSR NAT/G CHIEF ECO/TAC ADMIN LEAD WAR POPULISM...POLICY 19/20 LENIN/VI BOLSHEVISM. PAGE 157 H3148 SOCISM POL/PAR TOP/EX REV

L65
LASSWELL H.D.,"THE POLICY SCIENCES OF DEVELOPMENT." CULTURE SOCIETY EX/STRUC CREATE ADMIN ATTIT KNOWL ...SOC CONCPT SIMUL GEN/METH. PAGE 92 H1835 PWR METH/CNCPT DIPLOM

L65
MATTHEWS D.G.,"A CURRENT BIBLIOGRAPHY ON ETHIOPIAN AFFAIRS: A SELECT BIBLIOGRAPHY FROM 1950-1964." ETHIOPIA LAW CULTURE ECO/UNDEV INDUS LABOR SECT FORCES DIPLOM CIVMIL/REL RACE/REL...LING STAT 20. PAGE 105 H2093 BIBLIOG/A ADMIN POL/PAR NAT/G

S65
"FURTHER READING." INDIA NAT/G ADMIN 20. PAGE 2 H0045 BIBLIOG EDU/PROP SCHOOL ACADEM

S65
"FURTHER READING." INDIA ADMIN COLONIAL WAR GOV/REL ATTIT 20. PAGE 2 H0046 BIBLIOG DIPLOM NAT/G POLICY

S65
ASHFORD D.E.,"BUREAUCRATS AND CITIZENS." MOROCCO PAKISTAN PARTIC 20 TUNIS. PAGE 9 H0172 GOV/COMP ADMIN EX/STRUC ROLE

S65
HAYTER T.,"FRENCH AID TO AFRICA* ITS SCOPE AND ACHIEVEMENTS." CULTURE ECO/TAC INT/TRADE ADMIN REGION CENTRAL FEDERAL LOVE PWR SOVEREIGN EEC. PAGE 68 H1370 AFR FRANCE FOR/AID COLONIAL

S65
HUGHES T.L.,"SCHOLARS AND FOREIGN POLICY* VARIETIES OF RESEARCH EXPERIENCE." COM/IND DIPLOM ADMIN EXEC ROUTINE...MGT OBS CONGRESS PRESIDENT CAMELOT. PAGE 75 H1491 ACT/RES ACADEM CONTROL NAT/G

N65
MOTE M.E.,SOVIET LOCAL AND REPUBLIC ELECTIONS. COM USSR NAT/G PLAN PARTIC GOV/REL TOTALISM PWR ...CHARTS 20. PAGE 114 H2270 CHOOSE ADMIN CONTROL LOC/G

B66
ADAMS J.C.,THE GOVERNMENT OF REPUBLICAN ITALY (2ND ED.). ITALY LOC/G POL/PAR DELIB/GP LEGIS WORKER ADMIN CT/SYS FASCISM...CHARTS BIBLIOG 20 PARLIAMENT. PAGE 3 H0064 NAT/G CHOOSE EX/STRUC CONSTN

B66
ANDERSON S.V.,CANADIAN OMBUDSMAN PROPOSALS. CANADA LEGIS DEBATE PARL/PROC...MAJORIT JURID TIME/SEQ IDEA/COMP 20 OMBUDSMAN PARLIAMENT. PAGE 7 H0133 NAT/G CREATE ADMIN POL/PAR

B66
ASHRAF A.,THE CITY GOVERNMENT OF CALCUTTA: A STUDY OF INERTIA. INDIA ELITES INDUS NAT/G EX/STRUC ACT/RES PLAN PROB/SOLV LEAD HABITAT...BIBLIOG 20 CALCUTTA. PAGE 9 H0175 LOC/G MUNIC ADMIN ECO/UNDEV

B66
BHALERAO C.N.,PUBLIC SERVICE COMMISSIONS OF INDIA: A STUDY. INDIA SERV/IND EX/STRUC ROUTINE CHOOSE GOV/REL INGP/REL...KNO/TEST EXHIBIT 20. PAGE 16 H0326 NAT/G OP/RES LOC/G ADMIN

B66
BIRKHEAD G.S.,ADMINISTRATIVE PROBLEMS IN PAKISTAN. PAKISTAN AGRI FINAN INDUS LG/CO ECO/TAC CONTROL PWR ...CHARTS ANTHOL 20. PAGE 17 H0340 ADMIN NAT/G ORD/FREE ECO/UNDEV

B66
BRAIBANTI R.,ASIAN BUREAUCRATIC SYSTEMS EMERGENT FROM THE BRITISH IMPERIAL TRADITION. BURMA CEYLON INDIA PAKISTAN UK ELITES ECO/UNDEV NAT/G...MGT SOC CHARTS ANTHOL 19/20. PAGE 20 H0401 GOV/COMP COLONIAL ADMIN S/ASIA

B66
BRAIBANTI R.,RESEARCH ON THE BUREAUCRACY OF PAKISTAN. PAKISTAN LAW CULTURE INTELL ACADEM LOC/G SECT PRESS CT/SYS...LING CHARTS 20 BUREAUCRCY. PAGE 20 H0402 HABITAT NAT/G ADMIN CONSTN

B66
CHAPMAN B.,THE PROFESSION OF GOVERNMENT: THE PUBLIC SERVICE IN EUROPE. CONSTN NAT/G POL/PAR EX/STRUC LEGIS TOP/EX PROB/SOLV DEBATE EXEC PARL/PROC PARTIC 20. PAGE 29 H0581 BIBLIOG ADMIN EUR+WWI GOV/COMP

B66
DARLING M.,APPRENTICE TO POWER INDIA 1904-1908. INDIA LEAD GP/REL PERSON...GEOG 20. PAGE 37 H0742 OBS SOCIETY ADMIN NAT/G

B66
DEUTSCHER I.,STALIN: A POLITICAL BIOGRAPHY. EUR+WWI USSR POL/PAR FORCES DIPLOM ADMIN LEAD REV WAR TOTALISM PERSON 20 STALIN/J ROOSEVLT/F LENIN/VI HITLER/A. PAGE 40 H0807 BIOG MARXISM TOP/EX PWR

B66
DUNCOMBE H.S.,COUNTY GOVERNMENT IN AMERICA. USA+45 FINAN MUNIC ADMIN ROUTINE GOV/REL...GOV/COMP 20. PAGE 43 H0863 LOC/G PROVS CT/SYS TOP/EX

B66
EPSTEIN F.T.,THE AMERICAN BIBLIOGRAPHY OF RUSSIAN AND EAST EUROPEAN STUDIES FOR 1964. USSR LOC/G NAT/G POL/PAR FORCES ADMIN ARMS/CONT...JURID CONCPT 20 UN. PAGE 47 H0933 BIBLIOG COM MARXISM DIPLOM

B66
FISK E.K.,NEW GUINEA ON THE THRESHOLD; ASPECTS OF SOCIAL, POLITICAL, AND ECONOMIC DEVELOPMENT. AGRI ECO/UNDEV SOCIETY

NAT/G INT/TRADE ADMIN ADJUST LITERACY ROLE...CHARTS ANTHOL 20 NEW/GUINEA. PAGE 51 H1015

B66
FOX K.A.,THE THEORY OF QUANTITATIVE ECONOMIC POLICY WITH APPLICATIONS TO ECONOMIC GROWTH AND STABILIZATION. ECO/DEV AGRI NAT/G PLAN ADMIN RISK ...DECISION IDEA/COMP SIMUL T. PAGE 52 H1045 — ECO/TAC ECOMETRIC EQUILIB GEN/LAWS

B66
GERARD-LIBOIS J.,KATANGA SECESSION. INT/ORG FORCES DIPLOM ADMIN CONTROL WAR CHOOSE PWR...CHARTS 20 KATANGA TSHOMBE/M UN. PAGE 56 H1114 — NAT/G REGION ORD/FREE REV

B66
GLAZER M.,THE FEDERAL GOVERNMENT AND THE UNIVERSITY. CHILE PROB/SOLV DIPLOM GIVE ADMIN WAR ...POLICY SOC 20. PAGE 57 H1140 — BIBLIOG/A NAT/G PLAN ACADEM

B66
HANKE L.,HANDBOOK OF LATIN AMERICAN STUDIES. ECO/UNDEV ADMIN LEAD...HUM SOC 20. PAGE 65 H1313 — BIBLIOG/A L/A+17C INDEX NAT/G

B66
HARMON R.B.,SOURCES AND PROBLEMS OF BIBLIOGRAPHY IN POLITICAL SCIENCE (PAMPHLET). INT/ORG LOC/G MUNIC POL/PAR ADMIN GOV/REL ALL/IDEOS...JURID MGT CONCPT 19/20. PAGE 67 H1335 — BIBLIOG DIPLOM INT/LAW NAT/G

B66
HEADY F.,PUBLIC ADMINISTRATION: A COMPARATIVE PERSPECTIVE. ECO/DEV ECO/UNDEV...GOV/COMP 20 BUREAUCRCY. PAGE 69 H1376 — ADMIN NAT/COMP NAT/G CIVMIL/REL

B66
HOLT R.T.,THE POLITICAL BASIS OF ECONOMIC DEVELOPMENT. STRATA STRUCT NAT/G DIPLOM ADMIN...SOC NAT/COMP BIBLIOG 20. PAGE 73 H1458 — ECO/TAC GOV/COMP CONSTN EX/STRUC

B66
INTERPARLIAMENTARY UNION,PARLIAMENTS: COMPARATIVE STUDY ON STRUCTURE AND FUNCTIONING OF REPRESENTATIVE INSTITUTIONS IN FIFTY-FIVE COUNTRIES. WOR+45 POL/PAR DELIB/GP BUDGET ADMIN CONTROL CHOOSE. PAGE 78 H1560 — PARL/PROC LEGIS GOV/COMP EX/STRUC

B66
JOHNSON N.,PARLIAMENT AND ADMINISTRATION: THE ESTIMATES COMMITTEE 1945-65. FUT UK NAT/G EX/STRUC PLAN BUDGET ORD/FREE...T 20 PARLIAMENT HOUSE/CMNS. PAGE 81 H1625 — LEGIS ADMIN FINAN DELIB/GP

B66
KAUNDA K.,ZAMBIA: INDEPENDENCE AND BEYOND: THE SPEECHES OF KENNETH KAUNDA. AFR FUT ZAMBIA SOCIETY ECO/UNDEV NAT/G PROB/SOLV ECO/TAC ADMIN RACE/REL SOVEREIGN 20. PAGE 84 H1670 — ORD/FREE COLONIAL CONSTN LEAD

B66
KIRDAR U.,THE STRUCTURE OF UNITED NATIONS ECONOMIC AID TO UNDERDEVELOPED COUNTRIES. AGRI FINAN INDUS NAT/G EX/STRUC PLAN GIVE TASK...POLICY 20 UN. PAGE 86 H1721 — INT/ORG FOR/AID ECO/UNDEV ADMIN

B66
KIRKENDALL R.S.,SOCIAL SCIENTISTS AND FARM POLITICS IN THE AGE OF ROOSEVELT. ACADEM PLAN ECO/TAC GIVE ADMIN CONTROL PRODUC...SOC 20 NEW/DEAL ROOSEVLT/F BURAGR/ECO. PAGE 86 H1722 — AGRI INTELL POLICY NAT/G

B66
MACFARQUHAR R.,CHINA UNDER MAO: POLITICS TAKES COMMAND. CHINA/COM COM AGRI INDUS CHIEF FORCES DIPLOM INT/TRADE EDU/PROP TASK REV ADJUST...ANTHOL 20 MAO. PAGE 100 H1992 — ECO/UNDEV TEC/DEV ECO/TAC ADMIN

B66
O'NEILL C.E.,CHURCH AND STATE IN FRENCH COLONIAL LOUISIANA: POLICY AND POLITICS TO 1732. PROVS VOL/ASSN DELIB/GP ADJUD ADMIN GP/REL ATTIT DRIVE ...POLICY BIBLIOG 17/18 LOUISIANA CHURCH/STA. PAGE 120 H2390 — COLONIAL NAT/G SECT PWR

B66
RAEFF M.,ORIGINS OF THE RUSSIAN INTELLIGENTSIA: THE EIGHTEENTH-CENTURY NOBILITY. RUSSIA FAM NAT/G EDU/PROP ADMIN PERS/REL ATTIT...HUM BIOG 18. PAGE 129 H2580 — INTELL ELITES STRATA CONSERVE

B66
RAY A.,INTER-GOVERNMENTAL RELATIONS IN INDIA: A STUDY OF INDIAN FEDERALISM. CANADA INDIA SWITZERLND USA+45 USSR ADMIN GOV/REL...NAT/COMP BIBLIOG. PAGE 130 H2599 — CONSTN FEDERAL SOVEREIGN NAT/G

B66
SCHURMANN F.,IDEOLOGY AND ORGANIZATION IN COMMUNIST CHINA. CHINA/COM LOC/G MUNIC POL/PAR ECO/TAC CONTROL ATTIT...MGT STERTYP 20 COM/PARTY. PAGE 140 H2805 — MARXISM STRUCT ADMIN NAT/G

B66
SILBERMAN B.S.,MODERN JAPANESE LEADERSHIP; TRANSITION AND CHANGE. NAT/G POL/PAR CHIEF ADMIN REPRESENT GP/REL ADJUST RIGID/FLEX...SOC METH/COMP ANTHOL 19/20 CHINJAP CHRISTIAN. PAGE 144 H2873 — LEAD CULTURE ELITES MUNIC

B66
SMITH H.E.,READINGS IN ECONOMIC DEVELOPMENT AND ADMINISTRATION IN TANZANIA. TANZANIA FINAN INDUS LABOR NAT/G PLAN PROB/SOLV INT/TRADE COLONIAL REGION...ANTHOL BIBLIOG 20 AFRICA/E. PAGE 146 H2910 — TEC/DEV ADMIN GOV/REL

B66
SYMONDS R.,THE BRITISH AND THEIR SUCCESSORS. AFR CEYLON INDIA UK SCHOOL FORCES EDU/PROP ADMIN PARTIC ...NAT/COMP BIBLIOG 20 AFRICA/W AFRICA/E. PAGE 151 H3024 — NAT/G ECO/UNDEV POLICY COLONIAL

B66
US LIBRARY OF CONGRESS,NIGERIA: A GUIDE TO OFFICIAL PUBLICATIONS. CAMEROON NIGERIA UK DIPLOM...POLICY 19/20 UN LEAGUE/NAT. PAGE 161 H3215 — BIBLIOG ADMIN NAT/G COLONIAL

B66
WILLNER A.R.,THE NEOTRADITIONAL ACCOMMODATION TO POLITICAL INDEPENDENCE* THE CASE OF INDONESIA * RESEARCH MONOGRAPH NO. 26. CULTURE ECO/UNDEV CREATE PROB/SOLV FOR/AID LEGIT COLONIAL EFFICIENCY NAT/LISM ALL/VALS SOC. PAGE 168 H3371 — INDONESIA CONSERVE ELITES ADMIN

B66
ZINKIN T.,CHALLENGES IN INDIA. INDIA PAKISTAN LAW AGRI FINAN INDUS TOP/EX TEC/DEV CONTROL ROUTINE ORD/FREE PWR 20 NEHRU/J SHASTRI/LB CIVIL/SERV. PAGE 173 H3458 — NAT/G ECO/TAC POLICY ADMIN

L66
SEYLER W.C.,"DOCTORAL DISSERTATIONS IN POLITICAL SCIENCE IN UNIVERSITIES OF THE UNITED STATES AND CANADA." INT/ORG LOC/G ADMIN...INT/LAW MGT GOV/COMP. PAGE 142 H2836 — BIBLIOG LAW NAT/G

S66
"FURTHER READING." INDIA LOC/G NAT/G PLAN ADMIN WEALTH...GEOG SOC CONCPT CENSUS 20. PAGE 2 H0049 — BIBLIOG ECO/UNDEV TEC/DEV PROVS

S66
FLEMING W.G.,"AUTHORITY, EFFICIENCY, AND ROLE STRESS: PROBLEMS IN THE DEVELOPMENT OF EAST AFRICAN BUREAUCRACIES." AFR UGANDA STRUCT PROB/SOLV ROUTINE INGP/REL ROLE...MGT SOC GP/COMP GOV/COMP 20 TANGANYIKA AFRICA/E. PAGE 51 H1024 — DOMIN EFFICIENCY COLONIAL ADMIN

S66
HAIGH G.,"FIELD TRAINING IN HUMAN RELATIONS FOR THE PEACE CORPS." CONSULT CREATE EDU/PROP ADMIN TASK GP/REL ATTIT PERSON...PSY OBS SOC/EXP PEACE/CORP. PAGE 64 H1276 — CULTURE PERS/REL FOR/AID ADJUST

S66
MATTHEWS D.G.,"ETHIOPIAN OUTLINE: A BIBLIOGRAPHIC RESEARCH GUIDE." ETHIOPIA LAW STRUCT ECO/UNDEV AGRI LABOR SECT CHIEF DELIB/GP EX/STRUC ADMIN...LING ORG/CHARTS 20. PAGE 105 H2095 — BIBLIOG NAT/G DIPLOM POL/PAR

S66
MATTHEWS D.G.,"PRELUDE-COUP D'ETAT-MILITARY GOVERNMENT: A BIBLIOGRAPHICAL AND RESEARCH GUIDE TO NIGERIAN POL AND GOVT, JAN, 1965-66." AFR NIGER LAW CONSTN POL/PAR LEGIS CIVMIL/REL GOV/REL...STAT 20. PAGE 105 H2096 — BIBLIOG NAT/G ADMIN CHOOSE

S66
ROTHCHILD D.,"THE LIMITS OF FEDERALISM: AN EXAMINATION OF POLITICAL INSTITUTIONAL TRANSFER IN AFRICA." AFR CONSTN CULTURE ELITES ECO/UNDEV KIN PROB/SOLV ADMIN ORD/FREE PWR...POLICY 20. PAGE 135 H2695 — FEDERAL NAT/G NAT/LISM COLONIAL

B67
AMERICAN FRIENDS SERVICE COMM,IN PLACE OF WAR. NAT/G ACT/RES DIPLOM ADMIN NUC/PWR EFFICIENCY ...POLICY 20. PAGE 6 H0122 — PEACE PACIFISM WAR DETER

B67
ANDERSON C.W.,POLITICS AND ECONOMIC CHANGE IN LATIN AMERICA. L/A+17C INDUS NAT/G OP/RES ADMIN DEMAND ...POLICY STAT CHARTS NAT/COMP 20. PAGE 6 H0125 — ECO/UNDEV PROB/SOLV PLAN ECO/TAC

B67
ARIKPO O.,THE DEVELOPMENT OF MODERN NIGERIA. AFR NIGERIA SOCIETY ECO/UNDEV KIN ADMIN FEDERAL NAT/LISM ORD/FREE WEALTH...POLICY GEOG BIBLIOG 19/20. PAGE 8 H0163 — NAT/G CULTURE CONSTN COLONIAL

B67
DICKSON P.G.M.,THE FINANCIAL REVOLUTION IN ENGLAND. UK NAT/G TEC/DEV ADMIN GOV/REL...SOC METH/CNCPT CHARTS GP/COMP BIBLIOG 17/18. PAGE 41 H0823 — ECO/DEV FINAN CAP/ISM MGT

B67
EVANS R.H.,COEXISTENCE: COMMUNISM AND ITS PRACTICE IN BOLOGNA, 1945-1965. ITALY CAP/ISM ADMIN CHOOSE PEACE ORD/FREE...SOC STAT DEEP/INT SAMP CHARTS BIBLIOG 20. PAGE 48 H0952 — MARXISM CULTURE MUNIC POL/PAR

B67
FIELD M.G.,SOVIET SOCIALIZED MEDICINE. USSR FINAN R+D PROB/SOLV ADMIN SOCISM...MGT SOC CONCPT 20. PAGE 50 H0993 — PUB/INST HEALTH NAT/G MARXISM

B67
GELLHORN W.,OMBUDSMEN AND OTHERS: CITIZENS' PROTECTORS IN NINE COUNTRIES. WOR+45 LAW CONSTN LEGIS INSPECT ADJUD ADMIN CONTROL CT/SYS CHOOSE — NAT/COMP REPRESENT INGP/REL

PERS/REL...STAT CHARTS 20. PAGE 55 H1109 PROB/SOLV

B67
GIFFORD P.,BRITAIN AND GERMANY IN AFRICA. AFR GERMANY UK ECO/UNDEV LEAD WAR NAT/LISM ATTIT ...POLICY HIST/WRIT METH/COMP ANTHOL BIBLIOG 19/20 WWI. PAGE 56 H1123 COLONIAL ADMIN DIPLOM NAT/COMP

B67
GROSS B.M.,ACTION UNDER PLANNING: THE GUIDANCE OF ECONOMIC DEVELOPMENT. STRUCT R+D NAT/G ACT/RES HABITAT...DECISION 20. PAGE 62 H1232 ECO/UNDEV PLAN ADMIN MGT

B67
JAIN R.K.,MANAGEMENT OF STATE ENTERPRISES. INDIA SOCIETY FINAN WORKER BUDGET ADMIN CONTROL OWN 20. PAGE 79 H1584 NAT/G SOCISM INDUS MGT

B67
KONCZACKI Z.A.,PUBLIC FINANCE AND ECONOMIC DEVELOPMENT OF NATAL 1893-1910. TAX ADMIN COLONIAL ...STAT CHARTS BIBLIOG 19/20 NATAL. PAGE 88 H1755 ECO/TAC FINAN NAT/G ECO/UNDEV

B67
LAMBERT J.,LATIN AMERICA: SOCIAL STRUCTURES AND POLITICAL INSTITUTIONS. STRUCT TEC/DEV DIPLOM ADMIN COLONIAL LEAD ATTIT...SOC CLASSIF NAT/COMP 17/20. PAGE 90 H1801 L/A+17C NAT/G ECO/UNDEV SOCIETY

B67
LENG S.C.,JUSTICE IN COMMUNIST CHINA: A SURVEY OF THE JUDICIAL SYSTEM OF THE CHINESE PEOPLE'S REPUBLIC. CHINA/COM LAW CONSTN LOC/G NAT/G PROF/ORG CONSULT FORCES ADMIN CRIME ORD/FREE...BIBLIOG 20 MAO. PAGE 94 H1877 CT/SYS ADJUD JURID MARXISM

B67
MICKIEWICZ E.P.,SOVIET POLITICAL SCHOOLS: THE COMMUNIST PARTY ADULT INSTRUCTION SYSTEM. COM USSR INTELL SCHOOL WORKER CREATE PRESS ADMIN CONTROL ATTIT KNOWL...PROG/TEAC SOC/INTEG 20 COM/PARTY. PAGE 110 H2200 NAT/G EDU/PROP AGE/A MARXISM

B67
MILNE R.S.,GOVERNMENT AND POLITICS IN MALAYSIA. INDONESIA MALAYSIA LOC/G EX/STRUC FORCES DIPLOM GP/REL 20 SINGAPORE. PAGE 111 H2217 NAT/G LEGIS ADMIN

B67
MORRIS A.J.A.,PARLIAMENTARY DEMOCRACY IN THE NINETEENTH CENTURY. UK INDUS LOC/G NAT/G POL/PAR CONSULT LEGIS INT/TRADE ADMIN CHOOSE SUFF SOVEREIGN 19 PARLIAMENT. PAGE 113 H2261 TIME/SEQ CONSTN PARL/PROC POPULISM

B67
NESS G.D.,BUREAUCRACY AND RURAL DEVELOPMENT IN MALAYSIA. MALAYSIA UK SOCIETY FINAN INDUS WORKER TEC/DEV ECO/TAC COLONIAL EQUILIB ORD/FREE...STAT CHARTS 20. PAGE 117 H2330 ECO/UNDEV PLAN NAT/G ADMIN

B67
OVERSEAS DEVELOPMENT INSTIT,EFFECTIVE AID. WOR+45 INT/ORG TEC/DEV DIPLOM INT/TRADE ADMIN. PAGE 122 H2434 FOR/AID ECO/UNDEV ECO/TAC NAT/COMP

B67
POSNER M.V.,ITALIAN PUBLIC ENTERPRISE. ITALY ECO/DEV FINAN INDUS CREATE ECO/TAC ADMIN CONTROL EFFICIENCY PRODUC...TREND CHARTS 20. PAGE 127 H2545 NAT/G PLAN CAP/ISM SOCISM

B67
RAVKIN A.,THE NEW STATES OF AFRICA (HEADLINE SERIES, NO. 183((PAMPHLET). CULTURE STRUCT INDUS COLONIAL NAT/LISM...SOC 20. PAGE 130 H2597 AFR ECO/UNDEV SOCIETY ADMIN

B67
ROELOFS H.M.,THE LANGUAGE OF MODERN POLITICS: AN INTRODUCTION TO THE STUDY OF GOVERNMENT. DIPLOM ADMIN MARXISM NEW/LIB...JURID CONCPT METH/COMP T 20. PAGE 133 H2657 LEAD NAT/COMP PERS/REL NAT/G

B67
RUDMAN H.C.,THE SCHOOL AND STATE IN THE USSR. COM USSR ACADEM LABOR LOC/G PUB/INST EDU/PROP GP/REL ROLE...POLICY DECISION MGT CHARTS 20. PAGE 136 H2712 SCHOOL ADMIN NAT/G POL/PAR

B67
SCHWARTZ M.A.,PUBLIC OPINION AND CANADIAN IDENTITY. CANADA SOCIETY LOC/G DIPLOM ADMIN LEAD REGION GP/REL SAMP. PAGE 141 H2812 ATTIT NAT/G NAT/LISM POL/PAR

B67
VENKATESWARAN R.J.,CABINET GOVERNMENT IN INDIA. INDIA UK SOCIETY OP/RES COLONIAL LEAD EFFICIENCY ORD/FREE 20. PAGE 162 H3241 DELIB/GP ADMIN CONSTN NAT/G

B67
WARREN S.,THE AMERICAN PRESIDENT. POL/PAR FORCES LEGIS DIPLOM ECO/TAC ADMIN EXEC PWR...ANTHOL 18/20 ROOSEVLT/F KENNEDY/JF JOHNSON/LB TRUMAN/HS WILSON/W. PAGE 165 H3312 CHIEF LEAD NAT/G CONSTN

B67
ZALESKI E.,PLANNING REFORMS IN THE SOVIET UNION 1962-1966. COM USSR NAT/G CONFER CONTROL EFFICIENCY MARXISM...POLICY DECISION 20. PAGE 172 H3446 ECO/DEV PLAN ADMIN

CENTRAL

L67
"A PROPOS DES INCITATIONS FINANCIERES AUX GROUPEMENTS DES COMMUNES: ESSAI D'INTERPRETATION." FRANCE NAT/G LEGIS ADMIN GOV/REL CENTRAL 20. PAGE 3 H0051 LOC/G ECO/TAC APPORT ADJUD

L67
AUSTIN D.A.,"POLITICAL CONFLICT IN AFRICA." CONSTN NAT/G CREATE ADMIN COLONIAL ORD/FREE MARXISM POPULISM SOCISM...NAT/COMP ANTHOL 20. PAGE 9 H0180 ANOMIE AFR POL/PAR

L67
PICKERING J.F.,"RECRUITMENT TO THE ADMINISTRATIVE CLASS, 1960-1964: PART 2" UK STRATA NAT/G WORKER ...STAT CHARTS 20. PAGE 125 H2505 PERS/COMP ADMIN KNO/TEST EDU/PROP

L67
RUTH J.M.,"THE ADMINISTRATION OF WATER RESOURCES IN GUATEMALA." GUATEMALA L/A+17C DIST/IND LOC/G NAT/G EX/STRUC ADMIN GOV/REL DEMAND EQUILIB WEALTH...GEOG MGT 20. PAGE 136 H2723 EFFICIENCY ECO/UNDEV PLAN ACT/RES

L67
TAMBIAH S.J.,"THE POLITICS OF LANGUAGE IN INDIA AND CEYLON." CEYLON INDIA NAT/G DOMIN ADMIN...SOC 20. PAGE 152 H3039 POL/PAR LING NAT/LISM REGION

S67
ALEXANDER A.,"CANADA'S PARLIAMENTARY SECRETARIES: THEIR POLITICAL AND CONSTITUTIONAL POSITION." CANADA UK NAT/G POL/PAR GOV/REL...GOV/COMP 20. PAGE 5 H0099 CONSTN ADMIN EX/STRUC DELIB/GP

S67
ANDERSON L.G.,"ADMINISTERING A GOVERNMENT SOCIAL SERVICE" NEW/ZEALND EX/STRUC TASK ROLE 20. PAGE 6 H0129 ADMIN NAT/G DELIB/GP SOC/WK

S67
BERLINER J.S.,"RUSSIA'S BUREAUCRATS - WHY THEY'RE REACTIONARY." USSR NAT/G OP/RES PROB/SOLV TEC/DEV CONTROL SANCTION EFFICIENCY DRIVE PERSON...TECHNIC SOC 20. PAGE 15 H0308 CREATE ADMIN INDUS PRODUC

S67
BOSHER J.F.,"GOVERNMENT AND PRIVATE INTERESTS IN NEW FRANCE." CANADA FRANCE INDUS LG/CO SML/CO CAP/ISM INT/TRADE COLONIAL GP/REL...HIST/WRIT 17/18. PAGE 19 H0381 NAT/G FINAN ADMIN CONTROL

S67
BRADLEY A.W.,"CONSTITUTION-MAKING IN UGANDA." UGANDA LAW CHIEF DELIB/GP LEGIS ADMIN EXEC PARL/PROC RACE/REL ORD/FREE...GOV/COMP 20. PAGE 20 H0397 NAT/G CREATE CONSTN FEDERAL

S67
COLLINS B.A.,"SOME NOTES ON PUBLIC SERVICE COMMISSIONS IN THE COMMONWEALTH CARIBBEAN." JAMAICA L/A+17C TRINIDAD UK NAT/G OP/RES DOMIN SENIOR COLONIAL CONTROL INGP/REL CENTRAL EFFICIENCY PWR ...DECISION 20. PAGE 31 H0631 ADMIN EX/STRUC ECO/UNDEV CHOOSE

S67
DIAMANT A.,"EUROPEAN MODELS OF BUREAUCRACY AND DEVELOPMENT." EX/STRUC PLAN ADMIN CONTROL ROUTINE GOV/REL CENTRAL...DECISION TIME/SEQ CHARTS. PAGE 41 H0818 NAT/G EQUILIB ACT/RES NAT/COMP

S67
DRYDEN S.,"LOCAL GOVERNMENT IN TANZANIA PART II" TANZANIA LAW NAT/G POL/PAR CONTROL PARTIC REPRESENT ...DECISION 20. PAGE 42 H0850 LOC/G GOV/REL ADMIN STRUCT

S67
GRANT C.H.,"RURAL LOCAL GOVERNMENT IN GUYANA AND BRITISH HONDURAS." GUYANA HONDURAS L/A+17C AGRI NAT/G EX/STRUC ACT/RES REGION GOV/REL EFFICIENCY ORD/FREE 20. PAGE 60 H1196 ECO/UNDEV LOC/G ADMIN MUNIC

S67
HEBAL J.J.,"APPROACHES TO REGIONAL AND METROPOLITAN GOVERNMENTS IN THE UNITED STATES AND CANADA." CANADA FUT USA+45 MUNIC...TREND 20. PAGE 69 H1380 ADMIN REGION LOC/G NAT/COMP

S67
HOFMANN W.,"THE PUBLIC INTEREST PRESSURE GROUP: THE CASE OF THE DEUTSCHE STADTETAG." GERMANY GERMANY/W CONSTN STRUCT NAT/G CENTRAL FEDERAL PWR...TIME/SEQ 20. PAGE 72 H1447 LOC/G VOL/ASSN LOBBY ADMIN

S67
JOINER C.A.,"THE UBIQUITY OF THE ADMINISTRATIVE ROLE IN COUNTERINSURGENC. VIETNAM/S SOCIETY STRUCT NAT/G GP/REL EFFICIENCY 20. PAGE 81 H1627 ADMIN POLICY REV ATTIT

S67
KROLL M.,"POLITICAL LEADERSHIP AND ADMINISTRATIVE COMMUNICATIONS IN NEW NATION STATES* CASE STUDY OF TRINIDAD AND TOBAGO." L/A+17C TRINIDAD INTELL OP/RES DOMIN COLONIAL LEAD GP/REL CENTRAL EFFICIENCY...DECISION OBS METH/COMP 20. PAGE 89 H1774 NAT/G ADMIN EDU/PROP CONTROL

S67
LEVCIK B.,"WAGES AND EMPLOYMENT PROBLEMS IN THE NEW SYSTEM OF PLANNED MANAGEMENT IN CZECHOSLOVAKIA." MARXISM WORKER

CZECHOSLVK EUR+WWI NAT/G OP/RES PLAN ADMIN ROUTINE INGP/REL CENTRAL EFFICIENCY PRODUC DECISION. PAGE 95 H1895 — MGT PAY

S67

MALLORY J.R.,"THE MINISTER'S OFFICE STAFF* AN UNREFORMED PART OF PUBLIC SERVICE." CONSTN ELITES STRATA NAT/G PROB/SOLV TASK CHOOSE PERS/REL EFFICIENCY...DECISION 20. PAGE 102 H2033 — CANADA ADMIN EX/STRUC STRUCT

S67

READ J.S.,"CENSORED." UGANDA CONSTN INTELL SOCIETY NAT/G DIPLOM PRESS WRITING ADJUD ADMIN COLONIAL RISK...IDEA/COMP 20. PAGE 130 H2602 — EDU/PROP AFR CREATE

S67

SCOVILLE W.J.,"GOVERNMENT REGULATION AND GROWTH IN THE FRENCH PAPER INDUSTRY DURING THE EIGHTEENTH CENTURY." FRANCE MOD/EUR FINAN CAP/ISM TAX ADMIN CONTROL PRIVIL LAISSEZ...POLICY 18. PAGE 141 H2818 — NAT/G PROC/MFG ECO/DEV INGP/REL

S67

SUBRAMANIAM V.,"REPRESENTATIVE BUREAUCRACY: A REASSESSMENT." USA+45 ELITES LOC/G NAT/G ADMIN GOV/REL PRIVIL DRIVE ROLE...POLICY CENSUS 20 CIVIL/SERV BUREAUCRCY. PAGE 150 H3006 — STRATA GP/REL MGT GOV/COMP

S67

THIEN T.T.,"VIETNAM: A CASE OF SOCIAL ALIENATION." VIETNAM AGRI FORCES FOR/AID ADMIN REPRESENT INGP/REL PWR 19/20. PAGE 154 H3071 — NAT/G ELITES WORKER STRANGE

S67

TIKHOMIROV I.A.,"DIVISION OF POWERS OR DIVISION OF LABOR?" USSR NAT/G DELIB/GP ADJUD GP/REL MARXISM SOCISM 20. PAGE 155 H3093 — BAL/PWR WORKER STRATA ADMIN

S67

TIVEY L.,"THE POLITICAL CONSEQUENCES OF ECONOMIC PLANNING." UK CONSTN INDUS ACT/RES ADMIN CONTROL LOBBY REPRESENT EFFICIENCY SUPEGO SOVEREIGN ...DECISION 20. PAGE 155 H3108 — PLAN POLICY NAT/G

S67

VON LAUE T.H.,"WESTERNIZATION, REVOLUTION AND THE SEARCH FOR A BASIS OF AUTHORITY - RUSSIA IN 1917." USSR ELITES INTELL ECO/UNDEV NAT/G WORKER ECO/TAC TAX ADMIN LEAD AUTHORIT 20 LENIN/VI. PAGE 164 H3274 — MARXISM REV COM DOMIN

S67

WHITE W.L.,"THE TREASURY BOARD AND PARLIAMENT." CANADA CONSTN CONSULT LEGIS LEAD PARL/PROC GP/REL ...DECISION 20. PAGE 167 H3351 — FINAN DELIB/GP NAT/G ADMIN

S67

WRAITH R.E.,"ADMINISTRATIVE CHANGE IN THE NEW AFRICA." AFR LG/CO ADJUD INGP/REL PWR...RECORD GP/COMP 20. PAGE 171 H3416 — ADMIN NAT/G LOC/G ECO/UNDEV

B82

MACDONALD D.,AFRICANA; OR, THE HEART OF HEATHEN AFRICA, VOL. II: MISSION LIFE. SOCIETY STRATA KIN CREATE EDU/PROP ADMIN COERCE LITERACY HEALTH...MYTH WORSHIP 19 LIVNGSTN/D MISSION NEGRO. PAGE 100 H1990 — SECT AFR CULTURE ORD/FREE

B87

KINNEAR J.B.,PRINCIPLES OF CIVIL GOVERNMENT. MOD/EUR USA-45 CONSTN LOC/G EX/STRUC ADMIN PARL/PROC RACE/REL...CONCPT 18/19. PAGE 86 H1718 — POL/PAR NAT/G GOV/COMP REPRESENT

B89

ASHBEE H.S.,A BIBLIOGRAPHY OF TUNISIA FROM THE EARLIEST TIMES TO THE END OF 1888. AGRI ADMIN ...GEOG TUNIS. PAGE 8 H0171 — BIBLIOG COLONIAL CULTURE NAT/G

ADMINISTRATIVE STAFF COLLEGE H0070

ADMINISTRATIVE MANAGEMENT....SEE MGT

ADNITT F.W. H0071

ADOKO A. H0072

ADOLESCENCE....SEE AGE/Y

ADRIAN C.R. H0073

ADU A.L. H0074

ADVERT/ADV....ADVERTISING ADVISORY COMMISSION

ADVERTISING....SEE SERV/IND+EDU/PROP; SEE ALSO TV, PRESS

AEA....ATOMIC ENERGY AUTHORITY OF UN; SEE ALSO NUC/PWR

AEC....ATOMIC ENERGY COMMISSION; SEE ALSO NUC/PWR

B63

US ATOMIC ENERGY COMMISSION,ATOMIC ENERGY IN THE SOVIET UNION: TRIP REPORT OF THE US ATOMIC ENERGY DELEGATION, MAY 1933. USSR R+D NAT/G CONSULT CREATE DIPLOM ADMIN ROUTINE EFFICIENCY PRODUC KNOWL SKILL ...NAT/COMP 20 AEC TRAVEL TREATY. PAGE 159 H3176 — METH/COMP OP/RES TEC/DEV NUC/PWR

AFGHANISTN....SEE ALSO ISLAM, ASIA

B55

UN ECONOMIC COMN ASIA & FAR E,ECONOMIC SURVEY OF ASIA AND THE FAR EAST, 1954. AFGHANISTN CEYLON INDIA PHILIPPINE S/ASIA ECO/DEV FINAN INDUS INT/TRADE PRODUC WEALTH...STAT CHARTS 20 CHINJAP. PAGE 158 H3158 — ECO/UNDEV PRICE NAT/COMP ASIA

B56

WILBER D.N.,ANNOTATED BIBLIOGRAPHY OF AFGHANISTAN. AFGHANISTN...ART/METH GEOG HUM SOC CON/ANAL 19/20. PAGE 168 H3358 — BIBLIOG/A SOCIETY NAT/G ASIA

B57

CENTRAL ASIAN RESEARCH CENTRE,BIBLIOGRAPHY OF RECENT SOVIET SOURCE MATERIAL ON SOVIET CENTRAL ASIA AND THE BORDERLANDS. AFGHANISTN INDIA PAKISTAN UAR USSR ECO/UNDEV AGRI EXTR/IND INDUS ACADEM ADMIN ...HEAL HUM LING CON/ANAL 20. PAGE 28 H0567 — BIBLIOG/A COM CULTURE NAT/G

B66

US DEPARTMENT OF THE ARMY,SOUTH ASIA: A STRATEGIC SURVEY (PAMPHLET NO. 550-3). AFGHANISTN INDIA NEPAL PAKISTAN ECO/UNDEV INT/ORG POL/PAR FORCES FOR/AID INT/TRADE LEAD WAR...POLICY SOC TREND 20. PAGE 160 H3195 — BIBLIOG/A S/ASIA DIPLOM NAT/G

AFL/CIO....AMERICAN FEDERATION OF LABOR, CONGRESS OF INDUSTRIAL ORGANIZATIONS

B39

MARQUAND H.A.,ORGANIZED LABOUR IN FOUR CONTINENTS. EUR+WWI USA-45 INDUS NAT/G PAY GP/REL TOTALISM ATTIT WEALTH ALL/IDEOS...TREND NAT/COMP 20 ILO AFL/CIO EUROPE CHINJAP MEXIC/AMER. PAGE 103 H2055 — LABOR WORKER CONCPT ANTHOL

AFLAK/M....MICHEL AFLAK

AFR....AFRICA

N

BROCKWAY A.F.,AFRICAN SOCIALISM. EUR+WWI GHANA ISLAM UAR ECO/UNDEV CAP/ISM INT/TRADE COLONIAL COERCE GOV/REL DISCRIM 20 NEGRO NKRUMAH/K NASSER/G. PAGE 21 H0423 — AFR SOCISM MARXISM

N

SCHADERA I.,SELECT BIBLIOGRAPHY OF SOUTH AFRICAN NATIVE LIFE AND PROBLEMS. SOUTH/AFR LAW CULTURE ECO/UNDEV COLONIAL PARTIC...POLICY LING 20. PAGE 138 H2768 — BIBLIOG/A SOC AFR STRUCT

N

TOTEMEYER G.,SOUTH AFRICA; SOUTHWEST AFRICA: A BIBLIOGRAPHY, 1945-1963. AFR SOUTH/AFR PRESS...SOC 20. PAGE 157 H3134 — BIBLIOG CULTURE NAT/G EDU/PROP

N

NEUE POLITISCHE LITERATUR. AFR ASIA EUR+WWI GERMANY RUSSIA SOCIETY ECO/DEV ECO/UNDEV PLAN PROB/SOLV LEAD MARXISM...PHIL/SCI CONCPT 20. PAGE 1 H0008 — BIBLIOG DIPLOM COM NAT/G

N

AFRICAN RESEARCH BULLETIN. AFR CULTURE NAT/G COLONIAL...SOC 20. PAGE 1 H0010 — BIBLIOG/A DIPLOM PRESS

N

THE MIDDLE EAST AND NORTH AFRICA. AFR ISLAM CULTURE ECO/UNDEV AGRI NAT/G TEC/DEV FOR/AID INT/TRADE EDU/PROP...CHARTS 20. PAGE 2 H0026 — INDEX INDUS FINAN STAT

N

AFRICAN BIBLIOGRAPHIC CENTER,A CURRENT BIBLIOGRAPHY ON AFRICAN AFFAIRS. LAW CULTURE ECO/UNDEV LABOR SECT DIPLOM FOR/AID COLONIAL NAT/LISM...LING 20. PAGE 4 H0075 — BIBLIOG/A AFR NAT/G REGION

N

HOOVER INSTITUTION,UNITED STATES AND CANADIAN PUBLICATIONS ON AFRICA. CULTURE ECO/UNDEV AGRI TEC/DEV EDU/PROP COLONIAL RACE/REL NAT/LISM ATTIT HEALTH...SOC SOC/WK 20. PAGE 73 H1464 — BIBLIOG DIPLOM NAT/G AFR

N

NORTHWESTERN UNIVERSITY LIB,JOINT ACQUISITIONS LIST OF AFRICANA. AFR SOCIETY STRUCT EDU/PROP COLONIAL GP/REL RACE/REL NAT/LISM SOVEREIGN...SOC 20. PAGE 119 H2377 — BIBLIOG CULTURE ECO/UNDEV INDUS

NCO

CARRINGTON C.E.,THE COMMONWEALTH IN AFRICA (PAMPHLET). UK STRUCT NAT/G COLONIAL REPRESENT GOV/REL RACE/REL NAT/LISM...MAJORIT 20 EEC NEGRO COLD/WAR. PAGE 27 H0540 — ECO/UNDEV AFR DIPLOM PLAN

B00

MOCKLER-FERRYMAN A.,BRITISH WEST AFRICA. FRANCE GERMANY NIGER SIER/LEONE UK CULTURE DIPLOM WAR RACE/REL PRODUC PROFIT WEALTH...POLICY PREDICT 19. — AFR COLONIAL INT/TRADE

PAGE 112 H2232
CAP/ISM

B10
MENDELSSOHN S.,SOUTH AFRICAN BIBLIOGRAPHY (2 VOLS.). SOUTH/AFR EXTR/IND LABOR SECT DIPLOM INT/TRADE COLONIAL RACE/REL DISCRIM...GEOG 20. PAGE 109 H2172
BIBLIOG/A AFR NAT/G NAT/LISM

B12
SONOLET L.,L'AFRIQUE OCCIDENTALE FRANCAISE. FRANCE AGRI INDUS NAT/G SECT FORCES INT/TRADE EDU/PROP RACE/REL HEALTH ORD/FREE...CHARTS 19/20 NEGRO AFRICA/W. PAGE 147 H2933
DOMIN ADMIN COLONIAL AFR

B16
CALVERT A.F.,SOUTHWEST AFRICA 1884-1914 (2ND ED.). GERMANY EXTR/IND NAT/G FORCES...GEOG AUD/VIS CHARTS 19/20 RESOURCE/N AFRICA/SW. PAGE 25 H0508
COLONIAL ECO/UNDEV AFR

N19
HANNA A.J.,EUROPEAN RULE IN AFRICA (PAMPHLET). BELGIUM FRANCE MOD/EUR UK WOR+45 WOR-45 ECO/UNDEV NAT/G PARTIC SOVEREIGN...NAT/COMP 19/20. PAGE 66 H1314
DIPLOM COLONIAL AFR NAT/LISM

N19
PROVISIONS SECTION OAU,ORGANIZATION OF AFRICAN UNITY: BASIC DOCUMENTS AND RESOLUTIONS (PAMPHLET). AFR CULTURE ECO/UNDEV DIPLOM ECO/TAC EDU/PROP COLONIAL ARMS/CONT NUC/PWR RACE/REL DISCRIM NAT/LISM 20 UN OAU. PAGE 128 H2564
CONSTN EX/STRUC SOVEREIGN INT/ORG

N19
SALKEVER L.R.,SUB-SAHARA AFRICA (PAMPHLET). AFR USSR EXTR/IND NAT/G SCHOOL DIPLOM COLONIAL WEALTH ...GEOG CHARTS 16/20. PAGE 137 H2742
ECO/UNDEV TEC/DEV TASK INT/TRADE

N19
SENGHOR L.S.,AFRICAN SOCIALISM (PAMPHLET). AFR FRANCE MALI USSR ELITES ECO/UNDEV NAT/G DIPLOM DOMIN EDU/PROP ATTIT 20 NEGRO. PAGE 141 H2827
SOCISM MARXISM ORD/FREE NAT/LISM

B23
WILLOUGHBY W.C.,RACE PROBLEMS IN THE NEW AFRICA: A STUDY OF THE RELATION OF BANTU AND BRITONS IN THOSE PARTS OF BANTU AFRICA... AFR STRUCT SECT DOMIN EDU/PROP GP/REL ATTIT WORSHIP 20 BANTU EUROPE MISSION CHRISTIAN. PAGE 168 H3372
KIN COLONIAL RACE/REL CULTURE

B24
WALKER F.D.,AFRICA AND HER PEOPLES. ISLAM STRUCT FAM SECT EDU/PROP INGP/REL RACE/REL HABITAT...GEOG SOC IDEA/COMP WORSHIP 20 NEGRO. PAGE 164 H3292
CULTURE AFR GP/COMP KIN

B25
WILLIAMS B.,THE SELBORNE MEMORANDUM. AFR FUT SOUTH/AFR UK NAT/G BUDGET DIPLOM REGION GOV/REL SOVEREIGN...POLICY CHARTS 20 UNIFICA SELBORNE/W. PAGE 168 H3365
COLONIAL PROVS

B26
MCPHEE A.,THE ECONOMIC REVOLUTION IN BRITISH WEST AFRICA. AFR UK CULTURE DIST/IND FINAN INDUS PLAN GP/REL RACE/REL 20 AFRICA/W. PAGE 107 H2148
ECO/UNDEV INT/TRADE COLONIAL GEOG

B27
SMITH E.W.,THE GOLDEN STOOL: SOME ASPECTS OF THE CONFLICT OF CULTURES IN AFRICA. AFR FINAN INDUS SECT INT/TRADE COERCE CHOOSE RACE/REL ATTIT...GEOG LING 20 NEGRO. PAGE 145 H2907
COLONIAL CULTURE GP/REL EDU/PROP

B28
BUELL R.,THE NATIVE PROBLEM IN AFRICA. KIN LABOR LOC/G ECO/TAC ROUTINE ORD/FREE...REC/INT KNO/TEST CENSUS TREND CHARTS SOC/EXP STERTYP 20. PAGE 23 H0466
AFR CULTURE

B29
ROBERTS S.H.,HISTORY OF FRENCH COLONIAL POLICY. AFR ASIA L/A+17C S/ASIA CULTURE ECO/DEV ECO/UNDEV FINAN NAT/G PLAN ECO/TAC DOMIN ROUTINE SOVEREIGN...OBS HIST/WRIT TREND CHARTS VAL/FREE 19/20. PAGE 132 H2642
INT/ORG ACT/RES FRANCE COLONIAL

B30
OLDMAN J.H.,WHITE AND BLACK IN AFRICA. AFR STRUCT COLONIAL PARTIC DISCRIM ISOLAT PRIVIL 20 SMUTS/JAN NEGRO WHITE/SUP. PAGE 121 H2412
SOVEREIGN ORD/FREE RACE/REL NAT/G

B30
SMUTS J.C.,AFRICA AND SOME WORLD PROBLEMS. RHODESIA SOUTH/AFR CULTURE ECO/UNDEV INDUS INT/ORG SECT PROB/SOLV REGION GOV/REL DISCRIM ATTIT 19/20 LEAGUE/NAT LIVNGSTN/D NEGRO. PAGE 146 H2921
LEGIS AFR COLONIAL RACE/REL

B32
CARDINALL AW,A BIBLIOGRAPHY OF THE GOLD COAST. AFR UK NAT/G EX/STRUC ATTIT...POLICY 19/20. PAGE 26 H0527
BIBLIOG ADMIN COLONIAL DIPLOM

B35
GORER G.,AFRICA DANCES: A BOOK ABOUT WEST AFRICAN NEGROES. STRUCT LOC/G SECT FORCES TAX ADMIN COLONIAL...ART/METH MYTH WORSHIP 20 NEGRO AFRICA/W CHRISTIAN RITUAL. PAGE 59 H1181
AFR ATTIT CULTURE SOCIETY

B37
DE KIEWIET C.W.,THE IMPERIAL FACTOR IN SOUTH AFRICA. AFR SOUTH/AFR UK WAR...POLICY SOC 19. PAGE 38 H0759
DIPLOM COLONIAL CULTURE

B38
COUPLAND R.,EAST AFRICA AND ITS INVADERS. AFR ISLAM STRATA SECT FORCES DIPLOM TRIBUTE CONTROL DISCRIM NAT/LISM 19 AFRICA/E EUROPE MISSION. PAGE 34 H0680
CULTURE ELITES COLONIAL MARKET

B39
HILL R.L.,A BIBLIOGRAPHY OF THE ANGLO-EGYPTIAN SUDAN FROM THE EARLIEST TIMES TO 1937. AFR ETHIOPIA SUDAN UAR LAW COM/IND SECT RACE/REL...GEOG HEAL SOC LING 19/20 NEGRO. PAGE 71 H1417
BIBLIOG CULTURE NAT/COMP GP/COMP

B40
MEEK C.K.,EUROPE AND WEST AFRICA. AFR EUR+WWI EXTR/IND DIPLOM INT/TRADE EDU/PROP GP/REL...SOC 20. PAGE 108 H2158
CULTURE TEC/DEV ECO/UNDEV COLONIAL

B42
CONOVER H.F.,FRENCH COLONIES IN AFRICA: A LIST OF REFERENCES. ALGERIA FRANCE MOROCCO SOMALIA SUDAN CULTURE AGRI LOC/G SECT FORCES DIPLOM INT/TRADE NAT/LISM HEALTH...CON/ANAL 20. PAGE 32 H0641
BIBLIOG AFR ECO/UNDEV COLONIAL

B43
LEWIN E.,ROYAL EMPIRE SOCIETY BIBLIOGRAPHIES NO. 9: SUB-SAHARA AFRICA. ECO/UNDEV TEC/DEV DIPLOM ADMIN COLONIAL LEAD 20. PAGE 96 H1908
BIBLIOG AFR NAT/G SOCIETY

L44
HUXLEY J.,"THE FUTURE OF THE COLONIES." AFR SOCIETY NAT/G PLAN DOMIN COERCE ATTIT DRIVE ORD/FREE PWR WEALTH...TIME/SEQ TREND AUD/VIS CHARTS 20. PAGE 76 H1511
ECO/UNDEV FUT COLONIAL

B47
CROCKER W.R.,ON GOVERNING COLONIES: BEING AN OUTLINE OF THE REAL ISSUES AND A COMPARISON OF THE BRITISH, FRENCH, AND BELGIAN... AFR BELGIUM FRANCE UK CULTURE SOVEREIGN...OBS 20. PAGE 35 H0705
COLONIAL POLICY GOV/COMP ADMIN

B48
MINISTERE FINANCES ET ECO,BULLETIN BIBLIOGRAPHIQUE. AFR EUR+WWI FRANCE CULTURE STRUCT FINAN NAT/G ACT/RES INT/TRADE ADMIN REGION PRODUC STAT. PAGE 111 H2224
BIBLIOG/A ECO/UNDEV TEC/DEV COLONIAL

B50
HARLEY G.W.,MASKS AS AGENTS OF SOCIAL CONTROL IN NORTHEAST LIBERIA. AFR LIBERIA LAW CULTURE ADJUST CONSEN MORAL...GEOG SOC WORSHIP 20. PAGE 66 H1332
CONTROL ECO/UNDEV SECT CHIEF

B50
SMITH E.W.,AFRICAN IDEAS OF GOD. ATTIT...CONCPT MYTH IDEA/COMP ANTHOL BIBLIOG. PAGE 145 H2908
SOC AFR CULTURE SECT

B51
CARRINGTON C.E.,THE LIQUIDATION OF THE BRITISH EMPIRE. AFR NAT/G INT/TRADE COLONIAL RACE/REL ATTIT ORD/FREE...POLICY NAT/COMP 20 CMN/WLTH. PAGE 27 H0541
SOVEREIGN NAT/LISM DIPLOM GP/REL

B51
INTERNATIONAL AFRICAN INST,ETHNOGRAPHIC SURVEY OF AFRICA: WEST CENTRAL AFRICA (VOLS. I-III, 1951-1953). AFR RHODESIA CULTURE ECO/UNDEV HEREDITY ...GEOG SOC CHARTS BIBLIOG WORSHIP 20 CONGO/LEOP. PAGE 77 H1543
STRUCT KIN INGP/REL HABITAT

B52
FORDE L.D.,HABITAT, ECONOMY AND SOCIETY. AFR L/A+17C S/ASIA STRUCT AGRI INGP/REL...GEOG OBS BIBLIOG 20. PAGE 52 H1037
SOC HABITAT CULTURE ECO/UNDEV

B52
INTERNATIONAL AFRICAN INST,ETHNOGRAPHIC SURVEY OF AFRICA: SOUTHERN AFRICA (VOLS. I-III, 1952-1954). AFR SOUTH/AFR CULTURE ECO/UNDEV GOV/REL HEREDITY ...GEOG SOC CHARTS BIBLIOG WORSHIP 20. PAGE 77 H1544
STRUCT KIN INGP/REL HABITAT

B52
ISAACS H.R.,AFRICA: NEW CRISES IN THE MAKING (PAMPHLET). EUR+WWI USA+45 ELITES ECO/UNDEV WAR DISCRIM NAT/LISM ATTIT...POLICY NEW/IDEA CHARTS GOV/COMP 20 NEGRO COLD/WAR. PAGE 78 H1570
COLONIAL AFR RACE/REL ORD/FREE

B52
JULIEN C.A.,L'AFRIQUE DU NORD EN MARCHE: NATIONALISMES MUSULMANS ET SOUVERAINETE FRANCAISE (2ND ED). AFR ALGERIA FRANCE ISLAM MOROCCO NAT/G CONTROL ORD/FREE...POLICY 19/20 TUNIS MUSLIM. PAGE 82 H1641
NAT/LISM COERCE DOMIN COLONIAL

B52
US LIBRARY OF CONGRESS,INTRODUCTION TO AFRICA; A SELECTIVE GUIDE TO BACKGROUND READING. ECO/UNDEV COLONIAL GP/REL...SOC 19/20. PAGE 160 H3208
BIBLIOG/A AFR CULTURE NAT/G

B53
DAVIDSON B.,THE NEW WEST AFRICA: PROBLEMS OF INDEPENDENCE. UK AGRI TEC/DEV DIPLOM GP/REL RACE/REL SOVEREIGN...ANTHOL 20 AFRICA/W. PAGE 37 H0744
AFR COLONIAL ECO/UNDEV NAT/G

B54
FORDE C.D.,AFRICAN WORLDS. AFR CULTURE ROUTINE
SOCIETY

GP/REL PERS/REL ATTIT DRIVE ALL/VALS...OBS ANTHOL WORSHIP 20. PAGE 52 H1036 — KIN SOC

B54
PARRINDER G.,AFRICAN TRADITIONAL RELIGION. AFR SOCIETY EDU/PROP GP/REL PWR...SOC CONCPT IDEA/COMP WORSHIP 20 DEITY. PAGE 124 H2469 — SECT MYTH ATTIT CULTURE

B54
US LIBRARY OF CONGRESS,RESEARCH AND INFORMATION ON AFRICA: CONTINUING SOURCES. ISLAM ECO/UNDEV AGRI INDUS R+D ACADEM NAT/G INT/TRADE...SOC 20. PAGE 161 H3210 — BIBLIOG/A AFR PRESS COM/IND

S54
BALANDIER G.,"SOCIOLOGIE DE LA COLONISATION ET RELATIONS ENTRE SOCIETES GLOBALES." AFR SOCIETY ECO/UNDEV KIN DOMIN EDU/PROP RIGID/FLEX PWR...PSY CONCPT TREND TOT/POP. PAGE 10 H0203 — CULTURE SOC COLONIAL

B55
APTER D.E.,THE GOLD COAST IN TRANSITION. FUT CONSTN CULTURE SOCIETY ECO/UNDEV FAM KIN LOC/G NAT/G POL/PAR LEGIS TOP/EX EDU/PROP LEGIT ADMIN ATTIT PERSON PWR...CONCPT STAT INT CENSUS TOT/POP VAL/FREE. PAGE 7 H0149 — AFR SOVEREIGN

B55
INTERNATIONAL AFRICAN INST,ETHNOGRAPHIC SURVEY OF AFRICA: NORTH EASTERN AFRICA (VOLUMES 1-2, 1955-56). AFR ETHIOPIA CULTURE ECO/UNDEV KIN GOV/REL ATTIT HEREDITY...GEOG CHARTS BIBLIOG WORSHIP 20. PAGE 77 H1545 — STRUCT ECO/TAC INGP/REL HABITAT

B55
INTERNATIONAL AFRICAN INST,ETHNOGRAPHIC SURVEY OF AFRICA: WESTERN AFRICA: PEOPLES OF THE NIGER-BENUE CONFLUENCE. AFR NIGER CULTURE ECO/UNDEV KIN GOV/REL GP/REL ATTIT HEREDITY...CHARTS BIBLIOG WORSHIP 20. PAGE 77 H1546 — STRUCT GEOG HABITAT INGP/REL

S55
DE SMITH S.A.,"CONSTITUTIONAL MONARCHY IN BURGANDA." AFR UGANDA UK STRUCT CHIEF REGION INGP/REL ADJUST NAT/LISM SOVEREIGN CONSERVE ...POLICY 19/20 BURGANDA. PAGE 38 H0769 — NAT/G DIPLOM CONSTN COLONIAL

C55
APTER D.E.,"THE GOLD COAST IN TRANSITION." AFR CONSTN LOC/G LEGIS DIPLOM COLONIAL CONTROL GOV/REL ...CHARTS BIBLIOG 20 CMN/WLTH. PAGE 7 H0150 — ORD/FREE REPRESENT PARL/PROC NAT/G

B56
CENTRAL AFRICAN ARCHIVES,A GUIDE TO THE PUBLIC RECORDS OF SOUTHERN RHODESIA UNDER THE REGIME OF THE BRITISH SOUTH AFRICA COMPANY, 1890-1923. UK STRUCT NAT/G WRITING GP/REL 19/20. PAGE 28 H0566 — BIBLIOG/A COLONIAL ADMIN AFR

B56
GLUCKMAN M.,CUSTOM AND CONFLICT IN AFRICA. AFR FAM KIN NAT/G DOMIN DISCRIM DRIVE MORAL PWR...SOC BIBLIOG WORSHIP 20. PAGE 57 H1145 — CULTURE CREATE PERS/REL GP/COMP

B56
HATCH J.C.,NEW FROM AFRICA. AFR FUT UK NAT/G GUERRILLA ATTIT ORD/FREE PWR...AUD/VIS CHARTS 20. PAGE 68 H1354 — NAT/LISM COLONIAL RACE/REL

B56
INTERNATIONAL AFRICAN INST,SELECT ANNOTATED BIBLIOGRAPHY OF TROPICAL AFRICA. NAT/G EDU/PROP ADMIN HEALTH. PAGE 77 H1547 — BIBLIOG/A AFR SOC HABITAT

B56
INTERNATIONAL AFRICAN INST,SOCIAL IMPLICATIONS OF INDUSTRIALIZATION AND URBANIZATION IN AFRICA SOUTH OF THE SAHARA. SOUTH/AFR INDUS LABOR MUNIC WORKER TEC/DEV...SOC OBS TREND ANTHOL 20. PAGE 77 H1549 — AFR ECO/UNDEV ADJUST CULTURE

B56
MANNONI D.O.,PROSPERO AND CALIBAN: THE PSYCHOLOGY OF COLONIZATION. AFR EUR+WWI FAM KIN MUNIC SECT DOMIN ADMIN ATTIT DRIVE LOVE PWR RESPECT...PSY SOC CONCPT MYTH OBS DEEP/INT BIOG GEN/METH MALAGASY 20. PAGE 102 H2040 — CULTURE COLONIAL

B56
PADMORE G.,PAN-AFRICANISM OR COMMUNISM. AFR FUT NIGERIA INTELL NAT/G COLONIAL FEDERAL ATTIT DRIVE PWR RESPECT WEALTH MARXISM...CONCPT AUD/VIS STERTYP 20. PAGE 122 H2440 — POL/PAR NAT/LISM

B56
READ M.,EDUCATION AND SOCIAL CHANGE IN TROPICAL AREAS. AFR L/A+17C SOCIETY LITERACY PERCEPT PERSON WEALTH...HEAL PHIL/SCI SOC 20. PAGE 130 H2603 — EDU/PROP HABITAT DRIVE CULTURE

S56
KHAMA T.,"POLITICAL CHANGE IN AFRICAN SOCIETY." CONSTN SOCIETY LOC/G NAT/G POL/PAR EX/STRUC LEGIS LEGIT ADMIN CHOOSE REPRESENT NAT/LISM MORAL ORD/FREE PWR...CONCPT OBS TREND GEN/METH CMN/WLTH 17/20. PAGE 85 H1706 — AFR ELITES

N56
US HOUSE COMM FOREIGN AFFAIRS,REPORT OF THE SPECIAL STUDY MISSION TO AFRICA, SOUTH AND EAST OF THE SAHARA (PAMPHLET). AFR SOUTH/AFR USA+45 STRUCT INT/TRADE PARL/PROC NAT/LISM ATTIT ALL/VALS HEALTH ...POLICY 20 CONGRESS. PAGE 160 H3197 — FOR/AID COLONIAL ECO/UNDEV DIPLOM

B57
CONOVER H.F.,NORTH AND NORTHEAST AFRICA; A SELECTED ANNOTATED LIST OF WRITINGS. ALGERIA MOROCCO SUDAN UAR CULTURE INT/ORG PROB/SOLV ADJUD NAT/LISM PWR WEALTH...SOC 20 UN. PAGE 32 H0649 — BIBLIOG/A DIPLOM AFR ECO/UNDEV

B57
DEAN V.M.,THE NATURE OF THE NON-WESTERN WORLD. AFR ASIA L/A+17C S/ASIA CULTURE SOCIETY STRATA ECO/DEV DIPLOM ECO/TAC FOR/AID ATTIT DRIVE ALL/VALS ...RELATIV SOC CONCPT TIME/SEQ TREND TOT/POP 20. PAGE 39 H0778 — ECO/UNDEV STERTYP NAT/LISM

B57
HODGKIN T.,NATIONALISM IN COLONIAL AFRICA. STRATA STRUCT MUNIC NAT/G POL/PAR LEGIS ATTIT SOVEREIGN ...POLICY TREND BIBLIOG 20. PAGE 72 H1444 — AFR COLONIAL NAT/LISM DIPLOM

B57
INTERNATIONAL AFRICAN INST,ETHNOGRAPHIC SURVEY OF AFRICA: WESTERN AFRICA: THE BENIN KINGDOM. AFR NIGERIA CULTURE ECO/UNDEV KIN ECO/TAC GOV/REL AGE ATTIT HEREDITY...CHARTS BIBLIOG WORSHIP 20. PAGE 77 H1550 — STRUCT INGP/REL GEOG HABITAT

B57
INTERNATIONAL AFRICAN INST,ETHNOGRAPHIC SURVEY OF AFRICA: WESTERN AFRICA: THE WOLOF OF SENEGAMBIA. AFR SENEGAL CULTURE ECO/UNDEV FAM KIN REGION ...CHARTS GP/COMP BIBLIOG WORSHIP 20. PAGE 78 H1551 — STRUCT GEOG HABITAT INGP/REL

B57
RUMEU DE ARMAS A.,ESPANA EEN EL AFRICA ATLANTICA. AFR CHRIST-17C PORTUGAL SPAIN DIPLOM ECO/TAC CONTROL 14/16 AFRICA/W. PAGE 136 H2717 — NAT/G COLONIAL CHIEF PWR

B57
TAYLOR J.V.,CHRISTIANITY AND POLITICS IN AFRICA. AFR CONTROL PARTIC GP/REL RACE/REL ATTIT...POLICY BIBLIOG/A WORSHIP 20. PAGE 153 H3055 — SECT NAT/G NAT/LISM

B57
US SENATE SPEC COMM FOR AID,COMPILATION OF STUDIES AND SURVEYS. AFR ASIA L/A+17C USA+45 ECO/UNDEV AGRI INT/ORG CONSULT TEC/DEV CONFER TOTALISM...NAT/COMP 20 CONGRESS. PAGE 161 H3216 — FOR/AID DIPLOM ORD/FREE DELIB/GP

S57
HAILEY,"TOMORROW IN AFRICA." CONSTN SOCIETY LOC/G NAT/G DOMIN ADJUD ADMIN GP/REL DISCRIM NAT/LISM ATTIT MORAL ORD/FREE...PSY SOC CONCPT OBS RECORD TREND GEN/LAWS CMN/WLTH 20. PAGE 64 H1277 — AFR PERSON ELITES RACE/REL

S57
KILSON M.L.,"LAND AND POLITICS IN KENYA: AN ANALYSIS OF AFRICAN POLITICS IN A PLURAL SOCIETY." FUT LAW CULTURE KIN NAT/G ECO/TAC DOMIN REV NAT/LISM ORD/FREE PWR RESPECT SOVEREIGN WEALTH ...SOC OBS TREND WORK VAL/FREE CMN/WLTH 20. PAGE 86 H1710 — AFR ECO/UNDEV

B58
CARTER G.M.,TRANSITION IN AFRICA; STUDIES IN POLITICAL ADAPTATION. AFR CENTRL/AFR GHANA NIGERIA CONSTN LOC/G POL/PAR ADMIN GP/REL FEDERAL...MAJORIT BIBLIOG 20. PAGE 27 H0543 — NAT/COMP PWR CONTROL NAT/G

B58
COLEMAN J.S.,NIGERIA: BACKGROUND TO NATIONALISM. AFR SOCIETY ECO/DEV KIN LOC/G POL/PAR TEC/DEV DOMIN ADMIN DRIVE PWR RESPECT...TRADIT SOC INT SAMP TIME/SEQ 20. PAGE 31 H0627 — NAT/G NAT/LISM NIGERIA

B58
COWAN L.G.,LOCAL GOVERNMENT IN WEST AFRICA. AFR FRANCE UK CULTURE KIN POL/PAR CHIEF LEGIS CREATE ADMIN PARTIC GOV/REL GP/REL...METH/COMP 20. PAGE 34 H0682 — LOC/G COLONIAL SOVEREIGN REPRESENT

B58
GLUCKMAN M.,ANALYSIS OF A SOCIAL SITUATION IN MODERN ZULULAND. AFR PERS/REL ADJUST DISCRIM EQUILIB NAT/LISM...SOC RECORD AUD/VIS 20 ZULULAND. PAGE 57 H1146 — CULTURE RACE/REL STRUCT GP/REL

B58
HANCE W.A.,AFRICAN ECONOMIC DEVELOPMENT. AGRI DIST/IND INDUS R+D ACT/RES PLAN CAP/ISM FOR/AID ...GOV/COMP BIBLIOG 20. PAGE 65 H1312 — AFR ECO/UNDEV PROB/SOLV TEC/DEV

B58
HANSARD SOCIETY PARL GOVT,WHAT ARE THE PROBLEMS OF PARLIAMENTARY GOVERNMENT IN WEST AFRICA? PROB/SOLV DIPLOM GP/REL 20 PARLIAMENT AFRICA/W. PAGE 66 H1317 — PARL/PROC POL/PAR AFR NAT/G

B58
NICULESCU B.,COLONIAL PLANNING: A COMPARATIVE STUDY. AFR AGRI LOC/G MUNIC NAT/G DELIB/GP COLONIAL 20. PAGE 118 H2356 — PLAN ECO/UNDEV TEC/DEV NAT/COMP

S58
MAIR L.P.,"REPRESENTATIVE LOCAL GOVERNMENT AS A PROBLEM IN SOCIAL CHANGE." ECO/UNDEV KIN LOC/G NAT/G SCHOOL JUDGE ADMIN ROUTINE REPRESENT RIGID/FLEX RESPECT...CONCPT STERTYP CMN/WLTH 20. PAGE 101 H2025 — AFR PWR ELITES

S58
PYE L.W.,"THE NON-WESTERN POLITICAL PROCESS" (BMR)" AFR ASIA ISLAM S/ASIA DIPLOM ADMIN LEAD LOBBY ROUTINE CONSEN...DECISION 20. PAGE 128 H2567
CULTURE POL/PAR NAT/G LOC/G

B59
CARPENTER G.W.,THE WAY IN AFRICA. AFR INDUS MUNIC DIPLOM DOMIN EDU/PROP COERCE DISCRIM NAT/LISM ORD/FREE 20 NEGRO CHRISTIAN. PAGE 27 H0535
CULTURE SECT ECO/UNDEV COLONIAL

B59
KITTLER G.D.,EQUATORIAL AFRICA: THE NEW WORLD OF TOMORROW. CENTRL/AFR INDUS KIN SECT CHIEF EDU/PROP CHOOSE HEALTH...GEOG WORSHIP 20. PAGE 87 H1730
RACE/REL AFR ECO/UNDEV CULTURE

B59
MAC MILLAN W.M.,THE ROAD TO SELF-RULE. SOUTH/AFR UK CULTURE SOCIETY AGRI LABOR NAT/G INT/TRADE CONTROL GP/REL...SOC 19/20. PAGE 100 H1988
AFR COLONIAL SOVEREIGN POLICY

B59
MURDOCK G.P.,AFRICA: ITS PEOPLES AND THEIR CULTURE HISTORY. AFR CULTURE AGRI LOC/G INGP/REL HABITAT ...GEOG SOC LING CHARTS BIBLIOG 20 NEGRO EGYPT/ANC. PAGE 115 H2293
SOCIETY ECO/TAC GP/COMP KIN

B59
PANIKKAR K.M.,THE AFRO-ASIAN STATES AND THEIR PROBLEMS. COM CULTURE KIN POL/PAR SECT DIPLOM EDU/PROP COLONIAL SOVEREIGN...TECHNIC GOV/COMP 20. PAGE 123 H2458
AFR S/ASIA ECO/UNDEV

B59
SENGHOR L.S.,RAPPORT SUR LA DOCTRINE ET LA PROGRAMME DU PART I. FRANCE MALI CONSTN POL/PAR PLAN CHOOSE OWN ORD/FREE MARXISM...SOCIALIST 20 NEGRO. PAGE 141 H2828
ATTIT NAT/G AFR SOCISM

B59
SITHOLE N.,AFRICAN NATIONALISM. UNIV CULTURE SECT ADMIN COLONIAL CHOOSE. PAGE 145 H2892
RACE/REL AFR NAT/LISM PERSON

B59
WRAITH R.E.,EAST AFRICAN CITIZEN. AFR GHANA UK AGRI INDUS LOC/G POL/PAR PROB/SOLV CONTROL REGION REPRESENT NAT/LISM PWR...OBS 20 AFRICA/E AFRICA/W. PAGE 171 H3415
ECO/UNDEV RACE/REL NAT/G NAT/COMP

S59
LEVINE R.A.,"ANTI-EUROPEAN VIOLENCE IN AFRICA: A COMPARATIVE ANALYSIS." AFR CULTURE NAT/G DIPLOM EDU/PROP COLONIAL REGION COERCE ATTIT PWR...PSY CONCPT TIME/SEQ TREND HYPO/EXP SOC/EXP STERTYP GEN/METH COLD/WAR 20. PAGE 95 H1903
DRIVE ORD/FREE REV

S59
SILBERMAN L.,"CHANGE AND CONFLICT IN THE HORN OF AFRICA." EUR+WWI ITALY UK CULTURE FORCES ECO/TAC ADJUD COLONIAL ATTIT ORD/FREE PWR...DECISION METH/CNCPT HIST/WRIT SOMALI 20. PAGE 144 H2874
AFR TIME/SEQ

B60
ALMOND G.A.,THE POLITICS OF THE DEVELOPING AREAS. AFR ISLAM L/A+17C S/ASIA SOCIETY ECO/UNDEV NAT/G ADMIN PERCEPT KNOWL SOVEREIGN...CONCPT GEN/LAWS 20. PAGE 6 H0112
EX/STRUC ATTIT NAT/LISM

B60
BRIGGS L.C.,TRIBES OF THE SAHARA. AFR MOROCCO STRATA AGRI GP/REL HEALTH...GEOG SOC MYTH LING BIBLIOG 13/20 ARABS. PAGE 21 H0418
CULTURE HABITAT KIN SELF/OBS

B60
CARTER G.M.,INDEPENDENCE FOR AFRICA. AFR FUT SOCIETY STRATA ECO/DEV POL/PAR DELIB/GP PLAN DOMIN EDU/PROP COLONIAL REGION ATTIT DRIVE SOVEREIGN ...RECORD INT TIME/SEQ CHARTS 20. PAGE 27 H0544
NAT/G PWR NAT/LISM

B60
CHATTERJI S.K.,AFRICANISM: THE AFRICAN PERSONALITY. KIN NAT/G SECT CREATE DIPLOM COLONIAL GP/REL ATTIT ORD/FREE...LING WORSHIP 20. PAGE 29 H0585
PERSON NAT/LISM AFR CULTURE

B60
CONOVER H.F.,OFFICIAL PUBLICATIONS OF FRENCH WEST AFRICA, 1946-1958. DAHOMEY IVORY/CST NIGER SENEGAL UPPER/VOLT CONSTN AGRI PRESS...CON/ANAL 20. PAGE 33 H0651
BIBLIOG COLONIAL NAT/G AFR

B60
DIA M.,REFLEXIONS SUR L'ECONOMIE DE L'AFRIQUE NOIRE (REV. ED.). CULTURE ECO/UNDEV CREATE TEC/DEV DIPLOM INT/TRADE OPTIMAL ATTIT...POLICY 20. PAGE 41 H0816
AFR ECO/TAC SOCISM PLAN

B60
EASTON S.C.,THE TWILIGHT OF EUROPEAN COLONIALISM. AFR S/ASIA CONSTN SOCIETY STRUCT ECO/UNDEV INDUS NAT/G FORCES ECO/TAC COLONIAL CT/SYS ATTIT KNOWL ORD/FREE PWR...SOCIALIST TIME/SEQ TREND CON/ANAL 20. PAGE 44 H0882
FINAN ADMIN

B60
EMERSON R.,FROM EMPIRE TO NATION: THE RISE TO SELF-ASSERTION OF ASIAN AND AFRICAN PEOPLES. S/ASIA CULTURE NAT/G SECT DIPLOM ATTIT SOVEREIGN MARXISM ...POLICY BIBLIOG 19/20. PAGE 46 H0919
NAT/LISM COLONIAL AFR ASIA

B60
INTERNATIONAL AFRICAN INST,ETHNOGRAPHIC SURVEY OF AFRICA: WESTERN AFRICA: PEOPLES OF THE MIDDLE NIGER REGION, NORTHERN NIGERIA. AFR NIGER CULTURE ECO/UNDEV KIN NEIGH GOV/REL GP/REL ATTIT HEREDITY ...CHARTS BIBLIOG WORSHIP 20. PAGE 78 H1552
STRUCT GEOG HABITAT INGP/REL

B60
LEYDER J.,BIBLIOGRAPHIE DE L'ENSEIGNEMENT SUPERIEUR ET DE LA RECHERCHE SCIENTIFIQUE EN AFRIQUE INTERTROPICALE (2 VOLS.). AFR CULTURE ECO/UNDEV AGRI PLAN EDU/PROP ADMIN COLONIAL...GEOG SOC/INTEG 20 NEGRO. PAGE 96 H1918
BIBLIOG/A ACT/RES ACADEM R+D

B60
OTTENBERG S.,CULTURES AND SOCIETIES OF AFRICA. AFR KIN TEC/DEV GP/REL MARRIAGE ATTIT HABITAT HEREDITY ...ANTHOL BIBLIOG T WORSHIP 20. PAGE 122 H2433
SOCIETY INGP/REL STRUCT CULTURE

B60
PITCHER G.M.,BIBLIOGRAPHY OF GHANA. AFR GHANA NAT/G 20. PAGE 126 H2517
BIBLIOG/A SOC

B60
THEOBOLD R.,THE NEW NATIONS OF WEST AFRICA. GHANA NIGERIA CULTURE INT/ORG ECO/TAC FOR/AID COLONIAL RACE/REL POPULISM...ANTHOL BIBLIOG 20 UN. PAGE 153 H3068
AFR SOVEREIGN ECO/UNDEV DIPLOM

S60
APTER D.E.,"THE ROLE OF TRADITIONALISM IN THE POLITICAL MODERNIZATION OF GHANA AND UGANDA" (BMR)" AFR GHANA UGANDA CULTURE NAT/G POL/PAR NAT/LISM ...CON/ANAL 20. PAGE 8 H0152
CONSERVE ADMIN GOV/COMP PROB/SOLV

S60
BERG E.J.,"ECONOMIC BASIS OF POLITICAL CHOICE IN FRENCH WEST AFRICA." FRANCE ECO/UNDEV AGRI INDUS NAT/G PLAN LEGIT COLONIAL REGION ATTIT PWR WEALTH ...CONCPT 20. PAGE 15 H0299
AFR ECO/TAC

S60
EMERSON R.,"THE EROSION OF DEMOCRACY." AFR FUT LAW CULTURE INTELL SOCIETY ECO/UNDEV FAM LOC/G NAT/G FORCES PLAN TEC/DEV ECO/TAC ADMIN CT/SYS ATTIT ORD/FREE PWR...SOCIALIST SOC CONCPT STAND/INT TIME/SEQ WORK 20. PAGE 46 H0918
S/ASIA POL/PAR

S60
FRANKEL S.H.,"ECONOMIC ASPECTS OF POLITICAL INDEPENDENCE IN AFRICA." AFR FUT SOCIETY ECO/UNDEV COM/IND FINAN LEGIS PLAN TEC/DEV CAP/ISM ECO/TAC INT/TRADE ADMIN ATTIT DRIVE RIGID/FLEX PWR WEALTH ...MGT NEW/IDEA MATH TIME/SEQ VAL/FREE 20. PAGE 53 H1052
NAT/G FOR/AID

S60
JAFFEE A.J.,"POPULATION TRENDS AND CONTROLS IN UNDERDEVELOPED COUNTRIES." AFR FUT ISLAM L/A+17C S/ASIA CULTURE R+D FAM ACT/RES PLAN EDU/PROP BIO/SOC RIGID/FLEX HEALTH...SOC STAT OBS CHARTS 20. PAGE 79 H1582
ECO/UNDEV GEOG

S60
LEVINE R.A.,"THE INTERNALIZATION OF POLITICAL VALUES IN STATELESS SOCIETIES." AFR FAM KIN LOC/G PROVS JUDGE PERSON RIGID/FLEX...DECISION SOC TIME/SEQ 20. PAGE 95 H1904
CULTURE ATTIT

S60
RIVKIN A.,"AFRICAN ECONOMIC DEVELOPMENT: ADVANCED TECHNOLOGY AND THE STAGES OF GROWTH." CULTURE ECO/UNDEV AGRI COM/IND EXTR/IND PLAN ECO/TAC ATTIT DRIVE RIGID/FLEX SKILL WEALTH...MGT SOC GEN/LAWS WORK TOT/POP 20. PAGE 132 H2634
AFR TEC/DEV FOR/AID

S60
SHILS E.,"THE INTELLECTUALS IN THE POLITICAL DEVELOPMENT OF THE NEW STATES." AFR ASIA S/ASIA ELITES LOC/G NAT/G CONSULT EX/STRUC CREATE PLAN ECO/TAC DOMIN LEGIT DRIVE PWR...TRADIT CONCPT STERTYP GEN/LAWS 20. PAGE 143 H2861
POL/PAR INTELL NAT/LISM

S60
SPIRO H.J.,"NEW CONSTITUTIONAL FORMS IN AFRICA." FUT CULTURE SOCIETY ECO/UNDEV NAT/G POL/PAR VOL/ASSN EDU/PROP ATTIT DRIVE ORD/FREE PWR RESPECT ...POLICY CONCPT OBS TREND CON/ANAL STERTYP GEN/LAWS VAL/FREE. PAGE 148 H2950
AFR CONSTN FOR/AID NAT/LISM

S60
TIRYAKIAN E.A.,"APARTHEID AND POLITICS IN SOUTH AFRICA." SOUTH/AFR CULTURE STRATA ECO/DEV NAT/G POL/PAR ROUTINE CHOOSE GP/REL RACE/REL DISCRIM ATTIT ALL/VALS...CONCPT OBS TIME/SEQ VAL/FREE 20. PAGE 155 H3105
AFR DIPLOM

C60
SMITH T.E.,"ELECTIONS IN DEVELOPING COUNTRIES: A STUDY OF ELECTORAL PROCEDURES USED IN TOPICAL AFRICA, SOUTH-EAST ASIA..." AFR S/ASIA UK ROUTINE GOV/REL RACE/REL...GOV/COMP BIBLIOG 20. PAGE 146 H2918
ECO/UNDEV CHOOSE REPRESENT ADMIN

B61
ANSPRENGER F.,POLITIK IM SCHWARZEN AFRIKA. FRANCE NAT/G DIPLOM REGION REV NAT/LISM...CHARTS BIBLIOG 19/20. PAGE 7 H0141
AFR COLONIAL SOVEREIGN

B61
ATTLEE C.R.,EMPIRE INTO COMMONWEALTH. AFR ASIA
DIPLOM

CANADA UK NAT/G WAR NAT/LISM ATTIT...POLICY 20 AUSTRAL. PAGE 9 H0179 — GP/REL COLONIAL SOVEREIGN

B61
BIEBUYCK D.,CONGO TRIBES AND PARTIES. AFR CONGO/BRAZ CONSTN NAT/G COLONIAL CHOOSE FEDERAL 20 CONGO/LEOP. PAGE 17 H0333 — KIN POL/PAR GP/REL SOVEREIGN

B61
BONNEFOUS M.,EUROPE ET TIERS MONDE. EUR+WWI SOCIETY INT/ORG NAT/G VOL/ASSN ACT/RES TEC/DEV CAP/ISM ECO/TAC ATTIT ORD/FREE SOVEREIGN...POLICY CONCPT TREND 20. PAGE 19 H0373 — AFR ECO/UNDEV FOR/AID INT/TRADE

B61
CARNELL F.,THE POLITICS OF THE NEW STATES: A SELECT ANNOTATED BIBLIOGRAPHY WITH SPECIAL REFERENCE TO THE COMMONWEALTH. CONSTN ELITES LABOR NAT/G POL/PAR EX/STRUC DIPLOM ADJUD ADMIN...GOV/COMP 20 COMMONWLTH. PAGE 27 H0534 — BIBLIOG/A AFR ASIA COLONIAL

B61
CONOVER H.F.,SERIALS FOR AFRICAN STUDIES. ECO/UNDEV DIPLOM LEAD NAT/LISM ATTIT...SOC 20. PAGE 33 H0653 — BIBLIOG AFR NAT/G

B61
DIA M.,THE AFRICAN NATIONS AND WORLD SOLIDARITY. ISLAM CULTURE ELITES ECO/DEV ECO/UNDEV INT/ORG NAT/G PLAN ECO/TAC INT/TRADE EDU/PROP NAT/LISM ATTIT DRIVE ORD/FREE WEALTH...SOCIALIST CONCPT CON/ANAL GEN/LAWS TOT/POP 20. PAGE 41 H0817 — AFR REGION SOCISM

B61
DOOB L.W.,COMMUNICATION IN AFRICA: A SEARCH FOR BOUNDARIES. CULTURE SOCIETY EDU/PROP WRITING INGP/REL DRIVE ORD/FREE...ART/METH SOC LING BIBLIOG 20. PAGE 42 H0837 — AFR FEEDBACK PERCEPT PERS/REL

B61
DUFFY J.,AFRICA SPEAKS. GHANA TOGO CULTURE ECO/UNDEV PROB/SOLV COLONIAL NEUTRAL DISCRIM NAT/LISM SOVEREIGN ALL/IDEOS...CONCPT ANTHOL SOC/INTEG 20 NEGRO THIRD/WRLD. PAGE 43 H0857 — AFR NAT/G FUT STRUCT

B61
HEMPSTONE S.,THE NEW AFRICA. AGRI INDUS KIN NAT/G COLONIAL MARXISM...SOC INT TREND NAT/COMP BIBLIOG/A 20. PAGE 69 H1392 — AFR ORD/FREE PERSON CULTURE

B61
HOLDSWORTH M.,SOVIET AFRICAN STUDIES 1918-1959. USSR ACADEM NAT/G DIPLOM REGION KNOWL 20. PAGE 72 H1448 — BIBLIOG/A AFR HABITAT NAT/COMP

B61
JONES R.,AFRICA BIBLIOGRAPHY SERIES: SOUTH EAST CENTRAL AFRICA AND MADAGASCAR. AFR MADAGASCAR RHODESIA SECT BIO/SOC...JURID NAT/COMP 20. PAGE 82 H1633 — BIBLIOG/A SOC CULTURE LING

B61
LA DOCUMENTATION FRANCAISE,L'AFRIQUE A TRAVERS LES PUBLICATIONS DE LA DOCUMENTATION FRANCAISE; BIBLIOGRAPHIE 1945-1961 (PAMPHLET). FRANCE 20. PAGE 90 H1791 — BIBLIOG AFR COLONIAL NAT/G

B61
LEHMAN R.L.,AFRICA SOUTH OF THE SAHARA (PAMPHLET). DIPLOM COLONIAL NAT/LISM. PAGE 93 H1863 — BIBLIOG/A AFR CULTURE NAT/G

B61
MACLURE M.,AFRICA: THE POLITICAL PATTERN. SOUTH/AFR CULTURE LEGIS DIPLOM COLONIAL RACE/REL 20. PAGE 100 H2005 — AFR POLICY NAT/G

B61
MERRIAM A.,CONGO: BACKGROUND OF CONFLICT. AFR FUT KIN MUNIC NAT/G POL/PAR PROVS DELIB/GP PLAN DOMIN COERCE ATTIT...TIME/SEQ CHARTS CONGO 20. PAGE 109 H2182 — CHOOSE GUERRILLA

B61
MIT CENTER INTERNATIONAL STU,OFFICIAL SERIAL PUBLICATIONS RELATING TO ECONOMIC DEVELOPMENT IN AFRICA SOUTH OF THE SAHARA. AFR SOCIETY AGRI FINAN INDUS LG/CO ADMIN 20. PAGE 111 H2228 — BIBLIOG ECO/UNDEV ECO/TAC NAT/G

B61
MUNGER E.S.,AFRICAN FIELD REPORTS 1952-1961. SOUTH/AFR SOCIETY ECO/UNDEV NAT/G POL/PAR COLONIAL EXEC PARL/PROC GUERRILLA RACE/REL ALL/IDEOS...SOC AUD/VIS 20. PAGE 114 H2288 — AFR DISCRIM RECORD

B61
PANIKKAR K.M.,REVOLUTION IN AFRICA. AFR GUINEA ECO/UNDEV POL/PAR DIPLOM COLONIAL EXEC LEAD SOVEREIGN...CHARTS 20. PAGE 123 H2461 — NAT/LISM NAT/G CHIEF

B61
RYDINGS H.A.,THE BIBLIOGRAPHIES OF WEST AFRICA (PAMPHLET). ECO/UNDEV NAT/G COLONIAL REGION ATTIT 20. PAGE 136 H2725 — BIBLIOG/A AFR NAT/COMP

B61
SCHNAPPER B.,LA POLITIQUE ET LE COMMERCE FRANCAIS DANS LE GOLFE DE GUINEE DE 1838 A 1871. FRANCE GUINEA UK SEA EXTR/IND NAT/G DELIB/GP LEGIS ADMIN ORD/FREE...POLICY GEOG CENSUS CHARTS BIBLIOG 19. PAGE 139 H2791 — COLONIAL INT/TRADE DOMIN AFR

B61
SEMINAR REPRESENTATIVE GOVT,AFRO-ASIAN ATTITUDES: SEMINAR ON REPRESENTATIVE GOVERNMENTSPUBLIC LIBERTIES IN STATES OF ASIA AND AFRICA, RHODES, 1958. AFR ASIA BURMA INDIA ISLAM UAR VIETNAM/S SOCIETY POL/PAR CHIEF EDU/PROP PRESS PERSON ...POLICY INT 20 TUNIS. PAGE 141 H2826 — CHOOSE ATTIT NAT/COMP ORD/FREE

B61
SOUTHALL A.,SOCIAL CHANGE IN MODERN AFRICA. CULTURE STRATA ECO/UNDEV AGRI FAM KIN MUNIC GP/REL INGP/REL MARRIAGE...GEOG ANTHOL 20. PAGE 147 H2940 — AFR TREND SOCIETY SOC

B61
TURNBULL C.M.,THE FOREST PEOPLE. EATING GP/REL INGP/REL RACE/REL ISOLAT HABITAT HEREDITY...GEOG SOC LING DICTIONARY WORSHIP 20 CONGO NEGRO BA/MBUTI. PAGE 157 H3138 — AFR CULTURE KIN RECORD

S61
MILLER E.,"LEGAL ASPECTS OF UN ACTION IN THE CONGO." AFR CULTURE ADMIN PEACE DRIVE RIGID/FLEX ORD/FREE...WELF/ST JURID OBS UN CONGO 20. PAGE 111 H2212 — INT/ORG LEGIT

S61
PADELFORD N.J.,"POLITICS AND THE FUTURE OF ECOSOC." AFR S/ASIA ECO/UNDEV INDUS NAT/G DELIB/GP ACT/RES ORD/FREE WEALTH...CONCPT CHARTS UN 20 ECOSOC. PAGE 122 H2438 — INT/ORG TEC/DEV

B62
ABRAHAM W.E.,THE MIND OF AFRICA. AFR SOCIETY STRATA KIN ECO/TAC DOMIN EDU/PROP LEGIT COERCE ATTIT ALL/VALS...MAJORIT SOC OBS HIST/WRIT TIME/SEQ TREND TOT/POP 20. PAGE 3 H0058 — CULTURE SIMUL GHANA

B62
AMERICAN SOCIETY AFR CULTURE,PAN-AFRICANISM RECONSIDERED. AFR SOCIETY STRUCT SCHOOL CAP/ISM EDU/PROP...ART/METH NEW/IDEA PREDICT ANTHOL 20 PANAF/FREE NEGRO. PAGE 6 H0123 — DIPLOM FEDERAL NAT/LISM CULTURE

B62
BAULIN J.,THE ARAB ROLE IN AFRICA. AFR ALGERIA FUT ISLAM MOROCCO UAR COLONIAL NEUTRAL REV...SOC 20 TUNIS BOURGUIBA. PAGE 12 H0240 — NAT/LISM DIPLOM NAT/G SECT

B62
BRETTON H.L.,POWER AND STABILITY IN NIGERIA: THE POLITICS OF DECOLONIZATION. AFR CONSTN INTELL ECO/UNDEV COM/IND KIN NAT/G POL/PAR PROVS VOL/ASSN LEGIS DOMIN EDU/PROP LEGIT EXEC ROUTINE CHOOSE NAT/LISM ATTIT PERCEPT ALL/VALS. PAGE 20 H0411 — CULTURE OBS NIGERIA

B62
BUSIA K.A.,THE CHALLENGE OF AFRICA. CULTURE KIN MUNIC NAT/G POL/PAR SCHOOL DELIB/GP PLAN ECO/TAC DOMIN EDU/PROP TOTALISM ATTIT PERSON ALL/VALS SOVEREIGN...SOC CONCPT STERTYP TOT/POP VAL/FREE 20. PAGE 25 H0496 — AFR ECO/UNDEV NAT/LISM

B62
CALVOCORESSI P.,WORLD ORDER AND NEW STATES: PROBLEMS OF KEEPING THE PEACE. AFR EUR+WWI S/ASIA ELITES NAT/G ECO/TAC FOR/AID EDU/PROP COERCE ATTIT DRIVE ALL/VALS...GEN/LAWS COLD/WAR 20 UN. PAGE 25 H0509 — INT/ORG PEACE

B62
CARTER G.M.,AFRICAN ONE-PARTY STATES. ISLAM IVORY/CST LIBERIA CONSTN CULTURE SOCIETY POL/PAR PLAN DOMIN EDU/PROP EXEC REGION CHOOSE ATTIT ALL/VALS...CONCPT TIME/SEQ CHARTS VAL/FREE 20 TANGANYIKA. PAGE 27 H0545 — AFR NAT/LISM

B62
CARY J.,THE CASE FOR AFRICAN FREEDOM AND OTHER WRITINGS ON AFRICA. AFR UK INDUS LOC/G NAT/G SECT INT/TRADE EDU/PROP GOV/REL RACE/REL ORD/FREE ...CONCPT ANTHOL 19/20. PAGE 27 H0552 — NAT/LISM COLONIAL TREND ECO/UNDEV

B62
DUROSELLE J.B.,LES NOUVEAUX ETATS DANS LES RELATIONS INTERNATIONALES. AFR CHINA/COM FRANCE MOROCCO S/ASIA USSR ECO/UNDEV INT/ORG PLAN ECO/TAC EDU/PROP ATTIT DRIVE...TREND TOT/POP TUNIS 20. PAGE 44 H0872 — NAT/G CONSTN DIPLOM

B62
EVANS-PRITCHARD E.E.,ESSAYS IN SOCIAL ANTHROPOLOGY. AFR KIN REGION INGP/REL DRIVE HABITAT...OBS METH 20 ZANDE. PAGE 48 H0954 — SOCIETY CULTURE SOC STRUCT

B62
FEIT E.,SOUTH AFRICA, THE DYNAMICS OF THE AFRICAN NATIONAL CONGRESS. AFR SOUTH/AFR LAW INTELL STRATA KIN NAT/G POL/PAR ECO/TAC DOMIN RISK COERCE 20 NEGRO. PAGE 49 H0984 — RACE/REL ELITES CONTROL STRUCT

B62
GREEN L.P.,DEVELOPMENT IN AFRICA. AFR CENTRL/AFR GHANA RHODESIA SOUTH/AFR AGRI PROC/MFG INT/TRADE DEMAND NAT/LISM PRODUC WEALTH...GEOG METH/CNCPT CHARTS BIBLIOG 20. PAGE 60 H1206 — CULTURE ECO/UNDEV GOV/REL TREND

B62
GUENA Y.,HISTORIQUE DE LA COMMUNAUTE. FUT ECO/UNDEV NAT/G PLAN EDU/PROP COLONIAL REGION NAT/LISM — AFR VOL/ASSN

ALL/VALS SOVEREIGN...CONCPT OBS CHARTS 20. PAGE 62 H1244 FOR/AID FRANCE

B62
HATCH J.,AFRICA TODAY-AND TOMORROW: AN OUTLINE OF BASIC FACTS AND MAJOR PROBLEMS. AFR FUT ISLAM STRATA ECO/UNDEV INT/ORG NAT/G POL/PAR DELIB/GP TOP/EX EDU/PROP LEGIT CHOOSE ATTIT...TIME/SEQ TOT/POP COLD/WAR 20. PAGE 67 H1353 PLAN CONSTN NAT/LISM

B62
HUNTER G.,THE NEW SOCIETIES OF TROPICAL AFRICA. CULTURE INDUS KIN MUNIC WORKER INT/TRADE EDU/PROP ORD/FREE...INT TREND 20. PAGE 75 H1500 AFR GOV/COMP ECO/UNDEV SOCIETY

B62
INGHAM K.,A HISTORY OF EAST AFRICA. NAT/G DIPLOM ADMIN WAR NAT/LISM...SOC BIOG BIBLIOG. PAGE 77 H1534 AFR CONSTN COLONIAL

B62
JOHNSON J.J.,THE ROLE OF THE MILITARY IN UNDERDEVELOPED COUNTRIES. AFR BURMA INDONESIA ISLAM ISRAEL L/A+17C S/ASIA THAILAND CULTURE ECO/UNDEV KIN PROVS CONSULT ACT/RES COERCE REV DRIVE RIGID/FLEX ORD/FREE...RECORD ANTHOL 20. PAGE 81 H1622 FORCES CONCPT

B62
LEGUM C.,PAN-AFRICANISM: A SHORT POLITICAL GUIDE. ISLAM CULTURE INTELL ECO/DEV NAT/G POL/PAR DELIB/GP PLAN EDU/PROP FEDERAL NAT/LISM ATTIT DRIVE PERSON ...RECORD TIME/SEQ CHARTS STERTYP 20. PAGE 93 H1861 AFR CONCPT

B62
LOWENSTEIN A.K.,BRUTAL MANDATE: A JOURNEY TO SOUTH WEST AFRICA. CULTURE INT/ORG NAT/G DIPLOM...GEOG 20 UN AFRICA/SW. PAGE 99 H1975 AFR POLICY RACE/REL PROB/SOLV

B62
MELADY T.,THE WHITE MAN'S FUTURE IN BLACK AFRICA. FUT CULTURE SOCIETY NAT/G POL/PAR PLAN ECO/TAC DOMIN EDU/PROP LEGIT COLONIAL RACE/REL ATTIT DRIVE ALL/VALS...PSY SOC CONCPT TIME/SEQ TOT/POP VAL/FREE 20. PAGE 108 H2167 AFR STRATA ELITES

B62
NASRI A.R.,A BIBLIOGRAPHY OF THE SUDAN 1938-1958. AFR SUDAN CREATE...SOC 20. PAGE 116 H2316 BIBLIOG ECO/UNDEV NAT/G SOCIETY

B62
TAYLOR D.,THE BRITISH IN AFRICA. UK CULTURE ECO/UNDEV INDUS DIPLOM INT/TRADE ADMIN WAR RACE/REL ORD/FREE SOVEREIGN...POLICY BIBLIOG 15/20 CMN/WLTH. PAGE 153 H3053 AFR COLONIAL DOMIN

B62
TILMAN R.O.,THE NIGERIAN POLITICAL SXENE. NIGERIA DIPLOM COLONIAL PARTIC...POLICY SOC OBS PREDICT ANTHOL 20. PAGE 155 H3096 NAT/G AFR ECO/UNDEV FEDERAL

B62
TURNBULL C.M.,THE LONELY AFRICAN. AFR MUNIC SECT ANOMIE ALL/VALS...DECISION 20. PAGE 157 H3139 CULTURE ISOLAT KIN TRADIT

B62
UNECA LIBRARY,BOOKS ON AFRICA IN THE UNECA LIBRARY. WOR+45 AGRI INT/ORG NAT/G PLAN WRITING REGION...SOC STAT UN. PAGE 158 H3160 BIBLIOG AFR ECO/UNDEV TEC/DEV

B62
UNECA LIBRARY,NEW ACQUISITIONS IN THE UNECA LIBRARY. LAW NAT/G PLAN PROB/SOLV TEC/DEV ADMIN REGION...GEOG SOC 20 UN. PAGE 158 H3161 BIBLIOG AFR ECO/UNDEV INT/ORG

B62
US LIBRARY OF CONGRESS,A LIST OF AMERICAN DOCTORAL DISSERTATIONS ON AFRICA. SOCIETY SECT DIPLOM EDU/PROP ADMIN...GEOG 19/20. PAGE 161 H3212 BIBLIOG AFR ACADEM CULTURE

B62
VERHAEGEN P.,BIBLIOGRAPHIE DE L'URBANISATION DE L'AFRIQUE NOIRE: SON CADRE, SES CAUSES, ET SES CONSEQUENCES ECONOMIQUES, SOCIALES... AFR...SOC 20. PAGE 162 H3244 BIBLIOG ECO/UNDEV MUNIC CULTURE

B62
VILAKAZI A.,ZULU TRANSFORMATIONS: A STUDY OF THE DYNAMICS OF SOCIAL CHANGE. AFR CULTURE ECO/UNDEV KIN NEIGH SEX...GEOG QU TREND CHARTS BIBLIOG 19/20. PAGE 163 H3254 MARRIAGE SECT SOC EDU/PROP

L62
"AMERICAN BEHAVIORAL SCIENTIST." USSR LAW NAT/G ...SOC 20 UN. PAGE 2 H0039 BIBLIOG AFR R+D

L62
COHEN R.,"POWER IN COMPLEX SOCIETIES IN AFRICA." AFR KIN MUNIC POL/PAR DELIB/GP DOMIN ROUTINE ATTIT ALL/VALS...SOC STAT OBS INT QU CHARTS ANTHOL 20. PAGE 31 H0617 CULTURE STRATA ELITES

L62
MURACCIOLE L.,"LA BANQUE CENTRALE DES ETATS DE L'AFRIQUE DE L'OUEST." AFR LAW ECO/UNDEV INT/ORG NAT/G CONSULT ECO/TAC ROUTINE...CHARTS 20. PAGE 115 H2292 ISLAM FINAN INT/TRADE

L62
ORDONNEAU P.,"LES PROBLEMES POSES PAR L'INDEPENDANCE DES NOUVEAUX ETATS AFRICAINS ET MALGACHE SUR LE PLAN DU CONTENTIEUX." FRANCE ISLAM MADAGASCAR LAW STRATA ECO/UNDEV NAT/G LEGIS LEGIT ...JURID TIME/SEQ 20. PAGE 121 H2425 AFR ADJUD COLONIAL SOVEREIGN

S62
ANSPRENGER F.,"NATIONALISM, COMMUNISM, AND THE UNCOMMITTED NATIONS: AMERICAN PROFILES." FUT ISLAM CULTURE SOCIETY ECO/UNDEV NAT/G POL/PAR PLAN ECO/TAC EDU/PROP COERCE CHOOSE ALL/VALS MARXISM SOCISM...SOC CONCPT BIOG TREND 20. PAGE 7 H0142 AFR COM NAT/LISM

S62
KOLARZ W.,"THE IMPACT OF COMMUNISM ON WEST AFRICA." AFR FUT SOCIETY INT/ORG NAT/G CREATE PLAN DOMIN EDU/PROP COERCE NAT/LISM ATTIT RIGID/FLEX SOCISM ...POLICY CONCPT TREND MARX/KARL 20. PAGE 88 H1751 COM POL/PAR COLONIAL

S62
LEGUM C.,"THE DANGERS OF INDEPENDENCE" AFR UGANDA NAT/G DIPLOM DOMIN REGION CENTRAL ATTIT POPULISM 20. PAGE 93 H1862 ORD/FREE SOVEREIGN NAT/LISM GOV/COMP

S62
MBOYA T.,"RELATIONS BETWEEN THE PRESS AND GOVERNMENT IN AFRICA." AFR DIPLOM EDU/PROP NAT/LISM ORD/FREE SOVEREIGN 20. PAGE 106 H2115 PRESS GP/REL ATTIT NAT/G

S62
MURACCIOLE L.,"LES CONSTITUTIONS DES ETATS AFRICAINS D'EXPRESSION FRANCAISE: LA CONSTITUTION DU 16 AVRIL 1962 DE LA REPUBLIQUE DU" AFR CHAD CHIEF LEGIS LEGIT COLONIAL EXEC ROUTINE ORD/FREE SOVEREIGN...SOC CONCPT 20. PAGE 115 H2291 NAT/G CONSTN

S62
PIQUEMAL M.,"LES PROBLEMES DES UNIONS D'ETATS EN AFRIQUE NOIRE." FRANCE SOCIETY INT/ORG NAT/G DELIB/GP PLAN LEGIT ADMIN COLONIAL ROUTINE ATTIT ORD/FREE PWR...GEOG METH/CNCPT 20. PAGE 126 H2515 AFR ECO/UNDEV REGION

S62
PISTRAK L.,"SOVIET VIEWS ON AFRICA." AFR COM FUT ISLAM USSR INTELL STRUCT KIN POL/PAR PLAN EDU/PROP RIGID/FLEX PWR MARXISM...TIME/SEQ WORK TOT/POP 20. PAGE 126 H2516 NAT/G ATTIT SOCISM

S62
RAZAFIMBAHINY J.,"L'ORGANISATION AFRICAINE ET MALGACHE DE COOPERATION ECONOMIQUE." AFR ISLAM MADAGASCAR NAT/G ACT/RES ECO/TAC ALL/VALS ...TIME/SEQ 20. PAGE 130 H2601 INT/ORG ECO/UNDEV

S62
ROTBERG R.,"THE RISE OF AFRICAN NATIONALISM: THE CASE OF EAST AND CENTRAL AFRICA." AFR CULTURE SOCIETY NEIGH DIPLOM DOMIN COLONIAL COERCE DISPL PERCEPT PWR SOVEREIGN...POLICY OBS/ENVIR TREND WORK 20. PAGE 135 H2690 ATTIT DRIVE NAT/LISM REV

S62
SHATTEN F.,"POLYCENTRISM: AFRICA: NATIONALISM AND COMMUNISM." ASIA COM FUT ISLAM CULTURE SOCIETY ECO/UNDEV NAT/G PLAN DOMIN COLONIAL COERCE CHOOSE RIGID/FLEX ALL/VALS MARXISM...CONCPT TREND 20. PAGE 143 H2852 AFR ATTIT NAT/LISM SOCISM

B63
BRZEZINSKI Z.K.,AFRICA AND THE COMMUNIST WORLD. AFR ASIA COM CULTURE SOCIETY INT/ORG DELIB/GP ACT/RES ECO/TAC COERCE ORD/FREE PWR WEALTH...STAT TOT/POP VAL/FREE 20. PAGE 23 H0461 ATTIT EDU/PROP DIPLOM USSR

B63
CARTER G.M.,FIVE AFRICAN STATES: RESPONSES TO DIVERSITY. CONSTN CULTURE STRATA LEGIS PLAN ECO/TAC DOMIN EDU/PROP CT/SYS EXEC CHOOSE ATTIT HEALTH ORD/FREE PWR...TIME/SEQ TOT/POP VAL/FREE. PAGE 27 H0547 AFR SOCIETY

B63
CONOVER H.F.,AFRICA SOUTH OF THE SAHARA. CULTURE SECT TEC/DEV...ART/METH GEOG SOC. PAGE 33 H0654 BIBLIOG/A AFR CON/ANAL

B63
DECOTTIGNIES R.,LES NATIONALITES AFRICAINES. AFR NAT/G PROB/SOLV DIPLOM COLONIAL ORD/FREE...CHARTS GOV/COMP 20. PAGE 39 H0781 NAT/LISM JURID LEGIS LAW

B63
ELIAS T.O.,GOVERNMENT AND POLITICS IN AFRICA. CONSTN CULTURE SOCIETY NAT/G POL/PAR DIPLOM REPRESENT PERSON...SOC TREND BIBLIOG 4/20. PAGE 45 H0906 AFR NAT/LISM COLONIAL LAW

B63
GARDINIER D.E.,CAMEROON: UNITED NATIONS CHALLENGE TO FRENCH POLICY. AFR CAMEROON FRANCE NAT/G LEGIS CONTROL SOVEREIGN 20 UN. PAGE 55 H1101 DIPLOM POLICY INT/ORG COLONIAL

B63
GEERTZ C.,OLD SOCIETIES AND NEW STATES: THE QUEST FOR MODERNITY IN ASIA AND AFRICA. AFR ASIA LAW ECO/UNDEV TEC/DEV

CULTURE SECT EDU/PROP REV...GOV/COMP NAT/COMP 20. PAGE 55 H1107 — NAT/LISM SOVEREIGN

B63
GLUCKMAN M.,ORDER AND REBELLION IN TRIBAL AFRICA. EUR+WWI LAW CULTURE STRATA KIN MUNIC DELIB/GP ACT/RES DOMIN EDU/PROP LEGIT ADMIN COERCE CHOOSE ATTIT PERSON ORD/FREE PWR...SOC CHARTS GEN/LAWS TOT/POP VAL/FREE. PAGE 57 H1147 — AFR SOCIETY

B63
GOODE W.J.,WORLD REVOLUTION AND FAMILY PATTERNS. AFR CHINA/COM INDIA UAR CREATE ADJUST ATTIT SEX ...SOC 20 CHINJAP. PAGE 58 H1169 — FAM NAT/COMP CULTURE MARRIAGE

B63
HAILEY L.,THE REPUBLIC OF SOUTH AFRICA AND THE HIGH COMMISSION TERRITORIES. AFR SOUTH/AFR UK INT/ORG NAT/G PROVS RACE/REL SOVEREIGN...CHARTS 19/20 COMMONWLTH. PAGE 64 H1278 — COLONIAL DIPLOM ATTIT

B63
HUGHES A.J.,EAST AFRICA: THE SEARCH FOR UNITY- KENYA, TANGANYIKA, UGANDA, AND ZANZIBAR. TANZANIA UGANDA CONSTN POL/PAR SECT CHIEF DELIB/GP LEGIS WAR CHOOSE NAT/LISM MARXISM...POLICY CHARTS 20 NEGRO UN. PAGE 74 H1488 — NAT/G DOMIN LOC/G AFR

B63
HUNTER G.,EDUCATION FOR A DEVELOPING REGION; A STUDY IN EAST AFRICA. AFR TANZANIA UGANDA NAT/G TEC/DEV INGP/REL ADJUST LITERACY ATTIT 20 AFRICA/E. PAGE 75 H1501 — EDU/PROP POLICY ECO/UNDEV EFFICIENCY

B63
INTERNATIONAL ASSOCIATION RES,AFRICAN STUDIES IN INCOME AND WEALTH. AFR NAT/G PROB/SOLV DEMAND INCOME...ECOMETRIC METH/COMP 20. PAGE 78 H1553 — WEALTH PLAN ECO/UNDEV BUDGET

B63
JENNINGS W.I.,DEMOCRACY IN AFRICA. UK CULTURE STRUCT ECO/UNDEV DIPLOM COLONIAL GP/REL ADJUST NAT/LISM ORD/FREE...GOV/COMP 20 THIRD/WRLD. PAGE 81 H1613 — PROB/SOLV AFR CONSTN POPULISM

B63
JUDD P.,AFRICAN INDEPENDENCE: THE EXPLODING EMERGENCE OF THE NEW AFRICAN NATIONS. AFR UK LAW CONSTN CULTURE KIN DIPLOM ATTIT...CHARTS BIBLIOG 20 UN DEGAULLE/C NEGRO THIRD/WRLD. PAGE 82 H1640 — ORD/FREE POLICY DOMIN LOC/G

B63
JUNOD V.,HANDBOOK OF AFRICA. AFR ISLAM CONSTN SOCIETY NAT/G POL/PAR...GEOG SOC STAT CHARTS WORK 20. PAGE 82 H1642 — ECO/UNDEV REGION

B63
KURZMAN D.,SUBVERSION OF THE INNOCENTS: PATTERNS OF COMMUNIST PENETRATION OF AFRICA, THE MIDDLE EAST AND AFRICA. AFR ASIA ISLAM S/ASIA CULTURE NAT/G FORCES PLAN EDU/PROP ADMIN ATTIT...CONCPT INT UNPLAN/INT TIME/SEQ. PAGE 89 H1785 — COM COERCE

B63
MAC MILLAN W.M.,BANTU, BOER, AND BRITON: THE MAKING OF THE SOUTH AFRICAN NATIVE PROBLEM. SOUTH/AFR UK LAW KIN NAT/G SECT LEGIS COLONIAL ISOLAT ATTIT ...BIOG 18/20 BANTU NEGRO PHILIP/J MISSION. PAGE 100 H1989 — AFR RACE/REL ELITES

B63
MAIR L.,NEW NATIONS. AFR FAM MUNIC SECT DOMIN CHOOSE NAT/LISM ORD/FREE...SOC 19/20. PAGE 101 H2022 — COLONIAL CULTURE TEC/DEV ECO/UNDEV

B63
NKRUMAH K.,AFRICA MUST UNITE. AFR FUT GHANA CONSTN CULTURE SOCIETY NAT/G POL/PAR DELIB/GP TOP/EX PLAN DOMIN EDU/PROP ATTIT DRIVE...TIME/SEQ CHARTS TOT/POP 20. PAGE 118 H2364 — CONCPT GEN/LAWS REGION

B63
PADELFORD N.J.,AFRICA AND WORLD ORDER. AFR COLONIAL SOVEREIGN...ANTHOL BIBLIOG 20 UN UNIFICA COMMONWLTH. PAGE 122 H2439 — DIPLOM NAT/G ORD/FREE

B63
QUAISON-SACKEY A.,AFRICA UNBOUND: REFLECTIONS OF AN AFRICAN STATESMAN. ISLAM CULTURE INTELL INT/ORG POL/PAR TOP/EX DOMIN EDU/PROP LEGIT ATTIT PERSON ...CONCPT OBS TIME/SEQ CHARTS STERTYP 20 UN. PAGE 129 H2571 — AFR BIOG

B63
REYNOLDS B.,MAGIC, DIVINATION AND WITCHCRAFT AMONG THE BAROTSE OF NORTHERN RHODESIA. RHODESIA CULTURE KIN CREATE LEGIT PARTIC DEATH DREAM STRANGE HABITAT PERSON...AUD/VIS WORSHIP 20. PAGE 131 H2619 — AFR SOC MYTH SECT

B63
RIVKIN A.,THE AFRICAN PRESENCE IN WORLD AFFAIRS. ECO/UNDEV AGRI INT/ORG LOC/G NAT/LISM...OBS PREDICT GOV/COMP 20. PAGE 132 H2635 — AFR NAT/G DIPLOM BAL/PWR

B63
SCHECHTMAN J.B.,THE REFUGEE IN THE WORLD: DISPLACEMENT AND INTEGRATION. AFR ASIA EUR+WWI ISLAM L/A+17C S/ASIA CULTURE STRATA LOC/G EX/STRUC PLAN ECO/TAC ROUTINE...CONCPT TIME/SEQ VAL/FREE 20. PAGE 139 H2779 — INT/ORG SOC

B63
SKLAR R.L.,NIGERIAN POLITICAL PARTIES: POWER IN AN EMERGENT AFRICAN NATION. AFR EUR+WWI CULTURE STRATA NAT/G DELIB/GP EX/STRUC LEGIS DOMIN EDU/PROP ROUTINE CHOOSE ATTIT PERCEPT ORD/FREE PWR...SOC CONCPT OBS TOT/POP VAL/FREE. PAGE 145 H2898 — POL/PAR SOCIETY NAT/LISM NIGERIA

B63
STIRNIMANN H.,NGUNI UND GNONI; EINE KULTURGESCHICHTLICHE STUDIE (ACTA ETHNOLOGICA ET LINGUISTICA, NUMBER 6). AFR MALAWI SOUTH/AFR FORCES HABITAT...RECORD CHARTS BIBLIOG WORSHIP 19/20 NATAL. PAGE 149 H2987 — CULTURE GP/COMP SOCIETY

B63
TOUVAL S.,SOMALI NATIONALISM: INTERNATIONAL POLITICS AND THE DRIVE FOR UNITY IN THE HORN OF AFRICA. AFR CULTURE PROVS LEGIS EDU/PROP REGION COERCE ATTIT...MYTH UNPLAN/INT TIME/SEQ SOMALI VAL/FREE 20. PAGE 156 H3118 — SOCIETY EXEC NAT/LISM

B63
VIARD R.,LA FIN DE L'EMPIRE COLONIAL FRANCAIS. AFR FUT S/ASIA ECO/UNDEV NAT/G CONSULT PLAN ECO/TAC EDU/PROP REGION NAT/LISM ALL/VALS...CONCPT TIME/SEQ TREND VAL/FREE 20. PAGE 162 H3248 — VOL/ASSN COLONIAL FRANCE

B63
WILSON U.,EDUCATION AND CHANGING WEST AFRICAN CULTURE. AFR MOD/EUR UK CULTURE ECO/UNDEV MUNIC CONSULT 19/20 CMN/WLTH AFRICA/W. PAGE 169 H3384 — COLONIAL POLICY SCHOOL

B63
WODDIS J.,AFRICA, THE WAY AHEAD. AFR FUT ELITES POL/PAR CAP/ISM DIPLOM DOMIN RACE/REL ATTIT ORD/FREE SOVEREIGN SOCISM 20 PANAF/FREE. PAGE 170 H3394 — REV COLONIAL ECO/UNDEV NAT/G

B63
ZARTMAN I.W.,GOVERNMENT AND POLITICS IN NORTHERN AFRICA. AFR ALGERIA ISLAM LIBYA MOROCCO UAR ELITES SOCIETY PLAN ECO/TAC DOMIN EDU/PROP LEGIT ATTIT ...GEOG CONCPT TIME/SEQ 20 TUNIS. PAGE 172 H3448 — CULTURE DRIVE NAT/LISM

S63
BANFIELD J.,"FEDERATION IN EAST-AFRICA." AFR UGANDA ELITES INT/ORG NAT/G VOL/ASSN LEGIS ECO/TAC FEDERAL ATTIT SOVEREIGN TOT/POP 20 TANGANYIKA. PAGE 10 H0210 — EX/STRUC PWR REGION

S63
CRUTCHER J.,"PAN AFRICANISM: AFRICAN ODYSSEY." AFR NAT/G POL/PAR PROF/ORG VOL/ASSN TOP/EX CREATE REGION RACE/REL ALL/VALS...CONCPT TIME/SEQ TREND CON/ANAL 20. PAGE 36 H0716 — PROVS DELIB/GP COLONIAL

S63
DUDLEY B.J.,"THE NOMINATION OF PARLIAMENTARY CANDIDATES IN NORTHERN NIGERIA." AFR CONSTN CULTURE ELITES STRATA DELIB/GP LEGIS DOMIN EDU/PROP COERCE ATTIT SUPEGO PWR...STAT VAL/FREE 20. PAGE 43 H0854 — POL/PAR CHOOSE NIGERIA

S63
GLUCKMAN M.,"CIVIL WAR AND THEORIES OF POWER IN BAROTSE-LAND: AFRICAN AND MEDIEVAL ANALOGIES." AFR CHRIST-17C LAW CONSTN CULTURE STRATA KIN DELIB/GP FORCES DOMIN LEGIT COERCE PERCEPT ORD/FREE...SOC INT TIME/SEQ GEN/LAWS VAL/FREE. PAGE 57 H1148 — TOP/EX PWR WAR

S63
LEE J.M.,"PARLIAMENT IN REPUBLICAN GHANA." AFR CONSTN CULTURE SOCIETY STRATA POL/PAR DELIB/GP TOP/EX DOMIN EDU/PROP LEGIT COERCE CHOOSE ATTIT ALL/VALS...CONCPT STAT TIME/SEQ VAL/FREE 20. PAGE 93 H1857 — LEGIS GHANA

S63
LIGOT M.,"LA COOPERATION MILITAIRE DANS LES ACCORDS, PASSES ENTRE LA FRANCE ET LES ETATS AFRICAINS ET MALGACHE D'EXPRESSION." ECO/UNDEV INT/ORG NAT/G VOL/ASSN...CONCPT TIME/SEQ 20. PAGE 97 H1931 — AFR FORCES FOR/AID FRANCE

S63
MAZRUI A.A.,"ON THE CONCEPT 'WE ARE ALL AFRICANS'." AFR CULTURE KIN LOC/G NAT/G DOMIN EDU/PROP LEGIT ATTIT PERCEPT PERSON KNOWL ORD/FREE...TIME/SEQ TOT/POP 20. PAGE 106 H2110 — PROVS INT/ORG NAT/LISM

S63
MBOYA T.,"AFRICAN SOCIALISM." ECO/UNDEV INT/ORG DIPLOM FOR/AID INT/TRADE REGION GP/REL ATTIT ORD/FREE EACM. PAGE 106 H2116 — AFR SOCISM CULTURE NAT/LISM

S63
MORISON D.,"AFRICAN STUDIES IN THE SOVIET UNION." AFR COM CULTURE INTELL REGION ATTIT KNOWL...HUM TREND 20. PAGE 113 H2258 — EDU/PROP USSR

S63
OGOT B.,"FROM CHIEF TO PRESIDENT." AFR SECT REGION NAT/LISM...SOC GOV/COMP NAT/COMP 20 PRESIDENT. PAGE 121 H2410 — CHIEF CULTURE LEAD ORD/FREE

S63
ROGIN M.,"ROUSSEAU IN AFRICA." AFR MARXISM POPULISM SOCISM 20 ROUSSEAU/J. PAGE 133 H2661 — IDEA/COMP CULTURE CONSTN ORD/FREE

S63
ZOLBERG A.R.,"MASS PARTIES AND NATIONAL — POL/PAR

INTEGRATION: THE CASE OF THE IVORY COAST" (BMR)" AFR IVORY/CST CONSTN VOL/ASSN DIPLOM LEAD GP/REL INGP/REL 20. PAGE 173 H3461
ECO/UNDEV NAT/G ADJUST

N63
LIBRARY HUNGARIAN ACADEMY SCI,HUNGARIAN PUBLICATIONS ON ASIA AND AFRICA, 1950-1962: A SELECTED BIBLIOGRAPHY (PAMPHLET). AFR ASIA HUNGARY S/ASIA ECO/UNDEV NAT/G EDU/PROP ATTIT 20 UNESCO. PAGE 96 H1922
BIBLIOG REGION DIPLOM WRITING

B64
AFRO ASIAN SOLIDARITY AGAINST IMPERIALISM. AFR ISLAM S/ASIA ECO/UNDEV NAT/G POL/PAR TOP/EX PRESS ...INT ANTHOL 20 CHOU/ENLAI. PAGE 2 H0043
MARXISM DIPLOM EDU/PROP CHIEF

B64
ALDEFER H.F.,A BIBLIOGRAPHY OF AFRICAN GOVERNMENT: 1950-1964. ALGERIA GUINEA LIBERIA UAR ECO/UNDEV POL/PAR LEGIS COLONIAL LEAD PARL/PROC NAT/LISM 20. PAGE 5 H0098
BIBLIOG AFR LOC/G NAT/G

B64
BALOGH T.,THE ECONOMIC IMPACT OF MONETARY AND COMMERCIAL INSTITUTIONS OF A EUROPEAN ORIGIN IN AFRICA. AFR UAR INDUS FOR/AID COLONIAL CONTROL ...NAT/COMP 20. PAGE 10 H0205
TEC/DEV FINAN ECO/UNDEV ECO/TAC

B64
BOSTON UNIVERSITY LIBRARIES,CATALOG OF AFRICAN GOVERNMENT DOCUMENTS AND AFRICAN AREA INDEX. AFR NAT/G...SOC 20. PAGE 19 H0384
BIBLIOG ACADEM

B64
BROWN C.V.,GOVERNMENT AND BANKING IN WESTERN NIGERIA. AFR NIGERIA GOV/REL GP/REL...POLICY 20. PAGE 22 H0440
ADMIN ECO/UNDEV FINAN NAT/G

B64
BURKE F.G.,AFRICA'S QUEST FOR ORDER. AFR CULTURE KIN MUNIC NAT/G DIPLOM COLONIAL REV DISCRIM NAT/LISM AGE/Y 20. PAGE 24 H0488
ORD/FREE CONSEN RACE/REL LEAD

B64
COWAN L.G.,THE DILEMMAS OF AFRICAN INDEPENDENCE. AFR INDUS NAT/G SECT DIPLOM ECO/TAC REGION MARXISM ...CHARTS BIBLIOG 20 MAPS. PAGE 34 H0683
ORD/FREE COLONIAL REV ECO/UNDEV

B64
CURRIE D.P.,FEDERALISM AND THE NEW NATIONS OF AFRICA. CANADA USA+45 INT/TRADE TAX GP/REL ...NAT/COMP SOC/INTEG 20. PAGE 36 H0725
FEDERAL AFR ECO/UNDEV INT/LAW

B64
CURTIN P.D.,THE IMAGE OF AFRICA: BRITISH IDEAS AND ACTION, 1780-1850. MOD/EUR SOCIETY FORCES ACT/RES DOMIN EDU/PROP COERCE ATTIT PERCEPT RIGID/FLEX SUPEGO HEALTH KNOWL MORAL ORD/FREE WEALTH...CONCPT WORK VAL/FREE. PAGE 36 H0726
AFR CULTURE UK DIPLOM

B64
DE SMITH S.A.,THE NEW COMMONWEALTH AND ITS CONSTITUTIONS. AFR CYPRUS PAKISTAN S/ASIA INT/ORG NAT/G LEGIS LEGIT RIGID/FLEX PWR...CONCPT TIME/SEQ CMN/WLTH 20. PAGE 38 H0770
EX/STRUC CONSTN SOVEREIGN

B64
FRANCK T.M.,EAST AFRICAN UNITY THROUGH LAW. MALAWI TANZANIA UGANDA UK ZAMBIA CONSTN INT/ORG NAT/G ADMIN ROUTINE TASK NAT/LISM ATTIT SOVEREIGN ...RECORD IDEA/COMP NAT/COMP. PAGE 52 H1048
AFR FEDERAL REGION INT/LAW

B64
FRIEDLAND W.H.,AFRICAN SOCIALISM. ECO/UNDEV MARKET LABOR NAT/G POL/PAR PLAN CAP/ISM ECO/TAC EDU/PROP CHOOSE ATTIT DRIVE PWR WEALTH...POLICY CONCPT RECORD STERTYP 20. PAGE 53 H1063
AFR SOCISM

B64
GLUCKMANN M.,CLOSED SYSTEMS AND OPEN MINDS: THE LIMITS OF NAIVETY IN SOCIAL ANTHROPOLOGY. AFR INDIA MUNIC...IDEA/COMP METH/COMP ANTHOL. PAGE 57 H1149
CULTURE OBS SOC

B64
GREEN M.M.,IBO VILLAGE AFFAIRS. AFR FORCES PERS/REL ADJUST ISOLAT ATTIT HABITAT PERSON ALL/VALS...JURID RECORD SOC/INTEG 20 IBO. PAGE 60 H1207
MUNIC CULTURE ECO/UNDEV SOC

B64
HANNA W.J.,POLITICS IN BLACK AFRICA: A SELECTIVE BIBLIOGRAPHY OF RELEVANT PERIODICAL LITERATURE. AFR LAW LOC/G MUNIC NAT/G POL/PAR LOBBY CHOOSE RACE/REL SOVEREIGN 20. PAGE 66 H1315
BIBLIOG NAT/LISM COLONIAL

B64
HERRICK M.D.,CATALOG OF AFRICAN GOVERNMENT DOCUMENTS AND AFRICAN AREA INDEX (2ND REV. ED.) ....SOC INDEX METH 20. PAGE 70 H1405
BIBLIOG ECO/UNDEV AFR NAT/G

B64
HERSKOVITS M.J.,ECONOMIC TRANSITION IN AFRICA. FUT INT/ORG NAT/G WORKER PROB/SOLV TEC/DEV INT/TRADE EQUILIB INCOME...ANTHOL 20. PAGE 70 H1408
AFR ECO/UNDEV PLAN ADMIN

B64
HILL C.R.,BANTUSTANS: THE FRAGMENTATION OF SOUTH AFRICA. AFR SOUTH/AFR ELITES SOCIETY KIN CONTROL DISCRIM ANOMIE ATTIT...POLICY CHARTS GOV/COMP 20 NEGRO BANTUSTANS TRANSKEI NATAL. PAGE 71 H1416
RACE/REL CULTURE LOC/G ORD/FREE

B64
JUCKER-FLEETWOOD E.,MONEY AND FINANCE IN AFRICA. ISLAM ECO/UNDEV SERV/IND NAT/G EX/STRUC PLAN ECO/TAC ROUTINE WEALTH...MGT TOT/POP 20. PAGE 82 H1639
AFR FINAN

B64
KAUFMANN R.,MILLENARISME ET ACCULTURATION. SOCIETY DOMIN COLONIAL NAT/LISM ATTIT...SOC BIBLIOG 20 JEHOVA/WIT SEVENTHDAY. PAGE 84 H1669
AFR SECT MYTH CULTURE

B64
KITCHEN H.,A HANDBOOK OF AFRICAN AFFAIRS. ECO/UNDEV CREATE DIPLOM COLONIAL RACE/REL...ART/METH GEOG CHARTS 20. PAGE 87 H1729
AFR NAT/G INT/ORG FORCES

B64
LEBRUN J.,BIBLIOGRAPHIE DE LA FERTILITE DES SOLS ET ELEMENTS DE SOCIOLOGIE RURALE EN AFRIQUE AU SUD DU SAHARA. AFR PLAN TEC/DEV EFFICIENCY PRODUC...GEOG SOC NAT/COMP 20. PAGE 93 H1850
BIBLIOG/A ECO/UNDEV HABITAT AGRI

B64
LEWIN P.,THE FOREIGN TRADE OF COMMUNIST CHINA* ITS IMPACT ON THE FREE WORLD. AFR EUR+WWI L/A+17C S/ASIA ECO/UNDEV CREATE FOR/AID...STAT NET/THEORY TREND CHARTS. PAGE 96 H1910
ASIA INT/TRADE NAT/COMP USSR

B64
MATTHEWS D.G.,A CURRENT VIEW OF AFRICANA (PAMPHLET). CULTURE ECO/UNDEV DIPLOM RACE/REL ATTIT 20. PAGE 105 H2092
BIBLIOG/A AFR NAT/G NAT/LISM

B64
MCCALL D.F.,AFRICA IN TIME PERSPECTIVE. AFR EXTR/IND KIN SECT CREATE PERS/REL HABITAT...GEOG METH/CNCPT LING BIBLIOG/A TIME 20. PAGE 106 H2124
HIST/WRIT OBS/ENVIR CULTURE

B64
MELADY T.,FACES OF AFRICA. AFR FUT ISLAM NAT/G POL/PAR SCHOOL DELIB/GP PLAN ECO/TAC EDU/PROP ATTIT ALL/VALS...CHARTS TOT/POP VAL/FREE 20. PAGE 108 H2168
ECO/UNDEV TREND NAT/LISM

B64
MORGENTHAU R.S.,POLITICAL PARTIES IN FRENCH-SPEAKING WEST AFRICA. AFR FRANCE GUINEA IVORY/CST MALI SENEGAL CONSTN LEGIS CREATE PLAN LOBBY PARTIC GP/REL...POLICY BIBLIOG 20. PAGE 113 H2257
POL/PAR NAT/G SOVEREIGN COLONIAL

B64
MOUMOUNI A.,L'EDUCATION EN AFRIQUE. UNIV CULTURE ELITES INTELL EDU/PROP ADMIN COLONIAL...LING TREND BIBLIOG 20. PAGE 114 H2271
SCHOOL AFR PROB/SOLV

B64
NICOL D.,AFRICA - A SUBJECTIVE VIEW. AFR INT/ORG PLAN ADMIN COLONIAL PARL/PROC PARTIC REGION GOV/REL LITERACY ATTIT...BIBLIOG 20 CIVIL/SERV. PAGE 118 H2350
NAT/G LEAD CULTURE ACADEM

B64
PHILLIPS C.S.,THE DEVELOPMENT OF NIGERIAN FOREIGN POLICY. AFR CONSTN CULTURE STRATA NAT/G LEGIS DOMIN LEGIT EXEC...RELATIV SOC TIME/SEQ TREND TOT/POP 20. PAGE 125 H2502
CHOOSE POLICY DIPLOM NIGERIA

B64
QUIGG P.W.,AFRICA: A FOREIGN AFFAIRS READER. AFR FRANCE PORTUGAL UK DIPLOM LEAD PARL/PROC MARXISM ...MAJORIT METH/CNCPT GOV/COMP IDEA/COMP ANTHOL 19/20. PAGE 129 H2575
COLONIAL SOVEREIGN NAT/LISM RACE/REL

B64
SCHNITGER F.M.,FORGOTTEN KINGDOMS IN SUMATRA. FAM SECT LEISURE HABITAT...OBS AUD/VIS WORSHIP 20 SUMATRA. PAGE 140 H2793
CULTURE AFR SOCIETY STRUCT

B64
SEGAL R.,SANCTIONS AGAINST SOUTH AFRICA. AFR SOUTH/AFR NAT/G INT/TRADE RACE/REL PEACE PWR ...INT/LAW ANTHOL 20 UN. PAGE 141 H2821
SANCTION DISCRIM ECO/TAC POLICY

B64
SKINNER E.P.,THE MOSSI OF UPPER VOLTA: THE POLITICAL DEVELOPMENT OF A SUDANESE PEOPLE. AFR LAW AGRI FAM KIN POL/PAR PROVS SECT DELIB/GP EX/STRUC FORCES TOP/EX DOMIN EDU/PROP LEGIT CT/SYS COERCE CHOOSE ORD/FREE PWR WEALTH...SOC MYTH VAL/FREE. PAGE 145 H2897
CULTURE OBS UPPER/VOLT

B64
THORNTON T.P.,THE THIRD WORLD IN SOVIET PERSPECTIVE: STUDIES BY SOVIET WRITERS ON THE DEVELOPING AREAS. AFR L/A+17C S/ASIA STRATA AGRI INDUS MARKET NAT/G POL/PAR ECO/TAC COLONIAL PERCEPT PWR WEALTH...MARXIST STAT CHARTS WORK MARX/KARL 20. PAGE 155 H3090
ECO/UNDEV ACT/RES USSR DIPLOM

B64
WALLBANK T.W.,DOCUMENTS ON MODERN AFRICA. NAT/G COLONIAL GP/REL ATTIT PWR...BIBLIOG 19/20. PAGE 165 H3294
AFR NAT/LISM ECO/UNDEV DIPLOM

B64
WITHERELL J.W.,OFFICIAL PUBLICATIONS OF FRENCH
BIBLIOG/A

EQUATORIAL AFRICA, FRENCH CAMEROONS, AND TOGO, 1946-1958 (PAMPHLET). CAMEROON CHAD FRANCE GABON TOGO LAW ECO/UNDEV EXTR/IND INT/TRADE...GEOG HEAL 20. PAGE 169 H3392
AFR NAT/G ADMIN

L64
MACKINTOSH J.P.,"NIGERIA'S EXTERNAL AFFAIRS." UK CULTURE ECO/UNDEV NAT/G VOL/ASSN EDU/PROP LEGIT ADMIN ATTIT ORD/FREE PWR 20. PAGE 100 H2002
AFR DIPLOM NIGERIA

L64
ROTBERG R.,"THE FEDERATION MOVEMENT IN BRITISH EAST AND CENTRAL AFRICA." AFR RHODESIA UGANDA ECO/UNDEV NAT/G POL/PAR FORCES DOMIN LEGIT ADMIN COERCE ATTIT ...CONCPT TREND 20 TANGANYIKA. PAGE 135 H2691
VOL/ASSN PWR REGION

L64
SYMONDS R.,"REFLECTIONS IN LOCALISATION." AFR S/ASIA UK STRATA INT/ORG NAT/G SCHOOL EDU/PROP LEGIT KNOWL ORD/FREE PWR RESPECT CMN/WLTH 20. PAGE 151 H3023
ADMIN MGT COLONIAL

S64
BENSON M.,"SOUTH AFRICA AND WORLD OPINION." AFR SOUTH/AFR INTELL SOCIETY TOP/EX ECO/TAC DOMIN COERCE DISCRIM ATTIT PWR WEALTH...POLICY RECORD 20. PAGE 14 H0285
NAT/G RIGID/FLEX RACE/REL

S64
CLIFFE L.,"TANGANYIKA'S TWO YEARS OF INDEPENDENCE." AFR INDUS MARKET NAT/G POL/PAR DELIB/GP CREATE ECO/TAC LEGIT DRIVE ALL/VALS...METH/CNCPT RECORD 20 TANGANYIKA. PAGE 30 H0604
ECO/UNDEV PLAN

S64
CLIGNET R.,"POTENTIAL ELITES IN GHANA AND THE IVORY COAST: A PRELIMINARY SURVEY." AFR CULTURE ELITES STRATA KIN NAT/G SECT DOMIN EXEC ORD/FREE RESPECT SKILL...POLICY RELATIV GP/COMP NAT/COMP 20. PAGE 30 H0605
PWR LEGIT IVORY/CST GHANA

S64
DE GAULLE C.,"FRENCH WORLD VIEW." AFR ASIA CHINA/COM EUR+WWI ISLAM ECO/UNDEV INT/ORG NAT/G VOL/ASSN ACT/RES DIPLOM ECO/TAC EDU/PROP ATTIT DRIVE WEALTH 20. PAGE 37 H0751
TOP/EX PWR FOR/AID FRANCE

S64
GARMARNIKOW M.,"INFLUENCE-BUYING IN WEST AFRICA." COM FUT USSR INTELL NAT/G PLAN TEC/DEV ECO/TAC DOMIN EDU/PROP REGION NAT/LISM ATTIT DRIVE ALL/VALS SOVEREIGN...POLICY PSY SOC CONCPT TREND STERTYP WORK COLD/WAR 20. PAGE 55 H1102
AFR ECO/UNDEV FOR/AID SOCISM

S64
IRELE A.,"A DEFENSE OF NEGRITUDE." AFR NAT/LISM ...HUM 20 NEGRO. PAGE 78 H1566
CONCPT CULTURE NAT/COMP KIN

S64
KANOUTE P.,"AFRICAN SOCIALISM." AFR CONSTN NAT/G COLONIAL ORD/FREE...GOV/COMP METH/COMP 20 EUROPE. PAGE 83 H1655
SOCISM CULTURE STRUCT IDEA/COMP

S64
LOW D.A.,"LION RAMPANT." EUR+WWI MOD/EUR S/ASIA ECO/UNDEV NAT/G FORCES TEC/DEV ECO/TAC LEGIT ADMIN COLONIAL COERCE ORD/FREE RESPECT 19/20. PAGE 99 H1972
AFR DOMIN DIPLOM UK

S64
MARTELLI G.,"PORTUGAL AND THE UNITED NATIONS." AFR EUR+WWI ELITES INT/ORG NAT/G PROVS PLAN DIPLOM ECO/TAC DOMIN COLONIAL RIGID/FLEX MORAL ORD/FREE PWR WEALTH...MYTH UN 20. PAGE 103 H2060
ATTIT PORTUGAL

S64
MC WILLIAM M.,"THE WORLD BANK AND THE TRANSFER OF POWER IN KENYA." AFR ECO/UNDEV CONSULT ACT/RES TEC/DEV PERCEPT PWR SKILL WEALTH...CONCPT OBS TREND 20. PAGE 106 H2119
NAT/G ECO/TAC

S64
TOUVAL S.,"THE SOMALI REPUBLIC." AFR ISLAM SOMALIA FAM KIN NAT/G CREATE FOR/AID LEGIT ATTIT ALL/VALS ...RECORD TREND 20. PAGE 156 H3119
ECO/UNDEV RIGID/FLEX

N64
KENYA MINISTRY ECO PLAN DEV,AFRICAN SOCIALISM AND ITS APPLICATION TO PLANNING IN KENYA (PAMPHLET). AFR AGRI INDUS WORKER TAX COLONIAL WEALTH 20. PAGE 85 H1691
NAT/G SOCISM PLAN ECO/UNDEV

B65
ADAM T.R.,GOVERNMENT AND POLITICS IN AFRICA SOUTH OF THE SAHARA. AFR EUR+WWI CONSTN CULTURE INTELL POL/PAR TOP/EX LEGIT REGION DRIVE...OBS TREND CMN/WLTH 20. PAGE 3 H0062
NAT/G TIME/SEQ RACE/REL COLONIAL

B65
ADU A.L.,THE CIVIL SERVICE IN NEW AFRICAN STATES. AFR GHANA FINAN SOVEREIGN...POLICY 20 CIVIL/SERV AFRICA/E AFRICA/W. PAGE 4 H0074
ECO/UNDEV ADMIN COLONIAL NAT/G

B65
APTER D.E.,THE POLITICS OF MODERNIZATION. AFR L/A+17C CULTURE NAT/G POL/PAR ADMIN COLONIAL NAT/LISM ATTIT RIGID/FLEX PWR...SOC CONCPT. PAGE 8 H0154
ECO/UNDEV GEN/LAWS STRATA CREATE

B65
BRIDGMAN J.,GERMAN AFRICA: A SELECT ANNOTATED BIBLIOGRAPHY. AFR AGRI DIPLOM REPAR WAR FASCISM 20. PAGE 21 H0414
BIBLIOG/A COLONIAL NAT/G EDU/PROP

B65
COWAN L.G.,EDUCATION AND NATION-BUILDING IN AFRICA. AFR CULTURE ECO/UNDEV POL/PAR ACT/RES LEAD SOVEREIGN...METH/COMP ANTHOL BIBLIOG 20. PAGE 34 H0684
EDU/PROP COLONIAL ACADEM NAT/LISM

B65
CRABB C.V. JR.,THE ELEPHANTS AND THE GRASS* A STUDY OF NONALIGNMENT. AFR ASIA INDIA S/ASIA USA+45 USSR BAL/PWR NEUTRAL ATTIT...TREND NAT/COMP COLD/WAR. PAGE 34 H0691
ECO/UNDEV DIPLOM CONCPT

B65
GHAI D.P.,PORTRAIT OF A MINORITY: ASIANS IN EAST AFRICA. S/ASIA TANZANIA UGANDA COLONIAL...SOC OBS PREDICT ANTHOL 20. PAGE 56 H1119
RACE/REL GP/REL CULTURE AFR

B65
GIBBS S.L.,PEOPLES OF AFRICA. AFR INGP/REL HABITAT ...GEOG ANTHOL 20. PAGE 56 H1122
CULTURE AGRI FAM KIN

B65
GINIEWSKI P.,THE TWO FACES OF APARTHEID. AFR SOUTH/AFR STRATA AGRI INDUS COLONIAL PARTIC SOVEREIGN...CONCPT GOV/COMP NAT/COMP 19/20 NEGRO. PAGE 56 H1131
DISCRIM NAT/G RACE/REL STRUCT

B65
HAEFELE E.T.,GOVERNMENT CONTROLS ON TRANSPORT. AFR RHODESIA TANZANIA DIPLOM ECO/TAC TARIFFS PRICE ADJUD CONTROL REGION EFFICIENCY...POLICY 20 CONGO. PAGE 64 H1274
ECO/UNDEV DIST/IND FINAN NAT/G

B65
HAPGOOD D.,AFRICA: FROM INDEPENDENCE TO TOMARROW. AFR GUINEA SENEGAL CULTURE ELITES ECO/UNDEV AGRI SCHOOL FOR/AID COLONIAL MARXISM...TREND 20. PAGE 66 H1323
ECO/TAC SOCIETY NAT/G

B65
HARBISON F.,MANPOWER AND EDUCATION. AFR CHINA/COM IRAN L/A+17C S/ASIA TEC/DEV ADJUST OPTIMAL SKILL ...ANTHOL 20. PAGE 66 H1325
ECO/UNDEV EDU/PROP WORKER NAT/COMP

B65
HARRIS R.L.,POLITICAL ORGANIZATION OF THE MBEMBE NIGERIA. AFR NIGERIA SOCIETY AGRI SECT WORKER PAY ...SOC WORSHIP 20 MBEMBE. PAGE 67 H1345
STRUCT CHIEF CULTURE

B65
HORNE A.J.,THE COMMONWEALTH TODAY. AFR ASIA CANADA UK STRUCT ECO/UNDEV NAT/G SECT GP/REL 20 AUSTRAL CMN/WLTH. PAGE 73 H1470
BIBLIOG/A SOCIETY CULTURE

B65
INST INTL DES CIVILISATION DIF,THE CONSTITUTIONS AND ADMINISTRATIVE INSTITUTIONS OF THE NEW STATES. AFR ISLAM S/ASIA NAT/G POL/PAR DELIB/GP EX/STRUC CONFER EFFICIENCY NAT/LISM...JURID SOC 20. PAGE 77 H1535
CONSTN ADMIN ADJUD ECO/UNDEV

B65
KIRKWOOD K.,BRITAIN AND AFRICA. AFR UK ECO/UNDEV ECO/TAC WAR NAT/LISM SOVEREIGN 19/20. PAGE 86 H1725
NAT/G DIPLOM POLICY COLONIAL

B65
KOHN H.,AFRICAN NATIONALISM IN THE TWENTIETH CENTURY. AFR NAT/G POL/PAR COLONIAL REGION DISCRIM SOVEREIGN 20. PAGE 87 H1747
NAT/LISM CULTURE ATTIT

B65
KUPER H.,URBANIZATION AND MIGRATION IN WEST AFRICA. UPPER/VOLT CULTURE ECO/UNDEV WORKER REGION GOV/REL ...LING ANTHOL SOC/INTEG 20 AFRICA/W OSHOGBO MOSSI MIGRATION. PAGE 89 H1781
AFR HABITAT MUNIC GEOG

B65
LEWIS W.A.,POLITICS IN WEST AFRICA. AFR BAL/PWR DIPLOM REPRESENT...POLICY 20. PAGE 96 H1916
POL/PAR ELITES NAT/G ECO/UNDEV

B65
MEYER F.S.,THE AFRICAN NETTLE. SOUTH/AFR NAT/LISM SOVEREIGN...ANTHOL 20 EUROPE. PAGE 110 H2191
AFR COLONIAL RACE/REL ECO/UNDEV

B65
NEWBURY C.W.,BRITISH POLICY TOWARDS WEST AFRICA: SELECT DOCUMENTS 1786-1874. AFR UK INT/TRADE DOMIN ADMIN COLONIAL CT/SYS COERCE ORD/FREE...BIBLIOG/A 18/19. PAGE 117 H2345
DIPLOM POLICY NAT/G WRITING

B65
NYE J.S. JR.,PAN-AFRICANISM AND EAST AFRICAN INTEGRATION. TANZANIA UGANDA STRUCT ECO/UNDEV NAT/G DIPLOM FEDERAL NAT/LISM...STAT SOC/EXP BIBLIOG EEC OAU. PAGE 119 H2382
REGION ATTIT GEN/LAWS AFR

B65
OBUKAR C.,THE MODERN AFRICAN. AGRI INDUS WORKER CAP/ISM EDU/PROP PARTIC RACE/REL NAT/LISM ALL/VALS MARXISM...SOC IDEA/COMP 20. PAGE 120 H2393
AFR ECO/UNDEV CULTURE SOVEREIGN

B65
ONUOHA B.,THE ELEMENTS OF AFRICAN SOCIALISM. AFR FINAN SECT TEC/DEV FOR/AID GP/REL OWN LAISSEZ MARXISM...CONCPT BIBLIOG 20. PAGE 121 H2419
SOCISM ECO/UNDEV NAT/G EX/STRUC

B65
PEASLEE A.J.,CONSTITUTIONS OF NATIONS* THIRD REVISED EDITION (VOLUME I* AFRICA). LAW EX/STRUC LEGIS TOP/EX LEGIT CT/SYS ROUTINE ORD/FREE PWR SOVEREIGN...CON/ANAL CHARTS. PAGE 124 H2481
AFR CHOOSE CONSTN NAT/G

B65
ROTBERG R.I.,A POLITICAL HISTORY OF TROPICAL AFRICA. EX/STRUC DIPLOM INT/TRADE DOMIN ADMIN RACE/REL NAT/LISM PWR SOVEREIGN...GEOG TIME/SEQ BIBLIOG 1/20. PAGE 135 H2692
AFR CULTURE COLONIAL

B65
SIMMS R.P.,URBANIZATION IN WEST AFRICA; A REVIEW OF CURRENT LITERATURE. AFR PLAN TEC/DEV...SOC OBS NAT/COMP 20. PAGE 144 H2878
BIBLIOG/A MUNIC ECO/DEV ECO/UNDEV

B65
SPENCER P.,THE SAMBURU: A STUDY OF GERONTOCRACY IN A NOMADIC TRIBE. AFR SOCIETY ECO/UNDEV AGRI FAM NEIGH SECT GP/REL MARRIAGE WORSHIP 20 SAMBURU. PAGE 147 H2945
KIN STRUCT AGE/O CULTURE

B65
VAN DEN BERGHE P.L.,SOUTH AFRICA: A STUDY IN CONFLICT. AFR CULTURE SOCIETY STRATA STRUCT COERCE SEGREGAT. PAGE 161 H3227
DOMIN RACE/REL DISCRIM

B65
VAN DEN BERGHE P.L.,AFRICA: SOCIAL PROBLEMS OF CHANGE AND CONFLICT. ELITES STRATA ECO/UNDEV KIN MUNIC DIPLOM GP/REL RACE/REL NAT/LISM...ANTHOL BIBLIOG 20. PAGE 161 H3228
SOC CULTURE AFR STRUCT

B65
VATCHER W.H. JR.,WHITE LAAGER: THE RISE OF AFRIKANER NATIONALISM. AFR SOUTH/AFR CULTURE TOTALISM 20. PAGE 162 H3235
NAT/LISM POL/PAR RACE/REL DISCRIM

B65
VON RENESSE E.A.,UNVOLLENDETE DEMOKRATIEN. AFR ISLAM S/ASIA SOCIETY ACT/RES COLONIAL...JURID CHARTS BIBLIOG METH 13/20. PAGE 164 H3276
ECO/UNDEV NAT/COMP SOVEREIGN

B65
WALKER A.A.,THE RHODESIAS AND NYASALAND: A GUIDE TO OFFICIAL PUBLICATIONS. RHODESIA UK OP/RES PLAN PROB/SOLV DIPLOM...POLICY SOC CON/ANAL 19/20 NYASALAND. PAGE 164 H3291
BIBLIOG NAT/G COLONIAL AFR

L65
SCHAFFER B.B.,"THE CONCEPT OF PREPARATION* SOME QUESTIONS ABOUT THE TRANSFER OF SYSTEMS OF GOVERNMENT." AFR ASIA CANADA ELITES NAT/G POL/PAR COLONIAL RIGID/FLEX IDEA/COMP. PAGE 138 H2769
ECO/UNDEV UK RECORD

S65
HAYTER T.,"FRENCH AID TO AFRICA* ITS SCOPE AND ACHIEVEMENTS." CULTURE ECO/TAC INT/TRADE ADMIN REGION CENTRAL FEDERAL LOVE PWR SOVEREIGN EEC. PAGE 68 H1370
AFR FRANCE FOR/AID COLONIAL

S65
MULLER A.L.,"SOME NON-ECONOMIC DETERMINANTS OF THE ECONOMIC STATUS OF ASIANS IN AFRICA." AFR SOUTH/AFR CULTURE 20. PAGE 114 H2283
DISCRIM RACE/REL LABOR SECT

B66
AFRIFA A.A.,THE GHANA COUP. AFR GHANA ELITES NAT/G DIPLOM DOMIN 20 NKRUMAH/K. PAGE 4 H0076
TOP/EX REV FORCES POL/PAR

B66
BARNETT D.L.,MAU MAU FROM WITHIN. AFR UK POL/PAR LEAD GUERRILLA AUTHORIT ORD/FREE...SOC BIOG 20 NEGRO MAU/MAU. PAGE 11 H0225
REV CULTURE NAT/G

B66
BASDEN G.T.,NIGER IBOS. NIGERIA STRUCT SECT CHIEF COLONIAL HABITAT...POLICY SOC MYTH OBS WORSHIP 20 IBO. PAGE 12 H0233
CULTURE AFR SOCIETY

B66
BIRMINGHAM W.,A STUDY OF CONTEMPORARY GHANA VOL I: THE ECONOMY OF GHANA. AFR GHANA PLAN...POLICY STAT CHARTS ANTHOL BIBLIOG 20. PAGE 17 H0342
ECO/UNDEV ECO/TAC NAT/G PRODUC

B66
CROWDER M.,A SHORT HISTORY OF NIGERIA. AFR NIGERIA UK ECO/UNDEV CHIEF INT/TRADE RACE/REL NAT/LISM ORD/FREE...GEOG SOC CHARTS BIBLIOG 14/20. PAGE 36 H0711
COLONIAL NAT/G CULTURE

B66
DIAMOND S.,THE TRANSFORMATION OF EAST AFRICA. NAT/G SCHOOL CREATE PROB/SOLV COLONIAL REGION RACE/REL FEDERAL...SOC ANTHOL WORSHIP 20 AFRICA/E. PAGE 41 H0819
CULTURE AFR TEC/DEV INDUS

B66
DODGE D.,AFRICAN POLITICS IN PERSPECTIVE. ELITES POL/PAR PROB/SOLV LEAD...POLICY 20 THIRD/WRLD. PAGE 41 H0831
AFR NAT/G COLONIAL SOVEREIGN

B66
ELLIS A.B.,THE EWE-SPEAKING PEOPLES OF THE SLAVE COAST OF WEST AFRICA. AFR FORCES ADJUST...LING RECORD GP/COMP WORSHIP 20 AFRICA/W DEITY. PAGE 45 H0910
MYTH CULTURE HABITAT

B66
FLINT J.E.,NIGERIA AND GHANA. AFR GHANA NIGERIA UK NAT/G DOMIN DISCRIM...CHARTS BIBLIOG/A 15/20 NEGRO MAPS. PAGE 51 H1026
CULTURE COLONIAL NAT/LISM

B66
HAHN C.H.L.,THE NATIVE TRIBES OF SOUTH WEST AFRICA. LAW FAM SECT HABITAT SKILL...SOC AUD/VIS WORSHIP RITUAL 20 AFRICA/SW. PAGE 64 H1275
CULTURE SOCIETY STRUCT AFR

B66
HOWE R.W.,BLACK AFRICA: FROM PRE-HISTORY TO THE EVE OF THE COLONIAL ERA. ECO/UNDEV KIN PROVS SECT INT/TRADE EDU/PROP COLONIAL...BIBLIOG WORSHIP. PAGE 74 H1482
AFR CULTURE SOC

B66
JONES D.H.,AFRICA BIBLIOGRAPHY SERIES: EAST AFRICA. AFR UGANDA SECT BIO/SOC...JURID NAT/COMP 20. PAGE 82 H1630
BIBLIOG/A SOC CULTURE LING

B66
KASUNMU A.B.,NIGERIAN FAMILY LAW. NIGERIA KIN LEGIT ILLEGIT MARRIAGE AGE DRIVE HABITAT ALL/VALS...JURID IDEA/COMP T 20 ENGLSH/LAW. PAGE 83 H1667
FAM LAW CULTURE AFR

B66
KAUNDA K.,ZAMBIA: INDEPENDENCE AND BEYOND: THE SPEECHES OF KENNETH KAUNDA. AFR FUT ZAMBIA SOCIETY ECO/UNDEV NAT/G PROB/SOLV ECO/TAC ADMIN RACE/REL SOVEREIGN 20. PAGE 84 H1670
ORD/FREE COLONIAL CONSTN LEAD

B66
KEAY E.A.,THE NATIVE AND CUSTOMARY COURTS OF NIGERIA. NIGERIA CONSTN ELITES NAT/G TOP/EX PARTIC REGION...DECISION JURID 19/20. PAGE 84 H1673
AFR ADJUD LAW

B66
KEITH G.,THE FADING COLOUR BAR. AFR CENTRL/AFR UK ZAMBIA CULTURE SCHOOL EDU/PROP PERS/REL DISCRIM AGE ...AUD/VIS NAT/COMP SOC/INTEG 20 NEGRO. PAGE 84 H1682
RACE/REL STRUCT ATTIT NAT/G

B66
MATTHEWS R.,AFRICAN POWDER KEG: REVOLT AND DISSENT IN SIX EMERGENT NATIONS. AFR ALGERIA DAHOMEY GABON GHANA MALAWI GAMBLE LEAD PARTIC REV DRIVE...BIOG TREND GOV/COMP 20. PAGE 105 H2098
ELITES ECO/UNDEV TOP/EX CONTROL

B66
MCKAY V.,AFRICAN DIPLOMACY STUDIES IN THE DETERMINANTS OF FOREIGN POLICY. AFR SOUTH/AFR CULTURE NEUTRAL REGION SOVEREIGN...INT/LAW GOV/COMP ANTHOL 20. PAGE 107 H2138
ECO/UNDEV RACE/REL CIVMIL/REL DIPLOM

B66
MULLER C.F.J.,A SELECT BIBLIOGRAPHY OF SOUTH AFRICAN HISTORY; A GUIDE FOR HISTORICAL RESEARCH. SOUTH/AFR UK LAW CONSTN SOCIETY STRUCT AGRI SECT DIPLOM COLONIAL LEAD RACE/REL...POLICY 17/20 NEGRO. PAGE 114 H2284
BIBLIOG AFR NAT/G

B66
SCHATTEN F.,COMMUNISM IN AFRICA. AFR GHANA GUINEA MALI CULTURE ECO/UNDEV LABOR SECT ECO/TAC EDU/PROP REV 20. PAGE 139 H2774
COLONIAL NAT/LISM MARXISM DIPLOM

B66
SYMONDS R.,THE BRITISH AND THEIR SUCCESSORS. AFR CEYLON INDIA UK SCHOOL FORCES EDU/PROP ADMIN PARTIC ...NAT/COMP BIBLIOG 20 AFRICA/W AFRICA/E. PAGE 151 H3024
NAT/G ECO/UNDEV POLICY COLONIAL

B66
WEINSTEIN B.,GABON: NATION-BUILDING ON THE OGOOUE. AFR GABON WOR+45 CULTURE SOCIETY PLAN DIPLOM COLONIAL INGP/REL ANOMIE HABITAT SUPEGO 20. PAGE 166 H3329
ECO/UNDEV GP/REL LEAD NAT/G

B66
ZABLOCKI C.J.,SINO-SOVIET RIVALRY. AFR ASIA CHINA/COM CUBA EUR+WWI L/A+17C USA+45 USSR WOR+45 POL/PAR FORCES COERCE NUC/PWR...GOV/COMP IDEA/COMP 20 MAO KHRUSH/N. PAGE 172 H3444
DIPLOM MARXISM COM

B66
ZOLBERG A.R.,CREATING POLITICAL ORDER. AFR CONGO/BRAZ GHANA NIGER KIN NAT/G DOMIN COLONIAL REGION CENTRAL NAT/LISM ATTIT PWR 20 CONGO/LEOP. PAGE 173 H3462
SOVEREIGN ORD/FREE CONSTN POL/PAR

L66
LEMARCHAND R.,"SOCIAL CHANGE AND POLITICAL MODERNISATION IN BURUNDI." AFR BURUNDI STRATA CHIEF EX/STRUC RIGID/FLEX PWR...SOC 20. PAGE 94 H1874
NAT/G STRUCT ELITES CONSERVE

L66
MCAUSLAN J.P.W.,"CONSTITUTIONAL INNOVATION AND POLITICAL STABILITY IN TANZANIA: A PRELIMINARY ASSESSMENT." AFR TANZANIA ELITES CHIEF EX/STRUC RIGID/FLEX PWR 20 PRESIDENT BUREAUCRCY. PAGE 106 H2122
CONSTN NAT/G EXEC POL/PAR

S66
COWAN L.G.,"THE MILITARY AND AFRICAN POLITICS." AFR FUT NAT/G POL/PAR PARTIC REV 20. PAGE 34 H0685
CIVMIL/REL FORCES PWR LEAD

S66
FLEMING W.G.,"AUTHORITY, EFFICIENCY, AND ROLE STRESS: PROBLEMS IN THE DEVELOPMENT OF EAST AFRICAN BUREAUCRACIES." AFR UGANDA STRUCT PROB/SOLV ROUTINE INGP/REL ROLE...MGT SOC GP/COMP GOV/COMP 20 TANGANYIKA AFRICA/E. PAGE 51 H1024
DOMIN EFFICIENCY COLONIAL ADMIN

S66
GRUNDY K.W.,"RECENT CONTRIBUTIONS TO THE STUDY OF AFRICAN POLITICAL THOUGHT." DIPLOM NAT/LISM ALL/IDEOS...NEW/IDEA GOV/COMP 20. PAGE 62 H1239
BIBLIOG/A AFR ATTIT IDEA/COMP

S66
KAPIL R.L.,"ON THE CONFLICT POTENTIAL OF INHERITED BOUNDARIES IN AFRICA." MOD/EUR MOROCCO UAR EX/STRUC DIPLOM LEGIT REGION ADJUST...RECORD NAT/COMP GEN/LAWS. PAGE 83 H1658
AFR COLONIAL PREDICT GEOG

S66
MARTZ J.D.,"THE PLACE OF LATIN AMERICA IN THE STUDY OF COMPARATIVE POLITICS." AFR ASIA CULTURE STRUCT ECO/UNDEV ACADEM CREATE...CLASSIF NAT/COMP. PAGE 104 H2072
L/A+17C GOV/COMP STERTYP GEN/LAWS

S66
MATTHEWS D.G.,"PRELUDE-COUP D'ETAT-MILITARY GOVERNMENT: A BIBLIOGRAPHICAL AND RESEARCH GUIDE TO NIGERIAN POL AND GOVT, JAN, 1965-66." AFR NIGER LAW CONSTN POL/PAR LEGIS CIVMIL/REL GOV/REL...STAT 20. PAGE 105 H2096
BIBLIOG NAT/G ADMIN CHOOSE

S66
MCLANE C.B.,"SOVIET DOCTRINE AND THE MILITARY COUPS IN AFRICA." ALGERIA GHANA COLONIAL NAT/LISM RIGID/FLEX SOVEREIGN MARXISM...DECISION NAT/COMP. PAGE 107 H2140
USSR ATTIT AFR FORCES

S66
MERRITT R.L.,"SELECTED ARTICLES AND DOCUMENTS ON COMPARATIVE GOVERNMENT AND CROSS-NATIONAL RESEARCH." AFR ASIA EUR+WWI L/A+17C MOD/EUR ELITES R+D ACT/RES DIPLOM PWR...SOC CONCPT 18/20. PAGE 109 H2185
BIBLIOG GOV/COMP NAT/G GOV/REL

S66
O'BRIEN W.V.,"EVENTS AND TRENDS: PATTERNS OF AFRICAN INTERNATIONAL POLITICAL BEHAVIOR." CULTURE SOCIETY NAT/G NAT/LISM SOCISM. PAGE 119 H2386
BIBLIOG/A AFR TREND DIPLOM

S66
ROTHCHILD D.,"THE LIMITS OF FEDERALISM: AN EXAMINATION OF POLITICAL INSTITUTIONAL TRANSFER IN AFRICA." AFR CONSTN CULTURE ELITES ECO/UNDEV KIN PROB/SOLV ADMIN ORD/FREE PWR...POLICY 20. PAGE 135 H2695
FEDERAL NAT/G NAT/LISM COLONIAL

S66
TOUVAL S.,"AFRICA'S FRONTIERS* REACTIONS TO A COLONIAL LEGACY." L/A+17C CONFER ADJUD COLONIAL APPORT CONSEN NAT/LISM RESPECT...RECORD NAT/COMP. PAGE 156 H3120
AFR GEOG SOVEREIGN WAR

C66
ROSENBERG C.G. JR.,"THE MYTH OF "MAU-MAU:" NATIONALISM IN KENYA." AFR CULTURE NAT/G POL/PAR COERCE REV RACE/REL ATTIT ORD/FREE SOVEREIGN...MYTH BIBLIOG 20. PAGE 134 H2678
NAT/LISM COLONIAL MAJORIT LEAD

B67
ARIKPO O.,THE DEVELOPMENT OF MODERN NIGERIA. AFR NIGERIA SOCIETY ECO/UNDEV KIN ADMIN FEDERAL NAT/LISM ORD/FREE WEALTH...POLICY GEOG BIBLIOG 19/20. PAGE 8 H0163
NAT/G CULTURE CONSTN COLONIAL

B67
CHILCOTE R.H.,PORTUGUESE AFRICA. PORTUGAL CULTURE SOCIETY ECO/UNDEV DOMIN NAT/LISM...TREND IDEA/COMP NAT/COMP BIBLIOG 15/20. PAGE 29 H0589
AFR COLONIAL ORD/FREE PROB/SOLV

B67
CURTIN P.D.,AFRICA REMEMBERED. NIGERIA SENEGAL CULTURE DIPLOM INT/TRADE GP/REL RACE/REL...RECORD ANTHOL 18/19 NEGRO. PAGE 36 H0727
DOMIN ORD/FREE AFR DISCRIM

B67
FANON F.,TOWARD THE AFRICAN REVOLUTION. AFR FRANCE CULTURE ELITES LEAD REV GP/REL ORD/FREE SOVEREIGN 20. PAGE 49 H0969
COLONIAL DOMIN ECO/UNDEV RACE/REL

B67
GIFFORD P.,BRITAIN AND GERMANY IN AFRICA. AFR GERMANY UK ECO/UNDEV LEAD WAR NAT/LISM ATTIT ...POLICY HIST/WRIT METH/COMP ANTHOL BIBLIOG 19/20 WWI. PAGE 56 H1123
COLONIAL ADMIN DIPLOM NAT/COMP

B67
MAZRUI A.A.,THE ANGLO-AFRICAN COMMONWEALTH; POLITICAL FRICTION AND CULTURAL FUSION. AFR INT/ORG VOL/ASSN CHIEF GP/REL INGP/REL RACE/REL NAT/LISM 20 CMN/WLTH EEC. PAGE 106 H2111
COLONIAL SOVEREIGN DIPLOM CULTURE

B67
MUNGER E.S.,AFRIKANER AND AFRICAN NATIONALISM: SOUTH AFRICAN PARALLELS AND PARAMETERS. SOUTH/AFR WOR+45 CULTURE ELITES STRUCT NAT/G PROB/SOLV DOMIN CONTROL PERS/REL NAT/LISM...SOC 20. PAGE 115 H2289
AFR RACE/REL

B67
NYERERE J.K.,FREEDOM AND UNITY/UHURU NA UMOJA: A SELECTION FROM WRITINGS AND SPEECHES, 1952-65. TANZANIA ELITES ECO/UNDEV INT/ORG NAT/G CREATE DIPLOM COLONIAL REGION RACE/REL...ANTHOL 20. PAGE 119 H2383
SOVEREIGN AFR TREND ORD/FREE

B67
ODINGA O.,NOT YET UHURU. NAT/G POL/PAR PROB/SOLV COERCE REV WAR PERS/REL PERSON ORD/FREE...POLICY 20 ODINGA/O KENYATTA. PAGE 120 H2395
ATTIT BIOG LEAD AFR

B67
OLIVER R.,AFRICA SINCE 1800. AFR ISLAM CULTURE ECO/UNDEV SECT DOMIN RACE/REL DISCRIM SOVEREIGN 19/20. PAGE 121 H2414
DIPLOM COLONIAL REGION

B67
RAVKIN A.,THE NEW STATES OF AFRICA (HEADLINE SERIES, NO. 183((PAMPHLET). CULTURE STRUCT INDUS COLONIAL NAT/LISM...SOC 20. PAGE 130 H2597
AFR ECO/UNDEV SOCIETY ADMIN

B67
SPIRO H.S.,PATTERNS OF AFRICAN DEVLOPMENT: FIVE COMPARISONS. STRUCT ECO/UNDEV NAT/G CONSERVE SOCISM ...PREDICT NAT/COMP 20 CHINJAP. PAGE 148 H2951
AFR CONSTN NAT/LISM TREND

B67
WILLS A.J.,AN INTRODUCTION TO THE HISTORY OF CENTRAL AFRICA. RHODESIA ZAMBIA CULTURE SOCIETY ECO/UNDEV TEC/DEV DOMIN WAR ALL/VALS...POLICY TREND BIBLIOG T 14/20 NYASALAND. PAGE 169 H3375
AFR COLONIAL ORD/FREE

B67
WINTER E.H.,CONTEMPORARY CHANGE IN TRADITIONAL SOCIETIES: VOLUME I INTRODUCTION AND AFRICAN TRIBES. NIGERIA AGRI LOC/G NAT/G CREATE DOMIN COLONIAL CONTROL GP/REL PWR SOVEREIGN...SOC OBS 20 TANGANYIKA. PAGE 169 H3389
SOCIETY AFR CONSERVE KIN

L67
AUSTIN D.A.,"POLITICAL CONFLICT IN AFRICA." CONSTN NAT/G CREATE ADMIN COLONIAL ORD/FREE MARXISM POPULISM SOCISM...NAT/COMP ANTHOL 20. PAGE 9 H0180
ANOMIE AFR POL/PAR

L67
SEGAL A.,"THE INTEGRATION OF DEVELOPING COUNTRIES: SOME THOUGHTS ON EAST AFRICA AND CENTRAL AMERICA." AFR L/A+17C INT/ORG NAT/G VOL/ASSN FOR/AID INT/TRADE EQUILIB NAT/LISM PWR 20. PAGE 141 H2820
ECO/UNDEV DIPLOM REGION

L67
TABORSKY E.,"THE COMMUNIST PARTIES OF THE 'THIRD WORLD' IN SOVIET STRATEGY." AFR ASIA L/A+17C USSR INTELL NAT/G WORKER PLAN CONTROL LEAD PARTIC REV ...GOV/COMP 20 COM/PARTY THIRD/WRLD. PAGE 152 H3032
POL/PAR MARXISM ECO/UNDEV DIPLOM

L67
TOUVAL S.,"THE ORGANIZATION OF AFRICAN UNITY AND AFRICAN BORDERS." DEBATE REGION TASK REV ATTIT ORD/FREE...DECISION UN 20 OAU. PAGE 156 H3121
AFR NAT/G COLONIAL NAT/LISM

S67
ADOKO A.,"THE CONSTITUTION OF UGANDA." AFR UGANDA LOC/G CHIEF FORCES LEGIS ADJUD EXEC CHOOSE NAT/LISM ...IDEA/COMP 20. PAGE 4 H0072
NAT/G CONSTN ORD/FREE LAW

S67
COHEN R.,"ANTHROPOLOGY AND POLITICAL SCIENCE: COURTSHIP OR MARRIAGE?" CULTURE STRATA STRUCT MUNIC REGION UTOPIA...NEW/IDEA TREND IDEA/COMP METH/COMP 20. PAGE 31 H0618
SOC INGP/REL AFR

S67
FLETCHER-COOKE J.,"THE EMERGING AFRICAN STATE." AFR GP/REL NAT/LISM. PAGE 51 H1025
ECO/UNDEV NAT/COMP DIPLOM ATTIT

S67
GRUNDY K.W.,"AFRICA IN THE WORLD ARENA." ECO/UNDEV BAL/PWR FOR/AID NEUTRAL REV NAT/LISM GOV/COMP. PAGE 62 H1240
AFR DIPLOM INT/ORG COLONIAL

S67
HAMMOND R.J.,"RACE ATTITUDES AND POLICIES IN PORTUGUESE AFRICA IN THE NINETEENTH AND TWENTIETH CENTURIES." AFR PORTUGAL NAT/G SECT EDU/PROP COLONIAL ATTIT RIGID/FLEX SEX MORAL RESPECT 19/20 NEGRO. PAGE 65 H1309
POLICY RACE/REL DISCRIM SOCIETY

S67
IDENBURG P.J.,"POLITICAL STRUCTURAL DEVELOPMENT IN TROPICAL AFRICA." UK ECO/UNDEV KIN POL/PAR CHIEF EX/STRUC CREATE COLONIAL CONTROL REPRESENT RACE/REL ...MAJORIT TREND 20. PAGE 76 H1521
AFR CONSTN NAT/G GOV/COMP

S67
LOFCHIE M.F.,"OKELLO'S REVOLUTION." TANZANIA NAT/G POL/PAR FORCES PLAN CONTROL 20. PAGE 98 H1954
AFR REV LEAD CHIEF

S67
MAIR L.,"BUSOGA LOCAL GOVERNMENT" AFR UGANDA UK
LOC/G

CONSTN GP/REL...GOV/COMP METH/COMP 20. PAGE 101 H2024 — COLONIAL LAW ATTIT

S67
MAYANJA A.,"THE GOVERNMENT'S PROPOSALS ON THE NEW CONSTITUTION." AFR UGANDA LAW CHIEF LEGIS ADJUD REPRESENT FEDERAL PWR 20. PAGE 105 H2105 — CONSTN CONFER ORD/FREE NAT/G

S67
READ J.S.,"CENSORED." UGANDA CONSTN INTELL SOCIETY NAT/G DIPLOM PRESS WRITING ADJUD ADMIN COLONIAL RISK...IDEA/COMP 20. PAGE 130 H2602 — EDU/PROP AFR CREATE

S67
ROTBERG R.I.,"COLONIALISM AND AFTER: THE POLITICAL LITERATURE OF CENTRAL AFRICA - A BIBLIOGRAPHIC ESSAY." AFR CHIEF EX/STRUC REV INGP/REL RACE/REL SOVEREIGN 20. PAGE 135 H2693 — BIBLIOG/A COLONIAL DIPLOM NAT/G

S67
THEROUX P.,"HATING THE ASIANS." TANZANIA UGANDA CONSTN INDUS NAT/G POL/PAR WORKER ECO/TAC HABITAT LOVE...POLICY GEOG 20 MIGRATION. PAGE 154 H3069 — AFR RACE/REL SOVEREIGN ATTIT

S67
VINCENT S.,"SHOULD BIAFRA SURVIVE?" NIGERIA ECO/UNDEV CHIEF FORCES ECO/TAC GP/REL DISCRIM PEACE ORD/FREE SOC/INTEG 20 BIAFRA IBO. PAGE 163 H3256 — AFR REV REGION NAT/G

S67
WRAITH R.E.,"ADMINISTRATIVE CHANGE IN THE NEW AFRICA." AFR LG/CO ADJUD INGP/REL PWR...RECORD GP/COMP 20. PAGE 171 H3416 — ADMIN NAT/G LOC/G ECO/UNDEV

S67
ZARTMAN I.W.," NAT/G POL/PAR VOL/ASSN NAT/LISM ORD/FREE PWR...CONCPT NAT/COMP ORG/CHARTS OAU MAGHREB. PAGE 172 H3451 — AFR ISLAM DIPLOM REGION

C67
LING D.L.,"TUNISIA: FROM PROTECTORATE TO REPUBLIC." CULTURE NAT/G POL/PAR CHIEF DIPLOM COERCE WAR PWR ...BIBLIOG 19/20 TUNIS. PAGE 97 H1934 — AFR NAT/LISM COLONIAL PROB/SOLV

L68
CURRENT HISTORY,"AFRICA, 1968." ETHIOPIA GHANA NIGERIA SOUTH/AFR CULTURE ECO/UNDEV KIN SECT CHIEF EX/STRUC WAR WEAPON CHOOSE CIVMIL/REL...GOV/COMP 20 AFRICA/E. PAGE 36 H0724 — RACE/REL NAT/LISM FORCES AFR

S68
CHAPMAN A.R.,"THE CIVIL WAR IN NIGERIA." AFR NIGERIA NAT/G PLAN ECO/TAC EDU/PROP COERCE WAR GOV/REL INGP/REL ORD/FREE PWR WEALTH SOC/INTEG 20 BIAFRA. PAGE 29 H0579 — REV RACE/REL

S68
DUGARD J.,"THE REVOCATION OF THE MANDATE FOR SOUTH WEST AFRICA." SOUTH/AFR WOR+45 STRATA NAT/G DELIB/GP DIPLOM ADJUD SANCTION CHOOSE RACE/REL ...POLICY NAT/COMP 20 AFRICA/SW UN TRUST/TERR LEAGUE/NAT. PAGE 43 H0858 — AFR INT/ORG DISCRIM COLONIAL

S68
LAWRIE G.,"WHAT WILL CHANGE SOUTH AFRICA?" AFR SOUTH/AFR ELITES DOMIN CONTROL REPRESENT...TIME/SEQ TREND 20. PAGE 93 H1848 — RACE/REL DIPLOM NAT/G POLICY

B82
MACDONALD D.,AFRICANA; OR, THE HEART OF HEATHEN AFRICA, VOL. II: MISSION LIFE. SOCIETY STRATA KIN CREATE EDU/PROP ADMIN COERCE LITERACY HEALTH...MYTH WORSHIP 19 LIVNGSTN/D MISSION NEGRO. PAGE 100 H1990 — SECT AFR CULTURE ORD/FREE

B98
FORTES M.,AFRICAN POLITICAL SYSTEMS. ECO/UNDEV KIN LOC/G NEIGH POL/PAR SECT LEAD GP/REL ORD/FREE...SOC 20 NEGRO. PAGE 52 H1039 — AFR CULTURE STRUCT

B99
BROOKS S.,BRITAIN AND THE BOERS. AFR SOUTH/AFR UK CULTURE INSPECT LEGIT...INT/LAW 19/20 BOER/WAR. PAGE 22 H0433 — WAR DIPLOM NAT/G

B99
KINGSLEY M.H.,WEST AFRICAN STUDIES. GHANA NIGERIA SIER/LEONE LAW EXTR/IND SECT DIPLOM INT/TRADE DOMIN RACE/REL OWN HEALTH...SOC 19. PAGE 86 H1717 — AFR HEREDITY COLONIAL CULTURE

AFR/STATES....ORGANIZATION OF AFRICAN STATES

AFRICA/CEN....CENTRAL AFRICA

AFRICA/E....EAST AFRICA

B38
COUPLAND R.,EAST AFRICA AND ITS INVADERS. AFR ISLAM STRATA SECT FORCES DIPLOM TRIBUTE CONTROL DISCRIM NAT/LISM 19 AFRICA/E EUROPE MISSION. PAGE 34 H0680 — CULTURE ELITES COLONIAL MARKET

B59
WRAITH R.E.,EAST AFRICAN CITIZEN. AFR GHANA UK AGRI INDUS LOC/G POL/PAR PROB/SOLV CONTROL REGION REPRESENT NAT/LISM PWR...OBS 20 AFRICA/E AFRICA/W. PAGE 171 H3415 — ECO/UNDEV RACE/REL NAT/G NAT/COMP

B63
HUNTER G.,EDUCATION FOR A DEVELOPING REGION; A STUDY IN EAST AFRICA. AFR TANZANIA UGANDA NAT/G TEC/DEV INGP/REL ADJUST LITERACY ATTIT 20 AFRICA/E. PAGE 75 H1501 — EDU/PROP POLICY ECO/UNDEV EFFICIENCY

B65
ADU A.L.,THE CIVIL SERVICE IN NEW AFRICAN STATES. AFR GHANA FINAN SOVEREIGN...POLICY 20 CIVIL/SERV AFRICA/E AFRICA/W. PAGE 4 H0074 — ECO/UNDEV ADMIN COLONIAL NAT/G

B66
DIAMOND S.,THE TRANSFORMATION OF EAST AFRICA. NAT/G SCHOOL CREATE PROB/SOLV COLONIAL REGION RACE/REL FEDERAL...SOC ANTHOL WORSHIP 20 AFRICA/E. PAGE 41 H0819 — CULTURE AFR TEC/DEV INDUS

B66
SMITH H.E.,READINGS IN ECONOMIC DEVELOPMENT AND ADMINISTRATION IN TANZANIA. TANZANIA FINAN INDUS LABOR NAT/G PLAN PROB/SOLV INT/TRADE COLONIAL REGION...ANTHOL BIBLIOG 20 AFRICA/E. PAGE 146 H2910 — TEC/DEV ADMIN GOV/REL

B66
SYMONDS R.,THE BRITISH AND THEIR SUCCESSORS. AFR CEYLON INDIA UK SCHOOL FORCES EDU/PROP ADMIN PARTIC ...NAT/COMP BIBLIOG 20 AFRICA/W AFRICA/E. PAGE 151 H3024 — NAT/G ECO/UNDEV POLICY COLONIAL

S66
FLEMING W.G.,"AUTHORITY, EFFICIENCY, AND ROLE STRESS: PROBLEMS IN THE DEVELOPMENT OF EAST AFRICAN BUREAUCRACIES." AFR UGANDA STRUCT PROB/SOLV ROUTINE INGP/REL ROLE...MGT SOC GP/COMP GOV/COMP 20 TANGANYIKA AFRICA/E. PAGE 51 H1024 — DOMIN EFFICIENCY COLONIAL ADMIN

L68
CURRENT HISTORY,"AFRICA, 1968." ETHIOPIA GHANA NIGERIA SOUTH/AFR CULTURE ECO/UNDEV KIN SECT CHIEF EX/STRUC WAR WEAPON CHOOSE CIVMIL/REL...GOV/COMP 20 AFRICA/E. PAGE 36 H0724 — RACE/REL NAT/LISM FORCES AFR

AFRICA/N....NORTH AFRICA

AFRICA/SW....SOUTH WEST AFRICA

B16
CALVERT A.F.,SOUTHWEST AFRICA 1884-1914 (2ND ED.). GERMANY EXTR/IND NAT/G FORCES...GEOG AUD/VIS CHARTS 19/20 RESOURCE/N AFRICA/SW. PAGE 25 H0508 — COLONIAL ECO/UNDEV AFR

N19
SOUTH AFRICA COMMISSION ON FUT,INTERIM AND FINAL REPORTS ON FUTURE FORM OF GOVERNMENT IN THE SOUTH-WEST AFRICAN PROTECTORATE (PAMPHLET). SOUTH/AFR NAT/G FORCES CONFER COLONIAL CONTROL 20 AFRICA/SW. PAGE 147 H2936 — CONSTN REPRESENT ADMIN PROB/SOLV

B37
UNION OF SOUTH AFRICA,REPORT CONCERNING ADMINISTRATION OF SOUTH WEST AFRICA (6 VOLS.). SOUTH/AFR INDUS PUB/INST FORCES LEGIS BUDGET DIPLOM EDU/PROP ADJUD CT/SYS...GEOG CHARTS 20 AFRICA/SW LEAGUE/NAT. PAGE 158 H3166 — NAT/G ADMIN COLONIAL CONSTN

B60
THE AFRICA 1960 COMMITTEE,MANDATE IN TRUST; THE PROBLEM OF SOUTH WEST AFRICA. GERMANY STRUCT REGION SANCTION CHOOSE DISCRIM...INT/LAW 20 AFRICA/SW UN LEAGUE/NAT TRUST/TERR. PAGE 153 H3066 — NAT/G DIPLOM COLONIAL RACE/REL

B62
LOWENSTEIN A.K.,BRUTAL MANDATE: A JOURNEY TO SOUTH WEST AFRICA. CULTURE INT/ORG NAT/G DIPLOM...GEOG 20 UN AFRICA/SW. PAGE 99 H1975 — AFR POLICY RACE/REL PROB/SOLV

B63
FIRST R.,SOUTH WEST AFRICA. SOUTH/AFR INT/ORG KIN NAT/G WORKER COLONIAL WAR...POLICY 20 UN TRUST/TERR AFRICA/SW. PAGE 50 H1006 — DISCRIM ORD/FREE RACE/REL CONTROL

B66
HAHN C.H.L.,THE NATIVE TRIBES OF SOUTH WEST AFRICA. LAW FAM SECT HABITAT SKILL...SOC AUD/VIS WORSHIP RITUAL 20 AFRICA/SW. PAGE 64 H1275 — CULTURE SOCIETY STRUCT AFR

S68
DUGARD J.,"THE REVOCATION OF THE MANDATE FOR SOUTH WEST AFRICA." SOUTH/AFR WOR+45 STRATA NAT/G DELIB/GP DIPLOM ADJUD SANCTION CHOOSE RACE/REL ...POLICY NAT/COMP 20 AFRICA/SW UN TRUST/TERR LEAGUE/NAT. PAGE 43 H0858 — AFR INT/ORG DISCRIM COLONIAL

AFRICA/W....WEST AFRICA

B12
SONOLET L.,L'AFRIQUE OCCIDENTALE FRANCAISE. FRANCE AGRI INDUS NAT/G SECT FORCES INT/TRADE EDU/PROP RACE/REL HEALTH ORD/FREE...CHARTS 19/20 NEGRO AFRICA/W. PAGE 147 H2933 — DOMIN ADMIN COLONIAL AFR

B26
MCPHEE A.,THE ECONOMIC REVOLUTION IN BRITISH WEST AFRICA. AFR UK CULTURE DIST/IND FINAN INDUS PLAN — ECO/UNDEV INT/TRADE

GP/REL RACE/REL 20 AFRICA/W. PAGE 107 H2148
COLONIAL GEOG

B35
GORER G.,AFRICA DANCES: A BOOK ABOUT WEST AFRICAN NEGROES. STRUCT LOC/G SECT FORCES TAX ADMIN COLONIAL...ART/METH MYTH WORSHIP 20 NEGRO AFRICA/W CHRISTIAN RITUAL. PAGE 59 H1181
AFR ATTIT CULTURE SOCIETY

B53
DAVIDSON B.,THE NEW WEST AFRICA: PROBLEMS OF INDEPENDENCE. UK AGRI TEC/DEV DIPLOM GP/REL RACE/REL SOVEREIGN...ANTHOL 20 AFRICA/W. PAGE 37 H0744
AFR COLONIAL ECO/UNDEV NAT/G

B57
RUMEU DE ARMAS A.,ESPANA EEN EL AFRICA ATLANTICA. AFR CHRIST-17C PORTUGAL SPAIN DIPLOM ECO/TAC CONTROL 14/16 AFRICA/W. PAGE 136 H2717
NAT/G COLONIAL CHIEF PWR

B58
HANSARD SOCIETY PARL GOVT,WHAT ARE THE PROBLEMS OF PARLIAMENTARY GOVERNMENT IN WEST AFRICA? PROB/SOLV DIPLOM GP/REL 20 PARLIAMENT AFRICA/W. PAGE 66 H1317
PARL/PROC POL/PAR AFR NAT/G

B59
WRAITH R.E.,EAST AFRICAN CITIZEN. AFR GHANA UK AGRI INDUS LOC/G POL/PAR PROB/SOLV CONTROL REGION REPRESENT NAT/LISM PWR...OBS 20 AFRICA/E AFRICA/W. PAGE 171 H3415
ECO/UNDEV RACE/REL NAT/G NAT/COMP

B63
WILSON U.,EDUCATION AND CHANGING WEST AFRICAN CULTURE. AFR MOD/EUR UK CULTURE ECO/UNDEV MUNIC CONSULT 19/20 CMN/WLTH AFRICA/W. PAGE 169 H3384
COLONIAL POLICY SCHOOL

B65
ADU A.L.,THE CIVIL SERVICE IN NEW AFRICAN STATES. AFR GHANA FINAN SOVEREIGN...POLICY 20 CIVIL/SERV AFRICA/E AFRICA/W. PAGE 4 H0074
ECO/UNDEV ADMIN COLONIAL NAT/G

B65
KUPER H.,URBANIZATION AND MIGRATION IN WEST AFRICA. AFR UPPER/VOLT CULTURE ECO/UNDEV WORKER REGION GOV/REL ...LING ANTHOL SOC/INTEG 20 AFRICA/W OSHOGBO MOSSI MIGRATION. PAGE 89 H1781
AFR HABITAT MUNIC GEOG

B65
WARD W.E.,GOVERNMENT IN WEST AFRICA. WOR+45 POL/PAR EX/STRUC PLAN PARTIC GP/REL SOVEREIGN 20 AFRICA/W. PAGE 165 H3308
GOV/COMP CONSTN COLONIAL ECO/UNDEV

B66
ELLIS A.B.,THE EWE-SPEAKING PEOPLES OF THE SLAVE COAST OF WEST AFRICA. AFR FORCES ADJUST...LING RECORD GP/COMP WORSHIP 20 AFRICA/W DEITY. PAGE 45 H0910
MYTH CULTURE HABITAT

B66
SYMONDS R.,THE BRITISH AND THEIR SUCCESSORS. AFR CEYLON INDIA UK SCHOOL FORCES EDU/PROP ADMIN PARTIC ...NAT/COMP BIBLIOG 20 AFRICA/W AFRICA/E. PAGE 151 H3024
NAT/G ECO/UNDEV POLICY COLONIAL

AFRICAN BIBLIOGRAPHIC CENTER H0075

AFRIFA A.A. H0076

AFTA....ATLANTIC FREE TRADE AREA

AGE....AGE FACTORS

N19
INTERNATIONAL LABOUR OFFICE,EMPLOYMENT, UNEMPLOYMENT AND LABOUR FORCE STATISTICS (PAMPHLET). EUR+WWI STRATA AGRI INDUS NAT/G PROB/SOLV PAY AGE SEX...SAMP NAT/COMP METH 20 ILO. PAGE 78 H1557
WORKER LABOR STAT ECO/DEV

B37
TINGSTEN H.,POLITICAL BEHAVIOR. EUR+WWI STRATA NAT/G POL/PAR ACT/RES AGE...TREND CHARTS 20 FEMALE/SEX. PAGE 155 H3100
CHOOSE ATTIT PARTIC

B51
BERNATZIK H.A.,THE SPIRITS OF THE YELLOW LEAVES. BURMA LAOS S/ASIA THAILAND VIETNAM SOCIETY AGRI COLONIAL LEISURE GP/REL PERS/REL ISOLAT AGE HABITAT SEX WORSHIP 20. PAGE 16 H0310
SOC KIN ECO/UNDEV CULTURE

B55
DUVERGER M.,THE POLITICAL ROLE OF WOMEN. FRANCE GERMANY/W NORWAY YUGOSLAVIA STRATA LOBBY AGE ATTIT ROLE...STAT SAMP CHARTS METH/COMP NAT/COMP HYPO/EXP FEMALE/SEX. PAGE 44 H0875
SEX LEAD PARTIC CHOOSE

B55
RODNICK D.,THE NORWEGIANS: A STUDY IN NATIONAL CULTURE. NORWAY FAM INGP/REL PERS/REL AGE...PSY SOC SELF/OBS WORSHIP 20. PAGE 133 H2655
CULTURE INT RECORD ATTIT

B57
INTERNATIONAL AFRICAN INST,ETHNOGRAPHIC SURVEY OF AFRICA: WESTERN AFRICA: THE BENIN KINGDOM. AFR NIGERIA CULTURE ECO/UNDEV KIN ECO/TAC GOV/REL AGE ATTIT HEREDITY...CHARTS BIBLIOG WORSHIP 20. PAGE 77 H1550
STRUCT INGP/REL GEOG HABITAT

B61
BLAKE J.,FAMILY STRUCTURE IN JAMAICA. JAMAICA CULTURE SOCIETY ACT/RES CONTROL MARRIAGE AGE ...POLICY SOC BIBLIOG 20. PAGE 18 H0351
FAM SEX STRUCT ATTIT

B62
FALKENBERG J.,KIN AND TOTEM; GROUP RELATIONS OF AUSTRALIAN ABORIGINES IN THE PORT KEATS DISTRICT. SOCIETY STRATA STRUCT GP/REL PERS/REL MARRIAGE AGE ATTIT SEX...SOC STAT CHARTS AUSTRAL ABORIGINES. PAGE 48 H0964
KIN INGP/REL CULTURE FAM

B66
KASUNMU A.B.,NIGERIAN FAMILY LAW. NIGERIA KIN LEGIT ILLEGIT MARRIAGE AGE DRIVE HABITAT ALL/VALS...JURID IDEA/COMP T 20 ENGLSH/LAW. PAGE 83 H1667
FAM LAW CULTURE AFR

B66
KEITH G.,THE FADING COLOUR BAR. AFR CENTRL/AFR UK ZAMBIA CULTURE SCHOOL EDU/PROP PERS/REL DISCRIM AGE ...AUD/VIS NAT/COMP SOC/INTEG 20 NEGRO. PAGE 84 H1682
RACE/REL STRUCT ATTIT NAT/G

B66
UN ECONOMIC AND SOCIAL COUNCIL,WORLD POPULATION PROSPECTS AS ASSESSED IN 1963. FUT WOR+45 DEATH AGE ...TREND CHARTS UN. PAGE 158 H3157
PREDICT CENSUS GEOG NAT/COMP

S67
BASOV V.,"THE DEVELOPMENT OF PUBLIC EDUCATION AND THE BUDGET." USSR NAT/G CONTROL REV COST AGE...STAT 20. PAGE 12 H0235
BUDGET GIVE EDU/PROP SCHOOL

AGE/A....ADULTS

B57
KOENTJARANINGRAT R.,A PRELIMINARY DESCRIPTION OF THE JAVANESE KINSHIP SYSTEM. INDONESIA STRATA FAM INGP/REL ADJUST MARRIAGE AGE/C AGE/Y AGE/A PERSON ...OBS CHARTS DICTIONARY 20 JAVA. PAGE 87 H1736
KIN STRUCT ELITES CULTURE

B65
KLEIN J.,SAMPLES FROM ENGLISH CULTURES (2 VOLS.). UK STRATA FAM NEIGH WORKER ETIQUET ISOLAT AGE/C AGE/A HABITAT RIGID/FLEX...NET/THEORY CHARTS 20. PAGE 87 H1732
CULTURE INGP/REL ATTIT SOC

B66
KEIL S.,SEXUALITAT - ERKENNTNISSE UND MASS-STABE. CULTURE DOMIN MARRIAGE AGE/Y AGE/A PERSON SUPEGO PLURISM 17/20. PAGE 84 H1681
SEX ATTIT STRUCT SOCIETY

B66
TSURUMI K.,ADULT SOCIALIZATION AND SOCIAL CHANGE: JAPAN BEFORE AND AFTER DEFEAT IN WORLD WAR II. FAM DEATH SUPEGO...PSY SOC 20 CHINJAP. PAGE 157 H3133
SOCIETY AGE/A WAR PERSON

B67
MICKIEWICZ E.P.,SOVIET POLITICAL SCHOOLS: THE COMMUNIST PARTY ADULT INSTRUCTION SYSTEM. COM USSR INTELL SCHOOL WORKER CREATE PRESS ADMIN CONTROL ATTIT KNOWL...PROG/TEAC SOC/INTEG 20 COM/PARTY. PAGE 110 H2200
NAT/G EDU/PROP AGE/A MARXISM

AGE/C....INFANTS AND CHILDREN

B49
GORER G.,THE PEOPLE OF GREAT RUSSIA: A PSYCHOLOGICAL STUDY. RUSSIA USSR NAT/G DIPLOM LEAD AGE/C ANOMIE ATTIT DRIVE...POLICY 20. PAGE 59 H1182
ISOLAT PERSON PSY SOCIETY

B55
SHUMSKY A.,THE CLASH OF CULTURES IN ISRAEL: A PROBLEM FOR EDUCATION. ISRAEL CULTURE INTELL NAT/G ACT/RES DISCRIM AGE/Y...BIBLIOG 20 JEWS. PAGE 143 H2867
GP/REL EDU/PROP SCHOOL AGE/C

B57
KOENTJARANINGRAT R.,A PRELIMINARY DESCRIPTION OF THE JAVANESE KINSHIP SYSTEM. INDONESIA STRATA FAM INGP/REL ADJUST MARRIAGE AGE/C AGE/Y AGE/A PERSON ...OBS CHARTS DICTIONARY 20 JAVA. PAGE 87 H1736
KIN STRUCT ELITES CULTURE

S59
LYNN D.B.,"THE EFFECTS OF FATHER-ABSENCE ON NORWEGIAN BOYS AND GIRLS." NORWAY CULTURE PERS/REL ADJUST DISPL LOVE...PSY CORREL STAT INT CON/ANAL CHARTS SOC/INTEG 20. PAGE 99 H1983
SOC FAM AGE/C ANOMIE

S63
ROBINSON W.C.,"URBANIZATION AND FERTILITY: THE NON-WESTERN EXPERIENCE (BMR)" DEATH MARRIAGE AGE/C BIO/SOC...STAT CENSUS CON/ANAL CHARTS NAT/COMP 20 THIRD/WRLD. PAGE 133 H2651
GEOG MUNIC FAM ECO/UNDEV

B64
PINNICK A.W.,COUNTRY PLANNERS IN ACTION. UK FINAN SERV/IND NAT/G CONSULT DELIB/GP PRICE CONTROL ROUTINE LEISURE AGE/C...GEOG 20 URBAN/RNWL. PAGE 126 H2512
MUNIC PLAN INDUS ATTIT

B65
KLEIN J.,SAMPLES FROM ENGLISH CULTURES (2 VOLS.). UK STRATA FAM NEIGH WORKER ETIQUET ISOLAT AGE/C
CULTURE INGP/REL

AGE/A HABITAT RIGID/FLEX...NET/THEORY CHARTS 20. PAGE 87 H1732 ATTIT SOC

B67
CHANDRASEKHAR S.,ASIA'S POPULATION PROBLEMS. ASIA ECO/UNDEV PLAN AGE/C...OBS CHARTS BIBLIOG 18/20 AUSTRAL. PAGE 29 H0575 PROB/SOLV NAT/COMP GEOG TREND

B67
COWLES M.,PERSPECTIVES IN THE EDUCATION OF DISADVANTAGED CHILDREN. CULTURE OP/RES PLAN PERS/REL ADJUST HABITAT PERCEPT KNOWL WEALTH ...SOC/WK IDEA/COMP ANTHOL 20. PAGE 34 H0686 EDU/PROP AGE/C TEC/DEV SCHOOL

B67
LAMBERT W.E.,CHILDREN'S VIEWS OF FOREIGN PEOPLES: A CROSS-NATIONAL STUDY. UNIV CULTURE EDU/PROP RACE/REL ATTIT PERCEPT ROLE...STAT STAND/INT CHARTS GP/COMP NAT/COMP. PAGE 90 H1802 AGE/C STRANGE GP/REL STERTYP

AGE/O....OLD PEOPLE

B62
HARRINGTON M.,THE OTHER AMERICA: POVERTY IN THE UNITED STATES. WORKER CREATE REPRESENT RACE/REL AGE/O DRIVE POLICY. PAGE 67 H1338 WEALTH WELF/ST INCOME CULTURE

B63
GORDON M.S.,THE ECONOMICS OF WELFARE POLICIES. INDUS LOC/G NAT/G LEGIS WORKER INCOME AGE/O SKILL WEALTH...METH/COMP NAT/COMP 20. PAGE 59 H1180 METH/CNCPT ECO/TAC POLICY

B64
RAPHAEL M.,PENSIONS AND PUBLIC SERVANTS. UK NAT/G PLAN INGP/REL COST EFFICIENCY ATTIT...POLICY 17/20 CIVIL/SERV. PAGE 130 H2593 RECEIVE ADMIN INCOME AGE/O

B65
SPENCER P.,THE SAMBURU: A STUDY OF GERONTOCRACY IN A NOMADIC TRIBE. AFR SOCIETY ECO/UNDEV AGRI FAM NEIGH SECT GP/REL MARRIAGE WORSHIP 20 SAMBURU. PAGE 147 H2945 KIN STRUCT AGE/O CULTURE

AGE/Y....YOUTH AND ADOLESCENCE

N
DEUTSCHE BUCHEREI,DEUTSCHE NATIONALBIBLIOGRAPHIE. GERMANY ECO/DEV DIPLOM AGE/Y ATTIT...PHIL/SCI SOC 20. PAGE 40 H0803 BIBLIOG NAT/G LEAD POLICY

N19
BARRES M.,"THE WAR AND THE SPIRIT OF YOUTH" (PAMPHLET). FRANCE FORCES DOMIN LEAD DEATH AGE/Y ATTIT RESPECT...FASCIST 20 WWI. PAGE 11 H0228 WAR NAT/LISM CULTURE MYSTIC

B31
DUFFIELD M.,KING LEGION. NAT/G PROVS SECT LEGIS EDU/PROP PRESS GP/REL AGE/Y MARXISM POLICY. PAGE 43 H0856 SUPEGO FORCES VOL/ASSN LOBBY

B55
SHUMSKY A.,THE CLASH OF CULTURES IN ISRAEL: A PROBLEM FOR EDUCATION. ISRAEL CULTURE INTELL NAT/G ACT/RES DISCRIM AGE/Y...BIBLIOG 20 JEWS. PAGE 143 H2867 GP/REL EDU/PROP SCHOOL AGE/C

B57
KOENTJARANINGRAT R.,A PRELIMINARY DESCRIPTION OF THE JAVANESE KINSHIP SYSTEM. INDONESIA STRATA FAM INGP/REL ADJUST MARRIAGE AGE/C AGE/Y AGE/A PERSON ...OBS CHARTS DICTIONARY 20 JAVA. PAGE 87 H1736 KIN STRUCT ELITES CULTURE

B59
EPSTEIN F.T.,EAST GERMANY: A SELECTED BIBLIOGRAPHY (PAMPHLET). COM GERMANY/E LAW AGRI FINAN INDUS LABOR POL/PAR EDU/PROP ADMIN AGE/Y 20. PAGE 47 H0932 BIBLIOG/A INTELL MARXISM NAT/G

S60
TURNER R.H.,"SPONSORED AND CONTEST MOBILITY IN THE SCHOOL SYSTEM." UK USA+45 ELITES STRATA ACADEM FACE/GP EDU/PROP CONTROL INGP/REL ADJUST ATTIT PERSON...METH/COMP 20. PAGE 157 H3142 AGE/Y NAT/COMP SCHOOL STRUCT

B61
ALSTON P.L.,STATE EDUCATION AND SOCIAL CHANGE IN THE RUSSIAN EMPIRE 1871-1914 (PAPER). RUSSIA ELITES PROF/ORG EDU/PROP CONTROL PRIVIL AGE/Y...BIBLIOG 19/20. PAGE 6 H0115 SCHOOL SOCIETY NAT/G GP/REL

B61
EMMET C.,THE VANISHING SWASTIKA. GERMANY/W ELITES CRIME WAR...SAMP 20. PAGE 46 H0922 FASCISM ATTIT AGE/Y NAT/G

B61
STAHL W.,EDUCATION FOR DEMOCRACY IN WEST GERMANY: ACHIEVEMENT SHORTCOMINGS - PROSPECTS. GERMANY/W SOCIETY NAT/G FORCES PLAN PROB/SOLV PRESS ALL/VALS ...POLICY MAJORIT CONCPT ANTHOL 20. PAGE 148 H2967 EDU/PROP POPULISM AGE/Y ADJUST

C63
HSU F.L.,"COHESION AND DIVISION IN THE AMERICAN WORLD" HSU FL. CLAN, CASTE, AND CLUB." CULTURE EDU/PROP CONFER SANCTION PERSON...PSY GP/COMP. PAGE 74 H1484 PERS/REL AGE/Y ADJUST VOL/ASSN

B64
BURKE F.G.,AFRICA'S QUEST FOR ORDER. AFR CULTURE KIN MUNIC NAT/G DIPLOM COLONIAL REV DISCRIM NAT/LISM AGE/Y 20. PAGE 24 H0488 ORD/FREE CONSEN RACE/REL LEAD

B64
DOOLIN D.J.,COMMUNIST CHINA: THE POLITICS OF STUDENT OPPOSITION. CHINA/COM ELITES STRATA ACADEM NAT/G WRITING CT/SYS LEAD PARTIC COERCE TOTALISM 20. PAGE 42 H0838 MARXISM DEBATE AGE/Y PWR

B66
KEIL S.,SEXUALITAT - ERKENNTNISSE UND MASS-STABE. CULTURE DOMIN MARRIAGE AGE/Y AGE/A PERSON SUPEGO PLURISM 17/20. PAGE 84 H1681 SEX ATTIT STRUCT SOCIETY

B66
ZEINE Z.N.,THE EMERGENCE OF ARAB NATIONALISM (REV. ED.). TURKEY UK NAT/G SECT TEC/DEV LEAD REV WAR AGE/Y ROLE ORD/FREE...TRADIT CHARTS BIBLIOG 20 ARABS OTTOMAN. PAGE 173 H3453 ISLAM NAT/LISM DIPLOM

S66
BLANC N.,"SPAIN: LEARNING THROUGH STRUGGLE" SPAIN STRATA STRUCT SECT FORCES PROB/SOLV AGE/Y ATTIT ORD/FREE PWR WEALTH MARXISM SOCISM 19/20 FRANCO/F SUCCESSION. PAGE 18 H0352 NAT/G FUT SOCIALIST TOTALISM

L67
GLAZER M.,"LAS ACTITUDES Y ACTIVIDADES POLITICAS DE LOS ESTUDIANTES DE LA UNIVERSIDAD DE CHILE." CHILE NAT/G POL/PAR EDU/PROP LOBBY ATTIT 20. PAGE 57 H1141 ACADEM AGE/Y PARTIC ELITES

L67
GRAUBARD S.R.,"TOWARD THE YEAR 2000: WORK IN PROGRESS." FUT ACADEM SECT DELIB/GP DIPLOM EDU/PROP AGE/Y PERSON ROLE...PSY ANTHOL. PAGE 60 H1199 PREDICT PROB/SOLV SOCIETY CULTURE

L67
ISRAEL J.,"THE RED GUARDS IN HISTORICAL PERSPECTIVE: CONTINUITY AND CHANGE IN THE CHINESE YOUTH MOVEMENT." CHINA/COM FUT POL/PAR CONTROL REV GP/REL 20. PAGE 79 H1572 AGE/Y LOBBY MARXISM NAT/G

AGEE W.K. H0920

AGGARWALA R.C. H0077

AGGARWALA R.N. H0078

AGGER R.E. H0079

AGGRESSION....SEE COERCE+DIPLOMN

AGGRESSION, PHYSICAL....SEE COERCE, DRIVE

AGREE....AGREEMENTS, CONTRACTS, TREATIES, CONCORDATS, INTERSTATE COMPACTS

B13
KROPOTKIN P.,THE CONQUEST OF BREAD. SOCIETY STRATA AGRI INDUS WORKER REV HAPPINESS INCOME PRODUC HEALTH MORAL ORD/FREE. PAGE 89 H1775 ANARCH SOCIALIST OWN AGREE

B16
PUFENDORF S.,LAW OF NATURE AND OF NATIONS (ABRIDGED). UNIV LAW NAT/G DIPLOM AGREE WAR PERSON ALL/VALS PWR...POLICY 18 DEITY NATURL/LAW. PAGE 128 H2565 CONCPT INT/LAW SECT MORAL

N19
BENTHAM J.,A PLAN FOR AN UNIVERSAL AND PERPETUAL PEACE (1838) (PAMPHLET). NAT/G FORCES BAL/PWR INT/TRADE ADMIN AGREE CT/SYS ARMS/CONT SOVEREIGN WEALTH GEN/LAWS. PAGE 14 H0288 INT/ORG INT/LAW PEACE COLONIAL

N19
WEBB L.C.,CHURCH AND STATE IN ITALY: 1947-1957 (PAMPHLET). GERMANY ITALY CONSTN POL/PAR AGREE CONTROL PARTIC CHOOSE ATTIT ORD/FREE FASCISM MARXISM 20 CHURCH/STA MARITAIN/J SALO. PAGE 166 H3316 SECT CATHISM NAT/G GP/REL

B28
HOBBES T.,THE ELEMENTS OF LAW, NATURAL AND POLITIC (1650). STRATA NAT/G SECT CHIEF AGREE ATTIT ALL/VALS MORAL ORD/FREE POPULISM...POLICY CONCPT. PAGE 71 H1432 PERSON LAW SOVEREIGN CONSERVE

B29
LANGER W.L.,THE FRANCO-RUSSIAN ALLIANCE: 1890-1894. FRANCE MOD/EUR UK USSR NAT/G CHIEF FORCES BAL/PWR AGREE WAR PEACE PWR...TIME/SEQ TREATY 19 BISMARCK/O. PAGE 91 H1809 DIPLOM

B30
BURLAMAQUI J.J.,PRINCIPLES OF NATURAL AND POLITIC LAW (2 VOLS.) (1747-51). EX/STRUC LEGIS AGREE CT/SYS CHOOSE ROLE SOVEREIGN 18 NATURL/LAW. PAGE 24 H0490 LAW NAT/G ORD/FREE CONCPT

B32
BLUM L.,PEACE AND DISARMAMENT (TRANS. BY A. WERTH). NAT/G FORCES WORKER DIPLOM AGREE WAR ATTIT AUTHORIT SOCIALIST PEACE

ORD/FREE. PAGE 18 H0360 INT/ORG ARMS/CONT

B35
RAM J.,THE SCIENCE OF LEGAL JUDGMENT: A TREATISE... UK CONSTN NAT/G LEGIS CREATE PROB/SOLV AGREE CT/SYS ...INT/LAW CONCPT 19 ENGLSH/LAW CANON/LAW CIVIL/LAW CTS/WESTM. PAGE 129 H2584 LAW JURID EX/STRUC ADJUD

B36
VICO G.B.,DIRITTO UNIVERSALE (1722) (VOL. 2, PARTS 1,2, AND 3, OF G.B. VICO, OPERE). UNIV DIPLOM AGREE WAR OWN KNOWL ORD/FREE SOVEREIGN DEITY. PAGE 162 H3249 JURID SECT CONCPT NAT/G

B38
MCNAIR A.D.,THE LAW OF TREATIES: BRITISH PRACTICE AND OPINIONS. UK CREATE DIPLOM LEGIT WRITING ADJUD WAR...INT/LAW JURID TREATY. PAGE 107 H2144 AGREE LAW CT/SYS NAT/G

B38
SAINT-PIERRE C.I.,SCHEME FOR LASTING PEACE (TRANS. BY H. BELLOT). INDUS NAT/G CHIEF FORCES INT/TRADE CT/SYS WAR PWR SOVEREIGN WEALTH...POLICY 18. PAGE 137 H2732 INT/ORG PEACE AGREE INT/LAW

B39
CARR E.H.,PROPAGANDA IN INTERNATIONAL POLITICS (PAMPHLET). EUR+WWI GERMANY MOD/EUR NAT/G AGREE WAR MORAL...POLICY 20 TREATY. PAGE 27 H0536 DIPLOM EDU/PROP CONTROL ATTIT

B40
BROGAN D.W.,THE DEVELOPMENT OF MODERN FRANCE (1870-1939). FRANCE GERMANY UK USSR CONSTN CHIEF LEGIS DIPLOM AGREE COLONIAL WAR NAT/LISM PEACE SOCISM 19/20 TREATY. PAGE 21 H0428 MOD/EUR NAT/G

B40
WOLFERS A.,BRITAIN AND FRANCE BETWEEN TWO WORLD WARS. FRANCE UK INT/ORG NAT/G PLAN BARGAIN ECO/TAC AGREE ISOLAT ALL/IDEOS...DECISION GEOG 20 TREATY VERSAILLES INTERVENT. PAGE 170 H3402 DIPLOM WAR POLICY

B42
HEGEL G.W.F.,PHILOSOPHY OF RIGHT. UNIV FAM SECT CHIEF AGREE WAR MARRIAGE OWN ORD/FREE...POLICY CONCPT. PAGE 69 H1383 NAT/G LAW RATIONAL

B47
LOCKE J.,TWO TREATISES OF GOVERNMENT (1690). UK LAW SOCIETY LEGIS LEGIT AGREE REV OWN HEREDITY MORAL CONSERVE...POLICY MAJORIT 17 WILLIAM/3 NATURL/LAW. PAGE 97 H1946 CONCPT ORD/FREE NAT/G CONSEN

B50
ALBRECHT-CARRIE R.,ITALY FROM NAPOLEON TO MUSSOLINI. GERMANY ITALY SPAIN SOCIETY ECO/DEV POL/PAR LEGIS AGREE CONTROL WAR NAT/LISM TOTALISM PWR SOCISM...SOC 19/20 TREATY. PAGE 5 H0095 FASCISM NAT/G

B50
BERMAN H.J.,JUSTICE IN RUSSIA; AN INTERPRETATION OF SOVIET LAW. USSR LAW STRUCT LABOR FORCES AGREE GP/REL ORD/FREE SOCISM...TIME/SEQ 20. PAGE 15 H0309 JURID ADJUD MARXISM COERCE

B50
GATZKE H.W.,GERMANY'S DRIVE TO THE WEST. BELGIUM GERMANY MOD/EUR AGRI INDUS POL/PAR FORCES DOMIN AGREE CONTROL REGION COERCE 20 TREATY WWI. PAGE 55 H1104 WAR POLICY NAT/G DIPLOM

B50
GLEASON J.H.,THE GENESIS OF RUSSOPHOBIA IN GREAT BRITAIN: A STUDY OF THE INTERACTION OF POLICY AND OPINION. ASIA RUSSIA UK NAT/G AGREE CONTROL REV WAR LOVE PWR TREATY 19. PAGE 57 H1142 DIPLOM POLICY DOMIN COLONIAL

B55
SVARLIEN O.,AN INTRODUCTION TO THE LAW OF NATIONS. SEA AIR INT/ORG NAT/G CHIEF ADMIN AGREE WAR PRIVIL ORD/FREE SOVEREIGN...BIBLIOG 16/20. PAGE 151 H3012 INT/LAW DIPLOM

B61
FULLER J.F.C.,THE CONDUCT OF WAR, 1789-1961. FRANCE RUSSIA SOCIETY NAT/G FORCES PROB/SOLV AGREE NUC/PWR WEAPON PEACE...SOC 18/20 TREATY COLD/WAR. PAGE 54 H1076 WAR POLICY REV ROLE

B61
LAHAYE R.,LES ENTREPRISES PUBLIQUES AU MAROC. FRANCE MOROCCO LAW DIST/IND EXTR/IND FINAN CONSULT PLAN TEC/DEV ADMIN AGREE CONTROL OWN...POLICY 20. PAGE 90 H1796 NAT/G INDUS ECO/UNDEV ECO/TAC

B62
ROUSSEAU J.J.,THE SOCIAL CONTRACT. LAW CONSTN CHIEF DOMIN REPRESENT GP/REL ORD/FREE POPULISM...MAJORIT GOV/COMP 18. PAGE 135 H2700 GEN/LAWS AGREE REV

B62
SCHECHTMAN J.B.,POSTWAR POPULATION TRANSFERS IN EUROPE: 1945-1955. COM CZECHOSLVK GERMANY POLAND USSR CULTURE SOCIETY PROB/SOLV AGREE NAT/LISM...SOC STAT TREND CHARTS METH/COMP 20 MIGRATION. PAGE 139 H2778 GEOG CENSUS EUR+WWI HABITAT

L63
BOLGAR V.,"THE PUBLIC INTEREST: A JURISPRUDENTIAL AND COMPARATIVE OVERVIEW OF SYMPOSIUM ON FUNDAMENTAL CONCEPTS OF PUBLIC LAW" COM FRANCE GERMANY SWITZERLND LAW ADJUD ADMIN AGREE LAISSEZ ...JURID GEN/LAWS 20 EUROPE/E. PAGE 18 H0369 CONCPT ORD/FREE CONTROL NAT/COMP

B66
COLE A.B.,SOCIALIST PARTIES IN POSTWAR JAPAN. STRATA AGRI LABOR PLAN DIPLOM ECO/TAC AGREE LEAD CHOOSE ATTIT...CHARTS 20 CHINJAP SOC/DEMPAR. PAGE 31 H0620 POL/PAR POLICY SOCISM NAT/G

B66
PAN S.,VIETNAM CRISIS. ASIA FRANCE USA+45 USA-45 VIETNAM CULTURE SOCIETY INT/ORG ECO/TAC AGREE CONTROL WAR MARXISM 20. PAGE 123 H2454 ECO/UNDEV POLICY DIPLOM NAT/COMP

B66
THOMPSON J.M.,RUSSIA, BOLSHEVISM, AND THE VERSAILLES PEACE. RUSSIA USSR INT/ORG NAT/G DELIB/GP AGREE REV WAR PWR 20 TREATY VERSAILLES BOLSHEVISM. PAGE 154 H3083 DIPLOM PEACE MARXISM

B66
WEINSTEIN F.B.,VIETNAM'S UNHELD ELECTIONS: THE FAILURE TO CARRY OUT THE 1956 REUNIFICATION ELECTIONS... (MONOGRAPH). VIETNAM/S VIETNAM/N LEGIT CONFER ADJUD WAR PEACE 20 TREATY GENEVA/CON UNIFICA. PAGE 166 H3330 AGREE NAT/G CHOOSE DIPLOM

B67
PLANK J.,CUBA AND THE UNITED STATES: LONG RANGE PERSPECTIVES. CUBA L/A+17C USSR ECO/UNDEV NAT/G FORCES ECO/TAC INT/TRADE AGREE REV...PREDICT TREND ANTHOL 20 CASTRO/F COLD/WAR OAS. PAGE 126 H2520 DIPLOM

L67
KELLEHER G.W.,"THE COMMON MARKET ANTITRUST LAWS: THE FIRST TEN YEARS." EUR+WWI INDUS PRICE ADJUD AGREE CONTROL PROFIT...POLICY 20 EEC. PAGE 84 H1684 INT/ORG INT/TRADE MARKET NAT/G

L67
MCALLISTER J.T. JR.,"THE POSSIBILITIES FOR DIPLOMACY IN SOUTHEAST ASIA." LAOS VIETNAM INT/ORG NAT/G PROVS BAL/PWR DOMIN AGREE COLONIAL WAR PWR 17/20 TREATY. PAGE 106 H2121 DIPLOM S/ASIA

S67
GRIEB K.J.,"THE UNITED STATES AND THE CENTRAL AMERICAN CONFEDERATION." COSTA/RICA EL/SALVADR GUATEMALA HONDURAS L/A+17C NICARAGUA NAT/G FORCES CONFER AGREE EXEC ARMS/CONT REV WAR PEACE ATTIT 20. PAGE 60 H1212 INT/ORG DIPLOM POLICY REGION

S67
KINGSBURY E.C.,"LAW AS COMPACT: ANCIENT ISRAEL'S CONTRIBUTION TO THE UNDERSTANDING OF LAW." ISRAEL MEDIT-7 CULTURE KIN KNOWL...JURID CONCPT TREND IDEA/COMP METH/COMP WORSHIP JEWS DEITY. PAGE 86 H1716 LAW AGREE CONSTN INGP/REL

S67
ROOT W.,"REPORT FROM PARIS - DE GAULLE: WHICH WAY TO THE FUTURE?" CANADA FRANCE ISLAM UK INT/ORG CHIEF CREATE AGREE CONTROL ARMS/CONT NUC/PWR EQUILIB PEACE PWR 20 DEGAULLE/C NATO. PAGE 134 H2670 POLICY DIPLOM NAT/G BAL/PWR

B68
PROUDHON J.P.,IDEE GENERALE DE LA REVOLUTION AU XIXE SIECLE (1851). FRANCE UNIV NAT/G CREATE AGREE UTOPIA ORD/FREE...ANARCH 19. PAGE 128 H2563 REV SOCIETY WORKER LABOR

S68
GUZZARDI W.,"THE DECLINE OF THE STERLING CLUB." UK WOR+45 NAT/G PLAN DIPLOM INT/TRADE AGREE CONSEN EQUILIB SOVEREIGN...POLICY NEW/IDEA 20 COMMONWLTH GOLD/STAND. PAGE 63 H1259 FINAN ECO/TAC WEALTH NAT/COMP

S68
LUKASZEWSKI J.,"WESTERN INTEGRATION AND THE PEOPLE'S DEMOCRACIES." USSR ELITES ECO/DEV NAT/G VOL/ASSN INT/TRADE AGREE REV FEDERAL WEALTH SOCISM ...NAT/COMP SOC/INTEG 20 EEC. PAGE 99 H1977 DIPLOM INT/ORG COM REGION

S68
MILLAR T.B.,"THE COMMONWEALTH AND THE UN." UK DIPLOM TARIFFS AGREE COLONIAL CONTROL SOVEREIGN WEALTH...GP/COMP GOV/COMP 20 CMN/WLTH UN. PAGE 111 H2210 INT/ORG POLICY TREND ECO/TAC

B73
STEPHEN J.F.,LIBERTY, EQUALITY, FRATERNITY. UNIV SOCIETY NAT/G LEGIS DOMIN AGREE PERS/REL ATTIT MORAL...IDEA/COMP 19 MILL/JS. PAGE 149 H2978 ORD/FREE CONCPT COERCE SECT

B91
BENTHAM J.,A FRAGMENT ON GOVERNMENT (1776). CONSTN MUNIC NAT/G SECT AGREE HAPPINESS UTIL MORAL ORD/FREE...JURID CONCPT. PAGE 15 H0292 SOVEREIGN LAW DOMIN

B91
PAINE T.,RIGHTS OF MAN. FRANCE MOD/EUR CONSTN NAT/G CHIEF DOMIN LEGIT SOVEREIGN...MAJORIT IDEA/COMP 18 BURKE/EDM CIVIL/LIB. PAGE 122 H2446 GEN/LAWS ORD/FREE REV AGREE

B96
DE VATTEL E.,THE LAW OF NATIONS. AGRI FINAN CHIEF DIPLOM INT/TRADE AGREE OWN ALL/VALS MORAL ORD/FREE SOVEREIGN...GEN/LAWS 18 NATURL/LAW WOLFF/C. PAGE 39 H0774 LAW CONCPT NAT/G INT/LAW

B96
LOWELL A.L.,GOVERNMENTS AND PARTIES IN CONTINENTAL EUROPE, VOL. II. AUSTRIA GERMANY HUNGARY MOD/EUR POL/PAR NAT/G

SWITZERLND SOCIETY EX/STRUC LEGIS DIPLOM AGREE LEAD PARL/PROC PWR...POLICY 19. PAGE 99 H1974 — GOV/REL ELITES

B98
POLLOCK F.,THE HISTORY OF ENGLISH LAW BEFORE THE TIME OF EDWARD I (2 VOLS, 2ND ED.). UK CULTURE LOC/G LEGIS LICENSE AGREE CONTROL CT/SYS SANCTION CRIME...TIME/SEQ 13 COMMON/LAW CANON/LAW. PAGE 127 H2538 — LAW ADJUD JURID

AGRI....AGRICULTURE (INCLUDING HUNTING AND GATHERING)

N
CANADIAN GOVERNMENT PUBLICATIONS (1955-). CANADA AGRI FINAN LABOR FORCES INT/TRADE HEALTH...JURID 20 PARLIAMENT. PAGE 1 H0003 — BIBLIOG/A NAT/G DIPLOM INT/ORG

N
PEKING REVIEW. CHINA/COM CULTURE AGRI INDUS DIPLOM EDU/PROP GUERRILLA ATTIT MARXISM...BIBLIOG 20. PAGE 1 H0009 — MARXIST NAT/G POL/PAR PRESS

N
CHINA QUARTERLY. COM AGRI INDUS ACADEM POL/PAR INT/TRADE CONFER GOV/REL...TIME/SEQ CON/ANAL INDEX 20. PAGE 1 H0014 — BIBLIOG/A ASIA DIPLOM POLICY

N
THE MIDDLE EAST AND NORTH AFRICA. AFR ISLAM CULTURE ECO/UNDEV AGRI NAT/G TEC/DEV FOR/AID INT/TRADE EDU/PROP...CHARTS 20. PAGE 2 H0026 — INDEX INDUS FINAN STAT

N
"PROLOG",DIGEST OF THE SOVIET UKRANIAN PRESS. USSR LAW AGRI INDUS PROVS SCHOOL DIPLOM GOV/REL ATTIT ...HUM LING 20. PAGE 3 H0053 — BIBLIOG/A NAT/G PRESS COM

N
HOOVER INSTITUTION,UNITED STATES AND CANADIAN PUBLICATIONS ON AFRICA. CULTURE ECO/UNDEV AGRI TEC/DEV EDU/PROP COLONIAL RACE/REL NAT/LISM ATTIT HEALTH...SOC SOC/WK 20. PAGE 73 H1464 — BIBLIOG DIPLOM NAT/G AFR

N
KYRIAK T.E.,CHINA: A BIBLIOGRAPHY. ASIA CHINA/COM AGRI FINAN INDUS NAT/G INT/TRADE PRESS...SOC 20. PAGE 90 H1789 — BIBLIOG/A MARXISM TOP/EX POL/PAR

N
US DEPARTMENT OF STATE,BIBLIOGRAPHY (PAMPHLETS). AGRI INDUS INT/ORG FOR/AID EDU/PROP WAR MARXISM ...SOC GOV/COMP METH/COMP 20. PAGE 159 H3184 — BIBLIOG DIPLOM ECO/DEV NAT/G

N
US LIBRARY OF CONGRESS,ACCESSIONS LIST - INDIA. INDIA CULTURE AGRI LOC/G POL/PAR PLAN PROB/SOLV TEC/DEV DIPLOM EDU/PROP LEAD GP/REL ATTIT 20. PAGE 160 H3199 — BIBLIOG S/ASIA ECO/UNDEV NAT/G

N
US LIBRARY OF CONGRESS,SOUTHERN ASIA ACCESSIONS LIST. BURMA CEYLON INDIA NEPAL PAKISTAN S/ASIA THAILAND AGRI INDUS SCHOOL WORKER...ART/METH GEOG HEAL PHIL/SCI LING 20. PAGE 160 H3201 — BIBLIOG/A SOCIETY CULTURE ECO/UNDEV

B00
HOBSON J.A.,THE WAR IN SOUTH AFRICA: ITS CAUSES AND EFFECTS. NETHERLAND SOUTH/AFR UK ELITES AGRI EXTR/IND POL/PAR DIPLOM PRESS RACE/REL ATTIT ORD/FREE SOVEREIGN...INT 19 NEGRO. PAGE 72 H1439 — WAR DOMIN POLICY NAT/G

B05
PHILIPPINE ISLANDS BUREAU SCI,ETHNOLOGICAL SURVEY: THE BONTOC IGOROT. ECO/UNDEV AGRI FAM MARRIAGE HEALTH WEALTH...LING OBS AUD/VIS CHARTS WORSHIP 20 LUZON BONTOC. PAGE 125 H2500 — CULTURE INGP/REL KIN STRUCT

C06
MONTGOMERY H.,"A DICTIONARY OF POLITICAL PHRASES AND ILLUSIONS WITH A SHORT BIBLIOGRAPHY." EUR+WWI MOD/EUR UK AGRI LABOR LOC/G NAT/G COLONIAL CHOOSE RACE/REL. PAGE 112 H2245 — BIBLIOG DICTIONARY POLICY DIPLOM

B12
BRUNHES J.,LA GEOGRAPHIE HUMAINE: ESSAI DE CLASSIFICATION POSITIVE PRINCIPES ET EXEMPLES (2ND ED.). UNIV SEA AGRI EXTR/IND DRIVE...SOC CHARTS 20. PAGE 23 H0454 — GEOG HABITAT CULTURE

B12
SONOLET L.,L'AFRIQUE OCCIDENTALE FRANCAISE. FRANCE AGRI INDUS NAT/G SECT FORCES INT/TRADE EDU/PROP RACE/REL HEALTH ORD/FREE...CHARTS 19/20 NEGRO AFRICA/W. PAGE 147 H2933 — DOMIN ADMIN COLONIAL AFR

B13
KROPOTKIN P.,THE CONQUEST OF BREAD. SOCIETY STRATA AGRI INDUS WORKER REV HAPPINESS INCOME PRODUC HEALTH MORAL ORD/FREE. PAGE 89 H1775 — ANARCH SOCIALIST OWN AGREE

B14
CRAIG J.,ELEMENTS OF POLITICAL SCIENCE (3 VOLS.). CONSTN AGRI INDUS SCHOOL FORCES TAX CT/SYS SUFF MORAL WEALTH...CONCPT 19 CIVIL/LIB. PAGE 35 H0696 — PHIL/SCI NAT/G ORD/FREE

N19
INTERNATIONAL LABOUR OFFICE,EMPLOYMENT, UNEMPLOYMENT AND LABOUR FORCE STATISTICS (PAMPHLET). EUR+WWI STRATA AGRI INDUS NAT/G PROB/SOLV PAY AGE SEX...SAMP NAT/COMP METH 20 ILO. PAGE 78 H1557 — WORKER LABOR STAT ECO/DEV

N19
MAO TSE-TUNG,ON SOME IMPORTANT PROBLEMS OF THE PARTY'S PRESENT POLICY. CHINA/COM CONSTN ELITES INTELL AGRI DOMIN EDU/PROP REV REPRESENT GP/REL OWN PEACE ORD/FREE 20 COM/PARTY. PAGE 102 H2044 — POLICY NAT/G CHIEF LEGIT

B20
MALTHUS T.R.,PRINCIPLES OF POLITICAL ECONOMY. UK AGRI INDUS MARKET NAT/G DIPLOM PRICE CONTROL BAL/PAY COST OWN PWR LAISSEZ 18/19. PAGE 102 H2034 — GEN/LAWS DEMAND WEALTH

S21
MALINOWSKI B.,"THE PRIMITIVE ECONOMICS OF THE TROBRIAND ISLANDERS" (BMR)" CULTURE SOCIETY NAT/G CHIEF LEAD OWN...SOC MYTH WORSHIP 20 NEW/GUINEA TROBRIAND RESOURCE/N. PAGE 101 H2029 — ECO/UNDEV AGRI PRODUC STRUCT

B24
HOLDSWORTH W.S.,A HISTORY OF ENGLISH LAW; THE COMMON LAW AND ITS RIVALS (VOL. IV). UK SEA AGRI CHIEF ADJUD CONTROL CRIME GOV/REL...INT/LAW JURID NAT/COMP 16/17 PARLIAMENT COMMON/LAW CANON/LAW ENGLSH/LAW. PAGE 72 H1449 — LAW LEGIS CT/SYS CONSTN

B27
ENGELS F.,THE PEASANT WAR IN GERMANY (1850). GERMANY MOD/EUR AGRI WORKER LEAD COERCE INGP/REL ...TREND 16/19. PAGE 46 H0924 — WAR STRATA REV MARXIST

B27
WEBER M.,GENERAL ECONOMIC HISTORY. CHRIST-17C MOD/EUR STRUCT AGRI EXTR/IND FINAN INDUS MARKET FAM MUNIC NAT/G PROF/ORG SECT ECO/TAC 8/20. PAGE 166 H3319 — ECO/DEV CAP/ISM

S32
BEARD C.A.,"REPRESENTATIVE GOVERNMENT IN EVOLUTION" WOR-45 AGRI TEC/DEV DOMIN EFFICIENCY ORD/FREE CONSERVE...TIME/SEQ GOV/COMP IDEA/COMP GRECO/ROMN. PAGE 12 H0248 — REPRESENT POPULISM NAT/G PWR

B33
TANNENBAUM F.,PEACE BY REVOLUTION. ECO/UNDEV AGRI SECT WORKER DIPLOM EDU/PROP DISCRIM OWN WEALTH POPULISM 17/20 MEXIC/AMER INDIAN/AM. PAGE 152 H3043 — CULTURE COLONIAL RACE/REL REV

B38
CARVALHO C.M.,GEOGRAPHIA HUMANA; POLITICA E ECONOMICA (3RD ED.). BRAZIL CULTURE AGRI INDUS DIPLOM COLONIAL GP/REL RACE/REL...LING 20 RESOURCE/N. PAGE 27 H0551 — GEOG HABITAT

B38
HEIMANN E.,COMMUNISM, FASCISM, OR DEMOCRACY? WOR-45 CONSTN SOCIETY STRATA AGRI CAP/ISM MORAL ORD/FREE ...MAJORIT METH/COMP NAT/COMP 19/20. PAGE 69 H1384 — SOCISM MARXISM FASCISM PLURISM

B38
LAWLEY F.E.,THE GROWTH OF COLLECTIVE ECONOMY VOL. 1: NATIONAL. EUR+WWI AGRI INDUS NAT/G BARGAIN CAP/ISM ECO/TAC WAR OPTIMAL WEALTH...GOV/COMP METH/COMP 19/20 MONOPOLY. PAGE 92 H1844 — SOCISM PRICE CONTROL OWN

B38
LAWLEY F.E.,THE GROWTH OF COLLECTIVE ECONOMY VOL. 2: INTERNATIONAL. WOR-45 AGRI INDUS EQUILIB OPTIMAL OWN WEALTH...NAT/COMP 19/20 NAZI NEW/DEAL MONOPOLY. PAGE 92 H1845 — ECO/TAC SOCISM NAT/LISM CONTROL

B39
FIRTH R.,PRIMITIVE POLYNESIAN ECONOMY. SOCIETY DIST/IND SECT CHIEF CAP/ISM PRODUC WEALTH...SOC OBS METH WORSHIP 20 POLYNESIA. PAGE 50 H1007 — ECO/UNDEV CULTURE AGRI ECO/TAC

B39
VAN BILJON F.J.,STATE INTERFERENCE IN SOUTH AFRICA. SOUTH/AFR ECO/UNDEV AGRI INDUS WORKER RATION WEALTH ...JURID 20. PAGE 161 H3225 — ECO/TAC POLICY INT/TRADE NAT/G

S39
HECKSCHER G.,"GROUP ORGANIZATION IN SWEDEN." SWEDEN STRATA ECO/DEV AGRI INDUS LABOR NAT/G PROF/ORG ECO/TAC CENTRAL SOCISM...MGT 19/20. PAGE 69 H1382 — LAISSEZ SOC

B42
BLANCHARD L.R.,MARTINIQUE: A SELECTED LIST OF REFERENCES (PAMPHLET). WEST/IND AGRI LOC/G SCHOOL ...ART/METH GEOG JURID CHARTS 20. PAGE 18 H0353 — BIBLIOG/A SOCIETY CULTURE COLONIAL

B42
CONOVER H.F.,FRENCH COLONIES IN AFRICA: A LIST OF REFERENCES. ALGERIA FRANCE MOROCCO SOMALIA SUDAN CULTURE AGRI LOC/G SECT FORCES DIPLOM INT/TRADE NAT/LISM HEALTH...CON/ANAL 20. PAGE 32 H0641 — BIBLIOG AFR ECO/UNDEV COLONIAL

B42
CONOVER H.F.,THE NETHERLANDS EAST INDIES: A SELECTED LIST OF REFERENCES. ECO/UNDEV AGRI EXTR/IND LABOR SCHOOL SECT INT/TRADE COLONIAL HEALTH...GEOG 19/20. PAGE 32 H0642 — BIBLIOG S/ASIA CULTURE

B42
CONOVER H.F.,NEW ZEALAND: A SELECTED LIST OF REFERENCES (PAMPHLET). NEW/ZEALND ECO/UNDEV AGRI INDUS LABOR NAT/G SCHOOL FORCES DIPLOM COLONIAL WAR ...HUM 20. PAGE 32 H0643
BIBLIOG/A S/ASIA CULTURE

B43
BROWN A.D.,GREECE: SELECTED LIST OF REFERENCES. GREECE ECO/UNDEV AGRI FINAN INDUS LABOR SECT TEC/DEV INT/TRADE LEAD...SOC 20. PAGE 22 H0438
BIBLIOG/A WAR DIPLOM NAT/G

B43
US LIBRARY OF CONGRESS,BRITISH MALAYA AND BRITISH NORTH BORNEO. BORNEO MALAYSIA CONSTN AGRI COM/IND INDUS EDU/PROP 19/20. PAGE 160 H3203
BIBLIOG CULTURE

B44
FULLER G.H.,TURKEY: A SELECTED LIST OF REFERENCES. ISLAM TURKEY CULTURE ECO/UNDEV AGRI DIPLOM NAT/LISM CONSERVE...GEOG HUM INT/LAW SOC 7/20 MAPS. PAGE 54 H1075
BIBLIOG/A ALL/VALS

B44
SHELBY C.,LATIN AMERICAN PERIODICALS CURRENTLY RECEIVED IN THE LIBRARY OF CONGRESS AND IN LIBRARY OF DEPARTMENT OF AGRICULTURE. SOCIETY AGRI INDUS LABOR POL/PAR INT/TRADE...GEOG SOC 20. PAGE 143 H2856
BIBLIOG ECO/UNDEV CULTURE L/A+17C

B45
CLAGETT H.L.,COMMUNIST CHINA: RUTHLESS ENEMY OR PAPER TIGER (PAMPHLET). CHINA/COM ECO/UNDEV AGRI INDUS NAT/G POL/PAR ECO/TAC INT/TRADE GUERRILLA ATTIT...CHARTS NAT/COMP ORG/CHARTS 20. PAGE 30 H0602
BIBLIOG/A MARXISM DIPLOM COERCE

B45
MCBRYDE F.W.,CULTURAL AND HISTORICAL GEOGRAPHY OF SOUTHWEST GUATEMALA. GUATEMALA AGRI KIN PERSON ...GEOG AUD/VIS CHARTS 20. PAGE 106 H2123
HABITAT ISOLAT CULTURE ECO/UNDEV

B45
PERAZA SARAUSA F.,BIBLIOGRAFIAS CUBANAS. CUBA CULTURE ECO/UNDEV AGRI EDU/PROP PRESS CIVMIL/REL ...POLICY GEOG PHIL/SCI BIOG 19/20. PAGE 125 H2489
BIBLIOG/A L/A+17C NAT/G DIPLOM

B45
US LIBRARY OF CONGRESS,NETHERLANDS EAST INDIES. INDONESIA LAW CULTURE AGRI INDUS SCHOOL COLONIAL HEALTH...GEOG JURID SOC 19/20 NETH/IND. PAGE 160 H3205
BIBLIOG/A S/ASIA NAT/G

N46
HOBBS C.C.,SOUTHEAST ASIA, 1935-45: A SELECTED LIST OF REFERENCE BOOKS (PAMPHLET). S/ASIA AGRI INDUS NAT/G SECT DIPLOM WAR...ART/METH GEOG SOC LING 20. PAGE 72 H1435
BIBLIOG/A CULTURE HABITAT

B47
GITLOW A.L.,ECONOMICS OF THE MOUNT HAGEN TRIBES, NEW GUINEA. S/ASIA STRUCT AGRI FAM...GEOG MYTH 20 NEW/GUINEA. PAGE 57 H1137
HABITAT ECO/UNDEV CULTURE KIN

B48
WHITE C.L.,HUMAN GEOGRAPHY: AN ECOLOGICAL STUDY OF GEOGRAPHY. UNIV SEA CULTURE AGRI EXTR/IND RACE/REL PRODUC...CHARTS HYPO/EXP SIMUL GEN/LAWS T. PAGE 167 H3345
SOC HABITAT GEOG SOCIETY

B49
UNSTEAD J.F.,A WORLD SURVEY FROM THE HUMAN ASPECT. AGRI INDUS...SOC CENSUS CHARTS 20 MAPS MIGRATION. PAGE 159 H3172
CULTURE HABITAT GEOG ATTIT

B49
US DEPARTMENT OF STATE,SOVIET BIBLIOGRAPHY (PAMPHLET). CHINA/COM COM USSR LAW AGRI INT/ORG ECO/TAC EDU/PROP...POLICY GEOG 20. PAGE 159 H3185
BIBLIOG/A MARXISM CULTURE DIPLOM

B50
COUNCIL BRITISH NATIONAL BIB,BRITISH NATIONAL BIBLIOGRAPHY. UK AGRI CONSTRUC PERF/ART POL/PAR SECT CREATE INT/TRADE LEAD...HUM JURID PHIL/SCI 20. PAGE 34 H0677
BIBLIOG/A NAT/G TEC/DEV DIPLOM

B50
GATZKE H.W.,GERMANY'S DRIVE TO THE WEST. BELGIUM GERMANY MOD/EUR AGRI INDUS POL/PAR FORCES DOMIN AGREE CONTROL REGION COERCE 20 TREATY WWI. PAGE 55 H1104
WAR POLICY NAT/G DIPLOM

B50
HOBBS C.C.,INDOCHINA, A BIBLIOGRAPHY OF THE LAND AND PEOPLE. VIETNAM CULTURE AGRI INDUS NAT/G SECT ...ART/METH GEOG SOC LING 20. PAGE 72 H1436
BIBLIOG/A S/ASIA COLONIAL ECO/UNDEV

B50
LIPSET S.M.,AGRARIAN SOCIALISM. CANADA POL/PAR OP/RES ECO/TAC ADMIN ATTIT...TIME/SEQ NAT/COMP SOC/EXP 20 SASKATCH. PAGE 97 H1938
SOCISM AGRI METH/COMP STRUCT

B51
BERNATZIK H.A.,THE SPIRITS OF THE YELLOW LEAVES. BURMA LAOS S/ASIA THAILAND VIETNAM SOCIETY AGRI COLONIAL LEISURE GP/REL PERS/REL ISOLAT AGE HABITAT SEX WORSHIP 20. PAGE 16 H0310
SOC KIN ECO/UNDEV CULTURE

B51
BISSAINTHE M.,DICTIONNAIRE DE BIBLIOGRAPHIE HAITIENNE. HAITI ELITES AGRI LEGIS DIPLOM INT/TRADE WRITING ORD/FREE CATHISM...ART/METH GEOG 19/20 NEGRO TREATY. PAGE 17 H0347
BIBLIOG L/A+17C SOCIETY NAT/G

B51
GHANI A.R.,PAKISTAN: A SELECT BIBLIOGRAPHY. PAKISTAN S/ASIA CULTURE...GEOG 20. PAGE 56 H1120
BIBLIOG AGRI INDUS

B52
FORDE L.D.,HABITAT, ECONOMY AND SOCIETY. AFR L/A+17C S/ASIA STRUCT AGRI INGP/REL...GEOG OBS BIBLIOG 20. PAGE 52 H1037
SOC HABITAT CULTURE ECO/UNDEV

B52
SPICER E.H.,HUMAN PROBLEMS IN TECHNOLOGICAL CHANGE. ECO/UNDEV AGRI INDUS NAT/G ACT/RES LEAD GP/REL INGP/REL ROLE...INT METH 20 CASEBOOK. PAGE 147 H2947
TEC/DEV CULTURE STRUCT OP/RES

B53
DAVIDSON B.,THE NEW WEST AFRICA: PROBLEMS OF INDEPENDENCE. UK AGRI TEC/DEV DIPLOM GP/REL RACE/REL SOVEREIGN...ANTHOL 20 AFRICA/W. PAGE 37 H0744
AFR COLONIAL ECO/UNDEV NAT/G

B53
MEAD M.,CULTURAL PATTERNS AND TECHNICAL CHANGE. BURMA GREECE NIGERIA ECO/UNDEV AGRI INDUS SCHOOL SECT CREATE FEEDBACK HABITAT...PSY METH/COMP BIBLIOG 20 UN. PAGE 108 H2152
HEALTH TEC/DEV CULTURE ADJUST

B53
WAGLEY C.,AMAZON TOWN: A STUDY OF MAN IN THE TROPICS. BRAZIL L/A+17C STRATA STRUCT ECO/UNDEV AGRI EX/STRUC RACE/REL DISCRIM HABITAT WEALTH...OBS SOC/EXP 20. PAGE 164 H3285
SOC NEIGH CULTURE INGP/REL

B54
HAZARD B.H. JR.,KOREAN STUDIES GUIDE. KOREA CONSTN CULTURE AGRI FAM SECT CREATE WAR NAT/LISM HABITAT PWR...CHARTS 14/20. PAGE 68 H1371
BIBLIOG/A ELITES GP/REL

B54
MALINOWSKI B.,MAGIC, SCIENCE AND RELIGION. AGRI KIN GP/REL ALL/VALS...MYTH OBS RECORD IDEA/COMP WORSHIP 20 NEW/GUINEA. PAGE 102 H2031
CULTURE ATTIT SOC

B54
US LIBRARY OF CONGRESS,RESEARCH AND INFORMATION ON AFRICA: CONTINUING SOURCES. ISLAM ECO/UNDEV AGRI INDUS R+D ACADEM NAT/G INT/TRADE...SOC 20. PAGE 161 H3210
BIBLIOG/A AFR PRESS COM/IND

B55
JONES T.B.,A BIBLIOGRAPHY ON SOUTH AMERICAN ECONOMIC AFFAIRS: ARTICLES IN NINETEENTH CENTURY PERIODICALS (PAMPHLET). AGRI COM/IND DIST/IND EXTR/IND FINAN INDUS LABOR NAT/G 19. PAGE 82 H1634
BIBLIOG ECO/UNDEV L/A+17C TEC/DEV

B55
LIPSCOMB J.F.,WHITE AFRICANS. SOCIETY STRUCT AGRI ECO/TAC ADJUD COLONIAL COERCE PERS/REL ADJUST. PAGE 97 H1937
RACE/REL HABITAT ECO/UNDEV ORD/FREE

B55
RESHETAR J.S.,PROBLEMS OF ANALYZING AND PREDICTING SOVIET BEHAVIOR. USSR CULTURE ECO/DEV AGRI DIST/IND EXTR/IND PROC/MFG NAT/G SECT TOP/EX ACT/RES ADMIN PWR WEALTH...SOC METH TOT/POP VAL/FREE 20. PAGE 131 H2617
COM ATTIT

S55
GOODENOUGH W.H.,"A PROBLEM IN MALAYO-POLYNESIAN SOCIAL ORGANIZATION" (BMR)" MALAYSIA S/ASIA CULTURE AGRI PROB/SOLV OWN HABITAT...SOC 20 20 POLYNESIA. PAGE 58 H1170
KIN STRUCT FAM ECO/UNDEV

B57
CENTRAL ASIAN RESEARCH CENTRE,BIBLIOGRAPHY OF RECENT SOVIET SOURCE MATERIAL ON SOVIET CENTRAL ASIA AND THE BORDERLANDS. AFGHANISTN INDIA PAKISTAN UAR USSR ECO/UNDEV AGRI EXTR/IND INDUS ACADEM ADMIN ...HEAL HUM LING CON/ANAL 20. PAGE 28 H0567
BIBLIOG/A COM CULTURE NAT/G

B57
IKE N.,JAPANESE POLITICS. INTELL STRUCT AGRI INDUS FAM KIN LABOR PRESS CHOOSE ATTIT...DECISION BIBLIOG 19/20 CHINJAP. PAGE 76 H1523
NAT/G ADMIN POL/PAR CULTURE

B57
LOOMIS C.P.,RURAL SOCIOLOGY. CULTURE KIN NAT/G SECT VOL/ASSN ACT/RES EDU/PROP HEALTH. PAGE 98 H1963
SOC AGRI METH T

B57
NEUMARK S.D.,ECONOMIC INFLUENCES ON THE SOUTH AFRICAN FRONTIER, 1652-1836. SOUTH/AFR SEA AGRI NAT/G FORCES WORKER DIPLOM INT/TRADE PRICE DEMAND PRODUC...STAT CHARTS 17/19 FRONTIER. PAGE 117 H2341
COLONIAL ECO/UNDEV ECO/TAC MARKET

B57
PALACIOS A.L.,PETROLEO, MONOPOLIOS, Y LATIFUNDIOS. L/A+17C EXTR/IND NAT/G TEC/DEV ECO/TAC CONTROL PRODUC 20 ARGEN MONOPOLY RESOURCE/N. PAGE 123 H2448
ECO/UNDEV NAT/LISM INDUS AGRI

B57
PARK A.G.,BOLSHEVISM IN TURKESTAN 1917-1927. COM
REV

RUSSIA USSR CULTURE AGRI SECT DOMIN GP/REL INGP/REL NAT/LISM...BIBLIOG 20 TURKESTAN. PAGE 123 H2467 POLICY MARXISM ISLAM

B57
REAMAN G.E.,THE TRAIL OF THE BLACK WALNUT. CANADA AGRI COLONIAL...CHARTS BIBLIOG 18 GERMANS/PA. PAGE 130 H2604 STRANGE SECT CULTURE

B57
SHEIKH N.A.,SOME ASPECTS OF THE CONSTITUTION AND THE ECONOMICS OF ISLAM. PAKISTAN CULTURE AGRI FINAN LABOR NAT/G SECT INT/TRADE 20 MUSLIM. PAGE 143 H2855 ISLAM POLICY ECO/TAC CONSTN

B57
US SENATE SPEC COMM FOR AID,COMPILATION OF STUDIES AND SURVEYS. AFR ASIA L/A+17C USA+45 ECO/UNDEV AGRI INT/ORG CONSULT TEC/DEV CONFER TOTALISM...NAT/COMP 20 CONGRESS. PAGE 161 H3216 FOR/AID DIPLOM ORD/FREE DELIB/GP

B58
AVRAMOVIC D.,POSTWAR GROWTH IN INTERNATIONAL INDEBTEDNESS. WOR+45 AGRI INDUS CAP/ISM PRICE INCOME...NAT/COMP 20 GOLD/STAND SILVER. PAGE 9 H0184 INT/TRADE FINAN COST BAL/PAY

B58
BRIGGS L.C.,THE LIVING RACES OF THE SAHARA. STRATA AGRI KIN INT/TRADE HABITAT...GEOG AUD/VIS CHARTS BIBLIOG 20 SAHARA MIGRATION. PAGE 21 H0417 STRUCT SOCIETY SOC CULTURE

B58
HANCE W.A.,AFRICAN ECONOMIC DEVELOPMENT. AGRI DIST/IND INDUS R+D ACT/RES PLAN CAP/ISM FOR/AID ...GOV/COMP BIBLIOG 20. PAGE 65 H1312 AFR ECO/UNDEV PROB/SOLV TEC/DEV

B58
NICULESCU B.,COLONIAL PLANNING: A COMPARATIVE STUDY. AFR AGRI LOC/G MUNIC NAT/G DELIB/GP COLONIAL 20. PAGE 118 H2356 PLAN ECO/UNDEV TEC/DEV NAT/COMP

B58
SCOTT D.J.R.,RUSSIAN POLITICAL INSTITUTIONS. RUSSIA USSR CONSTN AGRI DELIB/GP PLAN EDU/PROP CONTROL CHOOSE EFFICIENCY ATTIT MARXISM...BIBLIOG/A 13/20. PAGE 141 H2813 NAT/G POL/PAR ADMIN DECISION

C58
BLANCHARD W.,"THAILAND." THAILAND CULTURE AGRI FINAN INDUS FAM LABOR INT/TRADE ATTIT...GEOG HEAL SOC BIBLIOG 20. PAGE 18 H0354 NAT/G DIPLOM ECO/UNDEV S/ASIA

B59
EAENZA L.,COMMUNISMO E CATTOLICESIMO IN UNA PARROCHIA DI CAMPAGNA. ITALY CULTURE ELITES ECO/DEV AGRI KIN POL/PAR DOMIN LEGIT RIGID/FLEX...DECISION OBS IDEA/COMP 20 COM/PARTY CHURCH/STA. PAGE 44 H0878 ATTIT CATHISM NEIGH MARXISM

B59
EPSTEIN F.T.,EAST GERMANY: A SELECTED BIBLIOGRAPHY (PAMPHLET). COM GERMANY/E LAW AGRI FINAN INDUS LABOR POL/PAR EDU/PROP ADMIN AGE/Y 20. PAGE 47 H0932 BIBLIOG/A INTELL MARXISM NAT/G

B59
LEMBERG E.,DIE VERTRIEBENEN IN WESTDEUTSCHLAND (3 VOLS.). GERMANY/W CULTURE STRUCT AGRI PROVS ADMIN ...JURID 20 MIGRATION. PAGE 94 H1875 GP/REL INGP/REL SOCIETY

B59
MAC MILLAN W.M.,THE ROAD TO SELF-RULE. SOUTH/AFR UK CULTURE SOCIETY AGRI LABOR NAT/G INT/TRADE CONTROL GP/REL...SOC 19/20. PAGE 100 H1988 AFR COLONIAL SOVEREIGN POLICY

B59
MURDOCK G.P.,AFRICA: ITS PEOPLES AND THEIR CULTURE HISTORY. AFR CULTURE AGRI LOC/G INGP/REL HABITAT ...GEOG SOC LING CHARTS BIBLIOG 20 NEGRO EGYPT/ANC. PAGE 115 H2293 SOCIETY ECO/TAC GP/COMP KIN

B59
WRAITH R.E.,EAST AFRICAN CITIZEN. AFR GHANA UK AGRI INDUS LOC/G POL/PAR PROB/SOLV CONTROL REGION REPRESENT NAT/LISM PWR...OBS 20 AFRICA/E AFRICA/W. PAGE 171 H3415 ECO/UNDEV RACE/REL NAT/G NAT/COMP

B60
BRIGGS L.C.,TRIBES OF THE SAHARA. AFR MOROCCO STRATA AGRI GP/REL HEALTH...GEOG SOC MYTH LING BIBLIOG 13/20 ARABS. PAGE 21 H0418 CULTURE HABITAT KIN SELF/OBS

B60
CONOVER H.F.,OFFICIAL PUBLICATIONS OF FRENCH WEST AFRICA, 1946-1958. DAHOMEY IVORY/CST NIGER SENEGAL UPPER/VOLT CONSTN AGRI PRESS...CON/ANAL 20. PAGE 33 H0651 BIBLIOG COLONIAL NAT/G AFR

B60
CONOVER H.F.,OFFICIAL PUBLICATIONS OF SOMALILAND, 1941-1959: A GUIDE. SOMALIA AGRI FINAN INT/ORG SCHOOL INT/TRADE PRESS CONFER COLONIAL PARL/PROC 20 CONGRESS. PAGE 33 H0652 BIBLIOG NAT/G CON/ANAL

B60
GONZALEZ NAVARRO M.,LA COLONIZACION EN MEXICO, 1877-1910. AGRI NAT/G PLAN PROB/SOLV INCOME ...POLICY JURID CENSUS 19/20 MEXIC/AMER MIGRATION. PAGE 58 H1164 ECO/UNDEV GEOG HABITAT COLONIAL

B60
HALBWACHS M.,POPULATION AND SOCIETY: INTRODUCTION TO SOCIAL MORPHOLOGY (TRANS. BY DUNCAN AND PFAUTZ). CULTURE SOCIETY AGRI INDUS HABITAT...CONCPT 20. PAGE 64 H1281 BIO/SOC GEOG NEIGH GP/COMP

B60
LEYDER J.,BIBLIOGRAPHIE DE L'ENSEIGNEMENT SUPERIEUR ET DE LA RECHERCHE SCIENTIFIQUE EN AFRIQUE INTERTROPICALE (2 VOLS.). AFR CULTURE ECO/UNDEV AGRI PLAN EDU/PROP ADMIN COLONIAL...GEOG SOC/INTEG 20 NEGRO. PAGE 96 H1918 BIBLIOG/A ACT/RES ACADEM R+D

B60
MC CLELLAN G.S.,INDIA. CHINA/COM INDIA CONSTN ELITES STRATA AGRI POL/PAR FOR/AID ARMS/CONT REV MARXISM...CENSUS BIBLIOG 20 COLD/WAR GANDHI/M NEHRU/J. PAGE 106 H2117 DIPLOM NAT/G SOCIETY ECO/UNDEV

B60
NICHOLLS W.H.,SOUTHERN TRADITION AND REGIONAL PROGRESS. STRATA STRUCT SCHOOL WORKER PARTIC REGION RACE/REL CONSEN ATTIT...SOC METH/CNCPT 19/20 SOUTH/US TVA. PAGE 118 H2349 RIGID/FLEX CONSERVE AGRI CULTURE

B60
PIERCE R.A.,RUSSIAN CENTRAL ASIA, 1867-1917. ASIA RUSSIA CULTURE AGRI INDUS EDU/PROP REV NAT/LISM ...CHARTS BIBLIOG 19/20 BOLSHEVISM INTERVENT. PAGE 125 H2509 COLONIAL DOMIN ADMIN ECO/UNDEV

B60
ROBINSON E.A.G.,ECONOMIC CONSEQUENCES OF THE SIZE OF NATIONS. AGRI INDUS DELIB/GP FOR/AID ADMIN EFFICIENCY...METH/COMP 20. PAGE 132 H2649 CONCPT INT/ORG NAT/COMP

B60
THE ECONOMIST (LONDON),THE COMMONWEALTH AND EUROPE. EUR+WWI WOR+45 AGRI FINAN INCOME...STAT CENSUS CHARTS CMN/WLTH EEC. PAGE 153 H3067 INT/TRADE INDUS INT/ORG NAT/COMP

B60
WILLIAMS L.E.,OVERSEAS CHINESE NATIONALISM: THE GENESIS OF THE PAN-CHINESE MOVEMENT IN INDONESIA, 1900-1916. ASIA COM INDONESIA AGRI INT/ORG LOC/G DIPLOM EDU/PROP HABITAT PWR POPULISM...GEOG LING CENSUS 20. PAGE 168 H3367 NAT/LISM GP/REL DECISION NAT/G

B60
WORLEY P.,ASIA TODAY (REV. ED.) (PAMPHLET). COM ECO/UNDEV AGRI FINAN INDUS POL/PAR FOR/AID ADMIN MARXISM 20. PAGE 170 H3411 BIBLIOG/A ASIA DIPLOM NAT/G

S60
BERG E.J.,"ECONOMIC BASIS OF POLITICAL CHOICE IN FRENCH WEST AFRICA." FRANCE ECO/UNDEV AGRI INDUS NAT/G PLAN LEGIT COLONIAL REGION ATTIT PWR WEALTH ...CONCPT 20. PAGE 15 H0299 AFR ECO/TAC

S60
RIVKIN A.,"AFRICAN ECONOMIC DEVELOPMENT: ADVANCED TECHNOLOGY AND THE STAGES OF GROWTH." CULTURE ECO/UNDEV AGRI COM/IND EXTR/IND PLAN ECO/TAC ATTIT DRIVE RIGID/FLEX SKILL WEALTH...MGT SOC GEN/LAWS WORK TOT/POP 20. PAGE 132 H2634 AFR TEC/DEV FOR/AID

B61
APTER D.E.,THE POLITICAL KINGDOM IN UGANDA. UGANDA CULTURE ECO/UNDEV AGRI KIN SECT TOP/EX REGION ATTIT HABITAT CONSERVE...GEOG AUD/VIS 20. PAGE 8 H0153 NAT/LISM POL/PAR COLONIAL ECO/TAC

B61
HADDAD J.A.,REVOLUCAO CUBANA E REVOLUCAO BRASILEIRA. BRAZIL CUBA L/A+17C STRATA AGRI WORKER EDU/PROP REGION...POLICY NAT/COMP 20. PAGE 63 H1272 REV ORD/FREE DIPLOM ECO/UNDEV

B61
HEMPSTONE S.,THE NEW AFRICA. AGRI INDUS KIN NAT/G COLONIAL MARXISM...SOC INT TREND NAT/COMP BIBLIOG/A 20. PAGE 69 H1392 AFR ORD/FREE PERSON CULTURE

B61
LUZ N.V.,A LUTA PELA INDUSTRIALIZACAO DO BRAZIL. BRAZIL L/A+17C AGRI NAT/G TEC/DEV COLONIAL 19/20. PAGE 99 H1981 ECO/UNDEV INDUS NAT/LISM POLICY

B61
MARX K.,THE COMMUNIST MANIFESTO. IN (MENDEL A. ESSENTIAL WORKS OF MARXISM, NEW YORK: BANTAM. FUT MOD/EUR CULTURE ECO/DEV ECO/UNDEV AGRI FINAN INDUS MARKET PROC/MFG LABOR MUNIC POL/PAR CONSULT FORCES CREATE PLAN ADMIN ATTIT DRIVE RIGID/FLEX ORD/FREE PWR RESPECT MARX/KARL WORK. PAGE 104 H2081 COM NEW/IDEA CAP/ISM REV

B61
MIT CENTER INTERNATIONAL STU,OFFICIAL SERIAL PUBLICATIONS RELATING TO ECONOMIC DEVELOPMENT IN AFRICA SOUTH OF THE SAHARA. AFR SOCIETY AGRI FINAN INDUS LG/CO ADMIN 20. PAGE 111 H2228 BIBLIOG ECO/UNDEV ECO/TAC NAT/G

B61
SANTHANAM K.,DEMOCRATIC PLANNING. INDIA AGRI FINAN LEGIS DIPLOM PARL/PROC ORD/FREE 20. PAGE 138 H2753 PLAN NAT/G CONSTN POLICY

B61
SOUTHALL A.,SOCIAL CHANGE IN MODERN AFRICA. CULTURE STRATA ECO/UNDEV AGRI FAM KIN MUNIC GP/REL INGP/REL MARRIAGE...GEOG ANTHOL 20. PAGE 147 H2940
AFR TREND SOCIETY SOC

B61
STARK H.,SOCIAL AND ECONOMIC FRONTIERS IN LATIN AMERICA (2ND ED.). CUBA FUT CULTURE AGRI INDUS ECO/TAC PRODUC ATTIT MARXISM...NAT/COMP BIBLIOG T 20. PAGE 149 H2971
L/A+17C SOCIETY DIPLOM ECO/UNDEV

L61
EZELLPH,"THE HISPANIC AGRICULTURATION OF THE GILA RIVER PIMAS." FAM TEC/DEV PERS/REL ADJUST...GEOG MYTH CHARTS BIBLIOG WORSHIP 17/20. PAGE 48 H0956
CULTURE SOC AGRI DRIVE

B62
THREE PRELIMINARY BIBLIOGRAPHIES OF WORKS RELATED TO THE SOCIAL SCIENCES IN LATIN AMERICA. BRAZIL CULTURE SOCIETY NAT/G PLAN PROB/SOLV...PSY 20 MEXIC/AMER. PAGE 2 H0040
BIBLIOG L/A+17C SOC AGRI

B62
BRUMBERG A.,RUSSIA UNDER KHRUSHCHEV. FUT USSR SOCIETY ECO/DEV AGRI PERF/ART WORKER PWR...SOC ANTHOL 20 KHRUSH/N. PAGE 22 H0453
COM MARXISM NAT/G CHIEF

B62
GALENSON W.,LABOR IN DEVELOPING COUNTRIES. BRAZIL INDONESIA ISRAEL PAKISTAN TURKEY AGRI INDUS WORKER PAY PRICE GP/REL WEALTH...MGT CHARTS METH/COMP NAT/COMP 20. PAGE 54 H1088
LABOR ECO/UNDEV BARGAIN POL/PAR

B62
GREEN L.P.,DEVELOPMENT IN AFRICA. AFR CENTRL/AFR GHANA RHODESIA SOUTH/AFR AGRI PROC/MFG INT/TRADE DEMAND NAT/LISM PRODUC WEALTH...GEOG METH/CNCPT CHARTS BIBLIOG 20. PAGE 60 H1206
CULTURE ECO/UNDEV GOV/REL TREND

B62
HUCKER C.O.,CHINA: A CRITICAL BIBLIOGRAPHY (PAMPHLET). ASIA STRUCT AGRI FINAN INDUS HABITAT MARXISM...EPIST HUM. PAGE 74 H1487
BIBLIOG/A CULTURE INTELL SOCIETY

B62
KOSAMBI D.D.,MYTH AND REALITY. INDIA AGRI KIN SECT HABITAT...SOC 20. PAGE 88 H1758
CULTURE SOCIETY MYTH ATTIT

B62
MARTINS A.F.,REVOLUCAO BRANCA NO CAMPO. L/A+17C SERV/IND DEMAND EFFICIENCY PRODUC...POLICY METH/COMP. PAGE 104 H2070
AGRI ECO/UNDEV TEC/DEV NAT/COMP

B62
ROBINSON A.D.,DUTCH ORGANIZED AGRICULTURE IN INTERNATIONAL POLITICS, 1945-1960. EUR+WWI NETHERLAND STRUCT ECO/DEV NAT/G VOL/ASSN CONSULT DELIB/GP PLAN TEC/DEV INT/TRADE EDU/PROP ATTIT RIGID/FLEX ALL/VALS...NEW/IDEA TREND EEC 20. PAGE 132 H2648
AGRI INT/ORG

B62
SILBERMAN B.S.,JAPAN AND KOREA; A CRITICAL BIBLIOGRAPHY. KOREA LAW STRATA STRUCT AGRI INDUS NAT/G POL/PAR SECT...HUM LING IDEA/COMP 5/20 CHINJAP. PAGE 144 H2872
BIBLIOG/A CULTURE S/ASIA

B62
SMITH M.G.,KINSHIP AND COMMUNITY IN CARRIACOU. WEST/IND STRATA AGRI FAM SECT WORKER MARRIAGE OWN HEREDITY WEALTH...SOC 18/20. PAGE 146 H2915
CULTURE HABITAT KIN STRUCT

B62
STARCKE V.,DENMARK IN WORLD HISTORY. DENMARK AGRI KIN WAR...BIBLIOG T 20. PAGE 149 H2970
GEOG CULTURE SOC

B62
TATZ C.M.,SHADOW AND SUBSTANCE IN SOUTH AFRICA. SOUTH/AFR AGRI NAT/G POL/PAR DOMIN GP/REL ATTIT PWR 20. PAGE 152 H3048
RACE/REL REPRESENT DISCRIM LEGIS

B62
UMENDRAS H.,LES SOCIETESRFRANCAISES; BIBLIOGRAPHIES FRANCAISES DE SCIENCE SOCIALES (VOL. III). FRANCE SECT WORKER 20. PAGE 158 H3154
BIBLIOG/A AGRI MUNIC CULTURE

B62
UNECA LIBRARY,BOOKS ON AFRICA IN THE UNECA LIBRARY. WOR+45 AGRI INT/ORG NAT/G PLAN WRITING REGION...SOC STAT UN. PAGE 158 H3160
BIBLIOG AFR ECO/UNDEV TEC/DEV

B62
WALSTON H.,AGRICULTURE UNDER COMMUNISM. CHINA/COM COM PROB/SOLV HAPPINESS RIGID/FLEX...POLICY METH/COMP 20. PAGE 165 H3295
AGRI MARXISM PLAN CREATE

B62
WHITING K.R.,THE SOVIET UNION TODAY: A CONCISE HANDBOOK. USSR ELITES AGRI INDUS POL/PAR FORCES DIPLOM EDU/PROP LEAD...GEOG TREND 19/20. PAGE 168 H3354
NAT/G ATTIT MARXISM POLICY

B63
BRITISH AID. UK AGRI DIST/IND INDUS SCHOOL TEC/DEV INT/TRADE COLONIAL DEMAND...TREND CHARTS 20. PAGE 2 H0041
FOR/AID ECO/UNDEV NAT/G FINAN

B63
BERGSON A.,ECONOMIC TRENDS IN THE SOVIET UNION. USSR ECO/UNDEV AGRI NAT/G FORCES PLAN TEC/DEV INT/TRADE BAL/PAY...POLICY ANTHOL 20. PAGE 15 H0302
ECO/DEV NAT/COMP INDUS LABOR

B63
DRIVER H.E.,ETHNOGRAPHY AND ACCULTURATION OF THE CHICHIMECA-JONAZ OF NORTHEAST MEXICO. ECO/UNDEV AGRI FAM KIN EDU/PROP MARRIAGE HEALTH...GEOG INT CHARTS WORSHIP 18/20 MEXIC/AMER. PAGE 42 H0848
CULTURE HABITAT STRUCT GP/REL

B63
ELWIN V.,A NEW DEAL FOR TRIBAL INDIA. INDIA AGRI COM/IND INDUS KIN TEC/DEV TAX EDU/PROP OWN HEALTH 20. PAGE 46 H0912
ECO/UNDEV CULTURE CONSTN SOC/WK

B63
ENKE S.,ECONOMICS FOR DEVELOPMENT. AGRI TEC/DEV CAP/ISM DIPLOM ECO/TAC TAX ATTIT DRIVE HABITAT WEALTH...GOV/COMP BIBLIOG 20. PAGE 46 H0928
ECO/UNDEV PHIL/SCI CON/ANAL

B63
FURTADO C.,THE ECONOMIC GROWTH OF BRAZIL: A SURVEY FROM COLONIAL TO MODERN TIMES. L/A+17C AGRI DIST/IND EXTR/IND INDUS WORKER COLONIAL RACE/REL OWN GOV/COMP. PAGE 54 H1082
ECO/UNDEV TEC/DEV LABOR DOMIN

B63
GAMBLE S.D.,NORTH CHINA VILLAGES: SOCIAL, POLITICAL, AND ECONOMIC ACTIVITIES BEFORE 1933. ASIA CULTURE STRUCT FAM DOMIN EDU/PROP WORSHIP 20. PAGE 55 H1093
MUNIC AGRI LEAD FINAN

B63
GLADE W.P. JR.,THE POLITICAL ECONOMY OF MEXICO. FUT L/A+17C CULTURE SOCIETY AGRI INDUS DELIB/GP ACT/RES ECO/TAC ATTIT HEALTH ORD/FREE...STAT TIME/SEQ TREND MEXIC/AMER TOT/POP VAL/FREE 20. PAGE 57 H1138
FINAN ECO/UNDEV

B63
GOURNAY B.,PUBLIC ADMINISTRATION. FRANCE LAW CONSTN AGRI FINAN LABOR SCHOOL EX/STRUC CHOOSE...MGT METH/COMP 20. PAGE 59 H1189
BIBLIOG/A ADMIN NAT/G LOC/G

B63
HAQ M.,THE STRATEGY OF ECONOMIC PLANNING. PAKISTAN AGRI FINAN INDUS NAT/G FOR/AID TAX CONTROL REGION PRODUC...POLICY CHARTS 20. PAGE 66 H1324
ECO/TAC ECO/UNDEV PLAN PROB/SOLV

B63
INDIAN INSTITUTE PUBLIC ADMIN,CASES IN INDIAN ADMINISTRATION. INDIA AGRI NAT/G PROB/SOLV TEC/DEV ECO/TAC ADMIN...ANTHOL METH 20. PAGE 77 H1532
DECISION PLAN MGT ECO/UNDEV

B63
ISSAWI C.,EGYPT IN REVOLUTION: AN ECONOMIC ANALYSIS. ISLAM STRUCT ECO/UNDEV AGRI FINAN INDUS PLAN EXEC REV NAT/LISM ATTIT RIGID/FLEX WEALTH SOCISM...STAT WORK 20. PAGE 79 H1573
NAT/G UAR

B63
KLEIMAN R.,ATLANTIC CRISIS; AMERICAN DIPLOMACY CONFRONTS A RESURGENT EUROPE. EUR+WWI USA+45 ECO/DEV AGRI NAT/G CHIEF FORCES PLAN LEAD ATTIT ...CONCPT 20 NATO KENNEDY/JF DEGAULLE/C EEC JOHNSON/LB. PAGE 87 H1731
DIPLOM REGION POLICY

B63
LETHBRIDGE H.J.,THE PEASANT AND THE COMMUNES. CHINA/COM COM USSR NEIGH PROB/SOLV ADJUST EFFICIENCY...POLICY METH/COMP NAT/COMP 20. PAGE 95 H1894
MARXISM ECO/TAC AGRI WORKER

B63
MOSELY P.E.,THE SOVIET UNION, 1922-1962: A FOREIGN AFFAIRS READER. ASIA POLAND USSR CULTURE INTELL AGRI POL/PAR WORKER INT/TRADE DOMIN WAR NAT/LISM MARXISM SOCISM 20 KHRUSH/N. PAGE 113 H2267
PWR POLICY DIPLOM

B63
NATIONAL OFF STATE GOVT THAI,STATISTICAL BIBLIOGRAPHY: AN ANNOTATED BIBLIOGRAPHY OF THAI GOVERNMENTAL STATISTICAL PUBLICATIONS. THAILAND AGRI 20. PAGE 116 H2321
BIBLIOG/A STAT NAT/G S/ASIA

B63
OLSON M. JR.,THE ECONOMICS OF WARTIME SHORTAGE. FRANCE GERMANY MOD/EUR UK AGRI PROB/SOLV ADMIN DEMAND WEALTH...POLICY OLD/LIB 17/20. PAGE 121 H2416
WAR ADJUST ECO/TAC NAT/COMP

B63
PEREZ ORTIZ R.,ANUARIO BIBLIOGRAFICO COLOMBIANO, 1961. AGRI...INT/LAW JURID SOC LING 20 COLOMB. PAGE 125 H2491
BIBLIOG L/A+17C NAT/G

B63
RIVKIN A.,THE AFRICAN PRESENCE IN WORLD AFFAIRS. ECO/UNDEV AGRI INT/ORG LOC/G NAT/LISM...OBS PREDICT GOV/COMP 20. PAGE 132 H2635
AFR NAT/G DIPLOM BAL/PWR

B63
SELF P.,THE STATE AND THE FARMER. UK ECO/DEV MARKET AGRI

WORKER PRICE CONTROL GP/REL...WELF/ST 20 DEPT/AGRI. NAT/G
PAGE 141 H2823 ADMIN
VOL/ASSN

B63
SPRING D.,THE ENGLISH LANDED ESTATE IN THE STRATA
NINETEENTH CENTURY: ITS ADMINISTRATION. UK ELITES PERS/REL
STRUCT AGRI NAT/G GP/REL OWN PWR WEALTH...BIBLIOG MGT
19 HOUSE/LORD. PAGE 148 H2954

B63
STEVENS G.G.,EGYPT YESTERDAY AND TODAY. CONSTN ISLAM
ECO/UNDEV AGRI INDUS NAT/G POL/PAR FORCES ECO/TAC TOP/EX
EDU/PROP COERCE WAR NAT/LISM DRIVE ALL/VALS REV
...TIME/SEQ WORK SUEZ 20. PAGE 149 H2983 UAR

S63
HARRIS R.L.,"COMMUNISM AND ASIA: ILLUSIONS AND PWR
MISCONCEPTIONS." ASIA COM FUT S/ASIA ECO/UNDEV AGRI GUERRILLA
NAT/G POL/PAR EX/STRUC EDU/PROP COERCE ATTIT
MARXISM COLD/WAR TOT/POP 20. PAGE 67 H1344

S63
HOSKINS H.L.,"ARAB SOCIALISM IN THE UAR." ISLAM ECO/DEV
USSR AGRI INDUS NAT/G TOP/EX CREATE DIPLOM EDU/PROP PLAN
DRIVE KNOWL PWR SOCISM...POLICY CONCPT TREND SUEZ UAR
20. PAGE 74 H1478

B64
BRZEZINSKI Z.,POLITICAL POWER: USA/USSR. USA+45 NAT/G
USSR AGRI POL/PAR FORCES CREATE CHOOSE ATTIT NAT/COMP
ORD/FREE PWR MARXISM...MYTH 20 KENNEDY/JF. PAGE 23 POLICY
H0457 LEAD

B64
FAINSOD M.,HOW RUSSIA IS RULED (REV. ED.). RUSSIA NAT/G
USSR AGRI PROC/MFG LABOR POL/PAR EX/STRUC CONTROL REV
PWR...POLICY BIBLIOG 19/20 KHRUSH/N COM/PARTY. MARXISM
PAGE 48 H0963

B64
GILLY A.,INSIDE THE CUBAN REVOLUTION. CUBA AGRI REV
INDUS LABOR CREATE DIPLOM...METH/COMP 20. PAGE 56 PLAN
H1129 MARXISM
ECO/UNDEV

B64
HAMILTON W.B.,THE TRANSFER OF INSTITUTIONS. CANADA NAT/COMP
INDIA UK LAW AGRI LABOR SECT COLONIAL 18/20. ECO/UNDEV
PAGE 65 H1301 EDU/PROP
CULTURE

B64
HARRIS M.,PATTERNS OF RACE IN THE AMERICAS. BRAZIL STRUCT
L/A+17C STRATA ECO/UNDEV AGRI KIN MUNIC SECT PRE/AMER
COLONIAL RACE/REL...SOC SOC/INTEG 17/20 NEGRO CULTURE
INDIAN/AM. PAGE 67 H1342 SOCIETY

B64
HAZLEWOOD A.,THE ECONOMICS OF DEVELOPMENT: AN BIBLIOG/A
ANNOTATED LIST OF BOOKS AND ARTICLES PUBLISHED ECO/UNDEV
1958-1962. AGRI FINAN INDUS LABOR NAT/G DIPLOM TEC/DEV
INT/TRADE INCOME...MGT 20. PAGE 69 H1374

B64
JOHNSON A.F.,BIBLIOGRAPHY OF GHANA: 1930-1961. BIBLIOG/A
GHANA LAW AGRI INDUS NAT/G INT/TRADE EDU/PROP CULTURE
HEALTH...GEOG AUD/VIS CHARTS 20. PAGE 81 H1618 SOC

B64
LEBRUN J.,BIBLIOGRAPHIE DE LA FERTILITE DES SOLS ET BIBLIOG/A
ELEMENTS DE SOCIOLOGIE RURALE EN AFRIQUE AU SUD DU ECO/UNDEV
SAHARA. AFR PLAN TEC/DEV EFFICIENCY PRODUC...GEOG HABITAT
SOC NAT/COMP 20. PAGE 93 H1850 AGRI

B64
LI C.M.,INDUSTRIAL DEVELOPMENT IN COMMUNIST CHINA. ASIA
CHINA/COM ECO/DEV ECO/UNDEV AGRI FINAN INDUS MARKET TEC/DEV
LABOR NAT/G ECO/TAC INT/TRADE EXEC ALL/VALS
...POLICY RELATIV TREND WORK TOT/POP VAL/FREE 20.
PAGE 96 H1921

B64
MORGAN H.W.,AMERICAN SOCIALISM 1900-1960. USA+45 SOCISM
USA-45 INTELL AGRI LABOR WORKER BARGAIN ECO/TAC POL/PAR
GP/REL RACE/REL 20 NEGRO MIGRATION GOLD/STAND. ECO/DEV
PAGE 113 H2254 STRATA

B64
MUSEUM FUR VOLKERKUNDE WIEN,ZENTRALAMERIKA MEXIKO SOCIETY
VOLKER UND KULTUREN. COSTA/RICA GUATEMALA L/A+17C STRUCT
PANAMA SECT WAR GP/REL SOVEREIGN...ART/METH 20 CULTURE
CENTRAL/AM MEXIC/AMER. PAGE 115 H2300 AGRI

B64
OECD,DEVELOPMENT ASSISTANCE EFFORTS - POLICIES OF INT/ORG
THE MEMBERS. AGRI INDUS BUDGET...GEOG NAT/COMP 20 FOR/AID
OECD. PAGE 120 H2398 ECO/UNDEV
TEC/DEV

B64
POWELSON J.P.,LATIN AMERICA: TODAY'S ECONOMIC AND ECO/UNDEV
SOCIAL REVOLUTION. L/A+17C INTELL SOCIETY STRUCT WEALTH
AGRI INDUS NAT/G DIPLOM ECO/TAC REV...POLICY 20. ADJUST
PAGE 128 H2552 PLAN

B64
SINGER M.R.,THE EMERGING ELITE: A STUDY OF TOP/EX
POLITICAL LEADERSHIP IN CEYLON. S/ASIA ECO/UNDEV STRATA
AGRI KIN NAT/G SECT EX/STRUC LEGIT ATTIT PWR NAT/LISM
RESPECT...SOC STAT CHARTS 20. PAGE 144 H2883 CEYLON

B64
SKINNER E.P.,THE MOSSI OF UPPER VOLTA: THE CULTURE
POLITICAL DEVELOPMENT OF A SUDANESE PEOPLE. AFR LAW OBS
AGRI FAM KIN POL/PAR PROVS SECT DELIB/GP EX/STRUC UPPER/VOLT
FORCES TOP/EX DOMIN EDU/PROP LEGIT CT/SYS COERCE
CHOOSE ORD/FREE PWR WEALTH...SOC MYTH VAL/FREE.
PAGE 145 H2897

B64
THAILAND NATIONAL ECO DEV,THE NATIONAL ECONOMIC ECO/UNDEV
DEVELOPMENT PLAN: 1961-66: SECOND PHASE 1964-66. ECO/TAC
THAILAND AGRI FINAN BUDGET EFFICIENCY INCOME...STAT PLAN
CHARTS 20. PAGE 153 H3065 NAT/G

B64
THORNTON T.P.,THE THIRD WORLD IN SOVIET ECO/UNDEV
PERSPECTIVE: STUDIES BY SOVIET WRITERS ON THE ACT/RES
DEVELOPING AREAS. AFR L/A+17C S/ASIA STRATA AGRI USSR
INDUS MARKET NAT/G POL/PAR ECO/TAC COLONIAL PERCEPT DIPLOM
PWR WEALTH...MARXIST STAT CHARTS WORK MARX/KARL 20.
PAGE 155 H3090

B64
WRIGHT G.,RURAL REVOLUTION IN FRANCE: THE PEASANTRY PWR
IN THE TWENTIETH CENTURY. EUR+WWI MOD/EUR LAW STRATA
CULTURE AGRI POL/PAR DELIB/GP LEGIS ECO/TAC FRANCE
EDU/PROP COERCE CHOOSE ATTIT RIGID/FLEX HEALTH REV
...STAT CENSUS CHARTS VAL/FREE 20. PAGE 171 H3419

B64
ZARTMAN I.W.,MOROCCO: PROBLEMS OF NEW POWER. ISLAM CHOOSE
CULTURE ECO/UNDEV AGRI POL/PAR SCHOOL FORCES ADMIN MOROCCO
...CONCPT STAT INT CENSUS TIME/SEQ CHARTS WORK DELIB/GP
VAL/FREE 20. PAGE 172 H3449 DECISION

S64
NASH M.,"SOCIAL PREREQUISITES TO ECONOMIC GROWTH IN ECO/DEV
LATIN AMERICA AND SOUTHEAST ASIA." L/A+17C S/ASIA PERCEPT
CULTURE SOCIETY ECO/UNDEV AGRI INDUS NAT/G PLAN
TEC/DEV EDU/PROP ROUTINE ALL/VALS...POLICY RELATIV
SOC NAT/COMP WORK TOT/POP 20. PAGE 116 H2314

S64
ZARTMAN I.W.,"LES RELATIONS ENTRE LA FRANCE ET ECO/UNDEV
L'ALGERIA DEPUIS LES ACCORDS D'EVIAN." EUR+WWI FUT ALGERIA
ISLAM CULTURE AGRI EXTR/IND FINAN INDUS POL/PAR FRANCE
DIPLOM ECO/TAC FOR/AID PEACE ATTIT DRIVE ALL/VALS
...TIME/SEQ VAL/FREE 20. PAGE 172 H3450

N64
KENYA MINISTRY ECO PLAN DEV,AFRICAN SOCIALISM AND NAT/G
ITS APPLICATION TO PLANNING IN KENYA (PAMPHLET). SOCISM
AFR AGRI INDUS WORKER TAX COLONIAL WEALTH 20. PLAN
PAGE 85 H1691 ECO/UNDEV

B65
APPLEMAN P.,THE SILENT EXPLOSION. WOR+45 ECO/DEV GEOG
ECO/UNDEV PLAN HEALTH ALL/IDEOS CATHISM...POLICY CENSUS
STAT RECORD GP/COMP IDEA/COMP NAT/COMP 20 BIRTH/CON AGRI
COM/PARTY. PAGE 7 H0148 BIO/SOC

B65
BARRY E.E.,NATIONALISATION IN BRITISH POLITICS: THE NAT/G
HISTORICAL BACKGROUND. UK AGRI DIST/IND EXTR/IND OWN
LABOR LG/CO ATTIT CONSERVE SOCISM 19/20 LABOR/PAR. INDUS
PAGE 12 H0231 POL/PAR

B65
BRIDGMAN J.,GERMAN AFRICA: A SELECT ANNOTATED BIBLIOG/A
BIBLIOGRAPHY. AFR AGRI DIPLOM REPAR WAR FASCISM 20. COLONIAL
PAGE 21 H0414 NAT/G
EDU/PROP

B65
BURLING R.,HILL FARMS AND PADI FIELDS. BURMA S/ASIA SOCIETY
THAILAND VIETNAM AGRI NEIGH SECT GP/REL NAT/LISM STRUCT
ORD/FREE 20 MID/EAST MIGRATION. PAGE 24 H0491 CULTURE
SOVEREIGN

B65
FILIPINIANA BOOK GUILD,THE COLONIZATION AND COLONIAL
CONQUEST OF THE PHILIPPINES BY SPAIN. PHILIPPINE COERCE
SPAIN ELITES AGRI KIN CHIEF DOMIN CONTROL ATTIT PWR CULTURE
...ANTHOL WORSHIP 16. PAGE 50 H1000 WAR

B65
FORM W.H.,INDUSTRIAL RELATIONS AND SOCIAL CHANGE IN INDUS
LATIN AMERICA. L/A+17C AGRI LABOR NAT/G PLAN GP/REL
PROB/SOLV DIPLOM...MGT SOC ANTHOL BIBLIOG/A METH NAT/COMP
20. PAGE 52 H1038 ECO/UNDEV

B65
GIBBS S.L.,PEOPLES OF AFRICA. AFR INGP/REL HABITAT CULTURE
...GEOG ANTHOL 20. PAGE 56 H1122 AGRI
FAM
KIN

B65
GINIEWSKI P.,THE TWO FACES OF APARTHEID. AFR DISCRIM
SOUTH/AFR STRATA AGRI INDUS COLONIAL PARTIC NAT/G
SOVEREIGN...CONCPT GOV/COMP NAT/COMP 19/20 NEGRO. RACE/REL
PAGE 56 H1131 STRUCT

B65
GUERIN D.,SUR LE FASCISME: FASCISME ET GRAND FASCISM
CAPITAL (VOL. II). GERMANY ITALY SOCIETY STRATA NAT/G
AGRI WORKER 20. PAGE 62 H1245 TOTALISM
EDU/PROP

B65
HADWIGER D.F.,PRESSURES AND PROTEST. NAT/G LEGIS AGRI
PLAN LEAD PARTIC ROUTINE ATTIT POLICY. PAGE 63 GP/REL
H1273 LOBBY
CHOOSE

B65
HAPGOOD D.,AFRICA: FROM INDEPENDENCE TO TOMARROW. ECO/TAC

AFR GUINEA SENEGAL CULTURE ELITES ECO/UNDEV AGRI SCHOOL FOR/AID COLONIAL MARXISM...TREND 20. PAGE 66 H1323 — SOCIETY NAT/G

B65
HARRIS R.L.,POLITICAL ORGANIZATION OF THE MBEMBE NIGERIA. AFR NIGERIA SOCIETY AGRI SECT WORKER PAY ...SOC WORSHIP 20 MBEMBE. PAGE 67 H1345 — STRUCT CHIEF CULTURE

B65
HERRICK B.H.,URBAN MIGRATION AND ECONOMIC DEVELOPMENT IN CHILE. CHILE AGRI INDUS LABOR NAT/G CENTRAL PRODUC...STAT SAMP CHARTS BIBLIOG/A 20 MIGRATION. PAGE 70 H1404 — HABITAT GEOG MUNIC ECO/UNDEV

B65
HLA MYINT U.,THE ECONOMICS OF THE DEVELOPING COUNTRIES. USA+45 WOR+45 AGRI FINAN NAT/G INT/TRADE ...CLASSIF CENSUS TREND NAT/COMP SIMUL GEN/LAWS. PAGE 71 H1430 — ECO/UNDEV FOR/AID GEOG

B65
HONDURAS CONSEJO NAC DE ECO,PLAN NACIONAL DE DESARROLLO ECONOMICO Y SOCIAL DE HONDURAS 1965-69. HONDURAS AGRI INDUS BAL/PAY INCOME 20. PAGE 73 H1459 — ECO/UNDEV NAT/G PLAN POLICY

B65
INT. BANK RECONSTR. DEVELOP.,ECONOMIC DEVELOPMENT OF KUWAIT. ISLAM KUWAIT AGRI FINAN MARKET EX/STRUC TEC/DEV ECO/TAC ADMIN WEALTH...OBS CON/ANAL CHARTS 20. PAGE 77 H1541 — INDUS NAT/G

B65
JAIN S.C.,THE STATE AND AGRICULTURE. INDIA S/ASIA ECO/UNDEV PROB/SOLV CAP/ISM MARXISM SOCISM 20. PAGE 79 H1586 — NAT/G POLICY AGRI ECO/TAC

B65
JASNY H.,KHRUSHCHEV'S CROP POLICY. USSR ECO/DEV PLAN MARXISM...STAT 20 KHRUSH/N RESOURCE/N. PAGE 80 H1593 — AGRI NAT/G POLICY ECO/TAC

B65
KUNSTADTER P.,THE LUA (LAWA) OF NORTHERN THAILAND: ASPECTS OF SOCIAL STRUCTURE, AGRICULTURE, AND RELIGION. THAILAND AGRI FAM KIN INGP/REL ISOLAT MARRIAGE HEALTH WORSHIP 20 BUDDHISM LUA. PAGE 89 H1780 — STRUCT ECO/UNDEV CULTURE

B65
THE STATE AND ECONOMIC ENTERPRISE IN JAPAN; ESSAYS IN THE POLITICAL ECONOMY OF GROWTH. AGRI INDUS DRIVE POPULISM...CHARTS NAT/COMP ANTHOL 19/20 CHINJAP. PAGE 98 H1949 — ECO/UNDEV ECO/DEV CAP/ISM ECO/TAC

B65
OBUKAR C.,THE MODERN AFRICAN. AGRI INDUS WORKER CAP/ISM EDU/PROP PARTIC RACE/REL NAT/LISM ALL/VALS MARXISM...SOC IDEA/COMP 20. PAGE 120 H2393 — AFR ECO/UNDEV CULTURE SOVEREIGN

B65
OECD,THE MEDITERRANEAN REGIONAL PROJECT: GREECE; EDUCATION AND DEVELOPMENT. FUT GREECE SOCIETY AGRI FINAN NAT/G PROF/ORG WORKER PLAN PROB/SOLV ADMIN DEMAND ATTIT 20 OECD. PAGE 120 H2401 — EDU/PROP SCHOOL ACADEM ECO/UNDEV

B65
ONSLOW C.,ASIAN ECONOMIC DEVELOPMENT. BURMA CEYLON INDIA MALAYSIA PAKISTAN S/ASIA AGRI INDUS MARKET PROB/SOLV CAP/ISM FOR/AID INT/TRADE DEMAND WEALTH ...POLICY ANTHOL 20. PAGE 121 H2418 — ECO/UNDEV ECO/TAC PLAN NAT/G

B65
ORGANSKI A.F.K.,THE STAGES OF POLITICAL DEVELOPMENT. STRATA AGRI INDUS NAT/G POL/PAR COLONIAL PWR WEALTH...CLASSIF TIME/SEQ. PAGE 121 H2428 — ECO/DEV ECO/UNDEV GEN/LAWS CREATE

B65
RANDALL F.B.,STALIN'S RUSSIA. USSR STRUCT AGRI NAT/G PLAN DIPLOM WAR TOTALISM MARXISM...BIBLIOG/A 19/20 STALIN/J. PAGE 129 H2590 — BIOG INDUS ECO/DEV

B65
SABLE M.H.,MASTER DIRECTORY FOR LATIN AMERICA. AGRI COM/IND FINAN R+D ACADEM LABOR NAT/G POL/PAR VOL/ASSN INT/TRADE EDU/PROP 20. PAGE 136 H2728 — INDEX L/A+17C INT/ORG DIPLOM

B65
SCHULER E.A.,THE PAKISTAN ACADEMIES FOR RURAL DEVELOPMENT COMILLA AND PESHAWAR 1959-1964. PAKISTAN S/ASIA SOCIETY STRUCT AGRI NAT/G TEC/DEV EDU/PROP 20. PAGE 140 H2801 — BIBLIOG PLAN ECO/TAC ECO/UNDEV

B65
SPENCER P.,THE SAMBURU: A STUDY OF GERONTOCRACY IN A NOMADIC TRIBE. AFR SOCIETY ECO/UNDEV AGRI FAM NEIGH SECT GP/REL MARRIAGE WORSHIP 20 SAMBURU. PAGE 147 H2945 — KIN STRUCT AGE/O CULTURE

B65
WUORINEN J.H.,SCANDINAVIA. DENMARK FINLAND ICELAND NORWAY SWEDEN SOCIETY AGRI INDUS DELIB/GP DIPLOM INT/TRADE NEUTRAL...GEOG CHARTS BIBLIOG TREATY. PAGE 171 H3428 — NAT/G POL/PAR TREND POLICY

B65
YOUNG A.N.,CHINA'S WARTIME FINANCE AND INFLATION. ASIA AGRI INDUS NAT/G ECO/TAC CONFER PRICE WAR COST 20. PAGE 172 H3437 — FINAN FOR/AID TAX

BUDGET

L65
MATTHEWS D.G.,"A CURRENT BIBLIOGRAPHY ON SUDANESE AFFAIRS; A SELECT BIBLIOGRAPHY FROM 1960-1964." SUDAN LAW CULTURE AGRI FINAN INDUS LABOR POL/PAR TEC/DEV FOR/AID RACE/REL LITERACY...LING 20. PAGE 105 H2094 — BIBLIOG ECO/UNDEV NAT/G DIPLOM

L65
WIONCZEK M.,"LATIN AMERICA FREE TRADE ASSOCIATION." AGRI DIST/IND FINAN INDUS INT/ORG LABOR NAT/G TEC/DEV ECO/TAC HEALTH SKILL WEALTH...POLICY RELATIV MGT LAFTA 20. PAGE 169 H3390 — L/A+17C MARKET REGION

S65
BRANDENBURG F.,"THE RELEVANCE OF MEXICAN EXPERIENCE TO LATIN AMERICAN DEVELOPMENT." BRAZIL CHILE VENEZUELA STRUCT ECO/UNDEV AGRI CREATE ECO/TAC ...STAT RECORD MEXIC/AMER ARGEN COLOMB. PAGE 20 H0405 — L/A+17C GOV/COMP

S65
HELMREICH E.C.,"KADAR'S HUNGARY." COM EUR+WWI HUNGARY USSR INTELL ECO/DEV AGRI INT/ORG TOP/EX DOMIN ALL/VALS WORK COLD/WAR 20. PAGE 69 H1390 — NAT/G RIGID/FLEX TOTALISM

S65
STAAR R.F.,"RETROGRESSION IN POLAND." COM USSR AGRI INDUS NAT/G CREATE EDU/PROP TOTALISM RIGID/FLEX ORD/FREE PWR SOCISM...RECORD CHARTS 20. PAGE 148 H2965 — TOP/EX ECO/TAC POLAND

S65
TABORSKY E.,"CHANGE IN CZECHOSLOVAKIA." COM USSR ELITES INTELL AGRI INDUS NAT/G DELIB/GP EX/STRUC ECO/TAC TOTALISM ATTIT RIGID/FLEX SOCISM...MGT CONCPT TREND 20. PAGE 152 H3031 — ECO/DEV PLAN CZECHOSLVK

C65
WUORINEN J.H.,"SCANDINAVIA." DENMARK FINLAND ICELAND NORWAY SWEDEN SOCIETY AGRI POL/PAR DELIB/GP DIPLOM INT/TRADE NEUTRAL WAR...CHARTS TREATY 20. PAGE 171 H3427 — BIBLIOG NAT/G POLICY

B66
AHMED Z.,DUSK AND DAWN IN VILLAGE INDIA. INDIA S/ASIA UK CULTURE SOCIETY NAT/G DOMIN COLONIAL HABITAT SOVEREIGN...SOC DICTIONARY 20. PAGE 4 H0080 — NEIGH ECO/UNDEV AGRI ADJUST

B66
BIRKHEAD G.S.,ADMINISTRATIVE PROBLEMS IN PAKISTAN. PAKISTAN AGRI FINAN INDUS LG/CO ECO/TAC CONTROL PWR ...CHARTS ANTHOL 20. PAGE 17 H0340 — ADMIN NAT/G ORD/FREE ECO/UNDEV

B66
BRECHER M.,SUCCESSION IN INDIA. INDIA USA+45 CONSTN AGRI POL/PAR PROVS SECT DELIB/GP FORCES PROB/SOLV ECO/TAC PWR...LING 20 CONGRESS NEHRU/J. PAGE 20 H0408 — CHIEF DECISION CHOOSE

B66
BROWN J.F.,THE NEW EASTERN EUROPE. ALBANIA BULGARIA HUNGARY POLAND ROMANIA CULTURE AGRI POL/PAR WAR NAT/LISM MARXISM...CHARTS BIBLIOG 20. PAGE 22 H0444 — DIPLOM COM NAT/G ECO/UNDEV

B66
BROWN L.C.,STATE AND SOCIETY IN INDEPENDENT NORTH AFRICA. ALGERIA LIBYA MOROCCO AGRI INDUS INT/ORG POL/PAR SECT PLAN DIPLOM COLONIAL...LING NAT/COMP ANTHOL BIBLIOG 20 TUNIS MUSLIM. PAGE 22 H0446 — NAT/G SOCIETY CULTURE ECO/UNDEV

B66
COLE A.B.,SOCIALIST PARTIES IN POSTWAR JAPAN. STRATA AGRI LABOR PLAN DIPLOM ECO/TAC AGREE LEAD CHOOSE ATTIT...CHARTS 20 CHINJAP SOC/DEMPAR. PAGE 31 H0620 — POL/PAR POLICY SOCISM NAT/G

B66
FISK E.K.,NEW GUINEA ON THE THRESHOLD; ASPECTS OF SOCIAL, POLITICAL, AND ECONOMIC DEVELOPMENT. AGRI NAT/G INT/TRADE ADMIN ADJUST LITERACY ROLE...CHARTS ANTHOL 20 NEW/GUINEA. PAGE 51 H1015 — ECO/UNDEV SOCIETY

B66
FOX K.A.,THE THEORY OF QUANTITATIVE ECONOMIC POLICY WITH APPLICATIONS TO ECONOMIC GROWTH AND STABILIZATION. ECO/DEV AGRI NAT/G PLAN ADMIN RISK ...DECISION IDEA/COMP SIMUL T. PAGE 52 H1045 — ECO/TAC ECOMETRIC EQUILIB GEN/LAWS

B66
GRAHAM B.D.,THE FORMATION OF THE AUSTRALIAN COUNTRY PARTIES. CANADA USA+45 USA-45 SOCIETY PLAN ECO/TAC ...NAT/COMP 20 AUSTRAL. PAGE 59 H1190 — POL/PAR AGRI REGION PARL/PROC

B66
JACKSON G.D.,COMINTERN AND PEASANT IN EAST EUROPE 1919-1930. BULGARIA COM CZECHOSLVK EUR+WWI POLAND ROMANIA YUGOSLAVIA STRATA AGRI VOL/ASSN DIPLOM CONTROL CROWD WEALTH...POLICY NAT/COMP 20. PAGE 79 H1575 — MARXISM ECO/UNDEV WORKER INT/ORG

B66
KIRDAR U.,THE STRUCTURE OF UNITED NATIONS ECONOMIC AID TO UNDERDEVELOPED COUNTRIES. AGRI FINAN INDUS NAT/G EX/STRUC PLAN GIVE TASK...POLICY 20 UN. PAGE 86 H1721 — INT/ORG FOR/AID ECO/UNDEV ADMIN

B66
KIRKENDALL R.S.,SOCIAL SCIENTISTS AND FARM POLITICS IN THE AGE OF ROOSEVELT. ACADEM PLAN ECO/TAC GIVE — AGRI INTELL

ADMIN CONTROL PRODUC...SOC 20 NEW/DEAL ROOSEVLT/F BURAGR/ECO. PAGE 86 H1722 [POLICY NAT/G]

B66
KUZNETS S.,MODERN ECONOMIC GROWTH. WOR+45 WOR-45 ECO/DEV ECO/UNDEV AGRI FINAN INDUS TEC/DEV EFFICIENCY INCOME...NAT/COMP 19/20. PAGE 89 H1786 [TIME/SEQ WEALTH PRODUC]

B66
LAVEN P.,RENAISSANCE ITALY: 1464-1534. ITALY AGRI EXTR/IND FINAN MUNIC INT/TRADE DRIVE...CATH GEOG CHARTS BIBLIOG/A 15. PAGE 92 H1841 [CULTURE HUM TEC/DEV KNOWL]

B66
MACFARQUHAR R.,CHINA UNDER MAO: POLITICS TAKES COMMAND. CHINA/COM COM AGRI INDUS CHIEF FORCES DIPLOM INT/TRADE EDU/PROP TASK REV ADJUST...ANTHOL 20 MAO. PAGE 100 H1992 [ECO/UNDEV TEC/DEV ECO/TAC ADMIN]

B66
MADAN G.R.,ECONOMIC THINKING IN INDIA. INDIA ECO/UNDEV AGRI FINAN INDUS LABOR PLAN CAP/ISM INT/TRADE MARXISM SOCISM...POLICY 1/20. PAGE 101 H2013 [ECO/TAC PHIL/SCI NAT/G POL/PAR]

B66
MASON E.S.,ECONOMIC DEVELOPMENT IN INDIA AND PAKISTAN. INDIA PAKISTAN AGRI FINAN PLAN BUDGET INT/TRADE WEALTH...POLICY STAT TREND CHARTS 20. PAGE 104 H2086 [NAT/COMP ECO/UNDEV ECO/TAC FOR/AID]

B66
MULLER C.F.J.,A SELECT BIBLIOGRAPHY OF SOUTH AFRICAN HISTORY; A GUIDE FOR HISTORICAL RESEARCH. SOUTH/AFR UK LAW CONSTN SOCIETY STRUCT AGRI SECT DIPLOM COLONIAL LEAD RACE/REL...POLICY 17/20 NEGRO. PAGE 114 H2284 [BIBLIOG AFR NAT/G]

B66
NAMBOODIRIPAD E.M.,ECONOMICS AND POLITICS OF INDIA'S SOCIALIST PATTERN. INDIA STRATA AGRI INDUS NAT/G PRICE ORD/FREE SOVEREIGN 20. PAGE 115 H2307 [ECO/UNDEV PLAN SOCISM CAP/ISM]

B66
THIESENHUSEN W.C.,CHILE'S EXPERIMENTS IN AGRARIAN REFORM. CHILE STRUCT NAT/G ACT/RES ECO/TAC GOV/REL COST SOCISM...TREND CHARTS SOC/EXP 20. PAGE 154 H3073 [AGRI ECO/UNDEV SOC TEC/DEV]

B66
WHITAKER A.P.,NATIONALISM IN CONTEMPORARY LATIN AMERICA. AGRI NAT/G WEALTH...POLICY SOC CONCPT OBS TREND 20. PAGE 167 H3344 [NAT/LISM L/A+17C DIPLOM ECO/UNDEV]

B66
ZINKIN T.,CHALLENGES IN INDIA. INDIA PAKISTAN LAW AGRI FINAN INDUS TOP/EX TEC/DEV CONTROL ROUTINE ORD/FREE PWR 20 NEHRU/J SHASTRI/LB CIVIL/SERV. PAGE 173 H3458 [NAT/G ECO/TAC POLICY ADMIN]

S66
MATTHEWS D.G.,"ETHIOPIAN OUTLINE: A BIBLIOGRAPHIC RESEARCH GUIDE." ETHIOPIA LAW STRUCT ECO/UNDEV AGRI LABOR SECT CHIEF DELIB/GP EX/STRUC ADMIN...LING ORG/CHARTS 20. PAGE 105 H2095 [BIBLIOG NAT/G DIPLOM POL/PAR]

B67
ALBA V.,THE MEXICANS; THE MAKING OF A NATION. SOCIETY ECO/UNDEV AGRI INDUS SECT STRANGE ATTIT ...GEOG 20 MEXIC/AMER. PAGE 4 H0091 [CONSTN NAT/G CULTURE ANOMIE]

B67
ALLWORTH E.,CENTRAL ASIA: A CENTURY OF RUSSIAN RULE. USSR INTELL SOCIETY AGRI INDUS COLONIAL REV WAR NAT/LISM...ART/METH GEOG LING 19/20. PAGE 5 H0108 [ASIA CULTURE NAT/G]

B67
CARTER G.M.,SOUTH AFRICA'S TRANSKEI: THE POLITICS OF DOMESTIC COLONIALISM. SOUTH/AFR ECO/UNDEV AGRI NAT/G PROVS PLAN DOMIN REPRESENT ADJUST DISCRIM ...OBS BIBLIOG 20 BANTUSTANS TRANSKEI. PAGE 27 H0550 [STRATA GOV/REL COLONIAL POLICY]

B67
COLLINS R.O.,EGYPT AND THE SUDAN. COM FRANCE ISLAM SUDAN UAR UK SOCIETY NAT/G COLONIAL NAT/LISM...GEOG SOC LING TREND SOC/INTEG 7/20 SUEZ. PAGE 32 H0635 [AGRI CULTURE ECO/UNDEV]

B67
DEGLER C.N.,THE AGE OF THE ECONOMIC REVOLUTION 1876-1900. USA-45 AGRI MUNIC POL/PAR SECT ECO/TAC CHOOSE...PHIL/SCI CHARTS NAT/COMP 19 NEGRO. PAGE 39 H0782 [INDUS SOCIETY ECO/DEV TEC/DEV]

B67
MENDEL A.P.,POLITICAL MEMOIRS 1905-1917 BY PAUL MILIUKOV (TRANS. BY CARL GOLDBERG). USSR AGRI DIPLOM ECO/TAC POPULISM...MAJORIT 20. PAGE 109 H2170 [BIOG LEAD NAT/G CONSTN]

B67
MOORE J.R.,THE ECONOMIC IMPACT OF THE TVA. AGRI INDUS PLAN BARGAIN CONTROL REGION GOV/REL DEMAND EFFICIENCY SOCISM 20 TVA. PAGE 112 H2249 [ECO/UNDEV ECO/DEV NAT/G CREATE]

B67
NASH M.,MACHINE AGE MAYA. GUATEMALA L/A+17C STRUCT AGRI WORKER CREATE INCOME ATTIT RIGID/FLEX ROLE ...IDEA/COMP SOC/EXP WORSHIP 20 INDIAN/AM. PAGE 116 H2315 [INDUS CULTURE SOC MUNIC]

B67
POMEROY W.J.,HALF A CENTURY OF SOCIALISM. USSR LAW AGRI INDUS NAT/G CREATE DIPLOM EDU/PROP PERSON ORD/FREE WEALTH...POLICY TREND 20. PAGE 127 H2541 [SOCISM MARXISM COM SOCIETY]

B67
SETON-WATSON H.,THE RUSSIAN EMPIRE, 1801-1917. COM RUSSIA STRATA ECO/DEV AGRI INDUS POL/PAR DIPLOM NAT/LISM MARXISM...IDEA/COMP BIBLIOG 19/20 MARX/KARL. PAGE 142 H2834 [SOCIETY NAT/G LEAD POLICY]

B67
WINTER E.H.,CONTEMPORARY CHANGE IN TRADITIONAL SOCIETIES: VOLUME I INTRODUCTION AND AFRICAN TRIBES. NIGERIA AGRI LOC/G NAT/G CREATE DOMIN COLONIAL CONTROL GP/REL PWR SOVEREIGN...SOC OBS 20 TANGANYIKA. PAGE 169 H3389 [SOCIETY AFR CONSERVE KIN]

L67
BERNSTEIN T.P.,"LEADERSHIP AND MASS MOBILIZATION IN THE SOVIET AND CHINESE COLLECTIVISATION CAMPAIGNS OF 1929-30, 1955-56: COMPARISON." CHINA/COM USSR WORKER CONTROL COERCE PRODUC ATTIT...NAT/COMP 20. PAGE 16 H0317 [FEDERAL PLAN AGRI NAT/G]

L67
LARKIN E.,"ECONOMIC GROWTH, CAPITAL INVESTMENT, AND THE ROMAN CATHOLIC CHURCH IN NINETEENTH-CENTURY IRELAND." IRELAND AGRI DIST/IND NAT/G GIVE OWN CATHISM...CHARTS 19. PAGE 91 H1823 [FINAN SECT WEALTH ECO/UNDEV]

L67
WILBER L.A.,"THE GOVERNMENTAL STRUCTURE OF MISSISSIPPI: ITS STRENGTHS AND WEAKNESSES." AGRI LOC/G SCHOOL EX/STRUC LEGIS TOP/EX BUDGET CT/SYS APPORT RACE/REL...GOV/COMP 20 MISSISSIPP. PAGE 168 H3359 [CONSTN PROVS STAT CON/ANAL]

S67
BAER W.,"THE INFLATION CONTROVERSY IN LATIN AMERICA: SURVEY." L/A+17C ECO/UNDEV AGRI FINAN INDUS PLAN PROB/SOLV TEC/DEV...BIBLIOG/A 20. PAGE 10 H0194 [NAT/G BAL/PAY ECO/TAC BUDGET]

S67
BRANCO R.,"LAND REFORM* THE ANSWER TO LATIN AMERICA'S AGRICULTURAL DEVELOPMENT?" L/A+17C NAT/G PLAN TEC/DEV BUDGET RENT EFFICIENCY 20. PAGE 20 H0404 [ECO/UNDEV AGRI TAX OWN]

S67
BUTTINGER J.,"VIETNAM* FRAUD OF THE 'OTHER WAR'." VIETNAM/S ELITES STRUCT AGRI NAT/G FOR/AID RENT TREND. PAGE 25 H0499 [PLAN WEALTH REV ECO/UNDEV]

S67
CARR E.H.,"REVOLUTION FROM ABOVE." USSR STRATA FINAN INDUS NAT/G DOMIN LEAD GP/REL INGP/REL OWN PRODUC PWR 20 STALIN/J. PAGE 27 H0538 [AGRI POLICY COM EFFICIENCY]

S67
CHU-YUAN CHENG,"THE CULTURAL REVOLUTION AND CHINA'S ECONOMY." CHINA/COM AGRI DIST/IND INDUS MARKET NAT/G WORKER PLAN INT/TRADE DOMIN DEMAND PRODUC ...CHARTS 20 MAO. PAGE 30 H0600 [ECO/DEV ECO/TAC REV SOCISM]

S67
DEWHURST A.,"THE WAGE MOVEMENT IN CANADA." CANADA AGRI NAT/G PARTIC COST PRODUC PROFIT 20. PAGE 41 H0811 [WORKER MARXIST INDUS LABOR]

S67
ELLISON H.J.,"THE SOCIALIST REVOLUTIONARIES." USSR ECO/UNDEV NAT/G INGP/REL EFFICIENCY ATTIT PWR MARXISM...CONCPT IDEA/COMP 20 SOC/REVPAR. PAGE 46 H0911 [POL/PAR REV AGRI]

S67
GRANT C.H.,"RURAL LOCAL GOVERNMENT IN GUYANA AND BRITISH HONDURAS." GUYANA HONDURAS L/A+17C AGRI NAT/G EX/STRUC ACT/RES REGION GOV/REL EFFICIENCY ORD/FREE 20. PAGE 60 H1196 [ECO/UNDEV LOC/G ADMIN MUNIC]

S67
HASSAN M.F.,"THE SECOND FOUR-YEAR PLAN OF VENEZUELA." L/A+17C VENEZUELA AGRI INDUS NAT/G PLAN RATION CONTROL HABITAT...MATH STAT 20. PAGE 67 H1352 [ECO/UNDEV FINAN BUDGET PROB/SOLV]

S67
NATSAGDORJ A.S.,"THE ECONOMIC BASIS OF FEUDALISM IN MONGOLIA." ASIA COM USSR OWN WEALTH CONSERVE...SOC 20 MONGOLIA. PAGE 116 H2324 [ECO/TAC AGRI NAT/COMP MARXISM]

S67
NUGENT J.B.,"ECONOMIC THOUGHT, INVESTMENT CRITERIA, AND DEVELOPMENT STRATEGIES IN GREECE* A POSTWAR SURVEY." GREECE AGRI INDUS INT/ORG NAT/G OP/RES DEMAND OPTIMAL PRODUC WEALTH 20 EEC. PAGE 119 H2379 [ECO/UNDEV PLAN FINAN]

S67
PERKINS D.H.,"ECONOMIC GROWTH IN CHINA AND THE CULTURAL REVOLUTION(1960APRIL 1967)" CHINA/COM FUT AGRI INDUS PLAN LEAD MARXISM...CHARTS 20 MAO. PAGE 125 H2493 [ECO/TAC CULTURE REV ECO/UNDEV]

S67
SANCHEZ J.D.,"DESARROLLO ECONOMICO Y FUTURO DE [ECO/UNDEV]

COLOMBIA." L/A+17C AGRI EXTR/IND FINAN INDUS MARKET INT/TRADE CONTROL...STAT TREND COLOMB. PAGE 137 H2748 — FUT NAT/G ECO/TAC

S67
SCHACHTER G.,"REGIONAL DEVELOPMENT IN THE ITALIAN DUAL ECONOMY" ITALY AGRI INDUS MARKET WORKER ECO/TAC CONTROL INCOME PRODUC 20. PAGE 138 H2767 — REGION ECO/UNDEV NAT/G PROB/SOLV

S67
SHIGEO N.,"THE GREAT CULTURAL REVOLUTION." ASIA ECO/UNDEV AGRI NAT/G CHIEF ECO/TAC EDU/PROP CONTROL LEAD PWR 20 MAO. PAGE 143 H2860 — CREATE REV CULTURE POL/PAR

S67
TAYLOR P.B. JR.,"PROGRESS IN VENEZUELA." L/A+17C VENEZUELA AGRI INDUS LG/CO NAT/G SML/CO CHOOSE ...POLICY 20. PAGE 153 H3057 — ECO/UNDEV ECO/TAC POL/PAR ORD/FREE

S67
THIEN T.T.,"VIETNAM: A CASE OF SOCIAL ALIENATION." VIETNAM AGRI FORCES FOR/AID ADMIN REPRESENT INGP/REL PWR 19/20. PAGE 154 H3071 — NAT/G ELITES WORKER STRANGE

S68
BOSSCHERE G D.E.,"A L'EST DU NOUVEAU." CZECHOSLVK HUNGARY POLAND ROMANIA YUGOSLAVIA AGRI CREATE ECO/TAC COERCE GP/REL ATTIT MARXISM SOCISM 20. PAGE 19 H0382 — ORD/FREE COM NAT/G DIPLOM

S68
LAPIERRE J.W.,"TRADITION ET MODERNITE A MADAGASCAR." ISLAM MADAGASCAR AGRI FINAN KIN NAT/G CREATE OP/RES GP/REL INGP/REL ATTIT CONSERVE...PSY 20. PAGE 91 H1813 — ECO/UNDEV FOR/AID CULTURE TEC/DEV

B82
RATZEL F.,ANTHROPO-GEOGRAPHIE. SEA AGRI NEIGH. PAGE 130 H2595 — GEOG CULTURE HABITAT

B89
ASHBEE H.S.,A BIBLIOGRAPHY OF TUNISIA FROM THE EARLIEST TIMES TO THE END OF 1888. AGRI ADMIN ...GEOG TUNIS. PAGE 8 H0171 — BIBLIOG COLONIAL CULTURE NAT/G

B91
MILL J.S.,SOCIALISM (1859). MOD/EUR AGRI INDUS NAT/G REV INCOME PRODUC ORD/FREE POPULISM SOCISM ...GOV/COMP METH/COMP 19. PAGE 110 H2209 — WEALTH SOCIALIST ECO/TAC OWN

C93
PLAYFAIR R.L.,"A BIBLIOGRAPHY OF MOROCCO." MOROCCO CULTURE AGRI FORCES DIPLOM WAR HEALTH...GEOG JURID SOC CHARTS. PAGE 126 H2526 — BIBLIOG ISLAM MEDIT-7

B96
DE VATTEL E.,THE LAW OF NATIONS. AGRI FINAN CHIEF DIPLOM INT/TRADE AGREE OWN ALL/VALS MORAL ORD/FREE SOVEREIGN...GEN/LAWS 18 NATURL/LAW WOLFF/C. PAGE 39 H0774 — LAW CONCPT NAT/G INT/LAW

AGRICULTURE....SEE AGRI

AHMED Z. H0080

AHN L.A. H0081

AHRCO....ALLEGHENY HOUSING REHABILITATION CORPORATION

AIKEN C. H0082

AIR....LOCALE OF SUBJECT ACTIVITY IS AERIAL

B55
SVARLIEN O.,AN INTRODUCTION TO THE LAW OF NATIONS. SEA AIR INT/ORG NAT/G CHIEF ADMIN AGREE WAR PRIVIL ORD/FREE SOVEREIGN...BIBLIOG 16/20. PAGE 151 H3012 — INT/LAW DIPLOM

B59
EMME E.M.,THE IMPACT OF AIR POWER - NATIONAL SECURITY AND WORLD POLITICS. USA+45 USSR FORCES DIPLOM WEAPON PEACE TOTALISM...POLICY NAT/COMP 20 EUROPE. PAGE 46 H0921 — DETER AIR WAR ORD/FREE

AIR FORCE ACADEMY ASSEMBLY H0083

AIR UNIVERSITY LIBRARY H0084

AIYAR S.P. H0085,H0086,H0087

AJAO/A....ADEROGBA AJAO

AKE C. H0088

AKIGA H0089

AKZIN B. H0090

ALABAMA....ALABAMA

ALASKA....ALASKA

ALBA V. H0091

ALBANIA....SEE ALSO COM

B56
WOLFF R.L.,THE BALKANS IN OUR TIME. ALBANIA FUT MOD/EUR USSR YUGOSLAVIA CULTURE INT/ORG SECT DIPLOM EDU/PROP COERCE WAR ORD/FREE...CHARTS 4/20 BALKANS COMINFORM. PAGE 170 H3403 — GEOG COM

B63
HAMM H.,ALBANIA - CHINA'S BEACHHEAD IN EUROPE. ALBANIA CHINA/COM USSR YUGOSLAVIA ELITES SOCIETY POL/PAR DELIB/GP FORCES ECO/TAC COERCE ISOLAT PEACE MARXISM...IDEA/COMP 20 MAO. PAGE 65 H1304 — DIPLOM REV NAT/G POLICY

B65
JELAVICH C.,THE BALKANS. ALBANIA BULGARIA GREECE ROMANIA YUGOSLAVIA ECO/UNDEV WAR SOVEREIGN MARXISM 6/20. PAGE 80 H1597 — NAT/LISM NAT/G

B66
BROWN J.F.,THE NEW EASTERN EUROPE. ALBANIA BULGARIA HUNGARY POLAND ROMANIA CULTURE AGRI POL/PAR WAR NAT/LISM MARXISM...CHARTS BIBLIOG 20. PAGE 22 H0444 — DIPLOM COM NAT/G ECO/UNDEV

S67
LOGERECI A.,"ALBANIA AND CHINA* THE INCONGRUOUS ALLIANCE." NAT/LISM PWR...GOV/COMP 20. PAGE 98 H1955 — ALBANIA CHINA/COM DIPLOM MARXISM

ALBERTA....ALBERTA

ALBI F. H0092

ALBINSKI H.S. H0093,H0094

ALBRECHT-CARRIE R. H0095,H0096

ALBRECHT M.C.H0097

ALCOHOLISM....SEE BIO/SOC

ALDERFER H.F.H0098

ALEMBERT/J....JEAN LE ROND D'ALEMBERT

ALEXANDER A. H0099

ALEXANDER L. H0100

ALEXANDER L.M. H0101

ALEXANDER R.J. H0102

ALFIERI D. H0103

ALGER C.F. H0104

ALGERIA....SEE ALSO ISLAM

B23
GRANT C.F.,STUDIES IN NORTH AFRICA. ALGERIA MOROCCO ROMAN/EMP CULTURE STRUCT NAT/G DIPLOM WAR ...NAT/COMP TUNIS EUROPE. PAGE 60 H1195 — ISLAM SECT DOMIN COLONIAL

B42
CONOVER H.F.,FRENCH COLONIES IN AFRICA: A LIST OF REFERENCES. ALGERIA FRANCE MOROCCO SOMALIA SUDAN CULTURE AGRI LOC/G SECT FORCES DIPLOM INT/TRADE NAT/LISM HEALTH...CON/ANAL 20. PAGE 32 H0641 — BIBLIOG AFR ECO/UNDEV COLONIAL

B48
MAUGHAM R.,NORTH AFRICAN NOTEBOOK. ALGERIA ISLAM LIBYA MOROCCO STRUCT ECO/UNDEV COLONIAL...SOC OBS AUD/VIS NAT/COMP WORSHIP 20 TUNIS. PAGE 105 H2102 — SOCIETY RECORD NAT/LISM

B52
JULIEN C.A.,L'AFRIQUE DU NORD EN MARCHE: NATIONALISMES MUSULMANS ET SOUVERAINETE FRANCAISE (2ND ED). AFR ALGERIA FRANCE ISLAM MOROCCO NAT/G CONTROL ORD/FREE...POLICY 19/20 TUNIS MUSLIM. PAGE 82 H1641 — NAT/LISM COERCE DOMIN COLONIAL

B57
CONOVER H.F.,NORTH AND NORTHEAST AFRICA; A SELECTED ANNOTATED LIST OF WRITINGS. ALGERIA MOROCCO SUDAN UAR CULTURE INT/ORG PROB/SOLV ADJUD NAT/LISM PWR WEALTH...SOC 20 UN. PAGE 32 H0649 — BIBLIOG/A DIPLOM AFR ECO/UNDEV

B58
TILLION G.,ALGERIA: THE REALITIES. ALGERIA FRANCE ISLAM CULTURE STRATA PROB/SOLV DOMIN REV NAT/LISM WEALTH MARXISM...GEOG 20. PAGE 155 H3094 — ECO/UNDEV SOC COLONIAL DIPLOM

B59
LEITES N.,ON THE GAME OF POLITICS IN FRANCE. ALGERIA FRANCE CONSTN SECT VOL/ASSN ECO/TAC INT/TRADE PARL/PROC WAR SOCISM 20 DEGAULLE/C EEC. PAGE 94 H1871 — POL/PAR NAT/G LEGIS IDEA/COMP

B60
MINER H.M.,OASIS AND CASBAH: ALGERIAN CULTURE AND PERSONALITY IN CHANGE. ALGERIA FRANCE SOCIETY MUNIC COLONIAL ATTIT...INT PROJ/TEST CHARTS 20. PAGE 111 H2221
GP/COMP PERSON CULTURE ADJUST

B60
PICKLES D.,THE FIFTH FRENCH REPUBLIC. ALGERIA FRANCE CHOOSE GOV/REL ATTIT CONSERVE...CHARTS 20 DEGAULLE/C. PAGE 125 H2506
CONSTN ADJUD NAT/G EFFICIENCY

S60
CROZIER B.,"FRANCE AND ALGERIA." ALGERIA EUR+WWI FRANCE FUT ISLAM ECO/UNDEV NEIGH CONSULT DELIB/GP ECO/TAC COLONIAL COERCE ATTIT...SOC INT CON/ANAL 20. PAGE 36 H0713
NAT/G FORCES GUERRILLA NAT/LISM

B61
BOURDIEU P.,THE ALGERIANS (TRANS. BY A.C. ROSS; REV. ED.). ALGERIA ISLAM CULTURE MUNIC CAP/ISM COLONIAL GP/REL ORD/FREE SOVEREIGN 20. PAGE 19 H0385
SOCIETY STRUCT ATTIT WAR

B61
LA PONCE J.A.,THE GOVERNMENT OF THE FIFTH REPUBLIC: FRENCH POLITICAL PARTIES AND THE CONSTITUTION. ALGERIA FRANCE LAW NAT/G DELIB/GP LEGIS ECO/TAC MARXISM SOCISM...CHARTS BIBLIOG/A 20 DEGAULLE/C. PAGE 90 H1794
PWR POL/PAR CONSTN CHIEF

B62
ANDREWS W.G.,FRENCH POLITICS AND ALGERIA: THE PROCESS OF POLICY FORMATION 1954-1962. ALGERIA FRANCE CONSTN ELITES POL/PAR CHIEF DELIB/GP LEGIS DIPLOM PRESS CHOOSE 20. PAGE 7 H0140
GOV/COMP EXEC COLONIAL

B62
BAULIN J.,THE ARAB ROLE IN AFRICA. AFR ALGERIA FUT ISLAM MOROCCO UAR COLONIAL NEUTRAL REV...SOC 20 TUNIS BOURGUIBA. PAGE 12 H0240
NAT/LISM DIPLOM NAT/G SECT

B63
ZARTMAN I.W.,GOVERNMENT AND POLITICS IN NORTHERN AFRICA. AFR ALGERIA ISLAM LIBYA MOROCCO UAR ELITES SOCIETY PLAN ECO/TAC DOMIN EDU/PROP LEGIT ATTIT ...GEOG CONCPT TIME/SEQ 20 TUNIS. PAGE 172 H3448
CULTURE DRIVE NAT/LISM

B64
ALDEFER H.F.,A BIBLIOGRAPHY OF AFRICAN GOVERNMENT: 1950-1964. ALGERIA GUINEA LIBERIA UAR ECO/UNDEV POL/PAR LEGIS COLONIAL LEAD PARL/PROC NAT/LISM 20. PAGE 5 H0098
BIBLIOG AFR LOC/G NAT/G

S64
ZARTMAN I.W.,"LES RELATIONS ENTRE LA FRANCE ET L'ALGERIA DEPUIS LES ACCORDS D'EVIAN." EUR+WWI FUT ISLAM CULTURE AGRI EXTR/IND FINAN INDUS POL/PAR DIPLOM ECO/TAC FOR/AID PEACE ATTIT DRIVE ALL/VALS ...TIME/SEQ VAL/FREE 20. PAGE 172 H3450
ECO/UNDEV ALGERIA FRANCE

B66
BROWN L.C.,STATE AND SOCIETY IN INDEPENDENT NORTH AFRICA. ALGERIA LIBYA MOROCCO AGRI INDUS INT/ORG POL/PAR SECT PLAN DIPLOM COLONIAL...LING NAT/COMP ANTHOL BIBLIOG 20 TUNIS MUSLIM. PAGE 22 H0446
NAT/G SOCIETY CULTURE ECO/UNDEV

B66
MATTHEWS R.,AFRICAN POWDER KEG: REVOLT AND DISSENT IN SIX EMERGENT NATIONS. AFR ALGERIA DAHOMEY GABON GHANA MALAWI GAMBLE LEAD PARTIC REV DRIVE...BIOG TREND GOV/COMP 20. PAGE 105 H2098
ELITES ECO/UNDEV TOP/EX CONTROL

S66
MCLANE C.B.,"SOVIET DOCTRINE AND THE MILITARY COUPS IN AFRICA." ALGERIA GHANA COLONIAL NAT/LISM RIGID/FLEX SOVEREIGN MARXISM...DECISION NAT/COMP. PAGE 107 H2140
USSR ATTIT AFR FORCES

B67
MENARD O.D.,THE ARMY AND THE FIFTH REPUBLIC. ALGERIA FRANCE VIETNAM ELITES STRATA COLONIAL CONTROL LOBBY WAR CIVMIL/REL ROLE PWR...POLICY 20 DEGAULLE/C. PAGE 108 H2169
FORCES ATTIT NAT/G

S68
KANET R.E.,"RECENT SOVIET REASSESSMENT OF DEVELOPMENTS IN THE THIRD WORLD." ALGERIA GHANA INDONESIA USSR WOR+45 CONSTN ELITES INTELL STRUCT DOMIN CONTROL REV PWR MARXISM...IDEA/COMP METH 20 THIRD/WRLD. PAGE 83 H1653
DIPLOM NEUTRAL NAT/G NAT/COMP

C89
PLAYFAIR R.L.,"A BIBLIOGRAPHY OF ALGERIA." ALGERIA CULTURE ECO/UNDEV DIST/IND EXTR/IND FINAN SECT CRIME 16/19. PAGE 126 H2525
BIBLIOG/A ISLAM GEOG

B93
ROYAL GEOGRAPHIC SOCIETY,BIBLIOGRAPHY OF BARBARY STATES (4 SUPPLEMENTARY PAPERS). ALGERIA LIBYA MOROCCO SOCIETY STRUCT DIPLOM LEAD 14/19 TUNIS. PAGE 135 H2706
BIBLIOG ISLAM NAT/G COLONIAL

ALGIER/CHR....CHARTER OF ALGIERS

ALIANZA POPULAR REVOLUCIONARIA AMERICANA (PERU)....SEE APRA

ALIENATION....SEE STRANGE

ALL/IDEOS....CONCERNS THREE OR MORE OF THE TERMS LISTED IN THE IDEOLOGICAL TOPIC INDEX, P. XIII

N
PUBLISHERS' TRADE LIST ANNUAL. LAW POL/PAR ADMIN PERSON ALL/IDEOS...HUM SOC 19/20. PAGE 1 H0020
BIBLIOG NAT/G DIPLOM POLICY

N
KYRIAK T.E.,ASIAN DEVELOPMENTS: A BIBLIOGRAPHY. INDONESIA KOREA/N VIETNAM/N CULTURE SOCIETY ECO/UNDEV NAT/G DIPLOM...SOC TREND 20 MONGOLIA. PAGE 90 H1788
BIBLIOG/A ALL/IDEOS S/ASIA ASIA

B28
BARKER E.,POLITICAL THOUGHT IN ENGLAND: FROM HERBERT SPENCER TO THE PRESENT DAY. UK ALL/IDEOS ...PHIL/SCI 19/20 SPENCER/H GREEN/TH BENTHAM/J MAITLAND/F. PAGE 11 H0217
INTELL GEN/LAWS IDEA/COMP

B32
THIBAUDET A.,LES IDEES POLITIQUES DE LA FRANCE. FRANCE NAT/G SECT PRESS REV NAT/LISM PEACE ATTIT ...PSY 19/20 JACOBINISM JAURES/JL. PAGE 154 H3070
IDEA/COMP ALL/IDEOS CATHISM

B39
MARQUAND H.A.,ORGANIZED LABOUR IN FOUR CONTINENTS. EUR+WWI USA-45 INDUS NAT/G PAY GP/REL TOTALISM ATTIT WEALTH ALL/IDEOS...TREND NAT/COMP 20 ILO AFL/CIO EUROPE CHINJAP MEXIC/AMER. PAGE 103 H2055
LABOR WORKER CONCPT ANTHOL

B39
OAKESHOTT M.,THE SOCIAL AND POLITICAL DOCTRINES OF CONTEMPORARY EUROPE. EUR+WWI RATIONAL CATHISM FASCISM MARXISM POPULISM...POLICY ANTHOL 20 NAZI. PAGE 120 H2392
IDEA/COMP GOV/COMP ALL/IDEOS NAT/G

B40
WOLFERS A.,BRITAIN AND FRANCE BETWEEN TWO WORLD WARS. FRANCE UK INT/ORG NAT/G PLAN BARGAIN ECO/TAC AGREE ISOLAT ALL/IDEOS...DECISION GEOG 20 TREATY VERSAILLES INTERVENT. PAGE 170 H3402
DIPLOM WAR POLICY

S46
TANNENBAUM F.,"THE BALANCE OF POWER IN SOCIETY." UNIV STRUCT FAM NAT/G SECT PERS/REL EQUILIB UTOPIA DRIVE ALL/IDEOS...OLD/LIB CONCPT. PAGE 152 H3044
SOCIETY ALL/VALS GP/REL PEACE

B50
CARR E.H.,STUDIES IN REVOLUTION. CREATE WAR PERSON ALL/IDEOS MARXISM SOCISM...PHIL/SCI METH/COMP ANTHOL 18/20 SAINTSIMON MARX/KARL PROUDHON/P LASSALLE/F PLEKHNV/GV. PAGE 27 H0537
REV IDEA/COMP COERCE BIOG

B51
MEYER E.W.,POLITICAL PARTIES IN WESTERN GERMANY (PAMPHLET). GERMANY/W MUNIC NAT/G GOV/REL ALL/IDEOS 20 UNIFICA BERLIN. PAGE 109 H2190
POL/PAR LOBBY CHOOSE CONSTN

S52
SABINE G.H.,"THE TWO DEMOCRATIC TRADITIONS" (BMR)" FRANCE UK USA-45 NAT/G CONTROL CHOOSE ALL/IDEOS ...PHIL/SCI CONCPT IDEA/COMP 20. PAGE 136 H2727
ORD/FREE POPULISM INGP/REL NAT/COMP

C52
EBENSTEIN W.,"INTRODUCTION TO POLITICAL PHILOSOPHY." COM CONSTN INTELL CONTROL PERSON NEW/LIB SOCISM...PSY GEN/LAWS BIBLIOG/A. PAGE 44 H0883
ALL/IDEOS PHIL/SCI IDEA/COMP NAT/G

S53
ARENDT H.,"IDEOLOGY AND TERROR: A NOVEL FORM OF GOVERNMENT." WOR-45 DOMIN STRANGE ATTIT SUPEGO MARXISM...GOV/COMP IDEA/COMP 20 NAZI. PAGE 8 H0160
TOTALISM ANOMIE ALL/IDEOS SOCIETY

B55
VIGON J.,TEORIA DEL MILITARISMO. NAT/G DIPLOM COLONIAL COERCE GUERRILLA CIVMIL/REL NAT/LISM MORAL ALL/IDEOS PACIFISM 18/20. PAGE 163 H3253
FORCES PHIL/SCI WAR POLICY

B56
ROBERTS H.L.,RUSSIA AND AMERICA. CHINA/COM S/ASIA USSR FORCES TEC/DEV FOR/AID NUC/PWR ALL/IDEOS ...MAJORIT TREND NAT/COMP 20 COLD/WAR UN NATO. PAGE 132 H2641
DIPLOM INT/ORG BAL/PWR TOTALISM

S56
ALMOND G.A.,"COMPARATIVE POLITICAL SYSTEMS" (BMR)" WOR+45 WOR-45 PROB/SOLV DIPLOM EFFICIENCY ...PHIL/SCI SOC METH 17/20. PAGE 5 H0111
GOV/COMP CONCPT ALL/IDEOS NAT/COMP

L57
LIPSET S.M.,"POLITICAL SOCIOLOGY." NAT/G POL/PAR ECO/TAC PARTIC CHOOSE PWR...BIBLIOG/A 20. PAGE 97 H1939
SOC ALL/IDEOS ACADEM

B59
BARRON R.,PARTIES AND POLITICS IN MODERN FRANCE. FRANCE LOC/G DELIB/GP LEGIS TOP/EX EDU/PROP LEGIT TV FEEDBACK 20. PAGE 12 H0230
POL/PAR ALL/IDEOS CHOOSE PARTIC

B59
WARNER W.L.,THE LIVING AND THE DEAD: A STUDY OF SYMBOLIC LIFE OF AMERICANS. INTELL KIN DEATH ALL/VALS ALL/IDEOS...CONCPT MYTH LING OBS/ENVIR CHARTS BIBLIOG WORSHIP 18/20. PAGE 165 H3311
CULTURE SOC TIME/SEQ IDEA/COMP

B60
BOZEMAN A.B.,POLITICS AND CULTURE IN INTERNATIONAL HISTORY. WOR-45 STRUCT SECT...SOC TIME/SEQ NAT/COMP
CULTURE DIPLOM

BIBLIOG. PAGE 20 H0393 GOV/COMP ALL/IDEOS

B60
JOHNSON H.M.,SOCIOLOGY: A SYSTEMATIC INTRODUCTION. MARKET FAM LABOR POL/PAR CHOOSE DISCRIM MARRIAGE ALL/IDEOS...BIBLIOG T WORSHIP. PAGE 81 H1620 SOC SOCIETY CULTURE GEN/LAWS

C60
EBENSTEIN W.,"MODERN POLITICAL THOUGHT (2ND ED.)" NAT/G CAP/ISM NAT/LISM PERSON ORD/FREE PWR ALL/IDEOS NEW/LIB SOCISM...TRADIT PSY BIBLIOG/A 18/20. PAGE 44 H0884 IDEA/COMP PHIL/SCI CONCPT GEN/LAWS

B61
BEARCE G.D.,BRITISH ATTITUDES TOWARDS INDIA 1784-1858. INDIA S/ASIA UK SECT ECO/TAC...POLICY HUM 18/19. PAGE 12 H0246 COLONIAL ATTIT ALL/IDEOS NAT/G

B61
DUFFY J.,AFRICA SPEAKS. GHANA TOGO CULTURE ECO/UNDEV PROB/SOLV COLONIAL NEUTRAL DISCRIM NAT/LISM SOVEREIGN ALL/IDEOS...CONCPT ANTHOL SOC/INTEG 20 NEGRO THIRD/WRLD. PAGE 43 H0857 AFR NAT/G FUT STRUCT

B61
HUNT E.F.,SOCIAL SCIENCE. DIPLOM ECO/TAC ROUTINE GP/REL DEMAND DISCRIM EFFICIENCY HABITAT ALL/IDEOS ...SOC T 20. PAGE 75 H1497 CULTURE ADJUST STRATA ROLE

B61
MUNGER E.S.,AFRICAN FIELD REPORTS 1952-1961. SOUTH/AFR SOCIETY ECO/UNDEV NAT/G POL/PAR COLONIAL EXEC PARL/PROC GUERRILLA RACE/REL ALL/IDEOS...SOC AUD/VIS 20. PAGE 114 H2288 AFR DISCRIM RECORD

B61
PALMER N.D.,THE INDIAN POLITICAL SYSTEM. INDIA ECO/UNDEV SECT CHIEF COLONIAL CHOOSE ALL/IDEOS SOCISM...CHARTS BIBLIOG/A 20. PAGE 123 H2452 NAT/LISM POL/PAR NAT/G DIPLOM

B62
HAY S.N.,SOUTHEAST ASIAN HISTORY: A BIBLIOGRAPHICAL GUIDE. STRATA KIN NAT/G REGION GUERRILLA REV WAR ADJUST HABITAT PERCEPT ALL/IDEOS...CHARTS 5/20. PAGE 68 H1365 BIBLIOG/A S/ASIA CULTURE

B62
JENNINGS I.,PARTY POLITICS: THE STUFF OF POLITICS (VOL.III). UK NAT/G SECT CHIEF INT/TRADE RECEIVE COLONIAL GP/REL NAT/LISM ORD/FREE SOCISM 19/20 CHURCH/STA WHIG/PARTY. PAGE 80 H1607 POL/PAR CONSTN PWR ALL/IDEOS

B62
SCHIEDER T.,THE STATE AND SOCIETY IN OUR TIMES (TRANS. BY C.A.M. SYM). SOCIETY NAT/G POL/PAR REV GP/REL ALL/IDEOS 19/20. PAGE 139 H2786 STRUCT PWR HIST/WRIT

B63
FRIED R.C.,THE ITALIAN PREFECTS. ITALY STRATA ECO/DEV NAT/LISM ALL/IDEOS...TREND CHARTS METH/COMP BIBLIOG 17/20 PREFECT. PAGE 53 H1061 ADMIN NAT/G EFFICIENCY

B63
LYON P.,NEUTRALISM. ECO/UNDEV EDU/PROP COLONIAL ALL/IDEOS...IDEA/COMP 20 COLD/WAR UN. PAGE 99 H1985 NAT/COMP NAT/LISM DIPLOM NEUTRAL

B63
NOMAD M.,POLITICAL HERETICS: FROM PLATO TO MAO TSE-TUNG. UNIV INGP/REL...SOC IDEA/COMP. PAGE 119 H2369 SOCIETY UTOPIA ALL/IDEOS CONCPT

B63
SCHELER M.,SCHRIFTEN ZUR SOZIOLOGIE UND WELTANSCHAUUNGSLEHRE (GESAMMELTE WERKE, BAND 6; 2ND ED.). SECT ALL/IDEOS...SOC CONCPT GP/COMP NAT/COMP 20. PAGE 139 H2783 SOCIETY IDEA/COMP PHIL/SCI

B63
SILVERT K.H.,EXPECTANT PEOPLES: NATIONALISM AND DEVELOPMENT. CULTURE STRATA SECT LEAD REGION RACE/REL ALL/IDEOS...GEN/LAWS SOC/INTEG 20. PAGE 144 H2877 NAT/LISM ECO/UNDEV ALL/VALS

B63
STUCKI C.W.,AMERICAN DOCTORAL DISSERTATIONS ON ASIA 1933-62 (A PAPER). PREHIST INDUS NAT/G GOV/REL ALL/IDEOS...ART/METH GEOG SOC LING 20. PAGE 150 H3002 BIBLIOG ASIA SOCIETY S/ASIA

B64
UTECHIN S.V.,RUSSIAN POLITICAL THOUGHT: A CONCISE HISTORY. RUSSIA USSR INTELL STRATA POL/PAR SECT LEGIS EDU/PROP REV WAR MARXISM...ANARCH BIBLIOG 9/20 REFORMERS SLAVS. PAGE 161 H3218 IDEA/COMP ATTIT ALL/IDEOS NAT/G

B64
VON STEIN L.J.,THE HISTORY OF THE SOCIAL MOVEMENT IN FRANCE, 1789-1850 (TRANS. BY K. MENGELBERG). COM FRANCE MOD/EUR NAT/G EX/STRUC INGP/REL ALL/IDEOS CONSERVE MARXISM...SOC BIBLIOG 18/19. PAGE 164 H3278 REV STRATA

B65
APPLEMAN P.,THE SILENT EXPLOSION. WOR+45 ECO/DEV ECO/UNDEV PLAN HEALTH ALL/IDEOS CATHISM...POLICY STAT RECORD GP/COMP IDEA/COMP NAT/COMP 20 BIRTH/CON COM/PARTY. PAGE 7 H0148 GEOG CENSUS AGRI BIO/SOC

B65
BROWNSON O.A.,THE AMERICAN REPUBLIC. NAT/G PROVS WAR GOV/REL PRIVIL ORD/FREE PWR ALL/IDEOS CONSERVE ...CONCPT 19 CIVIL/WAR. PAGE 22 H0452 CONSTN FEDERAL SOVEREIGN

B65
CARTER G.M.,GOVERNMENT AND POLITICS IN THE TWENTIETH CENTURY (REV. ED.). WOR+45 NAT/G POL/PAR LEGIS DIPLOM LEAD PARL/PROC CHOOSE TOTALISM 20. PAGE 27 H0549 GOV/COMP ECO/UNDEV ALL/IDEOS ECO/DEV

B65
RODRIGUEZ M.,CENTRAL AMERICA. COSTA/RICA GUATEMALA L/A+17C NICARAGUA DIPLOM COLONIAL REGION NAT/LISM ALL/IDEOS SOCISM...MAJORIT TIME/SEQ BIBLIOG 19/20. PAGE 133 H2656 CULTURE NAT/COMP NAT/G ECO/UNDEV

S65
CAIRNS J.C.,"FRANCE, DECEMBER 1965: END OF THE ELECTIVE MONARACHY" EUR+WWI FRANCE FUT CONSTN SOCIETY CHIEF BAL/PWR ATTIT ALL/IDEOS 20 DEGAULLE/C PRESIDENT. PAGE 25 H0505 CHOOSE NAT/G POL/PAR PWR

B66
CAUTE D.,THE LEFT IN EUROPE SINCE 1789. EUR+WWI MOD/EUR NAT/G POL/PAR REV...TIME/SEQ GEN/LAWS BIBLIOG 18/20. PAGE 28 H0564 ALL/IDEOS ORD/FREE CONCPT STRATA

B66
EMBREE A.T.,ASIA: A GUIDE TO BASIC BOOKS (PAMPHLET). ECO/UNDEV SECT FORCES DIPLOM ALL/IDEOS ...SOC 20. PAGE 46 H0914 BIBLIOG/A ASIA S/ASIA NAT/G

B66
FRANK E.,LAWMAKERS IN A CHANGING WORLD. FRANCE UK USSR WOR+45 PARTIC EFFICIENCY ROLE ALL/IDEOS ...CHARTS ANTHOL PARLIAMENT 20 UN COLD/WAR. PAGE 52 H1049 GOV/COMP LEGIS NAT/G DIPLOM

B66
FRIED R.C.,COMPARATIVE POLITICAL INSTITUTIONS. USSR EX/STRUC FORCES LEGIS JUDGE CONTROL REPRESENT ALL/IDEOS 20 CONGRESS BUREAUCRCY. PAGE 53 H1062 NAT/G PWR EFFICIENCY GOV/COMP

B66
HARMON R.B.,SOURCES AND PROBLEMS OF BIBLIOGRAPHY IN POLITICAL SCIENCE (PAMPHLET). INT/ORG LOC/G MUNIC POL/PAR ADMIN GOV/REL ALL/IDEOS...JURID MGT CONCPT 19/20. PAGE 67 H1335 BIBLIOG DIPLOM INT/LAW NAT/G

B66
MAC DONALD H.M.,THE INTELLECTUAL IN POLITICS. GERMANY PERU SWEDEN UK USSR NAT/G CONSULT PLAN EDU/PROP TASK INGP/REL EFFICIENCY RATIONAL ALL/VALS 20. PAGE 99 H1987 ALL/IDEOS INTELL POL/PAR PARTIC

B66
ODEGARD P.H.,POLITICAL POWER AND SOCIAL CHANGE. UNIV NAT/G CREATE ALL/IDEOS...POLICY GEOG SOC CENSUS TREND. PAGE 120 H2394 PWR TEC/DEV IDEA/COMP

B66
SETTON K.M.,GREAT PROBLEMS IN EUROPEAN CIVILIZATION. CHRIST-17C EUR+WWI MOD/EUR SECT GP/REL ALL/VALS ORD/FREE ALL/IDEOS...TREND ANTHOL T CHRISTIAN RENAISSAN PROTESTANT. PAGE 142 H2835 CULTURE CONCPT IDEA/COMP

S66
GRUNDY K.W.,"RECENT CONTRIBUTIONS TO THE STUDY OF AFRICAN POLITICAL THOUGHT." DIPLOM NAT/LISM ALL/IDEOS...NEW/IDEA GOV/COMP 20. PAGE 62 H1239 BIBLIOG/A AFR ATTIT IDEA/COMP

B67
MCNELLY T.,SOURCES IN MODERN EAST ASIAN HISTORY AND POLITICS. KOREA VIETNAM CULTURE DIPLOM COLONIAL REV WAR PWR ALL/IDEOS MARXISM...ANTHOL 20 CHINJAP. PAGE 107 H2147 NAT/COMP ASIA S/ASIA SOCIETY

B67
PYE L.W.,SOUTHEAST ASIA'S POLITICAL SYSTEMS. ASIA S/ASIA STRUCT ECO/UNDEV EX/STRUC CAP/ISM DIPLOM ALL/IDEOS...TREND CHARTS. PAGE 128 H2568 NAT/G POL/PAR GOV/COMP

B67
SHAPIRO P.S.,COMMUNICATIONS OR TRANSPORT: DECISION-MAKING IN DEVELOPING COUNTRIES. WOR+45 NAT/G PLAN ALL/IDEOS MARXISM...NAT/COMP GEN/LAWS. PAGE 142 H2844 BUDGET COM/IND DECISION ECO/DEV

S67
NIEBUHR R.,"THE SOCIAL MYTHS IN THE COLD WAR." USA+45 USSR VIETNAM PROB/SOLV BAL/PWR ARMS/CONT NAT/LISM PWR ALL/IDEOS CONCPT. PAGE 118 H2359 MYTH DIPLOM GOV/COMP

B91
SIDGWICK H.,THE ELEMENTS OF POLITICS. LOC/G NAT/G LEGIS DIPLOM ADJUD CONTROL EXEC PARL/PROC REPRESENT GOV/REL SOVEREIGN ALL/IDEOS 19 MILL/JS BENTHAM/J. PAGE 143 H2868 POLICY LAW CONCPT

ALL/PROG....ALLIANCE FOR PROGRESS

ALL/VALS....CONCERNS SIX OR MORE OF THE TERMS LISTED IN THE VALUES INDEX, P. XIII

B00
VOLPICELLI Z.,RUSSIA ON THE PACIFIC AND THE SIBERIAN RAILWAY. MOD/EUR ECO/UNDEV INT/ORG FORCES PLAN DOMIN COLONIAL ROUTINE ATTIT ALL/VALS...OBS NAT/G ACT/RES RUSSIA

HIST/WRIT TIME/SEQ TREND CON/ANAL AUD/VIS CHARTS 18/19. PAGE 163 H3261

B02
SEELEY J.R.,THE EXPANSION OF ENGLAND. MOD/EUR S/ASIA UK CULTURE NAT/G FORCES PLAN DOMIN EDU/PROP COLONIAL ROUTINE ATTIT ALL/VALS SOVEREIGN...CONCPT HIST/WRIT PARLIAMENT 18 CMN/WLTH. PAGE 141 H2819
INT/ORG ACT/RES CAP/ISM INDIA

B06
SUMNER W.G.,FOLKWAYS: STUDY OF THE SOCIOLOGICAL IMPORTANCE OF USAGES, MANNERS, CUSTOMS, MORES, AND MORALS. STRUCT KIN ETIQUET ROUTINE MURDER MARRIAGE PEACE SEX ALL/VALS WEALTH BIBLIOG. PAGE 150 H3008
CULTURE SOC SANCTION MORAL

B16
PUFENDORF S.,LAW OF NATURE AND OF NATIONS (ABRIDGED). UNIV LAW NAT/G DIPLOM AGREE WAR PERSON ALL/VALS PWR...POLICY 18 DEITY NATURL/LAW. PAGE 128 H2565
CONCPT INT/LAW SECT MORAL

B18
BARRES M.,THE FAITH OF FRANCE (TRANS. BY ELISABETH MARBURY). FRANCE FAM MUNIC NEIGH POL/PAR SECT ALL/VALS 20. PAGE 11 H0227
TRADIT CULTURE WAR GP/REL

B21
STUART G.H.,FRENCH FOREIGN POLICY. CONSTN INT/ORG NAT/G POL/PAR EX/STRUC FORCES PLAN ECO/TAC DOMIN EDU/PROP ADJUD COERCE ATTIT DRIVE RIGID/FLEX ALL/VALS...POLICY OBS RECORD BIOG TIME/SEQ TREND. PAGE 150 H3000
MOD/EUR DIPLOM FRANCE

B21
WALLAS G.,HUMAN NATURE IN POLITICS (3RD ED.). UNIV NAT/G LEAD CHOOSE REPRESENT GP/REL NAT/LISM RATIONAL BIO/SOC HEREDITY ALL/VALS MAJORIT. PAGE 165 H3293
PSY DRIVE PERSON

B23
FRANK T.,A HISTORY OF ROME. MEDIT-7 INTELL SOCIETY LOC/G NAT/G POL/PAR FORCES LEGIS DOMIN LEGIT ALL/VALS...POLICY CONCPT TIME/SEQ GEN/LAWS ROM/EMP ROM/EMP. PAGE 53 H1050
EXEC STRUCT ELITES

B26
HOCKING W.E.,PRESENT STATUS OF THE PHILOSOPHY OF LAW AND OF RIGHTS. UNIV CULTURE INTELL SOCIETY NAT/G CREATE LEGIT SANCTION ALL/VALS SOC/INTEG 18/20. PAGE 72 H1442
JURID PHIL/SCI ORD/FREE

B26
SMITH T.V.,THE DEMOCRATIC WAY OF LIFE. UNIV SOCIETY NAT/G WORKER TASK CHOOSE ALL/VALS...IDEA/COMP WORSHIP. PAGE 146 H2919
MAJORIT CONCPT ORD/FREE LEAD

B28
HOBBES T.,THE ELEMENTS OF LAW, NATURAL AND POLITIC (1650). STRATA NAT/G SECT CHIEF AGREE ATTIT ALL/VALS MORAL ORD/FREE POPULISM...POLICY CONCPT. PAGE 71 H1432
PERSON LAW SOVEREIGN CONSERVE

B31
KROEBER A.L.,SOURCE BOOK IN ANTHROPOLOGY. PREHIST SECT RACE/REL...LING GP/COMP ANTHOL. PAGE 89 H1770
SOC HEREDITY CULTURE ALL/VALS

B32
BRYCE J.,THE HOLY ROMAN EMPIRE. GERMANY ITALY MOD/EUR CULTURE SOCIETY STRUCT INT/ORG NAT/G SECT DIPLOM DOMIN WAR SUPEGO ALL/VALS SOVEREIGN...GEOG SOC TIME/SEQ CHARTS STERTYP. PAGE 23 H0456
CHRIST-17C NAT/LISM

B35
AQUINAS T.,ON THE GOVERNANCE OF RULERS (1265-66). UNIV SOCIETY STRATA FAM HABITAT PERSON ALL/VALS PWR SOVEREIGN CONSERVE...POLICY BIBLE. PAGE 8 H0155
CATH NAT/G CHIEF SUPEGO

B37
PARSONS T.,THE STRUCTURE OF SOCIAL ACTION. UNIV INTELL SOCIETY INDUS MARKET ECO/TAC ROUTINE CHOOSE ALL/VALS...CONCPT OBS BIOG TREND GEN/LAWS 20. PAGE 124 H2471
CULTURE ATTIT CAP/ISM

B40
THE GUIDE TO CATHOLIC LITERATURE, 1888-1940. ALL/VALS...POLICY MYSTIC HUM PHIL/SCI 19/20. PAGE 2 H0032
BIBLIOG/A CATHISM DIPLOM CULTURE

B43
EARLE E.M.,MAKERS OF MODERN STRATEGY: MILITARY THOUGHT FROM MACHIAVELLI TO HITLER. EUR+WWI MOD/EUR NAT/G ACT/RES BAL/PWR DOMIN COERCE ATTIT DRIVE RIGID/FLEX ALL/VALS...METH/CNCPT BIOG 16/20. PAGE 44 H0879
PLAN FORCES WAR

B43
JONES C.K.,A BIBLIOGRAPHY OF LATIN AMERICAN BIBLIOGRAPHIES (2ND ED.). CULTURE ALL/VALS...POLICY GEOG HUM SOC LING BIOG TREND 20. PAGE 82 H1629
BIBLIOG/A L/A+17C HIST/WRIT

B44
FULLER G.H.,TURKEY: A SELECTED LIST OF REFERENCES. ISLAM TURKEY CULTURE ECO/UNDEV AGRI DIPLOM NAT/LISM CONSERVE...GEOG HUM INT/LAW SOC 7/20 MAPS. PAGE 54 H1075
BIBLIOG/A ALL/VALS

B45
LINTON R.,THE CULTURAL BACKGROUND OF PERSONALITY. UNIV PERSON ALL/VALS...SOC CONCPT TIME/SEQ GEN/METH TOT/POP VAL/FREE. PAGE 97 H1935
CULTURE ATTIT

B46
GODWIN W.,ENQUIRY CONCERNING POLITICAL JUSTICE AND ITS INFLUENCE ON MORALS AND HAPPINESS (1793). UNIV SOCIETY NAT/G GP/REL INGP/REL HAPPINESS ALL/VALS CONCPT. PAGE 58 H1151
MORAL PERSON ORD/FREE

S46
TANNENBAUM F.,"THE BALANCE OF POWER IN SOCIETY." UNIV STRUCT FAM NAT/G SECT PERS/REL EQUILIB UTOPIA DRIVE ALL/IDEOS...OLD/LIB CONCPT. PAGE 152 H3044
SOCIETY ALL/VALS GP/REL PEACE

B48
HARRIS G.M.,COMPARATIVE LOCAL GOVERNMENT. FINAN CHOOSE ALL/VALS. PAGE 67 H1339
PARTIC GOV/REL LOC/G GOV/COMP

B48
LAUTERBACH A.,ECONOMIC SECURITY AND INDIVIDUAL FREEDOM: CAN WE HAVE BOTH? COM EUR+WWI MOD/EUR UNIV WOR+45 CAP/ISM TOTALISM ALL/VALS...GOV/COMP BIBLIOG 20. PAGE 92 H1840
ORD/FREE ECO/DEV DECISION INGP/REL

B49
SINGER K.,THE IDEA OF CONFLICT. UNIV INTELL INT/ORG NAT/G PLAN ROUTINE ATTIT DRIVE ALL/VALS...POLICY CONCPT TIME/SEQ. PAGE 144 H2882
ACT/RES SOC

B51
LOOS W.A.,RELIGIOUS FAITH AND WORLD CULTURE. INTELL SOCIETY SECT EDU/PROP ROUTINE ATTIT PERSON ALL/VALS MORAL...CONCPT GEN/LAWS VAL/FREE. PAGE 98 H1964
UNIV CULTURE PEACE

B51
MUMFORD L.,THE CONDUCT OF LIFE. UNIV SOCIETY CREATE ...TECHNIC METH/CNCPT TIME/SEQ TREND GEN/LAWS BIBLIOG/A. PAGE 114 H2286
ALL/VALS CULTURE PERSON CONCPT

B52
ULAM A.B.,TITOISM AND THE COMINFORM. USSR WOR+45 STRUCT INT/ORG NAT/G ACT/RES PLAN EXEC ATTIT DRIVE ALL/VALS...CONCPT OBS VAL/FREE 20 COMINTERN TITO/MARSH. PAGE 157 H3149
COM POL/PAR TOTALISM YUGOSLAVIA

B53
MURPHY G.,IN THE MINDS OF MEN: THE STUDY OF HUMAN BEHAVIOR AND SOCIAL TENSIONS IN INDIA. FUT S/ASIA FAM INT/ORG NAT/G DIPLOM EDU/PROP GP/REL ATTIT RIGID/FLEX ALL/VALS...SOC QU UNESCO 20. PAGE 115 H2297
SECT STRATA INDIA

B54
FORDE C.D.,AFRICAN WORLDS. AFR CULTURE ROUTINE GP/REL PERS/REL ATTIT DRIVE ALL/VALS...OBS ANTHOL WORSHIP 20. PAGE 52 H1036
SOCIETY KIN SOC

B54
MALINOWSKI B.,MAGIC, SCIENCE AND RELIGION. AGRI KIN GP/REL ALL/VALS...MYTH OBS RECORD IDEA/COMP WORSHIP 20 NEW/GUINEA. PAGE 102 H2031
CULTURE ATTIT SOC

B54
MATTHEWS D.R.,THE SOCIAL BACKGROUND OF POLITICAL DECISION-MAKERS. CULTURE SOCIETY STRATA FAM EX/STRUC LEAD ATTIT BIO/SOC DRIVE PERSON ALL/VALS HIST/WRIT. PAGE 105 H2097
DECISION BIOG SOC

S54
MIT CENTER INTERNATIONAL STU,"A PLAN OF RESEARCH IN INTERNATIONAL COMMUNICATION: A REPORT." UNIV CULTURE INTELL SOCIETY ACT/RES ALL/VALS...CONCPT METH/CNCPT. PAGE 111 H2227
R+D STYLE

B55
FRIEDMAN G.,INDUSTRIAL SOCIETY: THE EMERGENCE OF THE HUMAN PROBLEMS OF AUTOMATION. UNIV CULTURE ECO/DEV TEC/DEV INGP/REL HAPPINESS RATIONAL UTOPIA ROLE...HUM SOC TIME/SEQ 20. PAGE 53 H1064
AUTOMAT ADJUST ALL/VALS CONCPT

B55
KHADDURI M.,WAR AND PEACE IN THE LAW OF ISLAM. CONSTN CULTURE SOCIETY STRATA NAT/G PROVS SECT FORCES TOP/EX CREATE DOMIN EDU/PROP ADJUD COERCE ATTIT RIGID/FLEX ALL/VALS...CONCPT TIME/SEQ TOT/POP VAL/FREE. PAGE 85 H1702
ISLAM JURID PEACE WAR

B55
MAZZINI J.,THE DUTIES OF MAN. MOD/EUR LAW SOCIETY FAM NAT/G POL/PAR SECT VOL/ASSN EX/STRUC ACT/RES CREATE REV PEACE ATTIT ALL/VALS...GEN/LAWS WORK 19. PAGE 106 H2113
SUPEGO CONCPT NAT/LISM

L55
ROSTOW W.W.,"RUSSIA AND CHINA UNDER COMMUNISM." CHINA/COM USSR INTELL STRUCT INT/ORG NAT/G POL/PAR TOP/EX ACT/RES PLAN ADMIN ATTIT ALL/VALS MARXISM ...CONCPT OBS TIME/SEQ TREND GOV/COMP VAL/FREE 20. PAGE 134 H2689
COM ASIA

B56
EVANS-PRITCHARD E.E.,THE INSTITUTIONS OF PRIMITIVE SOCIETY. LAW SOCIETY KIN ACT/RES CREATE ALL/VALS ...ART/METH SOC METH/CNCPT WORSHIP 20. PAGE 48 H0953
STRUCT PHIL/SCI CULTURE CONCPT

B56
JENNINGS W.I.,THE APPROACH TO SELF-GOVERNMENT. CEYLON INDIA PAKISTAN S/ASIA UK SOCIETY POL/PAR DELIB/GP LEGIS ECO/TAC EDU/PROP ADMIN EXEC CHOOSE ATTIT ALL/VALS...JURID CONCPT GEN/METH TOT/POP 20. PAGE 81 H1610
NAT/G CONSTN COLONIAL

B56
MUMFORD L.,THE TRANSFORMATIONS OF MAN. UNIV CULTURE INGP/REL HABITAT HEREDITY ALL/VALS ORD/FREE...MYTH TIME/SEQ TREND WORSHIP. PAGE 114 H2287 — IDEA/COMP PERSON CONCPT

N56
US HOUSE COMM FOREIGN AFFAIRS,REPORT OF THE SPECIAL STUDY MISSION TO AFRICA, SOUTH AND EAST OF THE SAHARA (PAMPHLET). AFR SOUTH/AFR USA+45 STRUCT INT/TRADE PARL/PROC NAT/LISM ATTIT ALL/VALS HEALTH ...POLICY 20 CONGRESS. PAGE 160 H3197 — FOR/AID COLONIAL ECO/UNDEV DIPLOM

B57
DEAN V.M.,THE NATURE OF THE NON-WESTERN WORLD. AFR ASIA L/A+17C S/ASIA CULTURE SOCIETY STRATA ECO/DEV DIPLOM ECO/TAC FOR/AID ATTIT DRIVE ALL/VALS ...RELATIV SOC CONCPT TIME/SEQ TREND TOT/POP 20. PAGE 39 H0778 — ECO/UNDEV STERTYP NAT/LISM

B58
DUNAYEVSKAYA R.,MARXISM AND FREEDOM: FROM 1776 UNTIL TODAY. COM USSR WORKER CAP/ISM DOMIN REV GP/REL TOTALISM ALL/VALS...MYTH BIOG IDEA/COMP 18/20 MARX/KARL LENIN/VI STALIN/J. PAGE 43 H0861 — MARXISM CONCPT ORD/FREE

B58
EMMET D.M.,FUNCTION, PURPOSE AND POWERS. SECT ATTIT MORAL PWR...CONCPT MYTH. PAGE 46 H0923 — SOC CULTURE ALL/VALS GEN/LAWS

B59
WARNER W.L.,THE LIVING AND THE DEAD: A STUDY OF SYMBOLIC LIFE OF AMERICANS. INTELL KIN DEATH ALL/VALS ALL/IDEOS...CONCPT MYTH LING OBS/ENVIR CHARTS BIBLIOG WORSHIP 18/20. PAGE 165 H3311 — CULTURE SOC TIME/SEQ IDEA/COMP

B60
BLACK C.E.,THE TRANSFORMATION OF RUSSIAN SOCIETY. COM MOD/EUR RUSSIA SOCIETY EDU/PROP COERCE ALL/VALS 19/20. PAGE 17 H0349 — CULTURE RIGID/FLEX USSR

S60
FITZGIBBON R.H.,"DICTATORSHIP AND DEMOCRACY IN LATIN AMERICA." FUT ECO/DEV ECO/UNDEV INT/ORG LOC/G NAT/G TOP/EX PLAN TEC/DEV ECO/TAC CHOOSE ATTIT DRIVE PERSON ALL/VALS OAS TOT/POP 20. PAGE 51 H1019 — L/A+17C ACT/RES INT/TRADE

S60
TIRYAKIAN E.A.,"APARTHEID AND POLITICS IN SOUTH AFRICA." SOUTH/AFR CULTURE STRATA ECO/DEV NAT/G POL/PAR ROUTINE CHOOSE GP/REL RACE/REL DISCRIM ATTIT ALL/VALS...CONCPT OBS TIME/SEQ VAL/FREE 20. PAGE 155 H3105 — AFR DIPLOM

B61
BURDEAU G.,O PODER EXECUTIVO NA FRANCA. EUR+WWI FRANCE CONSTN DELIB/GP LEGIT ADMIN ATTIT ALL/VALS CONCPT. PAGE 24 H0478 — TOP/EX POL/PAR NAT/G LEGIS

B61
COBBAN A.,ROUSSEAU AND THE MODERN STATE. SOCIETY DOMIN INGP/REL HAPPINESS ALL/VALS...CON/ANAL 18/20 ROUSSEAU/J. PAGE 30 H0611 — ORD/FREE ROLE NAT/G POLICY

B61
LUNDBERG G.A.,CAN SCIENCE SAVE US. UNIV CULTURE INTELL SOCIETY ECO/DEV R+D PLAN EDU/PROP ROUTINE CHOOSE ATTIT PERCEPT ALL/VALS...TREND 20. PAGE 99 H1979 — ACT/RES CONCPT TOTALISM

B61
MACLEOD I.,NEVILLE CHAMBERLAIN. UK SOCIETY TOP/EX WAR PERSON ALL/VALS ORD/FREE PARLIAMENT 20 CHAMBRLN/N. PAGE 100 H2003 — BIOG NAT/G CREATE

B61
PATAI R.,CULTURES IN CONFLICT; AN INQUIRY INTO THE SOCIO-CULTURAL PROBLEMS OF ISRAEL AND HER NEIGHBORS (2ND REV. ED.). ISLAM ISRAEL SOCIETY STRUCT DIPLOM GP/REL ALL/VALS...SOC 20 JEWS ARABS. PAGE 124 H2475 — NAT/COMP CULTURE GP/COMP ATTIT

B61
STAHL W.,EDUCATION FOR DEMOCRACY IN WEST GERMANY: ACHIEVEMENT SHORTCOMINGS - PROSPECTS. GERMANY/W SOCIETY NAT/G FORCES PLAN PROB/SOLV PRESS ALL/VALS ...POLICY MAJORIT CONCPT ANTHOL 20. PAGE 148 H2967 — EDU/PROP POPULISM AGE/Y ADJUST

S61
DOGAN M.,"LES OFFICIERS DANS LA CARRIERE POLITIQUE DE MARECHAL MACMAHON AU GENERAL DE GAULLE." EUR+WWI FRANCE MOD/EUR ELITES STRATA POL/PAR LEGIT ATTIT ALL/VALS...SOC CONCPT 19/20. PAGE 42 H0833 — PROF/ORG FORCES NAT/G DELIB/GP

S61
SCHECHTMAN J.B.,"MINORITIES IN THE MIDDLE EAST." ISLAM INTELL SOCIETY STRATA KIN NAT/G VOL/ASSN EDU/PROP REGION GP/REL DISCRIM ATTIT BIO/SOC DISPL PERSON ALL/VALS...PSY SOC OBS SAMP GEN/LAWS 20. PAGE 139 H2776 — SECT CULTURE RACE/REL

S61
VALLET R.,"IRAN: KEY TO THE MIDDLE EAST." COM IRAQ ISLAM KUWAIT LEBANON SAUDI/ARAB TURKEY ELITES SOCIETY INDUS PROC/MFG POL/PAR TOP/EX PLAN BAL/PWR DIPLOM ECO/TAC ALL/VALS...TREND CENTO 20. PAGE 161 H3224 — NAT/G ECO/UNDEV IRAN

B62
ABRAHAM W.E.,THE MIND OF AFRICA. AFR SOCIETY STRATA KIN ECO/TAC DOMIN EDU/PROP LEGIT COERCE ATTIT ALL/VALS...MAJORIT SOC OBS HIST/WRIT TIME/SEQ TREND TOT/POP 20. PAGE 3 H0058 — CULTURE SIMUL GHANA

B62
BRETTON H.L.,POWER AND STABILITY IN NIGERIA: THE POLITICS OF DECOLONIZATION. AFR CONSTN INTELL ECO/UNDEV COM/IND KIN NAT/G POL/PAR PROVS VOL/ASSN LEGIS DOMIN EDU/PROP LEGIT EXEC ROUTINE CHOOSE NAT/LISM ATTIT PERCEPT ALL/VALS. PAGE 20 H0411 — CULTURE OBS NIGERIA

B62
BUSIA K.A.,THE CHALLENGE OF AFRICA. CULTURE KIN MUNIC NAT/G POL/PAR SCHOOL DELIB/GP PLAN ECO/TAC DOMIN EDU/PROP TOTALISM ATTIT PERSON ALL/VALS SOVEREIGN...SOC CONCPT STERTYP TOT/POP VAL/FREE 20. PAGE 25 H0496 — AFR ECO/UNDEV NAT/LISM

B62
CALVOCORESSI P.,WORLD ORDER AND NEW STATES: PROBLEMS OF KEEPING THE PEACE. AFR EUR+WWI S/ASIA ELITES NAT/G ECO/TAC FOR/AID EDU/PROP COERCE ATTIT DRIVE ALL/VALS...GEN/LAWS COLD/WAR 20 UN. PAGE 25 H0509 — INT/ORG PEACE

B62
CARTER G.M.,AFRICAN ONE-PARTY STATES. ISLAM IVORY/CST LIBERIA CONSTN CULTURE SOCIETY POL/PAR PLAN DOMIN EDU/PROP EXEC REGION CHOOSE ATTIT ALL/VALS...CONCPT TIME/SEQ CHARTS VAL/FREE 20 TANGANYIKA. PAGE 27 H0545 — AFR NAT/LISM

B62
CHAKRAVARTI P.C.,INDIA'S CHINA POLICY. ASIA CHINA/COM S/ASIA CULTURE NAT/G TOP/EX ACT/RES EDU/PROP DRIVE ALL/VALS...MYTH 20. PAGE 28 H0571 — RIGID/FLEX TREND INDIA

B62
DE MADARIAGA S.,L'AMERIQUE LATINE ENTRE L'OURS ET L'AIGLE. L/A+17C SOCIETY NAT/G ECO/TAC EDU/PROP REGION COERCE ATTIT ALL/VALS...MAJORIT TIME/SEQ STERTYP COLD/WAR OAS 20. PAGE 38 H0760 — POL/PAR ECO/UNDEV

B62
GUENA Y.,HISTORIQUE DE LA COMMUNAUTE. FUT ECO/UNDEV NAT/G PLAN EDU/PROP COLONIAL REGION NAT/LISM ALL/VALS SOVEREIGN...CONCPT OBS CHARTS 20. PAGE 62 H1244 — AFR VOL/ASSN FOR/AID FRANCE

B62
HO PING-TI,THE LADDER OF SUCCESS IN IMPERIAL CHINA: ASPECTS OF SOCIAL MOBILITY, 1368-1911. INTELL STRATA FAM KIN MUNIC NAT/G PROVS SCHOOL DELIB/GP DOMIN EDU/PROP ADMIN ROUTINE PERSON ALL/VALS...SOC STAT BIOG HIST/WRIT TIME/SEQ VAL/FREE. PAGE 71 H1431 — ASIA CULTURE

B62
HOOK S.,THE PARADOXES OF FREEDOM. UNIV CONSTN INTELL LEGIS CONTROL REV CHOOSE SUPEGO...POLICY JURID IDEA/COMP 19/20 CIV/RIGHTS. PAGE 73 H1461 — CONCPT MAJORIT ORD/FREE ALL/VALS

B62
MELADY T.,THE WHITE MAN'S FUTURE IN BLACK AFRICA. FUT CULTURE SOCIETY NAT/G POL/PAR PLAN ECO/TAC DOMIN EDU/PROP LEGIT COLONIAL RACE/REL ATTIT DRIVE ALL/VALS...PSY SOC CONCPT TIME/SEQ TOT/POP VAL/FREE 20. PAGE 108 H2167 — AFR STRATA ELITES

B62
ROBINSON A.D.,DUTCH ORGANIZED AGRICULTURE IN INTERNATIONAL POLITICS, 1945-1960. EUR+WWI NETHERLAND STRUCT ECO/DEV NAT/G VOL/ASSN CONSULT DELIB/GP PLAN TEC/DEV INT/TRADE EDU/PROP ATTIT RIGID/FLEX ALL/VALS...NEW/IDEA TREND EEC 20. PAGE 132 H2648 — AGRI INT/ORG

B62
TURNBULL C.M.,THE LONELY AFRICAN. AFR MUNIC SECT ANOMIE ALL/VALS...DECISION 20. PAGE 157 H3139 — CULTURE ISOLAT KIN TRADIT

L62
COHEN R.,"POWER IN COMPLEX SOCIETIES IN AFRICA." AFR KIN MUNIC POL/PAR DELIB/GP DOMIN ROUTINE ATTIT ALL/VALS...SOC STAT OBS INT QU CHARTS ANTHOL 20. PAGE 31 H0617 — CULTURE STRATA ELITES

L62
CORET A.,"L'INDEPENDANCE DU SAMOA OCCIDENTAL." S/ASIA LAW INT/ORG EXEC ALL/VALS SAMOA UN 20. PAGE 33 H0668 — NAT/G STRUCT SOVEREIGN

S62
ANSPRENGER F.,"NATIONALISM, COMMUNISM, AND THE UNCOMMITTED NATIONS: AMERICAN PROFILES." FUT ISLAM CULTURE SOCIETY ECO/UNDEV NAT/G POL/PAR PLAN ECO/TAC EDU/PROP COERCE CHOOSE ALL/VALS MARXISM SOCISM...SOC CONCPT BIOG TREND 20. PAGE 7 H0142 — AFR COM NAT/LISM

S62
FESLER J.W.,"FRENCH FIELD ADMINISTRATION: THE BEGINNINGS." CHRIST-17C CULTURE SOCIETY STRATA NAT/G ECO/TAC DOMIN EDU/PROP LEGIT ADJUD COERCE ATTIT ALL/VALS...TIME/SEQ CON/ANAL GEN/METH VAL/FREE 13/15. PAGE 49 H0988 — EX/STRUC FRANCE

S62
HYDE D.,"COMMUNISM IN LATIN AMERICA." L/A+17C ECO/DEV NAT/G SECT EDU/PROP ATTIT ALL/VALS MARXISM ...SOC CONCPT TOT/POP COLD/WAR OAS 20. PAGE 76 H1515 — COM POL/PAR REV

S62
RAZAFIMBAHINY J.,"L'ORGANISATION AFRICAINE ET MALGACHE DE COOPERATION ECONOMIQUE." AFR ISLAM MADAGASCAR NAT/G ACT/RES ECO/TAC ALL/VALS ...TIME/SEQ 20. PAGE 130 H2601
INT/ORG ECO/UNDEV

S62
SHATTEN F.,"POLYCENTRISM: AFRICA: NATIONALISM AND COMMUNISM." ASIA COM FUT ISLAM CULTURE SOCIETY ECO/UNDEV NAT/G PLAN DOMIN COLONIAL COERCE CHOOSE RIGID/FLEX ALL/VALS MARXISM...CONCPT TREND 20. PAGE 143 H2852
AFR ATTIT NAT/LISM SOCISM

S62
VIGNES D.,"L'AUTORITE DES TRAITES INTERNATIONAUX EN DROIT INTERNE." EUR+WWI UNIV LAW CONSTN INTELL NAT/G POL/PAR DIPLOM ATTIT PERCEPT ALL/VALS ...POLICY INT/LAW JURID CONCPT TIME/SEQ 20 TREATY. PAGE 163 H3252
STRUCT LEGIT FRANCE

B63
ARAZI A.,LE SYSTEME ELECTORAL ISRAELIEN. ISRAEL NAT/G ADMIN ALL/VALS PARLIAMENT. PAGE 8 H0158
LEGIS CHOOSE POL/PAR

B63
CREMEANS C.,THE ARABS AND THE WORLD: NASSER'S ARAB NATIONALIST POLICY. FUT ISLAM UAR USA+45 SOCIETY STRATA NAT/G POL/PAR PLAN DIPLOM EDU/PROP LEGIT DRIVE ALL/VALS...INT TIME/SEQ CHARTS 20 NASSER/G. PAGE 35 H0700
TOP/EX ATTIT REGION NAT/LISM

B63
DEBRAY P.,LE PORTUGAL ENTRE DEUX REVOLUTIONS. EUR+WWI PORTUGAL CONSTN LEGIT ADMIN ATTIT ALL/VALS ...DECISION CONCPT 20 SALAZAR/A. PAGE 39 H0779
NAT/G DELIB/GP TOP/EX

B63
FRANKEL J.,THE MAKING OF FOREIGN POLICY: AN ANALYSIS OF DECISION-MAKING. CHINA/COM EUR+WWI USA+45 ELITES INTELL FORCES LEGIS PLAN ATTIT ALL/VALS MORAL CONSERVE...GOV/COMP 20 PRESIDENT UN TREATY. PAGE 53 H1051
POLICY DECISION PROB/SOLV DIPLOM

B63
KAPP W.K.,HINDU CULTURE: ECONOMIC DEVELOPMENT AND ECONOMIC PLANNING IN INDIA. INDIA S/ASIA CULTURE ECO/TAC EDU/PROP ADMIN ALL/VALS...POLICY MGT TIME/SEQ VAL/FREE 20. PAGE 83 H1660
SECT ECO/UNDEV

B63
LARSON A.,A WARLESS WORLD. FUT CULTURE NAT/G VOL/ASSN FORCES CREATE DOMIN PEACE ALL/VALS...HUM STERTYP 20. PAGE 91 H1824
SOCIETY CONCPT ARMS/CONT

B63
RONNING C.N.,LAW AND POLITICS IN INTER-AMERICAN DIPLOMACY. L/A+17C ECO/UNDEV NAT/G CONSULT DELIB/GP CREATE CAP/ISM ECO/TAC LEGIT REGION RIGID/FLEX ...METH/CNCPT GEN/LAWS OAS 20. PAGE 133 H2668
VOL/ASSN ALL/VALS DIPLOM

B63
SILVERT K.H.,EXPECTANT PEOPLES: NATIONALISM AND DEVELOPMENT. CULTURE STRATA SECT LEAD REGION RACE/REL ALL/IDEOS...GEN/LAWS SOC/INTEG 20. PAGE 144 H2877
NAT/LISM ECO/UNDEV ALL/VALS

B63
STEVENS G.G.,EGYPT YESTERDAY AND TODAY. CONSTN ECO/UNDEV AGRI INDUS NAT/G POL/PAR FORCES ECO/TAC EDU/PROP COERCE WAR NAT/LISM DRIVE ALL/VALS ...TIME/SEQ WORK SUEZ 20. PAGE 149 H2983
ISLAM TOP/EX REV UAR

B63
VIARD R.,LA FIN DE L'EMPIRE COLONIAL FRANCAIS. AFR FUT S/ASIA ECO/UNDEV NAT/G CONSULT PLAN ECO/TAC EDU/PROP REGION NAT/LISM ALL/VALS...CONCPT TIME/SEQ TREND VAL/FREE 20. PAGE 162 H3248
VOL/ASSN COLONIAL FRANCE

S63
ANTHON C.G.,"THE END OF THE ADENAUER ERA." EUR+WWI GERMANY/W CONSTN EX/STRUC CREATE DIPLOM LEGIT ATTIT PERSON ALL/VALS...RECORD 20 ADENAUER/K. PAGE 7 H0144
NAT/G TOP/EX BAL/PWR GERMANY

S63
ARASTEH R.,"THE ROLE OF INTELLECTUALS IN ADMINISTRATIVE DEVELOPMENT AND SOCIAL CHANGE IN MODERN IRAN." ISLAM CULTURE NAT/G CONSULT ACT/RES EDU/PROP EXEC ATTIT BIO/SOC PERCEPT SUPEGO ALL/VALS ...POLICY MGT PSY SOC CONCPT 20. PAGE 8 H0157
INTELL ADMIN IRAN

S63
AYAL E.B.,"VALUE SYSTEM AND ECONOMIC DEVELOPMENT IN JAPAN AND THAILAND." ASIA S/ASIA THAILAND CULTURE ECO/DEV CAP/ISM DOMIN NAT/LISM DRIVE RIGID/FLEX SOCISM...WELF/ST OBS TREND CON/ANAL GEN/LAWS 20 CHINJAP. PAGE 9 H0185
ECO/UNDEV ALL/VALS

S63
CRUTCHER J.,"PAN AFRICANISM: AFRICAN ODYSSEY." AFR NAT/G POL/PAR PROF/ORG VOL/ASSN TOP/EX CREATE REGION RACE/REL ALL/VALS...CONCPT TIME/SEQ TREND CON/ANAL 20. PAGE 36 H0716
PROVS DELIB/GP COLONIAL

S63
HARRIS R.L.,"A COMPARATIVE ANALYSIS OF THE ADMINISTRATIVE SYSTEMS OF CANADA AND CEYLON." S/ASIA CULTURE SOCIETY STRATA TOP/EX ACT/RES DOMIN EDU/PROP LEGIT COERCE ATTIT SUPEGO ALL/VALS...MGT CHARTS GEN/LAWS VAL/FREE 20. PAGE 67 H1343
DELIB/GP EX/STRUC CANADA CEYLON

S63
LEE J.M.,"PARLIAMENT IN REPUBLICAN GHANA." AFR CONSTN CULTURE SOCIETY STRATA POL/PAR DELIB/GP TOP/EX DOMIN EDU/PROP LEGIT COERCE CHOOSE ATTIT ALL/VALS...CONCPT STAT TIME/SEQ VAL/FREE 20. PAGE 93 H1857
LEGIS GHANA

S63
LOPEZIBOR J.,"L'EUROPE, FORME DE VIE." CHRIST-17C EUR+WWI FUT MOD/EUR SOCIETY INT/ORG SECT EDU/PROP ATTIT RIGID/FLEX ALL/VALS...POLICY HUM SOC TIME/SEQ TREND GEN/LAWS. PAGE 98 H1966
NAT/G CULTURE

S63
NICHOLAS W.,"VILLAGE FACTIONS AND POLITICAL PARTIES IN RURAL WEST BENGAL." S/ASIA CULTURE STRATA FACE/GP KIN MUNIC DELIB/GP LEGIS DOMIN EDU/PROP COERCE CHOOSE ATTIT ALL/VALS...STAT TOT/POP VAL/FREE 20. PAGE 117 H2348
NEIGH POL/PAR

S63
RINTELEN F.,"L'HOMME EUROPEEN." EUR+WWI FUT CULTURE INTELL SECT EDU/PROP ATTIT ALL/VALS...HUM SOC METH/CNCPT TREND GEN/LAWS 20 WORSHIP. PAGE 132 H2631
SOCIETY PERSON

S63
SOEMARDJORN S.,"SOME SOCIAL AND CULTURAL IMPLICATIONS OF INDONESIA'S PLANNED AND UNPLANNED DEVELOPMENT." EUR+WWI FUT MOD/EUR S/ASIA CONSTN SOCIETY DELIB/GP ACT/RES PLAN ECO/TAC EDU/PROP COERCE ATTIT ALL/VALS...TIME/SEQ 20. PAGE 146 H2927
ECO/UNDEV CULTURE INDONESIA

B64
AGGER R.E.,THE RULERS AND THE RULED: POLITICAL POWER AND IMPOTENCE IN AMERICAN COMMUNITIES. CULTURE DOMIN CHOOSE ATTIT ALL/VALS...DECISION SOC CONCPT OBS QU CHARTS. PAGE 4 H0079
PWR STRUCT LOC/G MUNIC

B64
BEATTIE J.,OTHER CULTURES. UNIV LAW FAM POL/PAR SECT ADJUD OWN ALL/VALS WEALTH...SOC NAT/COMP SOC/INTEG 20. PAGE 13 H0251
METH/CNCPT CULTURE STRUCT

B64
GREEN M.M.,IBO VILLAGE AFFAIRS. AFR FORCES PERS/REL ADJUST ISOLAT ATTIT HABITAT PERSON ALL/VALS...JURID RECORD SOC/INTEG 20 IBO. PAGE 60 H1207
MUNIC CULTURE ECO/UNDEV SOC

B64
HEIMSATH C.H.,INDIAN NATIONALISM AND HINDU SOCIAL REFORM. S/ASIA LAW CULTURE SOCIETY STRATA PROVS VOL/ASSN DELIB/GP LEGIS TOP/EX DOMIN EDU/PROP LEGIT ATTIT ALL/VALS...POLICY SOC TIME/SEQ STERTYP VAL/FREE 19/20. PAGE 69 H1385
SECT NAT/G

B64
JOSEPHSON E.,MAN ALONE: ALIENATION IN MODERN SOCIETY. WOR+45 ECO/DEV WORKER WAR LEISURE RACE/REL ANOMIE ATTIT PERCEPT PERSON ALL/VALS...ANTHOL 20. PAGE 82 H1636
STRANGE CULTURE SOCIETY ADJUST

B64
KELLER J.W.,GERMANY, THE WALL AND BERLIN. EUR+WWI ECO/DEV NAT/G VOL/ASSN FORCES PLAN ECO/TAC EDU/PROP COERCE...POLICY CONCPT INT TREND COLD/WAR BER/BLOC 20 BERLIN. PAGE 84 H1685
ATTIT ALL/VALS DIPLOM GERMANY

B64
LAWRENCE P.,ROAD BELONG CARGO: A STUDY OF CARGO MOVEMENT IN SOUTHERN MADANG DISTRICT, NEW GUINEA. S/ASIA CULTURE ECO/UNDEV PROC/MFG KIN CHIEF COLONIAL COERCE GP/REL DRIVE WEALTH WORSHIP 20 NEW/GUINEA. PAGE 92 H1846
SOC SECT ALL/VALS MYTH

B64
LI C.M.,INDUSTRIAL DEVELOPMENT IN COMMUNIST CHINA. CHINA/COM ECO/DEV ECO/UNDEV AGRI FINAN INDUS MARKET LABOR NAT/G ECO/TAC INT/TRADE EXEC ALL/VALS ...POLICY RELATIV TREND WORK TOT/POP VAL/FREE 20. PAGE 96 H1921
ASIA TEC/DEV

B64
MELADY T.,FACES OF AFRICA. AFR FUT ISLAM NAT/G POL/PAR SCHOOL DELIB/GP PLAN ECO/TAC EDU/PROP ATTIT ALL/VALS...CHARTS TOT/POP VAL/FREE 20. PAGE 108 H2168
ECO/UNDEV TREND NAT/LISM

B64
PIPES R.,THE FORMATION OF THE SOVIET UNION. EUR+WWI MOD/EUR STRUCT ECO/UNDEV NAT/G LEGIS DOMIN LEGIT CT/SYS EXEC COERCE ALL/VALS...POLICY RELATIV HIST/WRIT TIME/SEQ TOT/POP 19/20. PAGE 126 H2514
COM USSR RUSSIA

B64
TAYLOR E.,RICHER BY ASIA. S/ASIA CULTURE VOL/ASSN ACT/RES ATTIT DISPL PERSON ALL/VALS...INT/LAW MYTH SELF/OBS 20. PAGE 153 H3054
SOCIETY RIGID/FLEX INDIA

B64
VOELKMANN K.,HERRSCHER VON MORGEN? BAL/PWR COLONIAL NEUTRAL REGION RACE/REL ALL/VALS SOVEREIGN...RECORD 20 COLD/WAR THIRD/WRLD. PAGE 163 H3259
DIPLOM ECO/UNDEV CONTROL NAT/COMP

B64
WARD R.E.,POLITICAL MODERNIZATION IN JAPAN AND TURKEY. ASIA ISLAM S/ASIA CONSTN CULTURE STRATA COM/IND POL/PAR FORCES ACT/RES ECO/TAC DOMIN EDU/PROP LEGIT ADMIN CHOOSE ATTIT ALL/VALS...STAT TIME/SEQ VAL/FREE CHINJAP. PAGE 165 H3307
SOCIETY TURKEY

B64
WHITEFORD A.H.,TWO CITIES OF LATIN AMERICA: A COMPARATIVE DESCRIPTION OF SOCIAL CLASSES. L/A+17C
STRATA SOC

CULTURE SOCIETY MUNIC DOMIN LEGIT ATTIT ALL/VALS ...STAT OBS VAL/FREE 20. PAGE 167 H3352

L64

BERELSON B.,"SAMPLE SURVEYS AND POPULATION CONTROL." ASIA FUT ISLAM L/A+17C CULTURE SOCIETY FAM NAT/G CONSULT PLAN EDU/PROP ATTIT DRIVE ALL/VALS...POLICY RELATIV HEAL PSY SOC CONCPT METH/CNCPT OBS OBS/ENVIR TOT/POP. PAGE 15 H0297 BIO/SOC SAMP

L64

FINDLATER R.,"US." EUR+WWI GERMANY USSR SOCIETY FACE/GP EDU/PROP PERCEPT PERSON ALL/VALS...PSY SOC CONCPT SELF/OBS SAMP TREND 20. PAGE 50 H1001 CULTURE ATTIT UK

S64

ADAMS R.,"POLITICS AND SOCIAL ANTHROPOLOGY IN SPANISH AMERICA." FUT CULTURE SOCIETY NAT/G PROF/ORG EDU/PROP ATTIT RIGID/FLEX ALL/VALS ...POLICY GEOG METH/CNCPT MYTH TREND VAL/FREE 20. PAGE 3 H0065 L/A+17C SOC

S64

CLIFFE L.,"TANGANYIKA'S TWO YEARS OF INDEPENDENCE." AFR INDUS MARKET NAT/G POL/PAR DELIB/GP CREATE ECO/TAC LEGIT DRIVE ALL/VALS...METH/CNCPT RECORD 20 TANGANYIKA. PAGE 30 H0604 ECO/UNDEV PLAN

S64

GARMARNIKOW M.,"INFLUENCE-BUYING IN WEST AFRICA." COM FUT USSR INTELL NAT/G PLAN TEC/DEV ECO/TAC DOMIN EDU/PROP REGION NAT/LISM ATTIT DRIVE ALL/VALS SOVEREIGN...POLICY PSY SOC CONCPT TREND STERTYP WORK COLD/WAR 20. PAGE 55 H1102 AFR ECO/UNDEV FOR/AID SOCISM

S64

GIROD R.,"LE SYSTEME DES PARTIS EN SUISSE." CONSTN LOC/G DELIB/GP FEDERAL ALL/VALS. PAGE 57 H1136 POL/PAR LEGIS NAT/G PARL/PROC

S64

LANGER P.F.,"JAPAN'S RELATIONS WITH CHINA." ASIA CHINA/COM KOREA S/ASIA ECO/DEV NAT/G POL/PAR EDU/PROP ATTIT ALL/VALS...METH/CNCPT TIME/SEQ TREND 20 CHINJAP. PAGE 91 H1808 RIGID/FLEX ECO/TAC

S64

LEWIS R.,"OPINION SURVEYING IN KOREA." ASIA FUT KOREA LEGIS EDU/PROP EXEC ALL/VALS...POLICY CONCPT MYTH TESTS CON/ANAL GEN/METH TOT/POP VAL/FREE 20. PAGE 96 H1915 NAT/G QU

S64

NASH M.,"SOCIAL PREREQUISITES TO ECONOMIC GROWTH IN LATIN AMERICA AND SOUTHEAST ASIA." L/A+17C S/ASIA CULTURE SOCIETY ECO/UNDEV AGRI INDUS NAT/G PLAN TEC/DEV EDU/PROP ROUTINE ALL/VALS...POLICY RELATIV SOC NAT/COMP WORK TOT/POP 20. PAGE 116 H2314 ECO/DEV PERCEPT

S64

NEEDHAM T.,"SCIENCE AND SOCIETY IN EAST AND WEST." INTELL STRATA R+D LOC/G NAT/G PROVS CONSULT ACT/RES CREATE PLAN TEC/DEV EDU/PROP ADMIN ATTIT ALL/VALS ...POLICY RELATIV MGT CONCPT NEW/IDEA TIME/SEQ WORK WORK. PAGE 116 H2327 ASIA STRUCT

S64

SAAB H.,"THE ARAB SEARCH FOR A FEDERAL UNION." SOCIETY INT/ORG NAT/G DELIB/GP FORCES ACT/RES TEC/DEV ECO/TAC DOMIN LEGIT REGION ROUTINE ATTIT DRIVE RIGID/FLEX ALL/VALS...SOC CONCPT NEW/IDEA TIME/SEQ TREND. PAGE 136 H2726 ISLAM PLAN

S64

SAYEED K.,"PATHAN REGIONALISM." ISLAM PAKISTAN S/ASIA CULTURE SOCIETY NAT/G NEIGH DIPLOM LEGIT COERCE CHOOSE ATTIT DISPL PERCEPT ALL/VALS SOVEREIGN...POLICY RELATIV SOC TIME/SEQ TOT/POP 20. PAGE 138 H2761 SECT NAT/LISM REGION

S64

TOUVAL S.,"THE SOMALI REPUBLIC." AFR ISLAM SOMALIA FAM KIN NAT/G CREATE FOR/AID LEGIT ATTIT ALL/VALS ...RECORD TREND 20. PAGE 156 H3119 ECO/UNDEV RIGID/FLEX

S64

ZARTMAN I.W.,"LES RELATIONS ENTRE LA FRANCE ET L'ALGERIA DEPUIS LES ACCORDS D'EVIAN." EUR+WWI FUT ISLAM CULTURE AGRI EXTR/IND FINAN INDUS POL/PAR DIPLOM ECO/TAC FOR/AID PEACE ATTIT DRIVE ALL/VALS ...TIME/SEQ VAL/FREE 20. PAGE 172 H3450 ECO/UNDEV ALGERIA FRANCE

B65

ARENSBERG C.M.,CULTURE AND COMMUNITY. UNIV FACE/GP ACT/RES EDU/PROP LEAD REGION GP/REL PERS/REL HABITAT ALL/VALS...SOC CONCPT 20. PAGE 8 H0162 SOCIETY CULTURE NEIGH NEW/IDEA

B65

BENTWICH J.S.,EDUCATION IN ISRAEL. ISRAEL CULTURE STRATA PROB/SOLV TEC/DEV ADJUST ALL/VALS 20 JEWS. PAGE 15 H0293 SECT EDU/PROP ACADEM SCHOOL

B65

CANTRIL H.,THE PATTERN OF HUMAN CONCERNS. ELITES ECO/DEV ECO/UNDEV...STAT CHARTS METH 20. PAGE 26 H0524 ATTIT ALL/VALS NAT/COMP CULTURE

B65

DOLCI D.,A NEW WORLD IN THE MAKING. GHANA SENEGAL USSR YUGOSLAVIA CULTURE INT/ORG PLAN EDU/PROP GP/REL PEACE MORAL...GEOG SOC 20 COLD/WAR. PAGE 42 H0834 SOCIETY ALL/VALS DRIVE PERSON

B65

FOSTER P.,EDUCATION AND SOCIAL CHANGE IN GHANA. GHANA CULTURE STRUCT ECO/UNDEV TEC/DEV REGION EFFICIENCY LITERACY ALL/VALS SOVEREIGN...STAT METH/COMP 19/20 GOLD/COAST. PAGE 52 H1043 SCHOOL CREATE SOCIETY

B65

HALEVY E.,THE ERA OF TYRANNIES (TRANS. BY R. K. WEBB). FRANCE MOD/EUR UK ECO/DEV LABOR NAT/G BAL/PWR FEDERAL ALL/VALS...OLD/LIB TREND 18/20 SAINTSIMON. PAGE 64 H1285 SOCISM CONCPT UTOPIA ORD/FREE

B65

OBUKAR C.,THE MODERN AFRICAN. AGRI INDUS WORKER CAP/ISM EDU/PROP PARTIC RACE/REL NAT/LISM ALL/VALS MARXISM...SOC IDEA/COMP 20. PAGE 120 H2393 AFR ECO/UNDEV CULTURE SOVEREIGN

B65

US DEPARTMENT OF DEFENSE,US SECURITY ARMS CONTROL, AND DISARMAMENT 1961-1965 (PAMPHLET). CHINA/COM COM GERMANY/W ISRAEL SPACE USA+45 USSR WOR+45 FORCES EDU/PROP DETER EQUILIB PEACE ALL/VALS...GOV/COMP 20 NATO. PAGE 159 H3183 BIBLIOG/A ARMS/CONT NUC/PWR DIPLOM

S65

HELMREICH E.C.,"KADAR'S HUNGARY." COM EUR+WWI HUNGARY USSR INTELL ECO/DEV AGRI INT/ORG TOP/EX DOMIN ALL/VALS WORK COLD/WAR 20. PAGE 69 H1390 NAT/G RIGID/FLEX TOTALISM

S65

RUBINSTEIN A.Z.,"YUGOSLAVIA'S OPENING SOCIETY." COM USSR INTELL NAT/G LEGIS TOP/EX LEGIT CT/SYS RIGID/FLEX ALL/VALS SOCISM...HUM TIME/SEQ TREND 20. PAGE 135 H2708 CONSTN EX/STRUC YUGOSLAVIA

S65

WRIGHT Q.,"THE ESCALATION OF INTERNATIONAL CONFLICTS." WOR+45 WOR-45 FORCES DIPLOM RISK COST ATTIT ALL/VALS...INT/LAW QUANT STAT NAT/COMP. PAGE 171 H3422 WAR PERCEPT PREDICT MATH

B66

AIR FORCE ACADEMY ASSEMBLY,CULTURAL AFFAIRS AND FOREIGN RELATIONS. NAT/G VOL/ASSN ALL/VALS. PAGE 4 H0083 CULTURE SOCIETY PERS/REL DIPLOM

B66

KASUNMU A.B.,NIGERIAN FAMILY LAW. NIGERIA KIN LEGIT ILLEGIT MARRIAGE AGE DRIVE HABITAT ALL/VALS...JURID IDEA/COMP T 20 ENGLSH/LAW. PAGE 83 H1667 FAM LAW CULTURE AFR

B66

KIRKLAND E.C.,A BIBLIOGRAPHY OF SOUTH ASIAN FOLKLORE. WRITING HABITAT ALL/VALS MYSTISM ...ART/METH GEOG PSY SOC MYTH WORSHIP 13/20. PAGE 86 H1723 BIBLIOG S/ASIA CULTURE CREATE

B66

MAC DONALD H.M.,THE INTELLECTUAL IN POLITICS. GERMANY PERU SWEDEN UK USSR NAT/G CONSULT PLAN EDU/PROP TASK INGP/REL EFFICIENCY RATIONAL ALL/VALS 20. PAGE 99 H1987 ALL/IDEOS INTELL POL/PAR PARTIC

B66

SETTON K.M.,GREAT PROBLEMS IN EUROPEAN CIVILIZATION. CHRIST-17C EUR+WWI MOD/EUR SECT GP/REL ALL/VALS ORD/FREE ALL/IDEOS...TREND ANTHOL T CHRISTIAN RENAISSAN PROTESTANT. PAGE 142 H2835 CULTURE CONCPT IDEA/COMP

B66

VOGT E.Z.,PEOPLE OF RIMROCK. STRATA STRUCT KIN SECT GP/REL HABITAT ALL/VALS...GEOG INT QU 20 TEXAS NAVAHO MORMON SPAN/AMER ZUNI. PAGE 163 H3260 CULTURE GP/COMP SOC SOCIETY

B66

WILLNER A.R.,THE NEOTRADITIONAL ACCOMMODATION TO POLITICAL INDEPENDENCE* THE CASE OF INDONESIA * RESEARCH MONOGRAPH NO. 26. CULTURE ECO/UNDEV CREATE PROB/SOLV FOR/AID LEGIT COLONIAL EFFICIENCY NAT/LISM ALL/VALS SOC. PAGE 168 H3371 INDONESIA CONSERVE ELITES ADMIN

S66

SNOW P.G.,"A SCALOGRAM ANALYSIS OF POLITICAL DEVELOPMENT." STRATA ECO/UNDEV POL/PAR REGION ALL/VALS PWR...SOC CHARTS. PAGE 146 H2924 L/A+17C NAT/COMP TESTS CLASSIF

B67

ANDERSON O.,A LIBERAL STATE AT WAR. MOD/EUR UK LAW CULTURE STRUCT ECO/DEV NAT/G DIPLOM PARL/PROC GP/REL ALL/VALS...CONCPT 19. PAGE 7 H0131 WAR FORCES

B67

BODENHEIMER E.,TREATISE ON JUSTICE. INT/ORG NAT/G PUB/INST ACT/RES RISK CRIME INGP/REL DISCRIM DRIVE LAISSEZ 20. PAGE 18 H0363 ALL/VALS STRUCT JURID CONCPT

B67

JOUVENEL B D.E.,THE ART OF CONJECTURE. FUT CONSULT EX/STRUC CHOOSE GOV/REL ALL/VALS. PAGE 82 H1638 PREDICT DELIB/GP PLAN NAT/G

B67

KING M.L. JR.,WHERE DO WE GO FROM HERE: CHAOS OR COMMUNITY? MUNIC NAT/G PARTIC INGP/REL ALL/VALS ...POLICY CONCPT BIOG 20. PAGE 86 H1715 RACE/REL DISCRIM STRUCT

PWR

B67
PIKE F.B.,FREEDOM AND REFORM IN LATIN AMERICA. BRAZIL URUGUAY CONSTN CULTURE SECT DIPLOM EDU/PROP PARTIC DRIVE ALL/VALS CATHISM...GEOG ANTHOL BIBLIOG REFORMERS BOLIV. PAGE 126 H2511 — L/A+17C ORD/FREE ECO/UNDEV REV

B67
THOMPSON E.T.,PERSPECTIVES ON THE SOUTH: AGENDA FOR RESEARCH. CULTURE ECO/UNDEV SECT GP/REL EFFICIENCY ALL/VALS...HUM SOC CONCPT LING 20 NEGRO. PAGE 154 H3080 — PROB/SOLV IDEA/COMP REGION ACT/RES

B67
WARD L.,LESTER WARD AND THE WELFARE STATE. SOCIETY NAT/G CREATE RECEIVE EQUILIB UTOPIA HABITAT HEREDITY PERSON...POLICY SOC BIOG 19/20 WARD/LEST. PAGE 165 H3303 — ALL/VALS NEW/IDEA WELF/ST CONCPT

B67
WILLS A.J.,AN INTRODUCTION TO THE HISTORY OF CENTRAL AFRICA. RHODESIA ZAMBIA CULTURE SOCIETY ECO/UNDEV TEC/DEV DOMIN WAR ALL/VALS...POLICY TREND BIBLIOG T 14/20 NYASALAND. PAGE 169 H3375 — AFR COLONIAL ORD/FREE

S67
HOPE M.,"THE RELUCTANT WAY: SELF-IMMOLATION IN VIETNAM." VIETNAM SOCIETY FAM KIN SECT DRIVE ALL/VALS...TRADIT OBS INT 20. PAGE 73 H1465 — CULTURE SUICIDE IDEA/COMP ATTIT

S67
WHITE J.W.,"MASS MOVEMENTS AND DEMOCRACY: SOKAGAKKAI IN JAPANESE POLITICS." NAT/G GP/REL ALL/VALS ORD/FREE WORSHIP 20 CHINJAP. PAGE 167 H3349 — SECT PWR ATTIT POL/PAR

B70
BOSSUET J.B.,"POLITIQUE TIREE DE L'ECRITURE SAINTE" (1679-1709) IN J.B. BOSSUET, OEVRES DE BOSSUET. NAT/G GP/REL AUTHORIT HEREDITY PERSON ALL/VALS SOVEREIGN 18 BIBLE DEITY CHRISTIAN. PAGE 19 H0383 — TRADIT CHIEF SECT CONCPT

B96
DE VATTEL E.,THE LAW OF NATIONS. AGRI FINAN CHIEF DIPLOM INT/TRADE AGREE OWN ALL/VALS MORAL ORD/FREE SOVEREIGN...GEN/LAWS 18 NATURL/LAW WOLFF/C. PAGE 39 H0774 — LAW CONCPT NAT/G INT/LAW

B99
DU BOIS W.E.B.,THE PHILADELPHIA NEGRO: A SOCIAL STUDY. CULTURE STRATA KIN CRIME SUFF ADJUST DISCRIM ISOLAT HABITAT HEREDITY ALL/VALS SOC/INTEG 17/19 NEGRO PHILADELPH. PAGE 42 H0851 — INGP/REL RACE/REL SOC CENSUS

ALLEN J.S. H0105

ALLEN W.S. H0106

ALLIANCE FOR PROGRESS....SEE ALL/PROG

ALLIANCES, MILITARY....SEE FORCES+DIPLOM.

ALLIGHAN G. H0107

ALLWORTH E. H0108

ALMAGRO BASCH M. H0109

ALMOND G.A. H0110,H0111,H0112,H0113

ALPANDER G.G. H0114

ALSTON J.P. H1143

ALSTON P.L. H0115

ALTBACH P. H0116

ALTO/ADIGE....ALTO-ADIGE REGION OF ITALY

ALTON T.P. H0117

ALVIM J.C. H0118

AM/LEGION....AMERICAN LEGION

AMA....AMERICAN MEDICAL ASSOCIATION

AMBITION....SEE DRIVE

AMEND/I....CONCERNED WITH FREEDOMS GRANTED IN THE FIRST AMENDMENT

AMEND/IV....CONCERNED WITH FREEDOMS GRANTED IN THE FOURTH AMENDMENT

AMEND/V....CONCERNED WITH FREEDOMS GRANTED IN THE FIFTH AMENDMENT

AMEND/VI....CONCERNED WITH FREEDOMS GRANTED IN THE SIXTH AMENDMENT

AMEND/XIV....CONCERNED WITH FREEDOMS GRANTED IN THE FOURTEENTH AMENDMENT

AMER ENTERPRISE INST PUB POL H0119

AMERASINGHE C.F. H0120

AMERICAN FARM BUREAU FEDERATION....SEE FARM/BUR

AMERICAN FEDERATION OF LABOR, CONGRESS OF INDUSTRIAL ORGANIZATIONS....SEE AFL/CIO, LABOR

AMERICAN INDIANS....SEE INDIAN/AM

AMERICAN LEGION....SEE AM/LEGION

AMERICAN POLITICAL SCIENCE ASSOCIATION....SEE APSA

AMERICAN TELEPHONE AND TELEGRAPH....SEE AT+T

AMERICAN COUNCIL LEARNED SOC H0121

AMERICAN FRIENDS SERVICE COMM H0122

AMERICAN SOCIETY AFR CULTURE H0123

AMERICAS, PRE/EUROPEAN....SEE PRE/AMER

AMMAN/MAX....MAX AMMAN

B64
HALE O.J.,THE CAPTIVE PRESS IN THE THIRD REICH. GERMANY CULTURE LG/CO NAT/G POL/PAR PLAN DOMIN TASK CENTRAL OWN TOTALISM PWR...BIBLIOG 20 HITLER/A NAZI AMMAN/MAX. PAGE 64 H1283 — COM/IND PRESS CONTROL FASCISM

AMOS S. H0124

ANARCH....ANARCHISM; SEE ALSO ATTIT, VALUES INDEX

B12
POLLOCK F.,THE GENIUS OF THE COMMON LAW. CHRIST-17C UK FINAN CHIEF ACT/RES ADMIN GP/REL ATTIT SOCISM ...ANARCH JURID. PAGE 127 H2537 — LAW CULTURE CREATE

B13
KROPOTKIN P.,THE CONQUEST OF BREAD. SOCIETY STRATA AGRI INDUS WORKER REV HAPPINESS INCOME PRODUC HEALTH MORAL ORD/FREE. PAGE 89 H1775 — ANARCH SOCIALIST OWN AGREE

B27
GOOCH G.P.,ENGLISH DEMOCRATIC IDEAS IN THE SEVENTEENTH CENTURY (2ND ED.). UK LAW SECT FORCES DIPLOM LEAD PARL/PROC REV ATTIT AUTHORIT...ANARCH CONCPT 17 PARLIAMENT CMN/WLTH REFORMERS. PAGE 58 H1167 — IDEA/COMP MAJORIT EX/STRUC CONSERVE

B37
BERDYAEV N.,THE ORIGIN OF RUSSIAN COMMUNISM. MOD/EUR RUSSIA USSR INTELL SECT REV...ANARCH HUM 19/20 ORTHO/RUSS COM/PARTY CHRISTIAN. PAGE 15 H0294 — MARXISM NAT/LISM CULTURE ATTIT

B43
LENIN V.I.,STATE AND REVOLUTION. USSR CAP/ISM ...ANARCH MARXIST PHIL/SCI IDEA/COMP 20. PAGE 94 H1878 — SOCIETY NAT/G REV MARXISM

B52
LOPEZ-AMO A.,LA MONARQUIA DE LA REFORMA SOCIAL. MOD/EUR SPAIN CONSTN NAT/G TASK EFFICIENCY CONSERVE ...ANARCH TRADIT SOC CONCPT IDEA/COMP 19/20. PAGE 98 H1967 — MARXISM REV LEGIT ORD/FREE

B53
MAXIMOFF G.P.,THE POLITICAL PHILOSOPHY OF BAKUNIN: SCIENTIFIC ANARCHISM. STRUCT INGP/REL FEDERAL MARXISM...ANARCH BIOG 19 BAKUNIN. PAGE 105 H2104 — SOCIETY PHIL/SCI NAT/G IDEA/COMP

B64
UTECHIN S.V.,RUSSIAN POLITICAL THOUGHT: A CONCISE HISTORY. RUSSIA USSR INTELL STRATA POL/PAR SECT LEGIS EDU/PROP REV WAR MARXISM...ANARCH BIBLIOG 9/20 REFORMERS SLAVS. PAGE 161 H3218 — IDEA/COMP ATTIT ALL/IDEOS NAT/G

B68
PROUDHON J.P.,IDEE GENERALE DE LA REVOLUTION AU XIXE SIECLE (1851). FRANCE UNIV NAT/G CREATE AGREE UTOPIA ORD/FREE...ANARCH 19. PAGE 128 H2563 — REV SOCIETY WORKER LABOR

B96
KROPOTKIN P.,L'ANARCHIE. NAT/G VOL/ASSN REV MORAL WEALTH...POLICY 19. PAGE 89 H1776 — SOCIETY ANARCH PERSON

CONCPT

ANARCHISM....SEE ANARCH

ANCIENT EGYPT....SEE EGYPT/ANC

ANCIENT GREECE....SEE GREECE/ANC

ANDALUSIA....SEE ALSO SPAIN

ANDERSON C.W. H0125,H0126,H1138

ANDERSON E.N. H0127

ANDERSON J. H0128

ANDERSON L.G. H0129

ANDERSON O. H0130,H0131

ANDERSON P.R. H0127,H0132

ANDERSON S.V. H0133,H0134

ANDERSON T. H0135

ANDERSON W. H0136

ANDORRA....SEE ALSO APPROPRIATE TIME/SPACE/CULTURE INDEX

ANDREN N. H0137

ANDREWS D.H. H0138

ANDREWS W.G. H0139,H0140,H0476

ANGLIN D. H2005

ANGLO/SAX....ANGLO-SAXON

ANGOLA....ANGOLA

ANNEXATION....ANNEXATION

ANOMIE....GENERALIZED PERSONAL ANXIETY; SEE DISPL

B22
OGBURN W.F.,SOCIAL CHANGE WITH RESPECT TO CULTURE AND ORIGINAL NATURE. ACT/RES OP/RES CRIME GP/REL ANOMIE BIO/SOC PWR...PSY SOC TIME/SEQ METH SOC/INTEG. PAGE 120 H2405
CULTURE CREATE TEC/DEV

B37
HORNEY K.,THE NEUROTIC PERSONALITY OF OUR TIME. SOCIETY PERS/REL ADJUST HAPPINESS ANOMIE ATTIT DRIVE SEX LOVE PWR CONCPT. PAGE 74 H1472
PSY PERSON STRANGE CULTURE

S38
MERTON R.K.,"SOCIAL STRUCTURE AND ANOMIE" (BMR)" UNIV CULTURE STRATA CREATE PARTIC ATTIT BIO/SOC PERSON...SOC CONCPT 20. PAGE 109 H2186
SOCIETY STRUCT ANOMIE DRIVE

B42
REDFIELD R.,THE FOLK CULTURE OF YUCATAN. STRATA FAM KIN MUNIC SECT DISCRIM ISOLAT ANOMIE HEALTH ...BIBLIOG 20 MEXIC/AMER. PAGE 130 H2605
CULTURE NEIGH GP/COMP SOCIETY

B49
GORER G.,THE PEOPLE OF GREAT RUSSIA: A PSYCHOLOGICAL STUDY. RUSSIA USSR NAT/G DIPLOM LEAD AGE/C ANOMIE ATTIT DRIVE...POLICY 20. PAGE 59 H1182
ISOLAT PERSON PSY SOCIETY

B51
LEMERT E.M.,SOCIAL PATHOLOGY. CULTURE BIO/SOC PERSON SEX 20 PROSTITUTN. PAGE 94 H1876
SOC ANOMIE CONCPT CRIME

S53
ARENDT H.,"IDEOLOGY AND TERROR: A NOVEL FORM OF GOVERNMENT." WOR-45 DOMIN STRANGE ATTIT SUPEGO MARXISM...GOV/COMP IDEA/COMP 20 NAZI. PAGE 8 H0160
TOTALISM ANOMIE ALL/IDEOS SOCIETY

B54
SPROTT W.J.H.,SCIENCE AND SOCIAL ACTION. STRUCT ACT/RES CRIME GP/REL INGP/REL ANOMIE...PSY SOC/INTEG 19/20. PAGE 148 H2956
SOC CULTURE PHIL/SCI

B56
SYKES G.M.,CRIME AND SOCIETY. LAW STRATA STRUCT ACT/RES ROUTINE ANOMIE WEALTH...POLICY SOC/INTEG 20. PAGE 151 H3021
CRIMLGY CRIME CULTURE INGP/REL

S56
BLAU P.M.,"SOCIAL MOBILITY AND INTERPERSONAL RELATIONS" (BMR)" UNIV CULTURE STRUCT WORKER ANOMIE ...SOC SOC/INTEG 19/20. PAGE 18 H0355
INGP/REL PERS/REL ORD/FREE STRATA

B59
LEIGHTON A.H.,MY NAME IS LEGION; FOUNDATIONS FOR A THEORY OF MAN IN RELATION TO CULTURE (VOL. I). CULTURE STRANGE ANOMIE...SOC CONCPT METH/CNCPT CHARTS BIBLIOG METH 20 NOVA/SCOT. PAGE 93 H1867
HEALTH PSY SOCIETY HABITAT

B59
VORSPAN A.,JUSTICE AND JUDAISM. FAM DIPLOM ECO/TAC EDU/PROP CRIME RACE/REL MARRIAGE ANOMIE ATTIT ORD/FREE...POLICY 20 UN. PAGE 164 H3279
SECT CULTURE ACT/RES GP/REL

S59
LYNN D.B.,"THE EFFECTS OF FATHER-ABSENCE ON NORWEGIAN BOYS AND GIRLS." NORWAY CULTURE PERS/REL ADJUST DISPL LOVE...PSY CORREL STAT INT CON/ANAL CHARTS SOC/INTEG 20. PAGE 99 H1983
SOC FAM AGE/C ANOMIE

B62
TURNBULL C.M.,THE LONELY AFRICAN. AFR MUNIC SECT ANOMIE ALL/VALS...DECISION 20. PAGE 157 H3139
CULTURE ISOLAT KIN TRADIT

B63
LEIGHTON D.C.,THE CHARACTER OF DANGER (VOL. III). SOCIETY STRUCT STRANGE ANOMIE...SOC STAT CHARTS GP/COMP SOC/EXP SOC/INTEG 20 NOVA/SCOT. PAGE 94 H1868
HEALTH PSY CULTURE

B64
HILL C.R.,BANTUSTANS: THE FRAGMENTATION OF SOUTH AFRICA. AFR SOUTH/AFR ELITES SOCIETY KIN CONTROL DISCRIM ANOMIE ATTIT...POLICY CHARTS GOV/COMP 20 NEGRO BANTUSTANS TRANSKEI NATAL. PAGE 71 H1416
RACE/REL CULTURE LOC/G ORD/FREE

B64
JOSEPHSON E.,MAN ALONE: ALIENATION IN MODERN SOCIETY. WOR+45 ECO/DEV WORKER WAR LEISURE RACE/REL ANOMIE ATTIT PERCEPT PERSON ALL/VALS...ANTHOL 20. PAGE 82 H1636
STRANGE CULTURE SOCIETY ADJUST

B65
COSTA H DE L.A.,THE BACKGROUND OF NATIONALISM AND OTHER ESSAYS. ASIA PHILIPPINE ATTIT PERCEPT CATHISM ...ANTHOL 20. PAGE 34 H0674
NAT/LISM CULTURE ANOMIE NAT/G

B66
WEINSTEIN B.,GABON: NATION-BUILDING ON THE OGOOUE. AFR GABON WOR+45 CULTURE SOCIETY PLAN DIPLOM COLONIAL INGP/REL ANOMIE HABITAT SUPEGO 20. PAGE 166 H3329
ECO/UNDEV GP/REL LEAD NAT/G

B67
ALBA V.,THE MEXICANS; THE MAKING OF A NATION. SOCIETY ECO/UNDEV AGRI INDUS SECT STRANGE ATTIT ...GEOG 20 MEXIC/AMER. PAGE 4 H0091
CONSTN NAT/G CULTURE ANOMIE

B67
KORNBERG A.,CANADIAN LEGISLATIVE BEHAVIOR: A STUDY OF THE 25TH PARLIAMENT. CANADA NAT/G POL/PAR PARL/PROC CHOOSE INGP/REL ADJUST ANOMIE RIGID/FLEX ...SOC STAND/INT CHARTS SOC/EXP 20 PARLIAMENT. PAGE 88 H1756
ATTIT LEGIS ROLE

B67
POLSKY N.,HUSTLERS, BEATS, AND OTHERS. FACE/GP PRESS CRIME ADJUST ANOMIE DRIVE WEALTH...PSY SOC 20. PAGE 127 H2540
CULTURE CRIMLGY NEW/IDEA STRUCT

L67
AUSTIN D.A.,"POLITICAL CONFLICT IN AFRICA." CONSTN NAT/G CREATE ADMIN COLONIAL ORD/FREE MARXISM POPULISM SOCISM...NAT/COMP ANTHOL 20. PAGE 9 H0180
ANOMIE AFR POL/PAR

L67
EGBERT D.D.,"THE IDEA OF 'AVANT-GARDE' IN ART AND POLITICS." USSR CULTURE INTELL POL/PAR CREATE EDU/PROP CONTROL REV ANOMIE DRIVE ROLE...IDEA/COMP 20. PAGE 45 H0895
ART/METH COM ATTIT

S67
BULLOUGH B.,"ALIENATION IN THE GHETTO." CULTURE NEIGH GP/REL INGP/REL ATTIT...PSY SOC SAMP. PAGE 23 H0471
DISCRIM ANOMIE ADJUST

S67
SOARES G.,"SOCIO-ECONOMIC VARIABLES AND VOTING FOR THE RADICAL LEFT: CHILE 1952." CHILE INDUS NAT/G WORKER ADJUST STRANGE ANOMIE WEALTH...METH/CNCPT CORREL 20. PAGE 146 H2925
STRATA POL/PAR CHOOSE STAT

ANSPRENGER F. H0141,H0142

ANTHEM T. H0143

ANTHOL....ANTHOLOGY, SYMPOSIUM, PANEL OF WRITERS

B13
DIE REKLAME IHRE KUNST UND WISSENSCHAFT. GERMANY POLAND SWITZERLND USA+45 TEC/DEV CAP/ISM DEMAND ...ART/METH EXHIBIT METH/COMP ANTHOL 20. PAGE 135 H2707
EDU/PROP MARKET NAT/COMP ATTIT

B18
EYBERS G.W.,SELECT CONSTITUTIONAL DOCUMENTS ILLUSTRATING SOUTH AFRICAN HISTORY 1795-1910.
CONSTN LAW

SOUTH/AFR LOC/G LEGIS CT/SYS...JURID ANTHOL 18/20 NATAL CAPE/HOPE ORANGE/STA. PAGE 48 H0955 NAT/G COLONIAL N19

BUSINESS ECONOMISTS' GROUP,INCOME POLICIES (PAMPHLET). UK INDUS LABOR TOP/EX PAY COST PRODUC ...ECOMETRIC GOV/COMP SIMUL ANTHOL 20. PAGE 25 H0497 INCOME WORKER WEALTH POLICY B21

BALFOUR A.J.,ESSAYS SPECULATIVE AND POLITICAL. SEA CULTURE CREATE WAR NAT/LISM PEACE LOVE...ART/METH INT/LAW CONCPT ANTHOL 20 JEWS. PAGE 10 H0204 PHIL/SCI SOCIETY DIPLOM B28

LODGE H.C.,THE HISTORY OF NATIONS (25 VOLS.). UNIV LEAD...ANTHOL BIBLIOG INDEX. PAGE 98 H1951 DIPLOM SOCIETY NAT/G B31

KROEBER A.L.,SOURCE BOOK IN ANTHROPOLOGY. PREHIST SECT RACE/REL...LING GP/COMP ANTHOL. PAGE 89 H1770 SOC HEREDITY CULTURE ALL/VALS B33

PUBLIC OPINION AND WORLD POLITICS. UNIV LAW CULTURE NAT/G PRESS REV GP/REL...MAJORIT METH/COMP ANTHOL 20. PAGE 171 H3420 DIPLOM EDU/PROP ATTIT MAJORITY B37

THOMPSON J.W.,SECRET DIPLOMACY: A RECORD OF ESPIONAGE AND DOUBLE-DEALING: 1500-1815. CHRIST-17C MOD/EUR NAT/G WRITING RISK MORAL...ANTHOL BIBLIOG 16/19 ESPIONAGE. PAGE 154 H3084 DIPLOM CRIME B38

DUNHAM W.H. JR.,COMPLAINT AND REFORM IN ENGLAND 1436-1714. UK LAW ACADEM NAT/G POL/PAR SCHOOL PRESS COLONIAL PARL/PROC MORAL...SOC/WK ANTHOL 15/18 HAKLUYT/R COWPER/W. PAGE 43 H0865 ATTIT SOCIETY SECT B39

MARQUAND H.A.,ORGANIZED LABOUR IN FOUR CONTINENTS. EUR+WWI USA-45 INDUS NAT/G PAY GP/REL TOTALISM ATTIT WEALTH ALL/IDEOS...TREND NAT/COMP 20 ILO AFL/CIO EUROPE CHINJAP MEXIC/AMER. PAGE 103 H2055 LABOR WORKER CONCPT ANTHOL B39

OAKESHOTT M.,THE SOCIAL AND POLITICAL DOCTRINES OF CONTEMPORARY EUROPE. EUR+WWI RATIONAL CATHISM FASCISM MARXISM POPULISM...POLICY ANTHOL 20 NAZI. PAGE 120 H2392 IDEA/COMP GOV/COMP ALL/IDEOS NAT/G B44

WOLFE D.M.,LEVELLER MANIFESTOES OF THE PURITAN REVOLUTION. UK CONSTN NAT/G SECT...CONCPT ANTHOL 17 LEVELLERS DECLAR/IND PURITAN LOCKE/JOHN. PAGE 170 H3400 POL/PAR REV ORD/FREE ATTIT B48

GRIFFITH E.S.,RESEARCH IN POLITICAL SCIENCE: THE WORK OF PANELS OF RESEARCH COMMITTEE, APSA. WOR+45 WOR-45 COM/IND R+D FORCES ACT/RES WAR...GOV/COMP ANTHOL 20. PAGE 61 H1220 BIBLIOG PHIL/SCI DIPLOM JURID B49

MCLEAN J.M.,THE PUBLIC SERVICE AND UNIVERSITY EDUCATION. UK USA-45 DELIB/GP EX/STRUC TOP/EX ADMIN ...GOV/COMP METH/COMP NAT/COMP ANTHOL 20. PAGE 107 H2142 ACADEM NAT/G EXEC EDU/PROP B50

CANTRIL H.,TENSIONS THAT CAUSE WAR. UNIV CULTURE R+D CREATE EDU/PROP DRIVE PERSON KNOWL ORD/FREE ...HUM PSY SOC OBS CENSUS TREND CON/ANAL SOC/EXP SIMUL GEN/METH ANTHOL COLD/WAR TOT/POP. PAGE 26 H0523 SOCIETY PHIL/SCI PEACE B50

CARR E.H.,STUDIES IN REVOLUTION. CREATE WAR PERSON ALL/IDEOS MARXISM SOCISM...PHIL/SCI METH/COMP ANTHOL 18/20 SAINTSIMON MARX/KARL PROUDHON/P LASSALLE/F PLEKHNV/GV. PAGE 27 H0537 REV IDEA/COMP COERCE BIOG B50

SMITH E.W.,AFRICAN IDEAS OF GOD. ATTIT...CONCPT MYTH IDEA/COMP ANTHOL BIBLIOG. PAGE 145 H2908 SOC AFR CULTURE SECT B50

US DEPARTMENT OF STATE,DOCUMENTS ON GERMAN FOREIGN POLICY, 1918-1945 (13 VOLS.). EUR+WWI GERMANY NAT/G PLAN DIPLOM DOMIN EDU/PROP CONTROL NAT/LISM ...ANTHOL 20. PAGE 159 H3186 BIBLIOG/A WAR POLICY FASCIST B50

WHITE R.J.,THE CONSERVATIVE TRADITION. UK POL/PAR SUPEGO PWR RESPECT...POLICY ANTHOL 19. PAGE 167 H3350 CONSERVE CONCPT NAT/G ORD/FREE B51

HUXLEY J.,FREEDOM AND CULTURE. UNIV LAW SOCIETY R+D ACADEM SCHOOL CREATE SANCTION ATTIT KNOWL...HUM ANTHOL 20. PAGE 76 H1512 CULTURE ORD/FREE PHIL/SCI IDEA/COMP B51

MORLEY C.,GUIDE TO RESEARCH IN RUSSIAN HISTORY. USSR MARXISM...BIOG HIST/WRIT ANTHOL DICTIONARY. PAGE 113 H2259 BIBLIOG/A R+D NAT/G COM B51

PARSONS T.,TOWARD A GENERAL THEORY OF ACTION. CULTURE PERSON...PSY SIMUL ANTHOL SOC/INTEG 20. PAGE 124 H2472 SOC PHIL/SCI DRIVE ACT/RES B52

BAILEY S.D.,THE BRITISH PARTY SYSTEM. UK LEGIS ...POLICY GP/COMP ANTHOL 11/20. PAGE 10 H0200 POL/PAR LOC/G NAT/G DELIB/GP B52

TAX S.,HERITAGE OF CONQUEST. L/A+17C ECO/UNDEV LOC/G WEALTH...POLICY ANTHOL WORSHIP 20 MEXIC/AMER CENTRAL/AM. PAGE 153 H3052 PHIL/SCI CULTURE SOCIETY B53

BROWN D.M.,THE WHITE UMBRELLA: INDIAN POLITICAL THOUGHT FROM MANU TO GANDHI. INDIA LAW NAT/G SECT WRITING NAT/LISM...ANTHOL BIBLIOG 20 HINDU GANDHI/M MANU. PAGE 22 H0442 CONCPT DOMIN CONSERVE B53

DAVIDSON B.,THE NEW WEST AFRICA: PROBLEMS OF INDEPENDENCE. UK AGRI TEC/DEV DIPLOM GP/REL RACE/REL SOVEREIGN...ANTHOL 20 AFRICA/W. PAGE 37 H0744 AFR COLONIAL ECO/UNDEV NAT/G B54

FORDE C.D.,AFRICAN WORLDS. AFR CULTURE ROUTINE GP/REL PERS/REL ATTIT DRIVE ALL/VALS...OBS ANTHOL WORSHIP 20. PAGE 52 H1036 SOCIETY KIN SOC B54

FRIEDMAN W.,THE PUBLIC CORPORATION: A COMPARATIVE SYMPOSIUM (UNIVERSITY OF TORONTO SCHOOL OF LAW COMPARATIVE LAW SERIES, VOL. I). SWEDEN USA+45 INDUS INT/ORG NAT/G REGION CENTRAL FEDERAL...POLICY JURID IDEA/COMP NAT/COMP ANTHOL 20 COMMONWLTH MONOPOLY EUROPE. PAGE 53 H1065 LAW SOCISM LG/CO OWN B54

GERMANY FOREIGN MINISTRY,DOCUMENTS ON GERMAN FOREIGN POLICY 1918-1945, SERIES C (1933-1937) VOLS. I-V. GERMANY MOD/EUR FORCES PLAN ECO/TAC ...FASCIST CHARTS ANTHOL 20. PAGE 56 H1115 NAT/G DIPLOM POLICY B55

BAILEY S.K.,RESEARCH FRONTIERS IN POLITICS AND GOVERNMENT. CONSTN LEGIS ADMIN REV CHOOSE...CONCPT IDEA/COMP GAME ANTHOL 20. PAGE 10 H0201 R+D METH NAT/G B55

CHARMATZ J.P.,COMPARATIVE STUDIES IN COMMUNITY PROPERTY LAW. FRANCE USA+45...JURID GOV/COMP ANTHOL 20. PAGE 29 H0583 MARRIAGE LAW OWN MUNIC B55

KHADDURI M.,LAW IN THE MIDDLE EAST. LAW CONSTN ACADEM FAM EDU/PROP CT/SYS SANCTION CRIME...INT/LAW GOV/COMP ANTHOL 6/20 MID/EAST. PAGE 85 H1703 ADJUD JURID ISLAM B55

MID-EUROPEAN LAW PROJECT,CHURCH AND STATE BEHIND THE IRON CURTAIN. COM CZECHOSLVK HUNGARY POLAND USSR CULTURE SECT EDU/PROP GOV/REL CATHISM...CHARTS ANTHOL BIBLIOG WORSHIP 20 CHURCH/STA. PAGE 110 H2202 LAW MARXISM POLICY B56

INTERNATIONAL AFRICAN INST,SOCIAL IMPLICATIONS OF INDUSTRIALIZATION AND URBANIZATION IN AFRICA SOUTH OF THE SAHARA. SOUTH/AFR INDUS LABOR MUNIC WORKER TEC/DEV...SOC OBS TREND ANTHOL 20. PAGE 77 H1549 AFR ECO/UNDEV ADJUST CULTURE B56

KALLEN H.M.,CULTURAL PLURALISM AND THE AMERICAN IDEA. RACE/REL ADJUST PERSON ORD/FREE LAISSEZ ...PLURIST GEN/LAWS ANTHOL. PAGE 83 H1652 PLURISM CULTURE GP/REL SECT B56

SHAPIRO H.L.,MAN, CULTURE, AND SOCIETY. STRUCT FAM SECT GP/REL INGP/REL...ART/METH GEOG PSY LING ANTHOL BIBLIOG. PAGE 142 H2842 CULTURE PERSON SOC C56

NEUMANN S.,"MODERN POLITICAL PARTIES: APPROACHES TO COMPARATIVE POLITIC. FRANCE UK EX/STRUC DOMIN ADMIN LEAD REPRESENT TOTALISM ATTIT...POLICY TREND METH/COMP ANTHOL BIBLIOG/A 20 CMN/WLTH. PAGE 117 H2338 POL/PAR GOV/COMP ELITES MAJORIT B57

BULLOCK A.,THE LIBERAL TRADITION FROM FOX TO KEYNES. UK CULTURE INTELL CREATE WRITING COLONIAL PERS/REL ATTIT ORD/FREE...POLICY OLD/LIB TRADIT CONCPT 18/20 CHURCHLL/W MILL/JS KEYNES/JM ASQUITH/HH. PAGE 23 H0469 ANTHOL DEBATE LAISSEZ B58

BRIERLY J.L.,THE BASIS OF OBLIGATION IN INTERNATIONAL LAW, AND OTHER PAPERS. WOR+45 WOR-45 LEGIS...JURID CONCPT NAT/COMP ANTHOL 20. PAGE 21 H0415 INT/LAW DIPLOM ADJUD SOVEREIGN B58

GURVITCH G.,TRAITE DE SOCIOLOGIE (2 VOLS.). FRANCE CULTURE INDUS GP/REL INGP/REL...PSY BIBLIOG 20. PAGE 63 H1256 ANTHOL SOC METH/COMP METH/CNCPT

B58
HENLE P.,LANGUAGE, THOUGHT AND CULTURE. CULTURE GP/REL PERCEPT...PSY TREND ANTHOL 20. PAGE 70 H1397
LING RATIONAL CONCPT SOC

B58
JACOBSSON P.,SOME MONETARY PROBLEMS, INTERNATIONAL AND NATIONAL. WOR+45 WOR-45 ECO/DEV FORCES WORKER PROB/SOLV DIPLOM INT/TRADE...ANTHOL 20. PAGE 79 H1580
FINAN PLAN ECO/TAC NAT/COMP

B58
LOWER A.R.M.,EVOLVING CANADIAN FEDERALISM. CANADA WEST/IND CONSTN PROB/SOLV COLONIAL REGION NAT/LISM ...ANTHOL 20. PAGE 99 H1976
FEDERAL NAT/G DIPLOM RACE/REL

B58
PALMER E.E.,"POLITICAL MAN" IN E. PALMER, PROBLEMS IN DEMOCRATIC CITIZENSHIP. LOC/G NAT/G LEGIS PRESS CHOOSE REPRESENT GP/REL...DECISION SOC IDEA/COMP ANTHOL 20. PAGE 123 H2449
PARTIC POL/PAR EDU/PROP MAJORIT

B58
PALMER E.E.,THE COMMUNIST CHALLENGE. COM USA+45 USA-45 ECO/DEV ECO/UNDEV NEUTRAL ORD/FREE POPULISM ...CONCPT NAT/COMP ANTHOL 19/20 LENIN/VI STALIN/J MAO MARX/KARL COM/PARTY. PAGE 123 H2450
MARXISM DIPLOM IDEA/COMP POLICY

B58
STRAUSZ-HUPE R.,THE IDEA OF COLONIALISM. WOR+45 WOR-45 BAL/PWR GOV/REL...POLICY CLASSIF TIME/SEQ GOV/COMP ANTHOL 20 UN. PAGE 150 H2996
IDEA/COMP COLONIAL CONTROL CONCPT

B58
WOODS H.D.,PATTERNS OF INDUSTRIAL DISPUTE SETTLEMENT IN FIVE CANADIAN INDUSTRIES. CANADA USA+45 CONSULT ADJUD GP/REL...JURID GOV/COMP METH/COMP ANTHOL 20. PAGE 170 H3408
BARGAIN INDUS LABOR NAT/G

B59
BRIGGS A.,CHARTIST STUDIES. UK LAW NAT/G WORKER EDU/PROP COERCE SUFF GP/REL ATTIT...ANTHOL 19. PAGE 21 H0416
INDUS STRATA LABOR POLICY

B59
GINSBURG M.,LAW AND OPINION IN ENGLAND. UK CULTURE KIN LABOR LEGIS EDU/PROP ADMIN CT/SYS CRIME OWN HEALTH...ANTHOL 20 ENGLSH/LAW. PAGE 56 H1132
JURID POLICY ECO/TAC

B59
HENDEL S.,THE SOVIET CRUCIBLE. USSR LEAD COERCE NAT/LISM UTOPIA PWR...POLICY CONCPT ANTHOL 20 STALIN/J LENIN/VI MARX/KARL BOLSHEVIK. PAGE 70 H1393
COM MARXISM REV TOTALISM

B59
JACOBS N.,CULTURE FOR THE MILLIONS? INTELL SOCIETY NAT/G...POLICY SOC OBS ANTHOL 20. PAGE 79 H1579
CULTURE COM/IND PERF/ART CONCPT

B59
MEYER A.J.,MIDDLE EASTERN CAPITALISM: NINE ESSAYS. ISLAM CULTURE ECO/UNDEV INDUS MARKET NAT/G PLAN ATTIT RIGID/FLEX...STAT OBS TREND GEN/LAWS. PAGE 109 H2188
TEC/DEV ECO/TAC ANTHOL

B60
JUNZ A.J.,PRESENT TRENDS IN AMERICAN NATIONAL GOVERNMENT. LEGIS DIPLOM ADMIN CT/SYS ORD/FREE ...CONCPT ANTHOL 20 CONGRESS PRESIDENT SUPREME/CT. PAGE 3 H0052
POL/PAR CHOOSE CONSTN NAT/G

B60
MANIS J.G.,MAN AND SOCIETY. STRATA LEAD INGP/REL PERS/REL ATTIT PWR...PSY ANTHOL T SOC/INTEG MARX/KARL MILL/JS FREUD/S CHURCHLL/W SPENCER/H RUSSELL/B. PAGE 102 H2036
SOC SOCIETY STRUCT CULTURE

B60
OTTENBERG S.,CULTURES AND SOCIETIES OF AFRICA. AFR KIN TEC/DEV GP/REL MARRIAGE ATTIT HABITAT HEREDITY ...ANTHOL BIBLIOG T WORSHIP 20. PAGE 122 H2433
SOCIETY INGP/REL STRUCT CULTURE

B60
SAKAI R.K.,STUDIES ON ASIA, 1960. ASIA CHINA/COM S/ASIA COM/IND ECO/TAC...ANTHOL 17/20 MALAYA. PAGE 137 H2733
ECO/UNDEV SOC

B60
SCANLON D.G.,INTERNATIONAL EDUCATION: A DOCUMENTARY HISTORY. ADMIN CONTROL ATTIT PERCEPT...BIOG ANTHOL METH 20. PAGE 138 H2765
EDU/PROP INT/ORG NAT/COMP DIPLOM

B60
THEOBOLD R.,THE NEW NATIONS OF WEST AFRICA. GHANA NIGERIA CULTURE INT/ORG ECO/TAC FOR/AID COLONIAL RACE/REL POPULISM...ANTHOL BIBLIOG 20 UN. PAGE 153 H3068
AFR SOVEREIGN ECO/UNDEV DIPLOM

B61
DUFFY J.,AFRICA SPEAKS. GHANA TOGO CULTURE ECO/UNDEV PROB/SOLV COLONIAL NEUTRAL DISCRIM NAT/LISM SOVEREIGN ALL/IDEOS...CONCPT ANTHOL SOC/INTEG 20 NEGRO THIRD/WRLD. PAGE 43 H0857
AFR NAT/G FUT STRUCT

B61
NARASIMHAN V.K.,THE PRESS, THE PUBLIC AND THE ADMINISTRATION (PAMPHLET). INDIA COM/IND CONTROL REPRESENT GOV/REL EFFICIENCY...ANTHOL 20. PAGE 116 H2312
NAT/G ADMIN PRESS NEW/LIB

B61
PANIKKAR K.M.,THE VOICE OF FREEDOM: SELECTED SPEECHES OF PANDIT MOTILAL NEHRU. INDIA UK CONSTN FINAN FORCES LEGIS DIPLOM TAX COLONIAL...POLICY MAJORIT ANTHOL 20 NEHRU/PM. PAGE 123 H2460
NAT/LISM ORD/FREE CHIEF NAT/G

B61
SAKAI R.K.,STUDIES ON ASIA, 1961. ASIA BURMA INDIA S/ASIA FINAN ECO/TAC NAT/LISM SOCISM...POLICY ANTHOL 19/20 CHINJAP. PAGE 137 H2734
ECO/UNDEV SECT

B61
SOUTHALL A.,SOCIAL CHANGE IN MODERN AFRICA. CULTURE STRATA ECO/UNDEV AGRI FAM KIN MUNIC GP/REL INGP/REL MARRIAGE...GEOG ANTHOL 20. PAGE 147 H2940
AFR TREND SOCIETY SOC

B61
STAHL W.,EDUCATION FOR DEMOCRACY IN WEST GERMANY: ACHIEVEMENT SHORTCOMINGS - PROSPECTS. GERMANY/W SOCIETY NAT/G FORCES PLAN PROB/SOLV PRESS ALL/VALS ...POLICY MAJORIT CONCPT ANTHOL 20. PAGE 148 H2967
EDU/PROP POPULISM AGE/Y ADJUST

B62
AMERICAN SOCIETY AFR CULTURE,PAN-AFRICANISM RECONSIDERED. AFR SOCIETY STRUCT SCHOOL CAP/ISM EDU/PROP...ART/METH NEW/IDEA PREDICT ANTHOL 20 PANAF/FREE NEGRO. PAGE 6 H0123
DIPLOM FEDERAL NAT/LISM CULTURE

B62
BROWN S.D.,STUDIES ON ASIA, 1962. ASIA BURMA INDIA ISLAM ISRAEL S/ASIA ECO/UNDEV POL/PAR SECT ECO/TAC ...ANTHOL 20 CHINJAP. PAGE 22 H0450
PWR PARL/PROC

B62
BRUMBERG A.,RUSSIA UNDER KHRUSHCHEV. FUT USSR SOCIETY ECO/DEV AGRI PERF/ART WORKER PWR...SOC ANTHOL 20 KHRUSH/N. PAGE 22 H0453
COM MARXISM NAT/G CHIEF

B62
CARY J.,THE CASE FOR AFRICAN FREEDOM AND OTHER WRITINGS ON AFRICA. AFR UK INDUS LOC/G NAT/G SECT INT/TRADE EDU/PROP GOV/REL RACE/REL ORD/FREE ...CONCPT ANTHOL 19/20. PAGE 27 H0552
NAT/LISM COLONIAL TREND ECO/UNDEV

B62
COUNCIL ON WORLD TENSIONS,RESTLESS NATIONS. WOR+45 STRUCT INT/ORG NAT/G PLAN ECO/TAC...NAT/COMP ANTHOL 20. PAGE 34 H0678
ECO/UNDEV POLICY DIPLOM TASK

B62
HAIM S.G.,ARAB NATIONALISM. ISLAM CONSTN GP/REL ...ANTHOL BIBLIOG JEWS 20 MID/EAST ARABS. PAGE 64 H1279
NAT/LISM REV SECT DIPLOM

B62
INAYATULLAH,BUREAUCRACY AND DEVELOPMENT IN PAKISTAN. PAKISTAN ECO/UNDEV EDU/PROP CONFER ...ANTHOL DICTIONARY 20 BUREAUCRCY. PAGE 76 H1526
EX/STRUC ADMIN NAT/G LOC/G

B62
JOHNSON J.J.,THE ROLE OF THE MILITARY IN UNDERDEVELOPED COUNTRIES. AFR BURMA INDONESIA ISLAM ISRAEL L/A+17C S/ASIA THAILAND CULTURE ECO/UNDEV KIN PROVS CONSULT ACT/RES COERCE REV DRIVE RIGID/FLEX ORD/FREE...RECORD ANTHOL 20. PAGE 81 H1622
FORCES CONCPT

B62
LAQUEUR W.,THE FUTURE OF COMMUNIST SOCIETY. CHINA/COM USSR LAW ECO/DEV NAT/G POL/PAR PLAN PROB/SOLV DIPLOM LEAD...POLICY CONCPT IDEA/COMP ANTHOL 20. PAGE 91 H1820
MARXISM COM FUT SOCIETY

B62
LAQUEUR W.,POLYCENTRISM. CHINA/COM COM USSR WOR+45 INT/ORG NAT/G ECO/TAC DOMIN LEAD ATTIT PWR SOVEREIGN...ANTHOL 20. PAGE 91 H1821
MARXISM DIPLOM BAL/PWR POLICY

B62
PHELPS E.S.,THE GOAL OF ECONOMIC GROWTH: SOURCES, COSTS, BENEFITS. USA+45 USSR FINAN TAX CONTROL DEMAND WEALTH...POLICY NAT/COMP ANTHOL BIBLIOG 20. PAGE 125 H2499
ECO/TAC ECO/DEV NAT/G FUT

B62
TILMAN R.O.,THE NIGERIAN POLITICAL SXENE. NIGERIA DIPLOM COLONIAL PARTIC...POLICY SOC OBS PREDICT ANTHOL 20. PAGE 155 H3096
NAT/G AFR ECO/UNDEV FEDERAL

L62
COHEN R.,"POWER IN COMPLEX SOCIETIES IN AFRICA." AFR KIN MUNIC POL/PAR DELIB/GP DOMIN ROUTINE ATTIT ALL/VALS...SOC STAT OBS INT QU CHARTS ANTHOL 20. PAGE 31 H0617
CULTURE STRATA ELITES

B63
BERGSON A.,ECONOMIC TRENDS IN THE SOVIET UNION. USSR ECO/UNDEV AGRI NAT/G FORCES PLAN TEC/DEV INT/TRADE BAL/PAY...POLICY ANTHOL 20. PAGE 15 H0302
ECO/DEV NAT/COMP INDUS LABOR

B63
COLUMBIA U SCHOOL OF LAW,PUBLIC INTERNATIONAL DEVELOPMENT FINANCING IN SENEGAL. SENEGAL FINAN DELIB/GP GIVE EFFICIENCY...CHARTS GOV/COMP ANTHOL
FOR/AID PLAN RECEIVE

20. PAGE 32 H0636 ECO/UNDEV

B63
CONFERENCE ABORIGINAL STUDIES,AUSTRALIAN ABORIGINAL STUDIES. ECO/UNDEV INT/TRADE COLONIAL ADJUST HABITAT HEREDITY...GEOG PSY LING SOC/EXP ANTHOL WORSHIP 20 AUSTRAL ABORIGINES. PAGE 32 H0638 SOC SOCIETY CULTURE STRUCT

B63
DALAND R.T.,PERSPECTIVES OF BRAZILIAN PUBLIC ADMINISTRATION (VOL. I). BRAZIL LAW ECO/UNDEV SCHOOL CHIEF TEC/DEV CONFER CONTROL GP/REL ATTIT ROLE PWR...ANTHOL 20. PAGE 37 H0735 ADMIN NAT/G PLAN GOV/REL

B63
DE VRIES E.,SOCIAL ASPECTS OF ECONOMIC DEVELOPMENT IN LATIN AMERICA. CULTURE SOCIETY STRATA FINAN INDUS INT/ORG DELIB/GP ACT/RES ECO/TAC EDU/PROP ADMIN ATTIT SUPEGO HEALTH KNOWL ORD/FREE...SOC STAT TREND ANTHOL TOT/POP VAL/FREE. PAGE 39 H0777 L/A+17C ECO/UNDEV

B63
ECKSTEIN H.,COMPARATIVE POLITICS. POL/PAR LEGIS CT/SYS CHOOSE TOTALISM PWR POPULISM...METH/COMP GEN/METH ANTHOL BIBLIOG 20. PAGE 44 H0886 NAT/COMP CONSTN REPRESENT NAT/G

B63
FLECHTHEIM O.K.,DOKUMENTE ZUR PARTEIPOLITISCHEN ENTWICKLUNG IN DEUTSCHLAND SEIT 1945 (2 VOLS.). EUR+WWI GERMANY/W...CONCPT ANTHOL 20. PAGE 51 H1023 POL/PAR ELITES NAT/G TIME/SEQ

B63
INDIAN INSTITUTE PUBLIC ADMIN,CASES IN INDIAN ADMINISTRATION. INDIA AGRI NAT/G PROB/SOLV TEC/DEV ECO/TAC ADMIN...ANTHOL METH 20. PAGE 77 H1532 DECISION PLAN MGT ECO/UNDEV

B63
JELAVICH C.,THE BALKANS IN TRANSITION: ESSAYS ON THE DEVELOPMENT OF BALKAN LIFE AND POLITICS SINCE THE EIGHTEENTH CENTURY. COM GREECE TURKEY ECO/UNDEV NAT/G SECT ATTIT...GEOG SOC CONCPT TIME/SEQ ANTHOL 18/20. PAGE 80 H1596 CULTURE RIGID/FLEX

B63
LERNER R.,MEDIEVAL POLITICAL PHILOSOPHY. ISLAM MORAL PWR CATHISM...CATH CONCPT OBS IDEA/COMP ANTHOL 9/15 JEWS CHRISTIAN BACON/R AQUINAS/T. PAGE 95 H1890 KNOWL PHIL/SCI

B63
MENZEL J.M.,THE CHINESE CIVIL SERVICE: CAREER OPEN TO TALENT? ASIA ROUTINE INGP/REL DISCRIM ATTIT ROLE KNOWL ANTHOL. PAGE 109 H2177 ADMIN NAT/G DECISION ELITES

B63
PADELFORD N.J.,AFRICA AND WORLD ORDER. AFR COLONIAL SOVEREIGN...ANTHOL BIBLIOG 20 UN UNIFICA COMMONWLTH. PAGE 122 H2439 DIPLOM NAT/G ORD/FREE

B63
SAKAI R.K.,STUDIES ON ASIA, 1963. ASIA INDIA ISRAEL S/ASIA USA+45 PERF/ART POL/PAR SECT REGION NAT/LISM ...SOC LING TREND ANTHOL 19/20 CHINJAP. PAGE 137 H2735 PWR CULTURE

B63
SHANKS M.,THE LESSONS OF PUBLIC ENTERPRISE. UK LEGIS WORKER ECO/TAC ADMIN PARL/PROC GOV/REL ATTIT ...POLICY MGT METH/COMP NAT/COMP ANTHOL 20 PARLIAMENT. PAGE 142 H2840 SOCISM OWN NAT/G INDUS

B63
STRAUSS L.,HISTORY OF POLITICAL PHILOSOPHY. LAW SOCIETY CAP/ISM MARXISM 19 AQUINAS/T BACON/F HEGEL/GWF MILL/JS NIETZSCH/F. PAGE 150 H2995 IDEA/COMP PHIL/SCI ANTHOL

B63
SWEARER H.R.,CONTEMPORARY COMMUNISM: THEORY AND PRACTICE. COM USSR SOCIETY ECO/DEV POL/PAR FORCES PLAN ADMIN LEAD NAT/LISM...POLICY ANTHOL 20 LENIN/VI COM/PARTY. PAGE 151 H3015 MARXISM CONCPT DIPLOM NAT/G

B63
WEINER M.,POLITICAL CHANGE IN SOUTH ASIA. CEYLON INDIA PAKISTAN S/ASIA CULTURE ELITES ECO/UNDEV EX/STRUC ADMIN CONTROL CHOOSE CONSERVE...GOV/COMP ANTHOL 20. PAGE 166 H3328 NAT/G CONSTN TEC/DEV

L63
NASH M.,"PSYCHO-CULTURAL FACTORS IN ASIAN ECONOMIC GROWTH." ASIA ISLAM S/ASIA CULTURE ECO/UNDEV DELIB/GP EDU/PROP COERCE ATTIT PERSON HEALTH KNOWL ORD/FREE...PSY SOC STAT TREND ANTHOL VAL/FREE 20. PAGE 116 H2313 SOCIETY ECO/TAC

L63
ROSE R.,"COMPARATIVE STUDIES IN POLITICAL FINANCE: A SYMPOSIUM." ASIA EUR+WWI S/ASIA LAW CULTURE DELIB/GP LEGIS ACT/RES ECO/TAC EDU/PROP CHOOSE ATTIT RIGID/FLEX SUPEGO PWR SKILL WEALTH...STAT ANTHOL VAL/FREE. PAGE 134 H2674 FINAN POL/PAR

B64
AFRO ASIAN SOLIDARITY AGAINST IMPERIALISM. AFR ISLAM S/ASIA ECO/UNDEV NAT/G POL/PAR TOP/EX PRESS ...INT ANTHOL 20 CHOU/ENLAI. PAGE 2 H0043 MARXISM DIPLOM EDU/PROP CHIEF

B64
COUNT E.W.,FACT AND THEORY IN SOCIAL SCIENCE. UNIV HABITAT...BIOG TREND CHARTS ANTHOL BIBLIOG. PAGE 34 H0679 STRUCT SOC CULTURE ADJUST

B64
GLUCKMANN M.,CLOSED SYSTEMS AND OPEN MINDS: THE LIMITS OF NAIVETY IN SOCIAL ANTHROPOLOGY. AFR INDIA MUNIC...IDEA/COMP METH/COMP ANTHOL. PAGE 57 H1149 CULTURE OBS SOC

B64
GRIFFITH W.E.,COMMUNISM IN EUROPE (2 VOLS.). CZECHOSLVK USSR WOR+45 WOR-45 YUGOSLAVIA INGP/REL MARXISM SOCISM...ANTHOL 20 EUROPE/E. PAGE 61 H1225 COM POL/PAR DIPLOM GOV/COMP

B64
HELMREICH E.,A FREE CHURCH IN A FREE STATE? FRANCE GERMANY ITALY SECT LEAD PWR CATHISM...POLICY ANTHOL WORSHIP 19/20 CHURCH/STA. PAGE 69 H1389 GP/REL NAT/G

B64
HERSKOVITS M.J.,ECONOMIC TRANSITION IN AFRICA. FUT INT/ORG NAT/G WORKER PROB/SOLV TEC/DEV INT/TRADE EQUILIB INCOME...ANTHOL 20. PAGE 70 H1408 AFR ECO/UNDEV PLAN ADMIN

B64
INTL CONF ON POPULATION,POPULATION DYNAMICS: INTERNATIONAL ACTION AND TRAINING PROGRAMS. INDIA KOREA L/A+17C TAIWAN USA+45 WOR+45 FAM PLAN CONFER ...NEW/IDEA ANTHOL 20 CHINJAP BIRTH/CON. PAGE 78 H1561 NAT/COMP CONTROL ATTIT EDU/PROP

B64
JOHNSON J.J.,CONTINUITY AND CHANGE IN LATIN AMERICA. L/A+17C INTELL FORCES WORKER CIVMIL/REL CHINJAP. PAGE 81 H1623 ANTHOL CULTURE STRATA GP/COMP

B64
JOSEPHSON E.,MAN ALONE: ALIENATION IN MODERN SOCIETY. WOR+45 ECO/DEV WORKER WAR LEISURE RACE/REL ANOMIE ATTIT PERCEPT PERSON ALL/VALS...ANTHOL 20. PAGE 82 H1636 STRANGE CULTURE SOCIETY ADJUST

B64
LEDERMAN W.R.,THE COURTS AND THE CANDIAN CONSTITUTION. CANADA PARL/PROC...POLICY JURID GOV/COMP ANTHOL 19/20 SUPREME/CT PARLIAMENT. PAGE 93 H1854 CONSTN CT/SYS LEGIS LAW

B64
ON CULTURE AND SOCIAL CHANGE. FAM NAT/G ACT/RES ECO/TAC RACE/REL...PSY TIME/SEQ TREND IDEA/COMP METH/COMP ANTHOL BIBLIOG 20. PAGE 120 H2406 CULTURE TEC/DEV STRUCT CREATE

B64
QUIGG P.W.,AFRICA: A FOREIGN AFFAIRS READER. AFR FRANCE PORTUGAL UK DIPLOM LEAD PARL/PROC MARXISM ...MAJORIT METH/CNCPT GOV/COMP IDEA/COMP ANTHOL 19/20. PAGE 129 H2575 COLONIAL SOVEREIGN NAT/LISM RACE/REL

B64
SANDEE J.,EUROPE'S FUTURE CONSUMPTION. EUR+WWI FUT EDU/PROP...IDEA/COMP NAT/COMP ANTHOL 20 EUROPE. PAGE 137 H2750 MARKET ECO/DEV PREDICT PRICE

B64
SEGAL R.,SANCTIONS AGAINST SOUTH AFRICA. AFR SOUTH/AFR NAT/G INT/TRADE RACE/REL PEACE PWR ...INT/LAW ANTHOL 20 UN. PAGE 141 H2821 SANCTION DISCRIM ECO/TAC POLICY

B64
ZOLLSCHAN G.K.,EXPLORATIONS IN SOCIAL CHANGE. SOCIETY STRATA STRUCT ECO/UNDEV EX/STRUC...PSY ANTHOL 20. PAGE 173 H3463 ORD/FREE SIMUL CONCPT CULTURE

C64
GOLDMAN M.I.,"COMPARATIVE ECONOMIC SYSTEMS: A READER." COM ECO/UNDEV NAT/G BUDGET CAP/ISM ADMIN TOTALISM MARXISM SOCISM...MGT ANTHOL BIBLIOG 19/20. PAGE 58 H1157 NAT/COMP CONTROL IDEA/COMP

B65
AIYAR S.P.,STUDIES IN INDIAN DEMOCRACY. INDIA STRATA ECO/UNDEV LABOR POL/PAR LEGIS DIPLOM LOBBY REGION CHOOSE ATTIT SOCISM...ANTHOL 20. PAGE 4 H0086 ORD/FREE REPRESENT ADMIN NAT/G

B65
BERNDT R.M.,ABORIGINAL MAN IN AUSTRALIA. LAW DOMIN ADMIN COLONIAL MARRIAGE HABITAT ORD/FREE...LING CHARTS ANTHOL BIBLIOG WORSHIP 20 AUSTRAL ABORIGINES MUSIC ELKIN/AP. PAGE 16 H0312 SOC CULTURE SOCIETY STRUCT

B65
BLITZ L.F.,THE POLITICS AND ADMINISTRATION OF NIGERIAN GOVERNMENT. NIGER CULTURE LOC/G LEGIS DIPLOM COLONIAL CT/SYS SOVEREIGN...GEOG SOC ANTHOL 20. PAGE 18 H0357 NAT/G GOV/REL POL/PAR

B65
CARTER G.M.,POLITICS IN EUROPE. EUR+WWI FRANCE GERMANY/W UK USSR LAW CONSTN POL/PAR VOL/ASSN PRESS LOBBY PWR...ANTHOL SOC/INTEG EEC. PAGE 27 H0548 GOV/COMP OP/RES ECO/DEV

B65
COSTA H DE L.A.,THE BACKGROUND OF NATIONALISM AND OTHER ESSAYS. ASIA PHILIPPINE ATTIT PERCEPT CATHISM ...ANTHOL 20. PAGE 34 H0674 NAT/LISM CULTURE ANOMIE NAT/G

B65
COWAN L.G.,EDUCATION AND NATION-BUILDING IN AFRICA. AFR CULTURE ECO/UNDEV POL/PAR ACT/RES LEAD SOVEREIGN...METH/COMP ANTHOL BIBLIOG 20. PAGE 34 H0684
EDU/PROP COLONIAL ACADEM NAT/LISM

B65
FILIPINIANA BOOK GUILD,THE COLONIZATION AND CONQUEST OF THE PHILIPPINES BY SPAIN. PHILIPPINE SPAIN ELITES AGRI KIN CHIEF DOMIN CONTROL ATTIT PWR ...ANTHOL WORSHIP 16. PAGE 50 H1000
COLONIAL COERCE CULTURE WAR

B65
FORM W.H.,INDUSTRIAL RELATIONS AND SOCIAL CHANGE IN LATIN AMERICA. L/A+17C AGRI LABOR NAT/G PLAN PROB/SOLV DIPLOM...MGT SOC ANTHOL BIBLIOG/A METH 20. PAGE 52 H1038
INDUS GP/REL NAT/COMP ECO/UNDEV

B65
GHAI D.P.,PORTRAIT OF A MINORITY: ASIANS IN EAST AFRICA. S/ASIA TANZANIA UGANDA COLONIAL...SOC OBS PREDICT ANTHOL 20. PAGE 56 H1119
RACE/REL GP/REL CULTURE AFR

B65
GIBBS S.L.,PEOPLES OF AFRICA. AFR INGP/REL HABITAT ...GEOG ANTHOL 20. PAGE 56 H1122
CULTURE AGRI FAM KIN

B65
HAMIL H.M.,DICTATORSHIP IN SPANISH AMERICA. NAT/G COERCE MORAL ORD/FREE...POLICY PSY SOC ANTHOL 18/20. PAGE 65 H1300
TOTALISM CHIEF L/A+17C FASCISM

B65
HARBISON F.,MANPOWER AND EDUCATION. AFR CHINA/COM IRAN L/A+17C S/ASIA TEC/DEV ADJUST OPTIMAL SKILL ...ANTHOL 20. PAGE 66 H1325
ECO/UNDEV EDU/PROP WORKER NAT/COMP

B65
HUNT G.L.,CALVINISM AND THE POLITICAL ORDER. NAT/G LEAD...POLICY IDEA/COMP ANTHOL WORSHIP 20. PAGE 75 H1498
SECT CONCPT

B65
HYMES D.,THE USE OF COMPUTERS IN ANTHROPOLOGY. CULTURE PROF/ORG CONSULT CREATE EFFICIENCY PERCEPT ...CLASSIF LING CON/ANAL COMPUT/IR METH/COMP ANTHOL 20. PAGE 76 H1517
METH COMPUTER TEC/DEV SOC

B65
KUPER H.,URBANIZATION AND MIGRATION IN WEST AFRICA. UPPER/VOLT CULTURE ECO/UNDEV WORKER REGION GOV/REL ...LING ANTHOL SOC/INTEG 20 AFRICA/W OSHOGBO MOSSI MIGRATION. PAGE 89 H1781
AFR HABITAT MUNIC GEOG

B65
LAWRENCE P.,GODS, GHOSTS, AND MEN IN MELANESIA: SOME RELIGIONS OF AUSTRALIAN NEW GUINEA AND THE NEW HEBRIDES. SOCIETY ECO/UNDEV FAM GP/REL INGP/REL HABITAT PERSON...GEOG SOC ANTHOL BIBLIOG WORSHIP 20 NEW/GUINEA. PAGE 92 H1847
MYTH S/ASIA SECT CULTURE

B65
THE STATE AND ECONOMIC ENTERPRISE IN JAPAN; ESSAYS IN THE POLITICAL ECONOMY OF GROWTH. AGRI INDUS DRIVE POPULISM...CHARTS NAT/COMP ANTHOL 19/20 CHINJAP. PAGE 98 H1949
ECO/UNDEV ECO/DEV CAP/ISM ECO/TAC

B65
MEYER F.S.,THE AFRICAN NETTLE. SOUTH/AFR NAT/LISM SOVEREIGN...ANTHOL 20 EUROPE. PAGE 110 H2191
AFR COLONIAL RACE/REL ECO/UNDEV

B65
MURDOCK G.P.,CULTURE AND SOCIETY. SOCIETY STRATA STRUCT SECT CREATE CONTROL ORD/FREE...GP/COMP ANTHOL 20. PAGE 115 H2294
CULTURE PHIL/SCI METH IDEA/COMP

B65
O'BRIEN W.V.,THE NEW NATIONS IN INTERNATIONAL LAW AND DIPLOMACY* THE YEAR BOOK OF WORLD POLITY* VOLUME III. USA+45 ECO/UNDEV INT/ORG FORCES DIPLOM COLONIAL NEUTRAL REV NAT/LISM ATTIT RESPECT. PAGE 119 H2385
INT/LAW CULTURE SOVEREIGN ANTHOL

B65
ONSLOW C.,ASIAN ECONOMIC DEVELOPMENT. BURMA CEYLON INDIA MALAYSIA PAKISTAN S/ASIA AGRI INDUS MARKET PROB/SOLV CAP/ISM FOR/AID INT/TRADE DEMAND WEALTH ...POLICY ANTHOL 20. PAGE 121 H2418
ECO/UNDEV ECO/TAC PLAN NAT/G

B65
PADELFORD N.,THE UNITED NATIONS IN THE BALANCE* ACCOMPLISHMENTS AND PROSPECTS. NAT/G VOL/ASSN DIPLOM ADMIN COLONIAL CT/SYS REGION WAR ORD/FREE ...ANTHOL UN. PAGE 122 H2437
INT/ORG CONTROL

B65
RIVLIN B.,THE CONTEMPORARY MIDDLE EAST* TRADITION AND INNOVATION. CULTURE SOCIETY ECO/UNDEV NAT/G TREND. PAGE 132 H2636
ANTHOL ISLAM NAT/LISM DIPLOM

B65
ROWAT D.C.,THE OMBUDSMAN: CITIZEN'S DEFENDER. DENMARK FINLAND NEW/ZEALND NORWAY SWEDEN CONSULT PROB/SOLV FEEDBACK PARTIC GP/REL...SOC CONCPT NEW/IDEA METH/COMP ANTHOL BIBLIOG 20. PAGE 135 H2701
INSPECT CONSTN NAT/G ADMIN

B65
RUBINSTEIN A.Z.,THE CHALLENGE OF POLITICS: IDEAS AND ISSUES (2ND ED.). UNIV ELITES SOCIETY EX/STRUC BAL/PWR PARL/PROC AUTHORIT...DECISION ANTHOL 20. PAGE 136 H2709
NAT/G DIPLOM GP/REL ORD/FREE

B65
VAN DEN BERGHE P.L.,AFRICA: SOCIAL PROBLEMS OF CHANGE AND CONFLICT. ELITES STRATA ECO/UNDEV KIN MUNIC DIPLOM GP/REL RACE/REL NAT/LISM...ANTHOL BIBLIOG 20. PAGE 161 H3228
SOC CULTURE AFR STRUCT

B65
ZIOCK H.,SIND DIE DEUTSCHEN WIRKLICH SO? GERMANY SOCIETY...NAT/COMP ANTHOL 19/20. PAGE 173 H3460
PERSON ATTIT CULTURE STRUCT

C65
COLEMAN J.S.,"EDUCATION AND POLITICAL DEVELOPMENT." COM CULTURE INTELL STRUCT SCHOOL PERSON SOVEREIGN ...POLICY ANTHOL BIBLIOG/A METH 20. PAGE 31 H0629
ECO/UNDEV NAT/LISM EDU/PROP TEC/DEV

B66
AIYAR S.P.,PERSPECTIVES ON THE WELFARE STATE. INDIA S/ASIA UK CONSTN ECO/UNDEV NAT/G INGP/REL CENTRAL NAT/LISM ATTIT...CONCPT ANTHOL BIBLIOG 20. PAGE 4 H0087
NEW/LIB WELF/ST IDEA/COMP ADJUST

B66
BERELSON B.,READER IN PUBLIC OPINION AND COMMUNICATION (2ND ED.). UNIV NAT/G PRESS GP/REL PERS/REL PERCEPT RIGID/FLEX...MAJORIT QUANT METH/COMP ANTHOL BIBLIOG 20. PAGE 15 H0298
EDU/PROP ATTIT CONCPT COM/IND

B66
BIRKHEAD G.S.,ADMINISTRATIVE PROBLEMS IN PAKISTAN. PAKISTAN AGRI FINAN INDUS LG/CO ECO/TAC CONTROL PWR ...CHARTS ANTHOL 20. PAGE 17 H0340
ADMIN NAT/G ORD/FREE ECO/UNDEV

B66
BIRMINGHAM W.,A STUDY OF CONTEMPORARY GHANA VOL I: THE ECONOMY OF GHANA. AFR GHANA PLAN...POLICY STAT CHARTS ANTHOL BIBLIOG 20. PAGE 17 H0342
ECO/UNDEV ECO/TAC NAT/G PRODUC

B66
BRAIBANTI R.,ASIAN BUREAUCRATIC SYSTEMS EMERGENT FROM THE BRITISH IMPERIAL TRADITION. BURMA CEYLON INDIA PAKISTAN UK ELITES ECO/UNDEV NAT/G...MGT SOC CHARTS ANTHOL 19/20. PAGE 20 H0401
GOV/COMP COLONIAL ADMIN S/ASIA

B66
BROWN L.C.,STATE AND SOCIETY IN INDEPENDENT NORTH AFRICA. ALGERIA LIBYA MOROCCO AGRI INDUS INT/ORG POL/PAR SECT PLAN DIPLOM COLONIAL...LING NAT/COMP ANTHOL BIBLIOG 20 TUNIS MUSLIM. PAGE 22 H0446
NAT/G SOCIETY CULTURE ECO/UNDEV

B66
COLEMAN-NORTON P.R.,ROMAN STATE AND CHRISTIAN CHURCH: A COLLECTION OF LEGAL DOCUMENTS TO A.D. 535 (3 VOLS.). CHRIST-17C ROMAN/EMP...ANTHOL DICTIONARY 6 CHRISTIAN CHURCH/STA. PAGE 31 H0630
GP/REL NAT/G SECT LAW

B66
DAHL R.A.,POLITICAL OPPOSITIONS IN WESTERN DEMOCRACIES. EUR+WWI USA+45 USA-45 SOCIETY STRATA ECO/DEV NAT/G LEGIS REPRESENT...TREND NAT/COMP ANTHOL 20. PAGE 37 H0732
POL/PAR CHOOSE PARTIC PLURISM

B66
DALLIN A.,POLITICS IN THE SOVIET UNION: 7 CASES. COM USSR LAW POL/PAR CHIEF FORCES WRITING CONTROL PARL/PROC CIVMIL/REL TOTALISM...ANTHOL 20 KHRUSH/N STALIN/J CASEBOOK COM/PARTY. PAGE 37 H0736
MARXISM DOMIN ORD/FREE GOV/REL

B66
DIAMOND S.,THE TRANSFORMATION OF EAST AFRICA. NAT/G SCHOOL CREATE PROB/SOLV COLONIAL REGION RACE/REL FEDERAL...SOC ANTHOL WORSHIP 20 AFRICA/E. PAGE 41 H0819
CULTURE AFR TEC/DEV INDUS

B66
FARRELL R.B.,APPROACHES TO COMPARATIVE AND INTERNATIONAL POLITICS. RUSSIA SOCIETY ACADEM GOV/REL GP/REL...METH/CNCPT NET/THEORY GOV/COMP HYPO/EXP SOC/EXP GEN/METH ANTHOL. PAGE 49 H0973
DIPLOM NAT/COMP NAT/G

B66
FISK E.K.,NEW GUINEA ON THE THRESHOLD; ASPECTS OF SOCIAL, POLITICAL, AND ECONOMIC DEVELOPMENT. AGRI NAT/G INT/TRADE ADMIN ADJUST LITERACY ROLE...CHARTS ANTHOL 20 NEW/GUINEA. PAGE 51 H1015
ECO/UNDEV SOCIETY

B66
FRANK E.,LAWMAKERS IN A CHANGING WORLD. FRANCE UK USSR WOR+45 PARTIC EFFICIENCY ROLE ALL/IDEOS ...CHARTS ANTHOL PARLIAMENT 20 UN COLD/WAR. PAGE 52 H1049
GOV/COMP LEGIS NAT/G DIPLOM

B66
FRIEDRICH C.J.,REVOLUTION: NOMOS VIII. NAT/G SOCISM ...OBS TREND IDEA/COMP ANTHOL 18/20. PAGE 54 H1070
REV MARXISM CONCPT DIPLOM

B66
HAMILTON W.B.,A DECADE OF THE COMMONWEALTH, 1955-1964. UK LAW ELITES FINAN FOR/AID CONFER COLONIAL PWR...GEOG CHARTS ANTHOL 20 CMN/WLTH UN. PAGE 65 H1302
INT/ORG INGP/REL DIPLOM NAT/G

B66
HANSON J.W.,EDUCATION AND THE DEVELOPMENT OF NATIONS. DIPLOM TASK ADJUST EFFICIENCY...POLICY ANTHOL 20. PAGE 66 H1322
ECO/UNDEV EDU/PROP NAT/G PLAN

B66
INTL CONF ON WORLD POLITICS-5,EASTERN EUROPE IN TRANSITION. EUR+WWI USSR ECO/TAC NAT/LISM ATTIT SOVEREIGN...CHARTS ANTHOL 20 TREATY WARSAW/P. PAGE 78 H1562
COM NAT/COMP MARXISM DIPLOM

B66
IOWA STATE U CTR AGRI AND ECO,RESEARCH AND EDUCATION FOR REGIONAL AND AREA DEVELOPMENT. FUT LAW CULTURE R+D LOC/G PLAN KNOWL...POLICY CHARTS ANTHOL 20. PAGE 78 H1565
REGION ACT/RES ECO/TAC INDUS

B66
LEONTIEF W.,ESSAYS IN ECONOMICS. ECO/UNDEV INDUS NAT/G CAP/ISM FOR/AID AUTOMAT MARXISM...ECOMETRIC CHARTS ANTHOL METH 20 KEYNES/JM. PAGE 94 H1886
CONCPT METH/CNCPT METH/COMP

B66
LONDON K.,EASTERN EUROPE IN TRANSITION. CHINA/COM USSR DOMIN COLONIAL CENTRAL RIGID/FLEX PWR...SOC ANTHOL 20. PAGE 98 H1958
SOVEREIGN COM NAT/LISM DIPLOM

B66
MACFARQUHAR R.,CHINA UNDER MAO: POLITICS TAKES COMMAND. CHINA/COM COM AGRI INDUS CHIEF FORCES DIPLOM INT/TRADE EDU/PROP TASK REV ADJUST...ANTHOL 20 MAO. PAGE 100 H1992
ECO/UNDEV TEC/DEV ECO/TAC ADMIN

B66
MCKAY V.,AFRICAN DIPLOMACY STUDIES IN THE DETERMINANTS OF FOREIGN POLICY. AFR SOUTH/AFR CULTURE NEUTRAL REGION SOVEREIGN...INT/LAW GOV/COMP ANTHOL 20. PAGE 107 H2138
ECO/UNDEV RACE/REL CIVMIL/REL DIPLOM

B66
MERRITT R.L.,COMPARING NATIONS* THE USE OF QUANTITATIVE DATA IN CROSSNATIONAL RESEARCH. ACADEM DIPLOM GP/REL...PHIL/SCI STAT TREND GP/COMP PERS/COMP GEN/METH ANTHOL BIBLIOG INDEX. PAGE 109 H2184
NAT/COMP MATH COMPUT/IR QUANT

B66
ROGGER H.,THE EUROPEAN RIGHT. EUR+WWI CONSERVE ...ANTHOL BIBLIOG 20. PAGE 133 H2660
NAT/COMP POL/PAR IDEA/COMP TRADIT

B66
ROSS A.M.,INDUSTRIAL RELATIONS AND ECONOMIC DEVELOPMENT. POL/PAR LEGIS WORKER BARGAIN PRICE EXEC LOBBY INCOME PWR...DECISION ANTHOL BIBLIOG 20. PAGE 134 H2686
ECO/UNDEV LABOR NAT/G GP/REL

B66
SETTON K.M.,GREAT PROBLEMS IN EUROPEAN CIVILIZATION. CHRIST-17C EUR+WWI MOD/EUR SECT GP/REL ALL/VALS ORD/FREE ALL/IDEOS...TREND ANTHOL T CHRISTIAN RENAISSAN PROTESTANT. PAGE 142 H2835
CULTURE CONCPT IDEA/COMP

B66
SILBERMAN B.S.,MODERN JAPANESE LEADERSHIP; TRANSITION AND CHANGE. NAT/G POL/PAR CHIEF ADMIN REPRESENT GP/REL ADJUST RIGID/FLEX...SOC METH/COMP ANTHOL 19/20 CHINJAP CHRISTIAN. PAGE 144 H2873
LEAD CULTURE ELITES MUNIC

B66
SMELSER N.J.,SOCIAL STRUCTURE AND MOBILITY IN ECONOMIC DEVELOPMENT. CULTURE SOCIETY CONFER...PSY SOC CHARTS METH/COMP NAT/COMP ANTHOL METH 20. PAGE 145 H2904
STRUCT STRATA ECO/UNDEV ECO/DEV

B66
SMITH H.E.,READINGS IN ECONOMIC DEVELOPMENT AND ADMINISTRATION IN TANZANIA. TANZANIA FINAN INDUS LABOR NAT/G PLAN PROB/SOLV INT/TRADE COLONIAL REGION...ANTHOL BIBLIOG 20 AFRICA/E. PAGE 146 H2910
TEC/DEV ADMIN GOV/REL

B66
SWARTZ M.J.,POLITICAL ANTHROPOLOGY. WOR+45 POL/PAR ACT/RES REV GP/REL DRIVE...SOC CONCPT TIME/SEQ GP/COMP ANTHOL WORSHIP 20. PAGE 151 H3013
PARTIC RIGID/FLEX LOC/G CREATE

B66
SWEARINGEN A.R.,SOVIET AND CHINESE COMMUNIST POWER IN THE WORLD TODAY. COM USA+45 ECO/UNDEV CREATE LEAD WAR ADJUST...TREND NAT/COMP ANTHOL COLD/WAR KHRUSH/N. PAGE 151 H3017
USSR ASIA DIPLOM ATTIT

B66
THOMPSON J.H.,MODERNIZATION OF THE ARAB WORLD. FUT ISRAEL STRUCT ECO/UNDEV DIPLOM INGP/REL ATTIT ...CENSUS ANTHOL 20 ARABS. PAGE 154 H3082
ADJUST ISLAM PROB/SOLV NAT/COMP

L66
"FEDERAL, STATE AND LOCAL GOVERNMENT PUBLICATIONS." ACADEM LOC/G NAT/G PROVS SCHOOL EFFICIENCY ...PHIL/SCI ANTHOL. PAGE 143 H2854
BIBLIOG OP/RES METH

B67
ALBINSKI H.S.,EUROPEAN POLITICAL PROCESSES: ESSAYS AND READINGS. EUR+WWI FRANCE GERMANY MOD/EUR UK ELITES POL/PAR PWR...CHARTS ANTHOL 18/20. PAGE 5 H0094
NAT/COMP POLICY IDEA/COMP

B67
BOHANNAN P.,LAW AND WARFARE. CULTURE CT/SYS COERCE REV PEACE...JURID SOC CONCPT ANTHOL 20. PAGE 18 H0367
METH/COMP ADJUD WAR LAW

B67
CANTOR N.F.,THE ENGLISH TRADITION* TWENTIETH-CENTURY VIEWS OF ENGLISH HISTORY (2VOLS.). UK STRATA NAT/G SECT WAR...POLICY GOV/COMP IDEA/COMP ANTHOL T PARLIAMENT CMN/WLTH. PAGE 26 H0522
CT/SYS LAW POL/PAR

B67
CORDIER A.W.,COLUMBIA ESSAYS IN INTERNATIONAL AFFAIRS. ASIA CHINA/COM FRANCE S/ASIA SPAIN UAR ECO/UNDEV LOC/G ECO/TAC GUERRILLA PWR...BIOG ANTHOL 18/20 MAU/MAU. PAGE 33 H0663
NAT/G DIPLOM MARXISM POLICY

B67
COWLES M.,PERSPECTIVES IN THE EDUCATION OF DISADVANTAGED CHILDREN. CULTURE OP/RES PLAN PERS/REL ADJUST HABITAT PERCEPT KNOWL WEALTH ...SOC/WK IDEA/COMP ANTHOL 20. PAGE 34 H0686
EDU/PROP AGE/C TEC/DEV SCHOOL

B67
CURTIN P.D.,AFRICA REMEMBERED. NIGERIA SENEGAL CULTURE DIPLOM INT/TRADE GP/REL RACE/REL...RECORD ANTHOL 18/19 NEGRO. PAGE 36 H0727
DOMIN ORD/FREE AFR DISCRIM

B67
DALTON G.,TRIBAL AND PEASANT ECONOMIES. SOCIETY FINAN FAM INT/TRADE RATION ADJUST WEALTH...CHARTS ANTHOL BIBLIOG T. PAGE 37 H0738
SOC ECO/UNDEV NAT/COMP

B67
FALL B.B.,HO CHI MINH ON REVOLUTION: SELECTED WRITINGS, 1920-66. COM VIETNAM ELITES NAT/G COERCE GUERRILLA RACE/REL MARXISM...MARXIST ANTHOL 20. PAGE 48 H0968
REV COLONIAL ECO/UNDEV S/ASIA

B67
FISHEL L.H. JR.,THE NEGRO AMERICAN: A DOCUMENTARY HISTORY. SOCIETY NAT/G ROLE...POLICY ANTHOL 15/20 NEGRO. PAGE 51 H1013
ORD/FREE DISCRIM RACE/REL STRATA

B67
GIFFORD P.,BRITAIN AND GERMANY IN AFRICA. AFR GERMANY UK ECO/UNDEV LEAD WAR NAT/LISM ATTIT ...POLICY HIST/WRIT METH/COMP ANTHOL BIBLIOG 19/20 WWI. PAGE 56 H1123
COLONIAL ADMIN DIPLOM NAT/COMP

B67
MACRIDIS R.C.,FOREIGN POLICY IN WORLD POLITICS (3RD ED.). EX/STRUC BAL/PWR COLONIAL NAT/LISM SKILL SOVEREIGN WEALTH...CONCPT TIME/SEQ ANTHOL 20 COLD/WAR. PAGE 101 H2011
DIPLOM POLICY NAT/G IDEA/COMP

B67
MCNELLY T.,SOURCES IN MODERN EAST ASIAN HISTORY AND POLITICS. KOREA VIETNAM CULTURE DIPLOM COLONIAL REV WAR PWR ALL/IDEOS MARXISM...ANTHOL 20 CHINJAP. PAGE 107 H2147
NAT/COMP ASIA S/ASIA SOCIETY

B67
NYERERE J.K.,FREEDOM AND UNITY/UHURU NA UMOJA: A SELECTION FROM WRITINGS AND SPEECHES, 1952-65. TANZANIA ELITES ECO/UNDEV INT/ORG NAT/G CREATE DIPLOM COLONIAL REGION RACE/REL...ANTHOL 20. PAGE 119 H2383
SOVEREIGN AFR TREND ORD/FREE

B67
PIKE F.B.,FREEDOM AND REFORM IN LATIN AMERICA. BRAZIL URUGUAY CONSTN CULTURE SECT DIPLOM EDU/PROP PARTIC DRIVE ALL/VALS CATHISM...GEOG ANTHOL BIBLIOG REFORMERS BOLIV. PAGE 126 H2511
L/A+17C ORD/FREE ECO/UNDEV REV

B67
PLANK J.,CUBA AND THE UNITED STATES: LONG RANGE PERSPECTIVES. CUBA L/A+17C USSR ECO/UNDEV NAT/G FORCES ECO/TAC INT/TRADE AGREE REV...PREDICT TREND ANTHOL 20 CASTRO/F COLD/WAR OAS. PAGE 126 H2520
DIPLOM

B67
SHAFFER H.G.,THE COMMUNIST WORLD: MARXIST AND NON-MARXIST VIEWS. WOR+45 SOCIETY DIPLOM ECO/TAC CONTROL SOCISM...MARXIST ANTHOL BIBLIOG/A 20. PAGE 142 H2838
MARXISM NAT/COMP IDEA/COMP COM

B67
WARREN S.,THE AMERICAN PRESIDENT. POL/PAR FORCES LEGIS DIPLOM ECO/TAC ADMIN EXEC PWR...ANTHOL 18/20 ROOSEVLT/F KENNEDY/JF JOHNSON/LB TRUMAN/HS WILSON/W. PAGE 165 H3312
CHIEF LEAD NAT/G CONSTN

L67
AUSTIN D.A.,"POLITICAL CONFLICT IN AFRICA." CONSTN NAT/G CREATE ADMIN COLONIAL ORD/FREE MARXISM POPULISM SOCISM...NAT/COMP ANTHOL 20. PAGE 9 H0180
ANOMIE AFR POL/PAR

L67
GRAUBARD S.R.,"TOWARD THE YEAR 2000: WORK IN PROGRESS." FUT ACADEM SECT DELIB/GP DIPLOM EDU/PROP AGE/Y PERSON ROLE...PSY ANTHOL. PAGE 60 H1199
PREDICT PROB/SOLV SOCIETY CULTURE

L67
LATIN AMERICAN STUDIES ASSN,"RESEARCH ON EDUCATION IN LATIN AMERICA." L/A+17C NAT/G HABITAT...GOV/COMP ANTHOL 20. PAGE 92 H1836
EDU/PROP SCHOOL ACADEM R+D

L67
SCALAPINO R.A.,"A SURVEY OF ASIA IN 1966." ASIA S/ASIA CONSTN SOCIETY POL/PAR CHIEF WAR...ANTHOL 20. PAGE 138 H2764
DIPLOM

S67
BEVEL D.N.,"JOURNEY TO NORTH VIETNAM." VIETNAM/N CONSTN NAT/G FORCES PROB/SOLV DEATH CIVMIL/REL PEACE MORAL...ANTHOL 20 NEGRO. PAGE 16 H0325
ATTIT DIPLOM ORD/FREE WAR

B79
BRODERICK G.C.,POLITICAL STUDIES. IRELAND UK ROMAN/EMP LAW ACADEM LOC/G NAT/G DIPLOM PARL/PROC SUFF GP/REL LAISSEZ...ANTHOL. PAGE 21 H0424
CONSTN COLONIAL

ANTHON C.G. H0144

ANTHROPOLOGY, PSYCHOLOGICAL....SEE PSY

ANTI/SEMIT....ANTI-SEMITISM; SEE ALSO JEWS, GP/REL

B66
ROSNER J.,DER FASCHISMUS. AUSTRIA GERMANY ITALY STRATA NAT/G POL/PAR COERCE RACE/REL TOTALISM ATTIT AUTHORIT...IDEA/COMP 20 NAZI ANTI/SEMIT. PAGE 134 H2684
NAT/LISM FASCISM ORD/FREE WAR

ANTIBALLISTIC MISSILE DEFENSE SYSTEMS....SEE ABM/DEFSYS

ANTI-SEMITISM....SEE JEWS, GP/REL, ANTI/SEMIT

ANTI-TRUST ACTIONS....SEE MONOPOLY, INDUS, CONTROL

ANXIETY....SEE ANOMIE

APACHE....APACHE INDIANS

APARTHEID....APARTHEID

APPADORAI A. H0145

APPALACHIA

APPELLATE COURT SYSTEM....SEE CT/SYS

APPERT K. H0146

APPLEBY P.H. H0147

APPLEMAN P. H0148

APPORT....DELINEATION OF LEGISLATIVE DISTRICTS

N19
OPERATIONS AND POLICY RESEARCH,PERU ELECTION MEMORANDA (PAMPHLET). L/A+17C PERU POL/PAR LEGIS EXEC APPORT REPRESENT 20. PAGE 121 H2421
CHOOSE CONSTN SUFF NAT/G

N19
ROWE J.W.,THE ARGENTINE ELECTIONS OF 1963 (PAMPHLET). L/A+17C LOC/G NAT/G LEGIS REPRESENT 20 ARGEN. PAGE 135 H2703
CHOOSE CONSTN APPORT POL/PAR

B32
MCKISACK M.,THE PARLIAMENTARY REPRESENTATION OF THE ENGLISH BOROUGHS DURING THE MIDDLE AGES. UK CONSTN CULTURE ELITES EX/STRUC TAX PAY ADJUD PARL/PROC APPORT FEDERAL...POLICY 13/15 PARLIAMENT. PAGE 107 H2139
NAT/G MUNIC LEGIS CHOOSE

B58
WILMERDING L. JR.,THE ELECTORAL COLLEGE. CONSTN NAT/G POL/PAR DELIB/GP LEGIS PROB/SOLV CONFER EXEC LEAD APPORT REPRESENT. PAGE 169 H3377
CHOOSE DECISION ACT/RES

B59
BROWN D.F.,THE GROWTH OF DEMOCRATIC GOVERNMENT. WOR+45 BARGAIN EDU/PROP LOBBY APPORT CHOOSE 20. PAGE 22 H0441
GOV/COMP LEGIS POL/PAR CHIEF

S66
TOUVAL S.,"AFRICA'S FRONTIERS* REACTIONS TO A COLONIAL LEGACY." L/A+17C CONFER ADJUD COLONIAL APPORT CONSEN NAT/LISM RESPECT...RECORD NAT/COMP. PAGE 156 H3120
AFR GEOG SOVEREIGN WAR

B67
RAE D.,THE POLITICAL CONSEQUENCES OF ELECTORAL LAWS. EUR+WWI ICELAND ISRAEL NEW/ZEALND UK USA+45 ADJUD APPORT GP/REL MAJORITY...MATH STAT CENSUS CHARTS BIBLIOG 20 AUSTRAL. PAGE 129 H2579
POL/PAR CHOOSE NAT/COMP REPRESENT

L67
"A PROPOS DES INCITATIONS FINANCIERES AUX GROUPEMENTS DES COMMUNES: ESSAI D'INTERPRETATION." FRANCE NAT/G LEGIS ADMIN GOV/REL CENTRAL 20. PAGE 3 H0051
LOC/G ECO/TAC APPORT ADJUD

L67
WILBER L.A.,"THE GOVERNMENTAL STRUCTURE OF MISSISSIPPI: ITS STRENGTHS AND WEAKNESSES." AGRI LOC/G SCHOOL EX/STRUC LEGIS TOP/EX BUDGET CT/SYS APPORT RACE/REL...GOV/COMP 20 MISSISSIPP. PAGE 168 H3359
CONSTN PROVS STAT CON/ANAL

APRA....ALIANZA POPULAR REVOLUCIONARIA AMERICANA, A PERUVIAN POLITICAL PARTY

B56
HERNANDEZ URBINA A.,LOS PARTIDOS Y LA CRISIS DEL APRA. PERU NAT/G LEAD LOBBY CHOOSE SOCISM...POLICY DECISION 20 COM/PARTY APRA CONGRESS. PAGE 70 H1402
POL/PAR PARTIC PARL/PROC GP/REL

APSA....AMERICAN POLITICAL SCIENCE ASSOCIATION

APT/TEST....APTITUDE TESTS

APTER D.E. H0149,H0150,H0151,H0152,H0153,H0154,H0886

APTITUDE TESTS....SEE APT/TEST

AQUINAS T. H0155

AQUINAS/T....SAINT THOMAS AQUINAS

B63
LERNER R.,MEDIEVAL POLITICAL PHILOSOPHY. ISLAM MORAL PWR CATHISM...CATH CONCPT OBS IDEA/COMP ANTHOL 9/15 JEWS CHRISTIAN BACON/R AQUINAS/T. PAGE 95 H1890
KNOWL PHIL/SCI

B63
STRAUSS L.,HISTORY OF POLITICAL PHILOSOPHY. LAW SOCIETY CAP/ISM MARXISM 19 AQUINAS/T BACON/F HEGEL/GWF MILL/JS NIETZSCH/F. PAGE 150 H2995
IDEA/COMP PHIL/SCI ANTHOL

ARA....AREA REDEVELOPMENT ACT

ARABIA/SOU....SOUTH ARABIA

ARABS....ARAB WORLD, INCLUDING ITS CULTURE

B60
BRIGGS L.C.,TRIBES OF THE SAHARA. AFR MOROCCO STRATA AGRI GP/REL HEALTH...GEOG SOC MYTH LING BIBLIOG 13/20 ARABS. PAGE 21 H0418
CULTURE HABITAT KIN SELF/OBS

B60
HAMADY S.,TEMPERAMENT AND CHARACTER OF THE ARABS. FAM NAT/G SECT DIPLOM NAT/LISM...POLICY 20 ARABS. PAGE 65 H1299
NAT/COMP PERSON CULTURE ISLAM

B61
PATAI R.,CULTURES IN CONFLICT; AN INQUIRY INTO THE SOCIO-CULTURAL PROBLEMS OF ISRAEL AND HER NEIGHBORS (2ND REV. ED.). ISLAM ISRAEL SOCIETY STRUCT DIPLOM GP/REL ALL/VALS...SOC 20 JEWS ARABS. PAGE 124 H2475
NAT/COMP CULTURE GP/COMP ATTIT

B61
SCHECHTMAN J.B.,ON WINGS OF EAGLES: THE PLIGHT, EXODUS, AND HOMECOMING OF ORIENTAL JEWRY. ASIA ISLAM ISRAEL VOL/ASSN DIPLOM CONTROL ORD/FREE ...GEOG WORSHIP SOC/INTEG 20 JEWS ARABS MIGRATION. PAGE 139 H2777
CULTURE HABITAT KIN SECT

B62
BERGER M.,THE ARAB WORLD TODAY. CULTURE FAM INT/ORG NAT/G SECT FORCES ECO/TAC NAT/LISM HABITAT...CHARTS BIBLIOG 20 ARABS. PAGE 15 H0301
ISLAM PERSON STRUCT SOCIETY

B62
HAIM S.G.,ARAB NATIONALISM. ISLAM CONSTN GP/REL ...ANTHOL BIBLIOG JEWS 20 MID/EAST ARABS. PAGE 64 H1279
NAT/LISM REV SECT DIPLOM

B63
BADI J.,THE GOVERNMENT OF THE STATE OF ISRAEL: A CRITICAL ACCOUNT OF ITS PARLIAMENT, EXECUTIVE, AND JUDICIARY. ISRAEL ECO/DEV CHIEF DELIB/GP LEGIS DIPLOM CT/SYS INGP/REL PEACE ORD/FREE...BIBLIOG 20 PARLIAMENT ARABS MIGRATION. PAGE 10 H0193
NAT/G CONSTN EX/STRUC POL/PAR

B63
HARDY M.J.L.,BLOOD FEUDS AND THE PAYMENT OF BLOOD MONEY IN THE MIDDLE EAST. ISLAM SOCIETY SECT REGION SANCTION COERCE DEATH MURDER 7/20 ARABS. PAGE 66 H1329
KIN TRIBUTE LAW CULTURE

B64
LEMARCHAND R.,POLITICAL AWAKENING IN THE BELGIAN CONGO. ECO/UNDEV VOL/ASSN DOMIN CHOOSE GP/REL INGP/REL DISCRIM ORD/FREE PWR...CHARTS 20 CONGO ARABS. PAGE 94 H1873
NAT/LISM COLONIAL POL/PAR RACE/REL

B64
VON GRUNEBAUM G.E.,MODERN ISLAM: THE SEARCH FOR CULTURAL IDENTITY. ACADEM NEIGH WRITING NAT/LISM ...HUM CONCPT 19/20 MUSLIM MID/EAST ARABS. PAGE 163 H3269
ISLAM CULTURE CREATE SECT

B66
RIZK C.,LE REGIME POLITIQUE LIBANAIS. ISLAM LEBANON STRUCT POL/PAR SECT LOBBY GP/REL 20 ARABS MUSLIM CHRISTIAN. PAGE 132 H2637
ECO/UNDEV NAT/G CULTURE

B66
THOMPSON J.H.,MODERNIZATION OF THE ARAB WORLD. FUT ISRAEL STRUCT ECO/UNDEV DIPLOM INGP/REL ATTIT
ADJUST ISLAM

...CENSUS ANTHOL 20 ARABS. PAGE 154 H3082 PROB/SOLV NAT/COMP

B66
ZEINE Z.N.,THE EMERGENCE OF ARAB NATIONALISM (REV. ED.). TURKEY UK NAT/G SECT TEC/DEV LEAD REV WAR AGE/Y ROLE ORD/FREE...TRADIT CHARTS BIBLIOG 20 ARABS OTTOMAN. PAGE 173 H3453 ISLAM NAT/LISM DIPLOM

ARASARATNAM S. H0156

ARASTEH R. H0157

ARAZI A. H0158

ARBITRATION....SEE DELIB/GP, CONSULT, AND FUNCTIONAL GROUP CONCERNED (E.G., LABOR)

ARCHER P. H0159

ARENDT H. H0160,H0161

ARENSBERG C.M. H0162

ARGENTINA....SEE ALSO L/A&17C

N19
ROWE J.W.,THE ARGENTINE ELECTIONS OF 1963 (PAMPHLET). L/A+17C LOC/G NAT/G LEGIS REPRESENT 20 ARGEN. PAGE 135 H2703 CHOOSE CONSTN APPORT POL/PAR

B31
KIRKPATRICK F.A.,A HISTORY OF THE ARGENTINE REPUBLIC. SPAIN UK CONSTN SOCIETY ECO/UNDEV EX/STRUC DIPLOM FOR/AID LEAD WAR ATTIT...BIOG CHARTS 16/20 ARGEN SAN/MARTIN. PAGE 86 H1724 NAT/G L/A+17C COLONIAL

B41
CHILDS J.B.,A GUIDE TO THE OFFICIAL PUBLICATIONS OF THE OTHER AMERICAN REPUBLICS: ARGENTINA. CHIEF DIPLOM GOV/REL...BIBLIOG 18/19 ARGEN. PAGE 30 H0594 NAT/G EX/STRUC METH/CNCPT LEGIS

B47
BEHAR D.,BIBLIOGRAFIA HISPANOAMERICANA. LIBROS ANTIGUOS Y MODERNOS REFERENTES A AMERICA Y ESPANA. PORTUGAL SPAIN CONSTN NAT/G SECT CREATE REV WAR GOV/REL...ART/METH GEOG PHIL/SCI LING 20 ARGEN. PAGE 13 H0260 BIBLIOG L/A+17C CULTURE

B56
WHITAKER A.P.,ARGENTINE UPHEAVAL. STRUCT FORCES DIPLOM COERCE PWR 20 ARGEN. PAGE 167 H3343 REV POL/PAR STRATA NAT/G

B57
HERNANDEZ-ARREGU J.,IMPERIALISMO Y CULTURA (LA POLITICA EN LA INTELIGENCIA ARGENTINA). L/A+17C CULTURE ELITES WRITING COLONIAL CROWD ATTIT FASCISM MARXISM SOCISM...BIOG IDEA/COMP 20 ARGEN PERON/JUAN COM/PARTY. PAGE 70 H1403 INTELL CREATE ART/METH HUM

B57
PALACIOS A.L.,PETROLEO, MONOPOLIOS, Y LATIFUNDIOS. L/A+17C EXTR/IND NAT/G TEC/DEV ECO/TAC CONTROL PRODUC 20 ARGEN MONOPOLY RESOURCE/N. PAGE 123 H2448 ECO/UNDEV NAT/LISM INDUS AGRI

B59
CUCCORESE H.J.,HISTORIA DE LA CONVERSION DEL PAPEL MONEDA EN BUENOS AIRES, 1861-1867. LAW LOC/G NAT/G ATTIT...POLICY BIBLIOG 19 ARGEN BUENOS/AIR GOLD/STAND. PAGE 36 H0717 FINAN PLAN LEGIS

B59
SZLUC T.,TWILIGHT OF THE TYRANTS. BRAZIL L/A+17C PERU VENEZUELA NAT/G FORCES CONTROL PERSON MORAL ORD/FREE PWR...CONCPT 20 ARGEN COLOMB. PAGE 151 H3028 TOTALISM CHIEF REV FASCISM

B64
IMAZ J.L.,LOS QUE MANDAN. INDUS LABOR NAT/G POL/PAR PROVS SECT CHIEF TOP/EX CONTROL 20 ARGEN. PAGE 76 H1524 LEAD FORCES ELITES ATTIT

S65
BRANDENBURG F.,"THE RELEVANCE OF MEXICAN EXPERIENCE TO LATIN AMERICAN DEVELOPMENT." BRAZIL CHILE VENEZUELA STRUCT ECO/UNDEV AGRI CREATE ECO/TAC ...STAT RECORD MEXIC/AMER ARGEN COLOMB. PAGE 20 H0405 L/A+17C GOV/COMP

S65
TENDLER J.D.,"TECHNOLOGY AND ECONOMIC DEVELOPMENT* THE CASE OF HYDRO VS THERMAL POWER." CONSTRUC DIST/IND CREATE TEC/DEV INT/TRADE CENTRAL PWR SKILL WEALTH...MGT NAT/COMP ARGEN. PAGE 153 H3061 BRAZIL INDUS ECO/UNDEV

L67
WRIGHT W.R.,"FOREIGN-OWNED RAILWAYS IN ARGENTINA: A CASE STUDY OF ECONOMIC NATIONALISM." L/A+17C UK ECO/UNDEV SERV/IND LG/CO NAT/G TEC/DEV BAL/PWR EQUILIB ARGEN. PAGE 171 H3423 NAT/LISM CAP/ISM ECO/TAC COLONIAL

S67
COHEN A.,"REVOLUTION IN ARGENTINA?" L/A+17C NAT/G POL/PAR CHIEF PROB/SOLV ECO/TAC 20 ARGEN. PAGE 31 H0615 REV ECO/UNDEV CONTROL BIOG

S67
DANA MONTANO S.M.,"APLICACIONES CONCRETAS DE LAS RESOLUCIONES Y RECOMENDACIONES DE LAS CONFERENCIAS INTERAMERICANAS DE ABOGADOS" L/A+17C NAT/G PROVS GOV/REL PERCEPT 20 ARGEN. PAGE 37 H0739 JURID CT/SYS ORD/FREE BAL/PWR

ARIKPO O. H0163

ARISTOCRATIC....SEE TRADIT, STRATA, ELITES

ARISTOTLE....ARISTOTLE

B95
HAMMOND B.E.,THE POLITICAL INSTITUTIONS OF THE ANCIENT GREEKS. GREECE MUNIC PROVS COERCE WAR ORD/FREE ARISTOTLE. PAGE 65 H1307 GOV/COMP NAT/G IDEA/COMP CONCPT

ARIZONA....ARIZONA

ARKANSAS....ARKANSAS

ARMED FORCES....SEE FORCES

ARMENIA ....SEE ALSO USSR

B63
NALBANDIAN L.,THE ARMENIAN REVOLUTIONARY MOVEMENT. MOD/EUR RUSSIA...IDEA/COMP NAT/COMP BIBLIOG 19 ARMENIA OTTOMAN. PAGE 115 H2306 NAT/LISM REV POL/PAR ORD/FREE

ARMS CONTROL....SEE ARMS/CONT

ARMS/CONT....ARMS CONTROL, DISARMAMENT

B15
FARIES J.C.,THE RISE OF INTERNATIONALISM. ASIA MOD/EUR NAT/G VOL/ASSN DELIB/GP BAL/PWR EDU/PROP ARMS/CONT RIGID/FLEX TREND. PAGE 49 H0971 INT/ORG DIPLOM PEACE

N19
BENTHAM J.,A PLAN FOR AN UNIVERSAL AND PERPETUAL PEACE (1838) (PAMPHLET). NAT/G FORCES BAL/PWR INT/TRADE ADMIN AGREE CT/SYS ARMS/CONT SOVEREIGN WEALTH GEN/LAWS. PAGE 14 H0288 INT/ORG INT/LAW PEACE COLONIAL

N19
PROVISIONS SECTION OAU,ORGANIZATION OF AFRICAN UNITY: BASIC DOCUMENTS AND RESOLUTIONS (PAMPHLET). AFR CULTURE ECO/UNDEV DIPLOM ECO/TAC EDU/PROP COLONIAL ARMS/CONT NUC/PWR RACE/REL DISCRIM NAT/LISM 20 UN OAU. PAGE 128 H2564 CONSTN EX/STRUC SOVEREIGN INT/ORG

B32
BLUM L.,PEACE AND DISARMAMENT (TRANS. BY A. WERTH). NAT/G FORCES WORKER DIPLOM AGREE WAR ATTIT AUTHORIT ORD/FREE. PAGE 18 H0360 SOCIALIST PEACE INT/ORG ARMS/CONT

B51
LEONARD L.L.,INTERNATIONAL ORGANIZATION. WOR+45 WOR-45 EX/STRUC FORCES LEGIS ECO/TAC INT/TRADE COLONIAL ARMS/CONT...SOC/WK GOV/COMP BIBLIOG. PAGE 94 H1884 NAT/G DIPLOM INT/ORG DELIB/GP

C52
FIFIELD R.H.,"WOODROW WILSON AND THE FAR EAST." ASIA CHIEF DELIB/GP BAL/PWR CONFER COLONIAL ARMS/CONT WAR...TIME/SEQ NAT/COMP 19/20 WILSON/W LEAGUE/NAT. PAGE 50 H0995 BIBLIOG DIPLOM INT/ORG

B60
ALBRECHT-CARRIE R.,FRANCE, EUROPE AND THE TWO WORLD WARS. EUR+WWI FRANCE GERMANY MOD/EUR UK ECO/DEV NAT/G FORCES BAL/PWR DOMIN ARMS/CONT PEACE PWR 20 TREATY EUROPE. PAGE 5 H0096 DIPLOM WAR

B60
FISCHER L.,THE SOVIETS IN WORLD AFFAIRS. CHINA/COM COM EUR+WWI USSR INT/ORG CONFER LEAD ARMS/CONT REV PWR...CHARTS 20 TREATY VERSAILLES. PAGE 51 H1010 DIPLOM NAT/G POLICY MARXISM

B60
MC CLELLAN G.S.,INDIA. CHINA/COM INDIA CONSTN ELITES STRATA AGRI POL/PAR FOR/AID ARMS/CONT REV MARXISM...CENSUS BIBLIOG 20 COLD/WAR GANDHI/M NEHRU/J. PAGE 106 H2117 DIPLOM NAT/G SOCIETY ECO/UNDEV

S60
WOLFE T.W.,"KHRUSHCHEV'S DISARMAMENT STRATEGY." COM NAT/G TOP/EX PLAN BAL/PWR DIPLOM ARMS/CONT COERCE ATTIT...POLICY CONCPT RECORD TREND CON/ANAL COLD/WAR 20 KHRUSH/N. PAGE 170 H3401 PWR GEN/LAWS USSR

B61
KISSINGER H.A.,THE NECESSITY FOR CHOICE. FUT USA+45 ECO/UNDEV NAT/G PLAN BAL/PWR ECO/TAC ARMS/CONT DETER NUC/PWR ATTIT...POLICY CONCPT RECORD GEN/LAWS COLD/WAR 20. PAGE 87 H1728
TOP/EX TREND DIPLOM

S61
SCHELLING T.C.,"NUCLEAR STRATEGY IN EUROPE." COM EUR+WWI USSR NAT/G FORCES NUC/PWR DRIVE ORD/FREE PWR...DECISION CONCPT OBS TREND HYPO/EXP 20. PAGE 139 H2784
FUT COERCE ARMS/CONT WAR

S62
MARTIN L.W.,"THE MARKET FOR STRATEGIC IDEAS IN BRITAIN: THE 'SANDYS ERA'" UK ARMS/CONT WAR GOV/REL OPTIMAL...POLICY DECISION GOV/COMP COLD/WAR CMN/WLTH. PAGE 103 H2063
DIPLOM COERCE FORCES PWR

B63
GONZALEZ PEDRERO E.,ANATOMIA DE UN CONFLICTO. WOR+45 ECO/DEV ECO/UNDEV ECO/TAC FOR/AID CONTROL ARMS/CONT GOV/REL...NAT/COMP 20 COLD/WAR. PAGE 58 H1166
DIPLOM DETER BAL/PWR

B63
LARSON A.,A WARLESS WORLD. FUT CULTURE NAT/G VOL/ASSN FORCES CREATE DOMIN PEACE ALL/VALS...HUM STERTYP 20. PAGE 91 H1824
SOCIETY CONCPT ARMS/CONT

S63
BECHHOEFER B.G.,"SOVIET ATTITUDE TOWARD DISARMAMENT." COM USSR NAT/G ACT/RES TEC/DEV NUC/PWR ATTIT DISPL RIGID/FLEX PWR...METH/CNCPT TREND GEN/LAWS COLD/WAR 20. PAGE 13 H0252
FORCES EDU/PROP ARMS/CONT

B64
BROWN N.,NUCLEAR WAR* THE IMPENDING STRATEGIC DEADLOCK. USA+45 USSR TEC/DEV BUDGET RISK ARMS/CONT NUC/PWR WEAPON COST BIO/SOC...GEOG IDEA/COMP NAT/COMP GAME NATO WARSAW/P. PAGE 22 H0448
FORCES OP/RES WAR GEN/LAWS

B64
ROBERTS HL,FOREIGN AFFAIRS BIBLIOGRAPHY, 1952-1962. ECO/DEV SECT PLAN FOR/AID INT/TRADE ARMS/CONT NAT/LISM ATTIT...INT/LAW GOV/COMP IDEA/COMP 20. PAGE 132 H2643
BIBLIOG/A DIPLOM INT/ORG WAR

B65
ADENAUER K.,MEINE ERINNERUNGEN, 1945-53 (VOL. I), 1953-55 (VOL. II). EUR+WWI GERMANY CHIEF FORCES PROB/SOLV DIPLOM ARMS/CONT INGP/REL PEACE SOVEREIGN ...OBS/ENVIR RECORD 20. PAGE 3 H0069
NAT/G BIOG SELF/OBS

B65
HALPERIN M.H.,COMMUNIST CHINA AND ARMS CONTROL. CHINA/COM FUT USA+45 CULTURE FORCES TEC/DEV ECO/TAC WAR PEACE ORD/FREE MARXISM 20 COLD/WAR. PAGE 64 H1292
ATTIT POLICY ARMS/CONT NUC/PWR

B65
US DEPARTMENT OF DEFENSE,US SECURITY ARMS CONTROL, AND DISARMAMENT 1961-1965 (PAMPHLET). CHINA/COM COM GERMANY/W ISRAEL SPACE USA+45 USSR WOR+45 FORCES EDU/PROP DETER EQUILIB PEACE ALL/VALS...GOV/COMP 20 NATO. PAGE 159 H3183
BIBLIOG/A ARMS/CONT NUC/PWR DIPLOM

S65
BIRNBAUM K.,"SWEDEN'S NUCLEAR POLICY." WOR+45 POL/PAR CREATE TEC/DEV NEUTRAL RISK WAR ORD/FREE ...DECISION IDEA/COMP NAT/COMP TIME. PAGE 17 H0343
SWEDEN NUC/PWR DIPLOM ARMS/CONT

S65
GORDON M.,"THE SETTING FOR EUROPEAN ARMS CONTROLS* POLITICAL AND STRATEGIC CHOICES OF EUROPEAN ELITES." FRANCE GERMANY UK USA+45 USSR ARMS/CONT DETER ATTIT ORD/FREE...SAMP NAT/COMP NATO. PAGE 59 H1179
REC/INT ELITES RISK WAR

S65
JENSEN L.,"MILITARY CAPABILITIES AND BARGAINING BEHAVIOR." USA+45 USSR ARMS/CONT DETER COST ATTIT ...METH/CNCPT STAT SYS/QU CON/ANAL CHARTS NAT/COMP. PAGE 81 H1614
DIPLOM DRIVE PWR STERTYP

S65
WEDGE B.,"PSYCHOLOGICAL FACTORS IN SOVIET DISARMAMENT NEGOTIATION." USA+45 CONFER ATTIT PERCEPT PERSON...PSY NAT/COMP. PAGE 166 H3324
USSR DIPLOM ARMS/CONT

B66
EPSTEIN F.T.,THE AMERICAN BIBLIOGRAPHY OF RUSSIAN AND EAST EUROPEAN STUDIES FOR 1964. USSR LOC/G NAT/G POL/PAR FORCES ADMIN ARMS/CONT...JURID CONCPT 20 UN. PAGE 47 H0933
BIBLIOG COM MARXISM DIPLOM

B66
GRAHAM I.C.C.,PUBLICATIONS OF THE SOCIAL SCIENCE DEPARTMENT, THE RAND CORPORATION, 1948-1966. USSR WOR+45 NAT/G ARMS/CONT DETER WAR NAT/LISM...SOC GOV/COMP. PAGE 60 H1192
BIBLIOG DIPLOM NUC/PWR FORCES

B67
DEUTSCH K.W.,FRANCE, GERMANY AND THE WESTERN ALLIANCE. FRANCE GERMANY/W INT/ORG ARMS/CONT NAT/LISM SOVEREIGN...INT NAT/COMP 20. PAGE 40 H0801
ELITES ATTIT DIPLOM POLICY

B67
RAMUNDO B.A.,PEACEFUL COEXISTENCE: INTERNATIONAL LAW IN THE BUILDING OF COMMUNISM. USSR INT/ORG DIPLOM COLONIAL ARMS/CONT ROLE SOVEREIGN...POLICY METH/COMP NAT/COMP BIBLIOG. PAGE 129 H2588
INT/LAW PEACE MARXISM METH/CNCPT

B67
REES D.,THE AGE OF CONTAINMENT. WOR+45 FORCES ARMS/CONT ATTIT PWR...CONCPT TREND METH/COMP BIBLIOG/A 20. PAGE 130 H2608
DIPLOM NUC/PWR MARXISM GOV/COMP

B67
ROSENBLUTH G.,THE CANADIAN ECONOMY AND DISARMAMENT. CANADA FUT ECO/DEV INDUS R+D DELIB/GP DIPLOM ECO/TAC CIVMIL/REL PEACE...POLICY BIBLIOG PACIFIST 20. PAGE 134 H2679
ARMS/CONT STAT PLAN NAT/G

S67
GRIEB K.J.,"THE UNITED STATES AND THE CENTRAL AMERICAN CONFEDERATION." COSTA/RICA EL/SALVADR GUATEMALA HONDURAS L/A+17C NICARAGUA NAT/G FORCES CONFER AGREE EXEC ARMS/CONT REV WAR PEACE ATTIT 20. PAGE 60 H1212
INT/ORG DIPLOM POLICY REGION

S67
JAIN G.,"INDIA REJECTS THE POWER RACE* REALISM ABOUT NUCLEAR WEAPONS." FORCES PROB/SOLV FOR/AID ARMS/CONT COST PWR...GOV/COMP 20. PAGE 79 H1583
INDIA CHINA/COM NUC/PWR DIPLOM

S67
LALL B.G.,"GAPS IN THE ABM DEBATE." NAT/G DIPLOM DETER CIVMIL/REL 20. PAGE 90 H1798
NUC/PWR ARMS/CONT EX/STRUC FORCES

S67
MENDL W.,"FRENCH ATTITUDES ON DISARMAMENT." FRANCE CULTURE CHIEF FORCES DIPLOM LEAD WAR...TIME/SEQ 20 DEGAULLE/C. PAGE 109 H2175
NUC/PWR WEAPON ARMS/CONT POLICY

S67
NIEBUHR R.,"THE SOCIAL MYTHS IN THE COLD WAR." USA+45 USSR VIETNAM PROB/SOLV BAL/PWR ARMS/CONT NAT/LISM PWR ALL/IDEOS CONCPT. PAGE 118 H2359
MYTH DIPLOM GOV/COMP

S67
ROOT W.,"REPORT FROM PARIS - DE GAULLE: WHICH WAY TO THE FUTURE?" CANADA FRANCE ISLAM UK INT/ORG CHIEF CREATE AGREE CONTROL ARMS/CONT NUC/PWR EQUILIB PEACE PWR 20 DEGAULLE/C NATO. PAGE 134 H2670
POLICY DIPLOM NAT/G BAL/PWR

C67
GEHLEN M.P.,"THE POLITICS OF COEXISTENCE: SOVIET METHODS AND MOTIVES." COM USSR NAT/G INT/TRADE EDU/PROP ARMS/CONT DETER KNOWL...CHARTS IDEA/COMP 20 COLD/WAR. PAGE 55 H1108
BIBLIOG PEACE DIPLOM MARXISM

ARMY....ARMY (ALL NATIONS)

ARNE S. H0165

ARNOLD M. H0166,H0167

ARNOLD/M....MATTHEW ARNOLD

ARON R. H0168,H0169,H0170

ART/METH....FINE AND PERFORMING ARTS

N
ACAD RUMANIAN SCI DOC CTR,RUMANIAN SCIENTIFIC ABSTRACTS: SOCIAL SCIENCES. ROMANIA FINAN HABITAT ...ART/METH GEOG HUM JURID PSY 20. PAGE 3 H0059
BIBLIOG/A CULTURE LING LAW

N
INADA S.,INTRODUCTION TO SCIENTIFIC WORKS IN HUMANITIES AND SOCIAL SCIENCES PUBLISHED IN JAPAN. LAW CULTURE ACADEM EDU/PROP...ART/METH HUM 20 CHINJAP. PAGE 76 H1525
BIBLIOG/A NAT/G SOC S/ASIA

N
US LIBRARY OF CONGRESS,SOUTHERN ASIA ACCESSIONS LIST. BURMA CEYLON INDIA NEPAL PAKISTAN S/ASIA THAILAND AGRI INDUS SCHOOL WORKER...ART/METH GEOG HEAL PHIL/SCI LING 20. PAGE 160 H3201
BIBLIOG/A SOCIETY CULTURE ECO/UNDEV

B13
DIE REKLAME IHRE KUNST UND WISSENSCHAFT. GERMANY POLAND SWITZERLND USA+45 TEC/DEV CAP/ISM DEMAND ...ART/METH EXHIBIT METH/COMP ANTHOL 20. PAGE 135 H2707
EDU/PROP MARKET NAT/COMP ATTIT

N13
H T.,GRUNDZUGE DES CHINESISCHEN VOLKSCHARACTERS. ASIA CULTURE SOCIETY...HUM 19/20. PAGE 63 H1262
ATTIT PERSON ART/METH LING

B21
BALFOUR A.J.,ESSAYS SPECULATIVE AND POLITICAL. SEA CULTURE CREATE WAR NAT/LISM PEACE LOVE...ART/METH INT/LAW CONCPT ANTHOL 20 JEWS. PAGE 10 H0204
PHIL/SCI SOCIETY DIPLOM

B22
FICHTE J.G.,ADDRESSES TO THE GERMAN NATION. GERMANY PRUSSIA ELITES NAT/G SECT CREATE INT/TRADE HEREDITY ...ART/METH LING 19 FRANK/PARL. PAGE 50 H0989
NAT/LISM CULTURE EDU/PROP REGION

B27
QUERARD J.M.,LA FRANCE LITTERAIRE (12 VOLS.). FRANCE CULTURE...HUM SOC 16/19. PAGE 129 H2573
BIBLIOG/A BIOG

ART/METH

B35
GORER G.,AFRICA DANCES: A BOOK ABOUT WEST AFRICAN NEGROES. STRUCT LOC/G SECT FORCES TAX ADMIN COLONIAL...ART/METH MYTH WORSHIP 20 NEGRO AFRICA/W CHRISTIAN RITUAL. PAGE 59 H1181
AFR ATTIT CULTURE SOCIETY

B38
RAWLINSON H.G.,INDIA: A SHORT CULTURAL HISTORY. INDIA LAW STRATA FORCES INT/TRADE ADMIN COLONIAL PERSON...GEOG HUM BIBLIOG WORSHIP 20. PAGE 130 H2598
CULTURE SECT MYTH ART/METH

B41
GRISMER R.,A NEW BIBLIOGRAPHY OF THE LITERATURES OF SPAIN AND SPANISH AMERICA. CHRIST-17C MOD/EUR PRE/AMER SPAIN CULTURE DIPLOM EDU/PROP...ART/METH GEOG HUM PHIL/SCI 20. PAGE 61 H1229
BIBLIOG LAW NAT/G ECO/UNDEV

B42
BLANCHARD L.R.,MARTINIQUE: A SELECTED LIST OF REFERENCES (PAMPHLET). WEST/IND AGRI LOC/G SCHOOL ...ART/METH GEOG JURID CHARTS 20. PAGE 18 H0353
BIBLIOG/A SOCIETY CULTURE COLONIAL

B42
SINGTON D.,THE GOEBBELS EXPERIMENT. GERMANY MOD/EUR NAT/G EX/STRUC FORCES CONTROL ROUTINE WAR TOTALISM PWR...ART/METH HUM 20 NAZI GOEBBELS/J. PAGE 144 H2886
FASCISM EDU/PROP ATTIT COM/IND

B44
US LIBRARY OF CONGRESS,RUSSIA: A CHECK LIST PRELIMINARY TO A BASIC BIBLIOGRAPHY OF MATERIALS IN THE RUSSIAN LANGUAGE. COM USSR CULTURE EDU/PROP MARXISM...ART/METH HUM LING 19/20. PAGE 160 H3204
BIBLIOG LAW SECT

N46
HOBBS C.C.,SOUTHEAST ASIA, 1935-45: A SELECTED LIST OF REFERENCE BOOKS (PAMPHLET). S/ASIA AGRI INDUS NAT/G SECT DIPLOM WAR...ART/METH GEOG SOC LING 20. PAGE 72 H1435
BIBLIOG/A CULTURE HABITAT

B47
BEHAR D.,BIBLIOGRAFIA HISPANOAMERICANA. LIBROS ANTIGUOS Y MODERNOS REFERENTES A AMERICA Y ESPANA. PORTUGAL SPAIN CONSTN NAT/G SECT CREATE REV WAR GOV/REL...ART/METH GEOG PHIL/SCI LING 20 ARGEN. PAGE 13 H0260
BIBLIOG L/A+17C CULTURE

B48
FLOREN LOZANO L.,BIBLIOGRAFIA DE LA BIBLIOGRAFIA DOMINICANA. DOMIN/REP NAT/G DIPLOM EDU/PROP CIVMIL/REL...POLICY ART/METH GEOG PHIL/SCI HIST/WRIT 20. PAGE 51 H1027
BIBLIOG/A BIOG L/A+17C CULTURE

B48
YAKOBSON S.,FIVE HUNDRED RUSSIAN WORKS FOR COLLEGE LIBRARIES (PAMPHLET). MOD/EUR USSR MARXISM SOCISM ...ART/METH GEOG HUM JURID SOC 13/20. PAGE 171 H3431
BIBLIOG NAT/G CULTURE COM

B50
CONOVER H.F.,INTRODUCTION TO EUROPE: A SELECTIVE GUIDE TO BACKGROUND READING. COM EUR+WWI NAT/G KNOWL...ART/METH GEOG SOC. PAGE 32 H0648
BIBLIOG/A MOD/EUR HIST/WRIT

B50
FITZGERALD C.P.,CHINA, A SHORT CULTURAL HISTORY. ASIA DIPLOM INT/TRADE...ART/METH SOC MANCHU/DYN. PAGE 51 H1016
NAT/G SOCIETY

B50
HOBBS C.C.,INDOCHINA, A BIBLIOGRAPHY OF THE LAND AND PEOPLE. VIETNAM CULTURE AGRI INDUS NAT/G SECT ...ART/METH GEOG SOC LING 20. PAGE 72 H1436
BIBLIOG/A S/ASIA COLONIAL ECO/UNDEV

B50
JONES H.D.,KOREA, AN ANNOTATED BIBLIOGRAPHY OF PUBLICATIONS IN WESTERN LANGUAGES. KOREA CULTURE MUNIC SECT FORCES DIPLOM HEALTH WEALTH...ART/METH GEOG SOC LING 20. PAGE 82 H1632
BIBLIOG/A ASIA NAT/G ECO/UNDEV

B51
BISSAINTHE M.,DICTIONNAIRE DE BIBLIOGRAPHIE HAITIENNE. HAITI ELITES AGRI LEGIS DIPLOM INT/TRADE WRITING ORD/FREE CATHISM...ART/METH GEOG 19/20 NEGRO TREATY. PAGE 17 H0347
BIBLIOG L/A+17C SOCIETY NAT/G

B51
WABEKE B.H.,A GUIDE TO DUTCH BIBLIOGRAPHIES. BELGIUM INDONESIA NETHERLAND DIPLOM INT/TRADE WAR NAT/LISM KNOWL...ART/METH HUM JURID CON/ANAL 14/20. PAGE 164 H3282
BIBLIOG/A NAT/G CULTURE COLONIAL

B52
ETTINGHAUSEN R.,SELECTED AND ANNOTATED BIBLIOGRAPHY OF BOOKS AND PERIODICALS IN WESTERN LANGUAGES DEALING WITH NEAR AND MIDDLE EAST. LAW CULTURE SECT ...ART/METH GEOG SOC. PAGE 47 H0944
BIBLIOG/A ISLAM MEDIT-7

B54
GIRALSO JARAMLLO G.,BIBLIOGRAFIA DE BIBLIOGRAFIAS COLOMBIANAS. L/A+17C ACADEM SECT CREATE EDU/PROP ...ART/METH GEOG LING TREND 20 COLOMB. PAGE 57 H1135
BIBLIOG/A CULTURE PHIL/SCI ECO/UNDEV

B56
EVANS-PRITCHARD E.E.,THE INSTITUTIONS OF PRIMITIVE SOCIETY. LAW SOCIETY KIN ACT/RES CREATE ALL/VALS ...ART/METH SOC METH/CNCPT WORSHIP 20. PAGE 48 H0953
STRUCT PHIL/SCI CULTURE CONCPT

B56
SHAPIRO H.L.,MAN, CULTURE, AND SOCIETY. STRUCT FAM SECT GP/REL INGP/REL...ART/METH GEOG PSY LING ANTHOL BIBLIOG. PAGE 142 H2842
CULTURE PERSON SOC

B56
WILBER D.N.,ANNOTATED BIBLIOGRAPHY OF AFGHANISTAN. AFGHANISTN...ART/METH GEOG HUM SOC CON/ANAL 19/20. PAGE 168 H3358
BIBLIOG/A SOCIETY NAT/G ASIA

B57
BYRNES R.F.,BIBLIOGRAPHY OF AMERICAN PUBLICATIONS ON EAST CENTRAL EUROPE, 1945-1957 (VOL. XXII). SECT DIPLOM EDU/PROP RACE/REL...ART/METH GEOG JURID SOC LING 20 JEWS. PAGE 25 H0503
BIBLIOG/A COM MARXISM NAT/G

B57
HERNANDEZ-ARREGU J.,IMPERIALISMO Y CULTURA (LA POLITICA EN LA INTELIGENCIA ARGENTINA). L/A+17C CULTURE ELITES WRITING COLONIAL CROWD ATTIT FASCISM MARXISM SOCISM...BIOG IDEA/COMP 20 ARGEN PERON/JUAN COM/PARTY. PAGE 70 H1403
INTELL CREATE ART/METH HUM

B57
KANTOROWICZ E.,THE KING'S TWO BODIES; A STUDY IN MEDIEVAL POLITICAL THEOLOGY. UK LAW CONSTN NAT/G CT/SYS...ART/METH HUM CONCPT MYTH TIME/SEQ BIBLIOG 4/17 ELIZABTH/I POPE CHURCH/STA. PAGE 83 H1657
JURID SECT CHIEF SOVEREIGN

B58
KURL S.,ESTONIA: A SELECTED BIBLIOGRAPHY. USSR ESTONIA LAW INTELL SECT...ART/METH GEOG HUM SOC 20. PAGE 89 H1784
BIBLIOG CULTURE NAT/G

B58
YUAN TUNG-LI,CHINA IN WESTERN LITERATURE. SECT DIPLOM...ART/METH GEOG JURID SOC BIOG CON/ANAL. PAGE 172 H3441
BIBLIOG ASIA CULTURE HUM

B60
SZTARAY Z.,BIBLIOGRAPHY ON HUNGARY. HUNGARY MOD/EUR CULTURE INDUS SECT DIPLOM REV...ART/METH SOC LING 18/20. PAGE 151 H3029
BIBLIOG NAT/G COM MARXISM

S60
ARENDT H.,"SOCIETY AND CULTURE." FUT CULTURE INTELL STRATA EDU/PROP ATTIT PERSON KNOWL...ART/METH HUM 20. PAGE 8 H0161
SOCIETY CREATE

B61
ACOSTA SAIGNES M.,ESTUDIOS DE ETNOLOGIA ANTIGUA DE VENEZUELA (2ND ED.). PRE/AMER VENEZUELA...ART/METH SOC BIBLIOG INDIAN/AM. PAGE 3 H0061
CULTURE STRUCT GP/REL HABITAT

B61
DOOB L.W.,COMMUNICATION IN AFRICA: A SEARCH FOR BOUNDARIES. CULTURE SOCIETY EDU/PROP WRITING INGP/REL DRIVE ORD/FREE...ART/METH SOC LING BIBLIOG 20. PAGE 42 H0837
AFR FEEDBACK PERCEPT PERS/REL

B61
FREYRE G.,THE PORTUGUESE AND THE TROPICS. L/A+17C PORTUGAL SOCIETY PERF/ART ADMIN TASK GP/REL ...ART/METH CONCPT SOC/INTEG 20. PAGE 53 H1060
COLONIAL METH PLAN CULTURE

B62
AMERICAN SOCIETY AFR CULTURE,PAN-AFRICANISM RECONSIDERED. AFR SOCIETY STRUCT SCHOOL CAP/ISM EDU/PROP...ART/METH NEW/IDEA PREDICT ANTHOL 20 PANAF/FREE NEGRO. PAGE 6 H0123
DIPLOM FEDERAL NAT/LISM CULTURE

B62
HACHMANN R.,VOLKER ZWISCHEN GERMANEN UND KELTEN. GERMANY CULTURE STRUCT MUNIC...ART/METH CHARTS MAPS. PAGE 63 H1269
LING SOC KIN GP/REL

B62
KIDDER F.E.,THESES ON PAN AMERICAN TOPICS. LAW CULTURE NAT/G SECT DIPLOM HEALTH...ART/METH GEOG SOC 13/20. PAGE 86 H1709
BIBLIOG CHRIST-17C L/A+17C SOCIETY

B62
MICHAEL H.N.,STUDIES IN SIBERIAN ETHNOGENESIS. USSR KIN...ART/METH SOC 20 SIBERIA. PAGE 110 H2196
HABITAT HEREDITY CULTURE LING

B63
CONOVER H.F.,AFRICA SOUTH OF THE SAHARA. CULTURE SECT TEC/DEV...ART/METH GEOG SOC. PAGE 33 H0654
BIBLIOG/A AFR CON/ANAL

B63
JAIRAZBHOY R.A.,FOREIGN INFLUENCE IN ANCIENT INDIA. INDIA ELITES SECT DIPLOM EDU/PROP COLONIAL REGION GP/REL...ART/METH LING WORSHIP +/14 GRECO/ROMN MESOPOTAM PERSIA PARTH/SASS. PAGE 79 H1587
CULTURE SOCIETY COERCE DOMIN

B63
STUCKI C.W.,AMERICAN DOCTORAL DISSERTATIONS ON ASIA 1933-62 (A PAPER). PREHIST INDUS NAT/G GOV/REL ALL/IDEOS...ART/METH GEOG SOC LING 20. PAGE 150 H3002
BIBLIOG ASIA SOCIETY S/ASIA

B64
ANDREWS D.H.,LATIN AMERICA: A BIBLIOGRAPHY OF PAPERBACK BOOKS. SECT INT/TRADE EDU/PROP WAR GOV/REL ADJUST NAT/LISM ATTIT...ART/METH LING BIOG
BIBLIOG L/A+17C CULTURE

20. PAGE 7 H0138 — NAT/G

B64
GRIFFITH W.,THE WELSH (2ND ED.). UK SOCIETY STRUCT SECT WRITING NAT/LISM...ART/METH MODAL OBS/ENVIR TREND SOC/INTEG WALES PURITAN MUSIC. PAGE 61 H1223 — CULTURE SOC LING

B64
KITCHEN H.,A HANDBOOK OF AFRICAN AFFAIRS. ECO/UNDEV CREATE DIPLOM COLONIAL RACE/REL...ART/METH GEOG CHARTS 20. PAGE 87 H1729 — AFR NAT/G INT/ORG FORCES

B64
MUSEUM FUR VOLKERKUNDE WIEN,ZENTRALAMERIKA MEXIKO VOLKER UND KULTUREN. COSTA/RICA GUATEMALA L/A+17C PANAMA SECT WAR GP/REL SOVEREIGN...ART/METH 20 CENTRAL/AM MEXIC/AMER. PAGE 115 H2300 — SOCIETY STRUCT CULTURE AGRI

B64
RAGHAVAN M.D.,INDIA IN CEYLONESE HISTORY, SOCIETY AND CULTURE. CEYLON INDIA S/ASIA LAW SOCIETY INT/TRADE ATTIT...ART/METH JURID SOC LING 20. PAGE 129 H2581 — DIPLOM CULTURE SECT STRUCT

B65
STERN F.,THE POLITICS OF CULTURAL DESPAIR. EUR+WWI GERMANY POL/PAR SECT RACE/REL STRANGE TOTALISM ...ART/METH MYTH BIBLIOG 20 JEWS. PAGE 149 H2980 — CULTURE ATTIT NAT/LISM FASCISM

B66
KIRKLAND E.C.,A BIBLIOGRAPHY OF SOUTH ASIAN FOLKLORE. WRITING HABITAT ALL/VALS MYSTISM ...ART/METH GEOG PSY SOC MYTH WORSHIP 13/20. PAGE 86 H1723 — BIBLIOG S/ASIA CULTURE CREATE

B67
ALLWORTH E.,CENTRAL ASIA: A CENTURY OF RUSSIAN RULE. USSR INTELL SOCIETY AGRI INDUS COLONIAL REV WAR NAT/LISM...ART/METH GEOG LING 19/20. PAGE 5 H0108 — ASIA CULTURE NAT/G

B67
RIESMAN D.,CONVERSATIONS IN JAPAN: MODERNIZATION, POLITICS, AND CULTURE. CHINA/COM STRATA STRUCT ECO/DEV INDUS ACADEM EDU/PROP...ART/METH SOC MODAL INT IDEA/COMP SOC/INTEG 20 CHINJAP HIROSHIMA. PAGE 131 H2629 — CULTURE SOCIETY ASIA

L67
EGBERT D.D.,"THE IDEA OF 'AVANT-GARDE' IN ART AND POLITICS." USSR CULTURE INTELL POL/PAR CREATE EDU/PROP CONTROL REV ANOMIE DRIVE ROLE...IDEA/COMP 20. PAGE 45 H0895 — ART/METH COM ATTIT

S67
EGBERT D.D.,"POLITICS AND ART IN COMMUNIST BULGARIA" BULGARIA COM USSR CULTURE DIPLOM INGP/REL TOTALISM...TREND 20. PAGE 45 H0894 — CREATE ART/METH CONTROL MARXISM

ARTHUR/CA....PRESIDENT CHESTER ALAN ARTHUR

ARTISTIC ACHIEVEMENT....SEE CREATE

ASHBEE H.S. H0171

ASHFORD D.E. H0172,H0173

ASHLEY M.P. H0174

ASHRAF A. H0175

ASIA....SEE ALSO APPROPRIATE TIME/SPACE/CULTURE INDEX

N
JOURNAL OF ASIAN STUDIES. CULTURE ECO/DEV SECT DIPLOM EDU/PROP WAR NAT/LISM...PHIL/SCI SOC 20. PAGE 1 H0005 — BIBLIOG ASIA S/ASIA NAT/G

N
NEUE POLITISCHE LITERATUR. AFR ASIA EUR+WWI GERMANY RUSSIA SOCIETY ECO/DEV ECO/UNDEV PLAN PROB/SOLV LEAD MARXISM...PHIL/SCI CONCPT 20. PAGE 1 H0008 — BIBLIOG DIPLOM COM NAT/G

N
DAILY SUMMARY OF THE JAPANESE PRESS. NAT/G DIPLOM LEAD 20 CHINJAP. PAGE 1 H0013 — BIBLIOG PRESS ASIA ATTIT

N
CHINA QUARTERLY. COM AGRI INDUS ACADEM POL/PAR INT/TRADE CONFER GOV/REL...TIME/SEQ CON/ANAL INDEX 20. PAGE 1 H0014 — BIBLIOG/A ASIA DIPLOM POLICY

N
SUMMARIES OF SELECTED JAPANESE MAGAZINES. LAW CULTURE ADMIN LEAD 20 CHINJAP. PAGE 2 H0025 — BIBLIOG/A ATTIT NAT/G ASIA

N
ASIA FOUNDATION,LIBRARY NOTES. LAW CONSTN CULTURE SOCIETY ECO/UNDEV INT/ORG NAT/G COLONIAL LEAD REGION NAT/LISM ATTIT 20 UN. PAGE 9 H0176 — BIBLIOG/A ASIA S/ASIA DIPLOM

N
CORDIER H.,BIBLIOTECA SINICA. SOCIETY STRUCT SECT DIPLOM COLONIAL...GEOG SOC CON/ANAL. PAGE 33 H0664 — BIBLIOG/A NAT/G CULTURE ASIA

N
KYRIAK T.E.,ASIAN DEVELOPMENTS: A BIBLIOGRAPHY. INDONESIA KOREA/N VIETNAM/N CULTURE SOCIETY ECO/UNDEV NAT/G DIPLOM...SOC TREND 20 MONGOLIA. PAGE 90 H1788 — BIBLIOG/A ALL/IDEOS S/ASIA ASIA

N
KYRIAK T.E.,CHINA: A BIBLIOGRAPHY. ASIA CHINA/COM AGRI FINAN INDUS NAT/G INT/TRADE PRESS...SOC 20. PAGE 90 H1789 — BIBLIOG/A MARXISM TOP/EX POL/PAR

N
US CONSULATE GENERAL HONG KONG,REVIEW OF THE HONG KONG CHINESE PRESS. ECO/UNDEV LOC/G NAT/G PLAN DIPLOM EDU/PROP LEAD GP/REL MARXISM...POLICY INDEX 20. PAGE 159 H3178 — BIBLIOG/A ASIA PRESS ATTIT

N
US CONSULATE GENERAL HONG KONG,CURRENT BACKGROUND. CHINA/COM ECO/UNDEV LOC/G NAT/G PLAN DIPLOM EDU/PROP LEAD REV ATTIT...POLICY INDEX 20. PAGE 159 H3179 — BIBLIOG/A MARXIST ASIA PRESS

N
US CONSULATE GENERAL HONG KONG,EXTRACTS FROM CHINA MAINLAND MAGAZINES. ASIA CHINA/COM ECO/UNDEV NAT/G CHIEF LEAD ATTIT...MARXIST INDEX 20. PAGE 159 H3180 — BIBLIOG MARXISM PRESS

N
US CONSULATE GENERAL HONG KONG,SURVEY OF CHINA MAINLAND PRESS. CHINA/COM ECO/UNDEV LOC/G NAT/G PLAN DIPLOM EDU/PROP LEAD REV ATTIT...POLICY INDEX 20. PAGE 159 H3181 — BIBLIOG/A MARXIST ASIA PRESS

N
US CONSULATE GENERAL HONG KONG,US CONSULATE GENERAL, HONG KONG, PRESS SUMMARIES. CHINA/COM ECO/UNDEV LOC/G NAT/G PLAN DIPLOM EDU/PROP LEAD REV ATTIT...POLICY INDEX 20. PAGE 159 H3182 — BIBLIOG/A MARXIST ASIA PRESS

N13
H T.,GRUNDZUGE DES CHINESISCHEN VOLKSCHARACTERS. ASIA CULTURE SOCIETY...HUM 19/20. PAGE 63 H1262 — ATTIT PERSON ART/METH LING

B15
FARIES J.C.,THE RISE OF INTERNATIONALISM. ASIA MOD/EUR NAT/G VOL/ASSN DELIB/GP BAL/PWR EDU/PROP ARMS/CONT RIGID/FLEX TREND. PAGE 49 H0971 — INT/ORG DIPLOM PEACE

B18
YUKIO O.,THE VOICE OF JAPANESE DEMOCRACY, AN ESSAY ON CONSTITUTIONAL LOYALTY (TRANS BY J. E. BECKER). ASIA POL/PAR DELIB/GP EX/STRUC RIGID/FLEX ORD/FREE PWR...POLICY JURID METH/COMP 19/20 CHINJAP. PAGE 172 H3443 — CONSTN MAJORIT CHOOSE NAT/G

N19
GOODMAN G.K.,IMPERIAL JAPAN AND ASIA: A REASSESSMENT (PAMPHLET). ASIA S/ASIA ECO/DEV FORCES LEAD WAR NAT/LISM ATTIT...DECISION CONCPT BIBLIOG 19/20 CHINJAP. PAGE 59 H1172 — DIPLOM NAT/G POLICY COLONIAL

B28
YANG KUNG-SUN,THE BOOK OF LORD SHANG. LAW ECO/UNDEV LOC/G NAT/G NEIGH PLAN ECO/TAC LEGIT ATTIT SKILL ...CONCPT CON/ANAL WORK TOT/POP. PAGE 172 H3434 — ASIA JURID

B29
ROBERTS S.H.,HISTORY OF FRENCH COLONIAL POLICY. AFR ASIA L/A+17C S/ASIA CULTURE ECO/DEV ECO/UNDEV FINAN NAT/G PLAN ECO/TAC DOMIN ROUTINE SOVEREIGN...OBS HIST/WRIT TREND CHARTS VAL/FREE 19/20. PAGE 132 H2642 — INT/ORG ACT/RES FRANCE COLONIAL

B35
TAKEUCHI T.,WAR AND DIPLOMACY IN THE JAPANESE EMPIRE. ASIA ELITES STRATA NAT/G SECT LEGIS ACT/RES PLAN LEGIT PARL/PROC ROUTINE WAR...MGT BIOG CHINJAP TOT/POP 19/20 CHINJAP. PAGE 152 H3038 — EXEC STRUCT

B39
KERNER R.J.,NORTHEAST ASIA: A SELECTED BIBLIOGRAPHY (2 VOLS.). KOREA RUSSIA NAT/G DIPLOM...GEOG 19/20 CHINJAP. PAGE 85 H1696 — BIBLIOG ASIA SOCIETY CULTURE

B39
TAGGART F.J.,ROME AND CHINA. MEDIT-7 INT/ORG NAT/G FORCES LEGIS TOP/EX PLAN PWR SOVEREIGN...CHARTS TOT/POP ROM/EMP. PAGE 152 H3034 — ASIA WAR

B40
CONOVER H.F.,JAPAN-ECONOMIC DEVELOPMENT AND FOREIGN POLICY, A SELECTED LIST OF REFERENCES (PAMPHLET). CULTURE FINAN INDUS NAT/G FORCES INT/TRADE WAR ...SOC TREND 20 CHINJAP. PAGE 32 H0640 — BIBLIOG ASIA ECO/DEV DIPLOM

C40
FAHS C.B.,"GOVERNMENT IN JAPAN." FINAN FORCES LEGIS TOP/EX BUDGET INT/TRADE EDU/PROP SOVEREIGN ...CON/ANAL BIBLIOG/A 20 CHINJAP. PAGE 48 H0962 — ASIA DIPLOM NAT/G ADMIN

B45
LASKER B.,ASIA ON THE MOVE. ASIA BURMA S/ASIA THAILAND USSR ECO/UNDEV FAM KIN WAR NAT/LISM ATTIT ...GEOG CENSUS TREND AUSTRAL 20. PAGE 91 H1826
CULTURE RIGID/FLEX

B48
CLYDE P.H.,THE FAR EAST: A HISTORY OF THE IMPACT OF THE WEST ON EASTERN ASIA. CHINA/COM CULTURE INT/TRADE DOMIN COLONIAL WAR PWR...CHARTS BIBLIOG 19/20 CHINJAP. PAGE 30 H0609
DIPLOM ASIA

B48
PELCOVITS N.A.,OLD CHINA HANDS AND THE FOREIGN OFFICE. ASIA BURMA UK ECO/UNDEV NAT/G ECO/TAC FOR/AID TARIFFS DOMIN COLONIAL GOV/REL SOVEREIGN 19 HONG/KONG TREATY. PAGE 124 H2483
INT/TRADE ATTIT DIPLOM

B50
FITZGERALD C.P.,CHINA, A SHORT CULTURAL HISTORY. ASIA DIPLOM INT/TRADE...ART/METH SOC MANCHU/DYN. PAGE 51 H1016
NAT/G SOCIETY

B50
GLEASON J.H.,THE GENESIS OF RUSSOPHOBIA IN GREAT BRITAIN: A STUDY OF THE INTERACTION OF POLICY AND OPINION. ASIA RUSSIA UK NAT/G AGREE CONTROL REV WAR LOVE PWR TREATY 19. PAGE 57 H1142
DIPLOM POLICY DOMIN COLONIAL

B50
JONES H.D.,KOREA, AN ANNOTATED BIBLIOGRAPHY OF PUBLICATIONS IN WESTERN LANGUAGES. KOREA CULTURE MUNIC SECT FORCES DIPLOM HEALTH WEALTH...ART/METH GEOG SOC LING 20. PAGE 82 H1632
BIBLIOG/A ASIA NAT/G ECO/UNDEV

B50
TENG S.,AN ANNOTATED BIBLIOGRAPHY OF SELECTED CHINESE REFERENCE WORKS (REV. ED.). CULTURE ECO/UNDEV LEAD MARXISM...LING INDEX 3/20. PAGE 153 H3062
BIBLIOG/A ASIA NAT/G

B50
WARD R.E.,A GUIDE TO JAPANESE REFERENCE AND RESEARCH MATERIALS IN THE FIELD OF POLITICAL SCIENCE. LAW CONSTN LOC/G PRESS ADMIN...SOC CON/ANAL METH 19/20 CHINJAP. PAGE 165 H3305
BIBLIOG/A ASIA NAT/G

S51
NORTHROP F.S.C.,"ASIAN MENTALITY AND UNITED STATES FOREIGN POLICY." ASIA ISLAM USA+45 CULTURE SOCIETY SECT EDU/PROP LEGIT COERCE DRIVE MORAL ORD/FREE ...POLICY RELATIV TOT/POP 20. PAGE 119 H2376
S/ASIA ATTIT DIPLOM

C52
FIFIELD R.H.,"WOODROW WILSON AND THE FAR EAST." ASIA CHIEF DELIB/GP BAL/PWR CONFER COLONIAL ARMS/CONT WAR...TIME/SEQ NAT/COMP 19/20 WILSON/W LEAGUE/NAT. PAGE 50 H0995
BIBLIOG DIPLOM INT/ORG

B53
HUNTER E.,BRAIN-WASHING IN RED CHINA. ASIA CHINA/COM CULTURE SOCIETY FORCES WAR TOTALISM ATTIT BIO/SOC DISPL DRIVE PERSON SUPEGO KNOWL ORD/FREE ...INT REC/INT COLD/WAR 20. PAGE 75 H1499
EDU/PROP COERCE

C53
KRACKE E.A. JR.,"CIVIL SERVICE IN EARLY SUNG CHINA, 960-1067." ASIA GP/REL...BIBLIOG/A 10/11. PAGE 88 H1762
ADMIN NAT/G WORKER CONTROL

B54
CHECKLIST OF ARCHIVES IN THE JAPANESE MINISTRY OF FOREIGN AFFAIRS....GEOG SOC METH 19/20 CHINJAP. PAGE 161 H3219
BIBLIOG/A NAT/G ASIA

B55
QUAN K.L.,INTRODUCTION TO ASIA: A SELECTIVE GUIDE TO BACKGROUND READING. ECO/UNDEV NAT/G PROB/SOLV DIPLOM ATTIT 20. PAGE 129 H2572
BIBLIOG/A S/ASIA CULTURE ASIA

B55
TAN C.C.,THE BOXER CATASTROPHE. ASIA UK USSR ELITES POL/PAR VOL/ASSN FORCES PROB/SOLV DIPLOM ADMIN COLONIAL NAT/LISM PEACE TREATY 19/20 BOXER/REBL. PAGE 152 H3040
REV NAT/G WAR

B55
UN ECONOMIC COMN ASIA & FAR E,ECONOMIC SURVEY OF ASIA AND THE FAR EAST, 1954. AFGHANISTN CEYLON INDIA PHILIPPINE S/ASIA ECO/DEV FINAN INDUS INT/TRADE PRODUC WEALTH...STAT CHARTS 20 CHINJAP. PAGE 158 H3158
ECO/UNDEV PRICE NAT/COMP ASIA

L55
ROSTOW W.W.,"RUSSIA AND CHINA UNDER COMMUNISM." CHINA/COM USSR INTELL STRUCT INT/ORG NAT/G POL/PAR TOP/EX ACT/RES PLAN ADMIN ATTIT ALL/VALS MARXISM ...CONCPT OBS TIME/SEQ TREND GOV/COMP VAL/FREE 20. PAGE 134 H2689
COM ASIA

B56
EGGAN F.,SELECTED BIBLIOGRAPHY OF THE PHILIPPINES. PHILIPPINE ATTIT...SOC NAT/COMP 20. PAGE 45 H0896
BIBLIOG/A ASIA CULTURE SOCIETY

B56
LEVIN M.G.,THE PEOPLES OF SIBERIA. PREHIST ECO/UNDEV KIN SECT HABITAT...CLASSIF AUD/VIS WORSHIP 20 SIBERIA. PAGE 95 H1900
CULTURE SOCIETY ASIA

B56
SMEDLEY A.,THE GREAT ROAD: THE LIFE AND TIMES OF CHU TEH. ASIA USSR NAT/G POL/PAR DIPLOM COERCE GUERRILLA CIVMIL/REL NAT/LISM PERSON SKILL MARXISM ...BIOG 20 CHINJAP MAO. PAGE 145 H2903
REV WAR FORCES

B56
WILBER D.N.,ANNOTATED BIBLIOGRAPHY OF AFGHANISTAN. AFGHANISTN...ART/METH GEOG HUM SOC CON/ANAL 19/20. PAGE 168 H3358
BIBLIOG/A SOCIETY NAT/G ASIA

L56
EISENTADT S.N.,"POLITICAL STRUGGLE IN BUREAUCRATIC SOCIETIES" ASIA CULTURE ADJUD SANCTION PWR BUREAUCRCY OTTOMAN BYZANTINE. PAGE 45 H0901
ADMIN CHIEF CONTROL ROUTINE

B57
AMERICAN COUNCIL LEARNED SOC,GOVERNMENT UNDER LAW AND THE INDIVIDUAL. ASIA ISLAM USSR NAT/G...POLICY SOC NAT/COMP 20. PAGE 6 H0121
SOCIETY ORD/FREE CONCPT IDEA/COMP

B57
DEAN V.M.,THE NATURE OF THE NON-WESTERN WORLD. AFR ASIA L/A+17C S/ASIA CULTURE SOCIETY STRATA ECO/DEV DIPLOM ECO/TAC FOR/AID ATTIT DRIVE ALL/VALS ...RELATIV SOC CONCPT TIME/SEQ TREND TOT/POP 20. PAGE 39 H0778
ECO/UNDEV STERTYP NAT/LISM

B57
HALLGARTEN G.W.,DAMONEN ODER RETTER. ASIA L/A+17C CAP/ISM ATTIT MARXISM SOCISM...NAT/COMP. PAGE 64 H1289
TOTALISM FASCISM COERCE DOMIN

B57
HOUN F.W.,CENTRAL GOVERNMENT OF CHINA, 1912-1928. ASIA CONSTN CHIEF LEGIS CONTROL PWR...BIBLIOG 20. PAGE 74 H1480
POL/PAR ATTIT NAT/G PLAN

B57
KENNEDY M.D.,A SHORT HISTORY OF COMMUNISM IN ASIA. ASIA BURMA INDIA S/ASIA THAILAND NAT/G POL/PAR LEAD REV WAR MARXISM SOCISM...POLICY 20 CHINJAP. PAGE 85 H1688
DIPLOM NAT/LISM TOTALISM COERCE

B57
US SENATE SPEC COMM FOR AID,COMPILATION OF STUDIES AND SURVEYS. AFR ASIA L/A+17C USA+45 ECO/UNDEV AGRI INT/ORG CONSULT TEC/DEV CONFER TOTALISM...NAT/COMP 20 CONGRESS. PAGE 161 H3216
FOR/AID DIPLOM ORD/FREE DELIB/GP

B57
VON HIPPEL E.,GESCHICHTE DER STAATSPHILOSOPHIE (2 VOLS.). ASIA GREECE INDIA PRE/AMER UAR NAT/LISM ORD/FREE MARXISM. PAGE 164 H3272
CULTURE CONCPT NAT/G

C57
WITTFOGEL K.A.,"ORIENTAL DESPOTISM: A COMPARATIVE STUDY OF TOTAL POWER." ASIA CULTURE STRATA NAT/G LEAD OWN ORD/FREE PWR...CONCPT TREND BIBLIOG 20. PAGE 170 H3393
TOTALISM HABITAT DOMIN ELITES

N57
JENNINGS W.I.,NATIONALISM, COLONIALISM, AND NEUTRALISM (PAMPHLET). ASIA INDIA S/ASIA UK INTELL ACADEM POL/PAR 20. PAGE 81 H1611
NAT/LISM COLONIAL NEUTRAL ATTIT

B58
CHANG H.,WITHIN THE FOUR SEAS. ASIA WAR MORAL MARXISM...IDEA/COMP NAT/COMP 20 CONFUCIUS. PAGE 29 H0577
PEACE DIPLOM KNOWL CULTURE

B58
HSU U.T.,THE INVISIBLE CONFLICT. ASIA USSR ELITES NAT/G CONTROL LEAD COERCE REV WAR NAT/LISM ORD/FREE PWR 20 COM/PARTY ESPIONAGE. PAGE 74 H1485
MARXISM POL/PAR EDU/PROP FORCES

B58
VARG P.A.,MISSIONARIES, CHINESE, AND DIPLOMATS: THE AMERICAN PROTESTANT MISSIONARY MOVEMENT IN CHINA, 1890-1952. ASIA ECO/UNDEV NAT/G PROB/SOLV CAP/ISM EDU/PROP COLONIAL NAT/LISM ATTIT MARXISM...NAT/COMP STERTYP 20 CHINJAP PROTESTANT MISSION. PAGE 162 H3234
CULTURE DIPLOM SECT

B58
YUAN TUNG-LI,CHINA IN WESTERN LITERATURE. SECT DIPLOM...ART/METH GEOG JURID SOC BIOG CON/ANAL. PAGE 172 H3441
BIBLIOG ASIA CULTURE HUM

S58
PYE L.W.,"THE NON-WESTERN POLITICAL PROCESS" (BMR)" AFR ASIA ISLAM S/ASIA DIPLOM ADMIN LEAD LOBBY ROUTINE CONSEN...DECISION 20. PAGE 128 H2567
CULTURE POL/PAR NAT/G LOC/G

B59
CAREW-HUNT R.C.,BOOKS ON COMMUNISM. NAT/G POL/PAR DIPLOM REV...BIOG 19/20. PAGE 26 H0528
BIBLIOG/A MARXISM COM ASIA

B59
ISRAEL J.,THE CHINESE STUDENT MOVEMENT, 1927-1937; A BIBLIOGRAPHICAL ESSAY BASED ON THE RESOURCES OF THE HOOVER INSTITUTION. ASIA INTELL NAT/G EDU/PROP 20. PAGE 79 H1571
BIBLIOG/A ACADEM ATTIT

B59
NAHM A.C.,JAPANESE PENETRATION OF KOREA, 1894-1910.
BIBLIOG/A

ASIA KOREA NAT/G...POLICY 20 CHINJAP. PAGE 115 H2303 DIPLOM WAR COLONIAL

B59
PHADINIS U.,DOCUMENTS ON ASIAN AFFAIRS: A SELECT BIBLIOGRAPHY. ASIA...SOC 20. PAGE 125 H2498 BIBLIOG NAT/G DIPLOM

B59
VINACKE H.M.,A HISTORY OF THE FAR EAST IN MODERN TIMES (6TH ED.). KOREA S/ASIA USSR CONSTN CULTURE STRATA ECO/UNDEV NAT/G CHIEF FOR/AID INT/TRADE GP/REL...SOC NAT/COMP 19/20 CHINJAP. PAGE 163 H3255 STRUCT ASIA

B60
COUGHLIN R.,DOUBLE IDENTITY: THE CHINESE AND MODERN THAILAND. CHINA/COM S/ASIA THAILAND ECO/UNDEV EXTR/IND FINAN INDUS KIN MUNIC NAT/G PROF/ORG SCHOOL SECT ATTIT DRIVE...CONCPT OBS 20. PAGE 34 H0676 ASIA FAM CULTURE

B60
EMERSON R.,FROM EMPIRE TO NATION: THE RISE TO SELF-ASSERTION OF ASIAN AND AFRICAN PEOPLES. S/ASIA CULTURE NAT/G SECT DIPLOM ATTIT SOVEREIGN MARXISM ...POLICY BIBLIOG 19/20. PAGE 46 H0919 NAT/LISM COLONIAL AFR ASIA

B60
MACFARQUHAR R.,THE HUNDRED FLOWERS. ASIA NAT/G WORKER GP/REL ORD/FREE MARXISM 20 MAO. PAGE 100 H1991 DEBATE PRESS POL/PAR ATTIT

B60
MORAES F.,THE REVOLT IN TIBET. ASIA CHINA/COM INDIA CULTURE CONTROL COERCE WAR TOTALISM...POLICY SOC WORSHIP 20 TIBET INTERVENT. PAGE 113 H2252 COLONIAL FORCES DIPLOM ORD/FREE

B60
MORRIS I.,NATIONALISM AND THE RIGHT WING IN JAPAN: A STUDY OF POST WAR TRENDS. ASIA ELITES NAT/G DELIB/GP FORCES TOP/EX CHOOSE ATTIT...INT GEN/LAWS CONGRESS 20 CHINJAP. PAGE 113 H2262 POL/PAR TREND NAT/LISM

B60
NAKAMURA H.,THE WAYS OF THINKING OF EASTERN PEOPLES. ASIA INDIA PERSON...HUM SOC LING LOG WORSHIP CHINJAP. PAGE 115 H2305 CULTURE SECT ATTIT

B60
PIERCE R.A.,RUSSIAN CENTRAL ASIA, 1867-1917. ASIA RUSSIA CULTURE AGRI INDUS EDU/PROP REV NAT/LISM ...CHARTS BIBLIOG 19/20 BOLSHEVISM INTERVENT. PAGE 125 H2509 COLONIAL DOMIN ADMIN ECO/UNDEV

B60
SAKAI R.K.,STUDIES ON ASIA, 1960. ASIA CHINA/COM S/ASIA COM/IND ECO/TAC...ANTHOL 17/20 MALAYA. PAGE 137 H2733 ECO/UNDEV SOC

B60
SALETORE B.A.,INDIA'S DIPLOMATIC RELATIONS WITH THE EAST. ASIA CEYLON INDIA NEPAL S/ASIA CULTURE 7/14 PERSIA. PAGE 137 H2740 DIPLOM NAT/COMP ETIQUET

B60
WILLIAMS L.E.,OVERSEAS CHINESE NATIONALISM: THE GENESIS OF THE PAN-CHINESE MOVEMENT IN INDONESIA, 1900-1916. ASIA COM INDONESIA AGRI INT/ORG LOC/G DIPLOM EDU/PROP HABITAT PWR POPULISM...GEOG LING CENSUS 20. PAGE 168 H3367 NAT/LISM GP/REL DECISION NAT/G

B60
WORLEY P.,ASIA TODAY (REV. ED.) (PAMPHLET). COM ECO/UNDEV AGRI FINAN INDUS POL/PAR FOR/AID ADMIN MARXISM 20. PAGE 170 H3411 BIBLIOG/A ASIA DIPLOM NAT/G

B60
ZENKOVSKY S.A.,PAN-TURKISM AND ISLAM IN RUSSIA. ASIA RUSSIA USSR CULTURE POL/PAR DOMIN REV GP/REL MARXISM...LING GP/COMP BIBLIOG 19/20 TURKIC. PAGE 173 H3454 SECT NAT/LISM COM ISLAM

S60
BRZEZINSKI Z.K.,"PATTERNS AND LIMITS OF THE SINO-SOVIET DISPUTE." ASIA CHINA/COM COM FUT STRATA NAT/G EX/STRUC FORCES BAL/PWR DIPLOM ECO/TAC DOMIN EDU/PROP ADMIN COERCE WAR ATTIT RIGID/FLEX ...GEN/LAWS VAL/FREE 20. PAGE 23 H0459 POL/PAR PWR REV USSR

S60
GINSBURGS G.,"PEKING-LHASA-NEW DELHI." CHINA/COM FUT INDIA S/ASIA KIN NAT/G PROVS SECT FORCES BAL/PWR ECO/TAC DOMIN EDU/PROP LEGIT ADMIN REGION GUERRILLA PWR...TREND TIBET 20. PAGE 57 H1134 ASIA COERCE DIPLOM

S60
KEYFITZ N.,"WESTERN PERSPECTIVES AND ASIAN PROBLEMS." ASIA EUR+WWI S/ASIA SOCIETY FOR/AID ...POLICY SOC CONCPT STERTYP WORK TOT/POP 20. PAGE 85 H1701 CULTURE ATTIT

S60
MURPHEY R.,"ECONOMIC CONFLICTS IN SOUTH ASIA." ASIA CULTURE INTELL ECO/TAC REGION ATTIT DRIVE KNOWL ...METH/CNCPT TIME/SEQ STERTYP TOT/POP VAL/FREE 20. PAGE 115 H2296 S/ASIA ECO/UNDEV

S60
NORTH R.C.,"THE NEW EXPANSIONISM." ASIA CHINA/COM FUT INDIA CULTURE SOCIETY NAT/G TOP/EX DOMIN COERCE PWR MARXISM...CONCPT TIME/SEQ TREND GEN/LAWS COLD/WAR 20 MAO. PAGE 119 H2372 ATTIT DRIVE NAT/LISM

S60
NORTH R.C.,"DIE DISKREPANZ ZWISCHEN REALITAT UND WUNSCHBILD ALS INNENPOLITISCHER FAKTOR." ASIA CHINA/COM COM FUT ECO/UNDEV NAT/G PLAN DOMIN ADMIN COERCE PERCEPT...SOC MYTH GEN/METH WORK TOT/POP 20. PAGE 119 H2373 SOCIETY ECO/TAC

S60
SHILS E.,"THE INTELLECTUALS IN THE POLITICAL DEVELOPMENT OF THE NEW STATES." AFR ASIA S/ASIA ELITES LOC/G NAT/G CONSULT EX/STRUC CREATE PLAN ECO/TAC DOMIN LEGIT DRIVE PWR...TRADIT CONCPT STERTYP GEN/LAWS 20. PAGE 143 H2861 POL/PAR INTELL NAT/LISM

C60
WRIGGINS W.H.,"CEYLON: DILEMMAS OF A NEW NATION." ASIA CEYLON CONSTN STRUCT POL/PAR SECT FORCES DIPLOM GOV/REL NAT/LISM...CHARTS BIBLIOG 20. PAGE 171 H3417 PROB/SOLV NAT/G ECO/UNDEV

B61
ATTLEE C.R.,EMPIRE INTO COMMONWEALTH. AFR ASIA CANADA UK NAT/G WAR NAT/LISM ATTIT...POLICY 20 AUSTRAL. PAGE 9 H0179 DIPLOM GP/REL COLONIAL SOVEREIGN

B61
CARNELL F.,THE POLITICS OF THE NEW STATES: A SELECT ANNOTATED BIBLIOGRAPHY WITH SPECIAL REFERENCE TO THE COMMONWEALTH. CONSTN ELITES LABOR NAT/G POL/PAR EX/STRUC DIPLOM ADJUD ADMIN...GOV/COMP 20 COMMONWLTH. PAGE 27 H0534 BIBLIOG/A AFR ASIA COLONIAL

B61
CHAKRABARTI A.,NEHRU: HIS DEMOCRACY AND INDIA. ASIA INDIA UK CONSTN ECO/UNDEV SECT DIPLOM COLONIAL PEACE WEALTH...BIBLIOG 20 CONGRESS NEHRU/J GANDHI/M. PAGE 28 H0570 ORD/FREE STRATA NAT/G CHIEF

B61
DALLIN D.J.,SOVIET FOREIGN POLICY AFTER STALIN. ASIA CHINA/COM EUR+WWI GERMANY IRAN UK YUGOSLAVIA INT/ORG NAT/G VOL/ASSN FORCES TOP/EX BAL/PWR DOMIN EDU/PROP COERCE ATTIT PWR 20. PAGE 37 H0737 COM DIPLOM USSR

B61
GOULD S.H.,SCIENCES IN COMMUNIST CHINA. CHINA/COM FUT INDUS NAT/G TOTALISM...RECORD TOT/POP 20. PAGE 59 H1187 ASIA TEC/DEV

B61
SAKAI R.K.,STUDIES ON ASIA, 1961. ASIA BURMA INDIA S/ASIA FINAN ECO/TAC NAT/LISM SOCISM...POLICY ANTHOL 19/20 CHINJAP. PAGE 137 H2734 ECO/UNDEV SECT

B61
SCHECHTMAN J.B.,ON WINGS OF EAGLES: THE PLIGHT, EXODUS, AND HOMECOMING OF ORIENTAL JEWRY. ASIA ISLAM ISRAEL VOL/ASSN DIPLOM CONTROL ORD/FREE ...GEOG WORSHIP SOC/INTEG 20 JEWS ARABS MIGRATION. PAGE 139 H2777 CULTURE HABITAT KIN SECT

B61
SEMINAR REPRESENTATIVE GOVT,AFRO-ASIAN ATTITUDES: SEMINAR ON REPRESENTATIVE GOVERNMENTSPUBLIC LIBERTIES IN STATES OF ASIA AND AFRICA, RHODES, 1958. AFR ASIA BURMA INDIA ISLAM UAR VIETNAM/S SOCIETY POL/PAR CHIEF EDU/PROP PRESS PERSON ...POLICY INT 20 TUNIS. PAGE 141 H2826 CHOOSE ATTIT NAT/COMP ORD/FREE

B61
SETON-WATSON H.,FROM LENIN TO KHRUSHCHEV: THE HISTORY OF WORLD COMMUNISM. ASIA COM EUR+WWI ISLAM S/ASIA ECO/DEV ECO/UNDEV NAT/G POL/PAR DIPLOM ECO/TAC EDU/PROP COERCE GUERRILLA ATTIT DRIVE WORK TOT/POP NAZI 20. PAGE 141 H2832 PWR REV USSR

B61
SSU-YU T.,JAPANESE STUDIES ON JAPAN AND THE FAR EAST: A SHORT BIOGRAPHICAL AND BIBLIOGRAPHICAL INTRODUCTION. ASIA CULTURE ECO/UNDEV NAT/G DIPLOM 20 CHINJAP. PAGE 148 H2962 BIBLIOG SOC

B61
STANLEY C.J.,LATE CH'ING FINANCE: HU KUANG-YUNG AS AN INNOVATOR. ASIA NAT/G FORCES BUDGET TAX WAR GOV/REL COST...POLICY BIOG CHARTS BIBLIOG 19. PAGE 148 H2969 FINAN ECO/TAC CIVMIL/REL ADMIN

B61
VAN GULIK R.H.,SEXUAL LIFE IN ANCIENT CHINA. ASIA LEISURE...CHARTS. PAGE 161 H3230 SEX CULTURE MARRIAGE LOVE

B61
YUAN TUNG-LI,A GUIDE TO DOCTORAL DISSERTATIONS BY CHINESE STUDENTS IN AMERICA, 1905-1960. ASIA CULTURE SOCIETY ECO/UNDEV NAT/G PROB/SOLV DIPLOM LEAD ATTIT...HUM SOC STAT 20. PAGE 172 H3442 BIBLIOG ACADEM ACT/RES OP/RES

S61
ZAGORIA D.S.,"THE FUTURE OF SINO-SOVIET RELATIONS." CHINA/COM INT/ORG NAT/G POL/PAR VOL/ASSN ACT/RES PLAN PERSON...METH/CNCPT TIME/SEQ TOT/POP VAL/FREE 20 MAO KHRUSH/N. PAGE 172 H3445 ASIA COM TOTALISM USSR

B62
BROWN S.D.,STUDIES ON ASIA, 1962. ASIA BURMA INDIA ISLAM ISRAEL S/ASIA ECO/UNDEV POL/PAR SECT ECO/TAC ...ANTHOL 20 CHINJAP. PAGE 22 H0450 PWR PARL/PROC

B62
CHAKRAVARTI P.C.,INDIA'S CHINA POLICY. ASIA CHINA/COM S/ASIA CULTURE NAT/G TOP/EX ACT/RES EDU/PROP DRIVE ALL/VALS...MYTH 20. PAGE 28 H0571 RIGID/FLEX TREND INDIA

B62
HO PING-TI,THE LADDER OF SUCCESS IN IMPERIAL CHINA: ASPECTS OF SOCIAL MOBILITY, 1368-1911. INTELL STRATA FAM KIN MUNIC NAT/G PROVS SCHOOL DELIB/GP DOMIN EDU/PROP ADMIN ROUTINE PERSON ALL/VALS...SOC STAT BIOG HIST/WRIT TIME/SEQ VAL/FREE. PAGE 71 H1431 ASIA CULTURE

B62
HUCKER C.O.,CHINA: A CRITICAL BIBLIOGRAPHY (PAMPHLET). ASIA STRUCT AGRI FINAN INDUS HABITAT MARXISM...EPIST HUM. PAGE 74 H1487 BIBLIOG/A CULTURE INTELL SOCIETY

B62
JACKSON W.A.D.,RUSSO-CHINESE BORDERLANDS. ASIA COM USSR NAT/G PROVS EX/STRUC FORCES DOMIN COERCE PEACE ATTIT PWR SOVEREIGN WEALTH...CONCPT TREND CHARTS STERTYP VAL/FREE. PAGE 79 H1576 GEOG DIPLOM RUSSIA

B62
MODELSKI G.,SEATO-SIX STUDIES. ASIA CHINA/COM INDIA S/ASIA INT/ORG NAT/G ECO/TAC DETER ATTIT ORD/FREE PWR...TIME/SEQ COLD/WAR TOT/POP 20 SEATO. PAGE 112 H2234 MARKET ECO/UNDEV INT/TRADE

B62
PENTONY D.E.,RED WORLD IN TUMULT: COMMUNIST FOREIGN POLICIES. CHINA/COM COM NAT/G EDU/PROP COERCE ATTIT PWR RESPECT...SOC CHARTS 20. PAGE 124 H2488 ECO/UNDEV DOMIN USSR ASIA

B62
US DEPARTMENT OF THE ARMY,GUIDE TO JAPANESE MONOGRAPHS AND JAPANESE STUDIES ON MANCHURIA: 1945-1960. CHINA/COM NAT/G DIPLOM LEAD COERCE WAR ...CHARTS 19/20 CHINJAP. PAGE 160 H3193 BIBLIOG/A FORCES ASIA S/ASIA

S62
CROAN M.,"POLYCENTRISM: COMMUNIST INTERNATIONAL RELATIONS." ASIA STRUCT INT/ORG NAT/G POL/PAR CONSULT PLAN DOMIN EDU/PROP COERCE ATTIT RIGID/FLEX SOCISM...POLICY CONCPT TREND CON/ANAL GEN/LAWS MARX/KARL. PAGE 35 H0703 COM CREATE DIPLOM NAT/LISM

S62
LONDON K.,"SINO-SOVIET RELATIONS IN THE CONTEXT OF THE 'WORLD SOCIALIST SYSTEM'." ASIA CHINA/COM COM USSR INT/ORG NAT/G TOP/EX BAL/PWR DIPLOM DOMIN ATTIT PERCEPT RIGID/FLEX PWR MARXISM...METH/CNCPT TREND 20. PAGE 98 H1957 DELIB/GP CONCPT SOCISM

S62
MU FU-SHENG,"THE WILTING OF THE HUNDRED FLOWERS: FREE THOUGHT IN CHINA TODAY." ASIA CHINA/COM CULTURE FAM NAT/G EDU/PROP REV TOTALISM ATTIT PERSON RESPECT...GEOG INT UNPLAN/INT COLD/WAR 20. PAGE 114 H2278 INTELL ELITES

S62
PASSIN H.,"THE SOURCES OF PROTEST IN JAPAN." CULTURE SOCIETY EDU/PROP COERCE NAT/LISM DISPL DRIVE PWR RESPECT...POLICY SOC TREND 20 CHINJAP. PAGE 124 H2473 ASIA ATTIT REV

S62
SARKISYANZ E.,"NATIONALISM, CAPITALISM, AND THE UNCOMMITED NATIONS: MARXISM AND ASIAN CULTURAL TRADITIONS." ASIA BURMA CHINA/COM COM CULTURE SOCIETY NAT/G POL/PAR PLAN DOMIN EDU/PROP COLONIAL COERCE ATTIT RIGID/FLEX...CONCPT TREND MARX/KARL 20 TIBET BUDDHISM. PAGE 138 H2755 S/ASIA SECT NAT/LISM CAP/ISM

S62
SHATTEN F.,"POLYCENTRISM: AFRICA: NATIONALISM AND COMMUNISM." ASIA COM FUT ISLAM CULTURE SOCIETY ECO/UNDEV NAT/G PLAN DOMIN COLONIAL COERCE CHOOSE RIGID/FLEX ALL/VALS MARXISM...CONCPT TREND 20. PAGE 143 H2852 AFR ATTIT NAT/LISM SOCISM

S62
STRACHEY J.,"COMMUNIST INTENTIONS." ASIA USSR YUGOSLAVIA INT/ORG NAT/G FORCES DOMIN EDU/PROP COERCE NUC/PWR NAT/LISM PEACE RIGID/FLEX PWR MARXISM...CONCPT MYTH OBS TIME/SEQ TREND COLD/WAR TOT/POP 20. PAGE 150 H2992 COM ATTIT WAR

B63
BARNETT A.D.,COMMUNIST STRATEGIES IN ASIA: A COMPARATIVE ANALYSIS OF GOVERNMENTS AND PARTIES. COM FUT S/ASIA CULTURE SOCIETY STRATA NAT/G DELIB/GP ACT/RES ECO/TAC EDU/PROP COERCE CHOOSE ATTIT RIGID/FLEX ORD/FREE PWR SKILL...SIMUL VAL/FREE 20. PAGE 11 H0223 ASIA POL/PAR DIPLOM USSR

B63
BRECHER M.,THE NEW STATES OF ASIA. ASIA S/ASIA INT/ORG BAL/PWR COLONIAL NEUTRAL ORD/FREE PWR 20 UN. PAGE 20 H0407 NAT/G ECO/UNDEV DIPLOM POLICY

B63
BRZEZINSKI Z.K.,AFRICA AND THE COMMUNIST WORLD. AFR ASIA COM CULTURE SOCIETY INT/ORG DELIB/GP ACT/RES ECO/TAC COERCE ORD/FREE PWR WEALTH...STAT TOT/POP VAL/FREE 20. PAGE 23 H0461 ATTIT EDU/PROP DIPLOM USSR

B63
CHEN N.-R.,THE ECONOMY OF MAINLAND CHINA, 1949-1963: A BIBLIOGRAPHY OF MATERIALS IN ENGLISH. CHINA/COM ECO/UNDEV PRESS 20. PAGE 29 H0586 BIBLIOG MARXISM NAT/G ASIA

B63
CHOU S.H.,THE CHINESE INFLATION 1937-1949. ASIA SOCIETY POL/PAR FOR/AID INT/TRADE BAL/PAY WEALTH MARXISM...STAT CHARTS 20 COM/PARTY GOLD/STAND. PAGE 30 H0597 FINAN ECO/TAC BUDGET NAT/G

B63
GAMBLE S.D.,NORTH CHINA VILLAGES: SOCIAL, POLITICAL, AND ECONOMIC ACTIVITIES BEFORE 1933. ASIA CULTURE STRUCT FAM DOMIN EDU/PROP WORSHIP 20. PAGE 55 H1093 MUNIC AGRI LEAD FINAN

B63
GEERTZ C.,OLD SOCIETIES AND NEW STATES: THE QUEST FOR MODERNITY IN ASIA AND AFRICA. AFR ASIA LAW CULTURE SECT EDU/PROP REV...GOV/COMP NAT/COMP 20. PAGE 55 H1107 ECO/UNDEV TEC/DEV NAT/LISM SOVEREIGN

B63
KAHIN G.M.,MAJOR GOVERNMENTS OF ASIA (2ND ED.). ASIA INDIA INDONESIA PAKISTAN S/ASIA DIPLOM...SOC 20 CHINJAP. PAGE 83 H1650 GOV/COMP POL/PAR ELITES

B63
KURZMAN D.,SUBVERSION OF THE INNOCENTS: PATTERNS OF COMMUNIST PENETRATION OF AFRICA, THE MIDDLE EAST AND AFRICA. AFR ASIA ISLAM S/ASIA CULTURE NAT/G FORCES PLAN EDU/PROP ADMIN ATTIT...CONCPT INT UNPLAN/INT TIME/SEQ. PAGE 89 H1785 COM COERCE

B63
MENZEL J.M.,THE CHINESE CIVIL SERVICE: CAREER OPEN TO TALENT? ASIA ROUTINE INGP/REL DISCRIM ATTIT ROLE KNOWL ANTHOL. PAGE 109 H2177 ADMIN NAT/G DECISION ELITES

B63
MOSELY P.E.,THE SOVIET UNION, 1922-1962: A FOREIGN AFFAIRS READER. ASIA POLAND USSR CULTURE INTELL AGRI POL/PAR WORKER INT/TRADE DOMIN WAR NAT/LISM MARXISM SOCISM 20 KHRUSH/N. PAGE 113 H2267 PWR POLICY DIPLOM

B63
PRICE A.G.,THE WESTERN INVASIONS OF THE PACIFIC AND ITS CONTINENTS. ASIA PRE/AMER S/ASIA ECO/UNDEV KIN NAT/G SECT FORCES DOMIN HEALTH...SOC 16/20. PAGE 128 H2560 COLONIAL CULTURE GEOG HABITAT

B63
SAKAI R.K.,STUDIES ON ASIA, 1963. ASIA INDIA ISRAEL S/ASIA USA+45 PERF/ART POL/PAR SECT REGION NAT/LISM ...SOC LING TREND ANTHOL 19/20 CHINJAP. PAGE 137 H2735 PWR CULTURE

B63
SCHECHTMAN J.B.,THE REFUGEE IN THE WORLD: DISPLACEMENT AND INTEGRATION. AFR ASIA EUR+WWI ISLAM L/A+17C S/ASIA CULTURE STRATA LOC/G EX/STRUC PLAN ECO/TAC ROUTINE...CONCPT TIME/SEQ VAL/FREE 20. PAGE 139 H2779 INT/ORG SOC

B63
SINOR D.,INTRODUCTION A L'ETUDE DE L'EURASIE CENTRALE. ASIA CULTURE KIN. PAGE 144 H2887 BIBLIOG SOC LING

B63
STUCKI C.W.,AMERICAN DOCTORAL DISSERTATIONS ON ASIA 1933-62 (A PAPER). PREHIST INDUS NAT/G GOV/REL ALL/IDEOS...ART/METH GEOG SOC LING 20. PAGE 150 H3002 BIBLIOG ASIA SOCIETY S/ASIA

L63
MICHAEL F.,"KHRUSHCHEV'S DISLOYAL OPPOSITION: STRUCTURAL CHANGE AND POWER STRUGGLE IN COMMUNIST BLOC." ASIA CHINA/COM FUT NAT/G POL/PAR CONSULT PLAN DOMIN ATTIT...POLICY CONCPT TREND MARX/KARL 20 KHRUSH/N. PAGE 110 H2195 COM STRUCT NAT/LISM USSR

L63
NASH M.,"PSYCHO-CULTURAL FACTORS IN ASIAN ECONOMIC GROWTH." ASIA ISLAM S/ASIA CULTURE ECO/UNDEV DELIB/GP EDU/PROP COERCE ATTIT PERSON HEALTH KNOWL ORD/FREE...PSY SOC STAT TREND ANTHOL VAL/FREE 20. PAGE 116 H2313 SOCIETY ECO/TAC

L63
ROSE R.,"COMPARATIVE STUDIES IN POLITICAL FINANCE: A SYMPOSIUM." ASIA EUR+WWI S/ASIA LAW CULTURE DELIB/GP LEGIS ACT/RES ECO/TAC EDU/PROP CHOOSE ATTIT RIGID/FLEX SUPEGO PWR SKILL WEALTH...STAT ANTHOL VAL/FREE. PAGE 134 H2674 FINAN POL/PAR

S63
AYAL E.B.,"VALUE SYSTEM AND ECONOMIC DEVELOPMENT IN JAPAN AND THAILAND." ASIA S/ASIA THAILAND CULTURE ECO/DEV CAP/ISM DOMIN NAT/LISM DRIVE RIGID/FLEX SOCISM...WELF/ST OBS TREND CON/ANAL GEN/LAWS 20 CHINJAP. PAGE 9 H0185 ECO/UNDEV ALL/VALS

S63
DUTT V.P.,"CHINA: JEALOUS NEIGHBOR." ASIA CHINA/COM INDIA S/ASIA NAT/G TOP/EX DOMIN COERCE REV ATTIT ...POLICY COLD/WAR 20. PAGE 44 H0874 FORCES PWR DIPLOM

S63
HALPERN A.M.,"THE EMERGENCE OF AN ASIAN COMMUNIST BLOC." ASIA CHINA/COM COM FUT KOREA/N S/ASIA POL/PAR EDU/PROP

VIETNAM/N STRATA NAT/G DELIB/GP FORCES TOP/EX PLAN BAL/PWR COERCE DETER PWR COLD/WAR WORK 20. PAGE 65 H1295 DIPLOM

S63
HARRIS R.L.,"COMMUNISM AND ASIA: ILLUSIONS AND MISCONCEPTIONS." ASIA COM FUT S/ASIA ECO/UNDEV AGRI NAT/G POL/PAR EX/STRUC EDU/PROP COERCE ATTIT MARXISM COLD/WAR TOT/POP 20. PAGE 67 H1344 PWR GUERRILLA

S63
TANG P.S.H.,"SINO-SOVIET TENSIONS." ASIA CHINA/COM COM CUBA KOREA/N VIETNAM/N NAT/G VOL/ASSN DELIB/GP PEACE PERCEPT PWR...METH/CNCPT MYTH RECORD TREND GEN/LAWS 20. PAGE 152 H3041 ACT/RES EDU/PROP REV

N63
LIBRARY HUNGARIAN ACADEMY SCI,HUNGARIAN PUBLICATIONS ON ASIA AND AFRICA, 1950-1962: A SELECTED BIBLIOGRAPHY (PAMPHLET). AFR ASIA HUNGARY S/ASIA ECO/UNDEV NAT/G EDU/PROP ATTIT 20 UNESCO. PAGE 96 H1922 BIBLIOG REGION DIPLOM WRITING

B64
BEDERMAN S.H.,THE ETHNOLOGICAL CONTRIBUTIONS OF JOHN LEDYARD (PAMPHLET). ASIA PRE/AMER S/ASIA...SOC 18 LEDYARD/J KAMCHATKA TAHITI TARTARS INDIAN/AM. PAGE 13 H0256 CULTURE BIOG METH/CNCPT STRUCT

B64
CLUBB O.E. JR.,TWENTIETH CENTURY CHINA. ASIA CHINA/COM INTELL NAT/G POL/PAR VOL/ASSN ACT/RES EDU/PROP COERCE REV PWR...TIME/SEQ 20. PAGE 30 H0608 TOP/EX DRIVE

B64
EMBREE A.T.,A GUIDE TO PAPERBACKS ON ASIA: SELECTED AND ANNOTATED (PAMPHLET). CULTURE SOCIETY ECO/UNDEV SECT DIPLOM COLONIAL MARXISM...SOC 20. PAGE 46 H0913 BIBLIOG/A ASIA S/ASIA NAT/G

B64
GRIFFITH W.E.,THE SINO-SOVIET RIFT. ASIA CHINA/COM COM CUBA USSR YUGOSLAVIA NAT/G POL/PAR VOL/ASSN DELIB/GP FORCES TOP/EX DIPLOM EDU/PROP DRIVE PERSON PWR...TREND 20 TREATY. PAGE 61 H1224 ATTIT TIME/SEQ BAL/PWR SOCISM

B64
LATOURETTE K.S.,CHINA. ASIA CHINA/COM FUT USSR ECO/UNDEV ECO/TAC WAR 19/20. PAGE 92 H1838 MARXISM NAT/G POLICY DIPLOM

B64
LEWIN P.,THE FOREIGN TRADE OF COMMUNIST CHINA* ITS IMPACT ON THE FREE WORLD. AFR EUR+WWI L/A+17C S/ASIA ECO/UNDEV CREATE FOR/AID...STAT NET/THEORY TREND CHARTS. PAGE 96 H1910 ASIA INT/TRADE NAT/COMP USSR

B64
LI C.M.,INDUSTRIAL DEVELOPMENT IN COMMUNIST CHINA. CHINA/COM ECO/DEV ECO/UNDEV AGRI FINAN INDUS MARKET LABOR NAT/G ECO/TAC INT/TRADE EXEC ALL/VALS ...POLICY RELATIV TREND WORK TOT/POP VAL/FREE 20. PAGE 96 H1921 ASIA TEC/DEV

B64
PERKINS D.,THE AMERICAN DEMOCRACY: ITS RISE TO POWER. ASIA USSR LAW CULTURE FINAN EDU/PROP COLONIAL CHOOSE...POLICY CHARTS BIBLIOG WORSHIP PRESIDENT 15/20 NEGRO. PAGE 125 H2492 LOC/G ECO/TAC WAR DIPLOM

B64
SAKAI R.K.,STUDIES ON ASIA, 1964. ASIA CHINA/COM ISRAEL MALAYSIA S/ASIA USA+45 USSR ECO/UNDEV FAM POL/PAR SECT CONSULT NAT/LISM...POLICY SOC 20 CHINJAP. PAGE 137 H2736 PWR DIPLOM

B64
SINAI I.R.,THE CHALLENGE OF MODERNISATION* THE WEST'S IMPACT ON THE NON-WESTERN WORLD. EUR+WWI CULTURE ELITES SECT CONSERVE SOCISM...GP/COMP IDEA/COMP NAT/COMP GEN/LAWS. PAGE 144 H2881 ASIA S/ASIA ECO/UNDEV CREATE

B64
WARD R.E.,POLITICAL MODERNIZATION IN JAPAN AND TURKEY. ASIA ISLAM S/ASIA CONSTN CULTURE STRATA COM/IND POL/PAR FORCES ACT/RES ECO/TAC DOMIN EDU/PROP LEGIT ADMIN CHOOSE ATTIT ALL/VALS...STAT TIME/SEQ VAL/FREE CHINJAP. PAGE 165 H3307 SOCIETY TURKEY

B64
WILCOX W.A.,INDIA, PAKISTAN AND THE RISE OF CHINA. ASIA BURMA CEYLON CHINA/COM INDIA PAKISTAN S/ASIA NAT/G VOL/ASSN FORCES TOP/EX ACT/RES DOMIN REGION RIGID/FLEX ORD/FREE...POLICY GEN/LAWS COLD/WAR 20. PAGE 168 H3362 CULTURE ATTIT DIPLOM

L64
BERELSON B.,"SAMPLE SURVEYS AND POPULATION CONTROL." ASIA FUT ISLAM L/A+17C CULTURE SOCIETY FAM NAT/G CONSULT PLAN EDU/PROP ATTIT DRIVE ALL/VALS...POLICY RELATIV HEAL PSY SOC CONCPT METH/CNCPT OBS OBS/ENVIR TOT/POP. PAGE 15 H0297 BIO/SOC SAMP

S64
DE GAULLE C.,"FRENCH WORLD VIEW." AFR ASIA CHINA/COM EUR+WWI ISLAM ECO/UNDEV INT/ORG NAT/G VOL/ASSN ACT/RES DIPLOM ECO/TAC EDU/PROP ATTIT DRIVE WEALTH 20. PAGE 37 H0751 TOP/EX PWR FOR/AID FRANCE

S64
HIRAI N.,"SHINTO AND INTERNATIONAL PROBLEMS." SOCIETY NAT/G PLAN EDU/PROP RACE/REL PEACE ATTIT PERCEPT LOVE MORAL...HUM MYTH RECORD SAMP TREND STERTYP TOT/POP 20 UN CHINJAP SHINTO. PAGE 71 H1423 ASIA SECT

S64
KOVNER M.,"THE SINO-SOVIET DISPUTE: COMMUNISM AT THE CROSSROADS." ASIA CHINA/COM COM USSR ECO/UNDEV NAT/G TOP/EX CREATE BAL/PWR DOMIN EDU/PROP PWR ...CONCPT COMECON 20. PAGE 88 H1760 ATTIT TREND

S64
LANGER P.F.,"JAPAN'S RELATIONS WITH CHINA." ASIA CHINA/COM KOREA S/ASIA ECO/DEV NAT/G POL/PAR EDU/PROP ATTIT ALL/VALS...METH/CNCPT TIME/SEQ TREND 20 CHINJAP. PAGE 91 H1808 RIGID/FLEX ECO/TAC

S64
LEVI W.,"INDIAN NEUTRALISM RECONSIDERED." ASIA CHINA/COM S/ASIA SOCIETY NAT/G ACT/RES LEGIT NEUTRAL COERCE ATTIT DRIVE PERCEPT RIGID/FLEX HEALTH LOVE PWR...DECISION RECORD TREND STERTYP 20. PAGE 95 H1896 ORD/FREE CONCPT INDIA

S64
LEWIS R.,"OPINION SURVEYING IN KOREA." ASIA FUT KOREA LEGIS EDU/PROP EXEC ALL/VALS...POLICY CONCPT MYTH TESTS CON/ANAL GEN/METH TOT/POP VAL/FREE 20. PAGE 96 H1915 NAT/G QU

S64
MOZINGO D.P.,"CHINA'S RELATIONS WITH HER ASIAN NEIGHBORS." ASIA CHINA/COM S/ASIA VIETNAM NAT/G DELIB/GP FORCES CREATE DOMIN EDU/PROP REV RIGID/FLEX PWR...TIME/SEQ GEN/LAWS COLD/WAR 20. PAGE 114 H2277 VOL/ASSN POLICY DIPLOM

S64
NEEDHAM T.,"SCIENCE AND SOCIETY IN EAST AND WEST." INTELL STRATA R+D LOC/G NAT/G PROVS CONSULT ACT/RES CREATE PLAN TEC/DEV EDU/PROP ADMIN ATTIT ALL/VALS ...POLICY RELATIV MGT CONCPT NEW/IDEA TIME/SEQ WORK WORK. PAGE 116 H2327 ASIA STRUCT

S64
POWELL R.L.,"COMMUNIST CHINA'S MILITARY POTENTIAL." ASIA CHINA/COM NAT/G EX/STRUC EDU/PROP COERCE GUERRILLA NUC/PWR WAR...RECORD CON/ANAL 20. PAGE 128 H2551 FORCES PWR

B65
CHUNG Y.S.,KOREA: A SELECTED BIBLIOGRAPHY 1959-1963. ASIA KOREA NAT/G DIPLOM 20. PAGE 30 H0601 BIBLIOG/A SOC

B65
COSTA H DE L.A.,THE BACKGROUND OF NATIONALISM AND OTHER ESSAYS. ASIA PHILIPPINE ATTIT PERCEPT CATHISM ...ANTHOL 20. PAGE 34 H0674 NAT/LISM CULTURE ANOMIE NAT/G

B65
CRABB C.V. JR.,THE ELEPHANTS AND THE GRASS* A STUDY OF NONALIGNMENT. AFR ASIA INDIA S/ASIA USA+45 USSR BAL/PWR NEUTRAL ATTIT...TREND NAT/COMP COLD/WAR. PAGE 34 H0691 ECO/UNDEV DIPLOM CONCPT

B65
GRETTON P.,MARITIME STRATEGY - A STUDY OF DEFENSE PROBLEMS. ASIA UK USSR DIPLOM COERCE DETER NUC/PWR WEAPON...CONCPT NAT/COMP 20. PAGE 60 H1211 FORCES PLAN WAR SEA

B65
HESS A.G.,CHASING THE DRAGON: A REPORT ON DRUG ADDICTION IN HONG KONG. ASIA CULTURE PROB/SOLV TRIBUTE...POLICY PSY SOC CLASSIF STAT 17/20 HONG/KONG. PAGE 70 H1411 BIO/SOC CRIME SOCIETY LAW

B65
HORNE A.J.,THE COMMONWEALTH TODAY. AFR ASIA CANADA UK STRUCT ECO/UNDEV NAT/G SECT GP/REL 20 AUSTRAL CMN/WLTH. PAGE 73 H1470 BIBLIOG/A SOCIETY CULTURE

B65
JANSEN M.B.,CHANGING JAPANESE ATTITUDES TOWARD MODERNIZATION. ASIA CHINA/COM S/ASIA INTELL SOCIETY KIN NAT/G SECT PERCEPT RIGID/FLEX...SOC CONCPT TIME/SEQ TREND TOT/POP 19/20 CHINJAP. PAGE 80 H1591 TEC/DEV ATTIT INDIA

B65
LARUS J.,COMPARATIVE WORLD POLITICS. ASIA INDIA WOR+45 WOR-45 BAL/PWR WAR PEACE RATIONAL MORAL PWR ...REALPOL INT/LAW MUSLIM. PAGE 91 H1825 GOV/COMP IDEA/COMP DIPLOM NAT/COMP

B65
ROMEIN J.,THE ASIAN CENTURY. ASIA COM S/ASIA DIPLOM COLONIAL TIME 20. PAGE 133 H2666 REV NAT/LISM CULTURE MARXISM

B65
SAKAI R.K.,STUDIES ON ASIA, 1965. INDIA KOREA S/ASIA USA+45 CONSTN KIN SECT PARTIC SUFF NAT/LISM ...POLICY SOC 19/20 CHINJAP. PAGE 137 H2737 PARL/PROC ASIA

B65
SCALAPINO R.A.,THE COMMUNIST REVOLUTION IN ASIA* TACTICS, GOALS, AND ACHIEVEMENTS. INDIA INTELL POL/PAR FORCES DOMIN EDU/PROP LEGIT COERCE REV ATTIT CHINJAP. PAGE 138 H2763 ASIA S/ASIA MARXISM NAT/COMP

B65
WINT G.,ASIA: A HANDBOOK. ASIA COM INDIA USSR CULTURE INTELL NAT/G...GEOG STAT CENSUS NAT/COMP WORSHIP 20 TREATY CHINJAP. PAGE 169 H3387 DIPLOM SOC

B65
YOUNG A.N.,CHINA'S WARTIME FINANCE AND INFLATION. ASIA AGRI INDUS NAT/G ECO/TAC CONFER PRICE WAR COST 20. PAGE 172 H3437 — FINAN FOR/AID TAX BUDGET

L65
HOUN F.S.,"THE COMMUNIST MONOLITH VERSUS THE CHINESE TRADITION." CULTURE INTELL SOCIETY STRUCT DOMIN GP/REL ORD/FREE CONSERVE PLURISM...GOV/COMP WORSHIP. PAGE 74 H1479 — ASIA MARXISM TOTALISM

L65
SCHAFFER B.B.,"THE CONCEPT OF PREPARATION* SOME QUESTIONS ABOUT THE TRANSFER OF SYSTEMS OF GOVERNMENT." AFR ASIA CANADA ELITES NAT/G POL/PAR COLONIAL RIGID/FLEX IDEA/COMP. PAGE 138 H2769 — ECO/UNDEV UK RECORD

L65
SHARMA S.P.,"THE INDIA-CHINA BORDER DISPUTE: AN INDIAN PERSPECTIVE." ASIA CHINA/COM S/ASIA NAT/G LEGIT CT/SYS NAT/LISM DRIVE MORAL ORD/FREE PWR 20. PAGE 142 H2850 — LAW ATTIT SOVEREIGN INDIA

S65
GRIFFITH S.B.,"COMMUNIST CHINA'S CAPACITY TO MAKE WAR." CHINA/COM COM NAT/G TOP/EX PLAN DOMIN COERCE NUC/PWR ATTIT RESPECT SKILL...CONCPT MYTH TIME/SEQ TREND COLD/WAR 20. PAGE 61 H1221 — FORCES PWR WEAPON ASIA

S65
PRABHAKAR P.,"SURVEY OF RESEARCH AND SOURCE MATERIALS; THE SINO-INDIAN BORDER DISPUTE." CHINA/COM INDIA LAW NAT/G PLAN BAL/PWR WAR...POLICY 20 COLD/WAR. PAGE 128 H2553 — BIBLIOG ASIA S/ASIA DIPLOM

B66
BESSON W.,DIE GROSSEN MACHTE - STRUKTURFRAGEN DER GEGENWARTIGEN WELTPOLITIK. ASIA USSR WOR+45 ATTIT ...IDEA/COMP 20 KENNEDY/JF. PAGE 16 H0321 — NAT/COMP DIPLOM STRUCT

B66
EMBREE A.T.,ASIA: A GUIDE TO BASIC BOOKS (PAMPHLET). ECO/UNDEV SECT FORCES DIPLOM ALL/IDEOS ...SOC 20. PAGE 46 H0914 — BIBLIOG/A ASIA S/ASIA NAT/G

B66
FITZGERALD C.P.,A CONCISE HISTORY OF EAST ASIA. ASIA KOREA S/ASIA INT/TRADE REGION MARXISM 20 CHINJAP. PAGE 51 H1017 — ECO/UNDEV COLONIAL CULTURE

B66
FITZGERALD C.P.,THE BIRTH OF COMMUNIST CHINA (2ND ED.). ASIA CHINA/COM STRUCT BAL/PWR DIPLOM ECO/TAC INT/TRADE WEALTH 20. PAGE 51 H1018 — REV MARXISM ECO/UNDEV

B66
HINTON W.,FANSHEN: A DOCUMENTARY OF REVOLUTION IN A CHINESE VILLAGE. ASIA ELITES MUNIC NAT/G POL/PAR SECT WORKER LEAD WAR PRIVIL PWR 20 MAO. PAGE 71 H1422 — MARXISM REV NEIGH OWN

B66
KOH S.J.,STAGES OF INDUSTRIAL DEVELOPMENT IN ASIA. ASIA INDIA KOREA STRATA STRUCT NAT/G INT/TRADE ...CHARTS 19/20 CHINJAP. PAGE 87 H1738 — INDUS ECO/UNDEV ECO/DEV LABOR

B66
PAN S.,VIETNAM CRISIS. ASIA FRANCE USA+45 USA-45 VIETNAM CULTURE SOCIETY INT/ORG ECO/TAC AGREE CONTROL WAR MARXISM 20. PAGE 123 H2454 — ECO/UNDEV POLICY DIPLOM NAT/COMP

B66
SCHRAM S.,MAO TSE-TUNG. ASIA CHINA/COM CONTROL REGION ATTIT...POLICY IDEA/COMP 20 MAO. PAGE 140 H2799 — BIOG MARXISM TOP/EX GUERRILLA

B66
SWEARINGEN A.R.,SOVIET AND CHINESE COMMUNIST POWER IN THE WORLD TODAY. COM USA+45 ECO/UNDEV CREATE LEAD WAR ADJUST...TREND NAT/COMP ANTHOL COLD/WAR KHRUSH/N. PAGE 151 H3017 — USSR ASIA DIPLOM ATTIT

B66
US DEPARTMENT OF STATE,RESEARCH ON AFRICA (EXTERNAL RESEARCH LIST NO 5-25). LAW CULTURE ECO/UNDEV POL/PAR DIPLOM EDU/PROP LEAD REGION MARXISM...GEOG LING WORSHIP 20. PAGE 159 H3188 — BIBLIOG/A ASIA S/ASIA NAT/G

B66
WANG Y.C.,CHINESE INTELLECTUALS AND THE WEST 1872-1949. ASIA ELITES LEAD STRANGE ROLE MARXISM ...CHARTS 19/20. PAGE 165 H3301 — INTELL EDU/PROP CULTURE SOCIETY

B66
ZABLOCKI C.J.,SINO-SOVIET RIVALRY. AFR ASIA CHINA/COM CUBA EUR+WWI L/A+17C USA+45 USSR WOR+45 POL/PAR FORCES COERCE NUC/PWR...GOV/COMP IDEA/COMP 20 MAO KHRUSH/N. PAGE 172 H3444 — DIPLOM MARXISM COM

L66
ZOPPO C.E.,"NUCLEAR TECHNOLOGY, MULTIPOLARITY, AND INTERNATIONAL STABILITY." ASIA RUSSIA USA+45 STRUCT TOP/EX BAL/PWR DIPLOM DETER CIVMIL/REL NAT/COMP. PAGE 173 H3464 — NET/THEORY ORD/FREE DECISION NUC/PWR

S66
CRANMER-BYNG J.L.,"THE CHINESE ATTITUDE TOWARDS EXTERNAL RELATIONS." ASIA CHINA/COM EXEC NAT/LISM MARXISM...POLICY 20. PAGE 35 H0699 — ATTIT DIPLOM NAT/G

S66
GILBERT S.P.,"WARS OF LIBERATION AND SOVIET MILITARY AID POLICY." ASIA INDIA INDONESIA UAR USA+45 STRATA WAR PERCEPT MARXISM...STAT NAT/COMP. PAGE 56 H1124 — USSR FOR/AID WEAPON DRIVE

S66
MARTZ J.D.,"THE PLACE OF LATIN AMERICA IN THE STUDY OF COMPARATIVE POLITICS." AFR ASIA CULTURE STRUCT ECO/UNDEV ACADEM CREATE...CLASSIF NAT/COMP. PAGE 104 H2072 — L/A+17C GOV/COMP STERTYP GEN/LAWS

S66
MERRITT R.L.,"SELECTED ARTICLES AND DOCUMENTS ON COMPARATIVE GOVERNMENT AND CROSS-NATIONAL RESEARCH." AFR ASIA EUR+WWI L/A+17C MOD/EUR ELITES R+D ACT/RES DIPLOM PWR...SOC CONCPT 18/20. PAGE 109 H2185 — BIBLIOG GOV/COMP NAT/G GOV/REL

S66
QUESTER G.H.,"ON THE IDENTIFICATION OF REAL AND PRETENDED COMMUNIST MILITARY DOCTRINE." ASIA USSR DETER WAR ATTIT DRIVE HEALTH TIME/SEQ. PAGE 129 H2574 — RATIONAL PERCEPT NUC/PWR NAT/COMP

S66
SCHWARTZ M.,"THE 1964 PRESIDENTIAL ELECTIONS THROUGH SOVIET EYES." ASIA POL/PAR DIPLOM ATTIT MARXISM...NAT/COMP COLD/WAR. PAGE 140 H2811 — USSR USA+45 PERCEPT

S66
STRAYER J.R.,"PROBLEMS OF DICTATORSHIP* THE RUSSIAN EXPERIENCE." ASIA MOD/EUR ELITES STRATA POL/PAR CREATE NAT/LISM MARXISM...GOV/COMP NAT/COMP. PAGE 150 H2997 — NAT/G GEN/LAWS USSR TOTALISM

C66
WINT G.,"ASIA: A HANDBOOK." ASIA S/ASIA INDUS LABOR SECT PRESS RACE/REL MARXISM...STAT CHARTS BIBLIOG 20. PAGE 169 H3388 — ECO/UNDEV DIPLOM NAT/G SOCIETY

B67
ALLWORTH E.,CENTRAL ASIA: A CENTURY OF RUSSIAN RULE. USSR INTELL SOCIETY AGRI INDUS COLONIAL REV WAR NAT/LISM...ART/METH GEOG LING 19/20. PAGE 5 H0108 — ASIA CULTURE NAT/G

B67
BURNHAM J.,THE WAR WE ARE IN, THE LAST DECADE AND THE NEXT. ASIA COM EUR+WWI S/ASIA WOR+45 ECO/UNDEV INT/ORG FORCES WAR...OLD/LIB TREND 20 COLD/WAR. PAGE 25 H0492 — POLICY NAT/G DIPLOM NAT/COMP

B67
CHANDRASEKHAR S.,ASIA'S POPULATION PROBLEMS. ASIA ECO/UNDEV PLAN AGE/C...OBS CHARTS BIBLIOG 18/20 AUSTRAL. PAGE 29 H0575 — PROB/SOLV NAT/COMP GEOG TREND

B67
CORDIER A.W.,COLUMBIA ESSAYS IN INTERNATIONAL AFFAIRS. ASIA CHINA/COM FRANCE S/ASIA SPAIN UAR ECO/UNDEV LOC/G ECO/TAC GUERRILLA PWR...BIOG ANTHOL 18/20 MAU/MAU. PAGE 33 H0663 — NAT/G DIPLOM MARXISM POLICY

B67
GILL R.T.,ECONOMIC DEVELOPMENT: PAST AND PRESENT (2ND ED.). ASIA INDIA USA+45 USA-45 WOR+45 WOR-45 DEMAND EFFICIENCY NAT/LISM WEALTH...GOV/COMP METH/COMP 18/20. PAGE 56 H1127 — ECO/DEV ECO/UNDEV PLAN PROB/SOLV

B67
MCNELLY T.,SOURCES IN MODERN EAST ASIAN HISTORY AND POLITICS. KOREA VIETNAM CULTURE DIPLOM COLONIAL REV WAR PWR ALL/IDEOS MARXISM...ANTHOL 20 CHINJAP. PAGE 107 H2147 — NAT/COMP ASIA S/ASIA SOCIETY

B67
PYE L.W.,SOUTHEAST ASIA'S POLITICAL SYSTEMS. ASIA S/ASIA STRUCT ECO/UNDEV EX/STRUC CAP/ISM DIPLOM ALL/IDEOS...TREND CHARTS. PAGE 128 H2568 — NAT/G POL/PAR GOV/COMP

B67
RIESMAN D.,CONVERSATIONS IN JAPAN: MODERNIZATION, POLITICS, AND CULTURE. CHINA/COM STRATA STRUCT ECO/DEV INDUS ACADEM EDU/PROP...ART/METH SOC MODAL INT IDEA/COMP SOC/INTEG 20 CHINJAP HIROSHIMA. PAGE 131 H2629 — CULTURE SOCIETY ASIA

B67
ROWLAND J.,A HISTORY OF SINO-INDIAN RELATIONS; HOSTILE CO-EXISTENCE. ASIA CHINA/COM INDIA NAT/G NUC/PWR PWR WEALTH...GEOG BIBLIOG 13/20 COLD/WAR. PAGE 135 H2704 — DIPLOM CENSUS IDEA/COMP

B67
YAMAMURA K.,ECONOMIC POLICY IN POSTWAR JAPAN. ASIA FINAN POL/PAR DIPLOM LEAD NAT/LISM ATTIT NEW/LIB POPULISM 20 CHINJAP. PAGE 171 H3432 — ECO/DEV POLICY NAT/G TEC/DEV

L67
HOSHII I.,"JAPAN'S STAKE IN ASIA." ASIA S/ASIA CAP/ISM ECO/TAC ROLE...GEOG 20 CHINJAP. PAGE 74 H1477 — DIPLOM REGION NAT/G INT/ORG

L67
SCALAPINO R.A.,"A SURVEY OF ASIA IN 1966." ASIA S/ASIA CONSTN SOCIETY POL/PAR CHIEF WAR...ANTHOL 20. PAGE 138 H2764 — DIPLOM

L67
TABORSKY E.,"THE COMMUNIST PARTIES OF THE 'THIRD — POL/PAR

WORLD' IN SOVIET STRATEGY." AFR ASIA L/A+17C USSR INTELL NAT/G WORKER PLAN CONTROL LEAD PARTIC REV ...GOV/COMP 20 COM/PARTY THIRD/WRLD. PAGE 152 H3032 MARXISM ECO/UNDEV DIPLOM

S67
MANGLAPUS R.S.,"ASIAN REVOLUTION AND AMERICAN IDEOLOGY." USA+45 SOCIETY CAP/ISM DIPLOM ADJUST CENTRAL...NAT/COMP 20. PAGE 102 H2035 REV POPULISM ATTIT ASIA

S67
NATSAGDORJ A.S.,"THE ECONOMIC BASIS OF FEUDALISM IN MONGOLIA." ASIA COM USSR OWN WEALTH CONSERVE...SOC 20 MONGOLIA. PAGE 116 H2324 ECO/TAC AGRI NAT/COMP MARXISM

S67
RICHMAN B.M.,"CAPITALISTS & MANAGERS IN COMMUNIST CHINA." ASIA CHINA/COM ECO/UNDEV NAT/G CONSULT EX/STRUC PLAN EFFICIENCY PRODUC WEALTH MARXISM ...MGT CHARTS 20. PAGE 131 H2623 CAP/ISM INDUS

S67
RONNING C.,"NANKING: 1950." ASIA CANADA CHINA/COM NAT/G PLAN ECO/TAC REV ADJUST 20. PAGE 133 H2667 DIPLOM ROLE PEACE

S67
ROSE S.,"ASIAN NATIONALISM* THE SECOND STAGE." ASIA COM ECO/UNDEV NAT/G PROB/SOLV DIPLOM FOR/AID DOMIN NEUTRAL REGION TASK...METH/COMP 20. PAGE 134 H2675 NAT/LISM S/ASIA BAL/PWR COLONIAL

S67
SHIGEO N.,"THE GREAT CULTURAL REVOLUTION." ASIA ECO/UNDEV AGRI NAT/G CHIEF ECO/TAC EDU/PROP CONTROL LEAD PWR 20 MAO. PAGE 143 H2860 CREATE REV CULTURE POL/PAR

S67
TANTER R.,"A THEORY OF REVOLUTION." ASIA CUBA L/A+17C S/ASIA SOCIETY NAT/G ADJUST...CONCPT CHARTS. PAGE 152 H3046 REV ECO/UNDEV EDU/PROP METH/COMP

ASIA FOUNDATION H0176

ASIANS....ASIANS, ASIAN MINORITIES

ASQUITH/HH....HERBERT HENRY ASQUITH

B57
BULLOCK A.,THE LIBERAL TRADITION FROM FOX TO KEYNES. UK CULTURE INTELL CREATE WRITING COLONIAL PERS/REL ATTIT ORD/FREE...POLICY OLD/LIB TRADIT CONCPT 18/20 CHURCHLL/W MILL/JS KEYNES/JM ASQUITH/HH. PAGE 23 H0469 ANTHOL DEBATE LAISSEZ

ASSASSINATION....SEE MURDER

ASSIMILATION....SEE GP/REL+INGP/REL

ASSOCIATIONS....SEE VOL/ASSN

AT+T....AMERICAN TELEPHONE AND TELEGRAPH

ATATURK/MK....MUSTAFA KEMAL ATATURK

ATHENS....ATHENS, GREECE

B30
HATTERSLEY A.F.,A SHORT HISTORY OF DEMOCRACY. WOR-45 CONSTN NAT/G SECT DOMIN WAR CHOOSE ORD/FREE PWR...CONCPT GOV/COMP BIBLIOG ATHENS ROME. PAGE 68 H1355 REPRESENT MAJORIT POPULISM

ATLAN/ALL....ATLANTIC ALLIANCE

ATLANTA....ATLANTA, GEORGIA

ATLANTIC ALLIANCE....SEE ATLAN/ALL

ATLASES....SEE MAPS

ATMORE A. H2414

ATOM BOMB....SEE NUC/PWR

ATOMIC ENERGY COMMISSION....SEE AEC + COUNTRY'S NAME

ATTENTION....SEE PERCEPT

ATTIA G.E.D. H0177,H0178

ATTIT....ATTITUDES, OPINIONS, IDEOLOGY

ATTLEE C.R. H0179

ATTLEE/C....CLEMENT ATLEE

ATTORNEY GENERAL....SEE ATTRNY/GEN

ATTRNY/GEN....ATTORNEY GENERAL

AUD/VIS....FILM AND SOUND (INCLUDING PHOTOGRAPHY)

N
HERSKOVITS M.V.,CULTURAL ANTHROPOLOGY. UNIV SOCIETY STRUCT FAM...AUD/VIS BIBLIOG. PAGE 70 H1410 CULTURE SOC INGP/REL GEOG

B00
VOLPICELLI Z.,RUSSIA ON THE PACIFIC AND THE SIBERIAN RAILWAY. MOD/EUR ECO/UNDEV INT/ORG FORCES PLAN DOMIN COLONIAL ROUTINE ATTIT ALL/VALS...OBS HIST/WRIT TIME/SEQ TREND CON/ANAL AUD/VIS CHARTS 18/19. PAGE 163 H3261 NAT/G ACT/RES RUSSIA

B04
REED W.A.,ETHNOLOGICAL SURVEY PUBLICATIONS (VOL. II). PHILIPPINE STRUCT INDUS SECT DEATH LEISURE HABITAT...AUD/VIS CHARTS WORSHIP 20 NABOLOI NEGRITO BATAK. PAGE 130 H2607 CULTURE SOCIETY SOC OBS

B05
PHILIPPINE ISLANDS BUREAU SCI,ETHNOLOGICAL SURVEY: THE BONTOC IGOROT. ECO/UNDEV AGRI FAM MARRIAGE HEALTH WEALTH...LING OBS AUD/VIS CHARTS WORSHIP 20 LUZON BONTOC. PAGE 125 H2500 CULTURE INGP/REL KIN STRUCT

B16
CALVERT A.F.,SOUTHWEST AFRICA 1884-1914 (2ND ED.). GERMANY EXTR/IND NAT/G FORCES...GEOG AUD/VIS CHARTS 19/20 RESOURCE/N AFRICA/SW. PAGE 25 H0508 COLONIAL ECO/UNDEV AFR

L44
HUXLEY J.,"THE FUTURE OF THE COLONIES." AFR SOCIETY NAT/G PLAN DOMIN COERCE ATTIT DRIVE ORD/FREE PWR WEALTH...TIME/SEQ TREND AUD/VIS CHARTS 20. PAGE 76 H1511 ECO/UNDEV FUT COLONIAL

B45
MCBRYDE F.W.,CULTURAL AND HISTORICAL GEOGRAPHY OF SOUTHWEST GUATEMALA. GUATEMALA AGRI KIN PERSON ...GEOG AUD/VIS CHARTS 20. PAGE 106 H2123 HABITAT ISOLAT CULTURE ECO/UNDEV

B47
HERSKOVITS M.U.,MAN AND HIS WORK. UNIV SECT TEC/DEV PARTIC...PHIL/SCI LING AUD/VIS BIBLIOG. PAGE 70 H1409 SOC CULTURE INGP/REL HABITAT

B48
MAUGHAM R.,NORTH AFRICAN NOTEBOOK. ALGERIA ISLAM LIBYA MOROCCO STRUCT ECO/UNDEV COLONIAL...SOC OBS AUD/VIS NAT/COMP WORSHIP 20 TUNIS. PAGE 105 H2102 SOCIETY RECORD NAT/LISM

B53
NELSON G.R.,FREEDOM AND WELFARE: SOCIAL PATTERNS IN THE NORTHERN COUNTRIES OF EUROPE. EUR+WWI ECO/DEV NAT/G EDU/PROP LEGIT HEALTH ORD/FREE SKILL WEALTH ...STAT AUD/VIS SCANDINAV WORK TOT/POP 20. PAGE 116 H2329 PLAN ECO/TAC

B56
HATCH J.C.,NEW FROM AFRICA. AFR FUT UK NAT/G GUERRILLA ATTIT ORD/FREE PWR...AUD/VIS CHARTS 20. PAGE 68 H1354 NAT/LISM COLONIAL RACE/REL

B56
KUPER L.,PASSIVE RESISTANCE IN SOUTH AFRICA. SOUTH/AFR LAW NAT/G POL/PAR VOL/ASSN DISCRIM ...POLICY SOC AUD/VIS 20. PAGE 89 H1782 ORD/FREE RACE/REL ATTIT

B56
LEVIN M.G.,THE PEOPLES OF SIBERIA. PREHIST ECO/UNDEV KIN SECT HABITAT...CLASSIF AUD/VIS WORSHIP 20 SIBERIA. PAGE 95 H1900 CULTURE SOCIETY ASIA

B56
PADMORE G.,PAN-AFRICANISM OR COMMUNISM. AFR FUT NIGERIA INTELL NAT/G COLONIAL FEDERAL ATTIT DRIVE PWR RESPECT WEALTH MARXISM...CONCPT AUD/VIS STERTYP 20. PAGE 122 H2440 POL/PAR NAT/LISM

B58
BRIGGS L.C.,THE LIVING RACES OF THE SAHARA. STRATA AGRI KIN INT/TRADE HABITAT...GEOG AUD/VIS CHARTS BIBLIOG 20 SAHARA MIGRATION. PAGE 21 H0417 STRUCT SOCIETY SOC CULTURE

B58
GLUCKMAN M.,ANALYSIS OF A SOCIAL SITUATION IN MODERN ZULULAND. AFR PERS/REL ADJUST DISCRIM EQUILIB NAT/LISM...SOC RECORD AUD/VIS 20 ZULULAND. PAGE 57 H1146 CULTURE RACE/REL STRUCT GP/REL

B61
APTER D.E.,THE POLITICAL KINGDOM IN UGANDA. UGANDA CULTURE ECO/UNDEV AGRI KIN SECT TOP/EX REGION ATTIT HABITAT CONSERVE...GEOG AUD/VIS 20. PAGE 8 H0153 NAT/LISM POL/PAR COLONIAL ECO/TAC

B61
MUNGER E.S.,AFRICAN FIELD REPORTS 1952-1961. SOUTH/AFR SOCIETY ECO/UNDEV NAT/G POL/PAR COLONIAL EXEC PARL/PROC GUERRILLA RACE/REL ALL/IDEOS...SOC AUD/VIS 20. PAGE 114 H2288 AFR DISCRIM RECORD

B63
EICH H.,THE UNLOVED GERMANS. EUR+WWI GERMANY PERS/REL RACE/REL DISCRIM HABITAT SUPEGO FASCISM ...PSY SOC AUD/VIS 19/20 JEWS. PAGE 45 H0898
STERTYP PERSON CULTURE ATTIT

B63
REYNOLDS B.,MAGIC, DIVINATION AND WITCHCRAFT AMONG THE BAROTSE OF NORTHERN RHODESIA. RHODESIA CULTURE KIN CREATE LEGIT PARTIC DEATH DREAM STRANGE HABITAT PERSON...AUD/VIS WORSHIP 20. PAGE 131 H2619
AFR SOC MYTH SECT

B64
HOPKINSON T.,SOUTH AFRICA. SOUTH/AFR UK NAT/G POL/PAR LEGIS ECO/TAC PARL/PROC WAR...JURID AUD/VIS 19/20. PAGE 73 H1467
SOCIETY RACE/REL DISCRIM

B64
HUXLEY M.,FAREWILL TO EDEN. SOCIETY ACT/RES EDU/PROP HEALTH...SOC AUD/VIS. PAGE 76 H1513
ECO/UNDEV SECT CULTURE ADJUST

B64
JOHNSON A.F.,BIBLIOGRAPHY OF GHANA: 1930-1961. GHANA LAW AGRI INDUS NAT/G INT/TRADE EDU/PROP HEALTH...GEOG AUD/VIS CHARTS 20. PAGE 81 H1618
BIBLIOG/A CULTURE SOC

B64
MORRIS J.,THE PRESENCE OF SPAIN. SPAIN MUNIC NAT/G FORCES ATTIT CATHISM...AUD/VIS 16/20. PAGE 113 H2263
CULTURE HABITAT SOCIETY GEOG

B64
SCHNITGER F.M.,FORGOTTEN KINGDOMS IN SUMATRA. FAM SECT LEISURE HABITAT...OBS AUD/VIS WORSHIP 20 SUMATRA. PAGE 140 H2793
CULTURE AFR SOCIETY STRUCT

S64
SOLOVEYTCHIK G.,"BOOKS ON RUSSIA." USSR ELITES NAT/G PERF/ART REV GOV/REL MARXISM...AUD/VIS 20. PAGE 147 H2929
BIBLIOG/A COM CULTURE

B65
CAMPBELL G.A.,THE CIVIL SERVICE IN BRITAIN (2ND ED.). UK DELIB/GP FORCES WORKER CREATE PLAN ...POLICY AUD/VIS 19/20 CIVIL/SERV. PAGE 26 H0515
ADMIN LEGIS NAT/G FINAN

B66
HAHN C.H.L.,THE NATIVE TRIBES OF SOUTH WEST AFRICA. LAW FAM SECT HABITAT SKILL...SOC AUD/VIS WORSHIP RITUAL 20 AFRICA/SW. PAGE 64 H1275
CULTURE SOCIETY STRUCT AFR

B66
KEITH G.,THE FADING COLOUR BAR. AFR CENTRL/AFR UK ZAMBIA CULTURE SCHOOL EDU/PROP PERS/REL DISCRIM AGE ...AUD/VIS NAT/COMP SOC/INTEG 20 NEGRO. PAGE 84 H1682
RACE/REL STRUCT ATTIT NAT/G

B67
DIX R.H.,COLOMBIA: THE POLITICAL DIMENSIONS OF CHANGE. ELITES POL/PAR DOMIN REV...AUD/VIS 20 COLOMB. PAGE 41 H0828
L/A+17C NAT/G TEC/DEV LEAD

AUGUSTINE....SAINT AUGUSTINE

AULT P.H. H0920

AUST/HUNG....AUSTRIA-HUNGARY

B62
HANAK H.,GREAT BRITAIN AND AUSTRIA-HUNGARY DURING THE FIRST WORLD WAR: A STUDY IN THE FORMATION OF PUBLIC OPINION. CZECHOSLVK UK NAT/G GIVE DOMIN EDU/PROP CONSERVE...BIBLIOG 20 AUST/HUNG WWI. PAGE 65 H1311
WAR DIPLOM ATTIT PRESS

S64
REISS I.,"LE DECLENCHEMENT DE LA PREMIERE GUERRE MONDIALE." GERMANY RUSSIA NAT/G FORCES DOMIN EDU/PROP COERCE RIGID/FLEX PWR SOVEREIGN...RELATIV HIST/WRIT TOT/POP AUST/HUNG SERBIA 20. PAGE 131 H2612
MOD/EUR BAL/PWR DIPLOM WAR

AUSTIN D.A. H0180

AUSTRALIA....SEE ALSO S/ASIA, COMMONWLTH

N
AUSTRALIAN NATIONAL RES COUN,AUSTRALIAN SOCIAL SCIENCE ABSTRACTS. NEW/ZEALND CULTURE SOCIETY LOC/G CT/SYS PARL/PROC...HEAL JURID PSY SOC 20 AUSTRAL. PAGE 9 H0181
BIBLIOG/A POLICY NAT/G ADMIN

N
AUSTRALIAN PUBLIC AFFAIRS INFORMATION SERVICE. LAW ...HEAL HUM MGT SOC CON/ANAL 20 AUSTRAL. PAGE 1 H0011
BIBLIOG NAT/G CULTURE DIPLOM

B30
CANAWAY A.P.,THE FAILURE OF FEDERALISM IN AUSTRALIA. UK PROB/SOLV ADMIN EFFICIENCY ATTIT ...POLICY NAT/COMP 20 AUSTRAL. PAGE 26 H0518
FEDERAL NAT/G CONSTN OP/RES

B32
LUNT D.C.,THE ROAD TO THE LAW. UK USA-45 LEGIS EDU/PROP OWN ORD/FREE...DECISION TIME/SEQ NAT/COMP 16/20 AUSTRAL ENGLSH/LAW COMMON/LAW. PAGE 99 H1980
ADJUD LAW JURID CT/SYS

B45
LASKER B.,ASIA ON THE MOVE. ASIA BURMA S/ASIA THAILAND USSR ECO/UNDEV FAM KIN WAR NAT/LISM ATTIT ...GEOG CENSUS TREND AUSTRAL 20. PAGE 91 H1826
CULTURE RIGID/FLEX

B57
SCARROW H.A.,THE HIGHER PUBLIC SERVICE OF THE COMMONWEALTH OF AUSTRALIA. LAW SENIOR LOBBY ROLE 20 AUSTRAL CIVIL/SERV COMMONWLTH. PAGE 138 H2766
ADMIN NAT/G EX/STRUC GOV/COMP

B58
BRADY A.,DEMOCRACY IN THE DOMINIONS (3RD ED.). CANADA NEW/ZEALND SOUTH/AFR WOR+45 LAW EX/STRUC DOMIN COLONIAL PARL/PROC REPRESENT RACE/REL NAT/LISM WEALTH 20 AUSTRAL CMN/WLTH. PAGE 20 H0399
GOV/COMP POL/PAR POPULISM NAT/G

B58
WARNER W.L.,A BLACK CIVILIZATION - A SOCIAL STUDY OF AN AUSTRALIAN TRIBE. SOCIETY FAM MARRIAGE...PSY SOC MYTH CHARTS 20 AUSTRAL MAPS MURNGIN RITUAL. PAGE 165 H3310
CULTURE KIN STRUCT DEATH

S59
MENDELSON W.,"JUDICIAL REVIEW AND PARTY POLITICS" (BMR)" UK USA+45 USA-45 NAT/G LEGIS PROB/SOLV EDU/PROP ADJUD EFFICIENCY...POLICY NAT/COMP 19/20 AUSTRAL SUPREME/CT. PAGE 109 H2171
CT/SYS POL/PAR BAL/PWR JURID

B61
AIYAR S.P.,FEDERALISM AND SOCIAL CHANGE. CANADA CULTURE STRUCT PLAN PROB/SOLV TEC/DEV ECO/TAC ORD/FREE...TIME/SEQ 18/20 AUSTRAL. PAGE 4 H0085
FEDERAL NAT/G CENTRAL GOV/COMP

B61
ATTLEE C.R.,EMPIRE INTO COMMONWEALTH. AFR ASIA CANADA UK NAT/G WAR NAT/LISM ATTIT...POLICY 20 AUSTRAL. PAGE 9 H0179
DIPLOM GP/REL COLONIAL SOVEREIGN

B62
DILLING A.R.,ABORIGINE CULTURE HISTORY - A SURVEY OF PUBLICATIONS 1954-1957. GUINEA...SOC CHARTS NAT/COMP BIBLIOG/A AUSTRAL ABORIGINES. PAGE 41 H0825
S/ASIA HIST/WRIT CULTURE KIN

B62
FALKENBERG J.,KIN AND TOTEM; GROUP RELATIONS OF AUSTRALIAN ABORIGINES IN THE PORT KEATS DISTRICT. SOCIETY STRATA STRUCT GP/REL PERS/REL MARRIAGE AGE ATTIT SEX...SOC STAT CHARTS AUSTRAL ABORIGINES. PAGE 48 H0964
KIN INGP/REL CULTURE FAM

B62
MEGGITT M.J.,DESERT PEOPLE. ECO/UNDEV KIN CREATE PROB/SOLV CONTROL DRIVE ROLE...GEOG SOC MYTH CHARTS BIBLIOG 20 AUSTRAL. PAGE 108 H2159
ADJUST CULTURE INGP/REL HABITAT

S62
CORET A.,"LE STATUT DE L'ILE CHRISTMAS DE L'OCEAN INDIEN." FUT S/ASIA ECO/DEV ECO/UNDEV VOL/ASSN DELIB/GP PLAN...RELATIV OBS TIME/SEQ TREND AUSTRAL 20. PAGE 33 H0667
NAT/G INT/ORG NEW/ZEALND

B63
CONFERENCE ABORIGINAL STUDIES,AUSTRALIAN ABORIGINAL STUDIES. ECO/UNDEV INT/TRADE COLONIAL ADJUST HABITAT HEREDITY...GEOG PSY LING SOC/EXP ANTHOL WORSHIP 20 AUSTRAL ABORIGINES. PAGE 32 H0638
SOC SOCIETY CULTURE STRUCT

B63
LIVINGSTON W.S.,FEDERALISM IN THE COMMONWEALTH - A BIBLIOGRAPHICAL COMMENTARY. CANADA INDIA PAKISTAN UK STRUCT LOC/G NAT/G POL/PAR...NAT/COMP 20 AUSTRAL. PAGE 97 H1943
BIBLIOG JURID FEDERAL CONSTN

B63
TINDALE N.B.,ABORIGINAL AUSTRALIANS. KIN CREATE ROLE...SOC MYTH TREND 20 AUSTRAL ABORIGINES MIGRATION. PAGE 155 H3099
CULTURE DRIVE ECO/UNDEV HABITAT

B64
BERNDT R.M.,THE WORLD OF THE FIRST AUSTRALIANS. S/ASIA ECO/UNDEV WORKER PROB/SOLV EFFICIENCY ROLE ...SOC MYTH WORSHIP AUSTRAL ABORIGINES. PAGE 16 H0311
CULTURE KIN STRUCT DRIVE

B64
ELKIN A.P.,THE AUSTRALIAN ABORIGINES - HOW TO UNDERSTAND THEM (4TH ED.). FAM NEIGH DEATH MARRIAGE ATTIT BIO/SOC HABITAT...PSY SOC MYTH WORSHIP AUSTRAL ABORIGINES. PAGE 45 H0908
CULTURE STRUCT SOCIETY KIN

B64
HORNE D.,THE LUCKY COUNTRY: AUSTRALIA TODAY. UK CULTURE STRATA ATTIT PWR PLURISM...GOV/COMP 20 AUSTRAL. PAGE 73 H1471
RACE/REL DIPLOM NAT/G STRUCT

B65
BERNDT R.M.,ABORIGINAL MAN IN AUSTRALIA. LAW DOMIN ADMIN COLONIAL MARRIAGE HABITAT ORD/FREE...LING CHARTS ANTHOL BIBLIOG WORSHIP 20 AUSTRAL ABORIGINES MUSIC ELKIN/AP. PAGE 16 H0312
SOC CULTURE SOCIETY STRUCT

B65
HORNE A.J.,THE COMMONWEALTH TODAY. AFR ASIA CANADA UK STRUCT ECO/UNDEV NAT/G SECT GP/REL 20 AUSTRAL CMN/WLTH. PAGE 73 H1470
BIBLIOG/A SOCIETY CULTURE

B65
MCWHINNEY E.,JUDICIAL REVIEW IN THE ENGLISH-SPEAKING WORLD (3RD ED.). CANADA UK WOR+45 LEGIS CONTROL EXEC PARTIC...JURID 20 AUSTRAL. PAGE 108 H2151
GOV/COMP CT/SYS ADJUD CONSTN

B65
TEW B.,WEALTH AND INCOME. UK BUDGET INT/TRADE PRICE BAL/PAY DEMAND...CHARTS GOV/COMP 20 AUSTRAL. PAGE 153 H3064
FINAN ECO/DEV WEALTH INCOME

B66
BARRETT J.,THAT BETTER COUNTRY: RELIGIOUS ASPECT OF LIFE IN EASTERN AUSTRALIA, 1835-1850. LAW ECO/UNDEV SCHOOL TEC/DEV EDU/PROP CONTROL HABITAT MORAL WORSHIP 19 AUSTRAL CHURCH/STA. PAGE 11 H0229
SECT CULTURE GOV/REL

B66
FORD P.,CARDINAL MORAN AND THE A. L. P. NAT/G POL/PAR SECT DELIB/GP LOBBY REV CHOOSE ORD/FREE MARXISM 19/20 AUSTRAL PROTESTANT LABOR/PAR. PAGE 52 H1035
CATHISM SOCISM LABOR SOCIETY

B66
GRAHAM B.D.,THE FORMATION OF THE AUSTRALIAN COUNTRY PARTIES. CANADA USA+45 USA-45 SOCIETY PLAN ECO/TAC ...NAT/COMP 20 AUSTRAL. PAGE 59 H1190
POL/PAR AGRI REGION PARL/PROC

B66
LEIBLER I.,SOVIET JEWRY AND HUMAN RIGHTS. USSR INTELL NAT/G DOMIN ATTIT 20 AUSTRAL JEWS. PAGE 93 H1865
DISCRIM RACE/REL MARXISM POL/PAR

B66
LOVEDAY P.,PARLIAMENT FACTIONS AND PARTIES: THE FIRST THIRTY YEARS OF RESPONSIBLE GOVERNMENT IN NEW SOUTH WALES, 1856-1889. PROVS LEAD PARL/PROC PARTIC GP/REL INGP/REL MAJORITY PWR...GP/COMP 19 AUSTRAL. PAGE 99 H1970
POL/PAR ELITES NAT/G LEGIS

B66
WINKS R.W.,THE HISTORIOGRAPHY OF THE BRITISH EMPIRE-COMMONWEALTH. CANADA INDIA PAKISTAN UK CULTURE SOCIETY STRUCT POL/PAR...CONCPT NAT/COMP 20 AUSTRAL. PAGE 169 H3386
HIST/WRIT TREND IDEA/COMP METH/COMP

S66
"RESEARCH WORK 1965-1966." NEW/ZEALND ELITES ACADEM LOC/G MUNIC POL/PAR PROVS DIPLOM COLONIAL...SOC 20 AUSTRAL. PAGE 2 H0047
BIBLIOG NAT/G CULTURE S/ASIA

B67
CHANDRASEKHAR S.,ASIA'S POPULATION PROBLEMS. ASIA ECO/UNDEV PLAN AGE/C...OBS CHARTS BIBLIOG 18/20 AUSTRAL. PAGE 29 H0575
PROB/SOLV NAT/COMP GEOG TREND

B67
MCLAUGHLIN M.R.,RELIGIOUS EDUCATION AND THE STATE: DEMOCRACY FINDS A WAY. CANADA EUR+WWI GP/REL POPULISM...CATH NAT/COMP 20 AUSTRAL. PAGE 107 H2141
SECT NAT/G EDU/PROP POLICY

B67
RAE D.,THE POLITICAL CONSEQUENCES OF ELECTORAL LAWS. EUR+WWI ICELAND ISRAEL NEW/ZEALND UK USA+45 ADJUD APPORT GP/REL MAJORITY...MATH STAT CENSUS CHARTS BIBLIOG 20 AUSTRAL. PAGE 129 H2579
POL/PAR CHOOSE NAT/COMP REPRESENT

S67
FUSARO A.,"THE EFFECT OF PROPORTIONAL REPRESENTATION ON VOTING IN THE AUSTRALIAN SENATE." S/ASIA CONSTN POL/PAR CONTROL GP/REL PWR...CHARTS 20 AUSTRAL HOUSE/REP SENATE. PAGE 54 H1083
LEGIS CHOOSE REPRESENT NAT/G

S67
SHELDON C.H.,"PUBLIC OPINION AND HIGH COURTS: COMMUNIST PARTY CASES IN FOUR CONSTITUTIONAL SYSTEMS." CANADA GERMANY/W WOR+45 POL/PAR MARXISM ...METH/COMP NAT/COMP 20 AUSTRAL. PAGE 143 H2857
ATTIT CT/SYS CONSTN DECISION

AUSTRALIAN NATIONAL RES COUN H0181

AUSTRIA....SEE ALSO APPROPRIATE TIME/SPACE/CULTURE INDEX

N
DEUTSCHE BUCHEREI,JAHRESVERZEICHNIS DES DEUTSCHEN SCHRIFTUMS. AUSTRIA EUR+WWI GERMANY SWITZERLND LAW LOC/G DIPLOM ADMIN...MGT SOC 19/20. PAGE 40 H0804
BIBLIOG WRITING NAT/G

B50
KANN R.A.,THE MULTINATIONAL EMPIRE (2 VOLS.). AUSTRIA CZECHOSLVK GERMANY HUNGARY CULTURE NAT/G POL/PAR PROVS REGION REV FEDERAL...GEOG TREND CHARTS IDEA/COMP NAT/COMP 19/20. PAGE 83 H1654
NAT/LISM MOD/EUR

B55
FRANZ G.,KULTURKAMPF. AUSTRIA GERMANY PRUSSIA SWITZERLND POL/PAR DIPLOM GP/REL ATTIT ORD/FREE 18/19 CHURCH/STA. PAGE 53 H1053
NAT/LISM CATHISM NAT/G REV

B61
BEDFORD S.,THE FACES OF JUSTICE: A TRAVELLER'S REPORT. AUSTRIA FRANCE GERMANY/W SWITZERLND UK UNIV WOR+45 WOR-45 CULTURE PARTIC GOV/REL MORAL...JURID OBS GOV/COMP 20. PAGE 13 H0257
CT/SYS ORD/FREE PERSON LAW

B61
KEE R.,REFUGEE WORLD. AUSTRIA EUR+WWI GERMANY NEIGH EX/STRUC WORKER PROB/SOLV ECO/TAC RENT EDU/PROP INGP/REL COST LITERACY HABITAT 20 MIGRATION. PAGE 84 H1676
NAT/G GIVE WEALTH STRANGE

B62
BROWN B.E.,NEW DIRECTIONS IN COMPARATIVE POLITICS. AUSTRIA FRANCE GERMANY UK WOR+45 EX/STRUC LEGIS ORD/FREE 20. PAGE 22 H0439
NAT/COMP METH POL/PAR FORCES

B65
SALVADORI M.,ITALY. AUSTRIA FRANCE GERMANY ITALY SPAIN CULTURE NAT/G POL/PAR DIPLOM WAR FASCISM LAISSEZ MARXISM...TIME/SEQ CHARTS BIBLIOG/A. PAGE 137 H2744
NAT/LISM CATHISM SOCIETY

B66
HOEVELER H.J.,INTERNATIONALE BEKAMPFUNG DES VERBRECHENS. AUSTRIA SWITZERLND WOR+45 INT/ORG CONTROL BIO/SOC...METH/COMP NAT/COMP 20 MAFIA SCOT/YARD FBI. PAGE 72 H1446
CRIMLGY CRIME DIPLOM INT/LAW

B66
RINGHOFER K.,STRUKTURPROBLEME DES RECHTES. AUSTRIA ATTIT ORD/FREE...IDEA/COMP 20. PAGE 132 H2630
JURID PROVS NAT/G NAT/LISM

B66
ROSNER J.,DER FASCHISMUS. AUSTRIA GERMANY ITALY STRATA NAT/G POL/PAR COERCE RACE/REL TOTALISM ATTIT AUTHORIT...IDEA/COMP 20 NAZI ANTI/SEMIT. PAGE 134 H2684
NAT/LISM FASCISM ORD/FREE WAR

B66
STADLER K.R.,THE BIRTH OF THE AUSTRIAN REPUBLIC, 1918-1921. AUSTRIA PLAN TASK PEACE...POLICY DECISION 20. PAGE 148 H2966
NAT/G DIPLOM WAR DELIB/GP

S67
BURGHART A.,"CATHOLIC SOCIAL THOUGHT IN AUSTRIA." AUSTRIA EUR+WWI NAT/G PAY PERS/REL OWN MARXISM SOCISM...SOC 20. PAGE 24 H0482
CATHISM ATTIT TREND SOCIETY

B96
LOWELL A.L.,GOVERNMENTS AND PARTIES IN CONTINENTAL EUROPE, VOL. II. AUSTRIA GERMANY HUNGARY MOD/EUR SWITZERLND SOCIETY EX/STRUC LEGIS DIPLOM AGREE LEAD PARL/PROC PWR...POLICY 19. PAGE 99 H1974
POL/PAR NAT/G GOV/REL ELITES

AUSTRIA-HUNGARY....SEE AUST/HUNG

AUSTRUY J. H0182

AUTHORIT....AUTHORITARIANISM, PERSONAL; SEE ALSO DOMIN

NSY
MACKENZIE K.R.,THE ENGLISH PARLIAMENT. UK POL/PAR CHIEF DIPLOM TAX TASK WAR AUTHORIT...POLICY TREND 12/20 PARLIAMENT. PAGE 100 H2000
ORD/FREE LEGIS NAT/G

B22
URE P.N.,THE ORIGIN OF TYRANNY. MEDIT-7 FINAN INDUS CHIEF FORCES ECO/TAC WEALTH. PAGE 159 H3174
AUTHORIT PWR NAT/G MARKET

B25
MAURRAS C.,ENQUETE SUR LA MONARCHIE (1909). FRANCE CONTROL REPRESENT DISCRIM HEREDITY PWR CONSERVE 20 BUREAUCRCY. PAGE 105 H2103
TRADIT AUTHORIT NAT/G CHIEF

B26
MCIVER R.M.,THE MODERN STATE. UNIV LAW AUTHORIT SOVEREIGN IDEA/COMP. PAGE 107 H2136
GEN/LAWS CONSTN NAT/G PWR

B27
GOOCH G.P.,ENGLISH DEMOCRATIC IDEAS IN THE SEVENTEENTH CENTURY (2ND ED.). UK LAW SECT FORCES DIPLOM LEAD PARL/PROC REV ATTIT AUTHORIT...ANARCH CONCPT 17 PARLIAMENT CMN/WLTH REFORMERS. PAGE 58 H1167
IDEA/COMP MAJORIT EX/STRUC CONSERVE

B32
BLUM L.,PEACE AND DISARMAMENT (TRANS. BY A. WERTH). NAT/G FORCES WORKER DIPLOM AGREE WAR ATTIT AUTHORIT ORD/FREE. PAGE 18 H0360
SOCIALIST PEACE INT/ORG ARMS/CONT

B34
GONZALEZ PALENCIA A,ESTUDIO HISTORICO SOBRE LA CENSURA GUBERNATIVA EN ESPANA 1800-1833. NAT/G COERCE INGP/REL ATTIT AUTHORIT KNOWL...POLICY JURID 19. PAGE 58 H1165
LEGIT EDU/PROP PRESS CONTROL

B38
FIELD G.L.,THE SYNDICAL AND CORPORATIVE INSTITUTIONS OF ITALIAN FASCISM. ITALY CONSTN STRATA LABOR EX/STRUC TOP/EX ADJUD ADMIN LEAD
FASCISM INDUS NAT/G

TOTALISM AUTHORIT...MGT 20 MUSSOLIN/B. PAGE 50 H0991 — WORKER

B39
MCILWAIN C.H.,CONSTITUTIONALISM AND THE CHANGING WORLD. UK USA-45 LEGIS PRIVIL AUTHORIT SOVEREIGN ...GOV/COMP 15/20 MAGNA/CART HOUSE/CMNS. PAGE 107 H2133 — CONSTN POLICY JURID

B40
LEDERER E.,STATE OF THE MASSES. GERMANY ITALY SOCIETY NAT/G ECO/TAC EDU/PROP LEAD TOTALISM ...SOCIALIST PSY 20. PAGE 93 H1852 — CROWD FASCISM AUTHORIT PERSON

B40
MCILWAIN C.H.,CONSTITUTIONALISM, ANCIENT AND MODERN. CHRIST-17C MOD/EUR NAT/G CHIEF PROB/SOLV INSPECT AUTHORIT ORD/FREE PWR...TIME/SEQ ROMAN/REP. PAGE 107 H2134 — CONSTN GEN/LAWS LAW

B42
BARKER E.,REFLECTIONS ON GOVERNMENT. EUR+WWI SOCIETY LEGIS EDU/PROP ADMIN LEAD PARTIC CHOOSE TOTALISM AUTHORIT ORD/FREE SOCISM 20. PAGE 11 H0218 — NAT/G POPULISM ACT/RES GEN/LAWS

C43
BENTHAM J.,"ON THE LIBERTY OF THE PRESS, AND PUBLIC DISCUSSION" IN J. BOWRING, ED., THE WORKS OF JEREMY BENTHAM." SPAIN UK LAW ELITES NAT/G LEGIS INSPECT LEGIT WRITING CONTROL PRIVIL TOTALISM AUTHORIT ...TRADIT 19 FREE/SPEE. PAGE 15 H0290 — ORD/FREE PRESS CONFER CONSERVE

B44
BERDYAEV N.,SLAVERY AND FREEDOM. NAT/G REV WAR NAT/LISM OWN AUTHORIT SEX CONSERVE SOCISM...TRADIT PHIL/SCI CIVIL/LIB. PAGE 15 H0295 — ORD/FREE PERSON ELITES SOCIETY

B48
ROSSITER C.L.,CONSTITUTIONAL DICTATORSHIP; CRISIS GOVERNMENT IN THE MODERN DEMOCRACIES. FRANCE GERMANY UK USA-45 WOR-45 EX/STRUC BAL/PWR CONTROL COERCE WAR CENTRAL ORD/FREE...DECISION 19/20. PAGE 134 H2688 — NAT/G AUTHORIT CONSTN TOTALISM

L48
SHILS E.A.,"COHESION AND DISINTEGRATION IN THE WEHRMACHT IN WORLD WAR II." GERMANY STRUCT DOMIN WAR INGP/REL ISOLAT NAT/LISM ATTIT AUTHORIT SUPEGO RESPECT...PSY CON/ANAL 20 NAZI. PAGE 143 H2862 — EDU/PROP DRIVE PERS/REL FORCES

B49
DE JOUVENEL B.,ON POWER: ITS NATURE AND THE HISTORY OF ITS GROWTH. SOCIETY CHIEF REV WAR ATTIT AUTHORIT ORD/FREE SOVEREIGN CONSERVE POPULISM CONCPT. PAGE 38 H0757 — PWR NAT/G DOMIN CONTROL

B54
BERGER M.,FREEDOM AND CONTROL IN MODERN SOCIETY. LABOR NAT/G VOL/ASSN AUTHORIT DRIVE PLURISM ...METH/CNCPT CLASSIF. PAGE 15 H0300 — ORD/FREE CONTROL INGP/REL

B55
VERGNAUD P.,L'IDEE DE LA NATIONALITE ET DE LA LIBRE DISPOSITION DES PEUPLES DANS SES RAPPORTS AVEC L'IDEE DE L'ETAT. STRATA NAT/G EDU/PROP RACE/REL AUTHORIT FASCISM MARXISM MYTH. PAGE 162 H3243 — NAT/LISM DISCRIM ORD/FREE

B56
RIESENBERG P.N.,INALIENABILITY OF SOVEREIGNTY IN MEDIEVAL POLITICAL THOUGHT. CHRIST-17C INTELL NAT/G SECT CHIEF LEGIS SANCTION AUTHORIT ORD/FREE CONSERVE...IDEA/COMP BIBLIOG 12/16. PAGE 131 H2627 — SOVEREIGN ATTIT

B58
OGILVIE C.,THE KING'S GOVERNMENT AND THE COMMON LAW, 1471-1641. UK STRUCT NAT/G CHIEF LEGIS WORKER BAL/PWR GP/REL AUTHORIT 15/17 COMMON/LAW. PAGE 120 H2408 — CONSTN ELITES DOMIN

B59
PAGE S.W.,LENIN AND WORLD REVOLUTION. COM USSR NAT/G DOMIN COERCE CROWD UTOPIA ATTIT AUTHORIT DRIVE PWR...CONCPT MYTH 19/20 LENIN/VI MARX/KARL. PAGE 122 H2441 — REV PERSON MARXISM BIOG

B60
MOORE W.E.,LABOR COMMITMENT AND SOCIAL CHANGE IN DEVELOPING AREAS. SOCIETY STRATA ECO/UNDEV MARKET VOL/ASSN WORKER AUTHORIT SKILL...MGT NAT/COMP SOC/INTEG 20. PAGE 113 H2250 — LABOR ORD/FREE ATTIT INDUS

B61
ALLIGHAN G.,VERWOERD - THE END. SOUTH/AFR TOP/EX DIPLOM COLONIAL DISCRIM TOTALISM ATTIT AUTHORIT ...BIOG 20 NEGRO VERWOERD/H. PAGE 5 H0107 — CONTROL CHIEF RACE/REL NAT/G

S61
MACRIDIS R.C.,"INTEREST GROUPS IN COMPARATIVE ANALYSIS." CULTURE OP/RES LOBBY REPRESENT GP/REL AUTHORIT ORD/FREE PWR...POLICY DECISION METH/CNCPT CLASSIF. PAGE 101 H2010 — GP/COMP CONCPT PLURISM

B62
BODIN J.,THE SIX BOOKES OF A COMMONWEALE (1576) (FACSIMILE REPRINT OF 1606 ENGLISH TRANSLATION). AUTHORIT ORD/FREE SOVEREIGN...TRADIT CONCPT. PAGE 18 H0364 — PWR CONSERVE CHIEF NAT/G

B62
TINKER H.,INDIA AND PAKISTAN. INDIA PAKISTAN NAT/G POL/PAR...OLD/LIB TRADIT TREND CHARTS BIBLIOG 20. PAGE 155 H3102 — ORD/FREE STRATA REPRESENT AUTHORIT

B64
BENDIX R.,NATION-BUILDING AND CITIZENSHIP: STUDIES OF OUR CHANGING SOCIAL ORDER. WOR+45 CULTURE LOC/G GOV/REL INGP/REL ORD/FREE PWR 20. PAGE 14 H0275 — PARTIC NAT/COMP ADMIN AUTHORIT

B64
ETZIONI A.,MODERN ORGANIZATIONS. CLIENT STRUCT DOMIN CONTROL LEAD PERS/REL AUTHORIT...CLASSIF BUREAUCRCY. PAGE 47 H0946 — MGT ADMIN PLAN CULTURE

B65
ALLEN W.S.,THE NAZI SEIZURE OF POWER. GERMANY NAT/G CHIEF LEAD COERCE CHOOSE REPRESENT GOV/REL AUTHORIT ...DECISION 20 HITLER/A NAZI. PAGE 5 H0106 — MUNIC FASCISM TOTALISM LOC/G

B65
FAGG J.E.,CUBA, HAITI, AND THE DOMINICAN REPUBLIC. CUBA DOMIN/REP HAITI L/A+17C NAT/G DIPLOM ECO/TAC DOMIN CHOOSE AUTHORIT ROLE SOVEREIGN POPULISM 17/20. PAGE 48 H0959 — COLONIAL ECO/UNDEV REV GOV/COMP

B65
RUBINSTEIN A.Z.,THE CHALLENGE OF POLITICS: IDEAS AND ISSUES (2ND ED.). UNIV ELITES SOCIETY EX/STRUC BAL/PWR PARL/PROC AUTHORIT...DECISION ANTHOL 20. PAGE 136 H2709 — NAT/G DIPLOM GP/REL ORD/FREE

B66
BARNETT D.L.,MAU MAU FROM WITHIN. AFR UK POL/PAR LEAD GUERRILLA AUTHORIT ORD/FREE...SOC BIOG 20 NEGRO MAU/MAU. PAGE 11 H0225 — REV CULTURE NAT/G

B66
BRACKMAN A.C.,SOUTHEAST ASIA'S SECOND FRONT: THE POWER STRUGGLE IN THE MALAY ARCHIPELAGO. CHINA/COM INDONESIA MALAYSIA ECO/UNDEV INT/ORG NAT/G FORCES DIPLOM EDU/PROP REGION COERCE GUERRILLA AUTHORIT POPULISM...MAJORIT 20 KENNEDY/JF SEATO. PAGE 20 H0396 — S/ASIA MARXISM REV

B66
DE VORE B.B.,LAND AND LIBERTY; A HISTORY OF THE MEXICAN REVOLUTION. CONSTN INTELL NAT/G CONTROL LEAD CHOOSE TOTALISM AUTHORIT...BIBLIOG 19/20 MEXIC/AMER DIAZ/P LIB/PARTY MAGON/F MADERO/F. PAGE 39 H0776 — REV CHIEF POL/PAR

B66
ROSNER J.,DER FASCHISMUS. AUSTRIA GERMANY ITALY STRATA NAT/G POL/PAR COERCE RACE/REL TOTALISM ATTIT AUTHORIT...IDEA/COMP 20 NAZI ANTI/SEMIT. PAGE 134 H2684 — NAT/LISM FASCISM ORD/FREE WAR

B67
RUSTOW D.A.,A WORLD OF NATIONS; PROBLEMS OF POLITICAL MODERNIZATION. CONSTN NAT/G POL/PAR FORCES DIPLOM LEAD AUTHORIT...CHARTS IDEA/COMP 20. PAGE 136 H2722 — PROB/SOLV ECO/UNDEV CONCPT NAT/COMP

S67
AKE C.,"POLITICAL INTEGRATION AND POLITICAL STABILITY." ELITES POL/PAR LEAD ADJUST EFFICIENCY ATTIT AUTHORIT DRIVE...CONCPT 20. PAGE 4 H0088 — CULTURE NAT/G CONTROL GP/REL

S67
FINLAY D.J.,"THE GHANA COUP...ONE YEAR LATER." GHANA FORCES FOR/AID PRESS CONTROL CIVMIL/REL NAT/LISM AUTHORIT PWR...PREDICT 20. PAGE 50 H1005 — REV NAT/G ATTIT ECO/UNDEV

S67
VON LAUE T.H.,"WESTERNIZATION, REVOLUTION AND THE SEARCH FOR A BASIS OF AUTHORITY - RUSSIA IN 1917." USSR ELITES INTELL ECO/UNDEV NAT/G WORKER ECO/TAC TAX ADMIN LEAD AUTHORIT 20 LENIN/VI. PAGE 164 H3274 — MARXISM REV COM DOMIN

L68
CURRENT HISTORY,"DE GAULLE'S FRANCE." FRANCE MOD/EUR WOR+45 INDUS MARKET INT/ORG BUDGET DIPLOM AUTHORIT DRIVE...GOV/COMP IDEA/COMP 20 DEGAULLE/C EEC. PAGE 36 H0723 — INT/TRADE PERSON LEAD NAT/LISM

B70
BOSSUET J.B.,"POLITIQUE TIREE DE L'ECRITURE SAINTE" (1679-1709) IN J.B. BOSSUET, OEVRES DE BOSSUET. NAT/G GP/REL AUTHORIT HEREDITY PERSON ALL/VALS SOVEREIGN 18 BIBLE DEITY CHRISTIAN. PAGE 19 H0383 — TRADIT CHIEF SECT CONCPT

AUTHORITY....SEE DOMIN

AUTOMAT....AUTOMATION; SEE ALSO COMPUTER, PLAN

B42
BARNES H.E.,SOCIAL INSTITUTIONS IN AN ERA OF WORLD UPHEAVAL. INDUS FAM NAT/G PERF/ART SECT AUTOMAT PERSON MORAL...PREDICT 20. PAGE 11 H0221 — SOCIETY CULTURE TECHRACY TREND

B55
FRIEDMAN G.,INDUSTRIAL SOCIETY: THE EMERGENCE OF THE HUMAN PROBLEMS OF AUTOMATION. UNIV CULTURE ECO/DEV TEC/DEV INGP/REL HAPPINESS RATIONAL UTOPIA ROLE...HUM SOC TIME/SEQ 20. PAGE 53 H1064 — AUTOMAT ADJUST ALL/VALS CONCPT

B64
BRIGHT J.R.,RESEARCH, DEVELOPMENT AND TECHNOLOGICAL — TEC/DEV

INNOVATION. CULTURE R+D CREATE PLAN PROB/SOLV AUTOMAT RISK PERSON...DECISION CONCPT PREDICT BIBLIOG. PAGE 21 H0419 — NEW/IDEA INDUS MGT

B64
WERNETTE J.P.,GOVERNMENT AND BUSINESS. LABOR CAP/ISM ECO/TAC INT/TRADE TAX ADMIN AUTOMAT NUC/PWR CIVMIL/REL DEMAND...MGT 20 MONOPOLY. PAGE 167 H3333 — NAT/G FINAN ECO/DEV CONTROL

B66
LEONTIEF W.,ESSAYS IN ECONOMICS. ECO/UNDEV INDUS NAT/G CAP/ISM FOR/AID AUTOMAT MARXISM...ECOMETRIC CHARTS ANTHOL METH 20 KEYNES/JM. PAGE 94 H1886 — CONCPT METH/CNCPT METH/COMP

AUTOMOBILE....AUTOMOBILE

AVASTHI A. H0183

AVERAGE....MEAN, AVERAGE BEHAVIORS

AVRAMOVIC D. H0184

AYAL E.B. H0185

AYEARST M. H0186

AYLMER G. H0187

AZERBAIJAN....AZERBAIJAN, IRAN

AZEVEDO T. H0188

B

BA/MBUTI....BA MBUTI - THE FOREST PEOPLE (CONGO)

B61
TURNBULL C.M.,THE FOREST PEOPLE. EATING GP/REL INGP/REL RACE/REL ISOLAT HABITAT HEREDITY...GEOG SOC LING DICTIONARY WORSHIP 20 CONGO NEGRO BA/MBUTI. PAGE 157 H3138 — AFR CULTURE KIN RECORD

BABIES....SEE AGE/C

BABYLONIA

N
BURY J.B.,THE CAMBRIDGE ANCIENT HISTORY (12 VOLS.). MEDIT-7 DIPLOM COLONIAL WAR...HUM EGYPT/ANC ROME/EMP BABYLONIA GREECE/ANC. PAGE 25 H0495 — BIBLIOG/A SOCIETY CULTURE NAT/G

BACKUS/I....ISAAC BACKUS

BACON F. H0190,H0191

BACON/F....FRANCIS BACON

B63
STRAUSS L.,HISTORY OF POLITICAL PHILOSOPHY. LAW SOCIETY CAP/ISM MARXISM 19 AQUINAS/T BACON/F HEGEL/GWF MILL/JS NIETZSCH/F. PAGE 150 H2995 — IDEA/COMP PHIL/SCI ANTHOL

BACON/R

B63
LERNER R.,MEDIEVAL POLITICAL PHILOSOPHY. ISLAM MORAL PWR CATHISM...CATH CONCPT OBS IDEA/COMP ANTHOL 9/15 JEWS CHRISTIAN BACON/R AQUINAS/T. PAGE 95 H1890 — KNOWL PHIL/SCI

BADEN....BADEN

BADGLEY R.F. H0192

BADI J. H0193

BAER W. H0194

BAFFREY S.A. H0195

BAGBY P. H0196

BAGEHOT W. H0197,H0198

BAGHDAD....BAGHDAD, IRAQ

BAHAWALPUR....BAHAWALPUR, PAKISTAN

BAHIA....BAHIA

BAIKALOV A. H0199

BAIL....BAIL

BAILEY S.D. H0200

BAILEY S.K. H0201,H2775

BAILEY/JM....JOHN MORAN BAILEY

BAILEY/S....S. BAILEY

BAILEY/T....THOMAS BAILEY

BAIN C.A. H0202

BAKUBA....BAKUBA TRIBE

BAKUNIN.... MIKHAIL BAKUNIN

B53
MAXIMOFF G.P.,THE POLITICAL PHILOSOPHY OF BAKUNIN: SCIENTIFIC ANARCHISM. STRUCT INGP/REL FEDERAL MARXISM...ANARCH BIOG 19 BAKUNIN. PAGE 105 H2104 — SOCIETY PHIL/SCI NAT/G IDEA/COMP

BAL/PAY....BALANCE OF PAYMENTS

N19
HABERLER G.,A SURVEY OF INTERNATIONAL TRADE THEORY (PAMPHLET). FINAN NAT/G COST INCOME 18/20 MONEY HUME/D MARSHALL/A. PAGE 63 H1267 — INT/TRADE BAL/PAY GEN/LAWS POLICY

B20
MALTHUS T.R.,PRINCIPLES OF POLITICAL ECONOMY. UK AGRI INDUS MARKET NAT/G DIPLOM PRICE CONTROL BAL/PAY COST OWN PWR LAISSEZ 18/19. PAGE 102 H2034 — GEN/LAWS DEMAND WEALTH

B47
ENKE S.,INTERNATIONAL ECONOMICS. UK USA+45 USSR INT/ORG BAL/PWR BARGAIN CAP/ISM BAL/PAY...NAT/COMP 20 TREATY. PAGE 46 H0927 — INT/TRADE FINAN TARIFFS ECO/TAC

B58
AVRAMOVIC D.,POSTWAR GROWTH IN INTERNATIONAL INDEBTEDNESS. WOR+45 AGRI INDUS CAP/ISM PRICE INCOME...NAT/COMP 20 GOLD/STAND SILVER. PAGE 9 H0184 — INT/TRADE FINAN COST BAL/PAY

B59
GUDIN E.,INFLACAO (2ND ED.). INDUS NAT/G PLAN ECO/TAC CONTROL COST 20. PAGE 62 H1243 — ECO/UNDEV INT/TRADE BAL/PAY FINAN

B60
KENEN P.B.,BRITISH MONETARY POLICY AND THE BALANCE OF PAYMENTS 1951-57. UK PLAN BUDGET ECO/TAC INT/TRADE PAY PRICE COST ATTIT 20. PAGE 84 H1687 — BAL/PAY PROB/SOLV FINAN NAT/G

B61
ESTEBAN J.C.,IMPERIALISMO Y DESARROLLO ECONOMICO. L/A+17C FINAN INDUS NAT/G ECO/TAC CONTROL ROLE. PAGE 47 H0941 — ECO/UNDEV NAT/LISM DIPLOM BAL/PAY

B61
OECD,STATISTICS OF BALANCE OF PAYMENTS 1950-61. WOR+45 FINAN ECO/TAC INT/TRADE DEMAND WEALTH...STAT NAT/COMP 20 OEEC OECD. PAGE 120 H2396 — BAL/PAY ECO/DEV INT/ORG CHARTS

B62
KINDLEBERGER C.P.,FOREIGN TRADE AND THE NATIONAL ECONOMY. WOR+45 ECO/DEV ECO/UNDEV ECO/TAC COST DEMAND 20. PAGE 86 H1713 — INT/TRADE GOV/COMP BAL/PAY POLICY

B63
BANERJI A.K.,INDIA'S BALANCE OF PAYMENTS. INDIA NAT/G PRICE BAL/PAY COST INCOME 20. PAGE 10 H0208 — INT/TRADE DIPLOM FINAN BUDGET

B63
BERGSON A.,ECONOMIC TRENDS IN THE SOVIET UNION. USSR ECO/UNDEV AGRI NAT/G FORCES PLAN TEC/DEV INT/TRADE BAL/PAY...POLICY ANTHOL 20. PAGE 15 H0302 — ECO/DEV NAT/COMP INDUS LABOR

B63
CHOU S.H.,THE CHINESE INFLATION 1937-1949. ASIA SOCIETY POL/PAR FOR/AID INT/TRADE BAL/PAY WEALTH MARXISM...STAT CHARTS 20 COM/PARTY GOLD/STAND. PAGE 30 H0597 — FINAN ECO/TAC BUDGET NAT/G

B63
GUIMARAES A.P.,INFLACAO E MONOPOLIO NO BRASIL. BRAZIL FINAN NAT/G PLAN PAY...METH/COMP 20. PAGE 62 H1248 — ECO/UNDEV PRICE INT/TRADE BAL/PAY

N63
LEDERER W.,THE BALANCE ON FOREIGN TRANSACTIONS: PROBLEMS OF DEFINITION AND MEASUREMENT (PAMPHLET). USA+45 BUDGET DIPLOM ECO/TAC PRICE GOV/REL...POLICY STAT NAT/COMP METH 20. PAGE 93 H1853 — FINAN BAL/PAY INT/TRADE ECO/DEV

B64
KALDOR N.,ESSAYS ON ECONOMIC POLICY (VOL. II). CHILE GERMANY INDIA FINAN...GOV/COMP METH/COMP 20 KEYNES/JM. PAGE 83 H1651 — BAL/PAY INT/TRADE METH/CNCPT ECO/UNDEV

B64
US HOUSE COMM BANKING-CURR,INTERNATIONAL — BAL/PAY

DEVELOPMENT ASSOCIATION ACT AMENDMENT. CHINA/COM USA+45 USSR FINAN FORCES LEGIS DIPLOM CONFER EFFICIENCY...CHARTS GOV/COMP 20 PRESIDENT CONGRESS INTL/DEV. PAGE 160 H3196
FOR/AID RECORD ECO/TAC

EDELMAN M.,THE POLITICS OF WAGE-PRICE DECISIONS. GERMANY ITALY NETHERLAND UK INDUS LABOR POL/PAR PROB/SOLV BARGAIN PRICE ROUTINE BAL/PAY COST DEMAND 20. PAGE 44 H0888
B65 GOV/COMP CONTROL ECO/TAC PLAN

HONDURAS CONSEJO NAC DE ECO,PLAN NACIONAL DE DESARROLLO ECONOMICO Y SOCIAL DE HONDURAS 1965-69. HONDURAS AGRI INDUS BAL/PAY INCOME 20. PAGE 73 H1459
B65 ECO/UNDEV NAT/G PLAN POLICY

TEW B.,WEALTH AND INCOME. UK BUDGET INT/TRADE PRICE BAL/PAY DEMAND...CHARTS GOV/COMP 20 AUSTRAL. PAGE 153 H3064
B65 FINAN ECO/DEV WEALTH INCOME

HACKETT J.,L'ECONOMIE BRITANNIQUE: PROBLEMES ET PERSPECTIVES. FRANCE UK LABOR MUNIC NAT/G EX/STRUC PROB/SOLV BAL/PAY INCOME RIGID/FLEX...MGT PHIL/SCI CHARTS 20. PAGE 63 H1271
B66 ECO/DEV FINAN ECO/TAC PLAN

KOMIYA R.,POSTWAR ECONOMIC GROWTH IN JAPAN. ELITES NAT/G EX/STRUC TEC/DEV BUDGET DIPLOM CONTROL BAL/PAY PRODUC...BIBLIOG 20 CHINJAP. PAGE 88 H1754
B66 ECO/DEV POLICY PLAN ADJUST

YEAGER L.B.,INTERNATIONAL MONETARY RELATIONS: THEORY, HISTORY, AND POLICY. WOR+45 WOR-45 INT/TRADE BAL/PAY...NAT/COMP 18/20 MONEY. PAGE 172 H3435
B66 FINAN DIPLOM ECO/TAC IDEA/COMP

DILLARD D.,ECONOMIC DEVELOPMENT OF THE NORTH ATLANTIC COMMUNITY. EUR+WWI MOD/EUR USA+45 USA-45 ECO/UNDEV LABOR CAP/ISM WAR BAL/PAY...NAT/COMP 15/20. PAGE 41 H0824
B67 ECO/DEV INT/TRADE INDUS DIPLOM

HAWTREY R.,INCOMES AND MONEY. EUR+WWI FUT UK LABOR WORKER INT/TRADE TAX PAY BAL/PAY COST WEALTH 20. PAGE 68 H1363
B67 FINAN NAT/G POLICY ECO/DEV

RUEFF J.,BALANCE OF PAYMENTS. WOR+45 FINAN TEC/DEV DIPLOM TARIFFS PRICE CONTROL...POLICY CONCPT IDEA/COMP. PAGE 136 H2715
B67 INT/TRADE BAL/PAY ECO/TAC NAT/COMP

THOMAN R.S.,GEOGRAPHY OF INTERNATIONAL TRADE. WOR+45 ECO/DEV ECO/UNDEV INT/ORG LG/CO PLAN BAL/PAY ...STAT CHARTS NAT/COMP 20. PAGE 154 H3075
B67 INT/TRADE GEOG ECO/TAC DIPLOM

ROTH A.R.,"CAPITAL-MARKET DEVELOPMENT IN ISRAEL AND BRAZIL: TWO EXAMPLES OF THE ROLE OF LAW IN DEVELOPMENT." BRAZIL ISRAEL L/A+17C INDUS MARKET ECO/TAC FOR/AID INT/TRADE CONTROL BAL/PAY 20. PAGE 135 H2694
L67 LAW ECO/UNDEV NAT/COMP FINAN

BAER W.,"THE INFLATION CONTROVERSY IN LATIN AMERICA: SURVEY." L/A+17C ECO/UNDEV AGRI FINAN INDUS PLAN PROB/SOLV TEC/DEV...BIBLIOG/A 20. PAGE 10 H0194
S67 NAT/G BAL/PAY ECO/TAC BUDGET

FRENCH D.S.,"DOES THE U.S. EXPLOIT THE DEVELOPING NATIONS?" INT/ORG NAT/G CAP/ISM BAL/PAY WEALTH POLICY. PAGE 53 H1057
S67 ECO/UNDEV INT/TRADE ECO/TAC COLONIAL

BAL/PWR....BALANCE OF POWER

DE JOMINI A.H.,THE ART OF WAR. MOD/EUR NAT/G BAL/PWR DIPLOM DOMIN EXEC ROUTINE COERCE DRIVE PWR SKILL...POLICY CONCPT CHARTS STERTYP 19. PAGE 38 H0755
B00 PLAN FORCES WAR WEAPON

FIGGIS J.N.,CHURCHES IN THE MODERN STATE (2ND ED.). LAW CHIEF BAL/PWR PWR...CONCPT CHURCH/STA POPE. PAGE 50 H0998
B14 SECT NAT/G SOCIETY ORD/FREE

FARIES J.C.,THE RISE OF INTERNATIONALISM. ASIA MOD/EUR NAT/G VOL/ASSN DELIB/GP BAL/PWR EDU/PROP ARMS/CONT RIGID/FLEX TREND. PAGE 49 H0971
B15 INT/ORG DIPLOM PEACE

MICHELS R.,POLITICAL PARTIES. NAT/G BAL/PWR CHOOSE REPRESENT ATTIT SOCISM...PSY SOC CONCPT OBS 20 MONOPOLY. PAGE 110 H2198
B15 POL/PAR CENTRAL LEAD PWR

VEBLEN T.,IMPERIAL GERMANY AND THE INDUSTRIAL REVOLUTION. GERMANY MOD/EUR UK USA-45 NAT/G TEC/DEV CAP/ISM...MAJORIT NAT/COMP 19/20 CHINJAP. PAGE 162 H3236
B15 ECO/DEV INDUS TECHNIC BAL/PWR

BENTHAM J.,A PLAN FOR AN UNIVERSAL AND PERPETUAL PEACE (1838) (PAMPHLET). NAT/G FORCES BAL/PWR INT/TRADE ADMIN AGREE CT/SYS ARMS/CONT SOVEREIGN WEALTH GEN/LAWS. PAGE 14 H0288
N19 INT/ORG INT/LAW PEACE COLONIAL

BAGEHOT W.,THE ENGLISH CONSTITUTION AND OTHER POLITICAL ESSAYS. UK DELIB/GP BAL/PWR ADMIN CONTROL EXEC ROUTINE CONSERVE...METH PARLIAMENT 19/20. PAGE 10 H0197
B24 NAT/G STRUCT CONCPT

WEBSTER C.,THE FOREIGN POLICY OF CASTLEREAGH: 1815-1822. LAW NAT/G DELIB/GP TOP/EX BAL/PWR ORD/FREE PWR RESPECT 19. PAGE 166 H3322
B25 MOD/EUR DIPLOM UK

PANIKKAR K.M.,INDIAN STATES AND THE GOVERNMENT OF INDIA. INDIA UK CONSTN CONTROL TASK GP/REL SOVEREIGN WEALTH...TREND BIBLIOG 19. PAGE 123 H2457
B27 GOV/COMP COLONIAL BAL/PWR PROVS

LANGER W.L.,THE FRANCO-RUSSIAN ALLIANCE: 1890-1894. FRANCE MOD/EUR UK USSR NAT/G CHIEF FORCES BAL/PWR AGREE WAR PEACE PWR...TIME/SEQ TREATY 19 BISMARCK/O. PAGE 91 H1809
B29 DIPLOM

BYNKERSHOEK C.,QUAESTIONUM JURIS PUBLICI LIBRI DUO. CHRIST-17C MOD/EUR CONSTN ELITES SOCIETY NAT/G PROVS EX/STRUC FORCES TOP/EX BAL/PWR DIPLOM ATTIT MORAL...TRADIT CONCPT. PAGE 25 H0502
B30 INT/ORG LAW NAT/LISM INT/LAW

LASKI H.J.,LIBERTY IN THE MODERN STATE. UNIV SOCIETY STRATA CREATE BAL/PWR CONTROL RATIONAL ATTIT PWR 18/20. PAGE 91 H1828
B30 CONCPT ORD/FREE NAT/G DOMIN

BENES E.,INTERNATIONAL SECURITY. GERMANY UK NAT/G DELIB/GP PLAN BAL/PWR ATTIT ORD/FREE PWR LEAGUE/NAT 20 TREATY. PAGE 14 H0280
B39 EUR+WWI INT/ORG WAR

HITLER A.,MEIN KAMPF. EUR+WWI FUT MOD/EUR STRUCT INT/ORG LABOR NAT/G POL/PAR FORCES CREATE PLAN BAL/PWR DIPLOM ECO/TAC DOMIN EDU/PROP ADMIN COERCE ATTIT...SOCIALIST BIOG TREND NAZI. PAGE 71 H1428
B39 PWR NEW/IDEA WAR

SIEYES E.J.,LES DISCOURS DE SIEYES DANS LES DEBATS CONSTITUTIONNELS DE L'AN III (2 ET 18 THERMIDOR). FRANCE LAW NAT/G PROB/SOLV BAL/PWR GOV/REL 18 JURY. PAGE 144 H2871
B39 CONSTN ADJUD LEGIS EX/STRUC

HAUSHOFER K.,WEHR-GEOPOLITIK. EUR+WWI GERMANY MOD/EUR NAT/G ACT/RES BAL/PWR PWR...STAT TIME/SEQ CHARTS NAZI 20. PAGE 68 H1361
B41 FORCES GEOG WAR

EARLE E.M.,MAKERS OF MODERN STRATEGY: MILITARY THOUGHT FROM MACHIAVELLI TO HITLER. EUR+WWI MOD/EUR NAT/G ACT/RES BAL/PWR DOMIN COERCE ATTIT DRIVE RIGID/FLEX ALL/VALS...METH/CNCPT BIOG 16/20. PAGE 44 H0879
B43 PLAN FORCES WAR

NICOLSON H.,THE CONGRESS OF VIENNA. MOD/EUR NAT/G FORCES BAL/PWR DOMIN LEGIT COERCE PERSON PWR ...RECORD TIME/SEQ STERTYP 19 CONG/VIENN. PAGE 118 H2353
B46 CONCPT POLICY DIPLOM

ENKE S.,INTERNATIONAL ECONOMICS. UK USA+45 USSR INT/ORG BAL/PWR BARGAIN CAP/ISM BAL/PAY...NAT/COMP 20 TREATY. PAGE 46 H0927
B47 INT/TRADE FINAN TARIFFS ECO/TAC

ROSSITER C.L.,CONSTITUTIONAL DICTATORSHIP; CRISIS GOVERNMENT IN THE MODERN DEMOCRACIES. FRANCE GERMANY UK USA-45 WOR-45 EX/STRUC BAL/PWR CONTROL COERCE WAR CENTRAL ORD/FREE...DECISION 19/20. PAGE 134 H2688
B48 NAT/G AUTHORIT CONSTN TOTALISM

HINDEN R.,EMPIRE AND AFTER. UK POL/PAR BAL/PWR DIPLOM INT/TRADE WAR NAT/LISM PWR 17/20. PAGE 71 H1420
B49 NAT/G COLONIAL ATTIT POLICY

WORMUTH F.D.,THE ORIGINS OF MODERN CONSTITUTIONALISM. GREECE UK LEGIS CREATE TEC/DEV BAL/PWR DOMIN ADJUD REV WAR PWR...JURID ROMAN/REP CROMWELL/O. PAGE 170 H3412
B49 NAT/G CONSTN LAW

ROUSSEAU J.J.,"DISCOURSE ON THE ORIGIN OF INEQUALITY" (1755) IN THE SOCIAL CONTRACT AND DISCOURSES." UNIV NAT/G PLAN BAL/PWR HAPPINESS UTOPIA BIO/SOC HEREDITY MORAL...WELF/ST CONCPT. PAGE 135 H2698
C50 SOCIETY STRUCT PERSON GEN/LAWS

WEBSTER C.,THE FOREIGN POLICY OF PALMERSTON - 1830 TO 1841. MOD/EUR UK LAW CONSTN INTELL SOCIETY STRUCT NAT/G FORCES TOP/EX CREATE BAL/PWR PWR 19. PAGE 166 H3323
B51 ADMIN PERSON DIPLOM

C52
FIFIELD R.H.,"WOODROW WILSON AND THE FAR EAST." ASIA CHIEF DELIB/GP BAL/PWR CONFER COLONIAL ARMS/CONT WAR...TIME/SEQ NAT/COMP 19/20 WILSON/W LEAGUE/NAT. PAGE 50 H0995
BIBLIOG DIPLOM INT/ORG

B53
LENZ F.,DIE BEWEGUNGEN DER GROSSEN MACHTE. USA+45 USA-45 USSR SOCIETY STRATA STRUCT NAT/G PERSON MARXISM...CONCPT IDEA/COMP NAT/COMP 18/20. PAGE 94 H1883
BAL/PWR TREND DIPLOM HIST/WRIT

B53
MEYER P.,THE JEWS IN THE SOVIET SATELLITES. CZECHOSLVK POLAND SOCIETY STRATA NAT/G BAL/PWR ECO/TAC EDU/PROP LEGIT ADMIN COERCE ATTIT DISPL PERCEPT HEALTH PWR RESPECT WEALTH...METH/CNCPT JEWS VAL/FREE NAZI 20. PAGE 110 H2192
COM SECT TOTALISM USSR

S53
DRUCKER P.F.,"THE EMPLOYEE SOCIETY." STRUCT BAL/PWR PARTIC REPRESENT PWR...DECISION CONCPT. PAGE 42 H0849
LABOR MGT WORKER CULTURE

B54
SALVEMINI G.,PRELUDE TO WORLD WAR II. ITALY MOD/EUR INT/ORG BAL/PWR EDU/PROP CONTROL TOTALISM...TREND NAT/COMP BIBLIOG 19 HITLER/A LEAGUE/NAT MUSSOLIN/B. PAGE 137 H2745
WAR FASCISM LEAD PWR

B55
HELANDER S.,DAS AUTARKIEPROBLEM IN DER WELTWIRTSCHAFT. PROB/SOLV BAL/PWR BARGAIN CAP/ISM ECO/TAC SOVEREIGN 20. PAGE 69 H1388
NAT/COMP COLONIAL DIPLOM

B55
ROWE C.,VOLTAIRE AND THE STATE. FRANCE MOD/EUR BAL/PWR CONTROL TASK SUPEGO ORD/FREE PWR...CONCPT 18 VOLTAIRE. PAGE 135 H2702
NAT/G DIPLOM NAT/LISM ATTIT

B55
TOYNBEE A.,THE REALIGNMENT OF EUROPE. COM GREECE ITALY NAT/G BAL/PWR ECO/TAC EDU/PROP REV SOVEREIGN ...SOC TIME/SEQ TREND COLD/WAR 20. PAGE 156 H3123
EUR+WWI PLAN USSR

B56
ROBERTS H.L.,RUSSIA AND AMERICA. CHINA/COM S/ASIA USSR FORCES TEC/DEV FOR/AID NUC/PWR ALL/IDEOS ...MAJORIT TREND NAT/COMP 20 COLD/WAR UN NATO. PAGE 132 H2641
DIPLOM INT/ORG BAL/PWR TOTALISM

B56
VON HARPE W.,DIE SOWJETUNION FINNLAND UND SKANDANAVIEN, 1945-1955. EUR+WWI FINLAND GERMANY USSR WAR INGP/REL ORD/FREE SOVEREIGN MARXISM ...POLICY GOV/COMP BIBLIOG 20 STALIN/J. PAGE 163 H3270
DIPLOM COM NEUTRAL BAL/PWR

B57
BUCK P.W.,CONTOL OF FOREIGN RELATIONS IN MODERN NATIONS. FRANCE L/A+17C NETHERLAND USSR WOR+45 INT/ORG TOP/EX BAL/PWR DOMIN EDU/PROP COERCE PEACE ATTIT...CONCPT TREND 20 CMN/WLTH. PAGE 23 H0465
NAT/G PWR DIPLOM

B57
MEINECKE F.,MACHIAVELLISM. CHRIST-17C FRANCE GERMANY ITALY MOD/EUR BAL/PWR PARL/PROC TOTALISM ...PHIL/SCI 15/20 MACHIAVELL. PAGE 108 H2166
NAT/LISM NAT/G PWR

B57
PALMER N.D.,INTERNATIONAL RELATIONS. WOR+45 INT/ORG NAT/G ECO/TAC EDU/PROP COLONIAL WAR PWR SOVEREIGN ...POLICY T 20 TREATY. PAGE 123 H2451
DIPLOM BAL/PWR NAT/COMP

B58
GARTHOFF R.L.,SOVIET STRATEGY IN THE NUCLEAR AGE. FUT USSR R+D INT/ORG NAT/G ACT/RES TEC/DEV DOMIN DETER WAR ATTIT PWR...RELATIV METH/CNCPT SELF/OBS TREND CON/ANAL STERTYP GEN/LAWS 20. PAGE 55 H1103
COM FORCES BAL/PWR NUC/PWR

B58
OGILVIE C.,THE KING'S GOVERNMENT AND THE COMMON LAW, 1471-1641. UK STRUCT NAT/G CHIEF LEGIS WORKER BAL/PWR GP/REL AUTHORIT 15/17 COMMON/LAW. PAGE 120 H2408
CONSTN ELITES DOMIN

B58
STRAUSZ-HUPE R.,THE IDEA OF COLONIALISM. WOR+45 WOR-45 BAL/PWR GOV/REL...POLICY CLASSIF TIME/SEQ GOV/COMP ANTHOL 20 UN. PAGE 150 H2996
IDEA/COMP COLONIAL CONTROL CONCPT

B59
BLOOMFIELD L.P.,WESTERN EUROPE AND THE UN - TRENDS AND PROSPECTS. EUR+WWI BAL/PWR DIPLOM ECO/TAC COLONIAL ATTIT PWR...POLICY 20 UN EUROPE/W. PAGE 18 H0359
INT/ORG TREND FUT NAT/G

B59
DEHIO L.,GERMANY AND WORLD POLITICS IN THE TWENTIETH CENTURY. EUR+WWI FRANCE GERMANY MOD/EUR UK USSR NAT/G CHIEF BAL/PWR DOMIN COLONIAL CONTROL LEAD...IDEA/COMP 20 VERSAILLES. PAGE 39 H0783
DIPLOM WAR NAT/LISM SOVEREIGN

B59
FOX A.,THE POWER OF SMALL STATES: DIPLOMACY IN WORLD WAR TWO. EUR+WWI FINLAND NORWAY SPAIN SWEDEN TURKEY NAT/G TOP/EX DIPLOM PWR...HIST/WRIT 20. PAGE 52 H1044
CONCPT STERTYP BAL/PWR

B59
SANCHEZ A.L.,EL CONCEPTO DEL ESTADO EN EL PENSAMIENTO ESPANOL DEL SIGLO XVI. SPAIN LEGIS JUDGE BAL/PWR LEGIT EXEC WAR PWR...MAJORIT 16. PAGE 137 H2747
NAT/G PHIL/SCI LAW SOVEREIGN

B59
THOMAS D.H.,GUIDE TO THE DIPLOMATIC ARCHIVES OF WESTERN EUROPE. EUR+WWI ELITES INT/ORG NAT/G BAL/PWR INT/TRADE PEACE. PAGE 154 H3076
BIBLIOG DIPLOM CONFER

S59
MENDELSON W.,"JUDICIAL REVIEW AND PARTY POLITICS" (BMR)" UK USA+45 USA-45 NAT/G LEGIS PROB/SOLV EDU/PROP ADJUD EFFICIENCY...POLICY NAT/COMP 19/20 AUSTRAL SUPREME/CT. PAGE 109 H2171
CT/SYS POL/PAR BAL/PWR JURID

B60
ALBRECHT-CARRIE R.,FRANCE, EUROPE AND THE TWO WORLD WARS. EUR+WWI FRANCE GERMANY MOD/EUR UK ECO/DEV NAT/G FORCES BAL/PWR DOMIN ARMS/CONT PEACE PWR 20 TREATY EUROPE. PAGE 5 H0096
DIPLOM WAR

B60
FEIS H.,BETWEEN WAR AND PEACE: THE POTSDAM CONFERENCE. EUR+WWI NAT/G DELIB/GP PROB/SOLV REPAR WAR CIVMIL/REL...BIBLIOG 20. PAGE 49 H0983
DIPLOM CONFER BAL/PWR

B60
FURNIA A.H.,THE DIPLOMACY OF APPEASEMENT: ANGLO-FRENCH RELATIONS AND THE PRELUDE TO WORLD WAR II 1931-1938. FRANCE GERMANY UK ELITES NAT/G DELIB/GP FORCES WAR PEACE RIGID/FLEX 20. PAGE 54 H1077
DIPLOM BAL/PWR COERCE

B60
FURNISS E.S.,FRANCE, TROUBLED ALLY. EUR+WWI FUT CULTURE SOCIETY BAL/PWR ADMIN ATTIT DRIVE PWR ...TREND TOT/POP 20 DEGAULLE/C. PAGE 54 H1079
NAT/G FRANCE

B60
SETHE P.,SCHICKSALSSTUNDEN DER WELTGESCHICHTE (6TH ED.). NAT/G BAL/PWR DOMIN REV PWR...NAT/COMP 16/20. PAGE 141 H2831
DIPLOM WAR PEACE

B60
STOLPER W.F.,GERMANY BETWEEN EAST AND WEST: THE ECONOMICS OF COMPETITIVE COEXISTENCE. FUT GERMANY/E GERMANY/W WOR+45 FINAN POL/PAR BUDGET ECO/TAC FOR/AID INT/TRADE...STAT CHARTS METH/COMP 20 COLD/WAR. PAGE 150 H2989
ECO/DEV DIPLOM GOV/COMP BAL/PWR

B60
STRACHEY J.,THE END OF EMPIRE. UK WOR+45 WOR-45 DIPLOM INT/TRADE DOMIN ADJUST ORD/FREE WEALTH ...SOCIALIST GOV/COMP TIME COMMONWLTH. PAGE 150 H2991
COLONIAL ECO/DEV BAL/PWR LAISSEZ

S60
BRZEZINSKI Z.K.,"PATTERNS AND LIMITS OF THE SINO-SOVIET DISPUTE." ASIA CHINA/COM COM FUT STRATA NAT/G EX/STRUC FORCES BAL/PWR DIPLOM ECO/TAC DOMIN EDU/PROP ADMIN COERCE WAR ATTIT RIGID/FLEX ...GEN/LAWS VAL/FREE 20. PAGE 23 H0459
POL/PAR PWR REV USSR

S60
GINSBURGS G.,"PEKING-LHASA-NEW DELHI." CHINA/COM FUT INDIA S/ASIA KIN NAT/G PROVS SECT FORCES BAL/PWR ECO/TAC DOMIN EDU/PROP LEGIT ADMIN REGION GUERRILLA PWR...TREND TIBET 20. PAGE 57 H1134
ASIA COERCE DIPLOM

S60
WOLFE T.W.,"KHRUSHCHEV'S DISARMAMENT STRATEGY." COM NAT/G TOP/EX PLAN BAL/PWR DIPLOM ARMS/CONT COERCE ATTIT...POLICY CONCPT RECORD TREND CON/ANAL COLD/WAR 20 KHRUSH/N. PAGE 170 H3401
PWR GEN/LAWS USSR

B61
DALLIN D.J.,SOVIET FOREIGN POLICY AFTER STALIN. ASIA CHINA/COM EUR+WWI GERMANY IRAN UK YUGOSLAVIA INT/ORG NAT/G VOL/ASSN FORCES TOP/EX BAL/PWR DOMIN EDU/PROP COERCE ATTIT PWR 20. PAGE 37 H0737
COM DIPLOM USSR

B61
DONNISON F.S.V.,CIVIL AFFAIRS AND MILITARY GOVERNMENT NORTH-WEST EUROPE 1944-1946. EUR+WWI FRANCE GERMANY UK USSR LOC/G PROVS PLAN PROB/SOLV BAL/PWR ECO/TAC CONTROL PWR...CHARTS 20. PAGE 42 H0836
NAT/G WAR FORCES CIVMIL/REL

B61
KISSINGER H.A.,THE NECESSITY FOR CHOICE. FUT USA+45 ECO/UNDEV NAT/G PLAN BAL/PWR ECO/TAC ARMS/CONT DETER NUC/PWR ATTIT...POLICY CONCPT RECORD GEN/LAWS COLD/WAR 20. PAGE 87 H1728
TOP/EX TREND DIPLOM

B61
MILLIKAW M.F.,THE EMERGING NATIONS: THEIR GROWTH AND UNITED STATES POLICY. FUT USA+45 WOR+45 WOR-45 NAT/G PLAN TEC/DEV BAL/PWR GOV/REL PEACE ORD/FREE 20. PAGE 111 H2216
ECO/UNDEV POLICY DIPLOM FOR/AID

B61
MOLLAU G.,INTERNATIONAL COMMUNISM AND WORLD REVOLUTION: HISTORY AND METHODS. RUSSIA USSR INT/ORG NAT/G POL/PAR VOL/ASSN FORCES BAL/PWR DIPLOM EXEC REGION WAR ATTIT PWR MARXISM...CONCPT TIME/SEQ COLD/WAR 19/20. PAGE 112 H2237
COM REV

B61
PECKERT J.,DIE GROSSEN UND DIE KLEINEN MAECHTE. COM GERMANY/W ECO/DEV ECO/UNDEV NAT/G WAR RACE/REL PEACE...POLICY GP/COMP GOV/COMP 20 COLD/WAR. PAGE 124 H2482
DIPLOM ECO/TAC BAL/PWR

S61
VALLET R.,"IRAN: KEY TO THE MIDDLE EAST." COM IRAQ ISLAM KUWAIT LEBANON SAUDI/ARAB TURKEY ELITES SOCIETY INDUS PROC/MFG POL/PAR TOP/EX PLAN BAL/PWR
NAT/G ECO/UNDEV IRAN

DIPLOM ECO/TAC ALL/VALS...TREND CENTO 20. PAGE 161 H3224

B62
DEHIO L.,THE PRECARIOUS BALANCE: FOUR CENTURIES OF THE EUROPEAN POWER STRUGGLE. FRANCE GERMANY SPAIN NAT/G DOMIN PWR...GOV/COMP 8/20. PAGE 39 H0784
BAL/PWR WAR DIPLOM COERCE

B62
DUTOIT B.,LA NEUTRALITE SUISSE A L'HEURE EUROPEENNE. EUR+WWI MOD/EUR INT/ORG NAT/G VOL/ASSN PLAN BAL/PWR LEGIT NEUTRAL REGION PEACE ORD/FREE SOVEREIGN...CONCPT OBS TIME/SEQ TREND STERTYP VAL/FREE LEAGUE/NAT UN 20. PAGE 44 H0873
ATTIT DIPLOM SWITZERLND

B62
FINER S.E.,THE MAN ON HORSEBACK: ROLE OF THE MILITARY IN POLITICS. UNIV LAW CONSTN ELITES SOCIETY POL/PAR BAL/PWR DOMIN EDU/PROP LEGIT COERCE GUERRILLA REV WAR WEAPON DRIVE SUPEGO ORD/FREE PWR RESPECT...POLICY CONCPT GEN/METH. PAGE 50 H1003
NAT/G FORCES TOTALISM

B62
LAQUEUR W.,POLYCENTRISM. CHINA/COM COM USSR WOR+45 INT/ORG NAT/G ECO/TAC DOMIN LEAD ATTIT PWR SOVEREIGN...ANTHOL 20. PAGE 91 H1821
MARXISM DIPLOM BAL/PWR POLICY

B62
PHILLIPS O.H.,CONSTITUTIONAL AND ADMINISTRATIVE LAW (3RD ED.). UK INT/ORG LOC/G CHIEF EX/STRUC LEGIS BAL/PWR ADJUD COLONIAL CT/SYS PWR...CHARTS 20. PAGE 125 H2503
JURID ADMIN CONSTN NAT/G

B62
ZINKIN T.,REPORTING INDIA. INDIA PAKISTAN WOR+45 SOCIETY SECT FORCES EDU/PROP CROWD DISCRIM NAT/LISM MARXISM...POLICY 20. PAGE 173 H3457
STRATA COLONIAL BAL/PWR CONTROL

S62
LONDON K.,"SINO-SOVIET RELATIONS IN THE CONTEXT OF THE 'WORLD SOCIALIST SYSTEM'." ASIA CHINA/COM COM USSR INT/ORG NAT/G TOP/EX BAL/PWR DIPLOM DOMIN ATTIT PERCEPT RIGID/FLEX PWR MARXISM...METH/CNCPT TREND 20. PAGE 98 H1957
DELIB/GP CONCPT SOCISM

B63
BRECHER M.,THE NEW STATES OF ASIA. ASIA S/ASIA INT/ORG BAL/PWR COLONIAL NEUTRAL ORD/FREE PWR 20 UN. PAGE 20 H0407
NAT/G ECO/UNDEV DIPLOM POLICY

B63
FRANZ G.,TEILUNG UND WIEDERVEREINIGUNG. GERMANY IRELAND ITALY NETHERLAND POLAND CULTURE BAL/PWR CHOOSE NAT/LISM ORD/FREE SOVEREIGN 19/20. PAGE 53 H1054
DIPLOM WAR NAT/COMP ATTIT

B63
GONZALEZ PEDRERO E.,ANATOMIA DE UN CONFLICTO. WOR+45 ECO/DEV ECO/UNDEV ECO/TAC FOR/AID CONTROL ARMS/CONT GOV/REL...NAT/COMP 20 COLD/WAR. PAGE 58 H1166
DIPLOM DETER BAL/PWR

B63
KRAEHE E.,METTERNICH'S GERMAN POLICY: THE CONTEST WITH NAPOLEON, 1799-1814, VOL. 1. FRANCE MOD/EUR NAT/G CONSULT TOP/EX PLAN BAL/PWR DOMIN COERCE ATTIT DRIVE PERCEPT PERSON SKILL...CONCPT RECORD TIME/SEQ TREND 18/19. PAGE 88 H1764
BIOG GERMANY DIPLOM

B63
LEWIN J.,POLITICS AND LAW IN SOUTH AFRICA. SOUTH/AFR UK POL/PAR BAL/PWR ECO/TAC COLONIAL CONTROL GP/REL DISCRIM PWR 20 NEGRO. PAGE 96 H1909
NAT/LISM POLICY LAW RACE/REL

B63
MERKL P.H.,THE ORIGIN OF THE WEST GERMAN REPUBLIC. GERMANY/W WOR+45 POL/PAR DIPLOM LEAD LOBBY REPRESENT GP/REL NAT/LISM 20. PAGE 109 H2179
CONSTN PARL/PROC CONTROL BAL/PWR

B63
RIVKIN A.,THE AFRICAN PRESENCE IN WORLD AFFAIRS. ECO/UNDEV AGRI INT/ORG LOC/G NAT/LISM...OBS PREDICT GOV/COMP 20. PAGE 132 H2635
AFR NAT/G DIPLOM BAL/PWR

S63
ANTHON C.G.,"THE END OF THE ADENAUER ERA." EUR+WWI GERMANY/W CONSTN EX/STRUC CREATE DIPLOM LEGIT ATTIT PERSON ALL/VALS...RECORD 20 ADENAUER/K. PAGE 7 H0144
NAT/G TOP/EX BAL/PWR GERMANY

S63
HALPERN A.M.,"THE EMERGENCE OF AN ASIAN COMMUNIST BLOC." ASIA CHINA/COM COM FUT KOREA/N S/ASIA VIETNAM/N STRATA NAT/G DELIB/GP FORCES TOP/EX PLAN BAL/PWR COERCE DETER PWR COLD/WAR WORK 20. PAGE 65 H1295
POL/PAR EDU/PROP DIPLOM

S63
KOHN H.,"GERMANY IN WORLD POLITICS." EUR+WWI GERMANY GERMANY/W USSR NAT/G POL/PAR TOP/EX ATTIT ...CONCPT TREND GEN/LAWS 20 NATO ADENAUER/K. PAGE 87 H1746
ACT/RES ORD/FREE BAL/PWR

S63
LERNER D.,"WILL EUROPEAN UNION BRING ABOUT MERGED NATIONAL GOALS." EUR+WWI FRANCE GERMANY UK ECO/DEV NAT/G VOL/ASSN DELIB/GP BAL/PWR ECO/TAC NAT/LISM
ATTIT STERTYP ELITES

EEC 20 DEGAULLE/C. PAGE 95 H1889
REGION

B64
ALVIM J.C.,A REVOLUCAO SEM RUMO. BRAZIL NAT/G BAL/PWR DIPLOM INT/TRADE PARTIC WEALTH...POLICY SOC SOC/INTEG 20. PAGE 6 H0118
REV CIVMIL/REL ECO/UNDEV ORD/FREE

B64
BAGEHOT W.,THE ENGLISH CONSTITUTION. UK CHIEF CONSULT LEGIS BAL/PWR PWR...BIBLIOG 18/19 PARLIAMENT. PAGE 10 H0198
CONSTN PARL/PROC NAT/G CONCPT

B64
BELL C.,THE DEBATABLE ALLIANCE. COM UK USA+45 NAT/G FORCES PLAN BAL/PWR NUC/PWR WAR ATTIT...GOV/COMP 20. PAGE 13 H0263
DIPLOM PWR PEACE POLICY

B64
GRIFFITH W.E.,THE SINO-SOVIET RIFT. ASIA CHINA/COM COM CUBA USSR YUGOSLAVIA NAT/G POL/PAR VOL/ASSN DELIB/GP FORCES TOP/EX DIPLOM EDU/PROP DRIVE PERSON PWR...TREND 20 TREATY. PAGE 61 H1224
ATTIT TIME/SEQ BAL/PWR SOCISM

B64
HOROWITZ I.L.,REVOLUTION IN BRAZIL. BRAZIL L/A+17C ELITES STRATA NAT/G BAL/PWR PARTIC ATTIT 20. PAGE 74 H1473
ECO/UNDEV DIPLOM POLICY ORD/FREE

B64
REMAK J.,THE GENTLE CRITIC: THEODOR FONTANE AND GERMAN POLITICS, 1848-1898. GERMANY PRUSSIA CULTURE ELITES BAL/PWR DIPLOM WRITING GOV/REL...HUM BIOG 19 BISMARCK/O JUNKER FONTANE/T. PAGE 131 H2614
PERSON SOCIETY WORKER CHIEF

B64
ROSENAU J.N.,INTERNATIONAL ASPECTS OF CIVIL STRIFE. CHINA/COM CUBA EUR+WWI USA+45 USSR BAL/PWR EDU/PROP NEUTRAL COERCE MORAL...NAT/COMP 20 COLD/WAR UN. PAGE 134 H2676
POLICY DIPLOM REV WAR

B64
VOELKMANN K.,HERRSCHER VON MORGEN? BAL/PWR COLONIAL NEUTRAL REGION RACE/REL ALL/VALS SOVEREIGN...RECORD 20 COLD/WAR THIRD/WRLD. PAGE 163 H3259
DIPLOM ECO/UNDEV CONTROL NAT/COMP

B64
WHEARE K.C.,FEDERAL GOVERNMENT (4TH ED.). WOR+45 WOR-45 POL/PAR LEGIS BAL/PWR CT/SYS...POLICY JURID CONCPT GOV/COMP 17/20. PAGE 167 H3339
FEDERAL CONSTN EX/STRUC NAT/COMP

B64
WRIGHT Q.,A STUDY OF WAR. LAW NAT/G PROB/SOLV BAL/PWR NAT/LISM PEACE ATTIT SOVEREIGN...CENSUS SOC/INTEG. PAGE 171 H3421
WAR CONCPT DIPLOM CONTROL

S64
KOVNER M.,"THE SINO-SOVIET DISPUTE: COMMUNISM AT THE CROSSROADS." ASIA CHINA/COM COM USSR ECO/UNDEV NAT/G TOP/EX CREATE BAL/PWR DOMIN EDU/PROP PWR ...CONCPT COMECON 20. PAGE 88 H1760
ATTIT TREND

S64
REISS I.,"LE DECLENCHEMENT DE LA PREMIERE GUERRE MONDIALE." GERMANY RUSSIA NAT/G FORCES DOMIN EDU/PROP COERCE RIGID/FLEX PWR SOVEREIGN...RELATIV HIST/WRIT TOT/POP AUST/HUNG SERBIA 20. PAGE 131 H2612
MOD/EUR BAL/PWR DIPLOM WAR

S64
VANDENBOSCH A.,"POWER BALANCE IN INDONESIA." S/ASIA USSR NAT/G TOP/EX BAL/PWR DOMIN NEUTRAL ORD/FREE PWR...POLICY TIME/SEQ GEN/LAWS 20 SUKARNO/A. PAGE 162 H3233
FORCES TREND DIPLOM INDONESIA

B65
CHRIMES S.B.,ENGLISH CONSTITUTIONAL HISTORY (3RD ED.). UK CHIEF CONSULT DELIB/GP LEGIS CT/SYS 15/20 COMMON/LAW PARLIAMENT. PAGE 30 H0598
CONSTN BAL/PWR NAT/G

B65
CRABB C.V. JR.,THE ELEPHANTS AND THE GRASS* A STUDY OF NONALIGNMENT. AFR ASIA INDIA S/ASIA USA+45 USSR BAL/PWR NEUTRAL ATTIT...TREND NAT/COMP COLD/WAR. PAGE 34 H0691
ECO/UNDEV DIPLOM CONCPT

B65
GRAHAM G.S.,THE POLITICS OF NAVAL SUPREMACY; STUDIES IN BRITISH MARITIME ASCENDANCY. UK SEA NAT/G BAL/PWR LEAD WAR WEAPON PEACE...POLICY 18/19 COMMONWLTH. PAGE 60 H1191
FORCES PWR COLONIAL DIPLOM

B65
HALEVY E.,THE ERA OF TYRANNIES (TRANS. BY R. K. WEBB). FRANCE MOD/EUR UK ECO/DEV LABOR NAT/G BAL/PWR FEDERAL ALL/VALS...OLD/LIB TREND 18/20 SAINTSIMON. PAGE 64 H1285
SOCISM CONCPT UTOPIA ORD/FREE

B65
LARUS J.,COMPARATIVE WORLD POLITICS. ASIA INDIA WOR+45 WOR-45 BAL/PWR WAR PEACE RATIONAL MORAL PWR ...REALPOL INT/LAW MUSLIM. PAGE 91 H1825
GOV/COMP IDEA/COMP DIPLOM NAT/COMP

B65
LEWIS W.A.,POLITICS IN WEST AFRICA. AFR BAL/PWR DIPLOM REPRESENT...POLICY 20. PAGE 96 H1916
POL/PAR ELITES NAT/G ECO/UNDEV

B65
MENON K.P.S.,MANY WORLDS. INDIA BAL/PWR CAP/ISM COLONIAL REV ORD/FREE PWR MARXISM...POLICY 20 COLD/WAR. PAGE 109 H2176
BIOG DIPLOM NAT/G

B65
RUBINSTEIN A.Z.,THE CHALLENGE OF POLITICS: IDEAS AND ISSUES (2ND ED.). UNIV ELITES SOCIETY EX/STRUC BAL/PWR PARL/PROC AUTHORIT...DECISION ANTHOL 20. PAGE 136 H2709
NAT/G DIPLOM GP/REL ORD/FREE

S65
CAIRNS J.C.,"FRANCE, DECEMBER 1965: END OF THE ELECTIVE MONARACHY" EUR+WWI FRANCE FUT CONSTN SOCIETY CHIEF BAL/PWR ATTIT ALL/IDEOS 20 DEGAULLE/C PRESIDENT. PAGE 25 H0505
CHOOSE NAT/G POL/PAR PWR

S65
GOLDMAN M.I.,"A BALANCE SHEET OF SOVIET FOREIGN AID." USA+45 ECO/UNDEV BAL/PWR ECO/TAC RENT GIVE EDU/PROP CONTROL COST PROFIT GEN/METH. PAGE 58 H1158
USSR FOR/AID NAT/COMP EFFICIENCY

S65
PRABHAKAR P.,"SURVEY OF RESEARCH AND SOURCE MATERIALS: THE SINO-INDIAN BORDER DISPUTE." CHINA/COM INDIA LAW NAT/G PLAN BAL/PWR WAR...POLICY 20 COLD/WAR. PAGE 128 H2553
BIBLIOG ASIA S/ASIA DIPLOM

B66
FITZGERALD C.P.,THE BIRTH OF COMMUNIST CHINA (2ND ED.). ASIA CHINA/COM STRUCT BAL/PWR DIPLOM ECO/TAC INT/TRADE WEALTH 20. PAGE 51 H1018
REV MARXISM ECO/UNDEV

B66
HARRISON B.,SOUTH-EAST ASIA: A SHORT HISTORY (3RD ED.). ECO/UNDEV INDUS NAT/G SECT BAL/PWR NAT/LISM ...SOC 15/20 S/EASTASIA. PAGE 67 H1346
COLONIAL S/ASIA CULTURE

B66
HOYT E.C.,NATIONAL POLICY AND INTERNATIONAL LAW* CASE STUDIES FROM AMERICAN CANAL POLICY* MONOGRAPH NO. 1 -- 1966-1967. PANAMA UK ELITES BAL/PWR EFFICIENCY...CLASSIF NAT/COMP SOC/EXP COLOMB TREATY. PAGE 74 H1483
INT/LAW USA-45 DIPLOM PWR

L66
ZOPPO C.E.,"NUCLEAR TECHNOLOGY, MULTIPOLARITY, AND INTERNATIONAL STABILITY." ASIA RUSSIA USA+45 STRUCT TOP/EX BAL/PWR DIPLOM DETER CIVMIL/REL NAT/COMP. PAGE 173 H3464
NET/THEORY ORD/FREE DECISION NUC/PWR

B67
HILSMAN R.,TO MOVE A NATION: THE POLITICS OF FOREIGN POLICY IN THE ADMINISTRATION OF JOHN F. KENNEDY. CHINA/COM COM USSR VIETNAM NAT/G DELIB/GP FORCES PLAN PROB/SOLV BAL/PWR COLONIAL EXEC REV PWR 20 KENNEDY/JF PRESIDENT. PAGE 71 H1418
CHIEF DIPLOM

B67
MACRIDIS R.C.,FOREIGN POLICY IN WORLD POLITICS (3RD ED.). EX/STRUC BAL/PWR COLONIAL NAT/LISM SKILL SOVEREIGN WEALTH...CONCPT TIME/SEQ ANTHOL 20 COLD/WAR. PAGE 101 H2011
DIPLOM POLICY NAT/G IDEA/COMP

B67
MCCLINTOCK R.,THE MEANING OF LIMITED WAR. FUT WOR+45 NAT/G FORCES GUERRILLA REV...POLICY SAMP/SIZ TREND NAT/COMP 45 COLD/WAR. PAGE 106 H2126
WAR NUC/PWR BAL/PWR DIPLOM

B67
POGANY A.H.,POLITICAL SCIENCE AND INTERNATIONAL RELATIONS, BOOKS RECOMMENDED FOR AMERICAN CATHOLIC COLLEGE LIBRARIES. INT/ORG LOC/G NAT/G FORCES BAL/PWR ECO/TAC NUC/PWR...CATH INT/LAW TREATY 20. PAGE 127 H2532
BIBLIOG DIPLOM

L67
MCALLISTER J.T. JR.,"THE POSSIBILITIES FOR DIPLOMACY IN SOUTHEAST ASIA." LAOS VIETNAM INT/ORG NAT/G PROVS BAL/PWR DOMIN AGREE COLONIAL WAR PWR 17/20 TREATY. PAGE 106 H2121
DIPLOM S/ASIA

L67
VAN DER KROEF J.M.,"INDONESIA: THE BATTLE OF THE 'OLD' AND THE 'NEW ORDER'." INDONESIA ISLAM ELITES POL/PAR DOMIN INGP/REL NAT/LISM PWR...IDEA/COMP 20. PAGE 161 H3229
FORCES MARXISM NAT/G BAL/PWR

L67
WRIGHT W.R.,"FOREIGN-OWNED RAILWAYS IN ARGENTINA: A CASE STUDY OF ECONOMIC NATIONALISM." L/A+17C UK ECO/UNDEV SERV/IND LG/CO NAT/G TEC/DEV BAL/PWR EQUILIB ARGEN. PAGE 171 H3423
NAT/LISM CAP/ISM ECO/TAC COLONIAL

S67
BATOR V.,"ONE WAR* TWO VIETNAMS." S/ASIA VIETNAM DIPLOM SUFF ATTIT ORD/FREE 20. PAGE 12 H0236
WAR BAL/PWR NAT/G STRUCT

S67
DANA MONTANO S.M.,"APLICACIONES CONCRETAS DE LAS RESOLUCIONES Y RECOMENDACIONES DE LAS CONFERENCIAS INTERAMERICANAS DE ABOGADOS" L/A+17C NAT/G PROVS GOV/REL PERCEPT 20 ARGEN. PAGE 37 H0739
JURID CT/SYS ORD/FREE BAL/PWR

S67
GRUNDY K.W.,"AFRICA IN THE WORLD ARENA." ECO/UNDEV BAL/PWR FOR/AID NEUTRAL REV NAT/LISM GOV/COMP. PAGE 62 H1240
AFR DIPLOM INT/ORG COLONIAL

S67
HEASMAN D.J.,"THE GIBRALTAR AFFAIR." SPAIN UK NAT/G BAL/PWR CONSEN NAT/LISM ATTIT...REALPOL 20. PAGE 69 H1378
DIPLOM COLONIAL REGION

S67
NIEBUHR R.,"THE SOCIAL MYTHS IN THE COLD WAR." USA+45 USSR VIETNAM PROB/SOLV BAL/PWR ARMS/CONT NAT/LISM PWR ALL/IDEOS CONCPT. PAGE 118 H2359
MYTH DIPLOM GOV/COMP

S67
ROOT W.,"REPORT FROM PARIS - DE GAULLE: WHICH WAY TO THE FUTURE?" CANADA FRANCE ISLAM UK INT/ORG CHIEF CREATE AGREE CONTROL ARMS/CONT NUC/PWR EQUILIB PEACE PWR 20 DEGAULLE/C NATO. PAGE 134 H2670
POLICY DIPLOM NAT/G BAL/PWR

S67
ROSE S.,"ASIAN NATIONALISM* THE SECOND STAGE." ASIA COM ECO/UNDEV NAT/G PROB/SOLV DIPLOM FOR/AID DOMIN NEUTRAL REGION TASK...METH/COMP 20. PAGE 134 H2675
NAT/LISM S/ASIA BAL/PWR COLONIAL

S67
SOMMER T.,"BONN CHANGES COURSE." GERMANY/W NAT/G POL/PAR PROB/SOLV NAT/LISM 20 NATO BERLIN/BLO. PAGE 147 H2932
DIPLOM BAL/PWR INT/ORG

S67
SPINELLI A.,"EUROPEAN UNION IN THE RESISTANCE." NAT/G BAL/PWR DIPLOM CONFER REGION TOTALISM ORD/FREE POLICY. PAGE 147 H2948
NAT/LISM FEDERAL EUR+WWI INT/ORG

S67
STRAFFORD P.,"FRENCH ELECTIONS." FRANCE NAT/G CHIEF LEGIS BAL/PWR ECO/TAC PARL/PROC PARTIC ATTIT 20. PAGE 150 H2993
POL/PAR SOCISM CENTRAL MARXISM

S67
TIKHOMIROV I.A.,"DIVISION OF POWERS OR DIVISION OF LABOR?" USSR NAT/G DELIB/GP ADJUD GP/REL MARXISM SOCISM 20. PAGE 155 H3093
BAL/PWR WORKER STRATA ADMIN

L86
BURGESS J.W.,"THE RECENT CONSTITUTIONAL CRISIS IN NORWAY" MOD/EUR NORWAY SWEDEN LOC/G NAT/G CHIEF BAL/PWR NAT/LISM ORD/FREE 19. PAGE 24 H0481
CONSTN SOVEREIGN GOV/REL

B87
ADAMS J.,A DEFENSE OF THE CONSTITUTIONS OF GOVERNMENT OF THE UNITED STATES OF AMERICA. USA-45 STRATA CHIEF EX/STRUC LEGIS CT/SYS CONSERVE POPULISM...CONCPT CON/ANAL GOV/COMP. PAGE 3 H0063
CONSTN BAL/PWR PWR NAT/G

BALANCE OF PAYMENTS....SEE BAL/PAY

BALANCE OF POWER....SEE BAL/PWR

BALANDIER G. H0203

BALDWIN/J....JAMES BALDWIN

BALFOUR A.J. H0204

BALKANS....BALKANS

B18
CVIJIC J.,THE BALKAN PENINSULA. MOD/EUR COERCE ...SOC CHARTS GP/COMP NAT/COMP 20 BALKANS MAPS. PAGE 36 H0729
GEOG HABITAT GOV/COMP CULTURE

B56
WOLFF R.L.,THE BALKANS IN OUR TIME. ALBANIA FUT MOD/EUR USSR YUGOSLAVIA CULTURE INT/ORG SECT DIPLOM EDU/PROP COERCE WAR ORD/FREE...CHARTS 4/20 BALKANS COMINFORM. PAGE 170 H3403
GEOG COM

B63
VALJAVEC F.,AUSGEWAHLTE AUFSATZE. GERMANY HUNGARY STRUCT ATTIT...CONCPT IDEA/COMP 18/20 BALKANS. PAGE 161 H3223
SOCIETY CULTURE GP/REL NAT/LISM

BALLACHEY E.L. H1765

BALOGH T. H0205

BALTIMORE....BALTIMORE, MD.

BALYS J. H0206

BANDA/HK....H.K. BANDA, PRIME MINISTER OF MALAWI

BANERJEE D.N. H0207

BANERJI A.K. H0208

BANFIELD E.C. H0209

BANFIELD J. H0210

BANKS A.S. H0211

BANK/ENGL....THE BANK OF ENGLAND

BANKING....SEE FINAN

BANKRUPTCY....BANKRUPTCY

BANKWITZ P.C. H0212

BANTU....BANTU NATION AND CULTURE

B23
WILLOUGHBY W.C.,RACE PROBLEMS IN THE NEW AFRICA: A STUDY OF THE RELATION OF BANTU AND BRITONS IN THOSE PARTS OF BANTU AFRICA... AFR STRUCT SECT DOMIN EDU/PROP GP/REL ATTIT WORSHIP 20 BANTU EUROPE MISSION CHRISTIAN. PAGE 168 H3372 — KIN COLONIAL RACE/REL CULTURE

B63
MAC MILLAN W.M.,BANTU, BOER, AND BRITON: THE MAKING OF THE SOUTH AFRICAN NATIVE PROBLEM. SOUTH/AFR UK LAW KIN NAT/G SECT LEGIS COLONIAL ISOLAT ATTIT ...BIOG 18/20 BANTU NEGRO PHILIP/J MISSION. PAGE 100 H1989 — AFR RACE/REL ELITES

BANTUSTANS....BANTUSTANS, REPUBLIC OF SOUTH AFRICA

B64
HILL C.R.,BANTUSTANS: THE FRAGMENTATION OF SOUTH AFRICA. AFR SOUTH/AFR ELITES SOCIETY KIN CONTROL DISCRIM ANOMIE ATTIT...POLICY CHARTS GOV/COMP 20 NEGRO BANTUSTANS TRANSKEI NATAL. PAGE 71 H1416 — RACE/REL CULTURE LOC/G ORD/FREE

B67
CARTER G.M.,SOUTH AFRICA'S TRANSKEI: THE POLITICS OF DOMESTIC COLONIALISM. SOUTH/AFR ECO/UNDEV AGRI NAT/G PROVS PLAN DOMIN REPRESENT ADJUST DISCRIM ...OBS BIBLIOG 20 BANTUSTANS TRANSKEI. PAGE 27 H0550 — STRATA GOV/REL COLONIAL POLICY

BAO/DAI....BAO DAI

BARAN P.A. H0213

BARBARIAN....BARBARIAN

BARBU Z. H0214

BARDOUX J. H0215

BARGAIN....BARGAINING; SEE ALSO ECO/TAC, MARKET, DIPLOM

B31
CROOK W.H.,THE GENERAL STRIKE: A STUDY OF LABOR'S TRAGIC WEAPON IN THEORY AND PRACTICE. BELGIUM FRANCE SWEDEN UK WOR-45 PROB/SOLV ECO/TAC DOMIN PWR ...POLICY TIME/SEQ NAT/COMP GEN/LAWS 19/20 STRIKE. PAGE 35 H0707 — LABOR WORKER LG/CO BARGAIN

B38
LAWLEY F.E.,THE GROWTH OF COLLECTIVE ECONOMY VOL. 1: NATIONAL. EUR+WWI AGRI INDUS NAT/G BARGAIN CAP/ISM ECO/TAC WAR OPTIMAL WEALTH...GOV/COMP METH/COMP 19/20 MONOPOLY. PAGE 92 H1844 — SOCISM PRICE CONTROL OWN

B38
REICH N.,LABOR RELATIONS IN REPUBLICAN GERMANY. GERMANY CONSTN ECO/DEV INDUS NAT/G ADMIN CONTROL GP/REL FASCISM POPULISM 20 WEIMAR/REP. PAGE 130 H2609 — WORKER MGT LABOR BARGAIN

B40
WOLFERS A.,BRITAIN AND FRANCE BETWEEN TWO WORLD WARS. FRANCE UK INT/ORG NAT/G PLAN BARGAIN ECO/TAC AGREE ISOLAT ALL/IDEOS...DECISION GEOG 20 TREATY VERSAILLES INTERVENT. PAGE 170 H3402 — DIPLOM WAR POLICY

B40
WUNDERLICH F.,LABOR UNDER GERMAN DEMOCRACY, ARBITRATION 1918-1933. GERMANY NAT/G PAY REPAR ADJUD CT/SYS GP/REL...MAJORIT 20. PAGE 171 H3426 — LABOR WORKER INDUS BARGAIN

B42
ROBBINS J.J.,THE GOVERNMENT OF LABOR RELATIONS IN SWEDEN. SWEDEN LAW CONSTN ADJUD CT/SYS GP/REL ...JURID 20. PAGE 132 H2638 — NAT/G BARGAIN LABOR INDUS

B47
ENKE S.,INTERNATIONAL ECONOMICS. UK USA+45 USSR INT/ORG BAL/PWR BARGAIN CAP/ISM BAL/PAY...NAT/COMP 20 TREATY. PAGE 46 H0927 — INT/TRADE FINAN TARIFFS ECO/TAC

B55
HELANDER S.,DAS AUTARKIEPROBLEM IN DER WELTWIRTSCHAFT. PROB/SOLV BAL/PWR BARGAIN CAP/ISM ECO/TAC SOVEREIGN 20. PAGE 69 H1388 — NAT/COMP COLONIAL DIPLOM

B57
POPLAI S.L.,NATIONAL POLITICS AND 1957 ELECTIONS IN INDIA. INDIA BARGAIN PARL/PROC CONSEN NAT/LISM PWR WEALTH 20. PAGE 127 H2543 — POL/PAR CHOOSE POLICY NAT/G

B58
CUNNINGHAM W.B.,COMPULSORY CONCILIATION AND COLLECTIVE BARGAINING. CANADA NAT/G LEGIS ADJUD CT/SYS GP/REL...MGT 20 NEW/BRUNS STRIKE CASEBOOK. PAGE 36 H0722 — POLICY BARGAIN LABOR INDUS

B58
WOODS H.D.,PATTERNS OF INDUSTRIAL DISPUTE SETTLEMENT IN FIVE CANADIAN INDUSTRIES. CANADA USA+45 CONSULT ADJUD GP/REL...JURID GOV/COMP METH/COMP ANTHOL 20. PAGE 170 H3408 — BARGAIN INDUS LABOR NAT/G

B59
BROWN D.F.,THE GROWTH OF DEMOCRATIC GOVERNMENT. WOR+45 BARGAIN EDU/PROP LOBBY APPORT CHOOSE 20. PAGE 22 H0441 — GOV/COMP LEGIS POL/PAR CHIEF

B60
BOMBACH G.,STABILE PREISE IN WACHSENDER WIRTSCHAFT: DAS INFLATIONSPROBLEM. BARGAIN CAP/ISM PRICE COST ...NAT/COMP 20 GOLD/STAND. PAGE 19 H0371 — ECO/UNDEV PLAN FINAN ECO/TAC

B61
CARROTHERS A.W.R.,LABOR ARBITRATION IN CANADA. CANADA LAW NAT/G CONSULT LEGIS WORKER ADJUD ADMIN CT/SYS 20. PAGE 27 H0542 — LABOR MGT GP/REL BARGAIN

B62
GALENSON W.,LABOR IN DEVELOPING COUNTRIES. BRAZIL INDONESIA ISRAEL PAKISTAN TURKEY AGRI INDUS WORKER PAY PRICE GP/REL WEALTH...MGT CHARTS METH/COMP NAT/COMP 20. PAGE 54 H1088 — LABOR ECO/UNDEV BARGAIN POL/PAR

B62
WOODS H.D.,LABOUR POLICY AND LABOUR ECONOMICS IN CANADA. CANADA FUT NAT/G VOL/ASSN WORKER BARGAIN ECO/TAC PAY CONFER GP/REL 20. PAGE 170 H3409 — LABOR POLICY INDUS ECO/DEV

B64
MORGAN H.W.,AMERICAN SOCIALISM 1900-1960. USA+45 USA-45 INTELL AGRI LABOR WORKER BARGAIN ECO/TAC GP/REL RACE/REL 20 NEGRO MIGRATION GOLD/STAND. PAGE 113 H2254 — SOCISM POL/PAR ECO/DEV STRATA

B65
ALEXANDER R.J.,ORGANIZED LABOR IN LATIN AMERICA. L/A+17C INT/ORG LEGIS WORKER TEC/DEV BARGAIN INT/TRADE REV...NAT/COMP BIBLIOG 20. PAGE 5 H0102 — LABOR POL/PAR ECO/UNDEV POLICY

B65
BULMER-THOMAS I.,THE GROWTH OF THE BRITISH PARTY SYSTEM (VOL. II) 1924-1964. UK ECO/DEV BARGAIN WAR CHOOSE ATTIT ORD/FREE 20 LABOR/PAR CONSRV/PAR. PAGE 23 H0472 — CHIEF POL/PAR PARL/PROC NAT/G

B65
EDELMAN M.,THE POLITICS OF WAGE-PRICE DECISIONS. GERMANY ITALY NETHERLAND UK INDUS LABOR POL/PAR PROB/SOLV BARGAIN PRICE ROUTINE BAL/PAY COST DEMAND 20. PAGE 44 H0888 — GOV/COMP CONTROL ECO/TAC PLAN

B66
ROSS A.M.,INDUSTRIAL RELATIONS AND ECONOMIC DEVELOPMENT. POL/PAR LEGIS WORKER BARGAIN PRICE EXEC LOBBY INCOME PWR...DECISION ANTHOL BIBLIOG 20. PAGE 134 H2686 — ECO/UNDEV LABOR NAT/G GP/REL

B67
BADGLEY R.F.,DOCTORS' STRIKE; MEDICAL CARE AND CONFLICT IN SASKATCHEWAN. CANADA NAT/G PROF/ORG GP/REL ADJUST ATTIT...HEAL SOC 20. PAGE 10 H0192 — HEALTH PLAN LABOR BARGAIN

B67
MOORE J.R.,THE ECONOMIC IMPACT OF THE TVA. AGRI INDUS PLAN BARGAIN CONTROL REGION GOV/REL DEMAND EFFICIENCY SOCISM 20 TVA. PAGE 112 H2249 — ECO/UNDEV ECO/DEV NAT/G CREATE

BARIETY J. H0216

BARILE P. H0064

BARKER E. H0217,H0218,H0219

BARNES H.E. H0220,H0221

BARNETT A.D. H0222,H0223,H0224

BARNETT D.L. H0225

BARNETT/R....ROSS BARNETT

BAROTSE....BAROTSE TRIBE OF RHODESIA

BARRES M. H0226,H0227,H0228

BARRETT J. H0229

BARRON R. H0230

BARRY E.E. H0231

BARZEL R. H0232

BASDEN G.T. H0233

BASHILELE....BASHILELE TRIBE

BASKIN D.B. H0234

BASOV V. H0235

BASTID P. H2871

BATAK....BATAK TRIBE, PHILIPPINES

B04
REED W.A.,ETHNOLOGICAL SURVEY PUBLICATIONS (VOL. II). PHILIPPINE STRUCT INDUS SECT DEATH LEISURE HABITAT...AUD/VIS CHARTS WORSHIP 20 NABOLOI NEGRITO BATAK. PAGE 130 H2607 — CULTURE SOCIETY SOC OBS

BATISTA/J....JUAN BATISTA

BATOR V. H0236

BATTAGLIA F. H0237

BAUCHET P. H0238

BAUER R.A. H0239

BAULIN J. H0240

BAUMANN G. H0241

BAVARIA....BAVARIA

BAWONGO....BAWONGO TRIBE

BAYER H. H0242

BAYESIAN INFLUENCE....SEE SIMUL

BAYITCH S.A. H0243

BAYNE E.A. H0244

BAYNES N.H. H0245

BEARCE G.D. H0246

BEARD C.A. H0247,H0248

BEARD/CA....CHARLES A. BEARD

BEARDSLEY R.K. H0249

BEATTIE J. H0250,H0251

BECCARIA/C....CAESARE BONESARA BECCARIA

BECHHOEFER B.G. H0252

BECKER H. H0253

BECKER J. H0254

BECKER/E....ERNEST BECKER

BECKHAM R.S. H0255

BEDERMAN S.H. H0256

BEDFORD S. H0257

BEEGLE J.A. H1963

BEER S.H. H0258

BEFU H. H0259

BEHAR D. H0260

BEHAV/SCI....BEHAVIORAL SCIENCES

BEHAVIORAL SCIENCES....SEE BEHAV/SCI

BEHAVIORSM....BEHAVIORISM

B63
MARTINDALE D.,COMMUNITY, CHARACTER AND CIVILIZATION: STUDIES IN SOCIAL BEHAVIORISM. INTELL FAM NEIGH VOL/ASSN GP/REL NAT/LISM ATTIT PERSON ...CONCPT GP/COMP 20 BEHAVIORSM. PAGE 103 H2066 — SOC METH/COMP CULTURE STRUCT

BELFRAGE C. H0261

BELGION M. H0262

BELGIUM....BELGIUM

B00
BENEDETTI V.,STUDIES IN DIPLOMACY. BELGIUM FRANCE GERMANY MOD/EUR CONSTN NAT/G CONSULT TOP/EX DOMIN EDU/PROP COERCE ATTIT...CONCPT INT BIOG TREND 19. PAGE 14 H0276 — PWR GEN/LAWS DIPLOM

N19
HANNA A.J.,EUROPEAN RULE IN AFRICA (PAMPHLET). BELGIUM FRANCE MOD/EUR UK WOR+45 WOR-45 ECO/UNDEV NAT/G PARTIC SOVEREIGN...NAT/COMP 19/20. PAGE 66 H1314 — DIPLOM COLONIAL AFR NAT/LISM

B29
LEITZ F.,DIE PUBLIZITAT DER AKTIENGESELLSCHAFT. BELGIUM FRANCE GERMANY UK FINAN PRESS GP/REL PROFIT KNOWL 20. PAGE 94 H1872 — LG/CO JURID ECO/TAC NAT/COMP

B31
CROOK W.H.,THE GENERAL STRIKE: A STUDY OF LABOR'S TRAGIC WEAPON IN THEORY AND PRACTICE. BELGIUM FRANCE SWEDEN UK WOR-45 PROB/SOLV ECO/TAC DOMIN PWR ...POLICY TIME/SEQ NAT/COMP GEN/LAWS 19/20 STRIKE. PAGE 35 H0707 — LABOR WORKER LG/CO BARGAIN

B33
DAHLIN E.,FRENCH AND GERMAN PUBLIC OPINION ON DECLARED WAR AIMS 1914-1918. BELGIUM FRANCE GERMANY NAT/G POL/PAR DIPLOM COERCE REV WAR PEACE 20 WWI WILSON/W. PAGE 37 H0733 — ATTIT EDU/PROP DOMIN NAT/COMP

B47
CROCKER W.R.,ON GOVERNING COLONIES: BEING AN OUTLINE OF THE REAL ISSUES AND A COMPARISON OF THE BRITISH, FRENCH, AND BELGIAN... AFR BELGIUM FRANCE UK CULTURE SOVEREIGN...OBS 20. PAGE 35 H0705 — COLONIAL POLICY GOV/COMP ADMIN

B50
GATZKE H.W.,GERMANY'S DRIVE TO THE WEST. BELGIUM GERMANY MOD/EUR AGRI INDUS POL/PAR FORCES DOMIN AGREE CONTROL REGION COERCE 20 TREATY WWI. PAGE 55 H1104 — WAR POLICY NAT/G DIPLOM

B51
WABEKE B.H.,A GUIDE TO DUTCH BIBLIOGRAPHIES. BELGIUM INDONESIA NETHERLAND DIPLOM INT/TRADE WAR NAT/LISM KNOWL...ART/METH HUM JURID CON/ANAL 14/20. PAGE 164 H3282 — BIBLIOG/A NAT/G CULTURE COLONIAL

B62
MEADE J.E.,CASE STUDIES IN EUROPEAN ECONOMIC UNION. BELGIUM EUR+WWI LUXEMBOURG NAT/G INT/TRADE REGION ROUTINE WEALTH...METH/CNCPT STAT CHARTS ECSC TOT/POP OEEC EEC 20. PAGE 108 H2154 — INT/ORG ECO/TAC

BELIEF....SEE SECT

BELL C. H0263

BELL D. H0264,H0265

BELL W. H0266,H0267

BELLAS/HES....NATIONAL BELLAS HESS

BELLER I. H0268

BELLOC H. H0269,H0270

BELOFF M. H0271

BELSHAW C.S. H0272

BEN/BELLA....AHMED BEN BELLA

BENDIX R. H0273,H0274,H0275,H1939,H1940

BENEDETTI V. H0276

BENEDICT B. H0277

BENEDICT R. H0278,H0279

BENES E. H0280,H0281

BENESE....BENES

BENGAL....BENGAL + BENGALIS

BENIN....BENIN - DISTRICT IN NIGERIA

BENN S.I. H0282

BENOIST C. H0283

BENOIT E. H0284

BENSON M. H0285

BENTHAM A. H0286

BENTHAM J. H0287,H0288,H0289,H0290,H0291,H0292

BENTHAM/J....JEREMY BENTHAM

B28
BARKER E.,POLITICAL THOUGHT IN ENGLAND: FROM HERBERT SPENCER TO THE PRESENT DAY. UK ALL/IDEOS ...PHIL/SCI 19/20 SPENCER/H GREEN/TH BENTHAM/J MAITLAND/F. PAGE 11 H0217
INTELL GEN/LAWS IDEA/COMP

B36
SMITH T.V.,THE PROMISE OF AMERICAN POLITICS. USA-45 WOR-45 LAW CONSTN STRATA PARTIC FASCISM LAISSEZ MARXISM...MAJORIT METH/COMP 18/20 JEFFERSN/T LOCKE/JOHN BENTHAM/J. PAGE 146 H2920
CONCPT ORD/FREE IDEA/COMP NAT/COMP

B75
MAINE H.S.,LECTURES ON THE EARLY HISTORY OF INSTITUTIONS. IRELAND UK CONSTN ELITES STRUCT FAM KIN CHIEF LEGIS CT/SYS OWN SOVEREIGN...CONCPT 16 BENTHAM/J BREHON ROMAN/LAW. PAGE 101 H2021
CULTURE LAW INGP/REL

B91
SIDGWICK H.,THE ELEMENTS OF POLITICS. LOC/G NAT/G LEGIS DIPLOM ADJUD CONTROL EXEC PARL/PROC REPRESENT GOV/REL SOVEREIGN ALL/IDEOS 19 MILL/JS BENTHAM/J. PAGE 143 H2868
POLICY LAW CONCPT

BENTLEY/AF....ARTHUR F. BENTLEY

BENTWICH J.S. H0293

BERDYAEV N. H0294,H0295

BERDYAEV N.A. H0294,H0295,H0296

BERELSON B. H0297,H0298

BERG E.J. H0299

BERGER M. H0300,H0301

BERGSON A. H0302

BERGSON/H....HENRI BERGSON

BERGSON/WJ....W. JAMES BERGSON

BERGSTRASSER L. H0303

BERKELEY....BERKELEY, CALIFORNIA

BERKOWITZ L. H0305

BERLE A.A. H0306

BERLIN I. H0307

BERLIN....BERLIN

B51
MEYER E.W.,POLITICAL PARTIES IN WESTERN GERMANY (PAMPHLET). GERMANY/W MUNIC NAT/G GOV/REL ALL/IDEOS 20 UNIFICA BERLIN. PAGE 109 H2190
POL/PAR LOBBY CHOOSE CONSTN

B60
VON KOENIGSWALD H.,SIE SUCHEN ZUFLUCHT. GERMANY/E NAT/G PLAN ECO/TAC SOCISM...GEOG CENSUS 20 BERLIN. PAGE 164 H3273
GP/REL COERCE DOMIN PERSON

B64
KELLER J.W.,GERMANY, THE WALL AND BERLIN. EUR+WWI ECO/DEV NAT/G VOL/ASSN FORCES PLAN ECO/TAC EDU/PROP COERCE...POLICY CONCPT INT TREND COLD/WAR BER/BLOC 20 BERLIN. PAGE 84 H1685
ATTIT ALL/VALS DIPLOM GERMANY

S65
PLISCHKE E.,"INTEGRATING BERLIN AND THE FEDERAL REPUBLIC OF GERMANY." EUR+WWI GERMANY/W LEGIS TEC/DEV DOMIN ORD/FREE PWR...JURID 20 BERLIN. PAGE 126 H2528
DIPLOM NAT/G MUNIC

BERLIN/BLO....BERLIN BLOCKADE

S59
WARBURG J.P.,"THE CENTRAL EUROPEAN CRISIS: A PROPOSAL FOR WESTERN INITIATIVE." EUR+WWI INT/ORG NAT/G LEGIT DETER WAR...CONCPT BER/BLOC UN 20. PAGE 165 H3302
PLAN GERMANY

B64
KELLER J.W.,GERMANY, THE WALL AND BERLIN. EUR+WWI ECO/DEV NAT/G VOL/ASSN FORCES PLAN ECO/TAC EDU/PROP COERCE...POLICY CONCPT INT TREND COLD/WAR BER/BLOC 20 BERLIN. PAGE 84 H1685
ATTIT ALL/VALS DIPLOM GERMANY

S67
SOMMER T.,"BONN CHANGES COURSE." GERMANY/W NAT/G POL/PAR PROB/SOLV NAT/LISM 20 NATO BERLIN/BLO. PAGE 147 H2932
DIPLOM BAL/PWR INT/ORG

BERLINER J.S. H0308

BERMAN H.J. H0309

BERNATZIK H.A. H0310

BERNAYS/EL....EDWARD L. BERNAYS

BERNDT C.H. H0311,H0312

BERNDT R.M. H0311,H0312

BERNHARDI F. H0304,H0313

BERNOT R.M. H0314

BERNSTEIN H. H0315,H0316

BERNSTEIN T.P. H0317

BERREMAN G.D. H0318,H0319

BERRIEN W. H0374

BERRINGTON H. H0320

BESSARABIA....BESSARABIA; SEE ALSO USSR

B66
BECKER J.,BESSARABIEN UND SEIN DEUTSCHTUM. ROMANIA USSR STRUCT INDUS PROF/ORG SECT GP/REL INGP/REL 15/20 BESSARABIA. PAGE 13 H0254
PROVS CULTURE SOCIETY

BESSON W. H0321

BEST H. H0322

BETEILLE A. H0323

BETTISON D.G. H0324

BEVEL D.N. H0325

BHALERAO C.N. H0326

BHAMBHRI C.P. H0327

BHATNAGAR J.K. H0328

BHUMIBOL/A....BHUMIBOL ADULYADEJ

BHUTAN....SEE ALSO ASIA

BIAFRA....BIAFRA

S67
VINCENT S.,"SHOULD BIAFRA SURVIVE?" NIGERIA ECO/UNDEV CHIEF FORCES ECO/TAC GP/REL DISCRIM PEACE ORD/FREE SOC/INTEG 20 BIAFRA IBO. PAGE 163 H3256
AFR REV REGION NAT/G

S68
CHAPMAN A.R.,"THE CIVIL WAR IN NIGERIA." AFR NIGERIA NAT/G PLAN ECO/TAC EDU/PROP COERCE WAR GOV/REL INGP/REL ORD/FREE PWR WEALTH SOC/INTEG 20 BIAFRA. PAGE 29 H0579
REV RACE/REL

BIALEK R.W. H0329

BIBLE....BIBLE: OLD AND NEW TESTAMENTS

B35
AQUINAS T.,ON THE GOVERNANCE OF RULERS (1265-66). UNIV SOCIETY STRATA FAM HABITAT PERSON ALL/VALS PWR SOVEREIGN CONSERVE...POLICY BIBLE. PAGE 8 H0155
CATH NAT/G CHIEF SUPEGO

B60
MORRISON C.,THE POWERS THAT BE. NAT/G SUPEGO ...POLICY CONCPT IDEA/COMP WORSHIP 20 BIBLE. PAGE 113 H2265
HUM ORD/FREE

B70
BOSSUET J.B.,"POLITIQUE TIREE DE L'ECRITURE SAINTE" (1679-1709) IN J.B. BOSSUET, OEVRES DE BOSSUET. NAT/G GP/REL AUTHORIT HEREDITY PERSON ALL/VALS SOVEREIGN 18 BIBLE DEITY CHRISTIAN. PAGE 19 H0383
TRADIT CHIEF SECT CONCPT

BIBLIOG....BIBLIOGRAPHY OVER 50 ITEMS

N
HERSKOVITS M.V.,CULTURAL ANTHROPOLOGY. UNIV SOCIETY STRUCT FAM...AUD/VIS BIBLIOG. PAGE 70 H1410
CULTURE SOC INGP/REL GEOG

N
TOTEMEYER G.,SOUTH AFRICA; SOUTHWEST AFRICA: A
BIBLIOG

BIBLIOGRAPHY, 1945-1963. AFR SOUTH/AFR PRESS...SOC 20. PAGE 157 H3134 CULTURE NAT/G EDU/PROP

B
DEUTSCHE BIBLIOTH FRANKF A M,DEUTSCHE BIBLIOGRAPHIE. EUR+WWI GERMANY ECO/DEV FORCES DIPLOM LEAD...POLICY PHIL/SCI SOC 20. PAGE 40 H0802 BIBLIOG LAW ADMIN NAT/G

N
JOURNAL OF ASIAN STUDIES. CULTURE ECO/DEV SECT DIPLOM EDU/PROP WAR NAT/LISM...PHIL/SCI SOC 20. PAGE 1 H0005 BIBLIOG ASIA S/ASIA NAT/G

N
MIDDLE EAST JOURNAL. CULTURE SECT DIPLOM LEAD GOV/REL ATTIT...POLICY PHIL/SCI SOC LING BIOG 20. PAGE 1 H0007 BIBLIOG ISLAM NAT/G ECO/UNDEV

N
NEUE POLITISCHE LITERATUR. AFR ASIA EUR+WWI GERMANY RUSSIA SOCIETY ECO/DEV ECO/UNDEV PLAN PROB/SOLV LEAD MARXISM...PHIL/SCI CONCPT 20. PAGE 1 H0008 BIBLIOG DIPLOM COM NAT/G

N
PEKING REVIEW. CHINA/COM CULTURE AGRI INDUS DIPLOM EDU/PROP GUERRILLA ATTIT MARXISM...BIBLIOG 20. PAGE 1 H0009 MARXIST NAT/G POL/PAR PRESS

N
AUSTRALIAN PUBLIC AFFAIRS INFORMATION SERVICE. LAW ...HEAL HUM MGT SOC CON/ANAL 20 AUSTRAL. PAGE 1 H0011 BIBLIOG NAT/G CULTURE DIPLOM

N
DAILY SUMMARY OF THE JAPANESE PRESS. NAT/G DIPLOM LEAD 20 CHINJAP. PAGE 1 H0013 BIBLIOG PRESS ASIA ATTIT

N
INDIA: A REFERENCE ANNUAL. INDIA CULTURE COM/IND R+D FORCES PLAN RECEIVE EDU/PROP HEALTH...STAT CHARTS BIBLIOG 20. PAGE 1 H0017 CONSTN LABOR INT/ORG

N
LONDON TIMES OFFICIAL INDEX. UK LAW ECO/DEV NAT/G DIPLOM LEAD ATTIT 20. PAGE 1 H0018 BIBLIOG INDEX PRESS WRITING

N
PUBLISHERS' CIRCULAR, THE OFFICIAL ORGAN OF THE PUBLISHERS' ASSOCIATION OF GREAT BRITAIN AND IRELAND. EUR+WWI MOD/EUR UK LAW PROB/SOLV DIPLOM COLONIAL ATTIT...HUM 19/20 CMN/WLTH. PAGE 1 H0019 BIBLIOG NAT/G WRITING LEAD

N
PUBLISHERS' TRADE LIST ANNUAL. LAW POL/PAR ADMIN PERSON ALL/IDEOS...HUM SOC 19/20. PAGE 1 H0020 BIBLIOG NAT/G DIPLOM POLICY

N
SEMINAR: THE MONTHLY SYMPOSIUM. INDIA ACT/RES TEC/DEV DIPLOM ATTIT...BIBLIOG 20. PAGE 1 H0022 NAT/G ECO/UNDEV SOVEREIGN POLICY

N
THE STATESMAN'S YEARBOOK; STATISTICAL AND HISTORICAL ANNUAL OF THE STATES OF THE WORLD. WOR+45 WOR-45 COM/IND FINAN INDUS SECT FORCES TEC/DEV EDU/PROP...GEOG BIBLIOG 19/20. PAGE 1 H0023 NAT/COMP GOV/COMP STAT CONSTN

N
SUBJECT GUIDE TO BOOKS IN PRINT: AN INDEX TO THE PUBLISHERS' TRADE LIST ANNUAL. UNIV LAW LOC/G DIPLOM WRITING ADMIN LEAD PERSON...MGT SOC. PAGE 2 H0024 BIBLIOG ECO/DEV POL/PAR NAT/G

N
THE MIDDLE EAST. CULTURE...BIOG BIBLIOG. PAGE 2 H0028 ISLAM INDUS FINAN

N
AVTOREFERATY DISSERTATSII. USSR INTELL ACADEM NAT/G DIPLOM GOV/REL KNOWL CONCPT. PAGE 2 H0029 BIBLIOG MARXISM MARXIST COM

N
CARIBBEAN COMMISSION,CURRENT CARIBBEAN BIBLIOGRAPHY. FRANCE NETHERLAND UK CULTURE ECO/UNDEV PRESS LEAD ATTIT...GEOG SOC 20. PAGE 26 H0530 BIBLIOG NAT/G L/A+17C DIPLOM

N
CORNELL UNIVERSITY LIBRARY,SOUTHEAST ASIA ACCESSIONS LIST. LAW SOCIETY STRUCT ECO/UNDEV POL/PAR TEC/DEV DIPLOM LEAD REGION. PAGE 34 H0671 BIBLIOG S/ASIA NAT/G CULTURE

N
DEUTSCHE BUCHEREI,DEUTSCHE NATIONALBIBLIOGRAPHIE. GERMANY ECO/DEV DIPLOM AGE/Y ATTIT...PHIL/SCI SOC 20. PAGE 40 H0803 BIBLIOG NAT/G LEAD POLICY

N
DEUTSCHE BUCHEREI,JAHRESVERZEICHNIS DES DEUTSCHEN SCHRIFTUMS. AUSTRIA EUR+WWI GERMANY SWITZERLND LAW LOC/G DIPLOM ADMIN...MGT SOC 19/20. PAGE 40 H0804 BIBLIOG WRITING NAT/G

N
DEUTSCHE BUCHEREI,DEUTSCHES BUCHERVERZEICHNIS. GERMANY LAW CULTURE POL/PAR ADMIN LEAD ATTIT PERSON ...SOC 20. PAGE 40 H0805 BIBLIOG NAT/G DIPLOM ECO/DEV

N
EUROPA PUBLICATIONS LIMITED,THE EUROPA YEAR BOOK. CONSTN FINAN INDUS POL/PAR DIPLOM TV CT/SYS...STAT BIOG CHARTS WORSHIP 20. PAGE 47 H0949 BIBLIOG NAT/G PRESS INT/ORG

N
HOOVER INSTITUTION,UNITED STATES AND CANADIAN PUBLICATIONS ON AFRICA. CULTURE ECO/UNDEV AGRI TEC/DEV EDU/PROP COLONIAL RACE/REL NAT/LISM ATTIT HEALTH...SOC SOC/WK 20. PAGE 73 H1464 BIBLIOG DIPLOM NAT/G AFR

N
LONDON LIBRARY ASSOCIATION,ATHENAEUM SUBJECT INDEX. 1915-1918. NAT/G DIPLOM NAT/LISM 20. PAGE 98 H1960 BIBLIOG CON/ANAL SOC

N
MIDDLE EAST INSTITUTE,CURRENT RESEARCH ON THE MIDDLE EAST....PHIL/SCI PSY SOC LING 20. PAGE 110 H2201 BIBLIOG R+D ISLAM NAT/G

N
MINISTERE DE L'EDUC NATIONALE,CATALOGUE DES THESES DE DOCTORAT SOUTENNES DEVANT LES UNIVERSITAIRES FRANCAISES. FRANCE LAW DIPLOM ADMIN...HUM SOC 20. PAGE 111 H2223 BIBLIOG ACADEM KNOWL NAT/G

N
MINISTRY OF OVERSEAS DEVELOPME,TECHNICAL CO-OPERATION -- A BIBLIOGRAPHY. UK LAW SOCIETY DIPLOM ECO/TAC FOR/AID...STAT 20 CMN/WLTH. PAGE 111 H2225 BIBLIOG TEC/DEV ECO/DEV NAT/G

N
NORTHWESTERN UNIVERSITY LIB,JOINT ACQUISITIONS LIST OF AFRICANA. AFR SOCIETY STRUCT EDU/PROP COLONIAL GP/REL RACE/REL NAT/LISM SOVEREIGN...SOC 20. PAGE 119 H2377 BIBLIOG CULTURE ECO/UNDEV INDUS

N
PRESSE UNIVERSITAIRES,ANNEE SOCIOLOGIQUE. EUR+WWI FRANCE MOD/EUR FAM ACT/RES WAR INGP/REL PERS/REL CONSEN DRIVE MORAL...CON/ANAL 19/20. PAGE 128 H2557 BIBLIOG SOC CULTURE SOCIETY

N
SOUTH AFRICA STATE LIBRARY,SOUTH AFRICAN NATIONAL BIBLIOGRAPHY, SANB. SOUTH/AFR LAW NAT/G EDU/PROP ...MGT PSY SOC 20. PAGE 147 H2937 BIBLIOG PRESS WRITING

N
UNIVERSITY OF CALIFORNIA,STATISTICAL ABSTRACT OF LATIN AMERICA. L/A+17C DIPLOM 20. PAGE 158 H3169 BIBLIOG NAT/G ECO/UNDEV STAT

N
US CONSULATE GENERAL HONG KONG,EXTRACTS FROM CHINA MAINLAND MAGAZINES. ASIA CHINA/COM ECO/UNDEV NAT/G CHIEF LEAD ATTIT...MARXIST INDEX 20. PAGE 159 H3180 BIBLIOG MARXISM PRESS

N
US DEPARTMENT OF STATE,BIBLIOGRAPHY (PAMPHLETS). AGRI INDUS INT/ORG FOR/AID EDU/PROP WAR MARXISM ...SOC GOV/COMP METH/COMP 20. PAGE 159 H3184 BIBLIOG DIPLOM ECO/DEV NAT/G

N
US LIBRARY OF CONGRESS,ACCESSIONS LIST - INDIA. INDIA CULTURE AGRI LOC/G POL/PAR PLAN PROB/SOLV TEC/DEV DIPLOM EDU/PROP LEAD GP/REL ATTIT 20. PAGE 160 H3199 BIBLIOG S/ASIA ECO/UNDEV NAT/G

N
US LIBRARY OF CONGRESS,ACCESSIONS LIST -- ISRAEL. ISRAEL CULTURE ECO/UNDEV POL/PAR PLAN PROB/SOLV TEC/DEV DIPLOM EDU/PROP LEAD WAR ATTIT 20 JEWS. PAGE 160 H3200 BIBLIOG ISLAM NAT/G GP/REL

N
US LIBRARY OF CONGRESS,EAST EUROPEAN ACCESSIONS INDEX. NAT/G ISOLAT ATTIT KNOWL...POLICY 20. PAGE 160 H3202 BIBLIOG COM MARXIST DIPLOM

B03
FORTESCUE G.K.,SUBJECT INDEX OF THE MODERN WORKS ADDED TO THE LIBRARY OF THE BRITISH MUSEUM IN THE YEARS 1881-1900 (3 VOLS.). UK LAW CONSTN FINAN NAT/G FORCES INT/TRADE COLONIAL 19. PAGE 52 H1041 BIBLIOG INDEX WRITING

C05
DUNNING W.A.,"HISTORY OF POLITICAL THEORIES FROM LUTHER TO MONTESQUIEU." LAW NAT/G SECT DIPLOM REV WAR ORD/FREE SOVEREIGN CONSERVE...TRADIT BIBLIOG 16/18. PAGE 43 H0867 PHIL/SCI CONCPT GEN/LAWS

B06
SUMNER W.G.,FOLKWAYS: STUDY OF THE SOCIOLOGICAL IMPORTANCE OF USAGES, MANNERS, CUSTOMS, MORES, AND MORALS. STRUCT KIN ETIQUET ROUTINE MURDER MARRIAGE PEACE SEX ALL/VALS WEALTH BIBLIOG. PAGE 150 H3008 CULTURE SOC SANCTION MORAL

C06
MONTGOMERY H.,"A DICTIONARY OF POLITICAL PHRASES AND ILLUSIONS WITH A SHORT BIBLIOGRAPHY." EUR+WWI MOD/EUR UK AGRI LABOR LOC/G NAT/G COLONIAL CHOOSE RACE/REL. PAGE 112 H2245
BIBLIOG DICTIONARY POLICY DIPLOM

B08
NIRRNHEIM O.,DAS ERSTE JAHR DES MINISTERIUMS BISMARCK UND DIE OEFFENTLICHE MEINUNG (HEIDELBERGER ABHANDLUNGEN, 20. HEFT). GERMANY MOD/EUR LEGIS DIPLOM EDU/PROP INGP/REL...BIOG GOV/COMP IDEA/COMP BIBLIOG 19 BISMARCK/O. PAGE 118 H2363
CHIEF PRESS NAT/G ATTIT

B09
LOBINGIER C.S.,THE PEOPLE'S LAW OR POPULAR PARTICIPATION IN LAW-MAKING. FRANCE SWITZERLND UK LOC/G NAT/G PROVS LEGIS SUFF MAJORITY PWR POPULISM ...GOV/COMP BIBLIOG 19. PAGE 97 H1945
CONSTN LAW PARTIC

C09
SCHAPIRO J.S.,"SOCIAL REFORM AND THE REFORMATION." CHRIST-17C GERMANY LAW CONSTN LG/CO NAT/G WORKER PROB/SOLV CT/SYS REV...BIBLIOG 16. PAGE 138 H2770
ORD/FREE SECT ECO/TAC BIOG

B10
TEMPERLEY H.W.V.,SENATES AND UPPER CHAMBERS; THEIR USE AND FUNCTION IN THE MODERN STATE... UK WOR-45 CONSTN NAT/G POL/PAR PROVS SECT COLONIAL LEAD CHOOSE REPRESENT PWR...BIBLIOG 19/20 PARLIAMENT SENATE CMN/WLTH HOUSE/LORD. PAGE 153 H3059
PARL/PROC NAT/COMP LEGIS EX/STRUC

B12
HEINSIUS W.,ALLGEMEINES BUCHER-LEXICON ODER VOLLSTANDIGES ALPHABETISCHES VERZEICHNIS ALLER VON 1700 BIS ZU ENDE...(1892). GERMANY PERF/ART...HUM SOC 18/19. PAGE 69 H1387
BIBLIOG POLICY ATTIT NAT/G

B14
LEVINE L.,SYNDICALISM IN FRANCE (2ND ED.). FRANCE LAW SOCIETY ECO/DEV NAT/G ECO/TAC LEAD ATTIT ...POLICY CONCPT STAT BIBLIOG 18/20 REFORMERS. PAGE 95 H1902
LABOR INDUS SOCISM REV

B18
KERNER R.J.,SLAVIC EUROPE: A SELECTED BIBLIOGRAPHY IN THE WESTERN EUROPEAN LANGUAGES. BULGARIA CZECHOSLVK GERMANY/E POLAND RUSSIA YUGOSLAVIA NAT/G DIPLOM MARXISM...LING 19/20. PAGE 85 H1695
BIBLIOG SOCIETY CULTURE COM

N19
GOODMAN G.K.,IMPERIAL JAPAN AND ASIA: A REASSESSMENT (PAMPHLET). ASIA S/ASIA ECO/DEV FORCES LEAD WAR NAT/LISM ATTIT...DECISION CONCPT BIBLIOG 19/20 CHINJAP. PAGE 59 H1172
DIPLOM NAT/G POLICY COLONIAL

B20
COLE G.D.H.,SOCIAL THEORY. CULTURE LOC/G SECT REGION REPRESENT ATTIT DRIVE...PSY SOC BIBLIOG. PAGE 31 H0621
CONCPT NAT/G PHIL/SCI

C20
DUNNING W.A.,"A HISTORY OF POLITICAL THINKERS FROM ROUSSEAU TO SPENCER." NAT/G REV NAT/LISM UTIL CONSERVE MARXISM POPULISM...JURID BIBLIOG 18/19. PAGE 43 H0868
IDEA/COMP PHIL/SCI CONCPT GEN/LAWS

B27
PANIKKAR K.M.,INDIAN STATES AND THE GOVERNMENT OF INDIA. INDIA UK CONSTN CONTROL TASK GP/REL SOVEREIGN WEALTH...TREND BIBLIOG 19. PAGE 123 H2457
GOV/COMP COLONIAL BAL/PWR PROVS

B28
CHILDS J.B.,FOREIGN GOVERNMENT PUBLICATIONS (PAMPHLET). LEGIS DIPLOM 19/20. PAGE 29 H0591
BIBLIOG PRESS NAT/G

B28
LODGE H.C.,THE HISTORY OF NATIONS (25 VOLS.). UNIV LEAD...ANTHOL BIBLIOG INDEX. PAGE 98 H1951
DIPLOM SOCIETY NAT/G

C28
SCHNEIDER H.W.,"MAKING THE FASCIST STATE." ITALY CULTURE LABOR DIPLOM REV WAR NAT/LISM TOTALISM ATTIT DRIVE SOCISM...BIBLIOG PARLIAMENT 20. PAGE 140 H2792
FASCISM POLICY POL/PAR

C28
WARD P.W.,"SOVEREIGNTY: A STUDY OF A CONTEMPORARY POLITICAL NOTION." CONSTN NAT/G DIPLOM REPRESENT PLURISM...IDEA/COMP BIBLIOG. PAGE 165 H3304
SOVEREIGN CONCPT NAT/LISM

B29
PRATT I.A.,MODERN EGYPT: A LIST OF REFERENCES TO MATERIAL IN THE NEW YORK PUBLIC LIBRARY. UAR ECO/UNDEV...GEOG JURID SOC LING 20. PAGE 128 H2555
BIBLIOG ISLAM DIPLOM NAT/G

B30
HATTERSLEY A.F.,A SHORT HISTORY OF DEMOCRACY. WOR-45 CONSTN NAT/G SECT DOMIN WAR CHOOSE ORD/FREE PWR...CONCPT GOV/COMP BIBLIOG ATHENS ROME. PAGE 68 H1355
REPRESENT MAJORIT POPULISM

B31
MACIVER R.M.,SOCIETY: ITS STRUCTURE AND CHANGES. CULTURE STRATA FAM CROWD HABITAT ORD/FREE...PSY SOC CONCPT BIBLIOG 20. PAGE 100 H1998
STRUCT SOCIETY PERSON DRIVE

C31
MACLEOD W.C.,"THE ORIGIN AND HISTORY OF POLITICS." UNIV CULTURE NAT/G REPRESENT...SOC CONCPT TREND BIBLIOG. PAGE 100 H2004
METH STRUCT SOCIETY

B32
CATALOGUE OF BOOKS, MANSUCRIPTS, ETC. IN THE CARIBBEANA SECTION OF THE N.M. WILLIAMS MEMORIAL ETHNOLOGICAL COLLECTION. JAMAICA WEST/IND GP/REL ATTIT SOC. PAGE 2 H0031
BIBLIOG L/A+17C CULTURE SOCIETY

B32
CARDINALL AW,A BIBLIOGRAPHY OF THE GOLD COAST. AFR UK NAT/G EX/STRUC ATTIT...POLICY 19/20. PAGE 26 H0527
BIBLIOG ADMIN COLONIAL DIPLOM

B32
CHILDS J.B.,THE MEMORIAS OF THE REPUBLICS OF CENTRAL AMERICA AND OF THE ANTILLES. L/A+17C 19/20 CENTRAL/AM. PAGE 29 H0592
BIBLIOG GOV/REL NAT/G EX/STRUC

B32
MARRARO H.R.,AMERICAN OPINION ON THE UNIFICATION OF ITALY. ITALY FORCES DIPLOM SOVEREIGN CATHISM CONSERVE...CONCPT NAT/COMP BIBLIOG 19. PAGE 103 H2056
ORD/FREE NAT/LISM REV CONSTN

C33
MURET C.T.,"FRENCH ROYALIST DOCTRINES SINCE THE REVOLUTION." FRANCE CONSTN NAT/G SECT ADMIN LEAD SOVEREIGN...POLICY BIOG IDEA/COMP BIBLIOG 18/20. PAGE 115 H2295
POL/PAR ATTIT INTELL CONSERVE

B34
RIDLEY C.E.,THE CITY-MANAGER PROFESSION. CHIEF PLAN ADMIN CONTROL ROUTINE CHOOSE...TECHNIC CHARTS GOV/COMP BIBLIOG 20. PAGE 131 H2624
MUNIC EX/STRUC LOC/G EXEC

B34
SMITH P.,A HISTORY OF MODERN CULTURE (2 VOLS.). NAT/G...HUM SOC TREND. PAGE 146 H2916
BIBLIOG CULTURE CONCPT

B35
DOUGLASS H.P.,THE PROTESTANT CHURCH AS A SOCIAL INSTITUTION. CULTURE FINAN NEIGH PROF/ORG OP/RES ADMIN...POLICY SOC/WK STAT BIBLIOG. PAGE 42 H0843
SECT PARTIC INGP/REL GP/REL

B35
NORDSKOG J.E.,SOCIAL REFORM IN NORWAY. NORWAY INDUS NAT/G POL/PAR LEGIS ADJUD...SOC BIBLIOG SOC/INTEG 20. PAGE 119 H2371
LABOR ADJUST

B36
BATTAGLIA F.,LINEAMENTI DI STORIA DELLE DOCTRINE POLITICHE CON APPENDICI BIBLIOGRAFICHE. ITALY PROB/SOLV LEAD 20. PAGE 12 H0237
BIBLIOG PHIL/SCI CONCPT NAT/G

B36
PREVITE-ORTON C.W.,THE CAMBRIDGE MEDIEVAL HISTORY (8 VOLS.). CHRIST-17C NAT/G PROB/SOLV TEC/DEV LEAD ...POLICY CONCPT WORSHIP. PAGE 128 H2559
BIBLIOG IDEA/COMP TREND

B37
THOMPSON J.W.,SECRET DIPLOMACY: A RECORD OF ESPIONAGE AND DOUBLE-DEALING: 1500-1815. CHRIST-17C MOD/EUR NAT/G WRITING RISK MORAL...ANTHOL BIBLIOG 16/19 ESPIONAGE. PAGE 154 H3084
DIPLOM CRIME

B38
JESSOP T.E.,A BIBLIOGRAPHY OF DAVID HUME AND OF SCOTTISH PHILOSOPHY FROM FRANCIS HUTCHESON TO LORD BALFOUR. UK INTELL NAT/G ATTIT...CONCPT 17/20 HUME/D CMN/WLTH. PAGE 81 H1615
BIBLIOG EPIST PERCEPT BIOG

B38
RAWLINSON H.G.,INDIA: A SHORT CULTURAL HISTORY. INDIA LAW STRATA FORCES INT/TRADE ADMIN COLONIAL PERSON...GEOG HUM BIBLIOG WORSHIP 20. PAGE 130 H2598
CULTURE SECT MYTH ART/METH

B39
HILL R.L.,A BIBLIOGRAPHY OF THE ANGLO-EGYPTIAN SUDAN FROM THE EARLIEST TIMES TO 1937. AFR ETHIOPIA SUDAN UAR LAW COM/IND SECT RACE/REL...GEOG HEAL SOC LING 19/20 NEGRO. PAGE 71 H1417
BIBLIOG CULTURE NAT/COMP GP/COMP

B39
KERNER R.J.,NORTHEAST ASIA: A SELECTED BIBLIOGRAPHY (2 VOLS.). KOREA RUSSIA NAT/G DIPLOM...GEOG 19/20 CHINJAP. PAGE 85 H1696
BIBLIOG ASIA SOCIETY CULTURE

C39
REISCHAUER R.,"JAPAN'S GOVERNMENT--POLITICS." CONSTN STRATA POL/PAR FORCES LEGIS DIPLOM ADMIN EXEC CENTRAL...POLICY BIBLIOG 20 CHINJAP. PAGE 131 H2610
NAT/G S/ASIA CONCPT ROUTINE

B40
CONOVER H.F.,JAPAN-ECONOMIC DEVELOPMENT AND FOREIGN POLICY, A SELECTED LIST OF REFERENCES (PAMPHLET). CULTURE FINAN INDUS NAT/G FORCES INT/TRADE WAR ...SOC TREND 20 CHINJAP. PAGE 32 H0640
BIBLIOG ASIA ECO/DEV DIPLOM

B40
HERSKOVITS M.J.,THE ECONOMIC LIFE OF PRIMITIVE PEOPLES. INDUS OP/RES PLAN PROB/SOLV...BIBLIOG METH 20. PAGE 70 H1407
CULTURE ECO/TAC ECO/UNDEV PRODUC

B40
KER A.M.,MEXICAN GOVERNMENT PUBLICATIONS: A GUIDE TO THE MORE IMPORTANT PUBLICATIONS OF THE
BIBLIOG NAT/G

GOVERNMENT OF MEXICO, 1821-1936. CHIEF ADJUD 19/20 MEXIC/AMER. PAGE 85 H1693 — EXEC LEGIS

B40

MANNHEIM K.,MAN AND SOCIETY IN AN AGE OF RECONSTRUCTION. MOD/EUR CULTURE ECO/DEV PLAN TEC/DEV PERSON LAISSEZ NEW/LIB...NEW/IDEA IDEA/COMP BIBLIOG 19/20. PAGE 102 H2038 — CONCPT ATTIT SOCIETY TOTALISM

B41

CHILDS J.B.,COLOMBIAN GOVERNMENT PUBLICATIONS (PAMPHLET). L/A+17C SOCIETY 19/20 COLOMB. PAGE 30 H0593 — BIBLIOG GOV/REL NAT/G EX/STRUC

B41

CHILDS J.B.,A GUIDE TO THE OFFICIAL PUBLICATIONS OF THE OTHER AMERICAN REPUBLICS: ARGENTINA. CHIEF DIPLOM GOV/REL...BIBLIOG 18/19 ARGEN. PAGE 30 H0594 — NAT/G EX/STRUC METH/CNCPT LEGIS

B41

COHEN E.W.,THE GROWTH OF THE BRITISH CIVIL SERVICE 1780-1939. UK NAT/G SENIOR ROUTINE GOV/REL...MGT METH/COMP BIBLIOG 18/20. PAGE 31 H0616 — OP/RES TIME/SEQ CENTRAL ADMIN

B41

GILMORE M.P.,ARGUMENT FROM ROMAN LAW IN POLITICAL THOUGHT, 1200-1600. INTELL LICENSE CONTROL CT/SYS GOV/REL PRIVIL PWR...IDEA/COMP BIBLIOG 13/16. PAGE 56 H1130 — JURID LAW CONCPT NAT/G

B41

GRISMER R.,A NEW BIBLIOGRAPHY OF THE LITERATURES OF SPAIN AND SPANISH AMERICA. CHRIST-17C MOD/EUR PRE/AMER SPAIN CULTURE DIPLOM EDU/PROP...ART/METH GEOG HUM PHIL/SCI 20. PAGE 61 H1229 — BIBLIOG LAW NAT/G ECO/UNDEV

B41

STATIST REICHSAMTE,BIBLIOGRAPHIE DER STAATS- UND WIRSCHAFTSWISSENSCHAFTEN. EUR+WWI GERMANY FINAN ADMIN. PAGE 149 H2974 — BIBLIOG ECO/DEV NAT/G POLICY

C41

KLUCKHOHN C.,"PATTERNING AS EXEMPLIFIED IN NAVAHO CULTURE" IN EDWARD SAPIR, LANGUAGE, CULTURE, AND PERSONALITY (BMR)" KIN PERS/REL ATTIT PERSON...SOC CONCPT METH/CNCPT LING OBS/ENVIR CON/ANAL BIBLIOG SOC/INTEG 20 NAVAHO INDIAN/AM SAPIR/EDW. PAGE 87 H1733 — CULTURE INGP/REL STRUCT

C41

WASSERMAN L.,"HANDBOOK OF POLITICAL "ISMS" CAP/ISM REPRESENT TOTALISM MARXISM NEW/LIB SOCISM...MAJORIT BIBLIOG 20. PAGE 166 H3313 — IDEA/COMP PHIL/SCI OWN NAT/G

B42

CONOVER H.F.,FRENCH COLONIES IN AFRICA: A LIST OF REFERENCES. ALGERIA FRANCE MOROCCO SOMALIA SUDAN CULTURE AGRI LOC/G SECT FORCES DIPLOM INT/TRADE NAT/LISM HEALTH...CON/ANAL 20. PAGE 32 H0641 — BIBLIOG AFR ECO/UNDEV COLONIAL

B42

CONOVER H.F.,THE NETHERLANDS EAST INDIES: A SELECTED LIST OF REFERENCES. ECO/UNDEV AGRI EXTR/IND LABOR SCHOOL SECT INT/TRADE COLONIAL HEALTH...GEOG 19/20. PAGE 32 H0642 — BIBLIOG S/ASIA CULTURE

B42

CRAIG A.,ABOVE ALL LIBERTIES. FRANCE UK USA-45 LAW CONSTN CULTURE INTELL NAT/G SECT JUDGE...IDEA/COMP BIBLIOG 18/20. PAGE 35 H0692 — ORD/FREE MORAL WRITING EDU/PROP

B42

NEUMANN S.,PERMANENT REVOLUTION: THE TOTAL STATE IN A WORLD AT WAR. COM EUR+WWI GERMANY USSR EX/STRUC DIPLOM CONTROL COERCE REPRESENT MARXISM...SOC GOV/COMP BIBLIOG 20 HITLER/A STALIN/J. PAGE 117 H2337 — FASCISM TOTALISM DOMIN EDU/PROP

B42

REDFIELD R.,THE FOLK CULTURE OF YUCATAN. STRATA FAM KIN MUNIC SECT DISCRIM ISOLAT ANOMIE HEALTH ...BIBLIOG 20 MEXIC/AMER. PAGE 130 H2605 — CULTURE NEIGH GP/COMP SOCIETY

B42

SIMOES DOS REIS A.,BIBLIOGRAFIA DAS BIBLIOGRAFIAS BRASILEIRAS. BRAZIL ADMIN COLONIAL 20. PAGE 144 H2879 — BIBLIOG NAT/G DIPLOM L/A+17C

B43

BROWN A.D.,BRITISH POSSESSIONS IN THE CARIBBEAN AREA: A SELECTED LIST OF REFERENCES. UK NAT/G DIPLOM...GEOG 20 CARIBBEAN. PAGE 22 H0437 — BIBLIOG COLONIAL ECO/UNDEV L/A+17C

B43

CONOVER H.F.,SOVIET RUSSIA: SELECTED LIST OF REFERENCES. USSR CULTURE INDUS NAT/G TOP/EX TEC/DEV BUDGET WAR CIVMIL/REL EFFICIENCY MARXISM 20. PAGE 32 H0644 — BIBLIOG ECO/DEV COM DIPLOM

B43

DURON J.F.,REPERTORIO BIBLIOGRAFICO HONDURENO. HONDURAS WRITING. PAGE 44 H0871 — BIBLIOG NAT/G L/A+17C

B43

LEWIN E.,ROYAL EMPIRE SOCIETY BIBLIOGRAPHIES NO. 9: SUB-SAHARA AFRICA. ECO/UNDEV TEC/DEV DIPLOM ADMIN COLONIAL LEAD 20. PAGE 96 H1908 — BIBLIOG AFR NAT/G SOCIETY

B43

MC DOWELL R.B.,IRISH PUBLIC OPINION, 1750-1800. IRELAND CONSTN VOL/ASSN WORKER ORD/FREE CATHISM CONSERVE...POLICY IDEA/COMP BIBLIOG 18/ PARLIAMENT. PAGE 106 H2118 — ATTIT NAT/G DIPLOM REV

B43

US LIBRARY OF CONGRESS,BRITISH MALAYA AND BRITISH NORTH BORNEO. BORNEO MALAYSIA CONSTN AGRI COM/IND INDUS EDU/PROP 19/20. PAGE 160 H3203 — BIBLIOG CULTURE

B44

SHELBY C.,LATIN AMERICAN PERIODICALS CURRENTLY RECEIVED IN THE LIBRARY OF CONGRESS AND IN LIBRARY OF DEPARTMENT OF AGRICULTURE. SOCIETY AGRI INDUS LABOR POL/PAR INT/TRADE...GEOG SOC 20. PAGE 143 H2856 — BIBLIOG ECO/UNDEV CULTURE L/A+17C

B44

US LIBRARY OF CONGRESS,RUSSIA: A CHECK LIST PRELIMINARY TO A BASIC BIBLIOGRAPHY OF MATERIALS IN THE RUSSIAN LANGUAGE. COM USSR CULTURE EDU/PROP MARXISM...ART/METH HUM LING 19/20. PAGE 160 H3204 — BIBLIOG LAW SECT

C44

VAN VALKENBURG S.,"ELEMENTS OF POLITICAL GEOGRAPHY." FRANCE COM/IND INDUS NAT/G SECT RACE/REL...LING TREND GEN/LAWS BIBLIOG 20. PAGE 162 H3232 — GEOG DIPLOM COLONIAL

B45

CONOVER H.F.,THE GOVERNMENTS OF THE MAJOR FOREIGN POWERS: A BIBLIOGRAPHY. FRANCE GERMANY ITALY UK USSR CONSTN LOC/G POL/PAR EX/STRUC FORCES ADMIN CT/SYS CIVMIL/REL TOTALISM...POLICY 19/20. PAGE 32 H0645 — BIBLIOG NAT/G DIPLOM

B45

CONOVER H.F.,ITALY: ECONOMICS, POLITICS AND MILITARY AFFAIRS, 1940-1945. ITALY ELITES NAT/G POL/PAR EX/STRUC TOP/EX DIPLOM DOMIN CONTROL COERCE WAR CIVMIL/REL EFFICIENCY 20. PAGE 32 H0646 — BIBLIOG TOTALISM FORCES

B45

CONOVER H.F.,THE NAZI STATE: WAR CRIMES AND WAR CRIMINALS. GERMANY CULTURE NAT/G SECT FORCES DIPLOM INT/TRADE EDU/PROP...INT/LAW BIOG HIST/WRIT TIME/SEQ 20. PAGE 32 H0647 — BIBLIOG WAR CRIME

B46

HUTTON J.,THE CONSTITUTION OF THE UNION OF SOUTH AFRICA: BIBLIOGRAPHY (PAMPHLET). SOUTH/AFR MUNIC DIPLOM RACE/REL 20. PAGE 75 H1510 — BIBLIOG CONSTN NAT/G LOC/G

B47

BEHAR D.,BIBLIOGRAFIA HISPANOAMERICANA. LIBROS ANTIGUOS Y MODERNOS REFERENTES A AMERICA Y ESPANA. PORTUGAL SPAIN CONSTN NAT/G SECT CREATE REV WAR GOV/REL...ART/METH GEOG PHIL/SCI LING 20 ARGEN. PAGE 13 H0260 — BIBLIOG L/A+17C CULTURE

B47

HERSKOVITS M.U.,MAN AND HIS WORK. UNIV SECT TEC/DEV PARTIC...PHIL/SCI LING AUD/VIS BIBLIOG. PAGE 70 H1409 — SOC CULTURE INGP/REL HABITAT

B48

GUIDE TO THE RECORDS IN THE NATIONAL ARCHIVES. ECO/UNDEV ADMIN COLONIAL 16/20. PAGE 2 H0034 — BIBLIOG NAT/G L/A+17C DIPLOM

B48

CLYDE P.H.,THE FAR EAST: A HISTORY OF THE IMPACT OF THE WEST ON EASTERN ASIA. CHINA/COM CULTURE INT/TRADE DOMIN COLONIAL WAR PWR...CHARTS BIBLIOG 19/20 CHINJAP. PAGE 30 H0609 — DIPLOM ASIA

B48

GRIFFITH E.S.,RESEARCH IN POLITICAL SCIENCE: THE WORK OF PANELS OF RESEARCH COMMITTEE, APSA. WOR+45 WOR-45 COM/IND R+D FORCES ACT/RES WAR...GOV/COMP ANTHOL 20. PAGE 61 H1220 — BIBLIOG PHIL/SCI DIPLOM JURID

B48

LAUTERBACH A.,ECONOMIC SECURITY AND INDIVIDUAL FREEDOM: CAN WE HAVE BOTH? COM EUR+WWI MOD/EUR UNIV WOR+45 CAP/ISM TOTALISM ALL/VALS...GOV/COMP BIBLIOG 20. PAGE 92 H1840 — ORD/FREE ECO/DEV DECISION INGP/REL

B48

TOWSTER J.,POLITICAL POWER IN THE USSR: 1917-1947. USSR CONSTN CULTURE ELITES CREATE PLAN COERCE CENTRAL ATTIT RIGID/FLEX ORD/FREE...BIBLIOG SOC/INTEG 20 LENIN/VI STALIN/J. PAGE 156 H3122 — EX/STRUC NAT/G MARXISM PWR

B48

WRIGHT G.,THE RESHAPING OF FRENCH DEMOCRACY. FRANCE NAT/G POL/PAR SECT LEAD CHOOSE GP/REL INGP/REL MARXISM SOCISM...CHARTS BIBLIOG 20 DEGAULLE/C. PAGE 171 H3418 — CONSTN POPULISM CREATE LEGIS

B48

YAKOBSON S.,FIVE HUNDRED RUSSIAN WORKS FOR COLLEGE LIBRARIES (PAMPHLET). MOD/EUR USSR MARXISM SOCISM ...ART/METH GEOG HUM JURID SOC 13/20. PAGE 171 H3431 — BIBLIOG NAT/G CULTURE COM

B49
BORBA DE MORAES R.,MANUAL BIBLIOGRAFICO DE ESTUDOS BRASILEIROS. BRAZIL DIPLOM ADMIN LEAD...SOC 20. PAGE 19 H0374
BIBLIOG L/A+17C NAT/G ECO/UNDEV

B49
HEADLAM-MORLEY,BIBLIOGRAPHY IN POLITICS FOR THE HONOUR SCHOOL OF PHILOSOPHY, POLITICS AND ECONOMICS (PAMPHLET). UK CONSTN LABOR MUNIC DIPLOM ADMIN 19/20. PAGE 69 H1375
BIBLIOG NAT/G PHIL/SCI GOV/REL

B49
PELZER K.J.,SELECTED BIBLIOGRAPHY ON THE GEOGRAPHY OF SOUTHEAST ASIA (3 VOLS., 1949-1956). PHILIPPINE CULTURE...SOC 20 MALAYA. PAGE 124 H2486
BIBLIOG S/ASIA GEOG

B49
ROGERS C.B.,THE SPIRIT OF REVOLUTION IN 1789: A STUDY OF PUBLIC OPINION ...AT THE BEGINNING OF THE FRENCH REVOLUTION. FRANCE CULTURE ELITES EDU/PROP COERCE CROWD...BIBLIOG 18 MUSIC. PAGE 133 H2658
ATTIT POPULISM REV CREATE

C49
SCHAPIRO J.S.,"LIBERALISM AND THE CHALLENGE OF FASCISM." FRANCE UK STRATA PERSON...CONCPT BIOG IDEA/COMP BIBLIOG 18/20. PAGE 139 H2771
FASCISM LAISSEZ ATTIT

B50
DUCLOS P.,L'EVOLUTION DES RAPPORTS POLITIQUES DEPUIS 1750 (LIBERTE, INTEGRATION, UNITE). LAW INT/ORG FEDERAL TOTALISM ATTIT PWR...MAJORIT BIBLIOG 18/20 PARLIAMENT EUROPE. PAGE 43 H0852
ORD/FREE DIPLOM NAT/G GOV/COMP

B50
FIGANIERE J.C.,BIBLIOTHECA HISTORICA PORTUGUEZA. BRAZIL PORTUGAL SECT ADMIN. PAGE 50 H0997
BIBLIOG NAT/G DIPLOM COLONIAL

B50
GOFF F.R.,FIFTEENTH CENTURY BOOKS IN THE LIBRARY OF CONGRESS. CHRIST-17C GERMANY ITALY CULTURE INTELL SECT CREATE...PHIL/SCI CONCPT CLASSIF BIOG TIME/SEQ 15. PAGE 58 H1153
BIBLIOG KNOWL HUM

B50
LYONS F.S.L.,THE IRISH PARLIAMENTARY PARTY, 1890-1910: STUDIES IN IRISH HISTORY (VOL. 4). IRELAND DELIB/GP LEGIS PAY EDU/PROP ADMIN GP/REL ATTIT...BIBLIOG 19/20 PARLIAMENT PARNELL/CS DIRECT/NAT. PAGE 99 H1986
POL/PAR CHOOSE NAT/G POLICY

B50
SMITH E.W.,AFRICAN IDEAS OF GOD. ATTIT...CONCPT MYTH IDEA/COMP ANTHOL BIBLIOG. PAGE 145 H2908
SOC AFR CULTURE SECT

C50
NUMELIN R.,"THE BEGINNINGS OF DIPLOMACY." INT/TRADE WAR GP/REL PEACE STRANGE ATTIT...INT/LAW CONCPT BIBLIOG. PAGE 119 H2380
DIPLOM KIN CULTURE LAW

C50
STOKES W.S.,"HONDURAS: AN AREA STUDY IN GOVERNMENT." HONDURAS NAT/G POL/PAR COLONIAL CT/SYS ROUTINE CHOOSE REPRESENT...GEOG RECORD BIBLIOG 19/20. PAGE 149 H2988
CONSTN LAW L/A+17C ADMIN

B51
CATALOGO GENERAL DE LA LIBRERIA ESPANOLA E HISPANOAMERICANA 1901-1930; AUTORES (5 VOLS., 1932-1951). SPAIN COLONIAL GOV/REL...SOC 20. PAGE 2 H0036
BIBLIOG L/A+17C DIPLOM NAT/G

B51
BISSAINTHE M.,DICTIONNAIRE DE BIBLIOGRAPHIE HAITIENNE. HAITI ELITES AGRI LEGIS DIPLOM INT/TRADE WRITING ORD/FREE CATHISM...ART/METH GEOG 19/20 NEGRO TREATY. PAGE 17 H0347
BIBLIOG L/A+17C SOCIETY NAT/G

B51
GHANI A.R.,PAKISTAN: A SELECT BIBLIOGRAPHY. PAKISTAN S/ASIA CULTURE...GEOG 20. PAGE 56 H1120
BIBLIOG AGRI INDUS

B51
INTERNATIONAL AFRICAN INST,ETHNOGRAPHIC SURVEY OF AFRICA: WEST CENTRAL AFRICA (VOLS. I-III, 1951-1953). AFR RHODESIA CULTURE ECO/UNDEV HEREDITY ...GEOG SOC CHARTS BIBLIOG WORSHIP 20 CONGO/LEOP. PAGE 77 H1543
STRUCT KIN INGP/REL HABITAT

B51
LEONARD L.L.,INTERNATIONAL ORGANIZATION. WOR+45 WOR-45 EX/STRUC FORCES LEGIS ECO/TAC INT/TRADE COLONIAL ARMS/CONT...SOC/WK GOV/COMP BIBLIOG. PAGE 94 H1884
NAT/G DIPLOM INT/ORG DELIB/GP

B51
WHEARE K.C.,MODERN CONSTITUTIONS (HOME UNIVERSITY LIBRARY). UNIV LAW NAT/G LEGIS...CONCPT TREND BIBLIOG. PAGE 167 H3336
CONSTN CLASSIF PWR CREATE

C51
BEST H.,"THE SOVIET STATE AND ITS INCEPTION." USSR CULTURE INDUS DIPLOM WEALTH...GEOG SOC BIBLIOG 20. PAGE 16 H0322
COM GEN/METH REV MARXISM

C51
HAMMOND M.,"CITY-STATE AND WORLD STATE." CONSTN INTELL LOC/G LEGIT CENTRAL RATIONAL BIBLIOG. PAGE 65 H1308
NAT/G ATTIT REGION MEDIT-7

N51
MEYER E.W.,POLITICAL PARTIES IN WESTERN GERMANY (PAMPHLET). EUR+WWI GERMANY/W PRESS LEAD CHOOSE REPRESENT ATTIT 20. PAGE 109 H2189
BIBLIOG POL/PAR NAT/G VOL/ASSN

B52
APPADORAI A.,THE SUBSTANCE OF POLITICS (6TH ED.). EX/STRUC LEGIS DIPLOM CT/SYS CHOOSE FASCISM MARXISM SOCISM...BIBLIOG T. PAGE 7 H0145
PHIL/SCI NAT/G

B52
CALLOT E.,LA SOCIETE ET SON ENVIRONNEMENT: ESSAI SUR LES PRINCIPES DES SCIENCES SOCIALES. GP/REL ADJUST CONSEN ISOLAT HABITAT PERCEPT PERSON ...BIBLIOG SOC/INTEG 20. PAGE 25 H0507
SOCIETY PHIL/SCI CULTURE

B52
DILLON D.R.,LATIN AMERICA, 1935-1949; A SELECTED BIBLIOGRAPHY. LAW EDU/PROP...SOC 20. PAGE 41 H0826
BIBLIOG L/A+17C NAT/G DIPLOM

B52
FORDE L.D.,HABITAT, ECONOMY AND SOCIETY. AFR L/A+17C S/ASIA STRUCT AGRI INGP/REL...GEOG OBS BIBLIOG 20. PAGE 52 H1037
SOC HABITAT CULTURE ECO/UNDEV

B52
INTERNATIONAL AFRICAN INST,ETHNOGRAPHIC SURVEY OF AFRICA: SOUTHERN AFRICA (VOLS. I-III, 1952-1954). AFR SOUTH/AFR CULTURE ECO/UNDEV GOV/REL HEREDITY ...GEOG SOC CHARTS BIBLIOG WORSHIP 20. PAGE 77 H1544
STRUCT KIN INGP/REL HABITAT

B52
MONTAGU A.,MAN'S MOST DANGEROUS MYTH: THE FALLACY OF RACE. LAW PROB/SOLV WAR HABITAT POPULISM...PSY CONCPT CHARTS BIBLIOG NEGRO JEWS. PAGE 112 H2242
DISCRIM MYTH CULTURE RACE/REL

B52
UNESCO,DOCUMENTATION IN THE SOCIAL SCIENCES. CULTURE...GP/COMP METH 20 UNESCO. PAGE 158 H3162
BIBLIOG SOC

B52
US DEPARTMENT OF STATE,RESEARCH ON EASTERN EUROPE (EXCLUDING USSR). EUR+WWI LAW ECO/DEV NAT/G PROB/SOLV DIPLOM ADMIN LEAD MARXISM...TREND 19/20. PAGE 159 H3187
BIBLIOG R+D ACT/RES COM

C52
FIFIELD R.H.,"WOODROW WILSON AND THE FAR EAST." ASIA CHIEF DELIB/GP BAL/PWR CONFER COLONIAL ARMS/CONT WAR...TIME/SEQ NAT/COMP 19/20 WILSON/W LEAGUE/NAT. PAGE 50 H0995
BIBLIOG DIPLOM INT/ORG

C52
LEWIS B.W.,"BRITISH PLANNING AND NATIONALIZATION." UK INDUS SERV/IND LABOR NAT/G OP/RES TEC/DEV TAX WEALTH...CHARTS BIBLIOG 20. PAGE 96 H1912
NEW/LIB ECO/DEV POL/PAR PLAN

B53
BIDNEY D.,THEORETICAL ANTHROPOLOGY. DRIVE ROLE ORD/FREE...CONCPT METH/CNCPT MYTH CLASSIF OBS IDEA/COMP METH/COMP BIBLIOG METH 20. PAGE 17 H0331
CULTURE SOC PSY PHIL/SCI

B53
BROWN D.M.,THE WHITE UMBRELLA: INDIAN POLITICAL THOUGHT FROM MANU TO GANDHI. INDIA LAW NAT/G SECT WRITING NAT/LISM...ANTHOL BIBLIOG 20 HINDU GANDHI/M MANU. PAGE 22 H0442
CONCPT DOMIN CONSERVE

B53
CURTISS J.S.,THE RUSSIAN CHURCH AND THE SOVIET STATE 1917-1950. COM USSR CONTROL LEAD REV MARXISM ...POLICY BIBLIOG 20 CHURCH/STA ORTHO/RUSS. PAGE 36 H0728
GP/REL NAT/G SECT PWR

B53
ELAHI K.N.,A GUIDE TO WORKS OF REFERENCE PUBLISHED IN PAKISTAN (PAMPHLET). PAKISTAN DIPLOM COLONIAL LEAD. PAGE 45 H0903
BIBLIOG S/ASIA NAT/G

B53
KANTOR H.,A BIBLIOGRAPHY OF UNPUBLISHED DOCTORAL DISSERTATIONS AND MASTERS' THESES DEALING WITH GOVTS, POL, INT REL OF LAT AM. L/A+17C INT/ORG POL/PAR ACT/RES OP/RES CONFER ATTIT...INT/LAW PHIL/SCI 20. PAGE 83 H1656
BIBLIOG ACADEM DIPLOM NAT/G

B53
KEESING F.M.,CULTURE CHANGE: AN ANALYSIS AND BIBLIOGRAPHY OF ANTHROPOLOGICAL SOURCES TO 1952. CULTURE STRUCT...TIME/SEQ 19/20. PAGE 84 H1679
BIBLIOG SOC CREATE ORD/FREE

B53
MEAD M.,CULTURAL PATTERNS AND TECHNICAL CHANGE. BURMA GREECE NIGERIA ECO/UNDEV AGRI INDUS SCHOOL SECT CREATE FEEDBACK HABITAT...PSY METH/COMP BIBLIOG 20 UN. PAGE 108 H2152
HEALTH TEC/DEV CULTURE ADJUST

B53
MIT CENTER INTERNATIONAL STU,BIBLIOGRAPHY OF THE ECONOMIC AND POLITICAL DEVELOPMENT OF INDONESIA. INDONESIA STRUCT NAT/G COLONIAL LEAD...STAT 20. PAGE 111 H2226
BIBLIOG ECO/UNDEV TEC/DEV S/ASIA

B53
ORFIELD L.B.,THE GROWTH OF SCANDINAVIAN LAW. DENMARK ICELAND NORWAY SWEDEN LAW DIPLOM...BIBLIOG 9/20. PAGE 121 H2426
JURID CT/SYS NAT/G

B53
PIERCE R.A.,RUSSIAN CENTRAL ASIA, 1867-1917: A SELECTED BIBLIOGRAPHY (PAMPHLET). USSR LAW CULTURE NAT/G EDU/PROP WAR...GEOG SOC 19/20. PAGE 125 H2508
BIBLIOG COLONIAL ADMIN COM

B53
STOUT H.M.,BRITISH GOVERNMENT. UK FINAN LOC/G POL/PAR DELIB/GP DIPLOM ADMIN COLONIAL CHOOSE ORD/FREE...JURID BIBLIOG 20 COMMONWLTH. PAGE 150 H2990
NAT/G PARL/PROC CONSTN NEW/LIB

C53
BULNER-THOMAS I.,"THE PARTY SYSTEM IN GREAT BRITAIN." UK CONSTN SECT PRESS CONFER GP/REL ATTIT ...POLICY TREND BIBLIOG 19/20 PARLIAMENT. PAGE 23 H0473
NAT/G POL/PAR ADMIN ROUTINE

C53
DORWART R.A.,"THE ADMINISTRATIVE REFORMS OF FREDRICK WILLIAM I OF PRUSSIA. GERMANY MOD/EUR CHIEF CONTROL PWR...BIBLIOG 16/18. PAGE 42 H0839
ADMIN NAT/G CENTRAL GOV/REL

B54
SALVEMINI G.,PRELUDE TO WORLD WAR II. ITALY MOD/EUR INT/ORG BAL/PWR EDU/PROP CONTROL TOTALISM...TREND NAT/COMP BIBLIOG 19 HITLER/A LEAGUE/NAT MUSSOLIN/B. PAGE 137 H2745
WAR FASCISM LEAD PWR

B54
TITIEV M.,THE SCIENCE OF MAN. LAW STRATA KIN GP/REL PERS/REL HABITAT HEREDITY KNOWL...LING CHARTS BIBLIOG WORSHIP. PAGE 155 H3107
SOC PSY CULTURE

C54
DE GRAZIA A.,"THE COMPARATIVE SURVEY OF EUROPEAN-AMERICAN POLITICAL BEHAV IOR; A RESEARCH PROSPECTUS (PAPER)" EUR+WWI FRANCE GERMANY SPAIN UK USA+45 WOR+45 STRATA POL/PAR DIPLOM EDU/PROP COLONIAL LEAD WAR NAT/LISM CONCPT. PAGE 37 H0752
BIBLIOG R+D METH NAT/COMP

C54
GUINS G.C.,"SOVIET LAW AND SOVIET SOCIETY." COM USSR STRATA FAM NAT/G WORKER DOMIN RACE/REL ...BIBLIOG 20. PAGE 62 H1249
LAW STRUCT PLAN

C54
HAMMER E.J.,"THE STRUGGLE FOR INDOCHINA." COM VIETNAM POL/PAR REV CENTRAL NAT/LISM ATTIT...POLICY CHARTS BIBLIOG 20. PAGE 65 H1305
WAR COLONIAL S/ASIA NAT/G

C54
LANDAU J.M.,"PARLIAMENTS AND PARTIES IN EGYPT." UAR NAT/G SECT CONSULT LEGIS TOP/EX PROB/SOLV ADMIN COLONIAL...GEN/LAWS BIBLIOG 19/20. PAGE 90 H1804
ISLAM NAT/LISM PARL/PROC POL/PAR

B55
CRAIG G.A.,THE POLITICS OF THE PRUSSIAN ARMY 1640-1945. CHRIST-17C EUR+WWI MOD/EUR PRUSSIA STRUCT DIPLOM ADMIN REV WAR...SOC BIBLIOG 17/20. PAGE 35 H0694
FORCES NAT/G ROLE CHIEF

B55
DE ARAGAO J.G.,LA JURIDICTION ADMINISTRATIVE AU BRESIL. BRAZIL ADJUD COLONIAL CT/SYS REV FEDERAL ORD/FREE...BIBLIOG 19/20. PAGE 37 H0749
EX/STRUC ADMIN NAT/G

B55
INTERNATIONAL AFRICAN INST,ETHNOGRAPHIC SURVEY OF AFRICA: NORTH EASTERN AFRICA (VOLUMES 1-2, 1955-56). AFR ETHIOPIA CULTURE ECO/UNDEV KIN GOV/REL ATTIT HEREDITY...GEOG CHARTS BIBLIOG WORSHIP 20. PAGE 77 H1545
STRUCT ECO/TAC INGP/REL HABITAT

B55
INTERNATIONAL AFRICAN INST,ETHNOGRAPHIC SURVEY OF AFRICA: WESTERN AFRICA: PEOPLES OF THE NIGER-BENUE CONFLUENCE. AFR NIGER CULTURE ECO/UNDEV KIN GOV/REL GP/REL ATTIT HEREDITY...CHARTS BIBLIOG WORSHIP 20. PAGE 77 H1546
STRUCT GEOG HABITAT INGP/REL

B55
JONES T.B.,A BIBLIOGRAPHY ON SOUTH AMERICAN ECONOMIC AFFAIRS: ARTICLES IN NINETEENTH CENTURY PERIODICALS (PAMPHLET). AGRI COM/IND DIST/IND EXTR/IND FINAN INDUS LABOR NAT/G 19. PAGE 82 H1634
BIBLIOG ECO/UNDEV L/A+17C TEC/DEV

B55
MID-EUROPEAN LAW PROJECT,CHURCH AND STATE BEHIND THE IRON CURTAIN. COM CZECHOSLVK HUNGARY POLAND USSR CULTURE SECT EDU/PROP GOV/REL CATHISM...CHARTS ANTHOL BIBLIOG WORSHIP 20 CHURCH/STA. PAGE 110 H2202
LAW MARXISM POLICY

B55
SHAFER B.C.,NATIONALISM: MYTH AND REALITY. FRANCE UK USA+45 USA-45 CULTURE SOCIETY STRUCT ECO/DEV WAR PWR...NAT/COMP BIBLIOG 18/20. PAGE 142 H2837
NAT/LISM MYTH NAT/G CONCPT

B55
SHUMSKY A.,THE CLASH OF CULTURES IN ISRAEL: A PROBLEM FOR EDUCATION. ISRAEL CULTURE INTELL NAT/G ACT/RES DISCRIM AGE/Y...BIBLIOG 20 JEWS. PAGE 143 H2867
GP/REL EDU/PROP SCHOOL AGE/C

B55
STEWARD J.H.,THEORY OF CULTURE CHANGE; THE METHODOLOGY OF MULTILINEAR EVOLUTION. SOCIETY KIN SECT GP/REL INGP/REL...BIBLIOG SOC/INTEG 20. PAGE 149 H2984
CULTURE CONCPT METH/COMP HABITAT

B55
SVARLIEN O.,AN INTRODUCTION TO THE LAW OF NATIONS. SEA AIR INT/ORG NAT/G CHIEF ADMIN AGREE WAR PRIVIL ORD/FREE SOVEREIGN...BIBLIOG 16/20. PAGE 151 H3012
INT/LAW DIPLOM

B55
UN ECONOMIC AND SOCIAL COUNCIL,ANALYTICAL BIBLIOGRAPHY OF INTERNATIONAL MIGRATION STATISTICS, SELECTED COUNTRIES, 1925-1950. STRATA...CLASSIF CENSUS NAT/COMP 20. PAGE 158 H3156
BIBLIOG STAT GEOG HABITAT

B55
WOYTINSKY W.S.,WORLD COMMERCE AND GOVERNMENTS: TRENDS AND OUTLOOK. WOR+45 FINAN POL/PAR DIPLOM ECO/TAC FOR/AID DOMIN WAR CHOOSE...CHARTS BIBLIOG 20 LEAGUE/NAT UN ILO. PAGE 171 H3413
INT/TRADE DIST/IND NAT/COMP NAT/G

C55
APTER D.E.,"THE GOLD COAST IN TRANSITION." AFR CONSTN LOC/G LEGIS DIPLOM COLONIAL CONTROL GOV/REL ...CHARTS BIBLIOG 20 CMN/WLTH. PAGE 7 H0150
ORD/FREE REPRESENT PARL/PROC NAT/G

B56
BECKER H.,MAN IN RECIPROCITY: INTRODUCTORY LECTURES ON CULTURE, SOCIETY, AND PERSONALITY. LAW FAM SECT REGION GP/REL ADJUST ATTIT PERSON...BIBLIOG 20. PAGE 13 H0253
CULTURE STRUCT SOC PSY

B56
GLUCKMAN M.,CUSTOM AND CONFLICT IN AFRICA. AFR FAM KIN NAT/G DOMIN DISCRIM DRIVE MORAL PWR...SOC BIBLIOG WORSHIP 20. PAGE 57 H1145
CULTURE CREATE PERS/REL GP/COMP

B56
RIESENBERG P.N.,INALIENABILITY OF SOVEREIGNTY IN MEDIEVAL POLITICAL THOUGHT. CHRIST-17C INTELL NAT/G SECT CHIEF LEGIS SANCTION AUTHORIT ORD/FREE CONSERVE...IDEA/COMP BIBLIOG 12/16. PAGE 131 H2627
SOVEREIGN ATTIT

B56
SHAPIRO H.L.,MAN, CULTURE, AND SOCIETY. STRUCT FAM SECT GP/REL INGP/REL...ART/METH GEOG PSY LING ANTHOL BIBLIOG. PAGE 142 H2842
CULTURE PERSON SOC

B56
VON BECKERATH E.,HANDWORTERBUCH DER SOCIALWISSENSCHAFTEN (II VOLS.). EUR+WWI GERMANY POL/PAR WORKER DIPLOM LEAD CHOOSE SUFF WEALTH...SOC 20. PAGE 163 H3263
BIBLIOG INT/TRADE NAT/G ECO/DEV

B56
VON HARPE W.,DIE SOWJETUNION FINNLAND UND SKANDANAVIEN, 1945-1955. EUR+WWI FINLAND GERMANY USSR WAR INGP/REL ORD/FREE SOVEREIGN MARXISM ...POLICY GOV/COMP BIBLIOG 20 STALIN/J. PAGE 163 H3270
DIPLOM COM NEUTRAL BAL/PWR

B56
VUCINICH A.,THE SOVIET ACADEMY OF SCIENCES. USSR STRUCT ACADEM NAT/G EDU/PROP ADMIN LEAD ROLE ...BIBLIOG 20 ACADEM/SCI. PAGE 164 H3280
PHIL/SCI CREATE INTELL PROF/ORG

B56
WILSON P.,GOVERNMENT AND POLITICS OF INDIA AND PAKISTAN: 1885-1955; A BIBLIOGRAPHY OF WORKS IN WESTERN LANGUAGES. INDIA PAKISTAN CONSTN LOC/G POL/PAR FORCES DIPLOM ADMIN WAR CHOOSE...BIOG CON/ANAL 19/20. PAGE 169 H3380
BIBLIOG COLONIAL NAT/G S/ASIA

B57
BISHOP O.B.,PUBLICATIONS OF THE GOVERNMENTS OF NOVA SCOTIA, PRINCE EDWARD ISLAND, NEW BRUNSWICK 1758-1952. CANADA UK ADMIN COLONIAL LEAD...POLICY 18/20. PAGE 17 H0345
BIBLIOG NAT/G DIPLOM

B57
CARIBBEAN COMMISSION,A CATALOGUE OF CARIBBEAN COMMISSION PUBLICATIONS (PAMPHLET). WEST/IND CULTURE ECO/UNDEV LOC/G DIPLOM SOC. PAGE 26 H0531
BIBLIOG L/A+17C INT/ORG NAT/G

B57
HODGKIN T.,NATIONALISM IN COLONIAL AFRICA. STRATA STRUCT MUNIC NAT/G POL/PAR LEGIS ATTIT SOVEREIGN ...POLICY TREND BIBLIOG 20. PAGE 72 H1444
AFR COLONIAL NAT/LISM DIPLOM

B57
HOUN F.W.,CENTRAL GOVERNMENT OF CHINA, 1912-1928. ASIA CONSTN CHIEF LEGIS CONTROL PWR...BIBLIOG 20. PAGE 74 H1480
POL/PAR ATTIT NAT/G PLAN

B57
IKE N.,JAPANESE POLITICS. INTELL STRUCT AGRI INDUS FAM KIN LABOR PRESS CHOOSE ATTIT...DECISION BIBLIOG 19/20 CHINJAP. PAGE 76 H1523
NAT/G ADMIN POL/PAR CULTURE

B57
INTERNATIONAL AFRICAN INST,ETHNOGRAPHIC SURVEY OF AFRICA: WESTERN AFRICA: THE BENIN KINGDOM. AFR NIGERIA CULTURE ECO/UNDEV KIN ECO/TAC GOV/REL AGE ATTIT HEREDITY...CHARTS BIBLIOG WORSHIP 20. PAGE 77 H1550
STRUCT INGP/REL GEOG HABITAT

B57
INTERNATIONAL AFRICAN INST,ETHNOGRAPHIC SURVEY OF AFRICA: WESTERN AFRICA: THE WOLOF OF SENEGAMBIA. AFR SENEGAL CULTURE ECO/UNDEV FAM KIN REGION ...CHARTS GP/COMP BIBLIOG WORSHIP 20. PAGE 78 H1551 STRUCT GEOG HABITAT INGP/REL

B57
KANTOROWICZ E.,THE KING'S TWO BODIES; A STUDY IN MEDIEVAL POLITICAL THEOLOGY. UK LAW CONSTN NAT/G CT/SYS...ART/METH HUM CONCPT MYTH TIME/SEQ BIBLIOG 4/17 ELIZABTH/I POPE CHURCH/STA. PAGE 83 H1657 JURID SECT CHIEF SOVEREIGN

B57
LOUCKS W.N.,COMPARATIVE ECONOMIC SYSTEMS (5TH ED.). COM UK USSR INDUS POL/PAR PLAN CAP/ISM TOTALISM MARXISM...PHIL/SCI BIBLIOG 19/20. PAGE 99 H1969 NAT/COMP IDEA/COMP SOCISM

B57
NARAIN D.,HINDU CHARACTER (A FEW GLIMPSES). INDIA DIPLOM SUICIDE PERS/REL ATTIT...PSY NAT/COMP PERS/COMP BIBLIOG WORSHIP 20 HINDU. PAGE 116 H2310 PERSON STERTYP SUPEGO SECT

B57
PARK A.G.,BOLSHEVISM IN TURKESTAN 1917-1927. COM RUSSIA USSR CULTURE AGRI SECT DOMIN GP/REL INGP/REL NAT/LISM...BIBLIOG 20 TURKESTAN. PAGE 123 H2467 REV POLICY MARXISM ISLAM

B57
PLAYFAIR G.,THE OFFENDERS: THE CASE AGAINST LEGAL VENGEANCE. UNIV LAW SOCIETY NAT/G PROB/SOLV DEATH PERSON ORD/FREE...HEAL INT/LAW BIBLIOG 20 REFORMERS. PAGE 126 H2524 CRIME TEC/DEV SANCTION CT/SYS

B57
REAMAN G.E.,THE TRAIL OF THE BLACK WALNUT. CANADA AGRI COLONIAL...CHARTS BIBLIOG 18 GERMANS/PA. PAGE 130 H2604 STRANGE SECT CULTURE

B57
ROBERTSON H.M.,SOUTH AFRICA, ECONOMIC AND POLITICAL ASPECTS. SOUTH/AFR CONSTN CULTURE POL/PAR LEGIS DIPLOM DOMIN COLONIAL...SOC BIBLIOG 19/20. PAGE 132 H2647 RACE/REL ECO/UNDEV ECO/TAC DISCRIM

B57
WILSON P.,SOUTH ASIA; A SELECTED BIBLIOGRAPHY ON INDIA, PAKISTAN, CEYLON (PAMPHLET). CEYLON INDIA PAKISTAN LAW ECO/UNDEV PLAN DIPLOM 20. PAGE 169 H3381 BIBLIOG S/ASIA CULTURE NAT/G

C57
MORRIS-JONES W.H.,"PARLIAMENT IN INDIA." INDIA CONSTN LEGIS CONFER COLONIAL CHOOSE PRIVIL ATTIT ...GOV/COMP BIBLIOG 20. PAGE 113 H2264 PARL/PROC EX/STRUC NAT/G POL/PAR

C57
WITTFOGEL K.A.,"ORIENTAL DESPOTISM: A COMPARATIVE STUDY OF TOTAL POWER." ASIA CULTURE STRATA NAT/G LEAD OWN ORD/FREE PWR...CONCPT TREND BIBLIOG 20. PAGE 170 H3393 TOTALISM HABITAT DOMIN ELITES

B58
LIST OF PUBLICATIONS (PERIODICAL OR AD HOC) ISSUED BY VARIOUS MINISTRIES OF THE GOVERNMENT OF INDIA (3RD ED.). INDIA ECO/UNDEV PLAN...POLICY MGT 20. PAGE 2 H0037 BIBLIOG NAT/G ADMIN

B58
BAGBY P.,CULTURE AND HISTORY....PHIL/SCI CONCPT LING LOG IDEA/COMP GEN/LAWS BIBLIOG 20. PAGE 10 H0196 HIST/WRIT CULTURE GP/COMP NAT/COMP

B58
BRIGGS L.C.,THE LIVING RACES OF THE SAHARA. STRATA AGRI KIN INT/TRADE HABITAT...GEOG AUD/VIS CHARTS BIBLIOG 20 SAHARA MIGRATION. PAGE 21 H0417 STRUCT SOCIETY SOC CULTURE

B58
CARTER G.M.,TRANSITION IN AFRICA; STUDIES IN POLITICAL ADAPTATION. AFR CENTRL/AFR GHANA NIGERIA CONSTN LOC/G POL/PAR ADMIN GP/REL FEDERAL...MAJORIT BIBLIOG 20. PAGE 27 H0543 NAT/COMP PWR CONTROL NAT/G

B58
DWARKADAS R.,ROLE OF HIGHER CIVIL SERVICE IN INDIA. INDIA ECO/UNDEV LEGIS PROB/SOLV GP/REL PERS/REL ...POLICY WELF/ST DECISION ORG/CHARTS BIBLIOG 20 CIVIL/SERV INTRVN/ECO. PAGE 44 H0876 ADMIN NAT/G ROLE PLAN

B58
EUSDEN J.D.,PURITANS, LAWYERS, AND POLITICS IN EARLY SEVENTEENTH-CENTURY ENGLAND. UK CT/SYS PARL/PROC RATIONAL PWR SOVEREIGN...IDEA/COMP BIBLIOG 17 PURITAN COMMON/LAW. PAGE 48 H0951 GP/REL SECT NAT/G LAW

B58
GURVITCH G.,TRAITE DE SOCIOLOGIE (2 VOLS.). FRANCE CULTURE INDUS GP/REL INGP/REL...PSY BIBLIOG 20. PAGE 63 H1256 ANTHOL SOC METH/COMP METH/CNCPT

B58
HANCE W.A.,AFRICAN ECONOMIC DEVELOPMENT. AGRI DIST/IND INDUS R+D ACT/RES PLAN CAP/ISM FOR/AID ...GOV/COMP BIBLIOG 20. PAGE 65 H1312 AFR ECO/UNDEV PROB/SOLV TEC/DEV

B58
KURL S.,ESTONIA: A SELECTED BIBLIOGRAPHY. USSR ESTONIA LAW INTELL SECT...ART/METH GEOG HUM SOC 20. PAGE 89 H1784 BIBLIOG CULTURE NAT/G

B58
LAHBABI M.,LE GOUVERNEMENT MAROCAIN A L'AUBE DU XXE SIECLE. FRANCE MOROCCO CHIEF EX/STRUC LEGIS ORD/FREE PWR...JURID BIBLIOG 19/20. PAGE 90 H1797 NAT/G COLONIAL SOVEREIGN

B58
LEPOINTE G.,ELEMENTS DE BIBLIOGRAPHIE SUR L'HISTOIRE DES INSTITUTIONS ET DES FAITS SOCIAUX, 987-1875. FRANCE SOCIETY NAT/G PROVS SECT ...PHIL/SCI 19/20. PAGE 94 H1887 BIBLIOG LAW

B58
MACRO E.,BIBLIOGRAPHY OF THE ARABIAN PENINSULA (PAMPHLET). KUWAIT SAUDI/ARAB YEMEN COLONIAL...GEOG 19/20. PAGE 101 H2012 BIBLIOG ISLAM CULTURE NAT/G

B58
MCIVOR R.C.,CANADIAN MONETARY, BANKING, AND FISCAL DEVELOPMENT. CANADA INDUS LG/CO NAT/G SML/CO CONTROL WAR...GEN/LAWS BIBLIOG 17/20. PAGE 107 H2137 ECO/TAC FINAN ECO/DEV WEALTH

B58
MECRENSKY E.,SCIENTIFIC MANPOWER IN EUROPE. WOR+45 EDU/PROP GOV/REL SKILL...TECHNIC PHIL/SCI INT CHARTS BIBLIOG 20. PAGE 108 H2157 ECO/TAC TEC/DEV METH/COMP NAT/COMP

B58
PAN AMERICAN UNION,REPERTORIO DE PUBLICACIONES PERIODICAS ACTUALES LATINO-AMERICANAS. CULTURE ECO/UNDEV ADMIN LEAD GOV/REL 20 OAS. PAGE 123 H2455 BIBLIOG L/A+17C NAT/G DIPLOM

B58
SHAW S.J.,THE FINANCIAL AND ADMINISTRATIVE ORGANIZATION AND DEVELOPMENT OF OTTOMAN EGYPT 1517-1798. UAR LOC/G FORCES BUDGET INT/TRADE TAX EATING INCOME WEALTH...CHARTS BIBLIOG 16/18 OTTOMAN NAPOLEON/B. PAGE 143 H2853 FINAN ADMIN GOV/REL CULTURE

B58
STRONG C.F.,MODERN POLITICAL CONSTITUTIONS. LAW CHIEF DELIB/GP EX/STRUC LEGIS ADJUD CHOOSE FEDERAL POPULISM...CONCPT BIBLIOG 20 UN. PAGE 150 H2998 CONSTN IDEA/COMP NAT/G

B58
YUAN TUNG-LI,CHINA IN WESTERN LITERATURE. SECT DIPLOM...ART/METH GEOG JURID SOC BIOG CON/ANAL. PAGE 172 H3441 BIBLIOG ASIA CULTURE HUM

C58
BLANCHARD W.,"THAILAND." THAILAND CULTURE AGRI FINAN INDUS FAM LABOR INT/TRADE ATTIT...GEOG HEAL SOC BIBLIOG 20. PAGE 18 H0354 NAT/G DIPLOM ECO/UNDEV S/ASIA

C58
FIFIELD R.H.,"THE DIPLOMACY OF SOUTHEAST ASIA: 1945-1958." INT/ORG NAT/G COLONIAL REGION...CHARTS BIBLIOG 20 UN. PAGE 50 H0996 S/ASIA DIPLOM NAT/LISM

C58
GINSBURG N.,"MALAYA." MALAYSIA PROB/SOLV REGION NAT/LISM KNOWL WEALTH...GEOG SOC CHARTS BIBLIOG 20. PAGE 57 H1133 COM/IND ECO/UNDEV CULTURE NAT/G

C58
GOLAY J.F.,"THE FOUNDING OF THE FEDERAL REPUBLIC OF GERMANY." GERMANY/W CONSTN EX/STRUC DIPLOM ADMIN CHOOSE...DECISION BIBLIOG 20. PAGE 58 H1155 FEDERAL NAT/G PARL/PROC POL/PAR

C58
MORRALL J.B.,"POLITICAL THOUGHT IN MEDIEVAL TIMES." LAW NAT/G SECT DOMIN ATTIT PWR...BIOG HIST/WRIT BIBLIOG. PAGE 113 H2260 CHRIST-17C CONCPT

C58
WILDING N.,"AN ENCYCLOPEDIA OF PARLIAMENT." UK LAW CONSTN CHIEF PROB/SOLV DIPLOM DEBATE WAR INGP/REL PRIVIL...BIBLIOG DICTIONARY 13/20 CMN/WLTH PARLIAMENT. PAGE 168 H3363 PARL/PROC POL/PAR NAT/G ADMIN

B59
BOLTON A.R.,SOVIET MIDDLE EAST STUDIES: AN ANALYSIS AND BIBLIOGRAPHY. ISLAM JORDAN UAR USSR NAT/G SOC. PAGE 18 H0370 BIBLIOG NAT/COMP ECO/UNDEV

B59
BROSE O.J.,CHURCH AND PARLIAMENT: THE RESHAPING OF THE CHURCH OF ENGLAND 1828-1860. UK SOCIETY TEC/DEV ATTIT LAISSEZ...BIBLIOG 19 CHURCH/STA. PAGE 22 H0434 SECT LEGIS GP/REL NAT/G

B59
BUNDESMIN FUR VERTRIEBENE,ZEITTAFEL DER VORGESCHICHTE UND DES ABLAUFS DER VERTREIBUNG SOWIE DER UNTERBRINGUNG UND EINGLIEDERUNG DER (2 VOLS.). GERMANY/E GERMANY/W NAT/G PROVS PROB/SOLV DIPLOM PARL/PROC ATTIT...BIBLIOG SOC/INTEG 20 MIGRATION PARLIAMENT. PAGE 24 H0475 JURID GP/REL INT/LAW

B59
CONOVER H.F.,NIGERIAN OFFICIAL PUBLICATIONS, 1869-1959: A GUIDE. NIGER CONSTN FINAN ACADEM SCHOOL FORCES PRESS ADMIN COLONIAL...HIST/WRIT 19/20. PAGE 33 H0650 BIBLIOG NAT/G CON/ANAL

B59
CORDONA G.D.,INDICE BIBLIOGRAFICO GUATEMALTECO BIBLIOG

1958. GUATEMALA...SOC 20. PAGE 33 H0666 NAT/G LOC/G L/A+17C

B59
CUCCORESE H.J.,HISTORIA DE LA CONVERSION DEL PAPEL MONEDA EN BUENOS AIRES, 1861-1867. LAW LOC/G NAT/G ATTIT...POLICY BIBLIOG 19 ARGEN BUENOS/AIR GOLD/STAND. PAGE 36 H0717 FINAN PLAN LEGIS

B59
HEMMERLE J.,SUDETENDEUTSCHE BIBLIOGRAPHIE 1949-1953. CZECHOSLVK GERMANY SOCIETY STRUCT SECT ...GEOG JURID 20. PAGE 69 H1391 BIBLIOG PROVS GP/REL CULTURE

B59
HONINGMAN J.J.,THE WORLD OF MAN. CHRIST-17C MEDIT-7 PRE/AMER PREHIST CREATE INGP/REL BIO/SOC HABITAT ...PSY SOC BIBLIOG. PAGE 73 H1460 CULTURE METH PERSON STRUCT

B59
LANDAUER C.,EUROPEAN SOCIALISM (2 VOLS.). COM EUR+WWI MOD/EUR INTELL INDUS REV WAR...MAJORIT IDEA/COMP BIBLIOG 19/20 HITLER/A. PAGE 90 H1805 SOCISM NAT/COMP LABOR MARXISM

B59
LEIGHTON A.H.,MY NAME IS LEGION; FOUNDATIONS FOR A THEORY OF MAN IN RELATION TO CULTURE (VOL. I). CULTURE STRANGE ANOMIE...SOC CONCPT METH/CNCPT CHARTS BIBLIOG METH 20 NOVA/SCOT. PAGE 93 H1867 HEALTH PSY SOCIETY HABITAT

B59
LOPEZ M.M.,CATALOGOS DE PUBLICACIONES PERIODICAS MEXICANAS. L/A+17C CULTURE NAT/G DIPLOM 20 MEXIC/AMER. PAGE 98 H1965 BIBLIOG PRESS CON/ANAL

B59
MARTZ J.D.,CENTRAL AMERICA: THE CRISIS AND THE CHALLENGE. L/A+17C POL/PAR CHIEF CHOOSE SOVEREIGN ...BIOG TREND BIBLIOG 20 CENTRAL/AM. PAGE 104 H2071 NAT/G GOV/REL DIPLOM GOV/COMP

B59
MURDOCK G.P.,AFRICA: ITS PEOPLES AND THEIR CULTURE HISTORY. AFR CULTURE AGRI LOC/G INGP/REL HABITAT ...GEOG SOC LING CHARTS BIBLIOG 20 NEGRO EGYPT/ANC. PAGE 115 H2293 SOCIETY ECO/TAC GP/COMP KIN

B59
OVERSTREET G.D.,COMMUNISM IN INDIA. INDIA S/ASIA CONSTN INT/ORG LEAD GP/REL...CHARTS BIBLIOG 20. PAGE 122 H2435 MARXISM NAT/LISM POL/PAR WAR

B59
PANAMERICAN UNION,PUBLICATIONS: PAU AND OFFICIAL RECORDS OF THE OAS, IN ENGLISH, SPANISH, PORTUGUESE, AND FRENCH, 1958-59. NAT/G ATTIT...SOC 20 OAS. PAGE 123 H2456 BIBLIOG L/A+17C INT/LAW DIPLOM

B59
PHADINIS U.,DOCUMENTS ON ASIAN AFFAIRS: A SELECT BIBLIOGRAPHY. ASIA...SOC 20. PAGE 125 H2498 BIBLIOG NAT/G DIPLOM

B59
THOMAS D.H.,GUIDE TO THE DIPLOMATIC ARCHIVES OF WESTERN EUROPE. EUR+WWI ELITES INT/ORG NAT/G BAL/PWR INT/TRADE PEACE. PAGE 154 H3076 BIBLIOG DIPLOM CONFER

B59
WARNER W.L.,THE LIVING AND THE DEAD: A STUDY OF SYMBOLIC LIFE OF AMERICANS. INTELL KIN DEATH ALL/VALS ALL/IDEOS...CONCPT MYTH LING OBS/ENVIR CHARTS BIBLIOG WORSHIP 18/20. PAGE 165 H3311 CULTURE SOC TIME/SEQ IDEA/COMP

B59
WOOD H.B.,NEPAL BIBLIOGRAPHY. NEPAL S/ASIA NAT/G 20. PAGE 170 H3406 BIBLIOG CULTURE

C59
COLLINS I.,"THE GOVERNMENT AND THE NEWSPAPER PRESS IN FRANCE, 1814-1881. FRANCE LAW ADMIN CT/SYS ...CON/ANAL BIBLIOG 19. PAGE 32 H0634 PRESS ORD/FREE NAT/G EDU/PROP

C59
KARPAT K.H.,"TURKEY'S POLITICS: THE TRANSITION TO A MULTI-PARTY SYSTEM." COM TURKEY CULTURE ECO/UNDEV SECT TEC/DEV NAT/LISM ATTIT...SOC CON/ANAL BIBLIOG 20. PAGE 83 H1664 POL/PAR NAT/G

C59
KORNHAUSER W.,"THE POLITICS OF MASS SOCIETY." COM CULTURE ELITES INTELL STRATA POL/PAR ATTIT...SOC CHARTS GEN/LAWS BIBLIOG 20. PAGE 88 H1757 CROWD PLURISM CONSTN SOCIETY

B60
AUSTRUY J.,STRUCTURE ECONOMIQUE ET CIVILISATION: L'EGYPTE ET LE DESTIN ECONOMIQUE DE L'ISLAM. ISLAM UAR CREATE OP/RES ECO/TAC...SOC BIBLIOG 20 MUSLIM. PAGE 9 H0182 ECO/UNDEV CULTURE STRUCT

B60
AYEARST M.,THE BRITISH WEST INDIES: THE SEARCH FOR SELF-GOVERNMENT. FUT WEST/IND LOC/G POL/PAR EX/STRUC LEGIS CHOOSE FEDERAL...NAT/COMP BIBLIOG 17/20. PAGE 9 H0186 CONSTN COLONIAL REPRESENT NAT/G

B60
BEATTIE J.,BUNYORO, AN AFRICAN KINGDOM. UGANDA STRATA INGP/REL PERS/REL...SOC BIBLIOG 19/20. PAGE 13 H0250 CULTURE ELITES SECT KIN

B60
BOZEMAN A.B.,POLITICS AND CULTURE IN INTERNATIONAL HISTORY. WOR-45 STRUCT SECT...SOC TIME/SEQ NAT/COMP BIBLIOG. PAGE 20 H0393 CULTURE DIPLOM GOV/COMP ALL/IDEOS

B60
BRIGGS L.C.,TRIBES OF THE SAHARA. AFR MOROCCO STRATA AGRI GP/REL HEALTH...GEOG SOC MYTH LING BIBLIOG 13/20 ARABS. PAGE 21 H0418 CULTURE HABITAT KIN SELF/OBS

B60
CONOVER H.F.,OFFICIAL PUBLICATIONS OF FRENCH WEST AFRICA, 1946-1958. DAHOMEY IVORY/CST NIGER SENEGAL UPPER/VOLT CONSTN AGRI PRESS...CON/ANAL 20. PAGE 33 H0651 BIBLIOG COLONIAL NAT/G AFR

B60
CONOVER H.F.,OFFICIAL PUBLICATIONS OF SOMALILAND, 1941-1959: A GUIDE. SOMALIA AGRI FINAN INT/ORG SCHOOL INT/TRADE PRESS CONFER COLONIAL PARL/PROC 20 CONGRESS. PAGE 33 H0652 BIBLIOG NAT/G CON/ANAL

B60
DE HERRERA C.D.,LISTA BIBLIOGRAFICA DE LOS TRABAJOS DE GRADUACION Y TESIS PRESENTADOS EN LA UNIVERSIDAD, 1939-1960. PANAMA DIPLOM LEAD...SOC 20. PAGE 38 H0754 BIBLIOG L/A+17C NAT/G ACADEM

B60
EMERSON R.,FROM EMPIRE TO NATION: THE RISE TO SELF-ASSERTION OF ASIAN AND AFRICAN PEOPLES. S/ASIA CULTURE NAT/G SECT DIPLOM ATTIT SOVEREIGN MARXISM ...POLICY BIBLIOG 19/20. PAGE 46 H0919 NAT/LISM COLONIAL AFR ASIA

B60
FEIS H.,BETWEEN WAR AND PEACE: THE POTSDAM CONFERENCE. EUR+WWI NAT/G DELIB/GP PROB/SOLV REPAR WAR CIVMIL/REL...BIBLIOG 20. PAGE 49 H0983 DIPLOM CONFER BAL/PWR

B60
FLORES R.H.,CATALOGO DE TESIS DOCTORALES DE LAS FACULTADES DE LA UNIVERSIDAD DE EL SALVADOR. EL/SALVADR LAW DIPLOM ADMIN LEAD GOV/REL...SOC 19/20. PAGE 52 H1030 BIBLIOG ACADEM L/A+17C NAT/G

B60
HUGHES C.C.,PEOPLE OF COVE AND WOODLOT; COMMUNITIES FROM THE VIEWPOINT OF SOCIAL PSYCHIATRY. CULTURE FAM PROVS HABITAT...PSY QU SAMP/SIZ CHARTS BIBLIOG 20. PAGE 74 H1489 GEOG SOCIETY STRUCT HEALTH

B60
INTERNATIONAL AFRICAN INST,ETHNOGRAPHIC SURVEY OF AFRICA: WESTERN AFRICA: PEOPLES OF THE MIDDLE NIGER REGION, NORTHERN NIGERIA. AFR NIGER CULTURE ECO/UNDEV KIN NEIGH GOV/REL GP/REL ATTIT HEREDITY ...CHARTS BIBLIOG WORSHIP 20. PAGE 78 H1552 STRUCT GEOG HABITAT INGP/REL

B60
JOHNSON H.M.,SOCIOLOGY: A SYSTEMATIC INTRODUCTION. MARKET FAM LABOR POL/PAR CHOOSE DISCRIM MARRIAGE ALL/IDEOS...BIBLIOG T WORSHIP. PAGE 81 H1620 SOC SOCIETY CULTURE GEN/LAWS

B60
KERSELL J.E.,PARLIAMENTARY SUPERVISION OF DELEGATED LEGISLATION. UK EFFICIENCY PWR...POLICY CHARTS BIBLIOG METH 20 PARLIAMENT. PAGE 85 H1699 LEGIS CONTROL NAT/G EX/STRUC

B60
LA PONCE J.A.,THE PROTECTION OF MINORITIES. WOR+45 WOR-45 NAT/G POL/PAR SUFF...INT/LAW CLASSIF GP/COMP GOV/COMP BIBLIOG 17/20 CIVIL/LIB CIV/RIGHTS. PAGE 90 H1793 INGP/REL DOMIN SOCIETY RACE/REL

B60
MC CLELLAN G.S.,INDIA. CHINA/COM INDIA CONSTN ELITES STRATA AGRI POL/PAR FOR/AID ARMS/CONT REV MARXISM...CENSUS BIBLIOG 20 COLD/WAR GANDHI/M NEHRU/J. PAGE 106 H2117 DIPLOM NAT/G SOCIETY ECO/UNDEV

B60
OTTENBERG S.,CULTURES AND SOCIETIES OF AFRICA. AFR KIN TEC/DEV GP/REL MARRIAGE ATTIT HABITAT HEREDITY ...ANTHOL BIBLIOG T WORSHIP 20. PAGE 122 H2433 SOCIETY INGP/REL STRUCT CULTURE

B60
PIERCE R.A.,RUSSIAN CENTRAL ASIA, 1867-1917. ASIA RUSSIA CULTURE AGRI INDUS EDU/PROP REV NAT/LISM ...CHARTS BIBLIOG 19/20 BOLSHEVISM INTERVENT. PAGE 125 H2509 COLONIAL DOMIN ADMIN ECO/UNDEV

B60
ROSKAM K.L.,APARTHEID AND DISCRIMINATION. SOUTH/AFR SOCIETY STRUCT NAT/G POL/PAR GP/REL ISOLAT ...BIBLIOG 20. PAGE 134 H2683 DISCRIM RACE/REL CULTURE POLICY

B60
SAHLINS M.D.,EVOLUTION AND CULTURE. CREATE...MYTH METH/COMP BIBLIOG 20. PAGE 137 H2730 CULTURE NEW/IDEA CONCPT HABITAT

B60
SLOTKIN J.S.,FROM FIELD TO FACTORY; NEW INDUSTRIAL EMPLOYEES. HABITAT...MGT NEW/IDEA NAT/COMP BIBLIOG SOC/INTEG 20. PAGE 145 H2901 INDUS LABOR CULTURE

WORKER

B60
SZTARAY Z.,BIBLIOGRAPHY ON HUNGARY. HUNGARY MOD/EUR CULTURE INDUS SECT DIPLOM REV...ART/METH SOC LING 18/20. PAGE 151 H3029
BIBLIOG NAT/G COM MARXISM

B60
THEOBOLD R.,THE NEW NATIONS OF WEST AFRICA. GHANA NIGERIA CULTURE INT/ORG ECO/TAC FOR/AID COLONIAL RACE/REL POPULISM...ANTHOL BIBLIOG 20 UN. PAGE 153 H3068
AFR SOVEREIGN ECO/UNDEV DIPLOM

B60
ZENKOVSKY S.A.,PAN-TURKISM AND ISLAM IN RUSSIA. ASIA RUSSIA USSR CULTURE POL/PAR DOMIN REV GP/REL MARXISM...LING GP/COMP BIBLIOG 19/20 TURKIC. PAGE 173 H3454
SECT NAT/LISM COM ISLAM

S60
COOK R.C.,"THE WORLD'S GREAT CITIES: EVOLUTION OR DEVOLUTION?" WOR+45 WOR-45 ECO/DEV ECO/UNDEV ACT/RES PROB/SOLV...GEOG TREND CHARTS NAT/COMP BIBLIOG 20. PAGE 33 H0658
MUNIC HABITAT PLAN CENSUS

C60
BOGARDUS E.S.,"THE DEVELOPMENT OF SOCIAL THOUGHT." SOCIETY PERSON KNOWL...EPIST CONCPT BIBLIOG T. PAGE 18 H0365
INTELL CULTURE IDEA/COMP GP/COMP

C60
COX R.H.,"LOCKE ON WAR AND PEACE." UK DIPLOM DOMIN PWR...BIOG IDEA/COMP BIBLIOG 18. PAGE 34 H0689
CONCPT NAT/G PEACE WAR

C60
FITZSIMMONS T.,"USSR: ITS PEOPLE, ITS SOCIETY, ITS CULTURE." USSR FAM SECT DIPLOM EDU/PROP ADMIN RACE/REL ATTIT...POLICY CHARTS BIBLIOG 20. PAGE 51 H1021
CULTURE STRUCT SOCIETY COM

C60
HAZARD J.N.,"SETTLING DISPUTES IN SOVIET SOCIETY: THE FORMATIVE YEARS OF LEGAL INSTITUTIONS." USSR NAT/G PROF/ORG PROB/SOLV CONTROL CT/SYS ROUTINE REV CENTRAL...JURID BIBLIOG 20. PAGE 68 H1372
ADJUD LAW COM POLICY

C60
SMITH T.E.,"ELECTIONS IN DEVELOPING COUNTRIES: A STUDY OF ELECTORAL PROCEDURES USED IN TOPICAL AFRICA, SOUTH-EAST ASIA..." AFR S/ASIA UK ROUTINE GOV/REL RACE/REL...GOV/COMP BIBLIOG 20. PAGE 146 H2918
ECO/UNDEV CHOOSE REPRESENT ADMIN

C60
WRIGGINS W.H.,"CEYLON: DILEMMAS OF A NEW NATION." ASIA CEYLON CONSTN STRUCT POL/PAR SECT FORCES DIPLOM GOV/REL NAT/LISM...CHARTS BIBLIOG 20. PAGE 171 H3417
PROB/SOLV NAT/G ECO/UNDEV

N60
RHODESIA-NYASA NATL ARCHIVES,A SELECT BIBLIOGRAPHY OF RECENT PUBLICATIONS CONCERNING THE FEDERATION OF RHODESIA AND NYASALAND (PAMPHLET). MALAWI RHODESIA LAW CULTURE STRUCT ECO/UNDEV LEGIS...GEOG 20. PAGE 131 H2620
BIBLIOG ADMIN ORD/FREE NAT/G

B61
ACOSTA SAIGNES M.,ESTUDIOS DE ETNOLOGIA ANTIGUA DE VENEZUELA (2ND ED.). PRE/AMER VENEZUELA...ART/METH SOC BIBLIOG INDIAN/AM. PAGE 3 H0061
CULTURE STRUCT GP/REL HABITAT

B61
ALSTON P.L.,STATE EDUCATION AND SOCIAL CHANGE IN THE RUSSIAN EMPIRE 1871-1914 (PAPER). RUSSIA ELITES PROF/ORG EDU/PROP CONTROL PRIVIL AGE/Y...BIBLIOG 19/20. PAGE 6 H0115
SCHOOL SOCIETY NAT/G GP/REL

B61
ANSPRENGER F.,POLITIK IM SCHWARZEN AFRIKA. FRANCE NAT/G DIPLOM REGION REV NAT/LISM...CHARTS BIBLIOG 19/20. PAGE 7 H0141
AFR COLONIAL SOVEREIGN

B61
ASHLEY M.P.,GREAT BRITAIN TO 1688: A MODERN HISTORY. UK NAT/G CHIEF LEAD REV WAR...POLICY BIBLIOG 1/17. PAGE 9 H0174
DOMIN CONSERVE

B61
BALYS J.,LITHUANIA AND LITHUANIANS: A SELECTED BIBLIOGRAPHY. LITHUANIA SOC. PAGE 10 H0206
BIBLIOG POLICY NAT/G COM

B61
BAYITCH S.A.,LATIN AMERICA: A BIBLIOGRAPHICAL GUIDE. LAW CONSTN LEGIS JUDGE ADJUD CT/SYS 20. PAGE 12 H0243
BIBLIOG L/A+17C NAT/G JURID

B61
BLAKE J.,FAMILY STRUCTURE IN JAMAICA. JAMAICA CULTURE SOCIETY ACT/RES CONTROL MARRIAGE AGE ...POLICY SOC BIBLIOG 20. PAGE 18 H0351
FAM SEX STRUCT ATTIT

B61
BROWN D.M.,THE NATIONALIST MOVEMENT. INDIA CULTURE STRATA REV MORAL ORD/FREE...BIBLIOG 20 HINDU. PAGE 22 H0443
NAT/LISM LEAD CHIEF POL/PAR

B61
CASSINELLI C.W.,THE POLITICS OF FREEDOM. FUT UNIV LAW POL/PAR CHOOSE ORD/FREE...POLICY CONCPT MYTH BIBLIOG. PAGE 28 H0555
MAJORIT NAT/G PARL/PROC PARTIC

B61
CHAKRABARTI A.,NEHRU: HIS DEMOCRACY AND INDIA. ASIA INDIA UK CONSTN ECO/UNDEV SECT DIPLOM COLONIAL PEACE WEALTH...BIBLIOG 20 CONGRESS NEHRU/J GANDHI/M. PAGE 28 H0570
ORD/FREE STRATA NAT/G CHIEF

B61
CONOVER H.F.,SERIALS FOR AFRICAN STUDIES. ECO/UNDEV DIPLOM LEAD NAT/LISM ATTIT...SOC 20. PAGE 33 H0653
BIBLIOG AFR NAT/G

B61
DOOB L.W.,COMMUNICATION IN AFRICA: A SEARCH FOR BOUNDARIES. CULTURE SOCIETY EDU/PROP WRITING INGP/REL DRIVE ORD/FREE...ART/METH SOC LING BIBLIOG 20. PAGE 42 H0837
AFR FEEDBACK PERCEPT PERS/REL

B61
GRASES P.,ESTUDIOS BIBLIOGRAFICOS. VENEZUELA...SOC 20. PAGE 60 H1197
BIBLIOG NAT/G DIPLOM L/A+17C

B61
HISTORICAL RESEARCH INSTITUTE,A SHORT BIBLIOGRAPHY OF INDO-MUSLIM HISTORY. INDIA S/ASIA DIPLOM EDU/PROP COLONIAL LEAD NAT/LISM ATTIT...BIOG 19/20. PAGE 71 H1427
BIBLIOG NAT/G SECT POL/PAR

B61
INTL UNION LOCAL AUTHORITIES,METROPOLIS. WOR+45 DIST/IND FINAN GIVE EDU/PROP CRIME COST HEALTH WEALTH 20. PAGE 78 H1563
MUNIC GOV/COMP LOC/G BIBLIOG

B61
LA DOCUMENTATION FRANCAISE,L'AFRIQUE A TRAVERS LES PUBLICATIONS DE LA DOCUMENTATION FRANCAISE; BIBLIOGRAPHIE 1945-1961 (PAMPHLET). FRANCE 20. PAGE 90 H1791
BIBLIOG AFR COLONIAL NAT/G

B61
MARTINEZ RIOS J.,BIBLIOGRAFIA ANTROPOLOGICA Y SOCIOLOGICA DEL ESTADO DE OAXACA. WRITING...LING 12/20 INDIAN/AM MEXIC/AMER. PAGE 103 H2069
BIBLIOG SOC PROVS CULTURE

B61
MIT CENTER INTERNATIONAL STU,OFFICIAL SERIAL PUBLICATIONS RELATING TO ECONOMIC DEVELOPMENT IN AFRICA SOUTH OF THE SAHARA. AFR SOCIETY AGRI FINAN INDUS LG/CO ADMIN 20. PAGE 111 H2228
BIBLIOG ECO/UNDEV ECO/TAC NAT/G

B61
NEWMAN R.P.,RECOGNITION OF COMMUNIST CHINA? A STUDY IN ARGUMENT. CHINA/COM NAT/G PROB/SOLV RATIONAL ...INT/LAW LOG IDEA/COMP BIBLIOG 20. PAGE 117 H2347
MARXISM ATTIT DIPLOM POLICY

B61
NOVE A.,THE SOVIET ECONOMY. USSR ECO/DEV FINAN NAT/G ECO/TAC PRICE ADMIN EFFICIENCY MARXISM ...TREND BIBLIOG 20. PAGE 119 H2378
PLAN PRODUC POLICY

B61
SCHNAPPER B.,LA POLITIQUE ET LE COMMERCE FRANCAIS DANS LE GOLFE DE GUINEE DE 1838 A 1871. FRANCE GUINEA UK SEA EXTR/IND NAT/G DELIB/GP LEGIS ADMIN ORD/FREE...POLICY GEOG CENSUS CHARTS BIBLIOG 19. PAGE 139 H2791
COLONIAL INT/TRADE DOMIN AFR

B61
SOKOL A.E.,SEAPOWER IN THE NUCLEAR AGE. USA+45 USSR DIST/IND FORCES INT/TRADE DETER WAR...POLICY NAT/COMP BIBLIOG COLD/WAR. PAGE 146 H2928
SEA PWR WEAPON NUC/PWR

B61
SSU-YU T.,JAPANESE STUDIES ON JAPAN AND THE FAR EAST: A SHORT BIOGRAPHICAL AND BIBLIOGRAPHICAL INTRODUCTION. ASIA CULTURE ECO/UNDEV NAT/G DIPLOM 20 CHINJAP. PAGE 148 H2962
BIBLIOG SOC

B61
STANLEY C.J.,LATE CH'ING FINANCE: HU KUANG-YUNG AS AN INNOVATOR. ASIA NAT/G FORCES BUDGET TAX WAR GOV/REL COST...POLICY BIOG CHARTS BIBLIOG 19. PAGE 148 H2969
FINAN ECO/TAC CIVMIL/REL ADMIN

B61
STARK H.,SOCIAL AND ECONOMIC FRONTIERS IN LATIN AMERICA (2ND ED.). CUBA FUT CULTURE AGRI INDUS ECO/TAC PRODUC ATTIT MARXISM...NAT/COMP BIBLIOG T 20. PAGE 149 H2971
L/A+17C SOCIETY DIPLOM ECO/UNDEV

B61
UAR MINISTRY OF CULTURE,A BIBLIOGRAPHICAL LIST OF TUNISIA. ISLAM CULTURE NAT/G EDU/PROP COLONIAL ...GEOG 19/20 TUNIS. PAGE 157 H3146
BIBLIOG DIPLOM SECT

B61
YUAN TUNG-LI,A GUIDE TO DOCTORAL DISSERTATIONS BY CHINESE STUDENTS IN AMERICA, 1905-1960. ASIA CULTURE SOCIETY ECO/UNDEV NAT/G PROB/SOLV DIPLOM LEAD ATTIT...HUM SOC STAT 20. PAGE 172 H3442
BIBLIOG ACADEM ACT/RES OP/RES

L61
EZELLPH,"THE HISPANIC AGRICULTURATION OF THE GILA RIVER PIMAS." FAM TEC/DEV PERS/REL ADJUST...GEOG
CULTURE SOC

MYTH CHARTS BIBLIOG WORSHIP 17/20. PAGE 48 H0956 AGRI DRIVE

C61
MOODIE G.C.,"THE GOVERNMENT OF GREAT BRITAIN." UK LAW STRUCT LOC/G POL/PAR DIPLOM RECEIVE ADMIN COLONIAL CHOOSE...BIBLIOG 20 PARLIAMENT. PAGE 112 H2247 NAT/G SOCIETY PARL/PROC GOV/COMP

B62
THREE PRELIMINARY BIBLIOGRAPHIES OF WORKS RELATED TO THE SOCIAL SCIENCES IN LATIN AMERICA. BRAZIL CULTURE SOCIETY NAT/G PLAN PROB/SOLV...PSY 20 MEXIC/AMER. PAGE 2 H0040 BIBLIOG L/A+17C SOC AGRI

B62
BERGER M.,THE ARAB WORLD TODAY. CULTURE FAM INT/ORG NAT/G SECT FORCES ECO/TAC NAT/LISM HABITAT...CHARTS BIBLIOG 20 ARABS. PAGE 15 H0301 ISLAM PERSON STRUCT SOCIETY

B62
BROWN L.C.,LATIN AMERICA, A BIBLIOGRAPHY. EX/STRUC ADMIN LEAD ATTIT...POLICY 20. PAGE 22 H0445 BIBLIOG L/A+17C DIPLOM NAT/G

B62
DAVAR F.C.,IRAN AND INDIA THROUGH THE AGES. INDIA IRAN ELITES SECT CREATE ORD/FREE...LING BIBLIOG. PAGE 37 H0743 NAT/COMP DIPLOM CULTURE

B62
DIAZ J.S.,MANUAL DE BIBLIOGRAFIA DE LA LITERATURA ESPANOLA. PRE/AMER SPAIN ECO/UNDEV DIPLOM LEAD ATTIT...SOC 15/20. PAGE 41 H0820 BIBLIOG L/A+17C NAT/G COLONIAL

B62
FATOUROS A.A.,GOVERNMENT GUARANTEES TO FOREIGN INVESTORS. WOR+45 ECO/UNDEV INDUS WORKER ADJUD ...NAT/COMP BIBLIOG TREATY. PAGE 49 H0975 NAT/G FINAN INT/TRADE ECO/DEV

B62
GANJI M.,INTERNATIONAL PROTECTION OF HUMAN RIGHTS. WOR+45 CONSTN INT/TRADE CT/SYS SANCTION CRIME WAR RACE/REL...CHARTS IDEA/COMP NAT/COMP BIBLIOG 20 TREATY NEGRO LEAGUE/NAT UN CIVIL/LIB. PAGE 55 H1097 ORD/FREE DISCRIM LEGIS DELIB/GP

B62
GREEN L.P.,DEVELOPMENT IN AFRICA. AFR CENTRL/AFR GHANA RHODESIA SOUTH/AFR AGRI PROC/MFG INT/TRADE DEMAND NAT/LISM PRODUC WEALTH...GEOG METH/CNCPT CHARTS BIBLIOG 20. PAGE 60 H1206 CULTURE ECO/UNDEV GOV/REL TREND

B62
GROVE J.W.,GOVERNMENT AND INDUSTRY IN BRITAIN. UK FINAN LOC/G CONSULT DELIB/GP INT/TRADE ADMIN CONTROL...BIBLIOG 20. PAGE 62 H1237 ECO/TAC INDUS NAT/G GP/REL

B62
HAIM S.G.,ARAB NATIONALISM. ISLAM CONSTN GP/REL ...ANTHOL BIBLIOG JEWS 20 MID/EAST ARABS. PAGE 64 H1279 NAT/LISM REV SECT DIPLOM

B62
HANAK H.,GREAT BRITAIN AND AUSTRIA-HUNGARY DURING THE FIRST WORLD WAR: A STUDY IN THE FORMATION OF PUBLIC OPINION. CZECHOSLVK UK NAT/G GIVE DOMIN EDU/PROP CONSERVE...BIBLIOG 20 AUST/HUNG WWI. PAGE 65 H1311 WAR DIPLOM ATTIT PRESS

B62
HENDERSON W.O.,THE GENESIS OF THE COMMON MARKET. EUR+WWI FRANCE MOD/EUR UK SEA COM/IND EXTR/IND COLONIAL DISCRIM...TIME/SEQ CHARTS BIBLIOG 18/20 EEC TREATY. PAGE 70 H1395 ECO/DEV INT/TRADE DIPLOM

B62
HUNKIN P.,ENSEIGNEMENT ET POLITIQUE EN FRANCE ET EN ANGLETERRE. FRANCE UK CONSTN ACADEM SECT CHIEF DELIB/GP PROB/SOLV CONTROL REV ORD/FREE CONSERVE ...BIBLIOG 18/20. PAGE 75 H1496 EDU/PROP LEGIS IDEA/COMP NAT/G

B62
INGHAM K.,A HISTORY OF EAST AFRICA. NAT/G DIPLOM ADMIN WAR NAT/LISM...SOC BIOG BIBLIOG. PAGE 77 H1534 AFR CONSTN COLONIAL

B62
KEESING F.M.,THE ETHNOHISTORY OF NORTHERN LUZON. PHILIPPINE ECO/UNDEV FAM SECT CHIEF REGION GP/REL HABITAT...GEOG LING BIBLIOG WORSHIP 20. PAGE 84 H1680 CULTURE SOC KIN

B62
KENNEDY R.,BIBLIOGRAPHY OF INDONESIAN PEOPLES AND CULTURES (2ND REV. ED.). INDONESIA STRUCT ECO/UNDEV SCHOOL EDU/PROP COLONIAL...GEOG SOC LING NAT/COMP 20. PAGE 85 H1689 BIBLIOG S/ASIA CULTURE KIN

B62
KIDDER F.E.,THESES ON PAN AMERICAN TOPICS. LAW CULTURE NAT/G SECT DIPLOM HEALTH...ART/METH GEOG SOC 13/20. PAGE 86 H1709 BIBLIOG CHRIST-17C L/A+17C SOCIETY

B62
KRECH D.,INDIVIDUAL IN SOCIETY; A TEXTBOOK OF SOCIAL PSYCHOLOGY. UNIV CULTURE LEAD INGP/REL ATTIT DRIVE PERCEPT ROLE...PHIL/SCI BIBLIOG T. PAGE 88 H1765 PSY SOC SOCIETY PERS/REL

B62
MANNING H.T.,THE REVOLT OF FRENCH CANADA 1800-1835. CANADA UK CULTURE GOV/REL RACE/REL...BIBLIOG 19. PAGE 102 H2039 NAT/LISM COLONIAL GEOG

B62
STATE AND LOCAL GOVERNMENT. MUNIC NAT/G NEIGH PRESS CONTROL CHOOSE REPRESENT...BIBLIOG 20. PAGE 104 H2076 PROVS LOC/G GOV/REL PWR

B62
MEGGITT M.J.,DESERT PEOPLE. ECO/UNDEV KIN CREATE PROB/SOLV CONTROL DRIVE ROLE...GEOG SOC MYTH CHARTS BIBLIOG 20 AUSTRAL. PAGE 108 H2159 ADJUST CULTURE INGP/REL HABITAT

B62
MEYER A.G.,LENINISM. USSR STRUCT NAT/G CAP/ISM LEAD WAR PWR SOVEREIGN...BIBLIOG 20 LENIN/VI. PAGE 109 H2187 POL/PAR REV MARXISM PHIL/SCI

B62
MITCHELL B.R.,ABSTRACT OF BRITISH HISTORICAL STATISTICS. UK FINAN NAT/G 12/20. PAGE 111 H2229 BIBLIOG STAT INDEX ECO/DEV

B62
NASRI A.R.,A BIBLIOGRAPHY OF THE SUDAN 1938-1958. AFR SUDAN CREATE...SOC 20. PAGE 116 H2316 BIBLIOG ECO/UNDEV NAT/G SOCIETY

B62
NEW ZEALAND COMM OF ST SERVICE,THE STATE SERVICES IN NEW ZEALAND. NEW/ZEALND CONSULT EX/STRUC ACT/RES ...BIBLIOG 20. PAGE 117 H2343 ADMIN WORKER TEC/DEV NAT/G

B62
PAIKERT G.C.,THE GERMAN EXODUS. EUR+WWI GERMANY/W LAW CULTURE SOCIETY STRUCT INDUS NAT/LISM RESPECT SOVEREIGN...CHARTS BIBLIOG SOC/INTEG 20 MIGRATION. PAGE 122 H2444 INGP/REL STRANGE GEOG GP/REL

B62
PHELPS E.S.,THE GOAL OF ECONOMIC GROWTH: SOURCES, COSTS, BENEFITS. USA+45 USSR FINAN TAX CONTROL DEMAND WEALTH...POLICY NAT/COMP ANTHOL BIBLIOG 20. PAGE 125 H2499 ECO/TAC ECO/DEV NAT/G FUT

B62
STARCKE V.,DENMARK IN WORLD HISTORY. DENMARK AGRI KIN WAR...BIBLIOG T 20. PAGE 149 H2970 GEOG CULTURE SOC

B62
STARR R.E.,POLAND 1944-1962: THE SOVIETIZATION OF A CAPTIVE PEOPLE. COM POLAND USSR POL/PAR SECT LEGIS DIPLOM DOMIN EDU/PROP CHOOSE ORD/FREE...POLICY CHARTS BIBLIOG 20. PAGE 149 H2973 MARXISM NAT/G TOTALISM NAT/COMP

B62
TAYLOR D.,THE BRITISH IN AFRICA. UK CULTURE ECO/UNDEV INDUS DIPLOM INT/TRADE ADMIN WAR RACE/REL ORD/FREE SOVEREIGN...POLICY BIBLIOG 15/20 CMN/WLTH. PAGE 153 H3053 AFR COLONIAL DOMIN

B62
TINKER H.,INDIA AND PAKISTAN. INDIA PAKISTAN NAT/G POL/PAR...OLD/LIB TRADIT TREND CHARTS BIBLIOG 20. PAGE 155 H3102 ORD/FREE STRATA REPRESENT AUTHORIT

B62
UNECA LIBRARY,BOOKS ON AFRICA IN THE UNECA LIBRARY. WOR+45 AGRI INT/ORG NAT/G PLAN WRITING REGION...SOC STAT UN. PAGE 158 H3160 BIBLIOG AFR ECO/UNDEV TEC/DEV

B62
UNECA LIBRARY,NEW ACQUISITIONS IN THE UNECA LIBRARY. LAW NAT/G PLAN PROB/SOLV TEC/DEV ADMIN REGION...GEOG SOC 20 UN. PAGE 158 H3161 BIBLIOG AFR ECO/UNDEV INT/ORG

B62
US LIBRARY OF CONGRESS,A LIST OF AMERICAN DOCTORAL DISSERTATIONS ON AFRICA. SOCIETY SECT DIPLOM EDU/PROP ADMIN...GEOG 19/20. PAGE 161 H3212 BIBLIOG AFR ACADEM CULTURE

B62
VERHAEGEN P.,BIBLIOGRAPHIE DE L'URBANISATION DE L'AFRIQUE NOIRE: SON CADRE, SES CAUSES, ET SES CONSEQUENCES ECONOMIQUES, SOCIALES... AFR...SOC 20. PAGE 162 H3244 BIBLIOG ECO/UNDEV MUNIC CULTURE

B62
VILAKAZI A.,ZULU TRANSFORMATIONS: A STUDY OF THE DYNAMICS OF SOCIAL CHANGE. AFR CULTURE ECO/UNDEV KIN NEIGH SEX...GEOG QU TREND CHARTS BIBLIOG 19/20. PAGE 163 H3254 MARRIAGE SECT SOC EDU/PROP

B62
YU LIEN YEN CHIU,INDEX TO THE CLASSIFIED FILES ON COMMUNIST CHINA. CHINA/COM CULTURE ECO/UNDEV CIVMIL/REL PWR WEALTH MARXISM...PSY SOC METH 20. PAGE 172 H3440 BIBLIOG INDEX COM

L62
"AMERICAN BEHAVIORAL SCIENTIST." USSR LAW NAT/G ...SOC 20 UN. PAGE 2 H0039 BIBLIOG AFR

R+D

B63
ATTIA G.E.D.,LES FORCES ARMEES DES NATIONS UNIES EN COREE ET AU MOYENORIENT. KOREA CONSTN NAT/G DELIB/GP LEGIS PWR...IDEA/COMP NAT/COMP BIBLIOG UN SUEZ. PAGE 9 H0177
FORCES INT/LAW

B63
BADI J.,THE GOVERNMENT OF THE STATE OF ISRAEL: A CRITICAL ACCOUNT OF ITS PARLIAMENT, EXECUTIVE, AND JUDICIARY. ISRAEL ECO/DEV CHIEF DELIB/GP LEGIS DIPLOM CT/SYS INGP/REL PEACE ORD/FREE...BIBLIOG 20 PARLIAMENT ARABS MIGRATION. PAGE 10 H0193
NAT/G CONSTN EX/STRUC POL/PAR

B63
BIALEK R.W.,CATHOLIC POLITICS: A HISTORY BASED ON ECUADOR. ECUADOR SPAIN CULTURE STRUCT CONTROL REV PWR...BIBLIOG WORSHIP 18/20. PAGE 16 H0329
COLONIAL CATHISM GOV/REL HABITAT

B63
BISHOP O.B.,PUBLICATIONS OF THE GOVERNMENT OF THE PROVINCE OF CANADA 1841-1867. CANADA DIPLOM COLONIAL LEAD...POLICY 18. PAGE 17 H0346
BIBLIOG NAT/G ATTIT

B63
BLONDEL J.,VOTERS, PARTIES, AND LEADERS. UK ELITES LOC/G NAT/G PROVS ACT/RES DOMIN REPRESENT GP/REL INGP/REL...SOC BIBLIOG 20. PAGE 18 H0358
POL/PAR STRATA LEGIS ADMIN

B63
BOHANNAN P.,SOCIAL ANTHROPOLOGY. ECO/DEV GP/REL DEMAND MARRIAGE HABITAT...CHARTS GP/COMP BIBLIOG T WORSHIP 20. PAGE 18 H0366
SOC STRUCT FAM CULTURE

B63
CHEN N.-R.,THE ECONOMY OF MAINLAND CHINA, 1949-1963: A BIBLIOGRAPHY OF MATERIALS IN ENGLISH. CHINA/COM ECO/UNDEV PRESS 20. PAGE 29 H0586
BIBLIOG MARXISM NAT/G ASIA

B63
COMISION DE HISTORIO,GUIA DE LOS DOCUMENTOS MICROFOTOGRAFIADOS POR LA UNIDAD MOVIL DE LA UNESCO. SOCIETY ECO/UNDEV INT/ORG ADMIN...SOC 20 UNESCO. PAGE 32 H0637
BIBLIOG NAT/G L/A+17C DIPLOM

B63
ECKSTEIN H.,COMPARATIVE POLITICS. POL/PAR LEGIS CT/SYS CHOOSE TOTALISM PWR POPULISM...METH/COMP GEN/METH ANTHOL BIBLIOG 20. PAGE 44 H0886
NAT/COMP CONSTN REPRESENT NAT/G

B63
ELIAS T.O.,GOVERNMENT AND POLITICS IN AFRICA. CONSTN CULTURE SOCIETY NAT/G POL/PAR DIPLOM REPRESENT PERSON...SOC TREND BIBLIOG 4/20. PAGE 45 H0906
AFR NAT/LISM COLONIAL LAW

B63
ENKE S.,ECONOMICS FOR DEVELOPMENT. AGRI TEC/DEV CAP/ISM DIPLOM ECO/TAC TAX ATTIT DRIVE HABITAT WEALTH...GOV/COMP BIBLIOG 20. PAGE 46 H0928
ECO/UNDEV PHIL/SCI CON/ANAL

B63
FRIED R.C.,THE ITALIAN PREFECTS. ITALY STRATA ECO/DEV NAT/LISM ALL/IDEOS...TREND CHARTS METH/COMP BIBLIOG 17/20 PREFECT. PAGE 53 H1061
ADMIN NAT/G EFFICIENCY

B63
FRIEDRICH C.J.,MAN AND HIS GOVERNMENT: AN EMPIRICAL THEORY OF POLITICS. UNIV LOC/G NAT/G ADJUD REV INGP/REL DISCRIM PWR BIBLIOG. PAGE 53 H1069
PERSON ORD/FREE PARTIC CONTROL

B63
FRITZ H.E.,THE MOVEMENT FOR INDIAN ASSIMILATION, 1860-1890. SECT FORCES GP/REL RACE/REL DISCRIM FEDERAL CATHISM...BIBLIOG 19 INDIAN/AM PROTESTANT GRANT/US. PAGE 54 H1071
CULTURE NAT/G ECO/TAC ATTIT

B63
HOLLANDER P.,THE NEW MAN AND HIS ENEMIES: A STUDY OF THE STALINIST CONCEPTIONS OF GOOD AND EVIL PERSONIFIED (DOCTORAL THESIS). USSR SOCIETY ECO/DEV NAT/G EDU/PROP WRITING...SOC STERTYP BIBLIOG 20 STALIN/J. PAGE 73 H1455
CONTROL ATTIT TOTALISM MARXISM

B63
JUDD P.,AFRICAN INDEPENDENCE: THE EXPLODING EMERGENCE OF THE NEW AFRICAN NATIONS. AFR UK LAW CONSTN CULTURE KIN DIPLOM ATTIT...CHARTS BIBLIOG 20 UN DEGAULLE/C NEGRO THIRD/WRLD. PAGE 82 H1640
ORD/FREE POLICY DOMIN LOC/G

B63
LAMB B.P.,INDIA: A WORLD IN TRANSITION. INDIA ECO/UNDEV SECT EDU/PROP COLONIAL HABITAT ORD/FREE ...GEOG CHARTS BIBLIOG SOC/INTEG 20. PAGE 90 H1799
POL/PAR NAT/G DIPLOM STRATA

B63
LAVROFF D.-G.,LES LIBERTES PUBLIQUES EN UNION SOVIETIQUE (REV. ED.). USSR NAT/G WORKER SANCTION CRIME MARXISM NEW/LIB...JURID BIBLIOG WORSHIP 20. PAGE 92 H1843
ORD/FREE LAW ATTIT COM

B63
LIVINGSTON W.S.,FEDERALISM IN THE COMMONWEALTH - A BIBLIOGRAPHICAL COMMENTARY. CANADA INDIA PAKISTAN UK STRUCT LOC/G NAT/G POL/PAR...NAT/COMP 20 AUSTRAL. PAGE 97 H1943
BIBLIOG JURID FEDERAL CONSTN

B63
MAJUMDAR O.N.,AN INTRODUCTION TO SOCIAL ANTHROPOLOGY. INDIA LAW STRATA ECO/UNDEV KIN DEMAND MARRIAGE...GP/COMP BIBLIOG T WORSHIP 20. PAGE 101 H2026
SOC CULTURE STRUCT GP/REL

B63
MILLER W.J.,THE MEANING OF COMMUNISM. USSR SOCIETY ECO/DEV EX/STRUC WORKER TEC/DEV ADMIN TOTALISM ...POLICY CONCPT CHARTS BIBLIOG T 20 COLD/WAR LENIN/VI STALIN/J. PAGE 111 H2215
MARXISM TRADIT DIPLOM NAT/G

B63
NALBANDIAN L.,THE ARMENIAN REVOLUTIONARY MOVEMENT. MOD/EUR RUSSIA...IDEA/COMP NAT/COMP BIBLIOG 19 ARMENIA OTTOMAN. PAGE 115 H2306
NAT/LISM REV POL/PAR ORD/FREE

B63
O'LEARY T.J.,ETHNOGRAPHIC BIBLIOGRAPHY OF SOUTH AMERICA. SOCIETY KIN...GEOG 19/20 SOUTH/AMER. PAGE 120 H2389
SOC CULTURE L/A+17C BIBLIOG

B63
PADELFORD N.J.,AFRICA AND WORLD ORDER. AFR COLONIAL SOVEREIGN...ANTHOL BIBLIOG 20 UN UNIFICA COMMONWLTH. PAGE 122 H2439
DIPLOM NAT/G ORD/FREE

B63
PEREZ ORTIZ R.,ANUARIO BIBLIOGRAFICO COLOMBIANO, 1961. AGRI...INT/LAW JURID SOC LING 20 COLOMB. PAGE 125 H2491
BIBLIOG L/A+17C NAT/G

B63
RICHARDSON H.G.,THE ADMINISTRATION OF IRELAND 1172-1377. IRELAND CONSTN EX/STRUC LEGIS JUDGE CT/SYS PARL/PROC...CHARTS BIBLIOG 12/14. PAGE 131 H2621
ADMIN NAT/G PWR

B63
SINOR D.,INTRODUCTION A L'ETUDE DE L'EURASIE CENTRALE. ASIA CULTURE KIN. PAGE 144 H2887
BIBLIOG SOC LING

B63
SPRING D.,THE ENGLISH LANDED ESTATE IN THE NINETEENTH CENTURY: ITS ADMINISTRATION. UK ELITES STRUCT AGRI NAT/G GP/REL OWN PWR WEALTH...BIBLIOG 19 HOUSE/LORD. PAGE 148 H2954
STRATA PERS/REL MGT

B63
STIFEL L.D.,THE TEXTILE INDUSTRY - A CASE STUDY OF INDUSTRIAL DEVELOPMENT IN THE PHILIPPINES (PAPER). PHILIPPINE WORKER CAP/ISM INT/TRADE TARIFFS RECEIVE PRICE ADMIN COST EFFICIENCY WEALTH...BIBLIOG 20. PAGE 149 H2986
S/ASIA ECO/UNDEV PROC/MFG NAT/G

B63
STIRNIMANN H.,NGUNI UND GNONI; EINE KULTURGESCHICHTLICHE STUDIE (ACTA ETHNOLOGICA ET LINGUISTICA, NUMBER 6). AFR MALAWI SOUTH/AFR FORCES HABITAT...RECORD CHARTS BIBLIOG WORSHIP 19/20 NATAL. PAGE 149 H2987
CULTURE GP/COMP SOCIETY

B63
STUCKI C.W.,AMERICAN DOCTORAL DISSERTATIONS ON ASIA 1933-62 (A PAPER). PREHIST INDUS NAT/G GOV/REL ALL/IDEOS...ART/METH GEOG SOC LING 20. PAGE 150 H3002
BIBLIOG ASIA SOCIETY S/ASIA

B63
THOMPSON F.M.L.,ENGLISH LANDED SOCIETY IN THE NINETEENTH CENTURY. UK STRUCT MUNIC NAT/G CONTROL WAR GP/REL OWN WEALTH...BIBLIOG 18/20. PAGE 154 H3081
STRATA PWR ELITES GOV/REL

B63
UAR MINISTRY OF CULTURE,A BIBLIOGRAPHICAL LIST OF ARABIAN PENINSULA. ISLAM SAUDI/ARAB YEMEN FINAN NAT/G DIPLOM 19/20. PAGE 157 H3147
BIBLIOG GEOG INDUS SECT

B63
WALKER A.A.,OFFICIAL PUBLICATIONS OF SIERRA LEONE AND GAMBIA. GAMBIA SIER/LEONE UK LAW CONSTN LEGIS PLAN BUDGET DIPLOM...SOC SAMP CON/ANAL 20. PAGE 164 H3290
BIBLIOG NAT/G COLONIAL ADMIN

C63
ATTIA G.E.O.,"LES FORCES ARMEES DES NATIONS UNIES EN COREE ET AU MOYENORIENT." KOREA CONSTN DELIB/GP LEGIS PWR...IDEA/COMP NAT/COMP BIBLIOG UN SUEZ. PAGE 9 H0178
FORCES NAT/G INT/LAW

C63
BECKHAM R.S.,"A BASIC LIST OF BOOKS AND PERIODICALS FOR COLLEGE LIBRARIES." UNIV GP/REL...PSY SOC. PAGE 13 H0255
BIBLIOG SOCIETY CULTURE KNOWL

N63
LIBRARY HUNGARIAN ACADEMY SCI,HUNGARIAN PUBLICATIONS ON ASIA AND AFRICA, 1950-1962: A SELECTED BIBLIOGRAPHY (PAMPHLET). AFR ASIA HUNGARY S/ASIA ECO/UNDEV NAT/G EDU/PROP ATTIT 20 UNESCO. PAGE 96 H1922
BIBLIOG REGION DIPLOM WRITING

B64
AGGARWALA R.C.,CONSTITUTIONAL HISTORY OF INDIA AND NATIONAL MOVEMENT INCLUDING COMPARATIVE STUDY OF MODERN INDIA CONSTITUTION. INDIA S/ASIA SECT VOL/ASSN EX/STRUC LEGIS COERCE REV INGP/REL ORD/FREE...SOC BIBLIOG 18/20 CMN/WLTH. PAGE 4 H0077
CONSTN COLONIAL DOMIN NAT/G

B64
ALDEFER H.F.,A BIBLIOGRAPHY OF AFRICAN GOVERNMENT: 1950-1964. ALGERIA GUINEA LIBERIA UAR ECO/UNDEV POL/PAR LEGIS COLONIAL LEAD PARL/PROC NAT/LISM 20. PAGE 5 H0098
BIBLIOG AFR LOC/G NAT/G

B64
ANDREWS D.H.,LATIN AMERICA: A BIBLIOGRAPHY OF PAPERBACK BOOKS. SECT INT/TRADE EDU/PROP WAR GOV/REL ADJUST NAT/LISM ATTIT...ART/METH LING BIOG 20. PAGE 7 H0138
BIBLIOG L/A+17C CULTURE NAT/G

B64
BAGEHOT W.,THE ENGLISH CONSTITUTION. UK CHIEF CONSULT LEGIS BAL/PWR PWR...BIBLIOG 18/19 PARLIAMENT. PAGE 10 H0198
CONSTN PARL/PROC NAT/G CONCPT

B64
BOSTON UNIVERSITY LIBRARIES,CATALOG OF AFRICAN GOVERNMENT DOCUMENTS AND AFRICAN AREA INDEX. AFR NAT/G...SOC 20. PAGE 19 H0384
BIBLIOG ACADEM

B64
BRIGHT J.R.,RESEARCH, DEVELOPMENT AND TECHNOLOGICAL INNOVATION. CULTURE R+D CREATE PLAN PROB/SOLV AUTOMAT RISK PERSON...DECISION CONCPT PREDICT BIBLIOG. PAGE 21 H0419
TEC/DEV NEW/IDEA INDUS MGT

B64
COONDOO R.,THE DIVISION OF POWERS IN THE INDIAN CONSTITUTION. INDIA ECO/UNDEV FINAN TEC/DEV WAR CENTRAL EFFICIENCY NAT/LISM PWR WEALTH NEW/LIB ...BIBLIOG 18/20. PAGE 33 H0659
CONSTN LEGIS WELF/ST GOV/COMP

B64
CORFO,CHILE, A SELECTED BIBLIOGRAPHY IN ENGLISH (PAMPHLET). CHILE DIPLOM...SOC 20. PAGE 33 H0669
BIBLIOG NAT/G POLICY L/A+17C

B64
COUNT E.W.,FACT AND THEORY IN SOCIAL SCIENCE. UNIV HABITAT...BIOG TREND CHARTS ANTHOL BIBLIOG. PAGE 34 H0679
STRUCT SOC CULTURE ADJUST

B64
COWAN L.G.,THE DILEMMAS OF AFRICAN INDEPENDENCE. AFR INDUS NAT/G SECT DIPLOM ECO/TAC REGION MARXISM ...CHARTS BIBLIOG 20 MAPS. PAGE 34 H0683
ORD/FREE COLONIAL REV ECO/UNDEV

B64
FAINSOD M.,HOW RUSSIA IS RULED (REV. ED.). RUSSIA USSR AGRI PROC/MFG LABOR POL/PAR EX/STRUC CONTROL PWR...POLICY BIBLIOG 19/20 KHRUSH/N COM/PARTY. PAGE 48 H0963
NAT/G REV MARXISM

B64
FLORENCE P.S.,ECONOMICS AND SOCIOLOGY OF INDUSTRY; A REALISTIC ANALYSIS OF DEVELOPMENT. ECO/UNDEV LG/CO NAT/G PLAN...GEOG MGT BIBLIOG 20. PAGE 51 H1029
INDUS SOC ADMIN

B64
FORBES A.H.,CURRENT RESEARCH IN BRITISH STUDIES. UK CONSTN CULTURE POL/PAR SECT DIPLOM ADMIN...JURID BIOG WORSHIP 20. PAGE 52 H1034
BIBLIOG PERSON NAT/G PARL/PROC

B64
GOODNOW H.F.,THE CIVIL SERVICE OF PAKISTAN: BUREAUCRACY IN A NEW NATION. INDIA PAKISTAN S/ASIA ECO/UNDEV PROVS CHIEF PARTIC CHOOSE EFFICIENCY PWR ...BIBLIOG 20. PAGE 59 H1173
ADMIN GOV/REL LAW NAT/G

B64
HALE O.J.,THE CAPTIVE PRESS IN THE THIRD REICH. GERMANY CULTURE LG/CO NAT/G POL/PAR PLAN DOMIN TASK CENTRAL OWN TOTALISM PWR...BIBLIOG 20 HITLER/A NAZI AMMAN/MAX. PAGE 64 H1283
COM/IND PRESS CONTROL FASCISM

B64
HANNA W.J.,POLITICS IN BLACK AFRICA: A SELECTIVE BIBLIOGRAPHY OF RELEVANT PERIODICAL LITERATURE. AFR LAW LOC/G MUNIC NAT/G POL/PAR LOBBY CHOOSE RACE/REL SOVEREIGN 20. PAGE 66 H1315
BIBLIOG NAT/LISM COLONIAL

B64
HARRIS M.,THE NATURE OF CULTURAL THINGS. GP/REL PERS/REL DRIVE HABITAT PERSON ROLE...PHIL/SCI PSY SOC CHARTS BIBLIOG 20. PAGE 67 H1341
CULTURE OBS CLASSIF NEW/IDEA

B64
HERRICK M.D.,CATALOG OF AFRICAN GOVERNMENT DOCUMENTS AND AFRICAN AREA INDEX (2ND REV. ED.) ....SOC INDEX METH 20. PAGE 70 H1405
BIBLIOG ECO/UNDEV AFR NAT/G

B64
IBERO-AMERICAN INSTITUTES,IBEROAMERICANA. STRUCT ADMIN SOC. PAGE 76 H1519
BIBLIOG L/A+17C NAT/G DIPLOM

B64
KAUFMANN R.,MILLENARISME ET ACCULTURATION. SOCIETY DOMIN COLONIAL NAT/LISM ATTIT...SOC BIBLIOG 20 JEHOVA/WIT SEVENTHDAY. PAGE 84 H1669
AFR SECT MYTH CULTURE

B64
KIDD K.E.,BRIEF BIBLIOGRAPHY OF ONTARIO ANTHROPOLOGY (PAMPHLET). CANADA PREHIST HABITAT ...MYTH WORSHIP. PAGE 86 H1708
BIBLIOG SOC LING CULTURE

B64
KIS T.I.,LES PAYS DE L'EUROPE DE L'EST: LEURS RAPPORTS MUTUELS ET LE PROBLEME DE LEUR INTEGRATION DANS L'ORBITE DE L'USSR. EUR+WWI RUSSIA USSR INT/ORG NAT/G REV ATTIT...JURID SOC BIBLIOG WARSAW/P COMECON EUROPE/E. PAGE 86 H1727
DIPLOM COM MARXISM REGION

B64
MARTINEZ J.R.,THREE CASES OF COMMUNISM: CUBA, BRAZIL, AND MEXICO. BRAZIL CUBA L/A+17C CONSTN NAT/G DIPLOM ECO/TAC GP/REL INGP/REL...GP/COMP BIBLIOG 20 MEXIC/AMER COM/PARTY. PAGE 103 H2068
MARXISM BIOG REV NAT/COMP

B64
MORGENTHAU R.S.,POLITICAL PARTIES IN FRENCH-SPEAKING WEST AFRICA. AFR FRANCE GUINEA IVORY/CST MALI SENEGAL CONSTN LEGIS CREATE PLAN LOBBY PARTIC GP/REL...POLICY BIBLIOG 20. PAGE 113 H2257
POL/PAR NAT/G SOVEREIGN COLONIAL

B64
MOUMOUNI A.,L'EDUCATION EN AFRIQUE. UNIV CULTURE ELITES INTELL EDU/PROP ADMIN COLONIAL...LING TREND BIBLIOG 20. PAGE 114 H2271
SCHOOL AFR PROB/SOLV

B64
MUSSO AMBROSI L.A.,BIBLIOGRAFIA DE BIBLIOGRAFIAS URUGUAYAS. URUGUAY DIPLOM ADMIN ATTIT...SOC 20. PAGE 115 H2301
BIBLIOG NAT/G L/A+17C PRESS

B64
NICOL D.,AFRICA - A SUBJECTIVE VIEW. AFR INT/ORG PLAN ADMIN COLONIAL PARL/PROC PARTIC REGION GOV/REL LITERACY ATTIT...BIBLIOG 20 CIVIL/SERV. PAGE 118 H2350
NAT/G LEAD CULTURE ACADEM

B64
O'HEARN P.J.T.,PEACE, ORDER AND GOOD GOVERNMENT; A NEW CONSTITUTION FOR CANADA. CANADA EX/STRUC LEGIS CT/SYS PARL/PROC...BIBLIOG 20. PAGE 120 H2388
NAT/G CONSTN LAW CREATE

B64
ON CULTURE AND SOCIAL CHANGE. FAM NAT/G ACT/RES ECO/TAC RACE/REL...PSY TIME/SEQ TREND IDEA/COMP METH/COMP ANTHOL BIBLIOG 20. PAGE 120 H2406
CULTURE TEC/DEV STRUCT CREATE

B64
PERKINS D.,THE AMERICAN DEMOCRACY: ITS RISE TO POWER. ASIA USSR LAW CULTURE FINAN EDU/PROP COLONIAL CHOOSE...POLICY CHARTS BIBLIOG WORSHIP PRESIDENT 15/20 NEGRO. PAGE 125 H2492
LOC/G ECO/TAC WAR DIPLOM

B64
RIES J.C.,THE MANAGEMENT OF DEFENSE: ORGANIZATION AND CONTROL OF THE US ARMED SERVICES. PROF/ORG DELIB/GP EX/STRUC LEGIS GOV/REL PERS/REL CENTRAL RATIONAL PWR...POLICY TREND GOV/COMP BIBLIOG. PAGE 131 H2626
FORCES ACT/RES DECISION CONTROL

B64
SIEKANOWICZ P.,LEGAL SOURCES AND BIBLIOGRAPHY OF POLAND. COM POLAND CONSTN NAT/G PARL/PROC SANCTION CRIME MARXISM 16/20. PAGE 143 H2870
BIBLIOG ADJUD LAW JURID

B64
TILMAN R.O.,BUREAUCRATIC TRANSITION IN MALAYA. MALAYSIA S/ASIA UK NAT/G EX/STRUC DIPLOM...CHARTS BIBLIOG 20. PAGE 155 H3098
ADMIN COLONIAL SOVEREIGN EFFICIENCY

B64
TURNER M.C.,LIBROS EN VENTA EN HISPANOAMERICA Y ESPANA. SPAIN LAW CONSTN CULTURE ADMIN LEAD...HUM SOC 20. PAGE 157 H3141
BIBLIOG L/A+17C NAT/G DIPLOM

B64
UTECHIN S.V.,RUSSIAN POLITICAL THOUGHT: A CONCISE HISTORY. RUSSIA USSR INTELL STRATA POL/PAR SECT LEGIS EDU/PROP REV WAR MARXISM...ANARCH BIBLIOG 9/20 REFORMERS SLAVS. PAGE 161 H3218
IDEA/COMP ATTIT ALL/IDEOS NAT/G

B64
VON STEIN L.J.,THE HISTORY OF THE SOCIAL MOVEMENT IN FRANCE, 1789-1850 (TRANS. BY K. MENGELBERG). COM FRANCE MOD/EUR NAT/G EX/STRUC INGP/REL ALL/IDEOS CONSERVE MARXISM...SOC BIBLIOG 18/19. PAGE 164 H3278
REV STRATA

B64
WALLBANK T.W.,DOCUMENTS ON MODERN AFRICA. NAT/G COLONIAL GP/REL ATTIT PWR...BIBLIOG 19/20. PAGE 165 H3294
AFR NAT/LISM ECO/UNDEV DIPLOM

B64
WICKENS G.M.,PERSIA IN ISLAMIC TIMES: A PRACTICAL BIBLIOGRAPHY OF ITS HISTORY, CULTURE AND LANGUAGE (PAMPHLET). IRAN ISLAM SECT. PAGE 168 H3355
BIBLIOG CULTURE LING

S64
"FURTHER READING." INDIA ATTIT...POLICY 20 NEHRU/J. PAGE 2 H0042
BIBLIOG S/ASIA CHIEF NAT/G

S64
"FURTHER READING." INDIA PAKISTAN SECT WAR PEACE
BIBLIOG

ATTIT...POLICY 20. PAGE 2 H0044 GP/REL DIPLOM NAT/G

C64
GOLDMAN M.I.,"COMPARATIVE ECONOMIC SYSTEMS: A READER." COM ECO/UNDEV NAT/G BUDGET CAP/ISM ADMIN TOTALISM MARXISM SOCISM...MGT ANTHOL BIBLIOG 19/20. PAGE 58 H1157 NAT/COMP CONTROL IDEA/COMP

C64
HARRIS M.,"THE NATURE OF CULTURAL THINGS." GP/REL DRIVE HABITAT PERSON ROLE...PHIL/SCI 20. PAGE 67 H1340 BIBLIOG CULTURE PSY SOC

C64
SCOTT R.E.,"MEXICAN GOVERNMENT IN TRANSITION (REV ED)" CULTURE STRUCT POL/PAR CHIEF ADMIN LOBBY REV CHOOSE GP/REL DRIVE...BIBLIOG METH 20 MEXIC/AMER. PAGE 141 H2816 NAT/G L/A+17C ROUTINE CONSTN

B65
AIR UNIVERSITY LIBRARY,LATIN AMERICA, SELECTED REFERENCES. ECO/UNDEV FORCES EDU/PROP MARXISM 20 OAS. PAGE 4 H0084 BIBLIOG L/A+17C NAT/G DIPLOM

B65
ALEXANDER R.J.,ORGANIZED LABOR IN LATIN AMERICA. L/A+17C INT/ORG LEGIS WORKER TEC/DEV BARGAIN INT/TRADE REV...NAT/COMP BIBLIOG 20. PAGE 5 H0102 LABOR POL/PAR ECO/UNDEV POLICY

B65
BERNDT R.M.,ABORIGINAL MAN IN AUSTRALIA. LAW DOMIN ADMIN COLONIAL MARRIAGE HABITAT ORD/FREE...LING CHARTS ANTHOL BIBLIOG WORSHIP 20 AUSTRAL ABORIGINES MUSIC ELKIN/AP. PAGE 16 H0312 SOC CULTURE SOCIETY STRUCT

B65
BETTISON D.G.,THE PAPUA-GUINEA ELECTIONS 1964. S/ASIA CONSTN POL/PAR EDU/PROP PARTIC SUFF CENTRAL CONSEN...OBS CHARTS BIBLIOG 20. PAGE 16 H0324 NAT/G LEGIS CHOOSE REPRESENT

B65
BOISSEVAIN J.,SAINTS AND FIREWORKS: RELIGION AND POLITICS IN RURAL MALTA. MALTA STRUCT FAM NEIGH POL/PAR REPRESENT INGP/REL CENTRAL...CHARTS BIBLIOG 20. PAGE 18 H0368 GP/REL NAT/G SECT MUNIC

B65
BORTOLI G.,SOCIOLOGIE DU REFERENDUM DANS LA FRANCE MODERNE. FRANCE CONSTN EDU/PROP SUFF ATTIT ORD/FREE ...POLICY DECISION CHARTS BIBLIOG 20 DEGAULLE/C. PAGE 19 H0379 LEGIS SOCIETY PWR NAT/G

B65
CALLEO D.P.,EUROPE'S FUTURE: THE GRAND ALTERNATIVES. UK INT/ORG DIPLOM PWR SOVEREIGN ...CONCPT IDEA/COMP NAT/COMP BIBLIOG 20 EEC EUROPE DEGAULLE/C NATO. PAGE 25 H0506 FUT EUR+WWI FEDERAL NAT/LISM

B65
CHANDLER M.J.,A GUIDE TO RECORDS IN BARBADOS. WEST/IND PUB/INST SCHOOL SECT...HIST/WRIT 20. PAGE 28 H0573 BIBLIOG LOC/G L/A+17C NAT/G

B65
CHAO K.,THE RATE AND PATTERN OF INDUSTRIAL GROWTH IN COMMUNIST CHINA. CHINA/COM ECO/UNDEV TEC/DEV PRICE...NAT/COMP BIBLIOG 20. PAGE 29 H0578 INDUS INDEX STAT PRODUC

B65
CHENG C.-Y.,SCIENTIFIC AND ENGINEERING MANPOWER IN COMMUNIST CHINA, 1949-1963. CHINA/COM USSR ELITES ECO/DEV R+D ACADEM LABOR NAT/G EDU/PROP CONTROL UTIL...POLICY BIBLIOG 20. PAGE 29 H0588 WORKER CONSULT MARXISM BIOG

B65
COWAN L.G.,EDUCATION AND NATION-BUILDING IN AFRICA. AFR CULTURE ECO/UNDEV POL/PAR ACT/RES LEAD SOVEREIGN...METH/COMP ANTHOL BIBLIOG 20. PAGE 34 H0684 EDU/PROP COLONIAL ACADEM NAT/LISM

B65
EDINGER L.J.,KURT SCHUMACHER: A STUDY IN PERSONALITY AND POLITICAL BEHAVIOR. EUR+WWI GERMANY NAT/G DRIVE ROLE PWR SOCISM...BIBLIOG 20 SOC/DEMPAR SCHUMCHR/K. PAGE 44 H0889 TOP/EX LEAD PERSON BIOG

B65
HARMON R.B.,POLITICAL SCIENCE: A BIBLIOGRAPHICAL GUIDE TO THE LITERATURE. WOR+45 WOR-45 R+D INT/ORG LOC/G NAT/G DIPLOM ADMIN...CONCPT METH. PAGE 67 H1334 BIBLIOG POL/PAR LAW GOV/COMP

B65
HISPANIC SOCIETY OF AMERICA,CATALOGUE (10 VOLS.). PORTUGAL PRE/AMER SPAIN NAT/G ADMIN...POLICY SOC 15/20. PAGE 71 H1426 BIBLIOG L/A+17C COLONIAL DIPLOM

B65
LANDE C.H.,LEADERS, FACTIONS, AND PARTIES. PHILIPPINE CONSTN LOC/G NAT/G PARTIC...CHARTS BIBLIOG 20. PAGE 90 H1806 LEAD POL/PAR POLICY

B65
LAWRENCE P.,GODS, GHOSTS, AND MEN IN MELANESIA: SOME RELIGIONS OF AUSTRALIAN NEW GUINEA AND THE NEW HEBRIDES. SOCIETY ECO/UNDEV FAM GP/REL INGP/REL MYTH S/ASIA SECT

HABITAT PERSON...GEOG SOC ANTHOL BIBLIOG WORSHIP 20 NEW/GUINEA. PAGE 92 H1847 CULTURE

B65
MEHROTRA S.R.,INDIA AND THE COMMONWEALTH 1885-1929. INDIA UK INT/ORG VOL/ASSN GP/REL ATTIT...POLICY BIBLIOG 19/20 CMN/WLTH. PAGE 108 H2163 DIPLOM NAT/G POL/PAR NAT/LISM

B65
NATIONAL BOOK CENTRE PAKISTAN,BOOKS ON PAKISTAN: A BIBLIOGRAPHY. PAKISTAN CULTURE DIPLOM ADMIN ATTIT ...MAJORIT SOC CONCPT 20. PAGE 116 H2319 BIBLIOG CONSTN S/ASIA NAT/G

B65
NYE J.S. JR.,PAN-AFRICANISM AND EAST AFRICAN INTEGRATION. TANZANIA UGANDA STRUCT ECO/UNDEV NAT/G DIPLOM FEDERAL NAT/LISM...STAT SOC/EXP BIBLIOG EEC OAU. PAGE 119 H2382 REGION ATTIT GEN/LAWS AFR

B65
O'CONNELL M.R.,IRISH POLITICS AND SOCIAL CONFLICT IN THE AGE OF THE AMERICAN REVOLUTION. FRANCE IRELAND MOD/EUR STRATA SECT LEGIS DIPLOM INT/TRADE DOMIN REV WAR...BIBLIOG 18 PARLIAMENT. PAGE 119 H2387 CATHISM ATTIT NAT/G DELIB/GP

B65
ONUOHA B.,THE ELEMENTS OF AFRICAN SOCIALISM. AFR FINAN SECT TEC/DEV FOR/AID GP/REL OWN LAISSEZ MARXISM...CONCPT BIBLIOG 20. PAGE 121 H2419 SOCISM ECO/UNDEV NAT/G EX/STRUC

B65
RODRIGUEZ M.,CENTRAL AMERICA. COSTA/RICA GUATEMALA L/A+17C NICARAGUA DIPLOM COLONIAL REGION NAT/LISM ALL/IDEOS SOCISM...MAJORIT TIME/SEQ BIBLIOG 19/20. PAGE 133 H2656 CULTURE NAT/COMP NAT/G ECO/UNDEV

B65
ROTBERG R.I.,A POLITICAL HISTORY OF TROPICAL AFRICA. EX/STRUC DIPLOM INT/TRADE DOMIN ADMIN RACE/REL NAT/LISM PWR SOVEREIGN...GEOG TIME/SEQ BIBLIOG 1/20. PAGE 135 H2692 AFR CULTURE COLONIAL

B65
ROWAT D.C.,THE OMBUDSMAN: CITIZEN'S DEFENDER. DENMARK FINLAND NEW/ZEALND NORWAY SWEDEN CONSULT PROB/SOLV FEEDBACK PARTIC GP/REL...SOC CONCPT NEW/IDEA METH/COMP ANTHOL BIBLIOG 20. PAGE 135 H2701 INSPECT CONSTN NAT/G ADMIN

B65
SCHULER E.A.,THE PAKISTAN ACADEMIES FOR RURAL DEVELOPMENT COMILLA AND PESHAWAR 1959-1964. PAKISTAN S/ASIA SOCIETY STRUCT AGRI NAT/G TEC/DEV EDU/PROP 20. PAGE 140 H2801 BIBLIOG PLAN ECO/TAC ECO/UNDEV

B65
SHEPHERD W.G.,ECONOMIC PERFORMANCE UNDER PUBLIC OWNERSHIP: BRITISH FUEL AND POWER. UK BUDGET GP/REL ...METH/CNCPT CHARTS BIBLIOG 20. PAGE 143 H2858 PROC/MFG NAT/G OWN FINAN

B65
STERN F.,THE POLITICS OF CULTURAL DESPAIR. EUR+WWI GERMANY POL/PAR SECT RACE/REL STRANGE TOTALISM ...ART/METH MYTH BIBLIOG 20 JEWS. PAGE 149 H2980 CULTURE ATTIT NAT/LISM FASCISM

B65
TILLY C.,MEASURING POLITICAL UPHEAVAL* RESEARCH MONOGRAPH NO. 19. FRANCE INDUS NAT/G FORCES WORKER ...GEOG RECORD EXHIBIT GEN/METH BIBLIOG INDEX. PAGE 155 H3095 CLASSIF QUANT COERCE REV

B65
ULLMANN W.,A HISTORY OF POLITICAL THOUGHT: THE MIDDLE AGES. CHRIST-17C LOC/G NAT/G CENTRAL PWR ...PHIL/SCI LOG BIBLIOG 6/15. PAGE 158 H3153 IDEA/COMP SOVEREIGN SECT LAW

B65
VAN DEN BERGHE P.L.,AFRICA: SOCIAL PROBLEMS OF CHANGE AND CONFLICT. ELITES STRATA ECO/UNDEV KIN MUNIC DIPLOM GP/REL RACE/REL NAT/LISM...ANTHOL BIBLIOG 20. PAGE 161 H3228 SOC CULTURE AFR STRUCT

B65
VON RENESSE E.A.,UNVOLLENDETE DEMOKRATIEN. AFR ISLAM S/ASIA SOCIETY ACT/RES COLONIAL...JURID CHARTS BIBLIOG METH 13/20. PAGE 164 H3276 ECO/UNDEV NAT/COMP SOVEREIGN

B65
VON STACKELBERG K.,ALLE KRETER LUGEN VORURTEILE UBER MENSCHEN UND VOLKER. DIPLOM DOMIN RUMOR NAT/LISM PERSON KNOWL...SOC QU BIBLIOG 20. PAGE 164 H3277 NAT/COMP ATTIT EDU/PROP SAMP

B65
WAINWRIGHT M.D.,A GUIDE TO WESTERN MANUSCRIPTS AND DOCUMENTS IN THE BRITISH ISLES RELATING TO SOUTH AND SOUTHEAST ASIA. UK CULTURE...SOC 15/20. PAGE 164 H3288 BIBLIOG S/ASIA WRITING

B65
WALKER A.A.,THE RHODESIAS AND NYASALAND: A GUIDE TO OFFICIAL PUBLICATIONS. RHODESIA UK OP/RES PLAN PROB/SOLV DIPLOM...POLICY SOC CON/ANAL 19/20 NYASALAND. PAGE 164 H3291 BIBLIOG NAT/G COLONIAL AFR

B65
WUORINEN J.H.,SCANDINAVIA. DENMARK FINLAND ICELAND NORWAY SWEDEN SOCIETY AGRI INDUS DELIB/GP DIPLOM NAT/G POL/PAR

INT/TRADE NEUTRAL...GEOG CHARTS BIBLIOG TREATY. PAGE 171 H3428 — TREND POLICY

L65
MATTHEWS D.G.,"A CURRENT BIBLIOGRAPHY ON SUDANESE AFFAIRS; A SELECT BIBLIOGRAPHY FROM 1960-1964." SUDAN LAW CULTURE AGRI FINAN INDUS LABOR POL/PAR TEC/DEV FOR/AID RACE/REL LITERACY...LING 20. PAGE 105 H2094 — BIBLIOG ECO/UNDEV NAT/G DIPLOM

S65
"FURTHER READING." INDIA NAT/G ADMIN 20. PAGE 2 H0045 — BIBLIOG EDU/PROP SCHOOL ACADEM

S65
"FURTHER READING." INDIA ADMIN COLONIAL WAR GOV/REL ATTIT 20. PAGE 2 H0046 — BIBLIOG DIPLOM NAT/G POLICY

S65
GANGAL S.C.,"SURVEY OF RECENT RESEARCH: INDIA AND THE COMMONWEALTH" INDIA UK NAT/G INT/TRADE PARTIC GOV/REL ROLE 20 CMN/WLTH. PAGE 55 H1095 — BIBLIOG POLICY REGION DIPLOM

S65
PRABHAKAR P.,"SURVEY OF RESEARCH AND SOURCE MATERIALS; THE SINO-INDIAN BORDER DISPUTE." CHINA/COM INDIA LAW NAT/G PLAN BAL/PWR WAR...POLICY 20 COLD/WAR. PAGE 128 H2553 — BIBLIOG ASIA S/ASIA DIPLOM

C65
BORTOLI G.,"SOCIOLOGIE DU REFERENDUM DANS LA FRANCE MODERNE." FRANCE CONSTN NAT/G EDU/PROP SUFF ATTIT ORD/FREE...POLICY DECISION SOC CHARTS 20. PAGE 19 H0378 — BIBLIOG LEGIS SOCIETY PWR

C65
NEUMANN S.,"PERMANENT REVOLUTION: TOTALITARIANISM IN THE AGE OF INTERNA TIONAL CIVIL WAR (2ND ED.)" EUR+WWI ELITES POL/PAR DOMIN EDU/PROP LEAD CROWD REPRESENT...MAJORIT GOV/COMP BIBLIOG 20. PAGE 117 H2340 — TOTALISM REV FASCISM STRUCT

C65
STERN F.,"THE POLITICS OF CULTURAL DESPAIR." NAT/LISM...IDEA/COMP BIBLIOG 19/20. PAGE 149 H2979 — CULTURE PHIL/SCI CONSERVE TOTALISM

C65
WUORINEN J.H.,"SCANDINAVIA." DENMARK FINLAND ICELAND NORWAY SWEDEN SOCIETY AGRI POL/PAR DELIB/GP DIPLOM INT/TRADE NEUTRAL WAR...CHARTS TREATY 20. PAGE 171 H3427 — BIBLIOG NAT/G POLICY

B66
ADAMS J.C.,THE GOVERNMENT OF REPUBLICAN ITALY (2ND ED.). ITALY LOC/G POL/PAR DELIB/GP LEGIS WORKER ADMIN CT/SYS FASCISM...CHARTS BIBLIOG 20 PARLIAMENT. PAGE 3 H0064 — NAT/G CHOOSE EX/STRUC CONSTN

B66
AIYAR S.P.,PERSPECTIVES ON THE WELFARE STATE. INDIA S/ASIA UK CONSTN ECO/UNDEV NAT/G INGP/REL CENTRAL NAT/LISM ATTIT...CONCPT ANTHOL BIBLIOG 20. PAGE 4 H0087 — NEW/LIB WELF/ST IDEA/COMP ADJUST

B66
ASHRAF A.,THE CITY GOVERNMENT OF CALCUTTA: A STUDY OF INERTIA. INDIA ELITES INDUS NAT/G EX/STRUC ACT/RES PLAN PROB/SOLV LEAD HABITAT...BIBLIOG 20 CALCUTTA. PAGE 9 H0175 — LOC/G MUNIC ADMIN ECO/UNDEV

B66
BERELSON B.,READER IN PUBLIC OPINION AND COMMUNICATION (2ND ED.). UNIV NAT/G PRESS GP/REL PERS/REL PERCEPT RIGID/FLEX...MAJORIT QUANT METH/COMP ANTHOL BIBLIOG 20. PAGE 15 H0298 — EDU/PROP ATTIT CONCPT COM/IND

B66
BIRMINGHAM W.,A STUDY OF CONTEMPORARY GHANA VOL I: THE ECONOMY OF GHANA. AFR GHANA PLAN...POLICY STAT CHARTS ANTHOL BIBLIOG 20. PAGE 17 H0342 — ECO/UNDEV ECO/TAC NAT/G PRODUC

B66
BRODERSEN A.,THE SOVIET WORKER: LABOR AND GOVERNMENT IN SOVIET SOCIETY. USSR STRUCT INDUS LABOR PLAN PAY INGP/REL PRODUC...POLICY GEN/LAWS BIBLIOG 20 STALIN/J LENIN/VI BOLSHEVISM KHRUSH/N. PAGE 21 H0425 — WORKER ROLE NAT/G MARXISM

B66
BROWN J.F.,THE NEW EASTERN EUROPE. ALBANIA BULGARIA HUNGARY POLAND ROMANIA CULTURE AGRI POL/PAR WAR NAT/LISM MARXISM...CHARTS BIBLIOG 20. PAGE 22 H0444 — DIPLOM COM NAT/G ECO/UNDEV

B66
BROWN L.C.,STATE AND SOCIETY IN INDEPENDENT NORTH AFRICA. ALGERIA LIBYA MOROCCO AGRI INDUS INT/ORG POL/PAR SECT PLAN DIPLOM COLONIAL...LING NAT/COMP ANTHOL BIBLIOG 20 TUNIS MUSLIM. PAGE 22 H0446 — NAT/G SOCIETY CULTURE ECO/UNDEV

B66
CANNING HOUSE LIBRARY,AUTHOR AND SUBJECT CATALOGUES OF THE CANNING HOUSE LIBRARY (5 VOLS.). UK CULTURE LEAD...SOC 19/20. PAGE 26 H0520 — BIBLIOG L/A+17C NAT/G DIPLOM

B66
CAPELL A.,STUDIES IN SOCIO-LINGUISTICS. CULTURE ADJUST...CLASSIF IDEA/COMP SOC/EXP BIBLIOG 20. PAGE 26 H0525 — LING SOC PHIL/SCI CORREL

B66
CAUTE D.,THE LEFT IN EUROPE SINCE 1789. EUR+WWI MOD/EUR NAT/G POL/PAR REV...TIME/SEQ GEN/LAWS BIBLIOG 18/20. PAGE 28 H0564 — ALL/IDEOS ORD/FREE CONCPT STRATA

B66
CHAPMAN B.,THE PROFESSION OF GOVERNMENT: THE PUBLIC SERVICE IN EUROPE. CONSTN NAT/G POL/PAR EX/STRUC LEGIS TOP/EX PROB/SOLV DEBATE EXEC PARL/PROC PARTIC 20. PAGE 29 H0581 — BIBLIOG ADMIN EUR+WWI GOV/COMP

B66
CROWDER M.,A SHORT HISTORY OF NIGERIA. AFR NIGERIA UK ECO/UNDEV CHIEF INT/TRADE RACE/REL NAT/LISM ORD/FREE...GEOG SOC CHARTS BIBLIOG 14/20. PAGE 36 H0711 — COLONIAL NAT/G CULTURE

B66
DE VORE B.B.,LAND AND LIBERTY; A HISTORY OF THE MEXICAN REVOLUTION. CONSTN INTELL NAT/G CONTROL LEAD CHOOSE TOTALISM AUTHORIT...BIBLIOG 19/20 MEXIC/AMER DIAZ/P LIB/PARTY MAGON/F MADERO/F. PAGE 39 H0776 — REV CHIEF POL/PAR

B66
EPSTEIN F.T.,THE AMERICAN BIBLIOGRAPHY OF RUSSIAN AND EAST EUROPEAN STUDIES FOR 1964. USSR LOC/G NAT/G POL/PAR FORCES ADMIN ARMS/CONT...JURID CONCPT 20 UN. PAGE 47 H0933 — BIBLIOG COM MARXISM DIPLOM

B66
FARWELL G.,MASK OF ASIA: THE PHILIPPINES. PHILIPPINE SECT DIPLOM ATTIT...SOC RECORD PREDICT BIBLIOG 20. PAGE 49 H0974 — S/ASIA CULTURE

B66
GRAHAM I.C.C.,PUBLICATIONS OF THE SOCIAL SCIENCE DEPARTMENT, THE RAND CORPORATION, 1948-1966. USSR WOR+45 NAT/G ARMS/CONT DETER WAR NAT/LISM...SOC GOV/COMP. PAGE 60 H1192 — BIBLIOG DIPLOM NUC/PWR FORCES

B66
HARMON R.B.,SOURCES AND PROBLEMS OF BIBLIOGRAPHY IN POLITICAL SCIENCE (PAMPHLET). INT/ORG LOC/G MUNIC POL/PAR ADMIN GOV/REL ALL/IDEOS...JURID MGT CONCPT 19/20. PAGE 67 H1335 — BIBLIOG DIPLOM INT/LAW NAT/G

B66
HOLT R.T.,THE POLITICAL BASIS OF ECONOMIC DEVELOPMENT. STRATA STRUCT NAT/G DIPLOM ADMIN...SOC NAT/COMP BIBLIOG 20. PAGE 73 H1458 — ECO/TAC GOV/COMP CONSTN EX/STRUC

B66
HOWE R.W.,BLACK AFRICA: FROM PRE-HISTORY TO THE EVE OF THE COLONIAL ERA. ECO/UNDEV KIN PROVS SECT INT/TRADE EDU/PROP COLONIAL...BIBLIOG WORSHIP. PAGE 74 H1482 — AFR CULTURE SOC

B66
IBRAHIM-HILMY,THE LITERATURE OF EGYPT AND THE SOUDAN: FROM THE EARLIEST TIMES TO THE YEAR 1885 INCLUSIVE (2 VOLS.). MEDIT-7 SUDAN UAR LAW SOCIETY SECT ATTIT EGYPT/ANC. PAGE 76 H1520 — BIBLIOG CULTURE ISLAM NAT/G

B66
INDIA PUBLICATIONS BRANCH,CATALOGUE OF GOVERNMENT OF INDIA CIVIL PUBLICATIONS. INDIA...INDEX 20. PAGE 76 H1529 — BIBLIOG NAT/G WRITING

B66
KERR M.H.,ISLAMIC REFORM: THE POLITICAL AND LEGAL THEORIES OF MUHAMMAD 'ABDUH AND RASHID RIDA. NAT/G SECT LEAD SOVEREIGN CONSERVE...JURID BIBLIOG WORSHIP 20. PAGE 85 H1698 — LAW CONCPT ISLAM

B66
KIRKLAND E.C.,A BIBLIOGRAPHY OF SOUTH ASIAN FOLKLORE. WRITING HABITAT ALL/VALS MYSTISM ...ART/METH GEOG PSY SOC MYTH WORSHIP 13/20. PAGE 86 H1723 — BIBLIOG S/ASIA CULTURE CREATE

B66
KOMIYA R.,POSTWAR ECONOMIC GROWTH IN JAPAN. ELITES NAT/G EX/STRUC TEC/DEV BUDGET DIPLOM CONTROL BAL/PAY PRODUC...BIBLIOG 20 CHINJAP. PAGE 88 H1754 — ECO/DEV POLICY PLAN ADJUST

B66
LEIGH M.B.,CHECK LIST OF HOLDINGS ON BORNEO IN THE CORNELL UNIVERSITY LIBRARIES (PAMPHLET). BORNEO MALAYSIA LAW CONSTN GP/REL SOC. PAGE 93 H1866 — BIBLIOG S/ASIA DIPLOM NAT/G

B66
LEROY P.,L'ORGANIZATION CONSTITUTIONNELLE ET LES CRISES. FRANCE NAT/G ADJUD CONTROL PARL/PROC WAR ...POLICY BIBLIOG 20. PAGE 95 H1892 — CONSTN PWR EXEC LEGIS

B66
MERRITT R.L.,COMPARING NATIONS* THE USE OF QUANTITATIVE DATA IN CROSSNATIONAL RESEARCH. ACADEM DIPLOM GP/REL...PHIL/SCI STAT TREND GP/COMP PERS/COMP GEN/METH ANTHOL BIBLIOG INDEX. PAGE 109 H2184 — NAT/COMP MATH COMPUT/IR QUANT

B66
MULLER C.F.J.,A SELECT BIBLIOGRAPHY OF SOUTH AFRICAN HISTORY; A GUIDE FOR HISTORICAL RESEARCH. SOUTH/AFR UK LAW CONSTN SOCIETY STRUCT AGRI SECT DIPLOM COLONIAL LEAD RACE/REL...POLICY 17/20 NEGRO. PAGE 114 H2284
BIBLIOG AFR NAT/G

B66
NEUMANN R.G.,THE GOVERNMENT OF THE GERMAN FEDERAL REPUBLIC. EUR+WWI GERMANY/W LOC/G EX/STRUC LEGIS CT/SYS INGP/REL PWR...BIBLIOG 20 ADENAUER/K. PAGE 117 H2336
NAT/G POL/PAR DIPLOM CONSTN

B66
O'NEILL C.E.,CHURCH AND STATE IN FRENCH COLONIAL LOUISIANA: POLICY AND POLITICS TO 1732. PROVS VOL/ASSN DELIB/GP ADJUD ADMIN GP/REL ATTIT DRIVE ...POLICY BIBLIOG 17/18 LOUISIANA CHURCH/STA. PAGE 120 H2390
COLONIAL NAT/G SECT PWR

B66
O'NEILL R.J.,THE GERMAN ARMY AND THE NAZI PARTY, 1933-1939. GERMANY ELITES NAT/G EDU/PROP CONTROL LEAD COERCE WAR...POLICY INT TIME/SEQ BIBLIOG 20 HITLER/A NAZI. PAGE 120 H2391
CIVMIL/REL FORCES FASCISM POL/PAR

B66
RAY A.,INTER-GOVERNMENTAL RELATIONS IN INDIA: A STUDY OF INDIAN FEDERALISM. CANADA INDIA SWITZERLND USA+45 USSR ADMIN GOV/REL...NAT/COMP BIBLIOG. PAGE 130 H2599
CONSTN FEDERAL SOVEREIGN NAT/G

B66
RISTIC D.N.,YUGOSLAVIA'S REVOLUTION OF 1941. EUR+WWI YUGOSLAVIA NAT/G WAR ORD/FREE...RECORD BIBLIOG 20 HITLER/A TREATY. PAGE 132 H2633
REV ATTIT FASCISM DIPLOM

B66
ROGGER H.,THE EUROPEAN RIGHT. EUR+WWI CONSERVE ...ANTHOL BIBLIOG 20. PAGE 133 H2660
NAT/COMP POL/PAR IDEA/COMP TRADIT

B66
ROOS H.,A HISTORY OF MODERN POLAND FROM THE FOUNDATION OF THE STATE IN THE FIRST WORLD WAR TO THE PRESENT DAY. EUR+WWI POLAND INTELL SOCIETY ECO/TAC LEAD REV ATTIT ORD/FREE MARXISM...BIBLIOG 20 WWI PARTITION. PAGE 133 H2669
NAT/G WAR DIPLOM

B66
ROSS A.M.,INDUSTRIAL RELATIONS AND ECONOMIC DEVELOPMENT. POL/PAR LEGIS WORKER BARGAIN PRICE EXEC LOBBY INCOME PWR...DECISION ANTHOL BIBLIOG 20. PAGE 134 H2686
ECO/UNDEV LABOR NAT/G GP/REL

B66
SKILLING H.G.,THE GOVERNMENTS OF COMMUNIST EAST EUROPE. COM EUR+WWI ELITES FORCES DIPLOM ECO/TAC CONTROL HABITAT SOCISM...DECISION BIBLIOG 20 EUROPE/E COM/PARTY. PAGE 145 H2895
MARXISM NAT/COMP GP/COMP DOMIN

B66
SMITH H.E.,READINGS IN ECONOMIC DEVELOPMENT AND ADMINISTRATION IN TANZANIA. TANZANIA FINAN INDUS LABOR NAT/G PLAN PROB/SOLV INT/TRADE COLONIAL REGION...ANTHOL BIBLIOG 20 AFRICA/E. PAGE 146 H2910
TEC/DEV ADMIN GOV/REL

B66
SYMONDS R.,THE BRITISH AND THEIR SUCCESSORS. AFR CEYLON INDIA UK SCHOOL FORCES EDU/PROP ADMIN PARTIC ...NAT/COMP BIBLIOG 20 AFRICA/W AFRICA/E. PAGE 151 H3024
NAT/G ECO/UNDEV POLICY COLONIAL

B66
TYSON G.,NEHRU: THE YEARS OF POWER. INDIA UK STRATA ECO/UNDEV FINAN SECT TASK WAR ORD/FREE MARXISM ...POLICY BIBLIOG 20 NEHRU/J. PAGE 157 H3145
CHIEF PWR DIPLOM NAT/G

B66
US LIBRARY OF CONGRESS,NIGERIA: A GUIDE TO OFFICIAL PUBLICATIONS. CAMEROON NIGERIA UK DIPLOM...POLICY 19/20 UN LEAGUE/NAT. PAGE 161 H3215
BIBLIOG ADMIN NAT/G COLONIAL

B66
ZEINE Z.N.,THE EMERGENCE OF ARAB NATIONALISM (REV. ED.). TURKEY UK NAT/G SECT TEC/DEV LEAD REV WAR AGE/Y ROLE ORD/FREE...TRADIT CHARTS BIBLIOG 20 ARABS OTTOMAN. PAGE 173 H3453
ISLAM NAT/LISM DIPLOM

L66
SEYLER W.C.,"DOCTORAL DISSERTATIONS IN POLITICAL SCIENCE IN UNIVERSITIES OF THE UNITED STATES AND CANADA." INT/ORG LOC/G ADMIN...INT/LAW MGT GOV/COMP. PAGE 142 H2836
BIBLIOG LAW NAT/G

L66
"FEDERAL, STATE AND LOCAL GOVERNMENT PUBLICATIONS." ACADEM LOC/G NAT/G PROVS SCHOOL EFFICIENCY ...PHIL/SCI ANTHOL. PAGE 143 H2854
BIBLIOG OP/RES METH

S66
"RESEARCH WORK 1965-1966." NEW/ZEALND ELITES ACADEM LOC/G MUNIC POL/PAR PROVS DIPLOM COLONIAL...SOC 20 AUSTRAL. PAGE 2 H0047
BIBLIOG NAT/G CULTURE S/ASIA

S66
"FURTHER READING." INDIA LEAD ATTIT...CONCPT 20. PAGE 2 H0048
BIBLIOG NAT/G DIPLOM POLICY

S66
"FURTHER READING." INDIA LOC/G NAT/G PLAN ADMIN WEALTH...GEOG SOC CONCPT CENSUS 20. PAGE 2 H0049
BIBLIOG ECO/UNDEV TEC/DEV PROVS

S66
MATTHEWS D.G.,"ETHIOPIAN OUTLINE: A BIBLIOGRAPHIC RESEARCH GUIDE." ETHIOPIA LAW STRUCT ECO/UNDEV AGRI LABOR SECT CHIEF DELIB/GP EX/STRUC ADMIN...LING ORG/CHARTS 20. PAGE 105 H2095
BIBLIOG NAT/G DIPLOM POL/PAR

S66
MATTHEWS D.G.,"PRELUDE-COUP D'ETAT-MILITARY GOVERNMENT: A BIBLIOGRAPHICAL AND RESEARCH GUIDE TO NIGERIAN POL AND GOVT, JAN, 1965-66." AFR NIGER LAW CONSTN POL/PAR LEGIS CIVMIL/REL GOV/REL...STAT 20. PAGE 105 H2096
BIBLIOG NAT/G ADMIN CHOOSE

S66
MERRITT R.L.,"SELECTED ARTICLES AND DOCUMENTS ON COMPARATIVE GOVERNMENT AND CROSS-NATIONAL RESEARCH." AFR ASIA EUR+WWI L/A+17C MOD/EUR ELITES R+D ACT/RES DIPLOM PWR...SOC CONCPT 18/20. PAGE 109 H2185
BIBLIOG GOV/COMP NAT/G GOV/REL

C66
DEUTSCH K.W.,"NATIONALISM AND SOCIAL COMMUNICATION." CULTURE INGP/REL ATTIT PWR...PSY SOC CONCPT LING IDEA/COMP 20. PAGE 40 H0800
BIBLIOG NAT/LISM GEN/LAWS

C66
ROSENBERG C.G. JR.,"THE MYTH OF "MAU-MAU:" NATIONALISM IN KENYA." AFR CULTURE NAT/G POL/PAR COERCE REV RACE/REL ATTIT ORD/FREE SOVEREIGN...MYTH BIBLIOG 20. PAGE 134 H2678
NAT/LISM COLONIAL MAJORIT LEAD

C66
WINT G.,"ASIA: A HANDBOOK." ASIA S/ASIA INDUS LABOR SECT PRESS RACE/REL MARXISM...STAT CHARTS BIBLIOG 20. PAGE 169 H3388
ECO/UNDEV DIPLOM NAT/G SOCIETY

B67
ANDERSON E.N.,POLITICAL INSTITUTIONS AND SOCIAL CHANGE IN CONTINENTAL EUROPE IN THE NINETEENTH CENTURY. MOD/EUR LAW CONSTN SOCIETY POL/PAR TEC/DEV LEAD REV ATTIT...BIBLIOG 19. PAGE 6 H0127
NAT/G NAT/COMP METH/COMP INDUS

B67
ANDERSON S.V.,THE NORDIC COUNCIL: A STUDY OF SCANDINAVIAN REGIONALISM. DENMARK FINLAND ICELAND NORWAY SWEDEN MARKET NAT/G VOL/ASSN CONSULT PARL/PROC ATTIT...TIME/SEQ BIBLIOG 20. PAGE 7 H0134
INT/ORG REGION DIPLOM LEGIS

B67
ANDERSON T.,RUSSIAN POLITICAL THOUGHT; AN INTRODUCTION. USSR NAT/G POL/PAR CHIEF MARXISM ...TIME/SEQ BIBLIOG 9/20. PAGE 7 H0135
TREND CONSTN ATTIT

B67
ARIKPO O.,THE DEVELOPMENT OF MODERN NIGERIA. AFR NIGERIA SOCIETY ECO/UNDEV KIN ADMIN FEDERAL NAT/LISM ORD/FREE WEALTH...POLICY GEOG BIBLIOG 19/20. PAGE 8 H0163
NAT/G CULTURE CONSTN COLONIAL

B67
ASHFORD D.E.,NATIONAL DEVELOPMENT AND LOCAL REFORM: POLITICAL PARTICIPATION IN MOROCCO, TUNISIA, AND PAKISTAN. MOROCCO PAKISTAN CULTURE PROB/SOLV ATTIT ...POLICY SOC METH/COMP NAT/COMP BIBLIOG 20 TUNIS. PAGE 9 H0173
PARTIC ECO/UNDEV ADJUST NAT/G

B67
BANKWITZ P.C.,MAXINE WEYGAND AND CIVIL-MILITARY RELATIONS IN MODERN FRANCE. FRANCE LEAD WAR PWR ...INT BIBLIOG 20. PAGE 11 H0212
CIVMIL/REL FORCES NAT/G TOP/EX

B67
BROMKE A.,POLAND'S POLITICS: IDEALISM VS. REALISM. COM GERMANY POLAND RUSSIA USSR POL/PAR CATHISM ...BIBLIOG 19/20. PAGE 21 H0431
NAT/G DIPLOM MARXISM

B67
CARTER G.M.,SOUTH AFRICA'S TRANSKEI: THE POLITICS OF DOMESTIC COLONIALISM. SOUTH/AFR ECO/UNDEV AGRI NAT/G PROVS PLAN DOMIN REPRESENT ADJUST DISCRIM ...OBS BIBLIOG 20 BANTUSTANS TRANSKEI. PAGE 27 H0550
STRATA GOV/REL COLONIAL POLICY

B67
CHANDRASEKHAR S.,ASIA'S POPULATION PROBLEMS. ASIA ECO/UNDEV PLAN AGE/C...OBS CHARTS BIBLIOG 18/20 AUSTRAL. PAGE 29 H0575
PROB/SOLV NAT/COMP GEOG TREND

B67
CHILCOTE R.H.,PORTUGUESE AFRICA. PORTUGAL CULTURE SOCIETY ECO/UNDEV DOMIN NAT/LISM...TREND IDEA/COMP NAT/COMP BIBLIOG 15/20. PAGE 29 H0589
AFR COLONIAL ORD/FREE PROB/SOLV

B67
DALTON G.,TRIBAL AND PEASANT ECONOMIES. SOCIETY FINAN FAM INT/TRADE RATION ADJUST WEALTH...CHARTS ANTHOL BIBLIOG T. PAGE 37 H0738
SOC ECO/UNDEV NAT/COMP

B67
DENISON E.F.,WHY GROWTH RATES DIFFER; POSTWAR EXPERIENCE IN NINE WESTERN COUNTRIES. WOR+45 FINAN WORKER TEC/DEV EDU/PROP PRICE PRODUC WEALTH ...ECOMETRIC STAT CHARTS BIBLIOG. PAGE 40 H0791
METH NAT/COMP ECO/DEV ECO/TAC

B67
DICKSON P.G.M.,THE FINANCIAL REVOLUTION IN ENGLAND. UK NAT/G TEC/DEV ADMIN GOV/REL...SOC METH/CNCPT CHARTS GP/COMP BIBLIOG 17/18. PAGE 41 H0823
ECO/DEV FINAN CAP/ISM MGT

B67
ERDMAN H.L.,THE SWATANTRA PARTY AND INDIAN CONSERVATISM. INDIA S/ASIA SOCIETY STRATA LOC/G NAT/G LEAD PARTIC GP/REL ATTIT...CONCPT GP/COMP BIBLIOG 20 SWATANTRA. PAGE 47 H0938
POL/PAR CONSERVE CHOOSE POLICY

B67
EVANS R.H.,COEXISTENCE: COMMUNISM AND ITS PRACTICE IN BOLOGNA, 1945-1965. ITALY CAP/ISM ADMIN CHOOSE PEACE ORD/FREE...SOC STAT DEEP/INT SAMP CHARTS BIBLIOG 20. PAGE 48 H0952
MARXISM CULTURE MUNIC POL/PAR

B67
GIFFORD P.,BRITAIN AND GERMANY IN AFRICA. AFR GERMANY UK ECO/UNDEV LEAD WAR NAT/LISM ATTIT ...POLICY HIST/WRIT METH/COMP ANTHOL BIBLIOG 19/20 WWI. PAGE 56 H1123
COLONIAL ADMIN DIPLOM NAT/COMP

B67
KONCZACKI Z.A.,PUBLIC FINANCE AND ECONOMIC DEVELOPMENT OF NATAL 1893-1910. TAX ADMIN COLONIAL ...STAT CHARTS BIBLIOG 19/20 NATAL. PAGE 88 H1755
ECO/TAC FINAN NAT/G ECO/UNDEV

B67
LAQUER W.,THE FATE OF THE REVOLUTION: INTERPRETATIONS OF SOVIET HISTORY. RUSSIA NAT/G MARXISM...BIBLIOG 20 STALIN/J. PAGE 91 H1816
REV KNOWL HIST/WRIT IDEA/COMP

B67
LENG S.C.,JUSTICE IN COMMUNIST CHINA: A SURVEY OF THE JUDICIAL SYSTEM OF THE CHINESE PEOPLE'S REPUBLIC. CHINA/COM LAW CONSTN LOC/G NAT/G PROF/ORG CONSULT FORCES ADMIN CRIME ORD/FREE...BIBLIOG 20 MAO. PAGE 94 H1877
CT/SYS ADJUD JURID MARXISM

B67
LEVY J.-P.,THE ECONOMIC LIFE OF THE ANCIENT WORLD. CULTURE SOCIETY INT/TRADE COLONIAL WEALTH ...BIBLIOG. PAGE 95 H1906
ECO/TAC ECO/UNDEV FINAN MEDIT-7

B67
PENDLE G.,PARAGUAY: A RIVERSIDE NATION (3RD ED.). PARAGUAY CHIEF ISOLAT...HUM CHARTS BIBLIOG 16/20. PAGE 124 H2487
CULTURE GEOG ECO/UNDEV

B67
PIKE F.B.,FREEDOM AND REFORM IN LATIN AMERICA. BRAZIL URUGUAY CONSTN CULTURE SECT DIPLOM EDU/PROP PARTIC DRIVE ALL/VALS CATHISM...GEOG ANTHOL BIBLIOG REFORMERS BOLIV. PAGE 126 H2511
L/A+17C ORD/FREE ECO/UNDEV REV

B67
PLISCHKE E.,CONDUCT OF AMERICAN DIPLOMACY (3RD REV. ED.). INT/ORG NAT/G PROB/SOLV FOR/AID...CHARTS BIBLIOG T 20 DEPT/STATE. PAGE 126 H2529
DIPLOM RATIONAL PLAN

B67
POGANY A.H.,POLITICAL SCIENCE AND INTERNATIONAL RELATIONS, BOOKS RECOMMENDED FOR AMERICAN CATHOLIC COLLEGE LIBRARIES. INT/ORG LOC/G NAT/G FORCES BAL/PWR ECO/TAC NUC/PWR...CATH INT/LAW TREATY 20. PAGE 127 H2532
BIBLIOG DIPLOM

B67
RAE D.,THE POLITICAL CONSEQUENCES OF ELECTORAL LAWS. EUR+WWI ICELAND ISRAEL NEW/ZEALND UK USA+45 ADJUD APPORT GP/REL MAJORITY...MATH STAT CENSUS CHARTS BIBLIOG 20 AUSTRAL. PAGE 129 H2579
POL/PAR CHOOSE NAT/COMP REPRESENT

B67
RAMUNDO B.A.,PEACEFUL COEXISTENCE: INTERNATIONAL LAW IN THE BUILDING OF COMMUNISM. USSR INT/ORG DIPLOM COLONIAL ARMS/CONT ROLE SOVEREIGN...POLICY METH/COMP NAT/COMP BIBLIOG. PAGE 129 H2588
INT/LAW PEACE MARXISM METH/CNCPT

B67
ROSENBLUTH G.,THE CANADIAN ECONOMY AND DISARMAMENT. CANADA FUT ECO/DEV INDUS R+D DELIB/GP DIPLOM ECO/TAC CIVMIL/REL PEACE...POLICY BIBLIOG PACIFIST 20. PAGE 134 H2679
ARMS/CONT STAT PLAN NAT/G

B67
ROWLAND J.,A HISTORY OF SINO-INDIAN RELATIONS; HOSTILE CO-EXISTENCE. ASIA CHINA/COM INDIA NAT/G NUC/PWR PWR WEALTH...GEOG BIBLIOG 13/20 COLD/WAR. PAGE 135 H2704
DIPLOM CENSUS IDEA/COMP

B67
RYDER A.J.,THE GERMAN REVOLUTION OF 1918; A STUDY OF GERMAN SOCIALISM IN WAR AND REVOLT. GERMANY NAT/G POL/PAR GP/REL...BIBLIOG 20. PAGE 136 H2724
SOCISM WAR REV INGP/REL

B67
SCHECTER J.,THE NEW FACE OF BUDDHA: BUDDHISM AND POLITICAL POWER IN SOUTHEAST ASIA. S/ASIA NAT/G POL/PAR NAT/LISM ATTIT MARXISM...BIBLIOG 20. PAGE 139 H2780
SECT POLICY PWR LEAD

B67
SETON-WATSON H.,THE RUSSIAN EMPIRE, 1801-1917. COM RUSSIA STRATA ECO/DEV AGRI INDUS POL/PAR DIPLOM NAT/LISM MARXISM...IDEA/COMP BIBLIOG 19/20 MARX/KARL. PAGE 142 H2834
SOCIETY NAT/G LEAD POLICY

B67
SHAKABPA T.W.D.,TIBET: A POLITICAL HISTORY. CHINA/COM UK CHIEF LEAD...INT BIBLIOG 20 TIBET. PAGE 142 H2839
DIPLOM SECT NAT/G

B67
TOMPKINS S.R.,THE TRIUMPH OF BOLSHEVISM: REVOLUTION OR REACTION? USSR WORKER PRESS WEALTH MARXISM POPULISM...BIOG TREND IDEA/COMP BIBLIOG 19/20 LENIN/VI. PAGE 156 H3113
REV NAT/G POL/PAR NAT/LISM

B67
VALI F.A.,THE QUEST FOR A UNITED GERMANY. GERMANY PROB/SOLV DIPLOM ADJUST...BIBLIOG 20. PAGE 161 H3222
NAT/G ATTIT PLAN CENTRAL

B67
WIENER F.B.,CIVILIANS UNDER MILITARY JUSTICE; THE BRITISH PRACTICE SINCE 1689 ESPECIALLY IN NORTH AMERICA. UK USA-45 LAW CONSTN CRIME REV...DECISION CHARTS NAT/COMP BIBLIOG 17/20. PAGE 168 H3356
CT/SYS FORCES ADJUD

B67
WILLS A.J.,AN INTRODUCTION TO THE HISTORY OF CENTRAL AFRICA. RHODESIA ZAMBIA CULTURE SOCIETY ECO/UNDEV TEC/DEV DOMIN WAR ALL/VALS...POLICY TREND BIBLIOG T 14/20 NYASALAND. PAGE 169 H3375
AFR COLONIAL ORD/FREE

B67
WOODRUFF W.,IMPACT OF WESTERN MAN. ECO/DEV INDUS CREATE PLAN PROB/SOLV COLONIAL GOV/REL...CHARTS GOV/COMP BIBLIOG 18/20. PAGE 170 H3407
EUR+WWI MOD/EUR CAP/ISM

C67
GEHLEN M.P.,"THE POLITICS OF COEXISTENCE: SOVIET METHODS AND MOTIVES." COM USSR NAT/G INT/TRADE EDU/PROP ARMS/CONT DETER KNOWL...CHARTS IDEA/COMP 20 COLD/WAR. PAGE 55 H1108
BIBLIOG PEACE DIPLOM MARXISM

C67
LING D.L.,"TUNISIA: FROM PROTECTORATE TO REPUBLIC." CULTURE NAT/G POL/PAR CHIEF DIPLOM COERCE WAR PWR ...BIBLIOG 19/20 TUNIS. PAGE 97 H1934
AFR NAT/LISM COLONIAL PROB/SOLV

B89
ASHBEE H.S.,A BIBLIOGRAPHY OF TUNISIA FROM THE EARLIEST TIMES TO THE END OF 1888. AGRI ADMIN ...GEOG TUNIS. PAGE 8 H0171
BIBLIOG COLONIAL CULTURE NAT/G

B93
ROYAL GEOGRAPHIC SOCIETY,BIBLIOGRAPHY OF BARBARY STATES (4 SUPPLEMENTARY PAPERS). ALGERIA LIBYA MOROCCO SOCIETY STRUCT DIPLOM LEAD 14/19 TUNIS. PAGE 135 H2706
BIBLIOG ISLAM NAT/G COLONIAL

C93
PLAYFAIR R.L.,"A BIBLIOGRAPHY OF MOROCCO." MOROCCO CULTURE AGRI FORCES DIPLOM WAR HEALTH...GEOG JURID SOC CHARTS. PAGE 126 H2526
BIBLIOG ISLAM MEDIT-7

B97
JENKS E.J.,LAW AND POLITICS IN THE MIDDLE AGES. CHRIST-17C CULTURE STRUCT KIN NAT/G SECT CT/SYS GP/REL...CLASSIF CHARTS IDEA/COMP BIBLIOG 8/16. PAGE 80 H1603
LAW SOCIETY ADJUST

BIBLIOG/A....BIBLIOGRAPHY OVER 50 ITEMS ANNOTATED

N
ACAD RUMANIAN SCI DOC CTR,RUMANIAN SCIENTIFIC ABSTRACTS: SOCIAL SCIENCES. ROMANIA FINAN HABITAT ...ART/METH GEOG HUM JURID PSY 20. PAGE 3 H0059
BIBLIOG/A CULTURE LING LAW

N
AUSTRALIAN NATIONAL RES COUN,AUSTRALIAN SOCIAL SCIENCE ABSTRACTS. NEW/ZEALND CULTURE SOCIETY LOC/G CT/SYS PARL/PROC...HEAL JURID PSY SOC 20 AUSTRAL. PAGE 9 H0181
BIBLIOG/A POLICY NAT/G ADMIN

N
BIBLIOTECH NACIONAL,CATALOGO BREVE DE LA BIBLIOTECA AMERICANA DE JT MEDINA (2 VOLS.). CHILE NAT/G PERSON HUM. PAGE 16 H0330
BIBLIOG/A CHARTS L/A+17C

N
CONOVER H.F.,MADAGASCAR: A SELECTED LIST OF REFERENCES. MADAGASCAR STRUCT ECO/UNDEV NAT/G ADMIN ...SOC 19/20. PAGE 32 H0639
BIBLIOG/A SOCIETY CULTURE COLONIAL

N
SCHADERA I.,SELECT BIBLIOGRAPHY OF SOUTH AFRICAN NATIVE LIFE AND PROBLEMS. SOUTH/AFR LAW CULTURE ECO/UNDEV COLONIAL PARTIC...POLICY LING 20. PAGE 138 H2768
BIBLIOG/A SOC AFR STRUCT

N
UNIVERSITY OF FLORIDA LIBRARY,DOORS TO LATIN AMERICA; RECENT BOOKS AND PAMPHLETS. CONSTN CULTURE SOCIETY ECO/UNDEV COLONIAL LEAD GOV/REL NAT/LISM ATTIT...HUM SOC 20. PAGE 159 H3170
BIBLIOG/A L/A+17C DIPLOM NAT/G

N
AMERICAN POLITICAL SCIENCE REVIEW. USA+45 USA-45 WOR+45 WOR-45 INT/ORG ADMIN...INT/LAW PHIL/SCI CONCPT METH 20 UN. PAGE 1 H0001
BIBLIOG/A DIPLOM NAT/G GOV/COMP

N
BULLETIN ANALYTIQUE DE DOCUMENTATION POLITIQUE,
BIBLIOG/A

ECONOMIQUE, ET SOCIAL CONTEMPORAIRE. FRANCE WOR+45 SOCIETY ECO/DEV ECO/UNDEV INT/ORG LOC/G PROB/SOLV FOR/AID LEAD REGION SOC. PAGE 1 H0002
DIPLOM NAT/COMP NAT/G

N
CANADIAN GOVERNMENT PUBLICATIONS (1955-). CANADA AGRI FINAN LABOR FORCES INT/TRADE HEALTH...JURID 20 PARLIAMENT. PAGE 1 H0003
BIBLIOG/A NAT/G DIPLOM INT/ORG

N
INTERNATIONAL BIBLIOGRAPHIE DER DEUTSCHEN ZEITSCHRIFTENLITERATUR. EUR+WWI GERMANY MOD/EUR ECO/DEV POL/PAR LEAD WAR NAT/LISM ATTIT...EPIST PHIL/SCI 19/20. PAGE 1 H0004
BIBLIOG/A NAT/G PERSON CULTURE

N
JOURNAL OF MODERN HISTORY. WOR+45 WOR-45 LEAD WAR ...TIME/SEQ TREND NAT/COMP 20. PAGE 1 H0006
BIBLIOG/A DIPLOM NAT/G

N
AFRICAN RESEARCH BULLETIN. AFR CULTURE NAT/G COLONIAL...SOC 20. PAGE 1 H0010
BIBLIOG/A DIPLOM PRESS

N
BIBLIOGRAPHIE DE LA PHILOSOPHIE. LAW CULTURE SECT EDU/PROP MORAL...HUM METH/CNCPT 20. PAGE 1 H0012
BIBLIOG/A PHIL/SCI CONCPT LOG

N
CHINA QUARTERLY. COM AGRI INDUS ACADEM POL/PAR INT/TRADE CONFER GOV/REL...TIME/SEQ CON/ANAL INDEX 20. PAGE 1 H0014
BIBLIOG/A ASIA DIPLOM POLICY

N
CIVIL SERVICE JOURNAL. PARTIC INGP/REL PERS/REL ...MGT BIBLIOG/A 20. PAGE 1 H0015
ADMIN NAT/G SERV/IND WORKER

N
HANDBOOK OF LATIN AMERICAN STUDIES. LAW CULTURE ECO/UNDEV POL/PAR ADMIN LEAD...SOC 20. PAGE 1 H0016
BIBLIOG/A L/A+17C NAT/G DIPLOM

N
REVUE FRANCAISE DE SCIENCE POLITIQUE. FRANCE UK ...BIBLIOG/A 20. PAGE 1 H0021
NAT/G DIPLOM CONCPT ROUTINE

N
SUMMARIES OF SELECTED JAPANESE MAGAZINES. LAW CULTURE ADMIN LEAD 20 CHINJAP. PAGE 2 H0025
BIBLIOG/A ATTIT NAT/G ASIA

N
NEUE POLITISCHE LITERATUR; BERICHTE UBER DAS INTERNATIONALE SCHRIFTTUM ZUR POLITIK. WOR+45 LAW CONSTN POL/PAR ADMIN LEAD GOV/REL...POLICY IDEA/COMP. PAGE 2 H0027
BIBLIOG/A DIPLOM NAT/G NAT/COMP

N
"PROLOG",DIGEST OF THE SOVIET UKRANIAN PRESS. USSR LAW AGRI INDUS PROVS SCHOOL DIPLOM GOV/REL ATTIT ...HUM LING 20. PAGE 3 H0053
BIBLIOG/A NAT/G PRESS COM

N
AFRICAN BIBLIOGRAPHIC CENTER,A CURRENT BIBLIOGRAPHY ON AFRICAN AFFAIRS. LAW CULTURE ECO/UNDEV LABOR SECT DIPLOM FOR/AID COLONIAL NAT/LISM...LING 20. PAGE 4 H0075
BIBLIOG/A AFR NAT/G REGION

N
ASIA FOUNDATION,LIBRARY NOTES. LAW CONSTN CULTURE SOCIETY ECO/UNDEV INT/ORG NAT/G COLONIAL LEAD REGION NAT/LISM ATTIT 20 UN. PAGE 9 H0176
BIBLIOG/A ASIA S/ASIA DIPLOM

N
BURY J.B.,THE CAMBRIDGE ANCIENT HISTORY (12 VOLS.). MEDIT-7 DIPLOM COLONIAL WAR...HUM EGYPT/ANC ROME/EMP BABYLONIA GREECE/ANC. PAGE 25 H0495
BIBLIOG/A SOCIETY CULTURE NAT/G

N
CARNEGIE ENDOWMENT,CURRENT RESEARCH IN INTERNATIONAL AFFAIRS: SELECTED BIBLIOGRAPHY OF WORK IN PROGRESS BY PRIVATE RESEARCH AGENCIES. WOR+45 NAT/G ACT/RES GOV/COMP. PAGE 27 H0533
BIBLIOG/A DIPLOM R+D

N
CORDIER H.,BIBLIOTECA SINICA. SOCIETY STRUCT SECT DIPLOM COLONIAL...GEOG SOC CON/ANAL. PAGE 33 H0664
BIBLIOG/A NAT/G CULTURE ASIA

N
INADA S.,INTRODUCTION TO SCIENTIFIC WORKS IN HUMANITIES AND SOCIAL SCIENCES PUBLISHED IN JAPAN. LAW CULTURE ACADEM EDU/PROP...ART/METH HUM 20 CHINJAP. PAGE 76 H1525
BIBLIOG/A NAT/G SOC S/ASIA

N
INSTITUTE OF HISPANIC STUDIES,HISPANIC AMERICAN REPORT. EUR+WWI SPAIN LAW CONSTN ECO/UNDEV POL/PAR EX/STRUC LEGIS LEAD...HUM SOC 20. PAGE 77 H1538
BIBLIOG/A L/A+17C NAT/G DIPLOM

N
INTERNATIONAL CENTRE AFRICAN,BULLETIN OF INFORMATION ON THESES AND STUDIES IN PROGRESS OR PROPOSED. LAW CULTURE FINAN INDUS LABOR TEC/DEV EDU/PROP...GEOG SOC NAT/COMP 20. PAGE 78 H1554
BIBLIOG/A ACT/RES ACADEM INTELL

N
KYRIAK T.E.,ASIAN DEVELOPMENTS: A BIBLIOGRAPHY. INDONESIA KOREA/N VIETNAM/N CULTURE SOCIETY ECO/UNDEV NAT/G DIPLOM...SOC TREND 20 MONGOLIA. PAGE 90 H1788
BIBLIOG/A ALL/IDEOS S/ASIA ASIA

N
KYRIAK T.E.,CHINA: A BIBLIOGRAPHY. ASIA CHINA/COM AGRI FINAN INDUS NAT/G INT/TRADE PRESS...SOC 20. PAGE 90 H1789
BIBLIOG/A MARXISM TOP/EX POL/PAR

N
US CONSULATE GENERAL HONG KONG,REVIEW OF THE HONG KONG CHINESE PRESS. ECO/UNDEV LOC/G NAT/G PLAN DIPLOM EDU/PROP LEAD GP/REL MARXISM...POLICY INDEX 20. PAGE 159 H3178
BIBLIOG/A ASIA PRESS ATTIT

N
US CONSULATE GENERAL HONG KONG,CURRENT BACKGROUND. CHINA/COM ECO/UNDEV LOC/G NAT/G PLAN DIPLOM EDU/PROP LEAD REV ATTIT...POLICY INDEX 20. PAGE 159 H3179
BIBLIOG/A MARXIST ASIA PRESS

N
US CONSULATE GENERAL HONG KONG,SURVEY OF CHINA MAINLAND PRESS. CHINA/COM ECO/UNDEV LOC/G NAT/G PLAN DIPLOM EDU/PROP LEAD REV ATTIT...POLICY INDEX 20. PAGE 159 H3181
BIBLIOG/A MARXIST ASIA PRESS

N
US CONSULATE GENERAL HONG KONG,US CONSULATE GENERAL, HONG KONG, PRESS SUMMARIES. CHINA/COM ECO/UNDEV LOC/G NAT/G PLAN DIPLOM EDU/PROP LEAD REV ATTIT...POLICY INDEX 20. PAGE 159 H3182
BIBLIOG/A MARXIST ASIA PRESS

N
US LIBRARY OF CONGRESS,SOUTHERN ASIA ACCESSIONS LIST. BURMA CEYLON INDIA NEPAL PAKISTAN S/ASIA THAILAND AGRI INDUS SCHOOL WORKER...ART/METH GEOG HEAL PHIL/SCI LING 20. PAGE 160 H3201
BIBLIOG/A SOCIETY CULTURE ECO/UNDEV

B01
GRIFFIN A.P.C.,A LIST OF BOOKS ON THE DANISH WEST INDIES (PAMPHLET). L/A+17C WEST/IND CULTURE LOC/G ...GEOG MGT 18/20. PAGE 61 H1214
BIBLIOG/A SOCIETY COLONIAL ADMIN

B01
GRIFFIN A.P.C.,A LIST OF BOOKS ON PORTO RICO. PUERT/RICO CULTURE LOC/G...GEOG MGT 19/20. PAGE 61 H1215
BIBLIOG/A SOCIETY COLONIAL ADMIN

B03
GRIFFIN A.P.C.,LIST OF BOOKS ON THE CABINETS OF ENGLAND AND AMERICA (PAMPHLET). MOD/EUR UK USA-45 CONSTN NAT/G CONSULT EX/STRUC 19/20. PAGE 61 H1216
BIBLIOG/A GOV/COMP ADMIN DELIB/GP

B03
GRIFFIN A.P.C.,SELECT LIST OF REFERENCES ON GOVERNMENT OWNERSHIP OF RAILROADS (PAMPHLET). MOD/EUR NAT/G ADMIN...MGT GOV/COMP 19/20. PAGE 61 H1217
BIBLIOG/A SOCISM OWN DIST/IND

B04
GRIFFIN A.P.C.,LIST OF REFERENCES ON BUDGETS OF FOREIGN COUNTRIES (PAMPHLET). MOD/EUR FINAN MARKET TAX...MGT STAT 19/20. PAGE 61 H1218
BIBLIOG/A BUDGET NAT/G

B05
GRIFFIN A.P.C.,LIST OF BOOKS ON RAILROADS IN FOREIGN COUNTRIES. MOD/EUR ECO/DEV NAT/G CONTROL SOCISM...JURID 19/20 RAILROAD. PAGE 61 H1219
BIBLIOG/A SERV/IND ADMIN DIST/IND

B10
MENDELSSOHN S.,SOUTH AFRICAN BIBLIOGRAPHY (2 VOLS.). SOUTH/AFR EXTR/IND LABOR SECT DIPLOM INT/TRADE COLONIAL RACE/REL DISCRIM...GEOG 20. PAGE 109 H2172
BIBLIOG/A AFR NAT/G NAT/LISM

B10
MENDELSSOHN S.,MENDELSSOHN'S SOUTH AFRICA BIBLIOGRAPHY (VOL. I). SOUTH/AFR RACE/REL...GEOG JURID 19/20. PAGE 109 H2173
BIBLIOG/A CULTURE

B12
CORDIER H.,BIBLIOTHECA INDOSINICA: DICTIONAIRE BIBLIOGRAPHIQUE DES OUVRAGES RELATIFS A LA PENINSULE INDOCHINOISE. BURMA LAOS MALAYSIA S/ASIA THAILAND VIETNAM SECT...LING 20. PAGE 33 H0665
BIBLIOG/A GEOG NAT/G

B17
DOS SANTOS M.,BIBLIOGRAPHIA GERAL, A DESCRIPCAO BIBLIOGRAFICA DE LIVROS TANTO DE AUTORES PORTUGUEZES COMO BRASILEIROS... BRAZIL PORTUGAL NAT/G LEAD GP/REL 15/20. PAGE 42 H0840
BIBLIOG/A L/A+17C DIPLOM COLONIAL

C20
BLACHLY F.F.,"THE GOVERNMENT AND ADMINISTRATION OF GERMANY." GERMANY CONSTN LOC/G PROVS DELIB/GP EX/STRUC FORCES LEGIS TOP/EX CT/SYS...BIBLIOG/A 19/20. PAGE 17 H0348
NAT/G GOV/REL ADMIN PHIL/SCI

B27
CHILDS J.B.,AN ACCOUNT OF GOVERNMENT DOCUMENT BIBLIOGRAPHY IN THE UNITED STATES AND ELSEWHERE (A
BIBLIOG/A CON/ANAL

PAPER). LOC/G PRESS CENTRAL KNOWL...METH 19/20 LEAGUE/NAT. PAGE 29 H0590 NAT/G

B27
QUERARD J.M.,LA FRANCE LITTERAIRE (12 VOLS.). FRANCE CULTURE...HUM SOC 16/19. PAGE 129 H2573 BIBLIOG/A BIOG ART/METH

B29
CAM H.M.,BIBLIOGRAPHY OF ENGLISH CONSTITUTIONAL HISTORY (PAMPHLET). UK LAW LOC/G NAT/G POL/PAR SECT DELIB/GP ADJUD ORD/FREE 19/20 PARLIAMENT. PAGE 25 H0510 BIBLIOG/A CONSTN ADMIN PARL/PROC

B34
DE CENIVAL P.,BIBLIOGRAPHIE MAROCAINE: 1923-1933. FRANCE MOROCCO SECT ADMIN LEAD GP/REL ATTIT...LING 20. PAGE 37 H0750 BIBLIOG/A ISLAM NAT/G COLONIAL

B36
CULVER D.C.,METHODOLOGY OF SOCIAL SCIENCE RESEARCH: A BIBLIOGRAPHY. LAW CULTURE...CRIMLGY GEOG STAT OBS INT QU HIST/WRIT CHARTS 20. PAGE 36 H0719 BIBLIOG/A METH SOC

B37
BOURNE H.E.,THE WORLD WAR: A LIST OF THE MORE IMPORTANT BOOKS PUBLISHED BEFORE 1937 (PAMPHLET). EUR+WWI NAT/G DIPLOM ATTIT SOC. PAGE 19 H0386 BIBLIOG/A WAR FORCES PLAN

B38
DEL TORO J.,A BIBLIOGRAPHY OF THE COLLECTIVE BIOGRAPHY OF SPANISH AMERICA. ELITES NAT/G WRITING LEAD PERSON 19/20. PAGE 39 H0786 BIBLIOG/A L/A+17C BIOG

B40
THE GUIDE TO CATHOLIC LITERATURE, 1888-1940. ALL/VALS...POLICY MYSTIC HUM PHIL/SCI 19/20. PAGE 2 H0032 BIBLIOG/A CATHISM DIPLOM CULTURE

B40
BROWN A.D.,PANAMA CANAL AND PANAMA CANAL ZONE: A SELECTED LIST OF REFERENCES. PANAMA NAT/G SCHOOL DIPLOM HEALTH...GEOG SOC 20 CANAL/ZONE. PAGE 22 H0436 BIBLIOG/A ECO/UNDEV

C40
FAHS C.B.,"GOVERNMENT IN JAPAN." FINAN FORCES LEGIS TOP/EX BUDGET INT/TRADE EDU/PROP SOVEREIGN ...CON/ANAL BIBLIOG/A 20 CHINJAP. PAGE 48 H0962 ASIA DIPLOM NAT/G ADMIN

B42
BLANCHARD L.R.,MARTINIQUE: A SELECTED LIST OF REFERENCES (PAMPHLET). WEST/IND AGRI LOC/G SCHOOL ...ART/METH GEOG JURID CHARTS 20. PAGE 18 H0353 BIBLIOG/A SOCIETY CULTURE COLONIAL

B42
CONOVER H.F.,NEW ZEALAND: A SELECTED LIST OF REFERENCES (PAMPHLET). NEW/ZEALND ECO/UNDEV AGRI INDUS LABOR NAT/G SCHOOL FORCES DIPLOM COLONIAL WAR ...HUM 20. PAGE 32 H0643 BIBLIOG/A S/ASIA CULTURE

B42
NEUBURGER O.,OFFICIAL PUBLICATIONS OF PRESENT-DAY GERMANY: GOVERNMENT, CORPORATE ORGANIZATIONS, AND NATIONAL SOCIALIST PARTY. GERMANY CONSTN COM/IND POL/PAR EDU/PROP PRESS 20 NAZI. PAGE 117 H2332 BIBLIOG/A FASCISM NAT/G ADMIN

B42
PAGINSKY P.,GERMAN WORKS RELATING TO AMERICA, 1493-1800; A LIST COMPILED FROM THE COLLECTIONS OF THE NEW YORK PUBLIC LIBRARY. GERMANY PRE/AMER CULTURE COLONIAL ATTIT...POLICY SOC 15/19. PAGE 122 H2442 BIBLIOG/A NAT/G L/A+17C DIPLOM

C42
CRAIG A.,"ABOVE ALL LIBERTIES." FRANCE UK LAW CULTURE INTELL SECT ORD/FREE 18/20. PAGE 35 H0693 BIBLIOG/A EDU/PROP WRITING MORAL

B43
BROWN A.D.,GREECE: SELECTED LIST OF REFERENCES. GREECE ECO/UNDEV AGRI FINAN INDUS LABOR SECT TEC/DEV INT/TRADE LEAD...SOC 20. PAGE 22 H0438 BIBLIOG/A WAR DIPLOM NAT/G

B43
GRIERSON P.,BOOKS ON SOVIET RUSSIA 1917-42: A BIBLIOGRAPHY AND A GUIDE TO READING. USSR CULTURE ELITES NAT/G PLAN DIPLOM REV...GEOG 20. PAGE 61 H1213 BIBLIOG/A COM MARXISM LEAD

B43
JONES C.K.,A BIBLIOGRAPHY OF LATIN AMERICAN BIBLIOGRAPHIES (2ND ED.). CULTURE ALL/VALS...POLICY GEOG HUM SOC LING BIOG TREND 20. PAGE 82 H1629 BIBLIOG/A L/A+17C HIST/WRIT

B44
FULLER G.H.,TURKEY: A SELECTED LIST OF REFERENCES. ISLAM TURKEY CULTURE ECO/UNDEV AGRI DIPLOM NAT/LISM CONSERVE...GEOG HUM INT/LAW SOC 7/20 MAPS. PAGE 54 H1075 BIBLIOG/A ALL/VALS

N45
INDIA QUARTERLY, A JOURNAL OF INTERNATIONAL AFFAIRS. INDIA LAW CONSTN ECO/UNDEV INT/ORG POL/PAR COLONIAL LEAD PARL/PROC WAR ATTIT...SOC 20 CMN/WLTH. PAGE 2 H0033 BIBLIOG/A S/ASIA DIPLOM NAT/G

B45
CLAGETT H.L.,COMMUNIST CHINA: RUTHLESS ENEMY OR PAPER TIGER (PAMPHLET). CHINA/COM ECO/UNDEV AGRI INDUS NAT/G POL/PAR ECO/TAC INT/TRADE GUERRILLA ATTIT...CHARTS NAT/COMP ORG/CHARTS 20. PAGE 30 H0602 BIBLIOG/A MARXISM DIPLOM COERCE

B45
HARVARD WIDENER LIBRARY,INDOCHINA: A SELECTED LIST OF REFERENCES. CAMBODIA FRANCE S/ASIA VIETNAM COLONIAL...POLICY 19/20. PAGE 67 H1351 BIBLIOG/A ACADEM DIPLOM NAT/G

B45
PERAZA SARAUSA F.,BIBLIOGRAFIAS CUBANAS. CUBA CULTURE ECO/UNDEV AGRI EDU/PROP PRESS CIVMIL/REL ...POLICY GEOG PHIL/SCI BIOG 19/20. PAGE 125 H2489 BIBLIOG/A L/A+17C NAT/G DIPLOM

B45
US LIBRARY OF CONGRESS,NETHERLANDS EAST INDIES. INDONESIA LAW CULTURE AGRI INDUS SCHOOL COLONIAL HEALTH...GEOG JURID SOC 19/20 NETH/IND. PAGE 160 H3205 BIBLIOG/A S/ASIA NAT/G

B45
WOOLBERT R.G.,FOREIGN AFFAIRS BIBLIOGRAPHY, 1932-1942. INT/ORG SECT INT/TRADE COLONIAL RACE/REL NAT/LISM...GEOG INT/LAW GOV/COMP IDEA/COMP 20. PAGE 170 H3410 BIBLIOG/A DIPLOM WAR

N46
HOBBS C.C.,SOUTHEAST ASIA, 1935-45: A SELECTED LIST OF REFERENCE BOOKS (PAMPHLET). S/ASIA AGRI INDUS NAT/G SECT DIPLOM WAR...ART/METH GEOG SOC LING 20. PAGE 72 H1435 BIBLIOG/A CULTURE HABITAT

B47
BOWLE J.,WESTERN POLITICAL THOUGHT: AN HISTORICAL INTRODUCTION FROM THE ORIGINS TO ROUSSEAU. CONSTN NAT/G SECT CREATE RATIONAL ORD/FREE...SOC BIBLIOG/A. PAGE 19 H0391 ATTIT IDEA/COMP PHIL/SCI

B47
DE NOIA J.,GUIDE TO OFFICIAL PUBLICATIONS OF OTHER AMERICAN REPUBLICS: ECUADOR (VOL. IX). ECUADOR LAW FINAN LEGIS BUDGET CT/SYS 19/20. PAGE 38 H0763 BIBLIOG/A CONSTN NAT/G EDU/PROP

B47
DE NOIA J.,GUIDE TO OFFICIAL PUBLICATIONS OF THE OTHER AMERICAN REPUBLICS: EL SALVADOR. EL/SALVADR LAW LEGIS EDU/PROP CT/SYS 20. PAGE 38 H0764 BIBLIOG/A CONSTN NAT/G ADMIN

B47
DE NOIA J.,GUIDE TO OFFICIAL PUBLICATIONS OF THE OTHER AMERICAN REPUBLICS: NICARAGUA (VOL. XIV). NICARAGUA LAW LEGIS ADMIN CT/SYS...JURID 19/20. PAGE 38 H0765 BIBLIOG/A EDU/PROP NAT/G CONSTN

B47
DE NOIA J.,GUIDE TO OFFICIAL PUBLICATIONS OF THE OTHER AMERICAN REPUBLICS: PANAMA (VOL. XV). PANAMA LAW LEGIS EDU/PROP CT/SYS 20. PAGE 38 H0766 BIBLIOG/A CONSTN ADMIN NAT/G

B47
NEUBURGER O.,GUIDE TO OFFICIAL PUBLICATIONS OF OTHER AMERICAN REPUBLICS: HONDURAS (VOL. XIII). HONDURAS LAW LEGIS ADMIN CT/SYS...JURID 19/20. PAGE 117 H2333 BIBLIOG/A NAT/G EDU/PROP CONSTN

B47
NEUBURGER O.,GUIDE TO OFFICIAL PUBLICATIONS OF THE OTHER AMERICAN REPUBLICS: HAITI (VOL. XII). HAITI LAW FINAN LEGIS PRESS...JURID 20. PAGE 117 H2334 BIBLIOG/A CONSTN NAT/G EDU/PROP

B48
DE NOIA J.,GUIDE TO OFFICIAL PUBLICATIONS OF OTHER AMERICAN REPUBLICS: PERU (VOL. XVII). PERU LAW LEGIS ADMIN CT/SYS...JURID 19/20. PAGE 38 H0767 BIBLIOG/A CONSTN NAT/G EDU/PROP

B48
FLOREN LOZANO L.,BIBLIOGRAFIA DE LA BIBLIOGRAFIA DOMINICANA. DOMIN/REP NAT/G DIPLOM EDU/PROP CIVMIL/REL...POLICY ART/METH GEOG PHIL/SCI HIST/WRIT 20. PAGE 51 H1027 BIBLIOG/A BIOG L/A+17C CULTURE

B48
JONES H.D.,UNESCO: A SELECTED LIST OF REFERENCES. CULTURE CREATE PEACE ATTIT DRIVE 20 UNESCO UN. PAGE 82 H1631 BIBLIOG/A INT/ORG DIPLOM EDU/PROP

B48
MINISTERE FINANCES ET ECO,BULLETIN BIBLIOGRAPHIQUE. AFR EUR+WWI FRANCE CULTURE STRUCT FINAN NAT/G ACT/RES INT/TRADE ADMIN REGION PRODUC STAT. PAGE 111 H2224 BIBLIOG/A ECO/UNDEV TEC/DEV COLONIAL

B48
NEUBURGER O.,GUIDE TO OFFICIAL PUBLICATIONS OF THE OTHER AMERICAN REPUBLICS: VENEZUELA (VOL. XIX). VENEZUELA FINAN LEGIS PLAN BUDGET DIPLOM CT/SYS PARL/PROC 19/20. PAGE 117 H2335 BIBLIOG/A NAT/G CONSTN LAW

B48
US LIBRARY OF CONGRESS,BRAZIL: A GUIDE TO THE OFFICIAL PUBLICATIONS OF BRAZIL. BRAZIL L/A+17C CONSULT DELIB/GP LEGIS CT/SYS 19/20. PAGE 160 H3206 BIBLIOG/A NAT/G ADMIN TOP/EX

B49
BOZZA T.,SCRITTORI POLITICI ITALIANI DAL 1550 AL BIBLIOG/A

1650. CHRIST-17C ITALY DIPLOM DOMIN 16/17. PAGE 20 H0394 — NAT/G CONCPT WRITING

B49
US DEPARTMENT OF STATE,SOVIET BIBLIOGRAPHY (PAMPHLET). CHINA/COM COM USSR LAW AGRI INT/ORG ECO/TAC EDU/PROP...POLICY GEOG 20. PAGE 159 H3185 — BIBLIOG/A MARXISM CULTURE DIPLOM

B50
CONOVER H.F.,INTRODUCTION TO EUROPE: A SELECTIVE GUIDE TO BACKGROUND READING. COM EUR+WWI NAT/G KNOWL...ART/METH GEOG SOC. PAGE 32 H0648 — BIBLIOG/A MOD/EUR HIST/WRIT

B50
CORNELL U DEPT ASIAN STUDIES,SOUTHEAST ASIA PROGRAM DATA PAPER. BURMA CAMBODIA INDONESIA MALAYSIA VIETNAM SOCIETY STRUCT NAT/G SECT DIPLOM FOR/AID PWR WEALTH...SOC 20. PAGE 33 H0670 — BIBLIOG/A CULTURE S/ASIA ECO/UNDEV

B50
COUNCIL BRITISH NATIONAL BIB,BRITISH NATIONAL BIBLIOGRAPHY. UK AGRI CONSTRUC PERF/ART POL/PAR SECT CREATE INT/TRADE LEAD...HUM JURID PHIL/SCI 20. PAGE 34 H0677 — BIBLIOG/A NAT/G TEC/DEV DIPLOM

B50
EMBREE J.F.,BIBLIOGRAPHY OF THE PEOPLES AND CULTURES OF MAINLAND SOUTHEAST ASIA. CAMBODIA LAOS THAILAND VIETNAM LAW...GEOG HUM SOC MYTH LING CHARTS WORSHIP 20. PAGE 46 H0915 — BIBLIOG/A CULTURE S/ASIA

B50
HOBBS C.C.,INDOCHINA, A BIBLIOGRAPHY OF THE LAND AND PEOPLE. VIETNAM CULTURE AGRI INDUS NAT/G SECT ...ART/METH GEOG SOC LING 20. PAGE 72 H1436 — BIBLIOG/A S/ASIA COLONIAL ECO/UNDEV

B50
JONES H.D.,KOREA, AN ANNOTATED BIBLIOGRAPHY OF PUBLICATIONS IN WESTERN LANGUAGES. KOREA CULTURE MUNIC SECT FORCES DIPLOM HEALTH WEALTH...ART/METH GEOG SOC LING 20. PAGE 82 H1632 — BIBLIOG/A ASIA NAT/G ECO/UNDEV

B50
TENG S.,AN ANNOTATED BIBLIOGRAPHY OF SELECTED CHINESE REFERENCE WORKS (REV. ED.). CULTURE ECO/UNDEV LEAD MARXISM...LING INDEX 3/20. PAGE 153 H3062 — BIBLIOG/A ASIA NAT/G

B50
US DEPARTMENT OF STATE,DOCUMENTS ON GERMAN FOREIGN POLICY, 1918-1945 (13 VOLS.). EUR+WWI GERMANY NAT/G PLAN DIPLOM DOMIN EDU/PROP CONTROL NAT/LISM ...ANTHOL 20. PAGE 159 H3186 — BIBLIOG/A WAR POLICY FASCIST

B50
WARD R.E.,A GUIDE TO JAPANESE REFERENCE AND RESEARCH MATERIALS IN THE FIELD OF POLITICAL SCIENCE. LAW CONSTN LOC/G PRESS ADMIN...SOC CON/ANAL METH 19/20 CHINJAP. PAGE 165 H3305 — BIBLIOG/A ASIA NAT/G

B50
WILBUR C.M.,CHINESE SOURCES ON THE HISTORY OF THE CHINESE COMMUNIST MOVEMENT (PAMPHLET). CHINA/COM ECO/UNDEV PROVS FORCES WAR...PHIL/SCI 20. PAGE 168 H3360 — BIBLIOG/A MARXISM REV NAT/G

B51
MORLEY C.,GUIDE TO RESEARCH IN RUSSIAN HISTORY. USSR MARXISM...BIOG HIST/WRIT ANTHOL DICTIONARY. PAGE 113 H2259 — BIBLIOG/A R+D NAT/G COM

B51
MUMFORD L.,THE CONDUCT OF LIFE. UNIV SOCIETY CREATE ...TECHNIC METH/CNCPT TIME/SEQ TREND GEN/LAWS BIBLIOG/A. PAGE 114 H2286 — ALL/VALS CULTURE PERSON CONCPT

B51
US LIBRARY OF CONGRESS,EAST EUROPEAN ACCESSIONS LIST (VOL. I). POL/PAR DIPLOM ADMIN LEAD 20. PAGE 160 H3207 — BIBLIOG/A COM SOCIETY NAT/G

B51
WABEKE B.H.,A GUIDE TO DUTCH BIBLIOGRAPHIES. BELGIUM INDONESIA NETHERLAND DIPLOM INT/TRADE WAR NAT/LISM KNOWL...ART/METH HUM JURID CON/ANAL 14/20. PAGE 164 H3282 — BIBLIOG/A NAT/G CULTURE COLONIAL

B52
ETTINGHAUSEN R.,SELECTED AND ANNOTATED BIBLIOGRAPHY OF BOOKS AND PERIODICALS IN WESTERN LANGUAGES DEALING WITH NEAR AND MIDDLE EAST. LAW CULTURE SECT ...ART/METH GEOG SOC. PAGE 47 H0944 — BIBLIOG/A ISLAM MEDIT-7

B52
GURLAND A.R.L.,POLITICAL SCIENCE IN WESTERN GERMANY: THOUGHTS AND WRITINGS, 1950-1952 (PAMPHLET). EUR+WWI GERMANY/W ELITES SOCIETY NAT/G NAT/LISM TOTALISM 20. PAGE 63 H1253 — BIBLIOG/A DIPLOM CIVMIL/REL FASCISM

B52
SPENCER F.A.,WAR AND POSTWAR GREECE: AN ANALYSIS BASED ON GREEK WRITINGS. GREECE SOCIETY NAT/G POL/PAR FORCES CREATE DIPLOM LEAD MARXISM...SOC 20. PAGE 147 H2943 — BIBLIOG/A WAR REV

B52
THOM J.M.,GUIDE TO RESEARCH MATERIAL IN POLITICAL SCIENCE (PAMPHLET). ELITES LOC/G MUNIC NAT/G LEGIS DIPLOM ADJUD CIVMIL/REL GOV/REL PWR MGT. PAGE 154 H3074 — BIBLIOG/A KNOWL

B52
US LIBRARY OF CONGRESS,INTRODUCTION TO AFRICA; A SELECTIVE GUIDE TO BACKGROUND READING. ECO/UNDEV COLONIAL GP/REL...SOC 19/20. PAGE 160 H3208 — BIBLIOG/A AFR CULTURE NAT/G

B52
US LIBRARY OF CONGRESS,EGYPT AND THE ANGLO-EGYPTIAN SUDAN: A SELECTIVE GUIDE TO BACKGROUND READING (PAMPHLET). SUDAN UAR UK DIPLOM...POLICY 20. PAGE 160 H3209 — BIBLIOG/A COLONIAL ISLAM NAT/G

C52
EBENSTEIN W.,"INTRODUCTION TO POLITICAL PHILOSOPHY." COM CONSTN INTELL CONTROL PERSON NEW/LIB SOCISM...PSY GEN/LAWS BIBLIOG/A. PAGE 44 H0883 — ALL/IDEOS PHIL/SCI IDEA/COMP NAT/G

N52
COORDINATING COMM DOC SOC SCI,INTERNATIONAL REPERTORY OF SOCIAL SCIENCE DOCUMENTATION CENTERS (PAMPHLET). ACT/RES OP/RES WRITING KNOWL...CON/ANAL METH. PAGE 33 H0661 — BIBLIOG/A R+D NAT/G INT/ORG

B53
SHIRATO I.,JAPANESE SOURCES ON THE HISTORY OF THE CHINESE COMMUNIST MOVEMENT (PAMPHLET). CHINA/COM USSR CONSTRUC NAT/G POL/PAR FORCES DIPLOM DOMIN EDU/PROP CONTROL WAR TOTALISM SOCISM 20. PAGE 143 H2863 — BIBLIOG/A MARXISM ECO/UNDEV

C53
KRACKE E.A. JR.,"CIVIL SERVICE IN EARLY SUNG CHINA, 960-1067." ASIA GP/REL...BIBLIOG/A 10/11. PAGE 88 H1762 — ADMIN NAT/G WORKER CONTROL

B54
GIRALSO JARAMLLO G.,BIBLIOGRAFIA DE BIBLIOGRAFIAS COLOMBIANAS. L/A+17C ACADEM SECT CREATE EDU/PROP ...ART/METH GEOG LING TREND 20 COLOMB. PAGE 57 H1135 — BIBLIOG/A CULTURE PHIL/SCI ECO/UNDEV

B54
HAMSON C.J.,EXECUTIVE DISCRETION AND JUDICIAL CONTROL; AN ASPECT OF THE FRENCH CONSEIL D'ETAT. EUR+WWI FRANCE MOD/EUR UK NAT/G EX/STRUC PARTIC CONSERVE...JURID BIBLIOG/A 18/20 SUPREME/CT. PAGE 65 H1310 — ELITES ADJUD NAT/COMP

B54
HAZARD B.H. JR.,KOREAN STUDIES GUIDE. KOREA CONSTN CULTURE AGRI FAM SECT CREATE WAR NAT/LISM HABITAT PWR...CHARTS 14/20. PAGE 68 H1371 — BIBLIOG/A ELITES GP/REL

B54
LEWIS E.,MEDIEVAL POLITICAL IDEAS. LAW CULTURE SOCIETY ECO/UNDEV NAT/G SECT GOV/REL ATTIT ...BIBLIOG/A T 11/15. PAGE 96 H1913 — CHRIST-17C IDEA/COMP INTELL CONCPT

B54
TOTOK W.,HANDBUCH DER BIBLIOGRAPHISCHEN NACHSCHLAGEWERKE. GERMANY LAW CULTURE ADMIN...SOC 20. PAGE 156 H3117 — BIBLIOG/A NAT/G DIPLOM POLICY

B54
US LIBRARY OF CONGRESS,RESEARCH AND INFORMATION ON AFRICA: CONTINUING SOURCES. ISLAM ECO/UNDEV AGRI INDUS R+D ACADEM NAT/G INT/TRADE...SOC 20. PAGE 161 H3210 — BIBLIOG/A AFR PRESS COM/IND

B54
CHECKLIST OF ARCHIVES IN THE JAPANESE MINISTRY OF FOREIGN AFFAIRS....GEOG SOC METH 19/20 CHINJAP. PAGE 161 H3219 — BIBLIOG/A NAT/G ASIA

C54
BERLE A.A. JR.,"THE 20TH CENTURY CAPITALIST REVOLUTION." ECO/DEV NAT/G DIPLOM PRICE CONTROL ATTIT...BIBLIOG/A 20. PAGE 15 H0306 — LG/CO CAP/ISM MGT PWR

B55
BENEDICT B.,A SHORT ANNOTATED BIBLIOGRAPHY RELATING TO THE SOCIOLOGY OF MUSLIM PEOPLES. NAT/G...SOC 20. PAGE 14 H0277 — BIBLIOG/A ISLAM SECT CULTURE

B55
FOGARTY M.P.,ECONOMIC CONTROL. FUT UK ECO/DEV FINAN CONSULT INT/TRADE...CHARTS BIBLIOG/A 20. PAGE 52 H1033 — ECO/TAC NAT/G CONTROL PROB/SOLV

B55
INSTITUTE POLITISCHE WISSEN,POLITISCHE LITERATUR (3 VOLS.). INT/ORG LEAD WAR PEACE...CONCPT TREND NAT/COMP 20. PAGE 77 H1540 — BIBLIOG/A NAT/G DIPLOM POLICY

B55
PYRAH G.B.,IMPERIAL POLICY AND SOUTH AFRICA 1902-1910. SOUTH/AFR UK NAT/G WAR DISCRIM...CONCPT CHARTS BIBLIOG/A 19/20 CMN/WLTH. PAGE 129 H2570 — DIPLOM COLONIAL POLICY RACE/REL

B55
QUAN K.L.,INTRODUCTION TO ASIA: A SELECTIVE GUIDE TO BACKGROUND READING. ECO/UNDEV NAT/G PROB/SOLV DIPLOM ATTIT 20. PAGE 129 H2572 — BIBLIOG/A S/ASIA CULTURE ASIA

C55
GRASSMUCK G.L.,"A MANUAL OF LEBANESE ADMINISTRATION." LEBANON PLAN...CHARTS BIBLIOG/A 20. PAGE 60 H1198
ADMIN NAT/G ISLAM EX/STRUC

B56
BRITISH BORNEO RESEARCH PROJ,BIBLIOGRAPHY OF BRITISH BORNEO (PAMPHLET). UK COM/IND NAT/G EDU/PROP...GEOG 20. PAGE 21 H0421
BIBLIOG/A SOC

B56
CENTRAL AFRICAN ARCHIVES,A GUIDE TO THE PUBLIC RECORDS OF SOUTHERN RHODESIA UNDER THE REGIME OF THE BRITISH SOUTH AFRICA COMPANY, 1890-1923. UK STRUCT NAT/G WRITING GP/REL 19/20. PAGE 28 H0566
BIBLIOG/A COLONIAL ADMIN AFR

B56
DEUTSCH K.W.,AN INTERDISCIPLINARY BIBLIOGRAPHY ON NATIONALISM, 1935-1953. CULTURE SOCIETY SECT ATTIT HABITAT HEREDITY PERCEPT ROLE WEALTH...METH/CNCPT LING 20. PAGE 40 H0798
BIBLIOG/A NAT/LISM COLONIAL ADJUST

B56
EGGAN F.,SELECTED BIBLIOGRAPHY OF THE PHILIPPINES. PHILIPPINE ATTIT...SOC NAT/COMP 20. PAGE 45 H0896
BIBLIOG/A ASIA CULTURE SOCIETY

B56
INTERNATIONAL AFRICAN INST,SELECT ANNOTATED BIBLIOGRAPHY OF TROPICAL AFRICA. NAT/G EDU/PROP ADMIN HEALTH. PAGE 77 H1547
BIBLIOG/A AFR SOC HABITAT

B56
IRIKURA J.K.,SOUTHEAST ASIA: SELECTED ANNOTATED BIBLIOGRAPHY OF JAPANESE PUBLICATIONS. CULTURE ADMIN RACE/REL 20 CHINJAP. PAGE 78 H1567
BIBLIOG/A S/ASIA DIPLOM

B56
PHILIPPINE STUDIES PROGRAM,SELECTED BIBLIOGRAPHY ON THE PHILIPPINES, TOPICALLY ARRANGED AND ANNOTATED. PHILIPPINE SECT DIPLOM COLONIAL LEAD...SOC 18/20. PAGE 125 H2501
BIBLIOG/A S/ASIA NAT/G ECO/UNDEV

B56
TRAGER F.N.,ANNOTATED BIBLIOGRAPHY OF BURMA. BURMA STRUCT NAT/G...GEOG JURID MGT SOC 20. PAGE 156 H3127
BIBLIOG/A S/ASIA CULTURE SOCIETY

B56
WILBER D.N.,ANNOTATED BIBLIOGRAPHY OF AFGHANISTAN. AFGHANISTN...ART/METH GEOG HUM SOC CON/ANAL 19/20. PAGE 168 H3358
BIBLIOG/A SOCIETY NAT/G ASIA

C56
FALL B.B.,"THE VIET-MINH REGIME." VIETNAM LAW ECO/UNDEV POL/PAR FORCES DOMIN WAR ATTIT MARXISM ...BIOG PREDICT BIBLIOG/A 20. PAGE 48 H0967
NAT/G ADMIN EX/STRUC LEAD

C56
NEUMANN S.,"MODERN POLITICAL PARTIES: APPROACHES TO COMPARATIVE POLITIC. FRANCE UK EX/STRUC DOMIN ADMIN LEAD REPRESENT TOTALISM ATTIT...POLICY TREND METH/COMP ANTHOL BIBLIOG/A 20 CMN/WLTH. PAGE 117 H2338
POL/PAR GOV/COMP ELITES MAJORIT

B57
BYRNES R.F.,BIBLIOGRAPHY OF AMERICAN PUBLICATIONS ON EAST CENTRAL EUROPE, 1945-1957 (VOL. XXII). SECT DIPLOM EDU/PROP RACE/REL...ART/METH GEOG JURID SOC LING 20 JEWS. PAGE 25 H0503
BIBLIOG/A COM MARXISM NAT/G

B57
CENTRAL ASIAN RESEARCH CENTRE,BIBLIOGRAPHY OF RECENT SOVIET SOURCE MATERIAL ON SOVIET CENTRAL ASIA AND THE BORDERLANDS. AFGHANISTN INDIA PAKISTAN UAR USSR ECO/UNDEV AGRI EXTR/IND INDUS ACADEM ADMIN ...HEAL HUM LING CON/ANAL 20. PAGE 28 H0567
BIBLIOG/A COM CULTURE NAT/G

B57
CHANDRA S.,PARTIES AND POLITICS AT THE MUGHAL COURT: 1707-1740. INDIA CULTURE EX/STRUC CREATE PLAN PWR...BIBLIOG/A 18. PAGE 29 H0574
POL/PAR ELITES NAT/G

B57
CONOVER H.F.,NORTH AND NORTHEAST AFRICA; A SELECTED ANNOTATED LIST OF WRITINGS. ALGERIA MOROCCO SUDAN UAR CULTURE INT/ORG PROB/SOLV ADJUD NAT/LISM PWR WEALTH...SOC 20 UN. PAGE 32 H0649
BIBLIOG/A DIPLOM AFR ECO/UNDEV

B57
DONALDSON A.G.,SOME COMPARATIVE ASPECTS OF IRISH LAW. IRELAND NAT/G DIPLOM ADMIN CT/SYS LEAD ATTIT SOVEREIGN...JURID BIBLIOG/A 12/20 CMN/WLTH. PAGE 42 H0835
CONSTN LAW NAT/COMP INT/LAW

B57
HIRSCH F.E.,EUROPE TODAY; A BIBLIOGRAPHY (2ND ED.). EUR+WWI MOD/EUR NAT/G WAR 20. PAGE 71 H1424
BIBLIOG/A GEOG DIPLOM

B57
MOYER K.E.,FROM IRAN TO MORROCCO; FROM TURKEY TO THE SUDAN: A SELECTED AND ANNOTATED BIBLIOGRAPHY OF NORTH AFRICA AND NEAR EAST... ISLAM DIPLOM EDU/PROP 20. PAGE 114 H2274
BIBLIOG/A ECO/UNDEV SECT NAT/G

B57
SOUTH PACIFIC COMMISSION,INDEX OF SOCIAL SCIENCE RESEARCH THESES ON THE SOUTH PACIFIC. S/ASIA ACADEM ADMIN COLONIAL...SOC 20. PAGE 147 H2939
BIBLIOG/A ACT/RES SECT CULTURE

B57
TAYLOR J.V.,CHRISTIANITY AND POLITICS IN AFRICA. AFR CONTROL PARTIC GP/REL RACE/REL ATTIT...POLICY BIBLIOG/A WORSHIP 20. PAGE 153 H3055
SECT NAT/G NAT/LISM

L57
BENDIX R.,"POLITICAL SOCIOLOGY." CULTURE INTELL LABOR POL/PAR SECT LEGIS EDU/PROP ADMIN CHOOSE CIVMIL/REL ATTIT...IDEA/COMP 20. PAGE 14 H0274
BIBLIOG/A ACT/RES SOC

L57
LIPSET S.M.,"POLITICAL SOCIOLOGY." NAT/G POL/PAR ECO/TAC PARTIC CHOOSE PWR...BIBLIOG/A 20. PAGE 97 H1939
SOC ALL/IDEOS ACADEM

B58
HUMPHREYS R.A.,LATIN AMERICAN HISTORY: A GUIDE TO THE LITERATURE IN ENGLISH. CULTURE NAT/G DIPLOM BIOG. PAGE 75 H1495
BIBLIOG/A L/A+17C

B58
JOHNSON J.J.,POLITICAL CHANGE IN LATIN AMERICA: THE EMERGENCE OF THE MIDDLE SECTORS. INTELL STRATA STRUCT ECO/UNDEV MUNIC TEC/DEV LEAD REV...DECISION TREND GOV/COMP BIBLIOG/A 20. PAGE 81 H1621
L/A+17C ELITES GP/REL DOMIN

B58
MASON J.B.,THAILAND BIBLIOGRAPHY. S/ASIA THAILAND CULTURE EDU/PROP ADMIN...GEOG SOC LING 20. PAGE 104 H2087
BIBLIOG/A ECO/UNDEV DIPLOM NAT/G

B58
SCOTT D.J.R.,RUSSIAN POLITICAL INSTITUTIONS. RUSSIA USSR CONSTN AGRI DELIB/GP PLAN EDU/PROP CONTROL CHOOSE EFFICIENCY ATTIT MARXISM...BIBLIOG/A 13/20. PAGE 141 H2813
NAT/G POL/PAR ADMIN DECISION

B58
VON FURER-HAIMEN E.,AN ANTHROPOLOGICAL BIBLIOGRAPHY OF SOUTH ASIA (VOL. I). STRATA STRUCT KIN SECT ACT/RES CREATE HABITAT...GEOG OBS 19/20. PAGE 163 H3267
BIBLIOG/A CULTURE S/ASIA SOC

B58
WIGGIN L.M.,THE FACTION OF COUSINS: A POLITICAL ACCOUNT OF THE GRENVILLES, 1733-1763. UK STRUCT KIN NAT/G INGP/REL...CONCPT BIOG BIBLIOG/A 18 GRENVILLES. PAGE 168 H3357
FAM POL/PAR PWR

B59
CAREW-HUNT R.C.,BOOKS ON COMMUNISM. NAT/G POL/PAR DIPLOM REV...BIOG 19/20. PAGE 26 H0528
BIBLIOG/A MARXISM COM ASIA

B59
ELDRIDGE H.T.,THE MATERIALS OF DEMOGRAPHY: A SELECTED AND ANNOTATED BIBLIOGRAPHY. R+D DEATH ...SAMP METH/COMP NAT/COMP 20. PAGE 45 H0905
BIBLIOG/A GEOG STAT TREND

B59
EPSTEIN F.T.,EAST GERMANY: A SELECTED BIBLIOGRAPHY (PAMPHLET). COM GERMANY/E LAW AGRI FINAN INDUS LABOR POL/PAR EDU/PROP ADMIN AGE/Y 20. PAGE 47 H0932
BIBLIOG/A INTELL MARXISM NAT/G

B59
HENDERSON G.P.,REFERENCE MANUAL OF DIRECTORIES (16 VOLS.). MUNIC PROVS GOV/REL 20. PAGE 70 H1394
BIBLIOG/A NAT/COMP NAT/G INDUS

B59
INTERAMERICAN CULTURAL COUN,LISTA DE LIBROS REPRESENTAVOS DE AMERICA. CULTURE DIPLOM ADMIN 20. PAGE 77 H1542
BIBLIOG/A NAT/G L/A+17C SOC

B59
ISRAEL J.,THE CHINESE STUDENT MOVEMENT, 1927-1937; A BIBLIOGRAPHICAL ESSAY BASED ON THE RESOURCES OF THE HOOVER INSTITUTION. ASIA INTELL NAT/G EDU/PROP 20. PAGE 79 H1571
BIBLIOG/A ACADEM ATTIT

B59
NAHM A.C.,JAPANESE PENETRATION OF KOREA, 1894-1910. ASIA KOREA NAT/G...POLICY 20 CHINJAP. PAGE 115 H2303
BIBLIOG/A DIPLOM WAR COLONIAL

C59
EASTON D.,"POLITICAL ANTHROPOLOGY" IN BIENNIAL REVIEW OF ANTHROPOLOGY" UNIV LAW CULTURE ELITES SOCIETY CREATE...PSY CONCPT GP/COMP GEN/METH 20. PAGE 44 H0880
SOC BIBLIOG/A NEW/IDEA

B60
ABERNATHY G.L.,PAKISTAN: A SELECTED, ANNOTATED BIBLIOGRAPHY (2ND ED., PAMPHLET). PAKISTAN CULTURE LEAD 20. PAGE 3 H0056
BIBLIOG/A SOC

B60
EMERY E.,INTRODUCTION TO MASS COMMUNICATIONS. ACADEM PROF/ORG SCHOOL ACT/RES EDU/PROP ATTIT ...CONCPT BIBLIOG/A. PAGE 46 H0920
COM/IND PRESS CON/ANAL CULTURE

B60
LEYDER J.,BIBLIOGRAPHIE DE L'ENSEIGNEMENT SUPERIEUR ET DE LA RECHERCHE SCIENTIFIQUE EN AFRIQUE INTERTROPICALE (2 VOLS.). AFR CULTURE ECO/UNDEV
BIBLIOG/A ACT/RES ACADEM

AGRI PLAN EDU/PROP ADMIN COLONIAL...GEOG SOC/INTEG 20 NEGRO. PAGE 96 H1918
R+D

B60
MEYRIAT J.,LA SCIENCE POLITIQUE EN FRANCE, 1945-1958; BIBLIOGRAPHIES FRANCAISES DE SCIENCES SOCIALES (VOL. I). EUR+WWI FRANCE POL/PAR DIPLOM ADMIN CHOOSE ATTIT...IDEA/COMP METH/COMP NAT/COMP 20. PAGE 110 H2193
BIBLIOG/A NAT/G CONCPT PHIL/SCI

B60
PITCHER G.M.,BIBLIOGRAPHY OF GHANA. AFR GHANA NAT/G 20. PAGE 126 H2517
BIBLIOG/A SOC

B60
US LIBRARY OF CONGRESS,INDEX TO LATIN AMERICAN LEGISLATION: 1950-1960 (2 VOLS.). NAT/G DELIB/GP ADMIN PARL/PROC 20. PAGE 161 H3211
BIBLIOG/A LEGIS L/A+17C JURID

B60
WORLEY P.,ASIA TODAY (REV. ED.) (PAMPHLET). COM ECO/UNDEV AGRI FINAN INDUS POL/PAR FOR/AID ADMIN MARXISM 20. PAGE 170 H3411
BIBLIOG/A ASIA DIPLOM NAT/G

C60
EBENSTEIN W.,"MODERN POLITICAL THOUGHT (2ND ED.)" NAT/G CAP/ISM NAT/LISM PERSON ORD/FREE PWR ALL/IDEOS NEW/LIB SOCISM...TRADIT PSY BIBLIOG/A 18/20. PAGE 44 H0884
IDEA/COMP PHIL/SCI CONCPT GEN/LAWS

C60
HAZARD J.N.,"THE SOVIET SYSTEM OF GOVERNMENT." USSR SOCIETY INDUS NAT/G POL/PAR DIPLOM CT/SYS...JURID CHARTS BIBLIOG/A 20. PAGE 69 H1373
COM NAT/COMP STRUCT ADMIN

B61
BURDETTE F.L.,POLITICAL SCIENCE: A SELECTED BIBLIOGRAPHY OF BOOKS IN PRINT, WITH ANNOTATIONS (PAMPHLET). LAW LOC/G NAT/G POL/PAR PROVS DIPLOM EDU/PROP ADMIN CHOOSE ATTIT 20. PAGE 24 H0479
BIBLIOG/A GOV/COMP CONCPT ROUTINE

B61
CARNELL F.,THE POLITICS OF THE NEW STATES: A SELECT ANNOTATED BIBLIOGRAPHY WITH SPECIAL REFERENCE TO THE COMMONWEALTH. CONSTN ELITES LABOR NAT/G POL/PAR EX/STRUC DIPLOM ADJUD ADMIN...GOV/COMP 20 COMMONWLTH. PAGE 27 H0534
BIBLIOG/A AFR ASIA COLONIAL

B61
COHN B.S.,DEVELOPMENT AND IMPACT OF BRITISH ADMINISTRATION IN INDIA: A BIBLIOGRAPHIC ESSAY. INDIA UK ECO/UNDEV NAT/G DOMIN...POLICY MGT SOC 19/20. PAGE 31 H0619
BIBLIOG/A COLONIAL S/ASIA ADMIN

B61
HEMPSTONE S.,THE NEW AFRICA. AGRI INDUS KIN NAT/G COLONIAL MARXISM...SOC INT TREND NAT/COMP BIBLIOG/A 20. PAGE 69 H1392
AFR ORD/FREE PERSON CULTURE

B61
HOLDSWORTH M.,SOVIET AFRICAN STUDIES 1918-1959. USSR ACADEM NAT/G DIPLOM REGION KNOWL 20. PAGE 72 H1448
BIBLIOG/A AFR HABITAT NAT/COMP

B61
JONES R.,AFRICA BIBLIOGRAPHY SERIES: SOUTH EAST CENTRAL AFRICA AND MADAGASCAR. AFR MADAGASCAR RHODESIA SECT BIO/SOC...JURID NAT/COMP 20. PAGE 82 H1633
BIBLIOG/A SOC CULTURE LING

B61
LA PONCE J.A.,THE GOVERNMENT OF THE FIFTH REPUBLIC: FRENCH POLITICAL PARTIES AND THE CONSTITUTION. ALGERIA FRANCE LAW NAT/G DELIB/GP LEGIS ECO/TAC MARXISM SOCISM...CHARTS BIBLIOG/A 20 DEGAULLE/C. PAGE 90 H1794
PWR POL/PAR CONSTN CHIEF

B61
LEHMAN R.L.,AFRICA SOUTH OF THE SAHARA (PAMPHLET). DIPLOM COLONIAL NAT/LISM. PAGE 93 H1863
BIBLIOG/A AFR CULTURE NAT/G

B61
LEVIN L.A.,BIBLIOGRAFIIA BIBLIOGRAFII PROIZVEDENII K. MARKSA, F. ENGELSA, V.I. LENINA. COM USSR NAT/G POL/PAR WORKER LEAD REV ATTIT...POLICY IDEA/COMP 20 MARX/KARL LENIN/VI ENGELS. PAGE 95 H1899
BIBLIOG/A MARXISM MARXIST CONCPT

B61
PALMER N.D.,THE INDIAN POLITICAL SYSTEM. INDIA ECO/UNDEV SECT CHIEF COLONIAL CHOOSE ALL/IDEOS SOCISM...CHARTS BIBLIOG/A 20. PAGE 123 H2452
NAT/LISM POL/PAR NAT/G DIPLOM

B61
RYDINGS H.A.,THE BIBLIOGRAPHIES OF WEST AFRICA (PAMPHLET). ECO/UNDEV NAT/G COLONIAL REGION ATTIT 20. PAGE 136 H2725
BIBLIOG/A AFR NAT/COMP

B61
TACHAKKYO K.,BIBLIOGRAPHY OF KOREAN STUDIES: A BIBLIOGRAPHICAL GUIDE TO KOREAN PUBLICATIONS ON KOREAN STUDIES APPEARING 1945-1958. KOREA LAW...HUM JURID PHIL/SCI LING 19/20. PAGE 152 H3033
BIBLIOG/A SOCIETY CULTURE WAR

B61
WARD R.E.,JAPANESE POLITICAL SCIENCE: A GUIDE TO JAPANESE REFERENCE AND RESEARCH MATERIALS (2ND ED.). LAW CONSTN STRATA NAT/G POL/PAR DELIB/GP LEGIS ADMIN CHOOSE GP/REL...INT/LAW 19/20 CHINJAP. PAGE 165 H3306
BIBLIOG/A PHIL/SCI

B61
ZIMMERMAN I.,A GUIDE TO CURRENT LATIN AMERICAN PERIODICALS: HUMANITIES AND SOCIAL SCIENCES. LABOR SECT EDU/PROP...GEOG HUM SOC LING STAT NAT/COMP 20. PAGE 173 H3456
BIBLIOG/A DIPLOM L/A+17C PHIL/SCI

C61
LAPONCE J.A.,"THE GOVERNMENT OF THE FIFTH REPUBLIC." FRANCE CHIEF LEGIS PARL/PROC CHOOSE ...CHARTS GP/COMP IDEA/COMP BIBLIOG/A 20. PAGE 91 H1814
POL/PAR NAT/G CONSTN DOMIN

B62
COSTA RICA UNIVERSIDAD BIBL,LISTA DE TESIS DE GRADO DE LA UNIVERSIDAD DE COSTA RICA. COSTA/RICA LAW LOC/G ADMIN LEAD...SOC 20. PAGE 34 H0675
BIBLIOG/A NAT/G DIPLOM ECO/UNDEV

B62
DILLING A.R.,ABORIGINE CULTURE HISTORY - A SURVEY OF PUBLICATIONS 1954-1957. GUINEA...SOC CHARTS NAT/COMP BIBLIOG/A AUSTRAL ABORIGINES. PAGE 41 H0825
S/ASIA HIST/WRIT CULTURE KIN

B62
HAY S.N.,SOUTHEAST ASIAN HISTORY: A BIBLIOGRAPHICAL GUIDE. STRATA KIN NAT/G REGION GUERRILLA REV WAR ADJUST HABITAT PERCEPT ALL/IDEOS...CHARTS 5/20. PAGE 68 H1365
BIBLIOG/A S/ASIA CULTURE

B62
HUCKER C.O.,CHINA: A CRITICAL BIBLIOGRAPHY (PAMPHLET). ASIA STRUCT AGRI FINAN INDUS HABITAT MARXISM...EPIST HUM. PAGE 74 H1487
BIBLIOG/A CULTURE INTELL SOCIETY

B62
KIRPICEVA I.K.,HANDBUCH DER RUSSISCHEN UND SOWJETISCHEN BIBLIOGRAPHIEN (5 VOLS.). USSR STRUCT ECO/DEV DIPLOM LEAD ATTIT 18/20. PAGE 86 H1726
BIBLIOG/A NAT/G MARXISM COM

B62
SILBERMAN B.S.,JAPAN AND KOREA; A CRITICAL BIBLIOGRAPHY. KOREA LAW STRATA STRUCT AGRI INDUS NAT/G POL/PAR SECT...HUM LING IDEA/COMP 5/20 CHINJAP. PAGE 144 H2872
BIBLIOG/A CULTURE S/ASIA

B62
UMENDRAS H.,LES SOCIETESRFRANCAISES; BIBLIOGRAPHIES FRANCAISES DE SCIENCE SOCIALES (VOL. III). FRANCE SECT WORKER 20. PAGE 158 H3154
BIBLIOG/A AGRI MUNIC CULTURE

B62
US DEPARTMENT OF THE ARMY,GUIDE TO JAPANESE MONOGRAPHS AND JAPANESE STUDIES ON MANCHURIA: 1945-1960. CHINA/COM NAT/G DIPLOM LEAD COERCE WAR ...CHARTS 19/20 CHINJAP. PAGE 160 H3193
BIBLIOG/A FORCES ASIA S/ASIA

B63
BRODOWSKI J.H.,LATIN AMERICA TODAY. CULTURE LEAD ...SOC 20. PAGE 21 H0426
BIBLIOG/A L/A+17C NAT/G DIPLOM

B63
CONOVER H.F.,AFRICA SOUTH OF THE SAHARA. CULTURE SECT TEC/DEV...ART/METH GEOG SOC. PAGE 33 H0654
BIBLIOG/A AFR CON/ANAL

B63
FABER K.,DIE NATIONALISTISCHE PUBLIZISTIK DEUTSCHLANDS VON 1866 BIS 1871 (2 VOLS.). EUR+WWI GERMANY DIPLOM EDU/PROP 19. PAGE 48 H0957
BIBLIOG/A NAT/G NAT/LISM POL/PAR

B63
FISCHER-GALATI S.A.,RUMANIA; A BIBLIOGRAPHIC GUIDE (PAMPHLET). ROMANIA INTELL ECO/DEV LABOR SECT WEALTH...GEOG SOC/WK LING 20. PAGE 51 H1012
BIBLIOG/A NAT/G COM LAW

B63
GOURNAY B.,PUBLIC ADMINISTRATION. FRANCE LAW CONSTN AGRI FINAN LABOR SCHOOL EX/STRUC CHOOSE...MGT METH/COMP 20. PAGE 59 H1189
BIBLIOG/A ADMIN NAT/G LOC/G

B63
NATIONAL OFF STATE GOVT THAI,STATISTICAL BIBLIOGRAPHY: AN ANNOTATED BIBLIOGRAPHY OF THAI GOVERNMENTAL STATISTICAL PUBLICATIONS. THAILAND AGRI 20. PAGE 116 H2321
BIBLIOG/A STAT NAT/G S/ASIA

B64
ANDREN N.,GOVERNMENT AND POLITICS IN THE NORDIC COUNTRIES: DENMARK, FINLAND, ICELAND, NORWAY, SWEDEN. DENMARK FINLAND ICELAND NORWAY SWEDEN POL/PAR CHIEF LEGIS ADMIN REGION REPRESENT ATTIT CONSERVE...CHARTS BIBLIOG/A 20. PAGE 7 H0137
CONSTN NAT/G CULTURE GOV/COMP

B64
BERNSTEIN H.,A BOOKSHELF ON BRAZIL. BRAZIL ADMIN COLONIAL...HUM JURID SOC 20. PAGE 16 H0315
BIBLIOG/A NAT/G L/A+17C ECO/UNDEV

B64
EMBREE A.T.,A GUIDE TO PAPERBACKS ON ASIA; SELECTED AND ANNOTATED (PAMPHLET). CULTURE SOCIETY ECO/UNDEV SECT DIPLOM COLONIAL MARXISM...SOC 20. PAGE 46
BIBLIOG/A ASIA S/ASIA

H0913 NAT/G

B64
GESELLSCHAFT RECHTSVERGLEICH,BIBLIOGRAPHIE DES DEUTSCHEN RECHTS (BIBLIOGRAPHY OF GERMAN LAW, TRANS. BY COURTLAND PETERSON). GERMANY FINAN INDUS LABOR SECT FORCES CT/SYS PARL/PROC CRIME...INT/LAW SOC NAT/COMP 20. PAGE 56 H1117 BIBLIOG/A JURID CONSTN ADMIN

B64
HAZLEWOOD A.,THE ECONOMICS OF DEVELOPMENT: AN ANNOTATED LIST OF BOOKS AND ARTICLES PUBLISHED 1958-1962. AGRI FINAN INDUS LABOR NAT/G DIPLOM INT/TRADE INCOME...MGT 20. PAGE 69 H1374 BIBLIOG/A ECO/UNDEV TEC/DEV

B64
HOBBS C.C.,SOUTHEAST ASIA: AN ANNOTATED BIBLIOGRAPHY OF SELECTED REFERENCES IN WESTERN LANGUAGES (REV. ED.). CAMBODIA INDONESIA LAOS THAILAND VIETNAM CONSTN NAT/G...SOC WORSHIP 20. PAGE 72 H1437 BIBLIOG/A S/ASIA CULTURE SOCIETY

B64
JOHNSON A.F.,BIBLIOGRAPHY OF GHANA: 1930-1961. GHANA LAW AGRI INDUS NAT/G INT/TRADE EDU/PROP HEALTH...GEOG AUD/VIS CHARTS 20. PAGE 81 H1618 BIBLIOG/A CULTURE SOC

B64
KOLARZ W.,BOOKS ON COMMUNISM. USSR WOR+45 CULTURE NAT/G POL/PAR DIPLOM LEAD...CONCPT GOV/COMP IDEA/COMP. PAGE 88 H1752 BIBLIOG/A SOCIETY COM MARXISM

B64
LEBRUN J.,BIBLIOGRAPHIE DE LA FERTILITE DES SOLS ET ELEMENTS DE SOCIOLOGIE RURALE EN AFRIQUE AU SUD DU SAHARA. AFR PLAN TEC/DEV EFFICIENCY PRODUC...GEOG SOC NAT/COMP 20. PAGE 93 H1850 BIBLIOG/A ECO/UNDEV HABITAT AGRI

B64
MAHAR J.M.,INDIA: A CRITICAL BIBLIOGRAPHY. INDIA PAKISTAN CULTURE ECO/UNDEV LOC/G POL/PAR SECT PROB/SOLV DIPLOM ADMIN COLONIAL PARL/PROC ATTIT 20. PAGE 101 H2016 BIBLIOG/A S/ASIA NAT/G LEAD

B64
MATTHEWS D.G.,A CURRENT VIEW OF AFRICANA (PAMPHLET). CULTURE ECO/UNDEV DIPLOM RACE/REL ATTIT 20. PAGE 105 H2092 BIBLIOG/A AFR NAT/G NAT/LISM

B64
MCCALL D.F.,AFRICA IN TIME PERSPECTIVE. AFR EXTR/IND KIN SECT CREATE PERS/REL HABITAT...GEOG METH/CNCPT LING BIBLIOG/A TIME 20. PAGE 106 H2124 HIST/WRIT OBS/ENVIR CULTURE

B64
NATIONAL BOOK LEAGUE,THE COMMONWEALTH IN BOOKS: AN ANNOTATED LIST. CANADA UK LOC/G SECT ADMIN...SOC BIOG 20 CMN/WLTH. PAGE 116 H2320 BIBLIOG/A JURID NAT/G

B64
PERAZA SARAUSA F.,DIRECTORIO DE REVISTAS Y PERIODICOS DE CUBA. CUBA L/A+17C NAT/G ATTIT 20. PAGE 125 H2490 BIBLIOG/A PRESS SERV/IND LEAD

B64
ROBERTS HL,FOREIGN AFFAIRS BIBLIOGRAPHY, 1952-1962. ECO/DEV SECT PLAN FOR/AID INT/TRADE ARMS/CONT NAT/LISM ATTIT...INT/LAW GOV/COMP IDEA/COMP 20. PAGE 132 H2643 BIBLIOG/A DIPLOM INT/ORG WAR

B64
SZLADITS C.,BIBLIOGRAPHY ON FOREIGN AND COMPARATIVE LAW: BOOKS AND ARTICLES IN ENGLISH (SUPPLEMENT 1962). FINAN INDUS JUDGE LICENSE ADMIN CT/SYS PARL/PROC OWN...INT/LAW CLASSIF METH/COMP NAT/COMP 20. PAGE 151 H3027 BIBLIOG/A JURID ADJUD LAW

B64
TODD W.B.,A BIBLIOGRAPHY OF EDMUND BURKE. MOD/EUR UK NAT/G EDU/PROP ATTIT...HUM 18 BURKE/EDM. PAGE 156 H3110 BIBLIOG/A PHIL/SCI WRITING CONCPT

B64
US LIBRARY OF CONGRESS,SOUTHEAST ASIA. CULTURE ...SOC STAT 20. PAGE 161 H3213 BIBLIOG/A S/ASIA ECO/UNDEV NAT/G

B64
VON FURER-HAIMEN E.,AN ANTHROPOLOGICAL BIBLIOGRAPHY OF SOUTH ASIA (VOL. II). STRATA STRUCT KIN SECT ACT/RES CREATE HABITAT...GEOG OBS 20. PAGE 163 H3268 BIBLIOG/A CULTURE S/ASIA SOC

B64
WITHERELL J.W.,OFFICIAL PUBLICATIONS OF FRENCH EQUATORIAL AFRICA, FRENCH CAMEROONS, AND TOGO, 1946-1958 (PAMPHLET). CAMEROON CHAD FRANCE GABON TOGO LAW ECO/UNDEV EXTR/IND INT/TRADE...GEOG HEAL 20. PAGE 169 H3392 BIBLIOG/A AFR NAT/G ADMIN

S64
HORECKY P.L.,"LIBRARY OF CONGRESS PUBLICATIONS IN AID OF USSR AND EAST EUROPEAN RESEARCH." BULGARIA CZECHOSLVK POLAND USSR YUGOSLAVIA NAT/G POL/PAR DIPLOM ADMIN GOV/REL...CLASSIF 20. PAGE 73 H1468 BIBLIOG/A COM MARXISM

S64
SOLOVEYTCHIK G.,"BOOKS ON RUSSIA." USSR ELITES NAT/G PERF/ART REV GOV/REL MARXISM...AUD/VIS 20. PAGE 147 H2929 BIBLIOG/A COM CULTURE

B65
BRIDGMAN J.,GERMAN AFRICA: A SELECT ANNOTATED BIBLIOGRAPHY. AFR AGRI DIPLOM REPAR WAR FASCISM 20. PAGE 21 H0414 BIBLIOG/A COLONIAL NAT/G EDU/PROP

B65
BROCK C.,A GUIDE TO LIBRARY RESOURCES FOR POLITICAL SCIENCE STUDENTS AT THE UNIVERSITY OF NORTH CAROLINA (PAMPHLET). USA+45 WOR+45 PROVS ATTIT MARXISM...POLICY NAT/COMP UN. PAGE 21 H0422 BIBLIOG/A DIPLOM NAT/G INT/ORG

B65
CHUNG Y.S.,KOREA: A SELECTED BIBLIOGRAPHY 1959-1963. ASIA KOREA NAT/G DIPLOM 20. PAGE 30 H0601 BIBLIOG/A SOC

B65
FORM W.H.,INDUSTRIAL RELATIONS AND SOCIAL CHANGE IN LATIN AMERICA. L/A+17C AGRI LABOR NAT/G PLAN PROB/SOLV DIPLOM...MGT SOC ANTHOL BIBLIOG/A METH 20. PAGE 52 H1038 INDUS GP/REL NAT/COMP ECO/UNDEV

B65
GOPAL S.,BRITISH POLICY IN INDIA 1858-1905. INDIA UK ELITES CHIEF DELIB/GP ECO/TAC GP/REL DISCRIM ATTIT...IDEA/COMP NAT/COMP PERS/COMP BIBLIOG/A 19/20. PAGE 59 H1176 COLONIAL ADMIN POL/PAR ECO/UNDEV

B65
HERRICK B.H.,URBAN MIGRATION AND ECONOMIC DEVELOPMENT IN CHILE. CHILE AGRI INDUS LABOR NAT/G CENTRAL PRODUC...STAT SAMP CHARTS BIBLIOG/A 20 MIGRATION. PAGE 70 H1404 HABITAT GEOG MUNIC ECO/UNDEV

B65
HORNE A.J.,THE COMMONWEALTH TODAY. AFR ASIA CANADA UK STRUCT ECO/UNDEV NAT/G SECT GP/REL 20 AUSTRAL CMN/WLTH. PAGE 73 H1470 BIBLIOG/A SOCIETY CULTURE

B65
NEWBURY C.W.,BRITISH POLICY TOWARDS WEST AFRICA: SELECT DOCUMENTS 1786-1874. AFR UK INT/TRADE DOMIN ADMIN COLONIAL CT/SYS COERCE ORD/FREE...BIBLIOG/A 18/19. PAGE 117 H2345 DIPLOM POLICY NAT/G WRITING

B65
PUNDEEF M.V.,BULGARIA; A BIBLIOGRAPHIC GUIDE. BULGARIA LAW CULTURE INTELL ECO/DEV LEAD MARXISM 20. PAGE 128 H2566 BIBLIOG/A NAT/G COM SOCISM

B65
RANDALL F.B.,STALIN'S RUSSIA. USSR STRUCT AGRI NAT/G PLAN DIPLOM WAR TOTALISM MARXISM...BIBLIOG/A 19/20 STALIN/J. PAGE 129 H2590 BIOG INDUS ECO/DEV

B65
SALVADORI M.,ITALY. AUSTRIA FRANCE GERMANY ITALY SPAIN CULTURE NAT/G POL/PAR DIPLOM WAR FASCISM LAISSEZ MARXISM...TIME/SEQ CHARTS BIBLIOG/A. PAGE 137 H2744 NAT/LISM CATHISM SOCIETY

B65
SAUVAGET J.,INTRODUCTION TO THE HISTORY OF THE MIDDLE EAST (A BIBLIOGRAPHICAL GUIDE). LAW CULTURE GEOG. PAGE 138 H2757 BIBLIOG/A ISLAM GOV/COMP

B65
SIMMS R.P.,URBANIZATION IN WEST AFRICA; A REVIEW OF CURRENT LITERATURE. AFR PLAN TEC/DEV...SOC OBS NAT/COMP 20. PAGE 144 H2878 BIBLIOG/A MUNIC ECO/DEV ECO/UNDEV

B65
US DEPARTMENT OF DEFENSE,US SECURITY ARMS CONTROL, AND DISARMAMENT 1961-1965 (PAMPHLET). CHINA/COM COM GERMANY/W ISRAEL SPACE USA+45 USSR WOR+45 FORCES EDU/PROP DETER EQUILIB PEACE ALL/VALS...GOV/COMP 20 NATO. PAGE 159 H3183 BIBLIOG/A ARMS/CONT NUC/PWR DIPLOM

B65
US LIBRARY OF CONGRESS,RARE BOOKS DIVISION: GUIDE TO ITS COLLECTION AND SERVICES. LOC/G SECT WAR. PAGE 161 H3214 BIBLIOG/A NAT/G DIPLOM

L65
MATTHEWS D.G.,"A CURRENT BIBLIOGRAPHY ON ETHIOPIAN AFFAIRS: A SELECT BIBLIOGRAPHY FROM 1950-1964." ETHIOPIA LAW CULTURE ECO/UNDEV INDUS LABOR SECT FORCES DIPLOM CIVMIL/REL RACE/REL...LING STAT 20. PAGE 105 H2093 BIBLIOG/A ADMIN POL/PAR NAT/G

C65
COLEMAN J.S.,"EDUCATION AND POLITICAL DEVELOPMENT." COM CULTURE INTELL STRUCT SCHOOL PERSON SOVEREIGN ...POLICY ANTHOL BIBLIOG/A METH 20. PAGE 31 H0629 ECO/UNDEV NAT/LISM EDU/PROP TEC/DEV

B66
CHANG,THE PARTY AND THE NATIONAL QUESTION IN CHINA (TRANS. BY GEORGE MOSELEY). CHINA/COM CULTURE CONTROL NAT/LISM...CHARTS BIBLIOG/A 20. PAGE 29 H0576 GP/REL REGION ISOLAT MARXISM

B66
DOUMA J.,BIBLIOGRAPHY ON THE INTERNATIONAL COURT INCLUDING THE PERMANENT COURT, 1918-1964. WOR+45 WOR-45 DELIB/GP WAR PRIVIL...JURID NAT/COMP 20 UN LEAGUE/NAT. PAGE 42 H0844 BIBLIOG/A INT/ORG CT/SYS DIPLOM

B66
EMBREE A.T.,ASIA: A GUIDE TO BASIC BOOKS (PAMPHLET). ECO/UNDEV SECT FORCES DIPLOM ALL/IDEOS ...SOC 20. PAGE 46 H0914 BIBLIOG/A ASIA S/ASIA

NAT/G

B66
FLINT J.E.,NIGERIA AND GHANA. AFR GHANA NIGERIA UK NAT/G DOMIN DISCRIM...CHARTS BIBLIOG/A 15/20 NEGRO MAPS. PAGE 51 H1026 — CULTURE COLONIAL NAT/LISM

B66
GLAZER M.,THE FEDERAL GOVERNMENT AND THE UNIVERSITY. CHILE PROB/SOLV DIPLOM GIVE ADMIN WAR ...POLICY SOC 20. PAGE 57 H1140 — BIBLIOG/A NAT/G PLAN ACADEM

B66
HANKE L.,HANDBOOK OF LATIN AMERICAN STUDIES. ECO/UNDEV ADMIN LEAD...HUM SOC 20. PAGE 65 H1313 — BIBLIOG/A L/A+17C INDEX NAT/G

B66
HEYMANN F.G.,POLAND AND CZECHOSLOVAKIA. COM CZECHOSLVK POLAND...CHARTS BIBLIOG/A 9/20. PAGE 70 H1413 — CULTURE NAT/LISM ORD/FREE WAR

B66
HOPKINS J.F.K.,ARABIC PERIODICAL LITERATURE, 1961. ISLAM LAW CULTURE SECT...GEOG HEAL PHIL/SCI PSY SOC 20. PAGE 73 H1466 — BIBLIOG/A NAT/LISM TEC/DEV INDUS

B66
JONES D.H.,AFRICA BIBLIOGRAPHY SERIES: EAST AFRICA. AFR UGANDA SECT BIO/SOC...JURID NAT/COMP 20. PAGE 82 H1630 — BIBLIOG/A SOC CULTURE LING

B66
KEYES J.G.,A BIBLIOGRAPHY OF WESTERN LANGUAGE PUBLICATIONS CONCERNING NORTH VIETNAM IN THE CORNELL LIBRARY. VIETNAM/N NAT/G FORCES TEC/DEV DIPLOM LEAD RACE/REL...GEOG SOC 20. PAGE 85 H1700 — BIBLIOG/A CULTURE ECO/UNDEV S/ASIA

B66
LAVEN P.,RENAISSANCE ITALY: 1464-1534. ITALY AGRI EXTR/IND FINAN MUNIC INT/TRADE DRIVE...CATH GEOG CHARTS BIBLIOG/A 15. PAGE 92 H1841 — CULTURE HUM TEC/DEV KNOWL

B66
LEYBURN J.G.,THE HAITIAN PEOPLE (REV. ED.). HAITI SOCIETY FAM SECT DOMIN COLONIAL MARRIAGE...SOC CHARTS BIBLIOG/A 18/10. PAGE 96 H1917 — STRUCT STRATA INGP/REL CULTURE

B66
MAICHEL K.,CATALOG OF SOVIET AND RUSSIAN NEWSPAPERS AT THE HOOVER INSTITUTION OF WAR, REVOLUTION AND PEACE. USSR NAT/G EDU/PROP LEAD REV WAR PEACE ATTIT 19/20. PAGE 101 H2017 — BIBLIOG/A PRESS COM MARXISM

B66
SPULBER N.,THE STATE AND ECONOMIC DEVELOPMENT IN EASTERN EUROPE. BULGARIA COM CZECHOSLVK HUNGARY POLAND YUGOSLAVIA CULTURE PLAN CAP/ISM INT/TRADE CONTROL...POLICY CHARTS METH/COMP BIBLIOG/A 19/20. PAGE 148 H2958 — ECO/DEV ECO/UNDEV NAT/G TOTALISM

B66
US DEPARTMENT OF STATE,RESEARCH ON AFRICA (EXTERNAL RESEARCH LIST NO 5-25). LAW CULTURE ECO/UNDEV POL/PAR DIPLOM EDU/PROP LEAD REGION MARXISM...GEOG LING WORSHIP 20. PAGE 159 H3188 — BIBLIOG/A ASIA S/ASIA NAT/G

B66
US DEPARTMENT OF STATE,RESEARCH ON THE AMERICAN REPUBLICS (EXTERNAL RESEARCH LIST NO 6-25). CULTURE SOCIETY POL/PAR DIPLOM EDU/PROP MARXISM WORSHIP 20 OAS. PAGE 159 H3189 — BIBLIOG/A L/A+17C REGION NAT/G

B66
US DEPARTMENT OF STATE,RESEARCH ON THE MIDDLE EAST (EXTERNAL RESEARCH LIST NO 4-25). GREECE ISRAEL SYRIA UAR YEMEN CULTURE SOCIETY POL/PAR SECT DIPLOM EDU/PROP WAR NAT/LISM...GEOG GOV/COMP 20. PAGE 160 H3190 — BIBLIOG/A ISLAM NAT/G REGION

B66
US DEPARTMENT OF STATE,RESEARCH ON THE USSR AND EASTERN EUROPE (EXTERNAL RESEARCH LIST NO 1-25). USSR LAW CULTURE SOCIETY NAT/G TEC/DEV DIPLOM EDU/PROP REGION...GEOG LING. PAGE 160 H3191 — BIBLIOG/A EUR+WWI COM MARXISM

B66
US DEPARTMENT OF STATE,RESEARCH ON WESTERN EUROPE, GREAT BRITAIN, AND CANADA (EXTERNAL RESEARCH LIST NO 3-25). CANADA GERMANY/W UK LAW CULTURE NAT/G POL/PAR FORCES EDU/PROP REGION MARXISM...GEOG SOC WORSHIP 20 CMN/WLTH. PAGE 160 H3192 — BIBLIOG/A EUR+WWI DIPLOM

B66
US DEPARTMENT OF THE ARMY,COMMUNIST CHINA: A STRATEGIC SURVEY: A BIBLIOGRAPHY (PAMPHLET NO. 20-67). CHINA/COM COM INDIA USSR NAT/G POL/PAR EX/STRUC FORCES NUC/PWR REV ATTIT...POLICY GEOG CHARTS. PAGE 160 H3194 — BIBLIOG/A MARXISM S/ASIA DIPLOM

B66
US DEPARTMENT OF THE ARMY,SOUTH ASIA: A STRATEGIC SURVEY (PAMPHLET NO. 550-3). AFGHANISTN INDIA NEPAL PAKISTAN ECO/UNDEV INT/ORG POL/PAR FORCES FOR/AID INT/TRADE LEAD WAR...POLICY SOC TREND 20. PAGE 160 H3195 — BIBLIOG/A S/ASIA DIPLOM NAT/G

S66
GRUNDY K.W.,"RECENT CONTRIBUTIONS TO THE STUDY OF AFRICAN POLITICAL THOUGHT." DIPLOM NAT/LISM ALL/IDEOS...NEW/IDEA GOV/COMP 20. PAGE 62 H1239 — BIBLIOG/A AFR ATTIT IDEA/COMP

S66
O'BRIEN W.V.,"EVENTS AND TRENDS: PATTERNS OF AFRICAN INTERNATIONAL POLITICAL BEHAVIOR." CULTURE SOCIETY NAT/G NAT/LISM SOCISM. PAGE 119 H2386 — BIBLIOG/A AFR TREND DIPLOM

N66
HISPANIC LUSO-BRAZILIAN COUN,LATIN AMERICA; AN INTRODUCTION TO MODERN BOOKS IN ENGLISH CONCERNING THE COUNTRIES OF LATIN AMERICA (2ND ED., PAMPH). CULTURE GOV/REL GEOG. PAGE 71 H1425 — BIBLIOG/A ECO/UNDEV NAT/G L/A+17C

B67
KOLKOWICZ R.,THE SOVIET MILITARY AND THE COMMUNIST PARTY. COM USSR ELITES NAT/G CREATE CIVMIL/REL GP/REL...TREND BIBLIOG/A 20 COM/PARTY. PAGE 88 H1753 — MARXISM CONSTN FORCES POL/PAR

B67
REES D.,THE AGE OF CONTAINMENT. WOR+45 FORCES ARMS/CONT ATTIT PWR...CONCPT TREND METH/COMP BIBLIOG/A 20. PAGE 130 H2608 — DIPLOM NUC/PWR MARXISM GOV/COMP

B67
SCHWARTZ B.,THE ROOTS OF FREEDOM: A CONSTITUTIONAL HISTORY OF ENGLAND. UK LAW POL/PAR DELIB/GP LEGIS REV REPRESENT...JURID BIBLIOG/A 13/20. PAGE 140 H2809 — CONSTN PARL/PROC NAT/G

B67
SHAFFER H.G.,THE COMMUNIST WORLD: MARXIST AND NON-MARXIST VIEWS. WOR+45 SOCIETY DIPLOM ECO/TAC CONTROL SOCISM...MARXIST ANTHOL BIBLIOG/A 20. PAGE 142 H2838 — MARXISM NAT/COMP IDEA/COMP COM

B67
UNIVERSAL REFERENCE SYSTEM,COMPARATIVE GOVERNMENT AND CULTURES (VOLUME X). WOR+45 WOR-45 NAT/G POL/PAR ATTIT...CON/ANAL COMPUT/IR IDEA/COMP GEN/METH. PAGE 158 H3168 — BIBLIOG/A GOV/COMP CULTURE NAT/COMP

L67
EINAUDI L.,"ANNOTATED BIBLIOGRAPHY OF LATIN AMERICAN MILITARY JOURNALS" LAW TEC/DEV DOMIN EDU/PROP COERCE WAR CIVMIL/REL 20. PAGE 45 H0899 — BIBLIOG/A NAT/G FORCES L/A+17C

S67
BAER W.,"THE INFLATION CONTROVERSY IN LATIN AMERICA: SURVEY." L/A+17C ECO/UNDEV AGRI FINAN INDUS PLAN PROB/SOLV TEC/DEV...BIBLIOG/A 20. PAGE 10 H0194 — NAT/G BAL/PAY ECO/TAC BUDGET

S67
ROTBERG R.I.,"COLONIALISM AND AFTER: THE POLITICAL LITERATURE OF CENTRAL AFRICA - A BIBLIOGRAPHIC ESSAY." AFR CHIEF EX/STRUC REV INGP/REL RACE/REL SOVEREIGN 20. PAGE 135 H2693 — BIBLIOG/A COLONIAL DIPLOM NAT/G

C89
PLAYFAIR R.L.,"A BIBLIOGRAPHY OF ALGERIA." ALGERIA CULTURE ECO/UNDEV DIST/IND EXTR/IND FINAN SECT CRIME 16/19. PAGE 126 H2525 — BIBLIOG/A ISLAM GEOG

B99
RIPLEY W.Z.,A SELECTED BIBLIOGRAPHY OF THE ANTHROPOLOGY AND ETHNOLOGY OF EUROPE. SOCIETY STRATA STRUCT KIN SECT VOL/ASSN GP/REL INGP/REL HABITAT...GEOG 19. PAGE 132 H2632 — BIBLIOG/A MOD/EUR SOC CULTURE

BIBLIOTECA NACIONAL H0330

BICAMERALISM....SEE LEGIS, CONGRESS, HOUSE/REP, SENATE

BIDNEY D. H0331,H0332

BIEBUYCK D. H0333

BIERKAEMPER C. H3276

BIGGERSTAFF K. H3062

BIGLER/W....WILLIAM BIGLER

BILL J.A. H0334

BILL/RIGHT....BILL OF RIGHTS

BINANI G.D. H0335

BINDER L. H0336,H0337,H0338

BINNS/JJ....JOSEPH J. BINNS

BIO/SOC....BIO-SOCIAL PROCESSES, DRUGS, SEXUALITY

N
KRADER L.,SOCIAL ORGANIZATION OF THE MONGOL-TURKIC PASTORAL NOMADS. SOCIETY FAM KIN NEIGH GP/REL — BIO/SOC HABITAT

MARRIAGE 16/20 MONGOLIA TURKIC MIGRATION. PAGE 88 H1763 CULTURE STRUCT

B20
MACIVER R.M.,COMMUNITY: A SOCIOLOGICAL STUDY; BEING AN ATTEMPT TO SET OUT THE FUNDAMENTAL LAWS OF SOCIAL LIFE. UNIV STRUCT NAT/G CONTROL WAR BIO/SOC ...PSY SOC CONCPT GEN/LAWS. PAGE 100 H1996 REGION SOCIETY GP/REL

B21
WALLAS G.,HUMAN NATURE IN POLITICS (3RD ED.). UNIV NAT/G LEAD CHOOSE REPRESENT GP/REL NAT/LISM RATIONAL BIO/SOC HEREDITY ALL/VALS MAJORIT. PAGE 165 H3293 PSY DRIVE PERSON

B22
OGBURN W.F.,SOCIAL CHANGE WITH RESPECT TO CULTURE AND ORIGINAL NATURE. ACT/RES OP/RES CRIME GP/REL ANOMIE BIO/SOC PWR...PSY SOC TIME/SEQ METH SOC/INTEG. PAGE 120 H2405 CULTURE CREATE TEC/DEV

S38
MERTON R.K.,"SOCIAL STRUCTURE AND ANOMIE" (BMR)" UNIV CULTURE STRATA CREATE PARTIC ATTIT BIO/SOC PERSON...SOC CONCPT 20. PAGE 109 H2186 SOCIETY STRUCT ANOMIE DRIVE

B45
HUNTINGTON E.,MAINSPRINGS OF CIVILIZATION. UNIV CULTURE SOCIETY BIO/SOC PERSON KNOWL SKILL...PSY RECORD HIST/WRIT TREND CHARTS TOT/POP. PAGE 75 H1504 SOC GEOG

B49
SARGENT S.S.,CULTURE AND PERSONALITY. FUT UNIV SOCIETY FAM KIN NEIGH BIO/SOC DRIVE PERCEPT RIGID/FLEX LOVE RESPECT...PSY SOC CONCPT OBS TIME/SEQ TREND CON/ANAL CHARTS HYPO/EXP SIMUL TOT/POP. PAGE 138 H2754 CULTURE PERSON

S49
MACKENZIE R.D.,"ECOLOGY, HUMAN." UNIV CULTURE ECO/DEV ECO/UNDEV ATTIT...POLICY GEOG PSY CONCPT METH/CNCPT CONT/OBS TREND GEN/LAWS. PAGE 100 H2001 SOCIETY BIO/SOC

C50
ROUSSEAU J.J.,"DISCOURSE ON THE ORIGIN OF INEQUALITY" (1755) IN THE SOCIAL CONTRACT AND DISCOURSES." UNIV NAT/G PLAN BAL/PWR HAPPINESS UTOPIA BIO/SOC HEREDITY MORAL...WELF/ST CONCPT. PAGE 135 H2698 SOCIETY STRUCT PERSON GEN/LAWS

B51
LEMERT E.M.,SOCIAL PATHOLOGY. CULTURE BIO/SOC PERSON SEX 20 PROSTITUTN. PAGE 94 H1876 SOC ANOMIE CONCPT CRIME

B53
HUNTER E.,BRAIN-WASHING IN RED CHINA. ASIA CHINA/COM CULTURE SOCIETY FORCES WAR TOTALISM ATTIT BIO/SOC DISPL DRIVE PERSON SUPEGO KNOWL ORD/FREE ...INT REC/INT COLD/WAR 20. PAGE 75 H1499 EDU/PROP COERCE

B54
MATTHEWS D.R.,THE SOCIAL BACKGROUND OF POLITICAL DECISION-MAKERS. CULTURE SOCIETY STRATA FAM EX/STRUC LEAD ATTIT BIO/SOC DRIVE PERSON ALL/VALS HIST/WRIT. PAGE 105 H2097 DECISION BIOG SOC

B56
DRIVER H.E.,AN INTEGRATION OF FUNCTIONAL, EVOLUTIONARY AND HISTORICAL THEORY BY MEANS OF CORRELATIONS. INGP/REL BIO/SOC HABITAT...PHIL/SCI GEN/LAWS. PAGE 42 H0847 CULTURE METH SOC CORREL

B59
HONINGMAN J.J.,THE WORLD OF MAN. CHRIST-17C MEDIT-7 PRE/AMER PREHIST CREATE INGP/REL BIO/SOC HABITAT ...PSY SOC BIBLIOG. PAGE 73 H1460 CULTURE METH PERSON STRUCT

B60
HALBWACHS M.,POPULATION AND SOCIETY: INTRODUCTION TO SOCIAL MORPHOLOGY (TRANS. BY DUNCAN AND PFAUTZ). CULTURE SOCIETY AGRI INDUS HABITAT...CONCPT 20. PAGE 64 H1281 BIO/SOC GEOG NEIGH GP/COMP

S60
JAFFEE A.J.,"POPULATION TRENDS AND CONTROLS IN UNDERDEVELOPED COUNTRIES." AFR FUT ISLAM L/A+17C S/ASIA CULTURE R+D FAM ACT/RES PLAN EDU/PROP BIO/SOC RIGID/FLEX HEALTH...SOC STAT OBS CHARTS 20. PAGE 79 H1582 ECO/UNDEV GEOG

B61
JONES R.,AFRICA BIBLIOGRAPHY SERIES: SOUTH EAST CENTRAL AFRICA AND MADAGASCAR. AFR MADAGASCAR RHODESIA SECT BIO/SOC...JURID NAT/COMP 20. PAGE 82 H1633 BIBLIOG/A SOC CULTURE LING

B61
VON EICKSTEDT E.,TURKEN, KURDEN UND IRANER SEIT DEM ALTERTUM. IRAN TURKEY GP/REL BIO/SOC HABITAT...PSY 20 PERSIA. PAGE 163 H3266 CULTURE SOC SOCIETY STRUCT

S61
SCHECHTMAN J.B.,"MINORITIES IN THE MIDDLE EAST." ISLAM INTELL SOCIETY STRATA KIN NAT/G VOL/ASSN EDU/PROP REGION GP/REL DISCRIM ATTIT BIO/SOC DISPL PERSON ALL/VALS...PSY SOC OBS SAMP GEN/LAWS 20. PAGE 139 H2776 SECT CULTURE RACE/REL

S63
ARASTEH R.,"THE ROLE OF INTELLECTUALS IN ADMINISTRATIVE DEVELOPMENT AND SOCIAL CHANGE IN MODERN IRAN." ISLAM CULTURE NAT/G CONSULT ACT/RES EDU/PROP EXEC ATTIT BIO/SOC PERCEPT SUPEGO ALL/VALS ...POLICY MGT PSY SOC CONCPT 20. PAGE 8 H0157 INTELL ADMIN IRAN

S63
ROBINSON W.C.,"URBANIZATION AND FERTILITY: THE NON-WESTERN EXPERIENCE (BMR)" DEATH MARRIAGE AGE/C BIO/SOC...STAT CENSUS CON/ANAL CHARTS NAT/COMP 20 THIRD/WRLD. PAGE 133 H2651 GEOG MUNIC FAM ECO/UNDEV

B64
BROWN N.,NUCLEAR WAR* THE IMPENDING STRATEGIC DEADLOCK. USA+45 USSR TEC/DEV BUDGET RISK ARMS/CONT NUC/PWR WEAPON COST BIO/SOC...GEOG IDEA/COMP NAT/COMP GAME NATO WARSAW/P. PAGE 22 H0448 FORCES OP/RES WAR GEN/LAWS

B64
ELKIN A.P.,THE AUSTRALIAN ABORIGINES - HOW TO UNDERSTAND THEM (4TH ED.). FAM NEIGH DEATH MARRIAGE ATTIT BIO/SOC HABITAT...PSY SOC MYTH WORSHIP AUSTRAL ABORIGINES. PAGE 45 H0908 CULTURE STRUCT SOCIETY KIN

L64
BERELSON B.,"SAMPLE SURVEYS AND POPULATION CONTROL." ASIA FUT ISLAM L/A+17C CULTURE SOCIETY FAM NAT/G CONSULT PLAN EDU/PROP ATTIT DRIVE ALL/VALS...POLICY RELATIV HEAL PSY SOC CONCPT METH/CNCPT OBS OBS/ENVIR TOT/POP. PAGE 15 H0297 BIO/SOC SAMP

B65
APPLEMAN P.,THE SILENT EXPLOSION. WOR+45 ECO/DEV ECO/UNDEV PLAN HEALTH ALL/IDEOS CATHISM...POLICY STAT RECORD GP/COMP IDEA/COMP NAT/COMP 20 BIRTH/CON COM/PARTY. PAGE 7 H0148 GEOG CENSUS AGRI BIO/SOC

B65
HESS A.G.,CHASING THE DRAGON: A REPORT ON DRUG ADDICTION IN HONG KONG. ASIA CULTURE PROB/SOLV TRIBUTE...POLICY PSY SOC CLASSIF STAT 17/20 HONG/KONG. PAGE 70 H1411 BIO/SOC CRIME SOCIETY LAW

B66
HOEVELER H.J.,INTERNATIONALE BEKAMPFUNG DES VERBRECHENS. AUSTRIA SWITZERLND WOR+45 INT/ORG CONTROL BIO/SOC...METH/COMP NAT/COMP 20 MAFIA SCOT/YARD FBI. PAGE 72 H1446 CRIMLGY CRIME DIPLOM INT/LAW

B66
JONES D.H.,AFRICA BIBLIOGRAPHY SERIES: EAST AFRICA. AFR UGANDA SECT BIO/SOC...JURID NAT/COMP 20. PAGE 82 H1630 BIBLIOG/A SOC CULTURE LING

B66
RADIN P.,THE METHOD AND THEORY OF ETHNOLOGY. CULTURE STRUCT BIO/SOC HABITAT...HUM OBS/ENVIR METH/COMP GEN/LAWS 20 HUMANISM. PAGE 129 H2578 PHIL/SCI SOC METH SOCIETY

BIOG....BIOGRAPHY (INCLUDES PSYCHOANALYSIS)

N
MIDDLE EAST JOURNAL. CULTURE SECT DIPLOM LEAD GOV/REL ATTIT...POLICY PHIL/SCI SOC LING BIOG 20. PAGE 1 H0007 BIBLIOG ISLAM NAT/G ECO/UNDEV

N
THE MIDDLE EAST. CULTURE...BIOG BIBLIOG. PAGE 2 H0028 ISLAM INDUS FINAN

N
EUROPA PUBLICATIONS LIMITED,THE EUROPA YEAR BOOK. CONSTN FINAN INDUS POL/PAR DIPLOM TV CT/SYS...STAT BIOG CHARTS WORSHIP 20. PAGE 47 H0949 BIBLIOG NAT/G PRESS INT/ORG

B00
BENEDETTI V.,STUDIES IN DIPLOMACY. BELGIUM FRANCE GERMANY MOD/EUR CONSTN NAT/G CONSULT TOP/EX DOMIN EDU/PROP COERCE ATTIT...CONCPT INT BIOG TREND 19. PAGE 14 H0276 PWR GEN/LAWS DIPLOM

B08
NIRRNHEIM O.,DAS ERSTE JAHR DES MINISTERIUMS BISMARCK UND DIE OEFFENTLICHE MEINUNG (HEIDELBERGER ABHANDLUNGEN, 20. HEFT). GERMANY MOD/EUR LEGIS DIPLOM EDU/PROP INGP/REL...BIOG GOV/COMP IDEA/COMP BIBLIOG 19 BISMARCK/O. PAGE 118 H2363 CHIEF PRESS NAT/G ATTIT

C09
SCHAPIRO J.S.,"SOCIAL REFORM AND THE REFORMATION." CHRIST-17C GERMANY LAW CONSTN LG/CO NAT/G WORKER PROB/SOLV CT/SYS REV...BIBLIOG 16. PAGE 138 H2770 ORD/FREE SECT ECO/TAC BIOG

B19
DE MAN H.,THE REMAKING OF A MIND. EUR+WWI NAT/G ECO/TAC REGION ORD/FREE SOCISM...BIOG 20 WWI EUROPE. PAGE 38 H0762 PSY WAR SELF/OBS PARTIC

N19
OPERATIONS AND POLICY RESEARCH,URUGUAY: ELECTION FACTBOOK: NOVEMBER 27, 1966 (PAMPHLET). URUGUAY LAW NAT/G LEAD REPRESENT...STAT BIOG CHARTS 20. PAGE 121 H2422 POL/PAR CHOOSE PLAN ATTIT

B20
HALDANE R.B.,BEFORE THE WAR. MOD/EUR SOCIETY INT/ORG NAT/G DELIB/GP PLAN DOMIN EDU/PROP LEGIT ADMIN COERCE ATTIT DRIVE MORAL ORD/FREE PWR...SOC CONCPT SELF/OBS RECORD BIOG TIME/SEQ. PAGE 64 H1282 POLICY DIPLOM UK

B21
STUART G.H.,FRENCH FOREIGN POLICY. CONSTN INT/ORG NAT/G POL/PAR EX/STRUC FORCES PLAN ECO/TAC DOMIN EDU/PROP ADJUD COERCE ATTIT DRIVE RIGID/FLEX ALL/VALS...POLICY OBS RECORD BIOG TIME/SEQ TREND. PAGE 150 H3000 MOD/EUR DIPLOM FRANCE

B25
TEMPERLEY H.,THE FOREIGN POLICY OF CANNING: 1822-1827. MOD/EUR NAT/G TOP/EX EDU/PROP ROUTINE ATTIT RIGID/FLEX SUPEGO PWR SKILL...TIME/SEQ PARLIAMENT 20. PAGE 153 H3058 PERSON DIPLOM UK BIOG

B27
QUERARD J.M.,LA FRANCE LITTERAIRE (12 VOLS.). FRANCE CULTURE...HUM SOC 16/19. PAGE 129 H2573 BIBLIOG/A BIOG ART/METH

B28
HOLDSWORTH W.S.,THE HISTORIANS OF ANGLO-AMERICAN LAW. UK USA-45 INTELL LEGIS RESPECT...BIOG NAT/COMP 17/20 COMMON/LAW. PAGE 72 H1450 HIST/WRIT LAW JURID

B31
BONAR J.,THEORIES OF POPULATION FROM RALEIGH TO ARTHUR YOUNG. CHRIST-17C MOD/EUR CULTURE SOCIETY R+D CREATE ATTIT PERCEPT RIGID/FLEX...OLD/LIB CONCPT NEW/IDEA TIME/SEQ IDEA/COMP STERTYP GEN/LAWS. PAGE 19 H0372 GEOG BIOG

B31
KIRKPATRICK F.A.,A HISTORY OF THE ARGENTINE REPUBLIC. SPAIN UK CONSTN SOCIETY ECO/UNDEV EX/STRUC DIPLOM FOR/AID LEAD WAR ATTIT...BIOG CHARTS 16/20 ARGEN SAN/MARTIN. PAGE 86 H1724 NAT/G L/A+17C COLONIAL

C33
MURET C.T.,"FRENCH ROYALIST DOCTRINES SINCE THE REVOLUTION." FRANCE CONSTN NAT/G SECT ADMIN LEAD SOVEREIGN...POLICY BIOG IDEA/COMP BIBLIOG 18/20. PAGE 115 H2295 POL/PAR ATTIT INTELL CONSERVE

B35
TAKEUCHI T.,WAR AND DIPLOMACY IN THE JAPANESE EMPIRE. ASIA ELITES STRATA NAT/G SECT LEGIS ACT/RES PLAN LEGIT PARL/PROC ROUTINE WAR...MGT BIOG CHINJAP TOT/POP 19/20 CHINJAP. PAGE 152 H3038 EXEC STRUCT

B37
PARSONS T.,THE STRUCTURE OF SOCIAL ACTION. UNIV INTELL SOCIETY INDUS MARKET ECO/TAC ROUTINE CHOOSE ALL/VALS...CONCPT OBS BIOG TREND GEN/LAWS 20. PAGE 124 H2471 CULTURE ATTIT CAP/ISM

B38
DEL TORO J.,A BIBLIOGRAPHY OF THE COLLECTIVE BIOGRAPHY OF SPANISH AMERICA. ELITES NAT/G WRITING LEAD PERSON 19/20. PAGE 39 H0786 BIBLIOG/A L/A+17C BIOG

B38
JESSOP T.E.,A BIBLIOGRAPHY OF DAVID HUME AND OF SCOTTISH PHILOSOPHY FROM FRANCIS HUTCHESON TO LORD BALFOUR. UK INTELL NAT/G ATTIT...CONCPT 17/20 HUME/D CMN/WLTH. PAGE 81 H1615 BIBLIOG EPIST PERCEPT BIOG

B39
HITLER A.,MEIN KAMPF. EUR+WWI FUT MOD/EUR STRUCT INT/ORG LABOR NAT/G POL/PAR FORCES CREATE PLAN BAL/PWR DIPLOM ECO/TAC DOMIN EDU/PROP ADMIN COERCE ATTIT...SOCIALIST BIOG TREND NAZI. PAGE 71 H1428 PWR NEW/IDEA WAR

B39
NICOLSON H.,CURZON: THE LAST PHASE, 1919-1925. UK NAT/G DELIB/GP TOP/EX ROUTINE WAR RIGID/FLEX ...METH/CNCPT 20 CURZON/GN. PAGE 118 H2352 POLICY DIPLOM BIOG

B41
HITLER A.,MEIN KAMPF (UNABR. ENG. VERSION) (1925). GERMANY CONSTN TEC/DEV RACE/REL NAT/LISM TOTALISM SOVEREIGN...BIOG 20 HITLER/A TREATY. PAGE 71 H1429 EDU/PROP WAR PLAN FASCISM

B41
PALMER R.R.,TWELVE WHO RULED. MOD/EUR ELITES STRUCT NAT/G POL/PAR DELIB/GP DOMIN ATTIT SUPEGO PWR ...POLICY CONCPT 18. PAGE 123 H2453 TOP/EX BIOG REV FRANCE

B43
EARLE E.M.,MAKERS OF MODERN STRATEGY: MILITARY THOUGHT FROM MACHIAVELLI TO HITLER. EUR+WWI MOD/EUR NAT/G ACT/RES BAL/PWR DOMIN COERCE ATTIT DRIVE RIGID/FLEX ALL/VALS...METH/CNCPT BIOG 16/20. PAGE 44 H0879 PLAN FORCES WAR

B43
JONES C.K.,A BIBLIOGRAPHY OF LATIN AMERICAN BIBLIOGRAPHIES (2ND ED.). CULTURE ALL/VALS...POLICY GEOG HUM SOC LING BIBLIOG TREND 20. PAGE 82 H1629 BIBLIOG/A L/A+17C HIST/WRIT

B45
CONOVER H.F.,THE NAZI STATE: WAR CRIMES AND WAR CRIMINALS. GERMANY CULTURE NAT/G SECT FORCES DIPLOM INT/TRADE EDU/PROP...INT/LAW BIOG HIST/WRIT TIME/SEQ 20. PAGE 32 H0647 BIBLIOG WAR CRIME

B45
PERAZA SARAUSA F.,BIBLIOGRAFIAS CUBANAS. CUBA CULTURE ECO/UNDEV AGRI EDU/PROP PRESS CIVMIL/REL ...POLICY GEOG PHIL/SCI BIOG 19/20. PAGE 125 H2489 BIBLIOG/A L/A+17C NAT/G DIPLOM

B47
JURJI E.J.,THE GREAT RELIGIONS OF THE MODERN WORLD. CULTURE INTELL SOCIETY INT/ORG CONSULT CHOOSE ATTIT DRIVE PERSON RIGID/FLEX...HUM CONCPT OBS BIOG HIST/WRIT TREND GEN/LAWS 20 WORSHIP. PAGE 82 H1643 UNIV SECT

B48
FLOREN LOZANO L.,BIBLIOGRAFIA DE LA BIBLIOGRAFIA DOMINICANA. DOMIN/REP NAT/G DIPLOM EDU/PROP CIVMIL/REL...POLICY ART/METH GEOG PHIL/SCI HIST/WRIT 20. PAGE 51 H1027 BIBLIOG/A BIOG L/A+17C CULTURE

B48
WOLFE B.D.,THREE WHO MADE A REVOLUTION. USSR CONSTN NAT/G CAP/ISM EDU/PROP CONTROL WAR GP/REL INGP/REL PERS/REL ROLE 20 STALIN/J LENIN/VI TROTSKY/L BOLSHEVISM. PAGE 170 H3398 BIOG REV LEAD MARXISM

C49
SCHAPIRO J.S.,"LIBERALISM AND THE CHALLENGE OF FASCISM." FRANCE UK STRATA PERSON...CONCPT BIOG IDEA/COMP BIBLIOG 18/20. PAGE 139 H2771 FASCISM LAISSEZ ATTIT

B50
CARR E.H.,STUDIES IN REVOLUTION. CREATE WAR PERSON ALL/IDEOS MARXISM SOCISM...PHIL/SCI METH/COMP ANTHOL 18/20 SAINTSIMON MARX/KARL PROUDHON/P LASSALLE/F PLEKHNV/GV. PAGE 27 H0537 REV IDEA/COMP COERCE BIOG

B50
GOFF F.R.,FIFTEENTH CENTURY BOOKS IN THE LIBRARY OF CONGRESS. CHRIST-17C GERMANY ITALY CULTURE INTELL SECT CREATE...PHIL/SCI CONCPT CLASSIF BIOG TIME/SEQ 15. PAGE 58 H1153 BIBLIOG KNOWL HUM

B50
ROHEIM G.,PSYCHOANALYSIS AND ANTHROPOLOGY. UNIV FAM PERS/REL ATTIT HABITAT...SOC OBS WORSHIP. PAGE 133 H2663 PSY BIOG CULTURE PERSON

B51
MORLEY C.,GUIDE TO RESEARCH IN RUSSIAN HISTORY. USSR MARXISM...BIOG HIST/WRIT ANTHOL DICTIONARY. PAGE 113 H2259 BIBLIOG/A R+D NAT/G COM

B52
HIMMELFARB G.,LORD ACTON: A STUDY IN CONSCIENCE AND POLITICS. MOD/EUR NAT/G POL/PAR SECT LEGIS TOP/EX EDU/PROP ADMIN NAT/LISM ATTIT PERSON SUPEGO MORAL ORD/FREE...CONCPT PARLIAMENT 19 ACTON/LORD. PAGE 71 H1419 PWR BIOG

B53
MAXIMOFF G.P.,THE POLITICAL PHILOSOPHY OF BAKUNIN: SCIENTIFIC ANARCHISM. STRUCT INGP/REL FEDERAL MARXISM...ANARCH BIOG 19 BAKUNIN. PAGE 105 H2104 SOCIETY PHIL/SCI NAT/G IDEA/COMP

B54
GATZKE H.W.,STRESEMANN AND THE REARMAMENT OF GERMANY. EUR+WWI GERMANY USSR FINAN NAT/G ECO/TAC ATTIT...BIOG METH 20 STRESEMN/G. PAGE 55 H1105 FORCES INDUS PWR

B54
MATTHEWS D.R.,THE SOCIAL BACKGROUND OF POLITICAL DECISION-MAKERS. CULTURE SOCIETY STRATA FAM EX/STRUC LEAD ATTIT BIO/SOC DRIVE PERSON ALL/VALS HIST/WRIT. PAGE 105 H2097 DECISION BIOG SOC

B54
MITCHELL P.,AFRICAN AFTERTHOUGHTS. UGANDA CONSTN NAT/G ADJUD COERCE WAR 20 WWI MAU/MAU. PAGE 112 H2230 BIOG CHIEF COLONIAL DOMIN

B56
MANNONI D.O.,PROSPERO AND CALIBAN: THE PSYCHOLOGY OF COLONIZATION. AFR EUR+WWI FAM KIN MUNIC SECT DOMIN ADMIN ATTIT DRIVE LOVE PWR RESPECT...PSY SOC CONCPT MYTH OBS DEEP/INT BIOG GEN/METH MALAGASY 20. PAGE 102 H2040 CULTURE COLONIAL

B56
SMEDLEY A.,THE GREAT ROAD: THE LIFE AND TIMES OF CHU TEH. ASIA USSR NAT/G POL/PAR DIPLOM COERCE GUERRILLA CIVMIL/REL NAT/LISM PERSON SKILL MARXISM ...BIOG 20 CHINJAP MAO. PAGE 145 H2903 REV WAR FORCES

B56
WILSON P.,GOVERNMENT AND POLITICS OF INDIA AND PAKISTAN: 1885-1955; A BIBLIOGRAPHY OF WORKS IN WESTERN LANGUAGES. INDIA PAKISTAN CONSTN LOC/G POL/PAR FORCES DIPLOM ADMIN WAR CHOOSE...BIOG CON/ANAL 19/20. PAGE 169 H3380 BIBLIOG COLONIAL NAT/G S/ASIA

C56
FALL B.B.,"THE VIET-MINH REGIME." VIETNAM LAW ECO/UNDEV POL/PAR FORCES DOMIN WAR ATTIT MARXISM ...BIOG PREDICT BIBLIOG/A 20. PAGE 48 H0967 NAT/G ADMIN EX/STRUC LEAD

B57
HERNANDEZ-ARREGU J.,IMPERIALISMO Y CULTURA (LA POLITICA EN LA INTELIGENCIA ARGENTINA). L/A+17C CULTURE ELITES WRITING COLONIAL CROWD ATTIT FASCISM MARXISM SOCISM...BIOG IDEA/COMP 20 ARGEN PERON/JUAN COM/PARTY. PAGE 70 H1403 INTELL CREATE ART/METH HUM

B57
TOMASIC D.A.,NATIONAL COMMUNISM AND SOVIET COM

STRATEGY. UK USSR YUGOSLAVIA NAT/G POL/PAR CHIEF CREATE DOMIN REV WAR PWR...BIOG TREND 20 TITO/MARSH STALIN/J. PAGE 156 H3112
NAT/LISM
MARXISM
DIPLOM

B58
DUNAYEVSKAYA R.,MARXISM AND FREEDOM: FROM 1776 UNTIL TODAY. COM USSR WORKER CAP/ISM DOMIN REV GP/REL TOTALISM ALL/VALS...MYTH BIOG IDEA/COMP 18/20 MARX/KARL LENIN/VI STALIN/J. PAGE 43 H0861
MARXISM
CONCPT
ORD/FREE

B58
HAYCRAFT J.,BABEL IN SPAIN. SPAIN ATTIT...RELATIV 20. PAGE 68 H1367
CULTURE
PERSON
BIOG
GEOG

B58
HUMPHREYS R.A.,LATIN AMERICAN HISTORY: A GUIDE TO THE LITERATURE IN ENGLISH. CULTURE NAT/G DIPLOM BIOG. PAGE 75 H1495
BIBLIOG/A
L/A+17C

B58
ORNES G.E.,TRUJILLO: LITTLE CAESAR OF THE CARIBBEAN. DOMIN/REP FAM NAT/G FORCES BUDGET CRIME REV PERSON 20 TRUJILLO/R. PAGE 122 H2429
BIOG
PWR
TOTALISM
CHIEF

B58
WIGGIN L.M.,THE FACTION OF COUSINS: A POLITICAL ACCOUNT OF THE GRENVILLES, 1733-1763. UK STRUCT KIN NAT/G INGP/REL...CONCPT BIOG BIBLIOG/A 18 GRENVILLES. PAGE 168 H3357
FAM
POL/PAR
PWR

B58
YUAN TUNG-LI,CHINA IN WESTERN LITERATURE. SECT DIPLOM...ART/METH GEOG JURID SOC BIOG CON/ANAL. PAGE 172 H3441
BIBLIOG
ASIA
CULTURE
HUM

C58
MORRALL J.B.,"POLITICAL THOUGHT IN MEDIEVAL TIMES." LAW NAT/G SECT DOMIN ATTIT PWR...BIOG HIST/WRIT BIBLIOG. PAGE 113 H2260
CHRIST-17C
CONCPT

B59
CAREW-HUNT R.C.,BOOKS ON COMMUNISM. NAT/G POL/PAR DIPLOM REV...BIOG 19/20. PAGE 26 H0528
BIBLIOG/A
MARXISM
COM
ASIA

B59
MARTZ J.D.,CENTRAL AMERICA: THE CRISIS AND THE CHALLENGE. L/A+17C POL/PAR CHIEF CHOOSE SOVEREIGN ...BIOG TREND BIBLIOG 20 CENTRAL/AM. PAGE 104 H2071
NAT/G
GOV/REL
DIPLOM
GOV/COMP

B59
PAGE S.W.,LENIN AND WORLD REVOLUTION. COM USSR NAT/G DOMIN COERCE CROWD UTOPIA ATTIT AUTHORIT DRIVE PWR...CONCPT MYTH 19/20 LENIN/VI MARX/KARL. PAGE 122 H2441
REV
PERSON
MARXISM
BIOG

B59
PARK R.L.,LEADERSHIP AND POLITICAL INSTITUTIONS IN INDIA. S/ASIA CULTURE ECO/UNDEV LOC/G MUNIC PROVS LEGIS PLAN ADMIN LEAD ORD/FREE WEALTH...GEOG SOC BIOG TOT/POP VAL/FREE 20. PAGE 123 H2468
NAT/G
EXEC
INDIA

B60
JAECKH A.,WELTSAAT; ERLEBTES UND ERSTREBTES. GERMANY WOR+45 WOR-45 PLAN WAR...POLICY OBS/ENVIR NAT/COMP PERS/COMP 20. PAGE 79 H1581
BIOG
NAT/G
SELF/OBS
DIPLOM

B60
SCANLON D.G.,INTERNATIONAL EDUCATION: A DOCUMENTARY HISTORY. ADMIN CONTROL ATTIT PERCEPT...BIOG ANTHOL METH 20. PAGE 138 H2765
EDU/PROP
INT/ORG
NAT/COMP
DIPLOM

C60
COX R.H.,"LOCKE ON WAR AND PEACE." UK DIPLOM DOMIN PWR...BIOG IDEA/COMP BIBLIOG 18. PAGE 34 H0689
CONCPT
NAT/G
PEACE
WAR

B61
ALLIGHAN G.,VERWOERD - THE END. SOUTH/AFR TOP/EX DIPLOM COLONIAL DISCRIM TOTALISM ATTIT AUTHORIT ...BIOG 20 NEGRO VERWOERD/H. PAGE 5 H0107
CONTROL
CHIEF
RACE/REL
NAT/G

B61
BULLOCK A.,HITLER: A STUDY IN TYRANNY. EUR+WWI GERMANY SOCIETY STRUCT NAT/G POL/PAR FORCES CREATE DOMIN EDU/PROP EXEC COERCE WAR NAT/LISM DISPL DRIVE PERSON PWR...PSY NAZI 20 HITLER/A. PAGE 23 H0470
ATTIT
BIOG
TOTALISM

B61
GUEVARA E.,GUERRILLA WARFARE. L/A+17C ECO/UNDEV NAT/G POL/PAR VOL/ASSN PLAN DOMIN REV DRIVE PWR WEALTH...NEW/IDEA RECORD BIOG COLD/WAR MARX/KARL OAS 20. PAGE 62 H1247
FORCES
COERCE
GUERRILLA
CUBA

B61
HISTORICAL RESEARCH INSTITUTE,A SHORT BIBLIOGRAPHY OF INDO-MUSLIM HISTORY. INDIA S/ASIA DIPLOM EDU/PROP COLONIAL LEAD NAT/LISM ATTIT...BIOG 19/20. PAGE 71 H1427
BIBLIOG
NAT/G
SECT
POL/PAR

B61
MACLEOD I.,NEVILLE CHAMBERLAIN. UK SOCIETY TOP/EX WAR PERSON ALL/VALS ORD/FREE PARLIAMENT 20 CHAMBRLN/N. PAGE 100 H2003
BIOG
NAT/G
CREATE

B61
MARVICK D.,POLITICAL DECISION-MAKERS. INTELL STRATA NAT/G POL/PAR EX/STRUC LEGIS DOMIN EDU/PROP ATTIT PERSON PWR...PSY STAT OBS CONT/OBS STAND/INT UNPLAN/INT TIME/SEQ CHARTS STERTYP VAL/FREE. PAGE 104 H2073
TOP/EX
BIOG
ELITES

B61
STANLEY C.J.,LATE CH'ING FINANCE: HU KUANG-YUNG AS AN INNOVATOR. ASIA NAT/G FORCES BUDGET TAX WAR GOV/REL COST...POLICY BIOG CHARTS BIBLIOG 19. PAGE 148 H2969
FINAN
ECO/TAC
CIVMIL/REL
ADMIN

B62
ARNE S.,LE PRESIDENT DU CONSEIL DES MINISTRES SOUS LA IV REPUBLIQUE. EUR+WWI FRANCE LEGIT PWR...BIOG CHARTS. PAGE 8 H0165
DELIB/GP
POL/PAR
NAT/G
LEGIS

B62
HO PING-TI,THE LADDER OF SUCCESS IN IMPERIAL CHINA: ASPECTS OF SOCIAL MOBILITY, 1368-1911. INTELL STRATA FAM KIN MUNIC NAT/G PROVS SCHOOL DELIB/GP DOMIN EDU/PROP ADMIN ROUTINE PERSON ALL/VALS...SOC STAT BIOG HIST/WRIT TIME/SEQ VAL/FREE. PAGE 71 H1431
ASIA
CULTURE

B62
INGHAM K.,A HISTORY OF EAST AFRICA. NAT/G DIPLOM ADMIN WAR NAT/LISM...SOC BIOG BIBLIOG. PAGE 77 H1534
AFR
CONSTN
COLONIAL

B62
KINDERSLEY R.,THE FIRST RUSSIAN REVISIONISTS. COM USSR LAW ELITES INTELL NAT/G LEGIS ECO/TAC EDU/PROP CONTROL LEAD GP/REL SOCISM 19/20 MARX/KARL BOLSHEVISM. PAGE 86 H1712
CONSTN
MARXISM
POPULISM
BIOG

B62
ROSENZWEIG F.,HEGEL UND DER STAAT. GERMANY SOCIETY FAM POL/PAR NAT/LISM...BIOG 19. PAGE 134 H2682
JURID
NAT/G
CONCPT
PHIL/SCI

S62
ANSPRENGER F.,"NATIONALISM, COMMUNISM, AND THE UNCOMMITTED NATIONS: AMERICAN PROFILES." FUT ISLAM CULTURE SOCIETY ECO/UNDEV NAT/G POL/PAR PLAN ECO/TAC EDU/PROP COERCE CHOOSE ALL/VALS MARXISM SOCISM...SOC CONCPT BIOG TREND 20. PAGE 7 H0142
AFR
COM
NAT/LISM

B63
BERLIN I.,KARL MARX, HIS LIFE AND ENVIRONMENT (3RD ED.). MOD/EUR USSR INTELL EDU/PROP PARTIC REV ATTIT 19 MARX/KARL. PAGE 15 H0307
BIOG
PERSON
MARXISM
CONCPT

B63
FALL B.,THE TWO VIETNAMS. CULTURE SOCIETY ECO/UNDEV NAT/G TOP/EX ACT/RES PLAN ECO/TAC DOMIN EDU/PROP COERCE ATTIT DRIVE PERSON ORD/FREE PWR...SOC TIME/SEQ COLD/WAR 20. PAGE 48 H0965
S/ASIA
BIOG
VIETNAM

B63
KRAEHE E.,METTERNICH'S GERMAN POLICY: THE CONTEST WITH NAPOLEON, 1799-1814, VOL. 1. FRANCE MOD/EUR NAT/G CONSULT TOP/EX PLAN BAL/PWR DOMIN COERCE ATTIT DRIVE PERCEPT PERSON SKILL...CONCPT RECORD TIME/SEQ TREND 18/19. PAGE 88 H1764
BIOG
GERMANY
DIPLOM

B63
LOOMIE A.J.,THE SPANISH ELIZABETHANS: THE ENGLISH EXILES AT THE COURT OF PHILIP II. SPAIN UK WAR INGP/REL DRIVE HABITAT CATHISM...BIOG 16/17 MIGRATION. PAGE 98 H1962
NAT/G
STRANGE
POLICY
DIPLOM

B63
MAC MILLAN W.M.,BANTU, BOER, AND BRITON: THE MAKING OF THE SOUTH AFRICAN NATIVE PROBLEM. SOUTH/AFR UK LAW KIN NAT/G SECT LEGIS COLONIAL ISOLAT ATTIT ...BIOG 18/20 BANTU NEGRO PHILIP/J MISSION. PAGE 100 H1989
AFR
RACE/REL
ELITES

B63
MCNEAL R.H.,THE BOLSHEVIK TRADITION: LENIN, STALIN, KHRUSHCHEV. USSR NAT/G SUPEGO CONSERVE...IDEA/COMP GEN/LAWS 20 LENIN/VI STALIN/J KHRUSH/N. PAGE 107 H2145
INTELL
BIOG
PERS/COMP

B63
QUAISON-SACKEY A.,AFRICA UNBOUND: REFLECTIONS OF AN AFRICAN STATESMAN. ISLAM CULTURE INTELL INT/ORG POL/PAR TOP/EX DOMIN EDU/PROP LEGIT ATTIT PERSON ...CONCPT OBS TIME/SEQ CHARTS STERTYP 20 UN. PAGE 129 H2571
AFR
BIOG

L63
FREUND G.,"ADENAUER AND THE FUTURE OF GERMANY." EUR+WWI FUT GERMANY/W FORCES LEGIT ADMIN ROUTINE ATTIT DRIVE PERSON PWR...POLICY TIME/SEQ TREND VAL/FREE 20 ADENAUER/K. PAGE 53 H1058
NAT/G
BIOG
DIPLOM
GERMANY

B64
ANDREWS D.H.,LATIN AMERICA: A BIBLIOGRAPHY OF PAPERBACK BOOKS. SECT INT/TRADE EDU/PROP WAR GOV/REL ADJUST NAT/LISM ATTIT...ART/METH LING BIOG 20. PAGE 7 H0138
BIBLIOG
L/A+17C
CULTURE
NAT/G

B64
BEDERMAN S.H.,THE ETHNOLOGICAL CONTRIBUTIONS OF JOHN LEDYARD (PAMPHLET). ASIA PRE/AMER S/ASIA...SOC 18 LEDYARD/J KAMCHATKA TAHITI TARTARS INDIAN/AM. PAGE 13 H0256
CULTURE
BIOG
METH/CNCPT
STRUCT

B64
COUNT E.W.,FACT AND THEORY IN SOCIAL SCIENCE. UNIV HABITAT...BIOG TREND CHARTS ANTHOL BIBLIOG. PAGE 34 H0679 — STRUCT SOC CULTURE ADJUST

B64
FISCHER L.,THE LIFE OF LENIN. USSR LEAD REV WAR ...SOC 19/20 LENIN/VI COM/PARTY BOLSHEVISM. PAGE 51 H1011 — BIOG MARXISM PERSON CHIEF

B64
FORBES A.H.,CURRENT RESEARCH IN BRITISH STUDIES. UK CONSTN CULTURE POL/PAR SECT DIPLOM ADMIN...JURID BIOG WORSHIP 20. PAGE 52 H1034 — BIBLIOG PERSON NAT/G PARL/PROC

B64
MARTINEZ J.R.,THREE CASES OF COMMUNISM: CUBA, BRAZIL, AND MEXICO. BRAZIL CUBA L/A+17C CONSTN NAT/G DIPLOM ECO/TAC GP/REL INGP/REL...GP/COMP BIBLIOG 20 MEXIC/AMER COM/PARTY. PAGE 103 H2068 — MARXISM BIOG REV NAT/COMP

B64
NATIONAL BOOK LEAGUE,THE COMMONWEALTH IN BOOKS: AN ANNOTATED LIST. CANADA UK LOC/G SECT ADMIN...SOC BIOG 20 CMN/WLTH. PAGE 116 H2320 — BIBLIOG/A JURID NAT/G

B64
REMAK J.,THE GENTLE CRITIC: THEODOR FONTANE AND GERMAN POLITICS, 1848-1898. GERMANY PRUSSIA CULTURE ELITES BAL/PWR DIPLOM WRITING GOV/REL...HUM BIOG 19 BISMARCK/O JUNKER FONTANE/T. PAGE 131 H2614 — PERSON SOCIETY WORKER CHIEF

B64
WHITE D.S.,SEEDS OF DISCORD. EUR+WWI FRANCE NAT/G VOL/ASSN FORCES DIPLOM DOMIN NAT/LISM DISPL RIGID/FLEX PWR...RECORD INT BIOG 20 DEGAULLE/C ROOSEVLT/F CHURCHLL/W HULL. PAGE 167 H3347 — TOP/EX ATTIT

S64
LANGERHANS H.,"NEHRU'S BITTERNESS." FUT INDIA S/ASIA CONSTN CULTURE ECO/UNDEV ECO/TAC DOMIN EDU/PROP ATTIT PERCEPT PERSON...POLICY 20 NEHRU/J. PAGE 91 H1811 — ECO/DEV BIOG

S64
RUDOLPH L.I.,"GENERALS AND POLITICIANS IN INDIA." INDIA S/ASIA CULTURE STRATA NAT/G LEGIS TOP/EX EDU/PROP ATTIT ORD/FREE PWR RESPECT SKILL...POLICY BIOG TIME/SEQ STERTYP VAL/FREE 20. PAGE 136 H2713 — FORCES COERCE

S64
SMYTHE H.H.,"NEHRU AND INDIAN FOREIGN POLICY." S/ASIA ECO/UNDEV NAT/G POL/PAR CONSULT PLAN DIPLOM NEUTRAL COERCE ATTIT DRIVE PERSON MORAL ORD/FREE RESPECT...GEOG CONCPT TIME/SEQ TREND GEN/LAWS 20 NEHRU/J. PAGE 146 H2922 — TOP/EX BIOG INDIA

B65
ACHTERBERG E.,BERLINER HOCHFINANZ - KAISER, FURSTEN, MILLIONARE UM 1900. GERMANY NAT/G EDU/PROP PERSON...MGT 19/20. PAGE 3 H0060 — FINAN MUNIC BIOG ECO/TAC

B65
ADENAUER K.,MEMOIRS 1945-53. EUR+WWI GERMANY/W ECO/DEV CHIEF FORCES ECO/TAC WAR GOV/REL PWR SOVEREIGN 20 NATO ADENAUER/K. PAGE 3 H0068 — BIOG DIPLOM NAT/G PERS/REL

B65
ADENAUER K.,MEINE ERINNERUNGEN, 1945-53 (VOL. I), 1953-55 (VOL. II). EUR+WWI GERMANY CHIEF FORCES PROB/SOLV DIPLOM ARMS/CONT INGP/REL PEACE SOVEREIGN ...OBS/ENVIR RECORD 20. PAGE 3 H0069 — NAT/G BIOG SELF/OBS

B65
CHENG C.-Y.,SCIENTIFIC AND ENGINEERING MANPOWER IN COMMUNIST CHINA, 1949-1963. CHINA/COM USSR ELITES ECO/DEV R+D ACADEM LABOR NAT/G EDU/PROP CONTROL UTIL...POLICY BIBLIOG 20. PAGE 29 H0588 — WORKER CONSULT MARXISM BIOG

B65
EDINGER L.J.,KURT SCHUMACHER: A STUDY IN PERSONALITY AND POLITICAL BEHAVIOR. EUR+WWI GERMANY NAT/G DRIVE ROLE PWR SOCISM...BIBLIOG 20 SOC/DEMPAR SCHUMCHR/K. PAGE 44 H0889 — TOP/EX LEAD PERSON BIOG

B65
HART B.H.L.,THE MEMOIRS OF CAPTAIN LIDDELL HART (VOL. I). UK NAT/G PLAN TEC/DEV DIPLOM ADMIN WEAPON GOV/REL PERS/REL ATTIT PWR FASCISM...POLICY 20. PAGE 67 H1348 — FORCES BIOG LEAD WAR

B65
MENON K.P.S.,MANY WORLDS. INDIA BAL/PWR CAP/ISM COLONIAL REV ORD/FREE PWR MARXISM...POLICY 20 COLD/WAR. PAGE 109 H2176 — BIOG DIPLOM NAT/G

B65
PANJABI K.L.,THE CIVIL SERVANT IN INDIA. INDIA UK NAT/G CONSULT EX/STRUC REGION GP/REL RACE/REL 20. PAGE 123 H2462 — ADMIN WORKER BIOG COLONIAL

B65
RANDALL F.B.,STALIN'S RUSSIA. USSR STRUCT AGRI NAT/G PLAN DIPLOM WAR TOTALISM MARXISM...BIBLIOG/A 19/20 STALIN/J. PAGE 129 H2590 — BIOG INDUS ECO/DEV

B66
BARNETT D.L.,MAU MAU FROM WITHIN. AFR UK POL/PAR LEAD GUERRILLA AUTHORIT ORD/FREE...SOC BIOG 20 NEGRO MAU/MAU. PAGE 11 H0225 — REV CULTURE NAT/G

B66
DEUTSCHER I.,STALIN: A POLITICAL BIOGRAPHY. EUR+WWI USSR POL/PAR FORCES DIPLOM ADMIN LEAD REV WAR TOTALISM PERSON 20 STALIN/J ROOSEVLT/F LENIN/VI HITLER/A. PAGE 40 H0807 — BIOG MARXISM TOP/EX PWR

B66
HOLDSWORTH W.S.,A HISTORY OF ENGLISH LAW; THE CENTURIES OF SETTLEMENT AND REFORM (VOL. XVI). UK LOC/G NAT/G EX/STRUC LEGIS CT/SYS LEAD ATTIT ...POLICY DECISION JURID IDEA/COMP 18 PARLIAMENT. PAGE 73 H1454 — BIOG PERSON PROF/ORG LAW

B66
MATTHEWS R.,AFRICAN POWDER KEG: REVOLT AND DISSENT IN SIX EMERGENT NATIONS. AFR ALGERIA DAHOMEY GABON GHANA MALAWI GAMBLE LEAD PARTIC REV DRIVE...BIOG TREND GOV/COMP 20. PAGE 105 H2098 — ELITES ECO/UNDEV TOP/EX CONTROL

B66
NOEL G.E.,THE NEW BRITAIN AND HAROLD WILSON: INTERIM REPORT, 1966 GENERAL ELECTION. UK POL/PAR CONSULT PROB/SOLV BUDGET DIPLOM ECO/TAC LEAD CHOOSE ATTIT 20 WILSON/H PARLIAMENT. PAGE 118 H2366 — BIOG PERSON NAT/G CHIEF

B66
RAEFF M.,ORIGINS OF THE RUSSIAN INTELLIGENTSIA: THE EIGHTEENTH-CENTURY NOBILITY. RUSSIA FAM NAT/G EDU/PROP ADMIN PERS/REL ATTIT...HUM BIOG 18. PAGE 129 H2580 — INTELL ELITES STRATA CONSERVE

B66
SCHRAM S.,MAO TSE-TUNG. ASIA CHINA/COM CONTROL REGION ATTIT...POLICY IDEA/COMP 20 MAO. PAGE 140 H2799 — BIOG MARXISM TOP/EX GUERRILLA

B66
SPEARS E.L.,TWO MEN WHO SAVED FRANCE: PETAIN AND DE GAULLE. FRANCE CONSTN FORCES DIPLOM WAR PERSON 20 WWI PETAIN/HP DEGAULLE/C. PAGE 147 H2942 — BIOG LEAD CHIEF NAT/G

B66
WEBER J.,EOTVOS UND DIE UNGARISCHE NATIONALITATENFRAGE. HUNGARY CULTURE SOCIETY REV ORD/FREE SOVEREIGN...BIOG 19. PAGE 166 H3318 — NAT/LISM GP/REL ATTIT CONCPT

B67
CORDIER A.W.,COLUMBIA ESSAYS IN INTERNATIONAL AFFAIRS. ASIA CHINA/COM FRANCE S/ASIA SPAIN UAR ECO/UNDEV LOC/G ECO/TAC GUERRILLA PWR...BIOG ANTHOL 18/20 MAU/MAU. PAGE 33 H0663 — NAT/G DIPLOM MARXISM POLICY

B67
DAVIDSON E.,THE TRIAL OF THE GERMANS* NUREMBERG* 1946-48. EUR+WWI GERMANY CULTURE NAT/G LEAD PERSON HEALTH...CRIMLGY PSY SOC BIOG JEWS. PAGE 37 H0745 — FASCISM ADJUD TOTALISM WAR

B67
FANON F.,BLACK SKIN, WHITE MASKS: THE EXPERIENCES OF A BLACK MAN IN A WHITE WORLD. CULTURE COLONIAL HAPPINESS ISOLAT STRANGE ATTIT HABITAT RIGID/FLEX SEX...BIOG STERTYP SOC/INTEG 20 NEGRO. PAGE 49 H0970 — DISCRIM PERS/REL RACE/REL PSY

B67
KING M.L. JR.,WHERE DO WE GO FROM HERE: CHAOS OR COMMUNITY? MUNIC NAT/G PARTIC INGP/REL ALL/VALS ...POLICY CONCPT BIOG 20. PAGE 86 H1715 — RACE/REL DISCRIM STRUCT PWR

B67
MENDEL A.P.,POLITICAL MEMOIRS 1905-1917 BY PAUL MILIUKOV (TRANS. BY CARL GOLDBERG). USSR AGRI DIPLOM ECO/TAC POPULISM...MAJORIT 20. PAGE 109 H2170 — BIOG LEAD NAT/G CONSTN

B67
ODINGA O.,NOT YET UHURU. NAT/G POL/PAR PROB/SOLV COERCE REV WAR PERS/REL PERSON ORD/FREE...POLICY 20 ODINGA/O KENYATTA. PAGE 120 H2395 — ATTIT BIOG LEAD AFR

B67
OPERATIONS AND POLICY RESEARCH,NICARAGUA: ELECTION FACTBOOK: FEBRUARY 5, 1967 (PAMPHLET). NICARAGUA LAW NAT/G LEAD REPRESENT...STAT BIOG CHARTS 20. PAGE 121 H2423 — POL/PAR CHOOSE PLAN ATTIT

B67
THOMAS P.,DOWN THESE MEAN STREETS. GP/REL RACE/REL ADJUST...SOC SELF/OBS 20. PAGE 154 H3078 — DISCRIM KIN CULTURE BIOG

B67
TOMPKINS S.R.,THE TRIUMPH OF BOLSHEVISM: REVOLUTION OR REACTION? USSR WORKER PRESS WEALTH MARXISM POPULISM...BIOG TREND IDEA/COMP BIBLIOG 19/20 LENIN/VI. PAGE 156 H3113 — REV NAT/G POL/PAR NAT/LISM

B67
WARD L.,LESTER WARD AND THE WELFARE STATE. SOCIETY NAT/G CREATE RECEIVE EQUILIB UTOPIA HABITAT HEREDITY PERSON...POLICY SOC BIOG 19/20 WARD/LEST. PAGE 165 H3303 — ALL/VALS NEW/IDEA WELF/ST CONCPT

S67
ADNITT F.W.,"THE RISE OF ENGLISH RADICALISM -- PART 2." UK NAT/G WORKER INCOME WEALTH...BIOG 19 — LEGIS LOBBY

PARLIAMENT. PAGE 4 H0071

S67
COHEN A.,"REVOLUTION IN ARGENTINA?" L/A+17C NAT/G POL/PAR CHIEF PROB/SOLV ECO/TAC 20 ARGEN. PAGE 31 H0615 — REV ECO/UNDEV CONTROL BIOG

BIRCH/SOC....JOHN BIRCH SOCIETY

BIRKET-SMITH K.A.J. H0339

BIRKHEAD G.S. H0340

BIRMINGHAM D. H0341

BIRMINGHAM W. H0342

BIRNBAUM K. H0343

BIRTH/CON....BIRTH CONTROL POLICIES AND TECHNIQUES

B64
INTL CONF ON POPULATION,POPULATION DYNAMICS: INTERNATIONAL ACTION AND TRAINING PROGRAMS. INDIA KOREA L/A+17C TAIWAN USA+45 WOR+45 FAM PLAN CONFER ...NEW/IDEA ANTHOL 20 CHINJAP BIRTH/CON. PAGE 78 H1561 — NAT/COMP CONTROL ATTIT EDU/PROP

B65
APPLEMAN P.,THE SILENT EXPLOSION. WOR+45 ECO/DEV ECO/UNDEV PLAN HEALTH ALL/IDEOS CATHISM...POLICY STAT RECORD GP/COMP IDEA/COMP NAT/COMP 20 BIRTH/CON COM/PARTY. PAGE 7 H0148 — GEOG CENSUS AGRI BIO/SOC

BISHOP D.G. H0344

BISHOP O.B. H0345,H0346

BISMARCK/O....OTTO VON BISMARCK

B08
NIRRNHEIM O.,DAS ERSTE JAHR DES MINISTERIUMS BISMARCK UND DIE OEFFENTLICHE MEINUNG (HEIDELBERGER ABHANDLUNGEN, 20. HEFT). GERMANY MOD/EUR LEGIS DIPLOM EDU/PROP INGP/REL...BIOG GOV/COMP IDEA/COMP BIBLIOG 19 BISMARCK/O. PAGE 118 H2363 — CHIEF PRESS NAT/G ATTIT

B29
LANGER W.L.,THE FRANCO-RUSSIAN ALLIANCE: 1890-1894. FRANCE MOD/EUR UK USSR NAT/G CHIEF FORCES BAL/PWR AGREE WAR PEACE PWR...TIME/SEQ TREATY 19 BISMARCK/O. PAGE 91 H1809 — DIPLOM

B58
CRAIG G.A.,FROM BISMARCK TO ADENAUER: ASPECTS OF GERMAN STATECRAFT. GERMANY INTELL FORCES ECO/TAC CONFER COERCE WAR GP/REL ORD/FREE PWR CONSERVE 19/20 BISMARCK/O ADENAUER/K. PAGE 35 H0695 — DIPLOM LEAD NAT/G

B62
SCHMIDT-VOLKMAR E.,DER KULTURKAMPF IN DEUTSCHLAND 1871-1890. GERMANY PRUSSIA SOCIETY STRUCT SECT DIPLOM GP/REL NAT/LISM 19 CHURCH/STA BISMARCK/O. PAGE 139 H2789 — POL/PAR CATHISM ATTIT NAT/G

B63
JACOB H.,GERMAN ADMINISTRATION SINCE BISMARCK: CENTRAL AUTHORITY VERSUS LOCAL AUTONOMY. GERMANY GERMANY/W LAW POL/PAR CONTROL CENTRAL TOTALISM FASCISM...MAJORIT DECISION STAT CHARTS GOV/COMP 19/20 BISMARCK/O HITLER/A WEIMAR/REP. PAGE 79 H1577 — ADMIN NAT/G LOC/G POLICY

B64
REMAK J.,THE GENTLE CRITIC: THEODOR FONTANE AND GERMAN POLITICS, 1848-1898. GERMANY PRUSSIA CULTURE ELITES BAL/PWR DIPLOM WRITING GOV/REL...HUM BIOG 19 BISMARCK/O JUNKER FONTANE/T. PAGE 131 H2614 — PERSON SOCIETY WORKER CHIEF

B65
GILG P.,DIE ERNEUERUNG DES DEMOKRATISCHEN DENKENS IM WILHELMINISCHEN DEUTSCHLAND. GERMANY PARL/PROC CHOOSE REPRESENT...CONCPT 19/20 BISMARCK/O WILHELM/II. PAGE 56 H1126 — POL/PAR ORD/FREE NAT/G

BISSAINTHE M. H0347

BLACHLY F.F. H0348

BLACK C.E. H0349,H0350

BLACK/EUG....EUGENE BLACK

BLACK/HL....HUGO L. BLACK

BLACK/MUS....BLACK MUSLIMS

BLACK/PWR....BLACK POWER; SEE ALSO NEGRO

BLACK/ZION....BLACK ZIONISM

BLACKMER D.L.M. H2216

BLACKSTN/W....SIR WILLIAM BLACKSTONE

BLACKSTONE, SIR WILLIAM....SEE BLACKSTN/W

BLAKE J. H0351

BLANC N. H0352

BLANCHARD L.R. H0353

BLANCHARD W. H0354

BLAU P.M. H0355

BLISS P. H0356

BLITZ L.F. H0357

BLOCH/E....ERNEST BLOCH

BLONDEL J. H0358,H2625

BLOOMFIELD L.P. H0359

BLUM A.A. H1038

BLUM L. H0360,H0361

BLUNTSCHLI J.K. H0362

BMA....BRITISH MEDICAL ASSOCIATION

BOARD....SEE DELIB/GP

BOARD/MDCN....BOARD ON MEDICINE

BOAS/FRANZ....FRANZ BOAS

BODENHEIMER E. H0363

BODIN J. H0364

BODIN/JEAN....JEAN BODIN

BOER/WAR....BOER WAR

B00
MARKHAM V.R.,SOUTH AFRICA, PAST AND PRESENT. NETHERLAND SOUTH/AFR CULTURE LEGIS EDU/PROP COLONIAL CHOOSE REPRESENT DISCRIM ATTIT...OBS TIME/SEQ 17/19 NEGRO BOER/WAR. PAGE 103 H2054 — WAR LEAD RACE/REL

B99
BROOKS S.,BRITAIN AND THE BOERS. AFR SOUTH/AFR UK CULTURE INSPECT LEGIT...INT/LAW 19/20 BOER/WAR. PAGE 22 H0433 — WAR DIPLOM NAT/G

BOGARDUS E.S. H0365

BOGARDUS....BOGARDUS SCALE

BOHANNAN P. H0366,H0367

BOHANNAN T.R. H3221

BOHME/H....HELMUT BOHME

BOISSEVAIN J. H0368

BOLGAR V. H0369

BOLIVIA....SEE ALSO L/A+17C

S61
RANDALL F.B.,"COMMUNISM IN THE HIGH ANDES." L/A+17C PERU USSR SOCIETY PLAN EDU/PROP TOTALISM ATTIT RIGID/FLEX PWR WEALTH...HUM CONCPT GEN/LAWS 20 BOLIV EQUADOR. PAGE 129 H2589 — CULTURE DRIVE

B67
PIKE F.B.,FREEDOM AND REFORM IN LATIN AMERICA. BRAZIL URUGUAY CONSTN CULTURE SECT DIPLOM EDU/PROP PARTIC DRIVE ALL/VALS CATHISM...GEOG ANTHOL BIBLIOG REFORMERS BOLIV. PAGE 126 H2511 — L/A+17C ORD/FREE ECO/UNDEV REV

S67
HEATH D.B.,"BOLIVIA UNDER BARRIENTOS." L/A+17C NAT/G CHIEF DIPLOM ECO/TAC...POLICY 20 BOLIV. PAGE 69 H1379 — ECO/UNDEV POL/PAR REV CONSTN

BOLSHEVIK

B59
HENDEL S.,THE SOVIET CRUCIBLE. USSR LEAD COERCE NAT/LISM UTOPIA PWR...POLICY CONCPT ANTHOL 20 STALIN/J LENIN/VI MARX/KARL BOLSHEVIK. PAGE 70 — COM MARXISM REV

H1393 TOTALISM

BOLSHEVISM....BOLSHEVISM AND BOLSHEVISTS

B48
WOLFE B.D.,THREE WHO MADE A REVOLUTION. USSR CONSTN NAT/G CAP/ISM EDU/PROP CONTROL WAR GP/REL INGP/REL PERS/REL ROLE 20 STALIN/J LENIN/VI TROTSKY/L BOLSHEVISM. PAGE 170 H3398 BIOG REV LEAD MARXISM

S51
MACRAE D.G.,"THE BOLSHEVIK IDEOLOGY; THE INTELLECTUAL AND EMOTIONAL FACTORS IN COMMUNIST AFFILIATION" (BMR)" COM LEAD REV ATTIT ORD/FREE ...SOC CON/ANAL 20 BOLSHEVISM. PAGE 100 H2008 MARXISM INTELL PHIL/SCI SECT

B53
LEITES N.,A STUDY OF BOLSHEVISM. ELITES STRATA INT/ORG LOC/G POL/PAR WORKER EDU/PROP REV TOTALISM UTOPIA PWR...CONCPT 20 BOLSHEVISM. PAGE 94 H1870 MARXISM PLAN COM

B59
GOLDWIN R.A.,READINGS IN RUSSIAN FOREIGN POLICY. HUNGARY USSR YUGOSLAVIA ELITES INT/ORG NAT/G REV WAR NAT/LISM PERSON SOCISM...CHARTS 20 MAPS BOLSHEVISM. PAGE 58 H1160 COM MARXISM DIPLOM POLICY

B60
PIERCE R.A.,RUSSIAN CENTRAL ASIA, 1867-1917. ASIA RUSSIA CULTURE AGRI INDUS EDU/PROP REV NAT/LISM ...CHARTS BIBLIOG 19/20 BOLSHEVISM INTERVENT. PAGE 125 H2509 COLONIAL DOMIN ADMIN ECO/UNDEV

S61
TUCKER R.C.,"TOWARDS A COMPARATIVE POLITICS OF MOVEMENT-REGIMES" (BMR)" USSR CONSTN NAT/G CREATE PROB/SOLV DIPLOM DOMIN REV...GP/COMP IDEA/COMP METH 20 STALIN/J BOLSHEVISM. PAGE 157 H3135 MARXISM POLICY GEN/LAWS PWR

B62
KINDERSLEY R.,THE FIRST RUSSIAN REVISIONISTS. COM USSR LAW ELITES INTELL NAT/G LEGIS ECO/TAC EDU/PROP CONTROL LEAD GP/REL SOCISM 19/20 MARX/KARL BOLSHEVISM. PAGE 86 H1712 CONSTN MARXISM POPULISM BIOG

B64
FISCHER L.,THE LIFE OF LENIN. USSR LEAD REV WAR ...SOC 19/20 LENIN/VI COM/PARTY BOLSHEVISM. PAGE 51 H1011 BIOG MARXISM PERSON CHIEF

B65
ULAM A.,THE BOLSHEVIKS. COM USSR NAT/G CHIEF ECO/TAC ADMIN LEAD WAR POPULISM...POLICY 19/20 LENIN/VI BOLSHEVISM. PAGE 157 H3148 SOCISM POL/PAR TOP/EX REV

B66
BRODERSEN A.,THE SOVIET WORKER: LABOR AND GOVERNMENT IN SOVIET SOCIETY. USSR STRUCT INDUS LABOR PLAN PAY INGP/REL PRODUC...POLICY GEN/LAWS BIBLIOG 20 STALIN/J LENIN/VI BOLSHEVISM KHRUSH/N. PAGE 21 H0425 WORKER ROLE NAT/G MARXISM

B66
THOMPSON J.M.,RUSSIA, BOLSHEVISM, AND THE VERSAILLES PEACE. RUSSIA USSR INT/ORG NAT/G DELIB/GP AGREE REV WAR PWR 20 TREATY VERSAILLES BOLSHEVISM. PAGE 154 H3083 DIPLOM PEACE MARXISM

BOLTON A.R. H0370

BOMBACH G. H0371

BONAPART/L....LOUIS BONAPARTE (KING OF HOLLAND)

BONAR J. H0372

BONNEFOUS M. H0373

BONTOC....BONTOC, A MOUNTAIN TRIBE OF LUZON, PHILIPPINES

B05
PHILIPPINE ISLANDS BUREAU SCI,ETHNOLOGICAL SURVEY: THE BONTOC IGOROT. ECO/UNDEV AGRI FAM MARRIAGE HEALTH WEALTH...LING OBS AUD/VIS CHARTS WORSHIP 20 LUZON BONTOC. PAGE 125 H2500 CULTURE INGP/REL KIN STRUCT

BORBA DE MORAES R. H0374

BORDEN/R....SIR ROBERT BORDEN

BORGESE G.A. H0375

BORKENAU F. H0376,H0377

BORNEO....SEE ALSO S/ASIA

B43
US LIBRARY OF CONGRESS,BRITISH MALAYA AND BRITISH NORTH BORNEO. BORNEO MALAYSIA CONSTN AGRI COM/IND INDUS EDU/PROP 19/20. PAGE 160 H3203 BIBLIOG CULTURE

B66
LEIGH M.B.,CHECK LIST OF HOLDINGS ON BORNEO IN THE CORNELL UNIVERSITY LIBRARIES (PAMPHLET). BORNEO MALAYSIA LAW CONSTN GP/REL SOC. PAGE 93 H1866 BIBLIOG S/ASIA DIPLOM NAT/G

BORTOLI G. H0378,H0379

BOSANQUET B. H0380

BOSCH/JUAN....JUAN BOSCH

BOSHER J.F. H0381

BOSSCHERE G D.E. H0382

BOSSISM....BOSSISM; MONOPOLY OF POLITICAL POWER (U.S.)

BOSSUET J.B. H0383

BOSTON....BOSTON, MASSACHUSETTS

BOSTON UNIVERSITY LIBRARIES H0384

BOTSWANA....BOTSWANA

BOULDER....BOULDER, COLORADO

BOURASSA/H....HENRI BOURASSA

BOURDIEU P. H0385

BOURGUIBA

B62
BAULIN J.,THE ARAB ROLE IN AFRICA. AFR ALGERIA FUT ISLAM MOROCCO UAR COLONIAL NEUTRAL REV...SOC 20 TUNIS BOURGUIBA. PAGE 12 H0240 NAT/LISM DIPLOM NAT/G SECT

BOURNE H.E. H0386

BOUSCAREN A.T. H0387

BOUSSER M. H0750

BOUSTEDT O. H0388

BOWEN R.H. H0389

BOWLE J. H0391

BOWLES G.T. H0679

BOXER/REBL....BOXER REBELLION

B55
TAN C.C.,THE BOXER CATASTROPHE. ASIA UK USSR ELITES POL/PAR VOL/ASSN FORCES PROB/SOLV DIPLOM ADMIN COLONIAL NAT/LISM PEACE TREATY 19/20 BOXER/REBL. PAGE 152 H3040 REV NAT/G WAR

BOYCE A.N. H0392

BOZEMAN A.B. H0393

BOZZA T. H0394

BRACHER K.D. H0395

BRACKMAN A.C. H0396

BRADLEY A.W. H0397

BRADLEY C.P. H0398

BRADLEY/FH....FRANCIS HERBERT BRADLEY

BRADY A. H0399

BRAHMIN....BRAHMIN CASTE

BRAIBANTI R.J.D. H0400,H0401,H0402

BRAINWASHING....SEE EDU/PROP

BRAMSTED E.K. H0403

BRANCO R. H0404

BRANDEIS/L....LOUIS BRANDEIS

BRANDENBURG F. H0405

BRANNAN/C....CHARLES BRANNAN (SECRETARY OF AGRICULTURE)

BRASS P.R. H0406

BRAZIL....SEE ALSO L/A+17C

B17
DOS SANTOS M.,BIBLIOGRAPHIA GERAL, A DESCRIPCAO BIBLIOGRAFICA DE LIVROS TANTO DE AUTORES PORTUGUEZES COMO BRASILEIROS... BRAZIL PORTUGAL NAT/G LEAD GP/REL 15/20. PAGE 42 H0840 — BIBLIOG/A L/A+17C DIPLOM COLONIAL

B38
CARVALHO C.M.,GEOGRAPHIA HUMANA; POLITICA E ECONOMICA (3RD ED.). BRAZIL CULTURE AGRI INDUS DIPLOM COLONIAL GP/REL RACE/REL...LING 20 RESOURCE/N. PAGE 27 H0551 — GEOG HABITAT

B42
SIMOES DOS REIS A.,BIBLIOGRAFIA DAS BIBLIOGRAFIAS BRASILEIRAS. BRAZIL ADMIN COLONIAL 20. PAGE 144 H2879 — BIBLIOG NAT/G DIPLOM L/A+17C

B48
EDUARDO O.D.C.,THE NEGRO IN NORTHERN BRAZIL: A STUDY IN ACCULTURATION. BRAZIL ECO/UNDEV FAM SECT PAY REGION HABITAT CATHISM MYSTISM...GEOG OBS SOC/INTEG WORSHIP 20 NEGRO MARANHAO. PAGE 44 H0890 — CULTURE ADJUST GP/REL

B48
US LIBRARY OF CONGRESS,BRAZIL: A GUIDE TO THE OFFICIAL PUBLICATIONS OF BRAZIL. BRAZIL L/A+17C CONSULT DELIB/GP LEGIS CT/SYS 19/20. PAGE 160 H3206 — BIBLIOG/A NAT/G ADMIN TOP/EX

B49
BORBA DE MORAES R.,MANUAL BIBLIOGRAFICO DE ESTUDOS BRASILEIROS. BRAZIL DIPLOM ADMIN LEAD...SOC 20. PAGE 19 H0374 — BIBLIOG L/A+17C NAT/G ECO/UNDEV

B50
FIGANIERE J.C.,BIBLIOTHECA HISTORICA PORTUGUEZA. BRAZIL PORTUGAL SECT ADMIN. PAGE 50 H0997 — BIBLIOG NAT/G DIPLOM COLONIAL

B53
WAGLEY C.,AMAZON TOWN: A STUDY OF MAN IN THE TROPICS. BRAZIL L/A+17C STRATA STRUCT ECO/UNDEV AGRI EX/STRUC RACE/REL DISCRIM HABITAT WEALTH...OBS SOC/EXP 20. PAGE 164 H3285 — SOC NEIGH CULTURE INGP/REL

B55
DE ARAGAO J.G.,LA JURIDICTION ADMINISTRATIVE AU BRESIL. BRAZIL ADJUD COLONIAL CT/SYS REV FEDERAL ORD/FREE...BIBLIOG 19/20. PAGE 37 H0749 — EX/STRUC ADMIN NAT/G

B56
VIANNA F.J.,EVOLUCAO DE POVO BRASILEIRO (4TH ED.). BRAZIL TEC/DEV COLONIAL GP/REL ATTIT SOVEREIGN ...SOC SOC/INTEG 15/20. PAGE 162 H3247 — STRUCT RACE/REL NAT/G

B59
ROCHE J.,LA COLONISATION ALLEMANDE ET LE RIO GRANDE DO SUL. BRAZIL L/A+17C NAT/G PROVS INGP/REL RACE/REL DISCRIM HABITAT...GEOG SOC/INTEG 19/20 MIGRATION. PAGE 133 H2652 — ECO/UNDEV GP/REL ATTIT

B59
SZLUC T.,TWILIGHT OF THE TYRANTS. BRAZIL L/A+17C PERU VENEZUELA NAT/G FORCES CONTROL PERSON MORAL ORD/FREE PWR...CONCPT 20 ARGEN COLOMB. PAGE 151 H3028 — TOTALISM CHIEF REV FASCISM

B60
PINTO F.B.M.,ENRIQUECIMENTO ILICITO NO EXERCICIO DE CARGOS PUBLICOS. BRAZIL L/A+17C USA+45 ELITES TRIBUTE CONTROL INGP/REL ORD/FREE PWR...NAT/COMP 20. PAGE 126 H2513 — ADMIN NAT/G CRIME LAW

B61
HADDAD J.A.,REVOLUCAO CUBANA E REVOLUCAO BRASILEIRA. BRAZIL CUBA L/A+17C STRATA AGRI WORKER EDU/PROP REGION...POLICY NAT/COMP 20. PAGE 63 H1272 — REV ORD/FREE DIPLOM ECO/UNDEV

B61
LUZ N.V.,A LUTA PELA INDUSTRIALIZACAO DO BRAZIL. BRAZIL L/A+17C AGRI NAT/G TEC/DEV COLONIAL 19/20. PAGE 99 H1981 — ECO/UNDEV INDUS NAT/LISM POLICY

B62
THREE PRELIMINARY BIBLIOGRAPHIES OF WORKS RELATED TO THE SOCIAL SCIENCES IN LATIN AMERICA. BRAZIL CULTURE SOCIETY NAT/G PLAN PROB/SOLV...PSY 20 MEXIC/AMER. PAGE 2 H0040 — BIBLIOG L/A+17C SOC AGRI

B62
GALENSON W.,LABOR IN DEVELOPING COUNTRIES. BRAZIL INDONESIA ISRAEL PAKISTAN TURKEY AGRI INDUS WORKER PAY PRICE GP/REL WEALTH...MGT CHARTS METH/COMP NAT/COMP 20. PAGE 54 H1088 — LABOR ECO/UNDEV BARGAIN POL/PAR

B63
AZEVEDO T.,SOCIAL CHANGE IN BRAZIL. BRAZIL ECO/DEV COM/IND FAM NAT/G SECT GP/REL PERS/REL...CONCPT WORSHIP 20. PAGE 9 H0188 — TEC/DEV STRUCT SOC CULTURE

B63
DALAND R.T.,PERSPECTIVES OF BRAZILIAN PUBLIC ADMINISTRATION (VOL. I). BRAZIL LAW ECO/UNDEV SCHOOL CHIEF TEC/DEV CONFER CONTROL GP/REL ATTIT ROLE PWR...ANTHOL 20. PAGE 37 H0735 — ADMIN NAT/G PLAN GOV/REL

B63
GUIMARAES A.P.,INFLACAO E MONOPOLIO NO BRASIL. BRAZIL FINAN NAT/G PLAN PAY...METH/COMP 20. PAGE 62 H1248 — ECO/UNDEV PRICE INT/TRADE BAL/PAY

B63
WAGLEY C.,INTRODUCTION TO BRAZIL. BRAZIL L/A+17C FAM KIN SCHOOL SECT ATTIT WEALTH...GEOG SOC. PAGE 164 H3286 — ECO/UNDEV ELITES HABITAT STRATA

S63
POPPINO R.E.,"IMBALANCE IN BRAZIL." L/A+17C NAT/G TOP/EX PLAN DIPLOM LEGIT DRIVE WEALTH...CON/ANAL LAFTA 20. PAGE 127 H2544 — POL/PAR ECO/TAC BRAZIL

B64
ALVIM J.C.,A REVOLUCAO SEM RUMO. BRAZIL NAT/G BAL/PWR DIPLOM INT/TRADE PARTIC WEALTH...POLICY SOC SOC/INTEG 20. PAGE 6 H0118 — REV CIVMIL/REL ECO/UNDEV ORD/FREE

B64
BERNSTEIN H.,A BOOKSHELF ON BRAZIL. BRAZIL ADMIN COLONIAL...HUM JURID SOC 20. PAGE 16 H0315 — BIBLIOG/A NAT/G L/A+17C ECO/UNDEV

B64
HARRIS M.,PATTERNS OF RACE IN THE AMERICAS. BRAZIL L/A+17C STRATA ECO/UNDEV AGRI KIN MUNIC SECT COLONIAL RACE/REL...SOC SOC/INTEG 17/20 NEGRO INDIAN/AM. PAGE 67 H1342 — STRUCT PRE/AMER CULTURE SOCIETY

B64
HOROWITZ I.L.,REVOLUTION IN BRAZIL. BRAZIL L/A+17C ELITES STRATA NAT/G BAL/PWR PARTIC ATTIT 20. PAGE 74 H1473 — ECO/UNDEV DIPLOM POLICY ORD/FREE

B64
MAIER J.,POLITICS OF CHANGE IN LATIN AMERICA. BRAZIL L/A+17C STRATA INT/ORG NAT/G POL/PAR FOR/AID REV 20. PAGE 101 H2019 — SOCIETY NAT/LISM DIPLOM REGION

B64
MARTINEZ J.R.,THREE CASES OF COMMUNISM: CUBA, BRAZIL, AND MEXICO. BRAZIL CUBA L/A+17C CONSTN NAT/G DIPLOM ECO/TAC GP/REL INGP/REL...GP/COMP BIBLIOG 20 MEXIC/AMER COM/PARTY. PAGE 103 H2068 — MARXISM BIOG REV NAT/COMP

B65
FAUST J.J.,A REVOLUCAO DEVORA SEUS PRESIDENTES. BRAZIL NAT/G POL/PAR LEAD CHOOSE CIVMIL/REL ORD/FREE 20 PRESIDENT. PAGE 49 H0976 — PARTIC REV FORCES GP/REL

B65
HAVIGHURST R.J.,SOCIETY AND EDUCATION IN BRAZIL. BRAZIL PORTUGAL ECO/UNDEV INDUS NAT/G CREATE INSPECT COLONIAL ADJUST DEMAND LITERACY...CENSUS TREND CHARTS 16/20. PAGE 68 H1362 — SCHOOL ACADEM ACT/RES CULTURE

S65
BRANDENBURG F.,"THE RELEVANCE OF MEXICAN EXPERIENCE TO LATIN AMERICAN DEVELOPMENT." BRAZIL CHILE VENEZUELA STRUCT ECO/UNDEV AGRI CREATE ECO/TAC ...STAT RECORD MEXIC/AMER ARGEN COLOMB. PAGE 20 H0405 — L/A+17C GOV/COMP

S65
TENDLER J.D.,"TECHNOLOGY AND ECONOMIC DEVELOPMENT* THE CASE OF HYDRO VS THERMAL POWER." CONSTRUC DIST/IND CREATE TEC/DEV INT/TRADE CENTRAL PWR SKILL WEALTH...MGT NAT/COMP ARGEN. PAGE 153 H3061 — BRAZIL INDUS ECO/UNDEV

B67
PIKE F.B.,FREEDOM AND REFORM IN LATIN AMERICA. BRAZIL URUGUAY CONSTN CULTURE SECT DIPLOM EDU/PROP PARTIC DRIVE ALL/VALS CATHISM...GEOG ANTHOL BIBLIOG REFORMERS BOLIV. PAGE 126 H2511 — L/A+17C ORD/FREE ECO/UNDEV REV

L67
ROTH A.R.,"CAPITAL-MARKET DEVELOPMENT IN ISRAEL AND BRAZIL: TWO EXAMPLES OF THE ROLE OF LAW IN DEVELOPMENT." BRAZIL ISRAEL L/A+17C INDUS MARKET ECO/TAC FOR/AID INT/TRADE CONTROL BAL/PAY 20. PAGE 135 H2694 — LAW ECO/UNDEV NAT/COMP FINAN

S67
GRAHAM R.,"BRAZIL'S DILEMMA." BRAZIL FUT L/A+17C NAT/G CHIEF PROB/SOLV ECO/TAC PWR 20. PAGE 60 H1193 — ECO/UNDEV CONSTN POL/PAR POLICY

S67
LANE J.P.,"FUNCTIONS OF MASS MEDIA IN BRAZIL'S 1964 CRISIS." BRAZIL NAT/G FORCES TOP/EX PRESS TV ATTIT PWR...METH/CNCPT 20. PAGE 90 H1807 — CIVMIL/REL REV COM/IND EDU/PROP

BRECHER M. H0407,H0408

BRECHT A. H0409

BREDVOLD L.I. H0410

BREHON....BREHON LAW (ANCIENT CELTIC)

B75
MAINE H.S.,LECTURES ON THE EARLY HISTORY OF INSTITUTIONS. IRELAND UK CONSTN ELITES STRUCT FAM KIN CHIEF LEGIS CT/SYS OWN SOVEREIGN...CONCPT 16 BENTHAM/J BREHON ROMAN/LAW. PAGE 101 H2021 — CULTURE LAW INGP/REL

BREMBECK C.S. H1322

BRETTON H.L. H0411

BREWIS T.N. H0412

BRIAND/A....ARISTIDE BRIAND

BRIDGEPORT....BRIDGEPORT, CONNECTICUT

BRIDGHAM P. H0413

BRIDGMAN J. H0414

BRIERLY J.L. H0415

BRIGGS A. H0416

BRIGGS L.C. H0417,H0418

BRIGHT J.R. H0419

BRIMMELL G.H. H0420

BRINKMANN C. H3263

BRIT/COLUM....BRITISH COLUMBIA, CANADA

BRITISH COLUMBIA, CANADA....SEE BRIT/COLUM

BRITISH COMMONWEALTH OF NATIONS....SEE COMMONWLTH

BRITISH GUIANA....SEE GUIANA/BR + GUYANA

BRITISH BORNEO RESEARCH PROJ H0421

BROCK C. H0422

BROCKWAY A.F. H0423

BRODERICK G.C. H0424

BRODERSEN A. H0425

BRODOWSKI J.H. H0426

BROEKMEIJER M.W. H0427

BROGAN D.W. H0428,H0429

BROMAGE A.W. H0430

BROMAGE M.C. H0430

BROMKE A. H0431

BROOK/EDGR....EDGAR H. BROOKES

BROOKE Z.N. H2559

BROOKES E.H. H0432

BROOKINGS....BROOKINGS INSTITUTION, THE

BROOKS S. H0433

BROSE O.J. H0434

BROUGHTON M. H0435

BROWN A.D. H0436,H0437,H0438

BROWN B.E. H0439,H2009

BROWN C.V. H0440

BROWN D.F. H0441

BROWN D.M. H0442,H0443

BROWN J.F. H0444

BROWN L.C. H0445,H0446

BROWN L.N. H0447

BROWN N. H0448

BROWN R.T. H0449

BROWN S.D. H0450

BROWN W.M. H0451

BROWN W.O. H0543

BROWN/JOHN....JOHN BROWN

BROWNE G.S. H0697

BROWNELL/H....HERBERT BROWNELL

BROWNSON O.A. H0452

BRUGADA R.S. H2474

BRUMBERG A. H0453

BRUNHES J. H0454

BRUNNER E. H0843

BRYAN/WJ....WILLIAM JENNINGS BRYAN

BRYCE J. H0455,H0456

BRYCE/J....JAMES BRYCE

BRZEZINSKI Z.K. H0457,H0458,H0459,H0460,H0461,H0462,H0463,H1068

BRZEZNSK/Z....ZBIGNIEW K. BRZEZINSKI

BUCHANAN/J....PRESIDENT JAMES BUCHANAN

BUCHHEIM K. H0464

BUCK P.W. H0465

BUCKLEY/WF....WILLIAM F. BUCKLEY

BUDDHISM....BUDDHISM

B55
THOMPSON V.,MINORITY PROBLEMS IN SOUTHEAST ASIA. CAMBODIA CHINA/COM LAOS S/ASIA KIN NAT/G SECT PROB/SOLV EDU/PROP REGION GP/REL RACE/REL MARXISM ...SOC 20 BUDDHISM UN. PAGE 154 H3085 — INGP/REL GEOG DIPLOM STRUCT

S62
SARKISYANZ E.,"NATIONALISM, CAPITALISM, AND THE UNCOMMITED NATIONS: MARXISM AND ASIAN CULTURAL TRADITIONS." ASIA BURMA CHINA/COM COM CULTURE SOCIETY NAT/G POL/PAR PLAN DOMIN EDU/PROP COLONIAL COERCE ATTIT RIGID/FLEX...CONCPT TREND MARX/KARL 20 TIBET BUDDHISM. PAGE 138 H2755 — S/ASIA SECT NAT/LISM CAP/ISM

B65
KUNSTADTER P.,THE LUA (LAWA) OF NORTHERN THAILAND: ASPECTS OF SOCIAL STRUCTURE, AGRICULTURE, AND RELIGION. THAILAND AGRI FAM KIN INGP/REL ISOLAT MARRIAGE HEALTH WORSHIP 20 BUDDHISM LUA. PAGE 89 H1780 — STRUCT ECO/UNDEV CULTURE

B66
CADY J.F.,THAILAND, BURMA, LAOS AND CAMBODIA. FRANCE UK CULTURE NAT/G DOMIN GP/REL RACE/REL HABITAT...GEOG TREND CHINJAP BUDDHISM. PAGE 25 H0504 — S/ASIA COLONIAL REGION SECT

BUDGET....BUDGETING, BUDGETS, FISCAL PLANNING

B04
GRIFFIN A.P.C.,LIST OF REFERENCES ON BUDGETS OF FOREIGN COUNTRIES (PAMPHLET). MOD/EUR FINAN MARKET TAX...MGT STAT 19/20. PAGE 61 H1218 — BIBLIOG/A BUDGET NAT/G

B08
THE GOVERNMENT OF SOUTH AFRICA (VOL. II). SOUTH/AFR STRATA EXTR/IND EX/STRUC TOP/EX BUDGET ADJUD ADMIN CT/SYS PRODUC...CORREL CENSUS 19 RAILROAD CIVIL/SERV POSTAL/SYS. PAGE 2 H0030 — CONSTN FINAN LEGIS NAT/G

B13
BARDOUX J.,L'ANGLETERRE RADICALE; ESSAI DE LA PSYCHOLOGIE SOCIALE (1906-1913). UK CONSTN NAT/G WORKER CREATE BUDGET ECO/TAC ATTIT...POLICY 20 PARLIAMENT LABOR/PAR STRIKE NAVY. PAGE 11 H0215 — POL/PAR CHOOSE COLONIAL LEGIS

B19
NATHAN M.,THE SOUTH AFRICAN COMMONWEALTH: CONSTITUTION, PROBLEMS, SOCIAL CONDITIONS. SOUTH/AFR UK CULTURE INDUS EX/STRUC LEGIS BUDGET EDU/PROP ADMIN CT/SYS GP/REL RACE/REL...LING 19/20 CMN/WLTH. PAGE 116 H2317 — CONSTN NAT/G POL/PAR SOCIETY

N19
FIKS M.,PUBLIC ADMINISTRATION IN ISRAEL (PAMPHLET). ISRAEL SCHOOL EX/STRUC BUDGET PAY INGP/REL ...DECISION 20 CIVIL/SERV. PAGE 50 H0999 — EDU/PROP NAT/G ADMIN

WORKER

B25
WILLIAMS B.,THE SELBORNE MEMORANDUM. AFR FUT SOUTH/AFR UK NAT/G BUDGET DIPLOM REGION GOV/REL SOVEREIGN...POLICY CHARTS 20 UNIFICA SELBORNE/W. PAGE 168 H3365 COLONIAL PROVS

B27
WILLOUGHBY W.F.,PRINCIPLES OF PUBLIC ADMINISTRATION WITH SPECIAL REFERENCE TO THE NATIONAL AND STATE GOVERNMENTS OF THE UNITED STATES. FINAN PROVS CHIEF CONSULT LEGIS CREATE BUDGET EXEC ROUTINE GOV/REL CENTRAL...MGT 20 BUR/BUDGET CONGRESS PRESIDENT. PAGE 169 H3373 NAT/G EX/STRUC OP/RES ADMIN

B37
UNION OF SOUTH AFRICA,REPORT CONCERNING ADMINISTRATION OF SOUTH WEST AFRICA (6 VOLS.). SOUTH/AFR INDUS PUB/INST FORCES LEGIS BUDGET DIPLOM EDU/PROP ADJUD CT/SYS...GEOG CHARTS 20 AFRICA/SW LEAGUE/NAT. PAGE 158 H3166 NAT/G ADMIN COLONIAL CONSTN

B39
JENNINGS W.I.,PARLIAMENT. UK POL/PAR OP/RES BUDGET LEAD CHOOSE GP/REL...MGT 20 PARLIAMENT HOUSE/LORD HOUSE/CMNS. PAGE 80 H1609 PARL/PROC LEGIS CONSTN NAT/G

S39
COLE G.D.H.,"NAZI ECONOMICS: HOW DO THEY MANAGE IT?" GERMANY FORCES WORKER BUDGET INT/TRADE ROUTINE COERCE WAR 20 HITLER/A NAZI. PAGE 31 H0622 FASCISM ECO/TAC ATTIT PLAN

C40
FAHS C.B.,"GOVERNMENT IN JAPAN." FINAN FORCES LEGIS TOP/EX BUDGET INT/TRADE EDU/PROP SOVEREIGN ...CON/ANAL BIBLIOG/A 20 CHINJAP. PAGE 48 H0962 ASIA DIPLOM NAT/G ADMIN

B43
CONOVER H.F.,SOVIET RUSSIA: SELECTED LIST OF REFERENCES. USSR CULTURE INDUS NAT/G TOP/EX TEC/DEV BUDGET WAR CIVMIL/REL EFFICIENCY MARXISM 20. PAGE 32 H0644 BIBLIOG ECO/DEV COM DIPLOM

B47
DE NOIA J.,GUIDE TO OFFICIAL PUBLICATIONS OF OTHER AMERICAN REPUBLICS: ECUADOR (VOL. IX). ECUADOR LAW FINAN LEGIS BUDGET CT/SYS 19/20. PAGE 38 H0763 BIBLIOG/A CONSTN NAT/G EDU/PROP

B48
NEUBURGER O.,GUIDE TO OFFICIAL PUBLICATIONS OF THE OTHER AMERICAN REPUBLICS: VENEZUELA (VOL. XIX). VENEZUELA FINAN LEGIS PLAN BUDGET DIPLOM CT/SYS PARL/PROC 19/20. PAGE 117 H2335 BIBLIOG/A NAT/G CONSTN LAW

B52
SCHATTSCHNEIDER E.E.,A GUIDE TO THE STUDY OF PUBLIC AFFAIRS. LAW LOC/G NAT/G LEGIS BUDGET PRESS ADMIN LOBBY...JURID CHARTS 20. PAGE 139 H2775 ACT/RES INTELL ACADEM METH/COMP

B54
GRAYSON H.,ECONOMIC PLANNING UNDER FREE ENTERPRISE. CANADA FUT UK DELIB/GP BUDGET CONFER CONTROL ...POLICY DECISION 20. PAGE 60 H1200 PLAN ECO/TAC NAT/COMP NAT/G

B58
ORNES G.E.,TRUJILLO: LITTLE CAESAR OF THE CARIBBEAN. DOMIN/REP FAM NAT/G FORCES BUDGET CRIME REV PERSON 20 TRUJILLO/R. PAGE 122 H2429 BIOG PWR TOTALISM CHIEF

B58
SHAW S.J.,THE FINANCIAL AND ADMINISTRATIVE ORGANIZATION AND DEVELOPMENT OF OTTOMAN EGYPT 1517-1798. UAR LOC/G FORCES BUDGET INT/TRADE TAX EATING INCOME WEALTH...CHARTS BIBLIOG 16/18 OTTOMAN NAPOLEON/B. PAGE 143 H2853 FINAN ADMIN GOV/REL CULTURE

B59
JENNINGS W.I.,CABINET GOVERNMENT (3RD ED.). UK POL/PAR CHIEF BUDGET ADMIN CHOOSE GP/REL 20. PAGE 81 H1612 DELIB/GP NAT/G CONSTN OP/RES

B60
ALBI F.,TRATADO DE LOS MODOS DE GESTION DE LAS CORPORACIONES LOCALES. SPAIN FINAN NAT/G BUDGET CONTROL EXEC ROUTINE GOV/REL ORD/FREE SOVEREIGN ...MGT 20. PAGE 5 H0092 LOC/G LAW ADMIN MUNIC

B60
KENEN P.B.,BRITISH MONETARY POLICY AND THE BALANCE OF PAYMENTS 1951-57. UK PLAN BUDGET ECO/TAC INT/TRADE PAY PRICE COST ATTIT 20. PAGE 84 H1687 BAL/PAY PROB/SOLV FINAN NAT/G

B60
STOLPER W.F.,GERMANY BETWEEN EAST AND WEST: THE ECONOMICS OF COMPETITIVE COEXISTENCE. FUT GERMANY/E GERMANY/W WOR+45 FINAN POL/PAR BUDGET ECO/TAC FOR/AID INT/TRADE...STAT CHARTS METH/COMP 20 COLD/WAR. PAGE 150 H2989 ECO/DEV DIPLOM GOV/COMP BAL/PWR

B61
BREWIS T.N.,CANADIAN ECONOMIC POLICY. CANADA BUDGET CAP/ISM INT/TRADE RATION TARIFFS TAX PRICE CONTROL ROUTINE FEDERAL INCOME PRODUC 20 GOLD/STAND. PAGE 20 H0412 ECO/DEV ECO/TAC NAT/G PLAN

B61
ESTEVEZ A.,ASPECTOS ECONOMICO-FINANCIEROS DE LA CAMPANA SANMARITANA. L/A+17C SPAIN FINAN COLONIAL LEAD ROLE ORD/FREE WEALTH 19 SOUTH/AMER SAN/MARTIN. PAGE 47 H0942 ECO/UNDEV REV BUDGET NAT/G

B61
HAUSER M.,DIE URSACHEN DER FRANZOSISCHEN INFLATION IN DEN JAHREN 1946-1952. FRANCE INDUS NAT/G BUDGET DIPLOM ECO/TAC FOR/AID COST MONEY 20 GOLD/STAND. PAGE 68 H1357 ECO/DEV FINAN PRICE

B61
NATIONAL BANK OF LIBYA,INFLATION IN LIBYA (PAMPHLET). LIBYA SOCIETY NAT/G PLAN INT/TRADE ...STAT CHARTS 20 GOLD/STAND. PAGE 116 H2318 ECO/TAC ECO/UNDEV FINAN BUDGET

B61
SHARMA T.R.,THE WORKING OF STATE ENTERPRISES IN INDIA. INDIA DELIB/GP LEGIS WORKER BUDGET PRICE CONTROL GP/REL OWN ATTIT...MGT CHARTS 20. PAGE 142 H2851 NAT/G INDUS ADMIN SOCISM

B61
STANLEY C.J.,LATE CH'ING FINANCE: HU KUANG-YUNG AS AN INNOVATOR. ASIA NAT/G FORCES BUDGET TAX WAR GOV/REL COST...POLICY BIOG CHARTS BIBLIOG 19. PAGE 148 H2969 FINAN ECO/TAC CIVMIL/REL ADMIN

B62
MEIER R.L.,A COMMUNICATIONS THEORY OF URBAN GROWTH. CULTURE ECO/DEV COMPUTER BUDGET UTIL KNOWL...SOC CONCPT METH 20 OPEN/SPACE. PAGE 108 H2164 OP/RES COM/IND MUNIC CONTROL

B63
BANERJI A.K.,INDIA'S BALANCE OF PAYMENTS. INDIA NAT/G PRICE BAL/PAY COST INCOME 20. PAGE 10 H0208 INT/TRADE DIPLOM FINAN BUDGET

B63
CHOU S.H.,THE CHINESE INFLATION 1937-1949. ASIA SOCIETY POL/PAR FOR/AID INT/TRADE BAL/PAY WEALTH MARXISM...STAT CHARTS 20 COM/PARTY GOLD/STAND. PAGE 30 H0597 FINAN ECO/TAC BUDGET NAT/G

B63
DUE J.F.,STATE SALES TAX ADMINISTRATION. OP/RES BUDGET PAY ADMIN EXEC ROUTINE COST EFFICIENCY PROFIT...CHARTS METH/COMP 20. PAGE 43 H0855 PROVS TAX STAT GOV/COMP

B63
INTERNATIONAL ASSOCIATION RES,AFRICAN STUDIES IN INCOME AND WEALTH. AFR NAT/G PROB/SOLV DEMAND INCOME...ECOMETRIC METH/COMP 20. PAGE 78 H1553 WEALTH PLAN ECO/UNDEV BUDGET

B63
UN SECRETARY GENERAL,PLANNING FOR ECONOMIC DEVELOPMENT. ECO/UNDEV FINAN BUDGET INT/TRADE TARIFFS TAX ADMIN 20 UN. PAGE 158 H3159 PLAN ECO/TAC MGT NAT/COMP

B63
WALKER A.A.,OFFICIAL PUBLICATIONS OF SIERRA LEONE AND GAMBIA. GAMBIA SIER/LEONE UK LAW CONSTN LEGIS PLAN BUDGET DIPLOM...SOC SAMP CON/ANAL 20. PAGE 164 H3290 BIBLIOG NAT/G COLONIAL ADMIN

N63
LEDERER W.,THE BALANCE ON FOREIGN TRANSACTIONS: PROBLEMS OF DEFINITION AND MEASUREMENT (PAMPHLET). USA+45 BUDGET DIPLOM ECO/TAC PRICE GOV/REL...POLICY STAT NAT/COMP METH 20. PAGE 93 H1853 FINAN BAL/PAY INT/TRADE ECO/DEV

B64
BROWN N.,NUCLEAR WAR* THE IMPENDING STRATEGIC DEADLOCK. USA+45 USSR TEC/DEV BUDGET RISK ARMS/CONT NUC/PWR WEAPON COST BIO/SOC...GEOG IDEA/COMP NAT/COMP GAME NATO WARSAW/P. PAGE 22 H0448 FORCES OP/RES WAR GEN/LAWS

B64
HAAR C.M.,LAW AND LAND: ANGLO-AMERICAN PLANNING PRACTICE. UK USA+45 NAT/G TEC/DEV BUDGET CT/SYS INGP/REL EFFICIENCY OWN...JURID 20. PAGE 63 H1263 LAW PLAN MUNIC NAT/COMP

B64
OECD,DEVELOPMENT ASSISTANCE EFFORTS - POLICIES OF THE MEMBERS. AGRI INDUS BUDGET...GEOG NAT/COMP 20 OECD. PAGE 120 H2398 INT/ORG FOR/AID ECO/UNDEV TEC/DEV

B64
THAILAND NATIONAL ECO DEV,THE NATIONAL ECONOMIC DEVELOPMENT PLAN: 1961-66: SECOND PHASE 1964-66. THAILAND AGRI FINAN BUDGET EFFICIENCY INCOME...STAT CHARTS 20. PAGE 153 H3065 ECO/UNDEV ECO/TAC PLAN NAT/G

B64
WILSON T.,POLICIES FOR REGIONAL DEVELOPMENT. CANADA UK FINAN INDUS NAT/G BUDGET TAX GIVE COST ...NAT/COMP 20. PAGE 169 H3383 REGION PLAN ECO/DEV ECO/TAC

C64
GOLDMAN M.I.,"COMPARATIVE ECONOMIC SYSTEMS: A READER." COM ECO/UNDEV NAT/G BUDGET CAP/ISM ADMIN TOTALISM MARXISM SOCISM...MGT ANTHOL BIBLIOG 19/20. PAGE 58 H1157 NAT/COMP CONTROL IDEA/COMP

B65
DUGGAR G.S.,RENEWAL OF TOWN AND VILLAGE I: A WORLD-WIDE SURVEY OF LOCAL GOVERNMENT EXPERIENCE. WOR+45 CONSTRUC INDUS CREATE BUDGET REGION GOV/REL...QU NAT/COMP 20 URBAN/RNWL. PAGE 43 H0859 MUNIC NEIGH PLAN ADMIN

B65
OGILVY-WEBB M.,THE GOVERNMENT EXPLAINS: A STUDY OF THE INFORMATION SERVICES. UK DELIB/GP LEGIS WORKER BUDGET DIPLOM 20. PAGE 121 H2409 EDU/PROP ATTIT NAT/G ADMIN

B65
SHEPHERD W.G.,ECONOMIC PERFORMANCE UNDER PUBLIC OWNERSHIP: BRITISH FUEL AND POWER. UK BUDGET GP/REL ...METH/CNCPT CHARTS BIBLIOG 20. PAGE 143 H2858 PROC/MFG NAT/G OWN FINAN

B65
TEW B.,WEALTH AND INCOME. UK BUDGET INT/TRADE PRICE BAL/PAY DEMAND...CHARTS GOV/COMP 20 AUSTRAL. PAGE 153 H3064 FINAN ECO/DEV WEALTH INCOME

B65
YOUNG A.N.,CHINA'S WARTIME FINANCE AND INFLATION. ASIA AGRI INDUS NAT/G ECO/TAC CONFER PRICE WAR COST 20. PAGE 172 H3437 FINAN FOR/AID TAX BUDGET

S65
KEE W.S.,"CENTRAL CITY EXPENDITURES AND METROPOLITAN AREAS." PLAN BUDGET ECO/TAC TAX GP/REL WEALTH...CHARTS 20. PAGE 84 H1677 LOC/G MUNIC GOV/COMP NEIGH

S65
WOLF C. JR.,"THE POLITICAL EFFECTS OF SOME MILITARY PROGRAMS* SOME INDICATIONS FROM LATIN AMERICA." ELITES STRATA BUDGET FOR/AID WEAPON ATTIT PERCEPT PWR...REGRESS SYS/QU CHARTS NAT/COMP. PAGE 170 H3397 L/A+17C FORCES CIVMIL/REL PROBABIL

B66
AGGARWALA R.N.,FINANCIAL COMMITTEES OF THE INDIAN PARLIAMENT: A STUDY IN PARLIAMENTARY CONTROL OVER PUBLIC EXPENDITURE. INDIA FINAN NAT/G ROLE...CHARTS METH/COMP METH 20 PARLIAMENT. PAGE 4 H0078 PARL/PROC BUDGET CONTROL DELIB/GP

B66
GHOSH P.K.,THE CONSTITUTION OF INDIA: HOW IT HAS BEEN FRAMED. INDIA LOC/G DELIB/GP EX/STRUC PROB/SOLV BUDGET INT/TRADE CT/SYS CHOOSE...LING 20. PAGE 56 H1121 CONSTN NAT/G LEGIS FEDERAL

B66
INTERPARLIAMENTARY UNION,PARLIAMENTS: COMPARATIVE STUDY ON STRUCTURE AND FUNCTIONING OF REPRESENTATIVE INSTITUTIONS IN FIFTY-FIVE COUNTRIES. WOR+45 POL/PAR DELIB/GP BUDGET ADMIN CONTROL CHOOSE. PAGE 78 H1560 PARL/PROC LEGIS GOV/COMP EX/STRUC

B66
JOHNSON N.,PARLIAMENT AND ADMINISTRATION: THE ESTIMATES COMMITTEE 1945-65. FUT UK NAT/G EX/STRUC PLAN BUDGET ORD/FREE...T 20 PARLIAMENT HOUSE/CMNS. PAGE 81 H1625 LEGIS ADMIN FINAN DELIB/GP

B66
KOMIYA R.,POSTWAR ECONOMIC GROWTH IN JAPAN. ELITES NAT/G EX/STRUC TEC/DEV BUDGET DIPLOM CONTROL BAL/PAY PRODUC...BIBLIOG 20 CHINJAP. PAGE 88 H1754 ECO/DEV POLICY PLAN ADJUST

B66
MASON E.S.,ECONOMIC DEVELOPMENT IN INDIA AND PAKISTAN. INDIA PAKISTAN AGRI FINAN PLAN BUDGET INT/TRADE WEALTH...POLICY STAT TREND CHARTS 20. PAGE 104 H2086 NAT/COMP ECO/UNDEV ECO/TAC FOR/AID

B66
NOEL G.E.,THE NEW BRITAIN AND HAROLD WILSON: INTERIM REPORT, 1966 GENERAL ELECTION. UK POL/PAR CONSULT PROB/SOLV BUDGET DIPLOM ECO/TAC LEAD CHOOSE ATTIT 20 WILSON/H PARLIAMENT. PAGE 118 H2366 BIOG PERSON NAT/G CHIEF

B66
SASTRI K.V.S.,FEDERAL-STATE FISCAL RELATIONS IN INDIA: A STUDY OF THE FINANCE COMMISSION AND TECHNIQUES OF FINANCIAL ADJUSTMENT. INDIA PROVS DELIB/GP GOV/REL FEDERAL...MATH CHARTS 20. PAGE 138 H2756 TAX BUDGET FINAN NAT/G

S66
BENOIT J.,"WORLD DEFENSE EXPENDITURES." WOR+45 WEAPON COST PRODUC. PAGE 14 H0284 FORCES STAT NAT/COMP BUDGET

B67
JAIN R.K.,MANAGEMENT OF STATE ENTERPRISES. INDIA SOCIETY FINAN WORKER BUDGET ADMIN CONTROL OWN 20. PAGE 79 H1584 NAT/G SOCISM INDUS MGT

B67
SHAPIRO P.S.,COMMUNICATIONS OR TRANSPORT: DECISION-MAKING IN DEVELOPING COUNTRIES. WOR+45 NAT/G PLAN ALL/IDEOS MARXISM...NAT/COMP GEN/LAWS. PAGE 142 H2844 BUDGET COM/IND DECISION ECO/DEV

L67
WILBER L.A.,"THE GOVERNMENTAL STRUCTURE OF MISSISSIPPI: ITS STRENGTHS AND WEAKNESSES." AGRI LOC/G SCHOOL EX/STRUC LEGIS TOP/EX BUDGET CT/SYS APPORT RACE/REL...GOV/COMP 20 MISSISSIPP. PAGE 168 H3359 CONSTN PROVS STAT CON/ANAL

S67
ANTHEM T.,"CYPRUS* WHAT NOW?" CYPRUS GREECE TURKEY NAT/G BUDGET MAJORITY 20 NATO. PAGE 7 H0143 DIPLOM COERCE INT/TRADE ADJUD

S67
BAER W.,"THE INFLATION CONTROVERSY IN LATIN AMERICA: SURVEY." L/A+17C ECO/UNDEV AGRI FINAN INDUS PLAN PROB/SOLV TEC/DEV...BIBLIOG/A 20. PAGE 10 H0194 NAT/G BAL/PAY ECO/TAC BUDGET

S67
BASOV V.,"THE DEVELOPMENT OF PUBLIC EDUCATION AND THE BUDGET." USSR NAT/G CONTROL REV COST AGE...STAT 20. PAGE 12 H0235 BUDGET GIVE EDU/PROP SCHOOL

S67
BRANCO R.,"LAND REFORM* THE ANSWER TO LATIN AMERICA'S AGRICULTURAL DEVELOPMENT?" L/A+17C NAT/G PLAN TEC/DEV BUDGET RENT EFFICIENCY 20. PAGE 20 H0404 ECO/UNDEV AGRI TAX OWN

S67
DESHPANDE A.M.,"FEDERAL-STATE FISCAL RELATIONS IN INDIA" (REVIEW ARTICLE)" GERMANY USSR DELIB/GP PLAN BUDGET ECO/TAC INCOME 20 SOC/DEMPAR SOC/REVPAR. PAGE 40 H0795 FINAN NAT/G GOV/REL TAX

S67
HARBRON J.D.,"UNIFICATION IN CANADA: FAIT ACCOMPLI" CANADA STRATA NAT/G DELIB/GP BUDGET GP/REL 20 NAVY. PAGE 66 H1327 INGP/REL FORCES PLAN ATTIT

S67
HASSAN M.F.,"THE SECOND FOUR-YEAR PLAN OF VENEZUELA." L/A+17C VENEZUELA AGRI INDUS NAT/G PLAN RATION CONTROL HABITAT...MATH STAT 20. PAGE 67 H1352 ECO/UNDEV FINAN BUDGET PROB/SOLV

S67
MITCHELL W.C.,"THE SHAPE OF POLITICAL THEORY TO COME: FROM POLITICAL SOCIOLOGY TO POLITICAL ECONOMY." ACADEM NAT/G BUDGET TAX LEGIT LOBBY GOV/REL INGP/REL...SOC NEW/IDEA TREND CHARTS 20 MONEY. PAGE 112 H2231 ECO/TAC GEN/LAWS

S67
PAI G.A.,"TAXATION AND PLANNING IN INDIA: A BIRDS-EYE VIEW." INDIA ELITES NAT/G LEGIS BUDGET CONTROL LOBBY INCOME...STAT CHARTS 20. PAGE 122 H2443 TAX PLAN WEALTH STRATA

S67
SALYZYN V.,"FEDERAL-PROVINCIAL TAX SHARING SCHEMES." CANADA LOC/G PROB/SOLV TEC/DEV BUDGET GOV/REL EFFICIENCY 20. PAGE 137 H2746 PROVS TAX MUNIC NAT/G

S67
SHARKANSKY I.,"ECONOMIC AND POLITICAL CORRELATES OF STATE GOVERNMENT EXPENDITURE: GENERAL TENDENCIES AND DEVIANT CASES." USA+45 LOC/G NAT/G TAX GIVE INCOME...CENSUS CHARTS. PAGE 142 H2845 PROVS BUDGET GOV/COMP

L68
CURRENT HISTORY,"DE GAULLE'S FRANCE." FRANCE MOD/EUR WOR+45 INDUS MARKET INT/ORG BUDGET DIPLOM AUTHORIT DRIVE...GOV/COMP IDEA/COMP 20 DEGAULLE/C EEC. PAGE 36 H0723 INT/TRADE PERSON LEAD NAT/LISM

BUELL R. H0466

BUENOS/AIR....BUENOS AIRES, ARGENTINA

B59
CUCCORESE H.J.,HISTORIA DE LA CONVERSION DEL PAPEL MONEDA EN BUENOS AIRES, 1861-1867. LAW LOC/G NAT/G ATTIT...POLICY BIBLIOG 19 ARGEN BUENOS/AIR GOLD/STAND. PAGE 36 H0717 FINAN PLAN LEGIS

BUGANDA....BUGANDA, UGANDA

BUISSON L. H0467

BUKHARIN N. H0468

BUKHARIN/N....NIKOLAI BUKHARIN

BULGARIA....BULGARIA; SEE ALSO COM

B18
KERNER R.J.,SLAVIC EUROPE: A SELECTED BIBLIOGRAPHY IN THE WESTERN EUROPEAN LANGUAGES. BULGARIA CZECHOSLVK GERMANY/E POLAND RUSSIA YUGOSLAVIA NAT/G DIPLOM MARXISM...LING 19/20. PAGE 85 H1695 BIBLIOG SOCIETY CULTURE COM

B59
ETSCHMANN R.,DIE WAHRUNGS- UND DEVISENPOLITIK DES OSTBLOCKS UND IHRE AUSWIRKUNGEN AUF DIE WIRTSCHAFTSBEZIEHUNGEN ZWISCHEN OST U WEST. ECO/TAC FINAN POLICY

BULGARIA CZECHOSLVK HUNGARY POLAND USSR MARKET NAT/G PLAN DIPLOM...NAT/COMP 20. PAGE 47 H0943 INT/TRADE

B63
SHANNON R.T.,GLADSTONE AND THE BULGARIAN AGITATION OF 1876. BULGARIA TURKEY UK DIPLOM COERCE REV ATTIT 19 GLADSTON/W DISRAELI/B. PAGE 142 H2841 EDU/PROP NAT/G PWR CONSEN

S64
HORECKY P.L.,"LIBRARY OF CONGRESS PUBLICATIONS IN AID OF USSR AND EAST EUROPEAN RESEARCH." BULGARIA CZECHOSLVK POLAND USSR YUGOSLAVIA NAT/G POL/PAR DIPLOM ADMIN GOV/REL...CLASSIF 20. PAGE 73 H1468 BIBLIOG/A COM MARXISM

B65
JELAVICH C.,THE BALKANS. ALBANIA BULGARIA GREECE ROMANIA YUGOSLAVIA ECO/UNDEV WAR SOVEREIGN MARXISM 6/20. PAGE 80 H1597 NAT/LISM NAT/G

B65
PUNDEEF M.V.,BULGARIA; A BIBLIOGRAPHIC GUIDE. BULGARIA LAW CULTURE INTELL ECO/DEV LEAD MARXISM 20. PAGE 128 H2566 BIBLIOG/A NAT/G COM SOCISM

B66
BROWN J.F.,THE NEW EASTERN EUROPE. ALBANIA BULGARIA HUNGARY POLAND ROMANIA CULTURE AGRI POL/PAR WAR NAT/LISM MARXISM...CHARTS BIBLIOG 20. PAGE 22 H0444 DIPLOM COM NAT/G ECO/UNDEV

B66
JACKSON G.D.,COMINTERN AND PEASANT IN EAST EUROPE 1919-1930. BULGARIA COM CZECHOSLVK EUR+WWI POLAND ROMANIA YUGOSLAVIA STRATA AGRI VOL/ASSN DIPLOM CONTROL CROWD WEALTH...POLICY NAT/COMP 20. PAGE 79 H1575 MARXISM ECO/UNDEV WORKER INT/ORG

B66
SPULBER N.,THE STATE AND ECONOMIC DEVELOPMENT IN EASTERN EUROPE. BULGARIA COM CZECHOSLVK HUNGARY POLAND YUGOSLAVIA CULTURE PLAN CAP/ISM INT/TRADE CONTROL...POLICY CHARTS METH/COMP BIBLIOG/A 19/20. PAGE 148 H2958 ECO/DEV ECO/UNDEV NAT/G TOTALISM

B67
NATIONAL SCIENCE FOUNDATION,DIRECTORY OF SELECTED RESEARCH INSTITUTES IN EASTERN EUROPE. BULGARIA CZECHOSLVK HUNGARY POLAND ROMANIA INTELL ACADEM NAT/G ACT/RES 20. PAGE 116 H2323 INDEX R+D COM PHIL/SCI

S67
EGBERT D.D.,"POLITICS AND ART IN COMMUNIST BULGARIA" BULGARIA COM USSR CULTURE DIPLOM INGP/REL TOTALISM...TREND 20. PAGE 45 H0894 CREATE ART/METH CONTROL MARXISM

BULLITT/WC....WILLIAM C. BULLITT

BULLOCK A. H0469,H0470

BULLOUGH B. H0471

BULMER-THOMAS I. H0472,H0473

BUNCHE/R....RALPH BUNCHE

BUNDESMIN FUR VERTRIEBENE H0474,H0475

BUNDY/M....MCGEORGE BUNDY

BUNN R.F. H0476

BUNTING B.P. H0477

BUR/BUDGET....BUREAU OF THE BUDGET

B27
WILLOUGHBY W.F.,PRINCIPLES OF PUBLIC ADMINISTRATION WITH SPECIAL REFERENCE TO THE NATIONAL AND STATE GOVERNMENTS OF THE UNITED STATES. FINAN PROVS CHIEF CONSULT LEGIS CREATE BUDGET EXEC ROUTINE GOV/REL CENTRAL...MGT 20 BUR/BUDGET CONGRESS PRESIDENT. PAGE 169 H3373 NAT/G EX/STRUC OP/RES ADMIN

BUR/STNDRD....BUREAU OF STANDARDS

BURAGR/ECO....BUREAU OF AGRICULTURAL ECONOMICS

B66
KIRKENDALL R.S.,SOCIAL SCIENTISTS AND FARM POLITICS IN THE AGE OF ROOSEVELT. ACADEM PLAN ECO/TAC GIVE ADMIN CONTROL PRODUC...SOC 20 NEW/DEAL ROOSEVLT/F BURAGR/ECO. PAGE 86 H1722 AGRI INTELL POLICY NAT/G

BURDEAU G. H0478

BURDETTE F.L. H0479

BUREAU OF AGRICULTURAL ECONOMICS....SEE BURAGR/ECO

BUREAU OF STANDARDS....SEE BUR/STNDRD

BUREAU OF THE BUDGET....SEE BUR/BUDGET

BUREAUCRCY....BUREAUCRACY; SEE ALSO ADMIN

B25
MAURRAS C.,ENQUETE SUR LA MONARCHIE (1909). FRANCE CONTROL REPRESENT DISCRIM HEREDITY PWR CONSERVE 20 BUREAUCRCY. PAGE 105 H2103 TRADIT AUTHORIT NAT/G CHIEF

B48
ROSENFARB J.,FREEDOM AND THE ADMINISTRATIVE STATE. NAT/G ROUTINE EFFICIENCY PRODUC RATIONAL UTIL ...TECHNIC WELF/ST MGT 20 BUREAUCRCY. PAGE 134 H2680 ECO/DEV INDUS PLAN WEALTH

L56
EISENTADT S.N.,"POLITICAL STRUGGLE IN BUREAUCRATIC SOCIETIES" ASIA CULTURE ADJUD SANCTION PWR BUREAUCRCY OTTOMAN BYZANTINE. PAGE 45 H0901 ADMIN CHIEF CONTROL ROUTINE

S59
DUNCAN O.D.,"CULTURAL, BEHAVIORAL, AND ECOLOGICAL PERSPECTIVES IN THE STUDY OF SOCIAL ORGANIZATION" (BMR)" UNIV STRATA EX/STRUC PROB/SOLV ADMIN ATTIT SOC/INTEG 20 BUREAUCRCY. PAGE 43 H0862 CULTURE METH/COMP SOCIETY HABITAT

B61
ETZIONI A.,COMPLEX ORGANIZATIONS: A SOCIOLOGICAL READER. CLIENT CULTURE STRATA CREATE OP/RES ADMIN ...POLICY METH/CNCPT BUREAUCRCY. PAGE 47 H0945 VOL/ASSN STRUCT CLASSIF PROF/ORG

S61
EHRMANN H.W.,"FRENCH BUREAUCRACY AND ORGANIZED INTERESTS" (BMR)" FRANCE NAT/G DELIB/GP ROUTINE ...INT 20 BUREAUCRCY CIVIL/SERV. PAGE 45 H0897 ADMIN DECISION PLURISM LOBBY

B62
INAYATULLAH,BUREAUCRACY AND DEVELOPMENT IN PAKISTAN. PAKISTAN ECO/UNDEV EDU/PROP CONFER ...ANTHOL DICTIONARY 20 BUREAUCRCY. PAGE 76 H1526 EX/STRUC ADMIN NAT/G LOC/G

B64
ETZIONI A.,MODERN ORGANIZATIONS. CLIENT STRUCT DOMIN CONTROL LEAD PERS/REL AUTHORIT...CLASSIF BUREAUCRCY. PAGE 47 H0946 MGT ADMIN PLAN CULTURE

B65
GOLEMBIEWSKI R.T.,MEN, MANAGEMENT, AND MORALITY; TOWARD A NEW ORGANIZATIONAL ETHIC. CONSTN EX/STRUC CREATE ADMIN CONTROL INGP/REL PERSON SUPEGO MORAL PWR...GOV/COMP METH/COMP 20 BUREAUCRCY. PAGE 58 H1161 LG/CO MGT PROB/SOLV

B66
BRAIBANTI R.,RESEARCH ON THE BUREAUCRACY OF PAKISTAN. PAKISTAN LAW CULTURE INTELL ACADEM LOC/G SECT PRESS CT/SYS...LING CHARTS 20 BUREAUCRCY. PAGE 20 H0402 HABITAT NAT/G ADMIN CONSTN

B66
FRIED R.C.,COMPARATIVE POLITICAL INSTITUTIONS. USSR EX/STRUC FORCES LEGIS JUDGE CONTROL REPRESENT ALL/IDEOS 20 CONGRESS BUREAUCRCY. PAGE 53 H1062 NAT/G PWR EFFICIENCY GOV/COMP

B66
HEADY F.,PUBLIC ADMINISTRATION: A COMPARATIVE PERSPECTIVE. ECO/DEV ECO/UNDEV...GOV/COMP 20 BUREAUCRCY. PAGE 69 H1376 ADMIN NAT/COMP NAT/G CIVMIL/REL

L66
MCAUSLAN J.P.W.,"CONSTITUTIONAL INNOVATION AND POLITICAL STABILITY IN TANZANIA: A PRELIMINARY ASSESSMENT." AFR TANZANIA ELITES CHIEF EX/STRUC RIGID/FLEX PWR 20 PRESIDENT BUREAUCRCY. PAGE 106 H2122 CONSTN NAT/G EXEC POL/PAR

S67
SUBRAMANIAM V.,"REPRESENTATIVE BUREAUCRACY: A REASSESSMENT." USA+45 ELITES LOC/G NAT/G ADMIN GOV/REL PRIVIL DRIVE ROLE...POLICY CENSUS 20 CIVIL/SERV BUREAUCRCY. PAGE 150 H3006 STRATA GP/REL MGT GOV/COMP

BURGANDA

S55
DE SMITH S.A.,"CONSTITUTIONAL MONARCHY IN BURGANDA." AFR UGANDA UK STRUCT CHIEF REGION INGP/REL ADJUST NAT/LISM SOVEREIGN CONSERVE ...POLICY 19/20 BURGANDA. PAGE 38 H0769 NAT/G DIPLOM CONSTN COLONIAL

BURGESS J.W. H0480,H0481

BURGHART A. H0482

BURKE E. H0483,H0484,H0485,H0486,H0487

BURKE F.G. H0488

BURKE/EDM....EDMUND BURKE

N17
BURKE E.,THOUGHTS ON THE CAUSE OF THE PRESENT DISCONTENTS (PAMPHLET). MOD/EUR UK CONSTN CHIEF LEGIS DOMIN CONTROL EXEC REPRESENT POPULISM ...TRADIT NEW/IDEA METH/COMP 18 BURKE/EDM. PAGE 24 H0484
ORD/FREE REV PARL/PROC NAT/G

N17
BURKE E.,LETTER TO SIR HERCULES LANGRISHE (PAMPHLET). IRELAND UK NAT/G CHIEF DIPLOM DOMIN PARL/PROC COERCE ORD/FREE SOVEREIGN POPULISM ...TRADIT 18 BURKE/EDM. PAGE 24 H0485
POLICY COLONIAL SECT

C39
BURKE E.,"ON THE REFORM OF THE REPRESENTATION IN THE HOUSE OF COMMONS" (1782) IN COLLECTED WORKS (VOL. 5)" UK ELITES STRATA NAT/G REPRESENT ORD/FREE PWR POPULISM...POLICY NEW/IDEA GEN/LAWS 18 BURKE/EDM. PAGE 24 H0486
TRADIT CONSTN PARL/PROC LEGIS

B60
BREDVOLD L.I.,THE PHILOSOPHY OF EDMUND BURKE. POL/PAR PARL/PROC REPRESENT CONSERVE...JURID 18 BURKE/EDM. PAGE 20 H0410
PHIL/SCI NAT/G CONCPT

B64
COBBAN A.,ROUSSEAU AND THE MODERN STATE (2ND ED.). FRANCE PROB/SOLV NAT/LISM UTOPIA PERSON MORAL ...EPIST PHIL/SCI SOC IDEA/COMP 18 ROUSSEAU/J BURKE/EDM HOBBES/T HUME/D. PAGE 30 H0612
GEN/LAWS INGP/REL NAT/G ORD/FREE

B64
TODD W.B.,A BIBLIOGRAPHY OF EDMUND BURKE. MOD/EUR UK NAT/G EDU/PROP ATTIT...HUM 18 BURKE/EDM. PAGE 156 H3110
BIBLIOG/A PHIL/SCI WRITING CONCPT

B91
PAINE T.,RIGHTS OF MAN. FRANCE MOD/EUR CONSTN NAT/G CHIEF DOMIN LEGIT SOVEREIGN...MAJORIT IDEA/COMP 18 BURKE/EDM CIVIL/LIB. PAGE 122 H2446
GEN/LAWS ORD/FREE REV AGREE

BURKS R.V. H0489

BURLAMAQUI J.J. H0490

BURLING R. H0491

BURMA....BURMA

N
US LIBRARY OF CONGRESS,SOUTHERN ASIA ACCESSIONS LIST. BURMA CEYLON INDIA NEPAL PAKISTAN S/ASIA THAILAND AGRI INDUS SCHOOL WORKER...ART/METH GEOG HEAL PHIL/SCI LING 20. PAGE 160 H3201
BIBLIOG/A SOCIETY CULTURE ECO/UNDEV

B12
CORDIER H.,BIBLIOTHECA INDOSINICA: DICTIONAIRE BIBLIOGRAPHIQUE DES OUVRAGES RELATIFS A LA PENINSULE INDOCHINOISE. BURMA LAOS MALAYSIA S/ASIA THAILAND VIETNAM SECT...LING 20. PAGE 33 H0665
BIBLIOG/A GEOG NAT/G

N19
BRIMMELL G.H.,COMMUNISM IN SOUTHEAST ASIA (PAMPHLET). BURMA CAMBODIA COM INDIA INDONESIA LAOS MOD/EUR NAT/G POL/PAR FORCES CAP/ISM CONTROL WEALTH ...MYTH 20. PAGE 21 H0420
MARXISM S/ASIA REV ECO/UNDEV

B45
LASKER B.,ASIA ON THE MOVE. ASIA BURMA S/ASIA THAILAND USSR ECO/UNDEV FAM KIN WAR NAT/LISM ATTIT ...GEOG CENSUS TREND AUSTRAL 20. PAGE 91 H1826
CULTURE RIGID/FLEX

B48
FURNIVAL J.,COLONIAL POLICY AND PRACTICE A COMPARATIVE STUDY OF BURMA, AND NETHERLANDS INDIA. BURMA INDONESIA S/ASIA...GEOG OBS GOV/COMP METH/COMP 20. PAGE 54 H1080
COLONIAL NAT/LISM WEALTH SOVEREIGN

B48
PELCOVITS N.A.,OLD CHINA HANDS AND THE FOREIGN OFFICE. ASIA BURMA UK ECO/UNDEV NAT/G ECO/TAC FOR/AID TARIFFS DOMIN COLONIAL GOV/REL SOVEREIGN 19 HONG/KONG TREATY. PAGE 124 H2483
INT/TRADE ATTIT DIPLOM

B50
CORNELL U DEPT ASIAN STUDIES,SOUTHEAST ASIA PROGRAM DATA PAPER. BURMA CAMBODIA INDONESIA MALAYSIA VIETNAM SOCIETY STRUCT NAT/G SECT DIPLOM FOR/AID PWR WEALTH...SOC 20. PAGE 33 H0670
BIBLIOG/A CULTURE S/ASIA ECO/UNDEV

B50
TRAGER F.N.,MARXISM IN SOUTHEAST ASIA. BURMA INDONESIA THAILAND VIETNAM CULTURE SOCIETY NAT/G VOL/ASSN EXEC ROUTINE COERCE ATTIT RIGID/FLEX PWR ...METH/CNCPT TIME/SEQ STERTYP GEN/LAWS MARX/KARL VAL/FREE COLD/WAR NAM 20. PAGE 156 H3126
S/ASIA POL/PAR REV

B51
BERNATZIK H.A.,THE SPIRITS OF THE YELLOW LEAVES. BURMA LAOS S/ASIA THAILAND VIETNAM SOCIETY AGRI COLONIAL LEISURE GP/REL PERS/REL ISOLAT AGE HABITAT SEX WORSHIP 20. PAGE 16 H0310
SOC KIN ECO/UNDEV CULTURE

B53
MEAD M.,CULTURAL PATTERNS AND TECHNICAL CHANGE. BURMA GREECE NIGERIA ECO/UNDEV AGRI INDUS SCHOOL SECT CREATE FEEDBACK HABITAT...PSY METH/COMP BIBLIOG 20 UN. PAGE 108 H2152
HEALTH TEC/DEV CULTURE ADJUST

B56
TRAGER F.N.,ANNOTATED BIBLIOGRAPHY OF BURMA. BURMA STRUCT NAT/G...GEOG JURID MGT SOC 20. PAGE 156 H3127
BIBLIOG/A S/ASIA CULTURE SOCIETY

B57
KENNEDY M.D.,A SHORT HISTORY OF COMMUNISM IN ASIA. ASIA BURMA INDIA S/ASIA THAILAND NAT/G POL/PAR LEAD REV WAR MARXISM SOCISM...POLICY 20 CHINJAP. PAGE 85 H1688
DIPLOM NAT/LISM TOTALISM COERCE

B61
SAKAI R.K.,STUDIES ON ASIA, 1961. ASIA BURMA INDIA S/ASIA FINAN ECO/TAC NAT/LISM SOCISM...POLICY ANTHOL 19/20 CHINJAP. PAGE 137 H2734
ECO/UNDEV SECT

B61
SEMINAR REPRESENTATIVE GOVT,AFRO-ASIAN ATTITUDES: SEMINAR ON REPRESENTATIVE GOVERNMENTSPUBLIC LIBERTIES IN STATES OF ASIA AND AFRICA, RHODES, 1958. AFR ASIA BURMA INDIA ISLAM UAR VIETNAM/S SOCIETY POL/PAR CHIEF EDU/PROP PRESS PERSON ...POLICY INT 20 TUNIS. PAGE 141 H2826
CHOOSE ATTIT NAT/COMP ORD/FREE

B62
BROWN S.D.,STUDIES ON ASIA, 1962. ASIA BURMA INDIA ISLAM ISRAEL S/ASIA ECO/UNDEV POL/PAR SECT ECO/TAC ...ANTHOL 20 CHINJAP. PAGE 22 H0450
PWR PARL/PROC

B62
JOHNSON J.J.,THE ROLE OF THE MILITARY IN UNDERDEVELOPED COUNTRIES. AFR BURMA INDONESIA ISLAM ISRAEL L/A+17C S/ASIA THAILAND CULTURE ECO/UNDEV KIN PROVS CONSULT ACT/RES COERCE REV DRIVE RIGID/FLEX ORD/FREE...RECORD ANTHOL 20. PAGE 81 H1622
FORCES CONCPT

S62
SARKISYANZ E.,"NATIONALISM, CAPITALISM, AND THE UNCOMMITED NATIONS: MARXISM AND ASIAN CULTURAL TRADITIONS." ASIA BURMA CHINA/COM COM CULTURE SOCIETY NAT/G POL/PAR PLAN DOMIN EDU/PROP COLONIAL COERCE ATTIT RIGID/FLEX...CONCPT TREND MARX/KARL 20 TIBET BUDDHISM. PAGE 138 H2755
S/ASIA SECT NAT/LISM CAP/ISM

B63
VON DER MEHDEN F.R.,RELIGION AND NATIONALISM IN SOUTHEAST ASIA. BURMA PHILIPPINE S/ASIA INTELL SOCIETY DOMIN EDU/PROP LEGIT ATTIT MORAL ORD/FREE ...SOC CENSUS HIST/WRIT TOT/POP VAL/FREE 20 WORSHIP LONDON. PAGE 163 H3265
SECT CULTURE NAT/LISM

B64
NORTHROP F.S.,CROSS-CULTURAL UNDERSTANDING: EPISTEMOLOGY IN ANTHROPOLOGY. BURMA GREECE THAILAND HABITAT PERCEPT PERSON...PHIL/SCI SOC METH 20 MEXIC/AMER CHINJAP. PAGE 119 H2375
EPIST PSY CULTURE CONCPT

B64
WILCOX W.A.,INDIA, PAKISTAN AND THE RISE OF CHINA. ASIA BURMA CEYLON CHINA/COM INDIA PAKISTAN S/ASIA NAT/G VOL/ASSN FORCES TOP/EX ACT/RES DOMIN REGION RIGID/FLEX ORD/FREE...POLICY GEN/LAWS COLD/WAR 20. PAGE 168 H3362
CULTURE ATTIT DIPLOM

B65
BURLING R.,HILL FARMS AND PADI FIELDS. BURMA S/ASIA THAILAND VIETNAM AGRI NEIGH SECT GP/REL NAT/LISM ORD/FREE 20 MID/EAST MIGRATION. PAGE 24 H0491
SOCIETY STRUCT CULTURE SOVEREIGN

B65
ONSLOW C.,ASIAN ECONOMIC DEVELOPMENT. BURMA CEYLON INDIA MALAYSIA PAKISTAN S/ASIA AGRI INDUS MARKET PROB/SOLV CAP/ISM FOR/AID INT/TRADE DEMAND WEALTH ...POLICY ANTHOL 20. PAGE 121 H2418
ECO/UNDEV ECO/TAC PLAN NAT/G

B66
BRAIBANTI R.,ASIAN BUREAUCRATIC SYSTEMS EMERGENT FROM THE BRITISH IMPERIAL TRADITION. BURMA CEYLON INDIA PAKISTAN UK ELITES ECO/UNDEV NAT/G...MGT SOC CHARTS ANTHOL 19/20. PAGE 20 H0401
GOV/COMP COLONIAL ADMIN S/ASIA

B66
COEDES G.,THE MAKING OF SOUTH EAST ASIA. BURMA CAMBODIA LAOS S/ASIA THAILAND VIETNAM REV WAR CIVMIL/REL...GEOG 6/13. PAGE 31 H0614
CULTURE FORCES DOMIN

B67
ANDERSON C.W.,ISSUES OF POLITICAL DEVELOPMENT. BURMA WOR+45 CULTURE TOP/EX ECO/TAC MARXISM ...CHARTS NAT/COMP 20 COLOMB CONGO/LEOP. PAGE 6 H0126
NAT/LISM COERCE ECO/UNDEV SOCISM

BURNHAM J. H0492

BURR R.N. H0493

BURR/AARON....AARON BURR

BURRIDGE K. H0494

BURUNDI....SEE ALSO AFR

L66
LEMARCHAND R.,"SOCIAL CHANGE AND POLITICAL MODERNISATION IN BURUNDI." AFR BURUNDI STRATA CHIEF EX/STRUC RIGID/FLEX PWR...SOC 20. PAGE 94 H1874
NAT/G STRUCT ELITES CONSERVE

BURY J.B. H0495

BUSHONG H1709

BUSIA K.A. H0496

BUSINESS CYCLE....SEE FINAN

BUSINESS MANAGEMENT....SEE MGT

BUSINESS ECONOMISTS' GROUP H0497

BUTLER D.E. H0498

BUTTINGER J. H0499

BUTTRICK J.A. H3369

BUTWELL R. H0500

BUTZ O. H0501

BYNKERSHOEK C. H0502

BYRNES R.F. H0503

BYZANTINE....BYZANTINE EMPIRE

L56
EISENTADT S.N.,"POLITICAL STRUGGLE IN BUREAUCRATIC SOCIETIES" ASIA CULTURE ADJUD SANCTION PWR BUREAUCRCY OTTOMAN BYZANTINE. PAGE 45 H0901
ADMIN CHIEF CONTROL ROUTINE

B62
TYSKEVIC S.,DIE EINHEIT DER KIRCHE UND BYZANZ (TRANS. BY F.K. LIESNER). ROMAN/EMP ADJUD GP/REL 1/17 CHRISTIAN BYZANTINE. PAGE 157 H3144
SECT NAT/G CATHISM ATTIT

C

CAB....CIVIL AERONAUTICS BOARD

CABINET....SEE ALSO EX/STRUC, DELIB/GP, CONSULT

B36
CLOKIE H.M.,THE ORIGIN AND NATURE OF CONSTITUTIONAL GOVERNMENT. UK NAT/G POL/PAR CONSULT LEGIS ...GOV/COMP 14/20 CABINET PARLIAMENT. PAGE 30 H0606
CONCPT CONSTN PARL/PROC

CADY J.F. H0504

CAESAR/JUL....JULIUS CAESAR

CAHEN C. H2757

CAIRNS J.C. H0505

CAIRO....CAIRO, EGYPT

CALCUTTA....CALCUTTA, INDIA

B66
ASHRAF A.,THE CITY GOVERNMENT OF CALCUTTA: A STUDY OF INERTIA. INDIA ELITES INDUS NAT/G EX/STRUC ACT/RES PLAN PROB/SOLV LEAD HABITAT...BIBLIOG 20 CALCUTTA. PAGE 9 H0175
LOC/G MUNIC ADMIN ECO/UNDEV

CALHOUN/JC....JOHN C. CALHOUN

CALIFORNIA....CALIFORNIA

S67
WILSON J.Q.,"A GUIDE TO REAGAN COUNTRY* THE POLITICAL CULTURE OF SOUTHERN CALIFORNIA." NEIGH PROVS PARTIC CHOOSE ADJUST CONSEN PERSON CONSERVE CALIFORNIA REAGAN/RON. PAGE 169 H3379
CULTURE ATTIT MORAL

CALLEO D.P. H0506

CALLOT E. H0507

CALVERT A.F. H0508

CALVIN/J....JOHN CALVIN

B49
HAUSER R.,AUTORITAT UND MACHT. SOCIETY SECT PWR CATHISM...JURID CONCPT 16/20 PROTESTANT LUTHER/M CALVIN/J CHURCH/STA. PAGE 68 H1360
SOVEREIGN NAT/G LEGIT

CALVOCORESSI P. H0509

CAM H.M. H0510

CAMB/SOMER....CAMBRIDGE-SOMERVILLE YOUTH STUDY

CAMBODIA....SEE ALSO S/ASIA

N19
BRIMMELL G.H.,COMMUNISM IN SOUTHEAST ASIA (PAMPHLET). BURMA CAMBODIA COM INDIA INDONESIA LAOS MOD/EUR NAT/G POL/PAR FORCES CAP/ISM CONTROL WEALTH ...MYTH 20. PAGE 21 H0420
MARXISM S/ASIA REV ECO/UNDEV

B45
HARVARD WIDENER LIBRARY,INDOCHINA: A SELECTED LIST OF REFERENCES. CAMBODIA FRANCE S/ASIA VIETNAM COLONIAL...POLICY 19/20. PAGE 67 H1351
BIBLIOG/A ACADEM DIPLOM NAT/G

B50
CORNELL U DEPT ASIAN STUDIES,SOUTHEAST ASIA PROGRAM DATA PAPER. BURMA CAMBODIA INDONESIA MALAYSIA VIETNAM SOCIETY STRUCT NAT/G SECT DIPLOM FOR/AID PWR WEALTH...SOC 20. PAGE 33 H0670
BIBLIOG/A CULTURE S/ASIA ECO/UNDEV

B50
EMBREE J.F.,BIBLIOGRAPHY OF THE PEOPLES AND CULTURES OF MAINLAND SOUTHEAST ASIA. CAMBODIA LAOS THAILAND VIETNAM LAW...GEOG HUM SOC MYTH LING CHARTS WORSHIP 20. PAGE 46 H0915
BIBLIOG/A CULTURE S/ASIA

B55
THOMPSON V.,MINORITY PROBLEMS IN SOUTHEAST ASIA. CAMBODIA CHINA/COM LAOS S/ASIA KIN NAT/G SECT PROB/SOLV EDU/PROP REGION GP/REL RACE/REL MARXISM ...SOC 20 BUDDHISM UN. PAGE 154 H3085
INGP/REL GEOG DIPLOM STRUCT

B64
HOBBS C.C.,SOUTHEAST ASIA: AN ANNOTATED BIBLIOGRAPHY OF SELECTED REFERENCES IN WESTERN LANGUAGES (REV. ED.). CAMBODIA INDONESIA LAOS THAILAND VIETNAM CONSTN NAT/G...SOC WORSHIP 20. PAGE 72 H1437
BIBLIOG/A S/ASIA CULTURE SOCIETY

B65
SMITH R.M.,CAMBODIA'S FOREIGN POLICY. ECO/UNDEV NAT/G NEUTRAL ORD/FREE COLD/WAR VAL/FREE. PAGE 146 H2917
S/ASIA CAMBODIA DIPLOM

B66
COEDES G.,THE MAKING OF SOUTH EAST ASIA. BURMA CAMBODIA LAOS S/ASIA THAILAND VIETNAM REV WAR CIVMIL/REL...GEOG 6/13. PAGE 31 H0614
CULTURE FORCES DOMIN

CAMBRAY P.G. H2245

CAMBRIDGE-SOMERVILLE YOUTH STUDY....SEE CAMB/SOMER

CAMELOT....PROJECT CAMELOT (CHILE)

S65
HUGHES T.L.,"SCHOLARS AND FOREIGN POLICY* VARIETIES OF RESEARCH EXPERIENCE." COM/IND DIPLOM ADMIN EXEC ROUTINE...MGT OBS CONGRESS PRESIDENT CAMELOT. PAGE 75 H1491
ACT/RES ACADEM CONTROL NAT/G

CAMERON R. H0511,H0512

CAMERON W.J. H0513

CAMEROON....SEE ALSO AFR

B63
GARDINIER D.E.,CAMEROON: UNITED NATIONS CHALLENGE TO FRENCH POLICY. AFR CAMEROON FRANCE NAT/G LEGIS CONTROL SOVEREIGN 20 UN. PAGE 55 H1101
DIPLOM POLICY INT/ORG COLONIAL

B64
WITHERELL J.W.,OFFICIAL PUBLICATIONS OF FRENCH EQUATORIAL AFRICA, FRENCH CAMEROONS, AND TOGO, 1946-1958 (PAMPHLET). CAMEROON CHAD FRANCE GABON TOGO LAW ECO/UNDEV EXTR/IND INT/TRADE...GEOG HEAL 20. PAGE 169 H3392
BIBLIOG/A AFR NAT/G ADMIN

B66
US LIBRARY OF CONGRESS,NIGERIA: A GUIDE TO OFFICIAL PUBLICATIONS. CAMEROON NIGERIA UK DIPLOM...POLICY 19/20 UN LEAGUE/NAT. PAGE 161 H3215
BIBLIOG ADMIN NAT/G COLONIAL

CAMPANELLA T. H0514

CAMPBELL A. H2665

CAMPBELL G.A. H0515

CAMPBELL P. H0516

CANAD/CRWN....CANADIAN CROWN CORPORATIONS

CANADA....SEE ALSO COMMONWLTH

N
CANADIAN GOVERNMENT PUBLICATIONS (1955-). CANADA AGRI FINAN LABOR FORCES INT/TRADE HEALTH...JURID 20 PARLIAMENT. PAGE 1 H0003
BIBLIOG/A NAT/G DIPLOM INT/ORG

N19
CANADA CIVIL SERV COMM,THE ANALYSIS OF ORGANIZATION IN THE GOVERNMENT OF CANADA (PAMPHLET). CANADA CONSTN EX/STRUC LEGIS TOP/EX CREATE PLAN CONTROL
NAT/G MGT ADMIN

GP/REL 20. PAGE 26 H0517 DELIB/GP

N19

MASSEY V.,CANADIANS AND THEIR COMMONWEALTH: THE ROMANES LECTURE DELIVERED IN THE SHELDONIAN THEATRE JUNE 1, 1961 (PAMPHLET). CANADA UK CULTURE ECO/DEV REPRESENT NAT/LISM PEACE PWR CONSERVE 20 CMN/WLTH. PAGE 104 H2088 ATTIT DIPLOM NAT/G SOVEREIGN

N19

WILSON T.,FINANCIAL ASSISTANCE WITH REGIONAL DEVELOPMENT (PAMPHLET). CANADA INDUS NAT/G PLAN TAX CONTROL COST EFFICIENCY...POLICY CHARTS 20. PAGE 169 H3382 FINAN ECO/TAC REGION GOV/REL

B28

CORBETT P.E.,CANADA AND WORLD POLITICS. LAW CULTURE SOCIETY STRUCT MARKET INT/ORG FORCES ACT/RES PLAN ECO/TAC LEGIT ORD/FREE PWR RESPECT...SOC CONCPT TIME/SEQ TREND CMN/WLTH 20 LEAGUE/NAT. PAGE 33 H0662 NAT/G CANADA

B50

LIPSET S.M.,AGRARIAN SOCIALISM. CANADA POL/PAR OP/RES ECO/TAC ADMIN ATTIT...TIME/SEQ NAT/COMP SOC/EXP 20 SASKATCH. PAGE 97 H1938 SOCISM AGRI METH/COMP STRUCT

B50

MCHENRY D.E.,THE THIRD FORCE IN CANADA: THE COOPERATIVE COMMONWEALTH FEDERATION, 1932-1948. CANADA EX/STRUC LEGIS REPRESENT 20 LABOR/PAR. PAGE 107 H2131 POL/PAR ADMIN CHOOSE POLICY

B54

GRAYSON H.,ECONOMIC PLANNING UNDER FREE ENTERPRISE. CANADA FUT UK DELIB/GP BUDGET CONFER CONTROL ...POLICY DECISION 20. PAGE 60 H1200 PLAN ECO/TAC NAT/COMP NAT/G

B55

WRONG D.H.,AMERICAN AND CANADIAN VIEWPOINTS. CANADA USA+45 CONSTN STRATA FAM SECT WORKER ECO/TAC EDU/PROP ADJUD MARRIAGE...IDEA/COMP 20. PAGE 171 H3424 DIPLOM ATTIT NAT/COMP CULTURE

B57

BISHOP O.B.,PUBLICATIONS OF THE GOVERNMENTS OF NOVA SCOTIA, PRINCE EDWARD ISLAND, NEW BRUNSWICK 1758-1952. CANADA UK ADMIN COLONIAL LEAD...POLICY 18/20. PAGE 17 H0345 BIBLIOG NAT/G DIPLOM

B57

HAMMOND B.,BANKS AND POLITICS IN AMERICA FROM THE REVOLUTION TO THE CIVIL WAR. CANADA USA-45 STRATA ...NAT/COMP 18/19. PAGE 65 H1306 FINAN PWR POL/PAR NAT/G

B57

REAMAN G.E.,THE TRAIL OF THE BLACK WALNUT. CANADA AGRI COLONIAL...CHARTS BIBLIOG 18 GERMANS/PA. PAGE 130 H2604 STRANGE SECT CULTURE

S57

HODGETTS J.E.,"THE CIVIL SERVICE AND POLICY FORMATION." CANADA NAT/G EX/STRUC ROUTINE GOV/REL 20. PAGE 72 H1443 ADMIN DECISION EFFICIENCY POLICY

B58

BRADY A.,DEMOCRACY IN THE DOMINIONS (3RD ED.). CANADA NEW/ZEALND SOUTH/AFR WOR+45 LAW EX/STRUC DOMIN COLONIAL PARL/PROC REPRESENT RACE/REL NAT/LISM WEALTH 20 AUSTRAL CMN/WLTH. PAGE 20 H0399 GOV/COMP POL/PAR POPULISM NAT/G

B58

CUNNINGHAM W.B.,COMPULSORY CONCILIATION AND COLLECTIVE BARGAINING. CANADA NAT/G LEGIS ADJUD CT/SYS GP/REL...MGT 20 NEW/BRUNS STRIKE CASEBOOK. PAGE 36 H0722 POLICY BARGAIN LABOR INDUS

B58

LOWER A.R.M.,EVOLVING CANADIAN FEDERALISM. CANADA WEST/IND CONSTN PROB/SOLV COLONIAL REGION NAT/LISM ...ANTHOL 20. PAGE 99 H1976 FEDERAL NAT/G DIPLOM RACE/REL

B58

MCIVOR R.C.,CANADIAN MONETARY, BANKING, AND FISCAL DEVELOPMENT. CANADA INDUS LG/CO NAT/G SML/CO CONTROL WAR...GEN/LAWS BIBLIOG 17/20. PAGE 107 H2137 ECO/TAC FINAN ECO/DEV WEALTH

B58

WOODS H.D.,PATTERNS OF INDUSTRIAL DISPUTE SETTLEMENT IN FIVE CANADIAN INDUSTRIES. CANADA USA+45 CONSULT ADJUD GP/REL...JURID GOV/COMP METH/COMP ANTHOL 20. PAGE 170 H3408 BARGAIN INDUS LABOR NAT/G

B59

SISSONS C.B.,CHURCH AND STATE IN CANADIAN EDUCATION: AN HISTORICAL STUDY. CANADA ACADEM NAT/G SCHOOL LEGIS REGION MAJORITY...MAJORIT WORSHIP 18/20 CHURCH/STA. PAGE 145 H2891 SECT EDU/PROP PROVS GP/REL

S59

LEYS C.,"MODELS, THEORIES, AND THE THEORY OF POLITICAL PARTIES" CANADA LIECHTENST UK LOC/G NAT/G PARTIC REPRESENT GP/REL CONSEN EQUILIB MAJORITY ...NEW/IDEA MATH CHARTS 20. PAGE 96 H1919 POL/PAR CHOOSE METH/CNCPT SIMUL

B60

LASKIN B.,CANADIAN CONSTITUTIONAL LAW: TEXT AND NOTES ON DISTRIBUTION OF LEGISLATIVE POWER (2ND ED.). CANADA LOC/G ECO/TAC TAX CONTROL CT/SYS CRIME FEDERAL PWR...JURID 20 PARLIAMENT. PAGE 92 H1832 CONSTN NAT/G LAW LEGIS

B60

MINIFIE J.M.,PEACEMAKER OR POWDER-MONKEY. CANADA INT/ORG NAT/G FORCES LEAD WAR...PREDICT 20. PAGE 111 H2222 DIPLOM POLICY NEUTRAL PEACE

S60

TAYLOR M.G.,"THE ROLE OF THE MEDICAL PROFESSION IN THE FORMULATION AND EXECUTION OF PUBLIC POLICY" (BMR)" CANADA NAT/G CONSULT ADMIN REPRESENT GP/REL ROLE SOVEREIGN...DECISION 20 CMA. PAGE 153 H3056 PROF/ORG HEALTH LOBBY POLICY

B61

AIYAR S.P.,FEDERALISM AND SOCIAL CHANGE. CANADA CULTURE STRUCT PLAN PROB/SOLV TEC/DEV ECO/TAC ORD/FREE...TIME/SEQ 18/20 AUSTRAL. PAGE 4 H0085 FEDERAL NAT/G CENTRAL GOV/COMP

B61

ATTLEE C.R.,EMPIRE INTO COMMONWEALTH. AFR ASIA CANADA UK NAT/G WAR NAT/LISM ATTIT...POLICY 20 AUSTRAL. PAGE 9 H0179 DIPLOM GP/REL COLONIAL SOVEREIGN

B61

BREWIS T.N.,CANADIAN ECONOMIC POLICY. CANADA BUDGET CAP/ISM INT/TRADE RATION TARIFFS TAX PRICE CONTROL ROUTINE FEDERAL INCOME PRODUC 20 GOLD/STAND. PAGE 20 H0412 ECO/DEV ECO/TAC NAT/G PLAN

B61

CARROTHERS A.W.R.,LABOR ARBITRATION IN CANADA. CANADA LAW NAT/G CONSULT LEGIS WORKER ADJUD ADMIN CT/SYS 20. PAGE 27 H0542 LABOR MGT GP/REL BARGAIN

B62

MANNING H.T.,THE REVOLT OF FRENCH CANADA 1800-1835. CANADA UK CULTURE GOV/REL RACE/REL...BIBLIOG 19. PAGE 102 H2039 NAT/LISM COLONIAL GEOG

B62

WOODS H.D.,LABOUR POLICY AND LABOUR ECONOMICS IN CANADA. CANADA FUT NAT/G VOL/ASSN WORKER BARGAIN ECO/TAC PAY CONFER GP/REL 20. PAGE 170 H3409 LABOR POLICY INDUS ECO/DEV

B63

BISHOP O.B.,PUBLICATIONS OF THE GOVERNMENT OF THE PROVINCE OF CANADA 1841-1867. CANADA DIPLOM COLONIAL LEAD...POLICY 18. PAGE 17 H0346 BIBLIOG NAT/G ATTIT

B63

LIVINGSTON W.S.,FEDERALISM IN THE COMMONWEALTH - A BIBLIOGRAPHICAL COMMENTARY. CANADA INDIA PAKISTAN UK STRUCT LOC/G NAT/G POL/PAR...NAT/COMP 20 AUSTRAL. PAGE 97 H1943 BIBLIOG JURID FEDERAL CONSTN

B63

THORBURN H.G.,PARTY POLITICS IN CANADA. CANADA ELITES STRUCT INDUS PWR 20. PAGE 154 H3086 POL/PAR CONCPT NAT/G PROVS

S63

HARRIS R.L.,"A COMPARATIVE ANALYSIS OF THE ADMINISTRATIVE SYSTEMS OF CANADA AND CEYLON." S/ASIA CULTURE SOCIETY STRATA TOP/EX ACT/RES DOMIN EDU/PROP LEGIT COERCE ATTIT SUPEGO ALL/VALS...MGT CHARTS GEN/LAWS VAL/FREE 20. PAGE 67 H1343 DELIB/GP EX/STRUC CANADA CEYLON

B64

BROWN W.M.,THE EXTERNAL LIQUIDITY OF AN ADVANCED COUNTRY. CANADA FRANCE GERMANY/W SWEDEN UK USA+45 ECO/DEV DIPLOM PRICE...CONCPT STAT NAT/COMP 20. PAGE 22 H0451 FINAN INT/TRADE COST INCOME

B64

CURRIE D.P.,FEDERALISM AND THE NEW NATIONS OF AFRICA. CANADA USA+45 INT/TRADE TAX GP/REL ...NAT/COMP SOC/INTEG 20. PAGE 36 H0725 FEDERAL AFR ECO/UNDEV INT/LAW

B64

DICKEY J.S.,THE UNITED STATES AND CANADA. CANADA USA+45...SOC 20. PAGE 41 H0822 DIPLOM TREND GOV/COMP PROB/SOLV

B64

HAMILTON W.B.,THE TRANSFER OF INSTITUTIONS. CANADA INDIA UK LAW AGRI LABOR SECT COLONIAL 18/20. PAGE 65 H1301 NAT/COMP ECO/UNDEV EDU/PROP CULTURE

B64

KIDD K.E.,BRIEF BIBLIOGRAPHY OF ONTARIO ANTHROPOLOGY (PAMPHLET). CANADA PREHIST HABITAT ...MYTH WORSHIP. PAGE 86 H1708 BIBLIOG SOC LING CULTURE

B64

LEDERMAN W.R.,THE COURTS AND THE CANDIAN CONSTITUTION. CANADA PARL/PROC...POLICY JURID GOV/COMP ANTHOL 19/20 SUPREME/CT PARLIAMENT. PAGE 93 H1854 CONSTN CT/SYS LEGIS LAW

B64

NATIONAL BOOK LEAGUE,THE COMMONWEALTH IN BOOKS: AN ANNOTATED LIST. CANADA UK LOC/G SECT ADMIN...SOC BIOG 20 CMN/WLTH. PAGE 116 H2320 BIBLIOG/A JURID NAT/G

B64

O'HEARN P.J.T.,PEACE, ORDER AND GOOD GOVERNMENT; A NAT/G

NEW CONSTITUTION FOR CANADA. CANADA EX/STRUC LEGIS CT/SYS PARL/PROC...BIBLIOG 20. PAGE 120 H2388
CONSTN LAW CREATE

B64
WILSON T.,POLICIES FOR REGIONAL DEVELOPMENT. CANADA UK FINAN INDUS NAT/G BUDGET TAX GIVE COST ...NAT/COMP 20. PAGE 169 H3383
REGION PLAN ECO/DEV ECO/TAC

B65
GWYN R.J.,THE SHAPE OF SCANDAL: A STUDY OF A GOVERNMENT IN CRISIS. CANADA LEGIS ADJUD CT/SYS SANCTION CMN/WLTH 20 PEARSON/L. PAGE 63 H1260
ELITES NAT/G CRIME

B65
HORNE A.J.,THE COMMONWEALTH TODAY. AFR ASIA CANADA UK STRUCT ECO/UNDEV NAT/G SECT GP/REL 20 AUSTRAL CMN/WLTH. PAGE 73 H1470
BIBLIOG/A SOCIETY CULTURE

B65
MCWHINNEY E.,JUDICIAL REVIEW IN THE ENGLISH-SPEAKING WORLD (3RD ED.). CANADA UK WOR+45 LEGIS CONTROL EXEC PARTIC...JURID 20 AUSTRAL. PAGE 108 H2151
GOV/COMP CT/SYS ADJUD CONSTN

L65
SCHAFFER B.B.,"THE CONCEPT OF PREPARATION* SOME QUESTIONS ABOUT THE TRANSFER OF SYSTEMS OF GOVERNMENT." AFR ASIA CANADA ELITES NAT/G POL/PAR COLONIAL RIGID/FLEX IDEA/COMP. PAGE 138 H2769
ECO/UNDEV UK RECORD

S65
LAULICHT J.,"PUBLIC OPINION AND FOREIGN POLICY DECISIONS." CANADA ELITES NAT/G FOR/AID LEAD NUC/PWR PERCEPT...INT QU CHARTS UN COLD/WAR. PAGE 92 H1839
DIPLOM ATTIT CON/ANAL SAMP

B66
ANDERSON S.V.,CANADIAN OMBUDSMAN PROPOSALS. CANADA LEGIS DEBATE PARL/PROC...MAJORIT JURID TIME/SEQ IDEA/COMP 20 OMBUDSMAN PARLIAMENT. PAGE 7 H0133
NAT/G CREATE ADMIN POL/PAR

B66
GRAHAM B.D.,THE FORMATION OF THE AUSTRALIAN COUNTRY PARTIES. CANADA USA+45 USA-45 SOCIETY PLAN ECO/TAC ...NAT/COMP 20 AUSTRAL. PAGE 59 H1190
POL/PAR AGRI REGION PARL/PROC

B66
GUNN G.E.,THE POLITICAL HISTORY OF NEWFOUNDLAND 1832-1864. CANADA FINAN LEGIS CHOOSE REPRESENT ...CHARTS 19. PAGE 62 H1252
POL/PAR NAT/G CONSTN

B66
RAY A.,INTER-GOVERNMENTAL RELATIONS IN INDIA: A STUDY OF INDIAN FEDERALISM. CANADA INDIA SWITZERLND USA+45 USSR ADMIN GOV/REL...NAT/COMP BIBLIOG. PAGE 130 H2599
CONSTN FEDERAL SOVEREIGN NAT/G

B66
US DEPARTMENT OF STATE,RESEARCH ON WESTERN EUROPE, GREAT BRITAIN, AND CANADA (EXTERNAL RESEARCH LIST NO 3-25). CANADA GERMANY/W UK LAW CULTURE NAT/G POL/PAR FORCES EDU/PROP REGION MARXISM...GEOG SOC WORSHIP 20 CMN/WLTH. PAGE 160 H3192
BIBLIOG/A EUR+WWI DIPLOM

B66
WINKS R.W.,THE HISTORIOGRAPHY OF THE BRITISH EMPIRE-COMMONWEALTH. CANADA INDIA PAKISTAN UK CULTURE SOCIETY STRUCT POL/PAR...CONCPT NAT/COMP 20 AUSTRAL. PAGE 169 H3386
HIST/WRIT TREND IDEA/COMP METH/COMP

B67
BADGLEY R.F.,DOCTORS' STRIKE; MEDICAL CARE AND CONFLICT IN SASKATCHEWAN. CANADA NAT/G PROF/ORG GP/REL ADJUST ATTIT...HEAL SOC 20. PAGE 10 H0192
HEALTH PLAN LABOR BARGAIN

B67
JOHNSON H.G.,ECONOMIC NATIONALISM IN OLD AND NEW STATES. CANADA CHINA/COM MALI UK DIPLOM...SIMUL GEN/LAWS 19/20 MEXIC/AMER. PAGE 81 H1619
NAT/LISM ECO/UNDEV ECO/DEV NAT/COMP

B67
KORNBERG A.,CANADIAN LEGISLATIVE BEHAVIOR: A STUDY OF THE 25TH PARLIAMENT. CANADA NAT/G POL/PAR PARL/PROC CHOOSE INGP/REL ADJUST ANOMIE RIGID/FLEX ...SOC STAND/INT CHARTS SOC/EXP 20 PARLIAMENT. PAGE 88 H1756
ATTIT LEGIS ROLE

B67
MCLAUGHLIN M.R.,RELIGIOUS EDUCATION AND THE STATE: DEMOCRACY FINDS A WAY. CANADA EUR+WWI GP/REL POPULISM...CATH NAT/COMP 20 AUSTRAL. PAGE 107 H2141
SECT NAT/G EDU/PROP POLICY

B67
ROSENBLUTH G.,THE CANADIAN ECONOMY AND DISARMAMENT. CANADA FUT ECO/DEV INDUS R+D DELIB/GP DIPLOM ECO/TAC CIVMIL/REL PEACE...POLICY BIBLIOG PACIFIST 20. PAGE 134 H2679
ARMS/CONT STAT PLAN NAT/G

B67
SCHWARTZ M.A.,PUBLIC OPINION AND CANADIAN IDENTITY. CANADA SOCIETY LOC/G DIPLOM ADMIN LEAD REGION GP/REL SAMP. PAGE 141 H2812
ATTIT NAT/G NAT/LISM POL/PAR

S67
ALBINSKI H.S.,"POLITICS AND BICULTURISM IN CANADA: THE FLAG DEBATE." CANADA SOCIETY NAT/G PROVS DELIB/GP DEBATE REGION SOVEREIGN PLURISM...POLICY SOC/INTEG 20. PAGE 5 H0093
NAT/LISM GP/REL POL/PAR CULTURE

S67
ALEXANDER A.,"CANADA'S PARLIAMENTARY SECRETARIES: THEIR POLITICAL AND CONSTITUTIONAL POSITION." CANADA UK NAT/G POL/PAR GOV/REL...GOV/COMP 20. PAGE 5 H0099
CONSTN ADMIN EX/STRUC DELIB/GP

S67
BOSHER J.F.,"GOVERNMENT AND PRIVATE INTERESTS IN NEW FRANCE." CANADA FRANCE INDUS LG/CO SML/CO CAP/ISM INT/TRADE COLONIAL GP/REL...HIST/WRIT 17/18. PAGE 19 H0381
NAT/G FINAN ADMIN CONTROL

S67
DEWHURST A.,"THE WAGE MOVEMENT IN CANADA." CANADA AGRI NAT/G PARTIC COST PRODUC PROFIT 20. PAGE 41 H0811
WORKER MARXIST INDUS LABOR

S67
DOERN G.B.,"THE ROYAL COMMISSIONS IN THE GENERAL POLICY PROCESS AND IN FEDERAL-PROVINCIAL RELATIONS." CANADA CONSTN ACADEM PROVS CONSULT DELIB/GP LEGIS ACT/RES PROB/SOLV CONFER CONTROL EFFICIENCY...METH/COMP 20 SENATE ROYAL/COMM. PAGE 42 H0832
R+D EX/STRUC GOV/REL NAT/G

S67
HARBRON J.D.,"UNIFICATION IN CANADA: FAIT ACCOMPLI" CANADA STRATA NAT/G DELIB/GP BUDGET GP/REL 20 NAVY. PAGE 66 H1327
INGP/REL FORCES PLAN ATTIT

S67
HEBAL J.J.,"APPROACHES TO REGIONAL AND METROPOLITAN GOVERNMENTS IN THE UNITED STATES AND CANADA." CANADA FUT USA+45 MUNIC...TREND 20. PAGE 69 H1380
ADMIN REGION LOC/G NAT/COMP

S67
KNOWLES A.F.,"NOTES ON A CANADIAN MASS MEDIA POLICY." CANADA TV CONTROL ROLE...METH/COMP 20. PAGE 87 H1735
EDU/PROP COM/IND NAT/G POLICY

S67
MALLORY J.R.,"THE MINISTER'S OFFICE STAFF* AN UNREFORMED PART OF PUBLIC SERVICE." CONSTN ELITES STRATA NAT/G PROB/SOLV TASK CHOOSE PERS/REL EFFICIENCY...DECISION 20. PAGE 102 H2033
CANADA ADMIN EX/STRUC STRUCT

S67
PLUMPTRE A.F.W.,"PERSPECTIVE ON OUR AID TO OTHERS." CANADA CREATE 20. PAGE 127 H2530
FOR/AID DIPLOM NAT/G PLAN

S67
RONNING C.,"NANKING: 1950." ASIA CANADA CHINA/COM NAT/G PLAN ECO/TAC REV ADJUST 20. PAGE 133 H2667
DIPLOM ROLE PEACE

S67
ROOT W.,"REPORT FROM PARIS - DE GAULLE: WHICH WAY TO THE FUTURE?" CANADA FRANCE ISLAM UK INT/ORG CHIEF CREATE AGREE CONTROL ARMS/CONT NUC/PWR EQUILIB PEACE PWR 20 DEGAULLE/C NATO. PAGE 134 H2670
POLICY DIPLOM NAT/G BAL/PWR

S67
SALYZYN V.,"FEDERAL-PROVINCIAL TAX SHARING SCHEMES." CANADA LOC/G PROB/SOLV TEC/DEV BUDGET GOV/REL EFFICIENCY 20. PAGE 137 H2746
PROVS TAX MUNIC NAT/G

S67
SHELDON C.H.,"PUBLIC OPINION AND HIGH COURTS: COMMUNIST PARTY CASES IN FOUR CONSTITUTIONAL SYSTEMS." CANADA GERMANY/W WOR+45 POL/PAR MARXISM ...METH/COMP NAT/COMP 20 AUSTRAL. PAGE 143 H2857
ATTIT CT/SYS CONSTN DECISION

S67
WHITE W.L.,"THE TREASURY BOARD AND PARLIAMENT." CANADA CONSTN CONSULT LEGIS LEAD PARL/PROC GP/REL ...DECISION 20. PAGE 167 H3351
FINAN DELIB/GP NAT/G ADMIN

CANADA CIVIL SERV COMM H0517

CANADIAN MEDICAL ASSOCIATION....SEE CMA

CANAL/ZONE.... PANAMA CANAL ZONE

B40
BROWN A.D.,PANAMA CANAL AND PANAMA CANAL ZONE: A SELECTED LIST OF REFERENCES. PANAMA NAT/G SCHOOL DIPLOM HEALTH...GEOG SOC 20 CANAL/ZONE. PAGE 22 H0436
BIBLIOG/A ECO/UNDEV

CANAWAY A.P. H0518

CANELAS O.A. H0519

CANNING HOUSE LIBRARY H0520

CANNON J.P. H0521

CANNON/JG....JOSEPH G. CANNON

CANON/LAW....CANON LAW

B24
HOLDSWORTH W.S.,A HISTORY OF ENGLISH LAW; THE COMMON LAW AND ITS RIVALS (VOL. IV). UK SEA AGRI CHIEF ADJUD CONTROL CRIME GOV/REL...INT/LAW JURID NAT/COMP 16/17 PARLIAMENT COMMON/LAW CANON/LAW ENGLSH/LAW. PAGE 72 H1449 — LAW LEGIS CT/SYS CONSTN

B26
MALINOWSKI B.,CRIME AND CUSTOM IN SAVAGE SOCIETY. SOCIETY FAM SECT LEGIT SANCTION MARRIAGE MYSTISM ...PSY SOC 19/20 MELANESIA CANON/LAW. PAGE 102 H2030 — LAW CULTURE CRIME ADJUD

B35
RAM J.,THE SCIENCE OF LEGAL JUDGMENT: A TREATISE... UK CONSTN NAT/G LEGIS CREATE PROB/SOLV AGREE CT/SYS ...INT/LAW CONCPT 19 ENGLSH/LAW CANON/LAW CIVIL/LAW CTS/WESTM. PAGE 129 H2584 — LAW JURID EX/STRUC ADJUD

B98
POLLOCK F.,THE HISTORY OF ENGLISH LAW BEFORE THE TIME OF EDWARD I (2 VOLS, 2ND ED.). UK CULTURE LOC/G LEGIS LICENSE AGREE CONTROL CT/SYS SANCTION CRIME...TIME/SEQ 13 COMMON/LAW CANON/LAW. PAGE 127 H2538 — LAW ADJUD JURID

CANTOR N.F. H0522

CANTRIL H. H0523,H0524

CANTRIL/H....HADLEY CANTRIL

CAP/ISM....CAPITALISM

N
BROCKWAY A.F.,AFRICAN SOCIALISM. EUR+WWI GHANA ISLAM UAR ECO/UNDEV CAP/ISM INT/TRADE COLONIAL COERCE GOV/REL DISCRIM 20 NEGRO NKRUMAH/K NASSER/G. PAGE 21 H0423 — AFR SOCISM MARXISM

B00
MOCKLER-FERRYMAN A.,BRITISH WEST AFRICA. FRANCE GERMANY NIGER SIER/LEONE UK CULTURE DIPLOM WAR RACE/REL PRODUC PROFIT WEALTH...POLICY PREDICT 19. PAGE 112 H2232 — AFR COLONIAL INT/TRADE CAP/ISM

B02
SEELEY J.R.,THE EXPANSION OF ENGLAND. MOD/EUR S/ASIA UK CULTURE NAT/G FORCES PLAN DOMIN EDU/PROP COLONIAL ROUTINE ATTIT ALL/VALS SOVEREIGN...CONCPT HIST/WRIT PARLIAMENT 18 CMN/WLTH. PAGE 141 H2819 — INT/ORG ACT/RES CAP/ISM INDIA

B12
HOBSON J.A.,THE EVOLUTION OF MODERN CAPITALISM. MOD/EUR UK STRATA ECO/DEV INDUS INCOME UTIL WEALTH ...SOC GEN/LAWS 7/20. PAGE 72 H1440 — CAP/ISM WORKER TEC/DEV TIME/SEQ

B13
DIE REKLAME IHRE KUNST UND WISSENSCHAFT. GERMANY POLAND SWITZERLND USA+45 TEC/DEV CAP/ISM DEMAND ...ART/METH EXHIBIT METH/COMP ANTHOL 20. PAGE 135 H2707 — EDU/PROP MARKET NAT/COMP ATTIT

B14
OPPENHEIMER F.,THE STATE. FUT SOCIETY STRATA STRUCT WORKER CAP/ISM WAR GP/REL SOCISM...SOC NAT/COMP SOC/INTEG. PAGE 121 H2424 — ELITES OWN DOMIN NAT/G

B15
VEBLEN T.,IMPERIAL GERMANY AND THE INDUSTRIAL REVOLUTION. GERMANY MOD/EUR UK USA-45 NAT/G TEC/DEV CAP/ISM...MAJORIT NAT/COMP 19/20 CHINJAP. PAGE 162 H3236 — ECO/DEV INDUS TECHNIC BAL/PWR

N19
BRIMMELL G.H.,COMMUNISM IN SOUTHEAST ASIA (PAMPHLET). BURMA CAMBODIA COM INDIA INDONESIA LAOS MOD/EUR NAT/G POL/PAR FORCES CAP/ISM CONTROL WEALTH ...MYTH 20. PAGE 21 H0420 — MARXISM S/ASIA REV ECO/UNDEV

N19
LIEBKNECHT W.P.C.,SOCIALISM (2 PTS.; 1875, 1894) (PAMPHLET). WORKER CAP/ISM EDU/PROP WEALTH POPULISM. PAGE 97 H1927 — ECO/TAC STRATA SOCIALIST PARTIC

B26
TAWNEY R.H.,RELIGION AND THE RISE OF CAPITALISM. UK CULTURE NAT/G TEC/DEV OWN LAISSEZ...POLICY SOC TIME/SEQ 16/19. PAGE 153 H3050 — SECT WEALTH INDUS CAP/ISM

B27
BELLOC H.,THE SERVILE STATE (1912) (3RD ED.). PRUSSIA UK CULTURE STRATA INDUS NAT/G ECO/TAC CONTROL LEAD SUFF DISCRIM EQUILIB ORD/FREE WEALTH 20. PAGE 13 H0269 — WORKER CAP/ISM DOMIN CATH

B27
WEBER M.,GENERAL ECONOMIC HISTORY. CHRIST-17C MOD/EUR STRUCT AGRI EXTR/IND FINAN INDUS MARKET FAM MUNIC NAT/G PROF/ORG SECT ECO/TAC 8/20. PAGE 166 H3319 — ECO/DEV CAP/ISM

B35
LASKI H.J.,THE STATE IN THEORY AND PRACTICE. ELITES ECO/TAC REPRESENT ORD/FREE PWR WEALTH POPULISM ...GOV/COMP GEN/LAWS 19/20. PAGE 92 H1829 — CAP/ISM COERCE NAT/G FASCISM

B36
BELLOC H.,THE RESTORATION OF PROPERTY. UK STRATA NAT/G PROF/ORG DELIB/GP WORKER CREATE PROB/SOLV ECO/TAC PARTIC UTOPIA ORD/FREE SOCISM 20. PAGE 13 H0270 — CONTROL MAJORIT CAP/ISM OWN

B36
HUBERMAN L.,MAN'S WORLDLY GOODS: THE STORY OF THE WEALTH OF NATIONS. CHRIST-17C EUR+WWI MOD/EUR SOCIETY DOMIN REV ORD/FREE...TIME/SEQ METH/COMP. PAGE 74 H1486 — WEALTH CAP/ISM MARXISM CREATE

B36
MARITAIN J.,FREEDOM IN THE MODERN WORLD. CONSTN NAT/G SECT CAP/ISM MARXISM SOCISM...GOV/COMP IDEA/COMP 19/20 HUMANISM CHRISTIAN. PAGE 102 H2049 — GEN/LAWS POLICY ORD/FREE

B37
PARSONS T.,THE STRUCTURE OF SOCIAL ACTION. UNIV INTELL SOCIETY INDUS MARKET ECO/TAC ROUTINE CHOOSE ALL/VALS...CONCPT OBS BIOG TREND GEN/LAWS 20. PAGE 124 H2471 — CULTURE ATTIT CAP/ISM

B38
DAVIES E.,"NATIONAL" CAPITALISM: THE GOVERNMENT'S RECORD AS PROTECTOR OF PRIVATE MONOPOLY. UK ELITES SOCIETY STRATA POL/PAR WORKER PROB/SOLV CONTROL SOCISM 20 MONOPOLY LABOR/PAR CHAMBRLN/N. PAGE 37 H0747 — CAP/ISM NAT/G INDUS POLICY

B38
HEIMANN E.,COMMUNISM, FASCISM, OR DEMOCRACY? WOR-45 CONSTN SOCIETY STRATA AGRI CAP/ISM MORAL ORD/FREE ...MAJORIT METH/COMP NAT/COMP 19/20. PAGE 69 H1384 — SOCISM MARXISM FASCISM PLURISM

B38
LAWLEY F.E.,THE GROWTH OF COLLECTIVE ECONOMY VOL. 1: NATIONAL. EUR+WWI AGRI INDUS NAT/G BARGAIN CAP/ISM ECO/TAC WAR OPTIMAL WEALTH...GOV/COMP METH/COMP 19/20 MONOPOLY. PAGE 92 H1844 — SOCISM PRICE CONTROL OWN

S38
HALL R.C.,"REPRESENTATION OF BIG BUSINESS IN THE HOUSE OF COMMONS." UK ECO/DEV INDUS PROF/ORG LEGIS CAP/ISM ECO/TAC LAISSEZ...POLICY OLD/LIB PLURIST MGT 20 HOUSE/CMNS. PAGE 64 H1287 — LOBBY NAT/G

B39
FIRTH R.,PRIMITIVE POLYNESIAN ECONOMY. SOCIETY DIST/IND SECT CHIEF CAP/ISM PRODUC WEALTH...SOC OBS METH WORSHIP 20 POLYNESIA. PAGE 50 H1007 — ECO/UNDEV CULTURE AGRI ECO/TAC

C41
WASSERMAN L.,"HANDBOOK OF POLITICAL "ISMS" CAP/ISM REPRESENT TOTALISM MARXISM NEW/LIB SOCISM...MAJORIT BIBLIOG 20. PAGE 166 H3313 — IDEA/COMP PHIL/SCI OWN NAT/G

B43
LASKI H.J.,REFLECTIONS ON THE REVOLUTIONS OF OUR TIME. COM USSR NAT/G WORKER UTOPIA ORD/FREE WEALTH MARXISM SOCISM 19/20. PAGE 92 H1830 — CAP/ISM WELF/ST ECO/TAC POLICY

B43
LENIN V.I.,STATE AND REVOLUTION. USSR CAP/ISM ...ANARCH MARXIST PHIL/SCI IDEA/COMP 20. PAGE 94 H1878 — SOCIETY NAT/G REV MARXISM

B45
VENABLE V.,HUMAN NATURE: THE MARXIAN VIEW. UNIV STRATA CAP/ISM REV GP/REL PERS/REL PRODUC KNOWL ...PHIL/SCI CONCPT IDEA/COMP 19 MARX/KARL ENGELS/F. PAGE 162 H3240 — PERSON MARXISM WORKER UTOPIA

B46
ALLEN J.S.,WORLD MONOPOLY AND PEACE. GERMANY UK USSR FINAN INDUS LG/CO DOMIN CONTROL PEACE PWR WEALTH SOCISM...NAT/COMP 20 MONOPOLY. PAGE 5 H0105 — CAP/ISM DIPLOM WAR COLONIAL

B47
ENKE S.,INTERNATIONAL ECONOMICS. UK USA+45 USSR INT/ORG BAL/PWR BARGAIN CAP/ISM BAL/PAY...NAT/COMP 20 TREATY. PAGE 46 H0927 — INT/TRADE FINAN TARIFFS ECO/TAC

N47
CANNON J.P.,AMERICAN STALINISM AND ANTI-STALINISM (PAMPHLET). NAT/G WORKER DOMIN EDU/PROP REV GP/REL ...MARXIST CONCPT 20 STALIN/J TROTSKY/L. PAGE 26 H0521 — LABOR MARXISM CAP/ISM POL/PAR

B48
LAUTERBACH A.,ECONOMIC SECURITY AND INDIVIDUAL FREEDOM: CAN WE HAVE BOTH? COM EUR+WWI MOD/EUR UNIV WOR+45 CAP/ISM TOTALISM ALL/VALS...GOV/COMP BIBLIOG 20. PAGE 92 H1840 — ORD/FREE ECO/DEV DECISION INGP/REL

B48
TOYNBEE A.J.,CIVILIZATION ON TRIAL. FUT WOR-45 NAT/G CREATE CAP/ISM DIPLOM NUC/PWR CHOOSE MARXISM ...GEOG CONCPT WORSHIP. PAGE 156 H3125 — SOCIETY TIME/SEQ NAT/COMP

B48
WOLFE B.D.,THREE WHO MADE A REVOLUTION. USSR CONSTN — BIOG

NAT/G CAP/ISM EDU/PROP CONTROL WAR GP/REL INGP/REL PERS/REL ROLE 20 STALIN/J LENIN/VI TROTSKY/L BOLSHEVISM. PAGE 170 H3398 REV LEAD MARXISM

B50
SCHUMPETER J.A.,CAPITALISM, SOCIALISM, AND DEMOCRACY (3RD ED.). USA-45 USSR WOR+45 WOR-45 INTELL ECO/DEV ECO/UNDEV ECO/TAC WAR PRODUC ORD/FREE...MGT SOC 20 MARX/KARL. PAGE 140 H2804 SOCIALIST CAP/ISM MARXISM IDEA/COMP

B51
MARX K.,THE EIGHTEENTH BRUMAIRE OF LOUIS BONAPARTE (1852). FRANCE STRATA FINAN INDUS LABOR CHIEF FORCES WORKER CAP/ISM ECO/TAC PARL/PROC ORD/FREE ...MARXIST 19. PAGE 104 H2080 REV MARXISM ELITES NAT/G

B52
ROBBINS L.,THE THEORY OF ECONOMIC POLICY IN ENGLISH CLASSICAL POLITICAL ECONOMY. UK ECO/DEV WORKER PLAN CAP/ISM EDU/PROP CONTROL INCOME OWN HEALTH SOCISM ...POLICY 17/19. PAGE 132 H2639 ECO/TAC ORD/FREE IDEA/COMP NAT/G

B53
FLORENCE P.S.,THE LOGIC OF BRITISH AND AMERICAN INDUSTRY; A REALISTIC ANALYSIS OF ECONOMIC STRUCTURE AND GOVERNMENT. UK USA+45 USA-45 FINAN LABOR CAP/ISM INGP/REL EFFICIENCY...MGT CONCPT STAT CHARTS METH 20. PAGE 51 H1028 INDUS ECO/DEV NAT/G NAT/COMP

B53
SWEEZY P.M.,THE PRESENT AS HISTORY. NAT/G PLAN COLONIAL ATTIT...POLICY SOCIALIST 19/20. PAGE 151 H3019 ECO/DEV CAP/ISM SOCISM ECO/TAC

B54
LENIN V.I.,SELECTED WORKS (12 VOLS.). USSR INTELL SOCIETY STRATA STRUCT NAT/G POL/PAR WORKER CAP/ISM REV WAR...MARXIST PHIL/SCI 20 MARX/KARL LENIN/VI. PAGE 94 H1880 COM MARXISM

B54
MOSK S.A.,INDUSTRIAL REVOLUTION IN MEXICO. MARKET LABOR CREATE CAP/ISM ADMIN ATTIT SOCISM...POLICY 20 MEXIC/AMER. PAGE 113 H2268 INDUS TEC/DEV ECO/UNDEV NAT/G

C54
BERLE A.A. JR.,"THE 20TH CENTURY CAPITALIST REVOLUTION." ECO/DEV NAT/G DIPLOM PRICE CONTROL ATTIT...BIBLIOG/A 20. PAGE 15 H0306 LG/CO CAP/ISM MGT PWR

B55
HELANDER S.,DAS AUTARKIEPROBLEM IN DER WELTWIRTSCHAFT. PROB/SOLV BAL/PWR BARGAIN CAP/ISM ECO/TAC SOVEREIGN 20. PAGE 69 H1388 NAT/COMP COLONIAL DIPLOM

B55
MAYO H.B.,DEMOCRACY AND MARXISM. COM USSR STRATA NAT/G WORKER ECO/TAC REV MORAL...PHIL/SCI HIST/WRIT IDEA/COMP WORSHIP 20 MARX/KARL LENIN/VI STALIN/J TROTSKY/L. PAGE 105 H2108 MARXISM CAP/ISM

B57
ALEXANDER L.M.,WORLD POLITICAL PATTERNS. NAT/G PROVS CAP/ISM DIPLOM COLONIAL NAT/LISM...POLICY GEOG CHARTS METH/COMP NAT/COMP 20. PAGE 5 H0101 CONTROL METH GOV/COMP

B57
BARAN P.A.,THE POLITICAL ECONOMY OF GROWTH. MOD/EUR USA+45 USA-45 TEC/DEV TAX SOCISM...MGT CONCPT GOV/COMP. PAGE 11 H0213 CAP/ISM CONTROL ECO/UNDEV FINAN

B57
HALLGARTEN G.W.,DAMONEN ODER RETTER. ASIA L/A+17C CAP/ISM ATTIT MARXISM SOCISM...NAT/COMP. PAGE 64 H1289 TOTALISM FASCISM COERCE DOMIN

B57
LOUCKS W.N.,COMPARATIVE ECONOMIC SYSTEMS (5TH ED.). COM UK USSR INDUS POL/PAR PLAN CAP/ISM TOTALISM MARXISM...PHIL/SCI BIBLIOG 19/20. PAGE 99 H1969 NAT/COMP IDEA/COMP SOCISM

B58
AVRAMOVIC D.,POSTWAR GROWTH IN INTERNATIONAL INDEBTEDNESS. WOR+45 AGRI INDUS CAP/ISM PRICE INCOME...NAT/COMP 20 GOLD/STAND SILVER. PAGE 9 H0184 INT/TRADE FINAN COST BAL/PAY

B58
DUNAYEVSKAYA R.,MARXISM AND FREEDOM: FROM 1776 UNTIL TODAY. COM USSR WORKER CAP/ISM DOMIN REV GP/REL TOTALISM ALL/VALS...MYTH BIOG IDEA/COMP 18/20 MARX/KARL LENIN/VI STALIN/J. PAGE 43 H0861 MARXISM CONCPT ORD/FREE

B58
HANCE W.A.,AFRICAN ECONOMIC DEVELOPMENT. AGRI DIST/IND INDUS R+D ACT/RES PLAN CAP/ISM FOR/AID ...GOV/COMP BIBLIOG 20. PAGE 65 H1312 AFR ECO/UNDEV PROB/SOLV TEC/DEV

B58
VARG P.A.,MISSIONARIES, CHINESE, AND DIPLOMATS: THE AMERICAN PROTESTANT MISSIONARY MOVEMENT IN CHINA, 1890-1952. ASIA ECO/UNDEV NAT/G PROB/SOLV CAP/ISM EDU/PROP COLONIAL NAT/LISM ATTIT MARXISM...NAT/COMP STERTYP 20 CHINJAP PROTESTANT MISSION. PAGE 162 H3234 CULTURE DIPLOM SECT

B59
MADHOK B.,POLITICAL TRENDS IN INDIA. INDIA PAKISTAN UK STRATA ECO/UNDEV POL/PAR LEGIS CAP/ISM DIPLOM COLONIAL CHOOSE MARXISM...SOC TREND 20 GANDHI/M NEHRU/J. PAGE 101 H2014 GEOG NAT/G

B59
VERNEY D.V.,PUBLIC ENTERPRISE IN SWEDEN. FUT SWEDEN UK INDUS POL/PAR LEGIS PROB/SOLV CAP/ISM INT/TRADE CONTROL SOCISM...MGT CONCPT NAT/COMP 20 SOCDEM/PAR CIVIL/SERV. PAGE 162 H3246 ECO/DEV POLICY LG/CO NAT/G

B60
BAYER H.,WIRTSCHAFTSPROGNOSE UND WIRTSCHAFTSGESTALTUNG. GERMANY NETHERLAND MARKET PLAN CAP/ISM DEBATE...NAT/COMP 20. PAGE 12 H0242 ECO/DEV ECO/UNDEV FINAN POLICY

B60
BOMBACH G.,STABILE PREISE IN WACHSENDER WIRTSCHAFT: DAS INFLATIONSPROBLEM. BARGAIN CAP/ISM PRICE COST ...NAT/COMP 20 GOLD/STAND. PAGE 19 H0371 ECO/UNDEV PLAN FINAN ECO/TAC

S60
FRANKEL S.H.,"ECONOMIC ASPECTS OF POLITICAL INDEPENDENCE IN AFRICA." AFR FUT SOCIETY ECO/UNDEV COM/IND FINAN LEGIS PLAN TEC/DEV CAP/ISM ECO/TAC INT/TRADE ADMIN ATTIT DRIVE RIGID/FLEX PWR WEALTH ...MGT NEW/IDEA MATH TIME/SEQ VAL/FREE 20. PAGE 53 H1052 NAT/G FOR/AID

C60
EBENSTEIN W.,"MODERN POLITICAL THOUGHT (2ND ED.)" NAT/G CAP/ISM NAT/LISM PERSON ORD/FREE PWR ALL/IDEOS NEW/LIB SOCISM...TRADIT PSY BIBLIOG/A 18/20. PAGE 44 H0884 IDEA/COMP PHIL/SCI CONCPT GEN/LAWS

B61
BONNEFOUS M.,EUROPE ET TIERS MONDE. EUR+WWI SOCIETY INT/ORG NAT/G VOL/ASSN ACT/RES TEC/DEV CAP/ISM ECO/TAC ATTIT ORD/FREE SOVEREIGN...POLICY CONCPT TREND 20. PAGE 19 H0373 AFR ECO/UNDEV FOR/AID INT/TRADE

B61
BOURDIEU P.,THE ALGERIANS (TRANS. BY A.C. ROSS; REV. ED.). ALGERIA ISLAM CULTURE MUNIC CAP/ISM COLONIAL GP/REL ORD/FREE SOVEREIGN 20. PAGE 19 H0385 SOCIETY STRUCT ATTIT WAR

B61
BREWIS T.N.,CANADIAN ECONOMIC POLICY. CANADA BUDGET CAP/ISM INT/TRADE RATION TARIFFS TAX PRICE CONTROL ROUTINE FEDERAL INCOME PRODUC 20 GOLD/STAND. PAGE 20 H0412 ECO/DEV ECO/TAC NAT/G PLAN

B61
GANGULI B.N.,ECONOMIC INTEGRATION. FINAN LABOR CAP/ISM DIPLOM WEALTH...NAT/COMP 20. PAGE 55 H1096 ECO/TAC METH/CNCPT EQUILIB ECO/UNDEV

B61
LENIN V.I.,WHAT IS TO BE DONE? (1902). RUSSIA LABOR NAT/G POL/PAR WORKER CAP/ISM ECO/TAC ADMIN PARTIC ...MARXIST IDEA/COMP GEN/LAWS 19/20. PAGE 94 H1881 EDU/PROP PRESS MARXISM METH/COMP

B61
LICHTHEIM G.,MARXISM. GERMANY SOCIETY WORKER CAP/ISM ECO/TAC NAT/LISM POPULISM...TIME/SEQ GOV/COMP NAT/COMP 18/20 COM/PARTY. PAGE 96 H1924 MARXISM SOCISM IDEA/COMP CULTURE

B61
MARX K.,THE COMMUNIST MANIFESTO. IN (MENDEL A. ESSENTIAL WORKS OF MARXISM, NEW YORK: BANTAM. FUT MOD/EUR CULTURE ECO/DEV ECO/UNDEV AGRI FINAN INDUS MARKET PROC/MFG LABOR MUNIC POL/PAR CONSULT FORCES CREATE PLAN ADMIN ATTIT DRIVE RIGID/FLEX ORD/FREE PWR RESPECT MARX/KARL WORK. PAGE 104 H2081 COM NEW/IDEA CAP/ISM REV

B61
VEIT O.,GRUNDRISS DER WAHRUNGSPOLITIK. FRANCE GERMANY USSR DIPLOM INT/TRADE...NAT/COMP 19/20 GOLD/STAND SILVER. PAGE 162 H3239 FINAN POLICY ECO/TAC CAP/ISM

B62
AMERICAN SOCIETY AFR CULTURE,PAN-AFRICANISM RECONSIDERED. AFR SOCIETY STRUCT SCHOOL CAP/ISM EDU/PROP...ART/METH NEW/IDEA PREDICT ANTHOL 20 PANAF/FREE NEGRO. PAGE 6 H0123 DIPLOM FEDERAL NAT/LISM CULTURE

B62
BAFFREY S.A.,THE RED MYTH: A HISTORY OF COMMUNISM FROM MARX TO KHRUSHCHEV. USSR NAT/G CHIEF CAP/ISM DIPLOM EDU/PROP REV WAR PEACE TOTALISM...POLICY 20 STALIN/J KHRUSH/N. PAGE 10 H0195 CONCPT MARXISM TV

B62
BELL D.,THE END OF IDEOLOGY (REV. ED.). USA+45 USA-45 ELITES STRATA LABOR CREATE CRIME PWR MARXISM ...PHIL/SCI METH/COMP 20 EUROPE. PAGE 13 H0265 CROWD CAP/ISM SOCISM IDEA/COMP

B62
FRIEDMANN W.,METHODS AND POLICIES OF PRINCIPAL DONOR COUNTRIES IN PUBLIC INTERNATIONAL DEVELOPMENT FINANCING: PRELIMINARY APPRAISAL. FRANCE GERMANY/W UK USA+45 USSR WOR+45 FINAN TEC/DEV CAP/ISM DIPLOM ECO/TAC ATTIT 20 EEC. PAGE 53 H1066 INT/ORG FOR/AID NAT/COMP ADMIN

B62
MEYER A.G.,LENINISM. USSR STRUCT NAT/G CAP/ISM LEAD WAR PWR SOVEREIGN...BIBLIOG 20 LENIN/VI. PAGE 109 H2187 POL/PAR REV MARXISM

PHIL/SCI

B62
MOUSSA P.,THE UNDERPRIVILEGED NATIONS. FINAN INT/ORG PLAN PROB/SOLV CAP/ISM GIVE TASK WEALTH ...POLICY SOC 20. PAGE 114 H2273
ECO/UNDEV NAT/G DIPLOM FOR/AID

S62
IOVTCHOUK M.T.,"ON SOME THEORETICAL PRINCIPLES AND METHODS OF SOCIOLOGICAL INVESTIGATIONS (IN RUSSIAN)." FUT USA+45 STRATA R+D NAT/G POL/PAR TOP/EX ACT/RES PLAN ECO/TAC EDU/PROP ROUTINE ATTIT RIGID/FLEX MARXISM SOCISM...MARXIST METH/CNCPT OBS TREND NAT/COMP GEN/LAWS 20. PAGE 78 H1564
COM ECO/DEV CAP/ISM USSR

S62
SARKISYANZ E.,"NATIONALISM, CAPITALISM, AND THE UNCOMMITED NATIONS: MARXISM AND ASIAN CULTURAL TRADITIONS." ASIA BURMA CHINA/COM COM CULTURE SOCIETY NAT/G POL/PAR PLAN DOMIN EDU/PROP COLONIAL COERCE ATTIT RIGID/FLEX...CONCPT TREND MARX/KARL 20 TIBET BUDDHISM. PAGE 138 H2755
S/ASIA SECT NAT/LISM CAP/ISM

B63
AHN L.A.,FUNFZIG JAHRE ZWISCHEN INFLATION UND DEFLATION. GERMANY DIPLOM PRICE...CONCPT 20 GOLD/STAND. PAGE 4 H0081
FINAN CAP/ISM NAT/COMP ECO/TAC

B63
CRANKSHAW E.,THE NEW COLD WAR: MOSCOW V. PEKIN. CHINA/COM USSR INTELL POL/PAR DELIB/GP CAP/ISM COERCE REV NAT/LISM TOTALISM DRIVE...POLICY IDEA/COMP 20 KHRUSH/N. PAGE 35 H0698
ATTIT DIPLOM NAT/COMP MARXISM

B63
ENKE S.,ECONOMICS FOR DEVELOPMENT. AGRI TEC/DEV CAP/ISM DIPLOM ECO/TAC TAX ATTIT DRIVE HABITAT WEALTH...GOV/COMP BIBLIOG 20. PAGE 46 H0928
ECO/UNDEV PHIL/SCI CON/ANAL

B63
GRIMOND J.,THE LIBERAL CHALLENGE. UK SOCIETY INDUS POL/PAR LEGIS PLAN CAP/ISM DIPLOM EDU/PROP GOV/REL CONSERVE 20 PARLIAMENT REFORMERS. PAGE 61 H1227
NAT/G NEW/LIB ECO/DEV POLICY

B63
HYDE D.,THE PEACEFUL ASSAULT. COM UAR USSR ECO/DEV ECO/UNDEV NAT/G POL/PAR CAP/ISM PWR 20. PAGE 76 H1516
MARXISM CONTROL ECO/TAC DIPLOM

B63
RONNING C.N.,LAW AND POLITICS IN INTER-AMERICAN DIPLOMACY. L/A+17C ECO/UNDEV NAT/G CONSULT DELIB/GP CREATE CAP/ISM ECO/TAC LEGIT REGION RIGID/FLEX ...METH/CNCPT GEN/LAWS OAS 20. PAGE 133 H2668
VOL/ASSN ALL/VALS DIPLOM

B63
STIFEL L.D.,THE TEXTILE INDUSTRY - A CASE STUDY OF INDUSTRIAL DEVELOPMENT IN THE PHILIPPINES (PAPER). PHILIPPINE WORKER CAP/ISM INT/TRADE TARIFFS RECEIVE PRICE ADMIN COST EFFICIENCY WEALTH...BIBLIOG 20. PAGE 149 H2986
S/ASIA ECO/UNDEV PROC/MFG NAT/G

B63
STRAUSS L.,HISTORY OF POLITICAL PHILOSOPHY. LAW SOCIETY CAP/ISM MARXISM 19 AQUINAS/T BACON/F HEGEL/GWF MILL/JS NIETZSCH/F. PAGE 150 H2995
IDEA/COMP PHIL/SCI ANTHOL

B63
VON BECKERATH E.,PROBLEME DER NORMATIVEN OKONOMIK UND DER WIRTSCHAFTSPOLITISCHEN BERATUNG. GERMANY UK ELITES CAP/ISM EFFICIENCY...CONCPT GOV/COMP IDEA/COMP 20. PAGE 163 H3264
ECO/TAC DELIB/GP ECO/DEV CONSULT

B63
WODDIS J.,AFRICA, THE WAY AHEAD. AFR FUT ELITES POL/PAR CAP/ISM DIPLOM DOMIN RACE/REL ATTIT ORD/FREE SOVEREIGN SOCISM 20 PANAF/FREE. PAGE 170 H3394
REV COLONIAL ECO/UNDEV NAT/G

S63
AYAL E.B.,"VALUE SYSTEM AND ECONOMIC DEVELOPMENT IN JAPAN AND THAILAND." ASIA S/ASIA THAILAND CULTURE ECO/DEV CAP/ISM DOMIN NAT/LISM DRIVE RIGID/FLEX SOCISM...WELF/ST OBS TREND CON/ANAL GEN/LAWS 20 CHINJAP. PAGE 9 H0185
ECO/UNDEV ALL/VALS

B64
BAUCHET P.,ECONOMIC PLANNING. FRANCE STRATA LG/CO CAP/ISM ADMIN PARL/PROC DEMAND OPTIMAL ATTIT PWR SOCISM...POLICY CHARTS 20. PAGE 12 H0238
ECO/DEV NAT/G PLAN ECO/TAC

B64
FRIEDLAND W.H.,AFRICAN SOCIALISM. ECO/UNDEV MARKET LABOR NAT/G POL/PAR PLAN CAP/ISM ECO/TAC EDU/PROP CHOOSE ATTIT DRIVE PWR WEALTH...POLICY CONCPT RECORD STERTYP 20. PAGE 53 H1063
AFR SOCISM

B64
MILIBAND R.,THE SOCIALIST REGISTER: 1964. GERMANY/W ITALY UK LABOR POL/PAR ECO/TAC FOR/AID NUC/PWR ...POLICY SOCIALIST IDEA/COMP 20 MAO NASSER/G. PAGE 110 H2204
MARXISM SOCISM CAP/ISM PROB/SOLV

B64
WERNETTE J.P.,GOVERNMENT AND BUSINESS. LABOR CAP/ISM ECO/TAC INT/TRADE TAX ADMIN AUTOMAT NUC/PWR CIVMIL/REL DEMAND...MGT 20 MONOPOLY. PAGE 167 H3333
NAT/G FINAN ECO/DEV CONTROL

S64
SALVADORI M.,"EL CAPITALISMO EN LA EUROPA DE LA POSGUERRA." INT/ORG NAT/G POL/PAR PLAN ECO/TAC ATTIT ORD/FREE WEALTH...HIST/WRIT COLD/WAR EEC 20. PAGE 137 H2743
EUR+WWI ECO/DEV CAP/ISM

C64
GOLDMAN M.I.,"COMPARATIVE ECONOMIC SYSTEMS: A READER." COM ECO/UNDEV NAT/G BUDGET CAP/ISM ADMIN TOTALISM MARXISM SOCISM...MGT ANTHOL BIBLIOG 19/20. PAGE 58 H1157
NAT/COMP CONTROL IDEA/COMP

B65
JAIN S.C.,THE STATE AND AGRICULTURE. INDIA S/ASIA ECO/UNDEV PROB/SOLV CAP/ISM MARXISM SOCISM 20. PAGE 79 H1586
NAT/G POLICY AGRI ECO/TAC

B65
THE STATE AND ECONOMIC ENTERPRISE IN JAPAN; ESSAYS IN THE POLITICAL ECONOMY OF GROWTH. AGRI INDUS DRIVE POPULISM...CHARTS NAT/COMP ANTHOL 19/20 CHINJAP. PAGE 98 H1949
ECO/UNDEV ECO/DEV CAP/ISM ECO/TAC

B65
MENON K.P.S.,MANY WORLDS. INDIA BAL/PWR CAP/ISM COLONIAL REV ORD/FREE PWR MARXISM...POLICY 20 COLD/WAR. PAGE 109 H2176
BIOG DIPLOM NAT/G

B65
OBUKAR C.,THE MODERN AFRICAN. AGRI INDUS WORKER CAP/ISM EDU/PROP PARTIC RACE/REL NAT/LISM ALL/VALS MARXISM...SOC IDEA/COMP 20. PAGE 120 H2393
AFR ECO/UNDEV CULTURE SOVEREIGN

B65
ONSLOW C.,ASIAN ECONOMIC DEVELOPMENT. BURMA CEYLON INDIA MALAYSIA PAKISTAN S/ASIA AGRI INDUS MARKET PROB/SOLV CAP/ISM FOR/AID INT/TRADE DEMAND WEALTH ...POLICY ANTHOL 20. PAGE 121 H2418
ECO/UNDEV ECO/TAC PLAN NAT/G

B65
PROEHL P.O.,FOREIGN ENTERPRISE IN NIGERIA. NIGERIA FINAN LABOR NAT/G TAX 20. PAGE 128 H2562
ECO/UNDEV ECO/TAC JURID CAP/ISM

B65
WURFEL S.W.,FOREIGN ENTERPRISE IN COLOMBIA. FINAN LABOR NAT/G ECO/TAC TAX REGION 20 COLOMB. PAGE 171 H3429
ECO/UNDEV INT/TRADE JURID CAP/ISM

S65
VAN DEN BERG M.,"SOME METHODOLOGICAL ASPECTS OF SOUTH AFRICA'S FIRST E.D.P." SOUTH/AFR NAT/G CREATE TEC/DEV CAP/ISM INCOME PRODUC...CON/ANAL CHARTS 20. PAGE 161 H3226
ECO/DEV PLAN METH STAT

S65
WHITE J.,"WEST GERMAN AID TO DEVELOPING COUNTRIES." INT/ORG OP/RES GIVE CENTRAL ATTIT DRIVE...STAT NAT/COMP COLD/WAR. PAGE 167 H3348
GERMANY FOR/AID ECO/UNDEV CAP/ISM

B66
BUKHARIN N.,THE ABC OF COMMUNISM: A POPULAR EXPLANATION OF THE PROGRAM OF THE COMMUNIST PARTY OF RUSSIA. USSR STRATA SECT FORCES WORKER CAP/ISM RECEIVE EDU/PROP NAT/LISM TOTALISM 20. PAGE 23 H0468
MARXISM CONCPT POLICY REV

B66
COLE G.D.H.,THE MEANING OF MARXISM. USSR WOR+45 STRATA STRUCT NAT/G WORKER COST FASCISM...IDEA/COMP 20. PAGE 31 H0625
MARXISM CONCPT HIST/WRIT CAP/ISM

B66
EDWARDS C.D.,TRADE REGULATIONS OVERSEAS. IRELAND NEW/ZEALND SOUTH/AFR NAT/G CAP/ISM TARIFFS CONTROL ...POLICY JURID 20 EEC CHINJAP. PAGE 45 H0892
INT/TRADE DIPLOM INT/LAW ECO/TAC

B66
LEONTIEF W.,ESSAYS IN ECONOMICS. ECO/UNDEV INDUS NAT/G CAP/ISM FOR/AID AUTOMAT MARXISM...ECOMETRIC CHARTS ANTHOL METH 20 KEYNES/JM. PAGE 94 H1886
CONCPT METH/CNCPT METH/COMP

B66
MADAN G.R.,ECONOMIC THINKING IN INDIA. INDIA ECO/UNDEV AGRI FINAN INDUS LABOR PLAN CAP/ISM INT/TRADE MARXISM SOCISM...POLICY 1/20. PAGE 101 H2013
ECO/TAC PHIL/SCI NAT/G POL/PAR

B66
NAMBOODIRIPAD E.M.,ECONOMICS AND POLITICS OF INDIA'S SOCIALIST PATTERN. INDIA STRATA AGRI INDUS NAT/G PRICE ORD/FREE SOVEREIGN 20. PAGE 115 H2307
ECO/UNDEV PLAN SOCISM CAP/ISM

B66
SPULBER N.,THE STATE AND ECONOMIC DEVELOPMENT IN EASTERN EUROPE. BULGARIA COM CZECHOSLVK HUNGARY POLAND YUGOSLAVIA CULTURE PLAN CAP/ISM INT/TRADE CONTROL...POLICY CHARTS METH/COMP BIBLIOG/A 19/20. PAGE 148 H2958
ECO/DEV ECO/UNDEV NAT/G TOTALISM

S66
LODGE G.C.,"REVOLUTION IN LATIN AMERICA." USA+45 ELITES INDUS LABOR PROF/ORG SECT TEC/DEV CAP/ISM SKILL MARXISM...POLICY NAT/COMP. PAGE 98 H1950
ATTIT REV L/A+17C IDEA/COMP

B67
DICKSON P.G.M.,THE FINANCIAL REVOLUTION IN ENGLAND. UK NAT/G TEC/DEV ADMIN GOV/REL...SOC METH/CNCPT CHARTS GP/COMP BIBLIOG 17/18. PAGE 41 H0823
ECO/DEV FINAN CAP/ISM MGT

B67
DILLARD D.,ECONOMIC DEVELOPMENT OF THE NORTH ATLANTIC COMMUNITY. EUR+WWI MOD/EUR USA+45 USA-45 ECO/UNDEV LABOR CAP/ISM WAR BAL/PAY...NAT/COMP 15/20. PAGE 41 H0824
ECO/DEV INT/TRADE INDUS DIPLOM

B67
EVANS R.H.,COEXISTENCE: COMMUNISM AND ITS PRACTICE IN BOLOGNA, 1945-1965. ITALY CAP/ISM ADMIN CHOOSE PEACE ORD/FREE...SOC STAT DEEP/INT SAMP CHARTS BIBLIOG 20. PAGE 48 H0952
MARXISM CULTURE MUNIC POL/PAR

B67
GALBRAITH J.K.,THE NEW INDUSTRIAL STATE. INDUS LABOR LG/CO NAT/G POL/PAR SCHOOL OP/RES CAP/ISM EXEC TREND. PAGE 54 H1087
TEC/DEV ECO/DEV SOCIETY MARKET

B67
PAPANEK G.F.,PAKISTAN'S DEVELOPMENT: SOCIAL GOALS AND PRIVATE INCENTIVES. PAKISTAN INDUS NAT/G PROB/SOLV CONTROL EFFICIENCY SOCISM...CHARTS 20. PAGE 123 H2463
ECO/UNDEV PLAN CAP/ISM ECO/TAC

B67
POSNER M.V.,ITALIAN PUBLIC ENTERPRISE. ITALY ECO/DEV FINAN INDUS CREATE ECO/TAC ADMIN CONTROL EFFICIENCY PRODUC...TREND CHARTS 20. PAGE 127 H2545
NAT/G PLAN CAP/ISM SOCISM

B67
PYE L.W.,SOUTHEAST ASIA'S POLITICAL SYSTEMS. ASIA S/ASIA STRUCT ECO/UNDEV EX/STRUC CAP/ISM DIPLOM ALL/IDEOS...TREND CHARTS. PAGE 128 H2568
NAT/G POL/PAR GOV/COMP

B67
WOODRUFF W.,IMPACT OF WESTERN MAN. ECO/DEV INDUS CREATE PLAN PROB/SOLV COLONIAL GOV/REL...CHARTS GOV/COMP BIBLIOG 18/20. PAGE 170 H3407
EUR+WWI MOD/EUR CAP/ISM

L67
HOSHII I.,"JAPAN'S STAKE IN ASIA." ASIA S/ASIA CAP/ISM ECO/TAC ROLE...GEOG 20 CHINJAP. PAGE 74 H1477
DIPLOM REGION NAT/G INT/ORG

L67
WRIGHT W.R.,"FOREIGN-OWNED RAILWAYS IN ARGENTINA: A CASE STUDY OF ECONOMIC NATIONALISM." L/A+17C UK ECO/UNDEV SERV/IND LG/CO NAT/G TEC/DEV BAL/PWR EQUILIB ARGEN. PAGE 171 H3423
NAT/LISM CAP/ISM ECO/TAC COLONIAL

S67
BOSHER J.F.,"GOVERNMENT AND PRIVATE INTERESTS IN NEW FRANCE." CANADA FRANCE INDUS LG/CO SML/CO CAP/ISM INT/TRADE COLONIAL GP/REL...HIST/WRIT 17/18. PAGE 19 H0381
NAT/G FINAN ADMIN CONTROL

S67
FRENCH D.S.,"DOES THE U.S. EXPLOIT THE DEVELOPING NATIONS?" INT/ORG NAT/G CAP/ISM BAL/PAY WEALTH POLICY. PAGE 53 H1057
ECO/UNDEV INT/TRADE ECO/TAC COLONIAL

S67
GAMARNIKOW M.,"THE NEW ROLE OF PRIVATE ENTERPRISE." ECO/DEV INDUS NAT/G SML/CO CREATE PROB/SOLV MARXISM ...POLICY TREND IDEA/COMP 20. PAGE 55 H1092
ECO/TAC ATTIT CAP/ISM COM

S67
MANGLAPUS R.S.,"ASIAN REVOLUTION AND AMERICAN IDEOLOGY." USA+45 SOCIETY CAP/ISM DIPLOM ADJUST CENTRAL...NAT/COMP 20. PAGE 102 H2035
REV POPULISM ATTIT ASIA

S67
RICHMAN B.M.,"CAPITALISTS & MANAGERS IN COMMUNIST CHINA." ASIA CHINA/COM ECO/UNDEV NAT/G CONSULT EX/STRUC PLAN EFFICIENCY PRODUC WEALTH MARXISM ...MGT CHARTS 20. PAGE 131 H2623
CAP/ISM INDUS

S67
SCOVILLE W.J.,"GOVERNMENT REGULATION AND GROWTH IN THE FRENCH PAPER INDUSTRY DURING THE EIGHTEENTH CENTURY." FRANCE MOD/EUR FINAN CAP/ISM TAX ADMIN CONTROL PRIVIL LAISSEZ...POLICY 18. PAGE 141 H2818
NAT/G PROC/MFG ECO/DEV INGP/REL

S67
SOLT L.F.,"PURITANISM, CAPITALISM, DEMOCRACY, AND THE NEW SCIENCE." NAT/G GP/REL CONSERVE...IDEA/COMP GEN/LAWS. PAGE 147 H2931
SECT CAP/ISM RATIONAL POPULISM

B82
CUNNINGHAM W.,THE GROWTH OF ENGLISH INDUSTRY AND COMMERCE. FUT UK FINAN NAT/G CAP/ISM...POLICY 20 MERCANTLST CHRISTIAN POPE. PAGE 36 H0721
INDUS INT/TRADE SML/CO CONSERVE

B84
ENGELS F.,THE ORIGIN OF THE FAMILY, PRIVATE PROPERTY, AND THE STATE (TRANS. BY E. UNTERMANN). UNIV ELITES SOCIETY CAP/ISM ECO/TAC MARRIAGE ORD/FREE POPULISM...MARXIST SOC ENGELS. PAGE 46 H0926
FAM OWN WEALTH SOCISM

CAPA C. H1513

CAPE/HOPE....CAPE OF GOOD HOPE

B18
EYBERS G.W.,SELECT CONSTITUTIONAL DOCUMENTS ILLUSTRATING SOUTH AFRICAN HISTORY 1795-1910. SOUTH/AFR LOC/G LEGIS CT/SYS...JURID ANTHOL 18/20 NATAL CAPE/HOPE ORANGE/STA. PAGE 48 H0955
CONSTN LAW NAT/G COLONIAL

CAPELL A. H0525

CAPITAL....SEE FINAN

CAPITALISM....SEE CAP/ISM

CAPLOW T. H0526

CAPODIST/J....JOHN CAPODISTRIAS

CAPONE/AL....AL CAPONE

CARDINALL AW H0527

CARDOZA/JN....JACOB N. CARDOZA

CAREW-HUNT R.C. H0528

CARIAS B. H0529

CARIBBEAN COMMISSION H0530,H0531

CARIBBEAN....CARIBBEAN

B43
BROWN A.D.,BRITISH POSSESSIONS IN THE CARIBBEAN AREA: A SELECTED LIST OF REFERENCES. UK NAT/G DIPLOM...GEOG 20 CARIBBEAN. PAGE 22 H0437
BIBLIOG COLONIAL ECO/UNDEV L/A+17C

S62
SPRINGER H.W.,"FEDERATION IN THE CARIBBEAN: AN ATTEMPT THAT FAILED." L/A+17C ECO/UNDEV INT/ORG POL/PAR PROVS LEGIS CREATE PLAN LEGIT ADMIN FEDERAL ATTIT DRIVE PERSON ORD/FREE PWR...POLICY GEOG PSY CONCPT OBS CARIBBEAN CMN/WLTH 20. PAGE 148 H2955
VOL/ASSN NAT/G REGION

CARLYLE T. H0532

CARNEG/COM....CARNEGIE COMMISSION

CARNEGIE COMMISSION....SEE CARNEG/COM

CARNEGIE ENDOWMENT H0533

CARNELL F. H0534

CARPENTER G.W. H0535

CARR E.H. H0536,H0537,H0538

CARRANZA/V....VENUSTIANZO CARRANZA

CARRIL B. H0539

CARRINGTON C.E. H0540,H0541

CARROTHERS A.W.R. H0542

CARTER G.M. H0543,H0544,H0545,H0546,H0547,H0548,H0549,H0550

CARVALHO C.M. H0551

CARY J. H0552,H0553

CASE M.H. H1365

CASE STUDIES....CARRIED UNDER THE SPECIAL TECHNIQUES USED, OR TOPICS COVERED

CASEBOOK....CASEBOOK, SUCH AS LEGAL OR SOCIOLOGICAL CASEBOOK

B52
SPICER E.H.,HUMAN PROBLEMS IN TECHNOLOGICAL CHANGE. ECO/UNDEV AGRI INDUS NAT/G ACT/RES LEAD GP/REL INGP/REL ROLE...INT METH 20 CASEBOOK. PAGE 147 H2947
TEC/DEV CULTURE STRUCT OP/RES

B58
CUNNINGHAM W.B.,COMPULSORY CONCILIATION AND COLLECTIVE BARGAINING. CANADA NAT/G LEGIS ADJUD CT/SYS GP/REL...MGT 20 NEW/BRUNS STRIKE CASEBOOK. PAGE 36 H0722
POLICY BARGAIN LABOR INDUS

B66
DALLIN A.,POLITICS IN THE SOVIET UNION: 7 CASES. COM USSR LAW POL/PAR CHIEF FORCES WRITING CONTROL PARL/PROC CIVMIL/REL TOTALISM...ANTHOL 20 KHRUSH/N STALIN/J CASEBOOK COM/PARTY. PAGE 37 H0736
MARXISM DOMIN ORD/FREE GOV/REL

CASSINELLI C.W. H0554,H0555

CASSIRER E. H0556,H0557

CASTBERG F. H0558

CASTE....SEE INDIA + STRATA, HINDU

CASTRO/F....FIDEL CASTRO

B63
BELFRAGE C.,THE MAN AT THE DOOR WITH THE GUN. CUBA L/A+17C NAT/G LEAD PARTIC GP/REL PWR...POLICY 20 CASTRO/F. PAGE 13 H0261 — REGION ECO/UNDEV STRUCT ATTIT

B67
PLANK J.,CUBA AND THE UNITED STATES: LONG RANGE PERSPECTIVES. CUBA L/A+17C USSR ECO/UNDEV NAT/G FORCES ECO/TAC INT/TRADE AGREE REV...PREDICT TREND ANTHOL 20 CASTRO/F COLD/WAR OAS. PAGE 126 H2520 — DIPLOM

S67
GONZALEZ M.P.,"CUBA, UNA REVOLUCION EN MARCHA." CUBA L/A+17C USA+45 VIETNAM ECO/UNDEV FORCES DIPLOM DOMIN...POLICY MARXIST NAT/COMP CASTRO/F. PAGE 58 H1163 — REV NAT/G COLONIAL SOVEREIGN

CATEGORY (AS CONCEPT)....SEE METH/CNCPT

CATH....ROMAN CATHOLIC

B04
DANTE ALIGHIERI,DE MONARCHIA (CA .1310). CHRIST-17C ITALY DOMIN LEGIT ATTIT PWR...CATH CONCPT TIME/SEQ. PAGE 37 H0741 — SECT NAT/G SOVEREIGN

B17
DE MAISTRE J.,DU PAPE (1817). FRANCE LAW SOCIETY SECT DOMIN REV HAPPINESS PWR SOVEREIGN 18/19 PROTESTANT. PAGE 38 H0761 — CATH CHIEF LEGIT NAT/G

B21
KREY A.C.,THE FIRST CRUSADE. CHRIST-17C SOCIETY STRATA NAT/G SECT FORCES WORKER WRITING LEAD ATTIT ...CHARTS 11 CHRISTIAN CRUSADES. PAGE 88 H1767 — WAR CATH DIPLOM PARTIC

B27
BELLOC H.,THE SERVILE STATE (1912) (3RD ED.). PRUSSIA UK CULTURE STRATA INDUS NAT/G ECO/TAC CONTROL LEAD SUFF DISCRIM EQUILIB ORD/FREE WEALTH 20. PAGE 13 H0269 — WORKER CAP/ISM DOMIN CATH

B27
JOHN OF SALISBURY,THE STATESMAN'S BOOK (1159) (TRANS. BY J. DICKINSON). DOMIN GP/REL MORAL ORD/FREE PWR CONSERVE...CATH CONCPT 12. PAGE 81 H1617 — NAT/G SECT CHIEF LAW

B28
MARSILIUS/PADUA,DEFENSOR PACIS (1324). CHRIST-17C CONSTN NAT/G DIPLOM DOMIN LEGIT CONTROL WAR PEACE ORD/FREE SOVEREIGN POPULISM 14 POPE. PAGE 103 H2059 — CATH SECT GEN/LAWS

B35
AQUINAS T.,ON THE GOVERNANCE OF RULERS (1265-66). UNIV SOCIETY STRATA FAM HABITAT PERSON ALL/VALS PWR SOVEREIGN CONSERVE...POLICY BIBLE. PAGE 8 H0155 — CATH NAT/G CHIEF SUPEGO

B44
SUAREZ F.,A TREATISE ON LAWS AND GOD THE LAWGIVER (1612) IN SELECTIONS FROM THREE WORKS, VOL. II. FRANCE ITALY UK CULTURE NAT/G SECT CHIEF LEGIS DOMIN LEGIT CT/SYS ORD/FREE PWR WORSHIP 16/17. PAGE 150 H3004 — LAW JURID GEN/LAWS CATH

C44
SUAREZ F.,"ON WAR" (1621) IN SELECTIONS FROM THREE WORKS, VOL. I." NAT/G SECT CHIEF DIPLOM LEGIT MORAL PWR...POLICY INT/LAW 17. PAGE 150 H3005 — WAR REV ORD/FREE CATH

S48
ALMOND G.A.,"THE CHRISTIAN PARTIES OF WESTEN EUROPE." EUR+WWI NAT/G EDU/PROP LEGIT TOTALISM ORD/FREE PWR MARXISM...TREND CHARTS STERTYP GEN/LAWS COLD/WAR 20. PAGE 5 H0110 — POL/PAR CATH SOCISM

B63
LERNER R.,MEDIEVAL POLITICAL PHILOSOPHY. ISLAM MORAL PWR CATHISM...CATH CONCPT OBS IDEA/COMP ANTHOL 9/15 JEWS CHRISTIAN BACON/R AQUINAS/T. PAGE 95 H1890 — KNOWL PHIL/SCI

B66
LAVEN P.,RENAISSANCE ITALY: 1464-1534. ITALY AGRI EXTR/IND FINAN MUNIC INT/TRADE DRIVE...CATH GEOG CHARTS BIBLIOG/A 15. PAGE 92 H1841 — CULTURE HUM TEC/DEV KNOWL

B67
MCLAUGHLIN M.R.,RELIGIOUS EDUCATION AND THE STATE: DEMOCRACY FINDS A WAY. CANADA EUR+WWI GP/REL POPULISM...CATH NAT/COMP 20 AUSTRAL. PAGE 107 H2141 — SECT NAT/G EDU/PROP POLICY

B67
POGANY A.H.,POLITICAL SCIENCE AND INTERNATIONAL RELATIONS, BOOKS RECOMMENDED FOR AMERICAN CATHOLIC COLLEGE LIBRARIES. INT/ORG LOC/G NAT/G FORCES BAL/PWR ECO/TAC NUC/PWR...CATH INT/LAW TREATY 20. PAGE 127 H2532 — BIBLIOG DIPLOM

CATHERINE R. H0559

CATHISM....ROMAN CATHOLICISM

N19
COUTROT A.,THE FIGHT OVER THE 1959 PRIVATE EDUCATION LAW IN FRANCE (PAMPHLET). FRANCE NAT/G SECT GIVE EDU/PROP GP/REL ATTIT RIGID/FLEX ORD/FREE 20 CHURCH/STA. PAGE 34 H0681 — SCHOOL PARL/PROC CATHISM LAW

N19
WEBB L.C.,CHURCH AND STATE IN ITALY: 1947-1957 (PAMPHLET). GERMANY ITALY CONSTN POL/PAR AGREE CONTROL PARTIC CHOOSE ATTIT ORD/FREE FASCISM MARXISM 20 CHURCH/STA MARITAIN/J SALO. PAGE 166 H3316 — SECT CATHISM NAT/G GP/REL

B32
MARRARO H.R.,AMERICAN OPINION ON THE UNIFICATION OF ITALY. ITALY FORCES DIPLOM SOVEREIGN CATHISM CONSERVE...CONCPT NAT/COMP BIBLIOG 19. PAGE 103 H2056 — ORD/FREE NAT/LISM REV CONSTN

B32
THIBAUDET A.,LES IDEES POLITIQUES DE LA FRANCE. FRANCE NAT/G SECT PRESS REV NAT/LISM PEACE ATTIT ...PSY 19/20 JACOBINISM JAURES/JL. PAGE 154 H3070 — IDEA/COMP ALL/IDEOS CATHISM

C36
MAZZINI J.,"FROM THE COUNCIL TO GOD" (1870) IN J. MAZZINI, ESSAYS." ITALY NAT/G EDU/PROP PARTIC ORD/FREE PWR SOVEREIGN 19 POPE CHRISTIAN DEITY. PAGE 106 H2112 — CATHISM DOMIN NAT/LISM SUPEGO

B39
MARITAIN J.,SCHOLASTICISM AND POLITICS. CONSTN SOCIETY NAT/G INGP/REL PERSON CATHISM POPULISM 19/20 FREUD/S SCHOLASTIC CHURCH/STA CHRISTIAN. PAGE 103 H2050 — SECT GEN/LAWS ORD/FREE

B39
OAKESHOTT M.,THE SOCIAL AND POLITICAL DOCTRINES OF CONTEMPORARY EUROPE. EUR+WWI RATIONAL CATHISM FASCISM MARXISM POPULISM...POLICY ANTHOL 20 NAZI. PAGE 120 H2392 — IDEA/COMP GOV/COMP ALL/IDEOS NAT/G

B40
THE GUIDE TO CATHOLIC LITERATURE, 1888-1940. ALL/VALS...POLICY MYSTIC HUM PHIL/SCI 19/20. PAGE 2 H0032 — BIBLIOG/A CATHISM DIPLOM CULTURE

B40
HOBBES T.,BEHEMOTH (1668). UK CONSTN SECT DOMIN LEGIT UTIL ORD/FREE CATHISM...POLICY CONCPT GEN/LAWS 17 CHARLES/I CROMWELL/O PROTESTANT. PAGE 71 H1433 — REV NAT/G CHIEF

B43
MC DOWELL R.B.,IRISH PUBLIC OPINION, 1750-1800. IRELAND CONSTN VOL/ASSN WORKER ORD/FREE CATHISM CONSERVE...POLICY IDEA/COMP BIBLIOG 18/ PARLIAMENT. PAGE 106 H2118 — ATTIT NAT/G DIPLOM REV

B47
BOWEN R.H.,GERMAN THEORIES OF THE CORPORATIVE STATE, WITH SPECIAL REFERENCES TO THE PERIOD 1870-1919. GERMANY INDUS LG/CO CATHISM SOCISM...SOC 18/20. PAGE 19 H0389 — IDEA/COMP CENTRAL NAT/G POLICY

B48
EDUARDO O.D.C.,THE NEGRO IN NORTHERN BRAZIL: A STUDY IN ACCULTURATION. BRAZIL ECO/UNDEV FAM SECT PAY REGION HABITAT CATHISM MYSTISM...GEOG OBS SOC/INTEG WORSHIP 20 NEGRO MARANHAO. PAGE 44 H0890 — CULTURE ADJUST GP/REL

B49
HAUSER R.,AUTORITAT UND MACHT. SOCIETY SECT PWR CATHISM...JURID CONCPT 16/20 PROTESTANT LUTHER/M CALVIN/J CHURCH/STA. PAGE 68 H1360 — SOVEREIGN NAT/G LEGIT

B49
HOLLERAN M.P.,CHURCH AND STATE IN GUATEMALA. GUATEMALA LAW STRUCT CATHISM...SOC SOC/INTEG 17/20 CHURCH/STA. PAGE 73 H1456 — SECT NAT/G GP/REL CULTURE

B51
BISSAINTHE M.,DICTIONNAIRE DE BIBLIOGRAPHIE HAITIENNE. HAITI ELITES AGRI LEGIS DIPLOM INT/TRADE WRITING ORD/FREE CATHISM...ART/METH GEOG 19/20 NEGRO TREATY. PAGE 17 H0347 — BIBLIOG L/A+17C SOCIETY NAT/G

B55
FRANZ G.,KULTURKAMPF. AUSTRIA GERMANY PRUSSIA SWITZERLND POL/PAR DIPLOM GP/REL ATTIT ORD/FREE 18/19 CHURCH/STA. PAGE 53 H1053 — NAT/LISM CATHISM NAT/G REV

B55
MID-EUROPEAN LAW PROJECT,CHURCH AND STATE BEHIND THE IRON CURTAIN. COM CZECHOSLVK HUNGARY POLAND USSR CULTURE SECT EDU/PROP GOV/REL CATHISM...CHARTS ANTHOL BIBLIOG WORSHIP 20 CHURCH/STA. PAGE 110 H2202 — LAW MARXISM POLICY

B56
MYERS F.M.,THE WARFARE OF DEMOCRATIC IDEALS. SECT — POPULISM

KNOWL MORAL CATHISM...TRADIT CONCPT 20. PAGE 115 H2302
CHOOSE REPRESENT PERCEPT

B58
BUISSON L.,POTESTAS UND CARITAS. FRANCE GERMANY UK ORD/FREE...JURID IDEA/COMP NAT/COMP 12/16 POPE CHURCH/STA. PAGE 23 H0467
GP/REL PWR CATHISM NAT/G

B58
FLORES X.,LA TRADICION CATOLICA Y EL FUTURO POLITICO DE ESPANA (PAMPHLET). SPAIN NAT/G ACT/RES LEAD GP/REL CATHISM 20 CHRISTIAN CHURCH/STA. PAGE 52 H1031
SECT POL/PAR ATTIT ORD/FREE

B58
PAYNO M.,LA REFORMA SOCIAL EN ESPANA Y MEXICO. SPAIN ECO/TAC TAX LOBBY COERCE REV OWN CATHISM 19/20 MEXIC/AMER. PAGE 124 H2479
SECT NAT/G LAW ELITES

B59
EAENZA L.,COMMUNISMO E CATTOLICESIMO IN UNA PARROCHIA DI CAMPAGNA. ITALY CULTURE ELITES ECO/DEV AGRI KIN POL/PAR DOMIN LEGIT RIGID/FLEX...DECISION OBS IDEA/COMP 20 COM/PARTY CHURCH/STA. PAGE 44 H0878
ATTIT CATHISM NEIGH MARXISM

B59
MAIER H.,REVOLUTION UND KIRCHE. FRANCE MOD/EUR SECT REV ORD/FREE...IDEA/COMP 18/19. PAGE 101 H2018
NAT/G CATHISM ATTIT POL/PAR

B60
JEMOLO A.C.,CHURCH AND STATE IN ITALY 1850-1950 (TRANS. BY DAVID MOORE). ITALY CONSTN STRATA WAR FASCISM SOCISM...TIME/SEQ 19/20 CHURCH/STA CHRIS/DEM. PAGE 80 H1599
GP/REL NAT/G CATHISM POL/PAR

B61
RAHNER H.,KIRCHE UND STAAT IM FRUHEN CHRISTENTUM. INGP/REL ORD/FREE PWR CATHISM...JURID 1/9 CHURCH/STA CHRISTIAN. PAGE 129 H2582
NAT/G SECT ATTIT GP/REL

B62
SCHMIDT-VOLKMAR E.,DER KULTURKAMPF IN DEUTSCHLAND 1871-1890. GERMANY PRUSSIA SOCIETY STRUCT SECT DIPLOM GP/REL NAT/LISM 19 CHURCH/STA BISMARCK/O. PAGE 139 H2789
POL/PAR CATHISM ATTIT NAT/G

B62
THIERRY S.S.,LE VATICAN SECRET. CHRIST-17C EUR+WWI MOD/EUR VATICAN NAT/G SECT DELIB/GP DOMIN LEGIT SOVEREIGN. PAGE 154 H3072
ADMIN EX/STRUC CATHISM DECISION

B62
TYSKEVIC S.,DIE EINHEIT DER KIRCHE UND BYZANZ (TRANS. BY F.K. LIESNER). ROMAN/EMP ADJUD GP/REL 1/17 CHRISTIAN BYZANTINE. PAGE 157 H3144
SECT NAT/G CATHISM ATTIT

B63
BIALEK R.W.,CATHOLIC POLITICS: A HISTORY BASED ON ECUADOR. ECUADOR SPAIN CULTURE STRUCT CONTROL REV PWR...BIBLIOG WORSHIP 18/20. PAGE 16 H0329
COLONIAL CATHISM GOV/REL HABITAT

B63
FRITZ H.E.,THE MOVEMENT FOR INDIAN ASSIMILATION, 1860-1890. SECT FORCES GP/REL RACE/REL DISCRIM FEDERAL CATHISM...BIBLIOG 19 INDIAN/AM PROTESTANT GRANT/US. PAGE 54 H1071
CULTURE NAT/G ECO/TAC ATTIT

B63
LERNER R.,MEDIEVAL POLITICAL PHILOSOPHY. ISLAM MORAL PWR CATHISM...CATH CONCPT OBS IDEA/COMP ANTHOL 9/15 JEWS CHRISTIAN BACON/R AQUINAS/T. PAGE 95 H1890
KNOWL PHIL/SCI

B63
LOOMIE A.J.,THE SPANISH ELIZABETHANS: THE ENGLISH EXILES AT THE COURT OF PHILIP II. SPAIN UK WAR INGP/REL DRIVE HABITAT CATHISM...BIOG 16/17 MIGRATION. PAGE 98 H1962
NAT/G STRANGE POLICY DIPLOM

B64
FREISEN J.,STAAT UND KATHOLISCHE KIRCHE IN DEN DEUTSCHEN BUNDESSTAATEN (2 VOLS.). GERMANY LAW FAM NAT/G EDU/PROP GP/REL MARRIAGE WEALTH 19/20 CHURCH/STA. PAGE 53 H1056
SECT CATHISM JURID PROVS

B64
HELMREICH E.,A FREE CHURCH IN A FREE STATE? FRANCE GERMANY ITALY SECT LEAD PWR CATHISM...POLICY ANTHOL WORSHIP 19/20 CHURCH/STA. PAGE 69 H1389
GP/REL NAT/G

B64
MORRIS J.,THE PRESENCE OF SPAIN. SPAIN MUNIC NAT/G FORCES ATTIT CATHISM...AUD/VIS 16/20. PAGE 113 H2263
CULTURE HABITAT SOCIETY GEOG

B65
APPLEMAN P.,THE SILENT EXPLOSION. WOR+45 ECO/DEV ECO/UNDEV PLAN HEALTH ALL/IDEOS CATHISM...POLICY STAT RECORD GP/COMP IDEA/COMP NAT/COMP 20 BIRTH/CON COM/PARTY. PAGE 7 H0148
GEOG CENSUS AGRI BIO/SOC

B65
CHARNAY J.P.,LE SUFFRAGE POLITIQUE EN FRANCE; ELECTIONS PARLEMENTAIRES, ELECTION PRESIDENTIELLE, REFERENDUMS. FRANCE CONSTN CHIEF DELIB/GP ECO/TAC EDU/PROP CRIME INGP/REL MORAL ORD/FREE PWR CATHISM 20 PARLIAMENT PRESIDENT. PAGE 29 H0584
CHOOSE SUFF NAT/G LEGIS

B65
COSTA H DE L.A.,THE BACKGROUND OF NATIONALISM AND OTHER ESSAYS. ASIA PHILIPPINE ATTIT PERCEPT CATHISM ...ANTHOL 20. PAGE 34 H0674
NAT/LISM CULTURE ANOMIE NAT/G

B65
KAAS L.,DIE GEISTLICHE GERICHTSBARKEIT DER KATHOLISCHEN KIRCHE IN PREUSSEN (2 VOLS.). PRUSSIA CONSTN NAT/G PROVS SECT ADJUD ADMIN ATTIT 16/20. PAGE 82 H1647
JURID CATHISM GP/REL CT/SYS

B65
O'CONNELL M.R.,IRISH POLITICS AND SOCIAL CONFLICT IN THE AGE OF THE AMERICAN REVOLUTION. FRANCE IRELAND MOD/EUR STRATA SECT LEGIS DIPLOM INT/TRADE DOMIN REV WAR...BIBLIOG 18 PARLIAMENT. PAGE 119 H2387
CATHISM ATTIT NAT/G DELIB/GP

B65
SALVADORI M.,ITALY. AUSTRIA FRANCE GERMANY ITALY SPAIN CULTURE NAT/G POL/PAR DIPLOM WAR FASCISM LAISSEZ MARXISM...TIME/SEQ CHARTS BIBLIOG/A. PAGE 137 H2744
NAT/LISM CATHISM SOCIETY

B66
FORD P.,CARDINAL MORAN AND THE A. L. P. NAT/G POL/PAR SECT DELIB/GP LOBBY REV CHOOSE ORD/FREE MARXISM 19/20 AUSTRAL PROTESTANT LABOR/PAR. PAGE 52 H1035
CATHISM SOCISM LABOR SOCIETY

B67
BROMKE A.,POLAND'S POLITICS: IDEALISM VS. REALISM. COM GERMANY POLAND RUSSIA USSR POL/PAR CATHISM ...BIBLIOG 19/20. PAGE 21 H0431
NAT/G DIPLOM MARXISM

B67
PIKE F.B.,FREEDOM AND REFORM IN LATIN AMERICA. BRAZIL URUGUAY CONSTN CULTURE SECT DIPLOM EDU/PROP PARTIC DRIVE ALL/VALS CATHISM...GEOG ANTHOL BIBLIOG REFORMERS BOLIV. PAGE 126 H2511
L/A+17C ORD/FREE ECO/UNDEV REV

L67
LARKIN E.,"ECONOMIC GROWTH, CAPITAL INVESTMENT, AND THE ROMAN CATHOLIC CHURCH IN NINETEENTH-CENTURY IRELAND." IRELAND AGRI DIST/IND NAT/G GIVE OWN CATHISM...CHARTS 19. PAGE 91 H1823
FINAN SECT WEALTH ECO/UNDEV

S67
BURGHART A.,"CATHOLIC SOCIAL THOUGHT IN AUSTRIA." AUSTRIA EUR+WWI NAT/G PAY PERS/REL OWN MARXISM SOCISM...SOC 20. PAGE 24 H0482
CATHISM ATTIT TREND SOCIETY

S67
RAMA C.M.,"PASADO Y PRESENTE DE LA RELIGION EN AMERICA LATINA." L/A+17C ELITES SOCIETY STRATA MARXISM...STAT WORSHIP PROTESTANT. PAGE 129 H2585
SECT CATHISM STRUCT NAT/COMP

B75
NEWMAN J.H.,A LETTER ADDRESSED TO THE DUKE OF NORFOLK ON THE OCCASION OF MR. GLADSTONE'S RECENT EXPOSTULATION. NAT/G SECT CHIEF LEGIS CONTROL LEAD GP/REL SUPEGO SOC/INTEG WORSHIP 19 ENGLAND. PAGE 117 H2346
POLICY DOMIN SOVEREIGN CATHISM

CATHOLICISM....SEE CATH, CATHISM

CATTELL D.T. H0560,H0561,H0562

CAUCUS....SEE PARL/PROC

CAUTE D. H0563,H0564

CED....COMMITTEE FOR ECONOMIC DEVELOPMENT

CEFKIN J.L. H0565

CENSORSHIP....SEE EDU/PROP

CENSUS....POPULATION ENUMERATION

B08
THE GOVERNMENT OF SOUTH AFRICA (VOL. II). SOUTH/AFR STRATA EXTR/IND EX/STRUC TOP/EX BUDGET ADJUD ADMIN CT/SYS PRODUC...CORREL CENSUS 19 RAILROAD CIVIL/SERV POSTAL/SYS. PAGE 2 H0030
CONSTN FINAN LEGIS NAT/G

B28
BUELL R.,THE NATIVE PROBLEM IN AFRICA. KIN LABOR LOC/G ECO/TAC ROUTINE ORD/FREE...REC/INT KNO/TEST CENSUS TREND CHARTS SOC/EXP STERTYP 20. PAGE 23 H0466
AFR CULTURE

B31
HENNIG P.,GEOPOLITIK (2ND ED.). CULTURE MUNIC COLONIAL...CENSUS CHARTS 20. PAGE 70 H1398
GEOG HABITAT CREATE NEIGH

S31
HEINBERG J.G.,"THE PERSONNEL OF FRENCH CABINETS, 1871-1930." FRANCE STRATA CHIEF CHOOSE REPRESENT MAJORITY...STAT QU CENSUS TREND CHARTS PERS/COMP 19/20 CHAMBR/DEP. PAGE 69 H1386
ELITES NAT/G DELIB/GP TOP/EX

S42
TISDALE H.,"THE PROCESS OF URBANIZATION" (BMR)" UNIV CULTURE...CENSUS GEN/LAWS. PAGE 155 H3106
MUNIC GEOG CONCPT TEC/DEV

B45
LASKER B.,ASIA ON THE MOVE. ASIA BURMA S/ASIA THAILAND USSR ECO/UNDEV FAM KIN WAR NAT/LISM ATTIT ...GEOG CENSUS TREND AUSTRAL 20. PAGE 91 H1826
CULTURE RIGID/FLEX

B49
UNSTEAD J.F.,A WORLD SURVEY FROM THE HUMAN ASPECT. AGRI INDUS...SOC CENSUS CHARTS 20 MAPS MIGRATION. PAGE 159 H3172
CULTURE HABITAT GEOG ATTIT

B50
CANTRIL H.,TENSIONS THAT CAUSE WAR. UNIV CULTURE R+D CREATE EDU/PROP DRIVE PERSON KNOWL ORD/FREE ...HUM PSY SOC OBS CENSUS TREND CON/ANAL SOC/EXP SIMUL GEN/METH ANTHOL COLD/WAR TOT/POP. PAGE 26 H0523
SOCIETY PHIL/SCI PEACE

B52
LEBON J.H.C.,AN INTRODUCTION TO HUMAN GEOGRAPHY. CULTURE...GEOG SOC CONCPT CENSUS CHARTS 20 MIGRATION. PAGE 93 H1849
HABITAT GP/REL SOCIETY

B54
WILLIAMSON H.F.,ECONOMIC DEVELOPMENT - PRINCIPLES AND PATTERNS. INDIA KOREA CULTURE ECO/DEV ECO/UNDEV TEC/DEV...CENSUS NAT/COMP 20 CHINJAP MEXIC/AMER RESOURCE/N. PAGE 168 H3369
ECO/TAC GEOG LABOR

B55
APTER D.E.,THE GOLD COAST IN TRANSITION. FUT CONSTN CULTURE SOCIETY ECO/UNDEV FAM KIN LOC/G NAT/G POL/PAR LEGIS TOP/EX EDU/PROP LEGIT ADMIN ATTIT PERSON PWR...CONCPT STAT INT CENSUS TOT/POP VAL/FREE. PAGE 7 H0149
AFR SOVEREIGN

B55
UN ECONOMIC AND SOCIAL COUNCIL,ANALYTICAL BIBLIOGRAPHY OF INTERNATIONAL MIGRATION STATISTICS, SELECTED COUNTRIES, 1925-1950. STRATA...CLASSIF CENSUS NAT/COMP 20. PAGE 158 H3156
BIBLIOG STAT GEOG HABITAT

B58
INTERNATIONAL ECONOMIC ASSN,ECONOMICS OF INTERNATIONAL MIGRATION. WOR+45 WOR-45 ECO/UNDEV FINAN NAT/G REGION...NAT/COMP METH 20. PAGE 78 H1556
CENSUS GEOG DIPLOM ECO/TAC

B60
GONZALEZ NAVARRO M.,LA COLONIZACION EN MEXICO, 1877-1910. AGRI NAT/G PLAN PROB/SOLV INCOME ...POLICY JURID CENSUS 19/20 MEXIC/AMER MIGRATION. PAGE 58 H1164
ECO/UNDEV GEOG HABITAT COLONIAL

B60
MC CLELLAN G.S.,INDIA. CHINA/COM INDIA CONSTN ELITES STRATA AGRI POL/PAR FOR/AID ARMS/CONT REV MARXISM...CENSUS BIBLIOG 20 COLD/WAR GANDHI/M NEHRU/J. PAGE 106 H2117
DIPLOM NAT/G SOCIETY ECO/UNDEV

B60
THE ECONOMIST (LONDON),THE COMMONWEALTH AND EUROPE. EUR+WWI WOR+45 AGRI FINAN INCOME...STAT CENSUS CHARTS CMN/WLTH EEC. PAGE 153 H3067
INT/TRADE INDUS INT/ORG NAT/COMP

B60
VON KOENIGSWALD H.,SIE SUCHEN ZUFLUCHT. GERMANY/E NAT/G PLAN ECO/TAC SOCISM...GEOG CENSUS 20 BERLIN. PAGE 164 H3273
GP/REL COERCE DOMIN PERSON

B60
WILLIAMS L.E.,OVERSEAS CHINESE NATIONALISM: THE GENESIS OF THE PAN-CHINESE MOVEMENT IN INDONESIA, 1900-1916. ASIA COM INDONESIA AGRI INT/ORG LOC/G DIPLOM EDU/PROP HABITAT PWR POPULISM...GEOG LING CENSUS 20. PAGE 168 H3367
NAT/LISM GP/REL DECISION NAT/G

L60
WHEELER G.,"RACIAL PROBLEMS IN SOVIET MUSLIM ASIA." COM CULTURE SOCIETY NEIGH SECT DOMIN EDU/PROP DISCRIM DISPL DRIVE PWR SOVEREIGN...CENSUS SAMP TREND 20 MUSLIM. PAGE 167 H3340
PERSON ATTIT USSR RACE/REL

S60
BANFIELD E.C.,"THE POLITICAL IMPLICATIONS OF METROPOLITAN GROWTH" (BMR)" UK USA+45 LOC/G PROB/SOLV ADMIN GP/REL...METH/COMP NAT/COMP 20. PAGE 10 H0209
TASK MUNIC GOV/COMP CENSUS

S60
COOK R.C.,"THE WORLD'S GREAT CITIES: EVOLUTION OR DEVOLUTION?" WOR+45 WOR-45 ECO/DEV ECO/UNDEV ACT/RES PROB/SOLV...GEOG TREND CHARTS NAT/COMP BIBLIOG 20. PAGE 33 H0658
MUNIC HABITAT PLAN CENSUS

B61
SCHNAPPER B.,LA POLITIQUE ET LE COMMERCE FRANCAIS DANS LE GOLFE DE GUINEE DE 1838 A 1871. FRANCE GUINEA UK SEA EXTR/IND NAT/G DELIB/GP LEGIS ADMIN ORD/FREE...POLICY GEOG CENSUS CHARTS BIBLIOG 19. PAGE 139 H2791
COLONIAL INT/TRADE DOMIN AFR

B62
SCHECHTMAN J.B.,POSTWAR POPULATION TRANSFERS IN EUROPE: 1945-1955. COM CZECHOSLVK GERMANY POLAND USSR CULTURE SOCIETY PROB/SOLV AGREE NAT/LISM...SOC STAT TREND CHARTS METH/COMP 20 MIGRATION. PAGE 139 H2778
GEOG CENSUS EUR+WWI HABITAT

B63
GEERTZ C.,PEDDLERS AND PRINCES: SOCIAL DEVELOPMENT AND ECONOMIC CHANGE IN TWO INDONESIAN TOWNS. S/ASIA CULTURE SOCIETY STRATA FACE/GP MUNIC CREATE TEC/DEV ECO/TAC ORD/FREE WEALTH...OBS INT CENSUS CHARTS WORK TOT/POP VAL/FREE 20. PAGE 55 H1106
ECO/UNDEV SOC ELITES INDONESIA

B63
LEVIN M.G.,ETHNIC ORIGINS OF THE PEOPLES OF NORTHEASTERN ASIA. CONSTN LEGIS...STAT CENSUS CHARTS 20 TEXAS MAPS. PAGE 95 H1901
HEREDITY HABITAT CULTURE GEOG

B63
VON DER MEHDEN F.R.,RELIGION AND NATIONALISM IN SOUTHEAST ASIA. BURMA PHILIPPINE S/ASIA INTELL SOCIETY DOMIN EDU/PROP LEGIT ATTIT MORAL ORD/FREE ...SOC CENSUS HIST/WRIT TOT/POP VAL/FREE 20 WORSHIP LONDON. PAGE 163 H3265
SECT CULTURE NAT/LISM

S63
ROBINSON W.C.,"URBANIZATION AND FERTILITY: THE NON-WESTERN EXPERIENCE (BMR)" DEATH MARRIAGE AGE/C BIO/SOC...STAT CENSUS CON/ANAL CHARTS NAT/COMP 20 THIRD/WRLD. PAGE 133 H2651
GEOG MUNIC FAM ECO/UNDEV

B64
WRIGHT G.,RURAL REVOLUTION IN FRANCE: THE PEASANTRY IN THE TWENTIETH CENTURY. EUR+WWI MOD/EUR LAW CULTURE AGRI POL/PAR DELIB/GP LEGIS ECO/TAC EDU/PROP COERCE CHOOSE ATTIT RIGID/FLEX HEALTH ...STAT CENSUS CHARTS VAL/FREE 20. PAGE 171 H3419
PWR STRATA FRANCE REV

B64
WRIGHT Q.,A STUDY OF WAR. LAW NAT/G PROB/SOLV BAL/PWR NAT/LISM PEACE ATTIT SOVEREIGN...CENSUS SOC/INTEG. PAGE 171 H3421
WAR CONCPT DIPLOM CONTROL

B64
ZARTMAN I.W.,MOROCCO: PROBLEMS OF NEW POWER. ISLAM CULTURE ECO/UNDEV AGRI POL/PAR SCHOOL FORCES ADMIN ...CONCPT STAT INT CENSUS TIME/SEQ CHARTS WORK VAL/FREE 20. PAGE 172 H3449
CHOOSE MOROCCO DELIB/GP DECISION

B65
APPLEMAN P.,THE SILENT EXPLOSION. WOR+45 ECO/DEV ECO/UNDEV PLAN HEALTH ALL/IDEOS CATHISM...POLICY STAT RECORD GP/COMP IDEA/COMP NAT/COMP 20 BIRTH/CON COM/PARTY. PAGE 7 H0148
GEOG CENSUS AGRI BIO/SOC

B65
HAVIGHURST R.J.,SOCIETY AND EDUCATION IN BRAZIL. BRAZIL PORTUGAL ECO/UNDEV INDUS NAT/G CREATE INSPECT COLONIAL ADJUST DEMAND LITERACY...CENSUS TREND CHARTS 16/20. PAGE 68 H1362
SCHOOL ACADEM ACT/RES CULTURE

B65
HLA MYINT U.,THE ECONOMICS OF THE DEVELOPING COUNTRIES. USA+45 WOR+45 AGRI FINAN NAT/G INT/TRADE ...CLASSIF CENSUS TREND NAT/COMP SIMUL GEN/LAWS. PAGE 71 H1430
ECO/UNDEV FOR/AID GEOG

B65
WINT G.,ASIA: A HANDBOOK. ASIA COM INDIA USSR CULTURE INTELL NAT/G...GEOG STAT CENSUS NAT/COMP WORSHIP 20 TREATY CHINJAP. PAGE 169 H3387
DIPLOM SOC

B66
MILONE P.D.,URBAN AREAS IN INDONESIA. INDONESIA LABOR NAT/G COLONIAL GP/REL...CENSUS CHARTS 17/20. PAGE 111 H2218
MUNIC GEOG STRUCT SOCIETY

B66
ODEGARD P.H.,POLITICAL POWER AND SOCIAL CHANGE. UNIV NAT/G CREATE ALL/IDEOS...POLICY GEOG SOC CENSUS TREND. PAGE 120 H2394
PWR TEC/DEV IDEA/COMP

B66
THOMPSON J.H.,MODERNIZATION OF THE ARAB WORLD. FUT ISRAEL STRUCT ECO/UNDEV DIPLOM INGP/REL ATTIT ...CENSUS ANTHOL 20 ARABS. PAGE 154 H3082
ADJUST ISLAM PROB/SOLV NAT/COMP

B66
UN ECONOMIC AND SOCIAL COUNCIL,WORLD POPULATION PROSPECTS AS ASSESSED IN 1963. FUT WOR+45 DEATH AGE ...TREND CHARTS UN. PAGE 158 H3157
PREDICT CENSUS GEOG NAT/COMP

S66
"FURTHER READING." INDIA LOC/G NAT/G PLAN ADMIN WEALTH...GEOG SOC CONCPT CENSUS 20. PAGE 2 H0049
BIBLIOG ECO/UNDEV TEC/DEV PROVS

B67
RAE D.,THE POLITICAL CONSEQUENCES OF ELECTORAL LAWS. EUR+WWI ICELAND ISRAEL NEW/ZEALND UK USA+45 ADJUD APPORT GP/REL MAJORITY...MATH STAT CENSUS CHARTS BIBLIOG 20 AUSTRAL. PAGE 129 H2579
POL/PAR CHOOSE NAT/COMP REPRESENT

B67
ROWLAND J.,A HISTORY OF SINO-INDIAN RELATIONS; HOSTILE CO-EXISTENCE. ASIA CHINA/COM INDIA NAT/G NUC/PWR PWR WEALTH...GEOG BIBLIOG 13/20 COLD/WAR. PAGE 135 H2704
DIPLOM CENSUS IDEA/COMP

S67
CRITTENDEN J.,"DIMENSIONS OF MODERNIZATION IN THE AMERICAN STATES." USA+45 STRUCT MUNIC PROB/SOLV
PROVS GOV/COMP

CONTROL LITERACY HABITAT...CONCPT METH/CNCPT CORREL STAT
CONT/OBS CENSUS 20. PAGE 35 H0702 ECO/DEV

S67
SHARKANSKY I.,"ECONOMIC AND POLITICAL CORRELATES OF PROVS
STATE GOVERNMENT EXPENDITURE: GENERAL TENDENCIES BUDGET
AND DEVIANT CASES." USA+45 LOC/G NAT/G TAX GIVE GOV/COMP
INCOME...CENSUS CHARTS. PAGE 142 H2845

S67
SUBRAMANIAM V.,"REPRESENTATIVE BUREAUCRACY: A STRATA
REASSESSMENT." USA+45 ELITES LOC/G NAT/G ADMIN GP/REL
GOV/REL PRIVIL DRIVE ROLE...POLICY CENSUS 20 MGT
CIVIL/SERV BUREAUCRCY. PAGE 150 H3006 GOV/COMP

B86
MAS LATRIE L.,RELATIONS ET COMMERCE DE L'AFRIQUE ISLAM
SEPTENTRIONALE OU MAGREB AVEC LES NATIONS SECT
CHRETIENNES AU MOYEN AGE. CULTURE CHIEF FORCES WAR DIPLOM
...SOC CENSUS TREATY 10/16. PAGE 104 H2084 INT/TRADE

B99
DU BOIS W.E.B.,THE PHILADELPHIA NEGRO: A SOCIAL INGP/REL
STUDY. CULTURE STRATA KIN CRIME SUFF ADJUST DISCRIM RACE/REL
ISOLAT HABITAT HEREDITY ALL/VALS SOC/INTEG 17/19 SOC
NEGRO PHILADELPH. PAGE 42 H0851 CENSUS

CENTER/PAR....CENTER PARTY (ALL NATIONS)

CENTO....CENTRAL TREATY ORGANIZATION

S61
VALLET R.,"IRAN: KEY TO THE MIDDLE EAST." COM IRAQ NAT/G
ISLAM KUWAIT LEBANON SAUDI/ARAB TURKEY ELITES ECO/UNDEV
SOCIETY INDUS PROC/MFG POL/PAR TOP/EX PLAN BAL/PWR IRAN
DIPLOM ECO/TAC ALL/VALS...TREND CENTO 20. PAGE 161
H3224

CENTRAL AFRICAN REPUBLIC....SEE CENTRL/AFR

CENTRAL TREATY ORGANIZATION....SEE CENTO

CENTRAL....CENTRALIZATION

B15
MICHELS R.,POLITICAL PARTIES. NAT/G BAL/PWR CHOOSE POL/PAR
REPRESENT ATTIT SOCISM...PSY SOC CONCPT OBS 20 CENTRAL
MONOPOLY. PAGE 110 H2198 LEAD
PWR

N19
ANDERSON J.,THE ORGANIZATION OF ECONOMIC STUDIES IN ECO/TAC
RELATION TO THE PROBLEMS OF GOVERNMENT (PAMPHLET). ACT/RES
UK FINAN INDUS DELIB/GP PLAN PROB/SOLV ADMIN 20. NAT/G
PAGE 6 H0128 CENTRAL

B22
KRABBE H.,THE MODERN IDEA OF THE STATE. LAW CHIEF SOVEREIGN
DIPLOM DOMIN ADMIN REPRESENT CENTRAL ORD/FREE CONSTN
...NEW/IDEA GOV/COMP IDEA/COMP. PAGE 88 H1761 PHIL/SCI

B27
CHILDS J.B.,AN ACCOUNT OF GOVERNMENT DOCUMENT BIBLIOG/A
BIBLIOGRAPHY IN THE UNITED STATES AND ELSEWHERE (A CON/ANAL
PAPER). LOC/G PRESS CENTRAL KNOWL...METH 19/20 NAT/G
LEAGUE/NAT. PAGE 29 H0590

B27
WILLOUGHBY W.F.,PRINCIPLES OF PUBLIC ADMINISTRATION NAT/G
WITH SPECIAL REFERENCE TO THE NATIONAL AND STATE EX/STRUC
GOVERNMENTS OF THE UNITED STATES. FINAN PROVS CHIEF OP/RES
CONSULT LEGIS CREATE BUDGET EXEC ROUTINE GOV/REL ADMIN
CENTRAL...MGT 20 BUR/BUDGET CONGRESS PRESIDENT.
PAGE 169 H3373

B39
ANDERSON W.,LOCAL GOVERNMENT IN EUROPE. FRANCE GOV/COMP
GERMANY ITALY UK USSR MUNIC PROVS ADMIN GOV/REL NAT/COMP
CENTRAL SOVEREIGN 20. PAGE 7 H0136 LOC/G
CONSTN

S39
HECKSCHER G.,"GROUP ORGANIZATION IN SWEDEN." SWEDEN LAISSEZ
STRATA ECO/DEV AGRI INDUS LABOR NAT/G PROF/ORG SOC
ECO/TAC CENTRAL SOCISM...MGT 19/20. PAGE 69 H1382

C39
REISCHAUER R.,"JAPAN'S GOVERNMENT--POLITICS." NAT/G
CONSTN STRATA POL/PAR FORCES LEGIS DIPLOM ADMIN S/ASIA
EXEC CENTRAL...POLICY BIBLIOG 20 CHINJAP. PAGE 131 CONCPT
H2610 ROUTINE

B41
COHEN E.W.,THE GROWTH OF THE BRITISH CIVIL SERVICE OP/RES
1780-1939. UK NAT/G SENIOR ROUTINE GOV/REL...MGT TIME/SEQ
METH/COMP BIBLIOG 18/20. PAGE 31 H0616 CENTRAL
ADMIN

B44
KOHN H.,THE IDEA OF NATIONALISM. UNIV SOCIETY KIN NAT/LISM
CREATE REGION CENTRAL SOVEREIGN. PAGE 87 H1740 CONCPT
NAT/G
GP/REL

B47
BOWEN R.H.,GERMAN THEORIES OF THE CORPORATIVE IDEA/COMP
STATE, WITH SPECIAL REFERENCES TO THE PERIOD CENTRAL
1870-1919. GERMANY INDUS LG/CO CATHISM SOCISM...SOC NAT/G
18/20. PAGE 19 H0389 POLICY

B48
ROSSITER C.L.,CONSTITUTIONAL DICTATORSHIP; CRISIS NAT/G
GOVERNMENT IN THE MODERN DEMOCRACIES. FRANCE AUTHORIT
GERMANY UK USA-45 WOR-45 EX/STRUC BAL/PWR CONTROL CONSTN
COERCE WAR CENTRAL ORD/FREE...DECISION 19/20. TOTALISM
PAGE 134 H2688

B48
TOWSTER J.,POLITICAL POWER IN THE USSR: 1917-1947. EX/STRUC
USSR CONSTN CULTURE ELITES CREATE PLAN COERCE NAT/G
CENTRAL ATTIT RIGID/FLEX ORD/FREE...BIBLIOG MARXISM
SOC/INTEG 20 LENIN/VI STALIN/J. PAGE 156 H3122 PWR

C51
HAMMOND M.,"CITY-STATE AND WORLD STATE." CONSTN NAT/G
INTELL LOC/G LEGIT CENTRAL RATIONAL BIBLIOG. ATTIT
PAGE 65 H1308 REGION
MEDIT-7

B53
LIEBER F.,CIVIL LIBERTY AND SELF GOVERNMENT: VOLUME ORD/FREE
2. NAT/G CONTROL CHOOSE PERSON PWR 19 CIVIL/LIB. SOVEREIGN
PAGE 96 H1925 CENTRAL
CONCPT

C53
DORWART R.A.,"THE ADMINISTRATIVE REFORMS OF ADMIN
FREDRICK WILLIAM I OF PRUSSIA. GERMANY MOD/EUR NAT/G
CHIEF CONTROL PWR...BIBLIOG 16/18. PAGE 42 H0839 CENTRAL
GOV/REL

B54
FRIEDMAN W.,THE PUBLIC CORPORATION: A COMPARATIVE LAW
SYMPOSIUM (UNIVERSITY OF TORONTO SCHOOL OF LAW SOCISM
COMPARATIVE LAW SERIES, VOL. I). SWEDEN USA+45 LG/CO
INDUS INT/ORG NAT/G REGION CENTRAL FEDERAL...POLICY OWN
JURID IDEA/COMP NAT/COMP ANTHOL 20 COMMONWLTH
MONOPOLY EUROPE. PAGE 53 H1065

C54
HAMMER E.J.,"THE STRUGGLE FOR INDOCHINA." COM WAR
VIETNAM POL/PAR REV CENTRAL NAT/LISM ATTIT...POLICY COLONIAL
CHARTS BIBLIOG 20. PAGE 65 H1305 S/ASIA
NAT/G

B57
LONG H.A.,USURPERS - FOES OF FREE MAN. LAW NAT/G CT/SYS
CHIEF LEGIS DOMIN ADJUD REPRESENT GOV/REL ORD/FREE CENTRAL
LAISSEZ POPULISM...POLICY 18/20 SUPREME/CT FEDERAL
ROOSEVLT/F CONGRESS CON/INTERP. PAGE 98 H1961 CONSTN

S57
LEWIS E.G.,"PARLIAMENTARY CONTROL OF NATIONALIZED PWR
INDUSTRY IN FRANCE." FRANCE NAT/G DELIB/GP ACT/RES LEGIS
PLAN PROB/SOLV ECO/TAC DOMIN CENTRAL. PAGE 96 H1914 INDUS
CONTROL

B60
PRASAD B.,THE ORIGINS OF PROVINCIAL AUTONOMY. INDIA CENTRAL
UK FINAN LOC/G FORCES LEGIS CONTROL CT/SYS PWR PROVS
...JURID 19/20. PAGE 128 H2554 COLONIAL
NAT/G

C60
HAZARD J.N.,"SETTLING DISPUTES IN SOVIET SOCIETY: ADJUD
THE FORMATIVE YEARS OF LEGAL INSTITUTIONS." USSR LAW
NAT/G PROF/ORG PROB/SOLV CONTROL CT/SYS ROUTINE REV COM
CENTRAL...JURID BIBLIOG 20. PAGE 68 H1372 POLICY

B61
AIYAR S.P.,FEDERALISM AND SOCIAL CHANGE. CANADA FEDERAL
CULTURE STRUCT PLAN PROB/SOLV TEC/DEV ECO/TAC NAT/G
ORD/FREE...TIME/SEQ 18/20 AUSTRAL. PAGE 4 H0085 CENTRAL
GOV/COMP

B62
BINDER L.,IRAN: POLITICAL DEVELOPMENT IN A CHANGING LEGIT
SOCIETY. IRAN OP/RES REV GP/REL CENTRAL RATIONAL NAT/G
PWR...PHIL/SCI NAT/COMP GEN/LAWS 20. PAGE 17 H0337 ADMIN
STRUCT

S62
LEGUM C.,"THE DANGERS OF INDEPENDENCE" AFR UGANDA ORD/FREE
NAT/G DIPLOM DOMIN REGION CENTRAL ATTIT POPULISM SOVEREIGN
20. PAGE 93 H1862 NAT/LISM
GOV/COMP

B63
FAWCETT J.E.S.,THE BRITISH COMMONWEALTH IN INT/LAW
INTERNATIONAL LAW. LAW INT/ORG NAT/G VOL/ASSN STRUCT
OP/RES DIPLOM ADJUD CENTRAL CONSEN...NET/THEORY COLONIAL
CMN/WLTH TREATY. PAGE 49 H0977

B63
JACOB H.,GERMAN ADMINISTRATION SINCE BISMARCK: ADMIN
CENTRAL AUTHORITY VERSUS LOCAL AUTONOMY. GERMANY NAT/G
GERMANY/W LAW POL/PAR CONTROL CENTRAL TOTALISM LOC/G
FASCISM...MAJORIT DECISION STAT CHARTS GOV/COMP POLICY
19/20 BISMARCK/O HITLER/A WEIMAR/REP. PAGE 79 H1577

B64
COONDOO R.,THE DIVISION OF POWERS IN THE INDIAN CONSTN
CONSTITUTION. INDIA ECO/UNDEV FINAN TEC/DEV WAR LEGIS
CENTRAL EFFICIENCY NAT/LISM PWR WEALTH NEW/LIB WELF/ST
...BIBLIOG 18/20. PAGE 33 H0659 GOV/COMP

B64
HALE O.J.,THE CAPTIVE PRESS IN THE THIRD REICH. COM/IND
GERMANY CULTURE LG/CO NAT/G POL/PAR PLAN DOMIN TASK PRESS
CENTRAL OWN TOTALISM PWR...BIBLIOG 20 HITLER/A NAZI CONTROL

AMMAN/MAX. PAGE 64 H1283 FASCISM

B64
RIES J.C.,THE MANAGEMENT OF DEFENSE: ORGANIZATION AND CONTROL OF THE US ARMED SERVICES. PROF/ORG DELIB/GP EX/STRUC LEGIS GOV/REL PERS/REL CENTRAL RATIONAL PWR...POLICY TREND GOV/COMP BIBLIOG. PAGE 131 H2626 FORCES ACT/RES DECISION CONTROL

B65
BETTISON D.G.,THE PAPUA-GUINEA ELECTIONS 1964. S/ASIA CONSTN POL/PAR EDU/PROP PARTIC SUFF CENTRAL CONSEN...OBS CHARTS BIBLIOG 20. PAGE 16 H0324 NAT/G LEGIS CHOOSE REPRESENT

B65
BOISSEVAIN J.,SAINTS AND FIREWORKS: RELIGION AND POLITICS IN RURAL MALTA. MALTA STRUCT FAM NEIGH POL/PAR REPRESENT INGP/REL CENTRAL...CHARTS BIBLIOG 20. PAGE 18 H0368 GP/REL NAT/G SECT MUNIC

B65
BRASS P.R.,FACTIONAL POLITICS IN AN INDIAN STATE: THE CONGRESS PARTY IN UTTAR PRADESH. INDIA UK CONSTN CULTURE ECO/UNDEV LOC/G DOMIN COLONIAL CROWD GP/REL ADJUST CENTRAL RIGID/FLEX SOVEREIGN 20 UTTAR/PRAD CONGRESS/P. PAGE 20 H0406 POL/PAR PROVS LEGIS CHOOSE

B65
CHANDA A.,FEDERALISM IN INDIA. INDIA UK ELITES FINAN NAT/G POL/PAR EX/STRUC LEGIS DIPLOM TAX GOV/REL POPULISM...POLICY 20. PAGE 28 H0572 CONSTN CENTRAL FEDERAL

B65
HERRICK B.H.,URBAN MIGRATION AND ECONOMIC DEVELOPMENT IN CHILE. CHILE AGRI INDUS LABOR NAT/G CENTRAL PRODUC...STAT SAMP CHARTS BIBLIOG/A 20 MIGRATION. PAGE 70 H1404 HABITAT GEOG MUNIC ECO/UNDEV

B65
PARRIS H.W.,GOVERNMENT AND THE RAILWAYS IN NINETEENTH-CENTURY BRITAIN. UK DELIB/GP CONTROL LEAD CENTRAL 19 RAILROAD. PAGE 124 H2470 DIST/IND NAT/G PLAN GP/REL

B65
ULLMANN W.,A HISTORY OF POLITICAL THOUGHT: THE MIDDLE AGES. CHRIST-17C LOC/G NAT/G CENTRAL PWR ...PHIL/SCI LOG BIBLIOG 6/15. PAGE 158 H3153 IDEA/COMP SOVEREIGN SECT LAW

S65
HAYTER T.,"FRENCH AID TO AFRICA* ITS SCOPE AND ACHIEVEMENTS." CULTURE ECO/TAC INT/TRADE ADMIN REGION CENTRAL FEDERAL LOVE PWR SOVEREIGN EEC. PAGE 68 H1370 AFR FRANCE FOR/AID COLONIAL

S65
LEVI W.,"THE CONCEPT OF INTEGRATION IN RESEARCH ON PEACE." NAT/G VOL/ASSN DIPLOM TASK ADJUST NAT/LISM PEACE DRIVE LOVE...PSY NET/THEORY GEN/LAWS. PAGE 95 H1897 CONCPT IDEA/COMP INT/ORG CENTRAL

S65
TENDLER J.D.,"TECHNOLOGY AND ECONOMIC DEVELOPMENT* THE CASE OF HYDRO VS THERMAL POWER." CONSTRUC DIST/IND CREATE TEC/DEV INT/TRADE CENTRAL PWR SKILL WEALTH...MGT NAT/COMP ARGEN. PAGE 153 H3061 BRAZIL INDUS ECO/UNDEV

S65
WHITE J.,"WEST GERMAN AID TO DEVELOPING COUNTRIES." INT/ORG OP/RES GIVE CENTRAL ATTIT DRIVE...STAT NAT/COMP COLD/WAR. PAGE 167 H3348 GERMANY FOR/AID ECO/UNDEV CAP/ISM

B66
AIYAR S.P.,PERSPECTIVES ON THE WELFARE STATE. INDIA S/ASIA UK CONSTN ECO/UNDEV NAT/G INGP/REL CENTRAL NAT/LISM ATTIT...CONCPT ANTHOL BIBLIOG 20. PAGE 4 H0087 NEW/LIB WELF/ST IDEA/COMP ADJUST

B66
LONDON K.,EASTERN EUROPE IN TRANSITION. CHINA/COM USSR DOMIN COLONIAL CENTRAL RIGID/FLEX PWR...SOC ANTHOL 20. PAGE 98 H1958 SOVEREIGN COM NAT/LISM DIPLOM

B66
ZOLBERG A.R.,CREATING POLITICAL ORDER. AFR CONGO/BRAZ GHANA NIGER KIN NAT/G DOMIN COLONIAL REGION CENTRAL NAT/LISM ATTIT PWR 20 CONGO/LEOP. PAGE 173 H3462 SOVEREIGN ORD/FREE CONSTN POL/PAR

S66
FELD W.,"NATIONAL ECONOMIC INTEREST GROUPS AND POLICY FORMATION IN THE EEC." NAT/G POL/PAR REGION CENTRAL SOVEREIGN...INT NET/THEORY EEC. PAGE 49 H0985 LOBBY ELITES DECISION

B67
PLANCK C.R.,THE CHANGING STATUS OF GERMAN REUNIFICATION IN WESTERN DIPLOMACY, 1955-1966. GERMANY DELIB/GP PLAN PEACE...TREND 20 KENNEDY/JF DEGAULLE/C. PAGE 126 H2519 NAT/G DIPLOM CENTRAL

B67
TREADGOLD D.W.,SOVIET AND CHINESE COMMUNISM* SIMILARITIES AND DIFFERENCES. CHINA/COM COM NAT/G PLAN DIPLOM CENTRAL PWR MARXISM...POLICY 20. PAGE 156 H3128 CULTURE NAT/LISM

B67
VALI F.A.,THE QUEST FOR A UNITED GERMANY. GERMANY PROB/SOLV DIPLOM ADJUST...BIBLIOG 20. PAGE 161 H3222 NAT/G ATTIT PLAN CENTRAL

B67
ZALESKI E.,PLANNING REFORMS IN THE SOVIET UNION 1962-1966. COM USSR NAT/G CONFER CONTROL EFFICIENCY MARXISM...POLICY DECISION 20. PAGE 172 H3446 ECO/DEV PLAN ADMIN CENTRAL

L67
"A PROPOS DES INCITATIONS FINANCIERES AUX GROUPEMENTS DES COMMUNES: ESSAI D'INTERPRETATION." FRANCE NAT/G LEGIS ADMIN GOV/REL CENTRAL 20. PAGE 3 H0051 LOC/G ECO/TAC APPORT ADJUD

S67
COLLINS B.A.,"SOME NOTES ON PUBLIC SERVICE COMMISSIONS IN THE COMMONWEALTH CARIBBEAN." JAMAICA L/A+17C TRINIDAD UK NAT/G OP/RES DOMIN SENIOR COLONIAL CONTROL INGP/REL CENTRAL EFFICIENCY PWR ...DECISION 20. PAGE 31 H0631 ADMIN EX/STRUC ECO/UNDEV CHOOSE

S67
DIAMANT A.,"EUROPEAN MODELS OF BUREAUCRACY AND DEVELOPMENT." EX/STRUC PLAN ADMIN CONTROL ROUTINE GOV/REL CENTRAL...DECISION TIME/SEQ CHARTS. PAGE 41 H0818 NAT/G EQUILIB ACT/RES NAT/COMP

S67
HANSON A.H.,"INDIA AFTER THE ELECTIONS." INDIA ECO/UNDEV LEGIS TEC/DEV FOR/AID GP/REL FEDERAL ATTIT 20. PAGE 66 H1321 NAT/G POL/PAR REGION CENTRAL

S67
HOFMANN W.,"THE PUBLIC INTEREST PRESSURE GROUP: THE CASE OF THE DEUTSCHE STADTETAG." GERMANY GERMANY/W CONSTN STRUCT NAT/G CENTRAL FEDERAL PWR...TIME/SEQ 20. PAGE 72 H1447 LOC/G VOL/ASSN LOBBY ADMIN

S67
KROLL M.,"POLITICAL LEADERSHIP AND ADMINISTRATIVE COMMUNICATIONS IN NEW NATION STATES* CASE STUDY OF TRINIDAD AND TOBAGO." L/A+17C TRINIDAD INTELL OP/RES DOMIN COLONIAL LEAD GP/REL CENTRAL EFFICIENCY...DECISION OBS METH/COMP 20. PAGE 89 H1774 NAT/G ADMIN EDU/PROP CONTROL

S67
LEVCIK B.,"WAGES AND EMPLOYMENT PROBLEMS IN THE NEW SYSTEM OF PLANNED MANAGEMENT IN CZECHOSLOVAKIA." CZECHOSLVK EUR+WWI NAT/G OP/RES PLAN ADMIN ROUTINE INGP/REL CENTRAL EFFICIENCY PRODUC DECISION. PAGE 95 H1895 MARXISM WORKER MGT PAY

S67
MANGLAPUS R.S.,"ASIAN REVOLUTION AND AMERICAN IDEOLOGY." USA+45 SOCIETY CAP/ISM DIPLOM ADJUST CENTRAL...NAT/COMP 20. PAGE 102 H2035 REV POPULISM ATTIT ASIA

S67
STRAFFORD P.,"FRENCH ELECTIONS." FRANCE NAT/G CHIEF LEGIS BAL/PWR ECO/TAC PARL/PROC PARTIC ATTIT 20. PAGE 150 H2993 POL/PAR SOCISM CENTRAL MARXISM

B90
TAINE H.A.,MODERN REGIME (2 VOLS.). FRANCE FAM REV CENTRAL MARRIAGE PWR...TREND 19 NAPOLEON/B. PAGE 152 H3037 STRUCT NAT/G OLD/LIB MORAL

CENTRAL AFRICAN ARCHIVES H0566

CENTRAL ASIAN RESEARCH CENTRE H0567

CENTRAL GAZETTEERS UNIT H0568

CENTRAL/AM....CENTRAL AMERICA

B32
CHILDS J.B.,THE MEMORIAS OF THE REPUBLICS OF CENTRAL AMERICA AND OF THE ANTILLES. L/A+17C 19/20 CENTRAL/AM. PAGE 29 H0592 BIBLIOG GOV/REL NAT/G EX/STRUC

B52
TAX S.,HERITAGE OF CONQUEST. L/A+17C ECO/UNDEV LOC/G WEALTH...POLICY ANTHOL WORSHIP 20 MEXIC/AMER CENTRAL/AM. PAGE 153 H3052 PHIL/SCI CULTURE SOCIETY

B59
MARTZ J.D.,CENTRAL AMERICA: THE CRISIS AND THE CHALLENGE. L/A+17C POL/PAR CHIEF CHOOSE SOVEREIGN ...BIOG TREND BIBLIOG 20 CENTRAL/AM. PAGE 104 H2071 NAT/G GOV/REL DIPLOM GOV/COMP

B62
ESCUELA SUPERIOR DE ADMIN PUBL,INFORME DEL SEMINARIO SOBRE SERVICIO CIVIL O CARRERA ADMINISTRATIVA. L/A+17C ELITES STRATA CONFER CONTROL GOV/REL INGP/REL SUPEGO 20 CENTRAL/AM CIVIL/SERV. PAGE 47 H0939 ADMIN NAT/G PROB/SOLV ATTIT

S63
LAMBERT D.,"LA TRANSPOSITION DU REGIME PRESIDENTIEL HORS DES ETATSUNIS; LE CAS DE L'AMERIQUE LATINE." NAT/G EX/STRUC LEGIS PARL/PROC PWR 18/20 PRESIDENT CENTRAL/AM SOUTH/AMER. PAGE 90 H1800 DELIB/GP CHIEF L/A+17C GOV/REL

B64
MUSEUM FUR VOLKERKUNDE WIEN,ZENTRALAMERIKA MEXIKO SOCIETY

VOLKER UND KULTUREN. COSTA/RICA GUATEMALA L/A+17C PANAMA SECT WAR GP/REL SOVEREIGN...ART/METH 20 CENTRAL/AM MEXIC/AMER. PAGE 115 H2300 — STRUCT CULTURE AGRI

CENTRL/AFR....CENTRAL AFRICAN REPUBLIC

B58
CARTER G.M.,TRANSITION IN AFRICA; STUDIES IN POLITICAL ADAPTATION. AFR CENTRL/AFR GHANA NIGERIA CONSTN LOC/G POL/PAR ADMIN GP/REL FEDERAL...MAJORIT BIBLIOG 20. PAGE 27 H0543 — NAT/COMP PWR CONTROL NAT/G

B59
KITTLER G.D.,EQUATORIAL AFRICA: THE NEW WORLD OF TOMORROW. CENTRL/AFR INDUS KIN SECT CHIEF EDU/PROP CHOOSE HEALTH...GEOG WORSHIP 20. PAGE 87 H1730 — RACE/REL AFR ECO/UNDEV CULTURE

B62
GREEN L.P.,DEVELOPMENT IN AFRICA. AFR CENTRL/AFR GHANA RHODESIA SOUTH/AFR AGRI PROC/MFG INT/TRADE DEMAND NAT/LISM PRODUC WEALTH...GEOG METH/CNCPT CHARTS BIBLIOG 20. PAGE 60 H1206 — CULTURE ECO/UNDEV GOV/REL TREND

B66
KEITH G.,THE FADING COLOUR BAR. AFR CENTRL/AFR UK ZAMBIA CULTURE SCHOOL EDU/PROP PERS/REL DISCRIM AGE ...AUD/VIS NAT/COMP SOC/INTEG 20 NEGRO. PAGE 84 H1682 — RACE/REL STRUCT ATTIT NAT/G

CEPEDA U.A. H0569

CERMAK/AJ....ANTON J. CERMAK

CEWA....CEWA (AFRICAN TRIBE)

CEYLON....CEYLON

N
US LIBRARY OF CONGRESS,SOUTHERN ASIA ACCESSIONS LIST. BURMA CEYLON INDIA NEPAL PAKISTAN S/ASIA THAILAND AGRI INDUS SCHOOL WORKER...ART/METH GEOG HEAL PHIL/SCI LING 20. PAGE 160 H3201 — BIBLIOG/A SOCIETY CULTURE ECO/UNDEV

B51
JENNINGS I.,THE COMMONWEALTH IN ASIA. CEYLON INDIA PAKISTAN CULTURE STRATA NAT/G LEGIS DIPLOM COLONIAL ATTIT...DECISION 20 CMN/WLTH. PAGE 80 H1604 — CONSTN INT/ORG POLICY PLAN

B51
JENNINGS S.I.,THE COMMONWEALTH IN ASIA. CEYLON INDIA PAKISTAN S/ASIA UK CONSTN CULTURE SOCIETY STRATA STRUCT NAT/G POL/PAR EDU/PROP LEAD WAR 20 CMN/WLTH. PAGE 80 H1608 — NAT/LISM REGION COLONIAL DIPLOM

B55
UN ECONOMIC COMN ASIA & FAR E,ECONOMIC SURVEY OF ASIA AND THE FAR EAST, 1954. AFGHANISTN CEYLON INDIA PHILIPPINE S/ASIA ECO/DEV FINAN INDUS INT/TRADE PRODUC WEALTH...STAT CHARTS 20 CHINJAP. PAGE 158 H3158 — ECO/UNDEV PRICE NAT/COMP ASIA

B56
JENNINGS W.I.,THE APPROACH TO SELF-GOVERNMENT. CEYLON INDIA PAKISTAN S/ASIA UK SOCIETY POL/PAR DELIB/GP LEGIS ECO/TAC EDU/PROP ADMIN EXEC CHOOSE ATTIT ALL/VALS...JURID CONCPT GEN/METH TOT/POP 20. PAGE 81 H1610 — NAT/G CONSTN COLONIAL

B57
WILSON P.,SOUTH ASIA; A SELECTED BIBLIOGRAPHY ON INDIA, PAKISTAN, CEYLON (PAMPHLET). CEYLON INDIA PAKISTAN LAW ECO/UNDEV PLAN DIPLOM 20. PAGE 169 H3381 — BIBLIOG S/ASIA CULTURE NAT/G

B59
VITTACHIT,EMERGENCY '58. CEYLON UK STRUCT NAT/G FORCES ADJUD CRIME REV NAT/LISM 20. PAGE 163 H3258 — RACE/REL DISCRIM DIPLOM SOVEREIGN

B60
JEFFRIES C.,TRANSFER OF POWER: PROBLEMS OF THE PASSAGE TO SELFGOVERNMENT. CEYLON GHANA MALAYSIA NIGERIA UK INT/ORG CONSULT DELIB/GP LEGIS DIPLOM CONFER PARL/PROC 20. PAGE 80 H1595 — SOVEREIGN COLONIAL ORD/FREE NAT/G

B60
SALETORE B.A.,INDIA'S DIPLOMATIC RELATIONS WITH THE EAST. ASIA CEYLON INDIA NEPAL S/ASIA CULTURE 7/14 PERSIA. PAGE 137 H2740 — DIPLOM NAT/COMP ETIQUET

B60
WOLF C.,FOREIGN AID: THEORY AND PRACTICE IN SOUTHERN ASIA. CEYLON INDONESIA PHILIPPINE S/ASIA CULTURE STRATA ECO/UNDEV PLAN EDU/PROP ATTIT ...METH/CNCPT MATH QUANT STAT CONT/OBS TIME/SEQ SIMUL TOT/POP 20. PAGE 170 H3396 — ACT/RES ECO/TAC FOR/AID

C60
WRIGGINS W.H.,"CEYLON: DILEMMAS OF A NEW NATION." ASIA CEYLON CONSTN STRUCT POL/PAR SECT FORCES DIPLOM GOV/REL NAT/LISM...CHARTS BIBLIOG 20. PAGE 171 H3417 — PROB/SOLV NAT/G ECO/UNDEV

B63
FARMER B.H.,CEYLON: A DIVIDED NATION. CEYLON INDIA NETHERLAND PORTUGAL UK ELITES POL/PAR COLONIAL ...SOC MYTH CHARTS GOV/COMP WORSHIP 20. PAGE 49 H0972 — DOMIN ORD/FREE ECO/UNDEV POLICY

B63
WEINER M.,POLITICAL CHANGE IN SOUTH ASIA. CEYLON INDIA PAKISTAN S/ASIA CULTURE ELITES ECO/UNDEV EX/STRUC ADMIN CONTROL CHOOSE CONSERVE...GOV/COMP ANTHOL 20. PAGE 166 H3328 — NAT/G CONSTN TEC/DEV

S63
HARRIS R.L.,"A COMPARATIVE ANALYSIS OF THE ADMINISTRATIVE SYSTEMS OF CANADA AND CEYLON." S/ASIA CULTURE SOCIETY STRATA TOP/EX ACT/RES DOMIN EDU/PROP LEGIT COERCE ATTIT SUPEGO ALL/VALS...MGT CHARTS GEN/LAWS VAL/FREE 20. PAGE 67 H1343 — DELIB/GP EX/STRUC CANADA CEYLON

B64
ARASARATNAM S.,CEYLON. CEYLON NETHERLAND PORTUGAL S/ASIA UK STRUCT ECO/UNDEV SECT DIPLOM DOMIN RACE/REL NAT/LISM 17/20 CMN/WLTH. PAGE 8 H0156 — COLONIAL NAT/G PROB/SOLV CULTURE

B64
RAGHAVAN M.D.,INDIA IN CEYLONESE HISTORY, SOCIETY AND CULTURE. CEYLON INDIA S/ASIA LAW SOCIETY INT/TRADE ATTIT...ART/METH JURID SOC LING 20. PAGE 129 H2581 — DIPLOM CULTURE SECT STRUCT

B64
SINGER M.R.,THE EMERGING ELITE: A STUDY OF POLITICAL LEADERSHIP IN CEYLON. S/ASIA ECO/UNDEV AGRI KIN NAT/G SECT EX/STRUC LEGIT ATTIT PWR RESPECT...SOC STAT CHARTS 20. PAGE 144 H2883 — TOP/EX STRATA NAT/LISM CEYLON

B64
TINKER H.,BALLOT BOX AND BAYONET - PEOPLE AND GOVERNMENT IN EMERGENT ASIAN COUNTRIES. CEYLON INDIA INDONESIA PHILIPPINE POL/PAR ADMIN COLONIAL LEAD PARL/PROC CHOOSE CONSEN ORD/FREE SOVEREIGN PLURISM...GOV/COMP THIRD/WRLD. PAGE 155 H3104 — MYTH S/ASIA NAT/COMP NAT/LISM

B64
WILCOX W.A.,INDIA, PAKISTAN AND THE RISE OF CHINA. ASIA BURMA CEYLON CHINA/COM INDIA PAKISTAN S/ASIA NAT/G VOL/ASSN FORCES TOP/EX ACT/RES DOMIN REGION RIGID/FLEX ORD/FREE...POLICY GEN/LAWS COLD/WAR 20. PAGE 168 H3362 — CULTURE ATTIT DIPLOM

B65
ONSLOW C.,ASIAN ECONOMIC DEVELOPMENT. BURMA CEYLON INDIA MALAYSIA PAKISTAN S/ASIA AGRI INDUS MARKET PROB/SOLV CAP/ISM FOR/AID INT/TRADE DEMAND WEALTH ...POLICY ANTHOL 20. PAGE 121 H2418 — ECO/UNDEV ECO/TAC PLAN NAT/G

B66
BRAIBANTI R.,ASIAN BUREAUCRATIC SYSTEMS EMERGENT FROM THE BRITISH IMPERIAL TRADITION. BURMA CEYLON INDIA PAKISTAN UK ELITES ECO/UNDEV NAT/G...MGT SOC CHARTS ANTHOL 19/20. PAGE 20 H0401 — GOV/COMP COLONIAL ADMIN S/ASIA

B66
SAKAI R.K.,STUDIES ON ASIA, 1966. CEYLON INDIA USA-45 INDUS POL/PAR DIPLOM ECO/TAC MARXISM ...POLICY 19/20 CHINJAP. PAGE 137 H2738 — SECT ECO/UNDEV

B66
SYMONDS R.,THE BRITISH AND THEIR SUCCESSORS. AFR CEYLON INDIA UK SCHOOL FORCES EDU/PROP ADMIN PARTIC ...NAT/COMP BIBLIOG 20 AFRICA/W AFRICA/E. PAGE 151 H3024 — NAT/G ECO/UNDEV POLICY COLONIAL

L67
TAMBIAH S.J.,"THE POLITICS OF LANGUAGE IN INDIA AND CEYLON." CEYLON INDIA NAT/G DOMIN ADMIN...SOC 20. PAGE 152 H3039 — POL/PAR LING NAT/LISM REGION

CHACO/WAR....CHACO WAR

CHAD....SEE ALSO AFR

S62
MURACCIOLE L.,"LES CONSTITUTIONS DES ETATS AFRICAINS D'EXPRESSION FRANCAISE: LA CONSTITUTION DU 16 AVRIL 1962 DE LA REPUBLIQUE DU" AFR CHAD CHIEF LEGIS LEGIT COLONIAL EXEC ROUTINE ORD/FREE SOVEREIGN...SOC CONCPT 20. PAGE 115 H2291 — NAT/G CONSTN

B64
WITHERELL J.W.,OFFICIAL PUBLICATIONS OF FRENCH EQUATORIAL AFRICA, FRENCH CAMEROONS, AND TOGO, 1946-1958 (PAMPHLET). CAMEROON CHAD FRANCE GABON TOGO LAW ECO/UNDEV EXTR/IND INT/TRADE...GEOG HEAL 20. PAGE 169 H3392 — BIBLIOG/A AFR NAT/G ADMIN

CHAKRABARTI A. H0570

CHAKRAVARTI P.C. H0571

CHAMBERS/J....JORDAN CHAMBERS

CHAMBR/DEP....CHAMBER OF DEPUTIES (FRANCE)

S31
HEINBERG J.G.,"THE PERSONNEL OF FRENCH CABINETS, 1871-1930." FRANCE STRATA CHIEF CHOOSE REPRESENT MAJORITY...STAT QU CENSUS TREND CHARTS PERS/COMP 19/20 CHAMBR/DEP. PAGE 69 H1386 — ELITES NAT/G DELIB/GP TOP/EX

CHAMBRLN/J....JOSEPH CHAMBERLAIN

CHAMBRLN/N....NEVILLE CHAMBERLAIN

B38
DAVIES E.,"NATIONAL" CAPITALISM: THE GOVERNMENT'S RECORD AS PROTECTOR OF PRIVATE MONOPOLY. UK ELITES SOCIETY STRATA POL/PAR WORKER PROB/SOLV CONTROL SOCISM 20 MONOPOLY LABOR/PAR CHAMBRLN/N. PAGE 37 H0747 — CAP/ISM NAT/G INDUS POLICY

B61
MACLEOD I.,NEVILLE CHAMBERLAIN. UK SOCIETY TOP/EX WAR PERSON ALL/VALS ORD/FREE PARLIAMENT 20 CHAMBRLN/N. PAGE 100 H2003 — BIOG NAT/G CREATE

CHANDA A. H0572

CHANDLER M.J. H0573

CHANDRA S. H0574

CHANDRASEKHAR S. H0575

CHANG H0576

CHANG H. H0577

CHANGE (AS GOAL)....SEE ORD/FREE

CHANGE (AS INNOVATION)....SEE CREATE

CHANGE (SOCIAL MOBILITY)....SEE GEOG, STRATA

CHAO K. H0578

CHAPMAN A.R. H0579

CHAPMAN B. H0580,H0581

CHAPMAN R.M. H0582

CHARACTER....SEE PERSON

CHARISMA....CHARISMA

CHARLES/I....CHARLES I OF ENGLAND

B40
HOBBES T.,BEHEMOTH (1668). UK CONSTN SECT DOMIN LEGIT UTIL ORD/FREE CATHISM...POLICY CONCPT GEN/LAWS 17 CHARLES/I CROMWELL/O PROTESTANT. PAGE 71 H1433 — REV NAT/G CHIEF

B61
AYLMER G.,THE KING'S SERVANTS. UK ELITES CHIEF PAY CT/SYS WEALTH 17 CROMWELL/O CHARLES/I. PAGE 9 H0187 — ADMIN ROUTINE EX/STRUC NAT/G

CHARMATZ J.P. H0583

CHARNAY J.P. H0584

CHARTISM....CHARTISM

CHARTS....GRAPHS, CHARTS, DIAGRAMS, MAPS

CHASE/S....STUART CHASE

CHATEAUB/F....VICOMTE FRANCOIS RENE DE CHATEAUBRIAND

CHATTANOOG....CHATTANOOGA, TENNESSEE

CHATTERJI S.K. H0585

CHECKS AND BALANCES SYSTEM....SEE BAL/PWR

CHEN N-R. H0586

CHEN T.H. H0587

CHEN/YUN....CH'EN YUN

CHENG C-Y. H0588

CHIANG....CHIANG KAI-SHEK

CHICAGO....CHICAGO, ILLINOIS

CHIEF....PRESIDENT, MONARCH, PRESIDENCY, PREMIER, CHIEF OFFICER OF ANY GOVERNMENT

N
US CONSULATE GENERAL HONG KONG,EXTRACTS FROM CHINA MAINLAND MAGAZINES. ASIA CHINA/COM ECO/UNDEV NAT/G CHIEF LEAD ATTIT...MARXIST INDEX 20. PAGE 159 H3180 — BIBLIOG MARXISM PRESS

NSY
MACKENZIE K.R.,THE ENGLISH PARLIAMENT. UK POL/PAR CHIEF DIPLOM TAX TASK WAR AUTHORIT...POLICY TREND 12/20 PARLIAMENT. PAGE 100 H2000 — ORD/FREE LEGIS NAT/G

B08
NIRRNHEIM O.,DAS ERSTE JAHR DES MINISTERIUMS BISMARCK UND DIE OEFFENTLICHE MEINUNG (HEIDELBERGER ABHANDLUNGEN, 20. HEFT). GERMANY MOD/EUR LEGIS DIPLOM EDU/PROP INGP/REL...BIOG GOV/COMP IDEA/COMP BIBLIOG 19 BISMARCK/O. PAGE 118 H2363 — CHIEF PRESS NAT/G ATTIT

B12
POLLOCK F.,THE GENIUS OF THE COMMON LAW. CHRIST-17C UK FINAN CHIEF ACT/RES ADMIN GP/REL ATTIT SOCISM ...ANARCH JURID. PAGE 127 H2537 — LAW CULTURE CREATE

B14
FIGGIS J.N.,CHURCHES IN THE MODERN STATE (2ND ED.). LAW CHIEF BAL/PWR PWR...CONCPT CHURCH/STA POPE. PAGE 50 H0998 — SECT NAT/G SOCIETY ORD/FREE

N16
MILTON J.,THE READIE AND EASY WAY TO ESTABLISH A FREE COMMONWEALTH. CONSTN LEGIS PARL/PROC CONSERVE ...MAJORIT 17. PAGE 111 H2219 — ORD/FREE NAT/G CHIEF POPULISM

B17
DE MAISTRE J.,DU PAPE (1817). FRANCE LAW SOCIETY SECT DOMIN REV HAPPINESS PWR SOVEREIGN 18/19 PROTESTANT. PAGE 38 H0761 — CATH CHIEF LEGIT NAT/G

B17
DE VICTORIA F.,DE INDIS ET DE JURE BELLI (1557) IN F. DE VICTORIA, DE INDIS ET DE JURE BELLI REFLECTIONES. UNIV NAT/G SECT CHIEF PARTIC COERCE PEACE MORAL...POLICY 16 INDIAN/AM CHRISTIAN CONSCN/OBJ. PAGE 39 H0775 — WAR INT/LAW OWN

N17
BURKE E.,THOUGHTS ON THE PROSPECT OF A REGICIDE PEACE (PAMPHLET). FRANCE UK SECT DOMIN MURDER PEACE ORD/FREE SOVEREIGN POPULISM...POLICY GOV/COMP IDEA/COMP 18 JACOBINISM COEXIST. PAGE 24 H0483 — REV CHIEF NAT/G DIPLOM

N17
BURKE E.,THOUGHTS ON THE CAUSE OF THE PRESENT DISCONTENTS (PAMPHLET). MOD/EUR UK CONSTN CHIEF LEGIS DOMIN CONTROL EXEC REPRESENT POPULISM ...TRADIT NEW/IDEA METH/COMP 18 BURKE/EDM. PAGE 24 H0484 — ORD/FREE REV PARL/PROC NAT/G

N17
BURKE E.,LETTER TO SIR HERCULES LANGRISHE (PAMPHLET). IRELAND UK NAT/G CHIEF DIPLOM DOMIN PARL/PROC COERCE ORD/FREE SOVEREIGN POPULISM ...TRADIT 18 BURKE/EDM. PAGE 24 H0485 — POLICY COLONIAL SECT

B19
ROUSSEAU J.J.,A LASTING PEACE. INT/ORG NAT/G CHIEF DIPLOM DETER WAR POLICY. PAGE 135 H2697 — PLAN PEACE UTIL

N19
HARTUNG F.,ENLIGHTENED DESPOTISM (PAMPHLET). ORD/FREE SOVEREIGN CONSERVE...PHIL/SCI FREDERICK ENLIGHTNMT. PAGE 67 H1350 — NAT/G CHIEF CONCPT PWR

N19
MAO TSE-TUNG,ON SOME IMPORTANT PROBLEMS OF THE PARTY'S PRESENT POLICY. CHINA/COM CONSTN ELITES INTELL AGRI DOMIN EDU/PROP REV REPRESENT GP/REL OWN PEACE ORD/FREE 20 COM/PARTY. PAGE 102 H2044 — POLICY NAT/G CHIEF LEGIT

N19
TREVELYAN G.M.,THE TWO-PARTY SYSTEM IN ENGLISH POLITICAL HISTORY (PAMPHLET). UK CHIEF LEGIS COLONIAL EXEC REV CHOOSE 17/19. PAGE 157 H3131 — PARL/PROC POL/PAR NAT/G PWR

S21
MALINOWSKI B.,"THE PRIMITIVE ECONOMICS OF THE TROBRIAND ISLANDERS" (BMR)" CULTURE SOCIETY NAT/G CHIEF LEAD OWN...SOC MYTH WORSHIP 20 NEW/GUINEA TROBRIAND RESOURCE/N. PAGE 101 H2029 — ECO/UNDEV AGRI PRODUC STRUCT

B22
KRABBE H.,THE MODERN IDEA OF THE STATE. LAW CHIEF DIPLOM DOMIN ADMIN REPRESENT CENTRAL ORD/FREE ...NEW/IDEA GOV/COMP IDEA/COMP. PAGE 88 H1761 — SOVEREIGN CONSTN PHIL/SCI

B22
URE P.N.,THE ORIGIN OF TYRANNY. MEDIT-7 FINAN INDUS CHIEF FORCES ECO/TAC WEALTH. PAGE 159 H3174 — AUTHORIT PWR NAT/G MARKET

B24
HOLDSWORTH W.S.,A HISTORY OF ENGLISH LAW; THE COMMON LAW AND ITS RIVALS (VOL. IV). UK SEA AGRI CHIEF ADJUD CONTROL CRIME GOV/REL...INT/LAW JURID NAT/COMP 16/17 PARLIAMENT COMMON/LAW CANON/LAW ENGLSH/LAW. PAGE 72 H1449 — LAW LEGIS CT/SYS CONSTN

B25
MAURRAS C.,ENQUETE SUR LA MONARCHIE (1909). FRANCE CONTROL REPRESENT DISCRIM HEREDITY PWR CONSERVE 20 BUREAUCRCY. PAGE 105 H2103 — TRADIT AUTHORIT NAT/G CHIEF

B26
FORTESCUE J.,THE GOVERNANCE OF ENGLAND (1471-76). UK LAW FINAN SECT LEGIS PROB/SOLV TAX DOMIN ADMIN GP/REL COST ORD/FREE PWR 14/15. PAGE 52 H1042 — CONSERVE CONSTN CHIEF

NAT/G

B27
HOCART A.M.,KINGSHIP. UNIV CULTURE EX/STRUC TRIBUTE CHIEF
ROUTINE CHOOSE ROLE SOVEREIGN RITUAL 20 KING. MYTH
PAGE 72 H1441 IDEA/COMP

B27
JOHN OF SALISBURY,THE STATESMAN'S BOOK (1159) NAT/G
(TRANS. BY J. DICKINSON). DOMIN GP/REL MORAL SECT
ORD/FREE PWR CONSERVE...CATH CONCPT 12. PAGE 81 CHIEF
H1617 LAW

B27
WILLOUGHBY W.F.,PRINCIPLES OF PUBLIC ADMINISTRATION NAT/G
WITH SPECIAL REFERENCE TO THE NATIONAL AND STATE EX/STRUC
GOVERNMENTS OF THE UNITED STATES. FINAN PROVS CHIEF OP/RES
CONSULT LEGIS CREATE BUDGET EXEC ROUTINE GOV/REL ADMIN
CENTRAL...MGT 20 BUR/BUDGET CONGRESS PRESIDENT.
PAGE 169 H3373

B28
HOBBES T.,THE ELEMENTS OF LAW, NATURAL AND POLITIC PERSON
(1650). STRATA NAT/G SECT CHIEF AGREE ATTIT LAW
ALL/VALS MORAL ORD/FREE POPULISM...POLICY CONCPT. SOVEREIGN
PAGE 71 H1432 CONSERVE

B29
LANGER W.L.,THE FRANCO-RUSSIAN ALLIANCE: 1890-1894. DIPLOM
FRANCE MOD/EUR UK USSR NAT/G CHIEF FORCES BAL/PWR
AGREE WAR PEACE PWR...TIME/SEQ TREATY 19
BISMARCK/O. PAGE 91 H1809

S31
HEINBERG J.G.,"THE PERSONNEL OF FRENCH CABINETS, ELITES
1871-1930." FRANCE STRATA CHIEF CHOOSE REPRESENT NAT/G
MAJORITY...STAT QU CENSUS TREND CHARTS PERS/COMP DELIB/GP
19/20 CHAMBR/DEP. PAGE 69 H1386 TOP/EX

B34
RIDLEY C.E.,THE CITY-MANAGER PROFESSION. CHIEF PLAN MUNIC
ADMIN CONTROL ROUTINE CHOOSE...TECHNIC CHARTS EX/STRUC
GOV/COMP BIBLIOG 20. PAGE 131 H2624 LOC/G
EXEC

B35
AQUINAS T.,ON THE GOVERNANCE OF RULERS (1265-66). CATH
UNIV SOCIETY STRATA FAM HABITAT PERSON ALL/VALS PWR NAT/G
SOVEREIGN CONSERVE...POLICY BIBLE. PAGE 8 H0155 CHIEF
SUPEGO

B35
MARRIOTT J.A.,DICTATORSHIP AND DEMOCRACY. GERMANY TOTALISM
GREECE UK CHIEF DIPLOM DOMIN LEGIT PEACE ORD/FREE POPULISM
CONSERVE...TREND ROME HITLER/A. PAGE 103 H2057 PLURIST
NAT/G

B36
LAPRADE W.T.,PUBLIC OPINION AND POLITICS IN POLICY
EIGHTEENTH CENTURY ENGLAND. UK CULTURE POL/PAR ELITES
CHIEF TOP/EX LEAD REV NAT/LISM PWR 18 PROTESTANT ATTIT
PROTESTANT CHURCH/STA. PAGE 91 H1815 TIME/SEQ

B37
CARLYLE T.,THE FRENCH REVOLUTION (2 VOLS.). FRANCE REV
CONSTN NAT/G FORCES COERCE MURDER PEACE MORAL CHIEF
POPULISM...TIME/SEQ IDEA/COMP GEN/LAWS 18. PAGE 26 TRADIT
H0532

B38
HOLDSWORTH W.S.,A HISTORY OF ENGLISH LAW; THE LAW
CENTURIES OF SETTLEMENT AND REFORM (VOL. X). INDIA LOC/G
UK CONSTN NAT/G CHIEF LEGIS ADMIN COLONIAL CT/SYS EX/STRUC
CHOOSE ORD/FREE PWR...JURID 18 PARLIAMENT ADJUD
COMMONWLTH COMMON/LAW. PAGE 72 H1451

B38
SAINT-PIERRE C.I.,SCHEME FOR LASTING PEACE (TRANS. INT/ORG
BY H. BELLOT). INDUS NAT/G CHIEF FORCES INT/TRADE PEACE
CT/SYS WAR PWR SOVEREIGN WEALTH...POLICY 18. AGREE
PAGE 137 H2732 INT/LAW

B39
FIRTH R.,PRIMITIVE POLYNESIAN ECONOMY. SOCIETY ECO/UNDEV
DIST/IND SECT CHIEF CAP/ISM PRODUC WEALTH...SOC OBS CULTURE
METH WORSHIP 20 POLYNESIA. PAGE 50 H1007 AGRI
ECO/TAC

B39
KOHN H.,REVOLUTIONS AND DICTATORSHIPS. COM EUR+WWI NAT/LISM
ISLAM MOD/EUR NAT/G CHIEF FORCES WAR CIVMIL/REL PWR TOTALISM
MARXISM 18/20. PAGE 87 H1739 REV
FASCISM

B40
BROGAN D.W.,THE DEVELOPMENT OF MODERN FRANCE MOD/EUR
(1870-1939). FRANCE GERMANY UK USSR CONSTN CHIEF NAT/G
LEGIS DIPLOM AGREE COLONIAL WAR NAT/LISM PEACE
SOCISM 19/20 TREATY. PAGE 21 H0428

B40
HOBBES T.,BEHEMOTH (1668). UK CONSTN SECT DOMIN REV
LEGIT UTIL ORD/FREE CATHISM...POLICY CONCPT NAT/G
GEN/LAWS 17 CHARLES/I CROMWELL/O PROTESTANT. CHIEF
PAGE 71 H1433

B40
KER A.M.,MEXICAN GOVERNMENT PUBLICATIONS: A GUIDE BIBLIOG
TO THE MORE IMPORTANT PUBLICATIONS OF THE NAT/G
GOVERNMENT OF MEXICO, 1821-1936. CHIEF ADJUD 19/20 EXEC
MEXIC/AMER. PAGE 85 H1693 LEGIS

B40
MCILWAIN C.H.,CONSTITUTIONALISM, ANCIENT AND CONSTN
MODERN. CHRIST-17C MOD/EUR NAT/G CHIEF PROB/SOLV GEN/LAWS
INSPECT AUTHORIT ORD/FREE PWR...TIME/SEQ ROMAN/REP. LAW
PAGE 107 H2134

B40
SIMON Y.,NATURE AND FUNCTIONS OF AUTHORITY. UNIV ORD/FREE
SOCIETY NAT/G CHIEF CONCPT. PAGE 144 H2880 DOMIN
GEN/LAWS
PERSON

B41
CHILDS J.B.,A GUIDE TO THE OFFICIAL PUBLICATIONS OF NAT/G
THE OTHER AMERICAN REPUBLICS: ARGENTINA. CHIEF EX/STRUC
DIPLOM GOV/REL...BIBLIOG 18/19 ARGEN. PAGE 30 H0594 METH/CNCPT
LEGIS

B42
FEFFERO G.,THE PRINCIPLES OF POWER (TRANS. BY T. PWR
JAECKEL). MOD/EUR CONSTN NAT/G CHIEF CONTROL REV LEGIT
WAR ORD/FREE CONSERVE FASCISM POPULISM...GEN/LAWS TRADIT
18/20 EUROPE. PAGE 49 H0980 ELITES

B42
FORTESCU J.,IN PRAISE OF ENGLISH LAW (1464) (TRANS. LAW
BY S.B. CHRIMES). UK ELITES CHIEF FORCES CT/SYS CONSTN
COERCE CRIME GOV/REL ILLEGIT...JURID GOV/COMP LEGIS
GEN/LAWS 15. PAGE 52 H1040 ORD/FREE

B42
HEGEL G.W.F.,PHILOSOPHY OF RIGHT. UNIV FAM SECT NAT/G
CHIEF AGREE WAR MARRIAGE OWN ORD/FREE...POLICY LAW
CONCPT. PAGE 69 H1383 RATIONAL

B42
LA BOETIE E.,ANTI-DICTATOR (1548) (TRANS. BY H. PWR
KUNZ). CONSTN NAT/G CHIEF DOMIN LEGIT CONTROL ORD/FREE
POPULISM. PAGE 90 H1790 TOTALISM
GEN/LAWS

B43
LENIN V.I.,LEFT WING COMMUNISM: AN INFANTILE COM
DISORDER (1920). GERMANY MOD/EUR USSR STRUCT CHIEF MARXISM
DOMIN EDU/PROP LEGIT LEAD REPRESENT POPULISM NAT/G
...METH/COMP 19 LENIN/VI COM/PARTY MENSHEVIK. REV
PAGE 94 H1879

B44
SUAREZ F.,A TREATISE ON LAWS AND GOD THE LAWGIVER LAW
(1612) IN SELECTIONS FROM THREE WORKS, VOL. II. JURID
FRANCE ITALY UK CULTURE NAT/G SECT CHIEF LEGIS GEN/LAWS
DOMIN LEGIT CT/SYS ORD/FREE PWR WORSHIP 16/17. CATH
PAGE 150 H3004

C44
SUAREZ F.,"ON WAR" (1621) IN SELECTIONS FROM THREE WAR
WORKS, VOL. I." NAT/G SECT CHIEF DIPLOM LEGIT MORAL REV
PWR...POLICY INT/LAW 17. PAGE 150 H3005 ORD/FREE
CATH

B47
MARX F.M.,THE PRESIDENT AND HIS STAFF SERVICES CONSTN
PUBLIC ADMINISTRATION SERVICES NUMBER 98 CHIEF
(PAMPHLET). FINAN ADMIN CT/SYS REPRESENT PWR 20 NAT/G
PRESIDENT. PAGE 104 H2075 EX/STRUC

B47
MCILWAIN C.H.,CONSTITUTIONALISM: ANCIENT AND CONSTN
MODERN. USA+45 ROMAN/EMP LAW CHIEF LEGIS CT/SYS NAT/G
GP/REL ORD/FREE SOVEREIGN...POLICY TIME/SEQ PARL/PROC
ROMAN/REP EUROPE. PAGE 107 H2135 GOV/COMP

B49
DE JOUVENEL B.,ON POWER: ITS NATURE AND THE HISTORY PWR
OF ITS GROWTH. SOCIETY CHIEF REV WAR ATTIT AUTHORIT NAT/G
ORD/FREE SOVEREIGN CONSERVE POPULISM CONCPT. DOMIN
PAGE 38 H0757 CONTROL

B49
DENNING A.,FREEDOM UNDER THE LAW. MOD/EUR UK LAW ORD/FREE
SOCIETY CHIEF EX/STRUC LEGIS ADJUD CT/SYS PERS/REL JURID
PERSON 17/20 ENGLSH/LAW. PAGE 40 H0793 NAT/G

L49
BRECHT A.,"THE NEW GERMAN CONSTITUTION." GERMANY/W CONSTN
NAT/G CHIEF EX/STRUC LEGIS PROB/SOLV ADMIN DIPLOM
REPRESENT TOTALISM ORD/FREE PLURISM...MAJORIT SOVEREIGN
CHARTS 20. PAGE 20 H0409 FEDERAL

L49
LOEWENSTEIN K.,"THE PRESIDENCY OUTSIDE THE UNITED CHIEF
STATES: A STUDY IN COMPARATIVE POLITICAL CONSTN
INSTITUTIONS." WOR-45 LEGIS GP/REL...POLICY 18/20. GOV/COMP
PAGE 98 H1953 NAT/G

B50
HARLEY G.W.,MASKS AS AGENTS OF SOCIAL CONTROL IN CONTROL
NORTHEAST LIBERIA. AFR LIBERIA LAW CULTURE ADJUST ECO/UNDEV
CONSEN MORAL...GEOG SOC WORSHIP 20. PAGE 66 H1332 SECT
CHIEF

B50
HOOKER R.,OF THE LAWS OF ECCLESIASTICAL POLITY SECT
(1594) (ABR. BY J. S. MARSHALL). UK UNIV CHIEF CONCPT
PARTIC MORAL...JURID GEN/LAWS WORSHIP 16. PAGE 73 LAW
H1463 NAT/G

B50
MACHIAVELLI N.,THE DISCOURSES (1516). NAT/G SECT PWR
FORCES DOMIN LEGIT CONTROL LEAD COERCE TOTALISM GEN/LAWS
ORD/FREE. PAGE 100 H1995 CHIEF

B51
MARX K.,THE EIGHTEENTH BRUMAIRE OF LOUIS BONAPARTE REV
(1852). FRANCE STRATA FINAN INDUS LABOR CHIEF MARXISM
FORCES WORKER CAP/ISM ECO/TAC PARL/PROC ORD/FREE ELITES
...MARXIST 19. PAGE 104 H2080 NAT/G

C52
FIFIELD R.H.,"WOODROW WILSON AND THE FAR EAST." BIBLIOG
ASIA CHIEF DELIB/GP BAL/PWR CONFER COLONIAL DIPLOM
ARMS/CONT WAR...TIME/SEQ NAT/COMP 19/20 WILSON/W INT/ORG
LEAGUE/NAT. PAGE 50 H0995

C52
HUME D.,"IDEA OF A PERFECT COMMONWEALTH" IN D. CONSTN
HUME, POLITICAL DISCOURSES (1752)" UK NAT/G DOMIN CHIEF
GP/REL CONSERVE...POLICY CONCPT GEN/LAWS 18 SOCIETY
MORE/THOM PLATO. PAGE 75 H1494 GOV/COMP

C53
DORWART R.A.,"THE ADMINISTRATIVE REFORMS OF ADMIN
FREDRICK WILLIAM I OF PRUSSIA. GERMANY MOD/EUR NAT/G
CHIEF CONTROL PWR...BIBLIOG 16/18. PAGE 42 H0839 CENTRAL
GOV/REL

B54
CAMPANELLA T.,A DISCOURSE TOUCHING THE SPANISH CONSERVE
MONARCHY... (1640). SPAIN UNIV SEA STRATA FINAN CHIEF
SECT FORCES SUPEGO LOVE ORD/FREE...CONCPT 17. NAT/G
PAGE 26 H0514 DIPLOM

B54
JENNINGS I.,THE QUEEN'S GOVERNMENT. UK POL/PAR NAT/G
DELIB/GP ADJUD ADMIN CT/SYS PARL/PROC REPRESENT CONSTN
CONSERVE 13/20 PARLIAMENT. PAGE 80 H1605 LEGIS
CHIEF

B54
MITCHELL P.,AFRICAN AFTERTHOUGHTS. UGANDA CONSTN BIOG
NAT/G ADJUD COERCE WAR 20 WWI MAU/MAU. PAGE 112 CHIEF
H2230 COLONIAL
DOMIN

B55
ALFIERI D.,DICTATORS FACE TO FACE. NAT/G TOP/EX WAR
DIPLOM EXEC COERCE ORD/FREE FASCISM...POLICY OBS 20 CHIEF
HITLER/A MUSSOLIN/B. PAGE 5 H0103 TOTALISM
PERS/REL

B55
CRAIG G.A.,THE POLITICS OF THE PRUSSIAN ARMY FORCES
1640-1945. CHRIST-17C EUR+WWI MOD/EUR PRUSSIA NAT/G
STRUCT DIPLOM ADMIN REV WAR...SOC BIBLIOG 17/20. ROLE
PAGE 35 H0694 CHIEF

B55
SVARLIEN O.,AN INTRODUCTION TO THE LAW OF NATIONS. INT/LAW
SEA AIR INT/ORG NAT/G CHIEF ADMIN AGREE WAR PRIVIL DIPLOM
ORD/FREE SOVEREIGN...BIBLIOG 16/20. PAGE 151 H3012

S55
DE SMITH S.A.,"CONSTITUTIONAL MONARCHY IN NAT/G
BURGANDA." AFR UGANDA UK STRUCT CHIEF REGION DIPLOM
INGP/REL ADJUST NAT/LISM SOVEREIGN CONSERVE CONSTN
...POLICY 19/20 BURGANDA. PAGE 38 H0769 COLONIAL

B56
CEPEDA U.A.,EN TORNO AL CONCEPTO DEL ESTADO EN LOS NAT/G
REYES CATHOLICOS. SPAIN SOCIETY STRUCT SECT LEGIT PHIL/SCI
WAR ATTIT WORSHIP 15/17. PAGE 28 H0569 CHIEF
PWR

B56
RIESENBERG P.N.,INALIENABILITY OF SOVEREIGNTY IN SOVEREIGN
MEDIEVAL POLITICAL THOUGHT. CHRIST-17C INTELL NAT/G ATTIT
SECT CHIEF LEGIS SANCTION AUTHORIT ORD/FREE
CONSERVE...IDEA/COMP BIBLIOG 12/16. PAGE 131 H2627

L56
EISENTADT S.N.,"POLITICAL STRUGGLE IN BUREAUCRATIC ADMIN
SOCIETIES" ASIA CULTURE ADJUD SANCTION PWR CHIEF
BUREAUCRCY OTTOMAN BYZANTINE. PAGE 45 H0901 CONTROL
ROUTINE

B57
HOUN F.W.,CENTRAL GOVERNMENT OF CHINA, 1912-1928. POL/PAR
ASIA CONSTN CHIEF LEGIS CONTROL PWR...BIBLIOG 20. ATTIT
PAGE 74 H1480 NAT/G
PLAN

B57
KANTOROWICZ E.,THE KING'S TWO BODIES; A STUDY IN JURID
MEDIEVAL POLITICAL THEOLOGY. UK LAW CONSTN NAT/G SECT
CT/SYS...ART/METH HUM CONCPT MYTH TIME/SEQ BIBLIOG CHIEF
4/17 ELIZABTH/I POPE CHURCH/STA. PAGE 83 H1657 SOVEREIGN

B57
LONG H.A.,USURPERS - FOES OF FREE MAN. LAW NAT/G CT/SYS
CHIEF LEGIS DOMIN ADJUD REPRESENT GOV/REL ORD/FREE CENTRAL
LAISSEZ POPULISM...POLICY 18/20 SUPREME/CT FEDERAL
ROOSEVLT/F CONGRESS CON/INTERP. PAGE 98 H1961 CONSTN

B57
RUMEU DE ARMAS A.,ESPANA EEN EL AFRICA ATLANTICA. NAT/G
AFR CHRIST-17C PORTUGAL SPAIN DIPLOM ECO/TAC COLONIAL
CONTROL 14/16 AFRICA/W. PAGE 136 H2717 CHIEF
PWR

B57
SCHLESINGER J.A.,HOW THEY BECAME GOVERNOR; A STUDY PROVS
OF COMPARATIVE STATE POLITICS, 1870-1950. USA+45 CHIEF
USA-45 LAW POL/PAR LEGIS EDU/PROP REGION...STAT GOV/COMP
TREND CHARTS TIME 19/20 GOVERNOR. PAGE 139 H2788 CHOOSE

B57
TOMASIC D.A.,NATIONAL COMMUNISM AND SOVIET COM
STRATEGY. UK USSR YUGOSLAVIA NAT/G POL/PAR CHIEF NAT/LISM
CREATE DOMIN REV WAR PWR...BIOG TREND 20 TITO/MARSH MARXISM
STALIN/J. PAGE 156 H3112 DIPLOM

B58
COWAN L.G.,LOCAL GOVERNMENT IN WEST AFRICA. AFR LOC/G
FRANCE UK CULTURE KIN POL/PAR CHIEF LEGIS CREATE COLONIAL
ADMIN PARTIC GOV/REL GP/REL...METH/COMP 20. PAGE 34 SOVEREIGN
H0682 REPRESENT

B58
LAHBABI M.,LE GOUVERNEMENT MAROCAIN A L'AUBE DU XXE NAT/G
SIECLE. FRANCE MOROCCO CHIEF EX/STRUC LEGIS COLONIAL
ORD/FREE PWR...JURID BIBLIOG 19/20. PAGE 90 H1797 SOVEREIGN

B58
OGILVIE C.,THE KING'S GOVERNMENT AND THE COMMON CONSTN
LAW, 1471-1641. UK STRUCT NAT/G CHIEF LEGIS WORKER ELITES
BAL/PWR GP/REL AUTHORIT 15/17 COMMON/LAW. PAGE 120 DOMIN
H2408

B58
ORNES G.E.,TRUJILLO: LITTLE CAESAR OF THE BIOG
CARIBBEAN. DOMIN/REP FAM NAT/G FORCES BUDGET CRIME PWR
REV PERSON 20 TRUJILLO/R. PAGE 122 H2429 TOTALISM
CHIEF

B58
STRONG C.F.,MODERN POLITICAL CONSTITUTIONS. LAW CONSTN
CHIEF DELIB/GP EX/STRUC LEGIS ADJUD CHOOSE FEDERAL IDEA/COMP
POPULISM...CONCPT BIBLIOG 20 UN. PAGE 150 H2998 NAT/G

B58
SYME R.,COLONIAL ELITES: ROME, SPAIN, AND THE COLONIAL
AMERICAS. CHRIST-17C MOD/EUR SPAIN UK USA-45 ELITES
CULTURE NAT/G CHIEF TOP/EX...GOV/COMP IDEA/COMP DOMIN
NAT/COMP ROM/EMP GIBBON/EDW TOYNBEE/A. PAGE 151
H3022

C58
WILDING N.,"AN ENCYCLOPEDIA OF PARLIAMENT." UK LAW PARL/PROC
CONSTN CHIEF PROB/SOLV DIPLOM DEBATE WAR INGP/REL POL/PAR
PRIVIL...BIBLIOG DICTIONARY 13/20 CMN/WLTH NAT/G
PARLIAMENT. PAGE 168 H3363 ADMIN

B59
BROWN D.F.,THE GROWTH OF DEMOCRATIC GOVERNMENT. GOV/COMP
WOR+45 BARGAIN EDU/PROP LOBBY APPORT CHOOSE 20. LEGIS
PAGE 22 H0441 POL/PAR
CHIEF

B59
DEHIO L.,GERMANY AND WORLD POLITICS IN THE DIPLOM
TWENTIETH CENTURY. EUR+WWI FRANCE GERMANY MOD/EUR WAR
UK USSR NAT/G CHIEF BAL/PWR DOMIN COLONIAL CONTROL NAT/LISM
LEAD...IDEA/COMP 20 VERSAILLES. PAGE 39 H0783 SOVEREIGN

B59
JENNINGS W.I.,CABINET GOVERNMENT (3RD ED.). UK DELIB/GP
POL/PAR CHIEF BUDGET ADMIN CHOOSE GP/REL 20. NAT/G
PAGE 81 H1612 CONSTN
OP/RES

B59
KITTLER G.D.,EQUATORIAL AFRICA: THE NEW WORLD OF RACE/REL
TOMORROW. CENTRL/AFR INDUS KIN SECT CHIEF EDU/PROP AFR
CHOOSE HEALTH...GEOG WORSHIP 20. PAGE 87 H1730 ECO/UNDEV
CULTURE

B59
MARTZ J.D.,CENTRAL AMERICA: THE CRISIS AND THE NAT/G
CHALLENGE. L/A+17C POL/PAR CHIEF CHOOSE SOVEREIGN GOV/REL
...BIOG TREND BIBLIOG 20 CENTRAL/AM. PAGE 104 H2071 DIPLOM
GOV/COMP

B59
SZLUC T.,TWILIGHT OF THE TYRANTS. BRAZIL L/A+17C TOTALISM
PERU VENEZUELA NAT/G FORCES CONTROL PERSON MORAL CHIEF
ORD/FREE PWR...CONCPT 20 ARGEN COLOMB. PAGE 151 REV
H3028 FASCISM

B59
VINACKE H.M.,A HISTORY OF THE FAR EAST IN MODERN STRUCT
TIMES (6TH ED.). KOREA S/ASIA USSR CONSTN CULTURE ASIA
STRATA ECO/UNDEV NAT/G CHIEF FOR/AID INT/TRADE
GP/REL...SOC NAT/COMP 19/20 CHINJAP. PAGE 163 H3255

B60
BURRIDGE K.,MAMBU: A MELANESIAN MILLENNIUM. S/ASIA
ECO/UNDEV PROC/MFG FAM KIN CHIEF COLONIAL COERCE SECT
GP/REL DRIVE WEALTH WORSHIP 20 NEW/GUINEA. PAGE 25 CULTURE
H0494 MYTH

B60
CASTBERG F.,FREEDOM OF SPEECH IN THE WEST. FRANCE ORD/FREE
GERMANY USA+45 USA-45 LAW CONSTN CHIEF PRESS SANCTION
DISCRIM...CONCPT 18/20. PAGE 28 H0558 ADJUD
NAT/COMP

B61
ALLIGHAN G.,VERWOERD - THE END. SOUTH/AFR TOP/EX CONTROL
DIPLOM COLONIAL DISCRIM TOTALISM ATTIT AUTHORIT CHIEF
...BIOG 20 NEGRO VERWOERD/H. PAGE 5 H0107 RACE/REL
NAT/G

B61
ASHLEY M.P.,GREAT BRITAIN TO 1688: A MODERN DOMIN
HISTORY. UK NAT/G CHIEF LEAD REV WAR...POLICY CONSERVE
BIBLIOG 1/17. PAGE 9 H0174

B61
AYLMER G.,THE KING'S SERVANTS. UK ELITES CHIEF PAY ADMIN
CT/SYS WEALTH 17 CROMWELL/O CHARLES/I. PAGE 9 H0187 ROUTINE
EX/STRUC
NAT/G

B61
BROWN D.M.,THE NATIONALIST MOVEMENT. INDIA CULTURE NAT/LISM
STRATA REV MORAL ORD/FREE...BIBLIOG 20 HINDU. LEAD
PAGE 22 H0443 CHIEF
POL/PAR

B61
CHAKRABARTI A.,NEHRU: HIS DEMOCRACY AND INDIA. ASIA INDIA UK CONSTN ECO/UNDEV SECT DIPLOM COLONIAL PEACE WEALTH...BIBLIOG 20 CONGRESS NEHRU/J GANDHI/M. PAGE 28 H0570
ORD/FREE STRATA NAT/G CHIEF

B61
FIRTH R.,ELEMENTS OF SOCIAL ORGANIZATION (3RD ED.). STRATA STRUCT ECO/UNDEV NEIGH CHIEF INGP/REL ATTIT MORAL...PHIL/SCI GP/COMP WORSHIP SOC/INTEG 20. PAGE 50 H1009
SOC CULTURE SOCIETY KIN

B61
GUIZOT F.P.G.,HISTORY OF THE ORIGIN OF REPRESENTATIVE GOVERNMENT IN EUROPE. CHRIST-17C FRANCE MOD/EUR SPAIN UK LAW CHIEF FORCES POPULISM ...MAJORIT TIME/SEQ GOV/COMP NAT/COMP 4/19 PARLIAMENT. PAGE 62 H1250
LEGIS REPRESENT CONSTN NAT/G

B61
LA PONCE J.A.,THE GOVERNMENT OF THE FIFTH REPUBLIC: FRENCH POLITICAL PARTIES AND THE CONSTITUTION. ALGERIA FRANCE LAW NAT/G DELIB/GP LEGIS ECO/TAC MARXISM SOCISM...CHARTS BIBLIOG/A 20 DEGAULLE/C. PAGE 90 H1794
PWR POL/PAR CONSTN CHIEF

B61
PALMER N.D.,THE INDIAN POLITICAL SYSTEM. INDIA ECO/UNDEV SECT CHIEF COLONIAL CHOOSE ALL/IDEOS SOCISM...CHARTS BIBLIOG/A 20. PAGE 123 H2452
NAT/LISM POL/PAR NAT/G DIPLOM

B61
PANIKKAR K.M.,THE VOICE OF FREEDOM: SELECTED SPEECHES OF PANDIT MOTILAL NEHRU. INDIA UK CONSTN FINAN FORCES LEGIS DIPLOM TAX COLONIAL...POLICY MAJORIT ANTHOL 20 NEHRU/PM. PAGE 123 H2460
NAT/LISM ORD/FREE CHIEF NAT/G

B61
PANIKKAR K.M.,REVOLUTION IN AFRICA. AFR GUINEA ECO/UNDEV POL/PAR DIPLOM COLONIAL EXEC LEAD SOVEREIGN...CHARTS 20. PAGE 123 H2461
NAT/LISM NAT/G CHIEF

B61
SEMINAR REPRESENTATIVE GOVT,AFRO-ASIAN ATTITUDES: SEMINAR ON REPRESENTATIVE GOVERNMENTSPUBLIC LIBERTIES IN STATES OF ASIA AND AFRICA, RHODES, 1958. AFR ASIA BURMA INDIA ISLAM UAR VIETNAM/S SOCIETY POL/PAR CHIEF EDU/PROP PRESS PERSON ...POLICY INT 20 TUNIS. PAGE 141 H2826
CHOOSE ATTIT NAT/COMP ORD/FREE

B61
SHIELS W.E.,KING AND CHURCH: THE RISE AND FALL OF THE PATRONATO REAL. SPAIN INGP/REL...CONCPT WORSHIP 16/19 CHURCH/STA MISSION. PAGE 143 H2859
SECT NAT/G CHIEF POLICY

B61
ULLMAN W.,PRINCIPLES OF GOVERNMENT AND POLITICS IN THE MIDDLE AGES. LAW CONSTN DOMIN EDU/PROP LEGIT TOTALISM SOVEREIGN POPULISM...POLICY GOV/COMP IDEA/COMP 12/16 POPE KING CHURCH/STA. PAGE 158 H3152
SECT CHIEF NAT/G LEGIS

S61
LOEWENBERG G.,"PARLIAMENTARISM IN WESTERN GERMANY: THE FUNCTIONING OF THE BUNDESTAG" (BMR)" GERMANY/W NAT/G POL/PAR CHIEF LEAD 20 PARLIAMENT. PAGE 98 H1952
LEGIS CHOOSE CONSTN PARL/PROC

C61
LAPONCE J.A.,"THE GOVERNMENT OF THE FIFTH REPUBLIC." FRANCE CHIEF LEGIS PARL/PROC CHOOSE ...CHARTS GP/COMP IDEA/COMP BIBLIOG/A 20. PAGE 91 H1814
POL/PAR NAT/G CONSTN DOMIN

B62
ANDREWS W.G.,FRENCH POLITICS AND ALGERIA: THE PROCESS OF POLICY FORMATION 1954-1962. ALGERIA FRANCE CONSTN ELITES POL/PAR CHIEF DELIB/GP LEGIS DIPLOM PRESS CHOOSE 20. PAGE 7 H0140
GOV/COMP EXEC COLONIAL

B62
BAFFREY S.A.,THE RED MYTH: A HISTORY OF COMMUNISM FROM MARX TO KHRUSHCHEV. USSR NAT/G CHIEF CAP/ISM DIPLOM EDU/PROP REV WAR PEACE TOTALISM...POLICY 20 STALIN/J KHRUSH/N. PAGE 10 H0195
CONCPT MARXISM TV

B62
BODIN J.,THE SIX BOOKES OF A COMMONWEALE (1576) (FACSIMILE REPRINT OF 1606 ENGLISH TRANSLATION). AUTHORIT ORD/FREE SOVEREIGN...TRADIT CONCPT. PAGE 18 H0364
PWR CONSERVE CHIEF NAT/G

B62
BRUMBERG A.,RUSSIA UNDER KHRUSHCHEV. FUT USSR SOCIETY ECO/DEV AGRI PERF/ART WORKER PWR...SOC ANTHOL 20 KHRUSH/N. PAGE 22 H0453
COM MARXISM NAT/G CHIEF

B62
HUNKIN P.,ENSEIGNEMENT ET POLITIQUE EN FRANCE ET EN ANGLETERRE. FRANCE UK CONSTN ACADEM SECT CHIEF DELIB/GP PROB/SOLV CONTROL REV ORD/FREE CONSERVE ...BIBLIOG 18/20. PAGE 75 H1496
EDU/PROP LEGIS IDEA/COMP NAT/G

B62
JAIN R.S.,THE GROWTH AND DEVELOPMENT OF GOVERNOR-GENERAL'S EXECUTIVE COUNCIL 1858-1919. INDIA UK CONSTN EX/STRUC LEGIS ADJUD ADMIN INGP/REL ATTIT 19/20. PAGE 79 H1585
NAT/G DELIB/GP CHIEF CONSULT

B62
JENNINGS I.,PARTY POLITICS: THE STUFF OF POLITICS (VOL.III). UK NAT/G SECT CHIEF INT/TRADE RECEIVE COLONIAL GP/REL NAT/LISM ORD/FREE SOCISM 19/20 CHURCH/STA WHIG/PARTY. PAGE 80 H1607
POL/PAR CONSTN PWR ALL/IDEOS

B62
KASTARI P.,LA PRESIDENCE DE LA REPUBLIQUE EN FINLANDE. FINLAND CONSTN NAT/G POL/PAR LEGIS LEGIT ATTIT...JURID CONCPT 20 PRESIDENT. PAGE 83 H1666
PARL/PROC CHIEF PWR DECISION

B62
KEESING F.M.,THE ETHNOHISTORY OF NORTHERN LUZON. PHILIPPINE ECO/UNDEV FAM SECT CHIEF REGION GP/REL HABITAT...GEOG LING BIBLIOG WORSHIP 20. PAGE 84 H1680
CULTURE SOC KIN

B62
PHILLIPS O.H.,CONSTITUTIONAL AND ADMINISTRATIVE LAW (3RD ED.). UK INT/ORG LOC/G CHIEF EX/STRUC LEGIS BAL/PWR ADJUD COLONIAL CT/SYS PWR...CHARTS 20. PAGE 125 H2503
JURID ADMIN CONSTN NAT/G

B62
ROUSSEAU J.J.,THE SOCIAL CONTRACT. LAW CONSTN CHIEF DOMIN REPRESENT GP/REL ORD/FREE POPULISM...MAJORIT GOV/COMP 18. PAGE 135 H2700
GEN/LAWS AGREE REV

L62
NOLTE E.,"ZUR PHANOMENOLOGIE DES FASCHIMUS." EUR+WWI GERMANY ITALY TURKEY INTELL NAT/G CHIEF CONSULT FORCES CREATE DOMIN EDU/PROP COERCE WAR CHOOSE DRIVE FASCISM...PSY CONCPT MYTH GEN/METH LEAGUE/NAT NAZI 20. PAGE 118 H2367
ATTIT PWR

S62
MURACCIOLE L.,"LES CONSTITUTIONS DES ETATS AFRICAINS D'EXPRESSION FRANCAISE: LA CONSTITUTION DU 16 AVRIL 1962 DE LA REPUBLIQUE DU" AFR CHAD CHIEF LEGIS LEGIT COLONIAL EXEC ROUTINE ORD/FREE SOVEREIGN...SOC CONCPT 20. PAGE 115 H2291
NAT/G CONSTN

C62
BACON F.,"OF EMPIRE" (1612) IN F. BACON, ESSAYS." ELITES NAT/G PROB/SOLV DIPLOM ADMIN CONTROL WEALTH 16/17 KING. PAGE 9 H0190
PWR CHIEF DOMIN GEN/LAWS

C62
BACON F.,"OF SEDITIONS AND TROUBLES" (1625) IN F. BACON, ESSAYS." INDUS MARKET CHIEF ECO/TAC EDU/PROP CONTROL LEAD PEACE WEALTH 17 MACHIAVELL. PAGE 9 H0191
REV ORD/FREE NAT/G GEN/LAWS

B63
BADI J.,THE GOVERNMENT OF THE STATE OF ISRAEL: A CRITICAL ACCOUNT OF ITS PARLIAMENT, EXECUTIVE, AND JUDICIARY. ISRAEL ECO/DEV CHIEF DELIB/GP LEGIS DIPLOM CT/SYS INGP/REL PEACE ORD/FREE...BIBLIOG 20 PARLIAMENT ARABS MIGRATION. PAGE 10 H0193
NAT/G CONSTN EX/STRUC POL/PAR

B63
DALAND R.T.,PERSPECTIVES OF BRAZILIAN PUBLIC ADMINISTRATION (VOL. I). BRAZIL LAW ECO/UNDEV SCHOOL CHIEF TEC/DEV CONFER CONTROL GP/REL ATTIT ROLE PWR...ANTHOL 20. PAGE 37 H0735
ADMIN NAT/G PLAN GOV/REL

B63
HUGHES A.J.,EAST AFRICA: THE SEARCH FOR UNITY-KENYA, TANGANYIKA, UGANDA, AND ZANZIBAR. TANZANIA UGANDA CONSTN POL/PAR SECT CHIEF DELIB/GP LEGIS WAR CHOOSE NAT/LISM MARXISM...POLICY CHARTS 20 NEGRO UN. PAGE 74 H1488
NAT/G DOMIN LOC/G AFR

B63
KLEIMAN R.,ATLANTIC CRISIS; AMERICAN DIPLOMACY CONFRONTS A RESURGENT EUROPE. EUR+WWI USA+45 ECO/DEV AGRI NAT/G CHIEF FORCES PLAN LEAD ATTIT ...CONCPT 20 NATO KENNEDY/JF DEGAULLE/C EEC JOHNSON/LB. PAGE 87 H1731
DIPLOM REGION POLICY

B63
SILONE I.,THE SCHOOL FOR DICTATORS. EUR+WWI GERMANY ITALY SOCIETY NAT/G CHIEF EX/STRUC ATTIT MORAL PWR ...HIST/WRIT 20. PAGE 144 H2876
TOTALISM EDU/PROP ORD/FREE FASCISM

S63
LAMBERT D.,"LA TRANSPOSITION DU REGIME PRESIDENTIEL HORS DES ETATSUNIS; LE CAS DE L'AMERIQUE LATINE." NAT/G EX/STRUC LEGIS PARL/PROC PWR 18/20 PRESIDENT CENTRAL/AM SOUTH/AMER. PAGE 90 H1800
DELIB/GP CHIEF L/A+17C GOV/REL

S63
OGOT B.,"FROM CHIEF TO PRESIDENT." AFR SECT REGION NAT/LISM...SOC GOV/COMP NAT/COMP 20 PRESIDENT. PAGE 121 H2410
CHIEF CULTURE LEAD ORD/FREE

B64
AFRO ASIAN SOLIDARITY AGAINST IMPERIALISM. AFR ISLAM S/ASIA ECO/UNDEV NAT/G POL/PAR TOP/EX PRESS ...INT ANTHOL 20 CHOU/ENLAI. PAGE 2 H0043
MARXISM DIPLOM EDU/PROP CHIEF

B64
ANDREN N.,GOVERNMENT AND POLITICS IN THE NORDIC COUNTRIES: DENMARK, FINLAND, ICELAND, NORWAY, SWEDEN. DENMARK FINLAND ICELAND NORWAY SWEDEN POL/PAR CHIEF LEGIS ADMIN REGION REPRESENT ATTIT CONSERVE...CHARTS BIBLIOG/A 20. PAGE 7 H0137
CONSTN NAT/G CULTURE GOV/COMP

B64
BAGEHOT W.,THE ENGLISH CONSTITUTION. UK CHIEF CONSULT LEGIS BAL/PWR PWR...BIBLIOG 18/19
CONSTN PARL/PROC

PARLIAMENT. PAGE 10 H0198
NAT/G CONCPT

B64
FISCHER L.,THE LIFE OF LENIN. USSR LEAD REV WAR ...SOC 19/20 LENIN/VI COM/PARTY BOLSHEVISM. PAGE 51 H1011
BIOG MARXISM PERSON CHIEF

B64
GOODNOW H.F.,THE CIVIL SERVICE OF PAKISTAN: BUREAUCRACY IN A NEW NATION. INDIA PAKISTAN S/ASIA ECO/UNDEV PROVS CHIEF PARTIC CHOOSE EFFICIENCY PWR ...BIBLIOG 20. PAGE 59 H1173
ADMIN GOV/REL LAW NAT/G

B64
GROVES H.E.,THE CONSTITUTION OF MALAYSIA. MALAYSIA POL/PAR CHIEF CONSULT DELIB/GP CT/SYS PARL/PROC CHOOSE FEDERAL ORD/FREE 20. PAGE 62 H1238
CONSTN NAT/G LAW

B64
HALLER W.,DER SCHWEDISCHE JUSTITIEOMBUDSMAN. DENMARK FINLAND NORWAY SWEDEN LEGIS ADJUD CONTROL PERSON ORD/FREE...NAT/COMP 20 OMBUDSMAN. PAGE 64 H1288
JURID PARL/PROC ADMIN CHIEF

B64
HALPERIN S.W.,MUSSOLINI AND ITALIAN FASCISM. ITALY NAT/G POL/PAR SECT ECO/TAC LEAD PWR SOCISM...POLICY 20 MUSSOLIN/B. PAGE 64 H1294
FASCISM NAT/LISM EDU/PROP CHIEF

B64
HOLDSWORTH W.S.,A HISTORY OF ENGLISH LAW; THE CENTURIES OF DEVELOPMENT AND REFORM (VOL. XIV). UK CONSTN LOC/G NAT/G POL/PAR CHIEF EX/STRUC ADJUD COLONIAL ATTIT...INT/LAW JURID 18/19 TORY/PARTY COMMONWLTH WHIG/PARTY COMMON/LAW. PAGE 73 H1453
LAW LEGIS LEAD CT/SYS

B64
IMAZ J.L.,LOS QUE MANDAN. INDUS LABOR NAT/G POL/PAR PROVS SECT CHIEF TOP/EX CONTROL 20 ARGEN. PAGE 76 H1524
LEAD FORCES ELITES ATTIT

B64
LAWRENCE P.,ROAD BELONG CARGO: A STUDY OF CARGO MOVEMENT IN SOUTHERN MADANG DISTRICT, NEW GUINEA. S/ASIA CULTURE ECO/UNDEV PROC/MFG KIN CHIEF COLONIAL COERCE GP/REL DRIVE WEALTH WORSHIP 20 NEW/GUINEA. PAGE 92 H1846
SOC SECT ALL/VALS MYTH

B64
MINAR D.W.,IDEAS AND POLITICS: THE AMERICAN EXPERIENCE. SECT CHIEF LEGIS CREATE ADJUD EXEC REV PWR...PHIL/SCI CONCPT IDEA/COMP 18/20 HAMILTON/A JEFFERSN/T DECLAR/IND JACKSON/A PRESIDENT. PAGE 111 H2220
CONSTN NAT/G FEDERAL

B64
REMAK J.,THE GENTLE CRITIC: THEODOR FONTANE AND GERMAN POLITICS, 1848-1898. GERMANY PRUSSIA CULTURE ELITES BAL/PWR DIPLOM WRITING GOV/REL...HUM BIOG 19 BISMARCK/O JUNKER FONTANE/T. PAGE 131 H2614
PERSON SOCIETY WORKER CHIEF

B64
RESHETAR J.S. JR.,A CONCISE HISTORY OF THE COMMUNIST PARTY OF THE SOVIET UNION (REV. ED.). COM USSR NAT/G EXEC 19/20 LENIN/VI STALIN/J KHRUSH/N. PAGE 131 H2618
CHIEF POL/PAR MARXISM PWR

S64
"FURTHER READING." INDIA ATTIT...POLICY 20 NEHRU/J. PAGE 2 H0042
BIBLIOG S/ASIA CHIEF NAT/G

S64
SWEARER H.R.,"AFTER KHRUSHCHEV: WHAT NEXT." COM FUT USSR CONSTN ELITES NAT/G POL/PAR CHIEF DELIB/GP LEGIS DOMIN LEAD...RECORD TREND STERTYP GEN/METH 20. PAGE 151 H3016
EX/STRUC PWR

C64
SCOTT R.E.,"MEXICAN GOVERNMENT IN TRANSITION (REV ED)" CULTURE STRUCT POL/PAR CHIEF ADMIN LOBBY REV CHOOSE GP/REL DRIVE...BIBLIOG METH 20 MEXIC/AMER. PAGE 141 H2816
NAT/G L/A+17C ROUTINE CONSTN

B65
ADENAUER K.,MEMOIRS 1945-53. EUR+WWI GERMANY/W ECO/DEV CHIEF FORCES ECO/TAC WAR GOV/REL PWR SOVEREIGN 20 NATO ADENAUER/K. PAGE 3 H0068
BIOG DIPLOM NAT/G PERS/REL

B65
ADENAUER K.,MEINE ERINNERUNGEN, 1945-53 (VOL. I), 1953-55 (VOL. II). EUR+WWI GERMANY CHIEF FORCES PROB/SOLV DIPLOM ARMS/CONT INGP/REL PEACE SOVEREIGN ...OBS/ENVIR RECORD 20. PAGE 3 H0069
NAT/G BIOG SELF/OBS

B65
ALLEN W.S.,THE NAZI SEIZURE OF POWER. GERMANY NAT/G CHIEF LEAD COERCE CHOOSE REPRESENT GOV/REL AUTHORIT ...DECISION 20 HITLER/A NAZI. PAGE 5 H0106
MUNIC FASCISM TOTALISM LOC/G

B65
BULMER-THOMAS I.,THE GROWTH OF THE BRITISH PARTY SYSTEM (VOL. II) 1924-1964. UK ECO/DEV BARGAIN WAR CHOOSE ATTIT ORD/FREE 20 LABOR/PAR CONSRV/PAR. PAGE 23 H0472
CHIEF POL/PAR PARL/PROC NAT/G

B65
CHARNAY J.P.,LE SUFFRAGE POLITIQUE EN FRANCE; ELECTIONS PARLEMENTAIRES, ELECTION PRESIDENTIELLE, REFERENDUMS. FRANCE CONSTN CHIEF DELIB/GP ECO/TAC EDU/PROP CRIME INGP/REL MORAL ORD/FREE PWR CATHISM 20 PARLIAMENT PRESIDENT. PAGE 29 H0584
CHOOSE SUFF NAT/G LEGIS

B65
CHRIMES S.B.,ENGLISH CONSTITUTIONAL HISTORY (3RD ED.). UK CHIEF CONSULT DELIB/GP LEGIS CT/SYS 15/20 COMMON/LAW PARLIAMENT. PAGE 30 H0598
CONSTN BAL/PWR NAT/G

B65
FILIPINIANA BOOK GUILD,THE COLONIZATION AND CONQUEST OF THE PHILIPPINES BY SPAIN. PHILIPPINE SPAIN ELITES AGRI KIN CHIEF DOMIN CONTROL ATTIT PWR ...ANTHOL WORSHIP 16. PAGE 50 H1000
COLONIAL COERCE CULTURE WAR

B65
GOPAL S.,BRITISH POLICY IN INDIA 1858-1905. INDIA UK ELITES CHIEF DELIB/GP ECO/TAC GP/REL DISCRIM ATTIT...IDEA/COMP NAT/COMP PERS/COMP BIBLIOG/A 19/20. PAGE 59 H1176
COLONIAL ADMIN POL/PAR ECO/UNDEV

B65
GREGG J.L.,POLITICAL PARTIES AND PARTY SYSTEMS IN GUATEMALA, 1944-1963. GUATEMALA L/A+17C EX/STRUC FORCES CREATE CONTROL REV CHOOSE PWR...TREND IDEA/COMP 20. PAGE 60 H1209
LEAD POL/PAR NAT/G CHIEF

B65
HAMIL H.M.,DICTATORSHIP IN SPANISH AMERICA. NAT/G COERCE MORAL ORD/FREE...POLICY PSY SOC ANTHOL 18/20. PAGE 65 H1300
TOTALISM CHIEF L/A+17C FASCISM

B65
HARRIS R.L.,POLITICAL ORGANIZATION OF THE MBEMBE NIGERIA. AFR NIGERIA SOCIETY AGRI SECT WORKER PAY ...SOC WORSHIP 20 MBEMBE. PAGE 67 H1345
STRUCT CHIEF CULTURE

B65
JACOB H.,POLITICS IN THE AMERICAN STATES; A COMPARATIVE ANALYSIS. USA+45 POL/PAR CHIEF LEGIS TAX EDU/PROP CONTROL CT/SYS LOBBY PARTIC...DECISION CHARTS 20. PAGE 79 H1578
PROVS GOV/COMP PWR

B65
JOHNSON P.,KHRUSHCHEV AND THE ARTS: POLITICS OF SOVIET CULTURE, 1962-1964. COM USSR NAT/G PERF/ART CONFER DEBATE GP/REL PERS/REL UTIL ATTIT DRIVE 20 KHRUSH/N. PAGE 81 H1626
CULTURE MARXISM POLICY CHIEF

B65
MCSHERRY J.E.,RUSSIA AND THE UNITED STATES UNDER EISENHOWER, KHRUSHCHEV, AND KENNEDY. USSR EX/STRUC TOP/EX PRESS WAR...POLICY TREND 20. PAGE 108 H2150
DIPLOM CHIEF NAT/G PEACE

B65
MONTESQUIEU C DE S.,CONSIDERATIONS ON THE CAUSES OF THE GREATNESS OF THE ROMANS AND THEIR DECLINE (1748 TRANS. BY D. LOWENTHAL). ROMAN/EMP SECT CHIEF EX/STRUC FORCES LEGIS DOMIN WAR POPULISM...POLICY REALPOL ROME/ANC. PAGE 112 H2244
NAT/G PWR COLONIAL MORAL

B65
PELLING H.,A SHORT HISTORY OF THE LABOUR PARTY (2ND ED.). UK NAT/G CHIEF PARL/PROC GP/REL INGP/REL 20 LABOR/PAR PARLIAMENT WILSON/H. PAGE 124 H2484
POL/PAR NEW/LIB LEAD LABOR

B65
ULAM A.,THE BOLSHEVIKS. COM USSR NAT/G CHIEF ECO/TAC ADMIN LEAD WAR POPULISM...POLICY 19/20 LENIN/VI BOLSHEVISM. PAGE 157 H3148
SOCISM POL/PAR TOP/EX REV

S65
CAIRNS J.C.,"FRANCE, DECEMBER 1965: END OF THE ELECTIVE MONARACHY" EUR+WWI FRANCE FUT CONSTN SOCIETY CHIEF BAL/PWR ATTIT ALL/IDEOS 20 DEGAULLE/C PRESIDENT. PAGE 25 H0505
CHOOSE NAT/G POL/PAR PWR

B66
BASDEN G.T.,NIGER IBOS. NIGERIA STRUCT SECT CHIEF COLONIAL HABITAT...POLICY SOC MYTH OBS WORSHIP 20 IBO. PAGE 12 H0233
CULTURE AFR SOCIETY

B66
BRECHER M.,SUCCESSION IN INDIA. INDIA USA+45 CONSTN AGRI POL/PAR PROVS SECT DELIB/GP FORCES PROB/SOLV ECO/TAC PWR...LING 20 CONGRESS NEHRU/J. PAGE 20 H0408
CHIEF DECISION CHOOSE

B66
CROWDER M.,A SHORT HISTORY OF NIGERIA. AFR NIGERIA UK ECO/UNDEV CHIEF INT/TRADE RACE/REL NAT/LISM ORD/FREE...GEOG SOC CHARTS BIBLIOG 14/20. PAGE 36 H0711
COLONIAL NAT/G CULTURE

B66
DALLIN A.,POLITICS IN THE SOVIET UNION: 7 CASES. COM USSR LAW POL/PAR CHIEF FORCES WRITING CONTROL PARL/PROC CIVMIL/REL TOTALISM...ANTHOL 20 KHRUSH/N STALIN/J CASEBOOK COM/PARTY. PAGE 37 H0736
MARXISM DOMIN ORD/FREE GOV/REL

B66
DE VORE B.B.,LAND AND LIBERTY; A HISTORY OF THE MEXICAN REVOLUTION. CONSTN INTELL NAT/G CONTROL LEAD CHOOSE TOTALISM AUTHORIT...BIBLIOG 19/20 MEXIC/AMER DIAZ/P LIB/PARTY MAGON/F MADERO/F. PAGE 39 H0776
REV CHIEF POL/PAR

B66
MACFARQUHAR R.,CHINA UNDER MAO: POLITICS TAKES COMMAND. CHINA/COM COM AGRI INDUS CHIEF FORCES
ECO/UNDEV TEC/DEV

DIPLOM INT/TRADE EDU/PROP TASK REV ADJUST...ANTHOL 20 MAO. PAGE 100 H1992
ECO/TAC ADMIN
B66

NOEL G.E.,THE NEW BRITAIN AND HAROLD WILSON: INTERIM REPORT, 1966 GENERAL ELECTION. UK POL/PAR CONSULT PROB/SOLV BUDGET DIPLOM ECO/TAC LEAD CHOOSE ATTIT 20 WILSON/H PARLIAMENT. PAGE 118 H2366
BIOG PERSON NAT/G CHIEF
B66

SAINDERICHIN P.,HISTORIE SECRETE D'UNE ELECTION, DECEMBER 5-19, 1965. FRANCE NAT/G DELIB/GP LEGIS PLAN EDU/PROP TV SOCISM...MARXIST 20 DEGAULLE/C. PAGE 137 H2731
CHOOSE CHIEF PROB/SOLV POL/PAR
B66

SILBERMAN B.S.,MODERN JAPANESE LEADERSHIP; TRANSITION AND CHANGE. NAT/G POL/PAR CHIEF ADMIN REPRESENT GP/REL ADJUST RIGID/FLEX...SOC METH/COMP ANTHOL 19/20 CHINJAP CHRISTIAN. PAGE 144 H2873
LEAD CULTURE ELITES MUNIC
B66

SPEARS E.L.,TWO MEN WHO SAVED FRANCE: PETAIN AND DE GAULLE. FRANCE CONSTN FORCES DIPLOM WAR PERSON 20 WWI PETAIN/HP DEGAULLE/C. PAGE 147 H2942
BIOG LEAD CHIEF NAT/G
B66

TYSON G.,NEHRU: THE YEARS OF POWER. INDIA UK STRATA ECO/UNDEV FINAN SECT TASK WAR ORD/FREE MARXISM ...POLICY BIBLIOG 20 NEHRU/J. PAGE 157 H3145
CHIEF PWR DIPLOM NAT/G
B66

VON ARSENIEW W.,DIE GEISTIGEN SCHICKSALE DES RUSSISCHEN VOLKES. RUSSIA USSR SOCIETY STRUCT NAT/G SECT CHIEF REV 19/20. PAGE 163 H3262
ATTIT PERSON CULTURE DRIVE
B66

WUEST J.J.,NEW SOURCE BOOK IN MAJOR EUROPEAN GOVERNMENTS. CHRIST-17C EUR+WWI FRANCE GERMANY ITALY MOD/EUR UK USSR LOC/G POL/PAR CHIEF EX/STRUC CHOOSE CONSERVE MARXISM...JURID T 13/20. PAGE 171 H3425
NAT/G CONSTN LEGIS
L66

LEMARCHAND R.,"SOCIAL CHANGE AND POLITICAL MODERNISATION IN BURUNDI." AFR BURUNDI STRATA CHIEF EX/STRUC RIGID/FLEX PWR...SOC 20. PAGE 94 H1874
NAT/G STRUCT ELITES CONSERVE
L66

MCAUSLAN J.P.W.,"CONSTITUTIONAL INNOVATION AND POLITICAL STABILITY IN TANZANIA: A PRELIMINARY ASSESSMENT." AFR TANZANIA ELITES CHIEF EX/STRUC RIGID/FLEX PWR 20 PRESIDENT BUREAUCRCY. PAGE 106 H2122
CONSTN NAT/G EXEC POL/PAR
S66

GAMER R.E.,"URGENT SINGAPORE, PATIENT MALAYSIA." MALAYSIA S/ASIA ECO/UNDEV POL/PAR CHIEF TARIFFS TAX CONTROL LEAD REGION PWR 20 SINGAPORE. PAGE 55 H1094
DIPLOM NAT/G POLICY ECO/TAC
S66

MATTHEWS D.G.,"ETHIOPIAN OUTLINE: A BIBLIOGRAPHIC RESEARCH GUIDE." ETHIOPIA LAW STRUCT ECO/UNDEV AGRI LABOR SECT CHIEF DELIB/GP EX/STRUC ADMIN...LING ORG/CHARTS 20. PAGE 105 H2095
BIBLIOG NAT/G DIPLOM POL/PAR
B67

ANDERSON T.,RUSSIAN POLITICAL THOUGHT; AN INTRODUCTION. USSR NAT/G POL/PAR CHIEF MARXISM ...TIME/SEQ BIBLIOG 9/20. PAGE 7 H0135
TREND CONSTN ATTIT
B67

BRZEZINSKI Z.K.,THE SOVIET BLOC: UNITY AND CONFLICT (2ND ED., REV., ENLARGED). COM POLAND USSR INTELL CHIEF EX/STRUC CONTROL EXEC GOV/REL PWR MARXISM ...TREND IDEA/COMP 20 LENIN/VI MARX/KARL STALIN/J. PAGE 23 H0463
NAT/G DIPLOM
B67

HILSMAN R.,TO MOVE A NATION: THE POLITICS OF FOREIGN POLICY IN THE ADMINISTRATION OF JOHN F. KENNEDY. CHINA/COM COM USSR VIETNAM NAT/G DELIB/GP FORCES PLAN PROB/SOLV BAL/PWR COLONIAL EXEC REV PWR 20 KENNEDY/JF PRESIDENT. PAGE 71 H1418
CHIEF DIPLOM
B67

KENNETT L.,THE FRENCH ARMIES IN THE SEVEN YEARS' WAR. FRANCE NAT/G CONTROL LEAD WAR CIVMIL/REL EFFICIENCY ATTIT PWR SKILL CONSERVE 18. PAGE 85 H1690
FORCES CHIEF METH/COMP
B67

MAZRUI A.A.,THE ANGLO-AFRICAN COMMONWEALTH; POLITICAL FRICTION AND CULTURAL FUSION. AFR INT/ORG VOL/ASSN CHIEF GP/REL INGP/REL RACE/REL NAT/LISM 20 CMN/WLTH EEC. PAGE 106 H2111
COLONIAL SOVEREIGN DIPLOM CULTURE
B67

PENDLE G.,PARAGUAY: A RIVERSIDE NATION (3RD ED.). PARAGUAY CHIEF ISOLAT...HUM CHARTS BIBLIOG 16/20. PAGE 124 H2487
CULTURE GEOG ECO/UNDEV
B67

SHAKABPA T.W.D.,TIBET: A POLITICAL HISTORY. CHINA/COM UK CHIEF LEAD...INT BIBLIOG 20 TIBET. PAGE 142 H2839
DIPLOM SECT NAT/G
B67

WARREN S.,THE AMERICAN PRESIDENT. POL/PAR FORCES LEGIS DIPLOM ECO/TAC ADMIN EXEC PWR...ANTHOL 18/20 ROOSEVLT/F KENNEDY/JF JOHNSON/LB TRUMAN/HS WILSON/W. PAGE 165 H3312
CHIEF LEAD NAT/G CONSTN
L67

SCALAPINO R.A.,"A SURVEY OF ASIA IN 1966." ASIA S/ASIA CONSTN SOCIETY POL/PAR CHIEF WAR...ANTHOL 20. PAGE 138 H2764
DIPLOM
S67

ADOKO A.,"THE CONSTITUTION OF UGANDA." AFR UGANDA LOC/G CHIEF FORCES LEGIS ADJUD EXEC CHOOSE NAT/LISM ...IDEA/COMP 20. PAGE 4 H0072
NAT/G CONSTN ORD/FREE LAW
S67

BRADLEY A.W.,"CONSTITUTION-MAKING IN UGANDA." UGANDA LAW CHIEF DELIB/GP LEGIS ADMIN EXEC PARL/PROC RACE/REL ORD/FREE...GOV/COMP 20. PAGE 20 H0397
NAT/G CREATE CONSTN FEDERAL
S67

CATTELL D.T.,"THE FIFTIETH ANNIVERSARY: A SOVIET WATERSHED?" USSR CONSTN ECO/DEV NAT/G LEAD TOTALISM 20 KHRUSH/N. PAGE 28 H0562
MARXISM CHIEF POLICY ADJUST
S67

COHEN A.,"REVOLUTION IN ARGENTINA?" L/A+17C NAT/G POL/PAR CHIEF PROB/SOLV ECO/TAC 20 ARGEN. PAGE 31 H0615
REV ECO/UNDEV CONTROL BIOG
S67

GOODSELL J.N.,"BALAGUER'S DOMINICAN REPUBLIC." DOMIN/REP FUT L/A+17C POL/PAR PROB/SOLV ECO/TAC 20. PAGE 59 H1174
ECO/UNDEV CHIEF POLICY NAT/G
S67

GRAHAM R.,"BRAZIL'S DILEMMA." BRAZIL FUT L/A+17C NAT/G CHIEF PROB/SOLV ECO/TAC PWR 20. PAGE 60 H1193
ECO/UNDEV CONSTN POL/PAR POLICY
S67

HEATH D.B.,"BOLIVIA UNDER BARRIENTOS." L/A+17C NAT/G CHIEF DIPLOM ECO/TAC...POLICY 20 BOLIV. PAGE 69 H1379
ECO/UNDEV POL/PAR REV CONSTN
S67

IDENBURG P.J.,"POLITICAL STRUCTURAL DEVELOPMENT IN TROPICAL AFRICA." UK ECO/UNDEV KIN POL/PAR CHIEF EX/STRUC CREATE COLONIAL CONTROL REPRESENT RACE/REL ...MAJORIT TREND 20. PAGE 76 H1521
AFR CONSTN NAT/G GOV/COMP
S67

INDER S.,"AFTER THE CORONATION." CONSTN ECO/UNDEV EX/STRUC LEGIS INT/TRADE CONTROL SOVEREIGN ...TIME/SEQ 20 TONGA COMMONWLTH INAUGURATE. PAGE 76 H1527
CHIEF NAT/G POLICY
S67

LOFCHIE M.F.,"OKELLO'S REVOLUTION." TANZANIA NAT/G POL/PAR FORCES PLAN CONTROL 20. PAGE 98 H1954
AFR REV LEAD CHIEF
S67

MAYANJA A.,"THE GOVERNMENT'S PROPOSALS ON THE NEW CONSTITUTION." AFR UGANDA LAW CHIEF LEGIS ADJUD REPRESENT FEDERAL PWR 20. PAGE 105 H2105
CONSTN CONFER ORD/FREE NAT/G
S67

MENDL W.,"FRENCH ATTITUDES ON DISARMAMENT." FRANCE CULTURE CHIEF FORCES DIPLOM LEAD WAR...TIME/SEQ 20 DEGAULLE/C. PAGE 109 H2175
NUC/PWR WEAPON ARMS/CONT POLICY
S67

PAK H.,"CHINA'S MILITIA AND MAO TSE-TUNG'S 'PEOPLE'S WAR'." CHINA/COM SOCIETY POL/PAR EX/STRUC PROB/SOLV PARTIC COERCE WAR CIVMIL/REL ATTIT DRIVE MARXISM...METH/COMP 20 MAO. PAGE 122 H2447
FORCES NAT/G WORKER CHIEF
S67

PONOMARYOV B.,"THE OCTOBER REVOLUTION - BEGINNING OF THE EPOCH OF SOCIALISM AND COMMUNISM." COM FUT USSR WOR+45 SOCIETY STRATA CHIEF CREATE DIPLOM ECO/TAC EDU/PROP SOCISM...NAT/COMP 20. PAGE 127 H2542
MARXIST WORKER INT/ORG POLICY
S67

RENFIELD R.L.,"A POLICY FOR VIETNAM." COM VIETNAM NAT/G POL/PAR VOL/ASSN CHIEF DIPLOM EDU/PROP DETER REPRESENT ATTIT ORD/FREE 20. PAGE 131 H2615
WAR POLICY PLAN COERCE
S67

ROOT W.,"REPORT FROM PARIS - DE GAULLE: WHICH WAY TO THE FUTURE?" CANADA FRANCE ISLAM UK INT/ORG CHIEF CREATE AGREE CONTROL ARMS/CONT NUC/PWR EQUILIB PEACE PWR 20 DEGAULLE/C NATO. PAGE 134 H2670
POLICY DIPLOM NAT/G BAL/PWR
S67

ROTBERG R.I.,"COLONIALISM AND AFTER: THE POLITICAL LITERATURE OF CENTRAL AFRICA - A BIBLIOGRAPHIC ESSAY." AFR CHIEF EX/STRUC REV INGP/REL RACE/REL SOVEREIGN 20. PAGE 135 H2693
BIBLIOG/A COLONIAL DIPLOM NAT/G
S67

SHIGEO N.,"THE GREAT CULTURAL REVOLUTION." ASIA ECO/UNDEV AGRI NAT/G CHIEF ECO/TAC EDU/PROP CONTROL
CREATE REV

LEAD PWR 20 MAO. PAGE 143 H2860 CULTURE POL/PAR

S67
SMITH J.E.,"THE RED PRUSSIANISM OF THE GERMAN DEMOCRATIC REPUBLIC." GERMANY/E INTELL NAT/G SECT CHIEF...PREDICT TIME/SEQ 20. PAGE 146 H2913 MARXISM NAT/LISM GOV/COMP EDU/PROP

S67
STRAFFORD P.,"FRENCH ELECTIONS." FRANCE NAT/G CHIEF LEGIS BAL/PWR ECO/TAC PARL/PROC PARTIC ATTIT 20. PAGE 150 H2993 POL/PAR SOCISM CENTRAL MARXISM

S67
TATU M.,"URSS: LES FLOTTEMENTS DE LA DIRECTION COLLEGIALE." UAR USSR CHIEF LEAD INGP/REL EFFICIENCY...DECISION TREND 20 MID/EAST. PAGE 152 H3047 POLICY NAT/G EX/STRUC DIPLOM

S67
VINCENT S.,"SHOULD BIAFRA SURVIVE?" NIGERIA ECO/UNDEV CHIEF FORCES ECO/TAC GP/REL DISCRIM PEACE ORD/FREE SOC/INTEG 20 BIAFRA IBO. PAGE 163 H3256 AFR REV REGION NAT/G

C67
LING D.L.,"TUNISIA: FROM PROTECTORATE TO REPUBLIC." CULTURE NAT/G POL/PAR CHIEF DIPLOM COERCE WAR PWR ...BIBLIOG 19/20 TUNIS. PAGE 97 H1934 AFR NAT/LISM COLONIAL PROB/SOLV

B68
DE SPINOZA B.,TRACTATUS THEOLOGICO-POLITICUS (TRANS. BY R. WILLIS). UNIV CHIEF DOMIN PWR WORSHIP. PAGE 38 H0771 SECT NAT/G ORD/FREE

L68
CURRENT HISTORY,"AFRICA, 1968." ETHIOPIA GHANA NIGERIA SOUTH/AFR CULTURE ECO/UNDEV KIN SECT CHIEF EX/STRUC WAR WEAPON CHOOSE CIVMIL/REL...GOV/COMP 20 AFRICA/E. PAGE 36 H0724 RACE/REL NAT/LISM FORCES AFR

S68
VERAX,"L'EUROPE ET LA FRANCE SUR LA SELLETTE." FRANCE UK NAT/G CHIEF DIPLOM EDU/PROP GP/REL 20 EEC DEGAULLE/C. PAGE 162 H3242 INT/TRADE INT/ORG POLICY ECO/TAC

B70
BOSSUET J.B.,"POLITIQUE TIREE DE L'ECRITURE SAINTE" (1679-1709) IN J.B. BOSSUET, OEVRES DE BOSSUET. NAT/G GP/REL AUTHORIT HEREDITY PERSON ALL/VALS SOVEREIGN 18 BIBLE DEITY CHRISTIAN. PAGE 19 H0383 TRADIT CHIEF SECT CONCPT

B75
MAINE H.S.,LECTURES ON THE EARLY HISTORY OF INSTITUTIONS. IRELAND UK CONSTN ELITES STRUCT FAM KIN CHIEF LEGIS CT/SYS OWN SOVEREIGN...CONCPT 16 BENTHAM/J BREHON ROMAN/LAW. PAGE 101 H2021 CULTURE LAW INGP/REL

B75
NEWMAN J.H.,A LETTER ADDRESSED TO THE DUKE OF NORFOLK ON THE OCCASION OF MR. GLADSTONE'S RECENT EXPOSTULATION. NAT/G SECT CHIEF LEGIS CONTROL LEAD GP/REL SUPEGO SOC/INTEG WORSHIP 19 ENGLAND. PAGE 117 H2346 POLICY DOMIN SOVEREIGN CATHISM

N80
MILL J.S.,"AN ESSAY ON GOVERNMENT" (PAMPHLET). ELITES NAT/G CHIEF OWN ORD/FREE PWR WEALTH GEN/LAWS. PAGE 110 H2207 CONSTN POPULISM REPRESENT UTIL

B86
MAS LATRIE L.,RELATIONS ET COMMERCE DE L'AFRIQUE SEPTENTRIONALE OU MAGREB AVEC LES NATIONS CHRETIENNES AU MOYEN AGE. CULTURE CHIEF FORCES WAR ...SOC CENSUS TREATY 10/16. PAGE 104 H2084 ISLAM SECT DIPLOM INT/TRADE

L86
BURGESS J.W.,"THE RECENT CONSTITUTIONAL CRISIS IN NORWAY" MOD/EUR NORWAY SWEDEN LOC/G NAT/G CHIEF BAL/PWR NAT/LISM ORD/FREE 19. PAGE 24 H0481 CONSTN SOVEREIGN GOV/REL

B87
ADAMS J.,A DEFENSE OF THE CONSTITUTIONS OF GOVERNMENT OF THE UNITED STATES OF AMERICA. USA-45 STRATA CHIEF EX/STRUC LEGIS CT/SYS CONSERVE POPULISM...CONCPT CON/ANAL GOV/COMP. PAGE 3 H0063 CONSTN BAL/PWR PWR NAT/G

B90
BURKE E.,REFLECTIONS ON THE REVOLUTION IN FRANCE. FRANCE UK NAT/G DOMIN LEGIT PEACE PWR SOVEREIGN CONSERVE...POLICY GEN/LAWS 18. PAGE 24 H0487 REV ORD/FREE CHIEF TRADIT

B91
PAINE T.,RIGHTS OF MAN. FRANCE MOD/EUR CONSTN NAT/G CHIEF DOMIN LEGIT SOVEREIGN...MAJORIT IDEA/COMP 18 BURKE/EDM CIVIL/LIB. PAGE 122 H2446 GEN/LAWS ORD/FREE REV AGREE

B96
DE VATTEL E.,THE LAW OF NATIONS. AGRI FINAN CHIEF DIPLOM INT/TRADE AGREE OWN ALL/VALS MORAL ORD/FREE SOVEREIGN...GEN/LAWS 18 NATURL/LAW WOLFF/C. PAGE 39 H0774 LAW CONCPT NAT/G INT/LAW

B96
ESMEIN A.,ELEMENTS DE DROIT CONSTITUTIONNEL. FRANCE UK CHIEF EX/STRUC LEGIS ADJUD CT/SYS PARL/PROC REV GOV/REL ORD/FREE...JURID METH/COMP 18/19. PAGE 47 H0940 LAW CONSTN NAT/G CONCPT

B96
LOWELL A.L.,GOVERNMENTS AND PARTIES IN CONTINENTAL EUROPE (VOL. I). MOD/EUR LOC/G NAT/G SECT CHIEF LEGIS PARL/PROC GOV/REL...POLICY 19. PAGE 99 H1973 POL/PAR GOV/COMP CONSTN EX/STRUC

CHILCOTE R.H. H0589

CHILDREN....SEE AGE/C

CHILDS J.B. H0590,H0591,H0592,H0593,H0594,H0764

CHILDS/RS....RICHARD SPENCER CHILDS

CHILE....SEE ALSO L/A+17C

N
BIBLIOTECH NACIONAL,CATALOGO BREVE DE LA BIBLIOTECA AMERICANA DE JT MEDINA (2 VOLS.). CHILE NAT/G PERSON HUM. PAGE 16 H0330 BIBLIOG/A CHARTS L/A+17C

B29
DE REPARAZ G.,GEOGRAFIA Y POLITICA. CHILE SPAIN USSR NAT/G DIPLOM REV MARXISM...POLICY 19/20. PAGE 38 H0768 GEOG MOD/EUR

B64
CORFO,CHILE, A SELECTED BIBLIOGRAPHY IN ENGLISH (PAMPHLET). CHILE DIPLOM...SOC 20. PAGE 33 H0669 BIBLIOG NAT/G POLICY L/A+17C

B64
KALDOR N.,ESSAYS ON ECONOMIC POLICY (VOL. II). CHILE GERMANY INDIA FINAN...GOV/COMP METH/COMP 20 KEYNES/JM. PAGE 83 H1651 BAL/PAY INT/TRADE METH/CNCPT ECO/UNDEV

B65
HERRICK B.H.,URBAN MIGRATION AND ECONOMIC DEVELOPMENT IN CHILE. CHILE AGRI INDUS LABOR NAT/G CENTRAL PRODUC...STAT SAMP CHARTS BIBLIOG/A 20 MIGRATION. PAGE 70 H1404 HABITAT GEOG MUNIC ECO/UNDEV

S65
BRANDENBURG F.,"THE RELEVANCE OF MEXICAN EXPERIENCE TO LATIN AMERICAN DEVELOPMENT." BRAZIL CHILE VENEZUELA STRUCT ECO/UNDEV AGRI CREATE ECO/TAC ...STAT RECORD MEXIC/AMER ARGEN COLOMB. PAGE 20 H0405 L/A+17C GOV/COMP

B66
GLAZER M.,THE FEDERAL GOVERNMENT AND THE UNIVERSITY. CHILE PROB/SOLV DIPLOM GIVE ADMIN WAR ...POLICY SOC 20. PAGE 57 H1140 BIBLIOG/A NAT/G PLAN ACADEM

B66
THIESENHUSEN W.C.,CHILE'S EXPERIMENTS IN AGRARIAN REFORM. CHILE STRUCT NAT/G ACT/RES ECO/TAC GOV/REL COST SOCISM...TREND CHARTS SOC/EXP 20. PAGE 154 H3073 AGRI ECO/UNDEV SOC TEC/DEV

L67
GLAZER M.,"LAS ACTITUDES Y ACTIVIDADES POLITICAS DE LOS ESTUDIANTES DE LA UNIVERSIDAD DE CHILE." CHILE NAT/G POL/PAR EDU/PROP LOBBY ATTIT 20. PAGE 57 H1141 ACADEM AGE/Y PARTIC ELITES

S67
SOARES G.,"SOCIO-ECONOMIC VARIABLES AND VOTING FOR THE RADICAL LEFT: CHILE 1952." CHILE INDUS NAT/G WORKER ADJUST STRANGE ANOMIE WEALTH...METH/CNCPT CORREL 20. PAGE 146 H2925 STRATA POL/PAR CHOOSE STAT

CHIN R. H2313

CHINA....PEOPLE'S REPUBLIC OF CHINA: SEE CHINA/COM
REPUBLIC OF CHINA: SEE TAIWAN

CHINA/COM....COMMUNIST CHINA

N
PEKING REVIEW. CHINA/COM CULTURE AGRI INDUS DIPLOM EDU/PROP GUERRILLA ATTIT MARXISM...BIBLIOG 20. PAGE 1 H0009 MARXIST NAT/G POL/PAR PRESS

N
KYRIAK T.E.,CHINA: A BIBLIOGRAPHY. ASIA CHINA/COM AGRI FINAN INDUS NAT/G INT/TRADE PRESS...SOC 20. PAGE 90 H1789 BIBLIOG/A MARXISM TOP/EX POL/PAR

N
US CONSULATE GENERAL HONG KONG,CURRENT BACKGROUND. CHINA/COM ECO/UNDEV LOC/G NAT/G PLAN DIPLOM EDU/PROP LEAD REV ATTIT...POLICY INDEX 20. PAGE 159 H3179 BIBLIOG/A MARXIST ASIA PRESS

N
US CONSULATE GENERAL HONG KONG,EXTRACTS FROM CHINA MAINLAND MAGAZINES. ASIA CHINA/COM ECO/UNDEV NAT/G CHIEF LEAD ATTIT...MARXIST INDEX 20. PAGE 159 H3180 BIBLIOG MARXISM PRESS

N
US CONSULATE GENERAL HONG KONG,SURVEY OF CHINA MAINLAND PRESS. CHINA/COM ECO/UNDEV LOC/G NAT/G BIBLIOG/A MARXIST

PLAN DIPLOM EDU/PROP LEAD REV ATTIT...POLICY INDEX 20. PAGE 159 H3181
ASIA PRESS

N
US CONSULATE GENERAL HONG KONG,US CONSULATE GENERAL, HONG KONG, PRESS SUMMARIES. CHINA/COM ECO/UNDEV LOC/G NAT/G PLAN DIPLOM EDU/PROP LEAD REV ATTIT...POLICY INDEX 20. PAGE 159 H3182
BIBLIOG/A MARXIST ASIA PRESS

N19
MAO TSE-TUNG,ON SOME IMPORTANT PROBLEMS OF THE PARTY'S PRESENT POLICY. CHINA/COM CONSTN ELITES INTELL AGRI DOMIN EDU/PROP REV REPRESENT GP/REL OWN PEACE ORD/FREE 20 COM/PARTY. PAGE 102 H2044
POLICY NAT/G CHIEF LEGIT

B45
CLAGETT H.L.,COMMUNIST CHINA: RUTHLESS ENEMY OR PAPER TIGER (PAMPHLET). CHINA/COM ECO/UNDEV AGRI INDUS NAT/G POL/PAR ECO/TAC INT/TRADE GUERRILLA ATTIT...CHARTS NAT/COMP ORG/CHARTS 20. PAGE 30 H0602
BIBLIOG/A MARXISM DIPLOM COERCE

B48
CLYDE P.H.,THE FAR EAST: A HISTORY OF THE IMPACT OF THE WEST ON EASTERN ASIA. CHINA/COM CULTURE INT/TRADE DOMIN COLONIAL WAR PWR...CHARTS BIBLIOG 19/20 CHINJAP. PAGE 30 H0609
DIPLOM ASIA

B49
MAO TSE-TUNG,NEW DEMOCRACY. CHINA/COM NAT/G DIPLOM ECO/TAC EDU/PROP REV...CONCPT METH SOC/INTEG 20. PAGE 102 H2045
SOCISM MARXISM POPULISM CULTURE

B49
US DEPARTMENT OF STATE,SOVIET BIBLIOGRAPHY (PAMPHLET). CHINA/COM COM USSR LAW AGRI INT/ORG ECO/TAC EDU/PROP...POLICY GEOG 20. PAGE 159 H3185
BIBLIOG/A MARXISM CULTURE DIPLOM

B50
WILBUR C.M.,CHINESE SOURCES ON THE HISTORY OF THE CHINESE COMMUNIST MOVEMENT (PAMPHLET). CHINA/COM ECO/UNDEV PROVS FORCES WAR...PHIL/SCI 20. PAGE 168 H3360
BIBLIOG/A MARXISM REV NAT/G

B53
HUNTER E.,BRAIN-WASHING IN RED CHINA. ASIA CHINA/COM CULTURE SOCIETY FORCES WAR TOTALISM ATTIT BIO/SOC DISPL DRIVE PERSON SUPEGO KNOWL ORD/FREE ...INT REC/INT COLD/WAR 20. PAGE 75 H1499
EDU/PROP COERCE

B53
SHIRATO I.,JAPANESE SOURCES ON THE HISTORY OF THE CHINESE COMMUNIST MOVEMENT (PAMPHLET). CHINA/COM USSR CONSTRUC NAT/G POL/PAR FORCES DIPLOM DOMIN EDU/PROP CONTROL WAR TOTALISM SOCISM 20. PAGE 143 H2863
BIBLIOG/A MARXISM ECO/UNDEV

B55
THOMPSON V.,MINORITY PROBLEMS IN SOUTHEAST ASIA. CAMBODIA CHINA/COM LAOS S/ASIA KIN NAT/G SECT PROB/SOLV EDU/PROP REGION GP/REL RACE/REL MARXISM ...SOC 20 BUDDHISM UN. PAGE 154 H3085
INGP/REL GEOG DIPLOM STRUCT

L55
ROSTOW W.W.,"RUSSIA AND CHINA UNDER COMMUNISM." CHINA/COM USSR INTELL STRUCT INT/ORG NAT/G POL/PAR TOP/EX ACT/RES PLAN ADMIN ATTIT ALL/VALS MARXISM ...CONCPT OBS TIME/SEQ TREND GOV/COMP VAL/FREE 20. PAGE 134 H2689
COM ASIA

B56
ROBERTS H.L.,RUSSIA AND AMERICA. CHINA/COM S/ASIA USSR FORCES TEC/DEV FOR/AID NUC/PWR ALL/IDEOS ...MAJORIT TREND NAT/COMP 20 COLD/WAR UN NATO. PAGE 132 H2641
DIPLOM INT/ORG BAL/PWR TOTALISM

B58
STUBEL H.,THE MEWU FANTZU. CHINA/COM INDIA EDU/PROP ADJUD CRIME GP/REL OWN...OBS 20 TIBET. PAGE 150 H3001
CULTURE STRUCT SECT FAM

S59
SKILLING H.G.,"COMMUNISM: NATIONAL OR INTERNATIONAL." CHINA/COM USSR YUGOSLAVIA NAT/G POL/PAR VOL/ASSN DOMIN REGION COERCE ATTIT PWR MARXISM SOCISM...CONCPT TOT/POP 20 TITO/MARSH. PAGE 145 H2894
COM TREND

B60
COUGHLIN R.,DOUBLE IDENTITY: THE CHINESE AND MODERN THAILAND. CHINA/COM S/ASIA THAILAND ECO/UNDEV EXTR/IND FINAN INDUS KIN MUNIC NAT/G PROF/ORG SCHOOL SECT ATTIT DRIVE...CONCPT OBS 20. PAGE 34 H0676
ASIA FAM CULTURE

B60
FISCHER L.,THE SOVIETS IN WORLD AFFAIRS. CHINA/COM COM EUR+WWI USSR INT/ORG CONFER LEAD ARMS/CONT REV PWR...CHARTS 20 TREATY VERSAILLES. PAGE 51 H1010
DIPLOM NAT/G POLICY MARXISM

B60
MC CLELLAN G.S.,INDIA. CHINA/COM INDIA CONSTN ELITES STRATA AGRI POL/PAR FOR/AID ARMS/CONT REV MARXISM...CENSUS BIBLIOG 20 COLD/WAR GANDHI/M NEHRU/J. PAGE 106 H2117
DIPLOM NAT/G SOCIETY ECO/UNDEV

B60
MORAES F.,THE REVOLT IN TIBET. ASIA CHINA/COM INDIA CULTURE CONTROL COERCE WAR TOTALISM...POLICY SOC WORSHIP 20 TIBET INTERVENT. PAGE 113 H2252
COLONIAL FORCES DIPLOM ORD/FREE

B60
SAKAI R.K.,STUDIES ON ASIA, 1960. ASIA CHINA/COM S/ASIA COM/IND ECO/TAC...ANTHOL 17/20 MALAYA. PAGE 137 H2733
ECO/UNDEV SOC

S60
BRZEZINSKI Z.K.,"PATTERNS AND LIMITS OF THE SINO-SOVIET DISPUTE." ASIA CHINA/COM COM FUT STRATA NAT/G EX/STRUC FORCES BAL/PWR DIPLOM ECO/TAC DOMIN EDU/PROP ADMIN COERCE WAR ATTIT RIGID/FLEX ...GEN/LAWS VAL/FREE 20. PAGE 23 H0459
POL/PAR PWR REV USSR

S60
GINSBURGS G.,"PEKING-LHASA-NEW DELHI." CHINA/COM FUT INDIA S/ASIA KIN NAT/G PROVS SECT FORCES BAL/PWR ECO/TAC DOMIN EDU/PROP LEGIT ADMIN REGION GUERRILLA PWR...TREND TIBET 20. PAGE 57 H1134
ASIA COERCE DIPLOM

S60
NORTH R.C.,"THE NEW EXPANSIONISM." ASIA CHINA/COM FUT INDIA CULTURE SOCIETY NAT/G TOP/EX DOMIN COERCE PWR MARXISM...CONCPT TIME/SEQ TREND GEN/LAWS COLD/WAR 20 MAO. PAGE 119 H2372
ATTIT DRIVE NAT/LISM

S60
NORTH R.C.,"DIE DISKREPANZ ZWISCHEN REALITAT UND WUNSCHBILD ALS INNENPOLITISCHER FAKTOR." ASIA CHINA/COM COM FUT ECO/UNDEV NAT/G PLAN DOMIN ADMIN COERCE PERCEPT...SOC MYTH GEN/METH WORK TOT/POP 20. PAGE 119 H2373
SOCIETY ECO/TAC

B61
DALLIN D.J.,SOVIET FOREIGN POLICY AFTER STALIN. ASIA CHINA/COM EUR+WWI GERMANY IRAN UK YUGOSLAVIA INT/ORG NAT/G VOL/ASSN FORCES TOP/EX BAL/PWR DOMIN EDU/PROP COERCE ATTIT PWR 20. PAGE 37 H0737
COM DIPLOM USSR

B61
GOULD S.H.,SCIENCES IN COMMUNIST CHINA. CHINA/COM FUT INDUS NAT/G TOTALISM...RECORD TOT/POP 20. PAGE 59 H1187
ASIA TEC/DEV

B61
LETHBRIDGE H.J.,CHINA'S URBAN COMMUNES. CHINA/COM FUT ECO/UNDEV DIPLOM EDU/PROP DEMAND INCOME MARXISM ...POLICY 20. PAGE 95 H1893
MUNIC CONTROL ECO/TAC NAT/G

B61
NEWMAN R.P.,RECOGNITION OF COMMUNIST CHINA? A STUDY IN ARGUMENT. CHINA/COM NAT/G PROB/SOLV RATIONAL ...INT/LAW LOG IDEA/COMP BIBLIOG 20. PAGE 117 H2347
MARXISM ATTIT DIPLOM POLICY

S61
ZAGORIA D.S.,"THE FUTURE OF SINO-SOVIET RELATIONS." CHINA/COM INT/ORG NAT/G POL/PAR VOL/ASSN ACT/RES PLAN PERSON...METH/CNCPT TIME/SEQ TOT/POP VAL/FREE 20 MAO KHRUSH/N. PAGE 172 H3445
ASIA COM TOTALISM USSR

B62
BARNETT A.D.,COMMUNIST CHINA IN PERSPECTIVE. CHINA/COM FUT CULTURE ECO/UNDEV TEC/DEV CONTROL 20. PAGE 11 H0222
REV MARXISM TREND PLAN

B62
CHAKRAVARTI P.C.,INDIA'S CHINA POLICY. ASIA CHINA/COM S/ASIA CULTURE NAT/G TOP/EX ACT/RES EDU/PROP DRIVE ALL/VALS...MYTH 20. PAGE 28 H0571
RIGID/FLEX TREND INDIA

B62
DUROSELLE J.B.,LES NOUVEAUX ETATS DANS LES RELATIONS INTERNATIONALES. AFR CHINA/COM FRANCE MOROCCO S/ASIA USSR ECO/UNDEV INT/ORG PLAN ECO/TAC EDU/PROP ATTIT DRIVE...TREND TOT/POP TUNIS 20. PAGE 44 H0872
NAT/G CONSTN DIPLOM

B62
LAQUEUR W.,THE FUTURE OF COMMUNIST SOCIETY. CHINA/COM USSR LAW ECO/DEV NAT/G POL/PAR PLAN PROB/SOLV DIPLOM LEAD...POLICY CONCPT IDEA/COMP ANTHOL 20. PAGE 91 H1820
MARXISM COM FUT SOCIETY

B62
LAQUEUR W.,POLYCENTRISM. CHINA/COM COM USSR WOR+45 INT/ORG NAT/G ECO/TAC DOMIN LEAD ATTIT PWR SOVEREIGN...ANTHOL 20. PAGE 91 H1821
MARXISM DIPLOM BAL/PWR POLICY

B62
MODELSKI G.,SEATO-SIX STUDIES. ASIA CHINA/COM INDIA S/ASIA INT/ORG NAT/G ECO/TAC DETER ATTIT ORD/FREE PWR...TIME/SEQ COLD/WAR TOT/POP 20 SEATO. PAGE 112 H2234
MARKET ECO/UNDEV INT/TRADE

B62
PENTONY D.E.,RED WORLD IN TUMULT: COMMUNIST FOREIGN POLICIES. CHINA/COM COM NAT/G EDU/PROP COERCE ATTIT PWR RESPECT...SOC CHARTS 20. PAGE 124 H2488
ECO/UNDEV DOMIN USSR ASIA

B62
US DEPARTMENT OF THE ARMY,GUIDE TO JAPANESE MONOGRAPHS AND JAPANESE STUDIES ON MANCHURIA: 1945-1960. CHINA/COM NAT/G DIPLOM LEAD COERCE WAR ...CHARTS 19/20 CHINJAP. PAGE 160 H3193
BIBLIOG/A FORCES ASIA S/ASIA

B62
WALSTON H.,AGRICULTURE UNDER COMMUNISM. CHINA/COM COM PROB/SOLV HAPPINESS RIGID/FLEX...POLICY METH/COMP 20. PAGE 165 H3295
AGRI MARXISM PLAN CREATE

B62
YU LIEN YEN CHIU,INDEX TO THE CLASSIFIED FILES ON COMMUNIST CHINA. CHINA/COM CULTURE ECO/UNDEV CIVMIL/REL PWR WEALTH MARXISM...PSY SOC METH 20. PAGE 172 H3440
BIBLIOG INDEX COM

S62
LONDON K.,"SINO-SOVIET RELATIONS IN THE CONTEXT OF THE 'WORLD SOCIALIST SYSTEM'." ASIA CHINA/COM COM USSR INT/ORG NAT/G TOP/EX BAL/PWR DIPLOM DOMIN ATTIT PERCEPT RIGID/FLEX PWR MARXISM...METH/CNCPT TREND 20. PAGE 98 H1957
DELIB/GP CONCPT SOCISM

S62
MU FU-SHENG,"THE WILTING OF THE HUNDRED FLOWERS: FREE THOUGHT IN CHINA TODAY." ASIA CHINA/COM CULTURE FAM NAT/G EDU/PROP REV TOTALISM ATTIT PERSON RESPECT...GEOG INT UNPLAN/INT COLD/WAR 20. PAGE 114 H2278
INTELL ELITES

S62
SARKISYANZ E.,"NATIONALISM, CAPITALISM, AND THE UNCOMMITED NATIONS: MARXISM AND ASIAN CULTURAL TRADITIONS." ASIA BURMA CHINA/COM COM CULTURE SOCIETY NAT/G POL/PAR PLAN DOMIN EDU/PROP COLONIAL COERCE ATTIT RIGID/FLEX...CONCPT TREND MARX/KARL 20 TIBET BUDDHISM. PAGE 138 H2755
S/ASIA SECT NAT/LISM CAP/ISM

B63
CHEN N.-R.,THE ECONOMY OF MAINLAND CHINA, 1949-1963: A BIBLIOGRAPHY OF MATERIALS IN ENGLISH. CHINA/COM ECO/UNDEV PRESS 20. PAGE 29 H0586
BIBLIOG MARXISM NAT/G ASIA

B63
CRANKSHAW E.,THE NEW COLD WAR: MOSCOW V. PEKIN. CHINA/COM USSR INTELL POL/PAR DELIB/GP CAP/ISM COERCE REV NAT/LISM TOTALISM DRIVE...POLICY IDEA/COMP 20 KHRUSH/N. PAGE 35 H0698
ATTIT DIPLOM NAT/COMP MARXISM

B63
FRANKEL J.,THE MAKING OF FOREIGN POLICY: AN ANALYSIS OF DECISION-MAKING. CHINA/COM EUR+WWI USA+45 ELITES INTELL FORCES LEGIS PLAN ATTIT ALL/VALS MORAL CONSERVE...GOV/COMP 20 PRESIDENT UN TREATY. PAGE 53 H1051
POLICY DECISION PROB/SOLV DIPLOM

B63
GOODE W.J.,WORLD REVOLUTION AND FAMILY PATTERNS. AFR CHINA/COM INDIA UAR CREATE ADJUST ATTIT SEX ...SOC 20 CHINJAP. PAGE 58 H1169
FAM NAT/COMP CULTURE MARRIAGE

B63
HAMM H.,ALBANIA - CHINA'S BEACHHEAD IN EUROPE. ALBANIA CHINA/COM USSR YUGOSLAVIA ELITES SOCIETY POL/PAR DELIB/GP FORCES ECO/TAC COERCE ISOLAT PEACE MARXISM...IDEA/COMP 20 MAO. PAGE 65 H1304
DIPLOM REV NAT/G POLICY

B63
LETHBRIDGE H.J.,THE PEASANT AND THE COMMUNES. CHINA/COM COM USSR NEIGH PROB/SOLV ADJUST EFFICIENCY...POLICY METH/COMP NAT/COMP 20. PAGE 95 H1894
MARXISM ECO/TAC AGRI WORKER

L63
MICHAEL F.,"KHRUSHCHEV'S DISLOYAL OPPOSITION: STRUCTURAL CHANGE AND POWER STRUGGLE IN COMMUNIST BLOC." ASIA CHINA/COM FUT NAT/G POL/PAR CONSULT PLAN DOMIN ATTIT...POLICY CONCPT TREND MARX/KARL 20 KHRUSH/N. PAGE 110 H2195
COM STRUCT NAT/LISM USSR

S63
DUTT V.P.,"CHINA: JEALOUS NEIGHBOR." ASIA CHINA/COM INDIA S/ASIA NAT/G TOP/EX DOMIN COERCE REV ATTIT ...POLICY COLD/WAR 20. PAGE 44 H0874
FORCES PWR DIPLOM

S63
HALPERN A.M.,"THE EMERGENCE OF AN ASIAN COMMUNIST BLOC." ASIA CHINA/COM COM FUT KOREA/N S/ASIA VIETNAM/N STRATA NAT/G DELIB/GP FORCES TOP/EX PLAN BAL/PWR COERCE DETER PWR COLD/WAR WORK 20. PAGE 65 H1295
POL/PAR EDU/PROP DIPLOM

S63
TANG P.S.H.,"SINO-SOVIET TENSIONS." ASIA CHINA/COM COM CUBA KOREA/N VIETNAM/N NAT/G VOL/ASSN DELIB/GP PEACE PERCEPT PWR...METH/CNCPT MYTH RECORD TREND GEN/LAWS 20. PAGE 152 H3041
ACT/RES EDU/PROP REV

S63
WEISSBERG G.,"MAPS AS EVIDENCE IN INTERNATIONAL BOUNDARY DISPUTES: A REAPPRAISAL." CHINA/COM EUR+WWI INDIA MOD/EUR S/ASIA INT/ORG NAT/G LEGIT PERCEPT...JURID CHARTS 20. PAGE 166 H3331
LAW GEOG SOVEREIGN

B64
CLUBB O.E. JR.,TWENTIETH CENTURY CHINA. ASIA CHINA/COM INTELL NAT/G POL/PAR VOL/ASSN ACT/RES EDU/PROP COERCE REV PWR...TIME/SEQ 20. PAGE 30 H0608
TOP/EX DRIVE

B64
DEL VAYO J.A.,CHINA TRIUMPHS. CHINA/COM CULTURE DIPLOM HEALTH 20. PAGE 39 H0787
MARXISM CREATE ORD/FREE POLICY

B64
DOOLIN D.J.,COMMUNIST CHINA: THE POLITICS OF STUDENT OPPOSITION. CHINA/COM ELITES STRATA ACADEM NAT/G WRITING CT/SYS LEAD PARTIC COERCE TOTALISM 20. PAGE 42 H0838
MARXISM DEBATE AGE/Y PWR

B64
GRIFFITH W.E.,THE SINO-SOVIET RIFT. ASIA CHINA/COM COM CUBA USSR YUGOSLAVIA NAT/G POL/PAR VOL/ASSN DELIB/GP FORCES TOP/EX DIPLOM EDU/PROP DRIVE PERSON PWR...TREND 20 TREATY. PAGE 61 H1224
ATTIT TIME/SEQ BAL/PWR SOCISM

B64
LATOURETTE K.S.,CHINA. ASIA CHINA/COM FUT USSR ECO/UNDEV ECO/TAC WAR 19/20. PAGE 92 H1838
MARXISM NAT/G POLICY DIPLOM

B64
LI C.M.,INDUSTRIAL DEVELOPMENT IN COMMUNIST CHINA. CHINA/COM ECO/DEV ECO/UNDEV AGRI FINAN INDUS MARKET LABOR NAT/G ECO/TAC INT/TRADE EXEC ALL/VALS ...POLICY RELATIV TREND WORK TOT/POP VAL/FREE 20. PAGE 96 H1921
ASIA TEC/DEV

B64
ROSENAU J.N.,INTERNATIONAL ASPECTS OF CIVIL STRIFE. CHINA/COM CUBA EUR+WWI USA+45 USSR BAL/PWR EDU/PROP NEUTRAL COERCE MORAL...NAT/COMP 20 COLD/WAR UN. PAGE 134 H2676
POLICY DIPLOM REV WAR

B64
SAKAI R.K.,STUDIES ON ASIA, 1964. ASIA CHINA/COM ISRAEL MALAYSIA S/ASIA USA+45 USSR ECO/UNDEV FAM POL/PAR SECT CONSULT NAT/LISM...POLICY SOC 20 CHINJAP. PAGE 137 H2736
PWR DIPLOM

B64
US HOUSE COMM BANKING-CURR,INTERNATIONAL DEVELOPMENT ASSOCIATION ACT AMENDMENT. CHINA/COM USA+45 USSR FINAN FORCES LEGIS DIPLOM CONFER EFFICIENCY...CHARTS GOV/COMP 20 PRESIDENT CONGRESS INTL/DEV. PAGE 160 H3196
BAL/PAY FOR/AID RECORD ECO/TAC

B64
WILCOX W.A.,INDIA, PAKISTAN AND THE RISE OF CHINA. ASIA BURMA CEYLON CHINA/COM INDIA PAKISTAN S/ASIA NAT/G VOL/ASSN FORCES TOP/EX ACT/RES DOMIN REGION RIGID/FLEX ORD/FREE...POLICY GEN/LAWS COLD/WAR 20. PAGE 168 H3362
CULTURE ATTIT DIPLOM

S64
DE GAULLE C.,"FRENCH WORLD VIEW." AFR ASIA CHINA/COM EUR+WWI ISLAM ECO/UNDEV INT/ORG NAT/G VOL/ASSN ACT/RES DIPLOM ECO/TAC EDU/PROP ATTIT DRIVE WEALTH 20. PAGE 37 H0751
TOP/EX PWR FOR/AID FRANCE

S64
KOVNER M.,"THE SINO-SOVIET DISPUTE: COMMUNISM AT THE CROSSROADS." ASIA CHINA/COM COM USSR ECO/UNDEV NAT/G TOP/EX CREATE BAL/PWR DOMIN EDU/PROP PWR ...CONCPT COMECON 20. PAGE 88 H1760
ATTIT TREND

S64
LANGER P.F.,"JAPAN'S RELATIONS WITH CHINA." ASIA CHINA/COM KOREA S/ASIA ECO/DEV NAT/G POL/PAR EDU/PROP ATTIT ALL/VALS...METH/CNCPT TIME/SEQ TREND 20 CHINJAP. PAGE 91 H1808
RIGID/FLEX ECO/TAC

S64
LEVI W.,"INDIAN NEUTRALISM RECONSIDERED." ASIA CHINA/COM S/ASIA SOCIETY NAT/G ACT/RES LEGIT NEUTRAL COERCE ATTIT DRIVE PERCEPT RIGID/FLEX HEALTH LOVE PWR...DECISION RECORD TREND STERTYP 20. PAGE 95 H1896
ORD/FREE CONCPT INDIA

S64
MOZINGO D.P.,"CHINA'S RELATIONS WITH HER ASIAN NEIGHBORS." ASIA CHINA/COM S/ASIA VIETNAM NAT/G DELIB/GP FORCES CREATE DOMIN EDU/PROP REV RIGID/FLEX PWR...TIME/SEQ GEN/LAWS COLD/WAR 20. PAGE 114 H2277
VOL/ASSN POLICY DIPLOM

S64
POWELL R.L.,"COMMUNIST CHINA'S MILITARY POTENTIAL." ASIA CHINA/COM NAT/G EX/STRUC EDU/PROP COERCE GUERRILLA NUC/PWR WAR...RECORD CON/ANAL 20. PAGE 128 H2551
FORCES PWR

B65
CHAO K.,THE RATE AND PATTERN OF INDUSTRIAL GROWTH IN COMMUNIST CHINA. CHINA/COM ECO/UNDEV TEC/DEV PRICE...NAT/COMP BIBLIOG 20. PAGE 29 H0578
INDUS INDEX STAT PRODUC

B65
CHEN T.H.,THE CHINESE COMMUNIST REGIME: A DOCUMENTARY STUDY (2 VOLS.). CHINA/COM LAW CONSTN ELITES ECO/UNDEV LEGIS ECO/TAC ADMIN CONTROL PWR ...SOC 20. PAGE 29 H0587
MARXISM POL/PAR NAT/G

B65
CHENG C.-Y.,SCIENTIFIC AND ENGINEERING MANPOWER IN COMMUNIST CHINA, 1949-1963. CHINA/COM USSR ELITES ECO/DEV R+D ACADEM LABOR NAT/G EDU/PROP CONTROL UTIL...POLICY BIBLIOG 20. PAGE 29 H0588
WORKER CONSULT MARXISM BIOG

B65
CRAMER J.F.,CONTEMPORARY EDUCATION: A COMPARATIVE STUDY OF NATIONAL SYSTEMS (2ND ED.). CHINA/COM EUR+WWI INDIA USA+45 FINAN PROB/SOLV ADMIN CONTROL ATTIT...IDEA/COMP METH/COMP 20 CHINJAP. PAGE 35 H0697
EDU/PROP NAT/COMP SCHOOL ACADEM

B65
HALPERIN M.H.,COMMUNIST CHINA AND ARMS CONTROL. CHINA/COM FUT USA+45 CULTURE FORCES TEC/DEV ECO/TAC WAR PEACE ORD/FREE MARXISM 20 COLD/WAR. PAGE 64 H1292
ATTIT POLICY ARMS/CONT NUC/PWR

B65
HARBISON F.,MANPOWER AND EDUCATION. AFR CHINA/COM IRAN L/A+17C S/ASIA TEC/DEV ADJUST OPTIMAL SKILL ...ANTHOL 20. PAGE 66 H1325
ECO/UNDEV EDU/PROP WORKER NAT/COMP

B65
JANSEN M.B.,CHANGING JAPANESE ATTITUDES TOWARD MODERNIZATION. ASIA CHINA/COM S/ASIA INTELL SOCIETY KIN NAT/G SECT PERCEPT RIGID/FLEX...SOC CONCPT TIME/SEQ TREND TOT/POP 19/20 CHINJAP. PAGE 80 H1591
TEC/DEV ATTIT INDIA

B65
US DEPARTMENT OF DEFENSE,US SECURITY ARMS CONTROL, AND DISARMAMENT 1961-1965 (PAMPHLET). CHINA/COM COM GERMANY/W ISRAEL SPACE USA+45 USSR WOR+45 FORCES EDU/PROP DETER EQUILIB PEACE ALL/VALS...GOV/COMP 20 NATO. PAGE 159 H3183
BIBLIOG/A ARMS/CONT NUC/PWR DIPLOM

L65
SHARMA S.P.,"THE INDIA-CHINA BORDER DISPUTE: AN INDIAN PERSPECTIVE." ASIA CHINA/COM S/ASIA NAT/G LEGIT CT/SYS NAT/LISM DRIVE MORAL ORD/FREE PWR 20. PAGE 142 H2850
LAW ATTIT SOVEREIGN INDIA

S65
GRIFFITH S.B.,"COMMUNIST CHINA'S CAPACITY TO MAKE WAR." CHINA/COM COM NAT/G TOP/EX PLAN DOMIN COERCE NUC/PWR ATTIT RESPECT SKILL...CONCPT MYTH TIME/SEQ TREND COLD/WAR 20. PAGE 61 H1221
FORCES PWR WEAPON ASIA

S65
PRABHAKAR P.,"SURVEY OF RESEARCH AND SOURCE MATERIALS; THE SINO-INDIAN BORDER DISPUTE." CHINA/COM INDIA LAW NAT/G PLAN BAL/PWR WAR...POLICY 20 COLD/WAR. PAGE 128 H2553
BIBLIOG ASIA S/ASIA DIPLOM

B66
BRACKMAN A.C.,SOUTHEAST ASIA'S SECOND FRONT: THE POWER STRUGGLE IN THE MALAY ARCHIPELAGO. CHINA/COM INDONESIA MALAYSIA ECO/UNDEV INT/ORG NAT/G FORCES DIPLOM EDU/PROP REGION COERCE GUERRILLA AUTHORIT POPULISM...MAJORIT 20 KENNEDY/JF SEATO. PAGE 20 H0396
S/ASIA MARXISM REV

B66
CHANG,THE PARTY AND THE NATIONAL QUESTION IN CHINA (TRANS. BY GEORGE MOSELEY). CHINA/COM CULTURE CONTROL NAT/LISM...CHARTS BIBLIOG/A 20. PAGE 29 H0576
GP/REL REGION ISOLAT MARXISM

B66
FITZGERALD C.P.,THE BIRTH OF COMMUNIST CHINA (2ND ED.). ASIA CHINA/COM STRUCT BAL/PWR DIPLOM ECO/TAC INT/TRADE WEALTH 20. PAGE 51 H1018
REV MARXISM ECO/UNDEV

B66
LONDON K.,EASTERN EUROPE IN TRANSITION. CHINA/COM USSR DOMIN COLONIAL CENTRAL RIGID/FLEX PWR...SOC ANTHOL 20. PAGE 98 H1958
SOVEREIGN COM NAT/LISM DIPLOM

B66
MACFARQUHAR R.,CHINA UNDER MAO: POLITICS TAKES COMMAND. CHINA/COM COM AGRI INDUS CHIEF FORCES DIPLOM INT/TRADE EDU/PROP TASK REV ADJUST...ANTHOL 20 MAO. PAGE 100 H1992
ECO/UNDEV TEC/DEV ECO/TAC ADMIN

B66
SCHRAM S.,MAO TSE-TUNG. ASIA CHINA/COM CONTROL REGION ATTIT...POLICY IDEA/COMP 20 MAO. PAGE 140 H2799
BIOG MARXISM TOP/EX GUERRILLA

B66
SCHURMANN F.,IDEOLOGY AND ORGANIZATION IN COMMUNIST CHINA. CHINA/COM LOC/G MUNIC POL/PAR ECO/TAC CONTROL ATTIT...MGT STERTYP 20 COM/PARTY. PAGE 140 H2805
MARXISM STRUCT ADMIN NAT/G

B66
US DEPARTMENT OF THE ARMY,COMMUNIST CHINA: A STRATEGIC SURVEY: A BIBLIOGRAPHY (PAMPHLET NO. 20-67). CHINA/COM COM INDIA USSR NAT/G POL/PAR EX/STRUC FORCES NUC/PWR REV ATTIT...POLICY GEOG CHARTS. PAGE 160 H3194
BIBLIOG/A MARXISM S/ASIA DIPLOM

B66
ZABLOCKI C.J.,SINO-SOVIET RIVALRY. AFR ASIA CHINA/COM CUBA EUR+WWI L/A+17C USA+45 USSR WOR+45 POL/PAR FORCES COERCE NUC/PWR...GOV/COMP IDEA/COMP 20 MAO KHRUSH/N. PAGE 172 H3444
DIPLOM MARXISM COM

S66
CRANMER-BYNG J.L.,"THE CHINESE ATTITUDE TOWARDS EXTERNAL RELATIONS." ASIA CHINA/COM EXEC NAT/LISM MARXISM...POLICY 20. PAGE 35 H0699
ATTIT DIPLOM NAT/G

B67
BARNETT A.D.,CADRES, BUREAUCRACY, AND POLITICAL POWER IN COMMUNIST CHINA. CHINA/COM ELITES LOC/G NAT/G INGP/REL...SOC INT DICTIONARY 20. PAGE 11 H0224
GOV/REL STRUCT MARXISM EDU/PROP

B67
CORDIER A.W.,COLUMBIA ESSAYS IN INTERNATIONAL AFFAIRS. ASIA CHINA/COM FRANCE S/ASIA SPAIN UAR ECO/UNDEV LOC/G ECO/TAC GUERRILLA PWR...BIOG ANTHOL 18/20 MAU/MAU. PAGE 33 H0663
NAT/G DIPLOM MARXISM POLICY

B67
HILSMAN R.,TO MOVE A NATION: THE POLITICS OF FOREIGN POLICY IN THE ADMINISTRATION OF JOHN F. KENNEDY. CHINA/COM COM USSR VIETNAM NAT/G DELIB/GP FORCES PLAN PROB/SOLV BAL/PWR COLONIAL EXEC REV PWR 20 KENNEDY/JF PRESIDENT. PAGE 71 H1418
CHIEF DIPLOM

B67
JOHNSON H.G.,ECONOMIC NATIONALISM IN OLD AND NEW STATES. CANADA CHINA/COM MALI UK DIPLOM...SIMUL GEN/LAWS 19/20 MEXIC/AMER. PAGE 81 H1619
NAT/LISM ECO/UNDEV ECO/DEV NAT/COMP

B67
KAROL K.S.,CHINA, THE OTHER COMMUNISM (TRANS. BY TOM BAISTOW). CHINA/COM CULTURE INDUS FORCES DIPLOM EDU/PROP CONTROL EXEC NUC/PWR ATTIT...SOC CHARTS 20. PAGE 83 H1663
NAT/G POL/PAR MARXISM INGP/REL

B67
LENG S.C.,JUSTICE IN COMMUNIST CHINA: A SURVEY OF THE JUDICIAL SYSTEM OF THE CHINESE PEOPLE'S REPUBLIC. CHINA/COM LAW CONSTN LOC/G NAT/G PROF/ORG CONSULT FORCES ADMIN CRIME ORD/FREE...BIBLIOG 20 MAO. PAGE 94 H1877
CT/SYS ADJUD JURID MARXISM

B67
RIESMAN D.,CONVERSATIONS IN JAPAN: MODERNIZATION, POLITICS, AND CULTURE. CHINA/COM STRATA STRUCT ECO/DEV INDUS ACADEM EDU/PROP...ART/METH SOC MODAL INT IDEA/COMP SOC/INTEG 20 CHINJAP HIROSHIMA. PAGE 131 H2629
CULTURE SOCIETY ASIA

B67
ROWLAND J.,A HISTORY OF SINO-INDIAN RELATIONS; HOSTILE CO-EXISTENCE. ASIA CHINA/COM INDIA NAT/G NUC/PWR PWR WEALTH...GEOG BIBLIOG 13/20 COLD/WAR. PAGE 135 H2704
DIPLOM CENSUS IDEA/COMP

B67
SHAKABPA T.W.D.,TIBET: A POLITICAL HISTORY. CHINA/COM UK CHIEF LEAD...INT BIBLIOG 20 TIBET. PAGE 142 H2839
DIPLOM SECT NAT/G

B67
TREADGOLD D.W.,SOVIET AND CHINESE COMMUNISM* SIMILARITIES AND DIFFERENCES. CHINA/COM COM NAT/G PLAN DIPLOM CENTRAL PWR MARXISM...POLICY 20. PAGE 156 H3128
CULTURE NAT/LISM

L67
BERNSTEIN T.P.,"LEADERSHIP AND MASS MOBILIZATION IN THE SOVIET AND CHINESE COLLECTIVISATION CAMPAIGNS OF 1929-30, 1955-56: COMPARISON." CHINA/COM USSR WORKER CONTROL COERCE PRODUC ATTIT...NAT/COMP 20. PAGE 16 H0317
FEDERAL PLAN AGRI NAT/G

L67
BRIDGHAM P.,"MAO'S "CULTURAL REVOLUTION"* ORIGIN AND DEVELOPMENT." NAT/G LEAD CIVMIL/REL NAT/LISM TOTALISM ATTIT DRIVE PWR MARXISM 20. PAGE 21 H0413
CHINA/COM CULTURE REV CROWD

L67
ISRAEL J.,"THE RED GUARDS IN HISTORICAL PERSPECTIVE: CONTINUITY AND CHANGE IN THE CHINESE YOUTH MOVEMENT." CHINA/COM FUT POL/PAR CONTROL REV GP/REL 20. PAGE 79 H1572
AGE/Y LOBBY MARXISM NAT/G

L67
ROBINSON T.W.,"A NATIONAL INTEREST ANALYSIS OF SINO-SOVIET RELATIONS." CHINA/COM USSR NAT/G NUC/PWR ATTIT PWR...CONCPT CHARTS 20. PAGE 132 H2650
MARXISM DIPLOM SOVEREIGN GEN/LAWS

S67
CHIU S.M.,"CHINA'S MILITARY POSTURE." CHINA/COM ELITES NAT/G POL/PAR TEC/DEV ECO/TAC DOMIN CONTROL LEAD REV MARXISM 20 MAO. PAGE 30 H0595
FORCES CIVMIL/REL NUC/PWR DIPLOM

S67
CHU-YUAN CHENG,"THE CULTURAL REVOLUTION AND CHINA'S ECONOMY." CHINA/COM AGRI DIST/IND INDUS MARKET NAT/G WORKER PLAN INT/TRADE DOMIN DEMAND PRODUC ...CHARTS 20 MAO. PAGE 30 H0600
ECO/DEV ECO/TAC REV SOCISM

S67
JAIN G.,"INDIA REJECTS THE POWER RACE* REALISM ABOUT NUCLEAR WEAPONS." FORCES PROB/SOLV FOR/AID ARMS/CONT COST PWR...GOV/COMP 20. PAGE 79 H1583
INDIA CHINA/COM NUC/PWR DIPLOM

S67
LOGERECI A.,"ALBANIA AND CHINA* THE INCONGRUOUS ALLIANCE." NAT/LISM PWR...GOV/COMP 20. PAGE 98 H1955
ALBANIA CHINA/COM DIPLOM MARXISM

S67
MOZINGO D.,"CHINA AND INDONESIA." CHINA/COM INDONESIA POL/PAR 20. PAGE 114 H2276
MARXISM CONTROL DIPLOM NAT/G

S67
OJHA I.C.,"CHINA'S CAUTIOUS AMERICAN POLICY." CHINA/COM VIETNAM NAT/G NUC/PWR PEACE 20. PAGE 121 H2411
DIPLOM POLICY WAR DECISION

S67
PAK H.,"CHINA'S MILITIA AND MAO TSE-TUNG'S 'PEOPLE'S WAR'." CHINA/COM SOCIETY POL/PAR EX/STRUC PROB/SOLV PARTIC COERCE WAR CIVMIL/REL ATTIT DRIVE MARXISM...METH/COMP 20 MAO. PAGE 122 H2447
FORCES NAT/G WORKER CHIEF

S67
PERKINS D.H.,"ECONOMIC GROWTH IN CHINA AND THE
ECO/TAC

CULTURAL REVOLUTION(1960APRIL 1967)" CHINA/COM FUT AGRI INDUS PLAN LEAD MARXISM...CHARTS 20 MAO. PAGE 125 H2493 — CULTURE REV ECO/UNDEV

S67
RICHMAN B.M.,"CAPITALISTS & MANAGERS IN COMMUNIST CHINA." ASIA CHINA/COM ECO/UNDEV NAT/G CONSULT EX/STRUC PLAN EFFICIENCY PRODUC WEALTH MARXISM ...MGT CHARTS 20. PAGE 131 H2623 — CAP/ISM INDUS

S67
RONNING C.,"NANKING: 1950." ASIA CANADA CHINA/COM NAT/G PLAN ECO/TAC REV ADJUST 20. PAGE 133 H2667 — DIPLOM ROLE PEACE

CHINESE/AM....CHINESE IMMIGRANTS TO US AND THEIR DESCENDANTS

CHITTAGONG....CHITTAGONG HILL TRIBES

CHIU S.M. H0595

CHODOROV F. H0596

CHOICE (IN DECISION-MAKING)....SEE PROB/SOLV

CHOOSE....CHOICE, ELECTION

B00
MARKHAM V.R.,SOUTH AFRICA, PAST AND PRESENT. NETHERLAND SOUTH/AFR CULTURE LEGIS EDU/PROP COLONIAL CHOOSE REPRESENT DISCRIM ATTIT...OBS TIME/SEQ 17/19 NEGRO BOER/WAR. PAGE 103 H2054 — WAR LEAD RACE/REL

C06
MONTGOMERY H.,"A DICTIONARY OF POLITICAL PHRASES AND ILLUSIONS WITH A SHORT BIBLIOGRAPHY." EUR+WWI MOD/EUR UK AGRI LABOR LOC/G NAT/G COLONIAL CHOOSE RACE/REL. PAGE 112 H2245 — BIBLIOG DICTIONARY POLICY DIPLOM

B08
LLOYD H.D.,THE SWISS DEMOCRACY. SWITZERLND INDUS NAT/G WORKER CHOOSE OWN ORD/FREE SOCISM...PLURIST 19/20 MONOPOLY. PAGE 97 H1944 — NAT/COMP GOV/COMP REPRESENT POPULISM

B10
TEMPERLEY H.W.V.,SENATES AND UPPER CHAMBERS; THEIR USE AND FUNCTION IN THE MODERN STATE... UK WOR-45 CONSTN NAT/G POL/PAR PROVS SECT COLONIAL LEAD CHOOSE REPRESENT PWR...BIBLIOG 19/20 PARLIAMENT SENATE CMN/WLTH HOUSE/LORD. PAGE 153 H3059 — PARL/PROC NAT/COMP LEGIS EX/STRUC

B12
HARIOU M.,LA SOUVERAINTE NATIONALE. EX/STRUC FORCES LEGIS CHOOSE PWR JURID. PAGE 66 H1331 — SOVEREIGN CONCPT NAT/G REPRESENT

B13
BARDOUX J.,L'ANGLETERRE RADICALE; ESSAI DE LA PSYCHOLOGIE SOCIALE (1906-1913). UK CONSTN NAT/G WORKER CREATE BUDGET ECO/TAC ATTIT...POLICY 20 PARLIAMENT LABOR/PAR STRIKE NAVY. PAGE 11 H0215 — POL/PAR CHOOSE COLONIAL LEGIS

B15
MICHELS R.,POLITICAL PARTIES. NAT/G BAL/PWR CHOOSE REPRESENT ATTIT SOCISM...PSY SOC CONCPT OBS 20 MONOPOLY. PAGE 110 H2198 — POL/PAR CENTRAL LEAD PWR

B18
YUKIO O.,THE VOICE OF JAPANESE DEMOCRACY, AN ESSAY ON CONSTITUTIONAL LOYALTY (TRANS BY J. E. BECKER). ASIA POL/PAR DELIB/GP EX/STRUC RIGID/FLEX ORD/FREE PWR...POLICY JURID METH/COMP 19/20 CHINJAP. PAGE 172 H3443 — CONSTN MAJORIT CHOOSE NAT/G

N19
GRIFFITH W.,THE PUBLIC SERVICE (PAMPHLET). UK LAW LOC/G NAT/G PARTIC CHOOSE DRIVE ROLE SKILL...CHARTS 20 CIVIL/SERV. PAGE 61 H1222 — ADMIN EFFICIENCY EDU/PROP GOV/REL

N19
OPERATIONS AND POLICY RESEARCH,PERU ELECTION MEMORANDA (PAMPHLET). L/A+17C PERU POL/PAR LEGIS EXEC APPORT REPRESENT 20. PAGE 121 H2421 — CHOOSE CONSTN SUFF NAT/G

N19
OPERATIONS AND POLICY RESEARCH,URUGUAY: ELECTION FACTBOOK: NOVEMBER 27, 1966 (PAMPHLET). URUGUAY LAW NAT/G LEAD REPRESENT...STAT BIOG CHARTS 20. PAGE 121 H2422 — POL/PAR CHOOSE PLAN ATTIT

N19
ROWE J.W.,THE ARGENTINE ELECTIONS OF 1963 (PAMPHLET). L/A+17C LOC/G NAT/G LEGIS REPRESENT 20 ARGEN. PAGE 135 H2703 — CHOOSE CONSTN APPORT POL/PAR

N19
TREVELYAN G.M.,THE TWO-PARTY SYSTEM IN ENGLISH POLITICAL HISTORY (PAMPHLET). UK CHIEF LEGIS COLONIAL EXEC REV CHOOSE 17/19. PAGE 157 H3131 — PARL/PROC POL/PAR NAT/G PWR

N19
WEBB L.C.,CHURCH AND STATE IN ITALY: 1947-1957 (PAMPHLET). GERMANY ITALY CONSTN POL/PAR AGREE CONTROL PARTIC CHOOSE ATTIT ORD/FREE FASCISM MARXISM 20 CHURCH/STA MARITAIN/J SALO. PAGE 166 H3316 — SECT CATHISM NAT/G GP/REL

B21
WALLAS G.,HUMAN NATURE IN POLITICS (3RD ED.). UNIV NAT/G LEAD CHOOSE REPRESENT GP/REL NAT/LISM RATIONAL BIO/SOC HEREDITY ALL/VALS MAJORIT. PAGE 165 H3293 — PSY DRIVE PERSON

B23
DELBRUCK H.,GOVERNMENT AND THE WILL OF THE PEOPLE (TRANS. BY ROY S. MACELWEE). MOD/EUR NAT/G CHOOSE REPRESENT...CONCPT 19/20. PAGE 39 H0788 — SOVEREIGN ORD/FREE MAJORITY POL/PAR

B23
ROBERT H.M.,PARLIAMENTARY LAW. POL/PAR LEGIS PARTIC CHOOSE REPRESENT GP/REL. PAGE 132 H2640 — PARL/PROC DELIB/GP NAT/G JURID

B26
SMITH T.V.,THE DEMOCRATIC WAY OF LIFE. UNIV SOCIETY NAT/G WORKER TASK CHOOSE ALL/VALS...IDEA/COMP WORSHIP. PAGE 146 H2919 — MAJORIT CONCPT ORD/FREE LEAD

B27
HOCART A.M.,KINGSHIP. UNIV CULTURE EX/STRUC TRIBUTE ROUTINE CHOOSE ROLE SOVEREIGN RITUAL 20 KING. PAGE 72 H1441 — CHIEF MYTH IDEA/COMP

B27
SMITH E.W.,THE GOLDEN STOOL: SOME ASPECTS OF THE CONFLICT OF CULTURES IN AFRICA. AFR FINAN INDUS SECT INT/TRADE COERCE CHOOSE RACE/REL ATTIT...GEOG LING 20 NEGRO. PAGE 145 H2907 — COLONIAL CULTURE GP/REL EDU/PROP

B28
FYFE H.,THE BRITISH LIBERAL PARTY. UK SECT ADMIN LEAD CHOOSE GP/REL PWR SOCISM...MAJORIT TIME/SEQ 19/20 LIB/PARTY CONSRV/PAR. PAGE 54 H1084 — POL/PAR NAT/G REPRESENT POPULISM

B30
BURLAMAQUI J.J.,PRINCIPLES OF NATURAL AND POLITIC LAW (2 VOLS.) (1747-51). EX/STRUC LEGIS AGREE CT/SYS CHOOSE ROLE SOVEREIGN 18 NATURL/LAW. PAGE 24 H0490 — LAW NAT/G ORD/FREE CONCPT

B30
HATTERSLEY A.F.,A SHORT HISTORY OF DEMOCRACY. WOR-45 CONSTN NAT/G SECT DOMIN WAR CHOOSE ORD/FREE PWR...CONCPT GOV/COMP BIBLIOG ATHENS ROME. PAGE 68 H1355 — REPRESENT MAJORIT POPULISM

B30
MASON E.S.,THE PARIS COMMUNE: AN EPISODE IN THE HISTORY OF THE SOCIALIST MOVEMENT. FRANCE MOD/EUR ELITES SOCIETY STRATA ECO/DEV WORKER EDU/PROP CHOOSE INGP/REL SOCISM 19 MARX/KARL PARIS. PAGE 104 H2085 — NAT/G REV MARXISM

S31
HEINBERG J.G.,"THE PERSONNEL OF FRENCH CABINETS, 1871-1930." FRANCE STRATA CHIEF CHOOSE REPRESENT MAJORITY...STAT QU CENSUS TREND CHARTS PERS/COMP 19/20 CHAMBR/DEP. PAGE 69 H1386 — ELITES NAT/G DELIB/GP TOP/EX

B32
MCKISACK M.,THE PARLIAMENTARY REPRESENTATION OF THE ENGLISH BOROUGHS DURING THE MIDDLE AGES. UK CONSTN CULTURE ELITES EX/STRUC TAX PAY ADJUD PARL/PROC APPORT FEDERAL...POLICY 13/15 PARLIAMENT. PAGE 107 H2139 — NAT/G MUNIC LEGIS CHOOSE

B33
MOSS W.,POLITICAL PARTIES IN THE IRISH FREE STATE. IRELAND UK LAW FINAN LABOR DELIB/GP TOP/EX TARIFFS EDU/PROP...CHARTS GP/COMP 20. PAGE 113 H2269 — POL/PAR NAT/G CHOOSE POLICY

B34
RIDLEY C.E.,THE CITY-MANAGER PROFESSION. CHIEF PLAN ADMIN CONTROL ROUTINE CHOOSE...TECHNIC CHARTS GOV/COMP BIBLIOG 20. PAGE 131 H2624 — MUNIC EX/STRUC LOC/G EXEC

B37
PARSONS T.,THE STRUCTURE OF SOCIAL ACTION. UNIV INTELL SOCIETY INDUS MARKET ECO/TAC ROUTINE CHOOSE ALL/VALS...CONCPT OBS BIOG TREND GEN/LAWS 20. PAGE 124 H2471 — CULTURE ATTIT CAP/ISM

B37
TINGSTEN H.,POLITICAL BEHAVIOR. EUR+WWI STRATA NAT/G POL/PAR ACT/RES AGE...TREND CHARTS 20 FEMALE/SEX. PAGE 155 H3100 — CHOOSE ATTIT PARTIC

B38
HOLDSWORTH W.S.,A HISTORY OF ENGLISH LAW; THE CENTURIES OF SETTLEMENT AND REFORM (VOL. X). INDIA UK CONSTN NAT/G CHIEF LEGIS ADMIN COLONIAL CT/SYS CHOOSE ORD/FREE PWR...JURID 18 PARLIAMENT COMMONWLTH COMMON/LAW. PAGE 72 H1451 — LAW LOC/G EX/STRUC ADJUD

B38
IIZAWA S.,POLITICS AND POLITICAL PARTIES IN JAPAN. ELITES VOL/ASSN CHOOSE SUFF CIVMIL/REL GP/REL 19/20 CHINJAP. PAGE 76 H1522 — POL/PAR REPRESENT FORCES NAT/G

B39
DEWEY J.,FREEDOM AND CULTURE. FUT CONSTN CULTURE INTELL NAT/G CONSULT PLAN CHOOSE ATTIT...CONCPT — SOCIETY CREATE

GEN/METH 20. PAGE 40 H0810

B39
JENNINGS W.I.,PARLIAMENT. UK POL/PAR OP/RES BUDGET LEAD CHOOSE GP/REL...MGT 20 PARLIAMENT HOUSE/LORD HOUSE/CMNS. PAGE 80 H1609
PARL/PROC LEGIS CONSTN NAT/G

B40
MCHENRY D.E.,HIS MAJESTY'S OPPOSITION: STRUCTURE AND PROBLEMS OF THE BRITISH LABOUR PARTY 1931-1938. UK FINAN LABOR LOC/G DELIB/GP LEGIS EDU/PROP LEAD PARTIC CHOOSE GP/REL SOCISM...TREND 20 LABOR/PAR. PAGE 107 H2130
POL/PAR MGT NAT/G POLICY

B41
CROTHERS G.D.,THE GERMAN ELECTIONS OF 1907. GERMANY NAT/G EDU/PROP COLONIAL ATTIT. PAGE 35 H0709
CHOOSE PARL/PROC NAT/LISM POL/PAR

B42
BARKER E.,REFLECTIONS ON GOVERNMENT. EUR+WWI SOCIETY LEGIS EDU/PROP ADMIN LEAD PARTIC CHOOSE TOTALISM AUTHORIT ORD/FREE SOCISM 20. PAGE 11 H0218
NAT/G POPULISM ACT/RES GEN/LAWS

B45
MERRIAM C.E.,SYSTEMATIC POLITICS. FUT POL/PAR DELIB/GP DIPLOM ADJUD ADMIN LEAD CHOOSE ATTIT...MGT PHIL/SCI TREND. PAGE 109 H2183
NAT/G METH/CNCPT CREATE

S45
SPENCER R.C.,"PARTY GOVERNMENT AND THE SWEDISH RISKDAG." SWEDEN CHOOSE MAJORITY. PAGE 147 H2946
GOV/COMP NAT/G POL/PAR PARL/PROC

B46
BLUM L.,FOR ALL MANKIND (TRANS. BY W. PICKLES). FRANCE GERMANY USSR LAW SOCIETY STRUCT POL/PAR WORKER DIPLOM DOMIN CHOOSE ORD/FREE FASCISM 20. PAGE 18 H0361
POPULISM SOCIALIST NAT/G WAR

B47
JURJI E.J.,THE GREAT RELIGIONS OF THE MODERN WORLD. CULTURE INTELL SOCIETY INT/ORG CONSULT CHOOSE ATTIT DRIVE PERSON RIGID/FLEX...HUM CONCPT OBS BIOG HIST/WRIT TREND GEN/LAWS 20 WORSHIP. PAGE 82 H1643
UNIV SECT

B48
HARRIS G.M.,COMPARATIVE LOCAL GOVERNMENT. FINAN CHOOSE ALL/VALS. PAGE 67 H1339
PARTIC GOV/REL LOC/G GOV/COMP

B48
TOYNBEE A.J.,CIVILIZATION ON TRIAL. FUT WOR-45 NAT/G CREATE CAP/ISM DIPLOM NUC/PWR CHOOSE MARXISM ...GEOG CONCPT WORSHIP. PAGE 156 H3125
SOCIETY TIME/SEQ NAT/COMP

B48
WRIGHT G.,THE RESHAPING OF FRENCH DEMOCRACY. FRANCE NAT/G POL/PAR SECT LEAD CHOOSE GP/REL INGP/REL MARXISM SOCISM...CHARTS BIBLIOG 20 DEGAULLE/C. PAGE 171 H3418
CONSTN POPULISM CREATE LEGIS

B49
GRODZINS M.,AMERICANS BETRAYED: POLITICS AND THE JAPANESE EXPANSION. PROVS COERCE CHOOSE GOV/REL GP/REL INGP/REL ATTIT ORD/FREE...DECISION CHARTS 20 NISEI. PAGE 61 H1230
DISCRIM POLICY NAT/G WAR

B50
LYONS F.S.L.,THE IRISH PARLIAMENTARY PARTY, 1890-1910: STUDIES IN IRISH HISTORY (VOL. 4). IRELAND DELIB/GP LEGIS PAY EDU/PROP ADMIN GP/REL ATTIT...BIBLIOG 19/20 PARLIAMENT PARNELL/CS DIRECT/NAT. PAGE 99 H1986
POL/PAR CHOOSE NAT/G POLICY

B50
MCHENRY D.E.,THE THIRD FORCE IN CANADA: THE COOPERATIVE COMMONWEALTH FEDERATION, 1932-1948. CANADA EX/STRUC LEGIS REPRESENT 20 LABOR/PAR. PAGE 107 H2131
POL/PAR ADMIN CHOOSE POLICY

C50
STOKES W.S.,"HONDURAS: AN AREA STUDY IN GOVERNMENT." HONDURAS NAT/G POL/PAR COLONIAL CT/SYS ROUTINE CHOOSE REPRESENT...GEOG RECORD BIBLIOG 19/20. PAGE 149 H2988
CONSTN LAW L/A+17C ADMIN

B51
MEYER E.W.,POLITICAL PARTIES IN WESTERN GERMANY (PAMPHLET). GERMANY/W MUNIC NAT/G GOV/REL ALL/IDEOS 20 UNIFICA BERLIN. PAGE 109 H2190
POL/PAR LOBBY CHOOSE CONSTN

N51
MEYER E.W.,POLITICAL PARTIES IN WESTERN GERMANY (PAMPHLET). EUR+WWI GERMANY/W PRESS LEAD CHOOSE REPRESENT ATTIT 20. PAGE 109 H2189
BIBLIOG POL/PAR NAT/G VOL/ASSN

B52
APPADORAI A.,THE SUBSTANCE OF POLITICS (6TH ED.). EX/STRUC LEGIS DIPLOM CT/SYS CHOOSE FASCISM MARXISM SOCISM...BIBLIOG T. PAGE 7 H0145
PHIL/SCI NAT/G

S52
SABINE G.H.,"THE TWO DEMOCRATIC TRADITIONS" (BMR)" FRANCE UK USA-45 NAT/G CONTROL CHOOSE ALL/IDEOS ...PHIL/SCI CONCPT IDEA/COMP 20. PAGE 136 H2727
ORD/FREE POPULISM INGP/REL NAT/COMP

B53
LIEBER F.,CIVIL LIBERTY AND SELF GOVERNMENT: VOLUME 2. NAT/G CONTROL CHOOSE PERSON PWR 19 CIVIL/LIB. PAGE 96 H1925
ORD/FREE SOVEREIGN CENTRAL CONCPT

B53
STOUT H.M.,BRITISH GOVERNMENT. UK FINAN LOC/G POL/PAR DELIB/GP DIPLOM ADMIN COLONIAL CHOOSE ORD/FREE...JURID BIBLIOG 20 COMMONWLTH. PAGE 150 H2990
NAT/G PARL/PROC CONSTN NEW/LIB

B55
BAILEY S.K.,RESEARCH FRONTIERS IN POLITICS AND GOVERNMENT. CONSTN LEGIS ADMIN REV CHOOSE...CONCPT IDEA/COMP GAME ANTHOL 20. PAGE 10 H0201
R+D METH NAT/G

B55
DUVERGER M.,THE POLITICAL ROLE OF WOMEN. FRANCE GERMANY/W NORWAY YUGOSLAVIA STRATA LOBBY AGE ATTIT ROLE...STAT SAMP CHARTS METH/COMP NAT/COMP HYPO/EXP FEMALE/SEX. PAGE 44 H0875
SEX LEAD PARTIC CHOOSE

B55
HEYDTE A F.,SOZIOLOGIE DER DEUTSCHEN PARTEIEN. GERMANY/W CONSTN ELITES CHOOSE 20. PAGE 70 H1412
POL/PAR SOC STRUCT NAT/G

B55
INTERNATIONAL COMN JURISTS,JUSTICE ENSLAVED. COM CONSTN LABOR NAT/G CONTROL CHOOSE 20. PAGE 78 H1555
SOCISM TOTALISM ORD/FREE COERCE

B55
POLLOCK J.K.,GERMAN DEMOCRACY AT WORK. GERMANY/W LOC/G NAT/G DIPLOM PARL/PROC...OBS IDEA/COMP 20. PAGE 127 H2539
PARTIC POL/PAR CHOOSE EDU/PROP

B55
WOYTINSKY W.S.,WORLD COMMERCE AND GOVERNMENTS: TRENDS AND OUTLOOK. WOR+45 FINAN POL/PAR DIPLOM ECO/TAC FOR/AID DOMIN WAR CHOOSE...CHARTS BIBLIOG 20 LEAGUE/NAT UN ILO. PAGE 171 H3413
INT/TRADE DIST/IND NAT/COMP NAT/G

B56
HERNANDEZ URBINA A.,LOS PARTIDOS Y LA CRISIS DEL APRA. PERU NAT/G LEAD LOBBY CHOOSE SOCISM...POLICY DECISION 20 COM/PARTY APRA CONGRESS. PAGE 70 H1402
POL/PAR PARTIC PARL/PROC GP/REL

B56
JENNINGS W.I.,THE APPROACH TO SELF-GOVERNMENT. CEYLON INDIA PAKISTAN S/ASIA UK SOCIETY POL/PAR DELIB/GP LEGIS ECO/TAC EDU/PROP ADMIN EXEC CHOOSE ATTIT ALL/VALS...JURID CONCPT GEN/METH TOT/POP 20. PAGE 81 H1610
NAT/G CONSTN COLONIAL

B56
MYERS F.M.,THE WARFARE OF DEMOCRATIC IDEALS. SECT KNOWL MORAL CATHISM...TRADIT CONCPT 20. PAGE 115 H2302
POPULISM CHOOSE REPRESENT PERCEPT

B56
VON BECKERATH E.,HANDWORTERBUCH DER SOCIALWISSENSCHAFTEN (II VOLS.). EUR+WWI GERMANY POL/PAR WORKER DIPLOM LEAD CHOOSE SUFF WEALTH...SOC 20. PAGE 163 H3263
BIBLIOG INT/TRADE NAT/G ECO/DEV

B56
WILSON P.,GOVERNMENT AND POLITICS OF INDIA AND PAKISTAN: 1885-1955; A BIBLIOGRAPHY OF WORKS IN WESTERN LANGUAGES. INDIA PAKISTAN CONSTN LOC/G POL/PAR FORCES DIPLOM ADMIN WAR CHOOSE...BIOG CON/ANAL 19/20. PAGE 169 H3380
BIBLIOG COLONIAL NAT/G S/ASIA

L56
EPSTEIN L.D.,"BRITISH MASS PARTIES IN COMPARISON WITH AMERICAN PARTIES" UK USA+45 STRATA ECO/DEV LABOR...CON/ANAL 20. PAGE 47 H0936
POL/PAR NAT/COMP PARTIC CHOOSE

S56
KHAMA T.,"POLITICAL CHANGE IN AFRICAN SOCIETY." CONSTN SOCIETY LOC/G NAT/G POL/PAR EX/STRUC LEGIS LEGIT ADMIN CHOOSE REPRESENT NAT/LISM MORAL ORD/FREE PWR...CONCPT OBS TREND GEN/METH CMN/WLTH 17/20. PAGE 85 H1706
AFR ELITES

S56
MACRAE D. JR.,"ROLL CALL VOTES AND LEADERSHIP." ACT/RES LEAD CHOOSE DRIVE CONSERVE NEW/LIB...STAT STYLE. PAGE 100 H2007
POL/PAR GOV/COMP LEGIS SUPEGO

B57
IKE N.,JAPANESE POLITICS. INTELL STRUCT AGRI INDUS FAM KIN LABOR PRESS CHOOSE ATTIT...DECISION BIBLIOG 19/20 CHINJAP. PAGE 76 H1523
NAT/G ADMIN POL/PAR CULTURE

B57
POPLAI S.L.,NATIONAL POLITICS AND 1957 ELECTIONS IN INDIA. INDIA BARGAIN PARL/PROC CONSEN NAT/LISM PWR WEALTH 20. PAGE 127 H2543
POL/PAR CHOOSE POLICY NAT/G

B57
SCHLESINGER J.A.,HOW THEY BECAME GOVERNOR; A STUDY OF COMPARATIVE STATE POLITICS, 1870-1950. USA+45 USA-45 LAW POL/PAR LEGIS EDU/PROP REGION...STAT
PROVS CHIEF GOV/COMP

TREND CHARTS TIME 19/20 GOVERNOR. PAGE 139 H2788 — CHOOSE

L57
BENDIX R.,"POLITICAL SOCIOLOGY." CULTURE INTELL LABOR POL/PAR SECT LEGIS EDU/PROP ADMIN CHOOSE CIVMIL/REL ATTIT...IDEA/COMP 20. PAGE 14 H0274 — BIBLIOG/A ACT/RES SOC

L57
LIPSET S.M.,"POLITICAL SOCIOLOGY." NAT/G POL/PAR ECO/TAC PARTIC CHOOSE PWR...BIBLIOG/A 20. PAGE 97 H1939 — SOC ALL/IDEOS ACADEM

S57
MARCH J.C.,"PARTY LEGISLATIVE REPRESENTATION AS A FUNCTION OF ELECTION RESULTS." DRIVE...PROBABIL REGRESS STYLE CHARTS HYPO/EXP SIMUL. PAGE 102 H2046 — REPRESENT GOV/COMP LEGIS CHOOSE

C57
MORRIS-JONES W.H.,"PARLIAMENT IN INDIA." INDIA CONSTN LEGIS CONFER COLONIAL CHOOSE PRIVIL ATTIT ...GOV/COMP BIBLIOG 20. PAGE 113 H2264 — PARL/PROC EX/STRUC NAT/G POL/PAR

B58
CAMPBELL P.,FRENCH ELECTORAL SYSTEMS AND ELECTIONS SINCE 1789 (2ND ED.). FRANCE NAT/G EX/STRUC PWR ...CHARTS 18/20. PAGE 26 H0516 — REPRESENT CHOOSE POL/PAR SUFF

B58
HERMENS F.A.,THE REPRESENTATIVE REPUBLIC. USA-45 PLURISM GOV/COMP. PAGE 70 H1401 — POL/PAR CHOOSE REPRESENT

B58
OGDEN F.D.,THE POLL TAX IN THE SOUTH. USA+45 USA-45 CONSTN ADJUD ADMIN PARTIC CRIME...TIME/SEQ GOV/COMP METH/COMP 18/20 SOUTH/US. PAGE 120 H2407 — TAX CHOOSE RACE/REL DISCRIM

B58
PALMER E.E.,"POLITICAL MAN" IN E. PALMER, PROBLEMS IN DEMOCRATIC CITIZENSHIP. LOC/G NAT/G LEGIS PRESS CHOOSE REPRESENT GP/REL...DECISION SOC IDEA/COMP ANTHOL 20. PAGE 123 H2449 — PARTIC POL/PAR EDU/PROP MAJORIT

B58
SCHOEPS H.J.,KONSERVATIVE ERNEUERUNG IDEEN ZUR DEUTSCHEN POLITIK. GERMANY ELITES SOCIETY ACADEM CHOOSE SOCISM 19/20. PAGE 140 H2796 — POL/PAR IDEA/COMP CONSERVE NAT/G

B58
SCOTT D.J.R.,RUSSIAN POLITICAL INSTITUTIONS. RUSSIA USSR CONSTN AGRI DELIB/GP PLAN EDU/PROP CONTROL CHOOSE EFFICIENCY ATTIT MARXISM...BIBLIOG/A 13/20. PAGE 141 H2813 — NAT/G POL/PAR ADMIN DECISION

B58
STRONG C.F.,MODERN POLITICAL CONSTITUTIONS. LAW CHIEF DELIB/GP EX/STRUC LEGIS ADJUD CHOOSE FEDERAL POPULISM...CONCPT BIBLIOG 20 UN. PAGE 150 H2998 — CONSTN IDEA/COMP NAT/G

B58
WILMERDING L. JR.,THE ELECTORAL COLLEGE. CONSTN NAT/G POL/PAR DELIB/GP LEGIS PROB/SOLV CONFER EXEC LEAD APPORT REPRESENT. PAGE 169 H3377 — CHOOSE DECISION ACT/RES

S58
EULAV H.,"HD LASSWELL'S DEVELOPMENTAL ANALYSIS." FUT CULTURE TOP/EX PLAN CHOOSE SUPEGO PWR...TREND HYPO/EXP SIMUL GEN/METH VAL/FREE 20 LASSWELL/H. PAGE 47 H0948 — CONCPT NEW/IDEA ELITES

S58
STAAR R.F.,"ELECTIONS IN COMMUNIST POLAND." EUR+WWI SOCIETY INT/ORG NAT/G POL/PAR LEGIS ACT/RES ECO/TAC EDU/PROP ADJUD ADMIN ROUTINE COERCE TOTALISM ATTIT ORD/FREE PWR 20. PAGE 148 H2963 — COM CHOOSE POLAND

C58
GOLAY J.F.,"THE FOUNDING OF THE FEDERAL REPUBLIC OF GERMANY." GERMANY/W CONSTN EX/STRUC DIPLOM ADMIN CHOOSE...DECISION BIBLIOG 20. PAGE 58 H1155 — FEDERAL NAT/G PARL/PROC POL/PAR

B59
BARRON R.,PARTIES AND POLITICS IN MODERN FRANCE. FRANCE LOC/G DELIB/GP LEGIS TOP/EX EDU/PROP LEGIT TV FEEDBACK 20. PAGE 12 H0230 — POL/PAR ALL/IDEOS CHOOSE PARTIC

B59
BROWN D.F.,THE GROWTH OF DEMOCRATIC GOVERNMENT. WOR+45 BARGAIN EDU/PROP LOBBY APPORT CHOOSE 20. PAGE 22 H0441 — GOV/COMP LEGIS POL/PAR CHIEF

B59
JENNINGS W.I.,CABINET GOVERNMENT (3RD ED.). UK POL/PAR CHIEF BUDGET ADMIN CHOOSE GP/REL 20. PAGE 81 H1612 — DELIB/GP NAT/G CONSTN OP/RES

B59
KITTLER G.D.,EQUATORIAL AFRICA: THE NEW WORLD OF TOMORROW. CENTRL/AFR INDUS KIN SECT CHIEF EDU/PROP CHOOSE HEALTH...GEOG WORSHIP 20. PAGE 87 H1730 — RACE/REL AFR ECO/UNDEV CULTURE

B59
MADHOK B.,POLITICAL TRENDS IN INDIA. INDIA PAKISTAN UK STRATA ECO/UNDEV POL/PAR LEGIS CAP/ISM DIPLOM COLONIAL CHOOSE MARXISM...SOC TREND 20 GANDHI/M NEHRU/J. PAGE 101 H2014 — GEOG NAT/G

B59
MARTZ J.D.,CENTRAL AMERICA: THE CRISIS AND THE CHALLENGE. L/A+17C POL/PAR CHIEF CHOOSE SOVEREIGN ...BIOG TREND BIBLIOG 20 CENTRAL/AM. PAGE 104 H2071 — NAT/G GOV/REL DIPLOM GOV/COMP

B59
SENGHOR L.S.,RAPPORT SUR LA DOCTRINE ET LA PROGRAMME DU PART I. FRANCE MALI CONSTN POL/PAR PLAN CHOOSE OWN ORD/FREE MARXISM...SOCIALIST 20 NEGRO. PAGE 141 H2828 — ATTIT NAT/G AFR SOCISM

B59
SITHOLE N.,AFRICAN NATIONALISM. UNIV CULTURE SECT ADMIN COLONIAL CHOOSE. PAGE 145 H2892 — RACE/REL AFR NAT/LISM PERSON

S59
LEYS C.,"MODELS, THEORIES, AND THE THEORY OF POLITICAL PARTIES" CANADA LIECHTENST UK LOC/G NAT/G PARTIC REPRESENT GP/REL CONSEN EQUILIB MAJORITY ...NEW/IDEA MATH CHARTS 20. PAGE 96 H1919 — POL/PAR CHOOSE METH/CNCPT SIMUL

S59
MECHAM J.L.,"LATIN AMERICAN CONSTITUTIONS: NOMINAL AND REAL" (BMR)" L/A+17C REV...CON/ANAL NAT/COMP 20. PAGE 108 H2156 — CONSTN CHOOSE CONCPT NAT/G

S59
ZAUBERMAN A.,"SOVIET BLOC ECONOMIC INTEGRATION." COM CULTURE INTELL ECO/DEV INDUS TOP/EX ACT/RES PLAN ECO/TAC INT/TRADE ROUTINE CHOOSE ATTIT ...TIME/SEQ 20. PAGE 172 H3452 — MARKET INT/ORG USSR TOTALISM

B60
JUNZ A.J.,PRESENT TRENDS IN AMERICAN NATIONAL GOVERNMENT. LEGIS DIPLOM ADMIN CT/SYS ORD/FREE ...CONCPT ANTHOL 20 CONGRESS PRESIDENT SUPREME/CT. PAGE 3 H0052 — POL/PAR CHOOSE CONSTN NAT/G

B60
AYEARST M.,THE BRITISH WEST INDIES: THE SEARCH FOR SELF-GOVERNMENT. FUT WEST/IND LOC/G POL/PAR EX/STRUC LEGIS CHOOSE FEDERAL...NAT/COMP BIBLIOG 17/20. PAGE 9 H0186 — CONSTN COLONIAL REPRESENT NAT/G

B60
HARRISON S.S.,INDIA: THE MOST DANGEROUS DECADES. INDIA CONSTN STRATA POL/PAR SECT PLAN ADMIN CHOOSE GP/REL TOTALISM MARXISM...LING 20 NEHRU/J. PAGE 67 H1347 — CULTURE ECO/UNDEV PROB/SOLV REGION

B60
HAYEK F.A.,THE CONSTITUTION OF LIBERTY. UNIV LAW CONSTN WORKER TAX EDU/PROP ADMIN CT/SYS COERCE DISCRIM...IDEA/COMP 20. PAGE 68 H1369 — ORD/FREE CHOOSE NAT/G CONCPT

B60
JHA C.,INDIAN GOVERNMENT AND POLITICS. INDIA SERV/IND POL/PAR PROVS LEGIS CT/SYS CHOOSE GOV/REL FEDERAL 20. PAGE 81 H1616 — NAT/G PARL/PROC CONSTN ADJUST

B60
JOHNSON H.M.,SOCIOLOGY: A SYSTEMATIC INTRODUCTION. MARKET FAM LABOR POL/PAR CHOOSE DISCRIM MARRIAGE ALL/IDEOS...BIBLIOG T WORSHIP. PAGE 81 H1620 — SOC SOCIETY CULTURE GEN/LAWS

B60
MATTHIAS E.,DAS ENDE DER PARTEIEN 1933. GERMANY NAT/G COERCE CHOOSE ORD/FREE PWR 20. PAGE 105 H2100 — FASCISM POL/PAR DOMIN ATTIT

B60
MEYRIAT J.,LA SCIENCE POLITIQUE EN FRANCE, 1945-1958; BIBLIOGRAPHIES FRANCAISES DE SCIENCES SOCIALES (VOL. I). EUR+WWI FRANCE POL/PAR DIPLOM ADMIN CHOOSE ATTIT...IDEA/COMP METH/COMP NAT/COMP 20. PAGE 110 H2193 — BIBLIOG/A NAT/G CONCPT PHIL/SCI

B60
MORRIS I.,NATIONALISM AND THE RIGHT WING IN JAPAN: A STUDY OF POST WAR TRENDS. ASIA ELITES NAT/G DELIB/GP FORCES TOP/EX CHOOSE ATTIT...INT GEN/LAWS CONGRESS 20 CHINJAP. PAGE 113 H2262 — POL/PAR TREND NAT/LISM

B60
PICKLES D.,THE FIFTH FRENCH REPUBLIC. ALGERIA FRANCE CHOOSE GOV/REL ATTIT CONSERVE...CHARTS 20 DEGAULLE/C. PAGE 125 H2506 — CONSTN ADJUD NAT/G EFFICIENCY

B60
THE AFRICA 1960 COMMITTEE,MANDATE IN TRUST; THE PROBLEM OF SOUTH WEST AFRICA. GERMANY STRUCT REGION SANCTION CHOOSE DISCRIM...INT/LAW 20 AFRICA/SW UN LEAGUE/NAT TRUST/TERR. PAGE 153 H3066 — NAT/G DIPLOM COLONIAL RACE/REL

L60
HAAS E.B.,"CONSENSUS FORMATION IN THE COUNCIL OF EUROPE." EUR+WWI NAT/G DELIB/GP DIPLOM REGION CHOOSE PWR SOVEREIGN...RELATIV NEW/IDEA QUANT CHARTS INDEX TOT/POP OEEC 20 COUNCL/EUR. PAGE 63 H1265 — POL/PAR INT/ORG STAT

L60
ROKKAN S.,"NORWAY AND THE UNITED STATES OF AMERICA." NORWAY CHOOSE...SOC STAND/INT SAMP CHARTS GP/COMP METH/COMP 20. PAGE 133 H2665 — STRUCT NAT/G PARTIC

REPRESENT

S60
FITZGIBBON R.H.,"DICTATORSHIP AND DEMOCRACY IN LATIN AMERICA." FUT ECO/DEV ECO/UNDEV INT/ORG LOC/G NAT/G TOP/EX PLAN TEC/DEV ECO/TAC CHOOSE ATTIT DRIVE PERSON ALL/VALS OAS TOT/POP 20. PAGE 51 H1019 L/A+17C ACT/RES INT/TRADE

S60
NORTHEDGE F.S.,"BRITISH FOREIGN POLICY AND THE PARTY SYSTEM." EUR+WWI FUT INT/ORG NAT/G EDU/PROP ATTIT PWR...POLICY CONCPT MYTH TIME/SEQ TREND 20 UN. PAGE 119 H2374 POL/PAR CHOOSE DIPLOM UK

S60
PERLMANN H.,"UPHEAVAL IN TURKEY." EUR+WWI ISLAM NAT/G FORCES TOP/EX LEGIT COERCE CHOOSE DRIVE ORD/FREE PWR...TIME/SEQ TOT/POP 20. PAGE 125 H2494 CONSTN TURKEY

S60
TIRYAKIAN E.A.,"APARTHEID AND POLITICS IN SOUTH AFRICA." SOUTH/AFR CULTURE STRATA ECO/DEV NAT/G POL/PAR ROUTINE CHOOSE GP/REL RACE/REL DISCRIM ATTIT ALL/VALS...CONCPT OBS TIME/SEQ VAL/FREE 20. PAGE 155 H3105 AFR DIPLOM

S60
WYCKOFF T.,"THE ROLE OF THE MILITARY IN LATIN AMERICAN POLITICS." L/A+17C CONSTN CULTURE ECO/UNDEV POL/PAR FORCES LEGIS TOP/EX LEGIT GUERRILLA REV CHOOSE ORD/FREE PWR...TIME/SEQ VAL/FREE 20. PAGE 171 H3430 NAT/G COERCE TOTALISM

C60
SMITH T.E.,"ELECTIONS IN DEVELOPING COUNTRIES: A STUDY OF ELECTORAL PROCEDURES USED IN TOPICAL AFRICA, SOUTH-EAST ASIA..." AFR S/ASIA UK ROUTINE GOV/REL RACE/REL...GOV/COMP BIBLIOG 20. PAGE 146 H2918 ECO/UNDEV CHOOSE REPRESENT ADMIN

B61
BIEBUYCK D.,CONGO TRIBES AND PARTIES. AFR CONGO/BRAZ CONSTN NAT/G COLONIAL CHOOSE FEDERAL 20 CONGO/LEOP. PAGE 17 H0333 KIN POL/PAR GP/REL SOVEREIGN

B61
BINDER L.,RELIGION AND POLITICS IN PAKISTAN. ISLAM PAKISTAN NAT/G SECT LEGIS CREATE CHOOSE GP/REL ...MAJORIT TRADIT 20. PAGE 17 H0336 CONSTN CONFER NAT/LISM POL/PAR

B61
BURDETTE F.L.,POLITICAL SCIENCE: A SELECTED BIBLIOGRAPHY OF BOOKS IN PRINT, WITH ANNOTATIONS (PAMPHLET). LAW LOC/G NAT/G POL/PAR PROVS DIPLOM EDU/PROP ADMIN CHOOSE ATTIT 20. PAGE 24 H0479 BIBLIOG/A GOV/COMP CONCPT ROUTINE

B61
CASSINELLI C.W.,THE POLITICS OF FREEDOM. FUT UNIV LAW POL/PAR CHOOSE ORD/FREE...POLICY CONCPT MYTH BIBLIOG. PAGE 28 H0555 MAJORIT NAT/G PARL/PROC PARTIC

B61
HARE T.,A TREATISE ON THE ELECTION OF REPRESENTATIVES, PARLIAMENTARY AND MUNICIPAL. UK CONSTN NAT/G PARL/PROC CHOOSE ATTIT...MAJORIT 18/19 PARLIAMENT. PAGE 66 H1330 LEGIS GOV/REL CONSEN REPRESENT

B61
JENNINGS I.,PARTY POLITICS: THE GROWTH OF PARTIES (VOL. II). UK SOCIETY NAT/G LEGIS ATTIT 18/20 LABOR/PAR LIB/PARTY CONSRV/PAR. PAGE 80 H1606 CHOOSE POL/PAR PWR POLICY

B61
KHALIQUZZAMAN C.,PATHWAY TO PAKISTAN. INDIA PAKISTAN UK SECT LEGIS CHOOSE RACE/REL ATTIT ORD/FREE 20 MUSLIM. PAGE 85 H1705 GP/REL NAT/G COLONIAL SOVEREIGN

B61
LUNDBERG G.A.,CAN SCIENCE SAVE US. UNIV CULTURE INTELL SOCIETY ECO/DEV R+D PLAN EDU/PROP ROUTINE CHOOSE ATTIT PERCEPT ALL/VALS...TREND 20. PAGE 99 H1979 ACT/RES CONCPT TOTALISM

B61
LYFORD J.P.,THE AGREEABLE AUTOCRACIES. SOCIETY LABOR POL/PAR SECT DIPLOM CHOOSE...CONCPT 20 WHITE/T NIEBUHR/R. PAGE 99 H1982 ATTIT POPULISM PRESS NAT/G

B61
MERRIAM A.,CONGO: BACKGROUND OF CONFLICT. AFR FUT KIN MUNIC NAT/G POL/PAR PROVS DELIB/GP PLAN DOMIN COERCE ATTIT...TIME/SEQ CHARTS CONGO 20. PAGE 109 H2182 CHOOSE GUERRILLA

B61
NARAIN J.P.,SWARAJ FOR THE PEOPLE. INDIA CONSTN LOC/G MUNIC POL/PAR CHOOSE REPRESENT EFFICIENCY ATTIT PWR SOVEREIGN 20. PAGE 116 H2311 NAT/G ORD/FREE EDU/PROP EX/STRUC

B61
NIPPERDEY T.,DIE ORGANISATION DER DEUTSCHEN PARTEIEN VOR 1918. GERMANY CONSTN STRUCT TEC/DEV CHOOSE ADJUST ATTIT...CONCPT TIME/SEQ 19/20. PAGE 118 H2362 POL/PAR PARL/PROC NAT/G

B61
PALMER N.D.,THE INDIAN POLITICAL SYSTEM. INDIA ECO/UNDEV SECT CHIEF COLONIAL CHOOSE ALL/IDEOS SOCISM...CHARTS BIBLIOG/A 20. PAGE 123 H2452 NAT/LISM POL/PAR NAT/G DIPLOM

B61
SEMINAR REPRESENTATIVE GOVT,AFRO-ASIAN ATTITUDES: SEMINAR ON REPRESENTATIVE GOVERNMENTSPUBLIC LIBERTIES IN STATES OF ASIA AND AFRICA, RHODES, 1958. AFR ASIA BURMA INDIA ISLAM UAR VIETNAM/S SOCIETY POL/PAR CHIEF EDU/PROP PRESS PERSON ...POLICY INT 20 TUNIS. PAGE 141 H2826 CHOOSE ATTIT NAT/COMP ORD/FREE

B61
TREVE W.,DEUTSCHE PARTEIPROGRAMME 1861-1961. GERMANY GERMANY/W DELIB/GP CONFER CHOOSE REPRESENT 19/20. PAGE 157 H3130 POL/PAR NAT/G LEGIS PARL/PROC

B61
WARD R.E.,JAPANESE POLITICAL SCIENCE: A GUIDE TO JAPANESE REFERENCE AND RESEARCH MATERIALS (2ND ED.). LAW CONSTN STRATA NAT/G POL/PAR DELIB/GP LEGIS ADMIN CHOOSE GP/REL...INT/LAW 19/20 CHINJAP. PAGE 165 H3306 BIBLIOG/A PHIL/SCI

B61
WEST F.J.,POLITICAL ADVANCEMENT IN THE SOUTH PACIFIC. CONSTN CULTURE POL/PAR LEGIS DOMIN ADMIN CHOOSE SOVEREIGN VAL/FREE 20 FIJI TAHITI SAMOA. PAGE 167 H3335 S/ASIA LOC/G COLONIAL

S61
FITZGIBBON R.H.,"MEASUREMENT OF LATIN AMERICAN POLITICAL CHANGE." L/A+17C CONSTN CULTURE SOCIETY ECO/UNDEV NAT/G POL/PAR PUB/INST ACT/RES EDU/PROP PERCEPT KNOWL ORD/FREE SOVEREIGN...METH/CNCPT TREND OAS 20. PAGE 51 H1020 CHOOSE ATTIT

S61
LOEWENBERG G.,"PARLIAMENTARISM IN WESTERN GERMANY: THE FUNCTIONING OF THE BUNDESTAG" (BMR)" GERMANY/W NAT/G POL/PAR CHIEF LEAD 20 PARLIAMENT. PAGE 98 H1952 LEGIS CHOOSE CONSTN PARL/PROC

C61
LAPONCE J.A.,"THE GOVERNMENT OF THE FIFTH REPUBLIC." FRANCE CHIEF LEGIS PARL/PROC CHOOSE ...CHARTS GP/COMP IDEA/COMP BIBLIOG/A 20. PAGE 91 H1814 POL/PAR NAT/G CONSTN DOMIN

C61
MOODIE G.C.,"THE GOVERNMENT OF GREAT BRITAIN." UK LAW STRUCT LOC/G POL/PAR DIPLOM RECEIVE ADMIN COLONIAL CHOOSE...BIBLIOG 20 PARLIAMENT. PAGE 112 H2247 NAT/G SOCIETY PARL/PROC GOV/COMP

B62
ABOSCH H.,THE MENACE OF THE MIRACLE: GERMANY FROM HITLER TO ADENAUER. EUR+WWI GERMANY/W CULTURE FORCES PRESS NUC/PWR WAR CHOOSE 20 HITLER/A ADENAUER/K. PAGE 3 H0057 DIPLOM PEACE POLICY

B62
ANDREWS W.G.,EUROPEAN POLITICAL INSTITUTIONS. FRANCE GERMANY UK USSR TOP/EX LEAD PARL/PROC CHOOSE 20. PAGE 7 H0139 NAT/COMP POL/PAR EX/STRUC LEGIS

B62
ANDREWS W.G.,FRENCH POLITICS AND ALGERIA: THE PROCESS OF POLICY FORMATION 1954-1962. ALGERIA FRANCE CONSTN ELITES POL/PAR CHIEF DELIB/GP LEGIS DIPLOM PRESS CHOOSE 20. PAGE 7 H0140 GOV/COMP EXEC COLONIAL

B62
BRETTON H.L.,POWER AND STABILITY IN NIGERIA: THE POLITICS OF DECOLONIZATION. AFR CONSTN INTELL ECO/UNDEV COM/IND KIN NAT/G POL/PAR PROVS VOL/ASSN LEGIS DOMIN EDU/PROP LEGIT EXEC ROUTINE CHOOSE NAT/LISM ATTIT PERCEPT ALL/VALS. PAGE 20 H0411 CULTURE OBS NIGERIA

B62
CARTER G.M.,AFRICAN ONE-PARTY STATES. ISLAM IVORY/CST LIBERIA CONSTN CULTURE SOCIETY POL/PAR PLAN DOMIN EDU/PROP EXEC REGION CHOOSE ATTIT ALL/VALS...CONCPT TIME/SEQ CHARTS VAL/FREE 20 TANGANYIKA. PAGE 27 H0545 AFR NAT/LISM

B62
CHAPMAN R.M.,NEW ZEALAND POLITICS IN ACTION: THE 1960 GENERAL ELECTION. NEW/ZEALND LEGIS EDU/PROP PRESS TV LEAD ATTIT...STAND/INT 20. PAGE 29 H0582 NAT/G CHOOSE POL/PAR

B62
HATCH J.,AFRICA TODAY-AND TOMORROW: AN OUTLINE OF BASIC FACTS AND MAJOR PROBLEMS. AFR FUT ISLAM STRATA ECO/UNDEV INT/ORG NAT/G POL/PAR DELIB/GP TOP/EX EDU/PROP LEGIT CHOOSE ATTIT...TIME/SEQ TOT/POP COLD/WAR 20. PAGE 67 H1353 PLAN CONSTN NAT/LISM

B62
HOOK S.,THE PARADOXES OF FREEDOM. UNIV CONSTN INTELL LEGIS CONTROL REV CHOOSE SUPEGO...POLICY JURID IDEA/COMP 19/20 CIV/RIGHTS. PAGE 73 H1461 CONCPT MAJORIT ORD/FREE ALL/VALS

B62
STATE AND LOCAL GOVERNMENT. MUNIC NAT/G NEIGH PRESS CONTROL CHOOSE REPRESENT...BIBLIOG 20. PAGE 104 H2076 PROVS LOC/G GOV/REL PWR

B62
RANNEY A.,THE DOCTRINE OF RESPONSIBLE PARTY GOVERNMENT. USA+45 USA-45 CONSTN PLAN CHOOSE POL/PAR POLICY

...MAJORIT GOV/COMP IDEA/COMP 20. PAGE 130 H2591 REPRESENT NAT/G

B62
RUDE G.,WILKES AND LIBERTY. UK NAT/G POL/PAR REPRESENT ORD/FREE...SOC 18. PAGE 136 H2711 PARL/PROC CHOOSE STRATA STRUCT

B62
SCALAPINO R.A.,PARTIES AND POLITICS IN CONTEMPORARY JAPAN. EX/STRUC DIPLOM CHOOSE NAT/LISM ATTIT ...POLICY 20 CHINJAP. PAGE 138 H2762 POL/PAR PARL/PROC ELITES DECISION

B62
STARR R.E.,POLAND 1944-1962: THE SOVIETIZATION OF A CAPTIVE PEOPLE. COM POLAND USSR POL/PAR SECT LEGIS DIPLOM DOMIN EDU/PROP CHOOSE ORD/FREE...POLICY CHARTS BIBLIOG 20. PAGE 149 H2973 MARXISM NAT/G TOTALISM NAT/COMP

B62
VAN RENSBURG P.,GUILTY LAND: THE HISTORY OF APARTHEID. SOUTH/AFR NAT/G POL/PAR DOMIN CHOOSE ...SOC 19/20 NEGRO. PAGE 162 H3231 RACE/REL DISCRIM NAT/LISM POLICY

L62
NOLTE E.,"ZUR PHANOMENOLOGIE DES FASCHIMUS." EUR+WWI GERMANY ITALY TURKEY INTELL NAT/G CHIEF CONSULT FORCES CREATE DOMIN EDU/PROP COERCE WAR CHOOSE DRIVE FASCISM...PSY CONCPT MYTH GEN/METH LEAGUE/NAT NAZI 20. PAGE 118 H2367 ATTIT PWR

S62
ANSPRENGER F.,"NATIONALISM, COMMUNISM, AND THE UNCOMMITTED NATIONS: AMERICAN PROFILES." FUT ISLAM CULTURE SOCIETY ECO/UNDEV NAT/G POL/PAR PLAN ECO/TAC EDU/PROP COERCE CHOOSE ALL/VALS MARXISM SOCISM...SOC CONCPT BIOG TREND 20. PAGE 7 H0142 AFR COM NAT/LISM

S62
GUETZKOW H.,"THE POTENTIAL OF CASE STUDY IN ANALYZING INTERNATIONAL CONFLICT." EUR+WWI FUT GERMANY INTELL SOCIETY STRUCT INT/ORG LOC/G NAT/G CONSULT CREATE PLAN CHOOSE ATTIT RIGID/FLEX ...POLICY SAAR 20. PAGE 62 H1246 EDU/PROP METH/CNCPT COERCE FRANCE

S62
SHATTEN F.,"POLYCENTRISM: AFRICA: NATIONALISM AND COMMUNISM." ASIA COM FUT ISLAM CULTURE SOCIETY ECO/UNDEV NAT/G PLAN DOMIN COLONIAL COERCE CHOOSE RIGID/FLEX ALL/VALS MARXISM...CONCPT TREND 20. PAGE 143 H2852 AFR ATTIT NAT/LISM SOCISM

B63
ARAZI A.,LE SYSTEME ELECTORAL ISRAELIEN. ISRAEL NAT/G ADMIN ALL/VALS PARLIAMENT. PAGE 8 H0158 LEGIS CHOOSE POL/PAR

B63
BARNETT A.D.,COMMUNIST STRATEGIES IN ASIA: A COMPARATIVE ANALYSIS OF GOVERNMENTS AND PARTIES. COM FUT S/ASIA CULTURE SOCIETY STRATA NAT/G DELIB/GP ACT/RES ECO/TAC EDU/PROP COERCE CHOOSE ATTIT RIGID/FLEX ORD/FREE PWR SKILL...SIMUL VAL/FREE 20. PAGE 11 H0223 ASIA POL/PAR DIPLOM USSR

B63
CARTER G.M.,FIVE AFRICAN STATES: RESPONSES TO DIVERSITY. CONSTN CULTURE STRATA LEGIS PLAN ECO/TAC DOMIN EDU/PROP CT/SYS EXEC CHOOSE ATTIT HEALTH ORD/FREE PWR...TIME/SEQ TOT/POP VAL/FREE. PAGE 27 H0547 AFR SOCIETY

B63
ECKSTEIN H.,COMPARATIVE POLITICS. POL/PAR LEGIS CT/SYS CHOOSE TOTALISM PWR POPULISM...METH/COMP GEN/METH ANTHOL BIBLIOG 20. PAGE 44 H0886 NAT/COMP CONSTN REPRESENT NAT/G

B63
FRANZ G.,TEILUNG UND WIEDERVEREINIGUNG. GERMANY IRELAND ITALY NETHERLAND POLAND CULTURE BAL/PWR CHOOSE NAT/LISM ORD/FREE SOVEREIGN 19/20. PAGE 53 H1054 DIPLOM WAR NAT/COMP ATTIT

B63
GLUCKMAN M.,ORDER AND REBELLION IN TRIBAL AFRICA. EUR+WWI LAW CULTURE STRATA KIN MUNIC DELIB/GP ACT/RES DOMIN EDU/PROP LEGIT ADMIN COERCE CHOOSE ATTIT PERSON ORD/FREE PWR...SOC CHARTS GEN/LAWS TOT/POP VAL/FREE. PAGE 57 H1147 AFR SOCIETY

B63
GOURNAY B.,PUBLIC ADMINISTRATION. FRANCE LAW CONSTN AGRI FINAN LABOR SCHOOL EX/STRUC CHOOSE...MGT METH/COMP 20. PAGE 59 H1189 BIBLIOG/A ADMIN NAT/G LOC/G

B63
HUGHES A.J.,EAST AFRICA: THE SEARCH FOR UNITY-KENYA, TANGANYIKA, UGANDA, AND ZANZIBAR. TANZANIA UGANDA CONSTN POL/PAR SECT CHIEF DELIB/GP LEGIS WAR CHOOSE NAT/LISM MARXISM...POLICY CHARTS 20 NEGRO UN. PAGE 74 H1488 NAT/G DOMIN LOC/G AFR

B63
MAIR L.,NEW NATIONS. AFR FAM MUNIC SECT DOMIN CHOOSE NAT/LISM ORD/FREE...SOC 19/20. PAGE 101 H2022 COLONIAL CULTURE TEC/DEV ECO/UNDEV

B63
MCPHEE W.N.,FORMAL THEORIES OF MASS BEHAVIOR. CULTURE STRUCT DOMIN EDU/PROP CHOOSE...MATH 20. PAGE 108 H2149 SOC METH CONCPT ATTIT

B63
SKLAR R.L.,NIGERIAN POLITICAL PARTIES: POWER IN AN EMERGENT AFRICAN NATION. AFR EUR+WWI CULTURE STRATA NAT/G DELIB/GP EX/STRUC LEGIS DOMIN EDU/PROP ROUTINE CHOOSE ATTIT PERCEPT ORD/FREE PWR...SOC CONCPT OBS TOT/POP VAL/FREE. PAGE 145 H2898 POL/PAR SOCIETY NAT/LISM NIGERIA

B63
WEINER M.,POLITICAL CHANGE IN SOUTH ASIA. CEYLON INDIA PAKISTAN S/ASIA CULTURE ELITES ECO/UNDEV EX/STRUC ADMIN CONTROL CHOOSE CONSERVE...GOV/COMP ANTHOL 20. PAGE 166 H3328 NAT/G CONSTN TEC/DEV

L63
ROSE R.,"COMPARATIVE STUDIES IN POLITICAL FINANCE: A SYMPOSIUM." ASIA EUR+WWI S/ASIA LAW CULTURE DELIB/GP LEGIS ACT/RES ECO/TAC EDU/PROP CHOOSE ATTIT RIGID/FLEX SUPEGO PWR SKILL WEALTH...STAT ANTHOL VAL/FREE. PAGE 134 H2674 FINAN POL/PAR

S63
DUDLEY B.J.,"THE NOMINATION OF PARLIAMENTARY CANDIDATES IN NORTHERN NIGERIA." AFR CONSTN CULTURE ELITES STRATA DELIB/GP LEGIS DOMIN EDU/PROP COERCE ATTIT SUPEGO PWR...STAT VAL/FREE 20. PAGE 43 H0854 POL/PAR CHOOSE NIGERIA

S63
LEE J.M.,"PARLIAMENT IN REPUBLICAN GHANA." AFR CONSTN CULTURE SOCIETY STRATA POL/PAR DELIB/GP TOP/EX DOMIN EDU/PROP LEGIT COERCE CHOOSE ATTIT ALL/VALS...CONCPT STAT TIME/SEQ VAL/FREE 20. PAGE 93 H1857 LEGIS GHANA

S63
NICHOLAS W.,"VILLAGE FACTIONS AND POLITICAL PARTIES IN RURAL WEST BENGAL." S/ASIA CULTURE STRATA FACE/GP KIN MUNIC DELIB/GP LEGIS DOMIN EDU/PROP COERCE CHOOSE ATTIT ALL/VALS...STAT TOT/POP VAL/FREE 20. PAGE 117 H2348 NEIGH POL/PAR

S63
TILMAN R.O.,"MALAYSIA: THE PROBLEMS OF FEDERATION." ISLAM S/ASIA CONSTN PROVS SECT DELIB/GP DOMIN EDU/PROP LEGIT EXEC COERCE CHOOSE ATTIT HEALTH ORD/FREE PWR...STAT TOT/POP VAL/FREE 20. PAGE 155 H3097 NAT/G CULTURE MALAYSIA

S63
WELLS H.,"THE OAS AND THE DOMINICAN ELECTIONS." L/A+17C INT/ORG NAT/G POL/PAR TEC/DEV ECO/TAC EDU/PROP PERCEPT...TIME/SEQ OAS TOT/POP 20. PAGE 166 H3332 CONSULT CHOOSE DOMIN/REP

B64
AGGER R.E.,THE RULERS AND THE RULED: POLITICAL POWER AND IMPOTENCE IN AMERICAN COMMUNITIES. CULTURE DOMIN CHOOSE ATTIT ALL/VALS...DECISION SOC CONCPT OBS QU CHARTS. PAGE 4 H0079 PWR STRUCT LOC/G MUNIC

B64
BERRINGTON H.,HOW NATIONS ARE GOVERNED. FRANCE WOR+45 ECO/UNDEV INT/ORG POL/PAR CHOOSE TOTALISM KNOWL...MAJORIT T 20 UN COMMONWLTH THIRD/WRLD. PAGE 16 H0320 NAT/G GOV/COMP ECO/DEV CONSTN

B64
BRZEZINSKI Z.,POLITICAL POWER: USA/USSR. USA+45 USSR AGRI POL/PAR FORCES CREATE CHOOSE ATTIT ORD/FREE PWR MARXISM...MYTH 20 KENNEDY/JF. PAGE 23 H0457 NAT/G NAT/COMP POLICY LEAD

B64
BUTWELL R.,SOUTHEAST ASIA TODAY - AND TOMORROW. NAT/G COLONIAL LEAD REGION WAR CHOOSE WEALTH MARXISM 20. PAGE 25 H0500 S/ASIA DIPLOM ECO/UNDEV NAT/LISM

B64
FRIEDLAND W.H.,AFRICAN SOCIALISM. ECO/UNDEV MARKET LABOR NAT/G POL/PAR PLAN CAP/ISM ECO/TAC EDU/PROP CHOOSE ATTIT DRIVE PWR WEALTH...POLICY CONCPT RECORD STERTYP 20. PAGE 53 H1063 AFR SOCISM

B64
GOODNOW H.F.,THE CIVIL SERVICE OF PAKISTAN: BUREAUCRACY IN A NEW NATION. INDIA PAKISTAN S/ASIA ECO/UNDEV PROVS CHIEF PARTIC CHOOSE EFFICIENCY PWR ...BIBLIOG 20. PAGE 59 H1173 ADMIN GOV/REL LAW NAT/G

B64
GROSSER A.,THE FEDERAL REPUBLIC OF GERMANY: A CONCISE HISTORY. GERMANY/W STRUCT MORAL ORD/FREE POPULISM SOCISM...SOC CONCPT 20. PAGE 62 H1235 NAT/G POL/PAR CHOOSE DIPLOM

B64
GROVES H.E.,THE CONSTITUTION OF MALAYSIA. MALAYSIA POL/PAR CHIEF CONSULT DELIB/GP CT/SYS PARL/PROC CHOOSE FEDERAL ORD/FREE 20. PAGE 62 H1238 CONSTN NAT/G LAW

B64
HANNA W.J.,POLITICS IN BLACK AFRICA: A SELECTIVE BIBLIOGRAPHY OF RELEVANT PERIODICAL LITERATURE. AFR LAW LOC/G MUNIC NAT/G POL/PAR LOBBY CHOOSE RACE/REL SOVEREIGN 20. PAGE 66 H1315 BIBLIOG NAT/LISM COLONIAL

B64
KAACK H.,DIE PARTEIEN IN DER POL/PAR

VERFASSUNGSWIRKLICHKEIT DER BUNDESREPUBLIK. GERMANY/W ADMIN PARL/PROC CHOOSE...JURID 20. PAGE 82 H1646
PROVS NAT/G
B64

KRUEGER H.,ALLGEMEINE STAATSLEHRE. WOR+45 CONSTN SECT CHOOSE INGP/REL PWR NEW/LIB...JURID CLASSIF IDEA/COMP. PAGE 89 H1777
NAT/G GOV/COMP SOCIETY
B64

LEMARCHAND R.,POLITICAL AWAKENING IN THE BELGIAN CONGO. ECO/UNDEV VOL/ASSN DOMIN CHOOSE GP/REL INGP/REL DISCRIM ORD/FREE PWR...CHARTS 20 CONGO ARABS. PAGE 94 H1873
NAT/LISM COLONIAL POL/PAR RACE/REL
B64

PERKINS D.,THE AMERICAN DEMOCRACY: ITS RISE TO POWER. ASIA USSR LAW CULTURE FINAN EDU/PROP COLONIAL CHOOSE...POLICY CHARTS BIBLIOG WORSHIP PRESIDENT 15/20 NEGRO. PAGE 125 H2492
LOC/G ECO/TAC WAR DIPLOM
B64

PHILLIPS C.S.,THE DEVELOPMENT OF NIGERIAN FOREIGN POLICY. AFR CONSTN CULTURE STRATA NAT/G LEGIS DOMIN LEGIT EXEC...RELATIV SOC TIME/SEQ TREND TOT/POP 20. PAGE 125 H2502
CHOOSE POLICY DIPLOM NIGERIA
B64

SKINNER E.P.,THE MOSSI OF UPPER VOLTA: THE POLITICAL DEVELOPMENT OF A SUDANESE PEOPLE. AFR LAW AGRI FAM KIN POL/PAR PROVS SECT DELIB/GP EX/STRUC FORCES TOP/EX DOMIN EDU/PROP LEGIT CT/SYS COERCE CHOOSE ORD/FREE PWR WEALTH...SOC MYTH VAL/FREE. PAGE 145 H2897
CULTURE OBS UPPER/VOLT
B64

TINKER H.,BALLOT BOX AND BAYONET - PEOPLE AND GOVERNMENT IN EMERGENT ASIAN COUNTRIES. CEYLON INDIA INDONESIA PHILIPPINE POL/PAR ADMIN COLONIAL LEAD PARL/PROC CHOOSE CONSEN ORD/FREE SOVEREIGN PLURISM...GOV/COMP THIRD/WRLD. PAGE 155 H3104
MYTH S/ASIA NAT/COMP NAT/LISM
B64

WARD R.E.,POLITICAL MODERNIZATION IN JAPAN AND TURKEY. ASIA ISLAM S/ASIA CONSTN CULTURE STRATA COM/IND POL/PAR FORCES ACT/RES ECO/TAC DOMIN EDU/PROP LEGIT ADMIN CHOOSE ATTIT ALL/VALS...STAT TIME/SEQ VAL/FREE CHINJAP. PAGE 165 H3307
SOCIETY TURKEY
B64

WRIGHT G.,RURAL REVOLUTION IN FRANCE: THE PEASANTRY IN THE TWENTIETH CENTURY. EUR+WWI MOD/EUR LAW CULTURE AGRI POL/PAR DELIB/GP LEGIS ECO/TAC EDU/PROP COERCE CHOOSE ATTIT RIGID/FLEX HEALTH ...STAT CENSUS CHARTS VAL/FREE 20. PAGE 171 H3419
PWR STRATA FRANCE REV
B64

ZARTMAN I.W.,MOROCCO: PROBLEMS OF NEW POWER. ISLAM CULTURE ECO/UNDEV AGRI POL/PAR SCHOOL FORCES ADMIN ...CONCPT STAT INT CENSUS TIME/SEQ CHARTS WORK VAL/FREE 20. PAGE 172 H3449
CHOOSE MOROCCO DELIB/GP DECISION
S64

MERKL P.H.,"EUROPEAN ASSEMBLY PARTIES AND NATIONAL DELEGATIONS." INT/ORG DELIB/GP DOMIN EDU/PROP LEGIT CHOOSE PWR...STAT VAL/FREE 20. PAGE 109 H2180
EUR+WWI POL/PAR REGION
S64

SAYEED K.,"PATHAN REGIONALISM." ISLAM PAKISTAN S/ASIA CULTURE SOCIETY NAT/G NEIGH DIPLOM LEGIT COERCE CHOOSE ATTIT DISPL PERCEPT ALL/VALS SOVEREIGN...POLICY RELATIV SOC TIME/SEQ TOT/POP 20. PAGE 138 H2761
SECT NAT/LISM REGION
S64

SCHEFFLER H.W.,"THE GENESIS AND REPRESSION OF CONFLICT: CHOISEUL ISLAND." S/ASIA LOC/G NAT/G FORCES LEGIS DIPLOM DOMIN LEGIT EXEC CHOOSE ATTIT RESPECT SKILL...POLICY JURID OBS TREND GEN/METH 20. PAGE 139 H2781
PWR COERCE WAR
C64

SCOTT R.E.,"MEXICAN GOVERNMENT IN TRANSITION (REV ED)" CULTURE STRUCT POL/PAR CHIEF ADMIN LOBBY REV CHOOSE GP/REL DRIVE...BIBLIOG METH 20 MEXIC/AMER. PAGE 141 H2816
NAT/G L/A+17C ROUTINE CONSTN
B65

AIYAR S.P.,STUDIES IN INDIAN DEMOCRACY. INDIA STRATA ECO/UNDEV LABOR POL/PAR LEGIS DIPLOM LOBBY REGION CHOOSE ATTIT SOCISM...ANTHOL 20. PAGE 4 H0086
ORD/FREE REPRESENT ADMIN NAT/G
B65

ALLEN W.S.,THE NAZI SEIZURE OF POWER. GERMANY NAT/G CHIEF LEAD COERCE CHOOSE REPRESENT GOV/REL AUTHORIT ...DECISION 20 HITLER/A NAZI. PAGE 5 H0106
MUNIC FASCISM TOTALISM LOC/G
B65

BAYNE E.A.,FOUR WAYS OF POLITICS: STATE AND NATION IN ITALY, SOMALIA, ISRAEL, AND IRAN. IRAN ISRAEL ITALY SOMALIA LEAD CHOOSE MAJORITY GOV/COMP. PAGE 12 H0244
ECO/UNDEV NAT/G DECISION TOP/EX
B65

BETTISON D.G.,THE PAPUA-GUINEA ELECTIONS 1964. S/ASIA CONSTN POL/PAR EDU/PROP PARTIC SUFF CENTRAL CONSEN...OBS CHARTS BIBLIOG 20. PAGE 16 H0324
NAT/G LEGIS CHOOSE REPRESENT
B65

BRASS P.R.,FACTIONAL POLITICS IN AN INDIAN STATE: THE CONGRESS PARTY IN UTTAR PRADESH. INDIA UK CONSTN CULTURE ECO/UNDEV LOC/G DOMIN COLONIAL CROWD GP/REL ADJUST CENTRAL RIGID/FLEX SOVEREIGN 20 UTTAR/PRAD CONGRESS/P. PAGE 20 H0406
POL/PAR PROVS LEGIS CHOOSE
B65

BULMER-THOMAS I.,THE GROWTH OF THE BRITISH PARTY SYSTEM (VOL. II) 1924-1964. UK ECO/DEV BARGAIN WAR CHOOSE ATTIT ORD/FREE 20 LABOR/PAR CONSRV/PAR. PAGE 23 H0472
CHIEF POL/PAR PARL/PROC NAT/G
B65

CARTER G.M.,GOVERNMENT AND POLITICS IN THE TWENTIETH CENTURY (REV. ED.). WOR+45 NAT/G POL/PAR LEGIS DIPLOM LEAD PARL/PROC CHOOSE TOTALISM 20. PAGE 27 H0549
GOV/COMP ECO/UNDEV ALL/IDEOS ECO/DEV
B65

CHARNAY J.P.,LE SUFFRAGE POLITIQUE EN FRANCE; ELECTIONS PARLEMENTAIRES, ELECTION PRESIDENTIELLE, REFERENDUMS. FRANCE CONSTN CHIEF DELIB/GP ECO/TAC EDU/PROP CRIME INGP/REL MORAL ORD/FREE PWR CATHISM 20 PARLIAMENT PRESIDENT. PAGE 29 H0584
CHOOSE SUFF NAT/G LEGIS
B65

FAGG J.E.,CUBA, HAITI, AND THE DOMINICAN REPUBLIC. CUBA DOMIN/REP HAITI L/A+17C NAT/G DIPLOM ECO/TAC DOMIN CHOOSE AUTHORIT ROLE SOVEREIGN POPULISM 17/20. PAGE 48 H0959
COLONIAL ECO/UNDEV REV GOV/COMP
B65

FAUST J.J.,A REVOLUCAO DEVORA SEUS PRESIDENTES. BRAZIL NAT/G POL/PAR LEAD CHOOSE CIVMIL/REL ORD/FREE 20 PRESIDENT. PAGE 49 H0976
PARTIC REV FORCES GP/REL
B65

FREY F.W.,THE TURKISH POLITICAL ELITE. TURKEY CULTURE INTELL NAT/G EX/STRUC CHOOSE ATTIT PWR ...METH/CNCPT CHARTS WORSHIP 20. PAGE 53 H1059
ELITES SOCIETY POL/PAR
B65

GILG P.,DIE ERNEUERUNG DES DEMOKRATISCHEN DENKENS IM WILHELMINISCHEN DEUTSCHLAND. GERMANY PARL/PROC CHOOSE REPRESENT...CONCPT 19/20 BISMARCK/O WILHELM/II. PAGE 56 H1126
POL/PAR ORD/FREE NAT/G
B65

GREGG J.L.,POLITICAL PARTIES AND PARTY SYSTEMS IN GUATEMALA, 1944-1963. GUATEMALA L/A+17C EX/STRUC FORCES CREATE CONTROL REV CHOOSE PWR...TREND IDEA/COMP 20. PAGE 60 H1209
LEAD POL/PAR NAT/G CHIEF
B65

HADWIGER D.F.,PRESSURES AND PROTEST. NAT/G LEGIS PLAN LEAD PARTIC ROUTINE ATTIT POLICY. PAGE 63 H1273
AGRI GP/REL LOBBY CHOOSE
B65

HANSER C.J.,GUIDE TO DECISION: ROYAL COMMISSION. UK INTELL EXTR/IND SCHOOL PROB/SOLV EXEC ROUTINE CHOOSE GOV/REL GP/REL HEALTH...CHARTS 20. PAGE 66 H1318
NAT/G DELIB/GP EX/STRUC PWR
B65

NAMIER L.B.,THE STRUCTURE OF POLITICS AT THE ACCESSION OF GEORGE III. UK LOC/G TOP/EX COLONIAL LEAD PARTIC REV CHOOSE REPRESENT GOV/REL PERSON SOVEREIGN...GOV/COMP 18 PARLIAMENT. PAGE 115 H2309
PARL/PROC LEGIS NAT/G POL/PAR
B65

PEASLEE A.J.,CONSTITUTIONS OF NATIONS* THIRD REVISED EDITION (VOLUME I* AFRICA). LAW EX/STRUC LEGIS TOP/EX LEGIT CT/SYS ROUTINE ORD/FREE PWR SOVEREIGN...CON/ANAL CHARTS. PAGE 124 H2481
AFR CHOOSE CONSTN NAT/G
B65

SIRISKAR V.M.,POLITICAL BEHAVIOR IN INDIA. INDIA SOCIETY MUNIC NAT/G PROVS ACT/RES SUFF...OBS CHARTS 20 POONA. PAGE 144 H2889
CHOOSE POL/PAR PWR ATTIT
B65

STEINER K.,LOCAL GOVERNMENT IN JAPAN. CONSTN CULTURE NAT/G ADMIN CHOOSE...SOC STAT 20 CHINJAP. PAGE 149 H2976
LOC/G SOCIETY JURID ORD/FREE
S65

CAIRNS J.C.,"FRANCE, DECEMBER 1965: END OF THE ELECTIVE MONARACHY" EUR+WWI FRANCE FUT CONSTN SOCIETY CHIEF BAL/PWR ATTIT ALL/IDEOS 20 DEGAULLE/C PRESIDENT. PAGE 25 H0505
CHOOSE NAT/G POL/PAR PWR
N65

MOTE M.E.,SOVIET LOCAL AND REPUBLIC ELECTIONS. COM USSR NAT/G PLAN PARTIC GOV/REL TOTALISM PWR ...CHARTS 20. PAGE 114 H2270
CHOOSE ADMIN CONTROL LOC/G
B66

ADAMS J.C.,THE GOVERNMENT OF REPUBLICAN ITALY (2ND ED.). ITALY LOC/G POL/PAR DELIB/GP LEGIS WORKER ADMIN CT/SYS FASCISM...CHARTS BIBLIOG 20 PARLIAMENT. PAGE 3 H0064
NAT/G CHOOSE EX/STRUC CONSTN
B66

BEER S.H.,BRITISH POLITICS IN THE COLLECTIVIST AGE. UK NAT/G CONTROL CHOOSE GP/REL ATTIT PWR PLURISM ...MAJORIT WELF/ST 16/20. PAGE 13 H0258
POL/PAR SOCISM TRADIT GP/COMP
B66

BHALERAO C.N.,PUBLIC SERVICE COMMISSIONS OF INDIA: A STUDY. INDIA SERV/IND EX/STRUC ROUTINE CHOOSE
NAT/G OP/RES

GOV/REL INGP/REL...KNO/TEST EXHIBIT 20. PAGE 16 H0326 — LOC/G ADMIN

B66
BRECHER M.,SUCCESSION IN INDIA. INDIA USA+45 CONSTN AGRI POL/PAR PROVS SECT DELIB/GP FORCES PROB/SOLV ECO/TAC PWR...LING 20 CONGRESS NEHRU/J. PAGE 20 H0408 — CHIEF DECISION CHOOSE

B66
BUTLER D.E.,THE BRITISH GENERAL ELECTION OF 1966. UK LOC/G NAT/G OP/RES CONFER CHOOSE MAJORITY ATTIT ...CHARTS TIME 20. PAGE 25 H0498 — POL/PAR REPRESENT GP/REL PERS/REL

B66
COLE A.B.,SOCIALIST PARTIES IN POSTWAR JAPAN. STRATA AGRI LABOR PLAN DIPLOM ECO/TAC AGREE LEAD CHOOSE ATTIT...CHARTS 20 CHINJAP SOC/DEMPAR. PAGE 31 H0620 — POL/PAR POLICY SOCISM NAT/G

B66
DAHL R.A.,POLITICAL OPPOSITIONS IN WESTERN DEMOCRACIES. EUR+WWI USA+45 USA-45 SOCIETY STRATA ECO/DEV NAT/G LEGIS REPRESENT...TREND NAT/COMP ANTHOL 20. PAGE 37 H0732 — POL/PAR CHOOSE PARTIC PLURISM

B66
DE VORE B.B.,LAND AND LIBERTY; A HISTORY OF THE MEXICAN REVOLUTION. CONSTN INTELL NAT/G CONTROL LEAD CHOOSE TOTALISM AUTHORIT...BIBLIOG 19/20 MEXIC/AMER DIAZ/P LIB/PARTY MAGON/F MADERO/F. PAGE 39 H0776 — REV CHIEF POL/PAR

B66
DEUTSCHE INST ZEITGESCHICHTE,DIE WESTDEUTSCHEN PARTEIEN: 1945-1965. GERMANY/W CHOOSE PWR ...TIME/SEQ 20. PAGE 40 H0806 — POL/PAR CONCPT NAT/G PROVS

B66
FEINE H.E.,REICH UND KIRCHE. CHRIST-17C MOD/EUR ROMAN/EMP LAW CHOOSE ATTIT 10/19 CHURCH/STA ROMAN/LAW. PAGE 49 H0982 — JURID SECT NAT/G GP/REL

B66
FINER S.E.,ANONYMOUS EMPIRE: STUDY OF THE LOBBY IN GREAT BRITAIN. UK CONSTN LABOR POL/PAR SECT DOMIN EDU/PROP PRESS CHOOSE...CONCPT CHARTS 20 PARLIAMENT. PAGE 50 H1004 — LOBBY NAT/G LEGIS PWR

B66
FORD P.,CARDINAL MORAN AND THE A. L. P. NAT/G POL/PAR SECT DELIB/GP LOBBY REV CHOOSE ORD/FREE MARXISM 19/20 AUSTRAL PROTESTANT LABOR/PAR. PAGE 52 H1035 — CATHISM SOCISM LABOR SOCIETY

B66
GERARD-LIBOIS J.,KATANGA SECESSION. INT/ORG FORCES DIPLOM ADMIN CONTROL WAR CHOOSE PWR...CHARTS 20 KATANGA TSHOMBE/M UN. PAGE 56 H1114 — NAT/G REGION ORD/FREE REV

B66
GHOSH P.K.,THE CONSTITUTION OF INDIA: HOW IT HAS BEEN FRAMED. INDIA LOC/G DELIB/GP EX/STRUC PROB/SOLV BUDGET INT/TRADE CT/SYS CHOOSE...LING 20. PAGE 56 H1121 — CONSTN NAT/G LEGIS FEDERAL

B66
GUNN G.E.,THE POLITICAL HISTORY OF NEWFOUNDLAND 1832-1864. CANADA FINAN LEGIS CHOOSE REPRESENT ...CHARTS 19. PAGE 62 H1252 — POL/PAR NAT/G CONSTN

B66
INSTITUTE COMP STUDY POL SYS,DOMINICAN REPUBLIC ELECTION FACT BOOK. DOMIN/REP LAW LEGIS REPRESENT ...JURID CHARTS 20. PAGE 77 H1536 — SUFF CHOOSE POL/PAR NAT/G

B66
INTERPARLIAMENTARY UNION,PARLIAMENTS: COMPARATIVE STUDY ON STRUCTURE AND FUNCTIONING OF REPRESENTATIVE INSTITUTIONS IN FIFTY-FIVE COUNTRIES. WOR+45 POL/PAR DELIB/GP BUDGET ADMIN CONTROL CHOOSE. PAGE 78 H1560 — PARL/PROC LEGIS GOV/COMP EX/STRUC

B66
LONDON DAILY TELEGRAPH,ELECTION '66: GALLUP ANALYSIS OF THE VOTING RESULTS. UK LEGIS COMPUTER ATTIT...QU SAMP CHARTS 20 LABOR/PAR HOUSE/CMNS. PAGE 98 H1959 — STAT CHOOSE REPRESENT POL/PAR

B66
NOEL G.E.,THE NEW BRITAIN AND HAROLD WILSON: INTERIM REPORT, 1966 GENERAL ELECTION. UK POL/PAR CONSULT PROB/SOLV BUDGET DIPLOM ECO/TAC LEAD CHOOSE ATTIT 20 WILSON/H PARLIAMENT. PAGE 118 H2366 — BIOG PERSON NAT/G CHIEF

B66
SAINDERICHIN P.,HISTORIE SECRETE D'UNE ELECTION, DECEMBER 5-19, 1965. FRANCE NAT/G DELIB/GP LEGIS PLAN EDU/PROP TV SOCISM...MARXIST 20 DEGAULLE/C. PAGE 137 H2731 — CHOOSE CHIEF PROB/SOLV POL/PAR

B66
TORMIN W.,GESCHICHTE DER DEUTSCHEN PARTEIEN SEIT 1848. GERMANY CHOOSE PWR...CONCPT 19/20 WEIMAR/REP. PAGE 156 H3116 — POL/PAR CONSTN NAT/G TOTALISM

B66
WEINSTEIN F.B.,VIETNAM'S UNHELD ELECTIONS: THE FAILURE TO CARRY OUT THE 1956 REUNIFICATION ELECTIONS... (MONOGRAPH). VIETNAM/S VIETNAM/N LEGIT CONFER ADJUD WAR PEACE 20 TREATY GENEVA/CON UNIFICA. PAGE 166 H3330 — AGREE NAT/G CHOOSE DIPLOM

B66
WUEST J.J.,NEW SOURCE BOOK IN MAJOR EUROPEAN GOVERNMENTS. CHRIST-17C EUR+WWI FRANCE GERMANY ITALY MOD/EUR UK USSR LOC/G POL/PAR CHIEF EX/STRUC CHOOSE CONSERVE MARXISM...JURID T 13/20. PAGE 171 H3425 — NAT/G CONSTN LEGIS

S66
MATTHEWS D.G.,"PRELUDE-COUP D'ETAT-MILITARY GOVERNMENT: A BIBLIOGRAPHICAL AND RESEARCH GUIDE TO NIGERIAN POL AND GOVT, JAN, 1965-66." AFR NIGER LAW CONSTN POL/PAR LEGIS CIVMIL/REL GOV/REL...STAT 20. PAGE 105 H2096 — BIBLIOG NAT/G ADMIN CHOOSE

B67
DEGLER C.N.,THE AGE OF THE ECONOMIC REVOLUTION 1876-1900. USA-45 AGRI MUNIC POL/PAR SECT ECO/TAC CHOOSE...PHIL/SCI CHARTS NAT/COMP 19 NEGRO. PAGE 39 H0782 — INDUS SOCIETY ECO/DEV TEC/DEV

B67
ERDMAN H.L.,THE SWATANTRA PARTY AND INDIAN CONSERVATISM. INDIA S/ASIA SOCIETY STRATA LOC/G NAT/G LEAD PARTIC GP/REL ATTIT...CONCPT GP/COMP BIBLIOG 20 SWATANTRA. PAGE 47 H0938 — POL/PAR CONSERVE CHOOSE POLICY

B67
EVANS R.H.,COEXISTENCE: COMMUNISM AND ITS PRACTICE IN BOLOGNA, 1945-1965. ITALY CAP/ISM ADMIN CHOOSE PEACE ORD/FREE...SOC STAT DEEP/INT SAMP CHARTS BIBLIOG 20. PAGE 48 H0952 — MARXISM CULTURE MUNIC POL/PAR

B67
GELLHORN W.,OMBUDSMEN AND OTHERS: CITIZENS' PROTECTORS IN NINE COUNTRIES. WOR+45 LAW CONSTN LEGIS INSPECT ADJUD ADMIN CONTROL CT/SYS CHOOSE PERS/REL...STAT CHARTS 20. PAGE 55 H1109 — NAT/COMP REPRESENT INGP/REL PROB/SOLV

B67
JOUVENEL B D.E.,THE ART OF CONJECTURE. FUT CONSULT EX/STRUC CHOOSE GOV/REL ALL/VALS. PAGE 82 H1638 — PREDICT DELIB/GP PLAN NAT/G

B67
KORNBERG A.,CANADIAN LEGISLATIVE BEHAVIOR: A STUDY OF THE 25TH PARLIAMENT. CANADA NAT/G POL/PAR PARL/PROC CHOOSE INGP/REL ADJUST ANOMIE RIGID/FLEX ...SOC STAND/INT CHARTS SOC/EXP 20 PARLIAMENT. PAGE 88 H1756 — ATTIT LEGIS ROLE

B67
MORRIS A.J.A.,PARLIAMENTARY DEMOCRACY IN THE NINETEENTH CENTURY. UK INDUS LOC/G NAT/G POL/PAR CONSULT LEGIS INT/TRADE ADMIN CHOOSE SUFF SOVEREIGN 19 PARLIAMENT. PAGE 113 H2261 — TIME/SEQ CONSTN PARL/PROC POPULISM

B67
OPERATIONS AND POLICY RESEARCH,NICARAGUA: ELECTION FACTBOOK: FEBRUARY 5, 1967 (PAMPHLET). NICARAGUA LAW NAT/G LEAD REPRESENT...STAT BIOG CHARTS 20. PAGE 121 H2423 — POL/PAR CHOOSE PLAN ATTIT

B67
RAE D.,THE POLITICAL CONSEQUENCES OF ELECTORAL LAWS. EUR+WWI ICELAND ISRAEL NEW/ZEALND UK USA+45 ADJUD APPORT GP/REL MAJORITY...MATH STAT CENSUS CHARTS BIBLIOG 20 AUSTRAL. PAGE 129 H2579 — POL/PAR CHOOSE NAT/COMP REPRESENT

S67
ADOKO A.,"THE CONSTITUTION OF UGANDA." AFR UGANDA LOC/G CHIEF FORCES LEGIS ADJUD EXEC CHOOSE NAT/LISM ...IDEA/COMP 20. PAGE 4 H0072 — NAT/G CONSTN ORD/FREE LAW

S67
COLLINS B.A.,"SOME NOTES ON PUBLIC SERVICE COMMISSIONS IN THE COMMONWEALTH CARIBBEAN." JAMAICA L/A+17C TRINIDAD UK NAT/G OP/RES DOMIN SENIOR COLONIAL CONTROL INGP/REL CENTRAL EFFICIENCY PWR ...DECISION 20. PAGE 31 H0631 — ADMIN EX/STRUC ECO/UNDEV CHOOSE

S67
FUSARO A.,"THE EFFECT OF PROPORTIONAL REPRESENTATION ON VOTING IN THE AUSTRALIAN SENATE." S/ASIA CONSTN POL/PAR CONTROL GP/REL PWR...CHARTS 20 AUSTRAL HOUSE/REP SENATE. PAGE 54 H1083 — LEGIS CHOOSE REPRESENT NAT/G

S67
LAQUEUR W.,"BONN IS NOT WEIMAR* REFLECTIONS ON THE RADICAL RIGHT IN GER MANY." CULTURE LOC/G NAT/G PARTIC CHOOSE. PAGE 91 H1822 — GERMANY/W FASCISM NAT/LISM

S67
LEGRES A.,"LES FONCTIONS D'UN PARLEMENT MODERNE." FRANCE DEBATE PARL/PROC SANCTION ATTIT PWR 20 PARLIAMENT. PAGE 93 H1860 — NAT/G LAW LEGIS CHOOSE

S67
LEHMBRUCH G.,"WAHLREFORM UND POLITISCHES SYSTEM." NETHERLAND NAT/G LEGIS PARL/PROC...SOC 20. PAGE 93 H1864 — CHOOSE POL/PAR METH/CNCPT GP/COMP

S67
MALAN V.D.,"THE SILENT VILLAGE." KIN MUNIC NEIGH CHOOSE ISOLAT ROLE...SOC INDIAN/AM. PAGE 101 H2027 — CULTURE STRUCT PREDICT

S67
MALLORY J.R.,"THE MINISTER'S OFFICE STAFF* AN UNREFORMED PART OF PUBLIC SERVICE." CONSTN ELITES STRATA NAT/G PROB/SOLV TASK CHOOSE PERS/REL EFFICIENCY...DECISION 20. PAGE 102 H2033
CANADA ADMIN EX/STRUC STRUCT

S67
MARWICK A.,"THE LABOUR PARTY AND THE WELFARE STATE IN BRITAIN, 19001948." UK SOCIETY STRUCT ECO/DEV WORKER CREATE PRICE CHOOSE WEALTH NEW/LIB SOCISM ...POLICY HEAL 20 PARLIAMENT LABOR/PAR. PAGE 104 H2074
POL/PAR RECEIVE LEGIS NAT/G

S67
NEALE R.S.,"WORKING CLASS WOMEN AND WOMEN'S SUFFRAGE." UK LAW CONSTN LABOR NAT/G DELIB/GP LEGIS WORKER PAY PARTIC CHOOSE 19 FEMALE/SEX. PAGE 116 H2326
STRATA SEX SUFF DISCRIM

S67
NEUBAUER D.E.,"SOME CONDITIONS OF DEMOCRACY." ECO/DEV COM/IND DIST/IND POL/PAR EDU/PROP REPRESENT ...SOC STAT NAT/COMP 20. PAGE 117 H2331
NAT/G CHOOSE MAJORIT ECO/UNDEV

S67
OOSTEN F.,"SUDVIETNAM IM JAHR VOR DER ENTSCHEIDUNG." VIETNAM/S VIETNAM/N NAT/G DIPLOM COERCE CHOOSE 20. PAGE 121 H2420
FORCES WAR WEAPON ATTIT

S67
ROCHET W.,"THE OCTOBER REVOLUTION AND THE STRUGGLE OF THE FRENCH COMMUNISTS." COM FRANCE ELITES SOCIETY STRATA ECO/TAC EDU/PROP GP/REL WEALTH ...MARXIST IDEA/COMP NAT/COMP 20. PAGE 133 H2654
SOCISM CHOOSE METH/COMP NAT/G

S67
SIPPEL D.,"INDIENS UNSICHERE ZUKUNFT." INDIA CULTURE ACADEM POL/PAR LEGIS COLONIAL CHOOSE SOVEREIGN...JURID 20. PAGE 144 H2888
SOCIETY STRUCT ECO/UNDEV NAT/G

S67
SOARES G.,"SOCIO-ECONOMIC VARIABLES AND VOTING FOR THE RADICAL LEFT: CHILE 1952." CHILE INDUS NAT/G WORKER ADJUST STRANGE ANOMIE WEALTH...METH/CNCPT CORREL 20. PAGE 146 H2925
STRATA POL/PAR CHOOSE STAT

S67
TAYLOR P.B. JR.,"PROGRESS IN VENEZUELA." L/A+17C VENEZUELA AGRI INDUS LG/CO NAT/G SML/CO CHOOSE ...POLICY 20. PAGE 153 H3057
ECO/UNDEV ECO/TAC POL/PAR ORD/FREE

S67
WILLIAMS F.R.A.,"FUNDAMENTAL RIGHTS AND THE PROSPECT FOR DEMOCRACY IN NIGERIA." FUT NIGERIA SOCIETY ECO/UNDEV LEGIS ADJUD CHOOSE 20. PAGE 168 H3366
CONSTN LAW ORD/FREE NAT/G

S67
WILLIAMS P.M.,"THE FRENCH GENERAL ELECTION OF MARCH 1967." FRANCE INDUS WORKER NAT/LISM PWR SOCISM 20. PAGE 168 H3368
POL/PAR NAT/G ATTIT CHOOSE

S67
WILSON J.Q.,"A GUIDE TO REAGAN COUNTRY* THE POLITICAL CULTURE OF SOUTHERN CALIFORNIA." NEIGH PROVS PARTIC CHOOSE ADJUST CONSEN PERSON CONSERVE CALIFORNIA REAGAN/RON. PAGE 169 H3379
CULTURE ATTIT MORAL

L68
CURRENT HISTORY,"AFRICA, 1968." ETHIOPIA GHANA NIGERIA SOUTH/AFR CULTURE ECO/UNDEV KIN SECT CHIEF EX/STRUC WAR WEAPON CHOOSE CIVMIL/REL...GOV/COMP 20 AFRICA/E. PAGE 36 H0724
RACE/REL NAT/LISM FORCES AFR

S68
DUGARD J.,"THE REVOCATION OF THE MANDATE FOR SOUTH WEST AFRICA." SOUTH/AFR WOR+45 STRATA NAT/G DELIB/GP DIPLOM ADJUD SANCTION CHOOSE RACE/REL ...POLICY NAT/COMP 20 AFRICA/SW UN TRUST/TERR LEAGUE/NAT. PAGE 43 H0858
AFR INT/ORG DISCRIM COLONIAL

CHOU S.H. H0597

CHOU/ENLAI....CHOU EN-LAI

B64
AFRO ASIAN SOLIDARITY AGAINST IMPERIALISM. AFR ISLAM S/ASIA ECO/UNDEV NAT/G POL/PAR TOP/EX PRESS ...INT ANTHOL 20 CHOU/ENLAI. PAGE 2 H0043
MARXISM DIPLOM EDU/PROP CHIEF

CHRIMES S.B. H0598

CHRIS/DEM....CHRISTIAN DEMOCRATIC PARTY (ALL NATIONS)

S49
BOUSCAREN A.T.,"THE EUROPEAN CHRISTIAN DEMOCRATS" EUR+WWI NAT/G LEGIS 19/20 CHRIS/DEM EUROPE. PAGE 19 H0387
REPRESENT POL/PAR

B53
BARZEL R.,DIE DEUTSCHEN PARTEIEN. GERMANY MARXISM SOCISM...CONCPT IDEA/COMP 19/20 SOC/DEMPAR CHRIS/DEM. PAGE 12 H0232
POL/PAR NAT/G LAISSEZ

B53
BUCHHEIM K.,GESCHICHTE DER CHRISTLICHEN PARTEIEN IN DEUTSCHLAND. GERMANY CREATE ATTIT SUPEGO ORD/FREE ...TIME/SEQ IDEA/COMP 19/20 CHRIS/DEM. PAGE 23 H0464
POL/PAR NAT/G

B60
JEMOLO A.C.,CHURCH AND STATE IN ITALY 1850-1950 (TRANS. BY DAVID MOORE). ITALY CONSTN STRATA WAR FASCISM SOCISM...TIME/SEQ 19/20 CHURCH/STA CHRIS/DEM. PAGE 80 H1599
GP/REL NAT/G CATHISM POL/PAR

CHRISTENSEN A.N. H0599

CHRISTIAN DEMOCRATIC PARTY....SEE CHRIS/DEM

CHRISTIAN....CHRISTIAN BELIEFS OR CHURCHES

B17
DE VICTORIA F.,DE INDIS ET DE JURE BELLI (1557) IN F. DE VICTORIA, DE INDIS ET DE JURE BELLI REFLECTIONES. UNIV NAT/G SECT CHIEF PARTIC COERCE PEACE MORAL...POLICY 16 INDIAN/AM CHRISTIAN CONSCN/OBJ. PAGE 39 H0775
WAR INT/LAW OWN

B21
KREY A.C.,THE FIRST CRUSADE. CHRIST-17C SOCIETY STRATA NAT/G SECT FORCES WORKER WRITING LEAD ATTIT ...CHARTS 11 CHRISTIAN CRUSADES. PAGE 88 H1767
WAR CATH DIPLOM PARTIC

B23
WILLOUGHBY W.C.,RACE PROBLEMS IN THE NEW AFRICA: A STUDY OF THE RELATION OF BANTU AND BRITONS IN THOSE PARTS OF BANTU AFRICA... AFR STRUCT SECT DOMIN EDU/PROP GP/REL ATTIT WORSHIP 20 BANTU EUROPE MISSION CHRISTIAN. PAGE 168 H3372
KIN COLONIAL RACE/REL CULTURE

B33
BERDYAYEV N.,CHRISTIANITY AND CLASS WAR. UNIV SOCIETY WORKER CREATE PROB/SOLV ATTIT PERSON ORD/FREE...CONCPT CHRISTIAN. PAGE 15 H0296
SECT MARXISM STRATA GP/REL

B35
GORER G.,AFRICA DANCES: A BOOK ABOUT WEST AFRICAN NEGROES. STRUCT LOC/G SECT FORCES TAX ADMIN COLONIAL...ART/METH MYTH WORSHIP 20 NEGRO AFRICA/W CHRISTIAN RITUAL. PAGE 59 H1181
AFR ATTIT CULTURE SOCIETY

B36
MARITAIN J.,FREEDOM IN THE MODERN WORLD. CONSTN NAT/G SECT CAP/ISM MARXISM SOCISM...GOV/COMP IDEA/COMP 19/20 HUMANISM CHRISTIAN. PAGE 102 H2049
GEN/LAWS POLICY ORD/FREE

C36
MAZZINI J.,"FROM THE COUNCIL TO GOD" (1870) IN J. MAZZINI, ESSAYS." ITALY NAT/G EDU/PROP PARTIC ORD/FREE PWR SOVEREIGN 19 POPE CHRISTIAN DEITY. PAGE 106 H2112
CATHISM DOMIN NAT/LISM SUPEGO

B37
BERDYAEV N.,THE ORIGIN OF RUSSIAN COMMUNISM. MOD/EUR RUSSIA USSR INTELL SECT REV...ANARCH HUM 19/20 ORTHO/RUSS COM/PARTY CHRISTIAN. PAGE 15 H0294
MARXISM NAT/LISM CULTURE ATTIT

B39
MARITAIN J.,SCHOLASTICISM AND POLITICS. CONSTN SOCIETY NAT/G INGP/REL PERSON CATHISM POPULISM 19/20 FREUD/S SCHOLASTIC CHURCH/STA CHRISTIAN. PAGE 103 H2050
SECT GEN/LAWS ORD/FREE

B47
NIEBUHR R.,THE CHILDREN OF LIGHT AND THE CHILDREN OF DARKNESS: A VINDICATION OF DEMOCRACY AND CRITIQUE OF TRADITIONAL DEFENSE. UNIV STRUCT NAT/G SECT INGP/REL OWN PEACE ORD/FREE MARXISM ...IDEA/COMP GEN/LAWS 20 CHRISTIAN. PAGE 118 H2358
POPULISM DIPLOM NEIGH GP/REL

B58
FLORES X.,LA TRADICION CATOLICA Y EL FUTURO POLITICO DE ESPANA (PAMPHLET). SPAIN NAT/G ACT/RES LEAD GP/REL CATHISM 20 CHRISTIAN CHURCH/STA. PAGE 52 H1031
SECT POL/PAR ATTIT ORD/FREE

B59
CARPENTER G.W.,THE WAY IN AFRICA. AFR INDUS MUNIC DIPLOM DOMIN EDU/PROP COERCE DISCRIM NAT/LISM ORD/FREE 20 NEGRO CHRISTIAN. PAGE 27 H0535
CULTURE SECT ECO/UNDEV COLONIAL

B61
RAHNER H.,KIRCHE UND STAAT IM FRUHEN CHRISTENTUM. INGP/REL ORD/FREE PWR CATHISM...JURID 1/9 CHURCH/STA CHRISTIAN. PAGE 129 H2582
NAT/G SECT ATTIT GP/REL

B62
TYSKEVIC S.,DIE EINHEIT DER KIRCHE UND BYZANZ (TRANS. BY F.K. LIESNER). ROMAN/EMP ADJUD GP/REL 1/17 CHRISTIAN BYZANTINE. PAGE 157 H3144
SECT NAT/G CATHISM ATTIT

B63
LERNER R.,MEDIEVAL POLITICAL PHILOSOPHY. ISLAM MORAL PWR CATHISM...CATH CONCPT OBS IDEA/COMP ANTHOL 9/15 JEWS CHRISTIAN BACON/R AQUINAS/T. PAGE 95 H1890
KNOWL PHIL/SCI

B66
COLEMAN-NORTON P.R.,ROMAN STATE AND CHRISTIAN
GP/REL

CHURCH: A COLLECTION OF LEGAL DOCUMENTS TO A.D. 535 (3 VOLS.). CHRIST-17C ROMAN/EMP...ANTHOL DICTIONARY 6 CHRISTIAN CHURCH/STA. PAGE 31 H0630
NAT/G SECT LAW

B66

FUCHS W.P.,STAAT UND KIRCHE IM WANDEL DER JAHRHUNDERTE. EUR+WWI MOD/EUR UK REV...JURID CONCPT 4/20 EUROPE CHRISTIAN CHURCH/STA. PAGE 54 H1074
SECT NAT/G ORD/FREE GP/REL

B66

RIZK C.,LE REGIME POLITIQUE LIBANAIS. ISLAM LEBANON STRUCT POL/PAR SECT LOBBY GP/REL 20 ARABS MUSLIM CHRISTIAN. PAGE 132 H2637
ECO/UNDEV NAT/G CULTURE

B66

SETTON K.M.,GREAT PROBLEMS IN EUROPEAN CIVILIZATION. CHRIST-17C EUR+WWI MOD/EUR SECT GP/REL ALL/VALS ORD/FREE ALL/IDEOS...TREND ANTHOL T CHRISTIAN RENAISSAN PROTESTANT. PAGE 142 H2835
CULTURE CONCPT IDEA/COMP

B66

SILBERMAN B.S.,MODERN JAPANESE LEADERSHIP; TRANSITION AND CHANGE. NAT/G POL/PAR CHIEF ADMIN REPRESENT GP/REL ADJUST RIGID/FLEX...SOC METH/COMP ANTHOL 19/20 CHINJAP CHRISTIAN. PAGE 144 H2873
LEAD CULTURE ELITES MUNIC

B70

BOSSUET J.B.,"POLITIQUE TIREE DE L'ECRITURE SAINTE" (1679-1709) IN J.B. BOSSUET, OEVRES DE BOSSUET. NAT/G GP/REL AUTHORIT HEREDITY PERSON ALL/VALS SOVEREIGN 18 BIBLE DEITY CHRISTIAN. PAGE 19 H0383
TRADIT CHIEF SECT CONCPT

B82

CUNNINGHAM W.,THE GROWTH OF ENGLISH INDUSTRY AND COMMERCE. FUT UK FINAN NAT/G CAP/ISM...POLICY 20 MERCANTLST CHRISTIAN POPE. PAGE 36 H0721
INDUS INT/TRADE SML/CO CONSERVE

CHRIST-17C.... CHRISTENDOM TO 1700

B00

OMAN C.,A HISTORY OF THE ART OF WAR: THE MIDDLE AGES FROM THE FOURTH TO THE FOURTEENTH CENTURY. CHRIST-17C MEDIT-7 CULTURE SOCIETY INT/ORG ROUTINE PERSON...CONT/OBS HIST/WRIT CHARTS VAL/FREE. PAGE 121 H2417
FORCES SKILL WAR

B04

DANTE ALIGHIERI,DE MONARCHIA (CA .1310). CHRIST-17C ITALY DOMIN LEGIT ATTIT PWR...CATH CONCPT TIME/SEQ. PAGE 37 H0741
SECT NAT/G SOVEREIGN

B05

MACHIAVELLI N.,THE ART OF WAR. CHRIST-17C TOP/EX DRIVE ORD/FREE PWR SKILL...MGT CHARTS. PAGE 100 H1993
NAT/G FORCES WAR ITALY

C09

SCHAPIRO J.S.,"SOCIAL REFORM AND THE REFORMATION." CHRIST-17C GERMANY LAW CONSTN LG/CO NAT/G WORKER PROB/SOLV CT/SYS REV...BIBLIOG 16. PAGE 138 H2770
ORD/FREE SECT ECO/TAC BIOG

B12

POLLOCK F.,THE GENIUS OF THE COMMON LAW. CHRIST-17C UK FINAN CHIEF ACT/RES ADMIN GP/REL ATTIT SOCISM ...ANARCH JURID. PAGE 127 H2537
LAW CULTURE CREATE

N19

TEMPLE W.,AN ESSAY UPON THE ORIGINAL AND NATURE OF GOVERNMENT (PAMPHLET). CHRIST-17C UK FAM LOC/G LEGIT ORD/FREE CONSERVE 17. PAGE 153 H3060
NAT/G CONCPT PWR SOCIETY

B21

KREY A.C.,THE FIRST CRUSADE. CHRIST-17C SOCIETY STRATA NAT/G SECT FORCES WORKER WRITING LEAD ATTIT ...CHARTS 11 CHRISTIAN CRUSADES. PAGE 88 H1767
WAR CATH DIPLOM PARTIC

B27

WEBER M.,GENERAL ECONOMIC HISTORY. CHRIST-17C MOD/EUR STRUCT AGRI EXTR/IND FINAN INDUS MARKET FAM MUNIC NAT/G PROF/ORG SECT ECO/TAC 8/20. PAGE 166 H3319
ECO/DEV CAP/ISM

B28

MARSILIUS/PADUA,DEFENSOR PACIS (1324). CHRIST-17C CONSTN NAT/G DIPLOM DOMIN LEGIT CONTROL WAR PEACE ORD/FREE SOVEREIGN POPULISM 14 POPE. PAGE 103 H2059
CATH SECT GEN/LAWS

B30

BYNKERSHOEK C.,QUAESTIONUM JURIS PUBLICI LIBRI DUO. CHRIST-17C MOD/EUR CONSTN ELITES SOCIETY NAT/G PROVS EX/STRUC FORCES TOP/EX BAL/PWR DIPLOM ATTIT MORAL...TRADIT CONCPT. PAGE 25 H0502
INT/ORG LAW NAT/LISM INT/LAW

B31

BONAR J.,THEORIES OF POPULATION FROM RALEIGH TO ARTHUR YOUNG. CHRIST-17C MOD/EUR CULTURE SOCIETY R+D CREATE ATTIT PERCEPT RIGID/FLEX...OLD/LIB CONCPT NEW/IDEA TIME/SEQ IDEA/COMP STERTYP GEN/LAWS. PAGE 19 H0372
GEOG BIOG

B32

BRYCE J.,THE HOLY ROMAN EMPIRE. GERMANY ITALY MOD/EUR CULTURE SOCIETY STRUCT INT/ORG NAT/G SECT DIPLOM DOMIN WAR SUPEGO ALL/VALS SOVEREIGN...GEOG SOC TIME/SEQ CHARTS STERTYP. PAGE 23 H0456
CHRIST-17C NAT/LISM

B36

HUBERMAN L.,MAN'S WORLDLY GOODS: THE STORY OF THE WEALTH OF NATIONS. CHRIST-17C EUR+WWI MOD/EUR SOCIETY DOMIN REV ORD/FREE...TIME/SEQ METH/COMP. PAGE 74 H1486
WEALTH CAP/ISM MARXISM CREATE

B36

PREVITE-ORTON C.W.,THE CAMBRIDGE MEDIEVAL HISTORY (8 VOLS.). CHRIST-17C NAT/G PROB/SOLV TEC/DEV LEAD ...POLICY CONCPT WORSHIP. PAGE 128 H2559
BIBLIOG IDEA/COMP TREND

B37

THOMPSON J.W.,SECRET DIPLOMACY: A RECORD OF ESPIONAGE AND DOUBLE-DEALING: 1500-1815. CHRIST-17C MOD/EUR NAT/G WRITING RISK MORAL...ANTHOL BIBLIOG 16/19 ESPIONAGE. PAGE 154 H3084
DIPLOM CRIME

B40

JORDAN W.K.,THE DEVELOPMENT OF RELIGIOUS TOLERATION IN ENGLAND. CHRIST-17C CULTURE SOCIETY LEGIT ATTIT RESPECT...POLICY CONCPT RECORD TIME/SEQ STERTYP GEN/LAWS TOT/POP 16/17. PAGE 82 H1635
SECT UK

B40

MCILWAIN C.H.,CONSTITUTIONALISM, ANCIENT AND MODERN. CHRIST-17C MOD/EUR NAT/G CHIEF PROB/SOLV INSPECT AUTHORIT ORD/FREE PWR...TIME/SEQ ROMAN/REP. PAGE 107 H2134
CONSTN GEN/LAWS LAW

B41

GRISMER R.,A NEW BIBLIOGRAPHY OF THE LITERATURES OF SPAIN AND SPANISH AMERICA. CHRIST-17C MOD/EUR PRE/AMER SPAIN CULTURE DIPLOM EDU/PROP...ART/METH GEOG HUM PHIL/SCI 20. PAGE 61 H1229
BIBLIOG LAW NAT/G ECO/UNDEV

B49

BOZZA T.,SCRITTORI POLITICI ITALIANI DAL 1550 AL 1650. CHRIST-17C ITALY DIPLOM DOMIN 16/17. PAGE 20 H0394
BIBLIOG/A NAT/G CONCPT WRITING

B49

SCHONS D.,BOOK CENSORSHIP IN NEW SPAIN (NEW WORLD STUDIES, BOOK II). SPAIN LAW CULTURE INSPECT ADJUD CT/SYS SANCTION GP/REL ORD/FREE 14/17. PAGE 140 H2797
CHRIST-17C EDU/PROP CONTROL PRESS

B50

GOFF F.R.,FIFTEENTH CENTURY BOOKS IN THE LIBRARY OF CONGRESS. CHRIST-17C GERMANY ITALY CULTURE INTELL SECT CREATE...PHIL/SCI CONCPT CLASSIF BIOG TIME/SEQ 15. PAGE 58 H1153
BIBLIOG KNOWL HUM

B54

LEWIS E.,MEDIEVAL POLITICAL IDEAS. LAW CULTURE SOCIETY ECO/UNDEV NAT/G SECT GOV/REL ATTIT ...BIBLIOG/A T 11/15. PAGE 96 H1913
CHRIST-17C IDEA/COMP INTELL CONCPT

B55

CRAIG G.A.,THE POLITICS OF THE PRUSSIAN ARMY 1640-1945. CHRIST-17C EUR+WWI MOD/EUR PRUSSIA STRUCT DIPLOM ADMIN REV WAR...SOC BIBLIOG 17/20. PAGE 35 H0694
FORCES NAT/G ROLE CHIEF

B56

RIESENBERG P.N.,INALIENABILITY OF SOVEREIGNTY IN MEDIEVAL POLITICAL THOUGHT. CHRIST-17C INTELL NAT/G SECT CHIEF LEGIS SANCTION AUTHORIT ORD/FREE CONSERVE...IDEA/COMP BIBLIOG 12/16. PAGE 131 H2627
SOVEREIGN ATTIT

B57

MEINECKE F.,MACHIAVELLISM. CHRIST-17C FRANCE GERMANY ITALY MOD/EUR BAL/PWR PARL/PROC TOTALISM ...PHIL/SCI 15/20 MACHIAVELL. PAGE 108 H2166
NAT/LISM NAT/G PWR

B57

RUMEU DE ARMAS A.,ESPANA EEN EL AFRICA ATLANTICA. AFR CHRIST-17C PORTUGAL SPAIN DIPLOM ECO/TAC CONTROL 14/16 AFRICA/W. PAGE 136 H2717
NAT/G COLONIAL CHIEF PWR

B58

SYME R.,COLONIAL ELITES: ROME, SPAIN, AND THE AMERICAS. CHRIST-17C MOD/EUR SPAIN UK USA-45 CULTURE NAT/G CHIEF TOP/EX...GOV/COMP IDEA/COMP NAT/COMP ROM/EMP GIBBON/EDW TOYNBEE/A. PAGE 151 H3022
COLONIAL ELITES DOMIN

C58

MORRALL J.B.,"POLITICAL THOUGHT IN MEDIEVAL TIMES." LAW NAT/G SECT DOMIN ATTIT PWR...BIOG HIST/WRIT BIBLIOG. PAGE 113 H2260
CHRIST-17C CONCPT

B59

HONINGMAN J.J.,THE WORLD OF MAN. CHRIST-17C MEDIT-7 PRE/AMER PREHIST CREATE INGP/REL BIO/SOC HABITAT ...PSY SOC BIBLIOG. PAGE 73 H1460
CULTURE METH PERSON STRUCT

B61

GUIZOT F.P.G.,HISTORY OF THE ORIGIN OF REPRESENTATIVE GOVERNMENT IN EUROPE. CHRIST-17C FRANCE MOD/EUR SPAIN UK LAW CHIEF FORCES POPULISM ...MAJORIT TIME/SEQ GOV/COMP NAT/COMP 4/19 PARLIAMENT. PAGE 62 H1250
LEGIS REPRESENT CONSTN NAT/G

B62

KIDDER F.E.,THESES ON PAN AMERICAN TOPICS. LAW CULTURE NAT/G SECT DIPLOM HEALTH...ART/METH GEOG SOC 13/20. PAGE 86 H1709
BIBLIOG CHRIST-17C L/A+17C SOCIETY

B62

THIERRY S.S.,LE VATICAN SECRET. CHRIST-17C EUR+WWI MOD/EUR VATICAN NAT/G SECT DELIB/GP DOMIN LEGIT SOVEREIGN. PAGE 154 H3072
ADMIN EX/STRUC CATHISM

DECISION

S62
FESLER J.W.,"FRENCH FIELD ADMINISTRATION: THE BEGINNINGS." CHRIST-17C CULTURE SOCIETY STRATA NAT/G ECO/TAC DOMIN EDU/PROP LEGIT ADJUD COERCE ATTIT ALL/VALS...TIME/SEQ CON/ANAL GEN/METH VAL/FREE 13/15. PAGE 49 H0988
EX/STRUC FRANCE

S63
GLUCKMAN M.,"CIVIL WAR AND THEORIES OF POWER IN BAROTSE-LAND: AFRICAN AND MEDIEVAL ANALOGIES." AFR CHRIST-17C LAW CONSTN CULTURE STRATA KIN DELIB/GP FORCES DOMIN LEGIT COERCE PERCEPT ORD/FREE...SOC INT TIME/SEQ GEN/LAWS VAL/FREE. PAGE 57 H1148
TOP/EX PWR WAR

S63
LOPEZIBOR J.,"L'EUROPE, FORME DE VIE." CHRIST-17C EUR+WWI FUT MOD/EUR SOCIETY INT/ORG SECT EDU/PROP ATTIT RIGID/FLEX ALL/VALS...POLICY HUM SOC TIME/SEQ TREND GEN/LAWS. PAGE 98 H1966
NAT/G CULTURE

B65
ULLMANN W.,A HISTORY OF POLITICAL THOUGHT: THE MIDDLE AGES. CHRIST-17C LOC/G NAT/G CENTRAL PWR ...PHIL/SCI LOG BIBLIOG 6/15. PAGE 158 H3153
IDEA/COMP SOVEREIGN SECT LAW

B66
COLEMAN-NORTON P.R.,ROMAN STATE AND CHRISTIAN CHURCH: A COLLECTION OF LEGAL DOCUMENTS TO A.D. 535 (3 VOLS.). CHRIST-17C ROMAN/EMP...ANTHOL DICTIONARY 6 CHRISTIAN CHURCH/STA. PAGE 31 H0630
GP/REL NAT/G SECT LAW

B66
FEINE H.E.,REICH UND KIRCHE. CHRIST-17C MOD/EUR ROMAN/EMP LAW CHOOSE ATTIT 10/19 CHURCH/STA ROMAN/LAW. PAGE 49 H0982
JURID SECT NAT/G GP/REL

B66
MASUR G.,NATIONALISM IN LATIN AMERICA* DIVERSITY AND UNITY. CHRIST-17C PRE/AMER ELITES ECO/UNDEV CREATE DIPLOM INT/TRADE COLONIAL REV SOVEREIGN SOC. PAGE 105 H2089
L/A+17C NAT/LISM CULTURE

B66
SETTON K.M.,GREAT PROBLEMS IN EUROPEAN CIVILIZATION. CHRIST-17C EUR+WWI MOD/EUR SECT GP/REL ALL/VALS ORD/FREE ALL/IDEOS...TREND ANTHOL T CHRISTIAN RENAISSAN PROTESTANT. PAGE 142 H2835
CULTURE CONCPT IDEA/COMP

B66
WUEST J.J.,NEW SOURCE BOOK IN MAJOR EUROPEAN GOVERNMENTS. CHRIST-17C EUR+WWI FRANCE GERMANY ITALY MOD/EUR UK USSR LOC/G POL/PAR CHIEF EX/STRUC CHOOSE CONSERVE MARXISM...JURID T 13/20. PAGE 171 H3425
NAT/G CONSTN LEGIS

B67
LYON B.,MEDIEVAL FINANCE. CHRIST-17C...SOC 11/12. PAGE 99 H1984
FINAN METH/COMP ECO/TAC NAT/COMP

B97
JENKS E.J.,LAW AND POLITICS IN THE MIDDLE AGES. CHRIST-17C CULTURE STRUCT KIN NAT/G SECT CT/SYS GP/REL...CLASSIF CHARTS IDEA/COMP BIBLIOG 8/16. PAGE 80 H1603
LAW SOCIETY ADJUST

CHRONOLOGY....SEE TIME/SEQ

CHU-YUAN CHENG H0600

CHUNG Y.S. H0601

CHURCH....SEE SECT

CHURCH/STA....CHURCH-STATE RELATIONS (ALL NATIONS)

B14
FIGGIS J.N.,CHURCHES IN THE MODERN STATE (2ND ED.). LAW CHIEF BAL/PWR PWR...CONCPT CHURCH/STA POPE. PAGE 50 H0998
SECT NAT/G SOCIETY ORD/FREE

N19
COUTROT A.,THE FIGHT OVER THE 1959 PRIVATE EDUCATION LAW IN FRANCE (PAMPHLET). FRANCE NAT/G SECT GIVE EDU/PROP GP/REL ATTIT RIGID/FLEX ORD/FREE 20 CHURCH/STA. PAGE 34 H0681
SCHOOL PARL/PROC CATHISM LAW

N19
WEBB L.C.,CHURCH AND STATE IN ITALY: 1947-1957 (PAMPHLET). GERMANY ITALY CONSTN POL/PAR AGREE CONTROL PARTIC CHOOSE ATTIT ORD/FREE FASCISM MARXISM 20 CHURCH/STA MARITAIN/J SALO. PAGE 166 H3316
SECT CATHISM NAT/G GP/REL

B36
LAPRADE W.T.,PUBLIC OPINION AND POLITICS IN EIGHTEENTH CENTURY ENGLAND. UK CULTURE POL/PAR CHIEF TOP/EX LEAD REV NAT/LISM PWR 18 PROTESTANT PROTESTANT CHURCH/STA. PAGE 91 H1815
POLICY ELITES ATTIT TIME/SEQ

B39
MARITAIN J.,SCHOLASTICISM AND POLITICS. CONSTN SOCIETY NAT/G INGP/REL PERSON CATHISM POPULISM 19/20 FREUD/S SCHOLASTIC CHURCH/STA CHRISTIAN. PAGE 103 H2050
SECT GEN/LAWS ORD/FREE

B43
MARITAIN J.,THE RIGHTS OF MAN AND NATURAL LAW. CONSTN NAT/G DOMIN LEGIT INGP/REL TOTALISM MORAL POPULISM WORSHIP 19/20 CIVIL/LIB CHURCH/STA NATURL/LAW. PAGE 103 H2051
PLURIST ORD/FREE GEN/LAWS

B49
HAUSER R.,AUTORITAT UND MACHT. SOCIETY SECT PWR CATHISM...JURID CONCPT 16/20 PROTESTANT LUTHER/M CALVIN/J CHURCH/STA. PAGE 68 H1360
SOVEREIGN NAT/G LEGIT

B49
HOLLERAN M.P.,CHURCH AND STATE IN GUATEMALA. GUATEMALA LAW STRUCT CATHISM...SOC SOC/INTEG 17/20 CHURCH/STA. PAGE 73 H1456
SECT NAT/G GP/REL CULTURE

B53
CURTISS J.S.,THE RUSSIAN CHURCH AND THE SOVIET STATE 1917-1950. COM USSR CONTROL LEAD REV MARXISM ...POLICY BIBLIOG 20 CHURCH/STA ORTHO/RUSS. PAGE 36 H0728
GP/REL NAT/G SECT PWR

B53
MARITAIN J.,L'HOMME ET L'ETAT. SECT DIPLOM GP/REL PEACE ORD/FREE...IDEA/COMP 17/20 CHURCH/STA NATURL/LAW. PAGE 103 H2052
CONCPT NAT/G SOVEREIGN COERCE

B55
FRANZ G.,KULTURKAMPF. AUSTRIA GERMANY PRUSSIA SWITZERLND POL/PAR DIPLOM GP/REL ATTIT ORD/FREE 18/19 CHURCH/STA. PAGE 53 H1053
NAT/LISM CATHISM NAT/G REV

B55
MID-EUROPEAN LAW PROJECT,CHURCH AND STATE BEHIND THE IRON CURTAIN. COM CZECHOSLVK HUNGARY POLAND USSR CULTURE SECT EDU/PROP GOV/REL CATHISM...CHARTS ANTHOL BIBLIOG WORSHIP 20 CHURCH/STA. PAGE 110 H2202
LAW MARXISM POLICY

B57
KANTOROWICZ E.,THE KING'S TWO BODIES; A STUDY IN MEDIEVAL POLITICAL THEOLOGY. UK LAW CONSTN NAT/G CT/SYS...ART/METH HUM CONCPT MYTH TIME/SEQ BIBLIOG 4/17 ELIZABTH/I POPE CHURCH/STA. PAGE 83 H1657
JURID SECT CHIEF SOVEREIGN

B58
BUISSON L.,POTESTAS UND CARITAS. FRANCE GERMANY UK ORD/FREE...JURID IDEA/COMP NAT/COMP 12/16 POPE CHURCH/STA. PAGE 23 H0467
GP/REL PWR CATHISM NAT/G

B58
FLORES X.,LA TRADICION CATOLICA Y EL FUTURO POLITICO DE ESPANA (PAMPHLET). SPAIN NAT/G ACT/RES LEAD GP/REL CATHISM 20 CHRISTIAN CHURCH/STA. PAGE 52 H1031
SECT POL/PAR ATTIT ORD/FREE

B58
HERRMANN K.,DAS STAATSDENKEN BEI LEIBNIZ. GP/REL ATTIT ORD/FREE...CONCPT IDEA/COMP 17 LEIBNITZ/G CHURCH/STA. PAGE 70 H1406
NAT/G JURID SECT EDU/PROP

B59
BROSE O.J.,CHURCH AND PARLIAMENT: THE RESHAPING OF THE CHURCH OF ENGLAND 1828-1860. UK SOCIETY TEC/DEV ATTIT LAISSEZ...BIBLIOG 19 CHURCH/STA. PAGE 22 H0434
SECT LEGIS GP/REL NAT/G

B59
EAENZA L.,COMMUNISMO E CATTOLICESIMO IN UNA PARROCHIA DI CAMPAGNA. ITALY CULTURE ELITES ECO/DEV AGRI KIN POL/PAR DOMIN LEGIT RIGID/FLEX...DECISION OBS IDEA/COMP 20 COM/PARTY CHURCH/STA. PAGE 44 H0878
ATTIT CATHISM NEIGH MARXISM

B59
SISSONS C.B.,CHURCH AND STATE IN CANADIAN EDUCATION: AN HISTORICAL STUDY. CANADA ACADEM NAT/G SCHOOL LEGIS REGION MAJORITY...MAJORIT WORSHIP 18/20 CHURCH/STA. PAGE 145 H2891
SECT EDU/PROP PROVS GP/REL

B60
JEMOLO A.C.,CHURCH AND STATE IN ITALY 1850-1950 (TRANS. BY DAVID MOORE). ITALY CONSTN STRATA WAR FASCISM SOCISM...TIME/SEQ 19/20 CHURCH/STA CHRIS/DEM. PAGE 80 H1599
GP/REL NAT/G CATHISM POL/PAR

B60
MOCTEZUMA A.P.,EL CONFLICTO RELIGIOSO DE 1926 (2ND ED.). L/A+17C LAW NAT/G LOBBY COERCE GP/REL ATTIT ...POLICY 20 MEXIC/AMER CHURCH/STA. PAGE 112 H2233
SECT ORD/FREE DISCRIM REV

B61
RAHNER H.,KIRCHE UND STAAT IM FRUHEN CHRISTENTUM. INGP/REL ORD/FREE PWR CATHISM...JURID 1/9 CHURCH/STA CHRISTIAN. PAGE 129 H2582
NAT/G SECT ATTIT GP/REL

B61
SHIELS W.E.,KING AND CHURCH: THE RISE AND FALL OF THE PATRONATO REAL. SPAIN INGP/REL...CONCPT WORSHIP 16/19 CHURCH/STA MISSION. PAGE 143 H2859
SECT NAT/G CHIEF POLICY

B61
ULLMAN W.,PRINCIPLES OF GOVERNMENT AND POLITICS IN THE MIDDLE AGES. LAW CONSTN DOMIN EDU/PROP LEGIT TOTALISM SOVEREIGN POPULISM...POLICY GOV/COMP IDEA/COMP 12/16 POPE KING CHURCH/STA. PAGE 158
SECT CHIEF NAT/G LEGIS

H3152

B62
JENNINGS I.,PARTY POLITICS: THE STUFF OF POLITICS (VOL.III). UK NAT/G SECT CHIEF INT/TRADE RECEIVE COLONIAL GP/REL NAT/LISM ORD/FREE SOCISM 19/20 CHURCH/STA WHIG/PARTY. PAGE 80 H1607
POL/PAR CONSTN PWR ALL/IDEOS

B62
SCHMIDT-VOLKMAR E.,DER KULTURKAMPF IN DEUTSCHLAND 1871-1890. GERMANY PRUSSIA SOCIETY STRUCT SECT DIPLOM GP/REL NAT/LISM 19 CHURCH/STA BISMARCK/O. PAGE 139 H2789
POL/PAR CATHISM ATTIT NAT/G

B63
CRUICKSHANK M.,CHURCH AND STATE IN ENGLISH EDUCATION 1870 TO PRESENT. UK LEGIS TAX GIVE DOMIN LEGIT ORD/FREE 19/20 CHURCH/STA. PAGE 36 H0715
NAT/G SECT EDU/PROP GP/REL

B64
FREISEN J.,STAAT UND KATHOLISCHE KIRCHE IN DEN DEUTSCHEN BUNDESSTAATEN (2 VOLS.). GERMANY LAW FAM NAT/G EDU/PROP GP/REL MARRIAGE WEALTH 19/20 CHURCH/STA. PAGE 53 H1056
SECT CATHISM JURID PROVS

B64
HELMREICH E.,A FREE CHURCH IN A FREE STATE? FRANCE GERMANY ITALY SECT LEAD PWR CATHISM...POLICY ANTHOL WORSHIP 19/20 CHURCH/STA. PAGE 69 H1389
GP/REL NAT/G

B65
CONRING E.,KIRCHE UND STAAT NACH DER LEHRE DER NIEDERLANDISCHEN CALVINISTEN IN DER ERSTEN HALFTE DES 17. JAHRHUNDERTS. NETHERLAND GP/REL...CONCPT 17 CHURCH/STA. PAGE 33 H0656
SECT JURID NAT/G ORD/FREE

B65
POBEDONOSTSEV K.P.,REFLECTIONS OF A RUSSIAN STATESMAN. RUSSIA LAW ELITES EDU/PROP PRESS ADJUD MARRIAGE ATTIT PWR...MAJORIT TRADIT 19 CHURCH/STA. PAGE 127 H2531
TOTALISM POLICY CONSTN NAT/G

B66
BARRETT J.,THAT BETTER COUNTRY: RELIGIOUS ASPECT OF LIFE IN EASTERN AUSTRALIA, 1835-1850. LAW ECO/UNDEV SCHOOL TEC/DEV EDU/PROP CONTROL HABITAT MORAL WORSHIP 19 AUSTRAL CHURCH/STA. PAGE 11 H0229
SECT CULTURE GOV/REL

B66
COLEMAN-NORTON P.R.,ROMAN STATE AND CHRISTIAN CHURCH: A COLLECTION OF LEGAL DOCUMENTS TO A.D. 535 (3 VOLS.). CHRIST-17C ROMAN/EMP...ANTHOL DICTIONARY 6 CHRISTIAN CHURCH/STA. PAGE 31 H0630
GP/REL NAT/G SECT LAW

B66
FEINE H.E.,REICH UND KIRCHE. CHRIST-17C MOD/EUR ROMAN/EMP LAW CHOOSE ATTIT 10/19 CHURCH/STA ROMAN/LAW. PAGE 49 H0982
JURID SECT NAT/G GP/REL

B66
FUCHS W.P.,STAAT UND KIRCHE IM WANDEL DER JAHRHUNDERTE. EUR+WWI MOD/EUR UK REV...JURID CONCPT 4/20 EUROPE CHRISTIAN CHURCH/STA. PAGE 54 H1074
SECT NAT/G ORD/FREE GP/REL

B66
O'NEILL C.E.,CHURCH AND STATE IN FRENCH COLONIAL LOUISIANA: POLICY AND POLITICS TO 1732. PROVS VOL/ASSN DELIB/GP ADJUD ADMIN GP/REL ATTIT DRIVE ...POLICY BIBLIOG 17/18 LOUISIANA CHURCH/STA. PAGE 120 H2390
COLONIAL NAT/G SECT PWR

CHURCHLL/W....SIR WINSTON CHURCHILL

B57
BULLOCK A.,THE LIBERAL TRADITION FROM FOX TO KEYNES. UK CULTURE INTELL CREATE WRITING COLONIAL PERS/REL ATTIT ORD/FREE...POLICY OLD/LIB TRADIT CONCPT 18/20 CHURCHLL/W MILL/JS KEYNES/JM ASQUITH/HH. PAGE 23 H0469
ANTHOL DEBATE LAISSEZ

B60
MANIS J.G.,MAN AND SOCIETY. STRATA LEAD INGP/REL PERS/REL ATTIT PWR...PSY ANTHOL T SOC/INTEG MARX/KARL MILL/JS FREUD/S CHURCHLL/W SPENCER/H RUSSELL/B. PAGE 102 H2036
SOC SOCIETY STRUCT CULTURE

B64
WHITE D.S.,SEEDS OF DISCORD. EUR+WWI FRANCE NAT/G VOL/ASSN FORCES DIPLOM DOMIN NAT/LISM DISPL RIGID/FLEX PWR...RECORD INT BIOG 20 DEGAULLE/C ROOSEVLT/F CHURCHLL/W HULL. PAGE 167 H3347
TOP/EX ATTIT

CIA....CENTRAL INTELLIGENCE AGENCY

CICERO....CICERO

CINCINNATI....CINCINNATI, OHIO

CINEMA....SEE FILM

CITIES....SEE MUNIC

CITIZENSHIP....SEE CITIZENSHP

CITIZENSHP....CITIZENSHIP

CITY/MGT....CITY MANAGEMENT, CITY MANAGERS; SEE ALSO MUNIC, ADMIN, MGT, LOC/G

CIV/DEFENS....CIVIL DEFENSE (SYSTEMS, PLANNING, AND

B62
GOURE L.,CIVIL DEFENSE IN THE SOVIET UNION. COM USA+45 USSR MUNIC NAT/G DETER ATTIT MARXISM ...NAT/COMP 20 CIV/DEFENS. PAGE 59 H1188
PLAN FORCES WAR COERCE

CIV/DISOBD....CIVIL DISOBEDIENCE

CIV/RIGHTS....CIVIL RIGHTS: CONTEMPORARY CIVIL RIGHTS MOVEMENTS; SEE ALSO RACE/REL, CONSTN + LAW

B60
LA PONCE J.A.,THE PROTECTION OF MINORITIES. WOR+45 WOR-45 NAT/G POL/PAR SUFF...INT/LAW CLASSIF GP/COMP GOV/COMP BIBLIOG 17/20 CIVIL/LIB CIV/RIGHTS. PAGE 90 H1793
INGP/REL DOMIN SOCIETY RACE/REL

B62
HOOK S.,THE PARADOXES OF FREEDOM. UNIV CONSTN INTELL LEGIS CONTROL REV CHOOSE SUPEGO...POLICY JURID IDEA/COMP 19/20 CIV/RIGHTS. PAGE 73 H1461
CONCPT MAJORIT ORD/FREE ALL/VALS

CIVIL DEFENSE....SEE CIV/DEFENS

CIVIL RIGHTS....SEE CIV/RIGHTS

CIVIL SERVICE....SEE ADMIN

CIVIL/CODE....CIVIL CODE (FRANCE)

CIVIL/LAW....CIVIL LAW

B09
JUSTINIAN,THE DIGEST (DIGESTA CORPUS JURIS CIVILIS) (2 VOLS.) (TRANS. BY C. H. MONRO). ROMAN/EMP LAW FAM LOC/G LEGIS EDU/PROP CONTROL MARRIAGE OWN ROLE CIVIL/LAW. PAGE 82 H1645
JURID CT/SYS NAT/G STRATA

B33
ENSOR R.C.K.,COURTS AND JUDGES IN FRANCE, GERMANY, AND ENGLAND. FRANCE GERMANY UK LAW PROB/SOLV ADMIN ROUTINE CRIME ROLE...METH/COMP 20 CIVIL/LAW. PAGE 46 H0930
CT/SYS EX/STRUC ADJUD NAT/COMP

B35
RAM J.,THE SCIENCE OF LEGAL JUDGMENT: A TREATISE... UK CONSTN NAT/G LEGIS CREATE PROB/SOLV AGREE CT/SYS ...INT/LAW CONCPT 19 ENGLSH/LAW CANON/LAW CIVIL/LAW CTS/WESTM. PAGE 129 H2584
LAW JURID EX/STRUC ADJUD

CIVIL/LIB....CIVIL LIBERTIES; SEE ALSO CONSTN + LAW

B14
CRAIG J.,ELEMENTS OF POLITICAL SCIENCE (3 VOLS.). CONSTN AGRI INDUS SCHOOL FORCES TAX CT/SYS SUFF MORAL WEALTH...CONCPT 19 CIVIL/LIB. PAGE 35 H0696
PHIL/SCI NAT/G ORD/FREE

B43
MARITAIN J.,THE RIGHTS OF MAN AND NATURAL LAW. CONSTN NAT/G DOMIN LEGIT INGP/REL TOTALISM MORAL POPULISM WORSHIP 19/20 CIVIL/LIB CHURCH/STA NATURL/LAW. PAGE 103 H2051
PLURIST ORD/FREE GEN/LAWS

B44
BERDYAEV N.,SLAVERY AND FREEDOM. NAT/G REV WAR NAT/LISM OWN AUTHORIT SEX CONSERVE SOCISM...TRADIT PHIL/SCI CIVIL/LIB. PAGE 15 H0295
ORD/FREE PERSON ELITES SOCIETY

B53
LIEBER F.,CIVIL LIBERTY AND SELF GOVERNMENT: VOLUME 2. NAT/G CONTROL CHOOSE PERSON PWR 19 CIVIL/LIB. PAGE 96 H1925
ORD/FREE SOVEREIGN CENTRAL CONCPT

B60
LA PONCE J.A.,THE PROTECTION OF MINORITIES. WOR+45 WOR-45 NAT/G POL/PAR SUFF...INT/LAW CLASSIF GP/COMP GOV/COMP BIBLIOG 17/20 CIVIL/LIB CIV/RIGHTS. PAGE 90 H1793
INGP/REL DOMIN SOCIETY RACE/REL

B60
SCHEIBER H.N.,THE WILSON ADMINISTRATION AND CIVIL LIBERTIES 1917-1921. LAW GOV/REL ATTIT 20 WILSON/W CIVIL/LIB. PAGE 139 H2782
ORD/FREE WAR NAT/G CONTROL

B62
GANJI M.,INTERNATIONAL PROTECTION OF HUMAN RIGHTS. WOR+45 CONSTN INT/TRADE CT/SYS SANCTION CRIME WAR RACE/REL...CHARTS IDEA/COMP NAT/COMP BIBLIOG 20 TREATY NEGRO LEAGUE/NAT UN CIVIL/LIB. PAGE 55 H1097
ORD/FREE DISCRIM LEGIS DELIB/GP

B66
ARCHER P.,FREEDOM AT STAKE. UK LAW NAT/G LEGIS JUDGE CRIME MORAL...CONCPT 20 CIVIL/LIB. PAGE 8 H0159
ORD/FREE NAT/COMP POLICY

B66
SWEET E.C.,CIVIL LIBERTIES IN AMERICA. LAW CONSTN NAT/G PRESS CT/SYS DISCRIM ATTIT WORSHIP 20 CIVIL/LIB. PAGE 151 H3018 — ADJUD ORD/FREE SUFF COERCE

B91
PAINE T.,RIGHTS OF MAN. FRANCE MOD/EUR CONSTN NAT/G CHIEF DOMIN LEGIT SOVEREIGN...MAJORIT IDEA/COMP 18 BURKE/EDM CIVIL/LIB. PAGE 122 H2446 — GEN/LAWS ORD/FREE REV AGREE

CIVIL/SERV....CIVIL SERVICE; SEE ALSO ADMIN

B08
THE GOVERNMENT OF SOUTH AFRICA (VOL. II). SOUTH/AFR STRATA EXTR/IND EX/STRUC TOP/EX BUDGET ADJUD ADMIN CT/SYS PRODUC...CORREL CENSUS 19 RAILROAD CIVIL/SERV POSTAL/SYS. PAGE 2 H0030 — CONSTN FINAN LEGIS NAT/G

N19
FIKS M.,PUBLIC ADMINISTRATION IN ISRAEL (PAMPHLET). ISRAEL SCHOOL EX/STRUC BUDGET PAY INGP/REL ...DECISION 20 CIVIL/SERV. PAGE 50 H0999 — EDU/PROP NAT/G ADMIN WORKER

N19
GRIFFITH W.,THE PUBLIC SERVICE (PAMPHLET). UK LAW LOC/G NAT/G PARTIC CHOOSE DRIVE ROLE SKILL...CHARTS 20 CIVIL/SERV. PAGE 61 H1222 — ADMIN EFFICIENCY EDU/PROP GOV/REL

B57
SCARROW H.A.,THE HIGHER PUBLIC SERVICE OF THE COMMONWEALTH OF AUSTRALIA. LAW SENIOR LOBBY ROLE 20 AUSTRAL CIVIL/SERV COMMONWLTH. PAGE 138 H2766 — ADMIN NAT/G EX/STRUC GOV/COMP

B58
DWARKADAS R.,ROLE OF HIGHER CIVIL SERVICE IN INDIA. INDIA ECO/UNDEV LEGIS PROB/SOLV GP/REL PERS/REL ...POLICY WELF/ST DECISION ORG/CHARTS BIBLIOG 20 CIVIL/SERV INTRVN/ECO. PAGE 44 H0876 — ADMIN NAT/G ROLE PLAN

B59
VERNEY D.V.,PUBLIC ENTERPRISE IN SWEDEN. FUT SWEDEN UK INDUS POL/PAR LEGIS PROB/SOLV CAP/ISM INT/TRADE CONTROL SOCISM...MGT CONCPT NAT/COMP 20 SOCDEM/PAR CIVIL/SERV. PAGE 162 H3246 — ECO/DEV POLICY LG/CO NAT/G

B60
ROY N.C.,THE CIVIL SERVICE IN INDIA. INDIA POL/PAR ECO/TAC INCOME...JURID MGT 20 CIVIL/SERV. PAGE 135 H2705 — ADMIN NAT/G DELIB/GP CONFER

B61
CATHERINE R.,LE FONCTIONNAIRE FRANCAIS. FRANCE NAT/G INGP/REL ATTIT MORAL ORD/FREE...T CIVIL/SERV. PAGE 28 H0559 — ADMIN GP/REL LEAD SUPEGO

S61
EHRMANN H.W.,"FRENCH BUREAUCRACY AND ORGANIZED INTERESTS" (BMR)" FRANCE NAT/G DELIB/GP ROUTINE ...INT 20 BUREAUCRCY CIVIL/SERV. PAGE 45 H0897 — ADMIN DECISION PLURISM LOBBY

B62
ESCUELA SUPERIOR DE ADMIN PUBL,INFORME DEL SEMINARIO SOBRE SERVICIO CIVIL O CARRERA ADMINISTRATIVA. L/A+17C ELITES STRATA CONFER CONTROL GOV/REL INGP/REL SUPEGO 20 CENTRAL/AM CIVIL/SERV. PAGE 47 H0939 — ADMIN NAT/G PROB/SOLV ATTIT

B62
INSTITUTE OF PUBLIC ADMIN,A SHORT HISTORY OF THE PUBLIC SERVICE IN IRELAND. IRELAND UK DIST/IND INGP/REL FEDERAL 13/20 CIVIL/SERV. PAGE 77 H1539 — ADMIN WORKER GOV/REL NAT/G

B63
SINGH H.L.,PROBLEMS AND POLICIES OF THE BRITISH IN INDIA, 1885-1898. INDIA UK NAT/G FORCES LEGIS PROB/SOLV CONTROL RACE/REL ADJUST DISCRIM NAT/LISM RIGID/FLEX...MGT 19 CIVIL/SERV. PAGE 144 H2885 — COLONIAL PWR POLICY ADMIN

B64
NICOL D.,AFRICA - A SUBJECTIVE VIEW. AFR INT/ORG PLAN ADMIN COLONIAL PARL/PROC PARTIC REGION GOV/REL LITERACY ATTIT...BIBLIOG 20 CIVIL/SERV. PAGE 118 H2350 — NAT/G LEAD CULTURE ACADEM

B64
RAPHAEL M.,PENSIONS AND PUBLIC SERVANTS. UK NAT/G PLAN INGP/REL COST EFFICIENCY ATTIT...POLICY 17/20 CIVIL/SERV. PAGE 130 H2593 — RECEIVE ADMIN INCOME AGE/O

B65
ADU A.L.,THE CIVIL SERVICE IN NEW AFRICAN STATES. AFR GHANA FINAN SOVEREIGN...POLICY 20 CIVIL/SERV AFRICA/E AFRICA/W. PAGE 4 H0074 — ECO/UNDEV ADMIN COLONIAL NAT/G

B65
CAMPBELL G.A.,THE CIVIL SERVICE IN BRITAIN (2ND ED.). UK DELIB/GP FORCES WORKER CREATE PLAN ...POLICY AUD/VIS 19/20 CIVIL/SERV. PAGE 26 H0515 — ADMIN LEGIS NAT/G FINAN

B66
ZINKIN T.,CHALLENGES IN INDIA. INDIA PAKISTAN LAW AGRI FINAN INDUS TOP/EX TEC/DEV CONTROL ROUTINE ORD/FREE PWR 20 NEHRU/J SHASTRI/LB CIVIL/SERV. PAGE 173 H3458 — NAT/G ECO/TAC POLICY ADMIN

S67
SUBRAMANIAM V.,"REPRESENTATIVE BUREAUCRACY: A REASSESSMENT." USA+45 ELITES LOC/G NAT/G ADMIN GOV/REL PRIVIL DRIVE ROLE...POLICY CENSUS 20 CIVIL/SERV BUREAUCRCY. PAGE 150 H3006 — STRATA GP/REL MGT GOV/COMP

CIVIL/WAR....CIVIL WAR

B65
BROWNSON O.A.,THE AMERICAN REPUBLIC. NAT/G PROVS WAR GOV/REL PRIVIL ORD/FREE PWR ALL/IDEOS CONSERVE ...CONCPT 19 CIVIL/WAR. PAGE 22 H0452 — CONSTN FEDERAL SOVEREIGN

CIVIL-MILITARY RELATIONS....SEE CIVMIL/REL

CIVMIL/REL....CIVIL-MILITARY RELATIONS

B38
IIZAWA S.,POLITICS AND POLITICAL PARTIES IN JAPAN. ELITES VOL/ASSN CHOOSE SUFF CIVMIL/REL GP/REL 19/20 CHINJAP. PAGE 76 H1522 — POL/PAR REPRESENT FORCES NAT/G

B39
KOHN H.,REVOLUTIONS AND DICTATORSHIPS. COM EUR+WWI ISLAM MOD/EUR NAT/G CHIEF FORCES WAR CIVMIL/REL PWR MARXISM 18/20. PAGE 87 H1739 — NAT/LISM TOTALISM REV FASCISM

S41
DENNERY E.,"DEMOCRACY AND THE FRENCH ARMY." FRANCE NAT/G EX/STRUC LEAD REV ROLE 18/20. PAGE 40 H0792 — FORCES POPULISM STRATA CIVMIL/REL

B42
BAYNES N.H.,INTELLECTUAL LIBERTY AND TOTALITARIAN CLAIMS. EUR+WWI GERMANY ITALY INTELL POL/PAR CIVMIL/REL NAT/LISM SOCISM CONCPT. PAGE 12 H0245 — KNOWL FASCISM EDU/PROP ACADEM

B43
CONOVER H.F.,SOVIET RUSSIA: SELECTED LIST OF REFERENCES. USSR CULTURE INDUS NAT/G TOP/EX TEC/DEV BUDGET WAR CIVMIL/REL EFFICIENCY MARXISM 20. PAGE 32 H0644 — BIBLIOG ECO/DEV COM DIPLOM

B45
CONOVER H.F.,THE GOVERNMENTS OF THE MAJOR FOREIGN POWERS: A BIBLIOGRAPHY. FRANCE GERMANY ITALY UK USSR CONSTN LOC/G POL/PAR EX/STRUC FORCES ADMIN CT/SYS CIVMIL/REL TOTALISM...POLICY 19/20. PAGE 32 H0645 — BIBLIOG NAT/G DIPLOM

B45
CONOVER H.F.,ITALY: ECONOMICS, POLITICS AND MILITARY AFFAIRS, 1940-1945. ITALY ELITES NAT/G POL/PAR EX/STRUC TOP/EX DIPLOM DOMIN CONTROL COERCE WAR CIVMIL/REL EFFICIENCY 20. PAGE 32 H0646 — BIBLIOG TOTALISM FORCES

B45
PERAZA SARAUSA F.,BIBLIOGRAFIAS CUBANAS. CUBA CULTURE ECO/UNDEV AGRI EDU/PROP PRESS CIVMIL/REL ...POLICY GEOG PHIL/SCI BIOG 19/20. PAGE 125 H2489 — BIBLIOG/A L/A+17C NAT/G DIPLOM

B48
FLOREN LOZANO L.,BIBLIOGRAFIA DE LA BIBLIOGRAFIA DOMINICANA. DOMIN/REP NAT/G DIPLOM EDU/PROP CIVMIL/REL...POLICY ART/METH GEOG PHIL/SCI HIST/WRIT 20. PAGE 51 H1027 — BIBLIOG/A BIOG L/A+17C CULTURE

C49
YANAGA C.,"JAPAN SINCE PERRY." S/ASIA CULTURE ECO/DEV FORCES WAR 19/20 CHINJAP. PAGE 172 H3433 — DIPLOM POL/PAR CIVMIL/REL NAT/LISM

B52
GURLAND A.R.L.,POLITICAL SCIENCE IN WESTERN GERMANY: THOUGHTS AND WRITINGS, 1950-1952 (PAMPHLET). EUR+WWI GERMANY/W ELITES SOCIETY NAT/G NAT/LISM TOTALISM 20. PAGE 63 H1253 — BIBLIOG/A DIPLOM CIVMIL/REL FASCISM

B52
THOM J.M.,GUIDE TO RESEARCH MATERIAL IN POLITICAL SCIENCE (PAMPHLET). ELITES LOC/G MUNIC NAT/G LEGIS DIPLOM ADJUD CIVMIL/REL GOV/REL PWR MGT. PAGE 154 H3074 — BIBLIOG/A KNOWL

B55
VIGON J.,TEORIA DEL MILITARISMO. NAT/G DIPLOM COLONIAL COERCE GUERRILLA CIVMIL/REL NAT/LISM MORAL ALL/IDEOS PACIFISM 18/20. PAGE 163 H3253 — FORCES PHIL/SCI WAR POLICY

B56
SMEDLEY A.,THE GREAT ROAD: THE LIFE AND TIMES OF CHU TEH. ASIA USSR NAT/G POL/PAR DIPLOM COERCE GUERRILLA CIVMIL/REL NAT/LISM PERSON SKILL MARXISM ...BIOG 20 CHINJAP MAO. PAGE 145 H2903 — REV WAR FORCES

L57
BENDIX R.,"POLITICAL SOCIOLOGY." CULTURE INTELL LABOR POL/PAR SECT LEGIS EDU/PROP ADMIN CHOOSE CIVMIL/REL ATTIT...IDEA/COMP 20. PAGE 14 H0274 — BIBLIOG/A ACT/RES SOC

B59
MATHER F.C.,PUBLIC ORDER IN THE AGE OF THE CHARTISTS. UK CULTURE ADJUD CONTROL. PAGE 105 H2090
ORD/FREE FORCES COERCE CIVMIL/REL

B59
STERNBERG F.,THE MILITARY AND INDUSTRIAL REVOLUTION OF OUR TIME. USA+45 USSR WOR+45 WORKER COMPUTER PLAN TEC/DEV NUC/PWR GP/REL...POLICY NAT/COMP 20. PAGE 149 H2981
DIPLOM FORCES INDUS CIVMIL/REL

B60
FEIS H.,BETWEEN WAR AND PEACE: THE POTSDAM CONFERENCE. EUR+WWI NAT/G DELIB/GP PROB/SOLV REPAR WAR CIVMIL/REL...BIBLIOG 20. PAGE 49 H0983
DIPLOM CONFER BAL/PWR

B60
THORD-GRAY I.,GRINGO REBEL. L/A+17C NAT/G CONTROL LEAD ATTIT...OBS 20 MEXIC/AMER. PAGE 154 H3087
REV FORCES CIVMIL/REL ORD/FREE

B61
DONNISON F.S.V.,CIVIL AFFAIRS AND MILITARY GOVERNMENT NORTH-WEST EUROPE 1944-1946. EUR+WWI FRANCE GERMANY UK USSR LOC/G PROVS PLAN PROB/SOLV BAL/PWR ECO/TAC CONTROL PWR...CHARTS 20. PAGE 42 H0836
NAT/G WAR FORCES CIVMIL/REL

B61
STANLEY C.J.,LATE CH'ING FINANCE: HU KUANG-YUNG AS AN INNOVATOR. ASIA NAT/G FORCES BUDGET TAX WAR GOV/REL COST...POLICY BIOG CHARTS BIBLIOG 19. PAGE 148 H2969
FINAN ECO/TAC CIVMIL/REL ADMIN

B62
YU LIEN YEN CHIU,INDEX TO THE CLASSIFIED FILES ON COMMUNIST CHINA. CHINA/COM CULTURE ECO/UNDEV CIVMIL/REL PWR WEALTH MARXISM...PSY SOC METH 20. PAGE 172 H3440
BIBLIOG INDEX COM

B64
ALVIM J.C.,A REVOLUCAO SEM RUMO. BRAZIL NAT/G BAL/PWR DIPLOM INT/TRADE PARTIC WEALTH...POLICY SOC SOC/INTEG 20. PAGE 6 H0118
REV CIVMIL/REL ECO/UNDEV ORD/FREE

B64
GUTTERIDGE W.,MILITARY INSTITUTIONS AND POWER IN THE NEW STATES. WOR+45 INT/ORG FOR/AID NEUTRAL REV CIVMIL/REL ATTIT ROLE...GOV/COMP 20. PAGE 63 H1258
FORCES DIPLOM ECO/UNDEV ELITES

B64
JOHNSON J.J.,CONTINUITY AND CHANGE IN LATIN AMERICA. L/A+17C INTELL FORCES WORKER CIVMIL/REL CHINJAP. PAGE 81 H1623
ANTHOL CULTURE STRATA GP/COMP

B64
LIEVWEN E.,GENERALS VS PRESIDENTS: WEOMILITARISM IN LATIN AMERICA. L/A+17C FORCES DIPLOM FOR/AID LEAD ...NAT/COMP 20 PRESIDENT. PAGE 97 H1929
CIVMIL/REL REV CONSERVE ORD/FREE

B64
WALDMAN E.,THE GOOSE STEP IS VERBOTEN: THE GERMAN ARMY TODAY. GERMANY/W LAW CONSTN LEGIS PROB/SOLV DOMIN CONTROL CIVMIL/REL GOV/REL INGP/REL ATTIT ...DEEP/QU 20. PAGE 164 H3289
SOC FORCES NAT/G

B64
WERNETTE J.P.,GOVERNMENT AND BUSINESS. LABOR CAP/ISM ECO/TAC INT/TRADE TAX ADMIN AUTOMAT NUC/PWR CIVMIL/REL DEMAND...MGT 20 MONOPOLY. PAGE 167 H3333
NAT/G FINAN ECO/DEV CONTROL

B65
FAUST J.J.,A REVOLUCAO DEVORA SEUS PRESIDENTES. BRAZIL NAT/G POL/PAR LEAD CHOOSE CIVMIL/REL ORD/FREE 20 PRESIDENT. PAGE 49 H0976
PARTIC REV FORCES GP/REL

L65
MATTHEWS D.G.,"A CURRENT BIBLIOGRAPHY ON ETHIOPIAN AFFAIRS: A SELECT BIBLIOGRAPHY FROM 1950-1964." ETHIOPIA LAW CULTURE ECO/UNDEV INDUS LABOR SECT FORCES DIPLOM CIVMIL/REL RACE/REL...LING STAT 20. PAGE 105 H2093
BIBLIOG/A ADMIN POL/PAR NAT/G

S65
WOLF C. JR.,"THE POLITICAL EFFECTS OF SOME MILITARY PROGRAMS* SOME INDICATIONS FROM LATIN AMERICA." ELITES STRATA BUDGET FOR/AID WEAPON ATTIT PERCEPT PWR...REGRESS SYS/QU CHARTS NAT/COMP. PAGE 170 H3397
L/A+17C FORCES CIVMIL/REL PROBABIL

B66
COEDES G.,THE MAKING OF SOUTH EAST ASIA. BURMA CAMBODIA LAOS S/ASIA THAILAND VIETNAM REV WAR CIVMIL/REL...GEOG 6/13. PAGE 31 H0614
CULTURE FORCES DOMIN

B66
DALLIN A.,POLITICS IN THE SOVIET UNION: 7 CASES. COM USSR LAW POL/PAR CHIEF FORCES WRITING CONTROL PARL/PROC CIVMIL/REL TOTALISM...ANTHOL 20 KHRUSH/N STALIN/J CASEBOOK COM/PARTY. PAGE 37 H0736
MARXISM DOMIN ORD/FREE GOV/REL

B66
HEADY F.,PUBLIC ADMINISTRATION: A COMPARATIVE PERSPECTIVE. ECO/DEV ECO/UNDEV...GOV/COMP 20 BUREAUCRCY. PAGE 69 H1376
ADMIN NAT/COMP NAT/G CIVMIL/REL

B66
MCKAY V.,AFRICAN DIPLOMACY STUDIES IN THE DETERMINANTS OF FOREIGN POLICY. AFR SOUTH/AFR CULTURE NEUTRAL REGION SOVEREIGN...INT/LAW GOV/COMP ANTHOL 20. PAGE 107 H2138
ECO/UNDEV RACE/REL CIVMIL/REL DIPLOM

B66
O'NEILL R.J.,THE GERMAN ARMY AND THE NAZI PARTY, 1933-1939. GERMANY ELITES NAT/G EDU/PROP CONTROL LEAD COERCE WAR...POLICY INT TIME/SEQ BIBLIOG 20 HITLER/A NAZI. PAGE 120 H2391
CIVMIL/REL FORCES FASCISM POL/PAR

L66
ZOPPO C.E.,"NUCLEAR TECHNOLOGY, MULTIPOLARITY, AND INTERNATIONAL STABILITY." ASIA RUSSIA USA+45 STRUCT TOP/EX BAL/PWR DIPLOM DETER CIVMIL/REL NAT/COMP. PAGE 173 H3464
NET/THEORY ORD/FREE DECISION NUC/PWR

S66
COWAN L.G.,"THE MILITARY AND AFRICAN POLITICS." AFR FUT NAT/G POL/PAR PARTIC REV 20. PAGE 34 H0685
CIVMIL/REL FORCES PWR LEAD

S66
MATTHEWS D.G.,"PRELUDE-COUP D'ETAT-MILITARY GOVERNMENT: A BIBLIOGRAPHICAL AND RESEARCH GUIDE TO NIGERIAN POL AND GOVT, JAN, 1965-66." AFR NIGER LAW CONSTN POL/PAR LEGIS CIVMIL/REL GOV/REL...STAT 20. PAGE 105 H2096
BIBLIOG NAT/G ADMIN CHOOSE

B67
BANKWITZ P.C.,MAXINE WEYGAND AND CIVIL-MILITARY RELATIONS IN MODERN FRANCE. FRANCE LEAD WAR PWR ...INT BIBLIOG 20. PAGE 11 H0212
CIVMIL/REL FORCES NAT/G TOP/EX

B67
KENNETT L.,THE FRENCH ARMIES IN THE SEVEN YEARS' WAR. FRANCE NAT/G CONTROL LEAD WAR CIVMIL/REL EFFICIENCY ATTIT PWR SKILL CONSERVE 18. PAGE 85 H1690
FORCES CHIEF METH/COMP

B67
KOLKOWICZ R.,THE SOVIET MILITARY AND THE COMMUNIST PARTY. COM USSR ELITES NAT/G CREATE CIVMIL/REL GP/REL...TREND BIBLIOG/A 20 COM/PARTY. PAGE 88 H1753
MARXISM CONSTN FORCES POL/PAR

B67
MENARD O.D.,THE ARMY AND THE FIFTH REPUBLIC. ALGERIA FRANCE VIETNAM ELITES STRATA COLONIAL CONTROL LOBBY WAR CIVMIL/REL ROLE PWR...POLICY 20 DEGAULLE/C. PAGE 108 H2169
FORCES ATTIT NAT/G

B67
ROSENBLUTH G.,THE CANADIAN ECONOMY AND DISARMAMENT. CANADA FUT ECO/DEV INDUS R+D DELIB/GP DIPLOM ECO/TAC CIVMIL/REL PEACE...POLICY BIBLIOG PACIFIST 20. PAGE 134 H2679
ARMS/CONT STAT PLAN NAT/G

B67
SALISBURY H.E.,BEHIND THE LINES - HANOI. VIETNAM/N NAT/G GUERRILLA CIVMIL/REL NAT/LISM KNOWL 20. PAGE 137 H2741
WAR PROB/SOLV DIPLOM OBS

L67
BRIDGHAM P.,"MAO'S "CULTURAL REVOLUTION"* ORIGIN AND DEVELOPMENT." NAT/G LEAD CIVMIL/REL NAT/LISM TOTALISM ATTIT DRIVE PWR MARXISM 20. PAGE 21 H0413
CHINA/COM CULTURE REV CROWD

L67
EINAUDI L.,"ANNOTATED BIBLIOGRAPHY OF LATIN AMERICAN MILITARY JOURNALS" LAW TEC/DEV DOMIN EDU/PROP COERCE WAR CIVMIL/REL 20. PAGE 45 H0899
BIBLIOG/A NAT/G FORCES L/A+17C

S67
BEVEL D.N.,"JOURNEY TO NORTH VIETNAM." VIETNAM/N CONSTN NAT/G FORCES PROB/SOLV DEATH CIVMIL/REL PEACE MORAL...ANTHOL 20 NEGRO. PAGE 16 H0325
ATTIT DIPLOM ORD/FREE WAR

S67
CHIU S.M.,"CHINA'S MILITARY POSTURE." CHINA/COM ELITES NAT/G POL/PAR TEC/DEV ECO/TAC DOMIN CONTROL LEAD REV MARXISM 20 MAO. PAGE 30 H0595
FORCES CIVMIL/REL NUC/PWR DIPLOM

S67
FINLAY D.J.,"THE GHANA COUP...ONE YEAR LATER." GHANA FORCES FOR/AID PRESS CONTROL CIVMIL/REL NAT/LISM AUTHORIT PWR...PREDICT 20. PAGE 50 H1005
REV NAT/G ATTIT ECO/UNDEV

S67
LALL B.G.,"GAPS IN THE ABM DEBATE." NAT/G DIPLOM DETER CIVMIL/REL 20. PAGE 90 H1798
NUC/PWR ARMS/CONT EX/STRUC FORCES

S67
LANE J.P.,"FUNCTIONS OF MASS MEDIA IN BRAZIL'S 1964 CRISIS." BRAZIL NAT/G FORCES TOP/EX PRESS TV ATTIT PWR...METH/CNCPT 20. PAGE 90 H1807
CIVMIL/REL REV COM/IND EDU/PROP

S67
PAK H.,"CHINA'S MILITIA AND MAO TSE-TUNG'S 'PEOPLE'S WAR'." CHINA/COM SOCIETY POL/PAR EX/STRUC PROB/SOLV PARTIC COERCE WAR CIVMIL/REL ATTIT DRIVE MARXISM...METH/COMP 20 MAO. PAGE 122 H2447
FORCES NAT/G WORKER CHIEF

S67
SULLIVAN J.H.,"THE PRESS AND POLITICS IN INDONESIA." INDONESIA NAT/G WRITING REV...TREND GOV/COMP 20. PAGE 150 H3007
CIVMIL/REL KNOWL TOTALISM

S67
SUNG C.H.,"POLITICAL DIAGNOSIS OF KOREAN SOCIETY* A SURVEY OF MILITARY AND CIVILIAN VALUES." KOREA/S ECO/UNDEV NAT/G CIVMIL/REL...QU SAMP GP/COMP. PAGE 151 H3009
ELITES FORCES ATTIT ORD/FREE

L68
CURRENT HISTORY,"AFRICA, 1968." ETHIOPIA GHANA NIGERIA SOUTH/AFR CULTURE ECO/UNDEV KIN SECT CHIEF EX/STRUC WAR WEAPON CHOOSE CIVMIL/REL...GOV/COMP 20 AFRICA/E. PAGE 36 H0724
RACE/REL NAT/LISM FORCES AFR

CLAGETT H.L. H0602

CLAN....SEE KIN

CLARK S.I. H2036

CLARK/JB....JOHN BATES CLARK

CLARKE D.E. H0414

CLARKE M.V. H0603

CLASS DIVISION....SEE STRATA

CLASS, SOCIAL....SEE STRATA

CLASSIF....CLASSIFICATION, TYPOLOGY, SET THEORY

B23
POUND R.,INTERPRETATIONS OF LEGAL HISTORY. CULTURE ...PHIL/SCI NEW/IDEA CLASSIF SIMUL GEN/LAWS 19/20. PAGE 127 H2547
LAW IDEA/COMP JURID

B31
LORWIN L.L.,ADVISORY ECONOMIC COUNCILS. EUR+WWI FRANCE GERMANY PROB/SOLV INGP/REL...CLASSIF GP/COMP. PAGE 99 H1968
CONSULT DELIB/GP ECO/TAC NAT/G

B45
WARNER W.L.,THE SOCIAL SYSTEM OF AMERICAN ETHNIC GROUPS. STRATA FAM EDU/PROP ATTIT HABITAT RESPECT CLASSIF. PAGE 165 H3309
CULTURE VOL/ASSN SECT GP/COMP

B46
FEIBLEMAN J.,THE THEORY OF HUMAN CULTURE. UNIV CONSTN SOCIETY...CONCPT CLASSIF TIME/SEQ. PAGE 49 H0981
GEN/LAWS CULTURE SOC PHIL/SCI

B50
GOFF F.R.,FIFTEENTH CENTURY BOOKS IN THE LIBRARY OF CONGRESS. CHRIST-17C GERMANY ITALY CULTURE INTELL SECT CREATE...PHIL/SCI CONCPT CLASSIF BIOG TIME/SEQ 15. PAGE 58 H1153
BIBLIOG KNOWL HUM

B51
WHEARE K.C.,MODERN CONSTITUTIONS (HOME UNIVERSITY LIBRARY). UNIV LAW NAT/G LEGIS...CONCPT TREND BIBLIOG. PAGE 167 H3336
CONSTN CLASSIF PWR CREATE

B53
BIDNEY D.,THEORETICAL ANTHROPOLOGY. DRIVE ROLE ORD/FREE...CONCPT METH/CNCPT MYTH CLASSIF OBS IDEA/COMP METH/COMP BIBLIOG METH 20. PAGE 17 H0331
CULTURE SOC PSY PHIL/SCI

B54
BERGER M.,FREEDOM AND CONTROL IN MODERN SOCIETY. LABOR NAT/G VOL/ASSN AUTHORIT DRIVE PLURISM ...METH/CNCPT CLASSIF. PAGE 15 H0300
ORD/FREE CONTROL INGP/REL

B55
COLE G.D.H.,STUDIES IN CLASS STRUCTURE. UK NAT/G WORKER TEC/DEV EDU/PROP...CLASSIF CHARTS 20. PAGE 31 H0623
STRUCT STRATA ELITES CONCPT

B55
UN ECONOMIC AND SOCIAL COUNCIL,ANALYTICAL BIBLIOGRAPHY OF INTERNATIONAL MIGRATION STATISTICS, SELECTED COUNTRIES, 1925-1950. STRATA...CLASSIF CENSUS NAT/COMP 20. PAGE 158 H3156
BIBLIOG STAT GEOG HABITAT

B56
LEVIN M.G.,THE PEOPLES OF SIBERIA. PREHIST ECO/UNDEV KIN SECT HABITAT...CLASSIF AUD/VIS WORSHIP 20 SIBERIA. PAGE 95 H1900
CULTURE SOCIETY ASIA

B58
STRAUSZ-HUPE R.,THE IDEA OF COLONIALISM. WOR+45 WOR-45 BAL/PWR GOV/REL...POLICY CLASSIF TIME/SEQ GOV/COMP ANTHOL 20 UN. PAGE 150 H2996
IDEA/COMP COLONIAL CONTROL CONCPT

B59
DAHRENDORF R.,CLASS AND CLASS CONFLICT IN INDUSTRIAL SOCIETY. LABOR NAT/G COERCE ROLE PLURISM ...POLICY MGT CONCPT CLASSIF. PAGE 37 H0734
VOL/ASSN STRUCT SOC GP/REL

B60
LA PONCE J.A.,THE PROTECTION OF MINORITIES. WOR+45 WOR-45 NAT/G POL/PAR SUFF...INT/LAW CLASSIF GP/COMP GOV/COMP BIBLIOG 17/20 CIVIL/LIB CIV/RIGHTS. PAGE 90 H1793
INGP/REL DOMIN SOCIETY RACE/REL

B61
ETZIONI A.,COMPLEX ORGANIZATIONS: A SOCIOLOGICAL READER. CLIENT CULTURE STRATA CREATE OP/RES ADMIN ...POLICY METH/CNCPT BUREAUCRCY. PAGE 47 H0945
VOL/ASSN STRUCT CLASSIF PROF/ORG

B61
FIELD H.,ANCIENT AND MODERN MAN IN SOUTHWESTERN ASIA: II. CULTURE SOCIETY...CLASSIF MATH GP/COMP NAT/COMP 20. PAGE 50 H0992
STAT CHARTS PHIL/SCI RECORD

S61
MACRIDIS R.C.,"INTEREST GROUPS IN COMPARATIVE ANALYSIS." CULTURE OP/RES LOBBY REPRESENT GP/REL AUTHORIT ORD/FREE PWR...POLICY DECISION METH/CNCPT CLASSIF. PAGE 101 H2010
GP/COMP CONCPT PLURISM

N63
RUMMEL R.J.,A FOREIGN CONFLICT BEHAVIOR CODE SHEET. ACT/RES DIPLOM...NEW/IDEA CHARTS NAT/COMP. PAGE 136 H2718
QUANT WAR CLASSIF SIMUL

B64
ETZIONI A.,MODERN ORGANIZATIONS. CLIENT STRUCT DOMIN CONTROL LEAD PERS/REL AUTHORIT...CLASSIF BUREAUCRCY. PAGE 47 H0946
MGT ADMIN PLAN CULTURE

B64
HARRIS M.,THE NATURE OF CULTURAL THINGS. GP/REL PERS/REL DRIVE HABITAT PERSON ROLE...PHIL/SCI PSY SOC CHARTS BIBLIOG 20. PAGE 67 H1341
CULTURE OBS CLASSIF NEW/IDEA

B64
KRUEGER H.,ALLGEMEINE STAATSLEHRE. WOR+45 CONSTN SECT CHOOSE INGP/REL PWR NEW/LIB...JURID CLASSIF IDEA/COMP. PAGE 89 H1777
NAT/G GOV/COMP SOCIETY

B64
SZLADITS C.,BIBLIOGRAPHY ON FOREIGN AND COMPARATIVE LAW: BOOKS AND ARTICLES IN ENGLISH (SUPPLEMENT 1962). FINAN INDUS JUDGE LICENSE ADMIN CT/SYS PARL/PROC OWN...INT/LAW CLASSIF METH/COMP NAT/COMP 20. PAGE 151 H3027
BIBLIOG/A JURID ADJUD LAW

S64
HORECKY P.L.,"LIBRARY OF CONGRESS PUBLICATIONS IN AID OF USSR AND EAST EUROPEAN RESEARCH." BULGARIA CZECHOSLVK POLAND USSR YUGOSLAVIA NAT/G POL/PAR DIPLOM ADMIN GOV/REL...CLASSIF 20. PAGE 73 H1468
BIBLIOG/A COM MARXISM

B65
HESS A.G.,CHASING THE DRAGON: A REPORT ON DRUG ADDICTION IN HONG KONG. ASIA CULTURE PROB/SOLV TRIBUTE...POLICY PSY SOC CLASSIF STAT 17/20 HONG/KONG. PAGE 70 H1411
BIO/SOC CRIME SOCIETY LAW

B65
HLA MYINT U.,THE ECONOMICS OF THE DEVELOPING COUNTRIES. USA+45 WOR+45 AGRI FINAN NAT/G INT/TRADE ...CLASSIF CENSUS TREND NAT/COMP SIMUL GEN/LAWS. PAGE 71 H1430
ECO/UNDEV FOR/AID GEOG

B65
HYMES D.,THE USE OF COMPUTERS IN ANTHROPOLOGY. CULTURE PROF/ORG CONSULT CREATE EFFICIENCY PERCEPT ...CLASSIF LING CON/ANAL COMPUT/IR METH/COMP ANTHOL 20. PAGE 76 H1517
METH COMPUTER TEC/DEV SOC

B65
ORGANSKI A.F.K.,THE STAGES OF POLITICAL DEVELOPMENT. STRATA AGRI INDUS NAT/G POL/PAR COLONIAL PWR WEALTH...CLASSIF TIME/SEQ. PAGE 121 H2428
ECO/DEV ECO/UNDEV GEN/LAWS CREATE

B65
RENNER K.,MENSCH UND GESELLSCHAFT - GRUNDRISS EINER SOZIOLOGIE (2ND ED.). STRATA FAM LABOR PROF/ORG WAR ...JURID CLASSIF 20. PAGE 131 H2616
SOC STRUCT NAT/G SOCIETY

B65
TILLY C.,MEASURING POLITICAL UPHEAVAL* RESEARCH MONOGRAPH NO. 19. FRANCE INDUS NAT/G FORCES WORKER ...GEOG RECORD EXHIBIT GEN/METH BIBLIOG INDEX. PAGE 155 H3095
CLASSIF QUANT COERCE REV

B65
WHITEMAN M.M.,DIGEST OF INTERNATIONAL LAW* VOLUME 5, DEPARTMENT OF STATE PUBLICATION 7873. USA+45 WOR+45 OP/RES...CONCPT CLASSIF RECORD IDEA/COMP. PAGE 167 H3353
INT/LAW NAT/G NAT/COMP

S65
BANK A.S.,"GROUPING POLITICAL SYSTEMS* Q-FACTOR ANALYSIS OF A CROSSPOLITY SURVEY." CULTURE...CHARTS NAT/COMP. PAGE 11 H0211
CLASSIF NAT/G WOR+45 MATH

S65
POWELL J.D.,"MILITARY ASSISTANCE AND MILITARISM IN LATIN AMERICA." USA+45 INT/ORG NAT/G CONTROL REGION PRODUC WEALTH...CLASSIF STAT NAT/COMP CONGRESS. PAGE 128 H2550
L/A+17C FORCES FOR/AID PWR

B66
CAPELL A.,STUDIES IN SOCIO-LINGUISTICS. CULTURE ADJUST...CLASSIF IDEA/COMP SOC/EXP BIBLIOG 20. PAGE 26 H0525
LING SOC PHIL/SCI CORREL

B66
HOYT E.C.,NATIONAL POLICY AND INTERNATIONAL LAW* CASE STUDIES FROM AMERICAN CANAL POLICY* MONOGRAPH NO. 1 -- 1966-1967. PANAMA UK ELITES BAL/PWR EFFICIENCY...CLASSIF NAT/COMP SOC/EXP COLOMB TREATY. PAGE 74 H1483
INT/LAW USA-45 DIPLOM PWR

S66
MARTZ J.D.,"THE PLACE OF LATIN AMERICA IN THE STUDY OF COMPARATIVE POLITICS." AFR ASIA CULTURE STRUCT ECO/UNDEV ACADEM CREATE...CLASSIF NAT/COMP. PAGE 104 H2072
L/A+17C GOV/COMP STERTYP GEN/LAWS

S66
SNOW P.G.,"A SCALOGRAM ANALYSIS OF POLITICAL DEVELOPMENT." STRATA ECO/UNDEV POL/PAR REGION ALL/VALS PWR...SOC CHARTS. PAGE 146 H2924
L/A+17C NAT/COMP TESTS CLASSIF

B67
LAMBERT J.,LATIN AMERICA: SOCIAL STRUCTURES AND POLITICAL INSTITUTIONS. STRUCT TEC/DEV DIPLOM ADMIN COLONIAL LEAD ATTIT...SOC CLASSIF NAT/COMP 17/20. PAGE 90 H1801
L/A+17C NAT/G ECO/UNDEV SOCIETY

S67
CATTELL D.T.,"A NEO-MARXIST THEORY OF COMPARATIVE ANALYSIS." USSR STRATA INSPECT DOMIN CONTROL COERCE OWN TOTALISM PWR...FASCIST HYPO/EXP METH 20. PAGE 28 H0561
GOV/COMP MARXISM SIMUL CLASSIF

B97
JENKS E.J.,LAW AND POLITICS IN THE MIDDLE AGES. CHRIST-17C CULTURE STRUCT KIN NAT/G SECT CT/SYS GP/REL...CLASSIF CHARTS IDEA/COMP BIBLIOG 8/16. PAGE 80 H1603
LAW SOCIETY ADJUST

CLAUSWTZ/K....KARL VON CLAUSEWITZ

CLEMENCE/G....GEORGES CLEMENCEAU

CLEMENCEAU, GEORGES....SEE CLEMENCE/G

CLEMSON....CLEMSON UNIVERSITY

CLEVELAND....CLEVELAND, OHIO

CLEVELND/G....PRESIDENT GROVER CLEVELAND

CLIENT....CLIENTS, CLIENTELE (BUT NOT CUSTOMERS)

B61
ETZIONI A.,COMPLEX ORGANIZATIONS: A SOCIOLOGICAL READER. CLIENT CULTURE STRATA CREATE OP/RES ADMIN ...POLICY METH/CNCPT BUREAUCRCY. PAGE 47 H0945
VOL/ASSN STRUCT CLASSIF PROF/ORG

B64
ETZIONI A.,MODERN ORGANIZATIONS. CLIENT STRUCT DOMIN CONTROL LEAD PERS/REL AUTHORIT...CLASSIF BUREAUCRCY. PAGE 47 H0946
MGT ADMIN PLAN CULTURE

S67
HARNON E.,"CRIMINAL PROCEDURE IN ISRAEL - SOME COMPARATIVE ASPECTS." ISRAEL USA+45 CLIENT EX/STRUC LEGIS...JURID NAT/COMP 20. PAGE 67 H1336
ADJUD CONSTN CT/SYS CRIME

CLIFFE L. H0604

CLIFFORD/C....CLARK CLIFFORD

CLIGNET R. H0605

CLIQUES....SEE FACE/GP

CLOKIE H.M. H0606,H0607

CLUBB O.E. H0608

CLUBS....SEE VOL/ASSN, FACE/GP

CLYDE P.H. H0609

CMA....CANADIAN MEDICAL ASSOCIATION

S60
TAYLOR M.G.,"THE ROLE OF THE MEDICAL PROFESSION IN THE FORMULATION AND EXECUTION OF PUBLIC POLICY" (BMR)" CANADA NAT/G CONSULT ADMIN REPRESENT GP/REL ROLE SOVEREIGN...DECISION 20 CMA. PAGE 153 H3056
PROF/ORG HEALTH LOBBY POLICY

CMN/WLTH....BRITISH COMMONWEALTH OF NATIONS ;SEE ALSO VOL/ASSN, APPROPRIATE NATIONS, COMMONWLTH

N
PUBLISHERS' CIRCULAR, THE OFFICIAL ORGAN OF THE PUBLISHERS' ASSOCIATION OF GREAT BRITAIN AND IRELAND. EUR+WWI MOD/EUR UK LAW PROB/SOLV DIPLOM COLONIAL ATTIT...HUM 19/20 CMN/WLTH. PAGE 1 H0019
BIBLIOG NAT/G WRITING LEAD

N
MINISTRY OF OVERSEAS DEVELOPME,TECHNICAL CO-OPERATION -- A BIBLIOGRAPHY. UK LAW SOCIETY DIPLOM ECO/TAC FOR/AID...STAT 20 CMN/WLTH. PAGE 111 H2225
BIBLIOG TEC/DEV ECO/DEV NAT/G

B02
SEELEY J.R.,THE EXPANSION OF ENGLAND. MOD/EUR S/ASIA UK CULTURE NAT/G FORCES PLAN DOMIN EDU/PROP COLONIAL ROUTINE ATTIT ALL/VALS SOVEREIGN...CONCPT HIST/WRIT PARLIAMENT 18 CMN/WLTH. PAGE 141 H2819
INT/ORG ACT/RES CAP/ISM INDIA

B10
TEMPERLEY H.W.V.,SENATES AND UPPER CHAMBERS; THEIR USE AND FUNCTION IN THE MODERN STATE... UK WOR-45 CONSTN NAT/G POL/PAR PROVS SECT COLONIAL LEAD CHOOSE REPRESENT PWR...BIBLIOG 19/20 PARLIAMENT SENATE CMN/WLTH HOUSE/LORD. PAGE 153 H3059
PARL/PROC NAT/COMP LEGIS EX/STRUC

B19
NATHAN M.,THE SOUTH AFRICAN COMMONWEALTH: CONSTITUTION, PROBLEMS, SOCIAL CONDITIONS. SOUTH/AFR UK CULTURE INDUS EX/STRUC LEGIS BUDGET EDU/PROP ADMIN CT/SYS GP/REL RACE/REL...LING 19/20 CMN/WLTH. PAGE 116 H2317
CONSTN NAT/G POL/PAR SOCIETY

N19
MASSEY V.,CANADIANS AND THEIR COMMONWEALTH: THE ROMANES LECTURE DELIVERED IN THE SHELDONIAN THEATRE JUNE 1, 1961 (PAMPHLET). CANADA UK CULTURE ECO/DEV REPRESENT NAT/LISM PEACE PWR CONSERVE 20 CMN/WLTH. PAGE 104 H2088
ATTIT DIPLOM NAT/G SOVEREIGN

B23
LEES-SMITH H.B.,SECOND CHAMBERS IN THEORY AND PRACTICE. IRELAND NORWAY SOUTH/AFR UK LAW POL/PAR LEGIS CONTROL 20 CMN/WLTH. PAGE 93 H1858
PARL/PROC DELIB/GP REPRESENT GP/COMP

B26
POLLARD A.F.,THE EVOLUTION OF PARLIAMENT. UK CONSTN POL/PAR EX/STRUC GOV/REL INGP/REL PRIVIL RIGID/FLEX ...TIME/SEQ 11/20 CMN/WLTH PARLIAMENT. PAGE 127 H2536
LEGIS PARL/PROC NAT/G

B27
GOOCH G.P.,ENGLISH DEMOCRATIC IDEAS IN THE SEVENTEENTH CENTURY (2ND ED.). UK LAW SECT FORCES DIPLOM LEAD PARL/PROC REV ATTIT AUTHORIT...ANARCH CONCPT 17 PARLIAMENT CMN/WLTH REFORMERS. PAGE 58 H1167
IDEA/COMP MAJORIT EX/STRUC CONSERVE

B28
CORBETT P.E.,CANADA AND WORLD POLITICS. LAW CULTURE SOCIETY STRUCT MARKET INT/ORG FORCES ACT/RES PLAN ECO/TAC LEGIT ORD/FREE PWR RESPECT...SOC CONCPT TIME/SEQ TREND CMN/WLTH 20 LEAGUE/NAT. PAGE 33 H0662
NAT/G CANADA

B28
HURST C.,GREAT BRITAIN AND THE DOMINIONS. EUR+WWI CULTURE ECO/DEV INT/ORG NAT/G DIPLOM ECO/TAC COLONIAL ATTIT PWR SOVEREIGN...TIME/SEQ GEN/LAWS TOT/POP VAL/FREE 20 CMN/WLTH. PAGE 75 H1508
VOL/ASSN DOMIN UK

L37
NICOLSON H.,"THE MEANING OF PRESTIGE." EUR+WWI MOD/EUR UK CULTURE SOCIETY NAT/G DIPLOM DOMIN LEGIT ATTIT DRIVE PWR...METH/CNCPT RECORD TIME/SEQ GEN/METH CMN/WLTH TOT/POP 20. PAGE 118 H2351
CONCPT STERTYP

B38
HOLDSWORTH W.S.,A HISTORY OF ENGLISH LAW; THE CENTURIES OF SETTLEMENT AND REFORM (VOL. XI). UK CONSTN NAT/G EX/STRUC DIPLOM ADJUD CT/SYS LEAD CRIME ATTIT...INT/LAW JURID 18 CMN/WLTH PARLIAMENT ENGLSH/LAW. PAGE 73 H1452
LAW COLONIAL LEGIS PARL/PROC

B38
JESSOP T.E.,A BIBLIOGRAPHY OF DAVID HUME AND OF SCOTTISH PHILOSOPHY FROM FRANCIS HUTCHESON TO LORD BALFOUR. UK INTELL NAT/G ATTIT...CONCPT 17/20 HUME/D CMN/WLTH. PAGE 81 H1615
BIBLIOG EPIST PERCEPT BIOG

N45
INDIA QUARTERLY, A JOURNAL OF INTERNATIONAL AFFAIRS. INDIA LAW CONSTN ECO/UNDEV INT/ORG POL/PAR COLONIAL LEAD PARL/PROC WAR ATTIT...SOC 20 CMN/WLTH. PAGE 2 H0033
BIBLIOG/A S/ASIA DIPLOM NAT/G

B50
WADE E.C.S.,CONSTITUTIONAL LAW; AN OUTLINE OF THE LAW AND PRACTICE OF THE CONSTITUTION. UK LEGIS DOMIN ADMIN GP/REL 16/20 CMN/WLTH PARLIAMENT ENGLSH/LAW. PAGE 164 H3283
CONSTN NAT/G PARL/PROC LAW

B51
CARRINGTON C.E.,THE LIQUIDATION OF THE BRITISH EMPIRE. AFR NAT/G INT/TRADE COLONIAL RACE/REL ATTIT ORD/FREE...POLICY NAT/COMP 20 CMN/WLTH. PAGE 27 H0541
SOVEREIGN NAT/LISM DIPLOM GP/REL

B51
JENNINGS I.,THE COMMONWEALTH IN ASIA. CEYLON INDIA PAKISTAN CULTURE STRATA NAT/G LEGIS DIPLOM COLONIAL ATTIT...DECISION 20 CMN/WLTH. PAGE 80 H1604
CONSTN INT/ORG POLICY PLAN

B51
JENNINGS S.I.,THE COMMONWEALTH IN ASIA. CEYLON INDIA PAKISTAN S/ASIA UK CONSTN CULTURE SOCIETY
NAT/LISM REGION

STRATA STRUCT NAT/G POL/PAR EDU/PROP LEAD WAR 20 CMN/WLTH. PAGE 80 H1608
COLONIAL DIPLOM

B55
PYRAH G.B.,IMPERIAL POLICY AND SOUTH AFRICA 1902-1910. SOUTH/AFR UK NAT/G WAR DISCRIM...CONCPT CHARTS BIBLIOG/A 19/20 CMN/WLTH. PAGE 129 H2570
DIPLOM COLONIAL POLICY RACE/REL

C55
APTER D.E.,"THE GOLD COAST IN TRANSITION." AFR CONSTN LOC/G LEGIS DIPLOM COLONIAL CONTROL GOV/REL ...CHARTS BIBLIOG 20 CMN/WLTH. PAGE 7 H0150
ORD/FREE REPRESENT PARL/PROC NAT/G

S56
KHAMA T.,"POLITICAL CHANGE IN AFRICAN SOCIETY." CONSTN SOCIETY LOC/G NAT/G POL/PAR EX/STRUC LEGIS LEGIT ADMIN CHOOSE REPRESENT NAT/LISM MORAL ORD/FREE PWR...CONCPT OBS TREND GEN/METH CMN/WLTH 17/20. PAGE 85 H1706
AFR ELITES

C56
NEUMANN S.,"MODERN POLITICAL PARTIES: APPROACHES TO COMPARATIVE POLITIC. FRANCE UK EX/STRUC DOMIN ADMIN LEAD REPRESENT TOTALISM ATTIT...POLICY TREND METH/COMP ANTHOL BIBLIOG/A 20 CMN/WLTH. PAGE 117 H2338
POL/PAR GOV/COMP ELITES MAJORIT

B57
BUCK P.W.,CONTOL OF FOREIGN RELATIONS IN MODERN NATIONS. FRANCE L/A+17C NETHERLAND USSR WOR+45 INT/ORG TOP/EX BAL/PWR DOMIN EDU/PROP COERCE PEACE ATTIT...CONCPT TREND 20 CMN/WLTH. PAGE 23 H0465
NAT/G PWR DIPLOM

B57
DONALDSON A.G.,SOME COMPARATIVE ASPECTS OF IRISH LAW. IRELAND NAT/G DIPLOM ADMIN CT/SYS LEAD ATTIT SOVEREIGN...JURID BIBLIOG/A 12/20 CMN/WLTH. PAGE 42 H0835
CONSTN LAW NAT/COMP INT/LAW

S57
HAILEY,"TOMORROW IN AFRICA." CONSTN SOCIETY LOC/G NAT/G DOMIN ADJUD ADMIN GP/REL DISCRIM NAT/LISM ATTIT MORAL ORD/FREE...PSY SOC CONCPT OBS RECORD TREND GEN/LAWS CMN/WLTH 20. PAGE 64 H1277
AFR PERSON ELITES RACE/REL

S57
KILSON M.L.,"LAND AND POLITICS IN KENYA: AN ANALYSIS OF AFRICAN POLITICS IN A PLURAL SOCIETY." FUT LAW CULTURE KIN NAT/G ECO/TAC DOMIN REV NAT/LISM ORD/FREE PWR RESPECT SOVEREIGN WEALTH ...SOC OBS TREND WORK VAL/FREE CMN/WLTH 20. PAGE 86 H1710
AFR ECO/UNDEV

B58
BRADY A.,DEMOCRACY IN THE DOMINIONS (3RD ED.). CANADA NEW/ZEALND SOUTH/AFR WOR+45 LAW EX/STRUC DOMIN COLONIAL PARL/PROC REPRESENT RACE/REL NAT/LISM WEALTH 20 AUSTRAL CMN/WLTH. PAGE 20 H0399
GOV/COMP POL/PAR POPULISM NAT/G

B58
INDIAN COUNCIL WORLD AFFAIRS,DEFENCE AND SECURITY IN THE INDIAN OCEAN AREA. INDIA S/ASIA CULTURE CONSULT DELIB/GP FORCES PROB/SOLV DIPLOM INT/TRADE 20 CMN/WLTH. PAGE 77 H1531
GEOG HABITAT ECO/UNDEV ORD/FREE

S58
MAIR L.P.,"REPRESENTATIVE LOCAL GOVERNMENT AS A PROBLEM IN SOCIAL CHANGE." ECO/UNDEV KIN LOC/G NAT/G SCHOOL JUDGE ADMIN ROUTINE REPRESENT RIGID/FLEX RESPECT...CONCPT STERTYP CMN/WLTH 20. PAGE 101 H2025
AFR PWR ELITES

C58
WILDING N.,"AN ENCYCLOPEDIA OF PARLIAMENT." UK LAW CONSTN CHIEF PROB/SOLV DIPLOM DEBATE WAR INGP/REL PRIVIL...BIBLIOG DICTIONARY 13/20 CMN/WLTH PARLIAMENT. PAGE 168 H3363
PARL/PROC POL/PAR NAT/G ADMIN

B60
THE ECONOMIST (LONDON),THE COMMONWEALTH AND EUROPE. EUR+WWI WOR+45 AGRI FINAN INCOME...STAT CENSUS CHARTS CMN/WLTH EEC. PAGE 153 H3067
INT/TRADE INDUS INT/ORG NAT/COMP

B61
BELOFF M.,NEW DIMENSIONS IN FOREIGN POLICY: A STUDY IN BRITISH ADMINISTRATION. UK NAT/G ATTIT RIGID/FLEX ORD/FREE...GEN/LAWS EUR+WWI CMN/WLTH EEC 20. PAGE 14 H0271
INT/ORG DIPLOM

B61
HICKS U.K.,DEVELOPMENT FROM BELOW. UK INDUS ADMIN COLONIAL ROUTINE GOV/REL...POLICY METH/CNCPT CHARTS 19/20 CMN/WLTH. PAGE 71 H1414
ECO/UNDEV LOC/G GOV/COMP METH/COMP

S61
RAY J.,"THE EUROPEAN FREE-TRADE ASSOCIATION AND ITS IMPACT ON INDIA'S TRADE." EUR+WWI FRANCE GERMANY INDIA S/ASIA UK NAT/G VOL/ASSN PLAN INT/TRADE ROUTINE WEALTH...STAT CHARTS CMN/WLTH EEC OEEC 20 EFTA. PAGE 130 H2600
ECO/DEV ECO/TAC

B62
TAYLOR D.,THE BRITISH IN AFRICA. UK CULTURE ECO/UNDEV INDUS DIPLOM INT/TRADE ADMIN WAR RACE/REL ORD/FREE SOVEREIGN...POLICY BIBLIOG 15/20 CMN/WLTH. PAGE 153 H3053
AFR COLONIAL DOMIN

S62
LANGER W.L.,"FAREWELL TO EMPIRE." EUR+WWI MOD/EUR NAT/G DIPLOM EDU/PROP COLONIAL ATTIT ORD/FREE PWR SOVEREIGN WEALTH...CONCPT TIME/SEQ GEN/LAWS TOT/POP VAL/FREE CMN/WLTH 20. PAGE 91 H1810
DOMIN ECO/TAC NAT/LISM

S62
MARTIN L.W.,"THE MARKET FOR STRATEGIC IDEAS IN BRITAIN: THE 'SANDYS ERA'" UK ARMS/CONT WAR GOV/REL OPTIMAL...POLICY DECISION GOV/COMP COLD/WAR CMN/WLTH. PAGE 103 H2063
DIPLOM COERCE FORCES PWR

S62
SPRINGER H.W.,"FEDERATION IN THE CARIBBEAN: AN ATTEMPT THAT FAILED." L/A+17C ECO/UNDEV INT/ORG POL/PAR PROVS LEGIS CREATE PLAN LEGIT ADMIN FEDERAL ATTIT DRIVE PERSON ORD/FREE PWR...POLICY GEOG PSY CONCPT OBS CARIBBEAN CMN/WLTH 20. PAGE 148 H2955
VOL/ASSN NAT/G REGION

S62
THOMPSON D.,"THE UNITED KINGDOM AND THE TREATY OF ROME." EUR+WWI INT/ORG NAT/G DELIB/GP LEGIS INT/TRADE RIGID/FLEX...CONCPT EEC PARLIAMENT CMN/WLTH 20. PAGE 154 H3079
ADJUD JURID

B63
FAWCETT J.E.S.,THE BRITISH COMMONWEALTH IN INTERNATIONAL LAW. LAW INT/ORG NAT/G VOL/ASSN OP/RES DIPLOM ADJUD CENTRAL CONSEN...NET/THEORY CMN/WLTH TREATY. PAGE 49 H0977
INT/LAW STRUCT COLONIAL

B63
WILSON U.,EDUCATION AND CHANGING WEST AFRICAN CULTURE. AFR MOD/EUR UK CULTURE ECO/UNDEV MUNIC CONSULT 19/20 CMN/WLTH AFRICA/W. PAGE 169 H3384
COLONIAL POLICY SCHOOL

S63
MONROE A.D.,"BRITAIN AND THE EUROPEAN COMMUNITY." EUR+WWI FRANCE NAT/G DELIB/GP TOP/EX ECO/TAC DOMIN PWR...POLICY RECORD GEN/LAWS EEC EFTA 20 EFTA CMN/WLTH. PAGE 112 H2241
VOL/ASSN ATTIT UK

B64
AGGARWALA R.C.,CONSTITUTIONAL HISTORY OF INDIA AND NATIONAL MOVEMENT INCLUDING COMPARATIVE STUDY OF MODERN INDIA CONSTITUTION. INDIA S/ASIA SECT VOL/ASSN EX/STRUC LEGIS COERCE REV INGP/REL ORD/FREE...SOC BIBLIOG 18/20 CMN/WLTH. PAGE 4 H0077
CONSTN COLONIAL DOMIN NAT/G

B64
ARASARATNAM S.,CEYLON. CEYLON NETHERLAND PORTUGAL S/ASIA UK STRUCT ECO/UNDEV SECT DIPLOM DOMIN RACE/REL NAT/LISM 17/20 CMN/WLTH. PAGE 8 H0156
COLONIAL NAT/G PROB/SOLV CULTURE

B64
DE SMITH S.A.,THE NEW COMMONWEALTH AND ITS CONSTITUTIONS. AFR CYPRUS PAKISTAN S/ASIA INT/ORG NAT/G LEGIS LEGIT RIGID/FLEX PWR...CONCPT TIME/SEQ CMN/WLTH 20. PAGE 38 H0770
EX/STRUC CONSTN SOVEREIGN

B64
GREAT BRITAIN CENTRAL OFF INF,CONSTITUTIONAL DEVELOPMENT IN THE COMMONWEALTH. VOL/ASSN PLAN DIPLOM COLONIAL INGP/REL NAT/LISM ORD/FREE PWR 17/20 CMN/WLTH. PAGE 60 H1202
REGION CONSTN NAT/G SOVEREIGN

B64
NATIONAL BOOK LEAGUE,THE COMMONWEALTH IN BOOKS: AN ANNOTATED LIST. CANADA UK LOC/G SECT ADMIN...SOC BIOG 20 CMN/WLTH. PAGE 116 H2320
BIBLIOG/A JURID NAT/G

B64
WAINHOUSE D.W.,REMNANTS OF EMPIRE: THE UNITED NATIONS AND THE END OF COLONIALISM. FUT PORTUGAL WOR+45 NAT/G CONSULT DOMIN LEGIT ADMIN ROUTINE ATTIT ORD/FREE...POLICY JURID RECORD INT TIME/SEQ UN CMN/WLTH 20. PAGE 164 H3287
INT/ORG TREND COLONIAL

L64
SYMONDS R.,"REFLECTIONS IN LOCALISATION." AFR S/ASIA UK STRATA INT/ORG NAT/G SCHOOL EDU/PROP LEGIT KNOWL ORD/FREE PWR RESPECT CMN/WLTH 20. PAGE 151 H3023
ADMIN MGT COLONIAL

S64
GROSS J.A.,"WHITEHALL AND THE COMMONWEALTH." EUR+WWI MOD/EUR INT/ORG NAT/G CONSULT DELIB/GP LEGIS DOMIN ADMIN COLONIAL ROUTINE PWR CMN/WLTH 19/20. PAGE 62 H1233
EX/STRUC ATTIT TREND

B65
ADAM T.R.,GOVERNMENT AND POLITICS IN AFRICA SOUTH OF THE SAHARA. AFR EUR+WWI CONSTN CULTURE INTELL POL/PAR TOP/EX LEGIT REGION DRIVE...OBS TREND CMN/WLTH 20. PAGE 3 H0062
NAT/G TIME/SEQ RACE/REL COLONIAL

B65
CAMERON W.J.,NEW ZEALAND. NEW/ZEALND S/ASIA DIPLOM INT/TRADE WRITING COLONIAL PARL/PROC...GEOG CMN/WLTH. PAGE 26 H0513
SOCIETY GP/REL STRUCT

B65
GRIMAL H.,HISTOIRE DU COMMONWEALTH BRITANNIQUE. UK FINAN DOMIN ATTIT ORD/FREE...T 15/20 CMN/WLTH. PAGE 61 H1226
NAT/G COLONIAL DIPLOM INT/TRADE

B65
GWYN R.J.,THE SHAPE OF SCANDAL: A STUDY OF A GOVERNMENT IN CRISIS. CANADA LEGIS ADJUD CT/SYS SANCTION CMN/WLTH 20 PEARSON/L. PAGE 63 H1260
ELITES NAT/G CRIME

B65
HORNE A.J.,THE COMMONWEALTH TODAY. AFR ASIA CANADA UK STRUCT ECO/UNDEV NAT/G SECT GP/REL 20 AUSTRAL CMN/WLTH. PAGE 73 H1470
BIBLIOG/A SOCIETY CULTURE

MEHROTRA S.R.,INDIA AND THE COMMONWEALTH 1885-1929. INDIA UK INT/ORG VOL/ASSN GP/REL ATTIT...POLICY BIBLIOG 19/20 CMN/WLTH. PAGE 108 H2163 — B65 DIPLOM NAT/G POL/PAR NAT/LISM

SHRIMALI K.L.,EDUCATION IN CHANGING INDIA. INDIA CULTURE DIPLOM FOR/AID GP/REL RACE/REL ATTIT SOC/INTEG 20 UNESCO CMN/WLTH. PAGE 143 H2866 — B65 EDU/PROP PROF/ORG ACADEM

WILLIAMSON J.A.,GREAT BRITAIN AND THE COMMONWEALTH. UK DOMIN COLONIAL INGP/REL...POLICY 18/20 CMN/WLTH. PAGE 168 H3370 — B65 NAT/G DIPLOM INT/ORG SOVEREIGN

GANGAL S.C.,"SURVEY OF RECENT RESEARCH: INDIA AND THE COMMONWEALTH" INDIA UK NAT/G INT/TRADE PARTIC GOV/REL ROLE 20 CMN/WLTH. PAGE 55 H1095 — S65 BIBLIOG POLICY REGION DIPLOM

HAMILTON W.B.,A DECADE OF THE COMMONWEALTH, 1955-1964. UK LAW ELITES FINAN FOR/AID CONFER COLONIAL PWR...GEOG CHARTS ANTHOL 20 CMN/WLTH UN. PAGE 65 H1302 — B66 INT/ORG INGP/REL DIPLOM NAT/G

US DEPARTMENT OF STATE,RESEARCH ON WESTERN EUROPE, GREAT BRITAIN, AND CANADA (EXTERNAL RESEARCH LIST NO 3-25). CANADA GERMANY/W UK LAW CULTURE NAT/G POL/PAR FORCES EDU/PROP REGION MARXISM...GEOG SOC WORSHIP 20 CMN/WLTH. PAGE 160 H3192 — B66 BIBLIOG/A EUR+WWI DIPLOM

CANTOR N.F.,THE ENGLISH TRADITION* TWENTIETH-CENTURY VIEWS OF ENGLISH HISTORY (2VOLS.). UK STRATA NAT/G SECT WAR...POLICY GOV/COMP IDEA/COMP ANTHOL T PARLIAMENT CMN/WLTH. PAGE 26 H0522 — B67 CT/SYS LAW POL/PAR

MAZRUI A.A.,THE ANGLO-AFRICAN COMMONWEALTH; POLITICAL FRICTION AND CULTURAL FUSION. AFR INT/ORG VOL/ASSN CHIEF GP/REL INGP/REL RACE/REL NAT/LISM 20 CMN/WLTH EEC. PAGE 106 H2111 — B67 COLONIAL SOVEREIGN DIPLOM CULTURE

WISEMAN H.V.,BRITAIN AND THE COMMONWEALTH. EUR+WWI FUT UK ECO/DEV POL/PAR TEC/DEV INT/TRADE LEAD ROLE SOVEREIGN...SOC TREND 20 CMN/WLTH. PAGE 169 H3391 — B67 INT/ORG DIPLOM NAT/G NAT/COMP

MILLAR T.B.,"THE COMMONWEALTH AND THE UN." UK DIPLOM TARIFFS AGREE COLONIAL CONTROL SOVEREIGN WEALTH...GP/COMP GOV/COMP 20 CMN/WLTH UN. PAGE 111 H2210 — S68 INT/ORG POLICY TREND ECO/TAC

COALITIONS....SEE VOL/ASSN

COASTGUARD....COAST GUARD

COBB/HOWLL....HOWELL COBB

COBBAN A. H0610,H0611,H0612

COBLENTZ S.A. H0613

COEDES G. H0614

COERCE....COERCION, VIOLENCE; SEE ALSO FORCES, PROCESSES AND PRACTICES INDEX, PART G, P. XIII

BROCKWAY A.F.,AFRICAN SOCIALISM. EUR+WWI GHANA ISLAM UAR ECO/UNDEV CAP/ISM INT/TRADE COLONIAL COERCE GOV/REL DISCRIM 20 NEGRO NKRUMAH/K NASSER/G. PAGE 21 H0423 — N AFR SOCISM MARXISM

BENEDETTI V.,STUDIES IN DIPLOMACY. BELGIUM FRANCE GERMANY MOD/EUR CONSTN NAT/G CONSULT TOP/EX DOMIN EDU/PROP COERCE ATTIT...CONCPT INT BIOG TREND 19. PAGE 14 H0276 — B00 PWR GEN/LAWS DIPLOM

DE JOMINI A.H.,THE ART OF WAR. MOD/EUR NAT/G BAL/PWR DIPLOM DOMIN EXEC ROUTINE COERCE DRIVE PWR SKILL...POLICY CONCPT CHARTS STERTYP 19. PAGE 38 H0755 — B00 PLAN FORCES WAR WEAPON

BERHARDI F.,GERMANY AND THE NEXT WAR. MOD/EUR NAT/G SCHOOL FORCES ACT/RES DOMIN EDU/PROP SUPEGO PWR ...TIME/SEQ STERTYP TOT/POP 20 WWI. PAGE 15 H0304 — B14 DRIVE COERCE WAR GERMANY

DE VICTORIA F.,DE INDIS ET DE JURE BELLI (1557) IN F. DE VICTORIA, DE INDIS ET DE JURE BELLI REFLECTIONES. UNIV NAT/G SECT CHIEF PARTIC COERCE PEACE MORAL...POLICY 16 INDIAN/AM CHRISTIAN CONSCN/OBJ. PAGE 39 H0775 — B17 WAR INT/LAW OWN

BURKE E.,LETTER TO SIR HERCULES LANGRISHE (PAMPHLET). IRELAND UK NAT/G CHIEF DIPLOM DOMIN PARL/PROC COERCE ORD/FREE SOVEREIGN POPULISM ...TRADIT 18 BURKE/EDM. PAGE 24 H0485 — N17 POLICY COLONIAL SECT

CVIJIC J.,THE BALKAN PENINSULA. MOD/EUR COERCE ...SOC CHARTS GP/COMP NAT/COMP 20 BALKANS MAPS. PAGE 36 H0729 — B18 GEOG HABITAT GOV/COMP CULTURE

FREEMAN H.A.,COERCION OF STATES IN FEDERAL UNIONS (PAMPHLET). WOR-45 DIPLOM CONTROL COERCE PEACE ORD/FREE...GOV/COMP METH/COMP NAT/COMP PACIFIST 20. PAGE 53 H1055 — N19 FEDERAL WAR INT/ORG PACIFISM

MEZERIK A.G.,APARTHEID IN THE REPUBLIC OF SOUTH AFRICA (PAMPHLET). DIPLOM DOMIN CONTROL COERCE REPRESENT CONSEN ATTIT. PAGE 110 H2194 — N19 DISCRIM RACE/REL POL/PAR POLICY

HALDANE R.B.,BEFORE THE WAR. MOD/EUR SOCIETY INT/ORG NAT/G DELIB/GP PLAN DOMIN EDU/PROP LEGIT ADMIN COERCE ATTIT DRIVE MORAL ORD/FREE PWR...SOC CONCPT SELF/OBS RECORD BIOG TIME/SEQ. PAGE 64 H1282 — B20 POLICY DIPLOM UK

STUART G.H.,FRENCH FOREIGN POLICY. CONSTN INT/ORG NAT/G POL/PAR EX/STRUC FORCES PLAN ECO/TAC DOMIN EDU/PROP ADJUD COERCE ATTIT DRIVE RIGID/FLEX ALL/VALS...POLICY OBS RECORD BIOG TIME/SEQ TREND. PAGE 150 H3000 — B21 MOD/EUR DIPLOM FRANCE

EDWARDS L.P.,THE NATURAL HISTORY OF REVOLUTION. UNIV NAT/G VOL/ASSN COERCE DRIVE WEALTH...TREND GEN/LAWS. PAGE 45 H0893 — B27 PWR GUERRILLA REV

ENGELS F.,THE PEASANT WAR IN GERMANY (1850). GERMANY MOD/EUR AGRI WORKER LEAD COERCE INGP/REL ...TREND 16/19. PAGE 46 H0924 — B27 WAR STRATA REV MARXIST

FLOURNOY F.,PARLIAMENT AND WAR. MOD/EUR UK NAT/G FORCES LEGIS TOP/EX DIPLOM LEGIT DEBATE ATTIT RIGID/FLEX PWR...DECISION TIME/SEQ PARLIAMENT 19/20. PAGE 52 H1032 — B27 COERCE WAR

SMITH E.W.,THE GOLDEN STOOL: SOME ASPECTS OF THE CONFLICT OF CULTURES IN AFRICA. AFR FINAN INDUS SECT INT/TRADE COERCE CHOOSE RACE/REL ATTIT...GEOG LING 20 NEGRO. PAGE 145 H2907 — B27 COLONIAL CULTURE GP/REL EDU/PROP

DAVIE M.R.,THE EVOLUTION OF WAR. CULTURE KIN COERCE WAR ATTIT DRIVE...PSY SOC TIME/SEQ TREND GEN/LAWS. PAGE 37 H0746 — B29 FORCES STERTYP

BENTHAM J.,THE RATIONALE OF PUNISHMENT. UK LAW LOC/G NAT/G LEGIS CONTROL...JURID GEN/LAWS COURT/SYS 19. PAGE 14 H0289 — B30 CRIME SANCTION COERCE ORD/FREE

BEARD C.A.,"THE TEUTONIC ORIGINS OF REPRESENTATIVE GOVERNMENT" UK ROMAN/EMP TAX COERCE PWR IDEA/COMP. PAGE 12 H0247 — S32 REPRESENT NAT/G

DAHLIN E.,FRENCH AND GERMAN PUBLIC OPINION ON DECLARED WAR AIMS 1914-1918. BELGIUM FRANCE GERMANY NAT/G POL/PAR DIPLOM COERCE REV WAR PEACE 20 WWI WILSON/W. PAGE 37 H0733 — B33 ATTIT EDU/PROP DOMIN NAT/COMP

GONZALEZ PALENCIA A,ESTUDIO HISTORICO SOBRE LA CENSURA GUBERNATIVA EN ESPANA 1800-1833. NAT/G COERCE INGP/REL ATTIT AUTHORIT KNOWL...POLICY JURID 19. PAGE 58 H1165 — B34 LEGIT EDU/PROP PRESS CONTROL

LASKI H.J.,THE STATE IN THEORY AND PRACTICE. ELITES ECO/TAC REPRESENT ORD/FREE PWR WEALTH POPULISM ...GOV/COMP GEN/LAWS 19/20. PAGE 92 H1829 — B35 CAP/ISM COERCE NAT/G FASCISM

PARETO V.,THE MIND AND SOCIETY (4 VOLS.). ELITES SECT ECO/TAC COERCE PERSON ORD/FREE PWR SOVEREIGN FASCISM POPULISM...TRADIT 19/20. PAGE 123 H2465 — B35 GEN/LAWS SOC PSY

CARLYLE T.,THE FRENCH REVOLUTION (2 VOLS.). FRANCE CONSTN NAT/G FORCES COERCE MURDER PEACE MORAL POPULISM...TIME/SEQ IDEA/COMP GEN/LAWS 18. PAGE 26 H0532 — B37 REV CHIEF TRADIT

MUNZENBERG W.,PROPAGANDA ALS WAFFE. COM/IND PRESS COERCE WAR...PSY 20. PAGE 115 H2290 — B37 EDU/PROP DOMIN NAT/G LEAD

HITLER A.,MEIN KAMPF. EUR+WWI FUT MOD/EUR STRUCT INT/ORG LABOR NAT/G POL/PAR FORCES CREATE PLAN BAL/PWR DIPLOM ECO/TAC DOMIN EDU/PROP ADMIN COERCE ATTIT...SOCIALIST BIOG TREND NAZI. PAGE 71 H1428 — B39 PWR NEW/IDEA WAR

S39
COLE G.D.H.,"NAZI ECONOMICS: HOW DO THEY MANAGE IT?" GERMANY FORCES WORKER BUDGET INT/TRADE ROUTINE COERCE WAR 20 HITLER/A NAZI. PAGE 31 H0622
FASCISM ECO/TAC ATTIT PLAN

B40
HUNTER R.,REVOLUTION: WHY, HOW, WHEN? NAT/G ECO/TAC EDU/PROP COERCE ORD/FREE FASCISM POPULISM SOCISM 18/20 HITLER/A LENIN/VI. PAGE 75 H1502
REV METH/COMP LEAD CONSTN

B40
TONNIES F.,FUNDAMENTAL CONCEPTS OF SOCIOLOGY (1887) (TRANS. BY C. LOOMIS). LAW STRATA STRUCT FAM MUNIC NAT/G DOMIN LEGIT SANCTION COERCE CRIME PERSON 19. PAGE 156 H3115
CULTURE SOCIETY GEN/LAWS SOC

S41
ABEL T.,"THE ELEMENT OF DECISION IN THE PATTERN OF WAR." EUR+WWI FUT NAT/G TOP/EX DIPLOM ROUTINE COERCE DISPL PERCEPT PWR...SOC METH/CNCPT HIST/WRIT TREND GEN/LAWS 20. PAGE 3 H0055
TEC/DEV FORCES WAR

B42
FORTESCU J.,IN PRAISE OF ENGLISH LAW (1464) (TRANS. BY S.B. CHRIMES). UK ELITES CHIEF FORCES CT/SYS COERCE CRIME GOV/REL ILLEGIT...JURID GOV/COMP GEN/LAWS 15. PAGE 52 H1040
LAW CONSTN LEGIS ORD/FREE

B42
NEUMANN S.,PERMANENT REVOLUTION: THE TOTAL STATE IN A WORLD AT WAR. COM EUR+WWI GERMANY USSR EX/STRUC DIPLOM CONTROL COERCE REPRESENT MARXISM...SOC GOV/COMP BIBLIOG 20 HITLER/A STALIN/J. PAGE 117 H2337
FASCISM TOTALISM DOMIN EDU/PROP

B43
EARLE E.M.,MAKERS OF MODERN STRATEGY: MILITARY THOUGHT FROM MACHIAVELLI TO HITLER. EUR+WWI MOD/EUR NAT/G ACT/RES BAL/PWR DOMIN COERCE ATTIT DRIVE RIGID/FLEX ALL/VALS...METH/CNCPT BIOG 16/20. PAGE 44 H0879
PLAN FORCES WAR

B43
SERENI A.P.,THE ITALIAN CONCEPTION OF INTERNATIONAL LAW. EUR+WWI MOD/EUR INT/ORG NAT/G DOMIN COERCE ORD/FREE FASCISM...OBS/ENVIR TREND 20. PAGE 141 H2829
LAW TIME/SEQ INT/LAW ITALY

L44
HUXLEY J.,"THE FUTURE OF THE COLONIES." AFR SOCIETY NAT/G PLAN DOMIN COERCE ATTIT DRIVE ORD/FREE PWR WEALTH...TIME/SEQ TREND AUD/VIS CHARTS 20. PAGE 76 H1511
ECO/UNDEV FUT COLONIAL

B45
CLAGETT H.L.,COMMUNIST CHINA: RUTHLESS ENEMY OR PAPER TIGER (PAMPHLET). CHINA/COM ECO/UNDEV AGRI INDUS NAT/G POL/PAR ECO/TAC INT/TRADE GUERRILLA ATTIT...CHARTS NAT/COMP ORG/CHARTS 20. PAGE 30 H0602
BIBLIOG/A MARXISM DIPLOM COERCE

B45
CONOVER H.F.,ITALY: ECONOMICS, POLITICS AND MILITARY AFFAIRS, 1940-1945. ITALY ELITES NAT/G POL/PAR EX/STRUC TOP/EX DIPLOM DOMIN CONTROL COERCE WAR CIVMIL/REL EFFICIENCY 20. PAGE 32 H0646
BIBLIOG TOTALISM FORCES

B46
NICOLSON H.,THE CONGRESS OF VIENNA. MOD/EUR NAT/G FORCES BAL/PWR DOMIN LEGIT COERCE PERSON PWR ...RECORD TIME/SEQ STERTYP 19 CONG/VIENN. PAGE 118 H2353
CONCPT POLICY DIPLOM

B48
ROSSITER C.L.,CONSTITUTIONAL DICTATORSHIP; CRISIS GOVERNMENT IN THE MODERN DEMOCRACIES. FRANCE GERMANY UK USA-45 WOR-45 EX/STRUC BAL/PWR CONTROL COERCE WAR CENTRAL ORD/FREE...DECISION 19/20. PAGE 134 H2688
NAT/G AUTHORIT CONSTN TOTALISM

B48
TOWSTER J.,POLITICAL POWER IN THE USSR: 1917-1947. USSR CONSTN CULTURE ELITES CREATE PLAN COERCE CENTRAL ATTIT RIGID/FLEX ORD/FREE...BIBLIOG SOC/INTEG 20 LENIN/VI STALIN/J. PAGE 156 H3122
EX/STRUC NAT/G MARXISM PWR

S48
ALEXANDER L.,"WAR CRIMES, THEIR SOCIAL-PSYCHOLOGICAL ASPECTS." EUR+WWI GERMANY LAW CULTURE ELITES KIN POL/PAR PUB/INST FORCES DOMIN EDU/PROP COERCE CRIME ATTIT SUPEGO HEALTH MORAL PWR FASCISM ...PSY OBS TREND GEN/LAWS NAZI 20. PAGE 5 H0100
DRIVE WAR

B49
GRODZINS M.,AMERICANS BETRAYED: POLITICS AND THE JAPANESE EXPANSION. PROVS COERCE CHOOSE GOV/REL GP/REL INGP/REL ATTIT ORD/FREE...DECISION CHARTS 20 NISEI. PAGE 61 H1230
DISCRIM POLICY NAT/G WAR

B49
ROGERS C.B.,THE SPIRIT OF REVOLUTION IN 1789: A STUDY OF PUBLIC OPINION ...AT THE BEGINNING OF THE FRENCH REVOLUTION. FRANCE CULTURE ELITES EDU/PROP COERCE CROWD...BIBLIOG 18 MUSIC. PAGE 133 H2658
ATTIT POPULISM REV CREATE

B50
BERMAN H.J.,JUSTICE IN RUSSIA; AN INTERPRETATION OF SOVIET LAW. USSR LAW STRUCT LABOR FORCES AGREE GP/REL ORD/FREE SOCISM...TIME/SEQ 20. PAGE 15 H0309
JURID ADJUD MARXISM COERCE

B50
CARR E.H.,STUDIES IN REVOLUTION. CREATE WAR PERSON ALL/IDEOS MARXISM SOCISM...PHIL/SCI METH/COMP ANTHOL 18/20 SAINTSIMON MARX/KARL PROUDHON/P LASSALLE/F PLEKHNV/GV. PAGE 27 H0537
REV IDEA/COMP COERCE BIOG

B50
GATZKE H.W.,GERMANY'S DRIVE TO THE WEST. BELGIUM GERMANY MOD/EUR AGRI INDUS POL/PAR FORCES DOMIN AGREE CONTROL REGION COERCE 20 TREATY WWI. PAGE 55 H1104
WAR POLICY NAT/G DIPLOM

B50
IRION F.C.,PUBLIC OPINION AND PROPAGANDA. STRUCT COM/IND FAM SECT COERCE 20 FILM. PAGE 78 H1568
EDU/PROP ATTIT NAT/G PRESS

B50
MACHIAVELLI N.,THE DISCOURSES (1516). NAT/G SECT FORCES DOMIN LEGIT CONTROL LEAD COERCE TOTALISM ORD/FREE. PAGE 100 H1995
PWR GEN/LAWS CHIEF

B50
TRAGER F.N.,MARXISM IN SOUTHEAST ASIA. BURMA INDONESIA THAILAND VIETNAM CULTURE SOCIETY NAT/G VOL/ASSN EXEC ROUTINE COERCE ATTIT RIGID/FLEX PWR ...METH/CNCPT TIME/SEQ STERTYP GEN/LAWS MARX/KARL VAL/FREE COLD/WAR NAM 20. PAGE 156 H3126
S/ASIA POL/PAR REV

S51
NORTHROP F.S.C.,"ASIAN MENTALITY AND UNITED STATES FOREIGN POLICY." ASIA ISLAM USA+45 CULTURE SOCIETY SECT EDU/PROP LEGIT COERCE DRIVE MORAL ORD/FREE ...POLICY RELATIV TOT/POP 20. PAGE 119 H2376
S/ASIA ATTIT DIPLOM

B52
JULIEN C.A.,L'AFRIQUE DU NORD EN MARCHE: NATIONALISMES MUSULMANS ET SOUVERAINETE FRANCAISE (2ND ED). AFR ALGERIA FRANCE ISLAM MOROCCO NAT/G CONTROL ORD/FREE...POLICY 19/20 TUNIS MUSLIM. PAGE 82 H1641
NAT/LISM COERCE DOMIN COLONIAL

B52
KOLARZ W.,RUSSIA AND HER COLONIES. COM RUSSIA LAW CULTURE ECO/DEV KIN LOC/G SECT TEC/DEV ECO/TAC EDU/PROP REGION COERCE ATTIT PWR SOVEREIGN...SOC TIME/SEQ CON/ANAL VAL/FREE 19/20. PAGE 88 H1749
NAT/G DOMIN USSR COLONIAL

B52
LEYS W.,ETHICS FOR POLICY DECISIONS. INTELL NAT/G CONSULT PLAN DOMIN EDU/PROP LEGIT COERCE KNOWL MORAL PWR...HUM GEN/LAWS. PAGE 96 H1920
ACT/RES POLICY

B53
HUNTER E.,BRAIN-WASHING IN RED CHINA. ASIA CHINA/COM CULTURE SOCIETY FORCES WAR TOTALISM ATTIT BIO/SOC DISPL DRIVE PERSON SUPEGO KNOWL ORD/FREE ...INT REC/INT COLD/WAR 20. PAGE 75 H1499
EDU/PROP COERCE

B53
MARITAIN J.,L'HOMME ET L'ETAT. SECT DIPLOM GP/REL PEACE ORD/FREE...IDEA/COMP 17/20 CHURCH/STA NATURL/LAW. PAGE 103 H2052
CONCPT NAT/G SOVEREIGN COERCE

B53
MEYER P.,THE JEWS IN THE SOVIET SATELLITES. CZECHOSLVK POLAND SOCIETY STRATA NAT/G BAL/PWR ECO/TAC EDU/PROP LEGIT ADMIN COERCE ATTIT DISPL PERCEPT HEALTH PWR RESPECT WEALTH...METH/CNCPT JEWS VAL/FREE NAZI 20. PAGE 110 H2192
COM SECT TOTALISM USSR

B54
FRIEDRICH C.J.,TOTALITARIAN DICTATORSHIP AND AUTOCRACY. COM EUR+WWI GERMANY ITALY USSR INTELL ECO/DEV NAT/G POL/PAR FORCES TOP/EX ECO/TAC EDU/PROP LEGIT COERCE ATTIT ORD/FREE PWR FASCISM ...CONCPT TIME/SEQ GEN/LAWS NAZI 20. PAGE 53 H1068
SOCIETY DOMIN TOTALISM

B54
MITCHELL P.,AFRICAN AFTERTHOUGHTS. UGANDA CONSTN NAT/G ADJUD COERCE WAR 20 WWI MAU/MAU. PAGE 112 H2230
BIOG CHIEF COLONIAL DOMIN

L54
FRIEDRICH C.J.,"TOTALITARIANISM." COM EUR+WWI NAT/G POL/PAR SECT FORCES PLAN ECO/TAC DOMIN EDU/PROP EXEC COERCE REV ORD/FREE PWR...SOC CONCPT NAZI 20. PAGE 53 H1067
ATTIT TOTALISM

B55
ALFIERI D.,DICTATORS FACE TO FACE. NAT/G TOP/EX DIPLOM EXEC COERCE ORD/FREE FASCISM...POLICY OBS 20 HITLER/A MUSSOLIN/B. PAGE 5 H0103
WAR CHIEF TOTALISM PERS/REL

B55
INTERNATIONAL COMN JURISTS,JUSTICE ENSLAVED. COM CONSTN LABOR NAT/G CONTROL CHOOSE 20. PAGE 78 H1555
SOCISM TOTALISM ORD/FREE COERCE

B55
KHADDURI M.,WAR AND PEACE IN THE LAW OF ISLAM. CONSTN CULTURE SOCIETY STRATA NAT/G PROVS SECT FORCES TOP/EX CREATE DOMIN EDU/PROP ADJUD COERCE ATTIT RIGID/FLEX ALL/VALS...CONCPT TIME/SEQ TOT/POP VAL/FREE. PAGE 85 H1702
ISLAM JURID PEACE WAR

B55
KOHN H.,THE MIND OF MODERN RUSSIA. COM MOD/EUR USSR SOCIETY NAT/G SECT FORCES TOP/EX COERCE TOTALISM
INTELL GEN/LAWS

DRIVE RIGID/FLEX PWR SOVEREIGN...CONCPT TIME/SEQ WORK. PAGE 87 H1742
SOCISM RUSSIA

B55
LIPSCOMB J.F.,WHITE AFRICANS. SOCIETY STRUCT AGRI ECO/TAC ADJUD COLONIAL COERCE PERS/REL ADJUST. PAGE 97 H1937
RACE/REL HABITAT ECO/UNDEV ORD/FREE

B55
VIGON J.,TEORIA DEL MILITARISMO. NAT/G DIPLOM COLONIAL COERCE GUERRILLA CIVMIL/REL NAT/LISM MORAL ALL/IDEOS PACIFISM 18/20. PAGE 163 H3253
FORCES PHIL/SCI WAR POLICY

S55
BENN S.I.,"THE USES OF 'SOVEREIGNTY'." UNIV NAT/G LEGIS DIPLOM COERCE...METH/CNCPT GEN/LAWS. PAGE 14 H0282
SOVEREIGN IDEA/COMP CONCPT PWR

S55
GLADSTONE A.E.,"THE POSSIBILITY OF PREDICTING REACTIONS TO INTERNATIONAL EVENTS." UNIV SOCIETY NAT/G FORCES CREATE EDU/PROP COERCE WAR ATTIT PERSON KNOWL PWR SKILL...METH/CNCPT NEW/IDEA ORG/CHARTS. PAGE 57 H1139
PHIL/SCI CONCPT

B56
SMEDLEY A.,THE GREAT ROAD: THE LIFE AND TIMES OF CHU TEH. ASIA USSR NAT/G POL/PAR DIPLOM COERCE GUERRILLA CIVMIL/REL NAT/LISM PERSON SKILL MARXISM ...BIOG 20 CHINJAP MAO. PAGE 145 H2903
REV WAR FORCES

B56
SPINKA M.,THE CHURCH IN SOVIET RUSSIA. USSR CONTROL LEAD TASK COERCE 20. PAGE 147 H2949
GP/REL NAT/G SECT PWR

B56
WHITAKER A.P.,ARGENTINE UPHEAVAL. STRUCT FORCES DIPLOM COERCE PWR 20 ARGEN. PAGE 167 H3343
REV POL/PAR STRATA NAT/G

B56
WOLFF R.L.,THE BALKANS IN OUR TIME. ALBANIA FUT MOD/EUR USSR YUGOSLAVIA CULTURE INT/ORG SECT DIPLOM EDU/PROP COERCE WAR ORD/FREE...CHARTS 4/20 BALKANS COMINFORM. PAGE 170 H3403
GEOG COM

B57
BUCK P.W.,CONTOL OF FOREIGN RELATIONS IN MODERN NATIONS. FRANCE L/A+17C NETHERLAND USSR WOR+45 INT/ORG TOP/EX BAL/PWR DOMIN EDU/PROP COERCE PEACE ATTIT...CONCPT TREND 20 CMN/WLTH. PAGE 23 H0465
NAT/G PWR DIPLOM

B57
BUNDESMIN FUR VERTRIEBENE,DIE VERTREIBUNG DER DEUTSCHEN BEVOLKERUNG AUS DER TSCHECHOSLOWAKEI. CZECHOSLVK GERMANY NAT/G FORCES MURDER WAR INGP/REL ATTIT 20 MIGRATION. PAGE 24 H0474
GP/REL DOMIN COERCE DISCRIM

B57
HALLGARTEN G.W.,DAMONEN ODER RETTER. ASIA L/A+17C CAP/ISM ATTIT MARXISM SOCISM...NAT/COMP. PAGE 64 H1289
TOTALISM FASCISM COERCE DOMIN

B57
KENNEDY M.D.,A SHORT HISTORY OF COMMUNISM IN ASIA. ASIA BURMA INDIA S/ASIA THAILAND NAT/G POL/PAR LEAD REV WAR MARXISM SOCISM...POLICY 20 CHINJAP. PAGE 85 H1688
DIPLOM NAT/LISM TOTALISM COERCE

B57
LAQUER W.Z.,COMMUNISM AND NATIONALISM IN THE MIDDLE EAST. ELITES INTELL STRATA NAT/G POL/PAR SECT VOL/ASSN TOP/EX DOMIN LEGIT REGION COERCE ATTIT PERSON PWR...CONCPT HIST/WRIT TIME/SEQ TREND GEN/LAWS VAL/FREE. PAGE 91 H1817
ISLAM NAT/LISM

B58
CRAIG G.A.,FROM BISMARCK TO ADENAUER: ASPECTS OF GERMAN STATECRAFT. GERMANY INTELL FORCES ECO/TAC CONFER COERCE WAR GP/REL ORD/FREE PWR CONSERVE 19/20 BISMARCK/O ADENAUER/K. PAGE 35 H0695
DIPLOM LEAD NAT/G

B58
DUCLOUX L.,FROM BLACKMAIL TO TREASON. FRANCE PLAN DIPLOM EDU/PROP PRESS RUMOR NAT/LISM...CRIMLGY 20. PAGE 43 H0853
COERCE CRIME NAT/G PWR

B58
HSU U.T.,THE INVISIBLE CONFLICT. ASIA USSR ELITES NAT/G CONTROL LEAD COERCE REV WAR NAT/LISM ORD/FREE PWR 20 COM/PARTY ESPIONAGE. PAGE 74 H1485
MARXISM POL/PAR EDU/PROP FORCES

B58
PAYNO M.,LA REFORMA SOCIAL EN ESPANA Y MEXICO. SPAIN ECO/TAC TAX LOBBY COERCE REV OWN CATHISM 19/20 MEXIC/AMER. PAGE 124 H2479
SECT NAT/G LAW ELITES

S58
STAAR R.F.,"ELECTIONS IN COMMUNIST POLAND." EUR+WWI SOCIETY INT/ORG NAT/G POL/PAR LEGIS ACT/RES ECO/TAC EDU/PROP ADJUD ADMIN ROUTINE COERCE TOTALISM ATTIT ORD/FREE PWR 20. PAGE 148 H2963
COM CHOOSE POLAND

B59
BRIGGS A.,CHARTIST STUDIES. UK LAW NAT/G WORKER EDU/PROP COERCE SUFF GP/REL ATTIT...ANTHOL 19. PAGE 21 H0416
INDUS STRATA LABOR POLICY

B59
CARPENTER G.W.,THE WAY IN AFRICA. AFR INDUS MUNIC DIPLOM DOMIN EDU/PROP COERCE DISCRIM NAT/LISM ORD/FREE 20 NEGRO CHRISTIAN. PAGE 27 H0535
CULTURE SECT ECO/UNDEV COLONIAL

B59
DAHRENDORF R.,CLASS AND CLASS CONFLICT IN INDUSTRIAL SOCIETY. LABOR NAT/G COERCE ROLE PLURISM ...POLICY MGT CONCPT CLASSIF. PAGE 37 H0734
VOL/ASSN STRUCT SOC GP/REL

B59
GOPAL R.,INDIAN MUSLIMS: A POLITICAL HISTORY (1858-1947). INDIA ISLAM PAKISTAN NAT/G SECT LEGIS LEAD COERCE WAR REPRESENT ISOLAT ORD/FREE 19/20 HINDU MUSLIM. PAGE 59 H1175
COLONIAL GP/REL POL/PAR REGION

B59
HENDEL S.,THE SOVIET CRUCIBLE. USSR LEAD COERCE NAT/LISM UTOPIA PWR...POLICY CONCPT ANTHOL 20 STALIN/J LENIN/VI MARX/KARL BOLSHEVIK. PAGE 70 H1393
COM MARXISM REV TOTALISM

B59
MATHER F.C.,PUBLIC ORDER IN THE AGE OF THE CHARTISTS. UK CULTURE ADJUD CONTROL. PAGE 105 H2090
ORD/FREE FORCES COERCE CIVMIL/REL

B59
PAGE S.W.,LENIN AND WORLD REVOLUTION. COM USSR NAT/G DOMIN COERCE CROWD UTOPIA ATTIT AUTHORIT DRIVE PWR...CONCPT MYTH 19/20 LENIN/VI MARX/KARL. PAGE 122 H2441
REV PERSON MARXISM BIOG

S59
LEVINE R.A.,"ANTI-EUROPEAN VIOLENCE IN AFRICA: A COMPARATIVE ANALYSIS." AFR CULTURE NAT/G DIPLOM EDU/PROP COLONIAL REGION COERCE ATTIT PWR...PSY CONCPT TIME/SEQ TREND HYPO/EXP SOC/EXP STERTYP GEN/METH COLD/WAR 20. PAGE 95 H1903
DRIVE ORD/FREE REV

S59
SKILLING H.G.,"COMMUNISM: NATIONAL OR INTERNATIONAL." CHINA/COM USSR YUGOSLAVIA NAT/G POL/PAR VOL/ASSN DOMIN REGION COERCE ATTIT PWR MARXISM SOCISM...CONCPT TOT/POP 20 TITO/MARSH. PAGE 145 H2894
COM TREND

B60
BLACK C.E.,THE TRANSFORMATION OF RUSSIAN SOCIETY. COM MOD/EUR RUSSIA SOCIETY EDU/PROP COERCE ALL/VALS 19/20. PAGE 17 H0349
CULTURE RIGID/FLEX USSR

B60
BURRIDGE K.,MAMBU: A MELANESIAN MILLENNIUM. ECO/UNDEV PROC/MFG FAM KIN CHIEF COLONIAL COERCE GP/REL DRIVE WEALTH WORSHIP 20 NEW/GUINEA. PAGE 25 H0494
S/ASIA SECT CULTURE MYTH

B60
FURNIA A.H.,THE DIPLOMACY OF APPEASEMENT: ANGLO-FRENCH RELATIONS AND THE PRELUDE TO WORLD WAR II 1931-1938. FRANCE GERMANY UK ELITES NAT/G DELIB/GP FORCES WAR PEACE RIGID/FLEX 20. PAGE 54 H1077
DIPLOM BAL/PWR COERCE

B60
GOODMAN E.,SOVIET DESIGN FOR A WORLD STATE. COM USSR NAT/G TOP/EX DIPLOM ECO/TAC DOMIN EDU/PROP COERCE REV ATTIT ORD/FREE...CON/ANAL 20. PAGE 59 H1171
PLAN PWR SOCISM TOTALISM

B60
GRAMPP W.D.,THE MANCHESTER SCHOOL OF ECONOMICS. UK LAW ECO/DEV COERCE ATTIT ORD/FREE LAISSEZ ...PHIL/SCI IDEA/COMP 19/20 MANCHESTER CORN/LAWS. PAGE 60 H1194
ECO/TAC VOL/ASSN LOBBY NAT/G

B60
HAYEK F.A.,THE CONSTITUTION OF LIBERTY. UNIV LAW CONSTN WORKER TAX EDU/PROP ADMIN CT/SYS COERCE DISCRIM...IDEA/COMP 20. PAGE 68 H1369
ORD/FREE CHOOSE NAT/G CONCPT

B60
MATTHIAS E.,DAS ENDE DER PARTEIEN 1933. GERMANY NAT/G COERCE CHOOSE ORD/FREE PWR 20. PAGE 105 H2100
FASCISM POL/PAR DOMIN ATTIT

B60
MCCLOSKY H.,THE SOVIET DICTATORSHIP. FUT CONSTN CULTURE INTELL SOCIETY POL/PAR SECT VOL/ASSN FORCES PLAN TEC/DEV DOMIN EDU/PROP COERCE PWR MARXISM ...POLICY CONCPT MYTH STERTYP 20. PAGE 106 H2127
COM NAT/G TOTALISM USSR

B60
MOCTEZUMA A.P.,EL CONFLICTO RELIGIOSO DE 1926 (2ND ED.). L/A+17C LAW NAT/G LOBBY COERCE GP/REL ATTIT ...POLICY 20 MEXIC/AMER CHURCH/STA. PAGE 112 H2233
SECT ORD/FREE DISCRIM REV

B60
MORAES F.,THE REVOLT IN TIBET. ASIA CHINA/COM INDIA CULTURE CONTROL COERCE WAR TOTALISM...POLICY SOC WORSHIP 20 TIBET INTERVENT. PAGE 113 H2252
COLONIAL FORCES DIPLOM ORD/FREE

B60
SCHAPIRO L.,THE COMMUNIST PARTY OF THE SOVIET
INTELL

UNION. COM LAW SOCIETY STRATA STRUCT ECO/DEV LABOR PWR
NAT/G POL/PAR CREATE DOMIN EDU/PROP COERCE TOTALISM USSR
MARXISM...POLICY CONCPT MYTH TIME/SEQ WORK TOT/POP
20 LENIN/VI STALIN/J. PAGE 139 H2772

B60
SHIRER W.L.,THE RISE AND FALL OF THE THIRD REICH: A STRUCT
HISTORY OF NAZI GERMANY. EUR+WWI CULTURE ECO/DEV GERMANY
INDUS NAT/G POL/PAR FORCES PLAN TEC/DEV ECO/TAC TOTALISM
COERCE ATTIT DRIVE PERSON PWR...MYSTIC PSY SOC MYTH
STAT CHARTS EXHIBIT WORK VAL/FREE. PAGE 143 H2864

B60
SOUTH AFRICAN CONGRESS OF DEM,FACE THE FUTURE. RACE/REL
SOUTH/AFR ELITES LEGIS ADMIN REGION COERCE PEACE DISCRIM
ATTIT 20. PAGE 147 H2938 CONSTN
NAT/G

B60
VON KOENIGSWALD H.,SIE SUCHEN ZUFLUCHT. GERMANY/E GP/REL
NAT/G PLAN ECO/TAC SOCISM...GEOG CENSUS 20 BERLIN. COERCE
PAGE 164 H3273 DOMIN
PERSON

L60
KAPLAN M.A.,"COMMUNIST COUP IN CZECHOSLOVAKIA." COM STRUCT
EUR+WWI INTELL LABOR LOC/G NAT/G POL/PAR FORCES COERCE
EDU/PROP EXEC MARXISM...TIME/SEQ HYPO/EXP 20. CZECHOSLVK
PAGE 83 H1659

S60
BRZEZINSKI Z.K.,"PATTERNS AND LIMITS OF THE SINO- POL/PAR
SOVIET DISPUTE." ASIA CHINA/COM COM FUT STRATA PWR
NAT/G EX/STRUC FORCES BAL/PWR DIPLOM ECO/TAC DOMIN REV
EDU/PROP ADMIN COERCE WAR ATTIT RIGID/FLEX USSR
...GEN/LAWS VAL/FREE 20. PAGE 23 H0459

S60
CASSINELLI C.,"TOTALITARIANISM, IDEOLOGY AND ATTIT
PROPAGANDA." EUR+WWI CULTURE SOCIETY NAT/G DOMIN EDU/PROP
COERCE ORD/FREE FASCISM MARXISM...MARXIST CONCPT TOTALISM
STERTYP GEN/LAWS TOT/POP 20. PAGE 28 H0554

S60
CROZIER B.,"FRANCE AND ALGERIA." ALGERIA EUR+WWI NAT/G
FRANCE FUT ISLAM ECO/UNDEV NEIGH CONSULT DELIB/GP FORCES
ECO/TAC COLONIAL COERCE ATTIT...SOC INT CON/ANAL GUERRILLA
20. PAGE 36 H0713 NAT/LISM

S60
GINSBURGS G.,"PEKING-LHASA-NEW DELHI." CHINA/COM ASIA
FUT INDIA S/ASIA KIN NAT/G PROVS SECT FORCES COERCE
BAL/PWR ECO/TAC DOMIN EDU/PROP LEGIT ADMIN REGION DIPLOM
GUERRILLA PWR...TREND TIBET 20. PAGE 57 H1134

S60
NORTH R.C.,"THE NEW EXPANSIONISM." ASIA CHINA/COM ATTIT
FUT INDIA CULTURE SOCIETY NAT/G TOP/EX DOMIN COERCE DRIVE
PWR MARXISM...CONCPT TIME/SEQ TREND GEN/LAWS NAT/LISM
COLD/WAR 20 MAO. PAGE 119 H2372

S60
NORTH R.C.,"DIE DISKREPANZ ZWISCHEN REALITAT UND SOCIETY
WUNSCHBILD ALS INNENPOLITISCHER FAKTOR." ASIA ECO/TAC
CHINA/COM COM FUT ECO/UNDEV NAT/G PLAN DOMIN ADMIN
COERCE PERCEPT...SOC MYTH GEN/METH WORK TOT/POP 20.
PAGE 119 H2373

S60
PERLMANN H.,"UPHEAVAL IN TURKEY." EUR+WWI ISLAM CONSTN
NAT/G FORCES TOP/EX LEGIT COERCE CHOOSE DRIVE TURKEY
ORD/FREE PWR...TIME/SEQ TOT/POP 20. PAGE 125 H2494

S60
WOLFE T.W.,"KHRUSHCHEV'S DISARMAMENT STRATEGY." COM PWR
NAT/G TOP/EX PLAN BAL/PWR DIPLOM ARMS/CONT COERCE GEN/LAWS
ATTIT...POLICY CONCPT RECORD TREND CON/ANAL USSR
COLD/WAR 20 KHRUSH/N. PAGE 170 H3401

S60
WYCKOFF T.,"THE ROLE OF THE MILITARY IN LATIN NAT/G
AMERICAN POLITICS." L/A+17C CONSTN CULTURE COERCE
ECO/UNDEV POL/PAR FORCES LEGIS TOP/EX LEGIT TOTALISM
GUERRILLA REV CHOOSE ORD/FREE PWR...TIME/SEQ
VAL/FREE 20. PAGE 171 H3430

B61
BERKOWITZ L.,AGGRESSION: AS A SOCIAL PSYCHOLOGICAL SOCIETY
ANALYSIS. UNIV CULTURE FACE/GP FAM KIN NEIGH COERCE
EDU/PROP DISPL DRIVE HEALTH LOVE ORD/FREE...PSY SOC WAR
CONCPT OBS TREND. PAGE 15 H0305

B61
BISHOP D.G.,THE ADMINISTRATION OF BRITISH FOREIGN ROUTINE
RELATIONS. EUR+WWI MOD/EUR INT/ORG NAT/G POL/PAR PWR
DELIB/GP LEGIS TOP/EX ECO/TAC DOMIN EDU/PROP ADMIN DIPLOM
COERCE 20. PAGE 17 H0344 UK

B61
BULLOCK A.,HITLER: A STUDY IN TYRANNY. EUR+WWI ATTIT
GERMANY SOCIETY STRUCT NAT/G POL/PAR FORCES CREATE BIOG
DOMIN EDU/PROP EXEC COERCE WAR NAT/LISM DISPL DRIVE TOTALISM
PERSON PWR...PSY NAZI 20 HITLER/A. PAGE 23 H0470

B61
DALLIN D.J.,SOVIET FOREIGN POLICY AFTER STALIN. COM
ASIA CHINA/COM EUR+WWI GERMANY IRAN UK YUGOSLAVIA DIPLOM
INT/ORG NAT/G VOL/ASSN FORCES TOP/EX BAL/PWR DOMIN USSR
EDU/PROP COERCE ATTIT PWR 20. PAGE 37 H0737

B61
GUEVARA E.,GUERRILLA WARFARE. L/A+17C ECO/UNDEV FORCES
NAT/G POL/PAR VOL/ASSN PLAN DOMIN REV DRIVE PWR COERCE
WEALTH...NEW/IDEA RECORD BIOG COLD/WAR MARX/KARL GUERRILLA
OAS 20. PAGE 62 H1247 CUBA

B61
JUSTICE,THE CITIZEN AND THE ADMINISTRATION: THE INGP/REL
REDRESS OF GRIEVANCES (PAMPHLET). EUR+WWI UK LAW CONSULT
CONSTN STRATA NAT/G CT/SYS PARTIC COERCE...NEW/IDEA ADJUD
IDEA/COMP 20 OMBUDSMAN. PAGE 82 H1644 REPRESENT

B61
MERRIAM A.,CONGO: BACKGROUND OF CONFLICT. AFR FUT CHOOSE
KIN MUNIC NAT/G POL/PAR PROVS DELIB/GP PLAN DOMIN GUERRILLA
COERCE ATTIT...TIME/SEQ CHARTS CONGO 20. PAGE 109
H2182

B61
MONAS S.,THE THIRD SECTION: POLICE AND SOCIETY IN ORD/FREE
RUSSIA UNDER NICHOLAS I. MOD/EUR RUSSIA ELITES COM
STRUCT NAT/G EX/STRUC ADMIN CONTROL PWR CONSERVE FORCES
...DECISION 19 NICHOLAS/I. PAGE 112 H2238 COERCE

B61
SAFRAN M.,EGYPT IN SEARCH OF POLITICAL COMMUNITY: INTELL
AN ANALYSIS OF THE INTELLECTUAL AND POLITICAL NAT/LISM
EVOLUTION OF EGYPT, 1804-1952. ISLAM NAT/G SECT UAR
EDU/PROP COERCE ATTIT DRIVE KNOWL PWR...TIME/SEQ
20. PAGE 137 H2729

B61
SETON-WATSON H.,FROM LENIN TO KHRUSHCHEV: THE PWR
HISTORY OF WORLD COMMUNISM. ASIA COM EUR+WWI ISLAM REV
S/ASIA ECO/DEV ECO/UNDEV NAT/G POL/PAR DIPLOM USSR
ECO/TAC EDU/PROP COERCE GUERRILLA ATTIT DRIVE WORK
TOT/POP NAZI 20. PAGE 141 H2832

S61
BRZEZINSKI Z.K.,"THE ORGANIZATION OF THE COMMUNIST VOL/ASSN
CAMP." COM CZECHOSLVK COM/IND NAT/G DELIB/GP DIPLOM
INT/TRADE DOMIN EDU/PROP EXEC ROUTINE COERCE ATTIT USSR
PWR...MGT CONCPT TIME/SEQ CHARTS VAL/FREE 20
TREATY. PAGE 23 H0460

S61
SCHELLING T.C.,"NUCLEAR STRATEGY IN EUROPE." COM FUT
EUR+WWI USSR NAT/G FORCES NUC/PWR DRIVE ORD/FREE COERCE
PWR...DECISION CONCPT OBS TREND HYPO/EXP 20. ARMS/CONT
PAGE 139 H2784 WAR

B62
ABRAHAM W.E.,THE MIND OF AFRICA. AFR SOCIETY STRATA CULTURE
KIN ECO/TAC DOMIN EDU/PROP LEGIT COERCE ATTIT SIMUL
ALL/VALS...MAJORIT SOC OBS HIST/WRIT TIME/SEQ TREND GHANA
TOT/POP 20. PAGE 3 H0058

B62
BERNOT R.M.,EXCESS AND RESTRAINT: SOCIAL CONTROL SOCIETY
AMONG GUINEA MOUNTAIN PEOPLE. CULTURE FAM KIN CONTROL
CT/SYS COERCE WAR PERS/REL MARRIAGE HABITAT SEX STRUCT
...MYTH 20 NEW/GUINEA. PAGE 16 H0314 ADJUST

B62
CALVOCORESSI P.,WORLD ORDER AND NEW STATES: INT/ORG
PROBLEMS OF KEEPING THE PEACE. AFR EUR+WWI S/ASIA PEACE
ELITES NAT/G ECO/TAC FOR/AID EDU/PROP COERCE ATTIT
DRIVE ALL/VALS...GEN/LAWS COLD/WAR 20 UN. PAGE 25
H0509

B62
DE MADARIAGA S.,L'AMERIQUE LATINE ENTRE L'OURS ET POL/PAR
L'AIGLE. L/A+17C SOCIETY NAT/G ECO/TAC EDU/PROP ECO/UNDEV
REGION COERCE ATTIT ALL/VALS...MAJORIT TIME/SEQ
STERTYP COLD/WAR OAS 20. PAGE 38 H0760

B62
DEHIO L.,THE PRECARIOUS BALANCE: FOUR CENTURIES OF BAL/PWR
THE EUROPEAN POWER STRUGGLE. FRANCE GERMANY SPAIN WAR
NAT/G DOMIN PWR...GOV/COMP 8/20. PAGE 39 H0784 DIPLOM
COERCE

B62
FEIT E.,SOUTH AFRICA, THE DYNAMICS OF THE AFRICAN RACE/REL
NATIONAL CONGRESS. AFR SOUTH/AFR LAW INTELL STRATA ELITES
KIN NAT/G POL/PAR ECO/TAC DOMIN RISK COERCE 20 CONTROL
NEGRO. PAGE 49 H0984 STRUCT

B62
FINER S.E.,THE MAN ON HORSEBACK: ROLE OF THE NAT/G
MILITARY IN POLITICS. UNIV LAW CONSTN ELITES FORCES
SOCIETY POL/PAR BAL/PWR DOMIN EDU/PROP LEGIT COERCE TOTALISM
GUERRILLA REV WAR WEAPON DRIVE SUPEGO ORD/FREE PWR
RESPECT...POLICY CONCPT GEN/METH. PAGE 50 H1003

B62
GOURE L.,CIVIL DEFENSE IN THE SOVIET UNION. COM PLAN
USA+45 USSR MUNIC NAT/G DETER ATTIT MARXISM FORCES
...NAT/COMP 20 CIV/DEFENS. PAGE 59 H1188 WAR
COERCE

B62
JACKSON W.A.D.,RUSSO-CHINESE BORDERLANDS. ASIA COM GEOG
USSR NAT/G PROVS EX/STRUC FORCES DOMIN COERCE PEACE DIPLOM
ATTIT PWR SOVEREIGN WEALTH...CONCPT TREND CHARTS RUSSIA
STERTYP VAL/FREE. PAGE 79 H1576

B62
JOHNSON J.J.,THE ROLE OF THE MILITARY IN FORCES
UNDERDEVELOPED COUNTRIES. AFR BURMA INDONESIA ISLAM CONCPT
ISRAEL L/A+17C S/ASIA THAILAND CULTURE ECO/UNDEV
KIN PROVS CONSULT ACT/RES COERCE REV DRIVE
RIGID/FLEX ORD/FREE...RECORD ANTHOL 20. PAGE 81
H1622

B62
PENTONY D.E.,RED WORLD IN TUMULT: COMMUNIST FOREIGN ECO/UNDEV
POLICIES. CHINA/COM COM NAT/G EDU/PROP COERCE ATTIT DOMIN

PWR RESPECT...SOC CHARTS 20. PAGE 124 H2488 USSR ASIA

B62
US DEPARTMENT OF THE ARMY,GUIDE TO JAPANESE MONOGRAPHS AND JAPANESE STUDIES ON MANCHURIA: 1945-1960. CHINA/COM NAT/G DIPLOM LEAD COERCE WAR ...CHARTS 19/20 CHINJAP. PAGE 160 H3193 BIBLIOG/A FORCES ASIA S/ASIA

B62
VALERIANO N.D.,COUNTER-GUERRILLA OPERATIONS: THE PHILLIPINE EXPERIENCE. NAT/G CONSULT ACT/RES PLAN COERCE GUERRILLA ATTIT ORD/FREE PWR SKILL...GEOG NEW/IDEA TIME/SEQ CHARTS 20. PAGE 161 H3221 S/ASIA FORCES PHILIPPINE

L62
NOLTE E.,"ZUR PHANOMENOLOGIE DES FASCHIMUS." EUR+WWI GERMANY ITALY TURKEY INTELL NAT/G CHIEF CONSULT FORCES CREATE DOMIN EDU/PROP COERCE WAR CHOOSE DRIVE FASCISM...PSY CONCPT MYTH GEN/METH LEAGUE/NAT NAZI 20. PAGE 118 H2367 ATTIT PWR

S62
ANSPRENGER F.,"NATIONALISM, COMMUNISM, AND THE UNCOMMITTED NATIONS: AMERICAN PROFILES." FUT ISLAM CULTURE SOCIETY ECO/UNDEV NAT/G POL/PAR PLAN ECO/TAC EDU/PROP COERCE CHOOSE ALL/VALS MARXISM SOCISM...SOC CONCPT BIOG TREND 20. PAGE 7 H0142 AFR COM NAT/LISM

S62
CROAN M.,"POLYCENTRISM: COMMUNIST INTERNATIONAL RELATIONS." ASIA STRUCT INT/ORG NAT/G POL/PAR CONSULT PLAN DOMIN EDU/PROP COERCE ATTIT RIGID/FLEX SOCISM...POLICY CONCPT TREND CON/ANAL GEN/LAWS MARX/KARL. PAGE 35 H0703 COM CREATE DIPLOM NAT/LISM

S62
FESLER J.W.,"FRENCH FIELD ADMINISTRATION: THE BEGINNINGS." CHRIST-17C CULTURE SOCIETY STRATA NAT/G ECO/TAC DOMIN EDU/PROP LEGIT ADJUD COERCE ATTIT ALL/VALS...TIME/SEQ CON/ANAL GEN/METH VAL/FREE 13/15. PAGE 49 H0988 EX/STRUC FRANCE

S62
GUETZKOW H.,"THE POTENTIAL OF CASE STUDY IN ANALYZING INTERNATIONAL CONFLICT." EUR+WWI FUT GERMANY INTELL SOCIETY STRUCT INT/ORG LOC/G NAT/G CONSULT CREATE PLAN CHOOSE ATTIT RIGID/FLEX ...POLICY SAAR 20. PAGE 62 H1246 EDU/PROP METH/CNCPT COERCE FRANCE

S62
KOLARZ W.,"THE IMPACT OF COMMUNISM ON WEST AFRICA." AFR FUT SOCIETY INT/ORG NAT/G CREATE PLAN DOMIN EDU/PROP COERCE NAT/LISM ATTIT RIGID/FLEX SOCISM ...POLICY CONCPT TREND MARX/KARL 20. PAGE 88 H1751 COM POL/PAR COLONIAL

S62
MARTIN L.W.,"THE MARKET FOR STRATEGIC IDEAS IN BRITAIN: THE 'SANDYS ERA'" UK ARMS/CONT WAR GOV/REL OPTIMAL...POLICY DECISION GOV/COMP COLD/WAR CMN/WLTH. PAGE 103 H2063 DIPLOM COERCE FORCES PWR

S62
PASSIN H.,"THE SOURCES OF PROTEST IN JAPAN." CULTURE SOCIETY EDU/PROP COERCE NAT/LISM DISPL DRIVE PWR RESPECT...POLICY SOC TREND 20 CHINJAP. PAGE 124 H2473 ASIA ATTIT REV

S62
ROTBERG R.,"THE RISE OF AFRICAN NATIONALISM: THE CASE OF EAST AND CENTRAL AFRICA." AFR CULTURE SOCIETY NEIGH DIPLOM DOMIN COLONIAL COERCE DISPL PERCEPT PWR SOVEREIGN...POLICY OBS/ENVIR TREND WORK 20. PAGE 135 H2690 ATTIT DRIVE NAT/LISM REV

S62
SARKISYANZ E.,"NATIONALISM, CAPITALISM, AND THE UNCOMMITED NATIONS: MARXISM AND ASIAN CULTURAL TRADITIONS." ASIA BURMA CHINA/COM COM CULTURE SOCIETY NAT/G POL/PAR PLAN DOMIN EDU/PROP COLONIAL COERCE ATTIT RIGID/FLEX...CONCPT TREND MARX/KARL 20 TIBET BUDDHISM. PAGE 138 H2755 S/ASIA SECT NAT/LISM CAP/ISM

S62
SHATTEN F.,"POLYCENTRISM: AFRICA: NATIONALISM AND COMMUNISM." ASIA COM FUT ISLAM CULTURE SOCIETY ECO/UNDEV NAT/G PLAN DOMIN COLONIAL COERCE CHOOSE RIGID/FLEX ALL/VALS MARXISM...CONCPT TREND 20. PAGE 143 H2852 AFR ATTIT NAT/LISM SOCISM

S62
STRACHEY J.,"COMMUNIST INTENTIONS." ASIA USSR YUGOSLAVIA INT/ORG NAT/G FORCES DOMIN EDU/PROP COERCE NUC/PWR NAT/LISM PEACE RIGID/FLEX PWR MARXISM...CONCPT MYTH OBS TIME/SEQ TREND COLD/WAR TOT/POP 20. PAGE 150 H2992 COM ATTIT WAR

B63
BARNETT A.D.,COMMUNIST STRATEGIES IN ASIA: A COMPARATIVE ANALYSIS OF GOVERNMENTS AND PARTIES. COM FUT S/ASIA CULTURE SOCIETY STRATA NAT/G DELIB/GP ACT/RES ECO/TAC EDU/PROP COERCE CHOOSE ATTIT RIGID/FLEX ORD/FREE PWR SKILL...SIMUL VAL/FREE 20. PAGE 11 H0223 ASIA POL/PAR DIPLOM USSR

B63
BRZEZINSKI Z.K.,AFRICA AND THE COMMUNIST WORLD. AFR ASIA COM CULTURE SOCIETY INT/ORG DELIB/GP ACT/RES ECO/TAC COERCE ORD/FREE PWR WEALTH...STAT TOT/POP VAL/FREE 20. PAGE 23 H0461 ATTIT EDU/PROP DIPLOM USSR

B63
CRANKSHAW E.,THE NEW COLD WAR: MOSCOW V. PEKIN. CHINA/COM USSR INTELL POL/PAR DELIB/GP CAP/ISM COERCE REV NAT/LISM TOTALISM DRIVE...POLICY IDEA/COMP 20 KHRUSH/N. PAGE 35 H0698 ATTIT DIPLOM NAT/COMP MARXISM

B63
FALL B.,THE TWO VIETNAMS. CULTURE SOCIETY ECO/UNDEV NAT/G TOP/EX ACT/RES PLAN ECO/TAC DOMIN EDU/PROP COERCE ATTIT DRIVE PERSON ORD/FREE PWR...SOC TIME/SEQ COLD/WAR 20. PAGE 48 H0965 S/ASIA BIOG VIETNAM

B63
GLUCKMAN M.,ORDER AND REBELLION IN TRIBAL AFRICA. EUR+WWI LAW CULTURE STRATA KIN MUNIC DELIB/GP ACT/RES DOMIN EDU/PROP LEGIT ADMIN COERCE CHOOSE ATTIT PERSON ORD/FREE PWR...SOC CHARTS GEN/LAWS TOT/POP VAL/FREE. PAGE 57 H1147 AFR SOCIETY

B63
HAMM H.,ALBANIA - CHINA'S BEACHHEAD IN EUROPE. ALBANIA CHINA/COM USSR YUGOSLAVIA ELITES SOCIETY POL/PAR DELIB/GP FORCES ECO/TAC COERCE ISOLAT PEACE MARXISM...IDEA/COMP 20 MAO. PAGE 65 H1304 DIPLOM REV NAT/G POLICY

B63
HARDY M.J.L.,BLOOD FEUDS AND THE PAYMENT OF BLOOD MONEY IN THE MIDDLE EAST. ISLAM SOCIETY SECT REGION SANCTION COERCE DEATH MURDER 7/20 ARABS. PAGE 66 H1329 KIN TRIBUTE LAW CULTURE

B63
JAIRAZBHOY R.A.,FOREIGN INFLUENCE IN ANCIENT INDIA. INDIA ELITES SECT DIPLOM EDU/PROP COLONIAL REGION GP/REL...ART/METH LING WORSHIP +/14 GRECO/ROMN MESOPOTAM PERSIA PARTH/SASS. PAGE 79 H1587 CULTURE SOCIETY COERCE DOMIN

B63
KRAEHE E.,METTERNICH'S GERMAN POLICY: THE CONTEST WITH NAPOLEON, 1799-1814, VOL. 1. FRANCE MOD/EUR NAT/G CONSULT TOP/EX PLAN BAL/PWR DOMIN COERCE ATTIT DRIVE PERCEPT PERSON SKILL...CONCPT RECORD TIME/SEQ TREND 18/19. PAGE 88 H1764 BIOG GERMANY DIPLOM

B63
KURZMAN D.,SUBVERSION OF THE INNOCENTS: PATTERNS OF COMMUNIST PENETRATION OF AFRICA, THE MIDDLE EAST AND AFRICA. AFR ASIA ISLAM S/ASIA CULTURE NAT/G FORCES PLAN EDU/PROP ADMIN ATTIT...CONCPT INT UNPLAN/INT TIME/SEQ. PAGE 89 H1785 COM COERCE

B63
SETON-WATSON H.,THE NEW IMPERIALISM. COM EUR+WWI MOD/EUR ECO/UNDEV NAT/G FORCES DIPLOM DOMIN EDU/PROP LEGIT COLONIAL EXEC COERCE GP/REL RACE/REL DISCRIM ATTIT...TIME/SEQ 20. PAGE 142 H2833 ECO/TAC RUSSIA USSR

B63
SHANNON R.T.,GLADSTONE AND THE BULGARIAN AGITATION OF 1876. BULGARIA TURKEY UK DIPLOM COERCE REV ATTIT 19 GLADSTON/W DISRAELI/B. PAGE 142 H2841 EDU/PROP NAT/G PWR CONSEN

B63
STEVENS G.G.,EGYPT YESTERDAY AND TODAY. CONSTN ECO/UNDEV AGRI INDUS NAT/G POL/PAR FORCES ECO/TAC EDU/PROP COERCE WAR NAT/LISM DRIVE ALL/VALS ...TIME/SEQ WORK SUEZ 20. PAGE 149 H2983 ISLAM TOP/EX REV UAR

B63
THUCYDIDES,THE PELOPONESIAN WARS. MEDIT-7 CULTURE INT/ORG NAT/G FORCES TOP/EX PLAN ROUTINE PWR ...CONCPT. PAGE 155 H3091 ATTIT COERCE WAR

B63
TOUVAL S.,SOMALI NATIONALISM: INTERNATIONAL POLITICS AND THE DRIVE FOR UNITY IN THE HORN OF AFRICA. AFR CULTURE PROVS LEGIS EDU/PROP REGION COERCE ATTIT...MYTH UNPLAN/INT TIME/SEQ SOMALI VAL/FREE 20. PAGE 156 H3118 SOCIETY EXEC NAT/LISM

B63
TUCKER R.C.,THE SOVIET POLITICAL MIND. COM INTELL NAT/G TOP/EX EDU/PROP ADMIN COERCE TOTALISM ATTIT PWR MARXISM...PSY MYTH HYPO/EXP 20. PAGE 157 H3136 STRUCT RIGID/FLEX ELITES USSR

B63
ULAM A.B.,THE NEW FACE OF SOVIET TOTALITARIANISM. FUT INTELL NAT/G POL/PAR EX/STRUC TOP/EX DIPLOM ECO/TAC DOMIN EDU/PROP LEGIT COERCE ATTIT RIGID/FLEX...OBS HIST/WRIT TREND TOT/POP VAL/FREE COLD/WAR. PAGE 158 H3150 COM PWR TOTALISM USSR

L63
NASH M.,"PSYCHO-CULTURAL FACTORS IN ASIAN ECONOMIC GROWTH." ASIA ISLAM S/ASIA CULTURE ECO/UNDEV DELIB/GP EDU/PROP COERCE ATTIT PERSON HEALTH KNOWL ORD/FREE...PSY SOC STAT TREND ANTHOL VAL/FREE 20. PAGE 116 H2313 SOCIETY ECO/TAC

S63
BILL J.A.,"THE SOCIAL AND ECONOMIC FOUNDATIONS OF POWER IN CONTEMPORARY IRAN." ISLAM CULTURE NAT/G ECO/TAC DOMIN COERCE ATTIT PWR WEALTH...TREND VAL/FREE 20. PAGE 17 H0334 SOCIETY STRATA IRAN

S63
DUDLEY B.J.,"THE NOMINATION OF PARLIAMENTARY CANDIDATES IN NORTHERN NIGERIA." AFR CONSTN CULTURE ELITES STRATA DELIB/GP LEGIS DOMIN EDU/PROP COERCE ATTIT SUPEGO PWR...STAT VAL/FREE 20. PAGE 43 H0854 POL/PAR CHOOSE NIGERIA

S63
DUTT V.P.,"CHINA: JEALOUS NEIGHBOR." ASIA CHINA/COM INDIA S/ASIA NAT/G TOP/EX DOMIN COERCE REV ATTIT FORCES PWR

...POLICY COLD/WAR 20. PAGE 44 H0874 DIPLOM

S63

GLUCKMAN M.,"CIVIL WAR AND THEORIES OF POWER IN BAROTSE-LAND: AFRICAN AND MEDIEVAL ANALOGIES." AFR CHRIST-17C LAW CONSTN CULTURE STRATA KIN DELIB/GP FORCES DOMIN LEGIT COERCE PERCEPT ORD/FREE...SOC INT TIME/SEQ GEN/LAWS VAL/FREE. PAGE 57 H1148 TOP/EX PWR WAR

S63

HALPERN A.M.,"THE EMERGENCE OF AN ASIAN COMMUNIST BLOC." ASIA CHINA/COM COM FUT KOREA/N S/ASIA VIETNAM/N STRATA NAT/G DELIB/GP FORCES TOP/EX PLAN BAL/PWR COERCE DETER PWR COLD/WAR WORK 20. PAGE 65 H1295 POL/PAR EDU/PROP DIPLOM

S63

HARRIS R.L.,"A COMPARATIVE ANALYSIS OF THE ADMINISTRATIVE SYSTEMS OF CANADA AND CEYLON." S/ASIA CULTURE SOCIETY STRATA TOP/EX ACT/RES DOMIN EDU/PROP LEGIT COERCE ATTIT SUPEGO ALL/VALS...MGT CHARTS GEN/LAWS VAL/FREE 20. PAGE 67 H1343 DELIB/GP EX/STRUC CANADA CEYLON

S63

HARRIS R.L.,"COMMUNISM AND ASIA: ILLUSIONS AND MISCONCEPTIONS." ASIA COM FUT S/ASIA ECO/UNDEV AGRI NAT/G POL/PAR EX/STRUC EDU/PROP COERCE ATTIT MARXISM COLD/WAR TOT/POP 20. PAGE 67 H1344 PWR GUERRILLA

S63

LEE J.M.,"PARLIAMENT IN REPUBLICAN GHANA." AFR CONSTN CULTURE SOCIETY STRATA POL/PAR DELIB/GP TOP/EX DOMIN EDU/PROP LEGIT COERCE CHOOSE ATTIT ALL/VALS...CONCPT STAT TIME/SEQ VAL/FREE 20. PAGE 93 H1857 LEGIS GHANA

S63

NICHOLAS W.,"VILLAGE FACTIONS AND POLITICAL PARTIES IN RURAL WEST BENGAL." S/ASIA CULTURE STRATA FACE/GP KIN MUNIC DELIB/GP LEGIS DOMIN EDU/PROP COERCE CHOOSE ATTIT ALL/VALS...STAT TOT/POP VAL/FREE 20. PAGE 117 H2348 NEIGH POL/PAR

S63

RUSTOW D.A.,"THE MILITARY IN MIDDLE EASTERN SOCIETY AND POLITICS." FUT ISLAM CONSTN SOCIETY FACE/GP NAT/G POL/PAR PROF/ORG CONSULT DOMIN ADMIN EXEC REGION COERCE NAT/LISM ATTIT DRIVE PERSON ORD/FREE PWR...POLICY CONCPT OBS STERTYP 20. PAGE 136 H2721 FORCES ELITES

S63

SOEMARDJORN S.,"SOME SOCIAL AND CULTURAL IMPLICATIONS OF INDONESIA'S PLANNED AND UNPLANNED DEVELOPMENT." EUR+WWI FUT MOD/EUR S/ASIA CONSTN SOCIETY DELIB/GP ACT/RES PLAN ECO/TAC EDU/PROP COERCE ATTIT ALL/VALS...TIME/SEQ 20. PAGE 146 H2927 ECO/UNDEV CULTURE INDONESIA

S63

TILMAN R.O.,"MALAYSIA: THE PROBLEMS OF FEDERATION." ISLAM S/ASIA CONSTN PROVS SECT DELIB/GP DOMIN EDU/PROP LEGIT EXEC COERCE CHOOSE ATTIT HEALTH ORD/FREE PWR...STAT TOT/POP VAL/FREE 20. PAGE 155 H3097 NAT/G CULTURE MALAYSIA

B64

AGGARWALA R.C.,CONSTITUTIONAL HISTORY OF INDIA AND NATIONAL MOVEMENT INCLUDING COMPARATIVE STUDY OF MODERN INDIA CONSTITUTION. INDIA S/ASIA SECT VOL/ASSN EX/STRUC LEGIS COERCE REV INGP/REL ORD/FREE...SOC BIBLIOG 18/20 CMN/WLTH. PAGE 4 H0077 CONSTN COLONIAL DOMIN NAT/G

B64

CLUBB O.E. JR.,TWENTIETH CENTURY CHINA. ASIA CHINA/COM INTELL NAT/G POL/PAR VOL/ASSN ACT/RES EDU/PROP COERCE REV PWR...TIME/SEQ 20. PAGE 30 H0608 TOP/EX DRIVE

B64

CURTIN P.D.,THE IMAGE OF AFRICA: BRITISH IDEAS AND ACTION, 1780-1850. MOD/EUR SOCIETY FORCES ACT/RES DOMIN EDU/PROP COERCE ATTIT PERCEPT RIGID/FLEX SUPEGO HEALTH KNOWL MORAL ORD/FREE WEALTH...CONCPT WORK VAL/FREE. PAGE 36 H0726 AFR CULTURE UK DIPLOM

B64

DOOLIN D.J.,COMMUNIST CHINA: THE POLITICS OF STUDENT OPPOSITION. CHINA/COM ELITES STRATA ACADEM NAT/G WRITING CT/SYS LEAD PARTIC COERCE TOTALISM 20. PAGE 42 H0838 MARXISM DEBATE AGE/Y PWR

B64

FALL B.,STREET WITHOUT JOY. FRANCE USA+45 DIPLOM ECO/TAC FOR/AID GUERRILLA REV WEAPON...TREND 20. PAGE 48 H0966 WAR S/ASIA FORCES COERCE

B64

KELLER J.W.,GERMANY, THE WALL AND BERLIN. EUR+WWI ECO/DEV NAT/G VOL/ASSN FORCES PLAN ECO/TAC EDU/PROP COERCE...POLICY CONCPT INT TREND COLD/WAR BER/BLOC 20 BERLIN. PAGE 84 H1685 ATTIT ALL/VALS DIPLOM GERMANY

B64

LAPENNA I.,STATE AND LAW: SOVIET AND YUGOSLAV THEORY. USSR YUGOSLAVIA STRATA STRUCT NAT/G DOMIN COERCE MARXISM...GOV/COMP IDEA/COMP 20. PAGE 91 H1812 JURID COM LAW SOVEREIGN

B64

LAWRENCE P.,ROAD BELONG CARGO: A STUDY OF CARGO MOVEMENT IN SOUTHERN MADANG DISTRICT, NEW GUINEA. S/ASIA CULTURE ECO/UNDEV PROC/MFG KIN CHIEF COLONIAL COERCE GP/REL DRIVE WEALTH WORSHIP 20 NEW/GUINEA. PAGE 92 H1846 SOC SECT ALL/VALS MYTH

B64

MBEKI G.,SOUTH AFRICA: THE PEASANT'S REVOLT. SOUTH/AFR POL/PAR COERCE REV NAT/LISM ORD/FREE SOVEREIGN 20 NEGRO. PAGE 106 H2114 COLONIAL RACE/REL DISCRIM DOMIN

B64

PIKE F.B.,THE CONFLICT BETWEEN CHURCH AND STATE IN LATIN AMERICA. L/A+17C CULTURE SOCIETY STRATA DOMIN EDU/PROP LEGIT COERCE ATTIT ORD/FREE PWR WEALTH ...CONCPT TIME/SEQ TREND VAL/FREE. PAGE 125 H2510 SECT NAT/G

B64

PIPES R.,THE FORMATION OF THE SOVIET UNION. EUR+WWI MOD/EUR STRUCT ECO/UNDEV NAT/G LEGIS DOMIN LEGIT CT/SYS EXEC COERCE ALL/VALS...POLICY RELATIV HIST/WRIT TIME/SEQ TOT/POP 19/20. PAGE 126 H2514 COM USSR RUSSIA

B64

ROSENAU J.N.,INTERNATIONAL ASPECTS OF CIVIL STRIFE. CHINA/COM CUBA EUR+WWI USA+45 USSR BAL/PWR EDU/PROP NEUTRAL COERCE MORAL...NAT/COMP 20 COLD/WAR UN. PAGE 134 H2676 POLICY DIPLOM REV WAR

B64

SKINNER E.P.,THE MOSSI OF UPPER VOLTA: THE POLITICAL DEVELOPMENT OF A SUDANESE PEOPLE. AFR LAW AGRI FAM KIN POL/PAR PROVS SECT DELIB/GP EX/STRUC FORCES TOP/EX DOMIN EDU/PROP LEGIT CT/SYS COERCE CHOOSE ORD/FREE PWR WEALTH...SOC MYTH VAL/FREE. PAGE 145 H2897 CULTURE OBS UPPER/VOLT

B64

WRIGHT G.,RURAL REVOLUTION IN FRANCE: THE PEASANTRY IN THE TWENTIETH CENTURY. EUR+WWI MOD/EUR LAW CULTURE AGRI POL/PAR DELIB/GP LEGIS ECO/TAC EDU/PROP COERCE CHOOSE ATTIT RIGID/FLEX HEALTH ...STAT CENSUS CHARTS VAL/FREE 20. PAGE 171 H3419 PWR STRATA FRANCE REV

L64

ROTBERG R.,"THE FEDERATION MOVEMENT IN BRITISH EAST AND CENTRAL AFRICA." AFR RHODESIA UGANDA ECO/UNDEV NAT/G POL/PAR FORCES DOMIN LEGIT ADMIN COERCE ATTIT ...CONCPT TREND 20 TANGANYIKA. PAGE 135 H2691 VOL/ASSN PWR REGION

S64

BARIETY J.,"LA POLITIQUE EXTERIEURE ALLEMANDE DANS L'HIVER 1939-1940." COM FINLAND GERMANY ISLAM ITALY USSR NAT/G FORCES ECO/TAC DOMIN EDU/PROP COERCE WAR PWR WEALTH...HIST/WRIT NAZI TOT/POP VAL/FREE 20. PAGE 11 H0216 EUR+WWI DIPLOM

S64

BENSON M.,"SOUTH AFRICA AND WORLD OPINION." AFR SOUTH/AFR INTELL SOCIETY TOP/EX ECO/TAC DOMIN COERCE DISCRIM ATTIT PWR WEALTH...POLICY RECORD 20. PAGE 14 H0285 NAT/G RIGID/FLEX RACE/REL

S64

ENNIS T.E.,"VIETNAM: LAND WITHOUT LAUGHTER." S/ASIA VIETNAM VIETNAM/S INTELL SOCIETY SECT FORCES DIPLOM LEGIT COERCE WAR ATTIT RIGID/FLEX ORD/FREE COLD/WAR 20. PAGE 46 H0929 NAT/G TOP/EX GUERRILLA

S64

JOHNSON K.F.,"CAUSAL FACTORS IN LATIN AMERICAN POLITICAL INSTABILITY." CULTURE NAT/G VOL/ASSN EX/STRUC FORCES EDU/PROP LEGIT ADMIN COERCE REV ATTIT KNOWL PWR...STYLE RECORD CHARTS WORK 20. PAGE 81 H1624 L/A+17C PERCEPT ELITES

S64

LEVI W.,"INDIAN NEUTRALISM RECONSIDERED." ASIA CHINA/COM S/ASIA SOCIETY NAT/G ACT/RES LEGIT NEUTRAL COERCE ATTIT DRIVE PERCEPT RIGID/FLEX HEALTH LOVE PWR...DECISION RECORD TREND STERTYP 20. PAGE 95 H1896 ORD/FREE CONCPT INDIA

S64

LOW D.A.,"LION RAMPANT." EUR+WWI MOD/EUR S/ASIA ECO/UNDEV NAT/G FORCES TEC/DEV ECO/TAC LEGIT ADMIN COLONIAL COERCE ORD/FREE RESPECT 19/20. PAGE 99 H1972 AFR DOMIN DIPLOM UK

S64

POWELL R.L.,"COMMUNIST CHINA'S MILITARY POTENTIAL." ASIA CHINA/COM NAT/G EX/STRUC EDU/PROP COERCE GUERRILLA NUC/PWR WAR...RECORD CON/ANAL 20. PAGE 128 H2551 FORCES PWR

S64

REISS I.,"LE DECLENCHEMENT DE LA PREMIERE GUERRE MONDIALE." GERMANY RUSSIA NAT/G FORCES DOMIN EDU/PROP COERCE RIGID/FLEX PWR SOVEREIGN...RELATIV HIST/WRIT TOT/POP AUST/HUNG SERBIA 20. PAGE 131 H2612 MOD/EUR BAL/PWR DIPLOM WAR

S64

RUDOLPH L.I.,"GENERALS AND POLITICIANS IN INDIA." INDIA S/ASIA CULTURE STRATA NAT/G LEGIS TOP/EX EDU/PROP ATTIT ORD/FREE PWR RESPECT SKILL...POLICY BIOG TIME/SEQ STERTYP VAL/FREE 20. PAGE 136 H2713 FORCES COERCE

S64

SAYEED K.,"PATHAN REGIONALISM." ISLAM PAKISTAN S/ASIA CULTURE SOCIETY NAT/G NEIGH DIPLOM LEGIT COERCE CHOOSE ATTIT DISPL PERCEPT ALL/VALS SOVEREIGN...POLICY RELATIV SOC TIME/SEQ TOT/POP 20. PAGE 138 H2761 SECT NAT/LISM REGION

S64

SCHEFFLER H.W.,"THE GENESIS AND REPRESSION OF PWR

CONFLICT: CHOISEUL ISLAND." S/ASIA LOC/G NAT/G FORCES LEGIS DIPLOM DOMIN LEGIT EXEC CHOOSE ATTIT RESPECT SKILL...POLICY JURID OBS TREND GEN/METH 20. PAGE 139 H2781 — COERCE WAR

S64
SMYTHE H.H.,"NEHRU AND INDIAN FOREIGN POLICY." S/ASIA ECO/UNDEV NAT/G POL/PAR CONSULT PLAN DIPLOM NEUTRAL COERCE ATTIT DRIVE PERSON MORAL ORD/FREE RESPECT...GEOG CONCPT TIME/SEQ TREND GEN/LAWS 20 NEHRU/J. PAGE 146 H2922 — TOP/EX BIOG INDIA

B65
ALLEN W.S.,THE NAZI SEIZURE OF POWER. GERMANY NAT/G CHIEF LEAD COERCE CHOOSE REPRESENT GOV/REL AUTHORIT ...DECISION 20 HITLER/A NAZI. PAGE 5 H0106 — MUNIC FASCISM TOTALISM LOC/G

B65
DAHL R.A.,MODERN POLITICAL ANALYSIS. UNIV COERCE ...MAJORIT DECISION METH. PAGE 36 H0731 — CONCPT GOV/COMP PWR

B65
FILIPINIANA BOOK GUILD,THE COLONIZATION AND CONQUEST OF THE PHILIPPINES BY SPAIN. PHILIPPINE SPAIN ELITES AGRI KIN CHIEF DOMIN CONTROL ATTIT PWR ...ANTHOL WORSHIP 16. PAGE 50 H1000 — COLONIAL COERCE CULTURE WAR

B65
GEORGE M.,THE WARPED VISION. EUR+WWI UK NAT/G POL/PAR LEGIS PARL/PROC SANCTION COERCE WAR GOV/REL PEACE RESPECT 20 CONSRV/PAR. PAGE 56 H1113 — LEAD ATTIT DIPLOM POLICY

B65
GRETTON P.,MARITIME STRATEGY - A STUDY OF DEFENSE PROBLEMS. ASIA UK USSR DIPLOM COERCE DETER NUC/PWR WEAPON...CONCPT NAT/COMP 20. PAGE 60 H1211 — FORCES PLAN WAR SEA

B65
HALEVY E.,THE ERA OF TYRANNIES (TRANS. BY R. K. WEBB). WOR-45 ECO/DEV PROB/SOLV CONTROL COERCE REV WAR TOTALISM 20. PAGE 64 H1286 — SOCISM IDEA/COMP DOMIN

B65
HAMIL H.M.,DICTATORSHIP IN SPANISH AMERICA. NAT/G COERCE MORAL ORD/FREE...POLICY PSY SOC ANTHOL 18/20. PAGE 65 H1300 — TOTALISM CHIEF L/A+17C FASCISM

B65
JACKSON G.,THE SPANISH REPUBLIC AND THE CIVIL WAR, 1931-1939. EUR+WWI INTELL STRUCT COM/IND NAT/G POL/PAR LEGIS EDU/PROP EXEC COERCE NAT/LISM DRIVE PWR...INT TIME/SEQ TOT/POP 20. PAGE 79 H1574 — ATTIT GUERRILLA SPAIN

B65
NEWBURY C.W.,BRITISH POLICY TOWARDS WEST AFRICA: SELECT DOCUMENTS 1786-1874. AFR UK INT/TRADE DOMIN ADMIN COLONIAL CT/SYS COERCE ORD/FREE...BIBLIOG/A 18/19. PAGE 117 H2345 — DIPLOM POLICY NAT/G WRITING

B65
ROSENBERG A.,DEMOCRACY AND SOCIALISM. COM EUR+WWI FRANCE MOD/EUR STRUCT INT/ORG NAT/G POL/PAR TOP/EX EDU/PROP COERCE PERSON PWR FASCISM MARXISM...CONCPT TIME/SEQ MARX/KARL 19/20. PAGE 134 H2677 — ATTIT

B65
SCALAPINO R.A.,THE COMMUNIST REVOLUTION IN ASIA* TACTICS, GOALS, AND ACHIEVEMENTS. INDIA INTELL POL/PAR FORCES DOMIN EDU/PROP LEGIT COERCE REV ATTIT CHINJAP. PAGE 138 H2763 — ASIA S/ASIA MARXISM NAT/COMP

B65
SLATER J.,A REVALUATION OF COLLECTIVE SECURITY* THE OAS IN ACTION. L/A+17C USA+45 NAT/G ADMIN COERCE ORD/FREE PWR...GOV/COMP IDEA/COMP GEN/LAWS OAS. PAGE 145 H2899 — REGION INT/ORG FORCES

B65
TILLY C.,MEASURING POLITICAL UPHEAVAL* RESEARCH MONOGRAPH NO. 19. FRANCE INDUS NAT/G FORCES WORKER ...GEOG RECORD EXHIBIT GEN/METH BIBLIOG INDEX. PAGE 155 H3095 — CLASSIF QUANT COERCE REV

B65
UPTON A.F.,FINLAND IN CRISIS 1940-1941. NAT/G FORCES DIPLOM COERCE...DECISION GEOG. PAGE 159 H3173 — FINLAND GERMANY USSR WAR

B65
VAN DEN BERGHE P.L.,SOUTH AFRICA: A STUDY IN CONFLICT. AFR CULTURE SOCIETY STRATA STRUCT COERCE SEGREGAT. PAGE 161 H3227 — DOMIN RACE/REL DISCRIM

S65
COOPER P.,"THE DEVELOPMENT OF THE CONCEPT OF WAR." UK COERCE ATTIT PERCEPT PERSON...STAT CHARTS CHINJAP. PAGE 33 H0660 — CULTURE WAR SAMP STAND/INT

S65
GRIFFITH S.B.,"COMMUNIST CHINA'S CAPACITY TO MAKE WAR." CHINA/COM COM NAT/G TOP/EX PLAN DOMIN COERCE NUC/PWR ATTIT RESPECT SKILL...CONCPT MYTH TIME/SEQ TREND COLD/WAR 20. PAGE 61 H1221 — FORCES PWR WEAPON ASIA

S65
PLANK J.N.,"THE CARIBBEAN* INTERVENTION, WHEN AND HOW." CUBA GUATEMALA HAITI PANAMA USA+45 VENEZUELA FORCES PROB/SOLV RISK COERCE...NAT/COMP OAS TIME. PAGE 126 H2521 — SOVEREIGN MARXISM REV

S65
ROGGER H.,"EAST GERMANY: STABLE OR IMMOBILE." COM EUR+WWI GERMANY/E NAT/G INT/TRADE DOMIN EDU/PROP COERCE TOTALISM COLD/WAR 20. PAGE 133 H2659 — TOP/EX RIGID/FLEX GERMANY

S65
TRISKA J.F.,"SOVIET-AMERICAN RELATIONS* A MULTIPLE SYMMETRY MODEL." USA+45 USSR ACADEM ACT/RES EDU/PROP COERCE PERCEPT...NET/THEORY CHARTS NAT/COMP GEN/LAWS COLD/WAR. PAGE 157 H3132 — SIMUL EQUILIB DIPLOM

B66
BRACKMAN A.C.,SOUTHEAST ASIA'S SECOND FRONT: THE POWER STRUGGLE IN THE MALAY ARCHIPELAGO. CHINA/COM INDONESIA MALAYSIA ECO/UNDEV INT/ORG NAT/G FORCES DIPLOM EDU/PROP REGION COERCE GUERRILLA AUTHORIT POPULISM...MAJORIT 20 KENNEDY/JF SEATO. PAGE 20 H0396 — S/ASIA MARXISM REV

B66
GURR T.,NEW ERROR-COMPENSATED MEASURES FOR COMPARING NATIONS* SOME CORRELATES OF CIVIL VIOLENCE. WOR+45 SOCIETY REV ISOLAT...PHIL/SCI SOC QUANT TESTS SAMP/SIZ HYPO/EXP. PAGE 63 H1254 — NAT/COMP INDEX COERCE NEW/IDEA

B66
NOLTE E.,THREE FACES OF FASCISM. FRANCE GERMANY DOMIN LEGIT COERCE CROWD REV WAR GP/REL RACE/REL SOVEREIGN...GOV/COMP IDEA/COMP 19/20 HITLER/A MUSSOLIN/B MARX/KARL. PAGE 118 H2368 — FASCISM TOTALISM NAT/G POL/PAR

B66
O'NEILL R.J.,THE GERMAN ARMY AND THE NAZI PARTY, 1933-1939. GERMANY ELITES NAT/G EDU/PROP CONTROL LEAD COERCE WAR...POLICY INT TIME/SEQ BIBLIOG 20 HITLER/A NAZI. PAGE 120 H2391 — CIVMIL/REL FORCES FASCISM POL/PAR

B66
ROSNER J.,DER FASCHISMUS. AUSTRIA GERMANY ITALY STRATA NAT/G POL/PAR COERCE RACE/REL TOTALISM ATTIT AUTHORIT...IDEA/COMP 20 NAZI ANTI/SEMIT. PAGE 134 H2684 — NAT/LISM FASCISM ORD/FREE WAR

B66
SWEET E.C.,CIVIL LIBERTIES IN AMERICA. LAW CONSTN NAT/G PRESS CT/SYS DISCRIM ATTIT WORSHIP 20 CIVIL/LIB. PAGE 151 H3018 — ADJUD ORD/FREE SUFF COERCE

B66
ZABLOCKI C.J.,SINO-SOVIET RIVALRY. AFR ASIA CHINA/COM CUBA EUR+WWI L/A+17C USA+45 USSR WOR+45 POL/PAR FORCES COERCE NUC/PWR...GOV/COMP IDEA/COMP 20 MAO KHRUSH/N. PAGE 172 H3444 — DIPLOM MARXISM COM

S66
DETTER I.,"THE PROBLEM OF UNEQUAL TREATIES." CONSTN NAT/G LEGIS COLONIAL COERCE PWR...GEOG UN TIME TREATY. PAGE 40 H0796 — SOVEREIGN DOMIN INT/LAW ECO/UNDEV

S66
SCHOENBRON D.,"VIETNAM* THE CASE FOR EXTRICATION." NAT/G FORCES PROB/SOLV DIPLOM COLONIAL CONTROL COERCE...CONCPT 20. PAGE 140 H2795 — VIETNAM WAR GUERRILLA

C66
ROSENBERG C.G. JR.,"THE MYTH OF "MAU-MAU:" NATIONALISM IN KENYA." AFR CULTURE NAT/G POL/PAR COERCE REV RACE/REL ATTIT ORD/FREE SOVEREIGN...MYTH BIBLIOG 20. PAGE 134 H2678 — NAT/LISM COLONIAL MAJORIT LEAD

B67
ANDERSON C.W.,ISSUES OF POLITICAL DEVELOPMENT. BURMA WOR+45 CULTURE TOP/EX ECO/TAC MARXISM ...CHARTS NAT/COMP 20 COLOMB CONGO/LEOP. PAGE 6 H0126 — NAT/LISM COERCE ECO/UNDEV SOCISM

B67
BOHANNAN P.,LAW AND WARFARE. CULTURE CT/SYS COERCE REV PEACE...JURID SOC CONCPT ANTHOL 20. PAGE 18 H0367 — METH/COMP ADJUD WAR LAW

B67
FALL B.B.,HO CHI MINH ON REVOLUTION: SELECTED WRITINGS, 1920-66. COM VIETNAM ELITES NAT/G COERCE GUERRILLA RACE/REL MARXISM...MARXIST ANTHOL 20. PAGE 48 H0968 — REV COLONIAL ECO/UNDEV S/ASIA

B67
MEHDI M.T.,PEACE IN THE MIDDLE EAST. ISRAEL SOCIETY NAT/G PLAN EDU/PROP NAT/LISM DRIVE...IDEA/COMP 20 JEWS. PAGE 108 H2160 — ISLAM DIPLOM GP/REL COERCE

B67
ODINGA O.,NOT YET UHURU. NAT/G POL/PAR PROB/SOLV COERCE REV WAR PERS/REL PERSON ORD/FREE...POLICY 20 ODINGA/O KENYATTA. PAGE 120 H2395 — ATTIT BIOG LEAD AFR

L67
BERNSTEIN T.P.,"LEADERSHIP AND MASS MOBILIZATION IN THE SOVIET AND CHINESE COLLECTIVISATION CAMPAIGNS OF 1929-30, 1955-56: COMPARISON." CHINA/COM USSR WORKER CONTROL COERCE PRODUC ATTIT...NAT/COMP 20. PAGE 16 H0317 — FEDERAL PLAN AGRI NAT/G

L67
EINAUDI L.,"ANNOTATED BIBLIOGRAPHY OF LATIN AMERICAN MILITARY JOURNALS" LAW TEC/DEV DOMIN EDU/PROP COERCE WAR CIVMIL/REL 20. PAGE 45 H0899 — BIBLIOG/A NAT/G FORCES

L/A+17C

L67
UNESCO,"APARTHEID." SOUTH/AFR STRUCT KIN SCHOOL SECT WORKER DOMIN EDU/PROP REGION RACE/REL ISOLAT 20. PAGE 158 H3164
DISCRIM CULTURE COERCE COLONIAL

S67
ANTHEM T.,"CYPRUS* WHAT NOW?" CYPRUS GREECE TURKEY NAT/G BUDGET MAJORITY 20 NATO. PAGE 7 H0143
DIPLOM COERCE INT/TRADE ADJUD

S67
CATTELL D.T.,"A NEO-MARXIST THEORY OF COMPARATIVE ANALYSIS." USSR STRATA INSPECT DOMIN CONTROL COERCE OWN TOTALISM PWR...FASCIST HYPO/EXP METH 20. PAGE 28 H0561
GOV/COMP MARXISM SIMUL CLASSIF

S67
KYLE K.,"BACKGROUND TO THE CRISIS" ISLAM ISRAEL UAR UK USSR NAT/G PROB/SOLV LEGIT CONTROL REGION STRANGE MORAL 20 JEWS. PAGE 89 H1787
DIPLOM POLICY SOVEREIGN COERCE

S67
MATTHEWS R.O.,"THE SUEZ CANAL DISPUTE* A CASE STUDY IN PEACEFUL SETTLEMENT." FRANCE ISRAEL UAR UK NAT/G CONTROL LEAD COERCE WAR NAT/LISM ROLE ORD/FREE PWR ...INT/LAW UN 20. PAGE 105 H2099
PEACE DIPLOM ADJUD

S67
MCCLEERY W.,"AN INTERVIEW WITH J. DOUGLAS BROWN ON THE 'WAY' OF VIETNAM" COM VIETNAM INTELL ECO/DEV ACADEM NAT/G COERCE PERSON SUPEGO ORD/FREE 20. PAGE 106 H2125
ATTIT WAR COLONIAL MARXISM

S67
OOSTEN F.,"SUDVIETNAM IM JAHR VOR DER ENTSCHEIDUNG." VIETNAM/S VIETNAM/N NAT/G DIPLOM COERCE CHOOSE 20. PAGE 121 H2420
FORCES WAR WEAPON ATTIT

S67
PAK H.,"CHINA'S MILITIA AND MAO TSE-TUNG'S 'PEOPLE'S WAR'." CHINA/COM SOCIETY POL/PAR EX/STRUC PROB/SOLV PARTIC COERCE WAR CIVMIL/REL ATTIT DRIVE MARXISM...METH/COMP 20 MAO. PAGE 122 H2447
FORCES NAT/G WORKER CHIEF

S67
RENFIELD R.L.,"A POLICY FOR VIETNAM." COM VIETNAM NAT/G POL/PAR VOL/ASSN CHIEF DIPLOM EDU/PROP DETER REPRESENT ATTIT ORD/FREE 20. PAGE 131 H2615
WAR POLICY PLAN COERCE

S67
SYRKIN M.,"THE RIGHT TO BE ORDINARY." ISLAM ISRAEL NAT/G COERCE NAT/LISM RIGID/FLEX 20. PAGE 151 H3025
SOVEREIGN WAR FORCES DIPLOM

C67
LING D.L.,"TUNISIA: FROM PROTECTORATE TO REPUBLIC." CULTURE NAT/G POL/PAR CHIEF DIPLOM COERCE WAR PWR ...BIBLIOG 19/20 TUNIS. PAGE 97 H1934
AFR NAT/LISM COLONIAL PROB/SOLV

S68
BOSSCHERE G D.E.,"A L'EST DU NOUVEAU." CZECHOSLVK HUNGARY POLAND ROMANIA YUGOSLAVIA AGRI CREATE ECO/TAC COERCE GP/REL ATTIT MARXISM SOCISM 20. PAGE 19 H0382
ORD/FREE COM NAT/G DIPLOM

S68
CHAPMAN A.R.,"THE CIVIL WAR IN NIGERIA." AFR NIGERIA NAT/G PLAN ECO/TAC EDU/PROP COERCE WAR GOV/REL INGP/REL ORD/FREE PWR WEALTH SOC/INTEG 20 BIAFRA. PAGE 29 H0579
REV RACE/REL

B73
STEPHEN J.F.,LIBERTY, EQUALITY, FRATERNITY. UNIV SOCIETY NAT/G LEGIS DOMIN AGREE PERS/REL ATTIT MORAL...IDEA/COMP 19 MILL/JS. PAGE 149 H2978
ORD/FREE CONCPT COERCE SECT

B82
MACDONALD D.,AFRICANA; OR, THE HEART OF HEATHEN AFRICA, VOL. II: MISSION LIFE. SOCIETY STRATA KIN CREATE EDU/PROP ADMIN COERCE LITERACY HEALTH...MYTH WORSHIP 19 LIVNGSTN/D MISSION NEGRO. PAGE 100 H1990
SECT AFR CULTURE ORD/FREE

B95
HAMMOND B.E.,THE POLITICAL INSTITUTIONS OF THE ANCIENT GREEKS. GREECE MUNIC PROVS COERCE WAR ORD/FREE ARISTOTLE. PAGE 65 H1307
GOV/COMP NAT/G IDEA/COMP CONCPT

COERCION....SEE COERCE

COEXIST....COEXISTENCE; SEE ALSO COLD/WAR, PEACE

N17
BURKE E.,THOUGHTS ON THE PROSPECT OF A REGICIDE PEACE (PAMPHLET). FRANCE UK SECT DOMIN MURDER PEACE ORD/FREE SOVEREIGN POPULISM...POLICY GOV/COMP IDEA/COMP 18 JACOBINISM COEXIST. PAGE 24 H0483
REV CHIEF NAT/G DIPLOM

COEXISTENCE....SEE COLD/WAR, PEACE, COEXIST

COFFIN/WS....WILLIAM SLOANE COFFIN, JR.

COGNITION....SEE PERCEPT

COGNITIVE DISSONANCE....SEE PERCEPT, ROLE

COHEN A. H0615

COHEN E.W. H0616

COHEN R. H0617,H0618

COHESION....SEE CONSEN

COHN B.S. H0619

COLD/WAR....COLD WAR

NCO
CARRINGTON C.E.,THE COMMONWEALTH IN AFRICA (PAMPHLET). UK STRUCT NAT/G COLONIAL REPRESENT GOV/REL RACE/REL NAT/LISM...MAJORIT 20 EEC NEGRO COLD/WAR. PAGE 27 H0540
ECO/UNDEV AFR DIPLOM PLAN

N19
HAJDA J.,THE COLD WAR VIEWED AS A SOCIOLOGICAL PROBLEM (PAMPHLET). COM CZECHOSLVK EUR+WWI SOCIETY PLAN EDU/PROP CONTROL TASK ATTIT MARXISM...POLICY 20 COLD/WAR MIGRATION. PAGE 64 H1280
DIPLOM LEAD PWR NAT/G

S48
ALMOND G.A.,"THE CHRISTIAN PARTIES OF WESTEN EUROPE." EUR+WWI NAT/G EDU/PROP LEGIT TOTALISM ORD/FREE PWR MARXISM...TREND CHARTS STERTYP GEN/LAWS COLD/WAR 20. PAGE 5 H0110
POL/PAR CATH SOCISM

B50
CANTRIL H.,TENSIONS THAT CAUSE WAR. UNIV CULTURE R+D CREATE EDU/PROP DRIVE PERSON KNOWL ORD/FREE ...HUM PSY SOC OBS CENSUS TREND CON/ANAL SOC/EXP SIMUL GEN/METH ANTHOL COLD/WAR TOT/POP. PAGE 26 H0523
SOCIETY PHIL/SCI PEACE

B50
TRAGER F.N.,MARXISM IN SOUTHEAST ASIA. BURMA INDONESIA THAILAND VIETNAM CULTURE SOCIETY NAT/G VOL/ASSN EXEC ROUTINE COERCE ATTIT RIGID/FLEX PWR ...METH/CNCPT TIME/SEQ STERTYP GEN/LAWS MARX/KARL VAL/FREE COLD/WAR NAM 20. PAGE 156 H3126
S/ASIA POL/PAR REV

B52
ISAACS H.R.,AFRICA: NEW CRISES IN THE MAKING (PAMPHLET). EUR+WWI USA+45 ELITES ECO/UNDEV WAR DISCRIM NAT/LISM ATTIT...POLICY NEW/IDEA CHARTS GOV/COMP 20 NEGRO COLD/WAR. PAGE 78 H1570
COLONIAL AFR RACE/REL ORD/FREE

B53
HUNTER E.,BRAIN-WASHING IN RED CHINA. ASIA CHINA/COM CULTURE SOCIETY FORCES WAR TOTALISM ATTIT BIO/SOC DISPL DRIVE PERSON SUPEGO KNOWL ORD/FREE ...INT REC/INT COLD/WAR 20. PAGE 75 H1499
EDU/PROP COERCE

B54
BUTZ O.,GERMANY: DILEMMA FOR AMERICAN POLICY. GERMANY USA+45 USA-45 USSR WOR+45 INT/ORG FORCES NUC/PWR EFFICIENCY PEACE PWR...GOV/COMP 20 COLD/WAR. PAGE 25 H0501
DIPLOM NAT/G WAR POLICY

B55
TOYNBEE A.,THE REALIGNMENT OF EUROPE. COM GREECE ITALY NAT/G BAL/PWR ECO/TAC EDU/PROP REV SOVEREIGN ...SOC TIME/SEQ TREND COLD/WAR 20. PAGE 156 H3123
EUR+WWI PLAN USSR

B56
ROBERTS H.L.,RUSSIA AND AMERICA. CHINA/COM S/ASIA USSR FORCES TEC/DEV FOR/AID NUC/PWR ALL/IDEOS ...MAJORIT TREND NAT/COMP 20 COLD/WAR UN NATO. PAGE 132 H2641
DIPLOM INT/ORG BAL/PWR TOTALISM

B58
KINTNER W.R.,ORGANIZING FOR CONFLICT: A PROPOSAL. USSR STRUCT NAT/G LEGIS ADMIN EXEC PEACE ORD/FREE PWR...CONCPT OBS TREND NAT/COMP VAL/FREE COLD/WAR 20. PAGE 86 H1719
USA+45 PLAN DIPLOM

B58
LAQUER W.Z.,THE MIDDLE EAST IN TRANSITION. COM USSR ECO/UNDEV NAT/G VOL/ASSN EDU/PROP EXEC ATTIT DRIVE PWR MARXISM COLD/WAR TOT/POP 20. PAGE 91 H1818
ISLAM TREND NAT/LISM

B59
LAQUER W.Z.,THE SOVIET UNION AND THE MIDDLE EAST. COM UAR USSR ECO/UNDEV NAT/G VOL/ASSN ECO/TAC EDU/PROP COLONIAL EXEC PWR...TIME/SEQ TREND COLD/WAR 20. PAGE 91 H1819
ISLAM DRIVE FOR/AID NAT/LISM

S59
LEVINE R.A.,"ANTI-EUROPEAN VIOLENCE IN AFRICA: A COMPARATIVE ANALYSIS." AFR CULTURE NAT/G DIPLOM EDU/PROP COLONIAL REGION COERCE ATTIT PWR...PSY CONCPT TIME/SEQ TREND HYPO/EXP SOC/EXP STERTYP GEN/METH COLD/WAR 20. PAGE 95 H1903
DRIVE ORD/FREE REV

B60
MC CLELLAN G.S.,INDIA. CHINA/COM INDIA CONSTN ELITES STRATA AGRI POL/PAR FOR/AID ARMS/CONT REV MARXISM...CENSUS BIBLIOG 20 COLD/WAR GANDHI/M NEHRU/J. PAGE 106 H2117
DIPLOM NAT/G SOCIETY ECO/UNDEV

B60
STOLPER W.F.,GERMANY BETWEEN EAST AND WEST: THE ECONOMICS OF COMPETITIVE COEXISTENCE. FUT GERMANY/E GERMANY/W WOR+45 FINAN POL/PAR BUDGET ECO/TAC
ECO/DEV DIPLOM GOV/COMP

FOR/AID INT/TRADE...STAT CHARTS METH/COMP 20 COLD/WAR. PAGE 150 H2989 — BAL/PWR

S60
GROSSMAN G.,"SOVIET GROWTH: ROUTINE, INERTIA, AND PRESSURE." COM STRATA NAT/G DELIB/GP PLAN TEC/DEV ECO/TAC EDU/PROP ADMIN ROUTINE DRIVE WEALTH COLD/WAR 20. PAGE 62 H1236 — POL/PAR ECO/DEV USSR

S60
NORTH R.C.,"THE NEW EXPANSIONISM." ASIA CHINA/COM FUT INDIA CULTURE SOCIETY NAT/G TOP/EX DOMIN COERCE PWR MARXISM...CONCPT TIME/SEQ TREND GEN/LAWS COLD/WAR 20 MAO. PAGE 119 H2372 — ATTIT DRIVE NAT/LISM

S60
TAUBER K.,"ASPECTS OF NATIONALIST-COMMUNIST COLLABORATION IN POSTWAR GERMANY." COM EUR+WWI USSR NAT/G VOL/ASSN ATTIT DRIVE PWR...TIME/SEQ COLD/WAR TOT/POP 20. PAGE 152 H3049 — POL/PAR EDU/PROP GERMANY

S60
WOLFE T.W.,"KHRUSHCHEV'S DISARMAMENT STRATEGY." COM NAT/G TOP/EX PLAN BAL/PWR DIPLOM ARMS/CONT COERCE ATTIT...POLICY CONCPT RECORD TREND CON/ANAL COLD/WAR 20 KHRUSH/N. PAGE 170 H3401 — PWR GEN/LAWS USSR

B61
FULLER J.F.C.,THE CONDUCT OF WAR, 1789-1961. FRANCE RUSSIA SOCIETY NAT/G FORCES PROB/SOLV AGREE NUC/PWR WEAPON PEACE...SOC 18/20 TREATY COLD/WAR. PAGE 54 H1076 — WAR POLICY REV ROLE

B61
GUEVARA E.,GUERRILLA WARFARE. L/A+17C ECO/UNDEV NAT/G POL/PAR VOL/ASSN PLAN DOMIN REV DRIVE PWR WEALTH...NEW/IDEA RECORD BIOG COLD/WAR MARX/KARL OAS 20. PAGE 62 H1247 — FORCES COERCE GUERRILLA CUBA

B61
HARDT J.P.,THE COLD WAR ECONOMIC GAP. USA+45 USSR ECO/DEV FORCES INT/TRADE NUC/PWR PWR 20 COLD/WAR. PAGE 66 H1328 — DIPLOM ECO/TAC NAT/COMP POLICY

B61
KISSINGER H.A.,THE NECESSITY FOR CHOICE. FUT USA+45 ECO/UNDEV NAT/G PLAN BAL/PWR ECO/TAC ARMS/CONT DETER NUC/PWR ATTIT...POLICY CONCPT RECORD GEN/LAWS COLD/WAR 20. PAGE 87 H1728 — TOP/EX TREND DIPLOM

B61
MOLLAU G.,INTERNATIONAL COMMUNISM AND WORLD REVOLUTION: HISTORY AND METHODS. RUSSIA USSR INT/ORG NAT/G POL/PAR VOL/ASSN FORCES BAL/PWR DIPLOM EXEC REGION WAR ATTIT PWR MARXISM...CONCPT TIME/SEQ COLD/WAR 19/20. PAGE 112 H2237 — COM REV

B61
PECKERT J.,DIE GROSSEN UND DIE KLEINEN MAECHTE. COM GERMANY/W ECO/DEV ECO/UNDEV NAT/G WAR RACE/REL PEACE...POLICY GP/COMP GOV/COMP 20 COLD/WAR. PAGE 124 H2482 — DIPLOM ECO/TAC BAL/PWR

B61
SOKOL A.E.,SEAPOWER IN THE NUCLEAR AGE. USA+45 USSR DIST/IND FORCES INT/TRADE DETER WAR...POLICY NAT/COMP BIBLIOG COLD/WAR. PAGE 146 H2928 — SEA PWR WEAPON NUC/PWR

B62
CALVOCORESSI P.,WORLD ORDER AND NEW STATES: PROBLEMS OF KEEPING THE PEACE. AFR EUR+WWI S/ASIA ELITES NAT/G ECO/TAC FOR/AID EDU/PROP COERCE ATTIT DRIVE ALL/VALS...GEN/LAWS COLD/WAR 20 UN. PAGE 25 H0509 — INT/ORG PEACE

B62
DE MADARIAGA S.,L'AMERIQUE LATINE ENTRE L'OURS ET L'AIGLE. L/A+17C SOCIETY NAT/G ECO/TAC EDU/PROP REGION COERCE ATTIT ALL/VALS...MAJORIT TIME/SEQ STERTYP COLD/WAR OAS 20. PAGE 38 H0760 — POL/PAR ECO/UNDEV

B62
HATCH J.,AFRICA TODAY-AND TOMORROW: AN OUTLINE OF BASIC FACTS AND MAJOR PROBLEMS. AFR FUT ISLAM STRATA ECO/UNDEV INT/ORG NAT/G POL/PAR DELIB/GP TOP/EX EDU/PROP LEGIT CHOOSE ATTIT...TIME/SEQ TOT/POP COLD/WAR 20. PAGE 67 H1353 — PLAN CONSTN NAT/LISM

B62
MODELSKI G.,SEATO-SIX STUDIES. ASIA CHINA/COM INDIA S/ASIA INT/ORG NAT/G ECO/TAC DETER ATTIT ORD/FREE PWR...TIME/SEQ COLD/WAR TOT/POP 20 SEATO. PAGE 112 H2234 — MARKET ECO/UNDEV INT/TRADE

B62
MORGENSTERN O.,STRATEGIE - HEUTE (2ND ED.). USA+45 USSR ECO/DEV DELIB/GP WAR PEACE ORD/FREE...GOV/COMP NAT/COMP 20 COLD/WAR NATO. PAGE 113 H2256 — NUC/PWR DIPLOM FORCES TEC/DEV

S62
HYDE D.,"COMMUNISM IN LATIN AMERICA." L/A+17C ECO/DEV NAT/G SECT EDU/PROP ATTIT ALL/VALS MARXISM ...SOC CONCPT TOT/POP COLD/WAR OAS 20. PAGE 76 H1515 — COM POL/PAR REV

S62
MARTIN L.W.,"THE MARKET FOR STRATEGIC IDEAS IN BRITAIN: THE 'SANDYS ERA'" UK ARMS/CONT WAR GOV/REL OPTIMAL...POLICY DECISION GOV/COMP COLD/WAR CMN/WLTH. PAGE 103 H2063 — DIPLOM COERCE FORCES PWR

S62
MU FU-SHENG,"THE WILTING OF THE HUNDRED FLOWERS: FREE THOUGHT IN CHINA TODAY." ASIA CHINA/COM CULTURE FAM NAT/G EDU/PROP REV TOTALISM ATTIT PERSON RESPECT...GEOG INT UNPLAN/INT COLD/WAR 20. PAGE 114 H2278 — INTELL ELITES

S62
STRACHEY J.,"COMMUNIST INTENTIONS." ASIA USSR YUGOSLAVIA INT/ORG NAT/G FORCES DOMIN EDU/PROP COERCE NUC/PWR NAT/LISM PEACE RIGID/FLEX PWR MARXISM...CONCPT MYTH OBS TIME/SEQ TREND COLD/WAR TOT/POP 20. PAGE 150 H2992 — COM ATTIT WAR

B63
FALL B.,THE TWO VIETNAMS. CULTURE SOCIETY ECO/UNDEV NAT/G TOP/EX ACT/RES PLAN ECO/TAC DOMIN EDU/PROP COERCE ATTIT DRIVE PERSON ORD/FREE PWR...SOC TIME/SEQ COLD/WAR 20. PAGE 48 H0965 — S/ASIA BIOG VIETNAM

B63
GONZALEZ PEDRERO E.,ANATOMIA DE UN CONFLICTO. WOR+45 ECO/DEV ECO/UNDEV ECO/TAC FOR/AID CONTROL ARMS/CONT GOV/REL...NAT/COMP 20 COLD/WAR. PAGE 58 H1166 — DIPLOM DETER BAL/PWR

B63
LYON P.,NEUTRALISM. ECO/UNDEV EDU/PROP COLONIAL ALL/IDEOS...IDEA/COMP 20 COLD/WAR UN. PAGE 99 H1985 — NAT/COMP NAT/LISM DIPLOM NEUTRAL

B63
MILLER W.J.,THE MEANING OF COMMUNISM. USSR SOCIETY ECO/DEV EX/STRUC WORKER TEC/DEV ADMIN TOTALISM ...POLICY CONCPT CHARTS BIBLIOG T 20 COLD/WAR LENIN/VI STALIN/J. PAGE 111 H2215 — MARXISM TRADIT DIPLOM NAT/G

B63
ULAM A.B.,THE NEW FACE OF SOVIET TOTALITARIANISM. FUT INTELL NAT/G POL/PAR EX/STRUC TOP/EX DIPLOM ECO/TAC DOMIN EDU/PROP LEGIT COERCE ATTIT RIGID/FLEX...OBS HIST/WRIT TREND TOT/POP VAL/FREE COLD/WAR. PAGE 158 H3150 — COM PWR TOTALISM USSR

S63
BECHHOEFER B.G.,"SOVIET ATTITUDE TOWARD DISARMAMENT." COM USSR NAT/G ACT/RES TEC/DEV NUC/PWR ATTIT DISPL RIGID/FLEX PWR...METH/CNCPT TREND GEN/LAWS COLD/WAR 20. PAGE 13 H0252 — FORCES EDU/PROP ARMS/CONT

S63
DUTT V.P.,"CHINA: JEALOUS NEIGHBOR." ASIA CHINA/COM INDIA S/ASIA NAT/G TOP/EX DOMIN COERCE REV ATTIT ...POLICY COLD/WAR 20. PAGE 44 H0874 — FORCES PWR DIPLOM

S63
GROSSER A.,"FRANCE AND GERMANY IN THE ATLANTIC COMMUNITY." INT/ORG NAT/G TOP/EX DIPLOM REGION PEACE ATTIT ORD/FREE PWR...CONCPT RECORD TIME/SEQ GEN/LAWS VAL/FREE COLD/WAR 20. PAGE 62 H1234 — EUR+WWI VOL/ASSN FRANCE GERMANY

S63
HALPERN A.M.,"THE EMERGENCE OF AN ASIAN COMMUNIST BLOC." ASIA CHINA/COM COM FUT KOREA/N S/ASIA VIETNAM/N STRATA NAT/G DELIB/GP FORCES TOP/EX PLAN BAL/PWR COERCE DETER PWR COLD/WAR WORK 20. PAGE 65 H1295 — POL/PAR EDU/PROP DIPLOM

S63
HARRIS R.L.,"COMMUNISM AND ASIA: ILLUSIONS AND MISCONCEPTIONS." ASIA COM FUT S/ASIA ECO/UNDEV AGRI NAT/G POL/PAR EX/STRUC EDU/PROP COERCE ATTIT MARXISM COLD/WAR TOT/POP 20. PAGE 67 H1344 — PWR GUERRILLA

B64
KELLER J.W.,GERMANY, THE WALL AND BERLIN. EUR+WWI ECO/DEV NAT/G VOL/ASSN FORCES PLAN ECO/TAC EDU/PROP COERCE...POLICY CONCPT INT TREND COLD/WAR BER/BLOC 20 BERLIN. PAGE 84 H1685 — ATTIT ALL/VALS DIPLOM GERMANY

B64
ROSENAU J.N.,INTERNATIONAL ASPECTS OF CIVIL STRIFE. CHINA/COM CUBA EUR+WWI USA+45 USSR BAL/PWR EDU/PROP NEUTRAL COERCE MORAL...NAT/COMP 20 COLD/WAR UN. PAGE 134 H2676 — POLICY DIPLOM REV WAR

B64
VOELKMANN K.,HERRSCHER VON MORGEN? BAL/PWR COLONIAL NEUTRAL REGION RACE/REL ALL/VALS SOVEREIGN...RECORD 20 COLD/WAR THIRD/WRLD. PAGE 163 H3259 — DIPLOM ECO/UNDEV CONTROL NAT/COMP

B64
WILCOX W.A.,INDIA, PAKISTAN AND THE RISE OF CHINA. ASIA BURMA CEYLON CHINA/COM INDIA PAKISTAN S/ASIA NAT/G VOL/ASSN FORCES TOP/EX ACT/RES DOMIN REGION RIGID/FLEX ORD/FREE...POLICY GEN/LAWS COLD/WAR 20. PAGE 168 H3362 — CULTURE ATTIT DIPLOM

S64
CATTELL D.T.,"SOVIET POLICIES IN LATIN AMERICA." COM CUBA L/A+17C USSR SOCIETY NAT/G POL/PAR FORCES CREATE ECO/TAC EDU/PROP REGION REV RIGID/FLEX ...GEN/LAWS COLD/WAR 20. PAGE 28 H0560 — DRIVE PWR

S64
ENNIS T.E.,"VIETNAM: LAND WITHOUT LAUGHTER." S/ASIA VIETNAM VIETNAM/S INTELL SOCIETY SECT FORCES DIPLOM LEGIT COERCE WAR ATTIT RIGID/FLEX ORD/FREE COLD/WAR 20. PAGE 46 H0929 — NAT/G TOP/EX GUERRILLA

S64
GARMARNIKOW M.,"INFLUENCE-BUYING IN WEST AFRICA." — AFR

COM FUT USSR INTELL NAT/G PLAN TEC/DEV ECO/TAC DOMIN EDU/PROP REGION NAT/LISM ATTIT DRIVE ALL/VALS SOVEREIGN...POLICY PSY SOC CONCPT TREND STERTYP WORK COLD/WAR 20. PAGE 55 H1102
ECO/UNDEV FOR/AID SOCISM

S64
GOLDBERG A.,"THE MILITARY ORIGINS OF THE BRITISH NUCLEAR DETERRENT." EUR+WWI ECO/DEV NAT/G PLAN NUC/PWR ATTIT PWR...DECISION HIST/WRIT COLD/WAR 20. PAGE 58 H1156
FORCES CONCPT DETER UK

S64
LERNER W.,"THE HISTORICAL ORIGINS OF THE SOVIET DOCTRINE OF PEACEFUL COEXISTENCE." COM USSR INT/ORG NAT/G VOL/ASSN PLAN PEACE ATTIT RIGID/FLEX PWR MARXISM...TIME/SEQ COLD/WAR 20. PAGE 95 H1891
EDU/PROP DIPLOM

S64
MOZINGO D.P.,"CHINA'S RELATIONS WITH HER ASIAN NEIGHBORS." ASIA CHINA/COM S/ASIA VIETNAM NAT/G DELIB/GP FORCES CREATE DOMIN EDU/PROP REV RIGID/FLEX PWR...TIME/SEQ GEN/LAWS COLD/WAR 20. PAGE 114 H2277
VOL/ASSN POLICY DIPLOM

S64
SALVADORI M.,"EL CAPITALISMO EN LA EUROPA DE LA POSGUERRA." INT/ORG NAT/G POL/PAR PLAN ECO/TAC ATTIT ORD/FREE WEALTH...HIST/WRIT COLD/WAR EEC 20. PAGE 137 H2743
EUR+WWI ECO/DEV CAP/ISM

S64
TINKER H.,"POLITICS IN SOUTHEAST ASIA." INT/ORG NAT/G CREATE PLAN TEC/DEV GUERRILLA KNOWL ORD/FREE COLD/WAR. PAGE 155 H3103
S/ASIA ACT/RES REGION

B65
CRABB C.V. JR.,THE ELEPHANTS AND THE GRASS* A STUDY OF NONALIGNMENT. AFR ASIA INDIA S/ASIA USA+45 USSR BAL/PWR NEUTRAL ATTIT...TREND NAT/COMP COLD/WAR. PAGE 34 H0691
ECO/UNDEV DIPLOM CONCPT

B65
DOLCI D.,A NEW WORLD IN THE MAKING. GHANA SENEGAL USSR YUGOSLAVIA CULTURE INT/ORG PLAN EDU/PROP GP/REL PEACE MORAL...GEOG SOC 20 COLD/WAR. PAGE 42 H0834
SOCIETY ALL/VALS DRIVE PERSON

B65
HALPERIN M.H.,COMMUNIST CHINA AND ARMS CONTROL. CHINA/COM FUT USA+45 CULTURE FORCES TEC/DEV ECO/TAC WAR PEACE ORD/FREE MARXISM 20 COLD/WAR. PAGE 64 H1292
ATTIT POLICY ARMS/CONT NUC/PWR

B65
MENON K.P.S.,MANY WORLDS. INDIA BAL/PWR CAP/ISM COLONIAL REV ORD/FREE PWR MARXISM...POLICY 20 COLD/WAR. PAGE 109 H2176
BIOG DIPLOM NAT/G

B65
O'BRIEN F.,CRISIS IN WORLD COMMUNISM* MARXISM IN SEARCH OF EFFICIENCY. COM ECO/DEV PLAN INT/TRADE WAR ADJUST PEACE...STAT TIME/SEQ GOV/COMP NAT/COMP COLD/WAR. PAGE 119 H2384
MARXISM USSR DRIVE EFFICIENCY

B65
POLK W.R.,THE UNITED STATES AND THE ARAB WORLD. USA+45 ECO/UNDEV EXTR/IND SECT WAR NAT/LISM ATTIT ...NAT/COMP COLD/WAR. PAGE 127 H2535
ISLAM REGION CULTURE DIPLOM

B65
SMITH R.M.,CAMBODIA'S FOREIGN POLICY. ECO/UNDEV NAT/G NEUTRAL ORD/FREE COLD/WAR VAL/FREE. PAGE 146 H2917
S/ASIA CAMBODIA DIPLOM

S65
GRIFFITH S.B.,"COMMUNIST CHINA'S CAPACITY TO MAKE WAR." CHINA/COM COM NAT/G TOP/EX PLAN DOMIN COERCE NUC/PWR ATTIT RESPECT SKILL...CONCPT MYTH TIME/SEQ TREND COLD/WAR 20. PAGE 61 H1221
FORCES PWR WEAPON ASIA

S65
HELMREICH E.C.,"KADAR'S HUNGARY." COM EUR+WWI HUNGARY USSR INTELL ECO/DEV AGRI INT/ORG TOP/EX DOMIN ALL/VALS WORK COLD/WAR 20. PAGE 69 H1390
NAT/G RIGID/FLEX TOTALISM

S65
LAULICHT J.,"PUBLIC OPINION AND FOREIGN POLICY DECISIONS." CANADA ELITES NAT/G FOR/AID LEAD NUC/PWR PERCEPT...INT QU CHARTS UN COLD/WAR. PAGE 92 H1839
DIPLOM ATTIT CON/ANAL SAMP

S65
PRABHAKAR P.,"SURVEY OF RESEARCH AND SOURCE MATERIALS; THE SINO-INDIAN BORDER DISPUTE." CHINA/COM INDIA LAW NAT/G PLAN BAL/PWR WAR...POLICY 20 COLD/WAR. PAGE 128 H2553
BIBLIOG ASIA S/ASIA DIPLOM

S65
ROGGER H.,"EAST GERMANY: STABLE OR IMMOBILE." COM EUR+WWI GERMANY/E NAT/G INT/TRADE DOMIN EDU/PROP COERCE TOTALISM COLD/WAR 20. PAGE 133 H2659
TOP/EX RIGID/FLEX GERMANY

S65
TRISKA J.F.,"SOVIET-AMERICAN RELATIONS* A MULTIPLE SYMMETRY MODEL." USA+45 USSR ACADEM ACT/RES EDU/PROP COERCE PERCEPT...NET/THEORY CHARTS NAT/COMP GEN/LAWS COLD/WAR. PAGE 157 H3132
SIMUL EQUILIB DIPLOM

S65
WHITE J.,"WEST GERMAN AID TO DEVELOPING COUNTRIES." INT/ORG OP/RES GIVE CENTRAL ATTIT DRIVE...STAT NAT/COMP COLD/WAR. PAGE 167 H3348
GERMANY FOR/AID ECO/UNDEV CAP/ISM

B66
DAENIKER G.,STRATEGIE DES KLEIN STAATS. SWITZERLND ACT/RES CREATE DIPLOM NEUTRAL DETER WAR WEAPON PWR SOVEREIGN...IDEA/COMP 20 COLD/WAR. PAGE 36 H0730
NUC/PWR PLAN FORCES NAT/G

B66
FRANK E.,LAWMAKERS IN A CHANGING WORLD. FRANCE UK USSR WOR+45 PARTIC EFFICIENCY ROLE ALL/IDEOS ...CHARTS ANTHOL PARLIAMENT 20 UN COLD/WAR. PAGE 52 H1049
GOV/COMP LEGIS NAT/G DIPLOM

B66
MARTIN L.W.,DIPLOMACY IN MODERN EUROPEAN HISTORY. EUR+WWI MOD/EUR INT/ORG NAT/G EX/STRUC ROUTINE WAR PEACE TOTALISM PWR 15/20 COLD/WAR EUROPE/W. PAGE 103 H2064
DIPLOM POLICY

B66
SOBEL L.A.,SOUTH VIETNAM: US-COMMUNIST CONFRONTATION IN SOUTHEAST ASIA 1961-65. VIETNAM FOR/AID CROWD DETER REV PEACE...GEOG 20 INTERVENT DIEM COLD/WAR. PAGE 146 H2926
WAR TIME/SEQ FORCES NAT/G

B66
SWEARINGEN A.R.,SOVIET AND CHINESE COMMUNIST POWER IN THE WORLD TODAY. COM USA+45 ECO/UNDEV CREATE LEAD WAR ADJUST...TREND NAT/COMP ANTHOL COLD/WAR KHRUSH/N. PAGE 151 H3017
USSR ASIA DIPLOM ATTIT

S66
GALTUNG J.,"EAST-WEST INTERACTION PATTERNS." DIPLOM INT/TRADE...NET/THEORY CON/ANAL CHARTS NAT/COMP INDEX NATO COLD/WAR UN WARSAW/P. PAGE 55 H1090
STAT HYPO/EXP

S66
SCHWARTZ M.,"THE 1964 PRESIDENTIAL ELECTIONS THROUGH SOVIET EYES." ASIA POL/PAR DIPLOM ATTIT MARXISM...NAT/COMP COLD/WAR. PAGE 140 H2811
USSR USA+45 PERCEPT

B67
BURNHAM J.,THE WAR WE ARE IN, THE LAST DECADE AND THE NEXT. ASIA COM EUR+WWI S/ASIA WOR+45 ECO/UNDEV INT/ORG FORCES WAR...OLD/LIB TREND 20 COLD/WAR. PAGE 25 H0492
POLICY NAT/G DIPLOM NAT/COMP

B67
CEFKIN J.L.,THE BACKGROUND OF CURRENT WORLD PROBLEMS. NAT/G MARXISM...T 20 UN COLD/WAR. PAGE 28 H0565
DIPLOM NAT/LISM ECO/UNDEV

B67
MACRIDIS R.C.,FOREIGN POLICY IN WORLD POLITICS (3RD ED.). EX/STRUC BAL/PWR COLONIAL NAT/LISM SKILL SOVEREIGN WEALTH...CONCPT TIME/SEQ ANTHOL 20 COLD/WAR. PAGE 101 H2011
DIPLOM POLICY NAT/G IDEA/COMP

B67
MCCLINTOCK R.,THE MEANING OF LIMITED WAR. FUT WOR+45 NAT/G FORCES GUERRILLA REV...POLICY SAMP/SIZ TREND NAT/COMP 45 COLD/WAR. PAGE 106 H2126
WAR NUC/PWR BAL/PWR DIPLOM

B67
PLANK J.,CUBA AND THE UNITED STATES: LONG RANGE PERSPECTIVES. CUBA L/A+17C USSR ECO/UNDEV NAT/G FORCES ECO/TAC INT/TRADE AGREE REV...PREDICT TREND ANTHOL 20 CASTRO/F COLD/WAR OAS. PAGE 126 H2520
DIPLOM

B67
ROWLAND J.,A HISTORY OF SINO-INDIAN RELATIONS; HOSTILE CO-EXISTENCE. ASIA CHINA/COM INDIA NAT/G NUC/PWR PWR WEALTH...GEOG BIBLIOG 13/20 COLD/WAR. PAGE 135 H2704
DIPLOM CENSUS IDEA/COMP

S67
SAVER W.,"NATIONAL SOCIALISM: TOTALITARIANISM OR FASCISM?" GERMANY STRUCT POL/PAR PROB/SOLV MARXISM ...SOC CONCPT HIST/WRIT IDEA/COMP 20 HITLER/A COLD/WAR. PAGE 138 H2760
SOCISM NAT/G TOTALISM FASCISM

S67
WILPERT C.,"A LOOK IN THE MIRROR AND OVER THE WALL." GERMANY POL/PAR...KNO/TEST COLD/WAR. PAGE 169 H3378
NAT/G PLAN DIPLOM ATTIT

C67
GEHLEN M.P.,"THE POLITICS OF COEXISTENCE: SOVIET METHODS AND MOTIVES." COM USSR NAT/G INT/TRADE EDU/PROP ARMS/CONT DETER KNOWL...CHARTS IDEA/COMP 20 COLD/WAR. PAGE 55 H1108
BIBLIOG PEACE DIPLOM MARXISM

COLE A.B. H0620

COLE G.D.H. H0621,H0622,H0623,H0624,H0625

COLE T. H0626,H3096

COLE/GEO....GEORGE COLE

COLEMAN J.S. H0112,H0627,H0628,H0629

COLEMAN-NORTON P.R. H0630

COLLECTIVE BARGAINING....SEE BARGAIN+LABOR+GP/REL

COLLECTIVE SECURITY....SEE INT/ORG+FORCES

COLLEGES....SEE ACADEM

COLLINS B.A. H0631

COLLINS B.E. H0632

COLLINS H. H0633

COLLINS I. H0634

COLLINS R.O. H0635

COLOMBIA....SEE ALSO L/A&17C

B41
CHILDS J.B.,COLOMBIAN GOVERNMENT PUBLICATIONS (PAMPHLET). L/A+17C SOCIETY 19/20 COLOMB. PAGE 30 H0593
BIBLIOG GOV/REL NAT/G EX/STRUC

B54
GIRALSO JARAMLLO G.,BIBLIOGRAFIA DE BIBLIOGRAFIAS COLOMBIANAS. L/A+17C ACADEM SECT CREATE EDU/PROP ...ART/METH GEOG LING TREND 20 COLOMB. PAGE 57 H1135
BIBLIOG/A CULTURE PHIL/SCI ECO/UNDEV

B59
SZLUC T.,TWILIGHT OF THE TYRANTS. BRAZIL L/A+17C PERU VENEZUELA NAT/G FORCES CONTROL PERSON MORAL ORD/FREE PWR...CONCPT 20 ARGEN COLOMB. PAGE 151 H3028
TOTALISM CHIEF REV FASCISM

B63
PEREZ ORTIZ R.,ANUARIO BIBLIOGRAFICO COLOMBIANO, 1961. AGRI...INT/LAW JURID SOC LING 20 COLOMB. PAGE 125 H2491
BIBLIOG L/A+17C NAT/G

B64
BERNSTEIN H.,VENEZUELA AND COLOMBIA. L/A+17C VENEZUELA INTELL COLONIAL ATTIT 20 COLOMB. PAGE 16 H0316
CULTURE NAT/LISM LEAD

B65
WURFEL S.W.,FOREIGN ENTERPRISE IN COLOMBIA. FINAN LABOR NAT/G ECO/TAC TAX REGION 20 COLOMB. PAGE 171 H3429
ECO/UNDEV INT/TRADE JURID CAP/ISM

S65
BRANDENBURG F.,"THE RELEVANCE OF MEXICAN EXPERIENCE TO LATIN AMERICAN DEVELOPMENT." BRAZIL CHILE VENEZUELA STRUCT ECO/UNDEV AGRI CREATE ECO/TAC ...STAT RECORD MEXIC/AMER ARGEN COLOMB. PAGE 20 H0405
L/A+17C GOV/COMP

B66
HOYT E.C.,NATIONAL POLICY AND INTERNATIONAL LAW* CASE STUDIES FROM AMERICAN CANAL POLICY* MONOGRAPH NO. 1 -- 1966-1967. PANAMA UK ELITES BAL/PWR EFFICIENCY...CLASSIF NAT/COMP SOC/EXP COLOMB TREATY. PAGE 74 H1483
INT/LAW USA-45 DIPLOM PWR

B67
ANDERSON C.W.,ISSUES OF POLITICAL DEVELOPMENT. BURMA WOR+45 CULTURE TOP/EX ECO/TAC MARXISM ...CHARTS NAT/COMP 20 COLOMB CONGO/LEOP. PAGE 6 H0126
NAT/LISM COERCE ECO/UNDEV SOCISM

B67
DIX R.H.,COLOMBIA: THE POLITICAL DIMENSIONS OF CHANGE. ELITES POL/PAR DOMIN REV...AUD/VIS 20 COLOMB. PAGE 41 H0828
L/A+17C NAT/G TEC/DEV LEAD

S67
PETRAS J.,"GUERRILLA MOVEMENTS IN LATIN AMERICA - I." GUATEMALA PERU VENEZUELA NAT/G COLONIAL LEAD ATTIT PWR...TIME/SEQ METH/COMP 20 COLOMB. PAGE 125 H2497
GUERRILLA REV L/A+17C MARXISM

S67
SANCHEZ J.D.,"DESARROLLO ECONOMICO Y FUTURO DE COLOMBIA." L/A+17C AGRI EXTR/IND FINAN INDUS MARKET INT/TRADE CONTROL...STAT TREND COLOMB. PAGE 137 H2748
ECO/UNDEV FUT NAT/G ECO/TAC

COLONIAL AMERICA....SEE PRE/AMER

COLONIAL....COLONIALISM; SEE ALSO DOMIN

N
BROCKWAY A.F.,AFRICAN SOCIALISM. EUR+WWI GHANA ISLAM UAR ECO/UNDEV CAP/ISM INT/TRADE COLONIAL COERCE GOV/REL DISCRIM 20 NEGRO NKRUMAH/K NASSER/G. PAGE 21 H0423
AFR SOCISM MARXISM

N
CONOVER H.F.,MADAGASCAR: A SELECTED LIST OF REFERENCES. MADAGASCAR STRUCT ECO/UNDEV NAT/G ADMIN ...SOC 19/20. PAGE 32 H0639
BIBLIOG/A SOCIETY CULTURE COLONIAL

N
SCHADERA I.,SELECT BIBLIOGRAPHY OF SOUTH AFRICAN NATIVE LIFE AND PROBLEMS. SOUTH/AFR LAW CULTURE ECO/UNDEV COLONIAL PARTIC...POLICY LING 20. PAGE 138 H2768
BIBLIOG/A SOC AFR STRUCT

N
UNIVERSITY OF FLORIDA LIBRARY,DOORS TO LATIN AMERICA; RECENT BOOKS AND PAMPHLETS. CONSTN CULTURE SOCIETY ECO/UNDEV COLONIAL LEAD GOV/REL NAT/LISM ATTIT...HUM SOC 20. PAGE 159 H3170
BIBLIOG/A L/A+17C DIPLOM NAT/G

N
AFRICAN RESEARCH BULLETIN. AFR CULTURE NAT/G COLONIAL...SOC 20. PAGE 1 H0010
BIBLIOG/A DIPLOM PRESS

N
PUBLISHERS' CIRCULAR, THE OFFICIAL ORGAN OF THE PUBLISHERS' ASSOCIATION OF GREAT BRITAIN AND IRELAND. EUR+WWI MOD/EUR UK LAW PROB/SOLV DIPLOM COLONIAL ATTIT...HUM 19/20 CMN/WLTH. PAGE 1 H0019
BIBLIOG NAT/G WRITING LEAD

N
AFRICAN BIBLIOGRAPHIC CENTER,A CURRENT BIBLIOGRAPHY ON AFRICAN AFFAIRS. LAW CULTURE ECO/UNDEV LABOR SECT DIPLOM FOR/AID COLONIAL NAT/LISM...LING 20. PAGE 4 H0075
BIBLIOG/A AFR NAT/G REGION

N
ASIA FOUNDATION,LIBRARY NOTES. LAW CONSTN CULTURE SOCIETY ECO/UNDEV INT/ORG NAT/G COLONIAL LEAD REGION NAT/LISM ATTIT 20 UN. PAGE 9 H0176
BIBLIOG/A ASIA S/ASIA DIPLOM

N
BURY J.B.,THE CAMBRIDGE ANCIENT HISTORY (12 VOLS.). MEDIT-7 DIPLOM COLONIAL WAR...HUM EGYPT/ANC ROME/EMP BABYLONIA GREECE/ANC. PAGE 25 H0495
BIBLIOG/A SOCIETY CULTURE NAT/G

N
CORDIER H.,BIBLIOTECA SINICA. SOCIETY STRUCT SECT DIPLOM COLONIAL...GEOG SOC CON/ANAL. PAGE 33 H0664
BIBLIOG/A NAT/G CULTURE ASIA

N
HOOVER INSTITUTION,UNITED STATES AND CANADIAN PUBLICATIONS ON AFRICA. CULTURE ECO/UNDEV AGRI TEC/DEV EDU/PROP COLONIAL RACE/REL NAT/LISM ATTIT HEALTH...SOC SOC/WK 20. PAGE 73 H1464
BIBLIOG DIPLOM NAT/G AFR

N
NORTHWESTERN UNIVERSITY LIB,JOINT ACQUISITIONS LIST OF AFRICANA. AFR SOCIETY STRUCT EDU/PROP COLONIAL GP/REL RACE/REL NAT/LISM SOVEREIGN...SOC 20. PAGE 119 H2377
BIBLIOG CULTURE ECO/UNDEV INDUS

NCO
CARRINGTON C.E.,THE COMMONWEALTH IN AFRICA (PAMPHLET). UK STRUCT NAT/G COLONIAL REPRESENT GOV/REL RACE/REL NAT/LISM...MAJORIT 20 EEC NEGRO COLD/WAR. PAGE 27 H0540
ECO/UNDEV AFR DIPLOM PLAN

B00
MARKHAM V.R.,SOUTH AFRICA, PAST AND PRESENT. NETHERLAND SOUTH/AFR CULTURE LEGIS EDU/PROP COLONIAL CHOOSE REPRESENT DISCRIM ATTIT...OBS TIME/SEQ 17/19 NEGRO BOER/WAR. PAGE 103 H2054
WAR LEAD RACE/REL

B00
MOCKLER-FERRYMAN A.,BRITISH WEST AFRICA. FRANCE GERMANY NIGER SIER/LEONE UK CULTURE DIPLOM WAR RACE/REL PRODUC PROFIT WEALTH...POLICY PREDICT 19. PAGE 112 H2232
AFR COLONIAL INT/TRADE CAP/ISM

B00
VOLPICELLI Z.,RUSSIA ON THE PACIFIC AND THE SIBERIAN RAILWAY. MOD/EUR ECO/UNDEV INT/ORG FORCES PLAN DOMIN COLONIAL ROUTINE ATTIT ALL/VALS...OBS HIST/WRIT TIME/SEQ TREND CON/ANAL AUD/VIS CHARTS 18/19. PAGE 163 H3261
NAT/G ACT/RES RUSSIA

B01
GRIFFIN A.P.C.,A LIST OF BOOKS ON THE DANISH WEST INDIES (PAMPHLET). L/A+17C WEST/IND CULTURE LOC/G ...GEOG MGT 18/20. PAGE 61 H1214
BIBLIOG/A SOCIETY COLONIAL ADMIN

B01
GRIFFIN A.P.C.,A LIST OF BOOKS ON PORTO RICO. PUERT/RICO CULTURE LOC/G...GEOG MGT 19/20. PAGE 61 H1215
BIBLIOG/A SOCIETY COLONIAL ADMIN

B02
SEELEY J.R.,THE EXPANSION OF ENGLAND. MOD/EUR S/ASIA UK CULTURE NAT/G FORCES PLAN DOMIN EDU/PROP COLONIAL ROUTINE ATTIT ALL/VALS SOVEREIGN...CONCPT HIST/WRIT PARLIAMENT 18 CMN/WLTH. PAGE 141 H2819
INT/ORG ACT/RES CAP/ISM INDIA

B03
FORTESCUE G.K.,SUBJECT INDEX OF THE MODERN WORKS ADDED TO THE LIBRARY OF THE BRITISH MUSEUM IN THE YEARS 1881-1900 (3 VOLS.). UK LAW CONSTN FINAN NAT/G FORCES INT/TRADE COLONIAL 19. PAGE 52 H1041
BIBLIOG INDEX WRITING

C06
MONTGOMERY H.,"A DICTIONARY OF POLITICAL PHRASES AND ILLUSIONS WITH A SHORT BIBLIOGRAPHY." EUR+WWI MOD/EUR UK AGRI LABOR LOC/G NAT/G COLONIAL CHOOSE RACE/REL. PAGE 112 H2245
BIBLIOG DICTIONARY POLICY DIPLOM

B10
MENDELSSOHN S.,SOUTH AFRICAN BIBLIOGRAPHY (2 VOLS.). SOUTH/AFR EXTR/IND LABOR SECT DIPLOM INT/TRADE COLONIAL RACE/REL DISCRIM...GEOG 20. PAGE 109 H2172
BIBLIOG/A AFR NAT/G NAT/LISM

B10
TEMPERLEY H.W.V.,SENATES AND UPPER CHAMBERS; THEIR USE AND FUNCTION IN THE MODERN STATE... UK WOR-45
PARL/PROC NAT/COMP

CONSTN NAT/G POL/PAR PROVS SECT COLONIAL LEAD CHOOSE REPRESENT PWR...BIBLIOG 19/20 PARLIAMENT SENATE CMN/WLTH HOUSE/LORD. PAGE 153 H3059
LEGIS EX/STRUC

B12
SONOLET L.,L'AFRIQUE OCCIDENTALE FRANCAISE. FRANCE AGRI INDUS NAT/G SECT FORCES INT/TRADE EDU/PROP RACE/REL HEALTH ORD/FREE...CHARTS 19/20 NEGRO AFRICA/W. PAGE 147 H2933
DOMIN ADMIN COLONIAL AFR

B13
BARDOUX J.,L'ANGLETERRE RADICALE; ESSAI DE LA PSYCHOLOGIE SOCIALE (1906-1913). UK CONSTN NAT/G WORKER CREATE BUDGET ECO/TAC ATTIT...POLICY 20 PARLIAMENT LABOR/PAR STRIKE NAVY. PAGE 11 H0215
POL/PAR CHOOSE COLONIAL LEGIS

B16
CALVERT A.F.,SOUTHWEST AFRICA 1884-1914 (2ND ED.). GERMANY EXTR/IND NAT/G FORCES...GEOG AUD/VIS CHARTS 19/20 RESOURCE/N AFRICA/SW. PAGE 25 H0508
COLONIAL ECO/UNDEV AFR

B17
DOS SANTOS M.,BIBLIOGRAPHIA GERAL, A DESCRIPCAO BIBLIOGRAFICA DE LIVROS TANTO DE AUTORES PORTUGUEZES COMO BRASILEIROS... BRAZIL PORTUGAL NAT/G LEAD GP/REL 15/20. PAGE 42 H0840
BIBLIOG/A L/A+17C DIPLOM COLONIAL

B17
HARLOW R.V.,THE HISTORY OF LEGISLATIVE METHODS IN THE PERIOD BEFORE 1825. USA-45 EX/STRUC ADMIN COLONIAL LEAD PARL/PROC ROUTINE...GP/COMP GOV/COMP HOUSE/REP. PAGE 66 H1333
LEGIS DELIB/GP PROVS POL/PAR

N17
BURKE E.,LETTER TO SIR HERCULES LANGRISHE (PAMPHLET). IRELAND UK NAT/G CHIEF DIPLOM DOMIN PARL/PROC COERCE ORD/FREE SOVEREIGN POPULISM ...TRADIT 18 BURKE/EDM. PAGE 24 H0485
POLICY COLONIAL SECT

B18
EYBERS G.W.,SELECT CONSTITUTIONAL DOCUMENTS ILLUSTRATING SOUTH AFRICAN HISTORY 1795-1910. SOUTH/AFR LOC/G LEGIS CT/SYS...JURID ANTHOL 18/20 NATAL CAPE/HOPE ORANGE/STA. PAGE 48 H0955
CONSTN LAW NAT/G COLONIAL

N19
BENTHAM J.,A PLAN FOR AN UNIVERSAL AND PERPETUAL PEACE (1838) (PAMPHLET). NAT/G FORCES BAL/PWR INT/TRADE ADMIN AGREE CT/SYS ARMS/CONT SOVEREIGN WEALTH GEN/LAWS. PAGE 14 H0288
INT/ORG INT/LAW PEACE COLONIAL

N19
GOODMAN G.K.,IMPERIAL JAPAN AND ASIA: A REASSESSMENT (PAMPHLET). ASIA S/ASIA ECO/DEV FORCES LEAD WAR NAT/LISM ATTIT...DECISION CONCPT BIBLIOG 19/20 CHINJAP. PAGE 59 H1172
DIPLOM NAT/G POLICY COLONIAL

N19
HANNA A.J.,EUROPEAN RULE IN AFRICA (PAMPHLET). BELGIUM FRANCE MOD/EUR UK WOR+45 WOR-45 ECO/UNDEV NAT/G PARTIC SOVEREIGN...NAT/COMP 19/20. PAGE 66 H1314
DIPLOM COLONIAL AFR NAT/LISM

N19
PROVISIONS SECTION OAU,ORGANIZATION OF AFRICAN UNITY: BASIC DOCUMENTS AND RESOLUTIONS (PAMPHLET). AFR CULTURE ECO/UNDEV DIPLOM ECO/TAC EDU/PROP COLONIAL ARMS/CONT NUC/PWR RACE/REL DISCRIM NAT/LISM 20 UN OAU. PAGE 128 H2564
CONSTN EX/STRUC SOVEREIGN INT/ORG

N19
SALKEVER L.R.,SUB-SAHARA AFRICA (PAMPHLET). AFR USSR EXTR/IND NAT/G SCHOOL DIPLOM COLONIAL WEALTH ...GEOG CHARTS 16/20. PAGE 137 H2742
ECO/UNDEV TEC/DEV TASK INT/TRADE

N19
SOUTH AFRICA COMMISSION ON FUT,INTERIM AND FINAL REPORTS ON FUTURE FORM OF GOVERNMENT IN THE SOUTH-WEST AFRICAN PROTECTORATE (PAMPHLET). SOUTH/AFR NAT/G FORCES CONFER COLONIAL CONTROL 20 AFRICA/SW. PAGE 147 H2936
CONSTN REPRESENT ADMIN PROB/SOLV

N19
TREVELYAN G.M.,THE TWO-PARTY SYSTEM IN ENGLISH POLITICAL HISTORY (PAMPHLET). UK CHIEF LEGIS COLONIAL EXEC REV CHOOSE 17/19. PAGE 157 H3131
PARL/PROC POL/PAR NAT/G PWR

B23
GRANT C.F.,STUDIES IN NORTH AFRICA. ALGERIA MOROCCO ROMAN/EMP CULTURE STRUCT NAT/G DIPLOM WAR ...NAT/COMP TUNIS EUROPE. PAGE 60 H1195
ISLAM SECT DOMIN COLONIAL

B23
WILLOUGHBY W.C.,RACE PROBLEMS IN THE NEW AFRICA: A STUDY OF THE RELATION OF BANTU AND BRITONS IN THOSE PARTS OF BANTU AFRICA... AFR STRUCT SECT DOMIN EDU/PROP GP/REL ATTIT WORSHIP 20 BANTU EUROPE MISSION CHRISTIAN. PAGE 168 H3372
KIN COLONIAL RACE/REL CULTURE

B25
WILLIAMS B.,THE SELBORNE MEMORANDUM. AFR FUT SOUTH/AFR UK NAT/G BUDGET DIPLOM REGION GOV/REL SOVEREIGN...POLICY CHARTS 20 UNIFICA SELBORNE/W. PAGE 168 H3365
COLONIAL PROVS

B26
MCPHEE A.,THE ECONOMIC REVOLUTION IN BRITISH WEST AFRICA. AFR UK CULTURE DIST/IND FINAN INDUS PLAN GP/REL RACE/REL 20 AFRICA/W. PAGE 107 H2148
ECO/UNDEV INT/TRADE COLONIAL GEOG

B27
PANIKKAR K.M.,INDIAN STATES AND THE GOVERNMENT OF INDIA. INDIA UK CONSTN CONTROL TASK GP/REL SOVEREIGN WEALTH...TREND BIBLIOG 19. PAGE 123 H2457
GOV/COMP COLONIAL BAL/PWR PROVS

B27
SMITH E.W.,THE GOLDEN STOOL: SOME ASPECTS OF THE CONFLICT OF CULTURES IN AFRICA. AFR FINAN INDUS SECT INT/TRADE COERCE CHOOSE RACE/REL ATTIT...GEOG LING 20 NEGRO. PAGE 145 H2907
COLONIAL CULTURE GP/REL EDU/PROP

B28
HURST C.,GREAT BRITAIN AND THE DOMINIONS. EUR+WWI CULTURE ECO/DEV INT/ORG NAT/G DIPLOM ECO/TAC COLONIAL ATTIT PWR SOVEREIGN...TIME/SEQ GEN/LAWS TOT/POP VAL/FREE 20 CMN/WLTH. PAGE 75 H1508
VOL/ASSN DOMIN UK

B29
ROBERTS S.H.,HISTORY OF FRENCH COLONIAL POLICY. AFR ASIA L/A+17C S/ASIA CULTURE ECO/DEV ECO/UNDEV FINAN NAT/G PLAN ECO/TAC DOMIN ROUTINE SOVEREIGN...OBS HIST/WRIT TREND CHARTS VAL/FREE 19/20. PAGE 132 H2642
INT/ORG ACT/RES FRANCE COLONIAL

B30
HULL W.I.,INDIA'S POLITICAL CRISIS. INDIA UK INT/ORG LABOR SECT DELIB/GP LEGIS DIPLOM NEUTRAL REGION CROWD GOV/REL MAJORITY ATTIT 20 NEHRU/J GANDHI/M COMMONWLTH. PAGE 75 H1492
ORD/FREE NAT/G COLONIAL NAT/LISM

B30
OLDMAN J.H.,WHITE AND BLACK IN AFRICA. AFR STRUCT COLONIAL PARTIC DISCRIM ISOLAT PRIVIL 20 SMUTS/JAN NEGRO WHITE/SUP. PAGE 121 H2412
SOVEREIGN ORD/FREE RACE/REL NAT/G

B30
SMUTS J.C.,AFRICA AND SOME WORLD PROBLEMS. RHODESIA SOUTH/AFR CULTURE ECO/UNDEV INDUS INT/ORG SECT PROB/SOLV REGION GOV/REL DISCRIM ATTIT 19/20 LEAGUE/NAT LIVNGSTN/D NEGRO. PAGE 146 H2921
LEGIS AFR COLONIAL RACE/REL

B31
DEKAT A.D.A.,COLONIAL POLICY. S/ASIA CULTURE EX/STRUC ECO/TAC DOMIN ADMIN COLONIAL ROUTINE SOVEREIGN WEALTH...POLICY MGT RECORD KNO/TEST SAMP. PAGE 39 H0785
DRIVE PWR INDONESIA NETHERLAND

B31
HENNIG P.,GEOPOLITIK (2ND ED.). CULTURE MUNIC COLONIAL...CENSUS CHARTS 20. PAGE 70 H1398
GEOG HABITAT CREATE NEIGH

B31
KIRKPATRICK F.A.,A HISTORY OF THE ARGENTINE REPUBLIC. SPAIN UK CONSTN SOCIETY ECO/UNDEV EX/STRUC DIPLOM FOR/AID LEAD WAR ATTIT...BIOG CHARTS 16/20 ARGEN SAN/MARTIN. PAGE 86 H1724
NAT/G L/A+17C COLONIAL

C31
MOGI S.,"THE PROBLEM OF FEDERALISM: A STUDY IN THE HISTORY OF POLITICAL THEORY." CONSTN COLONIAL NAT/LISM SOVEREIGN LAISSEZ PLURISM 18/20. PAGE 112 H2235
FEDERAL CONCPT NAT/G

B32
CARDINALL AW,A BIBLIOGRAPHY OF THE GOLD COAST. AFR UK NAT/G EX/STRUC ATTIT...POLICY 19/20. PAGE 26 H0527
BIBLIOG ADMIN COLONIAL DIPLOM

B33
TANNENBAUM F.,PEACE BY REVOLUTION. ECO/UNDEV AGRI SECT WORKER DIPLOM EDU/PROP DISCRIM OWN WEALTH POPULISM 17/20 MEXIC/AMER INDIAN/AM. PAGE 152 H3043
CULTURE COLONIAL RACE/REL REV

B34
DE CENIVAL P.,BIBLIOGRAPHIE MAROCAINE: 1923-1933. FRANCE MOROCCO SECT ADMIN LEAD GP/REL ATTIT...LING 20. PAGE 37 H0750
BIBLIOG/A ISLAM NAT/G COLONIAL

B34
LOVELL R.I.,THE STRUGGLE FOR SOUTH AFRICA, 1875-1899. GERMANY RHODESIA SOUTH/AFR UK NAT/G ECO/TAC HABITAT WEALTH...POLICY 19. PAGE 99 H1971
COLONIAL DIPLOM WAR GP/REL

B35
GORER G.,AFRICA DANCES: A BOOK ABOUT WEST AFRICAN NEGROES. STRUCT LOC/G SECT FORCES TAX ADMIN COLONIAL...ART/METH MYTH WORSHIP 20 NEGRO AFRICA/W CHRISTIAN RITUAL. PAGE 59 H1181
AFR ATTIT CULTURE SOCIETY

B36
BOYCE A.N.,EUROPE AND SOUTH AFRICA. FRANCE GERMANY ITALY SOUTH/AFR UK INDUS NAT/G CONTROL REV WAR NAT/LISM...CONCPT HIST/WRIT 20. PAGE 20 H0392
COLONIAL GOV/COMP NAT/COMP DIPLOM

B37
DE KIEWIET C.W.,THE IMPERIAL FACTOR IN SOUTH AFRICA. AFR SOUTH/AFR UK WAR...POLICY SOC 19. PAGE 38 H0759
DIPLOM COLONIAL CULTURE

B37
UNION OF SOUTH AFRICA,REPORT CONCERNING ADMINISTRATION OF SOUTH WEST AFRICA (6 VOLS.). SOUTH/AFR INDUS PUB/INST FORCES LEGIS BUDGET DIPLOM EDU/PROP ADJUD CT/SYS...GEOG CHARTS 20 AFRICA/SW LEAGUE/NAT. PAGE 158 H3166
NAT/G ADMIN COLONIAL CONSTN

B38
CARVALHO C.M.,GEOGRAPHIA HUMANA; POLITICA E ECONOMICA (3RD ED.). BRAZIL CULTURE AGRI INDUS DIPLOM COLONIAL GP/REL RACE/REL...LING 20 RESOURCE/N. PAGE 27 H0551
GEOG HABITAT

B38
COUPLAND R.,EAST AFRICA AND ITS INVADERS. AFR ISLAM STRATA SECT FORCES DIPLOM TRIBUTE CONTROL DISCRIM NAT/LISM 19 AFRICA/E EUROPE MISSION. PAGE 34 H0680
CULTURE ELITES COLONIAL MARKET

B38
DUNHAM W.H. JR.,COMPLAINT AND REFORM IN ENGLAND 1436-1714. UK LAW ACADEM NAT/G POL/PAR SCHOOL PRESS COLONIAL PARL/PROC MORAL...SOC/WK ANTHOL 15/18 HAKLUYT/R COWPER/W. PAGE 43 H0865
ATTIT SOCIETY SECT

B38
HOLDSWORTH W.S.,A HISTORY OF ENGLISH LAW; THE CENTURIES OF SETTLEMENT AND REFORM (VOL. X). INDIA UK CONSTN NAT/G CHIEF LEGIS ADMIN COLONIAL CT/SYS CHOOSE ORD/FREE PWR...JURID 18 PARLIAMENT COMMONWLTH COMMON/LAW. PAGE 72 H1451
LAW LOC/G EX/STRUC ADJUD

B38
HOLDSWORTH W.S.,A HISTORY OF ENGLISH LAW; THE CENTURIES OF SETTLEMENT AND REFORM (VOL. XI). UK CONSTN NAT/G EX/STRUC DIPLOM ADJUD CT/SYS LEAD CRIME ATTIT...INT/LAW JURID 18 CMN/WLTH PARLIAMENT ENGLSH/LAW. PAGE 73 H1452
LAW COLONIAL LEGIS PARL/PROC

B38
RAWLINSON H.G.,INDIA: A SHORT CULTURAL HISTORY. INDIA LAW STRATA FORCES INT/TRADE ADMIN COLONIAL PERSON...GEOG HUM BIBLIOG WORSHIP 20. PAGE 130 H2598
CULTURE SECT MYTH ART/METH

B39
ANDERSON P.R.,THE BACKGROUND OF ANTI-ENGLISH FEELING IN GERMANY, 1890-1902. GERMANY MOD/EUR UK NAT/G POL/PAR TOP/EX WAR...IDEA/COMP 19/20. PAGE 7 H0132
DIPLOM EDU/PROP ATTIT COLONIAL

B39
FURNIVALL J.S.,NETHERLANDS INDIA. INDIA NETHERLAND CULTURE INDUS NAT/G DIPLOM ADMIN WEALTH...POLICY CHARTS 17/20. PAGE 54 H1081
COLONIAL ECO/UNDEV SOVEREIGN PLURISM

B40
BROGAN D.W.,THE DEVELOPMENT OF MODERN FRANCE (1870-1939). FRANCE GERMANY UK USSR CONSTN CHIEF LEGIS DIPLOM AGREE COLONIAL WAR NAT/LISM PEACE SOCISM 19/20 TREATY. PAGE 21 H0428
MOD/EUR NAT/G

B40
MEEK C.K.,EUROPE AND WEST AFRICA. AFR EUR+WWI EXTR/IND DIPLOM INT/TRADE EDU/PROP GP/REL...SOC 20. PAGE 108 H2158
CULTURE TEC/DEV ECO/UNDEV COLONIAL

B41
CROTHERS G.D.,THE GERMAN ELECTIONS OF 1907. GERMANY NAT/G EDU/PROP COLONIAL ATTIT. PAGE 35 H0709
CHOOSE PARL/PROC NAT/LISM POL/PAR

B42
BLANCHARD L.R.,MARTINIQUE: A SELECTED LIST OF REFERENCES (PAMPHLET). WEST/IND AGRI LOC/G SCHOOL ...ART/METH GEOG JURID CHARTS 20. PAGE 18 H0353
BIBLIOG/A SOCIETY CULTURE COLONIAL

B42
CONOVER H.F.,FRENCH COLONIES IN AFRICA: A LIST OF REFERENCES. ALGERIA FRANCE MOROCCO SOMALIA SUDAN CULTURE AGRI LOC/G SECT FORCES DIPLOM INT/TRADE NAT/LISM HEALTH...CON/ANAL 20. PAGE 32 H0641
BIBLIOG AFR ECO/UNDEV COLONIAL

B42
CONOVER H.F.,THE NETHERLANDS EAST INDIES: A SELECTED LIST OF REFERENCES. ECO/UNDEV AGRI EXTR/IND LABOR SCHOOL SECT INT/TRADE COLONIAL HEALTH...GEOG 19/20. PAGE 32 H0642
BIBLIOG S/ASIA CULTURE

B42
CONOVER H.F.,NEW ZEALAND: A SELECTED LIST OF REFERENCES (PAMPHLET). NEW/ZEALND ECO/UNDEV AGRI INDUS LABOR NAT/G SCHOOL FORCES DIPLOM COLONIAL WAR ...HUM 20. PAGE 32 H0643
BIBLIOG/A S/ASIA CULTURE

B42
JOSHI P.S.,THE TYRANNY OF COLOUR. INDIA SOUTH/AFR UK ECO/UNDEV NAT/G POL/PAR DIPLOM ECO/TAC WAR ...POLICY 19/20. PAGE 82 H1637
COLONIAL DISCRIM RACE/REL

B42
PAGINSKY P.,GERMAN WORKS RELATING TO AMERICA, 1493-1800; A LIST COMPILED FROM THE COLLECTIONS OF THE NEW YORK PUBLIC LIBRARY. GERMANY PRE/AMER CULTURE COLONIAL ATTIT...POLICY SOC 15/19. PAGE 122 H2442
BIBLIOG/A NAT/G L/A+17C DIPLOM

B42
SIMOES DOS REIS A.,BIBLIOGRAFIA DAS BIBLIOGRAFIAS BRASILEIRAS. BRAZIL ADMIN COLONIAL 20. PAGE 144 H2879
BIBLIOG NAT/G DIPLOM L/A+17C

B43
BROWN A.D.,BRITISH POSSESSIONS IN THE CARIBBEAN AREA: A SELECTED LIST OF REFERENCES. UK NAT/G DIPLOM...GEOG 20 CARIBBEAN. PAGE 22 H0437
BIBLIOG COLONIAL ECO/UNDEV L/A+17C

B43
LEWIN E.,ROYAL EMPIRE SOCIETY BIBLIOGRAPHIES NO. 9: SUB-SAHARA AFRICA. ECO/UNDEV TEC/DEV DIPLOM ADMIN COLONIAL LEAD 20. PAGE 96 H1908
BIBLIOG AFR NAT/G SOCIETY

B44
KNORR K.E.,BRITISH COLONIAL THEORIES 1570-1850. NAT/G DELIB/GP ECO/TAC PERCEPT PWR...WELF/ST METH/CNCPT CONT/OBS TIME/SEQ SIMUL TOT/POP 20. PAGE 87 H1734
ACT/RES DOMIN COLONIAL

L44
HUXLEY J.,"THE FUTURE OF THE COLONIES." AFR SOCIETY NAT/G PLAN DOMIN COERCE ATTIT DRIVE ORD/FREE PWR WEALTH...TIME/SEQ TREND AUD/VIS CHARTS 20. PAGE 76 H1511
ECO/UNDEV FUT COLONIAL

C44
VAN VALKENBURG S.,"ELEMENTS OF POLITICAL GEOGRAPHY." FRANCE COM/IND INDUS NAT/G SECT RACE/REL...LING TREND GEN/LAWS BIBLIOG 20. PAGE 162 H3232
GEOG DIPLOM COLONIAL

N45
INDIA QUARTERLY, A JOURNAL OF INTERNATIONAL AFFAIRS. INDIA LAW CONSTN ECO/UNDEV INT/ORG POL/PAR COLONIAL LEAD PARL/PROC WAR ATTIT...SOC 20 CMN/WLTH. PAGE 2 H0033
BIBLIOG/A S/ASIA DIPLOM NAT/G

B45
HARVARD WIDENER LIBRARY,INDOCHINA: A SELECTED LIST OF REFERENCES. CAMBODIA FRANCE S/ASIA VIETNAM COLONIAL...POLICY 19/20. PAGE 67 H1351
BIBLIOG/A ACADEM DIPLOM NAT/G

B45
US LIBRARY OF CONGRESS,NETHERLANDS EAST INDIES. INDONESIA LAW CULTURE AGRI INDUS SCHOOL COLONIAL HEALTH...GEOG JURID SOC 19/20 NETH/IND. PAGE 160 H3205
BIBLIOG/A S/ASIA NAT/G

B45
WOOLBERT R.G.,FOREIGN AFFAIRS BIBLIOGRAPHY, 1932-1942. INT/ORG SECT INT/TRADE COLONIAL RACE/REL NAT/LISM...GEOG INT/LAW GOV/COMP IDEA/COMP 20. PAGE 170 H3410
BIBLIOG/A DIPLOM WAR

B46
ALLEN J.S.,WORLD MONOPOLY AND PEACE. GERMANY UK USSR FINAN INDUS LG/CO DOMIN CONTROL PEACE PWR WEALTH SOCISM...NAT/COMP 20 MONOPOLY. PAGE 5 H0105
CAP/ISM DIPLOM WAR COLONIAL

B47
CROCKER W.R.,ON GOVERNING COLONIES: BEING AN OUTLINE OF THE REAL ISSUES AND A COMPARISON OF THE BRITISH, FRENCH, AND BELGIAN... AFR BELGIUM FRANCE UK CULTURE SOVEREIGN...OBS 20. PAGE 35 H0705
COLONIAL POLICY GOV/COMP ADMIN

B47
ISAAC J.,ECONOMICS OF MIGRATION. MOD/EUR CULTURE STRATA STRUCT NAT/G COLONIAL WEALTH...OLD/LIB TREND TIME 19/20 EUROPE/W MIGRATION. PAGE 78 H1569
HABITAT SOC GEOG

B48
GUIDE TO THE RECORDS IN THE NATIONAL ARCHIVES. ECO/UNDEV ADMIN COLONIAL 16/20. PAGE 2 H0034
BIBLIOG NAT/G L/A+17C DIPLOM

B48
CLYDE P.H.,THE FAR EAST: A HISTORY OF THE IMPACT OF THE WEST ON EASTERN ASIA. CHINA/COM CULTURE INT/TRADE DOMIN COLONIAL WAR PWR...CHARTS BIBLIOG 19/20 CHINJAP. PAGE 30 H0609
DIPLOM ASIA

B48
FURNIVAL J.,COLONIAL POLICY AND PRACTICE A COMPARATIVE STUDY OF BURMA, AND NETHERLANDS INDIA. BURMA INDONESIA S/ASIA...GEOG OBS GOV/COMP METH/COMP 20. PAGE 54 H1080
COLONIAL NAT/LISM WEALTH SOVEREIGN

B48
MAUGHAM R.,NORTH AFRICAN NOTEBOOK. ALGERIA ISLAM LIBYA MOROCCO STRUCT ECO/UNDEV COLONIAL...SOC OBS AUD/VIS NAT/COMP WORSHIP 20 TUNIS. PAGE 105 H2102
SOCIETY RECORD NAT/LISM

B48
MINISTERE FINANCES ET ECO,BULLETIN BIBLIOGRAPHIQUE. AFR EUR+WWI FRANCE CULTURE STRUCT FINAN NAT/G ACT/RES INT/TRADE ADMIN REGION PRODUC STAT. PAGE 111 H2224
BIBLIOG/A ECO/UNDEV TEC/DEV COLONIAL

B48
PELCOVITS N.A.,OLD CHINA HANDS AND THE FOREIGN OFFICE. ASIA BURMA UK ECO/UNDEV NAT/G ECO/TAC FOR/AID TARIFFS DOMIN COLONIAL GOV/REL SOVEREIGN 19 HONG/KONG TREATY. PAGE 124 H2483
INT/TRADE ATTIT DIPLOM

B49
HINDEN R.,EMPIRE AND AFTER. UK POL/PAR BAL/PWR DIPLOM INT/TRADE WAR NAT/LISM PWR 17/20. PAGE 71 H1420
NAT/G COLONIAL ATTIT POLICY

S49
DEXTER L.A.,"A DIALOGUE ON THE SOCIAL PSYCHOLOGY OF COLONIALISM AND ON CERTAIN PUERTO RICAN PROFESSIONAL PERSONALITY PATTERNS." L/A+17C PUERT/RICO STRATA STRUCT DOMIN ISOLAT DRIVE ...NAT/COMP PERS/COMP HYPO/EXP 20 JEWS NEGRO. PAGE 41 H0813
COLONIAL SOC PSY PERSON

S49
STEINMETZ H.,"THE PROBLEMS OF THE LANDRAT: A STUDY OF COUNTY GOVERNMENT IN THE US ZONE OF GERMANY." GERMANY/W USA+45 INDUS PLAN DIPLOM EDU/PROP CONTROL WAR GOV/REL FEDERAL WEALTH PLURISM...GOV/COMP 20 LANDRAT. PAGE 149 H2977
LOC/G COLONIAL MGT TOP/EX

B50
FIGANIERE J.C.,BIBLIOTHECA HISTORICA PORTUGUEZA. BRAZIL PORTUGAL SECT ADMIN. PAGE 50 H0997
BIBLIOG NAT/G DIPLOM COLONIAL

B50
GLEASON J.H.,THE GENESIS OF RUSSOPHOBIA IN GREAT BRITAIN: A STUDY OF THE INTERACTION OF POLICY AND OPINION. ASIA RUSSIA UK NAT/G AGREE CONTROL REV WAR LOVE PWR TREATY 19. PAGE 57 H1142
DIPLOM POLICY DOMIN COLONIAL

B50
HOBBS C.C.,INDOCHINA, A BIBLIOGRAPHY OF THE LAND AND PEOPLE. VIETNAM CULTURE AGRI INDUS NAT/G SECT ...ART/METH GEOG SOC LING 20. PAGE 72 H1436
BIBLIOG/A S/ASIA COLONIAL ECO/UNDEV

C50
STOKES W.S.,"HONDURAS: AN AREA STUDY IN GOVERNMENT." HONDURAS NAT/G POL/PAR COLONIAL CT/SYS ROUTINE CHOOSE REPRESENT...GEOG RECORD BIBLIOG 19/20. PAGE 149 H2988
CONSTN LAW L/A+17C ADMIN

B51
CATALOGO GENERAL DE LA LIBRERIA ESPANOLA E HISPANOAMERICANA 1901-1930; AUTORES (5 VOLS., 1932-1951). SPAIN COLONIAL GOV/REL...SOC 20. PAGE 2 H0036
BIBLIOG L/A+17C DIPLOM NAT/G

B51
BERNATZIK H.A.,THE SPIRITS OF THE YELLOW LEAVES. BURMA LAOS S/ASIA THAILAND VIETNAM SOCIETY AGRI COLONIAL LEISURE GP/REL PERS/REL ISOLAT AGE HABITAT SEX WORSHIP 20. PAGE 16 H0310
SOC KIN ECO/UNDEV CULTURE

B51
CARRINGTON C.E.,THE LIQUIDATION OF THE BRITISH EMPIRE. AFR NAT/G INT/TRADE COLONIAL RACE/REL ATTIT ORD/FREE...POLICY NAT/COMP 20 CMN/WLTH. PAGE 27 H0541
SOVEREIGN NAT/LISM DIPLOM GP/REL

B51
HALEVY E.,IMPERIALISM AND THE RISE OF LABOR (2ND ED.). UK NAT/G POL/PAR TOP/EX ATTIT ORD/FREE PWR 19/20 PARLIAMENT LABOR/PAR. PAGE 64 H1284
COLONIAL LABOR POLICY WAR

B51
JENNINGS I.,THE COMMONWEALTH IN ASIA. CEYLON INDIA PAKISTAN CULTURE STRATA NAT/G LEGIS DIPLOM COLONIAL ATTIT...DECISION 20 CMN/WLTH. PAGE 80 H1604
CONSTN INT/ORG POLICY PLAN

B51
JENNINGS S.I.,THE COMMONWEALTH IN ASIA. CEYLON INDIA PAKISTAN S/ASIA UK CONSTN CULTURE SOCIETY STRATA STRUCT NAT/G POL/PAR EDU/PROP LEAD WAR 20 CMN/WLTH. PAGE 80 H1608
NAT/LISM REGION COLONIAL DIPLOM

B51
LEONARD L.L.,INTERNATIONAL ORGANIZATION. WOR+45 WOR-45 EX/STRUC FORCES LEGIS ECO/TAC INT/TRADE COLONIAL ARMS/CONT...SOC/WK GOV/COMP BIBLIOG. PAGE 94 H1884
NAT/G DIPLOM INT/ORG DELIB/GP

B51
WABEKE B.H.,A GUIDE TO DUTCH BIBLIOGRAPHIES. BELGIUM INDONESIA NETHERLAND DIPLOM INT/TRADE WAR NAT/LISM KNOWL...ART/METH HUM JURID CON/ANAL 14/20. PAGE 164 H3282
BIBLIOG/A NAT/G CULTURE COLONIAL

B52
ISAACS H.R.,AFRICA: NEW CRISES IN THE MAKING (PAMPHLET). EUR+WWI USA+45 ELITES ECO/UNDEV WAR DISCRIM NAT/LISM ATTIT...POLICY NEW/IDEA CHARTS GOV/COMP 20 NEGRO COLD/WAR. PAGE 78 H1570
COLONIAL AFR RACE/REL ORD/FREE

B52
JULIEN C.A.,L'AFRIQUE DU NORD EN MARCHE: NATIONALISMES MUSULMANS ET SOUVERAINETE FRANCAISE (2ND ED). AFR ALGERIA FRANCE ISLAM MOROCCO NAT/G CONTROL ORD/FREE...POLICY 19/20 TUNIS MUSLIM. PAGE 82 H1641
NAT/LISM COERCE DOMIN COLONIAL

B52
KOLARZ W.,RUSSIA AND HER COLONIES. COM RUSSIA LAW CULTURE ECO/DEV KIN LOC/G SECT TEC/DEV ECO/TAC EDU/PROP REGION COERCE ATTIT PWR SOVEREIGN...SOC TIME/SEQ CON/ANAL VAL/FREE 19/20. PAGE 88 H1749
NAT/G DOMIN USSR COLONIAL

B52
US LIBRARY OF CONGRESS,INTRODUCTION TO AFRICA; A SELECTIVE GUIDE TO BACKGROUND READING. ECO/UNDEV COLONIAL GP/REL...SOC 19/20. PAGE 160 H3208
BIBLIOG/A AFR CULTURE NAT/G

B52
US LIBRARY OF CONGRESS,EGYPT AND THE ANGLO-EGYPTIAN SUDAN: A SELECTIVE GUIDE TO BACKGROUND READING (PAMPHLET). SUDAN UAR UK DIPLOM...POLICY 20. PAGE 160 H3209
BIBLIOG/A COLONIAL ISLAM NAT/G

C52
FIFIELD R.H.,"WOODROW WILSON AND THE FAR EAST." ASIA CHIEF DELIB/GP BAL/PWR CONFER COLONIAL ARMS/CONT WAR...TIME/SEQ NAT/COMP 19/20 WILSON/W LEAGUE/NAT. PAGE 50 H0995
BIBLIOG DIPLOM INT/ORG

B53
DAVIDSON B.,THE NEW WEST AFRICA: PROBLEMS OF INDEPENDENCE. UK AGRI TEC/DEV DIPLOM GP/REL RACE/REL SOVEREIGN...ANTHOL 20 AFRICA/W. PAGE 37 H0744
AFR COLONIAL ECO/UNDEV NAT/G

B53
ELAHI K.N.,A GUIDE TO WORKS OF REFERENCE PUBLISHED IN PAKISTAN (PAMPHLET). PAKISTAN DIPLOM COLONIAL LEAD. PAGE 45 H0903
BIBLIOG S/ASIA NAT/G

B53
MIT CENTER INTERNATIONAL STU,BIBLIOGRAPHY OF THE ECONOMIC AND POLITICAL DEVELOPMENT OF INDONESIA. INDONESIA STRUCT NAT/G COLONIAL LEAD...STAT 20. PAGE 111 H2226
BIBLIOG ECO/UNDEV TEC/DEV S/ASIA

B53
PIERCE R.A.,RUSSIAN CENTRAL ASIA, 1867-1917: A SELECTED BIBLIOGRAPHY (PAMPHLET). USSR LAW CULTURE NAT/G EDU/PROP WAR...GEOG SOC 19/20. PAGE 125 H2508
BIBLIOG COLONIAL ADMIN COM

B53
ROSCIO J.G.,OBRAS. L/A+17C SPAIN DIPLOM REV WAR NAT/LISM TOTALISM PWR SOVEREIGN 19. PAGE 134 H2671
ORD/FREE COLONIAL NAT/G PHIL/SCI

B53
STOUT H.M.,BRITISH GOVERNMENT. UK FINAN LOC/G POL/PAR DELIB/GP DIPLOM ADMIN COLONIAL CHOOSE ORD/FREE...JURID BIBLIOG 20 COMMONWLTH. PAGE 150 H2990
NAT/G PARL/PROC CONSTN NEW/LIB

B53
SWEEZY P.M.,THE PRESENT AS HISTORY. NAT/G PLAN COLONIAL ATTIT...POLICY SOCIALIST 19/20. PAGE 151 H3019
ECO/DEV CAP/ISM SOCISM ECO/TAC

B54
KOLARZ W.,THE PEOPLES OF THE SOVIET FAR EAST. RUSSIA USSR STRUCT LEAD ISOLAT NAT/LISM...CHARTS 20. PAGE 88 H1750
COLONIAL RACE/REL ADJUST CULTURE

B54
MITCHELL P.,AFRICAN AFTERTHOUGHTS. UGANDA CONSTN NAT/G ADJUD COERCE WAR 20 WWI MAU/MAU. PAGE 112 H2230
BIOG CHIEF COLONIAL DOMIN

S54
BALANDIER G.,"SOCIOLOGIE DE LA COLONISATION ET RELATIONS ENTRE SOCIETES GLOBALES." AFR SOCIETY ECO/UNDEV KIN DOMIN EDU/PROP RIGID/FLEX PWR...PSY CONCPT TREND TOT/POP. PAGE 10 H0203
CULTURE SOC COLONIAL

C54
DE GRAZIA A.,"THE COMPARATIVE SURVEY OF EUROPEAN-AMERICAN POLITICAL BEHAV IOR; A RESEARCH PROSPECTUS (PAPER)" EUR+WWI FRANCE GERMANY SPAIN UK USA+45 WOR+45 STRATA POL/PAR DIPLOM EDU/PROP COLONIAL LEAD WAR NAT/LISM CONCPT. PAGE 37 H0752
BIBLIOG R+D METH NAT/COMP

C54
HAMMER E.J.,"THE STRUGGLE FOR INDOCHINA." COM VIETNAM POL/PAR REV CENTRAL NAT/LISM ATTIT...POLICY CHARTS BIBLIOG 20. PAGE 65 H1305
WAR COLONIAL S/ASIA NAT/G

C54
LANDAU J.M.,"PARLIAMENTS AND PARTIES IN EGYPT." UAR NAT/G SECT CONSULT LEGIS TOP/EX PROB/SOLV ADMIN COLONIAL...GEN/LAWS BIBLIOG 19/20. PAGE 90 H1804
ISLAM NAT/LISM PARL/PROC POL/PAR

B55
DE ARAGAO J.G.,LA JURIDICTION ADMINISTRATIVE AU BRESIL. BRAZIL ADJUD COLONIAL CT/SYS REV FEDERAL ORD/FREE...BIBLIOG 19/20. PAGE 37 H0749
EX/STRUC ADMIN NAT/G

B55
HELANDER S.,DAS AUTARKIEPROBLEM IN DER WELTWIRTSCHAFT. PROB/SOLV BAL/PWR BARGAIN CAP/ISM ECO/TAC SOVEREIGN 20. PAGE 69 H1388
NAT/COMP COLONIAL DIPLOM

B55
LIPSCOMB J.F.,WHITE AFRICANS. SOCIETY STRUCT AGRI ECO/TAC ADJUD COLONIAL COERCE PERS/REL ADJUST. PAGE 97 H1937
RACE/REL HABITAT ECO/UNDEV ORD/FREE

B55
PYRAH G.B.,IMPERIAL POLICY AND SOUTH AFRICA 1902-1910. SOUTH/AFR UK NAT/G WAR DISCRIM...CONCPT CHARTS BIBLIOG/A 19/20 CMN/WLTH. PAGE 129 H2570
DIPLOM COLONIAL POLICY RACE/REL

B55
TAN C.C.,THE BOXER CATASTROPHE. ASIA UK USSR ELITES POL/PAR VOL/ASSN FORCES PROB/SOLV DIPLOM ADMIN COLONIAL NAT/LISM PEACE TREATY 19/20 BOXER/REBL. PAGE 152 H3040
REV NAT/G WAR

B55
VIGON J.,TEORIA DEL MILITARISMO. NAT/G DIPLOM COLONIAL COERCE GUERRILLA CIVMIL/REL NAT/LISM MORAL ALL/IDEOS PACIFISM 18/20. PAGE 163 H3253
FORCES PHIL/SCI WAR POLICY

S55
DE SMITH S.A.,"CONSTITUTIONAL MONARCHY IN
NAT/G

BURGANDA." AFR UGANDA UK STRUCT CHIEF REGION INGP/REL ADJUST NAT/LISM SOVEREIGN CONSERVE ...POLICY 19/20 BURGANDA. PAGE 38 H0769 DIPLOM CONSTN COLONIAL

C55

APTER D.E.,"THE GOLD COAST IN TRANSITION." AFR CONSTN LOC/G LEGIS DIPLOM COLONIAL CONTROL GOV/REL ...CHARTS BIBLIOG 20 CMN/WLTH. PAGE 7 H0150 ORD/FREE REPRESENT PARL/PROC NAT/G

B56

CENTRAL AFRICAN ARCHIVES,A GUIDE TO THE PUBLIC RECORDS OF SOUTHERN RHODESIA UNDER THE REGIME OF THE BRITISH SOUTH AFRICA COMPANY, 1890-1923. UK STRUCT NAT/G WRITING GP/REL 19/20. PAGE 28 H0566 BIBLIOG/A COLONIAL ADMIN AFR

B56

DEUTSCH K.W.,AN INTERDISCIPLINARY BIBLIOGRAPHY ON NATIONALISM, 1935-1953. CULTURE SOCIETY SECT ATTIT HABITAT HEREDITY PERCEPT ROLE WEALTH...METH/CNCPT LING 20. PAGE 40 H0798 BIBLIOG/A NAT/LISM COLONIAL ADJUST

B56

HATCH J.C.,NEW FROM AFRICA. AFR FUT UK NAT/G GUERRILLA ATTIT ORD/FREE PWR...AUD/VIS CHARTS 20. PAGE 68 H1354 NAT/LISM COLONIAL RACE/REL

B56

JENNINGS W.I.,THE APPROACH TO SELF-GOVERNMENT. CEYLON INDIA PAKISTAN S/ASIA UK SOCIETY POL/PAR DELIB/GP LEGIS ECO/TAC EDU/PROP ADMIN EXEC CHOOSE ATTIT ALL/VALS...JURID CONCPT GEN/METH TOT/POP 20. PAGE 81 H1610 NAT/G CONSTN COLONIAL

B56

MANNONI D.O.,PROSPERO AND CALIBAN: THE PSYCHOLOGY OF COLONIZATION. AFR EUR+WWI FAM KIN MUNIC SECT DOMIN ADMIN ATTIT DRIVE LOVE PWR RESPECT...PSY SOC CONCPT MYTH OBS DEEP/INT BIOG GEN/METH MALAGASY 20. PAGE 102 H2040 CULTURE COLONIAL

B56

PADMORE G.,PAN-AFRICANISM OR COMMUNISM. AFR FUT NIGERIA INTELL NAT/G COLONIAL FEDERAL ATTIT DRIVE PWR RESPECT WEALTH MARXISM...CONCPT AUD/VIS STERTYP 20. PAGE 122 H2440 POL/PAR NAT/LISM

B56

PHILIPPINE STUDIES PROGRAM,SELECTED BIBLIOGRAPHY ON THE PHILIPPINES, TOPICALLY ARRANGED AND ANNOTATED. PHILIPPINE SECT DIPLOM COLONIAL LEAD...SOC 18/20. PAGE 125 H2501 BIBLIOG/A S/ASIA NAT/G ECO/UNDEV

B56

VIANNA F.J.,EVOLUCAO DE POVO BRASILEIRO (4TH ED.). BRAZIL TEC/DEV COLONIAL GP/REL ATTIT SOVEREIGN ...SOC SOC/INTEG 15/20. PAGE 162 H3247 STRUCT RACE/REL NAT/G

B56

WILSON P.,GOVERNMENT AND POLITICS OF INDIA AND PAKISTAN: 1885-1955; A BIBLIOGRAPHY OF WORKS IN WESTERN LANGUAGES. INDIA PAKISTAN CONSTN LOC/G POL/PAR FORCES DIPLOM ADMIN WAR CHOOSE...BIOG CON/ANAL 19/20. PAGE 169 H3380 BIBLIOG COLONIAL NAT/G S/ASIA

N56

US HOUSE COMM FOREIGN AFFAIRS,REPORT OF THE SPECIAL STUDY MISSION TO AFRICA, SOUTH AND EAST OF THE SAHARA (PAMPHLET). AFR SOUTH/AFR USA+45 STRUCT INT/TRADE PARL/PROC NAT/LISM ATTIT ALL/VALS HEALTH ...POLICY 20 CONGRESS. PAGE 160 H3197 FOR/AID COLONIAL ECO/UNDEV DIPLOM

B57

ALEXANDER L.M.,WORLD POLITICAL PATTERNS. NAT/G PROVS CAP/ISM DIPLOM COLONIAL NAT/LISM...POLICY GEOG CHARTS METH/COMP NAT/COMP 20. PAGE 5 H0101 CONTROL METH GOV/COMP

B57

BISHOP O.B.,PUBLICATIONS OF THE GOVERNMENTS OF NOVA SCOTIA, PRINCE EDWARD ISLAND, NEW BRUNSWICK 1758-1952. CANADA UK ADMIN COLONIAL LEAD...POLICY 18/20. PAGE 17 H0345 BIBLIOG NAT/G DIPLOM

B57

BULLOCK A.,THE LIBERAL TRADITION FROM FOX TO KEYNES. UK CULTURE INTELL CREATE WRITING COLONIAL PERS/REL ATTIT ORD/FREE...POLICY OLD/LIB TRADIT CONCPT 18/20 CHURCHLL/W MILL/JS KEYNES/JM ASQUITH/HH. PAGE 23 H0469 ANTHOL DEBATE LAISSEZ

B57

HERNANDEZ-ARREGU J.,IMPERIALISMO Y CULTURA (LA POLITICA EN LA INTELIGENCIA ARGENTINA). L/A+17C CULTURE ELITES WRITING COLONIAL CROWD ATTIT FASCISM MARXISM SOCISM...BIOG IDEA/COMP 20 ARGEN PERON/JUAN COM/PARTY. PAGE 70 H1403 INTELL CREATE ART/METH HUM

B57

HODGKIN T.,NATIONALISM IN COLONIAL AFRICA. STRATA STRUCT MUNIC NAT/G POL/PAR LEGIS ATTIT SOVEREIGN ...POLICY TREND BIBLIOG 20. PAGE 72 H1444 AFR COLONIAL NAT/LISM DIPLOM

B57

KOHN H.,AMERICAN NATIONALISM. EUR+WWI USA+45 USA-45 COLONIAL REGION 18/20. PAGE 87 H1744 NAT/LISM NAT/COMP FEDERAL DIPLOM

B57

NEUMARK S.D.,ECONOMIC INFLUENCES ON THE SOUTH AFRICAN FRONTIER, 1652-1836. SOUTH/AFR SEA AGRI NAT/G FORCES WORKER DIPLOM INT/TRADE PRICE DEMAND PRODUC...STAT CHARTS 17/19 FRONTIER. PAGE 117 H2341 COLONIAL ECO/UNDEV ECO/TAC MARKET

B57

PALMER N.D.,INTERNATIONAL RELATIONS. WOR+45 INT/ORG NAT/G ECO/TAC EDU/PROP COLONIAL WAR PWR SOVEREIGN ...POLICY T 20 TREATY. PAGE 123 H2451 DIPLOM BAL/PWR NAT/COMP

B57

REAMAN G.E.,THE TRAIL OF THE BLACK WALNUT. CANADA AGRI COLONIAL...CHARTS BIBLIOG 18 GERMANS/PA. PAGE 130 H2604 STRANGE SECT CULTURE

B57

ROBERTSON H.M.,SOUTH AFRICA, ECONOMIC AND POLITICAL ASPECTS. SOUTH/AFR CONSTN CULTURE POL/PAR LEGIS DIPLOM DOMIN COLONIAL...SOC BIBLIOG 19/20. PAGE 132 H2647 RACE/REL ECO/UNDEV ECO/TAC DISCRIM

B57

RUMEU DE ARMAS A.,ESPANA EEN EL AFRICA ATLANTICA. AFR CHRIST-17C PORTUGAL SPAIN DIPLOM ECO/TAC CONTROL 14/16 AFRICA/W. PAGE 136 H2717 NAT/G COLONIAL CHIEF PWR

B57

SOUTH PACIFIC COMMISSION,INDEX OF SOCIAL SCIENCE RESEARCH THESES ON THE SOUTH PACIFIC. S/ASIA ACADEM ADMIN COLONIAL...SOC 20. PAGE 147 H2939 BIBLIOG/A ACT/RES SECT CULTURE

C57

MORRIS-JONES W.H.,"PARLIAMENT IN INDIA." INDIA CONSTN LEGIS CONFER COLONIAL CHOOSE PRIVIL ATTIT ...GOV/COMP BIBLIOG 20. PAGE 113 H2264 PARL/PROC EX/STRUC NAT/G POL/PAR

N57

JENNINGS W.I.,NATIONALISM, COLONIALISM, AND NEUTRALISM (PAMPHLET). ASIA INDIA S/ASIA UK INTELL ACADEM POL/PAR 20. PAGE 81 H1611 NAT/LISM COLONIAL NEUTRAL ATTIT

B58

BRADY A.,DEMOCRACY IN THE DOMINIONS (3RD ED.). CANADA NEW/ZEALND SOUTH/AFR WOR+45 LAW EX/STRUC DOMIN COLONIAL PARL/PROC REPRESENT RACE/REL NAT/LISM WEALTH 20 AUSTRAL CMN/WLTH. PAGE 20 H0399 GOV/COMP POL/PAR POPULISM NAT/G

B58

COWAN L.G.,LOCAL GOVERNMENT IN WEST AFRICA. AFR FRANCE UK CULTURE KIN POL/PAR CHIEF LEGIS CREATE ADMIN PARTIC GOV/REL GP/REL...METH/COMP 20. PAGE 34 H0682 LOC/G COLONIAL SOVEREIGN REPRESENT

B58

LAHBABI M.,LE GOUVERNEMENT MAROCAIN A L'AUBE DU XXE SIECLE. FRANCE MOROCCO CHIEF EX/STRUC LEGIS ORD/FREE PWR...JURID BIBLIOG 19/20. PAGE 90 H1797 NAT/G COLONIAL SOVEREIGN

B58

LOWER A.R.M.,EVOLVING CANADIAN FEDERALISM. CANADA WEST/IND CONSTN PROB/SOLV COLONIAL REGION NAT/LISM ...ANTHOL 20. PAGE 99 H1976 FEDERAL NAT/G DIPLOM RACE/REL

B58

MACRO E.,BIBLIOGRAPHY OF THE ARABIAN PENINSULA (PAMPHLET). KUWAIT SAUDI/ARAB YEMEN COLONIAL...GEOG 19/20. PAGE 101 H2012 BIBLIOG ISLAM CULTURE NAT/G

B58

NICULESCU B.,COLONIAL PLANNING: A COMPARATIVE STUDY. AFR AGRI LOC/G MUNIC NAT/G DELIB/GP COLONIAL 20. PAGE 118 H2356 PLAN ECO/UNDEV TEC/DEV NAT/COMP

B58

STRAUSZ-HUPE R.,THE IDEA OF COLONIALISM. WOR+45 WOR-45 BAL/PWR GOV/REL...POLICY CLASSIF TIME/SEQ GOV/COMP ANTHOL 20 UN. PAGE 150 H2996 IDEA/COMP COLONIAL CONTROL CONCPT

B58

SYME R.,COLONIAL ELITES: ROME, SPAIN, AND THE AMERICAS. CHRIST-17C MOD/EUR SPAIN UK USA-45 CULTURE NAT/G CHIEF TOP/EX...GOV/COMP IDEA/COMP NAT/COMP ROM/EMP GIBBON/EDW TOYNBEE/A. PAGE 151 H3022 COLONIAL ELITES DOMIN

B58

TILLION G.,ALGERIA: THE REALITIES. ALGERIA FRANCE ISLAM CULTURE STRATA PROB/SOLV DOMIN REV NAT/LISM WEALTH MARXISM...GEOG 20. PAGE 155 H3094 ECO/UNDEV SOC COLONIAL DIPLOM

B58

VARG P.A.,MISSIONARIES, CHINESE, AND DIPLOMATS: THE AMERICAN PROTESTANT MISSIONARY MOVEMENT IN CHINA, 1890-1952. ASIA ECO/UNDEV NAT/G PROB/SOLV CAP/ISM EDU/PROP COLONIAL NAT/LISM ATTIT MARXISM...NAT/COMP STERTYP 20 CHINJAP PROTESTANT MISSION. PAGE 162 H3234 CULTURE DIPLOM SECT

C58

FIFIELD R.H.,"THE DIPLOMACY OF SOUTHEAST ASIA: 1945-1958." INT/ORG NAT/G COLONIAL REGION...CHARTS BIBLIOG 20 UN. PAGE 50 H0996 S/ASIA DIPLOM NAT/LISM

B59

BLOOMFIELD L.P.,WESTERN EUROPE AND THE UN - TRENDS AND PROSPECTS. EUR+WWI BAL/PWR DIPLOM ECO/TAC COLONIAL ATTIT PWR...POLICY 20 UN EUROPE/W. PAGE 18 H0359 INT/ORG TREND FUT NAT/G

B59

CARPENTER G.W.,THE WAY IN AFRICA. AFR INDUS MUNIC CULTURE

DIPLOM DOMIN EDU/PROP COERCE DISCRIM NAT/LISM ORD/FREE 20 NEGRO CHRISTIAN. PAGE 27 H0535 SECT ECO/UNDEV COLONIAL

B59
CONOVER H.F.,NIGERIAN OFFICIAL PUBLICATIONS, 1869-1959: A GUIDE. NIGER CONSTN FINAN ACADEM SCHOOL FORCES PRESS ADMIN COLONIAL...HIST/WRIT 19/20. PAGE 33 H0650 BIBLIOG NAT/G CON/ANAL

B59
DEHIO L.,GERMANY AND WORLD POLITICS IN THE TWENTIETH CENTURY. EUR+WWI FRANCE GERMANY MOD/EUR UK USSR NAT/G CHIEF BAL/PWR DOMIN COLONIAL CONTROL LEAD...IDEA/COMP 20 VERSAILLES. PAGE 39 H0783 DIPLOM WAR NAT/LISM SOVEREIGN

B59
GOPAL R.,INDIAN MUSLIMS: A POLITICAL HISTORY (1858-1947). INDIA ISLAM PAKISTAN NAT/G SECT LEGIS LEAD COERCE WAR REPRESENT ISOLAT ORD/FREE 19/20 HINDU MUSLIM. PAGE 59 H1175 COLONIAL GP/REL POL/PAR REGION

B59
LAQUER W.Z.,THE SOVIET UNION AND THE MIDDLE EAST. COM UAR USSR ECO/UNDEV NAT/G VOL/ASSN ECO/TAC EDU/PROP COLONIAL EXEC PWR...TIME/SEQ TREND COLD/WAR 20. PAGE 91 H1819 ISLAM DRIVE FOR/AID NAT/LISM

B59
MAC MILLAN W.M.,THE ROAD TO SELF-RULE. SOUTH/AFR UK CULTURE SOCIETY AGRI LABOR NAT/G INT/TRADE CONTROL GP/REL...SOC 19/20. PAGE 100 H1988 AFR COLONIAL SOVEREIGN POLICY

B59
MADHOK B.,POLITICAL TRENDS IN INDIA. INDIA PAKISTAN UK STRATA ECO/UNDEV POL/PAR LEGIS CAP/ISM DIPLOM COLONIAL CHOOSE MARXISM...SOC TREND 20 GANDHI/M NEHRU/J. PAGE 101 H2014 GEOG NAT/G

B59
NAHM A.C.,JAPANESE PENETRATION OF KOREA, 1894-1910. ASIA KOREA NAT/G...POLICY 20 CHINJAP. PAGE 115 H2303 BIBLIOG/A DIPLOM WAR COLONIAL

B59
PANIKKAR K.M.,THE AFRO-ASIAN STATES AND THEIR PROBLEMS. COM CULTURE KIN POL/PAR SECT DIPLOM EDU/PROP COLONIAL SOVEREIGN...TECHNIC GOV/COMP 20. PAGE 123 H2458 AFR S/ASIA ECO/UNDEV

B59
SITHOLE N.,AFRICAN NATIONALISM. UNIV CULTURE SECT ADMIN COLONIAL CHOOSE. PAGE 145 H2892 RACE/REL AFR NAT/LISM PERSON

S59
LEVINE R.A.,"ANTI-EUROPEAN VIOLENCE IN AFRICA: A COMPARATIVE ANALYSIS." AFR CULTURE NAT/G DIPLOM EDU/PROP COLONIAL REGION COERCE ATTIT PWR...PSY CONCPT TIME/SEQ TREND HYPO/EXP SOC/EXP STERTYP GEN/METH COLD/WAR 20. PAGE 95 H1903 DRIVE ORD/FREE REV

S59
SILBERMAN L.,"CHANGE AND CONFLICT IN THE HORN OF AFRICA." EUR+WWI ITALY UK CULTURE FORCES ECO/TAC ADJUD COLONIAL ATTIT ORD/FREE PWR...DECISION METH/CNCPT HIST/WRIT SOMALI 20. PAGE 144 H2874 AFR TIME/SEQ

B60
AYEARST M.,THE BRITISH WEST INDIES: THE SEARCH FOR SELF-GOVERNMENT. FUT WEST/IND LOC/G POL/PAR EX/STRUC LEGIS CHOOSE FEDERAL...NAT/COMP BIBLIOG 17/20. PAGE 9 H0186 CONSTN COLONIAL REPRESENT NAT/G

B60
BURRIDGE K.,MAMBU: A MELANESIAN MILLENNIUM. ECO/UNDEV PROC/MFG FAM KIN CHIEF COLONIAL COERCE GP/REL DRIVE WEALTH WORSHIP 20 NEW/GUINEA. PAGE 25 H0494 S/ASIA SECT CULTURE MYTH

B60
CARTER G.M.,INDEPENDENCE FOR AFRICA. AFR FUT SOCIETY STRATA ECO/DEV POL/PAR DELIB/GP PLAN DOMIN EDU/PROP COLONIAL REGION ATTIT DRIVE SOVEREIGN ...RECORD INT TIME/SEQ CHARTS 20. PAGE 27 H0544 NAT/G PWR NAT/LISM

B60
CHATTERJI S.K.,AFRICANISM: THE AFRICAN PERSONALITY. KIN NAT/G SECT CREATE DIPLOM COLONIAL GP/REL ATTIT ORD/FREE...LING WORSHIP 20. PAGE 29 H0585 PERSON NAT/LISM AFR CULTURE

B60
CONOVER H.F.,OFFICIAL PUBLICATIONS OF FRENCH WEST AFRICA, 1946-1958. DAHOMEY IVORY/CST NIGER SENEGAL UPPER/VOLT CONSTN AGRI PRESS...CON/ANAL 20. PAGE 33 H0651 BIBLIOG COLONIAL NAT/G AFR

B60
CONOVER H.F.,OFFICIAL PUBLICATIONS OF SOMALILAND, 1941-1959: A GUIDE. SOMALIA AGRI FINAN INT/ORG SCHOOL INT/TRADE PRESS CONFER COLONIAL PARL/PROC 20 CONGRESS. PAGE 33 H0652 BIBLIOG NAT/G CON/ANAL

B60
EASTON S.C.,THE TWILIGHT OF EUROPEAN COLONIALISM. AFR S/ASIA CONSTN SOCIETY STRUCT ECO/UNDEV INDUS NAT/G FORCES ECO/TAC COLONIAL CT/SYS ATTIT KNOWL ORD/FREE PWR...SOCIALIST TIME/SEQ TREND CON/ANAL 20. PAGE 44 H0882 FINAN ADMIN

B60
EMERSON R.,FROM EMPIRE TO NATION: THE RISE TO SELF-ASSERTION OF ASIAN AND AFRICAN PEOPLES. S/ASIA CULTURE NAT/G SECT DIPLOM ATTIT SOVEREIGN MARXISM ...POLICY BIBLIOG 19/20. PAGE 46 H0919 NAT/LISM COLONIAL AFR ASIA

B60
GONZALEZ NAVARRO M.,LA COLONIZACION EN MEXICO, 1877-1910. AGRI NAT/G PLAN PROB/SOLV INCOME ...POLICY JURID CENSUS 19/20 MEXIC/AMER MIGRATION. PAGE 58 H1164 ECO/UNDEV GEOG HABITAT COLONIAL

B60
JEFFRIES C.,TRANSFER OF POWER: PROBLEMS OF THE PASSAGE TO SELFGOVERNMENT. CEYLON GHANA MALAYSIA NIGERIA UK INT/ORG CONSULT DELIB/GP LEGIS DIPLOM CONFER PARL/PROC 20. PAGE 80 H1595 SOVEREIGN COLONIAL ORD/FREE NAT/G

B60
LEYDER J.,BIBLIOGRAPHIE DE L'ENSEIGNEMENT SUPERIEUR ET DE LA RECHERCHE SCIENTIFIQUE EN AFRIQUE INTERTROPICALE (2 VOLS.). AFR CULTURE ECO/UNDEV AGRI PLAN EDU/PROP ADMIN COLONIAL...GEOG SOC/INTEG 20 NEGRO. PAGE 96 H1918 BIBLIOG/A ACT/RES ACADEM R+D

B60
LOMBARDO TOLEDANO V,EL NEONAZISMO; SUS CHARACTERISTICAS Y PELIGROS. GERMANY/W POL/PAR COLONIAL LEAD LOBBY ATTIT 20 NAZI. PAGE 98 H1956 NAT/G FASCISM POLICY DIPLOM

B60
MINER H.M.,OASIS AND CASBAH: ALGERIAN CULTURE AND PERSONALITY IN CHANGE. ALGERIA FRANCE SOCIETY MUNIC COLONIAL ATTIT...INT PROJ/TEST CHARTS 20. PAGE 111 H2221 GP/COMP PERSON CULTURE ADJUST

B60
MORAES F.,THE REVOLT IN TIBET. ASIA CHINA/COM INDIA CULTURE CONTROL COERCE WAR TOTALISM...POLICY SOC WORSHIP 20 TIBET INTERVENT. PAGE 113 H2252 COLONIAL FORCES DIPLOM ORD/FREE

B60
PIERCE R.A.,RUSSIAN CENTRAL ASIA, 1867-1917. ASIA RUSSIA CULTURE AGRI INDUS EDU/PROP REV NAT/LISM ...CHARTS BIBLIOG 19/20 BOLSHEVISM INTERVENT. PAGE 125 H2509 COLONIAL DOMIN ADMIN ECO/UNDEV

B60
PRASAD B.,THE ORIGINS OF PROVINCIAL AUTONOMY. INDIA UK FINAN LOC/G FORCES LEGIS CONTROL CT/SYS PWR ...JURID 19/20. PAGE 128 H2554 CENTRAL PROVS COLONIAL NAT/G

B60
SMITH M.G.,GOVERNMENT IN ZAZZAU 1800-1950. NIGERIA UK CULTURE SOCIETY LOC/G ADMIN COLONIAL ...METH/CNCPT NEW/IDEA METH 19/20. PAGE 146 H2914 REGION CONSTN KIN ECO/UNDEV

B60
STRACHEY J.,THE END OF EMPIRE. UK WOR+45 WOR-45 DIPLOM INT/TRADE DOMIN ADJUST ORD/FREE WEALTH ...SOCIALIST GOV/COMP TIME COMMONWLTH. PAGE 150 H2991 COLONIAL ECO/DEV BAL/PWR LAISSEZ

B60
THE AFRICA 1960 COMMITTEE,MANDATE IN TRUST; THE PROBLEM OF SOUTH WEST AFRICA. GERMANY STRUCT REGION SANCTION CHOOSE DISCRIM...INT/LAW 20 AFRICA/SW UN LEAGUE/NAT TRUST/TERR. PAGE 153 H3066 NAT/G DIPLOM COLONIAL RACE/REL

B60
THEOBOLD R.,THE NEW NATIONS OF WEST AFRICA. GHANA NIGERIA CULTURE INT/ORG ECO/TAC FOR/AID COLONIAL RACE/REL POPULISM...ANTHOL BIBLIOG 20 UN. PAGE 153 H3068 AFR SOVEREIGN ECO/UNDEV DIPLOM

S60
BERG E.J.,"ECONOMIC BASIS OF POLITICAL CHOICE IN FRENCH WEST AFRICA." FRANCE ECO/UNDEV AGRI INDUS NAT/G PLAN LEGIT COLONIAL REGION ATTIT PWR WEALTH ...CONCPT 20. PAGE 15 H0299 AFR ECO/TAC

S60
CROZIER B.,"FRANCE AND ALGERIA." ALGERIA EUR+WWI FRANCE FUT ISLAM ECO/UNDEV NEIGH CONSULT DELIB/GP ECO/TAC COLONIAL COERCE ATTIT...SOC INT CON/ANAL 20. PAGE 36 H0713 NAT/G FORCES GUERRILLA NAT/LISM

B61
ALLIGHAN G.,VERWOERD - THE END. SOUTH/AFR TOP/EX DIPLOM COLONIAL DISCRIM TOTALISM ATTIT AUTHORIT ...BIOG 20 NEGRO VERWOERD/H. PAGE 5 H0107 CONTROL CHIEF RACE/REL NAT/G

B61
ANSPRENGER F.,POLITIK IM SCHWARZEN AFRIKA. FRANCE NAT/G DIPLOM REGION REV NAT/LISM...CHARTS BIBLIOG 19/20. PAGE 7 H0141 AFR COLONIAL SOVEREIGN

B61
APTER D.E.,THE POLITICAL KINGDOM IN UGANDA. UGANDA CULTURE ECO/UNDEV AGRI KIN SECT TOP/EX REGION ATTIT HABITAT CONSERVE...GEOG AUD/VIS 20. PAGE 8 H0153 NAT/LISM POL/PAR COLONIAL ECO/TAC

B61
ATTLEE C.R.,EMPIRE INTO COMMONWEALTH. AFR ASIA CANADA UK NAT/G WAR NAT/LISM ATTIT...POLICY 20 AUSTRAL. PAGE 9 H0179 DIPLOM GP/REL COLONIAL SOVEREIGN

B61
BEARCE G.D.,BRITISH ATTITUDES TOWARDS INDIA 1784-1858. INDIA S/ASIA UK SECT ECO/TAC...POLICY HUM 18/19. PAGE 12 H0246 — COLONIAL ATTIT ALL/IDEOS NAT/G

B61
BIEBUYCK D.,CONGO TRIBES AND PARTIES. AFR CONGO/BRAZ CONSTN NAT/G COLONIAL CHOOSE FEDERAL 20 CONGO/LEOP. PAGE 17 H0333 — KIN POL/PAR GP/REL SOVEREIGN

B61
BOURDIEU P.,THE ALGERIANS (TRANS. BY A.C. ROSS; REV. ED.). ALGERIA ISLAM CULTURE MUNIC CAP/ISM COLONIAL GP/REL ORD/FREE SOVEREIGN 20. PAGE 19 H0385 — SOCIETY STRUCT ATTIT WAR

B61
BROUGHTON M.,PRESS AND POLITICS OF SOUTH AFRICA. SOUTH/AFR NAT/G COLONIAL GP/REL ADJUST 20. PAGE 22 H0435 — NAT/LISM PRESS PWR CULTURE

B61
CARNELL F.,THE POLITICS OF THE NEW STATES: A SELECT ANNOTATED BIBLIOGRAPHY WITH SPECIAL REFERENCE TO THE COMMONWEALTH. CONSTN ELITES LABOR NAT/G POL/PAR EX/STRUC DIPLOM ADJUD ADMIN...GOV/COMP 20 COMMONWLTH. PAGE 27 H0534 — BIBLIOG/A AFR ASIA COLONIAL

B61
CHAKRABARTI A.,NEHRU: HIS DEMOCRACY AND INDIA. ASIA INDIA UK CONSTN ECO/UNDEV SECT DIPLOM COLONIAL PEACE WEALTH...BIBLIOG 20 CONGRESS NEHRU/J GANDHI/M. PAGE 28 H0570 — ORD/FREE STRATA NAT/G CHIEF

B61
COHN B.S.,DEVELOPMENT AND IMPACT OF BRITISH ADMINISTRATION IN INDIA: A BIBLIOGRAPHIC ESSAY. INDIA UK ECO/UNDEV NAT/G DOMIN...POLICY MGT SOC 19/20. PAGE 31 H0619 — BIBLIOG/A COLONIAL S/ASIA ADMIN

B61
DUFFY J.,AFRICA SPEAKS. GHANA TOGO CULTURE ECO/UNDEV PROB/SOLV COLONIAL NEUTRAL DISCRIM NAT/LISM SOVEREIGN ALL/IDEOS...CONCPT ANTHOL SOC/INTEG 20 NEGRO THIRD/WRLD. PAGE 43 H0857 — AFR NAT/G FUT STRUCT

B61
ESTEVEZ A.,ASPECTOS ECONOMICO-FINANCIEROS DE LA CAMPANA SANMARITANA. L/A+17C SPAIN FINAN COLONIAL LEAD ROLE ORD/FREE WEALTH 19 SOUTH/AMER SAN/MARTIN. PAGE 47 H0942 — ECO/UNDEV REV BUDGET NAT/G

B61
FREYRE G.,THE PORTUGUESE AND THE TROPICS. L/A+17C PORTUGAL SOCIETY PERF/ART ADMIN TASK GP/REL ...ART/METH CONCPT SOC/INTEG 20. PAGE 53 H1060 — COLONIAL METH PLAN CULTURE

B61
HEMPSTONE S.,THE NEW AFRICA. AGRI INDUS KIN NAT/G COLONIAL MARXISM...SOC INT TREND NAT/COMP BIBLIOG/A 20. PAGE 69 H1392 — AFR ORD/FREE PERSON CULTURE

B61
HICKS U.K.,DEVELOPMENT FROM BELOW. UK INDUS ADMIN COLONIAL ROUTINE GOV/REL...POLICY METH/CNCPT CHARTS 19/20 CMN/WLTH. PAGE 71 H1414 — ECO/UNDEV LOC/G GOV/COMP METH/COMP

B61
HISTORICAL RESEARCH INSTITUTE,A SHORT BIBLIOGRAPHY OF INDO-MUSLIM HISTORY. INDIA S/ASIA DIPLOM EDU/PROP COLONIAL LEAD NAT/LISM ATTIT...BIOG 19/20. PAGE 71 H1427 — BIBLIOG NAT/G SECT POL/PAR

B61
KHALIQUZZAMAN C.,PATHWAY TO PAKISTAN. INDIA PAKISTAN UK SECT LEGIS CHOOSE RACE/REL ATTIT ORD/FREE 20 MUSLIM. PAGE 85 H1705 — GP/REL NAT/G COLONIAL SOVEREIGN

B61
LA DOCUMENTATION FRANCAISE,L'AFRIQUE A TRAVERS LES PUBLICATIONS DE LA DOCUMENTATION FRANCAISE; BIBLIOGRAPHIE 1945-1961 (PAMPHLET). FRANCE 20. PAGE 90 H1791 — BIBLIOG AFR COLONIAL NAT/G

B61
LEHMAN R.L.,AFRICA SOUTH OF THE SAHARA (PAMPHLET). DIPLOM COLONIAL NAT/LISM. PAGE 93 H1863 — BIBLIOG/A AFR CULTURE NAT/G

B61
LUZ N.V.,A LUTA PELA INDUSTRIALIZACAO DO BRAZIL. BRAZIL L/A+17C AGRI NAT/G TEC/DEV COLONIAL 19/20. PAGE 99 H1981 — ECO/UNDEV INDUS NAT/LISM POLICY

B61
MACLURE M.,AFRICA: THE POLITICAL PATTERN. SOUTH/AFR CULTURE LEGIS DIPLOM COLONIAL RACE/REL 20. PAGE 100 H2005 — AFR POLICY NAT/G

B61
MUNGER E.S.,AFRICAN FIELD REPORTS 1952-1961. SOUTH/AFR SOCIETY ECO/UNDEV NAT/G POL/PAR COLONIAL EXEC PARL/PROC GUERRILLA RACE/REL ALL/IDEOS...SOC AUD/VIS 20. PAGE 114 H2288 — AFR DISCRIM RECORD

B61
PALMER N.D.,THE INDIAN POLITICAL SYSTEM. INDIA ECO/UNDEV SECT CHIEF COLONIAL CHOOSE ALL/IDEOS SOCISM...CHARTS BIBLIOG/A 20. PAGE 123 H2452 — NAT/LISM POL/PAR NAT/G DIPLOM

B61
PANIKKAR K.M.,THE VOICE OF FREEDOM: SELECTED SPEECHES OF PANDIT MOTILAL NEHRU. INDIA UK CONSTN FINAN FORCES LEGIS DIPLOM TAX COLONIAL...POLICY MAJORIT ANTHOL 20 NEHRU/PM. PAGE 123 H2460 — NAT/LISM ORD/FREE CHIEF NAT/G

B61
PANIKKAR K.M.,REVOLUTION IN AFRICA. AFR GUINEA ECO/UNDEV POL/PAR DIPLOM COLONIAL EXEC LEAD SOVEREIGN...CHARTS 20. PAGE 123 H2461 — NAT/LISM NAT/G CHIEF

B61
PAZ O.,THE LABYRINTH OF SOLITUDE; LIFE AND THOUGHT IN MEXICO (TRANS. BY LYSANDER KEMP). INTELL COLONIAL REV...PSY SOC TIME/SEQ 16/20 MEXIC/AMER. PAGE 124 H2480 — CULTURE PERSON PERS/REL SOCIETY

B61
RAO K.V.,PARLIAMENTARY DEMOCRACY OF INDIA. INDIA EX/STRUC TOP/EX COLONIAL CT/SYS PARL/PROC ORD/FREE ...POLICY CONCPT TREND 20 PARLIAMENT. PAGE 130 H2592 — CONSTN ADJUD NAT/G FEDERAL

B61
ROIG E.,MARTI, ANTIIMPERIALISTA. CUBA L/A+17C DIPLOM DOMIN COLONIAL CONTROL LEAD PWR SOVEREIGN ...PHIL/SCI 19 MARTI/JOSE INTERVENT. PAGE 133 H2664 — PERSON NAT/LISM ECO/UNDEV ORD/FREE

B61
ROSE D.L.,THE VIETNAMESE CIVIL SERVICE. VIETNAM CONSULT DELIB/GP GIVE PAY EDU/PROP COLONIAL GOV/REL UTIL...CHARTS 20. PAGE 134 H2672 — ADMIN EFFICIENCY STAT NAT/G

B61
RYDINGS H.A.,THE BIBLIOGRAPHIES OF WEST AFRICA (PAMPHLET). ECO/UNDEV NAT/G COLONIAL REGION ATTIT 20. PAGE 136 H2725 — BIBLIOG/A AFR NAT/COMP

B61
SCHNAPPER B.,LA POLITIQUE ET LE COMMERCE FRANCAIS DANS LE GOLFE DE GUINEE DE 1838 A 1871. FRANCE GUINEA UK SEA EXTR/IND NAT/G DELIB/GP LEGIS ADMIN ORD/FREE...POLICY GEOG CENSUS CHARTS BIBLIOG 19. PAGE 139 H2791 — COLONIAL INT/TRADE DOMIN AFR

B61
UAR MINISTRY OF CULTURE,A BIBLIOGRAPHICAL LIST OF TUNISIA. ISLAM CULTURE NAT/G EDU/PROP COLONIAL ...GEOG 19/20 TUNIS. PAGE 157 H3146 — BIBLIOG DIPLOM SECT

B61
WEST F.J.,POLITICAL ADVANCEMENT IN THE SOUTH PACIFIC. CONSTN CULTURE POL/PAR LEGIS DOMIN ADMIN CHOOSE SOVEREIGN VAL/FREE 20 FIJI TAHITI SAMOA. PAGE 167 H3335 — S/ASIA LOC/G COLONIAL

C61
MOODIE G.C.,"THE GOVERNMENT OF GREAT BRITAIN." UK LAW STRUCT LOC/G POL/PAR DIPLOM RECEIVE ADMIN COLONIAL CHOOSE...BIBLIOG 20 PARLIAMENT. PAGE 112 H2247 — NAT/G SOCIETY PARL/PROC GOV/COMP

B62
ANDREWS W.G.,FRENCH POLITICS AND ALGERIA: THE PROCESS OF POLICY FORMATION 1954-1962. ALGERIA FRANCE CONSTN ELITES POL/PAR CHIEF DELIB/GP LEGIS DIPLOM PRESS CHOOSE 20. PAGE 7 H0140 — GOV/COMP EXEC COLONIAL

B62
BAULIN J.,THE ARAB ROLE IN AFRICA. AFR ALGERIA FUT ISLAM MOROCCO UAR COLONIAL NEUTRAL REV...SOC 20 TUNIS BOURGUIBA. PAGE 12 H0240 — NAT/LISM DIPLOM NAT/G SECT

B62
CARY J.,THE CASE FOR AFRICAN FREEDOM AND OTHER WRITINGS ON AFRICA. AFR UK INDUS LOC/G NAT/G SECT INT/TRADE EDU/PROP GOV/REL RACE/REL ORD/FREE ...CONCPT ANTHOL 19/20. PAGE 27 H0552 — NAT/LISM COLONIAL TREND ECO/UNDEV

B62
DIAZ J.S.,MANUAL DE BIBLIOGRAFIA DE LA LITERATURA ESPANOLA. PRE/AMER SPAIN ECO/UNDEV DIPLOM LEAD ATTIT...SOC 15/20. PAGE 41 H0820 — BIBLIOG L/A+17C NAT/G COLONIAL

B62
GUENA Y.,HISTORIQUE DE LA COMMUNAUTE. FUT ECO/UNDEV NAT/G PLAN EDU/PROP COLONIAL REGION NAT/LISM ALL/VALS SOVEREIGN...CONCPT OBS CHARTS 20. PAGE 62 H1244 — AFR VOL/ASSN FOR/AID FRANCE

B62
HENDERSON W.O.,THE GENESIS OF THE COMMON MARKET. EUR+WWI FRANCE MOD/EUR UK SEA COM/IND EXTR/IND COLONIAL DISCRIM...TIME/SEQ CHARTS BIBLIOG 18/20 EEC TREATY. PAGE 70 H1395 — ECO/DEV INT/TRADE DIPLOM

B62
INGHAM K.,A HISTORY OF EAST AFRICA. NAT/G DIPLOM ADMIN WAR NAT/LISM...SOC BIOG BIBLIOG. PAGE 77 H1534 — AFR CONSTN COLONIAL

B62
JENNINGS I.,PARTY POLITICS: THE STUFF OF POLITICS (VOL.III). UK NAT/G SECT CHIEF INT/TRADE RECEIVE COLONIAL GP/REL NAT/LISM ORD/FREE SOCISM 19/20 — POL/PAR CONSTN PWR

CHURCH/STA WHIG/PARTY. PAGE 80 H1607 ALL/IDEOS

B62
KENNEDY R.,BIBLIOGRAPHY OF INDONESIAN PEOPLES AND CULTURES (2ND REV. ED.). INDONESIA STRUCT ECO/UNDEV SCHOOL EDU/PROP COLONIAL...GEOG SOC LING NAT/COMP 20. PAGE 85 H1689 BIBLIOG S/ASIA CULTURE KIN

B62
MANNING H.T.,THE REVOLT OF FRENCH CANADA 1800-1835. CANADA UK CULTURE GOV/REL RACE/REL...BIBLIOG 19. PAGE 102 H2039 NAT/LISM COLONIAL GEOG

B62
MANSERGH N.,SOUTH AFRICA 1906-1961: THE PRICE OF MAGNANIMITY. SOUTH/AFR LEGIS LEGIT SUFF NAT/LISM ATTIT ORD/FREE 20 NEGRO 20. PAGE 102 H2041 COLONIAL DISCRIM NAT/G

B62
MANSUR F.,PROCESS OF INDEPENDENCE. GHANA INDIA INDONESIA PAKISTAN CONSTN ELITES INTELL STRUCT ACADEM NAT/G REV PWR 20. PAGE 102 H2043 NAT/COMP POL/PAR SOVEREIGN COLONIAL

B62
MELADY T.,THE WHITE MAN'S FUTURE IN BLACK AFRICA. FUT CULTURE SOCIETY NAT/G POL/PAR PLAN ECO/TAC DOMIN EDU/PROP LEGIT COLONIAL RACE/REL ATTIT DRIVE ALL/VALS...PSY SOC CONCPT TIME/SEQ TOT/POP VAL/FREE 20. PAGE 108 H2167 AFR STRATA ELITES

B62
PHILLIPS O.H.,CONSTITUTIONAL AND ADMINISTRATIVE LAW (3RD ED.). UK INT/ORG LOC/G CHIEF EX/STRUC LEGIS BAL/PWR ADJUD COLONIAL CT/SYS PWR...CHARTS 20. PAGE 125 H2503 JURID ADMIN CONSTN NAT/G

B62
SELOSOEMARDJAN O.,SOCIAL CHANGES IN JOGJAKARTA. INDONESIA NETHERLAND ELITES STRATA STRUCT FAM POL/PAR CREATE DIPLOM INT/TRADE EDU/PROP ADMIN GOV/REL...SOC 20 JAVA CHINJAP. PAGE 141 H2825 ECO/UNDEV CULTURE REV COLONIAL

B62
TAYLOR D.,THE BRITISH IN AFRICA. UK CULTURE ECO/UNDEV INDUS DIPLOM INT/TRADE ADMIN WAR RACE/REL ORD/FREE SOVEREIGN...POLICY BIBLIOG 15/20 CMN/WLTH. PAGE 153 H3053 AFR COLONIAL DOMIN

B62
TILMAN R.O.,THE NIGERIAN POLITICAL SXENE. NIGERIA DIPLOM COLONIAL PARTIC...POLICY SOC OBS PREDICT ANTHOL 20. PAGE 155 H3096 NAT/G AFR ECO/UNDEV FEDERAL

B62
ZINKIN T.,REPORTING INDIA. INDIA PAKISTAN WOR+45 SOCIETY SECT FORCES EDU/PROP CROWD DISCRIM NAT/LISM MARXISM...POLICY 20. PAGE 173 H3457 STRATA COLONIAL BAL/PWR CONTROL

L62
ORDONNEAU P.,"LES PROBLEMES POSES PAR L'INDEPENDANCE DES NOUVEAUX ETATS AFRICAINS ET MALGACHE SUR LE PLAN DU CONTENTIEUX." FRANCE ISLAM MADAGASCAR LAW STRATA ECO/UNDEV NAT/G LEGIS LEGIT ...JURID TIME/SEQ 20. PAGE 121 H2425 AFR ADJUD COLONIAL SOVEREIGN

S62
KOLARZ W.,"THE IMPACT OF COMMUNISM ON WEST AFRICA." AFR FUT SOCIETY INT/ORG NAT/G CREATE PLAN DOMIN EDU/PROP COERCE NAT/LISM ATTIT RIGID/FLEX SOCISM ...POLICY CONCPT TREND MARX/KARL 20. PAGE 88 H1751 COM POL/PAR COLONIAL

S62
LANGER W.L.,"FAREWELL TO EMPIRE." EUR+WWI MOD/EUR NAT/G DIPLOM EDU/PROP COLONIAL ATTIT ORD/FREE PWR SOVEREIGN WEALTH...CONCPT TIME/SEQ GEN/LAWS TOT/POP VAL/FREE CMN/WLTH 20. PAGE 91 H1810 DOMIN ECO/TAC NAT/LISM

S62
MURACCIOLE L.,"LES CONSTITUTIONS DES ETATS AFRICAINS D'EXPRESSION FRANCAISE: LA CONSTITUTION DU 16 AVRIL 1962 DE LA REPUBLIQUE DU" AFR CHAD CHIEF LEGIS LEGIT COLONIAL EXEC ROUTINE ORD/FREE SOVEREIGN...SOC CONCPT 20. PAGE 115 H2291 NAT/G CONSTN

S62
PIQUEMAL M.,"LES PROBLEMES DES UNIONS D'ETATS EN AFRIQUE NOIRE." FRANCE SOCIETY INT/ORG NAT/G DELIB/GP PLAN LEGIT ADMIN COLONIAL ROUTINE ATTIT ORD/FREE PWR...GEOG METH/CNCPT 20. PAGE 126 H2515 AFR ECO/UNDEV REGION

S62
ROTBERG R.,"THE RISE OF AFRICAN NATIONALISM: THE CASE OF EAST AND CENTRAL AFRICA." AFR CULTURE SOCIETY NEIGH DIPLOM DOMIN COLONIAL COERCE DISPL PERCEPT PWR SOVEREIGN...POLICY OBS/ENVIR TREND WORK 20. PAGE 135 H2690 ATTIT DRIVE NAT/LISM REV

S62
SARKISYANZ E.,"NATIONALISM, CAPITALISM, AND THE UNCOMMITED NATIONS: MARXISM AND ASIAN CULTURAL TRADITIONS." ASIA BURMA CHINA/COM COM CULTURE SOCIETY NAT/G POL/PAR PLAN DOMIN EDU/PROP COLONIAL COERCE ATTIT RIGID/FLEX...CONCPT TREND MARX/KARL 20 TIBET BUDDHISM. PAGE 138 H2755 S/ASIA SECT NAT/LISM CAP/ISM

S62
SHATTEN F.,"POLYCENTRISM: AFRICA: NATIONALISM AND COMMUNISM." ASIA COM FUT ISLAM CULTURE SOCIETY ECO/UNDEV NAT/G PLAN DOMIN COLONIAL COERCE CHOOSE RIGID/FLEX ALL/VALS MARXISM...CONCPT TREND 20. PAGE 143 H2852 AFR ATTIT NAT/LISM SOCISM

B63
BRITISH AID. UK AGRI DIST/IND INDUS SCHOOL TEC/DEV INT/TRADE COLONIAL DEMAND...TREND CHARTS 20. PAGE 2 H0041 FOR/AID ECO/UNDEV NAT/G FINAN

B63
BIALEK R.W.,CATHOLIC POLITICS: A HISTORY BASED ON ECUADOR. ECUADOR SPAIN CULTURE STRUCT CONTROL REV PWR...BIBLIOG WORSHIP 18/20. PAGE 16 H0329 COLONIAL CATHISM GOV/REL HABITAT

B63
BISHOP O.B.,PUBLICATIONS OF THE GOVERNMENT OF THE PROVINCE OF CANADA 1841-1867. CANADA DIPLOM COLONIAL LEAD...POLICY 18. PAGE 17 H0346 BIBLIOG NAT/G ATTIT

B63
BRECHER M.,THE NEW STATES OF ASIA. ASIA S/ASIA INT/ORG BAL/PWR COLONIAL NEUTRAL ORD/FREE PWR 20 UN. PAGE 20 H0407 NAT/G ECO/UNDEV DIPLOM POLICY

B63
CANELAS O.A.,RADIOGRAFIA DE LA ALIANZA PARA EL ATRASO. L/A+17C USA+45 ECO/TAC DOMIN COLONIAL NAT/LISM...SOCIALIST NAT/COMP 20. PAGE 26 H0519 REV DIPLOM ECO/UNDEV REGION

B63
CONFERENCE ABORIGINAL STUDIES,AUSTRALIAN ABORIGINAL STUDIES. ECO/UNDEV INT/TRADE COLONIAL ADJUST HABITAT HEREDITY...GEOG PSY LING SOC/EXP ANTHOL WORSHIP 20 AUSTRAL ABORIGINES. PAGE 32 H0638 SOC SOCIETY CULTURE STRUCT

B63
DECOTTIGNIES R.,LES NATIONALITES AFRICAINES. AFR NAT/G PROB/SOLV DIPLOM COLONIAL ORD/FREE...CHARTS GOV/COMP 20. PAGE 39 H0781 NAT/LISM JURID LEGIS LAW

B63
ELIAS T.O.,GOVERNMENT AND POLITICS IN AFRICA. CONSTN CULTURE SOCIETY NAT/G POL/PAR DIPLOM REPRESENT PERSON...SOC TREND BIBLIOG 4/20. PAGE 45 H0906 AFR NAT/LISM COLONIAL LAW

B63
FARMER B.H.,CEYLON: A DIVIDED NATION. CEYLON INDIA NETHERLAND PORTUGAL UK ELITES POL/PAR COLONIAL ...SOC MYTH CHARTS GOV/COMP WORSHIP 20. PAGE 49 H0972 DOMIN ORD/FREE ECO/UNDEV POLICY

B63
FAWCETT J.E.S.,THE BRITISH COMMONWEALTH IN INTERNATIONAL LAW. LAW INT/ORG NAT/G VOL/ASSN OP/RES DIPLOM ADJUD CENTRAL CONSEN...NET/THEORY CMN/WLTH TREATY. PAGE 49 H0977 INT/LAW STRUCT COLONIAL

B63
FIRST R.,SOUTH WEST AFRICA. SOUTH/AFR INT/ORG KIN NAT/G WORKER COLONIAL WAR...POLICY 20 UN TRUST/TERR AFRICA/SW. PAGE 50 H1006 DISCRIM ORD/FREE RACE/REL CONTROL

B63
FURTADO C.,THE ECONOMIC GROWTH OF BRAZIL: A SURVEY FROM COLONIAL TO MODERN TIMES. L/A+17C AGRI DIST/IND EXTR/IND INDUS WORKER COLONIAL RACE/REL OWN GOV/COMP. PAGE 54 H1082 ECO/UNDEV TEC/DEV LABOR DOMIN

B63
GARDINIER D.E.,CAMEROON: UNITED NATIONS CHALLENGE TO FRENCH POLICY. AFR CAMEROON FRANCE NAT/G LEGIS CONTROL SOVEREIGN 20 UN. PAGE 55 H1101 DIPLOM POLICY INT/ORG COLONIAL

B63
HAILEY L.,THE REPUBLIC OF SOUTH AFRICA AND THE HIGH COMMISSION TERRITORIES. AFR SOUTH/AFR UK INT/ORG NAT/G PROVS RACE/REL SOVEREIGN...CHARTS 19/20 COMMONWLTH. PAGE 64 H1278 COLONIAL DIPLOM ATTIT

B63
JAIRAZBHOY R.A.,FOREIGN INFLUENCE IN ANCIENT INDIA. INDIA ELITES SECT DIPLOM EDU/PROP COLONIAL REGION GP/REL...ART/METH LING WORSHIP +/14 GRECO/ROMN MESOPOTAM PERSIA PARTH/SASS. PAGE 79 H1587 CULTURE SOCIETY COERCE DOMIN

B63
JENNINGS W.I.,DEMOCRACY IN AFRICA. UK CULTURE STRUCT ECO/UNDEV DIPLOM COLONIAL GP/REL ADJUST NAT/LISM ORD/FREE...GOV/COMP 20 THIRD/WRLD. PAGE 81 H1613 PROB/SOLV AFR CONSTN POPULISM

B63
LAMB B.P.,INDIA: A WORLD IN TRANSITION. INDIA ECO/UNDEV SECT EDU/PROP COLONIAL HABITAT ORD/FREE ...GEOG CHARTS BIBLIOG SOC/INTEG 20. PAGE 90 H1799 POL/PAR NAT/G DIPLOM STRATA

B63
LEE C.,THE POLITICS OF KOREAN NATIONALISM. KOREA S/ASIA DIPLOM REV WAR 14/20 CHINJAP. PAGE 93 H1855 NAT/LISM SOVEREIGN COLONIAL

B63
LEWIN J.,POLITICS AND LAW IN SOUTH AFRICA. SOUTH/AFR UK POL/PAR BAL/PWR ECO/TAC COLONIAL CONTROL GP/REL DISCRIM PWR 20 NEGRO. PAGE 96 H1909 NAT/LISM POLICY LAW RACE/REL

B63
LYON P.,NEUTRALISM. ECO/UNDEV EDU/PROP COLONIAL ALL/IDEOS...IDEA/COMP 20 COLD/WAR UN. PAGE 99 H1985 NAT/COMP NAT/LISM

DIPLOM NEUTRAL

MAC MILLAN W.M.,BANTU, BOER, AND BRITON: THE MAKING OF THE SOUTH AFRICAN NATIVE PROBLEM. SOUTH/AFR UK LAW KIN NAT/G SECT LEGIS COLONIAL ISOLAT ATTIT ...BIOG 18/20 BANTU NEGRO PHILIP/J MISSION. PAGE 100 H1989 — B63 AFR RACE/REL ELITES

MAIR L.,NEW NATIONS. AFR FAM MUNIC SECT DOMIN CHOOSE NAT/LISM ORD/FREE...SOC 19/20. PAGE 101 H2022 — B63 COLONIAL CULTURE TEC/DEV ECO/UNDEV

OTERO L.M.,HONDURAS. HONDURAS SPAIN STRUCT SECT COLONIAL REV WAR ATTIT PWR...GEOG WORSHIP 16/20. PAGE 122 H2432 — B63 NAT/G SOCIETY NAT/LISM ECO/UNDEV

PADELFORD N.J.,AFRICA AND WORLD ORDER. AFR COLONIAL SOVEREIGN...ANTHOL BIBLIOG 20 UN UNIFICA COMMONWLTH. PAGE 122 H2439 — B63 DIPLOM NAT/G ORD/FREE

PRICE A.G.,THE WESTERN INVASIONS OF THE PACIFIC AND ITS CONTINENTS. ASIA PRE/AMER S/ASIA ECO/UNDEV KIN NAT/G SECT FORCES DOMIN HEALTH...SOC 16/20. PAGE 128 H2560 — B63 COLONIAL CULTURE GEOG HABITAT

SETON-WATSON H.,THE NEW IMPERIALISM. COM EUR+WWI MOD/EUR ECO/UNDEV NAT/G FORCES DIPLOM DOMIN EDU/PROP LEGIT COLONIAL EXEC COERCE GP/REL RACE/REL DISCRIM ATTIT...TIME/SEQ 20. PAGE 142 H2833 — B63 ECO/TAC RUSSIA USSR

SINGH H.L.,PROBLEMS AND POLICIES OF THE BRITISH IN INDIA, 1885-1898. INDIA UK NAT/G FORCES LEGIS PROB/SOLV CONTROL RACE/REL ADJUST DISCRIM NAT/LISM RIGID/FLEX...MGT 19 CIVIL/SERV. PAGE 144 H2885 — B63 COLONIAL PWR POLICY ADMIN

VIARD R.,LA FIN DE L'EMPIRE COLONIAL FRANCAIS. AFR FUT S/ASIA ECO/UNDEV NAT/G CONSULT PLAN ECO/TAC EDU/PROP REGION NAT/LISM ALL/VALS...CONCPT TIME/SEQ TREND VAL/FREE 20. PAGE 162 H3248 — B63 VOL/ASSN COLONIAL FRANCE

WALKER A.A.,OFFICIAL PUBLICATIONS OF SIERRA LEONE AND GAMBIA. GAMBIA SIER/LEONE UK LAW CONSTN LEGIS PLAN BUDGET DIPLOM...SOC SAMP CON/ANAL 20. PAGE 164 H3290 — B63 BIBLIOG NAT/G COLONIAL ADMIN

WILCOX W.A.,PAKISTAN; THE CONSOLIDATION OF A NATION. INDIA PAKISTAN CONSTN SECT PROB/SOLV COLONIAL PARTIC GP/REL FEDERAL...POLICY 19/20. PAGE 168 H3361 — B63 NAT/LISM ECO/UNDEV DIPLOM STRUCT

WILSON U.,EDUCATION AND CHANGING WEST AFRICAN CULTURE. AFR MOD/EUR UK CULTURE ECO/UNDEV MUNIC CONSULT 19/20 CMN/WLTH AFRICA/W. PAGE 169 H3384 — B63 COLONIAL POLICY SCHOOL

WODDIS J.,AFRICA, THE WAY AHEAD. AFR FUT ELITES POL/PAR CAP/ISM DIPLOM DOMIN RACE/REL ATTIT ORD/FREE SOVEREIGN SOCISM 20 PANAF/FREE. PAGE 170 H3394 — B63 REV COLONIAL ECO/UNDEV NAT/G

CRUTCHER J.,"PAN AFRICANISM: AFRICAN ODYSSEY." AFR NAT/G POL/PAR PROF/ORG VOL/ASSN TOP/EX CREATE REGION RACE/REL ALL/VALS...CONCPT TIME/SEQ TREND CON/ANAL 20. PAGE 36 H0716 — S63 PROVS DELIB/GP COLONIAL

ROUGEMONT D.,"LES NOUVELLES CHANCES DE L'EUROPE." EUR+WWI FUT ECO/DEV INT/ORG NAT/G ACT/RES PLAN TEC/DEV EDU/PROP ADMIN COLONIAL FEDERAL ATTIT PWR SKILL...TREND 20. PAGE 135 H2696 — S63 ECO/UNDEV PERCEPT

TANNER R.,"WHO GOES HOME?" CULTURE GP/REL SOC/INTEG 20 TANGANYIKA MIGRATION. PAGE 152 H3045 — S63 ADMIN COLONIAL NAT/G NAT/LISM

AGGARWALA R.C.,CONSTITUTIONAL HISTORY OF INDIA AND NATIONAL MOVEMENT INCLUDING COMPARATIVE STUDY OF MODERN INDIA CONSTITUTION. INDIA S/ASIA SECT VOL/ASSN EX/STRUC LEGIS COERCE REV INGP/REL ORD/FREE...SOC BIBLIOG 18/20 CMN/WLTH. PAGE 4 H0077 — B64 CONSTN COLONIAL DOMIN NAT/G

ALDEFER H.F.,A BIBLIOGRAPHY OF AFRICAN GOVERNMENT: 1950-1964. ALGERIA GUINEA LIBERIA UAR ECO/UNDEV POL/PAR LEGIS COLONIAL LEAD PARL/PROC NAT/LISM 20. PAGE 5 H0098 — B64 BIBLIOG AFR LOC/G NAT/G

ARASARATNAM S.,CEYLON. CEYLON NETHERLAND PORTUGAL S/ASIA UK STRUCT ECO/UNDEV SECT DIPLOM DOMIN RACE/REL NAT/LISM 17/20 CMN/WLTH. PAGE 8 H0156 — B64 COLONIAL NAT/G PROB/SOLV CULTURE

BALOGH T.,THE ECONOMIC IMPACT OF MONETARY AND COMMERCIAL INSTITUTIONS OF A EUROPEAN ORIGIN IN AFRICA. AFR UAR INDUS FOR/AID COLONIAL CONTROL ...NAT/COMP 20. PAGE 10 H0205 — B64 TEC/DEV FINAN ECO/UNDEV ECO/TAC

BELL W.,JAMAICAN LEADERS: POLITICAL ATTITUDES IN A NEW NATION. JAMAICA STRUCT ACT/RES CREATE PROB/SOLV DIPLOM COLONIAL LEAD...QU 20. PAGE 13 H0267 — B64 NAT/LISM ATTIT DRIVE SOVEREIGN

BERNSTEIN H.,A BOOKSHELF ON BRAZIL. BRAZIL ADMIN COLONIAL...HUM JURID SOC 20. PAGE 16 H0315 — B64 BIBLIOG/A NAT/G L/A+17C ECO/UNDEV

BERNSTEIN H.,VENEZUELA AND COLOMBIA. L/A+17C VENEZUELA INTELL COLONIAL ATTIT 20 COLOMB. PAGE 16 H0316 — B64 CULTURE NAT/LISM LEAD

BURKE F.G.,AFRICA'S QUEST FOR ORDER. AFR CULTURE KIN MUNIC NAT/G DIPLOM COLONIAL REV DISCRIM NAT/LISM AGE/Y 20. PAGE 24 H0488 — B64 ORD/FREE CONSEN RACE/REL LEAD

BUTWELL R.,SOUTHEAST ASIA TODAY - AND TOMORROW. NAT/G COLONIAL LEAD REGION WAR CHOOSE WEALTH MARXISM 20. PAGE 25 H0500 — B64 S/ASIA DIPLOM ECO/UNDEV NAT/LISM

COWAN L.G.,THE DILEMMAS OF AFRICAN INDEPENDENCE. AFR INDUS NAT/G SECT DIPLOM ECO/TAC REGION MARXISM ...CHARTS BIBLIOG 20 MAPS. PAGE 34 H0683 — B64 ORD/FREE COLONIAL REV ECO/UNDEV

EMBREE A.T.,A GUIDE TO PAPERBACKS ON ASIA; SELECTED AND ANNOTATED (PAMPHLET). CULTURE SOCIETY ECO/UNDEV SECT DIPLOM COLONIAL MARXISM...SOC 20. PAGE 46 H0913 — B64 BIBLIOG/A ASIA S/ASIA NAT/G

GREAT BRITAIN CENTRAL OFF INF,CONSTITUTIONAL DEVELOPMENT IN THE COMMONWEALTH. VOL/ASSN PLAN DIPLOM COLONIAL INGP/REL NAT/LISM ORD/FREE PWR 17/20 CMN/WLTH. PAGE 60 H1202 — B64 REGION CONSTN NAT/G SOVEREIGN

HAMILTON W.B.,THE TRANSFER OF INSTITUTIONS. CANADA INDIA UK LAW AGRI LABOR SECT COLONIAL 18/20. PAGE 65 H1301 — B64 NAT/COMP ECO/UNDEV EDU/PROP CULTURE

HANNA W.J.,POLITICS IN BLACK AFRICA: A SELECTIVE BIBLIOGRAPHY OF RELEVANT PERIODICAL LITERATURE. AFR LAW LOC/G MUNIC NAT/G POL/PAR LOBBY CHOOSE RACE/REL SOVEREIGN 20. PAGE 66 H1315 — B64 BIBLIOG NAT/LISM COLONIAL

HARRIS M.,PATTERNS OF RACE IN THE AMERICAS. BRAZIL L/A+17C STRATA ECO/UNDEV AGRI KIN MUNIC SECT COLONIAL RACE/REL...SOC SOC/INTEG 17/20 NEGRO INDIAN/AM. PAGE 67 H1342 — B64 STRUCT PRE/AMER CULTURE SOCIETY

HOLDSWORTH W.S.,A HISTORY OF ENGLISH LAW; THE CENTURIES OF DEVELOPMENT AND REFORM (VOL. XIV). UK CONSTN LOC/G NAT/G POL/PAR CHIEF EX/STRUC ADJUD COLONIAL ATTIT...INT/LAW JURID 18/19 TORY/PARTY COMMONWLTH WHIG/PARTY COMMON/LAW. PAGE 73 H1453 — B64 LAW LEGIS LEAD CT/SYS

KAUFMANN R.,MILLENARISME ET ACCULTURATION. SOCIETY DOMIN COLONIAL NAT/LISM ATTIT...SOC BIBLIOG 20 JEHOVA/WIT SEVENTHDAY. PAGE 84 H1669 — B64 AFR SECT MYTH CULTURE

KITCHEN H.,A HANDBOOK OF AFRICAN AFFAIRS. ECO/UNDEV CREATE DIPLOM COLONIAL RACE/REL...ART/METH GEOG CHARTS 20. PAGE 87 H1729 — B64 AFR NAT/G INT/ORG FORCES

LAWRENCE P.,ROAD BELONG CARGO: A STUDY OF CARGO MOVEMENT IN SOUTHERN MADANG DISTRICT, NEW GUINEA. S/ASIA CULTURE ECO/UNDEV PROC/MFG KIN CHIEF COLONIAL COERCE GP/REL DRIVE WEALTH WORSHIP 20 NEW/GUINEA. PAGE 92 H1846 — B64 SOC SECT ALL/VALS MYTH

LEMARCHAND R.,POLITICAL AWAKENING IN THE BELGIAN CONGO. ECO/UNDEV VOL/ASSN DOMIN CHOOSE GP/REL INGP/REL DISCRIM ORD/FREE PWR...CHARTS 20 CONGO ARABS. PAGE 94 H1873 — B64 NAT/LISM COLONIAL POL/PAR RACE/REL

MAHAR J.M.,INDIA: A CRITICAL BIBLIOGRAPHY. INDIA PAKISTAN CULTURE ECO/UNDEV LOC/G POL/PAR SECT PROB/SOLV DIPLOM ADMIN COLONIAL PARL/PROC ATTIT 20. PAGE 101 H2016 — B64 BIBLIOG/A S/ASIA NAT/G LEAD

MBEKI G.,SOUTH AFRICA: THE PEASANT'S REVOLT. SOUTH/AFR POL/PAR COERCE REV NAT/LISM ORD/FREE SOVEREIGN 20 NEGRO. PAGE 106 H2114 — B64 COLONIAL RACE/REL DISCRIM DOMIN

MORGENTHAU R.S.,POLITICAL PARTIES IN FRENCH-SPEAKING WEST AFRICA. AFR FRANCE GUINEA IVORY/CST MALI SENEGAL CONSTN LEGIS CREATE PLAN LOBBY PARTIC — B64 POL/PAR NAT/G SOVEREIGN

GP/REL...POLICY BIBLIOG 20. PAGE 113 H2257 COLONIAL

B64
MOUMOUNI A.,L'EDUCATION EN AFRIQUE. UNIV CULTURE ELITES INTELL EDU/PROP ADMIN COLONIAL...LING TREND BIBLIOG 20. PAGE 114 H2271 SCHOOL AFR PROB/SOLV

B64
NICOL D.,AFRICA - A SUBJECTIVE VIEW. AFR INT/ORG PLAN ADMIN COLONIAL PARL/PROC PARTIC REGION GOV/REL LITERACY ATTIT...BIBLIOG 20 CIVIL/SERV. PAGE 118 H2350 NAT/G LEAD CULTURE ACADEM

B64
PERKINS D.,THE AMERICAN DEMOCRACY: ITS RISE TO POWER. ASIA USSR LAW CULTURE FINAN EDU/PROP COLONIAL CHOOSE...POLICY CHARTS BIBLIOG WORSHIP PRESIDENT 15/20 NEGRO. PAGE 125 H2492 LOC/G ECO/TAC WAR DIPLOM

B64
QUIGG P.W.,AFRICA: A FOREIGN AFFAIRS READER. AFR FRANCE PORTUGAL UK DIPLOM LEAD PARL/PROC MARXISM ...MAJORIT METH/CNCPT GOV/COMP IDEA/COMP ANTHOL 19/20. PAGE 129 H2575 COLONIAL SOVEREIGN NAT/LISM RACE/REL

B64
THORNTON T.P.,THE THIRD WORLD IN SOVIET PERSPECTIVE: STUDIES BY SOVIET WRITERS ON THE DEVELOPING AREAS. AFR L/A+17C S/ASIA STRATA AGRI INDUS MARKET NAT/G POL/PAR ECO/TAC COLONIAL PERCEPT PWR WEALTH...MARXIST STAT CHARTS WORK MARX/KARL 20. PAGE 155 H3090 ECO/UNDEV ACT/RES USSR DIPLOM

B64
TILMAN R.O.,BUREAUCRATIC TRANSITION IN MALAYA. MALAYSIA S/ASIA UK NAT/G EX/STRUC DIPLOM...CHARTS BIBLIOG 20. PAGE 155 H3098 ADMIN COLONIAL SOVEREIGN EFFICIENCY

B64
TINKER H.,BALLOT BOX AND BAYONET - PEOPLE AND GOVERNMENT IN EMERGENT ASIAN COUNTRIES. CEYLON INDIA INDONESIA PHILIPPINE POL/PAR ADMIN COLONIAL LEAD PARL/PROC CHOOSE CONSEN ORD/FREE SOVEREIGN PLURISM...GOV/COMP THIRD/WRLD. PAGE 155 H3104 MYTH S/ASIA NAT/COMP NAT/LISM

B64
VOELKMANN K.,HERRSCHER VON MORGEN? BAL/PWR COLONIAL NEUTRAL REGION RACE/REL ALL/VALS SOVEREIGN...RECORD 20 COLD/WAR THIRD/WRLD. PAGE 163 H3259 DIPLOM ECO/UNDEV CONTROL NAT/COMP

B64
WAINHOUSE D.W.,REMNANTS OF EMPIRE: THE UNITED NATIONS AND THE END OF COLONIALISM. FUT PORTUGAL WOR+45 NAT/G CONSULT DOMIN LEGIT ADMIN ROUTINE ATTIT ORD/FREE...POLICY JURID RECORD INT TIME/SEQ UN CMN/WLTH 20. PAGE 164 H3287 INT/ORG TREND COLONIAL

B64
WALLBANK T.W.,DOCUMENTS ON MODERN AFRICA. NAT/G COLONIAL GP/REL ATTIT PWR...BIBLIOG 19/20. PAGE 165 H3294 AFR NAT/LISM ECO/UNDEV DIPLOM

L64
SYMONDS R.,"REFLECTIONS IN LOCALISATION." AFR S/ASIA UK STRATA INT/ORG NAT/G SCHOOL EDU/PROP LEGIT KNOWL ORD/FREE PWR RESPECT CMN/WLTH 20. PAGE 151 H3023 ADMIN MGT COLONIAL

S64
BRADLEY C.P.,"THE FORMATION OF MALAYSIA." INDIA S/ASIA POL/PAR VOL/ASSN TOP/EX LEGIT RACE/REL ORD/FREE 20. PAGE 20 H0398 NAT/G CREATE COLONIAL MALAYSIA

S64
GROSS J.A.,"WHITEHALL AND THE COMMONWEALTH." EUR+WWI MOD/EUR INT/ORG NAT/G CONSULT DELIB/GP LEGIS DOMIN ADMIN COLONIAL ROUTINE PWR CMN/WLTH 19/20. PAGE 62 H1233 EX/STRUC ATTIT TREND

S64
KANOUTE P.,"AFRICAN SOCIALISM." AFR CONSTN NAT/G COLONIAL ORD/FREE...GOV/COMP METH/COMP 20 EUROPE. PAGE 83 H1655 SOCISM CULTURE STRUCT IDEA/COMP

S64
LOW D.A.,"LION RAMPANT." EUR+WWI MOD/EUR S/ASIA ECO/UNDEV NAT/G FORCES TEC/DEV ECO/TAC LEGIT ADMIN COLONIAL COERCE ORD/FREE RESPECT 19/20. PAGE 99 H1972 AFR DOMIN DIPLOM UK

S64
MARTELLI G.,"PORTUGAL AND THE UNITED NATIONS." AFR EUR+WWI ELITES INT/ORG NAT/G PROVS PLAN DIPLOM ECO/TAC DOMIN COLONIAL RIGID/FLEX MORAL ORD/FREE PWR WEALTH...MYTH UN 20. PAGE 103 H2060 ATTIT PORTUGAL

S64
TOYNBEE A.,"BRITAIN AND THE ARABS: THE NEED FOR A NEW START." NAT/G CREATE COLONIAL ATTIT RIGID/FLEX MORAL PWR...POLICY HIST/WRIT 20. PAGE 156 H3124 ISLAM ECO/TAC DIPLOM UK

N64
KENYA MINISTRY ECO PLAN DEV,AFRICAN SOCIALISM AND ITS APPLICATION TO PLANNING IN KENYA (PAMPHLET). AFR AGRI INDUS WORKER TAX COLONIAL WEALTH 20. PAGE 85 H1691 NAT/G SOCISM PLAN ECO/UNDEV

B65
ADAM T.R.,GOVERNMENT AND POLITICS IN AFRICA SOUTH OF THE SAHARA. AFR EUR+WWI CONSTN CULTURE INTELL POL/PAR TOP/EX LEGIT REGION DRIVE...OBS TREND CMN/WLTH 20. PAGE 3 H0062 NAT/G TIME/SEQ RACE/REL COLONIAL

B65
ADU A.L.,THE CIVIL SERVICE IN NEW AFRICAN STATES. AFR GHANA FINAN SOVEREIGN...POLICY 20 CIVIL/SERV AFRICA/E AFRICA/W. PAGE 4 H0074 ECO/UNDEV ADMIN COLONIAL NAT/G

B65
APTER D.E.,THE POLITICS OF MODERNIZATION. AFR L/A+17C CULTURE NAT/G POL/PAR ADMIN COLONIAL NAT/LISM ATTIT RIGID/FLEX PWR...SOC CONCPT. PAGE 8 H0154 ECO/UNDEV GEN/LAWS STRATA CREATE

B65
BERNDT R.M.,ABORIGINAL MAN IN AUSTRALIA. LAW DOMIN ADMIN COLONIAL MARRIAGE HABITAT ORD/FREE...LING CHARTS ANTHOL BIBLIOG WORSHIP 20 AUSTRAL ABORIGINES MUSIC ELKIN/AP. PAGE 16 H0312 SOC CULTURE SOCIETY STRUCT

B65
BLITZ L.F.,THE POLITICS AND ADMINISTRATION OF NIGERIAN GOVERNMENT. NIGER CULTURE LOC/G LEGIS DIPLOM COLONIAL CT/SYS SOVEREIGN...GEOG SOC ANTHOL 20. PAGE 18 H0357 NAT/G GOV/REL POL/PAR

B65
BRASS P.R.,FACTIONAL POLITICS IN AN INDIAN STATE: THE CONGRESS PARTY IN UTTAR PRADESH. INDIA UK CONSTN CULTURE ECO/UNDEV LOC/G DOMIN COLONIAL CROWD GP/REL ADJUST CENTRAL RIGID/FLEX SOVEREIGN 20 UTTAR/PRAD CONGRESS/P. PAGE 20 H0406 POL/PAR PROVS LEGIS CHOOSE

B65
BRIDGMAN J.,GERMAN AFRICA: A SELECT ANNOTATED BIBLIOGRAPHY. AFR AGRI DIPLOM REPAR WAR FASCISM 20. PAGE 21 H0414 BIBLIOG/A COLONIAL NAT/G EDU/PROP

B65
CAMERON W.J.,NEW ZEALAND. NEW/ZEALND S/ASIA DIPLOM INT/TRADE WRITING COLONIAL PARL/PROC...GEOG CMN/WLTH. PAGE 26 H0513 SOCIETY GP/REL STRUCT

B65
COWAN L.G.,EDUCATION AND NATION-BUILDING IN AFRICA. AFR CULTURE ECO/UNDEV POL/PAR ACT/RES LEAD SOVEREIGN...METH/COMP ANTHOL BIBLIOG 20. PAGE 34 H0684 EDU/PROP COLONIAL ACADEM NAT/LISM

B65
FAGG J.E.,CUBA, HAITI, AND THE DOMINICAN REPUBLIC. CUBA DOMIN/REP HAITI L/A+17C NAT/G DIPLOM ECO/TAC DOMIN CHOOSE AUTHORIT ROLE SOVEREIGN POPULISM 17/20. PAGE 48 H0959 COLONIAL ECO/UNDEV REV GOV/COMP

B65
FILIPINIANA BOOK GUILD,THE COLONIZATION AND CONQUEST OF THE PHILIPPINES BY SPAIN. PHILIPPINE SPAIN ELITES AGRI KIN CHIEF DOMIN CONTROL ATTIT PWR ...ANTHOL WORSHIP 16. PAGE 50 H1000 COLONIAL COERCE CULTURE WAR

B65
GHAI D.P.,PORTRAIT OF A MINORITY: ASIANS IN EAST AFRICA. S/ASIA TANZANIA UGANDA COLONIAL...SOC OBS PREDICT ANTHOL 20. PAGE 56 H1119 RACE/REL GP/REL CULTURE AFR

B65
GINIEWSKI P.,THE TWO FACES OF APARTHEID. AFR SOUTH/AFR STRATA AGRI INDUS COLONIAL PARTIC SOVEREIGN...CONCPT GOV/COMP NAT/COMP 19/20 NEGRO. PAGE 56 H1131 DISCRIM NAT/G RACE/REL STRUCT

B65
GOPAL S.,BRITISH POLICY IN INDIA 1858-1905. INDIA UK ELITES CHIEF DELIB/GP ECO/TAC GP/REL DISCRIM ATTIT...IDEA/COMP NAT/COMP PERS/COMP BIBLIOG/A 19/20. PAGE 59 H1176 COLONIAL ADMIN POL/PAR ECO/UNDEV

B65
GRAHAM G.S.,THE POLITICS OF NAVAL SUPREMACY; STUDIES IN BRITISH MARITIME ASCENDANCY. UK SEA NAT/G BAL/PWR LEAD WAR WEAPON PEACE...POLICY 18/19 COMMONWLTH. PAGE 60 H1191 FORCES PWR COLONIAL DIPLOM

B65
GRIMAL H.,HISTOIRE DU COMMONWEALTH BRITANNIQUE. UK FINAN DOMIN ATTIT ORD/FREE...T 15/20 CMN/WLTH. PAGE 61 H1226 NAT/G COLONIAL DIPLOM INT/TRADE

B65
HAPGOOD D.,AFRICA: FROM INDEPENDENCE TO TOMARROW. AFR GUINEA SENEGAL CULTURE ELITES ECO/UNDEV AGRI SCHOOL FOR/AID COLONIAL MARXISM...TREND 20. PAGE 66 H1323 ECO/TAC SOCIETY NAT/G

B65
HAVIGHURST R.J.,SOCIETY AND EDUCATION IN BRAZIL. BRAZIL PORTUGAL ECO/UNDEV INDUS NAT/G CREATE INSPECT COLONIAL ADJUST DEMAND LITERACY...CENSUS TREND CHARTS 16/20. PAGE 68 H1362 SCHOOL ACADEM ACT/RES CULTURE

B65
HISPANIC SOCIETY OF AMERICA,CATALOGUE (10 VOLS.). PORTUGAL PRE/AMER SPAIN NAT/G ADMIN...POLICY SOC 15/20. PAGE 71 H1426 BIBLIOG L/A+17C COLONIAL DIPLOM

B65
KIRKWOOD K.,BRITAIN AND AFRICA. AFR UK ECO/UNDEV ECO/TAC WAR NAT/LISM SOVEREIGN 19/20. PAGE 86 H1725 NAT/G DIPLOM

POLICY COLONIAL B65

KOHN H.,AFRICAN NATIONALISM IN THE TWENTIETH CENTURY. AFR NAT/G POL/PAR COLONIAL REGION DISCRIM SOVEREIGN 20. PAGE 87 H1747 NAT/LISM CULTURE ATTIT B65

MENON K.P.S.,MANY WORLDS. INDIA BAL/PWR CAP/ISM COLONIAL REV ORD/FREE PWR MARXISM...POLICY 20 COLD/WAR. PAGE 109 H2176 BIOG DIPLOM NAT/G B65

MEYER F.S.,THE AFRICAN NETTLE. SOUTH/AFR NAT/LISM SOVEREIGN...ANTHOL 20 EUROPE. PAGE 110 H2191 AFR COLONIAL RACE/REL ECO/UNDEV B65

MONTESQUIEU C DE S.,CONSIDERATIONS ON THE CAUSES OF THE GREATNESS OF THE ROMANS AND THEIR DECLINE (1748 TRANS. BY D. LOWENTHAL). ROMAN/EMP SECT CHIEF EX/STRUC FORCES LEGIS DOMIN WAR POPULISM...POLICY REALPOL ROME/ANC. PAGE 112 H2244 NAT/G PWR COLONIAL MORAL B65

MOORE C.H.,TUNISIA SINCE INDEPENDENCE. ELITES LOC/G POL/PAR ADMIN COLONIAL CONTROL EXEC GOV/REL TOTALISM MARXISM...INT 20 TUNIS. PAGE 112 H2248 NAT/G EX/STRUC SOCISM B65

NAMIER L.B.,THE STRUCTURE OF POLITICS AT THE ACCESSION OF GEORGE III. UK LOC/G TOP/EX COLONIAL LEAD PARTIC REV CHOOSE REPRESENT GOV/REL PERSON SOVEREIGN...GOV/COMP 18 PARLIAMENT. PAGE 115 H2309 PARL/PROC LEGIS NAT/G POL/PAR B65

NEWBURY C.W.,BRITISH POLICY TOWARDS WEST AFRICA: SELECT DOCUMENTS 1786-1874. AFR UK INT/TRADE DOMIN ADMIN COLONIAL CT/SYS COERCE ORD/FREE...BIBLIOG/A 18/19. PAGE 117 H2345 DIPLOM POLICY NAT/G WRITING B65

O'BRIEN W.V.,THE NEW NATIONS IN INTERNATIONAL LAW AND DIPLOMACY* THE YEAR BOOK OF WORLD POLITY* VOLUME III. USA+45 ECO/UNDEV INT/ORG FORCES DIPLOM COLONIAL NEUTRAL REV NAT/LISM ATTIT RESPECT. PAGE 119 H2385 INT/LAW CULTURE SOVEREIGN ANTHOL B65

ORGANSKI A.F.K.,THE STAGES OF POLITICAL DEVELOPMENT. STRATA AGRI INDUS NAT/G POL/PAR COLONIAL PWR WEALTH...CLASSIF TIME/SEQ. PAGE 121 H2428 ECO/DEV ECO/UNDEV GEN/LAWS CREATE B65

PADELFORD N.,THE UNITED NATIONS IN THE BALANCE* ACCOMPLISHMENTS AND PROSPECTS. NAT/G VOL/ASSN DIPLOM ADMIN COLONIAL CT/SYS REGION WAR ORD/FREE ...ANTHOL UN. PAGE 122 H2437 INT/ORG CONTROL B65

PANJABI K.L.,THE CIVIL SERVANT IN INDIA. INDIA UK NAT/G CONSULT EX/STRUC REGION GP/REL RACE/REL 20. PAGE 123 H2462 ADMIN WORKER BIOG COLONIAL B65

PYLEE M.V.,CONSTITUTIONAL GOVERNMENT IN INDIA (2ND REV. ED.). INDIA POL/PAR EX/STRUC DIPLOM COLONIAL CT/SYS PARL/PROC PRIVIL...JURID 16/20. PAGE 128 H2569 CONSTN NAT/G PROVS FEDERAL B65

QURESHI I.H.,THE STRUGGLE FOR PAKISTAN. INDIA PAKISTAN UK CULTURE LEGIS DIPLOM EDU/PROP COLONIAL ATTIT SOVEREIGN 19/20 MUSLIM. PAGE 129 H2576 GP/REL RACE/REL WAR SECT B65

RODRIGUEZ M.,CENTRAL AMERICA. COSTA/RICA GUATEMALA L/A+17C NICARAGUA DIPLOM COLONIAL REGION NAT/LISM ALL/IDEOS SOCISM...MAJORIT TIME/SEQ BIBLIOG 19/20. PAGE 133 H2656 CULTURE NAT/COMP NAT/G ECO/UNDEV B65

ROMEIN J.,THE ASIAN CENTURY. ASIA COM S/ASIA DIPLOM COLONIAL TIME 20. PAGE 133 H2666 REV NAT/LISM CULTURE MARXISM B65

ROTBERG R.I.,A POLITICAL HISTORY OF TROPICAL AFRICA. EX/STRUC DIPLOM INT/TRADE DOMIN ADMIN RACE/REL NAT/LISM PWR SOVEREIGN...GEOG TIME/SEQ BIBLIOG 1/20. PAGE 135 H2692 AFR CULTURE COLONIAL B65

VON RENESSE E.A.,UNVOLLENDETE DEMOKRATIEN. AFR ISLAM S/ASIA SOCIETY ACT/RES COLONIAL...JURID CHARTS BIBLIOG METH 13/20. PAGE 164 H3276 ECO/UNDEV NAT/COMP SOVEREIGN B65

WALKER A.A.,THE RHODESIAS AND NYASALAND: A GUIDE TO OFFICIAL PUBLICATIONS. RHODESIA UK OP/RES PLAN PROB/SOLV DIPLOM...POLICY SOC CON/ANAL 19/20 NYASALAND. PAGE 164 H3291 BIBLIOG NAT/G COLONIAL AFR B65

WARD W.E.,GOVERNMENT IN WEST AFRICA. WOR+45 POL/PAR EX/STRUC PLAN PARTIC GP/REL SOVEREIGN 20 AFRICA/W. PAGE 165 H3308 GOV/COMP CONSTN COLONIAL ECO/UNDEV B65

WILLIAMSON J.A.,GREAT BRITAIN AND THE COMMONWEALTH. UK DOMIN COLONIAL INGP/REL...POLICY 18/20 CMN/WLTH. PAGE 168 H3370 NAT/G DIPLOM INT/ORG SOVEREIGN B65

WOLPERT S.,INDIA. INDIA UK ECO/UNDEV DIPLOM GP/REL WEALTH 20 NEHRU/J. PAGE 170 H3405 CULTURE COLONIAL NAT/LISM SECT L65

SCHAFFER B.B.,"THE CONCEPT OF PREPARATION* SOME QUESTIONS ABOUT THE TRANSFER OF SYSTEMS OF GOVERNMENT." AFR ASIA CANADA ELITES NAT/G POL/PAR COLONIAL RIGID/FLEX IDEA/COMP. PAGE 138 H2769 ECO/UNDEV UK RECORD S65

"FURTHER READING." INDIA ADMIN COLONIAL WAR GOV/REL ATTIT 20. PAGE 2 H0046 BIBLIOG DIPLOM NAT/G POLICY S65

HAYTER T.,"FRENCH AID TO AFRICA* ITS SCOPE AND ACHIEVEMENTS." CULTURE ECO/TAC INT/TRADE ADMIN REGION CENTRAL FEDERAL LOVE PWR SOVEREIGN EEC. PAGE 68 H1370 AFR FRANCE FOR/AID COLONIAL B66

AHMED Z.,DUSK AND DAWN IN VILLAGE INDIA. INDIA S/ASIA UK CULTURE SOCIETY NAT/G DOMIN COLONIAL HABITAT SOVEREIGN...SOC DICTIONARY 20. PAGE 4 H0080 NEIGH ECO/UNDEV AGRI ADJUST B66

BASDEN G.T.,NIGER IBOS. NIGERIA STRUCT SECT CHIEF COLONIAL HABITAT...POLICY SOC MYTH OBS WORSHIP 20 IBO. PAGE 12 H0233 CULTURE AFR SOCIETY B66

BIRMINGHAM D.,TRADE AND CONFLICT IN ANGOLA. PORTUGAL CULTURE FORCES DIPLOM GP/REL PROFIT HABITAT NAT/COMP. PAGE 17 H0341 WAR INT/TRADE ECO/UNDEV COLONIAL B66

BRAIBANTI R.,ASIAN BUREAUCRATIC SYSTEMS EMERGENT FROM THE BRITISH IMPERIAL TRADITION. BURMA CEYLON INDIA PAKISTAN UK ELITES ECO/UNDEV NAT/G...MGT SOC CHARTS ANTHOL 19/20. PAGE 20 H0401 GOV/COMP COLONIAL ADMIN S/ASIA B66

BROWN L.C.,STATE AND SOCIETY IN INDEPENDENT NORTH AFRICA. ALGERIA LIBYA MOROCCO AGRI INDUS INT/ORG POL/PAR SECT PLAN DIPLOM COLONIAL...LING NAT/COMP ANTHOL BIBLIOG 20 TUNIS MUSLIM. PAGE 22 H0446 NAT/G SOCIETY CULTURE ECO/UNDEV B66

CADY J.F.,THAILAND, BURMA, LAOS AND CAMBODIA. FRANCE UK CULTURE NAT/G DOMIN GP/REL RACE/REL HABITAT...GEOG TREND CHINJAP BUDDHISM. PAGE 25 H0504 S/ASIA COLONIAL REGION SECT B66

CROWDER M.,A SHORT HISTORY OF NIGERIA. AFR NIGERIA UK ECO/UNDEV CHIEF INT/TRADE RACE/REL NAT/LISM ORD/FREE...GEOG SOC CHARTS BIBLIOG 14/20. PAGE 36 H0711 COLONIAL NAT/G CULTURE B66

DIAMOND S.,THE TRANSFORMATION OF EAST AFRICA. NAT/G SCHOOL CREATE PROB/SOLV COLONIAL REGION RACE/REL FEDERAL...SOC ANTHOL WORSHIP 20 AFRICA/E. PAGE 41 H0819 CULTURE AFR TEC/DEV INDUS B66

DODGE D.,AFRICAN POLITICS IN PERSPECTIVE. ELITES POL/PAR PROB/SOLV LEAD...POLICY 20 THIRD/WRLD. PAGE 41 H0831 AFR NAT/G COLONIAL SOVEREIGN B66

FIELDHOUSE D.K.,THE COLONIAL EMPIRES: A COMPARATIVE SURVEY FROM THE 18TH CENTURY. UK WOR-45 REV HABITAT 17/18. PAGE 50 H0994 NAT/COMP COLONIAL NAT/G DOMIN B66

FITZGERALD C.P.,A CONCISE HISTORY OF EAST ASIA. ASIA KOREA S/ASIA INT/TRADE REGION MARXISM 20 CHINJAP. PAGE 51 H1017 ECO/UNDEV COLONIAL CULTURE B66

FLINT J.E.,NIGERIA AND GHANA. AFR GHANA NIGERIA UK NAT/G DOMIN DISCRIM...CHARTS BIBLIOG/A 15/20 NEGRO MAPS. PAGE 51 H1026 CULTURE COLONIAL NAT/LISM B66

HAMILTON W.B.,A DECADE OF THE COMMONWEALTH, 1955-1964. UK LAW ELITES FINAN FOR/AID CONFER COLONIAL PWR...GEOG CHARTS ANTHOL 20 CMN/WLTH UN. PAGE 65 H1302 INT/ORG INGP/REL DIPLOM NAT/G B66

HARRISON B.,SOUTH-EAST ASIA: A SHORT HISTORY (3RD ED.). ECO/UNDEV INDUS NAT/G SECT BAL/PWR NAT/LISM ...SOC 15/20 S/EASTASIA. PAGE 67 H1346 COLONIAL S/ASIA CULTURE B66

HOWE R.W.,BLACK AFRICA: FROM PRE-HISTORY TO THE EVE OF THE COLONIAL ERA. ECO/UNDEV KIN PROVS SECT INT/TRADE EDU/PROP COLONIAL...BIBLIOG WORSHIP. PAGE 74 H1482 AFR CULTURE SOC

B66
KAUNDA K.,ZAMBIA: INDEPENDENCE AND BEYOND: THE SPEECHES OF KENNETH KAUNDA. AFR FUT ZAMBIA SOCIETY ECO/UNDEV NAT/G PROB/SOLV ECO/TAC ADMIN RACE/REL SOVEREIGN 20. PAGE 84 H1670
ORD/FREE COLONIAL CONSTN LEAD

B66
LEYBURN J.G.,THE HAITIAN PEOPLE (REV. ED.). HAITI SOCIETY FAM SECT DOMIN COLONIAL MARRIAGE...SOC CHARTS BIBLIOG/A 18/10. PAGE 96 H1917
STRUCT STRATA INGP/REL CULTURE

B66
LONDON K.,EASTERN EUROPE IN TRANSITION. CHINA/COM USSR DOMIN COLONIAL CENTRAL RIGID/FLEX PWR...SOC ANTHOL 20. PAGE 98 H1958
SOVEREIGN COM NAT/LISM DIPLOM

B66
MASUR G.,NATIONALISM IN LATIN AMERICA* DIVERSITY AND UNITY. CHRIST-17C PRE/AMER ELITES ECO/UNDEV CREATE DIPLOM INT/TRADE COLONIAL REV SOVEREIGN SOC. PAGE 105 H2089
L/A+17C NAT/LISM CULTURE

B66
MILONE P.D.,URBAN AREAS IN INDONESIA. INDONESIA LABOR NAT/G COLONIAL GP/REL...CENSUS CHARTS 17/20. PAGE 111 H2218
MUNIC GEOG STRUCT SOCIETY

B66
MULLER C.F.J.,A SELECT BIBLIOGRAPHY OF SOUTH AFRICAN HISTORY; A GUIDE FOR HISTORICAL RESEARCH. SOUTH/AFR UK LAW CONSTN SOCIETY STRUCT AGRI SECT DIPLOM COLONIAL LEAD RACE/REL...POLICY 17/20 NEGRO. PAGE 114 H2284
BIBLIOG AFR NAT/G

B66
O'NEILL C.E.,CHURCH AND STATE IN FRENCH COLONIAL LOUISIANA: POLICY AND POLITICS TO 1732. PROVS VOL/ASSN DELIB/GP ADJUD ADMIN GP/REL ATTIT DRIVE ...POLICY BIBLIOG 17/18 LOUISIANA CHURCH/STA. PAGE 120 H2390
COLONIAL NAT/G SECT PWR

B66
SCHATTEN F.,COMMUNISM IN AFRICA. AFR GHANA GUINEA MALI CULTURE ECO/UNDEV LABOR SECT ECO/TAC EDU/PROP REV 20. PAGE 139 H2774
COLONIAL NAT/LISM MARXISM DIPLOM

B66
SMITH H.E.,READINGS IN ECONOMIC DEVELOPMENT AND ADMINISTRATION IN TANZANIA. TANZANIA FINAN INDUS LABOR NAT/G PLAN PROB/SOLV INT/TRADE COLONIAL REGION...ANTHOL BIBLIOG 20 AFRICA/E. PAGE 146 H2910
TEC/DEV ADMIN GOV/REL

B66
SYMONDS R.,THE BRITISH AND THEIR SUCCESSORS. AFR CEYLON INDIA UK SCHOOL FORCES EDU/PROP ADMIN PARTIC ...NAT/COMP BIBLIOG 20 AFRICA/W AFRICA/E. PAGE 151 H3024
NAT/G ECO/UNDEV POLICY COLONIAL

B66
US LIBRARY OF CONGRESS,NIGERIA: A GUIDE TO OFFICIAL PUBLICATIONS. CAMEROON NIGERIA UK DIPLOM...POLICY 19/20 UN LEAGUE/NAT. PAGE 161 H3215
BIBLIOG ADMIN NAT/G COLONIAL

B66
VIEN N.C.,SEEKING THE TRUTH. VIETNAM DELIB/GP DOMIN RISK MARXISM 20 KY/NGUYEN. PAGE 162 H3250
NAT/G COLONIAL PWR SOVEREIGN

B66
WEINSTEIN B.,GABON: NATION-BUILDING ON THE OGOOUE. AFR GABON WOR+45 CULTURE SOCIETY PLAN DIPLOM COLONIAL INGP/REL ANOMIE HABITAT SUPEGO 20. PAGE 166 H3329
ECO/UNDEV GP/REL LEAD NAT/G

B66
WHEELER G.,THE PEOPLES OF SOVIET CENTRAL ASIA: A BACKGROUND BOOK. ISLAM USSR STRATA STRUCT FORCES REV WAR HABITAT 7/20. PAGE 167 H3341
COLONIAL DOMIN CULTURE ADJUST

B66
WILLNER A.R.,THE NEOTRADITIONAL ACCOMMODATION TO POLITICAL INDEPENDENCE* THE CASE OF INDONESIA * RESEARCH MONOGRAPH NO. 26. CULTURE ECO/UNDEV CREATE PROB/SOLV FOR/AID LEGIT COLONIAL EFFICIENCY NAT/LISM ALL/VALS SOC. PAGE 168 H3371
INDONESIA CONSERVE ELITES ADMIN

B66
ZOLBERG A.R.,CREATING POLITICAL ORDER. AFR CONGO/BRAZ GHANA NIGER KIN NAT/G DOMIN COLONIAL REGION CENTRAL NAT/LISM ATTIT PWR 20 CONGO/LEOP. PAGE 173 H3462
SOVEREIGN ORD/FREE CONSTN POL/PAR

S66
"RESEARCH WORK 1965-1966." NEW/ZEALND ELITES ACADEM LOC/G MUNIC POL/PAR PROVS DIPLOM COLONIAL...SOC 20 AUSTRAL. PAGE 2 H0047
BIBLIOG NAT/G CULTURE S/ASIA

S66
DETTER I.,"THE PROBLEM OF UNEQUAL TREATIES." CONSTN NAT/G LEGIS COLONIAL COERCE PWR...GEOG UN TIME TREATY. PAGE 40 H0796
SOVEREIGN DOMIN INT/LAW ECO/UNDEV

S66
FLEMING W.G.,"AUTHORITY, EFFICIENCY, AND ROLE STRESS: PROBLEMS IN THE DEVELOPMENT OF EAST AFRICAN BUREAUCRACIES." AFR UGANDA STRUCT PROB/SOLV ROUTINE INGP/REL ROLE...MGT SOC GP/COMP GOV/COMP 20 TANGANYIKA AFRICA/E. PAGE 51 H1024
DOMIN EFFICIENCY COLONIAL ADMIN

S66
KAPIL R.L.,"ON THE CONFLICT POTENTIAL OF INHERITED BOUNDARIES IN AFRICA." MOD/EUR MOROCCO UAR EX/STRUC DIPLOM LEGIT REGION ADJUST...RECORD NAT/COMP GEN/LAWS. PAGE 83 H1658
AFR COLONIAL PREDICT GEOG

S66
MANSERGH N.,"THE PARTITION OF INDIA IN RETROSPECT." INDIA PAKISTAN S/ASIA UK DIPLOM COLONIAL GP/REL PWR 20. PAGE 102 H2042
NAT/G PARL/PROC POLICY POL/PAR

S66
MCLANE C.B.,"SOVIET DOCTRINE AND THE MILITARY COUPS IN AFRICA." ALGERIA GHANA COLONIAL NAT/LISM RIGID/FLEX SOVEREIGN MARXISM...DECISION NAT/COMP. PAGE 107 H2140
USSR ATTIT AFR FORCES

S66
ROTHCHILD D.,"THE LIMITS OF FEDERALISM: AN EXAMINATION OF POLITICAL INSTITUTIONAL TRANSFER IN AFRICA." AFR CONSTN CULTURE ELITES ECO/UNDEV KIN PROB/SOLV ADMIN ORD/FREE PWR...POLICY 20. PAGE 135 H2695
FEDERAL NAT/G NAT/LISM COLONIAL

S66
SCHOENBRON D.,"VIETNAM* THE CASE FOR EXTRICATION." NAT/G FORCES PROB/SOLV DIPLOM COLONIAL CONTROL COERCE...CONCPT 20. PAGE 140 H2795
VIETNAM WAR GUERRILLA

S66
TOUVAL S.,"AFRICA'S FRONTIERS* REACTIONS TO A COLONIAL LEGACY." L/A+17C CONFER ADJUD COLONIAL APPORT CONSEN NAT/LISM RESPECT...RECORD NAT/COMP. PAGE 156 H3120
AFR GEOG SOVEREIGN WAR

C66
ROSENBERG C.G. JR.,"THE MYTH OF "MAU-MAU:" NATIONALISM IN KENYA." AFR CULTURE NAT/G POL/PAR COERCE REV RACE/REL ATTIT ORD/FREE SOVEREIGN...MYTH BIBLIOG 20. PAGE 134 H2678
NAT/LISM COLONIAL MAJORIT LEAD

B67
ALLWORTH E.,CENTRAL ASIA: A CENTURY OF RUSSIAN RULE. USSR INTELL SOCIETY AGRI INDUS COLONIAL REV WAR NAT/LISM...ART/METH GEOG LING 19/20. PAGE 5 H0108
ASIA CULTURE NAT/G

B67
ARIKPO O.,THE DEVELOPMENT OF MODERN NIGERIA. AFR NIGERIA SOCIETY ECO/UNDEV KIN ADMIN FEDERAL NAT/LISM ORD/FREE WEALTH...POLICY GEOG BIBLIOG 19/20. PAGE 8 H0163
NAT/G CULTURE CONSTN COLONIAL

B67
BAIN C.A.,VIETNAM: THE ROOTS OF CONFLICT. FRANCE S/ASIA USSR VIETNAM POL/PAR SECT FORCES COLONIAL NAT/LISM PEACE ORD/FREE MARXISM...GEOG CHARTS 4/20. PAGE 10 H0202
NAT/G WAR CULTURE

B67
BURR R.N.,OUR TROUBLED HEMISPHERE: PERSPECTIVES ON UNITED STATES-LATIN AMERICAN RELATIONS. L/A+17C USA+45 USA-45 INT/ORG FOR/AID COLONIAL PWR 19/20 OAS. PAGE 25 H0493
DIPLOM NAT/COMP NAT/G POLICY

B67
CARTER G.M.,SOUTH AFRICA'S TRANSKEI: THE POLITICS OF DOMESTIC COLONIALISM. SOUTH/AFR ECO/UNDEV AGRI NAT/G PROVS PLAN DOMIN REPRESENT ADJUST DISCRIM ...OBS BIBLIOG 20 BANTUSTANS TRANSKEI. PAGE 27 H0550
STRATA GOV/REL COLONIAL POLICY

B67
CHILCOTE R.H.,PORTUGUESE AFRICA. PORTUGAL CULTURE SOCIETY ECO/UNDEV DOMIN NAT/LISM...TREND IDEA/COMP NAT/COMP BIBLIOG 15/20. PAGE 29 H0589
AFR COLONIAL ORD/FREE PROB/SOLV

B67
COLLINS R.O.,EGYPT AND THE SUDAN. COM FRANCE ISLAM SUDAN UAR UK SOCIETY NAT/G COLONIAL NAT/LISM...GEOG SOC LING TREND SOC/INTEG 7/20 SUEZ. PAGE 32 H0635
AGRI CULTURE ECO/UNDEV

B67
FALL B.B.,HO CHI MINH ON REVOLUTION: SELECTED WRITINGS, 1920-66. COM VIETNAM ELITES NAT/G COERCE GUERRILLA RACE/REL MARXISM...MARXIST ANTHOL 20. PAGE 48 H0968
REV COLONIAL ECO/UNDEV S/ASIA

B67
FANON F.,TOWARD THE AFRICAN REVOLUTION. AFR FRANCE CULTURE ELITES LEAD REV GP/REL ORD/FREE SOVEREIGN 20. PAGE 49 H0969
COLONIAL DOMIN ECO/UNDEV RACE/REL

B67
FANON F.,BLACK SKIN, WHITE MASKS: THE EXPERIENCES OF A BLACK MAN IN A WHITE WORLD. CULTURE COLONIAL HAPPINESS ISOLAT STRANGE ATTIT HABITAT RIGID/FLEX SEX...BIOG STERTYP SOC/INTEG 20 NEGRO. PAGE 49 H0970
DISCRIM PERS/REL RACE/REL PSY

B67
GIFFORD P.,BRITAIN AND GERMANY IN AFRICA. AFR GERMANY UK ECO/UNDEV LEAD WAR NAT/LISM ATTIT ...POLICY HIST/WRIT METH/COMP ANTHOL BIBLIOG 19/20 WWI. PAGE 56 H1123
COLONIAL ADMIN DIPLOM NAT/COMP

B67
HILSMAN R.,TO MOVE A NATION: THE POLITICS OF
CHIEF

FOREIGN POLICY IN THE ADMINISTRATION OF JOHN F. KENNEDY. CHINA/COM COM USSR VIETNAM NAT/G DELIB/GP FORCES PLAN PROB/SOLV BAL/PWR COLONIAL EXEC REV PWR 20 KENNEDY/JF PRESIDENT. PAGE 71 H1418 DIPLOM
B67

HUTCHINS F.G.,THE ILLUSION OF PERMANENCE: BRITISH IMPERIALISM IN INDIA. INDIA UK CULTURE STRUCT NAT/G REV GP/REL RACE/REL ADJUST DISCRIM ATTIT MORAL PWR SOC/INTEG 18/20. PAGE 75 H1509 COLONIAL CONTROL SOVEREIGN CONSERVE
B67

KONCZACKI Z.A.,PUBLIC FINANCE AND ECONOMIC DEVELOPMENT OF NATAL 1893-1910. TAX ADMIN COLONIAL ...STAT CHARTS BIBLIOG 19/20 NATAL. PAGE 88 H1755 ECO/TAC FINAN NAT/G ECO/UNDEV
B67

LAMBERT J.,LATIN AMERICA: SOCIAL STRUCTURES AND POLITICAL INSTITUTIONS. STRUCT TEC/DEV DIPLOM ADMIN COLONIAL LEAD ATTIT...SOC CLASSIF NAT/COMP 17/20. PAGE 90 H1801 L/A+17C NAT/G ECO/UNDEV SOCIETY
B67

LEVY J.-P.,THE ECONOMIC LIFE OF THE ANCIENT WORLD. CULTURE SOCIETY INT/TRADE COLONIAL WEALTH ...BIBLIOG. PAGE 95 H1906 ECO/TAC ECO/UNDEV FINAN MEDIT-7
B67

MACRIDIS R.C.,FOREIGN POLICY IN WORLD POLITICS (3RD ED.). EX/STRUC BAL/PWR COLONIAL NAT/LISM SKILL SOVEREIGN WEALTH...CONCPT TIME/SEQ ANTHOL 20 COLD/WAR. PAGE 101 H2011 DIPLOM POLICY NAT/G IDEA/COMP
B67

MAZRUI A.A.,THE ANGLO-AFRICAN COMMONWEALTH; POLITICAL FRICTION AND CULTURAL FUSION. AFR INT/ORG VOL/ASSN CHIEF GP/REL INGP/REL RACE/REL NAT/LISM 20 CMN/WLTH EEC. PAGE 106 H2111 COLONIAL SOVEREIGN DIPLOM CULTURE
B67

MCNELLY T.,SOURCES IN MODERN EAST ASIAN HISTORY AND POLITICS. KOREA VIETNAM CULTURE DIPLOM COLONIAL REV WAR PWR ALL/IDEOS MARXISM...ANTHOL 20 CHINJAP. PAGE 107 H2147 NAT/COMP ASIA S/ASIA SOCIETY
B67

MENARD O.D.,THE ARMY AND THE FIFTH REPUBLIC. ALGERIA FRANCE VIETNAM ELITES STRATA COLONIAL CONTROL LOBBY WAR CIVMIL/REL ROLE PWR...POLICY 20 DEGAULLE/C. PAGE 108 H2169 FORCES ATTIT NAT/G
B67

MUHAMMAD A.C.,THE EMERGENCE OF PAKISTAN. PAKISTAN S/ASIA CONSTN ECO/UNDEV NAT/G CONTROL NAT/LISM 20. PAGE 114 H2281 DIPLOM COLONIAL SECT PROB/SOLV
B67

NESS G.D.,BUREAUCRACY AND RURAL DEVELOPMENT IN MALAYSIA. MALAYSIA UK SOCIETY FINAN INDUS WORKER TEC/DEV ECO/TAC COLONIAL EQUILIB ORD/FREE...STAT CHARTS 20. PAGE 117 H2330 ECO/UNDEV PLAN NAT/G ADMIN
B67

NYERERE J.K.,FREEDOM AND UNITY/UHURU NA UMOJA: A SELECTION FROM WRITINGS AND SPEECHES, 1952-65. TANZANIA ELITES ECO/UNDEV INT/ORG NAT/G CREATE DIPLOM COLONIAL REGION RACE/REL...ANTHOL 20. PAGE 119 H2383 SOVEREIGN AFR TREND ORD/FREE
B67

OLIVER R.,AFRICA SINCE 1800. AFR ISLAM CULTURE ECO/UNDEV SECT DOMIN RACE/REL DISCRIM SOVEREIGN 19/20. PAGE 121 H2414 DIPLOM COLONIAL REGION
B67

RAMUNDO B.A.,PEACEFUL COEXISTENCE: INTERNATIONAL LAW IN THE BUILDING OF COMMUNISM. USSR INT/ORG DIPLOM COLONIAL ARMS/CONT ROLE SOVEREIGN...POLICY METH/COMP NAT/COMP BIBLIOG. PAGE 129 H2588 INT/LAW PEACE MARXISM METH/CNCPT
B67

RAVKIN A.,THE NEW STATES OF AFRICA (HEADLINE SERIES, NO. 183((PAMPHLET). CULTURE STRUCT INDUS COLONIAL NAT/LISM...SOC 20. PAGE 130 H2597 AFR ECO/UNDEV SOCIETY ADMIN
B67

VENKATESWARAN R.J.,CABINET GOVERNMENT IN INDIA. INDIA UK SOCIETY OP/RES COLONIAL LEAD EFFICIENCY ORD/FREE 20. PAGE 162 H3241 DELIB/GP ADMIN CONSTN NAT/G
B67

WILLS A.J.,AN INTRODUCTION TO THE HISTORY OF CENTRAL AFRICA. RHODESIA ZAMBIA CULTURE SOCIETY ECO/UNDEV TEC/DEV DOMIN WAR ALL/VALS...POLICY TREND BIBLIOG T 14/20 NYASALAND. PAGE 169 H3375 AFR COLONIAL ORD/FREE
B67

WINTER E.H.,CONTEMPORARY CHANGE IN TRADITIONAL SOCIETIES: VOLUME I INTRODUCTION AND AFRICAN TRIBES. NIGERIA AGRI LOC/G NAT/G CREATE DOMIN COLONIAL CONTROL GP/REL PWR SOVEREIGN...SOC OBS 20 TANGANYIKA. PAGE 169 H3389 SOCIETY AFR CONSERVE KIN
B67

WOODRUFF W.,IMPACT OF WESTERN MAN. ECO/DEV INDUS CREATE PLAN PROB/SOLV COLONIAL GOV/REL...CHARTS GOV/COMP BIBLIOG 18/20. PAGE 170 H3407 EUR+WWI MOD/EUR CAP/ISM
L67

AUSTIN D.A.,"POLITICAL CONFLICT IN AFRICA." CONSTN NAT/G CREATE ADMIN COLONIAL ORD/FREE MARXISM POPULISM SOCISM...NAT/COMP ANTHOL 20. PAGE 9 H0180 ANOMIE AFR POL/PAR
L67

MCALLISTER J.T. JR.,"THE POSSIBILITIES FOR DIPLOMACY IN SOUTHEAST ASIA." LAOS VIETNAM INT/ORG NAT/G PROVS BAL/PWR DOMIN AGREE COLONIAL WAR PWR 17/20 TREATY. PAGE 106 H2121 DIPLOM S/ASIA
L67

TOUVAL S.,"THE ORGANIZATION OF AFRICAN UNITY AND AFRICAN BORDERS." DEBATE REGION TASK REV ATTIT ORD/FREE...DECISION UN 20 OAU. PAGE 156 H3121 AFR NAT/G COLONIAL NAT/LISM
L67

UNESCO,"APARTHEID." SOUTH/AFR STRUCT KIN SCHOOL SECT WORKER DOMIN EDU/PROP REGION RACE/REL ISOLAT 20. PAGE 158 H3164 DISCRIM CULTURE COERCE COLONIAL
L67

WRIGHT W.R.,"FOREIGN-OWNED RAILWAYS IN ARGENTINA: A CASE STUDY OF ECONOMIC NATIONALISM." L/A+17C UK ECO/UNDEV SERV/IND LG/CO NAT/G TEC/DEV BAL/PWR EQUILIB ARGEN. PAGE 171 H3423 NAT/LISM CAP/ISM ECO/TAC COLONIAL
S67

"PROTEST AGAINST SOVIET INDUSTRIALIZATION ILLS IN LITHUANIA* A MEMORANDUM." USSR LITHUANIA NAT/G PROVS COST GEOG. PAGE 2 H0050 INDUS COLONIAL NAT/LISM PLAN
S67

BHATNAGAR J.K.,"THE VALUES AND ATTITUDES OF SOME INDIAN AND BRITISH STUDENTS." INDIA UK ECO/UNDEV LEGIT COLONIAL GP/REL SOVEREIGN...QU 20. PAGE 16 H0328 NAT/COMP ATTIT EDU/PROP ACADEM
S67

BOSHER J.F.,"GOVERNMENT AND PRIVATE INTERESTS IN NEW FRANCE." CANADA FRANCE INDUS LG/CO SML/CO CAP/ISM INT/TRADE COLONIAL GP/REL...HIST/WRIT 17/18. PAGE 19 H0381 NAT/G FINAN ADMIN CONTROL
S67

COLLINS B.A.,"SOME NOTES ON PUBLIC SERVICE COMMISSIONS IN THE COMMONWEALTH CARIBBEAN." JAMAICA L/A+17C TRINIDAD UK NAT/G OP/RES DOMIN SENIOR COLONIAL CONTROL INGP/REL CENTRAL EFFICIENCY PWR ...DECISION 20. PAGE 31 H0631 ADMIN EX/STRUC ECO/UNDEV CHOOSE
S67

FRENCH D.S.,"DOES THE U.S. EXPLOIT THE DEVELOPING NATIONS?" INT/ORG NAT/G CAP/ISM BAL/PAY WEALTH POLICY. PAGE 53 H1057 ECO/UNDEV INT/TRADE ECO/TAC COLONIAL
S67

GONZALEZ M.P.,"CUBA, UNA REVOLUCION EN MARCHA." CUBA L/A+17C USA+45 VIETNAM ECO/UNDEV FORCES DIPLOM DOMIN...POLICY MARXIST NAT/COMP CASTRO/F. PAGE 58 H1163 REV NAT/G COLONIAL SOVEREIGN
S67

GRUNDY K.W.,"AFRICA IN THE WORLD ARENA." ECO/UNDEV BAL/PWR FOR/AID NEUTRAL REV NAT/LISM GOV/COMP. PAGE 62 H1240 AFR DIPLOM INT/ORG COLONIAL
S67

HAMMOND R.J.,"RACE ATTITUDES AND POLICIES IN PORTUGUESE AFRICA IN THE NINETEENTH AND TWENTIETH CENTURIES." AFR PORTUGAL NAT/G SECT EDU/PROP COLONIAL ATTIT RIGID/FLEX SEX MORAL RESPECT 19/20 NEGRO. PAGE 65 H1309 POLICY RACE/REL DISCRIM SOCIETY
S67

HEASMAN D.J.,"THE GIBRALTAR AFFAIR." SPAIN UK NAT/G BAL/PWR CONSEN NAT/LISM ATTIT...REALPOL 20. PAGE 69 H1378 DIPLOM COLONIAL REGION
S67

IDENBURG P.J.,"POLITICAL STRUCTURAL DEVELOPMENT IN TROPICAL AFRICA." UK ECO/UNDEV KIN POL/PAR CHIEF EX/STRUC CREATE COLONIAL CONTROL REPRESENT RACE/REL ...MAJORIT TREND 20. PAGE 76 H1521 AFR CONSTN NAT/G GOV/COMP
S67

KROLL M.,"POLITICAL LEADERSHIP AND ADMINISTRATIVE COMMUNICATIONS IN NEW NATION STATES* CASE STUDY OF TRINIDAD AND TOBAGO." L/A+17C TRINIDAD INTELL OP/RES DOMIN COLONIAL LEAD GP/REL CENTRAL EFFICIENCY...DECISION OBS METH/COMP 20. PAGE 89 H1774 NAT/G ADMIN EDU/PROP CONTROL
S67

LEVI W.,"THE ELITIST NATURE OF NEW ASIA'S FOREIGN POLICY." CULTURE ECO/UNDEV NAT/G PROB/SOLV EDU/PROP COLONIAL CONTROL REGION NAT/LISM...NAT/COMP 20. PAGE 95 H1898 POLICY ELITES DIPLOM CREATE
S67

MAIR L.,"BUSOGA LOCAL GOVERNMENT" AFR UGANDA UK CONSTN GP/REL...GOV/COMP METH/COMP 20. PAGE 101 H2024 LOC/G COLONIAL LAW ATTIT
S67

MCCLEERY W.,"AN INTERVIEW WITH J. DOUGLAS BROWN ON THE 'WAY' OF VIETNAM" COM VIETNAM INTELL ECO/DEV ACADEM NAT/G COERCE PERSON SUPEGO ORD/FREE 20. PAGE 106 H2125 ATTIT WAR COLONIAL MARXISM

S67
PETRAS J.,"GUERRILLA MOVEMENTS IN LATIN AMERICA - I." GUATEMALA PERU VENEZUELA NAT/G COLONIAL LEAD ATTIT PWR...TIME/SEQ METH/COMP 20 COLOMB. PAGE 125 H2497
GUERRILLA REV L/A+17C MARXISM

S67
READ J.S.,"CENSORED." UGANDA CONSTN INTELL SOCIETY NAT/G DIPLOM PRESS WRITING ADJUD ADMIN COLONIAL RISK...IDEA/COMP 20. PAGE 130 H2602
EDU/PROP AFR CREATE

S67
ROSE S.,"ASIAN NATIONALISM* THE SECOND STAGE." ASIA COM ECO/UNDEV NAT/G PROB/SOLV DIPLOM FOR/AID DOMIN NEUTRAL REGION TASK...METH/COMP 20. PAGE 134 H2675
NAT/LISM S/ASIA BAL/PWR COLONIAL

S67
ROTBERG R.I.,"COLONIALISM AND AFTER: THE POLITICAL LITERATURE OF CENTRAL AFRICA - A BIBLIOGRAPHIC ESSAY." AFR CHIEF EX/STRUC REV INGP/REL RACE/REL SOVEREIGN 20. PAGE 135 H2693
BIBLIOG/A COLONIAL DIPLOM NAT/G

S67
SIPPEL D.,"INDIENS UNSICHERE ZUKUNFT." INDIA CULTURE ACADEM POL/PAR LEGIS COLONIAL CHOOSE SOVEREIGN...JURID 20. PAGE 144 H2888
SOCIETY STRUCT ECO/UNDEV NAT/G

S67
SNELLEN I.T.,"APARTHEID* CHECKS AND CHANGES." SOUTH/AFR NAT/G PROB/SOLV COLONIAL REGION TASK GP/REL RACE/REL EFFICIENCY PRIVIL ORD/FREE 20. PAGE 146 H2923
DISCRIM NAT/LISM EQUILIB CONTROL

C67
LING D.L.,"TUNISIA: FROM PROTECTORATE TO REPUBLIC." CULTURE NAT/G POL/PAR CHIEF DIPLOM COERCE WAR PWR ...BIBLIOG 19/20 TUNIS. PAGE 97 H1934
AFR NAT/LISM COLONIAL PROB/SOLV

S68
DOUGLAS-HOME C.,"A MISTAKEN POLICY IN ADEN." YEMEN CULTURE ECO/UNDEV INDUS FORCES WORKER DIPLOM ECO/TAC CONTROL 20 ADEN. PAGE 42 H0842
SOVEREIGN COLONIAL POLICY REGION

S68
DUGARD J.,"THE REVOCATION OF THE MANDATE FOR SOUTH WEST AFRICA." SOUTH/AFR WOR+45 STRATA NAT/G DELIB/GP DIPLOM ADJUD SANCTION CHOOSE RACE/REL ...POLICY NAT/COMP 20 AFRICA/SW UN TRUST/TERR LEAGUE/NAT. PAGE 43 H0858
AFR INT/ORG DISCRIM COLONIAL

S68
MILLAR T.B.,"THE COMMONWEALTH AND THE UN." UK DIPLOM TARIFFS AGREE COLONIAL CONTROL SOVEREIGN WEALTH...GP/COMP GOV/COMP 20 CMN/WLTH UN. PAGE 111 H2210
INT/ORG POLICY TREND ECO/TAC

B79
BRODERICK G.C.,POLITICAL STUDIES. IRELAND UK ROMAN/EMP LAW ACADEM LOC/G NAT/G DIPLOM PARL/PROC SUFF GP/REL LAISSEZ...ANTHOL. PAGE 21 H0424
CONSTN COLONIAL

B89
ASHBEE H.S.,A BIBLIOGRAPHY OF TUNISIA FROM THE EARLIEST TIMES TO THE END OF 1888. AGRI ADMIN ...GEOG TUNIS. PAGE 8 H0171
BIBLIOG COLONIAL CULTURE NAT/G

B93
ROYAL GEOGRAPHIC SOCIETY,BIBLIOGRAPHY OF BARBARY STATES (4 SUPPLEMENTARY PAPERS). ALGERIA LIBYA MOROCCO SOCIETY STRUCT DIPLOM LEAD 14/19 TUNIS. PAGE 135 H2706
BIBLIOG ISLAM NAT/G COLONIAL

B99
KINGSLEY M.H.,WEST AFRICAN STUDIES. GHANA NIGERIA SIER/LEONE LAW EXTR/IND SECT DIPLOM INT/TRADE DOMIN RACE/REL OWN HEALTH...SOC 19. PAGE 86 H1717
AFR HEREDITY COLONIAL CULTURE

COLORADO....COLORADO

COLUMBIA U SCHOOL OF LAW H0636

COLUMBIA/U....COLUMBIA UNIVERSITY

COM....COMMUNIST COUNTRIES, EXCEPT CHINA; SEE ALSO APPROPRIATE NATIONS, MARXISM

N
NEUE POLITISCHE LITERATUR. AFR ASIA EUR+WWI GERMANY RUSSIA SOCIETY ECO/DEV ECO/UNDEV PLAN PROB/SOLV LEAD MARXISM...PHIL/SCI CONCPT 20. PAGE 1 H0008
BIBLIOG DIPLOM COM NAT/G

N
CHINA QUARTERLY. COM AGRI INDUS ACADEM POL/PAR INT/TRADE CONFER GOV/REL...TIME/SEQ CON/ANAL INDEX 20. PAGE 1 H0014
BIBLIOG/A ASIA DIPLOM POLICY

N
AVTOREFERATY DISSERTATSII. USSR INTELL ACADEM NAT/G DIPLOM GOV/REL KNOWL CONCPT. PAGE 2 H0029
BIBLIOG MARXISM MARXIST COM

N
"PROLOG",DIGEST OF THE SOVIET UKRANIAN PRESS. USSR LAW AGRI INDUS PROVS SCHOOL DIPLOM GOV/REL ATTIT ...HUM LING 20. PAGE 3 H0053
BIBLIOG/A NAT/G PRESS COM

N
US LIBRARY OF CONGRESS,EAST EUROPEAN ACCESSIONS INDEX. NAT/G ISOLAT ATTIT KNOWL...POLICY 20. PAGE 160 H3202
BIBLIOG COM MARXIST DIPLOM

B18
KERNER R.J.,SLAVIC EUROPE: A SELECTED BIBLIOGRAPHY IN THE WESTERN EUROPEAN LANGUAGES. BULGARIA CZECHOSLVK GERMANY/E POLAND RUSSIA YUGOSLAVIA NAT/G DIPLOM MARXISM...LING 19/20. PAGE 85 H1695
BIBLIOG SOCIETY CULTURE COM

N19
BRIMMELL G.H.,COMMUNISM IN SOUTHEAST ASIA (PAMPHLET). BURMA CAMBODIA COM INDIA INDONESIA LAOS MOD/EUR NAT/G POL/PAR FORCES CAP/ISM CONTROL WEALTH ...MYTH 20. PAGE 21 H0420
MARXISM S/ASIA REV ECO/UNDEV

N19
HAJDA J.,THE COLD WAR VIEWED AS A SOCIOLOGICAL PROBLEM (PAMPHLET). COM CZECHOSLVK EUR+WWI SOCIETY PLAN EDU/PROP CONTROL TASK ATTIT MARXISM...POLICY 20 COLD/WAR MIGRATION. PAGE 64 H1280
DIPLOM LEAD PWR NAT/G

N19
TABORSKY E.,CONFORMITY UNDER COMMUNISM (PAMPHLET). CZECHOSLVK HUNGARY POLAND SCHOOL DOMIN PRESS ...TREND GOV/COMP 20. PAGE 152 H3030
COM CONTROL EDU/PROP NAT/G

B38
HARPER S.N.,THE GOVERNMENT OF THE SOVIET UNION. COM USSR LAW CONSTN ECO/DEV PLAN TEC/DEV DIPLOM INT/TRADE ADMIN REV NAT/LISM...POLICY 20. PAGE 67 H1337
MARXISM NAT/G LEAD POL/PAR

B39
KOHN H.,REVOLUTIONS AND DICTATORSHIPS. COM EUR+WWI ISLAM MOD/EUR NAT/G CHIEF FORCES WAR CIVMIL/REL PWR MARXISM 18/20. PAGE 87 H1739
NAT/LISM TOTALISM REV FASCISM

B42
NEUMANN S.,PERMANENT REVOLUTION: THE TOTAL STATE IN A WORLD AT WAR. COM EUR+WWI GERMANY USSR EX/STRUC DIPLOM CONTROL COERCE REPRESENT MARXISM...SOC GOV/COMP BIBLIOG 20 HITLER/A STALIN/J. PAGE 117 H2337
FASCISM TOTALISM DOMIN EDU/PROP

B43
CONOVER H.F.,SOVIET RUSSIA: SELECTED LIST OF REFERENCES. USSR CULTURE INDUS NAT/G TOP/EX TEC/DEV BUDGET WAR CIVMIL/REL EFFICIENCY MARXISM 20. PAGE 32 H0644
BIBLIOG ECO/DEV COM DIPLOM

B43
GRIERSON P.,BOOKS ON SOVIET RUSSIA 1917-42: A BIBLIOGRAPHY AND A GUIDE TO READING. USSR CULTURE ELITES NAT/G PLAN DIPLOM REV...GEOG 20. PAGE 61 H1213
BIBLIOG/A COM MARXISM LEAD

B43
LASKI H.J.,REFLECTIONS ON THE REVOLUTIONS OF OUR TIME. COM USSR NAT/G WORKER UTOPIA ORD/FREE WEALTH MARXISM SOCISM 19/20. PAGE 92 H1830
CAP/ISM WELF/ST ECO/TAC POLICY

B43
LENIN V.I.,LEFT WING COMMUNISM: AN INFANTILE DISORDER (1920). GERMANY MOD/EUR USSR STRUCT CHIEF DOMIN EDU/PROP LEGIT LEAD REPRESENT POPULISM ...METH/COMP 19 LENIN/VI COM/PARTY MENSHEVIK. PAGE 94 H1879
COM MARXISM NAT/G REV

B44
US LIBRARY OF CONGRESS,RUSSIA: A CHECK LIST PRELIMINARY TO A BASIC BIBLIOGRAPHY OF MATERIALS IN THE RUSSIAN LANGUAGE. COM USSR CULTURE EDU/PROP MARXISM...ART/METH HUM LING 19/20. PAGE 160 H3204
BIBLIOG LAW SECT

B48
LAUTERBACH A.,ECONOMIC SECURITY AND INDIVIDUAL FREEDOM: CAN WE HAVE BOTH? COM EUR+WWI MOD/EUR UNIV WOR+45 CAP/ISM TOTALISM ALL/VALS...GOV/COMP BIBLIOG 20. PAGE 92 H1840
ORD/FREE ECO/DEV DECISION INGP/REL

B48
YAKOBSON S.,FIVE HUNDRED RUSSIAN WORKS FOR COLLEGE LIBRARIES (PAMPHLET). MOD/EUR USSR MARXISM SOCISM ...ART/METH GEOG HUM JURID SOC 13/20. PAGE 171 H3431
BIBLIOG NAT/G CULTURE COM

B49
LASSWELL H.D.,LANGUAGE OF POLITICS. COM NAT/G ACT/RES ATTIT PWR...STAT RECORD CON/ANAL GEN/METH 20. PAGE 92 H1834
EDU/PROP METH/CNCPT

B49
US DEPARTMENT OF STATE,SOVIET BIBLIOGRAPHY (PAMPHLET). CHINA/COM COM USSR LAW AGRI INT/ORG ECO/TAC EDU/PROP...POLICY GEOG 20. PAGE 159 H3185
BIBLIOG/A MARXISM CULTURE DIPLOM

B50
CONOVER H.F.,INTRODUCTION TO EUROPE: A SELECTIVE GUIDE TO BACKGROUND READING. COM EUR+WWI NAT/G KNOWL...ART/METH GEOG SOC. PAGE 32 H0648
BIBLIOG/A MOD/EUR HIST/WRIT

B51
BORKENAU F.,EUROPEAN COMMUNISM. COM EUR+WWI GERMANY SPAIN USSR INT/ORG PLAN REV WAR ATTIT 20 STALIN/J
MARXISM POLICY

HITLER/A. PAGE 19 H0376 DIPLOM NAT/G

B51
MORLEY C.,GUIDE TO RESEARCH IN RUSSIAN HISTORY. USSR MARXISM...BIOG HIST/WRIT ANTHOL DICTIONARY. PAGE 113 H2259 BIBLIOG/A R+D NAT/G COM

B51
US LIBRARY OF CONGRESS,EAST EUROPEAN ACCESSIONS LIST (VOL. I). POL/PAR DIPLOM ADMIN LEAD 20. PAGE 160 H3207 BIBLIOG/A COM SOCIETY NAT/G

S51
GOULD J.,"THE KOMSOMOL AND THE HITLER JUGEND." COM EUR+WWI GERMANY SOCIETY NAT/G POL/PAR SCHOOL TOTALISM DRIVE PERCEPT KNOWL FASCISM...SOC NAZI TOT/POP 20. PAGE 59 H1185 EDU/PROP CON/ANAL SOCISM

S51
MACRAE D.G.,"THE BOLSHEVIK IDEOLOGY; THE INTELLECTUAL AND EMOTIONAL FACTORS IN COMMUNIST AFFILIATION" (BMR)" COM LEAD REV ATTIT ORD/FREE ...SOC CON/ANAL 20 BOLSHEVISM. PAGE 100 H2008 MARXISM INTELL PHIL/SCI SECT

C51
BEST H.,"THE SOVIET STATE AND ITS INCEPTION." USSR CULTURE INDUS DIPLOM WEALTH...GEOG SOC BIBLIOG 20. PAGE 16 H0322 COM GEN/METH REV MARXISM

B52
KOLARZ W.,RUSSIA AND HER COLONIES. COM RUSSIA LAW CULTURE ECO/DEV KIN LOC/G SECT TEC/DEV ECO/TAC EDU/PROP REGION COERCE ATTIT PWR SOVEREIGN...SOC TIME/SEQ CON/ANAL VAL/FREE 19/20. PAGE 88 H1749 NAT/G DOMIN USSR COLONIAL

B52
ULAM A.B.,TITOISM AND THE COMINFORM. USSR WOR+45 STRUCT INT/ORG NAT/G ACT/RES PLAN EXEC ATTIT DRIVE ALL/VALS...CONCPT OBS VAL/FREE 20 COMINTERN TITO/MARSH. PAGE 157 H3149 COM POL/PAR TOTALISM YUGOSLAVIA

B52
US DEPARTMENT OF STATE,RESEARCH ON EASTERN EUROPE (EXCLUDING USSR). EUR+WWI LAW ECO/DEV NAT/G PROB/SOLV DIPLOM ADMIN LEAD MARXISM...TREND 19/20. PAGE 159 H3187 BIBLIOG R+D ACT/RES COM

C52
EBENSTEIN W.,"INTRODUCTION TO POLITICAL PHILOSOPHY." COM CONSTN INTELL CONTROL PERSON NEW/LIB SOCISM...PSY GEN/LAWS BIBLIOG/A. PAGE 44 H0883 ALL/IDEOS PHIL/SCI IDEA/COMP NAT/G

B53
CURTISS J.S.,THE RUSSIAN CHURCH AND THE SOVIET STATE 1917-1950. COM USSR CONTROL LEAD REV MARXISM ...POLICY BIBLIOG 20 CHURCH/STA ORTHO/RUSS. PAGE 36 H0728 GP/REL NAT/G SECT PWR

B53
LEITES N.,A STUDY OF BOLSHEVISM. WOR+45 WOR-45 ELITES SOCIETY INT/ORG NAT/G EX/STRUC EDU/PROP EXEC ROUTINE ATTIT MORAL MARXISM...CONCPT OBS VAL/FREE 20. PAGE 94 H1869 COM POL/PAR USSR TOTALISM

B53
LEITES N.,A STUDY OF BOLSHEVISM. ELITES STRATA INT/ORG LOC/G POL/PAR WORKER EDU/PROP REV TOTALISM UTOPIA PWR...CONCPT 20 BOLSHEVISM. PAGE 94 H1870 MARXISM PLAN COM

B53
MEYER P.,THE JEWS IN THE SOVIET SATELLITES. CZECHOSLVK POLAND SOCIETY STRATA NAT/G BAL/PWR ECO/TAC EDU/PROP LEGIT ADMIN COERCE ATTIT DISPL PERCEPT HEALTH PWR RESPECT WEALTH...METH/CNCPT JEWS VAL/FREE NAZI 20. PAGE 110 H2192 COM SECT TOTALISM USSR

B53
PIERCE R.A.,RUSSIAN CENTRAL ASIA, 1867-1917: A SELECTED BIBLIOGRAPHY (PAMPHLET). USSR LAW CULTURE NAT/G EDU/PROP WAR...GEOG SOC 19/20. PAGE 125 H2508 BIBLIOG COLONIAL ADMIN COM

S53
BAUER R.A.,"WORD-OF-MOUTH COMMUNICATION IN THE SOVIET UNION." COM INTELL SOCIETY LABOR ATTIT KNOWL ...INT QU SAMP CHARTS 20. PAGE 12 H0239 CULTURE USSR

B54
FRIEDRICH C.J.,TOTALITARIAN DICTATORSHIP AND AUTOCRACY. COM EUR+WWI GERMANY ITALY USSR INTELL ECO/DEV NAT/G POL/PAR FORCES TOP/EX ECO/TAC EDU/PROP LEGIT COERCE ATTIT ORD/FREE PWR FASCISM ...CONCPT TIME/SEQ GEN/LAWS NAZI 20. PAGE 53 H1068 SOCIETY DOMIN TOTALISM

B54
LENIN V.I.,SELECTED WORKS (12 VOLS.). USSR INTELL SOCIETY STRATA STRUCT NAT/G POL/PAR WORKER CAP/ISM REV WAR...MARXIST PHIL/SCI 20 MARX/KARL LENIN/VI. PAGE 94 H1880 COM MARXISM

L54
FRIEDRICH C.J.,"TOTALITARIANISM." COM EUR+WWI NAT/G POL/PAR SECT FORCES PLAN ECO/TAC DOMIN EDU/PROP EXEC COERCE REV ORD/FREE PWR...SOC CONCPT NAZI 20. PAGE 53 H1067 ATTIT TOTALISM

C54
GUINS G.C.,"SOVIET LAW AND SOVIET SOCIETY." COM USSR STRATA FAM NAT/G WORKER DOMIN RACE/REL ...BIBLIOG 20. PAGE 62 H1249 LAW STRUCT PLAN

C54
HAMMER E.J.,"THE STRUGGLE FOR INDOCHINA." COM VIETNAM POL/PAR REV CENTRAL NAT/LISM ATTIT...POLICY CHARTS BIBLIOG 20. PAGE 65 H1305 WAR COLONIAL S/ASIA NAT/G

B55
INTERNATIONAL COMN JURISTS,JUSTICE ENSLAVED. COM CONSTN LABOR NAT/G CONTROL CHOOSE 20. PAGE 78 H1555 SOCISM TOTALISM ORD/FREE COERCE

B55
KOHN H.,THE MIND OF MODERN RUSSIA. COM MOD/EUR USSR SOCIETY NAT/G SECT FORCES TOP/EX COERCE TOTALISM DRIVE RIGID/FLEX PWR SOVEREIGN...CONCPT TIME/SEQ WORK. PAGE 87 H1742 INTELL GEN/LAWS SOCISM RUSSIA

B55
MAYO H.B.,DEMOCRACY AND MARXISM. COM USSR STRATA NAT/G WORKER ECO/TAC REV MORAL...PHIL/SCI HIST/WRIT IDEA/COMP WORSHIP 20 MARX/KARL LENIN/VI STALIN/J TROTSKY/L. PAGE 105 H2108 MARXISM CAP/ISM

B55
MID-EUROPEAN LAW PROJECT,CHURCH AND STATE BEHIND THE IRON CURTAIN. COM CZECHOSLVK HUNGARY POLAND USSR CULTURE SECT EDU/PROP GOV/REL CATHISM...CHARTS ANTHOL BIBLIOG WORSHIP 20 CHURCH/STA. PAGE 110 H2202 LAW MARXISM POLICY

B55
RESHETAR J.S.,PROBLEMS OF ANALYZING AND PREDICTING SOVIET BEHAVIOR. USSR CULTURE ECO/DEV AGRI DIST/IND EXTR/IND PROC/MFG NAT/G SECT TOP/EX ACT/RES ADMIN PWR WEALTH...SOC METH TOT/POP VAL/FREE 20. PAGE 131 H2617 COM ATTIT

B55
TOYNBEE A.,THE REALIGNMENT OF EUROPE. COM GREECE ITALY NAT/G BAL/PWR ECO/TAC EDU/PROP REV SOVEREIGN ...SOC TIME/SEQ TREND COLD/WAR 20. PAGE 156 H3123 EUR+WWI PLAN USSR

L55
ROSTOW W.W.,"RUSSIA AND CHINA UNDER COMMUNISM." CHINA/COM USSR INTELL STRUCT INT/ORG NAT/G POL/PAR TOP/EX ACT/RES PLAN ADMIN ATTIT ALL/VALS MARXISM ...CONCPT OBS TIME/SEQ TREND GOV/COMP VAL/FREE 20. PAGE 134 H2689 COM ASIA

B56
VON HARPE W.,DIE SOWJETUNION FINNLAND UND SKANDANAVIEN, 1945-1955. EUR+WWI FINLAND GERMANY USSR WAR INGP/REL ORD/FREE SOVEREIGN MARXISM ...POLICY GOV/COMP BIBLIOG 20 STALIN/J. PAGE 163 H3270 DIPLOM COM NEUTRAL BAL/PWR

B56
WATT D.C.,BRITAIN AND THE SUEZ CANAL. COM UAR UK ...INT/LAW 20 SUEZ TREATY. PAGE 166 H3314 DIPLOM INT/TRADE DIST/IND NAT/G

B56
WOLFF R.L.,THE BALKANS IN OUR TIME. ALBANIA FUT MOD/EUR USSR YUGOSLAVIA CULTURE INT/ORG SECT DIPLOM EDU/PROP COERCE WAR ORD/FREE...CHARTS 4/20 BALKANS COMINFORM. PAGE 170 H3403 GEOG COM

B57
BYRNES R.F.,BIBLIOGRAPHY OF AMERICAN PUBLICATIONS ON EAST CENTRAL EUROPE, 1945-1957 (VOL. XXII). SECT DIPLOM EDU/PROP RACE/REL...ART/METH GEOG JURID SOC LING 20 JEWS. PAGE 25 H0503 BIBLIOG/A COM MARXISM NAT/G

B57
CENTRAL ASIAN RESEARCH CENTRE,BIBLIOGRAPHY OF RECENT SOVIET SOURCE MATERIAL ON SOVIET CENTRAL ASIA AND THE BORDERLANDS. AFGHANISTN INDIA PAKISTAN UAR USSR ECO/UNDEV AGRI EXTR/IND INDUS ACADEM ADMIN ...HEAL HUM LING CON/ANAL 20. PAGE 28 H0567 BIBLIOG/A COM CULTURE NAT/G

B57
LOUCKS W.N.,COMPARATIVE ECONOMIC SYSTEMS (5TH ED.). COM UK USSR INDUS POL/PAR PLAN CAP/ISM TOTALISM MARXISM...PHIL/SCI BIBLIOG 19/20. PAGE 99 H1969 NAT/COMP IDEA/COMP SOCISM

B57
PARK A.G.,BOLSHEVISM IN TURKESTAN 1917-1927. COM RUSSIA USSR CULTURE AGRI SECT DOMIN GP/REL INGP/REL NAT/LISM...BIBLIOG 20 TURKESTAN. PAGE 123 H2467 REV POLICY MARXISM ISLAM

B57
TOMASIC D.A.,NATIONAL COMMUNISM AND SOVIET STRATEGY. UK USSR YUGOSLAVIA NAT/G POL/PAR CHIEF CREATE DOMIN REV WAR PWR...BIOG TREND 20 TITO/MARSH STALIN/J. PAGE 156 H3112 COM NAT/LISM MARXISM DIPLOM

B58
DUNAYEVSKAYA R.,MARXISM AND FREEDOM: FROM 1776 UNTIL TODAY. COM USSR WORKER CAP/ISM DOMIN REV GP/REL TOTALISM ALL/VALS...MYTH BIOG IDEA/COMP 18/20 MARX/KARL LENIN/VI STALIN/J. PAGE 43 H0861 MARXISM CONCPT ORD/FREE

B58
GARTHOFF R.L.,SOVIET STRATEGY IN THE NUCLEAR AGE. FUT USSR R+D INT/ORG NAT/G ACT/RES TEC/DEV DOMIN DETER WAR ATTIT PWR...RELATIV METH/CNCPT SELF/OBS TREND CON/ANAL STERTYP GEN/LAWS 20. PAGE 55 H1103 COM FORCES BAL/PWR NUC/PWR

B58
LAQUER W.Z.,THE MIDDLE EAST IN TRANSITION. COM USSR ECO/UNDEV NAT/G VOL/ASSN EDU/PROP EXEC ATTIT DRIVE ISLAM TREND

PWR MARXISM COLD/WAR TOT/POP 20. PAGE 91 H1818 NAT/LISM

B58
PALMER E.E.,THE COMMUNIST CHALLENGE. COM USA+45 USA-45 ECO/DEV ECO/UNDEV NEUTRAL ORD/FREE POPULISM ...CONCPT NAT/COMP ANTHOL 19/20 LENIN/VI STALIN/J MAO MARX/KARL COM/PARTY. PAGE 123 H2450 MARXISM DIPLOM IDEA/COMP POLICY

L58
BELL D.,"TEN THEORIES IN SEARCH OF REALITY: THE PREDICTION OF SOVIET BEHAVIOR IN THE SOCIAL SCIENCES" (BMR)" COM USSR...POLICY SOC METH/COMP 20. PAGE 13 H0264 MARXISM PREDICT IDEA/COMP

S58
STAAR R.F.,"ELECTIONS IN COMMUNIST POLAND." EUR+WWI SOCIETY INT/ORG NAT/G POL/PAR LEGIS ACT/RES ECO/TAC EDU/PROP ADJUD ADMIN ROUTINE COERCE TOTALISM ATTIT ORD/FREE PWR 20. PAGE 148 H2963 COM CHOOSE POLAND

B59
CAREW-HUNT R.C.,BOOKS ON COMMUNISM. NAT/G POL/PAR DIPLOM REV...BIOG 19/20. PAGE 26 H0528 BIBLIOG/A MARXISM COM ASIA

B59
EPSTEIN F.T.,EAST GERMANY: A SELECTED BIBLIOGRAPHY (PAMPHLET). COM GERMANY/E LAW AGRI FINAN INDUS LABOR POL/PAR EDU/PROP ADMIN AGE/Y 20. PAGE 47 H0932 BIBLIOG/A INTELL MARXISM NAT/G

B59
GOLDWIN R.A.,READINGS IN RUSSIAN FOREIGN POLICY. HUNGARY USSR YUGOSLAVIA ELITES INT/ORG NAT/G REV WAR NAT/LISM PERSON SOCISM...CHARTS 20 MAPS BOLSHEVISM. PAGE 58 H1160 COM MARXISM DIPLOM POLICY

B59
HENDEL S.,THE SOVIET CRUCIBLE. USSR LEAD COERCE NAT/LISM UTOPIA PWR...POLICY CONCPT ANTHOL 20 STALIN/J LENIN/VI MARX/KARL BOLSHEVIK. PAGE 70 H1393 COM MARXISM REV TOTALISM

B59
INTERNATIONAL PRESS INSTITUTE,THE PRESS IN AUTHORITARIAN COUNTRIES. COM PORTUGAL SPAIN UAR USSR NAT/G DOMIN LEGIT ORD/FREE FASCISM SOCISM 20. PAGE 78 H1559 PRESS CONTROL TOTALISM EDU/PROP

B59
LANDAUER C.,EUROPEAN SOCIALISM (2 VOLS.). COM EUR+WWI MOD/EUR INTELL INDUS REV WAR...MAJORIT IDEA/COMP BIBLIOG 19/20 HITLER/A. PAGE 90 H1805 SOCISM NAT/COMP LABOR MARXISM

B59
LAQUER W.Z.,THE SOVIET UNION AND THE MIDDLE EAST. COM UAR USSR ECO/UNDEV NAT/G VOL/ASSN ECO/TAC EDU/PROP COLONIAL EXEC PWR...TIME/SEQ TREND COLD/WAR 20. PAGE 91 H1819 ISLAM DRIVE FOR/AID NAT/LISM

B59
PAGE S.W.,LENIN AND WORLD REVOLUTION. COM USSR NAT/G DOMIN COERCE CROWD UTOPIA ATTIT AUTHORIT DRIVE PWR...CONCPT MYTH 19/20 LENIN/VI MARX/KARL. PAGE 122 H2441 REV PERSON MARXISM BIOG

B59
PANIKKAR K.M.,THE AFRO-ASIAN STATES AND THEIR PROBLEMS. COM CULTURE KIN POL/PAR SECT DIPLOM EDU/PROP COLONIAL SOVEREIGN...TECHNIC GOV/COMP 20. PAGE 123 H2458 AFR S/ASIA ECO/UNDEV

S59
LABEDZ L.,"IDEOLOGY: THE FOURTH STAGE." COM USSR NAT/G TOP/EX LEGIT ATTIT PWR MARXISM...METH/CNCPT HIST/WRIT STERTYP TOT/POP 20. PAGE 90 H1795 CONCPT GEN/LAWS

S59
SKILLING H.G.,"COMMUNISM: NATIONAL OR INTERNATIONAL." CHINA/COM USSR YUGOSLAVIA NAT/G POL/PAR VOL/ASSN DOMIN REGION COERCE ATTIT PWR MARXISM SOCISM...CONCPT TOT/POP 20 TITO/MARSH. PAGE 145 H2894 COM TREND

S59
ZAUBERMAN A.,"SOVIET BLOC ECONOMIC INTEGRATION." COM CULTURE INTELL ECO/DEV INDUS TOP/EX ACT/RES PLAN ECO/TAC INT/TRADE ROUTINE CHOOSE ATTIT ...TIME/SEQ 20. PAGE 172 H3452 MARKET INT/ORG USSR TOTALISM

C59
KARPAT K.H.,"TURKEY'S POLITICS: THE TRANSITION TO A MULTI-PARTY SYSTEM." COM TURKEY CULTURE ECO/UNDEV SECT TEC/DEV NAT/LISM ATTIT...SOC CON/ANAL BIBLIOG 20. PAGE 83 H1664 POL/PAR NAT/G

C59
KORNHAUSER W.,"THE POLITICS OF MASS SOCIETY." COM CULTURE ELITES INTELL STRATA POL/PAR ATTIT...SOC CHARTS GEN/LAWS BIBLIOG 20. PAGE 88 H1757 CROWD PLURISM CONSTN SOCIETY

B60
BLACK C.E.,THE TRANSFORMATION OF RUSSIAN SOCIETY. COM MOD/EUR RUSSIA SOCIETY EDU/PROP COERCE ALL/VALS 19/20. PAGE 17 H0349 CULTURE RIGID/FLEX USSR

B60
BRZEZINSKI Z.K.,THE SOVIET BLOC-UNITY AND CONFLICT. COM USSR CONSTN DOMIN ADMIN TOTALISM PWR...SOC MYTH RECORD TREND STERTYP GEN/LAWS GEN/METH TOT/POP 20. PAGE 23 H0458 ATTIT EDU/PROP

B60
FISCHER L.,THE SOVIETS IN WORLD AFFAIRS. CHINA/COM COM EUR+WWI USSR INT/ORG CONFER LEAD ARMS/CONT REV PWR...CHARTS 20 TREATY VERSAILLES. PAGE 51 H1010 DIPLOM NAT/G POLICY MARXISM

B60
GOODMAN E.,SOVIET DESIGN FOR A WORLD STATE. COM USSR NAT/G TOP/EX DIPLOM ECO/TAC DOMIN EDU/PROP COERCE REV ATTIT ORD/FREE...CON/ANAL 20. PAGE 59 H1171 PLAN PWR SOCISM TOTALISM

B60
KOHN H.,PAN-SLAVISM: ITS HISTORY AND IDEOLOGY. COM CZECHOSLVK EUR+WWI MOD/EUR USSR YUGOSLAVIA CULTURE ELITES INTELL KIN NAT/G EDU/PROP DRIVE SOVEREIGN ...HUM PHIL/SCI MYTH HIST/WRIT 19/20. PAGE 87 H1745 ATTIT CONCPT NAT/LISM

B60
MCCLOSKY H.,THE SOVIET DICTATORSHIP. FUT CONSTN CULTURE INTELL SOCIETY POL/PAR SECT VOL/ASSN FORCES PLAN TEC/DEV DOMIN EDU/PROP COERCE PWR MARXISM ...POLICY CONCPT MYTH STERTYP 20. PAGE 106 H2127 COM NAT/G TOTALISM USSR

B60
SCHAPIRO L.,THE COMMUNIST PARTY OF THE SOVIET UNION. COM LAW SOCIETY STRATA STRUCT ECO/DEV LABOR NAT/G POL/PAR CREATE DOMIN EDU/PROP COERCE TOTALISM MARXISM...POLICY CONCPT MYTH TIME/SEQ WORK TOT/POP 20 LENIN/VI STALIN/J. PAGE 139 H2772 INTELL PWR USSR

B60
SZTARAY Z.,BIBLIOGRAPHY ON HUNGARY. HUNGARY MOD/EUR CULTURE INDUS SECT DIPLOM REV...ART/METH SOC LING 18/20. PAGE 151 H3029 BIBLIOG NAT/G COM MARXISM

B60
WILLIAMS L.E.,OVERSEAS CHINESE NATIONALISM: THE GENESIS OF THE PAN-CHINESE MOVEMENT IN INDONESIA, 1900-1916. ASIA COM INDONESIA AGRI INT/ORG LOC/G DIPLOM EDU/PROP HABITAT PWR POPULISM...GEOG LING CENSUS 20. PAGE 168 H3367 NAT/LISM GP/REL DECISION NAT/G

B60
WORLEY P.,ASIA TODAY (REV. ED.) (PAMPHLET). COM ECO/UNDEV AGRI FINAN INDUS POL/PAR FOR/AID ADMIN MARXISM 20. PAGE 170 H3411 BIBLIOG/A ASIA DIPLOM NAT/G

B60
ZENKOVSKY S.A.,PAN-TURKISM AND ISLAM IN RUSSIA. ASIA RUSSIA USSR CULTURE POL/PAR DOMIN REV GP/REL MARXISM...LING GP/COMP BIBLIOG 19/20 TURKIC. PAGE 173 H3454 SECT NAT/LISM COM ISLAM

L60
KAPLAN M.A.,"COMMUNIST COUP IN CZECHOSLOVAKIA." COM EUR+WWI INTELL LABOR LOC/G NAT/G POL/PAR FORCES EDU/PROP EXEC MARXISM...TIME/SEQ HYPO/EXP 20. PAGE 83 H1659 STRUCT COERCE CZECHOSLVK

L60
WHEELER G.,"RACIAL PROBLEMS IN SOVIET MUSLIM ASIA." COM CULTURE SOCIETY NEIGH SECT DOMIN EDU/PROP DISCRIM DISPL DRIVE PWR SOVEREIGN...CENSUS SAMP TREND 20 MUSLIM. PAGE 167 H3340 PERSON ATTIT USSR RACE/REL

S60
BRZEZINSKI Z.K.,"PATTERNS AND LIMITS OF THE SINO-SOVIET DISPUTE." ASIA CHINA/COM COM FUT STRATA NAT/G EX/STRUC FORCES BAL/PWR DIPLOM ECO/TAC DOMIN EDU/PROP ADMIN COERCE WAR ATTIT RIGID/FLEX ...GEN/LAWS VAL/FREE 20. PAGE 23 H0459 POL/PAR PWR REV USSR

S60
GROSSMAN G.,"SOVIET GROWTH: ROUTINE, INERTIA, AND PRESSURE." COM STRATA NAT/G DELIB/GP PLAN TEC/DEV ECO/TAC EDU/PROP ADMIN ROUTINE DRIVE WEALTH COLD/WAR 20. PAGE 62 H1236 POL/PAR ECO/DEV USSR

S60
NORTH R.C.,"DIE DISKREPANZ ZWISCHEN REALITAT UND WUNSCHBILD ALS INNENPOLITISCHER FAKTOR." ASIA CHINA/COM COM FUT ECO/UNDEV NAT/G PLAN DOMIN ADMIN COERCE PERCEPT...SOC MYTH GEN/METH WORK TOT/POP 20. PAGE 119 H2373 SOCIETY ECO/TAC

S60
TAUBER K.,"ASPECTS OF NATIONALIST-COMMUNIST COLLABORATION IN POSTWAR GERMANY." COM EUR+WWI USSR NAT/G VOL/ASSN ATTIT DRIVE PWR...TIME/SEQ COLD/WAR TOT/POP 20. PAGE 152 H3049 POL/PAR EDU/PROP GERMANY

S60
WOLFE T.W.,"KHRUSHCHEV'S DISARMAMENT STRATEGY." COM NAT/G TOP/EX PLAN BAL/PWR DIPLOM ARMS/CONT COERCE ATTIT...POLICY CONCPT RECORD TREND CON/ANAL COLD/WAR 20 KHRUSH/N. PAGE 170 H3401 PWR GEN/LAWS USSR

C60
FITZSIMMONS T.,"USSR: ITS PEOPLE, ITS SOCIETY, ITS CULTURE." USSR FAM SECT DIPLOM EDU/PROP ADMIN RACE/REL ATTIT...POLICY CHARTS BIBLIOG 20. PAGE 51 H1021 CULTURE STRUCT SOCIETY COM

C60
HAZARD J.N.,"SETTLING DISPUTES IN SOVIET SOCIETY: THE FORMATIVE YEARS OF LEGAL INSTITUTIONS." USSR NAT/G PROF/ORG PROB/SOLV CONTROL CT/SYS ROUTINE REV CENTRAL...JURID BIBLIOG 20. PAGE 68 H1372 ADJUD LAW COM POLICY

C60
HAZARD J.N.,"THE SOVIET SYSTEM OF GOVERNMENT." USSR COM

SOCIETY INDUS NAT/G POL/PAR DIPLOM CT/SYS...JURID CHARTS BIBLIOG/A 20. PAGE 69 H1373
NAT/COMP STRUCT ADMIN

B61
BALYS J.,LITHUANIA AND LITHUANIANS: A SELECTED BIBLIOGRAPHY. LITHUANIA SOC. PAGE 10 H0206
BIBLIOG POLICY NAT/G COM

B61
BURKS R.V.,THE DYNAMICS OF COMMUNISM IN EASTERN EUROPE. COM YUGOSLAVIA POL/PAR RACE/REL ISOLAT ...CORREL CON/ANAL CHARTS GP/COMP DICTIONARY 20 EUROPE/E SLAV/MACED. PAGE 24 H0489
MARXISM STRUCT WORKER REPRESENT

B61
CONQUEST R.,POWER AND POLICY IN THE USSR. USSR NAT/G POL/PAR DIPLOM MARXISM 20. PAGE 33 H0655
COM HIST/WRIT GOV/REL PWR

B61
DALLIN D.J.,SOVIET FOREIGN POLICY AFTER STALIN. ASIA CHINA/COM COM EUR+WWI GERMANY IRAN UK YUGOSLAVIA INT/ORG NAT/G VOL/ASSN FORCES TOP/EX BAL/PWR DOMIN EDU/PROP COERCE ATTIT PWR 20. PAGE 37 H0737
COM DIPLOM USSR

B61
LEVIN L.A.,BIBLIOGRAFIIA BIBLIOGRAFII PROIZVEDENII K. MARKSA, F. ENGELSA, V.I. LENINA. COM USSR NAT/G POL/PAR WORKER LEAD REV ATTIT...POLICY IDEA/COMP 20 MARX/KARL LENIN/VI ENGELS. PAGE 95 H1899
BIBLIOG/A MARXISM MARXIST CONCPT

B61
MARX K.,THE COMMUNIST MANIFESTO. IN (MENDEL A. ESSENTIAL WORKS OF MARXISM, NEW YORK: BANTAM. FUT MOD/EUR CULTURE ECO/DEV ECO/UNDEV AGRI FINAN INDUS MARKET PROC/MFG LABOR MUNIC POL/PAR CONSULT FORCES CREATE PLAN ADMIN ATTIT DRIVE RIGID/FLEX ORD/FREE PWR RESPECT MARX/KARL WORK. PAGE 104 H2081
COM NEW/IDEA CAP/ISM REV

B61
MOLLAU G.,INTERNATIONAL COMMUNISM AND WORLD REVOLUTION: HISTORY AND METHODS. RUSSIA USSR INT/ORG NAT/G POL/PAR VOL/ASSN FORCES BAL/PWR DIPLOM EXEC REGION WAR ATTIT PWR MARXISM...CONCPT TIME/SEQ COLD/WAR 19/20. PAGE 112 H2237
COM REV

B61
MONAS S.,THE THIRD SECTION: POLICE AND SOCIETY IN RUSSIA UNDER NICHOLAS I. MOD/EUR RUSSIA ELITES STRUCT NAT/G EX/STRUC ADMIN CONTROL PWR CONSERVE ...DECISION 19 NICHOLAS/I. PAGE 112 H2238
ORD/FREE COM FORCES COERCE

B61
PECKERT J.,DIE GROSSEN UND DIE KLEINEN MAECHTE. COM GERMANY/W ECO/DEV ECO/UNDEV NAT/G WAR RACE/REL PEACE...POLICY GP/COMP GOV/COMP 20 COLD/WAR. PAGE 124 H2482
DIPLOM ECO/TAC BAL/PWR

B61
REISKY-DUBNIC V.,COMMUNIST PROPAGANDA METHODS. CULTURE POL/PAR VOL/ASSN ATTIT...CONCPT TOT/POP. PAGE 131 H2611
COM EDU/PROP TOTALISM

B61
SCHIEDER T.,DOCUMENTS ON THE EXPULSION OF THE GERMANS FROM EASTERN-CENTRAL-EUROPE (VOL. II/III). COM EUR+WWI GERMANY HUNGARY ROMANIA USSR DIPLOM RACE/REL 20 MIGRATION. PAGE 139 H2785
GEOG CULTURE

B61
SETON-WATSON H.,FROM LENIN TO KHRUSHCHEV: THE HISTORY OF WORLD COMMUNISM. ASIA COM EUR+WWI ISLAM S/ASIA ECO/DEV ECO/UNDEV NAT/G POL/PAR DIPLOM ECO/TAC EDU/PROP COERCE GUERRILLA ATTIT DRIVE WORK TOT/POP NAZI 20. PAGE 141 H2832
PWR REV USSR

S61
BRZEZINSKI Z.K.,"THE ORGANIZATION OF THE COMMUNIST CAMP." COM CZECHOSLVK COM/IND NAT/G DELIB/GP INT/TRADE DOMIN EDU/PROP EXEC ROUTINE COERCE ATTIT PWR...MGT CONCPT TIME/SEQ CHARTS VAL/FREE 20 TREATY. PAGE 23 H0460
VOL/ASSN DIPLOM USSR

S61
SCHAPIRO L.,"SOVIET GOVERNMENT TODAY." COM EUR+WWI INT/ORG POL/PAR VOL/ASSN ACT/RES PLAN PERCEPT ...CONCPT TREND TOT/POP VAL/FREE 20. PAGE 139 H2773
NAT/G TOTALISM USSR

S61
SCHELLING T.C.,"NUCLEAR STRATEGY IN EUROPE." COM EUR+WWI USSR NAT/G FORCES NUC/PWR DRIVE ORD/FREE PWR...DECISION CONCPT OBS TREND HYPO/EXP 20. PAGE 139 H2784
FUT COERCE ARMS/CONT WAR

S61
TOMASIC D.,"POLITICAL LEADERSHIP IN CONTEMPORARY POLAND." COM EUR+WWI GERMANY NAT/G POL/PAR SECT DELIB/GP PLAN ECO/TAC DOMIN EDU/PROP PWR MARXISM ...MARXIST GEOG MGT CONCPT TIME/SEQ STERTYP 20. PAGE 156 H3111
SOCIETY ROUTINE USSR POLAND

S61
VALLET R.,"IRAN: KEY TO THE MIDDLE EAST." COM IRAQ ISLAM KUWAIT LEBANON SAUDI/ARAB TURKEY ELITES SOCIETY INDUS PROC/MFG POL/PAR TOP/EX PLAN BAL/PWR DIPLOM ECO/TAC ALL/VALS...TREND CENTO 20. PAGE 161 H3224
NAT/G ECO/UNDEV IRAN

S61
ZAGORIA D.S.,"THE FUTURE OF SINO-SOVIET RELATIONS." CHINA/COM INT/ORG NAT/G POL/PAR VOL/ASSN ACT/RES PLAN PERSON...METH/CNCPT TIME/SEQ TOT/POP VAL/FREE 20 MAO KHRUSH/N. PAGE 172 H3445
ASIA COM TOTALISM USSR

B62
BRUMBERG A.,RUSSIA UNDER KHRUSHCHEV. FUT USSR SOCIETY ECO/DEV AGRI PERF/ART WORKER PWR...SOC ANTHOL 20 KHRUSH/N. PAGE 22 H0453
COM MARXISM NAT/G CHIEF

B62
GOURE L.,CIVIL DEFENSE IN THE SOVIET UNION. COM USA+45 USSR MUNIC NAT/G DETER ATTIT MARXISM ...NAT/COMP 20 CIV/DEFENS. PAGE 59 H1188
PLAN FORCES WAR COERCE

B62
INSTITUTE FOR STUDY OF USSR,YOUTH IN FERMENT. INTELL NAT/G PERF/ART POL/PAR SCHOOL VOL/ASSN FORCES EDU/PROP ATTIT DRIVE PERCEPT HEALTH KNOWL MORAL ORD/FREE RESPECT...SOC OBS HIST/WRIT VAL/FREE. PAGE 77 H1537
COM CULTURE USSR

B62
JACKSON W.A.D.,RUSSO-CHINESE BORDERLANDS. ASIA COM USSR NAT/G PROVS EX/STRUC FORCES DOMIN COERCE PEACE ATTIT PWR SOVEREIGN WEALTH...CONCPT TREND CHARTS STERTYP VAL/FREE. PAGE 79 H1576
GEOG DIPLOM RUSSIA

B62
KINDERSLEY R.,THE FIRST RUSSIAN REVISIONISTS. COM USSR LAW ELITES INTELL NAT/G LEGIS ECO/TAC EDU/PROP CONTROL LEAD GP/REL SOCISM 19/20 MARX/KARL BOLSHEVISM. PAGE 86 H1712
CONSTN MARXISM POPULISM BIOG

B62
KIRPICEVA I.K.,HANDBUCH DER RUSSISCHEN UND SOWJETISCHEN BIBLIOGRAPHIEN (5 VOLS.). USSR STRUCT ECO/DEV DIPLOM LEAD ATTIT 18/20. PAGE 86 H1726
BIBLIOG/A NAT/G MARXISM COM

B62
KRUGLAK T.E.,THE TWO FACES OF TASS. COM COM/IND NAT/G ACT/RES PLAN PRESS PERCEPT PERSON KNOWL 20. PAGE 89 H1778
PUB/INST EDU/PROP USSR

B62
LAQUEUR W.,THE FUTURE OF COMMUNIST SOCIETY. CHINA/COM USSR LAW ECO/DEV NAT/G POL/PAR PLAN PROB/SOLV DIPLOM LEAD...POLICY CONCPT IDEA/COMP ANTHOL 20. PAGE 91 H1820
MARXISM COM FUT SOCIETY

B62
LAQUEUR W.,POLYCENTRISM. CHINA/COM COM USSR WOR+45 INT/ORG NAT/G ECO/TAC DOMIN LEAD ATTIT PWR SOVEREIGN...ANTHOL 20. PAGE 91 H1821
MARXISM DIPLOM BAL/PWR POLICY

B62
LITT T.,FREIHEIT UND LEBENS ORDNUNG. COM NAT/G ATTIT KNOWL...POLICY 20. PAGE 97 H1942
ORD/FREE MARXISM CONCPT IDEA/COMP

B62
MEHNERT K.,SOVIET MAN AND HIS WORLD. COM USSR INTELL FAM WORKER PLAN EDU/PROP REV PRODUC MARXISM ...SOC TREND SOC/INTEG 20 LENIN/VI STALIN/J KHRUSH/N. PAGE 108 H2162
SOCIETY CULTURE ECO/DEV

B62
PENTONY D.E.,RED WORLD IN TUMULT: COMMUNIST FOREIGN POLICIES. CHINA/COM COM NAT/G EDU/PROP COERCE ATTIT PWR RESPECT...SOC CHARTS 20. PAGE 124 H2488
ECO/UNDEV DOMIN USSR ASIA

B62
SCHECHTMAN J.B.,POSTWAR POPULATION TRANSFERS IN EUROPE: 1945-1955. COM CZECHOSLVK GERMANY POLAND USSR CULTURE SOCIETY PROB/SOLV AGREE NAT/LISM...SOC STAT TREND CHARTS METH/COMP 20 MIGRATION. PAGE 139 H2778
GEOG CENSUS EUR+WWI HABITAT

B62
STARR R.E.,POLAND 1944-1962: THE SOVIETIZATION OF A CAPTIVE PEOPLE. COM POLAND USSR POL/PAR SECT LEGIS DIPLOM DOMIN EDU/PROP CHOOSE ORD/FREE...POLICY CHARTS BIBLIOG 20. PAGE 149 H2973
MARXISM NAT/G TOTALISM NAT/COMP

B62
WALSTON H.,AGRICULTURE UNDER COMMUNISM. CHINA/COM COM PROB/SOLV HAPPINESS RIGID/FLEX...POLICY METH/COMP 20. PAGE 165 H3295
AGRI MARXISM PLAN CREATE

B62
YU LIEN YEN CHIU,INDEX TO THE CLASSIFIED FILES ON COMMUNIST CHINA. CHINA/COM CULTURE ECO/UNDEV CIVMIL/REL PWR WEALTH MARXISM...PSY SOC METH 20. PAGE 172 H3440
BIBLIOG INDEX COM

S62
ANSPRENGER F.,"NATIONALISM, COMMUNISM, AND THE UNCOMMITTED NATIONS: AMERICAN PROFILES." FUT ISLAM CULTURE SOCIETY ECO/UNDEV NAT/G POL/PAR PLAN ECO/TAC EDU/PROP COERCE CHOOSE ALL/VALS MARXISM SOCISM...SOC CONCPT BIOG TREND 20. PAGE 7 H0142
AFR COM NAT/LISM

S62
CROAN M.,"POLYCENTRISM: COMMUNIST INTERNATIONAL RELATIONS." ASIA STRUCT INT/ORG NAT/G POL/PAR CONSULT PLAN DOMIN EDU/PROP COERCE ATTIT RIGID/FLEX SOCISM...POLICY CONCPT TREND CON/ANAL GEN/LAWS MARX/KARL. PAGE 35 H0703
COM CREATE DIPLOM NAT/LISM

S62

DUNN S.D.,"DIRECTED CULTURE CHANGE IN THE SOVIET UNION: SOME SOVIET STUDIES." SOCIETY ORD/FREE...SOC HIST/WRIT VAL/FREE 20. PAGE 43 H0866

COM CULTURE USSR

S62

HYDE D.,"COMMUNISM IN LATIN AMERICA." L/A+17C ECO/DEV NAT/G SECT EDU/PROP ATTIT ALL/VALS MARXISM ...SOC CONCPT TOT/POP COLD/WAR OAS 20. PAGE 76 H1515

COM POL/PAR REV

S62

IOVTCHOUK M.T.,"ON SOME THEORETICAL PRINCIPLES AND METHODS OF SOCIOLOGICAL INVESTIGATIONS (IN RUSSIAN)." FUT USA+45 STRATA R+D NAT/G POL/PAR TOP/EX ACT/RES PLAN ECO/TAC EDU/PROP ROUTINE ATTIT RIGID/FLEX MARXISM SOCISM...MARXIST METH/CNCPT OBS TREND NAT/COMP GEN/LAWS 20. PAGE 78 H1564

COM ECO/DEV CAP/ISM USSR

S62

KOLARZ W.,"THE IMPACT OF COMMUNISM ON WEST AFRICA." AFR FUT SOCIETY INT/ORG NAT/G CREATE PLAN DOMIN EDU/PROP COERCE NAT/LISM ATTIT RIGID/FLEX SOCISM ...POLICY CONCPT TREND MARX/KARL 20. PAGE 88 H1751

COM POL/PAR COLONIAL

S62

LONDON K.,"SINO-SOVIET RELATIONS IN THE CONTEXT OF THE 'WORLD SOCIALIST SYSTEM'." ASIA CHINA/COM COM USSR INT/ORG NAT/G TOP/EX BAL/PWR DIPLOM DOMIN ATTIT PERCEPT RIGID/FLEX PWR MARXISM...METH/CNCPT TREND 20. PAGE 98 H1957

DELIB/GP CONCPT SOCISM

S62

PISTRAK L.,"SOVIET VIEWS ON AFRICA." AFR COM FUT ISLAM USSR INTELL STRUCT KIN POL/PAR PLAN EDU/PROP RIGID/FLEX PWR MARXISM...TIME/SEQ WORK TOT/POP 20. PAGE 126 H2516

NAT/G ATTIT SOCISM

S62

SARKISYANZ E.,"NATIONALISM, CAPITALISM, AND THE UNCOMMITED NATIONS: MARXISM AND ASIAN CULTURAL TRADITIONS." ASIA BURMA CHINA/COM COM CULTURE SOCIETY NAT/G POL/PAR PLAN DOMIN EDU/PROP COLONIAL COERCE ATTIT RIGID/FLEX...CONCPT TREND MARX/KARL 20 TIBET BUDDHISM. PAGE 138 H2755

S/ASIA SECT NAT/LISM CAP/ISM

S62

SHATTEN F.,"POLYCENTRISM: AFRICA: NATIONALISM AND COMMUNISM." ASIA COM FUT ISLAM CULTURE SOCIETY ECO/UNDEV NAT/G PLAN DOMIN COLONIAL COERCE CHOOSE RIGID/FLEX ALL/VALS MARXISM...CONCPT TREND 20. PAGE 143 H2852

AFR ATTIT NAT/LISM SOCISM

S62

STRACHEY J.,"COMMUNIST INTENTIONS." ASIA USSR YUGOSLAVIA INT/ORG NAT/G FORCES DOMIN EDU/PROP COERCE NUC/PWR NAT/LISM PEACE RIGID/FLEX PWR MARXISM...CONCPT MYTH OBS TIME/SEQ TREND COLD/WAR TOT/POP 20. PAGE 150 H2992

COM ATTIT WAR

B63

BARNETT A.D.,COMMUNIST STRATEGIES IN ASIA: A COMPARATIVE ANALYSIS OF GOVERNMENTS AND PARTIES. COM FUT S/ASIA CULTURE SOCIETY STRATA NAT/G DELIB/GP ACT/RES ECO/TAC EDU/PROP COERCE CHOOSE ATTIT RIGID/FLEX ORD/FREE PWR SKILL...SIMUL VAL/FREE 20. PAGE 11 H0223

ASIA POL/PAR DIPLOM USSR

B63

BROGAN D.W.,POLITICAL PATTERNS IN TODAY'S WORLD. FRANCE USA+45 USSR WOR+45 CONSTN STRUCT PLAN DIPLOM ADMIN LEAD ROLE SUPEGO...PHIL/SCI 20. PAGE 21 H0429

NAT/COMP NEW/LIB COM TOTALISM

B63

BRZEZINSKI Z.K.,AFRICA AND THE COMMUNIST WORLD. AFR ASIA COM CULTURE SOCIETY INT/ORG DELIB/GP ACT/RES ECO/TAC COERCE ORD/FREE PWR WEALTH...STAT TOT/POP VAL/FREE 20. PAGE 23 H0461

ATTIT EDU/PROP DIPLOM USSR

B63

FISCHER-GALATI S.A.,RUMANIA; A BIBLIOGRAPHIC GUIDE (PAMPHLET). ROMANIA INTELL ECO/DEV LABOR SECT WEALTH...GEOG SOC/WK LING 20. PAGE 51 H1012

BIBLIOG/A NAT/G COM LAW

B63

HYDE D.,THE PEACEFUL ASSAULT. COM UAR USSR ECO/DEV ECO/UNDEV NAT/G POL/PAR CAP/ISM PWR 20. PAGE 76 H1516

MARXISM CONTROL ECO/TAC DIPLOM

B63

JELAVICH C.,THE BALKANS IN TRANSITION: ESSAYS ON THE DEVELOPMENT OF BALKAN LIFE AND POLITICS SINCE THE EIGHTEENTH CENTURY. COM GREECE TURKEY ECO/UNDEV NAT/G SECT ATTIT...GEOG SOC CONCPT TIME/SEQ ANTHOL 18/20. PAGE 80 H1596

CULTURE RIGID/FLEX

B63

KURZMAN D.,SUBVERSION OF THE INNOCENTS: PATTERNS OF COMMUNIST PENETRATION OF AFRICA, THE MIDDLE EAST AND AFRICA. AFR ASIA ISLAM S/ASIA CULTURE NAT/G FORCES PLAN EDU/PROP ADMIN ATTIT...CONCPT INT UNPLAN/INT TIME/SEQ. PAGE 89 H1785

COM COERCE

B63

LAVROFF D.-G.,LES LIBERTES PUBLIQUES EN UNION SOVIETIQUE (REV. ED.). USSR NAT/G WORKER SANCTION CRIME MARXISM NEW/LIB...JURID BIBLIOG WORSHIP 20. PAGE 92 H1843

ORD/FREE LAW ATTIT COM

B63

LETHBRIDGE H.J.,THE PEASANT AND THE COMMUNES. CHINA/COM COM USSR NEIGH PROB/SOLV ADJUST EFFICIENCY...POLICY METH/COMP NAT/COMP 20. PAGE 95 H1894

MARXISM ECO/TAC AGRI WORKER

B63

SETON-WATSON H.,THE NEW IMPERIALISM. COM EUR+WWI MOD/EUR ECO/UNDEV NAT/G FORCES DIPLOM DOMIN EDU/PROP LEGIT COLONIAL EXEC COERCE GP/REL RACE/REL DISCRIM ATTIT...TIME/SEQ 20. PAGE 142 H2833

ECO/TAC RUSSIA USSR

B63

SWEARER H.R.,CONTEMPORARY COMMUNISM: THEORY AND PRACTICE. COM USSR SOCIETY ECO/DEV POL/PAR FORCES PLAN ADMIN LEAD NAT/LISM...POLICY ANTHOL 20 LENIN/VI COM/PARTY. PAGE 151 H3015

MARXISM CONCPT DIPLOM NAT/G

B63

TUCKER R.C.,THE SOVIET POLITICAL MIND. COM INTELL NAT/G TOP/EX EDU/PROP ADMIN COERCE TOTALISM ATTIT PWR MARXISM...PSY MYTH HYPO/EXP 20. PAGE 157 H3136

STRUCT RIGID/FLEX ELITES USSR

B63

ULAM A.B.,THE NEW FACE OF SOVIET TOTALITARIANISM. FUT INTELL NAT/G POL/PAR EX/STRUC TOP/EX DIPLOM ECO/TAC DOMIN EDU/PROP LEGIT COERCE ATTIT RIGID/FLEX...OBS HIST/WRIT TREND TOT/POP VAL/FREE COLD/WAR. PAGE 158 H3150

COM PWR TOTALISM USSR

L63

BOLGAR V.,"THE PUBLIC INTEREST: A JURISPRUDENTIAL AND COMPARATIVE OVERVIEW OF SYMPOSIUM ON FUNDAMENTAL CONCEPTS OF PUBLIC LAW" COM FRANCE GERMANY SWITZERLND LAW ADJUD ADMIN AGREE LAISSEZ ...JURID GEN/LAWS 20 EUROPE/E. PAGE 18 H0369

CONCPT ORD/FREE CONTROL NAT/COMP

L63

MICHAEL F.,"KHRUSHCHEV'S DISLOYAL OPPOSITION: STRUCTURAL CHANGE AND POWER STRUGGLE IN COMMUNIST BLOC." ASIA CHINA/COM FUT NAT/G POL/PAR CONSULT PLAN DOMIN ATTIT...POLICY CONCPT TREND MARX/KARL 20 KHRUSH/N. PAGE 110 H2195

COM STRUCT NAT/LISM USSR

S63

BECHHOEFER B.G.,"SOVIET ATTITUDE TOWARD DISARMAMENT." COM USSR NAT/G ACT/RES TEC/DEV NUC/PWR ATTIT DISPL RIGID/FLEX PWR...METH/CNCPT TREND GEN/LAWS COLD/WAR 20. PAGE 13 H0252

FORCES EDU/PROP ARMS/CONT

S63

HALPERN A.M.,"THE EMERGENCE OF AN ASIAN COMMUNIST BLOC." ASIA CHINA/COM COM FUT KOREA/N S/ASIA VIETNAM/N STRATA NAT/G DELIB/GP FORCES TOP/EX PLAN BAL/PWR COERCE DETER PWR COLD/WAR WORK 20. PAGE 65 H1295

POL/PAR EDU/PROP DIPLOM

S63

HARRIS R.L.,"COMMUNISM AND ASIA: ILLUSIONS AND MISCONCEPTIONS." ASIA COM FUT S/ASIA ECO/UNDEV AGRI NAT/G POL/PAR EX/STRUC EDU/PROP COERCE ATTIT MARXISM COLD/WAR TOT/POP 20. PAGE 67 H1344

PWR GUERRILLA

S63

MORISON D.,"AFRICAN STUDIES IN THE SOVIET UNION." AFR COM CULTURE INTELL REGION ATTIT KNOWL...HUM TREND 20. PAGE 113 H2258

EDU/PROP USSR

S63

STAAR R.F.,"HOW STRONG IS THE SOVIET BLOC." COM USSR ECO/DEV NAT/G DELIB/GP ECO/TAC RIGID/FLEX ...CONCPT RECORD CHARTS 20. PAGE 148 H2964

FORCES MYTH TOTALISM

S63

TANG P.S.H.,"SINO-SOVIET TENSIONS." ASIA CHINA/COM COM CUBA KOREA/N VIETNAM/N NAT/G VOL/ASSN DELIB/GP PEACE PERCEPT PWR...METH/CNCPT MYTH RECORD TREND GEN/LAWS 20. PAGE 152 H3041

ACT/RES EDU/PROP REV

B64

BELL C.,THE DEBATABLE ALLIANCE. COM UK USA+45 NAT/G FORCES PLAN BAL/PWR NUC/PWR WAR ATTIT...GOV/COMP 20. PAGE 13 H0263

DIPLOM PWR PEACE POLICY

B64

CAUTE D.,COMMUNISM AND THE FRENCH INTELLECTUALS, 1914-1960. COM EUR+WWI MOD/EUR NAT/G PERF/ART PROF/ORG CREATE EDU/PROP ATTIT PERSON KNOWL MARXISM ...SOC TIME/SEQ MARX/KARL 20 MALRAUX/A GIDE/A SARTRE/J. PAGE 28 H0563

POL/PAR INTELL

B64

GRIFFITH W.E.,THE SINO-SOVIET RIFT. ASIA CHINA/COM COM CUBA USSR YUGOSLAVIA NAT/G POL/PAR VOL/ASSN DELIB/GP FORCES TOP/EX DIPLOM EDU/PROP DRIVE PERSON PWR...TREND 20 TREATY. PAGE 61 H1224

ATTIT TIME/SEQ BAL/PWR SOCISM

B64

GRIFFITH W.E.,COMMUNISM IN EUROPE (2 VOLS.). CZECHOSLVK USSR WOR+45 WOR-45 YUGOSLAVIA INGP/REL MARXISM SOCISM...ANTHOL 20 EUROPE/E. PAGE 61 H1225

COM POL/PAR DIPLOM GOV/COMP

B64

KIS T.I.,LES PAYS DE L'EUROPE DE L'EST: LEURS RAPPORTS MUTUELS ET LE PROBLEME DE LEUR INTEGRATION DANS L'ORBITE DE L'USSR. EUR+WWI RUSSIA USSR INT/ORG NAT/G REV ATTIT...JURID SOC BIBLIOG WARSAW/P COMECON EUROPE/E. PAGE 86 H1727

DIPLOM COM MARXISM REGION

B64

KOLARZ W.,BOOKS ON COMMUNISM. USSR WOR+45 CULTURE

BIBLIOG/A

NAT/G POL/PAR DIPLOM LEAD...CONCPT GOV/COMP IDEA/COMP. PAGE 88 H1752 — SOCIETY COM MARXISM

B64
LAPENNA I.,STATE AND LAW: SOVIET AND YUGOSLAV THEORY. USSR YUGOSLAVIA STRATA STRUCT NAT/G DOMIN COERCE MARXISM...GOV/COMP IDEA/COMP 20. PAGE 91 H1812 — JURID COM LAW SOVEREIGN

B64
MAUD J.,AID FOR DEVELOPING COUNTRIES. COM EUR+WWI UK INT/TRADE ORD/FREE...GOV/COMP 20. PAGE 105 H2101 — FOR/AID DIPLOM ECO/TAC ECO/UNDEV

B64
PIPES R.,THE FORMATION OF THE SOVIET UNION. EUR+WWI MOD/EUR STRUCT ECO/UNDEV NAT/G LEGIS DOMIN LEGIT CT/SYS EXEC COERCE ALL/VALS...POLICY RELATIV HIST/WRIT TIME/SEQ TOT/POP 19/20. PAGE 126 H2514 — COM USSR RUSSIA

B64
RESHETAR J.S. JR.,A CONCISE HISTORY OF THE COMMUNIST PARTY OF THE SOVIET UNION (REV. ED.). COM USSR NAT/G EXEC 19/20 LENIN/VI STALIN/J KHRUSH/N. PAGE 131 H2618 — CHIEF POL/PAR MARXISM PWR

B64
SIEKANOWICZ P.,LEGAL SOURCES AND BIBLIOGRAPHY OF POLAND. COM POLAND CONSTN NAT/G PARL/PROC SANCTION CRIME MARXISM 16/20. PAGE 143 H2870 — BIBLIOG ADJUD LAW JURID

B64
VON STEIN L.J.,THE HISTORY OF THE SOCIAL MOVEMENT IN FRANCE, 1789-1850 (TRANS. BY K. MENGELBERG). COM FRANCE MOD/EUR NAT/G EX/STRUC INGP/REL ALL/IDEOS CONSERVE MARXISM...SOC BIBLIOG 18/19. PAGE 164 H3278 — REV STRATA

S64
BARIETY J.,"LA POLITIQUE EXTERIEURE ALLEMANDE DANS L'HIVER 1939-1940." COM FINLAND GERMANY ISLAM ITALY USSR NAT/G FORCES ECO/TAC DOMIN EDU/PROP COERCE WAR PWR WEALTH...HIST/WRIT NAZI TOT/POP VAL/FREE 20. PAGE 11 H0216 — EUR+WWI DIPLOM

S64
CATTELL D.T.,"SOVIET POLICIES IN LATIN AMERICA." COM CUBA L/A+17C USSR SOCIETY NAT/G POL/PAR FORCES CREATE ECO/TAC EDU/PROP REGION REV RIGID/FLEX ...GEN/LAWS COLD/WAR 20. PAGE 28 H0560 — DRIVE PWR

S64
GARMARNIKOW M.,"INFLUENCE-BUYING IN WEST AFRICA." COM FUT USSR INTELL NAT/G PLAN TEC/DEV ECO/TAC DOMIN EDU/PROP REGION NAT/LISM ATTIT DRIVE ALL/VALS SOVEREIGN...POLICY PSY SOC CONCPT TREND STERTYP WORK COLD/WAR 20. PAGE 55 H1102 — AFR ECO/UNDEV FOR/AID SOCISM

S64
HORECKY P.L.,"LIBRARY OF CONGRESS PUBLICATIONS IN AID OF USSR AND EAST EUROPEAN RESEARCH." BULGARIA CZECHOSLVK POLAND USSR YUGOSLAVIA NAT/G POL/PAR DIPLOM ADMIN GOV/REL...CLASSIF 20. PAGE 73 H1468 — BIBLIOG/A COM MARXISM

S64
KOVNER M.,"THE SINO-SOVIET DISPUTE: COMMUNISM AT THE CROSSROADS." ASIA CHINA/COM COM USSR ECO/UNDEV NAT/G TOP/EX CREATE BAL/PWR DOMIN EDU/PROP PWR ...CONCPT COMECON 20. PAGE 88 H1760 — ATTIT TREND

S64
LERNER W.,"THE HISTORICAL ORIGINS OF THE SOVIET DOCTRINE OF PEACEFUL COEXISTENCE." COM USSR INT/ORG NAT/G VOL/ASSN PLAN PEACE ATTIT RIGID/FLEX PWR MARXISM...TIME/SEQ COLD/WAR 20. PAGE 95 H1891 — EDU/PROP DIPLOM

S64
MARES V.E.,"EAST EUROPE'S SECOND CHANCE." COM EUR+WWI HUNGARY ROMANIA USSR YUGOSLAVIA ECO/UNDEV NAT/G TOP/EX CREATE PLAN TEC/DEV REGION NAT/LISM RIGID/FLEX PWR...CONCPT STAT COMECON 20. PAGE 102 H2047 — VOL/ASSN ECO/TAC

S64
SOLOVEYTCHIK G.,"BOOKS ON RUSSIA." USSR ELITES NAT/G PERF/ART REV GOV/REL MARXISM...AUD/VIS 20. PAGE 147 H2929 — BIBLIOG/A COM CULTURE

S64
SWEARER H.R.,"AFTER KHRUSHCHEV: WHAT NEXT." COM FUT USSR CONSTN ELITES NAT/G POL/PAR CHIEF DELIB/GP LEGIS DOMIN LEAD...RECORD TREND STERTYP GEN/METH 20. PAGE 151 H3016 — EX/STRUC PWR

C64
GOLDMAN M.I.,"COMPARATIVE ECONOMIC SYSTEMS: A READER." COM ECO/UNDEV NAT/G BUDGET CAP/ISM ADMIN TOTALISM MARXISM SOCISM...MGT ANTHOL BIBLIOG 19/20. PAGE 58 H1157 — NAT/COMP CONTROL IDEA/COMP

B65
ALTON T.P.,POLISH NATIONAL INCOME AND PRODUCT IN 1954, 1955, AND 1956. POLAND FINAN EX/STRUC ECO/TAC PRICE COST WEALTH 20. PAGE 6 H0117 — COM INDUS NAT/G ECO/DEV

B65
JOHNSON P.,KHRUSHCHEV AND THE ARTS: POLITICS OF SOVIET CULTURE, 1962-1964. COM USSR NAT/G PERF/ART CONFER DEBATE GP/REL PERS/REL UTIL ATTIT DRIVE 20 KHRUSH/N. PAGE 81 H1626 — CULTURE MARXISM POLICY CHIEF

B65
O'BRIEN F.,CRISIS IN WORLD COMMUNISM* MARXISM IN SEARCH OF EFFICIENCY. COM ECO/DEV PLAN INT/TRADE WAR ADJUST PEACE...STAT TIME/SEQ GOV/COMP NAT/COMP COLD/WAR. PAGE 119 H2384 — MARXISM USSR DRIVE EFFICIENCY

B65
PUNDEEF M.V.,BULGARIA; A BIBLIOGRAPHIC GUIDE. BULGARIA LAW CULTURE INTELL ECO/DEV LEAD MARXISM 20. PAGE 128 H2566 — BIBLIOG/A NAT/G COM SOCISM

B65
ROMEIN J.,THE ASIAN CENTURY. ASIA COM S/ASIA DIPLOM COLONIAL TIME 20. PAGE 133 H2666 — REV NAT/LISM CULTURE MARXISM

B65
ROSENBERG A.,DEMOCRACY AND SOCIALISM. COM EUR+WWI FRANCE MOD/EUR STRUCT INT/ORG NAT/G POL/PAR TOP/EX EDU/PROP COERCE PERSON PWR FASCISM MARXISM...CONCPT TIME/SEQ MARX/KARL 19/20. PAGE 134 H2677 — ATTIT

B65
ULAM A.,THE BOLSHEVIKS. COM USSR NAT/G CHIEF ECO/TAC ADMIN LEAD WAR POPULISM...POLICY 19/20 LENIN/VI BOLSHEVISM. PAGE 157 H3148 — SOCISM POL/PAR TOP/EX REV

B65
US DEPARTMENT OF DEFENSE,US SECURITY ARMS CONTROL, AND DISARMAMENT 1961-1965 (PAMPHLET). CHINA/COM COM GERMANY/W ISRAEL SPACE USA+45 USSR WOR+45 FORCES EDU/PROP DETER EQUILIB PEACE ALL/VALS...GOV/COMP 20 NATO. PAGE 159 H3183 — BIBLIOG/A ARMS/CONT NUC/PWR DIPLOM

B65
WINT G.,ASIA: A HANDBOOK. ASIA COM INDIA USSR CULTURE INTELL NAT/G...GEOG STAT CENSUS NAT/COMP WORSHIP 20 TREATY CHINJAP. PAGE 169 H3387 — DIPLOM SOC

S65
GRIFFITH S.B.,"COMMUNIST CHINA'S CAPACITY TO MAKE WAR." CHINA/COM COM NAT/G TOP/EX PLAN DOMIN COERCE NUC/PWR ATTIT RESPECT SKILL...CONCPT MYTH TIME/SEQ TREND COLD/WAR 20. PAGE 61 H1221 — FORCES PWR WEAPON ASIA

S65
HELMREICH E.C.,"KADAR'S HUNGARY." COM EUR+WWI HUNGARY USSR INTELL ECO/DEV AGRI INT/ORG TOP/EX DOMIN ALL/VALS WORK COLD/WAR 20. PAGE 69 H1390 — NAT/G RIGID/FLEX TOTALISM

S65
ROGGER H.,"EAST GERMANY: STABLE OR IMMOBILE." COM EUR+WWI GERMANY/E NAT/G INT/TRADE DOMIN EDU/PROP COERCE TOTALISM COLD/WAR 20. PAGE 133 H2659 — TOP/EX RIGID/FLEX GERMANY

S65
RUBINSTEIN A.Z.,"YUGOSLAVIA'S OPENING SOCIETY." COM USSR INTELL NAT/G LEGIS TOP/EX LEGIT CT/SYS RIGID/FLEX ALL/VALS SOCISM...HUM TIME/SEQ TREND 20. PAGE 135 H2708 — CONSTN EX/STRUC YUGOSLAVIA

S65
STAAR R.F.,"RETROGRESSION IN POLAND." COM USSR AGRI INDUS NAT/G CREATE EDU/PROP TOTALISM RIGID/FLEX ORD/FREE PWR SOCISM...RECORD CHARTS 20. PAGE 148 H2965 — TOP/EX ECO/TAC POLAND

S65
TABORSKY E.,"CHANGE IN CZECHOSLOVAKIA." COM USSR ELITES INTELL AGRI INDUS NAT/G DELIB/GP EX/STRUC ECO/TAC TOTALISM ATTIT RIGID/FLEX SOCISM...MGT CONCPT TREND 20. PAGE 152 H3031 — ECO/DEV PLAN CZECHOSLVK

S65
VUCINICH W.S.,"WHITHER RUMANIA." COM USSR YUGOSLAVIA NAT/G VOL/ASSN DELIB/GP TOP/EX LEGIT NAT/LISM TOTALISM ATTIT DRIVE RIGID/FLEX ORD/FREE WEALTH SOCISM...TIME/SEQ TREND 20. PAGE 164 H3281 — ECO/DEV CREATE ROMANIA

C65
COLEMAN J.S.,"EDUCATION AND POLITICAL DEVELOPMENT." COM CULTURE INTELL STRUCT SCHOOL PERSON SOVEREIGN ...POLICY ANTHOL BIBLIOG/A METH 20. PAGE 31 H0629 — ECO/UNDEV NAT/LISM EDU/PROP TEC/DEV

N65
MOTE M.E.,SOVIET LOCAL AND REPUBLIC ELECTIONS. COM USSR NAT/G PLAN PARTIC GOV/REL TOTALISM PWR ...CHARTS 20. PAGE 114 H2270 — CHOOSE ADMIN CONTROL LOC/G

B66
BROWN J.F.,THE NEW EASTERN EUROPE. ALBANIA BULGARIA HUNGARY POLAND ROMANIA CULTURE AGRI POL/PAR WAR NAT/LISM MARXISM...CHARTS BIBLIOG 20. PAGE 22 H0444 — DIPLOM COM NAT/G ECO/UNDEV

B66
DALLIN A.,POLITICS IN THE SOVIET UNION: 7 CASES. COM USSR LAW POL/PAR CHIEF FORCES WRITING CONTROL PARL/PROC CIVMIL/REL TOTALISM...ANTHOL 20 KHRUSH/N STALIN/J CASEBOOK COM/PARTY. PAGE 37 H0736 — MARXISM DOMIN ORD/FREE GOV/REL

B66
EPSTEIN F.T.,THE AMERICAN BIBLIOGRAPHY OF RUSSIAN AND EAST EUROPEAN STUDIES FOR 1964. USSR LOC/G NAT/G POL/PAR FORCES ADMIN ARMS/CONT...JURID CONCPT 20 UN. PAGE 47 H0933 — BIBLIOG COM MARXISM DIPLOM

B66
HEYMANN F.G.,POLAND AND CZECHOSLOVAKIA. COM CZECHOSLVK POLAND...CHARTS BIBLIOG/A 9/20. PAGE 70 — CULTURE NAT/LISM

H1413 ORD/FREE WAR

B66
INTL CONF ON WORLD POLITICS-5,EASTERN EUROPE IN TRANSITION. EUR+WWI USSR ECO/TAC NAT/LISM ATTIT SOVEREIGN...CHARTS ANTHOL 20 TREATY WARSAW/P. PAGE 78 H1562 COM NAT/COMP MARXISM DIPLOM

B66
JACKSON G.D.,COMINTERN AND PEASANT IN EAST EUROPE 1919-1930. BULGARIA COM CZECHOSLVK EUR+WWI POLAND ROMANIA YUGOSLAVIA STRATA AGRI VOL/ASSN DIPLOM CONTROL CROWD WEALTH...POLICY NAT/COMP 20. PAGE 79 H1575 MARXISM ECO/UNDEV WORKER INT/ORG

B66
LONDON K.,EASTERN EUROPE IN TRANSITION. CHINA/COM USSR DOMIN COLONIAL CENTRAL RIGID/FLEX PWR...SOC ANTHOL 20. PAGE 98 H1958 SOVEREIGN COM NAT/LISM DIPLOM

B66
MACFARQUHAR R.,CHINA UNDER MAO: POLITICS TAKES COMMAND. CHINA/COM COM AGRI INDUS CHIEF FORCES DIPLOM INT/TRADE EDU/PROP TASK REV ADJUST...ANTHOL 20 MAO. PAGE 100 H1992 ECO/UNDEV TEC/DEV ECO/TAC ADMIN

B66
MAICHEL K.,CATALOG OF SOVIET AND RUSSIAN NEWSPAPERS AT THE HOOVER INSTITUTION OF WAR, REVOLUTION AND PEACE. USSR NAT/G EDU/PROP LEAD REV WAR PEACE ATTIT 19/20. PAGE 101 H2017 BIBLIOG/A PRESS COM MARXISM

B66
SKILLING H.G.,THE GOVERNMENTS OF COMMUNIST EAST EUROPE. COM EUR+WWI ELITES FORCES DIPLOM ECO/TAC CONTROL HABITAT SOCISM...DECISION BIBLIOG 20 EUROPE/E COM/PARTY. PAGE 145 H2895 MARXISM NAT/COMP GP/COMP DOMIN

B66
SPULBER N.,THE STATE AND ECONOMIC DEVELOPMENT IN EASTERN EUROPE. BULGARIA COM CZECHOSLVK HUNGARY POLAND YUGOSLAVIA CULTURE PLAN CAP/ISM INT/TRADE CONTROL...POLICY CHARTS METH/COMP BIBLIOG/A 19/20. PAGE 148 H2958 ECO/DEV ECO/UNDEV NAT/G TOTALISM

B66
SWEARINGEN A.R.,SOVIET AND CHINESE COMMUNIST POWER IN THE WORLD TODAY. COM USA+45 ECO/UNDEV CREATE LEAD WAR ADJUST...TREND NAT/COMP ANTHOL COLD/WAR KHRUSH/N. PAGE 151 H3017 USSR ASIA DIPLOM ATTIT

B66
US DEPARTMENT OF STATE,RESEARCH ON THE USSR AND EASTERN EUROPE (EXTERNAL RESEARCH LIST NO 1-25). USSR LAW CULTURE SOCIETY NAT/G TEC/DEV DIPLOM EDU/PROP REGION...GEOG LING. PAGE 160 H3191 BIBLIOG/A EUR+WWI COM MARXISM

B66
US DEPARTMENT OF THE ARMY,COMMUNIST CHINA: A STRATEGIC SURVEY: A BIBLIOGRAPHY (PAMPHLET NO. 20-67). CHINA/COM COM INDIA USSR NAT/G POL/PAR EX/STRUC FORCES NUC/PWR REV ATTIT...POLICY GEOG CHARTS. PAGE 160 H3194 BIBLIOG/A MARXISM S/ASIA DIPLOM

B66
ZABLOCKI C.J.,SINO-SOVIET RIVALRY. AFR ASIA CHINA/COM CUBA EUR+WWI L/A+17C USA+45 USSR WOR+45 POL/PAR FORCES COERCE NUC/PWR...GOV/COMP IDEA/COMP 20 MAO KHRUSH/N. PAGE 172 H3444 DIPLOM MARXISM COM

S66
SKILLING H.G.,"THE RUMANIAN NATIONAL COURSE." COM EUR+WWI ROMANIA NAT/G ECO/TAC PWR 20. PAGE 145 H2896 NAT/LISM POLICY DIPLOM MARXISM

B67
BROMKE A.,POLAND'S POLITICS: IDEALISM VS. REALISM. COM GERMANY POLAND RUSSIA USSR POL/PAR CATHISM ...BIBLIOG 19/20. PAGE 21 H0431 NAT/G DIPLOM MARXISM

B67
BRZEZINSKI Z.K.,THE SOVIET BLOC: UNITY AND CONFLICT (2ND ED., REV., ENLARGED). COM POLAND USSR INTELL CHIEF EX/STRUC CONTROL EXEC GOV/REL PWR MARXISM ...TREND IDEA/COMP 20 LENIN/VI MARX/KARL STALIN/J. PAGE 23 H0463 NAT/G DIPLOM

B67
BURNHAM J.,THE WAR WE ARE IN, THE LAST DECADE AND THE NEXT. ASIA COM EUR+WWI S/ASIA WOR+45 ECO/UNDEV INT/ORG FORCES WAR...OLD/LIB TREND 20 COLD/WAR. PAGE 25 H0492 POLICY NAT/G DIPLOM NAT/COMP

B67
COLLINS R.O.,EGYPT AND THE SUDAN. COM FRANCE ISLAM SUDAN UAR UK SOCIETY NAT/G COLONIAL NAT/LISM...GEOG SOC LING TREND SOC/INTEG 7/20 SUEZ. PAGE 32 H0635 AGRI CULTURE ECO/UNDEV

B67
FALL B.B.,HO CHI MINH ON REVOLUTION: SELECTED WRITINGS, 1920-66. COM VIETNAM ELITES NAT/G COERCE GUERRILLA RACE/REL MARXISM...MARXIST ANTHOL 20. PAGE 48 H0968 REV COLONIAL ECO/UNDEV S/ASIA

B67
HILSMAN R.,TO MOVE A NATION: THE POLITICS OF FOREIGN POLICY IN THE ADMINISTRATION OF JOHN F. KENNEDY. CHINA/COM COM USSR VIETNAM NAT/G DELIB/GP FORCES PLAN PROB/SOLV BAL/PWR COLONIAL EXEC REV PWR 20 KENNEDY/JF PRESIDENT. PAGE 71 H1418 CHIEF DIPLOM

B67
KOLKOWICZ R.,THE SOVIET MILITARY AND THE COMMUNIST PARTY. COM USSR ELITES NAT/G CREATE CIVMIL/REL GP/REL...TREND BIBLIOG/A 20 COM/PARTY. PAGE 88 H1753 MARXISM CONSTN FORCES POL/PAR

B67
MICKIEWICZ E.P.,SOVIET POLITICAL SCHOOLS: THE COMMUNIST PARTY ADULT INSTRUCTION SYSTEM. COM USSR INTELL SCHOOL WORKER CREATE PRESS ADMIN CONTROL ATTIT KNOWL...PROG/TEAC SOC/INTEG 20 COM/PARTY. PAGE 110 H2200 NAT/G EDU/PROP AGE/A MARXISM

B67
NATIONAL SCIENCE FOUNDATION,DIRECTORY OF SELECTED RESEARCH INSTITUTES IN EASTERN EUROPE. BULGARIA CZECHOSLVK HUNGARY POLAND ROMANIA INTELL ACADEM NAT/G ACT/RES 20. PAGE 116 H2323 INDEX R+D COM PHIL/SCI

B67
POMEROY W.J.,HALF A CENTURY OF SOCIALISM. USSR LAW AGRI INDUS NAT/G CREATE DIPLOM EDU/PROP PERSON ORD/FREE WEALTH...POLICY TREND 20. PAGE 127 H2541 SOCISM MARXISM COM SOCIETY

B67
RUDMAN H.C.,THE SCHOOL AND STATE IN THE USSR. COM USSR ACADEM LABOR LOC/G PUB/INST EDU/PROP GP/REL ROLE...POLICY DECISION MGT CHARTS 20. PAGE 136 H2712 SCHOOL ADMIN NAT/G POL/PAR

B67
SETON-WATSON H.,THE RUSSIAN EMPIRE, 1801-1917. COM RUSSIA STRATA ECO/DEV AGRI INDUS POL/PAR DIPLOM NAT/LISM MARXISM...IDEA/COMP BIBLIOG 19/20 MARX/KARL. PAGE 142 H2834 SOCIETY NAT/G LEAD POLICY

B67
SHAFFER H.G.,THE COMMUNIST WORLD: MARXIST AND NON-MARXIST VIEWS. WOR+45 SOCIETY DIPLOM ECO/TAC CONTROL SOCISM...MARXIST ANTHOL BIBLIOG/A 20. PAGE 142 H2838 MARXISM NAT/COMP IDEA/COMP COM

B67
TREADGOLD D.W.,SOVIET AND CHINESE COMMUNISM* SIMILARITIES AND DIFFERENCES. CHINA/COM COM NAT/G PLAN DIPLOM CENTRAL PWR MARXISM...POLICY 20. PAGE 156 H3128 CULTURE NAT/LISM

B67
ZALESKI E.,PLANNING REFORMS IN THE SOVIET UNION 1962-1966. COM USSR NAT/G CONFER CONTROL EFFICIENCY MARXISM...POLICY DECISION 20. PAGE 172 H3446 ECO/DEV PLAN ADMIN CENTRAL

L67
EGBERT D.D.,"THE IDEA OF 'AVANT-GARDE' IN ART AND POLITICS." USSR CULTURE INTELL POL/PAR CREATE EDU/PROP CONTROL REV ANOMIE DRIVE ROLE...IDEA/COMP 20. PAGE 45 H0895 ART/METH COM ATTIT

S67
CARR E.H.,"REVOLUTION FROM ABOVE." USSR STRATA FINAN INDUS NAT/G DOMIN LEAD GP/REL INGP/REL OWN PRODUC PWR 20 STALIN/J. PAGE 27 H0538 AGRI POLICY COM EFFICIENCY

S67
EGBERT D.D.,"POLITICS AND ART IN COMMUNIST BULGARIA" BULGARIA COM USSR CULTURE DIPLOM INGP/REL TOTALISM...TREND 20. PAGE 45 H0894 CREATE ART/METH CONTROL MARXISM

S67
FRANCIS M.J.,"THE US PRESS AND CASTRO: A STUDY IN DECLINING RELATIONS." COM DIPLOM WAR TOTALISM ATTIT SOCISM...POLICY IDEA/COMP 20. PAGE 52 H1046 PRESS LEAD REV NAT/G

S67
GAMARNIKOW M.,"THE NEW ROLE OF PRIVATE ENTERPRISE." ECO/DEV INDUS NAT/G SML/CO CREATE PROB/SOLV MARXISM ...POLICY TREND IDEA/COMP 20. PAGE 55 H1092 ECO/TAC ATTIT CAP/ISM COM

S67
JANICKE M.,"MONOPOLISMUS UND PLURALISMUS IM KOMMUNISTISCHEN HERRSCHAFTSSYSTEM" COM CZECHOSLVK USSR YUGOSLAVIA SOCIETY CONTROL RIGID/FLEX...CONCPT NAT/COMP 20. PAGE 79 H1589 TOTALISM POL/PAR ATTIT PLURISM

S67
MCCLEERY W.,"AN INTERVIEW WITH J. DOUGLAS BROWN ON THE 'WAY' OF VIETNAM" COM VIETNAM INTELL ECO/DEV ACADEM NAT/G COERCE PERSON SUPEGO ORD/FREE 20. PAGE 106 H2125 ATTIT WAR COLONIAL MARXISM

S67
NATSAGDORJ A.S.,"THE ECONOMIC BASIS OF FEUDALISM IN MONGOLIA." ASIA COM USSR OWN WEALTH CONSERVE...SOC 20 MONGOLIA. PAGE 116 H2324 ECO/TAC AGRI NAT/COMP MARXISM

S67
PONOMARYOV B.,"THE OCTOBER REVOLUTION - BEGINNING OF THE EPOCH OF SOCIALISM AND COMMUNISM." COM FUT USSR WOR+45 SOCIETY STRATA CHIEF CREATE DIPLOM ECO/TAC EDU/PROP SOCISM...NAT/COMP 20. PAGE 127 H2542 MARXIST WORKER INT/ORG POLICY

S67
RENFIELD R.L.,"A POLICY FOR VIETNAM." COM VIETNAM NAT/G POL/PAR VOL/ASSN CHIEF DIPLOM EDU/PROP DETER REPRESENT ATTIT ORD/FREE 20. PAGE 131 H2615 WAR POLICY PLAN

COERCE

S67
ROCHET W.,"THE OCTOBER REVOLUTION AND THE STRUGGLE OF THE FRENCH COMMUNISTS." COM FRANCE ELITES SOCIETY STRATA ECO/TAC EDU/PROP GP/REL WEALTH ...MARXIST IDEA/COMP NAT/COMP 20. PAGE 133 H2654
SOCISM CHOOSE METH/COMP NAT/G

S67
ROSE S.,"ASIAN NATIONALISM* THE SECOND STAGE." ASIA COM ECO/UNDEV NAT/G PROB/SOLV DIPLOM FOR/AID DOMIN NEUTRAL REGION TASK...METH/COMP 20. PAGE 134 H2675
NAT/LISM S/ASIA BAL/PWR COLONIAL

S67
SPITTMANN I.,"EAST GERMANY: THE SWINGING PENDULUM." COM GERMANY/E NAT/G EFFICIENCY MARXISM 20. PAGE 148 H2952
PRODUC POL/PAR WEALTH ATTIT

S67
SZALAY L.B.,"SOVIET DOMESTIC PROPAGANDA AND LIBERALIZATION." COM USSR SOCIETY COM/IND NAT/G POL/PAR EX/STRUC TEC/DEV LEAD ATTIT ROLE MARXISM ...METH/COMP 20. PAGE 151 H3026
EDU/PROP TOTALISM PERSON PERCEPT

S67
ULC O.,"CLASS STRUGGLE AND SOCIALIST JUSTICE: THE CASE OF CZECHOSLOVAKIA." COM CZECHOSLVK LAW CONSTN ELITES STRUCT NAT/G CRIME GP/REL MARXISM 20. PAGE 158 H3151
TOTALISM CT/SYS ADJUD STRATA

S67
VON LAUE T.H.,"WESTERNIZATION, REVOLUTION AND THE SEARCH FOR A BASIS OF AUTHORITY - RUSSIA IN 1917." USSR ELITES INTELL ECO/UNDEV NAT/G WORKER ECO/TAC TAX ADMIN LEAD AUTHORIT 20 LENIN/VI. PAGE 164 H3274
MARXISM REV COM DOMIN

C67
GEHLEN M.P.,"THE POLITICS OF COEXISTENCE: SOVIET METHODS AND MOTIVES." COM USSR NAT/G INT/TRADE EDU/PROP ARMS/CONT DETER KNOWL...CHARTS IDEA/COMP 20 COLD/WAR. PAGE 55 H1108
BIBLIOG PEACE DIPLOM MARXISM

S68
BOSSCHERE G D.E.,"A L'EST DU NOUVEAU." CZECHOSLVK HUNGARY POLAND ROMANIA YUGOSLAVIA AGRI CREATE ECO/TAC COERCE GP/REL ATTIT MARXISM SOCISM 20. PAGE 19 H0382
ORD/FREE COM NAT/G DIPLOM

S68
LUKASZEWSKI J.,"WESTERN INTEGRATION AND THE PEOPLE'S DEMOCRACIES." USSR ELITES ECO/DEV NAT/G VOL/ASSN INT/TRADE AGREE REV FEDERAL WEALTH SOCISM ...NAT/COMP SOC/INTEG 20 EEC. PAGE 99 H1977
DIPLOM INT/ORG COM REGION

COM/IND....COMMUNICATIONS INDUSTRY

N
INDIA: A REFERENCE ANNUAL. INDIA CULTURE COM/IND R+D FORCES PLAN RECEIVE EDU/PROP HEALTH...STAT CHARTS BIBLIOG 20. PAGE 1 H0017
CONSTN LABOR INT/ORG

N
THE STATESMAN'S YEARBOOK; STATISTICAL AND HISTORICAL ANNUAL OF THE STATES OF THE WORLD. WOR+45 WOR-45 COM/IND FINAN INDUS SECT FORCES TEC/DEV EDU/PROP...GEOG BIBLIOG 19/20. PAGE 1 H0023
NAT/COMP GOV/COMP STAT CONSTN

B22
TONNIES F.,KRITIK DER OFFENTLICHEN MEINUNG. FRANCE UK CULTURE COM/IND DOMIN PRESS RUMOR ROLE NAT/COMP. PAGE 156 H3114
SOCIETY SOC ATTIT

B36
WANDERSCHECK H.,WELTKRIEG UND PROPAGANDA. GERMANY MOD/EUR UK COM/IND NAT/G DOMIN PRESS ATTIT...POLICY 20 HITLER/A. PAGE 165 H3299
EDU/PROP PSY WAR KNOWL

B37
MUNZENBERG W.,PROPAGANDA ALS WAFFE. COM/IND PRESS COERCE WAR...PSY 20. PAGE 115 H2290
EDU/PROP DOMIN NAT/G LEAD

B39
HILL R.L.,A BIBLIOGRAPHY OF THE ANGLO-EGYPTIAN SUDAN FROM THE EARLIEST TIMES TO 1937. AFR ETHIOPIA SUDAN UAR LAW COM/IND SECT RACE/REL...GEOG HEAL SOC LING 19/20 NEGRO. PAGE 71 H1417
BIBLIOG CULTURE NAT/COMP GP/COMP

B41
BAUMANN G.,GRUNDLAGEN UND PRAXIS DER INTERNATIONALEN PROPAGANDA. FRANCE GERMANY UK CULTURE COM/IND PRESS PWR...PSY METH/COMP 20. PAGE 12 H0241
EDU/PROP DOMIN ATTIT DIPLOM

B42
NEUBURGER O.,OFFICIAL PUBLICATIONS OF PRESENT-DAY GERMANY: GOVERNMENT, CORPORATE ORGANIZATIONS, AND NATIONAL SOCIALIST PARTY. GERMANY CONSTN COM/IND POL/PAR EDU/PROP PRESS 20 NAZI. PAGE 117 H2332
BIBLIOG/A FASCISM NAT/G ADMIN

B42
SINGTON D.,THE GOEBBELS EXPERIMENT. GERMANY MOD/EUR NAT/G EX/STRUC FORCES CONTROL ROUTINE WAR TOTALISM PWR...ART/METH HUM 20 NAZI GOEBBELS/J. PAGE 144 H2886
FASCISM EDU/PROP ATTIT COM/IND

B43
US LIBRARY OF CONGRESS,BRITISH MALAYA AND BRITISH NORTH BORNEO. BORNEO MALAYSIA CONSTN AGRI COM/IND INDUS EDU/PROP 19/20. PAGE 160 H3203
BIBLIOG CULTURE

C44
VAN VALKENBURG S.,"ELEMENTS OF POLITICAL GEOGRAPHY." FRANCE COM/IND INDUS NAT/G SECT RACE/REL...LING TREND GEN/LAWS BIBLIOG 20. PAGE 162 H3232
GEOG DIPLOM COLONIAL

B48
GRIFFITH E.S.,RESEARCH IN POLITICAL SCIENCE: THE WORK OF PANELS OF RESEARCH COMMITTEE, APSA. WOR+45 WOR-45 COM/IND R+D FORCES ACT/RES WAR...GOV/COMP ANTHOL 20. PAGE 61 H1220
BIBLIOG PHIL/SCI DIPLOM JURID

B48
LINEBARGER P.,PSYCHOLOGICAL WARFARE. NAT/G PLAN DIPLOM DOMIN ATTIT...POLICY CONCPT EXHIBIT 20 WWI. PAGE 97 H1933
EDU/PROP PSY WAR COM/IND

B48
TURNER A.C.,FREE SPEECH AND BROADCASTING. UK USA+45 ORD/FREE NAT/COMP. PAGE 157 H3140
COM/IND NAT/G CONTROL METH/COMP

B50
IRION F.C.,PUBLIC OPINION AND PROPAGANDA. STRUCT COM/IND FAM SECT COERCE 20 FILM. PAGE 78 H1568
EDU/PROP ATTIT NAT/G PRESS

B54
BINANI G.D.,INDIA AT A GLANCE (REV. ED.). INDIA COM/IND FINAN INDUS LABOR PROVS SCHOOL PLAN DIPLOM INT/TRADE ADMIN...JURID 20. PAGE 17 H0335
INDEX CON/ANAL NAT/G ECO/UNDEV

B54
SCHRAMM W.,THE PROCESS AND EFFECTS OF MASS COMMUNICATION. CULTURE INTELL SOCIETY COM/IND DRIVE PERCEPT PERSON RIGID/FLEX KNOWL...PSY SOC CONCPT CHARTS. PAGE 140 H2800
ATTIT EDU/PROP

B54
US LIBRARY OF CONGRESS,RESEARCH AND INFORMATION ON AFRICA: CONTINUING SOURCES. ISLAM ECO/UNDEV AGRI INDUS R+D ACADEM NAT/G INT/TRADE...SOC 20. PAGE 161 H3210
BIBLIOG/A AFR PRESS COM/IND

B55
JONES T.B.,A BIBLIOGRAPHY ON SOUTH AMERICAN ECONOMIC AFFAIRS: ARTICLES IN NINETEENTH CENTURY PERIODICALS (PAMPHLET). AGRI COM/IND DIST/IND EXTR/IND FINAN INDUS LABOR NAT/G 19. PAGE 82 H1634
BIBLIOG ECO/UNDEV L/A+17C TEC/DEV

B56
BRITISH BORNEO RESEARCH PROJ,BIBLIOGRAPHY OF BRITISH BORNEO (PAMPHLET). UK COM/IND NAT/G EDU/PROP...GEOG 20. PAGE 21 H0421
BIBLIOG/A SOC

B58
STEINBERG C.S.,THE MASS COMMUNICATORS: PUBLIC RELATIONS, PUBLIC OPINION, AND MASS MEDIA. CULTURE CONSULT ACT/RES FEEDBACK DISPL WEALTH 20. PAGE 149 H2975
EDU/PROP ATTIT COM/IND PERCEPT

C58
GINSBURG N.,"MALAYA." MALAYSIA PROB/SOLV REGION NAT/LISM KNOWL WEALTH...GEOG SOC CHARTS BIBLIOG 20. PAGE 57 H1133
COM/IND ECO/UNDEV CULTURE NAT/G

B59
JACOBS N.,CULTURE FOR THE MILLIONS? INTELL SOCIETY NAT/G...POLICY SOC OBS ANTHOL 20. PAGE 79 H1579
CULTURE COM/IND PERF/ART CONCPT

B60
EMERY E.,INTRODUCTION TO MASS COMMUNICATIONS. ACADEM PROF/ORG SCHOOL ACT/RES EDU/PROP ATTIT ...CONCPT BIBLIOG/A. PAGE 46 H0920
COM/IND PRESS CON/ANAL CULTURE

B60
SAKAI R.K.,STUDIES ON ASIA, 1960. ASIA CHINA/COM S/ASIA COM/IND ECO/TAC...ANTHOL 17/20 MALAYA. PAGE 137 H2733
ECO/UNDEV SOC

S60
FRANKEL S.H.,"ECONOMIC ASPECTS OF POLITICAL INDEPENDENCE IN AFRICA." AFR FUT SOCIETY ECO/UNDEV COM/IND FINAN LEGIS PLAN TEC/DEV CAP/ISM ECO/TAC INT/TRADE ADMIN ATTIT DRIVE RIGID/FLEX PWR WEALTH ...MGT NEW/IDEA MATH TIME/SEQ VAL/FREE 20. PAGE 53 H1052
NAT/G FOR/AID

S60
RIVKIN A.,"AFRICAN ECONOMIC DEVELOPMENT: ADVANCED TECHNOLOGY AND THE STAGES OF GROWTH." CULTURE ECO/UNDEV AGRI COM/IND EXTR/IND PLAN ECO/TAC ATTIT DRIVE RIGID/FLEX SKILL WEALTH...MGT SOC GEN/LAWS WORK TOT/POP 20. PAGE 132 H2634
AFR TEC/DEV FOR/AID

B61
NARASIMHAN V.K.,THE PRESS, THE PUBLIC AND THE ADMINISTRATION (PAMPHLET). INDIA COM/IND CONTROL REPRESENT GOV/REL EFFICIENCY...ANTHOL 20. PAGE 116 H2312
NAT/G ADMIN PRESS NEW/LIB

S61
BRZEZINSKI Z.K.,"THE ORGANIZATION OF THE COMMUNIST CAMP." COM CZECHOSLVK COM/IND NAT/G DELIB/GP INT/TRADE DOMIN EDU/PROP EXEC ROUTINE COERCE ATTIT PWR...MGT CONCPT TIME/SEQ CHARTS VAL/FREE 20
VOL/ASSN DIPLOM USSR

TREATY. PAGE 23 H0460

B62
BRETTON H.L.,POWER AND STABILITY IN NIGERIA: THE POLITICS OF DECOLONIZATION. AFR CONSTN INTELL ECO/UNDEV COM/IND KIN NAT/G POL/PAR PROVS VOL/ASSN LEGIS DOMIN EDU/PROP LEGIT EXEC ROUTINE CHOOSE NAT/LISM ATTIT PERCEPT ALL/VALS. PAGE 20 H0411 CULTURE OBS NIGERIA

B62
HENDERSON W.O.,THE GENESIS OF THE COMMON MARKET. EUR+WWI FRANCE MOD/EUR UK SEA COM/IND EXTR/IND COLONIAL DISCRIM...TIME/SEQ CHARTS BIBLIOG 18/20 EEC TREATY. PAGE 70 H1395 ECO/DEV INT/TRADE DIPLOM

B62
KRUGLAK T.E.,THE TWO FACES OF TASS. COM COM/IND NAT/G ACT/RES PLAN PRESS PERCEPT PERSON KNOWL 20. PAGE 89 H1778 PUB/INST EDU/PROP USSR

B62
MEIER R.L.,A COMMUNICATIONS THEORY OF URBAN GROWTH. CULTURE ECO/DEV COMPUTER BUDGET UTIL KNOWL...SOC CONCPT METH 20 OPEN/SPACE. PAGE 108 H2164 OP/RES COM/IND MUNIC CONTROL

B63
AZEVEDO T.,SOCIAL CHANGE IN BRAZIL. BRAZIL ECO/DEV COM/IND FAM NAT/G SECT GP/REL PERS/REL...CONCPT WORSHIP 20. PAGE 9 H0188 TEC/DEV STRUCT SOC CULTURE

B63
ELWIN V.,A NEW DEAL FOR TRIBAL INDIA. INDIA AGRI COM/IND INDUS KIN TEC/DEV TAX EDU/PROP OWN HEALTH 20. PAGE 46 H0912 ECO/UNDEV CULTURE CONSTN SOC/WK

S63
DEUTSCHMANN P.J.,"THE MASS MEDIA IN AN UNDERDEVELOPED VILLAGE." L/A+17C EDU/PROP PERCEPT KNOWL ORD/FREE...SOC INT VAL/FREE 20. PAGE 40 H0809 COM/IND CULTURE

B64
HALE O.J.,THE CAPTIVE PRESS IN THE THIRD REICH. GERMANY CULTURE LG/CO NAT/G POL/PAR PLAN DOMIN TASK CENTRAL OWN TOTALISM PWR...BIBLIOG 20 HITLER/A NAZI AMMAN/MAX. PAGE 64 H1283 COM/IND PRESS CONTROL FASCISM

B64
RUSSET B.M.,WORLD HANDBOOK OF POLITICAL AND SOCIAL INDICATORS. WOR+45 COM/IND ADMIN WEALTH...GEOG 20. PAGE 136 H2719 DIPLOM STAT NAT/G NAT/COMP

B64
UNESCO,WORLD COMMUNICATIONS: PRESS, RADIO, TELEVISION, FILM (4TH ED.). WOR+45 DIPLOM TV PEACE ...NAT/COMP SOC/INTEG 20 FILM. PAGE 158 H3163 COM/IND EDU/PROP PRESS TEC/DEV

B64
WARD R.E.,POLITICAL MODERNIZATION IN JAPAN AND TURKEY. ASIA ISLAM S/ASIA CONSTN CULTURE STRATA COM/IND POL/PAR FORCES ACT/RES ECO/TAC DOMIN EDU/PROP LEGIT ADMIN CHOOSE ATTIT ALL/VALS...STAT TIME/SEQ VAL/FREE CHINJAP. PAGE 165 H3307 SOCIETY TURKEY

B65
BRAMSTED E.K.,GOEBBELS AND NATIONAL SOCIALIST PROPAGANDA, 1925-1945. EUR+WWI GERMANY UK USSR NAT/G FORCES WAR FASCISM...TIME/SEQ 20 GOEBBELS/J NAZI. PAGE 20 H0403 EDU/PROP PSY COM/IND

B65
JACKSON G.,THE SPANISH REPUBLIC AND THE CIVIL WAR, 1931-1939. EUR+WWI INTELL STRUCT COM/IND NAT/G POL/PAR LEGIS EDU/PROP EXEC COERCE NAT/LISM DRIVE PWR...INT TIME/SEQ TOT/POP 20. PAGE 79 H1574 ATTIT GUERRILLA SPAIN

B65
SABLE M.H.,MASTER DIRECTORY FOR LATIN AMERICA. AGRI COM/IND FINAN R+D ACADEM LABOR NAT/G POL/PAR VOL/ASSN INT/TRADE EDU/PROP 20. PAGE 136 H2728 INDEX L/A+17C INT/ORG DIPLOM

S65
HUGHES T.L.,"SCHOLARS AND FOREIGN POLICY* VARIETIES OF RESEARCH EXPERIENCE." COM/IND DIPLOM ADMIN EXEC ROUTINE...MGT OBS CONGRESS PRESIDENT CAMELOT. PAGE 75 H1491 ACT/RES ACADEM CONTROL NAT/G

B66
BERELSON B.,READER IN PUBLIC OPINION AND COMMUNICATION (2ND ED.). UNIV NAT/G PRESS GP/REL PERS/REL PERCEPT RIGID/FLEX...MAJORIT QUANT METH/COMP ANTHOL BIBLIOG 20. PAGE 15 H0298 EDU/PROP ATTIT CONCPT COM/IND

B66
FAGEN R.R.,POLITICS AND COMMUNICATION. WOR+45 ECO/DEV NAT/G CONTROL ATTIT 20. PAGE 48 H0958 COM/IND GOV/COMP PWR EDU/PROP

B67
SHAPIRO P.S.,COMMUNICATIONS OR TRANSPORT: DECISION-MAKING IN DEVELOPING COUNTRIES. WOR+45 NAT/G PLAN ALL/IDEOS MARXISM...NAT/COMP GEN/LAWS. PAGE 142 H2844 BUDGET COM/IND DECISION ECO/DEV

S67
KNOWLES A.F.,"NOTES ON A CANADIAN MASS MEDIA POLICY." CANADA TV CONTROL ROLE...METH/COMP 20. PAGE 87 H1735 EDU/PROP COM/IND NAT/G POLICY

S67
LANE J.P.,"FUNCTIONS OF MASS MEDIA IN BRAZIL'S 1964 CRISIS." BRAZIL NAT/G FORCES TOP/EX PRESS TV ATTIT PWR...METH/CNCPT 20. PAGE 90 H1807 CIVMIL/REL REV COM/IND EDU/PROP

S67
NEUBAUER D.E.,"SOME CONDITIONS OF DEMOCRACY." ECO/DEV COM/IND DIST/IND POL/PAR EDU/PROP REPRESENT ...SOC STAT NAT/COMP 20. PAGE 117 H2331 NAT/G CHOOSE MAJORIT ECO/UNDEV

S67
SZALAY L.B.,"SOVIET DOMESTIC PROPAGANDA AND LIBERALIZATION." COM USSR SOCIETY COM/IND NAT/G POL/PAR EX/STRUC TEC/DEV LEAD ATTIT ROLE MARXISM ...METH/COMP 20. PAGE 151 H3026 EDU/PROP TOTALISM PERSON PERCEPT

COM/PARTY....COMMUNIST PARTY (ALL NATIONS)

N19
MAO TSE-TUNG,ON SOME IMPORTANT PROBLEMS OF THE PARTY'S PRESENT POLICY. CHINA/COM CONSTN ELITES INTELL AGRI DOMIN EDU/PROP REV REPRESENT GP/REL OWN PEACE ORD/FREE 20 COM/PARTY. PAGE 102 H2044 POLICY NAT/G CHIEF LEGIT

B37
BERDYAEV N.,THE ORIGIN OF RUSSIAN COMMUNISM. MOD/EUR RUSSIA USSR INTELL SECT REV...ANARCH HUM 19/20 ORTHO/RUSS COM/PARTY CHRISTIAN. PAGE 15 H0294 MARXISM NAT/LISM CULTURE ATTIT

B43
LENIN V.I.,LEFT WING COMMUNISM: AN INFANTILE DISORDER (1920). GERMANY MOD/EUR USSR STRUCT CHIEF DOMIN EDU/PROP LEGIT LEAD REPRESENT POPULISM ...METH/COMP 19 LENIN/VI COM/PARTY MENSHEVIK. PAGE 94 H1879 COM MARXISM NAT/G REV

B56
HERNANDEZ URBINA A.,LOS PARTIDOS Y LA CRISIS DEL APRA. PERU NAT/G LEAD LOBBY CHOOSE SOCISM...POLICY DECISION 20 COM/PARTY APRA CONGRESS. PAGE 70 H1402 POL/PAR PARTIC PARL/PROC GP/REL

B57
ARON R.,THE OPIUM OF THE INTELLECTUALS (TRANS. BY TERENCE KILMARTIN). FRANCE USSR WOR+45 CULTURE POL/PAR PLAN DOMIN EDU/PROP REV ATTIT ORD/FREE ...IDEA/COMP METH/COMP NAT/COMP 20 COM/PARTY. PAGE 8 H0169 INTELL UTOPIA MYTH MARXISM

B57
HERNANDEZ-ARREGU J.,IMPERIALISMO Y CULTURA (LA POLITICA EN LA INTELIGENCIA ARGENTINA). L/A+17C CULTURE ELITES WRITING COLONIAL CROWD ATTIT FASCISM MARXISM SOCISM...BIOG IDEA/COMP 20 ARGEN PERON/JUAN COM/PARTY. PAGE 70 H1403 INTELL CREATE ART/METH HUM

B58
HSU U.T.,THE INVISIBLE CONFLICT. ASIA USSR ELITES NAT/G CONTROL LEAD COERCE REV WAR NAT/LISM ORD/FREE PWR 20 COM/PARTY ESPIONAGE. PAGE 74 H1485 MARXISM POL/PAR EDU/PROP FORCES

B58
PALMER E.E.,THE COMMUNIST CHALLENGE. COM USA+45 USA-45 ECO/DEV ECO/UNDEV NEUTRAL ORD/FREE POPULISM ...CONCPT NAT/COMP ANTHOL 19/20 LENIN/VI STALIN/J MAO MARX/KARL COM/PARTY. PAGE 123 H2450 MARXISM DIPLOM IDEA/COMP POLICY

B59
EAENZA L.,COMMUNISMO E CATTOLICESIMO IN UNA PARROCHIA DI CAMPAGNA. ITALY CULTURE ELITES ECO/DEV AGRI KIN POL/PAR DOMIN LEGIT RIGID/FLEX...DECISION OBS IDEA/COMP 20 COM/PARTY CHURCH/STA. PAGE 44 H0878 ATTIT CATHISM NEIGH MARXISM

B61
LICHTHEIM G.,MARXISM. GERMANY SOCIETY WORKER CAP/ISM ECO/TAC NAT/LISM POPULISM...TIME/SEQ GOV/COMP NAT/COMP 18/20 COM/PARTY. PAGE 96 H1924 MARXISM SOCISM IDEA/COMP CULTURE

B62
CARTER G.M.,THE GOVERNMENT OF THE SOVIET UNION. USSR CULTURE LOC/G DIPLOM ECO/TAC ADJUD CT/SYS LEAD WEALTH...CHARTS T 20 COM/PARTY. PAGE 27 H0546 NAT/G MARXISM POL/PAR EX/STRUC

B63
CHOU S.H.,THE CHINESE INFLATION 1937-1949. ASIA SOCIETY POL/PAR FOR/AID INT/TRADE BAL/PAY WEALTH MARXISM...STAT CHARTS 20 COM/PARTY GOLD/STAND. PAGE 30 H0597 FINAN ECO/TAC BUDGET NAT/G

B63
SWEARER H.R.,CONTEMPORARY COMMUNISM: THEORY AND PRACTICE. COM USSR SOCIETY ECO/DEV POL/PAR FORCES PLAN ADMIN LEAD NAT/LISM...POLICY ANTHOL 20 LENIN/VI COM/PARTY. PAGE 151 H3015 MARXISM CONCPT DIPLOM NAT/G

B64
FAINSOD M.,HOW RUSSIA IS RULED (REV. ED.). RUSSIA USSR AGRI PROC/MFG LABOR POL/PAR EX/STRUC CONTROL PWR...POLICY BIBLIOG 19/20 KHRUSH/N COM/PARTY. PAGE 48 H0963 NAT/G REV MARXISM

B64
FISCHER L.,THE LIFE OF LENIN. USSR LEAD REV WAR ...SOC 19/20 LENIN/VI COM/PARTY BOLSHEVISM. PAGE 51 H1011 BIOG MARXISM PERSON

CHIEF

B64
MARTINEZ J.R.,THREE CASES OF COMMUNISM: CUBA, BRAZIL, AND MEXICO. BRAZIL CUBA L/A+17C CONSTN NAT/G DIPLOM ECO/TAC GP/REL INGP/REL...GP/COMP BIBLIOG 20 MEXIC/AMER COM/PARTY. PAGE 103 H2068 — MARXISM BIOG REV NAT/COMP

B65
APPLEMAN P.,THE SILENT EXPLOSION. WOR+45 ECO/DEV ECO/UNDEV PLAN HEALTH ALL/IDEOS CATHISM...POLICY STAT RECORD GP/COMP IDEA/COMP NAT/COMP 20 BIRTH/CON COM/PARTY. PAGE 7 H0148 — GEOG CENSUS AGRI BIO/SOC

B65
KOUSOULAS D.G.,REVOLUTION AND DEFEAT; THE STORY OF THE GREEK COMMUNIST PARTY. GREECE INT/ORG EX/STRUC DIPLOM FOR/AID EDU/PROP PARL/PROC ADJUST ATTIT 20 COM/PARTY. PAGE 88 H1759 — REV MARXISM POL/PAR ORD/FREE

B66
DALLIN A.,POLITICS IN THE SOVIET UNION: 7 CASES. COM USSR LAW POL/PAR CHIEF FORCES WRITING CONTROL PARL/PROC CIVMIL/REL TOTALISM...ANTHOL 20 KHRUSH/N STALIN/J CASEBOOK COM/PARTY. PAGE 37 H0736 — MARXISM DOMIN ORD/FREE GOV/REL

B66
SCHURMANN F.,IDEOLOGY AND ORGANIZATION IN COMMUNIST CHINA. CHINA/COM LOC/G MUNIC POL/PAR ECO/TAC CONTROL ATTIT...MGT STERTYP 20 COM/PARTY. PAGE 140 H2805 — MARXISM STRUCT ADMIN NAT/G

B66
SKILLING H.G.,THE GOVERNMENTS OF COMMUNIST EAST EUROPE. COM EUR+WWI ELITES FORCES DIPLOM ECO/TAC CONTROL HABITAT SOCISM...DECISION BIBLIOG 20 EUROPE/E COM/PARTY. PAGE 145 H2895 — MARXISM NAT/COMP GP/COMP DOMIN

B67
KOLKOWICZ R.,THE SOVIET MILITARY AND THE COMMUNIST PARTY. COM USSR ELITES NAT/G CREATE CIVMIL/REL GP/REL...TREND BIBLIOG/A 20 COM/PARTY. PAGE 88 H1753 — MARXISM CONSTN FORCES POL/PAR

B67
MICKIEWICZ E.P.,SOVIET POLITICAL SCHOOLS: THE COMMUNIST PARTY ADULT INSTRUCTION SYSTEM. COM USSR INTELL SCHOOL WORKER CREATE PRESS ADMIN CONTROL ATTIT KNOWL...PROG/TEAC SOC/INTEG 20 COM/PARTY. PAGE 110 H2200 — NAT/G EDU/PROP AGE/A MARXISM

L67
TABORSKY E.,"THE COMMUNIST PARTIES OF THE 'THIRD WORLD' IN SOVIET STRATEGY." AFR ASIA L/A+17C USSR INTELL NAT/G WORKER PLAN CONTROL LEAD PARTIC REV ...GOV/COMP 20 COM/PARTY THIRD/WRLD. PAGE 152 H3032 — POL/PAR MARXISM ECO/UNDEV DIPLOM

COM/SCITEC....COMMITTEE ON SCIENCE AND TECHNOLOGY (OF

COMECON....COMMUNIST ECONOMIC ORGANIZATION EAST EUROPE

B64
KIS T.I.,LES PAYS DE L'EUROPE DE L'EST: LEURS RAPPORTS MUTUELS ET LE PROBLEME DE LEUR INTEGRATION DANS L'ORBITE DE L'USSR. EUR+WWI RUSSIA USSR INT/ORG NAT/G REV ATTIT...JURID SOC BIBLIOG WARSAW/P COMECON EUROPE/E. PAGE 86 H1727 — DIPLOM COM MARXISM REGION

S64
KOVNER M.,"THE SINO-SOVIET DISPUTE: COMMUNISM AT THE CROSSROADS." ASIA CHINA/COM COM USSR ECO/UNDEV NAT/G TOP/EX CREATE BAL/PWR DOMIN EDU/PROP PWR ...CONCPT COMECON 20. PAGE 88 H1760 — ATTIT TREND

S64
MARES V.E.,"EAST EUROPE'S SECOND CHANCE." COM EUR+WWI HUNGARY ROMANIA USSR YUGOSLAVIA ECO/UNDEV NAT/G TOP/EX CREATE PLAN TEC/DEV REGION NAT/LISM RIGID/FLEX PWR...CONCPT STAT COMECON 20. PAGE 102 H2047 — VOL/ASSN ECO/TAC

COMINFORM....COMMUNIST INFORMATION BUREAU

B56
WOLFF R.L.,THE BALKANS IN OUR TIME. ALBANIA FUT MOD/EUR USSR YUGOSLAVIA CULTURE INT/ORG SECT DIPLOM EDU/PROP COERCE WAR ORD/FREE...CHARTS 4/20 BALKANS COMINFORM. PAGE 170 H3403 — GEOG COM

COMINTERN....COMMUNIST THIRD INTERNATIONAL

B52
ULAM A.B.,TITOISM AND THE COMINFORM. USSR WOR+45 STRUCT INT/ORG NAT/G ACT/RES PLAN EXEC ATTIT DRIVE ALL/VALS...CONCPT OBS VAL/FREE 20 COMINTERN TITO/MARSH. PAGE 157 H3149 — COM POL/PAR TOTALISM YUGOSLAVIA

COMISION DE HISTORIA H0637

COMM/SPACE....COMMITTEE ON SPACE RESEARCH

COMMAGER H.S. H3303

COMMANDS....SEE LEAD, DOMIN

COMMISSIONS....SEE CONFER, DELIB/GP

COMMITTEE ON SCIENCE AND TECHNOLOGY (OF THE BRITISH PARLIAMENT)....SEE COM/SCITEC

COMMITTEES....SEE CONFER, DELIB/GP

COMMON/LAW....COMMON LAW

B24
HOLDSWORTH W.S.,A HISTORY OF ENGLISH LAW; THE COMMON LAW AND ITS RIVALS (VOL. IV). UK SEA AGRI CHIEF ADJUD CONTROL CRIME GOV/REL...INT/LAW JURID NAT/COMP 16/17 PARLIAMENT COMMON/LAW CANON/LAW ENGLSH/LAW. PAGE 72 H1449 — LAW LEGIS CT/SYS CONSTN

B28
HOLDSWORTH W.S.,THE HISTORIANS OF ANGLO-AMERICAN LAW. UK USA-45 INTELL LEGIS RESPECT...BIOG NAT/COMP 17/20 COMMON/LAW. PAGE 72 H1450 — HIST/WRIT LAW JURID

B32
LUNT D.C.,THE ROAD TO THE LAW. UK USA-45 LEGIS EDU/PROP OWN ORD/FREE...DECISION TIME/SEQ NAT/COMP 16/20 AUSTRAL ENGLSH/LAW COMMON/LAW. PAGE 99 H1980 — ADJUD LAW JURID CT/SYS

B38
HOLDSWORTH W.S.,A HISTORY OF ENGLISH LAW; THE CENTURIES OF SETTLEMENT AND REFORM (VOL. X). INDIA UK CONSTN NAT/G CHIEF LEGIS ADMIN COLONIAL CT/SYS CHOOSE ORD/FREE PWR...JURID 18 PARLIAMENT COMMONWLTH COMMON/LAW. PAGE 72 H1451 — LAW LOC/G EX/STRUC ADJUD

B58
EUSDEN J.D.,PURITANS, LAWYERS, AND POLITICS IN EARLY SEVENTEENTH-CENTURY ENGLAND. UK CT/SYS PARL/PROC RATIONAL PWR SOVEREIGN...IDEA/COMP BIBLIOG 17 PURITAN COMMON/LAW. PAGE 48 H0951 — GP/REL SECT NAT/G LAW

B58
OGILVIE C.,THE KING'S GOVERNMENT AND THE COMMON LAW, 1471-1641. UK STRUCT NAT/G CHIEF LEGIS WORKER BAL/PWR GP/REL AUTHORIT 15/17 COMMON/LAW. PAGE 120 H2408 — CONSTN ELITES DOMIN

B63
EDDY J.P.,JUSTICE OF THE PEACE. UK LAW CONSTN CULTURE 14/20 COMMON/LAW. PAGE 44 H0887 — CRIME JURID CT/SYS ADJUD

B64
HOLDSWORTH W.S.,A HISTORY OF ENGLISH LAW; THE CENTURIES OF DEVELOPMENT AND REFORM (VOL. XIV). UK CONSTN LOC/G NAT/G POL/PAR CHIEF EX/STRUC ADJUD COLONIAL ATTIT...INT/LAW JURID 18/19 TORY/PARTY COMMONWLTH WHIG/PARTY COMMON/LAW. PAGE 73 H1453 — LAW LEGIS LEAD CT/SYS

B65
CHRIMES S.B.,ENGLISH CONSTITUTIONAL HISTORY (3RD ED.). UK CHIEF CONSULT DELIB/GP LEGIS CT/SYS 15/20 COMMON/LAW PARLIAMENT. PAGE 30 H0598 — CONSTN BAL/PWR NAT/G

B98
POLLOCK F.,THE HISTORY OF ENGLISH LAW BEFORE THE TIME OF EDWARD I (2 VOLS, 2ND ED.). UK CULTURE LOC/G LEGIS LICENSE AGREE CONTROL CT/SYS SANCTION CRIME...TIME/SEQ 13 COMMON/LAW CANON/LAW. PAGE 127 H2538 — LAW ADJUD JURID

COMMONWEALTH....SEE COMMONWLTH

COMMONWLTH....BRITISH COMMONWEALTH OF NATIONS; SEE ALSO VOL/ASSN, APPROPRIATE NATIONS, CMN/WLTH

B30
HULL W.I.,INDIA'S POLITICAL CRISIS. INDIA UK INT/ORG LABOR SECT DELIB/GP LEGIS DIPLOM NEUTRAL REGION CROWD GOV/REL MAJORITY ATTIT 20 NEHRU/J GANDHI/M COMMONWLTH. PAGE 75 H1492 — ORD/FREE NAT/G COLONIAL NAT/LISM

B38
HOLDSWORTH W.S.,A HISTORY OF ENGLISH LAW; THE CENTURIES OF SETTLEMENT AND REFORM (VOL. X). INDIA UK CONSTN NAT/G CHIEF LEGIS ADMIN COLONIAL CT/SYS CHOOSE ORD/FREE PWR...JURID 18 PARLIAMENT COMMONWLTH COMMON/LAW. PAGE 72 H1451 — LAW LOC/G EX/STRUC ADJUD

B53
STOUT H.M.,BRITISH GOVERNMENT. UK FINAN LOC/G POL/PAR DELIB/GP DIPLOM ADMIN COLONIAL CHOOSE ORD/FREE...JURID BIBLIOG 20 COMMONWLTH. PAGE 150 H2990 — NAT/G PARL/PROC CONSTN NEW/LIB

B54
FRIEDMAN W.,THE PUBLIC CORPORATION: A COMPARATIVE SYMPOSIUM (UNIVERSITY OF TORONTO SCHOOL OF LAW COMPARATIVE LAW SERIES, VOL. I). SWEDEN USA+45 INDUS INT/ORG NAT/G REGION CENTRAL FEDERAL...POLICY JURID IDEA/COMP NAT/COMP ANTHOL 20 COMMONWLTH MONOPOLY EUROPE. PAGE 53 H1065 — LAW SOCISM LG/CO OWN

B57
SCARROW H.A.,THE HIGHER PUBLIC SERVICE OF THE COMMONWEALTH OF AUSTRALIA. LAW SENIOR LOBBY ROLE 20 AUSTRAL CIVIL/SERV COMMONWLTH. PAGE 138 H2766 — ADMIN NAT/G EX/STRUC GOV/COMP

B60
BANERJEE D.N.,OUR FUNDAMENTAL RIGHTS: THEIR NATURE AND EXTENT (AS JUDICIALLY DETERMINED). INDIA UK CULTURE STRATA NAT/G WORKER EDU/PROP CONTROL DISCRIM OWN...IDEA/COMP WORSHIP 20 REFORMERS COMMONWLTH. PAGE 10 H0207 CONSTN ORD/FREE LEGIS POLICY

B60
STRACHEY J.,THE END OF EMPIRE. UK WOR+45 WOR-45 DIPLOM INT/TRADE DOMIN ADJUST ORD/FREE WEALTH ...SOCIALIST GOV/COMP TIME COMMONWLTH. PAGE 150 H2991 COLONIAL ECO/DEV BAL/PWR LAISSEZ

B61
CARNELL F.,THE POLITICS OF THE NEW STATES: A SELECT ANNOTATED BIBLIOGRAPHY WITH SPECIAL REFERENCE TO THE COMMONWEALTH. CONSTN ELITES LABOR NAT/G POL/PAR EX/STRUC DIPLOM ADJUD ADMIN...GOV/COMP 20 COMMONWLTH. PAGE 27 H0534 BIBLIOG/A AFR ASIA COLONIAL

B63
HAILEY L.,THE REPUBLIC OF SOUTH AFRICA AND THE HIGH COMMISSION TERRITORIES. AFR SOUTH/AFR UK INT/ORG NAT/G PROVS RACE/REL SOVEREIGN...CHARTS 19/20 COMMONWLTH. PAGE 64 H1278 COLONIAL DIPLOM ATTIT

B63
PADELFORD N.J.,AFRICA AND WORLD ORDER. AFR COLONIAL SOVEREIGN...ANTHOL BIBLIOG 20 UN UNIFICA COMMONWLTH. PAGE 122 H2439 DIPLOM NAT/G ORD/FREE

B64
BERRINGTON H.,HOW NATIONS ARE GOVERNED. FRANCE WOR+45 ECO/UNDEV INT/ORG POL/PAR CHOOSE TOTALISM KNOWL...MAJORIT T 20 UN COMMONWLTH THIRD/WRLD. PAGE 16 H0320 NAT/G GOV/COMP ECO/DEV CONSTN

B64
HOLDSWORTH W.S.,A HISTORY OF ENGLISH LAW; THE CENTURIES OF DEVELOPMENT AND REFORM (VOL. XIV). UK CONSTN LOC/G NAT/G POL/PAR CHIEF EX/STRUC ADJUD COLONIAL ATTIT...INT/LAW JURID 18/19 TORY/PARTY COMMONWLTH WHIG/PARTY COMMON/LAW. PAGE 73 H1453 LAW LEGIS LEAD CT/SYS

B65
GRAHAM G.S.,THE POLITICS OF NAVAL SUPREMACY; STUDIES IN BRITISH MARITIME ASCENDANCY. UK SEA NAT/G BAL/PWR LEAD WAR WEAPON PEACE...POLICY 18/19 COMMONWLTH. PAGE 60 H1191 FORCES PWR COLONIAL DIPLOM

S67
INDER S.,"AFTER THE CORONATION." CONSTN ECO/UNDEV EX/STRUC LEGIS INT/TRADE CONTROL SOVEREIGN ...TIME/SEQ 20 TONGA COMMONWLTH INAUGURATE. PAGE 76 H1527 CHIEF NAT/G POLICY

S68
GUZZARDI W.,"THE DECLINE OF THE STERLING CLUB." UK WOR+45 NAT/G PLAN DIPLOM INT/TRADE AGREE CONSEN EQUILIB SOVEREIGN...POLICY NEW/IDEA 20 COMMONWLTH GOLD/STAND. PAGE 63 H1259 FINAN ECO/TAC WEALTH NAT/COMP

COMMUN/DEV....COMMUNITY DEVELOPMENT MOVEMENT IN INDIA

COMMUNES....COMMUNES

COMMUNICATION, MASS....SEE EDU/PROP

COMMUNICATION, PERSONAL....SEE PERS/REL

COMMUNICATION, POLITICAL....SEE EDU/PROP

COMMUNICATIONS INDUSTRY....SEE COM/IND

COMMUNISM....SEE MARXISM

COMMUNIST CHINA....SEE CHINA/COM

COMMUNIST COUNTRIES (EXCEPT CHINA)....SEE COM

COMMUNIST ECONOMIC ORGANIZATION....SEE COMECON

COMMUNIST INFORMATION BUREAU....SEE COMINFORM

COMMUNIST THIRD INTERNATIONAL....SEE COMINTERN

COMMUNITY....SEE NEIGH

COMPANY, LARGE....SEE LG/CO

COMPANY, SMALL....SEE SML/CO

COMPARATIVE....SEE APPROPRIATE COMPARATIVE ANALYSIS INDEX

COMPETITION....SEE APPROPRIATE RELATIONS AND VALUES INDEXES

COMPNY/ACT....COMPANIES ACT (U.K., 1882)

COMPUT/IR....INFORMATION RETRIEVAL

B65
HYMES D.,THE USE OF COMPUTERS IN ANTHROPOLOGY. CULTURE PROF/ORG CONSULT CREATE EFFICIENCY PERCEPT ...CLASSIF LING CON/ANAL COMPUT/IR METH/COMP ANTHOL 20. PAGE 76 H1517 METH COMPUTER TEC/DEV SOC

B66
MERRITT R.L.,COMPARING NATIONS* THE USE OF QUANTITATIVE DATA IN CROSSNATIONAL RESEARCH. ACADEM DIPLOM GP/REL...PHIL/SCI STAT TREND GP/COMP PERS/COMP GEN/METH ANTHOL BIBLIOG INDEX. PAGE 109 H2184 NAT/COMP MATH COMPUT/IR QUANT

B67
UNIVERSAL REFERENCE SYSTEM,COMPARATIVE GOVERNMENT AND CULTURES (VOLUME X). WOR+45 WOR-45 NAT/G POL/PAR ATTIT...CON/ANAL COMPUT/IR IDEA/COMP GEN/METH. PAGE 158 H3168 BIBLIOG/A GOV/COMP CULTURE NAT/COMP

COMPUTER....COMPUTER TECHNIQUES AND TECHNOLOGY

B59
STERNBERG F.,THE MILITARY AND INDUSTRIAL REVOLUTION OF OUR TIME. USA+45 USSR WOR+45 WORKER COMPUTER PLAN TEC/DEV NUC/PWR GP/REL...POLICY NAT/COMP 20. PAGE 149 H2981 DIPLOM FORCES INDUS CIVMIL/REL

B62
MEIER R.L.,A COMMUNICATIONS THEORY OF URBAN GROWTH. CULTURE ECO/DEV COMPUTER BUDGET UTIL KNOWL...SOC CONCPT METH 20 OPEN/SPACE. PAGE 108 H2164 OP/RES COM/IND MUNIC CONTROL

B65
HYMES D.,THE USE OF COMPUTERS IN ANTHROPOLOGY. CULTURE PROF/ORG CONSULT CREATE EFFICIENCY PERCEPT ...CLASSIF LING CON/ANAL COMPUT/IR METH/COMP ANTHOL 20. PAGE 76 H1517 METH COMPUTER TEC/DEV SOC

B66
LONDON DAILY TELEGRAPH,ELECTION '66: GALLUP ANALYSIS OF THE VOTING RESULTS. UK LEGIS COMPUTER ATTIT...QU SAMP CHARTS 20 LABOR/PAR HOUSE/CMNS. PAGE 98 H1959 STAT CHOOSE REPRESENT POL/PAR

COMTE/A....AUGUST COMTE

CON/ANAL....QUANTITATIVE CONTENT ANALYSIS

N
AUSTRALIAN PUBLIC AFFAIRS INFORMATION SERVICE. LAW ...HEAL HUM MGT SOC CON/ANAL 20 AUSTRAL. PAGE 1 H0011 BIBLIOG NAT/G CULTURE DIPLOM

N
CHINA QUARTERLY. COM AGRI INDUS ACADEM POL/PAR INT/TRADE CONFER GOV/REL...TIME/SEQ CON/ANAL INDEX 20. PAGE 1 H0014 BIBLIOG/A ASIA DIPLOM POLICY

N
CORDIER H.,BIBLIOTECA SINICA. SOCIETY STRUCT SECT DIPLOM COLONIAL...GEOG SOC CON/ANAL. PAGE 33 H0664 BIBLIOG/A NAT/G CULTURE ASIA

N
LONDON LIBRARY ASSOCIATION,ATHENAEUM SUBJECT INDEX. 1915-1918. NAT/G DIPLOM NAT/LISM 20. PAGE 98 H1960 BIBLIOG CON/ANAL SOC

N
PRESSE UNIVERSITAIRES,ANNEE SOCIOLOGIQUE. EUR+WWI FRANCE MOD/EUR FAM ACT/RES WAR INGP/REL PERS/REL CONSEN DRIVE MORAL...CON/ANAL 19/20. PAGE 128 H2557 BIBLIOG SOC CULTURE SOCIETY

B00
MAINE H.S.,ANCIENT LAW. MEDIT-7 CULTURE SOCIETY KIN SECT LEGIS LEGIT ROUTINE...JURID HIST/WRIT CON/ANAL TOT/POP VAL/FREE. PAGE 101 H2020 FAM LAW

B00
VOLPICELLI Z.,RUSSIA ON THE PACIFIC AND THE SIBERIAN RAILWAY. MOD/EUR ECO/UNDEV INT/ORG FORCES PLAN DOMIN COLONIAL ROUTINE ATTIT ALL/VALS...OBS HIST/WRIT TIME/SEQ TREND CON/ANAL AUD/VIS CHARTS 18/19. PAGE 163 H3261 NAT/G ACT/RES RUSSIA

B11
PHILLIPSON C.,THE INTERNATIONAL LAW AND CUSTOM OF ANCIENT GREECE AND ROME. MEDIT-7 UNIV INTELL SOCIETY STRUCT NAT/G LEGIS EXEC PERSON...CONCPT OBS CON/ANAL ROM/EMP. PAGE 125 H2504 INT/ORG LAW INT/LAW

B27
CHILDS J.B.,AN ACCOUNT OF GOVERNMENT DOCUMENT BIBLIOGRAPHY IN THE UNITED STATES AND ELSEWHERE (A PAPER). LOC/G PRESS CENTRAL KNOWL...METH 19/20 LEAGUE/NAT. PAGE 29 H0590 BIBLIOG/A CON/ANAL NAT/G

B28
YANG KUNG-SUN,THE BOOK OF LORD SHANG. LAW ECO/UNDEV LOC/G NAT/G NEIGH PLAN ECO/TAC LEGIT ATTIT SKILL ...CONCPT CON/ANAL WORK TOT/POP. PAGE 172 H3434 ASIA JURID

C40
FAHS C.B.,"GOVERNMENT IN JAPAN." FINAN FORCES LEGIS TOP/EX BUDGET INT/TRADE EDU/PROP SOVEREIGN ...CON/ANAL BIBLIOG/A 20 CHINJAP. PAGE 48 H0962 ASIA DIPLOM NAT/G ADMIN

C41
KLUCKHOHN C.,"PATTERNING AS EXEMPLIFIED IN NAVAHO CULTURE

CULTURE" IN EDWARD SAPIR, LANGUAGE, CULTURE, AND PERSONALITY (BMR)" KIN PERS/REL ATTIT PERSON...SOC CONCPT METH/CNCPT LING OBS/ENVIR CON/ANAL BIBLIOG SOC/INTEG 20 NAVAHO INDIAN/AM SAPIR/EDW. PAGE 87 H1733
INGP/REL STRUCT

B42
CONOVER H.F.,FRENCH COLONIES IN AFRICA: A LIST OF REFERENCES. ALGERIA FRANCE MOROCCO SOMALIA SUDAN CULTURE AGRI LOC/G SECT FORCES DIPLOM INT/TRADE NAT/LISM HEALTH...CON/ANAL 20. PAGE 32 H0641
BIBLIOG AFR ECO/UNDEV COLONIAL

B44
KRIS E.,GERMAN RADIO PROPAGANDA: REPORT ON HOME BROADCASTS DURING THE WAR. EUR+WWI GERMANY CULTURE CONSULT PROB/SOLV FEEDBACK TASK INGP/REL DRIVE PWR FASCISM...CON/ANAL METH/COMP 20. PAGE 89 H1768
EDU/PROP DOMIN ACT/RES ATTIT

L48
SHILS E.A.,"COHESION AND DISINTEGRATION IN THE WEHRMACHT IN WORLD WAR II." GERMANY STRUCT DOMIN WAR INGP/REL ISOLAT NAT/LISM ATTIT AUTHORIT SUPEGO RESPECT...PSY CON/ANAL 20 NAZI. PAGE 143 H2862
EDU/PROP DRIVE PERS/REL FORCES

B49
LASSWELL H.D.,LANGUAGE OF POLITICS. COM NAT/G ACT/RES ATTIT PWR...STAT RECORD CON/ANAL GEN/METH 20. PAGE 92 H1834
EDU/PROP METH/CNCPT

B49
SARGENT S.S.,CULTURE AND PERSONALITY. FUT UNIV SOCIETY FAM KIN NEIGH BIO/SOC DRIVE PERCEPT RIGID/FLEX LOVE RESPECT...PSY SOC CONCPT OBS TIME/SEQ TREND CON/ANAL CHARTS HYPO/EXP SIMUL TOT/POP. PAGE 138 H2754
CULTURE PERSON

B50
CANTRIL H.,TENSIONS THAT CAUSE WAR. UNIV CULTURE R+D CREATE EDU/PROP DRIVE PERSON KNOWL ORD/FREE ...HUM PSY SOC OBS CENSUS TREND CON/ANAL SOC/EXP SIMUL GEN/METH ANTHOL COLD/WAR TOT/POP. PAGE 26 H0523
SOCIETY PHIL/SCI PEACE

B50
WARD R.E.,A GUIDE TO JAPANESE REFERENCE AND RESEARCH MATERIALS IN THE FIELD OF POLITICAL SCIENCE. LAW CONSTN LOC/G PRESS ADMIN...SOC CON/ANAL METH 19/20 CHINJAP. PAGE 165 H3305
BIBLIOG/A ASIA NAT/G

B51
WABEKE B.H.,A GUIDE TO DUTCH BIBLIOGRAPHIES. BELGIUM INDONESIA NETHERLAND DIPLOM INT/TRADE WAR NAT/LISM KNOWL...ART/METH HUM JURID CON/ANAL 14/20. PAGE 164 H3282
BIBLIOG/A NAT/G CULTURE COLONIAL

S51
GOULD J.,"THE KOMSOMOL AND THE HITLER JUGEND." COM EUR+WWI GERMANY SOCIETY NAT/G POL/PAR SCHOOL TOTALISM DRIVE PERCEPT KNOWL FASCISM...SOC NAZI TOT/POP 20. PAGE 59 H1185
EDU/PROP CON/ANAL SOCISM

S51
MACRAE D.G.,"THE BOLSHEVIK IDEOLOGY; THE INTELLECTUAL AND EMOTIONAL FACTORS IN COMMUNIST AFFILIATION" (BMR)" COM LEAD REV ATTIT ORD/FREE ...SOC CON/ANAL 20 BOLSHEVISM. PAGE 100 H2008
MARXISM INTELL PHIL/SCI SECT

B52
KOLARZ W.,RUSSIA AND HER COLONIES. COM RUSSIA LAW CULTURE ECO/DEV KIN LOC/G SECT TEC/DEV ECO/TAC EDU/PROP REGION COERCE ATTIT PWR SOVEREIGN...SOC TIME/SEQ CON/ANAL VAL/FREE 19/20. PAGE 88 H1749
NAT/G DOMIN USSR COLONIAL

N52
COORDINATING COMM DOC SOC SCI,INTERNATIONAL REPERTORY OF SOCIAL SCIENCE DOCUMENTATION CENTERS (PAMPHLET). ACT/RES OP/RES WRITING KNOWL...CON/ANAL METH. PAGE 33 H0661
BIBLIOG/A R+D NAT/G INT/ORG

B54
BINANI G.D.,INDIA AT A GLANCE (REV. ED.). INDIA COM/IND FINAN INDUS LABOR PROVS SCHOOL PLAN DIPLOM INT/TRADE ADMIN...JURID 20. PAGE 17 H0335
INDEX CON/ANAL NAT/G ECO/UNDEV

S54
DODD S.C.,"THE SCIENTIFIC MEASUREMENT OF FITNESS FOR SELF-GOVERNMENT." FUT CONSTN ECO/UNDEV INT/ORG PLAN PWR...CONCPT QUANT CON/ANAL SOC/EXP UN LEAGUE/NAT 20. PAGE 41 H0830
NAT/G STAT SOVEREIGN

C55
STEWARD J.H.,"THE CONCEPT AND METHOD OF CULTURAL ECOLOGY" IN T.H. STEWARD'S THEORY OF CULTURAL CHANGE." SOCIETY INGP/REL...CONCPT CON/ANAL METH/COMP 20. PAGE 149 H2985
HABITAT CULTURE CREATE ADJUST

B56
WILBER D.N.,ANNOTATED BIBLIOGRAPHY OF AFGHANISTAN. AFGHANISTN...ART/METH GEOG HUM SOC CON/ANAL 19/20. PAGE 168 H3358
BIBLIOG/A SOCIETY NAT/G ASIA

B56
WILSON P.,GOVERNMENT AND POLITICS OF INDIA AND PAKISTAN: 1885-1955; A BIBLIOGRAPHY OF WORKS IN WESTERN LANGUAGES. INDIA PAKISTAN CONSTN LOC/G POL/PAR FORCES DIPLOM ADMIN WAR CHOOSE...BIOG CON/ANAL 19/20. PAGE 169 H3380
BIBLIOG COLONIAL NAT/G S/ASIA

L56
EPSTEIN L.D.,"BRITISH MASS PARTIES IN COMPARISON WITH AMERICAN PARTIES" UK USA+45 STRATA ECO/DEV LABOR...CON/ANAL 20. PAGE 47 H0936
POL/PAR NAT/COMP PARTIC

CHOOSE

B57
CENTRAL ASIAN RESEARCH CENTRE,BIBLIOGRAPHY OF RECENT SOVIET SOURCE MATERIAL ON SOVIET CENTRAL ASIA AND THE BORDERLANDS. AFGHANISTN INDIA PAKISTAN UAR USSR ECO/UNDEV AGRI EXTR/IND INDUS ACADEM ADMIN ...HEAL HUM LING CON/ANAL 20. PAGE 28 H0567
BIBLIOG/A COM CULTURE NAT/G

B57
COLE G.D.H.,THE POST WAR CONDITIONS OF BRITAIN. EUR+WWI STRUCT NAT/G PLAN EDU/PROP LEGIT RIGID/FLEX ORD/FREE WEALTH...SOCIALIST WELF/ST STAT TREND CON/ANAL CHARTS PARLIAMENT WORK 20. PAGE 31 H0624
ECO/DEV UK

B58
GARTHOFF R.L.,SOVIET STRATEGY IN THE NUCLEAR AGE. FUT USSR R+D INT/ORG NAT/G ACT/RES TEC/DEV DOMIN DETER WAR ATTIT PWR...RELATIV METH/CNCPT SELF/OBS TREND CON/ANAL STERTYP GEN/LAWS 20. PAGE 55 H1103
COM FORCES BAL/PWR NUC/PWR

B58
YUAN TUNG-LI,CHINA IN WESTERN LITERATURE. SECT DIPLOM...ART/METH GEOG JURID SOC BIOG CON/ANAL. PAGE 172 H3441
BIBLIOG ASIA CULTURE HUM

B59
CONOVER H.F.,NIGERIAN OFFICIAL PUBLICATIONS, 1869-1959: A GUIDE. NIGER CONSTN FINAN ACADEM SCHOOL FORCES PRESS ADMIN COLONIAL...HIST/WRIT 19/20. PAGE 33 H0650
BIBLIOG NAT/G CON/ANAL

B59
LOPEZ M.M.,CATALOGOS DE PUBLICACIONES PERIODICAS MEXICANAS. L/A+17C CULTURE NAT/G DIPLOM 20 MEXIC/AMER. PAGE 98 H1965
BIBLIOG PRESS CON/ANAL

S59
LYNN D.B.,"THE EFFECTS OF FATHER-ABSENCE ON NORWEGIAN BOYS AND GIRLS." NORWAY CULTURE PERS/REL ADJUST DISPL LOVE...PSY CORREL STAT INT CON/ANAL CHARTS SOC/INTEG 20. PAGE 99 H1983
SOC FAM AGE/C ANOMIE

S59
MECHAM J.L.,"LATIN AMERICAN CONSTITUTIONS: NOMINAL AND REAL" (BMR)" L/A+17C REV...CON/ANAL NAT/COMP 20. PAGE 108 H2156
CONSTN CHOOSE CONCPT NAT/G

C59
COLLINS I.,"THE GOVERNMENT AND THE NEWSPAPER PRESS IN FRANCE, 1814-1881. FRANCE LAW ADMIN CT/SYS ...CON/ANAL BIBLIOG 19. PAGE 32 H0634
PRESS ORD/FREE NAT/G EDU/PROP

C59
KARPAT K.H.,"TURKEY'S POLITICS: THE TRANSITION TO A MULTI-PARTY SYSTEM." COM TURKEY CULTURE ECO/UNDEV SECT TEC/DEV NAT/LISM ATTIT...SOC CON/ANAL BIBLIOG 20. PAGE 83 H1664
POL/PAR NAT/G

B60
CONOVER H.F.,OFFICIAL PUBLICATIONS OF FRENCH WEST AFRICA, 1946-1958. DAHOMEY IVORY/CST NIGER SENEGAL UPPER/VOLT CONSTN AGRI PRESS...CON/ANAL 20. PAGE 33 H0651
BIBLIOG COLONIAL NAT/G AFR

B60
CONOVER H.F.,OFFICIAL PUBLICATIONS OF SOMALILAND, 1941-1959: A GUIDE. SOMALIA AGRI FINAN INT/ORG SCHOOL INT/TRADE PRESS CONFER COLONIAL PARL/PROC 20 CONGRESS. PAGE 33 H0652
BIBLIOG NAT/G CON/ANAL

B60
EASTON S.C.,THE TWILIGHT OF EUROPEAN COLONIALISM. AFR S/ASIA CONSTN SOCIETY STRUCT ECO/UNDEV INDUS NAT/G FORCES ECO/TAC COLONIAL CT/SYS ATTIT KNOWL ORD/FREE PWR...SOCIALIST TIME/SEQ TREND CON/ANAL 20. PAGE 44 H0882
FINAN ADMIN

B60
EMERY E.,INTRODUCTION TO MASS COMMUNICATIONS. ACADEM PROF/ORG SCHOOL ACT/RES EDU/PROP ATTIT ...CONCPT BIBLIOG/A. PAGE 46 H0920
COM/IND PRESS CON/ANAL CULTURE

B60
GOODMAN E.,SOVIET DESIGN FOR A WORLD STATE. COM USSR NAT/G TOP/EX DIPLOM ECO/TAC DOMIN EDU/PROP COERCE REV ATTIT ORD/FREE...CON/ANAL 20. PAGE 59 H1171
PLAN PWR SOCISM TOTALISM

S60
APTER D.E.,"THE ROLE OF TRADITIONALISM IN THE POLITICAL MODERNIZATION OF GHANA AND UGANDA" (BMR)" AFR GHANA UGANDA CULTURE NAT/G POL/PAR NAT/LISM ...CON/ANAL 20. PAGE 8 H0152
CONSERVE ADMIN GOV/COMP PROB/SOLV

S60
CROZIER B.,"FRANCE AND ALGERIA." ALGERIA EUR+WWI FRANCE FUT ISLAM ECO/UNDEV NEIGH CONSULT DELIB/GP ECO/TAC COLONIAL COERCE ATTIT...SOC INT CON/ANAL 20. PAGE 36 H0713
NAT/G FORCES GUERRILLA NAT/LISM

S60
SPIRO H.J.,"NEW CONSTITUTIONAL FORMS IN AFRICA." FUT CULTURE SOCIETY ECO/UNDEV NAT/G POL/PAR VOL/ASSN EDU/PROP ATTIT DRIVE ORD/FREE PWR RESPECT ...POLICY CONCPT OBS TREND CON/ANAL STERTYP GEN/LAWS VAL/FREE. PAGE 148 H2950
AFR CONSTN FOR/AID NAT/LISM

S60
WOLFE T.W.,"KHRUSHCHEV'S DISARMAMENT STRATEGY." COM NAT/G TOP/EX PLAN BAL/PWR DIPLOM ARMS/CONT COERCE
PWR GEN/LAWS

ATTIT...POLICY CONCPT RECORD TREND CON/ANAL COLD/WAR 20 KHRUSH/N. PAGE 170 H3401 USSR

B61
BURKS R.V.,THE DYNAMICS OF COMMUNISM IN EASTERN EUROPE. COM YUGOSLAVIA POL/PAR RACE/REL ISOLAT ...CORREL CON/ANAL CHARTS GP/COMP DICTIONARY 20 EUROPE/E SLAV/MACED. PAGE 24 H0489 MARXISM STRUCT WORKER REPRESENT

B61
COBBAN A.,ROUSSEAU AND THE MODERN STATE. SOCIETY DOMIN INGP/REL HAPPINESS ALL/VALS...CON/ANAL 18/20 ROUSSEAU/J. PAGE 30 H0611 ORD/FREE ROLE NAT/G POLICY

B61
DIA M.,THE AFRICAN NATIONS AND WORLD SOLIDARITY. ISLAM CULTURE ELITES ECO/DEV ECO/UNDEV INT/ORG NAT/G PLAN ECO/TAC INT/TRADE EDU/PROP NAT/LISM ATTIT DRIVE ORD/FREE WEALTH...SOCIALIST CONCPT CON/ANAL GEN/LAWS TOT/POP 20. PAGE 41 H0817 AFR REGION SOCISM

S61
LIEBERSON S.,"THE IMPACT OF RESIDENTIAL SEGREGATION ON ETHNIC ASSIMILATION" (BMR)" CULTURE MUNIC GP/REL RACE/REL DISCRIM...GEOG STAT CON/ANAL CHARTS SOC/INTEG 20 MIGRATION. PAGE 96 H1926 HABITAT ISOLAT NEIGH

S62
CROAN M.,"POLYCENTRISM: COMMUNIST INTERNATIONAL RELATIONS." ASIA STRUCT INT/ORG NAT/G POL/PAR CONSULT PLAN DOMIN EDU/PROP COERCE ATTIT RIGID/FLEX SOCISM...POLICY CONCPT TREND CON/ANAL GEN/LAWS MARX/KARL. PAGE 35 H0703 COM CREATE DIPLOM NAT/LISM

S62
FESLER J.W.,"FRENCH FIELD ADMINISTRATION: THE BEGINNINGS." CHRIST-17C CULTURE SOCIETY STRATA NAT/G ECO/TAC DOMIN EDU/PROP LEGIT ADJUD COERCE ATTIT ALL/VALS...TIME/SEQ CON/ANAL GEN/METH VAL/FREE 13/15. PAGE 49 H0988 EX/STRUC FRANCE

B63
CONOVER H.F.,AFRICA SOUTH OF THE SAHARA. CULTURE SECT TEC/DEV...ART/METH GEOG SOC. PAGE 33 H0654 BIBLIOG/A AFR CON/ANAL

B63
ENKE S.,ECONOMICS FOR DEVELOPMENT. AGRI TEC/DEV CAP/ISM DIPLOM ECO/TAC TAX ATTIT DRIVE HABITAT WEALTH...GOV/COMP BIBLIOG 20. PAGE 46 H0928 ECO/UNDEV PHIL/SCI CON/ANAL

B63
WALKER A.A.,OFFICIAL PUBLICATIONS OF SIERRA LEONE AND GAMBIA. GAMBIA SIER/LEONE UK LAW CONSTN LEGIS PLAN BUDGET DIPLOM...SOC SAMP CON/ANAL 20. PAGE 164 H3290 BIBLIOG NAT/G COLONIAL ADMIN

S63
AYAL E.B.,"VALUE SYSTEM AND ECONOMIC DEVELOPMENT IN JAPAN AND THAILAND." ASIA S/ASIA THAILAND CULTURE ECO/DEV CAP/ISM DOMIN NAT/LISM DRIVE RIGID/FLEX SOCISM...WELF/ST OBS TREND CON/ANAL GEN/LAWS 20 CHINJAP. PAGE 9 H0185 ECO/UNDEV ALL/VALS

S63
CRUTCHER J.,"PAN AFRICANISM: AFRICAN ODYSSEY." AFR NAT/G POL/PAR PROF/ORG VOL/ASSN TOP/EX CREATE REGION RACE/REL ALL/VALS...CONCPT TIME/SEQ TREND CON/ANAL 20. PAGE 36 H0716 PROVS DELIB/GP COLONIAL

S63
POPPINO R.E.,"IMBALANCE IN BRAZIL." L/A+17C NAT/G TOP/EX PLAN DIPLOM LEGIT DRIVE WEALTH...CON/ANAL LAFTA 20. PAGE 127 H2544 POL/PAR ECO/TAC BRAZIL

S63
ROBINSON W.C.,"URBANIZATION AND FERTILITY: THE NON-WESTERN EXPERIENCE (BMR)" DEATH MARRIAGE AGE/C BIO/SOC...STAT CENSUS CON/ANAL CHARTS NAT/COMP 20 THIRD/WRLD. PAGE 133 H2651 GEOG MUNIC FAM ECO/UNDEV

S64
GRUNER E.,"PRENSA, PARTIDOS POLITICOS, Y GRUPOS DE PRESION EN SUIZA." EUR+WWI MOD/EUR NAT/G EDU/PROP LEGIT PRESS ATTIT KNOWL ORD/FREE...CONCPT STAT CON/ANAL CHARTS 20. PAGE 62 H1241 POL/PAR SWITZERLND

S64
LEWIS R.,"OPINION SURVEYING IN KOREA." ASIA FUT KOREA LEGIS EDU/PROP EXEC ALL/VALS...POLICY CONCPT MYTH TESTS CON/ANAL GEN/METH TOT/POP VAL/FREE 20. PAGE 96 H1915 NAT/G QU

S64
POWELL R.L.,"COMMUNIST CHINA'S MILITARY POTENTIAL." ASIA CHINA/COM NAT/G EX/STRUC EDU/PROP COERCE GUERRILLA NUC/PWR WAR...RECORD CON/ANAL 20. PAGE 128 H2551 FORCES PWR

B65
HYMES D.,THE USE OF COMPUTERS IN ANTHROPOLOGY. CULTURE PROF/ORG CONSULT CREATE EFFICIENCY PERCEPT ...CLASSIF LING CON/ANAL COMPUT/IR METH/COMP ANTHOL 20. PAGE 76 H1517 METH COMPUTER TEC/DEV SOC

B65
INT. BANK RECONSTR. DEVELOP.,ECONOMIC DEVELOPMENT OF KUWAIT. ISLAM KUWAIT AGRI FINAN MARKET EX/STRUC TEC/DEV ECO/TAC ADMIN WEALTH...OBS CON/ANAL CHARTS 20. PAGE 77 H1541 INDUS NAT/G

B65
PEASLEE A.J.,CONSTITUTIONS OF NATIONS* THIRD REVISED EDITION (VOLUME I* AFRICA). LAW EX/STRUC LEGIS TOP/EX LEGIT CT/SYS ROUTINE ORD/FREE PWR SOVEREIGN...CON/ANAL CHARTS. PAGE 124 H2481 AFR CHOOSE CONSTN NAT/G

B65
WALKER A.A.,THE RHODESIAS AND NYASALAND: A GUIDE TO OFFICIAL PUBLICATIONS. RHODESIA UK OP/RES PLAN PROB/SOLV DIPLOM...POLICY SOC CON/ANAL 19/20 NYASALAND. PAGE 164 H3291 BIBLIOG NAT/G COLONIAL AFR

S65
JENSEN L.,"MILITARY CAPABILITIES AND BARGAINING BEHAVIOR." USA+45 USSR ARMS/CONT DETER COST ATTIT ...METH/CNCPT STAT SYS/QU CON/ANAL CHARTS NAT/COMP. PAGE 81 H1614 DIPLOM DRIVE PWR STERTYP

S65
LAULICHT J.,"PUBLIC OPINION AND FOREIGN POLICY DECISIONS." CANADA ELITES NAT/G FOR/AID LEAD NUC/PWR PERCEPT...INT QU CHARTS UN COLD/WAR. PAGE 92 H1839 DIPLOM ATTIT CON/ANAL SAMP

S65
VAN DEN BERG M.,"SOME METHODOLOGICAL ASPECTS OF SOUTH AFRICA'S FIRST E.D.P." SOUTH/AFR NAT/G CREATE TEC/DEV CAP/ISM INCOME PRODUC...CON/ANAL CHARTS 20. PAGE 161 H3226 ECO/DEV PLAN METH STAT

S66
GALTUNG J.,"EAST-WEST INTERACTION PATTERNS." DIPLOM INT/TRADE...NET/THEORY CON/ANAL CHARTS NAT/COMP INDEX NATO COLD/WAR UN WARSAW/P. PAGE 55 H1090 STAT HYPO/EXP

B67
UNIVERSAL REFERENCE SYSTEM,COMPARATIVE GOVERNMENT AND CULTURES (VOLUME X). WOR+45 WOR-45 NAT/G POL/PAR ATTIT...CON/ANAL COMPUT/IR IDEA/COMP GEN/METH. PAGE 158 H3168 BIBLIOG/A GOV/COMP CULTURE NAT/COMP

L67
WILBER L.A.,"THE GOVERNMENTAL STRUCTURE OF MISSISSIPPI: ITS STRENGTHS AND WEAKNESSES." AGRI LOC/G SCHOOL EX/STRUC LEGIS TOP/EX BUDGET CT/SYS APPORT RACE/REL...GOV/COMP 20 MISSISSIPP. PAGE 168 H3359 CONSTN PROVS STAT CON/ANAL

B87
ADAMS J.,A DEFENSE OF THE CONSTITUTIONS OF GOVERNMENT OF THE UNITED STATES OF AMERICA. USA-45 STRATA CHIEF EX/STRUC LEGIS CT/SYS CONSERVE POPULISM...CONCPT CON/ANAL GOV/COMP. PAGE 3 H0063 CONSTN BAL/PWR PWR NAT/G

CON/INTERP....CONSTITUTIONAL INTERPRETATION

B57
LONG H.A.,USURPERS - FOES OF FREE MAN. LAW NAT/G CHIEF LEGIS DOMIN ADJUD REPRESENT GOV/REL ORD/FREE LAISSEZ POPULISM...POLICY 18/20 SUPREME/CT ROOSEVLT/F CONGRESS CON/INTERP. PAGE 98 H1961 CT/SYS CENTRAL FEDERAL CONSTN

CONCEN/CMP....CONCENTRATION CAMPS

CONCEPT....SEE CONCPT

CONCPT....SUBJECT-MATTER CONCEPTS

CONDEMNATION OF LAND OR PROPERTY....SEE CONDEMNATN

CONDEMNATN....CONDEMNATION OF LAND OR PROPERTY

CONDOTTIER....CONDOTTIERI - HIRED MILITIA

CONFER....CONFERENCES; SEE ALSO DELIB/GP

N
CHINA QUARTERLY. COM AGRI INDUS ACADEM POL/PAR INT/TRADE CONFER GOV/REL...TIME/SEQ CON/ANAL INDEX 20. PAGE 1 H0014 BIBLIOG/A ASIA DIPLOM POLICY

N19
SOUTH AFRICA COMMISSION ON FUT,INTERIM AND FINAL REPORTS ON FUTURE FORM OF GOVERNMENT IN THE SOUTH-WEST AFRICAN PROTECTORATE (PAMPHLET). SOUTH/AFR NAT/G FORCES CONFER COLONIAL CONTROL 20 AFRICA/SW. PAGE 147 H2936 CONSTN REPRESENT ADMIN PROB/SOLV

B27
MCCOWN A.C.,THE CONGRESSIONAL CONFERENCE COMMITTEE. FACE/GP CONTROL. PAGE 106 H2128 DELIB/GP GOV/COMP LEGIS CONFER

B37
CLOKIE H.M.,ROYAL COMMISSIONS OF INQUIRY; THE SIGNIFICANCE OF INVESTIGATIONS IN BRITISH POLITICS. UK POL/PAR CONFER ROUTINE...POLICY DECISION TIME/SEQ 16/20. PAGE 30 H0607 NAT/G DELIB/GP INSPECT

C43
BENTHAM J.,"ON THE LIBERTY OF THE PRESS, AND PUBLIC DISCUSSION" IN J. BOWRING, ED., THE WORKS OF JEREMY BENTHAM." SPAIN UK LAW ELITES NAT/G LEGIS INSPECT LEGIT WRITING CONTROL PRIVIL TOTALISM AUTHORIT ...TRADIT 19 FREE/SPEE. PAGE 15 H0290 ORD/FREE PRESS CONFER CONSERVE

C52
FIFIELD R.H.,"WOODROW WILSON AND THE FAR EAST." ASIA CHIEF DELIB/GP BAL/PWR CONFER COLONIAL ARMS/CONT WAR...TIME/SEQ NAT/COMP 19/20 WILSON/W BIBLIOG DIPLOM INT/ORG

LEAGUE/NAT. PAGE 50 H0995

B53
KANTOR H.,A BIBLIOGRAPHY OF UNPUBLISHED DOCTORAL DISSERTATIONS AND MASTERS' THESES DEALING WITH GOVTS, POL, INT REL OF LAT AM. L/A+17C INT/ORG POL/PAR ACT/RES OP/RES CONFER ATTIT...INT/LAW PHIL/SCI 20. PAGE 83 H1656
BIBLIOG ACADEM DIPLOM NAT/G

C53
BULNER-THOMAS I.,"THE PARTY SYSTEM IN GREAT BRITAIN." UK CONSTN SECT PRESS CONFER GP/REL ATTIT ...POLICY TREND BIBLIOG 19/20 PARLIAMENT. PAGE 23 H0473
NAT/G POL/PAR ADMIN ROUTINE

B54
GRAYSON H.,ECONOMIC PLANNING UNDER FREE ENTERPRISE. CANADA FUT UK DELIB/GP BUDGET CONFER CONTROL ...POLICY DECISION 20. PAGE 60 H1200
PLAN ECO/TAC NAT/COMP NAT/G

B55
WHEARE K.C.,GOVERNMENT BY COMMITTEE; AN ESSAY ON THE BRITISH CONSTITUTION. UK NAT/G LEGIS INSPECT CONFER ADJUD ADMIN CONTROL TASK EFFICIENCY ROLE POPULISM 20. PAGE 167 H3337
DELIB/GP CONSTN LEAD GP/COMP

B57
US SENATE SPEC COMM FOR AID,COMPILATION OF STUDIES AND SURVEYS. AFR ASIA L/A+17C USA+45 ECO/UNDEV AGRI INT/ORG CONSULT TEC/DEV CONFER TOTALISM...NAT/COMP 20 CONGRESS. PAGE 161 H3216
FOR/AID DIPLOM ORD/FREE DELIB/GP

C57
MORRIS-JONES W.H.,"PARLIAMENT IN INDIA." INDIA CONSTN LEGIS CONFER COLONIAL CHOOSE PRIVIL ATTIT ...GOV/COMP BIBLIOG 20. PAGE 113 H2264
PARL/PROC EX/STRUC NAT/G POL/PAR

B58
CRAIG G.A.,FROM BISMARCK TO ADENAUER: ASPECTS OF GERMAN STATECRAFT. GERMANY INTELL FORCES ECO/TAC CONFER COERCE WAR GP/REL ORD/FREE PWR CONSERVE 19/20 BISMARCK/O ADENAUER/K. PAGE 35 H0695
DIPLOM LEAD NAT/G

B58
INDIA (REPUBLIC) PARLIAMENT,CLASSIFIED LIST OF PUBLIC UNDERTAKINGS AND OTHER BODIES IN INDIA. INDIA ACADEM LG/CO CONSULT LEGIT CONFER GOV/REL 20. PAGE 76 H1528
NAT/G LEGIS LICENSE PROF/ORG

B58
WILMERDING L. JR.,THE ELECTORAL COLLEGE. CONSTN NAT/G POL/PAR DELIB/GP LEGIS PROB/SOLV CONFER EXEC LEAD APPORT REPRESENT. PAGE 169 H3377
CHOOSE DECISION ACT/RES

B59
THOMAS D.H.,GUIDE TO THE DIPLOMATIC ARCHIVES OF WESTERN EUROPE. EUR+WWI ELITES INT/ORG NAT/G BAL/PWR INT/TRADE PEACE. PAGE 154 H3076
BIBLIOG DIPLOM CONFER

B60
CONOVER H.F.,OFFICIAL PUBLICATIONS OF SOMALILAND, 1941-1959: A GUIDE. SOMALIA AGRI FINAN INT/ORG SCHOOL INT/TRADE PRESS CONFER COLONIAL PARL/PROC 20 CONGRESS. PAGE 33 H0652
BIBLIOG NAT/G CON/ANAL

B60
FEIS H.,BETWEEN WAR AND PEACE: THE POTSDAM CONFERENCE. EUR+WWI NAT/G DELIB/GP PROB/SOLV REPAR WAR CIVMIL/REL...BIBLIOG 20. PAGE 49 H0983
DIPLOM CONFER BAL/PWR

B60
FISCHER L.,THE SOVIETS IN WORLD AFFAIRS. CHINA/COM COM EUR+WWI USSR INT/ORG CONFER LEAD ARMS/CONT REV PWR...CHARTS 20 TREATY VERSAILLES. PAGE 51 H1010
DIPLOM NAT/G POLICY MARXISM

B60
JEFFRIES C.,TRANSFER OF POWER: PROBLEMS OF THE PASSAGE TO SELFGOVERNMENT. CEYLON GHANA MALAYSIA NIGERIA UK INT/ORG CONSULT DELIB/GP LEGIS DIPLOM CONFER PARL/PROC 20. PAGE 80 H1595
SOVEREIGN COLONIAL ORD/FREE NAT/G

B60
ROY N.C.,THE CIVIL SERVICE IN INDIA. INDIA POL/PAR ECO/TAC INCOME...JURID MGT 20 CIVIL/SERV. PAGE 135 H2705
ADMIN NAT/G DELIB/GP CONFER

B61
BINDER L.,RELIGION AND POLITICS IN PAKISTAN. ISLAM PAKISTAN NAT/G SECT LEGIS CREATE CHOOSE GP/REL ...MAJORIT TRADIT 20. PAGE 17 H0336
CONSTN CONFER NAT/LISM POL/PAR

B61
INDIAN NATIONAL CONGRESS,SOUVENIR, 66TH SESSION. INDIA S/ASIA CONSTN CULTURE LEGIS CREATE TEC/DEV LEAD TASK...GEOG CHARTS 20. PAGE 77 H1533
CONFER PLAN NAT/G POLICY

B61
TREVE W.,DEUTSCHE PARTEIPROGRAMME 1861-1961. GERMANY GERMANY/W DELIB/GP CONFER CHOOSE REPRESENT 19/20. PAGE 157 H3130
POL/PAR NAT/G LEGIS PARL/PROC

B62
ESCUELA SUPERIOR DE ADMIN PUBL,INFORME DEL SEMINARIO SOBRE SERVICIO CIVIL O CARRERA ADMINISTRATIVA. L/A+17C ELITES STRATA CONFER CONTROL GOV/REL INGP/REL SUPEGO 20 CENTRAL/AM CIVIL/SERV. PAGE 47 H0939
ADMIN NAT/G PROB/SOLV ATTIT

B62
INAYATULLAH,BUREAUCRACY AND DEVELOPMENT IN PAKISTAN. PAKISTAN ECO/UNDEV EDU/PROP CONFER ...ANTHOL DICTIONARY 20 BUREAUCRCY. PAGE 76 H1526
EX/STRUC ADMIN NAT/G LOC/G

B62
WOODS H.D.,LABOUR POLICY AND LABOUR ECONOMICS IN CANADA. CANADA FUT NAT/G VOL/ASSN WORKER BARGAIN ECO/TAC PAY CONFER GP/REL 20. PAGE 170 H3409
LABOR POLICY INDUS ECO/DEV

B63
DALAND R.T.,PERSPECTIVES OF BRAZILIAN PUBLIC ADMINISTRATION (VOL. I). BRAZIL LAW ECO/UNDEV SCHOOL CHIEF TEC/DEV CONFER CONTROL GP/REL ATTIT ROLE PWR...ANTHOL 20. PAGE 37 H0735
ADMIN NAT/G PLAN GOV/REL

B63
NICOLSON H.,DIPLOMACY (3RD ED.). INT/ORG NAT/G CONSULT DELIB/GP CONFER 19/20 LEAGUE/NAT UN. PAGE 118 H2354
DIPLOM CONCPT NAT/COMP

C63
HSU F.L.,"COHESION AND DIVISION IN THE AMERICAN WORLD" HSU FL. CLAN, CASTE, AND CLUB." CULTURE EDU/PROP CONFER SANCTION PERSON...PSY GP/COMP. PAGE 74 H1484
PERS/REL AGE/Y ADJUST VOL/ASSN

B64
INTL CONF ON POPULATION,POPULATION DYNAMICS: INTERNATIONAL ACTION AND TRAINING PROGRAMS. INDIA KOREA L/A+17C TAIWAN USA+45 WOR+45 FAM PLAN CONFER ...NEW/IDEA ANTHOL 20 CHINJAP BIRTH/CON. PAGE 78 H1561
NAT/COMP CONTROL ATTIT EDU/PROP

B64
US HOUSE COMM BANKING-CURR,INTERNATIONAL DEVELOPMENT ASSOCIATION ACT AMENDMENT. CHINA/COM USA+45 USSR FINAN FORCES LEGIS DIPLOM CONFER EFFICIENCY...CHARTS GOV/COMP 20 PRESIDENT CONGRESS INTL/DEV. PAGE 160 H3196
BAL/PAY FOR/AID RECORD ECO/TAC

B65
INST INTL DES CIVILISATION DIF,THE CONSTITUTIONS AND ADMINISTRATIVE INSTITUTIONS OF THE NEW STATES. AFR ISLAM S/ASIA NAT/G POL/PAR DELIB/GP EX/STRUC CONFER EFFICIENCY NAT/LISM...JURID SOC 20. PAGE 77 H1535
CONSTN ADMIN ADJUD ECO/UNDEV

B65
JOHNSON P.,KHRUSHCHEV AND THE ARTS: POLITICS OF SOVIET CULTURE, 1962-1964. COM USSR NAT/G PERF/ART CONFER DEBATE GP/REL PERS/REL UTIL ATTIT DRIVE 20 KHRUSH/N. PAGE 81 H1626
CULTURE MARXISM POLICY CHIEF

B65
YOUNG A.N.,CHINA'S WARTIME FINANCE AND INFLATION. ASIA AGRI INDUS NAT/G ECO/TAC CONFER PRICE WAR COST 20. PAGE 172 H3437
FINAN FOR/AID TAX BUDGET

S65
WEDGE B.,"PSYCHOLOGICAL FACTORS IN SOVIET DISARMAMENT NEGOTIATION." USA+45 CONFER ATTIT PERCEPT PERSON...PSY NAT/COMP. PAGE 166 H3324
USSR DIPLOM ARMS/CONT

B66
BUTLER D.E.,THE BRITISH GENERAL ELECTION OF 1966. UK LOC/G NAT/G OP/RES CONFER CHOOSE MAJORITY ATTIT ...CHARTS TIME 20. PAGE 25 H0498
POL/PAR REPRESENT GP/REL PERS/REL

B66
HAMILTON W.B.,A DECADE OF THE COMMONWEALTH, 1955-1964. UK LAW ELITES FINAN FOR/AID CONFER COLONIAL PWR...GEOG CHARTS ANTHOL 20 CMN/WLTH UN. PAGE 65 H1302
INT/ORG INGP/REL DIPLOM NAT/G

B66
SMELSER N.J.,SOCIAL STRUCTURE AND MOBILITY IN ECONOMIC DEVELOPMENT. CULTURE SOCIETY CONFER...PSY SOC CHARTS METH/COMP NAT/COMP ANTHOL METH 20. PAGE 145 H2904
STRUCT STRATA ECO/UNDEV ECO/DEV

B66
WEINSTEIN F.B.,VIETNAM'S UNHELD ELECTIONS: THE FAILURE TO CARRY OUT THE 1956 REUNIFICATION ELECTIONS... (MONOGRAPH). VIETNAM/S VIETNAM/N LEGIT CONFER ADJUD WAR PEACE 20 TREATY GENEVA/CON UNIFICA. PAGE 166 H3330
AGREE NAT/G CHOOSE DIPLOM

S66
TOUVAL S.,"AFRICA'S FRONTIERS* REACTIONS TO A COLONIAL LEGACY." L/A+17C CONFER ADJUD COLONIAL APPORT CONSEN NAT/LISM RESPECT...RECORD NAT/COMP. PAGE 156 H3120
AFR GEOG SOVEREIGN WAR

B67
FAY S.B.,THE ORIGINS OF THE WORLD WAR (2ND REV. ED. 2 VOLS.). NAT/G FORCES DIPLOM CONFER LEAD PEACE ...REALPOL GOV/COMP 19/20. PAGE 49 H0978
MOD/EUR WAR REGION INT/ORG

B67
SCHUTZ W.W.,RETHINKING GERMAN POLICY; NEW APPROACHES TO REUNIFICATION. GERMANY USSR PLAN CONFER...POLICY 20. PAGE 140 H2806
REGION NAT/G DIPLOM PROB/SOLV

B67
UNESCO,PRINCIPLES AND PROBLEMS OF NATIONAL SCIENCE POLICIES. WOR+45 ECO/DEV ECO/UNDEV R+D INT/ORG PROB/SOLV CONFER...PHIL/SCI CHARTS 20 UNESCO UN.
NAT/COMP POLICY TEC/DEV

PAGE 158 H3165 CREATE

B67
ZALESKI E.,PLANNING REFORMS IN THE SOVIET UNION 1962-1966. COM USSR NAT/G CONFER CONTROL EFFICIENCY MARXISM...POLICY DECISION 20. PAGE 172 H3446 ECO/DEV PLAN ADMIN CENTRAL

S67
CUMMINS L.,"THE FORMULATION OF THE "PLATT" AMENDMENT." CUBA L/A+17C NAT/G DELIB/GP CONFER ...POLICY 20. PAGE 36 H0720 DIPLOM INT/LAW LEGIS

S67
DOERN G.B.,"THE ROYAL COMMISSIONS IN THE GENERAL POLICY PROCESS AND IN FEDERAL-PROVINCIAL RELATIONS." CANADA CONSTN ACADEM PROVS CONSULT DELIB/GP LEGIS ACT/RES PROB/SOLV CONFER CONTROL EFFICIENCY...METH/COMP 20 SENATE ROYAL/COMM. PAGE 42 H0832 R+D EX/STRUC GOV/REL NAT/G

S67
GRIEB K.J.,"THE UNITED STATES AND THE CENTRAL AMERICAN CONFEDERATION." COSTA/RICA EL/SALVADR GUATEMALA HONDURAS L/A+17C NICARAGUA NAT/G FORCES CONFER AGREE EXEC ARMS/CONT REV WAR PEACE ATTIT 20. PAGE 60 H1212 INT/ORG DIPLOM POLICY REGION

S67
KASFIR N.,"THE UGANDA CONSTITUENT ASSEMBLY DEBATE." UGANDA REPRESENT FEDERAL ORD/FREE POPULISM...POLICY DECISION 20. PAGE 83 H1665 CONSTN CONFER LAW NAT/G

S67
MAYANJA A.,"THE GOVERNMENT'S PROPOSALS ON THE NEW CONSTITUTION." AFR UGANDA LAW CHIEF LEGIS ADJUD REPRESENT FEDERAL PWR 20. PAGE 105 H2105 CONSTN CONFER ORD/FREE NAT/G

S67
NIEBUHR R.,"THE ETHICS OF WAR AND PEACE IN THE NUCLEAR AGE." VIETNAM INTELL CONFER CONTROL WAR GOV/REL PERS/REL ORD/FREE...POLICY INT GOV/COMP NAT/COMP 20 UN. PAGE 118 H2360 MORAL PEACE NUC/PWR DIPLOM

S67
SPINELLI A.,"EUROPEAN UNION IN THE RESISTANCE." NAT/G BAL/PWR DIPLOM CONFER REGION TOTALISM ORD/FREE POLICY. PAGE 147 H2948 NAT/LISM FEDERAL EUR+WWI INT/ORG

N67
US HOUSE COMM SCI ASTRONAUT,GOVERNMENT, SCIENCE, AND INTERNATIONAL POLICY (PAMPHLET). INDIA NETHERLAND ECO/DEV ECO/UNDEV R+D ACADEM PLAN DIPLOM FOR/AID CONFER...PREDICT 20 CHINJAP. PAGE 160 H3198 NAT/G POLICY CREATE TEC/DEV

CONFERENCE ABORIGINAL STUDIES H0638

CONFERENCES....SEE CONFER, DELIB/GP

CONFIDENCE, PERSONAL....SEE SUPEGO

CONFLICT, MILITARY....SEE WAR, FORCES+COERCE

CONFLICT, PERSONAL....SEE PERS/REL, ROLE

CONFLICT....CONFLICT THEORY

CONFORMITY....SEE CONSEN, DOMIN

CONFRONTATION....SEE CONFRONTN

CONFRONTN....CONFRONTATION

CONFUCIUS....CONFUCIUS

B58
CHANG H.,WITHIN THE FOUR SEAS. ASIA WAR MORAL MARXISM...IDEA/COMP NAT/COMP 20 CONFUCIUS. PAGE 29 H0577 PEACE DIPLOM KNOWL CULTURE

CONG/VIENN....CONGRESS OF VIENNA

B46
NICOLSON H.,THE CONGRESS OF VIENNA. MOD/EUR NAT/G FORCES BAL/PWR DOMIN LEGIT COERCE PERSON PWR ...RECORD TIME/SEQ STERTYP 19 CONG/VIENN. PAGE 118 H2353 CONCPT POLICY DIPLOM

CONGO....CONGO, PRE-INDEPENDENCE OR GENERAL

B61
MERRIAM A.,CONGO: BACKGROUND OF CONFLICT. AFR FUT KIN MUNIC NAT/G POL/PAR PROVS DELIB/GP PLAN DOMIN COERCE ATTIT...TIME/SEQ CHARTS CONGO 20. PAGE 109 H2182 CHOOSE GUERRILLA

B61
TURNBULL C.M.,THE FOREST PEOPLE. EATING GP/REL INGP/REL RACE/REL ISOLAT HABITAT HEREDITY...GEOG SOC LING DICTIONARY WORSHIP 20 CONGO NEGRO BA/MBUTI. PAGE 157 H3138 AFR CULTURE KIN RECORD

S61
MILLER E.,"LEGAL ASPECTS OF UN ACTION IN THE CONGO." AFR CULTURE ADMIN PEACE DRIVE RIGID/FLEX ORD/FREE...WELF/ST JURID OBS UN CONGO 20. PAGE 111 H2212 INT/ORG LEGIT

B64
LEMARCHAND R.,POLITICAL AWAKENING IN THE BELGIAN CONGO. ECO/UNDEV VOL/ASSN DOMIN CHOOSE GP/REL INGP/REL DISCRIM ORD/FREE PWR...CHARTS 20 CONGO ARABS. PAGE 94 H1873 NAT/LISM COLONIAL POL/PAR RACE/REL

B65
HAEFELE E.T.,GOVERNMENT CONTROLS ON TRANSPORT. AFR RHODESIA TANZANIA DIPLOM ECO/TAC TARIFFS PRICE ADJUD CONTROL REGION EFFICIENCY...POLICY 20 CONGO. PAGE 64 H1274 ECO/UNDEV DIST/IND FINAN NAT/G

CONGO/BRAZ....CONGO, BRAZZAVILLE; SEE ALSO AFR

B61
BIEBUYCK D.,CONGO TRIBES AND PARTIES. AFR CONGO/BRAZ CONSTN NAT/G COLONIAL CHOOSE FEDERAL 20 CONGO/LEOP. PAGE 17 H0333 KIN POL/PAR GP/REL SOVEREIGN

B66
ZOLBERG A.R.,CREATING POLITICAL ORDER. AFR CONGO/BRAZ GHANA NIGER KIN NAT/G DOMIN COLONIAL REGION CENTRAL NAT/LISM ATTIT PWR 20 CONGO/LEOP. PAGE 173 H3462 SOVEREIGN ORD/FREE CONSTN POL/PAR

CONGO/KINS....CONGO, KINSHASA; SEE ALSO AFR

B51
INTERNATIONAL AFRICAN INST,ETHNOGRAPHIC SURVEY OF AFRICA: WEST CENTRAL AFRICA (VOLS. I-III, 1951-1953). AFR RHODESIA CULTURE ECO/UNDEV HEREDITY ...GEOG SOC CHARTS BIBLIOG WORSHIP 20 CONGO/KINS. PAGE 77 H1543 STRUCT KIN INGP/REL HABITAT

B61
BIEBUYCK D.,CONGO TRIBES AND PARTIES. AFR CONGO/BRAZ CONSTN NAT/G COLONIAL CHOOSE FEDERAL 20 CONGO/KINS. PAGE 17 H0333 KIN POL/PAR GP/REL SOVEREIGN

B66
ZOLBERG A.R.,CREATING POLITICAL ORDER. AFR CONGO/BRAZ GHANA NIGER KIN NAT/G DOMIN COLONIAL REGION CENTRAL NAT/LISM ATTIT PWR 20 CONGO/KINS. PAGE 173 H3462 SOVEREIGN ORD/FREE CONSTN POL/PAR

B67
ANDERSON C.W.,ISSUES OF POLITICAL DEVELOPMENT. BURMA WOR+45 CULTURE TOP/EX ECO/TAC MARXISM ...CHARTS NAT/COMP 20 COLOMB CONGO/KINS. PAGE 6 H0126 NAT/LISM COERCE ECO/UNDEV SOCISM

CONGRESS OF RACIAL EQUALITY....SEE CORE

CONGRESS....CONGRESS (ALL NATIONS); SEE ALSO LEGIS, HOUSE/REP, SENATE, DELIB/GP

B27
WILLOUGHBY W.F.,PRINCIPLES OF PUBLIC ADMINISTRATION WITH SPECIAL REFERENCE TO THE NATIONAL AND STATE GOVERNMENTS OF THE UNITED STATES. FINAN PROVS CHIEF CONSULT LEGIS CREATE BUDGET EXEC ROUTINE GOV/REL CENTRAL...MGT 20 BUR/BUDGET CONGRESS PRESIDENT. PAGE 169 H3373 NAT/G EX/STRUC OP/RES ADMIN

S43
PRICE D.K.,"THE PARLIAMENTARY AND PRESIDENTIAL SYSTEMS" (BMR)" USA-45 NAT/G EX/STRUC PARL/PROC GOV/REL PWR 20 PRESIDENT CONGRESS PARLIAMENT. PAGE 128 H2561 LEGIS REPRESENT ADMIN GOV/COMP

B55
GALLOWAY G.B.,CONGRESS AND PARLIAMENT: THEIR ORGANIZATION AND OPERATION IN THE US AND THE UK: PLANNING PAMPHLET NO. 93. POL/PAR EX/STRUC DEBATE CONTROL LEAD ROUTINE EFFICIENCY PWR...POLICY CONGRESS PARLIAMENT. PAGE 54 H1089 DELIB/GP LEGIS PARL/PROC GOV/COMP

B56
HERNANDEZ URBINA A.,LOS PARTIDOS Y LA CRISIS DEL APRA. PERU NAT/G LEAD LOBBY CHOOSE SOCISM...POLICY DECISION 20 COM/PARTY APRA CONGRESS. PAGE 70 H1402 POL/PAR PARTIC PARL/PROC GP/REL

N56
US HOUSE COMM FOREIGN AFFAIRS,REPORT OF THE SPECIAL STUDY MISSION TO AFRICA, SOUTH AND EAST OF THE SAHARA (PAMPHLET). AFR SOUTH/AFR USA+45 STRUCT INT/TRADE PARL/PROC NAT/LISM ATTIT ALL/VALS HEALTH ...POLICY 20 CONGRESS. PAGE 160 H3197 FOR/AID COLONIAL ECO/UNDEV DIPLOM

B57
LONG H.A.,USURPERS - FOES OF FREE MAN. LAW NAT/G CHIEF LEGIS DOMIN ADJUD REPRESENT GOV/REL ORD/FREE LAISSEZ POPULISM...POLICY 18/20 SUPREME/CT ROOSEVLT/F CONGRESS CON/INTERP. PAGE 98 H1961 CT/SYS CENTRAL FEDERAL CONSTN

B57
US SENATE SPEC COMM FOR AID,COMPILATION OF STUDIES FOR/AID

AND SURVEYS. AFR ASIA L/A+17C USA+45 ECO/UNDEV AGRI INT/ORG CONSULT TEC/DEV CONFER TOTALISM...NAT/COMP 20 CONGRESS. PAGE 161 H3216 DIPLOM ORD/FREE DELIB/GP

B57
US SENATE SPEC COMM FOR AID,HEARINGS BEFORE THE SPECIAL COMMITTEE TO STUDY THE FOREIGN AID PROGRAM. USA+45 USSR ECO/UNDEV INT/ORG FORCES WEAPON TOTALISM ATTIT SUPEGO...NAT/COMP CONGRESS. PAGE 161 H3217 FOR/AID DIPLOM ORD/FREE TEC/DEV

L59
JANIS I.L.,"DECISIONAL CONFLICT: A THEORETICAL ANALYSIS." INTELL NAT/G POL/PAR DELIB/GP LEGIS TOP/EX PLAN...DECISION CONGRESS NAZI 20 WWI. PAGE 80 H1590 ACT/RES PSY DIPLOM

B60
JUNZ A.J.,PRESENT TRENDS IN AMERICAN NATIONAL GOVERNMENT. LEGIS DIPLOM ADMIN CT/SYS ORD/FREE ...CONCPT ANTHOL 20 CONGRESS PRESIDENT SUPREME/CT. PAGE 3 H0052 POL/PAR CHOOSE CONSTN NAT/G

B60
CONOVER H.F.,OFFICIAL PUBLICATIONS OF SOMALILAND, 1941-1959: A GUIDE. SOMALIA AGRI FINAN INT/ORG SCHOOL INT/TRADE PRESS CONFER COLONIAL PARL/PROC 20 CONGRESS. PAGE 33 H0652 BIBLIOG NAT/G CON/ANAL

B60
MORRIS I.,NATIONALISM AND THE RIGHT WING IN JAPAN: A STUDY OF POST WAR TRENDS. ASIA ELITES NAT/G DELIB/GP FORCES TOP/EX CHOOSE ATTIT...INT GEN/LAWS CONGRESS 20 CHINJAP. PAGE 113 H2262 POL/PAR TREND NAT/LISM

B61
CHAKRABARTI A.,NEHRU: HIS DEMOCRACY AND INDIA. ASIA INDIA UK CONSTN ECO/UNDEV SECT DIPLOM COLONIAL PEACE WEALTH...BIBLIOG 20 CONGRESS NEHRU/J GANDHI/M. PAGE 28 H0570 ORD/FREE STRATA NAT/G CHIEF

N62
US CONGRESS JT ATOM ENRGY COMM,PEACEFUL USES OF ATOMIC ENERGY, HEARING. USA+45 USSR TEC/DEV ATTIT RIGID/FLEX...TESTS CHARTS EXHIBIT METH/COMP 20 CONGRESS. PAGE 159 H3177 NUC/PWR ACADEM SCHOOL NAT/COMP

B64
US HOUSE COMM BANKING-CURR,INTERNATIONAL DEVELOPMENT ASSOCIATION ACT AMENDMENT. CHINA/COM USA+45 USSR FINAN FORCES LEGIS DIPLOM CONFER EFFICIENCY...CHARTS GOV/COMP 20 PRESIDENT CONGRESS INTL/DEV. PAGE 160 H3196 BAL/PAY FOR/AID RECORD ECO/TAC

S65
HUGHES T.L.,"SCHOLARS AND FOREIGN POLICY* VARIETIES OF RESEARCH EXPERIENCE." COM/IND DIPLOM ADMIN EXEC ROUTINE...MGT OBS CONGRESS PRESIDENT CAMELOT. PAGE 75 H1491 ACT/RES ACADEM CONTROL NAT/G

S65
POWELL J.D.,"MILITARY ASSISTANCE AND MILITARISM IN LATIN AMERICA." USA+45 INT/ORG NAT/G CONTROL REGION PRODUC WEALTH...CLASSIF STAT NAT/COMP CONGRESS. PAGE 128 H2550 L/A+17C FORCES FOR/AID PWR

B66
BRECHER M.,SUCCESSION IN INDIA. INDIA USA+45 CONSTN AGRI POL/PAR PROVS SECT DELIB/GP FORCES PROB/SOLV ECO/TAC PWR...LING 20 CONGRESS NEHRU/J. PAGE 20 H0408 CHIEF DECISION CHOOSE

B66
FRIED R.C.,COMPARATIVE POLITICAL INSTITUTIONS. USSR EX/STRUC FORCES LEGIS JUDGE CONTROL REPRESENT ALL/IDEOS 20 CONGRESS BUREAUCRCY. PAGE 53 H1062 NAT/G PWR EFFICIENCY GOV/COMP

CONGRESS/P....CONGRESS PARTY (ALL NATIONS)

B65
BRASS P.R.,FACTIONAL POLITICS IN AN INDIAN STATE: THE CONGRESS PARTY IN UTTAR PRADESH. INDIA UK CONSTN CULTURE ECO/UNDEV LOC/G DOMIN COLONIAL CROWD GP/REL ADJUST CENTRAL RIGID/FLEX SOVEREIGN 20 UTTAR/PRAD CONGRESS/P. PAGE 20 H0406 POL/PAR PROVS LEGIS CHOOSE

CONKLING E.C. H3075

CONNECTICT....CONNECTICUT

CONOVER H.F. H0639,H0640,H0641,H0642,H0643,H0644,H0645,H0646 , H0647,H0648,H0649,H0650,H0651,H0652,H0653,H0654

CONQUEST R. H0655

CONRAD/JOS....JOSEPH CONRAD

CONRING E. H0656

CONSCIENCE....SEE SUPEGO

CONSCN/OBJ....CONSCIENTIOUS OBJECTION TO WAR AND KILLING

B17
DE VICTORIA F.,DE INDIS ET DE JURE BELLI (1557) IN F. DE VICTORIA, DE INDIS ET DE JURE BELLI REFLECTIONES. UNIV NAT/G SECT CHIEF PARTIC COERCE PEACE MORAL...POLICY 16 INDIAN/AM CHRISTIAN CONSCN/OBJ. PAGE 39 H0775 WAR INT/LAW OWN

CONSCRIPTN....CONSCRIPTION

CONSEN....CONSENSUS

N
PRESSE UNIVERSITAIRES,ANNEE SOCIOLOGIQUE. EUR+WWI FRANCE MOD/EUR FAM ACT/RES WAR INGP/REL PERS/REL CONSEN DRIVE MORAL...CON/ANAL 19/20. PAGE 128 H2557 BIBLIOG SOC CULTURE SOCIETY

N19
ADMINISTRATIVE STAFF COLLEGE,THE ACCOUNTABILITY OF GOVERNMENT DEPARTMENTS (PAMPHLET) (REV. ED.). UK CONSTN FINAN NAT/G CONSULT ADMIN INGP/REL CONSEN PRIVIL 20 PARLIAMENT. PAGE 3 H0070 PARL/PROC ELITES SANCTION PROB/SOLV

N19
MEZERIK A.G.,APARTHEID IN THE REPUBLIC OF SOUTH AFRICA (PAMPHLET). DIPLOM DOMIN CONTROL COERCE REPRESENT CONSEN ATTIT. PAGE 110 H2194 DISCRIM RACE/REL POL/PAR POLICY

B39
MILLER P.,THE NEW ENGLAND MIND: THE SEVENTEENTH CENTURY. CULTURE DOMIN WRITING INGP/REL CONSEN MAJORITY PERCEPT KNOWL MORAL...CONCPT LING WORSHIP 17 NEW/ENGLND PROTESTANT. PAGE 111 H2214 SECT REGION SOC ATTIT

B47
LOCKE J.,TWO TREATISES OF GOVERNMENT (1690). UK LAW SOCIETY LEGIS LEGIT AGREE REV OWN HEREDITY MORAL CONSERVE...POLICY MAJORIT 17 WILLIAM/3 NATURL/LAW. PAGE 97 H1946 CONCPT ORD/FREE NAT/G CONSEN

B50
HARLEY G.W.,MASKS AS AGENTS OF SOCIAL CONTROL IN NORTHEAST LIBERIA. AFR LIBERIA LAW CULTURE ADJUST CONSEN MORAL...GEOG SOC WORSHIP 20. PAGE 66 H1332 CONTROL ECO/UNDEV SECT CHIEF

C50
ROUSSEAU J.J.,"A DISCOURSE ON POLITICAL ECONOMY" (1755) IN THE SOCIAL CONTRACT AND DISCOURSES." UNIV SOCIETY STRATA STRUCT CONSEN EQUILIB HAPPINESS UTOPIA HEALTH WEALTH...POLICY WELF/ST. PAGE 135 H2699 NAT/G ECO/TAC TAX GEN/LAWS

B52
CALLOT E.,LA SOCIETE ET SON ENVIRONNEMENT: ESSAI SUR LES PRINCIPES DES SCIENCES SOCIALES. GP/REL ADJUST CONSEN ISOLAT HABITAT PERCEPT PERSON ...BIBLIOG SOC/INTEG 20. PAGE 25 H0507 SOCIETY PHIL/SCI CULTURE

B57
POPLAI S.L.,NATIONAL POLITICS AND 1957 ELECTIONS IN INDIA. INDIA BARGAIN PARL/PROC CONSEN NAT/LISM PWR WEALTH 20. PAGE 127 H2543 POL/PAR CHOOSE POLICY NAT/G

S58
PYE L.W.,"THE NON-WESTERN POLITICAL PROCESS" (BMR)" AFR ASIA ISLAM S/ASIA DIPLOM ADMIN LEAD LOBBY ROUTINE CONSEN...DECISION 20. PAGE 128 H2567 CULTURE POL/PAR NAT/G LOC/G

B59
MILLER A.S.,PRIVATE GOVERNMENTS AND THE CONSTITUTION (PAMPHLET). LAW LABOR NAT/G ROLE PWR PLURISM...POLICY DECISION. PAGE 111 H2211 FEDERAL CONSTN VOL/ASSN CONSEN

S59
LEYS C.,"MODELS, THEORIES, AND THE THEORY OF POLITICAL PARTIES" CANADA LIECHTENST UK LOC/G NAT/G PARTIC REPRESENT GP/REL CONSEN EQUILIB MAJORITY ...NEW/IDEA MATH CHARTS 20. PAGE 96 H1919 POL/PAR CHOOSE METH/CNCPT SIMUL

B60
NICHOLLS W.H.,SOUTHERN TRADITION AND REGIONAL PROGRESS. STRATA STRUCT SCHOOL WORKER PARTIC REGION RACE/REL CONSEN ATTIT...SOC METH/CNCPT 19/20 SOUTH/US TVA. PAGE 118 H2349 RIGID/FLEX CONSERVE AGRI CULTURE

B61
HARE T.,A TREATISE ON THE ELECTION OF REPRESENTATIVES, PARLIAMENTARY AND MUNICIPAL. UK CONSTN NAT/G PARL/PROC CHOOSE ATTIT...MAJORIT 18/19 PARLIAMENT. PAGE 66 H1330 LEGIS GOV/REL CONSEN REPRESENT

B63
FAWCETT J.E.S.,THE BRITISH COMMONWEALTH IN INTERNATIONAL LAW. LAW INT/ORG NAT/G VOL/ASSN OP/RES DIPLOM ADJUD CENTRAL CONSEN...NET/THEORY CMN/WLTH TREATY. PAGE 49 H0977 INT/LAW STRUCT COLONIAL

B63
HARTLEY A.,A STATE OF ENGLAND. UK ELITES SOCIETY ACADEM NAT/G SCHOOL INGP/REL CONSEN ORD/FREE NEW/LIB...POLICY 20. PAGE 67 H1349 DIPLOM ATTIT INTELL ECO/DEV

B63
SHANNON R.T.,GLADSTONE AND THE BULGARIAN AGITATION OF 1876. BULGARIA TURKEY UK DIPLOM COERCE REV ATTIT 19 GLADSTON/W DISRAELI/B. PAGE 142 H2841 EDU/PROP NAT/G PWR CONSEN

B64
BURKE F.G.,AFRICA'S QUEST FOR ORDER. AFR CULTURE KIN MUNIC NAT/G DIPLOM COLONIAL REV DISCRIM ORD/FREE CONSEN

NAT/LISM AGE/Y 20. PAGE 24 H0488 RACE/REL LEAD

B64
TINKER H.,BALLOT BOX AND BAYONET - PEOPLE AND GOVERNMENT IN EMERGENT ASIAN COUNTRIES. CEYLON INDIA INDONESIA PHILIPPINE POL/PAR ADMIN COLONIAL LEAD PARL/PROC CHOOSE CONSEN ORD/FREE SOVEREIGN PLURISM...GOV/COMP THIRD/WRLD. PAGE 155 H3104 MYTH S/ASIA NAT/COMP NAT/LISM

B65
BETTISON D.G.,THE PAPUA-GUINEA ELECTIONS 1964. S/ASIA CONSTN POL/PAR EDU/PROP PARTIC SUFF CENTRAL CONSEN...OBS CHARTS BIBLIOG 20. PAGE 16 H0324 NAT/G LEGIS CHOOSE REPRESENT

B65
GEWIRTH A.,POLITICAL PHILOSOPHY. UNIV SOCIETY NAT/G GP/REL INGP/REL CONSEN PWR...IDEA/COMP GEN/LAWS 17/19 HOBBES/T LOCKE/JOHN MARX/KARL MILL/JS ROUSSEAU/J. PAGE 56 H1118 ORD/FREE SOVEREIGN PHIL/SCI

B65
LAMBIRI I.,SOCIAL CHANGE IN A GREEK COUNTRY TOWN. GREECE FAM PROB/SOLV ROUTINE TASK LEISURE INGP/REL CONSEN ORD/FREE...SOC INT QU CHARTS 20. PAGE 90 H1803 INDUS WORKER CULTURE NEIGH

B65
TINGSTEN H.,THE PROBLEM OF DEMOCRACY. ELITES SOCIETY STRATA NAT/G CONSEN TOTALISM WELF/ST. PAGE 155 H3101 IDEA/COMP GOV/COMP POPULISM SOCISM

S65
SPAAK P.H.,"THE SEARCH FOR CONSENSUS: A NEW EFFORT TO BUILD EUROPE." FRANCE GERMANY ECO/DEV NAT/G CONSULT FORCES PLAN EDU/PROP REGION CONSEN ATTIT ...SOC METH/CNCPT OBS TREND EEC NATO WORK 20. PAGE 147 H2941 EUR+WWI INT/ORG

B66
MERILLAT H.C.L.,LEGAL ADVISERS AND INTERNATIONAL ORGANIZATIONS. LAW NAT/G CONSULT OP/RES ADJUD SANCTION TASK CONSEN ORG/CHARTS. PAGE 109 H2178 INT/ORG INT/LAW CREATE OBS

S66
TOUVAL S.,"AFRICA'S FRONTIERS* REACTIONS TO A COLONIAL LEGACY." L/A+17C CONFER ADJUD COLONIAL APPORT CONSEN NAT/LISM RESPECT...RECORD NAT/COMP. PAGE 156 H3120 AFR GEOG SOVEREIGN WAR

B67
HANRIEDER W.F.,WEST GERMAN FOREIGN POLICY 1949-1963: INTERNATIONAL PRESSURE AND DOMESTIC RESPONSE. EUR+WWI GERMANY/W POL/PAR LOBBY CONSEN 20. PAGE 66 H1316 DIPLOM POLICY NAT/G ATTIT

L67
GOOD E.M.,"CAPITAL PUNISHMENT AND ITS ALTERNATIVES IN ANCIENT NEAR EASTERN LAW." SOCIETY SECT INGP/REL CONSEN ATTIT SEX MORAL...CRIMLGY GP/COMP. PAGE 58 H1168 MEDIT-7 LAW JURID CULTURE

S67
GLENN N.D.,"RURAL-URBAN DIFFERENCES IN REPORTED ATTITUDES AND BEHAVIOR" STRATA GP/REL CONSEN HABITAT RIGID/FLEX SAMP. PAGE 57 H1143 CULTURE ATTIT KIN CHARTS

S67
HEASMAN D.J.,"THE GIBRALTAR AFFAIR." SPAIN UK NAT/G BAL/PWR CONSEN NAT/LISM ATTIT...REALPOL 20. PAGE 69 H1378 DIPLOM COLONIAL REGION

S67
WILSON J.Q.,"A GUIDE TO REAGAN COUNTRY* THE POLITICAL CULTURE OF SOUTHERN CALIFORNIA." NEIGH PROVS PARTIC CHOOSE ADJUST CONSEN PERSON CONSERVE CALIFORNIA REAGAN/RON. PAGE 169 H3379 CULTURE ATTIT MORAL

S68
GUZZARDI W.,"THE DECLINE OF THE STERLING CLUB." UK WOR+45 NAT/G PLAN DIPLOM INT/TRADE AGREE CONSEN EQUILIB SOVEREIGN...POLICY NEW/IDEA 20 COMMONWLTH GOLD/STAND. PAGE 63 H1259 FINAN ECO/TAC WEALTH NAT/COMP

CONSENSUS....SEE CONSEN

CONSERVATISM....SEE CONSERVE

CONSERVE....TRADITIONALISM

B03
FAGUET E.,LE LIBERALISME. FRANCE PRESS ADJUD ADMIN DISCRIM CONSERVE SOCISM...TRADIT SOC LING WORSHIP PARLIAMENT. PAGE 48 H0960 ORD/FREE EDU/PROP NAT/G LAW

C05
DUNNING W.A.,"HISTORY OF POLITICAL THEORIES FROM LUTHER TO MONTESQUIEU." LAW NAT/G SECT DIPLOM REV WAR ORD/FREE SOVEREIGN CONSERVE...TRADIT BIBLIOG 16/18. PAGE 43 H0867 PHIL/SCI CONCPT GEN/LAWS

N16
MILTON J.,THE READIE AND EASY WAY TO ESTABLISH A FREE COMMONWEALTH. CONSTN LEGIS PARL/PROC CONSERVE ...MAJORIT 17. PAGE 111 H2219 ORD/FREE NAT/G CHIEF POPULISM

N19
HARTUNG F.,ENLIGHTENED DESPOTISM (PAMPHLET). ORD/FREE SOVEREIGN CONSERVE...PHIL/SCI FREDERICK ENLIGHTNMT. PAGE 67 H1350 NAT/G CHIEF CONCPT PWR

N19
MASSEY V.,CANADIANS AND THEIR COMMONWEALTH: THE ROMANES LECTURE DELIVERED IN THE SHELDONIAN THEATRE JUNE 1, 1961 (PAMPHLET). CANADA UK CULTURE ECO/DEV REPRESENT NAT/LISM PEACE PWR CONSERVE 20 CMN/WLTH. PAGE 104 H2088 ATTIT DIPLOM NAT/G SOVEREIGN

N19
TEMPLE W.,AN ESSAY UPON THE ORIGINAL AND NATURE OF GOVERNMENT (PAMPHLET). CHRIST-17C UK FAM LOC/G LEGIT ORD/FREE CONSERVE 17. PAGE 153 H3060 NAT/G CONCPT PWR SOCIETY

C20
DUNNING W.A.,"A HISTORY OF POLITICAL THINKERS FROM ROUSSEAU TO SPENCER." NAT/G REV NAT/LISM UTIL CONSERVE MARXISM POPULISM...JURID BIBLIOG 18/19. PAGE 43 H0868 IDEA/COMP PHIL/SCI CONCPT GEN/LAWS

B21
BERGSTRASSER L.,GESCHICHTE DER POLITISCHEN PARTEIEN. GERMANY MOD/EUR NAT/G PRESS PWR ...TIME/SEQ 17/20. PAGE 15 H0303 POL/PAR LAISSEZ CONSERVE

B24
BAGEHOT W.,THE ENGLISH CONSTITUTION AND OTHER POLITICAL ESSAYS. UK DELIB/GP BAL/PWR ADMIN CONTROL EXEC ROUTINE CONSERVE...METH PARLIAMENT 19/20. PAGE 10 H0197 NAT/G STRUCT CONCPT

B25
MAURRAS C.,ENQUETE SUR LA MONARCHIE (1909). FRANCE CONTROL REPRESENT DISCRIM HEREDITY PWR CONSERVE 20 BUREAUCRCY. PAGE 105 H2103 TRADIT AUTHORIT NAT/G CHIEF

B26
FORTESCUE J.,THE GOVERNANCE OF ENGLAND (1471-76). UK LAW FINAN SECT LEGIS PROB/SOLV TAX DOMIN ADMIN GP/REL COST ORD/FREE PWR 14/15. PAGE 52 H1042 CONSERVE CONSTN CHIEF NAT/G

B27
GOOCH G.P.,ENGLISH DEMOCRATIC IDEAS IN THE SEVENTEENTH CENTURY (2ND ED.). UK LAW SECT FORCES DIPLOM LEAD PARL/PROC REV ATTIT AUTHORIT...ANARCH CONCPT 17 PARLIAMENT CMN/WLTH REFORMERS. PAGE 58 H1167 IDEA/COMP MAJORIT EX/STRUC CONSERVE

B27
JOHN OF SALISBURY,THE STATESMAN'S BOOK (1159) (TRANS. BY J. DICKINSON). DOMIN GP/REL MORAL ORD/FREE PWR CONSERVE...CATH CONCPT 12. PAGE 81 H1617 NAT/G SECT CHIEF LAW

B28
HOBBES T.,THE ELEMENTS OF LAW, NATURAL AND POLITIC (1650). STRATA NAT/G SECT CHIEF AGREE ATTIT ALL/VALS MORAL ORD/FREE POPULISM...POLICY CONCPT. PAGE 71 H1432 PERSON LAW SOVEREIGN CONSERVE

B32
MARRARO H.R.,AMERICAN OPINION ON THE UNIFICATION OF ITALY. ITALY FORCES DIPLOM SOVEREIGN CATHISM CONSERVE...CONCPT NAT/COMP BIBLIOG 19. PAGE 103 H2056 ORD/FREE NAT/LISM REV CONSTN

S32
BEARD C.A.,"REPRESENTATIVE GOVERNMENT IN EVOLUTION" WOR-45 AGRI TEC/DEV DOMIN EFFICIENCY ORD/FREE CONSERVE...TIME/SEQ GOV/COMP IDEA/COMP GRECO/ROMN. PAGE 12 H0248 REPRESENT POPULISM NAT/G PWR

B33
FERRERO G.,PEACE AND WAR (TRANS. BY BERTHA PRITCHARD). CULTURE FINAN SECT ATTIT SUPEGO MORAL ORD/FREE CONSERVE POPULISM SOCISM POLICY. PAGE 49 H0987 WAR PEACE DIPLOM PROB/SOLV

C33
MURET C.T.,"FRENCH ROYALIST DOCTRINES SINCE THE REVOLUTION." FRANCE CONSTN NAT/G SECT ADMIN LEAD SOVEREIGN...POLICY BIOG IDEA/COMP BIBLIOG 18/20. PAGE 115 H2295 POL/PAR ATTIT INTELL CONSERVE

B34
MARX K.,THE CLASS STRUGGLES IN FRANCE. FRANCE INDUS WORKER CONSERVE...TREND GEN/LAWS 19. PAGE 104 H2077 MARXIST STRATA REV INT/TRADE

B35
AQUINAS T.,ON THE GOVERNANCE OF RULERS (1265-66). UNIV SOCIETY STRATA FAM HABITAT PERSON ALL/VALS PWR SOVEREIGN CONSERVE...POLICY BIBLE. PAGE 8 H0155 CATH NAT/G CHIEF SUPEGO

B35
MARRIOTT J.A.,DICTATORSHIP AND DEMOCRACY. GERMANY GREECE UK CHIEF DIPLOM DOMIN LEGIT PEACE ORD/FREE CONSERVE...TREND ROME HITLER/A. PAGE 103 H2057 TOTALISM POPULISM PLURIST NAT/G

B42
FEFFERO G.,THE PRINCIPLES OF POWER (TRANS. BY T. JAECKEL). MOD/EUR CONSTN NAT/G CHIEF CONTROL REV WAR ORD/FREE CONSERVE FASCISM POPULISM...GEN/LAWS 18/20 EUROPE. PAGE 49 H0980 PWR LEGIT TRADIT ELITES

B43
MC DOWELL R.B.,IRISH PUBLIC OPINION, 1750-1800. ATTIT
IRELAND CONSTN VOL/ASSN WORKER ORD/FREE CATHISM NAT/G
CONSERVE...POLICY IDEA/COMP BIBLIOG 18/ PARLIAMENT. DIPLOM
PAGE 106 H2118 REV

C43
BENTHAM J.,"ON THE LIBERTY OF THE PRESS, AND PUBLIC ORD/FREE
DISCUSSION" IN J. BOWRING, ED., THE WORKS OF JEREMY PRESS
BENTHAM." SPAIN UK LAW ELITES NAT/G LEGIS INSPECT CONFER
LEGIT WRITING CONTROL PRIVIL TOTALISM AUTHORIT CONSERVE
...TRADIT 19 FREE/SPEE. PAGE 15 H0290

B44
BERDYAEV N.,SLAVERY AND FREEDOM. NAT/G REV WAR ORD/FREE
NAT/LISM OWN AUTHORIT SEX CONSERVE SOCISM...TRADIT PERSON
PHIL/SCI CIVIL/LIB. PAGE 15 H0295 ELITES
SOCIETY

B44
FULLER G.H.,TURKEY: A SELECTED LIST OF REFERENCES. BIBLIOG/A
ISLAM TURKEY CULTURE ECO/UNDEV AGRI DIPLOM NAT/LISM ALL/VALS
CONSERVE...GEOG HUM INT/LAW SOC 7/20 MAPS. PAGE 54
H1075

B47
LOCKE J.,TWO TREATISES OF GOVERNMENT (1690). UK LAW CONCPT
SOCIETY LEGIS LEGIT AGREE REV OWN HEREDITY MORAL ORD/FREE
CONSERVE...POLICY MAJORIT 17 WILLIAM/3 NATURL/LAW. NAT/G
PAGE 97 H1946 CONSEN

B49
DE JOUVENEL B.,ON POWER: ITS NATURE AND THE HISTORY PWR
OF ITS GROWTH. SOCIETY CHIEF REV WAR ATTIT AUTHORIT NAT/G
ORD/FREE SOVEREIGN CONSERVE POPULISM CONCPT. DOMIN
PAGE 38 H0757 CONTROL

B49
VIERECK P.,CONSERVATISM REVISITED: THE REVOLT CONSERVE
AGAINST REVOLT 1815-1949. EUR+WWI ELITES NAT/G MARXISM
FORCES PARTIC GOV/REL NAT/LISM...MAJORIT CONCPT REALPOL
GOV/COMP METTRNCH/K. PAGE 163 H3251

B50
WHITE R.J.,THE CONSERVATIVE TRADITION. UK POL/PAR CONSERVE
SUPEGO PWR RESPECT...POLICY ANTHOL 19. PAGE 167 CONCPT
H3350 NAT/G
ORD/FREE

B52
LOPEZ-AMO A.,LA MONARQUIA DE LA REFORMA SOCIAL. MARXISM
MOD/EUR SPAIN CONSTN NAT/G TASK EFFICIENCY CONSERVE REV
...ANARCH TRADIT SOC CONCPT IDEA/COMP 19/20. LEGIT
PAGE 98 H1967 ORD/FREE

C52
HUME D.,"IDEA OF A PERFECT COMMONWEALTH" IN D. CONSTN
HUME, POLITICAL DISCOURSES (1752)" UK NAT/G DOMIN CHIEF
GP/REL CONSERVE...POLICY CONCPT GEN/LAWS 18 SOCIETY
MORE/THOM PLATO. PAGE 75 H1494 GOV/COMP

B53
BROWN D.M.,THE WHITE UMBRELLA: INDIAN POLITICAL CONCPT
THOUGHT FROM MANU TO GANDHI. INDIA LAW NAT/G SECT DOMIN
WRITING NAT/LISM...ANTHOL BIBLIOG 20 HINDU GANDHI/M CONSERVE
MANU. PAGE 22 H0442

B54
CAMPANELLA T.,A DISCOURSE TOUCHING THE SPANISH CONSERVE
MONARCHY... (1640). SPAIN UNIV SEA STRATA FINAN CHIEF
SECT FORCES SUPEGO LOVE ORD/FREE...CONCPT 17. NAT/G
PAGE 26 H0514 DIPLOM

B54
HAMSON C.J.,EXECUTIVE DISCRETION AND JUDICIAL ELITES
CONTROL; AN ASPECT OF THE FRENCH CONSEIL D'ETAT. ADJUD
EUR+WWI FRANCE MOD/EUR UK NAT/G EX/STRUC PARTIC NAT/COMP
CONSERVE...JURID BIBLIOG/A 18/20 SUPREME/CT.
PAGE 65 H1310

B54
JENNINGS I.,THE QUEEN'S GOVERNMENT. UK POL/PAR NAT/G
DELIB/GP ADJUD ADMIN CT/SYS PARL/PROC REPRESENT CONSTN
CONSERVE 13/20 PARLIAMENT. PAGE 80 H1605 LEGIS
CHIEF

S55
DE SMITH S.A.,"CONSTITUTIONAL MONARCHY IN NAT/G
BURGANDA." AFR UGANDA UK STRUCT CHIEF REGION DIPLOM
INGP/REL ADJUST NAT/LISM SOVEREIGN CONSERVE CONSTN
...POLICY 19/20 BURGANDA. PAGE 38 H0769 COLONIAL

C55
SANTAYANA G.,"REASON IN SOCIETY" IN G. SANTAYANA, RATIONAL
THE LIFE OF REASON." INDUS FAM NAT/G WAR GP/REL SOCIETY
HAPPINESS PRODUC LOVE WEALTH CONSERVE POPULISM CULTURE
CONCPT. PAGE 138 H2752 ATTIT

B56
RIESENBERG P.N.,INALIENABILITY OF SOVEREIGNTY IN SOVEREIGN
MEDIEVAL POLITICAL THOUGHT. CHRIST-17C INTELL NAT/G ATTIT
SECT CHIEF LEGIS SANCTION AUTHORIT ORD/FREE
CONSERVE...IDEA/COMP BIBLIOG 12/16. PAGE 131 H2627

B56
WEBER M.,STAATSSOZIOLOGIE. STRUCT LEGIT ADMIN SOC
PARL/PROC SUPEGO CONSERVE JURID. PAGE 166 H3320 NAT/G
POL/PAR
LEAD

S56
MACRAE D. JR.,"ROLL CALL VOTES AND LEADERSHIP." POL/PAR
ACT/RES LEAD CHOOSE DRIVE CONSERVE NEW/LIB...STAT GOV/COMP
STYLE. PAGE 100 H2007 LEGIS

SUPEGO

B58
CRAIG G.A.,FROM BISMARCK TO ADENAUER: ASPECTS OF DIPLOM
GERMAN STATECRAFT. GERMANY INTELL FORCES ECO/TAC LEAD
CONFER COERCE WAR GP/REL ORD/FREE PWR CONSERVE NAT/G
19/20 BISMARCK/O ADENAUER/K. PAGE 35 H0695

B58
ORTEGA Y GASSET J.,MAN AND CRISIS. SECT CREATE PHIL/SCI
PERSON CONSERVE...GEN/LAWS RENAISSAN. PAGE 122 CULTURE
H2430 CONCPT

B58
SCHOEPS H.J.,KONSERVATIVE ERNEUERUNG IDEEN ZUR POL/PAR
DEUTSCHEN POLITIK. GERMANY ELITES SOCIETY ACADEM IDEA/COMP
CHOOSE SOCISM 19/20. PAGE 140 H2796 CONSERVE
NAT/G

B60
BREDVOLD L.I.,THE PHILOSOPHY OF EDMUND BURKE. PHIL/SCI
POL/PAR PARL/PROC REPRESENT CONSERVE...JURID 18 NAT/G
BURKE/EDM. PAGE 20 H0410 CONCPT

B60
NICHOLLS W.H.,SOUTHERN TRADITION AND REGIONAL RIGID/FLEX
PROGRESS. STRATA STRUCT SCHOOL WORKER PARTIC REGION CONSERVE
RACE/REL CONSEN ATTIT...SOC METH/CNCPT 19/20 AGRI
SOUTH/US TVA. PAGE 118 H2349 CULTURE

B60
PICKLES D.,THE FIFTH FRENCH REPUBLIC. ALGERIA CONSTN
FRANCE CHOOSE GOV/REL ATTIT CONSERVE...CHARTS 20 ADJUD
DEGAULLE/C. PAGE 125 H2506 NAT/G
EFFICIENCY

S60
APTER D.E.,"THE ROLE OF TRADITIONALISM IN THE CONSERVE
POLITICAL MODERNIZATION OF GHANA AND UGANDA" (BMR)" ADMIN
AFR GHANA UGANDA CULTURE NAT/G POL/PAR NAT/LISM GOV/COMP
...CON/ANAL 20. PAGE 8 H0152 PROB/SOLV

B61
APTER D.E.,THE POLITICAL KINGDOM IN UGANDA. UGANDA NAT/LISM
CULTURE ECO/UNDEV AGRI KIN SECT TOP/EX REGION ATTIT POL/PAR
HABITAT CONSERVE...GEOG AUD/VIS 20. PAGE 8 H0153 COLONIAL
ECO/TAC

B61
ASHLEY M.P.,GREAT BRITAIN TO 1688: A MODERN DOMIN
HISTORY. UK NAT/G CHIEF LEAD REV WAR...POLICY CONSERVE
BIBLIOG 1/17. PAGE 9 H0174

B61
MONAS S.,THE THIRD SECTION: POLICE AND SOCIETY IN ORD/FREE
RUSSIA UNDER NICHOLAS I. MOD/EUR RUSSIA ELITES COM
STRUCT NAT/G EX/STRUC ADMIN CONTROL PWR CONSERVE FORCES
...DECISION 19 NICHOLAS/I. PAGE 112 H2238 COERCE

B62
BODIN J.,THE SIX BOOKES OF A COMMONWEALE (1576) PWR
(FACSIMILE REPRINT OF 1606 ENGLISH TRANSLATION). CONSERVE
AUTHORIT ORD/FREE SOVEREIGN...TRADIT CONCPT. CHIEF
PAGE 18 H0364 NAT/G

B62
HANAK H.,GREAT BRITAIN AND AUSTRIA-HUNGARY DURING WAR
THE FIRST WORLD WAR: A STUDY IN THE FORMATION OF DIPLOM
PUBLIC OPINION. CZECHOSLVK UK NAT/G GIVE DOMIN ATTIT
EDU/PROP CONSERVE...BIBLIOG 20 AUST/HUNG WWI. PRESS
PAGE 65 H1311

B62
HUNKIN P.,ENSEIGNEMENT ET POLITIQUE EN FRANCE ET EN EDU/PROP
ANGLETERRE. FRANCE UK CONSTN ACADEM SECT CHIEF LEGIS
DELIB/GP PROB/SOLV CONTROL REV ORD/FREE CONSERVE IDEA/COMP
...BIBLIOG 18/20. PAGE 75 H1496 NAT/G

B63
BORKENAU F.,THE SPANISH COCKPIT. SPAIN ELITES REV
STRATA POL/PAR ACT/RES CROWD WAR GP/REL INGP/REL CONSERVE
...SOC NAT/COMP 20. PAGE 19 H0377 SOCISM
FORCES

B63
FRANKEL J.,THE MAKING OF FOREIGN POLICY: AN POLICY
ANALYSIS OF DECISION-MAKING. CHINA/COM EUR+WWI DECISION
USA+45 ELITES INTELL FORCES LEGIS PLAN ATTIT PROB/SOLV
ALL/VALS MORAL CONSERVE...GOV/COMP 20 PRESIDENT UN DIPLOM
TREATY. PAGE 53 H1051

B63
GRIMOND J.,THE LIBERAL CHALLENGE. UK SOCIETY INDUS NAT/G
POL/PAR LEGIS PLAN CAP/ISM DIPLOM EDU/PROP GOV/REL NEW/LIB
CONSERVE 20 PARLIAMENT REFORMERS. PAGE 61 H1227 ECO/DEV
POLICY

B63
MCNEAL R.H.,THE BOLSHEVIK TRADITION: LENIN, STALIN, INTELL
KHRUSHCHEV. USSR NAT/G SUPEGO CONSERVE...IDEA/COMP BIOG
GEN/LAWS 20 LENIN/VI STALIN/J KHRUSH/N. PAGE 107 PERS/COMP
H2145

B63
WEINER M.,POLITICAL CHANGE IN SOUTH ASIA. CEYLON NAT/G
INDIA PAKISTAN S/ASIA CULTURE ELITES ECO/UNDEV CONSTN
EX/STRUC ADMIN CONTROL CHOOSE CONSERVE...GOV/COMP TEC/DEV
ANTHOL 20. PAGE 166 H3328

B64
ANDREN N.,GOVERNMENT AND POLITICS IN THE NORDIC CONSTN
COUNTRIES: DENMARK, FINLAND, ICELAND, NORWAY, NAT/G
SWEDEN. DENMARK FINLAND ICELAND NORWAY SWEDEN CULTURE
POL/PAR CHIEF LEGIS ADMIN REGION REPRESENT ATTIT GOV/COMP
CONSERVE...CHARTS BIBLIOG/A 20. PAGE 7 H0137

B64
LIEVWEN E.,GENERALS VS PRESIDENTS: WEOMILITARISM IN LATIN AMERICA. L/A+17C FORCES DIPLOM FOR/AID LEAD ...NAT/COMP 20 PRESIDENT. PAGE 97 H1929
CIVMIL/REL REV CONSERVE ORD/FREE

B64
RAISON T.,WHY CONSERVATIVE? UK FORCES DIPLOM ECO/TAC GIVE EDU/PROP ORD/FREE WEALTH LAISSEZ ...GOV/COMP 20 TORY/PARTY CONSRV/PAR. PAGE 129 H2583
PLURISM CONSERVE POL/PAR NAT/G

B64
SINAI I.R.,THE CHALLENGE OF MODERNISATION* THE WEST'S IMPACT ON THE NON-WESTERN WORLD. EUR+WWI CULTURE ELITES SECT CONSERVE SOCISM...GP/COMP IDEA/COMP NAT/COMP GEN/LAWS. PAGE 144 H2881
ASIA S/ASIA ECO/UNDEV CREATE

B64
TIERNEY B.,THE CRISIS OF CHURCH AND STATE 1050-1300. DOMIN EDU/PROP CONTROL PWR CONSERVE 11/14. PAGE 155 H3092
SECT NAT/G GP/REL

B64
VON STEIN L.J.,THE HISTORY OF THE SOCIAL MOVEMENT IN FRANCE, 1789-1850 (TRANS. BY K. MENGELBERG). COM FRANCE MOD/EUR NAT/G EX/STRUC INGP/REL ALL/IDEOS CONSERVE MARXISM...SOC BIBLIOG 18/19. PAGE 164 H3278
REV STRATA

B65
BARRY E.E.,NATIONALISATION IN BRITISH POLITICS: THE HISTORICAL BACKGROUND. UK AGRI DIST/IND EXTR/IND LABOR LG/CO ATTIT CONSERVE SOCISM 19/20 LABOR/PAR. PAGE 12 H0231
NAT/G OWN INDUS POL/PAR

B65
BROWNSON O.A.,THE AMERICAN REPUBLIC. NAT/G PROVS WAR GOV/REL PRIVIL ORD/FREE PWR ALL/IDEOS CONSERVE ...CONCPT 19 CIVIL/WAR. PAGE 22 H0452
CONSTN FEDERAL SOVEREIGN

L65
HOUN F.S.,"THE COMMUNIST MONOLITH VERSUS THE CHINESE TRADITION." CULTURE INTELL SOCIETY STRUCT DOMIN GP/REL ORD/FREE CONSERVE PLURISM...GOV/COMP WORSHIP. PAGE 74 H1479
ASIA MARXISM TOTALISM

C65
STERN F.,"THE POLITICS OF CULTURAL DESPAIR." NAT/LISM...IDEA/COMP BIBLIOG 19/20. PAGE 149 H2979
CULTURE PHIL/SCI CONSERVE TOTALISM

B66
KERR M.H.,ISLAMIC REFORM: THE POLITICAL AND LEGAL THEORIES OF MUHAMMAD 'ABDUH AND RASHID RIDA. NAT/G SECT LEAD SOVEREIGN CONSERVE...JURID BIBLIOG WORSHIP 20. PAGE 85 H1698
LAW CONCPT ISLAM

B66
RAEFF M.,ORIGINS OF THE RUSSIAN INTELLIGENTSIA: THE EIGHTEENTH-CENTURY NOBILITY. RUSSIA FAM NAT/G EDU/PROP ADMIN PERS/REL ATTIT...HUM BIOG 18. PAGE 129 H2580
INTELL ELITES STRATA CONSERVE

B66
ROGGER H.,THE EUROPEAN RIGHT. EUR+WWI CONSERVE ...ANTHOL BIBLIOG 20. PAGE 133 H2660
NAT/COMP POL/PAR IDEA/COMP TRADIT

B66
WILLNER A.R.,THE NEOTRADITIONAL ACCOMMODATION TO POLITICAL INDEPENDENCE* THE CASE OF INDONESIA * RESEARCH MONOGRAPH NO. 26. CULTURE ECO/UNDEV CREATE PROB/SOLV FOR/AID LEGIT COLONIAL EFFICIENCY NAT/LISM ALL/VALS SOC. PAGE 168 H3371
INDONESIA CONSERVE ELITES ADMIN

B66
WUEST J.J.,NEW SOURCE BOOK IN MAJOR EUROPEAN GOVERNMENTS. CHRIST-17C EUR+WWI FRANCE GERMANY ITALY MOD/EUR UK USSR LOC/G POL/PAR CHIEF EX/STRUC CHOOSE CONSERVE MARXISM...JURID T 13/20. PAGE 171 H3425
NAT/G CONSTN LEGIS

L66
HUNTINGTON S.P.,"POLITICAL MODERNIZATION* AMERICA VS EUROPE." EUR+WWI MOD/EUR UK USA+45 LAW ECO/UNDEV PWR SOVEREIGN CONSERVE LAISSEZ GOV/COMP. PAGE 75 H1505
STRUCT CREATE OBS

L66
LEMARCHAND R.,"SOCIAL CHANGE AND POLITICAL MODERNISATION IN BURUNDI." AFR BURUNDI STRATA CHIEF EX/STRUC RIGID/FLEX PWR...SOC 20. PAGE 94 H1874
NAT/G STRUCT ELITES CONSERVE

S66
MALENBAUM W.,"GOVERNMENT, ENTREPRENEURSHIP, AND ECONOMIC GROWTH IN POOR LANDS." ELITES ECO/UNDEV INDUS CREATE DRIVE. PAGE 101 H2028
ECO/TAC PLAN CONSERVE NAT/G

B67
ERDMAN H.L.,THE SWATANTRA PARTY AND INDIAN CONSERVATISM. INDIA S/ASIA SOCIETY STRATA LOC/G NAT/G LEAD PARTIC GP/REL ATTIT...CONCPT GP/COMP BIBLIOG 20 SWATANTRA. PAGE 47 H0938
POL/PAR CONSERVE CHOOSE POLICY

B67
HUTCHINS F.G.,THE ILLUSION OF PERMANENCE: BRITISH IMPERIALISM IN INDIA. INDIA UK CULTURE STRUCT NAT/G REV GP/REL RACE/REL ADJUST DISCRIM ATTIT MORAL PWR SOC/INTEG 18/20. PAGE 75 H1509
COLONIAL CONTROL SOVEREIGN CONSERVE

B67
KENNETT L.,THE FRENCH ARMIES IN THE SEVEN YEARS' WAR. FRANCE NAT/G CONTROL LEAD WAR CIVMIL/REL EFFICIENCY ATTIT PWR SKILL CONSERVE 18. PAGE 85 H1690
FORCES CHIEF METH/COMP

B67
SPIRO H.S.,PATTERNS OF AFRICAN DEVLOPMENT: FIVE COMPARISONS. STRUCT ECO/UNDEV NAT/G CONSERVE SOCISM ...PREDICT NAT/COMP 20 CHINJAP. PAGE 148 H2951
AFR CONSTN NAT/LISM TREND

B67
WALTZ K.N.,FOREIGN POLICY AND DEMOCRATIC POLITICS: THE AMERICAN AND BRITISH EXPERIENCE. FRANCE UK USA+45 PARL/PROC GOV/REL CONSERVE...DECISION 20. PAGE 165 H3298
POLICY DIPLOM NAT/G GOV/COMP

B67
WINTER E.H.,CONTEMPORARY CHANGE IN TRADITIONAL SOCIETIES: VOLUME I INTRODUCTION AND AFRICAN TRIBES. NIGERIA AGRI LOC/G NAT/G CREATE DOMIN COLONIAL CONTROL GP/REL PWR SOVEREIGN...SOC OBS 20 TANGANYIKA. PAGE 169 H3389
SOCIETY AFR CONSERVE KIN

S67
KOHN W.S.G.,"THE SOVEREIGNTY OF LIECHTENSTEIN." LIECHTENST SWITZERLND USSR CONSTN DEBATE WAR CONSERVE 18/20 UN. PAGE 88 H1748
SOVEREIGN NAT/G PWR DIPLOM

S67
NATSAGDORJ A.S.,"THE ECONOMIC BASIS OF FEUDALISM IN MONGOLIA." ASIA COM USSR OWN WEALTH CONSERVE...SOC 20 MONGOLIA. PAGE 116 H2324
ECO/TAC AGRI NAT/COMP MARXISM

S67
SAVELYEV N.,"MONOPOLY DRIVE IN INDIA." INDIA INDUS NAT/G INT/TRADE NEUTRAL SANCTION GOV/REL CONSERVE ...MARXIST 20. PAGE 138 H2759
ECO/UNDEV POL/PAR ECO/TAC CONTROL

S67
SOLT L.F.,"PURITANISM, CAPITALISM, DEMOCRACY, AND THE NEW SCIENCE." NAT/G GP/REL CONSERVE...IDEA/COMP GEN/LAWS. PAGE 147 H2931
SECT CAP/ISM RATIONAL POPULISM

S67
WILSON J.Q.,"A GUIDE TO REAGAN COUNTRY* THE POLITICAL CULTURE OF SOUTHERN CALIFORNIA." NEIGH PROVS PARTIC CHOOSE ADJUST CONSEN PERSON CONSERVE CALIFORNIA REAGAN/RON. PAGE 169 H3379
CULTURE ATTIT MORAL

S68
LAPIERRE J.W.,"TRADITION ET MODERNITE A MADAGASCAR." ISLAM MADAGASCAR AGRI FINAN KIN NAT/G CREATE OP/RES GP/REL INGP/REL ATTIT CONSERVE...PSY 20. PAGE 91 H1813
ECO/UNDEV FOR/AID CULTURE TEC/DEV

B76
TAINE H.A.,THE ANCIENT REGIME. FRANCE STRATA FORCES PARTIC EQUILIB WEALTH CONSERVE POPULISM...GOV/COMP SOC/INTEG 18/19. PAGE 152 H3035
NAT/G GOV/REL TAX REV

B82
CUNNINGHAM W.,THE GROWTH OF ENGLISH INDUSTRY AND COMMERCE. FUT UK FINAN NAT/G CAP/ISM...POLICY 20 MERCANTLST CHRISTIAN POPE. PAGE 36 H0721
INDUS INT/TRADE SML/CO CONSERVE

B85
BLISS P.,OF SOVEREIGNTY. NAT/G PROVS GOV/REL PRIVIL ORD/FREE PWR CONSERVE...CONCPT 19. PAGE 18 H0356
CONSTN SOVEREIGN FEDERAL

B85
BLUNTSCHLI J.K.,THE THEORY OF THE STATE. GERMANY CONSTN INGP/REL NAT/LISM PERSON SOVEREIGN CONSERVE ...SOC. PAGE 18 H0362
CONCPT LEGIS NAT/G

B87
ADAMS J.,A DEFENSE OF THE CONSTITUTIONS OF GOVERNMENT OF THE UNITED STATES OF AMERICA. USA-45 STRATA CHIEF EX/STRUC LEGIS CT/SYS CONSERVE POPULISM...CONCPT CON/ANAL GOV/COMP. PAGE 3 H0063
CONSTN BAL/PWR PWR NAT/G

B90
BURKE E.,REFLECTIONS ON THE REVOLUTION IN FRANCE. FRANCE UK NAT/G DOMIN LEGIT PEACE PWR SOVEREIGN CONSERVE...POLICY GEN/LAWS 18. PAGE 24 H0487
REV ORD/FREE CHIEF TRADIT

B99
LECKY W.E.H.,DEMOCRACY AND LIBERTY (2 VOLS.). LAW CONSTN STRATA POL/PAR SECT WORKER DIPLOM ADJUD REPRESENT NAT/LISM CONSERVE. PAGE 93 H1851
LEGIS NAT/G POPULISM ORD/FREE

CONSRV/PAR....CONSERVATIVE PARTY (ALL NATIONS)

B28
FYFE H.,THE BRITISH LIBERAL PARTY. UK SECT ADMIN LEAD CHOOSE GP/REL PWR SOCISM...MAJORIT TIME/SEQ 19/20 LIB/PARTY CONSRV/PAR. PAGE 54 H1084
POL/PAR NAT/G REPRESENT POPULISM

B54
EPSTEIN L.D.,BRITAIN - UNEASY ALLY. KOREA UK USA+45 NAT/G POL/PAR ECO/TAC FOR/AID INT/TRADE WAR LABOR/PAR CONSRV/PAR. PAGE 47 H0934
DIPLOM ATTIT POLICY

NAT/COMP
B61
JENNINGS I.,PARTY POLITICS: THE GROWTH OF PARTIES (VOL. II). UK SOCIETY NAT/G LEGIS ATTIT 18/20 LABOR/PAR LIB/PARTY CONSRV/PAR. PAGE 80 H1606
CHOOSE POL/PAR PWR POLICY

B64
RAISON T.,WHY CONSERVATIVE? UK FORCES DIPLOM ECO/TAC GIVE EDU/PROP ORD/FREE WEALTH LAISSEZ ...GOV/COMP 20 TORY/PARTY CONSRV/PAR. PAGE 129 H2583
PLURISM CONSERVE POL/PAR NAT/G

B65
BULMER-THOMAS I.,THE GROWTH OF THE BRITISH PARTY SYSTEM (VOL. II) 1924-1964. UK ECO/DEV BARGAIN WAR CHOOSE ATTIT ORD/FREE 20 LABOR/PAR CONSRV/PAR. PAGE 23 H0472
CHIEF POL/PAR PARL/PROC NAT/G

B65
GEORGE M.,THE WARPED VISION. EUR+WWI UK NAT/G POL/PAR LEGIS PARL/PROC SANCTION COERCE WAR GOV/REL PEACE RESPECT 20 CONSRV/PAR. PAGE 56 H1113
LEAD ATTIT DIPLOM POLICY

CONSTITUTION....SEE CONSTN

CONSTN....CONSTITUTIONS

N
UNIVERSITY OF FLORIDA LIBRARY,DOORS TO LATIN AMERICA; RECENT BOOKS AND PAMPHLETS. CONSTN CULTURE SOCIETY ECO/UNDEV COLONIAL LEAD GOV/REL NAT/LISM ATTIT...HUM SOC 20. PAGE 159 H3170
BIBLIOG/A L/A+17C DIPLOM NAT/G

N
INDIA: A REFERENCE ANNUAL. INDIA CULTURE COM/IND R+D FORCES PLAN RECEIVE EDU/PROP HEALTH...STAT CHARTS BIBLIOG 20. PAGE 1 H0017
CONSTN LABOR INT/ORG

N
THE STATESMAN'S YEARBOOK; STATISTICAL AND HISTORICAL ANNUAL OF THE STATES OF THE WORLD. WOR+45 WOR-45 COM/IND FINAN INDUS SECT FORCES TEC/DEV EDU/PROP...GEOG BIBLIOG 19/20. PAGE 1 H0023
NAT/COMP GOV/COMP STAT CONSTN

N
NEUE POLITISCHE LITERATUR; BERICHTE UBER DAS INTERNATIONALE SCHRIFTTUM ZUR POLITIK. WOR+45 LAW CONSTN POL/PAR ADMIN LEAD GOV/REL...POLICY IDEA/COMP. PAGE 2 H0027
BIBLIOG/A DIPLOM NAT/G NAT/COMP

N
ASIA FOUNDATION,LIBRARY NOTES. LAW CONSTN CULTURE SOCIETY ECO/UNDEV INT/ORG NAT/G COLONIAL LEAD REGION NAT/LISM ATTIT 20 UN. PAGE 9 H0176
BIBLIOG/A ASIA S/ASIA DIPLOM

N
EUROPA PUBLICATIONS LIMITED,THE EUROPA YEAR BOOK. CONSTN FINAN INDUS POL/PAR DIPLOM TV CT/SYS...STAT BIOG CHARTS WORSHIP 20. PAGE 47 H0949
BIBLIOG NAT/G PRESS INT/ORG

N
INSTITUTE OF HISPANIC STUDIES,HISPANIC AMERICAN REPORT. EUR+WWI SPAIN LAW CONSTN ECO/UNDEV POL/PAR EX/STRUC LEGIS LEAD...HUM SOC 20. PAGE 77 H1538
BIBLIOG/A L/A+17C NAT/G DIPLOM

B00
BENEDETTI V.,STUDIES IN DIPLOMACY. BELGIUM FRANCE GERMANY MOD/EUR CONSTN NAT/G CONSULT TOP/EX DOMIN EDU/PROP COERCE ATTIT...CONCPT INT BIOG TREND 19. PAGE 14 H0276
PWR GEN/LAWS DIPLOM

B01
BRYCE J.,STUDIES IN HISTORY AND JURISPRUDENCE (2 VOLS.). ICELAND SOUTH/AFR UK LAW PROB/SOLV SOVEREIGN...PHIL/SCI NAT/COMP ROME/ANC ROMAN/LAW. PAGE 23 H0455
IDEA/COMP CONSTN JURID

B03
FORTESCUE G.K.,SUBJECT INDEX OF THE MODERN WORKS ADDED TO THE LIBRARY OF THE BRITISH MUSEUM IN THE YEARS 1881-1900 (3 VOLS.). UK LAW CONSTN FINAN NAT/G FORCES INT/TRADE COLONIAL 19. PAGE 52 H1041
BIBLIOG INDEX WRITING

B03
GRIFFIN A.P.C.,LIST OF BOOKS ON THE CABINETS OF ENGLAND AND AMERICA (PAMPHLET). MOD/EUR UK USA-45 CONSTN NAT/G CONSULT EX/STRUC 19/20. PAGE 61 H1216
BIBLIOG/A GOV/COMP ADMIN DELIB/GP

B07
BENTHAM J.,AN INTRODUCTION TO THE PRINCIPLES OF MORALS AND LEGISLATION. UNIV CONSTN CULTURE SOCIETY NAT/G CONSULT LEGIS JUDGE ADJUD CT/SYS...JURID CONCPT NEW/IDEA. PAGE 14 H0287
LAW GEN/LAWS

B08
THE GOVERNMENT OF SOUTH AFRICA (VOL. II). SOUTH/AFR STRATA EXTR/IND EX/STRUC TOP/EX BUDGET ADJUD ADMIN CT/SYS PRODUC...CORREL CENSUS 19 RAILROAD CIVIL/SERV POSTAL/SYS. PAGE 2 H0030
CONSTN FINAN LEGIS NAT/G

B09
LOBINGIER C.S.,THE PEOPLE'S LAW OR POPULAR PARTICIPATION IN LAW-MAKING. FRANCE SWITZERLND UK LOC/G NAT/G PROVS LEGIS SUFF MAJORITY PWR POPULISM ...GOV/COMP BIBLIOG 19. PAGE 97 H1945
CONSTN LAW PARTIC

C09
SCHAPIRO J.S.,"SOCIAL REFORM AND THE REFORMATION." CHRIST-17C GERMANY LAW CONSTN LG/CO NAT/G WORKER PROB/SOLV CT/SYS REV...BIBLIOG 16. PAGE 138 H2770
ORD/FREE SECT ECO/TAC BIOG

B10
MCILWAIN C.H.,THE HIGH COURT OF PARLIAMENT AND ITS SUPREMACY B1910 1878 408. UK EX/STRUC PARL/PROC GOV/REL INGP/REL PRIVIL 12/20 PARLIAMENT ENGLSH/LAW. PAGE 107 H2132
LAW LEGIS CONSTN NAT/G

B10
TEMPERLEY H.W.V.,SENATES AND UPPER CHAMBERS; THEIR USE AND FUNCTION IN THE MODERN STATE... UK WOR-45 CONSTN NAT/G POL/PAR PROVS SECT COLONIAL LEAD CHOOSE REPRESENT PWR...BIBLIOG 19/20 PARLIAMENT SENATE CMN/WLTH HOUSE/LORD. PAGE 153 H3059
PARL/PROC NAT/COMP LEGIS EX/STRUC

B13
BARDOUX J.,L'ANGLETERRE RADICALE; ESSAI DE LA PSYCHOLOGIE SOCIALE (1906-1913). UK CONSTN NAT/G WORKER CREATE BUDGET ECO/TAC ATTIT...POLICY 20 PARLIAMENT LABOR/PAR STRIKE NAVY. PAGE 11 H0215
POL/PAR CHOOSE COLONIAL LEGIS

B14
CRAIG J.,ELEMENTS OF POLITICAL SCIENCE (3 VOLS.). CONSTN AGRI INDUS SCHOOL FORCES TAX CT/SYS SUFF MORAL WEALTH...CONCPT 19 CIVIL/LIB. PAGE 35 H0696
PHIL/SCI NAT/G ORD/FREE

N16
MILTON J.,THE READIE AND EASY WAY TO ESTABLISH A FREE COMMONWEALTH. CONSTN LEGIS PARL/PROC CONSERVE ...MAJORIT 17. PAGE 111 H2219
ORD/FREE NAT/G CHIEF POPULISM

N17
BURKE E.,THOUGHTS ON THE CAUSE OF THE PRESENT DISCONTENTS (PAMPHLET). MOD/EUR UK CONSTN CHIEF LEGIS DOMIN CONTROL EXEC REPRESENT POPULISM ...TRADIT NEW/IDEA METH/COMP 18 BURKE/EDM. PAGE 24 H0484
ORD/FREE REV PARL/PROC NAT/G

B18
EYBERS G.W.,SELECT CONSTITUTIONAL DOCUMENTS ILLUSTRATING SOUTH AFRICAN HISTORY 1795-1910. SOUTH/AFR LOC/G LEGIS CT/SYS...JURID ANTHOL 18/20 NATAL CAPE/HOPE ORANGE/STA. PAGE 48 H0955
CONSTN LAW NAT/G COLONIAL

B18
WILSON W.,THE STATE: ELEMENTS OF HISTORICAL AND PRACTICAL POLITICS. FRANCE GERMANY ITALY UK USSR CONSTN EX/STRUC LEGIS CT/SYS WAR PWR...POLICY GOV/COMP 20. PAGE 169 H3385
NAT/G JURID CONCPT NAT/COMP

B18
YUKIO O.,THE VOICE OF JAPANESE DEMOCRACY, AN ESSAY ON CONSTITUTIONAL LOYALTY (TRANS BY J. E. BECKER). ASIA POL/PAR DELIB/GP EX/STRUC RIGID/FLEX ORD/FREE PWR...POLICY JURID METH/COMP 19/20 CHINJAP. PAGE 172 H3443
CONSTN MAJORIT CHOOSE NAT/G

B19
DUGUIT L.,LAW IN THE MODERN STATE (TRANS. BY FRIDA AND HAROLD LASKI). CONSTN SOCIETY STRUCT MORAL ORD/FREE SOVEREIGN 20. PAGE 43 H0860
GEN/LAWS CONCPT NAT/G LAW

B19
NATHAN M.,THE SOUTH AFRICAN COMMONWEALTH: CONSTITUTION, PROBLEMS, SOCIAL CONDITIONS. SOUTH/AFR UK CULTURE INDUS EX/STRUC LEGIS BUDGET EDU/PROP ADMIN CT/SYS GP/REL RACE/REL...LING 19/20 CMN/WLTH. PAGE 116 H2317
CONSTN NAT/G POL/PAR SOCIETY

N19
ADMINISTRATIVE STAFF COLLEGE,THE ACCOUNTABILITY OF GOVERNMENT DEPARTMENTS (PAMPHLET) (REV. ED.). UK CONSTN FINAN NAT/G CONSULT ADMIN INGP/REL CONSEN PRIVIL 20 PARLIAMENT. PAGE 3 H0070
PARL/PROC ELITES SANCTION PROB/SOLV

N19
CANADA CIVIL SERV COMM,THE ANALYSIS OF ORGANIZATION IN THE GOVERNMENT OF CANADA (PAMPHLET). CANADA CONSTN EX/STRUC LEGIS TOP/EX CREATE PLAN CONTROL GP/REL 20. PAGE 26 H0517
NAT/G MGT ADMIN DELIB/GP

N19
MAO TSE-TUNG,ON SOME IMPORTANT PROBLEMS OF THE PARTY'S PRESENT POLICY. CHINA/COM CONSTN ELITES INTELL AGRI DOMIN EDU/PROP REV REPRESENT GP/REL OWN PEACE ORD/FREE 20 COM/PARTY. PAGE 102 H2044
POLICY NAT/G CHIEF LEGIT

N19
OPERATIONS AND POLICY RESEARCH,PERU ELECTION MEMORANDA (PAMPHLET). L/A+17C PERU POL/PAR LEGIS EXEC APPORT REPRESENT 20. PAGE 121 H2421
CHOOSE CONSTN SUFF NAT/G

N19
PROVISIONS SECTION OAU,ORGANIZATION OF AFRICAN UNITY: BASIC DOCUMENTS AND RESOLUTIONS (PAMPHLET). AFR CULTURE ECO/UNDEV DIPLOM ECO/TAC EDU/PROP COLONIAL ARMS/CONT NUC/PWR RACE/REL DISCRIM NAT/LISM 20 UN OAU. PAGE 128 H2564
CONSTN EX/STRUC SOVEREIGN INT/ORG

N19
ROWE J.W.,THE ARGENTINE ELECTIONS OF 1963 (PAMPHLET). L/A+17C LOC/G NAT/G LEGIS REPRESENT 20 ARGEN. PAGE 135 H2703
CHOOSE CONSTN APPORT POL/PAR

N19
SOUTH AFRICA COMMISSION ON FUT,INTERIM AND FINAL
CONSTN

REPORTS ON FUTURE FORM OF GOVERNMENT IN THE SOUTH-WEST AFRICAN PROTECTORATE (PAMPHLET). SOUTH/AFR NAT/G FORCES CONFER COLONIAL CONTROL 20 AFRICA/SW. PAGE 147 H2936 REPRESENT ADMIN PROB/SOLV N19

WEBB L.C.,CHURCH AND STATE IN ITALY: 1947-1957 (PAMPHLET). GERMANY ITALY CONSTN POL/PAR AGREE CONTROL PARTIC CHOOSE ATTIT ORD/FREE FASCISM MARXISM 20 CHURCH/STA MARITAIN/J SALO. PAGE 166 H3316 SECT CATHISM NAT/G GP/REL B20

BOSANQUET B.,THE PHILOSOPHICAL THEORY OF THE STATE (3RD ED.). SECT LEGIS EDU/PROP ORD/FREE...POLICY SOC GOV/COMP IDEA/COMP NAT/COMP. PAGE 19 H0380 GEN/LAWS CONSTN NAT/G C20

BLACHLY F.F.,"THE GOVERNMENT AND ADMINISTRATION OF GERMANY." GERMANY CONSTN LOC/G PROVS DELIB/GP EX/STRUC FORCES LEGIS TOP/EX CT/SYS...BIBLIOG/A 19/20. PAGE 17 H0348 NAT/G GOV/REL ADMIN PHIL/SCI B21

STUART G.H.,FRENCH FOREIGN POLICY. CONSTN INT/ORG NAT/G POL/PAR EX/STRUC FORCES PLAN ECO/TAC DOMIN EDU/PROP ADJUD COERCE ATTIT DRIVE RIGID/FLEX ALL/VALS...POLICY OBS RECORD BIOG TIME/SEQ TREND. PAGE 150 H3000 MOD/EUR DIPLOM FRANCE B22

KRABBE H.,THE MODERN IDEA OF THE STATE. LAW CHIEF DIPLOM DOMIN ADMIN REPRESENT CENTRAL ORD/FREE ...NEW/IDEA GOV/COMP IDEA/COMP. PAGE 88 H1761 SOVEREIGN CONSTN PHIL/SCI B23

FINER H.,REPRESENTATIVE GOVERNMENT AND A PARLIAMENT OF INDUSTRY. A STUDY OF THE GERMAN FEDERAL ECONOMIC COUNCIL. GERMANY UK CONSTN INDUS PARL/PROC ...NAT/COMP 20. PAGE 50 H1002 DELIB/GP ECO/TAC WAR REV B24

HOLDSWORTH W.S.,A HISTORY OF ENGLISH LAW; THE COMMON LAW AND ITS RIVALS (VOL. IV). UK SEA AGRI CHIEF ADJUD CONTROL CRIME GOV/REL...INT/LAW JURID NAT/COMP 16/17 PARLIAMENT COMMON/LAW CANON/LAW ENGLSH/LAW. PAGE 72 H1449 LAW LEGIS CT/SYS CONSTN B26

FORTESCUE J.,THE GOVERNANCE OF ENGLAND (1471-76). UK LAW FINAN SECT LEGIS PROB/SOLV TAX DOMIN ADMIN GP/REL COST ORD/FREE PWR 14/15. PAGE 52 H1042 CONSERVE CONSTN CHIEF NAT/G B26

MCIVER R.M.,THE MODERN STATE. UNIV LAW AUTHORIT SOVEREIGN IDEA/COMP. PAGE 107 H2136 GEN/LAWS CONSTN NAT/G PWR B26

POLLARD A.F.,THE EVOLUTION OF PARLIAMENT. UK CONSTN POL/PAR EX/STRUC GOV/REL INGP/REL PRIVIL RIGID/FLEX ...TIME/SEQ 11/20 CMN/WLTH PARLIAMENT. PAGE 127 H2536 LEGIS PARL/PROC NAT/G B27

PANIKKAR K.M.,INDIAN STATES AND THE GOVERNMENT OF INDIA. INDIA UK CONSTN CONTROL TASK GP/REL SOVEREIGN WEALTH...TREND BIBLIOG 19. PAGE 123 H2457 GOV/COMP COLONIAL BAL/PWR PROVS B28

MARSILIUS/PADUA,DEFENSOR PACIS (1324). CHRIST-17C CONSTN NAT/G DIPLOM DOMIN LEGIT CONTROL WAR PEACE ORD/FREE SOVEREIGN POPULISM 14 POPE. PAGE 103 H2059 CATH SECT GEN/LAWS C28

WARD P.W.,"SOVEREIGNTY: A STUDY OF A CONTEMPORARY POLITICAL NOTION." CONSTN NAT/G DIPLOM REPRESENT PLURISM...IDEA/COMP BIBLIOG. PAGE 165 H3304 SOVEREIGN CONCPT NAT/LISM B29

CAM H.M.,BIBLIOGRAPHY OF ENGLISH CONSTITUTIONAL HISTORY (PAMPHLET). UK LAW LOC/G NAT/G POL/PAR SECT DELIB/GP ADJUD ORD/FREE 19/20 PARLIAMENT. PAGE 25 H0510 BIBLIOG/A CONSTN ADMIN PARL/PROC B30

BYNKERSHOEK C.,QUAESTIONUM JURIS PUBLICI LIBRI DUO. CHRIST-17C MOD/EUR CONSTN ELITES SOCIETY NAT/G PROVS EX/STRUC FORCES TOP/EX BAL/PWR DIPLOM ATTIT MORAL...TRADIT CONCPT. PAGE 25 H0502 INT/ORG LAW NAT/LISM INT/LAW B30

CANAWAY A.P.,THE FAILURE OF FEDERALISM IN AUSTRALIA. UK PROB/SOLV ADMIN EFFICIENCY ATTIT ...POLICY NAT/COMP 20 AUSTRAL. PAGE 26 H0518 FEDERAL NAT/G CONSTN OP/RES B30

HATTERSLEY A.F.,A SHORT HISTORY OF DEMOCRACY. WOR-45 CONSTN NAT/G SECT DOMIN WAR CHOOSE ORD/FREE PWR...CONCPT GOV/COMP BIBLIOG ATHENS ROME. PAGE 68 H1355 REPRESENT MAJORIT POPULISM B30

WILLOUGHBY W.W.,THE ETHICAL BASIS OF POLITICAL AUTHORITY. NAT/G LEGIS PARL/PROC INGP/REL UTOPIA ORD/FREE 16/20. PAGE 169 H3374 MORAL POLICY CONSTN B31

KIRKPATRICK F.A.,A HISTORY OF THE ARGENTINE REPUBLIC. SPAIN UK CONSTN SOCIETY ECO/UNDEV EX/STRUC DIPLOM FOR/AID LEAD WAR ATTIT...BIOG CHARTS 16/20 ARGEN SAN/MARTIN. PAGE 86 H1724 NAT/G L/A+17C COLONIAL C31

MOGI S.,"THE PROBLEM OF FEDERALISM: A STUDY IN THE HISTORY OF POLITICAL THEORY." CONSTN COLONIAL NAT/LISM SOVEREIGN LAISSEZ PLURISM 18/20. PAGE 112 H2235 FEDERAL CONCPT NAT/G B32

GREAT BRIT COMM MINISTERS PWR,REPORT. UK LAW CONSTN CONSULT LEGIS PARL/PROC SANCTION SOVEREIGN ...DECISION JURID 20 PARLIAMENT. PAGE 60 H1201 EX/STRUC NAT/G PWR CONTROL B32

MARRARO H.R.,AMERICAN OPINION ON THE UNIFICATION OF ITALY. ITALY FORCES DIPLOM SOVEREIGN CATHISM CONSERVE...CONCPT NAT/COMP BIBLIOG 19. PAGE 103 H2056 ORD/FREE NAT/LISM REV CONSTN B32

MCKISACK M.,THE PARLIAMENTARY REPRESENTATION OF THE ENGLISH BOROUGHS DURING THE MIDDLE AGES. UK CONSTN CULTURE ELITES EX/STRUC TAX PAY ADJUD PARL/PROC APPORT FEDERAL...POLICY 13/15 PARLIAMENT. PAGE 107 H2139 NAT/G MUNIC LEGIS CHOOSE C33

MURET C.T.,"FRENCH ROYALIST DOCTRINES SINCE THE REVOLUTION." FRANCE CONSTN NAT/G SECT ADMIN LEAD SOVEREIGN...POLICY BIOG IDEA/COMP BIBLIOG 18/20. PAGE 115 H2295 POL/PAR ATTIT INTELL CONSERVE L34

GOSNELL H.F.,"BRITISH ROYAL COMMISSIONS OF INQUIRY" UK CONSTN LEGIS PRESS ADMIN PARL/PROC...DECISION 20 PARLIAMENT. PAGE 59 H1184 DELIB/GP INSPECT POLICY NAT/G B35

DE TOCQUEVILLE A.,DEMOCRACY IN AMERICA (4 VOLS.) (TRANS. BY HENRY REEVE). CONSTN STRUCT LOC/G NAT/G POL/PAR PROVS ETIQUET CT/SYS MAJORITY ATTIT 18/19. PAGE 39 H0772 POPULISM MAJORIT ORD/FREE SOCIETY B35

RAM J.,THE SCIENCE OF LEGAL JUDGMENT: A TREATISE... UK CONSTN NAT/G LEGIS CREATE PROB/SOLV AGREE CT/SYS ...INT/LAW CONCPT 19 ENGLSH/LAW CANON/LAW CIVIL/LAW CTS/WESTM. PAGE 129 H2584 LAW JURID EX/STRUC ADJUD B36

CLOKIE H.M.,THE ORIGIN AND NATURE OF CONSTITUTIONAL GOVERNMENT. UK NAT/G POL/PAR CONSULT LEGIS ...GOV/COMP 14/20 CABINET PARLIAMENT. PAGE 30 H0606 CONCPT CONSTN PARL/PROC B36

MARITAIN J.,FREEDOM IN THE MODERN WORLD. CONSTN NAT/G SECT CAP/ISM MARXISM SOCISM...GOV/COMP IDEA/COMP 19/20 HUMANISM CHRISTIAN. PAGE 102 H2049 GEN/LAWS POLICY ORD/FREE B36

RAPPARD W.E.,THE GOVERNMENT OF SWITZERLAND. SWITZERLND INT/ORG POL/PAR EX/STRUC DIPLOM NEUTRAL PARL/PROC REGION WAR HABITAT SOVEREIGN...NAT/COMP SOC/INTEG 20 LEAGUE/NAT WWI. PAGE 130 H2594 CONSTN NAT/G CULTURE FEDERAL B36

SMITH T.V.,THE PROMISE OF AMERICAN POLITICS. USA-45 WOR-45 LAW CONSTN STRATA PARTIC FASCISM LAISSEZ MARXISM...MAJORIT METH/COMP 18/20 JEFFERSN/T LOCKE/JOHN BENTHAM/J. PAGE 146 H2920 CONCPT ORD/FREE IDEA/COMP NAT/COMP B37

CARLYLE T.,THE FRENCH REVOLUTION (2 VOLS.). FRANCE CONSTN NAT/G FORCES COERCE MURDER PEACE MORAL POPULISM...TIME/SEQ IDEA/COMP GEN/LAWS 18. PAGE 26 H0532 REV CHIEF TRADIT B37

HAMILTON W.H.,THE POWER TO GOVERN. ECO/DEV FINAN INDUS ECO/TAC INT/TRADE TARIFFS TAX CONTROL CT/SYS WAR COST PWR 18/20 SUPREME/CT. PAGE 65 H1303 LING CONSTN NAT/G POLICY B37

UNION OF SOUTH AFRICA,REPORT CONCERNING ADMINISTRATION OF SOUTH WEST AFRICA (6 VOLS.). SOUTH/AFR INDUS PUB/INST FORCES LEGIS BUDGET DIPLOM EDU/PROP ADJUD CT/SYS...GEOG CHARTS 20 AFRICA/SW LEAGUE/NAT. PAGE 158 H3166 NAT/G ADMIN COLONIAL CONSTN B38

FIELD G.L.,THE SYNDICAL AND CORPORATIVE INSTITUTIONS OF ITALIAN FASCISM. ITALY CONSTN STRATA LABOR EX/STRUC TOP/EX ADJUD ADMIN LEAD TOTALISM AUTHORIT...MGT 20 MUSSOLIN/B. PAGE 50 H0991 FASCISM INDUS NAT/G WORKER B38

HARPER S.N.,THE GOVERNMENT OF THE SOVIET UNION. COM USSR LAW CONSTN ECO/DEV PLAN TEC/DEV DIPLOM INT/TRADE ADMIN REV NAT/LISM...POLICY 20. PAGE 67 H1337 MARXISM NAT/G LEAD POL/PAR B38

HEIMANN E.,COMMUNISM, FASCISM, OR DEMOCRACY? WOR-45 CONSTN SOCIETY STRATA AGRI CAP/ISM MORAL ORD/FREE ...MAJORIT METH/COMP NAT/COMP 19/20. PAGE 69 H1384 SOCISM MARXISM FASCISM PLURISM B38

HOLDSWORTH W.S.,A HISTORY OF ENGLISH LAW; THE CENTURIES OF SETTLEMENT AND REFORM (VOL. X). INDIA UK CONSTN NAT/G CHIEF LEGIS ADMIN COLONIAL CT/SYS LAW LOC/G EX/STRUC

CHOOSE ORD/FREE PWR...JURID 18 PARLIAMENT COMMONWLTH COMMON/LAW. PAGE 72 H1451 ADJUD
B38

HOLDSWORTH W.S.,A HISTORY OF ENGLISH LAW; THE CENTURIES OF SETTLEMENT AND REFORM (VOL. XI). UK CONSTN NAT/G EX/STRUC DIPLOM ADJUD CT/SYS LEAD CRIME ATTIT...INT/LAW JURID 18 CMN/WLTH PARLIAMENT ENGLSH/LAW. PAGE 73 H1452 LAW COLONIAL LEGIS PARL/PROC
B38

POUND R.,THE FORMATIVE ERA OF AMERICAN LAW. CULTURE NAT/G PROVS LEGIS ADJUD CT/SYS PERSON SOVEREIGN ...POLICY IDEA/COMP GEN/LAWS 18/19. PAGE 127 H2548 CONSTN LAW CREATE JURID
B38

REICH N.,LABOR RELATIONS IN REPUBLICAN GERMANY. GERMANY CONSTN ECO/DEV INDUS NAT/G ADMIN CONTROL GP/REL FASCISM POPULISM 20 WEIMAR/REP. PAGE 130 H2609 WORKER MGT LABOR BARGAIN
B39

ANDERSON W.,LOCAL GOVERNMENT IN EUROPE. FRANCE GERMANY ITALY UK USSR MUNIC PROVS ADMIN GOV/REL CENTRAL SOVEREIGN 20. PAGE 7 H0136 GOV/COMP NAT/COMP LOC/G CONSTN
B39

DEWEY J.,FREEDOM AND CULTURE. FUT CONSTN CULTURE INTELL NAT/G CONSULT PLAN CHOOSE ATTIT...CONCPT GEN/METH 20. PAGE 40 H0810 SOCIETY CREATE
B39

JENNINGS W.I.,PARLIAMENT. UK POL/PAR OP/RES BUDGET LEAD CHOOSE GP/REL...MGT 20 PARLIAMENT HOUSE/LORD HOUSE/CMNS. PAGE 80 H1609 PARL/PROC LEGIS CONSTN NAT/G
B39

MARITAIN J.,SCHOLASTICISM AND POLITICS. CONSTN SOCIETY NAT/G INGP/REL PERSON CATHISM POPULISM 19/20 FREUD/S SCHOLASTIC CHURCH/STA CHRISTIAN. PAGE 103 H2050 SECT GEN/LAWS ORD/FREE
B39

MCILWAIN C.H.,CONSTITUTIONALISM AND THE CHANGING WORLD. UK USA-45 LEGIS PRIVIL AUTHORIT SOVEREIGN ...GOV/COMP 15/20 MAGNA/CART HOUSE/CMNS. PAGE 107 H2133 CONSTN POLICY JURID
B39

SIEYES E.J.,LES DISCOURS DE SIEYES DANS LES DEBATS CONSTITUTIONNELS DE L'AN III (2 ET 18 THERMIDOR). FRANCE LAW NAT/G PROB/SOLV BAL/PWR GOV/REL 18 JURY. PAGE 144 H2871 CONSTN ADJUD LEGIS EX/STRUC
C39

BURKE E.,"ON THE REFORM OF THE REPRESENTATION IN THE HOUSE OF COMMONS" (1782) IN COLLECTED WORKS (VOL. 5)" UK ELITES STRATA NAT/G REPRESENT ORD/FREE PWR POPULISM...POLICY NEW/IDEA GEN/LAWS 18 BURKE/EDM. PAGE 24 H0486 TRADIT CONSTN PARL/PROC LEGIS
C39

REISCHAUER R.,"JAPAN'S GOVERNMENT--POLITICS." CONSTN STRATA POL/PAR FORCES LEGIS DIPLOM ADMIN EXEC CENTRAL...POLICY BIBLIOG 20 CHINJAP. PAGE 131 H2610 NAT/G S/ASIA CONCPT ROUTINE
B40

BROGAN D.W.,THE DEVELOPMENT OF MODERN FRANCE (1870-1939). FRANCE GERMANY UK USSR CONSTN CHIEF LEGIS DIPLOM AGREE COLONIAL WAR NAT/LISM PEACE SOCISM 19/20 TREATY. PAGE 21 H0428 MOD/EUR NAT/G
B40

HOBBES T.,BEHEMOTH (1668). UK CONSTN SECT DOMIN LEGIT UTIL ORD/FREE CATHISM...POLICY CONCPT GEN/LAWS 17 CHARLES/I CROMWELL/O PROTESTANT. PAGE 71 H1433 REV NAT/G CHIEF
B40

HUNTER R.,REVOLUTION: WHY, HOW, WHEN? NAT/G ECO/TAC EDU/PROP COERCE ORD/FREE FASCISM POPULISM SOCISM 18/20 HITLER/A LENIN/VI. PAGE 75 H1502 REV METH/COMP LEAD CONSTN
B40

MCILWAIN C.H.,CONSTITUTIONALISM, ANCIENT AND MODERN. CHRIST-17C MOD/EUR NAT/G CHIEF PROB/SOLV INSPECT AUTHORIT ORD/FREE PWR...TIME/SEQ ROMAN/REP. PAGE 107 H2134 CONSTN GEN/LAWS LAW
B41

GREEN T.H.,PRINCIPLES OF PUBLIC ADMINISTRATION. UNIV CONSTN VOL/ASSN INGP/REL MORAL ORD/FREE ...GOV/COMP IDEA/COMP GEN/LAWS 20. PAGE 60 H1208 POLICY LAISSEZ MAJORIT
B41

HITLER A.,MEIN KAMPF (UNABR. ENG. VERSION) (1925). GERMANY CONSTN TEC/DEV RACE/REL NAT/LISM TOTALISM SOVEREIGN...BIOG 20 HITLER/A TREATY. PAGE 71 H1429 EDU/PROP WAR PLAN FASCISM
B42

CRAIG A.,ABOVE ALL LIBERTIES. FRANCE UK USA-45 LAW CONSTN CULTURE INTELL NAT/G SECT JUDGE...IDEA/COMP BIBLIOG 18/20. PAGE 35 H0692 ORD/FREE MORAL WRITING EDU/PROP
B42

FEFFERO G.,THE PRINCIPLES OF POWER (TRANS. BY T. JAECKEL). MOD/EUR CONSTN NAT/G CHIEF CONTROL REV WAR ORD/FREE CONSERVE FASCISM POPULISM...GEN/LAWS 18/20 EUROPE. PAGE 49 H0980 PWR LEGIT TRADIT ELITES
B42

FORTESCU J.,IN PRAISE OF ENGLISH LAW (1464) (TRANS. BY S.B. CHRIMES). UK ELITES CHIEF FORCES CT/SYS COERCE CRIME GOV/REL ILLEGIT...JURID GOV/COMP GEN/LAWS 15. PAGE 52 H1040 LAW CONSTN LEGIS ORD/FREE
B42

LA BOETIE E.,ANTI-DICTATOR (1548) (TRANS. BY H. KUNZ). CONSTN NAT/G CHIEF DOMIN LEGIT CONTROL POPULISM. PAGE 90 H1790 PWR ORD/FREE TOTALISM GEN/LAWS
B42

NEUBURGER O.,OFFICIAL PUBLICATIONS OF PRESENT-DAY GERMANY: GOVERNMENT, CORPORATE ORGANIZATIONS, AND NATIONAL SOCIALIST PARTY. GERMANY CONSTN COM/IND POL/PAR EDU/PROP PRESS 20 NAZI. PAGE 117 H2332 BIBLIOG/A FASCISM NAT/G ADMIN
B42

ROBBINS J.J.,THE GOVERNMENT OF LABOR RELATIONS IN SWEDEN. SWEDEN LAW CONSTN ADJUD CT/SYS GP/REL ...JURID 20. PAGE 132 H2638 NAT/G BARGAIN LABOR INDUS
B43

MARITAIN J.,THE RIGHTS OF MAN AND NATURAL LAW. CONSTN NAT/G DOMIN LEGIT INGP/REL TOTALISM MORAL POPULISM WORSHIP 19/20 CIVIL/LIB CHURCH/STA NATURL/LAW. PAGE 103 H2051 PLURIST ORD/FREE GEN/LAWS
B43

MC DOWELL R.B.,IRISH PUBLIC OPINION, 1750-1800. IRELAND CONSTN VOL/ASSN WORKER ORD/FREE CATHISM CONSERVE...POLICY IDEA/COMP BIBLIOG 18/ PARLIAMENT. PAGE 106 H2118 ATTIT NAT/G DIPLOM REV
B43

US LIBRARY OF CONGRESS,BRITISH MALAYA AND BRITISH NORTH BORNEO. BORNEO MALAYSIA CONSTN AGRI COM/IND INDUS EDU/PROP 19/20. PAGE 160 H3203 BIBLIOG CULTURE
B44

WOLFE D.M.,LEVELLER MANIFESTOES OF THE PURITAN REVOLUTION. UK CONSTN NAT/G SECT...CONCPT ANTHOL 17 LEVELLERS DECLAR/IND PURITAN LOCKE/JOHN. PAGE 170 H3400 POL/PAR REV ORD/FREE ATTIT
N45

INDIA QUARTERLY, A JOURNAL OF INTERNATIONAL AFFAIRS. INDIA LAW CONSTN ECO/UNDEV INT/ORG POL/PAR COLONIAL LEAD PARL/PROC WAR ATTIT...SOC 20 CMN/WLTH. PAGE 2 H0033 BIBLIOG/A S/ASIA DIPLOM NAT/G
B45

CONOVER H.F.,THE GOVERNMENTS OF THE MAJOR FOREIGN POWERS: A BIBLIOGRAPHY. FRANCE GERMANY ITALY UK USSR CONSTN LOC/G POL/PAR EX/STRUC FORCES ADMIN CT/SYS CIVMIL/REL TOTALISM...POLICY 19/20. PAGE 32 H0645 BIBLIOG NAT/G DIPLOM
B46

FEIBLEMAN J.,THE THEORY OF HUMAN CULTURE. UNIV CONSTN SOCIETY...CONCPT CLASSIF TIME/SEQ. PAGE 49 H0981 GEN/LAWS CULTURE SOC PHIL/SCI
B46

HUTTON J.,THE CONSTITUTION OF THE UNION OF SOUTH AFRICA: BIBLIOGRAPHY (PAMPHLET). SOUTH/AFR MUNIC DIPLOM RACE/REL 20. PAGE 75 H1510 BIBLIOG CONSTN NAT/G LOC/G
B47

BEHAR D.,BIBLIOGRAFIA HISPANOAMERICANA. LIBROS ANTIGUOS Y MODERNOS REFERENTES A AMERICA Y ESPANA. PORTUGAL SPAIN CONSTN NAT/G SECT CREATE REV WAR GOV/REL...ART/METH GEOG PHIL/SCI LING 20 ARGEN. PAGE 13 H0260 BIBLIOG L/A+17C CULTURE
B47

BOWLE J.,WESTERN POLITICAL THOUGHT: AN HISTORICAL INTRODUCTION FROM THE ORIGINS TO ROUSSEAU. CONSTN NAT/G SECT CREATE RATIONAL ORD/FREE...SOC BIBLIOG/A. PAGE 19 H0391 ATTIT IDEA/COMP PHIL/SCI
B47

DE NOIA J.,GUIDE TO OFFICIAL PUBLICATIONS OF OTHER AMERICAN REPUBLICS: ECUADOR (VOL. IX). ECUADOR LAW FINAN LEGIS BUDGET CT/SYS 19/20. PAGE 38 H0763 BIBLIOG/A CONSTN NAT/G EDU/PROP
B47

DE NOIA J.,GUIDE TO OFFICIAL PUBLICATIONS OF THE OTHER AMERICAN REPUBLICS: EL SALVADOR. EL/SALVADR LAW LEGIS EDU/PROP CT/SYS 20. PAGE 38 H0764 BIBLIOG/A CONSTN NAT/G ADMIN
B47

DE NOIA J.,GUIDE TO OFFICIAL PUBLICATIONS OF THE OTHER AMERICAN REPUBLICS: NICARAGUA (VOL. XIV). NICARAGUA LAW LEGIS ADMIN CT/SYS...JURID 19/20. PAGE 38 H0765 BIBLIOG/A EDU/PROP NAT/G CONSTN
B47

DE NOIA J.,GUIDE TO OFFICIAL PUBLICATIONS OF THE OTHER AMERICAN REPUBLICS: PANAMA (VOL. XV). PANAMA LAW LEGIS EDU/PROP CT/SYS 20. PAGE 38 H0766 BIBLIOG/A CONSTN ADMIN NAT/G
B47

MARX F.M.,THE PRESIDENT AND HIS STAFF SERVICES PUBLIC ADMINISTRATION SERVICES NUMBER 98 (PAMPHLET). FINAN ADMIN CT/SYS REPRESENT PWR 20 CONSTN CHIEF NAT/G

PRESIDENT. PAGE 104 H2075 — EX/STRUC

B47
MCILWAIN C.H.,CONSTITUTIONALISM: ANCIENT AND MODERN. USA+45 ROMAN/EMP LAW CHIEF LEGIS CT/SYS GP/REL ORD/FREE SOVEREIGN...POLICY TIME/SEQ ROMAN/REP EUROPE. PAGE 107 H2135
CONSTN NAT/G PARL/PROC GOV/COMP

B47
NEUBURGER O.,GUIDE TO OFFICIAL PUBLICATIONS OF OTHER AMERICAN REPUBLICS: HONDURAS (VOL. XIII). HONDURAS LAW LEGIS ADMIN CT/SYS...JURID 19/20. PAGE 117 H2333
BIBLIOG/A NAT/G EDU/PROP CONSTN

B47
NEUBURGER O.,GUIDE TO OFFICIAL PUBLICATIONS OF THE OTHER AMERICAN REPUBLICS: HAITI (VOL. XII). HAITI LAW FINAN LEGIS PRESS...JURID 20. PAGE 117 H2334
BIBLIOG/A CONSTN NAT/G EDU/PROP

B48
DE NOIA J.,GUIDE TO OFFICIAL PUBLICATIONS OF OTHER AMERICAN REPUBLICS: PERU (VOL. XVII). PERU LAW LEGIS ADMIN CT/SYS...JURID 19/20. PAGE 38 H0767
BIBLIOG/A CONSTN NAT/G EDU/PROP

B48
NEUBURGER O.,GUIDE TO OFFICIAL PUBLICATIONS OF THE OTHER AMERICAN REPUBLICS: VENEZUELA (VOL. XIX). VENEZUELA FINAN LEGIS PLAN BUDGET DIPLOM CT/SYS PARL/PROC 19/20. PAGE 117 H2335
BIBLIOG/A NAT/G CONSTN LAW

B48
ROSSITER C.L.,CONSTITUTIONAL DICTATORSHIP; CRISIS GOVERNMENT IN THE MODERN DEMOCRACIES. FRANCE GERMANY UK USA-45 WOR-45 EX/STRUC BAL/PWR CONTROL COERCE WAR CENTRAL ORD/FREE...DECISION 19/20. PAGE 134 H2688
NAT/G AUTHORIT CONSTN TOTALISM

B48
TOWSTER J.,POLITICAL POWER IN THE USSR: 1917-1947. USSR CONSTN CULTURE ELITES CREATE PLAN COERCE CENTRAL ATTIT RIGID/FLEX ORD/FREE...BIBLIOG SOC/INTEG 20 LENIN/VI STALIN/J. PAGE 156 H3122
EX/STRUC NAT/G MARXISM PWR

B48
WOLFE B.D.,THREE WHO MADE A REVOLUTION. USSR CONSTN NAT/G CAP/ISM EDU/PROP CONTROL WAR GP/REL INGP/REL PERS/REL ROLE 20 STALIN/J LENIN/VI TROTSKY/L BOLSHEVISM. PAGE 170 H3398
BIOG REV LEAD MARXISM

B48
WRIGHT G.,THE RESHAPING OF FRENCH DEMOCRACY. FRANCE NAT/G POL/PAR SECT LEAD CHOOSE GP/REL INGP/REL MARXISM SOCISM...CHARTS BIBLIOG 20 DEGAULLE/C. PAGE 171 H3418
CONSTN POPULISM CREATE LEGIS

B49
HEADLAM-MORLEY,BIBLIOGRAPHY IN POLITICS FOR THE HONOUR SCHOOL OF PHILOSOPHY, POLITICS AND ECONOMICS (PAMPHLET). UK CONSTN LABOR MUNIC DIPLOM ADMIN 19/20. PAGE 69 H1375
BIBLIOG NAT/G PHIL/SCI GOV/REL

B49
WORMUTH F.D.,THE ORIGINS OF MODERN CONSTITUTIONALISM. GREECE UK LEGIS CREATE TEC/DEV BAL/PWR DOMIN ADJUD REV WAR PWR...JURID ROMAN/REP CROMWELL/O. PAGE 170 H3412
NAT/G CONSTN LAW

L49
BRECHT A.,"THE NEW GERMAN CONSTITUTION." GERMANY/W NAT/G CHIEF EX/STRUC LEGIS PROB/SOLV ADMIN REPRESENT TOTALISM ORD/FREE PLURISM...MAJORIT CHARTS 20. PAGE 20 H0409
CONSTN DIPLOM SOVEREIGN FEDERAL

L49
LOEWENSTEIN K.,"THE PRESIDENCY OUTSIDE THE UNITED STATES: A STUDY IN COMPARATIVE POLITICAL INSTITUTIONS." WOR-45 LEGIS GP/REL...POLICY 18/20. PAGE 98 H1953
CHIEF CONSTN GOV/COMP NAT/G

B50
HALLOWELL J.H.,MAIN CURRENTS IN MODERN POLITICAL THOUGHT. CONSTN SECT LEGIS...MAJORIT CONCPT 17/20 MARX/KARL MILL/JS HOBBES/T LENIN/VI. PAGE 64 H1290
IDEA/COMP POPULISM SOCISM

B50
HOBBES T.,LEVIATHAN. UNIV CONSTN SOCIETY LOC/G NAT/G CONSULT TOP/EX DOMIN DRIVE PERSON PWR ...PHIL/SCI CONCPT SELF/OBS GEN/LAWS TOT/POP. PAGE 72 H1434
LAW ORD/FREE

B50
MACIVER R.M.,GREAT EXPRESSIONS OF HUMAN RIGHTS. LAW CONSTN CULTURE INTELL SOCIETY R+D INT/ORG ATTIT DRIVE...JURID OBS HIST/WRIT GEN/LAWS. PAGE 100 H1999
UNIV CONCPT

B50
WADE E.C.S.,CONSTITUTIONAL LAW; AN OUTLINE OF THE LAW AND PRACTICE OF THE CONSTITUTION. UK LEGIS DOMIN ADMIN GP/REL 16/20 CMN/WLTH PARLIAMENT ENGLSH/LAW. PAGE 164 H3283
CONSTN NAT/G PARL/PROC LAW

B50
WARD R.E.,A GUIDE TO JAPANESE REFERENCE AND RESEARCH MATERIALS IN THE FIELD OF POLITICAL SCIENCE. LAW CONSTN LOC/G PRESS ADMIN...SOC CON/ANAL METH 19/20 CHINJAP. PAGE 165 H3305
BIBLIOG/A ASIA NAT/G

C50
STOKES W.S.,"HONDURAS: AN AREA STUDY IN GOVERNMENT." HONDURAS NAT/G POL/PAR COLONIAL CT/SYS ROUTINE CHOOSE REPRESENT...GEOG RECORD BIBLIOG 19/20. PAGE 149 H2988
CONSTN LAW L/A+17C ADMIN

B51
CHRISTENSEN A.N.,THE EVOLUTION OF LATIN AMERICAN GOVERNMENT: A BOOK OF READINGS. ECO/UNDEV INDUS LOC/G POL/PAR EX/STRUC LEGIS FOR/AID CT/SYS ...SOC/WK 20 SOUTH/AMER. PAGE 30 H0599
NAT/G CONSTN DIPLOM L/A+17C

B51
JENNINGS I.,THE COMMONWEALTH IN ASIA. CEYLON INDIA PAKISTAN CULTURE STRATA NAT/G LEGIS DIPLOM COLONIAL ATTIT...DECISION 20 CMN/WLTH. PAGE 80 H1604
CONSTN INT/ORG POLICY PLAN

B51
JENNINGS S.I.,THE COMMONWEALTH IN ASIA. CEYLON INDIA PAKISTAN S/ASIA UK CONSTN CULTURE SOCIETY STRATA STRUCT NAT/G POL/PAR EDU/PROP LEAD WAR 20 CMN/WLTH. PAGE 80 H1608
NAT/LISM REGION COLONIAL DIPLOM

B51
MEYER E.W.,POLITICAL PARTIES IN WESTERN GERMANY (PAMPHLET). GERMANY/W MUNIC NAT/G GOV/REL ALL/IDEOS 20 UNIFICA BERLIN. PAGE 109 H2190
POL/PAR LOBBY CHOOSE CONSTN

B51
WEBSTER C.,THE FOREIGN POLICY OF PALMERSTON - 1830 TO 1841. MOD/EUR UK LAW CONSTN INTELL SOCIETY STRUCT NAT/G FORCES TOP/EX CREATE BAL/PWR PWR 19. PAGE 166 H3323
ADMIN PERSON DIPLOM

B51
WHEARE K.C.,MODERN CONSTITUTIONS (HOME UNIVERSITY LIBRARY). UNIV LAW NAT/G LEGIS...CONCPT TREND BIBLIOG. PAGE 167 H3336
CONSTN CLASSIF PWR CREATE

C51
HAMMOND M.,"CITY-STATE AND WORLD STATE." CONSTN INTELL LOC/G LEGIT CENTRAL RATIONAL BIBLIOG. PAGE 65 H1308
NAT/G ATTIT REGION MEDIT-7

B52
LOPEZ-AMO A.,LA MONARQUIA DE LA REFORMA SOCIAL. MOD/EUR SPAIN CONSTN NAT/G TASK EFFICIENCY CONSERVE ...ANARCH TRADIT SOC CONCPT IDEA/COMP 19/20. PAGE 98 H1967
MARXISM REV LEGIT ORD/FREE

B52
WALTERS F.P.,A HISTORY OF THE LEAGUE OF NATIONS. EUR+WWI CONSTN NAT/G LEGIS TOP/EX ACT/RES PLAN EDU/PROP LEGIT ROUTINE ATTIT...TREND LEAGUE/NAT 20 CHINJAP. PAGE 165 H3297
INT/ORG TIME/SEQ NAT/LISM

C52
EBENSTEIN W.,"INTRODUCTION TO POLITICAL PHILOSOPHY." COM CONSTN INTELL CONTROL PERSON NEW/LIB SOCISM...PSY GEN/LAWS BIBLIOG/A. PAGE 44 H0883
ALL/IDEOS PHIL/SCI IDEA/COMP NAT/G

C52
HUME D.,"IDEA OF A PERFECT COMMONWEALTH" IN D. HUME, POLITICAL DISCOURSES (1752)" UK NAT/G DOMIN GP/REL CONSERVE...POLICY CONCPT GEN/LAWS 18 MORE/THOM PLATO. PAGE 75 H1494
CONSTN CHIEF SOCIETY GOV/COMP

B53
STOUT H.M.,BRITISH GOVERNMENT. UK FINAN LOC/G POL/PAR DELIB/GP DIPLOM ADMIN COLONIAL CHOOSE ORD/FREE...JURID BIBLIOG 20 COMMONWLTH. PAGE 150 H2990
NAT/G PARL/PROC CONSTN NEW/LIB

C53
BULNER-THOMAS I.,"THE PARTY SYSTEM IN GREAT BRITAIN." UK CONSTN SECT PRESS CONFER GP/REL ATTIT ...POLICY TREND BIBLIOG 19/20 PARLIAMENT. PAGE 23 H0473
NAT/G POL/PAR ADMIN ROUTINE

B54
HAZARD B.H. JR.,KOREAN STUDIES GUIDE. KOREA CONSTN CULTURE AGRI FAM SECT CREATE WAR NAT/LISM HABITAT PWR...CHARTS 14/20. PAGE 68 H1371
BIBLIOG/A ELITES GP/REL

B54
JENNINGS I.,THE QUEEN'S GOVERNMENT. UK POL/PAR DELIB/GP ADJUD ADMIN CT/SYS PARL/PROC REPRESENT CONSERVE 13/20 PARLIAMENT. PAGE 80 H1605
NAT/G CONSTN LEGIS CHIEF

B54
MITCHELL P.,AFRICAN AFTERTHOUGHTS. UGANDA CONSTN NAT/G ADJUD COERCE WAR 20 WWI MAU/MAU. PAGE 112 H2230
BIOG CHIEF COLONIAL DOMIN

S54
DODD S.C.,"THE SCIENTIFIC MEASUREMENT OF FITNESS FOR SELF-GOVERNMENT." FUT CONSTN ECO/UNDEV INT/ORG PLAN PWR...CONCPT QUANT CON/ANAL SOC/EXP UN LEAGUE/NAT 20. PAGE 41 H0830
NAT/G STAT SOVEREIGN

B55
APTER D.E.,THE GOLD COAST IN TRANSITION. FUT CONSTN CULTURE SOCIETY ECO/UNDEV FAM KIN LOC/G NAT/G POL/PAR LEGIS TOP/EX EDU/PROP LEGIT ADMIN ATTIT PERSON PWR...CONCPT STAT INT CENSUS TOT/POP VAL/FREE. PAGE 7 H0149
AFR SOVEREIGN

B55
BAILEY S.K.,RESEARCH FRONTIERS IN POLITICS AND GOVERNMENT. CONSTN LEGIS ADMIN REV CHOOSE...CONCPT IDEA/COMP GAME ANTHOL 20. PAGE 10 H0201
R+D METH NAT/G

B55
FLECHTHEIM O.K.,DIE DEUTSCHEN PARTEIEN SEIT 1945.
POL/PAR

GERMANY/W CONSTN STRUCT FINAN ATTIT 20. PAGE 51 H1022 — NAT/G GP/COMP

B55
HEYDTE A F.,SOZIOLOGIE DER DEUTSCHEN PARTEIEN. GERMANY/W CONSTN ELITES CHOOSE 20. PAGE 70 H1412 — POL/PAR SOC STRUCT NAT/G

B55
INTERNATIONAL COMN JURISTS,JUSTICE ENSLAVED. COM CONSTN LABOR NAT/G CONTROL CHOOSE 20. PAGE 78 H1555 — SOCISM TOTALISM ORD/FREE COERCE

B55
KHADDURI M.,WAR AND PEACE IN THE LAW OF ISLAM. CONSTN CULTURE SOCIETY STRATA NAT/G PROVS SECT FORCES TOP/EX CREATE DOMIN EDU/PROP ADJUD COERCE ATTIT RIGID/FLEX ALL/VALS...CONCPT TIME/SEQ TOT/POP VAL/FREE. PAGE 85 H1702 — ISLAM JURID PEACE WAR

B55
KHADDURI M.,LAW IN THE MIDDLE EAST. LAW CONSTN ACADEM FAM EDU/PROP CT/SYS SANCTION CRIME...INT/LAW GOV/COMP ANTHOL 6/20 MID/EAST. PAGE 85 H1703 — ADJUD JURID ISLAM

B55
SERRANO MOSCOSO E.,A STATEMENT OF THE LAWS OF ECUADOR IN MATTERS AFFECTING BUSINESS (2ND ED.). ECUADOR INDUS LABOR LG/CO NAT/G LEGIS TAX CONTROL MARRIAGE 20. PAGE 141 H2830 — FINAN ECO/UNDEV LAW CONSTN

B55
SMITH G.,A CONSTITUTIONAL AND LEGAL HISTORY OF ENGLAND. UK ELITES NAT/G LEGIS ADJUD OWN HABITAT POPULISM...JURID 20 ENGLSH/LAW. PAGE 145 H2909 — CONSTN PARTIC LAW CT/SYS

B55
WHEARE K.C.,GOVERNMENT BY COMMITTEE; AN ESSAY ON THE BRITISH CONSTITUTION. UK NAT/G LEGIS INSPECT CONFER ADJUD ADMIN CONTROL TASK EFFICIENCY ROLE POPULISM 20. PAGE 167 H3337 — DELIB/GP CONSTN LEAD GP/COMP

B55
WRONG D.H.,AMERICAN AND CANADIAN VIEWPOINTS. CANADA USA+45 CONSTN STRATA FAM SECT WORKER ECO/TAC EDU/PROP ADJUD MARRIAGE...IDEA/COMP 20. PAGE 171 H3424 — DIPLOM ATTIT NAT/COMP CULTURE

S55
DE SMITH S.A.,"CONSTITUTIONAL MONARCHY IN BURGANDA." AFR UGANDA UK STRUCT CHIEF REGION INGP/REL ADJUST NAT/LISM SOVEREIGN CONSERVE ...POLICY 19/20 BURGANDA. PAGE 38 H0769 — NAT/G DIPLOM CONSTN COLONIAL

C55
APTER D.E.,"THE GOLD COAST IN TRANSITION." AFR CONSTN LOC/G LEGIS DIPLOM COLONIAL CONTROL GOV/REL ...CHARTS BIBLIOG 20 CMN/WLTH. PAGE 7 H0150 — ORD/FREE REPRESENT PARL/PROC NAT/G

B56
CARRIL B.,PROBLEMAS DE LA REVOLUCION Y LA DEMOCRACIA. CONSTN FORCES DOMIN CONTROL TOTALISM PWR 20. PAGE 27 H0539 — REV ORD/FREE LEGIT NAT/G

B56
DOUGLAS W.O.,WE THE JUDGES. INDIA USA+45 USA-45 LAW NAT/G SECT LEGIS PRESS CRIME FEDERAL ORD/FREE ...POLICY GOV/COMP 19/20 WARRN/EARL MARSHALL/J SUPREME/CT. PAGE 42 H0841 — ADJUD CT/SYS CONSTN GOV/REL

B56
EMDEN C.S.,THE PEOPLE AND THE CONSTITUTION (2ND ED.). UK LEGIS POPULISM 17/20 PARLIAMENT. PAGE 46 H0916 — CONSTN PARL/PROC NAT/G LAW

B56
JENNINGS W.I.,THE APPROACH TO SELF-GOVERNMENT. CEYLON INDIA PAKISTAN S/ASIA UK SOCIETY POL/PAR DELIB/GP LEGIS ECO/TAC EDU/PROP ADMIN EXEC CHOOSE ATTIT ALL/VALS...JURID CONCPT GEN/METH TOT/POP 20. PAGE 81 H1610 — NAT/G CONSTN COLONIAL

B56
WILSON P.,GOVERNMENT AND POLITICS OF INDIA AND PAKISTAN: 1885-1955; A BIBLIOGRAPHY OF WORKS IN WESTERN LANGUAGES. INDIA PAKISTAN CONSTN LOC/G POL/PAR FORCES DIPLOM ADMIN WAR CHOOSE...BIOG CON/ANAL 19/20. PAGE 169 H3380 — BIBLIOG COLONIAL NAT/G S/ASIA

S56
KHAMA T.,"POLITICAL CHANGE IN AFRICAN SOCIETY." CONSTN SOCIETY LOC/G NAT/G POL/PAR EX/STRUC LEGIS LEGIT ADMIN CHOOSE REPRESENT NAT/LISM MORAL ORD/FREE PWR...CONCPT OBS TREND GEN/METH CMN/WLTH 17/20. PAGE 85 H1706 — AFR ELITES

B57
DONALDSON A.G.,SOME COMPARATIVE ASPECTS OF IRISH LAW. IRELAND NAT/G DIPLOM ADMIN CT/SYS LEAD ATTIT SOVEREIGN...JURID BIBLIOG/A 12/20 CMN/WLTH. PAGE 42 H0835 — CONSTN LAW NAT/COMP INT/LAW

B57
HOUN F.W.,CENTRAL GOVERNMENT OF CHINA, 1912-1928. ASIA CONSTN CHIEF LEGIS CONTROL PWR...BIBLIOG 20. PAGE 74 H1480 — POL/PAR ATTIT NAT/G PLAN

B57
KANTOROWICZ E.,THE KING'S TWO BODIES; A STUDY IN MEDIEVAL POLITICAL THEOLOGY. UK LAW CONSTN NAT/G CT/SYS...ART/METH HUM CONCPT MYTH TIME/SEQ BIBLIOG 4/17 ELIZABTH/I POPE CHURCH/STA. PAGE 83 H1657 — JURID SECT CHIEF SOVEREIGN

B57
LONG H.A.,USURPERS - FOES OF FREE MAN. LAW NAT/G CHIEF LEGIS DOMIN ADJUD REPRESENT GOV/REL ORD/FREE LAISSEZ POPULISM...POLICY 18/20 SUPREME/CT ROOSEVLT/F CONGRESS CON/INTERP. PAGE 98 H1961 — CT/SYS CENTRAL FEDERAL CONSTN

B57
MUELLER-DEHAM A.,HUMAN RELATIONS AND POWER; SOCIO-POLITICAL ANALYSIS AND SYNTHESIS. CONSTN SOCIETY NAT/G POL/PAR PROVS LEGIS POPULISM...SOC NEW/IDEA. PAGE 114 H2280 — GEN/LAWS PERS/REL PWR CONCPT

B57
ROBERTSON H.M.,SOUTH AFRICA, ECONOMIC AND POLITICAL ASPECTS. SOUTH/AFR CONSTN CULTURE POL/PAR LEGIS DIPLOM DOMIN COLONIAL...SOC BIBLIOG 19/20. PAGE 132 H2647 — RACE/REL ECO/UNDEV ECO/TAC DISCRIM

B57
SHEIKH N.A.,SOME ASPECTS OF THE CONSTITUTION AND THE ECONOMICS OF ISLAM. PAKISTAN CULTURE AGRI FINAN LABOR NAT/G SECT INT/TRADE 20 MUSLIM. PAGE 143 H2855 — ISLAM POLICY ECO/TAC CONSTN

S57
HAILEY,"TOMORROW IN AFRICA." CONSTN SOCIETY LOC/G NAT/G DOMIN ADJUD ADMIN GP/REL DISCRIM NAT/LISM ATTIT MORAL ORD/FREE...PSY SOC CONCPT OBS RECORD TREND GEN/LAWS CMN/WLTH 20. PAGE 64 H1277 — AFR PERSON ELITES RACE/REL

C57
MORRIS-JONES W.H.,"PARLIAMENT IN INDIA." INDIA CONSTN LEGIS CONFER COLONIAL CHOOSE PRIVIL ATTIT ...GOV/COMP BIBLIOG 20. PAGE 113 H2264 — PARL/PROC EX/STRUC NAT/G POL/PAR

B58
ARON R.,SOCIOLOGIE DES SOCIETES INDUSTRIELLES: ESQUISSE D'UNE THEORIE DES REGIMES POLITIQUES. FRANCE SOCIETY NAT/G PROB/SOLV ATTIT RIGID/FLEX MARXISM POPULISM...POLICY SOC T 20 MARX/KARL TOCQUEVILL. PAGE 8 H0170 — TOTALISM INDUS CONSTN GOV/COMP

B58
CARTER G.M.,TRANSITION IN AFRICA; STUDIES IN POLITICAL ADAPTATION. AFR CENTRL/AFR GHANA NIGERIA CONSTN LOC/G POL/PAR ADMIN GP/REL FEDERAL...MAJORIT BIBLIOG 20. PAGE 27 H0543 — NAT/COMP PWR CONTROL NAT/G

B58
LOWER A.R.M.,EVOLVING CANADIAN FEDERALISM. CANADA WEST/IND CONSTN PROB/SOLV COLONIAL REGION NAT/LISM ...ANTHOL 20. PAGE 99 H1976 — FEDERAL NAT/G DIPLOM RACE/REL

B58
OGDEN F.D.,THE POLL TAX IN THE SOUTH. USA+45 USA-45 CONSTN ADJUD ADMIN PARTIC CRIME...TIME/SEQ GOV/COMP METH/COMP 18/20 SOUTH/US. PAGE 120 H2407 — TAX CHOOSE RACE/REL DISCRIM

B58
OGILVIE C.,THE KING'S GOVERNMENT AND THE COMMON LAW, 1471-1641. UK STRUCT NAT/G CHIEF LEGIS WORKER BAL/PWR GP/REL AUTHORIT 15/17 COMMON/LAW. PAGE 120 H2408 — CONSTN ELITES DOMIN

B58
SCOTT D.J.R.,RUSSIAN POLITICAL INSTITUTIONS. RUSSIA USSR CONSTN AGRI DELIB/GP PLAN EDU/PROP CONTROL CHOOSE EFFICIENCY ATTIT MARXISM...BIBLIOG/A 13/20. PAGE 141 H2813 — NAT/G POL/PAR ADMIN DECISION

B58
STRONG C.F.,MODERN POLITICAL CONSTITUTIONS. LAW CHIEF DELIB/GP EX/STRUC LEGIS ADJUD CHOOSE FEDERAL POPULISM...CONCPT BIBLIOG 20 UN. PAGE 150 H2998 — CONSTN IDEA/COMP NAT/G

B58
WILMERDING L. JR.,THE ELECTORAL COLLEGE. CONSTN NAT/G POL/PAR DELIB/GP LEGIS PROB/SOLV CONFER EXEC LEAD APPORT REPRESENT. PAGE 169 H3377 — CHOOSE DECISION ACT/RES

S58
ELKIN A.B.,"OEEC-ITS STRUCTURE AND POWERS." EUR+WWI CONSTN INDUS INT/ORG NAT/G VOL/ASSN DELIB/GP ACT/RES PLAN ORD/FREE WEALTH...CHARTS ORG/CHARTS OEEC 20. PAGE 45 H0907 — ECO/DEV EX/STRUC

C58
GOLAY J.F.,"THE FOUNDING OF THE FEDERAL REPUBLIC OF GERMANY." GERMANY/W CONSTN EX/STRUC DIPLOM ADMIN CHOOSE...DECISION BIBLIOG 20. PAGE 58 H1155 — FEDERAL NAT/G PARL/PROC POL/PAR

C58
WILDING N.,"AN ENCYCLOPEDIA OF PARLIAMENT." UK LAW CONSTN CHIEF PROB/SOLV DIPLOM DEBATE WAR INGP/REL PRIVIL...BIBLIOG DICTIONARY 13/20 CMN/WLTH PARLIAMENT. PAGE 168 H3363 — PARL/PROC POL/PAR NAT/G ADMIN

B59
CONOVER H.F.,NIGERIAN OFFICIAL PUBLICATIONS, 1869-1959: A GUIDE. NIGER CONSTN FINAN ACADEM SCHOOL FORCES PRESS ADMIN COLONIAL...HIST/WRIT 19/20. PAGE 33 H0650 — BIBLIOG NAT/G CON/ANAL

B59
JENNINGS W.I.,CABINET GOVERNMENT (3RD ED.). UK — DELIB/GP

POL/PAR CHIEF BUDGET ADMIN CHOOSE GP/REL 20. PAGE 81 H1612
NAT/G CONSTN OP/RES

B59
LEFEVRE R.,THE NATURE OF MAN AND HIS GOVERNMENT. EUR+WWI MOD/EUR CONSTN CULTURE MORAL MARXISM ...POLICY 18/20. PAGE 93 H1859
NAT/G TASK ORD/FREE ATTIT

B59
LEITES N.,ON THE GAME OF POLITICS IN FRANCE. ALGERIA FRANCE CONSTN SECT VOL/ASSN ECO/TAC INT/TRADE PARL/PROC WAR SOCISM 20 DEGAULLE/C EEC. PAGE 94 H1871
POL/PAR NAT/G LEGIS IDEA/COMP

B59
MILLER A.S.,PRIVATE GOVERNMENTS AND THE CONSTITUTION (PAMPHLET). LAW LABOR NAT/G ROLE PWR PLURISM...POLICY DECISION. PAGE 111 H2211
FEDERAL CONSTN VOL/ASSN CONSEN

B59
OVERSTREET G.D.,COMMUNISM IN INDIA. INDIA S/ASIA CONSTN INT/ORG LEAD GP/REL...CHARTS BIBLIOG 20. PAGE 122 H2435
MARXISM NAT/LISM POL/PAR WAR

B59
SENGHOR L.S.,RAPPORT SUR LA DOCTRINE ET LA PROGRAMME DU PART I. FRANCE MALI CONSTN POL/PAR PLAN CHOOSE OWN ORD/FREE MARXISM...SOCIALIST 20 NEGRO. PAGE 141 H2828
ATTIT NAT/G AFR SOCISM

B59
VINACKE H.M.,A HISTORY OF THE FAR EAST IN MODERN TIMES (6TH ED.). KOREA S/ASIA USSR CONSTN CULTURE STRATA ECO/UNDEV NAT/G CHIEF FOR/AID INT/TRADE GP/REL...SOC NAT/COMP 19/20 CHINJAP. PAGE 163 H3255
STRUCT ASIA

S59
JENKS C.W.,"THE CHALLENGE OF UNIVERSALITY." FUT UNIV CONSTN CULTURE CONSULT CREATE PLAN LEGIT ATTIT MORAL ORD/FREE RESPECT...MAJORIT JURID 20. PAGE 80 H1602
INT/ORG LAW PEACE INT/LAW

S59
MECHAM J.L.,"LATIN AMERICAN CONSTITUTIONS: NOMINAL AND REAL" (BMR)" L/A+17C REV...CON/ANAL NAT/COMP 20. PAGE 108 H2156
CONSTN CHOOSE CONCPT NAT/G

C59
KORNHAUSER W.,"THE POLITICS OF MASS SOCIETY." COM CULTURE ELITES INTELL STRATA POL/PAR ATTIT...SOC CHARTS GEN/LAWS BIBLIOG 20. PAGE 88 H1757
CROWD PLURISM CONSTN SOCIETY

B60
JUNZ A.J.,PRESENT TRENDS IN AMERICAN NATIONAL GOVERNMENT. LEGIS DIPLOM ADMIN CT/SYS ORD/FREE ...CONCPT ANTHOL 20 CONGRESS PRESIDENT SUPREME/CT. PAGE 3 H0052
POL/PAR CHOOSE CONSTN NAT/G

B60
AYEARST M.,THE BRITISH WEST INDIES: THE SEARCH FOR SELF-GOVERNMENT. FUT WEST/IND LOC/G POL/PAR EX/STRUC LEGIS CHOOSE FEDERAL...NAT/COMP BIBLIOG 17/20. PAGE 9 H0186
CONSTN COLONIAL REPRESENT NAT/G

B60
BANERJEE D.N.,OUR FUNDAMENTAL RIGHTS: THEIR NATURE AND EXTENT (AS JUDICIALLY DETERMINED). INDIA UK CULTURE STRATA NAT/G WORKER EDU/PROP CONTROL DISCRIM OWN...IDEA/COMP WORSHIP 20 REFORMERS COMMONWLTH. PAGE 10 H0207
CONSTN ORD/FREE LEGIS POLICY

B60
BRZEZINSKI Z.K.,THE SOVIET BLOC-UNITY AND CONFLICT. COM USSR CONSTN DOMIN ADMIN TOTALISM PWR...SOC MYTH RECORD TREND STERTYP GEN/LAWS GEN/METH TOT/POP 20. PAGE 23 H0458
ATTIT EDU/PROP

B60
CASTBERG F.,FREEDOM OF SPEECH IN THE WEST. FRANCE GERMANY USA+45 USA-45 LAW CONSTN CHIEF PRESS DISCRIM...CONCPT 18/20. PAGE 28 H0558
ORD/FREE SANCTION ADJUD NAT/COMP

B60
CONOVER H.F.,OFFICIAL PUBLICATIONS OF FRENCH WEST AFRICA, 1946-1958. DAHOMEY IVORY/CST NIGER SENEGAL UPPER/VOLT CONSTN AGRI PRESS...CON/ANAL 20. PAGE 33 H0651
BIBLIOG COLONIAL NAT/G AFR

B60
EASTON S.C.,THE TWILIGHT OF EUROPEAN COLONIALISM. AFR S/ASIA CONSTN SOCIETY STRUCT ECO/UNDEV INDUS NAT/G FORCES ECO/TAC COLONIAL CT/SYS ATTIT KNOWL ORD/FREE PWR...SOCIALIST TIME/SEQ TREND CON/ANAL 20. PAGE 44 H0882
FINAN ADMIN

B60
HARRISON S.S.,INDIA: THE MOST DANGEROUS DECADES. INDIA CONSTN STRATA POL/PAR SECT PLAN ADMIN CHOOSE GP/REL TOTALISM MARXISM...LING 20 NEHRU/J. PAGE 67 H1347
CULTURE ECO/UNDEV PROB/SOLV REGION

B60
HAYEK F.A.,THE CONSTITUTION OF LIBERTY. UNIV LAW CONSTN WORKER TAX EDU/PROP ADMIN CT/SYS COERCE DISCRIM...IDEA/COMP 20. PAGE 68 H1369
ORD/FREE CHOOSE NAT/G CONCPT

B60
JEMOLO A.C.,CHURCH AND STATE IN ITALY 1850-1950 (TRANS. BY DAVID MOORE). ITALY CONSTN STRATA WAR FASCISM SOCISM...TIME/SEQ 19/20 CHURCH/STA CHRIS/DEM. PAGE 80 H1599
GP/REL NAT/G CATHISM POL/PAR

B60
JHA C.,INDIAN GOVERNMENT AND POLITICS. INDIA SERV/IND POL/PAR PROVS LEGIS CT/SYS CHOOSE GOV/REL FEDERAL 20. PAGE 81 H1616
NAT/G PARL/PROC CONSTN ADJUST

B60
LASKIN B.,CANADIAN CONSTITUTIONAL LAW: TEXT AND NOTES ON DISTRIBUTION OF LEGISLATIVE POWER (2ND ED.). CANADA LOC/G ECO/TAC TAX CONTROL CT/SYS CRIME FEDERAL PWR...JURID 20 PARLIAMENT. PAGE 92 H1832
CONSTN NAT/G LAW LEGIS

B60
MC CLELLAN G.S.,INDIA. CHINA/COM INDIA CONSTN ELITES STRATA AGRI POL/PAR FOR/AID ARMS/CONT REV MARXISM...CENSUS BIBLIOG 20 COLD/WAR GANDHI/M NEHRU/J. PAGE 106 H2117
DIPLOM NAT/G SOCIETY ECO/UNDEV

B60
MCCLOSKY H.,THE SOVIET DICTATORSHIP. FUT CONSTN CULTURE INTELL SOCIETY POL/PAR SECT VOL/ASSN FORCES PLAN TEC/DEV DOMIN EDU/PROP COERCE PWR MARXISM ...POLICY CONCPT MYTH STERTYP 20. PAGE 106 H2127
COM NAT/G TOTALISM USSR

B60
PICKLES D.,THE FIFTH FRENCH REPUBLIC. ALGERIA FRANCE CHOOSE GOV/REL ATTIT CONSERVE...CHARTS 20 DEGAULLE/C. PAGE 125 H2506
CONSTN ADJUD NAT/G EFFICIENCY

B60
SMITH M.G.,GOVERNMENT IN ZAZZAU 1800-1950. NIGERIA UK CULTURE SOCIETY LOC/G ADMIN COLONIAL ...METH/CNCPT NEW/IDEA METH 19/20. PAGE 146 H2914
REGION CONSTN KIN ECO/UNDEV

B60
SOUTH AFRICAN CONGRESS OF DEM,FACE THE FUTURE. SOUTH/AFR ELITES LEGIS ADMIN REGION COERCE PEACE ATTIT 20. PAGE 147 H2938
RACE/REL DISCRIM CONSTN NAT/G

S60
PERLMANN H.,"UPHEAVAL IN TURKEY." EUR+WWI ISLAM NAT/G FORCES TOP/EX LEGIT COERCE CHOOSE DRIVE ORD/FREE PWR...TIME/SEQ TOT/POP 20. PAGE 125 H2494
CONSTN TURKEY

S60
SPIRO H.J.,"NEW CONSTITUTIONAL FORMS IN AFRICA." FUT CULTURE SOCIETY ECO/UNDEV NAT/G POL/PAR VOL/ASSN EDU/PROP ATTIT DRIVE ORD/FREE PWR RESPECT ...POLICY CONCPT OBS TREND CON/ANAL STERTYP GEN/LAWS VAL/FREE. PAGE 148 H2950
AFR CONSTN FOR/AID NAT/LISM

S60
WYCKOFF T.,"THE ROLE OF THE MILITARY IN LATIN AMERICAN POLITICS." L/A+17C CONSTN CULTURE ECO/UNDEV POL/PAR FORCES LEGIS TOP/EX LEGIT GUERRILLA REV CHOOSE ORD/FREE PWR...TIME/SEQ VAL/FREE 20. PAGE 171 H3430
NAT/G COERCE TOTALISM

C60
WRIGGINS W.H.,"CEYLON: DILEMMAS OF A NEW NATION." ASIA CEYLON CONSTN STRUCT POL/PAR SECT FORCES DIPLOM GOV/REL NAT/LISM...CHARTS BIBLIOG 20. PAGE 171 H3417
PROB/SOLV NAT/G ECO/UNDEV

B61
BAYITCH S.A.,LATIN AMERICA: A BIBLIOGRAPHICAL GUIDE. LAW CONSTN LEGIS JUDGE ADJUD CT/SYS 20. PAGE 12 H0243
BIBLIOG L/A+17C NAT/G JURID

B61
BIEBUYCK D.,CONGO TRIBES AND PARTIES. AFR CONGO/BRAZ CONSTN NAT/G COLONIAL CHOOSE FEDERAL 20 CONGO/LEOP. PAGE 17 H0333
KIN POL/PAR GP/REL SOVEREIGN

B61
BINDER L.,RELIGION AND POLITICS IN PAKISTAN. ISLAM PAKISTAN NAT/G SECT LEGIS CREATE CHOOSE GP/REL ...MAJORIT TRADIT 20. PAGE 17 H0336
CONSTN CONFER NAT/LISM POL/PAR

B61
BURDEAU G.,O PODER EXECUTIVO NA FRANCA. EUR+WWI FRANCE CONSTN DELIB/GP LEGIT ADMIN ATTIT ALL/VALS CONCPT. PAGE 24 H0478
TOP/EX POL/PAR NAT/G LEGIS

B61
CARNELL F.,THE POLITICS OF THE NEW STATES: A SELECT ANNOTATED BIBLIOGRAPHY WITH SPECIAL REFERENCE TO THE COMMONWEALTH. CONSTN ELITES LABOR NAT/G POL/PAR EX/STRUC DIPLOM ADJUD ADMIN...GOV/COMP 20 COMMONWLTH. PAGE 27 H0534
BIBLIOG/A AFR ASIA COLONIAL

B61
CHAKRABARTI A.,NEHRU: HIS DEMOCRACY AND INDIA. ASIA INDIA UK CONSTN ECO/UNDEV SECT DIPLOM COLONIAL PEACE WEALTH...BIBLIOG 20 CONGRESS NEHRU/J GANDHI/M. PAGE 28 H0570
ORD/FREE STRATA NAT/G CHIEF

B61
DRAGNICH A.N.,MAJOR EUROPEAN GOVERNMENTS. FRANCE GERMANY/W UK USSR LOC/G EX/STRUC CT/SYS PARL/PROC ATTIT MARXISM...JURID MGT NAT/COMP 19/20. PAGE 42
NAT/G LEGIS CONSTN

H0846 POL/PAR

B61
GUIZOT F.P.G.,HISTORY OF THE ORIGIN OF REPRESENTATIVE GOVERNMENT IN EUROPE. CHRIST-17C FRANCE MOD/EUR SPAIN UK LAW CHIEF FORCES POPULISM ...MAJORIT TIME/SEQ GOV/COMP NAT/COMP 4/19 PARLIAMENT. PAGE 62 H1250
LEGIS REPRESENT CONSTN NAT/G

B61
HARE T.,A TREATISE ON THE ELECTION OF REPRESENTATIVES, PARLIAMENTARY AND MUNICIPAL. UK CONSTN NAT/G PARL/PROC CHOOSE ATTIT...MAJORIT 18/19 PARLIAMENT. PAGE 66 H1330
LEGIS GOV/REL CONSEN REPRESENT

B61
INDIAN NATIONAL CONGRESS,SOUVENIR, 66TH SESSION. INDIA S/ASIA CONSTN CULTURE LEGIS CREATE TEC/DEV LEAD TASK...GEOG CHARTS 20. PAGE 77 H1533
CONFER PLAN NAT/G POLICY

B61
JUSTICE,THE CITIZEN AND THE ADMINISTRATION: THE REDRESS OF GRIEVANCES (PAMPHLET). EUR+WWI UK LAW CONSTN STRATA NAT/G CT/SYS PARTIC COERCE...NEW/IDEA IDEA/COMP 20 OMBUDSMAN. PAGE 82 H1644
INGP/REL CONSULT ADJUD REPRESENT

B61
LA PONCE J.A.,THE GOVERNMENT OF THE FIFTH REPUBLIC: FRENCH POLITICAL PARTIES AND THE CONSTITUTION. ALGERIA FRANCE LAW NAT/G DELIB/GP LEGIS ECO/TAC MARXISM SOCISM...CHARTS BIBLIOG/A 20 DEGAULLE/C. PAGE 90 H1794
PWR POL/PAR CONSTN CHIEF

B61
NARAIN J.P.,SWARAJ FOR THE PEOPLE. INDIA CONSTN LOC/G MUNIC POL/PAR CHOOSE REPRESENT EFFICIENCY ATTIT PWR SOVEREIGN 20. PAGE 116 H2311
NAT/G ORD/FREE EDU/PROP EX/STRUC

B61
NIPPERDEY T.,DIE ORGANISATION DER DEUTSCHEN PARTEIEN VOR 1918. GERMANY CONSTN STRUCT TEC/DEV CHOOSE ADJUST ATTIT...CONCPT TIME/SEQ 19/20. PAGE 118 H2362
POL/PAR PARL/PROC NAT/G

B61
PANIKKAR K.M.,THE VOICE OF FREEDOM: SELECTED SPEECHES OF PANDIT MOTILAL NEHRU. INDIA UK CONSTN FINAN FORCES LEGIS DIPLOM TAX COLONIAL...POLICY MAJORIT ANTHOL 20 NEHRU/PM. PAGE 123 H2460
NAT/LISM ORD/FREE CHIEF NAT/G

B61
RAO K.V.,PARLIAMENTARY DEMOCRACY OF INDIA. INDIA EX/STRUC TOP/EX COLONIAL CT/SYS PARL/PROC ORD/FREE ...POLICY CONCPT TREND 20 PARLIAMENT. PAGE 130 H2592
CONSTN ADJUD NAT/G FEDERAL

B61
SANTHANAM K.,DEMOCRATIC PLANNING. INDIA AGRI FINAN LEGIS DIPLOM PARL/PROC ORD/FREE 20. PAGE 138 H2753
PLAN NAT/G CONSTN POLICY

B61
ULLMAN W.,PRINCIPLES OF GOVERNMENT AND POLITICS IN THE MIDDLE AGES. LAW CONSTN DOMIN EDU/PROP LEGIT TOTALISM SOVEREIGN POPULISM...POLICY GOV/COMP IDEA/COMP 12/16 POPE KING CHURCH/STA. PAGE 158 H3152
SECT CHIEF NAT/G LEGIS

B61
WARD R.E.,JAPANESE POLITICAL SCIENCE: A GUIDE TO JAPANESE REFERENCE AND RESEARCH MATERIALS (2ND ED.). LAW CONSTN STRATA NAT/G POL/PAR DELIB/GP LEGIS ADMIN CHOOSE GP/REL...INT/LAW 19/20 CHINJAP. PAGE 165 H3306
BIBLIOG/A PHIL/SCI

B61
WEST F.J.,POLITICAL ADVANCEMENT IN THE SOUTH PACIFIC. CONSTN CULTURE POL/PAR LEGIS DOMIN ADMIN CHOOSE SOVEREIGN VAL/FREE 20 FIJI TAHITI SAMOA. PAGE 167 H3335
S/ASIA LOC/G COLONIAL

B61
WILLSON F.M.G.,ADMINISTRATORS IN ACTION. UK MARKET TEC/DEV PARL/PROC 20. PAGE 169 H3376
ADMIN NAT/G CONSTN

L61
KAUPER P.G.,"CHURCH AND STATE: COOPERATIVE SEPARATISM." NAT/G LEGIS OP/RES TAX EDU/PROP GP/REL TREND. PAGE 84 H1671
SECT CONSTN LAW POLICY

S61
FITZGIBBON R.H.,"MEASUREMENT OF LATIN AMERICAN POLITICAL CHANGE." L/A+17C CONSTN CULTURE SOCIETY ECO/UNDEV NAT/G POL/PAR PUB/INST ACT/RES EDU/PROP PERCEPT KNOWL ORD/FREE SOVEREIGN...METH/CNCPT TREND OAS 20. PAGE 51 H1020
CHOOSE ATTIT

S61
LOEWENBERG G.,"PARLIAMENTARISM IN WESTERN GERMANY: THE FUNCTIONING OF THE BUNDESTAG" (BMR)" GERMANY/W NAT/G POL/PAR CHIEF LEAD 20 PARLIAMENT. PAGE 98 H1952
LEGIS CHOOSE CONSTN PARL/PROC

S61
TUCKER R.C.,"TOWARDS A COMPARATIVE POLITICS OF MOVEMENT-REGIMES" (BMR)" USSR CONSTN NAT/G CREATE PROB/SOLV DIPLOM DOMIN REV...GP/COMP IDEA/COMP METH 20 STALIN/J BOLSHEVISM. PAGE 157 H3135
MARXISM POLICY GEN/LAWS PWR

C61
LAPONCE J.A.,"THE GOVERNMENT OF THE FIFTH REPUBLIC." FRANCE CHIEF LEGIS PARL/PROC CHOOSE ...CHARTS GP/COMP IDEA/COMP BIBLIOG/A 20. PAGE 91 H1814
POL/PAR NAT/G CONSTN DOMIN

B62
ANDREWS W.G.,FRENCH POLITICS AND ALGERIA: THE PROCESS OF POLICY FORMATION 1954-1962. ALGERIA FRANCE CONSTN ELITES POL/PAR CHIEF DELIB/GP LEGIS DIPLOM PRESS CHOOSE 20. PAGE 7 H0140
GOV/COMP EXEC COLONIAL

B62
BRETTON H.L.,POWER AND STABILITY IN NIGERIA: THE POLITICS OF DECOLONIZATION. AFR CONSTN INTELL ECO/UNDEV COM/IND KIN NAT/G POL/PAR PROVS VOL/ASSN LEGIS DOMIN EDU/PROP LEGIT EXEC ROUTINE CHOOSE NAT/LISM ATTIT PERCEPT ALL/VALS. PAGE 20 H0411
CULTURE OBS NIGERIA

B62
CARTER G.M.,AFRICAN ONE-PARTY STATES. ISLAM IVORY/CST LIBERIA CONSTN CULTURE SOCIETY POL/PAR PLAN DOMIN EDU/PROP EXEC REGION CHOOSE ATTIT ALL/VALS...CONCPT TIME/SEQ CHARTS VAL/FREE 20 TANGANYIKA. PAGE 27 H0545
AFR NAT/LISM

B62
DUROSELLE J.B.,LES NOUVEAUX ETATS DANS LES RELATIONS INTERNATIONALES. AFR CHINA/COM FRANCE MOROCCO S/ASIA USSR ECO/UNDEV INT/ORG PLAN ECO/TAC EDU/PROP ATTIT DRIVE...TREND TOT/POP TUNIS 20. PAGE 44 H0872
NAT/G CONSTN DIPLOM

B62
FINER S.E.,THE MAN ON HORSEBACK: ROLE OF THE MILITARY IN POLITICS. UNIV LAW CONSTN ELITES SOCIETY POL/PAR BAL/PWR DOMIN EDU/PROP LEGIT COERCE GUERRILLA REV WAR WEAPON DRIVE SUPEGO ORD/FREE PWR RESPECT...POLICY CONCPT GEN/METH. PAGE 50 H1003
NAT/G FORCES TOTALISM

B62
GANJI M.,INTERNATIONAL PROTECTION OF HUMAN RIGHTS. WOR+45 CONSTN INT/TRADE CT/SYS SANCTION CRIME WAR RACE/REL...CHARTS IDEA/COMP NAT/COMP BIBLIOG 20 TREATY NEGRO LEAGUE/NAT UN CIVIL/LIB. PAGE 55 H1097
ORD/FREE DISCRIM LEGIS DELIB/GP

B62
HAIM S.G.,ARAB NATIONALISM. ISLAM CONSTN GP/REL ...ANTHOL BIBLIOG JEWS 20 MID/EAST ARABS. PAGE 64 H1279
NAT/LISM REV SECT DIPLOM

B62
HATCH J.,AFRICA TODAY-AND TOMORROW: AN OUTLINE OF BASIC FACTS AND MAJOR PROBLEMS. AFR FUT ISLAM STRATA ECO/UNDEV INT/ORG NAT/G POL/PAR DELIB/GP TOP/EX EDU/PROP LEGIT CHOOSE ATTIT...TIME/SEQ TOT/POP COLD/WAR 20. PAGE 67 H1353
PLAN CONSTN NAT/LISM

B62
HOOK S.,THE PARADOXES OF FREEDOM. UNIV CONSTN INTELL LEGIS CONTROL REV CHOOSE SUPEGO...POLICY JURID IDEA/COMP 19/20 CIV/RIGHTS. PAGE 73 H1461
CONCPT MAJORIT ORD/FREE ALL/VALS

B62
HUNKIN P.,ENSEIGNEMENT ET POLITIQUE EN FRANCE ET EN ANGLETERRE. FRANCE UK CONSTN ACADEM SECT CHIEF DELIB/GP PROB/SOLV CONTROL REV ORD/FREE CONSERVE ...BIBLIOG 18/20. PAGE 75 H1496
EDU/PROP LEGIS IDEA/COMP NAT/G

B62
INGHAM K.,A HISTORY OF EAST AFRICA. NAT/G DIPLOM ADMIN WAR NAT/LISM...SOC BIOG BIBLIOG. PAGE 77 H1534
AFR CONSTN COLONIAL

B62
JAIN R.S.,THE GROWTH AND DEVELOPMENT OF GOVERNOR-GENERAL'S EXECUTIVE COUNCIL 1858-1919. INDIA UK CONSTN EX/STRUC LEGIS ADJUD ADMIN INGP/REL ATTIT 19/20. PAGE 79 H1585
NAT/G DELIB/GP CHIEF CONSULT

B62
JENNINGS I.,PARTY POLITICS: THE STUFF OF POLITICS (VOL.III). UK NAT/G SECT CHIEF INT/TRADE RECEIVE COLONIAL GP/REL NAT/LISM ORD/FREE SOCISM 19/20 CHURCH/STA WHIG/PARTY. PAGE 80 H1607
POL/PAR CONSTN PWR ALL/IDEOS

B62
KASTARI P.,LA PRESIDENCE DE LA REPUBLIQUE EN FINLANDE. FINLAND CONSTN NAT/G POL/PAR LEGIS LEGIT ATTIT...JURID CONCPT 20 PRESIDENT. PAGE 83 H1666
PARL/PROC CHIEF PWR DECISION

B62
KINDERSLEY R.,THE FIRST RUSSIAN REVISIONISTS. COM USSR LAW ELITES INTELL NAT/G LEGIS ECO/TAC EDU/PROP CONTROL LEAD GP/REL SOCISM 19/20 MARX/KARL BOLSHEVISM. PAGE 86 H1712
CONSTN MARXISM POPULISM BIOG

B62
MANSUR F.,PROCESS OF INDEPENDENCE. GHANA INDIA INDONESIA PAKISTAN CONSTN ELITES INTELL STRUCT ACADEM NAT/G REV PWR 20. PAGE 102 H2043
NAT/COMP POL/PAR SOVEREIGN COLONIAL

B62
OLLE-LAPRUNE J.,LA STABILITE DES MINISTRES SOUS LA TROISIEME REPUBLIQUE, 1879-1940. FRANCE CONSTN POL/PAR LEAD WAR INGP/REL RIGID/FLEX PWR...POLICY CHARTS 19/20. PAGE 121 H2415
LEGIS NAT/G ADMIN PERSON

B62
PASTOR R.S.,A STATEMENT OF THE LAWS OF PARAGUAY IN
FINAN

MATTERS AFFECTING BUSINESS (2ND ED.). PARAGUAY INDUS FAM LABOR LG/CO NAT/G LEGIS TAX CONTROL MARRIAGE 20. PAGE 124 H2474 — ECO/UNDEV LAW CONSTN

B62
PHILLIPS O.H.,CONSTITUTIONAL AND ADMINISTRATIVE LAW (3RD ED.). UK INT/ORG LOC/G CHIEF EX/STRUC LEGIS BAL/PWR ADJUD COLONIAL CT/SYS PWR...CHARTS 20. PAGE 125 H2503 — JURID ADMIN CONSTN NAT/G

B62
RANNEY A.,THE DOCTRINE OF RESPONSIBLE PARTY GOVERNMENT. USA+45 USA-45 CONSTN PLAN CHOOSE ...MAJORIT GOV/COMP IDEA/COMP 20. PAGE 130 H2591 — POL/PAR POLICY REPRESENT NAT/G

B62
ROUSSEAU J.J.,THE SOCIAL CONTRACT. LAW CONSTN CHIEF DOMIN REPRESENT GP/REL ORD/FREE POPULISM...MAJORIT GOV/COMP 18. PAGE 135 H2700 — GEN/LAWS AGREE REV

S62
MONNIER J.P.,"LA SUCCESSION D'ETATS EN MATIERE DE RESPONSABILITE INTERNATIONALE." UNIV CONSTN INTELL SOCIETY ADJUD ROUTINE PERCEPT SUPEGO...GEN/LAWS TOT/POP 20. PAGE 112 H2240 — NAT/G JURID INT/LAW

S62
MURACCIOLE L.,"LES CONSTITUTIONS DES ETATS AFRICAINS D'EXPRESSION FRANCAISE: LA CONSTITUTION DU 16 AVRIL 1962 DE LA REPUBLIQUE DU" AFR CHAD CHIEF LEGIS LEGIT COLONIAL EXEC ROUTINE ORD/FREE SOVEREIGN...SOC CONCPT 20. PAGE 115 H2291 — NAT/G CONSTN

S62
VIGNES D.,"L'AUTORITE DES TRAITES INTERNATIONAUX EN DROIT INTERNE." EUR+WWI UNIV LAW CONSTN INTELL NAT/G POL/PAR DIPLOM ATTIT PERCEPT ALL/VALS ...POLICY INT/LAW JURID CONCPT TIME/SEQ 20 TREATY. PAGE 163 H3252 — STRUCT LEGIT FRANCE

B63
ADRIAN C.R.,GOVERNING OVER FIFTY STATES AND THEIR COMMUNITIES. USA+45 CONSTN FINAN MUNIC NAT/G POL/PAR EX/STRUC LEGIS ADMIN CONTROL CT/SYS ...CHARTS 20. PAGE 4 H0073 — PROVS LOC/G GOV/REL GOV/COMP

B63
ATTIA G.E.D.,LES FORCES ARMEES DES NATIONS UNIES EN COREE ET AU MOYENORIENT. KOREA CONSTN NAT/G DELIB/GP LEGIS PWR...IDEA/COMP NAT/COMP BIBLIOG UN SUEZ. PAGE 9 H0177 — FORCES INT/LAW

B63
BADI J.,THE GOVERNMENT OF THE STATE OF ISRAEL: A CRITICAL ACCOUNT OF ITS PARLIAMENT, EXECUTIVE, AND JUDICIARY. ISRAEL ECO/DEV CHIEF DELIB/GP LEGIS DIPLOM CT/SYS INGP/REL PEACE ORD/FREE...BIBLIOG 20 PARLIAMENT ARABS MIGRATION. PAGE 10 H0193 — NAT/G CONSTN EX/STRUC POL/PAR

B63
BROGAN D.W.,POLITICAL PATTERNS IN TODAY'S WORLD. FRANCE USA+45 USSR WOR+45 CONSTN STRUCT PLAN DIPLOM ADMIN LEAD ROLE SUPEGO...PHIL/SCI 20. PAGE 21 H0429 — NAT/COMP NEW/LIB COM TOTALISM

B63
CARTER G.M.,FIVE AFRICAN STATES: RESPONSES TO DIVERSITY. CONSTN CULTURE STRATA LEGIS PLAN ECO/TAC DOMIN EDU/PROP CT/SYS EXEC CHOOSE ATTIT HEALTH ORD/FREE PWR...TIME/SEQ TOT/POP VAL/FREE. PAGE 27 H0547 — AFR SOCIETY

B63
DEBRAY P.,LE PORTUGAL ENTRE DEUX REVOLUTIONS. EUR+WWI PORTUGAL CONSTN LEGIT ADMIN ATTIT ALL/VALS ...DECISION CONCPT 20 SALAZAR/A. PAGE 39 H0779 — NAT/G DELIB/GP TOP/EX

B63
ECKSTEIN H.,COMPARATIVE POLITICS. POL/PAR LEGIS CT/SYS CHOOSE TOTALISM PWR POPULISM...METH/COMP GEN/METH ANTHOL BIBLIOG 20. PAGE 44 H0886 — NAT/COMP CONSTN REPRESENT NAT/G

B63
EDDY J.P.,JUSTICE OF THE PEACE. UK LAW CONSTN CULTURE 14/20 COMMON/LAW. PAGE 44 H0887 — CRIME JURID CT/SYS ADJUD

B63
ELIAS T.O.,GOVERNMENT AND POLITICS IN AFRICA. CONSTN CULTURE SOCIETY NAT/G POL/PAR DIPLOM REPRESENT PERSON...SOC TREND BIBLIOG 4/20. PAGE 45 H0906 — AFR NAT/LISM COLONIAL LAW

B63
ELWIN V.,A NEW DEAL FOR TRIBAL INDIA. INDIA AGRI COM/IND INDUS KIN TEC/DEV TAX EDU/PROP OWN HEALTH 20. PAGE 46 H0912 — ECO/UNDEV CULTURE CONSTN SOC/WK

B63
GOURNAY B.,PUBLIC ADMINISTRATION. FRANCE LAW CONSTN AGRI FINAN LABOR SCHOOL EX/STRUC CHOOSE...MGT METH/COMP 20. PAGE 59 H1189 — BIBLIOG/A ADMIN NAT/G LOC/G

B63
HUGHES A.J.,EAST AFRICA: THE SEARCH FOR UNITY- KENYA, TANGANYIKA, UGANDA, AND ZANZIBAR. TANZANIA UGANDA CONSTN POL/PAR SECT CHIEF DELIB/GP LEGIS WAR CHOOSE NAT/LISM MARXISM...POLICY CHARTS 20 NEGRO UN. PAGE 74 H1488 — NAT/G DOMIN LOC/G AFR

B63
JENNINGS W.I.,DEMOCRACY IN AFRICA. UK CULTURE STRUCT ECO/UNDEV DIPLOM COLONIAL GP/REL ADJUST NAT/LISM ORD/FREE...GOV/COMP 20 THIRD/WRLD. PAGE 81 H1613 — PROB/SOLV AFR CONSTN POPULISM

B63
JUDD P.,AFRICAN INDEPENDENCE: THE EXPLODING EMERGENCE OF THE NEW AFRICAN NATIONS. AFR UK LAW CONSTN CULTURE KIN DIPLOM ATTIT...CHARTS BIBLIOG 20 UN DEGAULLE/C NEGRO THIRD/WRLD. PAGE 82 H1640 — ORD/FREE POLICY DOMIN LOC/G

B63
JUNOD V.,HANDBOOK OF AFRICA. AFR ISLAM CONSTN SOCIETY NAT/G POL/PAR...GEOG SOC STAT CHARTS WORK 20. PAGE 82 H1642 — ECO/UNDEV REGION

B63
LEVIN M.G.,ETHNIC ORIGINS OF THE PEOPLES OF NORTHEASTERN ASIA. CONSTN LEGIS...STAT CENSUS CHARTS 20 TEXAS MAPS. PAGE 95 H1901 — HEREDITY HABITAT CULTURE GEOG

B63
LIVINGSTON W.S.,FEDERALISM IN THE COMMONWEALTH - A BIBLIOGRAPHICAL COMMENTARY. CANADA INDIA PAKISTAN UK STRUCT LOC/G NAT/G POL/PAR...NAT/COMP 20 AUSTRAL. PAGE 97 H1943 — BIBLIOG JURID FEDERAL CONSTN

B63
MAYNE R.,THE COMMUNITY OF EUROPE. UK CONSTN NAT/G CONSULT DELIB/GP CREATE PLAN ECO/TAC LEGIT ADMIN ROUTINE ORD/FREE PWR WEALTH...CONCPT TIME/SEQ EEC EURATOM 20. PAGE 105 H2107 — EUR+WWI INT/ORG REGION

B63
MERKL P.H.,THE ORIGIN OF THE WEST GERMAN REPUBLIC. GERMANY/W WOR+45 POL/PAR DIPLOM LEAD LOBBY REPRESENT GP/REL NAT/LISM 20. PAGE 109 H2179 — CONSTN PARL/PROC CONTROL BAL/PWR

B63
NKRUMAH K.,AFRICA MUST UNITE. AFR FUT GHANA CONSTN CULTURE SOCIETY NAT/G POL/PAR DELIB/GP TOP/EX PLAN DOMIN EDU/PROP ATTIT DRIVE...TIME/SEQ CHARTS TOT/POP 20. PAGE 118 H2364 — CONCPT GEN/LAWS REGION

B63
RICHARDSON H.G.,THE ADMINISTRATION OF IRELAND 1172-1377. IRELAND CONSTN EX/STRUC LEGIS JUDGE CT/SYS PARL/PROC...CHARTS BIBLIOG 12/14. PAGE 131 H2621 — ADMIN NAT/G PWR

B63
ROBERTSON A.H.,HUMAN RIGHTS IN EUROPE. CONSTN SOCIETY INT/ORG NAT/G VOL/ASSN DELIB/GP ACT/RES PLAN ADJUD REGION ROUTINE ATTIT LOVE ORD/FREE RESPECT...JURID SOC CONCPT SOC/EXP UN 20. PAGE 132 H2645 — EUR+WWI PERSON

B63
SCHUMAN S.I.,LEGAL POSITIVISM: ITS SCOPE AND LIMITATIONS. CONSTN NAT/G DIPLOM PARTIC UTOPIA ...POLICY DECISION PHIL/SCI CONCPT 20. PAGE 140 H2802 — GEN/METH LAW METH/COMP

B63
STEVENS G.G.,EGYPT YESTERDAY AND TODAY. CONSTN ECO/UNDEV AGRI INDUS NAT/G POL/PAR FORCES ECO/TAC EDU/PROP COERCE WAR NAT/LISM DRIVE ALL/VALS ...TIME/SEQ WORK SUEZ 20. PAGE 149 H2983 — ISLAM TOP/EX REV UAR

B63
WALKER A.A.,OFFICIAL PUBLICATIONS OF SIERRA LEONE AND GAMBIA. GAMBIA SIER/LEONE UK LAW CONSTN LEGIS PLAN BUDGET DIPLOM...SOC SAMP CON/ANAL 20. PAGE 164 H3290 — BIBLIOG NAT/G COLONIAL ADMIN

B63
WEINER M.,POLITICAL CHANGE IN SOUTH ASIA. CEYLON INDIA PAKISTAN S/ASIA CULTURE ELITES ECO/UNDEV EX/STRUC ADMIN CONTROL CHOOSE CONSERVE...GOV/COMP ANTHOL 20. PAGE 166 H3328 — NAT/G CONSTN TEC/DEV

B63
WILCOX W.A.,PAKISTAN; THE CONSOLIDATION OF A NATION. INDIA PAKISTAN CONSTN SECT PROB/SOLV COLONIAL PARTIC GP/REL FEDERAL...POLICY 19/20. PAGE 168 H3361 — NAT/LISM ECO/UNDEV DIPLOM STRUCT

S63
ANTHON C.G.,"THE END OF THE ADENAUER ERA." EUR+WWI GERMANY/W CONSTN EX/STRUC CREATE DIPLOM LEGIT ATTIT PERSON ALL/VALS...RECORD 20 ADENAUER/K. PAGE 7 H0144 — NAT/G TOP/EX BAL/PWR GERMANY

S63
DUDLEY B.J.,"THE NOMINATION OF PARLIAMENTARY CANDIDATES IN NORTHERN NIGERIA." AFR CONSTN CULTURE ELITES STRATA DELIB/GP LEGIS DOMIN EDU/PROP COERCE ATTIT SUPEGO PWR...STAT VAL/FREE 20. PAGE 43 H0854 — POL/PAR CHOOSE NIGERIA

S63
GLUCKMAN M.,"CIVIL WAR AND THEORIES OF POWER IN BAROTSE-LAND: AFRICAN AND MEDIEVAL ANALOGIES." AFR CHRIST-17C LAW CONSTN CULTURE STRATA KIN DELIB/GP FORCES DOMIN LEGIT COERCE PERCEPT ORD/FREE...SOC INT TIME/SEQ GEN/LAWS VAL/FREE. PAGE 57 H1148 — TOP/EX PWR WAR

S63
LEE J.M.,"PARLIAMENT IN REPUBLICAN GHANA." AFR CONSTN CULTURE SOCIETY STRATA POL/PAR DELIB/GP TOP/EX DOMIN EDU/PROP LEGIT COERCE CHOOSE ATTIT ALL/VALS...CONCPT STAT TIME/SEQ VAL/FREE 20. — LEGIS GHANA

PAGE 93 H1857

S63
ROGIN M.,"ROUSSEAU IN AFRICA." AFR MARXISM POPULISM SOCISM 20 ROUSSEAU/J. PAGE 133 H2661
IDEA/COMP CULTURE CONSTN ORD/FREE

S63
RUSTOW D.A.,"THE MILITARY IN MIDDLE EASTERN SOCIETY AND POLITICS." FUT ISLAM CONSTN SOCIETY FACE/GP NAT/G POL/PAR PROF/ORG CONSULT DOMIN ADMIN EXEC REGION COERCE NAT/LISM ATTIT DRIVE PERSON ORD/FREE PWR...POLICY CONCPT OBS STERTYP 20. PAGE 136 H2721
FORCES ELITES

S63
SOEMARDJORN S.,"SOME SOCIAL AND CULTURAL IMPLICATIONS OF INDONESIA'S PLANNED AND UNPLANNED DEVELOPMENT." EUR+WWI FUT MOD/EUR S/ASIA CONSTN SOCIETY DELIB/GP ACT/RES PLAN ECO/TAC EDU/PROP COERCE ATTIT ALL/VALS...TIME/SEQ 20. PAGE 146 H2927
ECO/UNDEV CULTURE INDONESIA

S63
TILMAN R.O.,"MALAYSIA: THE PROBLEMS OF FEDERATION." ISLAM S/ASIA CONSTN PROVS SECT DELIB/GP DOMIN EDU/PROP LEGIT EXEC COERCE CHOOSE ATTIT HEALTH ORD/FREE PWR...STAT TOT/POP VAL/FREE 20. PAGE 155 H3097
NAT/G CULTURE MALAYSIA

S63
ZOLBERG A.R.,"MASS PARTIES AND NATIONAL INTEGRATION: THE CASE OF THE IVORY COAST" (BMR)" AFR IVORY/CST CONSTN VOL/ASSN DIPLOM LEAD GP/REL INGP/REL 20. PAGE 173 H3461
POL/PAR ECO/UNDEV NAT/G ADJUST

C63
ATTIA G.E.O.,"LES FORCES ARMEES DES NATIONS UNIES EN COREE ET AU MOYENORIENT." KOREA CONSTN DELIB/GP LEGIS PWR...IDEA/COMP NAT/COMP BIBLIOG UN SUEZ. PAGE 9 H0178
FORCES NAT/G INT/LAW

B64
AGGARWALA R.C.,CONSTITUTIONAL HISTORY OF INDIA AND NATIONAL MOVEMENT INCLUDING COMPARATIVE STUDY OF MODERN INDIA CONSTITUTION. INDIA S/ASIA SECT VOL/ASSN EX/STRUC LEGIS COERCE REV INGP/REL ORD/FREE...SOC BIBLIOG 18/20 CMN/WLTH. PAGE 4 H0077
CONSTN COLONIAL DOMIN NAT/G

B64
ANDREN N.,GOVERNMENT AND POLITICS IN THE NORDIC COUNTRIES: DENMARK, FINLAND, ICELAND, NORWAY, SWEDEN. DENMARK FINLAND ICELAND NORWAY SWEDEN POL/PAR CHIEF LEGIS ADMIN REGION REPRESENT ATTIT CONSERVE...CHARTS BIBLIOG/A 20. PAGE 7 H0137
CONSTN NAT/G CULTURE GOV/COMP

B64
BAGEHOT W.,THE ENGLISH CONSTITUTION. UK CHIEF CONSULT LEGIS BAL/PWR PWR...BIBLIOG 18/19 PARLIAMENT. PAGE 10 H0198
CONSTN PARL/PROC NAT/G CONCPT

B64
BERRINGTON H.,HOW NATIONS ARE GOVERNED. FRANCE WOR+45 ECO/UNDEV INT/ORG POL/PAR CHOOSE TOTALISM KNOWL...MAJORIT T 20 UN COMMONWLTH THIRD/WRLD. PAGE 16 H0320
NAT/G GOV/COMP ECO/DEV CONSTN

B64
COONDOO R.,THE DIVISION OF POWERS IN THE INDIAN CONSTITUTION. INDIA ECO/UNDEV FINAN TEC/DEV WAR CENTRAL EFFICIENCY NAT/LISM PWR WEALTH NEW/LIB ...BIBLIOG 18/20. PAGE 33 H0659
CONSTN LEGIS WELF/ST GOV/COMP

B64
DE SMITH S.A.,THE NEW COMMONWEALTH AND ITS CONSTITUTIONS. AFR CYPRUS PAKISTAN S/ASIA INT/ORG NAT/G LEGIS LEGIT RIGID/FLEX PWR...CONCPT TIME/SEQ CMN/WLTH 20. PAGE 38 H0770
EX/STRUC CONSTN SOVEREIGN

B64
FORBES A.H.,CURRENT RESEARCH IN BRITISH STUDIES. UK CONSTN CULTURE POL/PAR SECT DIPLOM ADMIN...JURID BIOG WORSHIP 20. PAGE 52 H1034
BIBLIOG PERSON NAT/G PARL/PROC

B64
FRANCK T.M.,EAST AFRICAN UNITY THROUGH LAW. MALAWI TANZANIA UGANDA UK ZAMBIA CONSTN INT/ORG NAT/G ADMIN ROUTINE TASK NAT/LISM ATTIT SOVEREIGN ...RECORD IDEA/COMP NAT/COMP. PAGE 52 H1048
AFR FEDERAL REGION INT/LAW

B64
GESELLSCHAFT RECHTSVERGLEICH,BIBLIOGRAPHIE DES DEUTSCHEN RECHTS (BIBLIOGRAPHY OF GERMAN LAW, TRANS. BY COURTLAND PETERSON). GERMANY FINAN INDUS LABOR SECT FORCES CT/SYS PARL/PROC CRIME...INT/LAW SOC NAT/COMP 20. PAGE 56 H1117
BIBLIOG/A JURID CONSTN ADMIN

B64
GREAT BRITAIN CENTRAL OFF INF,CONSTITUTIONAL DEVELOPMENT IN THE COMMONWEALTH. VOL/ASSN PLAN DIPLOM COLONIAL INGP/REL NAT/LISM ORD/FREE PWR 17/20 CMN/WLTH. PAGE 60 H1202
REGION CONSTN NAT/G SOVEREIGN

B64
GROVES H.E.,THE CONSTITUTION OF MALAYSIA. MALAYSIA POL/PAR CHIEF CONSULT DELIB/GP CT/SYS PARL/PROC CHOOSE FEDERAL ORD/FREE 20. PAGE 62 H1238
CONSTN NAT/G LAW

B64
HOBBS C.C.,SOUTHEAST ASIA: AN ANNOTATED BIBLIOGRAPHY OF SELECTED REFERENCES IN WESTERN LANGUAGES (REV. ED.). CAMBODIA INDONESIA LAOS THAILAND VIETNAM CONSTN NAT/G...SOC WORSHIP 20. PAGE 72 H1437
BIBLIOG/A S/ASIA CULTURE SOCIETY

B64
HOLDSWORTH W.S.,A HISTORY OF ENGLISH LAW; THE CENTURIES OF DEVELOPMENT AND REFORM (VOL. XIV). UK CONSTN LOC/G NAT/G POL/PAR CHIEF EX/STRUC ADJUD COLONIAL ATTIT...INT/LAW JURID 18/19 TORY/PARTY COMMONWLTH WHIG/PARTY COMMON/LAW. PAGE 73 H1453
LAW LEGIS LEAD CT/SYS

B64
KARIEL H.S.,IN SEARCH OF AUTHORITY: TWENTIETH-CENTURY POLITICAL THOUGHT. WOR+45 WOR-45 NAT/G EX/STRUC TOTALISM DRIVE PWR...MGT PHIL/SCI GEN/LAWS 19/20 NIETZSCH/F FREUD/S WEBER/MAX NIEBUHR/R MARITAIN/J. PAGE 83 H1661
CONSTN CONCPT ORD/FREE IDEA/COMP

B64
KRUEGER H.,ALLGEMEINE STAATSLEHRE. WOR+45 CONSTN SECT CHOOSE INGP/REL PWR NEW/LIB...JURID CLASSIF IDEA/COMP. PAGE 89 H1777
NAT/G GOV/COMP SOCIETY

B64
LEDERMAN W.R.,THE COURTS AND THE CANDIAN CONSTITUTION. CANADA PARL/PROC...POLICY JURID GOV/COMP ANTHOL 19/20 SUPREME/CT PARLIAMENT. PAGE 93 H1854
CONSTN CT/SYS LEGIS LAW

B64
LIGGETT E.,BRITISH POLITICAL ISSUES: VOLUME 1. UK LAW CONSTN LOC/G NAT/G ADJUD 20. PAGE 97 H1930
POL/PAR GOV/REL CT/SYS DIPLOM

B64
MARSH D.C.,THE FUTURE OF THE WELFARE STATE. UK CONSTN NAT/G POL/PAR...POLICY WELF/ST 20. PAGE 103 H2058
NEW/LIB ADMIN CONCPT INSPECT

B64
MARTINEZ J.R.,THREE CASES OF COMMUNISM: CUBA, BRAZIL, AND MEXICO. BRAZIL CUBA L/A+17C CONSTN NAT/G DIPLOM ECO/TAC GP/REL INGP/REL...GP/COMP BIBLIOG 20 MEXIC/AMER COM/PARTY. PAGE 103 H2068
MARXISM BIOG REV NAT/COMP

B64
MINAR D.W.,IDEAS AND POLITICS: THE AMERICAN EXPERIENCE. SECT CHIEF LEGIS CREATE ADJUD EXEC REV PWR...PHIL/SCI CONCPT IDEA/COMP 18/20 HAMILTON/A JEFFERSN/T DECLAR/IND JACKSON/A PRESIDENT. PAGE 111 H2220
CONSTN NAT/G FEDERAL

B64
MORGENTHAU R.S.,POLITICAL PARTIES IN FRENCH-SPEAKING WEST AFRICA. AFR FRANCE GUINEA IVORY/CST MALI SENEGAL CONSTN LEGIS CREATE PLAN LOBBY PARTIC GP/REL...POLICY BIBLIOG 20. PAGE 113 H2257
POL/PAR NAT/G SOVEREIGN COLONIAL

B64
O'HEARN P.J.T.,PEACE, ORDER AND GOOD GOVERNMENT; A NEW CONSTITUTION FOR CANADA. CANADA EX/STRUC LEGIS CT/SYS PARL/PROC...BIBLIOG 20. PAGE 120 H2388
NAT/G CONSTN LAW CREATE

B64
PHILLIPS C.S.,THE DEVELOPMENT OF NIGERIAN FOREIGN POLICY. AFR CONSTN CULTURE STRATA NAT/G LEGIS DOMIN LEGIT EXEC...RELATIV SOC TIME/SEQ TREND TOT/POP 20. PAGE 125 H2502
CHOOSE POLICY DIPLOM NIGERIA

B64
SIEKANOWICZ P.,LEGAL SOURCES AND BIBLIOGRAPHY OF POLAND. COM POLAND CONSTN NAT/G PARL/PROC SANCTION CRIME MARXISM 16/20. PAGE 143 H2870
BIBLIOG ADJUD LAW JURID

B64
STRONG C.F.,HISTORY OF MODERN POLITICAL CONSTITUTIONS. STRUCT INT/ORG NAT/G LEGIS TEC/DEV DIPLOM INT/TRADE CT/SYS EXEC...METH/COMP T 12/20 UN. PAGE 150 H2999
CONSTN CONCPT

B64
TURNER M.C.,LIBROS EN VENTA EN HISPANOAMERICA Y ESPANA. SPAIN LAW CONSTN CULTURE ADMIN LEAD...HUM SOC 20. PAGE 157 H3141
BIBLIOG L/A+17C NAT/G DIPLOM

B64
VECCHIO G.D.,L'ETAT ET LE DROIT. ITALY CONSTN EX/STRUC LEGIS DIPLOM CT/SYS...JURID 20 UN. PAGE 162 H3238
NAT/G SOVEREIGN CONCPT INT/LAW

B64
WALDMAN E.,THE GOOSE STEP IS VERBOTEN: THE GERMAN ARMY TODAY. GERMANY/W LAW CONSTN LEGIS PROB/SOLV DOMIN CONTROL CIVMIL/REL GOV/REL INGP/REL ATTIT ...DEEP/QU 20. PAGE 164 H3289
SOC FORCES NAT/G

B64
WARD R.E.,POLITICAL MODERNIZATION IN JAPAN AND TURKEY. ASIA ISLAM S/ASIA CONSTN CULTURE STRATA COM/IND POL/PAR FORCES ACT/RES ECO/TAC DOMIN EDU/PROP LEGIT ADMIN CHOOSE ATTIT ALL/VALS...STAT TIME/SEQ VAL/FREE CHINJAP. PAGE 165 H3307
SOCIETY TURKEY

B64
WHEARE K.C.,FEDERAL GOVERNMENT (4TH ED.). WOR+45 WOR-45 POL/PAR LEGIS BAL/PWR CT/SYS...POLICY JURID CONCPT GOV/COMP 17/20. PAGE 167 H3339
FEDERAL CONSTN EX/STRUC NAT/COMP

S64
GIROD R.,"LE SYSTEME DES PARTIS EN SUISSE." CONSTN
POL/PAR

LOC/G DELIB/GP FEDERAL ALL/VALS. PAGE 57 H1136 LEGIS NAT/G PARL/PROC

S64
KANOUTE P.,"AFRICAN SOCIALISM." AFR CONSTN NAT/G COLONIAL ORD/FREE...GOV/COMP METH/COMP 20 EUROPE. PAGE 83 H1655 SOCISM CULTURE STRUCT IDEA/COMP

S64
LANGERHANS H.,"NEHRU'S BITTERNESS." FUT INDIA S/ASIA CONSTN CULTURE ECO/UNDEV ECO/TAC DOMIN EDU/PROP ATTIT PERCEPT PERSON...POLICY 20 NEHRU/J. PAGE 91 H1811 ECO/DEV BIOG

S64
LEWIS B.,"THE QUEST FOR FREEDOM--A SAD STORY OF THE MIDDLE EAST." ISLAM ISRAEL LEBANON TURKEY CULTURE NAT/G SECT LEGIS TOP/EX DOMIN EDU/PROP LEGIT ORD/FREE PWR RESPECT...POLICY TIME/SEQ VAL/FREE 20. PAGE 96 H1911 CONSTN ATTIT NAT/LISM

S64
SWEARER H.R.,"AFTER KHRUSHCHEV: WHAT NEXT." COM FUT USSR CONSTN ELITES NAT/G POL/PAR CHIEF DELIB/GP LEGIS DOMIN LEAD...RECORD TREND STERTYP GEN/METH 20. PAGE 151 H3016 EX/STRUC PWR

C64
SCOTT R.E.,"MEXICAN GOVERNMENT IN TRANSITION (REV ED)" CULTURE STRUCT POL/PAR CHIEF ADMIN LOBBY REV CHOOSE GP/REL DRIVE...BIBLIOG METH 20 MEXIC/AMER. PAGE 141 H2816 NAT/G L/A+17C ROUTINE CONSTN

B65
ADAM T.R.,GOVERNMENT AND POLITICS IN AFRICA SOUTH OF THE SAHARA. AFR EUR+WWI CONSTN CULTURE INTELL POL/PAR TOP/EX LEGIT REGION DRIVE...OBS TREND CMN/WLTH 20. PAGE 3 H0062 NAT/G TIME/SEQ RACE/REL COLONIAL

B65
BETTISON D.G.,THE PAPUA-GUINEA ELECTIONS 1964. S/ASIA CONSTN POL/PAR EDU/PROP PARTIC SUFF CENTRAL CONSEN...OBS CHARTS BIBLIOG 20. PAGE 16 H0324 NAT/G LEGIS CHOOSE REPRESENT

B65
BORTOLI G.,SOCIOLOGIE DU REFERENDUM DANS LA FRANCE MODERNE. FRANCE CONSTN EDU/PROP SUFF ATTIT ORD/FREE ...POLICY DECISION CHARTS BIBLIOG 20 DEGAULLE/C. PAGE 19 H0379 LEGIS SOCIETY PWR NAT/G

B65
BRASS P.R.,FACTIONAL POLITICS IN AN INDIAN STATE: THE CONGRESS PARTY IN UTTAR PRADESH. INDIA UK CONSTN CULTURE ECO/UNDEV LOC/G DOMIN COLONIAL CROWD GP/REL ADJUST CENTRAL RIGID/FLEX SOVEREIGN 20 UTTAR/PRAD CONGRESS/P. PAGE 20 H0406 POL/PAR PROVS LEGIS CHOOSE

B65
BROWNSON O.A.,THE AMERICAN REPUBLIC. NAT/G PROVS WAR GOV/REL PRIVIL ORD/FREE PWR ALL/IDEOS CONSERVE ...CONCPT 19 CIVIL/WAR. PAGE 22 H0452 CONSTN FEDERAL SOVEREIGN

B65
CARTER G.M.,POLITICS IN EUROPE. EUR+WWI FRANCE GERMANY/W UK USSR LAW CONSTN POL/PAR VOL/ASSN PRESS LOBBY PWR...ANTHOL SOC/INTEG EEC. PAGE 27 H0548 GOV/COMP OP/RES ECO/DEV

B65
CHANDA A.,FEDERALISM IN INDIA. INDIA UK ELITES FINAN NAT/G POL/PAR EX/STRUC LEGIS DIPLOM TAX GOV/REL POPULISM...POLICY 20. PAGE 28 H0572 CONSTN CENTRAL FEDERAL

B65
CHARNAY J.P.,LE SUFFRAGE POLITIQUE EN FRANCE; ELECTIONS PARLEMENTAIRES, ELECTION PRESIDENTIELLE, REFERENDUMS. FRANCE CONSTN CHIEF DELIB/GP ECO/TAC EDU/PROP CRIME INGP/REL MORAL ORD/FREE PWR CATHISM 20 PARLIAMENT PRESIDENT. PAGE 29 H0584 CHOOSE SUFF NAT/G LEGIS

B65
CHEN T.H.,THE CHINESE COMMUNIST REGIME: A DOCUMENTARY STUDY (2 VOLS.). CHINA/COM LAW CONSTN ELITES ECO/UNDEV LEGIS ECO/TAC ADMIN CONTROL PWR ...SOC 20. PAGE 29 H0587 MARXISM POL/PAR NAT/G

B65
CHRIMES S.B.,ENGLISH CONSTITUTIONAL HISTORY (3RD ED.). UK CHIEF CONSULT DELIB/GP LEGIS CT/SYS 15/20 COMMON/LAW PARLIAMENT. PAGE 30 H0598 CONSTN BAL/PWR NAT/G

B65
GAJENDRAGADKAR P.B.,LAW, LIBERTY AND SOCIAL JUSTICE. INDIA CONSTN NAT/G SECT PLAN ECO/TAC PRESS POPULISM...SOC METH/COMP 20 HINDU. PAGE 54 H1086 ORD/FREE LAW ADJUD JURID

B65
GOLEMBIEWSKI R.T.,MEN, MANAGEMENT, AND MORALITY; TOWARD A NEW ORGANIZATIONAL ETHIC. CONSTN EX/STRUC CREATE ADMIN CONTROL INGP/REL PERSON SUPEGO MORAL PWR...GOV/COMP METH/COMP 20 BUREAUCRCY. PAGE 58 H1161 LG/CO MGT PROB/SOLV

B65
INST INTL DES CIVILISATION DIF,THE CONSTITUTIONS AND ADMINISTRATIVE INSTITUTIONS OF THE NEW STATES. AFR ISLAM S/ASIA NAT/G POL/PAR DELIB/GP EX/STRUC CONFER EFFICIENCY NAT/LISM...JURID SOC 20. PAGE 77 H1535 CONSTN ADMIN ADJUD ECO/UNDEV

B65
KAAS L.,DIE GEISTLICHE GERICHTSBARKEIT DER KATHOLISCHEN KIRCHE IN PREUSSEN (2 VOLS.). PRUSSIA CONSTN NAT/G PROVS SECT ADJUD ADMIN ATTIT 16/20. PAGE 82 H1647 JURID CATHISM GP/REL CT/SYS

B65
LANDE C.H.,LEADERS, FACTIONS, AND PARTIES. PHILIPPINE CONSTN LOC/G NAT/G PARTIC...CHARTS BIBLIOG 20. PAGE 90 H1806 LEAD POL/PAR POLICY

B65
MCWHINNEY E.,JUDICIAL REVIEW IN THE ENGLISH-SPEAKING WORLD (3RD ED.). CANADA UK WOR+45 LEGIS CONTROL EXEC PARTIC...JURID 20 AUSTRAL. PAGE 108 H2151 GOV/COMP CT/SYS ADJUD CONSTN

B65
NATIONAL BOOK CENTRE PAKISTAN,BOOKS ON PAKISTAN: A BIBLIOGRAPHY. PAKISTAN CULTURE DIPLOM ADMIN ATTIT ...MAJORIT SOC CONCPT 20. PAGE 116 H2319 BIBLIOG CONSTN S/ASIA NAT/G

B65
PEASLEE A.J.,CONSTITUTIONS OF NATIONS* THIRD REVISED EDITION (VOLUME I* AFRICA). LAW EX/STRUC LEGIS TOP/EX LEGIT CT/SYS ROUTINE ORD/FREE PWR SOVEREIGN...CON/ANAL CHARTS. PAGE 124 H2481 AFR CHOOSE CONSTN NAT/G

B65
POBEDONOSTSEV K.P.,REFLECTIONS OF A RUSSIAN STATESMAN. RUSSIA LAW ELITES EDU/PROP PRESS ADJUD MARRIAGE ATTIT PWR...MAJORIT TRADIT 19 CHURCH/STA. PAGE 127 H2531 TOTALISM POLICY CONSTN NAT/G

B65
PYLEE M.V.,CONSTITUTIONAL GOVERNMENT IN INDIA (2ND REV. ED.). INDIA POL/PAR EX/STRUC DIPLOM COLONIAL CT/SYS PARL/PROC PRIVIL...JURID 16/20. PAGE 128 H2569 CONSTN NAT/G PROVS FEDERAL

B65
ROWAT D.C.,THE OMBUDSMAN: CITIZEN'S DEFENDER. DENMARK FINLAND NEW/ZEALND NORWAY SWEDEN CONSULT PROB/SOLV FEEDBACK PARTIC GP/REL...SOC CONCPT NEW/IDEA METH/COMP ANTHOL BIBLIOG 20. PAGE 135 H2701 INSPECT CONSTN NAT/G ADMIN

B65
SAKAI R.K.,STUDIES ON ASIA, 1965. INDIA KOREA S/ASIA USA+45 CONSTN KIN SECT PARTIC SUFF NAT/LISM ...POLICY SOC 19/20 CHINJAP. PAGE 137 H2737 PARL/PROC ASIA

B65
SHARMA S.A.,PARLIAMENTARY GOVERNMENT IN INDIA. INDIA FINAN LOC/G PROVS DELIB/GP PLAN ADMIN CT/SYS FEDERAL...JURID 20. PAGE 142 H2849 NAT/G CONSTN PARL/PROC LEGIS

B65
STEINER K.,LOCAL GOVERNMENT IN JAPAN. CONSTN CULTURE NAT/G ADMIN CHOOSE...SOC STAT 20 CHINJAP. PAGE 149 H2976 LOC/G SOCIETY JURID ORD/FREE

B65
WARD W.E.,GOVERNMENT IN WEST AFRICA. WOR+45 POL/PAR EX/STRUC PLAN PARTIC GP/REL SOVEREIGN 20 AFRICA/W. PAGE 165 H3308 GOV/COMP CONSTN COLONIAL ECO/UNDEV

S65
CAIRNS J.C.,"FRANCE, DECEMBER 1965: END OF THE ELECTIVE MONARACHY" EUR+WWI FRANCE FUT CONSTN SOCIETY CHIEF BAL/PWR ATTIT ALL/IDEOS 20 DEGAULLE/C PRESIDENT. PAGE 25 H0505 CHOOSE NAT/G POL/PAR PWR

S65
RUBINSTEIN A.Z.,"YUGOSLAVIA'S OPENING SOCIETY." COM USSR INTELL NAT/G LEGIS TOP/EX LEGIT CT/SYS RIGID/FLEX ALL/VALS SOCISM...HUM TIME/SEQ TREND 20. PAGE 135 H2708 CONSTN EX/STRUC YUGOSLAVIA

C65
BORTOLI G.,"SOCIOLOGIE DU REFERENDUM DANS LA FRANCE MODERNE." FRANCE CONSTN NAT/G EDU/PROP SUFF ATTIT ORD/FREE...POLICY DECISION SOC CHARTS 20. PAGE 19 H0378 BIBLIOG LEGIS SOCIETY PWR

B66
ADAMS J.C.,THE GOVERNMENT OF REPUBLICAN ITALY (2ND ED.). ITALY LOC/G POL/PAR DELIB/GP LEGIS WORKER ADMIN CT/SYS FASCISM...CHARTS BIBLIOG 20 PARLIAMENT. PAGE 3 H0064 NAT/G CHOOSE EX/STRUC CONSTN

B66
AIYAR S.P.,PERSPECTIVES ON THE WELFARE STATE. INDIA S/ASIA UK CONSTN ECO/UNDEV NAT/G INGP/REL CENTRAL NAT/LISM ATTIT...CONCPT ANTHOL BIBLIOG 20. PAGE 4 H0087 NEW/LIB WELF/ST IDEA/COMP ADJUST

B66
BRAIBANTI R.,RESEARCH ON THE BUREAUCRACY OF PAKISTAN. PAKISTAN LAW CULTURE INTELL ACADEM LOC/G SECT PRESS CT/SYS...LING CHARTS 20 BUREAUCRCY. PAGE 20 H0402 HABITAT NAT/G ADMIN CONSTN

B66
BRECHER M.,SUCCESSION IN INDIA. INDIA USA+45 CONSTN AGRI POL/PAR PROVS SECT DELIB/GP FORCES PROB/SOLV ECO/TAC PWR...LING 20 CONGRESS NEHRU/J. PAGE 20 H0408 CHIEF DECISION CHOOSE

B66
CHAPMAN B.,THE PROFESSION OF GOVERNMENT: THE PUBLIC SERVICE IN EUROPE. CONSTN NAT/G POL/PAR EX/STRUC LEGIS TOP/EX PROB/SOLV DEBATE EXEC PARL/PROC PARTIC BIBLIOG ADMIN EUR+WWI

20. PAGE 29 H0581 — GOV/COMP

B66

DE TOCQUEVILLE A,DEMOCRACY IN AMERICA (1834-1840) (2 VOLS. IN I; TRANS. BY G. LAWRENCE). FRANCE CULTURE STRATA POL/PAR CT/SYS REPRESENT FEDERAL ORD/FREE SOVEREIGN...MAJORIT TREND GEN/LAWS 18/19. PAGE 39 H0773
POPULISM USA-45 CONSTN NAT/COMP

B66

DE VORE B.B.,LAND AND LIBERTY; A HISTORY OF THE MEXICAN REVOLUTION. CONSTN INTELL NAT/G CONTROL LEAD CHOOSE TOTALISM AUTHORIT...BIBLIOG 19/20 MEXIC/AMER DIAZ/P LIB/PARTY MAGON/F MADERO/F. PAGE 39 H0776
REV CHIEF POL/PAR

B66

FINER S.E.,ANONYMOUS EMPIRE: STUDY OF THE LOBBY IN GREAT BRITAIN. UK CONSTN LABOR POL/PAR SECT DOMIN EDU/PROP PRESS CHOOSE...CONCPT CHARTS 20 PARLIAMENT. PAGE 50 H1004
LOBBY NAT/G LEGIS PWR

B66

GHOSH P.K.,THE CONSTITUTION OF INDIA: HOW IT HAS BEEN FRAMED. INDIA LOC/G DELIB/GP EX/STRUC PROB/SOLV BUDGET INT/TRADE CT/SYS CHOOSE...LING 20. PAGE 56 H1121
CONSTN NAT/G LEGIS FEDERAL

B66

GUNN G.E.,THE POLITICAL HISTORY OF NEWFOUNDLAND 1832-1864. CANADA FINAN LEGIS CHOOSE REPRESENT ...CHARTS 19. PAGE 62 H1252
POL/PAR NAT/G CONSTN

B66

HIDAYATULLAH M.,DEMOCRACY IN INDIA AND THE JUDICIAL PROCESS. INDIA EX/STRUC LEGIS LEAD GOV/REL ATTIT ORD/FREE...MAJORIT CONCPT 20 NEHRU/J. PAGE 71 H1415
NAT/G CT/SYS CONSTN JURID

B66

HOLT R.T.,THE POLITICAL BASIS OF ECONOMIC DEVELOPMENT. STRATA STRUCT NAT/G DIPLOM ADMIN...SOC NAT/COMP BIBLIOG 20. PAGE 73 H1458
ECO/TAC GOV/COMP CONSTN EX/STRUC

B66

KAUNDA K.,ZAMBIA: INDEPENDENCE AND BEYOND: THE SPEECHES OF KENNETH KAUNDA. AFR FUT ZAMBIA SOCIETY ECO/UNDEV NAT/G PROB/SOLV ECO/TAC ADMIN RACE/REL SOVEREIGN 20. PAGE 84 H1670
ORD/FREE COLONIAL CONSTN LEAD

B66

KEAY E.A.,THE NATIVE AND CUSTOMARY COURTS OF NIGERIA. NIGERIA CONSTN ELITES NAT/G TOP/EX PARTIC REGION...DECISION JURID 19/20. PAGE 84 H1673
AFR ADJUD LAW

B66

LEIGH M.B.,CHECK LIST OF HOLDINGS ON BORNEO IN THE CORNELL UNIVERSITY LIBRARIES (PAMPHLET). BORNEO MALAYSIA LAW CONSTN GP/REL SOC. PAGE 93 H1866
BIBLIOG S/ASIA DIPLOM NAT/G

B66

LEROY P.,L'ORGANIZATION CONSTITUTIONNELLE ET LES CRISES. FRANCE NAT/G ADJUD CONTROL PARL/PROC WAR ...POLICY BIBLIOG 20. PAGE 95 H1892
CONSTN PWR EXEC LEGIS

B66

LOCKE J.,THE SECOND TREATISE OF GOVERNMENT: AN ESSAY CONCERNING THE TRUE ORIGINAL EXTENT AND END OF CIVIL GOVERNMENT (3RD ED.). CONSTN SOCIETY CONTROL OWN...PHIL/SCI 17 NATURL/LAW. PAGE 97 H1947
NAT/G PWR GEN/LAWS ORD/FREE

B66

MULLER C.F.J.,A SELECT BIBLIOGRAPHY OF SOUTH AFRICAN HISTORY; A GUIDE FOR HISTORICAL RESEARCH. SOUTH/AFR UK LAW CONSTN SOCIETY STRUCT AGRI SECT DIPLOM COLONIAL LEAD RACE/REL...POLICY 17/20 NEGRO. PAGE 114 H2284
BIBLIOG AFR NAT/G

B66

NEUMANN R.G.,THE GOVERNMENT OF THE GERMAN FEDERAL REPUBLIC. EUR+WWI GERMANY/W LOC/G EX/STRUC LEGIS CT/SYS INGP/REL PWR...BIBLIOG 20 ADENAUER/K. PAGE 117 H2336
NAT/G POL/PAR DIPLOM CONSTN

B66

PLATE H.,PARTEIFINANZIERUNG UND GRUNDESETZ. GERMANY NAT/G PLAN GIVE PAY INCOME WEALTH...JURID 20. PAGE 126 H2522
POL/PAR CONSTN FINAN

B66

POLE J.R.,POLITICAL REPRESENTATION IN ENGLAND AND THE ORIGINS OF THE AMERICAN REPUBLIC. UK USA-45 CONSTN ELITES NAT/G POL/PAR LEGIS PARL/PROC ...MAJORIT 17/19. PAGE 127 H2534
REPRESENT GOV/COMP

B66

RAY A.,INTER-GOVERNMENTAL RELATIONS IN INDIA: A STUDY OF INDIAN FEDERALISM. CANADA INDIA SWITZERLND USA+45 USSR ADMIN GOV/REL...NAT/COMP BIBLIOG. PAGE 130 H2599
CONSTN FEDERAL SOVEREIGN NAT/G

B66

SHARMA B.M.,THE REPUBLIC OF INDIA; CONSTITUTION AND GOVERNMENT. INDIA POL/PAR LEGIS EFFICIENCY ...TIME/SEQ GOV/COMP 20. PAGE 142 H2846
PROVS NAT/G CONSTN

B66

SPEARS E.L.,TWO MEN WHO SAVED FRANCE: PETAIN AND DE GAULLE. FRANCE CONSTN FORCES DIPLOM WAR PERSON 20 WWI PETAIN/HP DEGAULLE/C. PAGE 147 H2942
BIOG LEAD CHIEF NAT/G

B66

SWEET E.C.,CIVIL LIBERTIES IN AMERICA. LAW CONSTN NAT/G PRESS CT/SYS DISCRIM ATTIT WORSHIP 20 CIVIL/LIB. PAGE 151 H3018
ADJUD ORD/FREE SUFF COERCE

B66

TORMIN W.,GESCHICHTE DER DEUTSCHEN PARTEIEN SEIT 1848. GERMANY CHOOSE PWR...CONCPT 19/20 WEIMAR/REP. PAGE 156 H3116
POL/PAR CONSTN NAT/G TOTALISM

B66

WUEST J.J.,NEW SOURCE BOOK IN MAJOR EUROPEAN GOVERNMENTS. CHRIST-17C EUR+WWI FRANCE GERMANY ITALY MOD/EUR UK USSR LOC/G POL/PAR CHIEF EX/STRUC CHOOSE CONSERVE MARXISM...JURID T 13/20. PAGE 171 H3425
NAT/G CONSTN LEGIS

B66

ZOLBERG A.R.,CREATING POLITICAL ORDER. AFR CONGO/BRAZ GHANA NIGER KIN NAT/G DOMIN COLONIAL REGION CENTRAL NAT/LISM ATTIT PWR 20 CONGO/LEOP. PAGE 173 H3462
SOVEREIGN ORD/FREE CONSTN POL/PAR

L66

MCAUSLAN J.P.W.,"CONSTITUTIONAL INNOVATION AND POLITICAL STABILITY IN TANZANIA: A PRELIMINARY ASSESSMENT." AFR TANZANIA ELITES CHIEF EX/STRUC RIGID/FLEX PWR 20 PRESIDENT BUREAUCRCY. PAGE 106 H2122
CONSTN NAT/G EXEC POL/PAR

S66

ADAMS T.W.,"THE FIRST REPUBLIC OF CYPRUS: A REVIEW OF AN UNWORKABLE CONSTITUTION." CYPRUS FUT PLAN NAT/LISM POPULISM 20. PAGE 3 H0067
CONSTN NAT/G PROB/SOLV

S66

DETTER I.,"THE PROBLEM OF UNEQUAL TREATIES." CONSTN NAT/G LEGIS COLONIAL COERCE PWR...GEOG UN TIME TREATY. PAGE 40 H0796
SOVEREIGN DOMIN INT/LAW ECO/UNDEV

S66

MATTHEWS D.G.,"PRELUDE-COUP D'ETAT-MILITARY GOVERNMENT: A BIBLIOGRAPHICAL AND RESEARCH GUIDE TO NIGERIAN POL AND GOVT, JAN, 1965-66." AFR NIGER LAW CONSTN POL/PAR LEGIS CIVMIL/REL GOV/REL...STAT 20. PAGE 105 H2096
BIBLIOG NAT/G ADMIN CHOOSE

S66

ROTHCHILD D.,"THE LIMITS OF FEDERALISM: AN EXAMINATION OF POLITICAL INSTITUTIONAL TRANSFER IN AFRICA." AFR CONSTN CULTURE ELITES ECO/UNDEV KIN PROB/SOLV ADMIN ORD/FREE PWR...POLICY 20. PAGE 135 H2695
FEDERAL NAT/G NAT/LISM COLONIAL

B67

ALBA V.,THE MEXICANS; THE MAKING OF A NATION. SOCIETY ECO/UNDEV AGRI INDUS SECT STRANGE ATTIT ...GEOG 20 MEXIC/AMER. PAGE 4 H0091
CONSTN NAT/G CULTURE ANOMIE

B67

ANDERSON E.N.,POLITICAL INSTITUTIONS AND SOCIAL CHANGE IN CONTINENTAL EUROPE IN THE NINETEENTH CENTURY. MOD/EUR LAW CONSTN SOCIETY POL/PAR TEC/DEV LEAD REV ATTIT...BIBLIOG 19. PAGE 6 H0127
NAT/G NAT/COMP METH/COMP INDUS

B67

ANDERSON T.,RUSSIAN POLITICAL THOUGHT; AN INTRODUCTION. USSR NAT/G POL/PAR CHIEF MARXISM ...TIME/SEQ BIBLIOG 9/20. PAGE 7 H0135
TREND CONSTN ATTIT

B67

ARIKPO O.,THE DEVELOPMENT OF MODERN NIGERIA. AFR NIGERIA SOCIETY ECO/UNDEV KIN ADMIN FEDERAL NAT/LISM ORD/FREE WEALTH...POLICY GEOG BIBLIOG 19/20. PAGE 8 H0163
NAT/G CULTURE CONSTN COLONIAL

B67

BROWN L.N.,FRENCH ADMINISTRATIVE LAW. FRANCE UK CONSTN NAT/G LEGIS DOMIN CONTROL EXEC PARL/PROC PWR ...JURID METH/COMP GEN/METH. PAGE 22 H0447
EX/STRUC LAW IDEA/COMP CT/SYS

B67

BUNN R.F.,POLITICS AND CIVIL LIBERTIES IN EUROPE: FOUR CASE STUDIES. FRANCE GERMANY/W UK USSR NAT/G PRESS CRIME CROWD PRIVIL ATTIT 20. PAGE 24 H0476
ORD/FREE CONSTN NAT/COMP LAW

B67

GELLHORN W.,OMBUDSMEN AND OTHERS: CITIZENS' PROTECTORS IN NINE COUNTRIES. WOR+45 LAW CONSTN LEGIS INSPECT ADJUD ADMIN CONTROL CT/SYS CHOOSE PERS/REL...STAT CHARTS 20. PAGE 55 H1109
NAT/COMP REPRESENT INGP/REL PROB/SOLV

B67

KOLKOWICZ R.,THE SOVIET MILITARY AND THE COMMUNIST PARTY. COM USSR ELITES NAT/G CREATE CIVMIL/REL GP/REL...TREND BIBLIOG/A 20 COM/PARTY. PAGE 88 H1753
MARXISM CONSTN FORCES POL/PAR

B67

LENG S.C.,JUSTICE IN COMMUNIST CHINA: A SURVEY OF THE JUDICIAL SYSTEM OF THE CHINESE PEOPLE'S REPUBLIC. CHINA/COM LAW CONSTN LOC/G NAT/G PROF/ORG CONSULT FORCES ADMIN CRIME ORD/FREE...BIBLIOG 20 MAO. PAGE 94 H1877
CT/SYS ADJUD JURID MARXISM

B67

MENDEL A.P.,POLITICAL MEMOIRS 1905-1917 BY PAUL MILIUKOV (TRANS. BY CARL GOLDBERG). USSR AGRI
BIOG LEAD

DIPLOM ECO/TAC POPULISM...MAJORIT 20. PAGE 109 NAT/G
H2170 CONSTN

B67
MORRIS A.J.A.,PARLIAMENTARY DEMOCRACY IN THE TIME/SEQ
NINETEENTH CENTURY. UK INDUS LOC/G NAT/G POL/PAR CONSTN
CONSULT LEGIS INT/TRADE ADMIN CHOOSE SUFF SOVEREIGN PARL/PROC
19 PARLIAMENT. PAGE 113 H2261 POPULISM

B67
MUHAMMAD A.C.,THE EMERGENCE OF PAKISTAN. PAKISTAN DIPLOM
S/ASIA CONSTN ECO/UNDEV NAT/G CONTROL NAT/LISM 20. COLONIAL
PAGE 114 H2281 SECT
PROB/SOLV

B67
PIKE F.B.,FREEDOM AND REFORM IN LATIN AMERICA. L/A+17C
BRAZIL URUGUAY CONSTN CULTURE SECT DIPLOM EDU/PROP ORD/FREE
PARTIC DRIVE ALL/VALS CATHISM...GEOG ANTHOL BIBLIOG ECO/UNDEV
REFORMERS BOLIV. PAGE 126 H2511 REV

B67
RUSTOW D.A.,A WORLD OF NATIONS; PROBLEMS OF PROB/SOLV
POLITICAL MODERNIZATION. CONSTN NAT/G POL/PAR ECO/UNDEV
FORCES DIPLOM LEAD AUTHORIT...CHARTS IDEA/COMP 20. CONCPT
PAGE 136 H2722 NAT/COMP

B67
SCHWARTZ B.,THE ROOTS OF FREEDOM: A CONSTITUTIONAL CONSTN
HISTORY OF ENGLAND. UK LAW POL/PAR DELIB/GP LEGIS PARL/PROC
REV REPRESENT...JURID BIBLIOG/A 13/20. PAGE 140 NAT/G
H2809

B67
SPIRO H.S.,PATTERNS OF AFRICAN DEVLOPMENT: FIVE AFR
COMPARISONS. STRUCT ECO/UNDEV NAT/G CONSERVE SOCISM CONSTN
...PREDICT NAT/COMP 20 CHINJAP. PAGE 148 H2951 NAT/LISM
TREND

B67
VENKATESWARAN R.J.,CABINET GOVERNMENT IN INDIA. DELIB/GP
INDIA UK SOCIETY OP/RES COLONIAL LEAD EFFICIENCY ADMIN
ORD/FREE 20. PAGE 162 H3241 CONSTN
NAT/G

B67
WARREN S.,THE AMERICAN PRESIDENT. POL/PAR FORCES CHIEF
LEGIS DIPLOM ECO/TAC ADMIN EXEC PWR...ANTHOL 18/20 LEAD
ROOSEVLT/F KENNEDY/JF JOHNSON/LB TRUMAN/HS NAT/G
WILSON/W. PAGE 165 H3312 CONSTN

B67
WIENER F.B.,CIVILIANS UNDER MILITARY JUSTICE; THE CT/SYS
BRITISH PRACTICE SINCE 1689 ESPECIALLY IN NORTH FORCES
AMERICA. UK USA-45 LAW CONSTN CRIME REV...DECISION ADJUD
CHARTS NAT/COMP BIBLIOG 17/20. PAGE 168 H3356

L67
AUSTIN D.A.,"POLITICAL CONFLICT IN AFRICA." CONSTN ANOMIE
NAT/G CREATE ADMIN COLONIAL ORD/FREE MARXISM AFR
POPULISM SOCISM...NAT/COMP ANTHOL 20. PAGE 9 H0180 POL/PAR

L67
SCALAPINO R.A.,"A SURVEY OF ASIA IN 1966." ASIA DIPLOM
S/ASIA CONSTN SOCIETY POL/PAR CHIEF WAR...ANTHOL
20. PAGE 138 H2764

L67
WILBER L.A.,"THE GOVERNMENTAL STRUCTURE OF CONSTN
MISSISSIPPI: ITS STRENGTHS AND WEAKNESSES." AGRI PROVS
LOC/G SCHOOL EX/STRUC LEGIS TOP/EX BUDGET CT/SYS STAT
APPORT RACE/REL...GOV/COMP 20 MISSISSIPP. PAGE 168 CON/ANAL
H3359

S67
ADOKO A.,"THE CONSTITUTION OF UGANDA." AFR UGANDA NAT/G
LOC/G CHIEF FORCES LEGIS ADJUD EXEC CHOOSE NAT/LISM CONSTN
...IDEA/COMP 20. PAGE 4 H0072 ORD/FREE
LAW

S67
ALEXANDER A.,"CANADA'S PARLIAMENTARY SECRETARIES: CONSTN
THEIR POLITICAL AND CONSTITUTIONAL POSITION." ADMIN
CANADA UK NAT/G POL/PAR GOV/REL...GOV/COMP 20. EX/STRUC
PAGE 5 H0099 DELIB/GP

S67
BEVEL D.N.,"JOURNEY TO NORTH VIETNAM." VIETNAM/N ATTIT
CONSTN NAT/G FORCES PROB/SOLV DEATH CIVMIL/REL DIPLOM
PEACE MORAL...ANTHOL 20 NEGRO. PAGE 16 H0325 ORD/FREE
WAR

S67
BRADLEY A.W.,"CONSTITUTION-MAKING IN UGANDA." NAT/G
UGANDA LAW CHIEF DELIB/GP LEGIS ADMIN EXEC CREATE
PARL/PROC RACE/REL ORD/FREE...GOV/COMP 20. PAGE 20 CONSTN
H0397 FEDERAL

S67
CATTELL D.T.,"THE FIFTIETH ANNIVERSARY: A SOVIET MARXISM
WATERSHED?" USSR CONSTN ECO/DEV NAT/G LEAD TOTALISM CHIEF
20 KHRUSH/N. PAGE 28 H0562 POLICY
ADJUST

S67
DOERN G.B.,"THE ROYAL COMMISSIONS IN THE GENERAL R+D
POLICY PROCESS AND IN FEDERAL-PROVINCIAL EX/STRUC
RELATIONS." CANADA CONSTN ACADEM PROVS CONSULT GOV/REL
DELIB/GP LEGIS ACT/RES PROB/SOLV CONFER CONTROL NAT/G
EFFICIENCY...METH/COMP 20 SENATE ROYAL/COMM.
PAGE 42 H0832

S67
FUSARO A.,"THE EFFECT OF PROPORTIONAL LEGIS
REPRESENTATION ON VOTING IN THE AUSTRALIAN SENATE." CHOOSE
S/ASIA CONSTN POL/PAR CONTROL GP/REL PWR...CHARTS REPRESENT
20 AUSTRAL HOUSE/REP SENATE. PAGE 54 H1083 NAT/G

S67
GRAHAM R.,"BRAZIL'S DILEMMA." BRAZIL FUT L/A+17C ECO/UNDEV
NAT/G CHIEF PROB/SOLV ECO/TAC PWR 20. PAGE 60 H1193 CONSTN
POL/PAR
POLICY

S67
GREGORY R.,"THE MINISTER'S LINE: OR, THE M4 COMES DECISION
TO BERKSHIRE. PART I." UK CONSTN DIST/IND LEGIS CONSTRUC
TOP/EX PLAN ADJUD...GEOG 20. PAGE 60 H1210 NAT/G
DELIB/GP

S67
HARNON E.,"CRIMINAL PROCEDURE IN ISRAEL - SOME ADJUD
COMPARATIVE ASPECTS." ISRAEL USA+45 CLIENT EX/STRUC CONSTN
LEGIS...JURID NAT/COMP 20. PAGE 67 H1336 CT/SYS
CRIME

S67
HEATH D.B.,"BOLIVIA UNDER BARRIENTOS." L/A+17C ECO/UNDEV
NAT/G CHIEF DIPLOM ECO/TAC...POLICY 20 BOLIV. POL/PAR
PAGE 69 H1379 REV
CONSTN

S67
HOFMANN W.,"THE PUBLIC INTEREST PRESSURE GROUP: THE LOC/G
CASE OF THE DEUTSCHE STADTETAG." GERMANY GERMANY/W VOL/ASSN
CONSTN STRUCT NAT/G CENTRAL FEDERAL PWR...TIME/SEQ LOBBY
20. PAGE 72 H1447 ADMIN

S67
IDENBURG P.J.,"POLITICAL STRUCTURAL DEVELOPMENT IN AFR
TROPICAL AFRICA." UK ECO/UNDEV KIN POL/PAR CHIEF CONSTN
EX/STRUC CREATE COLONIAL CONTROL REPRESENT RACE/REL NAT/G
...MAJORIT TREND 20. PAGE 76 H1521 GOV/COMP

S67
INDER S.,"AFTER THE CORONATION." CONSTN ECO/UNDEV CHIEF
EX/STRUC LEGIS INT/TRADE CONTROL SOVEREIGN NAT/G
...TIME/SEQ 20 TONGA COMMONWLTH INAUGURATE. PAGE 76 POLICY
H1527

S67
KASFIR N.,"THE UGANDA CONSTITUENT ASSEMBLY DEBATE." CONSTN
UGANDA REPRESENT FEDERAL ORD/FREE POPULISM...POLICY CONFER
DECISION 20. PAGE 83 H1665 LAW
NAT/G

S67
KINGSBURY E.C.,"LAW AS COMPACT: ANCIENT ISRAEL'S LAW
CONTRIBUTION TO THE UNDERSTANDING OF LAW." ISRAEL AGREE
MEDIT-7 CULTURE KIN KNOWL...JURID CONCPT TREND CONSTN
IDEA/COMP METH/COMP WORSHIP JEWS DEITY. PAGE 86 INGP/REL
H1716

S67
KOHN W.S.G.,"THE SOVEREIGNTY OF LIECHTENSTEIN." SOVEREIGN
LIECHTENST SWITZERLND USSR CONSTN DEBATE WAR NAT/G
CONSERVE 18/20 UN. PAGE 88 H1748 PWR
DIPLOM

S67
KRISTOF L.K.D.,"THE STATE-IDEA, THE NATIONAL IDEA GEOG
AND THE IMAGE OF THE FATHERLAND." CONSTN CULTURE CONCPT
INTELL SOCIETY WORKER TASK DRIVE HABITAT...MYTH NAT/G
GOV/COMP IDEA/COMP. PAGE 89 H1769 PERCEPT

S67
MAIR L.,"BUSOGA LOCAL GOVERNMENT" AFR UGANDA UK LOC/G
CONSTN GP/REL...GOV/COMP METH/COMP 20. PAGE 101 COLONIAL
H2024 LAW
ATTIT

S67
MALLORY J.R.,"THE MINISTER'S OFFICE STAFF* AN CANADA
UNREFORMED PART OF PUBLIC SERVICE." CONSTN ELITES ADMIN
STRATA NAT/G PROB/SOLV TASK CHOOSE PERS/REL EX/STRUC
EFFICIENCY...DECISION 20. PAGE 102 H2033 STRUCT

S67
MAYANJA A.,"THE GOVERNMENT'S PROPOSALS ON THE NEW CONSTN
CONSTITUTION." AFR UGANDA LAW CHIEF LEGIS ADJUD CONFER
REPRESENT FEDERAL PWR 20. PAGE 105 H2105 ORD/FREE
NAT/G

S67
NEALE R.S.,"WORKING CLASS WOMEN AND WOMEN'S STRATA
SUFFRAGE." UK LAW CONSTN LABOR NAT/G DELIB/GP LEGIS SEX
WORKER PAY PARTIC CHOOSE 19 FEMALE/SEX. PAGE 116 SUFF
H2326 DISCRIM

S67
READ J.S.,"CENSORED." UGANDA CONSTN INTELL SOCIETY EDU/PROP
NAT/G DIPLOM PRESS WRITING ADJUD ADMIN COLONIAL AFR
RISK...IDEA/COMP 20. PAGE 130 H2602 CREATE

S67
SHELDON C.H.,"PUBLIC OPINION AND HIGH COURTS: ATTIT
COMMUNIST PARTY CASES IN FOUR CONSTITUTIONAL CT/SYS
SYSTEMS." CANADA GERMANY/W WOR+45 POL/PAR MARXISM CONSTN
...METH/COMP NAT/COMP 20 AUSTRAL. PAGE 143 H2857 DECISION

S67
THEROUX P.,"HATING THE ASIANS." TANZANIA UGANDA AFR
CONSTN INDUS NAT/G POL/PAR WORKER ECO/TAC HABITAT RACE/REL
LOVE...POLICY GEOG 20 MIGRATION. PAGE 154 H3069 SOVEREIGN
ATTIT

S67
TIVEY L.,"THE POLITICAL CONSEQUENCES OF ECONOMIC PLAN
PLANNING." UK CONSTN INDUS ACT/RES ADMIN CONTROL POLICY
LOBBY REPRESENT EFFICIENCY SUPEGO SOVEREIGN NAT/G

...DECISION 20. PAGE 155 H3108

S67
ULC O.,"CLASS STRUGGLE AND SOCIALIST JUSTICE: THE CASE OF CZECHOSLOVAKIA." COM CZECHOSLVK LAW CONSTN ELITES STRUCT NAT/G CRIME GP/REL MARXISM 20. PAGE 158 H3151 — TOTALISM CT/SYS ADJUD STRATA

S67
WHITE W.L.,"THE TREASURY BOARD AND PARLIAMENT." CANADA CONSTN CONSULT LEGIS LEAD PARL/PROC GP/REL ...DECISION 20. PAGE 167 H3351 — FINAN DELIB/GP NAT/G ADMIN

S67
WILLIAMS F.R.A.,"FUNDAMENTAL RIGHTS AND THE PROSPECT FOR DEMOCRACY IN NIGERIA." FUT NIGERIA SOCIETY ECO/UNDEV LEGIS ADJUD CHOOSE 20. PAGE 168 H3366 — CONSTN LAW ORD/FREE NAT/G

S68
BURGESS J.W.,"VON HOLST'S PUBLIC LAW OF THE UNITED STATES" USA-45 LAW GOV/REL...GOV/COMP IDEA/COMP 19. PAGE 24 H0480 — CONSTN FEDERAL NAT/G JURID

S68
KANET R.E.,"RECENT SOVIET REASSESSMENT OF DEVELOPMENTS IN THE THIRD WORLD." ALGERIA GHANA INDONESIA USSR WOR+45 CONSTN ELITES INTELL STRUCT DOMIN CONTROL REV PWR MARXISM...IDEA/COMP METH 20 THIRD/WRLD. PAGE 83 H1653 — DIPLOM NEUTRAL NAT/G NAT/COMP

B75
MAINE H.S.,LECTURES ON THE EARLY HISTORY OF INSTITUTIONS. IRELAND UK CONSTN ELITES STRUCT FAM KIN CHIEF LEGIS CT/SYS OWN SOVEREIGN...CONCPT 16 BENTHAM/J BREHON ROMAN/LAW. PAGE 101 H2021 — CULTURE LAW INGP/REL

B79
BRODERICK G.C.,POLITICAL STUDIES. IRELAND UK ROMAN/EMP LAW ACADEM LOC/G NAT/G DIPLOM PARL/PROC SUFF GP/REL LAISSEZ...ANTHOL. PAGE 21 H0424 — CONSTN COLONIAL

N80
MILL J.S.,"AN ESSAY ON GOVERNMENT" (PAMPHLET). ELITES NAT/G CHIEF OWN ORD/FREE PWR WEALTH GEN/LAWS. PAGE 110 H2207 — CONSTN POPULISM REPRESENT UTIL

B83
AMOS S.,THE SCIENCE OF POLITICS. MOD/EUR CONSTN LOC/G NAT/G EX/STRUC LEGIS DIPLOM...METH/COMP 19/20. PAGE 6 H0124 — NEW/IDEA PHIL/SCI CONCPT

B85
BLISS P.,OF SOVEREIGNTY. NAT/G PROVS GOV/REL PRIVIL ORD/FREE PWR CONSERVE...CONCPT 19. PAGE 18 H0356 — CONSTN SOVEREIGN FEDERAL

B85
BLUNTSCHLI J.K.,THE THEORY OF THE STATE. GERMANY CONSTN INGP/REL NAT/LISM PERSON SOVEREIGN CONSERVE ...SOC. PAGE 18 H0362 — CONCPT LEGIS NAT/G

L86
BURGESS J.W.,"THE RECENT CONSTITUTIONAL CRISIS IN NORWAY" MOD/EUR NORWAY SWEDEN LOC/G NAT/G CHIEF BAL/PWR NAT/LISM ORD/FREE 19. PAGE 24 H0481 — CONSTN SOVEREIGN GOV/REL

B87
ADAMS J.,A DEFENSE OF THE CONSTITUTIONS OF GOVERNMENT OF THE UNITED STATES OF AMERICA. USA-45 STRATA CHIEF EX/STRUC LEGIS CT/SYS CONSERVE POPULISM...CONCPT CON/ANAL GOV/COMP. PAGE 3 H0063 — CONSTN BAL/PWR PWR NAT/G

B87
KINNEAR J.B.,PRINCIPLES OF CIVIL GOVERNMENT. MOD/EUR USA-45 CONSTN LOC/G EX/STRUC ADMIN PARL/PROC RACE/REL...CONCPT 18/19. PAGE 86 H1718 — POL/PAR NAT/G GOV/COMP REPRESENT

B89
FERNEUIL T.,LES PRINCIPES DE 1789 ET LA SCIENCE SOCIALE. FRANCE NAT/G REV ATTIT...CONCPT TREND IDEA/COMP 18/19. PAGE 49 H0986 — CONSTN POLICY LAW

B91
BENTHAM J.,A FRAGMENT ON GOVERNMENT (1776). CONSTN MUNIC NAT/G SECT AGREE HAPPINESS UTIL MORAL ORD/FREE...JURID CONCPT. PAGE 15 H0292 — SOVEREIGN LAW DOMIN

B91
PAINE T.,RIGHTS OF MAN. FRANCE MOD/EUR CONSTN NAT/G CHIEF DOMIN LEGIT SOVEREIGN...MAJORIT IDEA/COMP 18 BURKE/EDM CIVIL/LIB. PAGE 122 H2446 — GEN/LAWS ORD/FREE REV AGREE

B96
ESMEIN A.,ELEMENTS DE DROIT CONSTITUTIONNEL. FRANCE UK CHIEF EX/STRUC LEGIS ADJUD CT/SYS PARL/PROC REV GOV/REL ORD/FREE...JURID METH/COMP 18/19. PAGE 47 H0940 — LAW CONSTN NAT/G CONCPT

B96
LOWELL A.L.,GOVERNMENTS AND PARTIES IN CONTINENTAL EUROPE (VOL. I). MOD/EUR LOC/G NAT/G SECT CHIEF LEGIS PARL/PROC GOV/REL...POLICY 19. PAGE 99 H1973 — POL/PAR GOV/COMP CONSTN EX/STRUC

B96
MARX K.,REVOLUTION AND COUNTER-REVOLUTION. GERMANY CONSTN ELITES INDUS NAT/G DIPLOM ECO/TAC WEALTH. PAGE 104 H2083 — MARXIST REV PWR STRATA

B99
LECKY W.E.H.,DEMOCRACY AND LIBERTY (2 VOLS.). LAW CONSTN STRATA POL/PAR SECT WORKER DIPLOM ADJUD REPRESENT NAT/LISM CONSERVE. PAGE 93 H1851 — LEGIS NAT/G POPULISM ORD/FREE

CONSTN/CNV....CONSTITUTIONAL CONVENTION

CONSTRUC....CONSTRUCTION INDUSTRY

B50
COUNCIL BRITISH NATIONAL BIB,BRITISH NATIONAL BIBLIOGRAPHY. UK AGRI CONSTRUC PERF/ART POL/PAR SECT CREATE INT/TRADE LEAD...HUM JURID PHIL/SCI 20. PAGE 34 H0677 — BIBLIOG/A NAT/G TEC/DEV DIPLOM

B53
SHIRATO I.,JAPANESE SOURCES ON THE HISTORY OF THE CHINESE COMMUNIST MOVEMENT (PAMPHLET). CHINA/COM USSR CONSTRUC NAT/G POL/PAR FORCES DIPLOM DOMIN EDU/PROP CONTROL WAR TOTALISM SOCISM 20. PAGE 143 H2863 — BIBLIOG/A MARXISM ECO/UNDEV

B64
GREBLER L.,URBAN RENEWAL IN EUROPEAN COUNTRIES: ITS EMERGENCE AND POTENTIALS. EUR+WWI UK ECO/DEV LOC/G NEIGH CREATE ADMIN ATTIT...TREND NAT/COMP 20 URBAN/RNWL. PAGE 60 H1205 — MUNIC PLAN CONSTRUC NAT/G

B65
DUGGAR G.S.,RENEWAL OF TOWN AND VILLAGE I: A WORLD-WIDE SURVEY OF LOCAL GOVERNMENT EXPERIENCE. WOR+45 CONSTRUC INDUS CREATE BUDGET REGION GOV/REL...QU NAT/COMP 20 URBAN/RNWL. PAGE 43 H0859 — MUNIC NEIGH PLAN ADMIN

S65
TENDLER J.D.,"TECHNOLOGY AND ECONOMIC DEVELOPMENT* THE CASE OF HYDRO VS THERMAL POWER." CONSTRUC DIST/IND CREATE TEC/DEV INT/TRADE CENTRAL PWR SKILL WEALTH...MGT NAT/COMP ARGEN. PAGE 153 H3061 — BRAZIL INDUS ECO/UNDEV

S67
GREGORY R.,"THE MINISTER'S LINE: OR, THE M4 COMES TO BERKSHIRE. PART I." UK CONSTN DIST/IND LEGIS TOP/EX PLAN ADJUD...GEOG 20. PAGE 60 H1210 — DECISION CONSTRUC NAT/G DELIB/GP

S67
LICHFIELD N.,"THE EVALUATION OF CAPITAL INVESTMENT PROJECTS IN TOWN CENTRE REDEVELOPMENT." UK CONSTRUC MUNIC CONSULT COST...METH/CNCPT IDEA/COMP 20. PAGE 96 H1923 — PLAN ECO/TAC NAT/G DECISION

CONSTRUCTION INDUSTRY....SEE CONSTRUC

CONSULT....CONSULTANTS

B00
BENEDETTI V.,STUDIES IN DIPLOMACY. BELGIUM FRANCE GERMANY MOD/EUR CONSTN NAT/G CONSULT TOP/EX DOMIN EDU/PROP COERCE ATTIT...CONCPT INT BIOG TREND 19. PAGE 14 H0276 — PWR GEN/LAWS DIPLOM

B03
GRIFFIN A.P.C.,LIST OF BOOKS ON THE CABINETS OF ENGLAND AND AMERICA (PAMPHLET). MOD/EUR UK USA-45 CONSTN NAT/G CONSULT EX/STRUC 19/20. PAGE 61 H1216 — BIBLIOG/A GOV/COMP ADMIN DELIB/GP

B07
BENTHAM J.,AN INTRODUCTION TO THE PRINCIPLES OF MORALS AND LEGISLATION. UNIV CONSTN CULTURE SOCIETY NAT/G CONSULT LEGIS JUDGE ADJUD CT/SYS...JURID CONCPT NEW/IDEA. PAGE 14 H0287 — LAW GEN/LAWS

N19
ADMINISTRATIVE STAFF COLLEGE,THE ACCOUNTABILITY OF GOVERNMENT DEPARTMENTS (PAMPHLET) (REV. ED.). UK CONSTN FINAN NAT/G CONSULT ADMIN INGP/REL CONSEN PRIVIL 20 PARLIAMENT. PAGE 3 H0070 — PARL/PROC ELITES SANCTION PROB/SOLV

B27
WILLOUGHBY W.F.,PRINCIPLES OF PUBLIC ADMINISTRATION WITH SPECIAL REFERENCE TO THE NATIONAL AND STATE GOVERNMENTS OF THE UNITED STATES. FINAN PROVS CHIEF CONSULT LEGIS CREATE BUDGET EXEC ROUTINE GOV/REL CENTRAL...MGT 20 BUR/BUDGET CONGRESS PRESIDENT. PAGE 169 H3373 — NAT/G EX/STRUC OP/RES ADMIN

B31
LORWIN L.L.,ADVISORY ECONOMIC COUNCILS. EUR+WWI FRANCE GERMANY PROB/SOLV INGP/REL...CLASSIF GP/COMP. PAGE 99 H1968 — CONSULT DELIB/GP ECO/TAC NAT/G

B32
GREAT BRIT COMM MINISTERS PWR,REPORT. UK LAW CONSTN CONSULT LEGIS PARL/PROC SANCTION SOVEREIGN ...DECISION JURID 20 PARLIAMENT. PAGE 60 H1201 — EX/STRUC NAT/G PWR CONTROL

B36
CLOKIE H.M.,THE ORIGIN AND NATURE OF CONSTITUTIONAL GOVERNMENT. UK NAT/G POL/PAR CONSULT LEGIS ...GOV/COMP 14/20 CABINET PARLIAMENT. PAGE 30 H0606 — CONCPT CONSTN PARL/PROC

B39
DEWEY J.,FREEDOM AND CULTURE. FUT CONSTN CULTURE INTELL NAT/G CONSULT PLAN CHOOSE ATTIT...CONCPT GEN/METH 20. PAGE 40 H0810 — SOCIETY CREATE

B44
KRIS E.,GERMAN RADIO PROPAGANDA: REPORT ON HOME BROADCASTS DURING THE WAR. EUR+WWI GERMANY CULTURE CONSULT PROB/SOLV FEEDBACK TASK INGP/REL DRIVE PWR FASCISM...CON/ANAL METH/COMP 20. PAGE 89 H1768
EDU/PROP DOMIN ACT/RES ATTIT

S46
SILBERNER E.,"THE PROBLEM OF WAR IN NINETEENTH CENTURY ECONOMIC THOUGHT." EUR+WWI MOD/EUR UNIV LAW ECO/DEV ECO/UNDEV FINAN INDUS MARKET INT/ORG NAT/G CONSULT FORCES...CONCPT GEN/LAWS GEN/METH 19. PAGE 144 H2875
ATTIT ECO/TAC WAR

B47
JURJI E.J.,THE GREAT RELIGIONS OF THE MODERN WORLD. CULTURE INTELL SOCIETY INT/ORG CONSULT CHOOSE ATTIT DRIVE PERSON RIGID/FLEX...HUM CONCPT OBS BIOG HIST/WRIT TREND GEN/LAWS 20 WORSHIP. PAGE 82 H1643
UNIV SECT

B48
US LIBRARY OF CONGRESS,BRAZIL: A GUIDE TO THE OFFICIAL PUBLICATIONS OF BRAZIL. BRAZIL L/A+17C CONSULT DELIB/GP LEGIS CT/SYS 19/20. PAGE 160 H3206
BIBLIOG/A NAT/G ADMIN TOP/EX

B50
HOBBES T.,LEVIATHAN. UNIV CONSTN SOCIETY LOC/G NAT/G CONSULT TOP/EX DOMIN DRIVE PERSON PWR ...PHIL/SCI CONCPT SELF/OBS GEN/LAWS TOT/POP. PAGE 72 H1434
LAW ORD/FREE

B52
LEYS W.,ETHICS FOR POLICY DECISIONS. INTELL NAT/G CONSULT PLAN DOMIN EDU/PROP LEGIT COERCE KNOWL MORAL PWR...HUM GEN/LAWS. PAGE 96 H1920
ACT/RES POLICY

S52
MCDOUGAL M.S.,"THE COMPARATIVE STUDY OF LAW FOR POLICY PURPOSES." FUT NAT/G POL/PAR CONSULT ADJUD PWR SOVEREIGN...METH/CNCPT IDEA/COMP SIMUL 20. PAGE 106 H2129
PLAN JURID NAT/LISM

C54
LANDAU J.M.,"PARLIAMENTS AND PARTIES IN EGYPT." UAR NAT/G SECT CONSULT LEGIS TOP/EX PROB/SOLV ADMIN COLONIAL...GEN/LAWS BIBLIOG 19/20. PAGE 90 H1804
ISLAM NAT/LISM PARL/PROC POL/PAR

B55
FOGARTY M.P.,ECONOMIC CONTROL. FUT UK ECO/DEV FINAN CONSULT INT/TRADE...CHARTS BIBLIOG/A 20. PAGE 52 H1033
ECO/TAC NAT/G CONTROL PROB/SOLV

S56
GORDON L.,"THE ORGANIZATION FOR EUROPEAN ECONOMIC COOPERATION." EUR+WWI INDUS INT/ORG NAT/G CONSULT DELIB/GP ACT/RES CREATE PLAN TEC/DEV EDU/PROP LEGIT WEALTH OEEC 20. PAGE 59 H1178
VOL/ASSN ECO/DEV

B57
US SENATE SPEC COMM FOR AID,COMPILATION OF STUDIES AND SURVEYS. AFR ASIA L/A+17C USA+45 ECO/UNDEV AGRI INT/ORG CONSULT TEC/DEV CONFER TOTALISM...NAT/COMP 20 CONGRESS. PAGE 161 H3216
FOR/AID DIPLOM ORD/FREE DELIB/GP

B58
CROWE S.,THE LANDSCAPE OF POWER. UK CULTURE SERV/IND NAT/G CONSULT PARTIC NUC/PWR LEISURE...SOC EXHIBIT 20. PAGE 36 H0712
HABITAT TEC/DEV PLAN CONTROL

B58
INDIA (REPUBLIC) PARLIAMENT,CLASSIFIED LIST OF PUBLIC UNDERTAKINGS AND OTHER BODIES IN INDIA. INDIA ACADEM LG/CO CONSULT LEGIT CONFER GOV/REL 20. PAGE 76 H1528
NAT/G LEGIS LICENSE PROF/ORG

B58
INDIAN COUNCIL WORLD AFFAIRS,DEFENCE AND SECURITY IN THE INDIAN OCEAN AREA. INDIA S/ASIA CULTURE CONSULT DELIB/GP FORCES PROB/SOLV DIPLOM INT/TRADE 20 CMN/WLTH. PAGE 77 H1531
GEOG HABITAT ECO/UNDEV ORD/FREE

B58
STEINBERG C.S.,THE MASS COMMUNICATORS: PUBLIC RELATIONS, PUBLIC OPINION, AND MASS MEDIA. CULTURE CONSULT ACT/RES FEEDBACK DISPL WEALTH 20. PAGE 149 H2975
EDU/PROP ATTIT COM/IND PERCEPT

B58
WOODS H.D.,PATTERNS OF INDUSTRIAL DISPUTE SETTLEMENT IN FIVE CANADIAN INDUSTRIES. CANADA USA+45 CONSULT ADJUD GP/REL...JURID GOV/COMP METH/COMP ANTHOL 20. PAGE 170 H3408
BARGAIN INDUS LABOR NAT/G

S59
CHAPMAN B.,"THE FRENCH CONSEIL D'ETAT." FRANCE NAT/G CONSULT OP/RES PROB/SOLV PWR...OBS 20. PAGE 29 H0580
ADMIN LAW CT/SYS LEGIS

S59
JENKS C.W.,"THE CHALLENGE OF UNIVERSALITY." FUT UNIV CONSTN CULTURE CONSULT CREATE PLAN LEGIT ATTIT MORAL ORD/FREE RESPECT...MAJORIT JURID 20. PAGE 80 H1602
INT/ORG LAW PEACE INT/LAW

B60
DICHTER E.,THE STRATEGY OF DESIRE. UNIV CULTURE ACT/RES ATTIT DRIVE 20. PAGE 41 H0821
EDU/PROP PSY CONSULT PERSON

B60
JEFFRIES C.,TRANSFER OF POWER: PROBLEMS OF THE PASSAGE TO SELFGOVERNMENT. CEYLON GHANA MALAYSIA NIGERIA UK INT/ORG CONSULT DELIB/GP LEGIS DIPLOM CONFER PARL/PROC 20. PAGE 80 H1595
SOVEREIGN COLONIAL ORD/FREE NAT/G

S60
CROZIER B.,"FRANCE AND ALGERIA." ALGERIA EUR+WWI FRANCE FUT ISLAM ECO/UNDEV NEIGH CONSULT DELIB/GP ECO/TAC COLONIAL COERCE ATTIT...SOC INT CON/ANAL 20. PAGE 36 H0713
NAT/G FORCES GUERRILLA NAT/LISM

S60
SHILS E.,"THE INTELLECTUALS IN THE POLITICAL DEVELOPMENT OF THE NEW STATES." AFR ASIA S/ASIA ELITES LOC/G NAT/G CONSULT EX/STRUC CREATE PLAN ECO/TAC DOMIN LEGIT DRIVE PWR...TRADIT CONCPT STERTYP GEN/LAWS 20. PAGE 143 H2861
POL/PAR INTELL NAT/LISM

S60
TAYLOR M.G.,"THE ROLE OF THE MEDICAL PROFESSION IN THE FORMULATION AND EXECUTION OF PUBLIC POLICY" (BMR)" CANADA NAT/G CONSULT ADMIN REPRESENT GP/REL ROLE SOVEREIGN...DECISION 20 CMA. PAGE 153 H3056
PROF/ORG HEALTH LOBBY POLICY

B61
CARROTHERS A.W.R.,LABOR ARBITRATION IN CANADA. CANADA LAW NAT/G CONSULT LEGIS WORKER ADJUD ADMIN CT/SYS 20. PAGE 27 H0542
LABOR MGT GP/REL BARGAIN

B61
JUSTICE,THE CITIZEN AND THE ADMINISTRATION: THE REDRESS OF GRIEVANCES (PAMPHLET). EUR+WWI UK LAW CONSTN STRATA NAT/G CT/SYS PARTIC COERCE...NEW/IDEA IDEA/COMP 20 OMBUDSMAN. PAGE 82 H1644
INGP/REL CONSULT ADJUD REPRESENT

B61
LAHAYE R.,LES ENTREPRISES PUBLIQUES AU MAROC. FRANCE MOROCCO LAW DIST/IND EXTR/IND FINAN CONSULT PLAN TEC/DEV ADMIN AGREE CONTROL OWN...POLICY 20. PAGE 90 H1796
NAT/G INDUS ECO/UNDEV ECO/TAC

B61
MARX K.,THE COMMUNIST MANIFESTO. IN (MENDEL A. ESSENTIAL WORKS OF MARXISM, NEW YORK: BANTAM. FUT MOD/EUR CULTURE ECO/DEV ECO/UNDEV AGRI FINAN INDUS MARKET PROC/MFG LABOR MUNIC POL/PAR CONSULT FORCES CREATE PLAN ADMIN ATTIT DRIVE RIGID/FLEX ORD/FREE PWR RESPECT MARX/KARL WORK. PAGE 104 H2081
COM NEW/IDEA CAP/ISM REV

B61
ROSE D.L.,THE VIETNAMESE CIVIL SERVICE. VIETNAM CONSULT DELIB/GP GIVE PAY EDU/PROP COLONIAL GOV/REL UTIL...CHARTS 20. PAGE 134 H2672
ADMIN EFFICIENCY STAT NAT/G

B62
GROVE J.W.,GOVERNMENT AND INDUSTRY IN BRITAIN. UK FINAN LOC/G CONSULT DELIB/GP INT/TRADE ADMIN CONTROL...BIBLIOG 20. PAGE 62 H1237
ECO/TAC INDUS NAT/G GP/REL

B62
JAIN R.S.,THE GROWTH AND DEVELOPMENT OF GOVERNOR-GENERAL'S EXECUTIVE COUNCIL 1858-1919. INDIA UK CONSTN EX/STRUC LEGIS ADJUD ADMIN INGP/REL ATTIT 19/20. PAGE 79 H1585
NAT/G DELIB/GP CHIEF CONSULT

B62
JOHNSON J.J.,THE ROLE OF THE MILITARY IN UNDERDEVELOPED COUNTRIES. AFR BURMA INDONESIA ISLAM ISRAEL L/A+17C S/ASIA THAILAND CULTURE ECO/UNDEV KIN PROVS CONSULT ACT/RES COERCE REV DRIVE RIGID/FLEX ORD/FREE...RECORD ANTHOL 20. PAGE 81 H1622
FORCES CONCPT

B62
NEW ZEALAND COMM OF ST SERVICE,THE STATE SERVICES IN NEW ZEALAND. NEW/ZEALND CONSULT EX/STRUC ACT/RES ...BIBLIOG 20. PAGE 117 H2343
ADMIN WORKER TEC/DEV NAT/G

B62
ROBINSON A.D.,DUTCH ORGANIZED AGRICULTURE IN INTERNATIONAL POLITICS, 1945-1960. EUR+WWI NETHERLAND STRUCT ECO/DEV NAT/G VOL/ASSN CONSULT DELIB/GP PLAN TEC/DEV INT/TRADE EDU/PROP ATTIT RIGID/FLEX ALL/VALS...NEW/IDEA TREND EEC 20. PAGE 132 H2648
AGRI INT/ORG

B62
VALERIANO N.D.,COUNTER-GUERRILLA OPERATIONS: THE PHILLIPINE EXPERIENCE. NAT/G CONSULT ACT/RES PLAN COERCE GUERRILLA ATTIT ORD/FREE PWR SKILL...GEOG NEW/IDEA TIME/SEQ CHARTS 20. PAGE 161 H3221
S/ASIA FORCES PHILIPPINE

L62
MURACCIOLE L.,"LA BANQUE CENTRALE DES ETATS DE L'AFRIQUE DE L'OUEST." AFR LAW ECO/UNDEV INT/ORG NAT/G CONSULT ECO/TAC ROUTINE...CHARTS 20. PAGE 115 H2292
ISLAM FINAN INT/TRADE

L62
NOLTE E.,"ZUR PHANOMENOLOGIE DES FASCHIMUS." EUR+WWI GERMANY ITALY TURKEY INTELL NAT/G CHIEF CONSULT FORCES CREATE DOMIN EDU/PROP COERCE WAR CHOOSE DRIVE FASCISM...PSY CONCPT MYTH GEN/METH LEAGUE/NAT NAZI 20. PAGE 118 H2367
ATTIT PWR

S62
CROAN M.,"POLYCENTRISM: COMMUNIST INTERNATIONAL RELATIONS." ASIA STRUCT INT/ORG NAT/G POL/PAR
COM CREATE

CONSULT PLAN DOMIN EDU/PROP COERCE ATTIT RIGID/FLEX SOCISM...POLICY CONCPT TREND CON/ANAL GEN/LAWS MARX/KARL. PAGE 35 H0703
DIPLOM NAT/LISM

S62
GUETZKOW H.,"THE POTENTIAL OF CASE STUDY IN ANALYZING INTERNATIONAL CONFLICT." EUR+WWI FUT GERMANY INTELL SOCIETY STRUCT INT/ORG LOC/G NAT/G CONSULT CREATE PLAN CHOOSE ATTIT RIGID/FLEX ...POLICY SAAR 20. PAGE 62 H1246
EDU/PROP METH/CNCPT COERCE FRANCE

B63
KRAEHE E.,METTERNICH'S GERMAN POLICY: THE CONTEST WITH NAPOLEON, 1799-1814, VOL. 1. FRANCE MOD/EUR NAT/G CONSULT TOP/EX PLAN BAL/PWR DOMIN COERCE ATTIT DRIVE PERCEPT PERSON SKILL...CONCPT RECORD TIME/SEQ TREND 18/19. PAGE 88 H1764
BIOG GERMANY DIPLOM

B63
MAYNE R.,THE COMMUNITY OF EUROPE. UK CONSTN NAT/G CONSULT DELIB/GP CREATE PLAN ECO/TAC LEGIT ADMIN ROUTINE ORD/FREE PWR WEALTH...CONCPT TIME/SEQ EEC EURATOM 20. PAGE 105 H2107
EUR+WWI INT/ORG REGION

B63
NICOLSON H.,DIPLOMACY (3RD ED.). INT/ORG NAT/G CONSULT DELIB/GP CONFER 19/20 LEAGUE/NAT UN. PAGE 118 H2354
DIPLOM CONCPT NAT/COMP

B63
RONNING C.N.,LAW AND POLITICS IN INTER-AMERICAN DIPLOMACY. L/A+17C ECO/UNDEV NAT/G CONSULT DELIB/GP CREATE CAP/ISM ECO/TAC LEGIT REGION RIGID/FLEX ...METH/CNCPT GEN/LAWS OAS 20. PAGE 133 H2668
VOL/ASSN ALL/VALS DIPLOM

B63
US ATOMIC ENERGY COMMISSION,ATOMIC ENERGY IN THE SOVIET UNION: TRIP REPORT OF THE US ATOMIC ENERGY DELEGATION, MAY 1933. USSR R+D NAT/G CONSULT CREATE DIPLOM ADMIN ROUTINE EFFICIENCY PRODUC KNOWL SKILL ...NAT/COMP 20 AEC TRAVEL TREATY. PAGE 159 H3176
METH/COMP OP/RES TEC/DEV NUC/PWR

B63
VIARD R.,LA FIN DE L'EMPIRE COLONIAL FRANCAIS. AFR FUT S/ASIA ECO/UNDEV NAT/G CONSULT PLAN ECO/TAC EDU/PROP REGION NAT/LISM ALL/VALS...CONCPT TIME/SEQ TREND VAL/FREE 20. PAGE 162 H3248
VOL/ASSN COLONIAL FRANCE

B63
VON BECKERATH E.,PROBLEME DER NORMATIVEN OKONOMIK UND DER WIRTSCHAFTSPOLITISCHEN BERATUNG. GERMANY UK ELITES CAP/ISM EFFICIENCY...CONCPT GOV/COMP IDEA/COMP 20. PAGE 163 H3264
ECO/TAC DELIB/GP ECO/DEV CONSULT

B63
WILSON U.,EDUCATION AND CHANGING WEST AFRICAN CULTURE. AFR MOD/EUR UK CULTURE ECO/UNDEV MUNIC CONSULT 19/20 CMN/WLTH AFRICA/W. PAGE 169 H3384
COLONIAL POLICY SCHOOL

L63
MICHAEL F.,"KHRUSHCHEV'S DISLOYAL OPPOSITION: STRUCTURAL CHANGE AND POWER STRUGGLE IN COMMUNIST BLOC." ASIA CHINA/COM FUT NAT/G POL/PAR CONSULT PLAN DOMIN ATTIT...POLICY CONCPT TREND MARX/KARL 20 KHRUSH/N. PAGE 110 H2195
COM STRUCT NAT/LISM USSR

S63
ARASTEH R.,"THE ROLE OF INTELLECTUALS IN ADMINISTRATIVE DEVELOPMENT AND SOCIAL CHANGE IN MODERN IRAN." ISLAM CULTURE NAT/G CONSULT ACT/RES EDU/PROP EXEC ATTIT BIO/SOC PERCEPT SUPEGO ALL/VALS ...POLICY MGT PSY SOC CONCPT 20. PAGE 8 H0157
INTELL ADMIN IRAN

S63
RUSTOW D.A.,"THE MILITARY IN MIDDLE EASTERN SOCIETY AND POLITICS." FUT ISLAM CONSTN SOCIETY FACE/GP NAT/G POL/PAR PROF/ORG CONSULT DOMIN ADMIN EXEC REGION COERCE NAT/LISM ATTIT DRIVE PERSON ORD/FREE PWR...POLICY CONCPT OBS STERTYP 20. PAGE 136 H2721
FORCES ELITES

S63
WELLS H.,"THE OAS AND THE DOMINICAN ELECTIONS." L/A+17C INT/ORG NAT/G POL/PAR TEC/DEV ECO/TAC EDU/PROP PERCEPT...TIME/SEQ OAS TOT/POP 20. PAGE 166 H3332
CONSULT CHOOSE DOMIN/REP

B64
BAGEHOT W.,THE ENGLISH CONSTITUTION. UK CHIEF CONSULT LEGIS BAL/PWR PWR...BIBLIOG 18/19 PARLIAMENT. PAGE 10 H0198
CONSTN PARL/PROC NAT/G CONCPT

B64
CULLINGWORTH J.B.,TOWN AND COUNTRY PLANNING IN ENGLAND AND WALES. UK LAW SOCIETY CONSULT ACT/RES ADMIN ROUTINE LEISURE INGP/REL ADJUST PWR...GEOG 20 OPEN/SPACE URBAN/RNWL. PAGE 36 H0718
MUNIC PLAN NAT/G PROB/SOLV

B64
GROVES H.E.,THE CONSTITUTION OF MALAYSIA. MALAYSIA POL/PAR CHIEF CONSULT DELIB/GP CT/SYS PARL/PROC CHOOSE FEDERAL ORD/FREE 20. PAGE 62 H1238
CONSTN NAT/G LAW

B64
PINNICK A.W.,COUNTRY PLANNERS IN ACTION. UK FINAN SERV/IND NAT/G CONSULT DELIB/GP PRICE CONTROL ROUTINE LEISURE AGE/C...GEOG 20 URBAN/RNWL. PAGE 126 H2512
MUNIC PLAN INDUS ATTIT

B64
SAKAI R.K.,STUDIES ON ASIA, 1964. ASIA CHINA/COM ISRAEL MALAYSIA S/ASIA USA+45 USSR ECO/UNDEV FAM POL/PAR SECT CONSULT NAT/LISM...POLICY SOC 20 CHINJAP. PAGE 137 H2736
PWR DIPLOM

B64
WAINHOUSE D.W.,REMNANTS OF EMPIRE: THE UNITED NATIONS AND THE END OF COLONIALISM. FUT PORTUGAL WOR+45 NAT/G CONSULT DOMIN LEGIT ADMIN ROUTINE ATTIT ORD/FREE...POLICY JURID RECORD INT TIME/SEQ UN CMN/WLTH 20. PAGE 164 H3287
INT/ORG TREND COLONIAL

L64
BERELSON B.,"SAMPLE SURVEYS AND POPULATION CONTROL." ASIA FUT ISLAM L/A+17C CULTURE SOCIETY FAM NAT/G CONSULT PLAN EDU/PROP ATTIT DRIVE ALL/VALS...POLICY RELATIV HEAL PSY SOC CONCPT METH/CNCPT OBS OBS/ENVIR TOT/POP. PAGE 15 H0297
BIO/SOC SAMP

S64
GROSS J.A.,"WHITEHALL AND THE COMMONWEALTH." EUR+WWI MOD/EUR INT/ORG NAT/G CONSULT DELIB/GP LEGIS DOMIN ADMIN COLONIAL ROUTINE PWR CMN/WLTH 19/20. PAGE 62 H1233
EX/STRUC ATTIT TREND

S64
MC WILLIAM M.,"THE WORLD BANK AND THE TRANSFER OF POWER IN KENYA." AFR ECO/UNDEV CONSULT ACT/RES TEC/DEV PERCEPT PWR SKILL WEALTH...CONCPT OBS TREND 20. PAGE 106 H2119
NAT/G ECO/TAC

S64
NEEDHAM T.,"SCIENCE AND SOCIETY IN EAST AND WEST." INTELL STRATA R+D LOC/G NAT/G PROVS CONSULT ACT/RES CREATE PLAN TEC/DEV EDU/PROP ADMIN ATTIT ALL/VALS ...POLICY RELATIV MGT CONCPT NEW/IDEA TIME/SEQ WORK WORK. PAGE 116 H2327
ASIA STRUCT

S64
SMYTHE H.H.,"NEHRU AND INDIAN FOREIGN POLICY." S/ASIA ECO/UNDEV NAT/G POL/PAR CONSULT PLAN DIPLOM NEUTRAL COERCE ATTIT DRIVE PERSON MORAL ORD/FREE RESPECT...GEOG CONCPT TIME/SEQ TREND GEN/LAWS 20 NEHRU/J. PAGE 146 H2922
TOP/EX BIOG INDIA

B65
CHENG C.-Y.,SCIENTIFIC AND ENGINEERING MANPOWER IN COMMUNIST CHINA, 1949-1963. CHINA/COM USSR ELITES ECO/DEV R+D ACADEM LABOR NAT/G EDU/PROP CONTROL UTIL...POLICY BIBLIOG 20. PAGE 29 H0588
WORKER CONSULT MARXISM BIOG

B65
CHRIMES S.B.,ENGLISH CONSTITUTIONAL HISTORY (3RD ED.). UK CHIEF CONSULT DELIB/GP LEGIS CT/SYS 15/20 COMMON/LAW PARLIAMENT. PAGE 30 H0598
CONSTN BAL/PWR NAT/G

B65
HYMES D.,THE USE OF COMPUTERS IN ANTHROPOLOGY. CULTURE PROF/ORG CONSULT CREATE EFFICIENCY PERCEPT ...CLASSIF LING CON/ANAL COMPUT/IR METH/COMP ANTHOL 20. PAGE 76 H1517
METH COMPUTER TEC/DEV SOC

B65
PANJABI K.L.,THE CIVIL SERVANT IN INDIA. INDIA UK NAT/G CONSULT EX/STRUC REGION GP/REL RACE/REL 20. PAGE 123 H2462
ADMIN WORKER BIOG COLONIAL

B65
ROWAT D.C.,THE OMBUDSMAN: CITIZEN'S DEFENDER. DENMARK FINLAND NEW/ZEALND NORWAY SWEDEN CONSULT PROB/SOLV FEEDBACK PARTIC GP/REL...SOC CONCPT NEW/IDEA METH/COMP ANTHOL BIBLIOG 20. PAGE 135 H2701
INSPECT CONSTN NAT/G ADMIN

S65
SPAAK P.H.,"THE SEARCH FOR CONSENSUS: A NEW EFFORT TO BUILD EUROPE." FRANCE GERMANY ECO/DEV NAT/G CONSULT FORCES PLAN EDU/PROP REGION CONSEN ATTIT ...SOC METH/CNCPT OBS TREND EEC NATO WORK 20. PAGE 147 H2941
EUR+WWI INT/ORG

B66
MAC DONALD H.M.,THE INTELLECTUAL IN POLITICS. GERMANY PERU SWEDEN UK USSR NAT/G CONSULT PLAN EDU/PROP TASK INGP/REL EFFICIENCY RATIONAL ALL/VALS 20. PAGE 99 H1987
ALL/IDEOS INTELL POL/PAR PARTIC

B66
MERILLAT H.C.L.,LEGAL ADVISERS AND INTERNATIONAL ORGANIZATIONS. LAW NAT/G CONSULT OP/RES ADJUD SANCTION TASK CONSEN ORG/CHARTS. PAGE 109 H2178
INT/ORG INT/LAW CREATE OBS

B66
NOEL G.E.,THE NEW BRITAIN AND HAROLD WILSON: INTERIM REPORT, 1966 GENERAL ELECTION. UK POL/PAR CONSULT PROB/SOLV BUDGET DIPLOM ECO/TAC LEAD CHOOSE ATTIT 20 WILSON/H PARLIAMENT. PAGE 118 H2366
BIOG PERSON NAT/G CHIEF

S66
HAIGH G.,"FIELD TRAINING IN HUMAN RELATIONS FOR THE PEACE CORPS." CONSULT CREATE EDU/PROP ADMIN TASK GP/REL ATTIT PERSON...PSY OBS SOC/EXP PEACE/CORP. PAGE 64 H1276
CULTURE PERS/REL FOR/AID ADJUST

B67
ANDERSON S.V.,THE NORDIC COUNCIL: A STUDY OF SCANDINAVIAN REGIONALISM. DENMARK FINLAND ICELAND NORWAY SWEDEN MARKET NAT/G VOL/ASSN CONSULT PARL/PROC ATTIT...TIME/SEQ BIBLIOG 20. PAGE 7 H0134
INT/ORG REGION DIPLOM LEGIS

B67
JOUVENEL B D.E.,THE ART OF CONJECTURE. FUT CONSULT EX/STRUC CHOOSE GOV/REL ALL/VALS. PAGE 82 H1638
PREDICT DELIB/GP PLAN NAT/G

B67
LENG S.C.,JUSTICE IN COMMUNIST CHINA: A SURVEY OF THE JUDICIAL SYSTEM OF THE CHINESE PEOPLE'S REPUBLIC. CHINA/COM LAW CONSTN LOC/G NAT/G PROF/ORG CONSULT FORCES ADMIN CRIME ORD/FREE...BIBLIOG 20 MAO. PAGE 94 H1877 CT/SYS ADJUD JURID MARXISM

B67
MORRIS A.J.A.,PARLIAMENTARY DEMOCRACY IN THE NINETEENTH CENTURY. UK INDUS LOC/G NAT/G POL/PAR CONSULT LEGIS INT/TRADE ADMIN CHOOSE SUFF SOVEREIGN 19 PARLIAMENT. PAGE 113 H2261 TIME/SEQ CONSTN PARL/PROC POPULISM

S67
ADAMS R.N.,"ETHICS AND THE SOCIAL ANTHROPOLOGIST IN LATIN AMERICA." USA+45 INTELL PROB/SOLV ECO/TAC LEAD...DECISION SOC NAT/COMP PERS/COMP. PAGE 3 H0066 L/A+17C POLICY ECO/UNDEV CONSULT

S67
DOERN G.B.,"THE ROYAL COMMISSIONS IN THE GENERAL POLICY PROCESS AND IN FEDERAL-PROVINCIAL RELATIONS." CANADA CONSTN ACADEM PROVS CONSULT DELIB/GP LEGIS ACT/RES PROB/SOLV CONFER CONTROL EFFICIENCY...METH/COMP 20 SENATE ROYAL/COMM. PAGE 42 H0832 R+D EX/STRUC GOV/REL NAT/G

S67
GLOBERSON A.,"SOCIAL GROWTH IN THE DEVELOPING COUNTRIES." CULTURE SOCIETY CONSULT PROB/SOLV SOC. PAGE 57 H1144 ECO/UNDEV FOR/AID EDU/PROP PLAN

S67
LICHFIELD N.,"THE EVALUATION OF CAPITAL INVESTMENT PROJECTS IN TOWN CENTRE REDEVELOPMENT." UK CONSTRUC MUNIC CONSULT COST...METH/CNCPT IDEA/COMP 20. PAGE 96 H1923 PLAN ECO/TAC NAT/G DECISION

S67
RICHMAN B.M.,"CAPITALISTS & MANAGERS IN COMMUNIST CHINA." ASIA CHINA/COM ECO/UNDEV NAT/G CONSULT EX/STRUC PLAN EFFICIENCY PRODUC WEALTH MARXISM ...MGT CHARTS 20. PAGE 131 H2623 CAP/ISM INDUS

S67
WHITE W.L.,"THE TREASURY BOARD AND PARLIAMENT." CANADA CONSTN CONSULT LEGIS LEAD PARL/PROC GP/REL ...DECISION 20. PAGE 167 H3351 FINAN DELIB/GP NAT/G ADMIN

CONSULTANTS....SEE CONSULT

CONSUMER....SEE MARKET

CONT/OBS....CONTROLLED DIRECT OBSERVATION

B00
OMAN C.,A HISTORY OF THE ART OF WAR: THE MIDDLE AGES FROM THE FOURTH TO THE FOURTEENTH CENTURY. CHRIST-17C MEDIT-7 CULTURE SOCIETY INT/ORG ROUTINE PERSON...CONT/OBS HIST/WRIT CHARTS VAL/FREE. PAGE 121 H2417 FORCES SKILL WAR

B44
KNORR K.E.,BRITISH COLONIAL THEORIES 1570-1850. NAT/G DELIB/GP ECO/TAC PERCEPT PWR...WELF/ST METH/CNCPT CONT/OBS TIME/SEQ SIMUL TOT/POP 20. PAGE 87 H1734 ACT/RES DOMIN COLONIAL

S49
MACKENZIE R.D.,"ECOLOGY, HUMAN." UNIV CULTURE ECO/DEV ECO/UNDEV ATTIT...POLICY GEOG PSY CONCPT METH/CNCPT CONT/OBS TREND GEN/LAWS. PAGE 100 H2001 SOCIETY BIO/SOC

S59
SCOTT W.A.,"EMPIRICAL ASSESSMENT OF VALUES AND IDEOLOGIES." CULTURE SOCIETY SECT CREATE DRIVE PERSON MORAL PWR...SOC METH/CNCPT STAT CONT/OBS DEEP/INT DEEP/QU CHARTS VAL/FREE. PAGE 141 H2817 ATTIT PSY

B60
WOLF C.,FOREIGN AID: THEORY AND PRACTICE IN SOUTHERN ASIA. CEYLON INDONESIA PHILIPPINE S/ASIA CULTURE STRATA ECO/UNDEV PLAN EDU/PROP ATTIT ...METH/CNCPT MATH QUANT STAT CONT/OBS TIME/SEQ SIMUL TOT/POP 20. PAGE 170 H3396 ACT/RES ECO/TAC FOR/AID

B61
MARVICK D.,POLITICAL DECISION-MAKERS. INTELL STRATA NAT/G POL/PAR EX/STRUC LEGIS DOMIN EDU/PROP ATTIT PERSON PWR...PSY STAT OBS CONT/OBS STAND/INT UNPLAN/INT TIME/SEQ CHARTS STERTYP VAL/FREE. PAGE 104 H2073 TOP/EX BIOG ELITES

S67
CRITTENDEN J.,"DIMENSIONS OF MODERNIZATION IN THE AMERICAN STATES." USA+45 STRUCT MUNIC PROB/SOLV CONTROL LITERACY HABITAT...CONCPT METH/CNCPT CORREL CONT/OBS CENSUS 20. PAGE 35 H0702 PROVS GOV/COMP STAT ECO/DEV

CONTEMPT....SEE RESPECT

CONTENT ANALYSIS....SEE CON/ANAL

CONTROL....CONTROL OF HUMAN GROUP OPERATIONS

B05
GRIFFIN A.P.C.,LIST OF BOOKS ON RAILROADS IN FOREIGN COUNTRIES. MOD/EUR ECO/DEV NAT/G CONTROL SOCISM...JURID 19/20 RAILROAD. PAGE 61 H1219 BIBLIOG/A SERV/IND ADMIN DIST/IND

B09
JUSTINIAN,THE DIGEST (DIGESTA CORPUS JURIS CIVILIS) (2 VOLS.) (TRANS. BY C. H. MONRO). ROMAN/EMP LAW FAM LOC/G LEGIS EDU/PROP CONTROL MARRIAGE OWN ROLE CIVIL/LAW. PAGE 82 H1645 JURID CT/SYS NAT/G STRATA

B10
MILL J.S.,UTILITARIANISM, LIBERTY, AND REPRESENTATIVE GOVERNMENT. CONTROL PERCEPT PERSON MORAL...CONCPT GEN/LAWS. PAGE 110 H2205 HAPPINESS ORD/FREE REPRESENT NAT/G

N17
BURKE E.,THOUGHTS ON THE CAUSE OF THE PRESENT DISCONTENTS (PAMPHLET). MOD/EUR UK CONSTN CHIEF LEGIS DOMIN CONTROL EXEC REPRESENT POPULISM ...TRADIT NEW/IDEA METH/COMP 18 BURKE/EDM. PAGE 24 H0484 ORD/FREE REV PARL/PROC NAT/G

N19
BRIMMELL G.H.,COMMUNISM IN SOUTHEAST ASIA (PAMPHLET). BURMA CAMBODIA COM INDIA INDONESIA LAOS MOD/EUR NAT/G POL/PAR FORCES CAP/ISM CONTROL WEALTH ...MYTH 20. PAGE 21 H0420 MARXISM S/ASIA REV ECO/UNDEV

N19
CANADA CIVIL SERV COMM,THE ANALYSIS OF ORGANIZATION IN THE GOVERNMENT OF CANADA (PAMPHLET). CANADA CONSTN EX/STRUC LEGIS TOP/EX CREATE PLAN CONTROL GP/REL 20. PAGE 26 H0517 NAT/G MGT ADMIN DELIB/GP

N19
FREEMAN H.A.,COERCION OF STATES IN FEDERAL UNIONS (PAMPHLET). WOR-45 DIPLOM CONTROL COERCE PEACE ORD/FREE...GOV/COMP METH/COMP NAT/COMP PACIFIST 20. PAGE 53 H1055 FEDERAL WAR INT/ORG PACIFISM

N19
GORWALA A.D.,THE ADMINISTRATIVE JUNGLE (PAMPHLET). INDIA NAT/G LEGIS ECO/TAC CONTROL GOV/REL ...METH/COMP 20. PAGE 59 H1183 ADMIN POLICY PLAN ECO/UNDEV

N19
HACKETT J.,ECONOMIC PLANNING IN FRANCE; ITS RELATION TO THE POLICIES OF THE DEVELOPED COUNTRIES OF WESTERN EUROPE (PAMPHLET). EUR+WWI FRANCE ECO/DEV PROB/SOLV CONTROL...POLICY 20 EUROPE/W. PAGE 63 H1270 ECO/TAC NAT/G PLAN INSPECT

N19
HAJDA J.,THE COLD WAR VIEWED AS A SOCIOLOGICAL PROBLEM (PAMPHLET). COM CZECHOSLVK EUR+WWI SOCIETY PLAN EDU/PROP CONTROL TASK ATTIT MARXISM...POLICY 20 COLD/WAR MIGRATION. PAGE 64 H1280 DIPLOM LEAD PWR NAT/G

N19
MEZERIK A.G.,APARTHEID IN THE REPUBLIC OF SOUTH AFRICA (PAMPHLET). DIPLOM DOMIN CONTROL COERCE REPRESENT CONSEN ATTIT. PAGE 110 H2194 DISCRIM RACE/REL POL/PAR POLICY

N19
SOUTH AFRICA COMMISSION ON FUT,INTERIM AND FINAL REPORTS ON FUTURE FORM OF GOVERNMENT IN THE SOUTH-WEST AFRICAN PROTECTORATE (PAMPHLET). SOUTH/AFR NAT/G FORCES CONFER COLONIAL CONTROL 20 AFRICA/SW. PAGE 147 H2936 CONSTN REPRESENT ADMIN PROB/SOLV

N19
TABORSKY E.,CONFORMITY UNDER COMMUNISM (PAMPHLET). CZECHOSLVK HUNGARY POLAND SCHOOL DOMIN PRESS ...TREND GOV/COMP 20. PAGE 152 H3030 COM CONTROL EDU/PROP NAT/G

N19
WEBB L.C.,CHURCH AND STATE IN ITALY: 1947-1957 (PAMPHLET). GERMANY ITALY CONSTN POL/PAR AGREE CONTROL PARTIC CHOOSE ATTIT ORD/FREE FASCISM MARXISM 20 CHURCH/STA MARITAIN/J SALO. PAGE 166 H3316 SECT CATHISM NAT/G GP/REL

N19
WILSON T.,FINANCIAL ASSISTANCE WITH REGIONAL DEVELOPMENT (PAMPHLET). CANADA INDUS NAT/G PLAN TAX CONTROL COST EFFICIENCY...POLICY CHARTS 20. PAGE 169 H3382 FINAN ECO/TAC REGION GOV/REL

B20
MACIVER R.M.,COMMUNITY: A SOCIOLOGICAL STUDY; BEING AN ATTEMPT TO SET OUT THE FUNDAMENTAL LAWS OF SOCIAL LIFE. UNIV STRUCT NAT/G CONTROL WAR BIO/SOC ...PSY SOC CONCPT GEN/LAWS. PAGE 100 H1996 REGION SOCIETY GP/REL

B20
MALTHUS T.R.,PRINCIPLES OF POLITICAL ECONOMY. UK AGRI INDUS MARKET NAT/G DIPLOM PRICE CONTROL BAL/PAY COST OWN PWR LAISSEZ 18/19. PAGE 102 H2034 GEN/LAWS DEMAND WEALTH

B23
LEES-SMITH H.B.,SECOND CHAMBERS IN THEORY AND PRACTICE. IRELAND NORWAY SOUTH/AFR UK LAW POL/PAR LEGIS CONTROL 20 CMN/WLTH. PAGE 93 H1858 PARL/PROC DELIB/GP REPRESENT GP/COMP

B24
BAGEHOT W.,THE ENGLISH CONSTITUTION AND OTHER POLITICAL ESSAYS. UK DELIB/GP BAL/PWR ADMIN CONTROL EXEC ROUTINE CONSERVE...METH PARLIAMENT 19/20. PAGE 10 H0197 NAT/G STRUCT CONCPT

B24
HOLDSWORTH W.S.,A HISTORY OF ENGLISH LAW; THE COMMON LAW AND ITS RIVALS (VOL. IV). UK SEA AGRI CHIEF ADJUD CONTROL CRIME GOV/REL...INT/LAW JURID NAT/COMP 16/17 PARLIAMENT COMMON/LAW CANON/LAW ENGLSH/LAW. PAGE 72 H1449
LAW LEGIS CT/SYS CONSTN

B25
MAURRAS C.,ENQUETE SUR LA MONARCHIE (1909). FRANCE CONTROL REPRESENT DISCRIM HEREDITY PWR CONSERVE 20 BUREAUCRCY. PAGE 105 H2103
TRADIT AUTHORIT NAT/G CHIEF

B27
BELLOC H.,THE SERVILE STATE (1912) (3RD ED.). PRUSSIA UK CULTURE STRATA INDUS NAT/G ECO/TAC CONTROL LEAD SUFF DISCRIM EQUILIB ORD/FREE WEALTH 20. PAGE 13 H0269
WORKER CAP/ISM DOMIN CATH

B27
MCCOWN A.C.,THE CONGRESSIONAL CONFERENCE COMMITTEE. FACE/GP CONTROL. PAGE 106 H2128
DELIB/GP GOV/COMP LEGIS CONFER

B27
PANIKKAR K.M.,INDIAN STATES AND THE GOVERNMENT OF INDIA. INDIA UK CONSTN CONTROL TASK GP/REL SOVEREIGN WEALTH...TREND BIBLIOG 19. PAGE 123 H2457
GOV/COMP COLONIAL BAL/PWR PROVS

B28
MARSILIUS/PADUA,DEFENSOR PACIS (1324). CHRIST-17C CONSTN NAT/G DIPLOM DOMIN LEGIT CONTROL WAR PEACE ORD/FREE SOVEREIGN POPULISM 14 POPE. PAGE 103 H2059
CATH SECT GEN/LAWS

B29
STURZO L.,THE INTERNATIONAL COMMUNITY AND THE RIGHT OF WAR (TRANS. BY BARBARA BARCLAY CARTER). CULTURE CREATE PROB/SOLV DIPLOM ADJUD CONTROL PEACE PERSON ORD/FREE...INT/LAW IDEA/COMP PACIFIST 20 LEAGUE/NAT. PAGE 150 H3003
INT/ORG PLAN WAR CONCPT

B30
BENTHAM J.,THE RATIONALE OF PUNISHMENT. UK LAW LOC/G NAT/G LEGIS CONTROL...JURID GEN/LAWS COURT/SYS 19. PAGE 14 H0289
CRIME SANCTION COERCE ORD/FREE

B30
LASKI H.J.,LIBERTY IN THE MODERN STATE. UNIV SOCIETY STRATA CREATE BAL/PWR CONTROL RATIONAL ATTIT PWR 18/20. PAGE 91 H1828
CONCPT ORD/FREE NAT/G DOMIN

B32
GREAT BRIT COMM MINISTERS PWR,REPORT. UK LAW CONSTN CONSULT LEGIS PARL/PROC SANCTION SOVEREIGN ...DECISION JURID 20 PARLIAMENT. PAGE 60 H1201
EX/STRUC NAT/G PWR CONTROL

B34
GONZALEZ PALENCIA A,ESTUDIO HISTORICO SOBRE LA CENSURA GUBERNATIVA EN ESPANA 1800-1833. NAT/G COERCE INGP/REL ATTIT AUTHORIT KNOWL...POLICY JURID 19. PAGE 58 H1165
LEGIT EDU/PROP PRESS CONTROL

B34
RIDLEY C.E.,THE CITY-MANAGER PROFESSION. CHIEF PLAN ADMIN CONTROL ROUTINE CHOOSE...TECHNIC CHARTS GOV/COMP BIBLIOG 20. PAGE 131 H2624
MUNIC EX/STRUC LOC/G EXEC

B34
STALIN J.,PROBLEMS OF LENINISM. USSR STRATA INDUS LOC/G POL/PAR ECO/TAC CONTROL TOTALISM PWR SOCISM LENIN/VI STALIN/J. PAGE 148 H2968
MARXISM REV ELITES NAT/G

B36
BELLOC H.,THE RESTORATION OF PROPERTY. UK STRATA NAT/G PROF/ORG DELIB/GP WORKER CREATE PROB/SOLV ECO/TAC PARTIC UTOPIA ORD/FREE SOCISM 20. PAGE 13 H0270
CONTROL MAJORIT CAP/ISM OWN

B36
BOYCE A.N.,EUROPE AND SOUTH AFRICA. FRANCE GERMANY ITALY SOUTH/AFR UK INDUS NAT/G CONTROL REV WAR NAT/LISM...CONCPT HIST/WRIT 20. PAGE 20 H0392
COLONIAL GOV/COMP NAT/COMP DIPLOM

B37
HAMILTON W.H.,THE POWER TO GOVERN. ECO/DEV FINAN INDUS ECO/TAC INT/TRADE TARIFFS TAX CONTROL CT/SYS WAR COST PWR 18/20 SUPREME/CT. PAGE 65 H1303
LING CONSTN NAT/G POLICY

B38
COUPLAND R.,EAST AFRICA AND ITS INVADERS. AFR ISLAM STRATA SECT FORCES DIPLOM TRIBUTE CONTROL DISCRIM NAT/LISM 19 AFRICA/E EUROPE MISSION. PAGE 34 H0680
CULTURE ELITES COLONIAL MARKET

B38
DAVIES E.,"NATIONAL" CAPITALISM: THE GOVERNMENT'S RECORD AS PROTECTOR OF PRIVATE MONOPOLY. UK ELITES SOCIETY STRATA POL/PAR WORKER PROB/SOLV CONTROL SOCISM 20 MONOPOLY LABOR/PAR CHAMBRLN/N. PAGE 37 H0747
CAP/ISM NAT/G INDUS POLICY

B38
LAWLEY F.E.,THE GROWTH OF COLLECTIVE ECONOMY VOL. 1: NATIONAL. EUR+WWI AGRI INDUS NAT/G BARGAIN CAP/ISM ECO/TAC WAR OPTIMAL WEALTH...GOV/COMP METH/COMP 19/20 MONOPOLY. PAGE 92 H1844
SOCISM PRICE CONTROL OWN

B38
LAWLEY F.E.,THE GROWTH OF COLLECTIVE ECONOMY VOL. 2: INTERNATIONAL. WOR-45 AGRI INDUS EQUILIB OPTIMAL OWN WEALTH...NAT/COMP 19/20 NAZI NEW/DEAL MONOPOLY. PAGE 92 H1845
ECO/TAC SOCISM NAT/LISM CONTROL

B38
REICH N.,LABOR RELATIONS IN REPUBLICAN GERMANY. GERMANY CONSTN ECO/DEV INDUS NAT/G ADMIN CONTROL GP/REL FASCISM POPULISM 20 WEIMAR/REP. PAGE 130 H2609
WORKER MGT LABOR BARGAIN

B39
CARR E.H.,PROPAGANDA IN INTERNATIONAL POLITICS (PAMPHLET). EUR+WWI GERMANY MOD/EUR NAT/G AGREE WAR MORAL...POLICY 20 TREATY. PAGE 27 H0536
DIPLOM EDU/PROP CONTROL ATTIT

B41
GILMORE M.P.,ARGUMENT FROM ROMAN LAW IN POLITICAL THOUGHT, 1200-1600. INTELL LICENSE CONTROL CT/SYS GOV/REL PRIVIL PWR...IDEA/COMP BIBLIOG 13/16. PAGE 56 H1130
JURID LAW CONCPT NAT/G

B42
FEFFERO G.,THE PRINCIPLES OF POWER (TRANS. BY T. JAECKEL). MOD/EUR CONSTN NAT/G CHIEF CONTROL REV WAR ORD/FREE CONSERVE FASCISM POPULISM...GEN/LAWS 18/20 EUROPE. PAGE 49 H0980
PWR LEGIT TRADIT ELITES

B42
LA BOETIE E.,ANTI-DICTATOR (1548) (TRANS. BY H. KUNZ). CONSTN NAT/G CHIEF DOMIN LEGIT CONTROL POPULISM. PAGE 90 H1790
PWR ORD/FREE TOTALISM GEN/LAWS

B42
NEUMANN S.,PERMANENT REVOLUTION: THE TOTAL STATE IN A WORLD AT WAR. COM EUR+WWI GERMANY USSR EX/STRUC DIPLOM CONTROL COERCE REPRESENT MARXISM...SOC GOV/COMP BIBLIOG 20 HITLER/A STALIN/J. PAGE 117 H2337
FASCISM TOTALISM DOMIN EDU/PROP

B42
SINGTON D.,THE GOEBBELS EXPERIMENT. GERMANY MOD/EUR NAT/G EX/STRUC FORCES CONTROL ROUTINE WAR TOTALISM PWR...ART/METH HUM 20 NAZI GOEBBELS/J. PAGE 144 H2886
FASCISM EDU/PROP ATTIT COM/IND

C43
BENTHAM J.,"ON THE LIBERTY OF THE PRESS, AND PUBLIC DISCUSSION" IN J. BOWRING, ED., THE WORKS OF JEREMY BENTHAM." SPAIN UK LAW ELITES NAT/G LEGIS INSPECT LEGIT WRITING CONTROL PRIVIL TOTALISM AUTHORIT ...TRADIT 19 FREE/SPEE. PAGE 15 H0290
ORD/FREE PRESS CONFER CONSERVE

C43
BENTHAM J.,"PRINCIPLES OF INTERNATIONAL LAW" IN J. BOWRING, ED., THE WORKS OF JEREMY BENTHAM." UNIV NAT/G PLAN PROB/SOLV DIPLOM CONTROL SANCTION MORAL ORD/FREE PWR SOVEREIGN 19. PAGE 15 H0291
INT/LAW JURID WAR PEACE

B44
BARKER E.,THE DEVELOPMENT OF PUBLIC SERVICES IN WESTERN WUROPE: 1660-1930. FRANCE GERMANY UK SCHOOL CONTROL REPRESENT ROLE...WELF/ST 17/20. PAGE 11 H0219
GOV/COMP ADMIN EX/STRUC

B45
CONOVER H.F.,ITALY: ECONOMICS, POLITICS AND MILITARY AFFAIRS, 1940-1945. ITALY ELITES NAT/G POL/PAR EX/STRUC TOP/EX DIPLOM DOMIN CONTROL COERCE WAR CIVMIL/REL EFFICIENCY 20. PAGE 32 H0646
BIBLIOG TOTALISM FORCES

B45
HORN O.B.,BRITISH PUBLIC OPINION AND THE FIRST PARTITION OF POLAND. POLAND UK LEGIS PRESS RUMOR CONTROL PARTIC NAT/LISM SOVEREIGN 18/19. PAGE 73 H1469
DIPLOM POLICY ATTIT NAT/G

B46
ALLEN J.S.,WORLD MONOPOLY AND PEACE. GERMANY UK USSR FINAN INDUS LG/CO DOMIN CONTROL PEACE PWR WEALTH SOCISM...NAT/COMP 20 MONOPOLY. PAGE 5 H0105
CAP/ISM DIPLOM WAR COLONIAL

B46
DAVIES E.,NATIONAL ENTERPRISE: THE DEVELOPMENT OF THE PUBLIC CORPORATION. UK LG/CO EX/STRUC WORKER PROB/SOLV COST ATTIT SOCISM 20. PAGE 37 H0748
ADMIN NAT/G CONTROL INDUS

B46
MILL J.S.,ON LIBERTY. NAT/G LEGIT CONTROL PERS/REL PERCEPT...CONCPT 19. PAGE 110 H2206
ORD/FREE SOCIETY PERSON GEN/LAWS

S46
DE GRE G.,"FREEDOM AND SOCIAL STRUCTURE" (BMR)" UNIV SOCIETY DOMIN CONTROL TOTALISM PLURISM...SOC CHARTS. PAGE 38 H0753
ORD/FREE STRUCT CONCPT GP/REL

B48
ROSSITER C.L.,CONSTITUTIONAL DICTATORSHIP; CRISIS GOVERNMENT IN THE MODERN DEMOCRACIES. FRANCE GERMANY UK USA-45 WOR-45 EX/STRUC BAL/PWR CONTROL COERCE WAR CENTRAL ORD/FREE...DECISION 19/20. PAGE 134 H2688
NAT/G AUTHORIT CONSTN TOTALISM

B48
TURNER A.C.,FREE SPEECH AND BROADCASTING. UK USA+45
COM/IND

ORD/FREE NAT/COMP. PAGE 157 H3140 NAT/G CONTROL METH/COMP

B48
WOLFE B.D.,THREE WHO MADE A REVOLUTION. USSR CONSTN NAT/G CAP/ISM EDU/PROP CONTROL WAR GP/REL INGP/REL PERS/REL ROLE 20 STALIN/J LENIN/VI TROTSKY/L BOLSHEVISM. PAGE 170 H3398 BIOG REV LEAD MARXISM

B49
DE JOUVENEL B.,ON POWER: ITS NATURE AND THE HISTORY OF ITS GROWTH. SOCIETY CHIEF REV WAR ATTIT AUTHORIT ORD/FREE SOVEREIGN CONSERVE POPULISM CONCPT. PAGE 38 H0757 PWR NAT/G DOMIN CONTROL

B49
SCHONS D.,BOOK CENSORSHIP IN NEW SPAIN (NEW WORLD STUDIES, BOOK II). SPAIN LAW CULTURE INSPECT ADJUD CT/SYS SANCTION GP/REL ORD/FREE 14/17. PAGE 140 H2797 CHRIST-17C EDU/PROP CONTROL PRESS

B49
SCHWARTZ B.,LAW AND THE EXECUTIVE IN BRITAIN: A COMPARATIVE STUDY. UK USA+45 LAW EX/STRUC PWR ...GOV/COMP 20. PAGE 140 H2807 ADMIN EXEC CONTROL REPRESENT

S49
STEINMETZ H.,"THE PROBLEMS OF THE LANDRAT: A STUDY OF COUNTY GOVERNMENT IN THE US ZONE OF GERMANY." GERMANY/W USA+45 INDUS PLAN DIPLOM EDU/PROP CONTROL WAR GOV/REL FEDERAL WEALTH PLURISM...GOV/COMP 20 LANDRAT. PAGE 149 H2977 LOC/G COLONIAL MGT TOP/EX

B50
ALBRECHT-CARRIE R.,ITALY FROM NAPOLEON TO MUSSOLINI. GERMANY ITALY SPAIN SOCIETY ECO/DEV POL/PAR LEGIS AGREE CONTROL WAR NAT/LISM TOTALISM PWR SOCISM...SOC 19/20 TREATY. PAGE 5 H0095 FASCISM NAT/G

B50
GATZKE H.W.,GERMANY'S DRIVE TO THE WEST. BELGIUM GERMANY MOD/EUR AGRI INDUS POL/PAR FORCES DOMIN AGREE CONTROL REGION COERCE 20 TREATY WWI. PAGE 55 H1104 WAR POLICY NAT/G DIPLOM

B50
GLEASON J.H.,THE GENESIS OF RUSSOPHOBIA IN GREAT BRITAIN: A STUDY OF THE INTERACTION OF POLICY AND OPINION. ASIA RUSSIA UK NAT/G AGREE CONTROL REV WAR LOVE PWR TREATY 19. PAGE 57 H1142 DIPLOM POLICY DOMIN COLONIAL

B50
HARLEY G.W.,MASKS AS AGENTS OF SOCIAL CONTROL IN NORTHEAST LIBERIA. AFR LIBERIA LAW CULTURE ADJUST CONSEN MORAL...GEOG SOC WORSHIP 20. PAGE 66 H1332 CONTROL ECO/UNDEV SECT CHIEF

B50
MACHIAVELLI N.,THE DISCOURSES (1516). NAT/G SECT FORCES DOMIN LEGIT CONTROL LEAD COERCE TOTALISM ORD/FREE. PAGE 100 H1995 PWR GEN/LAWS CHIEF

B50
ORTON W.A.,THE ECONOMIC ROLE OF THE STATE. INTELL ECO/UNDEV PLAN CONTROL PWR SOVEREIGN...POLICY 17/20. PAGE 122 H2431 ECO/DEV NAT/G ECO/TAC ORD/FREE

B50
US DEPARTMENT OF STATE,DOCUMENTS ON GERMAN FOREIGN POLICY, 1918-1945 (13 VOLS.). EUR+WWI GERMANY NAT/G PLAN DIPLOM DOMIN EDU/PROP CONTROL NAT/LISM ...ANTHOL 20. PAGE 159 H3186 BIBLIOG/A WAR POLICY FASCIST

B52
JULIEN C.A.,L'AFRIQUE DU NORD EN MARCHE: NATIONALISMES MUSULMANS ET SOUVERAINETE FRANCAISE (2ND ED). AFR ALGERIA FRANCE ISLAM MOROCCO NAT/G CONTROL ORD/FREE...POLICY 19/20 TUNIS MUSLIM. PAGE 82 H1641 NAT/LISM COERCE DOMIN COLONIAL

B52
ROBBINS L.,THE THEORY OF ECONOMIC POLICY IN ENGLISH CLASSICAL POLITICAL ECONOMY. UK ECO/DEV WORKER PLAN CAP/ISM EDU/PROP CONTROL INCOME OWN HEALTH SOCISM ...POLICY 17/19. PAGE 132 H2639 ECO/TAC ORD/FREE IDEA/COMP NAT/G

S52
SABINE G.H.,"THE TWO DEMOCRATIC TRADITIONS" (BMR)" FRANCE UK USA-45 NAT/G CONTROL CHOOSE ALL/IDEOS ...PHIL/SCI CONCPT IDEA/COMP 20. PAGE 136 H2727 ORD/FREE POPULISM INGP/REL NAT/COMP

C52
EBENSTEIN W.,"INTRODUCTION TO POLITICAL PHILOSOPHY." COM CONSTN INTELL CONTROL PERSON NEW/LIB SOCISM...PSY GEN/LAWS BIBLIOG/A. PAGE 44 H0883 ALL/IDEOS PHIL/SCI IDEA/COMP NAT/G

B53
CURTISS J.S.,THE RUSSIAN CHURCH AND THE SOVIET STATE 1917-1950. COM USSR CONTROL LEAD REV MARXISM ...POLICY BIBLIOG 20 CHURCH/STA ORTHO/RUSS. PAGE 36 H0728 GP/REL NAT/G SECT PWR

B53
LIEBER F.,CIVIL LIBERTY AND SELF GOVERNMENT: VOLUME 2. NAT/G CONTROL CHOOSE PERSON PWR 19 CIVIL/LIB. PAGE 96 H1925 ORD/FREE SOVEREIGN CENTRAL CONCPT

B53
SHIRATO I.,JAPANESE SOURCES ON THE HISTORY OF THE CHINESE COMMUNIST MOVEMENT (PAMPHLET). CHINA/COM USSR CONSTRUC NAT/G POL/PAR FORCES DIPLOM DOMIN EDU/PROP CONTROL WAR TOTALISM SOCISM 20. PAGE 143 H2863 BIBLIOG/A MARXISM ECO/UNDEV

B53
SQUIRES J.D.,BRITISH PROPAGANDA AT HOME AND IN THE UNITED STATES FROM 1914 TO 1917. UK NAT/G PROB/SOLV DOMIN PRESS EFFICIENCY...PSY PREDICT 20 WWI INTERVENT PSY/WAR. PAGE 148 H2960 EDU/PROP CONTROL WAR DIPLOM

C53
DORWART R.A.,"THE ADMINISTRATIVE REFORMS OF FREDRICK WILLIAM I OF PRUSSIA. GERMANY MOD/EUR CHIEF CONTROL PWR...BIBLIOG 16/18. PAGE 42 H0839 ADMIN NAT/G CENTRAL GOV/REL

C53
KRACKE E.A. JR.,"CIVIL SERVICE IN EARLY SUNG CHINA, 960-1067." ASIA GP/REL...BIBLIOG/A 10/11. PAGE 88 H1762 ADMIN NAT/G WORKER CONTROL

N53
VITO F.,"RECENT DEVELOPMENTS IN THE THEORY OF DEMOCRATIC ADMIN" INTL POL SCI ASS'N CONFERENCE ON PUBLIC ADMINISTRATION... FRANCE ITALY UK REPRESENT EFFICIENCY NEW/LIB SOCISM...WELF/ST 20. PAGE 163 H3257 GOV/COMP CONTROL EX/STRUC

B54
BERGER M.,FREEDOM AND CONTROL IN MODERN SOCIETY. LABOR NAT/G VOL/ASSN AUTHORIT DRIVE PLURISM ...METH/CNCPT CLASSIF. PAGE 15 H0300 ORD/FREE CONTROL INGP/REL

B54
GRAYSON H.,ECONOMIC PLANNING UNDER FREE ENTERPRISE. CANADA FUT UK DELIB/GP BUDGET CONFER CONTROL ...POLICY DECISION 20. PAGE 60 H1200 PLAN ECO/TAC NAT/COMP NAT/G

B54
SALVEMINI G.,PRELUDE TO WORLD WAR II. ITALY MOD/EUR INT/ORG BAL/PWR EDU/PROP CONTROL TOTALISM...TREND NAT/COMP BIBLIOG 19 HITLER/A LEAGUE/NAT MUSSOLIN/B. PAGE 137 H2745 WAR FASCISM LEAD PWR

C54
BERLE A.A. JR.,"THE 20TH CENTURY CAPITALIST REVOLUTION." ECO/DEV NAT/G DIPLOM PRICE CONTROL ATTIT...BIBLIOG/A 20. PAGE 15 H0306 LG/CO CAP/ISM MGT PWR

B55
FOGARTY M.P.,ECONOMIC CONTROL. FUT UK ECO/DEV FINAN CONSULT INT/TRADE...CHARTS BIBLIOG/A 20. PAGE 52 H1033 ECO/TAC NAT/G CONTROL PROB/SOLV

B55
GALLOWAY G.B.,CONGRESS AND PARLIAMENT: THEIR ORGANIZATION AND OPERATION IN THE US AND THE UK: PLANNING PAMPHLET NO. 93. POL/PAR EX/STRUC DEBATE CONTROL LEAD ROUTINE EFFICIENCY PWR...POLICY CONGRESS PARLIAMENT. PAGE 54 H1089 DELIB/GP LEGIS PARL/PROC GOV/COMP

B55
INTERNATIONAL COMN JURISTS,JUSTICE ENSLAVED. COM CONSTN LABOR NAT/G CONTROL CHOOSE 20. PAGE 78 H1555 SOCISM TOTALISM ORD/FREE COERCE

B55
ROWE C.,VOLTAIRE AND THE STATE. FRANCE MOD/EUR BAL/PWR CONTROL TASK SUPEGO ORD/FREE PWR...CONCPT 18 VOLTAIRE. PAGE 135 H2702 NAT/G DIPLOM NAT/LISM ATTIT

B55
SERRANO MOSCOSO E.,A STATEMENT OF THE LAWS OF ECUADOR IN MATTERS AFFECTING BUSINESS (2ND ED.). ECUADOR INDUS LABOR LG/CO NAT/G LEGIS TAX CONTROL MARRIAGE 20. PAGE 141 H2830 FINAN ECO/UNDEV LAW CONSTN

B55
WHEARE K.C.,GOVERNMENT BY COMMITTEE; AN ESSAY ON THE BRITISH CONSTITUTION. UK NAT/G LEGIS INSPECT CONFER ADJUD ADMIN CONTROL TASK EFFICIENCY ROLE POPULISM 20. PAGE 167 H3337 DELIB/GP CONSTN LEAD GP/COMP

C55
APTER D.E.,"THE GOLD COAST IN TRANSITION." AFR CONSTN LOC/G LEGIS DIPLOM COLONIAL CONTROL GOV/REL ...CHARTS BIBLIOG 20 CMN/WLTH. PAGE 7 H0150 ORD/FREE REPRESENT PARL/PROC NAT/G

C55
OLIVER D.L.,"A LEADER IN ACTION," IN D. A. OLIVER, SOLOMON ISLAND SOCIETY." S/ASIA SOCIETY STRUCT CONTROL TASK PWR...OBS/ENVIR WORSHIP 20. PAGE 121 H2413 LEAD RESPECT CULTURE KIN

B56
CARRIL B.,PROBLEMAS DE LA REVOLUCION Y LA DEMOCRACIA. CONSTN FORCES DOMIN CONTROL TOTALISM PWR 20. PAGE 27 H0539 REV ORD/FREE LEGIT NAT/G

B56
SPINKA M.,THE CHURCH IN SOVIET RUSSIA. USSR CONTROL LEAD TASK COERCE 20. PAGE 147 H2949 GP/REL NAT/G SECT PWR

L56
EISENTADT S.N.,"POLITICAL STRUGGLE IN BUREAUCRATIC SOCIETIES" ASIA CULTURE ADJUD SANCTION PWR BUREAUCRCY OTTOMAN BYZANTINE. PAGE 45 H0901
ADMIN CHIEF CONTROL ROUTINE

B57
ALEXANDER L.M.,WORLD POLITICAL PATTERNS. NAT/G PROVS CAP/ISM DIPLOM COLONIAL NAT/LISM...POLICY GEOG CHARTS METH/COMP NAT/COMP 20. PAGE 5 H0101
CONTROL METH GOV/COMP

B57
BARAN P.A.,THE POLITICAL ECONOMY OF GROWTH. MOD/EUR USA+45 USA-45 TEC/DEV TAX SOCISM...MGT CONCPT GOV/COMP. PAGE 11 H0213
CAP/ISM CONTROL ECO/UNDEV FINAN

B57
HOUN F.W.,CENTRAL GOVERNMENT OF CHINA, 1912-1928. ASIA CONSTN CHIEF LEGIS CONTROL PWR...BIBLIOG 20. PAGE 74 H1480
POL/PAR ATTIT NAT/G PLAN

B57
PALACIOS A.L.,PETROLEO, MONOPOLIOS, Y LATIFUNDIOS. L/A+17C EXTR/IND NAT/G TEC/DEV ECO/TAC CONTROL PRODUC 20 ARGEN MONOPOLY RESOURCE/N. PAGE 123 H2448
ECO/UNDEV NAT/LISM INDUS AGRI

B57
RUMEU DE ARMAS A.,ESPANA EEN EL AFRICA ATLANTICA. AFR CHRIST-17C PORTUGAL SPAIN DIPLOM ECO/TAC CONTROL 14/16 AFRICA/W. PAGE 136 H2717
NAT/G COLONIAL CHIEF PWR

B57
TAYLOR J.V.,CHRISTIANITY AND POLITICS IN AFRICA. AFR CONTROL PARTIC GP/REL RACE/REL ATTIT...POLICY BIBLIOG/A WORSHIP 20. PAGE 153 H3055
SECT NAT/G NAT/LISM

S57
LEWIS E.G.,"PARLIAMENTARY CONTROL OF NATIONALIZED INDUSTRY IN FRANCE." FRANCE NAT/G DELIB/GP ACT/RES PLAN PROB/SOLV ECO/TAC DOMIN CENTRAL. PAGE 96 H1914
PWR LEGIS INDUS CONTROL

B58
CARTER G.M.,TRANSITION IN AFRICA; STUDIES IN POLITICAL ADAPTATION. AFR CENTRL/AFR GHANA NIGERIA CONSTN LOC/G POL/PAR ADMIN GP/REL FEDERAL...MAJORIT BIBLIOG 20. PAGE 27 H0543
NAT/COMP PWR CONTROL NAT/G

B58
CROWE S.,THE LANDSCAPE OF POWER. UK CULTURE SERV/IND NAT/G CONSULT PARTIC NUC/PWR LEISURE...SOC EXHIBIT 20. PAGE 36 H0712
HABITAT TEC/DEV PLAN CONTROL

B58
HSU U.T.,THE INVISIBLE CONFLICT. ASIA USSR ELITES NAT/G CONTROL LEAD COERCE REV WAR NAT/LISM ORD/FREE PWR 20 COM/PARTY ESPIONAGE. PAGE 74 H1485
MARXISM POL/PAR EDU/PROP FORCES

B58
MCIVOR R.C.,CANADIAN MONETARY, BANKING, AND FISCAL DEVELOPMENT. CANADA INDUS LG/CO NAT/G SML/CO CONTROL WAR...GEN/LAWS BIBLIOG 17/20. PAGE 107 H2137
ECO/TAC FINAN ECO/DEV WEALTH

B58
SCOTT D.J.R.,RUSSIAN POLITICAL INSTITUTIONS. RUSSIA USSR CONSTN AGRI DELIB/GP PLAN EDU/PROP CONTROL CHOOSE EFFICIENCY ATTIT MARXISM...BIBLIOG/A 13/20. PAGE 141 H2813
NAT/G POL/PAR ADMIN DECISION

B58
STRAUSZ-HUPE R.,THE IDEA OF COLONIALISM. WOR+45 WOR-45 BAL/PWR GOV/REL...POLICY CLASSIF TIME/SEQ GOV/COMP ANTHOL 20 UN. PAGE 150 H2996
IDEA/COMP COLONIAL CONTROL CONCPT

S58
LOCKWOOD W.W.,"THE SOCIALISTIC SOCIETY: INDIA AND JAPAN." INDIA ECO/DEV ECO/UNDEV INDUS NAT/G CONTROL LEAD PRODUC WEALTH 20 CHINJAP. PAGE 98 H1948
ECO/TAC NAT/COMP FINAN SOCISM

B59
CHODOROV F.,THE RISE AND FALL OF SOCIETY. NAT/G CONTROL ORD/FREE...TIME/SEQ 20. PAGE 30 H0596
SOC INGP/REL ECO/DEV ATTIT

B59
DEHIO L.,GERMANY AND WORLD POLITICS IN THE TWENTIETH CENTURY. EUR+WWI FRANCE GERMANY MOD/EUR UK USSR NAT/G CHIEF BAL/PWR DOMIN COLONIAL CONTROL LEAD...IDEA/COMP 20 VERSAILLES. PAGE 39 H0783
DIPLOM WAR NAT/LISM SOVEREIGN

B59
GUDIN E.,INFLACAO (2ND ED.). INDUS NAT/G PLAN ECO/TAC CONTROL COST 20. PAGE 62 H1243
ECO/UNDEV INT/TRADE BAL/PAY FINAN

B59
HANSON A.H.,THE STRUCTURE AND CONTROL OF STATE ENTERPRISES IN TURKEY. TURKEY LAW ADMIN GOV/REL EFFICIENCY...CHARTS 20. PAGE 66 H1319
NAT/G LG/CO OWN CONTROL

B59
INTERNATIONAL PRESS INSTITUTE,THE PRESS IN AUTHORITARIAN COUNTRIES. COM PORTUGAL SPAIN UAR USSR NAT/G DOMIN LEGIT ORD/FREE FASCISM SOCISM 20. PAGE 78 H1559
PRESS CONTROL TOTALISM EDU/PROP

B59
JENKINS C.,POWER AT THE TOP: A CRITICAL SURVEY OF THE NATIONALIZED INDUSTRIES. UK POL/PAR CONTROL ...WELF/ST CHARTS 20 LABOR/PAR. PAGE 80 H1601
NAT/G OWN INDUS NEW/LIB

B59
MAC MILLAN W.M.,THE ROAD TO SELF-RULE. SOUTH/AFR UK CULTURE SOCIETY AGRI LABOR NAT/G INT/TRADE CONTROL GP/REL...SOC 19/20. PAGE 100 H1988
AFR COLONIAL SOVEREIGN POLICY

B59
MATHER F.C.,PUBLIC ORDER IN THE AGE OF THE CHARTISTS. UK CULTURE ADJUD CONTROL. PAGE 105 H2090
ORD/FREE FORCES COERCE CIVMIL/REL

B59
SZLUC T.,TWILIGHT OF THE TYRANTS. BRAZIL L/A+17C PERU VENEZUELA NAT/G FORCES CONTROL PERSON MORAL ORD/FREE PWR...CONCPT 20 ARGEN COLOMB. PAGE 151 H3028
TOTALISM CHIEF REV FASCISM

B59
VERNEY D.V.,PUBLIC ENTERPRISE IN SWEDEN. FUT SWEDEN UK INDUS POL/PAR LEGIS PROB/SOLV CAP/ISM INT/TRADE CONTROL SOCISM...MGT CONCPT NAT/COMP 20 SOCDEM/PAR CIVIL/SERV. PAGE 162 H3246
ECO/DEV POLICY LG/CO NAT/G

B59
WRAITH R.E.,EAST AFRICAN CITIZEN. AFR GHANA UK AGRI INDUS LOC/G POL/PAR PROB/SOLV CONTROL REGION REPRESENT NAT/LISM PWR...OBS 20 AFRICA/E AFRICA/W. PAGE 171 H3415
ECO/UNDEV RACE/REL NAT/G NAT/COMP

B60
ALBI F.,TRATADO DE LOS MODOS DE GESTION DE LAS CORPORACIONES LOCALES. SPAIN FINAN NAT/G BUDGET CONTROL EXEC ROUTINE GOV/REL ORD/FREE SOVEREIGN ...MGT 20. PAGE 5 H0092
LOC/G LAW ADMIN MUNIC

B60
BANERJEE D.N.,OUR FUNDAMENTAL RIGHTS: THEIR NATURE AND EXTENT (AS JUDICIALLY DETERMINED). INDIA UK CULTURE STRATA NAT/G WORKER EDU/PROP CONTROL DISCRIM OWN...IDEA/COMP WORSHIP 20 REFORMERS COMMONWLTH. PAGE 10 H0207
CONSTN ORD/FREE LEGIS POLICY

B60
BHAMBHRI C.P.,PARLIAMENTARY CONTROL OVER STATE ENTERPRISE IN INDIA. INDIA DELIB/GP ADMIN CONTROL INGP/REL EFFICIENCY 20 PARLIAMENT. PAGE 16 H0327
NAT/G OWN INDUS PARL/PROC

B60
KERSELL J.E.,PARLIAMENTARY SUPERVISION OF DELEGATED LEGISLATION. UK EFFICIENCY PWR...POLICY CHARTS BIBLIOG METH 20 PARLIAMENT. PAGE 85 H1699
LEGIS CONTROL NAT/G EX/STRUC

B60
LASKIN B.,CANADIAN CONSTITUTIONAL LAW: TEXT AND NOTES ON DISTRIBUTION OF LEGISLATIVE POWER (2ND ED.). CANADA LOC/G ECO/TAC TAX CONTROL CT/SYS CRIME FEDERAL PWR...JURID 20 PARLIAMENT. PAGE 92 H1832
CONSTN NAT/G LAW LEGIS

B60
MORAES F.,THE REVOLT IN TIBET. ASIA CHINA/COM INDIA CULTURE CONTROL COERCE WAR TOTALISM...POLICY SOC WORSHIP 20 TIBET INTERVENT. PAGE 113 H2252
COLONIAL FORCES DIPLOM ORD/FREE

B60
PINTO F.B.M.,ENRIQUECIMENTO ILICITO NO EXERCICIO DE CARGOS PUBLICOS. BRAZIL L/A+17C USA+45 ELITES TRIBUTE CONTROL INGP/REL ORD/FREE PWR...NAT/COMP 20. PAGE 126 H2513
ADMIN NAT/G CRIME LAW

B60
PRASAD B.,THE ORIGINS OF PROVINCIAL AUTONOMY. INDIA UK FINAN LOC/G FORCES LEGIS CONTROL CT/SYS PWR ...JURID 19/20. PAGE 128 H2554
CENTRAL PROVS COLONIAL NAT/G

B60
ROBERTSON D.,THE CONTROL OF INDUSTRY. UK MARKET LABOR WORKER PRICE CONTROL GP/REL COST DEMAND ORD/FREE WEALTH NEW/LIB SOCISM 20. PAGE 132 H2646
INDUS FINAN NAT/G ECO/DEV

B60
SCANLON D.G.,INTERNATIONAL EDUCATION: A DOCUMENTARY HISTORY. ADMIN CONTROL ATTIT PERCEPT...BIOG ANTHOL METH 20. PAGE 138 H2765
EDU/PROP INT/ORG NAT/COMP DIPLOM

B60
SCHEIBER H.N.,THE WILSON ADMINISTRATION AND CIVIL LIBERTIES 1917-1921. LAW GOV/REL ATTIT 20 WILSON/W CIVIL/LIB. PAGE 139 H2782
ORD/FREE WAR NAT/G CONTROL

B60
THORD-GRAY I.,GRINGO REBEL. L/A+17C NAT/G CONTROL LEAD ATTIT...OBS 20 MEXIC/AMER. PAGE 154 H3087
REV FORCES CIVMIL/REL ORD/FREE

B60
WEINER H.E.,BRITISH LABOR AND PUBLIC OWNERSHIP. UK SERV/IND LG/CO WORKER CONTROL OWN 20. PAGE 166
LABOR NAT/G

H3327 INDUS ATTIT

B60
RUDD J.,TABOO, A STUDY OF MALAGASY CUSTOMS AND BELIEFS. MADAGASCAR LAW FAM CONTROL CRIME PERSON ...CONCPT 20. PAGE 173 H3466 CULTURE DOMIN SECT SANCTION

S60
TURNER R.H.,"SPONSORED AND CONTEST MOBILITY IN THE SCHOOL SYSTEM." UK USA+45 ELITES STRATA ACADEM FACE/GP EDU/PROP CONTROL INGP/REL ADJUST ATTIT PERSON...METH/COMP 20. PAGE 157 H3142 AGE/Y NAT/COMP SCHOOL STRUCT

C60
HAZARD J.N.,"SETTLING DISPUTES IN SOVIET SOCIETY: THE FORMATIVE YEARS OF LEGAL INSTITUTIONS." USSR NAT/G PROF/ORG PROB/SOLV CONTROL CT/SYS ROUTINE REV CENTRAL...JURID BIBLIOG 20. PAGE 68 H1372 ADJUD LAW COM POLICY

B61
ALLIGHAN G.,VERWOERD - THE END. SOUTH/AFR TOP/EX DIPLOM COLONIAL DISCRIM TOTALISM ATTIT AUTHORIT ...BIOG 20 NEGRO VERWOERD/H. PAGE 5 H0107 CONTROL CHIEF RACE/REL NAT/G

B61
ALSTON P.L.,STATE EDUCATION AND SOCIAL CHANGE IN THE RUSSIAN EMPIRE 1871-1914 (PAPER). RUSSIA ELITES PROF/ORG EDU/PROP CONTROL PRIVIL AGE/Y...BIBLIOG 19/20. PAGE 6 H0115 SCHOOL SOCIETY NAT/G GP/REL

B61
BLAKE J.,FAMILY STRUCTURE IN JAMAICA. JAMAICA CULTURE SOCIETY ACT/RES CONTROL MARRIAGE AGE ...POLICY SOC BIBLIOG 20. PAGE 18 H0351 FAM SEX STRUCT ATTIT

B61
BREWIS T.N.,CANADIAN ECONOMIC POLICY. CANADA BUDGET CAP/ISM INT/TRADE RATION TARIFFS TAX PRICE CONTROL ROUTINE FEDERAL INCOME PRODUC 20 GOLD/STAND. PAGE 20 H0412 ECO/DEV ECO/TAC NAT/G PLAN

B61
DONNISON F.S.V.,CIVIL AFFAIRS AND MILITARY GOVERNMENT NORTH-WEST EUROPE 1944-1946. EUR+WWI FRANCE GERMANY UK USSR LOC/G PROVS PLAN PROB/SOLV BAL/PWR ECO/TAC CONTROL PWR...CHARTS 20. PAGE 42 H0836 NAT/G WAR FORCES CIVMIL/REL

B61
ESTEBAN J.C.,IMPERIALISMO Y DESARROLLO ECONOMICO. L/A+17C FINAN INDUS NAT/G ECO/TAC CONTROL ROLE. PAGE 47 H0941 ECO/UNDEV NAT/LISM DIPLOM BAL/PAY

B61
LAHAYE R.,LES ENTREPRISES PUBLIQUES AU MAROC. FRANCE MOROCCO LAW DIST/IND EXTR/IND FINAN CONSULT PLAN TEC/DEV ADMIN AGREE CONTROL OWN...POLICY 20. PAGE 90 H1796 NAT/G INDUS ECO/UNDEV ECO/TAC

B61
LETHBRIDGE H.J.,CHINA'S URBAN COMMUNES. CHINA/COM FUT ECO/UNDEV DIPLOM EDU/PROP DEMAND INCOME MARXISM ...POLICY 20. PAGE 95 H1893 MUNIC CONTROL ECO/TAC NAT/G

B61
MONAS S.,THE THIRD SECTION: POLICE AND SOCIETY IN RUSSIA UNDER NICHOLAS I. MOD/EUR RUSSIA ELITES STRUCT NAT/G EX/STRUC ADMIN CONTROL PWR CONSERVE ...DECISION 19 NICHOLAS/I. PAGE 112 H2238 ORD/FREE COM FORCES COERCE

B61
NARASIMHAN V.K.,THE PRESS, THE PUBLIC AND THE ADMINISTRATION (PAMPHLET). INDIA COM/IND CONTROL REPRESENT GOV/REL EFFICIENCY...ANTHOL 20. PAGE 116 H2312 NAT/G ADMIN PRESS NEW/LIB

B61
ROIG E.,MARTI, ANTIIMPERIALISTA. CUBA L/A+17C DIPLOM DOMIN COLONIAL CONTROL LEAD PWR SOVEREIGN ...PHIL/SCI 19 MARTI/JOSE INTERVENT. PAGE 133 H2664 PERSON NAT/LISM ECO/UNDEV ORD/FREE

B61
SCHECHTMAN J.B.,ON WINGS OF EAGLES: THE PLIGHT, EXODUS, AND HOMECOMING OF ORIENTAL JEWRY. ASIA ISLAM ISRAEL VOL/ASSN DIPLOM CONTROL ORD/FREE ...GEOG WORSHIP SOC/INTEG 20 JEWS ARABS MIGRATION. PAGE 139 H2777 CULTURE HABITAT KIN SECT

B61
SHARMA T.R.,THE WORKING OF STATE ENTERPRISES IN INDIA. INDIA DELIB/GP LEGIS WORKER BUDGET PRICE CONTROL GP/REL OWN ATTIT...MGT CHARTS 20. PAGE 142 H2851 NAT/G INDUS ADMIN SOCISM

B62
BARNETT A.D.,COMMUNIST CHINA IN PERSPECTIVE. CHINA/COM FUT CULTURE ECO/UNDEV TEC/DEV CONTROL 20. PAGE 11 H0222 REV MARXISM TREND PLAN

B62
BERNOT R.M.,EXCESS AND RESTRAINT: SOCIAL CONTROL AMONG GUINEA MOUNTAIN PEOPLE. CULTURE FAM KIN CT/SYS COERCE WAR PERS/REL MARRIAGE HABITAT SEX ...MYTH 20 NEW/GUINEA. PAGE 16 H0314 SOCIETY CONTROL STRUCT ADJUST

B62
EBENSTEIN W.,TWO WAYS OF LIFE. USA+45 CULTURE ECO/DEV PLAN EDU/PROP CONTROL ORD/FREE...GOV/COMP IDEA/COMP T 20 MARX/KARL ENGELS/F LENIN/VI LOCKE/JOHN MILL/JS. PAGE 44 H0885 MARXISM POPULISM ECO/TAC DIPLOM

B62
EDWARDS A.C.,THE OVIMBUNDU UNDER TWO SOVEREIGNTIES. CULTURE STRUCT FAM MARRIAGE HABITAT...SOC 19/20 OVIMBUNDU. PAGE 45 H0891 KIN NEIGH SOCIETY CONTROL

B62
ESCUELA SUPERIOR DE ADMIN PUBL,INFORME DEL SEMINARIO SOBRE SERVICIO CIVIL O CARRERA ADMINISTRATIVA. L/A+17C ELITES STRATA CONFER CONTROL GOV/REL INGP/REL SUPEGO 20 CENTRAL/AM CIVIL/SERV. PAGE 47 H0939 ADMIN NAT/G PROB/SOLV ATTIT

B62
FEIT E.,SOUTH AFRICA, THE DYNAMICS OF THE AFRICAN NATIONAL CONGRESS. AFR SOUTH/AFR LAW INTELL STRATA KIN NAT/G POL/PAR ECO/TAC DOMIN RISK COERCE 20 NEGRO. PAGE 49 H0984 RACE/REL ELITES CONTROL STRUCT

B62
FRYKLUND R.,100 MILLION LIVES: MAXIMUM SURVIVAL IN A NUCLEAR WAR. USA+45 USSR CONTROL WEAPON ...IDEA/COMP NAT/COMP 20. PAGE 54 H1073 NUC/PWR WAR PLAN DETER

B62
GROGAN V.,ADMINISTRATIVE TRIBUNALS IN THE PUBLIC SERVICE. IRELAND UK NAT/G CONTROL CT/SYS...JURID GOV/COMP 20. PAGE 61 H1231 ADMIN LAW ADJUD DELIB/GP

B62
GROVE J.W.,GOVERNMENT AND INDUSTRY IN BRITAIN. UK FINAN LOC/G CONSULT DELIB/GP INT/TRADE ADMIN CONTROL...BIBLIOG 20. PAGE 62 H1237 ECO/TAC INDUS NAT/G GP/REL

B62
GRZYBOWSKI K.,SOVIET LEGAL INSTITUTIONS. USA+45 USSR ECO/DEV NAT/G EDU/PROP CONTROL CT/SYS CRIME OWN ATTIT PWR SOCISM...NAT/COMP 20. PAGE 62 H1242 ADJUD LAW JURID

B62
HOOK S.,THE PARADOXES OF FREEDOM. UNIV CONSTN INTELL LEGIS CONTROL REV CHOOSE SUPEGO...POLICY JURID IDEA/COMP 19/20 CIV/RIGHTS. PAGE 73 H1461 CONCPT MAJORIT ORD/FREE ALL/VALS

B62
HUNKIN P.,ENSEIGNEMENT ET POLITIQUE EN FRANCE ET EN ANGLETERRE. FRANCE UK CONSTN ACADEM SECT CHIEF DELIB/GP PROB/SOLV CONTROL REV ORD/FREE CONSERVE ...BIBLIOG 18/20. PAGE 75 H1496 EDU/PROP LEGIS IDEA/COMP NAT/G

B62
KAGZI M.C.,THE INDIAN ADMINISTRATIVE LAW. INDIA LG/CO CONTROL CT/SYS...CONCPT 20. PAGE 83 H1649 JURID ADJUD DELIB/GP NAT/G

B62
KARNJAHAPRAKORN C.,MUNICIPAL GOVERNMENT IN THAILAND AS AN INSTITUTION AND PROCESS OF SELF-GOVERNMENT. THAILAND CULTURE FINAN EX/STRUC LEGIS PLAN CONTROL GOV/REL EFFICIENCY ATTIT...POLICY 20. PAGE 83 H1662 LOC/G MUNIC ORD/FREE ADMIN

B62
KINDERSLEY R.,THE FIRST RUSSIAN REVISIONISTS. COM USSR LAW ELITES INTELL NAT/G LEGIS ECO/TAC EDU/PROP CONTROL LEAD GP/REL SOCISM 19/20 MARX/KARL BOLSHEVISM. PAGE 86 H1712 CONSTN MARXISM POPULISM BIOG

B62
STATE AND LOCAL GOVERNMENT. MUNIC NAT/G NEIGH PRESS CONTROL CHOOSE REPRESENT...BIBLIOG 20. PAGE 104 H2076 PROVS LOC/G GOV/REL PWR

B62
MEGGITT M.J.,DESERT PEOPLE. ECO/UNDEV KIN CREATE PROB/SOLV CONTROL DRIVE ROLE...GEOG SOC MYTH CHARTS BIBLIOG 20 AUSTRAL. PAGE 108 H2159 ADJUST CULTURE INGP/REL HABITAT

B62
MEIER R.L.,A COMMUNICATIONS THEORY OF URBAN GROWTH. CULTURE ECO/DEV COMPUTER BUDGET UTIL KNOWL...SOC CONCPT METH 20 OPEN/SPACE. PAGE 108 H2164 OP/RES COM/IND MUNIC CONTROL

B62
NOBECOURT R.G.,LES SECRETS DE LA PROPAGANDE EN FRANCE OCCUPEE. FRANCE ELITES NAT/G DIPLOM GP/REL NAT/LISM TOTALISM ORD/FREE 20 VICHY VICHY. PAGE 118 H2365 METH/COMP EDU/PROP WAR CONTROL

B62
PASTOR R.S.,A STATEMENT OF THE LAWS OF PARAGUAY IN MATTERS AFFECTING BUSINESS (2ND ED.). PARAGUAY INDUS FAM LABOR LG/CO NAT/G LEGIS TAX CONTROL MARRIAGE 20. PAGE 124 H2474 FINAN ECO/UNDEV LAW CONSTN

B62
PHELPS E.S.,THE GOAL OF ECONOMIC GROWTH: SOURCES, COSTS, BENEFITS. USA+45 USSR FINAN TAX CONTROL DEMAND WEALTH...POLICY NAT/COMP ANTHOL BIBLIOG 20. PAGE 125 H2499 ECO/TAC ECO/DEV NAT/G FUT

B62
SWAYZE H.,POLITICAL CONTROL OF LITERATURE IN THE USSR, 1946-1959. USSR NAT/G CREATE LICENSE...JURID MARXISM WRITING

20. PAGE 151 H3014
CONTROL DOMIN

B62
ZINKIN T.,REPORTING INDIA. INDIA PAKISTAN WOR+45 SOCIETY SECT FORCES EDU/PROP CROWD DISCRIM NAT/LISM MARXISM...POLICY 20. PAGE 173 H3457
STRATA COLONIAL BAL/PWR CONTROL

S62
BRAIBANTI R.,"REFLECTIONS ON BUREAUCRATIC CORRPUTION." LAW REPRESENT 20. PAGE 20 H0400
CONTROL MORAL ADMIN GOV/COMP

C62
BACON F.,"OF EMPIRE" (1612) IN F. BACON, ESSAYS." ELITES NAT/G PROB/SOLV DIPLOM ADMIN CONTROL WEALTH 16/17 KING. PAGE 9 H0190
PWR CHIEF DOMIN GEN/LAWS

C62
BACON F.,"OF SEDITIONS AND TROUBLES" (1625) IN F. BACON, ESSAYS." INDUS MARKET CHIEF ECO/TAC EDU/PROP CONTROL LEAD PEACE WEALTH 17 MACHIAVELL. PAGE 9 H0191
REV ORD/FREE NAT/G GEN/LAWS

B63
ADRIAN C.R.,GOVERNING OVER FIFTY STATES AND THEIR COMMUNITIES. USA+45 CONSTN FINAN MUNIC NAT/G POL/PAR EX/STRUC LEGIS ADMIN CONTROL CT/SYS ...CHARTS 20. PAGE 4 H0073
PROVS LOC/G GOV/REL GOV/COMP

B63
BIALEK R.W.,CATHOLIC POLITICS: A HISTORY BASED ON ECUADOR. ECUADOR SPAIN CULTURE STRUCT CONTROL REV PWR...BIBLIOG WORSHIP 18/20. PAGE 16 H0329
COLONIAL CATHISM GOV/REL HABITAT

B63
DALAND R.T.,PERSPECTIVES OF BRAZILIAN PUBLIC ADMINISTRATION (VOL. I). BRAZIL LAW ECO/UNDEV SCHOOL CHIEF TEC/DEV CONFER CONTROL GP/REL ATTIT ROLE PWR...ANTHOL 20. PAGE 37 H0735
ADMIN NAT/G PLAN GOV/REL

B63
DE JOUVENEL B.,THE PURE THEORY OF POLITICS. NAT/G DIPLOM CONTROL GP/REL PERS/REL PERSON PWR OBJECTIVE CONCPT. PAGE 38 H0758
GEN/LAWS SOCIETY METH/CNCPT

B63
DEUTSCH K.W.,THE NERVES OF GOVERNMENT. NAT/G CREATE EDU/PROP CONTROL LEAD PWR...CONCPT GEN/LAWS 20. PAGE 40 H0799
DECISION GAME SIMUL OP/RES

B63
FIRST R.,SOUTH WEST AFRICA. SOUTH/AFR INT/ORG KIN NAT/G WORKER COLONIAL WAR...POLICY 20 UN TRUST/TERR AFRICA/SW. PAGE 50 H1006
DISCRIM ORD/FREE RACE/REL CONTROL

B63
FRIEDRICH C.J.,MAN AND HIS GOVERNMENT: AN EMPIRICAL THEORY OF POLITICS. UNIV LOC/G NAT/G ADJUD REV INGP/REL DISCRIM PWR BIBLIOG. PAGE 53 H1069
PERSON ORD/FREE PARTIC CONTROL

B63
GARDINIER D.E.,CAMEROON: UNITED NATIONS CHALLENGE TO FRENCH POLICY. AFR CAMEROON FRANCE NAT/G LEGIS CONTROL SOVEREIGN 20 UN. PAGE 55 H1101
DIPLOM POLICY INT/ORG COLONIAL

B63
GERSCHENKRON A.,THE STABILITY OF DICTATORSHIPS. NAT/G EDU/PROP TASK ATTIT PERSON...POLICY PSY SOC METH 19/20. PAGE 56 H1116
TOTALISM CONCPT CONTROL ORD/FREE

B63
GONZALEZ PEDRERO E.,ANATOMIA DE UN CONFLICTO. WOR+45 ECO/DEV ECO/UNDEV ECO/TAC FOR/AID CONTROL ARMS/CONT GOV/REL...NAT/COMP 20 COLD/WAR. PAGE 58 H1166
DIPLOM DETER BAL/PWR

B63
HAQ M.,THE STRATEGY OF ECONOMIC PLANNING. PAKISTAN AGRI FINAN INDUS NAT/G FOR/AID TAX CONTROL REGION PRODUC...POLICY CHARTS 20. PAGE 66 H1324
ECO/TAC ECO/UNDEV PLAN PROB/SOLV

B63
HOLLANDER P.,THE NEW MAN AND HIS ENEMIES: A STUDY OF THE STALINIST CONCEPTIONS OF GOOD AND EVIL PERSONIFIED (DOCTORAL THESIS). USSR SOCIETY ECO/DEV NAT/G EDU/PROP WRITING...SOC STERTYP BIBLIOG 20 STALIN/J. PAGE 73 H1455
CONTROL ATTIT TOTALISM MARXISM

B63
HYDE D.,THE PEACEFUL ASSAULT. COM UAR USSR ECO/DEV ECO/UNDEV NAT/G POL/PAR CAP/ISM PWR 20. PAGE 76 H1516
MARXISM CONTROL ECO/TAC DIPLOM

B63
JACOB H.,GERMAN ADMINISTRATION SINCE BISMARCK: CENTRAL AUTHORITY VERSUS LOCAL AUTONOMY. GERMANY GERMANY/W LAW POL/PAR CONTROL CENTRAL TOTALISM FASCISM...MAJORIT DECISION STAT CHARTS GOV/COMP 19/20 BISMARCK/O HITLER/A WEIMAR/REP. PAGE 79 H1577
ADMIN NAT/G LOC/G POLICY

B63
LEWIN J.,POLITICS AND LAW IN SOUTH AFRICA. SOUTH/AFR UK POL/PAR BAL/PWR ECO/TAC COLONIAL CONTROL GP/REL DISCRIM PWR 20 NEGRO. PAGE 96 H1909
NAT/LISM POLICY LAW RACE/REL

B63
MERKL P.H.,THE ORIGIN OF THE WEST GERMAN REPUBLIC. GERMANY/W WOR+45 POL/PAR DIPLOM LEAD LOBBY REPRESENT GP/REL NAT/LISM 20. PAGE 109 H2179
CONSTN PARL/PROC CONTROL BAL/PWR

B63
SELF P.,THE STATE AND THE FARMER. UK ECO/DEV MARKET WORKER PRICE CONTROL GP/REL...WELF/ST 20 DEPT/AGRI. PAGE 141 H2823
AGRI NAT/G ADMIN VOL/ASSN

B63
SINGH H.L.,PROBLEMS AND POLICIES OF THE BRITISH IN INDIA, 1885-1898. INDIA UK NAT/G FORCES LEGIS PROB/SOLV CONTROL RACE/REL ADJUST DISCRIM NAT/LISM RIGID/FLEX...MGT 19 CIVIL/SERV. PAGE 144 H2885
COLONIAL PWR POLICY ADMIN

B63
THOMPSON F.M.L.,ENGLISH LANDED SOCIETY IN THE NINETEENTH CENTURY. UK STRUCT MUNIC NAT/G CONTROL WAR GP/REL OWN WEALTH...BIBLIOG 18/20. PAGE 154 H3081
STRATA PWR ELITES GOV/REL

B63
WEINER M.,POLITICAL CHANGE IN SOUTH ASIA. CEYLON INDIA PAKISTAN S/ASIA CULTURE ELITES ECO/UNDEV EX/STRUC ADMIN CONTROL CHOOSE CONSERVE...GOV/COMP ANTHOL 20. PAGE 166 H3328
NAT/G CONSTN TEC/DEV

L63
BOLGAR V.,"THE PUBLIC INTEREST: A JURISPRUDENTIAL AND COMPARATIVE OVERVIEW OF SYMPOSIUM ON FUNDAMENTAL CONCEPTS OF PUBLIC LAW" COM FRANCE GERMANY SWITZERLND LAW ADJUD ADMIN AGREE LAISSEZ ...JURID GEN/LAWS 20 EUROPE/E. PAGE 18 H0369
CONCPT ORD/FREE CONTROL NAT/COMP

B64
BALOGH T.,THE ECONOMIC IMPACT OF MONETARY AND COMMERCIAL INSTITUTIONS OF A EUROPEAN ORIGIN IN AFRICA. AFR UAR INDUS FOR/AID COLONIAL CONTROL ...NAT/COMP 20. PAGE 10 H0205
TEC/DEV FINAN ECO/UNDEV ECO/TAC

B64
BUNTING B.P.,THE RISE OF THE SOUTH AFRICAN REICH. SOUTH/AFR INT/ORG NAT/G FORCES DIPLOM CONTROL WAR TOTALISM ATTIT...GOV/COMP 19/20. PAGE 24 H0477
RACE/REL DISCRIM NAT/LISM TREND

B64
ETZIONI A.,MODERN ORGANIZATIONS. CLIENT STRUCT DOMIN CONTROL LEAD PERS/REL AUTHORIT...CLASSIF BUREAUCRCY. PAGE 47 H0946
MGT ADMIN PLAN CULTURE

B64
FAINSOD M.,HOW RUSSIA IS RULED (REV. ED.). RUSSIA USSR AGRI PROC/MFG LABOR POL/PAR EX/STRUC CONTROL PWR...POLICY BIBLIOG 19/20 KHRUSH/N COM/PARTY. PAGE 48 H0963
NAT/G REV MARXISM

B64
HALE O.J.,THE CAPTIVE PRESS IN THE THIRD REICH. GERMANY CULTURE LG/CO NAT/G POL/PAR PLAN DOMIN TASK CENTRAL OWN TOTALISM PWR...BIBLIOG 20 HITLER/A NAZI AMMAN/MAX. PAGE 64 H1283
COM/IND PRESS CONTROL FASCISM

B64
HALLER W.,DER SCHWEDISCHE JUSTITIEOMBUDSMAN. DENMARK FINLAND NORWAY SWEDEN LEGIS ADJUD CONTROL PERSON ORD/FREE...NAT/COMP 20 OMBUDSMAN. PAGE 64 H1288
JURID PARL/PROC ADMIN CHIEF

B64
HILL C.R.,BANTUSTANS: THE FRAGMENTATION OF SOUTH AFRICA. AFR SOUTH/AFR ELITES SOCIETY KIN CONTROL DISCRIM ANOMIE ATTIT...POLICY CHARTS GOV/COMP 20 NEGRO BANTUSTANS TRANSKEI NATAL. PAGE 71 H1416
RACE/REL CULTURE LOC/G ORD/FREE

B64
IMAZ J.L.,LOS QUE MANDAN. INDUS LABOR NAT/G POL/PAR PROVS SECT CHIEF TOP/EX CONTROL 20 ARGEN. PAGE 76 H1524
LEAD FORCES ELITES ATTIT

B64
INTERNATIONAL LABOUR OFFICE,EMPLOYMENT AND ECONOMIC GROWTH. ECO/DEV ECO/UNDEV NAT/G PLAN DIPLOM INT/TRADE CONTROL INCOME PRODUC WEALTH...STAT NAT/COMP 20 ILO. PAGE 78 H1558
WORKER METH/COMP ECO/TAC OPTIMAL

B64
INTL CONF ON POPULATION,POPULATION DYNAMICS: INTERNATIONAL ACTION AND TRAINING PROGRAMS. INDIA KOREA L/A+17C TAIWAN USA+45 WOR+45 FAM PLAN CONFER ...NEW/IDEA ANTHOL 20 CHINJAP BIRTH/CON. PAGE 78 H1561
NAT/COMP CONTROL ATTIT EDU/PROP

B64
PINNICK A.W.,COUNTRY PLANNERS IN ACTION. UK FINAN SERV/IND NAT/G CONSULT DELIB/GP PRICE CONTROL ROUTINE LEISURE AGE/C...GEOG 20 URBAN/RNWL. PAGE 126 H2512
MUNIC PLAN INDUS ATTIT

B64
RIDLEY F.,PUBLIC ADMINISTRATION IN FRANCE. FRANCE UK EX/STRUC CONTROL PARTIC EFFICIENCY 20. PAGE 131 H2625
ADMIN REPRESENT GOV/COMP PWR

B64
RIES J.C.,THE MANAGEMENT OF DEFENSE: ORGANIZATION
FORCES

AND CONTROL OF THE US ARMED SERVICES. PROF/ORG DELIB/GP EX/STRUC LEGIS GOV/REL PERS/REL CENTRAL RATIONAL PWR...POLICY TREND GOV/COMP BIBLIOG. PAGE 131 H2626 — ACT/RES DECISION CONTROL

B64
TIERNEY B.,THE CRISIS OF CHURCH AND STATE 1050-1300. DOMIN EDU/PROP CONTROL PWR CONSERVE 11/14. PAGE 155 H3092 — SECT NAT/G GP/REL

B64
VOELKMANN K.,HERRSCHER VON MORGEN? BAL/PWR COLONIAL NEUTRAL REGION RACE/REL ALL/VALS SOVEREIGN...RECORD 20 COLD/WAR THIRD/WRLD. PAGE 163 H3259 — DIPLOM ECO/UNDEV CONTROL NAT/COMP

B64
WALDMAN E.,THE GOOSE STEP IS VERBOTEN: THE GERMAN ARMY TODAY. GERMANY/W LAW CONSTN LEGIS PROB/SOLV DOMIN CONTROL CIVMIL/REL GOV/REL INGP/REL ATTIT ...DEEP/QU 20. PAGE 164 H3289 — SOC FORCES NAT/G

B64
WERNETTE J.P.,GOVERNMENT AND BUSINESS. LABOR CAP/ISM ECO/TAC INT/TRADE TAX ADMIN AUTOMAT NUC/PWR CIVMIL/REL DEMAND...MGT 20 MONOPOLY. PAGE 167 H3333 — NAT/G FINAN ECO/DEV CONTROL

B64
WRIGHT Q.,A STUDY OF WAR. LAW NAT/G PROB/SOLV BAL/PWR NAT/LISM PEACE ATTIT SOVEREIGN...CENSUS SOC/INTEG. PAGE 171 H3421 — WAR CONCPT DIPLOM CONTROL

C64
GOLDMAN M.I.,"COMPARATIVE ECONOMIC SYSTEMS: A READER." COM ECO/UNDEV NAT/G BUDGET CAP/ISM ADMIN TOTALISM MARXISM SOCISM...MGT ANTHOL BIBLIOG 19/20. PAGE 58 H1157 — NAT/COMP CONTROL IDEA/COMP

B65
CHEN T.H.,THE CHINESE COMMUNIST REGIME: A DOCUMENTARY STUDY (2 VOLS.). CHINA/COM LAW CONSTN ELITES ECO/UNDEV LEGIS ECO/TAC ADMIN CONTROL PWR ...SOC 20. PAGE 29 H0587 — MARXISM POL/PAR NAT/G

B65
CHENG C.-Y.,SCIENTIFIC AND ENGINEERING MANPOWER IN COMMUNIST CHINA, 1949-1963. CHINA/COM USSR ELITES ECO/DEV R+D ACADEM LABOR NAT/G EDU/PROP CONTROL UTIL...POLICY BIBLIOG 20. PAGE 29 H0588 — WORKER CONSULT MARXISM BIOG

B65
CRAMER J.F.,CONTEMPORARY EDUCATION: A COMPARATIVE STUDY OF NATIONAL SYSTEMS (2ND ED.). CHINA/COM EUR+WWI INDIA USA+45 FINAN PROB/SOLV ADMIN CONTROL ATTIT...IDEA/COMP METH/COMP 20 CHINJAP. PAGE 35 H0697 — EDU/PROP NAT/COMP SCHOOL ACADEM

B65
EDELMAN M.,THE POLITICS OF WAGE-PRICE DECISIONS. GERMANY ITALY NETHERLAND UK INDUS LABOR POL/PAR PROB/SOLV BARGAIN PRICE ROUTINE BAL/PAY COST DEMAND 20. PAGE 44 H0888 — GOV/COMP CONTROL ECO/TAC PLAN

B65
FILIPINIANA BOOK GUILD,THE COLONIZATION AND CONQUEST OF THE PHILIPPINES BY SPAIN. PHILIPPINE SPAIN ELITES AGRI KIN CHIEF DOMIN CONTROL ATTIT PWR ...ANTHOL WORSHIP 16. PAGE 50 H1000 — COLONIAL COERCE CULTURE WAR

B65
GOLEMBIEWSKI R.T.,MEN, MANAGEMENT, AND MORALITY; TOWARD A NEW ORGANIZATIONAL ETHIC. CONSTN EX/STRUC CREATE ADMIN CONTROL INGP/REL PERSON SUPEGO MORAL PWR...GOV/COMP METH/COMP 20 BUREAUCRCY. PAGE 58 H1161 — LG/CO MGT PROB/SOLV

B65
GREGG J.L.,POLITICAL PARTIES AND PARTY SYSTEMS IN GUATEMALA, 1944-1963. GUATEMALA L/A+17C EX/STRUC FORCES CREATE CONTROL REV CHOOSE PWR...TREND IDEA/COMP 20. PAGE 60 H1209 — LEAD POL/PAR NAT/G CHIEF

B65
HAEFELE E.T.,GOVERNMENT CONTROLS ON TRANSPORT. AFR RHODESIA TANZANIA DIPLOM ECO/TAC TARIFFS PRICE ADJUD CONTROL REGION EFFICIENCY...POLICY 20 CONGO. PAGE 64 H1274 — ECO/UNDEV DIST/IND FINAN NAT/G

B65
HALEVY E.,THE ERA OF TYRANNIES (TRANS. BY R. K. WEBB). WOR-45 ECO/DEV PROB/SOLV CONTROL COERCE REV WAR TOTALISM 20. PAGE 64 H1286 — SOCISM IDEA/COMP DOMIN

B65
JACOB H.,POLITICS IN THE AMERICAN STATES; A COMPARATIVE ANALYSIS. USA+45 POL/PAR CHIEF LEGIS TAX EDU/PROP CONTROL CT/SYS LOBBY PARTIC...DECISION CHARTS 20. PAGE 79 H1578 — PROVS GOV/COMP PWR

B65
MCWHINNEY E.,JUDICIAL REVIEW IN THE ENGLISH-SPEAKING WORLD (3RD ED.). CANADA UK WOR+45 LEGIS CONTROL EXEC PARTIC...JURID 20 AUSTRAL. PAGE 108 H2151 — GOV/COMP CT/SYS ADJUD CONSTN

B65
MOORE C.H.,TUNISIA SINCE INDEPENDENCE. ELITES LOC/G POL/PAR ADMIN COLONIAL CONTROL EXEC GOV/REL TOTALISM MARXISM...INT 20 TUNIS. PAGE 112 H2248 — NAT/G EX/STRUC SOCISM

B65
MURDOCK G.P.,CULTURE AND SOCIETY. SOCIETY STRATA STRUCT SECT CREATE CONTROL ORD/FREE...GP/COMP ANTHOL 20. PAGE 115 H2294 — CULTURE PHIL/SCI METH IDEA/COMP

B65
PADELFORD N.,THE UNITED NATIONS IN THE BALANCE* ACCOMPLISHMENTS AND PROSPECTS. NAT/G VOL/ASSN DIPLOM ADMIN COLONIAL CT/SYS REGION WAR ORD/FREE ...ANTHOL UN. PAGE 122 H2437 — INT/ORG CONTROL

B65
PARRIS H.W.,GOVERNMENT AND THE RAILWAYS IN NINETEENTH-CENTURY BRITAIN. UK DELIB/GP CONTROL LEAD CENTRAL 19 RAILROAD. PAGE 124 H2470 — DIST/IND NAT/G PLAN GP/REL

S65
GOLDMAN M.I.,"A BALANCE SHEET OF SOVIET FOREIGN AID." USA+45 ECO/UNDEV BAL/PWR ECO/TAC RENT GIVE EDU/PROP CONTROL COST PROFIT GEN/METH. PAGE 58 H1158 — USSR FOR/AID NAT/COMP EFFICIENCY

S65
HUGHES T.L.,"SCHOLARS AND FOREIGN POLICY* VARIETIES OF RESEARCH EXPERIENCE." COM/IND DIPLOM ADMIN EXEC ROUTINE...MGT OBS CONGRESS PRESIDENT CAMELOT. PAGE 75 H1491 — ACT/RES ACADEM CONTROL NAT/G

S65
POWELL J.D.,"MILITARY ASSISTANCE AND MILITARISM IN LATIN AMERICA." USA+45 INT/ORG NAT/G CONTROL REGION PRODUC WEALTH...CLASSIF STAT NAT/COMP CONGRESS. PAGE 128 H2550 — L/A+17C FORCES FOR/AID PWR

N65
MOTE M.E.,SOVIET LOCAL AND REPUBLIC ELECTIONS. COM USSR NAT/G PLAN PARTIC GOV/REL TOTALISM PWR ...CHARTS 20. PAGE 114 H2270 — CHOOSE ADMIN CONTROL LOC/G

B66
AGGARWALA R.N.,FINANCIAL COMMITTEES OF THE INDIAN PARLIAMENT: A STUDY IN PARLIAMENTARY CONTROL OVER PUBLIC EXPENDITURE. INDIA FINAN NAT/G ROLE...CHARTS METH/COMP METH 20 PARLIAMENT. PAGE 4 H0078 — PARL/PROC BUDGET CONTROL DELIB/GP

B66
BARRETT J.,THAT BETTER COUNTRY: RELIGIOUS ASPECT OF LIFE IN EASTERN AUSTRALIA, 1835-1850. LAW ECO/UNDEV SCHOOL TEC/DEV EDU/PROP CONTROL HABITAT MORAL WORSHIP 19 AUSTRAL CHURCH/STA. PAGE 11 H0229 — SECT CULTURE GOV/REL

B66
BEER S.H.,BRITISH POLITICS IN THE COLLECTIVIST AGE. UK NAT/G CONTROL CHOOSE GP/REL ATTIT PWR PLURISM ...MAJORIT WELF/ST 16/20. PAGE 13 H0258 — POL/PAR SOCISM TRADIT GP/COMP

B66
BIRKHEAD G.S.,ADMINISTRATIVE PROBLEMS IN PAKISTAN. PAKISTAN AGRI FINAN INDUS LG/CO ECO/TAC CONTROL PWR ...CHARTS ANTHOL 20. PAGE 17 H0340 — ADMIN NAT/G ORD/FREE ECO/UNDEV

B66
CHANG,THE PARTY AND THE NATIONAL QUESTION IN CHINA (TRANS. BY GEORGE MOSELEY). CHINA/COM CULTURE CONTROL NAT/LISM...CHARTS BIBLIOG/A 20. PAGE 29 H0576 — GP/REL REGION ISOLAT MARXISM

B66
DALLIN A.,POLITICS IN THE SOVIET UNION: 7 CASES. COM USSR LAW POL/PAR CHIEF FORCES WRITING CONTROL PARL/PROC CIVMIL/REL TOTALISM...ANTHOL 20 KHRUSH/N STALIN/J CASEBOOK COM/PARTY. PAGE 37 H0736 — MARXISM DOMIN ORD/FREE GOV/REL

B66
DE VORE B.B.,LAND AND LIBERTY; A HISTORY OF THE MEXICAN REVOLUTION. CONSTN INTELL NAT/G CONTROL LEAD CHOOSE TOTALISM AUTHORIT...BIBLIOG 19/20 MEXIC/AMER DIAZ/P LIB/PARTY MAGON/F MADERO/F. PAGE 39 H0776 — REV CHIEF POL/PAR

B66
EDWARDS C.D.,TRADE REGULATIONS OVERSEAS. IRELAND NEW/ZEALND SOUTH/AFR NAT/G CAP/ISM TARIFFS CONTROL ...POLICY JURID 20 EEC CHINJAP. PAGE 45 H0892 — INT/TRADE DIPLOM INT/LAW ECO/TAC

B66
FAGEN R.R.,POLITICS AND COMMUNICATION. WOR+45 ECO/DEV NAT/G CONTROL ATTIT 20. PAGE 48 H0958 — COM/IND GOV/COMP PWR EDU/PROP

B66
FRIED R.C.,COMPARATIVE POLITICAL INSTITUTIONS. USSR EX/STRUC FORCES LEGIS JUDGE CONTROL REPRESENT ALL/IDEOS 20 CONGRESS BUREAUCRCY. PAGE 53 H1062 — NAT/G PWR EFFICIENCY GOV/COMP

B66
GERARD-LIBOIS J.,KATANGA SECESSION. INT/ORG FORCES DIPLOM ADMIN CONTROL WAR CHOOSE PWR...CHARTS 20 KATANGA TSHOMBE/M UN. PAGE 56 H1114 — NAT/G REGION ORD/FREE REV

B66
HOEVELER H.J.,INTERNATIONALE BEKAMPFUNG DES VERBRECHENS. AUSTRIA SWITZERLND WOR+45 INT/ORG CONTROL BIO/SOC...METH/COMP NAT/COMP 20 MAFIA SCOT/YARD FBI. PAGE 72 H1446 — CRIMLGY CRIME DIPLOM INT/LAW

B66
INTERPARLIAMENTARY UNION,PARLIAMENTS: COMPARATIVE STUDY ON STRUCTURE AND FUNCTIONING OF — PARL/PROC LEGIS

REPRESENTATIVE INSTITUTIONS IN FIFTY-FIVE COUNTRIES. WOR+45 POL/PAR DELIB/GP BUDGET ADMIN CONTROL CHOOSE. PAGE 78 H1560
GOV/COMP EX/STRUC

B66
JACKSON G.D.,COMINTERN AND PEASANT IN EAST EUROPE 1919-1930. BULGARIA COM CZECHOSLVK EUR+WWI POLAND ROMANIA YUGOSLAVIA STRATA AGRI VOL/ASSN DIPLOM CONTROL CROWD WEALTH...POLICY NAT/COMP 20. PAGE 79 H1575
MARXISM ECO/UNDEV WORKER INT/ORG

B66
KIRKENDALL R.S.,SOCIAL SCIENTISTS AND FARM POLITICS IN THE AGE OF ROOSEVELT. ACADEM PLAN ECO/TAC GIVE ADMIN CONTROL PRODUC...SOC 20 NEW/DEAL ROOSEVLT/F BURAGR/ECO. PAGE 86 H1722
AGRI INTELL POLICY NAT/G

B66
KOMIYA R.,POSTWAR ECONOMIC GROWTH IN JAPAN. ELITES NAT/G EX/STRUC TEC/DEV BUDGET DIPLOM CONTROL BAL/PAY PRODUC...BIBLIOG 20 CHINJAP. PAGE 88 H1754
ECO/DEV POLICY PLAN ADJUST

B66
LEROY P.,L'ORGANIZATION CONSTITUTIONNELLE ET LES CRISES. FRANCE NAT/G ADJUD CONTROL PARL/PROC WAR ...POLICY BIBLIOG 20. PAGE 95 H1892
CONSTN PWR EXEC LEGIS

B66
LOCKE J.,THE SECOND TREATISE OF GOVERNMENT: AN ESSAY CONCERNING THE TRUE ORIGINAL EXTENT AND END OF CIVIL GOVERNMENT (3RD ED.). CONSTN SOCIETY CONTROL OWN...PHIL/SCI 17 NATURL/LAW. PAGE 97 H1947
NAT/G PWR GEN/LAWS ORD/FREE

B66
MATTHEWS R.,AFRICAN POWDER KEG: REVOLT AND DISSENT IN SIX EMERGENT NATIONS. AFR ALGERIA DAHOMEY GABON GHANA MALAWI GAMBLE LEAD PARTIC REV DRIVE...BIOG TREND GOV/COMP 20. PAGE 105 H2098
ELITES ECO/UNDEV TOP/EX CONTROL

B66
NIEDERGANG M.,LA REVOLUTION DE SAINT-DOMINGUE. DOMIN/REP INT/ORG NAT/G CONTROL LEAD GP/REL ORD/FREE MARXISM 20. PAGE 118 H2361
REV FORCES DIPLOM

B66
O'NEILL R.J.,THE GERMAN ARMY AND THE NAZI PARTY, 1933-1939. GERMANY ELITES NAT/G EDU/PROP CONTROL LEAD COERCE WAR...POLICY INT TIME/SEQ BIBLIOG 20 HITLER/A NAZI. PAGE 120 H2391
CIVMIL/REL FORCES FASCISM POL/PAR

B66
PAN S.,VIETNAM CRISIS. ASIA FRANCE USA+45 USA-45 VIETNAM CULTURE SOCIETY INT/ORG ECO/TAC AGREE CONTROL WAR MARXISM 20. PAGE 123 H2454
ECO/UNDEV POLICY DIPLOM NAT/COMP

B66
SCHRAM S.,MAO TSE-TUNG. ASIA CHINA/COM CONTROL REGION ATTIT...POLICY IDEA/COMP 20 MAO. PAGE 140 H2799
BIOG MARXISM TOP/EX GUERRILLA

B66
SCHURMANN F.,IDEOLOGY AND ORGANIZATION IN COMMUNIST CHINA. CHINA/COM LOC/G MUNIC POL/PAR ECO/TAC CONTROL ATTIT...MGT STERTYP 20 COM/PARTY. PAGE 140 H2805
MARXISM STRUCT ADMIN NAT/G

B66
SKILLING H.G.,THE GOVERNMENTS OF COMMUNIST EAST EUROPE. COM EUR+WWI ELITES FORCES DIPLOM ECO/TAC CONTROL HABITAT SOCISM...DECISION BIBLIOG 20 EUROPE/E COM/PARTY. PAGE 145 H2895
MARXISM NAT/COMP GP/COMP DOMIN

B66
SPULBER N.,THE STATE AND ECONOMIC DEVELOPMENT IN EASTERN EUROPE. BULGARIA COM CZECHOSLVK HUNGARY POLAND YUGOSLAVIA CULTURE PLAN CAP/ISM INT/TRADE CONTROL...POLICY CHARTS METH/COMP BIBLIOG/A 19/20. PAGE 148 H2958
ECO/DEV ECO/UNDEV NAT/G TOTALISM

B66
TIVEY L.J.,NATIONALISATION IN BRITISH INDUSTRY. UK LEGIS PARL/PROC GP/REL OWN ATTIT SOCISM 20. PAGE 156 H3109
NAT/G INDUS CONTROL LG/CO

B66
ZINKIN T.,CHALLENGES IN INDIA. INDIA PAKISTAN LAW AGRI FINAN INDUS TOP/EX TEC/DEV CONTROL ROUTINE ORD/FREE PWR 20 NEHRU/J SHASTRI/LB CIVIL/SERV. PAGE 173 H3458
NAT/G ECO/TAC POLICY ADMIN

S66
GAMER R.E.,"URGENT SINGAPORE, PATIENT MALAYSIA." MALAYSIA S/ASIA ECO/UNDEV POL/PAR CHIEF TARIFFS TAX CONTROL LEAD REGION PWR 20 SINGAPORE. PAGE 55 H1094
DIPLOM NAT/G POLICY ECO/TAC

S66
SCHOENBRON D.,"VIETNAM* THE CASE FOR EXTRICATION." NAT/G FORCES PROB/SOLV DIPLOM COLONIAL CONTROL COERCE...CONCPT 20. PAGE 140 H2795
VIETNAM WAR GUERRILLA

B67
BROWN L.N.,FRENCH ADMINISTRATIVE LAW. FRANCE UK CONSTN NAT/G LEGIS DOMIN CONTROL EXEC PARL/PROC PWR ...JURID METH/COMP GEN/METH. PAGE 22 H0447
EX/STRUC LAW IDEA/COMP CT/SYS

B67
BRZEZINSKI Z.K.,THE SOVIET BLOC: UNITY AND CONFLICT (2ND ED., REV., ENLARGED). COM POLAND USSR INTELL CHIEF EX/STRUC CONTROL EXEC GOV/REL PWR MARXISM ...TREND IDEA/COMP 20 LENIN/VI MARX/KARL STALIN/J. PAGE 23 H0463
NAT/G DIPLOM

B67
GELLHORN W.,OMBUDSMEN AND OTHERS: CITIZENS' PROTECTORS IN NINE COUNTRIES. WOR+45 LAW CONSTN LEGIS INSPECT ADJUD ADMIN CONTROL CT/SYS CHOOSE PERS/REL...STAT CHARTS 20. PAGE 55 H1109
NAT/COMP REPRESENT INGP/REL PROB/SOLV

B67
HUTCHINS F.G.,THE ILLUSION OF PERMANENCE: BRITISH IMPERIALISM IN INDIA. INDIA UK CULTURE STRUCT NAT/G REV GP/REL RACE/REL ADJUST DISCRIM ATTIT MORAL PWR SOC/INTEG 18/20. PAGE 75 H1509
COLONIAL CONTROL SOVEREIGN CONSERVE

B67
JAIN R.K.,MANAGEMENT OF STATE ENTERPRISES. INDIA SOCIETY FINAN WORKER BUDGET ADMIN CONTROL OWN 20. PAGE 79 H1584
NAT/G SOCISM INDUS MGT

B67
KAROL K.S.,CHINA, THE OTHER COMMUNISM (TRANS. BY TOM BAISTOW). CHINA/COM CULTURE INDUS FORCES DIPLOM EDU/PROP CONTROL EXEC NUC/PWR ATTIT...SOC CHARTS 20. PAGE 83 H1663
NAT/G POL/PAR MARXISM INGP/REL

B67
KENNETT L.,THE FRENCH ARMIES IN THE SEVEN YEARS' WAR. FRANCE NAT/G CONTROL LEAD WAR CIVMIL/REL EFFICIENCY ATTIT PWR SKILL CONSERVE 18. PAGE 85 H1690
FORCES CHIEF METH/COMP

B67
MENARD O.D.,THE ARMY AND THE FIFTH REPUBLIC. ALGERIA FRANCE VIETNAM ELITES STRATA COLONIAL CONTROL LOBBY WAR CIVMIL/REL ROLE PWR...POLICY 20 DEGAULLE/C. PAGE 108 H2169
FORCES ATTIT NAT/G

B67
MICKIEWICZ E.P.,SOVIET POLITICAL SCHOOLS: THE COMMUNIST PARTY ADULT INSTRUCTION SYSTEM. COM USSR INTELL SCHOOL WORKER CREATE PRESS ADMIN CONTROL ATTIT KNOWL...PROG/TEAC SOC/INTEG 20 COM/PARTY. PAGE 110 H2200
NAT/G EDU/PROP AGE/A MARXISM

B67
MOORE J.R.,THE ECONOMIC IMPACT OF THE TVA. AGRI INDUS PLAN BARGAIN CONTROL REGION GOV/REL DEMAND EFFICIENCY SOCISM 20 TVA. PAGE 112 H2249
ECO/UNDEV ECO/DEV NAT/G CREATE

B67
MUHAMMAD A.C.,THE EMERGENCE OF PAKISTAN. PAKISTAN S/ASIA CONSTN ECO/UNDEV NAT/G CONTROL NAT/LISM 20. PAGE 114 H2281
DIPLOM COLONIAL SECT PROB/SOLV

B67
MUNGER E.S.,AFRIKANER AND AFRICAN NATIONALISM: SOUTH AFRICAN PARALLELS AND PARAMETERS. SOUTH/AFR WOR+45 CULTURE ELITES STRUCT NAT/G PROB/SOLV DOMIN CONTROL PERS/REL NAT/LISM...SOC 20. PAGE 115 H2289
AFR RACE/REL

B67
PAPANEK G.F.,PAKISTAN'S DEVELOPMENT: SOCIAL GOALS AND PRIVATE INCENTIVES. PAKISTAN INDUS NAT/G PROB/SOLV CONTROL EFFICIENCY SOCISM...CHARTS 20. PAGE 123 H2463
ECO/UNDEV PLAN CAP/ISM ECO/TAC

B67
POSNER M.V.,ITALIAN PUBLIC ENTERPRISE. ITALY ECO/DEV FINAN INDUS CREATE ECO/TAC ADMIN CONTROL EFFICIENCY PRODUC...TREND CHARTS 20. PAGE 127 H2545
NAT/G PLAN CAP/ISM SOCISM

B67
RUEFF J.,BALANCE OF PAYMENTS. WOR+45 FINAN TEC/DEV DIPLOM TARIFFS PRICE CONTROL...POLICY CONCPT IDEA/COMP. PAGE 136 H2715
INT/TRADE BAL/PAY ECO/TAC NAT/COMP

B67
SHAFFER H.G.,THE COMMUNIST WORLD: MARXIST AND NON-MARXIST VIEWS. WOR+45 SOCIETY DIPLOM ECO/TAC CONTROL SOCISM...MARXIST ANTHOL BIBLIOG/A 20. PAGE 142 H2838
MARXISM NAT/COMP IDEA/COMP COM

B67
WINTER E.H.,CONTEMPORARY CHANGE IN TRADITIONAL SOCIETIES: VOLUME I INTRODUCTION AND AFRICAN TRIBES. NIGERIA AGRI LOC/G NAT/G CREATE DOMIN COLONIAL CONTROL GP/REL PWR SOVEREIGN...SOC OBS 20 TANGANYIKA. PAGE 169 H3389
SOCIETY AFR CONSERVE KIN

B67
ZALESKI E.,PLANNING REFORMS IN THE SOVIET UNION 1962-1966. COM USSR NAT/G CONFER CONTROL EFFICIENCY MARXISM...POLICY DECISION 20. PAGE 172 H3446
ECO/DEV PLAN ADMIN CENTRAL

L67
BERNSTEIN T.P.,"LEADERSHIP AND MASS MOBILIZATION IN THE SOVIET AND CHINESE COLLECTIVISATION CAMPAIGNS OF 1929-30, 1955-56: COMPARISON." CHINA/COM USSR WORKER CONTROL COERCE PRODUC ATTIT...NAT/COMP 20. PAGE 16 H0317
FEDERAL PLAN AGRI NAT/G

L67
CRIBBET J.E.,"SOME REFLECTIONS ON THE LAW OF LAND - A VIEW FROM SCANDINAVIA." DENMARK NETHERLAND NORWAY SWEDEN INDUS MUNIC NEIGH RACE/REL ATTIT HABITAT ...IDEA/COMP 20. PAGE 35 H0701
LAW PLAN CONTROL NAT/G

L67
EGBERT D.D.,"THE IDEA OF 'AVANT-GARDE' IN ART AND POLITICS." USSR CULTURE INTELL POL/PAR CREATE EDU/PROP CONTROL REV ANOMIE DRIVE ROLE...IDEA/COMP 20. PAGE 45 H0895
ART/METH COM ATTIT

L67
ISRAEL J.,"THE RED GUARDS IN HISTORICAL PERSPECTIVE: CONTINUITY AND CHANGE IN THE CHINESE YOUTH MOVEMENT." CHINA/COM FUT POL/PAR CONTROL REV GP/REL 20. PAGE 79 H1572
AGE/Y LOBBY MARXISM NAT/G

L67
KELLEHER G.W.,"THE COMMON MARKET ANTITRUST LAWS: THE FIRST TEN YEARS." EUR+WWI INDUS PRICE ADJUD AGREE CONTROL PROFIT...POLICY 20 EEC. PAGE 84 H1684
INT/ORG INT/TRADE MARKET NAT/G

L67
ROTH A.R.,"CAPITAL-MARKET DEVELOPMENT IN ISRAEL AND BRAZIL: TWO EXAMPLES OF THE ROLE OF LAW IN DEVELOPMENT." BRAZIL ISRAEL L/A+17C INDUS MARKET ECO/TAC FOR/AID INT/TRADE CONTROL BAL/PAY 20. PAGE 135 H2694
LAW ECO/UNDEV NAT/COMP FINAN

L67
TABORSKY E.,"THE COMMUNIST PARTIES OF THE 'THIRD WORLD' IN SOVIET STRATEGY." AFR ASIA L/A+17C USSR INTELL NAT/G WORKER PLAN CONTROL LEAD PARTIC REV ...GOV/COMP 20 COM/PARTY THIRD/WRLD. PAGE 152 H3032
POL/PAR MARXISM ECO/UNDEV DIPLOM

S67
AKE C.,"POLITICAL INTEGRATION AND POLITICAL STABILITY." ELITES POL/PAR LEAD ADJUST EFFICIENCY ATTIT AUTHORIT DRIVE...CONCPT 20. PAGE 4 H0088
CULTURE NAT/G CONTROL GP/REL

S67
AMERASINGHE C.F.,"SOME LEGAL PROBLEMS OF STATE TRADING IN SOUTHEAST ASIA." PROB/SOLV ADJUD CONTROL CT/SYS GP/REL 20. PAGE 6 H0120
INT/TRADE NAT/G INT/LAW PRIVIL

S67
BASOV V.,"THE DEVELOPMENT OF PUBLIC EDUCATION AND THE BUDGET." USSR NAT/G CONTROL REV COST AGE...STAT 20. PAGE 12 H0235
BUDGET GIVE EDU/PROP SCHOOL

S67
BERLINER J.S.,"RUSSIA'S BUREAUCRATS - WHY THEY'RE REACTIONARY." USSR NAT/G OP/RES PROB/SOLV TEC/DEV CONTROL SANCTION EFFICIENCY DRIVE PERSON...TECHNIC SOC 20. PAGE 15 H0308
CREATE ADMIN INDUS PRODUC

S67
BOSHER J.F.,"GOVERNMENT AND PRIVATE INTERESTS IN NEW FRANCE." CANADA FRANCE INDUS LG/CO SML/CO CAP/ISM INT/TRADE COLONIAL GP/REL...HIST/WRIT 17/18. PAGE 19 H0381
NAT/G FINAN ADMIN CONTROL

S67
CARIAS B.,"EL CONTROL DE LAS EMPRESAS PUBLICAS POR GRUPOS DE INTERESES DE LA COMUNIDAD." FRANCE UK VENEZUELA INDUS NAT/G CONTROL OWN PWR...DECISION NAT/COMP 20. PAGE 26 H0529
WORKER REPRESENT MGT SOCISM

S67
CATTELL D.T.,"A NEO-MARXIST THEORY OF COMPARATIVE ANALYSIS." USSR STRATA INSPECT DOMIN CONTROL COERCE OWN TOTALISM PWR...FASCIST HYPO/EXP METH 20. PAGE 28 H0561
GOV/COMP MARXISM SIMUL CLASSIF

S67
CHIU S.M.,"CHINA'S MILITARY POSTURE." CHINA/COM ELITES NAT/G POL/PAR TEC/DEV ECO/TAC DOMIN CONTROL LEAD REV MARXISM 20 MAO. PAGE 30 H0595
FORCES CIVMIL/REL NUC/PWR DIPLOM

S67
COHEN A.,"REVOLUTION IN ARGENTINA?" L/A+17C NAT/G POL/PAR CHIEF PROB/SOLV ECO/TAC 20 ARGEN. PAGE 31 H0615
REV ECO/UNDEV CONTROL BIOG

S67
COLLINS B.A.,"SOME NOTES ON PUBLIC SERVICE COMMISSIONS IN THE COMMONWEALTH CARIBBEAN." JAMAICA L/A+17C TRINIDAD UK NAT/G OP/RES DOMIN SENIOR COLONIAL CONTROL INGP/REL CENTRAL EFFICIENCY PWR ...DECISION 20. PAGE 31 H0631
ADMIN EX/STRUC ECO/UNDEV CHOOSE

S67
CRITTENDEN J.,"DIMENSIONS OF MODERNIZATION IN THE AMERICAN STATES." USA+45 STRUCT MUNIC PROB/SOLV CONTROL LITERACY HABITAT...CONCPT METH/CNCPT CORREL CONT/OBS CENSUS 20. PAGE 35 H0702
PROVS GOV/COMP STAT ECO/DEV

S67
DIAMANT A.,"EUROPEAN MODELS OF BUREAUCRACY AND DEVELOPMENT." EX/STRUC PLAN ADMIN CONTROL ROUTINE GOV/REL CENTRAL...DECISION TIME/SEQ CHARTS. PAGE 41 H0818
NAT/G EQUILIB ACT/RES NAT/COMP

S67
DOERN G.B.,"THE ROYAL COMMISSIONS IN THE GENERAL POLICY PROCESS AND IN FEDERAL-PROVINCIAL RELATIONS." CANADA CONSTN ACADEM PROVS CONSULT DELIB/GP LEGIS ACT/RES PROB/SOLV CONFER CONTROL EFFICIENCY...METH/COMP 20 SENATE ROYAL/COMM. PAGE 42 H0832
R+D EX/STRUC GOV/REL NAT/G

S67
DRYDEN S.,"LOCAL GOVERNMENT IN TANZANIA PART II" TANZANIA LAW NAT/G POL/PAR CONTROL PARTIC REPRESENT ...DECISION 20. PAGE 42 H0850
LOC/G GOV/REL ADMIN STRUCT

S67
EGBERT D.D.,"POLITICS AND ART IN COMMUNIST BULGARIA" BULGARIA COM USSR CULTURE DIPLOM INGP/REL TOTALISM...TREND 20. PAGE 45 H0894
CREATE ART/METH CONTROL MARXISM

S67
FINLAY D.J.,"THE GHANA COUP...ONE YEAR LATER." GHANA FORCES FOR/AID PRESS CONTROL CIVMIL/REL NAT/LISM AUTHORIT PWR...PREDICT 20. PAGE 50 H1005
REV NAT/G ATTIT ECO/UNDEV

S67
FUSARO A.,"THE EFFECT OF PROPORTIONAL REPRESENTATION ON VOTING IN THE AUSTRALIAN SENATE." S/ASIA CONSTN POL/PAR CONTROL GP/REL PWR...CHARTS 20 AUSTRAL HOUSE/REP SENATE. PAGE 54 H1083
LEGIS CHOOSE REPRESENT NAT/G

S67
HASSAN M.F.,"THE SECOND FOUR-YEAR PLAN OF VENEZUELA." L/A+17C VENEZUELA AGRI INDUS NAT/G PLAN RATION CONTROL HABITAT...MATH STAT 20. PAGE 67 H1352
ECO/UNDEV FINAN BUDGET PROB/SOLV

S67
IDENBURG P.J.,"POLITICAL STRUCTURAL DEVELOPMENT IN TROPICAL AFRICA." UK ECO/UNDEV KIN POL/PAR CHIEF EX/STRUC CREATE COLONIAL CONTROL REPRESENT RACE/REL ...MAJORIT TREND 20. PAGE 76 H1521
AFR CONSTN NAT/G GOV/COMP

S67
INDER S.,"AFTER THE CORONATION." CONSTN ECO/UNDEV EX/STRUC LEGIS INT/TRADE CONTROL SOVEREIGN ...TIME/SEQ 20 TONGA COMMONWLTH INAUGURATE. PAGE 76 H1527
CHIEF NAT/G POLICY

S67
JANICKE M.,"MONOPOLISMUS UND PLURALISMUS IM KOMMUNISTISCHEN HERRSCHAFTSSYSTEM" COM CZECHOSLVK USSR YUGOSLAVIA SOCIETY CONTROL RIGID/FLEX...CONCPT NAT/COMP 20. PAGE 79 H1589
TOTALISM POL/PAR ATTIT PLURISM

S67
JENCKS C.E.,"SOCIAL STATUS OF COAL MINERS IN BRITAIN SINCE NATIONALIZATION." UK STRATA STRUCT LABOR RECEIVE GP/REL INCOME OWN ATTIT HABITAT...MGT T 20. PAGE 80 H1600
EXTR/IND WORKER CONTROL NAT/G

S67
KNOWLES A.F.,"NOTES ON A CANADIAN MASS MEDIA POLICY." CANADA TV CONTROL ROLE...METH/COMP 20. PAGE 87 H1735
EDU/PROP COM/IND NAT/G POLICY

S67
KROLL M.,"POLITICAL LEADERSHIP AND ADMINISTRATIVE COMMUNICATIONS IN NEW NATION STATES* CASE STUDY OF TRINIDAD AND TOBAGO." L/A+17C TRINIDAD INTELL OP/RES DOMIN COLONIAL LEAD GP/REL CENTRAL EFFICIENCY...DECISION OBS METH/COMP 20. PAGE 89 H1774
NAT/G ADMIN EDU/PROP CONTROL

S67
KYLE K.,"BACKGROUND TO THE CRISIS" ISLAM ISRAEL UAR UK USSR NAT/G PROB/SOLV LEGIT CONTROL REGION STRANGE MORAL 20 JEWS. PAGE 89 H1787
DIPLOM POLICY SOVEREIGN COERCE

S67
LEVI W.,"THE ELITIST NATURE OF NEW ASIA'S FOREIGN POLICY." CULTURE ECO/UNDEV NAT/G PROB/SOLV EDU/PROP COLONIAL CONTROL REGION NAT/LISM...NAT/COMP 20. PAGE 95 H1898
POLICY ELITES DIPLOM CREATE

S67
LOFCHIE M.F.,"OKELLO'S REVOLUTION." TANZANIA NAT/G POL/PAR FORCES PLAN CONTROL 20. PAGE 98 H1954
AFR REV LEAD CHIEF

S67
MATTHEWS R.O.,"THE SUEZ CANAL DISPUTE* A CASE STUDY IN PEACEFUL SETTLEMENT." FRANCE ISRAEL UAR UK NAT/G CONTROL LEAD COERCE WAR NAT/LISM ROLE ORD/FREE PWR ...INT/LAW UN 20. PAGE 105 H2099
PEACE DIPLOM ADJUD

S67
MOZINGO D.,"CONTAINMENT IN ASIA RECONSIDERED." NAT/G DIPLOM REV PEACE ORD/FREE 20. PAGE 114 H2275
ATTIT CONTROL NAT/LISM EFFICIENCY

S67
MOZINGO D.,"CHINA AND INDONESIA." CHINA/COM INDONESIA POL/PAR 20. PAGE 114 H2276
MARXISM CONTROL DIPLOM NAT/G

S67
NIEBUHR R.,"THE ETHICS OF WAR AND PEACE IN THE NUCLEAR AGE." VIETNAM INTELL CONFER CONTROL WAR GOV/REL PERS/REL ORD/FREE...POLICY INT GOV/COMP NAT/COMP 20 UN. PAGE 118 H2360
MORAL PEACE NUC/PWR DIPLOM

S67
PAI G.A.,"TAXATION AND PLANNING IN INDIA: A BIRDS-EYE VIEW." INDIA ELITES NAT/G LEGIS BUDGET CONTROL LOBBY INCOME...STAT CHARTS 20. PAGE 122 H2443
TAX PLAN WEALTH STRATA

S67
POWELL D.,"THE EFFECTIVENESS OF SOVIET ANTI-RELIGIOUS PROPAGANDA." USSR NAT/G DOMIN LEGIT NAT/LISM 20. PAGE 127 H2549
EDU/PROP ATTIT SECT CONTROL

S67
ROOT W.,"REPORT FROM PARIS - DE GAULLE: WHICH WAY TO THE FUTURE?" CANADA FRANCE ISLAM UK INT/ORG CHIEF CREATE AGREE CONTROL ARMS/CONT NUC/PWR EQUILIB PEACE PWR 20 DEGAULLE/C NATO. PAGE 134 H2670
POLICY DIPLOM NAT/G BAL/PWR

S67
SANCHEZ J.D.,"DESARROLLO ECONOMICO Y FUTURO DE COLOMBIA." L/A+17C AGRI EXTR/IND FINAN INDUS MARKET INT/TRADE CONTROL...STAT TREND COLOMB. PAGE 137 H2748
ECO/UNDEV FUT NAT/G ECO/TAC

S67
SAVELYEV N.,"MONOPOLY DRIVE IN INDIA." INDIA INDUS NAT/G INT/TRADE NEUTRAL SANCTION GOV/REL CONSERVE ...MARXIST 20. PAGE 138 H2759
ECO/UNDEV POL/PAR ECO/TAC CONTROL

S67
SCHACHTER G.,"REGIONAL DEVELOPMENT IN THE ITALIAN DUAL ECONOMY" ITALY AGRI INDUS MARKET WORKER ECO/TAC CONTROL INCOME PRODUC 20. PAGE 138 H2767
REGION ECO/UNDEV NAT/G PROB/SOLV

S67
SCOVILLE W.J.,"GOVERNMENT REGULATION AND GROWTH IN THE FRENCH PAPER INDUSTRY DURING THE EIGHTEENTH CENTURY." FRANCE MOD/EUR FINAN CAP/ISM TAX ADMIN CONTROL PRIVIL LAISSEZ...POLICY 18. PAGE 141 H2818
NAT/G PROC/MFG ECO/DEV INGP/REL

S67
SHIGEO N.,"THE GREAT CULTURAL REVOLUTION." ASIA ECO/UNDEV AGRI NAT/G CHIEF ECO/TAC EDU/PROP CONTROL LEAD PWR 20 MAO. PAGE 143 H2860
CREATE REV CULTURE POL/PAR

S67
SINGH B.,"ITALIAN EXPERIENCE IN REGIONAL ECONOMIC DEVELOPMENT AND LESSONS FOR OTHER COUNTRIES." EUR+WWI ITALY INDUS NAT/G ACT/RES REGION GP/REL EFFICIENCY EQUILIB PRODUC WEALTH. PAGE 144 H2884
ECO/UNDEV PLAN ECO/TAC CONTROL

S67
SMITH J.E.,"THE GERMAN DEMOCRATIC REPUBLIC AND THE WEST." GERMANY/E ECO/DEV NAT/G PROB/SOLV CONTROL REV TOTALISM...GOV/COMP 20. PAGE 146 H2911
DIPLOM PWR MARXISM

S67
SNELLEN I.T.,"APARTHEID* CHECKS AND CHANGES." SOUTH/AFR NAT/G PROB/SOLV COLONIAL REGION TASK GP/REL RACE/REL EFFICIENCY PRIVIL ORD/FREE 20. PAGE 146 H2923
DISCRIM NAT/LISM EQUILIB CONTROL

S67
TIVEY L.,"THE POLITICAL CONSEQUENCES OF ECONOMIC PLANNING." UK CONSTN INDUS ACT/RES ADMIN CONTROL LOBBY REPRESENT EFFICIENCY SUPEGO SOVEREIGN ...DECISION 20. PAGE 155 H3108
PLAN POLICY NAT/G

S68
DOUGLAS-HOME C.,"A MISTAKEN POLICY IN ADEN." YEMEN CULTURE ECO/UNDEV INDUS FORCES WORKER DIPLOM ECO/TAC CONTROL 20 ADEN. PAGE 42 H0842
SOVEREIGN COLONIAL POLICY REGION

S68
KANET R.E.,"RECENT SOVIET REASSESSMENT OF DEVELOPMENTS IN THE THIRD WORLD." ALGERIA GHANA INDONESIA USSR WOR+45 CONSTN ELITES INTELL STRUCT DOMIN CONTROL REV PWR MARXISM...IDEA/COMP METH 20 THIRD/WRLD. PAGE 83 H1653
DIPLOM NEUTRAL NAT/G NAT/COMP

S68
LAWRIE G.,"WHAT WILL CHANGE SOUTH AFRICA?" AFR SOUTH/AFR ELITES DOMIN CONTROL REPRESENT...TIME/SEQ TREND 20. PAGE 93 H1848
RACE/REL DIPLOM NAT/G POLICY

S68
MILLAR T.B.,"THE COMMONWEALTH AND THE UN." UK DIPLOM TARIFFS AGREE COLONIAL CONTROL SOVEREIGN WEALTH...GP/COMP GOV/COMP 20 CMN/WLTH UN. PAGE 111 H2210
INT/ORG POLICY TREND ECO/TAC

S68
SHAPIRO J.P.,"SOVIET HISTORIOGRAPHY AND THE MOSCOW TRIALS: AFTER THIRTY YEARS." USSR NAT/G LEGIT PRESS CONTROL LEAD ATTIT MARXISM...NEW/IDEA METH 20 TROTSKY/L STALIN/J KHRUSH/N. PAGE 142 H2843
HIST/WRIT EDU/PROP SANCTION ADJUD

B75
NEWMAN J.H.,A LETTER ADDRESSED TO THE DUKE OF NORFOLK ON THE OCCASION OF MR. GLADSTONE'S RECENT EXPOSTULATION. NAT/G SECT CHIEF LEGIS CONTROL LEAD GP/REL SUPEGO SOC/INTEG WORSHIP 19 ENGLAND. PAGE 117 H2346
POLICY DOMIN SOVEREIGN CATHISM

C82
MILL J.S.,"CIVILIZATION" IN DISSERTATIONS AND DISCUSSIONS." MOD/EUR UK ECO/DEV CONTROL MORAL ORD/FREE PWR...SOC IDEA/COMP 19. PAGE 110 H2208
SOCIETY NAT/G STRUCT CONCPT

B91
SIDGWICK H.,THE ELEMENTS OF POLITICS. LOC/G NAT/G LEGIS DIPLOM ADJUD CONTROL EXEC PARL/PROC REPRESENT GOV/REL SOVEREIGN ALL/IDEOS 19 MILL/JS BENTHAM/J. PAGE 143 H2868
POLICY LAW CONCPT

B95
SELIGMAN E.R.A.,ESSAYS IN TAXATION. NEW/ZEALND PRUSSIA UK USA-45 MARKET LOC/G CREATE PRICE CONTROL INCOME OWN WEALTH...GOV/COMP METH/COMP 19. PAGE 141 H2824
TAX TARIFFS INDUS NAT/G

B98
POLLOCK F.,THE HISTORY OF ENGLISH LAW BEFORE THE TIME OF EDWARD I (2 VOLS, 2ND ED.). UK CULTURE LOC/G LEGIS LICENSE AGREE CONTROL CT/SYS SANCTION CRIME...TIME/SEQ 13 COMMON/LAW CANON/LAW. PAGE 127 H2538
LAW ADJUD JURID

CONTROLLED DIRECT OBSERVATION....SEE CONT/OBS

CONV/LEASE....CONVICT LEASE SYSTEM IN SOUTH

CONVENTIONAL....SEE CONVNTL

CONVNTL....CONVENTIONAL

CONZE W. H0657

COOK R.C. H0658

COOK S.A. H0495

COOLIDGE/C....CALVIN COOLIDGE

COONDOO R. H0659

COOPER P. H0660

COOPERATION....SEE AGREE

COOPERATIVE....SEE VOL/ASSN

COORDINATING COMM DOC SOC SCI H0661

COORDINATION....SEE CENTRAL

COPYRIGHT....COPYRIGHT

CORBETT P.E. H0662

CORDIER A.W. H0663

CORDIER H. H0664,H0665

CORDONA G.D. H0666

CORE....CONGRESS OF RACIAL EQUALITY

CORET A. H0667,H0668

CORFO H0669

CORN/LAWS....CORN LAWS (U.K.)

B60
GRAMPP W.D.,THE MANCHESTER SCHOOL OF ECONOMICS. UK LAW ECO/DEV COERCE ATTIT ORD/FREE LAISSEZ ...PHIL/SCI IDEA/COMP 19/20 MANCHESTER CORN/LAWS. PAGE 60 H1194
ECO/TAC VOL/ASSN LOBBY NAT/G

CORNELL U DEPT ASIAN STUDIES H0670

CORNELL UNIVERSITY LIBRARY H0671

CORNELL/U....CORNELL UNIVERSITY

CORONATIONS....SEE INAUGURATE

CORPORATION....SEE CORPORATN

CORPORATN....CORPORATION

CORRECTIONAL INSTITUTION....SEE PUB/INST

CORREL....STATISTICAL CORRELATIONS

B08
THE GOVERNMENT OF SOUTH AFRICA (VOL. II). SOUTH/AFR STRATA EXTR/IND EX/STRUC TOP/EX BUDGET ADJUD ADMIN CT/SYS PRODUC...CORREL CENSUS 19 RAILROAD CIVIL/SERV POSTAL/SYS. PAGE 2 H0030
CONSTN FINAN LEGIS NAT/G

B56
DRIVER H.E.,AN INTEGRATION OF FUNCTIONAL, EVOLUTIONARY AND HISTORICAL THEORY BY MEANS OF CORRELATIONS. INGP/REL BIO/SOC HABITAT...PHIL/SCI GEN/LAWS. PAGE 42 H0847
CULTURE METH SOC CORREL

S59
LYNN D.B.,"THE EFFECTS OF FATHER-ABSENCE ON NORWEGIAN BOYS AND GIRLS." NORWAY CULTURE PERS/REL ADJUST DISPL LOVE...PSY CORREL STAT INT CON/ANAL CHARTS SOC/INTEG 20. PAGE 99 H1983
SOC FAM AGE/C ANOMIE

B61
BURKS R.V.,THE DYNAMICS OF COMMUNISM IN EASTERN EUROPE. COM YUGOSLAVIA POL/PAR RACE/REL ISOLAT ...CORREL CON/ANAL CHARTS GP/COMP DICTIONARY 20 EUROPE/E SLAV/MACED. PAGE 24 H0489 — MARXISM STRUCT WORKER REPRESENT

B66
CAPELL A.,STUDIES IN SOCIO-LINGUISTICS. CULTURE ADJUST...CLASSIF IDEA/COMP SOC/EXP BIBLIOG 20. PAGE 26 H0525 — LING SOC PHIL/SCI CORREL

S67
CRITTENDEN J.,"DIMENSIONS OF MODERNIZATION IN THE AMERICAN STATES." USA+45 STRUCT MUNIC PROB/SOLV CONTROL LITERACY HABITAT...CONCPT METH/CNCPT CORREL CONT/OBS CENSUS 20. PAGE 35 H0702 — PROVS GOV/COMP STAT ECO/DEV

S67
SOARES G.,"SOCIO-ECONOMIC VARIABLES AND VOTING FOR THE RADICAL LEFT: CHILE 1952." CHILE INDUS NAT/G WORKER ADJUST STRANGE ANOMIE WEALTH...METH/CNCPT CORREL 20. PAGE 146 H2925 — STRATA POL/PAR CHOOSE STAT

CORWIN A.F. H0672

COSER L.A. H0673

COST....ECONOMIC VALUE; SEE ALSO PROFIT, ECO

B17
VEBLEN T.B.,AN INQUIRY INTO THE NATURE OF PEACE AND THE TERMS OF ITS PERPETUATION. UNIV STRATA FINAN EDU/PROP PRICE COST DISCRIM NAT/LISM MORAL ORD/FREE PACIFIST 20 WORLDUNITY. PAGE 162 H3237 — PEACE DIPLOM WAR NAT/G

N19
BUSINESS ECONOMISTS' GROUP,INCOME POLICIES (PAMPHLET). UK INDUS LABOR TOP/EX PAY COST PRODUC ...ECOMETRIC GOV/COMP SIMUL ANTHOL 20. PAGE 25 H0497 — INCOME WORKER WEALTH POLICY

N19
HABERLER G.,A SURVEY OF INTERNATIONAL TRADE THEORY (PAMPHLET). FINAN NAT/G COST INCOME 18/20 MONEY HUME/D MARSHALL/A. PAGE 63 H1267 — INT/TRADE BAL/PAY GEN/LAWS POLICY

N19
WILSON T.,FINANCIAL ASSISTANCE WITH REGIONAL DEVELOPMENT (PAMPHLET). CANADA INDUS NAT/G PLAN TAX CONTROL COST EFFICIENCY...POLICY CHARTS 20. PAGE 169 H3382 — FINAN ECO/TAC REGION GOV/REL

B20
MALTHUS T.R.,PRINCIPLES OF POLITICAL ECONOMY. UK AGRI INDUS MARKET NAT/G DIPLOM PRICE CONTROL BAL/PAY COST OWN PWR LAISSEZ 18/19. PAGE 102 H2034 — GEN/LAWS DEMAND WEALTH

B26
FORTESCUE J.,THE GOVERNANCE OF ENGLAND (1471-76). UK LAW FINAN SECT LEGIS PROB/SOLV TAX DOMIN ADMIN GP/REL COST ORD/FREE PWR 14/15. PAGE 52 H1042 — CONSERVE CONSTN CHIEF NAT/G

B37
HAMILTON W.H.,THE POWER TO GOVERN. ECO/DEV FINAN INDUS ECO/TAC INT/TRADE TARIFFS TAX CONTROL CT/SYS WAR COST PWR 18/20 SUPREME/CT. PAGE 65 H1303 — LING CONSTN NAT/G POLICY

B46
DAVIES E.,NATIONAL ENTERPRISE: THE DEVELOPMENT OF THE PUBLIC CORPORATION. UK LG/CO EX/STRUC WORKER PROB/SOLV COST ATTIT SOCISM 20. PAGE 37 H0748 — ADMIN NAT/G CONTROL INDUS

C52
HUME D.,"OF TAXES" IN D. HUME, POLITICAL DISCOURSES (1752)" UK NAT/G COST INCOME LAISSEZ...GEN/LAWS 18. PAGE 75 H1493 — TAX FINAN WEALTH POLICY

B58
AVRAMOVIC D.,POSTWAR GROWTH IN INTERNATIONAL INDEBTEDNESS. WOR+45 AGRI INDUS CAP/ISM PRICE INCOME...NAT/COMP 20 GOLD/STAND SILVER. PAGE 9 H0184 — INT/TRADE FINAN COST BAL/PAY

B59
GUDIN E.,INFLACAO (2ND ED.). INDUS NAT/G PLAN ECO/TAC CONTROL COST 20. PAGE 62 H1243 — ECO/UNDEV INT/TRADE BAL/PAY FINAN

B60
BOMBACH G.,STABILE PREISE IN WACHSENDER WIRTSCHAFT: DAS INFLATIONSPROBLEM. BARGAIN CAP/ISM PRICE COST ...NAT/COMP 20 GOLD/STAND. PAGE 19 H0371 — ECO/UNDEV PLAN FINAN ECO/TAC

B60
KENEN P.B.,BRITISH MONETARY POLICY AND THE BALANCE OF PAYMENTS 1951-57. UK PLAN BUDGET ECO/TAC INT/TRADE PAY PRICE COST ATTIT 20. PAGE 84 H1687 — BAL/PAY PROB/SOLV FINAN NAT/G

B60
ROBERTSON D.,THE CONTROL OF INDUSTRY. UK MARKET LABOR WORKER PRICE CONTROL GP/REL COST DEMAND ORD/FREE WEALTH NEW/LIB SOCISM 20. PAGE 132 H2646 — INDUS FINAN NAT/G ECO/DEV

B61
HAUSER M.,DIE URSACHEN DER FRANZOSISCHEN INFLATION IN DEN JAHREN 1946-1952. FRANCE INDUS NAT/G BUDGET DIPLOM ECO/TAC FOR/AID COST MONEY 20 GOLD/STAND. PAGE 68 H1357 — ECO/DEV FINAN PRICE

B61
INTL UNION LOCAL AUTHORITIES,METROPOLIS. WOR+45 DIST/IND FINAN GIVE EDU/PROP CRIME COST HEALTH WEALTH 20. PAGE 78 H1563 — MUNIC GOV/COMP LOC/G BIBLIOG

B61
KEE R.,REFUGEE WORLD. AUSTRIA EUR+WWI GERMANY NEIGH EX/STRUC WORKER PROB/SOLV ECO/TAC RENT EDU/PROP INGP/REL COST LITERACY HABITAT 20 MIGRATION. PAGE 84 H1676 — NAT/G GIVE WEALTH STRANGE

B61
STANLEY C.J.,LATE CH'ING FINANCE: HU KUANG-YUNG AS AN INNOVATOR. ASIA NAT/G FORCES BUDGET TAX WAR GOV/REL COST...POLICY BIOG CHARTS BIBLIOG 19. PAGE 148 H2969 — FINAN ECO/TAC CIVMIL/REL ADMIN

B62
KINDLEBERGER C.P.,FOREIGN TRADE AND THE NATIONAL ECONOMY. WOR+45 ECO/DEV ECO/UNDEV ECO/TAC COST DEMAND 20. PAGE 86 H1713 — INT/TRADE GOV/COMP BAL/PAY POLICY

B63
BANERJI A.K.,INDIA'S BALANCE OF PAYMENTS. INDIA NAT/G PRICE BAL/PAY COST INCOME 20. PAGE 10 H0208 — INT/TRADE DIPLOM FINAN BUDGET

B63
DUE J.F.,STATE SALES TAX ADMINISTRATION. OP/RES BUDGET PAY ADMIN EXEC ROUTINE COST EFFICIENCY PROFIT...CHARTS METH/COMP 20. PAGE 43 H0855 — PROVS TAX STAT GOV/COMP

B63
STIFEL L.D.,THE TEXTILE INDUSTRY - A CASE STUDY OF INDUSTRIAL DEVELOPMENT IN THE PHILIPPINES (PAPER). PHILIPPINE WORKER CAP/ISM INT/TRADE TARIFFS RECEIVE PRICE ADMIN COST EFFICIENCY WEALTH...BIBLIOG 20. PAGE 149 H2986 — S/ASIA ECO/UNDEV PROC/MFG NAT/G

S63
NYE J.,"TANGANYIKA'S SELF-HELP." TANZANIA NAT/G GIVE COST EFFICIENCY NAT/LISM 20. PAGE 119 H2381 — ECO/TAC POL/PAR ECO/UNDEV WORKER

B64
BROWN N.,NUCLEAR WAR* THE IMPENDING STRATEGIC DEADLOCK. USA+45 USSR TEC/DEV BUDGET RISK ARMS/CONT NUC/PWR WEAPON COST BIO/SOC...GEOG IDEA/COMP NAT/COMP GAME NATO WARSAW/P. PAGE 22 H0448 — FORCES OP/RES WAR GEN/LAWS

B64
BROWN W.M.,THE EXTERNAL LIQUIDITY OF AN ADVANCED COUNTRY. CANADA FRANCE GERMANY/W SWEDEN UK USA+45 ECO/DEV DIPLOM PRICE...CONCPT STAT NAT/COMP 20. PAGE 22 H0451 — FINAN INT/TRADE COST INCOME

B64
RAPHAEL M.,PENSIONS AND PUBLIC SERVANTS. UK NAT/G PLAN INGP/REL COST EFFICIENCY ATTIT...POLICY 17/20 CIVIL/SERV. PAGE 130 H2593 — RECEIVE ADMIN INCOME AGE/O

B64
WILSON T.,POLICIES FOR REGIONAL DEVELOPMENT. CANADA UK FINAN INDUS NAT/G BUDGET TAX GIVE COST ...NAT/COMP 20. PAGE 169 H3383 — REGION PLAN ECO/DEV ECO/TAC

B65
ALTON T.P.,POLISH NATIONAL INCOME AND PRODUCT IN 1954, 1955, AND 1956. POLAND FINAN EX/STRUC ECO/TAC PRICE COST WEALTH 20. PAGE 6 H0117 — COM INDUS NAT/G ECO/DEV

B65
EDELMAN M.,THE POLITICS OF WAGE-PRICE DECISIONS. GERMANY ITALY NETHERLAND UK INDUS LABOR POL/PAR PROB/SOLV BARGAIN PRICE ROUTINE BAL/PAY COST DEMAND 20. PAGE 44 H0888 — GOV/COMP CONTROL ECO/TAC PLAN

B65
OECD,MEDITERRANEAN REGIONAL PROJECT: TURKEY; EDUCATION AND DEVELOPMENT. FUT TURKEY SOCIETY STRATA FINAN NAT/G PROF/ORG PLAN PROB/SOLV ADMIN COST...STAT CHARTS 20 OECD. PAGE 120 H2399 — EDU/PROP ACADEM SCHOOL ECO/UNDEV

B65
OECD,THE MEDITERRANEAN REGIONAL PROJECT: SPAIN; EDUCATION AND DEVELOPMENT. FUT SPAIN STRATA FINAN NAT/G WORKER PLAN PROB/SOLV ADMIN COST...POLICY STAT CHARTS 20 OECD. PAGE 120 H2402 — ECO/UNDEV EDU/PROP ACADEM SCHOOL

B65
ORG FOR ECO COOP AND DEVEL,THE MEDITERRANEAN REGIONAL PROJECT: AN EXPERIMENT IN PLANNING BY SIX COUNTRIES. FUT GREECE SPAIN TURKEY YUGOSLAVIA SOCIETY FINAN NAT/G PROF/ORG EDU/PROP ADMIN REGION COST...POLICY STAT CHARTS 20 OECD. PAGE 121 H2427 — PLAN ECO/UNDEV ACADEM SCHOOL

B65
YOUNG A.N.,CHINA'S WARTIME FINANCE AND INFLATION. ASIA AGRI INDUS NAT/G ECO/TAC CONFER PRICE WAR COST 20. PAGE 172 H3437 — FINAN FOR/AID TAX

BUDGET

S65
GOLDMAN M.I.,"A BALANCE SHEET OF SOVIET FOREIGN AID." USA+45 ECO/UNDEV BAL/PWR ECO/TAC RENT GIVE EDU/PROP CONTROL COST PROFIT GEN/METH. PAGE 58 H1158 — USSR FOR/AID NAT/COMP EFFICIENCY

S65
JENSEN L.,"MILITARY CAPABILITIES AND BARGAINING BEHAVIOR." USA+45 USSR ARMS/CONT DETER COST ATTIT ...METH/CNCPT STAT SYS/QU CON/ANAL CHARTS NAT/COMP. PAGE 81 H1614 — DIPLOM DRIVE PWR STERTYP

S65
WRIGHT Q.,"THE ESCALATION OF INTERNATIONAL CONFLICTS." WOR+45 WOR-45 FORCES DIPLOM RISK COST ATTIT ALL/VALS...INT/LAW QUANT STAT NAT/COMP. PAGE 171 H3422 — WAR PERCEPT PREDICT MATH

B66
COLE G.D.H.,THE MEANING OF MARXISM. USSR WOR+45 STRATA STRUCT NAT/G WORKER COST FASCISM...IDEA/COMP 20. PAGE 31 H0625 — MARXISM CONCPT HIST/WRIT CAP/ISM

B66
THIESENHUSEN W.C.,CHILE'S EXPERIMENTS IN AGRARIAN REFORM. CHILE STRUCT NAT/G ACT/RES ECO/TAC GOV/REL COST SOCISM...TREND CHARTS SOC/EXP 20. PAGE 154 H3073 — AGRI ECO/UNDEV SOC TEC/DEV

S66
BENOIT J.,"WORLD DEFENSE EXPENDITURES." WOR+45 WEAPON COST PRODUC. PAGE 14 H0284 — FORCES STAT NAT/COMP BUDGET

B67
HAWTREY R.,INCOMES AND MONEY. EUR+WWI FUT UK LABOR WORKER INT/TRADE TAX PAY BAL/PAY COST WEALTH 20. PAGE 68 H1363 — FINAN NAT/G POLICY ECO/DEV

B67
ZINN H.,VIETNAM THE LOGIC OF WITHDRAWAL. VIETNAM/S NAT/G DIPLOM DEATH MORAL 20. PAGE 173 H3459 — WAR COST PACIFISM ATTIT

S67
"PROTEST AGAINST SOVIET INDUSTRIALIZATION ILLS IN LITHUANIA* A MEMORANDUM." USSR LITHUANIA NAT/G PROVS COST GEOG. PAGE 2 H0050 — INDUS COLONIAL NAT/LISM PLAN

S67
BASOV V.,"THE DEVELOPMENT OF PUBLIC EDUCATION AND THE BUDGET." USSR NAT/G CONTROL REV COST AGE...STAT 20. PAGE 12 H0235 — BUDGET GIVE EDU/PROP SCHOOL

S67
BELLER I.,"ECONOMIC POLICY AND THE DEMANDS OF LABOR." PLAN TAX GIVE PRICE WAR COST PRODUC WEALTH. PAGE 13 H0268 — NAT/G ECO/TAC SOC/WK INCOME

S67
DENISON E.F.,"SOURCES OF GROWTH IN NINE WESTERN COUNTRIES." WORKER TEC/DEV COST PRODUC...TREND NAT/COMP. PAGE 39 H0790 — INCOME NAT/G EUR+WWI ECO/DEV

S67
DEWHURST A.,"THE WAGE MOVEMENT IN CANADA." CANADA AGRI NAT/G PARTIC COST PRODUC PROFIT 20. PAGE 41 H0811 — WORKER MARXIST INDUS LABOR

S67
JAIN G.,"INDIA REJECTS THE POWER RACE* REALISM ABOUT NUCLEAR WEAPONS." FORCES PROB/SOLV FOR/AID ARMS/CONT COST PWR...GOV/COMP 20. PAGE 79 H1583 — INDIA CHINA/COM NUC/PWR DIPLOM

S67
LICHFIELD N.,"THE EVALUATION OF CAPITAL INVESTMENT PROJECTS IN TOWN CENTRE REDEVELOPMENT." UK CONSTRUC MUNIC CONSULT COST...METH/CNCPT IDEA/COMP 20. PAGE 96 H1923 — PLAN ECO/TAC NAT/G DECISION

COSTA RICA UNIVERSIDAD BIBL H0675

COSTA/RICA....SEE ALSO L/A+17C

B62
COSTA RICA UNIVERSIDAD BIBL,LISTA DE TESIS DE GRADO DE LA UNIVERSIDAD DE COSTA RICA. COSTA/RICA LAW LOC/G ADMIN LEAD...SOC 20. PAGE 34 H0675 — BIBLIOG/A NAT/G DIPLOM ECO/UNDEV

B64
MUSEUM FUR VOLKERKUNDE WIEN,ZENTRALAMERIKA MEXIKO VOLKER UND KULTUREN. COSTA/RICA GUATEMALA L/A+17C PANAMA SECT WAR GP/REL SOVEREIGN...ART/METH 20 CENTRAL/AM MEXIC/AMER. PAGE 115 H2300 — SOCIETY STRUCT CULTURE AGRI

B65
RODRIGUEZ M.,CENTRAL AMERICA. COSTA/RICA GUATEMALA L/A+17C NICARAGUA DIPLOM COLONIAL REGION NAT/LISM ALL/IDEOS SOCISM...MAJORIT TIME/SEQ BIBLIOG 19/20. PAGE 133 H2656 — CULTURE NAT/COMP NAT/G ECO/UNDEV

S67
GRIEB K.J.,"THE UNITED STATES AND THE CENTRAL AMERICAN CONFEDERATION." COSTA/RICA EL/SALVADR GUATEMALA HONDURAS L/A+17C NICARAGUA NAT/G FORCES CONFER AGREE EXEC ARMS/CONT REV WAR PEACE ATTIT 20. PAGE 60 H1212 — INT/ORG DIPLOM POLICY REGION

COUGHLIN R. H0676

COUGHLIN/C....CHARLES EDWARD COUGHLIN

COUNCIL BRITISH NATIONAL BIB H0677

COUNCIL ON WORLD TENSIONS H0678

COUNCIL-MANAGER SYSTEM OF LOCAL GOVERNMENT....SEE COUNCL/MGR

COUNCL/EUR....COUNCIL OF EUROPE

L60
HAAS E.B.,"CONSENSUS FORMATION IN THE COUNCIL OF EUROPE." EUR+WWI NAT/G DELIB/GP DIPLOM REGION CHOOSE PWR SOVEREIGN...RELATIV NEW/IDEA QUANT CHARTS INDEX TOT/POP OEEC 20 COUNCL/EUR. PAGE 63 H1265 — POL/PAR INT/ORG STAT

COUNCL/MGR....COUNCIL-MANAGER SYSTEM OF LOCAL GOVERNMENT

COUNT E.W. H0679

COUNTIES....SEE LOC/G

COUNTY AGRICULTURAL AGENT....SEE COUNTY/AGT

COUNTY/AGT....COUNTY AGRICULTURAL AGENT

COUPLAND R. H0680

COURAGE....SEE DRIVE

COURT OF APPEALS....SEE CT/APPEALS

COURT SYSTEMS....SEE CT/SYS

COURT/DIST....DISTRICT COURTS

COURTS OF WESTMINSTER HALL....SEE CTS/WESTM

COUTROT A. H0681

COWAN L.G. H0682,H0683,H0684,H0685

COWLES M. H0686

COWPER/W....WILLIAM COWPER

B38
DUNHAM W.H. JR.,COMPLAINT AND REFORM IN ENGLAND 1436-1714. UK LAW ACADEM NAT/G POL/PAR SCHOOL PRESS COLONIAL PARL/PROC MORAL...SOC/WK ANTHOL 15/18 HAKLUYT/R COWPER/W. PAGE 43 H0865 — ATTIT SOCIETY SECT

COX H. H0687

COX O.C. H0688

COX R.H. H0689,H0690

CRABB C.V. H0691

CRAIG A. H0692,H0693

CRAIG G.A. H0694,H0695,H0879

CRAIG J. H0696

CRAMER J.F. H0697

CRANKSHAW E. H0698

CRANMER-BYNG J.L. H0699

CREATE....CREATIVE PROCESSES

B12
POLLOCK F.,THE GENIUS OF THE COMMON LAW. CHRIST-17C UK FINAN CHIEF ACT/RES ADMIN GP/REL ATTIT SOCISM ...ANARCH JURID. PAGE 127 H2537 — LAW CULTURE CREATE

B13
BARDOUX J.,L'ANGLETERRE RADICALE; ESSAI DE LA PSYCHOLOGIE SOCIALE (1906-1913). UK CONSTN NAT/G WORKER CREATE BUDGET ECO/TAC ATTIT...POLICY 20 PARLIAMENT LABOR/PAR STRIKE NAVY. PAGE 11 H0215 — POL/PAR CHOOSE COLONIAL LEGIS

N19
CANADA CIVIL SERV COMM,THE ANALYSIS OF ORGANIZATION IN THE GOVERNMENT OF CANADA (PAMPHLET). CANADA CONSTN EX/STRUC LEGIS TOP/EX CREATE PLAN CONTROL GP/REL 20. PAGE 26 H0517 — NAT/G MGT ADMIN DELIB/GP

B21
BALFOUR A.J.,ESSAYS SPECULATIVE AND POLITICAL. SEA CULTURE CREATE WAR NAT/LISM PEACE LOVE...ART/METH INT/LAW CONCPT ANTHOL 20 JEWS. PAGE 10 H0204 — PHIL/SCI SOCIETY DIPLOM

B22
FICHTE J.G.,ADDRESSES TO THE GERMAN NATION. GERMANY PRUSSIA ELITES NAT/G SECT CREATE INT/TRADE HEREDITY ...ART/METH LING 19 FRANK/PARL. PAGE 50 H0989 — NAT/LISM CULTURE EDU/PROP REGION

B22
OGBURN W.F.,SOCIAL CHANGE WITH RESPECT TO CULTURE AND ORIGINAL NATURE. ACT/RES OP/RES CRIME GP/REL ANOMIE BIO/SOC PWR...PSY SOC TIME/SEQ METH SOC/INTEG. PAGE 120 H2405 — CULTURE CREATE TEC/DEV

B26
HOCKING W.E.,PRESENT STATUS OF THE PHILOSOPHY OF LAW AND OF RIGHTS. UNIV CULTURE INTELL SOCIETY NAT/G CREATE LEGIT SANCTION ALL/VALS SOC/INTEG 18/20. PAGE 72 H1442 — JURID PHIL/SCI ORD/FREE

B27
WILLOUGHBY W.F.,PRINCIPLES OF PUBLIC ADMINISTRATION WITH SPECIAL REFERENCE TO THE NATIONAL AND STATE GOVERNMENTS OF THE UNITED STATES. FINAN PROVS CHIEF CONSULT LEGIS CREATE BUDGET EXEC ROUTINE GOV/REL CENTRAL...MGT 20 BUR/BUDGET CONGRESS PRESIDENT. PAGE 169 H3373 — NAT/G EX/STRUC OP/RES ADMIN

B29
STURZO L.,THE INTERNATIONAL COMMUNITY AND THE RIGHT OF WAR (TRANS. BY BARBARA BARCLAY CARTER). CULTURE CREATE PROB/SOLV DIPLOM ADJUD CONTROL PEACE PERSON ORD/FREE...INT/LAW IDEA/COMP PACIFIST 20 LEAGUE/NAT. PAGE 150 H3003 — INT/ORG PLAN WAR CONCPT

B30
LASKI H.J.,LIBERTY IN THE MODERN STATE. UNIV SOCIETY STRATA CREATE BAL/PWR CONTROL RATIONAL ATTIT PWR 18/20. PAGE 91 H1828 — CONCPT ORD/FREE NAT/G DOMIN

B31
BONAR J.,THEORIES OF POPULATION FROM RALEIGH TO ARTHUR YOUNG. CHRIST-17C MOD/EUR CULTURE SOCIETY R+D CREATE ATTIT PERCEPT RIGID/FLEX...OLD/LIB CONCPT NEW/IDEA TIME/SEQ IDEA/COMP STERTYP GEN/LAWS. PAGE 19 H0372 — GEOG BIOG

B31
HENNIG P.,GEOPOLITIK (2ND ED.). CULTURE MUNIC COLONIAL...CENSUS CHARTS 20. PAGE 70 H1398 — GEOG HABITAT CREATE NEIGH

B33
BERDYAYEV N.,CHRISTIANITY AND CLASS WAR. UNIV SOCIETY WORKER CREATE PROB/SOLV ATTIT PERSON ORD/FREE...CONCPT CHRISTIAN. PAGE 15 H0296 — SECT MARXISM STRATA GP/REL

B35
RAM J.,THE SCIENCE OF LEGAL JUDGMENT: A TREATISE... UK CONSTN NAT/G LEGIS CREATE PROB/SOLV AGREE CT/SYS ...INT/LAW CONCPT 19 ENGLSH/LAW CANON/LAW CIVIL/LAW CTS/WESTM. PAGE 129 H2584 — LAW JURID EX/STRUC ADJUD

B36
BELLOC H.,THE RESTORATION OF PROPERTY. UK STRATA NAT/G PROF/ORG DELIB/GP WORKER CREATE PROB/SOLV ECO/TAC PARTIC UTOPIA ORD/FREE SOCISM 20. PAGE 13 H0270 — CONTROL MAJORIT CAP/ISM OWN

B36
HUBERMAN L.,MAN'S WORLDLY GOODS: THE STORY OF THE WEALTH OF NATIONS. CHRIST-17C EUR+WWI MOD/EUR SOCIETY DOMIN REV ORD/FREE...TIME/SEQ METH/COMP. PAGE 74 H1486 — WEALTH CAP/ISM MARXISM CREATE

B38
MCNAIR A.D.,THE LAW OF TREATIES: BRITISH PRACTICE AND OPINIONS. UK CREATE DIPLOM LEGIT WRITING ADJUD WAR...INT/LAW JURID TREATY. PAGE 107 H2144 — AGREE LAW CT/SYS NAT/G

B38
POUND R.,THE FORMATIVE ERA OF AMERICAN LAW. CULTURE NAT/G PROVS LEGIS ADJUD CT/SYS PERSON SOVEREIGN ...POLICY IDEA/COMP GEN/LAWS 18/19. PAGE 127 H2548 — CONSTN LAW CREATE JURID

S38
LUNDBERG G.A.,"THE CONCEPT OF LAW IN THE SOCIAL SCIENCES"(BMR)" CULTURE INTELL SOCIETY STRUCT CREATE...NEW/IDEA 20. PAGE 99 H1978 — EPIST GEN/LAWS CONCPT

PHIL/SCI

S38
MERTON R.K.,"SOCIAL STRUCTURE AND ANOMIE" (BMR)" UNIV CULTURE STRATA CREATE PARTIC ATTIT BIO/SOC PERSON...SOC CONCPT 20. PAGE 109 H2186 — SOCIETY STRUCT ANOMIE DRIVE

B39
DEWEY J.,FREEDOM AND CULTURE. FUT CONSTN CULTURE INTELL NAT/G CONSULT PLAN CHOOSE ATTIT...CONCPT GEN/METH 20. PAGE 40 H0810 — SOCIETY CREATE

B39
HITLER A.,MEIN KAMPF. EUR+WWI FUT MOD/EUR STRUCT INT/ORG LABOR NAT/G POL/PAR FORCES CREATE PLAN BAL/PWR DIPLOM ECO/TAC DOMIN EDU/PROP ADMIN COERCE ATTIT...SOCIALIST BIOG TREND NAZI. PAGE 71 H1428 — PWR NEW/IDEA WAR

S39
LASSWELL H.D.,"PERSON, PERSONALITY, GROUP, CULTURE" (BMR)" UNIV CREATE EDU/PROP...EPIST CONCPT LING METH. PAGE 92 H1833 — PERSON GP/REL CULTURE PERS/REL

B44
CASSIRER E.,AN ESSAY ON MAN: AN INTRODUCTION TO A PHILOSOPHY OF HUMAN CULTURE. UNIV SECT CREATE EDU/PROP ATTIT KNOWL...HUM CONCPT MYTH TOT/POP. PAGE 28 H0556 — CULTURE SOC

B44
HAYEK F.A.,THE ROAD TO SERFDOM. NAT/G POL/PAR CREATE EDU/PROP ATTIT WEALTH LAISSEZ...OLD/LIB CONCPT TREND 20. PAGE 68 H1368 — FUT PLAN ECO/TAC SOCISM

B44
KOHN H.,THE IDEA OF NATIONALISM. UNIV SOCIETY KIN CREATE REGION CENTRAL SOVEREIGN. PAGE 87 H1740 — NAT/LISM CONCPT NAT/G GP/REL

B45
MERRIAM C.E.,SYSTEMATIC POLITICS. FUT POL/PAR DELIB/GP DIPLOM ADJUD ADMIN LEAD CHOOSE ATTIT...MGT PHIL/SCI TREND. PAGE 109 H2183 — NAT/G METH/CNCPT CREATE

B47
BEHAR D.,BIBLIOGRAFIA HISPANOAMERICANA. LIBROS ANTIGUOS Y MODERNOS REFERENTES A AMERICA Y ESPANA. PORTUGAL SPAIN CONSTN NAT/G SECT CREATE REV WAR GOV/REL...ART/METH GEOG PHIL/SCI LING 20 ARGEN. PAGE 13 H0260 — BIBLIOG L/A+17C CULTURE

B47
BOWLE J.,WESTERN POLITICAL THOUGHT: AN HISTORICAL INTRODUCTION FROM THE ORIGINS TO ROUSSEAU. CONSTN NAT/G SECT CREATE RATIONAL ORD/FREE...SOC BIBLIOG/A. PAGE 19 H0391 — ATTIT IDEA/COMP PHIL/SCI

B48
JONES H.D.,UNESCO: A SELECTED LIST OF REFERENCES. CULTURE CREATE PEACE ATTIT DRIVE 20 UNESCO UN. PAGE 82 H1631 — BIBLIOG/A INT/ORG DIPLOM EDU/PROP

B48
TOWSTER J.,POLITICAL POWER IN THE USSR: 1917-1947. USSR CONSTN CULTURE ELITES CREATE PLAN COERCE CENTRAL ATTIT RIGID/FLEX ORD/FREE...BIBLIOG SOC/INTEG 20 LENIN/VI STALIN/J. PAGE 156 H3122 — EX/STRUC NAT/G MARXISM PWR

B48
TOYNBEE A.J.,CIVILIZATION ON TRIAL. FUT WOR-45 NAT/G CREATE CAP/ISM DIPLOM NUC/PWR CHOOSE MARXISM ...GEOG CONCPT WORSHIP. PAGE 156 H3125 — SOCIETY TIME/SEQ NAT/COMP

B48
WRIGHT G.,THE RESHAPING OF FRENCH DEMOCRACY. FRANCE NAT/G POL/PAR SECT LEAD CHOOSE GP/REL INGP/REL MARXISM SOCISM...CHARTS BIBLIOG 20 DEGAULLE/C. PAGE 171 H3418 — CONSTN POPULISM CREATE LEGIS

B49
ROGERS C.B.,THE SPIRIT OF REVOLUTION IN 1789: A STUDY OF PUBLIC OPINION ...AT THE BEGINNING OF THE FRENCH REVOLUTION. FRANCE CULTURE ELITES EDU/PROP COERCE CROWD...BIBLIOG 18 MUSIC. PAGE 133 H2658 — ATTIT POPULISM REV CREATE

B49
WORMUTH F.D.,THE ORIGINS OF MODERN CONSTITUTIONALISM. GREECE UK LEGIS CREATE TEC/DEV BAL/PWR DOMIN ADJUD REV WAR PWR...JURID ROMAN/REP CROMWELL/O. PAGE 170 H3412 — NAT/G CONSTN LAW

B50
CANTRIL H.,TENSIONS THAT CAUSE WAR. UNIV CULTURE R+D CREATE EDU/PROP DRIVE PERSON KNOWL ORD/FREE ...HUM PSY SOC OBS CENSUS TREND CON/ANAL SOC/EXP SIMUL GEN/METH ANTHOL COLD/WAR TOT/POP. PAGE 26 H0523 — SOCIETY PHIL/SCI PEACE

B50
CARR E.H.,STUDIES IN REVOLUTION. CREATE WAR PERSON ALL/IDEOS MARXISM SOCISM...PHIL/SCI METH/COMP ANTHOL 18/20 SAINTSIMON MARX/KARL PROUDHON/P LASSALLE/F PLEKHNV/GV. PAGE 27 H0537 — REV IDEA/COMP COERCE BIOG

B50
COUNCIL BRITISH NATIONAL BIB,BRITISH NATIONAL BIBLIOGRAPHY. UK AGRI CONSTRUC PERF/ART POL/PAR SECT CREATE INT/TRADE LEAD...HUM JURID PHIL/SCI 20. PAGE 34 H0677 — BIBLIOG/A NAT/G TEC/DEV DIPLOM

B50
GOFF F.R.,FIFTEENTH CENTURY BOOKS IN THE LIBRARY OF CONGRESS. CHRIST-17C GERMANY ITALY CULTURE INTELL SECT CREATE...PHIL/SCI CONCPT CLASSIF BIOG TIME/SEQ 15. PAGE 58 H1153 — BIBLIOG KNOWL HUM

B51
HUXLEY J.,FREEDOM AND CULTURE. UNIV LAW SOCIETY R+D ACADEM SCHOOL CREATE SANCTION ATTIT KNOWL...HUM ANTHOL 20. PAGE 76 H1512 — CULTURE ORD/FREE PHIL/SCI IDEA/COMP

B51
MUMFORD L.,THE CONDUCT OF LIFE. UNIV SOCIETY CREATE ...TECHNIC METH/CNCPT TIME/SEQ TREND GEN/LAWS BIBLIOG/A. PAGE 114 H2286 — ALL/VALS CULTURE PERSON CONCPT

B51
WEBSTER C.,THE FOREIGN POLICY OF PALMERSTON - 1830 TO 1841. MOD/EUR UK LAW CONSTN INTELL SOCIETY STRUCT NAT/G FORCES TOP/EX CREATE BAL/PWR PWR 19. PAGE 166 H3323 — ADMIN PERSON DIPLOM

B51
WHEARE K.C.,MODERN CONSTITUTIONS (HOME UNIVERSITY LIBRARY). UNIV LAW NAT/G LEGIS...CONCPT TREND BIBLIOG. PAGE 167 H3336 — CONSTN CLASSIF PWR CREATE

B52
BENTHAM A.,HANDBOOK OF POLITICAL FALLACIES. FUT MOD/EUR LAW INTELL LOC/G MUNIC NAT/G DELIB/GP LEGIS CREATE EDU/PROP CT/SYS ATTIT RIGID/FLEX KNOWL PWR ...RELATIV PSY SOC CONCPT SELF/OBS TREND STERTYP TOT/POP. PAGE 14 H0286 — POL/PAR

B52
SPENCER F.A.,WAR AND POSTWAR GREECE: AN ANALYSIS BASED ON GREEK WRITINGS. GREECE SOCIETY NAT/G POL/PAR FORCES CREATE DIPLOM LEAD MARXISM...SOC 20. PAGE 147 H2943 — BIBLIOG/A WAR REV

S52
KECSKEMETI P.,"THE 'POLICY SCIENCES': ASPIRATION AND OUTLOOK." UNIV CULTURE INTELL SOCIETY STRUCT EDU/PROP ATTIT PERCEPT RIGID/FLEX KNOWL...PHIL/SCI METH/CNCPT OBS 20. PAGE 84 H1674 — CREATE NEW/IDEA

B53
BUCHHEIM K.,GESCHICHTE DER CHRISTLICHEN PARTEIEN IN DEUTSCHLAND. GERMANY CREATE ATTIT SUPEGO ORD/FREE ...TIME/SEQ IDEA/COMP 19/20 CHRIS/DEM. PAGE 23 H0464 — POL/PAR NAT/G

B53
KEESING F.M.,CULTURE CHANGE: AN ANALYSIS AND BIBLIOGRAPHY OF ANTHROPOLOGICAL SOURCES TO 1952. CULTURE STRUCT...TIME/SEQ 19/20. PAGE 84 H1679 — BIBLIOG SOC CREATE ORD/FREE

B53
MEAD M.,CULTURAL PATTERNS AND TECHNICAL CHANGE. BURMA GREECE NIGERIA ECO/UNDEV AGRI INDUS SCHOOL SECT CREATE FEEDBACK HABITAT...PSY METH/COMP BIBLIOG 20 UN. PAGE 108 H2152 — HEALTH TEC/DEV CULTURE ADJUST

B53
REDFIELD R.,THE PRIMITIVE WORLD AND ITS TRANSFORMATIONS. UNIV CULTURE ATTIT MORAL...CONCPT TREND. PAGE 130 H2606 — SOC CREATE PERSON SOCIETY

L53
DEUTSCH K.W.,"THE GROWTH OF NATIONS: SOME RECURRENT PATTERNS OF POLITICAL AND SOCIAL INTEGRATION" (BMR)" UNIV CULTURE SOCIETY ECO/DEV ECO/UNDEV NAT/G CREATE GP/REL...CONCPT GEN/LAWS SOC/INTEG 11/20. PAGE 40 H0797 — TREND NAT/LISM ORD/FREE

B54
GIRALSO JARAMLLO G.,BIBLIOGRAFIA DE BIBLIOGRAFIAS COLOMBIANAS. L/A+17C ACADEM SECT CREATE EDU/PROP ...ART/METH GEOG LING TREND 20 COLOMB. PAGE 57 H1135 — BIBLIOG/A CULTURE PHIL/SCI ECO/UNDEV

B54
HAZARD B.H. JR.,KOREAN STUDIES GUIDE. KOREA CONSTN CULTURE AGRI FAM SECT CREATE WAR NAT/LISM HABITAT PWR...CHARTS 14/20. PAGE 68 H1371 — BIBLIOG/A ELITES GP/REL

B54
MOSK S.A.,INDUSTRIAL REVOLUTION IN MEXICO. MARKET LABOR CREATE CAP/ISM ADMIN ATTIT SOCISM...POLICY 20 MEXIC/AMER. PAGE 113 H2268 — INDUS TEC/DEV ECO/UNDEV NAT/G

B55
KHADDURI M.,WAR AND PEACE IN THE LAW OF ISLAM. CONSTN CULTURE SOCIETY STRATA NAT/G PROVS SECT FORCES TOP/EX CREATE DOMIN EDU/PROP ADJUD COERCE ATTIT RIGID/FLEX ALL/VALS...CONCPT TIME/SEQ TOT/POP VAL/FREE. PAGE 85 H1702 — ISLAM JURID PEACE WAR

B55
MAZZINI J.,THE DUTIES OF MAN. MOD/EUR LAW SOCIETY FAM NAT/G POL/PAR SECT VOL/ASSN EX/STRUC ACT/RES CREATE REV PEACE ATTIT ALL/VALS...GEN/LAWS WORK 19. PAGE 106 H2113 — SUPEGO CONCPT NAT/LISM

S55
GLADSTONE A.E.,"THE POSSIBILITY OF PREDICTING REACTIONS TO INTERNATIONAL EVENTS." UNIV SOCIETY NAT/G FORCES CREATE EDU/PROP COERCE WAR ATTIT PERSON KNOWL PWR SKILL...METH/CNCPT NEW/IDEA ORG/CHARTS. PAGE 57 H1139 — PHIL/SCI CONCPT

C55
STEWARD J.H.,"THE CONCEPT AND METHOD OF CULTURAL ECOLOGY" IN T.H. STEWARD'S THEORY OF CULTURAL CHANGE." SOCIETY INGP/REL...CONCPT CON/ANAL METH/COMP 20. PAGE 149 H2985 — HABITAT CULTURE CREATE ADJUST

B56
EVANS-PRITCHARD E.E.,THE INSTITUTIONS OF PRIMITIVE SOCIETY. LAW SOCIETY KIN ACT/RES CREATE ALL/VALS ...ART/METH SOC METH/CNCPT WORSHIP 20. PAGE 48 H0953 — STRUCT PHIL/SCI CULTURE CONCPT

B56
GLUCKMAN M.,CUSTOM AND CONFLICT IN AFRICA. AFR FAM KIN NAT/G DOMIN DISCRIM DRIVE MORAL PWR...SOC BIBLIOG WORSHIP 20. PAGE 57 H1145 — CULTURE CREATE PERS/REL GP/COMP

B56
VUCINICH A.,THE SOVIET ACADEMY OF SCIENCES. USSR STRUCT ACADEM NAT/G EDU/PROP ADMIN LEAD ROLE ...BIBLIOG 20 ACADEM/SCI. PAGE 164 H3280 — PHIL/SCI CREATE INTELL PROF/ORG

S56
GORDON L.,"THE ORGANIZATION FOR EUROPEAN ECONOMIC COOPERATION." EUR+WWI INDUS INT/ORG NAT/G CONSULT DELIB/GP ACT/RES CREATE PLAN TEC/DEV EDU/PROP LEGIT WEALTH OEEC 20. PAGE 59 H1178 — VOL/ASSN ECO/DEV

B57
BULLOCK A.,THE LIBERAL TRADITION FROM FOX TO KEYNES. UK CULTURE INTELL CREATE WRITING COLONIAL PERS/REL ATTIT ORD/FREE...POLICY OLD/LIB TRADIT CONCPT 18/20 CHURCHLL/W MILL/JS KEYNES/JM ASQUITH/HH. PAGE 23 H0469 — ANTHOL DEBATE LAISSEZ

B57
CHANDRA S.,PARTIES AND POLITICS AT THE MUGHAL COURT: 1707-1740. INDIA CULTURE EX/STRUC CREATE PLAN PWR...BIBLIOG/A 18. PAGE 29 H0574 — POL/PAR ELITES NAT/G

B57
HERNANDEZ-ARREGU J.,IMPERIALISMO Y CULTURA (LA POLITICA EN LA INTELIGENCIA ARGENTINA). L/A+17C CULTURE ELITES WRITING COLONIAL CROWD ATTIT FASCISM MARXISM SOCISM...BIOG IDEA/COMP 20 ARGEN PERON/JUAN COM/PARTY. PAGE 70 H1403 — INTELL CREATE ART/METH HUM

B57
TOMASIC D.A.,NATIONAL COMMUNISM AND SOVIET STRATEGY. UK USSR YUGOSLAVIA NAT/G POL/PAR CHIEF CREATE DOMIN REV WAR PWR...BIOG TREND 20 TITO/MARSH STALIN/J. PAGE 156 H3112 — COM NAT/LISM MARXISM DIPLOM

B58
COWAN L.G.,LOCAL GOVERNMENT IN WEST AFRICA. AFR FRANCE UK CULTURE KIN POL/PAR CHIEF LEGIS CREATE ADMIN PARTIC GOV/REL GP/REL...METH/COMP 20. PAGE 34 H0682 — LOC/G COLONIAL SOVEREIGN REPRESENT

B58
ORTEGA Y GASSET J.,MAN AND CRISIS. SECT CREATE PERSON CONSERVE...GEN/LAWS RENAISSAN. PAGE 122 H2430 — PHIL/SCI CULTURE CONCPT

B58
VON FURER-HAIMEN E.,AN ANTHROPOLOGICAL BIBLIOGRAPHY OF SOUTH ASIA (VOL. I). STRATA STRUCT KIN SECT ACT/RES CREATE HABITAT...GEOG OBS 19/20. PAGE 163 H3267 — BIBLIOG/A CULTURE S/ASIA SOC

B59
GOLDSCHMIDT W.,UNDERSTANDING HUMAN SOCIETY. SOCIETY CREATE ATTIT...GEOG PHIL/SCI CONCPT GP/COMP. PAGE 58 H1159 — CULTURE STRUCT TEC/DEV PERSON

B59
HONINGMAN J.J.,THE WORLD OF MAN. CHRIST-17C MEDIT-7 PRE/AMER PREHIST CREATE INGP/REL BIO/SOC HABITAT ...PSY SOC BIBLIOG. PAGE 73 H1460 — CULTURE METH PERSON STRUCT

S59
JENKS C.W.,"THE CHALLENGE OF UNIVERSALITY." FUT UNIV CONSTN CULTURE CONSULT CREATE PLAN LEGIT ATTIT MORAL ORD/FREE RESPECT...MAJORIT JURID 20. PAGE 80 H1602 — INT/ORG LAW PEACE INT/LAW

S59
SCOTT W.A.,"EMPIRICAL ASSESSMENT OF VALUES AND IDEOLOGIES." CULTURE SOCIETY SECT CREATE DRIVE PERSON MORAL PWR...SOC METH/CNCPT STAT CONT/OBS DEEP/INT DEEP/QU CHARTS VAL/FREE. PAGE 141 H2817 — ATTIT PSY

C59
EASTON D.,"POLITICAL ANTHROPOLOGY" IN BIENNIAL REVIEW OF ANTHROPOLOGY" UNIV LAW CULTURE ELITES SOCIETY CREATE...PSY CONCPT GP/COMP GEN/METH 20. PAGE 44 H0880 — SOC BIBLIOG/A NEW/IDEA

B60
AUSTRUY J.,STRUCTURE ECONOMIQUE ET CIVILISATION: L'EGYPTE ET LE DESTIN ECONOMIQUE DE L'ISLAM. ISLAM UAR CREATE OP/RES ECO/TAC...SOC BIBLIOG 20 MUSLIM. PAGE 9 H0182 — ECO/UNDEV CULTURE STRUCT

B60
CHATTERJI S.K.,AFRICANISM: THE AFRICAN PERSONALITY. KIN NAT/G SECT CREATE DIPLOM COLONIAL GP/REL ATTIT ORD/FREE...LING WORSHIP 20. PAGE 29 H0585 — PERSON NAT/LISM AFR

CULTURE

B60

DIA M.,REFLEXIONS SUR L'ECONOMIE DE L'AFRIQUE NOIRE (REV. ED.). CULTURE ECO/UNDEV CREATE TEC/DEV DIPLOM INT/TRADE OPTIMAL ATTIT...POLICY 20. PAGE 41 H0816
AFR ECO/TAC SOCISM PLAN

B60

SAHLINS M.D.,EVOLUTION AND CULTURE. CREATE...MYTH METH/COMP BIBLIOG 20. PAGE 137 H2730
CULTURE NEW/IDEA CONCPT HABITAT

B60

SCHAPIRO L.,THE COMMUNIST PARTY OF THE SOVIET UNION. COM LAW SOCIETY STRATA STRUCT ECO/DEV LABOR NAT/G POL/PAR CREATE DOMIN EDU/PROP COERCE TOTALISM MARXISM...POLICY CONCPT MYTH TIME/SEQ WORK TOT/POP 20 LENIN/VI STALIN/J. PAGE 139 H2772
INTELL PWR USSR

S60

ARENDT H.,"SOCIETY AND CULTURE." FUT CULTURE INTELL STRATA EDU/PROP ATTIT PERSON KNOWL...ART/METH HUM 20. PAGE 8 H0161
SOCIETY CREATE

S60

HALSEY A.H.,"THE CHANGING FUNCTIONS OF UNIVERSITIES IN ADVANCED INDUSTRIAL SOCIETIES." R+D EDU/PROP REPRESENT ROLE ORD/FREE PWR TREND. PAGE 65 H1298
ACADEM CREATE CULTURE ADJUST

S60

SHILS E.,"THE INTELLECTUALS IN THE POLITICAL DEVELOPMENT OF THE NEW STATES." AFR ASIA S/ASIA ELITES LOC/G NAT/G CONSULT EX/STRUC CREATE PLAN ECO/TAC DOMIN LEGIT DRIVE PWR...TRADIT CONCPT STERTYP GEN/LAWS 20. PAGE 143 H2861
POL/PAR INTELL NAT/LISM

B61

BINDER L.,RELIGION AND POLITICS IN PAKISTAN. ISLAM PAKISTAN NAT/G SECT LEGIS CREATE CHOOSE GP/REL ...MAJORIT TRADIT 20. PAGE 17 H0336
CONSTN CONFER NAT/LISM POL/PAR

B61

BULLOCK A.,HITLER: A STUDY IN TYRANNY. EUR+WWI GERMANY SOCIETY STRUCT NAT/G POL/PAR FORCES CREATE DOMIN EDU/PROP EXEC COERCE WAR NAT/LISM DISPL DRIVE PERSON PWR...PSY NAZI 20 HITLER/A. PAGE 23 H0470
ATTIT BIOG TOTALISM

B61

ETZIONI A.,COMPLEX ORGANIZATIONS: A SOCIOLOGICAL READER. CLIENT CULTURE STRATA CREATE OP/RES ADMIN ...POLICY METH/CNCPT BUREAUCRCY. PAGE 47 H0945
VOL/ASSN STRUCT CLASSIF PROF/ORG

B61

INDIAN NATIONAL CONGRESS,SOUVENIR, 66TH SESSION. INDIA S/ASIA CONSTN CULTURE LEGIS CREATE TEC/DEV LEAD TASK...GEOG CHARTS 20. PAGE 77 H1533
CONFER PLAN NAT/G POLICY

B61

KEDOURIE E.,NATIONALISM (REV. ED.). MOD/EUR SOVEREIGN...CONCPT 19/20. PAGE 84 H1675
NAT/LISM NAT/G CREATE REV

B61

MACLEOD I.,NEVILLE CHAMBERLAIN. UK SOCIETY TOP/EX WAR PERSON ALL/VALS ORD/FREE PARLIAMENT 20 CHAMBRLN/N. PAGE 100 H2003
BIOG NAT/G CREATE

B61

MARX K.,THE COMMUNIST MANIFESTO. IN (MENDEL A. ESSENTIAL WORKS OF MARXISM, NEW YORK: BANTAM. FUT MOD/EUR CULTURE ECO/DEV ECO/UNDEV AGRI FINAN INDUS MARKET PROC/MFG LABOR MUNIC POL/PAR CONSULT FORCES CREATE PLAN ADMIN ATTIT DRIVE RIGID/FLEX ORD/FREE PWR RESPECT MARX/KARL WORK. PAGE 104 H2081
COM NEW/IDEA CAP/ISM REV

B61

MAYNE A.,DESIGNING AND ADMINISTERING A REGIONAL ECONOMIC DEVELOPMENT PLAN WITH SPECIFIC REFERENCE TO PUERTO RICO (PAMPHLET). PUERT/RICO SOCIETY NAT/G DELIB/GP REGION...DECISION 20. PAGE 105 H2106
ECO/UNDEV PLAN CREATE ADMIN

B61

VON MERING O.,A GRAMMAR OF HUMAN VALUES. WOR+45 CULTURE FACE/GP NEIGH CREATE EDU/PROP LEGIT ATTIT DRIVE PERSON ORD/FREE...PSY SOC METH/CNCPT OBS RECORD INT REC/INT STAND/INT QU CHARTS VAL/FREE. PAGE 164 H3275
SOCIETY MORAL

S61

TUCKER R.C.,"TOWARDS A COMPARATIVE POLITICS OF MOVEMENT-REGIMES" (BMR)" USSR CONSTN NAT/G CREATE PROB/SOLV DIPLOM DOMIN REV...GP/COMP IDEA/COMP METH 20 STALIN/J BOLSHEVISM. PAGE 157 H3135
MARXISM POLICY GEN/LAWS PWR

B62

BELL D.,THE END OF IDEOLOGY (REV. ED.). USA+45 USA-45 ELITES STRATA LABOR CREATE CRIME PWR MARXISM ...PHIL/SCI METH/COMP 20 EUROPE. PAGE 13 H0265
CROWD CAP/ISM SOCISM IDEA/COMP

B62

DAVAR F.C.,IRAN AND INDIA THROUGH THE AGES. INDIA IRAN ELITES SECT CREATE ORD/FREE...LING BIBLIOG. PAGE 37 H0743
NAT/COMP DIPLOM CULTURE

B62

HARRINGTON M.,THE OTHER AMERICA: POVERTY IN THE UNITED STATES. WORKER CREATE REPRESENT RACE/REL AGE/O DRIVE POLICY. PAGE 67 H1338
WEALTH WELF/ST INCOME CULTURE

B62

MEGGITT M.J.,DESERT PEOPLE. ECO/UNDEV KIN CREATE PROB/SOLV CONTROL DRIVE ROLE...GEOG SOC MYTH CHARTS BIBLIOG 20 AUSTRAL. PAGE 108 H2159
ADJUST CULTURE INGP/REL HABITAT

B62

NASRI A.R.,A BIBLIOGRAPHY OF THE SUDAN 1938-1958. AFR SUDAN CREATE...SOC 20. PAGE 116 H2316
BIBLIOG ECO/UNDEV NAT/G SOCIETY

B62

SELOSOEMARDJAN O.,SOCIAL CHANGES IN JOGJAKARTA. INDONESIA NETHERLAND ELITES STRATA STRUCT FAM POL/PAR CREATE DIPLOM INT/TRADE EDU/PROP ADMIN GOV/REL...SOC 20 JAVA CHINJAP. PAGE 141 H2825
ECO/UNDEV CULTURE REV COLONIAL

B62

SWAYZE H.,POLITICAL CONTROL OF LITERATURE IN THE USSR, 1946-1959. USSR NAT/G CREATE LICENSE...JURID 20. PAGE 151 H3014
MARXISM WRITING CONTROL DOMIN

B62

WALSTON H.,AGRICULTURE UNDER COMMUNISM. CHINA/COM COM PROB/SOLV HAPPINESS RIGID/FLEX...POLICY METH/COMP 20. PAGE 165 H3295
AGRI MARXISM PLAN CREATE

L62

NOLTE E.,"ZUR PHANOMENOLOGIE DES FASCHIMUS." EUR+WWI GERMANY ITALY TURKEY INTELL NAT/G CHIEF CONSULT FORCES CREATE DOMIN EDU/PROP COERCE WAR CHOOSE DRIVE FASCISM...PSY CONCPT MYTH GEN/METH LEAGUE/NAT NAZI 20. PAGE 118 H2367
ATTIT PWR

S62

CROAN M.,"POLYCENTRISM: COMMUNIST INTERNATIONAL RELATIONS." ASIA STRUCT INT/ORG NAT/G POL/PAR CONSULT PLAN DOMIN EDU/PROP COERCE ATTIT RIGID/FLEX SOCISM...POLICY CONCPT TREND CON/ANAL GEN/LAWS MARX/KARL. PAGE 35 H0703
COM CREATE DIPLOM NAT/LISM

S62

GUETZKOW H.,"THE POTENTIAL OF CASE STUDY IN ANALYZING INTERNATIONAL CONFLICT." EUR+WWI FUT GERMANY INTELL SOCIETY STRUCT INT/ORG LOC/G NAT/G CONSULT CREATE PLAN CHOOSE ATTIT RIGID/FLEX ...POLICY SAAR 20. PAGE 62 H1246
EDU/PROP METH/CNCPT COERCE FRANCE

S62

KOLARZ W.,"THE IMPACT OF COMMUNISM ON WEST AFRICA." AFR FUT SOCIETY INT/ORG NAT/G CREATE PLAN DOMIN EDU/PROP COERCE NAT/LISM ATTIT RIGID/FLEX SOCISM ...POLICY CONCPT TREND MARX/KARL 20. PAGE 88 H1751
COM POL/PAR COLONIAL

S62

MARIAS J.,"A PROGRAM FOR EUROPE." EUR+WWI INT/ORG NAT/G PLAN DIPLOM DOMIN PWR...STERTYP TOT/POP 20. PAGE 102 H2048
VOL/ASSN CREATE REGION

S62

SPRINGER H.W.,"FEDERATION IN THE CARIBBEAN: AN ATTEMPT THAT FAILED." L/A+17C ECO/UNDEV INT/ORG POL/PAR PROVS LEGIS CREATE PLAN LEGIT ADMIN FEDERAL ATTIT DRIVE PERSON ORD/FREE PWR...POLICY GEOG PSY CONCPT OBS CARIBBEAN CMN/WLTH 20. PAGE 148 H2955
VOL/ASSN NAT/G REGION

B63

BIDNEY D.,THE CONCEPT OF FREEDOM IN ANTHROPOLOGY. UNIV CULTURE STRATA SECT CREATE NAT/LISM ...METH/COMP 20. PAGE 17 H0332
SOC PERSON ORD/FREE CONCPT

B63

DEUTSCH K.W.,THE NERVES OF GOVERNMENT. NAT/G CREATE EDU/PROP CONTROL LEAD PWR...CONCPT GEN/LAWS 20. PAGE 40 H0799
DECISION GAME SIMUL OP/RES

B63

GEERTZ C.,PEDDLERS AND PRINCES: SOCIAL DEVELOPMENT AND ECONOMIC CHANGE IN TWO INDONESIAN TOWNS. S/ASIA CULTURE SOCIETY STRATA FACE/GP MUNIC CREATE TEC/DEV ECO/TAC ORD/FREE WEALTH...OBS INT CENSUS CHARTS WORK TOT/POP VAL/FREE 20. PAGE 55 H1106
ECO/UNDEV SOC ELITES INDONESIA

B63

GOODE W.J.,WORLD REVOLUTION AND FAMILY PATTERNS. AFR CHINA/COM INDIA UAR CREATE ADJUST ATTIT SEX ...SOC 20 CHINJAP. PAGE 58 H1169
FAM NAT/COMP CULTURE MARRIAGE

B63

LARSON A.,A WARLESS WORLD. FUT CULTURE NAT/G VOL/ASSN FORCES CREATE DOMIN PEACE ALL/VALS...HUM STERTYP 20. PAGE 91 H1824
SOCIETY CONCPT ARMS/CONT

B63

MAYNE R.,THE COMMUNITY OF EUROPE. UK CONSTN NAT/G CONSULT DELIB/GP CREATE PLAN ECO/TAC LEGIT ADMIN ROUTINE ORD/FREE PWR WEALTH...CONCPT TIME/SEQ EEC EURATOM 20. PAGE 105 H2107
EUR+WWI INT/ORG REGION

B63

MULLER H.J.,FREEDOM IN THE WESTERN WORLD. PREHIST CULTURE SECT CREATE TEC/DEV DOMIN PWR WEALTH ...MAJORIT SOC CONCPT. PAGE 114 H2285
ORD/FREE TIME/SEQ SOCIETY

B63

REYNOLDS B.,MAGIC, DIVINATION AND WITCHCRAFT AMONG
AFR

THE BAROTSE OF NORTHERN RHODESIA. RHODESIA CULTURE KIN CREATE LEGIT PARTIC DEATH DREAM STRANGE HABITAT PERSON...AUD/VIS WORSHIP 20. PAGE 131 H2619 — SOC MYTH SECT

B63
RONNING C.N.,LAW AND POLITICS IN INTER-AMERICAN DIPLOMACY. L/A+17C ECO/UNDEV NAT/G CONSULT DELIB/GP CREATE CAP/ISM ECO/TAC LEGIT REGION RIGID/FLEX ...METH/CNCPT GEN/LAWS OAS 20. PAGE 133 H2668 — VOL/ASSN ALL/VALS DIPLOM

B63
TINDALE N.B.,ABORIGINAL AUSTRALIANS. KIN CREATE ROLE...SOC MYTH TREND 20 AUSTRAL ABORIGINES MIGRATION. PAGE 155 H3099 — CULTURE DRIVE ECO/UNDEV HABITAT

B63
US ATOMIC ENERGY COMMISSION,ATOMIC ENERGY IN THE SOVIET UNION: TRIP REPORT OF THE US ATOMIC ENERGY DELEGATION, MAY 1933. USSR R+D NAT/G CONSULT CREATE DIPLOM ADMIN ROUTINE EFFICIENCY PRODUC KNOWL SKILL ...NAT/COMP 20 AEC TRAVEL TREATY. PAGE 159 H3176 — METH/COMP OP/RES TEC/DEV NUC/PWR

S63
ANTHON C.G.,"THE END OF THE ADENAUER ERA." EUR+WWI GERMANY/W CONSTN EX/STRUC CREATE DIPLOM LEGIT ATTIT PERSON ALL/VALS...RECORD 20 ADENAUER/K. PAGE 7 H0144 — NAT/G TOP/EX BAL/PWR GERMANY

S63
CRUTCHER J.,"PAN AFRICANISM: AFRICAN ODYSSEY." AFR NAT/G POL/PAR PROF/ORG VOL/ASSN TOP/EX CREATE REGION RACE/REL ALL/VALS...CONCPT TIME/SEQ TREND CON/ANAL 20. PAGE 36 H0716 — PROVS DELIB/GP COLONIAL

S63
HOSKINS H.L.,"ARAB SOCIALISM IN THE UAR." ISLAM USSR AGRI INDUS NAT/G TOP/EX CREATE DIPLOM EDU/PROP DRIVE KNOWL PWR SOCISM...POLICY CONCPT TREND SUEZ 20. PAGE 74 H1478 — ECO/DEV PLAN UAR

B64
BELL W.,JAMAICAN LEADERS: POLITICAL ATTITUDES IN A NEW NATION. JAMAICA STRUCT ACT/RES CREATE PROB/SOLV DIPLOM COLONIAL LEAD...QU 20. PAGE 13 H0267 — NAT/LISM ATTIT DRIVE SOVEREIGN

B64
BRIGHT J.R.,RESEARCH, DEVELOPMENT AND TECHNOLOGICAL INNOVATION. CULTURE R+D CREATE PLAN PROB/SOLV AUTOMAT RISK PERSON...DECISION CONCPT PREDICT BIBLIOG. PAGE 21 H0419 — TEC/DEV NEW/IDEA INDUS MGT

B64
BRZEZINSKI Z.,POLITICAL POWER: USA/USSR. USA+45 USSR AGRI POL/PAR FORCES CREATE CHOOSE ATTIT ORD/FREE PWR MARXISM...MYTH 20 KENNEDY/JF. PAGE 23 H0457 — NAT/G NAT/COMP POLICY LEAD

B64
CAPLOW T.,PRINCIPLES OF ORGANIZATION. UNIV CULTURE STRUCT CREATE INGP/REL UTOPIA...GEN/LAWS TIME. PAGE 26 H0526 — VOL/ASSN CONCPT SIMUL EX/STRUC

B64
CAUTE D.,COMMUNISM AND THE FRENCH INTELLECTUALS, 1914-1960. COM EUR+WWI MOD/EUR NAT/G PERF/ART PROF/ORG CREATE EDU/PROP ATTIT PERSON KNOWL MARXISM ...SOC TIME/SEQ MARX/KARL 20 MALRAUX/A GIDE/A SARTRE/J. PAGE 28 H0563 — POL/PAR INTELL

B64
DEL VAYO J.A.,CHINA TRIUMPHS. CHINA/COM CULTURE DIPLOM HEALTH 20. PAGE 39 H0787 — MARXISM CREATE ORD/FREE POLICY

B64
GILLY A.,INSIDE THE CUBAN REVOLUTION. CUBA AGRI INDUS LABOR CREATE DIPLOM...METH/COMP 20. PAGE 56 H1129 — REV PLAN MARXISM ECO/UNDEV

B64
GREBLER L.,URBAN RENEWAL IN EUROPEAN COUNTRIES: ITS EMERGENCE AND POTENTIALS. EUR+WWI UK ECO/DEV LOC/G NEIGH CREATE ADMIN ATTIT...TREND NAT/COMP 20 URBAN/RNWL. PAGE 60 H1205 — MUNIC PLAN CONSTRUC NAT/G

B64
KITCHEN H.,A HANDBOOK OF AFRICAN AFFAIRS. ECO/UNDEV CREATE DIPLOM COLONIAL RACE/REL...ART/METH GEOG CHARTS 20. PAGE 87 H1729 — AFR NAT/G INT/ORG FORCES

B64
LEWIN P.,THE FOREIGN TRADE OF COMMUNIST CHINA* ITS IMPACT ON THE FREE WORLD. AFR EUR+WWI L/A+17C S/ASIA ECO/UNDEV CREATE FOR/AID...STAT NET/THEORY TREND CHARTS. PAGE 96 H1910 — ASIA INT/TRADE NAT/COMP USSR

B64
MARTINET G.,MARXISM OF OUR TIME: OR THE CONTRADICTIONS OF SOCIALISM. FRANCE NAT/G OPTIMAL RIGID/FLEX SOCISM...IDEA/COMP 20. PAGE 103 H2067 — MARXISM MARXIST PROB/SOLV CREATE

B64
MCCALL D.F.,AFRICA IN TIME PERSPECTIVE. AFR EXTR/IND KIN SECT CREATE PERS/REL HABITAT...GEOG METH/CNCPT LING BIBLIOG/A TIME 20. PAGE 106 H2124 — HIST/WRIT OBS/ENVIR CULTURE

B64
MINAR D.W.,IDEAS AND POLITICS: THE AMERICAN EXPERIENCE. SECT CHIEF LEGIS CREATE ADJUD EXEC REV PWR...PHIL/SCI CONCPT IDEA/COMP 18/20 HAMILTON/A JEFFERSN/T DECLAR/IND JACKSON/A PRESIDENT. PAGE 111 H2220 — CONSTN NAT/G FEDERAL

B64
MORGENTHAU R.S.,POLITICAL PARTIES IN FRENCH-SPEAKING WEST AFRICA. AFR FRANCE GUINEA IVORY/CST MALI SENEGAL CONSTN LEGIS CREATE PLAN LOBBY PARTIC GP/REL...POLICY BIBLIOG 20. PAGE 113 H2257 — POL/PAR NAT/G SOVEREIGN COLONIAL

B64
O'HEARN P.J.T.,PEACE, ORDER AND GOOD GOVERNMENT; A NEW CONSTITUTION FOR CANADA. CANADA EX/STRUC LEGIS CT/SYS PARL/PROC...BIBLIOG 20. PAGE 120 H2388 — NAT/G CONSTN LAW CREATE

B64
ON CULTURE AND SOCIAL CHANGE. FAM NAT/G ACT/RES ECO/TAC RACE/REL...PSY TIME/SEQ TREND IDEA/COMP METH/COMP ANTHOL BIBLIOG 20. PAGE 120 H2406 — CULTURE TEC/DEV STRUCT CREATE

B64
SINAI I.R.,THE CHALLENGE OF MODERNISATION* THE WEST'S IMPACT ON THE NON-WESTERN WORLD. EUR+WWI CULTURE ELITES SECT CONSERVE SOCISM...GP/COMP IDEA/COMP NAT/COMP GEN/LAWS. PAGE 144 H2881 — ASIA S/ASIA ECO/UNDEV CREATE

B64
VON FURER-HAIMEN E.,AN ANTHROPOLOGICAL BIBLIOGRAPHY OF SOUTH ASIA (VOL. II). STRATA STRUCT KIN SECT ACT/RES CREATE HABITAT...GEOG OBS 20. PAGE 163 H3268 — BIBLIOG/A CULTURE S/ASIA SOC

B64
VON GRUNEBAUM G.E.,MODERN ISLAM: THE SEARCH FOR CULTURAL IDENTITY. ACADEM NEIGH WRITING NAT/LISM ...HUM CONCPT 19/20 MUSLIM MID/EAST ARABS. PAGE 163 H3269 — ISLAM CULTURE CREATE SECT

L64
HAAS E.B.,"ECONOMICS AND DIFFERENTIAL PATTERNS OF POLITICAL INTEGRATION: PROJECTIONS ABOUT UNITY IN LATIN AMERICA." SOCIETY NAT/G DELIB/GP ACT/RES CREATE PLAN ECO/TAC REGION ROUTINE ATTIT DRIVE PWR WEALTH...CONCPT TREND CHARTS LAFTA 20. PAGE 63 H1266 — L/A+17C INT/ORG MARKET

S64
BRADLEY C.P.,"THE FORMATION OF MALAYSIA." INDIA S/ASIA POL/PAR VOL/ASSN TOP/EX LEGIT RACE/REL ORD/FREE 20. PAGE 20 H0398 — NAT/G CREATE COLONIAL MALAYSIA

S64
CATTELL D.T.,"SOVIET POLICIES IN LATIN AMERICA." COM CUBA L/A+17C USSR SOCIETY NAT/G POL/PAR FORCES CREATE ECO/TAC EDU/PROP REGION REV RIGID/FLEX ...GEN/LAWS COLD/WAR 20. PAGE 28 H0560 — DRIVE PWR

S64
CLIFFE L.,"TANGANYIKA'S TWO YEARS OF INDEPENDENCE." AFR INDUS MARKET NAT/G POL/PAR DELIB/GP CREATE ECO/TAC LEGIT DRIVE ALL/VALS...METH/CNCPT RECORD 20 TANGANYIKA. PAGE 30 H0604 — ECO/UNDEV PLAN

S64
EISTER A.W.,"PERSPECTIVE ON FUNCTIONS OF RELIGION IN A DEVELOPING COUNTRY: ISLAM IN PAKISTAN." ISLAM CULTURE MUNIC ACT/RES CREATE PROB/SOLV TEC/DEV WORSHIP. PAGE 45 H0902 — ATTIT SECT ECO/DEV

S64
KOVNER M.,"THE SINO-SOVIET DISPUTE: COMMUNISM AT THE CROSSROADS." ASIA CHINA/COM COM USSR ECO/UNDEV NAT/G TOP/EX CREATE BAL/PWR DOMIN EDU/PROP PWR ...CONCPT COMECON 20. PAGE 88 H1760 — ATTIT TREND

S64
MARES V.E.,"EAST EUROPE'S SECOND CHANCE." COM EUR+WWI HUNGARY ROMANIA USSR YUGOSLAVIA ECO/UNDEV NAT/G TOP/EX CREATE PLAN TEC/DEV REGION NAT/LISM RIGID/FLEX PWR...CONCPT STAT COMECON 20. PAGE 102 H2047 — VOL/ASSN ECO/TAC

S64
MOZINGO D.P.,"CHINA'S RELATIONS WITH HER ASIAN NEIGHBORS." ASIA CHINA/COM S/ASIA VIETNAM NAT/G DELIB/GP FORCES CREATE DOMIN EDU/PROP REV RIGID/FLEX PWR...TIME/SEQ GEN/LAWS COLD/WAR 20. PAGE 114 H2277 — VOL/ASSN POLICY DIPLOM

S64
NEEDHAM T.,"SCIENCE AND SOCIETY IN EAST AND WEST." INTELL STRATA R+D LOC/G NAT/G PROVS CONSULT ACT/RES CREATE PLAN TEC/DEV EDU/PROP ADMIN ATTIT ALL/VALS ...POLICY RELATIV MGT CONCPT NEW/IDEA TIME/SEQ WORK WORK. PAGE 116 H2327 — ASIA STRUCT

S64
TINKER H.,"POLITICS IN SOUTHEAST ASIA." INT/ORG NAT/G CREATE PLAN TEC/DEV GUERRILLA KNOWL ORD/FREE COLD/WAR. PAGE 155 H3103 — S/ASIA ACT/RES REGION

S64
TOUVAL S.,"THE SOMALI REPUBLIC." AFR ISLAM SOMALIA FAM KIN NAT/G CREATE FOR/AID LEGIT ATTIT ALL/VALS ...RECORD TREND 20. PAGE 156 H3119 — ECO/UNDEV RIGID/FLEX

S64
TOYNBEE A.,"BRITAIN AND THE ARABS: THE NEED FOR A NEW START." NAT/G CREATE COLONIAL ATTIT RIGID/FLEX MORAL PWR...POLICY HIST/WRIT 20. PAGE 156 H3124 — ISLAM ECO/TAC DIPLOM

UK

UNRUH J.M.,"SCIENTIFIC INPUTS TO LEGISLATIVE DECISION-MAKING (SUPPLEMENT)" USA+45 ACADEM NAT/G PROVS GOV/REL GOV/COMP. PAGE 159 H3171 — S64 — CREATE DECISION LEGIS PARTIC

APTER D.E.,THE POLITICS OF MODERNIZATION. AFR L/A+17C CULTURE NAT/G POL/PAR ADMIN COLONIAL NAT/LISM ATTIT RIGID/FLEX PWR...SOC CONCPT. PAGE 8 H0154 — B65 — ECO/UNDEV GEN/LAWS STRATA CREATE

CAMPBELL G.A.,THE CIVIL SERVICE IN BRITAIN (2ND ED.). UK DELIB/GP FORCES WORKER CREATE PLAN ...POLICY AUD/VIS 19/20 CIVIL/SERV. PAGE 26 H0515 — B65 — ADMIN LEGIS NAT/G FINAN

DUGGAR G.S.,RENEWAL OF TOWN AND VILLAGE I: A WORLD-WIDE SURVEY OF LOCAL GOVERNMENT EXPERIENCE. WOR+45 CONSTRUC INDUS CREATE BUDGET REGION GOV/REL...QU NAT/COMP 20 URBAN/RNWL. PAGE 43 H0859 — B65 — MUNIC NEIGH PLAN ADMIN

FOSTER P.,EDUCATION AND SOCIAL CHANGE IN GHANA. GHANA CULTURE STRUCT ECO/UNDEV TEC/DEV REGION EFFICIENCY LITERACY ALL/VALS SOVEREIGN...STAT METH/COMP 19/20 GOLD/COAST. PAGE 52 H1043 — B65 — SCHOOL CREATE SOCIETY

GOLEMBIEWSKI R.T.,MEN, MANAGEMENT, AND MORALITY; TOWARD A NEW ORGANIZATIONAL ETHIC. CONSTN EX/STRUC CREATE ADMIN CONTROL INGP/REL PERSON SUPEGO MORAL PWR...GOV/COMP METH/COMP 20 BUREAUCRCY. PAGE 58 H1161 — B65 — LG/CO MGT PROB/SOLV

GREGG J.L.,POLITICAL PARTIES AND PARTY SYSTEMS IN GUATEMALA, 1944-1963. GUATEMALA L/A+17C EX/STRUC FORCES CREATE CONTROL REV CHOOSE PWR...TREND IDEA/COMP 20. PAGE 60 H1209 — B65 — LEAD POL/PAR NAT/G CHIEF

HAVIGHURST R.J.,SOCIETY AND EDUCATION IN BRAZIL. BRAZIL PORTUGAL ECO/UNDEV INDUS NAT/G CREATE INSPECT COLONIAL ADJUST DEMAND LITERACY...CENSUS TREND CHARTS 16/20. PAGE 68 H1362 — B65 — SCHOOL ACADEM ACT/RES CULTURE

HOSELITZ B.F.,ECONOMICS AND THE IDEA OF MANKIND. UNIV ECO/DEV ECO/UNDEV DIST/IND INDUS INT/ORG NAT/G ACT/RES ECO/TAC WEALTH...CONCPT STAT. PAGE 74 H1476 — B65 — CREATE INT/TRADE

HYMES D.,THE USE OF COMPUTERS IN ANTHROPOLOGY. CULTURE PROF/ORG CONSULT CREATE EFFICIENCY PERCEPT ...CLASSIF LING CON/ANAL COMPUT/IR METH/COMP ANTHOL 20. PAGE 76 H1517 — B65 — METH COMPUTER TEC/DEV SOC

MEIER R.L.,DEVELOPMENTAL PLANNING. PUERT/RICO INDUS PUB/INST SCHOOL CREATE ECO/TAC FOR/AID...NAT/COMP 20. PAGE 108 H2165 — B65 — PLAN ECO/UNDEV GOV/COMP TEC/DEV

MURDOCK G.P.,CULTURE AND SOCIETY. SOCIETY STRATA STRUCT SECT CREATE CONTROL ORD/FREE...GP/COMP ANTHOL 20. PAGE 115 H2294 — B65 — CULTURE PHIL/SCI METH IDEA/COMP

ORGANSKI A.F.K.,THE STAGES OF POLITICAL DEVELOPMENT. STRATA AGRI INDUS NAT/G POL/PAR COLONIAL PWR WEALTH...CLASSIF TIME/SEQ. PAGE 121 H2428 — B65 — ECO/DEV ECO/UNDEV GEN/LAWS CREATE

SLOTKIN J.S.,READINGS IN EARLY ANTHROPOLOGY. INTELL SECT CREATE ATTIT KNOWL...HUM PHIL/SCI PSY LING 1/18. PAGE 145 H2902 — B65 — SOC CULTURE GP/COMP

VERMOT-GAUCHY M.,L'EDUCATION NATIONALE DANS LA FRANCE DE 1975. FRANCE FUT CULTURE ELITES R+D SCHOOL PLAN EDU/PROP EFFICIENCY...POLICY PREDICT CHARTS INDEX 20. PAGE 162 H3245 — B65 — ACADEM CREATE TREND INTELL

LASSWELL H.D.,"THE POLICY SCIENCES OF DEVELOPMENT." CULTURE SOCIETY EX/STRUC CREATE ADMIN ATTIT KNOWL ...SOC CONCPT SIMUL GEN/METH. PAGE 92 H1835 — L65 — PWR METH/CNCPT DIPLOM

BIRNBAUM K.,"SWEDEN'S NUCLEAR POLICY." WOR+45 POL/PAR CREATE TEC/DEV NEUTRAL RISK WAR ORD/FREE ...DECISION IDEA/COMP NAT/COMP TIME. PAGE 17 H0343 — S65 — SWEDEN NUC/PWR DIPLOM ARMS/CONT

BRANDENBURG F.,"THE RELEVANCE OF MEXICAN EXPERIENCE TO LATIN AMERICAN DEVELOPMENT." BRAZIL CHILE VENEZUELA STRUCT ECO/UNDEV AGRI CREATE ECO/TAC ...STAT RECORD MEXIC/AMER ARGEN COLOMB. PAGE 20 H0405 — S65 — L/A+17C GOV/COMP

MARK M.,"MUST WE FIGHT SOCIAL REVOLUTIONS OF THE LEFT?" L/A+17C USA+45 ECO/UNDEV DIPLOM ADJUST PERCEPT...IDEA/COMP NAT/COMP. PAGE 103 H2053 — S65 — NAT/LISM REV MARXISM CREATE

MCALISTER L.N.,"CHANGING CONCEPTS OF THE ROLE OF THE MILITARY IN LATIN AMERICA." CULTURE NAT/G CREATE REGION NAT/LISM ATTIT SOVEREIGN...NAT/COMP GEN/LAWS. PAGE 106 H2120 — S65 — L/A+17C FORCES IDEA/COMP PWR

SANDERS R.,"MASS SUPPORT AND COMMUNIST INSURRECTION." GREECE MALAYSIA PHILIPPINE VIETNAM STRUCT ECO/UNDEV POL/PAR FORCES CREATE REV ...GP/COMP IDEA/COMP. PAGE 138 H2751 — S65 — GUERRILLA MARXISM GOV/COMP

STAAR R.F.,"RETROGRESSION IN POLAND." COM USSR AGRI INDUS NAT/G CREATE EDU/PROP TOTALISM RIGID/FLEX ORD/FREE PWR SOCISM...RECORD CHARTS 20. PAGE 148 H2965 — S65 — TOP/EX ECO/TAC POLAND

TENDLER J.D.,"TECHNOLOGY AND ECONOMIC DEVELOPMENT* THE CASE OF HYDRO VS THERMAL POWER." CONSTRUC DIST/IND CREATE TEC/DEV INT/TRADE CENTRAL PWR SKILL WEALTH...MGT NAT/COMP ARGEN. PAGE 153 H3061 — S65 — BRAZIL INDUS ECO/UNDEV

THOMAS F.C. JR.,"THE PEACE CORPS IN MOROCCO." CULTURE MUNIC PROVS CREATE ROUTINE TASK ADJUST STRANGE...OBS PEACE/CORP. PAGE 154 H3077 — S65 — MOROCCO FRANCE FOR/AID EDU/PROP

VAN DEN BERG M.,"SOME METHODOLOGICAL ASPECTS OF SOUTH AFRICA'S FIRST E.D.P." SOUTH/AFR NAT/G CREATE TEC/DEV CAP/ISM INCOME PRODUC...CON/ANAL CHARTS 20. PAGE 161 H3226 — S65 — ECO/DEV PLAN METH STAT

VUCINICH W.S.,"WHITHER RUMANIA." COM USSR YUGOSLAVIA NAT/G VOL/ASSN DELIB/GP TOP/EX LEGIT NAT/LISM TOTALISM ATTIT DRIVE RIGID/FLEX ORD/FREE WEALTH SOCISM...TIME/SEQ TREND 20. PAGE 164 H3281 — S65 — ECO/DEV CREATE ROMANIA

ANDERSON S.V.,CANADIAN OMBUDSMAN PROPOSALS. CANADA LEGIS DEBATE PARL/PROC...MAJORIT JURID TIME/SEQ IDEA/COMP 20 OMBUDSMAN PARLIAMENT. PAGE 7 H0133 — B66 — NAT/G CREATE ADMIN POL/PAR

DAENIKER G.,STRATEGIE DES KLEIN STAATS. SWITZERLND ACT/RES CREATE DIPLOM NEUTRAL DETER WAR WEAPON PWR SOVEREIGN...IDEA/COMP 20 COLD/WAR. PAGE 36 H0730 — B66 — NUC/PWR PLAN FORCES NAT/G

DIAMOND S.,THE TRANSFORMATION OF EAST AFRICA. NAT/G SCHOOL CREATE PROB/SOLV COLONIAL REGION RACE/REL FEDERAL...SOC ANTHOL WORSHIP 20 AFRICA/E. PAGE 41 H0819 — B66 — CULTURE AFR TEC/DEV INDUS

KIRKLAND E.C.,A BIBLIOGRAPHY OF SOUTH ASIAN FOLKLORE. WRITING HABITAT ALL/VALS MYSTISM ...ART/METH GEOG PSY SOC MYTH WORSHIP 13/20. PAGE 86 H1723 — B66 — BIBLIOG S/ASIA CULTURE CREATE

MASUR G.,NATIONALISM IN LATIN AMERICA* DIVERSITY AND UNITY. CHRIST-17C PRE/AMER ELITES ECO/UNDEV CREATE DIPLOM INT/TRADE COLONIAL REV SOVEREIGN SOC. PAGE 105 H2089 — B66 — L/A+17C NAT/LISM CULTURE

MERILLAT H.C.L.,LEGAL ADVISERS AND INTERNATIONAL ORGANIZATIONS. LAW NAT/G CONSULT OP/RES ADJUD SANCTION TASK CONSEN ORG/CHARTS. PAGE 109 H2178 — B66 — INT/ORG INT/LAW CREATE OBS

ODEGARD P.H.,POLITICAL POWER AND SOCIAL CHANGE. UNIV NAT/G CREATE ALL/IDEOS...POLICY GEOG SOC CENSUS TREND. PAGE 120 H2394 — B66 — PWR TEC/DEV IDEA/COMP

SWARTZ M.J.,POLITICAL ANTHROPOLOGY. WOR+45 POL/PAR ACT/RES REV GP/REL DRIVE...SOC CONCPT TIME/SEQ GP/COMP ANTHOL WORSHIP 20. PAGE 151 H3013 — B66 — PARTIC RIGID/FLEX LOC/G CREATE

SWEARINGEN A.R.,SOVIET AND CHINESE COMMUNIST POWER IN THE WORLD TODAY. COM USA+45 ECO/UNDEV CREATE LEAD WAR ADJUST...TREND NAT/COMP ANTHOL COLD/WAR KHRUSH/N. PAGE 151 H3017 — B66 — USSR ASIA DIPLOM ATTIT

WILLNER A.R.,THE NEOTRADITIONAL ACCOMMODATION TO POLITICAL INDEPENDENCE* THE CASE OF INDONESIA * RESEARCH MONOGRAPH NO. 26. CULTURE ECO/UNDEV CREATE PROB/SOLV FOR/AID LEGIT COLONIAL EFFICIENCY NAT/LISM ALL/VALS SOC. PAGE 168 H3371 — B66 — INDONESIA CONSERVE ELITES ADMIN

HUNTINGTON S.P.,"POLITICAL MODERNIZATION* AMERICA VS EUROPE." EUR+WWI MOD/EUR UK USA+45 LAW ECO/UNDEV PWR SOVEREIGN CONSERVE LAISSEZ GOV/COMP. PAGE 75 H1505 — L66 — STRUCT CREATE OBS

KRENZ F.E.,"THE REFUGEE AS A SUBJECT OF INTERNATIONAL LAW." FUT LAW NAT/G CREATE ADJUD ISOLAT STRANGE...RECORD UN. PAGE 88 H1766 — L66 — INT/LAW DISCRIM NEW/IDEA

HAIGH G.,"FIELD TRAINING IN HUMAN RELATIONS FOR THE — S66 — CULTURE

PEACE CORPS." CONSULT CREATE EDU/PROP ADMIN TASK GP/REL ATTIT PERSON...PSY OBS SOC/EXP PEACE/CORP. PAGE 64 H1276 PERS/REL FOR/AID ADJUST

S66
HEAPHEY J.,"THE ORGANIZATION OF EGYPT* INADEQUACIES OF A NONPOLITICAL MODEL FOR NATION-BUILDING." STRATA NAT/G CREATE PROB/SOLV ECO/TAC NAT/LISM SOCISM RECORD. PAGE 69 H1377 UAR ECO/UNDEV OBS

S66
MALENBAUM W.,"GOVERNMENT, ENTREPRENEURSHIP, AND ECONOMIC GROWTH IN POOR LANDS." ELITES ECO/UNDEV INDUS CREATE DRIVE. PAGE 101 H2028 ECO/TAC PLAN CONSERVE NAT/G

S66
MARTZ J.D.,"THE PLACE OF LATIN AMERICA IN THE STUDY OF COMPARATIVE POLITICS." AFR ASIA CULTURE STRUCT ECO/UNDEV ACADEM CREATE...CLASSIF NAT/COMP. PAGE 104 H2072 L/A+17C GOV/COMP STERTYP GEN/LAWS

S66
STRAYER J.R.,"PROBLEMS OF DICTATORSHIP* THE RUSSIAN EXPERIENCE." ASIA MOD/EUR ELITES STRATA POL/PAR CREATE NAT/LISM MARXISM...GOV/COMP NAT/COMP. PAGE 150 H2997 NAT/G GEN/LAWS USSR TOTALISM

B67
KOLKOWICZ R.,THE SOVIET MILITARY AND THE COMMUNIST PARTY. COM USSR ELITES NAT/G CREATE CIVMIL/REL GP/REL...TREND BIBLIOG/A 20 COM/PARTY. PAGE 88 H1753 MARXISM CONSTN FORCES POL/PAR

B67
MICKIEWICZ E.P.,SOVIET POLITICAL SCHOOLS: THE COMMUNIST PARTY ADULT INSTRUCTION SYSTEM. COM USSR INTELL SCHOOL WORKER CREATE PRESS ADMIN CONTROL ATTIT KNOWL...PROG/TEAC SOC/INTEG 20 COM/PARTY. PAGE 110 H2200 NAT/G EDU/PROP AGE/A MARXISM

B67
MOORE J.R.,THE ECONOMIC IMPACT OF THE TVA. AGRI INDUS PLAN BARGAIN CONTROL REGION GOV/REL DEMAND EFFICIENCY SOCISM 20 TVA. PAGE 112 H2249 ECO/UNDEV ECO/DEV NAT/G CREATE

B67
NASH M.,MACHINE AGE MAYA. GUATEMALA L/A+17C STRUCT AGRI WORKER CREATE INCOME ATTIT RIGID/FLEX ROLE ...IDEA/COMP SOC/EXP WORSHIP 20 INDIAN/AM. PAGE 116 H2315 INDUS CULTURE SOC MUNIC

B67
NYERERE J.K.,FREEDOM AND UNITY/UHURU NA UMOJA: A SELECTION FROM WRITINGS AND SPEECHES, 1952-65. TANZANIA ELITES ECO/UNDEV INT/ORG NAT/G CREATE DIPLOM COLONIAL REGION RACE/REL...ANTHOL 20. PAGE 119 H2383 SOVEREIGN AFR TREND ORD/FREE

B67
POMEROY W.J.,HALF A CENTURY OF SOCIALISM. USSR LAW AGRI INDUS NAT/G CREATE DIPLOM EDU/PROP PERSON ORD/FREE WEALTH...POLICY TREND 20. PAGE 127 H2541 SOCISM MARXISM COM SOCIETY

B67
POSNER M.V.,ITALIAN PUBLIC ENTERPRISE. ITALY ECO/DEV FINAN INDUS CREATE ECO/TAC ADMIN CONTROL EFFICIENCY PRODUC...TREND CHARTS 20. PAGE 127 H2545 NAT/G PLAN CAP/ISM SOCISM

B67
UNESCO,PRINCIPLES AND PROBLEMS OF NATIONAL SCIENCE POLICIES. WOR+45 ECO/DEV ECO/UNDEV R+D INT/ORG PROB/SOLV CONFER...PHIL/SCI CHARTS 20 UNESCO UN. PAGE 158 H3165 NAT/COMP POLICY TEC/DEV CREATE

B67
WARD L.,LESTER WARD AND THE WELFARE STATE. SOCIETY NAT/G CREATE RECEIVE EQUILIB UTOPIA HABITAT HEREDITY PERSON...POLICY SOC BIOG 19/20 WARD/LEST. PAGE 165 H3303 ALL/VALS NEW/IDEA WELF/ST CONCPT

B67
WINTER E.H.,CONTEMPORARY CHANGE IN TRADITIONAL SOCIETIES: VOLUME I INTRODUCTION AND AFRICAN TRIBES. NIGERIA AGRI LOC/G NAT/G CREATE DOMIN COLONIAL CONTROL GP/REL PWR SOVEREIGN...SOC OBS 20 TANGANYIKA. PAGE 169 H3389 SOCIETY AFR CONSERVE KIN

B67
WOODRUFF W.,IMPACT OF WESTERN MAN. ECO/DEV INDUS CREATE PLAN PROB/SOLV COLONIAL GOV/REL...CHARTS GOV/COMP BIBLIOG 18/20. PAGE 170 H3407 EUR+WWI MOD/EUR CAP/ISM

L67
AUSTIN D.A.,"POLITICAL CONFLICT IN AFRICA." CONSTN NAT/G CREATE ADMIN COLONIAL ORD/FREE MARXISM POPULISM SOCISM...NAT/COMP ANTHOL 20. PAGE 9 H0180 ANOMIE AFR POL/PAR

L67
EGBERT D.D.,"THE IDEA OF 'AVANT-GARDE' IN ART AND POLITICS." USSR CULTURE INTELL POL/PAR CREATE EDU/PROP CONTROL REV ANOMIE DRIVE ROLE...IDEA/COMP 20. PAGE 45 H0895 ART/METH COM ATTIT

S67
ABDEL-MALEK A.,"THE CRISIS IN NASSER'S EGYPT." ISLAM UAR STRUCT POL/PAR EX/STRUC CREATE PLAN WAR ATTIT ORD/FREE PWR...POLICY DECISION 20. PAGE 3 H0054 FORCES LEAD PROB/SOLV NAT/G

S67
BERLINER J.S.,"RUSSIA'S BUREAUCRATS - WHY THEY'RE REACTIONARY." USSR NAT/G OP/RES PROB/SOLV TEC/DEV CONTROL SANCTION EFFICIENCY DRIVE PERSON...TECHNIC SOC 20. PAGE 15 H0308 CREATE ADMIN INDUS PRODUC

S67
BRADLEY A.W.,"CONSTITUTION-MAKING IN UGANDA." UGANDA LAW CHIEF DELIB/GP LEGIS ADMIN EXEC PARL/PROC RACE/REL ORD/FREE...GOV/COMP 20. PAGE 20 H0397 NAT/G CREATE CONSTN FEDERAL

S67
EGBERT D.D.,"POLITICS AND ART IN COMMUNIST BULGARIA" BULGARIA COM USSR CULTURE DIPLOM INGP/REL TOTALISM...TREND 20. PAGE 45 H0894 CREATE ART/METH CONTROL MARXISM

S67
GAMARNIKOW M.,"THE NEW ROLE OF PRIVATE ENTERPRISE." ECO/DEV INDUS NAT/G SML/CO CREATE PROB/SOLV MARXISM ...POLICY TREND IDEA/COMP 20. PAGE 55 H1092 ECO/TAC ATTIT CAP/ISM COM

S67
IDENBURG P.J.,"POLITICAL STRUCTURAL DEVELOPMENT IN TROPICAL AFRICA." UK ECO/UNDEV KIN POL/PAR CHIEF EX/STRUC CREATE COLONIAL CONTROL REPRESENT RACE/REL ...MAJORIT TREND 20. PAGE 76 H1521 AFR CONSTN NAT/G GOV/COMP

S67
LEVI W.,"THE ELITIST NATURE OF NEW ASIA'S FOREIGN POLICY." CULTURE ECO/UNDEV NAT/G PROB/SOLV EDU/PROP COLONIAL CONTROL REGION NAT/LISM...NAT/COMP 20. PAGE 95 H1898 POLICY ELITES DIPLOM CREATE

S67
MARWICK A.,"THE LABOUR PARTY AND THE WELFARE STATE IN BRITAIN, 19001948." UK SOCIETY STRUCT ECO/DEV WORKER CREATE PRICE CHOOSE WEALTH NEW/LIB SOCISM ...POLICY HEAL 20 PARLIAMENT LABOR/PAR. PAGE 104 H2074 POL/PAR RECEIVE LEGIS NAT/G

S67
PLUMPTRE A.F.W.,"PERSPECTIVE ON OUR AID TO OTHERS." CANADA CREATE 20. PAGE 127 H2530 FOR/AID DIPLOM NAT/G PLAN

S67
PONOMARYOV B.,"THE OCTOBER REVOLUTION - BEGINNING OF THE EPOCH OF SOCIALISM AND COMMUNISM." COM FUT USSR WOR+45 SOCIETY STRATA CHIEF CREATE DIPLOM ECO/TAC EDU/PROP SOCISM...NAT/COMP 20. PAGE 127 H2542 MARXIST WORKER INT/ORG POLICY

S67
READ J.S.,"CENSORED." UGANDA CONSTN INTELL SOCIETY NAT/G DIPLOM PRESS WRITING ADJUD ADMIN COLONIAL RISK...IDEA/COMP 20. PAGE 130 H2602 EDU/PROP AFR CREATE

S67
ROOT W.,"REPORT FROM PARIS - DE GAULLE: WHICH WAY TO THE FUTURE?" CANADA FRANCE ISLAM UK INT/ORG CHIEF CREATE AGREE CONTROL ARMS/CONT NUC/PWR EQUILIB PEACE PWR 20 DEGAULLE/C NATO. PAGE 134 H2670 POLICY DIPLOM NAT/G BAL/PWR

S67
SHIGEO N.,"THE GREAT CULTURAL REVOLUTION." ASIA ECO/UNDEV AGRI NAT/G CHIEF ECO/TAC EDU/PROP CONTROL LEAD PWR 20 MAO. PAGE 143 H2860 CREATE REV CULTURE POL/PAR

S67
SLOAN P.,"FIFTY YEARS OF SOVIET RULE." USSR INDUS EDU/PROP EFFICIENCY PRODUC HEALTH KNOWL MORAL WEALTH MARXISM...POLICY 20. PAGE 145 H2900 CREATE NAT/G PLAN INSPECT

N67
US HOUSE COMM SCI ASTRONAUT,GOVERNMENT, SCIENCE, AND INTERNATIONAL POLICY (PAMPHLET). INDIA NETHERLAND ECO/DEV ECO/UNDEV R+D ACADEM PLAN DIPLOM FOR/AID CONFER...PREDICT 20 CHINJAP. PAGE 160 H3198 NAT/G POLICY CREATE TEC/DEV

B68
PROUDHON J.P.,IDEE GENERALE DE LA REVOLUTION AU XIXE SIECLE (1851). FRANCE UNIV NAT/G CREATE AGREE UTOPIA ORD/FREE...ANARCH 19. PAGE 128 H2563 REV SOCIETY WORKER LABOR

S68
BOSSCHERE G D.E.,"A L'EST DU NOUVEAU." CZECHOSLVK HUNGARY POLAND ROMANIA YUGOSLAVIA AGRI CREATE ECO/TAC COERCE GP/REL ATTIT MARXISM SOCISM 20. PAGE 19 H0382 ORD/FREE COM NAT/G DIPLOM

S68
LAPIERRE J.W.,"TRADITION ET MODERNITE A MADAGASCAR." ISLAM MADAGASCAR AGRI FINAN KIN NAT/G CREATE OP/RES GP/REL INGP/REL ATTIT CONSERVE...PSY 20. PAGE 91 H1813 ECO/UNDEV FOR/AID CULTURE TEC/DEV

B82
MACDONALD D.,AFRICANA; OR, THE HEART OF HEATHEN AFRICA, VOL. II: MISSION LIFE. SOCIETY STRATA KIN CREATE EDU/PROP ADMIN COERCE LITERACY HEALTH...MYTH WORSHIP 19 LIVNGSTN/D MISSION NEGRO. PAGE 100 H1990 SECT AFR CULTURE ORD/FREE

B95
SELIGMAN E.R.A.,ESSAYS IN TAXATION. NEW/ZEALND PRUSSIA UK USA-45 MARKET LOC/G CREATE PRICE CONTROL INCOME OWN WEALTH...GOV/COMP METH/COMP 19. PAGE 141 H2824 TAX TARIFFS INDUS NAT/G

B22
OGBURN W.F.,SOCIAL CHANGE WITH RESPECT TO CULTURE AND ORIGINAL NATURE. ACT/RES OP/RES CRIME GP/REL ANOMIE BIO/SOC PWR...PSY SOC TIME/SEQ METH SOC/INTEG. PAGE 120 H2405 — CULTURE CREATE TEC/DEV

B24
HOLDSWORTH W.S.,A HISTORY OF ENGLISH LAW; THE COMMON LAW AND ITS RIVALS (VOL. IV). UK SEA AGRI CHIEF ADJUD CONTROL CRIME GOV/REL...INT/LAW JURID NAT/COMP 16/17 PARLIAMENT COMMON/LAW CANON/LAW ENGLSH/LAW. PAGE 72 H1449 — LAW LEGIS CT/SYS CONSTN

B26
MALINOWSKI B.,CRIME AND CUSTOM IN SAVAGE SOCIETY. SOCIETY FAM SECT LEGIT SANCTION MARRIAGE MYSTISM ...PSY SOC 19/20 MELANESIA CANON/LAW. PAGE 102 H2030 — LAW CULTURE CRIME ADJUD

B30
BENTHAM J.,THE RATIONALE OF PUNISHMENT. UK LAW LOC/G NAT/G LEGIS CONTROL...JURID GEN/LAWS COURT/SYS 19. PAGE 14 H0289 — CRIME SANCTION COERCE ORD/FREE

B33
ENSOR R.C.K.,COURTS AND JUDGES IN FRANCE, GERMANY, AND ENGLAND. FRANCE GERMANY UK LAW PROB/SOLV ADMIN ROUTINE CRIME ROLE...METH/COMP 20 CIVIL/LAW. PAGE 46 H0930 — CT/SYS EX/STRUC ADJUD NAT/COMP

B37
THOMPSON J.W.,SECRET DIPLOMACY: A RECORD OF ESPIONAGE AND DOUBLE-DEALING: 1500-1815. CHRIST-17C MOD/EUR NAT/G WRITING RISK MORAL...ANTHOL BIBLIOG 16/19 ESPIONAGE. PAGE 154 H3084 — DIPLOM CRIME

B38
HOLDSWORTH W.S.,A HISTORY OF ENGLISH LAW; THE CENTURIES OF SETTLEMENT AND REFORM (VOL. XI). UK CONSTN NAT/G EX/STRUC DIPLOM ADJUD CT/SYS LEAD CRIME ATTIT...INT/LAW JURID 18 CMN/WLTH PARLIAMENT ENGLSH/LAW. PAGE 73 H1452 — LAW COLONIAL LEGIS PARL/PROC

B39
BARNES H.E.,SOCIETY IN TRANSITION: PROBLEMS OF A CHANGING ERA. USA-45 INDUS MUNIC PUB/INST EDU/PROP CRIME RACE/REL...SOC MYTH NAT/COMP. PAGE 11 H0220 — SOCIETY CULTURE TECHRACY TEC/DEV

B40
TONNIES F.,FUNDAMENTAL CONCEPTS OF SOCIOLOGY (1887) (TRANS. BY C. LOOMIS). LAW STRATA STRUCT FAM MUNIC NAT/G DOMIN LEGIT SANCTION COERCE CRIME PERSON 19. PAGE 156 H3115 — CULTURE SOCIETY GEN/LAWS SOC

B42
FORTESCU J.,IN PRAISE OF ENGLISH LAW (1464) (TRANS. BY S.B. CHRIMES). UK ELITES CHIEF FORCES CT/SYS COERCE CRIME GOV/REL ILLEGIT...JURID GOV/COMP GEN/LAWS 15. PAGE 52 H1040 — LAW CONSTN LEGIS ORD/FREE

B45
CONOVER H.F.,THE NAZI STATE: WAR CRIMES AND WAR CRIMINALS. GERMANY CULTURE NAT/G SECT FORCES DIPLOM INT/TRADE EDU/PROP...INT/LAW BIOG HIST/WRIT TIME/SEQ 20. PAGE 32 H0647 — BIBLIOG WAR CRIME

S48
ALEXANDER L.,"WAR CRIMES, THEIR SOCIAL-PSYCHOLOGICAL ASPECTS." EUR+WWI GERMANY LAW CULTURE ELITES KIN POL/PAR PUB/INST FORCES DOMIN EDU/PROP COERCE CRIME ATTIT SUPEGO HEALTH MORAL PWR FASCISM ...PSY OBS TREND GEN/LAWS NAZI 20. PAGE 5 H0100 — DRIVE WAR

B51
LEMERT E.M.,SOCIAL PATHOLOGY. CULTURE BIO/SOC PERSON SEX 20 PROSTITUTN. PAGE 94 H1876 — SOC ANOMIE CONCPT CRIME

B54
SPROTT W.J.H.,SCIENCE AND SOCIAL ACTION. STRUCT ACT/RES CRIME GP/REL INGP/REL ANOMIE...PSY SOC/INTEG 19/20. PAGE 148 H2956 — SOC CULTURE PHIL/SCI

B55
KHADDURI M.,LAW IN THE MIDDLE EAST. LAW CONSTN ACADEM FAM EDU/PROP CT/SYS SANCTION CRIME...INT/LAW GOV/COMP ANTHOL 6/20 MID/EAST. PAGE 85 H1703 — ADJUD JURID ISLAM

B56
DOUGLAS W.O.,WE THE JUDGES. INDIA USA+45 USA-45 LAW NAT/G SECT LEGIS PRESS CRIME FEDERAL ORD/FREE ...POLICY GOV/COMP 19/20 WARRN/EARL MARSHALL/J SUPREME/CT. PAGE 42 H0841 — ADJUD CT/SYS CONSTN GOV/REL

B56
SYKES G.M.,CRIME AND SOCIETY. LAW STRATA STRUCT ACT/RES ROUTINE ANOMIE WEALTH...POLICY SOC/INTEG 20. PAGE 151 H3021 — CRIMLGY CRIME CULTURE INGP/REL

B57
PLAYFAIR G.,THE OFFENDERS: THE CASE AGAINST LEGAL VENGEANCE. UNIV LAW SOCIETY NAT/G PROB/SOLV DEATH PERSON ORD/FREE...HEAL INT/LAW BIBLIOG 20 REFORMERS. PAGE 126 H2524 — CRIME TEC/DEV SANCTION CT/SYS

S57
DEXTER L.A.,"A SOCIAL THEORY OF MENTAL DEFICIENCY." CULTURE PUB/INST PROB/SOLV CRIME PERS/REL STRANGE PERSON SUPEGO SKILL...EPIST SOC/WK HYPO/EXP. PAGE 41 H0814 — SOC PSY HEALTH ROLE

B58
DUCLOUX L.,FROM BLACKMAIL TO TREASON. FRANCE PLAN DIPLOM EDU/PROP PRESS RUMOR NAT/LISM...CRIMLGY 20. PAGE 43 H0853 — COERCE CRIME NAT/G PWR

B58
OGDEN F.D.,THE POLL TAX IN THE SOUTH. USA+45 USA-45 CONSTN ADJUD ADMIN PARTIC CRIME...TIME/SEQ GOV/COMP METH/COMP 18/20 SOUTH/US. PAGE 120 H2407 — TAX CHOOSE RACE/REL DISCRIM

B58
ORNES G.E.,TRUJILLO: LITTLE CAESAR OF THE CARIBBEAN. DOMIN/REP FAM NAT/G FORCES BUDGET CRIME REV PERSON 20 TRUJILLO/R. PAGE 122 H2429 — BIOG PWR TOTALISM CHIEF

B58
STUBEL H.,THE MEWU FANTZU. CHINA/COM INDIA EDU/PROP ADJUD CRIME GP/REL OWN...OBS 20 TIBET. PAGE 150 H3001 — CULTURE STRUCT SECT FAM

B59
GINSBURG M.,LAW AND OPINION IN ENGLAND. UK CULTURE KIN LABOR LEGIS EDU/PROP ADMIN CT/SYS CRIME OWN HEALTH...ANTHOL 20 ENGLSH/LAW. PAGE 56 H1132 — JURID POLICY ECO/TAC

B59
HOBSBAWM E.J.,PRIMITIVE REBELS; STUDIES IN ARCHAIC FORMS OF SOCIAL MOVEMENT IN THE 19TH AND 20TH CENTURIES. ITALY SPAIN CULTURE VOL/ASSN RISK CROWD GP/REL INGP/REL ISOLAT TOTALISM...PSY SOC 18/20. PAGE 72 H1438 — SOCIETY CRIME REV GUERRILLA

B59
VITTACHIT,EMERGENCY '58. CEYLON UK STRUCT NAT/G FORCES ADJUD CRIME REV NAT/LISM 20. PAGE 163 H3258 — RACE/REL DISCRIM DIPLOM SOVEREIGN

B59
VORSPAN A.,JUSTICE AND JUDAISM. FAM DIPLOM ECO/TAC EDU/PROP CRIME RACE/REL MARRIAGE ANOMIE ATTIT ORD/FREE...POLICY 20 UN. PAGE 164 H3279 — SECT CULTURE ACT/RES GP/REL

B60
LASKIN B.,CANADIAN CONSTITUTIONAL LAW: TEXT AND NOTES ON DISTRIBUTION OF LEGISLATIVE POWER (2ND ED.). CANADA LOC/G ECO/TAC TAX CONTROL CT/SYS CRIME FEDERAL PWR...JURID 20 PARLIAMENT. PAGE 92 H1832 — CONSTN NAT/G LAW LEGIS

B60
PINTO F.B.M.,ENRIQUECIMENTO ILICITO NO EXERCICIO DE CARGOS PUBLICOS. BRAZIL L/A+17C USA+45 ELITES TRIBUTE CONTROL INGP/REL ORD/FREE PWR...NAT/COMP 20. PAGE 126 H2513 — ADMIN NAT/G CRIME LAW

B60
RUDD J.,TABOO, A STUDY OF MALAGASY CUSTOMS AND BELIEFS. MADAGASCAR LAW FAM CONTROL CRIME PERSON ...CONCPT 20. PAGE 173 H3466 — CULTURE DOMIN SECT SANCTION

B61
EMMET C.,THE VANISHING SWASTIKA. GERMANY/W ELITES CRIME WAR...SAMP 20. PAGE 46 H0922 — FASCISM ATTIT AGE/Y NAT/G

B61
INTL UNION LOCAL AUTHORITIES,METROPOLIS. WOR+45 DIST/IND FINAN GIVE EDU/PROP CRIME COST HEALTH WEALTH 20. PAGE 78 H1563 — MUNIC GOV/COMP LOC/G BIBLIOG

B62
BELL D.,THE END OF IDEOLOGY (REV. ED.). USA+45 USA-45 ELITES STRATA LABOR CREATE CRIME PWR MARXISM ...PHIL/SCI METH/COMP 20 EUROPE. PAGE 13 H0265 — CROWD CAP/ISM SOCISM IDEA/COMP

B62
GANJI M.,INTERNATIONAL PROTECTION OF HUMAN RIGHTS. WOR+45 CONSTN INT/TRADE CT/SYS SANCTION CRIME WAR RACE/REL...CHARTS IDEA/COMP NAT/COMP BIBLIOG 20 TREATY NEGRO LEAGUE/NAT UN CIVIL/LIB. PAGE 55 H1097 — ORD/FREE DISCRIM LEGIS DELIB/GP

B62
GRZYBOWSKI K.,SOVIET LEGAL INSTITUTIONS. USA+45 USSR ECO/DEV NAT/G EDU/PROP CONTROL CT/SYS CRIME OWN ATTIT PWR SOCISM...NAT/COMP 20. PAGE 62 H1242 — ADJUD LAW JURID

B63
EDDY J.P.,JUSTICE OF THE PEACE. UK LAW CONSTN CULTURE 14/20 COMMON/LAW. PAGE 44 H0887 — CRIME JURID CT/SYS ADJUD

B63
LAVROFF D.-G.,LES LIBERTES PUBLIQUES EN UNION SOVIETIQUE (REV. ED.). USSR NAT/G WORKER SANCTION CRIME MARXISM NEW/LIB...JURID BIBLIOG WORSHIP 20. — ORD/FREE LAW ATTIT

PAGE 92 H1843 COM

B64
GESELLSCHAFT RECHTSVERGLEICH,BIBLIOGRAPHIE DES DEUTSCHEN RECHTS (BIBLIOGRAPHY OF GERMAN LAW, TRANS. BY COURTLAND PETERSON). GERMANY FINAN INDUS LABOR SECT FORCES CT/SYS PARL/PROC CRIME...INT/LAW SOC NAT/COMP 20. PAGE 56 H1117 BIBLIOG/A JURID CONSTN ADMIN

B64
INDIAN COMM PREVENTION CORRUPT,REPORT, 1964. INDIA NAT/G GOV/REL ATTIT ORD/FREE...CRIMLGY METH 20. PAGE 76 H1530 CRIME ADMIN LEGIS LOC/G

B64
SIEKANOWICZ P.,LEGAL SOURCES AND BIBLIOGRAPHY OF POLAND. COM POLAND CONSTN NAT/G PARL/PROC SANCTION CRIME MARXISM 16/20. PAGE 143 H2870 BIBLIOG ADJUD LAW JURID

B64
WRAITH R.,CORRUPTION IN DEVELOPING COUNTRIES. NIGERIA UK LAW ELITES STRATA INDUS LOC/G NAT/G SECT FORCES EDU/PROP ADMIN PWR WEALTH 18/20. PAGE 171 H3414 ECO/UNDEV CRIME SANCTION ATTIT

B65
CHARNAY J.P.,LE SUFFRAGE POLITIQUE EN FRANCE; ELECTIONS PARLEMENTAIRES, ELECTION PRESIDENTIELLE, REFERENDUMS. FRANCE CONSTN CHIEF DELIB/GP ECO/TAC EDU/PROP CRIME INGP/REL MORAL ORD/FREE PWR CATHISM 20 PARLIAMENT PRESIDENT. PAGE 29 H0584 CHOOSE SUFF NAT/G LEGIS

B65
GWYN R.J.,THE SHAPE OF SCANDAL: A STUDY OF A GOVERNMENT IN CRISIS. CANADA LEGIS ADJUD CT/SYS SANCTION CMN/WLTH 20 PEARSON/L. PAGE 63 H1260 ELITES NAT/G CRIME

B65
HESS A.G.,CHASING THE DRAGON: A REPORT ON DRUG ADDICTION IN HONG KONG. ASIA CULTURE PROB/SOLV TRIBUTE...POLICY PSY SOC CLASSIF STAT 17/20 HONG/KONG. PAGE 70 H1411 BIO/SOC CRIME SOCIETY LAW

B66
ARCHER P.,FREEDOM AT STAKE. UK LAW NAT/G LEGIS JUDGE CRIME MORAL...CONCPT 20 CIVIL/LIB. PAGE 8 H0159 ORD/FREE NAT/COMP POLICY

B66
HOEVELER H.J.,INTERNATIONALE BEKAMPFUNG DES VERBRECHENS. AUSTRIA SWITZERLND WOR+45 INT/ORG CONTROL BIO/SOC...METH/COMP NAT/COMP 20 MAFIA SCOT/YARD FBI. PAGE 72 H1446 CRIMLGY CRIME DIPLOM INT/LAW

B67
BODENHEIMER E.,TREATISE ON JUSTICE. INT/ORG NAT/G PUB/INST ACT/RES RISK CRIME INGP/REL DISCRIM DRIVE LAISSEZ 20. PAGE 18 H0363 ALL/VALS STRUCT JURID CONCPT

B67
BUNN R.F.,POLITICS AND CIVIL LIBERTIES IN EUROPE: FOUR CASE STUDIES. FRANCE GERMANY/W UK USSR NAT/G PRESS CRIME CROWD PRIVIL ATTIT 20. PAGE 24 H0476 ORD/FREE CONSTN NAT/COMP LAW

B67
LENG S.C.,JUSTICE IN COMMUNIST CHINA: A SURVEY OF THE JUDICIAL SYSTEM OF THE CHINESE PEOPLE'S REPUBLIC. CHINA/COM LAW CONSTN LOC/G NAT/G PROF/ORG CONSULT FORCES ADMIN CRIME ORD/FREE...BIBLIOG 20 MAO. PAGE 94 H1877 CT/SYS ADJUD JURID MARXISM

B67
POLSKY N.,HUSTLERS, BEATS, AND OTHERS. FACE/GP PRESS CRIME ADJUST ANOMIE DRIVE WEALTH...PSY SOC 20. PAGE 127 H2540 CULTURE CRIMLGY NEW/IDEA STRUCT

B67
WIENER F.B.,CIVILIANS UNDER MILITARY JUSTICE; THE BRITISH PRACTICE SINCE 1689 ESPECIALLY IN NORTH AMERICA. UK USA-45 LAW CONSTN CRIME REV...DECISION CHARTS NAT/COMP BIBLIOG 17/20. PAGE 168 H3356 CT/SYS FORCES ADJUD

S67
HARNON E.,"CRIMINAL PROCEDURE IN ISRAEL - SOME COMPARATIVE ASPECTS." ISRAEL USA+45 CLIENT EX/STRUC LEGIS...JURID NAT/COMP 20. PAGE 67 H1336 ADJUD CONSTN CT/SYS CRIME

S67
ULC O.,"CLASS STRUGGLE AND SOCIALIST JUSTICE: THE CASE OF CZECHOSLOVAKIA." COM CZECHOSLVK LAW CONSTN ELITES STRUCT NAT/G CRIME GP/REL MARXISM 20. PAGE 158 H3151 TOTALISM CT/SYS ADJUD STRATA

C89
PLAYFAIR R.L.,"A BIBLIOGRAPHY OF ALGERIA." ALGERIA CULTURE ECO/UNDEV DIST/IND EXTR/IND FINAN SECT CRIME 16/19. PAGE 126 H2525 BIBLIOG/A ISLAM GEOG

B98
POLLOCK F.,THE HISTORY OF ENGLISH LAW BEFORE THE TIME OF EDWARD I (2 VOLS, 2ND ED.). UK CULTURE LOC/G LEGIS LICENSE AGREE CONTROL CT/SYS SANCTION CRIME...TIME/SEQ 13 COMMON/LAW CANON/LAW. PAGE 127 H2538 LAW ADJUD JURID

B99
DU BOIS W.E.B.,THE PHILADELPHIA NEGRO: A SOCIAL STUDY. CULTURE STRATA KIN CRIME SUFF ADJUST DISCRIM ISOLAT HABITAT HEREDITY ALL/VALS SOC/INTEG 17/19 NEGRO PHILADELPH. PAGE 42 H0851 INGP/REL RACE/REL SOC CENSUS

CRIMINOLOGY....SEE CRIMLGY

CRIMLGY....CRIMINOLOGY

B36
CULVER D.C.,METHODOLOGY OF SOCIAL SCIENCE RESEARCH: A BIBLIOGRAPHY. LAW CULTURE...CRIMLGY GEOG STAT OBS INT QU HIST/WRIT CHARTS 20. PAGE 36 H0719 BIBLIOG/A METH SOC

B56
SYKES G.M.,CRIME AND SOCIETY. LAW STRATA STRUCT ACT/RES ROUTINE ANOMIE WEALTH...POLICY SOC/INTEG 20. PAGE 151 H3021 CRIMLGY CRIME CULTURE INGP/REL

B58
DUCLOUX L.,FROM BLACKMAIL TO TREASON. FRANCE PLAN DIPLOM EDU/PROP PRESS RUMOR NAT/LISM...CRIMLGY 20. PAGE 43 H0853 COERCE CRIME NAT/G PWR

B64
INDIAN COMM PREVENTION CORRUPT,REPORT, 1964. INDIA NAT/G GOV/REL ATTIT ORD/FREE...CRIMLGY METH 20. PAGE 76 H1530 CRIME ADMIN LEGIS LOC/G

B66
HOEVELER H.J.,INTERNATIONALE BEKAMPFUNG DES VERBRECHENS. AUSTRIA SWITZERLND WOR+45 INT/ORG CONTROL BIO/SOC...METH/COMP NAT/COMP 20 MAFIA SCOT/YARD FBI. PAGE 72 H1446 CRIMLGY CRIME DIPLOM INT/LAW

B67
DAVIDSON E.,THE TRIAL OF THE GERMANS* NUREMBERG* 1946-48. EUR+WWI GERMANY CULTURE NAT/G LEAD PERSON HEALTH...CRIMLGY PSY SOC BIOG JEWS. PAGE 37 H0745 FASCISM ADJUD TOTALISM WAR

B67
POLSKY N.,HUSTLERS, BEATS, AND OTHERS. FACE/GP PRESS CRIME ADJUST ANOMIE DRIVE WEALTH...PSY SOC 20. PAGE 127 H2540 CULTURE CRIMLGY NEW/IDEA STRUCT

L67
GOOD E.M.,"CAPITAL PUNISHMENT AND ITS ALTERNATIVES IN ANCIENT NEAR EASTERN LAW." SOCIETY SECT INGP/REL CONSEN ATTIT SEX MORAL...CRIMLGY GP/COMP. PAGE 58 H1168 MEDIT-7 LAW JURID CULTURE

CRIMNL/LAW....CRIMINAL LAW

CRITTENDEN J. H0702

CROAN M. H0703

CROCE B. H0704

CROCKER W.R. H0705

CROCKETT D.G. H0706

CROMWELL/O....OLIVER CROMWELL

B40
HOBBES T.,BEHEMOTH (1668). UK CONSTN SECT DOMIN LEGIT UTIL ORD/FREE CATHISM...POLICY CONCPT GEN/LAWS 17 CHARLES/I CROMWELL/O PROTESTANT. PAGE 71 H1433 REV NAT/G CHIEF

B49
WORMUTH F.D.,THE ORIGINS OF MODERN CONSTITUTIONALISM. GREECE UK LEGIS CREATE TEC/DEV BAL/PWR DOMIN ADJUD REV WAR PWR...JURID ROMAN/REP CROMWELL/O. PAGE 170 H3412 NAT/G CONSTN LAW

B61
AYLMER G.,THE KING'S SERVANTS. UK ELITES CHIEF PAY CT/SYS WEALTH 17 CROMWELL/O CHARLES/I. PAGE 9 H0187 ADMIN ROUTINE EX/STRUC NAT/G

CROOK W.H. H0707

CROPSEY J. H2995

CROSS C. H0708

CROSS-PRESSURES .... SEE ROLE

CROSSLEY H.M. H1915

CROTHERS G.D. H0709

CROUZET F. H0710

CROWD....MOB BEHAVIOR, MASS BEHAVIOR

B30
HULL W.I.,INDIA'S POLITICAL CRISIS. INDIA UK INT/ORG LABOR SECT DELIB/GP LEGIS DIPLOM NEUTRAL REGION CROWD GOV/REL MAJORITY ATTIT 20 NEHRU/J ORD/FREE NAT/G COLONIAL

GANDHI/M COMMONWLTH. PAGE 75 H1492 NAT/LISM

B31
MACIVER R.M.,SOCIETY: ITS STRUCTURE AND CHANGES. CULTURE STRATA FAM CROWD HABITAT ORD/FREE...PSY SOC CONCPT BIBLIOG 20. PAGE 100 H1998
STRUCT SOCIETY PERSON DRIVE

B40
LEDERER E.,STATE OF THE MASSES. GERMANY ITALY SOCIETY NAT/G ECO/TAC EDU/PROP LEAD TOTALISM ...SOCIALIST PSY 20. PAGE 93 H1852
CROWD FASCISM AUTHORIT PERSON

B49
ROGERS C.B.,THE SPIRIT OF REVOLUTION IN 1789: A STUDY OF PUBLIC OPINION ...AT THE BEGINNING OF THE FRENCH REVOLUTION. FRANCE CULTURE ELITES EDU/PROP COERCE CROWD...BIBLIOG 18 MUSIC. PAGE 133 H2658
ATTIT POPULISM REV CREATE

B53
COBLENTZ S.A.,FROM ARROW TO ATOM BOMB: THE PSYCHOLOGICAL HISTORY OF WAR. PREHIST CULTURE CROWD PEACE DRIVE MORAL PWR...GP/COMP IDEA/COMP. PAGE 31 H0613
WAR PSY SOCIETY

B57
HERNANDEZ-ARREGU J.,IMPERIALISMO Y CULTURA (LA POLITICA EN LA INTELIGENCIA ARGENTINA). L/A+17C CULTURE ELITES WRITING COLONIAL CROWD ATTIT FASCISM MARXISM SOCISM...BIOG IDEA/COMP 20 ARGEN PERON/JUAN COM/PARTY. PAGE 70 H1403
INTELL CREATE ART/METH HUM

B57
MENDIETTA Y NUNE L.,THEORIE DES GROUPEMENT SOCIAUX SUIVI D'UNE ETUDE SUR LE DROIT SOCIAL. ELITES FAM KIN NAT/G PROB/SOLV CROWD ISOLAT ATTIT PERSON ...JURID CONCPT SOC/INTEG. PAGE 109 H2174
SOC STRATA STRUCT DISCRIM

B59
HOBSBAWM E.J.,PRIMITIVE REBELS; STUDIES IN ARCHAIC FORMS OF SOCIAL MOVEMENT IN THE 19TH AND 20TH CENTURIES. ITALY SPAIN CULTURE VOL/ASSN RISK CROWD GP/REL INGP/REL ISOLAT TOTALISM...PSY SOC 18/20. PAGE 72 H1438
SOCIETY CRIME REV GUERRILLA

B59
PAGE S.W.,LENIN AND WORLD REVOLUTION. COM USSR NAT/G DOMIN COERCE CROWD UTOPIA ATTIT AUTHORIT DRIVE PWR...CONCPT MYTH 19/20 LENIN/VI MARX/KARL. PAGE 122 H2441
REV PERSON MARXISM BIOG

C59
KORNHAUSER W.,"THE POLITICS OF MASS SOCIETY." COM CULTURE ELITES INTELL STRATA POL/PAR ATTIT...SOC CHARTS GEN/LAWS BIBLIOG 20. PAGE 88 H1757
CROWD PLURISM CONSTN SOCIETY

S60
GRIMSHAW A.D.,"URBAN RACIAL VIOLENCE IN THE UNITED STATES: CHANGING ECOLOGICAL CONSIDERATIONS." STRUCT MUNIC FORCES PARTIC DISCRIM ATTIT HABITAT ...IDEA/COMP 20 NEGRO. PAGE 61 H1228
CROWD RACE/REL GOV/COMP NEIGH

B62
BELL D.,THE END OF IDEOLOGY (REV. ED.). USA+45 USA-45 ELITES STRATA LABOR CREATE CRIME PWR MARXISM ...PHIL/SCI METH/COMP 20 EUROPE. PAGE 13 H0265
CROWD CAP/ISM SOCISM IDEA/COMP

B62
ZINKIN T.,REPORTING INDIA. INDIA PAKISTAN WOR+45 SOCIETY SECT FORCES EDU/PROP CROWD DISCRIM NAT/LISM MARXISM...POLICY 20. PAGE 173 H3457
STRATA COLONIAL BAL/PWR CONTROL

B63
BORKENAU F.,THE SPANISH COCKPIT. SPAIN ELITES STRATA POL/PAR ACT/RES CROWD WAR GP/REL INGP/REL ...SOC NAT/COMP 20. PAGE 19 H0377
REV CONSERVE SOCISM FORCES

B65
BRASS P.R.,FACTIONAL POLITICS IN AN INDIAN STATE: THE CONGRESS PARTY IN UTTAR PRADESH. INDIA UK CONSTN CULTURE ECO/UNDEV LOC/G DOMIN COLONIAL CROWD GP/REL ADJUST CENTRAL RIGID/FLEX SOVEREIGN 20 UTTAR/PRAD CONGRESS/P. PAGE 20 H0406
POL/PAR PROVS LEGIS CHOOSE

C65
NEUMANN S.,"PERMANENT REVOLUTION: TOTALITARIANISM IN THE AGE OF INTERNA TIONAL CIVIL WAR (2ND ED.)" EUR+WWI ELITES POL/PAR DOMIN EDU/PROP LEAD CROWD REPRESENT...MAJORIT GOV/COMP BIBLIOG 20. PAGE 117 H2340
TOTALISM REV FASCISM STRUCT

B66
JACKSON G.D.,COMINTERN AND PEASANT IN EAST EUROPE 1919-1930. BULGARIA COM CZECHOSLVK EUR+WWI POLAND ROMANIA YUGOSLAVIA STRATA AGRI VOL/ASSN DIPLOM CONTROL CROWD WEALTH...POLICY NAT/COMP 20. PAGE 79 H1575
MARXISM ECO/UNDEV WORKER INT/ORG

B66
NOLTE E.,THREE FACES OF FASCISM. FRANCE GERMANY DOMIN LEGIT COERCE CROWD REV WAR GP/REL RACE/REL SOVEREIGN...GOV/COMP IDEA/COMP 19/20 HITLER/A MUSSOLIN/B MARX/KARL. PAGE 118 H2368
FASCISM TOTALISM NAT/G POL/PAR

B66
SOBEL L.A.,SOUTH VIETNAM: US-COMMUNIST CONFRONTATION IN SOUTHEAST ASIA 1961-65. VIETNAM FOR/AID CROWD DETER REV PEACE...GEOG 20 INTERVENT DIEM COLD/WAR. PAGE 146 H2926
WAR TIME/SEQ FORCES NAT/G

B67
BUNN R.F.,POLITICS AND CIVIL LIBERTIES IN EUROPE: FOUR CASE STUDIES. FRANCE GERMANY/W UK USSR NAT/G PRESS CRIME CROWD PRIVIL ATTIT 20. PAGE 24 H0476
ORD/FREE CONSTN NAT/COMP LAW

L67
BRIDGHAM P.,"MAO'S "CULTURAL REVOLUTION"* ORIGIN AND DEVELOPMENT." NAT/G LEAD CIVMIL/REL NAT/LISM TOTALISM ATTIT DRIVE PWR MARXISM 20. PAGE 21 H0413
CHINA/COM CULTURE REV CROWD

CROWDER M. H0711

CROWE S. H0712

CROZIER B. H0713,H0714

CRUICKSHANK M. H0715

CRUSADES....CRUSADES, CRUSADERS OF HOLY WARS; ALSO KNIGHTS

B21
KREY A.C.,THE FIRST CRUSADE. CHRIST-17C SOCIETY STRATA NAT/G SECT FORCES WORKER WRITING LEAD ATTIT ...CHARTS 11 CHRISTIAN CRUSADES. PAGE 88 H1767
WAR CATH DIPLOM PARTIC

CRUTCHER J. H0716

CRUTCHFIELD R.S. H1765

CT/SYS....COURT SYSTEMS

N
AUSTRALIAN NATIONAL RES COUN,AUSTRALIAN SOCIAL SCIENCE ABSTRACTS. NEW/ZEALND CULTURE SOCIETY LOC/G CT/SYS PARL/PROC...HEAL JURID PSY SOC 20 AUSTRAL. PAGE 9 H0181
BIBLIOG/A POLICY NAT/G ADMIN

N
EUROPA PUBLICATIONS LIMITED,THE EUROPA YEAR BOOK. CONSTN FINAN INDUS POL/PAR DIPLOM TV CT/SYS...STAT BIOG CHARTS WORSHIP 20. PAGE 47 H0949
BIBLIOG NAT/G PRESS INT/ORG

B07
BENTHAM J.,AN INTRODUCTION TO THE PRINCIPLES OF MORALS AND LEGISLATION. UNIV CONSTN CULTURE SOCIETY NAT/G CONSULT LEGIS JUDGE ADJUD CT/SYS...JURID CONCPT NEW/IDEA. PAGE 14 H0287
LAW GEN/LAWS

B08
THE GOVERNMENT OF SOUTH AFRICA (VOL. II). SOUTH/AFR STRATA EXTR/IND EX/STRUC TOP/EX BUDGET ADJUD ADMIN CT/SYS PRODUC...CORREL CENSUS 19 RAILROAD CIVIL/SERV POSTAL/SYS. PAGE 2 H0030
CONSTN FINAN LEGIS NAT/G

B09
JUSTINIAN,THE DIGEST (DIGESTA CORPUS JURIS CIVILIS) (2 VOLS.) (TRANS. BY C. H. MONRO). ROMAN/EMP LAW FAM LOC/G LEGIS EDU/PROP CONTROL MARRIAGE OWN ROLE CIVIL/LAW. PAGE 82 H1645
JURID CT/SYS NAT/G STRATA

C09
SCHAPIRO J.S.,"SOCIAL REFORM AND THE REFORMATION." CHRIST-17C GERMANY LAW CONSTN LG/CO NAT/G WORKER PROB/SOLV CT/SYS REV...BIBLIOG 16. PAGE 138 H2770
ORD/FREE SECT ECO/TAC BIOG

B14
CRAIG J.,ELEMENTS OF POLITICAL SCIENCE (3 VOLS.). CONSTN AGRI INDUS SCHOOL FORCES TAX CT/SYS SUFF MORAL WEALTH...CONCPT 19 CIVIL/LIB. PAGE 35 H0696
PHIL/SCI NAT/G ORD/FREE

B18
EYBERS G.W.,SELECT CONSTITUTIONAL DOCUMENTS ILLUSTRATING SOUTH AFRICAN HISTORY 1795-1910. SOUTH/AFR LOC/G LEGIS CT/SYS...JURID ANTHOL 18/20 NATAL CAPE/HOPE ORANGE/STA. PAGE 48 H0955
CONSTN LAW NAT/G COLONIAL

B18
WILSON W.,THE STATE: ELEMENTS OF HISTORICAL AND PRACTICAL POLITICS. FRANCE GERMANY ITALY UK USSR CONSTN EX/STRUC LEGIS CT/SYS WAR PWR...POLICY GOV/COMP 20. PAGE 169 H3385
NAT/G JURID CONCPT NAT/COMP

B19
NATHAN M.,THE SOUTH AFRICAN COMMONWEALTH: CONSTITUTION, PROBLEMS, SOCIAL CONDITIONS. SOUTH/AFR UK CULTURE INDUS EX/STRUC LEGIS BUDGET EDU/PROP ADMIN CT/SYS GP/REL RACE/REL...LING 19/20 CMN/WLTH. PAGE 116 H2317
CONSTN NAT/G POL/PAR SOCIETY

N19
BENTHAM J.,A PLAN FOR AN UNIVERSAL AND PERPETUAL PEACE (1838) (PAMPHLET). NAT/G FORCES BAL/PWR INT/TRADE ADMIN AGREE CT/SYS ARMS/CONT SOVEREIGN WEALTH GEN/LAWS. PAGE 14 H0288
INT/ORG INT/LAW PEACE COLONIAL

N19
POUND R.,ORGANIZATION OF THE COURTS (PAMPHLET). MOD/EUR UK USA-45 ADJUD PWR...GOV/COMP 10/20 EUROPE. PAGE 127 H2546
CT/SYS JURID STRUCT ADMIN

C20
BLACHLY F.F.,"THE GOVERNMENT AND ADMINISTRATION OF GERMANY." GERMANY CONSTN LOC/G PROVS DELIB/GP EX/STRUC FORCES LEGIS TOP/EX CT/SYS...BIBLIOG/A
NAT/G GOV/REL ADMIN

19/20. PAGE 17 H0348 PHIL/SCI

B24
HOLDSWORTH W.S.,A HISTORY OF ENGLISH LAW; THE COMMON LAW AND ITS RIVALS (VOL. IV). UK SEA AGRI CHIEF ADJUD CONTROL CRIME GOV/REL...INT/LAW JURID NAT/COMP 16/17 PARLIAMENT COMMON/LAW CANON/LAW ENGLSH/LAW. PAGE 72 H1449
LAW LEGIS CT/SYS CONSTN

B30
BENTHAM J.,THE RATIONALE OF PUNISHMENT. UK LAW LOC/G NAT/G LEGIS CONTROL...JURID GEN/LAWS COURT/SYS 19. PAGE 14 H0289
CRIME SANCTION COERCE ORD/FREE

B30
BURLAMAQUI J.J.,PRINCIPLES OF NATURAL AND POLITIC LAW (2 VOLS.) (1747-51). EX/STRUC LEGIS AGREE CT/SYS CHOOSE ROLE SOVEREIGN 18 NATURL/LAW. PAGE 24 H0490
LAW NAT/G ORD/FREE CONCPT

B32
LUNT D.C.,THE ROAD TO THE LAW. UK USA-45 LEGIS EDU/PROP OWN ORD/FREE...DECISION TIME/SEQ NAT/COMP 16/20 AUSTRAL ENGLSH/LAW COMMON/LAW. PAGE 99 H1980
ADJUD LAW JURID CT/SYS

B33
ENSOR R.C.K.,COURTS AND JUDGES IN FRANCE, GERMANY, AND ENGLAND. FRANCE GERMANY UK LAW PROB/SOLV ADMIN ROUTINE CRIME ROLE...METH/COMP 20 CIVIL/LAW. PAGE 46 H0930
CT/SYS EX/STRUC ADJUD NAT/COMP

B35
DE TOCQUEVILLE A.,DEMOCRACY IN AMERICA (4 VOLS.) (TRANS. BY HENRY REEVE). CONSTN STRUCT LOC/G NAT/G POL/PAR PROVS ETIQUET CT/SYS MAJORITY ATTIT 18/19. PAGE 39 H0772
POPULISM MAJORIT ORD/FREE SOCIETY

B35
RAM J.,THE SCIENCE OF LEGAL JUDGMENT: A TREATISE... UK CONSTN NAT/G LEGIS CREATE PROB/SOLV AGREE CT/SYS ...INT/LAW CONCPT 19 ENGLSH/LAW CANON/LAW CIVIL/LAW CTS/WESTM. PAGE 129 H2584
LAW JURID EX/STRUC ADJUD

B37
HAMILTON W.H.,THE POWER TO GOVERN. ECO/DEV FINAN INDUS ECO/TAC INT/TRADE TARIFFS TAX CONTROL CT/SYS WAR COST PWR 18/20 SUPREME/CT. PAGE 65 H1303
LING CONSTN NAT/G POLICY

B37
UNION OF SOUTH AFRICA,REPORT CONCERNING ADMINISTRATION OF SOUTH WEST AFRICA (6 VOLS.). SOUTH/AFR INDUS PUB/INST FORCES LEGIS BUDGET DIPLOM EDU/PROP ADJUD CT/SYS...GEOG CHARTS 20 AFRICA/SW LEAGUE/NAT. PAGE 158 H3166
NAT/G ADMIN COLONIAL CONSTN

B38
HOLDSWORTH W.S.,A HISTORY OF ENGLISH LAW; THE CENTURIES OF SETTLEMENT AND REFORM (VOL. X). INDIA UK CONSTN NAT/G CHIEF LEGIS ADMIN COLONIAL CT/SYS CHOOSE ORD/FREE PWR...JURID 18 PARLIAMENT COMMONWLTH COMMON/LAW. PAGE 72 H1451
LAW LOC/G EX/STRUC ADJUD

B38
HOLDSWORTH W.S.,A HISTORY OF ENGLISH LAW; THE CENTURIES OF SETTLEMENT AND REFORM (VOL. XI). UK CONSTN NAT/G EX/STRUC DIPLOM ADJUD CT/SYS LEAD CRIME ATTIT...INT/LAW JURID 18 CMN/WLTH PARLIAMENT ENGLSH/LAW. PAGE 73 H1452
LAW COLONIAL LEGIS PARL/PROC

B38
MCNAIR A.D.,THE LAW OF TREATIES: BRITISH PRACTICE AND OPINIONS. UK CREATE DIPLOM LEGIT WRITING ADJUD WAR...INT/LAW JURID TREATY. PAGE 107 H2144
AGREE LAW CT/SYS NAT/G

B38
POUND R.,THE FORMATIVE ERA OF AMERICAN LAW. CULTURE NAT/G PROVS LEGIS ADJUD CT/SYS PERSON SOVEREIGN ...POLICY IDEA/COMP GEN/LAWS 18/19. PAGE 127 H2548
CONSTN LAW CREATE JURID

B38
SAINT-PIERRE C.I.,SCHEME FOR LASTING PEACE (TRANS. BY H. BELLOT). INDUS NAT/G CHIEF FORCES INT/TRADE CT/SYS WAR PWR SOVEREIGN WEALTH...POLICY 18. PAGE 137 H2732
INT/ORG PEACE AGREE INT/LAW

B40
WUNDERLICH F.,LABOR UNDER GERMAN DEMOCRACY. ARBITRATION 1918-1933. GERMANY NAT/G PAY REPAR ADJUD CT/SYS GP/REL...MAJORIT 20. PAGE 171 H3426
LABOR WORKER INDUS BARGAIN

B41
GILMORE M.P.,ARGUMENT FROM ROMAN LAW IN POLITICAL THOUGHT, 1200-1600. INTELL LICENSE CONTROL CT/SYS GOV/REL PRIVIL PWR...IDEA/COMP BIBLIOG 13/16. PAGE 56 H1130
JURID LAW CONCPT NAT/G

B42
FORTESCU J.,IN PRAISE OF ENGLISH LAW (1464) (TRANS. BY S.B. CHRIMES). UK ELITES CHIEF FORCES CT/SYS COERCE CRIME GOV/REL ILLEGIT...JURID GOV/COMP GEN/LAWS 15. PAGE 52 H1040
LAW CONSTN LEGIS ORD/FREE

B42
ROBBINS J.J.,THE GOVERNMENT OF LABOR RELATIONS IN SWEDEN. SWEDEN LAW CONSTN ADJUD CT/SYS GP/REL ...JURID 20. PAGE 132 H2638
NAT/G BARGAIN LABOR INDUS

B44
SUAREZ F.,A TREATISE ON LAWS AND GOD THE LAWGIVER (1612) IN SELECTIONS FROM THREE WORKS, VOL. II. FRANCE ITALY UK CULTURE NAT/G SECT CHIEF LEGIS DOMIN LEGIT CT/SYS ORD/FREE PWR WORSHIP 16/17. PAGE 150 H3004
LAW JURID GEN/LAWS CATH

B45
CONOVER H.F.,THE GOVERNMENTS OF THE MAJOR FOREIGN POWERS: A BIBLIOGRAPHY. FRANCE GERMANY ITALY UK USSR CONSTN LOC/G POL/PAR EX/STRUC FORCES ADMIN CT/SYS CIVMIL/REL TOTALISM...POLICY 19/20. PAGE 32 H0645
BIBLIOG NAT/G DIPLOM

B47
DE NOIA J.,GUIDE TO OFFICIAL PUBLICATIONS OF OTHER AMERICAN REPUBLICS: ECUADOR (VOL. IX). ECUADOR LAW FINAN LEGIS BUDGET CT/SYS 19/20. PAGE 38 H0763
BIBLIOG/A CONSTN NAT/G EDU/PROP

B47
DE NOIA J.,GUIDE TO OFFICIAL PUBLICATIONS OF THE OTHER AMERICAN REPUBLICS: EL SALVADOR. EL/SALVADR LAW LEGIS EDU/PROP CT/SYS 20. PAGE 38 H0764
BIBLIOG/A CONSTN NAT/G ADMIN

B47
DE NOIA J.,GUIDE TO OFFICIAL PUBLICATIONS OF THE OTHER AMERICAN REPUBLICS: NICARAGUA (VOL. XIV). NICARAGUA LAW LEGIS ADMIN CT/SYS...JURID 19/20. PAGE 38 H0765
BIBLIOG/A EDU/PROP NAT/G CONSTN

B47
DE NOIA J.,GUIDE TO OFFICIAL PUBLICATIONS OF THE OTHER AMERICAN REPUBLICS: PANAMA (VOL. XV). PANAMA LAW LEGIS EDU/PROP CT/SYS 20. PAGE 38 H0766
BIBLIOG/A CONSTN ADMIN NAT/G

B47
MARX F.M.,THE PRESIDENT AND HIS STAFF SERVICES PUBLIC ADMINISTRATION SERVICES NUMBER 98 (PAMPHLET). FINAN ADMIN CT/SYS REPRESENT PWR 20 PRESIDENT. PAGE 104 H2075
CONSTN CHIEF NAT/G EX/STRUC

B47
MCILWAIN C.H.,CONSTITUTIONALISM: ANCIENT AND MODERN. USA+45 ROMAN/EMP LAW CHIEF LEGIS CT/SYS GP/REL ORD/FREE SOVEREIGN...POLICY TIME/SEQ ROMAN/REP EUROPE. PAGE 107 H2135
CONSTN NAT/G PARL/PROC GOV/COMP

B47
NEUBURGER O.,GUIDE TO OFFICIAL PUBLICATIONS OF OTHER AMERICAN REPUBLICS: HONDURAS (VOL. XIII). HONDURAS LAW LEGIS ADMIN CT/SYS...JURID 19/20. PAGE 117 H2333
BIBLIOG/A NAT/G EDU/PROP CONSTN

B48
DE NOIA J.,GUIDE TO OFFICIAL PUBLICATIONS OF OTHER AMERICAN REPUBLICS: PERU (VOL. XVII). PERU LAW LEGIS ADMIN CT/SYS...JURID 19/20. PAGE 38 H0767
BIBLIOG/A CONSTN NAT/G EDU/PROP

B48
NEUBURGER O.,GUIDE TO OFFICIAL PUBLICATIONS OF THE OTHER AMERICAN REPUBLICS: VENEZUELA (VOL. XIX). VENEZUELA FINAN LEGIS PLAN BUDGET DIPLOM CT/SYS PARL/PROC 19/20. PAGE 117 H2335
BIBLIOG/A NAT/G CONSTN LAW

B48
US LIBRARY OF CONGRESS,BRAZIL: A GUIDE TO THE OFFICIAL PUBLICATIONS OF BRAZIL. BRAZIL L/A+17C CONSULT DELIB/GP LEGIS CT/SYS 19/20. PAGE 160 H3206
BIBLIOG/A NAT/G ADMIN TOP/EX

B49
DENNING A.,FREEDOM UNDER THE LAW. MOD/EUR UK LAW SOCIETY CHIEF EX/STRUC LEGIS ADJUD CT/SYS PERS/REL PERSON 17/20 ENGLSH/LAW. PAGE 40 H0793
ORD/FREE JURID NAT/G

B49
SCHONS D.,BOOK CENSORSHIP IN NEW SPAIN (NEW WORLD STUDIES, BOOK II). SPAIN LAW CULTURE INSPECT ADJUD CT/SYS SANCTION GP/REL ORD/FREE 14/17. PAGE 140 H2797
CHRIST-17C EDU/PROP CONTROL PRESS

C50
STOKES W.S.,"HONDURAS: AN AREA STUDY IN GOVERNMENT." HONDURAS NAT/G POL/PAR COLONIAL CT/SYS ROUTINE CHOOSE REPRESENT...GEOG RECORD BIBLIOG 19/20. PAGE 149 H2988
CONSTN LAW L/A+17C ADMIN

B51
CHRISTENSEN A.N.,THE EVOLUTION OF LATIN AMERICAN GOVERNMENT: A BOOK OF READINGS. ECO/UNDEV INDUS LOC/G POL/PAR EX/STRUC LEGIS FOR/AID CT/SYS ...SOC/WK 20 SOUTH/AMER. PAGE 30 H0599
NAT/G CONSTN DIPLOM L/A+17C

B52
APPADORAI A.,THE SUBSTANCE OF POLITICS (6TH ED.). EX/STRUC LEGIS DIPLOM CT/SYS CHOOSE FASCISM MARXISM SOCISM...BIBLIOG T. PAGE 7 H0145
PHIL/SCI NAT/G

B52
BENTHAM A.,HANDBOOK OF POLITICAL FALLACIES. FUT MOD/EUR LAW INTELL LOC/G MUNIC NAT/G DELIB/GP LEGIS CREATE EDU/PROP CT/SYS ATTIT RIGID/FLEX KNOWL PWR ...RELATIV PSY SOC CONCPT SELF/OBS TREND STERTYP TOT/POP. PAGE 14 H0286
POL/PAR

B53
ORFIELD L.B.,THE GROWTH OF SCANDINAVIAN LAW. DENMARK ICELAND NORWAY SWEDEN LAW DIPLOM...BIBLIOG 9/20. PAGE 121 H2426
JURID CT/SYS NAT/G

B54
JENNINGS I.,THE QUEEN'S GOVERNMENT. UK POL/PAR DELIB/GP ADJUD ADMIN CT/SYS PARL/PROC REPRESENT CONSERVE 13/20 PARLIAMENT. PAGE 80 H1605
NAT/G CONSTN LEGIS CHIEF

B54
SCHWARTZ B.,FRENCH ADMINISTRATIVE LAW AND THE COMMON-LAW WORLD. FRANCE CULTURE LOC/G NAT/G PROVS DELIB/GP EX/STRUC LEGIS PROB/SOLV CT/SYS EXEC GOV/REL...IDEA/COMP ENGLSH/LAW. PAGE 140 H2808
JURID LAW METH/COMP ADJUD

B55
DE ARAGAO J.G.,LA JURIDICTION ADMINISTRATIVE AU BRESIL. BRAZIL ADJUD COLONIAL CT/SYS REV FEDERAL ORD/FREE...BIBLIOG 19/20. PAGE 37 H0749
EX/STRUC ADMIN NAT/G

B55
KHADDURI M.,LAW IN THE MIDDLE EAST. LAW CONSTN ACADEM FAM EDU/PROP CT/SYS SANCTION CRIME...INT/LAW GOV/COMP ANTHOL 6/20 MID/EAST. PAGE 85 H1703
ADJUD JURID ISLAM

B55
SMITH G.,A CONSTITUTIONAL AND LEGAL HISTORY OF ENGLAND. UK ELITES NAT/G LEGIS ADJUD OWN HABITAT POPULISM...JURID 20 ENGLSH/LAW. PAGE 145 H2909
CONSTN PARTIC LAW CT/SYS

B56
DOUGLAS W.O.,WE THE JUDGES. INDIA USA+45 USA-45 LAW NAT/G SECT LEGIS PRESS CRIME FEDERAL ORD/FREE ...POLICY GOV/COMP 19/20 WARRN/EARL MARSHALL/J SUPREME/CT. PAGE 42 H0841
ADJUD CT/SYS CONSTN GOV/REL

B57
DONALDSON A.G.,SOME COMPARATIVE ASPECTS OF IRISH LAW. IRELAND NAT/G DIPLOM ADMIN CT/SYS LEAD ATTIT SOVEREIGN...JURID BIBLIOG/A 12/20 CMN/WLTH. PAGE 42 H0835
CONSTN LAW NAT/COMP INT/LAW

B57
KANTOROWICZ E.,THE KING'S TWO BODIES; A STUDY IN MEDIEVAL POLITICAL THEOLOGY. UK LAW CONSTN NAT/G CT/SYS...ART/METH HUM CONCPT MYTH TIME/SEQ BIBLIOG 4/17 ELIZABTH/I POPE CHURCH/STA. PAGE 83 H1657
JURID SECT CHIEF SOVEREIGN

B57
LONG H.A.,USURPERS - FOES OF FREE MAN. LAW NAT/G CHIEF LEGIS DOMIN ADJUD REPRESENT GOV/REL ORD/FREE LAISSEZ POPULISM...POLICY 18/20 SUPREME/CT ROOSEVLT/F CONGRESS CON/INTERP. PAGE 98 H1961
CT/SYS CENTRAL FEDERAL CONSTN

B57
PLAYFAIR G.,THE OFFENDERS: THE CASE AGAINST LEGAL VENGEANCE. UNIV LAW SOCIETY NAT/G PROB/SOLV DEATH PERSON ORD/FREE...HEAL INT/LAW BIBLIOG 20 REFORMERS. PAGE 126 H2524
CRIME TEC/DEV SANCTION CT/SYS

B58
CUNNINGHAM W.B.,COMPULSORY CONCILIATION AND COLLECTIVE BARGAINING. CANADA NAT/G LEGIS ADJUD CT/SYS GP/REL...MGT 20 NEW/BRUNS STRIKE CASEBOOK. PAGE 36 H0722
POLICY BARGAIN LABOR INDUS

B58
EUSDEN J.D.,PURITANS, LAWYERS, AND POLITICS IN EARLY SEVENTEENTH-CENTURY ENGLAND. UK CT/SYS PARL/PROC RATIONAL PWR SOVEREIGN...IDEA/COMP BIBLIOG 17 PURITAN COMMON/LAW. PAGE 48 H0951
GP/REL SECT NAT/G LAW

B59
GINSBURG M.,LAW AND OPINION IN ENGLAND. UK CULTURE KIN LABOR LEGIS EDU/PROP ADMIN CT/SYS CRIME OWN HEALTH...ANTHOL 20 ENGLSH/LAW. PAGE 56 H1132
JURID POLICY ECO/TAC

B59
SCHORN H.,DER RICHTER IM DRITTEN REICH; GESCHICHTE UND DOKUMENTE. GERMANY NAT/G LEGIT CT/SYS INGP/REL MORAL ORD/FREE RESPECT...JURID GP/COMP 20. PAGE 140 H2798
ADJUD JUDGE FASCISM

B59
SQUIBB G.D.,THE HIGH COURT OF CHIVALRY. UK NAT/G FORCES ADJUD WAR 14/20 PARLIAMENT ENGLSH/LAW. PAGE 148 H2959
CT/SYS PARL/PROC JURID

S59
CHAPMAN B.,"THE FRENCH CONSEIL D'ETAT." FRANCE NAT/G CONSULT OP/RES PROB/SOLV PWR...OBS 20. PAGE 29 H0580
ADMIN LAW CT/SYS LEGIS

S59
MENDELSON W.,"JUDICIAL REVIEW AND PARTY POLITICS" (BMR)" UK USA+45 USA-45 NAT/G LEGIS PROB/SOLV EDU/PROP ADJUD EFFICIENCY...POLICY NAT/COMP 19/20 AUSTRAL SUPREME/CT. PAGE 109 H2171
CT/SYS POL/PAR BAL/PWR JURID

C59
COLLINS I.,"THE GOVERNMENT AND THE NEWSPAPER PRESS IN FRANCE, 1814-1881. FRANCE LAW ADMIN CT/SYS ...CON/ANAL BIBLIOG 19. PAGE 32 H0634
PRESS ORD/FREE NAT/G EDU/PROP

B60
JUNZ A.J.,PRESENT TRENDS IN AMERICAN NATIONAL GOVERNMENT. LEGIS DIPLOM ADMIN CT/SYS ORD/FREE ...CONCPT ANTHOL 20 CONGRESS PRESIDENT SUPREME/CT. PAGE 3 H0052
POL/PAR CHOOSE CONSTN NAT/G

B60
EASTON S.C.,THE TWILIGHT OF EUROPEAN COLONIALISM. AFR S/ASIA CONSTN SOCIETY STRUCT ECO/UNDEV INDUS NAT/G FORCES ECO/TAC COLONIAL CT/SYS ATTIT KNOWL ORD/FREE PWR...SOCIALIST TIME/SEQ TREND CON/ANAL 20. PAGE 44 H0882
FINAN ADMIN

B60
HAYEK F.A.,THE CONSTITUTION OF LIBERTY. UNIV LAW CONSTN WORKER TAX EDU/PROP ADMIN CT/SYS COERCE DISCRIM...IDEA/COMP 20. PAGE 68 H1369
ORD/FREE CHOOSE NAT/G CONCPT

B60
JHA C.,INDIAN GOVERNMENT AND POLITICS. INDIA SERV/IND POL/PAR PROVS LEGIS CT/SYS CHOOSE GOV/REL FEDERAL 20. PAGE 81 H1616
NAT/G PARL/PROC CONSTN ADJUST

B60
LASKIN B.,CANADIAN CONSTITUTIONAL LAW: TEXT AND NOTES ON DISTRIBUTION OF LEGISLATIVE POWER (2ND ED.). CANADA LOC/G ECO/TAC TAX CONTROL CT/SYS CRIME FEDERAL PWR...JURID 20 PARLIAMENT. PAGE 92 H1832
CONSTN NAT/G LAW LEGIS

B60
PRASAD B.,THE ORIGINS OF PROVINCIAL AUTONOMY. INDIA UK FINAN LOC/G FORCES LEGIS CONTROL CT/SYS PWR ...JURID 19/20. PAGE 128 H2554
CENTRAL PROVS COLONIAL NAT/G

S60
EMERSON R.,"THE EROSION OF DEMOCRACY." AFR FUT LAW CULTURE INTELL SOCIETY ECO/UNDEV FAM LOC/G NAT/G FORCES PLAN TEC/DEV ECO/TAC ADMIN CT/SYS ATTIT ORD/FREE PWR...SOCIALIST SOC CONCPT STAND/INT TIME/SEQ WORK 20. PAGE 46 H0918
S/ASIA POL/PAR

C60
HAZARD J.N.,"SETTLING DISPUTES IN SOVIET SOCIETY: THE FORMATIVE YEARS OF LEGAL INSTITUTIONS." USSR NAT/G PROF/ORG PROB/SOLV CONTROL CT/SYS ROUTINE REV CENTRAL...JURID BIBLIOG 20. PAGE 68 H1372
ADJUD LAW COM POLICY

C60
HAZARD J.N.,"THE SOVIET SYSTEM OF GOVERNMENT." USSR SOCIETY INDUS NAT/G POL/PAR DIPLOM CT/SYS...JURID CHARTS BIBLIOG/A 20. PAGE 69 H1373
COM NAT/COMP STRUCT ADMIN

B61
AYLMER G.,THE KING'S SERVANTS. UK ELITES CHIEF PAY CT/SYS WEALTH 17 CROMWELL/O CHARLES/I. PAGE 9 H0187
ADMIN ROUTINE EX/STRUC NAT/G

B61
BAYITCH S.A.,LATIN AMERICA: A BIBLIOGRAPHICAL GUIDE. LAW CONSTN LEGIS JUDGE ADJUD CT/SYS 20. PAGE 12 H0243
BIBLIOG L/A+17C NAT/G JURID

B61
BEDFORD S.,THE FACES OF JUSTICE: A TRAVELLER'S REPORT. AUSTRIA FRANCE GERMANY/W SWITZERLND UK UNIV WOR+45 WOR-45 CULTURE PARTIC GOV/REL MORAL...JURID OBS GOV/COMP 20. PAGE 13 H0257
CT/SYS ORD/FREE PERSON LAW

B61
CARROTHERS A.W.R.,LABOR ARBITRATION IN CANADA. CANADA LAW NAT/G CONSULT LEGIS WORKER ADJUD ADMIN CT/SYS 20. PAGE 27 H0542
LABOR MGT GP/REL BARGAIN

B61
DRAGNICH A.N.,MAJOR EUROPEAN GOVERNMENTS. FRANCE GERMANY/W UK USSR LOC/G EX/STRUC CT/SYS PARL/PROC ATTIT MARXISM...JURID MGT NAT/COMP 19/20. PAGE 42 H0846
NAT/G LEGIS CONSTN POL/PAR

B61
JUSTICE,THE CITIZEN AND THE ADMINISTRATION: THE REDRESS OF GRIEVANCES (PAMPHLET). EUR+WWI UK LAW CONSTN STRATA NAT/G CT/SYS PARTIC COERCE...NEW/IDEA IDEA/COMP 20 OMBUDSMAN. PAGE 82 H1644
INGP/REL CONSULT ADJUD REPRESENT

B61
RAO K.V.,PARLIAMENTARY DEMOCRACY OF INDIA. INDIA EX/STRUC TOP/EX COLONIAL CT/SYS PARL/PROC ORD/FREE ...POLICY CONCPT TREND 20 PARLIAMENT. PAGE 130 H2592
CONSTN ADJUD NAT/G FEDERAL

B61
ROCHE J.P.,COURTS AND RIGHTS: THE AMERICAN JUDICIARY IN ACTION (2ND ED.). UK USA+45 USA-45 STRUCT TEC/DEV SANCTION PERS/REL RACE/REL ORD/FREE ...METH/CNCPT GOV/COMP METH/COMP T 13/20. PAGE 133 H2653
JURID CT/SYS NAT/G PROVS

N61
PLATO,APOLOGY" IN PLATO, THE COLLECTED DIALOGUES, ED. BY E. HAMILTON AND H. CAIRNS (TRANS. BY H. TREDENNICK). GREECE SOCIETY NAT/G...CONCPT GEN/LAWS SOCRATES. PAGE 126 H2523
DEATH CT/SYS ATTIT MORAL

B62
BERNOT R.M.,EXCESS AND RESTRAINT: SOCIAL CONTROL AMONG GUINEA MOUNTAIN PEOPLE. CULTURE FAM KIN CT/SYS COERCE WAR PERS/REL MARRIAGE HABITAT SEX ...MYTH 20 NEW/GUINEA. PAGE 16 H0314
SOCIETY CONTROL STRUCT ADJUST

B62
CARTER G.M.,THE GOVERNMENT OF THE SOVIET UNION. USSR CULTURE LOC/G DIPLOM ECO/TAC ADJUD CT/SYS LEAD WEALTH...CHARTS T 20 COM/PARTY. PAGE 27 H0546
NAT/G MARXISM POL/PAR EX/STRUC

B62
GANJI M.,INTERNATIONAL PROTECTION OF HUMAN RIGHTS. WOR+45 CONSTN INT/TRADE CT/SYS SANCTION CRIME WAR
ORD/FREE DISCRIM

RACE/REL...CHARTS IDEA/COMP NAT/COMP BIBLIOG 20 TREATY NEGRO LEAGUE/NAT UN CIVIL/LIB. PAGE 55 H1097 LEGIS DELIB/GP B62

GROGAN V.,ADMINISTRATIVE TRIBUNALS IN THE PUBLIC SERVICE. IRELAND UK NAT/G CONTROL CT/SYS...JURID GOV/COMP 20. PAGE 61 H1231 ADMIN LAW ADJUD DELIB/GP B62

GRZYBOWSKI K.,SOVIET LEGAL INSTITUTIONS. USA+45 USSR ECO/DEV NAT/G EDU/PROP CONTROL CT/SYS CRIME OWN ATTIT PWR SOCISM...NAT/COMP 20. PAGE 62 H1242 ADJUD LAW JURID B62

KAGZI M.C.,THE INDIAN ADMINISTRATIVE LAW. INDIA LG/CO CONTROL CT/SYS...CONCPT 20. PAGE 83 H1649 JURID ADJUD DELIB/GP NAT/G B62

PHILLIPS O.H.,CONSTITUTIONAL AND ADMINISTRATIVE LAW (3RD ED.). UK INT/ORG LOC/G CHIEF EX/STRUC LEGIS BAL/PWR ADJUD COLONIAL CT/SYS PWR...CHARTS 20. PAGE 125 H2503 JURID ADMIN CONSTN NAT/G B63

ADRIAN C.R.,GOVERNING OVER FIFTY STATES AND THEIR COMMUNITIES. USA+45 CONSTN FINAN MUNIC NAT/G POL/PAR EX/STRUC LEGIS ADMIN CONTROL CT/SYS ...CHARTS 20. PAGE 4 H0073 PROVS LOC/G GOV/REL GOV/COMP B63

BADI J.,THE GOVERNMENT OF THE STATE OF ISRAEL: A CRITICAL ACCOUNT OF ITS PARLIAMENT, EXECUTIVE, AND JUDICIARY. ISRAEL ECO/DEV CHIEF DELIB/GP LEGIS DIPLOM CT/SYS INGP/REL PEACE ORD/FREE...BIBLIOG 20 PARLIAMENT ARABS MIGRATION. PAGE 10 H0193 NAT/G CONSTN EX/STRUC POL/PAR B63

CARTER G.M.,FIVE AFRICAN STATES: RESPONSES TO DIVERSITY. CONSTN CULTURE STRATA LEGIS PLAN ECO/TAC DOMIN EDU/PROP CT/SYS EXEC CHOOSE ATTIT HEALTH ORD/FREE PWR...TIME/SEQ TOT/POP VAL/FREE. PAGE 27 H0547 AFR SOCIETY B63

ECKSTEIN H.,COMPARATIVE POLITICS. POL/PAR LEGIS CT/SYS CHOOSE TOTALISM PWR POPULISM...METH/COMP GEN/METH ANTHOL BIBLIOG 20. PAGE 44 H0886 NAT/COMP CONSTN REPRESENT NAT/G B63

EDDY J.P.,JUSTICE OF THE PEACE. UK LAW CONSTN CULTURE 14/20 COMMON/LAW. PAGE 44 H0887 CRIME JURID CT/SYS ADJUD B63

RICHARDSON H.G.,THE ADMINISTRATION OF IRELAND 1172-1377. IRELAND CONSTN EX/STRUC LEGIS JUDGE CT/SYS PARL/PROC...CHARTS BIBLIOG 12/14. PAGE 131 H2621 ADMIN NAT/G PWR B64

DOOLIN D.J.,COMMUNIST CHINA: THE POLITICS OF STUDENT OPPOSITION. CHINA/COM ELITES STRATA ACADEM NAT/G WRITING CT/SYS LEAD PARTIC COERCE TOTALISM 20. PAGE 42 H0838 MARXISM DEBATE AGE/Y PWR B64

GESELLSCHAFT RECHTSVERGLEICH,BIBLIOGRAPHIE DES DEUTSCHEN RECHTS (BIBLIOGRAPHY OF GERMAN LAW, TRANS. BY COURTLAND PETERSON). GERMANY FINAN INDUS LABOR SECT FORCES CT/SYS PARL/PROC CRIME...INT/LAW SOC NAT/COMP 20. PAGE 56 H1117 BIBLIOG/A JURID CONSTN ADMIN B64

GROVES H.E.,THE CONSTITUTION OF MALAYSIA. MALAYSIA POL/PAR CHIEF CONSULT DELIB/GP CT/SYS PARL/PROC CHOOSE FEDERAL ORD/FREE 20. PAGE 62 H1238 CONSTN NAT/G LAW B64

HAAR C.M.,LAW AND LAND: ANGLO-AMERICAN PLANNING PRACTICE. UK USA+45 NAT/G TEC/DEV BUDGET CT/SYS INGP/REL EFFICIENCY OWN...JURID 20. PAGE 63 H1263 LAW PLAN MUNIC NAT/COMP B64

HOLDSWORTH W.S.,A HISTORY OF ENGLISH LAW; THE CENTURIES OF DEVELOPMENT AND REFORM (VOL. XIV). UK CONSTN LOC/G NAT/G POL/PAR CHIEF EX/STRUC ADJUD COLONIAL ATTIT...INT/LAW JURID 18/19 TORY/PARTY COMMONWLTH WHIG/PARTY COMMON/LAW. PAGE 73 H1453 LAW LEGIS LEAD CT/SYS B64

LEDERMAN W.R.,THE COURTS AND THE CANDIAN CONSTITUTION. CANADA PARL/PROC...POLICY JURID GOV/COMP ANTHOL 19/20 SUPREME/CT PARLIAMENT. PAGE 93 H1854 CONSTN CT/SYS LEGIS LAW B64

LIGGETT E.,BRITISH POLITICAL ISSUES: VOLUME 1. UK LAW CONSTN LOC/G NAT/G ADJUD 20. PAGE 97 H1930 POL/PAR GOV/REL CT/SYS DIPLOM B64

NEWARK F.H.,NOTES ON IRISH LEGAL HISTORY (2ND ED.). IRELAND UK PARL/PROC ORD/FREE SOVEREIGN 12/20 ENGLSH/LAW. PAGE 117 H2344 CT/SYS JURID ADJUD NAT/G B64

O'HEARN P.J.T.,PEACE, ORDER AND GOOD GOVERNMENT; A NEW CONSTITUTION FOR CANADA. CANADA EX/STRUC LEGIS CT/SYS PARL/PROC...BIBLIOG 20. PAGE 120 H2388 NAT/G CONSTN LAW CREATE B64

PIPES R.,THE FORMATION OF THE SOVIET UNION. EUR+WWI MOD/EUR STRUCT ECO/UNDEV NAT/G LEGIS DOMIN LEGIT CT/SYS EXEC COERCE ALL/VALS...POLICY RELATIV HIST/WRIT TIME/SEQ TOT/POP 19/20. PAGE 126 H2514 COM USSR RUSSIA B64

SKINNER E.P.,THE MOSSI OF UPPER VOLTA: THE POLITICAL DEVELOPMENT OF A SUDANESE PEOPLE. AFR LAW AGRI FAM KIN POL/PAR PROVS SECT DELIB/GP EX/STRUC FORCES TOP/EX DOMIN EDU/PROP LEGIT CT/SYS COERCE CHOOSE ORD/FREE PWR WEALTH...SOC MYTH VAL/FREE. PAGE 145 H2897 CULTURE OBS UPPER/VOLT B64

STRONG C.F.,HISTORY OF MODERN POLITICAL CONSTITUTIONS. STRUCT INT/ORG NAT/G LEGIS TEC/DEV DIPLOM INT/TRADE CT/SYS EXEC...METH/COMP T 12/20 UN. PAGE 150 H2999 CONSTN CONCPT B64

SZLADITS C.,BIBLIOGRAPHY ON FOREIGN AND COMPARATIVE LAW: BOOKS AND ARTICLES IN ENGLISH (SUPPLEMENT 1962). FINAN INDUS JUDGE LICENSE ADMIN CT/SYS PARL/PROC OWN...INT/LAW CLASSIF METH/COMP NAT/COMP 20. PAGE 151 H3027 BIBLIOG/A JURID ADJUD LAW B64

VECCHIO G.D.,L'ETAT ET LE DROIT. ITALY CONSTN EX/STRUC LEGIS DIPLOM CT/SYS...JURID 20 UN. PAGE 162 H3238 NAT/G SOVEREIGN CONCPT INT/LAW B64

WHEARE K.C.,FEDERAL GOVERNMENT (4TH ED.). WOR+45 WOR-45 POL/PAR LEGIS BAL/PWR CT/SYS...POLICY JURID CONCPT GOV/COMP 17/20. PAGE 167 H3339 FEDERAL CONSTN EX/STRUC NAT/COMP B65

BLITZ L.F.,THE POLITICS AND ADMINISTRATION OF NIGERIAN GOVERNMENT. NIGER CULTURE LOC/G LEGIS DIPLOM COLONIAL CT/SYS SOVEREIGN...GEOG SOC ANTHOL 20. PAGE 18 H0357 NAT/G GOV/REL POL/PAR B65

CHRIMES S.B.,ENGLISH CONSTITUTIONAL HISTORY (3RD ED.). UK CHIEF CONSULT DELIB/GP LEGIS CT/SYS 15/20 COMMON/LAW PARLIAMENT. PAGE 30 H0598 CONSTN BAL/PWR NAT/G B65

GWYN R.J.,THE SHAPE OF SCANDAL: A STUDY OF A GOVERNMENT IN CRISIS. CANADA LEGIS ADJUD CT/SYS SANCTION CMN/WLTH 20 PEARSON/L. PAGE 63 H1260 ELITES NAT/G CRIME B65

JACOB H.,POLITICS IN THE AMERICAN STATES; A COMPARATIVE ANALYSIS. USA+45 POL/PAR CHIEF LEGIS TAX EDU/PROP CONTROL CT/SYS LOBBY PARTIC...DECISION CHARTS 20. PAGE 79 H1578 PROVS GOV/COMP PWR B65

KAAS L.,DIE GEISTLICHE GERICHTSBARKEIT DER KATHOLISCHEN KIRCHE IN PREUSSEN (2 VOLS.). PRUSSIA CONSTN NAT/G PROVS SECT ADJUD ADMIN ATTIT 16/20. PAGE 82 H1647 JURID CATHISM GP/REL CT/SYS B65

MCWHINNEY E.,JUDICIAL REVIEW IN THE ENGLISH-SPEAKING WORLD (3RD ED.). CANADA UK WOR+45 LEGIS CONTROL EXEC PARTIC...JURID 20 AUSTRAL. PAGE 108 H2151 GOV/COMP CT/SYS ADJUD CONSTN B65

NEWBURY C.W.,BRITISH POLICY TOWARDS WEST AFRICA: SELECT DOCUMENTS 1786-1874. AFR UK INT/TRADE DOMIN ADMIN COLONIAL CT/SYS COERCE ORD/FREE...BIBLIOG/A 18/19. PAGE 117 H2345 DIPLOM POLICY NAT/G WRITING B65

NORDEN A.,WAR AND NAZI CRIMINALS IN WEST GERMANY: STATE, ECONOMY, ADMINISTRATION, ARMY, JUSTICE, SCIENCE. GERMANY GERMANY/W MOD/EUR ECO/DEV ACADEM EX/STRUC FORCES DOMIN ADMIN CT/SYS...POLICY MAJORIT PACIFIST 20. PAGE 119 H2370 FASCIST WAR NAT/G TOP/EX B65

PADELFORD N.,THE UNITED NATIONS IN THE BALANCE* ACCOMPLISHMENTS AND PROSPECTS. NAT/G VOL/ASSN DIPLOM ADMIN COLONIAL CT/SYS REGION WAR ORD/FREE ...ANTHOL UN. PAGE 122 H2437 INT/ORG CONTROL B65

PEASLEE A.J.,CONSTITUTIONS OF NATIONS* THIRD REVISED EDITION (VOLUME I* AFRICA). LAW EX/STRUC LEGIS TOP/EX LEGIT CT/SYS ROUTINE ORD/FREE PWR SOVEREIGN...CON/ANAL CHARTS. PAGE 124 H2481 AFR CHOOSE CONSTN NAT/G B65

PYLEE M.V.,CONSTITUTIONAL GOVERNMENT IN INDIA (2ND REV. ED.). INDIA POL/PAR EX/STRUC DIPLOM COLONIAL CT/SYS PARL/PROC PRIVIL...JURID 16/20. PAGE 128 H2569 CONSTN NAT/G PROVS FEDERAL B65

SHARMA S.A.,PARLIAMENTARY GOVERNMENT IN INDIA. INDIA FINAN LOC/G PROVS DELIB/GP PLAN ADMIN CT/SYS FEDERAL...JURID 20. PAGE 142 H2849 NAT/G CONSTN PARL/PROC LEGIS

L65
SHARMA S.P.,"THE INDIA-CHINA BORDER DISPUTE: AN INDIAN PERSPECTIVE." ASIA CHINA/COM S/ASIA NAT/G LEGIT CT/SYS NAT/LISM DRIVE MORAL ORD/FREE PWR 20. PAGE 142 H2850 — LAW ATTIT SOVEREIGN INDIA

S65
RUBINSTEIN A.Z.,"YUGOSLAVIA'S OPENING SOCIETY." COM USSR INTELL NAT/G LEGIS TOP/EX LEGIT CT/SYS RIGID/FLEX ALL/VALS SOCISM...HUM TIME/SEQ TREND 20. PAGE 135 H2708 — CONSTN EX/STRUC YUGOSLAVIA

B66
ADAMS J.C.,THE GOVERNMENT OF REPUBLICAN ITALY (2ND ED.). ITALY LOC/G POL/PAR DELIB/GP LEGIS WORKER ADMIN CT/SYS FASCISM...CHARTS BIBLIOG 20 PARLIAMENT. PAGE 3 H0064 — NAT/G CHOOSE EX/STRUC CONSTN

B66
BRAIBANTI R.,RESEARCH ON THE BUREAUCRACY OF PAKISTAN. PAKISTAN LAW CULTURE INTELL ACADEM LOC/G SECT PRESS CT/SYS...LING CHARTS 20 BUREAUCRCY. PAGE 20 H0402 — HABITAT NAT/G ADMIN CONSTN

B66
DE TOCQUEVILLE A,DEMOCRACY IN AMERICA (1834-1840) (2 VOLS. IN I; TRANS. BY G. LAWRENCE). FRANCE CULTURE STRATA POL/PAR CT/SYS REPRESENT FEDERAL ORD/FREE SOVEREIGN...MAJORIT TREND GEN/LAWS 18/19. PAGE 39 H0773 — POPULISM USA-45 CONSTN NAT/COMP

B66
DOUMA J.,BIBLIOGRAPHY ON THE INTERNATIONAL COURT INCLUDING THE PERMANENT COURT, 1918-1964. WOR+45 WOR-45 DELIB/GP WAR PRIVIL...JURID NAT/COMP 20 UN LEAGUE/NAT. PAGE 42 H0844 — BIBLIOG/A INT/ORG CT/SYS DIPLOM

B66
DUNCOMBE H.S.,COUNTY GOVERNMENT IN AMERICA. USA+45 FINAN MUNIC ADMIN ROUTINE GOV/REL...GOV/COMP 20. PAGE 43 H0863 — LOC/G PROVS CT/SYS TOP/EX

B66
GARCON M.,LETTRE OUVERTE A LA JUSTICE. FRANCE NAT/G PROB/SOLV PAY EFFICIENCY MORAL 20. PAGE 55 H1100 — ORD/FREE ADJUD CT/SYS

B66
GHOSH P.K.,THE CONSTITUTION OF INDIA: HOW IT HAS BEEN FRAMED. INDIA LOC/G DELIB/GP EX/STRUC PROB/SOLV BUDGET INT/TRADE CT/SYS CHOOSE...LING 20. PAGE 56 H1121 — CONSTN NAT/G LEGIS FEDERAL

B66
HIDAYATULLAH M.,DEMOCRACY IN INDIA AND THE JUDICIAL PROCESS. INDIA EX/STRUC LEGIS LEAD GOV/REL ATTIT ORD/FREE...MAJORIT CONCPT 20 NEHRU/J. PAGE 71 H1415 — NAT/G CT/SYS CONSTN JURID

B66
HOLDSWORTH W.S.,A HISTORY OF ENGLISH LAW; THE CENTURIES OF SETTLEMENT AND REFORM (VOL. XVI). UK LOC/G NAT/G EX/STRUC LEGIS CT/SYS LEAD ATTIT ...POLICY DECISION JURID IDEA/COMP 18 PARLIAMENT. PAGE 73 H1454 — BIOG PERSON PROF/ORG LAW

B66
NEUMANN R.G.,THE GOVERNMENT OF THE GERMAN FEDERAL REPUBLIC. EUR+WWI GERMANY/W LOC/G EX/STRUC LEGIS CT/SYS INGP/REL PWR...BIBLIOG 20 ADENAUER/K. PAGE 117 H2336 — NAT/G POL/PAR DIPLOM CONSTN

B66
SWEET E.C.,CIVIL LIBERTIES IN AMERICA. LAW CONSTN NAT/G PRESS CT/SYS DISCRIM ATTIT WORSHIP 20 CIVIL/LIB. PAGE 151 H3018 — ADJUD ORD/FREE SUFF COERCE

B67
BOHANNAN P.,LAW AND WARFARE. CULTURE CT/SYS COERCE REV PEACE...JURID SOC CONCPT ANTHOL 20. PAGE 18 H0367 — METH/COMP ADJUD WAR LAW

B67
BROWN L.N.,FRENCH ADMINISTRATIVE LAW. FRANCE UK CONSTN NAT/G LEGIS DOMIN CONTROL EXEC PARL/PROC PWR ...JURID METH/COMP GEN/METH. PAGE 22 H0447 — EX/STRUC LAW IDEA/COMP CT/SYS

B67
CANTOR N.F.,THE ENGLISH TRADITION* TWENTIETH-CENTURY VIEWS OF ENGLISH HISTORY (2VOLS.). UK STRATA NAT/G SECT WAR...POLICY GOV/COMP IDEA/COMP ANTHOL T PARLIAMENT CMN/WLTH. PAGE 26 H0522 — CT/SYS LAW POL/PAR

B67
GELLHORN W.,OMBUDSMEN AND OTHERS: CITIZENS' PROTECTORS IN NINE COUNTRIES. WOR+45 LAW CONSTN LEGIS INSPECT ADJUD ADMIN CONTROL CT/SYS CHOOSE PERS/REL...STAT CHARTS 20. PAGE 55 H1109 — NAT/COMP REPRESENT INGP/REL PROB/SOLV

B67
LENG S.C.,JUSTICE IN COMMUNIST CHINA: A SURVEY OF THE JUDICIAL SYSTEM OF THE CHINESE PEOPLE'S REPUBLIC. CHINA/COM LAW CONSTN LOC/G NAT/G PROF/ORG CONSULT FORCES ADMIN CRIME ORD/FREE...BIBLIOG 20 MAO. PAGE 94 H1877 — CT/SYS ADJUD JURID MARXISM

B67
WIENER F.B.,CIVILIANS UNDER MILITARY JUSTICE; THE BRITISH PRACTICE SINCE 1689 ESPECIALLY IN NORTH AMERICA. UK USA-45 LAW CONSTN CRIME REV...DECISION CHARTS NAT/COMP BIBLIOG 17/20. PAGE 168 H3356 — CT/SYS FORCES ADJUD

L67
WAELBROECK M.,"THE APPLICATION OF EEC LAW BY NATIONAL COURTS." EUR+WWI INT/ORG CT/SYS...JURID EEC TREATY. PAGE 164 H3284 — INT/LAW NAT/G LAW PROB/SOLV

L67
WILBER L.A.,"THE GOVERNMENTAL STRUCTURE OF MISSISSIPPI: ITS STRENGTHS AND WEAKNESSES." AGRI LOC/G SCHOOL EX/STRUC LEGIS TOP/EX BUDGET CT/SYS APPORT RACE/REL...GOV/COMP 20 MISSISSIPP. PAGE 168 H3359 — CONSTN PROVS STAT CON/ANAL

S67
AMERASINGHE C.F.,"SOME LEGAL PROBLEMS OF STATE TRADING IN SOUTHEAST ASIA." PROB/SOLV ADJUD CONTROL CT/SYS GP/REL 20. PAGE 6 H0120 — INT/TRADE NAT/G INT/LAW PRIVIL

S67
DANA MONTANO S.M.,"APLICACIONES CONCRETAS DE LAS RESOLUCIONES Y RECOMENDACIONES DE LAS CONFERENCIAS INTERAMERICANAS DE ABOGADOS" L/A+17C NAT/G PROVS GOV/REL PERCEPT 20 ARGEN. PAGE 37 H0739 — JURID CT/SYS ORD/FREE BAL/PWR

S67
HARNON E.,"CRIMINAL PROCEDURE IN ISRAEL - SOME COMPARATIVE ASPECTS." ISRAEL USA+45 CLIENT EX/STRUC LEGIS...JURID NAT/COMP 20. PAGE 67 H1336 — ADJUD CONSTN CT/SYS CRIME

S67
RUCKER B.W.,"WHAT SOLUTIONS DO PEOPLE ENDORSE IN FREE PRESS-FAIR TRIAL DILEMMA?" LAW NAT/G CT/SYS ATTIT...NET/THEORY SAMP CHARTS IDEA/COMP METH 20. PAGE 136 H2710 — CONCPT PRESS ADJUD ORD/FREE

S67
SEIDLER G.L.,"MARXIST LEGAL THOUGHT IN POLAND." POLAND SOCIETY R+D LOC/G NAT/G ACT/RES ADJUD CT/SYS SUPEGO PWR...SOC TREND 20 MARX/KARL. PAGE 141 H2822 — MARXISM LAW CONCPT EFFICIENCY

S67
SHELDON C.H.,"PUBLIC OPINION AND HIGH COURTS: COMMUNIST PARTY CASES IN FOUR CONSTITUTIONAL SYSTEMS." CANADA GERMANY/W WOR+45 POL/PAR MARXISM ...METH/COMP NAT/COMP 20 AUSTRAL. PAGE 143 H2857 — ATTIT CT/SYS CONSTN DECISION

S67
ULC O.,"CLASS STRUGGLE AND SOCIALIST JUSTICE: THE CASE OF CZECHOSLOVAKIA." COM CZECHOSLVK LAW CONSTN ELITES STRUCT NAT/G CRIME GP/REL MARXISM 20. PAGE 158 H3151 — TOTALISM CT/SYS ADJUD STRATA

B75
MAINE H.S.,LECTURES ON THE EARLY HISTORY OF INSTITUTIONS. IRELAND UK CONSTN ELITES STRUCT FAM KIN CHIEF LEGIS CT/SYS OWN SOVEREIGN...CONCPT 16 BENTHAM/J BREHON ROMAN/LAW. PAGE 101 H2021 — CULTURE LAW INGP/REL

B87
ADAMS J.,A DEFENSE OF THE CONSTITUTIONS OF GOVERNMENT OF THE UNITED STATES OF AMERICA. USA-45 STRATA CHIEF EX/STRUC LEGIS CT/SYS CONSERVE POPULISM...CONCPT CON/ANAL GOV/COMP. PAGE 3 H0063 — CONSTN BAL/PWR PWR NAT/G

B96
ESMEIN A.,ELEMENTS DE DROIT CONSTITUTIONNEL. FRANCE UK CHIEF EX/STRUC LEGIS ADJUD CT/SYS PARL/PROC REV GOV/REL ORD/FREE...JURID METH/COMP 18/19. PAGE 47 H0940 — LAW CONSTN NAT/G CONCPT

B97
JENKS E.J.,LAW AND POLITICS IN THE MIDDLE AGES. CHRIST-17C CULTURE STRUCT KIN NAT/G SECT CT/SYS GP/REL...CLASSIF CHARTS IDEA/COMP BIBLIOG 8/16. PAGE 80 H1603 — LAW SOCIETY ADJUST

B98
POLLOCK F.,THE HISTORY OF ENGLISH LAW BEFORE THE TIME OF EDWARD I (2 VOLS, 2ND ED.). UK CULTURE LOC/G LEGIS LICENSE AGREE CONTROL CT/SYS SANCTION CRIME...TIME/SEQ 13 COMMON/LAW CANON/LAW. PAGE 127 H2538 — LAW ADJUD JURID

CTS/WESTM....COURTS OF WESTMINSTER HALL

B35
RAM J.,THE SCIENCE OF LEGAL JUDGMENT: A TREATISE... UK CONSTN NAT/G LEGIS CREATE PROB/SOLV AGREE CT/SYS ...INT/LAW CONCPT 19 ENGLSH/LAW CANON/LAW CIVIL/LAW CTS/WESTM. PAGE 129 H2584 — LAW JURID EX/STRUC ADJUD

CUBA....SEE ALSO L/A+17C

B45
PERAZA SARAUSA F.,BIBLIOGRAFIAS CUBANAS. CUBA CULTURE ECO/UNDEV AGRI EDU/PROP PRESS CIVMIL/REL ...POLICY GEOG PHIL/SCI BIOG 19/20. PAGE 125 H2489 — BIBLIOG/A L/A+17C NAT/G DIPLOM

B61
GUEVARA E.,GUERRILLA WARFARE. L/A+17C ECO/UNDEV NAT/G POL/PAR VOL/ASSN PLAN DOMIN REV DRIVE PWR WEALTH...NEW/IDEA RECORD BIOG COLD/WAR MARX/KARL OAS 20. PAGE 62 H1247 — FORCES COERCE GUERRILLA CUBA

B61
HADDAD J.A.,REVOLUCAO CUBANA E REVOLUCAO — REV

BRASILEIRA. BRAZIL CUBA L/A+17C STRATA AGRI WORKER EDU/PROP REGION...POLICY NAT/COMP 20. PAGE 63 H1272 ORD/FREE DIPLOM ECO/UNDEV

B61
ROIG E.,MARTI, ANTIIMPERIALISTA. CUBA L/A+17C DIPLOM DOMIN COLONIAL CONTROL LEAD PWR SOVEREIGN ...PHIL/SCI 19 MARTI/JOSE INTERVENT. PAGE 133 H2664 PERSON NAT/LISM ECO/UNDEV ORD/FREE

B61
STARK H.,SOCIAL AND ECONOMIC FRONTIERS IN LATIN AMERICA (2ND ED.). CUBA FUT CULTURE AGRI INDUS ECO/TAC PRODUC ATTIT MARXISM...NAT/COMP BIBLIOG T 20. PAGE 149 H2971 L/A+17C SOCIETY DIPLOM ECO/UNDEV

B63
BELFRAGE C.,THE MAN AT THE DOOR WITH THE GUN. CUBA L/A+17C NAT/G LEAD PARTIC GP/REL PWR...POLICY 20 CASTRO/F. PAGE 13 H0261 REGION ECO/UNDEV STRUCT ATTIT

S63
TANG P.S.H.,"SINO-SOVIET TENSIONS." ASIA CHINA/COM COM CUBA KOREA/N VIETNAM/N NAT/G VOL/ASSN DELIB/GP PEACE PERCEPT PWR...METH/CNCPT MYTH RECORD TREND GEN/LAWS 20. PAGE 152 H3041 ACT/RES EDU/PROP REV

B64
GILLY A.,INSIDE THE CUBAN REVOLUTION. CUBA AGRI INDUS LABOR CREATE DIPLOM...METH/COMP 20. PAGE 56 H1129 REV PLAN MARXISM ECO/UNDEV

B64
GRIFFITH W.E.,THE SINO-SOVIET RIFT. ASIA CHINA/COM COM CUBA USSR YUGOSLAVIA NAT/G POL/PAR VOL/ASSN DELIB/GP FORCES TOP/EX DIPLOM EDU/PROP DRIVE PERSON PWR...TREND 20 TREATY. PAGE 61 H1224 ATTIT TIME/SEQ BAL/PWR SOCISM

B64
MARTINEZ J.R.,THREE CASES OF COMMUNISM: CUBA, BRAZIL, AND MEXICO. BRAZIL CUBA L/A+17C CONSTN NAT/G DIPLOM ECO/TAC GP/REL INGP/REL...GP/COMP BIBLIOG 20 MEXIC/AMER COM/PARTY. PAGE 103 H2068 MARXISM BIOG REV NAT/COMP

B64
PERAZA SARAUSA F.,DIRECTORIO DE REVISTAS Y PERIODICOS DE CUBA. CUBA L/A+17C NAT/G ATTIT 20. PAGE 125 H2490 BIBLIOG/A PRESS SERV/IND LEAD

B64
ROSENAU J.N.,INTERNATIONAL ASPECTS OF CIVIL STRIFE. CHINA/COM CUBA EUR+WWI USA+45 USSR BAL/PWR EDU/PROP NEUTRAL COERCE MORAL...NAT/COMP 20 COLD/WAR UN. PAGE 134 H2676 POLICY DIPLOM REV WAR

S64
CATTELL D.T.,"SOVIET POLICIES IN LATIN AMERICA." COM CUBA L/A+17C USSR SOCIETY NAT/G POL/PAR FORCES CREATE ECO/TAC EDU/PROP REGION REV RIGID/FLEX ...GEN/LAWS COLD/WAR 20. PAGE 28 H0560 DRIVE PWR

B65
FAGG J.E.,CUBA, HAITI, AND THE DOMINICAN REPUBLIC. CUBA DOMIN/REP HAITI L/A+17C NAT/G DIPLOM ECO/TAC DOMIN CHOOSE AUTHORIT ROLE SOVEREIGN POPULISM 17/20. PAGE 48 H0959 COLONIAL ECO/UNDEV REV GOV/COMP

S65
PLANK J.N.,"THE CARIBBEAN* INTERVENTION, WHEN AND HOW." CUBA GUATEMALA HAITI PANAMA USA+45 VENEZUELA FORCES PROB/SOLV RISK COERCE...NAT/COMP OAS TIME. PAGE 126 H2521 SOVEREIGN MARXISM REV

S65
WOHLSTETTER R.,"CUBA AND PEARL HARBOR* HINDSIGHT AND FORESIGHT." USSR FORCES OP/RES TEC/DEV ATTIT PERCEPT...DECISION IDEA/COMP NAT/COMP STERTYP TIME. PAGE 170 H3395 CUBA RISK WAR ACT/RES

B66
ZABLOCKI C.J.,SINO-SOVIET RIVALRY. AFR ASIA CHINA/COM CUBA EUR+WWI L/A+17C USA+45 USSR WOR+45 POL/PAR FORCES COERCE NUC/PWR...GOV/COMP IDEA/COMP 20 MAO KHRUSH/N. PAGE 172 H3444 DIPLOM MARXISM COM

B67
PLANK J.,CUBA AND THE UNITED STATES: LONG RANGE PERSPECTIVES. CUBA L/A+17C USSR ECO/UNDEV NAT/G FORCES ECO/TAC INT/TRADE AGREE REV...PREDICT TREND ANTHOL 20 CASTRO/F COLD/WAR OAS. PAGE 126 H2520 DIPLOM

S67
CUMMINS L.,"THE FORMULATION OF THE "PLATT" AMENDMENT." CUBA L/A+17C NAT/G DELIB/GP CONFER ...POLICY 20. PAGE 36 H0720 DIPLOM INT/LAW LEGIS

S67
GONZALEZ M.P.,"CUBA, UNA REVOLUCION EN MARCHA." CUBA L/A+17C USA+45 VIETNAM ECO/UNDEV FORCES DIPLOM DOMIN...POLICY MARXIST NAT/COMP CASTRO/F. PAGE 58 H1163 REV NAT/G COLONIAL SOVEREIGN

S67
TANTER R.,"A THEORY OF REVOLUTION." ASIA CUBA L/A+17C S/ASIA SOCIETY NAT/G ADJUST...CONCPT CHARTS. PAGE 152 H3046 REV ECO/UNDEV EDU/PROP METH/COMP

CUBAN CRISIS....SEE INT/REL+APPROPRIATE NATIONS+COLD WAR

CUCCORESE H.J. H0717

CULLINGWORTH J.B. H0718

CULTS....SEE SECT

CULTUR/REV....CULTURAL REVOLUTION IN CHINA

CULTURAL REVOLUTION IN CHINA....SEE CULTUR/REV

CULTURE....CULTURAL PATTERNS

CULVER D.C. H0719

CUMMINS L. H0720

CUNNINGHAM W. H0721

CUNNINGHAM W.B. H0722

CURLEY/JM....JAMES M. CURLEY

CURRENT EVENTS....SEE HIST

CURRENT HISTORY H0723,H0724

CURRIE D.P. H0725

CURTIN P.D. H0726,H0727

CURTISS J.S. H0728

CURZON/GN....GEORGE NATHANIEL CURZON

B39
NICOLSON H.,CURZON: THE LAST PHASE, 1919-1925. UK NAT/G DELIB/GP TOP/EX ROUTINE WAR RIGID/FLEX ...METH/CNCPT 20 CURZON/GN. PAGE 118 H2352 POLICY DIPLOM BIOG

CVIJIC J. H0729

CYBERNETICS....SEE FEEDBACK, SIMUL, CONTROL

CYCLES....SEE TIME/SEQ

CYPRUS....SEE ALSO APPROPRIATE TIME/SPACE/CULTURE INDEX

B64
DE SMITH S.A.,THE NEW COMMONWEALTH AND ITS CONSTITUTIONS. AFR CYPRUS PAKISTAN S/ASIA INT/ORG NAT/G LEGIS LEGIT RIGID/FLEX PWR...CONCPT TIME/SEQ CMN/WLTH 20. PAGE 38 H0770 EX/STRUC CONSTN SOVEREIGN

S66
ADAMS T.W.,"THE FIRST REPUBLIC OF CYPRUS: A REVIEW OF AN UNWORKABLE CONSTITUTION." CYPRUS FUT PLAN NAT/LISM POPULISM 20. PAGE 3 H0067 CONSTN NAT/G PROB/SOLV

S67
ANTHEM T.,"CYPRUS* WHAT NOW?" CYPRUS GREECE TURKEY NAT/G BUDGET MAJORITY 20 NATO. PAGE 7 H0143 DIPLOM COERCE INT/TRADE ADJUD

CZECHOSLVK....CZECHOSLOVAKIA; SEE ALSO COM

B18
KERNER R.J.,SLAVIC EUROPE: A SELECTED BIBLIOGRAPHY IN THE WESTERN EUROPEAN LANGUAGES. BULGARIA CZECHOSLVK GERMANY/E POLAND RUSSIA YUGOSLAVIA NAT/G DIPLOM MARXISM...LING 19/20. PAGE 85 H1695 BIBLIOG SOCIETY CULTURE COM

N19
HAJDA J.,THE COLD WAR VIEWED AS A SOCIOLOGICAL PROBLEM (PAMPHLET). COM CZECHOSLVK EUR+WWI SOCIETY PLAN EDU/PROP CONTROL TASK ATTIT MARXISM...POLICY 20 COLD/WAR MIGRATION. PAGE 64 H1280 DIPLOM LEAD PWR NAT/G

N19
TABORSKY E.,CONFORMITY UNDER COMMUNISM (PAMPHLET). CZECHOSLVK HUNGARY POLAND SCHOOL DOMIN PRESS ...TREND GOV/COMP 20. PAGE 152 H3030 COM CONTROL EDU/PROP NAT/G

B50
KANN R.A.,THE MULTINATIONAL EMPIRE (2 VOLS.). AUSTRIA CZECHOSLVK GERMANY HUNGARY CULTURE NAT/G POL/PAR PROVS REGION REV FEDERAL...GEOG TREND CHARTS IDEA/COMP NAT/COMP 19/20. PAGE 83 H1654 NAT/LISM MOD/EUR

B53
MEYER P.,THE JEWS IN THE SOVIET SATELLITES. CZECHOSLVK POLAND SOCIETY STRATA NAT/G BAL/PWR ECO/TAC EDU/PROP LEGIT ADMIN COERCE ATTIT DISPL PERCEPT HEALTH PWR RESPECT WEALTH...METH/CNCPT JEWS VAL/FREE NAZI 20. PAGE 110 H2192 COM SECT TOTALISM USSR

B55
MID-EUROPEAN LAW PROJECT,CHURCH AND STATE BEHIND THE IRON CURTAIN. COM CZECHOSLVK HUNGARY POLAND USSR CULTURE SECT EDU/PROP GOV/REL CATHISM...CHARTS ANTHOL BIBLIOG WORSHIP 20 CHURCH/STA. PAGE 110 H2202 LAW MARXISM POLICY

B57
BUNDESMIN FUR VERTRIEBENE,DIE VERTREIBUNG DER GP/REL

DEUTSCHEN BEVOLKERUNG AUS DER TSCHECHOSLOWAKEI. CZECHOSLVK GERMANY NAT/G FORCES MURDER WAR INGP/REL ATTIT 20 MIGRATION. PAGE 24 H0474 — DOMIN COERCE DISCRIM

B59
ETSCHMANN R.,DIE WAHRUNGS- UND DEVISENPOLITIK DES OSTBLOCKS UND IHRE AUSWIRKUNGEN AUF DIE WIRTSCHAFTSBEZIEHUNGEN ZWISCHEN OST U WEST. BULGARIA CZECHOSLVK HUNGARY POLAND USSR MARKET NAT/G PLAN DIPLOM...NAT/COMP 20. PAGE 47 H0943 — ECO/TAC FINAN POLICY INT/TRADE

B59
HEMMERLE J.,SUDETENDEUTSCHE BIBLIOGRAPHIE 1949-1953. CZECHOSLVK GERMANY SOCIETY STRUCT SECT ...GEOG JURID 20. PAGE 69 H1391 — BIBLIOG PROVS GP/REL CULTURE

B60
KOHN H.,PAN-SLAVISM: ITS HISTORY AND IDEOLOGY. COM CZECHOSLVK EUR+WWI MOD/EUR USSR YUGOSLAVIA CULTURE ELITES INTELL KIN NAT/G EDU/PROP DRIVE SOVEREIGN ...HUM PHIL/SCI MYTH HIST/WRIT 19/20. PAGE 87 H1745 — ATTIT CONCPT NAT/LISM

L60
KAPLAN M.A.,"COMMUNIST COUP IN CZECHOSLOVAKIA." COM EUR+WWI INTELL LABOR LOC/G NAT/G POL/PAR FORCES EDU/PROP EXEC MARXISM...TIME/SEQ HYPO/EXP 20. PAGE 83 H1659 — STRUCT COERCE CZECHOSLVK

S61
BRZEZINSKI Z.K.,"THE ORGANIZATION OF THE COMMUNIST CAMP." COM CZECHOSLVK COM/IND NAT/G DELIB/GP INT/TRADE DOMIN EDU/PROP EXEC ROUTINE COERCE ATTIT PWR...MGT CONCPT TIME/SEQ CHARTS VAL/FREE 20 TREATY. PAGE 23 H0460 — VOL/ASSN DIPLOM USSR

B62
HANAK H.,GREAT BRITAIN AND AUSTRIA-HUNGARY DURING THE FIRST WORLD WAR: A STUDY IN THE FORMATION OF PUBLIC OPINION. CZECHOSLVK UK NAT/G GIVE DOMIN EDU/PROP CONSERVE...BIBLIOG 20 AUST/HUNG WWI. PAGE 65 H1311 — WAR DIPLOM ATTIT PRESS

B62
SCHECHTMAN J.B.,POSTWAR POPULATION TRANSFERS IN EUROPE: 1945-1955. COM CZECHOSLVK GERMANY POLAND USSR CULTURE SOCIETY PROB/SOLV AGREE NAT/LISM...SOC STAT TREND CHARTS METH/COMP 20 MIGRATION. PAGE 139 H2778 — GEOG CENSUS EUR+WWI HABITAT

B64
GRIFFITH W.E.,COMMUNISM IN EUROPE (2 VOLS.). CZECHOSLVK USSR WOR+45 WOR-45 YUGOSLAVIA INGP/REL MARXISM SOCISM...ANTHOL 20 EUROPE/E. PAGE 61 H1225 — COM POL/PAR DIPLOM GOV/COMP

S64
HORECKY P.L.,"LIBRARY OF CONGRESS PUBLICATIONS IN AID OF USSR AND EAST EUROPEAN RESEARCH." BULGARIA CZECHOSLVK POLAND USSR YUGOSLAVIA NAT/G POL/PAR DIPLOM ADMIN GOV/REL...CLASSIF 20. PAGE 73 H1468 — BIBLIOG/A COM MARXISM

S65
TABORSKY E.,"CHANGE IN CZECHOSLOVAKIA." COM USSR ELITES INTELL AGRI INDUS NAT/G DELIB/GP EX/STRUC ECO/TAC TOTALISM ATTIT RIGID/FLEX SOCISM...MGT CONCPT TREND 20. PAGE 152 H3031 — ECO/DEV PLAN CZECHOSLVK

B66
HEYMANN F.G.,POLAND AND CZECHOSLOVAKIA. COM CZECHOSLVK POLAND...CHARTS BIBLIOG/A 9/20. PAGE 70 H1413 — CULTURE NAT/LISM ORD/FREE WAR

B66
JACKSON G.D.,COMINTERN AND PEASANT IN EAST EUROPE 1919-1930. BULGARIA COM CZECHOSLVK EUR+WWI POLAND ROMANIA YUGOSLAVIA STRATA AGRI VOL/ASSN DIPLOM CONTROL CROWD WEALTH...POLICY NAT/COMP 20. PAGE 79 H1575 — MARXISM ECO/UNDEV WORKER INT/ORG

B66
SPULBER N.,THE STATE AND ECONOMIC DEVELOPMENT IN EASTERN EUROPE. BULGARIA COM CZECHOSLVK HUNGARY POLAND YUGOSLAVIA CULTURE PLAN CAP/ISM INT/TRADE CONTROL...POLICY CHARTS METH/COMP BIBLIOG/A 19/20. PAGE 148 H2958 — ECO/DEV ECO/UNDEV NAT/G TOTALISM

B67
NATIONAL SCIENCE FOUNDATION,DIRECTORY OF SELECTED RESEARCH INSTITUTES IN EASTERN EUROPE. BULGARIA CZECHOSLVK HUNGARY POLAND ROMANIA INTELL ACADEM NAT/G ACT/RES 20. PAGE 116 H2323 — INDEX R+D COM PHIL/SCI

S67
JANICKE M.,"MONOPOLISMUS UND PLURALISMUS IM KOMMUNISTISCHEN HERRSCHAFTSSYSTEM" COM CZECHOSLVK USSR YUGOSLAVIA SOCIETY CONTROL RIGID/FLEX...CONCPT NAT/COMP 20. PAGE 79 H1589 — TOTALISM POL/PAR ATTIT PLURISM

S67
LEVCIK B.,"WAGES AND EMPLOYMENT PROBLEMS IN THE NEW SYSTEM OF PLANNED MANAGEMENT IN CZECHOSLOVAKIA." CZECHOSLVK EUR+WWI NAT/G OP/RES PLAN ADMIN ROUTINE INGP/REL CENTRAL EFFICIENCY PRODUC DECISION. PAGE 95 H1895 — MARXISM WORKER MGT PAY

S67
ULC O.,"CLASS STRUGGLE AND SOCIALIST JUSTICE: THE CASE OF CZECHOSLOVAKIA." COM CZECHOSLVK LAW CONSTN ELITES STRUCT NAT/G CRIME GP/REL MARXISM 20. PAGE 158 H3151 — TOTALISM CT/SYS ADJUD STRATA

S68
BOSSCHERE G D.E.,"A L'EST DU NOUVEAU." CZECHOSLVK HUNGARY POLAND ROMANIA YUGOSLAVIA AGRI CREATE ECO/TAC COERCE GP/REL ATTIT MARXISM SOCISM 20. PAGE 19 H0382 — ORD/FREE COM NAT/G DIPLOM

D

DAC....DEVELOPMENT ASSISTANCE COMMITTEE (PART OF OECD)

DAENIKER G. H0730

DAGGETT H.S. H0583

DAHL R.A. H0731,H0732

DAHLIN E. H0733

DAHOMEY....SEE ALSO AFR

B60
CONOVER H.F.,OFFICIAL PUBLICATIONS OF FRENCH WEST AFRICA, 1946-1958. DAHOMEY IVORY/CST NIGER SENEGAL UPPER/VOLT CONSTN AGRI PRESS...CON/ANAL 20. PAGE 33 H0651 — BIBLIOG COLONIAL NAT/G AFR

B66
MATTHEWS R.,AFRICAN POWDER KEG: REVOLT AND DISSENT IN SIX EMERGENT NATIONS. AFR ALGERIA DAHOMEY GABON GHANA MALAWI GAMBLE LEAD PARTIC REV DRIVE...BIOG TREND GOV/COMP 20. PAGE 105 H2098 — ELITES ECO/UNDEV TOP/EX CONTROL

DAHRENDORF R. H0734

DAKAR....DAKAR, SENEGAL

DALAND R.T. H0735

DALLIN A. H0736

DALLIN D.J. H0737

DALTON G. H0738

DANA MONTANO S.M. H0739

DANIEL/Y....YULI DANIEL

DANIELS R.V. H0740

DANTE....DANTE ALIGHIERI

B37
BORGESE G.A.,GOLIATH: THE MARCH OF FASCISM. GERMANY ITALY LAW POL/PAR SECT DIPLOM SOCISM...JURID MYTH 20 DANTE MACHIAVELL MUSSOLIN/B. PAGE 19 H0375 — POLICY NAT/LISM FASCISM NAT/G

DANTE ALIGHIERI H0741

DARLING M. H0742

DARWIN/C....CHARLES DARWIN

DATA ANALYSIS....SEE CON/ANAL, STAT, MATH, COMPUTER

DAVAR F.C. H0743

DAVIDSON B. H0744

DAVIDSON E. H0745

DAVIE M.R. H0746

DAVIES E. H0747,H0748

DAVIS/JEFF....JEFFERSON DAVIS

DAVIS/W....WARREN DAVIS

DE ARAGAO J.G. H0749

DE BIEVILLE, MARC H0781

DE CENIVAL P. H0750

DE GAULLE C. H0751

DE GRAZIA A. H0752

DE GRE G. H0753

DE HERRERA C.D. H0754

DE JOMINI A.H. H0755

DE JONG L. H0756

DE JOUVENEL B. H0757,H0758

DE KIEWIET C.W. H0759

DE LA COSTA H. H0674

DE MADARIAGA S. H0760

DE MAISTRE J. H0761

DE MAN H. H0762

DE NOIA J. H0763,H0764,H0765,H0766,H0767

DE REPARAZ G. H0768

DE SMITH S.A. H0769,H0770

DE SPINOZA B. H0771

DE TOCQUEVILLE A. H0772,H0773

DE VATTEL E. H0774

DE VICTORIA F. H0775

DE VORE B.B. H0776

DE VOS G. H2221

DE VRIES E. H0777

DEAN V.M. H0778

DEANE P. H1511

DEATH....DEATH

B04
REED W.A.,ETHNOLOGICAL SURVEY PUBLICATIONS (VOL. II). PHILIPPINE STRUCT INDUS SECT DEATH LEISURE HABITAT...AUD/VIS CHARTS WORSHIP 20 NABOLOI NEGRITO BATAK. PAGE 130 H2607 — CULTURE SOCIETY SOC OBS

B17
BARRES M.,THE UNDYING SPIRIT OF FRANCE (TRANS. BY M. CORWIN). FRANCE DOMIN LEAD DEATH ATTIT RESPECT ...NAT/COMP 20 WWI. PAGE 11 H0226 — NAT/LISM FORCES WAR CULTURE

N19
BARRES M.,"THE WAR AND THE SPIRIT OF YOUTH" (PAMPHLET). FRANCE FORCES DOMIN LEAD DEATH AGE/Y ATTIT RESPECT...FASCIST 20 WWI. PAGE 11 H0228 — WAR NAT/LISM CULTURE MYSTIC

B57
PLAYFAIR G.,THE OFFENDERS: THE CASE AGAINST LEGAL VENGEANCE. UNIV LAW SOCIETY NAT/G PROB/SOLV DEATH PERSON ORD/FREE...HEAL INT/LAW BIBLIOG 20 REFORMERS. PAGE 126 H2524 — CRIME TEC/DEV SANCTION CT/SYS

B58
WARNER W.L.,A BLACK CIVILIZATION - A SOCIAL STUDY OF AN AUSTRALIAN TRIBE. SOCIETY FAM MARRIAGE...PSY SOC MYTH CHARTS 20 AUSTRAL MAPS MURNGIN RITUAL. PAGE 165 H3310 — CULTURE KIN STRUCT DEATH

B59
ELDRIDGE H.T.,THE MATERIALS OF DEMOGRAPHY: A SELECTED AND ANNOTATED BIBLIOGRAPHY. R+D DEATH ...SAMP METH/COMP NAT/COMP 20. PAGE 45 H0905 — BIBLIOG/A GEOG STAT TREND

B59
WARNER W.L.,THE LIVING AND THE DEAD: A STUDY OF SYMBOLIC LIFE OF AMERICANS. INTELL KIN DEATH ALL/VALS ALL/IDEOS...CONCPT MYTH LING OBS/ENVIR CHARTS BIBLIOG WORSHIP 18/20. PAGE 165 H3311 — CULTURE SOC TIME/SEQ IDEA/COMP

N61
PLATO,APOLOGY" IN PLATO, THE COLLECTED DIALOGUES, ED. BY E. HAMILTON AND H. CAIRNS (TRANS. BY H. TREDENNICK). GREECE SOCIETY NAT/G...CONCPT GEN/LAWS SOCRATES. PAGE 126 H2523 — DEATH CT/SYS ATTIT MORAL

B63
HARDY M.J.L.,BLOOD FEUDS AND THE PAYMENT OF BLOOD MONEY IN THE MIDDLE EAST. ISLAM SOCIETY SECT REGION SANCTION COERCE DEATH MURDER 7/20 ARABS. PAGE 66 H1329 — KIN TRIBUTE LAW CULTURE

B63
REYNOLDS B.,MAGIC, DIVINATION AND WITCHCRAFT AMONG THE BAROTSE OF NORTHERN RHODESIA. RHODESIA CULTURE KIN CREATE LEGIT PARTIC DEATH DREAM STRANGE HABITAT PERSON...AUD/VIS WORSHIP 20. PAGE 131 H2619 — AFR SOC MYTH SECT

S63
ROBINSON W.C.,"URBANIZATION AND FERTILITY: THE NON-WESTERN EXPERIENCE (BMR)" DEATH MARRIAGE AGE/C BIO/SOC...STAT CENSUS CON/ANAL CHARTS NAT/COMP 20 THIRD/WRLD. PAGE 133 H2651 — GEOG MUNIC FAM ECO/UNDEV

B64
ELKIN A.P.,THE AUSTRALIAN ABORIGINES - HOW TO UNDERSTAND THEM (4TH ED.). FAM NEIGH DEATH MARRIAGE ATTIT BIO/SOC HABITAT...PSY SOC MYTH WORSHIP AUSTRAL ABORIGINES. PAGE 45 H0908 — CULTURE STRUCT SOCIETY KIN

B66
TSURUMI K.,ADULT SOCIALIZATION AND SOCIAL CHANGE: JAPAN BEFORE AND AFTER DEFEAT IN WORLD WAR II. FAM DEATH SUPEGO...PSY SOC 20 CHINJAP. PAGE 157 H3133 — SOCIETY AGE/A WAR PERSON

B66
UN ECONOMIC AND SOCIAL COUNCIL,WORLD POPULATION PROSPECTS AS ASSESSED IN 1963. FUT WOR+45 DEATH AGE ...TREND CHARTS UN. PAGE 158 H3157 — PREDICT CENSUS GEOG NAT/COMP

B67
ZINN H.,VIETNAM THE LOGIC OF WITHDRAWAL. VIETNAM/S NAT/G DIPLOM DEATH MORAL 20. PAGE 173 H3459 — WAR COST PACIFISM ATTIT

S67
BEVEL D.N.,"JOURNEY TO NORTH VIETNAM." VIETNAM/N CONSTN NAT/G FORCES PROB/SOLV DEATH CIVMIL/REL PEACE MORAL...ANTHOL 20 NEGRO. PAGE 16 H0325 — ATTIT DIPLOM ORD/FREE WAR

DEBATE....ORGANIZED COLLECTIVE ARGUMENT

B27
FLOURNOY F.,PARLIAMENT AND WAR. MOD/EUR UK NAT/G FORCES LEGIS TOP/EX DIPLOM LEGIT DEBATE ATTIT RIGID/FLEX PWR...DECISION TIME/SEQ PARLIAMENT 19/20. PAGE 52 H1032 — COERCE WAR

B55
GALLOWAY G.B.,CONGRESS AND PARLIAMENT: THEIR ORGANIZATION AND OPERATION IN THE US AND THE UK: PLANNING PAMPHLET NO. 93. POL/PAR EX/STRUC DEBATE CONTROL LEAD ROUTINE EFFICIENCY PWR...POLICY CONGRESS PARLIAMENT. PAGE 54 H1089 — DELIB/GP LEGIS PARL/PROC GOV/COMP

B57
BULLOCK A.,THE LIBERAL TRADITION FROM FOX TO KEYNES. UK CULTURE INTELL CREATE WRITING COLONIAL PERS/REL ATTIT ORD/FREE...POLICY OLD/LIB TRADIT CONCPT 18/20 CHURCHLL/W MILL/JS KEYNES/JM ASQUITH/HH. PAGE 23 H0469 — ANTHOL DEBATE LAISSEZ

C58
WILDING N.,"AN ENCYCLOPEDIA OF PARLIAMENT." UK LAW CONSTN CHIEF PROB/SOLV DIPLOM DEBATE WAR INGP/REL PRIVIL...BIBLIOG DICTIONARY 13/20 CMN/WLTH PARLIAMENT. PAGE 168 H3363 — PARL/PROC POL/PAR NAT/G ADMIN

B60
BAYER H.,WIRTSCHAFTSPROGNOSE UND WIRTSCHAFTSGESTALTUNG. GERMANY NETHERLAND MARKET PLAN CAP/ISM DEBATE...NAT/COMP 20. PAGE 12 H0242 — ECO/DEV ECO/UNDEV FINAN POLICY

B60
MACFARQUHAR R.,THE HUNDRED FLOWERS. ASIA NAT/G WORKER GP/REL ORD/FREE MARXISM 20 MAO. PAGE 100 H1991 — DEBATE PRESS POL/PAR ATTIT

B64
DOOLIN D.J.,COMMUNIST CHINA: THE POLITICS OF STUDENT OPPOSITION. CHINA/COM ELITES STRATA ACADEM NAT/G WRITING CT/SYS LEAD PARTIC COERCE TOTALISM 20. PAGE 42 H0838 — MARXISM DEBATE AGE/Y PWR

B65
JOHNSON P.,KHRUSHCHEV AND THE ARTS: POLITICS OF SOVIET CULTURE, 1962-1964. COM USSR NAT/G PERF/ART CONFER DEBATE GP/REL PERS/REL UTIL ATTIT DRIVE 20 KHRUSH/N. PAGE 81 H1626 — CULTURE MARXISM POLICY CHIEF

B66
ANDERSON S.V.,CANADIAN OMBUDSMAN PROPOSALS. CANADA LEGIS DEBATE PARL/PROC...MAJORIT JURID TIME/SEQ IDEA/COMP 20 OMBUDSMAN PARLIAMENT. PAGE 7 H0133 — NAT/G CREATE ADMIN POL/PAR

B66
CHAPMAN B.,THE PROFESSION OF GOVERNMENT: THE PUBLIC SERVICE IN EUROPE. CONSTN NAT/G POL/PAR EX/STRUC LEGIS TOP/EX PROB/SOLV DEBATE EXEC PARL/PROC PARTIC 20. PAGE 29 H0581 — BIBLIOG ADMIN EUR+WWI GOV/COMP

L67
TOUVAL S.,"THE ORGANIZATION OF AFRICAN UNITY AND AFRICAN BORDERS." DEBATE REGION TASK REV ATTIT ORD/FREE...DECISION UN 20 OAU. PAGE 156 H3121 — AFR NAT/G COLONIAL NAT/LISM

S67
ALBINSKI H.S.,"POLITICS AND BICULTURISM IN CANADA: THE FLAG DEBATE." CANADA SOCIETY NAT/G PROVS DELIB/GP DEBATE REGION SOVEREIGN PLURISM...POLICY SOC/INTEG 20. PAGE 5 H0093 — NAT/LISM GP/REL POL/PAR CULTURE

S67
KOHN W.S.G.,"THE SOVEREIGNTY OF LIECHTENSTEIN." LIECHTENST SWITZERLND USSR CONSTN DEBATE WAR CONSERVE 18/20 UN. PAGE 88 H1748 — SOVEREIGN NAT/G PWR DIPLOM

S67
LEGRES A.,"LES FONCTIONS D'UN PARLEMENT MODERNE." FRANCE DEBATE PARL/PROC SANCTION ATTIT PWR 20 PARLIAMENT. PAGE 93 H1860 — NAT/G LAW LEGIS CHOOSE

DEBRAY P. H0779

DEBS/E....EUGENE DEBS

DEBT....PUBLIC DEBT, INCLUDING NATIONAL DEBT

DEBUYST F. H0780

DECISION....DECISION-MAKING AND GAME THEORY; SEE ALSO GAME

N19
FIKS M.,PUBLIC ADMINISTRATION IN ISRAEL (PAMPHLET). ISRAEL SCHOOL EX/STRUC BUDGET PAY INGP/REL ...DECISION 20 CIVIL/SERV. PAGE 50 H0999
EDU/PROP NAT/G ADMIN WORKER

N19
GOODMAN G.K.,IMPERIAL JAPAN AND ASIA: A REASSESSMENT (PAMPHLET). ASIA S/ASIA ECO/DEV FORCES LEAD WAR NAT/LISM ATTIT...DECISION CONCPT BIBLIOG 19/20 CHINJAP. PAGE 59 H1172
DIPLOM NAT/G POLICY COLONIAL

B27
FLOURNOY F.,PARLIAMENT AND WAR. MOD/EUR UK NAT/G FORCES LEGIS TOP/EX DIPLOM LEGIT DEBATE ATTIT RIGID/FLEX PWR...DECISION TIME/SEQ PARLIAMENT 19/20. PAGE 52 H1032
COERCE WAR

B32
GREAT BRIT COMM MINISTERS PWR,REPORT. UK LAW CONSTN CONSULT LEGIS PARL/PROC SANCTION SOVEREIGN ...DECISION JURID 20 PARLIAMENT. PAGE 60 H1201
EX/STRUC NAT/G PWR CONTROL

B32
LUNT D.C.,THE ROAD TO THE LAW. UK USA-45 LEGIS EDU/PROP OWN ORD/FREE...DECISION TIME/SEQ NAT/COMP 16/20 AUSTRAL ENGLSH/LAW COMMON/LAW. PAGE 99 H1980
ADJUD LAW JURID CT/SYS

L34
GOSNELL H.F.,"BRITISH ROYAL COMMISSIONS OF INQUIRY" UK CONSTN LEGIS PRESS ADMIN PARL/PROC...DECISION 20 PARLIAMENT. PAGE 59 H1184
DELIB/GP INSPECT POLICY NAT/G

B37
CLOKIE H.M.,ROYAL COMMISSIONS OF INQUIRY; THE SIGNIFICANCE OF INVESTIGATIONS IN BRITISH POLITICS. UK POL/PAR CONFER ROUTINE...POLICY DECISION TIME/SEQ 16/20. PAGE 30 H0607
NAT/G DELIB/GP INSPECT

B40
WOLFERS A.,BRITAIN AND FRANCE BETWEEN TWO WORLD WARS. FRANCE UK INT/ORG NAT/G PLAN BARGAIN ECO/TAC AGREE ISOLAT ALL/IDEOS...DECISION GEOG 20 TREATY VERSAILLES INTERVENT. PAGE 170 H3402
DIPLOM WAR POLICY

B48
LAUTERBACH A.,ECONOMIC SECURITY AND INDIVIDUAL FREEDOM: CAN WE HAVE BOTH? COM EUR+WWI MOD/EUR UNIV WOR+45 CAP/ISM TOTALISM ALL/VALS...GOV/COMP BIBLIOG 20. PAGE 92 H1840
ORD/FREE ECO/DEV DECISION INGP/REL

B48
ROSSITER C.L.,CONSTITUTIONAL DICTATORSHIP; CRISIS GOVERNMENT IN THE MODERN DEMOCRACIES. FRANCE GERMANY UK USA-45 WOR-45 EX/STRUC BAL/PWR CONTROL COERCE WAR CENTRAL ORD/FREE...DECISION 19/20. PAGE 134 H2688
NAT/G AUTHORIT CONSTN TOTALISM

B49
GRODZINS M.,AMERICANS BETRAYED: POLITICS AND THE JAPANESE EXPANSION. PROVS COERCE CHOOSE GOV/REL GP/REL INGP/REL ATTIT ORD/FREE...DECISION CHARTS 20 NISEI. PAGE 61 H1230
DISCRIM POLICY NAT/G WAR

B51
JENNINGS I.,THE COMMONWEALTH IN ASIA. CEYLON INDIA PAKISTAN CULTURE STRATA NAT/G LEGIS DIPLOM COLONIAL ATTIT...DECISION 20 CMN/WLTH. PAGE 80 H1604
CONSTN INT/ORG POLICY PLAN

S53
DRUCKER P.F.,"THE EMPLOYEE SOCIETY." STRUCT BAL/PWR PARTIC REPRESENT PWR...DECISION CONCPT. PAGE 42 H0849
LABOR MGT WORKER CULTURE

B54
GRAYSON H.,ECONOMIC PLANNING UNDER FREE ENTERPRISE. CANADA FUT UK DELIB/GP BUDGET CONFER CONTROL ...POLICY DECISION 20. PAGE 60 H1200
PLAN ECO/TAC NAT/COMP NAT/G

B54
MATTHEWS D.R.,THE SOCIAL BACKGROUND OF POLITICAL DECISION-MAKERS. CULTURE SOCIETY STRATA FAM EX/STRUC LEAD ATTIT BIO/SOC DRIVE PERSON ALL/VALS HIST/WRIT. PAGE 105 H2097
DECISION BIOG SOC

B56
HERNANDEZ URBINA A.,LOS PARTIDOS Y LA CRISIS DEL APRA. PERU NAT/G LEAD LOBBY CHOOSE SOCISM...POLICY DECISION 20 COM/PARTY APRA CONGRESS. PAGE 70 H1402
POL/PAR PARTIC PARL/PROC GP/REL

B57
IKE N.,JAPANESE POLITICS. INTELL STRUCT AGRI INDUS FAM KIN LABOR PRESS CHOOSE ATTIT...DECISION BIBLIOG 19/20 CHINJAP. PAGE 76 H1523
NAT/G ADMIN POL/PAR CULTURE

S57
HODGETTS J.E.,"THE CIVIL SERVICE AND POLICY FORMATION." CANADA NAT/G EX/STRUC ROUTINE GOV/REL 20. PAGE 72 H1443
ADMIN DECISION EFFICIENCY POLICY

S57
SPROUT H.,"ENVIRONMENTAL FACTORS IN THE STUDY OF INTERNATIONAL POLITICS." UNIV SOCIETY ECO/DEV NAT/G DELIB/GP TOP/EX ROUTINE ATTIT PERCEPT...POLICY GEOG CONCPT MYTH TIME/SEQ. PAGE 148 H2957
DECISION GEN/LAWS DIPLOM

B58
DWARKADAS R.,ROLE OF HIGHER CIVIL SERVICE IN INDIA. INDIA ECO/UNDEV LEGIS PROB/SOLV GP/REL PERS/REL ...POLICY WELF/ST DECISION ORG/CHARTS BIBLIOG 20 CIVIL/SERV INTRVN/ECO. PAGE 44 H0876
ADMIN NAT/G ROLE PLAN

B58
JOHNSON J.J.,POLITICAL CHANGE IN LATIN AMERICA: THE EMERGENCE OF THE MIDDLE SECTORS. INTELL STRATA STRUCT ECO/UNDEV MUNIC TEC/DEV LEAD REV...DECISION TREND GOV/COMP BIBLIOG/A 20. PAGE 81 H1621
L/A+17C ELITES GP/REL DOMIN

B58
PALMER E.E.,"POLITICAL MAN" IN E. PALMER, PROBLEMS IN DEMOCRATIC CITIZENSHIP. LOC/G NAT/G LEGIS PRESS CHOOSE REPRESENT GP/REL...DECISION SOC IDEA/COMP ANTHOL 20. PAGE 123 H2449
PARTIC POL/PAR EDU/PROP MAJORIT

B58
SCOTT D.J.R.,RUSSIAN POLITICAL INSTITUTIONS. RUSSIA USSR CONSTN AGRI DELIB/GP PLAN EDU/PROP CONTROL CHOOSE EFFICIENCY ATTIT MARXISM...BIBLIOG/A 13/20. PAGE 141 H2813
NAT/G POL/PAR ADMIN DECISION

B58
WILMERDING L. JR.,THE ELECTORAL COLLEGE. CONSTN NAT/G POL/PAR DELIB/GP LEGIS PROB/SOLV CONFER EXEC LEAD APPORT REPRESENT. PAGE 169 H3377
CHOOSE DECISION ACT/RES

S58
PYE L.W.,"THE NON-WESTERN POLITICAL PROCESS" (BMR)" AFR ASIA ISLAM S/ASIA DIPLOM ADMIN LEAD LOBBY ROUTINE CONSEN...DECISION 20. PAGE 128 H2567
CULTURE POL/PAR NAT/G LOC/G

C58
GOLAY J.F.,"THE FOUNDING OF THE FEDERAL REPUBLIC OF GERMANY." GERMANY/W CONSTN EX/STRUC DIPLOM ADMIN CHOOSE...DECISION BIBLIOG 20. PAGE 58 H1155
FEDERAL NAT/G PARL/PROC POL/PAR

B59
EAENZA L.,COMMUNISMO E CATTOLICESIMO IN UNA PARROCHIA DI CAMPAGNA. ITALY CULTURE ELITES ECO/DEV AGRI KIN POL/PAR DOMIN LEGIT RIGID/FLEX...DECISION OBS IDEA/COMP 20 COM/PARTY CHURCH/STA. PAGE 44 H0878
ATTIT CATHISM NEIGH MARXISM

B59
MILLER A.S.,PRIVATE GOVERNMENTS AND THE CONSTITUTION (PAMPHLET). LAW LABOR NAT/G ROLE PWR PLURISM...POLICY DECISION. PAGE 111 H2211
FEDERAL CONSTN VOL/ASSN CONSEN

B59
SISSON C.H.,THE SPIRIT OF BRITISH ADMINISTRATION AND SOME EUROPEAN COMPARISONS. FRANCE GERMANY/W SWEDEN UK LAW EX/STRUC INGP/REL EFFICIENCY ORD/FREE ...DECISION 20. PAGE 144 H2890
GOV/COMP ADMIN ELITES ATTIT

L59
JANIS I.L.,"DECISIONAL CONFLICT: A THEORETICAL ANALYSIS." INTELL NAT/G POL/PAR DELIB/GP LEGIS TOP/EX PLAN...DECISION CONGRESS NAZI 20 WWI. PAGE 80 H1590
ACT/RES PSY DIPLOM

S59
SILBERMAN L.,"CHANGE AND CONFLICT IN THE HORN OF AFRICA." EUR+WWI ITALY UK CULTURE FORCES ECO/TAC ADJUD COLONIAL ATTIT ORD/FREE PWR...DECISION METH/CNCPT HIST/WRIT SOMALI 20. PAGE 144 H2874
AFR TIME/SEQ

B60
FRANCIS R.G.,THE PREDICTIVE PROCESS. PLAN MARXISM ...DECISION SOC CONCPT NAT/COMP 19/20. PAGE 52 H1047
PREDICT PHIL/SCI TREND

B60
WILLIAMS L.E.,OVERSEAS CHINESE NATIONALISM: THE GENESIS OF THE PAN-CHINESE MOVEMENT IN INDONESIA, 1900-1916. ASIA COM INDONESIA AGRI INT/ORG LOC/G DIPLOM EDU/PROP HABITAT PWR POPULISM...GEOG LING CENSUS 20. PAGE 168 H3367
NAT/LISM GP/REL DECISION NAT/G

S60
LEVINE R.A.,"THE INTERNALIZATION OF POLITICAL VALUES IN STATELESS SOCIETIES." AFR FAM KIN LOC/G PROVS JUDGE PERSON RIGID/FLEX...DECISION SOC TIME/SEQ 20. PAGE 95 H1904
CULTURE ATTIT

S60
TAYLOR M.G.,"THE ROLE OF THE MEDICAL PROFESSION IN THE FORMULATION AND EXECUTION OF PUBLIC POLICY" (BMR)" CANADA NAT/G CONSULT ADMIN REPRESENT GP/REL ROLE SOVEREIGN...DECISION 20 CMA. PAGE 153 H3056
PROF/ORG HEALTH LOBBY POLICY

B61
DELEFORTRIE-SOU N.,LES DIRIGEANTS DE L'INDUSTRIE FRANCAISE. FRANCE CULTURE ELITES PROB/SOLV ...DECISION STAT CHARTS 20. PAGE 39 H0789
INDUS STRATA TOP/EX LEAD

B61
GARCIA E.,LA ADMINISTRACION ESPANOLA. SPAIN GOV/REL ...CONCPT METH/COMP 20. PAGE 55 H1099
ADMIN NAT/G LOC/G DECISION

B61
MAYNE A.,DESIGNING AND ADMINISTERING A REGIONAL ECONOMIC DEVELOPMENT PLAN WITH SPECIFIC REFERENCE TO PUERTO RICO (PAMPHLET). PUERT/RICO SOCIETY NAT/G DELIB/GP REGION...DECISION 20. PAGE 105 H2106
ECO/UNDEV PLAN CREATE ADMIN

B61
MONAS S.,THE THIRD SECTION: POLICE AND SOCIETY IN RUSSIA UNDER NICHOLAS I. MOD/EUR RUSSIA ELITES STRUCT NAT/G EX/STRUC ADMIN CONTROL PWR CONSERVE ...DECISION 19 NICHOLAS/I. PAGE 112 H2238
ORD/FREE COM FORCES COERCE

S61
EHRMANN H.W.,"FRENCH BUREAUCRACY AND ORGANIZED INTERESTS" (BMR)" FRANCE NAT/G DELIB/GP ROUTINE ...INT 20 BUREAUCRCY CIVIL/SERV. PAGE 45 H0897
ADMIN DECISION PLURISM LOBBY

S61
MACRIDIS R.C.,"INTEREST GROUPS IN COMPARATIVE ANALYSIS." CULTURE OP/RES LOBBY REPRESENT GP/REL AUTHORIT ORD/FREE PWR...POLICY DECISION METH/CNCPT CLASSIF. PAGE 101 H2010
GP/COMP CONCPT PLURISM

S61
SCHELLING T.C.,"NUCLEAR STRATEGY IN EUROPE." COM EUR+WWI USSR NAT/G FORCES NUC/PWR DRIVE ORD/FREE PWR...DECISION CONCPT OBS TREND HYPO/EXP 20. PAGE 139 H2784
FUT COERCE ARMS/CONT WAR

B62
KASTARI P.,LA PRESIDENCE DE LA REPUBLIQUE EN FINLANDE. FINLAND CONSTN NAT/G POL/PAR LEGIS LEGIT ATTIT...JURID CONCPT 20 PRESIDENT. PAGE 83 H1666
PARL/PROC CHIEF PWR DECISION

B62
SCALAPINO R.A.,PARTIES AND POLITICS IN CONTEMPORARY JAPAN. EX/STRUC DIPLOM CHOOSE NAT/LISM ATTIT ...POLICY 20 CHINJAP. PAGE 138 H2762
POL/PAR PARL/PROC ELITES DECISION

B62
THIERRY S.S.,LE VATICAN SECRET. CHRIST-17C EUR+WWI MOD/EUR VATICAN NAT/G SECT DELIB/GP DOMIN LEGIT SOVEREIGN. PAGE 154 H3072
ADMIN EX/STRUC CATHISM DECISION

B62
TURNBULL C.M.,THE LONELY AFRICAN. AFR MUNIC SECT ANOMIE ALL/VALS...DECISION 20. PAGE 157 H3139
CULTURE ISOLAT KIN TRADIT

S62
MARTIN L.W.,"THE MARKET FOR STRATEGIC IDEAS IN BRITAIN: THE 'SANDYS ERA'" UK ARMS/CONT WAR GOV/REL OPTIMAL...POLICY DECISION GOV/COMP COLD/WAR CMN/WLTH. PAGE 103 H2063
DIPLOM COERCE FORCES PWR

B63
DEBRAY P.,LE PORTUGAL ENTRE DEUX REVOLUTIONS. EUR+WWI PORTUGAL CONSTN LEGIT ADMIN ATTIT ALL/VALS ...DECISION CONCPT 20 SALAZAR/A. PAGE 39 H0779
NAT/G DELIB/GP TOP/EX

B63
DEUTSCH K.W.,THE NERVES OF GOVERNMENT. NAT/G CREATE EDU/PROP CONTROL LEAD PWR...CONCPT GEN/LAWS 20. PAGE 40 H0799
DECISION GAME SIMUL OP/RES

B63
FRANKEL J.,THE MAKING OF FOREIGN POLICY: AN ANALYSIS OF DECISION-MAKING. CHINA/COM EUR+WWI USA+45 ELITES INTELL FORCES LEGIS PLAN ATTIT ALL/VALS MORAL CONSERVE...GOV/COMP 20 PRESIDENT UN TREATY. PAGE 53 H1051
POLICY DECISION PROB/SOLV DIPLOM

B63
INDIAN INSTITUTE PUBLIC ADMIN,CASES IN INDIAN ADMINISTRATION. INDIA AGRI NAT/G PROB/SOLV TEC/DEV ECO/TAC ADMIN...ANTHOL METH 20. PAGE 77 H1532
DECISION PLAN MGT ECO/UNDEV

B63
JACOB H.,GERMAN ADMINISTRATION SINCE BISMARCK: CENTRAL AUTHORITY VERSUS LOCAL AUTONOMY. GERMANY GERMANY/W LAW POL/PAR CONTROL CENTRAL TOTALISM FASCISM...MAJORIT DECISION STAT CHARTS GOV/COMP 19/20 BISMARCK/O HITLER/A WEIMAR/REP. PAGE 79 H1577
ADMIN NAT/G LOC/G POLICY

B63
KOGAN N.,THE POLITICS OF ITALIAN FOREIGN POLICY. EUR+WWI LEGIS DOMIN LEGIT EXEC PWR RESPECT SKILL ...POLICY DECISION HUM SOC METH/CNCPT OBS INT CHARTS 20. PAGE 87 H1737
NAT/G ROUTINE DIPLOM ITALY

B63
MENZEL J.M.,THE CHINESE CIVIL SERVICE: CAREER OPEN TO TALENT? ASIA ROUTINE INGP/REL DISCRIM ATTIT ROLE KNOWL ANTHOL. PAGE 109 H2177
ADMIN NAT/G DECISION ELITES

B63
SCHUMAN S.I.,LEGAL POSITIVISM: ITS SCOPE AND LIMITATIONS. CONSTN NAT/G DIPLOM PARTIC UTOPIA ...POLICY DECISION PHIL/SCI CONCPT 20. PAGE 140 H2802
GEN/METH LAW METH/COMP

B64
AGGER R.E.,THE RULERS AND THE RULED: POLITICAL POWER AND IMPOTENCE IN AMERICAN COMMUNITIES. CULTURE DOMIN CHOOSE ATTIT ALL/VALS...DECISION SOC CONCPT OBS QU CHARTS. PAGE 4 H0079
PWR STRUCT LOC/G MUNIC

B64
BRIGHT J.R.,RESEARCH, DEVELOPMENT AND TECHNOLOGICAL INNOVATION. CULTURE R+D CREATE PLAN PROB/SOLV AUTOMAT RISK PERSON...DECISION CONCPT PREDICT BIBLIOG. PAGE 21 H0419
TEC/DEV NEW/IDEA INDUS MGT

B64
COLLINS B.E.,A SOCIAL PSYCHOLOGY OF GROUP PROCESSES FOR DECISION-MAKING. PROB/SOLV ROUTINE...SOC CHARTS HYPO/EXP. PAGE 32 H0632
FACE/GP DECISION NAT/G INDUS

B64
DANIELS R.V.,RUSSIA. RUSSIA USSR STRUCT NAT/LISM TOTALISM ORD/FREE WEALTH...POLICY DECISION TREND. PAGE 37 H0740
MARXISM REV ECO/DEV DIPLOM

B64
DOWNIE R.S.,GOVERNMENT ACTION AND MORALITY: SOME PRINCIPLES AND CONCEPTS OF LIBERAL-DEMOCRACY. UK PARL/PROC ATTIT ROLE...MAJORIT DECISION CONCPT 20. PAGE 42 H0845
NAT/G MORAL POLICY GEN/LAWS

B64
RIES J.C.,THE MANAGEMENT OF DEFENSE: ORGANIZATION AND CONTROL OF THE US ARMED SERVICES. PROF/ORG DELIB/GP EX/STRUC LEGIS GOV/REL PERS/REL CENTRAL RATIONAL PWR...POLICY TREND GOV/COMP BIBLIOG. PAGE 131 H2626
FORCES ACT/RES DECISION CONTROL

B64
ZARTMAN I.W.,MOROCCO: PROBLEMS OF NEW POWER. ISLAM CULTURE ECO/UNDEV AGRI POL/PAR SCHOOL FORCES ADMIN ...CONCPT STAT INT CENSUS TIME/SEQ CHARTS WORK VAL/FREE 20. PAGE 172 H3449
CHOOSE MOROCCO DELIB/GP DECISION

S64
COLEMAN J.S.,"COLLECTIVE DECISIONS." CULTURE ATTIT PERCEPT PWR SOC. PAGE 31 H0628
DECISION INGP/REL PERSON METH/COMP

S64
GOLDBERG A.,"THE MILITARY ORIGINS OF THE BRITISH NUCLEAR DETERRENT." EUR+WWI ECO/DEV NAT/G PLAN NUC/PWR ATTIT PWR...DECISION HIST/WRIT COLD/WAR 20. PAGE 58 H1156
FORCES CONCPT DETER UK

S64
LEVI W.,"INDIAN NEUTRALISM RECONSIDERED." ASIA CHINA/COM S/ASIA SOCIETY NAT/G ACT/RES LEGIT NEUTRAL COERCE ATTIT DRIVE PERCEPT RIGID/FLEX HEALTH LOVE PWR...DECISION RECORD TREND STERTYP 20. PAGE 95 H1896
ORD/FREE CONCPT INDIA

S64
UNRUH J.M.,"SCIENTIFIC INPUTS TO LEGISLATIVE DECISION-MAKING (SUPPLEMENT)" USA+45 ACADEM NAT/G PROVS GOV/REL GOV/COMP. PAGE 159 H3171
CREATE DECISION LEGIS PARTIC

B65
ALLEN W.S.,THE NAZI SEIZURE OF POWER. GERMANY NAT/G CHIEF LEAD COERCE CHOOSE REPRESENT GOV/REL AUTHORIT ...DECISION 20 HITLER/A NAZI. PAGE 5 H0106
MUNIC FASCISM TOTALISM LOC/G

B65
BAYNE E.A.,FOUR WAYS OF POLITICS: STATE AND NATION IN ITALY, SOMALIA, ISRAEL, AND IRAN. IRAN ISRAEL ITALY SOMALIA LEAD CHOOSE MAJORITY GOV/COMP. PAGE 12 H0244
ECO/UNDEV NAT/G DECISION TOP/EX

B65
BORTOLI G.,SOCIOLOGIE DU REFERENDUM DANS LA FRANCE MODERNE. FRANCE CONSTN EDU/PROP SUFF ATTIT ORD/FREE ...POLICY DECISION CHARTS BIBLIOG 20 DEGAULLE/C. PAGE 19 H0379
LEGIS SOCIETY PWR NAT/G

B65
DAHL R.A.,MODERN POLITICAL ANALYSIS. UNIV COERCE ...MAJORIT DECISION METH. PAGE 36 H0731
CONCPT GOV/COMP PWR

B65
JACOB H.,POLITICS IN THE AMERICAN STATES; A COMPARATIVE ANALYSIS. USA+45 POL/PAR CHIEF LEGIS TAX EDU/PROP CONTROL CT/SYS LOBBY PARTIC...DECISION CHARTS 20. PAGE 79 H1578
PROVS GOV/COMP PWR

B65
RUBINSTEIN A.Z.,THE CHALLENGE OF POLITICS: IDEAS AND ISSUES (2ND ED.). UNIV ELITES SOCIETY EX/STRUC BAL/PWR PARL/PROC AUTHORIT...DECISION ANTHOL 20. PAGE 136 H2709
NAT/G DIPLOM GP/REL ORD/FREE

B65
UPTON A.F.,FINLAND IN CRISIS 1940-1941. NAT/G FORCES DIPLOM COERCE...DECISION GEOG. PAGE 159 H3173
FINLAND GERMANY USSR WAR

S65
BIRNBAUM K.,"SWEDEN'S NUCLEAR POLICY." WOR+45 POL/PAR CREATE TEC/DEV NEUTRAL RISK WAR ORD/FREE ...DECISION IDEA/COMP NAT/COMP TIME. PAGE 17 H0343
SWEDEN NUC/PWR DIPLOM ARMS/CONT

S65
WOHLSTETTER R.,"CUBA AND PEARL HARBOR* HINDSIGHT AND FORESIGHT." USSR FORCES OP/RES TEC/DEV ATTIT PERCEPT...DECISION IDEA/COMP NAT/COMP STERTYP TIME. PAGE 170 H3395
CUBA RISK WAR ACT/RES

C65
BORTOLI G.,"SOCIOLOGIE DU REFERENDUM DANS LA FRANCE MODERNE." FRANCE CONSTN NAT/G EDU/PROP SUFF ATTIT ORD/FREE...POLICY DECISION SOC CHARTS 20. PAGE 19 H0378
BIBLIOG LEGIS SOCIETY PWR

B66
AMER ENTERPRISE INST PUB POL,SIGNIFICANT ISSUES IN ECONOMIC AID TO DEVELOPING COUNTRIES. FINAN INT/ORG NAT/G PLAN PROB/SOLV GIVE TASK WEALTH...DECISION 20. PAGE 6 H0119
ECO/UNDEV FOR/AID DIPLOM POLICY

B66
BRECHER M.,SUCCESSION IN INDIA. INDIA USA+45 CONSTN AGRI POL/PAR PROVS SECT DELIB/GP FORCES PROB/SOLV ECO/TAC PWR...LING 20 CONGRESS NEHRU/J. PAGE 20 H0408
CHIEF DECISION CHOOSE

B66
FOX K.A.,THE THEORY OF QUANTITATIVE ECONOMIC POLICY WITH APPLICATIONS TO ECONOMIC GROWTH AND STABILIZATION. ECO/DEV AGRI NAT/G PLAN ADMIN RISK ...DECISION IDEA/COMP SIMUL T. PAGE 52 H1045
ECO/TAC ECOMETRIC EQUILIB GEN/LAWS

B66
HOLDSWORTH W.S.,A HISTORY OF ENGLISH LAW; THE CENTURIES OF SETTLEMENT AND REFORM (VOL. XVI). UK LOC/G NAT/G EX/STRUC LEGIS CT/SYS LEAD ATTIT ...POLICY DECISION JURID IDEA/COMP 18 PARLIAMENT. PAGE 73 H1454
BIOG PERSON PROF/ORG LAW

B66
KEAY E.A.,THE NATIVE AND CUSTOMARY COURTS OF NIGERIA. NIGERIA CONSTN ELITES NAT/G TOP/EX PARTIC REGION...DECISION JURID 19/20. PAGE 84 H1673
AFR ADJUD LAW

B66
OWEN G.,INDUSTRY IN THE UNITED STATES. UK USA+45 NAT/G WEALTH...DECISION NAT/COMP 20. PAGE 122 H2436
METH/COMP INDUS MGT PROB/SOLV

B66
ROSS A.M.,INDUSTRIAL RELATIONS AND ECONOMIC DEVELOPMENT. POL/PAR LEGIS WORKER BARGAIN PRICE EXEC LOBBY INCOME PWR...DECISION ANTHOL BIBLIOG 20. PAGE 134 H2686
ECO/UNDEV LABOR NAT/G GP/REL

B66
SKILLING H.G.,THE GOVERNMENTS OF COMMUNIST EAST EUROPE. COM EUR+WWI ELITES FORCES DIPLOM ECO/TAC CONTROL HABITAT SOCISM...DECISION BIBLIOG 20 EUROPE/E COM/PARTY. PAGE 145 H2895
MARXISM NAT/COMP GP/COMP DOMIN

B66
STADLER K.R.,THE BIRTH OF THE AUSTRIAN REPUBLIC, 1918-1921. AUSTRIA PLAN TASK PEACE...POLICY DECISION 20. PAGE 148 H2966
NAT/G DIPLOM WAR DELIB/GP

L66
ZOPPO C.E.,"NUCLEAR TECHNOLOGY, MULTIPOLARITY, AND INTERNATIONAL STABILITY." ASIA RUSSIA USA+45 STRUCT TOP/EX BAL/PWR DIPLOM DETER CIVMIL/REL NAT/COMP. PAGE 173 H3464
NET/THEORY ORD/FREE DECISION NUC/PWR

S66
FELD W.,"NATIONAL ECONOMIC INTEREST GROUPS AND POLICY FORMATION IN THE EEC." NAT/G POL/PAR REGION CENTRAL SOVEREIGN...INT NET/THEORY EEC. PAGE 49 H0985
LOBBY ELITES DECISION

S66
MCLANE C.B.,"SOVIET DOCTRINE AND THE MILITARY COUPS IN AFRICA." ALGERIA GHANA COLONIAL NAT/LISM RIGID/FLEX SOVEREIGN MARXISM...DECISION NAT/COMP. PAGE 107 H2140
USSR ATTIT AFR FORCES

B67
GROSS B.M.,ACTION UNDER PLANNING: THE GUIDANCE OF ECONOMIC DEVELOPMENT. STRUCT R+D NAT/G ACT/RES HABITAT...DECISION 20. PAGE 62 H1232
ECO/UNDEV PLAN ADMIN MGT

B67
RUDMAN H.C.,THE SCHOOL AND STATE IN THE USSR. COM USSR ACADEM LABOR LOC/G PUB/INST EDU/PROP GP/REL ROLE...POLICY DECISION MGT CHARTS 20. PAGE 136 H2712
SCHOOL ADMIN NAT/G POL/PAR

B67
SHAPIRO P.S.,COMMUNICATIONS OR TRANSPORT: DECISION-MAKING IN DEVELOPING COUNTRIES. WOR+45 NAT/G PLAN ALL/IDEOS MARXISM...NAT/COMP GEN/LAWS. PAGE 142 H2844
BUDGET COM/IND DECISION ECO/DEV

B67
WALTZ K.N.,FOREIGN POLICY AND DEMOCRATIC POLITICS: THE AMERICAN AND BRITISH EXPERIENCE. FRANCE UK USA+45 PARL/PROC GOV/REL CONSERVE...DECISION 20. PAGE 165 H3298
POLICY DIPLOM NAT/G GOV/COMP

B67
WIENER F.B.,CIVILIANS UNDER MILITARY JUSTICE; THE BRITISH PRACTICE SINCE 1689 ESPECIALLY IN NORTH AMERICA. UK USA-45 LAW CONSTN CRIME REV...DECISION CHARTS NAT/COMP BIBLIOG 17/20. PAGE 168 H3356
CT/SYS FORCES ADJUD

B67
ZALESKI E.,PLANNING REFORMS IN THE SOVIET UNION 1962-1966. COM USSR NAT/G CONFER CONTROL EFFICIENCY MARXISM...POLICY DECISION 20. PAGE 172 H3446
ECO/DEV PLAN ADMIN CENTRAL

L67
TOUVAL S.,"THE ORGANIZATION OF AFRICAN UNITY AND AFRICAN BORDERS." DEBATE REGION TASK REV ATTIT ORD/FREE...DECISION UN 20 OAU. PAGE 156 H3121
AFR NAT/G COLONIAL NAT/LISM

S67
ABDEL-MALEK A.,"THE CRISIS IN NASSER'S EGYPT." ISLAM UAR STRUCT POL/PAR EX/STRUC CREATE PLAN WAR ATTIT ORD/FREE PWR...POLICY DECISION 20. PAGE 3 H0054
FORCES LEAD PROB/SOLV NAT/G

S67
ADAMS R.N.,"ETHICS AND THE SOCIAL ANTHROPOLOGIST IN LATIN AMERICA." USA+45 INTELL PROB/SOLV ECO/TAC LEAD...DECISION SOC NAT/COMP PERS/COMP. PAGE 3 H0066
L/A+17C POLICY ECO/UNDEV CONSULT

S67
CAMERON R.,"SOME LESSONS OF HISTORY FOR DEVELOPING NATIONS." WOR+45 WOR-45 FINAN NAT/G WORKER EDU/PROP PARTIC ROLE...DECISION METH/COMP 18/20. PAGE 25 H0511
ECO/UNDEV NAT/COMP POLICY CONCPT

S67
CARIAS B.,"EL CONTROL DE LAS EMPRESAS PUBLICAS POR GRUPOS DE INTERESES DE LA COMUNIDAD." FRANCE UK VENEZUELA INDUS NAT/G CONTROL OWN PWR...DECISION NAT/COMP 20. PAGE 26 H0529
WORKER REPRESENT MGT SOCISM

S67
COLLINS B.A.,"SOME NOTES ON PUBLIC SERVICE COMMISSIONS IN THE COMMONWEALTH CARIBBEAN." JAMAICA L/A+17C TRINIDAD UK NAT/G OP/RES DOMIN SENIOR COLONIAL CONTROL INGP/REL CENTRAL EFFICIENCY PWR ...DECISION 20. PAGE 31 H0631
ADMIN EX/STRUC ECO/UNDEV CHOOSE

S67
CROCKETT D.G.,"THE MP AND HIS CONSTITUENTS." UK POL/PAR...DECISION 20. PAGE 35 H0706
EXEC NAT/G PERS/REL REPRESENT

S67
DIAMANT A.,"EUROPEAN MODELS OF BUREAUCRACY AND DEVELOPMENT." EX/STRUC PLAN ADMIN CONTROL ROUTINE GOV/REL CENTRAL...DECISION TIME/SEQ CHARTS. PAGE 41 H0818
NAT/G EQUILIB ACT/RES NAT/COMP

S67
DRYDEN S.,"LOCAL GOVERNMENT IN TANZANIA PART II" TANZANIA LAW NAT/G POL/PAR CONTROL PARTIC REPRESENT ...DECISION 20. PAGE 42 H0850
LOC/G GOV/REL ADMIN STRUCT

S67
GREGORY R.,"THE MINISTER'S LINE: OR, THE M4 COMES TO BERKSHIRE. PART I." UK CONSTN DIST/IND LEGIS TOP/EX PLAN ADJUD...GEOG 20. PAGE 60 H1210
DECISION CONSTRUC NAT/G DELIB/GP

S67
KASFIR N.,"THE UGANDA CONSTITUENT ASSEMBLY DEBATE." UGANDA REPRESENT FEDERAL ORD/FREE POPULISM...POLICY DECISION 20. PAGE 83 H1665
CONSTN CONFER LAW NAT/G

S67
KROLL M.,"POLITICAL LEADERSHIP AND ADMINISTRATIVE COMMUNICATIONS IN NEW NATION STATES* CASE STUDY OF TRINIDAD AND TOBAGO." L/A+17C TRINIDAD INTELL OP/RES DOMIN COLONIAL LEAD GP/REL CENTRAL EFFICIENCY...DECISION OBS METH/COMP 20. PAGE 89 H1774
NAT/G ADMIN EDU/PROP CONTROL

S67
LEVCIK B.,"WAGES AND EMPLOYMENT PROBLEMS IN THE NEW SYSTEM OF PLANNED MANAGEMENT IN CZECHOSLOVAKIA." CZECHOSLVK EUR+WWI NAT/G OP/RES PLAN ADMIN ROUTINE INGP/REL CENTRAL EFFICIENCY PRODUC DECISION. PAGE 95 H1895
MARXISM WORKER MGT PAY

S67
LICHFIELD N.,"THE EVALUATION OF CAPITAL INVESTMENT PROJECTS IN TOWN CENTRE REDEVELOPMENT." UK CONSTRUC MUNIC CONSULT COST...METH/CNCPT IDEA/COMP 20. PAGE 96 H1923
PLAN ECO/TAC NAT/G DECISION

S67
MALLORY J.R.,"THE MINISTER'S OFFICE STAFF* AN UNREFORMED PART OF PUBLIC SERVICE." CONSTN ELITES STRATA NAT/G PROB/SOLV TASK CHOOSE PERS/REL EFFICIENCY...DECISION 20. PAGE 102 H2033
CANADA ADMIN EX/STRUC STRUCT

S67
OJHA I.C.,"CHINA'S CAUTIOUS AMERICAN POLICY." CHINA/COM VIETNAM NAT/G NUC/PWR PEACE 20. PAGE 121 H2411
DIPLOM POLICY WAR DECISION

S67
SHELDON C.H.,"PUBLIC OPINION AND HIGH COURTS: COMMUNIST PARTY CASES IN FOUR CONSTITUTIONAL SYSTEMS." CANADA GERMANY/W WOR+45 POL/PAR MARXISM ...METH/COMP NAT/COMP 20 AUSTRAL. PAGE 143 H2857
ATTIT CT/SYS CONSTN DECISION

S67
TATU M.,"URSS: LES FLOTTEMENTS DE LA DIRECTION
POLICY

COLLEGIALE." UAR USSR CHIEF LEAD INGP/REL EFFICIENCY...DECISION TREND 20 MID/EAST. PAGE 152 H3047 — NAT/G EX/STRUC DIPLOM

S67
TIVEY L.,"THE POLITICAL CONSEQUENCES OF ECONOMIC PLANNING." UK CONSTN INDUS ACT/RES ADMIN CONTROL LOBBY REPRESENT EFFICIENCY SUPEGO SOVEREIGN ...DECISION 20. PAGE 155 H3108 — PLAN POLICY NAT/G

S67
WHITE W.L.,"THE TREASURY BOARD AND PARLIAMENT." CANADA CONSTN CONSULT LEGIS LEAD PARL/PROC GP/REL ...DECISION 20. PAGE 167 H3351 — FINAN DELIB/GP NAT/G ADMIN

DECISION-MAKING, DISIPLINE....SEE DECISION

DECISION-MAKING, INDIVIDUAL....SEE PROB/SOLV, PWR

DECISION-MAKING, PROCEDURAL....SEE PROB/SOLV

DECISION-MAKING, THEORY....SEE GAME

DECLAR/IND....DECLARATION OF INDEPENDENCE (U.S.)

B44
WOLFE D.M.,LEVELLER MANIFESTOES OF THE PURITAN REVOLUTION. UK CONSTN NAT/G SECT...CONCPT ANTHOL 17 LEVELLERS DECLAR/IND PURITAN LOCKE/JOHN. PAGE 170 H3400 — POL/PAR REV ORD/FREE ATTIT

B64
MINAR D.W.,IDEAS AND POLITICS: THE AMERICAN EXPERIENCE. SECT CHIEF LEGIS CREATE ADJUD EXEC REV PWR...PHIL/SCI CONCPT IDEA/COMP 18/20 HAMILTON/A JEFFERSN/T DECLAR/IND JACKSON/A PRESIDENT. PAGE 111 H2220 — CONSTN NAT/G FEDERAL

DECOTTIGNIES R. H0781

DEEP/INT....DEPTH INTERVIEWS

B56
MANNONI D.O.,PROSPERO AND CALIBAN: THE PSYCHOLOGY OF COLONIZATION. AFR EUR+WWI FAM KIN MUNIC SECT DOMIN ADMIN ATTIT DRIVE LOVE PWR RESPECT...PSY SOC CONCPT MYTH OBS DEEP/INT BIOG GEN/METH MALAGASY 20. PAGE 102 H2040 — CULTURE COLONIAL

S59
SCOTT W.A.,"EMPIRICAL ASSESSMENT OF VALUES AND IDEOLOGIES." CULTURE SOCIETY SECT CREATE DRIVE PERSON MORAL PWR...SOC METH/CNCPT STAT CONT/OBS DEEP/INT DEEP/QU CHARTS VAL/FREE. PAGE 141 H2817 — ATTIT PSY

B63
ALMOND G.A.,THE CIVIC CULTURE: POLITICAL ATTITUDES AND DEMOCRACY IN FIVE NATIONS. GERMANY/W ITALY UK USA+45 SOCIETY STRUCT PARTIC...SOC DEEP/INT SAMP 20 MEXIC/AMER. PAGE 6 H0113 — POPULISM CULTURE NAT/COMP ATTIT

B67
EVANS R.H.,COEXISTENCE: COMMUNISM AND ITS PRACTICE IN BOLOGNA, 1945-1965. ITALY CAP/ISM ADMIN CHOOSE PEACE ORD/FREE...SOC STAT DEEP/INT SAMP CHARTS BIBLIOG 20. PAGE 48 H0952 — MARXISM CULTURE MUNIC POL/PAR

DEEP/QU....DEPTH QUESTIONNAIRES

S59
SCOTT W.A.,"EMPIRICAL ASSESSMENT OF VALUES AND IDEOLOGIES." CULTURE SOCIETY SECT CREATE DRIVE PERSON MORAL PWR...SOC METH/CNCPT STAT CONT/OBS DEEP/INT DEEP/QU CHARTS VAL/FREE. PAGE 141 H2817 — ATTIT PSY

B64
WALDMAN E.,THE GOOSE STEP IS VERBOTEN: THE GERMAN ARMY TODAY. GERMANY/W LAW CONSTN LEGIS PROB/SOLV DOMIN CONTROL CIVMIL/REL GOV/REL INGP/REL ATTIT ...DEEP/QU 20. PAGE 164 H3289 — SOC FORCES NAT/G

DEFENSE....SEE DETER, PLAN, FORCES, WAR, COERCE

DEFENSE DEPARTMENT....SEE DEPT/DEFEN

DEFINETT/B....BRUNO DEFINETTI

DEFLATION....DEFLATION

DEGAULLE/C....CHARLES DE GAULLE

B48
WRIGHT G.,THE RESHAPING OF FRENCH DEMOCRACY. FRANCE NAT/G POL/PAR SECT LEAD CHOOSE GP/REL INGP/REL MARXISM SOCISM...CHARTS BIBLIOG 20 DEGAULLE/C. PAGE 171 H3418 — CONSTN POPULISM CREATE LEGIS

B59
LEITES N.,ON THE GAME OF POLITICS IN FRANCE. ALGERIA FRANCE CONSTN SECT VOL/ASSN ECO/TAC INT/TRADE PARL/PROC WAR SOCISM 20 DEGAULLE/C EEC. PAGE 94 H1871 — POL/PAR NAT/G LEGIS IDEA/COMP

B60
FURNISS E.S.,FRANCE, TROUBLED ALLY. EUR+WWI FUT CULTURE SOCIETY BAL/PWR ADMIN ATTIT DRIVE PWR ...TREND TOT/POP 20 DEGAULLE/C. PAGE 54 H1079 — NAT/G FRANCE

B60
MACRIDIS R.C.,THE DE GAULLE REPUBLIC: QUEST FOR UNITY. EUR+WWI NAT/G POL/PAR LEGIS LEGIT NAT/LISM ATTIT RIGID/FLEX ORD/FREE PWR...JURID CONCPT TIME/SEQ 20 DEGAULLE/C. PAGE 100 H2009 — TOP/EX STRUCT FRANCE

B60
PICKLES D.,THE FIFTH FRENCH REPUBLIC. ALGERIA FRANCE CHOOSE GOV/REL ATTIT CONSERVE...CHARTS 20 DEGAULLE/C. PAGE 125 H2506 — CONSTN ADJUD NAT/G EFFICIENCY

B61
LA PONCE J.A.,THE GOVERNMENT OF THE FIFTH REPUBLIC: FRENCH POLITICAL PARTIES AND THE CONSTITUTION. ALGERIA FRANCE LAW NAT/G DELIB/GP LEGIS ECO/TAC MARXISM SOCISM...CHARTS BIBLIOG/A 20 DEGAULLE/C. PAGE 90 H1794 — PWR POL/PAR CONSTN CHIEF

B63
JUDD P.,AFRICAN INDEPENDENCE: THE EXPLODING EMERGENCE OF THE NEW AFRICAN NATIONS. AFR UK LAW CONSTN CULTURE KIN DIPLOM ATTIT...CHARTS BIBLIOG 20 UN DEGAULLE/C NEGRO THIRD/WRLD. PAGE 82 H1640 — ORD/FREE POLICY DOMIN LOC/G

B63
KLEIMAN R.,ATLANTIC CRISIS; AMERICAN DIPLOMACY CONFRONTS A RESURGENT EUROPE. EUR+WWI USA+45 ECO/DEV AGRI NAT/G CHIEF FORCES PLAN LEAD ATTIT ...CONCPT 20 NATO KENNEDY/JF DEGAULLE/C EEC JOHNSON/LB. PAGE 87 H1731 — DIPLOM REGION POLICY

S63
LERNER D.,"WILL EUROPEAN UNION BRING ABOUT MERGED NATIONAL GOALS." EUR+WWI FRANCE GERMANY UK ECO/DEV NAT/G VOL/ASSN DELIB/GP BAL/PWR ECO/TAC NAT/LISM EEC 20 DEGAULLE/C. PAGE 95 H1889 — ATTIT STERTYP ELITES REGION

B64
WHITE D.S.,SEEDS OF DISCORD. EUR+WWI FRANCE NAT/G VOL/ASSN FORCES DIPLOM DOMIN NAT/LISM DISPL RIGID/FLEX PWR...RECORD INT BIOG 20 DEGAULLE/C ROOSEVLT/F CHURCHLL/W HULL. PAGE 167 H3347 — TOP/EX ATTIT

B65
BORTOLI G.,SOCIOLOGIE DU REFERENDUM DANS LA FRANCE MODERNE. FRANCE CONSTN EDU/PROP SUFF ATTIT ORD/FREE ...POLICY DECISION CHARTS BIBLIOG 20 DEGAULLE/C. PAGE 19 H0379 — LEGIS SOCIETY PWR NAT/G

B65
CALLEO D.P.,EUROPE'S FUTURE: THE GRAND ALTERNATIVES. UK INT/ORG DIPLOM PWR SOVEREIGN ...CONCPT IDEA/COMP NAT/COMP BIBLIOG 20 EEC EUROPE DEGAULLE/C NATO. PAGE 25 H0506 — FUT EUR+WWI FEDERAL NAT/LISM

S65
CAIRNS J.C.,"FRANCE, DECEMBER 1965: END OF THE ELECTIVE MONARACHY" EUR+WWI FRANCE FUT CONSTN SOCIETY CHIEF BAL/PWR ATTIT ALL/IDEOS 20 DEGAULLE/C PRESIDENT. PAGE 25 H0505 — CHOOSE NAT/G POL/PAR PWR

B66
SAINDERICHIN P.,HISTORIE SECRETE D'UNE ELECTION, DECEMBER 5-19, 1965. FRANCE NAT/G DELIB/GP LEGIS PLAN EDU/PROP TV SOCISM...MARXIST 20 DEGAULLE/C. PAGE 137 H2731 — CHOOSE CHIEF PROB/SOLV POL/PAR

B66
SPEARS E.L.,TWO MEN WHO SAVED FRANCE: PETAIN AND DE GAULLE. FRANCE CONSTN FORCES DIPLOM WAR PERSON 20 WWI PETAIN/HP DEGAULLE/C. PAGE 147 H2942 — BIOG LEAD CHIEF NAT/G

B67
MENARD O.D.,THE ARMY AND THE FIFTH REPUBLIC. ALGERIA FRANCE VIETNAM ELITES STRATA COLONIAL CONTROL LOBBY WAR CIVMIL/REL ROLE PWR...POLICY 20 DEGAULLE/C. PAGE 108 H2169 — FORCES ATTIT NAT/G

B67
PLANCK C.R.,THE CHANGING STATUS OF GERMAN REUNIFICATION IN WESTERN DIPLOMACY, 1955-1966. GERMANY DELIB/GP PLAN PEACE...TREND 20 KENNEDY/JF DEGAULLE/C. PAGE 126 H2519 — NAT/G DIPLOM CENTRAL

S67
MENDL W.,"FRENCH ATTITUDES ON DISARMAMENT." FRANCE CULTURE CHIEF FORCES DIPLOM LEAD WAR...TIME/SEQ 20 DEGAULLE/C. PAGE 109 H2175 — NUC/PWR WEAPON ARMS/CONT POLICY

S67
ROOT W.,"REPORT FROM PARIS - DE GAULLE: WHICH WAY TO THE FUTURE?" CANADA FRANCE ISLAM UK INT/ORG CHIEF CREATE AGREE CONTROL ARMS/CONT NUC/PWR EQUILIB PEACE PWR 20 DEGAULLE/C NATO. PAGE 134 H2670 — POLICY DIPLOM NAT/G BAL/PWR

L68
CURRENT HISTORY,"DE GAULLE'S FRANCE." FRANCE MOD/EUR WOR+45 INDUS MARKET INT/ORG BUDGET DIPLOM AUTHORIT DRIVE...GOV/COMP IDEA/COMP 20 DEGAULLE/C EEC. PAGE 36 H0723 — INT/TRADE PERSON LEAD NAT/LISM

S68
VERAX,"L'EUROPE ET LA FRANCE SUR LA SELLETTE." FRANCE UK NAT/G CHIEF DIPLOM EDU/PROP GP/REL 20 EEC DEGAULLE/C. PAGE 162 H3242 — INT/TRADE INT/ORG POLICY

ECO/TAC

DEGLER C.N. H0782

DEHIO L. H0783,H0784

DEITY....DEITY: GOD AND GODS

B16
PUFENDORF S.,LAW OF NATURE AND OF NATIONS (ABRIDGED). UNIV LAW NAT/G DIPLOM AGREE WAR PERSON ALL/VALS PWR...POLICY 18 DEITY NATURL/LAW. PAGE 128 H2565 — CONCPT INT/LAW SECT MORAL

B36
VICO G.B.,DIRITTO UNIVERSALE (1722) (VOL. 2, PARTS 1,2, AND 3, OF G.B. VICO, OPERE). UNIV DIPLOM AGREE WAR OWN KNOWL ORD/FREE SOVEREIGN DEITY. PAGE 162 H3249 — JURID SECT CONCPT NAT/G

C36
MAZZINI J.,"FROM THE COUNCIL TO GOD" (1870) IN J. MAZZINI, ESSAYS." ITALY NAT/G EDU/PROP PARTIC ORD/FREE PWR SOVEREIGN 19 POPE CHRISTIAN DEITY. PAGE 106 H2112 — CATHISM DOMIN NAT/LISM SUPEGO

B54
PARRINDER G.,AFRICAN TRADITIONAL RELIGION. AFR SOCIETY EDU/PROP GP/REL PWR...SOC CONCPT IDEA/COMP WORSHIP 20 DEITY. PAGE 124 H2469 — SECT MYTH ATTIT CULTURE

B66
ELLIS A.B.,THE EWE-SPEAKING PEOPLES OF THE SLAVE COAST OF WEST AFRICA. AFR FORCES ADJUST...LING RECORD GP/COMP WORSHIP 20 AFRICA/W DEITY. PAGE 45 H0910 — MYTH CULTURE HABITAT

S67
KINGSBURY E.C.,"LAW AS COMPACT: ANCIENT ISRAEL'S CONTRIBUTION TO THE UNDERSTANDING OF LAW." ISRAEL MEDIT-7 CULTURE KIN KNOWL...JURID CONCPT TREND IDEA/COMP METH/COMP WORSHIP JEWS DEITY. PAGE 86 H1716 — LAW AGREE CONSTN INGP/REL

B70
BOSSUET J.B.,"POLITIQUE TIREE DE L'ECRITURE SAINTE" (1679-1709) IN J.B. BOSSUET, OEVRES DE BOSSUET. NAT/G GP/REL AUTHORIT HEREDITY PERSON ALL/VALS SOVEREIGN 18 BIBLE DEITY CHRISTIAN. PAGE 19 H0383 — TRADIT CHIEF SECT CONCPT

DE-STALINIZATION....SEE DESTALIN

DEKAT A.D.A. H0785

DEL TORO J. H0786

DEL VAYO J.A. H0787

DELAWARE....DELAWARE

DELBRUCK H. H0788

DELEFORTRIE-SOU N. H0789

DELEGATION OF POWER....SEE EX/STRUC

DELIB/GP....CONFERENCES, COMMITTEES, BOARDS, CABINETS

B03
GRIFFIN A.P.C.,LIST OF BOOKS ON THE CABINETS OF ENGLAND AND AMERICA (PAMPHLET). MOD/EUR UK USA-45 CONSTN NAT/G CONSULT EX/STRUC 19/20. PAGE 61 H1216 — BIBLIOG/A GOV/COMP ADMIN DELIB/GP

B15
FARIES J.C.,THE RISE OF INTERNATIONALISM. ASIA MOD/EUR NAT/G VOL/ASSN DELIB/GP BAL/PWR EDU/PROP ARMS/CONT RIGID/FLEX TREND. PAGE 49 H0971 — INT/ORG DIPLOM PEACE

B17
HARLOW R.V.,THE HISTORY OF LEGISLATIVE METHODS IN THE PERIOD BEFORE 1825. USA-45 EX/STRUC ADMIN COLONIAL LEAD PARL/PROC ROUTINE...GP/COMP GOV/COMP HOUSE/REP. PAGE 66 H1333 — LEGIS DELIB/GP PROVS POL/PAR

B18
YUKIO O.,THE VOICE OF JAPANESE DEMOCRACY, AN ESSAY ON CONSTITUTIONAL LOYALTY (TRANS BY J. E. BECKER). ASIA POL/PAR DELIB/GP EX/STRUC RIGID/FLEX ORD/FREE PWR...POLICY JURID METH/COMP 19/20 CHINJAP. PAGE 172 H3443 — CONSTN MAJORIT CHOOSE NAT/G

N19
ANDERSON J.,THE ORGANIZATION OF ECONOMIC STUDIES IN RELATION TO THE PROBLEMS OF GOVERNMENT (PAMPHLET). UK FINAN INDUS DELIB/GP PLAN PROB/SOLV ADMIN 20. PAGE 6 H0128 — ECO/TAC ACT/RES NAT/G CENTRAL

N19
CANADA CIVIL SERV COMM,THE ANALYSIS OF ORGANIZATION IN THE GOVERNMENT OF CANADA (PAMPHLET). CANADA CONSTN EX/STRUC LEGIS TOP/EX CREATE PLAN CONTROL GP/REL 20. PAGE 26 H0517 — NAT/G MGT ADMIN DELIB/GP

B20
HALDANE R.B.,BEFORE THE WAR. MOD/EUR SOCIETY INT/ORG NAT/G DELIB/GP PLAN DOMIN EDU/PROP LEGIT ADMIN COERCE ATTIT DRIVE MORAL ORD/FREE PWR...SOC CONCPT SELF/OBS RECORD BIOG TIME/SEQ. PAGE 64 H1282 — POLICY DIPLOM UK

C20
BLACHLY F.F.,"THE GOVERNMENT AND ADMINISTRATION OF GERMANY." GERMANY CONSTN LOC/G PROVS DELIB/GP EX/STRUC FORCES LEGIS TOP/EX CT/SYS...BIBLIOG/A 19/20. PAGE 17 H0348 — NAT/G GOV/REL ADMIN PHIL/SCI

B23
FINER H.,REPRESENTATIVE GOVERNMENT AND A PARLIAMENT OF INDUSTRY. A STUDY OF THE GERMAN FEDERAL ECONOMIC COUNCIL. GERMANY UK CONSTN INDUS PARL/PROC ...NAT/COMP 20. PAGE 50 H1002 — DELIB/GP ECO/TAC WAR REV

B23
LEES-SMITH H.B.,SECOND CHAMBERS IN THEORY AND PRACTICE. IRELAND NORWAY SOUTH/AFR UK LAW POL/PAR LEGIS CONTROL 20 CMN/WLTH. PAGE 93 H1858 — PARL/PROC DELIB/GP REPRESENT GP/COMP

B23
ROBERT H.M.,PARLIAMENTARY LAW. POL/PAR LEGIS PARTIC CHOOSE REPRESENT GP/REL. PAGE 132 H2640 — PARL/PROC DELIB/GP NAT/G JURID

B24
BAGEHOT W.,THE ENGLISH CONSTITUTION AND OTHER POLITICAL ESSAYS. UK DELIB/GP BAL/PWR ADMIN CONTROL EXEC ROUTINE CONSERVE...METH PARLIAMENT 19/20. PAGE 10 H0197 — NAT/G STRUCT CONCPT

B24
MARTIN B.K.,THE TRIUMPH OF LORD PALMERSTON. MOD/EUR RUSSIA TURKEY UK NAT/G DELIB/GP 19. PAGE 103 H2061 — ATTIT WAR POL/PAR POLICY

B25
WEBSTER C.,THE FOREIGN POLICY OF CASTLEREAGH: 1815-1822. LAW NAT/G DELIB/GP TOP/EX BAL/PWR ORD/FREE PWR RESPECT 19. PAGE 166 H3322 — MOD/EUR DIPLOM UK

B27
MCCOWN A.C.,THE CONGRESSIONAL CONFERENCE COMMITTEE. FACE/GP CONTROL. PAGE 106 H2128 — DELIB/GP GOV/COMP LEGIS CONFER

B29
CAM H.M.,BIBLIOGRAPHY OF ENGLISH CONSTITUTIONAL HISTORY (PAMPHLET). UK LAW LOC/G NAT/G POL/PAR SECT DELIB/GP ADJUD ORD/FREE 19/20 PARLIAMENT. PAGE 25 H0510 — BIBLIOG/A CONSTN ADMIN PARL/PROC

B30
HULL W.I.,INDIA'S POLITICAL CRISIS. INDIA UK INT/ORG LABOR SECT DELIB/GP LEGIS DIPLOM NEUTRAL REGION CROWD GOV/REL MAJORITY ATTIT 20 NEHRU/J GANDHI/M COMMONWLTH. PAGE 75 H1492 — ORD/FREE NAT/G COLONIAL NAT/LISM

B31
LORWIN L.L.,ADVISORY ECONOMIC COUNCILS. EUR+WWI FRANCE GERMANY PROB/SOLV INGP/REL...CLASSIF GP/COMP. PAGE 99 H1968 — CONSULT DELIB/GP ECO/TAC NAT/G

S31
HEINBERG J.G.,"THE PERSONNEL OF FRENCH CABINETS, 1871-1930." FRANCE STRATA CHIEF CHOOSE REPRESENT MAJORITY...STAT QU CENSUS TREND CHARTS PERS/COMP 19/20 CHAMBR/DEP. PAGE 69 H1386 — ELITES NAT/G DELIB/GP TOP/EX

B33
MOSS W.,POLITICAL PARTIES IN THE IRISH FREE STATE. IRELAND UK LAW FINAN LABOR DELIB/GP TOP/EX TARIFFS EDU/PROP...CHARTS GP/COMP 20. PAGE 113 H2269 — POL/PAR NAT/G CHOOSE POLICY

L34
GOSNELL H.F.,"BRITISH ROYAL COMMISSIONS OF INQUIRY" UK CONSTN LEGIS PRESS ADMIN PARL/PROC...DECISION 20 PARLIAMENT. PAGE 59 H1184 — DELIB/GP INSPECT POLICY NAT/G

B36
BELLOC H.,THE RESTORATION OF PROPERTY. UK STRATA NAT/G PROF/ORG DELIB/GP WORKER CREATE PROB/SOLV ECO/TAC PARTIC UTOPIA ORD/FREE SOCISM 20. PAGE 13 H0270 — CONTROL MAJORIT CAP/ISM OWN

B37
CLOKIE H.M.,ROYAL COMMISSIONS OF INQUIRY; THE SIGNIFICANCE OF INVESTIGATIONS IN BRITISH POLITICS. UK POL/PAR CONFER ROUTINE...POLICY DECISION TIME/SEQ 16/20. PAGE 30 H0607 — NAT/G DELIB/GP INSPECT

B39
BENES E.,INTERNATIONAL SECURITY. GERMANY UK NAT/G DELIB/GP PLAN BAL/PWR ATTIT ORD/FREE PWR LEAGUE/NAT 20 TREATY. PAGE 14 H0280 — EUR+WWI INT/ORG WAR

B39
BENES E.,DEMOCRACY TODAY AND TOMORROW. EUR+WWI SOCIETY ECO/DEV DELIB/GP ECO/TAC REGION ATTIT PWR FASCISM...CONCPT LEAGUE/NAT 20. PAGE 14 H0281 — NAT/G LEGIT NAT/LISM

B39
NICOLSON H.,CURZON: THE LAST PHASE, 1919-1925. UK NAT/G DELIB/GP TOP/EX ROUTINE WAR RIGID/FLEX ...METH/CNCPT 20 CURZON/GN. PAGE 118 H2352 — POLICY DIPLOM BIOG

B40
MCHENRY D.E.,HIS MAJESTY'S OPPOSITION: STRUCTURE AND PROBLEMS OF THE BRITISH LABOUR PARTY 1931-1938. — POL/PAR MGT

UK FINAN LABOR LOC/G DELIB/GP LEGIS EDU/PROP LEAD PARTIC CHOOSE GP/REL SOCISM...TREND 20 LABOR/PAR. PAGE 107 H2130
NAT/G POLICY

B41
PALMER R.R.,TWELVE WHO RULED. MOD/EUR ELITES STRUCT NAT/G POL/PAR DELIB/GP DOMIN ATTIT SUPEGO PWR ...POLICY CONCPT 18. PAGE 123 H2453
TOP/EX BIOG REV FRANCE

B44
KNORR K.E.,BRITISH COLONIAL THEORIES 1570-1850. NAT/G DELIB/GP ECO/TAC PERCEPT PWR...WELF/ST METH/CNCPT CONT/OBS TIME/SEQ SIMUL TOT/POP 20. PAGE 87 H1734
ACT/RES DOMIN COLONIAL

B45
MERRIAM C.E.,SYSTEMATIC POLITICS. FUT POL/PAR DELIB/GP DIPLOM ADJUD ADMIN LEAD CHOOSE ATTIT...MGT PHIL/SCI TREND. PAGE 109 H2183
NAT/G METH/CNCPT CREATE

B48
US LIBRARY OF CONGRESS,BRAZIL: A GUIDE TO THE OFFICIAL PUBLICATIONS OF BRAZIL. BRAZIL L/A+17C CONSULT DELIB/GP LEGIS CT/SYS 19/20. PAGE 160 H3206
BIBLIOG/A NAT/G ADMIN TOP/EX

B49
MCLEAN J.M.,THE PUBLIC SERVICE AND UNIVERSITY EDUCATION. UK USA-45 DELIB/GP EX/STRUC TOP/EX ADMIN ...GOV/COMP METH/COMP NAT/COMP ANTHOL 20. PAGE 107 H2142
ACADEM NAT/G EXEC EDU/PROP

B50
LYONS F.S.L.,THE IRISH PARLIAMENTARY PARTY, 1890-1910: STUDIES IN IRISH HISTORY (VOL. 4). IRELAND DELIB/GP LEGIS PAY EDU/PROP ADMIN GP/REL ATTIT...BIBLIOG 19/20 PARLIAMENT PARNELL/CS DIRECT/NAT. PAGE 99 H1986
POL/PAR CHOOSE NAT/G POLICY

B51
LEONARD L.L.,INTERNATIONAL ORGANIZATION. WOR+45 WOR-45 EX/STRUC FORCES LEGIS ECO/TAC INT/TRADE COLONIAL ARMS/CONT...SOC/WK GOV/COMP BIBLIOG. PAGE 94 H1884
NAT/G DIPLOM INT/ORG DELIB/GP

B52
BAILEY S.D.,THE BRITISH PARTY SYSTEM. UK LEGIS ...POLICY GP/COMP ANTHOL 11/20. PAGE 10 H0200
POL/PAR LOC/G NAT/G DELIB/GP

B52
BENTHAM A.,HANDBOOK OF POLITICAL FALLACIES. FUT MOD/EUR LAW INTELL LOC/G MUNIC NAT/G DELIB/GP LEGIS CREATE EDU/PROP CT/SYS ATTIT RIGID/FLEX KNOWL PWR ...RELATIV PSY SOC CONCPT SELF/OBS TREND STERTYP TOT/POP. PAGE 14 H0286
POL/PAR

C52
FIFIELD R.H.,"WOODROW WILSON AND THE FAR EAST." ASIA CHIEF DELIB/GP BAL/PWR CONFER COLONIAL ARMS/CONT WAR...TIME/SEQ NAT/COMP 19/20 WILSON/W LEAGUE/NAT. PAGE 50 H0995
BIBLIOG DIPLOM INT/ORG

B53
STOUT H.M.,BRITISH GOVERNMENT. UK FINAN LOC/G POL/PAR DELIB/GP DIPLOM ADMIN COLONIAL CHOOSE ORD/FREE...JURID BIBLIOG 20 COMMONWLTH. PAGE 150 H2990
NAT/G PARL/PROC CONSTN NEW/LIB

B54
GRAYSON H.,ECONOMIC PLANNING UNDER FREE ENTERPRISE. CANADA FUT UK DELIB/GP BUDGET CONFER CONTROL ...POLICY DECISION 20. PAGE 60 H1200
PLAN ECO/TAC NAT/COMP NAT/G

B54
JENNINGS I.,THE QUEEN'S GOVERNMENT. UK POL/PAR DELIB/GP ADJUD ADMIN CT/SYS PARL/PROC REPRESENT CONSERVE 13/20 PARLIAMENT. PAGE 80 H1605
NAT/G CONSTN LEGIS CHIEF

B54
SCHWARTZ B.,FRENCH ADMINISTRATIVE LAW AND THE COMMON-LAW WORLD. FRANCE CULTURE LOC/G NAT/G PROVS DELIB/GP EX/STRUC LEGIS PROB/SOLV CT/SYS EXEC GOV/REL...IDEA/COMP ENGLSH/LAW. PAGE 140 H2808
JURID LAW METH/COMP ADJUD

B55
GALLOWAY G.B.,CONGRESS AND PARLIAMENT: THEIR ORGANIZATION AND OPERATION IN THE US AND THE UK: PLANNING PAMPHLET NO. 93. POL/PAR EX/STRUC DEBATE CONTROL LEAD ROUTINE EFFICIENCY PWR...POLICY CONGRESS PARLIAMENT. PAGE 54 H1089
DELIB/GP LEGIS PARL/PROC GOV/COMP

B55
WHEARE K.C.,GOVERNMENT BY COMMITTEE; AN ESSAY ON THE BRITISH CONSTITUTION. UK NAT/G LEGIS INSPECT CONFER ADJUD ADMIN CONTROL TASK EFFICIENCY ROLE POPULISM 20. PAGE 167 H3337
DELIB/GP CONSTN LEAD GP/COMP

B56
JENNINGS W.I.,THE APPROACH TO SELF-GOVERNMENT. CEYLON INDIA PAKISTAN S/ASIA UK SOCIETY POL/PAR DELIB/GP LEGIS ECO/TAC EDU/PROP ADMIN EXEC CHOOSE ATTIT ALL/VALS...JURID CONCPT GEN/METH TOT/POP 20. PAGE 81 H1610
NAT/G CONSTN COLONIAL

S56
GORDON L.,"THE ORGANIZATION FOR EUROPEAN ECONOMIC COOPERATION." EUR+WWI INDUS INT/ORG NAT/G CONSULT DELIB/GP ACT/RES CREATE PLAN TEC/DEV EDU/PROP LEGIT WEALTH OEEC 20. PAGE 59 H1178
VOL/ASSN ECO/DEV

B57
US SENATE SPEC COMM FOR AID,COMPILATION OF STUDIES AND SURVEYS. AFR ASIA L/A+17C USA+45 ECO/UNDEV AGRI INT/ORG CONSULT TEC/DEV CONFER TOTALISM...NAT/COMP 20 CONGRESS. PAGE 161 H3216
FOR/AID DIPLOM ORD/FREE DELIB/GP

S57
LEWIS E.G.,"PARLIAMENTARY CONTROL OF NATIONALIZED INDUSTRY IN FRANCE." FRANCE NAT/G DELIB/GP ACT/RES PLAN PROB/SOLV ECO/TAC DOMIN CENTRAL. PAGE 96 H1914
PWR LEGIS INDUS CONTROL

S57
SPROUT H.,"ENVIRONMENTAL FACTORS IN THE STUDY OF INTERNATIONAL POLITICS." UNIV SOCIETY ECO/DEV NAT/G DELIB/GP TOP/EX ROUTINE ATTIT PERCEPT...POLICY GEOG CONCPT MYTH TIME/SEQ. PAGE 148 H2957
DECISION GEN/LAWS DIPLOM

B58
INDIAN COUNCIL WORLD AFFAIRS,DEFENCE AND SECURITY IN THE INDIAN OCEAN AREA. INDIA S/ASIA CULTURE CONSULT DELIB/GP FORCES PROB/SOLV DIPLOM INT/TRADE 20 CMN/WLTH. PAGE 77 H1531
GEOG HABITAT ECO/UNDEV ORD/FREE

B58
NICULESCU B.,COLONIAL PLANNING: A COMPARATIVE STUDY. AFR AGRI LOC/G MUNIC NAT/G DELIB/GP COLONIAL 20. PAGE 118 H2356
PLAN ECO/UNDEV TEC/DEV NAT/COMP

B58
SCOTT D.J.R.,RUSSIAN POLITICAL INSTITUTIONS. RUSSIA USSR CONSTN AGRI DELIB/GP PLAN EDU/PROP CONTROL CHOOSE EFFICIENCY ATTIT MARXISM...BIBLIOG/A 13/20. PAGE 141 H2813
NAT/G POL/PAR ADMIN DECISION

B58
SHARMA M.P.,PUBLIC ADMINISTRATION IN THEORY AND PRACTICE. INDIA UK USA+45 USA-45 EX/STRUC ADJUD ...POLICY CONCPT NAT/COMP 20. PAGE 142 H2847
MGT ADMIN DELIB/GP JURID

B58
STRONG C.F.,MODERN POLITICAL CONSTITUTIONS. LAW CHIEF DELIB/GP EX/STRUC LEGIS ADJUD CHOOSE FEDERAL POPULISM...CONCPT BIBLIOG 20 UN. PAGE 150 H2998
CONSTN IDEA/COMP NAT/G

B58
WILMERDING L. JR.,THE ELECTORAL COLLEGE. CONSTN NAT/G POL/PAR DELIB/GP LEGIS PROB/SOLV CONFER EXEC LEAD APPORT REPRESENT. PAGE 169 H3377
CHOOSE DECISION ACT/RES

S58
ELKIN A.B.,"OEEC-ITS STRUCTURE AND POWERS." EUR+WWI CONSTN INDUS INT/ORG NAT/G VOL/ASSN DELIB/GP ACT/RES PLAN ORD/FREE WEALTH...CHARTS ORG/CHARTS OEEC 20. PAGE 45 H0907
ECO/DEV EX/STRUC

S58
SCHUMM S.,"INTEREST REPRESENTATION IN FRANCE AND GERMANY." EUR+WWI FRANCE GERMANY INSPECT PARL/PROC REPRESENT 20 WEIMAR/REP. PAGE 140 H2803
LOBBY DELIB/GP NAT/G

B59
BARRON R.,PARTIES AND POLITICS IN MODERN FRANCE. FRANCE LOC/G DELIB/GP LEGIS TOP/EX EDU/PROP LEGIT TV FEEDBACK 20. PAGE 12 H0230
POL/PAR ALL/IDEOS CHOOSE PARTIC

B59
JENNINGS W.I.,CABINET GOVERNMENT (3RD ED.). UK POL/PAR CHIEF BUDGET ADMIN CHOOSE GP/REL 20. PAGE 81 H1612
DELIB/GP NAT/G CONSTN OP/RES

B59
SHARMA R.S.,ASPECTS OF POLITICAL IDEAS AND INSTITUTIONS IN ANCIENT INDIA. INDIA SOCIETY STRUCT FAM VOL/ASSN TAX DOMIN...CONCPT HIST/WRIT 7. PAGE 142 H2848
CULTURE JURID DELIB/GP SECT

B59
WILDNER H.,DIE TECHNIK DER DIPLOMATIE. TOP/EX ROLE ORD/FREE...INT/LAW JURID IDEA/COMP NAT/COMP 20. PAGE 168 H3364
DIPLOM POLICY DELIB/GP NAT/G

L59
JANIS I.L.,"DECISIONAL CONFLICT: A THEORETICAL ANALYSIS." INTELL NAT/G POL/PAR DELIB/GP LEGIS TOP/EX PLAN...DECISION CONGRESS NAZI 20 WWI. PAGE 80 H1590
ACT/RES PSY DIPLOM

B60
BHAMBHRI C.P.,PARLIAMENTARY CONTROL OVER STATE ENTERPRISE IN INDIA. INDIA DELIB/GP ADMIN CONTROL INGP/REL EFFICIENCY 20 PARLIAMENT. PAGE 16 H0327
NAT/G OWN INDUS PARL/PROC

B60
CARTER G.M.,INDEPENDENCE FOR AFRICA. AFR FUT SOCIETY STRATA ECO/DEV POL/PAR DELIB/GP PLAN DOMIN EDU/PROP COLONIAL REGION ATTIT DRIVE SOVEREIGN ...RECORD INT TIME/SEQ CHARTS 20. PAGE 27 H0544
NAT/G PWR NAT/LISM

B60
FEIS H.,BETWEEN WAR AND PEACE: THE POTSDAM CONFERENCE. EUR+WWI NAT/G DELIB/GP PROB/SOLV REPAR WAR CIVMIL/REL...BIBLIOG 20. PAGE 49 H0983
DIPLOM CONFER BAL/PWR

B60
FURNIA A.H.,THE DIPLOMACY OF APPEASEMENT: ANGLO-FRENCH RELATIONS AND THE PRELUDE TO WORLD WAR II 1931-1938. FRANCE GERMANY UK ELITES NAT/G DELIB/GP FORCES WAR PEACE RIGID/FLEX 20. PAGE 54 H1077
DIPLOM BAL/PWR COERCE

B60
JEFFRIES C.,TRANSFER OF POWER: PROBLEMS OF THE PASSAGE TO SELFGOVERNMENT. CEYLON GHANA MALAYSIA NIGERIA UK INT/ORG CONSULT DELIB/GP LEGIS DIPLOM CONFER PARL/PROC 20. PAGE 80 H1595
SOVEREIGN COLONIAL ORD/FREE NAT/G

B60
LISTER L.,EUROPE'S COAL AND STEEL COMMUNITY. FRANCE GERMANY STRUCT ECO/DEV EXTR/IND INDUS MARKET NAT/G DELIB/GP ECO/TAC INT/TRADE EDU/PROP ATTIT RIGID/FLEX ORD/FREE PWR WEALTH...CONCPT STAT TIME/SEQ CHARTS ECSC 20. PAGE 97 H1941
EUR+WWI INT/ORG REGION

B60
MORRIS I.,NATIONALISM AND THE RIGHT WING IN JAPAN: A STUDY OF POST WAR TRENDS. ASIA ELITES NAT/G DELIB/GP FORCES TOP/EX CHOOSE ATTIT...INT GEN/LAWS CONGRESS 20 CHINJAP. PAGE 113 H2262
POL/PAR TREND NAT/LISM

B60
ROBINSON E.A.G.,ECONOMIC CONSEQUENCES OF THE SIZE OF NATIONS. AGRI INDUS DELIB/GP FOR/AID ADMIN EFFICIENCY...METH/COMP 20. PAGE 132 H2649
CONCPT INT/ORG NAT/COMP

B60
ROY N.C.,THE CIVIL SERVICE IN INDIA. INDIA POL/PAR ECO/TAC INCOME...JURID MGT 20 CIVIL/SERV. PAGE 135 H2705
ADMIN NAT/G DELIB/GP CONFER

B60
US LIBRARY OF CONGRESS,INDEX TO LATIN AMERICAN LEGISLATION: 1950-1960 (2 VOLS.). NAT/G DELIB/GP ADMIN PARL/PROC 20. PAGE 161 H3211
BIBLIOG/A LEGIS L/A+17C JURID

L60
HAAS E.B.,"CONSENSUS FORMATION IN THE COUNCIL OF EUROPE." EUR+WWI NAT/G DELIB/GP DIPLOM REGION CHOOSE PWR SOVEREIGN...RELATIV NEW/IDEA QUANT CHARTS INDEX TOT/POP OEEC 20 COUNCL/EUR. PAGE 63 H1265
POL/PAR INT/ORG STAT

S60
CROZIER B.,"FRANCE AND ALGERIA." ALGERIA EUR+WWI FRANCE FUT ISLAM ECO/UNDEV NEIGH CONSULT DELIB/GP ECO/TAC COLONIAL COERCE ATTIT...SOC INT CON/ANAL 20. PAGE 36 H0713
NAT/G FORCES GUERRILLA NAT/LISM

S60
GROSSMAN G.,"SOVIET GROWTH: ROUTINE, INERTIA, AND PRESSURE." COM STRATA NAT/G DELIB/GP PLAN TEC/DEV ECO/TAC EDU/PROP ADMIN ROUTINE DRIVE WEALTH COLD/WAR 20. PAGE 62 H1236
POL/PAR ECO/DEV USSR

B61
BISHOP D.G.,THE ADMINISTRATION OF BRITISH FOREIGN RELATIONS. EUR+WWI MOD/EUR INT/ORG NAT/G POL/PAR DELIB/GP LEGIS TOP/EX ECO/TAC DOMIN EDU/PROP ADMIN COERCE 20. PAGE 17 H0344
ROUTINE PWR DIPLOM UK

B61
BURDEAU G.,O PODER EXECUTIVO NA FRANCA. EUR+WWI FRANCE CONSTN DELIB/GP LEGIT ADMIN ATTIT ALL/VALS CONCPT. PAGE 24 H0478
TOP/EX POL/PAR NAT/G LEGIS

B61
HALPERIN S.,THE POLITICAL WORLD OF AMERICAN ZIONISM. ISRAEL FINAN LABOR VOL/ASSN GIVE LOBBY REPRESENT GP/REL ATTIT POLICY. PAGE 64 H1293
CULTURE SECT EDU/PROP DELIB/GP

B61
LA PONCE J.A.,THE GOVERNMENT OF THE FIFTH REPUBLIC: FRENCH POLITICAL PARTIES AND THE CONSTITUTION. ALGERIA FRANCE LAW NAT/G DELIB/GP LEGIS ECO/TAC MARXISM SOCISM...CHARTS BIBLIOG/A 20 DEGAULLE/C. PAGE 90 H1794
PWR POL/PAR CONSTN CHIEF

B61
MAYNE A.,DESIGNING AND ADMINISTERING A REGIONAL ECONOMIC DEVELOPMENT PLAN WITH SPECIFIC REFERENCE TO PUERTO RICO (PAMPHLET). PUERT/RICO SOCIETY NAT/G DELIB/GP REGION...DECISION 20. PAGE 105 H2106
ECO/UNDEV PLAN CREATE ADMIN

B61
MERRIAM A.,CONGO: BACKGROUND OF CONFLICT. AFR FUT KIN MUNIC NAT/G POL/PAR PROVS DELIB/GP PLAN DOMIN COERCE ATTIT...TIME/SEQ CHARTS CONGO 20. PAGE 109 H2182
CHOOSE GUERRILLA

B61
ROBERTSON A.H.,THE LAW OF INTERNATIONAL INSTITUTIONS IN EUROPE. EUR+WWI MOD/EUR INT/ORG NAT/G VOL/ASSN DELIB/GP...JURID TIME/SEQ TOT/POP 20 TREATY. PAGE 132 H2644
RIGID/FLEX ORD/FREE

B61
ROSE D.L.,THE VIETNAMESE CIVIL SERVICE. VIETNAM CONSULT DELIB/GP GIVE PAY EDU/PROP COLONIAL GOV/REL UTIL...CHARTS 20. PAGE 134 H2672
ADMIN EFFICIENCY STAT NAT/G

B61
SCHNAPPER B.,LA POLITIQUE ET LE COMMERCE FRANCAIS DANS LE GOLFE DE GUINEE DE 1838 A 1871. FRANCE GUINEA UK SEA EXTR/IND NAT/G DELIB/GP LEGIS ADMIN ORD/FREE...POLICY GEOG CENSUS CHARTS BIBLIOG 19. PAGE 139 H2791
COLONIAL INT/TRADE DOMIN AFR

B61
SHARMA T.R.,THE WORKING OF STATE ENTERPRISES IN INDIA. INDIA DELIB/GP LEGIS WORKER BUDGET PRICE CONTROL GP/REL OWN ATTIT...MGT CHARTS 20. PAGE 142 H2851
NAT/G INDUS ADMIN SOCISM

B61
TREVE W.,DEUTSCHE PARTEIPROGRAMME 1861-1961. GERMANY GERMANY/W DELIB/GP CONFER CHOOSE REPRESENT 19/20. PAGE 157 H3130
POL/PAR NAT/G LEGIS PARL/PROC

B61
WARD R.E.,JAPANESE POLITICAL SCIENCE: A GUIDE TO JAPANESE REFERENCE AND RESEARCH MATERIALS (2ND ED.). LAW CONSTN STRATA NAT/G POL/PAR DELIB/GP LEGIS ADMIN CHOOSE GP/REL...INT/LAW 19/20 CHINJAP. PAGE 165 H3306
BIBLIOG/A PHIL/SCI

S61
BRZEZINSKI Z.K.,"THE ORGANIZATION OF THE COMMUNIST CAMP." COM CZECHOSLVK COM/IND NAT/G DELIB/GP INT/TRADE DOMIN EDU/PROP EXEC ROUTINE COERCE ATTIT PWR...MGT CONCPT TIME/SEQ CHARTS VAL/FREE 20 TREATY. PAGE 23 H0460
VOL/ASSN DIPLOM USSR

S61
DOGAN M.,"LES OFFICIERS DANS LA CARRIERE POLITIQUE DE MARECHAL MACMAHON AU GENERAL DE GAULLE." EUR+WWI FRANCE MOD/EUR ELITES STRATA POL/PAR LEGIT ATTIT ALL/VALS...SOC CONCPT 19/20. PAGE 42 H0833
PROF/ORG FORCES NAT/G DELIB/GP

S61
EHRMANN H.W.,"FRENCH BUREAUCRACY AND ORGANIZED INTERESTS" (BMR)" FRANCE NAT/G DELIB/GP ROUTINE ...INT 20 BUREAUCRCY CIVIL/SERV. PAGE 45 H0897
ADMIN DECISION PLURISM LOBBY

S61
PADELFORD N.J.,"POLITICS AND THE FUTURE OF ECOSOC." AFR S/ASIA ECO/UNDEV INDUS NAT/G DELIB/GP ACT/RES ORD/FREE WEALTH...CONCPT CHARTS UN 20 ECOSOC. PAGE 122 H2438
INT/ORG TEC/DEV

S61
TOMASIC D.,"POLITICAL LEADERSHIP IN CONTEMPORARY POLAND." COM EUR+WWI GERMANY NAT/G POL/PAR SECT DELIB/GP PLAN ECO/TAC DOMIN EDU/PROP PWR MARXISM ...MARXIST GEOG MGT CONCPT TIME/SEQ STERTYP 20. PAGE 156 H3111
SOCIETY ROUTINE USSR POLAND

B62
ANDREWS W.G.,FRENCH POLITICS AND ALGERIA: THE PROCESS OF POLICY FORMATION 1954-1962. ALGERIA FRANCE CONSTN ELITES POL/PAR CHIEF DELIB/GP LEGIS DIPLOM PRESS CHOOSE 20. PAGE 7 H0140
GOV/COMP EXEC COLONIAL

B62
ARNE S.,LE PRESIDENT DU CONSEIL DES MINISTRES SOUS LA IV REPUBLIQUE. EUR+WWI FRANCE LEGIT PWR...BIOG CHARTS. PAGE 8 H0165
DELIB/GP POL/PAR NAT/G LEGIS

B62
BUSIA K.A.,THE CHALLENGE OF AFRICA. CULTURE KIN MUNIC NAT/G POL/PAR SCHOOL DELIB/GP PLAN ECO/TAC DOMIN EDU/PROP TOTALISM ATTIT PERSON ALL/VALS SOVEREIGN...SOC CONCPT STERTYP TOT/POP VAL/FREE 20. PAGE 25 H0496
AFR ECO/UNDEV NAT/LISM

B62
GANJI M.,INTERNATIONAL PROTECTION OF HUMAN RIGHTS. WOR+45 CONSTN INT/TRADE CT/SYS SANCTION CRIME WAR RACE/REL...CHARTS IDEA/COMP NAT/COMP BIBLIOG 20 TREATY NEGRO LEAGUE/NAT UN CIVIL/LIB. PAGE 55 H1097
ORD/FREE DISCRIM LEGIS DELIB/GP

B62
GROGAN V.,ADMINISTRATIVE TRIBUNALS IN THE PUBLIC SERVICE. IRELAND UK NAT/G CONTROL CT/SYS...JURID GOV/COMP 20. PAGE 61 H1231
ADMIN LAW ADJUD DELIB/GP

B62
GROVE J.W.,GOVERNMENT AND INDUSTRY IN BRITAIN. UK FINAN LOC/G CONSULT DELIB/GP INT/TRADE ADMIN CONTROL...BIBLIOG 20. PAGE 62 H1237
ECO/TAC INDUS NAT/G GP/REL

B62
HANSON A.H.,MANAGERIAL PROBLEMS IN PUBLIC ENTERPRISE. INDIA DELIB/GP GP/REL INGP/REL EFFICIENCY 20 PARLIAMENT. PAGE 66 H1320
MGT NAT/G INDUS PROB/SOLV

B62
HATCH J.,AFRICA TODAY-AND TOMORROW: AN OUTLINE OF BASIC FACTS AND MAJOR PROBLEMS. AFR FUT ISLAM STRATA ECO/UNDEV INT/ORG NAT/G POL/PAR DELIB/GP TOP/EX EDU/PROP LEGIT CHOOSE ATTIT...TIME/SEQ TOT/POP COLD/WAR 20. PAGE 67 H1353
PLAN CONSTN NAT/LISM

B62
HO PING-TI,THE LADDER OF SUCCESS IN IMPERIAL CHINA: ASPECTS OF SOCIAL MOBILITY, 1368-1911. INTELL STRATA FAM KIN MUNIC NAT/G PROVS SCHOOL DELIB/GP DOMIN EDU/PROP ADMIN ROUTINE PERSON ALL/VALS...SOC STAT BIOG HIST/WRIT TIME/SEQ VAL/FREE. PAGE 71 H1431
ASIA CULTURE

B62
HUNKIN P.,ENSEIGNEMENT ET POLITIQUE EN FRANCE ET EN ANGLETERRE. FRANCE UK CONSTN ACADEM SECT CHIEF DELIB/GP PROB/SOLV CONTROL REV ORD/FREE CONSERVE ...BIBLIOG 18/20. PAGE 75 H1496
EDU/PROP LEGIS IDEA/COMP NAT/G

B62
JAIN R.S.,THE GROWTH AND DEVELOPMENT OF GOVERNOR-
NAT/G

GENERAL'S EXECUTIVE COUNCIL 1858-1919. INDIA UK CONSTN EX/STRUC LEGIS ADJUD ADMIN INGP/REL ATTIT 19/20. PAGE 79 H1585 DELIB/GP CHIEF CONSULT

B62

KAGZI M.C.,THE INDIAN ADMINISTRATIVE LAW. INDIA LG/CO CONTROL CT/SYS...CONCPT 20. PAGE 83 H1649 JURID ADJUD DELIB/GP NAT/G

B62

LEGUM C.,PAN-AFRICANISM: A SHORT POLITICAL GUIDE. ISLAM CULTURE INTELL ECO/DEV NAT/G POL/PAR DELIB/GP PLAN EDU/PROP FEDERAL NAT/LISM ATTIT DRIVE PERSON ...RECORD TIME/SEQ CHARTS STERTYP 20. PAGE 93 H1861 AFR CONCPT

B62

MORGENSTERN O.,STRATEGIE - HEUTE (2ND ED.). USA+45 USSR ECO/DEV DELIB/GP WAR PEACE ORD/FREE...GOV/COMP NAT/COMP 20 COLD/WAR NATO. PAGE 113 H2256 NUC/PWR DIPLOM FORCES TEC/DEV

B62

ROBINSON A.D.,DUTCH ORGANIZED AGRICULTURE IN INTERNATIONAL POLITICS, 1945-1960. EUR+WWI NETHERLAND STRUCT ECO/DEV NAT/G VOL/ASSN CONSULT DELIB/GP PLAN TEC/DEV INT/TRADE EDU/PROP ATTIT RIGID/FLEX ALL/VALS...NEW/IDEA TREND EEC 20. PAGE 132 H2648 AGRI INT/ORG

B62

THIERRY S.S.,LE VATICAN SECRET. CHRIST-17C EUR+WWI MOD/EUR VATICAN NAT/G SECT DELIB/GP DOMIN LEGIT SOVEREIGN. PAGE 154 H3072 ADMIN EX/STRUC CATHISM DECISION

L62

COHEN R.,"POWER IN COMPLEX SOCIETIES IN AFRICA." AFR KIN MUNIC POL/PAR DELIB/GP DOMIN ROUTINE ATTIT ALL/VALS...SOC STAT OBS INT QU CHARTS ANTHOL 20. PAGE 31 H0617 CULTURE STRATA ELITES

S62

CORET A.,"LE STATUT DE L'ILE CHRISTMAS DE L'OCEAN INDIEN." FUT S/ASIA ECO/DEV ECO/UNDEV VOL/ASSN DELIB/GP PLAN...RELATIV OBS TIME/SEQ TREND AUSTRAL 20. PAGE 33 H0667 NAT/G INT/ORG NEW/ZEALND

S62

LONDON K.,"SINO-SOVIET RELATIONS IN THE CONTEXT OF THE 'WORLD SOCIALIST SYSTEM'." ASIA CHINA/COM COM USSR INT/ORG NAT/G TOP/EX BAL/PWR DIPLOM DOMIN ATTIT PERCEPT RIGID/FLEX PWR MARXISM...METH/CNCPT TREND 20. PAGE 98 H1957 DELIB/GP CONCPT SOCISM

S62

PIQUEMAL M.,"LES PROBLEMES DES UNIONS D'ETATS EN AFRIQUE NOIRE." FRANCE SOCIETY INT/ORG NAT/G DELIB/GP PLAN LEGIT ADMIN COLONIAL ROUTINE ATTIT ORD/FREE PWR...GEOG METH/CNCPT 20. PAGE 126 H2515 AFR ECO/UNDEV REGION

S62

THOMPSON D.,"THE UNITED KINGDOM AND THE TREATY OF ROME." EUR+WWI INT/ORG NAT/G DELIB/GP LEGIS INT/TRADE RIGID/FLEX...CONCPT EEC PARLIAMENT CMN/WLTH 20. PAGE 154 H3079 ADJUD JURID

B63

ATTIA G.E.D.,LES FORCES ARMEES DES NATIONS UNIES EN COREE ET AU MOYENORIENT. KOREA CONSTN NAT/G DELIB/GP LEGIS PWR...IDEA/COMP NAT/COMP BIBLIOG UN SUEZ. PAGE 9 H0177 FORCES INT/LAW

B63

BADI J.,THE GOVERNMENT OF THE STATE OF ISRAEL: A CRITICAL ACCOUNT OF ITS PARLIAMENT, EXECUTIVE, AND JUDICIARY. ISRAEL ECO/DEV CHIEF DELIB/GP LEGIS DIPLOM CT/SYS INGP/REL PEACE ORD/FREE...BIBLIOG 20 PARLIAMENT ARABS MIGRATION. PAGE 10 H0193 NAT/G CONSTN EX/STRUC POL/PAR

B63

BARNETT A.D.,COMMUNIST STRATEGIES IN ASIA: A COMPARATIVE ANALYSIS OF GOVERNMENTS AND PARTIES. COM FUT S/ASIA CULTURE SOCIETY STRATA NAT/G DELIB/GP ACT/RES ECO/TAC EDU/PROP COERCE CHOOSE ATTIT RIGID/FLEX ORD/FREE PWR SKILL...SIMUL VAL/FREE 20. PAGE 11 H0223 ASIA POL/PAR DIPLOM USSR

B63

BRZEZINSKI Z.K.,AFRICA AND THE COMMUNIST WORLD. AFR ASIA COM CULTURE SOCIETY INT/ORG DELIB/GP ACT/RES ECO/TAC COERCE ORD/FREE PWR WEALTH...STAT TOT/POP VAL/FREE 20. PAGE 23 H0461 ATTIT EDU/PROP DIPLOM USSR

B63

COLUMBIA U SCHOOL OF LAW,PUBLIC INTERNATIONAL DEVELOPMENT FINANCING IN SENEGAL. SENEGAL FINAN DELIB/GP GIVE EFFICIENCY...CHARTS GOV/COMP ANTHOL 20. PAGE 32 H0636 FOR/AID PLAN RECEIVE ECO/UNDEV

B63

CRANKSHAW E.,THE NEW COLD WAR: MOSCOW V. PEKIN. CHINA/COM USSR INTELL POL/PAR DELIB/GP CAP/ISM COERCE REV NAT/LISM TOTALISM DRIVE...POLICY IDEA/COMP 20 KHRUSH/N. PAGE 35 H0698 ATTIT DIPLOM NAT/COMP MARXISM

B63

DE VRIES E.,SOCIAL ASPECTS OF ECONOMIC DEVELOPMENT IN LATIN AMERICA. CULTURE SOCIETY STRATA FINAN INDUS INT/ORG DELIB/GP ACT/RES ECO/TAC EDU/PROP ADMIN ATTIT SUPEGO HEALTH KNOWL ORD/FREE...SOC STAT TREND ANTHOL TOT/POP VAL/FREE. PAGE 39 H0777 L/A+17C ECO/UNDEV

B63

DEBRAY P.,LE PORTUGAL ENTRE DEUX REVOLUTIONS. EUR+WWI PORTUGAL CONSTN LEGIT ADMIN ATTIT ALL/VALS ...DECISION CONCPT 20 SALAZAR/A. PAGE 39 H0779 NAT/G DELIB/GP TOP/EX

B63

GLADE W.P. JR.,THE POLITICAL ECONOMY OF MEXICO. FUT L/A+17C CULTURE SOCIETY AGRI INDUS DELIB/GP ACT/RES ECO/TAC ATTIT HEALTH ORD/FREE...STAT TIME/SEQ TREND MEXIC/AMER TOT/POP VAL/FREE 20. PAGE 57 H1138 FINAN ECO/UNDEV

B63

GLUCKMAN M.,ORDER AND REBELLION IN TRIBAL AFRICA. EUR+WWI LAW CULTURE STRATA KIN MUNIC DELIB/GP ACT/RES DOMIN EDU/PROP LEGIT ADMIN COERCE CHOOSE ATTIT PERSON ORD/FREE PWR...SOC CHARTS GEN/LAWS TOT/POP VAL/FREE. PAGE 57 H1147 AFR SOCIETY

B63

HAMM H.,ALBANIA - CHINA'S BEACHHEAD IN EUROPE. ALBANIA CHINA/COM USSR YUGOSLAVIA ELITES SOCIETY POL/PAR DELIB/GP FORCES ECO/TAC COERCE ISOLAT PEACE MARXISM...IDEA/COMP 20 MAO. PAGE 65 H1304 DIPLOM REV NAT/G POLICY

B63

HUGHES A.J.,EAST AFRICA: THE SEARCH FOR UNITY- KENYA, TANGANYIKA, UGANDA, AND ZANZIBAR. TANZANIA UGANDA CONSTN POL/PAR SECT CHIEF DELIB/GP LEGIS WAR CHOOSE NAT/LISM MARXISM...POLICY CHARTS 20 NEGRO UN. PAGE 74 H1488 NAT/G DOMIN LOC/G AFR

B63

MAYNE R.,THE COMMUNITY OF EUROPE. UK CONSTN NAT/G CONSULT DELIB/GP CREATE PLAN ECO/TAC LEGIT ADMIN ROUTINE ORD/FREE PWR WEALTH...CONCPT TIME/SEQ EEC EURATOM 20. PAGE 105 H2107 EUR+WWI INT/ORG REGION

B63

NICOLSON H.,DIPLOMACY (3RD ED.). INT/ORG NAT/G CONSULT DELIB/GP CONFER 19/20 LEAGUE/NAT UN. PAGE 118 H2354 DIPLOM CONCPT NAT/COMP

B63

NKRUMAH K.,AFRICA MUST UNITE. AFR FUT GHANA CONSTN CULTURE SOCIETY NAT/G POL/PAR DELIB/GP TOP/EX PLAN DOMIN EDU/PROP ATTIT DRIVE...TIME/SEQ CHARTS TOT/POP 20. PAGE 118 H2364 CONCPT GEN/LAWS REGION

B63

ROBERTSON A.H.,HUMAN RIGHTS IN EUROPE. CONSTN SOCIETY INT/ORG NAT/G VOL/ASSN DELIB/GP ACT/RES PLAN ADJUD REGION ROUTINE ATTIT LOVE ORD/FREE RESPECT...JURID SOC CONCPT SOC/EXP UN 20. PAGE 132 H2645 EUR+WWI PERSON

B63

RONNING C.N.,LAW AND POLITICS IN INTER-AMERICAN DIPLOMACY. L/A+17C ECO/UNDEV NAT/G CONSULT DELIB/GP CREATE CAP/ISM ECO/TAC LEGIT REGION RIGID/FLEX ...METH/CNCPT GEN/LAWS OAS 20. PAGE 133 H2668 VOL/ASSN ALL/VALS DIPLOM

B63

SKLAR R.L.,NIGERIAN POLITICAL PARTIES: POWER IN AN EMERGENT AFRICAN NATION. AFR EUR+WWI CULTURE STRATA NAT/G DELIB/GP EX/STRUC LEGIS DOMIN EDU/PROP ROUTINE CHOOSE ATTIT PERCEPT ORD/FREE PWR...SOC CONCPT OBS TOT/POP VAL/FREE. PAGE 145 H2898 POL/PAR SOCIETY NAT/LISM NIGERIA

B63

VON BECKERATH E.,PROBLEME DER NORMATIVEN OKONOMIK UND DER WIRTSCHAFTSPOLITISCHEN BERATUNG. GERMANY UK ELITES CAP/ISM EFFICIENCY...CONCPT GOV/COMP IDEA/COMP 20. PAGE 163 H3264 ECO/TAC DELIB/GP ECO/DEV CONSULT

B63

WHEARE K.C.,LEGISLATURES. POL/PAR DELIB/GP WAR PEACE CONCPT. PAGE 167 H3338 LEGIS PARL/PROC JURID GOV/COMP

L63

NASH M.,"PSYCHO-CULTURAL FACTORS IN ASIAN ECONOMIC GROWTH." ASIA ISLAM S/ASIA CULTURE ECO/UNDEV DELIB/GP EDU/PROP COERCE ATTIT PERSON HEALTH KNOWL ORD/FREE...PSY SOC STAT TREND ANTHOL VAL/FREE 20. PAGE 116 H2313 SOCIETY ECO/TAC

L63

ROSE R.,"COMPARATIVE STUDIES IN POLITICAL FINANCE: A SYMPOSIUM." ASIA EUR+WWI S/ASIA LAW CULTURE DELIB/GP LEGIS ACT/RES ECO/TAC EDU/PROP CHOOSE ATTIT RIGID/FLEX SUPEGO PWR SKILL WEALTH...STAT ANTHOL VAL/FREE. PAGE 134 H2674 FINAN POL/PAR

L63

ZARTMAN I.W.,"THE SAHARA--BRIDGE OR BARRIER." ISLAM CULTURE SOCIETY NAT/G DELIB/GP DOMIN EDU/PROP LEGIT ATTIT...HIST/WRIT TIME/SEQ CHARTS TOT/POP VAL/FREE 20. PAGE 172 H3447 INT/ORG PWR NAT/LISM

S63

CRUTCHER J.,"PAN AFRICANISM: AFRICAN ODYSSEY." AFR NAT/G POL/PAR PROF/ORG VOL/ASSN TOP/EX CREATE REGION RACE/REL ALL/VALS...CONCPT TIME/SEQ TREND CON/ANAL 20. PAGE 36 H0716 PROVS DELIB/GP COLONIAL

S63

DUDLEY B.J.,"THE NOMINATION OF PARLIAMENTARY CANDIDATES IN NORTHERN NIGERIA." AFR CONSTN CULTURE ELITES STRATA DELIB/GP LEGIS DOMIN EDU/PROP COERCE ATTIT SUPEGO PWR...STAT VAL/FREE 20. PAGE 43 H0854 POL/PAR CHOOSE NIGERIA

S63

EMERI C.,"LES FORCES POLITIQUES AU PARLEMENT" POL/PAR

EUR+WWI FRANCE ELITES DELIB/GP TOP/EX LEGIT ATTIT ...SOC 20 PARLIAMENT. PAGE 46 H0917 LEGIS PWR NAT/G

S63
GLUCKMAN M.,"CIVIL WAR AND THEORIES OF POWER IN BAROTSE-LAND: AFRICAN AND MEDIEVAL ANALOGIES." AFR CHRIST-17C LAW CONSTN CULTURE STRATA KIN DELIB/GP FORCES DOMIN LEGIT COERCE PERCEPT ORD/FREE...SOC INT TIME/SEQ GEN/LAWS VAL/FREE. PAGE 57 H1148 TOP/EX PWR WAR

S63
HALPERN A.M.,"THE EMERGENCE OF AN ASIAN COMMUNIST BLOC." ASIA CHINA/COM COM FUT KOREA/N S/ASIA VIETNAM/N STRATA NAT/G DELIB/GP FORCES TOP/EX PLAN BAL/PWR COERCE DETER PWR COLD/WAR WORK 20. PAGE 65 H1295 POL/PAR EDU/PROP DIPLOM

S63
HARRIS R.L.,"A COMPARATIVE ANALYSIS OF THE ADMINISTRATIVE SYSTEMS OF CANADA AND CEYLON." S/ASIA CULTURE SOCIETY STRATA TOP/EX ACT/RES DOMIN EDU/PROP LEGIT COERCE ATTIT SUPEGO ALL/VALS...MGT CHARTS GEN/LAWS VAL/FREE 20. PAGE 67 H1343 DELIB/GP EX/STRUC CANADA CEYLON

S63
LAMBERT D.,"LA TRANSPOSITION DU REGIME PRESIDENTIEL HORS DES ETATSUNIS; LE CAS DE L'AMERIQUE LATINE." NAT/G EX/STRUC LEGIS PARL/PROC PWR 18/20 PRESIDENT CENTRAL/AM SOUTH/AMER. PAGE 90 H1800 DELIB/GP CHIEF L/A+17C GOV/REL

S63
LEE J.M.,"PARLIAMENT IN REPUBLICAN GHANA." AFR CONSTN CULTURE SOCIETY STRATA POL/PAR DELIB/GP TOP/EX DOMIN EDU/PROP LEGIT COERCE CHOOSE ATTIT ALL/VALS...CONCPT STAT TIME/SEQ VAL/FREE 20. PAGE 93 H1857 LEGIS GHANA

S63
LERNER D.,"WILL EUROPEAN UNION BRING ABOUT MERGED NATIONAL GOALS." EUR+WWI FRANCE GERMANY UK ECO/DEV NAT/G VOL/ASSN DELIB/GP BAL/PWR ECO/TAC NAT/LISM EEC 20 DEGAULLE/C. PAGE 95 H1889 ATTIT STERTYP ELITES REGION

S63
MONROE A.D.,"BRITAIN AND THE EUROPEAN COMMUNITY." EUR+WWI FRANCE NAT/G DELIB/GP TOP/EX ECO/TAC DOMIN PWR...POLICY RECORD GEN/LAWS EEC EFTA 20 EFTA CMN/WLTH. PAGE 112 H2241 VOL/ASSN ATTIT UK

S63
NICHOLAS W.,"VILLAGE FACTIONS AND POLITICAL PARTIES IN RURAL WEST BENGAL." S/ASIA CULTURE STRATA FACE/GP KIN MUNIC DELIB/GP LEGIS DOMIN EDU/PROP COERCE CHOOSE ATTIT ALL/VALS...STAT TOT/POP VAL/FREE 20. PAGE 117 H2348 NEIGH POL/PAR

S63
SOEMARDJORN S.,"SOME SOCIAL AND CULTURAL IMPLICATIONS OF INDONESIA'S PLANNED AND UNPLANNED DEVELOPMENT." EUR+WWI FUT MOD/EUR S/ASIA CONSTN SOCIETY DELIB/GP ACT/RES PLAN ECO/TAC EDU/PROP COERCE ATTIT ALL/VALS...TIME/SEQ 20. PAGE 146 H2927 ECO/UNDEV CULTURE INDONESIA

S63
STAAR R.F.,"HOW STRONG IS THE SOVIET BLOC." COM USSR ECO/DEV NAT/G DELIB/GP ECO/TAC RIGID/FLEX ...CONCPT RECORD CHARTS 20. PAGE 148 H2964 FORCES MYTH TOTALISM

S63
TANG P.S.H.,"SINO-SOVIET TENSIONS." ASIA CHINA/COM COM CUBA KOREA/N VIETNAM/N NAT/G VOL/ASSN DELIB/GP PEACE PERCEPT PWR...METH/CNCPT MYTH RECORD TREND GEN/LAWS 20. PAGE 152 H3041 ACT/RES EDU/PROP REV

S63
TILMAN R.O.,"MALAYSIA: THE PROBLEMS OF FEDERATION." ISLAM S/ASIA CONSTN PROVS SECT DELIB/GP DOMIN EDU/PROP LEGIT EXEC COERCE CHOOSE ATTIT HEALTH ORD/FREE PWR...STAT TOT/POP VAL/FREE 20. PAGE 155 H3097 NAT/G CULTURE MALAYSIA

C63
ATTIA G.E.O.,"LES FORCES ARMEES DES NATIONS UNIES EN COREE ET AU MOYENORIENT." KOREA CONSTN DELIB/GP LEGIS PWR...IDEA/COMP NAT/COMP BIBLIOG UN SUEZ. PAGE 9 H0178 FORCES NAT/G INT/LAW

B64
AVASTHI A.,ASPECTS OF ADMINISTRATION. INDIA UK USA+45 FINAN ACADEM DELIB/GP LEGIS RECEIVE PARL/PROC PRIVIL...NAT/COMP 20. PAGE 9 H0183 MGT ADMIN SOC/WK ORD/FREE

B64
GRIFFITH W.E.,THE SINO-SOVIET RIFT. ASIA CHINA/COM COM CUBA USSR YUGOSLAVIA NAT/G POL/PAR VOL/ASSN DELIB/GP FORCES TOP/EX DIPLOM EDU/PROP DRIVE PERSON PWR...TREND 20 TREATY. PAGE 61 H1224 ATTIT TIME/SEQ BAL/PWR SOCISM

B64
GROVES H.E.,THE CONSTITUTION OF MALAYSIA. MALAYSIA POL/PAR CHIEF CONSULT DELIB/GP CT/SYS PARL/PROC CHOOSE FEDERAL ORD/FREE 20. PAGE 62 H1238 CONSTN NAT/G LAW

B64
HEIMSATH C.H.,INDIAN NATIONALISM AND HINDU SOCIAL REFORM. S/ASIA LAW CULTURE SOCIETY STRATA PROVS VOL/ASSN DELIB/GP LEGIS TOP/EX DOMIN EDU/PROP LEGIT ATTIT ALL/VALS...POLICY SOC TIME/SEQ STERTYP VAL/FREE 19/20. PAGE 69 H1385 SECT NAT/G

B64
MELADY T.,FACES OF AFRICA. AFR FUT ISLAM NAT/G ECO/UNDEV POL/PAR SCHOOL DELIB/GP PLAN ECO/TAC EDU/PROP ATTIT ALL/VALS...CHARTS TOT/POP VAL/FREE 20. PAGE 108 H2168 TREND NAT/LISM

B64
PINNICK A.W.,COUNTRY PLANNERS IN ACTION. UK FINAN SERV/IND NAT/G CONSULT DELIB/GP PRICE CONTROL ROUTINE LEISURE AGE/C...GEOG 20 URBAN/RNWL. PAGE 126 H2512 MUNIC PLAN INDUS ATTIT

B64
RIES J.C.,THE MANAGEMENT OF DEFENSE: ORGANIZATION AND CONTROL OF THE US ARMED SERVICES. PROF/ORG DELIB/GP EX/STRUC LEGIS GOV/REL PERS/REL CENTRAL RATIONAL PWR...POLICY TREND GOV/COMP BIBLIOG. PAGE 131 H2626 FORCES ACT/RES DECISION CONTROL

B64
SKINNER E.P.,THE MOSSI OF UPPER VOLTA: THE POLITICAL DEVELOPMENT OF A SUDANESE PEOPLE. AFR LAW AGRI FAM KIN POL/PAR PROVS SECT DELIB/GP EX/STRUC FORCES TOP/EX DOMIN EDU/PROP LEGIT CT/SYS COERCE CHOOSE ORD/FREE PWR WEALTH...SOC MYTH VAL/FREE. PAGE 145 H2897 CULTURE OBS UPPER/VOLT

B64
THORNBURG M.W.,PEOPLE AND POLICY IN THE MIDDLE EAST. ISLAM ECO/UNDEV FAM KIN MUNIC NAT/G NEIGH POL/PAR SECT DELIB/GP LEGIS PLAN ECO/TAC DOMIN ADMIN ATTIT HEALTH RESPECT...SOC CONCPT METH/CNCPT OBS TIME/SEQ TOT/POP VAL/FREE. PAGE 154 H3088 TEC/DEV CULTURE

B64
WRIGHT G.,RURAL REVOLUTION IN FRANCE: THE PEASANTRY IN THE TWENTIETH CENTURY. EUR+WWI MOD/EUR LAW CULTURE AGRI POL/PAR DELIB/GP LEGIS ECO/TAC EDU/PROP COERCE CHOOSE ATTIT RIGID/FLEX HEALTH ...STAT CENSUS CHARTS VAL/FREE 20. PAGE 171 H3419 PWR STRATA FRANCE REV

B64
ZARTMAN I.W.,MOROCCO: PROBLEMS OF NEW POWER. ISLAM CULTURE ECO/UNDEV AGRI POL/PAR SCHOOL FORCES ADMIN ...CONCPT STAT INT CENSUS TIME/SEQ CHARTS WORK VAL/FREE 20. PAGE 172 H3449 CHOOSE MOROCCO DELIB/GP DECISION

L64
HAAS E.B.,"ECONOMICS AND DIFFERENTIAL PATTERNS OF POLITICAL INTEGRATION: PROJECTIONS ABOUT UNITY IN LATIN AMERICA." SOCIETY NAT/G DELIB/GP ACT/RES CREATE PLAN ECO/TAC REGION ROUTINE ATTIT DRIVE PWR WEALTH...CONCPT TREND CHARTS LAFTA 20. PAGE 63 H1266 L/A+17C INT/ORG MARKET

S64
CLIFFE L.,"TANGANYIKA'S TWO YEARS OF INDEPENDENCE." AFR INDUS MARKET NAT/G POL/PAR DELIB/GP CREATE ECO/TAC LEGIT DRIVE ALL/VALS...METH/CNCPT RECORD 20 TANGANYIKA. PAGE 30 H0604 ECO/UNDEV PLAN

S64
GIROD R.,"LE SYSTEME DES PARTIS EN SUISSE." CONSTN LOC/G DELIB/GP FEDERAL ALL/VALS. PAGE 57 H1136 POL/PAR LEGIS NAT/G PARL/PROC

S64
GROSS J.A.,"WHITEHALL AND THE COMMONWEALTH." EUR+WWI MOD/EUR INT/ORG NAT/G CONSULT DELIB/GP LEGIS DOMIN ADMIN COLONIAL ROUTINE PWR CMN/WLTH 19/20. PAGE 62 H1233 EX/STRUC ATTIT TREND

S64
MERKL P.H.,"EUROPEAN ASSEMBLY PARTIES AND NATIONAL DELEGATIONS." INT/ORG DELIB/GP DOMIN EDU/PROP LEGIT CHOOSE PWR...STAT VAL/FREE 20. PAGE 109 H2180 EUR+WWI POL/PAR REGION

S64
MOZINGO D.P.,"CHINA'S RELATIONS WITH HER ASIAN NEIGHBORS." ASIA CHINA/COM S/ASIA VIETNAM NAT/G DELIB/GP FORCES CREATE DOMIN EDU/PROP REV RIGID/FLEX PWR...TIME/SEQ GEN/LAWS COLD/WAR 20. PAGE 114 H2277 VOL/ASSN POLICY DIPLOM

S64
SAAB H.,"THE ARAB SEARCH FOR A FEDERAL UNION." SOCIETY INT/ORG NAT/G DELIB/GP FORCES ACT/RES TEC/DEV ECO/TAC DOMIN LEGIT REGION ROUTINE ATTIT DRIVE RIGID/FLEX ALL/VALS...SOC CONCPT NEW/IDEA TIME/SEQ TREND. PAGE 136 H2726 ISLAM PLAN

S64
SWEARER H.R.,"AFTER KHRUSHCHEV: WHAT NEXT." COM FUT USSR CONSTN ELITES NAT/G POL/PAR CHIEF DELIB/GP LEGIS DOMIN LEAD...RECORD TREND STERTYP GEN/METH 20. PAGE 151 H3016 EX/STRUC PWR

B65
CAMPBELL G.A.,THE CIVIL SERVICE IN BRITAIN (2ND ED.). UK DELIB/GP FORCES WORKER CREATE PLAN ...POLICY AUD/VIS 19/20 CIVIL/SERV. PAGE 26 H0515 ADMIN LEGIS NAT/G FINAN

B65
CHARNAY J.P.,LE SUFFRAGE POLITIQUE EN FRANCE; ELECTIONS PARLEMENTAIRES, ELECTION PRESIDENTIELLE, REFERENDUMS. FRANCE CONSTN CHIEF DELIB/GP ECO/TAC EDU/PROP CRIME INGP/REL MORAL ORD/FREE PWR CATHISM 20 PARLIAMENT PRESIDENT. PAGE 29 H0584 CHOOSE SUFF NAT/G LEGIS

B65
CHRIMES S.B.,ENGLISH CONSTITUTIONAL HISTORY (3RD ED.). UK CHIEF CONSULT DELIB/GP LEGIS CT/SYS 15/20 COMMON/LAW PARLIAMENT. PAGE 30 H0598 CONSTN BAL/PWR NAT/G

B65
GOPAL S.,BRITISH POLICY IN INDIA 1858-1905. INDIA UK ELITES CHIEF DELIB/GP ECO/TAC GP/REL DISCRIM ATTIT...IDEA/COMP NAT/COMP PERS/COMP BIBLIOG/A 19/20. PAGE 59 H1176
COLONIAL ADMIN POL/PAR ECO/UNDEV

B65
HANSER C.J.,GUIDE TO DECISION: ROYAL COMMISSION. UK INTELL EXTR/IND SCHOOL PROB/SOLV EXEC ROUTINE CHOOSE GOV/REL GP/REL HEALTH...CHARTS 20. PAGE 66 H1318
NAT/G DELIB/GP EX/STRUC PWR

B65
INST INTL DES CIVILISATION DIF,THE CONSTITUTIONS AND ADMINISTRATIVE INSTITUTIONS OF THE NEW STATES. AFR ISLAM S/ASIA NAT/G POL/PAR DELIB/GP EX/STRUC CONFER EFFICIENCY NAT/LISM...JURID SOC 20. PAGE 77 H1535
CONSTN ADMIN ADJUD ECO/UNDEV

B65
MEAGHER R.F.,PUBLIC INTERNATIONAL DEVELOPMENT FINANCING IN SUDAN. SUDAN FINAN DELIB/GP GIVE ...CHARTS GOV/COMP 20. PAGE 108 H2155
FOR/AID PLAN RECEIVE ECO/UNDEV

B65
O'CONNELL M.R.,IRISH POLITICS AND SOCIAL CONFLICT IN THE AGE OF THE AMERICAN REVOLUTION. FRANCE IRELAND MOD/EUR STRATA SECT LEGIS DIPLOM INT/TRADE DOMIN REV WAR...BIBLIOG 18 PARLIAMENT. PAGE 119 H2387
CATHISM ATTIT NAT/G DELIB/GP

B65
OGILVY-WEBB M.,THE GOVERNMENT EXPLAINS: A STUDY OF THE INFORMATION SERVICES. UK DELIB/GP LEGIS WORKER BUDGET DIPLOM 20. PAGE 121 H2409
EDU/PROP ATTIT NAT/G ADMIN

B65
PARRIS H.W.,GOVERNMENT AND THE RAILWAYS IN NINETEENTH-CENTURY BRITAIN. UK DELIB/GP CONTROL LEAD CENTRAL 19 RAILROAD. PAGE 124 H2470
DIST/IND NAT/G PLAN GP/REL

B65
SHARMA S.A.,PARLIAMENTARY GOVERNMENT IN INDIA. INDIA FINAN LOC/G PROVS DELIB/GP PLAN ADMIN CT/SYS FEDERAL...JURID 20. PAGE 142 H2849
NAT/G CONSTN PARL/PROC LEGIS

B65
WUORINEN J.H.,SCANDINAVIA. DENMARK FINLAND ICELAND NORWAY SWEDEN SOCIETY AGRI INDUS DELIB/GP DIPLOM INT/TRADE NEUTRAL...GEOG CHARTS BIBLIOG TREATY. PAGE 171 H3428
NAT/G POL/PAR TREND POLICY

S65
TABORSKY E.,"CHANGE IN CZECHOSLOVAKIA." COM USSR ELITES INTELL AGRI INDUS NAT/G DELIB/GP EX/STRUC ECO/TAC TOTALISM ATTIT RIGID/FLEX SOCISM...MGT CONCPT TREND 20. PAGE 152 H3031
ECO/DEV PLAN CZECHOSLVK

S65
VUCINICH W.S.,"WHITHER RUMANIA." COM USSR YUGOSLAVIA NAT/G VOL/ASSN DELIB/GP TOP/EX LEGIT NAT/LISM TOTALISM ATTIT DRIVE RIGID/FLEX ORD/FREE WEALTH SOCISM...TIME/SEQ TREND 20. PAGE 164 H3281
ECO/DEV CREATE ROMANIA

C65
WUORINEN J.H.,"SCANDINAVIA." DENMARK FINLAND ICELAND NORWAY SWEDEN SOCIETY AGRI POL/PAR DELIB/GP DIPLOM INT/TRADE NEUTRAL WAR...CHARTS TREATY 20. PAGE 171 H3427
BIBLIOG NAT/G POLICY

B66
ADAMS J.C.,THE GOVERNMENT OF REPUBLICAN ITALY (2ND ED.). ITALY LOC/G POL/PAR DELIB/GP LEGIS WORKER ADMIN CT/SYS FASCISM...CHARTS BIBLIOG 20 PARLIAMENT. PAGE 3 H0064
NAT/G CHOOSE EX/STRUC CONSTN

B66
AGGARWALA R.N.,FINANCIAL COMMITTEES OF THE INDIAN PARLIAMENT: A STUDY IN PARLIAMENTARY CONTROL OVER PUBLIC EXPENDITURE. INDIA FINAN NAT/G ROLE...CHARTS METH/COMP METH 20 PARLIAMENT. PAGE 4 H0078
PARL/PROC BUDGET CONTROL DELIB/GP

B66
BRECHER M.,SUCCESSION IN INDIA. INDIA USA+45 CONSTN AGRI POL/PAR PROVS SECT DELIB/GP FORCES PROB/SOLV ECO/TAC PWR...LING 20 CONGRESS NEHRU/J. PAGE 20 H0408
CHIEF DECISION CHOOSE

B66
DOUMA J.,BIBLIOGRAPHY ON THE INTERNATIONAL COURT INCLUDING THE PERMANENT COURT, 1918-1964. WOR+45 WOR-45 DELIB/GP WAR PRIVIL...JURID NAT/COMP 20 UN LEAGUE/NAT. PAGE 42 H0844
BIBLIOG/A INT/ORG CT/SYS DIPLOM

B66
FORD P.,CARDINAL MORAN AND THE A. L. P. NAT/G POL/PAR SECT DELIB/GP LOBBY REV CHOOSE ORD/FREE MARXISM 19/20 AUSTRAL PROTESTANT LABOR/PAR. PAGE 52 H1035
CATHISM SOCISM LABOR SOCIETY

B66
GHOSH P.K.,THE CONSTITUTION OF INDIA: HOW IT HAS BEEN FRAMED. INDIA LOC/G DELIB/GP EX/STRUC PROB/SOLV BUDGET INT/TRADE CT/SYS CHOOSE...LING 20. PAGE 56 H1121
CONSTN NAT/G LEGIS FEDERAL

B66
INTERPARLIAMENTARY UNION,PARLIAMENTS: COMPARATIVE STUDY ON STRUCTURE AND FUNCTIONING OF REPRESENTATIVE INSTITUTIONS IN FIFTY-FIVE COUNTRIES. WOR+45 POL/PAR DELIB/GP BUDGET ADMIN CONTROL CHOOSE. PAGE 78 H1560
PARL/PROC LEGIS GOV/COMP EX/STRUC

B66
JOHNSON N.,PARLIAMENT AND ADMINISTRATION: THE ESTIMATES COMMITTEE 1945-65. FUT UK NAT/G EX/STRUC PLAN BUDGET ORD/FREE...T 20 PARLIAMENT HOUSE/CMNS. PAGE 81 H1625
LEGIS ADMIN FINAN DELIB/GP

B66
NEVITT A.A.,THE ECONOMIC PROBLEMS OF HOUSING. WOR+45 ECO/DEV ECO/UNDEV ACT/RES PROB/SOLV ECO/TAC RENT...OBS CHARTS 20. PAGE 117 H2342
HABITAT PROC/MFG DELIB/GP NAT/COMP

B66
O'NEILL C.E.,CHURCH AND STATE IN FRENCH COLONIAL LOUISIANA: POLICY AND POLITICS TO 1732. PROVS VOL/ASSN DELIB/GP ADJUD ADMIN GP/REL ATTIT DRIVE ...POLICY BIBLIOG 17/18 LOUISIANA CHURCH/STA. PAGE 120 H2390
COLONIAL NAT/G SECT PWR

B66
SAINDERICHIN P.,HISTORIE SECRETE D'UNE ELECTION, DECEMBER 5-19, 1965. FRANCE NAT/G DELIB/GP LEGIS PLAN EDU/PROP TV SOCISM...MARXIST 20 DEGAULLE/C. PAGE 137 H2731
CHOOSE CHIEF PROB/SOLV POL/PAR

B66
SASTRI K.V.S.,FEDERAL-STATE FISCAL RELATIONS IN INDIA: A STUDY OF THE FINANCE COMMISSION AND TECHNIQUES OF FINANCIAL ADJUSTMENT. INDIA PROVS DELIB/GP GOV/REL FEDERAL...MATH CHARTS 20. PAGE 138 H2756
TAX BUDGET FINAN NAT/G

B66
STADLER K.R.,THE BIRTH OF THE AUSTRIAN REPUBLIC, 1918-1921. AUSTRIA PLAN TASK PEACE...POLICY DECISION 20. PAGE 148 H2966
NAT/G DIPLOM WAR DELIB/GP

B66
THOMPSON J.M.,RUSSIA, BOLSHEVISM, AND THE VERSAILLES PEACE. RUSSIA USSR INT/ORG NAT/G DELIB/GP AGREE REV WAR PWR 20 TREATY VERSAILLES BOLSHEVISM. PAGE 154 H3083
DIPLOM PEACE MARXISM

B66
VIEN N.C.,SEEKING THE TRUTH. VIETNAM DELIB/GP DOMIN RISK MARXISM 20 KY/NGUYEN. PAGE 162 H3250
NAT/G COLONIAL PWR SOVEREIGN

S66
MATTHEWS D.G.,"ETHIOPIAN OUTLINE: A BIBLIOGRAPHIC RESEARCH GUIDE." ETHIOPIA LAW STRUCT ECO/UNDEV AGRI LABOR SECT CHIEF DELIB/GP EX/STRUC ADMIN...LING ORG/CHARTS 20. PAGE 105 H2095
BIBLIOG NAT/G DIPLOM POL/PAR

B67
HILSMAN R.,TO MOVE A NATION: THE POLITICS OF FOREIGN POLICY IN THE ADMINISTRATION OF JOHN F. KENNEDY. CHINA/COM COM USSR VIETNAM NAT/G DELIB/GP FORCES PLAN PROB/SOLV BAL/PWR COLONIAL EXEC REV PWR 20 KENNEDY/JF PRESIDENT. PAGE 71 H1418
CHIEF DIPLOM

B67
JOUVENEL B D.E.,THE ART OF CONJECTURE. FUT CONSULT EX/STRUC CHOOSE GOV/REL ALL/VALS. PAGE 82 H1638
PREDICT DELIB/GP PLAN NAT/G

B67
PLANCK C.R.,THE CHANGING STATUS OF GERMAN REUNIFICATION IN WESTERN DIPLOMACY, 1955-1966. GERMANY DELIB/GP PLAN PEACE...TREND 20 KENNEDY/JF DEGAULLE/C. PAGE 126 H2519
NAT/G DIPLOM CENTRAL

B67
ROSENBLUTH G.,THE CANADIAN ECONOMY AND DISARMAMENT. CANADA FUT ECO/DEV INDUS R+D DELIB/GP DIPLOM ECO/TAC CIVMIL/REL PEACE...POLICY BIBLIOG PACIFIST 20. PAGE 134 H2679
ARMS/CONT STAT PLAN NAT/G

B67
SCHWARTZ B.,THE ROOTS OF FREEDOM: A CONSTITUTIONAL HISTORY OF ENGLAND. UK LAW POL/PAR DELIB/GP LEGIS REV REPRESENT...JURID BIBLIOG/A 13/20. PAGE 140 H2809
CONSTN PARL/PROC NAT/G

B67
VENKATESWARAN R.J.,CABINET GOVERNMENT IN INDIA. INDIA UK SOCIETY OP/RES COLONIAL LEAD EFFICIENCY ORD/FREE 20. PAGE 162 H3241
DELIB/GP ADMIN CONSTN NAT/G

L67
GRAUBARD S.R.,"TOWARD THE YEAR 2000: WORK IN PROGRESS." FUT ACADEM SECT DELIB/GP DIPLOM EDU/PROP AGE/Y PERSON ROLE...PSY ANTHOL. PAGE 60 H1199
PREDICT PROB/SOLV SOCIETY CULTURE

S67
ALBINSKI H.S.,"POLITICS AND BICULTURISM IN CANADA: THE FLAG DEBATE." CANADA SOCIETY NAT/G PROVS DELIB/GP DEBATE REGION SOVEREIGN PLURISM...POLICY SOC/INTEG 20. PAGE 5 H0093
NAT/LISM GP/REL POL/PAR CULTURE

S67
ALEXANDER A.,"CANADA'S PARLIAMENTARY SECRETARIES: THEIR POLITICAL AND CONSTITUTIONAL POSITION." CANADA UK NAT/G POL/PAR GOV/REL...GOV/COMP 20. PAGE 5 H0099
CONSTN ADMIN EX/STRUC DELIB/GP

S67
ANDERSON L.G.,"ADMINISTERING A GOVERNMENT SOCIAL SERVICE" NEW/ZEALND EX/STRUC TASK ROLE 20. PAGE 6 H0129
ADMIN NAT/G DELIB/GP SOC/WK

S67
BRADLEY A.W.,"CONSTITUTION-MAKING IN UGANDA." UGANDA LAW CHIEF DELIB/GP LEGIS ADMIN EXEC PARL/PROC RACE/REL ORD/FREE...GOV/COMP 20. PAGE 20 H0397
NAT/G CREATE CONSTN FEDERAL

S67
CUMMINS L.,"THE FORMULATION OF THE "PLATT" AMENDMENT." CUBA L/A+17C NAT/G DELIB/GP CONFER ...POLICY 20. PAGE 36 H0720
DIPLOM INT/LAW LEGIS

S67
DESHPANDE A.M.,"FEDERAL-STATE FISCAL RELATIONS IN INDIA" (REVIEW ARTICLE)" GERMANY USSR DELIB/GP PLAN BUDGET ECO/TAC INCOME 20 SOC/DEMPAR SOC/REVPAR. PAGE 40 H0795
FINAN NAT/G GOV/REL TAX

S67
DOERN G.B.,"THE ROYAL COMMISSIONS IN THE GENERAL POLICY PROCESS AND IN FEDERAL-PROVINCIAL RELATIONS." CANADA CONSTN ACADEM PROVS CONSULT DELIB/GP LEGIS ACT/RES PROB/SOLV CONFER CONTROL EFFICIENCY...METH/COMP 20 SENATE ROYAL/COMM. PAGE 42 H0832
R+D EX/STRUC GOV/REL NAT/G

S67
GREGORY R.,"THE MINISTER'S LINE: OR, THE M4 COMES TO BERKSHIRE. PART I." UK CONSTN DIST/IND LEGIS TOP/EX PLAN ADJUD...GEOG 20. PAGE 60 H1210
DECISION CONSTRUC NAT/G DELIB/GP

S67
HARBRON J.D.,"UNIFICATION IN CANADA: FAIT ACCOMPLI" CANADA STRATA NAT/G DELIB/GP BUDGET GP/REL 20 NAVY. PAGE 66 H1327
INGP/REL FORCES PLAN ATTIT

S67
NEALE R.S.,"WORKING CLASS WOMEN AND WOMEN'S SUFFRAGE." UK LAW CONSTN LABOR NAT/G DELIB/GP LEGIS WORKER PAY PARTIC CHOOSE 19 FEMALE/SEX. PAGE 116 H2326
STRATA SEX SUFF DISCRIM

S67
TIKHOMIROV I.A.,"DIVISION OF POWERS OR DIVISION OF LABOR?" USSR NAT/G DELIB/GP ADJUD GP/REL MARXISM SOCISM 20. PAGE 155 H3093
BAL/PWR WORKER STRATA ADMIN

S67
WHITE W.L.,"THE TREASURY BOARD AND PARLIAMENT." CANADA CONSTN CONSULT LEGIS LEAD PARL/PROC GP/REL ...DECISION 20. PAGE 167 H3351
FINAN DELIB/GP NAT/G ADMIN

S68
DUGARD J.,"THE REVOCATION OF THE MANDATE FOR SOUTH WEST AFRICA." SOUTH/AFR WOR+45 STRATA NAT/G DELIB/GP DIPLOM ADJUD SANCTION CHOOSE RACE/REL ...POLICY NAT/COMP 20 AFRICA/SW UN TRUST/TERR LEAGUE/NAT. PAGE 43 H0858
AFR INT/ORG DISCRIM COLONIAL

DEMAND....ECONOMIC DEMAND

B13
DIE REKLAME IHRE KUNST UND WISSENSCHAFT. GERMANY POLAND SWITZERLND USA+45 TEC/DEV CAP/ISM DEMAND ...ART/METH EXHIBIT METH/COMP ANTHOL 20. PAGE 135 H2707
EDU/PROP MARKET NAT/COMP ATTIT

B20
MALTHUS T.R.,PRINCIPLES OF POLITICAL ECONOMY. UK AGRI INDUS MARKET NAT/G DIPLOM PRICE CONTROL BAL/PAY COST OWN PWR LAISSEZ 18/19. PAGE 102 H2034
GEN/LAWS DEMAND WEALTH

B57
NEUMARK S.D.,ECONOMIC INFLUENCES ON THE SOUTH AFRICAN FRONTIER, 1652-1836. SOUTH/AFR SEA AGRI NAT/G FORCES WORKER DIPLOM INT/TRADE PRICE DEMAND PRODUC...STAT CHARTS 17/19 FRONTIER. PAGE 117 H2341
COLONIAL ECO/UNDEV ECO/TAC MARKET

B60
ROBERTSON D.,THE CONTROL OF INDUSTRY. UK MARKET LABOR WORKER PRICE CONTROL GP/REL COST DEMAND ORD/FREE WEALTH NEW/LIB SOCISM 20. PAGE 132 H2646
INDUS FINAN NAT/G ECO/DEV

B61
HUNT E.F.,SOCIAL SCIENCE. DIPLOM ECO/TAC ROUTINE GP/REL DEMAND DISCRIM EFFICIENCY HABITAT ALL/IDEOS ...SOC T 20. PAGE 75 H1497
CULTURE ADJUST STRATA ROLE

B61
LETHBRIDGE H.J.,CHINA'S URBAN COMMUNES. CHINA/COM FUT ECO/UNDEV DIPLOM EDU/PROP DEMAND INCOME MARXISM ...POLICY 20. PAGE 95 H1893
MUNIC CONTROL ECO/TAC NAT/G

B61
OECD,STATISTICS OF BALANCE OF PAYMENTS 1950-61. WOR+45 FINAN ECO/TAC INT/TRADE DEMAND WEALTH...STAT NAT/COMP 20 OEEC OECD. PAGE 120 H2396
BAL/PAY ECO/DEV INT/ORG CHARTS

B62
GREEN L.P.,DEVELOPMENT IN AFRICA. AFR CENTRL/AFR GHANA RHODESIA SOUTH/AFR AGRI PROC/MFG INT/TRADE DEMAND NAT/LISM PRODUC WEALTH...GEOG METH/CNCPT CHARTS BIBLIOG 20. PAGE 60 H1206
CULTURE ECO/UNDEV GOV/REL TREND

B62
KINDLEBERGER C.P.,FOREIGN TRADE AND THE NATIONAL ECONOMY. WOR+45 ECO/DEV ECO/UNDEV ECO/TAC COST DEMAND 20. PAGE 86 H1713
INT/TRADE GOV/COMP BAL/PAY POLICY

B62
MARTINS A.F.,REVOLUCAO BRANCA NO CAMPO. L/A+17C SERV/IND DEMAND EFFICIENCY PRODUC...POLICY METH/COMP. PAGE 104 H2070
AGRI ECO/UNDEV TEC/DEV NAT/COMP

B62
PHELPS E.S.,THE GOAL OF ECONOMIC GROWTH: SOURCES, COSTS, BENEFITS. USA+45 USSR FINAN TAX CONTROL DEMAND WEALTH...POLICY NAT/COMP ANTHOL BIBLIOG 20. PAGE 125 H2499
ECO/TAC ECO/DEV NAT/G FUT

B63
BRITISH AID. UK AGRI DIST/IND INDUS SCHOOL TEC/DEV INT/TRADE COLONIAL DEMAND...TREND CHARTS 20. PAGE 2 H0041
FOR/AID ECO/UNDEV NAT/G FINAN

B63
BOHANNAN P.,SOCIAL ANTHROPOLOGY. ECO/DEV GP/REL DEMAND MARRIAGE HABITAT...CHARTS GP/COMP BIBLIOG T WORSHIP 20. PAGE 18 H0366
SOC STRUCT FAM CULTURE

B63
INTERNATIONAL ASSOCIATION RES,AFRICAN STUDIES IN INCOME AND WEALTH. AFR NAT/G PROB/SOLV DEMAND INCOME...ECOMETRIC METH/COMP 20. PAGE 78 H1553
WEALTH PLAN ECO/UNDEV BUDGET

B63
MAJUMDAR O.N.,AN INTRODUCTION TO SOCIAL ANTHROPOLOGY. INDIA LAW STRATA ECO/UNDEV KIN DEMAND MARRIAGE...GP/COMP BIBLIOG T WORSHIP 20. PAGE 101 H2026
SOC CULTURE STRUCT GP/REL

B63
OLSON M. JR.,THE ECONOMICS OF WARTIME SHORTAGE. FRANCE GERMANY MOD/EUR UK AGRI PROB/SOLV ADMIN DEMAND WEALTH...POLICY OLD/LIB 17/20. PAGE 121 H2416
WAR ADJUST ECO/TAC NAT/COMP

B64
BAUCHET P.,ECONOMIC PLANNING. FRANCE STRATA LG/CO CAP/ISM ADMIN PARL/PROC DEMAND OPTIMAL ATTIT PWR SOCISM...POLICY CHARTS 20. PAGE 12 H0238
ECO/DEV NAT/G PLAN ECO/TAC

B64
PARANJAPE H.K.,THE FLIGHT OF TECHNICAL PERSONNEL IN PUBLIC UNDERTAKINGS. INDIA PAY DEMAND HAPPINESS ORD/FREE...MGT QU 20 MIGRATION. PAGE 123 H2464
ADMIN NAT/G WORKER PLAN

B64
WERNETTE J.P.,GOVERNMENT AND BUSINESS. LABOR CAP/ISM ECO/TAC INT/TRADE TAX ADMIN AUTOMAT NUC/PWR CIVMIL/REL DEMAND...MGT 20 MONOPOLY. PAGE 167 H3333
NAT/G FINAN ECO/DEV CONTROL

B65
EDELMAN M.,THE POLITICS OF WAGE-PRICE DECISIONS. GERMANY ITALY NETHERLAND UK INDUS LABOR POL/PAR PROB/SOLV BARGAIN PRICE ROUTINE BAL/PAY COST DEMAND 20. PAGE 44 H0888
GOV/COMP CONTROL ECO/TAC PLAN

B65
HAVIGHURST R.J.,SOCIETY AND EDUCATION IN BRAZIL. BRAZIL PORTUGAL ECO/UNDEV INDUS NAT/G CREATE INSPECT COLONIAL ADJUST DEMAND LITERACY...CENSUS TREND CHARTS 16/20. PAGE 68 H1362
SCHOOL ACADEM ACT/RES CULTURE

B65
OECD,THE MEDITERRANEAN REGIONAL PROJECT: GREECE; EDUCATION AND DEVELOPMENT. FUT GREECE SOCIETY AGRI FINAN NAT/G PROF/ORG WORKER PLAN PROB/SOLV ADMIN DEMAND ATTIT 20 OECD. PAGE 120 H2401
EDU/PROP SCHOOL ACADEM ECO/UNDEV

B65
ONSLOW C.,ASIAN ECONOMIC DEVELOPMENT. BURMA CEYLON INDIA MALAYSIA PAKISTAN S/ASIA AGRI INDUS MARKET PROB/SOLV CAP/ISM FOR/AID INT/TRADE DEMAND WEALTH ...POLICY ANTHOL 20. PAGE 121 H2418
ECO/UNDEV ECO/TAC PLAN NAT/G

B65
TEW B.,WEALTH AND INCOME. UK BUDGET INT/TRADE PRICE BAL/PAY DEMAND...CHARTS GOV/COMP 20 AUSTRAL. PAGE 153 H3064
FINAN ECO/DEV WEALTH INCOME

B67
ANDERSON C.W.,POLITICS AND ECONOMIC CHANGE IN LATIN AMERICA. L/A+17C INDUS NAT/G OP/RES ADMIN DEMAND ...POLICY STAT CHARTS NAT/COMP 20. PAGE 6 H0125
ECO/UNDEV PROB/SOLV PLAN ECO/TAC

B67
GILL R.T.,ECONOMIC DEVELOPMENT: PAST AND PRESENT (2ND ED.). ASIA INDIA USA+45 USA-45 WOR+45 WOR-45 DEMAND EFFICIENCY NAT/LISM WEALTH...GOV/COMP METH/COMP 18/20. PAGE 56 H1127
ECO/DEV ECO/UNDEV PLAN PROB/SOLV

B67
MOORE J.R.,THE ECONOMIC IMPACT OF THE TVA. AGRI INDUS PLAN BARGAIN CONTROL REGION GOV/REL DEMAND
ECO/UNDEV ECO/DEV

B62
GOURE L.,CIVIL DEFENSE IN THE SOVIET UNION. COM USA+45 USSR MUNIC NAT/G DETER ATTIT MARXISM ...NAT/COMP 20 CIV/DEFENS. PAGE 59 H1188
PLAN FORCES WAR COERCE

B62
MODELSKI G.,SEATO-SIX STUDIES. ASIA CHINA/COM INDIA S/ASIA INT/ORG NAT/G ECO/TAC DETER ATTIT ORD/FREE PWR...TIME/SEQ COLD/WAR TOT/POP 20 SEATO. PAGE 112 H2234
MARKET ECO/UNDEV INT/TRADE

B63
GONZALEZ PEDRERO E.,ANATOMIA DE UN CONFLICTO. WOR+45 ECO/DEV ECO/UNDEV ECO/TAC FOR/AID CONTROL ARMS/CONT GOV/REL...NAT/COMP 20 COLD/WAR. PAGE 58 H1166
DIPLOM DETER BAL/PWR

S63
HALPERN A.M.,"THE EMERGENCE OF AN ASIAN COMMUNIST BLOC." ASIA CHINA/COM COM FUT KOREA/N S/ASIA VIETNAM/N STRATA NAT/G DELIB/GP FORCES TOP/EX PLAN BAL/PWR COERCE DETER PWR COLD/WAR WORK 20. PAGE 65 H1295
POL/PAR EDU/PROP DIPLOM

S64
GOLDBERG A.,"THE MILITARY ORIGINS OF THE BRITISH NUCLEAR DETERRENT." EUR+WWI ECO/DEV NAT/G PLAN NUC/PWR ATTIT PWR...DECISION HIST/WRIT COLD/WAR 20. PAGE 58 H1156
FORCES CONCPT DETER UK

B65
GRETTON P.,MARITIME STRATEGY - A STUDY OF DEFENSE PROBLEMS. ASIA UK USSR DIPLOM COERCE DETER NUC/PWR WEAPON...CONCPT NAT/COMP 20. PAGE 60 H1211
FORCES PLAN WAR SEA

B65
US DEPARTMENT OF DEFENSE,US SECURITY ARMS CONTROL, AND DISARMAMENT 1961-1965 (PAMPHLET). CHINA/COM COM GERMANY/W ISRAEL SPACE USA+45 USSR WOR+45 FORCES EDU/PROP DETER EQUILIB PEACE ALL/VALS...GOV/COMP 20 NATO. PAGE 159 H3183
BIBLIOG/A ARMS/CONT NUC/PWR DIPLOM

S65
GORDON M.,"THE SETTING FOR EUROPEAN ARMS CONTROLS* POLITICAL AND STRATEGIC CHOICES OF EUROPEAN ELITES." FRANCE GERMANY UK USA+45 USSR ARMS/CONT DETER ATTIT ORD/FREE...SAMP NAT/COMP NATO. PAGE 59 H1179
REC/INT ELITES RISK WAR

S65
JENSEN L.,"MILITARY CAPABILITIES AND BARGAINING BEHAVIOR." USA+45 USSR ARMS/CONT DETER COST ATTIT ...METH/CNCPT STAT SYS/QU CON/ANAL CHARTS NAT/COMP. PAGE 81 H1614
DIPLOM DRIVE PWR STERTYP

B66
DAENIKER G.,STRATEGIE DES KLEIN STAATS. SWITZERLND ACT/RES CREATE DIPLOM NEUTRAL DETER WAR WEAPON PWR SOVEREIGN...IDEA/COMP 20 COLD/WAR. PAGE 36 H0730
NUC/PWR PLAN FORCES NAT/G

B66
GRAHAM I.C.C.,PUBLICATIONS OF THE SOCIAL SCIENCE DEPARTMENT, THE RAND CORPORATION, 1948-1966. USSR WOR+45 NAT/G ARMS/CONT DETER WAR NAT/LISM...SOC GOV/COMP. PAGE 60 H1192
BIBLIOG DIPLOM NUC/PWR FORCES

B66
SOBEL L.A.,SOUTH VIETNAM: US-COMMUNIST CONFRONTATION IN SOUTHEAST ASIA 1961-65. VIETNAM FOR/AID CROWD DETER REV PEACE...GEOG 20 INTERVENT DIEM COLD/WAR. PAGE 146 H2926
WAR TIME/SEQ FORCES NAT/G

L66
ZOPPO C.E.,"NUCLEAR TECHNOLOGY, MULTIPOLARITY, AND INTERNATIONAL STABILITY." ASIA RUSSIA USA+45 STRUCT TOP/EX BAL/PWR DIPLOM DETER CIVMIL/REL NAT/COMP. PAGE 173 H3464
NET/THEORY ORD/FREE DECISION NUC/PWR

S66
QUESTER G.H.,"ON THE IDENTIFICATION OF REAL AND PRETENDED COMMUNIST MILITARY DOCTRINE." ASIA USSR DETER WAR ATTIT DRIVE HEALTH TIME/SEQ. PAGE 129 H2574
RATIONAL PERCEPT NUC/PWR NAT/COMP

B67
AMERICAN FRIENDS SERVICE COMM,IN PLACE OF WAR NAT/G ACT/RES DIPLOM ADMIN NUC/PWR EFFICIENCY ...POLICY 20. PAGE 6 H0122
PEACE PACIFISM WAR DETER

S67
LALL B.G.,"GAPS IN THE ABM DEBATE." NAT/G DIPLOM DETER CIVMIL/REL 20. PAGE 90 H1798
NUC/PWR ARMS/CONT EX/STRUC FORCES

S67
RENFIELD R.L.,"A POLICY FOR VIETNAM." COM VIETNAM NAT/G POL/PAR VOL/ASSN CHIEF DIPLOM EDU/PROP DETER REPRESENT ATTIT ORD/FREE 20. PAGE 131 H2615
WAR POLICY PLAN COERCE

C67
GEHLEN M.P.,"THE POLITICS OF COEXISTENCE: SOVIET METHODS AND MOTIVES." COM USSR NAT/G INT/TRADE EDU/PROP ARMS/CONT DETER KNOWL...CHARTS IDEA/COMP 20 COLD/WAR. PAGE 55 H1108
BIBLIOG PEACE DIPLOM MARXISM

DETERRENCE....SEE DETER

DETROIT....DETROIT, MICHIGAN

DETTER I. H0796

DEUTSCH K.W. H0797,H0798,H0799,H0800,H0801

DEUTSCHE BIBLIOTH FRANKF A M H0802

DEUTSCHE BUCHEREI H0803,H0804,H0805

DEUTSCHE INST ZEITGESCHICHTE H0806

DEUTSCHER I. H0807,H0808

DEUTSCHMANN P.J. H0809

DEV/ASSIST....DEVELOPMENT AND ASSISTANCE COMMITTEE

DEVELOPMENT....SEE CREATE+ECO/UNDEV

DEVELOPMENT AND ASSISTANCE COMMITTEE....SEE DEV/ASSIST

DEVELOPMNT....HUMAN DEVELOPMENTAL CHANGE, PSYCHOLOGICAL AND PHYSIOLOGICAL

DEVIANT BEHAVIOR....SEE ANOMIE, CRIME

DEWEY J. H0810

DEWEY/JOHN....JOHN DEWEY

DEWEY/THOM....THOMAS DEWEY

DEWHURST A. H0811

DEXTER L.A. H0813,H0814

DEXTER N.C. H0815

DIA M. H0816,H0817

DIAGRAMS....SEE CHARTS

DIAMANT A. H0818

DIAMOND S. H0819

DIAZ/P....PORFIRIO DIAZ

B66
DE VORE B.B.,LAND AND LIBERTY; A HISTORY OF THE MEXICAN REVOLUTION. CONSTN INTELL NAT/G CONTROL LEAD CHOOSE TOTALISM AUTHORIT...BIBLIOG 19/20 MEXIC/AMER DIAZ/P LIB/PARTY MAGON/F MADERO/F. PAGE 39 H0776
REV CHIEF POL/PAR

DICHTER E. H0821

DICKEY J.S. H0822

DICKSON P.G.M. H0823

DICTIONARY....DICTIONARY

C06
MONTGOMERY H.,"A DICTIONARY OF POLITICAL PHRASES AND ILLUSIONS WITH A SHORT BIBLIOGRAPHY." EUR+WWI MOD/EUR UK AGRI LABOR LOC/G NAT/G COLONIAL CHOOSE RACE/REL. PAGE 112 H2245
BIBLIOG DICTIONARY POLICY DIPLOM

B51
MORLEY C.,GUIDE TO RESEARCH IN RUSSIAN HISTORY. USSR MARXISM...BIOG HIST/WRIT ANTHOL DICTIONARY. PAGE 113 H2259
BIBLIOG/A R+D NAT/G COM

B57
KOENTJARANINGRAT R.,A PRELIMINARY DESCRIPTION OF THE JAVANESE KINSHIP SYSTEM. INDONESIA STRATA FAM INGP/REL ADJUST MARRIAGE AGE/C AGE/Y AGE/A PERSON ...OBS CHARTS DICTIONARY 20 JAVA. PAGE 87 H1736
KIN STRUCT ELITES CULTURE

C58
WILDING N.,"AN ENCYCLOPEDIA OF PARLIAMENT." UK LAW CONSTN CHIEF PROB/SOLV DIPLOM DEBATE WAR INGP/REL PRIVIL...BIBLIOG DICTIONARY 13/20 CMN/WLTH PARLIAMENT. PAGE 168 H3363
PARL/PROC POL/PAR NAT/G ADMIN

B61
BURKS R.V.,THE DYNAMICS OF COMMUNISM IN EASTERN EUROPE. COM YUGOSLAVIA POL/PAR RACE/REL ISOLAT ...CORREL CON/ANAL CHARTS GP/COMP DICTIONARY 20 EUROPE/E SLAV/MACED. PAGE 24 H0489
MARXISM STRUCT WORKER REPRESENT

B61
TURNBULL C.M.,THE FOREST PEOPLE. EATING GP/REL INGP/REL RACE/REL ISOLAT HABITAT HEREDITY...GEOG SOC LING DICTIONARY WORSHIP 20 CONGO NEGRO BA/MBUTI. PAGE 157 H3138
AFR CULTURE KIN RECORD

B62
INAYATULLAH,BUREAUCRACY AND DEVELOPMENT IN PAKISTAN. PAKISTAN ECO/UNDEV EDU/PROP CONFER ...ANTHOL DICTIONARY 20 BUREAUCRCY. PAGE 76 H1526 EX/STRUC ADMIN NAT/G LOC/G

B66
AHMED Z.,DUSK AND DAWN IN VILLAGE INDIA. INDIA S/ASIA UK CULTURE SOCIETY NAT/G DOMIN COLONIAL HABITAT SOVEREIGN...SOC DICTIONARY 20. PAGE 4 H0080 NEIGH ECO/UNDEV AGRI ADJUST

B66
COLEMAN-NORTON P.R.,ROMAN STATE AND CHRISTIAN CHURCH: A COLLECTION OF LEGAL DOCUMENTS TO A.D. 535 (3 VOLS.). CHRIST-17C ROMAN/EMP...ANTHOL DICTIONARY 6 CHRISTIAN CHURCH/STA. PAGE 31 H0630 GP/REL NAT/G SECT LAW

B67
BARNETT A.D.,CADRES, BUREAUCRACY, AND POLITICAL POWER IN COMMUNIST CHINA. CHINA/COM ELITES LOC/G NAT/G INGP/REL...SOC INT DICTIONARY 20. PAGE 11 H0224 GOV/REL STRUCT MARXISM EDU/PROP

DIDEROT/D....DENIS DIDEROT

DIEM....NGO DINH DIEM

B66
SOBEL L.A.,SOUTH VIETNAM: US-COMMUNIST CONFRONTATION IN SOUTHEAST ASIA 1961-65. VIETNAM FOR/AID CROWD DETER REV PEACE...GEOG 20 INTERVENT DIEM COLD/WAR. PAGE 146 H2926 WAR TIME/SEQ FORCES NAT/G

DILLARD D. H0824

DILLING A.R. H0825

DILLON D.R. H0826

DIPLOM....DIPLOMACY

N
UNIVERSITY OF FLORIDA LIBRARY,DOORS TO LATIN AMERICA; RECENT BOOKS AND PAMPHLETS. CONSTN CULTURE SOCIETY ECO/UNDEV COLONIAL LEAD GOV/REL NAT/LISM ATTIT...HUM SOC 20. PAGE 159 H3170 BIBLIOG/A L/A+17C DIPLOM NAT/G

B
DEUTSCHE BIBLIOTH FRANKF A M,DEUTSCHE BIBLIOGRAPHIE. EUR+WWI GERMANY ECO/DEV FORCES DIPLOM LEAD...POLICY PHIL/SCI SOC 20. PAGE 40 H0802 BIBLIOG LAW ADMIN NAT/G

N
AMERICAN POLITICAL SCIENCE REVIEW. USA+45 USA-45 WOR+45 WOR-45 INT/ORG ADMIN...INT/LAW PHIL/SCI CONCPT METH 20 UN. PAGE 1 H0001 BIBLIOG/A DIPLOM NAT/G GOV/COMP

N
BULLETIN ANALYTIQUE DE DOCUMENTATION POLITIQUE, ECONOMIQUE, ET SOCIAL CONTEMPORAIRE. FRANCE WOR+45 SOCIETY ECO/DEV ECO/UNDEV INT/ORG LOC/G PROB/SOLV FOR/AID LEAD REGION SOC. PAGE 1 H0002 BIBLIOG/A DIPLOM NAT/COMP NAT/G

N
CANADIAN GOVERNMENT PUBLICATIONS (1955-). CANADA AGRI FINAN LABOR FORCES INT/TRADE HEALTH...JURID 20 PARLIAMENT. PAGE 1 H0003 BIBLIOG/A NAT/G DIPLOM INT/ORG

N
JOURNAL OF ASIAN STUDIES. CULTURE ECO/DEV SECT DIPLOM EDU/PROP WAR NAT/LISM...PHIL/SCI SOC 20. PAGE 1 H0005 BIBLIOG ASIA S/ASIA NAT/G

N
JOURNAL OF MODERN HISTORY. WOR+45 WOR-45 LEAD WAR ...TIME/SEQ TREND NAT/COMP 20. PAGE 1 H0006 BIBLIOG/A DIPLOM NAT/G

N
MIDDLE EAST JOURNAL. CULTURE SECT DIPLOM LEAD GOV/REL ATTIT...POLICY PHIL/SCI SOC LING BIOG 20. PAGE 1 H0007 BIBLIOG ISLAM NAT/G ECO/UNDEV

N
NEUE POLITISCHE LITERATUR. AFR ASIA EUR+WWI GERMANY RUSSIA SOCIETY ECO/DEV ECO/UNDEV PLAN PROB/SOLV LEAD MARXISM...PHIL/SCI CONCPT 20. PAGE 1 H0008 BIBLIOG DIPLOM COM NAT/G

N
PEKING REVIEW. CHINA/COM CULTURE AGRI INDUS DIPLOM EDU/PROP GUERRILLA ATTIT MARXISM...BIBLIOG 20. PAGE 1 H0009 MARXIST NAT/G POL/PAR PRESS

N
AFRICAN RESEARCH BULLETIN. AFR CULTURE NAT/G COLONIAL...SOC 20. PAGE 1 H0010 BIBLIOG/A DIPLOM PRESS

N
AUSTRALIAN PUBLIC AFFAIRS INFORMATION SERVICE. LAW ...HEAL HUM MGT SOC CON/ANAL 20 AUSTRAL. PAGE 1 H0011 BIBLIOG NAT/G CULTURE

DIPLOM
N
DAILY SUMMARY OF THE JAPANESE PRESS. NAT/G DIPLOM LEAD 20 CHINJAP. PAGE 1 H0013 BIBLIOG PRESS ASIA ATTIT

N
CHINA QUARTERLY. COM AGRI INDUS ACADEM POL/PAR INT/TRADE CONFER GOV/REL...TIME/SEQ CON/ANAL INDEX 20. PAGE 1 H0014 BIBLIOG/A ASIA DIPLOM POLICY

N
HANDBOOK OF LATIN AMERICAN STUDIES. LAW CULTURE ECO/UNDEV POL/PAR ADMIN LEAD...SOC 20. PAGE 1 H0016 BIBLIOG/A L/A+17C NAT/G DIPLOM

N
LONDON TIMES OFFICIAL INDEX. UK LAW ECO/DEV NAT/G DIPLOM LEAD ATTIT 20. PAGE 1 H0018 BIBLIOG INDEX PRESS WRITING

N
PUBLISHERS' CIRCULAR, THE OFFICIAL ORGAN OF THE PUBLISHERS' ASSOCIATION OF GREAT BRITAIN AND IRELAND. EUR+WWI MOD/EUR UK LAW PROB/SOLV DIPLOM COLONIAL ATTIT...HUM 19/20 CMN/WLTH. PAGE 1 H0019 BIBLIOG NAT/G WRITING LEAD

N
PUBLISHERS' TRADE LIST ANNUAL. LAW POL/PAR ADMIN PERSON ALL/IDEOS...HUM SOC 19/20. PAGE 1 H0020 BIBLIOG NAT/G DIPLOM POLICY

N
REVUE FRANCAISE DE SCIENCE POLITIQUE. FRANCE UK ...BIBLIOG/A 20. PAGE 1 H0021 NAT/G DIPLOM CONCPT ROUTINE

N
SEMINAR: THE MONTHLY SYMPOSIUM. INDIA ACT/RES TEC/DEV DIPLOM ATTIT...BIBLIOG 20. PAGE 1 H0022 NAT/G ECO/UNDEV SOVEREIGN POLICY

N
SUBJECT GUIDE TO BOOKS IN PRINT: AN INDEX TO THE PUBLISHERS' TRADE LIST ANNUAL. UNIV LAW LOC/G DIPLOM WRITING ADMIN LEAD PERSON...MGT SOC. PAGE 2 H0024 BIBLIOG ECO/DEV POL/PAR NAT/G

N
NEUE POLITISCHE LITERATUR; BERICHTE UBER DAS INTERNATIONALE SCHRIFTTUM ZUR POLITIK. WOR+45 LAW CONSTN POL/PAR ADMIN LEAD GOV/REL...POLICY IDEA/COMP. PAGE 2 H0027 BIBLIOG/A DIPLOM NAT/G NAT/COMP

N
AVTOREFERATY DISSERTATSII. USSR INTELL ACADEM NAT/G DIPLOM GOV/REL KNOWL CONCPT. PAGE 2 H0029 BIBLIOG MARXISM MARXIST COM

N
"PROLOG",DIGEST OF THE SOVIET UKRANIAN PRESS. USSR LAW AGRI INDUS PROVS SCHOOL DIPLOM GOV/REL ATTIT ...HUM LING 20. PAGE 3 H0053 BIBLIOG/A NAT/G PRESS COM

N
AFRICAN BIBLIOGRAPHIC CENTER,A CURRENT BIBLIOGRAPHY ON AFRICAN AFFAIRS. LAW CULTURE ECO/UNDEV LABOR SECT DIPLOM FOR/AID COLONIAL NAT/LISM...LING 20. PAGE 4 H0075 BIBLIOG/A AFR NAT/G REGION

N
ASIA FOUNDATION,LIBRARY NOTES. LAW CONSTN CULTURE SOCIETY ECO/UNDEV INT/ORG NAT/G COLONIAL LEAD REGION NAT/LISM ATTIT 20 UN. PAGE 9 H0176 BIBLIOG/A ASIA S/ASIA DIPLOM

N
BURY J.B.,THE CAMBRIDGE ANCIENT HISTORY (12 VOLS.). MEDIT-7 DIPLOM COLONIAL WAR...HUM EGYPT/ANC ROME/EMP BABYLONIA GREECE/ANC. PAGE 25 H0495 BIBLIOG/A SOCIETY CULTURE NAT/G

N
CARIBBEAN COMMISSION,CURRENT CARIBBEAN BIBLIOGRAPHY. FRANCE NETHERLAND UK CULTURE ECO/UNDEV PRESS LEAD ATTIT...GEOG SOC 20. PAGE 26 H0530 BIBLIOG NAT/G L/A+17C DIPLOM

N
CARNEGIE ENDOWMENT,CURRENT RESEARCH IN INTERNATIONAL AFFAIRS: SELECTED BIBLIOGRAPHY OF WORK IN PROGRESS BY PRIVATE RESEARCH AGENCIES. WOR+45 NAT/G ACT/RES GOV/COMP. PAGE 27 H0533 BIBLIOG/A DIPLOM R+D

N
CORDIER H.,BIBLIOTECA SINICA. SOCIETY STRUCT SECT DIPLOM COLONIAL...GEOG SOC CON/ANAL. PAGE 33 H0664 BIBLIOG/A NAT/G CULTURE ASIA

N
CORNELL UNIVERSITY LIBRARY,SOUTHEAST ASIA ACCESSIONS LIST. LAW SOCIETY STRUCT ECO/UNDEV POL/PAR TEC/DEV DIPLOM LEAD REGION. PAGE 34 H0671 BIBLIOG S/ASIA NAT/G CULTURE

N
DEUTSCHE BUCHEREI,DEUTSCHE NATIONALBIBLIOGRAPHIE. GERMANY ECO/DEV DIPLOM AGE/Y ATTIT...PHIL/SCI SOC 20. PAGE 40 H0803
BIBLIOG NAT/G LEAD POLICY

N
DEUTSCHE BUCHEREI,JAHRESVERZEICHNIS DES DEUTSCHEN SCHRIFTUMS. AUSTRIA EUR+WWI GERMANY SWITZERLND LAW LOC/G DIPLOM ADMIN...MGT SOC 19/20. PAGE 40 H0804
BIBLIOG WRITING NAT/G

N
DEUTSCHE BUCHEREI,DEUTSCHES BUCHERVERZEICHNIS. GERMANY LAW CULTURE POL/PAR ADMIN LEAD ATTIT PERSON ...SOC 20. PAGE 40 H0805
BIBLIOG NAT/G DIPLOM ECO/DEV

N
EUROPA PUBLICATIONS LIMITED,THE EUROPA YEAR BOOK. CONSTN FINAN INDUS POL/PAR DIPLOM TV CT/SYS...STAT BIOG CHARTS WORSHIP 20. PAGE 47 H0949
BIBLIOG NAT/G PRESS INT/ORG

N
HOOVER INSTITUTION,UNITED STATES AND CANADIAN PUBLICATIONS ON AFRICA. CULTURE ECO/UNDEV AGRI TEC/DEV EDU/PROP COLONIAL RACE/REL NAT/LISM ATTIT HEALTH...SOC SOC/WK 20. PAGE 73 H1464
BIBLIOG DIPLOM NAT/G AFR

N
INSTITUTE OF HISPANIC STUDIES,HISPANIC AMERICAN REPORT. EUR+WWI SPAIN LAW CONSTN ECO/UNDEV POL/PAR EX/STRUC LEGIS LEAD...HUM SOC 20. PAGE 77 H1538
BIBLIOG/A L/A+17C NAT/G DIPLOM

N
KYRIAK T.E.,ASIAN DEVELOPMENTS: A BIBLIOGRAPHY. INDONESIA KOREA/N VIETNAM/N CULTURE SOCIETY ECO/UNDEV NAT/G DIPLOM...SOC TREND 20 MONGOLIA. PAGE 90 H1788
BIBLIOG/A ALL/IDEOS S/ASIA ASIA

N
LONDON LIBRARY ASSOCIATION,ATHENAEUM SUBJECT INDEX. 1915-1918. NAT/G DIPLOM NAT/LISM 20. PAGE 98 H1960
BIBLIOG CON/ANAL SOC

N
MINISTERE DE L'EDUC NATIONALE,CATALOGUE DES THESES DE DOCTORAT SOUTENNES DEVANT LES UNIVERSITAIRES FRANCAISES. FRANCE LAW DIPLOM ADMIN...HUM SOC 20. PAGE 111 H2223
BIBLIOG ACADEM KNOWL NAT/G

N
MINISTRY OF OVERSEAS DEVELOPME,TECHNICAL CO-OPERATION -- A BIBLIOGRAPHY. UK LAW SOCIETY DIPLOM ECO/TAC FOR/AID...STAT 20 CMN/WLTH. PAGE 111 H2225
BIBLIOG TEC/DEV ECO/DEV NAT/G

N
UNIVERSITY OF CALIFORNIA,STATISTICAL ABSTRACT OF LATIN AMERICA. L/A+17C DIPLOM 20. PAGE 158 H3169
BIBLIOG NAT/G ECO/UNDEV STAT

N
US CONSOLATE GENERAL HONG KONG,REVIEW OF THE HONG KONG CHINESE PRESS. ECO/UNDEV LOC/G NAT/G PLAN DIPLOM EDU/PROP LEAD GP/REL MARXISM...POLICY INDEX 20. PAGE 159 H3178
BIBLIOG/A ASIA PRESS ATTIT

N
US CONSULATE GENERAL HONG KONG,CURRENT BACKGROUND. CHINA/COM ECO/UNDEV LOC/G NAT/G PLAN DIPLOM EDU/PROP LEAD REV ATTIT...POLICY INDEX 20. PAGE 159 H3179
BIBLIOG/A MARXIST ASIA PRESS

N
US CONSULATE GENERAL HONG KONG,SURVEY OF CHINA MAINLAND PRESS. CHINA/COM ECO/UNDEV LOC/G NAT/G PLAN DIPLOM EDU/PROP LEAD REV ATTIT...POLICY INDEX 20. PAGE 159 H3181
BIBLIOG/A MARXIST ASIA PRESS

N
US CONSULATE GENERAL HONG KONG,US CONSULATE GENERAL, HONG KONG, PRESS SUMMARIES. CHINA/COM ECO/UNDEV LOC/G NAT/G PLAN DIPLOM EDU/PROP LEAD REV ATTIT...POLICY INDEX 20. PAGE 159 H3182
BIBLIOG/A MARXIST ASIA PRESS

N
US DEPARTMENT OF STATE,BIBLIOGRAPHY (PAMPHLETS). AGRI INDUS INT/ORG FOR/AID EDU/PROP WAR MARXISM ...SOC GOV/COMP METH/COMP 20. PAGE 159 H3184
BIBLIOG DIPLOM ECO/DEV NAT/G

N
US LIBRARY OF CONGRESS,ACCESSIONS LIST - INDIA. INDIA CULTURE AGRI LOC/G POL/PAR PLAN PROB/SOLV TEC/DEV DIPLOM EDU/PROP LEAD GP/REL ATTIT 20. PAGE 160 H3199
BIBLIOG S/ASIA ECO/UNDEV NAT/G

N
US LIBRARY OF CONGRESS,ACCESSIONS LIST -- ISRAEL. ISRAEL CULTURE ECO/UNDEV POL/PAR PLAN PROB/SOLV TEC/DEV DIPLOM EDU/PROP LEAD WAR ATTIT 20 JEWS. PAGE 160 H3200
BIBLIOG ISLAM NAT/G GP/REL

N
US LIBRARY OF CONGRESS,EAST EUROPEAN ACCESSIONS INDEX. NAT/G ISOLAT ATTIT KNOWL...POLICY 20. PAGE 160 H3202
BIBLIOG COM MARXIST DIPLOM

NCO
CARRINGTON C.E.,THE COMMONWEALTH IN AFRICA (PAMPHLET). UK STRUCT NAT/G COLONIAL REPRESENT GOV/REL RACE/REL NAT/LISM...MAJORIT 20 EEC NEGRO COLD/WAR. PAGE 27 H0540
ECO/UNDEV AFR DIPLOM PLAN

NSY
MACKENZIE K.R.,THE ENGLISH PARLIAMENT. UK POL/PAR CHIEF DIPLOM TAX TASK WAR AUTHORIT...POLICY TREND 12/20 PARLIAMENT. PAGE 100 H2000
ORD/FREE LEGIS NAT/G

B00
BENEDETTI V.,STUDIES IN DIPLOMACY. BELGIUM FRANCE GERMANY MOD/EUR CONSTN NAT/G CONSULT TOP/EX DOMIN EDU/PROP COERCE ATTIT...CONCPT INT BIOG TREND 19. PAGE 14 H0276
PWR GEN/LAWS DIPLOM

B00
DE JOMINI A.H.,THE ART OF WAR. MOD/EUR NAT/G BAL/PWR DIPLOM DOMIN EXEC ROUTINE COERCE DRIVE PWR SKILL...POLICY CONCPT CHARTS STERTYP 19. PAGE 38 H0755
PLAN FORCES WAR WEAPON

B00
HOBSON J.A.,THE WAR IN SOUTH AFRICA: ITS CAUSES AND EFFECTS. NETHERLAND SOUTH/AFR UK ELITES AGRI EXTR/IND POL/PAR DIPLOM PRESS RACE/REL ATTIT ORD/FREE SOVEREIGN...INT 19 NEGRO. PAGE 72 H1439
WAR DOMIN POLICY NAT/G

B00
MOCKLER-FERRYMAN A.,BRITISH WEST AFRICA. FRANCE GERMANY NIGER SIER/LEONE UK CULTURE DIPLOM WAR RACE/REL PRODUC PROFIT WEALTH...POLICY PREDICT 19. PAGE 112 H2232
AFR COLONIAL INT/TRADE CAP/ISM

C05
DUNNING W.A.,"HISTORY OF POLITICAL THEORIES FROM LUTHER TO MONTESQUIEU." LAW NAT/G SECT DIPLOM REV WAR ORD/FREE SOVEREIGN CONSERVE...TRADIT BIBLIOG 16/18. PAGE 43 H0867
PHIL/SCI CONCPT GEN/LAWS

C06
MONTGOMERY H.,"A DICTIONARY OF POLITICAL PHRASES AND ILLUSIONS WITH A SHORT BIBLIOGRAPHY." EUR+WWI MOD/EUR UK AGRI LABOR LOC/G NAT/G COLONIAL CHOOSE RACE/REL. PAGE 112 H2245
BIBLIOG DICTIONARY POLICY DIPLOM

B08
NIRRNHEIM O.,DAS ERSTE JAHR DES MINISTERIUMS BISMARCK UND DIE OEFFENTLICHE MEINUNG (HEIDELBERGER ABHANDLUNGEN, 20. HEFT). GERMANY MOD/EUR LEGIS DIPLOM EDU/PROP INGP/REL...BIOG GOV/COMP IDEA/COMP BIBLIOG 19 BISMARCK/O. PAGE 118 H2363
CHIEF PRESS NAT/G ATTIT

B10
MENDELSSOHN S.,SOUTH AFRICAN BIBLIOGRAPHY (2 VOLS.). SOUTH/AFR EXTR/IND LABOR SECT DIPLOM INT/TRADE COLONIAL RACE/REL DISCRIM...GEOG 20. PAGE 109 H2172
BIBLIOG/A AFR NAT/G NAT/LISM

B15
FARIES J.C.,THE RISE OF INTERNATIONALISM. ASIA MOD/EUR NAT/G VOL/ASSN DELIB/GP BAL/PWR EDU/PROP ARMS/CONT RIGID/FLEX TREND. PAGE 49 H0971
INT/ORG DIPLOM PEACE

B16
PUFENDORF S.,LAW OF NATURE AND OF NATIONS (ABRIDGED). UNIV LAW NAT/G DIPLOM AGREE WAR PERSON ALL/VALS PWR...POLICY 18 DEITY NATURL/LAW. PAGE 128 H2565
CONCPT INT/LAW SECT MORAL

B17
DOS SANTOS M.,BIBLIOGRAPHIA GERAL, A DESCRIPCAO BIBLIOGRAFICA DE LIVROS TANTO DE AUTORES PORTUGUEZES COMO BRASILEIROS... BRAZIL PORTUGAL NAT/G LEAD GP/REL 15/20. PAGE 42 H0840
BIBLIOG/A L/A+17C DIPLOM COLONIAL

B17
VEBLEN T.B.,AN INQUIRY INTO THE NATURE OF PEACE AND THE TERMS OF ITS PERPETUATION. UNIV STRATA FINAN EDU/PROP PRICE COST DISCRIM NAT/LISM MORAL ORD/FREE PACIFIST 20 WORLDUNITY. PAGE 162 H3237
PEACE DIPLOM WAR NAT/G

N17
BURKE E.,THOUGHTS ON THE PROSPECT OF A REGICIDE PEACE (PAMPHLET). FRANCE UK SECT DOMIN MURDER PEACE ORD/FREE SOVEREIGN POPULISM...POLICY GOV/COMP IDEA/COMP 18 JACOBINISM COEXIST. PAGE 24 H0483
REV CHIEF NAT/G DIPLOM

N17
BURKE E.,LETTER TO SIR HERCULES LANGRISHE (PAMPHLET). IRELAND UK NAT/G CHIEF DIPLOM DOMIN PARL/PROC COERCE ORD/FREE SOVEREIGN POPULISM ...TRADIT 18 BURKE/EDM. PAGE 24 H0485
POLICY COLONIAL SECT

B18
KERNER R.J.,SLAVIC EUROPE: A SELECTED BIBLIOGRAPHY IN THE WESTERN EUROPEAN LANGUAGES. BULGARIA CZECHOSLVK GERMANY/E POLAND RUSSIA YUGOSLAVIA NAT/G DIPLOM MARXISM...LING 19/20. PAGE 85 H1695
BIBLIOG SOCIETY CULTURE COM

B19
ROUSSEAU J.J.,A LASTING PEACE. INT/ORG NAT/G CHIEF DIPLOM DETER WAR POLICY. PAGE 135 H2697
PLAN PEACE UTIL

N19
FREEMAN H.A.,COERCION OF STATES IN FEDERAL UNIONS (PAMPHLET). WOR-45 DIPLOM CONTROL COERCE PEACE ORD/FREE...GOV/COMP METH/COMP NAT/COMP PACIFIST 20. PAGE 53 H1055
FEDERAL WAR INT/ORG PACIFISM

N19
GOODMAN G.K.,IMPERIAL JAPAN AND ASIA: A REASSESSMENT (PAMPHLET). ASIA S/ASIA ECO/DEV FORCES LEAD WAR NAT/LISM ATTIT...DECISION CONCPT BIBLIOG 19/20 CHINJAP. PAGE 59 H1172
DIPLOM NAT/G POLICY COLONIAL

N19
HAJDA J.,THE COLD WAR VIEWED AS A SOCIOLOGICAL PROBLEM (PAMPHLET). COM CZECHOSLVK EUR+WWI SOCIETY PLAN EDU/PROP CONTROL TASK ATTIT MARXISM...POLICY 20 COLD/WAR MIGRATION. PAGE 64 H1280
DIPLOM LEAD PWR NAT/G

N19
HANNA A.J.,EUROPEAN RULE IN AFRICA (PAMPHLET). BELGIUM FRANCE MOD/EUR UK WOR+45 WOR-45 ECO/UNDEV NAT/G PARTIC SOVEREIGN...NAT/COMP 19/20. PAGE 66 H1314
DIPLOM COLONIAL AFR NAT/LISM

N19
MASSEY V.,CANADIANS AND THEIR COMMONWEALTH: THE ROMANES LECTURE DELIVERED IN THE SHELDONIAN THEATRE JUNE 1, 1961 (PAMPHLET). CANADA UK CULTURE ECO/DEV REPRESENT NAT/LISM PEACE PWR CONSERVE 20 CMN/WLTH. PAGE 104 H2088
ATTIT DIPLOM NAT/G SOVEREIGN

N19
MEZERIK A.G.,APARTHEID IN THE REPUBLIC OF SOUTH AFRICA (PAMPHLET). DIPLOM DOMIN CONTROL COERCE REPRESENT CONSEN ATTIT. PAGE 110 H2194
DISCRIM RACE/REL POL/PAR POLICY

N19
PROVISIONS SECTION OAU,ORGANIZATION OF AFRICAN UNITY: BASIC DOCUMENTS AND RESOLUTIONS (PAMPHLET). AFR CULTURE ECO/UNDEV DIPLOM ECO/TAC EDU/PROP COLONIAL ARMS/CONT NUC/PWR RACE/REL DISCRIM NAT/LISM 20 UN OAU. PAGE 128 H2564
CONSTN EX/STRUC SOVEREIGN INT/ORG

N19
SALKEVER L.R.,SUB-SAHARA AFRICA (PAMPHLET). AFR USSR EXTR/IND NAT/G SCHOOL DIPLOM COLONIAL WEALTH ...GEOG CHARTS 16/20. PAGE 137 H2742
ECO/UNDEV TEC/DEV TASK INT/TRADE

N19
SENGHOR L.S.,AFRICAN SOCIALISM (PAMPHLET). AFR FRANCE MALI USSR ELITES ECO/UNDEV NAT/G DIPLOM DOMIN EDU/PROP ATTIT 20 NEGRO. PAGE 141 H2827
SOCISM MARXISM ORD/FREE NAT/LISM

N19
STEUBER F.A.,THE CONTRIBUTION OF SWITZERLAND TO THE ECONOMIC AND SOCIAL DEVELOPMENT OF LOW-INCOME COUNTRIES (PAMPHLET). SWITZERLND FINAN NAT/G VOL/ASSN INT/TRADE DRIVE...CHARTS 20. PAGE 149 H2982
FOR/AID ECO/UNDEV PLAN DIPLOM

B20
HALDANE R.B.,BEFORE THE WAR. MOD/EUR SOCIETY INT/ORG NAT/G DELIB/GP PLAN DOMIN EDU/PROP LEGIT ADMIN COERCE ATTIT DRIVE MORAL ORD/FREE PWR...SOC CONCPT SELF/OBS RECORD BIOG TIME/SEQ. PAGE 64 H1282
POLICY DIPLOM UK

B20
MALTHUS T.R.,PRINCIPLES OF POLITICAL ECONOMY. UK AGRI INDUS MARKET NAT/G DIPLOM PRICE CONTROL BAL/PAY COST OWN PWR LAISSEZ 18/19. PAGE 102 H2034
GEN/LAWS DEMAND WEALTH

B21
BALFOUR A.J.,ESSAYS SPECULATIVE AND POLITICAL. SEA CULTURE CREATE WAR NAT/LISM PEACE LOVE...ART/METH INT/LAW CONCPT ANTHOL 20 JEWS. PAGE 10 H0204
PHIL/SCI SOCIETY DIPLOM

B21
KREY A.C.,THE FIRST CRUSADE. CHRIST-17C SOCIETY STRATA NAT/G SECT FORCES WORKER WRITING LEAD ATTIT ...CHARTS 11 CHRISTIAN CRUSADES. PAGE 88 H1767
WAR CATH DIPLOM PARTIC

B21
STUART G.H.,FRENCH FOREIGN POLICY. CONSTN INT/ORG NAT/G POL/PAR EX/STRUC FORCES PLAN ECO/TAC DOMIN EDU/PROP ADJUD COERCE ATTIT DRIVE RIGID/FLEX ALL/VALS...POLICY OBS RECORD BIOG TIME/SEQ TREND. PAGE 150 H3000
MOD/EUR DIPLOM FRANCE

B22
KRABBE H.,THE MODERN IDEA OF THE STATE. LAW CHIEF DIPLOM DOMIN ADMIN REPRESENT CENTRAL ORD/FREE ...NEW/IDEA GOV/COMP IDEA/COMP. PAGE 88 H1761
SOVEREIGN CONSTN PHIL/SCI

B23
GRANT C.F.,STUDIES IN NORTH AFRICA. ALGERIA MOROCCO ROMAN/EMP CULTURE STRUCT NAT/G DIPLOM WAR ...NAT/COMP TUNIS EUROPE. PAGE 60 H1195
ISLAM SECT DOMIN COLONIAL

B23
KADEN E.H.,DER POLITISCHE CHARAKTER DER FRANZOSISCHEN KULTURPROPAGANDA AM RHEIN. FRANCE MOD/EUR DOMIN PRESS...GEOG METH/COMP 20. PAGE 82 H1648
EDU/PROP ATTIT DIPLOM NAT/G

B25
TEMPERLEY H.,THE FOREIGN POLICY OF CANNING: 1822-1827. MOD/EUR NAT/G TOP/EX EDU/PROP ROUTINE ATTIT RIGID/FLEX SUPEGO PWR SKILL...TIME/SEQ PARLIAMENT 20. PAGE 153 H3058
PERSON DIPLOM UK BIOG

B25
WEBSTER C.,THE FOREIGN POLICY OF CASTLEREAGH: 1815-1822. LAW NAT/G DELIB/GP TOP/EX BAL/PWR ORD/FREE PWR RESPECT 19. PAGE 166 H3322
MOD/EUR DIPLOM UK

B25
WILLIAMS B.,THE SELBORNE MEMORANDUM. AFR FUT SOUTH/AFR UK NAT/G BUDGET DIPLOM REGION GOV/REL SOVEREIGN...POLICY CHARTS 20 UNIFICA SELBORNE/W. PAGE 168 H3365
COLONIAL PROVS

B27
FLOURNOY F.,PARLIAMENT AND WAR. MOD/EUR UK NAT/G FORCES LEGIS TOP/EX DIPLOM LEGIT DEBATE ATTIT RIGID/FLEX PWR...DECISION TIME/SEQ PARLIAMENT 19/20. PAGE 52 H1032
COERCE WAR

B27
GOOCH G.P.,ENGLISH DEMOCRATIC IDEAS IN THE SEVENTEENTH CENTURY (2ND ED.). UK LAW SECT FORCES DIPLOM LEAD PARL/PROC REV ATTIT AUTHORIT...ANARCH CONCPT 17 PARLIAMENT CMN/WLTH REFORMERS. PAGE 58 H1167
IDEA/COMP MAJORIT EX/STRUC CONSERVE

B28
CHILDS J.B.,FOREIGN GOVERNMENT PUBLICATIONS (PAMPHLET). LEGIS DIPLOM 19/20. PAGE 29 H0591
BIBLIOG PRESS NAT/G

B28
HURST C.,GREAT BRITAIN AND THE DOMINIONS. EUR+WWI CULTURE ECO/DEV INT/ORG NAT/G DIPLOM ECO/TAC COLONIAL ATTIT PWR SOVEREIGN...TIME/SEQ GEN/LAWS TOT/POP VAL/FREE 20 CMN/WLTH. PAGE 75 H1508
VOL/ASSN DOMIN UK

B28
LODGE H.C.,THE HISTORY OF NATIONS (25 VOLS.). UNIV LEAD...ANTHOL BIBLIOG INDEX. PAGE 98 H1951
DIPLOM SOCIETY NAT/G

B28
MARSILIUS/PADUA,DEFENSOR PACIS (1324). CHRIST-17C CONSTN NAT/G DIPLOM DOMIN LEGIT CONTROL WAR PEACE ORD/FREE SOVEREIGN POPULISM 14 POPE. PAGE 103 H2059
CATH SECT GEN/LAWS

C28
SCHNEIDER H.W.,"MAKING THE FASCIST STATE." ITALY CULTURE LABOR DIPLOM REV WAR NAT/LISM TOTALISM ATTIT DRIVE SOCISM...BIBLIOG PARLIAMENT 20. PAGE 140 H2792
FASCISM POLICY POL/PAR

C28
WARD P.W.,"SOVEREIGNTY: A STUDY OF A CONTEMPORARY POLITICAL NOTION." CONSTN NAT/G DIPLOM REPRESENT PLURISM...IDEA/COMP BIBLIOG. PAGE 165 H3304
SOVEREIGN CONCPT NAT/LISM

B29
DE REPARAZ G.,GEOGRAFIA Y POLITICA. CHILE SPAIN USSR NAT/G DIPLOM REV MARXISM...POLICY 19/20. PAGE 38 H0768
GEOG MOD/EUR

B29
LANGER W.L.,THE FRANCO-RUSSIAN ALLIANCE: 1890-1894. FRANCE MOD/EUR UK USSR NAT/G CHIEF FORCES BAL/PWR AGREE WAR PEACE PWR...TIME/SEQ TREATY 19 BISMARCK/O. PAGE 91 H1809
DIPLOM

B29
PRATT I.A.,MODERN EGYPT: A LIST OF REFERENCES TO MATERIAL IN THE NEW YORK PUBLIC LIBRARY. UAR ECO/UNDEV...GEOG JURID SOC LING 20. PAGE 128 H2555
BIBLIOG ISLAM DIPLOM NAT/G

B29
STURZO L.,THE INTERNATIONAL COMMUNITY AND THE RIGHT OF WAR (TRANS. BY BARBARA BARCLAY CARTER). CULTURE CREATE PROB/SOLV DIPLOM ADJUD CONTROL PEACE PERSON ORD/FREE...INT/LAW IDEA/COMP PACIFIST 20 LEAGUE/NAT. PAGE 150 H3003
INT/ORG PLAN WAR CONCPT

B30
BYNKERSHOEK C.,QUAESTIONUM JURIS PUBLICI LIBRI DUO. CHRIST-17C MOD/EUR CONSTN ELITES SOCIETY NAT/G PROVS EX/STRUC FORCES TOP/EX BAL/PWR DIPLOM ATTIT MORAL...TRADIT CONCPT. PAGE 25 H0502
INT/ORG LAW NAT/LISM INT/LAW

B30
HULL W.I.,INDIA'S POLITICAL CRISIS. INDIA UK INT/ORG LABOR SECT DELIB/GP LEGIS DIPLOM NEUTRAL REGION CROWD GOV/REL MAJORITY ATTIT 20 NEHRU/J GANDHI/M COMMONWLTH. PAGE 75 H1492
ORD/FREE NAT/G COLONIAL NAT/LISM

B31
KIRKPATRICK F.A.,A HISTORY OF THE ARGENTINE REPUBLIC. SPAIN UK CONSTN SOCIETY ECO/UNDEV EX/STRUC DIPLOM FOR/AID LEAD WAR ATTIT...BIOG CHARTS 16/20 ARGEN SAN/MARTIN. PAGE 86 H1724
NAT/G L/A+17C COLONIAL

B32
BLUM L.,PEACE AND DISARMAMENT (TRANS. BY A. WERTH). NAT/G FORCES WORKER DIPLOM AGREE WAR ATTIT AUTHORIT ORD/FREE. PAGE 18 H0360
SOCIALIST PEACE INT/ORG ARMS/CONT

B32
BRYCE J.,THE HOLY ROMAN EMPIRE. GERMANY ITALY MOD/EUR CULTURE SOCIETY STRUCT INT/ORG NAT/G SECT DIPLOM DOMIN WAR SUPEGO ALL/VALS SOVEREIGN...GEOG SOC TIME/SEQ CHARTS STERTYP. PAGE 23 H0456
CHRIST-17C NAT/LISM

B32
CARDINALL AW,A BIBLIOGRAPHY OF THE GOLD COAST. AFR UK NAT/G EX/STRUC ATTIT...POLICY 19/20. PAGE 26 H0527
BIBLIOG ADMIN COLONIAL DIPLOM

B32
MARRARO H.R.,AMERICAN OPINION ON THE UNIFICATION OF ITALY. ITALY FORCES DIPLOM SOVEREIGN CATHISM CONSERVE...CONCPT NAT/COMP BIBLIOG 19. PAGE 103 H2056
ORD/FREE NAT/LISM REV CONSTN

B32
NIEBUHR R.,MORAL MAN AND IMMORAL SOCIETY* A STUDY IN ETHICS AND POLITICS. UNIV CULTURE SOCIETY STRUCT DIPLOM GOV/REL GP/REL PERS/REL...TREND IDEA/COMP.
MORAL PWR

PAGE 118 H2357

B33
DAHLIN E.,FRENCH AND GERMAN PUBLIC OPINION ON DECLARED WAR AIMS 1914-1918. BELGIUM FRANCE GERMANY NAT/G POL/PAR DIPLOM COERCE REV WAR PEACE 20 WWI WILSON/W. PAGE 37 H0733
ATTIT EDU/PROP DOMIN NAT/COMP

B33
FERRERO G.,PEACE AND WAR (TRANS. BY BERTHA PRITCHARD). CULTURE FINAN SECT ATTIT SUPEGO MORAL ORD/FREE CONSERVE POPULISM SOCISM POLICY. PAGE 49 H0987
WAR PEACE DIPLOM PROB/SOLV

B33
TANNENBAUM F.,PEACE BY REVOLUTION. ECO/UNDEV AGRI SECT WORKER DIPLOM EDU/PROP DISCRIM OWN WEALTH POPULISM 17/20 MEXIC/AMER INDIAN/AM. PAGE 152 H3043
CULTURE COLONIAL RACE/REL REV

B33
PUBLIC OPINION AND WORLD POLITICS. UNIV LAW CULTURE NAT/G PRESS REV GP/REL...MAJORIT METH/COMP ANTHOL 20. PAGE 171 H3420
DIPLOM EDU/PROP ATTIT MAJORITY

B34
LOVELL R.I.,THE STRUGGLE FOR SOUTH AFRICA, 1875-1899. GERMANY RHODESIA SOUTH/AFR UK NAT/G ECO/TAC HABITAT WEALTH...POLICY 19. PAGE 99 H1971
COLONIAL DIPLOM WAR GP/REL

B35
MARRIOTT J.A.,DICTATORSHIP AND DEMOCRACY. GERMANY GREECE UK CHIEF DIPLOM DOMIN LEGIT PEACE ORD/FREE CONSERVE...TREND ROME HITLER/A. PAGE 103 H2057
TOTALISM POPULISM PLURIST NAT/G

B36
BOYCE A.N.,EUROPE AND SOUTH AFRICA. FRANCE GERMANY ITALY SOUTH/AFR UK INDUS NAT/G CONTROL REV WAR NAT/LISM...CONCPT HIST/WRIT 20. PAGE 20 H0392
COLONIAL GOV/COMP NAT/COMP DIPLOM

B36
RAPPARD W.E.,THE GOVERNMENT OF SWITZERLAND. SWITZERLND INT/ORG POL/PAR EX/STRUC DIPLOM NEUTRAL PARL/PROC REGION WAR HABITAT SOVEREIGN...NAT/COMP SOC/INTEG 20 LEAGUE/NAT WWI. PAGE 130 H2594
CONSTN NAT/G CULTURE FEDERAL

B36
VICO G.B.,DIRITTO UNIVERSALE (1722) (VOL. 2, PARTS 1,2, AND 3, OF G.B. VICO, OPERE). UNIV DIPLOM AGREE WAR OWN KNOWL ORD/FREE SOVEREIGN DEITY. PAGE 162 H3249
JURID SECT CONCPT NAT/G

B37
BORGESE G.A.,GOLIATH: THE MARCH OF FASCISM. GERMANY ITALY LAW POL/PAR SECT DIPLOM SOCISM...JURID MYTH 20 DANTE MACHIAVELL MUSSOLIN/B. PAGE 19 H0375
POLICY NAT/LISM FASCISM NAT/G

B37
BOURNE H.E.,THE WORLD WAR: A LIST OF THE MORE IMPORTANT BOOKS PUBLISHED BEFORE 1937 (PAMPHLET). EUR+WWI NAT/G DIPLOM ATTIT SOC. PAGE 19 H0386
BIBLIOG/A WAR FORCES PLAN

B37
DE KIEWIET C.W.,THE IMPERIAL FACTOR IN SOUTH AFRICA. AFR SOUTH/AFR UK WAR...POLICY SOC 19. PAGE 38 H0759
DIPLOM COLONIAL CULTURE

B37
MARX K.,THE CIVIL WAR IN THE UNITED STATES. USA-45 WORKER DIPLOM INT/TRADE DOMIN RACE/REL ATTIT ...TREND 19. PAGE 104 H2078
WAR REV MARXIST ORD/FREE

B37
THOMPSON J.W.,SECRET DIPLOMACY: A RECORD OF ESPIONAGE AND DOUBLE-DEALING: 1500-1815. CHRIST-17C MOD/EUR NAT/G WRITING RISK MORAL...ANTHOL BIBLIOG 16/19 ESPIONAGE. PAGE 154 H3084
DIPLOM CRIME

B37
UNION OF SOUTH AFRICA,REPORT CONCERNING ADMINISTRATION OF SOUTH WEST AFRICA (6 VOLS.). SOUTH/AFR INDUS PUB/INST FORCES LEGIS BUDGET DIPLOM EDU/PROP ADJUD CT/SYS...GEOG CHARTS 20 AFRICA/SW LEAGUE/NAT. PAGE 158 H3166
NAT/G ADMIN COLONIAL CONSTN

B37
VON HAYEK F.A.,MONETARY NATIONALISM AND INTERNATIONAL STABILITY. WOR-45 ECO/DEV NAT/G PROB/SOLV INT/TRADE...POLICY CONCPT METH/COMP NAT/COMP 20. PAGE 163 H3271
ECO/TAC FINAN DIPLOM NAT/LISM

L37
NICOLSON H.,"THE MEANING OF PRESTIGE." EUR+WWI MOD/EUR UK CULTURE SOCIETY NAT/G DIPLOM DOMIN LEGIT ATTIT DRIVE PWR...METH/CNCPT RECORD TIME/SEQ GEN/METH CMN/WLTH TOT/POP 20. PAGE 118 H2351
CONCPT STERTYP

B38
CARVALHO C.M.,GEOGRAPHIA HUMANA; POLITICA E ECONOMICA (3RD ED.). BRAZIL CULTURE AGRI INDUS DIPLOM COLONIAL GP/REL RACE/REL...LING 20 RESOURCE/N. PAGE 27 H0551
GEOG HABITAT

B38
COUPLAND R.,EAST AFRICA AND ITS INVADERS. AFR ISLAM STRATA SECT FORCES DIPLOM TRIBUTE CONTROL DISCRIM NAT/LISM 19 AFRICA/E EUROPE MISSION. PAGE 34 H0680
CULTURE ELITES COLONIAL MARKET

B38
HARPER S.N.,THE GOVERNMENT OF THE SOVIET UNION. COM USSR LAW CONSTN ECO/DEV PLAN TEC/DEV DIPLOM INT/TRADE ADMIN REV NAT/LISM...POLICY 20. PAGE 67 H1337
MARXISM NAT/G LEAD POL/PAR

B38
HOLDSWORTH W.S.,A HISTORY OF ENGLISH LAW; THE CENTURIES OF SETTLEMENT AND REFORM (VOL. XI). UK CONSTN NAT/G EX/STRUC DIPLOM ADJUD CT/SYS LEAD CRIME ATTIT...INT/LAW JURID 18 CMN/WLTH PARLIAMENT ENGLSH/LAW. PAGE 73 H1452
LAW COLONIAL LEGIS PARL/PROC

B38
MCNAIR A.D.,THE LAW OF TREATIES: BRITISH PRACTICE AND OPINIONS. UK CREATE DIPLOM LEGIT WRITING ADJUD WAR...INT/LAW JURID TREATY. PAGE 107 H2144
AGREE LAW CT/SYS NAT/G

B39
ANDERSON P.R.,THE BACKGROUND OF ANTI-ENGLISH FEELING IN GERMANY, 1890-1902. GERMANY MOD/EUR UK NAT/G POL/PAR TOP/EX WAR...IDEA/COMP 19/20. PAGE 7 H0132
DIPLOM EDU/PROP ATTIT COLONIAL

B39
CARR E.H.,PROPAGANDA IN INTERNATIONAL POLITICS (PAMPHLET). EUR+WWI GERMANY MOD/EUR NAT/G AGREE WAR MORAL...POLICY 20 TREATY. PAGE 27 H0536
DIPLOM EDU/PROP CONTROL ATTIT

B39
FURNIVALL J.S.,NETHERLANDS INDIA. INDIA NETHERLAND CULTURE INDUS NAT/G DIPLOM ADMIN WEALTH...POLICY CHARTS 17/20. PAGE 54 H1081
COLONIAL ECO/UNDEV SOVEREIGN PLURISM

B39
HITLER A.,MEIN KAMPF. EUR+WWI FUT MOD/EUR STRUCT INT/ORG LABOR NAT/G POL/PAR FORCES CREATE PLAN BAL/PWR DIPLOM ECO/TAC DOMIN EDU/PROP ADMIN COERCE ATTIT...SOCIALIST BIOG TREND NAZI. PAGE 71 H1428
PWR NEW/IDEA WAR

B39
KERNER R.J.,NORTHEAST ASIA: A SELECTED BIBLIOGRAPHY (2 VOLS.). KOREA RUSSIA NAT/G DIPLOM...GEOG 19/20 CHINJAP. PAGE 85 H1696
BIBLIOG ASIA SOCIETY CULTURE

B39
NICOLSON H.,CURZON: THE LAST PHASE, 1919-1925. UK NAT/G DELIB/GP TOP/EX ROUTINE WAR RIGID/FLEX ...METH/CNCPT 20 CURZON/GN. PAGE 118 H2352
POLICY DIPLOM BIOG

C39
REISCHAUER R.,"JAPAN'S GOVERNMENT--POLITICS." CONSTN STRATA POL/PAR FORCES LEGIS DIPLOM ADMIN EXEC CENTRAL...POLICY BIBLIOG 20 CHINJAP. PAGE 131 H2610
NAT/G S/ASIA CONCPT ROUTINE

B40
THE GUIDE TO CATHOLIC LITERATURE, 1888-1940. ALL/VALS...POLICY MYSTIC HUM PHIL/SCI 19/20. PAGE 2 H0032
BIBLIOG/A CATHISM DIPLOM CULTURE

B40
BROGAN D.W.,THE DEVELOPMENT OF MODERN FRANCE (1870-1939). FRANCE GERMANY UK USSR CONSTN CHIEF LEGIS DIPLOM AGREE COLONIAL WAR NAT/LISM PEACE SOCISM 19/20 TREATY. PAGE 21 H0428
MOD/EUR NAT/G

B40
BROWN A.D.,PANAMA CANAL AND PANAMA CANAL ZONE: A SELECTED LIST OF REFERENCES. PANAMA NAT/G SCHOOL DIPLOM HEALTH...GEOG SOC 20 CANAL/ZONE. PAGE 22 H0436
BIBLIOG/A ECO/UNDEV

B40
CONOVER H.F.,JAPAN-ECONOMIC DEVELOPMENT AND FOREIGN POLICY, A SELECTED LIST OF REFERENCES (PAMPHLET). CULTURE FINAN INDUS NAT/G FORCES INT/TRADE WAR ...SOC TREND 20 CHINJAP. PAGE 32 H0640
BIBLIOG ASIA ECO/DEV DIPLOM

B40
MEEK C.K.,EUROPE AND WEST AFRICA. AFR EUR+WWI EXTR/IND DIPLOM INT/TRADE EDU/PROP GP/REL...SOC 20. PAGE 108 H2158
CULTURE TEC/DEV ECO/UNDEV COLONIAL

B40
WANDERSCHECK H.,FRANKREICHS PROPAGANDA GEGEN DEUTSCHLAND. FRANCE GERMANY MOD/EUR UK NAT/G DIPLOM WAR 20 JEWS. PAGE 165 H3300
EDU/PROP ATTIT DOMIN PRESS

B40
WOLFERS A.,BRITAIN AND FRANCE BETWEEN TWO WORLD WARS. FRANCE UK INT/ORG NAT/G PLAN BARGAIN ECO/TAC AGREE ISOLAT ALL/IDEOS...DECISION GEOG 20 TREATY VERSAILLES INTERVENT. PAGE 170 H3402
DIPLOM WAR POLICY

C40
FAHS C.B.,"GOVERNMENT IN JAPAN." FINAN FORCES LEGIS TOP/EX BUDGET INT/TRADE EDU/PROP SOVEREIGN ...CON/ANAL BIBLIOG/A 20 CHINJAP. PAGE 48 H0962
ASIA DIPLOM NAT/G ADMIN

B41
BAUMANN G.,GRUNDLAGEN UND PRAXIS DER INTERNATIONALEN PROPAGANDA. FRANCE GERMANY UK CULTURE COM/IND PRESS PWR...PSY METH/COMP 20. PAGE 12 H0241
EDU/PROP DOMIN ATTIT DIPLOM

B41
CHILDS J.B.,A GUIDE TO THE OFFICIAL PUBLICATIONS OF THE OTHER AMERICAN REPUBLICS: ARGENTINA. CHIEF DIPLOM GOV/REL...BIBLIOG 18/19 ARGEN. PAGE 30 H0594 NAT/G EX/STRUC METH/CNCPT LEGIS

B41
GRISMER R.,A NEW BIBLIOGRAPHY OF THE LITERATURES OF SPAIN AND SPANISH AMERICA. CHRIST-17C MOD/EUR PRE/AMER SPAIN CULTURE DIPLOM EDU/PROP...ART/METH GEOG HUM PHIL/SCI 20. PAGE 61 H1229 BIBLIOG LAW NAT/G ECO/UNDEV

B41
KEESING F.M.,THE SOUTH SEAS IN THE MODERN WORLD. INDONESIA STRUCT FAM SECT EDU/PROP LEAD INCOME WEALTH...HEAL SOC 20. PAGE 84 H1678 CULTURE ECO/UNDEV GOV/COMP DIPLOM

S41
ABEL T.,"THE ELEMENT OF DECISION IN THE PATTERN OF WAR." EUR+WWI FUT NAT/G TOP/EX DIPLOM ROUTINE COERCE DISPL PERCEPT PWR...SOC METH/CNCPT HIST/WRIT TREND GEN/LAWS 20. PAGE 3 H0055 TEC/DEV FORCES WAR

B42
CONOVER H.F.,FRENCH COLONIES IN AFRICA: A LIST OF REFERENCES. ALGERIA FRANCE MOROCCO SOMALIA SUDAN CULTURE AGRI LOC/G SECT FORCES DIPLOM INT/TRADE NAT/LISM HEALTH...CON/ANAL 20. PAGE 32 H0641 BIBLIOG AFR ECO/UNDEV COLONIAL

B42
CONOVER H.F.,NEW ZEALAND: A SELECTED LIST OF REFERENCES (PAMPHLET). NEW/ZEALND ECO/UNDEV AGRI INDUS LABOR NAT/G SCHOOL FORCES DIPLOM COLONIAL WAR ...HUM 20. PAGE 32 H0643 BIBLIOG/A S/ASIA CULTURE

B42
JOSHI P.S.,THE TYRANNY OF COLOUR. INDIA SOUTH/AFR UK ECO/UNDEV NAT/G POL/PAR DIPLOM ECO/TAC WAR ...POLICY 19/20. PAGE 82 H1637 COLONIAL DISCRIM RACE/REL

B42
NEUMANN S.,PERMANENT REVOLUTION: THE TOTAL STATE IN A WORLD AT WAR. COM EUR+WWI GERMANY USSR EX/STRUC DIPLOM CONTROL COERCE REPRESENT MARXISM...SOC GOV/COMP BIBLIOG 20 HITLER/A STALIN/J. PAGE 117 H2337 FASCISM TOTALISM DOMIN EDU/PROP

B42
PAGINSKY P.,GERMAN WORKS RELATING TO AMERICA, 1493-1800; A LIST COMPILED FROM THE COLLECTIONS OF THE NEW YORK PUBLIC LIBRARY. GERMANY PRE/AMER CULTURE COLONIAL ATTIT...POLICY SOC 15/19. PAGE 122 H2442 BIBLIOG/A NAT/G L/A+17C DIPLOM

B42
SIMOES DOS REIS A.,BIBLIOGRAFIA DAS BIBLIOGRAFIAS BRASILEIRAS. BRAZIL ADMIN COLONIAL 20. PAGE 144 H2879 BIBLIOG NAT/G DIPLOM L/A+17C

B43
BROWN A.D.,BRITISH POSSESSIONS IN THE CARIBBEAN AREA: A SELECTED LIST OF REFERENCES. UK NAT/G DIPLOM...GEOG 20 CARIBBEAN. PAGE 22 H0437 BIBLIOG COLONIAL ECO/UNDEV L/A+17C

B43
BROWN A.D.,GREECE: SELECTED LIST OF REFERENCES. GREECE ECO/UNDEV AGRI FINAN INDUS LABOR SECT TEC/DEV INT/TRADE LEAD...SOC 20. PAGE 22 H0438 BIBLIOG/A WAR DIPLOM NAT/G

B43
CONOVER H.F.,SOVIET RUSSIA: SELECTED LIST OF REFERENCES. USSR CULTURE INDUS NAT/G TOP/EX TEC/DEV BUDGET WAR CIVMIL/REL EFFICIENCY MARXISM 20. PAGE 32 H0644 BIBLIOG ECO/DEV COM DIPLOM

B43
GRIERSON P.,BOOKS ON SOVIET RUSSIA 1917-42: A BIBLIOGRAPHY AND A GUIDE TO READING. USSR CULTURE ELITES NAT/G PLAN DIPLOM REV...GEOG 20. PAGE 61 H1213 BIBLIOG/A COM MARXISM LEAD

B43
LEWIN E.,ROYAL EMPIRE SOCIETY BIBLIOGRAPHIES NO. 9: SUB-SAHARA AFRICA. ECO/UNDEV TEC/DEV DIPLOM ADMIN COLONIAL LEAD 20. PAGE 96 H1908 BIBLIOG AFR NAT/G SOCIETY

B43
MC DOWELL R.B.,IRISH PUBLIC OPINION, 1750-1800. IRELAND CONSTN VOL/ASSN WORKER ORD/FREE CATHISM CONSERVE...POLICY IDEA/COMP BIBLIOG 18/ PARLIAMENT. PAGE 106 H2118 ATTIT NAT/G DIPLOM REV

C43
BENTHAM J.,"PRINCIPLES OF INTERNATIONAL LAW" IN J. BOWRING, ED., THE WORKS OF JEREMY BENTHAM." UNIV NAT/G PLAN PROB/SOLV DIPLOM CONTROL SANCTION MORAL ORD/FREE PWR SOVEREIGN 19. PAGE 15 H0291 INT/LAW JURID WAR PEACE

B44
FULLER G.H.,TURKEY: A SELECTED LIST OF REFERENCES. ISLAM TURKEY CULTURE ECO/UNDEV AGRI DIPLOM NAT/LISM CONSERVE...GEOG HUM INT/LAW SOC 7/20 MAPS. PAGE 54 H1075 BIBLIOG/A ALL/VALS

C44
SUAREZ F.,"ON WAR" (1621) IN SELECTIONS FROM THREE WORKS, VOL. I." NAT/G SECT CHIEF DIPLOM LEGIT MORAL PWR...POLICY INT/LAW 17. PAGE 150 H3005 WAR REV ORD/FREE CATH

C44
VAN VALKENBURG S.,"ELEMENTS OF POLITICAL GEOGRAPHY." FRANCE COM/IND INDUS NAT/G SECT RACE/REL...LING TREND GEN/LAWS BIBLIOG 20. PAGE 162 H3232 GEOG DIPLOM COLONIAL

N45
INDIA QUARTERLY, A JOURNAL OF INTERNATIONAL AFFAIRS. INDIA LAW CONSTN ECO/UNDEV INT/ORG POL/PAR COLONIAL LEAD PARL/PROC WAR ATTIT...SOC 20 CMN/WLTH. PAGE 2 H0033 BIBLIOG/A S/ASIA DIPLOM NAT/G

B45
CLAGETT H.L.,COMMUNIST CHINA: RUTHLESS ENEMY OR PAPER TIGER (PAMPHLET). CHINA/COM ECO/UNDEV AGRI INDUS NAT/G POL/PAR ECO/TAC INT/TRADE GUERRILLA ATTIT...CHARTS NAT/COMP ORG/CHARTS 20. PAGE 30 H0602 BIBLIOG/A MARXISM DIPLOM COERCE

B45
CONOVER H.F.,THE GOVERNMENTS OF THE MAJOR FOREIGN POWERS: A BIBLIOGRAPHY. FRANCE GERMANY ITALY UK USSR CONSTN LOC/G POL/PAR EX/STRUC FORCES ADMIN CT/SYS CIVMIL/REL TOTALISM...POLICY 19/20. PAGE 32 H0645 BIBLIOG NAT/G DIPLOM

B45
CONOVER H.F.,ITALY: ECONOMICS, POLITICS AND MILITARY AFFAIRS, 1940-1945. ITALY ELITES NAT/G POL/PAR EX/STRUC TOP/EX DIPLOM DOMIN CONTROL COERCE WAR CIVMIL/REL EFFICIENCY 20. PAGE 32 H0646 BIBLIOG TOTALISM FORCES

B45
CONOVER H.F.,THE NAZI STATE: WAR CRIMES AND WAR CRIMINALS. GERMANY CULTURE NAT/G SECT FORCES DIPLOM INT/TRADE EDU/PROP...INT/LAW BIOG HIST/WRIT TIME/SEQ 20. PAGE 32 H0647 BIBLIOG WAR CRIME

B45
HARVARD WIDENER LIBRARY,INDOCHINA: A SELECTED LIST OF REFERENCES. CAMBODIA FRANCE S/ASIA VIETNAM COLONIAL...POLICY 19/20. PAGE 67 H1351 BIBLIOG/A ACADEM DIPLOM NAT/G

B45
HORN O.B.,BRITISH PUBLIC OPINION AND THE FIRST PARTITION OF POLAND. POLAND UK LEGIS PRESS RUMOR CONTROL PARTIC NAT/LISM SOVEREIGN 18/19. PAGE 73 H1469 DIPLOM POLICY ATTIT NAT/G

B45
MERRIAM C.E.,SYSTEMATIC POLITICS. FUT POL/PAR DELIB/GP DIPLOM ADJUD ADMIN LEAD CHOOSE ATTIT...MGT PHIL/SCI TREND. PAGE 109 H2183 NAT/G METH/CNCPT CREATE

B45
PERAZA SARAUSA F.,BIBLIOGRAFIAS CUBANAS. CUBA CULTURE ECO/UNDEV AGRI EDU/PROP PRESS CIVMIL/REL ...POLICY GEOG PHIL/SCI BIOG 19/20. PAGE 125 H2489 BIBLIOG/A L/A+17C NAT/G DIPLOM

B45
WOOLBERT R.G.,FOREIGN AFFAIRS BIBLIOGRAPHY, 1932-1942. INT/ORG SECT INT/TRADE COLONIAL RACE/REL NAT/LISM...GEOG INT/LAW GOV/COMP IDEA/COMP 20. PAGE 170 H3410 BIBLIOG/A DIPLOM WAR

B46
ALLEN J.S.,WORLD MONOPOLY AND PEACE. GERMANY UK USSR FINAN INDUS LG/CO DOMIN CONTROL PEACE PWR WEALTH SOCISM...NAT/COMP 20 MONOPOLY. PAGE 5 H0105 CAP/ISM DIPLOM WAR COLONIAL

B46
BLUM L.,FOR ALL MANKIND (TRANS. BY W. PICKLES). FRANCE GERMANY USSR LAW SOCIETY STRUCT POL/PAR WORKER DIPLOM DOMIN CHOOSE ORD/FREE FASCISM 20. PAGE 18 H0361 POPULISM SOCIALIST NAT/G WAR

B46
HUTTON J.,THE CONSTITUTION OF THE UNION OF SOUTH AFRICA: BIBLIOGRAPHY (PAMPHLET). SOUTH/AFR MUNIC DIPLOM RACE/REL 20. PAGE 75 H1510 BIBLIOG CONSTN NAT/G LOC/G

B46
NICOLSON H.,THE CONGRESS OF VIENNA. MOD/EUR NAT/G FORCES BAL/PWR DOMIN LEGIT COERCE PERSON PWR ...RECORD TIME/SEQ STERTYP 19 CONG/VIENN. PAGE 118 H2353 CONCPT POLICY DIPLOM

N46
HOBBS C.C.,SOUTHEAST ASIA, 1935-45: A SELECTED LIST OF REFERENCE BOOKS (PAMPHLET). S/ASIA AGRI INDUS NAT/G SECT DIPLOM WAR...ART/METH GEOG SOC LING 20. PAGE 72 H1435 BIBLIOG/A CULTURE HABITAT

B47
NIEBUHR R.,THE CHILDREN OF LIGHT AND THE CHILDREN OF DARKNESS: A VINDICATION OF DEMOCRACY AND CRITIQUE OF TRADITIONAL DEFENSE. UNIV STRUCT NAT/G SECT INGP/REL OWN PEACE ORD/FREE MARXISM ...IDEA/COMP GEN/LAWS 20 CHRISTIAN. PAGE 118 H2358 POPULISM DIPLOM NEIGH GP/REL

B48
GUIDE TO THE RECORDS IN THE NATIONAL ARCHIVES. ECO/UNDEV ADMIN COLONIAL 16/20. PAGE 2 H0034 BIBLIOG NAT/G L/A+17C DIPLOM

B48
CLYDE P.H.,THE FAR EAST: A HISTORY OF THE IMPACT OF THE WEST ON EASTERN ASIA. CHINA/COM CULTURE INT/TRADE DOMIN COLONIAL WAR PWR...CHARTS BIBLIOG DIPLOM ASIA

19/20 CHINJAP. PAGE 30 H0609

B48
FLOREN LOZANO L.,BIBLIOGRAFIA DE LA BIBLIOGRAFIA DOMINICANA. DOMIN/REP NAT/G DIPLOM EDU/PROP CIVMIL/REL...POLICY ART/METH GEOG PHIL/SCI HIST/WRIT 20. PAGE 51 H1027
BIBLIOG/A BIOG L/A+17C CULTURE

B48
GRIFFITH E.S.,RESEARCH IN POLITICAL SCIENCE: THE WORK OF PANELS OF RESEARCH COMMITTEE, APSA. WOR+45 WOR-45 COM/IND R+D FORCES ACT/RES WAR...GOV/COMP ANTHOL 20. PAGE 61 H1220
BIBLIOG PHIL/SCI DIPLOM JURID

B48
JONES H.D.,UNESCO: A SELECTED LIST OF REFERENCES. CULTURE CREATE PEACE ATTIT DRIVE 20 UNESCO UN. PAGE 82 H1631
BIBLIOG/A INT/ORG DIPLOM EDU/PROP

B48
LASKI H.S.,THE AMERICAN DEMOCRACY. CULTURE INDUS SECT WORKER DIPLOM EDU/PROP REPRESENT RACE/REL ORD/FREE PWR...NAT/COMP 18/20. PAGE 92 H1831
NAT/G LOC/G USA-45 POPULISM

B48
LINEBARGER P.,PSYCHOLOGICAL WARFARE. NAT/G PLAN DIPLOM DOMIN ATTIT...POLICY CONCPT EXHIBIT 20 WWI. PAGE 97 H1933
EDU/PROP PSY WAR COM/IND

B48
NEUBURGER O.,GUIDE TO OFFICIAL PUBLICATIONS OF THE OTHER AMERICAN REPUBLICS: VENEZUELA (VOL. XIX). VENEZUELA FINAN LEGIS PLAN BUDGET DIPLOM CT/SYS PARL/PROC 19/20. PAGE 117 H2335
BIBLIOG/A NAT/G CONSTN LAW

B48
PELCOVITS N.A.,OLD CHINA HANDS AND THE FOREIGN OFFICE. ASIA BURMA UK ECO/UNDEV NAT/G ECO/TAC FOR/AID TARIFFS DOMIN COLONIAL GOV/REL SOVEREIGN 19 HONG/KONG TREATY. PAGE 124 H2483
INT/TRADE ATTIT DIPLOM

B48
TOYNBEE A.J.,CIVILIZATION ON TRIAL. FUT WOR-45 NAT/G CREATE CAP/ISM DIPLOM NUC/PWR CHOOSE MARXISM ...GEOG CONCPT WORSHIP. PAGE 156 H3125
SOCIETY TIME/SEQ NAT/COMP

B49
BORBA DE MORAES R.,MANUAL BIBLIOGRAFICO DE ESTUDOS BRASILEIROS. BRAZIL DIPLOM ADMIN LEAD...SOC 20. PAGE 19 H0374
BIBLIOG L/A+17C NAT/G ECO/UNDEV

B49
BOZZA T.,SCRITTORI POLITICI ITALIANI DAL 1550 AL 1650. CHRIST-17C ITALY DIPLOM DOMIN 16/17. PAGE 20 H0394
BIBLIOG/A NAT/G CONCPT WRITING

B49
GORER G.,THE PEOPLE OF GREAT RUSSIA: A PSYCHOLOGICAL STUDY. RUSSIA USSR NAT/G DIPLOM LEAD AGE/C ANOMIE ATTIT DRIVE...POLICY 20. PAGE 59 H1182
ISOLAT PERSON PSY SOCIETY

B49
HEADLAM-MORLEY,BIBLIOGRAPHY IN POLITICS FOR THE HONOUR SCHOOL OF PHILOSOPHY, POLITICS AND ECONOMICS (PAMPHLET). UK CONSTN LABOR MUNIC DIPLOM ADMIN 19/20. PAGE 69 H1375
BIBLIOG NAT/G PHIL/SCI GOV/REL

B49
HINDEN R.,EMPIRE AND AFTER. UK POL/PAR BAL/PWR DIPLOM INT/TRADE WAR NAT/LISM PWR 17/20. PAGE 71 H1420
NAT/G COLONIAL ATTIT POLICY

B49
MAO TSE-TUNG,NEW DEMOCRACY. CHINA/COM NAT/G DIPLOM ECO/TAC EDU/PROP REV...CONCPT METH SOC/INTEG 20. PAGE 102 H2045
SOCISM MARXISM POPULISM CULTURE

B49
US DEPARTMENT OF STATE,SOVIET BIBLIOGRAPHY (PAMPHLET). CHINA/COM COM USSR LAW AGRI INT/ORG ECO/TAC EDU/PROP...POLICY GEOG 20. PAGE 159 H3185
BIBLIOG/A MARXISM CULTURE DIPLOM

L49
BRECHT A.,"THE NEW GERMAN CONSTITUTION." GERMANY/W NAT/G CHIEF EX/STRUC LEGIS PROB/SOLV ADMIN REPRESENT TOTALISM ORD/FREE PLURISM...MAJORIT CHARTS 20. PAGE 20 H0409
CONSTN DIPLOM SOVEREIGN FEDERAL

S49
STEINMETZ H.,"THE PROBLEMS OF THE LANDRAT: A STUDY OF COUNTY GOVERNMENT IN THE US ZONE OF GERMANY." GERMANY/W USA+45 INDUS PLAN DIPLOM EDU/PROP CONTROL WAR GOV/REL FEDERAL WEALTH PLURISM...GOV/COMP 20 LANDRAT. PAGE 149 H2977
LOC/G COLONIAL MGT TOP/EX

C49
YANAGA C.,"JAPAN SINCE PERRY." S/ASIA CULTURE ECO/DEV FORCES WAR 19/20 CHINJAP. PAGE 172 H3433
DIPLOM POL/PAR CIVMIL/REL NAT/LISM

B50
CORNELL U DEPT ASIAN STUDIES,SOUTHEAST ASIA PROGRAM DATA PAPER. BURMA CAMBODIA INDONESIA MALAYSIA VIETNAM SOCIETY STRUCT NAT/G SECT DIPLOM FOR/AID PWR WEALTH...SOC 20. PAGE 33 H0670
BIBLIOG/A CULTURE S/ASIA ECO/UNDEV

B50
COUNCIL BRITISH NATIONAL BIB,BRITISH NATIONAL BIBLIOGRAPHY. UK AGRI CONSTRUC PERF/ART POL/PAR SECT CREATE INT/TRADE LEAD...HUM JURID PHIL/SCI 20. PAGE 34 H0677
BIBLIOG/A NAT/G TEC/DEV DIPLOM

B50
DUCLOS P.,L'EVOLUTION DES RAPPORTS POLITIQUES DEPUIS 1750 (LIBERTE, INTEGRATION, UNITE). LAW INT/ORG FEDERAL TOTALISM ATTIT PWR...MAJORIT BIBLIOG 18/20 PARLIAMENT EUROPE. PAGE 43 H0852
ORD/FREE DIPLOM NAT/G GOV/COMP

B50
FIGANIERE J.C.,BIBLIOTHECA HISTORICA PORTUGUEZA. BRAZIL PORTUGAL SECT ADMIN. PAGE 50 H0997
BIBLIOG NAT/G DIPLOM COLONIAL

B50
FITZGERALD C.P.,CHINA, A SHORT CULTURAL HISTORY. ASIA DIPLOM INT/TRADE...ART/METH SOC MANCHU/DYN. PAGE 51 H1016
NAT/G SOCIETY

B50
GATZKE H.W.,GERMANY'S DRIVE TO THE WEST. BELGIUM GERMANY MOD/EUR AGRI INDUS POL/PAR FORCES DOMIN AGREE CONTROL REGION COERCE 20 TREATY WWI. PAGE 55 H1104
WAR POLICY NAT/G DIPLOM

B50
GLEASON J.H.,THE GENESIS OF RUSSOPHOBIA IN GREAT BRITAIN: A STUDY OF THE INTERACTION OF POLICY AND OPINION. ASIA RUSSIA UK NAT/G AGREE CONTROL REV WAR LOVE PWR TREATY 19. PAGE 57 H1142
DIPLOM POLICY DOMIN COLONIAL

B50
JONES H.D.,KOREA, AN ANNOTATED BIBLIOGRAPHY OF PUBLICATIONS IN WESTERN LANGUAGES. KOREA CULTURE MUNIC SECT FORCES DIPLOM HEALTH WEALTH...ART/METH GEOG SOC LING 20. PAGE 82 H1632
BIBLIOG/A ASIA NAT/G ECO/UNDEV

B50
US DEPARTMENT OF STATE,DOCUMENTS ON GERMAN FOREIGN POLICY, 1918-1945 (13 VOLS.). EUR+WWI GERMANY NAT/G PLAN DIPLOM DOMIN EDU/PROP CONTROL NAT/LISM ...ANTHOL 20. PAGE 159 H3186
BIBLIOG/A WAR POLICY FASCIST

C50
NUMELIN R.,"THE BEGINNINGS OF DIPLOMACY." INT/TRADE WAR GP/REL PEACE STRANGE ATTIT...INT/LAW CONCPT BIBLIOG. PAGE 119 H2380
DIPLOM KIN CULTURE LAW

B51
CATALOGO GENERAL DE LA LIBRERIA ESPANOLA E HISPANOAMERICANA 1901-1930; AUTORES (5 VOLS., 1932-1951). SPAIN COLONIAL GOV/REL...SOC 20. PAGE 2 H0036
BIBLIOG L/A+17C DIPLOM NAT/G

B51
BISSAINTHE M.,DICTIONNAIRE DE BIBLIOGRAPHIE HAITIENNE. HAITI ELITES AGRI LEGIS DIPLOM INT/TRADE WRITING ORD/FREE CATHISM...ART/METH GEOG 19/20 NEGRO TREATY. PAGE 17 H0347
BIBLIOG L/A+17C SOCIETY NAT/G

B51
BORKENAU F.,EUROPEAN COMMUNISM. COM EUR+WWI GERMANY SPAIN USSR INT/ORG PLAN REV WAR ATTIT 20 STALIN/J HITLER/A. PAGE 19 H0376
MARXISM POLICY DIPLOM NAT/G

B51
CARRINGTON C.E.,THE LIQUIDATION OF THE BRITISH EMPIRE. AFR NAT/G INT/TRADE COLONIAL RACE/REL ATTIT ORD/FREE...POLICY NAT/COMP 20 CMN/WLTH. PAGE 27 H0541
SOVEREIGN NAT/LISM DIPLOM GP/REL

B51
CHRISTENSEN A.N.,THE EVOLUTION OF LATIN AMERICAN GOVERNMENT: A BOOK OF READINGS. ECO/UNDEV INDUS LOC/G POL/PAR EX/STRUC LEGIS FOR/AID CT/SYS ...SOC/WK 20 SOUTH/AMER. PAGE 30 H0599
NAT/G CONSTN DIPLOM L/A+17C

B51
JENNINGS I.,THE COMMONWEALTH IN ASIA. CEYLON INDIA PAKISTAN CULTURE STRATA NAT/G LEGIS DIPLOM COLONIAL ATTIT...DECISION 20 CMN/WLTH. PAGE 80 H1604
CONSTN INT/ORG POLICY PLAN

B51
JENNINGS S.I.,THE COMMONWEALTH IN ASIA. CEYLON INDIA PAKISTAN S/ASIA UK CONSTN CULTURE SOCIETY STRATA STRUCT NAT/G POL/PAR EDU/PROP LEAD WAR 20 CMN/WLTH. PAGE 80 H1608
NAT/LISM REGION COLONIAL DIPLOM

B51
LEONARD L.L.,INTERNATIONAL ORGANIZATION. WOR+45 WOR-45 EX/STRUC FORCES LEGIS ECO/TAC INT/TRADE COLONIAL ARMS/CONT...SOC/WK GOV/COMP BIBLIOG. PAGE 94 H1884
NAT/G DIPLOM INT/ORG DELIB/GP

B51
US LIBRARY OF CONGRESS,EAST EUROPEAN ACCESSIONS LIST (VOL. I). POL/PAR DIPLOM ADMIN LEAD 20. PAGE 160 H3207
BIBLIOG/A COM SOCIETY NAT/G

B51
WABEKE B.H.,A GUIDE TO DUTCH BIBLIOGRAPHIES. BELGIUM INDONESIA NETHERLAND DIPLOM INT/TRADE WAR NAT/LISM KNOWL...ART/METH HUM JURID CON/ANAL 14/20. PAGE 164 H3282
BIBLIOG/A NAT/G CULTURE COLONIAL

B51
WEBSTER C.,THE FOREIGN POLICY OF PALMERSTON - 1830
ADMIN

TO 1841. MOD/EUR UK LAW CONSTN INTELL SOCIETY STRUCT NAT/G FORCES TOP/EX CREATE BAL/PWR PWR 19. PAGE 166 H3323 PERSON DIPLOM
B51

YOUNG T.C.,NEAR EASTERN CULTURE AND SOCIETY. ISLAM ECO/UNDEV SECT WRITING ATTIT HABITAT ORD/FREE 20. PAGE 172 H3439 CULTURE STRUCT REGION DIPLOM
S51

NORTHROP F.S.C.,"ASIAN MENTALITY AND UNITED STATES FOREIGN POLICY." ASIA ISLAM USA+45 CULTURE SOCIETY SECT EDU/PROP LEGIT COERCE DRIVE MORAL ORD/FREE ...POLICY RELATIV TOT/POP 20. PAGE 119 H2376 S/ASIA ATTIT DIPLOM
C51

BEST H.,"THE SOVIET STATE AND ITS INCEPTION." USSR CULTURE INDUS DIPLOM WEALTH...GEOG SOC BIBLIOG 20. PAGE 16 H0322 COM GEN/METH REV MARXISM
B52

APPADORAI A.,THE SUBSTANCE OF POLITICS (6TH ED.). EX/STRUC LEGIS DIPLOM CT/SYS CHOOSE FASCISM MARXISM SOCISM...BIBLIOG T. PAGE 7 H0145 PHIL/SCI NAT/G
B52

DILLON D.R.,LATIN AMERICA, 1935-1949; A SELECTED BIBLIOGRAPHY. LAW EDU/PROP...SOC 20. PAGE 41 H0826 BIBLIOG L/A+17C NAT/G DIPLOM
B52

GURLAND A.R.L.,POLITICAL SCIENCE IN WESTERN GERMANY: THOUGHTS AND WRITINGS, 1950-1952 (PAMPHLET). EUR+WWI GERMANY/W ELITES SOCIETY NAT/G NAT/LISM TOTALISM 20. PAGE 63 H1253 BIBLIOG/A DIPLOM CIVMIL/REL FASCISM
B52

SKALWEIT S.,FRANKREICH UND FRIEDRICH DER GROSSE. FRANCE GERMANY PRUSSIA NAT/G DOMIN WAR 18 FREDERICK. PAGE 145 H2893 ATTIT EDU/PROP DIPLOM SOC
B52

SPENCER F.A.,WAR AND POSTWAR GREECE: AN ANALYSIS BASED ON GREEK WRITINGS. GREECE SOCIETY NAT/G POL/PAR FORCES CREATE DIPLOM LEAD MARXISM...SOC 20. PAGE 147 H2943 BIBLIOG/A WAR REV
B52

THOM J.M.,GUIDE TO RESEARCH MATERIAL IN POLITICAL SCIENCE (PAMPHLET). ELITES LOC/G MUNIC NAT/G LEGIS DIPLOM ADJUD CIVMIL/REL GOV/REL PWR MGT. PAGE 154 H3074 BIBLIOG/A KNOWL
B52

US DEPARTMENT OF STATE,RESEARCH ON EASTERN EUROPE (EXCLUDING USSR). EUR+WWI LAW ECO/DEV NAT/G PROB/SOLV DIPLOM ADMIN LEAD MARXISM...TREND 19/20. PAGE 159 H3187 BIBLIOG R+D ACT/RES COM
B52

US LIBRARY OF CONGRESS,EGYPT AND THE ANGLO-EGYPTIAN SUDAN: A SELECTIVE GUIDE TO BACKGROUND READING (PAMPHLET). SUDAN UAR UK DIPLOM...POLICY 20. PAGE 160 H3209 BIBLIOG/A COLONIAL ISLAM NAT/G
C52

FIFIELD R.H.,"WOODROW WILSON AND THE FAR EAST." ASIA CHIEF DELIB/GP BAL/PWR CONFER COLONIAL ARMS/CONT WAR...TIME/SEQ NAT/COMP 19/20 WILSON/W LEAGUE/NAT. PAGE 50 H0995 BIBLIOG DIPLOM INT/ORG
B53

DAVIDSON B.,THE NEW WEST AFRICA: PROBLEMS OF INDEPENDENCE. UK AGRI TEC/DEV DIPLOM GP/REL RACE/REL SOVEREIGN...ANTHOL 20 AFRICA/W. PAGE 37 H0744 AFR COLONIAL ECO/UNDEV NAT/G
B53

ELAHI K.N.,A GUIDE TO WORKS OF REFERENCE PUBLISHED IN PAKISTAN (PAMPHLET). PAKISTAN DIPLOM COLONIAL LEAD. PAGE 45 H0903 BIBLIOG S/ASIA NAT/G
B53

KANTOR H.,A BIBLIOGRAPHY OF UNPUBLISHED DOCTORAL DISSERTATIONS AND MASTERS' THESES DEALING WITH GOVTS, POL, INT REL OF LAT AM. L/A+17C INT/ORG POL/PAR ACT/RES OP/RES CONFER ATTIT...INT/LAW PHIL/SCI 20. PAGE 83 H1656 BIBLIOG ACADEM DIPLOM NAT/G
B53

LENZ F.,DIE BEWEGUNGEN DER GROSSEN MACHTE. USA+45 USA-45 USSR SOCIETY STRATA STRUCT NAT/G PERSON MARXISM...CONCPT IDEA/COMP NAT/COMP 18/20. PAGE 94 H1883 BAL/PWR TREND DIPLOM HIST/WRIT
B53

MARITAIN J.,L'HOMME ET L'ETAT. SECT DIPLOM GP/REL PEACE ORD/FREE...IDEA/COMP 17/20 CHURCH/STA NATURL/LAW. PAGE 103 H2052 CONCPT NAT/G SOVEREIGN COERCE
B53

MURPHY G.,IN THE MINDS OF MEN: THE STUDY OF HUMAN BEHAVIOR AND SOCIAL TENSIONS IN INDIA. FUT S/ASIA FAM INT/ORG NAT/G DIPLOM EDU/PROP GP/REL ATTIT RIGID/FLEX ALL/VALS...SOC QU UNESCO 20. PAGE 115 H2297 SECT STRATA INDIA
B53

ORFIELD L.B.,THE GROWTH OF SCANDINAVIAN LAW. DENMARK ICELAND NORWAY SWEDEN LAW DIPLOM...BIBLIOG 9/20. PAGE 121 H2426 JURID CT/SYS NAT/G
B53

ROSCIO J.G.,OBRAS. L/A+17C SPAIN DIPLOM REV WAR NAT/LISM TOTALISM PWR SOVEREIGN 19. PAGE 134 H2671 ORD/FREE COLONIAL NAT/G PHIL/SCI
B53

SHIRATO I.,JAPANESE SOURCES ON THE HISTORY OF THE CHINESE COMMUNIST MOVEMENT (PAMPHLET). CHINA/COM USSR CONSTRUC NAT/G POL/PAR FORCES DIPLOM DOMIN EDU/PROP CONTROL WAR TOTALISM SOCISM 20. PAGE 143 H2863 BIBLIOG/A MARXISM ECO/UNDEV
B53

SQUIRES J.D.,BRITISH PROPAGANDA AT HOME AND IN THE UNITED STATES FROM 1914 TO 1917. UK NAT/G PROB/SOLV DOMIN PRESS EFFICIENCY...PSY PREDICT 20 WWI INTERVENT PSY/WAR. PAGE 148 H2960 EDU/PROP CONTROL WAR DIPLOM
B53

STOUT H.M.,BRITISH GOVERNMENT. UK FINAN LOC/G POL/PAR DELIB/GP DIPLOM ADMIN COLONIAL CHOOSE ORD/FREE...JURID BIBLIOG 20 COMMONWLTH. PAGE 150 H2990 NAT/G PARL/PROC CONSTN NEW/LIB
B54

BINANI G.D.,INDIA AT A GLANCE (REV. ED.). INDIA COM/IND FINAN INDUS LABOR PROVS SCHOOL PLAN DIPLOM INT/TRADE ADMIN...JURID 20. PAGE 17 H0335 INDEX CON/ANAL NAT/G ECO/UNDEV
B54

BUTZ O.,GERMANY: DILEMMA FOR AMERICAN POLICY. GERMANY USA+45 USA-45 USSR WOR+45 INT/ORG FORCES NUC/PWR EFFICIENCY PEACE PWR...GOV/COMP 20 COLD/WAR. PAGE 25 H0501 DIPLOM NAT/G WAR POLICY
B54

CAMPANELLA T.,A DISCOURSE TOUCHING THE SPANISH MONARCHY... (1640). SPAIN UNIV SEA STRATA FINAN SECT FORCES SUPEGO LOVE ORD/FREE...CONCPT 17. PAGE 26 H0514 CONSERVE CHIEF NAT/G DIPLOM
B54

EPSTEIN L.D.,BRITAIN - UNEASY ALLY. KOREA UK USA+45 NAT/G POL/PAR ECO/TAC FOR/AID INT/TRADE WAR LABOR/PAR CONSRV/PAR. PAGE 47 H0934 DIPLOM ATTIT POLICY NAT/COMP
B54

GERMANY FOREIGN MINISTRY,DOCUMENTS ON GERMAN FOREIGN POLICY 1918-1945, SERIES C (1933-1937) VOLS. I-V. GERMANY MOD/EUR FORCES PLAN ECO/TAC ...FASCIST CHARTS ANTHOL 20. PAGE 56 H1115 NAT/G DIPLOM POLICY
B54

TOTOK W.,HANDBUCH DER BIBLIOGRAPHISCHEN NACHSCHLAGEWERKE. GERMANY LAW CULTURE ADMIN...SOC 20. PAGE 156 H3117 BIBLIOG/A NAT/G DIPLOM POLICY
L54

FURNISS E.S.,"WEAKNESSES IN FRENCH FOREIGN POLICY-MAKING." EUR+WWI LEGIS LEGIT EXEC ATTIT RIGID/FLEX ORD/FREE...SOC CONCPT METH/CNCPT OBS 20. PAGE 54 H1078 NAT/G STRUCT DIPLOM FRANCE
S54

ALBRECT M.C.,"THE RELATIONSHIP OF LITERATURE AND SOCIETY." STRATA STRUCT DIPLOM...POLICY SOC/INTEG. PAGE 5 H0097 HUM CULTURE WRITING NAT/COMP
C54

BERLE A.A. JR.,"THE 20TH CENTURY CAPITALIST REVOLUTION." ECO/DEV NAT/G DIPLOM PRICE CONTROL ATTIT...BIBLIOG/A 20. PAGE 15 H0306 LG/CO CAP/ISM MGT PWR
C54

DE GRAZIA A.,"THE COMPARATIVE SURVEY OF EUROPEAN-AMERICAN POLITICAL BEHAV IOR; A RESEARCH PROSPECTUS (PAPER)" EUR+WWI FRANCE GERMANY SPAIN UK USA+45 WOR+45 STRATA POL/PAR DIPLOM EDU/PROP COLONIAL LEAD WAR NAT/LISM CONCPT. PAGE 37 H0752 BIBLIOG R+D METH NAT/COMP
B55

ALFIERI D.,DICTATORS FACE TO FACE. NAT/G TOP/EX DIPLOM EXEC COERCE ORD/FREE FASCISM...POLICY OBS 20 HITLER/A MUSSOLIN/B. PAGE 5 H0103 WAR CHIEF TOTALISM PERS/REL
B55

CRAIG G.A.,THE POLITICS OF THE PRUSSIAN ARMY 1640-1945. CHRIST-17C EUR+WWI MOD/EUR PRUSSIA STRUCT DIPLOM ADMIN REV WAR...SOC BIBLIOG 17/20. PAGE 35 H0694 FORCES NAT/G ROLE CHIEF
B55

FRANZ G.,KULTURKAMPF. AUSTRIA GERMANY PRUSSIA SWITZERLND POL/PAR DIPLOM GP/REL ATTIT ORD/FREE 18/19 CHURCH/STA. PAGE 53 H1053 NAT/LISM CATHISM NAT/G REV
B55

HELANDER S.,DAS AUTARKIEPROBLEM IN DER WELTWIRTSCHAFT. PROB/SOLV BAL/PWR BARGAIN CAP/ISM ECO/TAC SOVEREIGN 20. PAGE 69 H1388 NAT/COMP COLONIAL DIPLOM
B55

INSTITUTE POLITISCHE WISSEN,POLITISCHE LITERATUR (3 VOLS.). INT/ORG LEAD WAR PEACE...CONCPT TREND NAT/COMP 20. PAGE 77 H1540 BIBLIOG/A NAT/G DIPLOM

POLICY

B55
KOHN H.,NATIONALISM: ITS MEANING AND HISTORY. GP/REL INGP/REL ATTIT...CONCPT NAT/COMP 16/20 MACHIAVELL. PAGE 87 H1743
NAT/LISM DIPLOM FASCISM REV

B55
KRUSE H.,DAS STAATSANGEHORIGKEITSRECHT DER ARABISCHEN STAATEN. ISLAM JORDAN LIBYA SYRIA UAR NAT/G SECT RACE/REL...INT/LAW 6/20 TREATY. PAGE 89 H1779
JURID NAT/LISM DIPLOM GP/REL

B55
NAMIER L.,PERSONALITIES AND POWERS. EUR+WWI MOD/EUR NAT/G POL/PAR TOP/EX EDU/PROP KNOWL...GEOG 17/20. PAGE 115 H2308
TIME/SEQ DIPLOM UK

B55
POHLENZ M.,GRIECHISCHE FREIHEIT. GREECE DIPLOM WAR SUPEGO PWR RESPECT...IDEA/COMP. PAGE 127 H2533
ORD/FREE CONCPT JURID NAT/G

B55
POLLOCK J.K.,GERMAN DEMOCRACY AT WORK. GERMANY/W LOC/G NAT/G DIPLOM PARL/PROC...OBS IDEA/COMP 20. PAGE 127 H2539
PARTIC POL/PAR CHOOSE EDU/PROP

B55
PYRAH G.B.,IMPERIAL POLICY AND SOUTH AFRICA 1902-1910. SOUTH/AFR UK NAT/G WAR DISCRIM...CONCPT CHARTS BIBLIOG/A 19/20 CMN/WLTH. PAGE 129 H2570
DIPLOM COLONIAL POLICY RACE/REL

B55
QUAN K.L.,INTRODUCTION TO ASIA: A SELECTIVE GUIDE TO BACKGROUND READING. ECO/UNDEV NAT/G PROB/SOLV DIPLOM ATTIT 20. PAGE 129 H2572
BIBLIOG/A S/ASIA CULTURE ASIA

B55
ROWE C.,VOLTAIRE AND THE STATE. FRANCE MOD/EUR BAL/PWR CONTROL TASK SUPEGO ORD/FREE PWR...CONCPT 18 VOLTAIRE. PAGE 135 H2702
NAT/G DIPLOM NAT/LISM ATTIT

B55
SVARLIEN O.,AN INTRODUCTION TO THE LAW OF NATIONS. SEA AIR INT/ORG NAT/G CHIEF ADMIN AGREE WAR PRIVIL ORD/FREE SOVEREIGN...BIBLIOG 16/20. PAGE 151 H3012
INT/LAW DIPLOM

B55
TAN C.C.,THE BOXER CATASTROPHE. ASIA UK USSR ELITES POL/PAR VOL/ASSN FORCES PROB/SOLV DIPLOM ADMIN COLONIAL NAT/LISM PEACE TREATY 19/20 BOXER/REBL. PAGE 152 H3040
REV NAT/G WAR

B55
THOMPSON V.,MINORITY PROBLEMS IN SOUTHEAST ASIA. CAMBODIA CHINA/COM LAOS S/ASIA KIN NAT/G SECT PROB/SOLV EDU/PROP REGION GP/REL RACE/REL MARXISM ...SOC 20 BUDDHISM UN. PAGE 154 H3085
INGP/REL GEOG DIPLOM STRUCT

B55
VIGON J.,TEORIA DEL MILITARISMO. NAT/G DIPLOM COLONIAL COERCE GUERRILLA CIVMIL/REL NAT/LISM MORAL ALL/IDEOS PACIFISM 18/20. PAGE 163 H3253
FORCES PHIL/SCI WAR POLICY

B55
WOYTINSKY W.S.,WORLD COMMERCE AND GOVERNMENTS: TRENDS AND OUTLOOK. WOR+45 FINAN POL/PAR DIPLOM ECO/TAC FOR/AID DOMIN WAR CHOOSE...CHARTS BIBLIOG 20 LEAGUE/NAT UN ILO. PAGE 171 H3413
INT/TRADE DIST/IND NAT/COMP NAT/G

B55
WRONG D.H.,AMERICAN AND CANADIAN VIEWPOINTS. CANADA USA+45 CONSTN STRATA FAM SECT WORKER ECO/TAC EDU/PROP ADJUD MARRIAGE...IDEA/COMP 20. PAGE 171 H3424
DIPLOM ATTIT NAT/COMP CULTURE

S55
BENN S.I.,"THE USES OF 'SOVEREIGNTY'." UNIV NAT/G LEGIS DIPLOM COERCE...METH/CNCPT GEN/LAWS. PAGE 14 H0282
SOVEREIGN IDEA/COMP CONCPT PWR

S55
DE SMITH S.A.,"CONSTITUTIONAL MONARCHY IN BURGANDA." AFR UGANDA UK STRUCT CHIEF REGION INGP/REL ADJUST NAT/LISM SOVEREIGN CONSERVE ...POLICY 19/20 BURGANDA. PAGE 38 H0769
NAT/G DIPLOM CONSTN COLONIAL

C55
APTER D.E.,"THE GOLD COAST IN TRANSITION." AFR CONSTN LOC/G LEGIS DIPLOM COLONIAL CONTROL GOV/REL ...CHARTS BIBLIOG 20 CMN/WLTH. PAGE 7 H0150
ORD/FREE REPRESENT PARL/PROC NAT/G

B56
DE JONG L.,THE GERMAN FIFTH COLUMN IN THE SECOND WORLD WAR. EUR+WWI GERMANY NAT/G DIPLOM ATTIT FASCISM...MYTH 20 NAZI. PAGE 38 H0756
EDU/PROP WAR RUMOR

B56
FIELD G.C.,POLITICAL THEORY. POL/PAR REPRESENT MORAL SOVEREIGN...JURID IDEA/COMP. PAGE 50 H0990
CONCPT NAT/G ORD/FREE DIPLOM

B56
IRIKURA J.K.,SOUTHEAST ASIA: SELECTED ANNOTATED BIBLIOGRAPHY OF JAPANESE PUBLICATIONS. CULTURE ADMIN RACE/REL 20 CHINJAP. PAGE 78 H1567
BIBLIOG/A S/ASIA DIPLOM

B56
PHILIPPINE STUDIES PROGRAM,SELECTED BIBLIOGRAPHY ON THE PHILIPPINES, TOPICALLY ARRANGED AND ANNOTATED. PHILIPPINE SECT DIPLOM COLONIAL LEAD...SOC 18/20. PAGE 125 H2501
BIBLIOG/A S/ASIA NAT/G ECO/UNDEV

B56
ROBERTS H.L.,RUSSIA AND AMERICA. CHINA/COM S/ASIA USSR FORCES TEC/DEV FOR/AID NUC/PWR ALL/IDEOS ...MAJORIT TREND NAT/COMP 20 COLD/WAR UN NATO. PAGE 132 H2641
DIPLOM INT/ORG BAL/PWR TOTALISM

B56
SMEDLEY A.,THE GREAT ROAD: THE LIFE AND TIMES OF CHU TEH. ASIA USSR NAT/G POL/PAR DIPLOM COERCE GUERRILLA CIVMIL/REL NAT/LISM PERSON SKILL MARXISM ...BIOG 20 CHINJAP MAO. PAGE 145 H2903
REV WAR FORCES

B56
VON BECKERATH E.,HANDWORTERBUCH DER SOCIALWISSENSCHAFTEN (II VOLS.). EUR+WWI GERMANY POL/PAR WORKER DIPLOM LEAD CHOOSE SUFF WEALTH...SOC 20. PAGE 163 H3263
BIBLIOG INT/TRADE NAT/G ECO/DEV

B56
VON HARPE W.,DIE SOWJETUNION FINNLAND UND SKANDANAVIEN, 1945-1955. EUR+WWI FINLAND GERMANY USSR WAR INGP/REL ORD/FREE SOVEREIGN MARXISM ...POLICY GOV/COMP BIBLIOG 20 STALIN/J. PAGE 163 H3270
DIPLOM COM NEUTRAL BAL/PWR

B56
WATT D.C.,BRITAIN AND THE SUEZ CANAL. COM UAR UK ...INT/LAW 20 SUEZ TREATY. PAGE 166 H3314
DIPLOM INT/TRADE DIST/IND NAT/G

B56
WHITAKER A.P.,ARGENTINE UPHEAVAL. STRUCT FORCES DIPLOM COERCE PWR 20 ARGEN. PAGE 167 H3343
REV POL/PAR STRATA NAT/G

B56
WILSON P.,GOVERNMENT AND POLITICS OF INDIA AND PAKISTAN: 1885-1955; A BIBLIOGRAPHY OF WORKS IN WESTERN LANGUAGES. INDIA PAKISTAN CONSTN LOC/G POL/PAR FORCES DIPLOM ADMIN WAR CHOOSE...BIOG CON/ANAL 19/20. PAGE 169 H3380
BIBLIOG COLONIAL NAT/G S/ASIA

B56
WOLFF R.L.,THE BALKANS IN OUR TIME. ALBANIA FUT MOD/EUR USSR YUGOSLAVIA CULTURE INT/ORG SECT DIPLOM EDU/PROP COERCE WAR ORD/FREE...CHARTS 4/20 BALKANS COMINFORM. PAGE 170 H3403
GEOG COM

S56
ALMOND G.A.,"COMPARATIVE POLITICAL SYSTEMS" (BMR)" WOR+45 WOR-45 PROB/SOLV DIPLOM EFFICIENCY ...PHIL/SCI SOC METH 17/20. PAGE 5 H0111
GOV/COMP CONCPT ALL/IDEOS NAT/COMP

N56
US HOUSE COMM FOREIGN AFFAIRS,REPORT OF THE SPECIAL STUDY MISSION TO AFRICA, SOUTH AND EAST OF THE SAHARA (PAMPHLET). AFR SOUTH/AFR USA+45 STRUCT INT/TRADE PARL/PROC NAT/LISM ATTIT ALL/VALS HEALTH ...POLICY 20 CONGRESS. PAGE 160 H3197
FOR/AID COLONIAL ECO/UNDEV DIPLOM

B57
ALEXANDER L.M.,WORLD POLITICAL PATTERNS. NAT/G PROVS CAP/ISM DIPLOM COLONIAL NAT/LISM...POLICY GEOG CHARTS METH/COMP NAT/COMP 20. PAGE 5 H0101
CONTROL METH GOV/COMP

B57
BISHOP O.B.,PUBLICATIONS OF THE GOVERNMENTS OF NOVA SCOTIA, PRINCE EDWARD ISLAND, NEW BRUNSWICK 1758-1952. CANADA UK ADMIN COLONIAL LEAD...POLICY 18/20. PAGE 17 H0345
BIBLIOG NAT/G DIPLOM

B57
BUCK P.W.,CONTOL OF FOREIGN RELATIONS IN MODERN NATIONS. FRANCE L/A+17C NETHERLAND USSR WOR+45 INT/ORG TOP/EX BAL/PWR DOMIN EDU/PROP COERCE PEACE ATTIT...CONCPT TREND 20 CMN/WLTH. PAGE 23 H0465
NAT/G PWR DIPLOM

B57
BYRNES R.F.,BIBLIOGRAPHY OF AMERICAN PUBLICATIONS ON EAST CENTRAL EUROPE, 1945-1957 (VOL. XXII). SECT DIPLOM EDU/PROP RACE/REL...ART/METH GEOG JURID SOC LING 20 JEWS. PAGE 25 H0503
BIBLIOG/A COM MARXISM NAT/G

B57
CARIBBEAN COMMISSION,A CATALOGUE OF CARIBBEAN COMMISSION PUBLICATIONS (PAMPHLET). WEST/IND CULTURE ECO/UNDEV LOC/G DIPLOM SOC. PAGE 26 H0531
BIBLIOG L/A+17C INT/ORG NAT/G

B57
CONOVER H.F.,NORTH AND NORTHEAST AFRICA; A SELECTED ANNOTATED LIST OF WRITINGS. ALGERIA MOROCCO SUDAN UAR CULTURE INT/ORG PROB/SOLV ADJUD NAT/LISM PWR WEALTH...SOC 20 UN. PAGE 32 H0649
BIBLIOG/A DIPLOM AFR ECO/UNDEV

B57
DEAN V.M.,THE NATURE OF THE NON-WESTERN WORLD. AFR ASIA L/A+17C S/ASIA CULTURE SOCIETY STRATA ECO/DEV DIPLOM ECO/TAC FOR/AID ATTIT DRIVE ALL/VALS ...RELATIV SOC CONCPT TIME/SEQ TREND TOT/POP 20. PAGE 39 H0778
ECO/UNDEV STERTYP NAT/LISM

B57
DONALDSON A.G.,SOME COMPARATIVE ASPECTS OF IRISH
CONSTN

LAW. IRELAND NAT/G DIPLOM ADMIN CT/SYS LEAD ATTIT SOVEREIGN...JURID BIBLIOG/A 12/20 CMN/WLTH. PAGE 42 H0835 — LAW NAT/COMP INT/LAW

B57
HIRSCH F.E.,EUROPE TODAY; A BIBLIOGRAPHY (2ND ED.). EUR+WWI MOD/EUR NAT/G WAR 20. PAGE 71 H1424 — BIBLIOG/A GEOG DIPLOM

B57
HODGKIN T.,NATIONALISM IN COLONIAL AFRICA. STRATA STRUCT MUNIC NAT/G POL/PAR LEGIS ATTIT SOVEREIGN ...POLICY TREND BIBLIOG 20. PAGE 72 H1444 — AFR COLONIAL NAT/LISM DIPLOM

B57
KENNEDY M.D.,A SHORT HISTORY OF COMMUNISM IN ASIA. ASIA BURMA INDIA S/ASIA THAILAND NAT/G POL/PAR LEAD REV WAR MARXISM SOCISM...POLICY 20 CHINJAP. PAGE 85 H1688 — DIPLOM NAT/LISM TOTALISM COERCE

B57
KOHN H.,AMERICAN NATIONALISM. EUR+WWI USA+45 USA-45 COLONIAL REGION 18/20. PAGE 87 H1744 — NAT/LISM NAT/COMP FEDERAL DIPLOM

B57
MOYER K.E.,FROM IRAN TO MORROCCO; FROM TURKEY TO THE SUDAN: A SELECTED AND ANNOTATED BIBLIOGRAPHY OF NORTH AFRICA AND NEAR EAST... ISLAM DIPLOM EDU/PROP 20. PAGE 114 H2274 — BIBLIOG/A ECO/UNDEV SECT NAT/G

B57
NARAIN D.,HINDU CHARACTER (A FEW GLIMPSES). INDIA DIPLOM SUICIDE PERS/REL ATTIT...PSY NAT/COMP PERS/COMP BIBLIOG WORSHIP 20 HINDU. PAGE 116 H2310 — PERSON STERTYP SUPEGO SECT

B57
NEUMARK S.D.,ECONOMIC INFLUENCES ON THE SOUTH AFRICAN FRONTIER, 1652-1836. SOUTH/AFR SEA AGRI NAT/G FORCES WORKER DIPLOM INT/TRADE PRICE DEMAND PRODUC...STAT CHARTS 17/19 FRONTIER. PAGE 117 H2341 — COLONIAL ECO/UNDEV ECO/TAC MARKET

B57
PALMER N.D.,INTERNATIONAL RELATIONS. WOR+45 INT/ORG NAT/G ECO/TAC EDU/PROP COLONIAL WAR PWR SOVEREIGN ...POLICY T 20 TREATY. PAGE 123 H2451 — DIPLOM BAL/PWR NAT/COMP

B57
REISS J.,GEORGE KENNANS POLITIK DER EINDAMMUNG. USSR NAT/G FORCES TOTALISM ATTIT ORD/FREE...POLICY 20 NATO TRUMAN/HS MARSHL/PLN KENNAN/G. PAGE 131 H2613 — DIPLOM DETER PEACE

B57
ROBERTSON H.M.,SOUTH AFRICA, ECONOMIC AND POLITICAL ASPECTS. SOUTH/AFR CONSTN CULTURE POL/PAR LEGIS DIPLOM DOMIN COLONIAL...SOC BIBLIOG 19/20. PAGE 132 H2647 — RACE/REL ECO/UNDEV ECO/TAC DISCRIM

B57
RUMEU DE ARMAS A.,ESPANA EEN EL AFRICA ATLANTICA. AFR CHRIST-17C PORTUGAL SPAIN DIPLOM ECO/TAC CONTROL 14/16 AFRICA/W. PAGE 136 H2717 — NAT/G COLONIAL CHIEF PWR

B57
TOMASIC D.A.,NATIONAL COMMUNISM AND SOVIET STRATEGY. UK USSR YUGOSLAVIA NAT/G POL/PAR CHIEF CREATE DOMIN REV WAR PWR...BIOG TREND 20 TITO/MARSH STALIN/J. PAGE 156 H3112 — COM NAT/LISM MARXISM DIPLOM

B57
US SENATE SPEC COMM FOR AID,COMPILATION OF STUDIES AND SURVEYS. AFR ASIA L/A+17C USA+45 ECO/UNDEV AGRI INT/ORG CONSULT TEC/DEV CONFER TOTALISM...NAT/COMP 20 CONGRESS. PAGE 161 H3216 — FOR/AID DIPLOM ORD/FREE DELIB/GP

B57
US SENATE SPEC COMM FOR AID,HEARINGS BEFORE THE SPECIAL COMMITTEE TO STUDY THE FOREIGN AID PROGRAM. USA+45 USSR ECO/UNDEV INT/ORG FORCES WEAPON TOTALISM ATTIT SUPEGO...NAT/COMP CONGRESS. PAGE 161 H3217 — FOR/AID DIPLOM ORD/FREE TEC/DEV

B57
WILSON P.,SOUTH ASIA; A SELECTED BIBLIOGRAPHY ON INDIA, PAKISTAN, CEYLON (PAMPHLET). CEYLON INDIA PAKISTAN LAW ECO/UNDEV PLAN DIPLOM 20. PAGE 169 H3381 — BIBLIOG S/ASIA CULTURE NAT/G

S57
SPROUT H.,"ENVIRONMENTAL FACTORS IN THE STUDY OF INTERNATIONAL POLITICS." UNIV SOCIETY ECO/DEV NAT/G DELIB/GP TOP/EX ROUTINE ATTIT PERCEPT...POLICY GEOG CONCPT MYTH TIME/SEQ. PAGE 148 H2957 — DECISION GEN/LAWS DIPLOM

B58
BRIERLY J.L.,THE BASIS OF OBLIGATION IN INTERNATIONAL LAW, AND OTHER PAPERS. WOR+45 WOR-45 LEGIS...JURID CONCPT NAT/COMP ANTHOL 20. PAGE 21 H0415 — INT/LAW DIPLOM ADJUD SOVEREIGN

B58
CHANG H.,WITHIN THE FOUR SEAS. ASIA WAR MORAL MARXISM...IDEA/COMP NAT/COMP 20 CONFUCIUS. PAGE 29 H0577 — PEACE DIPLOM KNOWL CULTURE

B58
CRAIG G.A.,FROM BISMARCK TO ADENAUER: ASPECTS OF GERMAN STATECRAFT. GERMANY INTELL FORCES ECO/TAC CONFER COERCE WAR GP/REL ORD/FREE PWR CONSERVE 19/20 BISMARCK/O ADENAUER/K. PAGE 35 H0695 — DIPLOM LEAD NAT/G

B58
DUCLOUX L.,FROM BLACKMAIL TO TREASON. FRANCE PLAN DIPLOM EDU/PROP PRESS RUMOR NAT/LISM...CRIMLGY 20. PAGE 43 H0853 — COERCE CRIME NAT/G PWR

B58
HANSARD SOCIETY PARL GOVT,WHAT ARE THE PROBLEMS OF PARLIAMENTARY GOVERNMENT IN WEST AFRICA? PROB/SOLV DIPLOM GP/REL 20 PARLIAMENT AFRICA/W. PAGE 66 H1317 — PARL/PROC POL/PAR AFR NAT/G

B58
HUMPHREYS R.A.,LATIN AMERICAN HISTORY: A GUIDE TO THE LITERATURE IN ENGLISH. CULTURE NAT/G DIPLOM BIOG. PAGE 75 H1495 — BIBLIOG/A L/A+17C

B58
INDIAN COUNCIL WORLD AFFAIRS,DEFENCE AND SECURITY IN THE INDIAN OCEAN AREA. INDIA S/ASIA CULTURE CONSULT DELIB/GP FORCES PROB/SOLV DIPLOM INT/TRADE 20 CMN/WLTH. PAGE 77 H1531 — GEOG HABITAT ECO/UNDEV ORD/FREE

B58
INTERNATIONAL ECONOMIC ASSN,ECONOMICS OF INTERNATIONAL MIGRATION. WOR+45 WOR-45 ECO/UNDEV FINAN NAT/G REGION...NAT/COMP METH 20. PAGE 78 H1556 — CENSUS GEOG DIPLOM ECO/TAC

B58
JACOBSSON P.,SOME MONETARY PROBLEMS, INTERNATIONAL AND NATIONAL. WOR+45 WOR-45 ECO/DEV FORCES WORKER PROB/SOLV DIPLOM INT/TRADE...ANTHOL 20. PAGE 79 H1580 — FINAN PLAN ECO/TAC NAT/COMP

B58
KINTNER W.R.,ORGANIZING FOR CONFLICT: A PROPOSAL. USSR STRUCT NAT/G LEGIS ADMIN EXEC PEACE ORD/FREE PWR...CONCPT OBS TREND NAT/COMP VAL/FREE COLD/WAR 20. PAGE 86 H1719 — USA+45 PLAN DIPLOM

B58
LOWER A.R.M.,EVOLVING CANADIAN FEDERALISM. CANADA WEST/IND CONSTN PROB/SOLV COLONIAL REGION NAT/LISM ...ANTHOL 20. PAGE 99 H1976 — FEDERAL NAT/G DIPLOM RACE/REL

B58
MASON J.B.,THAILAND BIBLIOGRAPHY. S/ASIA THAILAND CULTURE EDU/PROP ADMIN...GEOG SOC LING 20. PAGE 104 H2087 — BIBLIOG/A ECO/UNDEV DIPLOM NAT/G

B58
PALMER E.E.,THE COMMUNIST CHALLENGE. COM USA+45 USA-45 ECO/DEV ECO/UNDEV NEUTRAL ORD/FREE POPULISM ...CONCPT NAT/COMP ANTHOL 19/20 LENIN/VI STALIN/J MAO MARX/KARL COM/PARTY. PAGE 123 H2450 — MARXISM DIPLOM IDEA/COMP POLICY

B58
PAN AMERICAN UNION,REPERTORIO DE PUBLICACIONES PERIODICAS ACTUALES LATINO-AMERICANAS. CULTURE ECO/UNDEV ADMIN LEAD GOV/REL 20 OAS. PAGE 123 H2455 — BIBLIOG L/A+17C NAT/G DIPLOM

B58
SALETORE B.A.,INDIA'S DIPLOMATIC RELATIONS WITH THE WEST. GREECE INDIA CULTURE ETIQUET...IDEA/COMP 3 ROM/EMP PERSIA. PAGE 137 H2739 — DIPLOM CONCPT INT/TRADE

B58
TILLION G.,ALGERIA: THE REALITIES. ALGERIA FRANCE ISLAM CULTURE STRATA PROB/SOLV DOMIN REV NAT/LISM WEALTH MARXISM...GEOG 20. PAGE 155 H3094 — ECO/UNDEV SOC COLONIAL DIPLOM

B58
VARG P.A.,MISSIONARIES, CHINESE, AND DIPLOMATS: THE AMERICAN PROTESTANT MISSIONARY MOVEMENT IN CHINA, 1890-1952. ASIA ECO/UNDEV NAT/G PROB/SOLV CAP/ISM EDU/PROP COLONIAL NAT/LISM ATTIT MARXISM...NAT/COMP STERTYP 20 CHINJAP PROTESTANT MISSION. PAGE 162 H3234 — CULTURE DIPLOM SECT

B58
YUAN TUNG-LI,CHINA IN WESTERN LITERATURE. SECT DIPLOM...ART/METH GEOG JURID SOC BIOG CON/ANAL. PAGE 172 H3441 — BIBLIOG ASIA CULTURE HUM

S58
PYE L.W.,"THE NON-WESTERN POLITICAL PROCESS" (BMR)" AFR ASIA ISLAM S/ASIA DIPLOM ADMIN LEAD LOBBY ROUTINE CONSEN...DECISION 20. PAGE 128 H2567 — CULTURE POL/PAR NAT/G LOC/G

C58
BLANCHARD W.,"THAILAND." THAILAND CULTURE AGRI FINAN INDUS FAM LABOR INT/TRADE ATTIT...GEOG HEAL SOC BIBLIOG 20. PAGE 18 H0354 — NAT/G DIPLOM ECO/UNDEV S/ASIA

C58
FIFIELD R.H.,"THE DIPLOMACY OF SOUTHEAST ASIA: 1945-1958." INT/ORG NAT/G COLONIAL REGION...CHARTS BIBLIOG 20 UN. PAGE 50 H0996 — S/ASIA DIPLOM NAT/LISM

C58
GOLAY J.F.,"THE FOUNDING OF THE FEDERAL REPUBLIC OF GERMANY." GERMANY/W CONSTN EX/STRUC DIPLOM ADMIN CHOOSE...DECISION BIBLIOG 20. PAGE 58 H1155 — FEDERAL NAT/G PARL/PROC POL/PAR

C58
WILDING N.,"AN ENCYCLOPEDIA OF PARLIAMENT." UK LAW CONSTN CHIEF PROB/SOLV DIPLOM DEBATE WAR INGP/REL PRIVIL...BIBLIOG DICTIONARY 13/20 CMN/WLTH PARLIAMENT. PAGE 168 H3363
PARL/PROC POL/PAR NAT/G ADMIN

B59
BLOOMFIELD L.P.,WESTERN EUROPE AND THE UN - TRENDS AND PROSPECTS. EUR+WWI BAL/PWR DIPLOM ECO/TAC COLONIAL ATTIT PWR...POLICY 20 UN EUROPE/W. PAGE 18 H0359
INT/ORG TREND FUT NAT/G

B59
BUNDESMIN FUR VERTRIEBENE,ZEITTAFEL DER VORGESCHICHTE UND DES ABLAUFS DER VERTREIBUNG SOWIE DER UNTERBRINGUNG UND EINGLIEDERUNG DER (2 VOLS.). GERMANY/E GERMANY/W NAT/G PROVS PROB/SOLV DIPLOM PARL/PROC ATTIT...BIBLIOG SOC/INTEG 20 MIGRATION PARLIAMENT. PAGE 24 H0475
JURID GP/REL INT/LAW

B59
CAREW-HUNT R.C.,BOOKS ON COMMUNISM. NAT/G POL/PAR DIPLOM REV...BIOG 19/20. PAGE 26 H0528
BIBLIOG/A MARXISM COM ASIA

B59
CARPENTER G.W.,THE WAY IN AFRICA. AFR INDUS MUNIC DIPLOM DOMIN EDU/PROP COERCE DISCRIM NAT/LISM ORD/FREE 20 NEGRO CHRISTIAN. PAGE 27 H0535
CULTURE SECT ECO/UNDEV COLONIAL

B59
DEHIO L.,GERMANY AND WORLD POLITICS IN THE TWENTIETH CENTURY. EUR+WWI FRANCE GERMANY MOD/EUR UK USSR NAT/G CHIEF BAL/PWR DOMIN COLONIAL CONTROL LEAD...IDEA/COMP 20 VERSAILLES. PAGE 39 H0783
DIPLOM WAR NAT/LISM SOVEREIGN

B59
EMME E.M.,THE IMPACT OF AIR POWER - NATIONAL SECURITY AND WORLD POLITICS. USA+45 USSR FORCES DIPLOM WEAPON PEACE TOTALISM...POLICY NAT/COMP 20 EUROPE. PAGE 46 H0921
DETER AIR WAR ORD/FREE

B59
ETSCHMANN R.,DIE WAHRUNGS- UND DEVISENPOLITIK DES OSTBLOCKS UND IHRE AUSWIRKUNGEN AUF DIE WIRTSCHAFTSBEZIEHUNGEN ZWISCHEN OST U WEST. BULGARIA CZECHOSLVK HUNGARY POLAND USSR MARKET NAT/G PLAN DIPLOM...NAT/COMP 20. PAGE 47 H0943
ECO/TAC FINAN POLICY INT/TRADE

B59
FOX A.,THE POWER OF SMALL STATES: DIPLOMACY IN WORLD WAR TWO. EUR+WWI FINLAND NORWAY SPAIN SWEDEN TURKEY NAT/G TOP/EX DIPLOM PWR...HIST/WRIT 20. PAGE 52 H1044
CONCPT STERTYP BAL/PWR

B59
GOLDWIN R.A.,READINGS IN RUSSIAN FOREIGN POLICY. HUNGARY USSR YUGOSLAVIA ELITES INT/ORG NAT/G REV WAR NAT/LISM PERSON SOCISM...CHARTS 20 MAPS BOLSHEVISM. PAGE 58 H1160
COM MARXISM DIPLOM POLICY

B59
INTERAMERICAN CULTURAL COUN,LISTA DE LIBROS REPRESENTAVOS DE AMERICA. CULTURE DIPLOM ADMIN 20. PAGE 77 H1542
BIBLIOG/A NAT/G L/A+17C SOC

B59
KIRCHHEIMER O.,GEGENWARTSPROBLEME DER ASYLGEWAHRUNG. DOMIN GP/REL ATTIT...NAT/COMP 20. PAGE 86 H1720
DIPLOM INT/LAW JURID ORD/FREE

B59
LOPEZ M.M.,CATALOGOS DE PUBLICACIONES PERIODICAS MEXICANAS. L/A+17C CULTURE NAT/G DIPLOM 20 MEXIC/AMER. PAGE 98 H1965
BIBLIOG PRESS CON/ANAL

B59
MADHOK B.,POLITICAL TRENDS IN INDIA. INDIA PAKISTAN UK STRATA ECO/UNDEV POL/PAR LEGIS CAP/ISM DIPLOM COLONIAL CHOOSE MARXISM...SOC TREND 20 GANDHI/M NEHRU/J. PAGE 101 H2014
GEOG NAT/G

B59
MARTZ J.D.,CENTRAL AMERICA: THE CRISIS AND THE CHALLENGE. L/A+17C POL/PAR CHIEF CHOOSE SOVEREIGN ...BIOG TREND BIBLIOG 20 CENTRAL/AM. PAGE 104 H2071
NAT/G GOV/REL DIPLOM GOV/COMP

B59
NAHM A.C.,JAPANESE PENETRATION OF KOREA, 1894-1910. ASIA KOREA NAT/G...POLICY 20 CHINJAP. PAGE 115 H2303
BIBLIOG/A DIPLOM WAR COLONIAL

B59
PANAMERICAN UNION,PUBLICATIONS: PAU AND OFFICIAL RECORDS OF THE OAS, IN ENGLISH, SPANISH, PORTUGUESE, AND FRENCH, 1958-59. NAT/G ATTIT...SOC 20 OAS. PAGE 123 H2456
BIBLIOG L/A+17C INT/LAW DIPLOM

B59
PANIKKAR K.M.,THE AFRO-ASIAN STATES AND THEIR PROBLEMS. COM CULTURE KIN POL/PAR SECT DIPLOM EDU/PROP COLONIAL SOVEREIGN...TECHNIC GOV/COMP 20. PAGE 123 H2458
AFR S/ASIA ECO/UNDEV

B59
PHADINIS U.,DOCUMENTS ON ASIAN AFFAIRS: A SELECT BIBLIOGRAPHY. ASIA...SOC 20. PAGE 125 H2498
BIBLIOG NAT/G DIPLOM

B59
STERNBERG F.,THE MILITARY AND INDUSTRIAL REVOLUTION OF OUR TIME. USA+45 USSR WOR+45 WORKER COMPUTER PLAN TEC/DEV NUC/PWR GP/REL...POLICY NAT/COMP 20. PAGE 149 H2981
DIPLOM FORCES INDUS CIVMIL/REL

B59
THOMAS D.H.,GUIDE TO THE DIPLOMATIC ARCHIVES OF WESTERN EUROPE. EUR+WWI ELITES INT/ORG NAT/G BAL/PWR INT/TRADE PEACE. PAGE 154 H3076
BIBLIOG DIPLOM CONFER

B59
VITTACHIT,EMERGENCY '58. CEYLON UK STRUCT NAT/G FORCES ADJUD CRIME REV NAT/LISM 20. PAGE 163 H3258
RACE/REL DISCRIM DIPLOM SOVEREIGN

B59
VORSPAN A.,JUSTICE AND JUDAISM. FAM DIPLOM ECO/TAC EDU/PROP CRIME RACE/REL MARRIAGE ANOMIE ATTIT ORD/FREE...POLICY 20 UN. PAGE 164 H3279
SECT CULTURE ACT/RES GP/REL

B59
WILDNER H.,DIE TECHNIK DER DIPLOMATIE. TOP/EX ROLE ORD/FREE...INT/LAW JURID IDEA/COMP NAT/COMP 20. PAGE 168 H3364
DIPLOM POLICY DELIB/GP NAT/G

L59
JANIS I.L.,"DECISIONAL CONFLICT: A THEORETICAL ANALYSIS." INTELL NAT/G POL/PAR DELIB/GP LEGIS TOP/EX PLAN...DECISION CONGRESS NAZI 20 WWI. PAGE 80 H1590
ACT/RES PSY DIPLOM

S59
LEVINE R.A.,"ANTI-EUROPEAN VIOLENCE IN AFRICA: A COMPARATIVE ANALYSIS." AFR CULTURE NAT/G DIPLOM EDU/PROP COLONIAL REGION COERCE ATTIT PWR...PSY CONCPT TIME/SEQ TREND HYPO/EXP SOC/EXP STERTYP GEN/METH COLD/WAR 20. PAGE 95 H1903
DRIVE ORD/FREE REV

B60
JUNZ A.J.,PRESENT TRENDS IN AMERICAN NATIONAL GOVERNMENT. LEGIS DIPLOM ADMIN CT/SYS ORD/FREE ...CONCPT ANTHOL 20 CONGRESS PRESIDENT SUPREME/CT. PAGE 3 H0052
POL/PAR CHOOSE CONSTN NAT/G

B60
ALBRECHT-CARRIE R.,FRANCE, EUROPE AND THE TWO WORLD WARS. EUR+WWI FRANCE GERMANY MOD/EUR UK ECO/DEV NAT/G FORCES BAL/PWR DOMIN ARMS/CONT PEACE PWR 20 TREATY EUROPE. PAGE 5 H0096
DIPLOM WAR

B60
BOZEMAN A.B.,POLITICS AND CULTURE IN INTERNATIONAL HISTORY. WOR-45 STRUCT SECT...SOC TIME/SEQ NAT/COMP BIBLIOG. PAGE 20 H0393
CULTURE DIPLOM GOV/COMP ALL/IDEOS

B60
CHATTERJI S.K.,AFRICANISM: THE AFRICAN PERSONALITY. KIN NAT/G SECT CREATE DIPLOM COLONIAL GP/REL ATTIT ORD/FREE...LING WORSHIP 20. PAGE 29 H0585
PERSON NAT/LISM AFR CULTURE

B60
DE HERRERA C.D.,LISTA BIBLIOGRAFICA DE LOS TRABAJOS DE GRADUACION Y TESIS PRESENTADOS EN LA UNIVERSIDAD, 1939-1960. PANAMA DIPLOM LEAD...SOC 20. PAGE 38 H0754
BIBLIOG L/A+17C NAT/G ACADEM

B60
DIA M.,REFLEXIONS SUR L'ECONOMIE DE L'AFRIQUE NOIRE (REV. ED.). CULTURE ECO/UNDEV CREATE TEC/DEV DIPLOM INT/TRADE OPTIMAL ATTIT...POLICY 20. PAGE 41 H0816
AFR ECO/TAC SOCISM PLAN

B60
EMERSON R.,FROM EMPIRE TO NATION: THE RISE TO SELF-ASSERTION OF ASIAN AND AFRICAN PEOPLES. S/ASIA CULTURE NAT/G SECT DIPLOM ATTIT SOVEREIGN MARXISM ...POLICY BIBLIOG 19/20. PAGE 46 H0919
NAT/LISM COLONIAL AFR ASIA

B60
FEIS H.,BETWEEN WAR AND PEACE: THE POTSDAM CONFERENCE. EUR+WWI NAT/G DELIB/GP PROB/SOLV REPAR WAR CIVMIL/REL...BIBLIOG 20. PAGE 49 H0983
DIPLOM CONFER BAL/PWR

B60
FISCHER L.,THE SOVIETS IN WORLD AFFAIRS. CHINA/COM COM EUR+WWI USSR INT/ORG CONFER LEAD ARMS/CONT REV PWR...CHARTS 20 TREATY VERSAILLES. PAGE 51 H1010
DIPLOM NAT/G POLICY MARXISM

B60
FLORES R.H.,CATALOGO DE TESIS DOCTORALES DE LAS FACULTADES DE LA UNIVERSIDAD DE EL SALVADOR. EL/SALVADR LAW DIPLOM ADMIN LEAD GOV/REL...SOC 19/20. PAGE 52 H1030
BIBLIOG ACADEM L/A+17C NAT/G

B60
FURNIA A.H.,THE DIPLOMACY OF APPEASEMENT: ANGLO-FRENCH RELATIONS AND THE PRELUDE TO WORLD WAR II 1931-1938. FRANCE GERMANY UK ELITES NAT/G DELIB/GP FORCES WAR PEACE RIGID/FLEX 20. PAGE 54 H1077
DIPLOM BAL/PWR COERCE

B60
GOODMAN E.,SOVIET DESIGN FOR A WORLD STATE. COM USSR NAT/G TOP/EX DIPLOM ECO/TAC DOMIN EDU/PROP COERCE REV ATTIT ORD/FREE...CON/ANAL 20. PAGE 59 H1171
PLAN PWR SOCISM TOTALISM

B60
HAMADY S.,TEMPERAMENT AND CHARACTER OF THE ARABS.
NAT/COMP

FAM NAT/G SECT DIPLOM NAT/LISM...POLICY 20 ARABS. PAGE 65 H1299 PERSON CULTURE ISLAM
B60

JAECKH A.,WELTSAAT; ERLEBTES UND ERSTREBTES. GERMANY WOR+45 WOR-45 PLAN WAR...POLICY OBS/ENVIR NAT/COMP PERS/COMP 20. PAGE 79 H1581 BIOG NAT/G SELF/OBS DIPLOM
B60

JEFFRIES C.,TRANSFER OF POWER: PROBLEMS OF THE PASSAGE TO SELFGOVERNMENT. CEYLON GHANA MALAYSIA NIGERIA UK INT/ORG CONSULT DELIB/GP LEGIS DIPLOM CONFER PARL/PROC 20. PAGE 80 H1595 SOVEREIGN COLONIAL ORD/FREE NAT/G
B60

LOMBARDO TOLEDANO V.EL NEONAZISMO; SUS CHARACTERISTICAS Y PELIGROS. GERMANY/W POL/PAR COLONIAL LEAD LOBBY ATTIT 20 NAZI. PAGE 98 H1956 NAT/G FASCISM POLICY DIPLOM
B60

MC CLELLAN G.S.,INDIA. CHINA/COM INDIA CONSTN ELITES STRATA AGRI POL/PAR FOR/AID ARMS/CONT REV MARXISM...CENSUS BIBLIOG 20 COLD/WAR GANDHI/M NEHRU/J. PAGE 106 H2117 DIPLOM NAT/G SOCIETY ECO/UNDEV
B60

MEYRIAT J.,LA SCIENCE POLITIQUE EN FRANCE, 1945-1958; BIBLIOGRAPHIES FRANCAISES DE SCIENCES SOCIALES (VOL. I). EUR+WWI FRANCE POL/PAR DIPLOM ADMIN CHOOSE ATTIT...IDEA/COMP METH/COMP NAT/COMP 20. PAGE 110 H2193 BIBLIOG/A NAT/G CONCPT PHIL/SCI
B60

MINIFIE J.M.,PEACEMAKER OR POWDER-MONKEY. CANADA INT/ORG NAT/G FORCES LEAD WAR...PREDICT 20. PAGE 111 H2222 DIPLOM POLICY NEUTRAL PEACE
B60

MORAES F.,THE REVOLT IN TIBET. ASIA CHINA/COM INDIA CULTURE CONTROL COERCE WAR TOTALISM...POLICY SOC WORSHIP 20 TIBET INTERVENT. PAGE 113 H2252 COLONIAL FORCES DIPLOM ORD/FREE
B60

NEALE A.D.,THE FLOW OF RESOURCES FROM RICH TO POOR. WOR+45 ECO/DEV ECO/UNDEV FINAN INDUS NAT/G PLAN EFFICIENCY WEALTH...POLICY NAT/COMP 20 RESOURCE/N. PAGE 116 H2325 FOR/AID DIPLOM METH/CNCPT
B60

SALETORE B.A.,INDIA'S DIPLOMATIC RELATIONS WITH THE EAST. ASIA CEYLON INDIA NEPAL S/ASIA CULTURE 7/14 PERSIA. PAGE 137 H2740 DIPLOM NAT/COMP ETIQUET
B60

SCANLON D.G.,INTERNATIONAL EDUCATION: A DOCUMENTARY HISTORY. ADMIN CONTROL ATTIT PERCEPT...BIOG ANTHOL METH 20. PAGE 138 H2765 EDU/PROP INT/ORG NAT/COMP DIPLOM
B60

SETHE P.,SCHICKSALSSTUNDEN DER WELTGESCHICHTE (6TH ED.). NAT/G BAL/PWR DOMIN REV PWR...NAT/COMP 16/20. PAGE 141 H2831 DIPLOM WAR PEACE
B60

STOLPER W.F.,GERMANY BETWEEN EAST AND WEST: THE ECONOMICS OF COMPETITIVE COEXISTENCE. FUT GERMANY/E GERMANY/W WOR+45 FINAN POL/PAR BUDGET ECO/TAC FOR/AID INT/TRADE...STAT CHARTS METH/COMP 20 COLD/WAR. PAGE 150 H2989 ECO/DEV DIPLOM GOV/COMP BAL/PWR
B60

STRACHEY J.,THE END OF EMPIRE. UK WOR+45 WOR-45 DIPLOM INT/TRADE DOMIN ADJUST ORD/FREE WEALTH ...SOCIALIST GOV/COMP TIME COMMONWLTH. PAGE 150 H2991 COLONIAL ECO/DEV BAL/PWR LAISSEZ
B60

SZTARAY Z.,BIBLIOGRAPHY ON HUNGARY. HUNGARY MOD/EUR CULTURE INDUS SECT DIPLOM REV...ART/METH SOC LING 18/20. PAGE 151 H3029 BIBLIOG NAT/G COM MARXISM
B60

THE AFRICA 1960 COMMITTEE,MANDATE IN TRUST; THE PROBLEM OF SOUTH WEST AFRICA. GERMANY STRUCT REGION SANCTION CHOOSE DISCRIM...INT/LAW 20 AFRICA/SW UN LEAGUE/NAT TRUST/TERR. PAGE 153 H3066 NAT/G DIPLOM COLONIAL RACE/REL
B60

THEOBOLD R.,THE NEW NATIONS OF WEST AFRICA. GHANA NIGERIA CULTURE INT/ORG ECO/TAC FOR/AID COLONIAL RACE/REL POPULISM...ANTHOL BIBLIOG 20 UN. PAGE 153 H3068 AFR SOVEREIGN ECO/UNDEV DIPLOM
B60

WILLIAMS L.E.,OVERSEAS CHINESE NATIONALISM: THE GENESIS OF THE PAN-CHINESE MOVEMENT IN INDONESIA, 1900-1916. ASIA COM INDONESIA AGRI INT/ORG LOC/G DIPLOM EDU/PROP HABITAT PWR POPULISM...GEOG LING CENSUS 20. PAGE 168 H3367 NAT/LISM GP/REL DECISION NAT/G
B60

WORLEY P.,ASIA TODAY (REV. ED.) (PAMPHLET). COM ECO/UNDEV AGRI FINAN INDUS POL/PAR FOR/AID ADMIN MARXISM 20. PAGE 170 H3411 BIBLIOG/A ASIA DIPLOM NAT/G
L60

HAAS E.B.,"CONSENSUS FORMATION IN THE COUNCIL OF EUROPE." EUR+WWI NAT/G DELIB/GP DIPLOM REGION CHOOSE PWR SOVEREIGN...RELATIV NEW/IDEA QUANT CHARTS INDEX TOT/POP OEEC 20 COUNCL/EUR. PAGE 63 H1265 POL/PAR INT/ORG STAT
S60

BRZEZINSKI Z.K.,"PATTERNS AND LIMITS OF THE SINO-SOVIET DISPUTE." ASIA CHINA/COM COM FUT STRATA NAT/G EX/STRUC FORCES BAL/PWR DIPLOM ECO/TAC DOMIN EDU/PROP ADMIN COERCE WAR ATTIT RIGID/FLEX ...GEN/LAWS VAL/FREE 20. PAGE 23 H0459 POL/PAR PWR REV USSR
S60

GINSBURGS G.,"PEKING-LHASA-NEW DELHI." CHINA/COM FUT INDIA S/ASIA KIN NAT/G PROVS SECT FORCES BAL/PWR ECO/TAC DOMIN EDU/PROP LEGIT ADMIN REGION GUERRILLA PWR...TREND TIBET 20. PAGE 57 H1134 ASIA COERCE DIPLOM
S60

HOWARD M.,"BRITAIN'S DEFENSE: COMMITMENTS AND CAPABILITIES." EUR+WWI ECO/DEV NAT/G FORCES LEGIS PLAN DETER ORD/FREE WEALTH...POLICY CONCPT TIME/SEQ GEN/METH 20. PAGE 74 H1481 FUT PWR DIPLOM UK
S60

NORTHEDGE F.S.,"BRITISH FOREIGN POLICY AND THE PARTY SYSTEM." EUR+WWI FUT INT/ORG NAT/G EDU/PROP ATTIT PWR...POLICY CONCPT MYTH TIME/SEQ TREND 20 UN. PAGE 119 H2374 POL/PAR CHOOSE DIPLOM UK
S60

TIRYAKIAN E.A.,"APARTHEID AND POLITICS IN SOUTH AFRICA." SOUTH/AFR CULTURE STRATA ECO/DEV NAT/G POL/PAR ROUTINE CHOOSE GP/REL RACE/REL DISCRIM ATTIT ALL/VALS...CONCPT OBS TIME/SEQ VAL/FREE 20. PAGE 155 H3105 AFR DIPLOM
S60

WOLFE T.W.,"KHRUSHCHEV'S DISARMAMENT STRATEGY." COM NAT/G TOP/EX PLAN BAL/PWR DIPLOM ARMS/CONT COERCE ATTIT...POLICY CONCPT RECORD TREND CON/ANAL COLD/WAR 20 KHRUSH/N. PAGE 170 H3401 PWR GEN/LAWS USSR
C60

COX R.H.,"LOCKE ON WAR AND PEACE." UK DIPLOM DOMIN PWR...BIOG IDEA/COMP BIBLIOG 18. PAGE 34 H0689 CONCPT NAT/G PEACE WAR
C60

FITZSIMMONS T.,"USSR: ITS PEOPLE, ITS SOCIETY, ITS CULTURE." USSR FAM SECT DIPLOM EDU/PROP ADMIN RACE/REL ATTIT...POLICY CHARTS BIBLIOG 20. PAGE 51 H1021 CULTURE STRUCT SOCIETY COM
C60

HAZARD J.N.,"THE SOVIET SYSTEM OF GOVERNMENT." USSR SOCIETY INDUS NAT/G POL/PAR DIPLOM CT/SYS...JURID CHARTS BIBLIOG/A 20. PAGE 69 H1373 COM NAT/COMP STRUCT ADMIN
C60

WRIGGINS W.H.,"CEYLON: DILEMMAS OF A NEW NATION." ASIA CEYLON CONSTN STRUCT POL/PAR SECT FORCES DIPLOM GOV/REL NAT/LISM...CHARTS BIBLIOG 20. PAGE 171 H3417 PROB/SOLV NAT/G ECO/UNDEV
B61

ALLIGHAN G.,VERWOERD - THE END. SOUTH/AFR TOP/EX DIPLOM COLONIAL DISCRIM TOTALISM ATTIT AUTHORIT ...BIOG 20 NEGRO VERWOERD/H. PAGE 5 H0107 CONTROL CHIEF RACE/REL NAT/G
B61

ANSPRENGER F.,POLITIK IM SCHWARZEN AFRIKA. FRANCE NAT/G DIPLOM REGION REV NAT/LISM...CHARTS BIBLIOG 19/20. PAGE 7 H0141 AFR COLONIAL SOVEREIGN
B61

ATTLEE C.R.,EMPIRE INTO COMMONWEALTH. AFR ASIA CANADA UK NAT/G WAR NAT/LISM ATTIT...POLICY 20 AUSTRAL. PAGE 9 H0179 DIPLOM GP/REL COLONIAL SOVEREIGN
B61

BELOFF M.,NEW DIMENSIONS IN FOREIGN POLICY: A STUDY IN BRITISH ADMINISTRATION. UK NAT/G ATTIT RIGID/FLEX ORD/FREE...GEN/LAWS EUR+WWI CMN/WLTH EEC 20. PAGE 14 H0271 INT/ORG DIPLOM
B61

BISHOP D.G.,THE ADMINISTRATION OF BRITISH FOREIGN RELATIONS. EUR+WWI MOD/EUR INT/ORG NAT/G POL/PAR DELIB/GP LEGIS TOP/EX ECO/TAC DOMIN EDU/PROP ADMIN COERCE 20. PAGE 17 H0344 ROUTINE PWR DIPLOM UK
B61

BURDETTE F.L.,POLITICAL SCIENCE: A SELECTED BIBLIOGRAPHY OF BOOKS IN PRINT, WITH ANNOTATIONS (PAMPHLET). LAW LOC/G NAT/G POL/PAR PROVS DIPLOM EDU/PROP ADMIN CHOOSE ATTIT 20. PAGE 24 H0479 BIBLIOG/A GOV/COMP CONCPT ROUTINE
B61

CARNELL F.,THE POLITICS OF THE NEW STATES: A SELECT ANNOTATED BIBLIOGRAPHY WITH SPECIAL REFERENCE TO THE COMMONWEALTH. CONSTN ELITES LABOR NAT/G POL/PAR EX/STRUC DIPLOM ADJUD ADMIN...GOV/COMP 20 COMMONWLTH. PAGE 27 H0534 BIBLIOG/A AFR ASIA COLONIAL
B61

CHAKRABARTI A.,NEHRU: HIS DEMOCRACY AND INDIA. ASIA INDIA UK CONSTN ECO/UNDEV SECT DIPLOM COLONIAL PEACE WEALTH...BIBLIOG 20 CONGRESS NEHRU/J GANDHI/M. PAGE 28 H0570 ORD/FREE STRATA NAT/G CHIEF

B61
CONOVER H.F.,SERIALS FOR AFRICAN STUDIES. ECO/UNDEV DIPLOM LEAD NAT/LISM ATTIT...SOC 20. PAGE 33 H0653 BIBLIOG AFR NAT/G

B61
CONQUEST R.,POWER AND POLICY IN THE USSR. USSR NAT/G POL/PAR DIPLOM MARXISM 20. PAGE 33 H0655 COM HIST/WRIT GOV/REL PWR

B61
DALLIN D.J.,SOVIET FOREIGN POLICY AFTER STALIN. ASIA CHINA/COM EUR+WWI GERMANY IRAN UK YUGOSLAVIA INT/ORG NAT/G VOL/ASSN FORCES TOP/EX BAL/PWR DOMIN EDU/PROP COERCE ATTIT PWR 20. PAGE 37 H0737 COM DIPLOM USSR

B61
ESTEBAN J.C.,IMPERIALISMO Y DESARROLLO ECONOMICO. L/A+17C FINAN INDUS NAT/G ECO/TAC CONTROL ROLE. PAGE 47 H0941 ECO/UNDEV NAT/LISM DIPLOM BAL/PAY

B61
GANGULI B.N.,ECONOMIC INTEGRATION. FINAN LABOR CAP/ISM DIPLOM WEALTH...NAT/COMP 20. PAGE 55 H1096 ECO/TAC METH/CNCPT EQUILIB ECO/UNDEV

B61
GRASES P.,ESTUDIOS BIBLIOGRAFICOS. VENEZUELA...SOC 20. PAGE 60 H1197 BIBLIOG NAT/G DIPLOM L/A+17C

B61
HADDAD J.A.,REVOLUCAO CUBANA E REVOLUCAO BRASILEIRA. BRAZIL CUBA L/A+17C STRATA AGRI WORKER EDU/PROP REGION...POLICY NAT/COMP 20. PAGE 63 H1272 REV ORD/FREE DIPLOM ECO/UNDEV

B61
HARDT J.P.,THE COLD WAR ECONOMIC GAP. USA+45 USSR ECO/DEV FORCES INT/TRADE NUC/PWR PWR 20 COLD/WAR. PAGE 66 H1328 DIPLOM ECO/TAC NAT/COMP POLICY

B61
HAUSER M.,DIE URSACHEN DER FRANZOSISCHEN INFLATION IN DEN JAHREN 1946-1952. FRANCE INDUS NAT/G BUDGET DIPLOM ECO/TAC FOR/AID COST MONEY 20 GOLD/STAND. PAGE 68 H1357 ECO/DEV FINAN PRICE

B61
HISTORICAL RESEARCH INSTITUTE,A SHORT BIBLIOGRAPHY OF INDO-MUSLIM HISTORY. INDIA S/ASIA DIPLOM EDU/PROP COLONIAL LEAD NAT/LISM ATTIT...BIOG 19/20. PAGE 71 H1427 BIBLIOG NAT/G SECT POL/PAR

B61
HOLDSWORTH M.,SOVIET AFRICAN STUDIES 1918-1959. USSR ACADEM NAT/G DIPLOM REGION KNOWL 20. PAGE 72 H1448 BIBLIOG/A AFR HABITAT NAT/COMP

B61
HUNT E.F.,SOCIAL SCIENCE. DIPLOM ECO/TAC ROUTINE GP/REL DEMAND DISCRIM EFFICIENCY HABITAT ALL/IDEOS ...SOC T 20. PAGE 75 H1497 CULTURE ADJUST STRATA ROLE

B61
JAKOBSON M.,THE DIPLOMACY OF THE WINTER WAR. EUR+WWI FINLAND GERMANY USSR INT/ORG NAT/G PEACE TOTALISM PWR...POLICY CONCPT 20 TREATY. PAGE 79 H1588 WAR ORD/FREE DIPLOM

B61
KHAN A.W.,INDIA WINS FREEDOM: THE OTHER SIDE. INDIA PAKISTAN CULTURE LEGIS DIPLOM PARL/PROC REV WAR NAT/LISM 20. PAGE 85 H1707 SOVEREIGN GP/REL RACE/REL ORD/FREE

B61
KISSINGER H.A.,THE NECESSITY FOR CHOICE. FUT USA+45 ECO/UNDEV NAT/G PLAN BAL/PWR ECO/TAC ARMS/CONT DETER NUC/PWR ATTIT...POLICY CONCPT RECORD GEN/LAWS COLD/WAR 20. PAGE 87 H1728 TOP/EX TREND DIPLOM

B61
LEHMAN R.L.,AFRICA SOUTH OF THE SAHARA (PAMPHLET). DIPLOM COLONIAL NAT/LISM. PAGE 93 H1863 BIBLIOG/A AFR CULTURE NAT/G

B61
LETHBRIDGE H.J.,CHINA'S URBAN COMMUNES. CHINA/COM FUT ECO/UNDEV DIPLOM EDU/PROP DEMAND INCOME MARXISM ...POLICY 20. PAGE 95 H1893 MUNIC CONTROL ECO/TAC NAT/G

B61
LYFORD J.P.,THE AGREEABLE AUTOCRACIES. SOCIETY LABOR POL/PAR SECT DIPLOM CHOOSE...CONCPT 20 WHITE/T NIEBUHR/R. PAGE 99 H1982 ATTIT POPULISM PRESS NAT/G

B61
MACLURE M.,AFRICA: THE POLITICAL PATTERN. SOUTH/AFR CULTURE LEGIS DIPLOM COLONIAL RACE/REL 20. PAGE 100 H2005 AFR POLICY NAT/G

B61
MILLIKAW M.F.,THE EMERGING NATIONS: THEIR GROWTH AND UNITED STATES POLICY. FUT USA+45 WOR+45 WOR-45 NAT/G PLAN TEC/DEV BAL/PWR GOV/REL PEACE ORD/FREE 20. PAGE 111 H2216 ECO/UNDEV POLICY DIPLOM FOR/AID

B61
MOLLAU G.,INTERNATIONAL COMMUNISM AND WORLD REVOLUTION: HISTORY AND METHODS. RUSSIA USSR INT/ORG NAT/G POL/PAR VOL/ASSN FORCES BAL/PWR DIPLOM EXEC REGION WAR ATTIT PWR MARXISM...CONCPT TIME/SEQ COLD/WAR 19/20. PAGE 112 H2237 COM REV

B61
NEWMAN R.P.,RECOGNITION OF COMMUNIST CHINA? A STUDY IN ARGUMENT. CHINA/COM NAT/G PROB/SOLV RATIONAL ...INT/LAW LOG IDEA/COMP BIBLIOG 20. PAGE 117 H2347 MARXISM ATTIT DIPLOM POLICY

B61
NICOLSON H.G.,THE OLD DIPLOMACY AND THE NEW. NAT/G PLAN PROB/SOLV...METH 20. PAGE 118 H2355 DIPLOM POLICY INT/ORG

B61
PALMER N.D.,THE INDIAN POLITICAL SYSTEM. INDIA ECO/UNDEV SECT CHIEF COLONIAL CHOOSE ALL/IDEOS SOCISM...CHARTS BIBLIOG/A 20. PAGE 123 H2452 NAT/LISM POL/PAR NAT/G DIPLOM

B61
PANIKKAR K.M.,THE VOICE OF FREEDOM: SELECTED SPEECHES OF PANDIT MOTILAL NEHRU. INDIA UK CONSTN FINAN FORCES LEGIS DIPLOM TAX COLONIAL...POLICY MAJORIT ANTHOL 20 NEHRU/PM. PAGE 123 H2460 NAT/LISM ORD/FREE CHIEF NAT/G

B61
PANIKKAR K.M.,REVOLUTION IN AFRICA. AFR GUINEA ECO/UNDEV POL/PAR DIPLOM COLONIAL EXEC LEAD SOVEREIGN...CHARTS 20. PAGE 123 H2461 NAT/LISM NAT/G CHIEF

B61
PATAI R.,CULTURES IN CONFLICT; AN INQUIRY INTO THE SOCIO-CULTURAL PROBLEMS OF ISRAEL AND HER NEIGHBORS (2ND REV. ED.). ISLAM ISRAEL SOCIETY STRUCT DIPLOM GP/REL ALL/VALS...SOC 20 JEWS ARABS. PAGE 124 H2475 NAT/COMP CULTURE GP/COMP ATTIT

B61
PECKERT J.,DIE GROSSEN UND DIE KLEINEN MAECHTE. COM GERMANY/W ECO/DEV ECO/UNDEV NAT/G WAR RACE/REL PEACE...POLICY GP/COMP GOV/COMP 20 COLD/WAR. PAGE 124 H2482 DIPLOM ECO/TAC BAL/PWR

B61
ROIG E.,MARTI, ANTIIMPERIALISTA. CUBA L/A+17C DIPLOM DOMIN COLONIAL CONTROL LEAD PWR SOVEREIGN ...PHIL/SCI 19 MARTI/JOSE INTERVENT. PAGE 133 H2664 PERSON NAT/LISM ECO/UNDEV ORD/FREE

B61
SANTHANAM K.,DEMOCRATIC PLANNING. INDIA AGRI FINAN LEGIS DIPLOM PARL/PROC ORD/FREE 20. PAGE 138 H2753 PLAN NAT/G CONSTN POLICY

B61
SCHECHTMAN J.B.,ON WINGS OF EAGLES: THE PLIGHT, EXODUS, AND HOMECOMING OF ORIENTAL JEWRY. ASIA ISLAM ISRAEL VOL/ASSN DIPLOM CONTROL ORD/FREE ...GEOG WORSHIP SOC/INTEG 20 JEWS ARABS MIGRATION. PAGE 139 H2777 CULTURE HABITAT KIN SECT

B61
SCHIEDER T.,DOCUMENTS ON THE EXPULSION OF THE GERMANS FROM EASTERN-CENTRAL-EUROPE (VOL. II/III). COM EUR+WWI GERMANY HUNGARY ROMANIA USSR DIPLOM RACE/REL 20 MIGRATION. PAGE 139 H2785 GEOG CULTURE

B61
SCHWARTZ H.,THE RED PHOENIX: RUSSIA SINCE WORLD WAR II. USA+45 WOR+45 ELITES POL/PAR TEC/DEV ECO/TAC MARXISM. PAGE 140 H2810 DIPLOM NAT/G ECO/DEV

B61
SETON-WATSON H.,FROM LENIN TO KHRUSHCHEV: THE HISTORY OF WORLD COMMUNISM. ASIA COM EUR+WWI ISLAM S/ASIA ECO/DEV ECO/UNDEV NAT/G POL/PAR DIPLOM ECO/TAC EDU/PROP COERCE GUERRILLA ATTIT DRIVE WORK TOT/POP NAZI 20. PAGE 141 H2832 PWR REV USSR

B61
SSU-YU T.,JAPANESE STUDIES ON JAPAN AND THE FAR EAST: A SHORT BIOGRAPHICAL AND BIBLIOGRAPHICAL INTRODUCTION. ASIA CULTURE ECO/UNDEV NAT/G DIPLOM 20 CHINJAP. PAGE 148 H2962 BIBLIOG SOC

B61
STARK H.,SOCIAL AND ECONOMIC FRONTIERS IN LATIN AMERICA (2ND ED.). CUBA FUT CULTURE AGRI INDUS ECO/TAC PRODUC ATTIT MARXISM...NAT/COMP BIBLIOG T 20. PAGE 149 H2971 L/A+17C SOCIETY DIPLOM ECO/UNDEV

B61
UAR MINISTRY OF CULTURE,A BIBLIOGRAPHICAL LIST OF TUNISIA. ISLAM CULTURE NAT/G EDU/PROP COLONIAL ...GEOG 19/20 TUNIS. PAGE 157 H3146 BIBLIOG DIPLOM SECT

B61
VEIT O.,GRUNDRISS DER WAHRUNGSPOLITIK. FRANCE GERMANY USSR DIPLOM INT/TRADE...NAT/COMP 19/20 GOLD/STAND SILVER. PAGE 162 H3239 FINAN POLICY ECO/TAC CAP/ISM

B61
YUAN TUNG-LI,A GUIDE TO DOCTORAL DISSERTATIONS BY CHINESE STUDENTS IN AMERICA, 1905-1960. ASIA CULTURE SOCIETY ECO/UNDEV NAT/G PROB/SOLV DIPLOM LEAD ATTIT...HUM SOC STAT 20. PAGE 172 H3442 BIBLIOG ACADEM ACT/RES OP/RES

B61
ZIMMERMAN I.,A GUIDE TO CURRENT LATIN AMERICAN PERIODICALS: HUMANITIES AND SOCIAL SCIENCES. LABOR SECT EDU/PROP...GEOG HUM SOC LING STAT NAT/COMP 20. PAGE 173 H3456 — BIBLIOG/A DIPLOM L/A+17C PHIL/SCI

S61
BRZEZINSKI Z.K.,"THE ORGANIZATION OF THE COMMUNIST CAMP." COM CZECHOSLVK COM/IND NAT/G DELIB/GP INT/TRADE DOMIN EDU/PROP EXEC ROUTINE COERCE ATTIT PWR...MGT CONCPT TIME/SEQ CHARTS VAL/FREE 20 TREATY. PAGE 23 H0460 — VOL/ASSN DIPLOM USSR

S61
TUCKER R.C.,"TOWARDS A COMPARATIVE POLITICS OF MOVEMENT-REGIMES" (BMR)" USSR CONSTN NAT/G CREATE PROB/SOLV DIPLOM DOMIN REV...GP/COMP IDEA/COMP METH 20 STALIN/J BOLSHEVISM. PAGE 157 H3135 — MARXISM POLICY GEN/LAWS PWR

S61
VALLET R.,"IRAN: KEY TO THE MIDDLE EAST." COM IRAQ ISLAM KUWAIT LEBANON SAUDI/ARAB TURKEY ELITES SOCIETY INDUS PROC/MFG POL/PAR TOP/EX PLAN BAL/PWR DIPLOM ECO/TAC ALL/VALS...TREND CENTO 20. PAGE 161 H3224 — NAT/G ECO/UNDEV IRAN

C61
MOODIE G.C.,"THE GOVERNMENT OF GREAT BRITAIN." UK LAW STRUCT LOC/G POL/PAR DIPLOM RECEIVE ADMIN COLONIAL CHOOSE...BIBLIOG 20 PARLIAMENT. PAGE 112 H2247 — NAT/G SOCIETY PARL/PROC GOV/COMP

B62
ABOSCH H.,THE MENACE OF THE MIRACLE: GERMANY FROM HITLER TO ADENAUER. EUR+WWI GERMANY/W CULTURE FORCES PRESS NUC/PWR WAR CHOOSE 20 HITLER/A ADENAUER/K. PAGE 3 H0057 — DIPLOM PEACE POLICY

B62
AMERICAN SOCIETY AFR CULTURE,PAN-AFRICANISM RECONSIDERED. AFR SOCIETY STRUCT SCHOOL CAP/ISM EDU/PROP...ART/METH NEW/IDEA PREDICT ANTHOL 20 PANAF/FREE NEGRO. PAGE 6 H0123 — DIPLOM FEDERAL NAT/LISM CULTURE

B62
ANDREWS W.G.,FRENCH POLITICS AND ALGERIA: THE PROCESS OF POLICY FORMATION 1954-1962. ALGERIA FRANCE CONSTN ELITES POL/PAR CHIEF DELIB/GP LEGIS DIPLOM PRESS CHOOSE 20. PAGE 7 H0140 — GOV/COMP EXEC COLONIAL

B62
BAFFREY S.A.,THE RED MYTH: A HISTORY OF COMMUNISM FROM MARX TO KHRUSHCHEV. USSR NAT/G CHIEF CAP/ISM DIPLOM EDU/PROP REV WAR PEACE TOTALISM...POLICY 20 STALIN/J KHRUSH/N. PAGE 10 H0195 — CONCPT MARXISM TV

B62
BAULIN J.,THE ARAB ROLE IN AFRICA. AFR ALGERIA FUT ISLAM MOROCCO UAR COLONIAL NEUTRAL REV...SOC 20 TUNIS BOURGUIBA. PAGE 12 H0240 — NAT/LISM DIPLOM NAT/G SECT

B62
BROWN L.C.,LATIN AMERICA, A BIBLIOGRAPHY. EX/STRUC ADMIN LEAD ATTIT...POLICY 20. PAGE 22 H0445 — BIBLIOG L/A+17C DIPLOM NAT/G

B62
CARTER G.M.,THE GOVERNMENT OF THE SOVIET UNION. USSR CULTURE LOC/G DIPLOM ECO/TAC ADJUD CT/SYS LEAD WEALTH...CHARTS T 20 COM/PARTY. PAGE 27 H0546 — NAT/G MARXISM POL/PAR EX/STRUC

B62
COSTA RICA UNIVERSIDAD BIBL,LISTA DE TESIS DE GRADO DE LA UNIVERSIDAD DE COSTA RICA. COSTA/RICA LAW LOC/G ADMIN LEAD...SOC 20. PAGE 34 H0675 — BIBLIOG/A NAT/G DIPLOM ECO/UNDEV

B62
COUNCIL ON WORLD TENSIONS,RESTLESS NATIONS. WOR+45 STRUCT INT/ORG NAT/G PLAN ECO/TAC...NAT/COMP ANTHOL 20. PAGE 34 H0678 — ECO/UNDEV POLICY DIPLOM TASK

B62
DAVAR F.C.,IRAN AND INDIA THROUGH THE AGES. INDIA IRAN ELITES SECT CREATE ORD/FREE...LING BIBLIOG. PAGE 37 H0743 — NAT/COMP DIPLOM CULTURE

B62
DEHIO L.,THE PRECARIOUS BALANCE: FOUR CENTURIES OF THE EUROPEAN POWER STRUGGLE. FRANCE GERMANY SPAIN NAT/G DOMIN PWR...GOV/COMP 8/20. PAGE 39 H0784 — BAL/PWR WAR DIPLOM COERCE

B62
DIAZ J.S.,MANUAL DE BIBLIOGRAFIA DE LA LITERATURA ESPANOLA. PRE/AMER SPAIN ECO/UNDEV DIPLOM LEAD ATTIT...SOC 15/20. PAGE 41 H0820 — BIBLIOG L/A+17C NAT/G COLONIAL

B62
DUROSELLE J.B.,LES NOUVEAUX ETATS DANS LES RELATIONS INTERNATIONALES. AFR CHINA/COM FRANCE MOROCCO S/ASIA USSR ECO/UNDEV INT/ORG PLAN ECO/TAC EDU/PROP ATTIT DRIVE...TREND TOT/POP TUNIS 20. PAGE 44 H0872 — NAT/G CONSTN DIPLOM

B62
DUTOIT B.,LA NEUTRALITE SUISSE A L'HEURE EUROPEENNE. EUR+WWI MOD/EUR INT/ORG NAT/G VOL/ASSN PLAN BAL/PWR LEGIT NEUTRAL REGION PEACE ORD/FREE SOVEREIGN...CONCPT OBS TIME/SEQ TREND STERTYP VAL/FREE LEAGUE/NAT UN 20. PAGE 44 H0873 — ATTIT DIPLOM SWITZERLND

B62
EBENSTEIN W.,TWO WAYS OF LIFE. USA+45 CULTURE ECO/DEV PLAN EDU/PROP CONTROL ORD/FREE...GOV/COMP IDEA/COMP T 20 MARX/KARL ENGELS/F LENIN/VI LOCKE/JOHN MILL/JS. PAGE 44 H0885 — MARXISM POPULISM ECO/TAC DIPLOM

B62
FRIEDMANN W.,METHODS AND POLICIES OF PRINCIPAL DONOR COUNTRIES IN PUBLIC INTERNATIONAL DEVELOPMENT FINANCING: PRELIMINARY APPRAISAL. FRANCE GERMANY/W UK USA+45 USSR WOR+45 FINAN TEC/DEV CAP/ISM DIPLOM ECO/TAC ATTIT 20 EEC. PAGE 53 H1066 — INT/ORG FOR/AID NAT/COMP ADMIN

B62
HAIM S.G.,ARAB NATIONALISM. ISLAM CONSTN GP/REL ...ANTHOL BIBLIOG JEWS 20 MID/EAST ARABS. PAGE 64 H1279 — NAT/LISM REV SECT DIPLOM

B62
HANAK H.,GREAT BRITAIN AND AUSTRIA-HUNGARY DURING THE FIRST WORLD WAR: A STUDY IN THE FORMATION OF PUBLIC OPINION. CZECHOSLVK UK NAT/G GIVE DOMIN EDU/PROP CONSERVE...BIBLIOG 20 AUST/HUNG WWI. PAGE 65 H1311 — WAR DIPLOM ATTIT PRESS

B62
HENDERSON W.O.,THE GENESIS OF THE COMMON MARKET. EUR+WWI FRANCE MOD/EUR UK SEA COM/IND EXTR/IND COLONIAL DISCRIM...TIME/SEQ CHARTS BIBLIOG 18/20 EEC TREATY. PAGE 70 H1395 — ECO/DEV INT/TRADE DIPLOM

B62
INGHAM K.,A HISTORY OF EAST AFRICA. NAT/G DIPLOM ADMIN WAR NAT/LISM...SOC BIOG BIBLIOG. PAGE 77 H1534 — AFR CONSTN COLONIAL

B62
JACKSON W.A.D.,RUSSO-CHINESE BORDERLANDS. ASIA COM USSR NAT/G PROVS EX/STRUC FORCES DOMIN COERCE PEACE ATTIT PWR SOVEREIGN WEALTH...CONCPT TREND CHARTS STERTYP VAL/FREE. PAGE 79 H1576 — GEOG DIPLOM RUSSIA

B62
KIDDER F.E.,THESES ON PAN AMERICAN TOPICS. LAW CULTURE NAT/G SECT DIPLOM HEALTH...ART/METH GEOG SOC 13/20. PAGE 86 H1709 — BIBLIOG CHRIST-17C L/A+17C SOCIETY

B62
KIRPICEVA I.K.,HANDBUCH DER RUSSISCHEN UND SOWJETISCHEN BIBLIOGRAPHIEN (5 VOLS.). USSR STRUCT ECO/DEV DIPLOM LEAD ATTIT 18/20. PAGE 86 H1726 — BIBLIOG/A NAT/G MARXISM COM

B62
LAQUEUR W.,THE FUTURE OF COMMUNIST SOCIETY. CHINA/COM USSR LAW ECO/DEV NAT/G POL/PAR PLAN PROB/SOLV DIPLOM LEAD...POLICY CONCPT IDEA/COMP ANTHOL 20. PAGE 91 H1820 — MARXISM COM FUT SOCIETY

B62
LAQUEUR W.,POLYCENTRISM. CHINA/COM COM USSR WOR+45 INT/ORG NAT/G ECO/TAC DOMIN LEAD ATTIT PWR SOVEREIGN...ANTHOL 20. PAGE 91 H1821 — MARXISM DIPLOM BAL/PWR POLICY

B62
LOWENSTEIN A.K.,BRUTAL MANDATE: A JOURNEY TO SOUTH WEST AFRICA. CULTURE INT/ORG NAT/G DIPLOM...GEOG 20 UN AFRICA/SW. PAGE 99 H1975 — AFR POLICY RACE/REL PROB/SOLV

B62
MORGENSTERN O.,STRATEGIE - HEUTE (2ND ED.). USA+45 USSR ECO/DEV DELIB/GP WAR PEACE ORD/FREE...GOV/COMP NAT/COMP 20 COLD/WAR NATO. PAGE 113 H2256 — NUC/PWR DIPLOM FORCES TEC/DEV

B62
MOUSSA P.,THE UNDERPRIVILEGED NATIONS. FINAN INT/ORG PLAN PROB/SOLV CAP/ISM GIVE TASK WEALTH ...POLICY SOC 20. PAGE 114 H2273 — ECO/UNDEV NAT/G DIPLOM FOR/AID

B62
NOBECOURT R.G.,LES SECRETS DE LA PROPAGANDE EN FRANCE OCCUPEE. FRANCE ELITES NAT/G DIPLOM GP/REL NAT/LISM TOTALISM ORD/FREE 20 VICHY VICHY. PAGE 118 H2365 — METH/COMP EDU/PROP WAR CONTROL

B62
SCALAPINO R.A.,PARTIES AND POLITICS IN CONTEMPORARY JAPAN. EX/STRUC DIPLOM CHOOSE NAT/LISM ATTIT ...POLICY 20 CHINJAP. PAGE 138 H2762 — POL/PAR PARL/PROC ELITES DECISION

B62
SCHMIDT-VOLKMAR E.,DER KULTURKAMPF IN DEUTSCHLAND 1871-1890. GERMANY PRUSSIA SOCIETY STRUCT SECT DIPLOM GP/REL NAT/LISM 19 CHURCH/STA BISMARCK/O. PAGE 139 H2789 — POL/PAR CATHISM ATTIT NAT/G

B62
SELOSOEMARDJAN O.,SOCIAL CHANGES IN JOGJAKARTA. INDONESIA NETHERLAND ELITES STRATA STRUCT FAM POL/PAR CREATE DIPLOM INT/TRADE EDU/PROP ADMIN GOV/REL...SOC 20 JAVA CHINJAP. PAGE 141 H2825 — ECO/UNDEV CULTURE REV COLONIAL

B62
STARR R.E.,POLAND 1944-1962: THE SOVIETIZATION OF A CAPTIVE PEOPLE. COM POLAND USSR POL/PAR SECT LEGIS — MARXISM NAT/G

DIPLOM DOMIN EDU/PROP CHOOSE ORD/FREE...POLICY CHARTS BIBLIOG 20. PAGE 149 H2973
TOTALISM NAT/COMP

B62
TAYLOR D.,THE BRITISH IN AFRICA. UK CULTURE ECO/UNDEV INDUS DIPLOM INT/TRADE ADMIN WAR RACE/REL ORD/FREE SOVEREIGN...POLICY BIBLIOG 15/20 CMN/WLTH. PAGE 153 H3053
AFR COLONIAL DOMIN

B62
TILMAN R.O.,THE NIGERIAN POLITICAL SXENE. NIGERIA DIPLOM COLONIAL PARTIC...POLICY SOC OBS PREDICT ANTHOL 20. PAGE 155 H3096
NAT/G AFR ECO/UNDEV FEDERAL

B62
US DEPARTMENT OF THE ARMY,GUIDE TO JAPANESE MONOGRAPHS AND JAPANESE STUDIES ON MANCHURIA: 1945-1960. CHINA/COM NAT/G DIPLOM LEAD COERCE WAR ...CHARTS 19/20 CHINJAP. PAGE 160 H3193
BIBLIOG/A FORCES ASIA S/ASIA

B62
US LIBRARY OF CONGRESS,A LIST OF AMERICAN DOCTORAL DISSERTATIONS ON AFRICA. SOCIETY SECT DIPLOM EDU/PROP ADMIN...GEOG 19/20. PAGE 161 H3212
BIBLIOG AFR ACADEM CULTURE

B62
WEHLER H.V.,SOZIALDEMOKRATIE UND NATIONALSTAAT. GERMANY POLAND USSR CULTURE SOCIETY STRUCT NAT/G POL/PAR DIPLOM ORD/FREE 19/20. PAGE 166 H3325
NAT/LISM SOVEREIGN GP/REL ATTIT

B62
WHITING K.R.,THE SOVIET UNION TODAY: A CONCISE HANDBOOK. USSR ELITES AGRI INDUS POL/PAR FORCES DIPLOM EDU/PROP LEAD...GEOG TREND 19/20. PAGE 168 H3354
NAT/G ATTIT MARXISM POLICY

S62
CROAN M.,"POLYCENTRISM: COMMUNIST INTERNATIONAL RELATIONS." ASIA STRUCT INT/ORG NAT/G POL/PAR CONSULT PLAN DOMIN EDU/PROP COERCE ATTIT RIGID/FLEX SOCISM...POLICY CONCPT TREND CON/ANAL GEN/LAWS MARX/KARL. PAGE 35 H0703
COM CREATE DIPLOM NAT/LISM

S62
LANGER W.L.,"FAREWELL TO EMPIRE." EUR+WWI MOD/EUR NAT/G DIPLOM EDU/PROP COLONIAL ATTIT ORD/FREE PWR SOVEREIGN WEALTH...CONCPT TIME/SEQ GEN/LAWS TOT/POP VAL/FREE CMN/WLTH 20. PAGE 91 H1810
DOMIN ECO/TAC NAT/LISM

S62
LEGUM C.,"THE DANGERS OF INDEPENDENCE" AFR UGANDA NAT/G DIPLOM DOMIN REGION CENTRAL ATTIT POPULISM 20. PAGE 93 H1862
ORD/FREE SOVEREIGN NAT/LISM GOV/COMP

S62
LONDON K.,"SINO-SOVIET RELATIONS IN THE CONTEXT OF THE 'WORLD SOCIALIST SYSTEM'." ASIA CHINA/COM COM USSR INT/ORG NAT/G TOP/EX BAL/PWR DIPLOM DOMIN ATTIT PERCEPT RIGID/FLEX PWR MARXISM...METH/CNCPT TREND 20. PAGE 98 H1957
DELIB/GP CONCPT SOCISM

S62
MARIAS J.,"A PROGRAM FOR EUROPE." EUR+WWI INT/ORG NAT/G PLAN DIPLOM DOMIN PWR...STERTYP TOT/POP 20. PAGE 102 H2048
VOL/ASSN CREATE REGION

S62
MARTIN L.W.,"THE MARKET FOR STRATEGIC IDEAS IN BRITAIN: THE 'SANDYS ERA'" UK ARMS/CONT WAR GOV/REL OPTIMAL...POLICY DECISION GOV/COMP COLD/WAR CMN/WLTH. PAGE 103 H2063
DIPLOM COERCE FORCES PWR

S62
MBOYA T.,"RELATIONS BETWEEN THE PRESS AND GOVERNMENT IN AFRICA." AFR DIPLOM EDU/PROP NAT/LISM ORD/FREE SOVEREIGN 20. PAGE 106 H2115
PRESS GP/REL ATTIT NAT/G

S62
ROTBERG R.,"THE RISE OF AFRICAN NATIONALISM: THE CASE OF EAST AND CENTRAL AFRICA." AFR CULTURE SOCIETY NEIGH DIPLOM DOMIN COLONIAL COERCE DISPL PERCEPT PWR SOVEREIGN...POLICY OBS/ENVIR TREND WORK 20. PAGE 135 H2690
ATTIT DRIVE NAT/LISM REV

S62
VIGNES D.,"L'AUTORITE DES TRAITES INTERNATIONAUX EN DROIT INTERNE." EUR+WWI UNIV LAW CONSTN INTELL NAT/G POL/PAR DIPLOM ATTIT PERCEPT ALL/VALS ...POLICY INT/LAW JURID CONCPT TIME/SEQ 20 TREATY. PAGE 163 H3252
STRUCT LEGIT FRANCE

C62
BACON F.,"OF EMPIRE" (1612) IN F. BACON, ESSAYS." ELITES NAT/G PROB/SOLV DIPLOM ADMIN CONTROL WEALTH 16/17 KING. PAGE 9 H0190
PWR CHIEF DOMIN GEN/LAWS

B63
AHN L.A.,FUNFZIG JAHRE ZWISCHEN INFLATION UND DEFLATION. GERMANY DIPLOM PRICE...CONCPT 20 GOLD/STAND. PAGE 4 H0081
FINAN CAP/ISM NAT/COMP ECO/TAC

B63
BADI J.,THE GOVERNMENT OF THE STATE OF ISRAEL: A CRITICAL ACCOUNT OF ITS PARLIAMENT, EXECUTIVE, AND JUDICIARY. ISRAEL ECO/DEV CHIEF DELIB/GP LEGIS DIPLOM CT/SYS INGP/REL PEACE ORD/FREE...BIBLIOG 20 PARLIAMENT ARABS MIGRATION. PAGE 10 H0193
NAT/G CONSTN EX/STRUC POL/PAR

B63
BANERJI A.K.,INDIA'S BALANCE OF PAYMENTS. INDIA NAT/G PRICE BAL/PAY COST INCOME 20. PAGE 10 H0208
INT/TRADE DIPLOM FINAN BUDGET

B63
BARNETT A.D.,COMMUNIST STRATEGIES IN ASIA: A COMPARATIVE ANALYSIS OF GOVERNMENTS AND PARTIES. COM FUT S/ASIA CULTURE SOCIETY STRATA NAT/G DELIB/GP ACT/RES ECO/TAC EDU/PROP COERCE CHOOSE ATTIT RIGID/FLEX ORD/FREE PWR SKILL...SIMUL VAL/FREE 20. PAGE 11 H0223
ASIA POL/PAR DIPLOM USSR

B63
BISHOP O.B.,PUBLICATIONS OF THE GOVERNMENT OF THE PROVINCE OF CANADA 1841-1867. CANADA DIPLOM COLONIAL LEAD...POLICY 18. PAGE 17 H0346
BIBLIOG NAT/G ATTIT

B63
BRECHER M.,THE NEW STATES OF ASIA. ASIA S/ASIA INT/ORG BAL/PWR COLONIAL NEUTRAL ORD/FREE PWR 20 UN. PAGE 20 H0407
NAT/G ECO/UNDEV DIPLOM POLICY

B63
BRODOWSKI J.H.,LATIN AMERICA TODAY. CULTURE LEAD ...SOC 20. PAGE 21 H0426
BIBLIOG/A L/A+17C NAT/G DIPLOM

B63
BROEKMEIJER M.W.,DEVELOPING COUNTRIES AND NATO. USSR FORCES DIPLOM NUC/PWR WAR PEACE TOTALISM 20 NATO. PAGE 21 H0427
ECO/UNDEV FOR/AID ORD/FREE NAT/G

B63
BROGAN D.W.,POLITICAL PATTERNS IN TODAY'S WORLD. FRANCE USA+45 USSR WOR+45 CONSTN STRUCT PLAN DIPLOM ADMIN LEAD ROLE SUPEGO...PHIL/SCI 20. PAGE 21 H0429
NAT/COMP NEW/LIB COM TOTALISM

B63
BRZEZINSKI Z.K.,AFRICA AND THE COMMUNIST WORLD. AFR ASIA COM CULTURE SOCIETY INT/ORG DELIB/GP ACT/RES ECO/TAC COERCE ORD/FREE PWR WEALTH...STAT TOT/POP VAL/FREE 20. PAGE 23 H0461
ATTIT EDU/PROP DIPLOM USSR

B63
CANELAS O.A.,RADIOGRAFIA DE LA ALIANZA PARA EL ATRASO. L/A+17C USA+45 ECO/TAC DOMIN COLONIAL NAT/LISM...SOCIALIST NAT/COMP 20. PAGE 26 H0519
REV DIPLOM ECO/UNDEV REGION

B63
COMISION DE HISTORIO,GUIA DE LOS DOCUMENTOS MICROFOTOGRAFIADOS POR LA UNIDAD MOVIL DE LA UNESCO. SOCIETY ECO/UNDEV INT/ORG ADMIN...SOC 20 UNESCO. PAGE 32 H0637
BIBLIOG NAT/G L/A+17C DIPLOM

B63
CRANKSHAW E.,THE NEW COLD WAR: MOSCOW V. PEKIN. CHINA/COM USSR INTELL POL/PAR DELIB/GP CAP/ISM COERCE REV NAT/LISM TOTALISM DRIVE...POLICY IDEA/COMP 20 KHRUSH/N. PAGE 35 H0698
ATTIT DIPLOM NAT/COMP MARXISM

B63
CREMEANS C.,THE ARABS AND THE WORLD: NASSER'S ARAB NATIONALIST POLICY. FUT ISLAM UAR USA+45 SOCIETY STRATA NAT/G POL/PAR PLAN DIPLOM EDU/PROP LEGIT DRIVE ALL/VALS...INT TIME/SEQ CHARTS 20 NASSER/G. PAGE 35 H0700
TOP/EX ATTIT REGION NAT/LISM

B63
DE JOUVENEL B.,THE PURE THEORY OF POLITICS. NAT/G DIPLOM CONTROL GP/REL PERS/REL PERSON PWR OBJECTIVE CONCPT. PAGE 38 H0758
GEN/LAWS SOCIETY METH/CNCPT

B63
DECOTTIGNIES R.,LES NATIONALITES AFRICAINES. AFR NAT/G PROB/SOLV DIPLOM COLONIAL ORD/FREE...CHARTS GOV/COMP 20. PAGE 39 H0781
NAT/LISM JURID LEGIS LAW

B63
ELIAS T.O.,GOVERNMENT AND POLITICS IN AFRICA. CONSTN CULTURE SOCIETY NAT/G POL/PAR DIPLOM REPRESENT PERSON...SOC TREND BIBLIOG 4/20. PAGE 45 H0906
AFR NAT/LISM COLONIAL LAW

B63
ELLIOT J.H.,THE REVOLT OF THE CATALANS. SPAIN LOC/G PROVS FORCES DIPLOM TASK WAR GOV/REL INGP/REL ...POLICY 17 OLIVARES. PAGE 45 H0909
REV NAT/G TOP/EX DOMIN

B63
ENKE S.,ECONOMICS FOR DEVELOPMENT. AGRI TEC/DEV CAP/ISM DIPLOM ECO/TAC TAX ATTIT DRIVE HABITAT WEALTH...GOV/COMP BIBLIOG 20. PAGE 46 H0928
ECO/UNDEV PHIL/SCI CON/ANAL

B63
FABER K.,DIE NATIONALISTISCHE PUBLIZISTIK DEUTSCHLANDS VON 1866 BIS 1871 (2 VOLS.). EUR+WWI GERMANY DIPLOM EDU/PROP 19. PAGE 48 H0957
BIBLIOG/A NAT/G NAT/LISM POL/PAR

B63
FAWCETT J.E.S.,THE BRITISH COMMONWEALTH IN INTERNATIONAL LAW. LAW INT/ORG NAT/G VOL/ASSN OP/RES DIPLOM ADJUD CENTRAL CONSEN...NET/THEORY CMN/WLTH TREATY. PAGE 49 H0977
INT/LAW STRUCT COLONIAL

B63
FRANKEL J.,THE MAKING OF FOREIGN POLICY: AN ANALYSIS OF DECISION-MAKING. CHINA/COM EUR+WWI USA+45 ELITES INTELL FORCES LEGIS PLAN ATTIT ALL/VALS MORAL CONSERVE...GOV/COMP 20 PRESIDENT UN TREATY. PAGE 53 H1051
POLICY DECISION PROB/SOLV DIPLOM

B63
FRANZ G.,TEILUNG UND WIEDERVEREINIGUNG. GERMANY IRELAND ITALY NETHERLAND POLAND CULTURE BAL/PWR CHOOSE NAT/LISM ORD/FREE SOVEREIGN 19/20. PAGE 53 H1054
DIPLOM WAR NAT/COMP ATTIT

B63
GARDINIER D.E.,CAMEROON: UNITED NATIONS CHALLENGE TO FRENCH POLICY. AFR CAMEROON FRANCE NAT/G LEGIS CONTROL SOVEREIGN 20 UN. PAGE 55 H1101
DIPLOM POLICY INT/ORG COLONIAL

B63
GONZALEZ PEDRERO E.,ANATOMIA DE UN CONFLICTO. WOR+45 ECO/DEV ECO/UNDEV ECO/TAC FOR/AID CONTROL ARMS/CONT GOV/REL...NAT/COMP 20 COLD/WAR. PAGE 58 H1166
DIPLOM DETER BAL/PWR

B63
GRIMOND J.,THE LIBERAL CHALLENGE. UK SOCIETY INDUS POL/PAR LEGIS PLAN CAP/ISM DIPLOM EDU/PROP GOV/REL CONSERVE 20 PARLIAMENT REFORMERS. PAGE 61 H1227
NAT/G NEW/LIB ECO/DEV POLICY

B63
HAILEY L.,THE REPUBLIC OF SOUTH AFRICA AND THE HIGH COMMISSION TERRITORIES. AFR SOUTH/AFR UK INT/ORG NAT/G PROVS RACE/REL SOVEREIGN...CHARTS 19/20 COMMONWLTH. PAGE 64 H1278
COLONIAL DIPLOM ATTIT

B63
HAMM H.,ALBANIA - CHINA'S BEACHHEAD IN EUROPE. ALBANIA CHINA/COM USSR YUGOSLAVIA ELITES SOCIETY POL/PAR DELIB/GP FORCES ECO/TAC COERCE ISOLAT PEACE MARXISM...IDEA/COMP 20 MAO. PAGE 65 H1304
DIPLOM REV NAT/G POLICY

B63
HARTLEY A.,A STATE OF ENGLAND. UK ELITES SOCIETY ACADEM NAT/G SCHOOL INGP/REL CONSEN ORD/FREE NEW/LIB...POLICY 20. PAGE 67 H1349
DIPLOM ATTIT INTELL ECO/DEV

B63
HYDE D.,THE PEACEFUL ASSAULT. COM UAR USSR ECO/DEV ECO/UNDEV NAT/G POL/PAR CAP/ISM PWR 20. PAGE 76 H1516
MARXISM CONTROL ECO/TAC DIPLOM

B63
JAIRAZBHOY R.A.,FOREIGN INFLUENCE IN ANCIENT INDIA. INDIA ELITES SECT DIPLOM EDU/PROP COLONIAL REGION GP/REL...ART/METH LING WORSHIP +/14 GRECO/ROMN MESOPOTAM PERSIA PARTH/SASS. PAGE 79 H1587
CULTURE SOCIETY COERCE DOMIN

B63
JENNINGS W.I.,DEMOCRACY IN AFRICA. UK CULTURE STRUCT ECO/UNDEV DIPLOM COLONIAL GP/REL ADJUST NAT/LISM ORD/FREE...GOV/COMP 20 THIRD/WRLD. PAGE 81 H1613
PROB/SOLV AFR CONSTN POPULISM

B63
JUDD P.,AFRICAN INDEPENDENCE: THE EXPLODING EMERGENCE OF THE NEW AFRICAN NATIONS. AFR UK LAW CONSTN CULTURE KIN DIPLOM ATTIT...CHARTS BIBLIOG 20 UN DEGAULLE/C NEGRO THIRD/WRLD. PAGE 82 H1640
ORD/FREE POLICY DOMIN LOC/G

B63
KAHIN G.M.,MAJOR GOVERNMENTS OF ASIA (2ND ED.). ASIA INDIA INDONESIA PAKISTAN S/ASIA DIPLOM...SOC 20 CHINJAP. PAGE 83 H1650
GOV/COMP POL/PAR ELITES

B63
KHADDURI M.,MODERN LIBYA: A STUDY IN POLITICAL DEVELOPMENT. EUR+WWI ISLAM LIBYA ELITES INT/ORG POL/PAR FORCES DIPLOM FOR/AID DOMIN EDU/PROP LEGIT NAT/LISM DRIVE RIGID/FLEX SKILL...CONCPT TIME/SEQ TREND 20. PAGE 85 H1704
NAT/G STRUCT

B63
KLEIMAN R.,ATLANTIC CRISIS; AMERICAN DIPLOMACY CONFRONTS A RESURGENT EUROPE. EUR+WWI USA+45 ECO/DEV AGRI NAT/G CHIEF FORCES PLAN LEAD ATTIT ...CONCPT 20 NATO KENNEDY/JF DEGAULLE/C EEC JOHNSON/LB. PAGE 87 H1731
DIPLOM REGION POLICY

B63
KOGAN N.,THE POLITICS OF ITALIAN FOREIGN POLICY. EUR+WWI LEGIS DOMIN LEGIT EXEC PWR RESPECT SKILL ...POLICY DECISION HUM SOC METH/CNCPT OBS INT CHARTS 20. PAGE 87 H1737
NAT/G ROUTINE DIPLOM ITALY

B63
KRAEHE E.,METTERNICH'S GERMAN POLICY: THE CONTEST WITH NAPOLEON, 1799-1814, VOL. 1. FRANCE MOD/EUR NAT/G CONSULT TOP/EX PLAN BAL/PWR DOMIN COERCE ATTIT DRIVE PERCEPT PERSON SKILL...CONCPT RECORD TIME/SEQ TREND 18/19. PAGE 88 H1764
BIOG GERMANY DIPLOM

B63
LAMB B.P.,INDIA: A WORLD IN TRANSITION. INDIA ECO/UNDEV SECT EDU/PROP COLONIAL HABITAT ORD/FREE ...GEOG CHARTS BIBLIOG SOC/INTEG 20. PAGE 90 H1799
POL/PAR NAT/G DIPLOM STRATA

B63
LEE C.,THE POLITICS OF KOREAN NATIONALISM. KOREA S/ASIA DIPLOM REV WAR 14/20 CHINJAP. PAGE 93 H1855
NAT/LISM SOVEREIGN

COLONIAL

B63
LOOMIE A.J.,THE SPANISH ELIZABETHANS: THE ENGLISH EXILES AT THE COURT OF PHILIP II. SPAIN UK WAR INGP/REL DRIVE HABITAT CATHISM...BIOG 16/17 MIGRATION. PAGE 98 H1962
NAT/G STRANGE POLICY DIPLOM

B63
LYON P.,NEUTRALISM. ECO/UNDEV EDU/PROP COLONIAL ALL/IDEOS...IDEA/COMP 20 COLD/WAR UN. PAGE 99 H1985
NAT/COMP NAT/LISM DIPLOM NEUTRAL

B63
MERKL P.H.,THE ORIGIN OF THE WEST GERMAN REPUBLIC. GERMANY/W WOR+45 POL/PAR DIPLOM LEAD LOBBY REPRESENT GP/REL NAT/LISM 20. PAGE 109 H2179
CONSTN PARL/PROC CONTROL BAL/PWR

B63
MILLER W.J.,THE MEANING OF COMMUNISM. USSR SOCIETY ECO/DEV EX/STRUC WORKER TEC/DEV ADMIN TOTALISM ...POLICY CONCPT CHARTS BIBLIOG T 20 COLD/WAR LENIN/VI STALIN/J. PAGE 111 H2215
MARXISM TRADIT DIPLOM NAT/G

B63
MONGER G.W.,THE END OF ISOLATION. FRANCE MOD/EUR RUSSIA UK NAT/G LEGIS TOP/EX GOV/REL PWR 20 TREATY CHINJAP. PAGE 112 H2239
DIPLOM POLICY WAR

B63
MOSELY P.E.,THE SOVIET UNION, 1922-1962: A FOREIGN AFFAIRS READER. ASIA POLAND USSR CULTURE INTELL AGRI POL/PAR WORKER INT/TRADE DOMIN WAR NAT/LISM MARXISM SOCISM 20 KHRUSH/N. PAGE 113 H2267
PWR POLICY DIPLOM

B63
NICOLSON H.,DIPLOMACY (3RD ED.). INT/ORG NAT/G CONSULT DELIB/GP CONFER 19/20 LEAGUE/NAT UN. PAGE 118 H2354
DIPLOM CONCPT NAT/COMP

B63
OECD,FOOD AID: ITS ROLE IN ECONOMIC DEVELOPMENT. FINAN NAT/G PLAN DIPLOM GIVE TASK WEALTH ...METH/COMP METH 20. PAGE 120 H2397
ECO/UNDEV FOR/AID INT/ORG POLICY

B63
PADELFORD N.J.,AFRICA AND WORLD ORDER. AFR COLONIAL SOVEREIGN...ANTHOL BIBLIOG 20 UN UNIFICA COMMONWLTH. PAGE 122 H2439
DIPLOM NAT/G ORD/FREE

B63
RIVKIN A.,THE AFRICAN PRESENCE IN WORLD AFFAIRS. ECO/UNDEV AGRI INT/ORG LOC/G NAT/LISM...OBS PREDICT GOV/COMP 20. PAGE 132 H2635
AFR NAT/G DIPLOM BAL/PWR

B63
RONNING C.N.,LAW AND POLITICS IN INTER-AMERICAN DIPLOMACY. L/A+17C ECO/UNDEV NAT/G CONSULT DELIB/GP CREATE CAP/ISM ECO/TAC LEGIT REGION RIGID/FLEX ...METH/CNCPT GEN/LAWS OAS 20. PAGE 133 H2668
VOL/ASSN ALL/VALS DIPLOM

B63
SCHUMAN S.I.,LEGAL POSITIVISM: ITS SCOPE AND LIMITATIONS. CONSTN NAT/G DIPLOM PARTIC UTOPIA ...POLICY DECISION PHIL/SCI CONCPT 20. PAGE 140 H2802
GEN/METH LAW METH/COMP

B63
SETON-WATSON H.,THE NEW IMPERIALISM. COM EUR+WWI MOD/EUR ECO/UNDEV NAT/G FORCES DIPLOM DOMIN EDU/PROP LEGIT COLONIAL EXEC COERCE GP/REL RACE/REL DISCRIM ATTIT...TIME/SEQ 20. PAGE 142 H2833
ECO/TAC RUSSIA USSR

B63
SHANNON R.T.,GLADSTONE AND THE BULGARIAN AGITATION OF 1876. BULGARIA TURKEY UK DIPLOM COERCE REV ATTIT 19 GLADSTON/W DISRAELI/B. PAGE 142 H2841
EDU/PROP NAT/G PWR CONSEN

B63
SWEARER H.R.,CONTEMPORARY COMMUNISM: THEORY AND PRACTICE. COM USSR SOCIETY ECO/DEV POL/PAR FORCES PLAN ADMIN LEAD NAT/LISM...POLICY ANTHOL 20 LENIN/VI COM/PARTY. PAGE 151 H3015
MARXISM CONCPT DIPLOM NAT/G

B63
UAR MINISTRY OF CULTURE,A BIBLIOGRAPHICAL LIST OF ARABIAN PENINSULA. ISLAM SAUDI/ARAB YEMEN FINAN NAT/G DIPLOM 19/20. PAGE 157 H3147
BIBLIOG GEOG INDUS SECT

B63
ULAM A.B.,THE NEW FACE OF SOVIET TOTALITARIANISM. FUT INTELL NAT/G POL/PAR EX/STRUC TOP/EX DIPLOM ECO/TAC DOMIN EDU/PROP LEGIT COERCE ATTIT RIGID/FLEX...OBS HIST/WRIT TREND TOT/POP VAL/FREE COLD/WAR. PAGE 158 H3150
COM PWR TOTALISM USSR

B63
US ATOMIC ENERGY COMMISSION,ATOMIC ENERGY IN THE SOVIET UNION: TRIP REPORT OF THE US ATOMIC ENERGY DELEGATION, MAY 1933. USSR R+D NAT/G CONSULT CREATE DIPLOM ADMIN ROUTINE EFFICIENCY PRODUC KNOWL SKILL ...NAT/COMP 20 AEC TRAVEL TREATY. PAGE 159 H3176
METH/COMP OP/RES TEC/DEV NUC/PWR

B63
WALKER A.A.,OFFICIAL PUBLICATIONS OF SIERRA LEONE AND GAMBIA. GAMBIA SIER/LEONE UK LAW CONSTN LEGIS PLAN BUDGET DIPLOM...SOC SAMP CON/ANAL 20. PAGE 164 H3290
BIBLIOG NAT/G COLONIAL ADMIN

B63
WILCOX W.A.,PAKISTAN; THE CONSOLIDATION OF A NATION. INDIA PAKISTAN CONSTN SECT PROB/SOLV COLONIAL PARTIC GP/REL FEDERAL...POLICY 19/20. PAGE 168 H3361
NAT/LISM ECO/UNDEV DIPLOM STRUCT

B63
WODDIS J.,AFRICA, THE WAY AHEAD. AFR FUT ELITES POL/PAR CAP/ISM DIPLOM DOMIN RACE/REL ATTIT ORD/FREE SOVEREIGN SOCISM 20 PANAF/FREE. PAGE 170 H3394
REV COLONIAL ECO/UNDEV NAT/G

L63
FREUND G.,"ADENAUER AND THE FUTURE OF GERMANY." EUR+WWI FUT GERMANY/W FORCES LEGIT ADMIN ROUTINE ATTIT DRIVE PERSON PWR...POLICY TIME/SEQ TREND VAL/FREE 20 ADENAUER/K. PAGE 53 H1058
NAT/G BIOG DIPLOM GERMANY

S63
ANTHON C.G.,"THE END OF THE ADENAUER ERA." EUR+WWI GERMANY/W CONSTN EX/STRUC CREATE DIPLOM LEGIT ATTIT PERSON ALL/VALS...RECORD 20 ADENAUER/K. PAGE 7 H0144
NAT/G TOP/EX BAL/PWR GERMANY

S63
DUTT V.P.,"CHINA: JEALOUS NEIGHBOR." ASIA CHINA/COM INDIA S/ASIA NAT/G TOP/EX DOMIN COERCE REV ATTIT ...POLICY COLD/WAR 20. PAGE 44 H0874
FORCES PWR DIPLOM

S63
GROSSER A.,"FRANCE AND GERMANY IN THE ATLANTIC COMMUNITY." INT/ORG NAT/G TOP/EX DIPLOM REGION PEACE ATTIT ORD/FREE PWR...CONCPT RECORD TIME/SEQ GEN/LAWS VAL/FREE COLD/WAR 20. PAGE 62 H1234
EUR+WWI VOL/ASSN FRANCE GERMANY

S63
HALPERN A.M.,"THE EMERGENCE OF AN ASIAN COMMUNIST BLOC." ASIA CHINA/COM COM FUT KOREA/N S/ASIA VIETNAM/N STRATA NAT/G DELIB/GP FORCES TOP/EX PLAN BAL/PWR COERCE DETER PWR COLD/WAR WORK 20. PAGE 65 H1295
POL/PAR EDU/PROP DIPLOM

S63
HOSKINS H.L.,"ARAB SOCIALISM IN THE UAR." ISLAM USSR AGRI INDUS NAT/G TOP/EX CREATE DIPLOM EDU/PROP DRIVE KNOWL PWR SOCISM...POLICY CONCPT TREND SUEZ 20. PAGE 74 H1478
ECO/DEV PLAN UAR

S63
MBOYA T.,"AFRICAN SOCIALISM." ECO/UNDEV INT/ORG DIPLOM FOR/AID INT/TRADE REGION GP/REL ATTIT ORD/FREE EACM. PAGE 106 H2116
AFR SOCISM CULTURE NAT/LISM

S63
POPPINO R.E.,"IMBALANCE IN BRAZIL." L/A+17C NAT/G TOP/EX PLAN DIPLOM LEGIT DRIVE WEALTH...CON/ANAL LAFTA 20. PAGE 127 H2544
POL/PAR ECO/TAC BRAZIL

S63
ZOLBERG A.R.,"MASS PARTIES AND NATIONAL INTEGRATION: THE CASE OF THE IVORY COAST" (BMR)" AFR IVORY/CST CONSTN VOL/ASSN DIPLOM LEAD GP/REL INGP/REL 20. PAGE 173 H3461
POL/PAR ECO/UNDEV NAT/G ADJUST

N63
LEDERER W.,THE BALANCE ON FOREIGN TRANSACTIONS: PROBLEMS OF DEFINITION AND MEASUREMENT (PAMPHLET). USA+45 BUDGET DIPLOM ECO/TAC PRICE GOV/REL...POLICY STAT NAT/COMP METH 20. PAGE 93 H1853
FINAN BAL/PAY INT/TRADE ECO/DEV

N63
LIBRARY HUNGARIAN ACADEMY SCI,HUNGARIAN PUBLICATIONS ON ASIA AND AFRICA, 1950-1962: A SELECTED BIBLIOGRAPHY (PAMPHLET). AFR ASIA HUNGARY S/ASIA ECO/UNDEV NAT/G EDU/PROP ATTIT 20 UNESCO. PAGE 96 H1922
BIBLIOG REGION DIPLOM WRITING

N63
RUMMEL R.J.,A FOREIGN CONFLICT BEHAVIOR CODE SHEET. ACT/RES DIPLOM...NEW/IDEA CHARTS NAT/COMP. PAGE 136 H2718
QUANT WAR CLASSIF SIMUL

B64
AFRO ASIAN SOLIDARITY AGAINST IMPERIALISM. AFR ISLAM S/ASIA ECO/UNDEV NAT/G POL/PAR TOP/EX PRESS ...INT ANTHOL 20 CHOU/ENLAI. PAGE 2 H0043
MARXISM DIPLOM EDU/PROP CHIEF

B64
AKZIN B.,STATE AND NATION. UNIV ECO/UNDEV DIPLOM RACE/REL NAT/LISM ATTIT PLURISM...CONCPT IDEA/COMP 20. PAGE 4 H0090
GP/REL NAT/G KIN

B64
ALVIM J.C.,A REVOLUCAO SEM RUMO. BRAZIL NAT/G BAL/PWR DIPLOM INT/TRADE PARTIC WEALTH...POLICY SOC SOC/INTEG 20. PAGE 6 H0118
REV CIVMIL/REL ECO/UNDEV ORD/FREE

B64
ARASARATNAM S.,CEYLON. CEYLON NETHERLAND PORTUGAL S/ASIA UK STRUCT ECO/UNDEV SECT DIPLOM DOMIN RACE/REL NAT/LISM 17/20 CMN/WLTH. PAGE 8 H0156
COLONIAL NAT/G PROB/SOLV CULTURE

B64
BELL C.,THE DEBATABLE ALLIANCE. COM UK USA+45 NAT/G FORCES PLAN BAL/PWR NUC/PWR WAR ATTIT...GOV/COMP 20. PAGE 13 H0263
DIPLOM PWR PEACE POLICY

B64
BELL W.,JAMAICAN LEADERS: POLITICAL ATTITUDES IN A NEW NATION. JAMAICA STRUCT ACT/RES CREATE PROB/SOLV DIPLOM COLONIAL LEAD...QU 20. PAGE 13 H0267
NAT/LISM ATTIT DRIVE SOVEREIGN

B64
BROWN W.M.,THE EXTERNAL LIQUIDITY OF AN ADVANCED COUNTRY. CANADA FRANCE GERMANY/W SWEDEN UK USA+45 ECO/DEV DIPLOM PRICE...CONCPT STAT NAT/COMP 20. PAGE 22 H0451
FINAN INT/TRADE COST INCOME

B64
BUNTING B.P.,THE RISE OF THE SOUTH AFRICAN REICH. SOUTH/AFR INT/ORG NAT/G FORCES DIPLOM CONTROL WAR TOTALISM ATTIT...GOV/COMP 19/20. PAGE 24 H0477
RACE/REL DISCRIM NAT/LISM TREND

B64
BURKE F.G.,AFRICA'S QUEST FOR ORDER. AFR CULTURE KIN MUNIC NAT/G DIPLOM COLONIAL REV DISCRIM NAT/LISM AGE/Y 20. PAGE 24 H0488
ORD/FREE CONSEN RACE/REL LEAD

B64
BUTWELL R.,SOUTHEAST ASIA TODAY - AND TOMORROW. NAT/G COLONIAL LEAD REGION WAR CHOOSE WEALTH MARXISM 20. PAGE 25 H0500
S/ASIA DIPLOM ECO/UNDEV NAT/LISM

B64
CORFO,CHILE, A SELECTED BIBLIOGRAPHY IN ENGLISH (PAMPHLET). CHILE DIPLOM...SOC 20. PAGE 33 H0669
BIBLIOG NAT/G POLICY L/A+17C

B64
COWAN L.G.,THE DILEMMAS OF AFRICAN INDEPENDENCE. AFR INDUS NAT/G SECT DIPLOM ECO/TAC REGION MARXISM ...CHARTS BIBLIOG 20 MAPS. PAGE 34 H0683
ORD/FREE COLONIAL REV ECO/UNDEV

B64
CURTIN P.D.,THE IMAGE OF AFRICA: BRITISH IDEAS AND ACTION, 1780-1850. MOD/EUR SOCIETY FORCES ACT/RES DOMIN EDU/PROP COERCE ATTIT PERCEPT RIGID/FLEX SUPEGO HEALTH KNOWL MORAL ORD/FREE WEALTH...CONCPT WORK VAL/FREE. PAGE 36 H0726
AFR CULTURE UK DIPLOM

B64
DANIELS R.V.,RUSSIA. RUSSIA USSR STRUCT NAT/LISM TOTALISM ORD/FREE WEALTH...POLICY DECISION TREND. PAGE 37 H0740
MARXISM REV ECO/DEV DIPLOM

B64
DEL VAYO J.A.,CHINA TRIUMPHS. CHINA/COM CULTURE DIPLOM HEALTH 20. PAGE 39 H0787
MARXISM CREATE ORD/FREE POLICY

B64
DICKEY J.S.,THE UNITED STATES AND CANADA. CANADA USA+45...SOC 20. PAGE 41 H0822
DIPLOM TREND GOV/COMP PROB/SOLV

B64
EMBREE A.T.,A GUIDE TO PAPERBACKS ON ASIA; SELECTED AND ANNOTATED (PAMPHLET). CULTURE SOCIETY ECO/UNDEV SECT DIPLOM COLONIAL MARXISM...SOC 20. PAGE 46 H0913
BIBLIOG/A ASIA S/ASIA NAT/G

B64
FALL B.,STREET WITHOUT JOY. FRANCE USA+45 DIPLOM ECO/TAC FOR/AID GUERRILLA REV WEAPON...TREND 20. PAGE 48 H0966
WAR S/ASIA FORCES COERCE

B64
FORBES A.H.,CURRENT RESEARCH IN BRITISH STUDIES. UK CONSTN CULTURE POL/PAR SECT DIPLOM ADMIN...JURID BIOG WORSHIP 20. PAGE 52 H1034
BIBLIOG PERSON NAT/G PARL/PROC

B64
GILLY A.,INSIDE THE CUBAN REVOLUTION. CUBA AGRI INDUS LABOR CREATE DIPLOM...METH/COMP 20. PAGE 56 H1129
REV PLAN MARXISM ECO/UNDEV

B64
GREAT BRITAIN CENTRAL OFF INF,CONSTITUTIONAL DEVELOPMENT IN THE COMMONWEALTH. VOL/ASSN PLAN DIPLOM COLONIAL INGP/REL NAT/LISM ORD/FREE PWR 17/20 CMN/WLTH. PAGE 60 H1202
REGION CONSTN NAT/G SOVEREIGN

B64
GRIFFITH W.E.,THE SINO-SOVIET RIFT. ASIA CHINA/COM COM CUBA USSR YUGOSLAVIA NAT/G POL/PAR VOL/ASSN DELIB/GP FORCES TOP/EX DIPLOM EDU/PROP DRIVE PERSON PWR...TREND 20 TREATY. PAGE 61 H1224
ATTIT TIME/SEQ BAL/PWR SOCISM

B64
GRIFFITH W.E.,COMMUNISM IN EUROPE (2 VOLS.). CZECHOSLVK USSR WOR+45 WOR-45 YUGOSLAVIA INGP/REL MARXISM SOCISM...ANTHOL 20 EUROPE/E. PAGE 61 H1225
COM POL/PAR DIPLOM GOV/COMP

B64
GROSSER A.,THE FEDERAL REPUBLIC OF GERMANY: A CONCISE HISTORY. GERMANY/W STRUCT MORAL ORD/FREE POPULISM SOCISM...SOC CONCPT 20. PAGE 62 H1235
NAT/G POL/PAR CHOOSE DIPLOM

B64
GUTTERIDGE W.,MILITARY INSTITUTIONS AND POWER IN
FORCES

THE NEW STATES. WOR+45 INT/ORG FOR/AID NEUTRAL REV CIVMIL/REL ATTIT ROLE...GOV/COMP 20. PAGE 63 H1258 DIPLOM ECO/UNDEV ELITES B64

HALPERN J.M.,GOVERNMENT, POLITICS, AND SOCIAL STRUCTURE IN LAOS. LAOS CULTURE SOCIETY STRATA STRUCT FAM DIPLOM DOMIN MARXISM...INT GOV/COMP WORSHIP SOC/INTEG 20. PAGE 65 H1297 NAT/G SOC LOC/G B64

HAZLEWOOD A.,THE ECONOMICS OF DEVELOPMENT: AN ANNOTATED LIST OF BOOKS AND ARTICLES PUBLISHED 1958-1962. AGRI FINAN INDUS LABOR NAT/G DIPLOM INT/TRADE INCOME...MGT 20. PAGE 69 H1374 BIBLIOG/A ECO/UNDEV TEC/DEV B64

HORNE D.,THE LUCKY COUNTRY: AUSTRALIA TODAY. UK CULTURE STRATA ATTIT PWR PLURISM...GOV/COMP 20 AUSTRAL. PAGE 73 H1471 RACE/REL DIPLOM NAT/G STRUCT B64

HOROWITZ I.L.,REVOLUTION IN BRAZIL. BRAZIL L/A+17C ELITES STRATA NAT/G BAL/PWR PARTIC ATTIT 20. PAGE 74 H1473 ECO/UNDEV DIPLOM POLICY ORD/FREE B64

IBERO-AMERICAN INSTITUTES,IBEROAMERICANA. STRUCT ADMIN SOC. PAGE 76 H1519 BIBLIOG L/A+17C NAT/G DIPLOM B64

INTERNATIONAL LABOUR OFFICE,EMPLOYMENT AND ECONOMIC GROWTH. ECO/DEV ECO/UNDEV NAT/G PLAN DIPLOM INT/TRADE CONTROL INCOME PRODUC WEALTH...STAT NAT/COMP 20 ILO. PAGE 78 H1558 WORKER METH/COMP ECO/TAC OPTIMAL B64

KELLER J.W.,GERMANY, THE WALL AND BERLIN. EUR+WWI ECO/DEV NAT/G VOL/ASSN FORCES PLAN ECO/TAC EDU/PROP COERCE...POLICY CONCPT INT TREND COLD/WAR BER/BLOC 20 BERLIN. PAGE 84 H1685 ATTIT ALL/VALS DIPLOM GERMANY B64

KIS T.I.,LES PAYS DE L'EUROPE DE L'EST: LEURS RAPPORTS MUTUELS ET LE PROBLEME DE LEUR INTEGRATION DANS L'ORBITE DE L'USSR. EUR+WWI RUSSIA USSR INT/ORG NAT/G REV ATTIT...JURID SOC BIBLIOG WARSAW/P COMECON EUROPE/E. PAGE 86 H1727 DIPLOM COM MARXISM REGION B64

KITCHEN H.,A HANDBOOK OF AFRICAN AFFAIRS. ECO/UNDEV CREATE DIPLOM COLONIAL RACE/REL...ART/METH GEOG CHARTS 20. PAGE 87 H1729 AFR NAT/G INT/ORG FORCES B64

KOLARZ W.,BOOKS ON COMMUNISM. USSR WOR+45 CULTURE NAT/G POL/PAR DIPLOM LEAD...CONCPT GOV/COMP IDEA/COMP. PAGE 88 H1752 BIBLIOG/A SOCIETY COM MARXISM B64

LATOURETTE K.S.,CHINA. ASIA CHINA/COM FUT USSR ECO/UNDEV ECO/TAC WAR 19/20. PAGE 92 H1838 MARXISM NAT/G POLICY DIPLOM B64

LIEVWEN E.,GENERALS VS PRESIDENTS: WEOMILITARISM IN LATIN AMERICA. L/A+17C FORCES DIPLOM FOR/AID LEAD ...NAT/COMP 20 PRESIDENT. PAGE 97 H1929 CIVMIL/REL REV CONSERVE ORD/FREE B64

LIGGETT E.,BRITISH POLITICAL ISSUES: VOLUME 1. UK LAW CONSTN LOC/G NAT/G ADJUD 20. PAGE 97 H1930 POL/PAR GOV/REL CT/SYS DIPLOM B64

MAHAR J.M.,INDIA: A CRITICAL BIBLIOGRAPHY. INDIA PAKISTAN CULTURE ECO/UNDEV LOC/G POL/PAR SECT PROB/SOLV DIPLOM ADMIN COLONIAL PARL/PROC ATTIT 20. PAGE 101 H2016 BIBLIOG/A S/ASIA NAT/G LEAD B64

MAIER J.,POLITICS OF CHANGE IN LATIN AMERICA. BRAZIL L/A+17C STRATA INT/ORG NAT/G POL/PAR FOR/AID REV 20. PAGE 101 H2019 SOCIETY NAT/LISM DIPLOM REGION B64

MARTINEZ J.R.,THREE CASES OF COMMUNISM: CUBA, BRAZIL, AND MEXICO. BRAZIL CUBA L/A+17C CONSTN NAT/G DIPLOM ECO/TAC GP/REL INGP/REL...GP/COMP BIBLIOG 20 MEXIC/AMER COM/PARTY. PAGE 103 H2068 MARXISM BIOG REV NAT/COMP B64

MATTHEWS D.G.,A CURRENT VIEW OF AFRICANA (PAMPHLET). CULTURE ECO/UNDEV DIPLOM RACE/REL ATTIT 20. PAGE 105 H2092 BIBLIOG/A AFR NAT/G NAT/LISM B64

MAUD J.,AID FOR DEVELOPING COUNTRIES. COM EUR+WWI UK INT/TRADE ORD/FREE...GOV/COMP 20. PAGE 105 H2101 FOR/AID DIPLOM ECO/TAC ECO/UNDEV B64

MUSSO AMBROSI L.A.,BIBLIOGRAFIA DE BIBLIOGRAFIAS URUGUAYAS. URUGUAY DIPLOM ADMIN ATTIT...SOC 20. PAGE 115 H2301 BIBLIOG NAT/G L/A+17C PRESS B64

PERKINS D.,THE AMERICAN DEMOCRACY: ITS RISE TO POWER. ASIA USSR LAW CULTURE FINAN EDU/PROP COLONIAL CHOOSE...POLICY CHARTS BIBLIOG WORSHIP PRESIDENT 15/20 NEGRO. PAGE 125 H2492 LOC/G ECO/TAC WAR DIPLOM B64

PHILLIPS C.S.,THE DEVELOPMENT OF NIGERIAN FOREIGN POLICY. AFR CONSTN CULTURE STRATA NAT/G LEGIS DOMIN LEGIT EXEC...RELATIV SOC TIME/SEQ TREND TOT/POP 20. PAGE 125 H2502 CHOOSE POLICY DIPLOM NIGERIA B64

PITTMAN J.,PEACEFUL COEXISTENCE. USSR NAT/G NUC/PWR WAR ATTIT 20. PAGE 126 H2518 DIPLOM PEACE POLICY FORCES B64

POWELSON J.P.,LATIN AMERICA: TODAY'S ECONOMIC AND SOCIAL REVOLUTION. L/A+17C INTELL SOCIETY STRUCT AGRI INDUS NAT/G DIPLOM ECO/TAC REV...POLICY 20. PAGE 128 H2552 ECO/UNDEV WEALTH ADJUST PLAN B64

QUIGG P.W.,AFRICA: A FOREIGN AFFAIRS READER. AFR FRANCE PORTUGAL UK DIPLOM LEAD PARL/PROC MARXISM ...MAJORIT METH/CNCPT GOV/COMP IDEA/COMP ANTHOL 19/20. PAGE 129 H2575 COLONIAL SOVEREIGN NAT/LISM RACE/REL B64

RAGHAVAN M.D.,INDIA IN CEYLONESE HISTORY, SOCIETY AND CULTURE. CEYLON INDIA S/ASIA LAW SOCIETY INT/TRADE ATTIT...ART/METH JURID SOC LING 20. PAGE 129 H2581 DIPLOM CULTURE SECT STRUCT B64

RAISON T.,WHY CONSERVATIVE? UK FORCES DIPLOM ECO/TAC GIVE EDU/PROP ORD/FREE WEALTH LAISSEZ ...GOV/COMP 20 TORY/PARTY CONSRV/PAR. PAGE 129 H2583 PLURISM CONSERVE POL/PAR NAT/G B64

REMAK J.,THE GENTLE CRITIC: THEODOR FONTANE AND GERMAN POLITICS, 1848-1898. GERMANY PRUSSIA CULTURE ELITES BAL/PWR DIPLOM WRITING GOV/REL...HUM BIOG 19 BISMARCK/O JUNKER FONTANE/T. PAGE 131 H2614 PERSON SOCIETY WORKER CHIEF B64

ROBERTS HL,FOREIGN AFFAIRS BIBLIOGRAPHY, 1952-1962. ECO/DEV SECT PLAN FOR/AID INT/TRADE ARMS/CONT NAT/LISM ATTIT...INT/LAW GOV/COMP IDEA/COMP 20. PAGE 132 H2643 BIBLIOG/A DIPLOM INT/ORG WAR B64

ROSENAU J.N.,INTERNATIONAL ASPECTS OF CIVIL STRIFE. CHINA/COM CUBA EUR+WWI USA+45 USSR BAL/PWR EDU/PROP NEUTRAL COERCE MORAL...NAT/COMP 20 COLD/WAR UN. PAGE 134 H2676 POLICY DIPLOM REV WAR B64

RUSSET B.M.,WORLD HANDBOOK OF POLITICAL AND SOCIAL INDICATORS. WOR+45 COM/IND ADMIN WEALTH...GEOG 20. PAGE 136 H2719 DIPLOM STAT NAT/G NAT/COMP B64

SAKAI R.K.,STUDIES ON ASIA, 1964. ASIA CHINA/COM ISRAEL MALAYSIA S/ASIA USA+45 USSR ECO/UNDEV FAM POL/PAR SECT CONSULT NAT/LISM...POLICY SOC 20 CHINJAP. PAGE 137 H2736 PWR DIPLOM B64

STRONG C.F.,HISTORY OF MODERN POLITICAL CONSTITUTIONS. STRUCT INT/ORG NAT/G LEGIS TEC/DEV DIPLOM INT/TRADE CT/SYS EXEC...METH/COMP T 12/20 UN. PAGE 150 H2999 CONSTN CONCPT B64

THORNTON T.P.,THE THIRD WORLD IN SOVIET PERSPECTIVE: STUDIES BY SOVIET WRITERS ON THE DEVELOPING AREAS. AFR L/A+17C S/ASIA STRATA AGRI INDUS MARKET NAT/G POL/PAR ECO/TAC COLONIAL PERCEPT PWR WEALTH...MARXIST STAT CHARTS WORK MARX/KARL 20. PAGE 155 H3090 ECO/UNDEV ACT/RES USSR DIPLOM B64

TILMAN R.O.,BUREAUCRATIC TRANSITION IN MALAYA. MALAYSIA S/ASIA UK NAT/G EX/STRUC DIPLOM...CHARTS BIBLIOG 20. PAGE 155 H3098 ADMIN COLONIAL SOVEREIGN EFFICIENCY B64

TURNER M.C.,LIBROS EN VENTA EN HISPANOAMERICA Y ESPANA. SPAIN LAW CONSTN CULTURE ADMIN LEAD...HUM SOC 20. PAGE 157 H3141 BIBLIOG L/A+17C NAT/G DIPLOM B64

UNESCO,WORLD COMMUNICATIONS: PRESS, RADIO, TELEVISION, FILM (4TH ED.). WOR+45 DIPLOM TV PEACE ...NAT/COMP SOC/INTEG 20 FILM. PAGE 158 H3163 COM/IND EDU/PROP PRESS TEC/DEV B64

URQUIDI V.L.,THE CHALLENGE OF DEVELOPMENT IN LATIN AMERICA. L/A+17C FINAN INT/ORG TEC/DEV DIPLOM INT/TRADE PRICE REGION PRODUC...CHARTS 20. PAGE 159 H3175 ECO/UNDEV ECO/TAC NAT/G TREND

B64
US HOUSE COMM BANKING-CURR,INTERNATIONAL DEVELOPMENT ASSOCIATION ACT AMENDMENT. CHINA/COM USA+45 USSR FINAN FORCES LEGIS DIPLOM CONFER EFFICIENCY...CHARTS GOV/COMP 20 PRESIDENT CONGRESS INTL/DEV. PAGE 160 H3196
BAL/PAY FOR/AID RECORD ECO/TAC

B64
VECCHIO G.D.,L'ETAT ET LE DROIT. ITALY CONSTN EX/STRUC LEGIS DIPLOM CT/SYS...JURID 20 UN. PAGE 162 H3238
NAT/G SOVEREIGN CONCPT INT/LAW

B64
VOELKMANN K.,HERRSCHER VON MORGEN? BAL/PWR COLONIAL NEUTRAL REGION RACE/REL ALL/VALS SOVEREIGN...RECORD 20 COLD/WAR THIRD/WRLD. PAGE 163 H3259
DIPLOM ECO/UNDEV CONTROL NAT/COMP

B64
WALLBANK T.W.,DOCUMENTS ON MODERN AFRICA. NAT/G COLONIAL GP/REL ATTIT PWR...BIBLIOG 19/20. PAGE 165 H3294
AFR NAT/LISM ECO/UNDEV DIPLOM

B64
WHITE D.S.,SEEDS OF DISCORD. EUR+WWI FRANCE NAT/G VOL/ASSN FORCES DIPLOM DOMIN NAT/LISM DISPL RIGID/FLEX PWR...RECORD INT BIOG 20 DEGAULLE/C ROOSEVLT/F CHURCHLL/W HULL. PAGE 167 H3347
TOP/EX ATTIT

B64
WILCOX W.A.,INDIA, PAKISTAN AND THE RISE OF CHINA. ASIA BURMA CEYLON CHINA/COM INDIA PAKISTAN S/ASIA NAT/G VOL/ASSN FORCES TOP/EX ACT/RES DOMIN REGION RIGID/FLEX ORD/FREE...POLICY GEN/LAWS COLD/WAR 20. PAGE 168 H3362
CULTURE ATTIT DIPLOM

B64
WRIGHT Q.,A STUDY OF WAR. LAW NAT/G PROB/SOLV BAL/PWR NAT/LISM PEACE ATTIT SOVEREIGN...CENSUS SOC/INTEG. PAGE 171 H3421
WAR CONCPT DIPLOM CONTROL

L64
MACKINTOSH J.P.,"NIGERIA'S EXTERNAL AFFAIRS." UK CULTURE ECO/UNDEV NAT/G VOL/ASSN EDU/PROP LEGIT ADMIN ATTIT ORD/FREE PWR 20. PAGE 100 H2002
AFR DIPLOM NIGERIA

S64
"FURTHER READING." INDIA PAKISTAN SECT WAR PEACE ATTIT...POLICY 20. PAGE 2 H0044
BIBLIOG GP/REL DIPLOM NAT/G

S64
BARIETY J.,"LA POLITIQUE EXTERIEURE ALLEMANDE DANS L'HIVER 1939-1940." COM FINLAND GERMANY ISLAM ITALY USSR NAT/G FORCES ECO/TAC DOMIN EDU/PROP COERCE WAR PWR WEALTH...HIST/WRIT NAZI TOT/POP VAL/FREE 20. PAGE 11 H0216
EUR+WWI DIPLOM

S64
CROZIER B.,"POUVOIR ET ORGANISATION." SOCIETY NAT/G DOMIN...PSY SOC CONCPT TOT/POP VAL/FREE 20. PAGE 36 H0714
PERSON PWR DIPLOM

S64
DE GAULLE C.,"FRENCH WORLD VIEW." AFR ASIA CHINA/COM EUR+WWI ISLAM ECO/UNDEV INT/ORG NAT/G VOL/ASSN ACT/RES DIPLOM ECO/TAC EDU/PROP ATTIT DRIVE WEALTH 20. PAGE 37 H0751
TOP/EX PWR FOR/AID FRANCE

S64
ENNIS T.E.,"VIETNAM: LAND WITHOUT LAUGHTER." S/ASIA VIETNAM VIETNAM/S INTELL SOCIETY SECT FORCES DIPLOM LEGIT COERCE WAR ATTIT RIGID/FLEX ORD/FREE COLD/WAR 20. PAGE 46 H0929
NAT/G TOP/EX GUERRILLA

S64
HORECKY P.L.,"LIBRARY OF CONGRESS PUBLICATIONS IN AID OF USSR AND EAST EUROPEAN RESEARCH." BULGARIA CZECHOSLVK POLAND USSR YUGOSLAVIA NAT/G POL/PAR DIPLOM ADMIN GOV/REL...CLASSIF 20. PAGE 73 H1468
BIBLIOG/A COM MARXISM

S64
LERNER W.,"THE HISTORICAL ORIGINS OF THE SOVIET DOCTRINE OF PEACEFUL COEXISTENCE." COM USSR INT/ORG NAT/G VOL/ASSN PLAN PEACE ATTIT RIGID/FLEX PWR MARXISM...TIME/SEQ COLD/WAR 20. PAGE 95 H1891
EDU/PROP DIPLOM

S64
LOW D.A.,"LION RAMPANT." EUR+WWI MOD/EUR S/ASIA ECO/UNDEV NAT/G FORCES TEC/DEV ECO/TAC LEGIT ADMIN COLONIAL COERCE ORD/FREE RESPECT 19/20. PAGE 99 H1972
AFR DOMIN DIPLOM UK

S64
MARTELLI G.,"PORTUGAL AND THE UNITED NATIONS." AFR EUR+WWI ELITES INT/ORG NAT/G PROVS PLAN DIPLOM ECO/TAC DOMIN COLONIAL RIGID/FLEX MORAL ORD/FREE PWR WEALTH...MYTH UN 20. PAGE 103 H2060
ATTIT PORTUGAL

S64
MOZINGO D.P.,"CHINA'S RELATIONS WITH HER ASIAN NEIGHBORS." ASIA CHINA/COM S/ASIA VIETNAM NAT/G DELIB/GP FORCES CREATE DOMIN EDU/PROP REV RIGID/FLEX PWR...TIME/SEQ GEN/LAWS COLD/WAR 20. PAGE 114 H2277
VOL/ASSN POLICY DIPLOM

S64
REISS I.,"LE DECLENCHEMENT DE LA PREMIERE GUERRE MONDIALE." GERMANY RUSSIA NAT/G FORCES DOMIN EDU/PROP COERCE RIGID/FLEX PWR SOVEREIGN...RELATIV HIST/WRIT TOT/POP AUST/HUNG SERBIA 20. PAGE 131 H2612
MOD/EUR BAL/PWR DIPLOM WAR

S64
SAYEED K.,"PATHAN REGIONALISM." ISLAM PAKISTAN S/ASIA CULTURE SOCIETY NAT/G NEIGH DIPLOM LEGIT COERCE CHOOSE ATTIT DISPL PERCEPT ALL/VALS SOVEREIGN...POLICY RELATIV SOC TIME/SEQ TOT/POP 20. PAGE 138 H2761
SECT NAT/LISM REGION

S64
SCHEFFLER H.W.,"THE GENESIS AND REPRESSION OF CONFLICT: CHOISEUL ISLAND." S/ASIA LOC/G NAT/G FORCES LEGIS DIPLOM DOMIN LEGIT EXEC CHOOSE ATTIT RESPECT SKILL...POLICY JURID OBS TREND GEN/METH 20. PAGE 139 H2781
PWR COERCE WAR

S64
SMYTHE H.H.,"NEHRU AND INDIAN FOREIGN POLICY." S/ASIA ECO/UNDEV NAT/G POL/PAR CONSULT PLAN DIPLOM NEUTRAL COERCE ATTIT DRIVE PERSON MORAL ORD/FREE RESPECT...GEOG CONCPT TIME/SEQ TREND GEN/LAWS 20 NEHRU/J. PAGE 146 H2922
TOP/EX BIOG INDIA

S64
TOYNBEE A.,"BRITAIN AND THE ARABS: THE NEED FOR A NEW START." NAT/G CREATE COLONIAL ATTIT RIGID/FLEX MORAL PWR...POLICY HIST/WRIT 20. PAGE 156 H3124
ISLAM ECO/TAC DIPLOM UK

S64
VANDENBOSCH A.,"POWER BALANCE IN INDONESIA." S/ASIA USSR NAT/G TOP/EX BAL/PWR DOMIN NEUTRAL ORD/FREE PWR...POLICY TIME/SEQ GEN/LAWS 20 SUKARNO/A. PAGE 162 H3233
FORCES TREND DIPLOM INDONESIA

S64
ZARTMAN I.W.,"LES RELATIONS ENTRE LA FRANCE ET L'ALGERIA DEPUIS LES ACCORDS D'EVIAN." EUR+WWI FUT ISLAM CULTURE AGRI EXTR/IND FINAN INDUS POL/PAR DIPLOM ECO/TAC FOR/AID PEACE ATTIT DRIVE ALL/VALS ...TIME/SEQ VAL/FREE 20. PAGE 172 H3450
ECO/UNDEV ALGERIA FRANCE

B65
ADENAUER K.,MEMOIRS 1945-53. EUR+WWI GERMANY/W ECO/DEV CHIEF FORCES ECO/TAC WAR GOV/REL PWR SOVEREIGN 20 NATO ADENAUER/K. PAGE 3 H0068
BIOG DIPLOM NAT/G PERS/REL

B65
ADENAUER K.,MEINE ERINNERUNGEN, 1945-53 (VOL. I), 1953-55 (VOL. II). EUR+WWI GERMANY CHIEF FORCES PROB/SOLV DIPLOM ARMS/CONT INGP/REL PEACE SOVEREIGN ...OBS/ENVIR RECORD 20. PAGE 3 H0069
NAT/G BIOG SELF/OBS

B65
AIR UNIVERSITY LIBRARY,LATIN AMERICA, SELECTED REFERENCES. ECO/UNDEV FORCES EDU/PROP MARXISM 20 OAS. PAGE 4 H0084
BIBLIOG L/A+17C NAT/G DIPLOM

B65
AIYAR S.P.,STUDIES IN INDIAN DEMOCRACY. INDIA STRATA ECO/UNDEV LABOR POL/PAR LEGIS DIPLOM LOBBY REGION CHOOSE ATTIT SOCISM...ANTHOL 20. PAGE 4 H0086
ORD/FREE REPRESENT ADMIN NAT/G

B65
BLITZ L.F.,THE POLITICS AND ADMINISTRATION OF NIGERIAN GOVERNMENT. NIGER CULTURE LOC/G LEGIS DIPLOM COLONIAL CT/SYS SOVEREIGN...GEOG SOC ANTHOL 20. PAGE 18 H0357
NAT/G GOV/REL POL/PAR

B65
BRIDGMAN J.,GERMAN AFRICA: A SELECT ANNOTATED BIBLIOGRAPHY. AFR AGRI DIPLOM REPAR WAR FASCISM 20. PAGE 21 H0414
BIBLIOG/A COLONIAL NAT/G EDU/PROP

B65
BROCK C.,A GUIDE TO LIBRARY RESOURCES FOR POLITICAL SCIENCE STUDENTS AT THE UNIVERSITY OF NORTH CAROLINA (PAMPHLET). USA+45 WOR+45 PROVS ATTIT MARXISM...POLICY NAT/COMP UN. PAGE 21 H0422
BIBLIOG/A DIPLOM NAT/G INT/ORG

B65
CALLEO D.P.,EUROPE'S FUTURE: THE GRAND ALTERNATIVES. UK INT/ORG DIPLOM PWR SOVEREIGN ...CONCPT IDEA/COMP NAT/COMP BIBLIOG 20 EEC EUROPE DEGAULLE/C NATO. PAGE 25 H0506
FUT EUR+WWI FEDERAL NAT/LISM

B65
CAMERON W.J.,NEW ZEALAND. NEW/ZEALND S/ASIA DIPLOM INT/TRADE WRITING COLONIAL PARL/PROC...GEOG CMN/WLTH. PAGE 26 H0513
SOCIETY GP/REL STRUCT

B65
CARTER G.M.,GOVERNMENT AND POLITICS IN THE TWENTIETH CENTURY (REV. ED.). WOR+45 NAT/G POL/PAR LEGIS DIPLOM LEAD PARL/PROC CHOOSE TOTALISM 20. PAGE 27 H0549
GOV/COMP ECO/UNDEV ALL/IDEOS ECO/DEV

B65
CHANDA A.,FEDERALISM IN INDIA. INDIA UK ELITES FINAN NAT/G POL/PAR EX/STRUC LEGIS DIPLOM TAX GOV/REL POPULISM...POLICY 20. PAGE 28 H0572
CONSTN CENTRAL FEDERAL

B65
CHUNG Y.S.,KOREA: A SELECTED BIBLIOGRAPHY 1959-1963. ASIA KOREA NAT/G DIPLOM 20. PAGE 30 H0601
BIBLIOG/A SOC

B65
COX R.H.,THE STATE IN INTERNATIONAL RELATIONS. INT/ORG DIPLOM REV WAR PEACE MARXISM...CONCPT
SOVEREIGN NAT/G

GOV/COMP. PAGE 34 H0690 FASCISM ORD/FREE

B65
CRABB C.V. JR.,THE ELEPHANTS AND THE GRASS* A STUDY OF NONALIGNMENT. AFR ASIA INDIA S/ASIA USA+45 USSR BAL/PWR NEUTRAL ATTIT...TREND NAT/COMP COLD/WAR. PAGE 34 H0691 ECO/UNDEV DIPLOM CONCPT

B65
FAGG J.E.,CUBA, HAITI, AND THE DOMINICAN REPUBLIC. CUBA DOMIN/REP HAITI L/A+17C NAT/G DIPLOM ECO/TAC DOMIN CHOOSE AUTHORIT ROLE SOVEREIGN POPULISM 17/20. PAGE 48 H0959 COLONIAL ECO/UNDEV REV GOV/COMP

B65
FORM W.H.,INDUSTRIAL RELATIONS AND SOCIAL CHANGE IN LATIN AMERICA. L/A+17C AGRI LABOR NAT/G PLAN PROB/SOLV DIPLOM...MGT SOC ANTHOL BIBLIOG/A METH 20. PAGE 52 H1038 INDUS GP/REL NAT/COMP ECO/UNDEV

B65
GEORGE M.,THE WARPED VISION. EUR+WWI UK NAT/G POL/PAR LEGIS PARL/PROC SANCTION COERCE WAR GOV/REL PEACE RESPECT 20 CONSRV/PAR. PAGE 56 H1113 LEAD ATTIT DIPLOM POLICY

B65
GOULD J.,PENGUIN SURVEY OF THE SOCIAL SCIENCES* 1965. CULTURE SOCIETY R+D FAM KIN MUNIC ACT/RES DIPLOM SKILL. PAGE 59 H1186 SOC PHIL/SCI USSR UK

B65
GRAHAM G.S.,THE POLITICS OF NAVAL SUPREMACY; STUDIES IN BRITISH MARITIME ASCENDANCY. UK SEA NAT/G BAL/PWR LEAD WAR WEAPON PEACE...POLICY 18/19 COMMONWLTH. PAGE 60 H1191 FORCES PWR COLONIAL DIPLOM

B65
GRETTON P.,MARITIME STRATEGY - A STUDY OF DEFENSE PROBLEMS. ASIA UK USSR DIPLOM COERCE DETER NUC/PWR WEAPON...CONCPT NAT/COMP 20. PAGE 60 H1211 FORCES PLAN WAR SEA

B65
GRIMAL H.,HISTOIRE DU COMMONWEALTH BRITANNIQUE. UK FINAN DOMIN ATTIT ORD/FREE...T 15/20 CMN/WLTH. PAGE 61 H1226 NAT/G COLONIAL DIPLOM INT/TRADE

B65
HAEFELE E.T.,GOVERNMENT CONTROLS ON TRANSPORT. AFR RHODESIA TANZANIA DIPLOM ECO/TAC TARIFFS PRICE ADJUD CONTROL REGION EFFICIENCY...POLICY 20 CONGO. PAGE 64 H1274 ECO/UNDEV DIST/IND FINAN NAT/G

B65
HARMON R.B.,POLITICAL SCIENCE: A BIBLIOGRAPHICAL GUIDE TO THE LITERATURE. WOR+45 WOR-45 R+D INT/ORG LOC/G NAT/G DIPLOM ADMIN...CONCPT METH. PAGE 67 H1334 BIBLIOG POL/PAR LAW GOV/COMP

B65
HART B.H.L.,THE MEMOIRS OF CAPTAIN LIDDELL HART (VOL. I). UK NAT/G PLAN TEC/DEV DIPLOM ADMIN WEAPON GOV/REL PERS/REL ATTIT PWR FASCISM...POLICY 20. PAGE 67 H1348 FORCES BIOG LEAD WAR

B65
HISPANIC SOCIETY OF AMERICA,CATALOGUE (10 VOLS.). PORTUGAL PRE/AMER SPAIN NAT/G ADMIN...POLICY SOC 15/20. PAGE 71 H1426 BIBLIOG L/A+17C COLONIAL DIPLOM

B65
KIRKWOOD K.,BRITAIN AND AFRICA. AFR UK ECO/UNDEV ECO/TAC WAR NAT/LISM SOVEREIGN 19/20. PAGE 86 H1725 NAT/G DIPLOM POLICY COLONIAL

B65
KOUSOULAS D.G.,REVOLUTION AND DEFEAT; THE STORY OF THE GREEK COMMUNIST PARTY. GREECE INT/ORG EX/STRUC DIPLOM FOR/AID EDU/PROP PARL/PROC ADJUST ATTIT 20 COM/PARTY. PAGE 88 H1759 REV MARXISM POL/PAR ORD/FREE

B65
LARUS J.,COMPARATIVE WORLD POLITICS. ASIA INDIA WOR+45 WOR-45 BAL/PWR WAR PEACE RATIONAL MORAL PWR ...REALPOL INT/LAW MUSLIM. PAGE 91 H1825 GOV/COMP IDEA/COMP DIPLOM NAT/COMP

B65
LEWIS W.A.,POLITICS IN WEST AFRICA. AFR BAL/PWR DIPLOM REPRESENT...POLICY 20. PAGE 96 H1916 POL/PAR ELITES NAT/G ECO/UNDEV

B65
MCSHERRY J.E.,RUSSIA AND THE UNITED STATES UNDER EISENHOWER, KHRUSHCHEV, AND KENNEDY. USSR EX/STRUC TOP/EX PRESS WAR...POLICY TREND 20. PAGE 108 H2150 DIPLOM CHIEF NAT/G PEACE

B65
MEHROTRA S.R.,INDIA AND THE COMMONWEALTH 1885-1929. INDIA UK INT/ORG VOL/ASSN GP/REL ATTIT...POLICY BIBLIOG 19/20 CMN/WLTH. PAGE 108 H2163 DIPLOM NAT/G POL/PAR NAT/LISM

B65
MENON K.P.S.,MANY WORLDS. INDIA BAL/PWR CAP/ISM COLONIAL REV ORD/FREE PWR MARXISM...POLICY 20 COLD/WAR. PAGE 109 H2176 BIOG DIPLOM NAT/G

B65
MERKL P.H.,GERMANY: YESTERDAY AND TOMORROW. GERMANY POL/PAR PLAN DIPLOM LEAD FEDERAL 19/20. PAGE 109 H2181 NAT/G FUT

B65
NATIONAL BOOK CENTRE PAKISTAN,BOOKS ON PAKISTAN: A BIBLIOGRAPHY. PAKISTAN CULTURE DIPLOM ADMIN ATTIT ...MAJORIT SOC CONCPT 20. PAGE 116 H2319 BIBLIOG CONSTN S/ASIA NAT/G

B65
NEWBURY C.W.,BRITISH POLICY TOWARDS WEST AFRICA: SELECT DOCUMENTS 1786-1874. AFR UK INT/TRADE DOMIN ADMIN COLONIAL CT/SYS COERCE ORD/FREE...BIBLIOG/A 18/19. PAGE 117 H2345 DIPLOM POLICY NAT/G WRITING

B65
NYE J.S. JR.,PAN-AFRICANISM AND EAST AFRICAN INTEGRATION. TANZANIA UGANDA STRUCT ECO/UNDEV NAT/G DIPLOM FEDERAL NAT/LISM...STAT SOC/EXP BIBLIOG EEC OAU. PAGE 119 H2382 REGION ATTIT GEN/LAWS AFR

B65
O'BRIEN W.V.,THE NEW NATIONS IN INTERNATIONAL LAW AND DIPLOMACY* THE YEAR BOOK OF WORLD POLITY* VOLUME III. USA+45 ECO/UNDEV INT/ORG FORCES DIPLOM COLONIAL NEUTRAL REV NAT/LISM ATTIT RESPECT. PAGE 119 H2385 INT/LAW CULTURE SOVEREIGN ANTHOL

B65
O'CONNELL M.R.,IRISH POLITICS AND SOCIAL CONFLICT IN THE AGE OF THE AMERICAN REVOLUTION. FRANCE IRELAND MOD/EUR STRATA SECT LEGIS DIPLOM INT/TRADE DOMIN REV WAR...BIBLIOG 18 PARLIAMENT. PAGE 119 H2387 CATHISM ATTIT NAT/G DELIB/GP

B65
OGILVY-WEBB M.,THE GOVERNMENT EXPLAINS: A STUDY OF THE INFORMATION SERVICES. UK DELIB/GP LEGIS WORKER BUDGET DIPLOM 20. PAGE 121 H2409 EDU/PROP ATTIT NAT/G ADMIN

B65
PADELFORD N.,THE UNITED NATIONS IN THE BALANCE* ACCOMPLISHMENTS AND PROSPECTS. NAT/G VOL/ASSN DIPLOM ADMIN COLONIAL CT/SYS REGION WAR ORD/FREE ...ANTHOL UN. PAGE 122 H2437 INT/ORG CONTROL

B65
POLK W.R.,THE UNITED STATES AND THE ARAB WORLD. USA+45 ECO/UNDEV EXTR/IND SECT WAR NAT/LISM ATTIT ...NAT/COMP COLD/WAR. PAGE 127 H2535 ISLAM REGION CULTURE DIPLOM

B65
PYLEE M.V.,CONSTITUTIONAL GOVERNMENT IN INDIA (2ND REV. ED.). INDIA POL/PAR EX/STRUC DIPLOM COLONIAL CT/SYS PARL/PROC PRIVIL...JURID 16/20. PAGE 128 H2569 CONSTN NAT/G PROVS FEDERAL

B65
QURESHI I.H.,THE STRUGGLE FOR PAKISTAN. INDIA PAKISTAN UK CULTURE LEGIS DIPLOM EDU/PROP COLONIAL ATTIT SOVEREIGN 19/20 MUSLIM. PAGE 129 H2576 GP/REL RACE/REL WAR SECT

B65
RANDALL F.B.,STALIN'S RUSSIA. USSR STRUCT AGRI NAT/G PLAN DIPLOM WAR TOTALISM MARXISM...BIBLIOG/A 19/20 STALIN/J. PAGE 129 H2590 BIOG INDUS ECO/DEV

B65
RIVLIN B.,THE CONTEMPORARY MIDDLE EAST* TRADITION AND INNOVATION. CULTURE SOCIETY ECO/UNDEV NAT/G TREND. PAGE 132 H2636 ANTHOL ISLAM NAT/LISM DIPLOM

B65
RODRIGUEZ M.,CENTRAL AMERICA. COSTA/RICA GUATEMALA L/A+17C NICARAGUA DIPLOM COLONIAL REGION NAT/LISM ALL/IDEOS SOCISM...MAJORIT TIME/SEQ BIBLIOG 19/20. PAGE 133 H2656 CULTURE NAT/COMP NAT/G ECO/UNDEV

B65
ROMEIN J.,THE ASIAN CENTURY. ASIA COM S/ASIA DIPLOM COLONIAL TIME 20. PAGE 133 H2666 REV NAT/LISM CULTURE MARXISM

B65
ROTBERG R.I.,A POLITICAL HISTORY OF TROPICAL AFRICA. EX/STRUC DIPLOM INT/TRADE DOMIN ADMIN RACE/REL NAT/LISM PWR SOVEREIGN...GEOG TIME/SEQ BIBLIOG 1/20. PAGE 135 H2692 AFR CULTURE COLONIAL

B65
RUBINSTEIN A.Z.,THE CHALLENGE OF POLITICS: IDEAS AND ISSUES (2ND ED.). UNIV ELITES SOCIETY EX/STRUC BAL/PWR PARL/PROC AUTHORIT...DECISION ANTHOL 20. PAGE 136 H2709 NAT/G DIPLOM GP/REL ORD/FREE

B65
SABLE M.H.,MASTER DIRECTORY FOR LATIN AMERICA. AGRI COM/IND FINAN R+D ACADEM LABOR NAT/G POL/PAR VOL/ASSN INT/TRADE EDU/PROP 20. PAGE 136 H2728 INDEX L/A+17C INT/ORG DIPLOM

B65
SALVADORI M.,ITALY. AUSTRIA FRANCE GERMANY ITALY SPAIN CULTURE NAT/G POL/PAR DIPLOM WAR FASCISM LAISSEZ MARXISM...TIME/SEQ CHARTS BIBLIOG/A. PAGE 137 H2744 NAT/LISM CATHISM SOCIETY

B65
SHRIMALI K.L.,EDUCATION IN CHANGING INDIA. INDIA CULTURE DIPLOM FOR/AID GP/REL RACE/REL ATTIT SOC/INTEG 20 UNESCO CMN/WLTH. PAGE 143 H2866
EDU/PROP PROF/ORG ACADEM

B65
SMITH R.M.,CAMBODIA'S FOREIGN POLICY. ECO/UNDEV NAT/G NEUTRAL ORD/FREE COLD/WAR VAL/FREE. PAGE 146 H2917
S/ASIA CAMBODIA DIPLOM

B65
UN,SPACE ACTIVITIES AND RESOURCES: REVIEW OF UNITED NATION'S NATIONAL AND INTERNATIONAL PROGRAMS. INT/ORG LABOR PLAN TEC/DEV DIPLOM EFFICIENCY HEALTH ...GOV/COMP 20 UN. PAGE 158 H3155
SPACE NUC/PWR FOR/AID PEACE

B65
UPTON A.F.,FINLAND IN CRISIS 1940-1941. NAT/G FORCES DIPLOM COERCE...DECISION GEOG. PAGE 159 H3173
FINLAND GERMANY USSR WAR

B65
US DEPARTMENT OF DEFENSE,US SECURITY ARMS CONTROL, AND DISARMAMENT 1961-1965 (PAMPHLET). CHINA/COM COM GERMANY/W ISRAEL SPACE USA+45 USSR WOR+45 FORCES EDU/PROP DETER EQUILIB PEACE ALL/VALS...GOV/COMP 20 NATO. PAGE 159 H3183
BIBLIOG/A ARMS/CONT NUC/PWR DIPLOM

B65
US LIBRARY OF CONGRESS,RARE BOOKS DIVISION: GUIDE TO ITS COLLECTION AND SERVICES. LOC/G SECT WAR. PAGE 161 H3214
BIBLIOG/A NAT/G DIPLOM

B65
VAN DEN BERGHE P.L.,AFRICA: SOCIAL PROBLEMS OF CHANGE AND CONFLICT. ELITES STRATA ECO/UNDEV KIN MUNIC DIPLOM GP/REL RACE/REL NAT/LISM...ANTHOL BIBLIOG 20. PAGE 161 H3228
SOC CULTURE AFR STRUCT

B65
VON STACKELBERG K.,ALLE KRETER LUGEN VORURTEILE UBER MENSCHEN UND VOLKER. DIPLOM DOMIN RUMOR NAT/LISM PERSON KNOWL...SOC QU BIBLIOG 20. PAGE 164 H3277
NAT/COMP ATTIT EDU/PROP SAMP

B65
WALKER A.A.,THE RHODESIAS AND NYASALAND: A GUIDE TO OFFICIAL PUBLICATIONS. RHODESIA UK OP/RES PLAN PROB/SOLV DIPLOM...POLICY SOC CON/ANAL 19/20 NYASALAND. PAGE 164 H3291
BIBLIOG NAT/G COLONIAL AFR

B65
WILLIAMSON J.A.,GREAT BRITAIN AND THE COMMONWEALTH. UK DOMIN COLONIAL INGP/REL...POLICY 18/20 CMN/WLTH. PAGE 168 H3370
NAT/G DIPLOM INT/ORG SOVEREIGN

B65
WINT G.,ASIA: A HANDBOOK. ASIA COM INDIA USSR CULTURE INTELL NAT/G...GEOG STAT CENSUS NAT/COMP WORSHIP 20 TREATY CHINJAP. PAGE 169 H3387
DIPLOM SOC

B65
WOLPERT S.,INDIA. INDIA UK ECO/UNDEV DIPLOM GP/REL WEALTH 20 NEHRU/J. PAGE 170 H3405
CULTURE COLONIAL NAT/LISM SECT

B65
WUORINEN J.H.,SCANDINAVIA. DENMARK FINLAND ICELAND NORWAY SWEDEN SOCIETY AGRI INDUS DELIB/GP DIPLOM INT/TRADE NEUTRAL...GEOG CHARTS BIBLIOG TREATY. PAGE 171 H3428
NAT/G POL/PAR TREND POLICY

L65
LASSWELL H.D.,"THE POLICY SCIENCES OF DEVELOPMENT." CULTURE SOCIETY EX/STRUC CREATE ADMIN ATTIT KNOWL ...SOC CONCPT SIMUL GEN/METH. PAGE 92 H1835
PWR METH/CNCPT DIPLOM

L65
MATTHEWS D.G.,"A CURRENT BIBLIOGRAPHY ON ETHIOPIAN AFFAIRS: A SELECT BIBLIOGRAPHY FROM 1950-1964." ETHIOPIA LAW CULTURE ECO/UNDEV INDUS LABOR SECT FORCES DIPLOM CIVMIL/REL RACE/REL...LING STAT 20. PAGE 105 H2093
BIBLIOG/A ADMIN POL/PAR NAT/G

L65
MATTHEWS D.G.,"A CURRENT BIBLIOGRAPHY ON SUDANESE AFFAIRS; A SELECT BIBLIOGRAPHY FROM 1960-1964." SUDAN LAW CULTURE AGRI FINAN INDUS LABOR POL/PAR TEC/DEV FOR/AID RACE/REL LITERACY...LING 20. PAGE 105 H2094
BIBLIOG ECO/UNDEV NAT/G DIPLOM

S65
"FURTHER READING." INDIA ADMIN COLONIAL WAR GOV/REL ATTIT 20. PAGE 2 H0046
BIBLIOG DIPLOM NAT/G POLICY

S65
BIRNBAUM K.,"SWEDEN'S NUCLEAR POLICY." WOR+45 POL/PAR CREATE TEC/DEV NEUTRAL RISK WAR ORD/FREE ...DECISION IDEA/COMP NAT/COMP TIME. PAGE 17 H0343
SWEDEN NUC/PWR DIPLOM ARMS/CONT

S65
GANGAL S.C.,"SURVEY OF RECENT RESEARCH: INDIA AND THE COMMONWEALTH" INDIA UK NAT/G INT/TRADE PARTIC GOV/REL ROLE 20 CMN/WLTH. PAGE 55 H1095
BIBLIOG POLICY REGION DIPLOM

S65
HUGHES T.L.,"SCHOLARS AND FOREIGN POLICY* VARIETIES OF RESEARCH EXPERIENCE." COM/IND DIPLOM ADMIN EXEC ROUTINE...MGT OBS CONGRESS PRESIDENT CAMELOT. PAGE 75 H1491
ACT/RES ACADEM CONTROL NAT/G

S65
JENSEN L.,"MILITARY CAPABILITIES AND BARGAINING BEHAVIOR." USA+45 USSR ARMS/CONT DETER COST ATTIT ...METH/CNCPT STAT SYS/QU CON/ANAL CHARTS NAT/COMP. PAGE 81 H1614
DIPLOM DRIVE PWR STERTYP

S65
LAULICHT J.,"PUBLIC OPINION AND FOREIGN POLICY DECISIONS." CANADA ELITES NAT/G FOR/AID LEAD NUC/PWR PERCEPT...INT QU CHARTS UN COLD/WAR. PAGE 92 H1839
DIPLOM ATTIT CON/ANAL SAMP

S65
LEVI W.,"THE CONCEPT OF INTEGRATION IN RESEARCH ON PEACE." NAT/G VOL/ASSN DIPLOM TASK ADJUST NAT/LISM PEACE DRIVE LOVE...PSY NET/THEORY GEN/LAWS. PAGE 95 H1897
CONCPT IDEA/COMP INT/ORG CENTRAL

S65
MARK M.,"MUST WE FIGHT SOCIAL REVOLUTIONS OF THE LEFT?" L/A+17C USA+45 ECO/UNDEV DIPLOM ADJUST PERCEPT...IDEA/COMP NAT/COMP. PAGE 103 H2053
NAT/LISM REV MARXISM CREATE

S65
PLISCHKE E.,"INTEGRATING BERLIN AND THE FEDERAL REPUBLIC OF GERMANY." EUR+WWI GERMANY/W LEGIS TEC/DEV DOMIN ORD/FREE PWR...JURID 20 BERLIN. PAGE 126 H2528
DIPLOM NAT/G MUNIC

S65
PRABHAKAR P.,"SURVEY OF RESEARCH AND SOURCE MATERIALS; THE SINO-INDIAN BORDER DISPUTE." CHINA/COM INDIA LAW NAT/G PLAN BAL/PWR WAR...POLICY 20 COLD/WAR. PAGE 128 H2553
BIBLIOG ASIA S/ASIA DIPLOM

S65
TRISKA J.F.,"SOVIET-AMERICAN RELATIONS* A MULTIPLE SYMMETRY MODEL." USA+45 USSR ACADEM ACT/RES EDU/PROP COERCE PERCEPT...NET/THEORY CHARTS NAT/COMP GEN/LAWS COLD/WAR. PAGE 157 H3132
SIMUL EQUILIB DIPLOM

S65
WATT D.C.,"RESTRICTIONS ON RESEARCH* THE FIFTY-YEAR RULE AND BRITISH FOREIGN POLICY." ACADEM PERCEPT ...HIST/WRIT NAT/COMP TIME. PAGE 166 H3315
UK USA+45 DIPLOM

S65
WEDGE B.,"PSYCHOLOGICAL FACTORS IN SOVIET DISARMAMENT NEGOTIATION." USA+45 CONFER ATTIT PERCEPT PERSON...PSY NAT/COMP. PAGE 166 H3324
USSR DIPLOM ARMS/CONT

S65
WRIGHT Q.,"THE ESCALATION OF INTERNATIONAL CONFLICTS." WOR+45 WOR-45 FORCES DIPLOM RISK COST ATTIT ALL/VALS...INT/LAW QUANT STAT NAT/COMP. PAGE 171 H3422
WAR PERCEPT PREDICT MATH

C65
WUORINEN J.H.,"SCANDINAVIA." DENMARK FINLAND ICELAND NORWAY SWEDEN SOCIETY AGRI POL/PAR DELIB/GP DIPLOM INT/TRADE NEUTRAL WAR...CHARTS TREATY 20. PAGE 171 H3427
BIBLIOG NAT/G POLICY

B66
AFRIFA A.A.,THE GHANA COUP. AFR GHANA ELITES NAT/G DIPLOM DOMIN 20 NKRUMAH/K. PAGE 4 H0076
TOP/EX REV FORCES POL/PAR

B66
AIR FORCE ACADEMY ASSEMBLY,CULTURAL AFFAIRS AND FOREIGN RELATIONS. NAT/G VOL/ASSN ALL/VALS. PAGE 4 H0083
CULTURE SOCIETY PERS/REL DIPLOM

B66
AMER ENTERPRISE INST PUB POL,SIGNIFICANT ISSUES IN ECONOMIC AID TO DEVELOPING COUNTRIES. FINAN INT/ORG NAT/G PLAN PROB/SOLV GIVE TASK WEALTH...DECISION 20. PAGE 6 H0119
ECO/UNDEV FOR/AID DIPLOM POLICY

B66
BESSON W.,DIE GROSSEN MACHTE - STRUKTURFRAGEN DER GEGENWARTIGEN WELTPOLITIK. ASIA USSR WOR+45 ATTIT ...IDEA/COMP 20 KENNEDY/JF. PAGE 16 H0321
NAT/COMP DIPLOM STRUCT

B66
BIRMINGHAM D.,TRADE AND CONFLICT IN ANGOLA. PORTUGAL CULTURE FORCES DIPLOM GP/REL PROFIT HABITAT NAT/COMP. PAGE 17 H0341
WAR INT/TRADE ECO/UNDEV COLONIAL

B66
BLACK C.E.,THE DYNAMICS OF MODERNIZATION: A STUDY IN COMPARATIVE HISTORY. STRUCT ECO/DEV ECO/UNDEV NAT/G DIPLOM LEAD REV...PREDICT TIME/SEQ TREND SOC/INTEG 17/20. PAGE 17 H0350
SOCIETY SOC NAT/COMP

B66
BRACKMAN A.C.,SOUTHEAST ASIA'S SECOND FRONT: THE POWER STRUGGLE IN THE MALAY ARCHIPELAGO. CHINA/COM INDONESIA MALAYSIA ECO/UNDEV INT/ORG NAT/G FORCES DIPLOM EDU/PROP REGION COERCE GUERRILLA AUTHORIT POPULISM...MAJORIT 20 KENNEDY/JF SEATO. PAGE 20 H0396
S/ASIA MARXISM REV

B66
BROWN J.F.,THE NEW EASTERN EUROPE. ALBANIA BULGARIA HUNGARY POLAND ROMANIA CULTURE AGRI POL/PAR WAR NAT/LISM MARXISM...CHARTS BIBLIOG 20. PAGE 22 H0444
DIPLOM COM NAT/G ECO/UNDEV

B66
BROWN L.C.,STATE AND SOCIETY IN INDEPENDENT NORTH AFRICA. ALGERIA LIBYA MOROCCO AGRI INDUS INT/ORG POL/PAR SECT PLAN DIPLOM COLONIAL...LING NAT/COMP ANTHOL BIBLIOG 20 TUNIS MUSLIM. PAGE 22 H0446
NAT/G SOCIETY CULTURE ECO/UNDEV

B66
BROWN R.T.,TRANSPORT AND THE ECONOMIC INTEGRATION OF SOUTH AMERICA. L/A+17C ECO/UNDEV NAT/G OP/RES DIPLOM INT/TRADE REGION WEALTH...ECOMETRIC GEOG STAT LAFTA TIME. PAGE 22 H0449
MARKET DIST/IND SIMUL

B66
CANNING HOUSE LIBRARY,AUTHOR AND SUBJECT CATALOGUES OF THE CANNING HOUSE LIBRARY (5 VOLS.). UK CULTURE LEAD...SOC 19/20. PAGE 26 H0520
BIBLIOG L/A+17C NAT/G DIPLOM

B66
COLE A.B.,SOCIALIST PARTIES IN POSTWAR JAPAN. STRATA AGRI LABOR PLAN DIPLOM ECO/TAC AGREE LEAD CHOOSE ATTIT...CHARTS 20 CHINJAP SOC/DEMPAR. PAGE 31 H0620
POL/PAR POLICY SOCISM NAT/G

B66
DAENIKER G.,STRATEGIE DES KLEIN STAATS. SWITZERLND ACT/RES CREATE DIPLOM NEUTRAL DETER WAR WEAPON PWR SOVEREIGN...IDEA/COMP 20 COLD/WAR. PAGE 36 H0730
NUC/PWR PLAN FORCES NAT/G

B66
DEUTSCHER I.,STALIN: A POLITICAL BIOGRAPHY. EUR+WWI USSR POL/PAR FORCES DIPLOM ADMIN LEAD REV WAR TOTALISM PERSON 20 STALIN/J ROOSEVLT/F LENIN/VI HITLER/A. PAGE 40 H0807
BIOG MARXISM TOP/EX PWR

B66
DOUMA J.,BIBLIOGRAPHY ON THE INTERNATIONAL COURT INCLUDING THE PERMANENT COURT, 1918-1964. WOR+45 WOR-45 DELIB/GP WAR PRIVIL...JURID NAT/COMP 20 UN LEAGUE/NAT. PAGE 42 H0844
BIBLIOG/A INT/ORG CT/SYS DIPLOM

B66
DYCK H.V.,WEIMAR GERMANY AND SOVIET RUSSIA 1926-1933. EUR+WWI GERMANY UK USSR ECO/TAC INT/TRADE NEUTRAL WAR ATTIT 20 WEIMAR/REP TREATY. PAGE 44 H0877
DIPLOM GOV/REL POLICY

B66
EDWARDS C.D.,TRADE REGULATIONS OVERSEAS. IRELAND NEW/ZEALND SOUTH/AFR NAT/G CAP/ISM TARIFFS CONTROL ...POLICY JURID 20 EEC CHINJAP. PAGE 45 H0892
INT/TRADE DIPLOM INT/LAW ECO/TAC

B66
EMBREE A.T.,ASIA: A GUIDE TO BASIC BOOKS (PAMPHLET). ECO/UNDEV SECT FORCES DIPLOM ALL/IDEOS ...SOC 20. PAGE 46 H0914
BIBLIOG/A ASIA S/ASIA NAT/G

B66
EPSTEIN F.T.,THE AMERICAN BIBLIOGRAPHY OF RUSSIAN AND EAST EUROPEAN STUDIES FOR 1964. USSR LOC/G NAT/G POL/PAR FORCES ADMIN ARMS/CONT...JURID CONCPT 20 UN. PAGE 47 H0933
BIBLIOG COM MARXISM DIPLOM

B66
FARRELL R.B.,APPROACHES TO COMPARATIVE AND INTERNATIONAL POLITICS. RUSSIA SOCIETY ACADEM GOV/REL GP/REL...METH/CNCPT NET/THEORY GOV/COMP HYPO/EXP SOC/EXP GEN/METH ANTHOL. PAGE 49 H0973
DIPLOM NAT/COMP NAT/G

B66
FARWELL G.,MASK OF ASIA: THE PHILIPPINES. PHILIPPINE SECT DIPLOM ATTIT...SOC RECORD PREDICT BIBLIOG 20. PAGE 49 H0974
S/ASIA CULTURE

B66
FITZGERALD C.P.,THE BIRTH OF COMMUNIST CHINA (2ND ED.). ASIA CHINA/COM STRUCT BAL/PWR DIPLOM ECO/TAC INT/TRADE WEALTH 20. PAGE 51 H1018
REV MARXISM ECO/UNDEV

B66
FRANK E.,LAWMAKERS IN A CHANGING WORLD. FRANCE UK USSR WOR+45 PARTIC EFFICIENCY ROLE ALL/IDEOS ...CHARTS ANTHOL PARLIAMENT 20 UN COLD/WAR. PAGE 52 H1049
GOV/COMP LEGIS NAT/G DIPLOM

B66
FRIEDRICH C.J.,REVOLUTION: NOMOS VIII. NAT/G SOCISM ...OBS TREND IDEA/COMP ANTHOL 18/20. PAGE 54 H1070
REV MARXISM CONCPT DIPLOM

B66
GERARD-LIBOIS J.,KATANGA SECESSION. INT/ORG FORCES DIPLOM ADMIN CONTROL WAR CHOOSE PWR...CHARTS 20 KATANGA TSHOMBE/M UN. PAGE 56 H1114
NAT/G REGION ORD/FREE REV

B66
GLAZER M.,THE FEDERAL GOVERNMENT AND THE UNIVERSITY. CHILE PROB/SOLV DIPLOM GIVE ADMIN WAR ...POLICY SOC 20. PAGE 57 H1140
BIBLIOG/A NAT/G PLAN ACADEM

B66
GORDON B.K.,THE DIMENSIONS OF CONFLICT IN SOUTHEAST ASIA. S/ASIA FORCES ADJUD REGION...CHARTS 20. PAGE 59 H1177
DIPLOM NAT/COMP INT/ORG VOL/ASSN

B66
GRAHAM I.C.C.,PUBLICATIONS OF THE SOCIAL SCIENCE DEPARTMENT, THE RAND CORPORATION, 1948-1966. USSR WOR+45 NAT/G ARMS/CONT DETER WAR NAT/LISM...SOC GOV/COMP. PAGE 60 H1192
BIBLIOG DIPLOM NUC/PWR FORCES

B66
HAMILTON W.B.,A DECADE OF THE COMMONWEALTH, 1955-1964. UK LAW ELITES FINAN FOR/AID CONFER COLONIAL PWR...GEOG CHARTS ANTHOL 20 CMN/WLTH UN. PAGE 65 H1302
INT/ORG INGP/REL DIPLOM NAT/G

B66
HANSON J.W.,EDUCATION AND THE DEVELOPMENT OF NATIONS. DIPLOM TASK ADJUST EFFICIENCY...POLICY ANTHOL 20. PAGE 66 H1322
ECO/UNDEV EDU/PROP NAT/G PLAN

B66
HARMON R.B.,SOURCES AND PROBLEMS OF BIBLIOGRAPHY IN POLITICAL SCIENCE (PAMPHLET). INT/ORG LOC/G MUNIC POL/PAR ADMIN GOV/REL ALL/IDEOS...JURID MGT CONCPT 19/20. PAGE 67 H1335
BIBLIOG DIPLOM INT/LAW NAT/G

B66
HAY P.,FEDERALISM AND SUPRANATIONAL ORGANIZATIONS: PATTERNS FOR NEW LEGAL STRUCTURES. EUR+WWI LAW NAT/G VOL/ASSN DIPLOM PWR...NAT/COMP TREATY EEC. PAGE 68 H1364
SOVEREIGN FEDERAL INT/ORG INT/LAW

B66
HENKYS R.,DEUTSCHLAND UND DIE OSTLICHEN NACHBARN. GERMANY POLAND NAT/G POL/PAR INGP/REL ATTIT 20 MIGRATION. PAGE 70 H1396
GP/REL JURID INT/LAW DIPLOM

B66
HOEVELER H.J.,INTERNATIONALE BEKAMPFUNG DES VERBRECHENS. AUSTRIA SWITZERLND WOR+45 INT/ORG CONTROL BIO/SOC...METH/COMP NAT/COMP 20 MAFIA SCOT/YARD FBI. PAGE 72 H1446
CRIMLGY CRIME DIPLOM INT/LAW

B66
HOLT R.T.,THE POLITICAL BASIS OF ECONOMIC DEVELOPMENT. STRATA STRUCT NAT/G DIPLOM ADMIN...SOC NAT/COMP BIBLIOG 20. PAGE 73 H1458
ECO/TAC GOV/COMP CONSTN EX/STRUC

B66
HOYT E.C.,NATIONAL POLICY AND INTERNATIONAL LAW* CASE STUDIES FROM AMERICAN CANAL POLICY* MONOGRAPH NO. 1 -- 1966-1967. PANAMA UK ELITES BAL/PWR EFFICIENCY...CLASSIF NAT/COMP SOC/EXP COLOMB TREATY. PAGE 74 H1483
INT/LAW USA-45 DIPLOM PWR

B66
INTL CONF ON WORLD POLITICS-5,EASTERN EUROPE IN TRANSITION. EUR+WWI USSR ECO/TAC NAT/LISM ATTIT SOVEREIGN...CHARTS ANTHOL 20 TREATY WARSAW/P. PAGE 78 H1562
COM NAT/COMP MARXISM DIPLOM

B66
JACKSON G.D.,COMINTERN AND PEASANT IN EAST EUROPE 1919-1930. BULGARIA COM CZECHOSLVK EUR+WWI POLAND ROMANIA YUGOSLAVIA STRATA AGRI VOL/ASSN DIPLOM CONTROL CROWD WEALTH...POLICY NAT/COMP 20. PAGE 79 H1575
MARXISM ECO/UNDEV WORKER INT/ORG

B66
KEYES J.G.,A BIBLIOGRAPHY OF WESTERN LANGUAGE PUBLICATIONS CONCERNING NORTH VIETNAM IN THE CORNELL LIBRARY. VIETNAM/N NAT/G FORCES TEC/DEV DIPLOM LEAD RACE/REL...GEOG SOC 20. PAGE 85 H1700
BIBLIOG/A CULTURE ECO/UNDEV S/ASIA

B66
KOMIYA R.,POSTWAR ECONOMIC GROWTH IN JAPAN. ELITES NAT/G EX/STRUC TEC/DEV BUDGET DIPLOM CONTROL BAL/PAY PRODUC...BIBLIOG 20 CHINJAP. PAGE 88 H1754
ECO/DEV POLICY PLAN ADJUST

B66
LEIGH M.B.,CHECK LIST OF HOLDINGS ON BORNEO IN THE CORNELL UNIVERSITY LIBRARIES (PAMPHLET). BORNEO MALAYSIA LAW CONSTN GP/REL SOC. PAGE 93 H1866
BIBLIOG S/ASIA DIPLOM NAT/G

B66
LONDON K.,EASTERN EUROPE IN TRANSITION. CHINA/COM USSR DOMIN COLONIAL CENTRAL RIGID/FLEX PWR...SOC ANTHOL 20. PAGE 98 H1958
SOVEREIGN COM NAT/LISM DIPLOM

B66
MACFARQUHAR R.,CHINA UNDER MAO: POLITICS TAKES COMMAND. CHINA/COM COM AGRI INDUS CHIEF FORCES DIPLOM INT/TRADE EDU/PROP TASK REV ADJUST...ANTHOL 20 MAO. PAGE 100 H1992
ECO/UNDEV TEC/DEV ECO/TAC ADMIN

B66
MARTIN L.W.,DIPLOMACY IN MODERN EUROPEAN HISTORY. EUR+WWI MOD/EUR INT/ORG NAT/G EX/STRUC ROUTINE WAR PEACE TOTALISM PWR 15/20 COLD/WAR EUROPE/W. PAGE 103 H2064
DIPLOM POLICY

B66
MASUR G.,NATIONALISM IN LATIN AMERICA* DIVERSITY AND UNITY. CHRIST-17C PRE/AMER ELITES ECO/UNDEV CREATE DIPLOM INT/TRADE COLONIAL REV SOVEREIGN SOC. PAGE 105 H2089
L/A+17C NAT/LISM CULTURE

B66
MCKAY V.,AFRICAN DIPLOMACY STUDIES IN THE DETERMINANTS OF FOREIGN POLICY. AFR SOUTH/AFR CULTURE NEUTRAL REGION SOVEREIGN...INT/LAW GOV/COMP ANTHOL 20. PAGE 107 H2138
ECO/UNDEV RACE/REL CIVMIL/REL DIPLOM

B66
MERRITT R.L.,COMPARING NATIONS* THE USE OF
NAT/COMP

QUANTITATIVE DATA IN CROSSNATIONAL RESEARCH. ACADEM DIPLOM GP/REL...PHIL/SCI STAT TREND GP/COMP PERS/COMP GEN/METH ANTHOL BIBLIOG INDEX. PAGE 109 H2184 MATH COMPUT/IR QUANT B66

MULLER C.F.J.,A SELECT BIBLIOGRAPHY OF SOUTH AFRICAN HISTORY; A GUIDE FOR HISTORICAL RESEARCH. SOUTH/AFR UK LAW CONSTN SOCIETY STRUCT AGRI SECT DIPLOM COLONIAL LEAD RACE/REL...POLICY 17/20 NEGRO. PAGE 114 H2284 BIBLIOG AFR NAT/G B66

NEUMANN R.G.,THE GOVERNMENT OF THE GERMAN FEDERAL REPUBLIC. EUR+WWI GERMANY/W LOC/G EX/STRUC LEGIS CT/SYS INGP/REL PWR...BIBLIOG 20 ADENAUER/K. PAGE 117 H2336 NAT/G POL/PAR DIPLOM CONSTN B66

NIEDERGANG M.,LA REVOLUTION DE SAINT-DOMINGUE. DOMIN/REP INT/ORG NAT/G CONTROL LEAD GP/REL ORD/FREE MARXISM 20. PAGE 118 H2361 REV FORCES DIPLOM B66

NOEL G.E.,THE NEW BRITAIN AND HAROLD WILSON: INTERIM REPORT, 1966 GENERAL ELECTION. UK POL/PAR CONSULT PROB/SOLV BUDGET DIPLOM ECO/TAC LEAD CHOOSE ATTIT 20 WILSON/H PARLIAMENT. PAGE 118 H2366 BIOG PERSON NAT/G CHIEF B66

PAN S.,VIETNAM CRISIS. ASIA FRANCE USA+45 USA-45 VIETNAM CULTURE SOCIETY INT/ORG ECO/TAC AGREE CONTROL WAR MARXISM 20. PAGE 123 H2454 ECO/UNDEV POLICY DIPLOM NAT/COMP B66

RISTIC D.N.,YUGOSLAVIA'S REVOLUTION OF 1941. EUR+WWI YUGOSLAVIA NAT/G WAR ORD/FREE...RECORD BIBLIOG 20 HITLER/A TREATY. PAGE 132 H2633 REV ATTIT FASCISM DIPLOM B66

ROOS H.,A HISTORY OF MODERN POLAND FROM THE FOUNDATION OF THE STATE IN THE FIRST WORLD WAR TO THE PRESENT DAY. EUR+WWI POLAND INTELL SOCIETY ECO/TAC LEAD REV ATTIT ORD/FREE MARXISM...BIBLIOG 20 WWI PARTITION. PAGE 133 H2669 NAT/G WAR DIPLOM B66

SAKAI R.K.,STUDIES ON ASIA, 1966. CEYLON INDIA USA-45 INDUS POL/PAR DIPLOM ECO/TAC MARXISM ...POLICY 19/20 CHINJAP. PAGE 137 H2738 SECT ECO/UNDEV B66

SCHATTEN F.,COMMUNISM IN AFRICA. AFR GHANA GUINEA MALI CULTURE ECO/UNDEV LABOR SECT ECO/TAC EDU/PROP REV 20. PAGE 139 H2774 COLONIAL NAT/LISM MARXISM DIPLOM B66

SKILLING H.G.,THE GOVERNMENTS OF COMMUNIST EAST EUROPE. COM EUR+WWI ELITES FORCES DIPLOM ECO/TAC CONTROL HABITAT SOCISM...DECISION BIBLIOG 20 EUROPE/E COM/PARTY. PAGE 145 H2895 MARXISM NAT/COMP GP/COMP DOMIN B66

SPEARS E.L.,TWO MEN WHO SAVED FRANCE: PETAIN AND DE GAULLE. FRANCE CONSTN FORCES DIPLOM WAR PERSON 20 WWI PETAIN/HP DEGAULLE/C. PAGE 147 H2942 BIOG LEAD CHIEF NAT/G B66

STADLER K.R.,THE BIRTH OF THE AUSTRIAN REPUBLIC, 1918-1921. AUSTRIA PLAN TASK PEACE...POLICY DECISION 20. PAGE 148 H2966 NAT/G DIPLOM WAR DELIB/GP B66

SWEARINGEN A.R.,SOVIET AND CHINESE COMMUNIST POWER IN THE WORLD TODAY. COM USA+45 ECO/UNDEV CREATE LEAD WAR ADJUST...TREND NAT/COMP ANTHOL COLD/WAR KHRUSH/N. PAGE 151 H3017 USSR ASIA DIPLOM ATTIT B66

THOMPSON J.H.,MODERNIZATION OF THE ARAB WORLD. FUT ISRAEL STRUCT ECO/UNDEV DIPLOM INGP/REL ATTIT ...CENSUS ANTHOL 20 ARABS. PAGE 154 H3082 ADJUST ISLAM PROB/SOLV NAT/COMP B66

THOMPSON J.M.,RUSSIA, BOLSHEVISM, AND THE VERSAILLES PEACE. RUSSIA USSR INT/ORG NAT/G DELIB/GP AGREE REV WAR PWR 20 TREATY VERSAILLES BOLSHEVISM. PAGE 154 H3083 DIPLOM PEACE MARXISM B66

THORNTON M.J.,NAZISM, 1918-1945. GERMANY INT/ORG DIPLOM REV PEACE FASCISM...CONCPT 20 HITLER/A WEIMAR/REP NAZI. PAGE 155 H3089 TOTALISM POL/PAR NAT/G WAR B66

TYSON G.,NEHRU: THE YEARS OF POWER. INDIA UK STRATA ECO/UNDEV FINAN SECT TASK WAR ORD/FREE MARXISM ...POLICY BIBLIOG 20 NEHRU/J. PAGE 157 H3145 CHIEF PWR DIPLOM NAT/G B66

US DEPARTMENT OF STATE,RESEARCH ON AFRICA (EXTERNAL RESEARCH LIST NO 5-25). LAW CULTURE ECO/UNDEV POL/PAR DIPLOM EDU/PROP LEAD REGION MARXISM...GEOG LING WORSHIP 20. PAGE 159 H3188 BIBLIOG/A ASIA S/ASIA NAT/G B66

US DEPARTMENT OF STATE,RESEARCH ON THE AMERICAN REPUBLICS (EXTERNAL RESEARCH LIST NO 6-25). CULTURE SOCIETY POL/PAR DIPLOM EDU/PROP MARXISM WORSHIP 20 OAS. PAGE 159 H3189 BIBLIOG/A L/A+17C REGION NAT/G B66

US DEPARTMENT OF STATE,RESEARCH ON THE MIDDLE EAST (EXTERNAL RESEARCH LIST NO 4-25). GREECE ISRAEL SYRIA UAR YEMEN CULTURE SOCIETY POL/PAR SECT DIPLOM EDU/PROP WAR NAT/LISM...GEOG GOV/COMP 20. PAGE 160 H3190 BIBLIOG/A ISLAM NAT/G REGION B66

US DEPARTMENT OF STATE,RESEARCH ON THE USSR AND EASTERN EUROPE (EXTERNAL RESEARCH LIST NO 1-25). USSR LAW CULTURE SOCIETY NAT/G TEC/DEV DIPLOM EDU/PROP REGION...GEOG LING. PAGE 160 H3191 BIBLIOG/A EUR+WWI COM MARXISM B66

US DEPARTMENT OF STATE,RESEARCH ON WESTERN EUROPE, GREAT BRITAIN, AND CANADA (EXTERNAL RESEARCH LIST NO 3-25). CANADA GERMANY/W UK LAW CULTURE NAT/G POL/PAR FORCES EDU/PROP REGION MARXISM...GEOG SOC WORSHIP 20 CMN/WLTH. PAGE 160 H3192 BIBLIOG/A EUR+WWI DIPLOM B66

US DEPARTMENT OF THE ARMY,COMMUNIST CHINA: A STRATEGIC SURVEY: A BIBLIOGRAPHY (PAMPHLET NO. 20-67). CHINA/COM COM INDIA USSR NAT/G POL/PAR EX/STRUC FORCES NUC/PWR REV ATTIT...POLICY GEOG CHARTS. PAGE 160 H3194 BIBLIOG/A MARXISM S/ASIA DIPLOM B66

US DEPARTMENT OF THE ARMY,SOUTH ASIA: A STRATEGIC SURVEY (PAMPHLET NO. 550-3). AFGHANISTN INDIA NEPAL PAKISTAN ECO/UNDEV INT/ORG POL/PAR FORCES FOR/AID INT/TRADE LEAD WAR...POLICY SOC TREND 20. PAGE 160 H3195 BIBLIOG/A S/ASIA DIPLOM NAT/G B66

US LIBRARY OF CONGRESS,NIGERIA: A GUIDE TO OFFICIAL PUBLICATIONS. CAMEROON NIGERIA UK DIPLOM...POLICY 19/20 UN LEAGUE/NAT. PAGE 161 H3215 BIBLIOG ADMIN NAT/G COLONIAL B66

WEINSTEIN B.,GABON: NATION-BUILDING ON THE OGOOUE. AFR GABON WOR+45 CULTURE SOCIETY PLAN DIPLOM COLONIAL INGP/REL ANOMIE HABITAT SUPEGO 20. PAGE 166 H3329 ECO/UNDEV GP/REL LEAD NAT/G B66

WEINSTEIN F.B.,VIETNAM'S UNHELD ELECTIONS: THE FAILURE TO CARRY OUT THE 1956 REUNIFICATION ELECTIONS... (MONOGRAPH). VIETNAM/S VIETNAM/N LEGIT CONFER ADJUD WAR PEACE 20 TREATY GENEVA/CON UNIFICA. PAGE 166 H3330 AGREE NAT/G CHOOSE DIPLOM B66

WHITAKER A.P.,NATIONALISM IN CONTEMPORARY LATIN AMERICA. AGRI NAT/G WEALTH...POLICY SOC CONCPT OBS TREND 20. PAGE 167 H3344 NAT/LISM L/A+17C DIPLOM ECO/UNDEV B66

YEAGER L.B.,INTERNATIONAL MONETARY RELATIONS: THEORY, HISTORY, AND POLICY. WOR+45 WOR-45 INT/TRADE BAL/PAY...NAT/COMP 18/20 MONEY. PAGE 172 H3435 FINAN DIPLOM ECO/TAC IDEA/COMP B66

ZABLOCKI C.J.,SINO-SOVIET RIVALRY. AFR ASIA CHINA/COM CUBA EUR+WWI L/A+17C USA+45 USSR WOR+45 POL/PAR FORCES COERCE NUC/PWR...GOV/COMP IDEA/COMP 20 MAO KHRUSH/N. PAGE 172 H3444 DIPLOM MARXISM COM B66

ZEINE Z.N.,THE EMERGENCE OF ARAB NATIONALISM (REV. ED.). TURKEY UK NAT/G SECT TEC/DEV LEAD REV WAR AGE/Y ROLE ORD/FREE...TRADIT CHARTS BIBLIOG 20 ARABS OTTOMAN. PAGE 173 H3453 ISLAM NAT/LISM DIPLOM L66

ZOPPO C.E.,"NUCLEAR TECHNOLOGY, MULTIPOLARITY, AND INTERNATIONAL STABILITY." ASIA RUSSIA USA+45 STRUCT TOP/EX BAL/PWR DIPLOM DETER CIVMIL/REL NAT/COMP. PAGE 173 H3464 NET/THEORY ORD/FREE DECISION NUC/PWR S66

"RESEARCH WORK 1965-1966." NEW/ZEALND ELITES ACADEM LOC/G MUNIC POL/PAR PROVS DIPLOM COLONIAL...SOC 20 AUSTRAL. PAGE 2 H0047 BIBLIOG NAT/G CULTURE S/ASIA S66

"FURTHER READING." INDIA LEAD ATTIT...CONCPT 20. PAGE 2 H0048 BIBLIOG NAT/G DIPLOM POLICY S66

CRANMER-BYNG J.L.,"THE CHINESE ATTITUDE TOWARDS EXTERNAL RELATIONS." ASIA CHINA/COM EXEC NAT/LISM MARXISM...POLICY 20. PAGE 35 H0699 ATTIT DIPLOM NAT/G S66

GALTUNG J.,"EAST-WEST INTERACTION PATTERNS." DIPLOM INT/TRADE...NET/THEORY CON/ANAL CHARTS NAT/COMP INDEX NATO COLD/WAR UN WARSAW/P. PAGE 55 H1090 STAT HYPO/EXP S66

GAMER R.E.,"URGENT SINGAPORE, PATIENT MALAYSIA." MALAYSIA S/ASIA ECO/UNDEV POL/PAR CHIEF TARIFFS TAX CONTROL LEAD REGION PWR 20 SINGAPORE. PAGE 55 H1094 DIPLOM NAT/G POLICY ECO/TAC

S66
GRUNDY K.W.,"RECENT CONTRIBUTIONS TO THE STUDY OF AFRICAN POLITICAL THOUGHT." DIPLOM NAT/LISM ALL/IDEOS...NEW/IDEA GOV/COMP 20. PAGE 62 H1239 BIBLIOG/A AFR ATTIT IDEA/COMP

S66
KAPIL R.L.,"ON THE CONFLICT POTENTIAL OF INHERITED BOUNDARIES IN AFRICA." MOD/EUR MOROCCO UAR EX/STRUC DIPLOM LEGIT REGION ADJUST...RECORD NAT/COMP GEN/LAWS. PAGE 83 H1658 AFR COLONIAL PREDICT GEOG

S66
MANSERGH N.,"THE PARTITION OF INDIA IN RETROSPECT." INDIA PAKISTAN S/ASIA UK DIPLOM COLONIAL GP/REL PWR 20. PAGE 102 H2042 NAT/G PARL/PROC POLICY POL/PAR

S66
MATTHEWS D.G.,"ETHIOPIAN OUTLINE: A BIBLIOGRAPHIC RESEARCH GUIDE." ETHIOPIA LAW STRUCT ECO/UNDEV AGRI LABOR SECT CHIEF DELIB/GP EX/STRUC ADMIN...LING ORG/CHARTS 20. PAGE 105 H2095 BIBLIOG NAT/G DIPLOM POL/PAR

S66
MERRITT R.L.,"SELECTED ARTICLES AND DOCUMENTS ON COMPARATIVE GOVERNMENT AND CROSS-NATIONAL RESEARCH." AFR ASIA EUR+WWI L/A+17C MOD/EUR ELITES R+D ACT/RES DIPLOM PWR...SOC CONCPT 18/20. PAGE 109 H2185 BIBLIOG GOV/COMP NAT/G GOV/REL

S66
O'BRIEN W.V.,"EVENTS AND TRENDS: PATTERNS OF AFRICAN INTERNATIONAL POLITICAL BEHAVIOR." CULTURE SOCIETY NAT/G NAT/LISM SOCISM. PAGE 119 H2386 BIBLIOG/A AFR TREND DIPLOM

S66
SCHOENBRON D.,"VIETNAM* THE CASE FOR EXTRICATION." NAT/G FORCES PROB/SOLV DIPLOM COLONIAL CONTROL COERCE...CONCPT 20. PAGE 140 H2795 VIETNAM WAR GUERRILLA

S66
SCHWARTZ M.,"THE 1964 PRESIDENTIAL ELECTIONS THROUGH SOVIET EYES." ASIA POL/PAR DIPLOM ATTIT MARXISM...NAT/COMP COLD/WAR. PAGE 140 H2811 USSR USA+45 PERCEPT

S66
SKILLING H.G.,"THE RUMANIAN NATIONAL COURSE." COM EUR+WWI ROMANIA NAT/G ECO/TAC PWR 20. PAGE 145 H2896 NAT/LISM POLICY DIPLOM MARXISM

S66
TURKEVICH J.,"SOVIET SCIENCE APPRAISED." USA+45 R+D ACADEM FORCES DIPLOM EDU/PROP WAR EFFICIENCY PEACE SKILL OBS. PAGE 157 H3137 USSR TEC/DEV NAT/COMP ATTIT

C66
WINT G.,"ASIA: A HANDBOOK." ASIA S/ASIA INDUS LABOR SECT PRESS RACE/REL MARXISM...STAT CHARTS BIBLIOG 20. PAGE 169 H3388 ECO/UNDEV DIPLOM NAT/G SOCIETY

B67
AMERICAN FRIENDS SERVICE COMM,IN PLACE OF WAR. NAT/G ACT/RES DIPLOM ADMIN NUC/PWR EFFICIENCY ...POLICY 20. PAGE 6 H0122 PEACE PACIFISM WAR DETER

B67
ANDERSON O.,A LIBERAL STATE AT WAR. MOD/EUR UK LAW CULTURE STRUCT ECO/DEV NAT/G DIPLOM PARL/PROC GP/REL ALL/VALS...CONCPT 19. PAGE 7 H0131 WAR FORCES

B67
ANDERSON S.V.,THE NORDIC COUNCIL: A STUDY OF SCANDINAVIAN REGIONALISM. DENMARK FINLAND ICELAND NORWAY SWEDEN MARKET NAT/G VOL/ASSN CONSULT PARL/PROC ATTIT...TIME/SEQ BIBLIOG 20. PAGE 7 H0134 INT/ORG REGION DIPLOM LEGIS

B67
BROMKE A.,POLAND'S POLITICS: IDEALISM VS. REALISM. COM GERMANY POLAND RUSSIA USSR POL/PAR CATHISM ...BIBLIOG 19/20. PAGE 21 H0431 NAT/G DIPLOM MARXISM

B67
BRZEZINSKI Z.K.,IDEOLOGY AND POWER IN SOVIET POLITICS. USSR NAT/G POL/PAR PWR...GEN/LAWS 19/20. PAGE 23 H0462 DIPLOM EX/STRUC MARXISM

B67
BRZEZINSKI Z.K.,THE SOVIET BLOC: UNITY AND CONFLICT (2ND ED., REV., ENLARGED). COM POLAND USSR INTELL CHIEF EX/STRUC CONTROL EXEC GOV/REL PWR MARXISM ...TREND IDEA/COMP 20 LENIN/VI MARX/KARL STALIN/J. PAGE 23 H0463 NAT/G DIPLOM

B67
BURNHAM J.,THE WAR WE ARE IN, THE LAST DECADE AND THE NEXT. ASIA COM EUR+WWI S/ASIA WOR+45 ECO/UNDEV INT/ORG FORCES WAR...OLD/LIB TREND 20 COLD/WAR. PAGE 25 H0492 POLICY NAT/G DIPLOM NAT/COMP

B67
BURR R.N.,OUR TROUBLED HEMISPHERE: PERSPECTIVES ON UNITED STATES-LATIN AMERICAN RELATIONS. L/A+17C USA+45 USA-45 INT/ORG FOR/AID COLONIAL PWR 19/20 OAS. PAGE 25 H0493 DIPLOM NAT/COMP NAT/G POLICY

B67
CEFKIN J.L.,THE BACKGROUND OF CURRENT WORLD PROBLEMS. NAT/G MARXISM...T 20 UN COLD/WAR. PAGE 28 H0565 DIPLOM NAT/LISM ECO/UNDEV

B67
CORDIER A.W.,COLUMBIA ESSAYS IN INTERNATIONAL AFFAIRS. ASIA CHINA/COM FRANCE S/ASIA SPAIN UAR ECO/UNDEV LOC/G ECO/TAC GUERRILLA PWR...BIOG ANTHOL 18/20 MAU/MAU. PAGE 33 H0663 NAT/G DIPLOM MARXISM POLICY

B67
CURTIN P.D.,AFRICA REMEMBERED. NIGERIA SENEGAL CULTURE DIPLOM INT/TRADE GP/REL RACE/REL...RECORD ANTHOL 18/19 NEGRO. PAGE 36 H0727 DOMIN ORD/FREE AFR DISCRIM

B67
DEUTSCH K.W.,FRANCE, GERMANY AND THE WESTERN ALLIANCE. FRANCE GERMANY/W INT/ORG ARMS/CONT NAT/LISM SOVEREIGN...INT NAT/COMP 20. PAGE 40 H0801 ELITES ATTIT DIPLOM POLICY

B67
DILLARD D.,ECONOMIC DEVELOPMENT OF THE NORTH ATLANTIC COMMUNITY. EUR+WWI MOD/EUR USA+45 USA-45 ECO/UNDEV LABOR CAP/ISM WAR BAL/PAY...NAT/COMP 15/20. PAGE 41 H0824 ECO/DEV INT/TRADE INDUS DIPLOM

B67
FAY S.B.,THE ORIGINS OF THE WORLD WAR (2ND REV. ED. 2 VOLS.). NAT/G FORCES DIPLOM CONFER LEAD PEACE ...REALPOL GOV/COMP 19/20. PAGE 49 H0978 MOD/EUR WAR REGION INT/ORG

B67
GIFFORD P.,BRITAIN AND GERMANY IN AFRICA. AFR GERMANY UK ECO/UNDEV LEAD WAR NAT/LISM ATTIT ...POLICY HIST/WRIT METH/COMP ANTHOL BIBLIOG 19/20 WWI. PAGE 56 H1123 COLONIAL ADMIN DIPLOM NAT/COMP

B67
HANRIEDER W.F.,WEST GERMAN FOREIGN POLICY 1949-1963: INTERNATIONAL PRESSURE AND DOMESTIC RESPONSE. EUR+WWI GERMANY/W POL/PAR LOBBY CONSEN 20. PAGE 66 H1316 DIPLOM POLICY NAT/G ATTIT

B67
HILSMAN R.,TO MOVE A NATION: THE POLITICS OF FOREIGN POLICY IN THE ADMINISTRATION OF JOHN F. KENNEDY. CHINA/COM COM USSR VIETNAM NAT/G DELIB/GP FORCES PLAN PROB/SOLV BAL/PWR COLONIAL EXEC REV PWR 20 KENNEDY/JF PRESIDENT. PAGE 71 H1418 CHIEF DIPLOM

B67
HOLLERMAN L.,JAPAN'S DEPENDENCE ON THE WORLD ECONOMY. INDUS MARKET LABOR NAT/G DIPLOM 20 CHINJAP. PAGE 73 H1457 PLAN ECO/DEV ECO/TAC INT/TRADE

B67
JOHNSON H.G.,ECONOMIC NATIONALISM IN OLD AND NEW STATES. CANADA CHINA/COM MALI UK DIPLOM...SIMUL GEN/LAWS 19/20 MEXIC/AMER. PAGE 81 H1619 NAT/LISM ECO/UNDEV ECO/DEV NAT/COMP

B67
KAROL K.S.,CHINA, THE OTHER COMMUNISM (TRANS. BY TOM BAISTOW). CHINA/COM CULTURE INDUS FORCES DIPLOM EDU/PROP CONTROL EXEC NUC/PWR ATTIT...SOC CHARTS 20. PAGE 83 H1663 NAT/G POL/PAR MARXISM INGP/REL

B67
LAMBERT J.,LATIN AMERICA: SOCIAL STRUCTURES AND POLITICAL INSTITUTIONS. STRUCT TEC/DEV DIPLOM ADMIN COLONIAL LEAD ATTIT...SOC CLASSIF NAT/COMP 17/20. PAGE 90 H1801 L/A+17C NAT/G ECO/UNDEV SOCIETY

B67
MACRIDIS R.C.,FOREIGN POLICY IN WORLD POLITICS (3RD ED.). EX/STRUC BAL/PWR COLONIAL NAT/LISM SKILL SOVEREIGN WEALTH...CONCPT TIME/SEQ ANTHOL 20 COLD/WAR. PAGE 101 H2011 DIPLOM POLICY NAT/G IDEA/COMP

B67
MAZRUI A.A.,THE ANGLO-AFRICAN COMMONWEALTH; POLITICAL FRICTION AND CULTURAL FUSION. AFR INT/ORG VOL/ASSN CHIEF GP/REL INGP/REL RACE/REL NAT/LISM 20 CMN/WLTH EEC. PAGE 106 H2111 COLONIAL SOVEREIGN DIPLOM CULTURE

B67
MCCLINTOCK R.,THE MEANING OF LIMITED WAR. FUT WOR+45 NAT/G FORCES GUERRILLA REV...POLICY SAMP/SIZ TREND NAT/COMP 45 COLD/WAR. PAGE 106 H2126 WAR NUC/PWR BAL/PWR DIPLOM

B67
MCNELLY T.,SOURCES IN MODERN EAST ASIAN HISTORY AND POLITICS. KOREA VIETNAM CULTURE DIPLOM COLONIAL REV WAR PWR ALL/IDEOS MARXISM...ANTHOL 20 CHINJAP. PAGE 107 H2147 NAT/COMP ASIA S/ASIA SOCIETY

B67
MEHDI M.T.,PEACE IN THE MIDDLE EAST. ISRAEL SOCIETY NAT/G PLAN EDU/PROP NAT/LISM DRIVE...IDEA/COMP 20 JEWS. PAGE 108 H2160 ISLAM DIPLOM GP/REL COERCE

B67
MENDEL A.P.,POLITICAL MEMOIRS 1905-1917 BY PAUL MILIUKOV (TRANS. BY CARL GOLDBERG). USSR AGRI DIPLOM ECO/TAC POPULISM...MAJORIT 20. PAGE 109 H2170 BIOG LEAD NAT/G CONSTN

B67
MILNE R.S.,GOVERNMENT AND POLITICS IN MALAYSIA. INDONESIA MALAYSIA LOC/G EX/STRUC FORCES DIPLOM GP/REL 20 SINGAPORE. PAGE 111 H2217 NAT/G LEGIS ADMIN

B67
MUHAMMAD A.C.,THE EMERGENCE OF PAKISTAN. PAKISTAN S/ASIA CONSTN ECO/UNDEV NAT/G CONTROL NAT/LISM 20. PAGE 114 H2281
DIPLOM COLONIAL SECT PROB/SOLV

B67
NYERERE J.K.,FREEDOM AND UNITY/UHURU NA UMOJA: A SELECTION FROM WRITINGS AND SPEECHES, 1952-65. TANZANIA ELITES ECO/UNDEV INT/ORG NAT/G CREATE DIPLOM COLONIAL REGION RACE/REL...ANTHOL 20. PAGE 119 H2383
SOVEREIGN AFR TREND ORD/FREE

B67
OLIVER R.,AFRICA SINCE 1800. AFR ISLAM CULTURE ECO/UNDEV SECT DOMIN RACE/REL DISCRIM SOVEREIGN 19/20. PAGE 121 H2414
DIPLOM COLONIAL REGION

B67
OVERSEAS DEVELOPMENT INSTIT,EFFECTIVE AID. WOR+45 INT/ORG TEC/DEV DIPLOM INT/TRADE ADMIN. PAGE 122 H2434
FOR/AID ECO/UNDEV ECO/TAC NAT/COMP

B67
PIKE F.B.,FREEDOM AND REFORM IN LATIN AMERICA. BRAZIL URUGUAY CONSTN CULTURE SECT DIPLOM EDU/PROP PARTIC DRIVE ALL/VALS CATHISM...GEOG ANTHOL BIBLIOG REFORMERS BOLIV. PAGE 126 H2511
L/A+17C ORD/FREE ECO/UNDEV REV

B67
PLANCK C.R.,THE CHANGING STATUS OF GERMAN REUNIFICATION IN WESTERN DIPLOMACY, 1955-1966. GERMANY DELIB/GP PLAN PEACE...TREND 20 KENNEDY/JF DEGAULLE/C. PAGE 126 H2519
NAT/G DIPLOM CENTRAL

B67
PLANK J.,CUBA AND THE UNITED STATES: LONG RANGE PERSPECTIVES. CUBA L/A+17C USSR ECO/UNDEV NAT/G FORCES ECO/TAC INT/TRADE AGREE REV...PREDICT TREND ANTHOL 20 CASTRO/F COLD/WAR OAS. PAGE 126 H2520
DIPLOM

B67
PLISCHKE E.,CONDUCT OF AMERICAN DIPLOMACY (3RD REV. ED.). INT/ORG NAT/G PROB/SOLV FOR/AID...CHARTS BIBLIOG T 20 DEPT/STATE. PAGE 126 H2529
DIPLOM RATIONAL PLAN

B67
POGANY A.H.,POLITICAL SCIENCE AND INTERNATIONAL RELATIONS, BOOKS RECOMMENDED FOR AMERICAN CATHOLIC COLLEGE LIBRARIES. INT/ORG LOC/G NAT/G FORCES BAL/PWR ECO/TAC NUC/PWR...CATH INT/LAW TREATY 20. PAGE 127 H2532
BIBLIOG DIPLOM

B67
POMEROY W.J.,HALF A CENTURY OF SOCIALISM. USSR LAW AGRI INDUS NAT/G CREATE DIPLOM EDU/PROP PERSON ORD/FREE WEALTH...POLICY TREND 20. PAGE 127 H2541
SOCISM MARXISM COM SOCIETY

B67
PYE L.W.,SOUTHEAST ASIA'S POLITICAL SYSTEMS. ASIA S/ASIA STRUCT ECO/UNDEV EX/STRUC CAP/ISM DIPLOM ALL/IDEOS...TREND CHARTS. PAGE 128 H2568
NAT/G POL/PAR GOV/COMP

B67
RAMUNDO B.A.,PEACEFUL COEXISTENCE: INTERNATIONAL LAW IN THE BUILDING OF COMMUNISM. USSR INT/ORG DIPLOM COLONIAL ARMS/CONT ROLE SOVEREIGN...POLICY METH/COMP NAT/COMP BIBLIOG. PAGE 129 H2588
INT/LAW PEACE MARXISM METH/CNCPT

B67
REES D.,THE AGE OF CONTAINMENT. WOR+45 FORCES ARMS/CONT ATTIT PWR...CONCPT TREND METH/COMP BIBLIOG/A 20. PAGE 130 H2608
DIPLOM NUC/PWR MARXISM GOV/COMP

B67
ROELOFS H.M.,THE LANGUAGE OF MODERN POLITICS: AN INTRODUCTION TO THE STUDY OF GOVERNMENT. DIPLOM ADMIN MARXISM NEW/LIB...JURID CONCPT METH/COMP T 20. PAGE 133 H2657
LEAD NAT/COMP PERS/REL NAT/G

B67
ROSENBLUTH G.,THE CANADIAN ECONOMY AND DISARMAMENT. CANADA FUT ECO/DEV INDUS R+D DELIB/GP DIPLOM ECO/TAC CIVMIL/REL PEACE...POLICY BIBLIOG PACIFIST 20. PAGE 134 H2679
ARMS/CONT STAT PLAN NAT/G

B67
ROWLAND J.,A HISTORY OF SINO-INDIAN RELATIONS; HOSTILE CO-EXISTENCE. ASIA CHINA/COM INDIA NAT/G NUC/PWR PWR WEALTH...GEOG BIBLIOG 13/20 COLD/WAR. PAGE 135 H2704
DIPLOM CENSUS IDEA/COMP

B67
RUEFF J.,BALANCE OF PAYMENTS. WOR+45 FINAN TEC/DEV DIPLOM TARIFFS PRICE CONTROL...POLICY CONCPT IDEA/COMP. PAGE 136 H2715
INT/TRADE BAL/PAY ECO/TAC NAT/COMP

B67
RUSTOW D.A.,A WORLD OF NATIONS; PROBLEMS OF POLITICAL MODERNIZATION. CONSTN NAT/G POL/PAR FORCES DIPLOM LEAD AUTHORIT...CHARTS IDEA/COMP 20. PAGE 136 H2722
PROB/SOLV ECO/UNDEV CONCPT NAT/COMP

B67
SALISBURY H.E.,BEHIND THE LINES - HANOI. VIETNAM/N NAT/G GUERRILLA CIVMIL/REL NAT/LISM KNOWL 20. PAGE 137 H2741
WAR PROB/SOLV DIPLOM OBS

B67
SCHUTZ W.W.,RETHINKING GERMAN POLICY; NEW APPROACHES TO REUNIFICATION. GERMANY USSR PLAN CONFER...POLICY 20. PAGE 140 H2806
REGION NAT/G DIPLOM PROB/SOLV

B67
SCHWARTZ M.A.,PUBLIC OPINION AND CANADIAN IDENTITY. CANADA SOCIETY LOC/G DIPLOM ADMIN LEAD REGION GP/REL SAMP. PAGE 141 H2812
ATTIT NAT/G NAT/LISM POL/PAR

B67
SETON-WATSON H.,THE RUSSIAN EMPIRE, 1801-1917. COM RUSSIA STRATA ECO/DEV AGRI INDUS POL/PAR DIPLOM NAT/LISM MARXISM...IDEA/COMP BIBLIOG 19/20 MARX/KARL. PAGE 142 H2834
SOCIETY NAT/G LEAD POLICY

B67
SHAFFER H.G.,THE COMMUNIST WORLD: MARXIST AND NON-MARXIST VIEWS. WOR+45 SOCIETY DIPLOM ECO/TAC CONTROL SOCISM...MARXIST ANTHOL BIBLIOG/A 20. PAGE 142 H2838
MARXISM NAT/COMP IDEA/COMP COM

B67
SHAKABPA T.W.D.,TIBET: A POLITICAL HISTORY. CHINA/COM UK CHIEF LEAD...INT BIBLIOG 20 TIBET. PAGE 142 H2839
DIPLOM SECT NAT/G

B67
THOMAN R.S.,GEOGRAPHY OF INTERNATIONAL TRADE. WOR+45 ECO/DEV ECO/UNDEV INT/ORG LG/CO PLAN BAL/PAY ...STAT CHARTS NAT/COMP 20. PAGE 154 H3075
INT/TRADE GEOG ECO/TAC DIPLOM

B67
TREADGOLD D.W.,SOVIET AND CHINESE COMMUNISM* SIMILARITIES AND DIFFERENCES. CHINA/COM COM NAT/G PLAN DIPLOM CENTRAL PWR MARXISM...POLICY 20. PAGE 156 H3128
CULTURE NAT/LISM

B67
VALI F.A.,THE QUEST FOR A UNITED GERMANY. GERMANY PROB/SOLV DIPLOM ADJUST...BIBLIOG 20. PAGE 161 H3222
NAT/G ATTIT PLAN CENTRAL

B67
WALTZ K.N.,FOREIGN POLICY AND DEMOCRATIC POLITICS: THE AMERICAN AND BRITISH EXPERIENCE. FRANCE UK USA+45 PARL/PROC GOV/REL CONSERVE...DECISION 20. PAGE 165 H3298
POLICY DIPLOM NAT/G GOV/COMP

B67
WARREN S.,THE AMERICAN PRESIDENT. POL/PAR FORCES LEGIS DIPLOM ECO/TAC ADMIN EXEC PWR...ANTHOL 18/20 ROOSEVLT/F KENNEDY/JF JOHNSON/LB TRUMAN/HS WILSON/W. PAGE 165 H3312
CHIEF LEAD NAT/G CONSTN

B67
WISEMAN H.V.,BRITAIN AND THE COMMONWEALTH. EUR+WWI FUT UK ECO/DEV POL/PAR TEC/DEV INT/TRADE LEAD ROLE SOVEREIGN...SOC TREND 20 CMN/WLTH. PAGE 169 H3391
INT/ORG DIPLOM NAT/G NAT/COMP

B67
YAMAMURA K.,ECONOMIC POLICY IN POSTWAR JAPAN. ASIA FINAN POL/PAR DIPLOM LEAD NAT/LISM ATTIT NEW/LIB POPULISM 20 CHINJAP. PAGE 171 H3432
ECO/DEV POLICY NAT/G TEC/DEV

B67
ZINN H.,VIETNAM THE LOGIC OF WITHDRAWAL. VIETNAM/S NAT/G DIPLOM DEATH MORAL 20. PAGE 173 H3459
WAR COST PACIFISM ATTIT

L67
GALTUNG J.,"ON THE EFFECTS OF INTERNATIONAL ECONOMIC SANCTIONS, WITH EXAMPLES FROM THE CASE OF RHODESIA." NAT/G DIPLOM EDU/PROP ADJUST EFFICIENCY ATTIT MORAL...OBS CHARTS 20. PAGE 55 H1091
SANCTION ECO/TAC INT/TRADE ECO/UNDEV

L67
GRAUBARD S.R.,"TOWARD THE YEAR 2000: WORK IN PROGRESS." FUT ACADEM SECT DELIB/GP DIPLOM EDU/PROP AGE/Y PERSON ROLE...PSY ANTHOL. PAGE 60 H1199
PREDICT PROB/SOLV SOCIETY CULTURE

L67
HOSHII I.,"JAPAN'S STAKE IN ASIA." ASIA S/ASIA CAP/ISM ECO/TAC ROLE...GEOG 20 CHINJAP. PAGE 74 H1477
DIPLOM REGION NAT/G INT/ORG

L67
MCALLISTER J.T. JR.,"THE POSSIBILITIES FOR DIPLOMACY IN SOUTHEAST ASIA." LAOS VIETNAM INT/ORG NAT/G PROVS BAL/PWR DOMIN AGREE COLONIAL WAR PWR 17/20 TREATY. PAGE 106 H2121
DIPLOM S/ASIA

L67
ROBINSON T.W.,"A NATIONAL INTEREST ANALYSIS OF SINO-SOVIET RELATIONS." CHINA/COM USSR NAT/G NUC/PWR ATTIT PWR...CONCPT CHARTS 20. PAGE 132 H2650
MARXISM DIPLOM SOVEREIGN GEN/LAWS

L67
SCALAPINO R.A.,"A SURVEY OF ASIA IN 1966." ASIA S/ASIA CONSTN SOCIETY POL/PAR CHIEF WAR...ANTHOL 20. PAGE 138 H2764
DIPLOM

L67
SEGAL A.,"THE INTEGRATION OF DEVELOPING COUNTRIES: SOME THOUGHTS ON EAST AFRICA AND CENTRAL AMERICA." AFR L/A+17C INT/ORG NAT/G VOL/ASSN FOR/AID INT/TRADE EQUILIB NAT/LISM PWR 20. PAGE 141 H2820
ECO/UNDEV DIPLOM REGION

L67
TABORSKY E.,"THE COMMUNIST PARTIES OF THE 'THIRD WORLD' IN SOVIET STRATEGY." AFR ASIA L/A+17C USSR INTELL NAT/G WORKER PLAN CONTROL LEAD PARTIC REV ...GOV/COMP 20 COM/PARTY THIRD/WRLD. PAGE 152 H3032 POL/PAR MARXISM ECO/UNDEV DIPLOM

S67
ALGER C.F.,"INTERNATIONALIZING COLLEGES AND UNIVERSITIES." WOR+45...NAT/COMP SIMUL. PAGE 5 H0104 DIPLOM EDU/PROP ACADEM GP/REL

S67
ANTHEM T.,"CYPRUS* WHAT NOW?" CYPRUS GREECE TURKEY NAT/G BUDGET MAJORITY 20 NATO. PAGE 7 H0143 DIPLOM COERCE INT/TRADE ADJUD

S67
BATOR V.,"ONE WAR* TWO VIETNAMS." S/ASIA VIETNAM DIPLOM SUFF ATTIT ORD/FREE 20. PAGE 12 H0236 WAR BAL/PWR NAT/G STRUCT

S67
BELGION M.,"THE CASE FOR REHABILITATING MARSHAL PETAIN." EUR+WWI FRANCE NAT/G DIPLOM ATTIT PERSON MORAL PETAIN/HP. PAGE 13 H0262 WAR FORCES LEAD

S67
BEVEL D.N.,"JOURNEY TO NORTH VIETNAM." VIETNAM/N CONSTN NAT/G FORCES PROB/SOLV DEATH CIVMIL/REL PEACE MORAL...ANTHOL 20 NEGRO. PAGE 16 H0325 ATTIT DIPLOM ORD/FREE WAR

S67
CHIU S.M.,"CHINA'S MILITARY POSTURE." CHINA/COM ELITES NAT/G POL/PAR TEC/DEV ECO/TAC DOMIN CONTROL LEAD REV MARXISM 20 MAO. PAGE 30 H0595 FORCES CIVMIL/REL NUC/PWR DIPLOM

S67
CUMMINS L.,"THE FORMULATION OF THE "PLATT" AMENDMENT." CUBA L/A+17C NAT/G DELIB/GP CONFER ...POLICY 20. PAGE 36 H0720 DIPLOM INT/LAW LEGIS

S67
EGBERT D.D.,"POLITICS AND ART IN COMMUNIST BULGARIA" BULGARIA COM USSR CULTURE DIPLOM INGP/REL TOTALISM...TREND 20. PAGE 45 H0894 CREATE ART/METH CONTROL MARXISM

S67
FLETCHER-COOKE J.,"THE EMERGING AFRICAN STATE." AFR GP/REL NAT/LISM. PAGE 51 H1025 ECO/UNDEV NAT/COMP DIPLOM ATTIT

S67
FRANCIS M.J.,"THE US PRESS AND CASTRO: A STUDY IN DECLINING RELATIONS." COM DIPLOM WAR TOTALISM ATTIT SOCISM...POLICY IDEA/COMP 20. PAGE 52 H1046 PRESS LEAD REV NAT/G

S67
GONZALEZ M.P.,"CUBA, UNA REVOLUCION EN MARCHA." CUBA L/A+17C USA+45 VIETNAM ECO/UNDEV FORCES DIPLOM DOMIN...POLICY MARXIST NAT/COMP CASTRO/F. PAGE 58 H1163 REV NAT/G COLONIAL SOVEREIGN

S67
GRIEB K.J.,"THE UNITED STATES AND THE CENTRAL AMERICAN CONFEDERATION." COSTA/RICA EL/SALVADR GUATEMALA HONDURAS L/A+17C NICARAGUA NAT/G FORCES CONFER AGREE EXEC ARMS/CONT REV WAR PEACE ATTIT 20. PAGE 60 H1212 INT/ORG DIPLOM POLICY REGION

S67
GRUNDY K.W.,"AFRICA IN THE WORLD ARENA." ECO/UNDEV BAL/PWR FOR/AID NEUTRAL REV NAT/LISM GOV/COMP. PAGE 62 H1240 AFR DIPLOM INT/ORG COLONIAL

S67
HALPERN B.,"THE ORIGINS OF THE CRISIS." ISLAM ISRAEL INT/ORG FORCES WEAPON PEACE ORD/FREE TREATY 20 UN. PAGE 65 H1296 WAR NAT/G DIPLOM

S67
HEASMAN D.J.,"THE GIBRALTAR AFFAIR." SPAIN UK NAT/G BAL/PWR CONSEN NAT/LISM ATTIT...REALPOL 20. PAGE 69 H1378 DIPLOM COLONIAL REGION

S67
HEATH D.B.,"BOLIVIA UNDER BARRIENTOS." L/A+17C NAT/G CHIEF DIPLOM ECO/TAC...POLICY 20 BOLIV. PAGE 69 H1379 ECO/UNDEV POL/PAR REV CONSTN

S67
JAIN G.,"INDIA REJECTS THE POWER RACE* REALISM ABOUT NUCLEAR WEAPONS." FORCES PROB/SOLV FOR/AID ARMS/CONT COST PWR...GOV/COMP 20. PAGE 79 H1583 INDIA CHINA/COM NUC/PWR DIPLOM

S67
KOHN W.S.G.,"THE SOVEREIGNTY OF LIECHTENSTEIN." LIECHTENST SWITZERLND USSR CONSTN DEBATE WAR CONSERVE 18/20 UN. PAGE 88 H1748 SOVEREIGN NAT/G PWR DIPLOM

S67
KYLE K.,"BACKGROUND TO THE CRISIS" ISLAM ISRAEL UAR UK USSR NAT/G PROB/SOLV LEGIT CONTROL REGION STRANGE MORAL 20 JEWS. PAGE 89 H1787 DIPLOM POLICY SOVEREIGN

COERCE

S67
LALL B.G.,"GAPS IN THE ABM DEBATE." NAT/G DIPLOM DETER CIVMIL/REL 20. PAGE 90 H1798 NUC/PWR ARMS/CONT EX/STRUC FORCES

S67
LEVI W.,"THE ELITIST NATURE OF NEW ASIA'S FOREIGN POLICY." CULTURE ECO/UNDEV NAT/G PROB/SOLV EDU/PROP COLONIAL CONTROL REGION NAT/LISM...NAT/COMP 20. PAGE 95 H1898 POLICY ELITES DIPLOM CREATE

S67
LOGERECI A.,"ALBANIA AND CHINA* THE INCONGRUOUS ALLIANCE." NAT/LISM PWR...GOV/COMP 20. PAGE 98 H1955 ALBANIA CHINA/COM DIPLOM MARXISM

S67
MANGLAPUS R.S.,"ASIAN REVOLUTION AND AMERICAN IDEOLOGY." USA+45 SOCIETY CAP/ISM DIPLOM ADJUST CENTRAL...NAT/COMP 20. PAGE 102 H2035 REV POPULISM ATTIT ASIA

S67
MATTHEWS R.O.,"THE SUEZ CANAL DISPUTE* A CASE STUDY IN PEACEFUL SETTLEMENT." FRANCE ISRAEL UAR UK NAT/G CONTROL LEAD COERCE WAR NAT/LISM ROLE ORD/FREE PWR ...INT/LAW UN 20. PAGE 105 H2099 PEACE DIPLOM ADJUD

S67
MENDL W.,"FRENCH ATTITUDES ON DISARMAMENT." FRANCE CULTURE CHIEF FORCES DIPLOM LEAD WAR...TIME/SEQ 20 DEGAULLE/C. PAGE 109 H2175 NUC/PWR WEAPON ARMS/CONT POLICY

S67
MOZINGO D.,"CONTAINMENT IN ASIA RECONSIDERED." NAT/G DIPLOM REV PEACE ORD/FREE 20. PAGE 114 H2275 ATTIT CONTROL NAT/LISM EFFICIENCY

S67
MOZINGO D.,"CHINA AND INDONESIA." CHINA/COM INDONESIA POL/PAR 20. PAGE 114 H2276 MARXISM CONTROL DIPLOM NAT/G

S67
NAHUMI M.,"THE POWERS IN THE MIDDLE EAST CONFLICT." ISLAM ISRAEL JORDAN UAR NAT/G PEACE ATTIT 20 JEWS. PAGE 115 H2304 DIPLOM WAR NAT/LISM

S67
NIEBUHR R.,"THE SOCIAL MYTHS IN THE COLD WAR." USA+45 USSR VIETNAM PROB/SOLV BAL/PWR ARMS/CONT NAT/LISM PWR ALL/IDEOS CONCPT. PAGE 118 H2359 MYTH DIPLOM GOV/COMP

S67
NIEBUHR R.,"THE ETHICS OF WAR AND PEACE IN THE NUCLEAR AGE." VIETNAM INTELL CONFER CONTROL WAR GOV/REL PERS/REL ORD/FREE...POLICY INT GOV/COMP NAT/COMP 20 UN. PAGE 118 H2360 MORAL PEACE NUC/PWR DIPLOM

S67
OJHA I.C.,"CHINA'S CAUTIOUS AMERICAN POLICY." CHINA/COM VIETNAM NAT/G NUC/PWR PEACE 20. PAGE 121 H2411 DIPLOM POLICY WAR DECISION

S67
OOSTEN F.,"SUDVIETNAM IM JAHR VOR DER ENTSCHEIDUNG." VIETNAM/S VIETNAM/N NAT/G DIPLOM COERCE CHOOSE 20. PAGE 121 H2420 FORCES WAR WEAPON ATTIT

S67
PLUMPTRE A.F.W.,"PERSPECTIVE ON OUR AID TO OTHERS." CANADA CREATE 20. PAGE 127 H2530 FOR/AID DIPLOM NAT/G PLAN

S67
PONOMARYOV B.,"THE OCTOBER REVOLUTION - BEGINNING OF THE EPOCH OF SOCIALISM AND COMMUNISM." COM FUT USSR WOR+45 SOCIETY STRATA CHIEF CREATE DIPLOM ECO/TAC EDU/PROP SOCISM...NAT/COMP 20. PAGE 127 H2542 MARXIST WORKER INT/ORG POLICY

S67
READ J.S.,"CENSORED." UGANDA CONSTN INTELL SOCIETY NAT/G DIPLOM PRESS WRITING ADJUD ADMIN COLONIAL RISK...IDEA/COMP 20. PAGE 130 H2602 EDU/PROP AFR CREATE

S67
RENFIELD R.L.,"A POLICY FOR VIETNAM." COM VIETNAM NAT/G POL/PAR VOL/ASSN CHIEF DIPLOM EDU/PROP DETER REPRESENT ATTIT ORD/FREE 20. PAGE 131 H2615 WAR POLICY PLAN COERCE

S67
RONNING C.,"NANKING: 1950." ASIA CANADA CHINA/COM NAT/G PLAN ECO/TAC REV ADJUST 20. PAGE 133 H2667 DIPLOM ROLE PEACE

S67
ROOT W.,"REPORT FROM PARIS - DE GAULLE: WHICH WAY TO THE FUTURE?" CANADA FRANCE ISLAM UK INT/ORG CHIEF CREATE AGREE CONTROL ARMS/CONT NUC/PWR EQUILIB PEACE PWR 20 DEGAULLE/C NATO. PAGE 134 H2670 POLICY DIPLOM NAT/G BAL/PWR

S67
ROSE S.,"ASIAN NATIONALISM* THE SECOND STAGE." ASIA NAT/LISM

COM ECO/UNDEV NAT/G PROB/SOLV DIPLOM FOR/AID DOMIN NEUTRAL REGION TASK...METH/COMP 20. PAGE 134 H2675
S/ASIA BAL/PWR COLONIAL

S67
ROTBERG R.I.,"COLONIALISM AND AFTER: THE POLITICAL LITERATURE OF CENTRAL AFRICA - A BIBLIOGRAPHIC ESSAY." AFR CHIEF EX/STRUC REV INGP/REL RACE/REL SOVEREIGN 20. PAGE 135 H2693
BIBLIOG/A COLONIAL DIPLOM NAT/G

S67
SMITH J.E.,"THE GERMAN DEMOCRATIC REPUBLIC AND THE WEST." GERMANY/E ECO/DEV NAT/G PROB/SOLV CONTROL REV TOTALISM...GOV/COMP 20. PAGE 146 H2911
DIPLOM PWR MARXISM

S67
SMITH J.E.,"RED PRUSSIANISM OF THE GERMAN DEMOCRATIC REPUBLIC." GERMANY/E INTELL TOP/EX WORKER PLAN DIPLOM PRODUC ATTIT WEALTH MARXISM. PAGE 146 H2912
NAT/G TOTALISM INDUS NAT/LISM

S67
SOMMER T.,"BONN CHANGES COURSE." GERMANY/W NAT/G POL/PAR PROB/SOLV NAT/LISM 20 NATO BERLIN/BLO. PAGE 147 H2932
DIPLOM BAL/PWR INT/ORG

S67
SPINELLI A.,"EUROPEAN UNION IN THE RESISTANCE." NAT/G BAL/PWR DIPLOM CONFER REGION TOTALISM ORD/FREE POLICY. PAGE 147 H2948
NAT/LISM FEDERAL EUR+WWI INT/ORG

S67
SYRKIN M.,"THE RIGHT TO BE ORDINARY." ISLAM ISRAEL NAT/G COERCE NAT/LISM RIGID/FLEX 20. PAGE 151 H3025
SOVEREIGN WAR FORCES DIPLOM

S67
TATU M.,"URSS: LES FLOTTEMENTS DE LA DIRECTION COLLEGIALE." UAR USSR CHIEF LEAD INGP/REL EFFICIENCY...DECISION TREND 20 MID/EAST. PAGE 152 H3047
POLICY NAT/G EX/STRUC DIPLOM

S67
WILPERT C.,"A LOOK IN THE MIRROR AND OVER THE WALL." GERMANY POL/PAR...KNO/TEST COLD/WAR. PAGE 169 H3378
NAT/G PLAN DIPLOM ATTIT

S67
YEFROMEV A.,"THE TRUE FACE OF THE WEST GERMAN NATIONAL-DEMOCRATS." GERMANY/W NAT/G DOMIN LEAD SANCTION WAR ATTIT PERSON...MARXIST 20. PAGE 172 H3436
POL/PAR TOTALISM PARL/PROC DIPLOM

S67
ZARTMAN I.W.," NAT/G POL/PAR VOL/ASSN NAT/LISM ORD/FREE PWR...CONCPT NAT/COMP ORG/CHARTS OAU MAGHREB. PAGE 172 H3451
AFR ISLAM DIPLOM REGION

C67
GEHLEN M.P.,"THE POLITICS OF COEXISTENCE: SOVIET METHODS AND MOTIVES." COM USSR NAT/G INT/TRADE EDU/PROP ARMS/CONT DETER KNOWL...CHARTS IDEA/COMP 20 COLD/WAR. PAGE 55 H1108
BIBLIOG PEACE DIPLOM MARXISM

C67
LING D.L.,"TUNISIA: FROM PROTECTORATE TO REPUBLIC." CULTURE NAT/G POL/PAR CHIEF DIPLOM COERCE WAR PWR ...BIBLIOG 19/20 TUNIS. PAGE 97 H1934
AFR NAT/LISM COLONIAL PROB/SOLV

N67
US HOUSE COMM SCI ASTRONAUT,GOVERNMENT, SCIENCE, AND INTERNATIONAL POLICY (PAMPHLET). INDIA NETHERLAND ECO/DEV ECO/UNDEV R+D ACADEM PLAN DIPLOM FOR/AID CONFER...PREDICT 20 CHINJAP. PAGE 160 H3198
NAT/G POLICY CREATE TEC/DEV

L68
CURRENT HISTORY,"DE GAULLE'S FRANCE." FRANCE MOD/EUR WOR+45 INDUS MARKET INT/ORG BUDGET DIPLOM AUTHORIT DRIVE...GOV/COMP IDEA/COMP 20 DEGAULLE/C EEC. PAGE 36 H0723
INT/TRADE PERSON LEAD NAT/LISM

S68
BOSSCHERE G D.E.,"A L'EST DU NOUVEAU." CZECHOSLVK HUNGARY POLAND ROMANIA YUGOSLAVIA AGRI CREATE ECO/TAC COERCE GP/REL ATTIT MARXISM SOCISM 20. PAGE 19 H0382
ORD/FREE COM NAT/G DIPLOM

S68
DOUGLAS-HOME C.,"A MISTAKEN POLICY IN ADEN." YEMEN CULTURE ECO/UNDEV INDUS FORCES WORKER DIPLOM ECO/TAC CONTROL 20 ADEN. PAGE 42 H0842
SOVEREIGN COLONIAL POLICY REGION

S68
DUGARD J.,"THE REVOCATION OF THE MANDATE FOR SOUTH WEST AFRICA." SOUTH/AFR WOR+45 STRATA NAT/G DELIB/GP DIPLOM ADJUD SANCTION CHOOSE RACE/REL ...POLICY NAT/COMP 20 AFRICA/SW UN TRUST/TERR LEAGUE/NAT. PAGE 43 H0858
AFR INT/ORG DISCRIM COLONIAL

S68
GUZZARDI W.,"THE DECLINE OF THE STERLING CLUB." UK WOR+45 NAT/G PLAN DIPLOM INT/TRADE AGREE CONSEN EQUILIB SOVEREIGN...POLICY NEW/IDEA 20 COMMONWLTH GOLD/STAND. PAGE 63 H1259
FINAN ECO/TAC WEALTH NAT/COMP

S68
KANET R.E.,"RECENT SOVIET REASSESSMENT OF DEVELOPMENTS IN THE THIRD WORLD." ALGERIA GHANA INDONESIA USSR WOR+45 CONSTN ELITES INTELL STRUCT DOMIN CONTROL REV PWR MARXISM...IDEA/COMP METH 20 THIRD/WRLD. PAGE 83 H1653
DIPLOM NEUTRAL NAT/G NAT/COMP

S68
LAVRIN J.,"THE TWO WORLDS." RUSSIA USSR SOCIETY STRUCT NAT/G DIPLOM ATTIT PERSON MARXISM...GEOG SOC IDEA/COMP PERS/COMP 18/20. PAGE 92 H1842
NAT/COMP NAT/LISM CULTURE

S68
LAWRIE G.,"WHAT WILL CHANGE SOUTH AFRICA?" AFR SOUTH/AFR ELITES DOMIN CONTROL REPRESENT...TIME/SEQ TREND 20. PAGE 93 H1848
RACE/REL DIPLOM NAT/G POLICY

S68
LUKASZEWSKI J.,"WESTERN INTEGRATION AND THE PEOPLE'S DEMOCRACIES." USSR ELITES ECO/DEV NAT/G VOL/ASSN INT/TRADE AGREE REV FEDERAL WEALTH SOCISM ...NAT/COMP SOC/INTEG 20 EEC. PAGE 99 H1977
DIPLOM INT/ORG COM REGION

S68
MILLAR T.B.,"THE COMMONWEALTH AND THE UN." UK DIPLOM TARIFFS AGREE COLONIAL CONTROL SOVEREIGN WEALTH...GP/COMP GOV/COMP 20 CMN/WLTH UN. PAGE 111 H2210
INT/ORG POLICY TREND ECO/TAC

S68
VERAX,"L'EUROPE ET LA FRANCE SUR LA SELLETTE." FRANCE UK NAT/G CHIEF DIPLOM EDU/PROP GP/REL 20 EEC DEGAULLE/C. PAGE 162 H3242
INT/TRADE INT/ORG POLICY ECO/TAC

B76
SMITH A.,THE WEALTH OF NATIONS. UK STRUCT WORKER DIPLOM ECO/TAC OPTIMAL DRIVE PERSON ORD/FREE ...OLD/LIB GEN/LAWS 17/18. PAGE 145 H2905
WEALTH PRODUC INDUS LAISSEZ

B79
BRODERICK G.C.,POLITICAL STUDIES. IRELAND UK ROMAN/EMP LAW ACADEM LOC/G NAT/G DIPLOM PARL/PROC SUFF GP/REL LAISSEZ...ANTHOL. PAGE 21 H0424
CONSTN COLONIAL

B83
AMOS S.,THE SCIENCE OF POLITICS. MOD/EUR CONSTN LOC/G NAT/G EX/STRUC LEGIS DIPLOM...METH/COMP 19/20. PAGE 6 H0124
NEW/IDEA PHIL/SCI CONCPT

B86
MAS LATRIE L.,RELATIONS ET COMMERCE DE L'AFRIQUE SEPTENTRIONALE OU MAGREB AVEC LES NATIONS CHRETIENNES AU MOYEN AGE. CULTURE CHIEF FORCES WAR ...SOC CENSUS TREATY 10/16. PAGE 104 H2084
ISLAM SECT DIPLOM INT/TRADE

B91
SIDGWICK H.,THE ELEMENTS OF POLITICS. LOC/G NAT/G LEGIS DIPLOM ADJUD CONTROL EXEC PARL/PROC REPRESENT GOV/REL SOVEREIGN ALL/IDEOS 19 MILL/JS BENTHAM/J. PAGE 143 H2868
POLICY LAW CONCPT

B93
ROYAL GEOGRAPHIC SOCIETY,BIBLIOGRAPHY OF BARBARY STATES (4 SUPPLEMENTARY PAPERS). ALGERIA LIBYA MOROCCO SOCIETY STRUCT DIPLOM LEAD 14/19 TUNIS. PAGE 135 H2706
BIBLIOG ISLAM NAT/G COLONIAL

C93
PLAYFAIR R.L.,"A BIBLIOGRAPHY OF MOROCCO." MOROCCO CULTURE AGRI FORCES DIPLOM WAR HEALTH...GEOG JURID SOC CHARTS. PAGE 126 H2526
BIBLIOG ISLAM MEDIT-7

B96
DE VATTEL E.,THE LAW OF NATIONS. AGRI FINAN CHIEF DIPLOM INT/TRADE AGREE OWN ALL/VALS MORAL ORD/FREE SOVEREIGN...GEN/LAWS 18 NATURL/LAW WOLFF/C. PAGE 39 H0774
LAW CONCPT NAT/G INT/LAW

B96
LOWELL A.L.,GOVERNMENTS AND PARTIES IN CONTINENTAL EUROPE, VOL. II. AUSTRIA GERMANY HUNGARY MOD/EUR SWITZERLND SOCIETY EX/STRUC LEGIS DIPLOM AGREE LEAD PARL/PROC PWR...POLICY 19. PAGE 99 H1974
POL/PAR NAT/G GOV/REL ELITES

B96
MARX K.,REVOLUTION AND COUNTER-REVOLUTION. GERMANY CONSTN ELITES INDUS NAT/G DIPLOM ECO/TAC WEALTH. PAGE 104 H2083
MARXIST REV PWR STRATA

B99
BROOKS S.,BRITAIN AND THE BOERS. AFR SOUTH/AFR UK CULTURE INSPECT LEGIT...INT/LAW 19/20 BOER/WAR. PAGE 22 H0433
WAR DIPLOM NAT/G

B99
KINGSLEY M.H.,WEST AFRICAN STUDIES. GHANA NIGERIA SIER/LEONE LAW EXTR/IND SECT DIPLOM INT/TRADE DOMIN RACE/REL OWN HEALTH...SOC 19. PAGE 86 H1717
AFR HEREDITY COLONIAL CULTURE

B99
LECKY W.E.H.,DEMOCRACY AND LIBERTY (2 VOLS.). LAW CONSTN STRATA POL/PAR SECT WORKER DIPLOM ADJUD REPRESENT NAT/LISM CONSERVE. PAGE 93 H1851
LEGIS NAT/G POPULISM ORD/FREE

DIPLOMACY....SEE DIPLOM

DIRECT/NAT....DIRECTORY NATIONAL (IRELAND)

B50
LYONS F.S.L.,THE IRISH PARLIAMENTARY PARTY, 1890-1910: STUDIES IN IRISH HISTORY (VOL. 4). IRELAND DELIB/GP LEGIS PAY EDU/PROP ADMIN GP/REL
POL/PAR CHOOSE NAT/G

ATTIT...BIBLIOG 19/20 PARLIAMENT PARNELL/CS DIRECT/NAT. PAGE 99 H1986
POLICY

DIRECTORY NATIONAL (IRELAND)....SEE DIRECT/NAT

DIRKSEN/E....EVERETT DIRKSEN

DISARMAMENT....SEE ARMS/CONT

DISCIPLINE....SEE EDU/PROP, CONTROL

DISCRIM....DISCRIMINATION; SEE ALSO GP/REL, RACE/REL, ISOLAT

N
BROCKWAY A.F.,AFRICAN SOCIALISM. EUR+WWI GHANA ISLAM UAR ECO/UNDEV CAP/ISM INT/TRADE COLONIAL COERCE GOV/REL DISCRIM 20 NEGRO NKRUMAH/K NASSER/G. PAGE 21 H0423
AFR SOCISM MARXISM

B00
MARKHAM V.R.,SOUTH AFRICA, PAST AND PRESENT. NETHERLAND SOUTH/AFR CULTURE LEGIS EDU/PROP COLONIAL CHOOSE REPRESENT DISCRIM ATTIT...OBS TIME/SEQ 17/19 NEGRO BOER/WAR. PAGE 103 H2054
WAR LEAD RACE/REL

B03
FAGUET E.,LE LIBERALISME. FRANCE PRESS ADJUD ADMIN DISCRIM CONSERVE SOCISM...TRADIT SOC LING WORSHIP PARLIAMENT. PAGE 48 H0960
ORD/FREE EDU/PROP NAT/G LAW

B10
MENDELSSOHN S.,SOUTH AFRICAN BIBLIOGRAPHY (2 VOLS.). SOUTH/AFR EXTR/IND LABOR SECT DIPLOM INT/TRADE COLONIAL RACE/REL DISCRIM...GEOG 20. PAGE 109 H2172
BIBLIOG/A AFR NAT/G NAT/LISM

B17
VEBLEN T.B.,AN INQUIRY INTO THE NATURE OF PEACE AND THE TERMS OF ITS PERPETUATION. UNIV STRATA FINAN EDU/PROP PRICE COST DISCRIM NAT/LISM MORAL ORD/FREE PACIFIST 20 WORLDUNITY. PAGE 162 H3237
PEACE DIPLOM WAR NAT/G

N19
MEZERIK A.G.,APARTHEID IN THE REPUBLIC OF SOUTH AFRICA (PAMPHLET). DIPLOM DOMIN CONTROL COERCE REPRESENT CONSEN ATTIT. PAGE 110 H2194
DISCRIM RACE/REL POL/PAR POLICY

N19
PROVISIONS SECTION OAU,ORGANIZATION OF AFRICAN UNITY: BASIC DOCUMENTS AND RESOLUTIONS (PAMPHLET). AFR CULTURE ECO/UNDEV DIPLOM ECO/TAC EDU/PROP COLONIAL ARMS/CONT NUC/PWR RACE/REL DISCRIM NAT/LISM 20 UN OAU. PAGE 128 H2564
CONSTN EX/STRUC SOVEREIGN INT/ORG

B25
MAURRAS C.,ENQUETE SUR LA MONARCHIE (1909). FRANCE CONTROL REPRESENT DISCRIM HEREDITY PWR CONSERVE 20 BUREAUCRCY. PAGE 105 H2103
TRADIT AUTHORIT NAT/G CHIEF

B27
BELLOC H.,THE SERVILE STATE (1912) (3RD ED.). PRUSSIA UK CULTURE STRATA INDUS NAT/G ECO/TAC CONTROL LEAD SUFF DISCRIM EQUILIB ORD/FREE WEALTH 20. PAGE 13 H0269
WORKER CAP/ISM DOMIN CATH

B30
OLDMAN J.H.,WHITE AND BLACK IN AFRICA. AFR STRUCT COLONIAL PARTIC DISCRIM ISOLAT PRIVIL 20 SMUTS/JAN NEGRO WHITE/SUP. PAGE 121 H2412
SOVEREIGN ORD/FREE RACE/REL NAT/G

B30
SMUTS J.C.,AFRICA AND SOME WORLD PROBLEMS. RHODESIA SOUTH/AFR CULTURE ECO/UNDEV INDUS INT/ORG SECT PROB/SOLV REGION GOV/REL DISCRIM ATTIT 19/20 LEAGUE/NAT LIVNGSTN/D NEGRO. PAGE 146 H2921
LEGIS AFR COLONIAL RACE/REL

B33
TANNENBAUM F.,PEACE BY REVOLUTION. ECO/UNDEV AGRI SECT WORKER DIPLOM EDU/PROP DISCRIM OWN WEALTH POPULISM 17/20 MEXIC/AMER INDIAN/AM. PAGE 152 H3043
CULTURE COLONIAL RACE/REL REV

B38
COUPLAND R.,EAST AFRICA AND ITS INVADERS. AFR ISLAM STRATA SECT FORCES DIPLOM TRIBUTE CONTROL DISCRIM NAT/LISM 19 AFRICA/E EUROPE MISSION. PAGE 34 H0680
CULTURE ELITES COLONIAL MARKET

B42
JOSHI P.S.,THE TYRANNY OF COLOUR. INDIA SOUTH/AFR UK ECO/UNDEV NAT/G POL/PAR DIPLOM ECO/TAC WAR ...POLICY 19/20. PAGE 82 H1637
COLONIAL DISCRIM RACE/REL

B42
REDFIELD R.,THE FOLK CULTURE OF YUCATAN. STRATA FAM KIN MUNIC SECT DISCRIM ISOLAT ANOMIE HEALTH ...BIBLIOG 20 MEXIC/AMER. PAGE 130 H2605
CULTURE NEIGH GP/COMP SOCIETY

B48
COX O.C.,CASTE, CLASS, AND RACE. INDIA WOR+45 WOR-45 SECT TEC/DEV MARRIAGE ROLE MARXISM...MAJORIT NAT/COMP SOC/INTEG 20 NEGRO HINDU. PAGE 34 H0688
RACE/REL STRUCT STRATA DISCRIM

B49
GRODZINS M.,AMERICANS BETRAYED: POLITICS AND THE JAPANESE EXPANSION. PROVS COERCE CHOOSE GOV/REL GP/REL INGP/REL ATTIT ORD/FREE...DECISION CHARTS 20 NISEI. PAGE 61 H1230
DISCRIM POLICY NAT/G WAR

S49
HUGHES E.C.,"SOCIAL CHANGE AND STATUS PROTEST: AN ESSAY ON THE MARGINAL MAN" (BMR)" EUR+WWI UK USA+45 CULTURE SOCIETY STRUCT RACE/REL...SOC NAT/COMP SOC/INTEG 19/20 NEGRO PARK/R. PAGE 74 H1490
STRATA ATTIT DISCRIM

B52
ISAACS H.R.,AFRICA: NEW CRISES IN THE MAKING (PAMPHLET). EUR+WWI USA+45 ELITES ECO/UNDEV WAR DISCRIM NAT/LISM ATTIT...POLICY NEW/IDEA CHARTS GOV/COMP 20 NEGRO COLD/WAR. PAGE 78 H1570
COLONIAL AFR RACE/REL ORD/FREE

B52
MONTAGU A.,MAN'S MOST DANGEROUS MYTH: THE FALLACY OF RACE. LAW PROB/SOLV WAR HABITAT POPULISM...PSY CONCPT CHARTS BIBLIOG NEGRO JEWS. PAGE 112 H2242
DISCRIM MYTH CULTURE RACE/REL

B53
WAGLEY C.,AMAZON TOWN: A STUDY OF MAN IN THE TROPICS. BRAZIL L/A+17C STRATA STRUCT ECO/UNDEV AGRI EX/STRUC RACE/REL DISCRIM HABITAT WEALTH...OBS SOC/EXP 20. PAGE 164 H3285
SOC NEIGH CULTURE INGP/REL

B55
PYRAH G.B.,IMPERIAL POLICY AND SOUTH AFRICA 1902-1910. SOUTH/AFR UK NAT/G WAR DISCRIM...CONCPT CHARTS BIBLIOG/A 19/20 CMN/WLTH. PAGE 129 H2570
DIPLOM COLONIAL POLICY RACE/REL

B55
SHUMSKY A.,THE CLASH OF CULTURES IN ISRAEL: A PROBLEM FOR EDUCATION. ISRAEL CULTURE INTELL NAT/G ACT/RES DISCRIM AGE/Y...BIBLIOG 20 JEWS. PAGE 143 H2867
GP/REL EDU/PROP SCHOOL AGE/C

B55
VERGNAUD P.,L'IDEE DE LA NATIONALITE ET DE LA LIBRE DISPOSITION DES PEUPLES DANS SES RAPPORTS AVEC L'IDEE DE L'ETAT. STRATA NAT/G EDU/PROP RACE/REL AUTHORIT FASCISM MARXISM MYTH. PAGE 162 H3243
NAT/LISM DISCRIM ORD/FREE

B56
GLUCKMAN M.,CUSTOM AND CONFLICT IN AFRICA. AFR FAM KIN NAT/G DOMIN DISCRIM DRIVE MORAL PWR...SOC BIBLIOG WORSHIP 20. PAGE 57 H1145
CULTURE CREATE PERS/REL GP/COMP

B56
KUPER L.,PASSIVE RESISTANCE IN SOUTH AFRICA. SOUTH/AFR LAW NAT/G POL/PAR VOL/ASSN DISCRIM ...POLICY SOC AUD/VIS 20. PAGE 89 H1782
ORD/FREE RACE/REL ATTIT

B57
BUNDESMIN FUR VERTRIEBENE,DIE VERTREIBUNG DER DEUTSCHEN BEVOLKERUNG AUS DER TSCHECHOSLOWAKEI. CZECHOSLVK GERMANY NAT/G FORCES MURDER WAR INGP/REL ATTIT 20 MIGRATION. PAGE 24 H0474
GP/REL DOMIN COERCE DISCRIM

B57
MENDIETTA Y NUNE L.,THEORIE DES GROUPEMENT SOCIAUX SUIVI D'UNE ETUDE SUR LE DROIT SOCIAL. ELITES FAM KIN NAT/G PROB/SOLV CROWD ISOLAT ATTIT PERSON ...JURID CONCPT SOC/INTEG. PAGE 109 H2174
SOC STRATA STRUCT DISCRIM

B57
ROBERTSON H.M.,SOUTH AFRICA, ECONOMIC AND POLITICAL ASPECTS. SOUTH/AFR CONSTN CULTURE POL/PAR LEGIS DIPLOM DOMIN COLONIAL...SOC BIBLIOG 19/20. PAGE 132 H2647
RACE/REL ECO/UNDEV ECO/TAC DISCRIM

S57
HAILEY,"TOMORROW IN AFRICA." CONSTN SOCIETY LOC/G NAT/G DOMIN ADJUD ADMIN GP/REL DISCRIM NAT/LISM ATTIT MORAL ORD/FREE...PSY SOC CONCPT OBS RECORD TREND GEN/LAWS CMN/WLTH 20. PAGE 64 H1277
AFR PERSON ELITES RACE/REL

B58
GLUCKMAN M.,ANALYSIS OF A SOCIAL SITUATION IN MODERN ZULULAND. AFR PERS/REL ADJUST DISCRIM EQUILIB NAT/LISM...SOC RECORD AUD/VIS 20 ZULULAND. PAGE 57 H1146
CULTURE RACE/REL STRUCT GP/REL

B58
OGDEN F.D.,THE POLL TAX IN THE SOUTH. USA+45 USA-45 CONSTN ADJUD ADMIN PARTIC CRIME...TIME/SEQ GOV/COMP METH/COMP 18/20 SOUTH/US. PAGE 120 H2407
TAX CHOOSE RACE/REL DISCRIM

B59
CARPENTER G.W.,THE WAY IN AFRICA. AFR INDUS MUNIC DIPLOM DOMIN EDU/PROP COERCE DISCRIM NAT/LISM ORD/FREE 20 NEGRO CHRISTIAN. PAGE 27 H0535
CULTURE SECT ECO/UNDEV COLONIAL

B59
ROCHE J.,LA COLONISATION ALLEMANDE ET LE RIO GRANDE DO SUL. BRAZIL L/A+17C NAT/G PROVS INGP/REL RACE/REL DISCRIM HABITAT...GEOG SOC/INTEG 19/20 MIGRATION. PAGE 133 H2652
ECO/UNDEV GP/REL ATTIT

B59
VITTACHIT,EMERGENCY '58. CEYLON UK STRUCT NAT/G FORCES ADJUD CRIME REV NAT/LISM 20. PAGE 163 H3258
RACE/REL DISCRIM DIPLOM SOVEREIGN

B60
BANERJEE D.N.,OUR FUNDAMENTAL RIGHTS: THEIR NATURE AND EXTENT (AS JUDICIALLY DETERMINED). INDIA UK CULTURE STRATA NAT/G WORKER EDU/PROP CONTROL
CONSTN ORD/FREE LEGIS

DISCRIM OWN...IDEA/COMP WORSHIP 20 REFORMERS COMMONWLTH. PAGE 10 H0207 — POLICY

B60
CASTBERG F.,FREEDOM OF SPEECH IN THE WEST. FRANCE GERMANY USA+45 USA-45 LAW CONSTN CHIEF PRESS DISCRIM...CONCPT 18/20. PAGE 28 H0558 — ORD/FREE SANCTION ADJUD NAT/COMP

B60
HAYEK F.A.,THE CONSTITUTION OF LIBERTY. UNIV LAW CONSTN WORKER TAX EDU/PROP ADMIN CT/SYS COERCE DISCRIM...IDEA/COMP 20. PAGE 68 H1369 — ORD/FREE CHOOSE NAT/G CONCPT

B60
JOHNSON H.M.,SOCIOLOGY: A SYSTEMATIC INTRODUCTION. MARKET FAM LABOR POL/PAR CHOOSE DISCRIM MARRIAGE ALL/IDEOS...BIBLIOG T WORSHIP. PAGE 81 H1620 — SOC SOCIETY CULTURE GEN/LAWS

B60
MOCTEZUMA A.P.,EL CONFLICTO RELIGIOSO DE 1926 (2ND ED.). L/A+17C LAW NAT/G LOBBY COERCE GP/REL ATTIT ...POLICY 20 MEXIC/AMER CHURCH/STA. PAGE 112 H2233 — SECT ORD/FREE DISCRIM REV

B60
ROSKAM K.L.,APARTHEID AND DISCRIMINATION. SOUTH/AFR SOCIETY STRUCT NAT/G POL/PAR GP/REL ISOLAT ...BIBLIOG 20. PAGE 134 H2683 — DISCRIM RACE/REL CULTURE POLICY

B60
SOUTH AFRICAN CONGRESS OF DEM,FACE THE FUTURE. SOUTH/AFR ELITES LEGIS ADMIN REGION COERCE PEACE ATTIT 20. PAGE 147 H2938 — RACE/REL DISCRIM CONSTN NAT/G

B60
THE AFRICA 1960 COMMITTEE,MANDATE IN TRUST; THE PROBLEM OF SOUTH WEST AFRICA. GERMANY STRUCT REGION SANCTION CHOOSE DISCRIM...INT/LAW 20 AFRICA/SW UN LEAGUE/NAT TRUST/TERR. PAGE 153 H3066 — NAT/G DIPLOM COLONIAL RACE/REL

L60
WHEELER G.,"RACIAL PROBLEMS IN SOVIET MUSLIM ASIA." COM CULTURE SOCIETY NEIGH SECT DOMIN EDU/PROP DISCRIM DISPL DRIVE PWR SOVEREIGN...CENSUS SAMP TREND 20 MUSLIM. PAGE 167 H3340 — PERSON ATTIT USSR RACE/REL

S60
BERREMAN G.D.,"CASTE IN INDIA AND THE UNITED STATES" (BMR)" INDIA USA+45 CULTURE SOCIETY STRUCT SECT GP/REL DISCRIM HEREDITY...SOC STERTYP 20 NEGRO HINDU. PAGE 16 H0318 — STRATA RACE/REL NAT/COMP ATTIT

S60
GRIMSHAW A.D.,"URBAN RACIAL VIOLENCE IN THE UNITED STATES: CHANGING ECOLOGICAL CONSIDERATIONS." STRUCT MUNIC FORCES PARTIC DISCRIM ATTIT HABITAT ...IDEA/COMP 20 NEGRO. PAGE 61 H1228 — CROWD RACE/REL GOV/COMP NEIGH

S60
TIRYAKIAN E.A.,"APARTHEID AND POLITICS IN SOUTH AFRICA." SOUTH/AFR CULTURE STRATA ECO/DEV NAT/G POL/PAR ROUTINE CHOOSE GP/REL RACE/REL DISCRIM ATTIT ALL/VALS...CONCPT OBS TIME/SEQ VAL/FREE 20. PAGE 155 H3105 — AFR DIPLOM

B61
ALLIGHAN G.,VERWOERD - THE END. SOUTH/AFR TOP/EX DIPLOM COLONIAL DISCRIM TOTALISM ATTIT AUTHORIT ...BIOG 20 NEGRO VERWOERD/H. PAGE 5 H0107 — CONTROL CHIEF RACE/REL NAT/G

B61
DUFFY J.,AFRICA SPEAKS. GHANA TOGO CULTURE ECO/UNDEV PROB/SOLV COLONIAL NEUTRAL DISCRIM NAT/LISM SOVEREIGN ALL/IDEOS...CONCPT ANTHOL SOC/INTEG 20 NEGRO THIRD/WRLD. PAGE 43 H0857 — AFR NAT/G FUT STRUCT

B61
HUNT E.F.,SOCIAL SCIENCE. DIPLOM ECO/TAC ROUTINE GP/REL DEMAND DISCRIM EFFICIENCY HABITAT ALL/IDEOS ...SOC T 20. PAGE 75 H1497 — CULTURE ADJUST STRATA ROLE

B61
MUNGER E.S.,AFRICAN FIELD REPORTS 1952-1961. SOUTH/AFR SOCIETY ECO/UNDEV NAT/G POL/PAR COLONIAL EXEC PARL/PROC GUERRILLA RACE/REL ALL/IDEOS...SOC AUD/VIS 20. PAGE 114 H2288 — AFR DISCRIM RECORD

B61
SPOONER F.P.,SOUTH AFRICAN PREDICAMENT. FUT SOUTH/AFR INDUS POL/PAR RACE/REL INCOME...CHARTS 20 NEGRO. PAGE 148 H2953 — ECO/DEV DISCRIM ECO/TAC POLICY

S61
LIEBERSON S.,"THE IMPACT OF RESIDENTIAL SEGREGATION ON ETHNIC ASSIMILATION" (BMR)" CULTURE MUNIC GP/REL RACE/REL DISCRIM...GEOG STAT CON/ANAL CHARTS SOC/INTEG 20 MIGRATION. PAGE 96 H1926 — HABITAT ISOLAT NEIGH

S61
SCHECHTMAN J.B.,"MINORITIES IN THE MIDDLE EAST." ISLAM INTELL SOCIETY STRATA KIN NAT/G VOL/ASSN EDU/PROP REGION GP/REL DISCRIM ATTIT BIO/SOC DISPL PERSON ALL/VALS...PSY SOC OBS SAMP GEN/LAWS 20. PAGE 139 H2776 — SECT CULTURE RACE/REL

B62
GANJI M.,INTERNATIONAL PROTECTION OF HUMAN RIGHTS. WOR+45 CONSTN INT/TRADE CT/SYS SANCTION CRIME WAR RACE/REL...CHARTS IDEA/COMP NAT/COMP BIBLIOG 20 TREATY NEGRO LEAGUE/NAT UN CIVIL/LIB. PAGE 55 H1097 — ORD/FREE DISCRIM LEGIS DELIB/GP

B62
HENDERSON W.O.,THE GENESIS OF THE COMMON MARKET. EUR+WWI FRANCE MOD/EUR UK SEA COM/IND EXTR/IND COLONIAL DISCRIM...TIME/SEQ CHARTS BIBLIOG 18/20 EEC TREATY. PAGE 70 H1395 — ECO/DEV INT/TRADE DIPLOM

B62
MANSERGH N.,SOUTH AFRICA 1906-1961: THE PRICE OF MAGNANIMITY. SOUTH/AFR LEGIS LEGIT SUFF NAT/LISM ATTIT ORD/FREE 20 NEGRO 20. PAGE 102 H2041 — COLONIAL DISCRIM NAT/G

B62
TATZ C.M.,SHADOW AND SUBSTANCE IN SOUTH AFRICA. SOUTH/AFR AGRI NAT/G POL/PAR DOMIN GP/REL ATTIT PWR 20. PAGE 152 H3048 — RACE/REL REPRESENT DISCRIM LEGIS

B62
VAN RENSBURG P.,GUILTY LAND: THE HISTORY OF APARTHEID. SOUTH/AFR NAT/G POL/PAR DOMIN CHOOSE ...SOC 19/20 NEGRO. PAGE 162 H3231 — RACE/REL DISCRIM NAT/LISM POLICY

B62
ZINKIN T.,REPORTING INDIA. INDIA PAKISTAN WOR+45 SOCIETY SECT FORCES EDU/PROP CROWD DISCRIM NAT/LISM MARXISM...POLICY 20. PAGE 173 H3457 — STRATA COLONIAL BAL/PWR CONTROL

B63
CROSS C.,THE FASCISTS IN BRITAIN. UK ELITES LABOR NAT/G DOMIN PARTIC DISCRIM TOTALISM ATTIT...STERTYP 20. PAGE 35 H0708 — POL/PAR FASCISM RACE/REL LEAD

B63
EICH H.,THE UNLOVED GERMANS. EUR+WWI GERMANY PERS/REL RACE/REL DISCRIM HABITAT SUPEGO FASCISM ...PSY SOC AUD/VIS 19/20 JEWS. PAGE 45 H0898 — STERTYP PERSON CULTURE ATTIT

B63
FIRST R.,SOUTH WEST AFRICA. SOUTH/AFR INT/ORG KIN NAT/G WORKER COLONIAL WAR...POLICY 20 UN TRUST/TERR AFRICA/SW. PAGE 50 H1006 — DISCRIM ORD/FREE RACE/REL CONTROL

B63
FRIEDRICH C.J.,MAN AND HIS GOVERNMENT: AN EMPIRICAL THEORY OF POLITICS. UNIV LOC/G NAT/G ADJUD REV INGP/REL DISCRIM PWR BIBLIOG. PAGE 53 H1069 — PERSON ORD/FREE PARTIC CONTROL

B63
FRITZ H.E.,THE MOVEMENT FOR INDIAN ASSIMILATION, 1860-1890. SECT FORCES GP/REL RACE/REL DISCRIM FEDERAL CATHISM...BIBLIOG 19 INDIAN/AM PROTESTANT GRANT/US. PAGE 54 H1071 — CULTURE NAT/G ECO/TAC ATTIT

B63
LEWIN J.,POLITICS AND LAW IN SOUTH AFRICA. SOUTH/AFR UK POL/PAR BAL/PWR ECO/TAC COLONIAL CONTROL GP/REL DISCRIM PWR 20 NEGRO. PAGE 96 H1909 — NAT/LISM POLICY LAW RACE/REL

B63
MENZEL J.M.,THE CHINESE CIVIL SERVICE: CAREER OPEN TO TALENT? ASIA ROUTINE INGP/REL DISCRIM ATTIT ROLE KNOWL ANTHOL. PAGE 109 H2177 — ADMIN NAT/G DECISION ELITES

B63
SETON-WATSON H.,THE NEW IMPERIALISM. COM EUR+WWI MOD/EUR ECO/UNDEV NAT/G FORCES DIPLOM DOMIN EDU/PROP LEGIT COLONIAL EXEC COERCE GP/REL RACE/REL DISCRIM ATTIT...TIME/SEQ 20. PAGE 142 H2833 — ECO/TAC RUSSIA USSR

B63
SINGH H.L.,PROBLEMS AND POLICIES OF THE BRITISH IN INDIA, 1885-1898. INDIA UK NAT/G FORCES LEGIS PROB/SOLV CONTROL RACE/REL ADJUST DISCRIM NAT/LISM RIGID/FLEX...MGT 19 CIVIL/SERV. PAGE 144 H2885 — COLONIAL PWR POLICY ADMIN

B64
BUNTING B.P.,THE RISE OF THE SOUTH AFRICAN REICH. SOUTH/AFR INT/ORG NAT/G FORCES DIPLOM CONTROL WAR TOTALISM ATTIT...GOV/COMP 19/20. PAGE 24 H0477 — RACE/REL DISCRIM NAT/LISM TREND

B64
BURKE F.G.,AFRICA'S QUEST FOR ORDER. AFR CULTURE KIN MUNIC NAT/G DIPLOM COLONIAL REV DISCRIM NAT/LISM AGE/Y 20. PAGE 24 H0488 — ORD/FREE CONSEN RACE/REL LEAD

B64
HILL C.R.,BANTUSTANS: THE FRAGMENTATION OF SOUTH AFRICA. AFR SOUTH/AFR ELITES SOCIETY KIN CONTROL DISCRIM ANOMIE ATTIT...POLICY CHARTS GOV/COMP 20 NEGRO BANTUSTANS TRANSKEI NATAL. PAGE 71 H1416 — RACE/REL CULTURE LOC/G ORD/FREE

B64
HOPKINSON T.,SOUTH AFRICA. SOUTH/AFR UK NAT/G POL/PAR LEGIS ECO/TAC PARL/PROC WAR...JURID AUD/VIS 19/20. PAGE 73 H1467 — SOCIETY RACE/REL DISCRIM

B64
LEMARCHAND R.,POLITICAL AWAKENING IN THE BELGIAN CONGO. ECO/UNDEV VOL/ASSN DOMIN CHOOSE GP/REL INGP/REL DISCRIM ORD/FREE PWR...CHARTS 20 CONGO ARABS. PAGE 94 H1873 — NAT/LISM COLONIAL POL/PAR RACE/REL

B64
MBEKI G.,SOUTH AFRICA: THE PEASANT'S REVOLT. SOUTH/AFR POL/PAR COERCE REV NAT/LISM ORD/FREE SOVEREIGN 20 NEGRO. PAGE 106 H2114
COLONIAL RACE/REL DISCRIM DOMIN

B64
SEGAL R.,SANCTIONS AGAINST SOUTH AFRICA. AFR SOUTH/AFR NAT/G INT/TRADE RACE/REL PEACE PWR ...INT/LAW ANTHOL 20 UN. PAGE 141 H2821
SANCTION DISCRIM ECO/TAC POLICY

S64
BENSON M.,"SOUTH AFRICA AND WORLD OPINION." AFR SOUTH/AFR INTELL SOCIETY TOP/EX ECO/TAC DOMIN COERCE DISCRIM ATTIT PWR WEALTH...POLICY RECORD 20. PAGE 14 H0285
NAT/G RIGID/FLEX RACE/REL

B65
GINIEWSKI P.,THE TWO FACES OF APARTHEID. AFR SOUTH/AFR STRATA AGRI INDUS COLONIAL PARTIC SOVEREIGN...CONCPT GOV/COMP NAT/COMP 19/20 NEGRO. PAGE 56 H1131
DISCRIM NAT/G RACE/REL STRUCT

B65
GOPAL S.,BRITISH POLICY IN INDIA 1858-1905. INDIA UK ELITES CHIEF DELIB/GP ECO/TAC GP/REL DISCRIM ATTIT...IDEA/COMP NAT/COMP PERS/COMP BIBLIOG/A 19/20. PAGE 59 H1176
COLONIAL ADMIN POL/PAR ECO/UNDEV

B65
KOHN H.,AFRICAN NATIONALISM IN THE TWENTIETH CENTURY. AFR NAT/G POL/PAR COLONIAL REGION DISCRIM SOVEREIGN 20. PAGE 87 H1747
NAT/LISM CULTURE ATTIT

B65
KUPER L.,AN AFRICAN BOURGEOISIE. SOUTH/AFR LAW INTELL NAT/G POL/PAR VOL/ASSN DISCRIM...POLICY 20. PAGE 89 H1783
RACE/REL SOC STRUCT

B65
VAN DEN BERGHE P.L.,SOUTH AFRICA: A STUDY IN CONFLICT. AFR CULTURE SOCIETY STRATA STRUCT COERCE SEGREGAT. PAGE 161 H3227
DOMIN RACE/REL DISCRIM

B65
VATCHER W.H. JR.,WHITE LAAGER: THE RISE OF AFRIKANER NATIONALISM. AFR SOUTH/AFR CULTURE TOTALISM 20. PAGE 162 H3235
NAT/LISM POL/PAR RACE/REL DISCRIM

S65
MULLER A.L.,"SOME NON-ECONOMIC DETERMINANTS OF THE ECONOMIC STATUS OF ASIANS IN AFRICA." AFR SOUTH/AFR CULTURE 20. PAGE 114 H2283
DISCRIM RACE/REL LABOR SECT

B66
FLINT J.E.,NIGERIA AND GHANA. AFR GHANA NIGERIA UK NAT/G DOMIN DISCRIM...CHARTS BIBLIOG/A 15/20 NEGRO MAPS. PAGE 51 H1026
CULTURE COLONIAL NAT/LISM

B66
KEITH G.,THE FADING COLOUR BAR. AFR CENTRL/AFR UK ZAMBIA CULTURE SCHOOL EDU/PROP PERS/REL DISCRIM AGE ...AUD/VIS NAT/COMP SOC/INTEG 20 NEGRO. PAGE 84 H1682
RACE/REL STRUCT ATTIT NAT/G

B66
LEIBLER I.,SOVIET JEWRY AND HUMAN RIGHTS. USSR INTELL NAT/G DOMIN ATTIT 20 AUSTRAL JEWS. PAGE 93 H1865
DISCRIM RACE/REL MARXISM POL/PAR

B66
SWEET E.C.,CIVIL LIBERTIES IN AMERICA. LAW CONSTN NAT/G PRESS CT/SYS DISCRIM ATTIT WORSHIP 20 CIVIL/LIB. PAGE 151 H3018
ADJUD ORD/FREE SUFF COERCE

L66
KRENZ F.E.,"THE REFUGEE AS A SUBJECT OF INTERNATIONAL LAW." FUT LAW NAT/G CREATE ADJUD ISOLAT STRANGE...RECORD UN. PAGE 88 H1766
INT/LAW DISCRIM NEW/IDEA

B67
BODENHEIMER E.,TREATISE ON JUSTICE. INT/ORG NAT/G PUB/INST ACT/RES RISK CRIME INGP/REL DISCRIM DRIVE LAISSEZ 20. PAGE 18 H0363
ALL/VALS STRUCT JURID CONCPT

B67
CARTER G.M.,SOUTH AFRICA'S TRANSKEI: THE POLITICS OF DOMESTIC COLONIALISM. SOUTH/AFR ECO/UNDEV AGRI NAT/G PROVS PLAN DOMIN REPRESENT ADJUST DISCRIM ...OBS BIBLIOG 20 BANTUSTANS TRANSKEI. PAGE 27 H0550
STRATA GOV/REL COLONIAL POLICY

B67
CURTIN P.D.,AFRICA REMEMBERED. NIGERIA SENEGAL CULTURE DIPLOM INT/TRADE GP/REL RACE/REL...RECORD ANTHOL 18/19 NEGRO. PAGE 36 H0727
DOMIN ORD/FREE AFR DISCRIM

B67
FANON F.,BLACK SKIN, WHITE MASKS: THE EXPERIENCES OF A BLACK MAN IN A WHITE WORLD. CULTURE COLONIAL HAPPINESS ISOLAT STRANGE ATTIT HABITAT RIGID/FLEX SEX...BIOG STERTYP SOC/INTEG 20 NEGRO. PAGE 49 H0970
DISCRIM PERS/REL RACE/REL PSY

B67
FISHEL L.H. JR.,THE NEGRO AMERICAN: A DOCUMENTARY HISTORY. SOCIETY NAT/G ROLE...POLICY ANTHOL 15/20 NEGRO. PAGE 51 H1013
ORD/FREE DISCRIM RACE/REL STRATA

B67
HUTCHINS F.G.,THE ILLUSION OF PERMANENCE: BRITISH IMPERIALISM IN INDIA. INDIA UK CULTURE STRUCT NAT/G REV GP/REL RACE/REL ADJUST DISCRIM ATTIT MORAL PWR SOC/INTEG 18/20. PAGE 75 H1509
COLONIAL CONTROL SOVEREIGN CONSERVE

B67
KING M.L. JR.,WHERE DO WE GO FROM HERE: CHAOS OR COMMUNITY? MUNIC NAT/G PARTIC INGP/REL ALL/VALS ...POLICY CONCPT BIOG 20. PAGE 86 H1715
RACE/REL DISCRIM STRUCT PWR

B67
OLIVER R.,AFRICA SINCE 1800. AFR ISLAM CULTURE ECO/UNDEV SECT DOMIN RACE/REL DISCRIM SOVEREIGN 19/20. PAGE 121 H2414
DIPLOM COLONIAL REGION

B67
THOMAS P.,DOWN THESE MEAN STREETS. GP/REL RACE/REL ADJUST...SOC SELF/OBS 20. PAGE 154 H3078
DISCRIM KIN CULTURE BIOG

L67
UNESCO,"APARTHEID." SOUTH/AFR STRUCT KIN SCHOOL SECT WORKER DOMIN EDU/PROP REGION RACE/REL ISOLAT 20. PAGE 158 H3164
DISCRIM CULTURE COERCE COLONIAL

S67
BASKIN D.B.,"NATIONALITY DOCTRINE AND ANTI-SEMITISM IN THE USSR." USSR CULTURE STRATA ISOLAT MAJORITY ATTIT RIGID/FLEX RESPECT...GP/COMP JEWS. PAGE 12 H0234
NAT/LISM MARXISM GP/REL DISCRIM

S67
BULLOUGH B.,"ALIENATION IN THE GHETTO." CULTURE NEIGH GP/REL INGP/REL ATTIT...PSY SOC SAMP. PAGE 23 H0471
DISCRIM ANOMIE ADJUST

S67
HAMMOND R.J.,"RACE ATTITUDES AND POLICIES IN PORTUGUESE AFRICA IN THE NINETEENTH AND TWENTIETH CENTURIES." AFR PORTUGAL NAT/G SECT EDU/PROP COLONIAL ATTIT RIGID/FLEX SEX MORAL RESPECT 19/20 NEGRO. PAGE 65 H1309
POLICY RACE/REL DISCRIM SOCIETY

S67
NEALE R.S.,"WORKING CLASS WOMEN AND WOMEN'S SUFFRAGE." UK LAW CONSTN LABOR NAT/G DELIB/GP LEGIS WORKER PAY PARTIC CHOOSE 19 FEMALE/SEX. PAGE 116 H2326
STRATA SEX SUFF DISCRIM

S67
SNELLEN I.T.,"APARTHEID* CHECKS AND CHANGES." SOUTH/AFR NAT/G PROB/SOLV COLONIAL REGION TASK GP/REL RACE/REL EFFICIENCY PRIVIL ORD/FREE 20. PAGE 146 H2923
DISCRIM NAT/LISM EQUILIB CONTROL

S67
VINCENT S.,"SHOULD BIAFRA SURVIVE?" NIGERIA ECO/UNDEV CHIEF FORCES ECO/TAC GP/REL DISCRIM PEACE ORD/FREE SOC/INTEG 20 BIAFRA IBO. PAGE 163 H3256
AFR REV REGION NAT/G

S68
DUGARD J.,"THE REVOCATION OF THE MANDATE FOR SOUTH WEST AFRICA." SOUTH/AFR WOR+45 STRATA NAT/G DELIB/GP DIPLOM ADJUD SANCTION CHOOSE RACE/REL ...POLICY NAT/COMP 20 AFRICA/SW UN TRUST/TERR LEAGUE/NAT. PAGE 43 H0858
AFR INT/ORG DISCRIM COLONIAL

B99
DU BOIS W.E.B.,THE PHILADELPHIA NEGRO: A SOCIAL STUDY. CULTURE STRATA KIN CRIME SUFF ADJUST DISCRIM ISOLAT HABITAT HEREDITY ALL/VALS SOC/INTEG 17/19 NEGRO PHILADELPH. PAGE 42 H0851
INGP/REL RACE/REL SOC CENSUS

DISCRIMINATION....SEE DISCRIM

DISEASE....SEE HEALTH

DISPL....DISPLACEMENT AND PROJECTION

S41
ABEL T.,"THE ELEMENT OF DECISION IN THE PATTERN OF WAR." EUR+WWI FUT NAT/G TOP/EX DIPLOM ROUTINE COERCE DISPL PERCEPT PWR...SOC METH/CNCPT HIST/WRIT TREND GEN/LAWS 20. PAGE 3 H0055
TEC/DEV FORCES WAR

B53
HUNTER E.,BRAIN-WASHING IN RED CHINA. ASIA CHINA/COM CULTURE SOCIETY FORCES WAR TOTALISM ATTIT BIO/SOC DISPL DRIVE PERSON SUPEGO KNOWL ORD/FREE ...INT REC/INT COLD/WAR 20. PAGE 75 H1499
EDU/PROP COERCE

B53
MEYER P.,THE JEWS IN THE SOVIET SATELLITES. CZECHOSLVK POLAND SOCIETY STRATA NAT/G BAL/PWR ECO/TAC EDU/PROP LEGIT ADMIN COERCE ATTIT DISPL PERCEPT HEALTH PWR RESPECT WEALTH...METH/CNCPT JEWS VAL/FREE NAZI 20. PAGE 110 H2192
COM SECT TOTALISM USSR

B58
SCOTT J.P.,AGGRESSION. CULTURE FAM SCHOOL ATTIT DISPL HEALTH...SOC CONCPT NEW/IDEA CHARTS LAB/EXP. PAGE 141 H2814
DRIVE PSY WAR

B58
STEINBERG C.S.,THE MASS COMMUNICATORS: PUBLIC RELATIONS, PUBLIC OPINION, AND MASS MEDIA. CULTURE
EDU/PROP ATTIT

CONSULT ACT/RES FEEDBACK DISPL WEALTH 20. PAGE 149 H2975 COM/IND PERCEPT

S59
LYNN D.B.,"THE EFFECTS OF FATHER-ABSENCE ON NORWEGIAN BOYS AND GIRLS." NORWAY CULTURE PERS/REL ADJUST DISPL LOVE...PSY CORREL STAT INT CON/ANAL CHARTS SOC/INTEG 20. PAGE 99 H1983 SOC FAM AGE/C ANOMIE

S59
MCNEIL E.B.,"PSYCHOLOGY AND AGGRESSION." CULTURE SOCIETY ACT/RES DISPL PERSON HEALTH. PAGE 107 H2146 DRIVE PSY

L60
WHEELER G.,"RACIAL PROBLEMS IN SOVIET MUSLIM ASIA." COM CULTURE SOCIETY NEIGH SECT DOMIN EDU/PROP DISCRIM DISPL DRIVE PWR SOVEREIGN...CENSUS SAMP TREND 20 MUSLIM. PAGE 167 H3340 PERSON ATTIT USSR RACE/REL

B61
BERKOWITZ L.,AGGRESSION: AS A SOCIAL PSYCHOLOGICAL ANALYSIS. UNIV CULTURE FACE/GP FAM KIN NEIGH EDU/PROP DISPL DRIVE HEALTH LOVE ORD/FREE...PSY SOC CONCPT OBS TREND. PAGE 15 H0305 SOCIETY COERCE WAR

B61
BULLOCK A.,HITLER: A STUDY IN TYRANNY. EUR+WWI GERMANY SOCIETY STRUCT NAT/G POL/PAR FORCES CREATE DOMIN EDU/PROP EXEC COERCE WAR NAT/LISM DISPL DRIVE PERSON PWR...PSY NAZI 20 HITLER/A. PAGE 23 H0470 ATTIT BIOG TOTALISM

S61
SCHECHTMAN J.B.,"MINORITIES IN THE MIDDLE EAST." ISLAM INTELL SOCIETY STRATA KIN NAT/G VOL/ASSN EDU/PROP REGION GP/REL DISCRIM ATTIT BIO/SOC DISPL PERSON ALL/VALS...PSY SOC OBS SAMP GEN/LAWS 20. PAGE 139 H2776 SECT CULTURE RACE/REL

S62
PASSIN H.,"THE SOURCES OF PROTEST IN JAPAN." CULTURE SOCIETY EDU/PROP COERCE NAT/LISM DISPL DRIVE PWR RESPECT...POLICY SOC TREND 20 CHINJAP. PAGE 124 H2473 ASIA ATTIT REV

S62
ROTBERG R.,"THE RISE OF AFRICAN NATIONALISM: THE CASE OF EAST AND CENTRAL AFRICA." AFR CULTURE SOCIETY NEIGH DIPLOM DOMIN COLONIAL COERCE DISPL PERCEPT PWR SOVEREIGN...POLICY OBS/ENVIR TREND WORK 20. PAGE 135 H2690 ATTIT DRIVE NAT/LISM REV

S63
BECHHOEFER B.G.,"SOVIET ATTITUDE TOWARD DISARMAMENT." COM USSR NAT/G ACT/RES TEC/DEV NUC/PWR ATTIT DISPL RIGID/FLEX PWR...METH/CNCPT TREND GEN/LAWS COLD/WAR 20. PAGE 13 H0252 FORCES EDU/PROP ARMS/CONT

B64
TAYLOR E.,RICHER BY ASIA. S/ASIA CULTURE VOL/ASSN ACT/RES ATTIT DISPL PERSON ALL/VALS...INT/LAW MYTH SELF/OBS 20. PAGE 153 H3054 SOCIETY RIGID/FLEX INDIA

B64
WHITE D.S.,SEEDS OF DISCORD. EUR+WWI FRANCE NAT/G VOL/ASSN FORCES DIPLOM DOMIN NAT/LISM DISPL RIGID/FLEX PWR...RECORD INT BIOG 20 DEGAULLE/C ROOSEVLT/F CHURCHLL/W HULL. PAGE 167 H3347 TOP/EX ATTIT

S64
SAYEED K.,"PATHAN REGIONALISM." ISLAM PAKISTAN S/ASIA CULTURE SOCIETY NAT/G NEIGH DIPLOM LEGIT COERCE CHOOSE ATTIT DISPL PERCEPT ALL/VALS SOVEREIGN...POLICY RELATIV SOC TIME/SEQ TOT/POP 20. PAGE 138 H2761 SECT NAT/LISM REGION

DISPLACEMENT....SEE DISPL

DISPUTE, RESOLUTION OF....SEE ADJUD

DISRAELI/B....BENJAMIN DISRAELI

B63
SHANNON R.T.,GLADSTONE AND THE BULGARIAN AGITATION OF 1876. BULGARIA TURKEY UK DIPLOM COERCE REV ATTIT 19 GLADSTON/W DISRAELI/B. PAGE 142 H2841 EDU/PROP NAT/G PWR CONSEN

DIST/IND....DISTRIBUTIVE SYSTEM

B03
GRIFFIN A.P.C.,SELECT LIST OF REFERENCES ON GOVERNMENT OWNERSHIP OF RAILROADS (PAMPHLET). MOD/EUR NAT/G ADMIN...MGT GOV/COMP 19/20. PAGE 61 H1217 BIBLIOG/A SOCISM OWN DIST/IND

B05
GRIFFIN A.P.C.,LIST OF BOOKS ON RAILROADS IN FOREIGN COUNTRIES. MOD/EUR ECO/DEV NAT/G CONTROL SOCISM...JURID 19/20 RAILROAD. PAGE 61 H1219 BIBLIOG/A SERV/IND ADMIN DIST/IND

B26
MCPHEE A.,THE ECONOMIC REVOLUTION IN BRITISH WEST AFRICA. AFR UK CULTURE DIST/IND FINAN INDUS PLAN GP/REL RACE/REL 20 AFRICA/W. PAGE 107 H2148 ECO/UNDEV INT/TRADE COLONIAL GEOG

B39
FIRTH R.,PRIMITIVE POLYNESIAN ECONOMY. SOCIETY DIST/IND SECT CHIEF CAP/ISM PRODUC WEALTH...SOC OBS METH WORSHIP 20 POLYNESIA. PAGE 50 H1007 ECO/UNDEV CULTURE AGRI ECO/TAC

B55
JONES T.B.,A BIBLIOGRAPHY ON SOUTH AMERICAN ECONOMIC AFFAIRS: ARTICLES IN NINETEENTH CENTURY PERIODICALS (PAMPHLET). AGRI COM/IND DIST/IND EXTR/IND FINAN INDUS LABOR NAT/G 19. PAGE 82 H1634 BIBLIOG ECO/UNDEV L/A+17C TEC/DEV

B55
RESHETAR J.S.,PROBLEMS OF ANALYZING AND PREDICTING SOVIET BEHAVIOR. USSR CULTURE ECO/DEV AGRI DIST/IND EXTR/IND PROC/MFG NAT/G SECT TOP/EX ACT/RES ADMIN PWR WEALTH...SOC METH TOT/POP VAL/FREE 20. PAGE 131 H2617 COM ATTIT

B55
WOYTINSKY W.S.,WORLD COMMERCE AND GOVERNMENTS: TRENDS AND OUTLOOK. WOR+45 FINAN POL/PAR DIPLOM ECO/TAC FOR/AID DOMIN WAR CHOOSE...CHARTS BIBLIOG 20 LEAGUE/NAT UN ILO. PAGE 171 H3413 INT/TRADE DIST/IND NAT/COMP NAT/G

B56
WATT D.C.,BRITAIN AND THE SUEZ CANAL. COM UAR UK ...INT/LAW 20 SUEZ TREATY. PAGE 166 H3314 DIPLOM INT/TRADE DIST/IND NAT/G

B58
HANCE W.A.,AFRICAN ECONOMIC DEVELOPMENT. AGRI DIST/IND INDUS R+D ACT/RES PLAN CAP/ISM FOR/AID ...GOV/COMP BIBLIOG 20. PAGE 65 H1312 AFR ECO/UNDEV PROB/SOLV TEC/DEV

L59
MURPHY J.C.,"SOME IMPLICATIONS OF EUROPE'S COMMON MARKET. IN (COOK P, ECONOMIC DEVELOPMENT AND INTERNATIONAL TRADE.." EUR+WWI ECO/DEV DIST/IND INDUS NAT/G PLAN ECO/TAC INT/TRADE WEALTH...STAT TREND OEEC TOT/POP 20 EEC. PAGE 115 H2298 MARKET INT/ORG REGION

S60
"THE EMERGING COMMON MARKETS IN LATIN AMERICA." FUT L/A+17C STRATA DIST/IND INDUS LABOR NAT/G LEGIS ECO/TAC ADMIN RIGID/FLEX HEALTH...NEW/IDEA TIME/SEQ OAS 20. PAGE 2 H0038 FINAN ECO/UNDEV INT/TRADE

B61
INTL UNION LOCAL AUTHORITIES,METROPOLIS. WOR+45 DIST/IND FINAN GIVE EDU/PROP CRIME COST HEALTH WEALTH 20. PAGE 78 H1563 MUNIC GOV/COMP LOC/G BIBLIOG

B61
LAHAYE R.,LES ENTREPRISES PUBLIQUES AU MAROC. FRANCE MOROCCO LAW DIST/IND EXTR/IND FINAN CONSULT PLAN TEC/DEV ADMIN AGREE CONTROL OWN...POLICY 20. PAGE 90 H1796 NAT/G INDUS ECO/UNDEV ECO/TAC

B61
SOKOL A.E.,SEAPOWER IN THE NUCLEAR AGE. USA+45 USSR DIST/IND FORCES INT/TRADE DETER WAR...POLICY NAT/COMP BIBLIOG COLD/WAR. PAGE 146 H2928 SEA PWR WEAPON NUC/PWR

B62
INSTITUTE OF PUBLIC ADMIN,A SHORT HISTORY OF THE PUBLIC SERVICE IN IRELAND. IRELAND UK DIST/IND INGP/REL FEDERAL 13/20 CIVIL/SERV. PAGE 77 H1539 ADMIN WORKER GOV/REL NAT/G

B63
BRITISH AID. UK AGRI DIST/IND INDUS SCHOOL TEC/DEV INT/TRADE COLONIAL DEMAND...TREND CHARTS 20. PAGE 2 H0041 FOR/AID ECO/UNDEV NAT/G FINAN

B63
FURTADO C.,THE ECONOMIC GROWTH OF BRAZIL: A SURVEY FROM COLONIAL TO MODERN TIMES. L/A+17C AGRI DIST/IND EXTR/IND INDUS WORKER COLONIAL RACE/REL OWN GOV/COMP. PAGE 54 H1082 ECO/UNDEV TEC/DEV LABOR DOMIN

B65
BARRY E.E.,NATIONALISATION IN BRITISH POLITICS: THE HISTORICAL BACKGROUND. UK AGRI DIST/IND EXTR/IND LABOR LG/CO ATTIT CONSERVE SOCISM 19/20 LABOR/PAR. PAGE 12 H0231 NAT/G OWN INDUS POL/PAR

B65
HAEFELE E.T.,GOVERNMENT CONTROLS ON TRANSPORT. AFR RHODESIA TANZANIA DIPLOM ECO/TAC TARIFFS PRICE ADJUD CONTROL REGION EFFICIENCY...POLICY 20 CONGO. PAGE 64 H1274 ECO/UNDEV DIST/IND FINAN NAT/G

B65
HOSELITZ B.F.,ECONOMICS AND THE IDEA OF MANKIND. UNIV ECO/DEV ECO/UNDEV DIST/IND INDUS INT/ORG NAT/G ACT/RES ECO/TAC WEALTH...CONCPT STAT. PAGE 74 H1476 CREATE INT/TRADE

B65
PARRIS H.W.,GOVERNMENT AND THE RAILWAYS IN NINETEENTH-CENTURY BRITAIN. UK DELIB/GP CONTROL LEAD CENTRAL 19 RAILROAD. PAGE 124 H2470 DIST/IND NAT/G PLAN GP/REL

L65
WIONCZEK M.,"LATIN AMERICA FREE TRADE ASSOCIATION." AGRI DIST/IND FINAN INDUS INT/ORG LABOR NAT/G TEC/DEV ECO/TAC HEALTH SKILL WEALTH...POLICY RELATIV MGT LAFTA 20. PAGE 169 H3390 L/A+17C MARKET REGION

S65
TENDLER J.D.,"TECHNOLOGY AND ECONOMIC DEVELOPMENT* THE CASE OF HYDRO VS THERMAL POWER." CONSTRUC DIST/IND CREATE TEC/DEV INT/TRADE CENTRAL PWR SKILL BRAZIL INDUS ECO/UNDEV

WEALTH...MGT NAT/COMP ARGEN. PAGE 153 H3061

BROWN R.T.,TRANSPORT AND THE ECONOMIC INTEGRATION OF SOUTH AMERICA. L/A+17C ECO/UNDEV NAT/G OP/RES DIPLOM INT/TRADE REGION WEALTH...ECOMETRIC GEOG STAT LAFTA TIME. PAGE 22 H0449 — B66 MARKET DIST/IND SIMUL

LARKIN E.,"ECONOMIC GROWTH, CAPITAL INVESTMENT, AND THE ROMAN CATHOLIC CHURCH IN NINETEENTH-CENTURY IRELAND." IRELAND AGRI DIST/IND NAT/G GIVE OWN CATHISM...CHARTS 19. PAGE 91 H1823 — L67 FINAN SECT WEALTH ECO/UNDEV

RUTH J.M.,"THE ADMINISTRATION OF WATER RESOURCES IN GUATEMALA." GUATEMALA L/A+17C DIST/IND LOC/G NAT/G EX/STRUC ADMIN GOV/REL DEMAND EQUILIB WEALTH...GEOG MGT 20. PAGE 136 H2723 — L67 EFFICIENCY ECO/UNDEV PLAN ACT/RES

CHU-YUAN CHENG,"THE CULTURAL REVOLUTION AND CHINA'S ECONOMY." CHINA/COM AGRI DIST/IND INDUS MARKET NAT/G WORKER PLAN INT/TRADE DOMIN DEMAND PRODUC ...CHARTS 20 MAO. PAGE 30 H0600 — S67 ECO/DEV ECO/TAC REV SOCISM

GREGORY R.,"THE MINISTER'S LINE: OR, THE M4 COMES TO BERKSHIRE. PART I." UK CONSTN DIST/IND LEGIS TOP/EX PLAN ADJUD...GEOG 20. PAGE 60 H1210 — S67 DECISION CONSTRUC NAT/G DELIB/GP

NEUBAUER D.E.,"SOME CONDITIONS OF DEMOCRACY." ECO/DEV COM/IND DIST/IND POL/PAR EDU/PROP REPRESENT ...SOC STAT NAT/COMP 20. PAGE 117 H2331 — S67 NAT/G CHOOSE MAJORIT ECO/UNDEV

PLAYFAIR R.L.,"A BIBLIOGRAPHY OF ALGERIA." ALGERIA CULTURE ECO/UNDEV DIST/IND EXTR/IND FINAN SECT CRIME 16/19. PAGE 126 H2525 — C89 BIBLIOG/A ISLAM GEOG

DISTRIBUTIVE SYSTEM....SEE DIST/IND

DISTRICT COURTS....SEE COURT/DIST

DISTRICTING...SEE APPORT

DITTMANN H0827

DIVORCE....DIVORCE

DIX R.H. H0828

DIXON/YATE....DIXON-YATES BILL

DOBB M. H0829

DOC/ANAL....CONVENTIONAL CONTENT ANALYSIS

DODD S.C. H0830

DODD/TJ....SENATOR THOMAS J. DODD

DODGE D. H0831

DOERN G.B. H0832

DOGAN M. H0833

DOLCI D. H0834

DOMIN....DOMINATION THROUGH USE OF ESTABLISHED POWER

BENEDETTI V.,STUDIES IN DIPLOMACY. BELGIUM FRANCE GERMANY MOD/EUR CONSTN NAT/G CONSULT TOP/EX DOMIN EDU/PROP COERCE ATTIT...CONCPT INT BIOG TREND 19. PAGE 14 H0276 — B00 PWR GEN/LAWS DIPLOM

DE JOMINI A.H.,THE ART OF WAR. MOD/EUR NAT/G BAL/PWR DIPLOM DOMIN EXEC ROUTINE COERCE DRIVE PWR SKILL...POLICY CONCPT CHARTS STERTYP 19. PAGE 38 H0755 — B00 PLAN FORCES WAR WEAPON

HOBSON J.A.,THE WAR IN SOUTH AFRICA: ITS CAUSES AND EFFECTS. NETHERLAND SOUTH/AFR UK ELITES AGRI EXTR/IND POL/PAR DIPLOM PRESS RACE/REL ATTIT ORD/FREE SOVEREIGN...INT 19 NEGRO. PAGE 72 H1439 — B00 WAR DOMIN POLICY NAT/G

VOLPICELLI Z.,RUSSIA ON THE PACIFIC AND THE SIBERIAN RAILWAY. MOD/EUR ECO/UNDEV INT/ORG FORCES PLAN DOMIN COLONIAL ROUTINE ATTIT ALL/VALS...OBS HIST/WRIT TIME/SEQ TREND CON/ANAL AUD/VIS CHARTS 18/19. PAGE 163 H3261 — B00 NAT/G ACT/RES RUSSIA

SEELEY J.R.,THE EXPANSION OF ENGLAND. MOD/EUR S/ASIA UK CULTURE NAT/G FORCES PLAN DOMIN EDU/PROP COLONIAL ROUTINE ATTIT ALL/VALS SOVEREIGN...CONCPT HIST/WRIT PARLIAMENT 18 CMN/WLTH. PAGE 141 H2819 — B02 INT/ORG ACT/RES CAP/ISM INDIA

DANTE ALIGHIERI,DE MONARCHIA (CA .1310). CHRIST-17C ITALY DOMIN LEGIT ATTIT PWR...CATH CONCPT TIME/SEQ. PAGE 37 H0741 — B04 SECT NAT/G SOVEREIGN

SONOLET L.,L'AFRIQUE OCCIDENTALE FRANCAISE. FRANCE AGRI INDUS NAT/G SECT FORCES INT/TRADE EDU/PROP RACE/REL HEALTH ORD/FREE...CHARTS 19/20 NEGRO AFRICA/W. PAGE 147 H2933 — B12 DOMIN ADMIN COLONIAL AFR

BERHARDI F.,GERMANY AND THE NEXT WAR. MOD/EUR NAT/G SCHOOL FORCES ACT/RES DOMIN EDU/PROP SUPEGO PWR ...TIME/SEQ STERTYP TOT/POP 20 WWI. PAGE 15 H0304 — B14 DRIVE COERCE WAR GERMANY

OPPENHEIMER F.,THE STATE. FUT SOCIETY STRATA STRUCT WORKER CAP/ISM WAR GP/REL SOCISM...SOC NAT/COMP SOC/INTEG. PAGE 121 H2424 — B14 ELITES OWN DOMIN NAT/G

TREITSCHKE H.,POLITICS. UNIV SOCIETY STRATA NAT/G EX/STRUC LEGIS DOMIN EDU/PROP ATTIT PWR RESPECT ...CONCPT TIME/SEQ GEN/LAWS TOT/POP 20. PAGE 157 H3129 — B16 EXEC ELITES GERMANY

BARRES M.,THE UNDYING SPIRIT OF FRANCE (TRANS. BY M. CORWIN). FRANCE DOMIN LEAD DEATH ATTIT RESPECT ...NAT/COMP 20 WWI. PAGE 11 H0226 — B17 NAT/LISM FORCES WAR CULTURE

DE MAISTRE J.,DU PAPE (1817). FRANCE LAW SOCIETY SECT DOMIN REV HAPPINESS PWR SOVEREIGN 18/19 PROTESTANT. PAGE 38 H0761 — B17 CATH CHIEF LEGIT NAT/G

BURKE E.,THOUGHTS ON THE PROSPECT OF A REGICIDE PEACE (PAMPHLET). FRANCE UK SECT DOMIN MURDER PEACE ORD/FREE SOVEREIGN POPULISM...POLICY GOV/COMP IDEA/COMP 18 JACOBINISM COEXIST. PAGE 24 H0483 — N17 REV CHIEF NAT/G DIPLOM

BURKE E.,THOUGHTS ON THE CAUSE OF THE PRESENT DISCONTENTS (PAMPHLET). MOD/EUR UK CONSTN CHIEF LEGIS DOMIN CONTROL EXEC REPRESENT POPULISM ...TRADIT NEW/IDEA METH/COMP 18 BURKE/EDM. PAGE 24 H0484 — N17 ORD/FREE REV PARL/PROC NAT/G

BURKE E.,LETTER TO SIR HERCULES LANGRISHE (PAMPHLET). IRELAND UK NAT/G CHIEF DIPLOM DOMIN PARL/PROC COERCE ORD/FREE SOVEREIGN POPULISM ...TRADIT 18 BURKE/EDM. PAGE 24 H0485 — N17 POLICY COLONIAL SECT

BARRES M.,"THE WAR AND THE SPIRIT OF YOUTH" (PAMPHLET). FRANCE FORCES DOMIN LEAD DEATH AGE/Y ATTIT RESPECT...FASCIST 20 WWI. PAGE 11 H0228 — N19 WAR NAT/LISM CULTURE MYSTIC

MAO TSE-TUNG,ON SOME IMPORTANT PROBLEMS OF THE PARTY'S PRESENT POLICY. CHINA/COM CONSTN ELITES INTELL AGRI DOMIN EDU/PROP REV REPRESENT GP/REL OWN PEACE ORD/FREE 20 COM/PARTY. PAGE 102 H2044 — N19 POLICY NAT/G CHIEF LEGIT

MEZERIK A.G.,APARTHEID IN THE REPUBLIC OF SOUTH AFRICA (PAMPHLET). DIPLOM DOMIN CONTROL COERCE REPRESENT CONSEN ATTIT. PAGE 110 H2194 — N19 DISCRIM RACE/REL POL/PAR POLICY

SENGHOR L.S.,AFRICAN SOCIALISM (PAMPHLET). AFR FRANCE MALI USSR ELITES ECO/UNDEV NAT/G DIPLOM DOMIN EDU/PROP ATTIT 20 NEGRO. PAGE 141 H2827 — N19 SOCISM MARXISM ORD/FREE NAT/LISM

TABORSKY E.,CONFORMITY UNDER COMMUNISM (PAMPHLET). CZECHOSLVK HUNGARY POLAND SCHOOL DOMIN PRESS ...TREND GOV/COMP 20. PAGE 152 H3030 — N19 COM CONTROL EDU/PROP NAT/G

HALDANE R.B.,BEFORE THE WAR. MOD/EUR SOCIETY INT/ORG NAT/G DELIB/GP PLAN DOMIN EDU/PROP LEGIT ADMIN COERCE ATTIT DRIVE MORAL ORD/FREE PWR...SOC CONCPT SELF/OBS RECORD BIOG TIME/SEQ. PAGE 64 H1282 — B20 POLICY DIPLOM UK

STUART G.H.,FRENCH FOREIGN POLICY. CONSTN INT/ORG NAT/G POL/PAR EX/STRUC FORCES PLAN ECO/TAC DOMIN EDU/PROP ADJUD COERCE ATTIT DRIVE RIGID/FLEX ALL/VALS...POLICY OBS RECORD BIOG TIME/SEQ TREND. PAGE 150 H3000 — B21 MOD/EUR DIPLOM FRANCE

KRABBE H.,THE MODERN IDEA OF THE STATE. LAW CHIEF DIPLOM DOMIN ADMIN REPRESENT CENTRAL ORD/FREE ...NEW/IDEA GOV/COMP IDEA/COMP. PAGE 88 H1761 — B22 SOVEREIGN CONSTN PHIL/SCI

TONNIES F.,KRITIK DER OFFENTLICHEN MEINUNG. FRANCE UK CULTURE COM/IND DOMIN PRESS RUMOR ROLE NAT/COMP. PAGE 156 H3114 — B22 SOCIETY SOC ATTIT

FRANK T.,A HISTORY OF ROME. MEDIT-7 INTELL SOCIETY — B23 EXEC

LOC/G NAT/G POL/PAR FORCES LEGIS DOMIN LEGIT ALL/VALS...POLICY CONCPT TIME/SEQ GEN/LAWS ROM/EMP ROM/EMP. PAGE 53 H1050
STRUCT ELITES

B23
GRANT C.F.,STUDIES IN NORTH AFRICA. ALGERIA MOROCCO ROMAN/EMP CULTURE STRUCT NAT/G DIPLOM WAR ...NAT/COMP TUNIS EUROPE. PAGE 60 H1195
ISLAM SECT DOMIN COLONIAL

B23
KADEN E.H.,DER POLITISCHE CHARAKTER DER FRANZOSISCHEN KULTURPROPAGANDA AM RHEIN. FRANCE MOD/EUR DOMIN PRESS...GEOG METH/COMP 20. PAGE 82 H1648
EDU/PROP ATTIT DIPLOM NAT/G

B23
WILLOUGHBY W.C.,RACE PROBLEMS IN THE NEW AFRICA: A STUDY OF THE RELATION OF BANTU AND BRITONS IN THOSE PARTS OF BANTU AFRICA... AFR STRUCT SECT DOMIN EDU/PROP GP/REL ATTIT WORSHIP 20 BANTU EUROPE MISSION CHRISTIAN. PAGE 168 H3372
KIN COLONIAL RACE/REL CULTURE

B26
FORTESCUE J.,THE GOVERNANCE OF ENGLAND (1471-76). UK LAW FINAN SECT LEGIS PROB/SOLV TAX DOMIN ADMIN GP/REL COST ORD/FREE PWR 14/15. PAGE 52 H1042
CONSERVE CONSTN CHIEF NAT/G

B27
BELLOC H.,THE SERVILE STATE (1912) (3RD ED.). PRUSSIA UK CULTURE STRATA INDUS NAT/G ECO/TAC CONTROL LEAD SUFF DISCRIM EQUILIB ORD/FREE WEALTH 20. PAGE 13 H0269
WORKER CAP/ISM DOMIN CATH

B27
JOHN OF SALISBURY,THE STATESMAN'S BOOK (1159) (TRANS. BY J. DICKINSON). DOMIN GP/REL MORAL ORD/FREE PWR CONSERVE...CATH CONCPT 12. PAGE 81 H1617
NAT/G SECT CHIEF LAW

B28
HURST C.,GREAT BRITAIN AND THE DOMINIONS. EUR+WWI CULTURE ECO/DEV INT/ORG NAT/G DIPLOM ECO/TAC COLONIAL ATTIT PWR SOVEREIGN...TIME/SEQ GEN/LAWS TOT/POP VAL/FREE 20 CMN/WLTH. PAGE 75 H1508
VOL/ASSN DOMIN UK

B28
MARSILIUS/PADUA,DEFENSOR PACIS (1324). CHRIST-17C CONSTN NAT/G DIPLOM DOMIN LEGIT CONTROL WAR PEACE ORD/FREE SOVEREIGN POPULISM 14 POPE. PAGE 103 H2059
CATH SECT GEN/LAWS

B29
ROBERTS S.H.,HISTORY OF FRENCH COLONIAL POLICY. AFR ASIA L/A+17C S/ASIA CULTURE ECO/DEV ECO/UNDEV FINAN NAT/G PLAN ECO/TAC DOMIN ROUTINE SOVEREIGN...OBS HIST/WRIT TREND CHARTS VAL/FREE 19/20. PAGE 132 H2642
INT/ORG ACT/RES FRANCE COLONIAL

B30
HATTERSLEY A.F.,A SHORT HISTORY OF DEMOCRACY. WOR-45 CONSTN NAT/G SECT DOMIN WAR CHOOSE ORD/FREE PWR...CONCPT GOV/COMP BIBLIOG ATHENS ROME. PAGE 68 H1355
REPRESENT MAJORIT POPULISM

B30
LASKI H.J.,LIBERTY IN THE MODERN STATE. UNIV SOCIETY STRATA CREATE BAL/PWR CONTROL RATIONAL ATTIT PWR 18/20. PAGE 91 H1828
CONCPT ORD/FREE NAT/G DOMIN

B31
CROOK W.H.,THE GENERAL STRIKE: A STUDY OF LABOR'S TRAGIC WEAPON IN THEORY AND PRACTICE. BELGIUM FRANCE SWEDEN UK WOR-45 PROB/SOLV ECO/TAC DOMIN PWR ...POLICY TIME/SEQ NAT/COMP GEN/LAWS 19/20 STRIKE. PAGE 35 H0707
LABOR WORKER LG/CO BARGAIN

B31
DEKAT A.D.A.,COLONIAL POLICY. S/ASIA CULTURE EX/STRUC ECO/TAC DOMIN ADMIN COLONIAL ROUTINE SOVEREIGN WEALTH...POLICY MGT RECORD KNO/TEST SAMP. PAGE 39 H0785
DRIVE PWR INDONESIA NETHERLAND

B32
BRYCE J.,THE HOLY ROMAN EMPIRE. GERMANY ITALY MOD/EUR CULTURE SOCIETY STRUCT INT/ORG NAT/G SECT DIPLOM DOMIN WAR SUPEGO ALL/VALS SOVEREIGN...GEOG SOC TIME/SEQ CHARTS STERTYP. PAGE 23 H0456
CHRIST-17C NAT/LISM

S32
BEARD C.A.,"REPRESENTATIVE GOVERNMENT IN EVOLUTION" WOR-45 AGRI TEC/DEV DOMIN EFFICIENCY ORD/FREE CONSERVE...TIME/SEQ GOV/COMP IDEA/COMP GRECO/ROMN. PAGE 12 H0248
REPRESENT POPULISM NAT/G PWR

B33
DAHLIN E.,FRENCH AND GERMAN PUBLIC OPINION ON DECLARED WAR AIMS 1914-1918. BELGIUM FRANCE GERMANY NAT/G POL/PAR DIPLOM COERCE REV WAR PEACE 20 WWI WILSON/W. PAGE 37 H0733
ATTIT EDU/PROP DOMIN NAT/COMP

B35
MARRIOTT J.A.,DICTATORSHIP AND DEMOCRACY. GERMANY GREECE UK CHIEF DIPLOM DOMIN LEGIT PEACE ORD/FREE CONSERVE...TREND ROME HITLER/A. PAGE 103 H2057
TOTALISM POPULISM PLURIST NAT/G

B36
HUBERMAN L.,MAN'S WORLDLY GOODS: THE STORY OF THE WEALTH OF NATIONS. CHRIST-17C EUR+WWI MOD/EUR SOCIETY DOMIN REV ORD/FREE...TIME/SEQ METH/COMP. PAGE 74 H1486
WEALTH CAP/ISM MARXISM CREATE

B36
WANDERSCHECK H.,WELTKRIEG UND PROPAGANDA. GERMANY MOD/EUR UK COM/IND NAT/G DOMIN PRESS ATTIT...POLICY 20 HITLER/A. PAGE 165 H3299
EDU/PROP PSY WAR KNOWL

C36
MAZZINI J.,"FROM THE COUNCIL TO GOD" (1870) IN J. MAZZINI, ESSAYS." ITALY NAT/G EDU/PROP PARTIC ORD/FREE PWR SOVEREIGN 19 POPE CHRISTIAN DEITY. PAGE 106 H2112
CATHISM DOMIN NAT/LISM SUPEGO

B37
MARX K.,THE CIVIL WAR IN THE UNITED STATES. USA-45 WORKER DIPLOM INT/TRADE DOMIN RACE/REL ATTIT ...TREND 19. PAGE 104 H2078
WAR REV MARXIST ORD/FREE

B37
MUNZENBERG W.,PROPAGANDA ALS WAFFE. COM/IND PRESS COERCE WAR...PSY 20. PAGE 115 H2290
EDU/PROP DOMIN NAT/G LEAD

L37
NICOLSON H.,"THE MEANING OF PRESTIGE." EUR+WWI MOD/EUR UK CULTURE SOCIETY NAT/G DIPLOM DOMIN LEGIT ATTIT DRIVE PWR...METH/CNCPT RECORD TIME/SEQ GEN/METH CMN/WLTH TOT/POP 20. PAGE 118 H2351
CONCPT STERTYP

B38
MARX K.,THE GERMAN IDEOLOGY, PARTS 1 AND 3 (1846). MOD/EUR LAW STRATA WORKER DOMIN REV UTOPIA SOCISM 19 MARX/KARL. PAGE 104 H2079
MARXIST OWN PRODUC ECO/TAC

B39
HITLER A.,MEIN KAMPF. EUR+WWI FUT MOD/EUR STRUCT INT/ORG LABOR NAT/G POL/PAR FORCES CREATE PLAN BAL/PWR DIPLOM ECO/TAC DOMIN EDU/PROP ADMIN COERCE ATTIT...SOCIALIST BIOG TREND NAZI. PAGE 71 H1428
PWR NEW/IDEA WAR

B39
MILLER P.,THE NEW ENGLAND MIND: THE SEVENTEENTH CENTURY. CULTURE DOMIN WRITING INGP/REL CONSEN MAJORITY PERCEPT KNOWL MORAL...CONCPT LING WORSHIP 17 NEW/ENGLND PROTESTANT. PAGE 111 H2214
SECT REGION SOC ATTIT

B39
SCHOCKEL E.,DAS POLITISCHE PLAKAT. EUR+WWI GERMANY NAT/G PWR FASCISM EXHIBIT. PAGE 140 H2794
EDU/PROP ATTIT DOMIN POL/PAR

B40
HOBBES T.,BEHEMOTH (1668). UK CONSTN SECT DOMIN LEGIT UTIL ORD/FREE CATHISM...POLICY CONCPT GEN/LAWS 17 CHARLES/I CROMWELL/O PROTESTANT. PAGE 71 H1433
REV NAT/G CHIEF

B40
SIMON Y.,NATURE AND FUNCTIONS OF AUTHORITY. UNIV SOCIETY NAT/G CHIEF CONCPT. PAGE 144 H2880
ORD/FREE DOMIN GEN/LAWS PERSON

B40
TONNIES F.,FUNDAMENTAL CONCEPTS OF SOCIOLOGY (1887) (TRANS. BY C. LOOMIS). LAW STRATA STRUCT FAM MUNIC NAT/G DOMIN LEGIT SANCTION COERCE CRIME PERSON 19. PAGE 156 H3115
CULTURE SOCIETY GEN/LAWS SOC

B40
WANDERSCHECK H.,FRANKREICHS PROPAGANDA GEGEN DEUTSCHLAND. FRANCE GERMANY MOD/EUR UK NAT/G DIPLOM WAR 20 JEWS. PAGE 165 H3300
EDU/PROP ATTIT DOMIN PRESS

B41
BAUMANN G.,GRUNDLAGEN UND PRAXIS DER INTERNATIONALEN PROPAGANDA. FRANCE GERMANY UK CULTURE COM/IND PRESS PWR...PSY METH/COMP 20. PAGE 12 H0241
EDU/PROP DOMIN ATTIT DIPLOM

B41
PALMER R.R.,TWELVE WHO RULED. MOD/EUR ELITES STRUCT NAT/G POL/PAR DELIB/GP DOMIN ATTIT SUPEGO PWR ...POLICY CONCPT 18. PAGE 123 H2453
TOP/EX BIOG REV FRANCE

B42
LA BOETIE E.,ANTI-DICTATOR (1548) (TRANS. BY H. KUNZ). CONSTN NAT/G CHIEF DOMIN LEGIT CONTROL POPULISM. PAGE 90 H1790
PWR ORD/FREE TOTALISM GEN/LAWS

B42
NEUMANN S.,PERMANENT REVOLUTION: THE TOTAL STATE IN A WORLD AT WAR. COM EUR+WWI GERMANY USSR EX/STRUC DIPLOM CONTROL COERCE REPRESENT MARXISM...SOC GOV/COMP BIBLIOG 20 HITLER/A STALIN/J. PAGE 117 H2337
FASCISM TOTALISM DOMIN EDU/PROP

B43
EARLE E.M.,MAKERS OF MODERN STRATEGY: MILITARY THOUGHT FROM MACHIAVELLI TO HITLER. EUR+WWI MOD/EUR NAT/G ACT/RES BAL/PWR DOMIN COERCE ATTIT DRIVE RIGID/FLEX ALL/VALS...METH/CNCPT BIOG 16/20. PAGE 44 H0879
PLAN FORCES WAR

B43
LENIN V.I.,LEFT WING COMMUNISM: AN INFANTILE DISORDER (1920). GERMANY MOD/EUR USSR STRUCT CHIEF DOMIN EDU/PROP LEGIT LEAD REPRESENT POPULISM
COM MARXISM NAT/G

...METH/COMP 19 LENIN/VI COM/PARTY MENSHEVIK. PAGE 94 H1879 — REV

B43
MARITAIN J.,THE RIGHTS OF MAN AND NATURAL LAW. CONSTN NAT/G DOMIN LEGIT INGP/REL TOTALISM MORAL POPULISM WORSHIP 19/20 CIVIL/LIB CHURCH/STA NATURL/LAW. PAGE 103 H2051 — PLURIST ORD/FREE GEN/LAWS

B43
SERENI A.P.,THE ITALIAN CONCEPTION OF INTERNATIONAL LAW. EUR+WWI MOD/EUR INT/ORG NAT/G DOMIN COERCE ORD/FREE FASCISM...OBS/ENVIR TREND 20. PAGE 141 H2829 — LAW TIME/SEQ INT/LAW ITALY

B44
GYORGY A.,GEOPOLITICS: THE NEW GERMAN SCIENCE. EUR+WWI GERMANY STRATA NAT/G PROVS DOMIN EDU/PROP ATTIT DRIVE FASCISM...GEOG NAZI 20. PAGE 63 H1261 — PWR LEGIT WAR

B44
KNORR K.E.,BRITISH COLONIAL THEORIES 1570-1850. NAT/G DELIB/GP ECO/TAC PERCEPT PWR...WELF/ST METH/CNCPT CONT/OBS TIME/SEQ SIMUL TOT/POP 20. PAGE 87 H1734 — ACT/RES DOMIN COLONIAL

B44
KRIS E.,GERMAN RADIO PROPAGANDA: REPORT ON HOME BROADCASTS DURING THE WAR. EUR+WWI GERMANY CULTURE CONSULT PROB/SOLV FEEDBACK TASK INGP/REL DRIVE PWR FASCISM...CON/ANAL METH/COMP 20. PAGE 89 H1768 — EDU/PROP DOMIN ACT/RES ATTIT

B44
SUAREZ F.,A TREATISE ON LAWS AND GOD THE LAWGIVER (1612) IN SELECTIONS FROM THREE WORKS, VOL. II. FRANCE ITALY UK CULTURE NAT/G SECT CHIEF LEGIS DOMIN LEGIT CT/SYS ORD/FREE PWR WORSHIP 16/17. PAGE 150 H3004 — LAW JURID GEN/LAWS CATH

L44
HUXLEY J.,"THE FUTURE OF THE COLONIES." AFR SOCIETY NAT/G PLAN DOMIN COERCE ATTIT DRIVE ORD/FREE PWR WEALTH...TIME/SEQ TREND AUD/VIS CHARTS 20. PAGE 76 H1511 — ECO/UNDEV FUT COLONIAL

B45
CONOVER H.F.,ITALY: ECONOMICS, POLITICS AND MILITARY AFFAIRS, 1940-1945. ITALY ELITES NAT/G POL/PAR EX/STRUC TOP/EX DIPLOM DOMIN CONTROL COERCE WAR CIVMIL/REL EFFICIENCY 20. PAGE 32 H0646 — BIBLIOG TOTALISM FORCES

C45
PAINE T.,"THE AGE OF REASON IN T. PAINE, THE COMPLETE WRITINGS OF THOMAS PAINE (VOL. 1) (1794-95)" CULTURE ACT/RES DOMIN UTOPIA ATTIT PERCEPT WORSHIP. PAGE 122 H2445 — SECT KNOWL PHIL/SCI ORD/FREE

B46
ALLEN J.S.,WORLD MONOPOLY AND PEACE. GERMANY UK USSR FINAN INDUS LG/CO DOMIN CONTROL PEACE PWR WEALTH SOCISM...NAT/COMP 20 MONOPOLY. PAGE 5 H0105 — CAP/ISM DIPLOM WAR COLONIAL

B46
BLUM L.,FOR ALL MANKIND (TRANS. BY W. PICKLES). FRANCE GERMANY USSR LAW SOCIETY STRUCT POL/PAR WORKER DIPLOM DOMIN CHOOSE ORD/FREE FASCISM 20. PAGE 18 H0361 — POPULISM SOCIALIST NAT/G WAR

B46
NICOLSON H.,THE CONGRESS OF VIENNA. MOD/EUR NAT/G FORCES BAL/PWR DOMIN LEGIT COERCE PERSON PWR ...RECORD TIME/SEQ STERTYP 19 CONG/VIENN. PAGE 118 H2353 — CONCPT POLICY DIPLOM

S46
DE GRE G.,"FREEDOM AND SOCIAL STRUCTURE" (BMR)" UNIV SOCIETY DOMIN CONTROL TOTALISM PLURISM...SOC CHARTS. PAGE 38 H0753 — ORD/FREE STRUCT CONCPT GP/REL

N47
CANNON J.P.,AMERICAN STALINISM AND ANTI-STALINISM (PAMPHLET). NAT/G WORKER DOMIN EDU/PROP REV GP/REL ...MARXIST CONCPT 20 STALIN/J TROTSKY/L. PAGE 26 H0521 — LABOR MARXISM CAP/ISM POL/PAR

B48
CLYDE P.H.,THE FAR EAST: A HISTORY OF THE IMPACT OF THE WEST ON EASTERN ASIA. CHINA/COM CULTURE INT/TRADE DOMIN COLONIAL WAR PWR...CHARTS BIBLIOG 19/20 CHINJAP. PAGE 30 H0609 — DIPLOM ASIA

B48
LINEBARGER P.,PSYCHOLOGICAL WARFARE. NAT/G PLAN DIPLOM DOMIN ATTIT...POLICY CONCPT EXHIBIT 20 WWI. PAGE 97 H1933 — EDU/PROP PSY WAR COM/IND

B48
PELCOVITS N.A.,OLD CHINA HANDS AND THE FOREIGN OFFICE. ASIA BURMA UK ECO/UNDEV NAT/G ECO/TAC FOR/AID TARIFFS DOMIN COLONIAL GOV/REL SOVEREIGN 19 HONG/KONG TREATY. PAGE 124 H2483 — INT/TRADE ATTIT DIPLOM

L48
SHILS E.A.,"COHESION AND DISINTEGRATION IN THE WEHRMACHT IN WORLD WAR II." GERMANY STRUCT DOMIN WAR INGP/REL ISOLAT NAT/LISM ATTIT AUTHORIT SUPEGO RESPECT...PSY CON/ANAL 20 NAZI. PAGE 143 H2862 — EDU/PROP DRIVE PERS/REL FORCES

S48
ALEXANDER L.,"WAR CRIMES, THEIR SOCIAL-PSYCHOLOGICAL ASPECTS." EUR+WWI GERMANY LAW CULTURE ELITES KIN POL/PAR PUB/INST FORCES DOMIN EDU/PROP COERCE CRIME ATTIT SUPEGO HEALTH MORAL PWR FASCISM ...PSY OBS TREND GEN/LAWS NAZI 20. PAGE 5 H0100 — DRIVE WAR

B49
BOZZA T.,SCRITTORI POLITICI ITALIANI DAL 1550 AL 1650. CHRIST-17C ITALY DIPLOM DOMIN 16/17. PAGE 20 H0394 — BIBLIOG/A NAT/G CONCPT WRITING

B49
DE JOUVENEL B.,ON POWER: ITS NATURE AND THE HISTORY OF ITS GROWTH. SOCIETY CHIEF REV WAR ATTIT AUTHORIT ORD/FREE SOVEREIGN CONSERVE POPULISM CONCPT. PAGE 38 H0757 — PWR NAT/G DOMIN CONTROL

B49
WORMUTH F.D.,THE ORIGINS OF MODERN CONSTITUTIONALISM. GREECE UK LEGIS CREATE TEC/DEV BAL/PWR DOMIN ADJUD REV WAR PWR...JURID ROMAN/REP CROMWELL/O. PAGE 170 H3412 — NAT/G CONSTN LAW

S49
DEXTER L.A.,"A DIALOGUE ON THE SOCIAL PSYCHOLOGY OF COLONIALISM AND ON CERTAIN PUERTO RICAN PROFESSIONAL PERSONALITY PATTERNS." L/A+17C PUERT/RICO STRATA STRUCT DOMIN ISOLAT DRIVE ...NAT/COMP PERS/COMP HYPO/EXP 20 JEWS NEGRO. PAGE 41 H0813 — COLONIAL SOC PSY PERSON

B50
GATZKE H.W.,GERMANY'S DRIVE TO THE WEST. BELGIUM GERMANY MOD/EUR AGRI INDUS POL/PAR FORCES DOMIN AGREE CONTROL REGION COERCE 20 TREATY WWI. PAGE 55 H1104 — WAR POLICY NAT/G DIPLOM

B50
GLEASON J.H.,THE GENESIS OF RUSSOPHOBIA IN GREAT BRITAIN: A STUDY OF THE INTERACTION OF POLICY AND OPINION. ASIA RUSSIA UK NAT/G AGREE CONTROL REV WAR LOVE PWR TREATY 19. PAGE 57 H1142 — DIPLOM POLICY DOMIN COLONIAL

B50
HOBBES T.,LEVIATHAN. UNIV CONSTN SOCIETY LOC/G NAT/G CONSULT TOP/EX DOMIN DRIVE PERSON PWR ...PHIL/SCI CONCPT SELF/OBS GEN/LAWS TOT/POP. PAGE 72 H1434 — LAW ORD/FREE

B50
MACHIAVELLI N.,THE DISCOURSES (1516). NAT/G SECT FORCES DOMIN LEGIT CONTROL LEAD COERCE TOTALISM ORD/FREE. PAGE 100 H1995 — PWR GEN/LAWS CHIEF

B50
US DEPARTMENT OF STATE,DOCUMENTS ON GERMAN FOREIGN POLICY, 1918-1945 (13 VOLS.). EUR+WWI GERMANY NAT/G PLAN DIPLOM DOMIN EDU/PROP CONTROL NAT/LISM ...ANTHOL 20. PAGE 159 H3186 — BIBLIOG/A WAR POLICY FASCIST

B50
WADE E.C.S.,CONSTITUTIONAL LAW; AN OUTLINE OF THE LAW AND PRACTICE OF THE CONSTITUTION. UK LEGIS DOMIN ADMIN GP/REL 16/20 CMN/WLTH PARLIAMENT ENGLSH/LAW. PAGE 164 H3283 — CONSTN NAT/G PARL/PROC LAW

B52
JULIEN C.A.,L'AFRIQUE DU NORD EN MARCHE: NATIONALISMES MUSULMANS ET SOUVERAINETE FRANCAISE (2ND ED). AFR ALGERIA FRANCE ISLAM MOROCCO NAT/G CONTROL ORD/FREE...POLICY 19/20 TUNIS MUSLIM. PAGE 82 H1641 — NAT/LISM COERCE DOMIN COLONIAL

B52
KOLARZ W.,RUSSIA AND HER COLONIES. COM RUSSIA LAW CULTURE ECO/DEV KIN LOC/G SECT TEC/DEV ECO/TAC EDU/PROP REGION COERCE ATTIT PWR SOVEREIGN...SOC TIME/SEQ CON/ANAL VAL/FREE 19/20. PAGE 88 H1749 — NAT/G DOMIN USSR COLONIAL

B52
LEYS W.,ETHICS FOR POLICY DECISIONS. INTELL NAT/G CONSULT PLAN DOMIN EDU/PROP LEGIT COERCE KNOWL MORAL PWR...HUM GEN/LAWS. PAGE 96 H1920 — ACT/RES POLICY

B52
SKALWEIT S.,FRANKREICH UND FRIEDRICH DER GROSSE. FRANCE GERMANY PRUSSIA NAT/G DOMIN WAR 18 FREDERICK. PAGE 145 H2893 — ATTIT EDU/PROP DIPLOM SOC

C52
HUME D.,"IDEA OF A PERFECT COMMONWEALTH" IN D. HUME, POLITICAL DISCOURSES (1752)" UK NAT/G DOMIN GP/REL CONSERVE...POLICY CONCPT GEN/LAWS 18 MORE/THOM PLATO. PAGE 75 H1494 — CONSTN CHIEF SOCIETY GOV/COMP

B53
BENDIX R.,CLASS, STATUS AND POWER: A READER IN SOCIAL STRATIFICATION. USA+45 SOCIETY ACT/RES DOMIN ATTIT RIGID/FLEX...PSY SOC CONCPT METH/COMP NAT/COMP 20. PAGE 14 H0273 — STRATA PWR STRUCT ROLE

B53
BROWN D.M.,THE WHITE UMBRELLA: INDIAN POLITICAL THOUGHT FROM MANU TO GANDHI. INDIA LAW NAT/G SECT WRITING NAT/LISM...ANTHOL BIBLIOG 20 HINDU GANDHI/M MANU. PAGE 22 H0442 — CONCPT DOMIN CONSERVE

B53
SHIRATO I.,JAPANESE SOURCES ON THE HISTORY OF THE CHINESE COMMUNIST MOVEMENT (PAMPHLET). CHINA/COM USSR CONSTRUC NAT/G POL/PAR FORCES DIPLOM DOMIN EDU/PROP CONTROL WAR TOTALISM SOCISM 20. PAGE 143 H2863 — BIBLIOG/A MARXISM ECO/UNDEV

B53
SQUIRES J.D.,BRITISH PROPAGANDA AT HOME AND IN THE — EDU/PROP

UNITED STATES FROM 1914 TO 1917. UK NAT/G PROB/SOLV DOMIN PRESS EFFICIENCY...PSY PREDICT 20 WWI INTERVENT PSY/WAR. PAGE 148 H2960 — CONTROL WAR DIPLOM

S53
ARENDT H.,"IDEOLOGY AND TERROR: A NOVEL FORM OF GOVERNMENT." WOR-45 DOMIN STRANGE ATTIT SUPEGO MARXISM...GOV/COMP IDEA/COMP 20 NAZI. PAGE 8 H0160 — TOTALISM ANOMIE ALL/IDEOS SOCIETY

B54
FRIEDRICH C.J.,TOTALITARIAN DICTATORSHIP AND AUTOCRACY. COM EUR+WWI GERMANY ITALY USSR INTELL ECO/DEV NAT/G POL/PAR FORCES TOP/EX ECO/TAC EDU/PROP LEGIT COERCE ATTIT ORD/FREE PWR FASCISM ...CONCPT TIME/SEQ GEN/LAWS NAZI 20. PAGE 53 H1068 — SOCIETY DOMIN TOTALISM

B54
MITCHELL P.,AFRICAN AFTERTHOUGHTS. UGANDA CONSTN NAT/G ADJUD COERCE WAR 20 WWI MAU/MAU. PAGE 112 H2230 — BIOG CHIEF COLONIAL DOMIN

L54
FRIEDRICH C.J.,"TOTALITARIANISM." COM EUR+WWI NAT/G POL/PAR SECT FORCES PLAN ECO/TAC DOMIN EDU/PROP EXEC COERCE REV ORD/FREE PWR...SOC CONCPT NAZI 20. PAGE 53 H1067 — ATTIT TOTALISM

S54
BALANDIER G.,"SOCIOLOGIE DE LA COLONISATION ET RELATIONS ENTRE SOCIETES GLOBALES." AFR SOCIETY ECO/UNDEV KIN DOMIN EDU/PROP RIGID/FLEX PWR...PSY CONCPT TREND TOT/POP. PAGE 10 H0203 — CULTURE SOC COLONIAL

C54
GUINS G.C.,"SOVIET LAW AND SOVIET SOCIETY." COM USSR STRATA FAM NAT/G WORKER DOMIN RACE/REL ...BIBLIOG 20. PAGE 62 H1249 — LAW STRUCT PLAN

B55
KHADDURI M.,WAR AND PEACE IN THE LAW OF ISLAM. CONSTN CULTURE SOCIETY STRATA NAT/G PROVS SECT FORCES TOP/EX CREATE DOMIN EDU/PROP ADJUD COERCE ATTIT RIGID/FLEX ALL/VALS...CONCPT TIME/SEQ TOT/POP VAL/FREE. PAGE 85 H1702 — ISLAM JURID PEACE WAR

B55
WOYTINSKY W.S.,WORLD COMMERCE AND GOVERNMENTS: TRENDS AND OUTLOOK. WOR+45 FINAN POL/PAR DIPLOM ECO/TAC FOR/AID DOMIN WAR CHOOSE...CHARTS BIBLIOG 20 LEAGUE/NAT UN ILO. PAGE 171 H3413 — INT/TRADE DIST/IND NAT/COMP NAT/G

B56
CARRIL B.,PROBLEMAS DE LA REVOLUCION Y LA DEMOCRACIA. CONSTN FORCES DOMIN CONTROL TOTALISM PWR 20. PAGE 27 H0539 — REV ORD/FREE LEGIT NAT/G

B56
GLUCKMAN M.,CUSTOM AND CONFLICT IN AFRICA. AFR FAM KIN NAT/G DOMIN DISCRIM DRIVE MORAL PWR...SOC BIBLIOG WORSHIP 20. PAGE 57 H1145 — CULTURE CREATE PERS/REL GP/COMP

B56
MANNONI D.O.,PROSPERO AND CALIBAN: THE PSYCHOLOGY OF COLONIZATION. AFR EUR+WWI FAM KIN MUNIC SECT DOMIN ADMIN ATTIT DRIVE LOVE PWR RESPECT...PSY SOC CONCPT MYTH OBS DEEP/INT BIOG GEN/METH MALAGASY 20. PAGE 102 H2040 — CULTURE COLONIAL

C56
FALL B.B.,"THE VIET-MINH REGIME." VIETNAM LAW ECO/UNDEV POL/PAR FORCES DOMIN WAR ATTIT MARXISM ...BIOG PREDICT BIBLIOG/A 20. PAGE 48 H0967 — NAT/G ADMIN EX/STRUC LEAD

C56
NEUMANN S.,"MODERN POLITICAL PARTIES: APPROACHES TO COMPARATIVE POLITIC. FRANCE UK EX/STRUC DOMIN ADMIN LEAD REPRESENT TOTALISM ATTIT...POLICY TREND METH/COMP ANTHOL BIBLIOG/A 20 CMN/WLTH. PAGE 117 H2338 — POL/PAR GOV/COMP ELITES MAJORIT

B57
ARON R.,THE OPIUM OF THE INTELLECTUALS (TRANS. BY TERENCE KILMARTIN). FRANCE USSR WOR+45 CULTURE POL/PAR PLAN DOMIN EDU/PROP REV ATTIT ORD/FREE ...IDEA/COMP METH/COMP NAT/COMP 20 COM/PARTY. PAGE 8 H0169 — INTELL UTOPIA MYTH MARXISM

B57
BUCK P.W.,CONTOL OF FOREIGN RELATIONS IN MODERN NATIONS. FRANCE L/A+17C NETHERLAND USSR WOR+45 INT/ORG TOP/EX BAL/PWR DOMIN EDU/PROP COERCE PEACE ATTIT...CONCPT TREND 20 CMN/WLTH. PAGE 23 H0465 — NAT/G PWR DIPLOM

B57
BUNDESMIN FUR VERTRIEBENE,DIE VERTREIBUNG DER DEUTSCHEN BEVOLKERUNG AUS DER TSCHECHOSLOWAKEI. CZECHOSLVK GERMANY NAT/G FORCES MURDER WAR INGP/REL ATTIT 20 MIGRATION. PAGE 24 H0474 — GP/REL DOMIN COERCE DISCRIM

B57
HALLGARTEN G.W.,DAMONEN ODER RETTER. ASIA L/A+17C CAP/ISM ATTIT MARXISM SOCISM...NAT/COMP. PAGE 64 H1289 — TOTALISM FASCISM COERCE DOMIN

B57
LAQUER W.Z.,COMMUNISM AND NATIONALISM IN THE MIDDLE EAST. ELITES INTELL STRATA NAT/G POL/PAR SECT VOL/ASSN TOP/EX DOMIN LEGIT REGION COERCE ATTIT PERSON PWR...CONCPT HIST/WRIT TIME/SEQ TREND GEN/LAWS VAL/FREE. PAGE 91 H1817 — ISLAM NAT/LISM

B57
LONG H.A.,USURPERS - FOES OF FREE MAN. LAW NAT/G CHIEF LEGIS DOMIN ADJUD REPRESENT GOV/REL ORD/FREE LAISSEZ POPULISM...POLICY 18/20 SUPREME/CT ROOSEVLT/F CONGRESS CON/INTERP. PAGE 98 H1961 — CT/SYS CENTRAL FEDERAL CONSTN

B57
PARK A.G.,BOLSHEVISM IN TURKESTAN 1917-1927. COM RUSSIA USSR CULTURE AGRI SECT DOMIN GP/REL INGP/REL NAT/LISM...BIBLIOG 20 TURKESTAN. PAGE 123 H2467 — REV POLICY MARXISM ISLAM

B57
ROBERTSON H.M.,SOUTH AFRICA, ECONOMIC AND POLITICAL ASPECTS. SOUTH/AFR CONSTN CULTURE POL/PAR LEGIS DIPLOM DOMIN COLONIAL...SOC BIBLIOG 19/20. PAGE 132 H2647 — RACE/REL ECO/UNDEV ECO/TAC DISCRIM

B57
TOMASIC D.A.,NATIONAL COMMUNISM AND SOVIET STRATEGY. UK USSR YUGOSLAVIA NAT/G POL/PAR CHIEF CREATE DOMIN REV WAR PWR...BIOG TREND 20 TITO/MARSH STALIN/J. PAGE 156 H3112 — COM NAT/LISM MARXISM DIPLOM

S57
HAILEY,"TOMORROW IN AFRICA." CONSTN SOCIETY LOC/G NAT/G DOMIN ADJUD ADMIN GP/REL DISCRIM NAT/LISM ATTIT MORAL ORD/FREE...PSY SOC CONCPT OBS RECORD TREND GEN/LAWS CMN/WLTH 20. PAGE 64 H1277 — AFR PERSON ELITES RACE/REL

S57
KILSON M.L.,"LAND AND POLITICS IN KENYA: AN ANALYSIS OF AFRICAN POLITICS IN A PLURAL SOCIETY." FUT LAW CULTURE KIN NAT/G ECO/TAC DOMIN REV NAT/LISM ORD/FREE PWR RESPECT SOVEREIGN WEALTH ...SOC OBS TREND WORK VAL/FREE CMN/WLTH 20. PAGE 86 H1710 — AFR ECO/UNDEV

S57
LEWIS E.G.,"PARLIAMENTARY CONTROL OF NATIONALIZED INDUSTRY IN FRANCE." FRANCE NAT/G DELIB/GP ACT/RES PLAN PROB/SOLV ECO/TAC DOMIN CENTRAL. PAGE 96 H1914 — PWR LEGIS INDUS CONTROL

C57
WITTFOGEL K.A.,"ORIENTAL DESPOTISM: A COMPARATIVE STUDY OF TOTAL POWER." ASIA CULTURE STRATA NAT/G LEAD OWN ORD/FREE PWR...CONCPT TREND BIBLIOG 20. PAGE 170 H3393 — TOTALISM HABITAT DOMIN ELITES

B58
BRADY A.,DEMOCRACY IN THE DOMINIONS (3RD ED.). CANADA NEW/ZEALND SOUTH/AFR WOR+45 LAW EX/STRUC DOMIN COLONIAL PARL/PROC REPRESENT RACE/REL NAT/LISM WEALTH 20 AUSTRAL CMN/WLTH. PAGE 20 H0399 — GOV/COMP POL/PAR POPULISM NAT/G

B58
COLEMAN J.S.,NIGERIA: BACKGROUND TO NATIONALISM. AFR SOCIETY ECO/DEV KIN LOC/G POL/PAR TEC/DEV DOMIN ADMIN DRIVE PWR RESPECT...TRADIT SOC INT SAMP TIME/SEQ 20. PAGE 31 H0627 — NAT/G NAT/LISM NIGERIA

B58
DUNAYEVSKAYA R.,MARXISM AND FREEDOM: FROM 1776 UNTIL TODAY. COM USSR WORKER CAP/ISM DOMIN REV GP/REL TOTALISM ALL/VALS...MYTH BIOG IDEA/COMP 18/20 MARX/KARL LENIN/VI STALIN/J. PAGE 43 H0861 — MARXISM CONCPT ORD/FREE

B58
GARTHOFF R.L.,SOVIET STRATEGY IN THE NUCLEAR AGE. FUT USSR R+D INT/ORG NAT/G ACT/RES TEC/DEV DOMIN DETER WAR ATTIT PWR...RELATIV METH/CNCPT SELF/OBS TREND CON/ANAL STERTYP GEN/LAWS 20. PAGE 55 H1103 — COM FORCES BAL/PWR NUC/PWR

B58
JOHNSON J.J.,POLITICAL CHANGE IN LATIN AMERICA: THE EMERGENCE OF THE MIDDLE SECTORS. INTELL STRATA STRUCT ECO/UNDEV MUNIC TEC/DEV LEAD REV...DECISION TREND GOV/COMP BIBLIOG/A 20. PAGE 81 H1621 — L/A+17C ELITES GP/REL DOMIN

B58
OGILVIE C.,THE KING'S GOVERNMENT AND THE COMMON LAW, 1471-1641. UK STRUCT NAT/G CHIEF LEGIS WORKER BAL/PWR GP/REL AUTHORIT 15/17 COMMON/LAW. PAGE 120 H2408 — CONSTN ELITES DOMIN

B58
SYME R.,COLONIAL ELITES: ROME, SPAIN, AND THE AMERICAS. CHRIST-17C MOD/EUR SPAIN UK USA-45 CULTURE NAT/G CHIEF TOP/EX...GOV/COMP IDEA/COMP NAT/COMP ROM/EMP GIBBON/EDW TOYNBEE/A. PAGE 151 H3022 — COLONIAL ELITES DOMIN

B58
TILLION G.,ALGERIA: THE REALITIES. ALGERIA FRANCE ISLAM CULTURE STRATA PROB/SOLV DOMIN REV NAT/LISM WEALTH MARXISM...GEOG 20. PAGE 155 H3094 — ECO/UNDEV SOC COLONIAL DIPLOM

C58
MORRALL J.B.,"POLITICAL THOUGHT IN MEDIEVAL TIMES." LAW NAT/G SECT DOMIN ATTIT PWR...BIOG HIST/WRIT BIBLIOG. PAGE 113 H2260 — CHRIST-17C CONCPT

B59
CARPENTER G.W.,THE WAY IN AFRICA. AFR INDUS MUNIC DIPLOM DOMIN EDU/PROP COERCE DISCRIM NAT/LISM ORD/FREE 20 NEGRO CHRISTIAN. PAGE 27 H0535 — CULTURE SECT ECO/UNDEV COLONIAL

B59
DEHIO L.,GERMANY AND WORLD POLITICS IN THE — DIPLOM

TWENTIETH CENTURY. EUR+WWI FRANCE GERMANY MOD/EUR UK USSR NAT/G CHIEF BAL/PWR DOMIN COLONIAL CONTROL LEAD...IDEA/COMP 20 VERSAILLES. PAGE 39 H0783 — WAR NAT/LISM SOVEREIGN

B59
EAENZA L.,COMMUNISMO E CATTOLICESIMO IN UNA PARROCHIA DI CAMPAGNA. ITALY CULTURE ELITES ECO/DEV AGRI KIN POL/PAR DOMIN LEGIT RIGID/FLEX...DECISION OBS IDEA/COMP 20 COM/PARTY CHURCH/STA. PAGE 44 H0878 — ATTIT CATHISM NEIGH MARXISM

B59
INTERNATIONAL PRESS INSTITUTE,THE PRESS IN AUTHORITARIAN COUNTRIES. COM PORTUGAL SPAIN UAR USSR NAT/G DOMIN LEGIT ORD/FREE FASCISM SOCISM 20. PAGE 78 H1559 — PRESS CONTROL TOTALISM EDU/PROP

B59
KIRCHHEIMER O.,GEGENWARTSPROBLEME DER ASYLGEWAHRUNG. DOMIN GP/REL ATTIT...NAT/COMP 20. PAGE 86 H1720 — DIPLOM INT/LAW JURID ORD/FREE

B59
PAGE S.W.,LENIN AND WORLD REVOLUTION. COM USSR NAT/G DOMIN COERCE CROWD UTOPIA ATTIT AUTHORIT DRIVE PWR...CONCPT MYTH 19/20 LENIN/VI MARX/KARL. PAGE 122 H2441 — REV PERSON MARXISM BIOG

B59
SHARMA R.S.,ASPECTS OF POLITICAL IDEAS AND INSTITUTIONS IN ANCIENT INDIA. INDIA SOCIETY STRUCT FAM VOL/ASSN TAX DOMIN...CONCPT HIST/WRIT 7. PAGE 142 H2848 — CULTURE JURID DELIB/GP SECT

S59
SKILLING H.G.,"COMMUNISM: NATIONAL OR INTERNATIONAL." CHINA/COM USSR YUGOSLAVIA NAT/G POL/PAR VOL/ASSN DOMIN REGION COERCE ATTIT PWR MARXISM SOCISM...CONCPT TOT/POP 20 TITO/MARSH. PAGE 145 H2894 — COM TREND

B60
ALBRECHT-CARRIE R.,FRANCE, EUROPE AND THE TWO WORLD WARS. EUR+WWI FRANCE GERMANY MOD/EUR UK ECO/DEV NAT/G FORCES BAL/PWR DOMIN ARMS/CONT PEACE PWR 20 TREATY EUROPE. PAGE 5 H0096 — DIPLOM WAR

B60
BRZEZINSKI Z.K.,THE SOVIET BLOC-UNITY AND CONFLICT. COM USSR CONSTN DOMIN ADMIN TOTALISM PWR...SOC MYTH RECORD TREND STERTYP GEN/LAWS GEN/METH TOT/POP 20. PAGE 23 H0458 — ATTIT EDU/PROP

B60
CARTER G.M.,INDEPENDENCE FOR AFRICA. AFR FUT SOCIETY STRATA ECO/DEV POL/PAR DELIB/GP PLAN DOMIN EDU/PROP COLONIAL REGION ATTIT DRIVE SOVEREIGN ...RECORD INT TIME/SEQ CHARTS 20. PAGE 27 H0544 — NAT/G PWR NAT/LISM

B60
GOODMAN E.,SOVIET DESIGN FOR A WORLD STATE. COM USSR NAT/G TOP/EX DIPLOM ECO/TAC DOMIN EDU/PROP COERCE REV ATTIT ORD/FREE...CON/ANAL 20. PAGE 59 H1171 — PLAN PWR SOCISM TOTALISM

B60
LA PONCE J.A.,THE PROTECTION OF MINORITIES. WOR+45 WOR-45 NAT/G POL/PAR SUFF...INT/LAW CLASSIF GP/COMP GOV/COMP BIBLIOG 17/20 CIVIL/LIB CIV/RIGHTS. PAGE 90 H1793 — INGP/REL DOMIN SOCIETY RACE/REL

B60
LINDSAY K.,EUROPEAN ASSEMBLIES: THE EXPERIMENTAL PERIOD 1949-1959. EUR+WWI ECO/DEV NAT/G POL/PAR LEGIS TOP/EX ACT/RES PLAN ECO/TAC DOMIN LEGIT ROUTINE ATTIT DRIVE ORD/FREE PWR SKILL...SOC CONCPT TREND CHARTS GEN/LAWS VAL/FREE. PAGE 97 H1932 — VOL/ASSN INT/ORG REGION

B60
MATTHIAS E.,DAS ENDE DER PARTEIEN 1933. GERMANY NAT/G COERCE CHOOSE ORD/FREE PWR 20. PAGE 105 H2100 — FASCISM POL/PAR DOMIN ATTIT

B60
MCCLOSKY H.,THE SOVIET DICTATORSHIP. FUT CONSTN CULTURE INTELL SOCIETY POL/PAR SECT VOL/ASSN FORCES PLAN TEC/DEV DOMIN EDU/PROP COERCE PWR MARXISM ...POLICY CONCPT MYTH STERTYP 20. PAGE 106 H2127 — COM NAT/G TOTALISM USSR

B60
PANIKKAR K.M.,THE STATE AND THE CITIZEN (2ND ED.). INDIA DOMIN ATTIT SUPEGO ORD/FREE WEALTH...GEOG CONCPT GP/COMP 20. PAGE 123 H2459 — TEC/DEV POL/PAR NAT/G EDU/PROP

B60
PIERCE R.A.,RUSSIAN CENTRAL ASIA, 1867-1917. ASIA RUSSIA CULTURE AGRI INDUS EDU/PROP REV NAT/LISM ...CHARTS BIBLIOG 19/20 BOLSHEVISM INTERVENT. PAGE 125 H2509 — COLONIAL DOMIN ADMIN ECO/UNDEV

B60
SCHAPIRO L.,THE COMMUNIST PARTY OF THE SOVIET UNION. COM LAW SOCIETY STRATA STRUCT ECO/DEV LABOR NAT/G POL/PAR CREATE DOMIN EDU/PROP COERCE TOTALISM MARXISM...POLICY CONCPT MYTH TIME/SEQ WORK TOT/POP 20 LENIN/VI STALIN/J. PAGE 139 H2772 — INTELL PWR USSR

B60
SETHE P.,SCHICKSALSSTUNDEN DER WELTGESCHICHTE (6TH ED.). NAT/G BAL/PWR DOMIN REV PWR...NAT/COMP 16/20. PAGE 141 H2831 — DIPLOM WAR PEACE

B60
STRACHEY J.,THE END OF EMPIRE. UK WOR+45 WOR-45 DIPLOM INT/TRADE DOMIN ADJUST ORD/FREE WEALTH ...SOCIALIST GOV/COMP TIME COMMONWLTH. PAGE 150 H2991 — COLONIAL ECO/DEV BAL/PWR LAISSEZ

B60
VON KOENIGSWALD H.,SIE SUCHEN ZUFLUCHT. GERMANY/E NAT/G PLAN ECO/TAC SOCISM...GEOG CENSUS 20 BERLIN. PAGE 164 H3273 — GP/REL COERCE DOMIN PERSON

B60
ZENKOVSKY S.A.,PAN-TURKISM AND ISLAM IN RUSSIA. ASIA RUSSIA USSR CULTURE POL/PAR DOMIN REV GP/REL MARXISM...LING GP/COMP BIBLIOG 19/20 TURKIC. PAGE 173 H3454 — SECT NAT/LISM COM ISLAM

B60
RUDD J.,TABOO, A STUDY OF MALAGASY CUSTOMS AND BELIEFS. MADAGASCAR LAW FAM CONTROL CRIME PERSON ...CONCPT 20. PAGE 173 H3466 — CULTURE DOMIN SECT SANCTION

L60
WHEELER G.,"RACIAL PROBLEMS IN SOVIET MUSLIM ASIA." COM CULTURE SOCIETY NEIGH SECT DOMIN EDU/PROP DISCRIM DISPL DRIVE PWR SOVEREIGN...CENSUS SAMP TREND 20 MUSLIM. PAGE 167 H3340 — PERSON ATTIT USSR RACE/REL

S60
BRZEZINSKI Z.K.,"PATTERNS AND LIMITS OF THE SINO-SOVIET DISPUTE." ASIA CHINA/COM COM FUT STRATA NAT/G EX/STRUC FORCES BAL/PWR DIPLOM ECO/TAC DOMIN EDU/PROP ADMIN COERCE WAR ATTIT RIGID/FLEX ...GEN/LAWS VAL/FREE 20. PAGE 23 H0459 — POL/PAR PWR REV USSR

S60
CASSINELLI C.,"TOTALITARIANISM, IDEOLOGY AND PROPAGANDA." EUR+WWI CULTURE SOCIETY NAT/G DOMIN COERCE ORD/FREE FASCISM MARXISM...MARXIST CONCPT STERTYP GEN/LAWS TOT/POP 20. PAGE 28 H0554 — ATTIT EDU/PROP TOTALISM

S60
GINSBURGS G.,"PEKING-LHASA-NEW DELHI." CHINA/COM FUT INDIA S/ASIA KIN NAT/G PROVS SECT FORCES BAL/PWR ECO/TAC DOMIN EDU/PROP LEGIT ADMIN REGION GUERRILLA PWR...TREND TIBET 20. PAGE 57 H1134 — ASIA COERCE DIPLOM

S60
MAGATHAN W.,"SOME BASES OF WEST GERMAN MILITARY POLICY." EUR+WWI FUT INT/ORG TOP/EX EÇO/TAC DOMIN DRIVE ORD/FREE PWR...TRADIT GEOG OBS TREND. PAGE 101 H2015 — NAT/G FORCES GERMANY

S60
NORTH R.C.,"THE NEW EXPANSIONISM." ASIA CHINA/COM FUT INDIA CULTURE SOCIETY NAT/G TOP/EX DOMIN COERCE PWR MARXISM...CONCPT TIME/SEQ TREND GEN/LAWS COLD/WAR 20 MAO. PAGE 119 H2372 — ATTIT DRIVE NAT/LISM

S60
NORTH R.C.,"DIE DISKREPANZ ZWISCHEN REALITAT UND WUNSCHBILD ALS INNENPOLITISCHER FAKTOR." ASIA CHINA/COM COM FUT ECO/UNDEV NAT/G PLAN DOMIN ADMIN COERCE PERCEPT...SOC MYTH GEN/METH WORK TOT/POP 20. PAGE 119 H2373 — SOCIETY ECO/TAC

S60
SHILS E.,"THE INTELLECTUALS IN THE POLITICAL DEVELOPMENT OF THE NEW STATES." AFR ASIA S/ASIA ELITES LOC/G NAT/G CONSULT EX/STRUC CREATE PLAN ECO/TAC DOMIN LEGIT DRIVE PWR...TRADIT CONCPT STERTYP GEN/LAWS 20. PAGE 143 H2861 — POL/PAR INTELL NAT/LISM

S60
WOLFINGER R.E.,"REPUTATION AND REALITY IN THE STUDY OF COMMUNITY POWER." STRUCT PROB/SOLV INGP/REL ATTIT OBJECTIVE...SOC METH/CNCPT PERS/COMP. PAGE 170 H3404 — CULTURE MUNIC DOMIN PWR

C60
COX R.H.,"LOCKE ON WAR AND PEACE." UK DIPLOM DOMIN PWR...BIOG IDEA/COMP BIBLIOG 18. PAGE 34 H0689 — CONCPT NAT/G PEACE WAR

B61
ASHLEY M.P.,GREAT BRITAIN TO 1688: A MODERN HISTORY. UK NAT/G CHIEF LEAD REV WAR...POLICY BIBLIOG 1/17. PAGE 9 H0174 — DOMIN CONSERVE

B61
BISHOP D.G.,THE ADMINISTRATION OF BRITISH FOREIGN RELATIONS. EUR+WWI MOD/EUR INT/ORG NAT/G POL/PAR DELIB/GP LEGIS TOP/EX ECO/TAC DOMIN EDU/PROP ADMIN COERCE 20. PAGE 17 H0344 — ROUTINE PWR DIPLOM UK

B61
BULLOCK A.,HITLER: A STUDY IN TYRANNY. EUR+WWI GERMANY SOCIETY STRUCT NAT/G POL/PAR FORCES CREATE DOMIN EDU/PROP EXEC COERCE WAR NAT/LISM DISPL DRIVE PERSON PWR...PSY NAZI 20 HITLER/A. PAGE 23 H0470 — ATTIT BIOG TOTALISM

B61
COBBAN A.,ROUSSEAU AND THE MODERN STATE. SOCIETY DOMIN INGP/REL HAPPINESS ALL/VALS...CON/ANAL 18/20 ROUSSEAU/J. PAGE 30 H0611 — ORD/FREE ROLE NAT/G POLICY

B61
COHN B.S.,DEVELOPMENT AND IMPACT OF BRITISH ADMINISTRATION IN INDIA: A BIBLIOGRAPHIC ESSAY. INDIA UK ECO/UNDEV NAT/G DOMIN...POLICY MGT SOC — BIBLIOG/A COLONIAL S/ASIA

19/20. PAGE 31 H0619 ADMIN

B61
DALLIN D.J.,SOVIET FOREIGN POLICY AFTER STALIN. ASIA CHINA/COM EUR+WWI GERMANY IRAN UK YUGOSLAVIA INT/ORG NAT/G VOL/ASSN FORCES TOP/EX BAL/PWR DOMIN EDU/PROP COERCE ATTIT PWR 20. PAGE 37 H0737
COM DIPLOM USSR

B61
GUEVARA E.,GUERRILLA WARFARE. L/A+17C ECO/UNDEV NAT/G POL/PAR VOL/ASSN PLAN DOMIN REV DRIVE PWR WEALTH...NEW/IDEA RECORD BIOG COLD/WAR MARX/KARL OAS 20. PAGE 62 H1247
FORCES COERCE GUERRILLA CUBA

B61
MARVICK D.,POLITICAL DECISION-MAKERS. INTELL STRATA NAT/G POL/PAR EX/STRUC LEGIS DOMIN EDU/PROP ATTIT PERSON PWR...PSY STAT OBS CONT/OBS STAND/INT UNPLAN/INT TIME/SEQ CHARTS STERTYP VAL/FREE. PAGE 104 H2073
TOP/EX BIOG ELITES

B61
MERRIAM A.,CONGO: BACKGROUND OF CONFLICT. AFR FUT KIN MUNIC NAT/G POL/PAR PROVS DELIB/GP PLAN DOMIN COERCE ATTIT...TIME/SEQ CHARTS CONGO 20. PAGE 109 H2182
CHOOSE GUERRILLA

B61
ROIG E.,MARTI, ANTIIMPERIALISTA. CUBA L/A+17C DIPLOM DOMIN COLONIAL CONTROL LEAD PWR SOVEREIGN ...PHIL/SCI 19 MARTI/JOSE INTERVENT. PAGE 133 H2664
PERSON NAT/LISM ECO/UNDEV ORD/FREE

B61
SCHNAPPER B.,LA POLITIQUE ET LE COMMERCE FRANCAIS DANS LE GOLFE DE GUINEE DE 1838 A 1871. FRANCE GUINEA UK SEA EXTR/IND NAT/G DELIB/GP LEGIS ADMIN ORD/FREE...POLICY GEOG CENSUS CHARTS BIBLIOG 19. PAGE 139 H2791
COLONIAL INT/TRADE DOMIN AFR

B61
ULLMAN W.,PRINCIPLES OF GOVERNMENT AND POLITICS IN THE MIDDLE AGES. LAW CONSTN DOMIN EDU/PROP LEGIT TOTALISM SOVEREIGN POPULISM...POLICY GOV/COMP IDEA/COMP 12/16 POPE KING CHURCH/STA. PAGE 158 H3152
SECT CHIEF NAT/G LEGIS

B61
WEST F.J.,POLITICAL ADVANCEMENT IN THE SOUTH PACIFIC. CONSTN CULTURE POL/PAR LEGIS DOMIN ADMIN CHOOSE SOVEREIGN VAL/FREE 20 FIJI TAHITI SAMOA. PAGE 167 H3335
S/ASIA LOC/G COLONIAL

S61
BRZEZINSKI Z.K.,"THE ORGANIZATION OF THE COMMUNIST CAMP." COM CZECHOSLVK COM/IND NAT/G DELIB/GP INT/TRADE DOMIN EDU/PROP EXEC ROUTINE COERCE ATTIT PWR...MGT CONCPT TIME/SEQ CHARTS VAL/FREE 20 TREATY. PAGE 23 H0460
VOL/ASSN DIPLOM USSR

S61
TOMASIC D.,"POLITICAL LEADERSHIP IN CONTEMPORARY POLAND." COM EUR+WWI GERMANY NAT/G POL/PAR SECT DELIB/GP PLAN ECO/TAC DOMIN EDU/PROP PWR MARXISM ...MARXIST GEOG MGT CONCPT TIME/SEQ STERTYP 20. PAGE 156 H3111
SOCIETY ROUTINE USSR POLAND

S61
TUCKER R.C.,"TOWARDS A COMPARATIVE POLITICS OF MOVEMENT-REGIMES" (BMR)" USSR CONSTN NAT/G CREATE PROB/SOLV DIPLOM DOMIN REV...GP/COMP IDEA/COMP METH 20 STALIN/J BOLSHEVISM. PAGE 157 H3135
MARXISM POLICY GEN/LAWS PWR

C61
LAPONCE J.A.,"THE GOVERNMENT OF THE FIFTH REPUBLIC." FRANCE CHIEF LEGIS PARL/PROC CHOOSE ...CHARTS GP/COMP IDEA/COMP BIBLIOG/A 20. PAGE 91 H1814
POL/PAR NAT/G CONSTN DOMIN

B62
ABRAHAM W.E.,THE MIND OF AFRICA. AFR SOCIETY STRATA KIN ECO/TAC DOMIN EDU/PROP LEGIT COERCE ATTIT ALL/VALS...MAJORIT SOC OBS HIST/WRIT TIME/SEQ TREND TOT/POP 20. PAGE 3 H0058
CULTURE 'SIMUL GHANA

B62
BRETTON H.L.,POWER AND STABILITY IN NIGERIA: THE POLITICS OF DECOLONIZATION. AFR CONSTN INTELL ECO/UNDEV COM/IND KIN NAT/G POL/PAR PROVS VOL/ASSN LEGIS DOMIN EDU/PROP LEGIT EXEC ROUTINE CHOOSE NAT/LISM ATTIT PERCEPT ALL/VALS. PAGE 20 H0411
CULTURE OBS NIGERIA

B62
BUSIA K.A.,THE CHALLENGE OF AFRICA. CULTURE KIN MUNIC NAT/G POL/PAR SCHOOL DELIB/GP PLAN ECO/TAC DOMIN EDU/PROP TOTALISM ATTIT PERSON ALL/VALS SOVEREIGN...SOC CONCPT STERTYP TOT/POP VAL/FREE 20. PAGE 25 H0496
AFR ECO/UNDEV NAT/LISM

B62
CARTER G.M.,AFRICAN ONE-PARTY STATES. ISLAM IVORY/CST LIBERIA CONSTN CULTURE SOCIETY POL/PAR PLAN DOMIN EDU/PROP EXEC REGION CHOOSE ATTIT ALL/VALS...CONCPT TIME/SEQ CHARTS VAL/FREE 20 TANGANYIKA. PAGE 27 H0545
AFR NAT/LISM

B62
DEHIO L.,THE PRECARIOUS BALANCE: FOUR CENTURIES OF THE EUROPEAN POWER STRUGGLE. FRANCE GERMANY SPAIN NAT/G DOMIN PWR...GOV/COMP 8/20. PAGE 39 H0784
BAL/PWR WAR DIPLOM COERCE

B62
FEIT E.,SOUTH AFRICA, THE DYNAMICS OF THE AFRICAN NATIONAL CONGRESS. AFR SOUTH/AFR LAW INTELL STRATA KIN NAT/G POL/PAR ECO/TAC DOMIN RISK COERCE 20 NEGRO. PAGE 49 H0984
RACE/REL ELITES CONTROL STRUCT

B62
FINER S.E.,THE MAN ON HORSEBACK: ROLE OF THE MILITARY IN POLITICS. UNIV LAW CONSTN ELITES SOCIETY POL/PAR BAL/PWR DOMIN EDU/PROP LEGIT COERCE GUERRILLA REV WAR WEAPON DRIVE SUPEGO ORD/FREE PWR RESPECT...POLICY CONCPT GEN/METH. PAGE 50 H1003
NAT/G FORCES TOTALISM

B62
HABERMAS J.,STRUKTURWANDEL DER OFFENTLICHKEIT. NAT/G EDU/PROP PRESS LEAD PARTIC PWR 20. PAGE 63 H1268
ATTIT CONCPT DOMIN

B62
HANAK H.,GREAT BRITAIN AND AUSTRIA-HUNGARY DURING THE FIRST WORLD WAR: A STUDY IN THE FORMATION OF PUBLIC OPINION. CZECHOSLVK UK NAT/G GIVE DOMIN EDU/PROP CONSERVE...BIBLIOG 20 AUST/HUNG WWI. PAGE 65 H1311
WAR DIPLOM ATTIT PRESS

B62
HO PING-TI,THE LADDER OF SUCCESS IN IMPERIAL CHINA: ASPECTS OF SOCIAL MOBILITY, 1368-1911. INTELL STRATA FAM KIN MUNIC NAT/G PROVS SCHOOL DELIB/GP DOMIN EDU/PROP ADMIN ROUTINE PERSON ALL/VALS...SOC STAT BIOG HIST/WRIT TIME/SEQ VAL/FREE. PAGE 71 H1431
ASIA CULTURE

B62
JACKSON W.A.D.,RUSSO-CHINESE BORDERLANDS. ASIA COM USSR NAT/G PROVS EX/STRUC FORCES DOMIN COERCE PEACE ATTIT PWR SOVEREIGN WEALTH...CONCPT TREND CHARTS STERTYP VAL/FREE. PAGE 79 H1576
GEOG DIPLOM RUSSIA

B62
LAQUEUR W.,POLYCENTRISM. CHINA/COM COM USSR WOR+45 INT/ORG NAT/G ECO/TAC DOMIN LEAD ATTIT PWR SOVEREIGN...ANTHOL 20. PAGE 91 H1821
MARXISM DIPLOM BAL/PWR POLICY

B62
MELADY T.,THE WHITE MAN'S FUTURE IN BLACK AFRICA. FUT CULTURE SOCIETY NAT/G POL/PAR PLAN ECO/TAC DOMIN EDU/PROP LEGIT COLONIAL RACE/REL ATTIT DRIVE ALL/VALS...PSY SOC CONCPT TIME/SEQ TOT/POP VAL/FREE 20. PAGE 108 H2167
AFR STRATA ELITES

B62
MILLER J.D.B.,THE NATURE OF POLITICS. NAT/G DOMIN LEGIT LEAD...CONCPT METH. PAGE 111 H2213
METH/COMP IDEA/COMP PHIL/SCI

B62
PENTONY D.E.,RED WORLD IN TUMULT: COMMUNIST FOREIGN POLICIES. CHINA/COM COM NAT/G EDU/PROP COERCE ATTIT PWR RESPECT...SOC CHARTS 20. PAGE 124 H2488
ECO/UNDEV DOMIN USSR ASIA

B62
ROUSSEAU J.J.,THE SOCIAL CONTRACT. LAW CONSTN CHIEF DOMIN REPRESENT GP/REL ORD/FREE POPULISM...MAJORIT GOV/COMP 18. PAGE 135 H2700
GEN/LAWS AGREE REV

B62
STARR R.E.,POLAND 1944-1962: THE SOVIETIZATION OF A CAPTIVE PEOPLE. COM POLAND USSR POL/PAR SECT LEGIS DIPLOM DOMIN EDU/PROP CHOOSE ORD/FREE...POLICY CHARTS BIBLIOG 20. PAGE 149 H2973
MARXISM NAT/G TOTALISM NAT/COMP

B62
SWAYZE H.,POLITICAL CONTROL OF LITERATURE IN THE USSR, 1946-1959. USSR NAT/G CREATE LICENSE...JURID 20. PAGE 151 H3014
MARXISM WRITING CONTROL DOMIN

B62
TATZ C.M.,SHADOW AND SUBSTANCE IN SOUTH AFRICA. SOUTH/AFR AGRI NAT/G POL/PAR DOMIN GP/REL ATTIT PWR 20. PAGE 152 H3048
RACE/REL REPRESENT DISCRIM LEGIS

B62
TAYLOR D.,THE BRITISH IN AFRICA. UK CULTURE ECO/UNDEV INDUS DIPLOM INT/TRADE ADMIN WAR RACE/REL ORD/FREE SOVEREIGN...POLICY BIBLIOG 15/20 CMN/WLTH. PAGE 153 H3053
AFR COLONIAL DOMIN

B62
THIERRY S.S.,LE VATICAN SECRET. CHRIST-17C EUR+WWI MOD/EUR VATICAN NAT/G SECT DELIB/GP DOMIN LEGIT SOVEREIGN. PAGE 154 H3072
ADMIN EX/STRUC CATHISM DECISION

B62
VAN RENSBURG P.,GUILTY LAND: THE HISTORY OF APARTHEID. SOUTH/AFR NAT/G POL/PAR DOMIN CHOOSE ...SOC 19/20 NEGRO. PAGE 162 H3231
RACE/REL DISCRIM NAT/LISM POLICY

L62
COHEN R.,"POWER IN COMPLEX SOCIETIES IN AFRICA." AFR KIN MUNIC POL/PAR DELIB/GP DOMIN ROUTINE ATTIT ALL/VALS...SOC STAT OBS INT QU CHARTS ANTHOL 20. PAGE 31 H0617
CULTURE STRATA ELITES

L62
NOLTE E.,"ZUR PHANOMENOLOGIE DES FASCHIMUS." EUR+WWI GERMANY ITALY TURKEY INTELL NAT/G CHIEF CONSULT FORCES CREATE DOMIN EDU/PROP COERCE WAR CHOOSE DRIVE FASCISM...PSY CONCPT MYTH GEN/METH LEAGUE/NAT NAZI 20. PAGE 118 H2367
ATTIT PWR

S62
CROAN M.,"POLYCENTRISM: COMMUNIST INTERNATIONAL RELATIONS." ASIA STRUCT INT/ORG NAT/G POL/PAR CONSULT PLAN DOMIN EDU/PROP COERCE ATTIT RIGID/FLEX SOCISM...POLICY CONCPT TREND CON/ANAL GEN/LAWS MARX/KARL. PAGE 35 H0703
COM CREATE DIPLOM NAT/LISM

S62
FESLER J.W.,"FRENCH FIELD ADMINISTRATION: THE BEGINNINGS." CHRIST-17C CULTURE SOCIETY STRATA NAT/G ECO/TAC DOMIN EDU/PROP LEGIT ADJUD COERCE ATTIT ALL/VALS...TIME/SEQ CON/ANAL GEN/METH VAL/FREE 13/15. PAGE 49 H0988
EX/STRUC FRANCE

S62
KOLARZ W.,"THE IMPACT OF COMMUNISM ON WEST AFRICA." AFR FUT SOCIETY INT/ORG NAT/G CREATE PLAN DOMIN EDU/PROP COERCE NAT/LISM ATTIT RIGID/FLEX SOCISM ...POLICY CONCPT TREND MARX/KARL 20. PAGE 88 H1751
COM POL/PAR COLONIAL

S62
LANGER W.L.,"FAREWELL TO EMPIRE." EUR+WWI MOD/EUR NAT/G DIPLOM EDU/PROP COLONIAL ATTIT ORD/FREE PWR SOVEREIGN WEALTH...CONCPT TIME/SEQ GEN/LAWS TOT/POP VAL/FREE CMN/WLTH 20. PAGE 91 H1810
DOMIN ECO/TAC NAT/LISM

S62
LEGUM C.,"THE DANGERS OF INDEPENDENCE" AFR UGANDA NAT/G DIPLOM DOMIN REGION CENTRAL ATTIT POPULISM 20. PAGE 93 H1862
ORD/FREE SOVEREIGN NAT/LISM GOV/COMP

S62
LONDON K.,"SINO-SOVIET RELATIONS IN THE CONTEXT OF THE 'WORLD SOCIALIST SYSTEM'." ASIA CHINA/COM COM USSR INT/ORG NAT/G TOP/EX BAL/PWR DIPLOM DOMIN ATTIT PERCEPT RIGID/FLEX PWR MARXISM...METH/CNCPT TREND 20. PAGE 98 H1957
DELIB/GP CONCPT SOCISM

S62
MARIAS J.,"A PROGRAM FOR EUROPE." EUR+WWI INT/ORG NAT/G PLAN DIPLOM DOMIN PWR...STERTYP TOT/POP 20. PAGE 102 H2048
VOL/ASSN CREATE REGION

S62
ROTBERG R.,"THE RISE OF AFRICAN NATIONALISM: THE CASE OF EAST AND CENTRAL AFRICA." AFR CULTURE SOCIETY NEIGH DIPLOM DOMIN COLONIAL COERCE DISPL PERCEPT PWR SOVEREIGN...POLICY OBS/ENVIR TREND WORK 20. PAGE 135 H2690
ATTIT DRIVE NAT/LISM REV

S62
SARKISYANZ E.,"NATIONALISM, CAPITALISM, AND THE UNCOMMITED NATIONS: MARXISM AND ASIAN CULTURAL TRADITIONS." ASIA BURMA CHINA/COM COM CULTURE SOCIETY NAT/G POL/PAR PLAN DOMIN EDU/PROP COLONIAL COERCE ATTIT RIGID/FLEX...CONCPT TREND MARX/KARL 20 TIBET BUDDHISM. PAGE 138 H2755
S/ASIA SECT NAT/LISM CAP/ISM

S62
SHATTEN F.,"POLYCENTRISM: AFRICA: NATIONALISM AND COMMUNISM." ASIA COM FUT ISLAM CULTURE SOCIETY ECO/UNDEV NAT/G PLAN DOMIN COLONIAL COERCE CHOOSE RIGID/FLEX ALL/VALS MARXISM...CONCPT TREND 20. PAGE 143 H2852
AFR ATTIT NAT/LISM SOCISM

S62
STRACHEY J.,"COMMUNIST INTENTIONS." ASIA USSR YUGOSLAVIA INT/ORG NAT/G FORCES DOMIN EDU/PROP COERCE NUC/PWR NAT/LISM PEACE RIGID/FLEX PWR MARXISM...CONCPT MYTH OBS TIME/SEQ TREND COLD/WAR TOT/POP 20. PAGE 150 H2992
COM ATTIT WAR

C62
BACON F.,"OF EMPIRE" (1612) IN F. BACON, ESSAYS." ELITES NAT/G PROB/SOLV DIPLOM ADMIN CONTROL WEALTH 16/17 KING. PAGE 9 H0190
PWR CHIEF DOMIN GEN/LAWS

B63
BLONDEL J.,VOTERS, PARTIES, AND LEADERS. UK ELITES LOC/G NAT/G PROVS ACT/RES DOMIN REPRESENT GP/REL INGP/REL...SOC BIBLIOG 20. PAGE 18 H0358
POL/PAR STRATA LEGIS ADMIN

B63
CANELAS O.A.,RADIOGRAFIA DE LA ALIANZA PARA EL ATRASO. L/A+17C USA+45 ECO/TAC DOMIN COLONIAL NAT/LISM...SOCIALIST NAT/COMP 20. PAGE 26 H0519
REV DIPLOM ECO/UNDEV REGION

B63
CARTER G.M.,FIVE AFRICAN STATES: RESPONSES TO DIVERSITY. CONSTN CULTURE STRATA LEGIS PLAN ECO/TAC DOMIN EDU/PROP CT/SYS EXEC CHOOSE ATTIT HEALTH ORD/FREE PWR...TIME/SEQ TOT/POP VAL/FREE. PAGE 27 H0547
AFR SOCIETY

B63
CROSS C.,THE FASCISTS IN BRITAIN. UK ELITES LABOR NAT/G DOMIN PARTIC DISCRIM TOTALISM ATTIT...STERTYP 20. PAGE 35 H0708
POL/PAR FASCISM RACE/REL LEAD

B63
CRUICKSHANK M.,CHURCH AND STATE IN ENGLISH EDUCATION 1870 TO PRESENT. UK LEGIS TAX GIVE DOMIN LEGIT ORD/FREE 19/20 CHURCH/STA. PAGE 36 H0715
NAT/G SECT EDU/PROP GP/REL

B63
ELLIOT J.H.,THE REVOLT OF THE CATALANS. SPAIN LOC/G PROVS FORCES DIPLOM TASK WAR GOV/REL INGP/REL ...POLICY 17 OLIVARES. PAGE 45 H0909
REV NAT/G TOP/EX DOMIN

B63
FALL B.,THE TWO VIETNAMS. CULTURE SOCIETY ECO/UNDEV NAT/G TOP/EX ACT/RES PLAN ECO/TAC DOMIN EDU/PROP COERCE ATTIT DRIVE PERSON ORD/FREE PWR...SOC TIME/SEQ COLD/WAR 20. PAGE 48 H0965
S/ASIA BIOG VIETNAM

B63
FARMER B.H.,CEYLON: A DIVIDED NATION. CEYLON INDIA NETHERLAND PORTUGAL UK ELITES POL/PAR COLONIAL ...SOC MYTH CHARTS GOV/COMP WORSHIP 20. PAGE 49 H0972
DOMIN ORD/FREE ECO/UNDEV POLICY

B63
FURTADO C.,THE ECONOMIC GROWTH OF BRAZIL: A SURVEY FROM COLONIAL TO MODERN TIMES. L/A+17C AGRI DIST/IND EXTR/IND INDUS WORKER COLONIAL RACE/REL OWN GOV/COMP. PAGE 54 H1082
ECO/UNDEV TEC/DEV LABOR DOMIN

B63
GAMBLE S.D.,NORTH CHINA VILLAGES: SOCIAL, POLITICAL, AND ECONOMIC ACTIVITIES BEFORE 1933. ASIA CULTURE STRUCT FAM DOMIN EDU/PROP WORSHIP 20. PAGE 55 H1093
MUNIC AGRI LEAD FINAN

B63
GLUCKMAN M.,ORDER AND REBELLION IN TRIBAL AFRICA. EUR+WWI LAW CULTURE STRATA KIN MUNIC DELIB/GP ACT/RES DOMIN EDU/PROP LEGIT ADMIN COERCE CHOOSE ATTIT PERSON ORD/FREE PWR...SOC CHARTS GEN/LAWS TOT/POP VAL/FREE. PAGE 57 H1147
AFR SOCIETY

B63
HUGHES A.J.,EAST AFRICA: THE SEARCH FOR UNITY- KENYA, TANGANYIKA, UGANDA, AND ZANZIBAR. TANZANIA UGANDA CONSTN POL/PAR SECT CHIEF DELIB/GP LEGIS WAR CHOOSE NAT/LISM MARXISM...POLICY CHARTS 20 NEGRO UN. PAGE 74 H1488
NAT/G DOMIN LOC/G AFR

B63
JAIRAZBHOY R.A.,FOREIGN INFLUENCE IN ANCIENT INDIA. INDIA ELITES SECT DIPLOM EDU/PROP COLONIAL REGION GP/REL...ART/METH LING WORSHIP +/14 GRECO/ROMN MESOPOTAM PERSIA PARTH/SASS. PAGE 79 H1587
CULTURE SOCIETY COERCE DOMIN

B63
JUDD P.,AFRICAN INDEPENDENCE: THE EXPLODING EMERGENCE OF THE NEW AFRICAN NATIONS. AFR UK LAW CONSTN CULTURE KIN DIPLOM ATTIT...CHARTS BIBLIOG 20 UN DEGAULLE/C NEGRO THIRD/WRLD. PAGE 82 H1640
ORD/FREE POLICY DOMIN LOC/G

B63
KHADDURI M.,MODERN LIBYA: A STUDY IN POLITICAL DEVELOPMENT. EUR+WWI ISLAM LIBYA ELITES INT/ORG POL/PAR FORCES DIPLOM FOR/AID DOMIN EDU/PROP LEGIT NAT/LISM DRIVE RIGID/FLEX SKILL...CONCPT TIME/SEQ TREND 20. PAGE 85 H1704
NAT/G STRUCT

B63
KOGAN N.,THE POLITICS OF ITALIAN FOREIGN POLICY. EUR+WWI LEGIS DOMIN LEGIT EXEC PWR RESPECT SKILL ...POLICY DECISION HUM SOC METH/CNCPT OBS INT CHARTS 20. PAGE 87 H1737
NAT/G ROUTINE DIPLOM ITALY

B63
KRAEHE E.,METTERNICH'S GERMAN POLICY: THE CONTEST WITH NAPOLEON, 1799-1814, VOL. 1. FRANCE MOD/EUR NAT/G CONSULT TOP/EX PLAN BAL/PWR DOMIN COERCE ATTIT DRIVE PERCEPT PERSON SKILL...CONCPT RECORD TIME/SEQ TREND 18/19. PAGE 88 H1764
BIOG GERMANY DIPLOM

B63
LARSON A.,A WARLESS WORLD. FUT CULTURE NAT/G VOL/ASSN FORCES CREATE DOMIN PEACE ALL/VALS...HUM STERTYP 20. PAGE 91 H1824
SOCIETY CONCPT ARMS/CONT

B63
MAIR L.,NEW NATIONS. AFR FAM MUNIC SECT DOMIN CHOOSE NAT/LISM ORD/FREE...SOC 19/20. PAGE 101 H2022
COLONIAL CULTURE TEC/DEV ECO/UNDEV

B63
MCPHEE W.N.,FORMAL THEORIES OF MASS BEHAVIOR. CULTURE STRUCT DOMIN EDU/PROP CHOOSE...MATH 20. PAGE 108 H2149
SOC METH CONCPT ATTIT

B63
MOSELY P.E.,THE SOVIET UNION, 1922-1962: A FOREIGN AFFAIRS READER. ASIA POLAND USSR CULTURE INTELL AGRI POL/PAR WORKER INT/TRADE DOMIN WAR NAT/LISM MARXISM SOCISM 20 KHRUSH/N. PAGE 113 H2267
PWR POLICY DIPLOM

B63
MULLER H.J.,FREEDOM IN THE WESTERN WORLD. PREHIST CULTURE SECT CREATE TEC/DEV DOMIN PWR WEALTH ...MAJORIT SOC CONCPT. PAGE 114 H2285
ORD/FREE TIME/SEQ SOCIETY

B63
NKRUMAH K.,AFRICA MUST UNITE. AFR FUT GHANA CONSTN CULTURE SOCIETY NAT/G POL/PAR DELIB/GP TOP/EX PLAN DOMIN EDU/PROP ATTIT DRIVE...TIME/SEQ CHARTS TOT/POP 20. PAGE 118 H2364
CONCPT GEN/LAWS REGION

B63
PRICE A.G.,THE WESTERN INVASIONS OF THE PACIFIC AND ITS CONTINENTS. ASIA PRE/AMER S/ASIA ECO/UNDEV KIN NAT/G SECT FORCES DOMIN HEALTH...SOC 16/20. PAGE 128 H2560
COLONIAL CULTURE GEOG HABITAT

B63
QUAISON-SACKEY A.,AFRICA UNBOUND: REFLECTIONS OF AN
AFR

AFRICAN STATESMAN. ISLAM CULTURE INTELL INT/ORG POL/PAR TOP/EX DOMIN EDU/PROP LEGIT ATTIT PERSON ...CONCPT OBS TIME/SEQ CHARTS STERTYP 20 UN. PAGE 129 H2571
BIOG

B63
SETON-WATSON H.,THE NEW IMPERIALISM. COM EUR+WWI MOD/EUR ECO/UNDEV NAT/G FORCES DIPLOM DOMIN EDU/PROP LEGIT COLONIAL EXEC COERCE GP/REL RACE/REL DISCRIM ATTIT...TIME/SEQ 20. PAGE 142 H2833
ECO/TAC RUSSIA USSR

B63
SKLAR R.L.,NIGERIAN POLITICAL PARTIES: POWER IN AN EMERGENT AFRICAN NATION. AFR EUR+WWI CULTURE STRATA NAT/G DELIB/GP EX/STRUC LEGIS DOMIN EDU/PROP ROUTINE CHOOSE ATTIT PERCEPT ORD/FREE PWR...SOC CONCPT OBS TOT/POP VAL/FREE. PAGE 145 H2898
POL/PAR SOCIETY NAT/LISM NIGERIA

B63
ULAM A.B.,THE NEW FACE OF SOVIET TOTALITARIANISM. FUT INTELL NAT/G POL/PAR EX/STRUC TOP/EX DIPLOM ECO/TAC DOMIN EDU/PROP LEGIT COERCE ATTIT RIGID/FLEX...OBS HIST/WRIT TREND TOT/POP VAL/FREE COLD/WAR. PAGE 158 H3150
COM PWR TOTALISM USSR

B63
VON DER MEHDEN F.R.,RELIGION AND NATIONALISM IN SOUTHEAST ASIA. BURMA PHILIPPINE S/ASIA INTELL SOCIETY DOMIN EDU/PROP LEGIT ATTIT MORAL ORD/FREE ...SOC CENSUS HIST/WRIT TOT/POP VAL/FREE 20 WORSHIP LONDON. PAGE 163 H3265
SECT CULTURE NAT/LISM

B63
WODDIS J.,AFRICA, THE WAY AHEAD. AFR FUT ELITES POL/PAR CAP/ISM DIPLOM DOMIN RACE/REL ATTIT ORD/FREE SOVEREIGN SOCISM 20 PANAF/FREE. PAGE 170 H3394
REV COLONIAL ECO/UNDEV NAT/G

B63
ZARTMAN I.W.,GOVERNMENT AND POLITICS IN NORTHERN AFRICA. AFR ALGERIA ISLAM LIBYA MOROCCO UAR ELITES SOCIETY PLAN ECO/TAC DOMIN EDU/PROP LEGIT ATTIT ...GEOG CONCPT TIME/SEQ 20 TUNIS. PAGE 172 H3448
CULTURE DRIVE NAT/LISM

L63
MICHAEL F.,"KHRUSHCHEV'S DISLOYAL OPPOSITION: STRUCTURAL CHANGE AND POWER STRUGGLE IN COMMUNIST BLOC." ASIA CHINA/COM FUT NAT/G POL/PAR CONSULT PLAN DOMIN ATTIT...POLICY CONCPT TREND MARX/KARL 20 KHRUSH/N. PAGE 110 H2195
COM STRUCT NAT/LISM USSR

L63
ZARTMAN I.W.,"THE SAHARA--BRIDGE OR BARRIER." ISLAM CULTURE SOCIETY NAT/G DELIB/GP DOMIN EDU/PROP LEGIT ATTIT...HIST/WRIT TIME/SEQ CHARTS TOT/POP VAL/FREE 20. PAGE 172 H3447
INT/ORG PWR NAT/LISM

S63
AYAL E.B.,"VALUE SYSTEM AND ECONOMIC DEVELOPMENT IN JAPAN AND THAILAND." ASIA S/ASIA THAILAND CULTURE ECO/DEV CAP/ISM DOMIN NAT/LISM DRIVE RIGID/FLEX SOCISM...WELF/ST OBS TREND CON/ANAL GEN/LAWS 20 CHINJAP. PAGE 9 H0185
ECO/UNDEV ALL/VALS

S63
BILL J.A.,"THE SOCIAL AND ECONOMIC FOUNDATIONS OF POWER IN CONTEMPORARY IRAN." ISLAM CULTURE NAT/G ECO/TAC DOMIN COERCE ATTIT PWR WEALTH...TREND VAL/FREE 20. PAGE 17 H0334
SOCIETY STRATA IRAN

S63
DUDLEY B.J.,"THE NOMINATION OF PARLIAMENTARY CANDIDATES IN NORTHERN NIGERIA." AFR CONSTN CULTURE ELITES STRATA DELIB/GP LEGIS DOMIN EDU/PROP COERCE ATTIT SUPEGO PWR...STAT VAL/FREE 20. PAGE 43 H0854
POL/PAR CHOOSE NIGERIA

S63
DUTT V.P.,"CHINA: JEALOUS NEIGHBOR." ASIA CHINA/COM INDIA S/ASIA NAT/G TOP/EX DOMIN COERCE REV ATTIT ...POLICY COLD/WAR 20. PAGE 44 H0874
FORCES PWR DIPLOM

S63
GLUCKMAN M.,"CIVIL WAR AND THEORIES OF POWER IN BAROTSE-LAND: AFRICAN AND MEDIEVAL ANALOGIES." AFR CHRIST-17C LAW CONSTN CULTURE STRATA KIN DELIB/GP FORCES DOMIN LEGIT COERCE PERCEPT ORD/FREE...SOC INT TIME/SEQ GEN/LAWS VAL/FREE. PAGE 57 H1148
TOP/EX PWR WAR

S63
HARRIS R.L.,"A COMPARATIVE ANALYSIS OF THE ADMINISTRATIVE SYSTEMS OF CANADA AND CEYLON." S/ASIA CULTURE SOCIETY STRATA TOP/EX ACT/RES DOMIN EDU/PROP LEGIT COERCE ATTIT SUPEGO ALL/VALS...MGT CHARTS GEN/LAWS VAL/FREE 20. PAGE 67 H1343
DELIB/GP EX/STRUC CANADA CEYLON

S63
HUREWITZ J.C.,"LEBANESE DEMOCRACY IN ITS INTERNATIONAL SETTING." FRANCE ISLAM UK LOC/G NAT/G SECT DOMIN EDU/PROP EXEC ATTIT PWR...TIME/SEQ 20. PAGE 75 H1507
STRUCT LEBANON

S63
LEE J.M.,"PARLIAMENT IN REPUBLICAN GHANA." AFR CONSTN CULTURE SOCIETY STRATA POL/PAR DELIB/GP TOP/EX DOMIN EDU/PROP LEGIT COERCE CHOOSE ATTIT ALL/VALS...CONCPT STAT TIME/SEQ VAL/FREE 20. PAGE 93 H1857
LEGIS GHANA

S63
MAZRUI A.A.,"ON THE CONCEPT 'WE ARE ALL AFRICANS'." AFR CULTURE KIN LOC/G NAT/G DOMIN EDU/PROP LEGIT ATTIT PERCEPT PERSON KNOWL ORD/FREE...TIME/SEQ TOT/POP 20. PAGE 106 H2110
PROVS INT/ORG NAT/LISM

S63
MONROE A.D.,"BRITAIN AND THE EUROPEAN COMMUNITY." EUR+WWI FRANCE NAT/G DELIB/GP TOP/EX ECO/TAC DOMIN PWR...POLICY RECORD GEN/LAWS EEC EFTA 20 EFTA CMN/WLTH. PAGE 112 H2241
VOL/ASSN ATTIT UK

S63
NICHOLAS W.,"VILLAGE FACTIONS AND POLITICAL PARTIES IN RURAL WEST BENGAL." S/ASIA CULTURE STRATA FACE/GP KIN MUNIC DELIB/GP LEGIS DOMIN EDU/PROP COERCE CHOOSE ATTIT ALL/VALS...STAT TOT/POP VAL/FREE 20. PAGE 117 H2348
NEIGH POL/PAR

S63
RUSTOW D.A.,"THE MILITARY IN MIDDLE EASTERN SOCIETY AND POLITICS." FUT ISLAM CONSTN SOCIETY FACE/GP NAT/G POL/PAR PROF/ORG CONSULT DOMIN ADMIN EXEC REGION COERCE NAT/LISM ATTIT DRIVE PERSON ORD/FREE PWR...POLICY CONCPT OBS STERTYP 20. PAGE 136 H2721
FORCES ELITES

S63
TILMAN R.O.,"MALAYSIA: THE PROBLEMS OF FEDERATION." ISLAM S/ASIA CONSTN PROVS SECT DELIB/GP DOMIN EDU/PROP LEGIT EXEC COERCE CHOOSE ATTIT HEALTH ORD/FREE PWR...STAT TOT/POP VAL/FREE 20. PAGE 155 H3097
NAT/G CULTURE MALAYSIA

B64
AGGARWALA R.C.,CONSTITUTIONAL HISTORY OF INDIA AND NATIONAL MOVEMENT INCLUDING COMPARATIVE STUDY OF MODERN INDIA CONSTITUTION. INDIA S/ASIA SECT VOL/ASSN EX/STRUC LEGIS COERCE REV INGP/REL ORD/FREE...SOC BIBLIOG 18/20 CMN/WLTH. PAGE 4 H0077
CONSTN COLONIAL DOMIN NAT/G

B64
AGGER R.E.,THE RULERS AND THE RULED: POLITICAL POWER AND IMPOTENCE IN AMERICAN COMMUNITIES. CULTURE DOMIN CHOOSE ATTIT ALL/VALS...DECISION SOC CONCPT OBS QU CHARTS. PAGE 4 H0079
PWR STRUCT LOC/G MUNIC

B64
ARASARATNAM S.,CEYLON. CEYLON NETHERLAND PORTUGAL S/ASIA UK STRUCT ECO/UNDEV SECT DIPLOM DOMIN RACE/REL NAT/LISM 17/20 CMN/WLTH. PAGE 8 H0156
COLONIAL NAT/G PROB/SOLV CULTURE

B64
CURTIN P.D.,THE IMAGE OF AFRICA: BRITISH IDEAS AND ACTION, 1780-1850. MOD/EUR SOCIETY FORCES ACT/RES DOMIN EDU/PROP COERCE ATTIT PERCEPT RIGID/FLEX SUPEGO HEALTH KNOWL MORAL ORD/FREE WEALTH...CONCPT WORK VAL/FREE. PAGE 36 H0726
AFR CULTURE UK DIPLOM

B64
ETZIONI A.,MODERN ORGANIZATIONS. CLIENT STRUCT DOMIN CONTROL LEAD PERS/REL AUTHORIT...CLASSIF BUREAUCRCY. PAGE 47 H0946
MGT ADMIN PLAN CULTURE

B64
HALE O.J.,THE CAPTIVE PRESS IN THE THIRD REICH. GERMANY CULTURE LG/CO NAT/G POL/PAR PLAN DOMIN TASK CENTRAL OWN TOTALISM PWR...BIBLIOG 20 HITLER/A NAZI AMMAN/MAX. PAGE 64 H1283
COM/IND PRESS CONTROL FASCISM

B64
HALPERN J.M.,GOVERNMENT, POLITICS, AND SOCIAL STRUCTURE IN LAOS. LAOS CULTURE SOCIETY STRATA STRUCT FAM DIPLOM DOMIN MARXISM...INT GOV/COMP WORSHIP SOC/INTEG 20. PAGE 65 H1297
NAT/G SOC LOC/G

B64
HEIMSATH C.H.,INDIAN NATIONALISM AND HINDU SOCIAL REFORM. S/ASIA LAW CULTURE SOCIETY STRATA PROVS VOL/ASSN DELIB/GP LEGIS TOP/EX DOMIN EDU/PROP LEGIT ATTIT ALL/VALS...POLICY SOC TIME/SEQ STERTYP VAL/FREE 19/20. PAGE 69 H1385
SECT NAT/G

B64
KAUFMANN R.,MILLENARISME ET ACCULTURATION. SOCIETY DOMIN COLONIAL NAT/LISM ATTIT...SOC BIBLIOG 20 JEHOVA/WIT SEVENTHDAY. PAGE 84 H1669
AFR SECT MYTH CULTURE

B64
LAPENNA I.,STATE AND LAW: SOVIET AND YUGOSLAV THEORY. USSR YUGOSLAVIA STRATA STRUCT NAT/G DOMIN COERCE MARXISM...GOV/COMP IDEA/COMP 20. PAGE 91 H1812
JURID COM LAW SOVEREIGN

B64
LEMARCHAND R.,POLITICAL AWAKENING IN THE BELGIAN CONGO. ECO/UNDEV VOL/ASSN DOMIN CHOOSE GP/REL INGP/REL DISCRIM ORD/FREE PWR...CHARTS 20 CONGO ARABS. PAGE 94 H1873
NAT/LISM COLONIAL POL/PAR RACE/REL

B64
MBEKI G.,SOUTH AFRICA: THE PEASANT'S REVOLT. SOUTH/AFR POL/PAR COERCE REV NAT/LISM ORD/FREE SOVEREIGN 20 NEGRO. PAGE 106 H2114
COLONIAL RACE/REL DISCRIM DOMIN

B64
PHILLIPS C.S.,THE DEVELOPMENT OF NIGERIAN FOREIGN POLICY. AFR CONSTN CULTURE STRATA NAT/G LEGIS DOMIN LEGIT EXEC...RELATIV SOC TIME/SEQ TREND TOT/POP 20. PAGE 125 H2502
CHOOSE POLICY DIPLOM NIGERIA

B64
PIKE F.B.,THE CONFLICT BETWEEN CHURCH AND STATE IN LATIN AMERICA. L/A+17C CULTURE SOCIETY STRATA DOMIN EDU/PROP LEGIT COERCE ATTIT ORD/FREE PWR WEALTH ...CONCPT TIME/SEQ TREND VAL/FREE. PAGE 125 H2510
SECT NAT/G

B64
PIPES R.,THE FORMATION OF THE SOVIET UNION. EUR+WWI MOD/EUR STRUCT ECO/UNDEV NAT/G LEGIS DOMIN LEGIT CT/SYS EXEC COERCE ALL/VALS...POLICY RELATIV HIST/WRIT TIME/SEQ TOT/POP 19/20. PAGE 126 H2514 — COM USSR RUSSIA

B64
SKINNER E.P.,THE MOSSI OF UPPER VOLTA: THE POLITICAL DEVELOPMENT OF A SUDANESE PEOPLE. AFR LAW AGRI FAM KIN POL/PAR PROVS SECT DELIB/GP EX/STRUC FORCES TOP/EX DOMIN EDU/PROP LEGIT CT/SYS COERCE CHOOSE ORD/FREE PWR WEALTH...SOC MYTH VAL/FREE. PAGE 145 H2897 — CULTURE OBS UPPER/VOLT

B64
THORNBURG M.W.,PEOPLE AND POLICY IN THE MIDDLE EAST. ISLAM ECO/UNDEV FAM KIN MUNIC NAT/G NEIGH POL/PAR SECT DELIB/GP LEGIS PLAN ECO/TAC DOMIN ADMIN ATTIT HEALTH RESPECT...SOC CONCPT METH/CNCPT OBS TIME/SEQ TOT/POP VAL/FREE. PAGE 154 H3088 — TEC/DEV CULTURE

B64
TIERNEY B.,THE CRISIS OF CHURCH AND STATE 1050-1300. DOMIN EDU/PROP CONTROL PWR CONSERVE 11/14. PAGE 155 H3092 — SECT NAT/G GP/REL

B64
WAINHOUSE D.W.,REMNANTS OF EMPIRE: THE UNITED NATIONS AND THE END OF COLONIALISM. FUT PORTUGAL WOR+45 NAT/G CONSULT DOMIN LEGIT ADMIN ROUTINE ATTIT ORD/FREE...POLICY JURID RECORD INT TIME/SEQ UN CMN/WLTH 20. PAGE 164 H3287 — INT/ORG TREND COLONIAL

B64
WALDMAN E.,THE GOOSE STEP IS VERBOTEN: THE GERMAN ARMY TODAY. GERMANY/W LAW CONSTN LEGIS PROB/SOLV DOMIN CONTROL CIVMIL/REL GOV/REL INGP/REL ATTIT ...DEEP/QU 20. PAGE 164 H3289 — SOC FORCES NAT/G

B64
WARD R.E.,POLITICAL MODERNIZATION IN JAPAN AND TURKEY. ASIA ISLAM S/ASIA CONSTN CULTURE STRATA COM/IND POL/PAR FORCES ACT/RES ECO/TAC DOMIN EDU/PROP LEGIT ADMIN CHOOSE ATTIT ALL/VALS...STAT TIME/SEQ VAL/FREE CHINJAP. PAGE 165 H3307 — SOCIETY TURKEY

B64
WHITE D.S.,SEEDS OF DISCORD. EUR+WWI FRANCE NAT/G VOL/ASSN FORCES DIPLOM DOMIN NAT/LISM DISPL RIGID/FLEX PWR...RECORD INT BIOG 20 DEGAULLE/C ROOSEVLT/F CHURCHLL/W HULL. PAGE 167 H3347 — TOP/EX ATTIT

B64
WHITEFORD A.H.,TWO CITIES OF LATIN AMERICA: A COMPARATIVE DESCRIPTION OF SOCIAL CLASSES. L/A+17C CULTURE SOCIETY MUNIC DOMIN LEGIT ATTIT ALL/VALS ...STAT OBS VAL/FREE 20. PAGE 167 H3352 — STRATA SOC

B64
WILCOX W.A.,INDIA, PAKISTAN AND THE RISE OF CHINA. ASIA BURMA CEYLON CHINA/COM INDIA PAKISTAN S/ASIA NAT/G VOL/ASSN FORCES TOP/EX ACT/RES DOMIN REGION RIGID/FLEX ORD/FREE...POLICY GEN/LAWS COLD/WAR 20. PAGE 168 H3362 — CULTURE ATTIT DIPLOM

L64
ROTBERG R.,"THE FEDERATION MOVEMENT IN BRITISH EAST AND CENTRAL AFRICA." AFR RHODESIA UGANDA ECO/UNDEV NAT/G POL/PAR FORCES DOMIN LEGIT ADMIN COERCE ATTIT ...CONCPT TREND 20 TANGANYIKA. PAGE 135 H2691 — VOL/ASSN PWR REGION

S64
BARIETY J.,"LA POLITIQUE EXTERIEURE ALLEMANDE DANS L'HIVER 1939-1940." COM FINLAND GERMANY ISLAM ITALY USSR NAT/G FORCES ECO/TAC DOMIN EDU/PROP COERCE WAR PWR WEALTH...HIST/WRIT NAZI TOT/POP VAL/FREE 20. PAGE 11 H0216 — EUR+WWI DIPLOM

S64
BENSON M.,"SOUTH AFRICA AND WORLD OPINION." AFR SOUTH/AFR INTELL SOCIETY TOP/EX ECO/TAC DOMIN COERCE DISCRIM ATTIT PWR WEALTH...POLICY RECORD 20. PAGE 14 H0285 — NAT/G RIGID/FLEX RACE/REL

S64
CLIGNET R.,"POTENTIAL ELITES IN GHANA AND THE IVORY COAST: A PRELIMINARY SURVEY." AFR CULTURE ELITES STRATA KIN NAT/G SECT DOMIN EXEC ORD/FREE RESPECT SKILL...POLICY RELATIV GP/COMP NAT/COMP 20. PAGE 30 H0605 — PWR LEGIT IVORY/CST GHANA

S64
CROZIER B.,"POUVOIR ET ORGANISATION." SOCIETY NAT/G DOMIN...PSY SOC CONCPT TOT/POP VAL/FREE 20. PAGE 36 H0714 — PERSON PWR DIPLOM

S64
GARMARNIKOW M.,"INFLUENCE-BUYING IN WEST AFRICA." COM FUT USSR INTELL NAT/G PLAN TEC/DEV ECO/TAC DOMIN EDU/PROP REGION NAT/LISM ATTIT DRIVE ALL/VALS SOVEREIGN...POLICY PSY SOC CONCPT TREND STERTYP WORK COLD/WAR 20. PAGE 55 H1102 — AFR ECO/UNDEV FOR/AID SOCISM

S64
GROSS J.A.,"WHITEHALL AND THE COMMONWEALTH." EUR+WWI MOD/EUR INT/ORG NAT/G CONSULT DELIB/GP LEGIS DOMIN ADMIN COLONIAL ROUTINE PWR CMN/WLTH 19/20. PAGE 62 H1233 — EX/STRUC ATTIT TREND

S64
KOVNER M.,"THE SINO-SOVIET DISPUTE: COMMUNISM AT THE CROSSROADS." ASIA CHINA/COM COM USSR ECO/UNDEV NAT/G TOP/EX CREATE BAL/PWR DOMIN EDU/PROP PWR ...CONCPT COMECON 20. PAGE 88 H1760 — ATTIT TREND

S64
LANGERHANS H.,"NEHRU'S BITTERNESS." FUT INDIA S/ASIA CONSTN CULTURE ECO/UNDEV ECO/TAC DOMIN EDU/PROP ATTIT PERCEPT PERSON...POLICY 20 NEHRU/J. PAGE 91 H1811 — ECO/DEV BIOG

S64
LEWIS B.,"THE QUEST FOR FREEDOM--A SAD STORY OF THE MIDDLE EAST." ISLAM ISRAEL LEBANON TURKEY CULTURE NAT/G SECT LEGIS TOP/EX DOMIN EDU/PROP LEGIT ORD/FREE PWR RESPECT...POLICY TIME/SEQ VAL/FREE 20. PAGE 96 H1911 — CONSTN ATTIT NAT/LISM

S64
LOW D.A.,"LION RAMPANT." EUR+WWI MOD/EUR S/ASIA ECO/UNDEV NAT/G FORCES TEC/DEV ECO/TAC LEGIT ADMIN COLONIAL COERCE ORD/FREE RESPECT 19/20. PAGE 99 H1972 — AFR DOMIN DIPLOM UK

S64
MARTELLI G.,"PORTUGAL AND THE UNITED NATIONS." AFR EUR+WWI ELITES INT/ORG NAT/G PROVS PLAN DIPLOM ECO/TAC DOMIN COLONIAL RIGID/FLEX MORAL ORD/FREE PWR WEALTH...MYTH UN 20. PAGE 103 H2060 — ATTIT PORTUGAL

S64
MERKL P.H.,"EUROPEAN ASSEMBLY PARTIES AND NATIONAL DELEGATIONS." INT/ORG DELIB/GP DOMIN EDU/PROP LEGIT CHOOSE PWR...STAT VAL/FREE 20. PAGE 109 H2180 — EUR+WWI POL/PAR REGION

S64
MOZINGO D.P.,"CHINA'S RELATIONS WITH HER ASIAN NEIGHBORS." ASIA CHINA/COM S/ASIA VIETNAM NAT/G DELIB/GP FORCES CREATE DOMIN EDU/PROP REV RIGID/FLEX PWR...TIME/SEQ GEN/LAWS COLD/WAR 20. PAGE 114 H2277 — VOL/ASSN POLICY DIPLOM

S64
REISS I.,"LE DECLENCHEMENT DE LA PREMIERE GUERRE MONDIALE." GERMANY RUSSIA NAT/G FORCES DOMIN EDU/PROP COERCE RIGID/FLEX PWR SOVEREIGN...RELATIV HIST/WRIT TOT/POP AUST/HUNG SERBIA 20. PAGE 131 H2612 — MOD/EUR BAL/PWR DIPLOM WAR

S64
SAAB H.,"THE ARAB SEARCH FOR A FEDERAL UNION." SOCIETY INT/ORG NAT/G DELIB/GP FORCES ACT/RES TEC/DEV ECO/TAC DOMIN LEGIT REGION ROUTINE ATTIT DRIVE RIGID/FLEX ALL/VALS...SOC CONCPT NEW/IDEA TIME/SEQ TREND. PAGE 136 H2726 — ISLAM PLAN

S64
SCHEFFLER H.W.,"THE GENESIS AND REPRESSION OF CONFLICT: CHOISEUL ISLAND." S/ASIA LOC/G NAT/G FORCES LEGIS DIPLOM DOMIN LEGIT EXEC CHOOSE ATTIT RESPECT SKILL...POLICY JURID OBS TREND GEN/METH 20. PAGE 139 H2781 — PWR COERCE WAR

S64
SWEARER H.R.,"AFTER KHRUSHCHEV: WHAT NEXT." COM FUT USSR CONSTN ELITES NAT/G POL/PAR CHIEF DELIB/GP LEGIS DOMIN LEAD...RECORD TREND STERTYP GEN/METH 20. PAGE 151 H3016 — EX/STRUC PWR

S64
VANDENBOSCH A.,"POWER BALANCE IN INDONESIA." S/ASIA USSR NAT/G TOP/EX BAL/PWR DOMIN NEUTRAL ORD/FREE PWR...POLICY TIME/SEQ GEN/LAWS 20 SUKARNO/A. PAGE 162 H3233 — FORCES TREND DIPLOM INDONESIA

B65
BERNDT R.M.,ABORIGINAL MAN IN AUSTRALIA. LAW DOMIN ADMIN COLONIAL MARRIAGE HABITAT ORD/FREE...LING CHARTS ANTHOL BIBLIOG WORSHIP 20 AUSTRAL ABORIGINES MUSIC ELKIN/AP. PAGE 16 H0312 — SOC CULTURE SOCIETY STRUCT

B65
BRASS P.R.,FACTIONAL POLITICS IN AN INDIAN STATE: THE CONGRESS PARTY IN UTTAR PRADESH. INDIA UK CONSTN CULTURE ECO/UNDEV LOC/G DOMIN COLONIAL CROWD GP/REL ADJUST CENTRAL RIGID/FLEX SOVEREIGN 20 UTTAR/PRAD CONGRESS/P. PAGE 20 H0406 — POL/PAR PROVS LEGIS CHOOSE

B65
FAGG J.E.,CUBA, HAITI, AND THE DOMINICAN REPUBLIC. CUBA DOMIN/REP HAITI L/A+17C NAT/G DIPLOM ECO/TAC DOMIN CHOOSE AUTHORIT ROLE SOVEREIGN POPULISM 17/20. PAGE 48 H0959 — COLONIAL ECO/UNDEV REV GOV/COMP

B65
FILIPINIANA BOOK GUILD,THE COLONIZATION AND CONQUEST OF THE PHILIPPINES BY SPAIN. PHILIPPINE SPAIN ELITES AGRI KIN CHIEF DOMIN CONTROL ATTIT PWR ...ANTHOL WORSHIP 16. PAGE 50 H1000 — COLONIAL COERCE CULTURE WAR

B65
GRIMAL H.,HISTOIRE DU COMMONWEALTH BRITANNIQUE. UK FINAN DOMIN ATTIT ORD/FREE...T 15/20 CMN/WLTH. PAGE 61 H1226 — NAT/G COLONIAL DIPLOM INT/TRADE

B65
HALEVY E.,THE ERA OF TYRANNIES (TRANS. BY R. K. WEBB). WOR-45 ECO/DEV PROB/SOLV CONTROL COERCE REV WAR TOTALISM 20. PAGE 64 H1286 — SOCISM IDEA/COMP DOMIN

B65
MONTESQUIEU C DE S.,CONSIDERATIONS ON THE CAUSES OF THE GREATNESS OF THE ROMANS AND THEIR DECLINE (1748 TRANS. BY D. LOWENTHAL). ROMAN/EMP SECT CHIEF EX/STRUC FORCES LEGIS DOMIN WAR POPULISM...POLICY REALPOL ROME/ANC. PAGE 112 H2244 — NAT/G PWR COLONIAL MORAL

B65
NEWBURY C.W.,BRITISH POLICY TOWARDS WEST AFRICA: SELECT DOCUMENTS 1786-1874. AFR UK INT/TRADE DOMIN ADMIN COLONIAL CT/SYS COERCE ORD/FREE...BIBLIOG/A 18/19. PAGE 117 H2345 DIPLOM POLICY NAT/G WRITING

B65
NORDEN A.,WAR AND NAZI CRIMINALS IN WEST GERMANY: STATE, ECONOMY, ADMINISTRATION, ARMY, JUSTICE, SCIENCE. GERMANY GERMANY/W MOD/EUR ECO/DEV ACADEM EX/STRUC FORCES DOMIN ADMIN CT/SYS...POLICY MAJORIT PACIFIST 20. PAGE 119 H2370 FASCIST WAR NAT/G TOP/EX

B65
O'CONNELL M.R.,IRISH POLITICS AND SOCIAL CONFLICT IN THE AGE OF THE AMERICAN REVOLUTION. FRANCE IRELAND MOD/EUR STRATA SECT LEGIS DIPLOM INT/TRADE DOMIN REV WAR...BIBLIOG 18 PARLIAMENT. PAGE 119 H2387 CATHISM ATTIT NAT/G DELIB/GP

B65
ROTBERG R.I.,A POLITICAL HISTORY OF TROPICAL AFRICA. EX/STRUC DIPLOM INT/TRADE DOMIN ADMIN RACE/REL NAT/LISM PWR SOVEREIGN...GEOG TIME/SEQ BIBLIOG 1/20. PAGE 135 H2692 AFR CULTURE COLONIAL

B65
SCALAPINO R.A.,THE COMMUNIST REVOLUTION IN ASIA* TACTICS, GOALS, AND ACHIEVEMENTS. INDIA INTELL POL/PAR FORCES DOMIN EDU/PROP LEGIT COERCE REV ATTIT CHINJAP. PAGE 138 H2763 ASIA S/ASIA MARXISM NAT/COMP

B65
VAN DEN BERGHE P.L.,SOUTH AFRICA: A STUDY IN CONFLICT. AFR CULTURE SOCIETY STRATA STRUCT COERCE SEGREGAT. PAGE 161 H3227 DOMIN RACE/REL DISCRIM

B65
VON STACKELBERG K.,ALLE KRETER LUGEN VORURTEILE UBER MENSCHEN UND VOLKER. DIPLOM DOMIN RUMOR NAT/LISM PERSON KNOWL...SOC QU BIBLIOG 20. PAGE 164 H3277 NAT/COMP ATTIT EDU/PROP SAMP

B65
WILLIAMSON J.A.,GREAT BRITAIN AND THE COMMONWEALTH. UK DOMIN COLONIAL INGP/REL...POLICY 18/20 CMN/WLTH. PAGE 168 H3370 NAT/G DIPLOM INT/ORG SOVEREIGN

L65
HOUN F.S.,"THE COMMUNIST MONOLITH VERSUS THE CHINESE TRADITION." CULTURE INTELL SOCIETY STRUCT DOMIN GP/REL ORD/FREE CONSERVE PLURISM...GOV/COMP WORSHIP. PAGE 74 H1479 ASIA MARXISM TOTALISM

S65
GRIFFITH S.B.,"COMMUNIST CHINA'S CAPACITY TO MAKE WAR." CHINA/COM COM NAT/G TOP/EX PLAN DOMIN COERCE NUC/PWR ATTIT RESPECT SKILL...CONCPT MYTH TIME/SEQ TREND COLD/WAR 20. PAGE 61 H1221 FORCES PWR WEAPON ASIA

S65
HELMREICH E.C.,"KADAR'S HUNGARY." COM EUR+WWI HUNGARY USSR INTELL ECO/DEV AGRI INT/ORG TOP/EX DOMIN ALL/VALS WORK COLD/WAR 20. PAGE 69 H1390 NAT/G RIGID/FLEX TOTALISM

S65
PLISCHKE E.,"INTEGRATING BERLIN AND THE FEDERAL REPUBLIC OF GERMANY." EUR+WWI GERMANY/W LEGIS TEC/DEV DOMIN ORD/FREE PWR...JURID 20 BERLIN. PAGE 126 H2528 DIPLOM NAT/G MUNIC

S65
ROGGER H.,"EAST GERMANY: STABLE OR IMMOBILE." COM EUR+WWI GERMANY/E NAT/G INT/TRADE DOMIN EDU/PROP COERCE TOTALISM COLD/WAR 20. PAGE 133 H2659 TOP/EX RIGID/FLEX GERMANY

C65
NEUMANN S.,"PERMANENT REVOLUTION: TOTALITARIANISM IN THE AGE OF INTERNA TIONAL CIVIL WAR (2ND ED.)" EUR+WWI ELITES POL/PAR DOMIN EDU/PROP LEAD CROWD REPRESENT...MAJORIT GOV/COMP BIBLIOG 20. PAGE 117 H2340 TOTALISM REV FASCISM STRUCT

B66
AFRIFA A.A.,THE GHANA COUP. AFR GHANA ELITES NAT/G DIPLOM DOMIN 20 NKRUMAH/K. PAGE 4 H0076 TOP/EX REV FORCES POL/PAR

B66
AHMED Z.,DUSK AND DAWN IN VILLAGE INDIA. INDIA S/ASIA UK CULTURE SOCIETY NAT/G DOMIN COLONIAL HABITAT SOVEREIGN...SOC DICTIONARY 20. PAGE 4 H0080 NEIGH ECO/UNDEV AGRI ADJUST

B66
CADY J.F.,THAILAND, BURMA, LAOS AND CAMBODIA. FRANCE UK CULTURE NAT/G DOMIN GP/REL RACE/REL HABITAT...GEOG TREND CHINJAP BUDDHISM. PAGE 25 H0504 S/ASIA COLONIAL REGION SECT

B66
COEDES G.,THE MAKING OF SOUTH EAST ASIA. BURMA CAMBODIA LAOS S/ASIA THAILAND VIETNAM REV WAR CIVMIL/REL...GEOG 6/13. PAGE 31 H0614 CULTURE FORCES DOMIN

B66
DALLIN A.,POLITICS IN THE SOVIET UNION: 7 CASES. COM USSR LAW POL/PAR CHIEF FORCES WRITING CONTROL PARL/PROC CIVMIL/REL TOTALISM...ANTHOL 20 KHRUSH/N STALIN/J CASEBOOK COM/PARTY. PAGE 37 H0736 MARXISM DOMIN ORD/FREE GOV/REL

B66
FIELDHOUSE D.K.,THE COLONIAL EMPIRES: A COMPARATIVE SURVEY FROM THE 18TH CENTURY. UK WOR-45 REV HABITAT 17/18. PAGE 50 H0994 NAT/COMP COLONIAL NAT/G DOMIN

B66
FINER S.E.,ANONYMOUS EMPIRE: STUDY OF THE LOBBY IN GREAT BRITAIN. UK CONSTN LABOR POL/PAR SECT DOMIN EDU/PROP PRESS CHOOSE...CONCPT CHARTS 20 PARLIAMENT. PAGE 50 H1004 LOBBY NAT/G LEGIS PWR

B66
FLINT J.E.,NIGERIA AND GHANA. AFR GHANA NIGERIA UK NAT/G DOMIN DISCRIM...CHARTS BIBLIOG/A 15/20 NEGRO MAPS. PAGE 51 H1026 CULTURE COLONIAL NAT/LISM

B66
KEIL S.,SEXUALITAT - ERKENNTNISSE UND MASS-STABE. CULTURE DOMIN MARRIAGE AGE/Y AGE/A PERSON SUPEGO PLURISM 17/20. PAGE 84 H1681 SEX ATTIT STRUCT SOCIETY

B66
LEIBLER I.,SOVIET JEWRY AND HUMAN RIGHTS. USSR INTELL NAT/G DOMIN ATTIT 20 AUSTRAL JEWS. PAGE 93 H1865 DISCRIM RACE/REL MARXISM POL/PAR

B66
LEYBURN J.G.,THE HAITIAN PEOPLE (REV. ED.). HAITI SOCIETY FAM SECT DOMIN COLONIAL MARRIAGE...SOC CHARTS BIBLIOG/A 18/10. PAGE 96 H1917 STRUCT STRATA INGP/REL CULTURE

B66
LONDON K.,EASTERN EUROPE IN TRANSITION. CHINA/COM USSR DOMIN COLONIAL CENTRAL RIGID/FLEX PWR...SOC ANTHOL 20. PAGE 98 H1958 SOVEREIGN COM NAT/LISM DIPLOM

B66
NOLTE E.,THREE FACES OF FASCISM. FRANCE GERMANY DOMIN LEGIT COERCE CROWD REV WAR GP/REL RACE/REL SOVEREIGN...GOV/COMP IDEA/COMP 19/20 HITLER/A MUSSOLIN/B MARX/KARL. PAGE 118 H2368 FASCISM TOTALISM NAT/G POL/PAR

B66
SKILLING H.G.,THE GOVERNMENTS OF COMMUNIST EAST EUROPE. COM EUR+WWI ELITES FORCES DIPLOM ECO/TAC CONTROL HABITAT SOCISM...DECISION BIBLIOG 20 EUROPE/E COM/PARTY. PAGE 145 H2895 MARXISM NAT/COMP GP/COMP DOMIN

B66
VIEN N.C.,SEEKING THE TRUTH. VIETNAM DELIB/GP DOMIN RISK MARXISM 20 KY/NGUYEN. PAGE 162 H3250 NAT/G COLONIAL PWR SOVEREIGN

B66
WHEELER G.,THE PEOPLES OF SOVIET CENTRAL ASIA: A BACKGROUND BOOK. ISLAM USSR STRATA STRUCT FORCES REV WAR HABITAT 7/20. PAGE 167 H3341 COLONIAL DOMIN CULTURE ADJUST

B66
ZOLBERG A.R.,CREATING POLITICAL ORDER. AFR CONGO/BRAZ GHANA NIGER KIN NAT/G DOMIN COLONIAL REGION CENTRAL NAT/LISM ATTIT PWR 20 CONGO/LEOP. PAGE 173 H3462 SOVEREIGN ORD/FREE CONSTN POL/PAR

S66
DETTER I.,"THE PROBLEM OF UNEQUAL TREATIES." CONSTN NAT/G LEGIS COLONIAL COERCE PWR...GEOG UN TIME TREATY. PAGE 40 H0796 SOVEREIGN DOMIN INT/LAW ECO/UNDEV

S66
FLEMING W.G.,"AUTHORITY, EFFICIENCY, AND ROLE STRESS: PROBLEMS IN THE DEVELOPMENT OF EAST AFRICAN BUREAUCRACIES." AFR UGANDA STRUCT PROB/SOLV ROUTINE INGP/REL ROLE...MGT SOC GP/COMP GOV/COMP 20 TANGANYIKA AFRICA/E. PAGE 51 H1024 DOMIN EFFICIENCY COLONIAL ADMIN

B67
BROWN L.N.,FRENCH ADMINISTRATIVE LAW. FRANCE UK CONSTN NAT/G LEGIS DOMIN CONTROL EXEC PARL/PROC PWR ...JURID METH/COMP GEN/METH. PAGE 22 H0447 EX/STRUC LAW IDEA/COMP CT/SYS

B67
CARTER G.M.,SOUTH AFRICA'S TRANSKEI: THE POLITICS OF DOMESTIC COLONIALISM. SOUTH/AFR ECO/UNDEV AGRI NAT/G PROVS PLAN DOMIN REPRESENT ADJUST DISCRIM ...OBS BIBLIOG 20 BANTUSTANS TRANSKEI. PAGE 27 H0550 STRATA GOV/REL COLONIAL POLICY

B67
CHILCOTE R.H.,PORTUGUESE AFRICA. PORTUGAL CULTURE SOCIETY ECO/UNDEV DOMIN NAT/LISM...TREND IDEA/COMP NAT/COMP BIBLIOG 15/20. PAGE 29 H0589 AFR COLONIAL ORD/FREE PROB/SOLV

B67
CURTIN P.D.,AFRICA REMEMBERED. NIGERIA SENEGAL CULTURE DIPLOM INT/TRADE GP/REL RACE/REL...RECORD ANTHOL 18/19 NEGRO. PAGE 36 H0727 DOMIN ORD/FREE AFR DISCRIM

B67
DIX R.H.,COLOMBIA: THE POLITICAL DIMENSIONS OF CHANGE. ELITES POL/PAR DOMIN REV...AUD/VIS 20 COLOMB. PAGE 41 H0828 L/A+17C NAT/G TEC/DEV LEAD

B67
FANON F.,TOWARD THE AFRICAN REVOLUTION. AFR FRANCE COLONIAL

CULTURE ELITES LEAD REV GP/REL ORD/FREE SOVEREIGN 20. PAGE 49 H0969 DOMIN ECO/UNDEV RACE/REL

B67
MUNGER E.S.,AFRIKANER AND AFRICAN NATIONALISM: SOUTH AFRICAN PARALLELS AND PARAMETERS. SOUTH/AFR WOR+45 CULTURE ELITES STRUCT NAT/G PROB/SOLV DOMIN CONTROL PERS/REL NAT/LISM...SOC 20. PAGE 115 H2289 AFR RACE/REL

B67
OLIVER R.,AFRICA SINCE 1800. AFR ISLAM CULTURE ECO/UNDEV SECT DOMIN RACE/REL DISCRIM SOVEREIGN 19/20. PAGE 121 H2414 DIPLOM COLONIAL REGION

B67
WILLS A.J.,AN INTRODUCTION TO THE HISTORY OF CENTRAL AFRICA. RHODESIA ZAMBIA CULTURE SOCIETY ECO/UNDEV TEC/DEV DOMIN WAR ALL/VALS...POLICY TREND BIBLIOG T 14/20 NYASALAND. PAGE 169 H3375 AFR COLONIAL ORD/FREE

B67
WINTER E.H.,CONTEMPORARY CHANGE IN TRADITIONAL SOCIETIES: VOLUME I INTRODUCTION AND AFRICAN TRIBES. NIGERIA AGRI LOC/G NAT/G CREATE DOMIN COLONIAL CONTROL GP/REL PWR SOVEREIGN...SOC OBS 20 TANGANYIKA. PAGE 169 H3389 SOCIETY AFR CONSERVE KIN

L67
EINAUDI L.,"ANNOTATED BIBLIOGRAPHY OF LATIN AMERICAN MILITARY JOURNALS" LAW TEC/DEV DOMIN EDU/PROP COERCE WAR CIVMIL/REL 20. PAGE 45 H0899 BIBLIOG/A NAT/G FORCES L/A+17C

L67
MCALLISTER J.T. JR.,"THE POSSIBILITIES FOR DIPLOMACY IN SOUTHEAST ASIA." LAOS VIETNAM INT/ORG NAT/G PROVS BAL/PWR DOMIN AGREE COLONIAL WAR PWR 17/20 TREATY. PAGE 106 H2121 DIPLOM S/ASIA

L67
TAMBIAH S.J.,"THE POLITICS OF LANGUAGE IN INDIA AND CEYLON." CEYLON INDIA NAT/G DOMIN ADMIN...SOC 20. PAGE 152 H3039 POL/PAR LING NAT/LISM REGION

L67
UNESCO,"APARTHEID." SOUTH/AFR STRUCT KIN SCHOOL SECT WORKER DOMIN EDU/PROP REGION RACE/REL ISOLAT 20. PAGE 158 H3164 DISCRIM CULTURE COERCE COLONIAL

L67
VAN DER KROEF J.M.,"INDONESIA: THE BATTLE OF THE 'OLD' AND THE 'NEW ORDER'." INDONESIA ISLAM ELITES POL/PAR DOMIN INGP/REL NAT/LISM PWR...IDEA/COMP 20. PAGE 161 H3229 FORCES MARXISM NAT/G BAL/PWR

S67
BEFU H.,"THE POLITICAL RELATION OF THE VILLAGE TO THE STATE." NAT/G DOMIN GOV/REL GP/REL MGT. PAGE 13 H0259 GOV/COMP NAT/LISM KIN MUNIC

S67
CARR E.H.,"REVOLUTION FROM ABOVE." USSR STRATA FINAN INDUS NAT/G DOMIN LEAD GP/REL INGP/REL OWN PRODUC PWR 20 STALIN/J. PAGE 27 H0538 AGRI POLICY COM EFFICIENCY

S67
CATTELL D.T.,"A NEO-MARXIST THEORY OF COMPARATIVE ANALYSIS." USSR STRATA INSPECT DOMIN CONTROL COERCE OWN TOTALISM PWR...FASCIST HYPO/EXP METH 20. PAGE 28 H0561 GOV/COMP MARXISM SIMUL CLASSIF

S67
CHIU S.M.,"CHINA'S MILITARY POSTURE." CHINA/COM ELITES NAT/G POL/PAR TEC/DEV ECO/TAC DOMIN CONTROL LEAD REV MARXISM 20 MAO. PAGE 30 H0595 FORCES CIVMIL/REL NUC/PWR DIPLOM

S67
CHU-YUAN CHENG,"THE CULTURAL REVOLUTION AND CHINA'S ECONOMY." CHINA/COM AGRI DIST/IND INDUS MARKET NAT/G WORKER PLAN INT/TRADE DOMIN DEMAND PRODUC ...CHARTS 20 MAO. PAGE 30 H0600 ECO/DEV ECO/TAC REV SOCISM

S67
COLLINS B.A.,"SOME NOTES ON PUBLIC SERVICE COMMISSIONS IN THE COMMONWEALTH CARIBBEAN." JAMAICA L/A+17C TRINIDAD UK NAT/G OP/RES DOMIN SENIOR COLONIAL CONTROL INGP/REL CENTRAL EFFICIENCY PWR ...DECISION 20. PAGE 31 H0631 ADMIN EX/STRUC ECO/UNDEV CHOOSE

S67
GONZALEZ M.P.,"CUBA, UNA REVOLUCION EN MARCHA." CUBA L/A+17C USA+45 VIETNAM ECO/UNDEV FORCES DIPLOM DOMIN...POLICY MARXIST NAT/COMP CASTRO/F. PAGE 58 H1163 REV NAT/G COLONIAL SOVEREIGN

S67
KROLL M.,"POLITICAL LEADERSHIP AND ADMINISTRATIVE COMMUNICATIONS IN NEW NATION STATES* CASE STUDY OF TRINIDAD AND TOBAGO." L/A+17C TRINIDAD INTELL OP/RES DOMIN COLONIAL LEAD GP/REL CENTRAL EFFICIENCY...DECISION OBS METH/COMP 20. PAGE 89 H1774 NAT/G ADMIN EDU/PROP CONTROL

S67
POWELL D.,"THE EFFECTIVENESS OF SOVIET ANTI-RELIGIOUS PROPAGANDA." USSR NAT/G DOMIN LEGIT NAT/LISM 20. PAGE 127 H2549 EDU/PROP ATTIT SECT CONTROL

S67
ROSE S.,"ASIAN NATIONALISM* THE SECOND STAGE." ASIA COM ECO/UNDEV NAT/G PROB/SOLV DIPLOM FOR/AID DOMIN NEUTRAL REGION TASK...METH/COMP 20. PAGE 134 H2675 NAT/LISM S/ASIA BAL/PWR COLONIAL

S67
VON LAUE T.H.,"WESTERNIZATION, REVOLUTION AND THE SEARCH FOR A BASIS OF AUTHORITY - RUSSIA IN 1917." USSR ELITES INTELL ECO/UNDEV NAT/G WORKER ECO/TAC TAX ADMIN LEAD AUTHORIT 20 LENIN/VI. PAGE 164 H3274 MARXISM REV COM DOMIN

S67
YEFROMEV A.,"THE TRUE FACE OF THE WEST GERMAN NATIONAL-DEMOCRATS." GERMANY/W NAT/G DOMIN LEAD SANCTION WAR ATTIT PERSON...MARXIST 20. PAGE 172 H3436 POL/PAR TOTALISM PARL/PROC DIPLOM

B68
DE SPINOZA B.,TRACTATUS THEOLOGICO-POLITICUS (TRANS. BY R. WILLIS). UNIV CHIEF DOMIN PWR WORSHIP. PAGE 38 H0771 SECT NAT/G ORD/FREE

S68
KANET R.E.,"RECENT SOVIET REASSESSMENT OF DEVELOPMENTS IN THE THIRD WORLD." ALGERIA GHANA INDONESIA USSR WOR+45 CONSTN ELITES INTELL STRUCT DOMIN CONTROL REV PWR MARXISM...IDEA/COMP METH 20 THIRD/WRLD. PAGE 83 H1653 DIPLOM NEUTRAL NAT/G NAT/COMP

S68
LAWRIE G.,"WHAT WILL CHANGE SOUTH AFRICA?" AFR SOUTH/AFR ELITES DOMIN CONTROL REPRESENT...TIME/SEQ TREND 20. PAGE 93 H1848 RACE/REL DIPLOM NAT/G POLICY

B73
STEPHEN J.F.,LIBERTY, EQUALITY, FRATERNITY. UNIV SOCIETY NAT/G LEGIS DOMIN AGREE PERS/REL ATTIT MORAL...IDEA/COMP 19 MILL/JS. PAGE 149 H2978 ORD/FREE CONCPT COERCE SECT

B75
NEWMAN J.H.,A LETTER ADDRESSED TO THE DUKE OF NORFOLK ON THE OCCASION OF MR. GLADSTONE'S RECENT EXPOSTULATION. NAT/G SECT CHIEF LEGIS CONTROL LEAD GP/REL SUPEGO SOC/INTEG WORSHIP 19 ENGLAND. PAGE 117 H2346 POLICY DOMIN SOVEREIGN CATHISM

B85
TAINE H.A.,THE FRENCH REVOLUTION (3 VOLS.) (TRANS. BY J. DURAND). FRANCE MOD/EUR SOCIETY STRATA POL/PAR ECO/TAC DOMIN EDU/PROP GP/REL PWR ...GOV/COMP IDEA/COMP 18. PAGE 152 H3036 REV NAT/G EX/STRUC LEAD

B90
BURKE E.,REFLECTIONS ON THE REVOLUTION IN FRANCE. FRANCE UK NAT/G DOMIN LEGIT PEACE PWR SOVEREIGN CONSERVE...POLICY GEN/LAWS 18. PAGE 24 H0487 REV ORD/FREE CHIEF TRADIT

B91
BENTHAM J.,A FRAGMENT ON GOVERNMENT (1776). CONSTN MUNIC NAT/G SECT AGREE HAPPINESS UTIL MORAL ORD/FREE...JURID CONCPT. PAGE 15 H0292 SOVEREIGN LAW DOMIN

B91
PAINE T.,RIGHTS OF MAN. FRANCE MOD/EUR CONSTN NAT/G CHIEF DOMIN LEGIT SOVEREIGN...MAJORIT IDEA/COMP 18 BURKE/EDM CIVIL/LIB. PAGE 122 H2446 GEN/LAWS ORD/FREE REV AGREE

B99
KINGSLEY M.H.,WEST AFRICAN STUDIES. GHANA NIGERIA SIER/LEONE LAW EXTR/IND SECT DIPLOM INT/TRADE DOMIN RACE/REL OWN HEALTH...SOC 19. PAGE 86 H1717 AFR HEREDITY COLONIAL CULTURE

DOMIN/REP....DOMINICAN REPUBLIC; SEE ALSO L/A + 17C

B48
FLOREN LOZANO L.,BIBLIOGRAFIA DE LA BIBLIOGRAFIA DOMINICANA. DOMIN/REP NAT/G DIPLOM EDU/PROP CIVMIL/REL...POLICY ART/METH GEOG PHIL/SCI HIST/WRIT 20. PAGE 51 H1027 BIBLIOG/A BIOG L/A+17C CULTURE

B58
ORNES G.E.,TRUJILLO: LITTLE CAESAR OF THE CARIBBEAN. DOMIN/REP FAM NAT/G FORCES BUDGET CRIME REV PERSON 20 TRUJILLO/R. PAGE 122 H2429 BIOG PWR TOTALISM CHIEF

S63
WELLS H.,"THE OAS AND THE DOMINICAN ELECTIONS." L/A+17C INT/ORG NAT/G POL/PAR TEC/DEV ECO/TAC EDU/PROP PERCEPT...TIME/SEQ OAS TOT/POP 20. PAGE 166 H3332 CONSULT CHOOSE DOMIN/REP

B65
FAGG J.E.,CUBA, HAITI, AND THE DOMINICAN REPUBLIC. CUBA DOMIN/REP HAITI L/A+17C NAT/G DIPLOM ECO/TAC DOMIN CHOOSE AUTHORIT ROLE SOVEREIGN POPULISM 17/20. PAGE 48 H0959 COLONIAL ECO/UNDEV REV GOV/COMP

B66
INSTITUTE COMP STUDY POL SYS,DOMINICAN REPUBLIC ELECTION FACT BOOK. DOMIN/REP LAW LEGIS REPRESENT ...JURID CHARTS 20. PAGE 77 H1536 SUFF CHOOSE POL/PAR NAT/G

B66
NIEDERGANG M.,LA REVOLUTION DE SAINT-DOMINGUE. DOMIN/REP INT/ORG NAT/G CONTROL LEAD GP/REL REV FORCES

ORD/FREE MARXISM 20. PAGE 118 H2361 DIPLOM

S67
GOODSELL J.N.,"BALAGUER'S DOMINICAN REPUBLIC." ECO/UNDEV
DOMIN/REP FUT L/A+17C POL/PAR PROB/SOLV ECO/TAC 20. CHIEF
PAGE 59 H1174 POLICY
NAT/G

DOMINATION....SEE DOMIN

DOMINICAN REPUBLIC....SEE DOMIN/REP

DOMINO....THE DOMINO THEORY

DONALDSON A.G. H0835

DONNELLY/I....IGNATIUS DONNELLY

DONNISON F.S.V. H0836

DOOB L.W. H0837

DOOLIN D.J. H0838

DORWART R.A. H0839

DOS SANTOS M. H0840

DOSTOYEV/F....FYODOR DOSTOYEVSKY

DOTSON L.O. H0915

DOUGLAS M. H0333

DOUGLAS W.O. H0841

DOUGLAS/P....PAUL DOUGLAS

DOUGLAS/WO....WILLIAM O. DOUGLAS

DOUGLAS-HOME C. H0842

DOUGLASS H.P. H0843

DOUMA J. H0844

DOWNIE R.S. H0845

DRAGNICH A.N. H0846

DRAPER/HAL....HAL DRAPER

DREAM....DREAMING

B63
REYNOLDS B.,MAGIC, DIVINATION AND WITCHCRAFT AMONG AFR
THE BAROTSE OF NORTHERN RHODESIA. RHODESIA CULTURE SOC
KIN CREATE LEGIT PARTIC DEATH DREAM STRANGE HABITAT MYTH
PERSON...AUD/VIS WORSHIP 20. PAGE 131 H2619 SECT

DREYFUS/A....ALFRED DREYFUS OR DREYFUS AFFAIR

DRIVE....DRIVE AND MORALE

N
PRESSE UNIVERSITAIRES,ANNEE SOCIOLOGIQUE. EUR+WWI BIBLIOG
FRANCE MOD/EUR FAM ACT/RES WAR INGP/REL PERS/REL SOC
CONSEN DRIVE MORAL...CON/ANAL 19/20. PAGE 128 H2557 CULTURE
SOCIETY

B00
DE JOMINI A.H.,THE ART OF WAR. MOD/EUR NAT/G PLAN
BAL/PWR DIPLOM DOMIN EXEC ROUTINE COERCE DRIVE PWR FORCES
SKILL...POLICY CONCPT CHARTS STERTYP 19. PAGE 38 WAR
H0755 WEAPON

B05
MACHIAVELLI N.,THE ART OF WAR. CHRIST-17C TOP/EX NAT/G
DRIVE ORD/FREE PWR SKILL...MGT CHARTS. PAGE 100 FORCES
H1993 WAR
ITALY

B12
BRUNHES J.,LA GEOGRAPHIE HUMAINE: ESSAI DE GEOG
CLASSIFICATION POSITIVE PRINCIPES ET EXEMPLES (2ND HABITAT
ED.). UNIV SEA AGRI EXTR/IND DRIVE...SOC CHARTS 20. CULTURE
PAGE 23 H0454

B14
BERHARDI F.,GERMANY AND THE NEXT WAR. MOD/EUR NAT/G DRIVE
SCHOOL FORCES ACT/RES DOMIN EDU/PROP SUPEGO PWR COERCE
...TIME/SEQ STERTYP TOT/POP 20 WWI. PAGE 15 H0304 WAR
GERMANY

N19
GRIFFITH W.,THE PUBLIC SERVICE (PAMPHLET). UK LAW ADMIN
LOC/G NAT/G PARTIC CHOOSE DRIVE ROLE SKILL...CHARTS EFFICIENCY
20 CIVIL/SERV. PAGE 61 H1222 EDU/PROP
GOV/REL

N19
STEUBER F.A.,THE CONTRIBUTION OF SWITZERLAND TO THE FOR/AID
ECONOMIC AND SOCIAL DEVELOPMENT OF LOW-INCOME ECO/UNDEV
COUNTRIES (PAMPHLET). SWITZERLND FINAN NAT/G PLAN
VOL/ASSN INT/TRADE DRIVE...CHARTS 20. PAGE 149 DIPLOM
H2982

B20
COLE G.D.H.,SOCIAL THEORY. CULTURE LOC/G SECT CONCPT
REGION REPRESENT ATTIT DRIVE...PSY SOC BIBLIOG. NAT/G
PAGE 31 H0621 PHIL/SCI

B20
HALDANE R.B.,BEFORE THE WAR. MOD/EUR SOCIETY POLICY
INT/ORG NAT/G DELIB/GP PLAN DOMIN EDU/PROP LEGIT DIPLOM
ADMIN COERCE ATTIT DRIVE MORAL ORD/FREE PWR...SOC UK
CONCPT SELF/OBS RECORD BIOG TIME/SEQ. PAGE 64 H1282

B21
STUART G.H.,FRENCH FOREIGN POLICY. CONSTN INT/ORG MOD/EUR
NAT/G POL/PAR EX/STRUC FORCES PLAN ECO/TAC DOMIN DIPLOM
EDU/PROP ADJUD COERCE ATTIT DRIVE RIGID/FLEX FRANCE
ALL/VALS...POLICY OBS RECORD BIOG TIME/SEQ TREND.
PAGE 150 H3000

B21
WALLAS G.,HUMAN NATURE IN POLITICS (3RD ED.). UNIV PSY
NAT/G LEAD CHOOSE REPRESENT GP/REL NAT/LISM DRIVE
RATIONAL BIO/SOC HEREDITY ALL/VALS MAJORIT. PERSON
PAGE 165 H3293

B27
EDWARDS L.P.,THE NATURAL HISTORY OF REVOLUTION. PWR
UNIV NAT/G VOL/ASSN COERCE DRIVE WEALTH...TREND GUERRILLA
GEN/LAWS. PAGE 45 H0893 REV

S27
MICHELS R.,"SOME REFLECTIONS ON THE SOCIOLOGICAL POL/PAR
CHARACTER OF POLITICAL PARTIES" (BMR)" WOR-45 PWR
STRATA MAJORITY DRIVE...GOV/COMP 20. PAGE 110 H2199 LEAD
CONCPT

B28
SOROKIN P.,CONTEMPORARY SOCIOLOGICAL THEORIES. CULTURE
MOD/EUR UNIV SOCIETY R+D SCHOOL ECO/TAC EDU/PROP SOC
ROUTINE ATTIT DRIVE...PSY CONCPT TIME/SEQ TREND WAR
GEN/LAWS 20. PAGE 147 H2934

C28
SCHNEIDER H.W.,"MAKING THE FASCIST STATE." ITALY FASCISM
CULTURE LABOR DIPLOM REV WAR NAT/LISM TOTALISM POLICY
ATTIT DRIVE SOCISM...BIBLIOG PARLIAMENT 20. POL/PAR
PAGE 140 H2792

B29
DAVIE M.R.,THE EVOLUTION OF WAR. CULTURE KIN COERCE FORCES
WAR ATTIT DRIVE...PSY SOC TIME/SEQ TREND GEN/LAWS. STERTYP
PAGE 37 H0746

B31
DEKAT A.D.A.,COLONIAL POLICY. S/ASIA CULTURE DRIVE
EX/STRUC ECO/TAC DOMIN ADMIN COLONIAL ROUTINE PWR
SOVEREIGN WEALTH...POLICY MGT RECORD KNO/TEST SAMP. INDONESIA
PAGE 39 H0785 NETHERLAND

B31
MACIVER R.M.,SOCIETY: ITS STRUCTURE AND CHANGES. STRUCT
CULTURE STRATA FAM CROWD HABITAT ORD/FREE...PSY SOC SOCIETY
CONCPT BIBLIOG 20. PAGE 100 H1998 PERSON
DRIVE

B37
HORNEY K.,THE NEUROTIC PERSONALITY OF OUR TIME. PSY
SOCIETY PERS/REL ADJUST HAPPINESS ANOMIE ATTIT PERSON
DRIVE SEX LOVE PWR CONCPT. PAGE 74 H1472 STRANGE
CULTURE

L37
NICOLSON H.,"THE MEANING OF PRESTIGE." EUR+WWI CONCPT
MOD/EUR UK CULTURE SOCIETY NAT/G DIPLOM DOMIN LEGIT STERTYP
ATTIT DRIVE PWR...METH/CNCPT RECORD TIME/SEQ
GEN/METH CMN/WLTH TOT/POP 20. PAGE 118 H2351

S38
MERTON R.K.,"SOCIAL STRUCTURE AND ANOMIE" (BMR)" SOCIETY
UNIV CULTURE STRATA CREATE PARTIC ATTIT BIO/SOC STRUCT
PERSON...SOC CONCPT 20. PAGE 109 H2186 ANOMIE
DRIVE

B43
EARLE E.M.,MAKERS OF MODERN STRATEGY: MILITARY PLAN
THOUGHT FROM MACHIAVELLI TO HITLER. EUR+WWI MOD/EUR FORCES
NAT/G ACT/RES BAL/PWR DOMIN COERCE ATTIT DRIVE WAR
RIGID/FLEX ALL/VALS...METH/CNCPT BIOG 16/20.
PAGE 44 H0879

B44
GYORGY A.,GEOPOLITICS: THE NEW GERMAN SCIENCE. PWR
EUR+WWI GERMANY STRATA NAT/G PROVS DOMIN EDU/PROP LEGIT
ATTIT DRIVE FASCISM...GEOG NAZI 20. PAGE 63 H1261 WAR

B44
KRIS E.,GERMAN RADIO PROPAGANDA: REPORT ON HOME EDU/PROP
BROADCASTS DURING THE WAR. EUR+WWI GERMANY CULTURE DOMIN
CONSULT PROB/SOLV FEEDBACK TASK INGP/REL DRIVE PWR ACT/RES
FASCISM...CON/ANAL METH/COMP 20. PAGE 89 H1768 ATTIT

L44
HUXLEY J.,"THE FUTURE OF THE COLONIES." AFR SOCIETY ECO/UNDEV
NAT/G PLAN DOMIN COERCE ATTIT DRIVE ORD/FREE PWR FUT
WEALTH...TIME/SEQ TREND AUD/VIS CHARTS 20. PAGE 76 COLONIAL
H1511

S46
TANNENBAUM F.,"THE BALANCE OF POWER IN SOCIETY." SOCIETY
UNIV STRUCT FAM NAT/G SECT PERS/REL EQUILIB UTOPIA ALL/VALS
DRIVE ALL/IDEOS...OLD/LIB CONCPT. PAGE 152 H3044 GP/REL
PEACE

B47
JURJI E.J.,THE GREAT RELIGIONS OF THE MODERN WORLD. UNIV
CULTURE INTELL SOCIETY INT/ORG CONSULT CHOOSE ATTIT SECT
DRIVE PERSON RIGID/FLEX...HUM CONCPT OBS BIOG
HIST/WRIT TREND GEN/LAWS 20 WORSHIP. PAGE 82 H1643

B48
JONES H.D.,UNESCO: A SELECTED LIST OF REFERENCES. BIBLIOG/A
CULTURE CREATE PEACE ATTIT DRIVE 20 UNESCO UN. INT/ORG
PAGE 82 H1631 DIPLOM
EDU/PROP

L48
SHILS E.A.,"COHESION AND DISINTEGRATION IN THE EDU/PROP
WEHRMACHT IN WORLD WAR II." GERMANY STRUCT DOMIN DRIVE
WAR INGP/REL ISOLAT NAT/LISM ATTIT AUTHORIT SUPEGO PERS/REL
RESPECT...PSY CON/ANAL 20 NAZI. PAGE 143 H2862 FORCES

S48
ALEXANDER L.,"WAR CRIMES, THEIR SOCIAL- DRIVE
PSYCHOLOGICAL ASPECTS." EUR+WWI GERMANY LAW CULTURE WAR
ELITES KIN POL/PAR PUB/INST FORCES DOMIN EDU/PROP
COERCE CRIME ATTIT SUPEGO HEALTH MORAL PWR FASCISM
...PSY OBS TREND GEN/LAWS NAZI 20. PAGE 5 H0100

B49
GORER G.,THE PEOPLE OF GREAT RUSSIA: A ISOLAT
PSYCHOLOGICAL STUDY. RUSSIA USSR NAT/G DIPLOM LEAD PERSON
AGE/C ANOMIE ATTIT DRIVE...POLICY 20. PAGE 59 H1182 PSY
SOCIETY

B49
SARGENT S.S.,CULTURE AND PERSONALITY. FUT UNIV CULTURE
SOCIETY FAM KIN NEIGH BIO/SOC DRIVE PERCEPT PERSON
RIGID/FLEX LOVE RESPECT...PSY SOC CONCPT OBS
TIME/SEQ TREND CON/ANAL CHARTS HYPO/EXP SIMUL
TOT/POP. PAGE 138 H2754

B49
SINGER K.,THE IDEA OF CONFLICT. UNIV INTELL INT/ORG ACT/RES
NAT/G PLAN ROUTINE ATTIT DRIVE ALL/VALS...POLICY SOC
CONCPT TIME/SEQ. PAGE 144 H2882

S49
DEXTER L.A.,"A DIALOGUE ON THE SOCIAL PSYCHOLOGY OF COLONIAL
COLONIALISM AND ON CERTAIN PUERTO RICAN SOC
PROFESSIONAL PERSONALITY PATTERNS." L/A+17C PSY
PUERT/RICO STRATA STRUCT DOMIN ISOLAT DRIVE PERSON
...NAT/COMP PERS/COMP HYPO/EXP 20 JEWS NEGRO.
PAGE 41 H0813

B50
CANTRIL H.,TENSIONS THAT CAUSE WAR. UNIV CULTURE SOCIETY
R+D CREATE EDU/PROP DRIVE PERSON KNOWL ORD/FREE PHIL/SCI
...HUM PSY SOC OBS CENSUS TREND CON/ANAL SOC/EXP PEACE
SIMUL GEN/METH ANTHOL COLD/WAR TOT/POP. PAGE 26
H0523

B50
HOBBES T.,LEVIATHAN. UNIV CONSTN SOCIETY LOC/G LAW
NAT/G CONSULT TOP/EX DOMIN DRIVE PERSON PWR ORD/FREE
...PHIL/SCI CONCPT SELF/OBS GEN/LAWS TOT/POP.
PAGE 72 H1434

B50
MACIVER R.M.,GREAT EXPRESSIONS OF HUMAN RIGHTS. LAW UNIV
CONSTN CULTURE INTELL SOCIETY R+D INT/ORG ATTIT CONCPT
DRIVE...JURID OBS HIST/WRIT GEN/LAWS. PAGE 100
H1999

B51
PARSONS T.,TOWARD A GENERAL THEORY OF ACTION. SOC
CULTURE PERSON...PSY SIMUL ANTHOL SOC/INTEG 20. PHIL/SCI
PAGE 124 H2472 DRIVE
ACT/RES

S51
GOULD J.,"THE KOMSOMOL AND THE HITLER JUGEND." COM EDU/PROP
EUR+WWI GERMANY SOCIETY NAT/G POL/PAR SCHOOL CON/ANAL
TOTALISM DRIVE PERCEPT KNOWL FASCISM...SOC NAZI SOCISM
TOT/POP 20. PAGE 59 H1185

S51
NORTHROP F.S.C.,"ASIAN MENTALITY AND UNITED STATES S/ASIA
FOREIGN POLICY." ASIA ISLAM USA+45 CULTURE SOCIETY ATTIT
SECT EDU/PROP LEGIT COERCE DRIVE MORAL ORD/FREE DIPLOM
...POLICY RELATIV TOT/POP 20. PAGE 119 H2376

B52
LEVY M.,THE STRUCTURE OF SOCIETY. CULTURE STRATA SOCIETY
DRIVE KNOWL...PSY CONCPT METH/CNCPT NEW/IDEA STYLE SOC
GEN/LAWS. PAGE 95 H1907

B52
ULAM A.B.,TITOISM AND THE COMINFORM. USSR WOR+45 COM
STRUCT INT/ORG NAT/G ACT/RES PLAN EXEC ATTIT DRIVE POL/PAR
ALL/VALS...CONCPT OBS VAL/FREE 20 COMINTERN TOTALISM
TITO/MARSH. PAGE 157 H3149 YUGOSLAVIA

S52
EISENSTADT S.N.,"THE PROCESS OF ABSORPTION OF NEW HABITAT
IMMIGRANTS IN ISRAEL" (BMR)" ISRAEL CULTURE SCHOOL ATTIT
WORKER PARTIC DRIVE ORD/FREE...STAT OBS INT CHARTS SAMP
SOC/INTEG 20 JEWS. PAGE 45 H0900

B53
BIDNEY D.,THEORETICAL ANTHROPOLOGY. DRIVE ROLE CULTURE
ORD/FREE...CONCPT METH/CNCPT MYTH CLASSIF OBS SOC
IDEA/COMP METH/COMP BIBLIOG METH 20. PAGE 17 H0331 PSY
PHIL/SCI

B53
COBLENTZ S.A.,FROM ARROW TO ATOM BOMB: THE WAR
PSYCHOLOGICAL HISTORY OF WAR. PREHIST CULTURE CROWD PSY
PEACE DRIVE MORAL PWR...GP/COMP IDEA/COMP. PAGE 31 SOCIETY
H0613

B53
HUNTER E.,BRAIN-WASHING IN RED CHINA. ASIA EDU/PROP
CHINA/COM CULTURE SOCIETY FORCES WAR TOTALISM ATTIT COERCE
BIO/SOC DISPL DRIVE PERSON SUPEGO KNOWL ORD/FREE
...INT REC/INT COLD/WAR 20. PAGE 75 H1499

B54
BERGER M.,FREEDOM AND CONTROL IN MODERN SOCIETY. ORD/FREE
LABOR NAT/G VOL/ASSN AUTHORIT DRIVE PLURISM CONTROL
...METH/CNCPT CLASSIF. PAGE 15 H0300 INGP/REL

B54
FORDE C.D.,AFRICAN WORLDS. AFR CULTURE ROUTINE SOCIETY
GP/REL PERS/REL ATTIT DRIVE ALL/VALS...OBS ANTHOL KIN
WORSHIP 20. PAGE 52 H1036 SOC

B54
MATTHEWS D.R.,THE SOCIAL BACKGROUND OF POLITICAL DECISION
DECISION-MAKERS. CULTURE SOCIETY STRATA FAM BIOG
EX/STRUC LEAD ATTIT BIO/SOC DRIVE PERSON ALL/VALS SOC
HIST/WRIT. PAGE 105 H2097

B54
SCHRAMM W.,THE PROCESS AND EFFECTS OF MASS ATTIT
COMMUNICATION. CULTURE INTELL SOCIETY COM/IND DRIVE EDU/PROP
PERCEPT PERSON RIGID/FLEX KNOWL...PSY SOC CONCPT
CHARTS. PAGE 140 H2800

B55
KOHN H.,THE MIND OF MODERN RUSSIA. COM MOD/EUR USSR INTELL
SOCIETY NAT/G SECT FORCES TOP/EX COERCE TOTALISM GEN/LAWS
DRIVE RIGID/FLEX PWR SOVEREIGN...CONCPT TIME/SEQ SOCISM
WORK. PAGE 87 H1742 RUSSIA

B56
GLUCKMAN M.,CUSTOM AND CONFLICT IN AFRICA. AFR FAM CULTURE
KIN NAT/G DOMIN DISCRIM DRIVE MORAL PWR...SOC CREATE
BIBLIOG WORSHIP 20. PAGE 57 H1145 PERS/REL
GP/COMP

B56
GOFFMAN E.,THE PRESENTATION OF SELF IN EVERYDAY PERS/COMP
LIFE. CULTURE INGP/REL ATTIT DRIVE...SOC OBS RECORD PERSON
20. PAGE 58 H1154 PERCEPT
ROLE

B56
MANNONI D.O.,PROSPERO AND CALIBAN: THE PSYCHOLOGY CULTURE
OF COLONIZATION. AFR EUR+WWI FAM KIN MUNIC SECT COLONIAL
DOMIN ADMIN ATTIT DRIVE LOVE PWR RESPECT...PSY SOC
CONCPT MYTH OBS DEEP/INT BIOG GEN/METH MALAGASY 20.
PAGE 102 H2040

B56
PADMORE G.,PAN-AFRICANISM OR COMMUNISM. AFR FUT POL/PAR
NIGERIA INTELL NAT/G COLONIAL FEDERAL ATTIT DRIVE NAT/LISM
PWR RESPECT WEALTH MARXISM...CONCPT AUD/VIS STERTYP
20. PAGE 122 H2440

B56
READ M.,EDUCATION AND SOCIAL CHANGE IN TROPICAL EDU/PROP
AREAS. AFR L/A+17C SOCIETY LITERACY PERCEPT PERSON HABITAT
WEALTH...HEAL PHIL/SCI SOC 20. PAGE 130 H2603 DRIVE
CULTURE

S56
MACRAE D. JR.,"ROLL CALL VOTES AND LEADERSHIP." POL/PAR
ACT/RES LEAD CHOOSE DRIVE CONSERVE NEW/LIB...STAT GOV/COMP
STYLE. PAGE 100 H2007 LEGIS
SUPEGO

B57
DEAN V.M.,THE NATURE OF THE NON-WESTERN WORLD. AFR ECO/UNDEV
ASIA L/A+17C S/ASIA CULTURE SOCIETY STRATA ECO/DEV STERTYP
DIPLOM ECO/TAC FOR/AID ATTIT DRIVE ALL/VALS NAT/LISM
...RELATIV SOC CONCPT TIME/SEQ TREND TOT/POP 20.
PAGE 39 H0778

S57
MARCH J.C.,"PARTY LEGISLATIVE REPRESENTATION AS A REPRESENT
FUNCTION OF ELECTION RESULTS." DRIVE...PROBABIL GOV/COMP
REGRESS STYLE CHARTS HYPO/EXP SIMUL. PAGE 102 H2046 LEGIS
CHOOSE

B58
COLEMAN J.S.,NIGERIA: BACKGROUND TO NATIONALISM. NAT/G
AFR SOCIETY ECO/DEV KIN LOC/G POL/PAR TEC/DEV DOMIN NAT/LISM
ADMIN DRIVE PWR RESPECT...TRADIT SOC INT SAMP NIGERIA
TIME/SEQ 20. PAGE 31 H0627

B58
HAAS E.B.,THE UNITING OF EUROPE. EUR+WWI INT/ORG VOL/ASSN
NAT/G POL/PAR TOP/EX ECO/TAC EDU/PROP LEGIT FEDERAL ECO/DEV
NAT/LISM DRIVE RIGID/FLEX ORD/FREE PWR PLURISM
...POLICY CONCPT INT GEN/LAWS ECSC EEC 20. PAGE 63
H1264

B58
LAQUER W.Z.,THE MIDDLE EAST IN TRANSITION. COM USSR ISLAM
ECO/UNDEV NAT/G VOL/ASSN EDU/PROP EXEC ATTIT DRIVE TREND
PWR MARXISM COLD/WAR TOT/POP 20. PAGE 91 H1818 NAT/LISM

B58
SCOTT J.P.,AGGRESSION. CULTURE FAM SCHOOL ATTIT DRIVE
DISPL HEALTH...SOC CONCPT NEW/IDEA CHARTS LAB/EXP. PSY
PAGE 141 H2814 WAR

B59
LAQUER W.Z.,THE SOVIET UNION AND THE MIDDLE EAST. ISLAM
COM UAR USSR ECO/UNDEV NAT/G VOL/ASSN ECO/TAC DRIVE
EDU/PROP COLONIAL EXEC PWR...TIME/SEQ TREND FOR/AID
COLD/WAR 20. PAGE 91 H1819 NAT/LISM

B59
LIPSET S.M.,SOCIAL MOBILITY IN INDUSTRIAL SOCIETY. EUR+WWI USA+45 USSR STRUCT INDUS WRITING GP/REL INGP/REL DRIVE...SOC CHARTS NAT/COMP SOC/INTEG 20 MARX/KARL ENGELS/F. PAGE 97 H1940
STRATA ECO/DEV SOCIETY

B59
PAGE S.W.,LENIN AND WORLD REVOLUTION. COM USSR NAT/G DOMIN COERCE CROWD UTOPIA ATTIT AUTHORIT DRIVE PWR...CONCPT MYTH 19/20 LENIN/VI MARX/KARL. PAGE 122 H2441
REV PERSON MARXISM BIOG

S59
LEVINE R.A.,"ANTI-EUROPEAN VIOLENCE IN AFRICA: A COMPARATIVE ANALYSIS." AFR CULTURE NAT/G DIPLOM EDU/PROP COLONIAL REGION COERCE ATTIT PWR...PSY CONCPT TIME/SEQ TREND HYPO/EXP SOC/EXP STERTYP GEN/METH COLD/WAR 20. PAGE 95 H1903
DRIVE ORD/FREE REV

S59
MCNEIL E.B.,"PSYCHOLOGY AND AGGRESSION." CULTURE SOCIETY ACT/RES DISPL PERSON HEALTH. PAGE 107 H2146
DRIVE PSY

S59
SCOTT W.A.,"EMPIRICAL ASSESSMENT OF VALUES AND IDEOLOGIES." CULTURE SOCIETY SECT CREATE DRIVE PERSON MORAL PWR...SOC METH/CNCPT STAT CONT/OBS DEEP/INT DEEP/QU CHARTS VAL/FREE. PAGE 141 H2817
ATTIT PSY

B60
BURRIDGE K.,MAMBU: A MELANESIAN MILLENNIUM. ECO/UNDEV PROC/MFG FAM KIN CHIEF COLONIAL COERCE GP/REL DRIVE WEALTH WORSHIP 20 NEW/GUINEA. PAGE 25 H0494
S/ASIA SECT CULTURE MYTH

B60
CARTER G.M.,INDEPENDENCE FOR AFRICA. AFR FUT SOCIETY STRATA ECO/DEV POL/PAR DELIB/GP PLAN DOMIN EDU/PROP COLONIAL REGION ATTIT DRIVE SOVEREIGN ...RECORD INT TIME/SEQ CHARTS 20. PAGE 27 H0544
NAT/G PWR NAT/LISM

B60
COUGHLIN R.,DOUBLE IDENTITY: THE CHINESE AND MODERN THAILAND. CHINA/COM S/ASIA THAILAND ECO/UNDEV EXTR/IND FINAN INDUS KIN MUNIC NAT/G PROF/ORG SCHOOL SECT ATTIT DRIVE...CONCPT OBS 20. PAGE 34 H0676
ASIA FAM CULTURE

B60
DICHTER E.,THE STRATEGY OF DESIRE. UNIV CULTURE ACT/RES ATTIT DRIVE 20. PAGE 41 H0821
EDU/PROP PSY CONSULT PERSON

B60
FURNISS E.S.,FRANCE, TROUBLED ALLY. EUR+WWI FUT CULTURE SOCIETY BAL/PWR ADMIN ATTIT DRIVE PWR ...TREND TOT/POP 20 DEGAULLE/C. PAGE 54 H1079
NAT/G FRANCE

B60
KOHN H.,PAN-SLAVISM: ITS HISTORY AND IDEOLOGY. COM CZECHOSLVK EUR+WWI MOD/EUR USSR YUGOSLAVIA CULTURE ELITES INTELL KIN NAT/G EDU/PROP DRIVE SOVEREIGN ...HUM PHIL/SCI MYTH HIST/WRIT 19/20. PAGE 87 H1745
ATTIT CONCPT NAT/LISM

B60
LINDSAY K.,EUROPEAN ASSEMBLIES: THE EXPERIMENTAL PERIOD 1949-1959. EUR+WWI ECO/DEV NAT/G POL/PAR LEGIS TOP/EX ACT/RES PLAN ECO/TAC DOMIN LEGIT ROUTINE ATTIT DRIVE ORD/FREE PWR SKILL...SOC CONCPT TREND CHARTS GEN/LAWS VAL/FREE. PAGE 97 H1932
VOL/ASSN INT/ORG REGION

B60
SHIRER W.L.,THE RISE AND FALL OF THE THIRD REICH: A HISTORY OF NAZI GERMANY. EUR+WWI CULTURE ECO/DEV INDUS NAT/G POL/PAR FORCES PLAN TEC/DEV ECO/TAC COERCE ATTIT DRIVE PERSON PWR...MYSTIC PSY SOC MYTH STAT CHARTS EXHIBIT WORK VAL/FREE. PAGE 143 H2864
STRUCT GERMANY TOTALISM

L60
WHEELER G.,"RACIAL PROBLEMS IN SOVIET MUSLIM ASIA." COM CULTURE SOCIETY NEIGH SECT DOMIN EDU/PROP DISCRIM DISPL DRIVE PWR SOVEREIGN...CENSUS SAMP TREND 20 MUSLIM. PAGE 167 H3340
PERSON ATTIT USSR RACE/REL

S60
FITZGIBBON R.H.,"DICTATORSHIP AND DEMOCRACY IN LATIN AMERICA." FUT ECO/DEV ECO/UNDEV INT/ORG LOC/G NAT/G TOP/EX PLAN TEC/DEV ECO/TAC CHOOSE ATTIT DRIVE PERSON ALL/VALS OAS TOT/POP 20. PAGE 51 H1019
L/A+17C ACT/RES INT/TRADE

S60
FRANKEL S.H.,"ECONOMIC ASPECTS OF POLITICAL INDEPENDENCE IN AFRICA." AFR FUT SOCIETY ECO/UNDEV COM/IND FINAN LEGIS PLAN TEC/DEV CAP/ISM ECO/TAC INT/TRADE ADMIN ATTIT DRIVE RIGID/FLEX PWR WEALTH ...MGT NEW/IDEA MATH TIME/SEQ VAL/FREE 20. PAGE 53 H1052
NAT/G FOR/AID

S60
GROSSMAN G.,"SOVIET GROWTH: ROUTINE, INERTIA, AND PRESSURE." COM STRATA NAT/G DELIB/GP PLAN TEC/DEV ECO/TAC EDU/PROP ADMIN ROUTINE DRIVE WEALTH COLD/WAR 20. PAGE 62 H1236
POL/PAR ECO/DEV USSR

S60
MAGATHAN W.,"SOME BASES OF WEST GERMAN MILITARY POLICY." EUR+WWI FUT INT/ORG TOP/EX ECO/TAC DOMIN DRIVE ORD/FREE PWR...TRADIT GEOG OBS TREND. PAGE 101 H2015
NAT/G FORCES GERMANY

S60
MURPHEY R.,"ECONOMIC CONFLICTS IN SOUTH ASIA." ASIA CULTURE INTELL ECO/TAC REGION ATTIT DRIVE KNOWL ...METH/CNCPT TIME/SEQ STERTYP TOT/POP VAL/FREE 20. PAGE 115 H2296
S/ASIA ECO/UNDEV

S60
NORTH R.C.,"THE NEW EXPANSIONISM." ASIA CHINA/COM FUT INDIA CULTURE SOCIETY NAT/G TOP/EX DOMIN COERCE PWR MARXISM...CONCPT TIME/SEQ TREND GEN/LAWS COLD/WAR 20 MAO. PAGE 119 H2372
ATTIT DRIVE NAT/LISM

S60
PERLMANN H.,"UPHEAVAL IN TURKEY." EUR+WWI ISLAM NAT/G FORCES TOP/EX LEGIT COERCE CHOOSE DRIVE ORD/FREE PWR...TIME/SEQ TOT/POP 20. PAGE 125 H2494
CONSTN TURKEY

S60
RIVKIN A.,"AFRICAN ECONOMIC DEVELOPMENT: ADVANCED TECHNOLOGY AND THE STAGES OF GROWTH." CULTURE ECO/UNDEV AGRI COM/IND EXTR/IND PLAN ECO/TAC ATTIT DRIVE RIGID/FLEX SKILL WEALTH...MGT SOC GEN/LAWS WORK TOT/POP 20. PAGE 132 H2634
AFR TEC/DEV FOR/AID

S60
SHILS E.,"THE INTELLECTUALS IN THE POLITICAL DEVELOPMENT OF THE NEW STATES." AFR ASIA S/ASIA ELITES LOC/G NAT/G CONSULT EX/STRUC CREATE PLAN ECO/TAC DOMIN LEGIT DRIVE PWR...TRADIT CONCPT STERTYP GEN/LAWS 20. PAGE 143 H2861
POL/PAR INTELL NAT/LISM

S60
SPIRO H.J.,"NEW CONSTITUTIONAL FORMS IN AFRICA." FUT CULTURE SOCIETY ECO/UNDEV NAT/G POL/PAR VOL/ASSN EDU/PROP ATTIT DRIVE ORD/FREE PWR RESPECT ...POLICY CONCPT OBS TREND CON/ANAL STERTYP GEN/LAWS VAL/FREE. PAGE 148 H2950
AFR CONSTN FOR/AID NAT/LISM

S60
TAUBER K.,"ASPECTS OF NATIONALIST-COMMUNIST COLLABORATION IN POSTWAR GERMANY." COM EUR+WWI USSR NAT/G VOL/ASSN ATTIT DRIVE PWR...TIME/SEQ COLD/WAR TOT/POP 20. PAGE 152 H3049
POL/PAR EDU/PROP GERMANY

B61
BERKOWITZ L.,AGGRESSION: AS A SOCIAL PSYCHOLOGICAL ANALYSIS. UNIV CULTURE FACE/GP FAM KIN NEIGH EDU/PROP DISPL DRIVE HEALTH LOVE ORD/FREE...PSY SOC CONCPT OBS TREND. PAGE 15 H0305
SOCIETY COERCE WAR

B61
BULLOCK A.,HITLER: A STUDY IN TYRANNY. EUR+WWI GERMANY SOCIETY STRUCT NAT/G POL/PAR FORCES CREATE DOMIN EDU/PROP EXEC COERCE WAR NAT/LISM DISPL DRIVE PERSON PWR...PSY NAZI 20 HITLER/A. PAGE 23 H0470
ATTIT BIOG TOTALISM

B61
DIA M.,THE AFRICAN NATIONS AND WORLD SOLIDARITY. ISLAM CULTURE ELITES ECO/DEV ECO/UNDEV INT/ORG NAT/G PLAN ECO/TAC INT/TRADE EDU/PROP NAT/LISM ATTIT DRIVE ORD/FREE WEALTH...SOCIALIST CONCPT CON/ANAL GEN/LAWS TOT/POP 20. PAGE 41 H0817
AFR REGION SOCISM

B61
DOOB L.W.,COMMUNICATION IN AFRICA: A SEARCH FOR BOUNDARIES. CULTURE SOCIETY EDU/PROP WRITING INGP/REL DRIVE ORD/FREE...ART/METH SOC LING BIBLIOG 20. PAGE 42 H0837
AFR FEEDBACK PERCEPT PERS/REL

B61
ERASMUS C.J.,MAN TAKES CONTROL: CULTURAL DEVELOPMENT AND AMERICAN AID. STRUCT OWN DRIVE PERCEPT...SOC 20 MEXIC/AMER. PAGE 47 H0937
ORD/FREE CULTURE ECO/UNDEV TEC/DEV

B61
GUEVARA E.,GUERRILLA WARFARE. L/A+17C ECO/UNDEV NAT/G POL/PAR VOL/ASSN PLAN DOMIN REV DRIVE PWR WEALTH...NEW/IDEA RECORD BIOG COLD/WAR MARX/KARL OAS 20. PAGE 62 H1247
FORCES COERCE GUERRILLA CUBA

B61
MARX K.,THE COMMUNIST MANIFESTO. IN (MENDEL A. ESSENTIAL WORKS OF MARXISM, NEW YORK: BANTAM. FUT MOD/EUR CULTURE ECO/DEV ECO/UNDEV AGRI FINAN INDUS MARKET PROC/MFG LABOR MUNIC POL/PAR CONSULT FORCES CREATE PLAN ADMIN ATTIT DRIVE RIGID/FLEX ORD/FREE PWR RESPECT MARX/KARL WORK. PAGE 104 H2081
COM NEW/IDEA CAP/ISM REV

B61
SAFRAN M.,EGYPT IN SEARCH OF POLITICAL COMMUNITY: AN ANALYSIS OF THE INTELLECTUAL AND POLITICAL EVOLUTION OF EGYPT, 1804-1952. ISLAM NAT/G SECT EDU/PROP COERCE ATTIT DRIVE KNOWL PWR...TIME/SEQ 20. PAGE 137 H2729
INTELL NAT/LISM UAR

B61
SETON-WATSON H.,FROM LENIN TO KHRUSHCHEV: THE HISTORY OF WORLD COMMUNISM. ASIA COM EUR+WWI ISLAM S/ASIA ECO/DEV ECO/UNDEV NAT/G POL/PAR DIPLOM ECO/TAC EDU/PROP COERCE GUERRILLA ATTIT DRIVE WORK TOT/POP NAZI 20. PAGE 141 H2832
PWR REV USSR

B61
VON MERING O.,A GRAMMAR OF HUMAN VALUES. WOR+45 CULTURE FACE/GP NEIGH CREATE EDU/PROP LEGIT ATTIT DRIVE PERSON ORD/FREE...PSY SOC METH/CNCPT OBS RECORD INT REC/INT STAND/INT QU CHARTS VAL/FREE. PAGE 164 H3275
SOCIETY MORAL

L61
EZELLPH,"THE HISPANIC AGRICULTURATION OF THE GILA RIVER PIMAS." FAM TEC/DEV PERS/REL ADJUST...GEOG MYTH CHARTS BIBLIOG WORSHIP 17/20. PAGE 48 H0956
CULTURE SOC AGRI DRIVE

S61
ANDERSON O.,"ECONOMIC WARFARE IN THE CRIMEAN WAR." EUR+WWI MOD/EUR NAT/G ACT/RES WAR DRIVE PWR 19/20. PAGE 6 H0130
ECO/TAC UK RUSSIA

S61
MILLER E.,"LEGAL ASPECTS OF UN ACTION IN THE CONGO." AFR CULTURE ADMIN PEACE DRIVE RIGID/FLEX ORD/FREE...WELF/ST JURID OBS UN CONGO 20. PAGE 111 H2212
INT/ORG LEGIT

S61
RANDALL F.B.,"COMMUNISM IN THE HIGH ANDES." L/A+17C PERU USSR SOCIETY PLAN EDU/PROP TOTALISM ATTIT RIGID/FLEX PWR WEALTH...HUM CONCPT GEN/LAWS 20 BOLIV EQUADOR. PAGE 129 H2589
CULTURE DRIVE

S61
SCHELLING T.C.,"NUCLEAR STRATEGY IN EUROPE." COM EUR+WWI USSR NAT/G FORCES NUC/PWR DRIVE ORD/FREE PWR...DECISION CONCPT OBS TREND HYPO/EXP 20. PAGE 139 H2784
FUT COERCE ARMS/CONT WAR

B62
CALVOCORESSI P.,WORLD ORDER AND NEW STATES: PROBLEMS OF KEEPING THE PEACE. AFR EUR+WWI S/ASIA ELITES NAT/G ECO/TAC FOR/AID EDU/PROP COERCE ATTIT DRIVE ALL/VALS...GEN/LAWS COLD/WAR 20 UN. PAGE 25 H0509
INT/ORG PEACE

B62
CHAKRAVARTI P.C.,INDIA'S CHINA POLICY. ASIA CHINA/COM S/ASIA CULTURE NAT/G TOP/EX ACT/RES EDU/PROP DRIVE ALL/VALS...MYTH 20. PAGE 28 H0571
RIGID/FLEX TREND INDIA

B62
DUROSELLE J.B.,LES NOUVEAUX ETATS DANS LES RELATIONS INTERNATIONALES. AFR CHINA/COM FRANCE MOROCCO S/ASIA USSR ECO/UNDEV INT/ORG PLAN ECO/TAC EDU/PROP ATTIT DRIVE...TREND TOT/POP TUNIS 20. PAGE 44 H0872
NAT/G CONSTN DIPLOM

B62
EVANS-PRITCHARD E.E.,ESSAYS IN SOCIAL ANTHROPOLOGY. AFR KIN REGION INGP/REL DRIVE HABITAT...OBS METH 20 ZANDE. PAGE 48 H0954
SOCIETY CULTURE SOC STRUCT

B62
FINER S.E.,THE MAN ON HORSEBACK: ROLE OF THE MILITARY IN POLITICS. UNIV LAW CONSTN ELITES SOCIETY POL/PAR BAL/PWR DOMIN EDU/PROP LEGIT COERCE GUERRILLA REV WAR WEAPON DRIVE SUPEGO ORD/FREE PWR RESPECT...POLICY CONCPT GEN/METH. PAGE 50 H1003
NAT/G FORCES TOTALISM

B62
HARRINGTON M.,THE OTHER AMERICA: POVERTY IN THE UNITED STATES. WORKER CREATE REPRESENT RACE/REL AGE/O DRIVE POLICY. PAGE 67 H1338
WEALTH WELF/ST INCOME CULTURE

B62
INSTITUTE FOR STUDY OF USSR,YOUTH IN FERMENT. INTELL NAT/G PERF/ART POL/PAR SCHOOL VOL/ASSN FORCES EDU/PROP ATTIT DRIVE PERCEPT HEALTH KNOWL MORAL ORD/FREE RESPECT...SOC OBS HIST/WRIT VAL/FREE. PAGE 77 H1537
COM CULTURE USSR

B62
JOHNSON J.J.,THE ROLE OF THE MILITARY IN UNDERDEVELOPED COUNTRIES. AFR BURMA INDONESIA ISLAM ISRAEL L/A+17C S/ASIA THAILAND CULTURE ECO/UNDEV KIN PROVS CONSULT ACT/RES COERCE REV DRIVE RIGID/FLEX ORD/FREE...RECORD ANTHOL 20. PAGE 81 H1622
FORCES CONCPT

B62
KRECH D.,INDIVIDUAL IN SOCIETY; A TEXTBOOK OF SOCIAL PSYCHOLOGY. UNIV CULTURE LEAD INGP/REL ATTIT DRIVE PERCEPT ROLE...PHIL/SCI BIBLIOG T. PAGE 88 H1765
PSY SOC SOCIETY PERS/REL

B62
LEGUM C.,PAN-AFRICANISM: A SHORT POLITICAL GUIDE. ISLAM CULTURE INTELL ECO/DEV NAT/G POL/PAR DELIB/GP PLAN EDU/PROP FEDERAL NAT/LISM ATTIT DRIVE PERSON ...RECORD TIME/SEQ CHARTS STERTYP 20. PAGE 93 H1861
AFR CONCPT

B62
MEGGITT M.J.,DESERT PEOPLE. ECO/UNDEV KIN CREATE PROB/SOLV CONTROL DRIVE ROLE...GEOG SOC MYTH CHARTS BIBLIOG 20 AUSTRAL. PAGE 108 H2159
ADJUST CULTURE INGP/REL HABITAT

B62
MELADY T.,THE WHITE MAN'S FUTURE IN BLACK AFRICA. FUT CULTURE SOCIETY NAT/G POL/PAR PLAN ECO/TAC DOMIN EDU/PROP LEGIT COLONIAL RACE/REL ATTIT DRIVE ALL/VALS...PSY SOC CONCPT TIME/SEQ TOT/POP VAL/FREE 20. PAGE 108 H2167
AFR STRATA ELITES

L62
NOLTE E.,"ZUR PHANOMENOLOGIE DES FASCHIMUS." EUR+WWI GERMANY ITALY TURKEY INTELL NAT/G CHIEF CONSULT FORCES CREATE DOMIN EDU/PROP COERCE WAR CHOOSE DRIVE FASCISM...PSY CONCPT MYTH GEN/METH LEAGUE/NAT NAZI 20. PAGE 118 H2367
ATTIT PWR

S62
PASSIN H.,"THE SOURCES OF PROTEST IN JAPAN." CULTURE SOCIETY EDU/PROP COERCE NAT/LISM DISPL DRIVE PWR RESPECT...POLICY SOC TREND 20 CHINJAP. PAGE 124 H2473
ASIA ATTIT REV

S62
ROTBERG R.,"THE RISE OF AFRICAN NATIONALISM: THE CASE OF EAST AND CENTRAL AFRICA." AFR CULTURE SOCIETY NEIGH DIPLOM DOMIN COLONIAL COERCE DISPL PERCEPT PWR SOVEREIGN...POLICY OBS/ENVIR TREND WORK 20. PAGE 135 H2690
ATTIT DRIVE NAT/LISM REV

S62
SPRINGER H.W.,"FEDERATION IN THE CARIBBEAN: AN ATTEMPT THAT FAILED." L/A+17C ECO/UNDEV INT/ORG POL/PAR PROVS LEGIS CREATE PLAN LEGIT ADMIN FEDERAL ATTIT DRIVE PERSON ORD/FREE PWR...POLICY GEOG PSY CONCPT OBS CARIBBEAN CMN/WLTH 20. PAGE 148 H2955
VOL/ASSN NAT/G REGION

B63
CRANKSHAW E.,THE NEW COLD WAR: MOSCOW V. PEKIN. CHINA/COM USSR INTELL POL/PAR DELIB/GP CAP/ISM COERCE REV NAT/LISM TOTALISM DRIVE...POLICY IDEA/COMP 20 KHRUSH/N. PAGE 35 H0698
ATTIT DIPLOM NAT/COMP MARXISM

B63
CREMEANS C.,THE ARABS AND THE WORLD: NASSER'S ARAB NATIONALIST POLICY. FUT ISLAM UAR USA+45 SOCIETY STRATA NAT/G POL/PAR PLAN DIPLOM EDU/PROP LEGIT DRIVE ALL/VALS...INT TIME/SEQ CHARTS 20 NASSER/G. PAGE 35 H0700
TOP/EX ATTIT REGION NAT/LISM

B63
ENKE S.,ECONOMICS FOR DEVELOPMENT. AGRI TEC/DEV CAP/ISM DIPLOM ECO/TAC TAX ATTIT DRIVE HABITAT WEALTH...GOV/COMP BIBLIOG 20. PAGE 46 H0928
ECO/UNDEV PHIL/SCI CON/ANAL

B63
FALL B.,THE TWO VIETNAMS. CULTURE SOCIETY ECO/UNDEV NAT/G TOP/EX ACT/RES PLAN ECO/TAC DOMIN EDU/PROP COERCE ATTIT DRIVE PERSON ORD/FREE PWR...SOC TIME/SEQ COLD/WAR 20. PAGE 48 H0965
S/ASIA BIOG VIETNAM

B63
KHADDURI M.,MODERN LIBYA: A STUDY IN POLITICAL DEVELOPMENT. EUR+WWI ISLAM LIBYA ELITES INT/ORG POL/PAR FORCES DIPLOM FOR/AID DOMIN EDU/PROP LEGIT NAT/LISM DRIVE RIGID/FLEX SKILL...CONCPT TIME/SEQ TREND 20. PAGE 85 H1704
NAT/G STRUCT

B63
KRAEHE E.,METTERNICH'S GERMAN POLICY: THE CONTEST WITH NAPOLEON, 1799-1814, VOL. 1. FRANCE MOD/EUR NAT/G CONSULT TOP/EX PLAN BAL/PWR DOMIN COERCE ATTIT DRIVE PERCEPT PERSON SKILL...CONCPT RECORD TIME/SEQ TREND 18/19. PAGE 88 H1764
BIOG GERMANY DIPLOM

B63
LOOMIE A.J.,THE SPANISH ELIZABETHANS: THE ENGLISH EXILES AT THE COURT OF PHILIP II. SPAIN UK WAR INGP/REL DRIVE HABITAT CATHISM...BIOG 16/17 MIGRATION. PAGE 98 H1962
NAT/G STRANGE POLICY DIPLOM

B63
NKRUMAH K.,AFRICA MUST UNITE. AFR FUT GHANA CONSTN CULTURE SOCIETY NAT/G POL/PAR DELIB/GP TOP/EX PLAN DOMIN EDU/PROP ATTIT DRIVE...TIME/SEQ CHARTS TOT/POP 20. PAGE 118 H2364
CONCPT GEN/LAWS REGION

B63
STEVENS G.G.,EGYPT YESTERDAY AND TODAY. CONSTN ECO/UNDEV AGRI INDUS NAT/G POL/PAR FORCES ECO/TAC EDU/PROP COERCE WAR NAT/LISM DRIVE ALL/VALS ...TIME/SEQ WORK SUEZ 20. PAGE 149 H2983
ISLAM TOP/EX REV UAR

B63
TINDALE N.B.,ABORIGINAL AUSTRALIANS. KIN CREATE ROLE...SOC MYTH TREND 20 AUSTRAL ABORIGINES MIGRATION. PAGE 155 H3099
CULTURE DRIVE ECO/UNDEV HABITAT

B63
ZARTMAN I.W.,GOVERNMENT AND POLITICS IN NORTHERN AFRICA. AFR ALGERIA ISLAM LIBYA MOROCCO UAR ELITES SOCIETY PLAN ECO/TAC DOMIN EDU/PROP LEGIT ATTIT ...GEOG CONCPT TIME/SEQ 20 TUNIS. PAGE 172 H3448
CULTURE DRIVE NAT/LISM

L63
FREUND G.,"ADENAUER AND THE FUTURE OF GERMANY." EUR+WWI FUT GERMANY/W FORCES LEGIT ADMIN ROUTINE ATTIT DRIVE PERSON PWR...POLICY TIME/SEQ TREND VAL/FREE 20 ADENAUER/K. PAGE 53 H1058
NAT/G BIOG DIPLOM GERMANY

S63
AYAL E.B.,"VALUE SYSTEM AND ECONOMIC DEVELOPMENT IN JAPAN AND THAILAND." ASIA S/ASIA THAILAND CULTURE ECO/DEV CAP/ISM DOMIN NAT/LISM DRIVE RIGID/FLEX SOCISM...WELF/ST OBS TREND CON/ANAL GEN/LAWS 20 CHINJAP. PAGE 9 H0185
ECO/UNDEV ALL/VALS

S63
HOSKINS H.L.,"ARAB SOCIALISM IN THE UAR." ISLAM USSR AGRI INDUS NAT/G TOP/EX CREATE DIPLOM EDU/PROP DRIVE KNOWL PWR SOCISM...POLICY CONCPT TREND SUEZ 20. PAGE 74 H1478
ECO/DEV PLAN UAR

S63
POPPINO R.E.,"IMBALANCE IN BRAZIL." L/A+17C NAT/G TOP/EX PLAN DIPLOM LEGIT DRIVE WEALTH...CON/ANAL LAFTA 20. PAGE 127 H2544
POL/PAR ECO/TAC BRAZIL

S63
RUSTOW D.A.,"THE MILITARY IN MIDDLE EASTERN SOCIETY AND POLITICS." FUT ISLAM CONSTN SOCIETY FACE/GP NAT/G POL/PAR PROF/ORG CONSULT DOMIN ADMIN EXEC REGION COERCE NAT/LISM ATTIT DRIVE PERSON ORD/FREE PWR...POLICY CONCPT OBS STERTYP 20. PAGE 136 H2721
FORCES ELITES

B64
BELL W.,JAMAICAN LEADERS: POLITICAL ATTITUDES IN A NEW NATION. JAMAICA STRUCT ACT/RES CREATE PROB/SOLV DIPLOM COLONIAL LEAD...QU 20. PAGE 13 H0267 NAT/LISM ATTIT DRIVE SOVEREIGN

B64
BERNDT R.M.,THE WORLD OF THE FIRST AUSTRALIANS. S/ASIA ECO/UNDEV WORKER PROB/SOLV EFFICIENCY ROLE ...SOC MYTH WORSHIP AUSTRAL ABORIGINES. PAGE 16 H0311 CULTURE KIN STRUCT DRIVE

B64
BINDER L.,THE IDEOLOGICAL REVOLUTION IN THE MIDDLE EAST. ISLAM STRUCT INT/ORG KIN SECT EX/STRUC TOP/EX PLAN ATTIT DRIVE RIGID/FLEX PWR...MYTH TOT/POP 20. PAGE 17 H0338 POL/PAR NAT/G NAT/LISM

B64
CLUBB O.E. JR.,TWENTIETH CENTURY CHINA. ASIA CHINA/COM INTELL NAT/G POL/PAR VOL/ASSN ACT/RES EDU/PROP COERCE REV PWR...TIME/SEQ 20. PAGE 30 H0608 TOP/EX DRIVE

B64
FRIEDLAND W.H.,AFRICAN SOCIALISM. ECO/UNDEV MARKET LABOR NAT/G POL/PAR PLAN CAP/ISM ECO/TAC EDU/PROP CHOOSE ATTIT DRIVE PWR WEALTH...POLICY CONCPT RECORD STERTYP 20. PAGE 53 H1063 AFR SOCISM

B64
GRIFFITH W.E.,THE SINO-SOVIET RIFT. ASIA CHINA/COM COM CUBA USSR YUGOSLAVIA NAT/G POL/PAR VOL/ASSN DELIB/GP FORCES TOP/EX DIPLOM EDU/PROP DRIVE PERSON PWR...TREND 20 TREATY. PAGE 61 H1224 ATTIT TIME/SEQ BAL/PWR SOCISM

B64
HARRIS M.,THE NATURE OF CULTURAL THINGS. GP/REL PERS/REL DRIVE HABITAT PERSON ROLE...PHIL/SCI PSY SOC CHARTS BIBLIOG 20. PAGE 67 H1341 CULTURE OBS CLASSIF NEW/IDEA

B64
KARIEL H.S.,IN SEARCH OF AUTHORITY: TWENTIETH-CENTURY POLITICAL THOUGHT. WOR+45 WOR-45 NAT/G EX/STRUC TOTALISM DRIVE PWR...MGT PHIL/SCI GEN/LAWS 19/20 NIETZSCH/F FREUD/S WEBER/MAX NIEBUHR/R MARITAIN/J. PAGE 83 H1661 CONSTN CONCPT ORD/FREE IDEA/COMP

B64
LAWRENCE P.,ROAD BELONG CARGO: A STUDY OF CARGO MOVEMENT IN SOUTHERN MADANG DISTRICT, NEW GUINEA. S/ASIA CULTURE ECO/UNDEV PROC/MFG KIN CHIEF COLONIAL COERCE GP/REL DRIVE WEALTH WORSHIP 20 NEW/GUINEA. PAGE 92 H1846 SOC SECT ALL/VALS MYTH

B64
MEAD M.,CONTINUITIES IN CULTURAL EVOLUTION. FACE/GP KIN ACT/RES EDU/PROP GP/REL INGP/REL DRIVE HEREDITY ROLE...TIME/SEQ TREND METH SOC/INTEG 20. PAGE 108 H2153 CULTURE SOC PERS/REL

B64
RAMAZANI R.K.,THE MIDDLE EAST AND THE EUROPEAN COMMON MARKET. EUR+WWI ISLAM ECO/DEV EXTR/IND MARKET PROC/MFG INT/ORG NAT/G TEC/DEV ECO/TAC REGION DRIVE WEALTH...STAT CHARTS EEC TOT/POP 20. PAGE 129 H2587 ECO/UNDEV ATTIT INT/TRADE

L64
BERELSON B.,"SAMPLE SURVEYS AND POPULATION CONTROL." ASIA FUT ISLAM L/A+17C CULTURE SOCIETY FAM NAT/G CONSULT PLAN EDU/PROP ATTIT DRIVE ALL/VALS...POLICY RELATIV HEAL PSY SOC CONCPT METH/CNCPT OBS OBS/ENVIR TOT/POP. PAGE 15 H0297 BIO/SOC SAMP

L64
HAAS E.B.,"ECONOMICS AND DIFFERENTIAL PATTERNS OF POLITICAL INTEGRATION: PROJECTIONS ABOUT UNITY IN LATIN AMERICA." SOCIETY NAT/G DELIB/GP ACT/RES CREATE PLAN ECO/TAC REGION ROUTINE ATTIT DRIVE PWR WEALTH...CONCPT TREND CHARTS LAFTA 20. PAGE 63 H1266 L/A+17C INT/ORG MARKET

S64
CATTELL D.T.,"SOVIET POLICIES IN LATIN AMERICA." COM CUBA L/A+17C USSR SOCIETY NAT/G POL/PAR FORCES CREATE ECO/TAC EDU/PROP REGION REV RIGID/FLEX ...GEN/LAWS COLD/WAR 20. PAGE 28 H0560 DRIVE PWR

S64
CLIFFE L.,"TANGANYIKA'S TWO YEARS OF INDEPENDENCE." AFR INDUS MARKET NAT/G POL/PAR DELIB/GP CREATE ECO/TAC LEGIT DRIVE ALL/VALS...METH/CNCPT RECORD 20 TANGANYIKA. PAGE 30 H0604 ECO/UNDEV PLAN

S64
DE GAULLE C.,"FRENCH WORLD VIEW." AFR ASIA CHINA/COM EUR+WWI ISLAM ECO/UNDEV INT/ORG NAT/G VOL/ASSN ACT/RES DIPLOM ECO/TAC EDU/PROP ATTIT DRIVE WEALTH 20. PAGE 37 H0751 TOP/EX PWR FOR/AID FRANCE

S64
GARMARNIKOW M.,"INFLUENCE-BUYING IN WEST AFRICA." COM FUT USSR INTELL NAT/G PLAN TEC/DEV ECO/TAC DOMIN EDU/PROP REGION NAT/LISM ATTIT DRIVE ALL/VALS SOVEREIGN...POLICY PSY SOC CONCPT TREND STERTYP WORK COLD/WAR 20. PAGE 55 H1102 AFR ECO/UNDEV FOR/AID SOCISM

S64
LEVI W.,"INDIAN NEUTRALISM RECONSIDERED." ASIA CHINA/COM S/ASIA SOCIETY NAT/G ACT/RES LEGIT NEUTRAL COERCE ATTIT DRIVE PERCEPT RIGID/FLEX HEALTH LOVE PWR...DECISION RECORD TREND STERTYP 20. PAGE 95 H1896 ORD/FREE CONCPT INDIA

S64
SAAB H.,"THE ARAB SEARCH FOR A FEDERAL UNION." SOCIETY INT/ORG NAT/G DELIB/GP FORCES ACT/RES TEC/DEV ECO/TAC DOMIN LEGIT REGION ROUTINE ATTIT DRIVE RIGID/FLEX ALL/VALS...SOC CONCPT NEW/IDEA TIME/SEQ TREND. PAGE 136 H2726 ISLAM PLAN

S64
SMYTHE H.H.,"NEHRU AND INDIAN FOREIGN POLICY." S/ASIA ECO/UNDEV NAT/G POL/PAR CONSULT PLAN DIPLOM NEUTRAL COERCE ATTIT DRIVE PERSON MORAL ORD/FREE RESPECT...GEOG CONCPT TIME/SEQ TREND GEN/LAWS 20 NEHRU/J. PAGE 146 H2922 TOP/EX BIOG INDIA

S64
ZARTMAN I.W.,"LES RELATIONS ENTRE LA FRANCE ET L'ALGERIA DEPUIS LES ACCORDS D'EVIAN." EUR+WWI FUT ISLAM CULTURE AGRI EXTR/IND FINAN INDUS POL/PAR DIPLOM ECO/TAC FOR/AID PEACE ATTIT DRIVE ALL/VALS ...TIME/SEQ VAL/FREE 20. PAGE 172 H3450 ECO/UNDEV ALGERIA FRANCE

C64
HARRIS M.,"THE NATURE OF CULTURAL THINGS." GP/REL DRIVE HABITAT PERSON ROLE...PHIL/SCI 20. PAGE 67 H1340 BIBLIOG CULTURE PSY SOC

C64
SCOTT R.E.,"MEXICAN GOVERNMENT IN TRANSITION (REV ED)" CULTURE STRUCT POL/PAR CHIEF ADMIN LOBBY REV CHOOSE GP/REL DRIVE...BIBLIOG METH 20 MEXIC/AMER. PAGE 141 H2816 NAT/G L/A+17C ROUTINE CONSTN

B65
ADAM T.R.,GOVERNMENT AND POLITICS IN AFRICA SOUTH OF THE SAHARA. AFR EUR+WWI CONSTN CULTURE INTELL POL/PAR TOP/EX LEGIT REGION DRIVE...OBS TREND CMN/WLTH 20. PAGE 3 H0062 NAT/G TIME/SEQ RACE/REL COLONIAL

B65
DOLCI D.,A NEW WORLD IN THE MAKING. GHANA SENEGAL USSR YUGOSLAVIA CULTURE INT/ORG PLAN EDU/PROP GP/REL PEACE MORAL...GEOG SOC 20 COLD/WAR. PAGE 42 H0834 SOCIETY ALL/VALS DRIVE PERSON

B65
EDINGER L.J.,KURT SCHUMACHER: A STUDY IN PERSONALITY AND POLITICAL BEHAVIOR. EUR+WWI GERMANY NAT/G DRIVE ROLE PWR SOCISM...BIBLIOG 20 SOC/DEMPAR SCHUMCHR/K. PAGE 44 H0889 TOP/EX LEAD PERSON BIOG

B65
JACKSON G.,THE SPANISH REPUBLIC AND THE CIVIL WAR, 1931-1939. EUR+WWI INTELL STRUCT COM/IND NAT/G POL/PAR LEGIS EDU/PROP EXEC COERCE NAT/LISM DRIVE PWR...INT TIME/SEQ TOT/POP 20. PAGE 79 H1574 ATTIT GUERRILLA SPAIN

B65
JOHNSON P.,KHRUSHCHEV AND THE ARTS: POLITICS OF SOVIET CULTURE, 1962-1964. COM USSR NAT/G PERF/ART CONFER DEBATE GP/REL PERS/REL UTIL ATTIT DRIVE 20 KHRUSH/N. PAGE 81 H1626 CULTURE MARXISM POLICY CHIEF

B65
THE STATE AND ECONOMIC ENTERPRISE IN JAPAN; ESSAYS IN THE POLITICAL ECONOMY OF GROWTH. AGRI INDUS DRIVE POPULISM...CHARTS NAT/COMP ANTHOL 19/20 CHINJAP. PAGE 98 H1949 ECO/UNDEV ECO/DEV CAP/ISM ECO/TAC

B65
O'BRIEN F.,CRISIS IN WORLD COMMUNISM* MARXISM IN SEARCH OF EFFICIENCY. COM ECO/DEV PLAN INT/TRADE WAR ADJUST PEACE...STAT TIME/SEQ GOV/COMP NAT/COMP COLD/WAR. PAGE 119 H2384 MARXISM USSR DRIVE EFFICIENCY

L65
SHARMA S.P.,"THE INDIA-CHINA BORDER DISPUTE: AN INDIAN PERSPECTIVE." ASIA CHINA/COM S/ASIA NAT/G LEGIT CT/SYS NAT/LISM DRIVE MORAL ORD/FREE PWR 20. PAGE 142 H2850 LAW ATTIT SOVEREIGN INDIA

S65
JENSEN L.,"MILITARY CAPABILITIES AND BARGAINING BEHAVIOR." USA+45 USSR ARMS/CONT DETER COST ATTIT ...METH/CNCPT STAT SYS/QU CON/ANAL CHARTS NAT/COMP. PAGE 81 H1614 DIPLOM DRIVE PWR STERTYP

S65
LEVI W.,"THE CONCEPT OF INTEGRATION IN RESEARCH ON PEACE." NAT/G VOL/ASSN DIPLOM TASK ADJUST NAT/LISM PEACE DRIVE LOVE...PSY NET/THEORY GEN/LAWS. PAGE 95 H1897 CONCPT IDEA/COMP INT/ORG CENTRAL

S65
STAROBIN J.R.,"COMMUNISM IN WESTERN EUROPE." FRANCE GERMANY ITALY USA+45 USSR ECO/DEV FEDERAL PEACE ATTIT DRIVE PWR TREND. PAGE 149 H2972 MARXISM EUR+WWI POL/PAR NAT/COMP

S65
VUCINICH W.S.,"WHITHER RUMANIA." COM USSR YUGOSLAVIA NAT/G VOL/ASSN DELIB/GP TOP/EX LEGIT NAT/LISM TOTALISM ATTIT DRIVE RIGID/FLEX ORD/FREE WEALTH SOCISM...TIME/SEQ TREND 20. PAGE 164 H3281 ECO/DEV CREATE ROMANIA

S65
WHITE J.,"WEST GERMAN AID TO DEVELOPING COUNTRIES." INT/ORG OP/RES GIVE CENTRAL ATTIT DRIVE...STAT NAT/COMP COLD/WAR. PAGE 167 H3348 GERMANY FOR/AID ECO/UNDEV CAP/ISM

B66
KASUNMU A.B.,NIGERIAN FAMILY LAW. NIGERIA KIN LEGIT ILLEGIT MARRIAGE AGE DRIVE HABITAT ALL/VALS...JURID IDEA/COMP T 20 ENGLSH/LAW. PAGE 83 H1667 — FAM LAW CULTURE AFR

B66
LAVEN P.,RENAISSANCE ITALY: 1464-1534. ITALY AGRI EXTR/IND FINAN MUNIC INT/TRADE DRIVE...CATH GEOG CHARTS BIBLIOG/A 15. PAGE 92 H1841 — CULTURE HUM TEC/DEV KNOWL

B66
MATTHEWS R.,AFRICAN POWDER KEG: REVOLT AND DISSENT IN SIX EMERGENT NATIONS. AFR ALGERIA DAHOMEY GABON GHANA MALAWI GAMBLE LEAD PARTIC REV DRIVE...BIOG TREND GOV/COMP 20. PAGE 105 H2098 — ELITES ECO/UNDEV TOP/EX CONTROL

B66
O'NEILL C.E.,CHURCH AND STATE IN FRENCH COLONIAL LOUISIANA: POLICY AND POLITICS TO 1732. PROVS VOL/ASSN DELIB/GP ADJUD ADMIN GP/REL ATTIT DRIVE ...POLICY BIBLIOG 17/18 LOUISIANA CHURCH/STA. PAGE 120 H2390 — COLONIAL NAT/G SECT PWR

B66
SWARTZ M.J.,POLITICAL ANTHROPOLOGY. WOR+45 POL/PAR ACT/RES REV GP/REL DRIVE...SOC CONCPT TIME/SEQ GP/COMP ANTHOL WORSHIP 20. PAGE 151 H3013 — PARTIC RIGID/FLEX LOC/G CREATE

B66
VON ARSENIEW W.,DIE GEISTIGEN SCHICKSALE DES RUSSISCHEN VOLKES. RUSSIA USSR SOCIETY STRUCT NAT/G SECT CHIEF REV 19/20. PAGE 163 H3262 — ATTIT PERSON CULTURE DRIVE

S66
GILBERT S.P.,"WARS OF LIBERATION AND SOVIET MILITARY AID POLICY." ASIA INDIA INDONESIA UAR USA+45 STRATA WAR PERCEPT MARXISM...STAT NAT/COMP. PAGE 56 H1124 — USSR FOR/AID WEAPON DRIVE

S66
MALENBAUM W.,"GOVERNMENT, ENTREPRENEURSHIP, AND ECONOMIC GROWTH IN POOR LANDS." ELITES ECO/UNDEV INDUS CREATE DRIVE. PAGE 101 H2028 — ECO/TAC PLAN CONSERVE NAT/G

S66
QUESTER G.H.,"ON THE IDENTIFICATION OF REAL AND PRETENDED COMMUNIST MILITARY DOCTRINE." ASIA USSR DETER WAR ATTIT DRIVE HEALTH TIME/SEQ. PAGE 129 H2574 — RATIONAL PERCEPT NUC/PWR NAT/COMP

B67
BODENHEIMER E.,TREATISE ON JUSTICE. INT/ORG NAT/G PUB/INST ACT/RES RISK CRIME INGP/REL DISCRIM DRIVE LAISSEZ 20. PAGE 18 H0363 — ALL/VALS STRUCT JURID CONCPT

B67
MEHDI M.T.,PEACE IN THE MIDDLE EAST. ISRAEL SOCIETY NAT/G PLAN EDU/PROP NAT/LISM DRIVE...IDEA/COMP 20 JEWS. PAGE 108 H2160 — ISLAM DIPLOM GP/REL COERCE

B67
PIKE F.B.,FREEDOM AND REFORM IN LATIN AMERICA. BRAZIL URUGUAY CONSTN CULTURE SECT DIPLOM EDU/PROP PARTIC DRIVE ALL/VALS CATHISM...GEOG ANTHOL BIBLIOG REFORMERS BOLIV. PAGE 126 H2511 — L/A+17C ORD/FREE ECO/UNDEV REV

B67
POLSKY N.,HUSTLERS, BEATS, AND OTHERS. FACE/GP PRESS CRIME ADJUST ANOMIE DRIVE WEALTH...PSY SOC 20. PAGE 127 H2540 — CULTURE CRIMLGY NEW/IDEA STRUCT

L67
BRIDGHAM P.,"MAO'S "CULTURAL REVOLUTION"* ORIGIN AND DEVELOPMENT." NAT/G LEAD CIVMIL/REL NAT/LISM TOTALISM ATTIT DRIVE PWR MARXISM 20. PAGE 21 H0413 — CHINA/COM CULTURE REV CROWD

L67
EGBERT D.D.,"THE IDEA OF 'AVANT-GARDE' IN ART AND POLITICS." USSR CULTURE INTELL POL/PAR CREATE EDU/PROP CONTROL REV ANOMIE DRIVE ROLE...IDEA/COMP 20. PAGE 45 H0895 — ART/METH COM ATTIT

S67
AKE C.,"POLITICAL INTEGRATION AND POLITICAL STABILITY." ELITES POL/PAR LEAD ADJUST EFFICIENCY ATTIT AUTHORIT DRIVE...CONCPT 20. PAGE 4 H0088 — CULTURE NAT/G CONTROL GP/REL

S67
ALPANDER G.G.,"ENTREPRENEURS AND PRIVATE ENTERPRISE IN TURKEY." TURKEY INDUS PROC/MFG EDU/PROP ATTIT DRIVE WEALTH...GEOG MGT SOC STAT TREND CHARTS 20. PAGE 6 H0114 — ECO/UNDEV LG/CO NAT/G POLICY

S67
BERLINER J.S.,"RUSSIA'S BUREAUCRATS - WHY THEY'RE REACTIONARY." USSR NAT/G OP/RES PROB/SOLV TEC/DEV CONTROL SANCTION EFFICIENCY DRIVE PERSON...TECHNIC SOC 20. PAGE 15 H0308 — CREATE ADMIN INDUS PRODUC

S67
HOPE M.,"THE RELUCTANT WAY: SELF-IMMOLATION IN VIETNAM." VIETNAM SOCIETY FAM KIN SECT DRIVE ALL/VALS...TRADIT OBS INT 20. PAGE 73 H1465 — CULTURE SUICIDE IDEA/COMP ATTIT

S67
KRISTOF L.K.D.,"THE STATE-IDEA, THE NATIONAL IDEA AND THE IMAGE OF THE FATHERLAND." CONSTN CULTURE INTELL SOCIETY WORKER TASK DRIVE HABITAT...MYTH GOV/COMP IDEA/COMP. PAGE 89 H1769 — GEOG CONCPT NAT/G PERCEPT

S67
PAK H.,"CHINA'S MILITIA AND MAO TSE-TUNG'S 'PEOPLE'S WAR'." CHINA/COM SOCIETY POL/PAR EX/STRUC PROB/SOLV PARTIC COERCE WAR CIVMIL/REL ATTIT DRIVE MARXISM...METH/COMP 20 MAO. PAGE 122 H2447 — FORCES NAT/G WORKER CHIEF

S67
RIESMAN D.,"SOME QUESTIONS ABOUT THE STUDY OF AMERICAN CHARACTER IN THE TWENTIETH CENTURY." STRATA PRESS PERSON RIGID/FLEX SOC. PAGE 131 H2628 — CULTURE ATTIT DRIVE GEN/LAWS

S67
SUBRAMANIAM V.,"REPRESENTATIVE BUREAUCRACY: A REASSESSMENT." USA+45 ELITES LOC/G NAT/G ADMIN GOV/REL PRIVIL DRIVE ROLE...POLICY CENSUS 20 CIVIL/SERV BUREAUCRCY. PAGE 150 H3006 — STRATA GP/REL MGT GOV/COMP

L68
CURRENT HISTORY,"DE GAULLE'S FRANCE." FRANCE MOD/EUR WOR+45 INDUS MARKET INT/ORG BUDGET DIPLOM AUTHORIT DRIVE...GOV/COMP IDEA/COMP 20 DEGAULLE/C EEC. PAGE 36 H0723 — INT/TRADE PERSON LEAD NAT/LISM

B76
SMITH A.,THE WEALTH OF NATIONS. UK STRUCT WORKER DIPLOM ECO/TAC OPTIMAL DRIVE PERSON ORD/FREE ...OLD/LIB GEN/LAWS 17/18. PAGE 145 H2905 — WEALTH PRODUC INDUS LAISSEZ

DRIVER H.E. H0847,H0848

DRIVER W. H0848

DRUCKER P.F. H0849

DRUG ADDICTION....SEE BIO/SOC, ANOMIE, CRIME

DRYDEN S. H0850

DU BOIS W.E.B. H0851

DUBCEK/A....ALEXANDER DUBCEK

DUBOIS/J....JULES DUBOIS

DUBOIS/WEB....W.E.B. DUBOIS

DUCLOS P. H0852

DUCLOUX L. H0853

DUDLEY B.J. H0854

DUE J.F. H0855

DUFFIELD M. H0856

DUFFY J. H0857

DUGARD J. H0858

DUGGAR G.S. H0859

DUGUIT L. H0860

DUGUIT/L....LEON DUGUIT

DUHRING/E....EUGEN DUHRING

DULLES/JF....JOHN FOSTER DULLES

DUNAYEVSKAYA R. H0861

DUNCAN O.D. H0862,H2406

DUNCOMBE H.S. H0863

DUNHAM H.W. H0864

DUNHAM W.H. H0865

DUNN E. H0866

DUNN S.D. H0866

DUNNING W.A. H0867,H0868

DUPONT....DUPONT CORPORATION (E.I. DUPONT DE NEMOURS)

DURKHEIM E. H0870

DURKHEIM/E....EMIL DURKHEIM

DURON J.F. H0871

DUROSELLE J.B. H0872

DUTOIT B. H0873

DUTT V.P. H0874

DUTY....SEE SUPEGO

DUVERGER M. H0875

DUVERGER/M....MAURICE DUVERGER

DWARKADAS R. H0876

DYCK H.V. H0877

E

EACM....EAST AFRICAN COMMON MARKET

S63
MBOYA T.,"AFRICAN SOCIALISM." ECO/UNDEV INT/ORG DIPLOM FOR/AID INT/TRADE REGION GP/REL ATTIT ORD/FREE EACM. PAGE 106 H2116
AFR SOCISM CULTURE NAT/LISM

EAENZA L. H0878

EARLE E.M. H0879

EAST AFRICA....SEE AFRICA/E

EAST GERMANY....SEE GERMANY/E

EASTERN EUROPE....SEE EUROPE/E

EASTON D. H0880,H0881

EASTON S.C. H0882

EATING....EATING, CUISINE

B58
SHAW S.J.,THE FINANCIAL AND ADMINISTRATIVE ORGANIZATION AND DEVELOPMENT OF OTTOMAN EGYPT 1517-1798. UAR LOC/G FORCES BUDGET INT/TRADE TAX EATING INCOME WEALTH...CHARTS BIBLIOG 16/18 OTTOMAN NAPOLEON/B. PAGE 143 H2853
FINAN ADMIN GOV/REL CULTURE

B61
TURNBULL C.M.,THE FOREST PEOPLE. EATING GP/REL INGP/REL RACE/REL ISOLAT HABITAT HEREDITY...GEOG SOC LING DICTIONARY WORSHIP 20 CONGO NEGRO BA/MBUTI. PAGE 157 H3138
AFR CULTURE KIN RECORD

EBENSTEIN W. H0883,H0884,H0885

ECHAVARRIA J.M. H0777

ECHR....EUROPEAN CONVENTION ON HUMAN RIGHTS

ECKSTEIN H. H0886

ECO....ECONOMICS

ECO/DEV....ECONOMIC SYSTEM IN DEVELOPED COUNTRIES

ECO/TAC....ECONOMIC MEASURES

N
MINISTRY OF OVERSEAS DEVELOPME,TECHNICAL CO-OPERATION -- A BIBLIOGRAPHY. UK LAW SOCIETY DIPLOM ECO/TAC FOR/AID...STAT 20 CMN/WLTH. PAGE 111 H2225
BIBLIOG TEC/DEV ECO/DEV NAT/G

C09
SCHAPIRO J.S.,"SOCIAL REFORM AND THE REFORMATION." CHRIST-17C GERMANY LAW CONSTN LG/CO NAT/G WORKER PROB/SOLV CT/SYS REV...BIBLIOG 16. PAGE 138 H2770
ORD/FREE SECT ECO/TAC BIOG

B13
BARDOUX J.,L'ANGLETERRE RADICALE; ESSAI DE LA PSYCHOLOGIE SOCIALE (1906-1913). UK CONSTN NAT/G WORKER CREATE BUDGET ECO/TAC ATTIT...POLICY 20 PARLIAMENT LABOR/PAR STRIKE NAVY. PAGE 11 H0215
POL/PAR CHOOSE COLONIAL LEGIS

B14
LEVINE L.,SYNDICALISM IN FRANCE (2ND ED.). FRANCE LAW SOCIETY ECO/DEV NAT/G ECO/TAC LEAD ATTIT ...POLICY CONCPT STAT BIBLIOG 18/20 REFORMERS. PAGE 95 H1902
LABOR INDUS SOCISM REV

B19
DE MAN H.,THE REMAKING OF A MIND. EUR+WWI NAT/G ECO/TAC REGION ORD/FREE SOCISM...BIOG 20 WWI EUROPE. PAGE 38 H0762
PSY WAR SELF/OBS PARTIC

N19
ANDERSON J.,THE ORGANIZATION OF ECONOMIC STUDIES IN RELATION TO THE PROBLEMS OF GOVERNMENT (PAMPHLET). UK FINAN INDUS DELIB/GP PLAN PROB/SOLV ADMIN 20. PAGE 6 H0128
ECO/TAC ACT/RES NAT/G CENTRAL

N19
GORWALA A.D.,THE ADMINISTRATIVE JUNGLE (PAMPHLET). INDIA NAT/G LEGIS ECO/TAC CONTROL GOV/REL ...METH/COMP 20. PAGE 59 H1183
ADMIN POLICY PLAN ECO/UNDEV

N19
HACKETT J.,ECONOMIC PLANNING IN FRANCE; ITS RELATION TO THE POLICIES OF THE DEVELOPED COUNTRIES OF WESTERN EUROPE (PAMPHLET). EUR+WWI FRANCE ECO/DEV PROB/SOLV CONTROL...POLICY 20 EUROPE/W. PAGE 63 H1270
ECO/TAC NAT/G PLAN INSPECT

N19
LIEBKNECHT W.P.C.,SOCIALISM (2 PTS.; 1875, 1894) (PAMPHLET). WORKER CAP/ISM EDU/PROP WEALTH POPULISM. PAGE 97 H1927
ECO/TAC STRATA SOCIALIST PARTIC

N19
PROVISIONS SECTION OAU,ORGANIZATION OF AFRICAN UNITY: BASIC DOCUMENTS AND RESOLUTIONS (PAMPHLET). AFR CULTURE ECO/UNDEV DIPLOM ECO/TAC EDU/PROP COLONIAL ARMS/CONT NUC/PWR RACE/REL DISCRIM NAT/LISM 20 UN OAU. PAGE 128 H2564
CONSTN EX/STRUC SOVEREIGN INT/ORG

N19
WILSON T.,FINANCIAL ASSISTANCE WITH REGIONAL DEVELOPMENT (PAMPHLET). CANADA INDUS NAT/G PLAN TAX CONTROL COST EFFICIENCY...POLICY CHARTS 20. PAGE 169 H3382
FINAN ECO/TAC REGION GOV/REL

B20
COX H.,ECONOMIC LIBERTY. UNIV LAW INT/TRADE RATION TARIFFS RACE/REL SOCISM POLICY. PAGE 34 H0687
NAT/G ORD/FREE ECO/TAC PERSON

B21
STUART G.H.,FRENCH FOREIGN POLICY. CONSTN INT/ORG NAT/G POL/PAR EX/STRUC FORCES PLAN ECO/TAC DOMIN EDU/PROP ADJUD COERCE ATTIT DRIVE RIGID/FLEX ALL/VALS...POLICY OBS RECORD BIOG TIME/SEQ TREND. PAGE 150 H3000
MOD/EUR DIPLOM FRANCE

B22
URE P.N.,THE ORIGIN OF TYRANNY. MEDIT-7 FINAN INDUS CHIEF FORCES ECO/TAC WEALTH. PAGE 159 H3174
AUTHORIT PWR NAT/G MARKET

B23
FINER H.,REPRESENTATIVE GOVERNMENT AND A PARLIAMENT OF INDUSTRY. A STUDY OF THE GERMAN FEDERAL ECONOMIC COUNCIL. GERMANY UK CONSTN INDUS PARL/PROC ...NAT/COMP 20. PAGE 50 H1002
DELIB/GP ECO/TAC WAR REV

B27
BELLOC H.,THE SERVILE STATE (1912) (3RD ED.). PRUSSIA UK CULTURE STRATA INDUS NAT/G ECO/TAC CONTROL LEAD SUFF DISCRIM EQUILIB ORD/FREE WEALTH 20. PAGE 13 H0269
WORKER CAP/ISM DOMIN CATH

B27
WEBER M.,GENERAL ECONOMIC HISTORY. CHRIST-17C MOD/EUR STRUCT AGRI EXTR/IND FINAN INDUS MARKET FAM MUNIC NAT/G PROF/ORG SECT ECO/TAC 8/20. PAGE 166 H3319
ECO/DEV CAP/ISM

B28
BUELL R.,THE NATIVE PROBLEM IN AFRICA. KIN LABOR LOC/G ECO/TAC ROUTINE ORD/FREE...REC/INT KNO/TEST CENSUS TREND CHARTS SOC/EXP STERTYP 20. PAGE 23 H0466
AFR CULTURE

B28
CORBETT P.E.,CANADA AND WORLD POLITICS. LAW CULTURE SOCIETY STRUCT MARKET INT/ORG FORCES ACT/RES PLAN ECO/TAC LEGIT ORD/FREE PWR RESPECT...SOC CONCPT TIME/SEQ TREND CMN/WLTH 20 LEAGUE/NAT. PAGE 33 H0662
NAT/G CANADA

B28
HURST C.,GREAT BRITAIN AND THE DOMINIONS. EUR+WWI CULTURE ECO/DEV INT/ORG NAT/G DIPLOM ECO/TAC COLONIAL ATTIT PWR SOVEREIGN...TIME/SEQ GEN/LAWS TOT/POP VAL/FREE 20 CMN/WLTH. PAGE 75 H1508
VOL/ASSN DOMIN UK

B28
SOROKIN P.,CONTEMPORARY SOCIOLOGICAL THEORIES. MOD/EUR UNIV SOCIETY R+D SCHOOL ECO/TAC EDU/PROP ROUTINE ATTIT DRIVE...PSY CONCPT TIME/SEQ TREND GEN/LAWS 20. PAGE 147 H2934
CULTURE SOC WAR

B28
YANG KUNG-SUN,THE BOOK OF LORD SHANG. LAW ECO/UNDEV LOC/G NAT/G NEIGH PLAN ECO/TAC LEGIT ATTIT SKILL ...CONCPT CON/ANAL WORK TOT/POP. PAGE 172 H3434
ASIA JURID

B29
LEITZ F.,DIE PUBLIZITAT DER AKTIENGESELLSCHAFT. BELGIUM FRANCE GERMANY UK FINAN PRESS GP/REL PROFIT KNOWL 20. PAGE 94 H1872
LG/CO JURID ECO/TAC NAT/COMP

B29
ROBERTS S.H.,HISTORY OF FRENCH COLONIAL POLICY. AFR ASIA L/A+17C S/ASIA CULTURE ECO/DEV ECO/UNDEV FINAN NAT/G PLAN ECO/TAC DOMIN ROUTINE SOVEREIGN...OBS HIST/WRIT TREND CHARTS VAL/FREE 19/20. PAGE 132 H2642
INT/ORG ACT/RES FRANCE COLONIAL

B31
CROOK W.H.,THE GENERAL STRIKE: A STUDY OF LABOR'S
LABOR

TRAGIC WEAPON IN THEORY AND PRACTICE. BELGIUM FRANCE SWEDEN UK WOR-45 PROB/SOLV ECO/TAC DOMIN PWR ...POLICY TIME/SEQ NAT/COMP GEN/LAWS 19/20 STRIKE. PAGE 35 H0707
WORKER LG/CO BARGAIN

B31
DEKAT A.D.A.,COLONIAL POLICY. S/ASIA CULTURE EX/STRUC ECO/TAC DOMIN ADMIN COLONIAL ROUTINE SOVEREIGN WEALTH...POLICY MGT RECORD KNO/TEST SAMP. PAGE 39 H0785
DRIVE PWR INDONESIA NETHERLAND

B31
LORWIN L.L.,ADVISORY ECONOMIC COUNCILS. EUR+WWI FRANCE GERMANY PROB/SOLV INGP/REL...CLASSIF GP/COMP. PAGE 99 H1968
CONSULT DELIB/GP ECO/TAC NAT/G

B34
LOVELL R.I.,THE STRUGGLE FOR SOUTH AFRICA, 1875-1899. GERMANY RHODESIA SOUTH/AFR UK NAT/G ECO/TAC HABITAT WEALTH...POLICY 19. PAGE 99 H1971
COLONIAL DIPLOM WAR GP/REL

B34
STALIN J.,PROBLEMS OF LENINISM. USSR STRATA INDUS LOC/G POL/PAR ECO/TAC CONTROL TOTALISM PWR SOCISM LENIN/VI STALIN/J. PAGE 148 H2968
MARXISM REV ELITES NAT/G

B35
LASKI H.J.,THE STATE IN THEORY AND PRACTICE. ELITES ECO/TAC REPRESENT ORD/FREE PWR WEALTH POPULISM ...GOV/COMP GEN/LAWS 19/20. PAGE 92 H1829
CAP/ISM COERCE NAT/G FASCISM

B35
MORE T.,UTOPIA (1516) (TRANS. BY R. ROBYNSON). LAW CULTURE SOCIETY STRUCT FAM SECT EDU/PROP WAR OWN UTIL KNOWL WEALTH 16. PAGE 113 H2253
UTOPIA NAT/G ECO/TAC GEN/LAWS

B35
PARETO V.,THE MIND AND SOCIETY (4 VOLS.). ELITES SECT ECO/TAC COERCE PERSON ORD/FREE PWR SOVEREIGN FASCISM POPULISM...TRADIT 19/20. PAGE 123 H2465
GEN/LAWS SOC PSY

B36
BELLOC H.,THE RESTORATION OF PROPERTY. UK STRATA NAT/G PROF/ORG DELIB/GP WORKER CREATE PROB/SOLV ECO/TAC PARTIC UTOPIA ORD/FREE SOCISM 20. PAGE 13 H0270
CONTROL MAJORIT CAP/ISM OWN

B37
HAMILTON W.H.,THE POWER TO GOVERN. ECO/DEV FINAN INDUS ECO/TAC INT/TRADE TARIFFS TAX CONTROL CT/SYS WAR COST PWR 18/20 SUPREME/CT. PAGE 65 H1303
LING CONSTN NAT/G POLICY

B37
PARSONS T.,THE STRUCTURE OF SOCIAL ACTION. UNIV INTELL SOCIETY INDUS MARKET ECO/TAC ROUTINE CHOOSE ALL/VALS...CONCPT OBS BIOG TREND GEN/LAWS 20. PAGE 124 H2471
CULTURE ATTIT CAP/ISM

B37
VON HAYEK F.A.,MONETARY NATIONALISM AND INTERNATIONAL STABILITY. WOR-45 ECO/DEV NAT/G PROB/SOLV INT/TRADE...POLICY CONCPT METH/COMP NAT/COMP 20. PAGE 163 H3271
ECO/TAC FINAN DIPLOM NAT/LISM

B38
LAWLEY F.E.,THE GROWTH OF COLLECTIVE ECONOMY VOL. 1: NATIONAL. EUR+WWI AGRI INDUS NAT/G BARGAIN CAP/ISM ECO/TAC WAR OPTIMAL WEALTH...GOV/COMP METH/COMP 19/20 MONOPOLY. PAGE 92 H1844
SOCISM PRICE CONTROL OWN

B38
LAWLEY F.E.,THE GROWTH OF COLLECTIVE ECONOMY VOL. 2: INTERNATIONAL. WOR-45 AGRI INDUS EQUILIB OPTIMAL OWN WEALTH...NAT/COMP 19/20 NAZI NEW/DEAL MONOPOLY. PAGE 92 H1845
ECO/TAC SOCISM NAT/LISM CONTROL

B38
MARX K.,THE GERMAN IDEOLOGY, PARTS 1 AND 3 (1846). MOD/EUR LAW STRATA WORKER DOMIN REV UTOPIA SOCISM 19 MARX/KARL. PAGE 104 H2079
MARXIST OWN PRODUC ECO/TAC

S38
HALL R.C.,"REPRESENTATION OF BIG BUSINESS IN THE HOUSE OF COMMONS." UK ECO/DEV INDUS PROF/ORG LEGIS CAP/ISM ECO/TAC LAISSEZ...POLICY OLD/LIB PLURIST MGT 20 HOUSE/CMNS. PAGE 64 H1287
LOBBY NAT/G

B39
BENES E.,DEMOCRACY TODAY AND TOMORROW. EUR+WWI SOCIETY ECO/DEV DELIB/GP ECO/TAC REGION ATTIT PWR FASCISM...CONCPT LEAGUE/NAT 20. PAGE 14 H0281
NAT/G LEGIT NAT/LISM

B39
ENGELS F.,HERRN EUGEN DUHRING'S REVOLUTION IN SCIENCE (1878). CULTURE STRATA STRUCT FAM SECT ECO/TAC REV WAR SOCISM...MARXIST 19. PAGE 46 H0925
PWR SOCIETY WEALTH GEN/LAWS

B39
FIRTH R.,PRIMITIVE POLYNESIAN ECONOMY. SOCIETY DIST/IND SECT CHIEF CAP/ISM PRODUC WEALTH...SOC OBS METH WORSHIP 20 POLYNESIA. PAGE 50 H1007
ECO/UNDEV CULTURE AGRI ECO/TAC

B39
HITLER A.,MEIN KAMPF. EUR+WWI FUT MOD/EUR STRUCT INT/ORG LABOR NAT/G POL/PAR FORCES CREATE PLAN BAL/PWR DIPLOM ECO/TAC DOMIN EDU/PROP ADMIN COERCE ATTIT...SOCIALIST BIOG TREND NAZI. PAGE 71 H1428
PWR NEW/IDEA WAR

B39
VAN BILJON F.J.,STATE INTERFERENCE IN SOUTH AFRICA. SOUTH/AFR ECO/UNDEV AGRI INDUS WORKER RATION WEALTH ...JURID 20. PAGE 161 H3225
ECO/TAC POLICY INT/TRADE NAT/G

S39
COLE G.D.H.,"NAZI ECONOMICS: HOW DO THEY MANAGE IT?" GERMANY FORCES WORKER BUDGET INT/TRADE ROUTINE COERCE WAR 20 HITLER/A NAZI. PAGE 31 H0622
FASCISM ECO/TAC ATTIT PLAN

S39
HECKSCHER G.,"GROUP ORGANIZATION IN SWEDEN." SWEDEN STRATA ECO/DEV AGRI INDUS LABOR NAT/G PROF/ORG ECO/TAC CENTRAL SOCISM...MGT 19/20. PAGE 69 H1382
LAISSEZ SOC

B40
HERSKOVITS M.J.,THE ECONOMIC LIFE OF PRIMITIVE PEOPLES. INDUS OP/RES PLAN PROB/SOLV...BIBLIOG METH 20. PAGE 70 H1407
CULTURE ECO/TAC ECO/UNDEV PRODUC

B40
HUNTER R.,REVOLUTION: WHY, HOW, WHEN? NAT/G ECO/TAC EDU/PROP COERCE ORD/FREE FASCISM POPULISM SOCISM 18/20 HITLER/A LENIN/VI. PAGE 75 H1502
REV METH/COMP LEAD CONSTN

B40
LEDERER E.,STATE OF THE MASSES. GERMANY ITALY SOCIETY NAT/G ECO/TAC EDU/PROP LEAD TOTALISM ...SOCIALIST PSY 20. PAGE 93 H1852
CROWD FASCISM AUTHORIT PERSON

B40
WOLFERS A.,BRITAIN AND FRANCE BETWEEN TWO WORLD WARS. FRANCE UK INT/ORG NAT/G PLAN BARGAIN ECO/TAC AGREE ISOLAT ALL/IDEOS...DECISION GEOG 20 TREATY VERSAILLES INTERVENT. PAGE 170 H3402
DIPLOM WAR POLICY

B40
ZWEIG F.,THE WORKER IN AN AFFLUENT SOCIETY: FAMILY LIFE AND INDUSTRY. UK STRATA LG/CO ECO/TAC LEISURE INGP/REL HAPPINESS HEALTH...PSY SOC/WK INT CHARTS WORSHIP 20 FEMALE/SEX. PAGE 173 H3465
MARRIAGE ATTIT FINAN CULTURE

B42
JOSHI P.S.,THE TYRANNY OF COLOUR. INDIA SOUTH/AFR UK ECO/UNDEV NAT/G POL/PAR DIPLOM ECO/TAC WAR ...POLICY 19/20. PAGE 82 H1637
COLONIAL DISCRIM RACE/REL

B43
LASKI H.J.,REFLECTIONS ON THE REVOLUTIONS OF OUR TIME. COM USSR NAT/G WORKER UTOPIA ORD/FREE WEALTH MARXISM SOCISM 19/20. PAGE 92 H1830
CAP/ISM WELF/ST ECO/TAC POLICY

B44
HAYEK F.A.,THE ROAD TO SERFDOM. NAT/G POL/PAR CREATE EDU/PROP ATTIT WEALTH LAISSEZ...OLD/LIB CONCPT TREND 20. PAGE 68 H1368
FUT PLAN ECO/TAC SOCISM

B44
KNORR K.E.,BRITISH COLONIAL THEORIES 1570-1850. NAT/G DELIB/GP ECO/TAC PERCEPT PWR...WELF/ST METH/CNCPT CONT/OBS TIME/SEQ SIMUL TOT/POP 20. PAGE 87 H1734
ACT/RES DOMIN COLONIAL

B45
CLAGETT H.L.,COMMUNIST CHINA: RUTHLESS ENEMY OR PAPER TIGER (PAMPHLET). CHINA/COM ECO/UNDEV AGRI INDUS NAT/G POL/PAR ECO/TAC INT/TRADE GUERRILLA ATTIT...CHARTS NAT/COMP ORG/CHARTS 20. PAGE 30 H0602
BIBLIOG/A MARXISM DIPLOM COERCE

B45
CROCE B.,POLITICS AND MORALS. UNIV NAT/G ECO/TAC ORD/FREE MARXISM POPULISM SOCISM...REALPOL 15/20 HEGEL/GWF ROUSSEAU/J. PAGE 35 H0704
MORAL GEN/LAWS IDEA/COMP

S46
SILBERNER E.,"THE PROBLEM OF WAR IN NINETEENTH CENTURY ECONOMIC THOUGHT." EUR+WWI MOD/EUR UNIV LAW ECO/DEV ECO/UNDEV FINAN INDUS MARKET INT/ORG NAT/G CONSULT FORCES...CONCPT GEN/LAWS GEN/METH 19. PAGE 144 H2875
ATTIT ECO/TAC WAR

B47
ENKE S.,INTERNATIONAL ECONOMICS. UK USA+45 USSR INT/ORG BAL/PWR BARGAIN CAP/ISM BAL/PAY...NAT/COMP 20 TREATY. PAGE 46 H0927
INT/TRADE FINAN TARIFFS ECO/TAC

B48
PELCOVITS N.A.,OLD CHINA HANDS AND THE FOREIGN OFFICE. ASIA BURMA UK ECO/UNDEV NAT/G ECO/TAC FOR/AID TARIFFS DOMIN COLONIAL GOV/REL SOVEREIGN 19 HONG/KONG TREATY. PAGE 124 H2483
INT/TRADE ATTIT DIPLOM

B49
MAO TSE-TUNG,NEW DEMOCRACY. CHINA/COM NAT/G DIPLOM ECO/TAC EDU/PROP REV...CONCPT METH SOC/INTEG 20. PAGE 102 H2045
SOCISM MARXISM POPULISM CULTURE

B49
US DEPARTMENT OF STATE,SOVIET BIBLIOGRAPHY (PAMPHLET). CHINA/COM COM USSR LAW AGRI INT/ORG ECO/TAC EDU/PROP...POLICY GEOG 20. PAGE 159 H3185
BIBLIOG/A MARXISM CULTURE DIPLOM

B50
LIPSET S.M.,AGRARIAN SOCIALISM. CANADA POL/PAR OP/RES ECO/TAC ADMIN ATTIT...TIME/SEQ NAT/COMP SOC/EXP 20 SASKATCH. PAGE 97 H1938
SOCISM AGRI METH/COMP STRUCT

B50
ORTON W.A.,THE ECONOMIC ROLE OF THE STATE. INTELL ECO/UNDEV PLAN CONTROL PWR SOVEREIGN...POLICY 17/20. PAGE 122 H2431
ECO/DEV NAT/G ECO/TAC ORD/FREE

B50
SCHUMPETER J.A.,CAPITALISM, SOCIALISM, AND DEMOCRACY (3RD ED.). USA-45 USSR WOR+45 WOR-45 INTELL ECO/DEV ECO/UNDEV ECO/TAC WAR PRODUC ORD/FREE...MGT SOC 20 MARX/KARL. PAGE 140 H2804
SOCIALIST CAP/ISM MARXISM IDEA/COMP

C50
ROUSSEAU J.J.,"A DISCOURSE ON POLITICAL ECONOMY" (1755) IN THE SOCIAL CONTRACT AND DISCOURSES." UNIV SOCIETY STRATA STRUCT CONSEN EQUILIB HAPPINESS UTOPIA HEALTH WEALTH...POLICY WELF/ST. PAGE 135 H2699
NAT/G ECO/TAC TAX GEN/LAWS

B51
EUCKEN W.,THIS UNSUCCESSFUL AGE. GERMANY NAT/G WORKER TEC/DEV ECO/TAC ORD/FREE 20. PAGE 47 H0947
ECO/DEV PLAN LAISSEZ NEW/LIB

B51
LEONARD L.L.,INTERNATIONAL ORGANIZATION. WOR+45 WOR-45 EX/STRUC FORCES LEGIS ECO/TAC INT/TRADE COLONIAL ARMS/CONT...SOC/WK GOV/COMP BIBLIOG. PAGE 94 H1884
NAT/G DIPLOM INT/ORG DELIB/GP

B51
MARX K.,THE EIGHTEENTH BRUMAIRE OF LOUIS BONAPARTE (1852). FRANCE STRATA FINAN INDUS LABOR CHIEF FORCES WORKER CAP/ISM ECO/TAC PARL/PROC ORD/FREE ...MARXIST 19. PAGE 104 H2080
REV MARXISM ELITES NAT/G

B52
KOLARZ W.,RUSSIA AND HER COLONIES. COM RUSSIA LAW CULTURE ECO/DEV KIN LOC/G SECT TEC/DEV ECO/TAC EDU/PROP REGION COERCE ATTIT PWR SOVEREIGN...SOC TIME/SEQ CON/ANAL VAL/FREE 19/20. PAGE 88 H1749
NAT/G DOMIN USSR COLONIAL

B52
ROBBINS L.,THE THEORY OF ECONOMIC POLICY IN ENGLISH CLASSICAL POLITICAL ECONOMY. UK ECO/DEV WORKER PLAN CAP/ISM EDU/PROP CONTROL INCOME OWN HEALTH SOCISM ...POLICY 17/19. PAGE 132 H2639
ECO/TAC ORD/FREE IDEA/COMP NAT/G

B53
MEYER P.,THE JEWS IN THE SOVIET SATELLITES. CZECHOSLVK POLAND SOCIETY STRATA NAT/G BAL/PWR ECO/TAC EDU/PROP LEGIT ADMIN COERCE ATTIT DISPL PERCEPT HEALTH PWR RESPECT WEALTH...METH/CNCPT JEWS VAL/FREE NAZI 20. PAGE 110 H2192
COM SECT TOTALISM USSR

B53
NELSON G.R.,FREEDOM AND WELFARE: SOCIAL PATTERNS IN THE NORTHERN COUNTRIES OF EUROPE. EUR+WWI ECO/DEV NAT/G EDU/PROP LEGIT HEALTH ORD/FREE SKILL WEALTH ...STAT AUD/VIS SCANDINAV WORK TOT/POP 20. PAGE 116 H2329
PLAN ECO/TAC

B53
SWEEZY P.M.,THE PRESENT AS HISTORY. NAT/G PLAN COLONIAL ATTIT...POLICY SOCIALIST 19/20. PAGE 151 H3019
ECO/DEV CAP/ISM SOCISM ECO/TAC

B54
EPSTEIN L.D.,BRITAIN - UNEASY ALLY. KOREA UK USA+45 NAT/G POL/PAR ECO/TAC FOR/AID INT/TRADE WAR LABOR/PAR CONSRV/PAR. PAGE 47 H0934
DIPLOM ATTIT POLICY NAT/COMP

B54
FRIEDRICH C.J.,TOTALITARIAN DICTATORSHIP AND AUTOCRACY. COM EUR+WWI GERMANY ITALY USSR INTELL ECO/DEV NAT/G POL/PAR FORCES TOP/EX ECO/TAC EDU/PROP LEGIT COERCE ATTIT ORD/FREE PWR FASCISM ...CONCPT TIME/SEQ GEN/LAWS NAZI 20. PAGE 53 H1068
SOCIETY DOMIN TOTALISM

B54
GATZKE H.W.,STRESEMANN AND THE REARMAMENT OF GERMANY. EUR+WWI GERMANY USSR FINAN NAT/G ECO/TAC ATTIT...BIOG METH 20 STRESEMN/G. PAGE 55 H1105
FORCES INDUS PWR

B54
GERMANY FOREIGN MINISTRY,DOCUMENTS ON GERMAN FOREIGN POLICY 1918-1945, SERIES C (1933-1937) VOLS. I-V. GERMANY MOD/EUR FORCES PLAN ECO/TAC ...FASCIST CHARTS ANTHOL 20. PAGE 56 H1115
NAT/G DIPLOM POLICY

B54
GRAYSON H.,ECONOMIC PLANNING UNDER FREE ENTERPRISE. CANADA FUT UK DELIB/GP BUDGET CONFER CONTROL ...POLICY DECISION 20. PAGE 60 H1200
PLAN ECO/TAC NAT/COMP NAT/G

B54
SPENCER H.,SOCIAL STATICS. MOD/EUR UNIV SOCIETY ECO/DEV NAT/G ACT/RES PLAN EDU/PROP PERSON...POLICY CONCPT. PAGE 147 H2944
MORAL ECO/TAC

B54
WILLIAMSON H.F.,ECONOMIC DEVELOPMENT - PRINCIPLES AND PATTERNS. INDIA KOREA CULTURE ECO/DEV ECO/UNDEV TEC/DEV...CENSUS NAT/COMP 20 CHINJAP MEXIC/AMER RESOURCE/N. PAGE 168 H3369
ECO/TAC GEOG LABOR

L54
FRIEDRICH C.J.,"TOTALITARIANISM." COM EUR+WWI NAT/G POL/PAR SECT FORCES PLAN ECO/TAC DOMIN EDU/PROP EXEC COERCE REV ORD/FREE PWR...SOC CONCPT NAZI 20. PAGE 53 H1067
ATTIT TOTALISM

B55
FOGARTY M.P.,ECONOMIC CONTROL. FUT UK ECO/DEV FINAN CONSULT INT/TRADE...CHARTS BIBLIOG/A 20. PAGE 52 H1033
ECO/TAC NAT/G CONTROL PROB/SOLV

B55
HELANDER S.,DAS AUTARKIEPROBLEM IN DER WELTWIRTSCHAFT. PROB/SOLV BAL/PWR BARGAIN CAP/ISM ECO/TAC SOVEREIGN 20. PAGE 69 H1388
NAT/COMP COLONIAL DIPLOM

B55
INTERNATIONAL AFRICAN INST,ETHNOGRAPHIC SURVEY OF AFRICA: NORTH EASTERN AFRICA (VOLUMES 1-2, 1955-56). AFR ETHIOPIA CULTURE ECO/UNDEV KIN GOV/REL ATTIT HEREDITY...GEOG CHARTS BIBLIOG WORSHIP 20. PAGE 77 H1545
STRUCT ECO/TAC INGP/REL HABITAT

B55
LIPSCOMB J.F.,WHITE AFRICANS. SOCIETY STRUCT AGRI ECO/TAC ADJUD COLONIAL COERCE PERS/REL ADJUST. PAGE 97 H1937
RACE/REL HABITAT ECO/UNDEV ORD/FREE

B55
MAYO H.B.,DEMOCRACY AND MARXISM. COM USSR STRATA NAT/G WORKER ECO/TAC REV MORAL...PHIL/SCI HIST/WRIT IDEA/COMP WORSHIP 20 MARX/KARL LENIN/VI STALIN/J TROTSKY/L. PAGE 105 H2108
MARXISM CAP/ISM

B55
RUSTOW D.A.,THE POLITICS OF COMPROMISE. SWEDEN LABOR EX/STRUC LEGIS PLAN REPRESENT SOCISM...SOC 19/20. PAGE 136 H2720
POL/PAR NAT/G POLICY ECO/TAC

B55
TOYNBEE A.,THE REALIGNMENT OF EUROPE. COM GREECE ITALY NAT/G BAL/PWR ECO/TAC EDU/PROP REV SOVEREIGN ...SOC TIME/SEQ TREND COLD/WAR 20. PAGE 156 H3123
EUR+WWI PLAN USSR

B55
WOYTINSKY W.S.,WORLD COMMERCE AND GOVERNMENTS: TRENDS AND OUTLOOK. WOR+45 FINAN POL/PAR DIPLOM ECO/TAC FOR/AID DOMIN WAR CHOOSE...CHARTS BIBLIOG 20 LEAGUE/NAT UN ILO. PAGE 171 H3413
INT/TRADE DIST/IND NAT/COMP NAT/G

B55
WRONG D.H.,AMERICAN AND CANADIAN VIEWPOINTS. CANADA USA+45 CONSTN STRATA FAM SECT WORKER ECO/TAC EDU/PROP ADJUD MARRIAGE...IDEA/COMP 20. PAGE 171 H3424
DIPLOM ATTIT NAT/COMP CULTURE

B56
INTERNATIONAL AFRICAN INST,ETHNOGRAPHIC SURVEY OF AFRICA; WESTERN AFRICA: PAGAN PEOPLES OF CENTRAL AREA OF NORTHERN NIGERIA (VOL. XII). NIGERIA FAM KIN SECT ECO/TAC GOV/REL GP/REL ATTIT...LING CHARTS 20. PAGE 77 H1548
STRUCT INGP/REL HABITAT CULTURE

B56
JENNINGS W.I.,THE APPROACH TO SELF-GOVERNMENT. CEYLON INDIA PAKISTAN S/ASIA UK SOCIETY POL/PAR DELIB/GP LEGIS ECO/TAC EDU/PROP ADMIN EXEC CHOOSE ATTIT ALL/VALS...JURID CONCPT GEN/METH TOT/POP 20. PAGE 81 H1610
NAT/G CONSTN COLONIAL

B57
ARON R.,L'UNIFICATION ECONOMIQUE DE L'EUROPE. EUR+WWI SWITZERLND UK INT/ORG NAT/G REGION NAT/LISM ORD/FREE PWR...CONCPT METH/CNCPT OBS TREND STERTYP GEN/LAWS EEC 20. PAGE 8 H0168
VOL/ASSN ECO/TAC

B57
DEAN V.M.,THE NATURE OF THE NON-WESTERN WORLD. AFR ASIA L/A+17C S/ASIA CULTURE SOCIETY STRATA ECO/DEV DIPLOM ECO/TAC FOR/AID ATTIT DRIVE ALL/VALS ...RELATIV SOC CONCPT TIME/SEQ TREND TOT/POP 20. PAGE 39 H0778
ECO/UNDEV STERTYP NAT/LISM

B57
INTERNATIONAL AFRICAN INST,ETHNOGRAPHIC SURVEY OF AFRICA: WESTERN AFRICA: THE BENIN KINGDOM. AFR NIGERIA CULTURE ECO/UNDEV KIN ECO/TAC GOV/REL AGE ATTIT HEREDITY...CHARTS BIBLIOG WORSHIP 20. PAGE 77 H1550
STRUCT INGP/REL GEOG HABITAT

B57
NEUMARK S.D.,ECONOMIC INFLUENCES ON THE SOUTH AFRICAN FRONTIER, 1652-1836. SOUTH/AFR SEA AGRI NAT/G FORCES WORKER DIPLOM INT/TRADE PRICE DEMAND PRODUC...STAT CHARTS 17/19 FRONTIER. PAGE 117 H2341
COLONIAL ECO/UNDEV ECO/TAC MARKET

B57
PALACIOS A.L.,PETROLEO, MONOPOLIOS, Y LATIFUNDIOS. L/A+17C EXTR/IND NAT/G TEC/DEV ECO/TAC CONTROL PRODUC 20 ARGEN MONOPOLY RESOURCE/N. PAGE 123 H2448
ECO/UNDEV NAT/LISM INDUS AGRI

B57
PALMER N.D.,INTERNATIONAL RELATIONS. WOR+45 INT/ORG NAT/G ECO/TAC EDU/PROP COLONIAL WAR PWR SOVEREIGN ...POLICY T 20 TREATY. PAGE 123 H2451
DIPLOM BAL/PWR NAT/COMP

B57
ROBERTSON H.M.,SOUTH AFRICA, ECONOMIC AND POLITICAL ASPECTS. SOUTH/AFR CONSTN CULTURE POL/PAR LEGIS
RACE/REL ECO/UNDEV

DIPLOM DOMIN COLONIAL...SOC BIBLIOG 19/20. PAGE 132 H2647
ECO/TAC DISCRIM

B57
RUMEU DE ARMAS A.,ESPANA EEN EL AFRICA ATLANTICA. AFR CHRIST-17C PORTUGAL SPAIN DIPLOM ECO/TAC CONTROL 14/16 AFRICA/W. PAGE 136 H2717
NAT/G COLONIAL CHIEF PWR

B57
SHEIKH N.A.,SOME ASPECTS OF THE CONSTITUTION AND THE ECONOMICS OF ISLAM. PAKISTAN CULTURE AGRI FINAN LABOR NAT/G SECT INT/TRADE 20 MUSLIM. PAGE 143 H2855
ISLAM POLICY ECO/TAC CONSTN

L57
LIPSET S.M.,"POLITICAL SOCIOLOGY." NAT/G POL/PAR ECO/TAC PARTIC CHOOSE PWR...BIBLIOG/A 20. PAGE 97 H1939
SOC ALL/IDEOS ACADEM

S57
KILSON M.L.,"LAND AND POLITICS IN KENYA: AN ANALYSIS OF AFRICAN POLITICS IN A PLURAL SOCIETY." FUT LAW CULTURE KIN NAT/G ECO/TAC DOMIN REV NAT/LISM ORD/FREE PWR RESPECT SOVEREIGN WEALTH ...SOC OBS TREND WORK VAL/FREE CMN/WLTH 20. PAGE 86 H1710
AFR ECO/UNDEV

S57
LEWIS E.G.,"PARLIAMENTARY CONTROL OF NATIONALIZED INDUSTRY IN FRANCE." FRANCE NAT/G DELIB/GP ACT/RES PLAN PROB/SOLV ECO/TAC DOMIN CENTRAL. PAGE 96 H1914
PWR LEGIS INDUS CONTROL

B58
CRAIG G.A.,FROM BISMARCK TO ADENAUER: ASPECTS OF GERMAN STATECRAFT. GERMANY INTELL FORCES ECO/TAC CONFER COERCE WAR GP/REL ORD/FREE PWR CONSERVE 19/20 BISMARCK/O ADENAUER/K. PAGE 35 H0695
DIPLOM LEAD NAT/G

B58
HAAS E.B.,THE UNITING OF EUROPE. EUR+WWI INT/ORG NAT/G POL/PAR TOP/EX ECO/TAC EDU/PROP LEGIT FEDERAL NAT/LISM DRIVE RIGID/FLEX ORD/FREE PWR PLURISM ...POLICY CONCPT INT GEN/LAWS ECSC EEC 20. PAGE 63 H1264
VOL/ASSN ECO/DEV

B58
INTERNATIONAL ECONOMIC ASSN,ECONOMICS OF INTERNATIONAL MIGRATION. WOR+45 WOR-45 ECO/UNDEV FINAN NAT/G REGION...NAT/COMP METH 20. PAGE 78 H1556
CENSUS GEOG DIPLOM ECO/TAC

B58
JACOBSSON P.,SOME MONETARY PROBLEMS, INTERNATIONAL AND NATIONAL. WOR+45 WOR-45 ECO/DEV FORCES WORKER PROB/SOLV DIPLOM INT/TRADE...ANTHOL 20. PAGE 79 H1580
FINAN PLAN ECO/TAC NAT/COMP

B58
MCIVOR R.C.,CANADIAN MONETARY, BANKING, AND FISCAL DEVELOPMENT. CANADA INDUS LG/CO NAT/G SML/CO CONTROL WAR...GEN/LAWS BIBLIOG 17/20. PAGE 107 H2137
ECO/TAC FINAN ECO/DEV WEALTH

B58
MECRENSKY E.,SCIENTIFIC MANPOWER IN EUROPE. WOR+45 EDU/PROP GOV/REL SKILL...TECHNIC PHIL/SCI INT CHARTS BIBLIOG 20. PAGE 108 H2157
ECO/TAC TEC/DEV METH/COMP NAT/COMP

B58
PAYNO M.,LA REFORMA SOCIAL EN ESPANA Y MEXICO. SPAIN ECO/TAC TAX LOBBY COERCE REV OWN CATHISM 19/20 MEXIC/AMER. PAGE 124 H2479
SECT NAT/G LAW ELITES

S58
LOCKWOOD W.W.,"THE SOCIALISTIC SOCIETY: INDIA AND JAPAN." INDIA ECO/DEV ECO/UNDEV INDUS NAT/G CONTROL LEAD PRODUC WEALTH 20 CHINJAP. PAGE 98 H1948
ECO/TAC NAT/COMP FINAN SOCISM

S58
STAAR R.F.,"ELECTIONS IN COMMUNIST POLAND." EUR+WWI SOCIETY INT/ORG NAT/G POL/PAR LEGIS ACT/RES ECO/TAC EDU/PROP ADJUD ADMIN ROUTINE COERCE TOTALISM ATTIT ORD/FREE PWR 20. PAGE 148 H2963
COM CHOOSE POLAND

B59
BLOOMFIELD L.P.,WESTERN EUROPE AND THE UN - TRENDS AND PROSPECTS. EUR+WWI BAL/PWR DIPLOM ECO/TAC COLONIAL ATTIT PWR...POLICY 20 UN EUROPE/W. PAGE 18 H0359
INT/ORG TREND FUT NAT/G

B59
ETSCHMANN R.,DIE WAHRUNGS- UND DEVISENPOLITIK DES OSTBLOCKS UND IHRE AUSWIRKUNGEN AUF DIE WIRTSCHAFTSBEZIEHUNGEN ZWISCHEN OST U WEST. BULGARIA CZECHOSLVK HUNGARY POLAND USSR MARKET NAT/G PLAN DIPLOM...NAT/COMP 20. PAGE 47 H0943
ECO/TAC FINAN POLICY INT/TRADE

B59
GINSBURG M.,LAW AND OPINION IN ENGLAND. UK CULTURE KIN LABOR LEGIS EDU/PROP ADMIN CT/SYS CRIME OWN HEALTH...ANTHOL 20 ENGLSH/LAW. PAGE 56 H1132
JURID POLICY ECO/TAC

B59
GUDIN E.,INFLACAO (2ND ED.). INDUS NAT/G PLAN ECO/TAC CONTROL COST 20. PAGE 62 H1243
ECO/UNDEV INT/TRADE BAL/PAY FINAN

B59
KELF-COHEN R.,NATIONALISATION IN BRITAIN: THE END OF DOGMA. EUR+WWI UK NAT/G POL/PAR WORKER ECO/TAC PARL/PROC WEALTH SOCISM...GOV/COMP 20. PAGE 84 H1683
NEW/LIB ECO/DEV INDUS OWN

B59
LAQUER W.Z.,THE SOVIET UNION AND THE MIDDLE EAST. COM UAR USSR ECO/UNDEV NAT/G VOL/ASSN ECO/TAC EDU/PROP COLONIAL EXEC PWR...TIME/SEQ TREND COLD/WAR 20. PAGE 91 H1819
ISLAM DRIVE FOR/AID NAT/LISM

B59
LEITES N.,ON THE GAME OF POLITICS IN FRANCE. ALGERIA FRANCE CONSTN SECT VOL/ASSN ECO/TAC INT/TRADE PARL/PROC WAR SOCISM 20 DEGAULLE/C EEC. PAGE 94 H1871
POL/PAR NAT/G LEGIS IDEA/COMP

B59
MEYER A.J.,MIDDLE EASTERN CAPITALISM: NINE ESSAYS. ISLAM CULTURE ECO/UNDEV INDUS MARKET NAT/G PLAN ATTIT RIGID/FLEX...STAT OBS TREND GEN/LAWS. PAGE 109 H2188
TEC/DEV ECO/TAC ANTHOL

B59
MURDOCK G.P.,AFRICA: ITS PEOPLES AND THEIR CULTURE HISTORY. AFR CULTURE AGRI LOC/G INGP/REL HABITAT ...GEOG SOC LING CHARTS BIBLIOG 20 NEGRO EGYPT/ANC. PAGE 115 H2293
SOCIETY ECO/TAC GP/COMP KIN

B59
VORSPAN A.,JUSTICE AND JUDAISM. FAM DIPLOM ECO/TAC EDU/PROP CRIME RACE/REL MARRIAGE ANOMIE ATTIT ORD/FREE...POLICY 20 UN. PAGE 164 H3279
SECT CULTURE ACT/RES GP/REL

L59
MURPHY J.C.,"SOME IMPLICATIONS OF EUROPE'S COMMON MARKET. IN (COOK P. ECONOMIC DEVELOPMENT AND INTERNATIONAL TRADE.." EUR+WWI ECO/DEV DIST/IND INDUS NAT/G PLAN ECO/TAC INT/TRADE WEALTH...STAT TREND OEEC TOT/POP 20 EEC. PAGE 115 H2298
MARKET INT/ORG REGION

S59
PLAZA G.,"FOR A REGIONAL MARKET IN LATIN AMERICA." FUT L/A+17C CULTURE INDUS NAT/G ECO/TAC INT/TRADE ATTIT WEALTH...NEW/IDEA TREND OAS 20. PAGE 126 H2527
MARKET INT/ORG REGION

S59
SILBERMAN L.,"CHANGE AND CONFLICT IN THE HORN OF AFRICA." EUR+WWI ITALY UK CULTURE FORCES ECO/TAC ADJUD COLONIAL ATTIT ORD/FREE PWR...DECISION METH/CNCPT HIST/WRIT SOMALI 20. PAGE 144 H2874
AFR TIME/SEQ

S59
ZAUBERMAN A.,"SOVIET BLOC ECONOMIC INTEGRATION." COM CULTURE INTELL ECO/DEV INDUS TOP/EX ACT/RES PLAN ECO/TAC INT/TRADE ROUTINE CHOOSE ATTIT ...TIME/SEQ 20. PAGE 172 H3452
MARKET INT/ORG USSR TOTALISM

B60
AUSTRUY J.,STRUCTURE ECONOMIQUE ET CIVILISATION: L'EGYPTE ET LE DESTIN ECONOMIQUE DE L'ISLAM. ISLAM UAR CREATE OP/RES ECO/TAC...SOC BIBLIOG 20 MUSLIM. PAGE 9 H0182
ECO/UNDEV CULTURE STRUCT

B60
BOMBACH G.,STABILE PREISE IN WACHSENDER WIRTSCHAFT: DAS INFLATIONSPROBLEM. BARGAIN CAP/ISM PRICE COST ...NAT/COMP 20 GOLD/STAND. PAGE 19 H0371
ECO/UNDEV PLAN FINAN ECO/TAC

B60
DIA M.,REFLEXIONS SUR L'ECONOMIE DE L'AFRIQUE NOIRE (REV. ED.). CULTURE ECO/UNDEV CREATE TEC/DEV DIPLOM INT/TRADE OPTIMAL ATTIT...POLICY 20. PAGE 41 H0816
AFR ECO/TAC SOCISM PLAN

B60
EASTON S.C.,THE TWILIGHT OF EUROPEAN COLONIALISM. AFR S/ASIA CONSTN SOCIETY STRUCT ECO/UNDEV INDUS NAT/G FORCES ECO/TAC COLONIAL CT/SYS ATTIT KNOWL ORD/FREE PWR...SOCIALIST TIME/SEQ TREND CON/ANAL 20. PAGE 44 H0882
FINAN ADMIN

B60
GOODMAN E.,SOVIET DESIGN FOR A WORLD STATE. COM USSR NAT/G TOP/EX DIPLOM ECO/TAC DOMIN EDU/PROP COERCE REV ATTIT ORD/FREE...CON/ANAL 20. PAGE 59 H1171
PLAN PWR SOCISM TOTALISM

B60
GRAMPP W.D.,THE MANCHESTER SCHOOL OF ECONOMICS. UK LAW ECO/DEV COERCE ATTIT ORD/FREE LAISSEZ ...PHIL/SCI IDEA/COMP 19/20 MANCHESTER CORN/LAWS. PAGE 60 H1194
ECO/TAC VOL/ASSN LOBBY NAT/G

B60
KENEN P.B.,BRITISH MONETARY POLICY AND THE BALANCE OF PAYMENTS 1951-57. UK PLAN BUDGET ECO/TAC INT/TRADE PAY PRICE COST ATTIT 20. PAGE 84 H1687
BAL/PAY PROB/SOLV FINAN NAT/G

B60
LASKIN B.,CANADIAN CONSTITUTIONAL LAW: TEXT AND NOTES ON DISTRIBUTION OF LEGISLATIVE POWER (2ND ED.). CANADA LOC/G ECO/TAC TAX CONTROL CT/SYS CRIME FEDERAL PWR...JURID 20 PARLIAMENT. PAGE 92 H1832
CONSTN NAT/G LAW LEGIS

B60
LINDSAY K.,EUROPEAN ASSEMBLIES: THE EXPERIMENTAL PERIOD 1949-1959. EUR+WWI ECO/DEV NAT/G POL/PAR LEGIS TOP/EX ACT/RES PLAN ECO/TAC DOMIN LEGIT ROUTINE ATTIT DRIVE ORD/FREE PWR SKILL...SOC CONCPT TREND CHARTS GEN/LAWS VAL/FREE. PAGE 97 H1932
VOL/ASSN INT/ORG REGION

B60
LISTER L.,EUROPE'S COAL AND STEEL COMMUNITY. FRANCE GERMANY STRUCT ECO/DEV EXTR/IND INDUS MARKET NAT/G DELIB/GP ECO/TAC INT/TRADE EDU/PROP ATTIT RIGID/FLEX ORD/FREE PWR WEALTH...CONCPT STAT TIME/SEQ CHARTS ECSC 20. PAGE 97 H1941 EUR+WWI INT/ORG REGION

B60
PETERSON W.C.,THE WELFARE STATE IN FRANCE. EUR+WWI FRANCE FUT STRATA PROB/SOLV TAX GIVE RECEIVE INCOME ORD/FREE PWR...CHARTS 20. PAGE 125 H2496 NEW/LIB ECO/TAC WEALTH NAT/G

B60
ROY N.C.,THE CIVIL SERVICE IN INDIA. INDIA POL/PAR ECO/TAC INCOME...JURID MGT 20 CIVIL/SERV. PAGE 135 H2705 ADMIN NAT/G DELIB/GP CONFER

B60
SAKAI R.K.,STUDIES ON ASIA, 1960. ASIA CHINA/COM S/ASIA COM/IND ECO/TAC...ANTHOL 17/20 MALAYA. PAGE 137 H2733 ECO/UNDEV SOC

B60
SHIRER W.L.,THE RISE AND FALL OF THE THIRD REICH: A HISTORY OF NAZI GERMANY. EUR+WWI CULTURE ECO/DEV INDUS NAT/G POL/PAR FORCES PLAN TEC/DEV ECO/TAC COERCE ATTIT DRIVE PERSON PWR...MYSTIC PSY SOC MYTH STAT CHARTS EXHIBIT WORK VAL/FREE. PAGE 143 H2864 STRUCT GERMANY TOTALISM

B60
STOLPER W.F.,GERMANY BETWEEN EAST AND WEST: THE ECONOMICS OF COMPETITIVE COEXISTENCE. FUT GERMANY/E GERMANY/W WOR+45 FINAN POL/PAR BUDGET ECO/TAC FOR/AID INT/TRADE...STAT CHARTS METH/COMP 20 COLD/WAR. PAGE 150 H2989 ECO/DEV DIPLOM GOV/COMP BAL/PWR

B60
THEOBOLD R.,THE NEW NATIONS OF WEST AFRICA. GHANA NIGERIA CULTURE INT/ORG ECO/TAC FOR/AID COLONIAL RACE/REL POPULISM...ANTHOL BIBLIOG 20 UN. PAGE 153 H3068 AFR SOVEREIGN ECO/UNDEV DIPLOM

B60
VON KOENIGSWALD H.,SIE SUCHEN ZUFLUCHT. GERMANY/E NAT/G PLAN ECO/TAC SOCISM...GEOG CENSUS 20 BERLIN. PAGE 164 H3273 GP/REL COERCE DOMIN PERSON

B60
WOLF C.,FOREIGN AID: THEORY AND PRACTICE IN SOUTHERN ASIA. CEYLON INDONESIA PHILIPPINE S/ASIA CULTURE STRATA ECO/UNDEV PLAN EDU/PROP ATTIT ...METH/CNCPT MATH QUANT STAT CONT/OBS TIME/SEQ SIMUL TOT/POP 20. PAGE 170 H3396 ACT/RES ECO/TAC FOR/AID

S60
"THE EMERGING COMMON MARKETS IN LATIN AMERICA." FUT L/A+17C STRATA DIST/IND INDUS LABOR NAT/G LEGIS ECO/TAC ADMIN RIGID/FLEX HEALTH...NEW/IDEA TIME/SEQ OAS 20. PAGE 2 H0038 FINAN ECO/UNDEV INT/TRADE

S60
BERG E.J.,"ECONOMIC BASIS OF POLITICAL CHOICE IN FRENCH WEST AFRICA." FRANCE ECO/UNDEV AGRI INDUS NAT/G PLAN LEGIT COLONIAL REGION ATTIT PWR WEALTH ...CONCPT 20. PAGE 15 H0299 AFR ECO/TAC

S60
BRZEZINSKI Z.K.,"PATTERNS AND LIMITS OF THE SINO-SOVIET DISPUTE." ASIA CHINA/COM COM FUT STRATA NAT/G EX/STRUC FORCES BAL/PWR DIPLOM ECO/TAC DOMIN EDU/PROP ADMIN COERCE WAR ATTIT RIGID/FLEX ...GEN/LAWS VAL/FREE 20. PAGE 23 H0459 POL/PAR PWR REV USSR

S60
CROZIER B.,"FRANCE AND ALGERIA." ALGERIA EUR+WWI FRANCE FUT ISLAM ECO/UNDEV NEIGH CONSULT DELIB/GP ECO/TAC COLONIAL COERCE ATTIT...SOC INT CON/ANAL 20. PAGE 36 H0713 NAT/G FORCES GUERRILLA NAT/LISM

S60
EMERSON R.,"THE EROSION OF DEMOCRACY." AFR FUT LAW CULTURE INTELL SOCIETY ECO/UNDEV FAM LOC/G NAT/G FORCES PLAN TEC/DEV ECO/TAC ADMIN CT/SYS ATTIT ORD/FREE PWR...SOCIALIST SOC CONCPT STAND/INT TIME/SEQ WORK 20. PAGE 46 H0918 S/ASIA POL/PAR

S60
FITZGIBBON R.H.,"DICTATORSHIP AND DEMOCRACY IN LATIN AMERICA." FUT ECO/DEV ECO/UNDEV INT/ORG LOC/G NAT/G TOP/EX PLAN TEC/DEV ECO/TAC CHOOSE ATTIT DRIVE PERSON ALL/VALS OAS TOT/POP 20. PAGE 51 H1019 L/A+17C ACT/RES INT/TRADE

S60
FRANKEL S.H.,"ECONOMIC ASPECTS OF POLITICAL INDEPENDENCE IN AFRICA." AFR FUT SOCIETY ECO/UNDEV COM/IND FINAN LEGIS PLAN TEC/DEV CAP/ISM ECO/TAC INT/TRADE ADMIN ATTIT DRIVE RIGID/FLEX PWR WEALTH ...MGT NEW/IDEA MATH TIME/SEQ VAL/FREE 20. PAGE 53 H1052 NAT/G FOR/AID

S60
GINSBURGS G.,"PEKING-LHASA-NEW DELHI." CHINA/COM FUT INDIA S/ASIA KIN NAT/G PROVS SECT FORCES BAL/PWR ECO/TAC DOMIN EDU/PROP LEGIT ADMIN REGION GUERRILLA PWR...TREND TIBET 20. PAGE 57 H1134 ASIA COERCE DIPLOM

S60
GROSSMAN G.,"SOVIET GROWTH: ROUTINE, INERTIA, AND PRESSURE." COM STRATA NAT/G DELIB/GP PLAN TEC/DEV ECO/TAC EDU/PROP ADMIN ROUTINE DRIVE WEALTH COLD/WAR 20. PAGE 62 H1236 POL/PAR ECO/DEV USSR

S60
MAGATHAN W.,"SOME BASES OF WEST GERMAN MILITARY POLICY." EUR+WWI FUT INT/ORG TOP/EX ECO/TAC DOMIN DRIVE ORD/FREE PWR...TRADIT GEOG OBS TREND. PAGE 101 H2015 NAT/G FORCES GERMANY

S60
MURPHEY R.,"ECONOMIC CONFLICTS IN SOUTH ASIA." ASIA CULTURE INTELL ECO/TAC REGION ATTIT DRIVE KNOWL ...METH/CNCPT TIME/SEQ STERTYP TOT/POP VAL/FREE 20. PAGE 115 H2296 S/ASIA ECO/UNDEV

S60
NORTH R.C.,"DIE DISKREPANZ ZWISCHEN REALITAT UND WUNSCHBILD ALS INNENPOLITISCHER FAKTOR." ASIA CHINA/COM COM FUT ECO/UNDEV NAT/G PLAN DOMIN ADMIN COERCE PERCEPT...SOC MYTH GEN/METH WORK TOT/POP 20. PAGE 119 H2373 SOCIETY ECO/TAC

S60
RIVKIN A.,"AFRICAN ECONOMIC DEVELOPMENT: ADVANCED TECHNOLOGY AND THE STAGES OF GROWTH." CULTURE ECO/UNDEV AGRI COM/IND EXTR/IND PLAN ECO/TAC ATTIT DRIVE RIGID/FLEX SKILL WEALTH...MGT SOC GEN/LAWS WORK TOT/POP 20. PAGE 132 H2634 AFR TEC/DEV FOR/AID

S60
SHILS E.,"THE INTELLECTUALS IN THE POLITICAL DEVELOPMENT OF THE NEW STATES." AFR ASIA S/ASIA ELITES LOC/G NAT/G CONSULT EX/STRUC CREATE PLAN ECO/TAC DOMIN LEGIT DRIVE PWR...TRADIT CONCPT STERTYP GEN/LAWS 20. PAGE 143 H2861 POL/PAR INTELL NAT/LISM

B61
AIYAR S.P.,FEDERALISM AND SOCIAL CHANGE. CANADA CULTURE STRUCT PLAN PROB/SOLV TEC/DEV ECO/TAC ORD/FREE...TIME/SEQ 18/20 AUSTRAL. PAGE 4 H0085 FEDERAL NAT/G CENTRAL GOV/COMP

B61
APTER D.E.,THE POLITICAL KINGDOM IN UGANDA. UGANDA CULTURE ECO/UNDEV AGRI KIN SECT TOP/EX REGION ATTIT HABITAT CONSERVE...GEOG AUD/VIS 20. PAGE 8 H0153 NAT/LISM POL/PAR COLONIAL ECO/TAC

B61
BEARCE G.D.,BRITISH ATTITUDES TOWARDS INDIA 1784-1858. INDIA S/ASIA UK SECT ECO/TAC...POLICY HUM 18/19. PAGE 12 H0246 COLONIAL ATTIT ALL/IDEOS NAT/G

B61
BISHOP D.G.,THE ADMINISTRATION OF BRITISH FOREIGN RELATIONS. EUR+WWI MOD/EUR INT/ORG NAT/G POL/PAR DELIB/GP LEGIS TOP/EX ECO/TAC DOMIN EDU/PROP ADMIN COERCE 20. PAGE 17 H0344 ROUTINE PWR DIPLOM UK

B61
BONNEFOUS M.,EUROPE ET TIERS MONDE. EUR+WWI SOCIETY INT/ORG NAT/G VOL/ASSN ACT/RES TEC/DEV CAP/ISM ECO/TAC ATTIT ORD/FREE SOVEREIGN...POLICY CONCPT TREND 20. PAGE 19 H0373 AFR ECO/UNDEV FOR/AID INT/TRADE

B61
BREWIS T.N.,CANADIAN ECONOMIC POLICY. CANADA BUDGET CAP/ISM INT/TRADE RATION TARIFFS TAX PRICE CONTROL ROUTINE FEDERAL INCOME PRODUC 20 GOLD/STAND. PAGE 20 H0412 ECO/DEV ECO/TAC NAT/G PLAN

B61
DIA M.,THE AFRICAN NATIONS AND WORLD SOLIDARITY. ISLAM CULTURE ELITES ECO/DEV ECO/UNDEV INT/ORG NAT/G PLAN ECO/TAC INT/TRADE EDU/PROP NAT/LISM ATTIT DRIVE ORD/FREE WEALTH...SOCIALIST CONCPT CON/ANAL GEN/LAWS TOT/POP 20. PAGE 41 H0817 AFR REGION SOCISM

B61
DONNISON F.S.V.,CIVIL AFFAIRS AND MILITARY GOVERNMENT NORTH-WEST EUROPE 1944-1946. EUR+WWI FRANCE GERMANY UK USSR LOC/G PROVS PLAN PROB/SOLV BAL/PWR ECO/TAC CONTROL PWR...CHARTS 20. PAGE 42 H0836 NAT/G WAR FORCES CIVMIL/REL

B61
ESTEBAN J.C.,IMPERIALISMO Y DESARROLLO ECONOMICO. L/A+17C FINAN INDUS NAT/G ECO/TAC CONTROL ROLE. PAGE 47 H0941 ECO/UNDEV NAT/LISM DIPLOM BAL/PAY

B61
GANGULI B.N.,ECONOMIC INTEGRATION. FINAN LABOR CAP/ISM DIPLOM WEALTH...NAT/COMP 20. PAGE 55 H1096 ECO/TAC METH/CNCPT EQUILIB ECO/UNDEV

B61
HARDT J.P.,THE COLD WAR ECONOMIC GAP. USA+45 USSR ECO/DEV FORCES INT/TRADE NUC/PWR PWR 20 COLD/WAR. PAGE 66 H1328 DIPLOM ECO/TAC NAT/COMP POLICY

B61
HAUSER M.,DIE URSACHEN DER FRANZOSISCHEN INFLATION IN DEN JAHREN 1946-1952. FRANCE INDUS NAT/G BUDGET DIPLOM ECO/TAC FOR/AID COST MONEY 20 GOLD/STAND. PAGE 68 H1357 ECO/DEV FINAN PRICE

B61
HUNT E.F.,SOCIAL SCIENCE. DIPLOM ECO/TAC ROUTINE GP/REL DEMAND DISCRIM EFFICIENCY HABITAT ALL/IDEOS ...SOC T 20. PAGE 75 H1497 CULTURE ADJUST STRATA ROLE

B61
KEE R.,REFUGEE WORLD. AUSTRIA EUR+WWI GERMANY NEIGH EX/STRUC WORKER PROB/SOLV ECO/TAC RENT EDU/PROP INGP/REL COST LITERACY HABITAT 20 MIGRATION. PAGE 84 H1676 — NAT/G GIVE WEALTH STRANGE

B61
KISSINGER H.A.,THE NECESSITY FOR CHOICE. FUT USA+45 ECO/UNDEV NAT/G PLAN BAL/PWR ECO/TAC ARMS/CONT DETER NUC/PWR ATTIT...POLICY CONCPT RECORD GEN/LAWS COLD/WAR 20. PAGE 87 H1728 — TOP/EX TREND DIPLOM

B61
LA PONCE J.A.,THE GOVERNMENT OF THE FIFTH REPUBLIC: FRENCH POLITICAL PARTIES AND THE CONSTITUTION. ALGERIA FRANCE LAW NAT/G DELIB/GP LEGIS ECO/TAC MARXISM SOCISM...CHARTS BIBLIOG/A 20 DEGAULLE/C. PAGE 90 H1794 — PWR POL/PAR CONSTN CHIEF

B61
LAHAYE R.,LES ENTREPRISES PUBLIQUES AU MAROC. FRANCE MOROCCO LAW DIST/IND EXTR/IND FINAN CONSULT PLAN TEC/DEV ADMIN AGREE CONTROL OWN...POLICY 20. PAGE 90 H1796 — NAT/G INDUS ECO/UNDEV ECO/TAC

B61
LENIN V.I.,WHAT IS TO BE DONE? (1902). RUSSIA LABOR NAT/G POL/PAR WORKER CAP/ISM ECO/TAC ADMIN PARTIC ...MARXIST IDEA/COMP GEN/LAWS 19/20. PAGE 94 H1881 — EDU/PROP PRESS MARXISM METH/COMP

B61
LETHBRIDGE H.J.,CHINA'S URBAN COMMUNES. CHINA/COM FUT ECO/UNDEV DIPLOM EDU/PROP DEMAND INCOME MARXISM ...POLICY 20. PAGE 95 H1893 — MUNIC CONTROL ECO/TAC NAT/G

B61
LICHTHEIM G.,MARXISM. GERMANY SOCIETY WORKER CAP/ISM ECO/TAC NAT/LISM POPULISM...TIME/SEQ GOV/COMP NAT/COMP 18/20 COM/PARTY. PAGE 96 H1924 — MARXISM SOCISM IDEA/COMP CULTURE

B61
MIT CENTER INTERNATIONAL STU,OFFICIAL SERIAL PUBLICATIONS RELATING TO ECONOMIC DEVELOPMENT IN AFRICA SOUTH OF THE SAHARA. AFR SOCIETY AGRI FINAN INDUS LG/CO ADMIN 20. PAGE 111 H2228 — BIBLIOG ECO/UNDEV ECO/TAC NAT/G

B61
NATIONAL BANK OF LIBYA,INFLATION IN LIBYA (PAMPHLET). LIBYA SOCIETY NAT/G PLAN INT/TRADE ...STAT CHARTS 20 GOLD/STAND. PAGE 116 H2318 — ECO/TAC ECO/UNDEV FINAN BUDGET

B61
NOVE A.,THE SOVIET ECONOMY. USSR ECO/DEV FINAN NAT/G ECO/TAC PRICE ADMIN EFFICIENCY MARXISM ...TREND BIBLIOG 20. PAGE 119 H2378 — PLAN PRODUC POLICY

B61
OECD,STATISTICS OF BALANCE OF PAYMENTS 1950-61. WOR+45 FINAN ECO/TAC INT/TRADE DEMAND WEALTH...STAT NAT/COMP 20 OEEC OECD. PAGE 120 H2396 — BAL/PAY ECO/DEV INT/ORG CHARTS

B61
PECKERT J.,DIE GROSSEN UND DIE KLEINEN MAECHTE. COM GERMANY/W ECO/DEV ECO/UNDEV NAT/G WAR RACE/REL PEACE...POLICY GP/COMP GOV/COMP 20 COLD/WAR. PAGE 124 H2482 — DIPLOM ECO/TAC BAL/PWR

B61
SAKAI R.K.,STUDIES ON ASIA, 1961. ASIA BURMA INDIA S/ASIA FINAN ECO/TAC NAT/LISM SOCISM...POLICY ANTHOL 19/20 CHINJAP. PAGE 137 H2734 — ECO/UNDEV SECT

B61
SCHWARTZ H.,THE RED PHOENIX: RUSSIA SINCE WORLD WAR II. USA+45 WOR+45 ELITES POL/PAR TEC/DEV ECO/TAC MARXISM. PAGE 140 H2810 — DIPLOM NAT/G ECO/DEV

B61
SETON-WATSON H.,FROM LENIN TO KHRUSHCHEV: THE HISTORY OF WORLD COMMUNISM. ASIA COM EUR+WWI ISLAM S/ASIA ECO/DEV ECO/UNDEV NAT/G POL/PAR DIPLOM ECO/TAC EDU/PROP COERCE GUERRILLA ATTIT DRIVE WORK TOT/POP NAZI 20. PAGE 141 H2832 — PWR REV USSR

B61
SPOONER F.P.,SOUTH AFRICAN PREDICAMENT. FUT SOUTH/AFR INDUS POL/PAR RACE/REL INCOME...CHARTS 20 NEGRO. PAGE 148 H2953 — ECO/DEV DISCRIM ECO/TAC POLICY

B61
STANLEY C.J.,LATE CH'ING FINANCE: HU KUANG-YUNG AS AN INNOVATOR. ASIA NAT/G FORCES BUDGET TAX WAR GOV/REL COST...POLICY BIOG CHARTS BIBLIOG 19. PAGE 148 H2969 — FINAN ECO/TAC CIVMIL/REL ADMIN

B61
STARK H.,SOCIAL AND ECONOMIC FRONTIERS IN LATIN AMERICA (2ND ED.). CUBA FUT CULTURE AGRI INDUS ECO/TAC PRODUC ATTIT MARXISM...NAT/COMP BIBLIOG T 20. PAGE 149 H2971 — L/A+17C SOCIETY DIPLOM ECO/UNDEV

B61
VEIT O.,GRUNDRISS DER WAHRUNGSPOLITIK. FRANCE GERMANY USSR DIPLOM INT/TRADE...NAT/COMP 19/20 GOLD/STAND SILVER. PAGE 162 H3239 — FINAN POLICY ECO/TAC CAP/ISM

S61
ANDERSON O.,"ECONOMIC WARFARE IN THE CRIMEAN WAR." EUR+WWI MOD/EUR NAT/G ACT/RES WAR DRIVE PWR 19/20. PAGE 6 H0130 — ECO/TAC UK RUSSIA

S61
RAY J.,"THE EUROPEAN FREE-TRADE ASSOCIATION AND ITS IMPACT ON INDIA'S TRADE." EUR+WWI FRANCE GERMANY INDIA S/ASIA UK NAT/G VOL/ASSN PLAN INT/TRADE ROUTINE WEALTH...STAT CHARTS CMN/WLTH EEC OEEC 20 EFTA. PAGE 130 H2600 — ECO/DEV ECO/TAC

S61
TANHAM B.K.,"COMMUNIST REVOLUTIONARY WARFARE: THE VIETMINH IN INDOCHINA." EUR+WWI S/ASIA VIETNAM NAT/G EDU/PROP LEGIT GUERRILLA ATTIT PWR...CONCPT GEN/LAWS 20. PAGE 152 H3042 — FORCES ECO/TAC WAR FRANCE

S61
TOMASIC D.,"POLITICAL LEADERSHIP IN CONTEMPORARY POLAND." COM EUR+WWI GERMANY NAT/G POL/PAR SECT DELIB/GP PLAN ECO/TAC DOMIN EDU/PROP PWR MARXISM ...MARXIST GEOG MGT CONCPT TIME/SEQ STERTYP 20. PAGE 156 H3111 — SOCIETY ROUTINE USSR POLAND

S61
VALLET R.,"IRAN: KEY TO THE MIDDLE EAST." COM IRAQ ISLAM KUWAIT LEBANON SAUDI/ARAB TURKEY ELITES SOCIETY INDUS PROC/MFG POL/PAR TOP/EX PLAN BAL/PWR DIPLOM ECO/TAC ALL/VALS...TREND CENTO 20. PAGE 161 H3224 — NAT/G ECO/UNDEV IRAN

B62
ABRAHAM W.E.,THE MIND OF AFRICA. AFR SOCIETY STRATA KIN ECO/TAC DOMIN EDU/PROP LEGIT COERCE ATTIT ALL/VALS...MAJORIT SOC OBS HIST/WRIT TIME/SEQ TREND TOT/POP 20. PAGE 3 H0058 — CULTURE SIMUL GHANA

B62
BERGER M.,THE ARAB WORLD TODAY. CULTURE FAM INT/ORG NAT/G SECT FORCES ECO/TAC NAT/LISM HABITAT...CHARTS BIBLIOG 20 ARABS. PAGE 15 H0301 — ISLAM PERSON STRUCT SOCIETY

B62
BROWN S.D.,STUDIES ON ASIA, 1962. ASIA BURMA INDIA ISLAM ISRAEL S/ASIA ECO/UNDEV POL/PAR SECT ECO/TAC ...ANTHOL 20 CHINJAP. PAGE 22 H0450 — PWR PARL/PROC

B62
BUSIA K.A.,THE CHALLENGE OF AFRICA. CULTURE KIN MUNIC NAT/G POL/PAR SCHOOL DELIB/GP PLAN ECO/TAC DOMIN EDU/PROP TOTALISM ATTIT PERSON ALL/VALS SOVEREIGN...SOC CONCPT STERTYP TOT/POP VAL/FREE 20. PAGE 25 H0496 — AFR ECO/UNDEV NAT/LISM

B62
CALVOCORESSI P.,WORLD ORDER AND NEW STATES: PROBLEMS OF KEEPING THE PEACE. AFR EUR+WWI S/ASIA ELITES NAT/G ECO/TAC FOR/AID EDU/PROP COERCE ATTIT DRIVE ALL/VALS...GEN/LAWS COLD/WAR 20 UN. PAGE 25 H0509 — INT/ORG PEACE

B62
CARTER G.M.,THE GOVERNMENT OF THE SOVIET UNION. USSR CULTURE LOC/G DIPLOM ECO/TAC ADJUD CT/SYS LEAD WEALTH...CHARTS T 20 COM/PARTY. PAGE 27 H0546 — NAT/G MARXISM POL/PAR EX/STRUC

B62
COUNCIL ON WORLD TENSIONS,RESTLESS NATIONS. WOR+45 STRUCT INT/ORG NAT/G PLAN ECO/TAC...NAT/COMP ANTHOL 20. PAGE 34 H0678 — ECO/UNDEV POLICY DIPLOM TASK

B62
DE MADARIAGA S.,L'AMERIQUE LATINE ENTRE L'OURS ET L'AIGLE. L/A+17C SOCIETY NAT/G ECO/TAC EDU/PROP REGION COERCE ATTIT ALL/VALS...MAJORIT TIME/SEQ STERTYP COLD/WAR OAS 20. PAGE 38 H0760 — POL/PAR ECO/UNDEV

B62
DUROSELLE J.B.,LES NOUVEAUX ETATS DANS LES RELATIONS INTERNATIONALES. AFR CHINA/COM FRANCE MOROCCO S/ASIA USSR ECO/UNDEV INT/ORG PLAN ECO/TAC EDU/PROP ATTIT DRIVE...TREND TOT/POP TUNIS 20. PAGE 44 H0872 — NAT/G CONSTN DIPLOM

B62
EBENSTEIN W.,TWO WAYS OF LIFE. USA+45 CULTURE ECO/DEV PLAN EDU/PROP CONTROL ORD/FREE...GOV/COMP IDEA/COMP T 20 MARX/KARL ENGELS/F LENIN/VI LOCKE/JOHN MILL/JS. PAGE 44 H0885 — MARXISM POPULISM ECO/TAC DIPLOM

B62
FEIT E.,SOUTH AFRICA, THE DYNAMICS OF THE AFRICAN NATIONAL CONGRESS. AFR SOUTH/AFR LAW INTELL STRATA KIN NAT/G POL/PAR ECO/TAC DOMIN RISK COERCE 20 NEGRO. PAGE 49 H0984 — RACE/REL ELITES CONTROL STRUCT

B62
FRIEDMANN W.,METHODS AND POLICIES OF PRINCIPAL DONOR COUNTRIES IN PUBLIC INTERNATIONAL DEVELOPMENT FINANCING: PRELIMINARY APPRAISAL. FRANCE GERMANY/W UK USA+45 USSR WOR+45 FINAN TEC/DEV CAP/ISM DIPLOM ECO/TAC ATTIT 20 EEC. PAGE 53 H1066 — INT/ORG FOR/AID NAT/COMP ADMIN

B62
GROVE J.W.,GOVERNMENT AND INDUSTRY IN BRITAIN. UK FINAN LOC/G CONSULT DELIB/GP INT/TRADE ADMIN CONTROL...BIBLIOG 20. PAGE 62 H1237 — ECO/TAC INDUS NAT/G GP/REL

B62
KINDERSLEY R.,THE FIRST RUSSIAN REVISIONISTS. COM USSR LAW ELITES INTELL NAT/G LEGIS ECO/TAC EDU/PROP — CONSTN MARXISM

CONTROL LEAD GP/REL SOCISM 19/20 MARX/KARL BOLSHEVISM. PAGE 86 H1712
POPULISM BIOG

B62
KINDLEBERGER C.P.,FOREIGN TRADE AND THE NATIONAL ECONOMY. WOR+45 ECO/DEV ECO/UNDEV ECO/TAC COST DEMAND 20. PAGE 86 H1713
INT/TRADE GOV/COMP BAL/PAY POLICY

B62
LAQUEUR W.,POLYCENTRISM. CHINA/COM COM USSR WOR+45 INT/ORG NAT/G ECO/TAC DOMIN LEAD ATTIT PWR SOVEREIGN...ANTHOL 20. PAGE 91 H1821
MARXISM DIPLOM BAL/PWR POLICY

B62
MEADE J.E.,CASE STUDIES IN EUROPEAN ECONOMIC UNION. BELGIUM EUR+WWI LUXEMBOURG NAT/G INT/TRADE REGION ROUTINE WEALTH...METH/CNCPT STAT CHARTS ECSC TOT/POP OEEC EEC 20. PAGE 108 H2154
INT/ORG ECO/TAC

B62
MELADY T.,THE WHITE MAN'S FUTURE IN BLACK AFRICA. FUT CULTURE SOCIETY NAT/G POL/PAR PLAN ECO/TAC DOMIN EDU/PROP LEGIT COLONIAL RACE/REL ATTIT DRIVE ALL/VALS...PSY SOC CONCPT TIME/SEQ TOT/POP VAL/FREE 20. PAGE 108 H2167
AFR STRATA ELITES

B62
MODELSKI G.,SEATO-SIX STUDIES. ASIA CHINA/COM INDIA S/ASIA INT/ORG NAT/G ECO/TAC DETER ATTIT ORD/FREE PWR...TIME/SEQ COLD/WAR TOT/POP 20 SEATO. PAGE 112 H2234
MARKET ECO/UNDEV INT/TRADE

B62
PHELPS E.S.,THE GOAL OF ECONOMIC GROWTH: SOURCES, COSTS, BENEFITS. USA+45 USSR FINAN TAX CONTROL DEMAND WEALTH...POLICY NAT/COMP ANTHOL BIBLIOG 20. PAGE 125 H2499
ECO/TAC ECO/DEV NAT/G FUT

B62
WOODS H.D.,LABOUR POLICY AND LABOUR ECONOMICS IN CANADA. CANADA FUT NAT/G VOL/ASSN WORKER BARGAIN ECO/TAC PAY CONFER GP/REL 20. PAGE 170 H3409
LABOR POLICY INDUS ECO/DEV

L62
MURACCIOLE L.,"LA BANQUE CENTRALE DES ETATS DE L'AFRIQUE DE L'OUEST." AFR LAW ECO/UNDEV INT/ORG NAT/G CONSULT ECO/TAC ROUTINE...CHARTS 20. PAGE 115 H2292
ISLAM FINAN INT/TRADE

S62
ANSPRENGER F.,"NATIONALISM, COMMUNISM, AND THE UNCOMMITTED NATIONS: AMERICAN PROFILES." FUT ISLAM CULTURE SOCIETY ECO/UNDEV NAT/G POL/PAR PLAN ECO/TAC EDU/PROP COERCE CHOOSE ALL/VALS MARXISM SOCISM...SOC CONCPT BIOG TREND 20. PAGE 7 H0142
AFR COM NAT/LISM

S62
FESLER J.W.,"FRENCH FIELD ADMINISTRATION: THE BEGINNINGS." CHRIST-17C CULTURE SOCIETY STRATA NAT/G ECO/TAC DOMIN EDU/PROP LEGIT ADJUD COERCE ATTIT ALL/VALS...TIME/SEQ CON/ANAL GEN/METH VAL/FREE 13/15. PAGE 49 H0988
EX/STRUC FRANCE

S62
IOVTCHOUK M.T.,"ON SOME THEORETICAL PRINCIPLES AND METHODS OF SOCIOLOGICAL INVESTIGATIONS (IN RUSSIAN)." FUT USA+45 STRATA R+D NAT/G POL/PAR TOP/EX ACT/RES PLAN ECO/TAC EDU/PROP ROUTINE ATTIT RIGID/FLEX MARXISM SOCISM...MARXIST METH/CNCPT OBS TREND NAT/COMP GEN/LAWS 20. PAGE 78 H1564
COM ECO/DEV CAP/ISM USSR

S62
LANGER W.L.,"FAREWELL TO EMPIRE." EUR+WWI MOD/EUR NAT/G DIPLOM EDU/PROP COLONIAL ATTIT ORD/FREE PWR SOVEREIGN WEALTH...CONCPT TIME/SEQ GEN/LAWS TOT/POP VAL/FREE CMN/WLTH 20. PAGE 91 H1810
DOMIN ECO/TAC NAT/LISM

S62
RAZAFIMBAHINY J.,"L'ORGANISATION AFRICAINE ET MALGACHE DE COOPERATION ECONOMIQUE." AFR ISLAM MADAGASCAR NAT/G ACT/RES ECO/TAC ALL/VALS ...TIME/SEQ 20. PAGE 130 H2601
INT/ORG ECO/UNDEV

C62
BACON F.,"OF SEDITIONS AND TROUBLES" (1625) IN F. BACON, ESSAYS." INDUS MARKET CHIEF ECO/TAC EDU/PROP CONTROL LEAD PEACE WEALTH 17 MACHIAVELL. PAGE 9 H0191
REV ORD/FREE NAT/G GEN/LAWS

B63
AHN L.A.,FUNFZIG JAHRE ZWISCHEN INFLATION UND DEFLATION. GERMANY DIPLOM PRICE...CONCPT 20 GOLD/STAND. PAGE 4 H0081
FINAN CAP/ISM NAT/COMP ECO/TAC

B63
BARNETT A.D.,COMMUNIST STRATEGIES IN ASIA: A COMPARATIVE ANALYSIS OF GOVERNMENTS AND PARTIES. COM FUT S/ASIA CULTURE SOCIETY STRATA NAT/G DELIB/GP ACT/RES ECO/TAC EDU/PROP COERCE CHOOSE ATTIT RIGID/FLEX ORD/FREE PWR SKILL...SIMUL VAL/FREE 20. PAGE 11 H0223
ASIA POL/PAR DIPLOM USSR

B63
BRZEZINSKI Z.K.,AFRICA AND THE COMMUNIST WORLD. AFR ASIA COM CULTURE SOCIETY INT/ORG DELIB/GP ACT/RES ECO/TAC COERCE ORD/FREE PWR WEALTH...STAT TOT/POP VAL/FREE 20. PAGE 23 H0461
ATTIT EDU/PROP DIPLOM USSR

B63
CANELAS O.A.,RADIOGRAFIA DE LA ALIANZA PARA EL ATRASO. L/A+17C USA+45 ECO/TAC DOMIN COLONIAL NAT/LISM...SOCIALIST NAT/COMP 20. PAGE 26 H0519
REV DIPLOM ECO/UNDEV REGION

B63
CARTER G.M.,FIVE AFRICAN STATES: RESPONSES TO DIVERSITY. CONSTN CULTURE STRATA LEGIS PLAN ECO/TAC DOMIN EDU/PROP CT/SYS EXEC CHOOSE ATTIT HEALTH ORD/FREE PWR...TIME/SEQ TOT/POP VAL/FREE. PAGE 27 H0547
AFR SOCIETY

B63
CHOU S.H.,THE CHINESE INFLATION 1937-1949. ASIA SOCIETY POL/PAR FOR/AID INT/TRADE BAL/PAY WEALTH MARXISM...STAT CHARTS 20 COM/PARTY GOLD/STAND. PAGE 30 H0597
FINAN ECO/TAC BUDGET NAT/G

B63
DE VRIES E.,SOCIAL ASPECTS OF ECONOMIC DEVELOPMENT IN LATIN AMERICA. CULTURE SOCIETY STRATA FINAN INDUS INT/ORG DELIB/GP ACT/RES ECO/TAC EDU/PROP ADMIN ATTIT SUPEGO HEALTH KNOWL ORD/FREE...SOC STAT TREND ANTHOL TOT/POP VAL/FREE. PAGE 39 H0777
L/A+17C ECO/UNDEV

B63
ENKE S.,ECONOMICS FOR DEVELOPMENT. AGRI TEC/DEV CAP/ISM DIPLOM ECO/TAC TAX ATTIT DRIVE HABITAT WEALTH...GOV/COMP BIBLIOG 20. PAGE 46 H0928
ECO/UNDEV PHIL/SCI CON/ANAL

B63
FALL B.,THE TWO VIETNAMS. CULTURE SOCIETY ECO/UNDEV NAT/G TOP/EX ACT/RES PLAN ECO/TAC DOMIN EDU/PROP COERCE ATTIT DRIVE PERSON ORD/FREE PWR...SOC TIME/SEQ COLD/WAR 20. PAGE 48 H0965
S/ASIA BIOG VIETNAM

B63
FRITZ H.E.,THE MOVEMENT FOR INDIAN ASSIMILATION, 1860-1890. SECT FORCES GP/REL RACE/REL DISCRIM FEDERAL CATHISM...BIBLIOG 19 INDIAN/AM PROTESTANT GRANT/US. PAGE 54 H1071
CULTURE NAT/G ECO/TAC ATTIT

B63
GEERTZ C.,PEDDLERS AND PRINCES: SOCIAL DEVELOPMENT AND ECONOMIC CHANGE IN TWO INDONESIAN TOWNS. S/ASIA CULTURE SOCIETY STRATA FACE/GP MUNIC CREATE TEC/DEV ECO/TAC ORD/FREE WEALTH...OBS INT CENSUS CHARTS WORK TOT/POP VAL/FREE 20. PAGE 55 H1106
ECO/UNDEV SOC ELITES INDONESIA

B63
GLADE W.P. JR.,THE POLITICAL ECONOMY OF MEXICO. FUT L/A+17C CULTURE SOCIETY AGRI INDUS DELIB/GP ACT/RES ECO/TAC ATTIT HEALTH ORD/FREE...STAT TIME/SEQ TREND MEXIC/AMER TOT/POP VAL/FREE 20. PAGE 57 H1138
FINAN ECO/UNDEV

B63
GONZALEZ PEDRERO E.,ANATOMIA DE UN CONFLICTO. WOR+45 ECO/DEV ECO/UNDEV ECO/TAC FOR/AID CONTROL ARMS/CONT GOV/REL...NAT/COMP 20 COLD/WAR. PAGE 58 H1166
DIPLOM DETER BAL/PWR

B63
GORDON M.S.,THE ECONOMICS OF WELFARE POLICIES. INDUS LOC/G NAT/G LEGIS WORKER INCOME AGE/O SKILL WEALTH...METH/COMP NAT/COMP 20. PAGE 59 H1180
METH/CNCPT ECO/TAC POLICY

B63
HAMM H.,ALBANIA - CHINA'S BEACHHEAD IN EUROPE. ALBANIA CHINA/COM USSR YUGOSLAVIA ELITES SOCIETY POL/PAR DELIB/GP FORCES ECO/TAC COERCE ISOLAT PEACE MARXISM...IDEA/COMP 20 MAO. PAGE 65 H1304
DIPLOM REV NAT/G POLICY

B63
HAQ M.,THE STRATEGY OF ECONOMIC PLANNING. PAKISTAN AGRI FINAN INDUS NAT/G FOR/AID TAX CONTROL REGION PRODUC...POLICY CHARTS 20. PAGE 66 H1324
ECO/TAC ECO/UNDEV PLAN PROB/SOLV

B63
HYDE D.,THE PEACEFUL ASSAULT. COM UAR USSR ECO/DEV ECO/UNDEV NAT/G POL/PAR CAP/ISM PWR 20. PAGE 76 H1516
MARXISM CONTROL ECO/TAC DIPLOM

B63
INDIAN INSTITUTE PUBLIC ADMIN,CASES IN INDIAN ADMINISTRATION. INDIA AGRI NAT/G PROB/SOLV TEC/DEV ECO/TAC ADMIN...ANTHOL METH 20. PAGE 77 H1532
DECISION PLAN MGT ECO/UNDEV

B63
KAPP W.K.,HINDU CULTURE: ECONOMIC DEVELOPMENT AND ECONOMIC PLANNING IN INDIA. INDIA S/ASIA CULTURE ECO/TAC EDU/PROP ADMIN ALL/VALS...POLICY MGT TIME/SEQ VAL/FREE 20. PAGE 83 H1660
SECT ECO/UNDEV

B63
LETHBRIDGE H.J.,THE PEASANT AND THE COMMUNES. CHINA/COM COM USSR NEIGH PROB/SOLV ADJUST EFFICIENCY...POLICY METH/COMP NAT/COMP 20. PAGE 95 H1894
MARXISM ECO/TAC AGRI WORKER

B63
LEWIN J.,POLITICS AND LAW IN SOUTH AFRICA. SOUTH/AFR UK POL/PAR BAL/PWR ECO/TAC COLONIAL CONTROL GP/REL DISCRIM PWR 20 NEGRO. PAGE 96 H1909
NAT/LISM POLICY LAW RACE/REL

B63
MAYNE R.,THE COMMUNITY OF EUROPE. UK CONSTN NAT/G CONSULT DELIB/GP CREATE PLAN ECO/TAC LEGIT ADMIN ROUTINE ORD/FREE PWR WEALTH...CONCPT TIME/SEQ EEC EURATOM 20. PAGE 105 H2107
EUR+WWI INT/ORG REGION

B63
OLSON M. JR.,THE ECONOMICS OF WARTIME SHORTAGE.
WAR

FRANCE GERMANY MOD/EUR UK AGRI PROB/SOLV ADMIN DEMAND WEALTH...POLICY OLD/LIB 17/20. PAGE 121 H2416 — ADJUST ECO/TAC NAT/COMP

B63
RONNING C.N.,LAW AND POLITICS IN INTER-AMERICAN DIPLOMACY. L/A+17C ECO/UNDEV NAT/G CONSULT DELIB/GP CREATE CAP/ISM ECO/TAC LEGIT REGION RIGID/FLEX ...METH/CNCPT GEN/LAWS OAS 20. PAGE 133 H2668 — VOL/ASSN ALL/VALS DIPLOM

B63
SCHECHTMAN J.B.,THE REFUGEE IN THE WORLD: DISPLACEMENT AND INTEGRATION. AFR ASIA EUR+WWI ISLAM L/A+17C S/ASIA CULTURE STRATA LOC/G EX/STRUC PLAN ECO/TAC ROUTINE...CONCPT TIME/SEQ VAL/FREE 20. PAGE 139 H2779 — INT/ORG SOC

B63
SETON-WATSON H.,THE NEW IMPERIALISM. COM EUR+WWI MOD/EUR ECO/UNDEV NAT/G FORCES DIPLOM DOMIN EDU/PROP LEGIT COLONIAL EXEC COERCE GP/REL RACE/REL DISCRIM ATTIT...TIME/SEQ 20. PAGE 142 H2833 — ECO/TAC RUSSIA USSR

B63
SHANKS M.,THE LESSONS OF PUBLIC ENTERPRISE. UK LEGIS WORKER ECO/TAC ADMIN PARL/PROC GOV/REL ATTIT ...POLICY MGT METH/COMP NAT/COMP ANTHOL 20 PARLIAMENT. PAGE 142 H2840 — SOCISM OWN NAT/G INDUS

B63
STEVENS G.G.,EGYPT YESTERDAY AND TODAY. CONSTN ECO/UNDEV AGRI INDUS NAT/G POL/PAR FORCES ECO/TAC EDU/PROP COERCE WAR NAT/LISM DRIVE ALL/VALS ...TIME/SEQ WORK SUEZ 20. PAGE 149 H2983 — ISLAM TOP/EX REV UAR

B63
ULAM A.B.,THE NEW FACE OF SOVIET TOTALITARIANISM. FUT INTELL NAT/G POL/PAR EX/STRUC TOP/EX DIPLOM ECO/TAC DOMIN EDU/PROP LEGIT COERCE ATTIT RIGID/FLEX...OBS HIST/WRIT TREND TOT/POP VAL/FREE COLD/WAR. PAGE 158 H3150 — COM PWR TOTALISM USSR

B63
UN SECRETARY GENERAL,PLANNING FOR ECONOMIC DEVELOPMENT. ECO/UNDEV FINAN BUDGET INT/TRADE TARIFFS TAX ADMIN 20 UN. PAGE 158 H3159 — PLAN ECO/TAC MGT NAT/COMP

B63
VIARD R.,LA FIN DE L'EMPIRE COLONIAL FRANCAIS. AFR FUT S/ASIA ECO/UNDEV NAT/G CONSULT PLAN ECO/TAC EDU/PROP REGION NAT/LISM ALL/VALS...CONCPT TIME/SEQ TREND VAL/FREE 20. PAGE 162 H3248 — VOL/ASSN COLONIAL FRANCE

B63
VON BECKERATH E.,PROBLEME DER NORMATIVEN OKONOMIK UND DER WIRTSCHAFTSPOLITISCHEN BERATUNG. GERMANY UK ELITES CAP/ISM EFFICIENCY...CONCPT GOV/COMP IDEA/COMP 20. PAGE 163 H3264 — ECO/TAC DELIB/GP ECO/DEV CONSULT

B63
ZARTMAN I.W.,GOVERNMENT AND POLITICS IN NORTHERN AFRICA. AFR ALGERIA ISLAM LIBYA MOROCCO UAR ELITES SOCIETY PLAN ECO/TAC DOMIN EDU/PROP LEGIT ATTIT ...GEOG CONCPT TIME/SEQ 20 TUNIS. PAGE 172 H3448 — CULTURE DRIVE NAT/LISM

L63
CORWIN A.F.,"CONTEMPORARY MEXICAN ATTITUDES TOWARD POPULATION, POVERTY, AND PUBLIC OPINION." L/A+17C CULTURE SOCIETY ACT/RES ECO/TAC EDU/PROP PERSON HEALTH KNOWL...GEOG PHIL/SCI STAT OBS INT SAMP MEXIC/AMER VAL/FREE 20. PAGE 34 H0672 — ATTIT QU

L63
NASH M.,"PSYCHO-CULTURAL FACTORS IN ASIAN ECONOMIC GROWTH." ASIA ISLAM S/ASIA CULTURE ECO/UNDEV DELIB/GP EDU/PROP COERCE ATTIT PERSON HEALTH KNOWL ORD/FREE...PSY SOC STAT TREND ANTHOL VAL/FREE 20. PAGE 116 H2313 — SOCIETY ECO/TAC

L63
ROSE R.,"COMPARATIVE STUDIES IN POLITICAL FINANCE: A SYMPOSIUM." ASIA EUR+WWI S/ASIA LAW CULTURE DELIB/GP LEGIS ACT/RES ECO/TAC EDU/PROP CHOOSE ATTIT RIGID/FLEX SUPEGO PWR SKILL WEALTH...STAT ANTHOL VAL/FREE. PAGE 134 H2674 — FINAN POL/PAR

S63
BANFIELD J.,"FEDERATION IN EAST-AFRICA." AFR UGANDA ELITES INT/ORG NAT/G VOL/ASSN LEGIS ECO/TAC FEDERAL ATTIT SOVEREIGN TOT/POP 20 TANGANYIKA. PAGE 10 H0210 — EX/STRUC PWR REGION

S63
BILL J.A.,"THE SOCIAL AND ECONOMIC FOUNDATIONS OF POWER IN CONTEMPORARY IRAN." ISLAM CULTURE NAT/G ECO/TAC DOMIN COERCE ATTIT PWR WEALTH...TREND VAL/FREE 20. PAGE 17 H0334 — SOCIETY STRATA IRAN

S63
HINDLEY D.,"FOREIGN AID TO INDONESIA AND ITS POLITICAL IMPLICATIONS." INDONESIA POL/PAR ATTIT SOVEREIGN...CHARTS 20. PAGE 71 H1421 — FOR/AID NAT/G WEALTH ECO/TAC

S63
LERNER D.,"WILL EUROPEAN UNION BRING ABOUT MERGED NATIONAL GOALS." EUR+WWI FRANCE GERMANY UK ECO/DEV NAT/G VOL/ASSN DELIB/GP BAL/PWR ECO/TAC NAT/LISM EEC 20 DEGAULLE/C. PAGE 95 H1889 — ATTIT STERTYP ELITES REGION

S63
MONROE A.D.,"BRITAIN AND THE EUROPEAN COMMUNITY." EUR+WWI FRANCE NAT/G DELIB/GP TOP/EX ECO/TAC DOMIN PWR...POLICY RECORD GEN/LAWS EEC EFTA 20 EFTA CMN/WLTH. PAGE 112 H2241 — VOL/ASSN ATTIT UK

S63
NYE J.,"TANGANYIKA'S SELF-HELP." TANZANIA NAT/G GIVE COST EFFICIENCY NAT/LISM 20. PAGE 119 H2381 — ECO/TAC POL/PAR ECO/UNDEV WORKER

S63
POPPINO R.E.,"IMBALANCE IN BRAZIL." L/A+17C NAT/G TOP/EX PLAN DIPLOM LEGIT DRIVE WEALTH...CON/ANAL LAFTA 20. PAGE 127 H2544 — POL/PAR ECO/TAC BRAZIL

S63
SOEMARDJORN S.,"SOME SOCIAL AND CULTURAL IMPLICATIONS OF INDONESIA'S PLANNED AND UNPLANNED DEVELOPMENT." EUR+WWI FUT MOD/EUR S/ASIA CONSTN SOCIETY DELIB/GP ACT/RES PLAN ECO/TAC EDU/PROP COERCE ATTIT ALL/VALS...TIME/SEQ 20. PAGE 146 H2927 — ECO/UNDEV CULTURE INDONESIA

S63
STAAR R.F.,"HOW STRONG IS THE SOVIET BLOC." COM USSR ECO/DEV NAT/G DELIB/GP ECO/TAC RIGID/FLEX ...CONCPT RECORD CHARTS 20. PAGE 148 H2964 — FORCES MYTH TOTALISM

S63
WELLS H.,"THE OAS AND THE DOMINICAN ELECTIONS." L/A+17C INT/ORG NAT/G POL/PAR TEC/DEV ECO/TAC EDU/PROP PERCEPT...TIME/SEQ OAS TOT/POP 20. PAGE 166 H3332 — CONSULT CHOOSE DOMIN/REP

N63
LEDERER W.,THE BALANCE ON FOREIGN TRANSACTIONS: PROBLEMS OF DEFINITION AND MEASUREMENT (PAMPHLET). USA+45 BUDGET DIPLOM ECO/TAC PRICE GOV/REL...POLICY STAT NAT/COMP METH 20. PAGE 93 H1853 — FINAN BAL/PAY INT/TRADE ECO/DEV

B64
BALOGH T.,THE ECONOMIC IMPACT OF MONETARY AND COMMERCIAL INSTITUTIONS OF A EUROPEAN ORIGIN IN AFRICA. AFR UAR INDUS FOR/AID COLONIAL CONTROL ...NAT/COMP 20. PAGE 10 H0205 — TEC/DEV FINAN ECO/UNDEV ECO/TAC

B64
BAUCHET P.,ECONOMIC PLANNING. FRANCE STRATA LG/CO CAP/ISM ADMIN PARL/PROC DEMAND OPTIMAL ATTIT PWR SOCISM...POLICY CHARTS 20. PAGE 12 H0238 — ECO/DEV NAT/G PLAN ECO/TAC

B64
COWAN L.G.,THE DILEMMAS OF AFRICAN INDEPENDENCE. AFR INDUS NAT/G SECT DIPLOM ECO/TAC REGION MARXISM ...CHARTS BIBLIOG 20 MAPS. PAGE 34 H0683 — ORD/FREE COLONIAL REV ECO/UNDEV

B64
FALL B.,STREET WITHOUT JOY. FRANCE USA+45 DIPLOM ECO/TAC FOR/AID GUERRILLA REV WEAPON...TREND 20. PAGE 48 H0966 — WAR S/ASIA FORCES COERCE

B64
FRIEDLAND W.H.,AFRICAN SOCIALISM. ECO/UNDEV MARKET LABOR NAT/G POL/PAR PLAN CAP/ISM ECO/TAC EDU/PROP CHOOSE ATTIT DRIVE PWR WEALTH...POLICY CONCPT RECORD STERTYP 20. PAGE 53 H1063 — AFR SOCISM

B64
HALPERIN S.W.,MUSSOLINI AND ITALIAN FASCISM. ITALY NAT/G POL/PAR SECT ECO/TAC LEAD PWR SOCISM...POLICY 20 MUSSOLIN/B. PAGE 64 H1294 — FASCISM NAT/LISM EDU/PROP CHIEF

B64
HOPKINSON T.,SOUTH AFRICA. SOUTH/AFR UK NAT/G POL/PAR LEGIS ECO/TAC PARL/PROC WAR...JURID AUD/VIS 19/20. PAGE 73 H1467 — SOCIETY RACE/REL DISCRIM

B64
INTERNATIONAL LABOUR OFFICE,EMPLOYMENT AND ECONOMIC GROWTH. ECO/DEV ECO/UNDEV NAT/G PLAN DIPLOM INT/TRADE CONTROL INCOME PRODUC WEALTH...STAT NAT/COMP 20 ILO. PAGE 78 H1558 — WORKER METH/COMP ECO/TAC OPTIMAL

B64
JUCKER-FLEETWOOD E.,MONEY AND FINANCE IN AFRICA. ISLAM ECO/UNDEV SERV/IND NAT/G EX/STRUC PLAN ECO/TAC ROUTINE WEALTH...MGT TOT/POP 20. PAGE 82 H1639 — AFR FINAN

B64
KELLER J.W.,GERMANY, THE WALL AND BERLIN. EUR+WWI ECO/DEV NAT/G VOL/ASSN FORCES PLAN ECO/TAC EDU/PROP COERCE...POLICY CONCPT INT TREND COLD/WAR BER/BLOC 20 BERLIN. PAGE 84 H1685 — ATTIT ALL/VALS DIPLOM GERMANY

B64
LATOURETTE K.S.,CHINA. ASIA CHINA/COM FUT USSR ECO/UNDEV ECO/TAC WAR 19/20. PAGE 92 H1838 — MARXISM NAT/G POLICY DIPLOM

B64
LI C.M.,INDUSTRIAL DEVELOPMENT IN COMMUNIST CHINA. CHINA/COM ECO/DEV ECO/UNDEV AGRI FINAN INDUS MARKET LABOR NAT/G ECO/TAC INT/TRADE EXEC ALL/VALS ...POLICY RELATIV TREND WORK TOT/POP VAL/FREE 20. PAGE 96 H1921 — ASIA TEC/DEV

B64
MARTINEZ J.R.,THREE CASES OF COMMUNISM: CUBA, BRAZIL, AND MEXICO. BRAZIL CUBA L/A+17C CONSTN NAT/G DIPLOM ECO/TAC GP/REL INGP/REL...GP/COMP BIBLIOG 20 MEXIC/AMER COM/PARTY. PAGE 103 H2068 — MARXISM BIOG REV NAT/COMP

B64
MAUD J.,AID FOR DEVELOPING COUNTRIES. COM EUR+WWI UK INT/TRADE ORD/FREE...GOV/COMP 20. PAGE 105 H2101 FOR/AID DIPLOM ECO/TAC ECO/UNDEV

B64
MELADY T.,FACES OF AFRICA. AFR FUT ISLAM NAT/G POL/PAR SCHOOL DELIB/GP PLAN ECO/TAC EDU/PROP ATTIT ALL/VALS...CHARTS TOT/POP VAL/FREE 20. PAGE 108 H2168 ECO/UNDEV TREND NAT/LISM

B64
MILIBAND R.,THE SOCIALIST REGISTER: 1964. GERMANY/W ITALY UK LABOR POL/PAR ECO/TAC FOR/AID NUC/PWR ...POLICY SOCIALIST IDEA/COMP 20 MAO NASSER/G. PAGE 110 H2204 MARXISM SOCISM CAP/ISM PROB/SOLV

B64
MORGAN H.W.,AMERICAN SOCIALISM 1900-1960. USA+45 USA-45 INTELL AGRI LABOR WORKER BARGAIN ECO/TAC GP/REL RACE/REL 20 NEGRO MIGRATION GOLD/STAND. PAGE 113 H2254 SOCISM POL/PAR ECO/DEV STRATA

B64
ON CULTURE AND SOCIAL CHANGE. FAM NAT/G ACT/RES ECO/TAC RACE/REL...PSY TIME/SEQ TREND IDEA/COMP METH/COMP ANTHOL BIBLIOG 20. PAGE 120 H2406 CULTURE TEC/DEV STRUCT CREATE

B64
PERKINS D.,THE AMERICAN DEMOCRACY: ITS RISE TO POWER. ASIA USSR LAW CULTURE FINAN EDU/PROP COLONIAL CHOOSE...POLICY CHARTS BIBLIOG WORSHIP PRESIDENT 15/20 NEGRO. PAGE 125 H2492 LOC/G ECO/TAC WAR DIPLOM

B64
POWELSON J.P.,LATIN AMERICA: TODAY'S ECONOMIC AND SOCIAL REVOLUTION. L/A+17C INTELL SOCIETY STRUCT AGRI INDUS NAT/G DIPLOM ECO/TAC REV...POLICY 20. PAGE 128 H2552 ECO/UNDEV WEALTH ADJUST PLAN

B64
RAISON T.,WHY CONSERVATIVE? UK FORCES DIPLOM ECO/TAC GIVE EDU/PROP ORD/FREE WEALTH LAISSEZ ...GOV/COMP 20 TORY/PARTY CONSRV/PAR. PAGE 129 H2583 PLURISM CONSERVE POL/PAR NAT/G

B64
RAMAZANI R.K.,THE MIDDLE EAST AND THE EUROPEAN COMMON MARKET. EUR+WWI ISLAM ECO/DEV EXTR/IND MARKET PROC/MFG INT/ORG NAT/G TEC/DEV ECO/TAC REGION DRIVE WEALTH...STAT CHARTS EEC TOT/POP 20. PAGE 129 H2587 ECO/UNDEV ATTIT INT/TRADE

B64
SEGAL R.,SANCTIONS AGAINST SOUTH AFRICA. AFR SOUTH/AFR NAT/G INT/TRADE RACE/REL PEACE PWR ...INT/LAW ANTHOL 20 UN. PAGE 141 H2821 SANCTION DISCRIM ECO/TAC POLICY

B64
SOLOW R.M.,THE NATURE AND SOURCES OF UNEMPLOYMENT IN THE UNITED STATES (PAMPHLET). USA+45 INDUS LABOR TEC/DEV ECO/TAC SKILL WEALTH...TREND NAT/COMP 20. PAGE 147 H2930 ECO/DEV WORKER STAT PRODUC

B64
TAWNEY R.H.,EQUALITY. UK CULTURE STRATA ECO/TAC EDU/PROP REPRESENT OWN NEW/LIB...MAJORIT WELF/ST SOC 20. PAGE 153 H3051 WEALTH STRUCT ELITES POPULISM

B64
TEPASKE J.J.,EXPLOSIVE FORCES IN LATIN AMERICA. CULTURE INTELL ECO/UNDEV INT/ORG NAT/G SECT FORCES ECO/TAC EDU/PROP PWR WEALTH SOC. PAGE 153 H3063 L/A+17C RIGID/FLEX FOR/AID USSR

B64
THAILAND NATIONAL ECO DEV,THE NATIONAL ECONOMIC DEVELOPMENT PLAN: 1961-66: SECOND PHASE 1964-66. THAILAND AGRI FINAN BUDGET EFFICIENCY INCOME...STAT CHARTS 20. PAGE 153 H3065 ECO/UNDEV ECO/TAC PLAN NAT/G

B64
THORNBURG M.W.,PEOPLE AND POLICY IN THE MIDDLE EAST. ISLAM ECO/UNDEV FAM KIN MUNIC NAT/G NEIGH POL/PAR SECT DELIB/GP LEGIS PLAN ECO/TAC DOMIN ADMIN ATTIT HEALTH RESPECT...SOC CONCPT METH/CNCPT OBS TIME/SEQ TOT/POP VAL/FREE. PAGE 154 H3088 TEC/DEV CULTURE

B64
THORNTON T.P.,THE THIRD WORLD IN SOVIET PERSPECTIVE: STUDIES BY SOVIET WRITERS ON THE DEVELOPING AREAS. AFR L/A+17C S/ASIA STRATA AGRI INDUS MARKET NAT/G POL/PAR ECO/TAC COLONIAL PERCEPT PWR WEALTH...MARXIST STAT CHARTS WORK MARX/KARL 20. PAGE 155 H3090 ECO/UNDEV ACT/RES USSR DIPLOM

B64
URQUIDI V.L.,THE CHALLENGE OF DEVELOPMENT IN LATIN AMERICA. L/A+17C FINAN INT/ORG TEC/DEV DIPLOM INT/TRADE PRICE REGION PRODUC...CHARTS 20. PAGE 159 H3175 ECO/UNDEV ECO/TAC NAT/G TREND

B64
US HOUSE COMM BANKING-CURR,INTERNATIONAL DEVELOPMENT ASSOCIATION ACT AMENDMENT. CHINA/COM USA+45 USSR FINAN FORCES LEGIS DIPLOM CONFER EFFICIENCY...CHARTS GOV/COMP 20 PRESIDENT CONGRESS INTL/DEV. PAGE 160 H3196 BAL/PAY FOR/AID RECORD ECO/TAC

B64
WARD R.E.,POLITICAL MODERNIZATION IN JAPAN AND TURKEY. ASIA ISLAM S/ASIA CONSTN CULTURE STRATA COM/IND POL/PAR FORCES ACT/RES ECO/TAC DOMIN EDU/PROP LEGIT ADMIN CHOOSE ATTIT ALL/VALS...STAT TIME/SEQ VAL/FREE CHINJAP. PAGE 165 H3307 SOCIETY TURKEY

B64
WERNETTE J.P.,GOVERNMENT AND BUSINESS. LABOR CAP/ISM ECO/TAC INT/TRADE TAX ADMIN AUTOMAT NUC/PWR CIVMIL/REL DEMAND...MGT 20 MONOPOLY. PAGE 167 H3333 NAT/G FINAN ECO/DEV CONTROL

B64
WILSON T.,POLICIES FOR REGIONAL DEVELOPMENT. CANADA UK FINAN INDUS NAT/G BUDGET TAX GIVE COST ...NAT/COMP 20. PAGE 169 H3383 REGION PLAN ECO/DEV ECO/TAC

B64
WRIGHT G.,RURAL REVOLUTION IN FRANCE: THE PEASANTRY IN THE TWENTIETH CENTURY. EUR+WWI MOD/EUR LAW CULTURE AGRI POL/PAR DELIB/GP LEGIS ECO/TAC EDU/PROP COERCE CHOOSE ATTIT RIGID/FLEX HEALTH ...STAT CENSUS CHARTS VAL/FREE 20. PAGE 171 H3419 PWR STRATA FRANCE REV

L64
HAAS E.B.,"ECONOMICS AND DIFFERENTIAL PATTERNS OF POLITICAL INTEGRATION: PROJECTIONS ABOUT UNITY IN LATIN AMERICA." SOCIETY NAT/G DELIB/GP ACT/RES CREATE PLAN ECO/TAC REGION ROUTINE ATTIT DRIVE PWR WEALTH...CONCPT TREND CHARTS LAFTA 20. PAGE 63 H1266 L/A+17C INT/ORG MARKET

S64
BARIETY J.,"LA POLITIQUE EXTERIEURE ALLEMANDE DANS L'HIVER 1939-1940." COM FINLAND GERMANY ISLAM ITALY USSR NAT/G FORCES ECO/TAC DOMIN EDU/PROP COERCE WAR PWR WEALTH...HIST/WRIT NAZI TOT/POP VAL/FREE 20. PAGE 11 H0216 EUR+WWI DIPLOM

S64
BENSON M.,"SOUTH AFRICA AND WORLD OPINION." AFR SOUTH/AFR INTELL SOCIETY TOP/EX ECO/TAC DOMIN COERCE DISCRIM ATTIT PWR WEALTH...POLICY RECORD 20. PAGE 14 H0285 NAT/G RIGID/FLEX RACE/REL

S64
CATTELL D.T.,"SOVIET POLICIES IN LATIN AMERICA." COM CUBA L/A+17C USSR SOCIETY NAT/G POL/PAR FORCES CREATE ECO/TAC EDU/PROP REGION REV RIGID/FLEX ...GEN/LAWS COLD/WAR 20. PAGE 28 H0560 DRIVE PWR

S64
CLIFFE L.,"TANGANYIKA'S TWO YEARS OF INDEPENDENCE." AFR INDUS MARKET NAT/G POL/PAR DELIB/GP CREATE ECO/TAC LEGIT DRIVE ALL/VALS...METH/CNCPT RECORD 20 TANGANYIKA. PAGE 30 H0604 ECO/UNDEV PLAN

S64
CROUZET F.,"WARS, BLOCKADE, AND ECONOMIC CHANGE IN EUROPE, 1792-1815." UK INDUS NAT/G TEC/DEV ECO/TAC WEALTH...POLICY RELATIV HIST/WRIT TIME/SEQ 18/19. PAGE 35 H0710 MOD/EUR MARKET

S64
DE GAULLE C.,"FRENCH WORLD VIEW." AFR ASIA CHINA/COM EUR+WWI ISLAM ECO/UNDEV INT/ORG NAT/G VOL/ASSN ACT/RES DIPLOM ECO/TAC EDU/PROP ATTIT DRIVE WEALTH 20. PAGE 37 H0751 TOP/EX PWR FOR/AID FRANCE

S64
GARMARNIKOW M.,"INFLUENCE-BUYING IN WEST AFRICA." COM FUT USSR INTELL NAT/G PLAN TEC/DEV ECO/TAC DOMIN EDU/PROP REGION NAT/LISM ATTIT DRIVE ALL/VALS SOVEREIGN...POLICY PSY SOC CONCPT TREND STERTYP WORK COLD/WAR 20. PAGE 55 H1102 AFR ECO/UNDEV FOR/AID SOCISM

S64
LANGER P.F.,"JAPAN'S RELATIONS WITH CHINA." ASIA CHINA/COM KOREA S/ASIA ECO/DEV NAT/G POL/PAR EDU/PROP ATTIT ALL/VALS...METH/CNCPT TIME/SEQ TREND 20 CHINJAP. PAGE 91 H1808 RIGID/FLEX ECO/TAC

S64
LANGERHANS H.,"NEHRU'S BITTERNESS." FUT INDIA S/ASIA CONSTN CULTURE ECO/UNDEV ECO/TAC DOMIN EDU/PROP ATTIT PERCEPT PERSON...POLICY 20 NEHRU/J. PAGE 91 H1811 ECO/DEV BIOG

S64
LOW D.A.,"LION RAMPANT." EUR+WWI MOD/EUR S/ASIA ECO/UNDEV NAT/G FORCES TEC/DEV ECO/TAC LEGIT ADMIN COLONIAL COERCE ORD/FREE RESPECT 19/20. PAGE 99 H1972 AFR DOMIN DIPLOM UK

S64
MARES V.E.,"EAST EUROPE'S SECOND CHANCE." COM EUR+WWI HUNGARY ROMANIA USSR YUGOSLAVIA ECO/UNDEV NAT/G TOP/EX CREATE PLAN TEC/DEV REGION NAT/LISM RIGID/FLEX PWR...CONCPT STAT COMECON 20. PAGE 102 H2047 VOL/ASSN ECO/TAC

S64
MARTELLI G.,"PORTUGAL AND THE UNITED NATIONS." AFR EUR+WWI ELITES INT/ORG NAT/G PROVS PLAN DIPLOM ECO/TAC DOMIN COLONIAL RIGID/FLEX MORAL ORD/FREE PWR WEALTH...MYTH UN 20. PAGE 103 H2060 ATTIT PORTUGAL

S64
MC WILLIAM M.,"THE WORLD BANK AND THE TRANSFER OF POWER IN KENYA." AFR ECO/UNDEV CONSULT ACT/RES TEC/DEV PERCEPT PWR SKILL WEALTH...CONCPT OBS TREND NAT/G ECO/TAC

20. PAGE 106 H2119

S64
SAAB H.,"THE ARAB SEARCH FOR A FEDERAL UNION." SOCIETY INT/ORG NAT/G DELIB/GP FORCES ACT/RES TEC/DEV ECO/TAC DOMIN LEGIT REGION ROUTINE ATTIT DRIVE RIGID/FLEX ALL/VALS...SOC CONCPT NEW/IDEA TIME/SEQ TREND. PAGE 136 H2726
ISLAM PLAN

S64
SALVADORI M.,"EL CAPITALISMO EN LA EUROPA DE LA POSGUERRA." INT/ORG NAT/G POL/PAR PLAN ECO/TAC ATTIT ORD/FREE WEALTH...HIST/WRIT COLD/WAR EEC 20. PAGE 137 H2743
EUR+WWI ECO/DEV CAP/ISM

S64
TOYNBEE A.,"BRITAIN AND THE ARABS: THE NEED FOR A NEW START." NAT/G CREATE COLONIAL ATTIT RIGID/FLEX MORAL PWR...POLICY HIST/WRIT 20. PAGE 156 H3124
ISLAM ECO/TAC DIPLOM UK

S64
ZARTMAN I.W.,"LES RELATIONS ENTRE LA FRANCE ET L'ALGERIA DEPUIS LES ACCORDS D'EVIAN." EUR+WWI FUT ISLAM CULTURE AGRI EXTR/IND FINAN INDUS POL/PAR DIPLOM ECO/TAC FOR/AID PEACE ATTIT DRIVE ALL/VALS ...TIME/SEQ VAL/FREE 20. PAGE 172 H3450
ECO/UNDEV ALGERIA FRANCE

B65
ACHTERBERG E.,BERLINER HOCHFINANZ - KAISER, FURSTEN, MILLIONARE UM 1900. GERMANY NAT/G EDU/PROP PERSON...MGT 19/20. PAGE 3 H0060
FINAN MUNIC BIOG ECO/TAC

B65
ADENAUER K.,MEMOIRS 1945-53. EUR+WWI GERMANY/W ECO/DEV CHIEF FORCES ECO/TAC WAR GOV/REL PWR SOVEREIGN 20 NATO ADENAUER/K. PAGE 3 H0068
BIOG DIPLOM NAT/G PERS/REL

B65
ALTON T.P.,POLISH NATIONAL INCOME AND PRODUCT IN 1954, 1955, AND 1956. POLAND FINAN EX/STRUC ECO/TAC PRICE COST WEALTH 20. PAGE 6 H0117
COM INDUS NAT/G ECO/DEV

B65
CHARNAY J.P.,LE SUFFRAGE POLITIQUE EN FRANCE; ELECTIONS PARLEMENTAIRES, ELECTION PRESIDENTIELLE, REFERENDUMS. FRANCE CONSTN CHIEF DELIB/GP ECO/TAC EDU/PROP CRIME INGP/REL MORAL ORD/FREE PWR CATHISM 20 PARLIAMENT PRESIDENT. PAGE 29 H0584
CHOOSE SUFF NAT/G LEGIS

B65
CHEN T.H.,THE CHINESE COMMUNIST REGIME: A DOCUMENTARY STUDY (2 VOLS.). CHINA/COM LAW CONSTN ELITES ECO/UNDEV LEGIS ECO/TAC ADMIN CONTROL PWR ...SOC 20. PAGE 29 H0587
MARXISM POL/PAR NAT/G

B65
EDELMAN M.,THE POLITICS OF WAGE-PRICE DECISIONS. GERMANY ITALY NETHERLAND UK INDUS LABOR POL/PAR PROB/SOLV BARGAIN PRICE ROUTINE BAL/PAY COST DEMAND 20. PAGE 44 H0888
GOV/COMP CONTROL ECO/TAC PLAN

B65
FAGG J.E.,CUBA, HAITI, AND THE DOMINICAN REPUBLIC. CUBA DOMIN/REP HAITI L/A+17C NAT/G DIPLOM ECO/TAC DOMIN CHOOSE AUTHORIT ROLE SOVEREIGN POPULISM 17/20. PAGE 48 H0959
COLONIAL ECO/UNDEV REV GOV/COMP

B65
GAJENDRAGADKAR P.B.,LAW, LIBERTY AND SOCIAL JUSTICE. INDIA CONSTN NAT/G SECT PLAN ECO/TAC PRESS POPULISM...SOC METH/COMP 20 HINDU. PAGE 54 H1086
ORD/FREE LAW ADJUD JURID

B65
GOPAL S.,BRITISH POLICY IN INDIA 1858-1905. INDIA UK ELITES CHIEF DELIB/GP ECO/TAC GP/REL DISCRIM ATTIT...IDEA/COMP NAT/COMP PERS/COMP BIBLIOG/A 19/20. PAGE 59 H1176
COLONIAL ADMIN POL/PAR ECO/UNDEV

B65
HAEFELE E.T.,GOVERNMENT CONTROLS ON TRANSPORT. AFR RHODESIA TANZANIA DIPLOM ECO/TAC TARIFFS PRICE ADJUD CONTROL REGION EFFICIENCY...POLICY 20 CONGO. PAGE 64 H1274
ECO/UNDEV DIST/IND FINAN NAT/G

B65
HALPERIN M.H.,COMMUNIST CHINA AND ARMS CONTROL. CHINA/COM FUT USA+45 CULTURE FORCES TEC/DEV ECO/TAC WAR PEACE ORD/FREE MARXISM 20 COLD/WAR. PAGE 64 H1292
ATTIT POLICY ARMS/CONT NUC/PWR

B65
HAPGOOD D.,AFRICA: FROM INDEPENDENCE TO TOMARROW. AFR GUINEA SENEGAL CULTURE ELITES ECO/UNDEV AGRI SCHOOL FOR/AID COLONIAL MARXISM...TREND 20. PAGE 66 H1323
ECO/TAC SOCIETY NAT/G

B65
HOSELITZ B.F.,ECONOMICS AND THE IDEA OF MANKIND. UNIV ECO/DEV ECO/UNDEV DIST/IND INDUS INT/ORG NAT/G ACT/RES ECO/TAC WEALTH...CONCPT STAT. PAGE 74 H1476
CREATE INT/TRADE

B65
IANNI O.,ESTADO E CAPITALISMO. L/A+17C FINAN TEC/DEV ECO/TAC ORD/FREE WEALTH POLICY. PAGE 76 H1518
ECO/UNDEV STRUCT INDUS NAT/G

B65
INT. BANK RECONSTR. DEVELOP.,ECONOMIC DEVELOPMENT OF KUWAIT. ISLAM KUWAIT AGRI FINAN MARKET EX/STRUC TEC/DEV ECO/TAC ADMIN WEALTH...OBS CON/ANAL CHARTS 20. PAGE 77 H1541
INDUS NAT/G

B65
JAIN S.C.,THE STATE AND AGRICULTURE. INDIA S/ASIA ECO/UNDEV PROB/SOLV CAP/ISM MARXISM SOCISM 20. PAGE 79 H1586
NAT/G POLICY AGRI ECO/TAC

B65
JASNY H.,KHRUSHCHEV'S CROP POLICY. USSR ECO/DEV PLAN MARXISM...STAT 20 KHRUSH/N RESOURCE/N. PAGE 80 H1593
AGRI NAT/G POLICY ECO/TAC

B65
KIRKWOOD K.,BRITAIN AND AFRICA. AFR UK ECO/UNDEV ECO/TAC WAR NAT/LISM SOVEREIGN 19/20. PAGE 86 H1725
NAT/G DIPLOM POLICY COLONIAL

B65
THE STATE AND ECONOMIC ENTERPRISE IN JAPAN; ESSAYS IN THE POLITICAL ECONOMY OF GROWTH. AGRI INDUS DRIVE POPULISM...CHARTS NAT/COMP ANTHOL 19/20 CHINJAP. PAGE 98 H1949
ECO/UNDEV ECO/DEV CAP/ISM ECO/TAC

B65
MEIER R.L.,DEVELOPMENTAL PLANNING. PUERT/RICO INDUS PUB/INST SCHOOL CREATE ECO/TAC FOR/AID...NAT/COMP 20. PAGE 108 H2165
PLAN ECO/UNDEV GOV/COMP TEC/DEV

B65
ONSLOW C.,ASIAN ECONOMIC DEVELOPMENT. BURMA CEYLON INDIA MALAYSIA PAKISTAN S/ASIA AGRI INDUS MARKET PROB/SOLV CAP/ISM FOR/AID INT/TRADE DEMAND WEALTH ...POLICY ANTHOL 20. PAGE 121 H2418
ECO/UNDEV ECO/TAC PLAN NAT/G

B65
PROEHL P.O.,FOREIGN ENTERPRISE IN NIGERIA. NIGERIA FINAN LABOR NAT/G TAX 20. PAGE 128 H2562
ECO/UNDEV ECO/TAC JURID CAP/ISM

B65
SCHULER E.A.,THE PAKISTAN ACADEMIES FOR RURAL DEVELOPMENT COMILLA AND PESHAWAR 1959-1964. PAKISTAN S/ASIA SOCIETY STRUCT AGRI NAT/G TEC/DEV EDU/PROP 20. PAGE 140 H2801
BIBLIOG PLAN ECO/TAC ECO/UNDEV

B65
ULAM A.,THE BOLSHEVIKS. COM USSR NAT/G CHIEF ECO/TAC ADMIN LEAD WAR POPULISM...POLICY 19/20 LENIN/VI BOLSHEVISM. PAGE 157 H3148
SOCISM POL/PAR TOP/EX REV

B65
WURFEL S.W.,FOREIGN ENTERPRISE IN COLOMBIA. FINAN LABOR NAT/G ECO/TAC TAX REGION 20 COLOMB. PAGE 171 H3429
ECO/UNDEV INT/TRADE JURID CAP/ISM

B65
YOUNG A.N.,CHINA'S WARTIME FINANCE AND INFLATION. ASIA AGRI INDUS NAT/G ECO/TAC CONFER PRICE WAR COST 20. PAGE 172 H3437
FINAN FOR/AID TAX BUDGET

L65
WIONCZEK M.,"LATIN AMERICA FREE TRADE ASSOCIATION." AGRI DIST/IND FINAN INDUS INT/ORG LABOR NAT/G TEC/DEV ECO/TAC HEALTH SKILL WEALTH...POLICY RELATIV MGT LAFTA 20. PAGE 169 H3390
L/A+17C MARKET REGION

S65
BRANDENBURG F.,"THE RELEVANCE OF MEXICAN EXPERIENCE TO LATIN AMERICAN DEVELOPMENT." BRAZIL CHILE VENEZUELA STRUCT ECO/UNDEV AGRI CREATE ECO/TAC ...STAT RECORD MEXIC/AMER ARGEN COLOMB. PAGE 20 H0405
L/A+17C GOV/COMP

S65
GOLDMAN M.I.,"A BALANCE SHEET OF SOVIET FOREIGN AID." USA+45 ECO/UNDEV BAL/PWR ECO/TAC RENT GIVE EDU/PROP CONTROL COST PROFIT GEN/METH. PAGE 58 H1158
USSR FOR/AID NAT/COMP EFFICIENCY

S65
HAYTER T.,"FRENCH AID TO AFRICA* ITS SCOPE AND ACHIEVEMENTS." CULTURE ECO/TAC INT/TRADE ADMIN REGION CENTRAL FEDERAL LOVE PWR SOVEREIGN EEC. PAGE 68 H1370
AFR FRANCE FOR/AID COLONIAL

S65
KEE W.S.,"CENTRAL CITY EXPENDITURES AND METROPOLITAN AREAS." PLAN BUDGET ECO/TAC TAX GP/REL WEALTH...CHARTS 20. PAGE 84 H1677
LOC/G MUNIC GOV/COMP NEIGH

S65
STAAR R.F.,"RETROGRESSION IN POLAND." COM USSR AGRI INDUS NAT/G CREATE EDU/PROP TOTALISM RIGID/FLEX ORD/FREE PWR SOCISM...RECORD CHARTS 20. PAGE 148 H2965
TOP/EX ECO/TAC POLAND

S65
TABORSKY E.,"CHANGE IN CZECHOSLOVAKIA." COM USSR ELITES INTELL AGRI INDUS NAT/G DELIB/GP EX/STRUC ECO/TAC TOTALISM ATTIT RIGID/FLEX SOCISM...MGT CONCPT TREND 20. PAGE 152 H3031
ECO/DEV PLAN CZECHOSLVK

B66
BIRKHEAD G.S.,ADMINISTRATIVE PROBLEMS IN PAKISTAN. PAKISTAN AGRI FINAN INDUS LG/CO ECO/TAC CONTROL PWR
ADMIN NAT/G

...CHARTS ANTHOL 20. PAGE 17 H0340
ORD/FREE ECO/UNDEV

B66
BIRMINGHAM W.,A STUDY OF CONTEMPORARY GHANA VOL I: THE ECONOMY OF GHANA. AFR GHANA PLAN...POLICY STAT CHARTS ANTHOL BIBLIOG 20. PAGE 17 H0342
ECO/UNDEV ECO/TAC NAT/G PRODUC

B66
BRECHER M.,SUCCESSION IN INDIA. INDIA USA+45 CONSTN AGRI POL/PAR PROVS SECT DELIB/GP FORCES PROB/SOLV ECO/TAC PWR...LING 20 CONGRESS NEHRU/J. PAGE 20 H0408
CHIEF DECISION CHOOSE

B66
COLE A.B.,SOCIALIST PARTIES IN POSTWAR JAPAN. STRATA AGRI LABOR PLAN DIPLOM ECO/TAC AGREE LEAD CHOOSE ATTIT...CHARTS 20 CHINJAP SOC/DEMPAR. PAGE 31 H0620
POL/PAR POLICY SOCISM NAT/G

B66
DOBB M.,SOVIET ECONOMIC DEVELOPMENT SINCE 1917. USSR ECO/DEV ECO/UNDEV LABOR NAT/G TEC/DEV ECO/TAC ROUTINE PRODUC MARXISM 20. PAGE 41 H0829
PLAN INDUS WORKER

B66
DYCK H.V.,WEIMAR GERMANY AND SOVIET RUSSIA 1926-1933. EUR+WWI GERMANY UK USSR ECO/TAC INT/TRADE NEUTRAL WAR ATTIT 20 WEIMAR/REP TREATY. PAGE 44 H0877
DIPLOM GOV/REL POLICY

B66
EDWARDS C.D.,TRADE REGULATIONS OVERSEAS. IRELAND NEW/ZEALND SOUTH/AFR NAT/G CAP/ISM TARIFFS CONTROL ...POLICY JURID 20 EEC CHINJAP. PAGE 45 H0892
INT/TRADE DIPLOM INT/LAW ECO/TAC

B66
FITZGERALD C.P.,THE BIRTH OF COMMUNIST CHINA (2ND ED.). ASIA CHINA/COM STRUCT BAL/PWR DIPLOM ECO/TAC INT/TRADE WEALTH 20. PAGE 51 H1018
REV MARXISM ECO/UNDEV

B66
FOX K.A.,THE THEORY OF QUANTITATIVE ECONOMIC POLICY WITH APPLICATIONS TO ECONOMIC GROWTH AND STABILIZATION. ECO/DEV AGRI NAT/G PLAN ADMIN RISK ...DECISION IDEA/COMP SIMUL T. PAGE 52 H1045
ECO/TAC ECOMETRIC EQUILIB GEN/LAWS

B66
GRAHAM B.D.,THE FORMATION OF THE AUSTRALIAN COUNTRY PARTIES. CANADA USA+45 USA-45 SOCIETY PLAN ECO/TAC ...NAT/COMP 20 AUSTRAL. PAGE 59 H1190
POL/PAR AGRI REGION PARL/PROC

B66
HACKETT J.,L'ECONOMIE BRITANNIQUE: PROBLEMES ET PERSPECTIVES. FRANCE UK LABOR MUNIC NAT/G EX/STRUC PROB/SOLV BAL/PAY INCOME RIGID/FLEX...MGT PHIL/SCI CHARTS 20. PAGE 63 H1271
ECO/DEV FINAN ECO/TAC PLAN

B66
HOLT R.T.,THE POLITICAL BASIS OF ECONOMIC DEVELOPMENT. STRATA STRUCT NAT/G DIPLOM ADMIN...SOC NAT/COMP BIBLIOG 20. PAGE 73 H1458
ECO/TAC GOV/COMP CONSTN EX/STRUC

B66
INTL CONF ON WORLD POLITICS-5,EASTERN EUROPE IN TRANSITION. EUR+WWI USSR ECO/TAC NAT/LISM ATTIT SOVEREIGN...CHARTS ANTHOL 20 TREATY WARSAW/P. PAGE 78 H1562
COM NAT/COMP MARXISM DIPLOM

B66
IOWA STATE U CTR AGRI AND ECO.RESEARCH AND EDUCATION FOR REGIONAL AND AREA DEVELOPMENT. FUT LAW CULTURE R+D LOC/G PLAN KNOWL...POLICY CHARTS ANTHOL 20. PAGE 78 H1565
REGION ACT/RES ECO/TAC INDUS

B66
KAUNDA K.,ZAMBIA: INDEPENDENCE AND BEYOND: THE SPEECHES OF KENNETH KAUNDA. AFR FUT ZAMBIA SOCIETY ECO/UNDEV NAT/G PROB/SOLV ECO/TAC ADMIN RACE/REL SOVEREIGN 20. PAGE 84 H1670
ORD/FREE COLONIAL CONSTN LEAD

B66
KIRKENDALL R.S.,SOCIAL SCIENTISTS AND FARM POLITICS IN THE AGE OF ROOSEVELT. ACADEM PLAN ECO/TAC GIVE ADMIN CONTROL PRODUC...SOC 20 NEW/DEAL ROOSEVLT/F BURAGR/ECO. PAGE 86 H1722
AGRI INTELL POLICY NAT/G

B66
MACFARQUHAR R.,CHINA UNDER MAO: POLITICS TAKES COMMAND. CHINA/COM COM AGRI INDUS CHIEF FORCES DIPLOM INT/TRADE EDU/PROP TASK REV ADJUST...ANTHOL 20 MAO. PAGE 100 H1992
ECO/UNDEV TEC/DEV ECO/TAC ADMIN

B66
MADAN G.R.,ECONOMIC THINKING IN INDIA. INDIA ECO/UNDEV AGRI FINAN INDUS LABOR PLAN CAP/ISM INT/TRADE MARXISM SOCISM...POLICY 1/20. PAGE 101 H2013
ECO/TAC PHIL/SCI NAT/G POL/PAR

B66
MASON E.S.,ECONOMIC DEVELOPMENT IN INDIA AND PAKISTAN. INDIA PAKISTAN AGRI FINAN PLAN BUDGET INT/TRADE WEALTH...POLICY STAT TREND CHARTS 20. PAGE 104 H2086
NAT/COMP ECO/UNDEV ECO/TAC FOR/AID

B66
NEVITT A.A.,THE ECONOMIC PROBLEMS OF HOUSING. WOR+45 ECO/DEV ECO/UNDEV ACT/RES PROB/SOLV ECO/TAC RENT...OBS CHARTS 20. PAGE 117 H2342
HABITAT PROC/MFG DELIB/GP NAT/COMP

B66
NOEL G.E.,THE NEW BRITAIN AND HAROLD WILSON: INTERIM REPORT, 1966 GENERAL ELECTION. UK POL/PAR CONSULT PROB/SOLV BUDGET DIPLOM ECO/TAC LEAD CHOOSE ATTIT 20 WILSON/H PARLIAMENT. PAGE 118 H2366
BIOG PERSON NAT/G CHIEF

B66
PAN S.,VIETNAM CRISIS. ASIA FRANCE USA+45 USA-45 VIETNAM CULTURE SOCIETY INT/ORG ECO/TAC AGREE CONTROL WAR MARXISM 20. PAGE 123 H2454
ECO/UNDEV POLICY DIPLOM NAT/COMP

B66
ROOS H.,A HISTORY OF MODERN POLAND FROM THE FOUNDATION OF THE STATE IN THE FIRST WORLD WAR TO THE PRESENT DAY. EUR+WWI POLAND INTELL SOCIETY ECO/TAC LEAD REV ATTIT ORD/FREE MARXISM...BIBLIOG 20 WWI PARTITION. PAGE 133 H2669
NAT/G WAR DIPLOM

B66
SAKAI R.K.,STUDIES ON ASIA, 1966. CEYLON INDIA USA-45 INDUS POL/PAR DIPLOM ECO/TAC MARXISM ...POLICY 19/20 CHINJAP. PAGE 137 H2738
SECT ECO/UNDEV

B66
SCHATTEN F.,COMMUNISM IN AFRICA. AFR GHANA GUINEA MALI CULTURE ECO/UNDEV LABOR SECT ECO/TAC EDU/PROP REV 20. PAGE 139 H2774
COLONIAL NAT/LISM MARXISM DIPLOM

B66
SCHURMANN F.,IDEOLOGY AND ORGANIZATION IN COMMUNIST CHINA. CHINA/COM LOC/G MUNIC POL/PAR ECO/TAC CONTROL ATTIT...MGT STERTYP 20 COM/PARTY. PAGE 140 H2805
MARXISM STRUCT ADMIN NAT/G

B66
SKILLING H.G.,THE GOVERNMENTS OF COMMUNIST EAST EUROPE. COM EUR+WWI ELITES FORCES DIPLOM ECO/TAC CONTROL HABITAT SOCISM...DECISION BIBLIOG 20 EUROPE/E COM/PARTY. PAGE 145 H2895
MARXISM NAT/COMP GP/COMP DOMIN

B66
THIESENHUSEN W.C.,CHILE'S EXPERIMENTS IN AGRARIAN REFORM. CHILE STRUCT NAT/G ACT/RES ECO/TAC GOV/REL COST SOCISM...TREND CHARTS SOC/EXP 20. PAGE 154 H3073
AGRI ECO/UNDEV SOC TEC/DEV

B66
YEAGER L.B.,INTERNATIONAL MONETARY RELATIONS: THEORY, HISTORY, AND POLICY. WOR+45 WOR-45 INT/TRADE BAL/PAY...NAT/COMP 18/20 MONEY. PAGE 172 H3435
FINAN DIPLOM ECO/TAC IDEA/COMP

B66
ZINKIN T.,CHALLENGES IN INDIA. INDIA PAKISTAN LAW AGRI FINAN INDUS TOP/EX TEC/DEV CONTROL ROUTINE ORD/FREE PWR 20 NEHRU/J SHASTRI/LB CIVIL/SERV. PAGE 173 H3458
NAT/G ECO/TAC POLICY ADMIN

S66
GAMER R.E.,"URGENT SINGAPORE, PATIENT MALAYSIA." MALAYSIA S/ASIA ECO/UNDEV POL/PAR CHIEF TARIFFS TAX CONTROL LEAD REGION PWR 20 SINGAPORE. PAGE 55 H1094
DIPLOM NAT/G POLICY ECO/TAC

S66
HEAPHEY J.,"THE ORGANIZATION OF EGYPT* INADEQUACIES OF A NONPOLITICAL MODEL FOR NATION-BUILDING." STRATA NAT/G CREATE PROB/SOLV ECO/TAC NAT/LISM SOCISM RECORD. PAGE 69 H1377
UAR ECO/UNDEV OBS

S66
MALENBAUM W.,"GOVERNMENT, ENTREPRENEURSHIP, AND ECONOMIC GROWTH IN POOR LANDS." ELITES ECO/UNDEV INDUS CREATE DRIVE. PAGE 101 H2028
ECO/TAC PLAN CONSERVE NAT/G

S66
SKILLING H.G.,"THE RUMANIAN NATIONAL COURSE." COM EUR+WWI ROMANIA NAT/G ECO/TAC PWR 20. PAGE 145 H2896
NAT/LISM POLICY DIPLOM MARXISM

B67
ANDERSON C.W.,POLITICS AND ECONOMIC CHANGE IN LATIN AMERICA. L/A+17C INDUS NAT/G OP/RES ADMIN DEMAND ...POLICY STAT CHARTS NAT/COMP 20. PAGE 6 H0125
ECO/UNDEV PROB/SOLV PLAN ECO/TAC

B67
ANDERSON C.W.,ISSUES OF POLITICAL DEVELOPMENT. BURMA WOR+45 CULTURE TOP/EX ECO/TAC MARXISM ...CHARTS NAT/COMP 20 COLOMB CONGO/LEOP. PAGE 6 H0126
NAT/LISM COERCE ECO/UNDEV SOCISM

B67
CORDIER A.W.,COLUMBIA ESSAYS IN INTERNATIONAL AFFAIRS. ASIA CHINA/COM FRANCE S/ASIA SPAIN UAR ECO/UNDEV LOC/G ECO/TAC GUERRILLA PWR...BIOG ANTHOL 18/20 MAU/MAU. PAGE 33 H0663
NAT/G DIPLOM MARXISM POLICY

B67
DEGLER C.N.,THE AGE OF THE ECONOMIC REVOLUTION 1876-1900. USA-45 AGRI MUNIC POL/PAR SECT ECO/TAC CHOOSE...PHIL/SCI CHARTS NAT/COMP 19 NEGRO. PAGE 39 H0782
INDUS SOCIETY ECO/DEV TEC/DEV

B67
DENISON E.F.,WHY GROWTH RATES DIFFER; POSTWAR EXPERIENCE IN NINE WESTERN COUNTRIES. WOR+45 FINAN WORKER TEC/DEV EDU/PROP PRICE PRODUC WEALTH ...ECOMETRIC STAT CHARTS BIBLIOG. PAGE 40 H0791
METH NAT/COMP ECO/DEV ECO/TAC

B67
HOLLERMAN L.,JAPAN'S DEPENDENCE ON THE WORLD ECONOMY. INDUS MARKET LABOR NAT/G DIPLOM 20 CHINJAP. PAGE 73 H1457
PLAN ECO/DEV ECO/TAC INT/TRADE

B67
KONCZACKI Z.A.,PUBLIC FINANCE AND ECONOMIC DEVELOPMENT OF NATAL 1893-1910. TAX ADMIN COLONIAL ...STAT CHARTS BIBLIOG 19/20 NATAL. PAGE 88 H1755
ECO/TAC FINAN NAT/G ECO/UNDEV

B67
LEVY J.-P.,THE ECONOMIC LIFE OF THE ANCIENT WORLD. CULTURE SOCIETY INT/TRADE COLONIAL WEALTH ...BIBLIOG. PAGE 95 H1906
ECO/TAC ECO/UNDEV FINAN MEDIT-7

B67
LYON B.,MEDIEVAL FINANCE. CHRIST-17C...SOC 11/12. PAGE 99 H1984
FINAN METH/COMP ECO/TAC NAT/COMP

B67
MENDEL A.P.,POLITICAL MEMOIRS 1905-1917 BY PAUL MILIUKOV (TRANS. BY CARL GOLDBERG). USSR AGRI DIPLOM ECO/TAC POPULISM...MAJORIT 20. PAGE 109 H2170
BIOG LEAD NAT/G CONSTN

B67
NESS G.D.,BUREAUCRACY AND RURAL DEVELOPMENT IN MALAYSIA. MALAYSIA UK SOCIETY FINAN INDUS WORKER TEC/DEV ECO/TAC COLONIAL EQUILIB ORD/FREE...STAT CHARTS 20. PAGE 117 H2330
ECO/UNDEV PLAN NAT/G ADMIN

B67
OVERSEAS DEVELOPMENT INSTIT,EFFECTIVE AID. WOR+45 INT/ORG TEC/DEV DIPLOM INT/TRADE ADMIN. PAGE 122 H2434
FOR/AID ECO/UNDEV ECO/TAC NAT/COMP

B67
PAPANEK G.F.,PAKISTAN'S DEVELOPMENT: SOCIAL GOALS AND PRIVATE INCENTIVES. PAKISTAN INDUS NAT/G PROB/SOLV CONTROL EFFICIENCY SOCISM...CHARTS 20. PAGE 123 H2463
ECO/UNDEV PLAN CAP/ISM ECO/TAC

B67
PLANK J.,CUBA AND THE UNITED STATES: LONG RANGE PERSPECTIVES. CUBA L/A+17C USSR ECO/UNDEV NAT/G FORCES ECO/TAC INT/TRADE AGREE REV...PREDICT TREND ANTHOL 20 CASTRO/F COLD/WAR OAS. PAGE 126 H2520
DIPLOM

B67
POGANY A.H.,POLITICAL SCIENCE AND INTERNATIONAL RELATIONS, BOOKS RECOMMENDED FOR AMERICAN CATHOLIC COLLEGE LIBRARIES. INT/ORG LOC/G NAT/G FORCES BAL/PWR ECO/TAC NUC/PWR...CATH INT/LAW TREATY 20. PAGE 127 H2532
BIBLIOG DIPLOM

B67
POSNER M.V.,ITALIAN PUBLIC ENTERPRISE. ITALY ECO/DEV FINAN INDUS CREATE ECO/TAC ADMIN CONTROL EFFICIENCY PRODUC...TREND CHARTS 20. PAGE 127 H2545
NAT/G PLAN CAP/ISM SOCISM

B67
ROSENBLUTH G.,THE CANADIAN ECONOMY AND DISARMAMENT. CANADA FUT ECO/DEV INDUS R+D DELIB/GP DIPLOM ECO/TAC CIVMIL/REL PEACE...POLICY BIBLIOG PACIFIST 20. PAGE 134 H2679
ARMS/CONT STAT PLAN NAT/G

B67
RUEFF J.,BALANCE OF PAYMENTS. WOR+45 FINAN TEC/DEV DIPLOM TARIFFS PRICE CONTROL...POLICY CONCPT IDEA/COMP. PAGE 136 H2715
INT/TRADE BAL/PAY ECO/TAC NAT/COMP

B67
SHAFFER H.G.,THE COMMUNIST WORLD: MARXIST AND NON-MARXIST VIEWS. WOR+45 SOCIETY DIPLOM ECO/TAC CONTROL SOCISM...MARXIST ANTHOL BIBLIOG/A 20. PAGE 142 H2838
MARXISM NAT/COMP IDEA/COMP COM

B67
THOMAN R.S.,GEOGRAPHY OF INTERNATIONAL TRADE. WOR+45 ECO/DEV ECO/UNDEV INT/ORG LG/CO PLAN BAL/PAY ...STAT CHARTS NAT/COMP 20. PAGE 154 H3075
INT/TRADE GEOG ECO/TAC DIPLOM

B67
WARREN S.,THE AMERICAN PRESIDENT. POL/PAR FORCES LEGIS DIPLOM ECO/TAC ADMIN EXEC PWR...ANTHOL 18/20 ROOSEVLT/F KENNEDY/JF JOHNSON/LB TRUMAN/HS WILSON/W. PAGE 165 H3312
CHIEF LEAD NAT/G CONSTN

L67
"A PROPOS DES INCITATIONS FINANCIERES AUX GROUPEMENTS DES COMMUNES: ESSAI D'INTERPRETATION." FRANCE NAT/G LEGIS ADMIN GOV/REL CENTRAL 20. PAGE 3 H0051
LOC/G ECO/TAC APPORT ADJUD

L67
GALTUNG J.,"ON THE EFFECTS OF INTERNATIONAL ECONOMIC SANCTIONS, WITH EXAMPLES FROM THE CASE OF RHODESIA." NAT/G DIPLOM EDU/PROP ADJUST EFFICIENCY ATTIT MORAL...OBS CHARTS 20. PAGE 55 H1091
SANCTION ECO/TAC INT/TRADE ECO/UNDEV

L67
HOSHII I.,"JAPAN'S STAKE IN ASIA." ASIA S/ASIA CAP/ISM ECO/TAC ROLE...GEOG 20 CHINJAP. PAGE 74 H1477
DIPLOM REGION NAT/G INT/ORG

L67
ROTH A.R.,"CAPITAL-MARKET DEVELOPMENT IN ISRAEL AND BRAZIL: TWO EXAMPLES OF THE ROLE OF LAW IN DEVELOPMENT." BRAZIL ISRAEL L/A+17C INDUS MARKET ECO/TAC FOR/AID INT/TRADE CONTROL BAL/PAY 20. PAGE 135 H2694
LAW ECO/UNDEV NAT/COMP FINAN

L67
WRIGHT W.R.,"FOREIGN-OWNED RAILWAYS IN ARGENTINA: A CASE STUDY OF ECONOMIC NATIONALISM." L/A+17C UK ECO/UNDEV SERV/IND LG/CO NAT/G TEC/DEV BAL/PWR EQUILIB ARGEN. PAGE 171 H3423
NAT/LISM CAP/ISM ECO/TAC COLONIAL

S67
ADAMS R.N.,"ETHICS AND THE SOCIAL ANTHROPOLOGIST IN LATIN AMERICA." USA+45 INTELL PROB/SOLV ECO/TAC LEAD...DECISION SOC NAT/COMP PERS/COMP. PAGE 3 H0066
L/A+17C POLICY ECO/UNDEV CONSULT

S67
BAER W.,"THE INFLATION CONTROVERSY IN LATIN AMERICA: SURVEY." L/A+17C ECO/UNDEV AGRI FINAN INDUS PLAN PROB/SOLV TEC/DEV...BIBLIOG/A 20. PAGE 10 H0194
NAT/G BAL/PAY ECO/TAC BUDGET

S67
BELLER I.,"ECONOMIC POLICY AND THE DEMANDS OF LABOR." PLAN TAX GIVE PRICE WAR COST PRODUC WEALTH. PAGE 13 H0268
NAT/G ECO/TAC SOC/WK INCOME

S67
CHIU S.M.,"CHINA'S MILITARY POSTURE." CHINA/COM ELITES NAT/G POL/PAR TEC/DEV ECO/TAC DOMIN CONTROL LEAD REV MARXISM 20 MAO. PAGE 30 H0595
FORCES CIVMIL/REL NUC/PWR DIPLOM

S67
CHU-YUAN CHENG,"THE CULTURAL REVOLUTION AND CHINA'S ECONOMY." CHINA/COM AGRI DIST/IND INDUS MARKET NAT/G WORKER PLAN INT/TRADE DOMIN DEMAND PRODUC ...CHARTS 20 MAO. PAGE 30 H0600
ECO/DEV ECO/TAC REV SOCISM

S67
COHEN A.,"REVOLUTION IN ARGENTINA?" L/A+17C NAT/G POL/PAR CHIEF PROB/SOLV ECO/TAC 20 ARGEN. PAGE 31 H0615
REV ECO/UNDEV CONTROL BIOG

S67
DESHPANDE A.M.,"FEDERAL-STATE FISCAL RELATIONS IN INDIA" (REVIEW ARTICLE)" GERMANY USSR DELIB/GP PLAN BUDGET ECO/TAC INCOME 20 SOC/DEMPAR SOC/REVPAR. PAGE 40 H0795
FINAN NAT/G GOV/REL TAX

S67
FRENCH D.S.,"DOES THE U.S. EXPLOIT THE DEVELOPING NATIONS?" INT/ORG NAT/G CAP/ISM BAL/PAY WEALTH POLICY. PAGE 53 H1057
ECO/UNDEV INT/TRADE ECO/TAC COLONIAL

S67
GAMARNIKOW M.,"THE NEW ROLE OF PRIVATE ENTERPRISE." ECO/DEV INDUS NAT/G SML/CO CREATE PROB/SOLV MARXISM ...POLICY TREND IDEA/COMP 20. PAGE 55 H1092
ECO/TAC ATTIT CAP/ISM COM

S67
GOODSELL J.N.,"BALAGUER'S DOMINICAN REPUBLIC." DOMIN/REP FUT L/A+17C POL/PAR PROB/SOLV ECO/TAC 20. PAGE 59 H1174
ECO/UNDEV CHIEF POLICY NAT/G

S67
GRAHAM R.,"BRAZIL'S DILEMMA." BRAZIL FUT L/A+17C NAT/G CHIEF PROB/SOLV ECO/TAC PWR 20. PAGE 60 H1193
ECO/UNDEV CONSTN POL/PAR POLICY

S67
HEATH D.B.,"BOLIVIA UNDER BARRIENTOS." L/A+17C NAT/G CHIEF DIPLOM ECO/TAC...POLICY 20 BOLIV. PAGE 69 H1379
ECO/UNDEV POL/PAR REV CONSTN

S67
LICHFIELD N.,"THE EVALUATION OF CAPITAL INVESTMENT PROJECTS IN TOWN CENTRE REDEVELOPMENT." UK CONSTRUC MUNIC CONSULT COST...METH/CNCPT IDEA/COMP 20. PAGE 96 H1923
PLAN ECO/TAC NAT/G DECISION

S67
MITCHELL W.C.,"THE SHAPE OF POLITICAL THEORY TO COME: FROM POLITICAL SOCIOLOGY TO POLITICAL ECONOMY." ACADEM NAT/G BUDGET TAX LEGIT LOBBY GOV/REL INGP/REL...SOC NEW/IDEA TREND CHARTS 20 MONEY. PAGE 112 H2231
ECO/TAC GEN/LAWS

S67
NATSAGDORJ A.S.,"THE ECONOMIC BASIS OF FEUDALISM IN MONGOLIA." ASIA COM USSR OWN WEALTH CONSERVE...SOC 20 MONGOLIA. PAGE 116 H2324
ECO/TAC AGRI NAT/COMP MARXISM

S67
PERKINS D.H.,"ECONOMIC GROWTH IN CHINA AND THE CULTURAL REVOLUTION(1960APRIL 1967)" CHINA/COM FUT AGRI INDUS PLAN LEAD MARXISM...CHARTS 20 MAO. PAGE 125 H2493
ECO/TAC CULTURE REV ECO/UNDEV

S67
PONOMARYOV B.,"THE OCTOBER REVOLUTION - BEGINNING OF THE EPOCH OF SOCIALISM AND COMMUNISM." COM FUT USSR WOR+45 SOCIETY STRATA CHIEF CREATE DIPLOM
MARXIST WORKER INT/ORG

ECO/TAC EDU/PROP SOCISM...NAT/COMP 20. PAGE 127 H2542 — POLICY

S67
ROCHET W.,"THE OCTOBER REVOLUTION AND THE STRUGGLE OF THE FRENCH COMMUNISTS." COM FRANCE ELITES SOCIETY STRATA ECO/TAC EDU/PROP GP/REL WEALTH ...MARXIST IDEA/COMP NAT/COMP 20. PAGE 133 H2654 — SOCISM CHOOSE METH/COMP NAT/G

S67
RONNING C.,"NANKING: 1950." ASIA CANADA CHINA/COM NAT/G PLAN ECO/TAC REV ADJUST 20. PAGE 133 H2667 — DIPLOM ROLE PEACE

S67
SANCHEZ J.D.,"DESARROLLO ECONOMICO Y FUTURO DE COLOMBIA." L/A+17C AGRI EXTR/IND FINAN INDUS MARKET INT/TRADE CONTROL...STAT TREND COLOMB. PAGE 137 H2748 — ECO/UNDEV FUT NAT/G ECO/TAC

S67
SAVELYEV N.,"MONOPOLY DRIVE IN INDIA." INDIA INDUS NAT/G INT/TRADE NEUTRAL SANCTION GOV/REL CONSERVE ...MARXIST 20. PAGE 138 H2759 — ECO/UNDEV POL/PAR ECO/TAC CONTROL

S67
SCHACHTER G.,"REGIONAL DEVELOPMENT IN THE ITALIAN DUAL ECONOMY" ITALY AGRI INDUS MARKET WORKER ECO/TAC CONTROL INCOME PRODUC 20. PAGE 138 H2767 — REGION ECO/UNDEV NAT/G PROB/SOLV

S67
SHIGEO N.,"THE GREAT CULTURAL REVOLUTION." ASIA ECO/UNDEV AGRI NAT/G CHIEF ECO/TAC EDU/PROP CONTROL LEAD PWR 20 MAO. PAGE 143 H2860 — CREATE REV CULTURE POL/PAR

S67
SINGH B.,"ITALIAN EXPERIENCE IN REGIONAL ECONOMIC DEVELOPMENT AND LESSONS FOR OTHER COUNTRIES." EUR+WWI ITALY INDUS NAT/G ACT/RES REGION GP/REL EFFICIENCY EQUILIB PRODUC WEALTH. PAGE 144 H2884 — ECO/UNDEV PLAN ECO/TAC CONTROL

S67
STRAFFORD P.,"FRENCH ELECTIONS." FRANCE NAT/G CHIEF LEGIS BAL/PWR ECO/TAC PARL/PROC PARTIC ATTIT 20. PAGE 150 H2993 — POL/PAR SOCISM CENTRAL MARXISM

S67
TAYLOR P.B. JR.,"PROGRESS IN VENEZUELA." L/A+17C VENEZUELA AGRI INDUS LG/CO NAT/G SML/CO CHOOSE ...POLICY 20. PAGE 153 H3057 — ECO/UNDEV ECO/TAC POL/PAR ORD/FREE

S67
THEROUX P.,"HATING THE ASIANS." TANZANIA UGANDA CONSTN INDUS NAT/G POL/PAR WORKER ECO/TAC HABITAT LOVE...POLICY GEOG 20 MIGRATION. PAGE 154 H3069 — AFR RACE/REL SOVEREIGN ATTIT

S67
VINCENT S.,"SHOULD BIAFRA SURVIVE?" NIGERIA ECO/UNDEV CHIEF FORCES ECO/TAC GP/REL DISCRIM PEACE ORD/FREE SOC/INTEG 20 BIAFRA IBO. PAGE 163 H3256 — AFR REV REGION NAT/G

S67
VON LAUE T.H.,"WESTERNIZATION, REVOLUTION AND THE SEARCH FOR A BASIS OF AUTHORITY - RUSSIA IN 1917." USSR ELITES INTELL ECO/UNDEV NAT/G WORKER ECO/TAC TAX ADMIN LEAD AUTHORIT 20 LENIN/VI. PAGE 164 H3274 — MARXISM REV COM DOMIN

S68
BOSSCHERE G D.E.,"A L'EST DU NOUVEAU." CZECHOSLVK HUNGARY POLAND ROMANIA YUGOSLAVIA AGRI CREATE ECO/TAC COERCE GP/REL ATTIT MARXISM SOCISM 20. PAGE 19 H0382 — ORD/FREE COM NAT/G DIPLOM

S68
CHAPMAN A.R.,"THE CIVIL WAR IN NIGERIA." AFR NIGERIA NAT/G PLAN ECO/TAC EDU/PROP COERCE WAR GOV/REL INGP/REL ORD/FREE PWR WEALTH SOC/INTEG 20 BIAFRA. PAGE 29 H0579 — REV RACE/REL

S68
DOUGLAS-HOME C.,"A MISTAKEN POLICY IN ADEN." YEMEN CULTURE ECO/UNDEV INDUS FORCES WORKER DIPLOM ECO/TAC CONTROL 20 ADEN. PAGE 42 H0842 — SOVEREIGN COLONIAL POLICY REGION

S68
GUZZARDI W.,"THE DECLINE OF THE STERLING CLUB." UK WOR+45 NAT/G PLAN DIPLOM INT/TRADE AGREE CONSEN EQUILIB SOVEREIGN...POLICY NEW/IDEA 20 COMMONWLTH GOLD/STAND. PAGE 63 H1259 — FINAN ECO/TAC WEALTH NAT/COMP

S68
MILLAR T.B.,"THE COMMONWEALTH AND THE UN." UK DIPLOM TARIFFS AGREE COLONIAL CONTROL SOVEREIGN WEALTH...GP/COMP GOV/COMP 20 CMN/WLTH UN. PAGE 111 H2210 — INT/ORG POLICY TREND ECO/TAC

S68
VERAX,"L'EUROPE ET LA FRANCE SUR LA SELLETTE." FRANCE UK NAT/G CHIEF DIPLOM EDU/PROP GP/REL 20 EEC DEGAULLE/C. PAGE 162 H3242 — INT/TRADE INT/ORG POLICY ECO/TAC

B76
SMITH A.,THE WEALTH OF NATIONS. UK STRUCT WORKER DIPLOM ECO/TAC OPTIMAL DRIVE PERSON ORD/FREE ...OLD/LIB GEN/LAWS 17/18. PAGE 145 H2905 — WEALTH PRODUC INDUS LAISSEZ

B84
ENGELS F.,THE ORIGIN OF THE FAMILY, PRIVATE PROPERTY, AND THE STATE (TRANS. BY E. UNTERMANN). UNIV ELITES SOCIETY CAP/ISM ECO/TAC MARRIAGE ORD/FREE POPULISM...MARXIST SOC ENGELS. PAGE 46 H0926 — FAM OWN WEALTH SOCISM

B85
TAINE H.A.,THE FRENCH REVOLUTION (3 VOLS.) (TRANS. BY J. DURAND). FRANCE MOD/EUR SOCIETY STRATA POL/PAR ECO/TAC DOMIN EDU/PROP GP/REL PWR ...GOV/COMP IDEA/COMP 18. PAGE 152 H3036 — REV NAT/G EX/STRUC LEAD

B91
MILL J.S.,SOCIALISM (1859). MOD/EUR AGRI INDUS NAT/G REV INCOME PRODUC ORD/FREE POPULISM SOCISM ...GOV/COMP METH/COMP 19. PAGE 110 H2209 — WEALTH SOCIALIST ECO/TAC OWN

L95
BELSHAW C.S.,"IN SEARCH OF WEALTH; STUDY OF EMERGENCE OF COMMERCIAL OPERA TIONS IN MELANESIAN SOCIETY OF SOUTHEASTERN PAPUA." S/ASIA CULTURE KIN ECO/TAC DEMAND INCOME 20 MELANESIA PAPUA. PAGE 14 H0272 — INT/TRADE ECO/UNDEV METH/COMP SOCIETY

B96
MARX K.,REVOLUTION AND COUNTER-REVOLUTION. GERMANY CONSTN ELITES INDUS NAT/G DIPLOM ECO/TAC WEALTH. PAGE 104 H2083 — MARXIST REV PWR STRATA

B96
SCHMOLLER G.,THE MERCANTILE SYSTEM AND ITS HISTORICAL SIGNIFICANCE: ILLUSTRATED CHIEFLY FROM PRUSSIAN HISTORY (TRANS.). PRUSSIA CULTURE INDUS KIN MUNIC NAT/G PROVS OP/RES ECO/TAC INT/TRADE SUPEGO PWR WEALTH 19 MERCANTLST. PAGE 139 H2790 — GEN/METH INGP/REL CONCPT

ECO/UNDEV....ECONOMIC SYSTEM IN DEVELOPING COUNTRIES

N
BROCKWAY A.F.,AFRICAN SOCIALISM. EUR+WWI GHANA ISLAM UAR ECO/UNDEV CAP/ISM INT/TRADE COLONIAL COERCE GOV/REL DISCRIM 20 NEGRO NKRUMAH/K NASSER/G. PAGE 21 H0423 — AFR SOCISM MARXISM

N
CONOVER H.F.,MADAGASCAR: A SELECTED LIST OF REFERENCES. MADAGASCAR STRUCT ECO/UNDEV NAT/G ADMIN ...SOC 19/20. PAGE 32 H0639 — BIBLIOG/A SOCIETY CULTURE COLONIAL

N
SCHADERA I.,SELECT BIBLIOGRAPHY OF SOUTH AFRICAN NATIVE LIFE AND PROBLEMS. SOUTH/AFR LAW CULTURE ECO/UNDEV COLONIAL PARTIC...POLICY LING 20. PAGE 138 H2768 — BIBLIOG/A SOC AFR STRUCT

N
UNIVERSITY OF FLORIDA LIBRARY,DOORS TO LATIN AMERICA; RECENT BOOKS AND PAMPHLETS. CONSTN CULTURE SOCIETY ECO/UNDEV COLONIAL LEAD GOV/REL NAT/LISM ATTIT...HUM SOC 20. PAGE 159 H3170 — BIBLIOG/A L/A+17C DIPLOM NAT/G

N
BULLETIN ANALYTIQUE DE DOCUMENTATION POLITIQUE, ECONOMIQUE, ET SOCIAL CONTEMPORAIRE. FRANCE WOR+45 SOCIETY ECO/DEV ECO/UNDEV INT/ORG LOC/G PROB/SOLV FOR/AID LEAD REGION SOC. PAGE 1 H0002 — BIBLIOG/A DIPLOM NAT/COMP NAT/G

N
MIDDLE EAST JOURNAL. CULTURE SECT DIPLOM LEAD GOV/REL ATTIT...POLICY PHIL/SCI SOC LING BIOG 20. PAGE 1 H0007 — BIBLIOG ISLAM NAT/G ECO/UNDEV

N
NEUE POLITISCHE LITERATUR. AFR ASIA EUR+WWI GERMANY RUSSIA SOCIETY ECO/DEV ECO/UNDEV PLAN PROB/SOLV LEAD MARXISM...PHIL/SCI CONCPT 20. PAGE 1 H0008 — BIBLIOG DIPLOM COM NAT/G

N
HANDBOOK OF LATIN AMERICAN STUDIES. LAW CULTURE ECO/UNDEV POL/PAR ADMIN LEAD...SOC 20. PAGE 1 H0016 — BIBLIOG/A L/A+17C NAT/G DIPLOM

N
SEMINAR: THE MONTHLY SYMPOSIUM. INDIA ACT/RES TEC/DEV DIPLOM ATTIT...BIBLIOG 20. PAGE 1 H0022 — NAT/G ECO/UNDEV SOVEREIGN POLICY

N
THE MIDDLE EAST AND NORTH AFRICA. AFR ISLAM CULTURE ECO/UNDEV AGRI NAT/G TEC/DEV FOR/AID INT/TRADE EDU/PROP...CHARTS 20. PAGE 2 H0026 — INDEX INDUS FINAN STAT

N
AFRICAN BIBLIOGRAPHIC CENTER,A CURRENT BIBLIOGRAPHY ON AFRICAN AFFAIRS. LAW CULTURE ECO/UNDEV LABOR SECT DIPLOM FOR/AID COLONIAL NAT/LISM...LING 20. PAGE 4 H0075 — BIBLIOG/A AFR NAT/G REGION

N
ASIA FOUNDATION,LIBRARY NOTES. LAW CONSTN CULTURE SOCIETY ECO/UNDEV INT/ORG NAT/G COLONIAL LEAD REGION NAT/LISM ATTIT 20 UN. PAGE 9 H0176 — BIBLIOG/A ASIA S/ASIA DIPLOM

N
CARIBBEAN COMMISSION,CURRENT CARIBBEAN BIBLIOGRAPHY. FRANCE NETHERLAND UK CULTURE ECO/UNDEV PRESS LEAD ATTIT...GEOG SOC 20. PAGE 26 H0530
BIBLIOG NAT/G L/A+17C DIPLOM

N
CORNELL UNIVERSITY LIBRARY,SOUTHEAST ASIA ACCESSIONS LIST. LAW SOCIETY STRUCT ECO/UNDEV POL/PAR TEC/DEV DIPLOM LEAD REGION. PAGE 34 H0671
BIBLIOG S/ASIA NAT/G CULTURE

N
HOOVER INSTITUTION,UNITED STATES AND CANADIAN PUBLICATIONS ON AFRICA. CULTURE ECO/UNDEV AGRI TEC/DEV EDU/PROP COLONIAL RACE/REL NAT/LISM ATTIT HEALTH...SOC SOC/WK 20. PAGE 73 H1464
BIBLIOG DIPLOM NAT/G AFR

N
INSTITUTE OF HISPANIC STUDIES,HISPANIC AMERICAN REPORT. EUR+WWI SPAIN LAW CONSTN ECO/UNDEV POL/PAR EX/STRUC LEGIS LEAD...HUM SOC 20. PAGE 77 H1538
BIBLIOG/A L/A+17C NAT/G DIPLOM

N
KYRIAK T.E.,ASIAN DEVELOPMENTS: A BIBLIOGRAPHY. INDONESIA KOREA/N VIETNAM/N CULTURE SOCIETY ECO/UNDEV NAT/G DIPLOM...SOC TREND 20 MONGOLIA. PAGE 90 H1788
BIBLIOG/A ALL/IDEOS S/ASIA ASIA

N
NORTHWESTERN UNIVERSITY LIB,JOINT ACQUISITIONS LIST OF AFRICANA. AFR SOCIETY STRUCT EDU/PROP COLONIAL GP/REL RACE/REL NAT/LISM SOVEREIGN...SOC 20. PAGE 119 H2377
BIBLIOG CULTURE ECO/UNDEV INDUS

N
UNIVERSITY OF CALIFORNIA,STATISTICAL ABSTRACT OF LATIN AMERICA. L/A+17C DIPLOM 20. PAGE 158 H3169
BIBLIOG NAT/G ECO/UNDEV STAT

N
US CONSOLATE GENERAL HONG KONG,REVIEW OF THE HONG KONG CHINESE PRESS. ECO/UNDEV LOC/G NAT/G PLAN DIPLOM EDU/PROP LEAD GP/REL MARXISM...POLICY INDEX 20. PAGE 159 H3178
BIBLIOG/A ASIA PRESS ATTIT

N
US CONSULATE GENERAL HONG KONG,CURRENT BACKGROUND. CHINA/COM ECO/UNDEV LOC/G NAT/G PLAN DIPLOM EDU/PROP LEAD REV ATTIT...POLICY INDEX 20. PAGE 159 H3179
BIBLIOG/A MARXIST ASIA PRESS

N
US CONSULATE GENERAL HONG KONG,EXTRACTS FROM CHINA MAINLAND MAGAZINES. ASIA CHINA/COM ECO/UNDEV NAT/G CHIEF LEAD ATTIT...MARXIST INDEX 20. PAGE 159 H3180
BIBLIOG MARXISM PRESS

N
US CONSULATE GENERAL HONG KONG,SURVEY OF CHINA MAINLAND PRESS. CHINA/COM ECO/UNDEV LOC/G NAT/G PLAN DIPLOM EDU/PROP LEAD REV ATTIT...POLICY INDEX 20. PAGE 159 H3181
BIBLIOG/A MARXIST ASIA PRESS

N
US CONSULATE GENERAL HONG KONG,US CONSULATE GENERAL, HONG KONG, PRESS SUMMARIES. CHINA/COM ECO/UNDEV LOC/G NAT/G PLAN DIPLOM EDU/PROP LEAD REV ATTIT...POLICY INDEX 20. PAGE 159 H3182
BIBLIOG/A MARXIST ASIA PRESS

N
US LIBRARY OF CONGRESS,ACCESSIONS LIST - INDIA. INDIA CULTURE AGRI LOC/G POL/PAR PLAN PROB/SOLV TEC/DEV DIPLOM EDU/PROP LEAD GP/REL ATTIT 20. PAGE 160 H3199
BIBLIOG S/ASIA ECO/UNDEV NAT/G

N
US LIBRARY OF CONGRESS,ACCESSIONS LIST -- ISRAEL. ISRAEL CULTURE ECO/UNDEV POL/PAR PLAN PROB/SOLV TEC/DEV DIPLOM EDU/PROP LEAD WAR ATTIT 20 JEWS. PAGE 160 H3200
BIBLIOG ISLAM NAT/G GP/REL

N
US LIBRARY OF CONGRESS,SOUTHERN ASIA ACCESSIONS LIST. BURMA CEYLON INDIA NEPAL PAKISTAN S/ASIA THAILAND AGRI INDUS SCHOOL WORKER...ART/METH GEOG HEAL PHIL/SCI LING 20. PAGE 160 H3201
BIBLIOG/A SOCIETY CULTURE ECO/UNDEV

NCO
CARRINGTON C.E.,THE COMMONWEALTH IN AFRICA (PAMPHLET). UK STRUCT NAT/G COLONIAL REPRESENT GOV/REL RACE/REL NAT/LISM...MAJORIT 20 EEC NEGRO COLD/WAR. PAGE 27 H0540
ECO/UNDEV AFR DIPLOM PLAN

B00
VOLPICELLI Z.,RUSSIA ON THE PACIFIC AND THE SIBERIAN RAILWAY. MOD/EUR ECO/UNDEV INT/ORG FORCES PLAN DOMIN COLONIAL ROUTINE ATTIT ALL/VALS...OBS HIST/WRIT TIME/SEQ TREND CON/ANAL AUD/VIS CHARTS 18/19. PAGE 163 H3261
NAT/G ACT/RES RUSSIA

B05
PHILIPPINE ISLANDS BUREAU SCI,ETHNOLOGICAL SURVEY: THE BONTOC IGOROT. ECO/UNDEV AGRI FAM MARRIAGE HEALTH WEALTH...LING OBS AUD/VIS CHARTS WORSHIP 20 LUZON BONTOC. PAGE 125 H2500
CULTURE INGP/REL KIN STRUCT

B16
CALVERT A.F.,SOUTHWEST AFRICA 1884-1914 (2ND ED.). GERMANY EXTR/IND NAT/G FORCES...GEOG AUD/VIS CHARTS 19/20 RESOURCE/N AFRICA/SW. PAGE 25 H0508
COLONIAL ECO/UNDEV AFR

N19
BRIMMELL G.H.,COMMUNISM IN SOUTHEAST ASIA (PAMPHLET). BURMA CAMBODIA COM INDIA INDONESIA LAOS MOD/EUR NAT/G POL/PAR FORCES CAP/ISM CONTROL WEALTH ...MYTH 20. PAGE 21 H0420
MARXISM S/ASIA REV ECO/UNDEV

N19
GORWALA A.D.,THE ADMINISTRATIVE JUNGLE (PAMPHLET). INDIA NAT/G LEGIS ECO/TAC CONTROL GOV/REL ...METH/COMP 20. PAGE 59 H1183
ADMIN POLICY PLAN ECO/UNDEV

N19
HANNA A.J.,EUROPEAN RULE IN AFRICA (PAMPHLET). BELGIUM FRANCE MOD/EUR UK WOR+45 WOR-45 ECO/UNDEV NAT/G PARTIC SOVEREIGN...NAT/COMP 19/20. PAGE 66 H1314
DIPLOM COLONIAL AFR NAT/LISM

N19
PROVISIONS SECTION OAU,ORGANIZATION OF AFRICAN UNITY: BASIC DOCUMENTS AND RESOLUTIONS (PAMPHLET). AFR CULTURE ECO/UNDEV DIPLOM ECO/TAC EDU/PROP COLONIAL ARMS/CONT NUC/PWR RACE/REL DISCRIM NAT/LISM 20 UN OAU. PAGE 128 H2564
CONSTN EX/STRUC SOVEREIGN INT/ORG

N19
SALKEVER L.R.,SUB-SAHARA AFRICA (PAMPHLET). AFR USSR EXTR/IND NAT/G SCHOOL DIPLOM COLONIAL WEALTH ...GEOG CHARTS 16/20. PAGE 137 H2742
ECO/UNDEV TEC/DEV TASK INT/TRADE

N19
SENGHOR L.S.,AFRICAN SOCIALISM (PAMPHLET). AFR FRANCE MALI USSR ELITES ECO/UNDEV NAT/G DIPLOM DOMIN EDU/PROP ATTIT 20 NEGRO. PAGE 141 H2827
SOCISM MARXISM ORD/FREE NAT/LISM

N19
STEUBER F.A.,THE CONTRIBUTION OF SWITZERLAND TO THE ECONOMIC AND SOCIAL DEVELOPMENT OF LOW-INCOME COUNTRIES (PAMPHLET). SWITZERLND FINAN NAT/G VOL/ASSN INT/TRADE DRIVE...CHARTS 20. PAGE 149 H2982
FOR/AID ECO/UNDEV PLAN DIPLOM

S21
MALINOWSKI B.,"THE PRIMITIVE ECONOMICS OF THE TROBRIAND ISLANDERS" (BMR)" CULTURE SOCIETY NAT/G CHIEF LEAD OWN...SOC MYTH WORSHIP 20 NEW/GUINEA TROBRIAND RESOURCE/N. PAGE 101 H2029
ECO/UNDEV AGRI PRODUC STRUCT

B26
MCPHEE A.,THE ECONOMIC REVOLUTION IN BRITISH WEST AFRICA. AFR UK CULTURE DIST/IND FINAN INDUS PLAN GP/REL RACE/REL 20 AFRICA/W. PAGE 107 H2148
ECO/UNDEV INT/TRADE COLONIAL GEOG

B28
YANG KUNG-SUN,THE BOOK OF LORD SHANG. LAW ECO/UNDEV LOC/G NAT/G NEIGH PLAN ECO/TAC LEGIT ATTIT SKILL ...CONCPT CON/ANAL WORK TOT/POP. PAGE 172 H3434
ASIA JURID

B29
PRATT I.A.,MODERN EGYPT: A LIST OF REFERENCES TO MATERIAL IN THE NEW YORK PUBLIC LIBRARY. UAR ECO/UNDEV...GEOG JURID SOC LING 20. PAGE 128 H2555
BIBLIOG ISLAM DIPLOM NAT/G

B29
ROBERTS S.H.,HISTORY OF FRENCH COLONIAL POLICY. AFR ASIA L/A+17C S/ASIA CULTURE ECO/DEV ECO/UNDEV FINAN NAT/G PLAN ECO/TAC DOMIN ROUTINE SOVEREIGN...OBS HIST/WRIT TREND CHARTS VAL/FREE 19/20. PAGE 132 H2642
INT/ORG ACT/RES FRANCE COLONIAL

B30
SMUTS J.C.,AFRICA AND SOME WORLD PROBLEMS. RHODESIA SOUTH/AFR CULTURE ECO/UNDEV INDUS INT/ORG SECT PROB/SOLV REGION GOV/REL DISCRIM ATTIT 19/20 LEAGUE/NAT LIVNGSTN/D NEGRO. PAGE 146 H2921
LEGIS AFR COLONIAL RACE/REL

B31
KIRKPATRICK F.A.,A HISTORY OF THE ARGENTINE REPUBLIC. SPAIN UK CONSTN SOCIETY ECO/UNDEV EX/STRUC DIPLOM FOR/AID LEAD WAR ATTIT...BIOG CHARTS 16/20 ARGEN SAN/MARTIN. PAGE 86 H1724
NAT/G L/A+17C COLONIAL

B33
TANNENBAUM F.,PEACE BY REVOLUTION. ECO/UNDEV AGRI SECT WORKER DIPLOM EDU/PROP DISCRIM OWN WEALTH POPULISM 17/20 MEXIC/AMER INDIAN/AM. PAGE 152 H3043
CULTURE COLONIAL RACE/REL REV

B39
AKIGA,AKIGA'S STORY: THE TIV TRIBE AS SEEN BY ONE OF ITS MEMBERS. NIGERIA LAW STRUCT ECO/UNDEV FAM LEAD GP/REL MARRIAGE...LING WORSHIP 20. PAGE 4 H0089
KIN SECT SOC CULTURE

B39
FIRTH R.,PRIMITIVE POLYNESIAN ECONOMY. SOCIETY DIST/IND SECT CHIEF CAP/ISM PRODUC WEALTH...SOC OBS METH WORSHIP 20 POLYNESIA. PAGE 50 H1007
ECO/UNDEV CULTURE AGRI ECO/TAC

B39
FURNIVALL J.S.,NETHERLANDS INDIA. INDIA NETHERLAND CULTURE INDUS NAT/G DIPLOM ADMIN WEALTH...POLICY CHARTS 17/20. PAGE 54 H1081
COLONIAL ECO/UNDEV SOVEREIGN PLURISM

B39
VAN BILJON F.J.,STATE INTERFERENCE IN SOUTH AFRICA. SOUTH/AFR ECO/UNDEV AGRI INDUS WORKER RATION WEALTH ...JURID 20. PAGE 161 H3225
ECO/TAC POLICY INT/TRADE NAT/G

B40
BROWN A.D.,PANAMA CANAL AND PANAMA CANAL ZONE: A SELECTED LIST OF REFERENCES. PANAMA NAT/G SCHOOL DIPLOM HEALTH...GEOG SOC 20 CANAL/ZONE. PAGE 22 H0436 — BIBLIOG/A ECO/UNDEV

B40
HERSKOVITS M.J.,THE ECONOMIC LIFE OF PRIMITIVE PEOPLES. INDUS OP/RES PLAN PROB/SOLV...BIBLIOG METH 20. PAGE 70 H1407 — CULTURE ECO/TAC ECO/UNDEV PRODUC

B40
MEEK C.K.,EUROPE AND WEST AFRICA. AFR EUR+WWI EXTR/IND DIPLOM INT/TRADE EDU/PROP GP/REL...SOC 20. PAGE 108 H2158 — CULTURE TEC/DEV ECO/UNDEV COLONIAL

B41
GRISMER R.,A NEW BIBLIOGRAPHY OF THE LITERATURES OF SPAIN AND SPANISH AMERICA. CHRIST-17C MOD/EUR PRE/AMER SPAIN CULTURE DIPLOM EDU/PROP...ART/METH GEOG HUM PHIL/SCI 20. PAGE 61 H1229 — BIBLIOG LAW NAT/G ECO/UNDEV

B41
KEESING F.M.,THE SOUTH SEAS IN THE MODERN WORLD. INDONESIA STRUCT FAM SECT EDU/PROP LEAD INCOME WEALTH...HEAL SOC 20. PAGE 84 H1678 — CULTURE ECO/UNDEV GOV/COMP DIPLOM

B42
CONOVER H.F.,FRENCH COLONIES IN AFRICA: A LIST OF REFERENCES. ALGERIA FRANCE MOROCCO SOMALIA SUDAN CULTURE AGRI LOC/G SECT FORCES DIPLOM INT/TRADE NAT/LISM HEALTH...CON/ANAL 20. PAGE 32 H0641 — BIBLIOG AFR ECO/UNDEV COLONIAL

B42
CONOVER H.F.,THE NETHERLANDS EAST INDIES: A SELECTED LIST OF REFERENCES. ECO/UNDEV AGRI EXTR/IND LABOR SCHOOL SECT INT/TRADE COLONIAL HEALTH...GEOG 19/20. PAGE 32 H0642 — BIBLIOG S/ASIA CULTURE

B42
CONOVER H.F.,NEW ZEALAND: A SELECTED LIST OF REFERENCES (PAMPHLET). NEW/ZEALND ECO/UNDEV AGRI INDUS LABOR NAT/G SCHOOL FORCES DIPLOM COLONIAL WAR ...HUM 20. PAGE 32 H0643 — BIBLIOG/A S/ASIA CULTURE

B42
JOSHI P.S.,THE TYRANNY OF COLOUR. INDIA SOUTH/AFR UK ECO/UNDEV NAT/G POL/PAR DIPLOM ECO/TAC WAR ...POLICY 19/20. PAGE 82 H1637 — COLONIAL DISCRIM RACE/REL

B43
BROWN A.D.,BRITISH POSSESSIONS IN THE CARIBBEAN AREA: A SELECTED LIST OF REFERENCES. UK NAT/G DIPLOM...GEOG 20 CARIBBEAN. PAGE 22 H0437 — BIBLIOG COLONIAL ECO/UNDEV L/A+17C

B43
BROWN A.D.,GREECE: SELECTED LIST OF REFERENCES. GREECE ECO/UNDEV AGRI FINAN INDUS LABOR SECT TEC/DEV INT/TRADE LEAD...SOC 20. PAGE 22 H0438 — BIBLIOG/A WAR DIPLOM NAT/G

B43
LEWIN E.,ROYAL EMPIRE SOCIETY BIBLIOGRAPHIES NO. 9: SUB-SAHARA AFRICA. ECO/UNDEV TEC/DEV DIPLOM ADMIN COLONIAL LEAD 20. PAGE 96 H1908 — BIBLIOG AFR NAT/G SOCIETY

B44
FULLER G.H.,TURKEY: A SELECTED LIST OF REFERENCES. ISLAM TURKEY CULTURE ECO/UNDEV AGRI DIPLOM NAT/LISM CONSERVE...GEOG HUM INT/LAW SOC 7/20 MAPS. PAGE 54 H1075 — BIBLIOG/A ALL/VALS

B44
SHELBY C.,LATIN AMERICAN PERIODICALS CURRENTLY RECEIVED IN THE LIBRARY OF CONGRESS AND IN LIBRARY OF DEPARTMENT OF AGRICULTURE. SOCIETY AGRI INDUS LABOR POL/PAR INT/TRADE...GEOG SOC 20. PAGE 143 H2856 — BIBLIOG ECO/UNDEV CULTURE L/A+17C

L44
HUXLEY J.,"THE FUTURE OF THE COLONIES." AFR SOCIETY NAT/G PLAN DOMIN COERCE ATTIT DRIVE ORD/FREE PWR WEALTH...TIME/SEQ TREND AUD/VIS CHARTS 20. PAGE 76 H1511 — ECO/UNDEV FUT COLONIAL

N45
INDIA QUARTERLY, A JOURNAL OF INTERNATIONAL AFFAIRS. INDIA LAW CONSTN ECO/UNDEV INT/ORG POL/PAR COLONIAL LEAD PARL/PROC WAR ATTIT...SOC 20 CMN/WLTH. PAGE 2 H0033 — BIBLIOG/A S/ASIA DIPLOM NAT/G

B45
CLAGETT H.L.,COMMUNIST CHINA: RUTHLESS ENEMY OR PAPER TIGER (PAMPHLET). CHINA/COM ECO/UNDEV AGRI INDUS NAT/G POL/PAR ECO/TAC INT/TRADE GUERRILLA ATTIT...CHARTS NAT/COMP ORG/CHARTS 20. PAGE 30 H0602 — BIBLIOG/A MARXISM DIPLOM COERCE

B45
LASKER B.,ASIA ON THE MOVE. ASIA BURMA S/ASIA THAILAND USSR ECO/UNDEV FAM KIN WAR NAT/LISM ATTIT ...GEOG CENSUS TREND AUSTRAL 20. PAGE 91 H1826 — CULTURE RIGID/FLEX

B45
MCBRYDE F.W.,CULTURAL AND HISTORICAL GEOGRAPHY OF SOUTHWEST GUATEMALA. GUATEMALA AGRI KIN PERSON ...GEOG AUD/VIS CHARTS 20. PAGE 106 H2123 — HABITAT ISOLAT CULTURE ECO/UNDEV

B45
PERAZA SARAUSA F.,BIBLIOGRAFIAS CUBANAS. CUBA CULTURE ECO/UNDEV AGRI EDU/PROP PRESS CIVMIL/REL ...POLICY GEOG PHIL/SCI BIOG 19/20. PAGE 125 H2489 — BIBLIOG/A L/A+17C NAT/G DIPLOM

S46
SILBERNER E.,"THE PROBLEM OF WAR IN NINETEENTH CENTURY ECONOMIC THOUGHT." EUR+WWI MOD/EUR UNIV LAW ECO/DEV ECO/UNDEV FINAN INDUS MARKET INT/ORG NAT/G CONSULT FORCES...CONCPT GEN/LAWS GEN/METH 19. PAGE 144 H2875 — ATTIT ECO/TAC WAR

B47
GITLOW A.L.,ECONOMICS OF THE MOUNT HAGEN TRIBES, NEW GUINEA. S/ASIA STRUCT AGRI FAM...GEOG MYTH 20 NEW/GUINEA. PAGE 57 H1137 — HABITAT ECO/UNDEV CULTURE KIN

B48
GUIDE TO THE RECORDS IN THE NATIONAL ARCHIVES. ECO/UNDEV ADMIN COLONIAL 16/20. PAGE 2 H0034 — BIBLIOG NAT/G L/A+17C DIPLOM

B48
EDUARDO O.D.C.,THE NEGRO IN NORTHERN BRAZIL: A STUDY IN ACCULTURATION. BRAZIL ECO/UNDEV FAM SECT PAY REGION HABITAT CATHISM MYSTISM...GEOG OBS SOC/INTEG WORSHIP 20 NEGRO MARANHAO. PAGE 44 H0890 — CULTURE ADJUST GP/REL

B48
MAUGHAM R.,NORTH AFRICAN NOTEBOOK. ALGERIA ISLAM LIBYA MOROCCO STRUCT ECO/UNDEV COLONIAL...SOC OBS AUD/VIS NAT/COMP WORSHIP 20 TUNIS. PAGE 105 H2102 — SOCIETY RECORD NAT/LISM

B48
MINISTERE FINANCES ET ECO,BULLETIN BIBLIOGRAPHIQUE. AFR EUR+WWI FRANCE CULTURE STRUCT FINAN NAT/G ACT/RES INT/TRADE ADMIN REGION PRODUC STAT. PAGE 111 H2224 — BIBLIOG/A ECO/UNDEV TEC/DEV COLONIAL

B48
PELCOVITS N.A.,OLD CHINA HANDS AND THE FOREIGN OFFICE. ASIA BURMA UK ECO/UNDEV NAT/G ECO/TAC FOR/AID TARIFFS DOMIN COLONIAL GOV/REL SOVEREIGN 19 HONG/KONG TREATY. PAGE 124 H2483 — INT/TRADE ATTIT DIPLOM

B49
BORBA DE MORAES R.,MANUAL BIBLIOGRAFICO DE ESTUDOS BRASILEIROS. BRAZIL DIPLOM ADMIN LEAD...SOC 20. PAGE 19 H0374 — BIBLIOG L/A+17C NAT/G ECO/UNDEV

S49
MACKENZIE R.D.,"ECOLOGY, HUMAN." UNIV CULTURE ECO/DEV ECO/UNDEV ATTIT...POLICY GEOG PSY CONCPT METH/CNCPT CONT/OBS TREND GEN/LAWS. PAGE 100 H2001 — SOCIETY BIO/SOC

B50
CORNELL U DEPT ASIAN STUDIES,SOUTHEAST ASIA PROGRAM DATA PAPER. BURMA CAMBODIA INDONESIA MALAYSIA VIETNAM SOCIETY STRUCT NAT/G SECT DIPLOM FOR/AID PWR WEALTH...SOC 20. PAGE 33 H0670 — BIBLIOG/A CULTURE S/ASIA ECO/UNDEV

B50
HARLEY G.W.,MASKS AS AGENTS OF SOCIAL CONTROL IN NORTHEAST LIBERIA. AFR LIBERIA LAW CULTURE ADJUST CONSEN MORAL...GEOG SOC WORSHIP 20. PAGE 66 H1332 — CONTROL ECO/UNDEV SECT CHIEF

B50
HOBBS C.C.,INDOCHINA, A BIBLIOGRAPHY OF THE LAND AND PEOPLE. VIETNAM CULTURE AGRI INDUS NAT/G SECT ...ART/METH GEOG SOC LING 20. PAGE 72 H1436 — BIBLIOG/A S/ASIA COLONIAL ECO/UNDEV

B50
JONES H.D.,KOREA, AN ANNOTATED BIBLIOGRAPHY OF PUBLICATIONS IN WESTERN LANGUAGES. KOREA CULTURE MUNIC SECT FORCES DIPLOM HEALTH WEALTH...ART/METH GEOG SOC LING 20. PAGE 82 H1632 — BIBLIOG/A ASIA NAT/G ECO/UNDEV

B50
ORTON W.A.,THE ECONOMIC ROLE OF THE STATE. INTELL ECO/UNDEV PLAN CONTROL PWR SOVEREIGN...POLICY 17/20. PAGE 122 H2431 — ECO/DEV NAT/G ECO/TAC ORD/FREE

B50
SCHUMPETER J.A.,CAPITALISM, SOCIALISM, AND DEMOCRACY (3RD ED.). USA-45 USSR WOR+45 WOR-45 INTELL ECO/DEV ECO/UNDEV ECO/TAC WAR PRODUC ORD/FREE...MGT SOC 20 MARX/KARL. PAGE 140 H2804 — SOCIALIST CAP/ISM MARXISM IDEA/COMP

B50
TENG S.,AN ANNOTATED BIBLIOGRAPHY OF SELECTED CHINESE REFERENCE WORKS (REV. ED.). CULTURE ECO/UNDEV LEAD MARXISM...LING INDEX 3/20. PAGE 153 H3062 — BIBLIOG/A ASIA NAT/G

B50
WILBUR C.M.,CHINESE SOURCES ON THE HISTORY OF THE CHINESE COMMUNIST MOVEMENT (PAMPHLET). CHINA/COM ECO/UNDEV PROVS FORCES WAR...PHIL/SCI 20. PAGE 168 H3360 — BIBLIOG/A MARXISM REV NAT/G

B51
BERNATZIK H.A.,THE SPIRITS OF THE YELLOW LEAVES. BURMA LAOS S/ASIA THAILAND VIETNAM SOCIETY AGRI COLONIAL LEISURE GP/REL PERS/REL ISOLAT AGE HABITAT SEX WORSHIP 20. PAGE 16 H0310 — SOC KIN ECO/UNDEV CULTURE

B51
CHRISTENSEN A.N.,THE EVOLUTION OF LATIN AMERICAN — NAT/G

GOVERNMENT: A BOOK OF READINGS. ECO/UNDEV INDUS LOC/G POL/PAR EX/STRUC LEGIS FOR/AID CT/SYS ...SOC/WK 20 SOUTH/AMER. PAGE 30 H0599
CONSTN DIPLOM L/A+17C

B51
INTERNATIONAL AFRICAN INST,ETHNOGRAPHIC SURVEY OF AFRICA: WEST CENTRAL AFRICA (VOLS. I-III, 1951-1953). AFR RHODESIA CULTURE ECO/UNDEV HEREDITY ...GEOG SOC CHARTS BIBLIOG WORSHIP 20 CONGO/LEOP. PAGE 77 H1543
STRUCT KIN INGP/REL HABITAT

B51
YOUNG T.C.,NEAR EASTERN CULTURE AND SOCIETY. ISLAM ECO/UNDEV SECT WRITING ATTIT HABITAT ORD/FREE 20. PAGE 172 H3439
CULTURE STRUCT REGION DIPLOM

B52
FORDE L.D.,HABITAT, ECONOMY AND SOCIETY. AFR L/A+17C S/ASIA STRUCT AGRI INGP/REL...GEOG OBS BIBLIOG 20. PAGE 52 H1037
SOC HABITAT CULTURE ECO/UNDEV

B52
INTERNATIONAL AFRICAN INST,ETHNOGRAPHIC SURVEY OF AFRICA: SOUTHERN AFRICA (VOLS. I-III, 1952-1954). AFR SOUTH/AFR CULTURE ECO/UNDEV GOV/REL HEREDITY ...GEOG SOC CHARTS BIBLIOG WORSHIP 20. PAGE 77 H1544
STRUCT KIN INGP/REL HABITAT

B52
ISAACS H.R.,AFRICA: NEW CRISES IN THE MAKING (PAMPHLET). EUR+WWI USA+45 ELITES ECO/UNDEV WAR DISCRIM NAT/LISM ATTIT...POLICY NEW/IDEA CHARTS GOV/COMP 20 NEGRO COLD/WAR. PAGE 78 H1570
COLONIAL AFR RACE/REL ORD/FREE

B52
SPICER E.H.,HUMAN PROBLEMS IN TECHNOLOGICAL CHANGE. ECO/UNDEV AGRI INDUS NAT/G ACT/RES LEAD GP/REL INGP/REL ROLE...INT METH 20 CASEBOOK. PAGE 147 H2947
TEC/DEV CULTURE STRUCT OP/RES

B52
TAX S.,HERITAGE OF CONQUEST. L/A+17C ECO/UNDEV LOC/G WEALTH...POLICY ANTHOL WORSHIP 20 MEXIC/AMER CENTRAL/AM. PAGE 153 H3052
PHIL/SCI CULTURE SOCIETY

B52
US LIBRARY OF CONGRESS,INTRODUCTION TO AFRICA; A SELECTIVE GUIDE TO BACKGROUND READING. ECO/UNDEV COLONIAL GP/REL...SOC 19/20. PAGE 160 H3208
BIBLIOG/A AFR CULTURE NAT/G

B53
DAVIDSON B.,THE NEW WEST AFRICA: PROBLEMS OF INDEPENDENCE. UK AGRI TEC/DEV DIPLOM GP/REL RACE/REL SOVEREIGN...ANTHOL 20 AFRICA/W. PAGE 37 H0744
AFR COLONIAL ECO/UNDEV NAT/G

B53
MEAD M.,CULTURAL PATTERNS AND TECHNICAL CHANGE. BURMA GREECE NIGERIA ECO/UNDEV AGRI INDUS SCHOOL SECT CREATE FEEDBACK HABITAT...PSY METH/COMP BIBLIOG 20 UN. PAGE 108 H2152
HEALTH TEC/DEV CULTURE ADJUST

B53
MIT CENTER INTERNATIONAL STU,BIBLIOGRAPHY OF THE ECONOMIC AND POLITICAL DEVELOPMENT OF INDONESIA. INDONESIA STRUCT NAT/G COLONIAL LEAD...STAT 20. PAGE 111 H2226
BIBLIOG ECO/UNDEV TEC/DEV S/ASIA

B53
SHIRATO I.,JAPANESE SOURCES ON THE HISTORY OF THE CHINESE COMMUNIST MOVEMENT (PAMPHLET). CHINA/COM USSR CONSTRUC NAT/G POL/PAR FORCES DIPLOM DOMIN EDU/PROP CONTROL WAR TOTALISM SOCISM 20. PAGE 143 H2863
BIBLIOG/A MARXISM ECO/UNDEV

B53
WAGLEY C.,AMAZON TOWN: A STUDY OF MAN IN THE TROPICS. BRAZIL L/A+17C STRATA STRUCT ECO/UNDEV AGRI EX/STRUC RACE/REL DISCRIM HABITAT WEALTH...OBS SOC/EXP 20. PAGE 164 H3285
SOC NEIGH CULTURE INGP/REL

L53
DEUTSCH K.W.,"THE GROWTH OF NATIONS: SOME RECURRENT PATTERNS OF POLITICAL AND SOCIAL INTEGRATION" (BMR)" UNIV CULTURE SOCIETY ECO/DEV ECO/UNDEV NAT/G CREATE GP/REL...CONCPT GEN/LAWS SOC/INTEG 11/20. PAGE 40 H0797
TREND NAT/LISM ORD/FREE

B54
BINANI G.D.,INDIA AT A GLANCE (REV. ED.). INDIA COM/IND FINAN INDUS LABOR PROVS SCHOOL PLAN DIPLOM INT/TRADE ADMIN...JURID 20. PAGE 17 H0335
INDEX CON/ANAL NAT/G ECO/UNDEV

B54
GIRALSO JARAMLLO G.,BIBLIOGRAFIA DE BIBLIOGRAFIAS COLOMBIANAS. L/A+17C ACADEM SECT CREATE EDU/PROP ...ART/METH GEOG LING TREND 20 COLOMB. PAGE 57 H1135
BIBLIOG/A CULTURE PHIL/SCI ECO/UNDEV

B54
LEWIS E.,MEDIEVAL POLITICAL IDEAS. LAW CULTURE SOCIETY ECO/UNDEV NAT/G SECT GOV/REL ATTIT ...BIBLIOG/A T 11/15. PAGE 96 H1913
CHRIST-17C IDEA/COMP INTELL CONCPT

B54
MOSK S.A.,INDUSTRIAL REVOLUTION IN MEXICO. MARKET LABOR CREATE CAP/ISM ADMIN ATTIT SOCISM...POLICY 20 MEXIC/AMER. PAGE 113 H2268
INDUS TEC/DEV ECO/UNDEV NAT/G

B54
US LIBRARY OF CONGRESS,RESEARCH AND INFORMATION ON AFRICA: CONTINUING SOURCES. ISLAM ECO/UNDEV AGRI INDUS R+D ACADEM NAT/G INT/TRADE...SOC 20. PAGE 161 H3210
BIBLIOG/A AFR PRESS COM/IND

B54
WILLIAMSON H.F.,ECONOMIC DEVELOPMENT - PRINCIPLES AND PATTERNS. INDIA KOREA CULTURE ECO/DEV ECO/UNDEV TEC/DEV...CENSUS NAT/COMP 20 CHINJAP MEXIC/AMER RESOURCE/N. PAGE 168 H3369
ECO/TAC GEOG LABOR

S54
BALANDIER G.,"SOCIOLOGIE DE LA COLONISATION ET RELATIONS ENTRE SOCIETES GLOBALES." AFR SOCIETY ECO/UNDEV KIN DOMIN EDU/PROP RIGID/FLEX PWR...PSY CONCPT TREND TOT/POP. PAGE 10 H0203
CULTURE SOC COLONIAL

S54
DODD S.C.,"THE SCIENTIFIC MEASUREMENT OF FITNESS FOR SELF-GOVERNMENT." FUT CONSTN ECO/UNDEV INT/ORG PLAN PWR...CONCPT QUANT CON/ANAL SOC/EXP UN LEAGUE/NAT 20. PAGE 41 H0830
NAT/G STAT SOVEREIGN

B55
APTER D.E.,THE GOLD COAST IN TRANSITION. FUT CONSTN CULTURE SOCIETY ECO/UNDEV FAM KIN LOC/G NAT/G POL/PAR LEGIS TOP/EX EDU/PROP LEGIT ADMIN ATTIT PERSON PWR...CONCPT STAT INT CENSUS TOT/POP VAL/FREE. PAGE 7 H0149
AFR SOVEREIGN

B55
INTERNATIONAL AFRICAN INST,ETHNOGRAPHIC SURVEY OF AFRICA: NORTH EASTERN AFRICA (VOLUMES 1-2, 1955-56). AFR ETHIOPIA CULTURE ECO/UNDEV KIN GOV/REL ATTIT HEREDITY...GEOG CHARTS BIBLIOG WORSHIP 20. PAGE 77 H1545
STRUCT ECO/TAC INGP/REL HABITAT

B55
INTERNATIONAL AFRICAN INST,ETHNOGRAPHIC SURVEY OF AFRICA: WESTERN AFRICA: PEOPLES OF THE NIGER-BENUE CONFLUENCE. AFR NIGER CULTURE ECO/UNDEV KIN GOV/REL GP/REL ATTIT HEREDITY...CHARTS BIBLIOG WORSHIP 20. PAGE 77 H1546
STRUCT GEOG HABITAT INGP/REL

B55
JONES T.B.,A BIBLIOGRAPHY ON SOUTH AMERICAN ECONOMIC AFFAIRS: ARTICLES IN NINETEENTH CENTURY PERIODICALS (PAMPHLET). AGRI COM/IND DIST/IND EXTR/IND FINAN INDUS LABOR NAT/G 19. PAGE 82 H1634
BIBLIOG ECO/UNDEV L/A+17C TEC/DEV

B55
LIPSCOMB J.F.,WHITE AFRICANS. SOCIETY STRUCT AGRI ECO/TAC ADJUD COLONIAL COERCE PERS/REL ADJUST. PAGE 97 H1937
RACE/REL HABITAT ECO/UNDEV ORD/FREE

B55
QUAN K.L.,INTRODUCTION TO ASIA: A SELECTIVE GUIDE TO BACKGROUND READING. ECO/UNDEV NAT/G PROB/SOLV DIPLOM ATTIT 20. PAGE 129 H2572
BIBLIOG/A S/ASIA CULTURE ASIA

B55
SERRANO MOSCOSO E.,A STATEMENT OF THE LAWS OF ECUADOR IN MATTERS AFFECTING BUSINESS (2ND ED.). ECUADOR INDUS LABOR LG/CO NAT/G LEGIS TAX CONTROL MARRIAGE 20. PAGE 141 H2830
FINAN ECO/UNDEV LAW CONSTN

B55
UN ECONOMIC COMN ASIA & FAR E,ECONOMIC SURVEY OF ASIA AND THE FAR EAST, 1954. AFGHANISTN CEYLON INDIA PHILIPPINE S/ASIA ECO/DEV FINAN INDUS INT/TRADE PRODUC WEALTH...STAT CHARTS 20 CHINJAP. PAGE 158 H3158
ECO/UNDEV PRICE NAT/COMP ASIA

S55
GOODENOUGH W.H.,"A PROBLEM IN MALAYO-POLYNESIAN SOCIAL ORGANIZATION" (BMR)" MALAYSIA S/ASIA CULTURE AGRI PROB/SOLV OWN HABITAT...SOC 20 20 POLYNESIA. PAGE 58 H1170
KIN STRUCT FAM ECO/UNDEV

B56
INTERNATIONAL AFRICAN INST,SOCIAL IMPLICATIONS OF INDUSTRIALIZATION AND URBANIZATION IN AFRICA SOUTH OF THE SAHARA. SOUTH/AFR INDUS LABOR MUNIC WORKER TEC/DEV...SOC OBS TREND ANTHOL 20. PAGE 77 H1549
AFR ECO/UNDEV ADJUST CULTURE

B56
LEVIN M.G.,THE PEOPLES OF SIBERIA. PREHIST ECO/UNDEV KIN SECT HABITAT...CLASSIF AUD/VIS WORSHIP 20 SIBERIA. PAGE 95 H1900
CULTURE SOCIETY ASIA

B56
PHILIPPINE STUDIES PROGRAM,SELECTED BIBLIOGRAPHY ON THE PHILIPPINES, TOPICALLY ARRANGED AND ANNOTATED. PHILIPPINE SECT DIPLOM COLONIAL LEAD...SOC 18/20. PAGE 125 H2501
BIBLIOG/A S/ASIA NAT/G ECO/UNDEV

C56
FALL B.B.,"THE VIET-MINH REGIME." VIETNAM LAW ECO/UNDEV POL/PAR FORCES DOMIN WAR ATTIT MARXISM ...BIOG PREDICT BIBLIOG/A 20. PAGE 48 H0967
NAT/G ADMIN EX/STRUC LEAD

N56
US HOUSE COMM FOREIGN AFFAIRS,REPORT OF THE SPECIAL STUDY MISSION TO AFRICA, SOUTH AND EAST OF THE SAHARA (PAMPHLET). AFR SOUTH/AFR USA+45 STRUCT INT/TRADE PARL/PROC NAT/LISM ATTIT ALL/VALS HEALTH ...POLICY 20 CONGRESS. PAGE 160 H3197
FOR/AID COLONIAL ECO/UNDEV DIPLOM

B57
BARAN P.A.,THE POLITICAL ECONOMY OF GROWTH. MOD/EUR
CAP/ISM

USA+45 USA-45 TEC/DEV TAX SOCISM...MGT CONCPT GOV/COMP. PAGE 11 H0213 CONTROL ECO/UNDEV FINAN

B57
CARIBBEAN COMMISSION,A CATALOGUE OF CARIBBEAN COMMISSION PUBLICATIONS (PAMPHLET). WEST/IND CULTURE ECO/UNDEV LOC/G DIPLOM SOC. PAGE 26 H0531 BIBLIOG L/A+17C INT/ORG NAT/G

B57
CENTRAL ASIAN RESEARCH CENTRE,BIBLIOGRAPHY OF RECENT SOVIET SOURCE MATERIAL ON SOVIET CENTRAL ASIA AND THE BORDERLANDS. AFGHANISTN INDIA PAKISTAN UAR USSR ECO/UNDEV AGRI EXTR/IND INDUS ACADEM ADMIN ...HEAL HUM LING CON/ANAL 20. PAGE 28 H0567 BIBLIOG/A COM CULTURE NAT/G

B57
CONOVER H.F.,NORTH AND NORTHEAST AFRICA; A SELECTED ANNOTATED LIST OF WRITINGS. ALGERIA MOROCCO SUDAN UAR CULTURE INT/ORG PROB/SOLV ADJUD NAT/LISM PWR WEALTH...SOC 20 UN. PAGE 32 H0649 BIBLIOG/A DIPLOM AFR ECO/UNDEV

B57
DEAN V.M.,THE NATURE OF THE NON-WESTERN WORLD. AFR ASIA L/A+17C S/ASIA CULTURE SOCIETY STRATA ECO/DEV DIPLOM ECO/TAC FOR/AID ATTIT DRIVE ALL/VALS ...RELATIV SOC CONCPT TIME/SEQ TREND TOT/POP 20. PAGE 39 H0778 ECO/UNDEV STERTYP NAT/LISM

B57
INTERNATIONAL AFRICAN INST,ETHNOGRAPHIC SURVEY OF AFRICA: WESTERN AFRICA: THE BENIN KINGDOM. AFR NIGERIA CULTURE ECO/UNDEV KIN ECO/TAC GOV/REL AGE ATTIT HEREDITY...CHARTS BIBLIOG WORSHIP 20. PAGE 77 H1550 STRUCT INGP/REL GEOG HABITAT

B57
INTERNATIONAL AFRICAN INST,ETHNOGRAPHIC SURVEY OF AFRICA: WESTERN AFRICA: THE WOLOF OF SENEGAMBIA. AFR SENEGAL CULTURE ECO/UNDEV FAM KIN REGION ...CHARTS GP/COMP BIBLIOG WORSHIP 20. PAGE 78 H1551 STRUCT GEOG HABITAT INGP/REL

B57
MOYER K.E.,FROM IRAN TO MORROCCO; FROM TURKEY TO THE SUDAN: A SELECTED AND ANNOTATED BIBLIOGRAPHY OF NORTH AFRICA AND NEAR EAST... ISLAM DIPLOM EDU/PROP 20. PAGE 114 H2274 BIBLIOG/A ECO/UNDEV SECT NAT/G

B57
NEUMARK S.D.,ECONOMIC INFLUENCES ON THE SOUTH AFRICAN FRONTIER, 1652-1836. SOUTH/AFR SEA AGRI NAT/G FORCES WORKER DIPLOM INT/TRADE PRICE DEMAND PRODUC...STAT CHARTS 17/19 FRONTIER. PAGE 117 H2341 COLONIAL ECO/UNDEV ECO/TAC MARKET

B57
PALACIOS A.L.,PETROLEO, MONOPOLIOS, Y LATIFUNDIOS. L/A+17C EXTR/IND NAT/G TEC/DEV ECO/TAC CONTROL PRODUC 20 ARGEN MONOPOLY RESOURCE/N. PAGE 123 H2448 ECO/UNDEV NAT/LISM INDUS AGRI

B57
ROBERTSON H.M.,SOUTH AFRICA, ECONOMIC AND POLITICAL ASPECTS. SOUTH/AFR CONSTN CULTURE POL/PAR LEGIS DIPLOM DOMIN COLONIAL...SOC BIBLIOG 19/20. PAGE 132 H2647 RACE/REL ECO/UNDEV ECO/TAC DISCRIM

B57
US SENATE SPEC COMM FOR AID,COMPILATION OF STUDIES AND SURVEYS. AFR ASIA L/A+17C USA+45 ECO/UNDEV AGRI INT/ORG CONSULT TEC/DEV CONFER TOTALISM...NAT/COMP 20 CONGRESS. PAGE 161 H3216 FOR/AID DIPLOM ORD/FREE DELIB/GP

B57
US SENATE SPEC COMM FOR AID,HEARINGS BEFORE THE SPECIAL COMMITTEE TO STUDY THE FOREIGN AID PROGRAM. USA+45 USSR ECO/UNDEV INT/ORG FORCES WEAPON TOTALISM ATTIT SUPEGO...NAT/COMP CONGRESS. PAGE 161 H3217 FOR/AID DIPLOM ORD/FREE TEC/DEV

B57
WILSON P.,SOUTH ASIA; A SELECTED BIBLIOGRAPHY ON INDIA, PAKISTAN, CEYLON (PAMPHLET). CEYLON INDIA PAKISTAN LAW ECO/UNDEV PLAN DIPLOM 20. PAGE 169 H3381 BIBLIOG S/ASIA CULTURE NAT/G

S57
KILSON M.L.,"LAND AND POLITICS IN KENYA: AN ANALYSIS OF AFRICAN POLITICS IN A PLURAL SOCIETY." FUT LAW CULTURE KIN NAT/G ECO/TAC DOMIN REV NAT/LISM ORD/FREE PWR RESPECT SOVEREIGN WEALTH ...SOC OBS TREND WORK VAL/FREE CMN/WLTH 20. PAGE 86 H1710 AFR ECO/UNDEV

B58
LIST OF PUBLICATIONS (PERIODICAL OR AD HOC) ISSUED BY VARIOUS MINISTRIES OF THE GOVERNMENT OF INDIA (3RD ED.). INDIA ECO/UNDEV PLAN...POLICY MGT 20. PAGE 2 H0037 BIBLIOG NAT/G ADMIN

B58
DWARKADAS R.,ROLE OF HIGHER CIVIL SERVICE IN INDIA. INDIA ECO/UNDEV LEGIS PROB/SOLV GP/REL PERS/REL ...POLICY WELF/ST DECISION ORG/CHARTS BIBLIOG 20 CIVIL/SERV INTRVN/ECO. PAGE 44 H0876 ADMIN NAT/G ROLE PLAN

B58
HANCE W.A.,AFRICAN ECONOMIC DEVELOPMENT. AGRI DIST/IND INDUS R+D ACT/RES PLAN CAP/ISM FOR/AID ...GOV/COMP BIBLIOG 20. PAGE 65 H1312 AFR ECO/UNDEV PROB/SOLV TEC/DEV

B58
INDIAN COUNCIL WORLD AFFAIRS,DEFENCE AND SECURITY IN THE INDIAN OCEAN AREA. INDIA S/ASIA CULTURE CONSULT DELIB/GP FORCES PROB/SOLV DIPLOM INT/TRADE 20 CMN/WLTH. PAGE 77 H1531 GEOG HABITAT ECO/UNDEV ORD/FREE

B58
INTERNATIONAL ECONOMIC ASSN,ECONOMICS OF INTERNATIONAL MIGRATION. WOR+45 WOR-45 ECO/UNDEV FINAN NAT/G REGION...NAT/COMP METH 20. PAGE 78 H1556 CENSUS GEOG DIPLOM ECO/TAC

B58
JOHNSON J.J.,POLITICAL CHANGE IN LATIN AMERICA: THE EMERGENCE OF THE MIDDLE SECTORS. INTELL STRATA STRUCT ECO/UNDEV MUNIC TEC/DEV LEAD REV...DECISION TREND GOV/COMP BIBLIOG/A 20. PAGE 81 H1621 L/A+17C ELITES GP/REL DOMIN

B58
LAQUER W.Z.,THE MIDDLE EAST IN TRANSITION. COM USSR ECO/UNDEV NAT/G VOL/ASSN EDU/PROP EXEC ATTIT DRIVE PWR MARXISM COLD/WAR TOT/POP 20. PAGE 91 H1818 ISLAM TREND NAT/LISM

B58
LERNER D.,THE PASSING OF TRADITIONAL SOCIETY: MODERNIZING THE MIDDLE EAST. IRAN ISLAM LEBANON SYRIA TURKEY UAR CULTURE INTELL STRATA KIN NAT/G NEIGH SECT EDU/PROP ATTIT PERSON...MYTH OBS 20. PAGE 95 H1888 ECO/UNDEV RIGID/FLEX

B58
MASON J.B.,THAILAND BIBLIOGRAPHY. S/ASIA THAILAND CULTURE EDU/PROP ADMIN...GEOG SOC LING 20. PAGE 104 H2087 BIBLIOG/A ECO/UNDEV DIPLOM NAT/G

B58
MATOS J.,LAS ACTUALES COMMUNIDADES DE INDIGENAS: HUAROCHIRI EN 1955. PERU FAM NAT/G SECT EDU/PROP ADJUD GP/REL INGP/REL 20 INDIAN/AM. PAGE 105 H2091 STRUCT NEIGH KIN ECO/UNDEV

B58
NICULESCU B.,COLONIAL PLANNING: A COMPARATIVE STUDY. AFR AGRI LOC/G MUNIC NAT/G DELIB/GP COLONIAL 20. PAGE 118 H2356 PLAN ECO/UNDEV TEC/DEV NAT/COMP

B58
PALMER E.E.,THE COMMUNIST CHALLENGE. COM USA+45 USA-45 ECO/DEV ECO/UNDEV NEUTRAL ORD/FREE POPULISM ...CONCPT NAT/COMP ANTHOL 19/20 LENIN/VI STALIN/J MAO MARX/KARL COM/PARTY. PAGE 123 H2450 MARXISM DIPLOM IDEA/COMP POLICY

B58
PAN AMERICAN UNION,REPERTORIO DE PUBLICACIONES PERIODICAS ACTUALES LATINO-AMERICANAS. CULTURE ECO/UNDEV ADMIN LEAD GOV/REL 20 OAS. PAGE 123 H2455 BIBLIOG L/A+17C NAT/G DIPLOM

B58
TILLION G.,ALGERIA: THE REALITIES. ALGERIA FRANCE ISLAM CULTURE STRATA PROB/SOLV DOMIN REV NAT/LISM WEALTH MARXISM...GEOG 20. PAGE 155 H3094 ECO/UNDEV SOC COLONIAL DIPLOM

B58
VARG P.A.,MISSIONARIES, CHINESE, AND DIPLOMATS: THE AMERICAN PROTESTANT MISSIONARY MOVEMENT IN CHINA, 1890-1952. ASIA ECO/UNDEV NAT/G PROB/SOLV CAP/ISM EDU/PROP COLONIAL NAT/LISM ATTIT MARXISM...NAT/COMP STERTYP 20 CHINJAP PROTESTANT MISSION. PAGE 162 H3234 CULTURE DIPLOM SECT

S58
LOCKWOOD W.W.,"THE SOCIALISTIC SOCIETY: INDIA AND JAPAN." INDIA ECO/DEV ECO/UNDEV INDUS NAT/G CONTROL LEAD PRODUC WEALTH 20 CHINJAP. PAGE 98 H1948 ECO/TAC NAT/COMP FINAN SOCISM

S58
MAIR L.P.,"REPRESENTATIVE LOCAL GOVERNMENT AS A PROBLEM IN SOCIAL CHANGE." ECO/UNDEV KIN LOC/G NAT/G SCHOOL JUDGE ADMIN ROUTINE REPRESENT RIGID/FLEX RESPECT...CONCPT STERTYP CMN/WLTH 20. PAGE 101 H2025 AFR PWR ELITES

C58
BLANCHARD W.,"THAILAND." THAILAND CULTURE AGRI FINAN INDUS FAM LABOR INT/TRADE ATTIT...GEOG HEAL SOC BIBLIOG 20. PAGE 18 H0354 NAT/G DIPLOM ECO/UNDEV S/ASIA

C58
GINSBURG N.,"MALAYA." MALAYSIA PROB/SOLV REGION NAT/LISM KNOWL WEALTH...GEOG SOC CHARTS BIBLIOG 20. PAGE 57 H1133 COM/IND ECO/UNDEV CULTURE NAT/G

B59
BOLTON A.R.,SOVIET MIDDLE EAST STUDIES: AN ANALYSIS AND BIBLIOGRAPHY. ISLAM JORDAN UAR USSR NAT/G SOC. PAGE 18 H0370 BIBLIOG NAT/COMP ECO/UNDEV

B59
CARPENTER G.W.,THE WAY IN AFRICA. AFR INDUS MUNIC DIPLOM DOMIN EDU/PROP COERCE DISCRIM NAT/LISM ORD/FREE 20 NEGRO CHRISTIAN. PAGE 27 H0535 CULTURE SECT ECO/UNDEV COLONIAL

B59
GUDIN E.,INFLACAO (2ND ED.). INDUS NAT/G PLAN ECO/TAC CONTROL COST 20. PAGE 62 H1243 ECO/UNDEV INT/TRADE BAL/PAY FINAN

B59
KITTLER G.D.,EQUATORIAL AFRICA: THE NEW WORLD OF TOMORROW. CENTRL/AFR INDUS KIN SECT CHIEF EDU/PROP CHOOSE HEALTH...GEOG WORSHIP 20. PAGE 87 H1730
RACE/REL AFR ECO/UNDEV CULTURE

B59
LAQUER W.Z.,THE SOVIET UNION AND THE MIDDLE EAST. COM UAR USSR ECO/UNDEV NAT/G VOL/ASSN ECO/TAC EDU/PROP COLONIAL EXEC PWR...TIME/SEQ TREND COLD/WAR 20. PAGE 91 H1819
ISLAM DRIVE FOR/AID NAT/LISM

B59
MADHOK B.,POLITICAL TRENDS IN INDIA. INDIA PAKISTAN UK STRATA ECO/UNDEV POL/PAR LEGIS CAP/ISM DIPLOM COLONIAL CHOOSE MARXISM...SOC TREND 20 GANDHI/M NEHRU/J. PAGE 101 H2014
GEOG NAT/G

B59
MEYER A.J.,MIDDLE EASTERN CAPITALISM: NINE ESSAYS. ISLAM CULTURE ECO/UNDEV INDUS MARKET NAT/G PLAN ATTIT RIGID/FLEX...STAT OBS TREND GEN/LAWS. PAGE 109 H2188
TEC/DEV ECO/TAC ANTHOL

B59
PANIKKAR K.M.,THE AFRO-ASIAN STATES AND THEIR PROBLEMS. COM CULTURE KIN POL/PAR SECT DIPLOM EDU/PROP COLONIAL SOVEREIGN...TECHNIC GOV/COMP 20. PAGE 123 H2458
AFR S/ASIA ECO/UNDEV

B59
PARK R.L.,LEADERSHIP AND POLITICAL INSTITUTIONS IN INDIA. S/ASIA CULTURE ECO/UNDEV LOC/G MUNIC PROVS LEGIS PLAN ADMIN LEAD ORD/FREE WEALTH...GEOG SOC BIOG TOT/POP VAL/FREE 20. PAGE 123 H2468
NAT/G EXEC INDIA

B59
ROCHE J.,LA COLONISATION ALLEMANDE ET LE RIO GRANDE DO SUL. BRAZIL L/A+17C NAT/G PROVS INGP/REL RACE/REL DISCRIM HABITAT...GEOG SOC/INTEG 19/20 MIGRATION. PAGE 133 H2652
ECO/UNDEV GP/REL ATTIT

B59
VINACKE H.M.,A HISTORY OF THE FAR EAST IN MODERN TIMES (6TH ED.). KOREA S/ASIA USSR CONSTN CULTURE STRATA ECO/UNDEV NAT/G CHIEF FOR/AID INT/TRADE GP/REL...SOC NAT/COMP 19/20 CHINJAP. PAGE 163 H3255
STRUCT ASIA

B59
WRAITH R.E.,EAST AFRICAN CITIZEN. AFR GHANA UK AGRI INDUS LOC/G POL/PAR PROB/SOLV CONTROL REGION REPRESENT NAT/LISM PWR...OBS 20 AFRICA/E AFRICA/W. PAGE 171 H3415
ECO/UNDEV RACE/REL NAT/G NAT/COMP

C59
KARPAT K.H.,"TURKEY'S POLITICS: THE TRANSITION TO A MULTI-PARTY SYSTEM." COM TURKEY CULTURE ECO/UNDEV SECT TEC/DEV NAT/LISM ATTIT...SOC CON/ANAL BIBLIOG 20. PAGE 83 H1664
POL/PAR NAT/G

B60
ALMOND G.A.,THE POLITICS OF THE DEVELOPING AREAS. AFR ISLAM L/A+17C S/ASIA SOCIETY ECO/UNDEV NAT/G ADMIN PERCEPT KNOWL SOVEREIGN...CONCPT GEN/LAWS 20. PAGE 6 H0112
EX/STRUC ATTIT NAT/LISM

B60
AUSTRUY J.,STRUCTURE ECONOMIQUE ET CIVILISATION: L'EGYPTE ET LE DESTIN ECONOMIQUE DE L'ISLAM. ISLAM UAR CREATE OP/RES ECO/TAC...SOC BIBLIOG 20 MUSLIM. PAGE 9 H0182
ECO/UNDEV CULTURE STRUCT

B60
BAYER H.,WIRTSCHAFTSPROGNOSE UND WIRTSCHAFTSGESTALTUNG. GERMANY NETHERLAND MARKET PLAN CAP/ISM DEBATE...NAT/COMP 20. PAGE 12 H0242
ECO/DEV ECO/UNDEV FINAN POLICY

B60
BOMBACH G.,STABILE PREISE IN WACHSENDER WIRTSCHAFT: DAS INFLATIONSPROBLEM. BARGAIN CAP/ISM PRICE COST ...NAT/COMP 20 GOLD/STAND. PAGE 19 H0371
ECO/UNDEV PLAN FINAN ECO/TAC

B60
BURRIDGE K.,MAMBU: A MELANESIAN MILLENNIUM. ECO/UNDEV PROC/MFG FAM KIN CHIEF COLONIAL COERCE GP/REL DRIVE WEALTH WORSHIP 20 NEW/GUINEA. PAGE 25 H0494
S/ASIA SECT CULTURE MYTH

B60
COUGHLIN R.,DOUBLE IDENTITY: THE CHINESE AND MODERN THAILAND. CHINA/COM S/ASIA THAILAND ECO/UNDEV EXTR/IND FINAN INDUS KIN MUNIC NAT/G PROF/ORG SCHOOL SECT ATTIT DRIVE...CONCPT OBS 20. PAGE 34 H0676
ASIA FAM CULTURE

B60
DIA M.,REFLEXIONS SUR L'ECONOMIE DE L'AFRIQUE NOIRE (REV. ED.). CULTURE ECO/UNDEV CREATE TEC/DEV DIPLOM INT/TRADE OPTIMAL ATTIT...POLICY 20. PAGE 41 H0816
AFR ECO/TAC SOCISM PLAN

B60
EASTON S.C.,THE TWILIGHT OF EUROPEAN COLONIALISM. AFR S/ASIA CONSTN SOCIETY STRUCT ECO/UNDEV INDUS NAT/G FORCES ECO/TAC COLONIAL CT/SYS ATTIT KNOWL ORD/FREE PWR...SOCIALIST TIME/SEQ TREND CON/ANAL 20. PAGE 44 H0882
FINAN ADMIN

B60
GONZALEZ NAVARRO M.,LA COLONIZACION EN MEXICO, 1877-1910. AGRI NAT/G PLAN PROB/SOLV INCOME ...POLICY JURID CENSUS 19/20 MEXIC/AMER MIGRATION. PAGE 58 H1164
ECO/UNDEV GEOG HABITAT COLONIAL

B60
HARRISON S.S.,INDIA: THE MOST DANGEROUS DECADES. INDIA CONSTN STRATA POL/PAR SECT PLAN ADMIN CHOOSE GP/REL TOTALISM MARXISM...LING 20 NEHRU/J. PAGE 67 H1347
CULTURE ECO/UNDEV PROB/SOLV REGION

B60
INTERNATIONAL AFRICAN INST,ETHNOGRAPHIC SURVEY OF AFRICA: WESTERN AFRICA: PEOPLES OF THE MIDDLE NIGER REGION, NORTHERN NIGERIA. AFR NIGER CULTURE ECO/UNDEV KIN NEIGH GOV/REL GP/REL ATTIT HEREDITY ...CHARTS BIBLIOG WORSHIP 20. PAGE 78 H1552
STRUCT GEOG HABITAT INGP/REL

B60
KERR C.,INDUSTRIALISM AND INDUSTRIAL MAN. CULTURE SOCIETY ECO/UNDEV NAT/G ADMIN PRODUC WEALTH ...PREDICT TREND NAT/COMP 19/20. PAGE 85 H1697
WORKER MGT ECO/DEV INDUS

B60
LEYDER J.,BIBLIOGRAPHIE DE L'ENSEIGNEMENT SUPERIEUR ET DE LA RECHERCHE SCIENTIFIQUE EN AFRIQUE INTERTROPICALE (2 VOLS.). AFR CULTURE ECO/UNDEV AGRI PLAN EDU/PROP ADMIN COLONIAL...GEOG SOC/INTEG 20 NEGRO. PAGE 96 H1918
BIBLIOG/A ACT/RES ACADEM R+D

B60
MC CLELLAN G.S.,INDIA. CHINA/COM INDIA CONSTN ELITES STRATA AGRI POL/PAR FOR/AID ARMS/CONT REV MARXISM...CENSUS BIBLIOG 20 COLD/WAR GANDHI/M NEHRU/J. PAGE 106 H2117
DIPLOM NAT/G SOCIETY ECO/UNDEV

B60
MOORE W.E.,LABOR COMMITMENT AND SOCIAL CHANGE IN DEVELOPING AREAS. SOCIETY STRATA ECO/UNDEV MARKET VOL/ASSN WORKER AUTHORIT SKILL...MGT NAT/COMP SOC/INTEG 20. PAGE 113 H2250
LABOR ORD/FREE ATTIT INDUS

B60
NEALE A.D.,THE FLOW OF RESOURCES FROM RICH TO POOR. WOR+45 ECO/DEV ECO/UNDEV FINAN INDUS NAT/G PLAN EFFICIENCY WEALTH...POLICY NAT/COMP 20 RESOURCE/N. PAGE 116 H2325
FOR/AID DIPLOM METH/CNCPT

B60
PIERCE R.A.,RUSSIAN CENTRAL ASIA, 1867-1917. ASIA RUSSIA CULTURE AGRI INDUS EDU/PROP REV NAT/LISM ...CHARTS BIBLIOG 19/20 BOLSHEVISM INTERVENT. PAGE 125 H2509
COLONIAL DOMIN ADMIN ECO/UNDEV

B60
SAKAI R.K.,STUDIES ON ASIA, 1960. ASIA CHINA/COM S/ASIA COM/IND ECO/TAC...ANTHOL 17/20 MALAYA. PAGE 137 H2733
ECO/UNDEV SOC

B60
SMITH M.G.,GOVERNMENT IN ZAZZAU 1800-1950. NIGERIA UK CULTURE SOCIETY LOC/G ADMIN COLONIAL ...METH/CNCPT NEW/IDEA METH 19/20. PAGE 146 H2914
REGION CONSTN KIN ECO/UNDEV

B60
THEOBOLD R.,THE NEW NATIONS OF WEST AFRICA. GHANA NIGERIA CULTURE INT/ORG ECO/TAC FOR/AID COLONIAL RACE/REL POPULISM...ANTHOL BIBLIOG 20 UN. PAGE 153 H3068
AFR SOVEREIGN ECO/UNDEV DIPLOM

B60
WOLF C.,FOREIGN AID: THEORY AND PRACTICE IN SOUTHERN ASIA. CEYLON INDONESIA PHILIPPINE S/ASIA CULTURE STRATA ECO/UNDEV PLAN EDU/PROP ATTIT ...METH/CNCPT MATH QUANT STAT CONT/OBS TIME/SEQ SIMUL TOT/POP 20. PAGE 170 H3396
ACT/RES ECO/TAC FOR/AID

B60
WORLEY P.,ASIA TODAY (REV. ED.) (PAMPHLET). COM ECO/UNDEV AGRI FINAN INDUS POL/PAR FOR/AID ADMIN MARXISM 20. PAGE 170 H3411
BIBLIOG/A ASIA DIPLOM NAT/G

S60
"THE EMERGING COMMON MARKETS IN LATIN AMERICA." FUT L/A+17C STRATA DIST/IND INDUS LABOR NAT/G LEGIS ECO/TAC ADMIN RIGID/FLEX HEALTH...NEW/IDEA TIME/SEQ OAS 20. PAGE 2 H0038
FINAN ECO/UNDEV INT/TRADE

S60
BERG E.J.,"ECONOMIC BASIS OF POLITICAL CHOICE IN FRENCH WEST AFRICA." FRANCE ECO/UNDEV AGRI INDUS NAT/G PLAN LEGIT COLONIAL REGION ATTIT PWR WEALTH ...CONCPT 20. PAGE 15 H0299
AFR ECO/TAC

S60
COOK R.C.,"THE WORLD'S GREAT CITIES: EVOLUTION OR DEVOLUTION?" WOR+45 WOR-45 ECO/DEV ECO/UNDEV ACT/RES PROB/SOLV...GEOG TREND CHARTS NAT/COMP BIBLIOG 20. PAGE 33 H0658
MUNIC HABITAT PLAN CENSUS

S60
CROZIER B.,"FRANCE AND ALGERIA." ALGERIA EUR+WWI FRANCE FUT ISLAM ECO/UNDEV NEIGH CONSULT DELIB/GP ECO/TAC COLONIAL COERCE ATTIT...SOC INT CON/ANAL 20. PAGE 36 H0713
NAT/G FORCES GUERRILLA NAT/LISM

S60
EMERSON R.,"THE EROSION OF DEMOCRACY." AFR FUT LAW CULTURE INTELL SOCIETY ECO/UNDEV FAM LOC/G NAT/G FORCES PLAN TEC/DEV ECO/TAC ADMIN CT/SYS ATTIT ORD/FREE PWR...SOCIALIST SOC CONCPT STAND/INT TIME/SEQ WORK 20. PAGE 46 H0918
S/ASIA POL/PAR

S60
FITZGIBBON R.H.,"DICTATORSHIP AND DEMOCRACY IN
L/A+17C

LATIN AMERICA." FUT ECO/DEV ECO/UNDEV INT/ORG LOC/G NAT/G TOP/EX PLAN TEC/DEV ECO/TAC CHOOSE ATTIT DRIVE PERSON ALL/VALS OAS TOT/POP 20. PAGE 51 H1019
ACT/RES INT/TRADE

S60

FRANKEL S.H.,"ECONOMIC ASPECTS OF POLITICAL INDEPENDENCE IN AFRICA." AFR FUT SOCIETY ECO/UNDEV COM/IND FINAN LEGIS PLAN TEC/DEV CAP/ISM ECO/TAC INT/TRADE ADMIN ATTIT DRIVE RIGID/FLEX PWR WEALTH ...MGT NEW/IDEA MATH TIME/SEQ VAL/FREE 20. PAGE 53 H1052
NAT/G FOR/AID

S60

JAFFEE A.J.,"POPULATION TRENDS AND CONTROLS IN UNDERDEVELOPED COUNTRIES." AFR FUT ISLAM L/A+17C S/ASIA CULTURE R+D FAM ACT/RES PLAN EDU/PROP BIO/SOC RIGID/FLEX HEALTH...SOC STAT OBS CHARTS 20. PAGE 79 H1582
ECO/UNDEV GEOG

S60

MURPHEY R.,"ECONOMIC CONFLICTS IN SOUTH ASIA." ASIA CULTURE INTELL ECO/TAC REGION ATTIT DRIVE KNOWL ...METH/CNCPT TIME/SEQ STERTYP TOT/POP VAL/FREE 20. PAGE 115 H2296
S/ASIA ECO/UNDEV

S60

NORTH R.C.,"DIE DISKREPANZ ZWISCHEN REALITAT UND WUNSCHBILD ALS INNENPOLITISCHER FAKTOR." ASIA CHINA/COM COM FUT ECO/UNDEV NAT/G PLAN DOMIN ADMIN COERCE PERCEPT...SOC MYTH GEN/METH WORK TOT/POP 20. PAGE 119 H2373
SOCIETY ECO/TAC

S60

RIVKIN A.,"AFRICAN ECONOMIC DEVELOPMENT: ADVANCED TECHNOLOGY AND THE STAGES OF GROWTH." CULTURE ECO/UNDEV AGRI COM/IND EXTR/IND PLAN ECO/TAC ATTIT DRIVE RIGID/FLEX SKILL WEALTH...MGT SOC GEN/LAWS WORK TOT/POP 20. PAGE 132 H2634
AFR TEC/DEV FOR/AID

S60

SPIRO H.J.,"NEW CONSTITUTIONAL FORMS IN AFRICA." FUT CULTURE SOCIETY ECO/UNDEV NAT/G POL/PAR VOL/ASSN EDU/PROP ATTIT DRIVE ORD/FREE PWR RESPECT ...POLICY CONCPT OBS TREND CON/ANAL STERTYP GEN/LAWS VAL/FREE. PAGE 148 H2950
AFR CONSTN FOR/AID NAT/LISM

S60

WYCKOFF T.,"THE ROLE OF THE MILITARY IN LATIN AMERICAN POLITICS." L/A+17C CONSTN CULTURE ECO/UNDEV POL/PAR FORCES LEGIS TOP/EX LEGIT GUERRILLA REV CHOOSE ORD/FREE PWR...TIME/SEQ VAL/FREE 20. PAGE 171 H3430
NAT/G COERCE TOTALISM

C60

HOSELITZ B.,"THE ROLE OF CITIES IN THE ECONOMIC GROWTH OF UNDERDEVELOPED COUNTRIES" IN "SOCIOLOGICAL ASPECTS OF ECONOMIC GROWTH"(BMR). CULTURE LOC/G ACT/RES...SOC IDEA/COMP METH/COMP METH 14/20 REDFIELD/R. PAGE 74 H1474
METH/CNCPT MUNIC TEC/DEV ECO/UNDEV

C60

SMITH T.E.,"ELECTIONS IN DEVELOPING COUNTRIES: A STUDY OF ELECTORAL PROCEDURES USED IN TOPICAL AFRICA, SOUTH-EAST ASIA..." AFR S/ASIA UK ROUTINE GOV/REL RACE/REL...GOV/COMP BIBLIOG 20. PAGE 146 H2918
ECO/UNDEV CHOOSE REPRESENT ADMIN

C60

WRIGGINS W.H.,"CEYLON: DILEMMAS OF A NEW NATION." ASIA CEYLON CONSTN STRUCT POL/PAR SECT FORCES DIPLOM GOV/REL NAT/LISM...CHARTS BIBLIOG 20. PAGE 171 H3417
PROB/SOLV NAT/G ECO/UNDEV

N60

RHODESIA-NYASA NATL ARCHIVES,A SELECT BIBLIOGRAPHY OF RECENT PUBLICATIONS CONCERNING THE FEDERATION OF RHODESIA AND NYASALAND (PAMPHLET). MALAWI RHODESIA LAW CULTURE STRUCT ECO/UNDEV LEGIS...GEOG 20. PAGE 131 H2620
BIBLIOG ADMIN ORD/FREE NAT/G

B61

APTER D.E.,THE POLITICAL KINGDOM IN UGANDA. UGANDA CULTURE ECO/UNDEV AGRI KIN SECT TOP/EX REGION ATTIT HABITAT CONSERVE...GEOG AUD/VIS 20. PAGE 8 H0153
NAT/LISM POL/PAR COLONIAL ECO/TAC

B61

BONNEFOUS M.,EUROPE ET TIERS MONDE. EUR+WWI SOCIETY INT/ORG NAT/G VOL/ASSN ACT/RES TEC/DEV CAP/ISM ECO/TAC ATTIT ORD/FREE SOVEREIGN...POLICY CONCPT TREND 20. PAGE 19 H0373
AFR ECO/UNDEV FOR/AID INT/TRADE

B61

CHAKRABARTI A.,NEHRU: HIS DEMOCRACY AND INDIA. ASIA INDIA UK CONSTN ECO/UNDEV SECT DIPLOM COLONIAL PEACE WEALTH...BIBLIOG 20 CONGRESS NEHRU/J GANDHI/M. PAGE 28 H0570
ORD/FREE STRATA NAT/G CHIEF

B61

COHN B.S.,DEVELOPMENT AND IMPACT OF BRITISH ADMINISTRATION IN INDIA: A BIBLIOGRAPHIC ESSAY. INDIA UK ECO/UNDEV NAT/G DOMIN...POLICY MGT SOC 19/20. PAGE 31 H0619
BIBLIOG/A COLONIAL S/ASIA ADMIN

B61

CONOVER H.F.,SERIALS FOR AFRICAN STUDIES. ECO/UNDEV DIPLOM LEAD NAT/LISM ATTIT...SOC 20. PAGE 33 H0653
BIBLIOG AFR NAT/G

B61

DIA M.,THE AFRICAN NATIONS AND WORLD SOLIDARITY. ISLAM CULTURE ELITES ECO/DEV ECO/UNDEV INT/ORG NAT/G PLAN ECO/TAC INT/TRADE EDU/PROP NAT/LISM ATTIT DRIVE ORD/FREE WEALTH...SOCIALIST CONCPT CON/ANAL GEN/LAWS TOT/POP 20. PAGE 41 H0817
AFR REGION SOCISM

B61

DUFFY J.,AFRICA SPEAKS. GHANA TOGO CULTURE ECO/UNDEV PROB/SOLV COLONIAL NEUTRAL DISCRIM NAT/LISM SOVEREIGN ALL/IDEOS...CONCPT ANTHOL SOC/INTEG 20 NEGRO THIRD/WRLD. PAGE 43 H0857
AFR NAT/G FUT STRUCT

B61

ERASMUS C.J.,MAN TAKES CONTROL: CULTURAL DEVELOPMENT AND AMERICAN AID. STRUCT OWN DRIVE PERCEPT...SOC 20 MEXIC/AMER. PAGE 47 H0937
ORD/FREE CULTURE ECO/UNDEV TEC/DEV

B61

ESTEBAN J.C.,IMPERIALISMO Y DESARROLLO ECONOMICO. L/A+17C FINAN INDUS NAT/G ECO/TAC CONTROL ROLE. PAGE 47 H0941
ECO/UNDEV NAT/LISM DIPLOM BAL/PAY

B61

ESTEVEZ A.,ASPECTOS ECONOMICO-FINANCIEROS DE LA CAMPANA SANMARITANA. L/A+17C SPAIN FINAN COLONIAL LEAD ROLE ORD/FREE WEALTH 19 SOUTH/AMER SAN/MARTIN. PAGE 47 H0942
ECO/UNDEV REV BUDGET NAT/G

B61

FIRTH R.,ELEMENTS OF SOCIAL ORGANIZATION (3RD ED.). STRATA STRUCT ECO/UNDEV NEIGH CHIEF INGP/REL ATTIT MORAL...PHIL/SCI GP/COMP WORSHIP SOC/INTEG 20. PAGE 50 H1009
SOC CULTURE SOCIETY KIN

B61

GANGULI B.N.,ECONOMIC INTEGRATION. FINAN LABOR CAP/ISM DIPLOM WEALTH...NAT/COMP 20. PAGE 55 H1096
ECO/TAC METH/CNCPT EQUILIB ECO/UNDEV

B61

GUEVARA E.,GUERRILLA WARFARE. L/A+17C ECO/UNDEV NAT/G POL/PAR VOL/ASSN PLAN DOMIN REV DRIVE PWR WEALTH...NEW/IDEA RECORD BIOG COLD/WAR MARX/KARL OAS 20. PAGE 62 H1247
FORCES COERCE GUERRILLA CUBA

B61

HADDAD J.A.,REVOLUCAO CUBANA E REVOLUCAO BRASILEIRA. BRAZIL CUBA L/A+17C STRATA AGRI WORKER EDU/PROP REGION...POLICY NAT/COMP 20. PAGE 63 H1272
REV ORD/FREE DIPLOM ECO/UNDEV

B61

HICKS U.K.,DEVELOPMENT FROM BELOW. UK INDUS ADMIN COLONIAL ROUTINE GOV/REL...POLICY METH/CNCPT CHARTS 19/20 CMN/WLTH. PAGE 71 H1414
ECO/UNDEV LOC/G GOV/COMP METH/COMP

B61

KEREKES T.,THE ARAB MIDDLE EAST AND MUSLIM AFRICA. ISLAM SOCIETY ECO/UNDEV SECT VOL/ASSN TOP/EX REGION ATTIT PWR...GEOG CONCPT TIME/SEQ GEN/LAWS 20. PAGE 85 H1694
NAT/G TREND NAT/LISM

B61

KISSINGER H.A.,THE NECESSITY FOR CHOICE. FUT USA+45 ECO/UNDEV NAT/G PLAN BAL/PWR ECO/TAC ARMS/CONT DETER NUC/PWR ATTIT...POLICY CONCPT RECORD GEN/LAWS COLD/WAR 20. PAGE 87 H1728
TOP/EX TREND DIPLOM

B61

LAHAYE R.,LES ENTREPRISES PUBLIQUES AU MAROC. FRANCE MOROCCO LAW DIST/IND EXTR/IND FINAN CONSULT PLAN TEC/DEV ADMIN AGREE CONTROL OWN...POLICY 20. PAGE 90 H1796
NAT/G INDUS ECO/UNDEV ECO/TAC

B61

LETHBRIDGE H.J.,CHINA'S URBAN COMMUNES. CHINA/COM FUT ECO/UNDEV DIPLOM EDU/PROP DEMAND INCOME MARXISM ...POLICY 20. PAGE 95 H1893
MUNIC CONTROL ECO/TAC NAT/G

B61

LUZ N.V.,A LUTA PELA INDUSTRIALIZACAO DO BRAZIL. BRAZIL L/A+17C AGRI NAT/G TEC/DEV COLONIAL 19/20. PAGE 99 H1981
ECO/UNDEV INDUS NAT/LISM POLICY

B61

MARX K.,THE COMMUNIST MANIFESTO. IN (MENDEL A. ESSENTIAL WORKS OF MARXISM, NEW YORK: BANTAM. FUT MOD/EUR CULTURE ECO/DEV ECO/UNDEV AGRI FINAN INDUS MARKET PROC/MFG LABOR MUNIC POL/PAR CONSULT FORCES CREATE PLAN ADMIN ATTIT DRIVE RIGID/FLEX ORD/FREE PWR RESPECT MARX/KARL WORK. PAGE 104 H2081
COM NEW/IDEA CAP/ISM REV

B61

MAYNE A.,DESIGNING AND ADMINISTERING A REGIONAL ECONOMIC DEVELOPMENT PLAN WITH SPECIFIC REFERENCE TO PUERTO RICO (PAMPHLET). PUERT/RICO SOCIETY NAT/G DELIB/GP REGION...DECISION 20. PAGE 105 H2106
ECO/UNDEV PLAN CREATE ADMIN

B61

MILLIKAW M.F.,THE EMERGING NATIONS: THEIR GROWTH AND UNITED STATES POLICY. FUT USA+45 WOR+45 WOR-45 NAT/G PLAN TEC/DEV BAL/PWR GOV/REL PEACE ORD/FREE 20. PAGE 111 H2216
ECO/UNDEV POLICY DIPLOM FOR/AID

B61

MIT CENTER INTERNATIONAL STU,OFFICIAL SERIAL PUBLICATIONS RELATING TO ECONOMIC DEVELOPMENT IN AFRICA SOUTH OF THE SAHARA. AFR SOCIETY AGRI FINAN INDUS LG/CO ADMIN 20. PAGE 111 H2228
BIBLIOG ECO/UNDEV ECO/TAC NAT/G

B61

MUNGER E.S.,AFRICAN FIELD REPORTS 1952-1961.
AFR

SOUTH/AFR SOCIETY ECO/UNDEV NAT/G POL/PAR COLONIAL EXEC PARL/PROC GUERRILLA RACE/REL ALL/IDEOS...SOC AUD/VIS 20. PAGE 114 H2288 DISCRIM RECORD

B61
NATIONAL BANK OF LIBYA,INFLATION IN LIBYA (PAMPHLET). LIBYA SOCIETY NAT/G PLAN INT/TRADE ...STAT CHARTS 20 GOLD/STAND. PAGE 116 H2318 ECO/TAC ECO/UNDEV FINAN BUDGET

B61
PALMER N.D.,THE INDIAN POLITICAL SYSTEM. INDIA ECO/UNDEV SECT CHIEF COLONIAL CHOOSE ALL/IDEOS SOCISM...CHARTS BIBLIOG/A 20. PAGE 123 H2452 NAT/LISM POL/PAR NAT/G DIPLOM

B61
PANIKKAR K.M.,REVOLUTION IN AFRICA. AFR GUINEA ECO/UNDEV POL/PAR DIPLOM COLONIAL EXEC LEAD SOVEREIGN...CHARTS 20. PAGE 123 H2461 NAT/LISM NAT/G CHIEF

B61
PECKERT J.,DIE GROSSEN UND DIE KLEINEN MAECHTE. COM GERMANY/W ECO/DEV ECO/UNDEV NAT/G WAR RACE/REL PEACE...POLICY GP/COMP GOV/COMP 20 COLD/WAR. PAGE 124 H2482 DIPLOM ECO/TAC BAL/PWR

B61
ROIG E.,MARTI, ANTIIMPERIALISTA. CUBA L/A+17C DIPLOM DOMIN COLONIAL CONTROL LEAD PWR SOVEREIGN ...PHIL/SCI 19 MARTI/JOSE INTERVENT. PAGE 133 H2664 PERSON NAT/LISM ECO/UNDEV ORD/FREE

B61
RYDINGS H.A.,THE BIBLIOGRAPHIES OF WEST AFRICA (PAMPHLET). ECO/UNDEV NAT/G COLONIAL REGION ATTIT 20. PAGE 136 H2725 BIBLIOG/A AFR NAT/COMP

B61
SAKAI R.K.,STUDIES ON ASIA, 1961. ASIA BURMA INDIA S/ASIA FINAN ECO/TAC NAT/LISM SOCISM...POLICY ANTHOL 19/20 CHINJAP. PAGE 137 H2734 ECO/UNDEV SECT

B61
SETON-WATSON H.,FROM LENIN TO KHRUSHCHEV: THE HISTORY OF WORLD COMMUNISM. ASIA COM EUR+WWI ISLAM S/ASIA ECO/DEV ECO/UNDEV NAT/G POL/PAR DIPLOM ECO/TAC EDU/PROP COERCE GUERRILLA ATTIT DRIVE WORK TOT/POP NAZI 20. PAGE 141 H2832 PWR REV USSR

B61
SOUTHALL A.,SOCIAL CHANGE IN MODERN AFRICA. CULTURE STRATA ECO/UNDEV AGRI FAM KIN MUNIC GP/REL INGP/REL MARRIAGE...GEOG ANTHOL 20. PAGE 147 H2940 AFR TREND SOCIETY SOC

B61
SSU-YU T.,JAPANESE STUDIES ON JAPAN AND THE FAR EAST: A SHORT BIOGRAPHICAL AND BIBLIOGRAPHICAL INTRODUCTION. ASIA CULTURE ECO/UNDEV NAT/G DIPLOM 20 CHINJAP. PAGE 148 H2962 BIBLIOG SOC

B61
STARK H.,SOCIAL AND ECONOMIC FRONTIERS IN LATIN AMERICA (2ND ED.). CUBA FUT CULTURE AGRI INDUS ECO/TAC PRODUC ATTIT MARXISM...NAT/COMP BIBLIOG T 20. PAGE 149 H2971 L/A+17C SOCIETY DIPLOM ECO/UNDEV

B61
YUAN TUNG-LI,A GUIDE TO DOCTORAL DISSERTATIONS BY CHINESE STUDENTS IN AMERICA, 1905-1960. ASIA CULTURE SOCIETY ECO/UNDEV NAT/G PROB/SOLV DIPLOM LEAD ATTIT...HUM SOC STAT 20. PAGE 172 H3442 BIBLIOG ACADEM ACT/RES OP/RES

S61
FITZGIBBON R.H.,"MEASUREMENT OF LATIN AMERICAN POLITICAL CHANGE." L/A+17C CONSTN CULTURE SOCIETY ECO/UNDEV NAT/G POL/PAR PUB/INST ACT/RES EDU/PROP PERCEPT KNOWL ORD/FREE SOVEREIGN...METH/CNCPT TREND OAS 20. PAGE 51 H1020 CHOOSE ATTIT

S61
HOSELITZ B.F.,"ECONOMIC DEVELOPMENT AND POLITICAL STABILITY IN INDIA" INDIA NAT/G GP/REL...POLICY 20. PAGE 74 H1475 ECO/UNDEV GEN/LAWS PROB/SOLV

S61
PADELFORD N.J.,"POLITICS AND THE FUTURE OF ECOSOC." AFR S/ASIA ECO/UNDEV INDUS NAT/G DELIB/GP ACT/RES ORD/FREE WEALTH...CONCPT CHARTS UN 20 ECOSOC. PAGE 122 H2438 INT/ORG TEC/DEV

S61
VALLET R.,"IRAN: KEY TO THE MIDDLE EAST." COM IRAQ ISLAM KUWAIT LEBANON SAUDI/ARAB TURKEY ELITES SOCIETY INDUS PROC/MFG POL/PAR TOP/EX PLAN BAL/PWR DIPLOM ECO/TAC ALL/VALS...TREND CENTO 20. PAGE 161 H3224 NAT/G ECO/UNDEV IRAN

B62
BARNETT A.D.,COMMUNIST CHINA IN PERSPECTIVE. CHINA/COM FUT CULTURE ECO/UNDEV TEC/DEV CONTROL 20. PAGE 11 H0222 REV MARXISM TREND PLAN

B62
BRETTON H.L.,POWER AND STABILITY IN NIGERIA: THE POLITICS OF DECOLONIZATION. AFR CONSTN INTELL ECO/UNDEV COM/IND KIN NAT/G POL/PAR PROVS VOL/ASSN LEGIS DOMIN EDU/PROP LEGIT EXEC ROUTINE CHOOSE NAT/LISM ATTIT PERCEPT ALL/VALS. PAGE 20 H0411 CULTURE OBS NIGERIA

B62
BROWN S.D.,STUDIES ON ASIA, 1962. ASIA BURMA INDIA ISLAM ISRAEL S/ASIA ECO/UNDEV POL/PAR SECT ECO/TAC ...ANTHOL 20 CHINJAP. PAGE 22 H0450 PWR PARL/PROC

B62
BUSIA K.A.,THE CHALLENGE OF AFRICA. CULTURE KIN MUNIC NAT/G POL/PAR SCHOOL DELIB/GP PLAN ECO/TAC DOMIN EDU/PROP TOTALISM ATTIT PERSON ALL/VALS SOVEREIGN...SOC CONCPT STERTYP TOT/POP VAL/FREE 20. PAGE 25 H0496 AFR ECO/UNDEV NAT/LISM

B62
CARY J.,THE CASE FOR AFRICAN FREEDOM AND OTHER WRITINGS ON AFRICA. AFR UK INDUS LOC/G NAT/G SECT INT/TRADE EDU/PROP GOV/REL RACE/REL ORD/FREE ...CONCPT ANTHOL 19/20. PAGE 27 H0552 NAT/LISM COLONIAL TREND ECO/UNDEV

B62
COSTA RICA UNIVERSIDAD BIBL,LISTA DE TESIS DE GRADO DE LA UNIVERSIDAD DE COSTA RICA. COSTA/RICA LAW LOC/G ADMIN LEAD...SOC 20. PAGE 34 H0675 BIBLIOG/A NAT/G DIPLOM ECO/UNDEV

B62
COUNCIL ON WORLD TENSIONS,RESTLESS NATIONS. WOR+45 STRUCT INT/ORG NAT/G PLAN ECO/TAC...NAT/COMP ANTHOL 20. PAGE 34 H0678 ECO/UNDEV POLICY DIPLOM TASK

B62
DE MADARIAGA S.,L'AMERIQUE LATINE ENTRE L'OURS ET L'AIGLE. L/A+17C SOCIETY NAT/G ECO/TAC EDU/PROP REGION COERCE ATTIT ALL/VALS...MAJORIT TIME/SEQ STERTYP COLD/WAR OAS 20. PAGE 38 H0760 POL/PAR ECO/UNDEV

B62
DIAZ J.S.,MANUAL DE BIBLIOGRAFIA DE LA LITERATURA ESPANOLA. PRE/AMER SPAIN ECO/UNDEV DIPLOM LEAD ATTIT...SOC 15/20. PAGE 41 H0820 BIBLIOG L/A+17C NAT/G COLONIAL

B62
DUROSELLE J.B.,LES NOUVEAUX ETATS DANS LES RELATIONS INTERNATIONALES. AFR CHINA/COM FRANCE MOROCCO S/ASIA USSR ECO/UNDEV INT/ORG PLAN ECO/TAC EDU/PROP ATTIT DRIVE...TREND TOT/POP TUNIS 20. PAGE 44 H0872 NAT/G CONSTN DIPLOM

B62
FATOUROS A.A.,GOVERNMENT GUARANTEES TO FOREIGN INVESTORS. WOR+45 ECO/UNDEV INDUS WORKER ADJUD ...NAT/COMP BIBLIOG TREATY. PAGE 49 H0975 NAT/G FINAN INT/TRADE ECO/DEV

B62
GALENSON W.,LABOR IN DEVELOPING COUNTRIES. BRAZIL INDONESIA ISRAEL PAKISTAN TURKEY AGRI INDUS WORKER PAY PRICE GP/REL WEALTH...MGT CHARTS METH/COMP NAT/COMP 20. PAGE 54 H1088 LABOR ECO/UNDEV BARGAIN POL/PAR

B62
GREEN L.P.,DEVELOPMENT IN AFRICA. AFR CENTRL/AFR GHANA RHODESIA SOUTH/AFR AGRI PROC/MFG INT/TRADE DEMAND NAT/LISM PRODUC WEALTH...GEOG METH/CNCPT CHARTS BIBLIOG 20. PAGE 60 H1206 CULTURE ECO/UNDEV GOV/REL TREND

B62
GUENA Y.,HISTORIQUE DE LA COMMUNAUTE. FUT ECO/UNDEV NAT/G PLAN EDU/PROP COLONIAL REGION NAT/LISM ALL/VALS SOVEREIGN...CONCPT OBS CHARTS 20. PAGE 62 H1244 AFR VOL/ASSN FOR/AID FRANCE

B62
HATCH J.,AFRICA TODAY-AND TOMORROW: AN OUTLINE OF BASIC FACTS AND MAJOR PROBLEMS. AFR FUT ISLAM STRATA ECO/UNDEV INT/ORG NAT/G POL/PAR DELIB/GP TOP/EX EDU/PROP LEGIT CHOOSE ATTIT...TIME/SEQ TOT/POP COLD/WAR 20. PAGE 67 H1353 PLAN CONSTN NAT/LISM

B62
HUNTER G.,THE NEW SOCIETIES OF TROPICAL AFRICA. CULTURE INDUS KIN MUNIC WORKER INT/TRADE EDU/PROP ORD/FREE...INT TREND 20. PAGE 75 H1500 AFR GOV/COMP ECO/UNDEV SOCIETY

B62
INAYATULLAH,BUREAUCRACY AND DEVELOPMENT IN PAKISTAN. PAKISTAN ECO/UNDEV EDU/PROP CONFER ...ANTHOL DICTIONARY 20 BUREAUCRCY. PAGE 76 H1526 EX/STRUC ADMIN NAT/G LOC/G

B62
JOHNSON J.J.,THE ROLE OF THE MILITARY IN UNDERDEVELOPED COUNTRIES. AFR BURMA INDONESIA ISLAM ISRAEL L/A+17C S/ASIA THAILAND CULTURE ECO/UNDEV KIN PROVS CONSULT ACT/RES COERCE REV DRIVE RIGID/FLEX ORD/FREE...RECORD ANTHOL 20. PAGE 81 H1622 FORCES CONCPT

B62
KEESING F.M.,THE ETHNOHISTORY OF NORTHERN LUZON. PHILIPPINE ECO/UNDEV FAM SECT CHIEF REGION GP/REL HABITAT...GEOG LING BIBLIOG WORSHIP 20. PAGE 84 H1680 CULTURE SOC KIN

B62
KENNEDY R.,BIBLIOGRAPHY OF INDONESIAN PEOPLES AND CULTURES (2ND REV. ED.). INDONESIA STRUCT ECO/UNDEV SCHOOL EDU/PROP COLONIAL...GEOG SOC LING NAT/COMP 20. PAGE 85 H1689 BIBLIOG S/ASIA CULTURE KIN

B62
KINDLEBERGER C.P.,FOREIGN TRADE AND THE NATIONAL ECONOMY. WOR+45 ECO/DEV ECO/UNDEV ECO/TAC COST DEMAND 20. PAGE 86 H1713 INT/TRADE GOV/COMP BAL/PAY POLICY

B62
MARTINS A.F.,REVOLUCAO BRANCA NO CAMPO. L/A+17C SERV/IND DEMAND EFFICIENCY PRODUC...POLICY METH/COMP. PAGE 104 H2070
AGRI ECO/UNDEV TEC/DEV NAT/COMP

B62
MEGGITT M.J.,DESERT PEOPLE. ECO/UNDEV KIN CREATE PROB/SOLV CONTROL DRIVE ROLE...GEOG SOC MYTH CHARTS BIBLIOG 20 AUSTRAL. PAGE 108 H2159
ADJUST CULTURE INGP/REL HABITAT

B62
MICHAELY M.,CONCENTRATION IN INTERNATIONAL TRADE. ECO/DEV ECO/UNDEV PRICE INCOME...CHARTS NAT/COMP 20. PAGE 110 H2197
INT/TRADE MARKET FINAN GEOG

B62
MODELSKI G.,SEATO-SIX STUDIES. ASIA CHINA/COM INDIA S/ASIA INT/ORG NAT/G ECO/TAC DETER ATTIT ORD/FREE PWR...TIME/SEQ COLD/WAR TOT/POP 20 SEATO. PAGE 112 H2234
MARKET ECO/UNDEV INT/TRADE

B62
MOUSSA P.,THE UNDERPRIVILEGED NATIONS. FINAN INT/ORG PLAN PROB/SOLV CAP/ISM GIVE TASK WEALTH ...POLICY SOC 20. PAGE 114 H2273
ECO/UNDEV NAT/G DIPLOM FOR/AID

B62
NASRI A.R.,A BIBLIOGRAPHY OF THE SUDAN 1938-1958. AFR SUDAN CREATE...SOC 20. PAGE 116 H2316
BIBLIOG ECO/UNDEV NAT/G SOCIETY

B62
PASTOR R.S.,A STATEMENT OF THE LAWS OF PARAGUAY IN MATTERS AFFECTING BUSINESS (2ND ED.). PARAGUAY INDUS FAM LABOR LG/CO NAT/G LEGIS TAX CONTROL MARRIAGE 20. PAGE 124 H2474
FINAN ECO/UNDEV LAW CONSTN

B62
PENTONY D.E.,RED WORLD IN TUMULT: COMMUNIST FOREIGN POLICIES. CHINA/COM COM NAT/G EDU/PROP COERCE ATTIT PWR RESPECT...SOC CHARTS 20. PAGE 124 H2488
ECO/UNDEV DOMIN USSR ASIA

B62
SELOSOEMARDJAN O.,SOCIAL CHANGES IN JOGJAKARTA. INDONESIA NETHERLAND ELITES STRATA STRUCT FAM POL/PAR CREATE DIPLOM INT/TRADE EDU/PROP ADMIN GOV/REL...SOC 20 JAVA CHINJAP. PAGE 141 H2825
ECO/UNDEV CULTURE REV COLONIAL

B62
TAYLOR D.,THE BRITISH IN AFRICA. UK CULTURE ECO/UNDEV INDUS DIPLOM INT/TRADE ADMIN WAR RACE/REL ORD/FREE SOVEREIGN...POLICY BIBLIOG 15/20 CMN/WLTH. PAGE 153 H3053
AFR COLONIAL DOMIN

B62
TILMAN R.O.,THE NIGERIAN POLITICAL SXENE. NIGERIA DIPLOM COLONIAL PARTIC...POLICY SOC OBS PREDICT ANTHOL 20. PAGE 155 H3096
NAT/G AFR ECO/UNDEV FEDERAL

B62
UNECA LIBRARY,BOOKS ON AFRICA IN THE UNECA LIBRARY. WOR+45 AGRI INT/ORG NAT/G PLAN WRITING REGION...SOC STAT UN. PAGE 158 H3160
BIBLIOG AFR ECO/UNDEV TEC/DEV

B62
UNECA LIBRARY,NEW ACQUISITIONS IN THE UNECA LIBRARY. LAW NAT/G PLAN PROB/SOLV TEC/DEV ADMIN REGION...GEOG SOC 20 UN. PAGE 158 H3161
BIBLIOG AFR ECO/UNDEV INT/ORG

B62
VERHAEGEN P.,BIBLIOGRAPHIE DE L'URBANISATION DE L'AFRIQUE NOIRE: SON CADRE, SES CAUSES, ET SES CONSEQUENCES ECONOMIQUES, SOCIALES... AFR...SOC 20. PAGE 162 H3244
BIBLIOG ECO/UNDEV MUNIC CULTURE

B62
VILAKAZI A.,ZULU TRANSFORMATIONS: A STUDY OF THE DYNAMICS OF SOCIAL CHANGE. AFR CULTURE ECO/UNDEV KIN NEIGH SEX...GEOG QU TREND CHARTS BIBLIOG 19/20. PAGE 163 H3254
MARRIAGE SECT SOC EDU/PROP

B62
YOUNG G.,THE HILL TRIBES OF NORTHERN THAILAND. S/ASIA THAILAND FAM KIN LOC/G GP/REL HABITAT...GEOG LING OBS 20. PAGE 172 H3438
CULTURE STRUCT ECO/UNDEV SECT

B62
YU LIEN YEN CHIU,INDEX TO THE CLASSIFIED FILES ON COMMUNIST CHINA. CHINA/COM CULTURE ECO/UNDEV CIVMIL/REL PWR WEALTH MARXISM...PSY SOC METH 20. PAGE 172 H3440
BIBLIOG INDEX COM

L62
MURACCIOLE L.,"LA BANQUE CENTRALE DES ETATS DE L'AFRIQUE DE L'OUEST." AFR LAW ECO/UNDEV INT/ORG NAT/G CONSULT ECO/TAC ROUTINE...CHARTS 20. PAGE 115 H2292
ISLAM FINAN INT/TRADE

L62
ORDONNEAU P.,"LES PROBLEMES POSES PAR L'INDEPENDANCE DES NOUVEAUX ETATS AFRICAINS ET MALGACHE SUR LE PLAN DU CONTENTIEUX." FRANCE ISLAM MADAGASCAR LAW STRATA ECO/UNDEV NAT/G LEGIS LEGIT ...JURID TIME/SEQ 20. PAGE 121 H2425
AFR ADJUD COLONIAL SOVEREIGN

S62
ANSPRENGER F.,"NATIONALISM, COMMUNISM, AND THE UNCOMMITTED NATIONS: AMERICAN PROFILES." FUT ISLAM CULTURE SOCIETY ECO/UNDEV NAT/G POL/PAR PLAN ECO/TAC EDU/PROP COERCE CHOOSE ALL/VALS MARXISM SOCISM...SOC CONCPT BIOG TREND 20. PAGE 7 H0142
AFR COM NAT/LISM

S62
CORET A.,"LE STATUT DE L'ILE CHRISTMAS DE L'OCEAN INDIEN." FUT S/ASIA ECO/DEV ECO/UNDEV VOL/ASSN DELIB/GP PLAN...RELATIV OBS TIME/SEQ TREND AUSTRAL 20. PAGE 33 H0667
NAT/G INT/ORG NEW/ZEALND

S62
PIQUEMAL M.,"LES PROBLEMES DES UNIONS D'ETATS EN AFRIQUE NOIRE." FRANCE SOCIETY INT/ORG NAT/G DELIB/GP PLAN LEGIT ADMIN COLONIAL ROUTINE ATTIT ORD/FREE PWR...GEOG METH/CNCPT 20. PAGE 126 H2515
AFR ECO/UNDEV REGION

S62
RAZAFIMBAHINY J.,"L'ORGANISATION AFRICAINE ET MALGACHE DE COOPERATION ECONOMIQUE." AFR ISLAM MADAGASCAR NAT/G ACT/RES ECO/TAC ALL/VALS ...TIME/SEQ 20. PAGE 130 H2601
INT/ORG ECO/UNDEV

S62
SHATTEN F.,"POLYCENTRISM: AFRICA: NATIONALISM AND COMMUNISM." ASIA COM FUT ISLAM CULTURE SOCIETY ECO/UNDEV NAT/G PLAN DOMIN COLONIAL COERCE CHOOSE RIGID/FLEX ALL/VALS MARXISM...CONCPT TREND 20. PAGE 143 H2852
AFR ATTIT NAT/LISM SOCISM

S62
SPRINGER H.W.,"FEDERATION IN THE CARIBBEAN: AN ATTEMPT THAT FAILED." L/A+17C ECO/UNDEV INT/ORG POL/PAR PROVS LEGIS CREATE PLAN LEGIT ADMIN FEDERAL ATTIT DRIVE PERSON ORD/FREE PWR...POLICY GEOG PSY CONCPT OBS CARIBBEAN CMN/WLTH 20. PAGE 148 H2955
VOL/ASSN NAT/G REGION

B63
BRITISH AID. UK AGRI DIST/IND INDUS SCHOOL TEC/DEV INT/TRADE COLONIAL DEMAND...TREND CHARTS 20. PAGE 2 H0041
FOR/AID ECO/UNDEV NAT/G FINAN

B63
BELFRAGE C.,THE MAN AT THE DOOR WITH THE GUN. CUBA L/A+17C NAT/G LEAD PARTIC GP/REL PWR...POLICY 20 CASTRO/F. PAGE 13 H0261
REGION ECO/UNDEV STRUCT ATTIT

B63
BERGSON A.,ECONOMIC TRENDS IN THE SOVIET UNION. USSR ECO/UNDEV AGRI NAT/G FORCES PLAN TEC/DEV INT/TRADE BAL/PAY...POLICY ANTHOL 20. PAGE 15 H0302
ECO/DEV NAT/COMP INDUS LABOR

B63
BERREMAN G.D.,HINDUS OF THE HIMALAYAS. INDIA STRATA STRUCT KIN MUNIC 20 HINDU. PAGE 16 H0319
CULTURE SECT GP/REL ECO/UNDEV

B63
BRECHER M.,THE NEW STATES OF ASIA. ASIA S/ASIA INT/ORG BAL/PWR COLONIAL NEUTRAL ORD/FREE PWR 20 UN. PAGE 20 H0407
NAT/G ECO/UNDEV DIPLOM POLICY

B63
BROEKMEIJER M.W.,DEVELOPING COUNTRIES AND NATO. USSR FORCES DIPLOM NUC/PWR WAR PEACE TOTALISM 20 NATO. PAGE 21 H0427
ECO/UNDEV FOR/AID ORD/FREE NAT/G

B63
CANELAS O.A.,RADIOGRAFIA DE LA ALIANZA PARA EL ATRASO. L/A+17C USA+45 ECO/TAC DOMIN COLONIAL NAT/LISM...SOCIALIST NAT/COMP 20. PAGE 26 H0519
REV DIPLOM ECO/UNDEV REGION

B63
CHEN N.-R.,THE ECONOMY OF MAINLAND CHINA, 1949-1963: A BIBLIOGRAPHY OF MATERIALS IN ENGLISH. CHINA/COM ECO/UNDEV PRESS 20. PAGE 29 H0586
BIBLIOG MARXISM NAT/G ASIA

B63
COLUMBIA U SCHOOL OF LAW,PUBLIC INTERNATIONAL DEVELOPMENT FINANCING IN SENEGAL. SENEGAL FINAN DELIB/GP GIVE EFFICIENCY...CHARTS GOV/COMP ANTHOL 20. PAGE 32 H0636
FOR/AID PLAN RECEIVE ECO/UNDEV

B63
COMISION DE HISTORIO,GUIA DE LOS DOCUMENTOS MICROFOTOGRAFIADOS POR LA UNIDAD MOVIL DE LA UNESCO. SOCIETY ECO/UNDEV INT/ORG ADMIN...SOC 20 UNESCO. PAGE 32 H0637
BIBLIOG NAT/G L/A+17C DIPLOM

B63
CONFERENCE ABORIGINAL STUDIES,AUSTRALIAN ABORIGINAL STUDIES. ECO/UNDEV INT/TRADE COLONIAL ADJUST HABITAT HEREDITY...GEOG PSY LING SOC/EXP ANTHOL WORSHIP 20 AUSTRAL ABORIGINES. PAGE 32 H0638
SOC SOCIETY CULTURE STRUCT

B63
DALAND R.T.,PERSPECTIVES OF BRAZILIAN PUBLIC ADMINISTRATION (VOL. I). BRAZIL LAW ECO/UNDEV SCHOOL CHIEF TEC/DEV CONFER CONTROL GP/REL ATTIT ROLE PWR...ANTHOL 20. PAGE 37 H0735
ADMIN NAT/G PLAN GOV/REL

B63
DE VRIES E.,SOCIAL ASPECTS OF ECONOMIC DEVELOPMENT IN LATIN AMERICA. CULTURE SOCIETY STRATA FINAN
L/A+17C ECO/UNDEV

INDUS INT/ORG DELIB/GP ACT/RES ECO/TAC EDU/PROP ADMIN ATTIT SUPEGO HEALTH KNOWL ORD/FREE...SOC STAT TREND ANTHOL TOT/POP VAL/FREE. PAGE 39 H0777

B63
DRIVER H.E.,ETHNOGRAPHY AND ACCULTURATION OF THE CHICHIMECA-JONAZ OF NORTHEAST MEXICO. ECO/UNDEV AGRI FAM KIN EDU/PROP MARRIAGE HEALTH...GEOG INT CHARTS WORSHIP 18/20 MEXIC/AMER. PAGE 42 H0848
CULTURE HABITAT STRUCT GP/REL

B63
ELWIN V.,A NEW DEAL FOR TRIBAL INDIA. INDIA AGRI COM/IND INDUS KIN TEC/DEV TAX EDU/PROP OWN HEALTH 20. PAGE 46 H0912
ECO/UNDEV CULTURE CONSTN SOC/WK

B63
ENKE S.,ECONOMICS FOR DEVELOPMENT. AGRI TEC/DEV CAP/ISM DIPLOM ECO/TAC TAX ATTIT DRIVE HABITAT WEALTH...GOV/COMP BIBLIOG 20. PAGE 46 H0928
ECO/UNDEV PHIL/SCI CON/ANAL

B63
FALL B.,THE TWO VIETNAMS. CULTURE SOCIETY ECO/UNDEV NAT/G TOP/EX ACT/RES PLAN ECO/TAC DOMIN EDU/PROP COERCE ATTIT DRIVE PERSON ORD/FREE PWR...SOC TIME/SEQ COLD/WAR 20. PAGE 48 H0965
S/ASIA BIOG VIETNAM

B63
FARMER B.H.,CEYLON: A DIVIDED NATION. CEYLON INDIA NETHERLAND PORTUGAL UK ELITES POL/PAR COLONIAL ...SOC MYTH CHARTS GOV/COMP WORSHIP 20. PAGE 49 H0972
DOMIN ORD/FREE ECO/UNDEV POLICY

B63
FURTADO C.,THE ECONOMIC GROWTH OF BRAZIL: A SURVEY FROM COLONIAL TO MODERN TIMES. L/A+17C AGRI DIST/IND EXTR/IND INDUS WORKER COLONIAL RACE/REL OWN GOV/COMP. PAGE 54 H1082
ECO/UNDEV TEC/DEV LABOR DOMIN

B63
GEERTZ C.,PEDDLERS AND PRINCES: SOCIAL DEVELOPMENT AND ECONOMIC CHANGE IN TWO INDONESIAN TOWNS. S/ASIA CULTURE SOCIETY STRATA FACE/GP MUNIC CREATE TEC/DEV ECO/TAC ORD/FREE WEALTH...OBS INT CENSUS CHARTS WORK TOT/POP VAL/FREE 20. PAGE 55 H1106
ECO/UNDEV SOC ELITES INDONESIA

B63
GEERTZ C.,OLD SOCIETIES AND NEW STATES: THE QUEST FOR MODERNITY IN ASIA AND AFRICA. AFR ASIA LAW CULTURE SECT EDU/PROP REV...GOV/COMP NAT/COMP 20. PAGE 55 H1107
ECO/UNDEV TEC/DEV NAT/LISM SOVEREIGN

B63
GLADE W.P. JR.,THE POLITICAL ECONOMY OF MEXICO. FUT L/A+17C CULTURE SOCIETY AGRI INDUS DELIB/GP ACT/RES ECO/TAC ATTIT HEALTH ORD/FREE...STAT TIME/SEQ TREND MEXIC/AMER TOT/POP VAL/FREE 20. PAGE 57 H1138
FINAN ECO/UNDEV

B63
GONZALEZ PEDRERO E.,ANATOMIA DE UN CONFLICTO. WOR+45 ECO/DEV ECO/UNDEV ECO/TAC FOR/AID CONTROL ARMS/CONT GOV/REL...NAT/COMP 20 COLD/WAR. PAGE 58 H1166
DIPLOM DETER BAL/PWR

B63
GUIMARAES A.P.,INFLACAO E MONOPOLIO NO BRASIL. BRAZIL FINAN NAT/G PLAN PAY...METH/COMP 20. PAGE 62 H1248
ECO/UNDEV PRICE INT/TRADE BAL/PAY

B63
HAQ M.,THE STRATEGY OF ECONOMIC PLANNING. PAKISTAN AGRI FINAN INDUS NAT/G FOR/AID TAX CONTROL REGION PRODUC...POLICY CHARTS 20. PAGE 66 H1324
ECO/TAC ECO/UNDEV PLAN PROB/SOLV

B63
HUNTER G.,EDUCATION FOR A DEVELOPING REGION; A STUDY IN EAST AFRICA. AFR TANZANIA UGANDA NAT/G TEC/DEV INGP/REL ADJUST LITERACY ATTIT 20 AFRICA/E. PAGE 75 H1501
EDU/PROP POLICY ECO/UNDEV EFFICIENCY

B63
HYDE D.,THE PEACEFUL ASSAULT. COM UAR USSR ECO/DEV ECO/UNDEV NAT/G POL/PAR CAP/ISM PWR 20. PAGE 76 H1516
MARXISM CONTROL ECO/TAC DIPLOM

B63
INDIAN INSTITUTE PUBLIC ADMIN,CASES IN INDIAN ADMINISTRATION. INDIA AGRI NAT/G PROB/SOLV TEC/DEV ECO/TAC ADMIN...ANTHOL METH 20. PAGE 77 H1532
DECISION PLAN MGT ECO/UNDEV

B63
INTERNATIONAL ASSOCIATION RES,AFRICAN STUDIES IN INCOME AND WEALTH. AFR NAT/G PROB/SOLV DEMAND INCOME...ECOMETRIC METH/COMP 20. PAGE 78 H1553
WEALTH PLAN ECO/UNDEV BUDGET

B63
ISSAWI C.,EGYPT IN REVOLUTION: AN ECONOMIC ANALYSIS. ISLAM STRUCT ECO/UNDEV AGRI FINAN INDUS PLAN EXEC REV NAT/LISM ATTIT RIGID/FLEX WEALTH SOCISM...STAT WORK 20. PAGE 79 H1573
NAT/G UAR

B63
JELAVICH C.,THE BALKANS IN TRANSITION: ESSAYS ON THE DEVELOPMENT OF BALKAN LIFE AND POLITICS SINCE THE EIGHTEENTH CENTURY. COM GREECE TURKEY ECO/UNDEV NAT/G SECT ATTIT...GEOG SOC CONCPT TIME/SEQ ANTHOL 18/20. PAGE 80 H1596
CULTURE RIGID/FLEX

B63
JENNINGS W.I.,DEMOCRACY IN AFRICA. UK CULTURE STRUCT ECO/UNDEV DIPLOM COLONIAL GP/REL ADJUST NAT/LISM ORD/FREE...GOV/COMP 20 THIRD/WRLD. PAGE 81 H1613
PROB/SOLV AFR CONSTN POPULISM

B63
JUNOD V.,HANDBOOK OF AFRICA. AFR ISLAM CONSTN SOCIETY NAT/G POL/PAR...GEOG SOC STAT CHARTS WORK 20. PAGE 82 H1642
ECO/UNDEV REGION

B63
KAPP W.K.,HINDU CULTURE: ECONOMIC DEVELOPMENT AND ECONOMIC PLANNING IN INDIA. INDIA S/ASIA CULTURE ECO/TAC EDU/PROP ADMIN ALL/VALS...POLICY MGT TIME/SEQ VAL/FREE 20. PAGE 83 H1660
SECT ECO/UNDEV

B63
LAMB B.P.,INDIA: A WORLD IN TRANSITION. INDIA ECO/UNDEV SECT EDU/PROP COLONIAL HABITAT ORD/FREE ...GEOG CHARTS BIBLIOG SOC/INTEG 20. PAGE 90 H1799
POL/PAR NAT/G DIPLOM STRATA

B63
LYON P.,NEUTRALISM. ECO/UNDEV EDU/PROP COLONIAL ALL/IDEOS...IDEA/COMP 20 COLD/WAR UN. PAGE 99 H1985
NAT/COMP NAT/LISM DIPLOM NEUTRAL

B63
MAIR L.,NEW NATIONS. AFR FAM MUNIC SECT DOMIN CHOOSE NAT/LISM ORD/FREE...SOC 19/20. PAGE 101 H2022
COLONIAL CULTURE TEC/DEV ECO/UNDEV

B63
MAJUMDAR D.N.,AN INTRODUCTION TO SOCIAL ANTHROPOLOGY. INDIA LAW STRATA ECO/UNDEV KIN DEMAND MARRIAGE...GP/COMP BIBLIOG T WORSHIP 20. PAGE 101 H2026
SOC CULTURE STRUCT GP/REL

B63
OECD,FOOD AID: ITS ROLE IN ECONOMIC DEVELOPMENT. FINAN NAT/G PLAN DIPLOM GIVE TASK WEALTH ...METH/COMP METH 20. PAGE 120 H2397
ECO/UNDEV FOR/AID INT/ORG POLICY

B63
OTERO L.M.,HONDURAS. HONDURAS SPAIN STRUCT SECT COLONIAL REV WAR ATTIT PWR...GEOG WORSHIP 16/20. PAGE 122 H2432
NAT/G SOCIETY NAT/LISM ECO/UNDEV

B63
PRICE A.G.,THE WESTERN INVASIONS OF THE PACIFIC AND ITS CONTINENTS. ASIA PRE/AMER S/ASIA ECO/UNDEV KIN NAT/G SECT FORCES DOMIN HEALTH...SOC 16/20. PAGE 128 H2560
COLONIAL CULTURE GEOG HABITAT

B63
RIVKIN A.,THE AFRICAN PRESENCE IN WORLD AFFAIRS. ECO/UNDEV AGRI INT/ORG LOC/G NAT/LISM...OBS PREDICT GOV/COMP 20. PAGE 132 H2635
AFR NAT/G DIPLOM BAL/PWR

B63
RONNING C.N.,LAW AND POLITICS IN INTER-AMERICAN DIPLOMACY. L/A+17C ECO/UNDEV NAT/G CONSULT DELIB/GP CREATE CAP/ISM ECO/TAC LEGIT REGION RIGID/FLEX ...METH/CNCPT GEN/LAWS OAS 20. PAGE 133 H2668
VOL/ASSN ALL/VALS DIPLOM

B63
SETON-WATSON H.,THE NEW IMPERIALISM. COM EUR+WWI MOD/EUR ECO/UNDEV NAT/G FORCES DIPLOM DOMIN EDU/PROP LEGIT COLONIAL EXEC COERCE GP/REL RACE/REL DISCRIM ATTIT...TIME/SEQ 20. PAGE 142 H2833
ECO/TAC RUSSIA USSR

B63
SILVERT K.H.,EXPECTANT PEOPLES: NATIONALISM AND DEVELOPMENT. CULTURE STRATA SECT LEAD REGION RACE/REL ALL/IDEOS...GEN/LAWS SOC/INTEG 20. PAGE 144 H2877
NAT/LISM ECO/UNDEV ALL/VALS

B63
STEVENS G.G.,EGYPT YESTERDAY AND TODAY. CONSTN ECO/UNDEV AGRI INDUS NAT/G POL/PAR FORCES ECO/TAC EDU/PROP COERCE WAR NAT/LISM DRIVE ALL/VALS ...TIME/SEQ WORK SUEZ 20. PAGE 149 H2983
ISLAM TOP/EX REV UAR

B63
STIFEL L.D.,THE TEXTILE INDUSTRY - A CASE STUDY OF INDUSTRIAL DEVELOPMENT IN THE PHILIPPINES (PAPER). PHILIPPINE WORKER CAP/ISM INT/TRADE TARIFFS RECEIVE PRICE ADMIN COST EFFICIENCY WEALTH...BIBLIOG 20. PAGE 149 H2986
S/ASIA ECO/UNDEV PROC/MFG NAT/G

B63
TINDALE N.B.,ABORIGINAL AUSTRALIANS. KIN CREATE ROLE...SOC MYTH TREND 20 AUSTRAL ABORIGINES MIGRATION. PAGE 155 H3099
CULTURE DRIVE ECO/UNDEV HABITAT

B63
UN SECRETARY GENERAL,PLANNING FOR ECONOMIC DEVELOPMENT. ECO/UNDEV FINAN BUDGET INT/TRADE TARIFFS TAX ADMIN 20 UN. PAGE 158 H3159
PLAN ECO/TAC MGT NAT/COMP

B63
VIARD R.,LA FIN DE L'EMPIRE COLONIAL FRANCAIS. AFR FUT S/ASIA ECO/UNDEV NAT/G CONSULT PLAN ECO/TAC EDU/PROP REGION NAT/LISM ALL/VALS...CONCPT TIME/SEQ TREND VAL/FREE 20. PAGE 162 H3248
VOL/ASSN COLONIAL FRANCE

B63
WAGLEY C.,INTRODUCTION TO BRAZIL. BRAZIL L/A+17C FAM KIN SCHOOL SECT ATTIT WEALTH...GEOG SOC.
ECO/UNDEV ELITES

PAGE 164 H3286
HABITAT STRATA

B63
WEINER M.,POLITICAL CHANGE IN SOUTH ASIA. CEYLON INDIA PAKISTAN S/ASIA CULTURE ELITES ECO/UNDEV EX/STRUC ADMIN CONTROL CHOOSE CONSERVE...GOV/COMP ANTHOL 20. PAGE 166 H3328
NAT/G CONSTN TEC/DEV

B63
WILCOX W.A.,PAKISTAN; THE CONSOLIDATION OF A NATION. INDIA PAKISTAN CONSTN SECT PROB/SOLV COLONIAL PARTIC GP/REL FEDERAL...POLICY 19/20. PAGE 168 H3361
NAT/LISM ECO/UNDEV DIPLOM STRUCT

B63
WILSON U.,EDUCATION AND CHANGING WEST AFRICAN CULTURE. AFR MOD/EUR UK CULTURE ECO/UNDEV MUNIC CONSULT 19/20 CMN/WLTH AFRICA/W. PAGE 169 H3384
COLONIAL POLICY SCHOOL

B63
WODDIS J.,AFRICA, THE WAY AHEAD. AFR FUT ELITES POL/PAR CAP/ISM DIPLOM DOMIN RACE/REL ATTIT ORD/FREE SOVEREIGN SOCISM 20 PANAF/FREE. PAGE 170 H3394
REV COLONIAL ECO/UNDEV NAT/G

L63
NASH M.,"PSYCHO-CULTURAL FACTORS IN ASIAN ECONOMIC GROWTH." ASIA ISLAM S/ASIA CULTURE ECO/UNDEV DELIB/GP EDU/PROP COERCE ATTIT PERSON HEALTH KNOWL ORD/FREE...PSY SOC STAT TREND ANTHOL VAL/FREE 20. PAGE 116 H2313
SOCIETY ECO/TAC

S63
AYAL E.B.,"VALUE SYSTEM AND ECONOMIC DEVELOPMENT IN JAPAN AND THAILAND." ASIA S/ASIA THAILAND CULTURE ECO/DEV CAP/ISM DOMIN NAT/LISM DRIVE RIGID/FLEX SOCISM...WELF/ST OBS TREND CON/ANAL GEN/LAWS 20 CHINJAP. PAGE 9 H0185
ECO/UNDEV ALL/VALS

S63
HARRIS R.L.,"COMMUNISM AND ASIA: ILLUSIONS AND MISCONCEPTIONS." ASIA COM FUT S/ASIA ECO/UNDEV AGRI NAT/G POL/PAR EX/STRUC EDU/PROP COERCE ATTIT MARXISM COLD/WAR TOT/POP 20. PAGE 67 H1344
PWR GUERRILLA

S63
LIGOT M.,"LA COOPERATION MILITAIRE DANS LES ACCORDS, PASSES ENTRE LA FRANCE ET LES ETATS AFRICAINS ET MALGACHE D'EXPRESSION." ECO/UNDEV INT/ORG NAT/G VOL/ASSN...CONCPT TIME/SEQ 20. PAGE 97 H1931
AFR FORCES FOR/AID FRANCE

S63
MBOYA T.,"AFRICAN SOCIALISM." ECO/UNDEV INT/ORG DIPLOM FOR/AID INT/TRADE REGION GP/REL ATTIT ORD/FREE EACM. PAGE 106 H2116
AFR SOCISM CULTURE NAT/LISM

S63
NYE J.,"TANGANYIKA'S SELF-HELP." TANZANIA NAT/G GIVE COST EFFICIENCY NAT/LISM 20. PAGE 119 H2381
ECO/TAC POL/PAR ECO/UNDEV WORKER

S63
ROBINSON W.C.,"URBANIZATION AND FERTILITY: THE NON-WESTERN EXPERIENCE (BMR)" DEATH MARRIAGE AGE/C BIO/SOC...STAT CENSUS CON/ANAL CHARTS NAT/COMP 20 THIRD/WRLD. PAGE 133 H2651
GEOG MUNIC FAM ECO/UNDEV

S63
ROUGEMONT D.,"LES NOUVELLES CHANCES DE L'EUROPE." EUR+WWI FUT ECO/DEV INT/ORG NAT/G ACT/RES PLAN TEC/DEV EDU/PROP ADMIN COLONIAL FEDERAL ATTIT PWR SKILL...TREND 20. PAGE 135 H2696
ECO/UNDEV PERCEPT

S63
SOEMARDJORN S.,"SOME SOCIAL AND CULTURAL IMPLICATIONS OF INDONESIA'S PLANNED AND UNPLANNED DEVELOPMENT." EUR+WWI FUT MOD/EUR S/ASIA CONSTN SOCIETY DELIB/GP ACT/RES PLAN ECO/TAC EDU/PROP COERCE ATTIT ALL/VALS...TIME/SEQ 20. PAGE 146 H2927
ECO/UNDEV CULTURE INDONESIA

S63
ZOLBERG A.R.,"MASS PARTIES AND NATIONAL INTEGRATION: THE CASE OF THE IVORY COAST" (BMR)" AFR IVORY/CST CONSTN VOL/ASSN DIPLOM LEAD GP/REL INGP/REL 20. PAGE 173 H3461
POL/PAR ECO/UNDEV NAT/G ADJUST

N63
LIBRARY HUNGARIAN ACADEMY SCI,HUNGARIAN PUBLICATIONS ON ASIA AND AFRICA, 1950-1962: A SELECTED BIBLIOGRAPHY (PAMPHLET). AFR ASIA HUNGARY S/ASIA ECO/UNDEV NAT/G EDU/PROP ATTIT 20 UNESCO. PAGE 96 H1922
BIBLIOG REGION DIPLOM WRITING

B64
AFRO ASIAN SOLIDARITY AGAINST IMPERIALISM. AFR ISLAM S/ASIA ECO/UNDEV NAT/G POL/PAR TOP/EX PRESS ...INT ANTHOL 20 CHOU/ENLAI. PAGE 2 H0043
MARXISM DIPLOM EDU/PROP CHIEF

B64
AKZIN B.,STATE AND NATION. UNIV ECO/UNDEV DIPLOM RACE/REL NAT/LISM ATTIT PLURISM...CONCPT IDEA/COMP 20. PAGE 4 H0090
GP/REL NAT/G KIN

B64
ALDEFER H.F.,A BIBLIOGRAPHY OF AFRICAN GOVERNMENT: 1950-1964. ALGERIA GUINEA LIBERIA UAR ECO/UNDEV POL/PAR LEGIS COLONIAL LEAD PARL/PROC NAT/LISM 20. PAGE 5 H0098
BIBLIOG AFR LOC/G NAT/G

B64
ALVIM J.C.,A REVOLUCAO SEM RUMO. BRAZIL NAT/G BAL/PWR DIPLOM INT/TRADE PARTIC WEALTH...POLICY SOC SOC/INTEG 20. PAGE 6 H0118
REV CIVMIL/REL ECO/UNDEV ORD/FREE

B64
ARASARATNAM S.,CEYLON. CEYLON NETHERLAND PORTUGAL S/ASIA UK STRUCT ECO/UNDEV SECT DIPLOM DOMIN RACE/REL NAT/LISM 17/20 CMN/WLTH. PAGE 8 H0156
COLONIAL NAT/G PROB/SOLV CULTURE

B64
BALOGH T.,THE ECONOMIC IMPACT OF MONETARY AND COMMERCIAL INSTITUTIONS OF A EUROPEAN ORIGIN IN AFRICA. AFR UAR INDUS FOR/AID COLONIAL CONTROL ...NAT/COMP 20. PAGE 10 H0205
TEC/DEV FINAN ECO/UNDEV ECO/TAC

B64
BERNDT R.M.,THE WORLD OF THE FIRST AUSTRALIANS. S/ASIA ECO/UNDEV WORKER PROB/SOLV EFFICIENCY ROLE ...SOC MYTH WORSHIP AUSTRAL ABORIGINES. PAGE 16 H0311
CULTURE KIN STRUCT DRIVE

B64
BERNSTEIN H.,A BOOKSHELF ON BRAZIL. BRAZIL ADMIN COLONIAL...HUM JURID SOC 20. PAGE 16 H0315
BIBLIOG/A NAT/G L/A+17C ECO/UNDEV

B64
BERRINGTON H.,HOW NATIONS ARE GOVERNED. FRANCE WOR+45 ECO/UNDEV INT/ORG POL/PAR CHOOSE TOTALISM KNOWL...MAJORIT T 20 UN COMMONWLTH THIRD/WRLD. PAGE 16 H0320
NAT/G GOV/COMP ECO/DEV CONSTN

B64
BROWN C.V.,GOVERNMENT AND BANKING IN WESTERN NIGERIA. AFR NIGERIA GOV/REL GP/REL...POLICY 20. PAGE 22 H0440
ADMIN ECO/UNDEV FINAN NAT/G

B64
BUTWELL R.,SOUTHEAST ASIA TODAY - AND TOMORROW. NAT/G COLONIAL LEAD REGION WAR CHOOSE WEALTH MARXISM 20. PAGE 25 H0500
S/ASIA DIPLOM ECO/UNDEV NAT/LISM

B64
COONDOO R.,THE DIVISION OF POWERS IN THE INDIAN CONSTITUTION. INDIA ECO/UNDEV FINAN TEC/DEV WAR CENTRAL EFFICIENCY NAT/LISM PWR WEALTH NEW/LIB ...BIBLIOG 18/20. PAGE 33 H0659
CONSTN LEGIS WELF/ST GOV/COMP

B64
COWAN L.G.,THE DILEMMAS OF AFRICAN INDEPENDENCE. AFR INDUS NAT/G SECT DIPLOM ECO/TAC REGION MARXISM ...CHARTS BIBLIOG 20 MAPS. PAGE 34 H0683
ORD/FREE COLONIAL REV ECO/UNDEV

B64
CURRIE D.P.,FEDERALISM AND THE NEW NATIONS OF AFRICA. CANADA USA+45 INT/TRADE TAX GP/REL ...NAT/COMP SOC/INTEG 20. PAGE 36 H0725
FEDERAL AFR ECO/UNDEV INT/LAW

B64
EMBREE A.T.,A GUIDE TO PAPERBACKS ON ASIA; SELECTED AND ANNOTATED (PAMPHLET). CULTURE SOCIETY ECO/UNDEV SECT DIPLOM COLONIAL MARXISM...SOC 20. PAGE 46 H0913
BIBLIOG/A ASIA S/ASIA NAT/G

B64
FLORENCE P.S.,ECONOMICS AND SOCIOLOGY OF INDUSTRY; A REALISTIC ANALYSIS OF DEVELOPMENT. ECO/UNDEV LG/CO NAT/G PLAN...GEOG MGT BIBLIOG 20. PAGE 51 H1029
INDUS SOC ADMIN

B64
FRIEDLAND W.H.,AFRICAN SOCIALISM. ECO/UNDEV MARKET LABOR NAT/G POL/PAR PLAN CAP/ISM ECO/TAC EDU/PROP CHOOSE ATTIT DRIVE PWR WEALTH...POLICY CONCPT RECORD STERTYP 20. PAGE 53 H1063
AFR SOCISM

B64
GILLY A.,INSIDE THE CUBAN REVOLUTION. CUBA AGRI INDUS LABOR CREATE DIPLOM...METH/COMP 20. PAGE 56 H1129
REV PLAN MARXISM ECO/UNDEV

B64
GOODNOW H.F.,THE CIVIL SERVICE OF PAKISTAN: BUREAUCRACY IN A NEW NATION. INDIA PAKISTAN S/ASIA ECO/UNDEV PROVS CHIEF PARTIC CHOOSE EFFICIENCY PWR ...BIBLIOG 20. PAGE 59 H1173
ADMIN GOV/REL LAW NAT/G

B64
GREEN M.M.,IBO VILLAGE AFFAIRS. AFR FORCES PERS/REL ADJUST ISOLAT ATTIT HABITAT PERSON ALL/VALS...JURID RECORD SOC/INTEG 20 IBO. PAGE 60 H1207
MUNIC CULTURE ECO/UNDEV SOC

B64
GUTTERIDGE W.,MILITARY INSTITUTIONS AND POWER IN THE NEW STATES. WOR+45 INT/ORG FOR/AID NEUTRAL REV CIVMIL/REL ATTIT ROLE...GOV/COMP 20. PAGE 63 H1258
FORCES DIPLOM ECO/UNDEV ELITES

B64
HAMILTON W.B.,THE TRANSFER OF INSTITUTIONS. CANADA INDIA UK LAW AGRI LABOR SECT COLONIAL 18/20. PAGE 65 H1301
NAT/COMP ECO/UNDEV EDU/PROP CULTURE

B64
HARBISON F.H.,EDUCATION, MANPOWER, AND ECONOMIC GROWTH. WOR+45 ECO/DEV ECO/UNDEV ACADEM LABOR SCHOOL WORKER UTIL...IDEA/COMP NAT/COMP. PAGE 66 H1326
PLAN TEC/DEV EDU/PROP SKILL

B64
HARRIS M.,PATTERNS OF RACE IN THE AMERICAS. BRAZIL L/A+17C STRATA ECO/UNDEV AGRI KIN MUNIC SECT COLONIAL RACE/REL...SOC SOC/INTEG 17/20 NEGRO INDIAN/AM. PAGE 67 H1342
STRUCT PRE/AMER CULTURE SOCIETY

B64
HAZLEWOOD A.,THE ECONOMICS OF DEVELOPMENT: AN ANNOTATED LIST OF BOOKS AND ARTICLES PUBLISHED 1958-1962. AGRI FINAN INDUS LABOR NAT/G DIPLOM INT/TRADE INCOME...MGT 20. PAGE 69 H1374
BIBLIOG/A ECO/UNDEV TEC/DEV

B64
HERRICK M.D.,CATALOG OF AFRICAN GOVERNMENT DOCUMENTS AND AFRICAN AREA INDEX (2ND REV. ED.) ....SOC INDEX METH 20. PAGE 70 H1405
BIBLIOG ECO/UNDEV AFR NAT/G

B64
HERSKOVITS M.J.,ECONOMIC TRANSITION IN AFRICA. FUT INT/ORG NAT/G WORKER PROB/SOLV TEC/DEV INT/TRADE EQUILIB INCOME...ANTHOL 20. PAGE 70 H1408
AFR ECO/UNDEV PLAN ADMIN

B64
HOROWITZ I.L.,REVOLUTION IN BRAZIL. BRAZIL L/A+17C ELITES STRATA NAT/G BAL/PWR PARTIC ATTIT 20. PAGE 74 H1473
ECO/UNDEV DIPLOM POLICY ORD/FREE

B64
HUXLEY M.,FAREWILL TO EDEN. SOCIETY ACT/RES EDU/PROP HEALTH...SOC AUD/VIS. PAGE 76 H1513
ECO/UNDEV SECT CULTURE ADJUST

B64
INTERNATIONAL LABOUR OFFICE,EMPLOYMENT AND ECONOMIC GROWTH. ECO/DEV ECO/UNDEV NAT/G PLAN DIPLOM INT/TRADE CONTROL INCOME PRODUC WEALTH...STAT NAT/COMP 20 ILO. PAGE 78 H1558
WORKER METH/COMP ECO/TAC OPTIMAL

B64
JUCKER-FLEETWOOD E.,MONEY AND FINANCE IN AFRICA. ISLAM ECO/UNDEV SERV/IND NAT/G EX/STRUC PLAN ECO/TAC ROUTINE WEALTH...MGT TOT/POP 20. PAGE 82 H1639
AFR FINAN

B64
KALDOR N.,ESSAYS ON ECONOMIC POLICY (VOL. II). CHILE GERMANY INDIA FINAN...GOV/COMP METH/COMP 20 KEYNES/JM. PAGE 83 H1651
BAL/PAY INT/TRADE METH/CNCPT ECO/UNDEV

B64
KITCHEN H.,A HANDBOOK OF AFRICAN AFFAIRS. ECO/UNDEV CREATE DIPLOM COLONIAL RACE/REL...ART/METH GEOG CHARTS 20. PAGE 87 H1729
AFR NAT/G INT/ORG FORCES

B64
LATOURETTE K.S.,CHINA. ASIA CHINA/COM FUT USSR ECO/UNDEV ECO/TAC WAR 19/20. PAGE 92 H1838
MARXISM NAT/G POLICY DIPLOM

B64
LAWRENCE P.,ROAD BELONG CARGO: A STUDY OF CARGO MOVEMENT IN SOUTHERN MADANG DISTRICT, NEW GUINEA. S/ASIA CULTURE ECO/UNDEV PROC/MFG KIN CHIEF COLONIAL COERCE GP/REL DRIVE WEALTH WORSHIP 20 NEW/GUINEA. PAGE 92 H1846
SOC SECT ALL/VALS MYTH

B64
LEBRUN J.,BIBLIOGRAPHIE DE LA FERTILITE DES SOLS ET ELEMENTS DE SOCIOLOGIE RURALE EN AFRIQUE AU SUD DU SAHARA. AFR PLAN TEC/DEV EFFICIENCY PRODUC...GEOG SOC NAT/COMP 20. PAGE 93 H1850
BIBLIOG/A ECO/UNDEV HABITAT AGRI

B64
LEMARCHAND R.,POLITICAL AWAKENING IN THE BELGIAN CONGO. ECO/UNDEV VOL/ASSN DOMIN CHOOSE GP/REL INGP/REL DISCRIM ORD/FREE PWR...CHARTS 20 CONGO ARABS. PAGE 94 H1873
NAT/LISM COLONIAL POL/PAR RACE/REL

B64
LEWIN P.,THE FOREIGN TRADE OF COMMUNIST CHINA* ITS IMPACT ON THE FREE WORLD. AFR EUR+WWI L/A+17C S/ASIA ECO/UNDEV CREATE FOR/AID...STAT NET/THEORY TREND CHARTS. PAGE 96 H1910
ASIA INT/TRADE NAT/COMP USSR

B64
LI C.M.,INDUSTRIAL DEVELOPMENT IN COMMUNIST CHINA. CHINA/COM ECO/DEV ECO/UNDEV AGRI FINAN INDUS MARKET LABOR NAT/G ECO/TAC INT/TRADE EXEC ALL/VALS ...POLICY RELATIV TREND WORK TOT/POP VAL/FREE 20. PAGE 96 H1921
ASIA TEC/DEV

B64
MAHAR J.M.,INDIA: A CRITICAL BIBLIOGRAPHY. INDIA PAKISTAN CULTURE ECO/UNDEV LOC/G POL/PAR SECT PROB/SOLV DIPLOM ADMIN COLONIAL PARL/PROC ATTIT 20. PAGE 101 H2016
BIBLIOG/A S/ASIA NAT/G LEAD

B64
MATTHEWS D.G.,A CURRENT VIEW OF AFRICANA (PAMPHLET). CULTURE ECO/UNDEV DIPLOM RACE/REL ATTIT 20. PAGE 105 H2092
BIBLIOG/A AFR NAT/G NAT/LISM

B64
MAUD J.,AID FOR DEVELOPING COUNTRIES. COM EUR+WWI UK INT/TRADE ORD/FREE...GOV/COMP 20. PAGE 105 H2101
FOR/AID DIPLOM ECO/TAC ECO/UNDEV

B64
MELADY T.,FACES OF AFRICA. AFR FUT ISLAM NAT/G POL/PAR SCHOOL DELIB/GP PLAN ECO/TAC EDU/PROP ATTIT ALL/VALS...CHARTS TOT/POP VAL/FREE 20. PAGE 108 H2168
ECO/UNDEV TREND NAT/LISM

B64
OECD,DEVELOPMENT ASSISTANCE EFFORTS - POLICIES OF THE MEMBERS. AGRI INDUS BUDGET...GEOG NAT/COMP 20 OECD. PAGE 120 H2398
INT/ORG FOR/AID ECO/UNDEV TEC/DEV

B64
OECD SEMINAR REGIONAL DEV,REGIONAL DEVELOPMENT IN ISRAEL. ISRAEL STRUCT ECO/UNDEV NAT/G REGION...GEOG 20. PAGE 120 H2404
ADMIN PROVS PLAN METH/COMP

B64
PIPES R.,THE FORMATION OF THE SOVIET UNION. EUR+WWI MOD/EUR STRUCT ECO/UNDEV NAT/G LEGIS DOMIN LEGIT CT/SYS EXEC COERCE ALL/VALS...POLICY RELATIV HIST/WRIT TIME/SEQ TOT/POP 19/20. PAGE 126 H2514
COM USSR RUSSIA

B64
POWELSON J.P.,LATIN AMERICA: TODAY'S ECONOMIC AND SOCIAL REVOLUTION. L/A+17C INTELL SOCIETY STRUCT AGRI INDUS NAT/G DIPLOM ECO/TAC REV...POLICY 20. PAGE 128 H2552
ECO/UNDEV WEALTH ADJUST PLAN

B64
RAMAZANI R.K.,THE MIDDLE EAST AND THE EUROPEAN COMMON MARKET. EUR+WWI ISLAM ECO/DEV EXTR/IND MARKET PROC/MFG INT/ORG NAT/G TEC/DEV ECO/TAC REGION DRIVE WEALTH...STAT CHARTS EEC TOT/POP 20. PAGE 129 H2587
ECO/UNDEV ATTIT INT/TRADE

B64
SAKAI R.K.,STUDIES ON ASIA, 1964. ASIA CHINA/COM ISRAEL MALAYSIA S/ASIA USA+45 USSR ECO/UNDEV FAM POL/PAR SECT CONSULT NAT/LISM...POLICY SOC 20 CHINJAP. PAGE 137 H2736
PWR DIPLOM

B64
SINAI I.R.,THE CHALLENGE OF MODERNISATION* THE WEST'S IMPACT ON THE NON-WESTERN WORLD. EUR+WWI CULTURE ELITES SECT CONSERVE SOCISM...GP/COMP IDEA/COMP NAT/COMP GEN/LAWS. PAGE 144 H2881
ASIA S/ASIA ECO/UNDEV CREATE

B64
SINGER M.R.,THE EMERGING ELITE: A STUDY OF POLITICAL LEADERSHIP IN CEYLON. S/ASIA ECO/UNDEV AGRI KIN NAT/G SECT EX/STRUC LEGIT ATTIT PWR RESPECT...SOC STAT CHARTS 20. PAGE 144 H2883
TOP/EX STRATA NAT/LISM CEYLON

B64
TEPASKE J.J.,EXPLOSIVE FORCES IN LATIN AMERICA. CULTURE INTELL ECO/UNDEV INT/ORG NAT/G SECT FORCES ECO/TAC EDU/PROP PWR WEALTH SOC. PAGE 153 H3063
L/A+17C RIGID/FLEX FOR/AID USSR

B64
THAILAND NATIONAL ECO DEV,THE NATIONAL ECONOMIC DEVELOPMENT PLAN: 1961-66: SECOND PHASE 1964-66. THAILAND AGRI FINAN BUDGET EFFICIENCY INCOME...STAT CHARTS 20. PAGE 153 H3065
ECO/UNDEV ECO/TAC PLAN NAT/G

B64
THORNBURG M.W.,PEOPLE AND POLICY IN THE MIDDLE EAST. ISLAM ECO/UNDEV FAM KIN MUNIC NAT/G NEIGH POL/PAR SECT DELIB/GP LEGIS PLAN ECO/TAC DOMIN ADMIN ATTIT HEALTH RESPECT...SOC CONCPT METH/CNCPT OBS TIME/SEQ TOT/POP VAL/FREE. PAGE 154 H3088
TEC/DEV CULTURE

B64
THORNTON T.P.,THE THIRD WORLD IN SOVIET PERSPECTIVE: STUDIES BY SOVIET WRITERS ON THE DEVELOPING AREAS. AFR L/A+17C S/ASIA STRATA AGRI INDUS MARKET NAT/G POL/PAR ECO/TAC COLONIAL PERCEPT PWR WEALTH...MARXIST STAT CHARTS WORK MARX/KARL 20. PAGE 155 H3090
ECO/UNDEV ACT/RES USSR DIPLOM

B64
URQUIDI V.L.,THE CHALLENGE OF DEVELOPMENT IN LATIN AMERICA. L/A+17C FINAN INT/ORG TEC/DEV DIPLOM INT/TRADE PRICE REGION PRODUC...CHARTS 20. PAGE 159 H3175
ECO/UNDEV ECO/TAC NAT/G TREND

B64
US LIBRARY OF CONGRESS,SOUTHEAST ASIA. CULTURE ...SOC STAT 20. PAGE 161 H3213
BIBLIOG/A S/ASIA ECO/UNDEV NAT/G

B64
VOELKMANN K.,HERRSCHER VON MORGEN? BAL/PWR COLONIAL NEUTRAL REGION RACE/REL ALL/VALS SOVEREIGN...RECORD 20 COLD/WAR THIRD/WRLD. PAGE 163 H3259
DIPLOM ECO/UNDEV CONTROL NAT/COMP

B64
WALLBANK T.W.,DOCUMENTS ON MODERN AFRICA. NAT/G COLONIAL GP/REL ATTIT PWR...BIBLIOG 19/20. PAGE 165 H3294
AFR NAT/LISM ECO/UNDEV DIPLOM

B64
WERTHEIM W.F.,EAST-WEST PARALLELS. INDONESIA S/ASIA SOC
NAT/G SECT...TIME/SEQ METH REFORMERS S/EASTASIA. ECO/UNDEV
PAGE 167 H3334 CULTURE
NAT/LISM

B64
WITHERELL J.W.,OFFICIAL PUBLICATIONS OF FRENCH BIBLIOG/A
EQUATORIAL AFRICA, FRENCH CAMEROONS, AND TOGO, AFR
1946-1958 (PAMPHLET). CAMEROON CHAD FRANCE GABON NAT/G
TOGO LAW ECO/UNDEV EXTR/IND INT/TRADE...GEOG HEAL ADMIN
20. PAGE 169 H3392

B64
WRAITH R.,CORRUPTION IN DEVELOPING COUNTRIES. ECO/UNDEV
NIGERIA UK LAW ELITES STRATA INDUS LOC/G NAT/G SECT CRIME
FORCES EDU/PROP ADMIN PWR WEALTH 18/20. PAGE 171 SANCTION
H3414 ATTIT

B64
ZARTMAN I.W.,MOROCCO: PROBLEMS OF NEW POWER. ISLAM CHOOSE
CULTURE ECO/UNDEV AGRI POL/PAR SCHOOL FORCES ADMIN MOROCCO
...CONCPT STAT INT CENSUS TIME/SEQ CHARTS WORK DELIB/GP
VAL/FREE 20. PAGE 172 H3449 DECISION

B64
ZOLLSCHAN G.K.,EXPLORATIONS IN SOCIAL CHANGE. ORD/FREE
SOCIETY STRATA STRUCT ECO/UNDEV EX/STRUC...PSY SIMUL
ANTHOL 20. PAGE 173 H3463 CONCPT
CULTURE

L64
MACKINTOSH J.P.,"NIGERIA'S EXTERNAL AFFAIRS." UK AFR
CULTURE ECO/UNDEV NAT/G VOL/ASSN EDU/PROP LEGIT DIPLOM
ADMIN ATTIT ORD/FREE PWR 20. PAGE 100 H2002 NIGERIA

L64
ROTBERG R.,"THE FEDERATION MOVEMENT IN BRITISH EAST VOL/ASSN
AND CENTRAL AFRICA." AFR RHODESIA UGANDA ECO/UNDEV PWR
NAT/G POL/PAR FORCES DOMIN LEGIT ADMIN COERCE ATTIT REGION
...CONCPT TREND 20 TANGANYIKA. PAGE 135 H2691

S64
CLIFFE L.,"TANGANYIKA'S TWO YEARS OF INDEPENDENCE." ECO/UNDEV
AFR INDUS MARKET NAT/G POL/PAR DELIB/GP CREATE PLAN
ECO/TAC LEGIT DRIVE ALL/VALS...METH/CNCPT RECORD 20
TANGANYIKA. PAGE 30 H0604

S64
DE GAULLE C.,"FRENCH WORLD VIEW." AFR ASIA TOP/EX
CHINA/COM EUR+WWI ISLAM ECO/UNDEV INT/ORG NAT/G PWR
VOL/ASSN ACT/RES DIPLOM ECO/TAC EDU/PROP ATTIT FOR/AID
DRIVE WEALTH 20. PAGE 37 H0751 FRANCE

S64
GARMARNIKOW M.,"INFLUENCE-BUYING IN WEST AFRICA." AFR
COM FUT USSR INTELL NAT/G PLAN TEC/DEV ECO/TAC ECO/UNDEV
DOMIN EDU/PROP REGION NAT/LISM ATTIT DRIVE ALL/VALS FOR/AID
SOVEREIGN...POLICY PSY SOC CONCPT TREND STERTYP SOCISM
WORK COLD/WAR 20. PAGE 55 H1102

S64
KOVNER M.,"THE SINO-SOVIET DISPUTE: COMMUNISM AT ATTIT
THE CROSSROADS." ASIA CHINA/COM COM USSR ECO/UNDEV TREND
NAT/G TOP/EX CREATE BAL/PWR DOMIN EDU/PROP PWR
...CONCPT COMECON 20. PAGE 88 H1760

S64
LANGERHANS H.,"NEHRU'S BITTERNESS." FUT INDIA ECO/DEV
S/ASIA CONSTN CULTURE ECO/UNDEV ECO/TAC DOMIN BIOG
EDU/PROP ATTIT PERCEPT PERSON...POLICY 20 NEHRU/J.
PAGE 91 H1811

S64
LOW D.A.,"LION RAMPANT." EUR+WWI MOD/EUR S/ASIA AFR
ECO/UNDEV NAT/G FORCES TEC/DEV ECO/TAC LEGIT ADMIN DOMIN
COLONIAL COERCE ORD/FREE RESPECT 19/20. PAGE 99 DIPLOM
H1972 UK

S64
MARES V.E.,"EAST EUROPE'S SECOND CHANCE." COM VOL/ASSN
EUR+WWI HUNGARY ROMANIA USSR YUGOSLAVIA ECO/UNDEV ECO/TAC
NAT/G TOP/EX CREATE PLAN TEC/DEV REGION NAT/LISM
RIGID/FLEX PWR...CONCPT STAT COMECON 20. PAGE 102
H2047

S64
MC WILLIAM M.,"THE WORLD BANK AND THE TRANSFER OF NAT/G
POWER IN KENYA." AFR ECO/UNDEV CONSULT ACT/RES ECO/TAC
TEC/DEV PERCEPT PWR SKILL WEALTH...CONCPT OBS TREND
20. PAGE 106 H2119

S64
NASH M.,"SOCIAL PREREQUISITES TO ECONOMIC GROWTH IN ECO/DEV
LATIN AMERICA AND SOUTHEAST ASIA." L/A+17C S/ASIA PERCEPT
CULTURE SOCIETY ECO/UNDEV AGRI INDUS NAT/G PLAN
TEC/DEV EDU/PROP ROUTINE ALL/VALS...POLICY RELATIV
SOC NAT/COMP WORK TOT/POP 20. PAGE 116 H2314

S64
SMYTHE H.H.,"NEHRU AND INDIAN FOREIGN POLICY." TOP/EX
S/ASIA ECO/UNDEV NAT/G POL/PAR CONSULT PLAN DIPLOM BIOG
NEUTRAL COERCE ATTIT DRIVE PERSON MORAL ORD/FREE INDIA
RESPECT...GEOG CONCPT TIME/SEQ TREND GEN/LAWS 20
NEHRU/J. PAGE 146 H2922

S64
TOUVAL S.,"THE SOMALI REPUBLIC." AFR ISLAM SOMALIA ECO/UNDEV
FAM KIN NAT/G CREATE FOR/AID LEGIT ATTIT ALL/VALS RIGID/FLEX
...RECORD TREND 20. PAGE 156 H3119

S64
ZARTMAN I.W.,"LES RELATIONS ENTRE LA FRANCE ET ECO/UNDEV
L'ALGERIA DEPUIS LES ACCORDS D'EVIAN." EUR+WWI FUT ALGERIA
ISLAM CULTURE AGRI EXTR/IND FINAN INDUS POL/PAR FRANCE
DIPLOM ECO/TAC FOR/AID PEACE ATTIT DRIVE ALL/VALS
...TIME/SEQ VAL/FREE 20. PAGE 172 H3450

C64
GOLDMAN M.I.,"COMPARATIVE ECONOMIC SYSTEMS: A NAT/COMP
READER." COM ECO/UNDEV NAT/G BUDGET CAP/ISM ADMIN CONTROL
TOTALISM MARXISM SOCISM...MGT ANTHOL BIBLIOG 19/20. IDEA/COMP
PAGE 58 H1157

N64
KENYA MINISTRY ECO PLAN DEV,AFRICAN SOCIALISM AND NAT/G
ITS APPLICATION TO PLANNING IN KENYA (PAMPHLET). SOCISM
AFR AGRI INDUS WORKER TAX COLONIAL WEALTH 20. PLAN
PAGE 85 H1691 ECO/UNDEV

B65
ADU A.L.,THE CIVIL SERVICE IN NEW AFRICAN STATES. ECO/UNDEV
AFR GHANA FINAN SOVEREIGN...POLICY 20 CIVIL/SERV ADMIN
AFRICA/E AFRICA/W. PAGE 4 H0074 COLONIAL
NAT/G

B65
AIR UNIVERSITY LIBRARY,LATIN AMERICA, SELECTED BIBLIOG
REFERENCES. ECO/UNDEV FORCES EDU/PROP MARXISM 20 L/A+17C
OAS. PAGE 4 H0084 NAT/G
DIPLOM

B65
AIYAR S.P.,STUDIES IN INDIAN DEMOCRACY. INDIA ORD/FREE
STRATA ECO/UNDEV LABOR POL/PAR LEGIS DIPLOM LOBBY REPRESENT
REGION CHOOSE ATTIT SOCISM...ANTHOL 20. PAGE 4 ADMIN
H0086 NAT/G

B65
ALEXANDER R.J.,ORGANIZED LABOR IN LATIN AMERICA. LABOR
L/A+17C INT/ORG LEGIS WORKER TEC/DEV BARGAIN POL/PAR
INT/TRADE REV...NAT/COMP BIBLIOG 20. PAGE 5 H0102 ECO/UNDEV
POLICY

B65
APPLEMAN P.,THE SILENT EXPLOSION. WOR+45 ECO/DEV GEOG
ECO/UNDEV PLAN HEALTH ALL/IDEOS CATHISM...POLICY CENSUS
STAT RECORD GP/COMP IDEA/COMP NAT/COMP 20 BIRTH/CON AGRI
COM/PARTY. PAGE 7 H0148 BIO/SOC

B65
APTER D.E.,THE POLITICS OF MODERNIZATION. AFR ECO/UNDEV
L/A+17C CULTURE NAT/G POL/PAR ADMIN COLONIAL GEN/LAWS
NAT/LISM ATTIT RIGID/FLEX PWR...SOC CONCPT. PAGE 8 STRATA
H0154 CREATE

B65
BAYNE E.A.,FOUR WAYS OF POLITICS: STATE AND NATION ECO/UNDEV
IN ITALY, SOMALIA, ISRAEL, AND IRAN. IRAN ISRAEL NAT/G
ITALY SOMALIA LEAD CHOOSE MAJORITY GOV/COMP. DECISION
PAGE 12 H0244 TOP/EX

B65
BRASS P.R.,FACTIONAL POLITICS IN AN INDIAN STATE: POL/PAR
THE CONGRESS PARTY IN UTTAR PRADESH. INDIA UK PROVS
CONSTN CULTURE ECO/UNDEV LOC/G DOMIN COLONIAL CROWD LEGIS
GP/REL ADJUST CENTRAL RIGID/FLEX SOVEREIGN 20 CHOOSE
UTTAR/PRAD CONGRESS/P. PAGE 20 H0406

B65
CANTRIL H.,THE PATTERN OF HUMAN CONCERNS. ELITES ATTIT
ECO/DEV ECO/UNDEV...STAT CHARTS METH 20. PAGE 26 ALL/VALS
H0524 NAT/COMP
CULTURE

B65
CARTER G.M.,GOVERNMENT AND POLITICS IN THE GOV/COMP
TWENTIETH CENTURY (REV. ED.). WOR+45 NAT/G POL/PAR ECO/UNDEV
LEGIS DIPLOM LEAD PARL/PROC CHOOSE TOTALISM 20. ALL/IDEOS
PAGE 27 H0549 ECO/DEV

B65
CHAO K.,THE RATE AND PATTERN OF INDUSTRIAL GROWTH INDUS
IN COMMUNIST CHINA. CHINA/COM ECO/UNDEV TEC/DEV INDEX
PRICE...NAT/COMP BIBLIOG 20. PAGE 29 H0578 STAT
PRODUC

B65
CHEN T.H.,THE CHINESE COMMUNIST REGIME: A MARXISM
DOCUMENTARY STUDY (2 VOLS.). CHINA/COM LAW CONSTN POL/PAR
ELITES ECO/UNDEV LEGIS ECO/TAC ADMIN CONTROL PWR NAT/G
...SOC 20. PAGE 29 H0587

B65
COWAN L.G.,EDUCATION AND NATION-BUILDING IN AFRICA. EDU/PROP
AFR CULTURE ECO/UNDEV POL/PAR ACT/RES LEAD COLONIAL
SOVEREIGN...METH/COMP ANTHOL BIBLIOG 20. PAGE 34 ACADEM
H0684 NAT/LISM

B65
CRABB C.V. JR.,THE ELEPHANTS AND THE GRASS* A STUDY ECO/UNDEV
OF NONALIGNMENT. AFR ASIA INDIA S/ASIA USA+45 USSR DIPLOM
BAL/PWR NEUTRAL ATTIT...TREND NAT/COMP COLD/WAR. CONCPT
PAGE 34 H0691

B65
EUROPEAN FREE TRADE ASSN,REGIONAL DEVELOPMENT EUR+WWI
POLICIES IN EFTA. ECO/UNDEV INT/ORG PLAN REGION ECO/DEV
...POLICY GEOG EFTA. PAGE 48 H0950 NAT/COMP
INT/TRADE

B65
FAGG J.E.,CUBA, HAITI, AND THE DOMINICAN REPUBLIC. COLONIAL
CUBA DOMIN/REP HAITI L/A+17C NAT/G DIPLOM ECO/TAC ECO/UNDEV
DOMIN CHOOSE AUTHORIT ROLE SOVEREIGN POPULISM REV
17/20. PAGE 48 H0959 GOV/COMP

B65
FORM W.H.,INDUSTRIAL RELATIONS AND SOCIAL CHANGE IN INDUS

LATIN AMERICA. L/A+17C AGRI LABOR NAT/G PLAN PROB/SOLV DIPLOM...MGT SOC ANTHOL BIBLIOG/A METH 20. PAGE 52 H1038
GP/REL NAT/COMP ECO/UNDEV
B65

FOSTER P.,EDUCATION AND SOCIAL CHANGE IN GHANA. GHANA CULTURE STRUCT ECO/UNDEV TEC/DEV REGION EFFICIENCY LITERACY ALL/VALS SOVEREIGN...STAT METH/COMP 19/20 GOLD/COAST. PAGE 52 H1043
SCHOOL CREATE SOCIETY
B65

GODECHOT J.,FRANCE AND THE ATLANTIC REVOLUTION OF THE EIGHTEENTH CENTURY 1770-1799. FRANCE CULTURE SOCIETY...GEOG 18. PAGE 57 H1150
MOD/EUR NAT/G REV ECO/UNDEV
B65

GOPAL S.,BRITISH POLICY IN INDIA 1858-1905. INDIA UK ELITES CHIEF DELIB/GP ECO/TAC GP/REL DISCRIM ATTIT...IDEA/COMP NAT/COMP PERS/COMP BIBLIOG/A 19/20. PAGE 59 H1176
COLONIAL ADMIN POL/PAR ECO/UNDEV
B65

HAEFELE E.T.,GOVERNMENT CONTROLS ON TRANSPORT. AFR RHODESIA TANZANIA DIPLOM ECO/TAC TARIFFS PRICE ADJUD CONTROL REGION EFFICIENCY...POLICY 20 CONGO. PAGE 64 H1274
ECO/UNDEV DIST/IND FINAN NAT/G
B65

HAPGOOD D.,AFRICA: FROM INDEPENDENCE TO TOMARROW. AFR GUINEA SENEGAL CULTURE ELITES ECO/UNDEV AGRI SCHOOL FOR/AID COLONIAL MARXISM...TREND 20. PAGE 66 H1323
ECO/TAC SOCIETY NAT/G
B65

HARBISON F.,MANPOWER AND EDUCATION. AFR CHINA/COM IRAN L/A+17C S/ASIA TEC/DEV ADJUST OPTIMAL SKILL ...ANTHOL 20. PAGE 66 H1325
ECO/UNDEV EDU/PROP WORKER NAT/COMP
B65

HAUSER P.M.,THE STUDY OF URBANIZATION. S/ASIA ECO/DEV ECO/UNDEV NEIGH ACT/RES GEOG. PAGE 68 H1359
CULTURE MUNIC SOC
B65

HAVIGHURST R.J.,SOCIETY AND EDUCATION IN BRAZIL. BRAZIL PORTUGAL ECO/UNDEV INDUS NAT/G CREATE INSPECT COLONIAL ADJUST DEMAND LITERACY...CENSUS TREND CHARTS 16/20. PAGE 68 H1362
SCHOOL ACADEM ACT/RES CULTURE
B65

HERRICK B.H.,URBAN MIGRATION AND ECONOMIC DEVELOPMENT IN CHILE. CHILE AGRI INDUS LABOR NAT/G CENTRAL PRODUC...STAT SAMP CHARTS BIBLIOG/A 20 MIGRATION. PAGE 70 H1404
HABITAT GEOG MUNIC ECO/UNDEV
B65

HLA MYINT U.,THE ECONOMICS OF THE DEVELOPING COUNTRIES. USA+45 WOR+45 AGRI FINAN NAT/G INT/TRADE ...CLASSIF CENSUS TREND NAT/COMP SIMUL GEN/LAWS. PAGE 71 H1430
ECO/UNDEV FOR/AID GEOG
B65

HONDURAS CONSEJO NAC DE ECO,PLAN NACIONAL DE DESARROLLO ECONOMICO Y SOCIAL DE HONDURAS 1965-69. HONDURAS AGRI INDUS BAL/PAY INCOME 20. PAGE 73 H1459
ECO/UNDEV NAT/G PLAN POLICY
B65

HORNE A.J.,THE COMMONWEALTH TODAY. AFR ASIA CANADA UK STRUCT ECO/UNDEV NAT/G SECT GP/REL 20 AUSTRAL CMN/WLTH. PAGE 73 H1470
BIBLIOG/A SOCIETY CULTURE
B65

HOSELITZ B.F.,ECONOMICS AND THE IDEA OF MANKIND. UNIV ECO/DEV ECO/UNDEV DIST/IND INDUS INT/ORG NAT/G ACT/RES ECO/TAC WEALTH...CONCPT STAT. PAGE 74 H1476
CREATE INT/TRADE
B65

IANNI O.,ESTADO E CAPITALISMO. L/A+17C FINAN TEC/DEV ECO/TAC ORD/FREE WEALTH POLICY. PAGE 76 H1518
ECO/UNDEV STRUCT INDUS NAT/G
B65

INST INTL DES CIVILISATION DIF,THE CONSTITUTIONS AND ADMINISTRATIVE INSTITUTIONS OF THE NEW STATES. AFR ISLAM S/ASIA NAT/G POL/PAR DELIB/GP EX/STRUC CONFER EFFICIENCY NAT/LISM...JURID SOC 20. PAGE 77 H1535
CONSTN ADMIN ADJUD ECO/UNDEV
B65

JAIN S.C.,THE STATE AND AGRICULTURE. INDIA S/ASIA ECO/UNDEV PROB/SOLV CAP/ISM MARXISM SOCISM 20. PAGE 79 H1586
NAT/G POLICY AGRI ECO/TAC
B65

JELAVICH C.,THE BALKANS. ALBANIA BULGARIA GREECE ROMANIA YUGOSLAVIA ECO/UNDEV WAR SOVEREIGN MARXISM 6/20. PAGE 80 H1597
NAT/LISM NAT/G
B65

KIRKWOOD K.,BRITAIN AND AFRICA. AFR UK ECO/UNDEV ECO/TAC WAR NAT/LISM SOVEREIGN 19/20. PAGE 86 H1725
NAT/G DIPLOM POLICY COLONIAL
B65

KUNSTADTER P.,THE LUA (LAWA) OF NORTHERN THAILAND: ASPECTS OF SOCIAL STRUCTURE, AGRICULTURE, AND RELIGION. THAILAND AGRI FAM KIN INGP/REL ISOLAT MARRIAGE HEALTH WORSHIP 20 BUDDHISM LUA. PAGE 89 H1780
STRUCT ECO/UNDEV CULTURE
B65

KUPER H.,URBANIZATION AND MIGRATION IN WEST AFRICA. UPPER/VOLT CULTURE ECO/UNDEV WORKER REGION GOV/REL ...LING ANTHOL SOC/INTEG 20 AFRICA/W OSHOGBO MOSSI MIGRATION. PAGE 89 H1781
AFR HABITAT MUNIC GEOG
B65

LAWRENCE P.,GODS, GHOSTS, AND MEN IN MELANESIA: SOME RELIGIONS OF AUSTRALIAN NEW GUINEA AND THE NEW HEBRIDES. SOCIETY ECO/UNDEV FAM GP/REL INGP/REL HABITAT PERSON...GEOG SOC ANTHOL BIBLIOG WORSHIP 20 NEW/GUINEA. PAGE 92 H1847
MYTH S/ASIA SECT CULTURE
B65

LEWIS W.A.,POLITICS IN WEST AFRICA. AFR BAL/PWR DIPLOM REPRESENT...POLICY 20. PAGE 96 H1916
POL/PAR ELITES NAT/G ECO/UNDEV
B65

THE STATE AND ECONOMIC ENTERPRISE IN JAPAN; ESSAYS IN THE POLITICAL ECONOMY OF GROWTH. AGRI INDUS DRIVE POPULISM...CHARTS NAT/COMP ANTHOL 19/20 CHINJAP. PAGE 98 H1949
ECO/UNDEV ECO/DEV CAP/ISM ECO/TAC
B65

MEAGHER R.F.,PUBLIC INTERNATIONAL DEVELOPMENT FINANCING IN SUDAN. SUDAN FINAN DELIB/GP GIVE ...CHARTS GOV/COMP 20. PAGE 108 H2155
FOR/AID PLAN RECEIVE ECO/UNDEV
B65

MEIER R.L.,DEVELOPMENTAL PLANNING. PUERT/RICO INDUS PUB/INST SCHOOL CREATE ECO/TAC FOR/AID...NAT/COMP 20. PAGE 108 H2165
PLAN ECO/UNDEV GOV/COMP TEC/DEV
B65

MEYER F.S.,THE AFRICAN NETTLE. SOUTH/AFR NAT/LISM SOVEREIGN...ANTHOL 20 EUROPE. PAGE 110 H2191
AFR COLONIAL RACE/REL ECO/UNDEV
B65

MOORE W.E.,THE IMPACT OF INDUSTRY. CULTURE STRUCT ORD/FREE...TREND 20. PAGE 113 H2251
INDUS MGT TEC/DEV ECO/UNDEV
B65

NYE J.S. JR.,PAN-AFRICANISM AND EAST AFRICAN INTEGRATION. TANZANIA UGANDA STRUCT ECO/UNDEV NAT/G DIPLOM FEDERAL NAT/LISM...STAT SOC/EXP BIBLIOG EEC OAU. PAGE 119 H2382
REGION ATTIT GEN/LAWS AFR
B65

O'BRIEN W.V.,THE NEW NATIONS IN INTERNATIONAL LAW AND DIPLOMACY* THE YEAR BOOK OF WORLD POLITY* VOLUME III. USA+45 ECO/UNDEV INT/ORG FORCES DIPLOM COLONIAL NEUTRAL REV NAT/LISM ATTIT RESPECT. PAGE 119 H2385
INT/LAW CULTURE SOVEREIGN ANTHOL
B65

OBUKAR C.,THE MODERN AFRICAN. AGRI INDUS WORKER CAP/ISM EDU/PROP PARTIC RACE/REL NAT/LISM ALL/VALS MARXISM...SOC IDEA/COMP 20. PAGE 120 H2393
AFR ECO/UNDEV CULTURE SOVEREIGN
B65

OECD,MEDITERRANEAN REGIONAL PROJECT: TURKEY; EDUCATION AND DEVELOPMENT. FUT TURKEY SOCIETY STRATA FINAN NAT/G PROF/ORG PLAN PROB/SOLV ADMIN COST...STAT CHARTS 20 OECD. PAGE 120 H2399
EDU/PROP ACADEM SCHOOL ECO/UNDEV
B65

OECD,THE MEDITERRANEAN REGIONAL PROJECT: ITALY; EDUCATION AND DEVELOPMENT. ITALY SOCIETY STRATA FINAN NAT/G PROF/ORG WORKER PLAN PROB/SOLV ADMIN ...STAT CHARTS METH 20 OECD. PAGE 120 H2400
SCHOOL EDU/PROP ECO/UNDEV ACADEM
B65

OECD,THE MEDITERRANEAN REGIONAL PROJECT: GREECE; EDUCATION AND DEVELOPMENT. FUT GREECE SOCIETY AGRI FINAN NAT/G PROF/ORG WORKER PLAN PROB/SOLV ADMIN DEMAND ATTIT 20 OECD. PAGE 120 H2401
EDU/PROP SCHOOL ACADEM ECO/UNDEV
B65

OECD,THE MEDITERRANEAN REGIONAL PROJECT: SPAIN; EDUCATION AND DEVELOPMENT. FUT SPAIN STRATA FINAN NAT/G WORKER PLAN PROB/SOLV ADMIN COST...POLICY STAT CHARTS 20 OECD. PAGE 120 H2402
ECO/UNDEV EDU/PROP ACADEM SCHOOL
B65

ONSLOW C.,ASIAN ECONOMIC DEVELOPMENT. BURMA CEYLON INDIA MALAYSIA PAKISTAN S/ASIA AGRI INDUS MARKET PROB/SOLV CAP/ISM FOR/AID INT/TRADE DEMAND WEALTH ...POLICY ANTHOL 20. PAGE 121 H2418
ECO/UNDEV ECO/TAC PLAN NAT/G
B65

ONUOHA B.,THE ELEMENTS OF AFRICAN SOCIALISM. AFR FINAN SECT TEC/DEV FOR/AID GP/REL OWN LAISSEZ MARXISM...CONCPT BIBLIOG 20. PAGE 121 H2419
SOCISM ECO/UNDEV NAT/G EX/STRUC
B65

ORG FOR ECO COOP AND DEVEL,THE MEDITERRANEAN REGIONAL PROJECT: AN EXPERIMENT IN PLANNING BY SIX COUNTRIES. FUT GREECE SPAIN TURKEY YUGOSLAVIA SOCIETY FINAN NAT/G PROF/ORG EDU/PROP ADMIN REGION COST...POLICY STAT CHARTS 20 OECD. PAGE 121 H2427
PLAN ECO/UNDEV ACADEM SCHOOL
B65

ORGANSKI A.F.K.,THE STAGES OF POLITICAL DEVELOPMENT. STRATA AGRI INDUS NAT/G POL/PAR
ECO/DEV ECO/UNDEV

COLONIAL PWR WEALTH...CLASSIF TIME/SEQ. PAGE 121 H2428 GEN/LAWS CREATE

B65
POLK W.R.,THE UNITED STATES AND THE ARAB WORLD. USA+45 ECO/UNDEV EXTR/IND SECT WAR NAT/LISM ATTIT ...NAT/COMP COLD/WAR. PAGE 127 H2535 ISLAM REGION CULTURE DIPLOM

B65
PROEHL P.O.,FOREIGN ENTERPRISE IN NIGERIA. NIGERIA FINAN LABOR NAT/G TAX 20. PAGE 128 H2562 ECO/UNDEV ECO/TAC JURID CAP/ISM

B65
RIVLIN B.,THE CONTEMPORARY MIDDLE EAST* TRADITION AND INNOVATION. CULTURE SOCIETY ECO/UNDEV NAT/G TREND. PAGE 132 H2636 ANTHOL ISLAM NAT/LISM DIPLOM

B65
RODRIGUEZ M.,CENTRAL AMERICA. COSTA/RICA GUATEMALA L/A+17C NICARAGUA DIPLOM COLONIAL REGION NAT/LISM ALL/IDEOS SOCISM...MAJORIT TIME/SEQ BIBLIOG 19/20. PAGE 133 H2656 CULTURE NAT/COMP NAT/G ECO/UNDEV

B65
SCHULER E.A.,THE PAKISTAN ACADEMIES FOR RURAL DEVELOPMENT COMILLA AND PESHAWAR 1959-1964. PAKISTAN S/ASIA SOCIETY STRUCT AGRI NAT/G TEC/DEV EDU/PROP 20. PAGE 140 H2801 BIBLIOG PLAN ECO/TAC ECO/UNDEV

B65
SIMMS R.P.,URBANIZATION IN WEST AFRICA; A REVIEW OF CURRENT LITERATURE. AFR PLAN TEC/DEV...SOC OBS NAT/COMP 20. PAGE 144 H2878 BIBLIOG/A MUNIC ECO/DEV ECO/UNDEV

B65
SMITH R.M.,CAMBODIA'S FOREIGN POLICY. ECO/UNDEV NAT/G NEUTRAL ORD/FREE COLD/WAR VAL/FREE. PAGE 146 H2917 S/ASIA CAMBODIA DIPLOM

B65
SPENCER P.,THE SAMBURU: A STUDY OF GERONTOCRACY IN A NOMADIC TRIBE. AFR SOCIETY ECO/UNDEV AGRI FAM NEIGH SECT GP/REL MARRIAGE WORSHIP 20 SAMBURU. PAGE 147 H2945 KIN STRUCT AGE/O CULTURE

B65
SWIFT M.G.,MALAY PEASANT SOCIETY IN JELEBU. MALAYSIA FAM INT/TRADE ADJUD OWN WEALTH...SOC WORSHIP 20. PAGE 151 H3020 STRUCT ECO/UNDEV CULTURE SOCIETY

B65
TUTSCH H.E.,FACETS OF ARAB NATIONALISM. ISLAM ISRAEL CULTURE STRUCT SECT RIGID/FLEX ORD/FREE MARXISM SOCISM 20. PAGE 157 H3143 ECO/UNDEV NAT/LISM TEC/DEV SOCIETY

B65
VAN DEN BERGHE P.L.,AFRICA: SOCIAL PROBLEMS OF CHANGE AND CONFLICT. ELITES STRATA ECO/UNDEV KIN MUNIC DIPLOM GP/REL RACE/REL NAT/LISM...ANTHOL BIBLIOG 20. PAGE 161 H3228 SOC CULTURE AFR STRUCT

B65
VON RENESSE E.A.,UNVOLLENDETE DEMOKRATIEN. AFR ISLAM S/ASIA SOCIETY ACT/RES COLONIAL...JURID CHARTS BIBLIOG METH 13/20. PAGE 164 H3276 ECO/UNDEV NAT/COMP SOVEREIGN

B65
WARD W.E.,GOVERNMENT IN WEST AFRICA. WOR+45 POL/PAR EX/STRUC PLAN PARTIC GP/REL SOVEREIGN 20 AFRICA/W. PAGE 165 H3308 GOV/COMP CONSTN COLONIAL ECO/UNDEV

B65
WOLPERT S.,INDIA. INDIA UK ECO/UNDEV DIPLOM GP/REL WEALTH 20 NEHRU/J. PAGE 170 H3405 CULTURE COLONIAL NAT/LISM SECT

B65
WURFEL S.W.,FOREIGN ENTERPRISE IN COLOMBIA. FINAN LABOR NAT/G ECO/TAC TAX REGION 20 COLOMB. PAGE 171 H3429 ECO/UNDEV INT/TRADE JURID CAP/ISM

L65
MATTHEWS D.G.,"A CURRENT BIBLIOGRAPHY ON ETHIOPIAN AFFAIRS: A SELECT BIBLIOGRAPHY FROM 1950-1964." ETHIOPIA LAW CULTURE ECO/UNDEV INDUS LABOR SECT FORCES DIPLOM CIVMIL/REL RACE/REL...LING STAT 20. PAGE 105 H2093 BIBLIOG/A ADMIN POL/PAR NAT/G

L65
MATTHEWS D.G.,"A CURRENT BIBLIOGRAPHY ON SUDANESE AFFAIRS; A SELECT BIBLIOGRAPHY FROM 1960-1964." SUDAN LAW CULTURE AGRI FINAN INDUS LABOR POL/PAR TEC/DEV FOR/AID RACE/REL LITERACY...LING 20. PAGE 105 H2094 BIBLIOG ECO/UNDEV NAT/G DIPLOM

L65
SCHAFFER B.B.,"THE CONCEPT OF PREPARATION* SOME QUESTIONS ABOUT THE TRANSFER OF SYSTEMS OF GOVERNMENT." AFR ASIA CANADA ELITES NAT/G POL/PAR COLONIAL RIGID/FLEX IDEA/COMP. PAGE 138 H2769 ECO/UNDEV UK RECORD

S65
BRANDENBURG F.,"THE RELEVANCE OF MEXICAN EXPERIENCE TO LATIN AMERICAN DEVELOPMENT." BRAZIL CHILE VENEZUELA STRUCT ECO/UNDEV AGRI CREATE ECO/TAC ...STAT RECORD MEXIC/AMER ARGEN COLOMB. PAGE 20 H0405 L/A+17C GOV/COMP

S65
GOLDMAN M.I.,"A BALANCE SHEET OF SOVIET FOREIGN AID." USA+45 ECO/UNDEV BAL/PWR ECO/TAC RENT GIVE EDU/PROP CONTROL COST PROFIT GEN/METH. PAGE 58 H1158 USSR FOR/AID NAT/COMP EFFICIENCY

S65
KINDLEBERGER C.P.,"MASS MIGRATION, THEN AND NOW." LAW ECO/DEV ECO/UNDEV INDUS LABOR INT/TRADE FEEDBACK REGION RIGID/FLEX...SOC NAT/COMP EEC. PAGE 86 H1714 EUR+WWI USA-45 WORKER IDEA/COMP

S65
MARK M.,"MUST WE FIGHT SOCIAL REVOLUTIONS OF THE LEFT?" L/A+17C USA+45 ECO/UNDEV DIPLOM ADJUST PERCEPT...IDEA/COMP NAT/COMP. PAGE 103 H2053 NAT/LISM REV MARXISM CREATE

S65
SANDERS R.,"MASS SUPPORT AND COMMUNIST INSURRECTION." GREECE MALAYSIA PHILIPPINE VIETNAM STRUCT ECO/UNDEV POL/PAR FORCES CREATE REV ...GP/COMP IDEA/COMP. PAGE 138 H2751 GUERRILLA MARXISM GOV/COMP

S65
TENDLER J.D.,"TECHNOLOGY AND ECONOMIC DEVELOPMENT* THE CASE OF HYDRO VS THERMAL POWER." CONSTRUC DIST/IND CREATE TEC/DEV INT/TRADE CENTRAL PWR SKILL WEALTH...MGT NAT/COMP ARGEN. PAGE 153 H3061 BRAZIL INDUS ECO/UNDEV

S65
WHITE J.,"WEST GERMAN AID TO DEVELOPING COUNTRIES." INT/ORG OP/RES GIVE CENTRAL ATTIT DRIVE...STAT NAT/COMP COLD/WAR. PAGE 167 H3348 GERMANY FOR/AID ECO/UNDEV CAP/ISM

C65
COLEMAN J.S.,"EDUCATION AND POLITICAL DEVELOPMENT." COM CULTURE INTELL STRUCT SCHOOL PERSON SOVEREIGN ...POLICY ANTHOL BIBLIOG/A METH 20. PAGE 31 H0629 ECO/UNDEV NAT/LISM EDU/PROP TEC/DEV

B66
AHMED Z.,DUSK AND DAWN IN VILLAGE INDIA. INDIA S/ASIA UK CULTURE SOCIETY NAT/G DOMIN COLONIAL HABITAT SOVEREIGN...SOC DICTIONARY 20. PAGE 4 H0080 NEIGH ECO/UNDEV AGRI ADJUST

B66
AIYAR S.P.,PERSPECTIVES ON THE WELFARE STATE. INDIA S/ASIA UK CONSTN ECO/UNDEV NAT/G INGP/REL CENTRAL NAT/LISM ATTIT...CONCPT ANTHOL BIBLIOG 20. PAGE 4 H0087 NEW/LIB WELF/ST IDEA/COMP ADJUST

B66
AMER ENTERPRISE INST PUB POL,SIGNIFICANT ISSUES IN ECONOMIC AID TO DEVELOPING COUNTRIES. FINAN INT/ORG NAT/G PLAN PROB/SOLV GIVE TASK WEALTH...DECISION 20. PAGE 6 H0119 ECO/UNDEV FOR/AID DIPLOM POLICY

B66
ASHRAF A.,THE CITY GOVERNMENT OF CALCUTTA: A STUDY OF INERTIA. INDIA ELITES INDUS NAT/G EX/STRUC ACT/RES PLAN PROB/SOLV LEAD HABITAT...BIBLIOG 20 CALCUTTA. PAGE 9 H0175 LOC/G MUNIC ADMIN ECO/UNDEV

B66
BARRETT J.,THAT BETTER COUNTRY: RELIGIOUS ASPECT OF LIFE IN EASTERN AUSTRALIA, 1835-1850. LAW ECO/UNDEV SCHOOL TEC/DEV EDU/PROP CONTROL HABITAT MORAL WORSHIP 19 AUSTRAL CHURCH/STA. PAGE 11 H0229 SECT CULTURE GOV/REL

B66
BIRKHEAD G.S.,ADMINISTRATIVE PROBLEMS IN PAKISTAN. PAKISTAN AGRI FINAN INDUS LG/CO ECO/TAC CONTROL PWR ...CHARTS ANTHOL 20. PAGE 17 H0340 ADMIN NAT/G ORD/FREE ECO/UNDEV

B66
BIRMINGHAM D.,TRADE AND CONFLICT IN ANGOLA. PORTUGAL CULTURE FORCES DIPLOM GP/REL PROFIT HABITAT NAT/COMP. PAGE 17 H0341 WAR INT/TRADE ECO/UNDEV COLONIAL

B66
BIRMINGHAM W.,A STUDY OF CONTEMPORARY GHANA VOL I: THE ECONOMY OF GHANA. AFR GHANA PLAN...POLICY STAT CHARTS ANTHOL BIBLIOG 20. PAGE 17 H0342 ECO/UNDEV ECO/TAC NAT/G PRODUC

B66
BLACK C.E.,THE DYNAMICS OF MODERNIZATION: A STUDY IN COMPARATIVE HISTORY. STRUCT ECO/DEV ECO/UNDEV NAT/G DIPLOM LEAD REV...PREDICT TIME/SEQ TREND SOC/INTEG 17/20. PAGE 17 H0350 SOCIETY SOC NAT/COMP

B66
BRACKMAN A.C.,SOUTHEAST ASIA'S SECOND FRONT: THE POWER STRUGGLE IN THE MALAY ARCHIPELAGO. CHINA/COM INDONESIA MALAYSIA ECO/UNDEV INT/ORG NAT/G FORCES DIPLOM EDU/PROP REGION COERCE GUERRILLA AUTHORIT POPULISM...MAJORIT 20 KENNEDY/JF SEATO. PAGE 20 H0396 S/ASIA MARXISM REV

B66
BRAIBANTI R.,ASIAN BUREAUCRATIC SYSTEMS EMERGENT FROM THE BRITISH IMPERIAL TRADITION. BURMA CEYLON INDIA PAKISTAN UK ELITES ECO/UNDEV NAT/G...MGT SOC CHARTS ANTHOL 19/20. PAGE 20 H0401 GOV/COMP COLONIAL ADMIN S/ASIA

B66
BROWN J.F.,THE NEW EASTERN EUROPE. ALBANIA BULGARIA DIPLOM

HUNGARY POLAND ROMANIA CULTURE AGRI POL/PAR WAR NAT/LISM MARXISM...CHARTS BIBLIOG 20. PAGE 22 H0444 COM NAT/G ECO/UNDEV

B66
BROWN L.C.,STATE AND SOCIETY IN INDEPENDENT NORTH AFRICA. ALGERIA LIBYA MOROCCO AGRI INDUS INT/ORG POL/PAR SECT PLAN DIPLOM COLONIAL...LING NAT/COMP ANTHOL BIBLIOG 20 TUNIS MUSLIM. PAGE 22 H0446 NAT/G SOCIETY CULTURE ECO/UNDEV

B66
BROWN R.T.,TRANSPORT AND THE ECONOMIC INTEGRATION OF SOUTH AMERICA. L/A+17C ECO/UNDEV NAT/G OP/RES DIPLOM INT/TRADE REGION WEALTH...ECOMETRIC GEOG STAT LAFTA TIME. PAGE 22 H0449 MARKET DIST/IND SIMUL

B66
CROWDER M.,A SHORT HISTORY OF NIGERIA. AFR NIGERIA UK ECO/UNDEV CHIEF INT/TRADE RACE/REL NAT/LISM ORD/FREE...GEOG SOC CHARTS BIBLIOG 14/20. PAGE 36 H0711 COLONIAL NAT/G CULTURE

B66
DOBB M.,SOVIET ECONOMIC DEVELOPMENT SINCE 1917. USSR ECO/DEV ECO/UNDEV LABOR NAT/G TEC/DEV ECO/TAC ROUTINE PRODUC MARXISM 20. PAGE 41 H0829 PLAN INDUS WORKER

B66
EMBREE A.T.,ASIA: A GUIDE TO BASIC BOOKS (PAMPHLET). ECO/UNDEV SECT FORCES DIPLOM ALL/IDEOS ...SOC 20. PAGE 46 H0914 BIBLIOG/A ASIA S/ASIA NAT/G

B66
FISK E.K.,NEW GUINEA ON THE THRESHOLD; ASPECTS OF SOCIAL, POLITICAL, AND ECONOMIC DEVELOPMENT. AGRI NAT/G INT/TRADE ADMIN ADJUST LITERACY ROLE...CHARTS ANTHOL 20 NEW/GUINEA. PAGE 51 H1015 ECO/UNDEV SOCIETY

B66
FITZGERALD C.P.,A CONCISE HISTORY OF EAST ASIA. ASIA KOREA S/ASIA INT/TRADE REGION MARXISM 20 CHINJAP. PAGE 51 H1017 ECO/UNDEV COLONIAL CULTURE

B66
FITZGERALD C.P.,THE BIRTH OF COMMUNIST CHINA (2ND ED.). ASIA CHINA/COM STRUCT BAL/PWR DIPLOM ECO/TAC INT/TRADE WEALTH 20. PAGE 51 H1018 REV MARXISM ECO/UNDEV

B66
HANKE L.,HANDBOOK OF LATIN AMERICAN STUDIES. ECO/UNDEV ADMIN LEAD...HUM SOC 20. PAGE 65 H1313 BIBLIOG/A L/A+17C INDEX NAT/G

B66
HANSON J.W.,EDUCATION AND THE DEVELOPMENT OF NATIONS. DIPLOM TASK ADJUST EFFICIENCY...POLICY ANTHOL 20. PAGE 66 H1322 ECO/UNDEV EDU/PROP NAT/G PLAN

B66
HARRISON B.,SOUTH-EAST ASIA: A SHORT HISTORY (3RD ED.). ECO/UNDEV INDUS NAT/G SECT BAL/PWR NAT/LISM ...SOC 15/20 S/EASTASIA. PAGE 67 H1346 COLONIAL S/ASIA CULTURE

B66
HEADY F.,PUBLIC ADMINISTRATION: A COMPARATIVE PERSPECTIVE. ECO/DEV ECO/UNDEV...GOV/COMP 20 BUREAUCRCY. PAGE 69 H1376 ADMIN NAT/COMP NAT/G CIVMIL/REL

B66
HOWE R.W.,BLACK AFRICA: FROM PRE-HISTORY TO THE EVE OF THE COLONIAL ERA. ECO/UNDEV KIN PROVS SECT INT/TRADE EDU/PROP COLONIAL...BIBLIOG WORSHIP. PAGE 74 H1482 AFR CULTURE SOC

B66
JACKSON G.D.,COMINTERN AND PEASANT IN EAST EUROPE 1919-1930. BULGARIA COM CZECHOSLVK EUR+WWI POLAND ROMANIA YUGOSLAVIA STRATA AGRI VOL/ASSN DIPLOM CONTROL CROWD WEALTH...POLICY NAT/COMP 20. PAGE 79 H1575 MARXISM ECO/UNDEV WORKER INT/ORG

B66
KAUNDA K.,ZAMBIA: INDEPENDENCE AND BEYOND: THE SPEECHES OF KENNETH KAUNDA. AFR FUT ZAMBIA SOCIETY ECO/UNDEV NAT/G PROB/SOLV ECO/TAC ADMIN RACE/REL SOVEREIGN 20. PAGE 84 H1670 ORD/FREE COLONIAL CONSTN LEAD

B66
KEYES J.G.,A BIBLIOGRAPHY OF WESTERN LANGUAGE PUBLICATIONS CONCERNING NORTH VIETNAM IN THE CORNELL LIBRARY. VIETNAM/N NAT/G FORCES TEC/DEV DIPLOM LEAD RACE/REL...GEOG SOC 20. PAGE 85 H1700 BIBLIOG/A CULTURE ECO/UNDEV S/ASIA

B66
KIRDAR U.,THE STRUCTURE OF UNITED NATIONS ECONOMIC AID TO UNDERDEVELOPED COUNTRIES. AGRI FINAN INDUS NAT/G EX/STRUC PLAN GIVE TASK...POLICY 20 UN. PAGE 86 H1721 INT/ORG FOR/AID ECO/UNDEV ADMIN

B66
KOH S.J.,STAGES OF INDUSTRIAL DEVELOPMENT IN ASIA. ASIA INDIA KOREA STRATA STRUCT NAT/G INT/TRADE ...CHARTS 19/20 CHINJAP. PAGE 87 H1738 INDUS ECO/UNDEV ECO/DEV LABOR

B66
KUZNETS S.,MODERN ECONOMIC GROWTH. WOR+45 WOR-45 ECO/DEV ECO/UNDEV AGRI FINAN INDUS TEC/DEV EFFICIENCY INCOME...NAT/COMP 19/20. PAGE 89 H1786 TIME/SEQ WEALTH PRODUC

B66
LENSKI G.E.,POWER AND PRIVILEGE: A THEORY OF SOCIAL STRATIFICATION. SWEDEN UK UNIV USSR CULTURE ECO/UNDEV PRIVIL PWR...PHIL/SCI CONCPT CHARTS IDEA/COMP HYPO/EXP METH MARX/KARL. PAGE 94 H1882 SOC STRATA STRUCT SOCIETY

B66
LEONTIEF W.,ESSAYS IN ECONOMICS. ECO/UNDEV INDUS NAT/G CAP/ISM FOR/AID AUTOMAT MARXISM...ECOMETRIC CHARTS ANTHOL METH 20 KEYNES/JM. PAGE 94 H1886 CONCPT METH/CNCPT METH/COMP

B66
MACFARQUHAR R.,CHINA UNDER MAO: POLITICS TAKES COMMAND. CHINA/COM COM AGRI INDUS CHIEF FORCES DIPLOM INT/TRADE EDU/PROP TASK REV ADJUST...ANTHOL 20 MAO. PAGE 100 H1992 ECO/UNDEV TEC/DEV ECO/TAC ADMIN

B66
MADAN G.R.,ECONOMIC THINKING IN INDIA. INDIA ECO/UNDEV AGRI FINAN INDUS LABOR PLAN CAP/ISM INT/TRADE MARXISM SOCISM...POLICY 1/20. PAGE 101 H2013 ECO/TAC PHIL/SCI NAT/G POL/PAR

B66
MASON E.S.,ECONOMIC DEVELOPMENT IN INDIA AND PAKISTAN. INDIA PAKISTAN AGRI FINAN PLAN BUDGET INT/TRADE WEALTH...POLICY STAT TREND CHARTS 20. PAGE 104 H2086 NAT/COMP ECO/UNDEV ECO/TAC FOR/AID

B66
MASUR G.,NATIONALISM IN LATIN AMERICA* DIVERSITY AND UNITY. CHRIST-17C PRE/AMER ELITES ECO/UNDEV CREATE DIPLOM INT/TRADE COLONIAL REV SOVEREIGN SOC. PAGE 105 H2089 L/A+17C NAT/LISM CULTURE

B66
MATTHEWS R.,AFRICAN POWDER KEG: REVOLT AND DISSENT IN SIX EMERGENT NATIONS. AFR ALGERIA DAHOMEY GABON GHANA MALAWI GAMBLE LEAD PARTIC REV DRIVE...BIOG TREND GOV/COMP 20. PAGE 105 H2098 ELITES ECO/UNDEV TOP/EX CONTROL

B66
MCKAY V.,AFRICAN DIPLOMACY STUDIES IN THE DETERMINANTS OF FOREIGN POLICY. AFR SOUTH/AFR CULTURE NEUTRAL REGION SOVEREIGN...INT/LAW GOV/COMP ANTHOL 20. PAGE 107 H2138 ECO/UNDEV RACE/REL CIVMIL/REL DIPLOM

B66
NAMBOODIRIPAD E.M.,ECONOMICS AND POLITICS OF INDIA'S SOCIALIST PATTERN. INDIA STRATA AGRI INDUS NAT/G PRICE ORD/FREE SOVEREIGN 20. PAGE 115 H2307 ECO/UNDEV PLAN SOCISM CAP/ISM

B66
NEVITT A.A.,THE ECONOMIC PROBLEMS OF HOUSING. WOR+45 ECO/DEV ECO/UNDEV ACT/RES PROB/SOLV ECO/TAC RENT...OBS CHARTS 20. PAGE 117 H2342 HABITAT PROC/MFG DELIB/GP NAT/COMP

B66
OECD DEVELOPMENT CENTRE,CATALOGUE OF SOCIAL AND ECONOMIC DEVELOPMENT INSTITUTES AND PROGRAMMES* RESEARCH. ACT/RES PLAN TEC/DEV EDU/PROP...SOC GP/COMP NAT/COMP. PAGE 120 H2403 ECO/UNDEV ECO/DEV R+D ACADEM

B66
PAN S.,VIETNAM CRISIS. ASIA FRANCE USA+45 USA-45 VIETNAM CULTURE SOCIETY INT/ORG ECO/TAC AGREE CONTROL WAR MARXISM 20. PAGE 123 H2454 ECO/UNDEV POLICY DIPLOM NAT/COMP

B66
RIZK C.,LE REGIME POLITIQUE LIBANAIS. ISLAM LEBANON STRUCT POL/PAR SECT LOBBY GP/REL 20 ARABS MUSLIM CHRISTIAN. PAGE 132 H2637 ECO/UNDEV NAT/G CULTURE

B66
ROSS A.M.,INDUSTRIAL RELATIONS AND ECONOMIC DEVELOPMENT. POL/PAR LEGIS WORKER BARGAIN PRICE EXEC LOBBY INCOME PWR...DECISION ANTHOL BIBLIOG 20. PAGE 134 H2686 ECO/UNDEV LABOR NAT/G GP/REL

B66
SAKAI R.K.,STUDIES ON ASIA, 1966. CEYLON INDIA USA-45 INDUS POL/PAR DIPLOM ECO/TAC MARXISM ...POLICY 19/20 CHINJAP. PAGE 137 H2738 SECT ECO/UNDEV

B66
SCHATTEN F.,COMMUNISM IN AFRICA. AFR GHANA GUINEA MALI CULTURE ECO/UNDEV LABOR SECT ECO/TAC EDU/PROP REV 20. PAGE 139 H2774 COLONIAL NAT/LISM MARXISM DIPLOM

B66
SMELSER N.J.,SOCIAL STRUCTURE AND MOBILITY IN ECONOMIC DEVELOPMENT. CULTURE SOCIETY CONFER...PSY SOC CHARTS METH/COMP NAT/COMP ANTHOL METH 20. PAGE 145 H2904 STRUCT STRATA ECO/UNDEV ECO/DEV

B66
SPULBER N.,THE STATE AND ECONOMIC DEVELOPMENT IN EASTERN EUROPE. BULGARIA COM CZECHOSLVK HUNGARY POLAND YUGOSLAVIA CULTURE PLAN CAP/ISM INT/TRADE CONTROL...POLICY CHARTS METH/COMP BIBLIOG/A 19/20. PAGE 148 H2958 ECO/DEV ECO/UNDEV NAT/G TOTALISM

B66
SRINIVAS M.N.,SOCIAL CHANGE IN MODERN INDIA. INDIA CULTURE SOCIETY STRUCT SECT TEC/DEV...METH/CNCPT SELF/OBS WORSHIP 20. PAGE 148 H2961 ORD/FREE STRATA SOC ECO/UNDEV

B66
SWEARINGEN A.R.,SOVIET AND CHINESE COMMUNIST POWER IN THE WORLD TODAY. COM USA+45 ECO/UNDEV CREATE LEAD WAR ADJUST...TREND NAT/COMP ANTHOL COLD/WAR KHRUSH/N. PAGE 151 H3017 USSR ASIA DIPLOM ATTIT

B66
SYMONDS R.,THE BRITISH AND THEIR SUCCESSORS. AFR CEYLON INDIA UK SCHOOL FORCES EDU/PROP ADMIN PARTIC ...NAT/COMP BIBLIOG 20 AFRICA/W AFRICA/E. PAGE 151 H3024
NAT/G ECO/UNDEV POLICY COLONIAL

B66
THIESENHUSEN W.C.,CHILE'S EXPERIMENTS IN AGRARIAN REFORM. CHILE STRUCT NAT/G ACT/RES ECO/TAC GOV/REL COST SOCISM...TREND CHARTS SOC/EXP 20. PAGE 154 H3073
AGRI ECO/UNDEV SOC TEC/DEV

B66
THOMPSON J.H.,MODERNIZATION OF THE ARAB WORLD. FUT ISRAEL STRUCT ECO/UNDEV DIPLOM INGP/REL ATTIT ...CENSUS ANTHOL 20 ARABS. PAGE 154 H3082
ADJUST ISLAM PROB/SOLV NAT/COMP

B66
TYSON G.,NEHRU: THE YEARS OF POWER. INDIA UK STRATA ECO/UNDEV FINAN SECT TASK WAR ORD/FREE MARXISM ...POLICY BIBLIOG 20 NEHRU/J. PAGE 157 H3145
CHIEF PWR DIPLOM NAT/G

B66
US DEPARTMENT OF STATE,RESEARCH ON AFRICA (EXTERNAL RESEARCH LIST NO 5-25). LAW CULTURE ECO/UNDEV POL/PAR DIPLOM EDU/PROP LEAD REGION MARXISM...GEOG LING WORSHIP 20. PAGE 159 H3188
BIBLIOG/A ASIA S/ASIA NAT/G

B66
US DEPARTMENT OF THE ARMY,SOUTH ASIA: A STRATEGIC SURVEY (PAMPHLET NO. 550-3). AFGHANISTN INDIA NEPAL PAKISTAN ECO/UNDEV INT/ORG POL/PAR FORCES FOR/AID INT/TRADE LEAD WAR...POLICY SOC TREND 20. PAGE 160 H3195
BIBLIOG/A S/ASIA DIPLOM NAT/G

B66
WEINSTEIN B.,GABON: NATION-BUILDING ON THE OGOOUE. AFR GABON WOR+45 CULTURE SOCIETY PLAN DIPLOM COLONIAL INGP/REL ANOMIE HABITAT SUPEGO 20. PAGE 166 H3329
ECO/UNDEV GP/REL LEAD NAT/G

B66
WHITAKER A.P.,NATIONALISM IN CONTEMPORARY LATIN AMERICA. AGRI NAT/G WEALTH...POLICY SOC CONCPT OBS TREND 20. PAGE 167 H3344
NAT/LISM L/A+17C DIPLOM ECO/UNDEV

B66
WILLNER A.R.,THE NEOTRADITIONAL ACCOMMODATION TO POLITICAL INDEPENDENCE* THE CASE OF INDONESIA * RESEARCH MONOGRAPH NO. 26. CULTURE ECO/UNDEV CREATE PROB/SOLV FOR/AID LEGIT COLONIAL EFFICIENCY NAT/LISM ALL/VALS SOC. PAGE 168 H3371
INDONESIA CONSERVE ELITES ADMIN

L66
HUNTINGTON S.P.,"POLITICAL MODERNIZATION* AMERICA VS EUROPE." EUR+WWI MOD/EUR UK USA+45 LAW ECO/UNDEV PWR SOVEREIGN CONSERVE LAISSEZ GOV/COMP. PAGE 75 H1505
STRUCT CREATE OBS

S66
"FURTHER READING." INDIA LOC/G NAT/G PLAN ADMIN WEALTH...GEOG SOC CONCPT CENSUS 20. PAGE 2 H0049
BIBLIOG ECO/UNDEV TEC/DEV PROVS

S66
DETTER I.,"THE PROBLEM OF UNEQUAL TREATIES." CONSTN NAT/G LEGIS COLONIAL COERCE PWR...GEOG UN TIME TREATY. PAGE 40 H0796
SOVEREIGN DOMIN INT/LAW ECO/UNDEV

S66
GAMER R.E.,"URGENT SINGAPORE, PATIENT MALAYSIA." MALAYSIA S/ASIA ECO/UNDEV POL/PAR CHIEF TARIFFS TAX CONTROL LEAD REGION PWR 20 SINGAPORE. PAGE 55 H1094
DIPLOM NAT/G POLICY ECO/TAC

S66
HEAPHEY J.,"THE ORGANIZATION OF EGYPT* INADEQUACIES OF A NONPOLITICAL MODEL FOR NATION-BUILDING." STRATA NAT/G CREATE PROB/SOLV ECO/TAC NAT/LISM SOCISM RECORD. PAGE 69 H1377
UAR ECO/UNDEV OBS

S66
MALENBAUM W.,"GOVERNMENT, ENTREPRENEURSHIP, AND ECONOMIC GROWTH IN POOR LANDS." ELITES ECO/UNDEV INDUS CREATE DRIVE. PAGE 101 H2028
ECO/TAC PLAN CONSERVE NAT/G

S66
MARTZ J.D.,"THE PLACE OF LATIN AMERICA IN THE STUDY OF COMPARATIVE POLITICS." AFR ASIA CULTURE STRUCT ECO/UNDEV ACADEM CREATE...CLASSIF NAT/COMP. PAGE 104 H2072
L/A+17C GOV/COMP STERTYP GEN/LAWS

S66
MATTHEWS D.G.,"ETHIOPIAN OUTLINE: A BIBLIOGRAPHIC RESEARCH GUIDE." ETHIOPIA LAW STRUCT ECO/UNDEV AGRI LABOR SECT CHIEF DELIB/GP EX/STRUC ADMIN...LING ORG/CHARTS 20. PAGE 105 H2095
BIBLIOG NAT/G DIPLOM POL/PAR

S66
ROTHCHILD D.,"THE LIMITS OF FEDERALISM: AN EXAMINATION OF POLITICAL INSTITUTIONAL TRANSFER IN AFRICA." AFR CONSTN CULTURE ELITES ECO/UNDEV KIN PROB/SOLV ADMIN ORD/FREE PWR...POLICY 20. PAGE 135 H2695
FEDERAL NAT/G NAT/LISM COLONIAL

S66
SNOW P.G.,"A SCALOGRAM ANALYSIS OF POLITICAL DEVELOPMENT." STRATA ECO/UNDEV POL/PAR REGION ALL/VALS PWR...SOC CHARTS. PAGE 146 H2924
L/A+17C NAT/COMP TESTS CLASSIF

C66
WINT G.,"ASIA: A HANDBOOK." ASIA S/ASIA INDUS LABOR SECT PRESS RACE/REL MARXISM...STAT CHARTS BIBLIOG 20. PAGE 169 H3388
ECO/UNDEV DIPLOM NAT/G SOCIETY

N66
HISPANIC LUSO-BRAZILIAN COUN,LATIN AMERICA; AN INTRODUCTION TO MODERN BOOKS IN ENGLISH CONCERNING THE COUNTRIES OF LATIN AMERICA (2ND ED., PAMPH). CULTURE GOV/REL GEOG. PAGE 71 H1425
BIBLIOG/A ECO/UNDEV NAT/G L/A+17C

B67
ALBA V.,THE MEXICANS; THE MAKING OF A NATION. SOCIETY ECO/UNDEV AGRI INDUS SECT STRANGE ATTIT ...GEOG 20 MEXIC/AMER. PAGE 4 H0091
CONSTN NAT/G CULTURE ANOMIE

B67
ANDERSON C.W.,POLITICS AND ECONOMIC CHANGE IN LATIN AMERICA. L/A+17C INDUS NAT/G OP/RES ADMIN DEMAND ...POLICY STAT CHARTS NAT/COMP 20. PAGE 6 H0125
ECO/UNDEV PROB/SOLV PLAN ECO/TAC

B67
ANDERSON C.W.,ISSUES OF POLITICAL DEVELOPMENT. BURMA WOR+45 CULTURE TOP/EX ECO/TAC MARXISM ...CHARTS NAT/COMP 20 COLOMB CONGO/LEOP. PAGE 6 H0126
NAT/LISM COERCE ECO/UNDEV SOCISM

B67
ARIKPO O.,THE DEVELOPMENT OF MODERN NIGERIA. AFR NIGERIA SOCIETY ECO/UNDEV KIN ADMIN FEDERAL NAT/LISM ORD/FREE WEALTH...POLICY GEOG BIBLIOG 19/20. PAGE 8 H0163
NAT/G CULTURE CONSTN COLONIAL

B67
ASHFORD D.E.,NATIONAL DEVELOPMENT AND LOCAL REFORM: POLITICAL PARTICIPATION IN MOROCCO, TUNISIA, AND PAKISTAN. MOROCCO PAKISTAN CULTURE PROB/SOLV ATTIT ...POLICY SOC METH/COMP NAT/COMP BIBLIOG 20 TUNIS. PAGE 9 H0173
PARTIC ECO/UNDEV ADJUST NAT/G

B67
BURNHAM J.,THE WAR WE ARE IN, THE LAST DECADE AND THE NEXT. ASIA COM EUR+WWI S/ASIA WOR+45 ECO/UNDEV INT/ORG FORCES WAR...OLD/LIB TREND 20 COLD/WAR. PAGE 25 H0492
POLICY NAT/G DIPLOM NAT/COMP

B67
CARTER G.M.,SOUTH AFRICA'S TRANSKEI: THE POLITICS OF DOMESTIC COLONIALISM. SOUTH/AFR ECO/UNDEV AGRI NAT/G PROVS PLAN DOMIN REPRESENT ADJUST DISCRIM ...OBS BIBLIOG 20 BANTUSTANS TRANSKEI. PAGE 27 H0550
STRATA GOV/REL COLONIAL POLICY

B67
CEFKIN J.L.,THE BACKGROUND OF CURRENT WORLD PROBLEMS. NAT/G MARXISM...T 20 UN COLD/WAR. PAGE 28 H0565
DIPLOM NAT/LISM ECO/UNDEV

B67
CHANDRASEKHAR S.,ASIA'S POPULATION PROBLEMS. ASIA ECO/UNDEV PLAN AGE/C...OBS CHARTS BIBLIOG 18/20 AUSTRAL. PAGE 29 H0575
PROB/SOLV NAT/COMP GEOG TREND

B67
CHILCOTE R.H.,PORTUGUESE AFRICA. PORTUGAL CULTURE SOCIETY ECO/UNDEV DOMIN NAT/LISM...TREND IDEA/COMP NAT/COMP BIBLIOG 15/20. PAGE 29 H0589
AFR COLONIAL ORD/FREE PROB/SOLV

B67
COLLINS R.O.,EGYPT AND THE SUDAN. COM FRANCE ISLAM SUDAN UAR UK SOCIETY NAT/G COLONIAL NAT/LISM...GEOG SOC LING TREND SOC/INTEG 7/20 SUEZ. PAGE 32 H0635
AGRI CULTURE ECO/UNDEV

B67
CORDIER A.W.,COLUMBIA ESSAYS IN INTERNATIONAL AFFAIRS. ASIA CHINA/COM FRANCE S/ASIA SPAIN UAR ECO/UNDEV LOC/G ECO/TAC GUERRILLA PWR...BIOG ANTHOL 18/20 MAU/MAU. PAGE 33 H0663
NAT/G DIPLOM MARXISM POLICY

B67
DALTON G.,TRIBAL AND PEASANT ECONOMIES. SOCIETY FINAN FAM INT/TRADE RATION ADJUST WEALTH...CHARTS ANTHOL BIBLIOG T. PAGE 37 H0738
SOC ECO/UNDEV NAT/COMP

B67
DILLARD D.,ECONOMIC DEVELOPMENT OF THE NORTH ATLANTIC COMMUNITY. EUR+WWI MOD/EUR USA+45 USA-45 ECO/UNDEV LABOR CAP/ISM WAR BAL/PAY...NAT/COMP 15/20. PAGE 41 H0824
ECO/DEV INT/TRADE INDUS DIPLOM

B67
FALL B.B.,HO CHI MINH ON REVOLUTION: SELECTED WRITINGS, 1920-66. COM VIETNAM ELITES NAT/G COERCE GUERRILLA RACE/REL MARXISM...MARXIST ANTHOL 20. PAGE 48 H0968
REV COLONIAL ECO/UNDEV S/ASIA

B67
FANON F.,TOWARD THE AFRICAN REVOLUTION. AFR FRANCE CULTURE ELITES LEAD REV GP/REL ORD/FREE SOVEREIGN 20. PAGE 49 H0969
COLONIAL DOMIN ECO/UNDEV RACE/REL

B67
GIFFORD P.,BRITAIN AND GERMANY IN AFRICA. AFR GERMANY UK ECO/UNDEV LEAD WAR NAT/LISM ATTIT ...POLICY HIST/WRIT METH/COMP ANTHOL BIBLIOG 19/20 WWI. PAGE 56 H1123
COLONIAL ADMIN DIPLOM NAT/COMP

B67
GILL R.T.,ECONOMIC DEVELOPMENT: PAST AND PRESENT (2ND ED.). ASIA INDIA USA+45 USA-45 WOR+45 WOR-45 DEMAND EFFICIENCY NAT/LISM WEALTH...GOV/COMP METH/COMP 18/20. PAGE 56 H1127
ECO/DEV ECO/UNDEV PLAN PROB/SOLV

B67
GROSS B.M.,ACTION UNDER PLANNING: THE GUIDANCE OF ECONOMIC DEVELOPMENT. STRUCT R+D NAT/G ACT/RES HABITAT...DECISION 20. PAGE 62 H1232
ECO/UNDEV PLAN ADMIN MGT

B67
JOHNSON H.G.,ECONOMIC NATIONALISM IN OLD AND NEW STATES. CANADA CHINA/COM MALI UK DIPLOM...SIMUL GEN/LAWS 19/20 MEXIC/AMER. PAGE 81 H1619
NAT/LISM ECO/UNDEV ECO/DEV NAT/COMP

B67
KONCZACKI Z.A.,PUBLIC FINANCE AND ECONOMIC DEVELOPMENT OF NATAL 1893-1910. TAX ADMIN COLONIAL ...STAT CHARTS BIBLIOG 19/20 NATAL. PAGE 88 H1755
ECO/TAC FINAN NAT/G ECO/UNDEV

B67
LAMBERT J.,LATIN AMERICA: SOCIAL STRUCTURES AND POLITICAL INSTITUTIONS. STRUCT TEC/DEV DIPLOM ADMIN COLONIAL LEAD ATTIT...SOC CLASSIF NAT/COMP 17/20. PAGE 90 H1801
L/A+17C NAT/G ECO/UNDEV SOCIETY

B67
LEVY J.-P.,THE ECONOMIC LIFE OF THE ANCIENT WORLD. CULTURE SOCIETY INT/TRADE COLONIAL WEALTH ...BIBLIOG. PAGE 95 H1906
ECO/TAC ECO/UNDEV FINAN MEDIT-7

B67
MOORE J.R.,THE ECONOMIC IMPACT OF THE TVA. AGRI INDUS PLAN BARGAIN CONTROL REGION GOV/REL DEMAND EFFICIENCY SOCISM 20 TVA. PAGE 112 H2249
ECO/UNDEV ECO/DEV NAT/G CREATE

B67
MUHAMMAD A.C.,THE EMERGENCE OF PAKISTAN. PAKISTAN S/ASIA CONSTN ECO/UNDEV NAT/G CONTROL NAT/LISM 20. PAGE 114 H2281
DIPLOM COLONIAL SECT PROB/SOLV

B67
NESS G.D.,BUREAUCRACY AND RURAL DEVELOPMENT IN MALAYSIA. MALAYSIA UK SOCIETY FINAN INDUS WORKER TEC/DEV ECO/TAC COLONIAL EQUILIB ORD/FREE...STAT CHARTS 20. PAGE 117 H2330
ECO/UNDEV PLAN NAT/G ADMIN

B67
NYERERE J.K.,FREEDOM AND UNITY/UHURU NA UMOJA: A SELECTION FROM WRITINGS AND SPEECHES, 1952-65. TANZANIA ELITES ECO/UNDEV INT/ORG NAT/G CREATE DIPLOM COLONIAL REGION RACE/PEL...ANTHOL 20. PAGE 119 H2383
SOVEREIGN AFR TREND ORD/FREE

B67
OLIVER R.,AFRICA SINCE 1800. AFR ISLAM CULTURE ECO/UNDEV SECT DOMIN RACE/REL DISCRIM SOVEREIGN 19/20. PAGE 121 H2414
DIPLOM COLONIAL REGION

B67
OVERSEAS DEVELOPMENT INSTIT,EFFECTIVE AID. WOR+45 INT/ORG TEC/DEV DIPLOM INT/TRADE ADMIN. PAGE 122 H2434
FOR/AID ECO/UNDEV ECO/TAC NAT/COMP

B67
PAPANEK G.F.,PAKISTAN'S DEVELOPMENT: SOCIAL GOALS AND PRIVATE INCENTIVES. PAKISTAN INDUS NAT/G PROB/SOLV CONTROL EFFICIENCY SOCISM...CHARTS 20. PAGE 123 H2463
ECO/UNDEV PLAN CAP/ISM ECO/TAC

B67
PENDLE G.,PARAGUAY: A RIVERSIDE NATION (3RD ED.). PARAGUAY CHIEF ISOLAT...HUM CHARTS BIBLIOG 16/20. PAGE 124 H2487
CULTURE GEOG ECO/UNDEV

B67
PIKE F.B.,FREEDOM AND REFORM IN LATIN AMERICA. BRAZIL URUGUAY CONSTN CULTURE SECT DIPLOM EDU/PROP PARTIC DRIVE ALL/VALS CATHISM...GEOG ANTHOL BIBLIOG REFORMERS BOLIV. PAGE 126 H2511
L/A+17C ORD/FREE ECO/UNDEV REV

B67
PLANK J.,CUBA AND THE UNITED STATES: LONG RANGE PERSPECTIVES. CUBA L/A+17C USSR ECO/UNDEV NAT/G FORCES ECO/TAC INT/TRADE AGREE REV...PREDICT TREND ANTHOL 20 CASTRO/F COLD/WAR OAS. PAGE 126 H2520
DIPLOM

B67
PYE L.W.,SOUTHEAST ASIA'S POLITICAL SYSTEMS. ASIA S/ASIA STRUCT ECO/UNDEV EX/STRUC CAP/ISM DIPLOM ALL/IDEOS...TREND CHARTS. PAGE 128 H2568
NAT/G POL/PAR GOV/COMP

B67
RAVKIN A.,THE NEW STATES OF AFRICA (HEADLINE SERIES, NO. 183((PAMPHLET). CULTURE STRUCT INDUS COLONIAL NAT/LISM...SOC 20. PAGE 130 H2597
AFR ECO/UNDEV SOCIETY ADMIN

B67
RUSTOW D.A.,A WORLD OF NATIONS; PROBLEMS OF POLITICAL MODERNIZATION. CONSTN NAT/G POL/PAR FORCES DIPLOM LEAD AUTHORIT...CHARTS IDEA/COMP 20. PAGE 136 H2722
PROB/SOLV ECO/UNDEV CONCPT NAT/COMP

B67
SPIRO H.S.,PATTERNS OF AFRICAN DEVLOPMENT: FIVE COMPARISONS. STRUCT ECO/UNDEV NAT/G CONSERVE SOCISM
AFR CONSTN

...PREDICT NAT/COMP 20 CHINJAP. PAGE 148 H2951
NAT/LISM TREND

B67
THOMAN R.S.,GEOGRAPHY OF INTERNATIONAL TRADE. WOR+45 ECO/DEV ECO/UNDEV INT/ORG LG/CO PLAN BAL/PAY ...STAT CHARTS NAT/COMP 20. PAGE 154 H3075
INT/TRADE GEOG ECO/TAC DIPLOM

B67
THOMPSON E.T.,PERSPECTIVES ON THE SOUTH: AGENDA FOR RESEARCH. CULTURE ECO/UNDEV SECT GP/REL EFFICIENCY ALL/VALS...HUM SOC CONCPT LING 20 NEGRO. PAGE 154 H3080
PROB/SOLV IDEA/COMP REGION ACT/RES

B67
UNESCO,PRINCIPLES AND PROBLEMS OF NATIONAL SCIENCE POLICIES. WOR+45 ECO/DEV ECO/UNDEV R+D INT/ORG PROB/SOLV CONFER...PHIL/SCI CHARTS 20 UNESCO UN. PAGE 158 H3165
NAT/COMP POLICY TEC/DEV CREATE

B67
WILLS A.J.,AN INTRODUCTION TO THE HISTORY OF CENTRAL AFRICA. RHODESIA ZAMBIA CULTURE SOCIETY ECO/UNDEV TEC/DEV DOMIN WAR ALL/VALS...POLICY TREND BIBLIOG T 14/20 NYASALAND. PAGE 169 H3375
AFR COLONIAL ORD/FREE

L67
GALTUNG J.,"ON THE EFFECTS OF INTERNATIONAL ECONOMIC SANCTIONS, WITH EXAMPLES FROM THE CASE OF RHODESIA." NAT/G DIPLOM EDU/PROP ADJUST EFFICIENCY ATTIT MORAL...OBS CHARTS 20. PAGE 55 H1091
SANCTION ECO/TAC INT/TRADE ECO/UNDEV

L67
LARKIN E.,"ECONOMIC GROWTH, CAPITAL INVESTMENT, AND THE ROMAN CATHOLIC CHURCH IN NINETEENTH-CENTURY IRELAND." IRELAND AGRI DIST/IND NAT/G GIVE OWN CATHISM...CHARTS 19. PAGE 91 H1823
FINAN SECT WEALTH ECO/UNDEV

L67
ROTH A.R.,"CAPITAL-MARKET DEVELOPMENT IN ISRAEL AND BRAZIL: TWO EXAMPLES OF THE ROLE OF LAW IN DEVELOPMENT." BRAZIL ISRAEL L/A+17C INDUS MARKET ECO/TAC FOR/AID INT/TRADE CONTROL BAL/PAY 20. PAGE 135 H2694
LAW ECO/UNDEV NAT/COMP FINAN

L67
RUTH J.M.,"THE ADMINISTRATION OF WATER RESOURCES IN GUATEMALA." GUATEMALA L/A+17C DIST/IND LOC/G NAT/G EX/STRUC ADMIN GOV/REL DEMAND EQUILIB WEALTH...GEOG MGT 20. PAGE 136 H2723
EFFICIENCY ECO/UNDEV PLAN ACT/RES

L67
SEGAL A.,"THE INTEGRATION OF DEVELOPING COUNTRIES: SOME THOUGHTS ON EAST AFRICA AND CENTRAL AMERICA." AFR L/A+17C INT/ORG NAT/G VOL/ASSN FOR/AID INT/TRADE EQUILIB NAT/LISM PWR 20. PAGE 141 H2820
ECO/UNDEV DIPLOM REGION

L67
TABORSKY E.,"THE COMMUNIST PARTIES OF THE 'THIRD WORLD' IN SOVIET STRATEGY." AFR ASIA L/A+17C USSR INTELL NAT/G WORKER PLAN CONTROL LEAD PARTIC REV ...GOV/COMP 20 COM/PARTY THIRD/WRLD. PAGE 152 H3032
POL/PAR MARXISM ECO/UNDEV DIPLOM

L67
WRIGHT W.R.,"FOREIGN-OWNED RAILWAYS IN ARGENTINA: A CASE STUDY OF ECONOMIC NATIONALISM." L/A+17C UK ECO/UNDEV SERV/IND LG/CO NAT/G TEC/DEV BAL/PWR EQUILIB ARGEN. PAGE 171 H3423
NAT/LISM CAP/ISM ECO/TAC COLONIAL

S67
ADAMS R.N.,"ETHICS AND THE SOCIAL ANTHROPOLOGIST IN LATIN AMERICA." USA+45 INTELL PROB/SOLV ECO/TAC LEAD...DECISION SOC NAT/COMP PERS/COMP. PAGE 3 H0066
L/A+17C POLICY ECO/UNDEV CONSULT

S67
ALPANDER G.G.,"ENTREPRENEURS AND PRIVATE ENTERPRISE IN TURKEY." TURKEY INDUS PROC/MFG EDU/PROP ATTIT DRIVE WEALTH...GEOG MGT SOC STAT TREND CHARTS 20. PAGE 6 H0114
ECO/UNDEV LG/CO NAT/G POLICY

S67
BAER W.,"THE INFLATION CONTROVERSY IN LATIN AMERICA: SURVEY." L/A+17C ECO/UNDEV AGRI FINAN INDUS PLAN PROB/SOLV TEC/DEV...BIBLIOG/A 20. PAGE 10 H0194
NAT/G BAL/PAY ECO/TAC BUDGET

S67
BHATNAGAR J.K.,"THE VALUES AND ATTITUDES OF SOME INDIAN AND BRITISH STUDENTS." INDIA UK ECO/UNDEV LEGIT COLONIAL GP/REL SOVEREIGN...QU 20. PAGE 16 H0328
NAT/COMP ATTIT EDU/PROP ACADEM

S67
BRANCO R.,"LAND REFORM* THE ANSWER TO LATIN AMERICA'S AGRICULTURAL DEVELOPMENT?" L/A+17C NAT/G PLAN TEC/DEV BUDGET RENT EFFICIENCY 20. PAGE 20 H0404
ECO/UNDEV AGRI TAX OWN

S67
BUTTINGER J.,"VIETNAM* FRAUD OF THE 'OTHER WAR'." VIETNAM/S ELITES STRUCT AGRI NAT/G FOR/AID RENT TREND. PAGE 25 H0499
PLAN WEALTH REV ECO/UNDEV

S67
CAMERON R.,"SOME LESSONS OF HISTORY FOR DEVELOPING NATIONS." WOR+45 WOR-45 FINAN NAT/G WORKER EDU/PROP PARTIC ROLE...DECISION METH/COMP 18/20. PAGE 25 H0511
ECO/UNDEV NAT/COMP POLICY CONCPT

S67
COHEN A.,"REVOLUTION IN ARGENTINA?" L/A+17C NAT/G POL/PAR CHIEF PROB/SOLV ECO/TAC 20 ARGEN. PAGE 31
REV ECO/UNDEV

H0615 CONTROL BIOG

S67

COLLINS B.A.,"SOME NOTES ON PUBLIC SERVICE COMMISSIONS IN THE COMMONWEALTH CARIBBEAN." JAMAICA L/A+17C TRINIDAD UK NAT/G OP/RES DOMIN SENIOR COLONIAL CONTROL INGP/REL CENTRAL EFFICIENCY PWR ...DECISION 20. PAGE 31 H0631 ADMIN EX/STRUC ECO/UNDEV CHOOSE

S67

ELLISON H.J.,"THE SOCIALIST REVOLUTIONARIES." USSR ECO/UNDEV NAT/G INGP/REL EFFICIENCY ATTIT PWR MARXISM...CONCPT IDEA/COMP 20 SOC/REVPAR. PAGE 46 H0911 POL/PAR REV AGRI

S67

FINLAY D.J.,"THE GHANA COUP...ONE YEAR LATER." GHANA FORCES FOR/AID PRESS CONTROL CIVMIL/REL NAT/LISM AUTHORIT PWR...PREDICT 20. PAGE 50 H1005 REV NAT/G ATTIT ECO/UNDEV

S67

FLETCHER-COOKE J.,"THE EMERGING AFRICAN STATE." AFR GP/REL NAT/LISM. PAGE 51 H1025 ECO/UNDEV NAT/COMP DIPLOM ATTIT

S67

FRENCH D.S.,"DOES THE U.S. EXPLOIT THE DEVELOPING NATIONS?" INT/ORG NAT/G CAP/ISM BAL/PAY WEALTH POLICY. PAGE 53 H1057 ECO/UNDEV INT/TRADE ECO/TAC COLONIAL

S67

GLOBERSON A.,"SOCIAL GROWTH IN THE DEVELOPING COUNTRIES." CULTURE SOCIETY CONSULT PROB/SOLV SOC. PAGE 57 H1144 ECO/UNDEV FOR/AID EDU/PROP PLAN

S67

GONZALEZ M.P.,"CUBA, UNA REVOLUCION EN MARCHA." CUBA L/A+17C USA+45 VIETNAM ECO/UNDEV FORCES DIPLOM DOMIN...POLICY MARXIST NAT/COMP CASTRO/F. PAGE 58 H1163 REV NAT/G COLONIAL SOVEREIGN

S67

GOODSELL J.N.,"BALAGUER'S DOMINICAN REPUBLIC." DOMIN/REP FUT L/A+17C POL/PAR PROB/SOLV ECO/TAC 20. PAGE 59 H1174 ECO/UNDEV CHIEF POLICY NAT/G

S67

GRAHAM R.,"BRAZIL'S DILEMMA." BRAZIL FUT L/A+17C NAT/G CHIEF PROB/SOLV ECO/TAC PWR 20. PAGE 60 H1193 ECO/UNDEV CONSTN POL/PAR POLICY

S67

GRANT C.H.,"RURAL LOCAL GOVERNMENT IN GUYANA AND BRITISH HONDURAS." GUYANA HONDURAS L/A+17C AGRI NAT/G EX/STRUC ACT/RES REGION GOV/REL EFFICIENCY ORD/FREE 20. PAGE 60 H1196 ECO/UNDEV LOC/G ADMIN MUNIC

S67

GRUNDY K.W.,"AFRICA IN THE WORLD ARENA." ECO/UNDEV BAL/PWR FOR/AID NEUTRAL REV NAT/LISM GOV/COMP. PAGE 62 H1240 AFR DIPLOM INT/ORG COLONIAL

S67

HANSON A.H.,"INDIA AFTER THE ELECTIONS." INDIA ECO/UNDEV LEGIS TEC/DEV FOR/AID GP/REL FEDERAL ATTIT 20. PAGE 66 H1321 NAT/G POL/PAR REGION CENTRAL

S67

HASSAN M.F.,"THE SECOND FOUR-YEAR PLAN OF VENEZUELA." L/A+17C VENEZUELA AGRI INDUS NAT/G PLAN RATION CONTROL HABITAT...MATH STAT 20. PAGE 67 H1352 ECO/UNDEV FINAN BUDGET PROB/SOLV

S67

HEATH D.B.,"BOLIVIA UNDER BARRIENTOS." L/A+17C NAT/G CHIEF DIPLOM ECO/TAC...POLICY 20 BOLIV. PAGE 69 H1379 ECO/UNDEV POL/PAR REV CONSTN

S67

IDENBURG P.J.,"POLITICAL STRUCTURAL DEVELOPMENT IN TROPICAL AFRICA." UK ECO/UNDEV KIN POL/PAR CHIEF EX/STRUC CREATE COLONIAL CONTROL REPRESENT RACE/REL ...MAJORIT TREND 20. PAGE 76 H1521 AFR CONSTN NAT/G GOV/COMP

S67

INDER S.,"AFTER THE CORONATION." CONSTN ECO/UNDEV EX/STRUC LEGIS INT/TRADE CONTROL SOVEREIGN ...TIME/SEQ 20 TONGA COMMONWLTH INAUGURATE. PAGE 76 H1527 CHIEF NAT/G POLICY

S67

LEVI W.,"THE ELITIST NATURE OF NEW ASIA'S FOREIGN POLICY." CULTURE ECO/UNDEV NAT/G PROB/SOLV EDU/PROP COLONIAL CONTROL REGION NAT/LISM...NAT/COMP 20. PAGE 95 H1898 POLICY ELITES DIPLOM CREATE

S67

NEUBAUER D.E.,"SOME CONDITIONS OF DEMOCRACY." ECO/DEV COM/IND DIST/IND POL/PAR EDU/PROP REPRESENT ...SOC STAT NAT/COMP 20. PAGE 117 H2331 NAT/G CHOOSE MAJORIT ECO/UNDEV

S67

NUGENT J.B.,"ECONOMIC THOUGHT, INVESTMENT CRITERIA, AND DEVELOPMENT STRATEGIES IN GREECE* A POSTWAR SURVEY." GREECE AGRI INDUS INT/ORG NAT/G OP/RES DEMAND OPTIMAL PRODUC WEALTH 20 EEC. PAGE 119 H2379 ECO/UNDEV PLAN FINAN

S67

PERKINS D.H.,"ECONOMIC GROWTH IN CHINA AND THE CULTURAL REVOLUTION(1960APRIL 1967)" CHINA/COM FUT AGRI INDUS PLAN LEAD MARXISM...CHARTS 20 MAO. PAGE 125 H2493 ECO/TAC CULTURE REV ECO/UNDEV

S67

RICHMAN B.M.,"CAPITALISTS & MANAGERS IN COMMUNIST CHINA." ASIA CHINA/COM ECO/UNDEV NAT/G CONSULT EX/STRUC PLAN EFFICIENCY PRODUC WEALTH MARXISM ...MGT CHARTS 20. PAGE 131 H2623 CAP/ISM INDUS

S67

ROSE S.,"ASIAN NATIONALISM* THE SECOND STAGE." ASIA COM ECO/UNDEV NAT/G PROB/SOLV DIPLOM FOR/AID DOMIN NEUTRAL REGION TASK...METH/COMP 20. PAGE 134 H2675 NAT/LISM S/ASIA BAL/PWR COLONIAL

S67

SANCHEZ J.D.,"DESARROLLO ECONOMICO Y FUTURO DE COLOMBIA." L/A+17C AGRI EXTR/IND FINAN INDUS MARKET INT/TRADE CONTROL...STAT TREND COLOMB. PAGE 137 H2748 ECO/UNDEV FUT NAT/G ECO/TAC

S67

SAVELYEV N.,"MONOPOLY DRIVE IN INDIA." INDIA INDUS NAT/G INT/TRADE NEUTRAL SANCTION GOV/REL CONSERVE ...MARXIST 20. PAGE 138 H2759 ECO/UNDEV POL/PAR ECO/TAC CONTROL

S67

SCHACHTER G.,"REGIONAL DEVELOPMENT IN THE ITALIAN DUAL ECONOMY" ITALY AGRI INDUS MARKET WORKER ECO/TAC CONTROL INCOME PRODUC 20. PAGE 138 H2767 REGION ECO/UNDEV NAT/G PROB/SOLV

S67

SCOTT J.W.,"SOURCES OF SOCIAL CHANGE IN COMMUNITY, FAMILY, AND FERTILITY IN A PUERTO RICAN TOWN." PUERT/RICO CULTURE STRUCT ECO/UNDEV INDUS PERS/REL ROLE...SOC STAND/INT. PAGE 141 H2815 FAM MARRIAGE LITERACY ATTIT

S67

SHIGEO N.,"THE GREAT CULTURAL REVOLUTION." ASIA ECO/UNDEV AGRI NAT/G CHIEF ECO/TAC EDU/PROP CONTROL LEAD PWR 20 MAO. PAGE 143 H2860 CREATE REV CULTURE POL/PAR

S67

SINGH B.,"ITALIAN EXPERIENCE IN REGIONAL ECONOMIC DEVELOPMENT AND LESSONS FOR OTHER COUNTRIES." EUR+WWI ITALY INDUS NAT/G ACT/RES REGION GP/REL EFFICIENCY EQUILIB PRODUC WEALTH. PAGE 144 H2884 ECO/UNDEV PLAN ECO/TAC CONTROL

S67

SIPPEL D.,"INDIENS UNSICHERE ZUKUNFT." INDIA CULTURE ACADEM POL/PAR LEGIS COLONIAL CHOOSE SOVEREIGN...JURID 20. PAGE 144 H2888 SOCIETY STRUCT ECO/UNDEV NAT/G

S67

SUNG C.H.,"POLITICAL DIAGNOSIS OF KOREAN SOCIETY* A SURVEY OF MILITARY AND CIVILIAN VALUES." KOREA/S ECO/UNDEV NAT/G CIVMIL/REL...QU SAMP GP/COMP. PAGE 151 H3009 ELITES FORCES ATTIT ORD/FREE

S67

TANTER R.,"A THEORY OF REVOLUTION." ASIA CUBA L/A+17C S/ASIA SOCIETY NAT/G ADJUST...CONCPT CHARTS. PAGE 152 H3046 REV ECO/UNDEV EDU/PROP METH/COMP

S67

TAYLOR P.B. JR.,"PROGRESS IN VENEZUELA." L/A+17C VENEZUELA AGRI INDUS LG/CO NAT/G SML/CO CHOOSE ...POLICY 20. PAGE 153 H3057 ECO/UNDEV ECO/TAC POL/PAR ORD/FREE

S67

VINCENT S.,"SHOULD BIAFRA SURVIVE?" NIGERIA ECO/UNDEV CHIEF FORCES ECO/TAC GP/REL DISCRIM PEACE ORD/FREE SOC/INTEG 20 BIAFRA IBO. PAGE 163 H3256 AFR REV REGION NAT/G

S67

VON LAUE T.H.,"WESTERNIZATION, REVOLUTION AND THE SEARCH FOR A BASIS OF AUTHORITY - RUSSIA IN 1917." USSR ELITES INTELL ECO/UNDEV NAT/G WORKER ECO/TAC TAX ADMIN LEAD AUTHORIT 20 LENIN/VI. PAGE 164 H3274 MARXISM REV COM DOMIN

S67

WILLIAMS F.R.A.,"FUNDAMENTAL RIGHTS AND THE PROSPECT FOR DEMOCRACY IN NIGERIA." FUT NIGERIA SOCIETY ECO/UNDEV LEGIS ADJUD CHOOSE 20. PAGE 168 H3366 CONSTN LAW ORD/FREE NAT/G

S67

WRAITH R.E.,"ADMINISTRATIVE CHANGE IN THE NEW AFRICA." AFR LG/CO ADJUD INGP/REL PWR...RECORD GP/COMP 20. PAGE 171 H3416 ADMIN NAT/G LOC/G ECO/UNDEV

N67

US HOUSE COMM SCI ASTRONAUT,GOVERNMENT, SCIENCE, AND INTERNATIONAL POLICY (PAMPHLET). INDIA NETHERLAND ECO/DEV ECO/UNDEV R+D ACADEM PLAN DIPLOM FOR/AID CONFER...PREDICT 20 CHINJAP. PAGE 160 H3198 NAT/G POLICY CREATE TEC/DEV

L68

CURRENT HISTORY,"AFRICA, 1968." ETHIOPIA GHANA NIGERIA SOUTH/AFR CULTURE ECO/UNDEV KIN SECT CHIEF EX/STRUC WAR WEAPON CHOOSE CIVMIL/REL...GOV/COMP 20 RACE/REL NAT/LISM FORCES

AFRICA/E. PAGE 36 H0724 — AFR

S68
DOUGLAS-HOME C.,"A MISTAKEN POLICY IN ADEN." YEMEN CULTURE ECO/UNDEV INDUS FORCES WORKER DIPLOM ECO/TAC CONTROL 20 ADEN. PAGE 42 H0842
SOVEREIGN COLONIAL POLICY REGION

S68
LAPIERRE J.W.,"TRADITION ET MODERNITE A MADAGASCAR." ISLAM MADAGASCAR AGRI FINAN KIN NAT/G CREATE OP/RES GP/REL INGP/REL ATTIT CONSERVE...PSY 20. PAGE 91 H1813
ECO/UNDEV FOR/AID CULTURE TEC/DEV

C89
PLAYFAIR R.L.,"A BIBLIOGRAPHY OF ALGERIA." ALGERIA CULTURE ECO/UNDEV DIST/IND EXTR/IND FINAN SECT CRIME 16/19. PAGE 126 H2525
BIBLIOG/A ISLAM GEOG

L95
BELSHAW C.S.,"IN SEARCH OF WEALTH; STUDY OF EMERGENCE OF COMMERCIAL OPERA TIONS IN MELANESIAN SOCIETY OF SOUTHEASTERN PAPUA." S/ASIA CULTURE KIN ECO/TAC DEMAND INCOME 20 MELANESIA PAPUA. PAGE 14 H0272
INT/TRADE ECO/UNDEV METH/COMP SOCIETY

B98
FORTES M.,AFRICAN POLITICAL SYSTEMS. ECO/UNDEV KIN LOC/G NEIGH POL/PAR SECT LEAD GP/REL ORD/FREE...SOC 20 NEGRO. PAGE 52 H1039
AFR CULTURE STRUCT

ECOLOGY....SEE HABITAT

ECOMETRIC....MATHEMATICAL ECONOMICS, ECONOMETRICS

N19
BUSINESS ECONOMISTS' GROUP,INCOME POLICIES (PAMPHLET). UK INDUS LABOR TOP/EX PAY COST PRODUC ...ECOMETRIC GOV/COMP SIMUL ANTHOL 20. PAGE 25 H0497
INCOME WORKER WEALTH POLICY

B63
INTERNATIONAL ASSOCIATION RES,AFRICAN STUDIES IN INCOME AND WEALTH. AFR NAT/G PROB/SOLV DEMAND INCOME...ECOMETRIC METH/COMP 20. PAGE 78 H1553
WEALTH PLAN ECO/UNDEV BUDGET

B66
BROWN R.T.,TRANSPORT AND THE ECONOMIC INTEGRATION OF SOUTH AMERICA. L/A+17C ECO/UNDEV NAT/G OP/RES DIPLOM INT/TRADE REGION WEALTH...ECOMETRIC GEOG STAT LAFTA TIME. PAGE 22 H0449
MARKET DIST/IND SIMUL

B66
FOX K.A.,THE THEORY OF QUANTITATIVE ECONOMIC POLICY WITH APPLICATIONS TO ECONOMIC GROWTH AND STABILIZATION. ECO/DEV AGRI NAT/G PLAN ADMIN RISK ...DECISION IDEA/COMP SIMUL T. PAGE 52 H1045
ECO/TAC ECOMETRIC EQUILIB GEN/LAWS

B66
LEONTIEF W.,ESSAYS IN ECONOMICS. ECO/UNDEV INDUS NAT/G CAP/ISM FOR/AID AUTOMAT MARXISM...ECOMETRIC CHARTS ANTHOL METH 20 KEYNES/JM. PAGE 94 H1886
CONCPT METH/CNCPT METH/COMP

B67
DENISON E.F.,WHY GROWTH RATES DIFFER; POSTWAR EXPERIENCE IN NINE WESTERN COUNTRIES. WOR+45 FINAN WORKER TEC/DEV EDU/PROP PRICE PRODUC WEALTH ...ECOMETRIC STAT CHARTS BIBLIOG. PAGE 40 H0791
METH NAT/COMP ECO/DEV ECO/TAC

ECONOMIC DETERMINISM....SEE GEN/LAWS

ECONOMIC WARFARE....SEE ECO/TAC

ECOSOC....UNITED NATIONS ECONOMIC AND SOCIAL COUNCIL

S61
PADELFORD N.J.,"POLITICS AND THE FUTURE OF ECOSOC." AFR S/ASIA ECO/UNDEV INDUS NAT/G DELIB/GP ACT/RES ORD/FREE WEALTH...CONCPT CHARTS UN 20 ECOSOC. PAGE 122 H2438
INT/ORG TEC/DEV

ECSC....EUROPEAN COAL AND STEEL COMMUNITY, SEE ALSO VOL/ASSN, INT/ORG

B58
HAAS E.B.,THE UNITING OF EUROPE. EUR+WWI INT/ORG NAT/G POL/PAR TOP/EX ECO/TAC EDU/PROP LEGIT FEDERAL NAT/LISM DRIVE RIGID/FLEX ORD/FREE PWR PLURISM ...POLICY CONCPT INT GEN/LAWS ECSC EEC 20. PAGE 63 H1264
VOL/ASSN ECO/DEV

B60
LISTER L.,EUROPE'S COAL AND STEEL COMMUNITY. FRANCE GERMANY STRUCT ECO/DEV EXTR/IND INDUS MARKET NAT/G DELIB/GP ECO/TAC INT/TRADE EDU/PROP ATTIT RIGID/FLEX ORD/FREE PWR WEALTH...CONCPT STAT TIME/SEQ CHARTS ECSC 20. PAGE 97 H1941
EUR+WWI INT/ORG REGION

B62
MEADE J.E.,CASE STUDIES IN EUROPEAN ECONOMIC UNION. BELGIUM EUR+WWI LUXEMBOURG NAT/G INT/TRADE REGION ROUTINE WEALTH...METH/CNCPT STAT CHARTS ECSC TOT/POP OEEC EEC 20. PAGE 108 H2154
INT/ORG ECO/TAC

ECUADOR....SEE ALSO L/A+17C

B47
DE NOIA J.,GUIDE TO OFFICIAL PUBLICATIONS OF OTHER AMERICAN REPUBLICS: ECUADOR (VOL. IX). ECUADOR LAW FINAN LEGIS BUDGET CT/SYS 19/20. PAGE 38 H0763
BIBLIOG/A CONSTN NAT/G EDU/PROP

B55
SERRANO MOSCOSO E.,A STATEMENT OF THE LAWS OF ECUADOR IN MATTERS AFFECTING BUSINESS (2ND ED.). ECUADOR INDUS LABOR LG/CO NAT/G LEGIS TAX CONTROL MARRIAGE 20. PAGE 141 H2830
FINAN ECO/UNDEV LAW CONSTN

S61
RANDALL F.B.,"COMMUNISM IN THE HIGH ANDES." L/A+17C PERU USSR SOCIETY PLAN EDU/PROP TOTALISM ATTIT RIGID/FLEX PWR WEALTH...HUM CONCPT GEN/LAWS 20 BOLIV EQUADOR. PAGE 129 H2589
CULTURE DRIVE

B63
BIALEK R.W.,CATHOLIC POLITICS: A HISTORY BASED ON ECUADOR. ECUADOR SPAIN CULTURE STRUCT CONTROL REV PWR...BIBLIOG WORSHIP 18/20. PAGE 16 H0329
COLONIAL CATHISM GOV/REL HABITAT

ECUMENIC....ECUMENICAL MOVEMENT OF CHURCHES

EDDING F. H1875

EDDY J.P. H0887

EDELMAN M. H0888

EDINGER L.J. H0889

EDU/PROP....EDUCATION, PROPAGANDA, PERSUASION

N
TOTEMEYER G.,SOUTH AFRICA; SOUTHWEST AFRICA: A BIBLIOGRAPHY, 1945-1963. AFR SOUTH/AFR PRESS...SOC 20. PAGE 157 H3134
BIBLIOG CULTURE NAT/G EDU/PROP

N
JOURNAL OF ASIAN STUDIES. CULTURE ECO/DEV SECT DIPLOM EDU/PROP WAR NAT/LISM...PHIL/SCI SOC 20. PAGE 1 H0005
BIBLIOG ASIA S/ASIA NAT/G

N
PEKING REVIEW. CHINA/COM CULTURE AGRI INDUS DIPLOM EDU/PROP GUERRILLA ATTIT MARXISM...BIBLIOG 20. PAGE 1 H0009
MARXIST NAT/G POL/PAR PRESS

N
BIBLIOGRAPHIE DE LA PHILOSOPHIE. LAW CULTURE SECT EDU/PROP MORAL...HUM METH/CNCPT 20. PAGE 1 H0012
BIBLIOG/A PHIL/SCI CONCPT LOG

N
INDIA: A REFERENCE ANNUAL. INDIA CULTURE COM/IND R+D FORCES PLAN RECEIVE EDU/PROP HEALTH...STAT CHARTS BIBLIOG 20. PAGE 1 H0017
CONSTN LABOR INT/ORG

N
THE STATESMAN'S YEARBOOK; STATISTICAL AND HISTORICAL ANNUAL OF THE STATES OF THE WORLD. WOR+45 WOR-45 COM/IND FINAN INDUS SECT FORCES TEC/DEV EDU/PROP...GEOG BIBLIOG 19/20. PAGE 1 H0023
NAT/COMP GOV/COMP STAT CONSTN

N
THE MIDDLE EAST AND NORTH AFRICA. AFR ISLAM CULTURE ECO/UNDEV AGRI NAT/G TEC/DEV FOR/AID INT/TRADE EDU/PROP...CHARTS 20. PAGE 2 H0026
INDEX INDUS FINAN STAT

N
HOOVER INSTITUTION,UNITED STATES AND CANADIAN PUBLICATIONS ON AFRICA. CULTURE ECO/UNDEV AGRI TEC/DEV EDU/PROP COLONIAL RACE/REL NAT/LISM ATTIT HEALTH...SOC SOC/WK 20. PAGE 73 H1464
BIBLIOG DIPLOM NAT/G AFR

N
INADA S.,INTRODUCTION TO SCIENTIFIC WORKS IN HUMANITIES AND SOCIAL SCIENCES PUBLISHED IN JAPAN. LAW CULTURE ACADEM EDU/PROP...ART/METH HUM 20 CHINJAP. PAGE 76 H1525
BIBLIOG/A NAT/G SOC S/ASIA

N
INTERNATIONAL CENTRE AFRICAN,BULLETIN OF INFORMATION ON THESES AND STUDIES IN PROGRESS OR PROPOSED. LAW CULTURE FINAN INDUS LABOR TEC/DEV EDU/PROP...GEOG SOC NAT/COMP 20. PAGE 78 H1554
BIBLIOG/A ACT/RES ACADEM INTELL

N
NORTHWESTERN UNIVERSITY LIB,JOINT ACQUISITIONS LIST OF AFRICANA. AFR SOCIETY STRUCT EDU/PROP COLONIAL GP/REL RACE/REL NAT/LISM SOVEREIGN...SOC 20. PAGE 119 H2377
BIBLIOG CULTURE ECO/UNDEV INDUS

N
SOUTH AFRICA STATE LIBRARY,SOUTH AFRICAN NATIONAL BIBLIOGRAPHY, SANB. SOUTH/AFR LAW NAT/G EDU/PROP ...MGT PSY SOC 20. PAGE 147 H2937
BIBLIOG PRESS WRITING

N
US CONSOLATE GENERAL HONG KONG,REVIEW OF THE HONG
BIBLIOG/A

KONG CHINESE PRESS. ECO/UNDEV LOC/G NAT/G PLAN DIPLOM EDU/PROP LEAD GP/REL MARXISM...POLICY INDEX 20. PAGE 159 H3178
ASIA PRESS ATTIT

N
US CONSULATE GENERAL HONG KONG,CURRENT BACKGROUND. CHINA/COM ECO/UNDEV LOC/G NAT/G PLAN DIPLOM EDU/PROP LEAD REV ATTIT...POLICY INDEX 20. PAGE 159 H3179
BIBLIOG/A MARXIST ASIA PRESS

N
US CONSULATE GENERAL HONG KONG,SURVEY OF CHINA MAINLAND PRESS. CHINA/COM ECO/UNDEV LOC/G NAT/G PLAN DIPLOM EDU/PROP LEAD REV ATTIT...POLICY INDEX 20. PAGE 159 H3181
BIBLIOG/A MARXIST ASIA PRESS

N
US CONSULATE GENERAL HONG KONG,US CONSULATE GENERAL, HONG KONG, PRESS SUMMARIES. CHINA/COM ECO/UNDEV LOC/G NAT/G PLAN DIPLOM EDU/PROP LEAD REV ATTIT...POLICY INDEX 20. PAGE 159 H3182
BIBLIOG/A MARXIST ASIA PRESS

N
US DEPARTMENT OF STATE,BIBLIOGRAPHY (PAMPHLETS). AGRI INDUS INT/ORG FOR/AID EDU/PROP WAR MARXISM ...SOC GOV/COMP METH/COMP 20. PAGE 159 H3184
BIBLIOG DIPLOM ECO/DEV NAT/G

N
US LIBRARY OF CONGRESS,ACCESSIONS LIST - INDIA. INDIA CULTURE AGRI LOC/G POL/PAR PLAN PROB/SOLV TEC/DEV DIPLOM EDU/PROP LEAD GP/REL ATTIT 20. PAGE 160 H3199
BIBLIOG S/ASIA ECO/UNDEV NAT/G

N
US LIBRARY OF CONGRESS,ACCESSIONS LIST -- ISRAEL. ISRAEL CULTURE ECO/UNDEV POL/PAR PLAN PROB/SOLV TEC/DEV DIPLOM EDU/PROP LEAD WAR ATTIT 20 JEWS. PAGE 160 H3200
BIBLIOG ISLAM NAT/G GP/REL

B00
BENEDETTI V.,STUDIES IN DIPLOMACY. BELGIUM FRANCE GERMANY MOD/EUR CONSTN NAT/G CONSULT TOP/EX DOMIN EDU/PROP COERCE ATTIT...CONCPT INT BIOG TREND 19. PAGE 14 H0276
PWR GEN/LAWS DIPLOM

B00
MARKHAM V.R.,SOUTH AFRICA, PAST AND PRESENT. NETHERLAND SOUTH/AFR CULTURE LEGIS EDU/PROP COLONIAL CHOOSE REPRESENT DISCRIM ATTIT...OBS TIME/SEQ 17/19 NEGRO BOER/WAR. PAGE 103 H2054
WAR LEAD RACE/REL

B02
SEELEY J.R.,THE EXPANSION OF ENGLAND. MOD/EUR S/ASIA UK CULTURE NAT/G FORCES PLAN DOMIN EDU/PROP COLONIAL ROUTINE ATTIT ALL/VALS SOVEREIGN...CONCPT HIST/WRIT PARLIAMENT 18 CMN/WLTH. PAGE 141 H2819
INT/ORG ACT/RES CAP/ISM INDIA

B03
FAGUET E.,LE LIBERALISME. FRANCE PRESS ADJUD ADMIN DISCRIM CONSERVE SOCISM...TRADIT SOC LING WORSHIP PARLIAMENT. PAGE 48 H0960
ORD/FREE EDU/PROP NAT/G LAW

B08
NIRRNHEIM O.,DAS ERSTE JAHR DES MINISTERIUMS BISMARCK UND DIE OEFFENTLICHE MEINUNG (HEIDELBERGER ABHANDLUNGEN, 20. HEFT). GERMANY MOD/EUR LEGIS DIPLOM EDU/PROP INGP/REL...BIOG GOV/COMP IDEA/COMP BIBLIOG 19 BISMARCK/O. PAGE 118 H2363
CHIEF PRESS NAT/G ATTIT

B09
JUSTINIAN,THE DIGEST (DIGESTA CORPUS JURIS CIVILIS) (2 VOLS.) (TRANS. BY C. H. MONRO). ROMAN/EMP LAW FAM LOC/G LEGIS EDU/PROP CONTROL MARRIAGE OWN ROLE CIVIL/LAW. PAGE 82 H1645
JURID CT/SYS NAT/G STRATA

B11
HUXLEY T.H.,METHOD AND RESULTS: ESSAYS. EDU/PROP REPRESENT OWN PERSON PWR WEALTH...PSY IDEA/COMP GEN/LAWS. PAGE 76 H1514
ORD/FREE NAT/G POPULISM PLURIST

B12
SONOLET L.,L'AFRIQUE OCCIDENTALE FRANCAISE. FRANCE AGRI INDUS NAT/G SECT FORCES INT/TRADE EDU/PROP RACE/REL HEALTH ORD/FREE...CHARTS 19/20 NEGRO AFRICA/W. PAGE 147 H2933
DOMIN ADMIN COLONIAL AFR

B13
DIE REKLAME IHRE KUNST UND WISSENSCHAFT. GERMANY POLAND SWITZERLND USA+45 TEC/DEV CAP/ISM DEMAND ...ART/METH EXHIBIT METH/COMP ANTHOL 20. PAGE 135 H2707
EDU/PROP MARKET NAT/COMP ATTIT

B14
BERHARDI F.,GERMANY AND THE NEXT WAR. MOD/EUR NAT/G SCHOOL FORCES ACT/RES DOMIN EDU/PROP SUPEGO PWR ...TIME/SEQ STERTYP TOT/POP 20 WWI. PAGE 15 H0304
DRIVE COERCE WAR GERMANY

B15
FARIES J.C.,THE RISE OF INTERNATIONALISM. ASIA MOD/EUR NAT/G VOL/ASSN DELIB/GP BAL/PWR EDU/PROP ARMS/CONT RIGID/FLEX TREND. PAGE 49 H0971
INT/ORG DIPLOM PEACE

B16
TREITSCHKE H.,POLITICS. UNIV SOCIETY STRATA NAT/G EX/STRUC LEGIS DOMIN EDU/PROP ATTIT PWR RESPECT ...CONCPT TIME/SEQ GEN/LAWS TOT/POP 20. PAGE 157 H3129
EXEC ELITES GERMANY

B17
VEBLEN T.B.,AN INQUIRY INTO THE NATURE OF PEACE AND THE TERMS OF ITS PERPETUATION. UNIV STRATA FINAN EDU/PROP PRICE COST DISCRIM NAT/LISM MORAL ORD/FREE PACIFIST 20 WORLDUNITY. PAGE 162 H3237
PEACE DIPLOM WAR NAT/G

B19
NATHAN M.,THE SOUTH AFRICAN COMMONWEALTH: CONSTITUTION, PROBLEMS, SOCIAL CONDITIONS. SOUTH/AFR UK CULTURE INDUS EX/STRUC LEGIS BUDGET EDU/PROP ADMIN CT/SYS GP/REL RACE/REL...LING 19/20 CMN/WLTH. PAGE 116 H2317
CONSTN NAT/G POL/PAR SOCIETY

N19
COUTROT A.,THE FIGHT OVER THE 1959 PRIVATE EDUCATION LAW IN FRANCE (PAMPHLET). FRANCE NAT/G SECT GIVE EDU/PROP GP/REL ATTIT RIGID/FLEX ORD/FREE 20 CHURCH/STA. PAGE 34 H0681
SCHOOL PARL/PROC CATHISM LAW

N19
FIKS M.,PUBLIC ADMINISTRATION IN ISRAEL (PAMPHLET). ISRAEL SCHOOL EX/STRUC BUDGET PAY INGP/REL ...DECISION 20 CIVIL/SERV. PAGE 50 H0999
EDU/PROP NAT/G ADMIN WORKER

N19
GRIFFITH W.,THE PUBLIC SERVICE (PAMPHLET). UK LAW LOC/G NAT/G PARTIC CHOOSE DRIVE ROLE SKILL...CHARTS 20 CIVIL/SERV. PAGE 61 H1222
ADMIN EFFICIENCY EDU/PROP GOV/REL

N19
HAJDA J.,THE COLD WAR VIEWED AS A SOCIOLOGICAL PROBLEM (PAMPHLET). COM CZECHOSLVK EUR+WWI SOCIETY PLAN EDU/PROP CONTROL TASK ATTIT MARXISM...POLICY 20 COLD/WAR MIGRATION. PAGE 64 H1280
DIPLOM LEAD PWR NAT/G

N19
LIEBKNECHT W.P.C.,SOCIALISM (2 PTS.; 1875, 1894) (PAMPHLET). WORKER CAP/ISM EDU/PROP WEALTH POPULISM. PAGE 97 H1927
ECO/TAC STRATA SOCIALIST PARTIC

N19
MAO TSE-TUNG,ON SOME IMPORTANT PROBLEMS OF THE PARTY'S PRESENT POLICY. CHINA/COM CONSTN ELITES INTELL AGRI DOMIN EDU/PROP REV REPRESENT GP/REL OWN PEACE ORD/FREE 20 COM/PARTY. PAGE 102 H2044
POLICY NAT/G CHIEF LEGIT

N19
PROVISIONS SECTION OAU,ORGANIZATION OF AFRICAN UNITY: BASIC DOCUMENTS AND RESOLUTIONS (PAMPHLET). AFR CULTURE ECO/UNDEV DIPLOM ECO/TAC EDU/PROP COLONIAL ARMS/CONT NUC/PWR RACE/REL DISCRIM NAT/LISM 20 UN OAU. PAGE 128 H2564
CONSTN EX/STRUC SOVEREIGN INT/ORG

N19
SENGHOR L.S.,AFRICAN SOCIALISM (PAMPHLET). AFR FRANCE MALI USSR ELITES ECO/UNDEV NAT/G DIPLOM DOMIN EDU/PROP ATTIT 20 NEGRO. PAGE 141 H2827
SOCISM MARXISM ORD/FREE NAT/LISM

N19
TABORSKY E.,CONFORMITY UNDER COMMUNISM (PAMPHLET). CZECHOSLVK HUNGARY POLAND SCHOOL DOMIN PRESS ...TREND GOV/COMP 20. PAGE 152 H3030
COM CONTROL EDU/PROP NAT/G

B20
BOSANQUET B.,THE PHILOSOPHICAL THEORY OF THE STATE (3RD ED.). SECT LEGIS EDU/PROP ORD/FREE...POLICY SOC GOV/COMP IDEA/COMP NAT/COMP. PAGE 19 H0380
GEN/LAWS CONSTN NAT/G

B20
HALDANE R.B.,BEFORE THE WAR. MOD/EUR SOCIETY INT/ORG NAT/G DELIB/GP PLAN DOMIN EDU/PROP LEGIT ADMIN COERCE ATTIT DRIVE MORAL ORD/FREE PWR...SOC CONCPT SELF/OBS RECORD BIOG TIME/SEQ. PAGE 64 H1282
POLICY DIPLOM UK

B21
STUART G.H.,FRENCH FOREIGN POLICY. CONSTN INT/ORG NAT/G POL/PAR EX/STRUC FORCES PLAN ECO/TAC DOMIN EDU/PROP ADJUD COERCE ATTIT DRIVE RIGID/FLEX ALL/VALS...POLICY OBS RECORD BIOG TIME/SEQ TREND. PAGE 150 H3000
MOD/EUR DIPLOM FRANCE

B22
FICHTE J.G.,ADDRESSES TO THE GERMAN NATION. GERMANY PRUSSIA ELITES NAT/G SECT CREATE INT/TRADE HEREDITY ...ART/METH LING 19 FRANK/PARL. PAGE 50 H0989
NAT/LISM CULTURE EDU/PROP REGION

B23
KADEN E.H.,DER POLITISCHE CHARAKTER DER FRANZOSISCHEN KULTURPROPAGANDA AM RHEIN. FRANCE MOD/EUR DOMIN PRESS...GEOG METH/COMP 20. PAGE 82 H1648
EDU/PROP ATTIT DIPLOM NAT/G

B23
WILLOUGHBY W.C.,RACE PROBLEMS IN THE NEW AFRICA: A STUDY OF THE RELATION OF BANTU AND BRITONS IN THOSE PARTS OF BANTU AFRICA... AFR STRUCT SECT DOMIN EDU/PROP GP/REL ATTIT WORSHIP 20 BANTU EUROPE MISSION CHRISTIAN. PAGE 168 H3372
KIN COLONIAL RACE/REL CULTURE

B24
WALKER F.D.,AFRICA AND HER PEOPLES. ISLAM STRUCT FAM SECT EDU/PROP INGP/REL RACE/REL HABITAT...GEOG SOC IDEA/COMP WORSHIP 20 NEGRO. PAGE 164 H3292
CULTURE AFR GP/COMP KIN

B25
TEMPERLEY H.,THE FOREIGN POLICY OF CANNING: 1822-1827. MOD/EUR NAT/G TOP/EX EDU/PROP ROUTINE ATTIT RIGID/FLEX SUPEGO PWR SKILL...TIME/SEQ PARLIAMENT 20. PAGE 153 H3058
PERSON DIPLOM UK BIOG

B27
SMITH E.W.,THE GOLDEN STOOL: SOME ASPECTS OF THE CONFLICT OF CULTURES IN AFRICA. AFR FINAN INDUS SECT INT/TRADE COERCE CHOOSE RACE/REL ATTIT...GEOG LING 20 NEGRO. PAGE 145 H2907
COLONIAL CULTURE GP/REL EDU/PROP

B28
SOROKIN P.,CONTEMPORARY SOCIOLOGICAL THEORIES. MOD/EUR UNIV SOCIETY R+D SCHOOL ECO/TAC EDU/PROP ROUTINE ATTIT DRIVE...PSY CONCPT TIME/SEQ TREND GEN/LAWS 20. PAGE 147 H2934
CULTURE SOC WAR

B30
MASON E.S.,THE PARIS COMMUNE: AN EPISODE IN THE HISTORY OF THE SOCIALIST MOVEMENT. FRANCE MOD/EUR ELITES SOCIETY STRATA ECO/DEV WORKER EDU/PROP CHOOSE INGP/REL SOCISM 19 MARX/KARL PARIS. PAGE 104 H2085
NAT/G REV MARXISM

B31
DUFFIELD M.,KING LEGION. NAT/G PROVS SECT LEGIS EDU/PROP PRESS GP/REL AGE/Y MARXISM POLICY. PAGE 43 H0856
SUPEGO FORCES VOL/ASSN LOBBY

B32
LUNT D.C.,THE ROAD TO THE LAW. UK USA-45 LEGIS EDU/PROP OWN ORD/FREE...DECISION TIME/SEQ NAT/COMP 16/20 AUSTRAL ENGLSH/LAW COMMON/LAW. PAGE 99 H1980
ADJUD LAW JURID CT/SYS

B33
DAHLIN E.,FRENCH AND GERMAN PUBLIC OPINION ON DECLARED WAR AIMS 1914-1918. BELGIUM FRANCE GERMANY NAT/G POL/PAR DIPLOM COERCE REV WAR PEACE 20 WWI WILSON/W. PAGE 37 H0733
ATTIT EDU/PROP DOMIN NAT/COMP

B33
MOSS W.,POLITICAL PARTIES IN THE IRISH FREE STATE. IRELAND UK LAW FINAN LABOR DELIB/GP TOP/EX TARIFFS EDU/PROP...CHARTS GP/COMP 20. PAGE 113 H2269
POL/PAR NAT/G CHOOSE POLICY

B33
TANNENBAUM F.,PEACE BY REVOLUTION. ECO/UNDEV AGRI SECT WORKER DIPLOM EDU/PROP DISCRIM OWN WEALTH POPULISM 17/20 MEXIC/AMER INDIAN/AM. PAGE 152 H3043
CULTURE COLONIAL RACE/REL REV

B33
PUBLIC OPINION AND WORLD POLITICS. UNIV LAW CULTURE NAT/G PRESS REV GP/REL...MAJORIT METH/COMP ANTHOL 20. PAGE 171 H3420
DIPLOM EDU/PROP ATTIT MAJORITY

B34
GONZALEZ PALENCIA A,ESTUDIO HISTORICO SOBRE LA CENSURA GUBERNATIVA EN ESPANA 1800-1833. NAT/G COERCE INGP/REL ATTIT AUTHORIT KNOWL...POLICY JURID 19. PAGE 58 H1165
LEGIT EDU/PROP PRESS CONTROL

B35
MORE T.,UTOPIA (1516) (TRANS. BY R. ROBYNSON). LAW CULTURE SOCIETY STRUCT FAM SECT EDU/PROP WAR OWN UTIL KNOWL WEALTH 16. PAGE 113 H2253
UTOPIA NAT/G ECO/TAC GEN/LAWS

B36
WANDERSCHECK H.,WELTKRIEG UND PROPAGANDA. GERMANY MOD/EUR UK COM/IND NAT/G DOMIN PRESS ATTIT...POLICY 20 HITLER/A. PAGE 165 H3299
EDU/PROP PSY WAR KNOWL

C36
MAZZINI J.,"FROM THE COUNCIL TO GOD" (1870) IN J. MAZZINI, ESSAYS." ITALY NAT/G EDU/PROP PARTIC ORD/FREE PWR SOVEREIGN 19 POPE CHRISTIAN DEITY. PAGE 106 H2112
CATHISM DOMIN NAT/LISM SUPEGO

B37
MUNZENBERG W.,PROPAGANDA ALS WAFFE. COM/IND PRESS COERCE WAR...PSY 20. PAGE 115 H2290
EDU/PROP DOMIN NAT/G LEAD

B37
UNION OF SOUTH AFRICA,REPORT CONCERNING ADMINISTRATION OF SOUTH WEST AFRICA (6 VOLS.). SOUTH/AFR INDUS PUB/INST FORCES LEGIS BUDGET DIPLOM EDU/PROP ADJUD CT/SYS...GEOG CHARTS 20 AFRICA/SW LEAGUE/NAT. PAGE 158 H3166
NAT/G ADMIN COLONIAL CONSTN

B39
ANDERSON P.R.,THE BACKGROUND OF ANTI-ENGLISH FEELING IN GERMANY, 1890-1902. GERMANY MOD/EUR UK NAT/G POL/PAR TOP/EX WAR...IDEA/COMP 19/20. PAGE 7 H0132
DIPLOM EDU/PROP ATTIT COLONIAL

B39
BARNES H.E.,SOCIETY IN TRANSITION: PROBLEMS OF A CHANGING ERA. USA-45 INDUS MUNIC PUB/INST EDU/PROP CRIME RACE/REL...SOC MYTH NAT/COMP. PAGE 11 H0220
SOCIETY CULTURE TECHRACY TEC/DEV

B39
CARR E.H.,PROPAGANDA IN INTERNATIONAL POLITICS (PAMPHLET). EUR+WWI GERMANY MOD/EUR NAT/G AGREE WAR MORAL...POLICY 20 TREATY. PAGE 27 H0536
DIPLOM EDU/PROP CONTROL ATTIT

B39
HITLER A.,MEIN KAMPF. EUR+WWI FUT MOD/EUR STRUCT INT/ORG LABOR NAT/G POL/PAR FORCES CREATE PLAN BAL/PWR DIPLOM ECO/TAC DOMIN EDU/PROP ADMIN COERCE ATTIT...SOCIALIST BIOG TREND NAZI. PAGE 71 H1428
PWR NEW/IDEA WAR

B39
SCHOCKEL E.,DAS POLITISCHE PLAKAT. EUR+WWI GERMANY NAT/G PWR FASCISM EXHIBIT. PAGE 140 H2794
EDU/PROP ATTIT DOMIN POL/PAR

S39
LASSWELL H.D.,"PERSON, PERSONALITY, GROUP, CULTURE" (BMR)" UNIV CREATE EDU/PROP...EPIST CONCPT LING METH. PAGE 92 H1833
PERSON GP/REL CULTURE PERS/REL

B40
HUNTER R.,REVOLUTION: WHY, HOW, WHEN? NAT/G ECO/TAC EDU/PROP COERCE ORD/FREE FASCISM POPULISM SOCISM 18/20 HITLER/A LENIN/VI. PAGE 75 H1502
REV METH/COMP LEAD CONSTN

B40
LEDERER E.,STATE OF THE MASSES. GERMANY ITALY SOCIETY NAT/G ECO/TAC EDU/PROP LEAD TOTALISM ...SOCIALIST PSY 20. PAGE 93 H1852
CROWD FASCISM AUTHORIT PERSON

B40
MCHENRY D.E.,HIS MAJESTY'S OPPOSITION: STRUCTURE AND PROBLEMS OF THE BRITISH LABOUR PARTY 1931-1938. UK FINAN LABOR LOC/G DELIB/GP LEGIS EDU/PROP LEAD PARTIC CHOOSE GP/REL SOCISM...TREND 20 LABOR/PAR. PAGE 107 H2130
POL/PAR MGT NAT/G POLICY

B40
MEEK C.K.,EUROPE AND WEST AFRICA. AFR EUR+WWI EXTR/IND DIPLOM INT/TRADE EDU/PROP GP/REL...SOC 20. PAGE 108 H2158
CULTURE TEC/DEV ECO/UNDEV COLONIAL

B40
WANDERSCHECK H.,FRANKREICHS PROPAGANDA GEGEN DEUTSCHLAND. FRANCE GERMANY MOD/EUR UK NAT/G DIPLOM WAR 20 JEWS. PAGE 165 H3300
EDU/PROP ATTIT DOMIN PRESS

C40
FAHS C.B.,"GOVERNMENT IN JAPAN." FINAN FORCES LEGIS TOP/EX BUDGET INT/TRADE EDU/PROP SOVEREIGN ...CON/ANAL BIBLIOG/A 20 CHINJAP. PAGE 48 H0962
ASIA DIPLOM NAT/G ADMIN

B41
BAUMANN G.,GRUNDLAGEN UND PRAXIS DER INTERNATIONALEN PROPAGANDA. FRANCE GERMANY UK CULTURE COM/IND PRESS PWR...PSY METH/COMP 20. PAGE 12 H0241
EDU/PROP DOMIN ATTIT DIPLOM

B41
CROTHERS G.D.,THE GERMAN ELECTIONS OF 1907. GERMANY NAT/G EDU/PROP COLONIAL ATTIT. PAGE 35 H0709
CHOOSE PARL/PROC NAT/LISM POL/PAR

B41
GRISMER R.,A NEW BIBLIOGRAPHY OF THE LITERATURES OF SPAIN AND SPANISH AMERICA. CHRIST-17C MOD/EUR PRE/AMER SPAIN CULTURE DIPLOM EDU/PROP...ART/METH GEOG HUM PHIL/SCI 20. PAGE 61 H1229
BIBLIOG LAW NAT/G ECO/UNDEV

B41
HAYAKAWA S.I.,LANGUAGE IN ACTION. CULTURE INTELL SOCIETY KNOWL...METH/CNCPT LING LOG RECORD STERTYP GEN/METH TOT/POP 20. PAGE 68 H1366
EDU/PROP SOC

B41
HITLER A.,MEIN KAMPF (UNABR. ENG. VERSION) (1925). GERMANY CONSTN TEC/DEV RACE/REL NAT/LISM TOTALISM SOVEREIGN...BIOG 20 HITLER/A TREATY. PAGE 71 H1429
EDU/PROP WAR PLAN FASCISM

B41
KEESING F.M.,THE SOUTH SEAS IN THE MODERN WORLD. INDONESIA STRUCT FAM SECT EDU/PROP LEAD INCOME WEALTH...HEAL SOC 20. PAGE 84 H1678
CULTURE ECO/UNDEV GOV/COMP DIPLOM

B42
BARKER E.,REFLECTIONS ON GOVERNMENT. EUR+WWI SOCIETY LEGIS EDU/PROP ADMIN LEAD PARTIC CHOOSE TOTALISM AUTHORIT ORD/FREE SOCISM 20. PAGE 11 H0218
NAT/G POPULISM ACT/RES GEN/LAWS

B42
BAYNES N.H.,INTELLECTUAL LIBERTY AND TOTALITARIAN CLAIMS. EUR+WWI GERMANY ITALY INTELL POL/PAR CIVMIL/REL NAT/LISM SOCISM CONCPT. PAGE 12 H0245
KNOWL FASCISM EDU/PROP ACADEM

B42
CRAIG A.,ABOVE ALL LIBERTIES. FRANCE UK USA-45 LAW CONSTN CULTURE INTELL NAT/G SECT JUDGE...IDEA/COMP BIBLIOG 18/20. PAGE 35 H0692
ORD/FREE MORAL WRITING EDU/PROP

B42
NEUBURGER O.,OFFICIAL PUBLICATIONS OF PRESENT-DAY GERMANY: GOVERNMENT, CORPORATE ORGANIZATIONS, AND NATIONAL SOCIALIST PARTY. GERMANY CONSTN COM/IND POL/PAR EDU/PROP PRESS 20 NAZI. PAGE 117 H2332
BIBLIOG/A FASCISM NAT/G ADMIN

B42
NEUMANN S.,PERMANENT REVOLUTION: THE TOTAL STATE IN A WORLD AT WAR. COM EUR+WWI GERMANY USSR EX/STRUC DIPLOM CONTROL COERCE REPRESENT MARXISM...SOC GOV/COMP BIBLIOG 20 HITLER/A STALIN/J. PAGE 117
FASCISM TOTALISM DOMIN EDU/PROP

H2337

B42
SINGTON D.,THE GOEBBELS EXPERIMENT. GERMANY MOD/EUR NAT/G EX/STRUC FORCES CONTROL ROUTINE WAR TOTALISM PWR...ART/METH HUM 20 NAZI GOEBBELS/J. PAGE 144 H2886
FASCISM EDU/PROP ATTIT COM/IND

C42
CRAIG A.,"ABOVE ALL LIBERTIES." FRANCE UK LAW CULTURE INTELL SECT ORD/FREE 18/20. PAGE 35 H0693
BIBLIOG/A EDU/PROP WRITING MORAL

B43
LENIN V.I.,LEFT WING COMMUNISM: AN INFANTILE DISORDER (1920). GERMANY MOD/EUR USSR STRUCT CHIEF DOMIN EDU/PROP LEGIT LEAD REPRESENT POPULISM ...METH/COMP 19 LENIN/VI COM/PARTY MENSHEVIK. PAGE 94 H1879
COM MARXISM NAT/G REV

B43
US LIBRARY OF CONGRESS,BRITISH MALAYA AND BRITISH NORTH BORNEO. BORNEO MALAYSIA CONSTN AGRI COM/IND INDUS EDU/PROP 19/20. PAGE 160 H3203
BIBLIOG CULTURE

B44
CASSIRER E.,AN ESSAY ON MAN: AN INTRODUCTION TO A PHILOSOPHY OF HUMAN CULTURE. UNIV SECT CREATE EDU/PROP ATTIT KNOWL...HUM CONCPT MYTH TOT/POP. PAGE 28 H0556
CULTURE SOC

B44
GYORGY A.,GEOPOLITICS: THE NEW GERMAN SCIENCE. EUR+WWI GERMANY STRATA NAT/G PROVS DOMIN EDU/PROP ATTIT DRIVE FASCISM...GEOG NAZI 20. PAGE 63 H1261
PWR LEGIT WAR

B44
HAYEK F.A.,THE ROAD TO SERFDOM. NAT/G POL/PAR CREATE EDU/PROP ATTIT WEALTH LAISSEZ...OLD/LIB CONCPT TREND 20. PAGE 68 H1368
FUT PLAN ECO/TAC SOCISM

B44
KRIS E.,GERMAN RADIO PROPAGANDA: REPORT ON HOME BROADCASTS DURING THE WAR. EUR+WWI GERMANY CULTURE CONSULT PROB/SOLV FEEDBACK TASK INGP/REL DRIVE PWR FASCISM...CON/ANAL METH/COMP 20. PAGE 89 H1768
EDU/PROP DOMIN ACT/RES ATTIT

B44
US LIBRARY OF CONGRESS,RUSSIA: A CHECK LIST PRELIMINARY TO A BASIC BIBLIOGRAPHY OF MATERIALS IN THE RUSSIAN LANGUAGE. COM USSR CULTURE EDU/PROP MARXISM...ART/METH HUM LING 19/20. PAGE 160 H3204
BIBLIOG LAW SECT

B45
CONOVER H.F.,THE NAZI STATE: WAR CRIMES AND WAR CRIMINALS. GERMANY CULTURE NAT/G SECT FORCES DIPLOM INT/TRADE EDU/PROP...INT/LAW BIOG HIST/WRIT TIME/SEQ 20. PAGE 32 H0647
BIBLIOG WAR CRIME

B45
PERAZA SARAUSA F.,BIBLIOGRAFIAS CUBANAS. CUBA CULTURE ECO/UNDEV AGRI EDU/PROP PRESS CIVMIL/REL ...POLICY GEOG PHIL/SCI BIOG 19/20. PAGE 125 H2489
BIBLIOG/A L/A+17C NAT/G DIPLOM

B45
WARNER W.L.,THE SOCIAL SYSTEM OF AMERICAN ETHNIC GROUPS. STRATA FAM EDU/PROP ATTIT HABITAT RESPECT CLASSIF. PAGE 165 H3309
CULTURE VOL/ASSN SECT GP/COMP

B47
DE NOIA J.,GUIDE TO OFFICIAL PUBLICATIONS OF OTHER AMERICAN REPUBLICS: ECUADOR (VOL. IX). ECUADOR LAW FINAN LEGIS BUDGET CT/SYS 19/20. PAGE 38 H0763
BIBLIOG/A CONSTN NAT/G EDU/PROP

B47
DE NOIA J.,GUIDE TO OFFICIAL PUBLICATIONS OF THE OTHER AMERICAN REPUBLICS: EL SALVADOR. EL/SALVADR LAW LEGIS EDU/PROP CT/SYS 20. PAGE 38 H0764
BIBLIOG/A CONSTN NAT/G ADMIN

B47
DE NOIA J.,GUIDE TO OFFICIAL PUBLICATIONS OF THE OTHER AMERICAN REPUBLICS: NICARAGUA (VOL. XIV). NICARAGUA LAW LEGIS ADMIN CT/SYS...JURID 19/20. PAGE 38 H0765
BIBLIOG/A EDU/PROP NAT/G CONSTN

B47
DE NOIA J.,GUIDE TO OFFICIAL PUBLICATIONS OF THE OTHER AMERICAN REPUBLICS: PANAMA (VOL. XV). PANAMA LAW LEGIS EDU/PROP CT/SYS 20. PAGE 38 H0766
BIBLIOG/A CONSTN ADMIN NAT/G

B47
NEUBURGER O.,GUIDE TO OFFICIAL PUBLICATIONS OF OTHER AMERICAN REPUBLICS: HONDURAS (VOL. XIII). HONDURAS LAW LEGIS ADMIN CT/SYS...JURID 19/20. PAGE 117 H2333
BIBLIOG/A NAT/G EDU/PROP CONSTN

B47
NEUBURGER O.,GUIDE TO OFFICIAL PUBLICATIONS OF THE OTHER AMERICAN REPUBLICS: HAITI (VOL. XII). HAITI LAW FINAN LEGIS PRESS...JURID 20. PAGE 117 H2334
BIBLIOG/A CONSTN NAT/G EDU/PROP

N47
CANNON J.P.,AMERICAN STALINISM AND ANTI-STALINISM (PAMPHLET). NAT/G WORKER DOMIN EDU/PROP REV GP/REL ...MARXIST CONCPT 20 STALIN/J TROTSKY/L. PAGE 26 H0521
LABOR MARXISM CAP/ISM POL/PAR

B48
DE NOIA J.,GUIDE TO OFFICIAL PUBLICATIONS OF OTHER AMERICAN REPUBLICS: PERU (VOL. XVII). PERU LAW LEGIS ADMIN CT/SYS...JURID 19/20. PAGE 38 H0767
BIBLIOG/A CONSTN NAT/G EDU/PROP

B48
FLOREN LOZANO L.,BIBLIOGRAFIA DE LA BIBLIOGRAFIA DOMINICANA. DOMIN/REP NAT/G DIPLOM EDU/PROP CIVMIL/REL...POLICY ART/METH GEOG PHIL/SCI HIST/WRIT 20. PAGE 51 H1027
BIBLIOG/A BIOG L/A+17C CULTURE

B48
JONES H.D.,UNESCO: A SELECTED LIST OF REFERENCES. CULTURE CREATE PEACE ATTIT DRIVE 20 UNESCO UN. PAGE 82 H1631
BIBLIOG/A INT/ORG DIPLOM EDU/PROP

B48
LASKI H.S.,THE AMERICAN DEMOCRACY. CULTURE INDUS SECT WORKER DIPLOM EDU/PROP REPRESENT RACE/REL ORD/FREE PWR...NAT/COMP 18/20. PAGE 92 H1831
NAT/G LOC/G USA-45 POPULISM

B48
LINEBARGER P.,PSYCHOLOGICAL WARFARE. NAT/G PLAN DIPLOM DOMIN ATTIT...POLICY CONCPT EXHIBIT 20 WWI. PAGE 97 H1933
EDU/PROP PSY WAR COM/IND

B48
WOLFE B.D.,THREE WHO MADE A REVOLUTION. USSR CONSTN NAT/G CAP/ISM EDU/PROP CONTROL WAR GP/REL INGP/REL PERS/REL ROLE 20 STALIN/J LENIN/VI TROTSKY/L BOLSHEVISM. PAGE 170 H3398
BIOG REV LEAD MARXISM

L48
SHILS E.A.,"COHESION AND DISINTEGRATION IN THE WEHRMACHT IN WORLD WAR II." GERMANY STRUCT DOMIN WAR INGP/REL ISOLAT NAT/LISM ATTIT AUTHORIT SUPEGO RESPECT...PSY CON/ANAL 20 NAZI. PAGE 143 H2862
EDU/PROP DRIVE PERS/REL FORCES

S48
ALEXANDER L.,"WAR CRIMES, THEIR SOCIAL-PSYCHOLOGICAL ASPECTS." EUR+WWI GERMANY LAW CULTURE ELITES KIN POL/PAR PUB/INST FORCES DOMIN EDU/PROP COERCE CRIME ATTIT SUPEGO HEALTH MORAL PWR FASCISM ...PSY OBS TREND GEN/LAWS NAZI 20. PAGE 5 H0100
DRIVE WAR

S48
ALMOND G.A.,"THE CHRISTIAN PARTIES OF WESTEN EUROPE." EUR+WWI NAT/G EDU/PROP LEGIT TOTALISM ORD/FREE PWR MARXISM...TREND CHARTS STERTYP GEN/LAWS COLD/WAR 20. PAGE 5 H0110
POL/PAR CATH SOCISM

B49
LASSWELL H.D.,LANGUAGE OF POLITICS. COM NAT/G ACT/RES ATTIT PWR...STAT RECORD CON/ANAL GEN/METH 20. PAGE 92 H1834
EDU/PROP METH/CNCPT

B49
MAO TSE-TUNG,NEW DEMOCRACY. CHINA/COM NAT/G DIPLOM ECO/TAC EDU/PROP REV...CONCPT METH SOC/INTEG 20. PAGE 102 H2045
SOCISM MARXISM POPULISM CULTURE

B49
MCLEAN J.M.,THE PUBLIC SERVICE AND UNIVERSITY EDUCATION. UK USA-45 DELIB/GP EX/STRUC TOP/EX ADMIN ...GOV/COMP METH/COMP NAT/COMP ANTHOL 20. PAGE 107 H2142
ACADEM NAT/G EXEC EDU/PROP

B49
ROGERS C.B.,THE SPIRIT OF REVOLUTION IN 1789: A STUDY OF PUBLIC OPINION ...AT THE BEGINNING OF THE FRENCH REVOLUTION. FRANCE CULTURE ELITES EDU/PROP COERCE CROWD...BIBLIOG 18 MUSIC. PAGE 133 H2658
ATTIT POPULISM REV CREATE

B49
SAUVY A.,LE POUVOIR ET L'OPINION. FRANCE STRATA NAT/G PERCEPT...POLICY PSY 20. PAGE 138 H2758
EDU/PROP MYTH PARTIC ATTIT

B49
SCHONS D.,BOOK CENSORSHIP IN NEW SPAIN (NEW WORLD STUDIES, BOOK II). SPAIN LAW CULTURE INSPECT ADJUD CT/SYS SANCTION GP/REL ORD/FREE 14/17. PAGE 140 H2797
CHRIST-17C EDU/PROP CONTROL PRESS

B49
US DEPARTMENT OF STATE,SOVIET BIBLIOGRAPHY (PAMPHLET). CHINA/COM COM USSR LAW AGRI INT/ORG ECO/TAC EDU/PROP...POLICY GEOG 20. PAGE 159 H3185
BIBLIOG/A MARXISM CULTURE DIPLOM

S49
STEINMETZ H.,"THE PROBLEMS OF THE LANDRAT: A STUDY OF COUNTY GOVERNMENT IN THE US ZONE OF GERMANY." GERMANY/W USA+45 INDUS PLAN DIPLOM EDU/PROP CONTROL WAR GOV/REL FEDERAL WEALTH PLURISM...GOV/COMP 20 LANDRAT. PAGE 149 H2977
LOC/G COLONIAL MGT TOP/EX

B50
CANTRIL H.,TENSIONS THAT CAUSE WAR. UNIV CULTURE R+D CREATE EDU/PROP DRIVE PERSON KNOWL ORD/FREE ...HUM PSY SOC OBS CENSUS TREND CON/ANAL SOC/EXP SIMUL GEN/METH ANTHOL COLD/WAR TOT/POP. PAGE 26 H0523
SOCIETY PHIL/SCI PEACE

B50
IRION F.C.,PUBLIC OPINION AND PROPAGANDA. STRUCT COM/IND FAM SECT COERCE 20 FILM. PAGE 78 H1568
EDU/PROP ATTIT NAT/G

PRESS

B50
LYONS F.S.L.,THE IRISH PARLIAMENTARY PARTY, 1890-1910: STUDIES IN IRISH HISTORY (VOL. 4). IRELAND DELIB/GP LEGIS PAY EDU/PROP ADMIN GP/REL ATTIT...BIBLIOG 19/20 PARLIAMENT PARNELL/CS DIRECT/NAT. PAGE 99 H1986 POL/PAR CHOOSE NAT/G POLICY

B50
US DEPARTMENT OF STATE,DOCUMENTS ON GERMAN FOREIGN POLICY, 1918-1945 (13 VOLS.). EUR+WWI GERMANY NAT/G PLAN DIPLOM DOMIN EDU/PROP CONTROL NAT/LISM ...ANTHOL 20. PAGE 159 H3186 BIBLIOG/A WAR POLICY FASCIST

B51
JENNINGS S.I.,THE COMMONWEALTH IN ASIA. CEYLON INDIA PAKISTAN S/ASIA UK CONSTN CULTURE SOCIETY STRATA STRUCT NAT/G POL/PAR EDU/PROP LEAD WAR 20 CMN/WLTH. PAGE 80 H1608 NAT/LISM REGION COLONIAL DIPLOM

B51
LOOS W.A.,RELIGIOUS FAITH AND WORLD CULTURE. INTELL SOCIETY SECT EDU/PROP ROUTINE ATTIT PERSON ALL/VALS MORAL...CONCPT GEN/LAWS VAL/FREE. PAGE 98 H1964 UNIV CULTURE PEACE

S51
GOULD J.,"THE KOMSOMOL AND THE HITLER JUGEND." COM EUR+WWI GERMANY SOCIETY NAT/G POL/PAR SCHOOL TOTALISM DRIVE PERCEPT KNOWL FASCISM...SOC NAZI TOT/POP 20. PAGE 59 H1185 EDU/PROP CON/ANAL SOCISM

S51
NORTHROP F.S.C.,"ASIAN MENTALITY AND UNITED STATES FOREIGN POLICY." ASIA ISLAM USA+45 CULTURE SOCIETY SECT EDU/PROP LEGIT COERCE DRIVE MORAL ORD/FREE ...POLICY RELATIV TOT/POP 20. PAGE 119 H2376 S/ASIA ATTIT DIPLOM

B52
BENTHAM A.,HANDBOOK OF POLITICAL FALLACIES. FUT MOD/EUR LAW INTELL LOC/G MUNIC NAT/G DELIB/GP LEGIS CREATE EDU/PROP CT/SYS ATTIT RIGID/FLEX KNOWL PWR ...RELATIV PSY SOC CONCPT SELF/OBS TREND STERTYP TOT/POP. PAGE 14 H0286 POL/PAR

B52
DILLON D.R.,LATIN AMERICA, 1935-1949; A SELECTED BIBLIOGRAPHY. LAW EDU/PROP...SOC 20. PAGE 41 H0826 BIBLIOG L/A+17C NAT/G DIPLOM

B52
HIMMELFARB G.,LORD ACTON: A STUDY IN CONSCIENCE AND POLITICS. MOD/EUR NAT/G POL/PAR SECT LEGIS TOP/EX EDU/PROP ADMIN NAT/LISM ATTIT PERSON SUPEGO MORAL ORD/FREE...CONCPT PARLIAMENT 19 ACTON/LORD. PAGE 71 H1419 PWR BIOG

B52
KOLARZ W.,RUSSIA AND HER COLONIES. COM RUSSIA LAW CULTURE ECO/DEV KIN LOC/G SECT TEC/DEV ECO/TAC EDU/PROP REGION COERCE ATTIT PWR SOVEREIGN...SOC TIME/SEQ CON/ANAL VAL/FREE 19/20. PAGE 88 H1749 NAT/G DOMIN USSR COLONIAL

B52
LEYS W.,ETHICS FOR POLICY DECISIONS. INTELL NAT/G CONSULT PLAN DOMIN EDU/PROP LEGIT COERCE KNOWL MORAL PWR...HUM GEN/LAWS. PAGE 96 H1920 ACT/RES POLICY

B52
ROBBINS L.,THE THEORY OF ECONOMIC POLICY IN ENGLISH CLASSICAL POLITICAL ECONOMY. UK ECO/DEV WORKER PLAN CAP/ISM EDU/PROP CONTROL INCOME OWN HEALTH SOCISM ...POLICY 17/19. PAGE 132 H2639 ECO/TAC ORD/FREE IDEA/COMP NAT/G

B52
SKALWEIT S.,FRANKREICH UND FRIEDRICH DER GROSSE. FRANCE GERMANY PRUSSIA NAT/G DOMIN WAR 18 FREDERICK. PAGE 145 H2893 ATTIT EDU/PROP DIPLOM SOC

B52
WALTERS F.P.,A HISTORY OF THE LEAGUE OF NATIONS. EUR+WWI CONSTN NAT/G LEGIS TOP/EX ACT/RES PLAN EDU/PROP LEGIT ROUTINE ATTIT...TREND LEAGUE/NAT 20 CHINJAP. PAGE 165 H3297 INT/ORG TIME/SEQ NAT/LISM

S52
KECSKEMETI P.,"THE 'POLICY SCIENCES': ASPIRATION AND OUTLOOK." UNIV CULTURE INTELL SOCIETY STRUCT EDU/PROP ATTIT PERCEPT RIGID/FLEX KNOWL...PHIL/SCI METH/CNCPT OBS 20. PAGE 84 H1674 CREATE NEW/IDEA

B53
HUNTER E.,BRAIN-WASHING IN RED CHINA. ASIA CHINA/COM CULTURE SOCIETY FORCES WAR TOTALISM ATTIT BIO/SOC DISPL DRIVE PERSON SUPEGO KNOWL ORD/FREE ...INT REC/INT COLD/WAR 20. PAGE 75 H1499 EDU/PROP COERCE

B53
LEITES N.,A STUDY OF BOLSHEVISM. WOR+45 WOR-45 ELITES SOCIETY INT/ORG NAT/G EX/STRUC EDU/PROP EXEC ROUTINE ATTIT MORAL MARXISM...CONCPT OBS VAL/FREE 20. PAGE 94 H1869 COM POL/PAR USSR TOTALISM

B53
LEITES N.,A STUDY OF BOLSHEVISM. ELITES STRATA INT/ORG LOC/G POL/PAR WORKER EDU/PROP REV TOTALISM UTOPIA PWR...CONCPT 20 BOLSHEVISM. PAGE 94 H1870 MARXISM PLAN COM

B53
MEYER P.,THE JEWS IN THE SOVIET SATELLITES. CZECHOSLVK POLAND SOCIETY STRATA NAT/G BAL/PWR ECO/TAC EDU/PROP LEGIT ADMIN COERCE ATTIT DISPL PERCEPT HEALTH PWR RESPECT WEALTH...METH/CNCPT JEWS VAL/FREE NAZI 20. PAGE 110 H2192 COM SECT TOTALISM USSR

B53
MURPHY G.,IN THE MINDS OF MEN: THE STUDY OF HUMAN BEHAVIOR AND SOCIAL TENSIONS IN INDIA. FUT S/ASIA FAM INT/ORG NAT/G DIPLOM EDU/PROP GP/REL ATTIT RIGID/FLEX ALL/VALS...SOC QU UNESCO 20. PAGE 115 H2297 SECT STRATA INDIA

B53
NELSON G.R.,FREEDOM AND WELFARE: SOCIAL PATTERNS IN THE NORTHERN COUNTRIES OF EUROPE. EUR+WWI ECO/DEV NAT/G EDU/PROP LEGIT HEALTH ORD/FREE SKILL WEALTH ...STAT AUD/VIS SCANDINAV WORK TOT/POP 20. PAGE 116 H2329 PLAN ECO/TAC

B53
PIERCE R.A.,RUSSIAN CENTRAL ASIA, 1867-1917: A SELECTED BIBLIOGRAPHY (PAMPHLET). USSR LAW CULTURE NAT/G EDU/PROP WAR...GEOG SOC 19/20. PAGE 125 H2508 BIBLIOG COLONIAL ADMIN COM

B53
SHIRATO I.,JAPANESE SOURCES ON THE HISTORY OF THE CHINESE COMMUNIST MOVEMENT (PAMPHLET). CHINA/COM USSR CONSTRUC NAT/G POL/PAR FORCES DIPLOM DOMIN EDU/PROP CONTROL WAR TOTALISM SOCISM 20. PAGE 143 H2863 BIBLIOG/A MARXISM ECO/UNDEV

B53
SQUIRES J.D.,BRITISH PROPAGANDA AT HOME AND IN THE UNITED STATES FROM 1914 TO 1917. UK NAT/G PROB/SOLV DOMIN PRESS EFFICIENCY...PSY PREDICT 20 WWI INTERVENT PSY/WAR. PAGE 148 H2960 EDU/PROP CONTROL WAR DIPLOM

B54
FRIEDRICH C.J.,TOTALITARIAN DICTATORSHIP AND AUTOCRACY. COM EUR+WWI GERMANY ITALY USSR INTELL ECO/DEV NAT/G POL/PAR FORCES TOP/EX ECO/TAC EDU/PROP LEGIT COERCE ATTIT ORD/FREE PWR FASCISM ...CONCPT TIME/SEQ GEN/LAWS NAZI 20. PAGE 53 H1068 SOCIETY DOMIN TOTALISM

B54
GIRALSO JARAMLLO G.,BIBLIOGRAFIA DE BIBLIOGRAFIAS COLOMBIANAS. L/A+17C ACADEM SECT CREATE EDU/PROP ...ART/METH GEOG LING TREND 20 COLOMB. PAGE 57 H1135 BIBLIOG/A CULTURE PHIL/SCI ECO/UNDEV

B54
PARRINDER G.,AFRICAN TRADITIONAL RELIGION. AFR SOCIETY EDU/PROP GP/REL PWR...SOC CONCPT IDEA/COMP WORSHIP 20 DEITY. PAGE 124 H2469 SECT MYTH ATTIT CULTURE

B54
SALVEMINI G.,PRELUDE TO WORLD WAR II. ITALY MOD/EUR INT/ORG BAL/PWR EDU/PROP CONTROL TOTALISM...TREND NAT/COMP BIBLIOG 19 HITLER/A LEAGUE/NAT MUSSOLIN/B. PAGE 137 H2745 WAR FASCISM LEAD PWR

B54
SCHRAMM W.,THE PROCESS AND EFFECTS OF MASS COMMUNICATION. CULTURE INTELL SOCIETY COM/IND DRIVE PERCEPT PERSON RIGID/FLEX KNOWL...PSY SOC CONCPT CHARTS. PAGE 140 H2800 ATTIT EDU/PROP

B54
SPENCER H.,SOCIAL STATICS. MOD/EUR UNIV SOCIETY ECO/DEV NAT/G ACT/RES PLAN EDU/PROP PERSON...POLICY CONCPT. PAGE 147 H2944 MORAL ECO/TAC

L54
FRIEDRICH C.J.,"TOTALITARIANISM." COM EUR+WWI NAT/G POL/PAR SECT FORCES PLAN ECO/TAC DOMIN EDU/PROP EXEC COERCE REV ORD/FREE PWR...SOC CONCPT NAZI 20. PAGE 53 H1067 ATTIT TOTALISM

S54
BALANDIER G.,"SOCIOLOGIE DE LA COLONISATION ET RELATIONS ENTRE SOCIETES GLOBALES." AFR SOCIETY ECO/UNDEV KIN DOMIN EDU/PROP RIGID/FLEX PWR...PSY CONCPT TREND TOT/POP. PAGE 10 H0203 CULTURE SOC COLONIAL

C54
DE GRAZIA A.,"THE COMPARATIVE SURVEY OF EUROPEAN-AMERICAN POLITICAL BEHAV IOR; A RESEARCH PROSPECTUS (PAPER)" EUR+WWI FRANCE GERMANY SPAIN UK USA+45 WOR+45 STRATA POL/PAR DIPLOM EDU/PROP COLONIAL LEAD WAR NAT/LISM CONCPT. PAGE 37 H0752 BIBLIOG R+D METH NAT/COMP

B55
APTER D.E.,THE GOLD COAST IN TRANSITION. FUT CONSTN CULTURE SOCIETY ECO/UNDEV FAM KIN LOC/G NAT/G POL/PAR LEGIS TOP/EX EDU/PROP LEGIT ADMIN ATTIT PERSON PWR...CONCPT STAT INT CENSUS TOT/POP VAL/FREE. PAGE 7 H0149 AFR SOVEREIGN

B55
COLE G.D.H.,STUDIES IN CLASS STRUCTURE. UK NAT/G WORKER TEC/DEV EDU/PROP...CLASSIF CHARTS 20. PAGE 31 H0623 STRUCT STRATA ELITES CONCPT

B55
KHADDURI M.,WAR AND PEACE IN THE LAW OF ISLAM. CONSTN CULTURE SOCIETY STRATA NAT/G PROVS SECT FORCES TOP/EX CREATE DOMIN EDU/PROP ADJUD COERCE ATTIT RIGID/FLEX ALL/VALS...CONCPT TIME/SEQ TOT/POP VAL/FREE. PAGE 85 H1702 ISLAM JURID PEACE WAR

B55
KHADDURI M.,LAW IN THE MIDDLE EAST. LAW CONSTN ACADEM FAM EDU/PROP CT/SYS SANCTION CRIME...INT/LAW GOV/COMP ANTHOL 6/20 MID/EAST. PAGE 85 H1703 ADJUD JURID ISLAM

B55
MID-EUROPEAN LAW PROJECT,CHURCH AND STATE BEHIND THE IRON CURTAIN. COM CZECHOSLVK HUNGARY POLAND USSR CULTURE SECT EDU/PROP GOV/REL CATHISM...CHARTS ANTHOL BIBLIOG WORSHIP 20 CHURCH/STA. PAGE 110 H2202
LAW MARXISM POLICY

B55
NAMIER L.,PERSONALITIES AND POWERS. EUR+WWI MOD/EUR NAT/G POL/PAR TOP/EX EDU/PROP KNOWL...GEOG 17/20. PAGE 115 H2308
TIME/SEQ DIPLOM UK

B55
POLLOCK J.K.,GERMAN DEMOCRACY AT WORK. GERMANY/W LOC/G NAT/G DIPLOM PARL/PROC...OBS IDEA/COMP 20. PAGE 127 H2539
PARTIC POL/PAR CHOOSE EDU/PROP

B55
SHUMSKY A.,THE CLASH OF CULTURES IN ISRAEL: A PROBLEM FOR EDUCATION. ISRAEL CULTURE INTELL NAT/G ACT/RES DISCRIM AGE/Y...BIBLIOG 20 JEWS. PAGE 143 H2867
GP/REL EDU/PROP SCHOOL AGE/C

B55
THOMPSON V.,MINORITY PROBLEMS IN SOUTHEAST ASIA. CAMBODIA CHINA/COM LAOS S/ASIA KIN NAT/G SECT PROB/SOLV EDU/PROP REGION GP/REL RACE/REL MARXISM ...SOC 20 BUDDHISM UN. PAGE 154 H3085
INGP/REL GEOG DIPLOM STRUCT

B55
TOYNBEE A.,THE REALIGNMENT OF EUROPE. COM GREECE ITALY NAT/G BAL/PWR ECO/TAC EDU/PROP REV SOVEREIGN ...SOC TIME/SEQ TREND COLD/WAR 20. PAGE 156 H3123
EUR+WWI PLAN USSR

B55
VERGNAUD P.,L'IDEE DE LA NATIONALITE ET DE LA LIBRE DISPOSITION DES PEUPLES DANS SES RAPPORTS AVEC L'IDEE DE L'ETAT. STRATA NAT/G EDU/PROP RACE/REL AUTHORIT FASCISM MARXISM MYTH. PAGE 162 H3243
NAT/LISM DISCRIM ORD/FREE

B55
WRONG D.H.,AMERICAN AND CANADIAN VIEWPOINTS. CANADA USA+45 CONSTN STRATA FAM SECT WORKER ECO/TAC EDU/PROP ADJUD MARRIAGE...IDEA/COMP 20. PAGE 171 H3424
DIPLOM ATTIT NAT/COMP CULTURE

S55
GLADSTONE A.E.,"THE POSSIBILITY OF PREDICTING REACTIONS TO INTERNATIONAL EVENTS." UNIV SOCIETY NAT/G FORCES CREATE EDU/PROP COERCE WAR ATTIT PERSON KNOWL PWR SKILL...METH/CNCPT NEW/IDEA ORG/CHARTS. PAGE 57 H1139
PHIL/SCI CONCPT

B56
BRITISH BORNEO RESEARCH PROJ,BIBLIOGRAPHY OF BRITISH BORNEO (PAMPHLET). UK COM/IND NAT/G EDU/PROP...GEOG 20. PAGE 21 H0421
BIBLIOG/A SOC

B56
DE JONG L.,THE GERMAN FIFTH COLUMN IN THE SECOND WORLD WAR. EUR+WWI GERMANY NAT/G DIPLOM ATTIT FASCISM...MYTH 20 NAZI. PAGE 38 H0756
EDU/PROP WAR RUMOR

B56
INTERNATIONAL AFRICAN INST,SELECT ANNOTATED BIBLIOGRAPHY OF TROPICAL AFRICA. NAT/G EDU/PROP ADMIN HEALTH. PAGE 77 H1547
BIBLIOG/A AFR SOC HABITAT

B56
JENNINGS W.I.,THE APPROACH TO SELF-GOVERNMENT. CEYLON INDIA PAKISTAN S/ASIA UK SOCIETY POL/PAR DELIB/GP LEGIS ECO/TAC EDU/PROP ADMIN EXEC CHOOSE ATTIT ALL/VALS...JURID CONCPT GEN/METH TOT/POP 20. PAGE 81 H1610
NAT/G CONSTN COLONIAL

B56
READ M.,EDUCATION AND SOCIAL CHANGE IN TROPICAL AREAS. AFR L/A+17C SOCIETY LITERACY PERCEPT PERSON WEALTH...HEAL PHIL/SCI SOC 20. PAGE 130 H2603
EDU/PROP HABITAT DRIVE CULTURE

B56
VUCINICH A.,THE SOVIET ACADEMY OF SCIENCES. USSR STRUCT ACADEM NAT/G EDU/PROP ADMIN LEAD ROLE ...BIBLIOG 20 ACADEM/SCI. PAGE 164 H3280
PHIL/SCI CREATE INTELL PROF/ORG

B56
WOLFF R.L.,THE BALKANS IN OUR TIME. ALBANIA FUT MOD/EUR USSR YUGOSLAVIA CULTURE INT/ORG SECT DIPLOM EDU/PROP COERCE WAR ORD/FREE...CHARTS 4/20 BALKANS COMINFORM. PAGE 170 H3403
GEOG COM

S56
GORDON L.,"THE ORGANIZATION FOR EUROPEAN ECONOMIC COOPERATION." EUR+WWI INDUS INT/ORG NAT/G CONSULT DELIB/GP ACT/RES CREATE PLAN TEC/DEV EDU/PROP LEGIT WEALTH OEEC 20. PAGE 59 H1178
VOL/ASSN ECO/DEV

B57
ARON R.,THE OPIUM OF THE INTELLECTUALS (TRANS. BY TERENCE KILMARTIN). FRANCE USSR WOR+45 CULTURE POL/PAR PLAN DOMIN EDU/PROP REV ATTIT ORD/FREE ...IDEA/COMP METH/COMP NAT/COMP 20 COM/PARTY. PAGE 8 H0169
INTELL UTOPIA MYTH MARXISM

B57
BUCK P.W.,CONTOL OF FOREIGN RELATIONS IN MODERN NATIONS. FRANCE L/A+17C NETHERLAND USSR WOR+45 INT/ORG TOP/EX BAL/PWR DOMIN EDU/PROP COERCE PEACE ATTIT...CONCPT TREND 20 CMN/WLTH. PAGE 23 H0465
NAT/G PWR DIPLOM

B57
BYRNES R.F.,BIBLIOGRAPHY OF AMERICAN PUBLICATIONS ON EAST CENTRAL EUROPE, 1945-1957 (VOL. XXII). SECT DIPLOM EDU/PROP RACE/REL...ART/METH GEOG JURID SOC LING 20 JEWS. PAGE 25 H0503
BIBLIOG/A COM MARXISM NAT/G

B57
COLE G.D.H.,THE POST WAR CONDITIONS OF BRITAIN. EUR+WWI STRUCT NAT/G PLAN EDU/PROP LEGIT RIGID/FLEX ORD/FREE WEALTH...SOCIALIST WELF/ST STAT TREND CON/ANAL CHARTS PARLIAMENT WORK 20. PAGE 31 H0624
ECO/DEV UK

B57
LOOMIS C.P.,RURAL SOCIOLOGY. CULTURE KIN NAT/G SECT VOL/ASSN ACT/RES EDU/PROP HEALTH. PAGE 98 H1963
SOC AGRI METH T

B57
MOYER K.E.,FROM IRAN TO MORROCCO; FROM TURKEY TO THE SUDAN: A SELECTED AND ANNOTATED BIBLIOGRAPHY OF NORTH AFRICA AND NEAR EAST... ISLAM DIPLOM EDU/PROP 20. PAGE 114 H2274
BIBLIOG/A ECO/UNDEV SECT NAT/G

B57
PALMER N.D.,INTERNATIONAL RELATIONS. WOR+45 INT/ORG NAT/G ECO/TAC EDU/PROP COLONIAL WAR PWR SOVEREIGN ...POLICY T 20 TREATY. PAGE 123 H2451
DIPLOM BAL/PWR NAT/COMP

B57
SCHLESINGER J.A.,HOW THEY BECAME GOVERNOR: A STUDY OF COMPARATIVE STATE POLITICS, 1870-1950. USA+45 USA-45 LAW POL/PAR LEGIS EDU/PROP REGION...STAT TREND CHARTS TIME 19/20 GOVERNOR. PAGE 139 H2788
PROVS CHIEF GOV/COMP CHOOSE

L57
BENDIX R.,"POLITICAL SOCIOLOGY." CULTURE INTELL LABOR POL/PAR SECT LEGIS EDU/PROP ADMIN CHOOSE CIVMIL/REL ATTIT...IDEA/COMP 20. PAGE 14 H0274
BIBLIOG/A ACT/RES SOC

B58
DUCLOUX L.,FROM BLACKMAIL TO TREASON. FRANCE PLAN DIPLOM EDU/PROP PRESS RUMOR NAT/LISM...CRIMLGY 20. PAGE 43 H0853
COERCE CRIME NAT/G PWR

B58
HAAS E.B.,THE UNITING OF EUROPE. EUR+WWI INT/ORG NAT/G POL/PAR TOP/EX ECO/TAC EDU/PROP LEGIT FEDERAL NAT/LISM DRIVE RIGID/FLEX ORD/FREE PWR PLURISM ...POLICY CONCPT INT GEN/LAWS ECSC EEC 20. PAGE 63 H1264
VOL/ASSN ECO/DEV

B58
HERRMANN K.,DAS STAATSDENKEN BEI LEIBNIZ. GP/REL ATTIT ORD/FREE...CONCPT IDEA/COMP 17 LEIBNITZ/G CHURCH/STA. PAGE 70 H1406
NAT/G JURID SECT EDU/PROP

B58
HSU U.T.,THE INVISIBLE CONFLICT. ASIA USSR ELITES NAT/G CONTROL LEAD COERCE REV WAR NAT/LISM ORD/FREE PWR 20 COM/PARTY ESPIONAGE. PAGE 74 H1485
MARXISM POL/PAR EDU/PROP FORCES

B58
LAQUER W.Z.,THE MIDDLE EAST IN TRANSITION. COM USSR ECO/UNDEV NAT/G VOL/ASSN EDU/PROP EXEC ATTIT DRIVE PWR MARXISM COLD/WAR TOT/POP 20. PAGE 91 H1818
ISLAM TREND NAT/LISM

B58
LERNER D.,THE PASSING OF TRADITIONAL SOCIETY: MODERNIZING THE MIDDLE EAST. IRAN ISLAM LEBANON SYRIA TURKEY UAR CULTURE INTELL STRATA KIN NAT/G NEIGH SECT EDU/PROP ATTIT PERSON...MYTH OBS 20. PAGE 95 H1888
ECO/UNDEV RIGID/FLEX

B58
MASON J.B.,THAILAND BIBLIOGRAPHY. S/ASIA THAILAND CULTURE EDU/PROP ADMIN...GEOG SOC LING 20. PAGE 104 H2087
BIBLIOG/A ECO/UNDEV DIPLOM NAT/G

B58
MATOS J.,LAS ACTUALES COMMUNIDADES DE INDIGENAS: HUAROCHIRI EN 1955. PERU FAM NAT/G SECT EDU/PROP ADJUD GP/REL INGP/REL 20 INDIAN/AM. PAGE 105 H2091
STRUCT NEIGH KIN ECO/UNDEV

B58
MECRENSKY E.,SCIENTIFIC MANPOWER IN EUROPE. WOR+45 EDU/PROP GOV/REL SKILL...TECHNIC PHIL/SCI INT CHARTS BIBLIOG 20. PAGE 108 H2157
ECO/TAC TEC/DEV METH/COMP NAT/COMP

B58
MEHNERT K.,DER SOWJETMENSCH. USSR NAT/G SECT EDU/PROP TOTALISM ORD/FREE 20. PAGE 108 H2161
SOCIETY ATTIT PERSON FAM

B58
PALMER E.E.,"POLITICAL MAN" IN E. PALMER, PROBLEMS IN DEMOCRATIC CITIZENSHIP. LOC/G NAT/G LEGIS PRESS CHOOSE REPRESENT GP/REL...DECISION SOC IDEA/COMP ANTHOL 20. PAGE 123 H2449
PARTIC POL/PAR EDU/PROP MAJORIT

B58
SCOTT D.J.R.,RUSSIAN POLITICAL INSTITUTIONS. RUSSIA USSR CONSTN AGRI DELIB/GP PLAN EDU/PROP CONTROL CHOOSE EFFICIENCY ATTIT MARXISM...BIBLIOG/A 13/20. PAGE 141 H2813
NAT/G POL/PAR ADMIN DECISION

B58
STEINBERG C.S.,THE MASS COMMUNICATORS: PUBLIC
EDU/PROP

RELATIONS, PUBLIC OPINION, AND MASS MEDIA. CULTURE CONSULT ACT/RES FEEDBACK DISPL WEALTH 20. PAGE 149 H2975 — ATTIT COM/IND PERCEPT

B58
STUBEL H.,THE MEWU FANTZU. CHINA/COM INDIA EDU/PROP ADJUD CRIME GP/REL OWN...OBS 20 TIBET. PAGE 150 H3001 — CULTURE STRUCT SECT FAM

B58
VARG P.A.,MISSIONARIES, CHINESE, AND DIPLOMATS: THE AMERICAN PROTESTANT MISSIONARY MOVEMENT IN CHINA, 1890-1952. ASIA ECO/UNDEV NAT/G PROB/SOLV CAP/ISM EDU/PROP COLONIAL NAT/LISM ATTIT MARXISM...NAT/COMP STERTYP 20 CHINJAP PROTESTANT MISSION. PAGE 162 H3234 — CULTURE DIPLOM SECT

S58
STAAR R.F.,"ELECTIONS IN COMMUNIST POLAND." EUR+WWI SOCIETY INT/ORG NAT/G POL/PAR LEGIS ACT/RES ECO/TAC EDU/PROP ADJUD ADMIN ROUTINE COERCE TOTALISM ATTIT ORD/FREE PWR 20. PAGE 148 H2963 — COM CHOOSE POLAND

B59
BARRON R.,PARTIES AND POLITICS IN MODERN FRANCE. FRANCE LOC/G DELIB/GP LEGIS TOP/EX EDU/PROP LEGIT TV FEEDBACK 20. PAGE 12 H0230 — POL/PAR ALL/IDEOS CHOOSE PARTIC

B59
BRIGGS A.,CHARTIST STUDIES. UK LAW NAT/G WORKER EDU/PROP COERCE SUFF GP/REL ATTIT...ANTHOL 19. PAGE 21 H0416 — INDUS STRATA LABOR POLICY

B59
BROWN D.F.,THE GROWTH OF DEMOCRATIC GOVERNMENT. WOR+45 BARGAIN EDU/PROP LOBBY APPORT CHOOSE 20. PAGE 22 H0441 — GOV/COMP LEGIS POL/PAR CHIEF

B59
CARPENTER G.W.,THE WAY IN AFRICA. AFR INDUS MUNIC DIPLOM DOMIN EDU/PROP COERCE DISCRIM NAT/LISM ORD/FREE 20 NEGRO CHRISTIAN. PAGE 27 H0535 — CULTURE SECT ECO/UNDEV COLONIAL

B59
EPSTEIN F.T.,EAST GERMANY: A SELECTED BIBLIOGRAPHY (PAMPHLET). COM GERMANY/E LAW AGRI FINAN INDUS LABOR POL/PAR EDU/PROP ADMIN AGE/Y 20. PAGE 47 H0932 — BIBLIOG/A INTELL MARXISM NAT/G

B59
GINSBURG M.,LAW AND OPINION IN ENGLAND. UK CULTURE KIN LABOR LEGIS EDU/PROP ADMIN CT/SYS CRIME OWN HEALTH...ANTHOL 20 ENGLSH/LAW. PAGE 56 H1132 — JURID POLICY ECO/TAC

B59
INTERNATIONAL PRESS INSTITUTE,THE PRESS IN AUTHORITARIAN COUNTRIES. COM PORTUGAL SPAIN UAR USSR NAT/G DOMIN LEGIT ORD/FREE FASCISM SOCISM 20. PAGE 78 H1559 — PRESS CONTROL TOTALISM EDU/PROP

B59
ISRAEL J.,THE CHINESE STUDENT MOVEMENT, 1927-1937; A BIBLIOGRAPHICAL ESSAY BASED ON THE RESOURCES OF THE HOOVER INSTITUTION. ASIA INTELL NAT/G EDU/PROP 20. PAGE 79 H1571 — BIBLIOG/A ACADEM ATTIT

B59
KITTLER G.D.,EQUATORIAL AFRICA: THE NEW WORLD OF TOMORROW. CENTRL/AFR INDUS KIN SECT CHIEF EDU/PROP CHOOSE HEALTH...GEOG WORSHIP 20. PAGE 87 H1730 — RACE/REL AFR ECO/UNDEV CULTURE

B59
LAQUER W.Z.,THE SOVIET UNION AND THE MIDDLE EAST. COM UAR USSR ECO/UNDEV NAT/G VOL/ASSN ECO/TAC EDU/PROP COLONIAL EXEC PWR...TIME/SEQ TREND COLD/WAR 20. PAGE 91 H1819 — ISLAM DRIVE FOR/AID NAT/LISM

B59
PANIKKAR K.M.,THE AFRO-ASIAN STATES AND THEIR PROBLEMS. COM CULTURE KIN POL/PAR SECT DIPLOM EDU/PROP COLONIAL SOVEREIGN...TECHNIC GOV/COMP 20. PAGE 123 H2458 — AFR S/ASIA ECO/UNDEV

B59
SISSONS C.B.,CHURCH AND STATE IN CANADIAN EDUCATION: AN HISTORICAL STUDY. CANADA ACADEM NAT/G SCHOOL LEGIS REGION MAJORITY...MAJORIT WORSHIP 18/20 CHURCH/STA. PAGE 145 H2891 — SECT EDU/PROP PROVS GP/REL

B59
SVALASTOGA K.,PRESTIGE, CLASS, AND MOBILITY. DENMARK UK EDU/PROP INCOME WEALTH...SOC SAMP 20. PAGE 151 H3010 — NAT/COMP STRATA STRUCT ELITES

B59
VORSPAN A.,JUSTICE AND JUDAISM. FAM DIPLOM ECO/TAC EDU/PROP CRIME RACE/REL MARRIAGE ANOMIE ATTIT ORD/FREE...POLICY 20 UN. PAGE 164 H3279 — SECT CULTURE ACT/RES GP/REL

S59
LEVINE R.A.,"ANTI-EUROPEAN VIOLENCE IN AFRICA: A COMPARATIVE ANALYSIS." AFR CULTURE NAT/G DIPLOM EDU/PROP COLONIAL REGION COERCE ATTIT PWR...PSY CONCPT TIME/SEQ TREND HYPO/EXP SOC/EXP STERTYP GEN/METH COLD/WAR 20. PAGE 95 H1903 — DRIVE ORD/FREE REV

S59
MENDELSON W.,"JUDICIAL REVIEW AND PARTY POLITICS" (BMR)" UK USA+45 USA-45 NAT/G LEGIS PROB/SOLV EDU/PROP ADJUD EFFICIENCY...POLICY NAT/COMP 19/20 AUSTRAL SUPREME/CT. PAGE 109 H2171 — CT/SYS POL/PAR BAL/PWR JURID

C59
COLLINS I.,"THE GOVERNMENT AND THE NEWSPAPER PRESS IN FRANCE, 1814-1881. FRANCE LAW ADMIN CT/SYS ...CON/ANAL BIBLIOG 19. PAGE 32 H0634 — PRESS ORD/FREE NAT/G EDU/PROP

B60
BANERJEE D.N.,OUR FUNDAMENTAL RIGHTS: THEIR NATURE AND EXTENT (AS JUDICIALLY DETERMINED). INDIA UK CULTURE STRATA NAT/G WORKER EDU/PROP CONTROL DISCRIM OWN...IDEA/COMP WORSHIP 20 REFORMERS COMMONWLTH. PAGE 10 H0207 — CONSTN ORD/FREE LEGIS POLICY

B60
BLACK C.E.,THE TRANSFORMATION OF RUSSIAN SOCIETY. COM MOD/EUR RUSSIA SOCIETY EDU/PROP COERCE ALL/VALS 19/20. PAGE 17 H0349 — CULTURE RIGID/FLEX USSR

B60
BRZEZINSKI Z.K.,THE SOVIET BLOC-UNITY AND CONFLICT. COM USSR CONSTN DOMIN ADMIN TOTALISM PWR...SOC MYTH RECORD TREND STERTYP GEN/LAWS GEN/METH TOT/POP 20. PAGE 23 H0458 — ATTIT EDU/PROP

B60
CARTER G.M.,INDEPENDENCE FOR AFRICA. AFR FUT SOCIETY STRATA ECO/DEV POL/PAR DELIB/GP PLAN DOMIN EDU/PROP COLONIAL REGION ATTIT DRIVE SOVEREIGN ...RECORD INT TIME/SEQ CHARTS 20. PAGE 27 H0544 — NAT/G PWR NAT/LISM

B60
DICHTER E.,THE STRATEGY OF DESIRE. UNIV CULTURE ACT/RES ATTIT DRIVE 20. PAGE 41 H0821 — EDU/PROP PSY CONSULT PERSON

B60
EMERY E.,INTRODUCTION TO MASS COMMUNICATIONS. ACADEM PROF/ORG SCHOOL ACT/RES EDU/PROP ATTIT ...CONCPT BIBLIOG/A. PAGE 46 H0920 — COM/IND PRESS CON/ANAL CULTURE

B60
GOODMAN E.,SOVIET DESIGN FOR A WORLD STATE. COM USSR NAT/G TOP/EX DIPLOM ECO/TAC DOMIN EDU/PROP COERCE REV ATTIT ORD/FREE...CON/ANAL 20. PAGE 59 H1171 — PLAN PWR SOCISM TOTALISM

B60
HAYEK F.A.,THE CONSTITUTION OF LIBERTY. UNIV LAW CONSTN WORKER TAX EDU/PROP ADMIN CT/SYS COERCE DISCRIM...IDEA/COMP 20. PAGE 68 H1369 — ORD/FREE CHOOSE NAT/G CONCPT

B60
KOHN H.,PAN-SLAVISM: ITS HISTORY AND IDEOLOGY. COM CZECHOSLVK EUR+WWI MOD/EUR USSR YUGOSLAVIA CULTURE ELITES INTELL KIN NAT/G EDU/PROP DRIVE SOVEREIGN ...HUM PHIL/SCI MYTH HIST/WRIT 19/20. PAGE 87 H1745 — ATTIT CONCPT NAT/LISM

B60
LEYDER J.,BIBLIOGRAPHIE DE L'ENSEIGNEMENT SUPERIEUR ET DE LA RECHERCHE SCIENTIFIQUE EN AFRIQUE INTERTROPICALE (2 VOLS.). AFR CULTURE ECO/UNDEV AGRI PLAN EDU/PROP ADMIN COLONIAL...GEOG SOC/INTEG 20 NEGRO. PAGE 96 H1918 — BIBLIOG/A ACT/RES ACADEM R+D

B60
LISTER L.,EUROPE'S COAL AND STEEL COMMUNITY. FRANCE GERMANY STRUCT ECO/DEV EXTR/IND INDUS MARKET NAT/G DELIB/GP ECO/TAC INT/TRADE EDU/PROP ATTIT RIGID/FLEX ORD/FREE PWR WEALTH...CONCPT STAT TIME/SEQ CHARTS ECSC 20. PAGE 97 H1941 — EUR+WWI INT/ORG REGION

B60
MCCLOSKY H.,THE SOVIET DICTATORSHIP. FUT CONSTN CULTURE INTELL SOCIETY POL/PAR SECT VOL/ASSN FORCES PLAN TEC/DEV DOMIN EDU/PROP COERCE PWR MARXISM ...POLICY CONCPT MYTH STERTYP 20. PAGE 106 H2127 — COM NAT/G TOTALISM USSR

B60
PANIKKAR K.M.,THE STATE AND THE CITIZEN (2ND ED.). INDIA DOMIN ATTIT SUPEGO ORD/FREE WEALTH...GEOG CONCPT GP/COMP 20. PAGE 123 H2459 — TEC/DEV POL/PAR NAT/G EDU/PROP

B60
PIERCE R.A.,RUSSIAN CENTRAL ASIA, 1867-1917. ASIA RUSSIA CULTURE AGRI INDUS EDU/PROP REV NAT/LISM ...CHARTS BIBLIOG 19/20 BOLSHEVISM INTERVENT. PAGE 125 H2509 — COLONIAL DOMIN ADMIN ECO/UNDEV

B60
SCANLON D.G.,INTERNATIONAL EDUCATION: A DOCUMENTARY HISTORY. ADMIN CONTROL ATTIT PERCEPT...BIOG ANTHOL METH 20. PAGE 138 H2765 — EDU/PROP INT/ORG NAT/COMP DIPLOM

B60
SCHAPIRO L.,THE COMMUNIST PARTY OF THE SOVIET UNION. COM LAW SOCIETY STRATA STRUCT ECO/DEV LABOR NAT/G POL/PAR CREATE DOMIN EDU/PROP COERCE TOTALISM MARXISM...POLICY CONCPT MYTH TIME/SEQ WORK TOT/POP 20 LENIN/VI STALIN/J. PAGE 139 H2772 — INTELL PWR USSR

B60
WILLIAMS L.E.,OVERSEAS CHINESE NATIONALISM: THE GENESIS OF THE PAN-CHINESE MOVEMENT IN INDONESIA, — NAT/LISM GP/REL

1900-1916. ASIA COM INDONESIA AGRI INT/ORG LOC/G DIPLOM EDU/PROP HABITAT PWR POPULISM...GEOG LING CENSUS 20. PAGE 168 H3367 — DECISION / NAT/G

B60
WOLF C.,FOREIGN AID: THEORY AND PRACTICE IN SOUTHERN ASIA. CEYLON INDONESIA PHILIPPINE S/ASIA CULTURE STRATA ECO/UNDEV PLAN EDU/PROP ATTIT ...METH/CNCPT MATH QUANT STAT CONT/OBS TIME/SEQ SIMUL TOT/POP 20. PAGE 170 H3396 — ACT/RES / ECO/TAC / FOR/AID

L60
KAPLAN M.A.,"COMMUNIST COUP IN CZECHOSLOVAKIA." COM EUR+WWI INTELL LABOR LOC/G NAT/G POL/PAR FORCES EDU/PROP EXEC MARXISM...TIME/SEQ HYPO/EXP 20. PAGE 83 H1659 — STRUCT / COERCE / CZECHOSLVK

L60
WHEELER G.,"RACIAL PROBLEMS IN SOVIET MUSLIM ASIA." COM CULTURE SOCIETY NEIGH SECT DOMIN EDU/PROP DISCRIM DISPL DRIVE PWR SOVEREIGN...CENSUS SAMP TREND 20 MUSLIM. PAGE 167 H3340 — PERSON / ATTIT / USSR / RACE/REL

S60
ARENDT H.,"SOCIETY AND CULTURE." FUT CULTURE INTELL STRATA EDU/PROP ATTIT PERSON KNOWL...ART/METH HUM 20. PAGE 8 H0161 — SOCIETY / CREATE

S60
BRZEZINSKI Z.K.,"PATTERNS AND LIMITS OF THE SINO-SOVIET DISPUTE." ASIA CHINA/COM COM FUT STRATA NAT/G EX/STRUC FORCES BAL/PWR DIPLOM ECO/TAC DOMIN EDU/PROP ADMIN COERCE WAR ATTIT RIGID/FLEX ...GEN/LAWS VAL/FREE 20. PAGE 23 H0459 — POL/PAR / PWR / REV / USSR

S60
CASSINELLI C.,"TOTALITARIANISM, IDEOLOGY AND PROPAGANDA." EUR+WWI CULTURE SOCIETY NAT/G DOMIN COERCE ORD/FREE FASCISM MARXISM...MARXIST CONCPT STERTYP GEN/LAWS TOT/POP 20. PAGE 28 H0554 — ATTIT / EDU/PROP / TOTALISM

S60
GINSBURGS G.,"PEKING-LHASA-NEW DELHI." CHINA/COM FUT INDIA S/ASIA KIN NAT/G PROVS SECT FORCES BAL/PWR ECO/TAC DOMIN EDU/PROP LEGIT ADMIN REGION GUERRILLA PWR...TREND TIBET 20. PAGE 57 H1134 — ASIA / COERCE / DIPLOM

S60
GROSSMAN G.,"SOVIET GROWTH: ROUTINE, INERTIA, AND PRESSURE." COM STRATA NAT/G DELIB/GP PLAN TEC/DEV ECO/TAC EDU/PROP ADMIN ROUTINE DRIVE WEALTH COLD/WAR 20. PAGE 62 H1236 — POL/PAR / ECO/DEV / USSR

S60
HALSEY A.H.,"THE CHANGING FUNCTIONS OF UNIVERSITIES IN ADVANCED INDUSTRIAL SOCIETIES." R+D EDU/PROP REPRESENT ROLE ORD/FREE PWR TREND. PAGE 65 H1298 — ACADEM / CREATE / CULTURE / ADJUST

S60
JAFFEE A.J.,"POPULATION TRENDS AND CONTROLS IN UNDERDEVELOPED COUNTRIES." AFR FUT ISLAM L/A+17C S/ASIA CULTURE R+D FAM ACT/RES PLAN EDU/PROP BIO/SOC RIGID/FLEX HEALTH...SOC STAT OBS CHARTS 20. PAGE 79 H1582 — ECO/UNDEV / GEOG

S60
NORTHEDGE F.S.,"BRITISH FOREIGN POLICY AND THE PARTY SYSTEM." EUR+WWI FUT INT/ORG NAT/G EDU/PROP ATTIT PWR...POLICY CONCPT MYTH TIME/SEQ TREND 20 UN. PAGE 119 H2374 — POL/PAR / CHOOSE / DIPLOM / UK

S60
SPIRO H.J.,"NEW CONSTITUTIONAL FORMS IN AFRICA." FUT CULTURE SOCIETY ECO/UNDEV NAT/G POL/PAR VOL/ASSN EDU/PROP ATTIT DRIVE ORD/FREE PWR RESPECT ...POLICY CONCPT OBS TREND CON/ANAL STERTYP GEN/LAWS VAL/FREE. PAGE 148 H2950 — AFR / CONSTN / FOR/AID / NAT/LISM

S60
TAUBER K.,"ASPECTS OF NATIONALIST-COMMUNIST COLLABORATION IN POSTWAR GERMANY." COM EUR+WWI USSR NAT/G VOL/ASSN ATTIT DRIVE PWR...TIME/SEQ COLD/WAR TOT/POP 20. PAGE 152 H3049 — POL/PAR / EDU/PROP / GERMANY

S60
TURNER R.H.,"SPONSORED AND CONTEST MOBILITY IN THE SCHOOL SYSTEM." UK USA+45 ELITES STRATA ACADEM FACE/GP EDU/PROP CONTROL INGP/REL ADJUST ATTIT PERSON...METH/COMP 20. PAGE 157 H3142 — AGE/Y / NAT/COMP / SCHOOL / STRUCT

C60
FITZSIMMONS T.,"USSR: ITS PEOPLE, ITS SOCIETY, ITS CULTURE." USSR FAM SECT DIPLOM EDU/PROP ADMIN RACE/REL ATTIT...POLICY CHARTS BIBLIOG 20. PAGE 51 H1021 — CULTURE / STRUCT / SOCIETY / COM

B61
ALSTON P.L.,STATE EDUCATION AND SOCIAL CHANGE IN THE RUSSIAN EMPIRE 1871-1914 (PAPER). RUSSIA ELITES PROF/ORG EDU/PROP CONTROL PRIVIL AGE/Y...BIBLIOG 19/20. PAGE 6 H0115 — SCHOOL / SOCIETY / NAT/G / GP/REL

B61
BERKOWITZ L.,AGGRESSION: AS A SOCIAL PSYCHOLOGICAL ANALYSIS. UNIV CULTURE FACE/GP FAM KIN NEIGH EDU/PROP DISPL DRIVE HEALTH LOVE ORD/FREE...PSY SOC CONCPT OBS TREND. PAGE 15 H0305 — SOCIETY / COERCE / WAR

B61
BISHOP D.G.,THE ADMINISTRATION OF BRITISH FOREIGN RELATIONS. EUR+WWI MOD/EUR INT/ORG NAT/G POL/PAR DELIB/GP LEGIS TOP/EX ECO/TAC DOMIN EDU/PROP ADMIN COERCE 20. PAGE 17 H0344 — ROUTINE / PWR / DIPLOM / UK

B61
BULLOCK A.,HITLER: A STUDY IN TYRANNY. EUR+WWI GERMANY SOCIETY STRUCT NAT/G POL/PAR FORCES CREATE DOMIN EDU/PROP EXEC COERCE WAR NAT/LISM DISPL DRIVE PERSON PWR...PSY NAZI 20 HITLER/A. PAGE 23 H0470 — ATTIT / BIOG / TOTALISM

B61
BURDETTE F.L.,POLITICAL SCIENCE: A SELECTED BIBLIOGRAPHY OF BOOKS IN PRINT, WITH ANNOTATIONS (PAMPHLET). LAW LOC/G NAT/G POL/PAR PROVS DIPLOM EDU/PROP ADMIN CHOOSE ATTIT 20. PAGE 24 H0479 — BIBLIOG/A / GOV/COMP / CONCPT / ROUTINE

B61
DALLIN D.J.,SOVIET FOREIGN POLICY AFTER STALIN. ASIA CHINA/COM EUR+WWI GERMANY IRAN UK YUGOSLAVIA INT/ORG NAT/G VOL/ASSN FORCES TOP/EX BAL/PWR DOMIN EDU/PROP COERCE ATTIT PWR 20. PAGE 37 H0737 — COM / DIPLOM / USSR

B61
DIA M.,THE AFRICAN NATIONS AND WORLD SOLIDARITY. ISLAM CULTURE ELITES ECO/DEV ECO/UNDEV INT/ORG NAT/G PLAN ECO/TAC INT/TRADE EDU/PROP NAT/LISM ATTIT DRIVE ORD/FREE WEALTH...SOCIALIST CONCPT CON/ANAL GEN/LAWS TOT/POP 20. PAGE 41 H0817 — AFR / REGION / SOCISM

B61
DOOB L.W.,COMMUNICATION IN AFRICA: A SEARCH FOR BOUNDARIES. CULTURE SOCIETY EDU/PROP WRITING INGP/REL DRIVE ORD/FREE...ART/METH SOC LING BIBLIOG 20. PAGE 42 H0837 — AFR / FEEDBACK / PERCEPT / PERS/REL

B61
HADDAD J.A.,REVOLUCAO CUBANA E REVOLUCAO BRASILEIRA. BRAZIL CUBA L/A+17C STRATA AGRI WORKER EDU/PROP REGION...POLICY NAT/COMP 20. PAGE 63 H1272 — REV / ORD/FREE / DIPLOM / ECO/UNDEV

B61
HALPERIN S.,THE POLITICAL WORLD OF AMERICAN ZIONISM. ISRAEL FINAN LABOR VOL/ASSN GIVE LOBBY REPRESENT GP/REL ATTIT POLICY. PAGE 64 H1293 — CULTURE / SECT / EDU/PROP / DELIB/GP

B61
HISTORICAL RESEARCH INSTITUTE,A SHORT BIBLIOGRAPHY OF INDO-MUSLIM HISTORY. INDIA S/ASIA DIPLOM EDU/PROP COLONIAL LEAD NAT/LISM ATTIT...BIOG 19/20. PAGE 71 H1427 — BIBLIOG / NAT/G / SECT / POL/PAR

B61
INTL UNION LOCAL AUTHORITIES,METROPOLIS. WOR+45 DIST/IND FINAN GIVE EDU/PROP CRIME COST HEALTH WEALTH 20. PAGE 78 H1563 — MUNIC / GOV/COMP / LOC/G / BIBLIOG

B61
KEE R.,REFUGEE WORLD. AUSTRIA EUR+WWI GERMANY NEIGH EX/STRUC WORKER PROB/SOLV ECO/TAC RENT EDU/PROP INGP/REL COST LITERACY HABITAT 20 MIGRATION. PAGE 84 H1676 — NAT/G / GIVE / WEALTH / STRANGE

B61
LENIN V.I.,WHAT IS TO BE DONE? (1902). RUSSIA LABOR NAT/G POL/PAR WORKER CAP/ISM ECO/TAC ADMIN PARTIC ...MARXIST IDEA/COMP GEN/LAWS 19/20. PAGE 94 H1881 — EDU/PROP / PRESS / MARXISM / METH/COMP

B61
LETHBRIDGE H.J.,CHINA'S URBAN COMMUNES. CHINA/COM FUT ECO/UNDEV DIPLOM EDU/PROP DEMAND INCOME MARXISM ...POLICY 20. PAGE 95 H1893 — MUNIC / CONTROL / ECO/TAC / NAT/G

B61
LUNDBERG G.A.,CAN SCIENCE SAVE US. UNIV CULTURE INTELL SOCIETY ECO/DEV R+D PLAN EDU/PROP ROUTINE CHOOSE ATTIT PERCEPT ALL/VALS...TREND 20. PAGE 99 H1979 — ACT/RES / CONCPT / TOTALISM

B61
MARVICK D.,POLITICAL DECISION-MAKERS. INTELL STRATA NAT/G POL/PAR EX/STRUC LEGIS DOMIN EDU/PROP ATTIT PERSON PWR...PSY STAT OBS CONT/OBS STAND/INT UNPLAN/INT TIME/SEQ CHARTS STERTYP VAL/FREE. PAGE 104 H2073 — TOP/EX / BIOG / ELITES

B61
NARAIN J.P.,SWARAJ FOR THE PEOPLE. INDIA CONSTN LOC/G MUNIC POL/PAR CHOOSE REPRESENT EFFICIENCY ATTIT PWR SOVEREIGN 20. PAGE 116 H2311 — NAT/G / ORD/FREE / EDU/PROP / EX/STRUC

B61
REISKY-DUBNIC V.,COMMUNIST PROPAGANDA METHODS. CULTURE POL/PAR VOL/ASSN ATTIT...CONCPT TOT/POP. PAGE 131 H2611 — COM / EDU/PROP / TOTALISM

B61
ROSE D.L.,THE VIETNAMESE CIVIL SERVICE. VIETNAM CONSULT DELIB/GP GIVE PAY EDU/PROP COLONIAL GOV/REL UTIL...CHARTS 20. PAGE 134 H2672 — ADMIN / EFFICIENCY / STAT / NAT/G

B61
SAFRAN M.,EGYPT IN SEARCH OF POLITICAL COMMUNITY: AN ANALYSIS OF THE INTELLECTUAL AND POLITICAL EVOLUTION OF EGYPT, 1804-1952. ISLAM NAT/G SECT EDU/PROP COERCE ATTIT DRIVE KNOWL PWR...TIME/SEQ 20. PAGE 137 H2729 — INTELL / NAT/LISM / UAR

B61
SEMINAR REPRESENTATIVE GOVT,AFRO-ASIAN ATTITUDES: SEMINAR ON REPRESENTATIVE GOVERNMENTSPUBLIC LIBERTIES IN STATES OF ASIA AND AFRICA, RHODES, — CHOOSE / ATTIT / NAT/COMP

1958. AFR ASIA BURMA INDIA ISLAM UAR VIETNAM/S SOCIETY POL/PAR CHIEF EDU/PROP PRESS PERSON ...POLICY INT 20 TUNIS. PAGE 141 H2826
ORD/FREE

B61
SETON-WATSON H.,FROM LENIN TO KHRUSHCHEV: THE HISTORY OF WORLD COMMUNISM. ASIA COM EUR+WWI ISLAM S/ASIA ECO/DEV ECO/UNDEV NAT/G POL/PAR DIPLOM ECO/TAC EDU/PROP COERCE GUERRILLA ATTIT DRIVE WORK TOT/POP NAZI 20. PAGE 141 H2832
PWR REV USSR

B61
STAHL W.,EDUCATION FOR DEMOCRACY IN WEST GERMANY: ACHIEVEMENT SHORTCOMINGS - PROSPECTS. GERMANY/W SOCIETY NAT/G FORCES PLAN PROB/SOLV PRESS ALL/VALS ...POLICY MAJORIT CONCPT ANTHOL 20. PAGE 148 H2967
EDU/PROP POPULISM AGE/Y ADJUST

B61
UAR MINISTRY OF CULTURE,A BIBLIOGRAPHICAL LIST OF TUNISIA. ISLAM CULTURE NAT/G EDU/PROP COLONIAL ...GEOG 19/20 TUNIS. PAGE 157 H3146
BIBLIOG DIPLOM SECT

B61
ULLMAN W.,PRINCIPLES OF GOVERNMENT AND POLITICS IN THE MIDDLE AGES. LAW CONSTN DOMIN EDU/PROP LEGIT TOTALISM SOVEREIGN POPULISM...POLICY GOV/COMP IDEA/COMP 12/16 POPE KING CHURCH/STA. PAGE 158 H3152
SECT CHIEF NAT/G LEGIS

B61
VON MERING O.,A GRAMMAR OF HUMAN VALUES. WOR+45 CULTURE FACE/GP NEIGH CREATE EDU/PROP LEGIT ATTIT DRIVE PERSON ORD/FREE...PSY SOC METH/CNCPT OBS RECORD INT REC/INT STAND/INT QU CHARTS VAL/FREE. PAGE 164 H3275
SOCIETY MORAL

B61
ZIMMERMAN I.,A GUIDE TO CURRENT LATIN AMERICAN PERIODICALS: HUMANITIES AND SOCIAL SCIENCES. LABOR SECT EDU/PROP...GEOG HUM SOC LING STAT NAT/COMP 20. PAGE 173 H3456
BIBLIOG/A DIPLOM L/A+17C PHIL/SCI

L61
KAUPER P.G.,"CHURCH AND STATE: COOPERATIVE SEPARATISM." NAT/G LEGIS OP/RES TAX EDU/PROP GP/REL TREND. PAGE 84 H1671
SECT CONSTN LAW POLICY

S61
BRZEZINSKI Z.K.,"THE ORGANIZATION OF THE COMMUNIST CAMP." COM CZECHOSLVK COM/IND NAT/G DELIB/GP INT/TRADE DOMIN EDU/PROP EXEC ROUTINE COERCE ATTIT PWR...MGT CONCPT TIME/SEQ CHARTS VAL/FREE 20 TREATY. PAGE 23 H0460
VOL/ASSN DIPLOM USSR

S61
ELAZAR D.J.,"CHURCHES AS MOLDERS OF AMERICAN POLITICS." STRATA MUNIC EDU/PROP RACE/REL ORD/FREE SOC. PAGE 45 H0904
SECT CULTURE REPRESENT LOC/G

S61
FITZGIBBON R.H.,"MEASUREMENT OF LATIN AMERICAN POLITICAL CHANGE." L/A+17C CONSTN CULTURE SOCIETY ECO/UNDEV NAT/G POL/PAR PUB/INST ACT/RES EDU/PROP PERCEPT KNOWL ORD/FREE SOVEREIGN...METH/CNCPT TREND OAS 20. PAGE 51 H1020
CHOOSE ATTIT

S61
RANDALL F.B.,"COMMUNISM IN THE HIGH ANDES." L/A+17C PERU USSR SOCIETY PLAN EDU/PROP TOTALISM ATTIT RIGID/FLEX PWR WEALTH...HUM CONCPT GEN/LAWS 20 BOLIV EQUADOR. PAGE 129 H2589
CULTURE DRIVE

S61
SCHECHTMAN J.B.,"MINORITIES IN THE MIDDLE EAST." ISLAM INTELL SOCIETY STRATA KIN NAT/G VOL/ASSN EDU/PROP REGION GP/REL DISCRIM ATTIT BIO/SOC DISPL PERSON ALL/VALS...PSY SOC OBS SAMP GEN/LAWS 20. PAGE 139 H2776
SECT CULTURE RACE/REL

S61
TANHAM B.K.,"COMMUNIST REVOLUTIONARY WARFARE: THE VIETMINH IN INDOCHINA." EUR+WWI S/ASIA VIETNAM NAT/G EDU/PROP LEGIT GUERRILLA ATTIT PWR...CONCPT GEN/LAWS 20. PAGE 152 H3042
FORCES ECO/TAC WAR FRANCE

S61
TOMASIC D.,"POLITICAL LEADERSHIP IN CONTEMPORARY POLAND." COM EUR+WWI GERMANY NAT/G POL/PAR SECT DELIB/GP PLAN ECO/TAC DOMIN EDU/PROP PWR MARXISM ...MARXIST GEOG MGT CONCPT TIME/SEQ STERTYP 20. PAGE 156 H3111
SOCIETY ROUTINE USSR POLAND

B62
ABRAHAM W.E.,THE MIND OF AFRICA. AFR SOCIETY STRATA KIN ECO/TAC DOMIN EDU/PROP LEGIT COERCE ATTIT ALL/VALS...MAJORIT SOC OBS HIST/WRIT TIME/SEQ TREND TOT/POP 20. PAGE 3 H0058
CULTURE SIMUL GHANA

B62
AMERICAN SOCIETY AFR CULTURE,PAN-AFRICANISM RECONSIDERED. AFR SOCIETY STRUCT SCHOOL CAP/ISM EDU/PROP...ART/METH NEW/IDEA PREDICT ANTHOL 20 PANAF/FREE NEGRO. PAGE 6 H0123
DIPLOM FEDERAL NAT/LISM CULTURE

B62
BAFFREY S.A.,THE RED MYTH: A HISTORY OF COMMUNISM FROM MARX TO KHRUSHCHEV. USSR NAT/G CHIEF CAP/ISM DIPLOM EDU/PROP REV WAR PEACE TOTALISM...POLICY 20 STALIN/J KHRUSH/N. PAGE 10 H0195
CONCPT MARXISM TV

B62
BRETTON H.L.,POWER AND STABILITY IN NIGERIA: THE POLITICS OF DECOLONIZATION. AFR CONSTN INTELL ECO/UNDEV COM/IND KIN NAT/G POL/PAR PROVS VOL/ASSN LEGIS DOMIN EDU/PROP LEGIT EXEC ROUTINE CHOOSE NAT/LISM ATTIT PERCEPT ALL/VALS. PAGE 20 H0411
CULTURE OBS NIGERIA

B62
BUSIA K.A.,THE CHALLENGE OF AFRICA. CULTURE KIN MUNIC NAT/G POL/PAR SCHOOL DELIB/GP PLAN ECO/TAC DOMIN EDU/PROP TOTALISM ATTIT PERSON ALL/VALS SOVEREIGN...SOC CONCPT STERTYP TOT/POP VAL/FREE 20. PAGE 25 H0496
AFR ECO/UNDEV NAT/LISM

B62
CALVOCORESSI P.,WORLD ORDER AND NEW STATES: PROBLEMS OF KEEPING THE PEACE. AFR EUR+WWI S/ASIA ELITES NAT/G ECO/TAC FOR/AID EDU/PROP COERCE ATTIT DRIVE ALL/VALS...GEN/LAWS COLD/WAR 20 UN. PAGE 25 H0509
INT/ORG PEACE

B62
CARTER G.M.,AFRICAN ONE-PARTY STATES. ISLAM IVORY/CST LIBERIA CONSTN CULTURE SOCIETY POL/PAR PLAN DOMIN EDU/PROP EXEC REGION CHOOSE ATTIT ALL/VALS...CONCPT TIME/SEQ CHARTS VAL/FREE 20 TANGANYIKA. PAGE 27 H0545
AFR NAT/LISM

B62
CARY J.,THE CASE FOR AFRICAN FREEDOM AND OTHER WRITINGS ON AFRICA. AFR UK INDUS LOC/G NAT/G SECT INT/TRADE EDU/PROP GOV/REL RACE/REL ORD/FREE ...CONCPT ANTHOL 19/20. PAGE 27 H0552
NAT/LISM COLONIAL TREND ECO/UNDEV

B62
CHAKRAVARTI P.C.,INDIA'S CHINA POLICY. ASIA CHINA/COM S/ASIA CULTURE NAT/G TOP/EX ACT/RES EDU/PROP DRIVE ALL/VALS...MYTH 20. PAGE 28 H0571
RIGID/FLEX TREND INDIA

B62
CHAPMAN R.M.,NEW ZEALAND POLITICS IN ACTION: THE 1960 GENERAL ELECTION. NEW/ZEALND LEGIS EDU/PROP PRESS TV LEAD ATTIT...STAND/INT 20. PAGE 29 H0582
NAT/G CHOOSE POL/PAR

B62
DE MADARIAGA S.,L'AMERIQUE LATINE ENTRE L'OURS ET L'AIGLE. L/A+17C SOCIETY NAT/G ECO/TAC EDU/PROP REGION COERCE ATTIT ALL/VALS...MAJORIT TIME/SEQ STERTYP COLD/WAR OAS 20. PAGE 38 H0760
POL/PAR ECO/UNDEV

B62
DEBUYST F.,LAS CLASES SOCIALES EN AMERICA LATINA. L/A+17C SOCIETY STRUCT WORKER EDU/PROP RACE/REL ATTIT HABITAT ROLE...GEOG SOC NAT/COMP SOC/INTEG 20. PAGE 39 H0780
STRATA GP/REL WEALTH

B62
DUROSELLE J.B.,LES NOUVEAUX ETATS DANS LES RELATIONS INTERNATIONALES. AFR CHINA/COM FRANCE MOROCCO S/ASIA USSR ECO/UNDEV INT/ORG PLAN ECO/TAC EDU/PROP ATTIT DRIVE...TREND TOT/POP TUNIS 20. PAGE 44 H0872
NAT/G CONSTN DIPLOM

B62
EBENSTEIN W.,TWO WAYS OF LIFE. USA+45 CULTURE ECO/DEV PLAN EDU/PROP CONTROL ORD/FREE...GOV/COMP IDEA/COMP T 20 MARX/KARL ENGELS/F LENIN/VI LOCKE/JOHN MILL/JS. PAGE 44 H0885
MARXISM POPULISM ECO/TAC DIPLOM

B62
FINER S.E.,THE MAN ON HORSEBACK: ROLE OF THE MILITARY IN POLITICS. UNIV LAW CONSTN ELITES SOCIETY POL/PAR BAL/PWR DOMIN EDU/PROP LEGIT COERCE GUERRILLA REV WAR WEAPON DRIVE SUPEGO ORD/FREE PWR RESPECT...POLICY CONCPT GEN/METH. PAGE 50 H1003
NAT/G FORCES TOTALISM

B62
GRZYBOWSKI K.,SOVIET LEGAL INSTITUTIONS. USA+45 USSR ECO/DEV NAT/G EDU/PROP CONTROL CT/SYS CRIME OWN ATTIT PWR SOCISM...NAT/COMP 20. PAGE 62 H1242
ADJUD LAW JURID

B62
GUENA Y.,HISTORIQUE DE LA COMMUNAUTE. FUT ECO/UNDEV NAT/G PLAN EDU/PROP COLONIAL REGION NAT/LISM ALL/VALS SOVEREIGN...CONCPT OBS CHARTS 20. PAGE 62 H1244
AFR VOL/ASSN FOR/AID FRANCE

B62
HABERMAS J.,STRUKTURWANDEL DER OFFENTLICHKEIT. NAT/G EDU/PROP PRESS LEAD PARTIC PWR 20. PAGE 63 H1268
ATTIT CONCPT DOMIN

B62
HANAK H.,GREAT BRITAIN AND AUSTRIA-HUNGARY DURING THE FIRST WORLD WAR: A STUDY IN THE FORMATION OF PUBLIC OPINION. CZECHOSLVK UK NAT/G GIVE DOMIN EDU/PROP CONSERVE...BIBLIOG 20 AUST/HUNG WWI. PAGE 65 H1311
WAR DIPLOM ATTIT PRESS

B62
HATCH J.,AFRICA TODAY-AND TOMORROW: AN OUTLINE OF BASIC FACTS AND MAJOR PROBLEMS. AFR FUT ISLAM STRATA ECO/UNDEV INT/ORG NAT/G POL/PAR DELIB/GP TOP/EX EDU/PROP LEGIT CHOOSE ATTIT...TIME/SEQ TOT/POP COLD/WAR 20. PAGE 67 H1353
PLAN CONSTN NAT/LISM

B62
HO PING-TI,THE LADDER OF SUCCESS IN IMPERIAL CHINA: ASPECTS OF SOCIAL MOBILITY, 1368-1911. INTELL STRATA FAM KIN MUNIC NAT/G PROVS SCHOOL DELIB/GP DOMIN EDU/PROP ADMIN ROUTINE PERSON ALL/VALS...SOC STAT BIOG HIST/WRIT TIME/SEQ VAL/FREE. PAGE 71 H1431
ASIA CULTURE

B62
HUNKIN P.,ENSEIGNEMENT ET POLITIQUE EN FRANCE ET EN
EDU/PROP

ANGLETERRE. FRANCE UK CONSTN ACADEM SECT CHIEF DELIB/GP PROB/SOLV CONTROL REV ORD/FREE CONSERVE ...BIBLIOG 18/20. PAGE 75 H1496
LEGIS IDEA/COMP NAT/G

B62
HUNTER G.,THE NEW SOCIETIES OF TROPICAL AFRICA. CULTURE INDUS KIN MUNIC WORKER INT/TRADE EDU/PROP ORD/FREE...INT TREND 20. PAGE 75 H1500
AFR GOV/COMP ECO/UNDEV SOCIETY

B62
INAYATULLAH,BUREAUCRACY AND DEVELOPMENT IN PAKISTAN. PAKISTAN ECO/UNDEV EDU/PROP CONFER ...ANTHOL DICTIONARY 20 BUREAUCRCY. PAGE 76 H1526
EX/STRUC ADMIN NAT/G LOC/G

B62
INSTITUTE FOR STUDY OF USSR,YOUTH IN FERMENT. INTELL NAT/G PERF/ART POL/PAR SCHOOL VOL/ASSN FORCES EDU/PROP ATTIT DRIVE PERCEPT HEALTH KNOWL MORAL ORD/FREE RESPECT...SOC OBS HIST/WRIT VAL/FREE. PAGE 77 H1537
COM CULTURE USSR

B62
KENNEDY R.,BIBLIOGRAPHY OF INDONESIAN PEOPLES AND CULTURES (2ND REV. ED.). INDONESIA STRUCT ECO/UNDEV SCHOOL EDU/PROP COLONIAL...GEOG SOC LING NAT/COMP 20. PAGE 85 H1689
BIBLIOG S/ASIA CULTURE KIN

B62
KINDERSLEY R.,THE FIRST RUSSIAN REVISIONISTS. COM USSR LAW ELITES INTELL NAT/G LEGIS ECO/TAC EDU/PROP CONTROL LEAD GP/REL SOCISM 19/20 MARX/KARL BOLSHEVISM. PAGE 86 H1712
CONSTN MARXISM POPULISM BIOG

B62
KRUGLAK T.E.,THE TWO FACES OF TASS. COM COM/IND NAT/G ACT/RES PLAN PRESS PERCEPT PERSON KNOWL 20. PAGE 89 H1778
PUB/INST EDU/PROP USSR

B62
LEGUM C.,PAN-AFRICANISM: A SHORT POLITICAL GUIDE. ISLAM CULTURE INTELL ECO/DEV NAT/G POL/PAR DELIB/GP PLAN EDU/PROP FEDERAL NAT/LISM ATTIT DRIVE PERSON ...RECORD TIME/SEQ CHARTS STERTYP 20. PAGE 93 H1861
AFR CONCPT

B62
MEHNERT K.,SOVIET MAN AND HIS WORLD. COM USSR INTELL FAM WORKER PLAN EDU/PROP REV PRODUC MARXISM ...SOC TREND SOC/INTEG 20 LENIN/VI STALIN/J KHRUSH/N. PAGE 108 H2162
SOCIETY CULTURE ECO/DEV

B62
MELADY T.,THE WHITE MAN'S FUTURE IN BLACK AFRICA. FUT CULTURE SOCIETY NAT/G POL/PAR PLAN ECO/TAC DOMIN EDU/PROP LEGIT COLONIAL RACE/REL ATTIT DRIVE ALL/VALS...PSY SOC CONCPT TIME/SEQ TOT/POP VAL/FREE 20. PAGE 108 H2167
AFR STRATA ELITES

B62
MUKERJI S.N.,ADMINISTRATION OF EDUCATION IN INDIA. ACADEM LOC/G PROVS ROUTINE...POLICY STAT CHARTS 20. PAGE 114 H2282
SCHOOL ADMIN NAT/G EDU/PROP

B62
NOBECOURT R.G.,LES SECRETS DE LA PROPAGANDE EN FRANCE OCCUPEE. FRANCE ELITES NAT/G DIPLOM GP/REL NAT/LISM TOTALISM ORD/FREE 20 VICHY VICHY. PAGE 118 H2365
METH/COMP EDU/PROP WAR CONTROL

B62
PENTONY D.E.,RED WORLD IN TUMULT: COMMUNIST FOREIGN POLICIES. CHINA/COM COM NAT/G EDU/PROP COERCE ATTIT PWR RESPECT...SOC CHARTS 20. PAGE 124 H2488
ECO/UNDEV DOMIN USSR ASIA

B62
ROBINSON A.D.,DUTCH ORGANIZED AGRICULTURE IN INTERNATIONAL POLITICS, 1945-1960. EUR+WWI NETHERLAND STRUCT ECO/DEV NAT/G VOL/ASSN CONSULT DELIB/GP PLAN TEC/DEV INT/TRADE EDU/PROP ATTIT RIGID/FLEX ALL/VALS...NEW/IDEA TREND EEC 20. PAGE 132 H2648
AGRI INT/ORG

B62
SELOSOEMARDJAN O.,SOCIAL CHANGES IN JOGJAKARTA. INDONESIA NETHERLAND ELITES STRATA STRUCT FAM POL/PAR CREATE DIPLOM INT/TRADE EDU/PROP ADMIN GOV/REL...SOC 20 JAVA CHINJAP. PAGE 141 H2825
ECO/UNDEV CULTURE REV COLONIAL

B62
STARR R.E.,POLAND 1944-1962: THE SOVIETIZATION OF A CAPTIVE PEOPLE. COM POLAND USSR POL/PAR SECT LEGIS DIPLOM DOMIN EDU/PROP CHOOSE ORD/FREE...POLICY CHARTS BIBLIOG 20. PAGE 149 H2973
MARXISM NAT/G TOTALISM NAT/COMP

B62
US LIBRARY OF CONGRESS,A LIST OF AMERICAN DOCTORAL DISSERTATIONS ON AFRICA. SOCIETY SECT DIPLOM EDU/PROP ADMIN...GEOG 19/20. PAGE 161 H3212
BIBLIOG AFR ACADEM CULTURE

B62
VILAKAZI A.,ZULU TRANSFORMATIONS: A STUDY OF THE DYNAMICS OF SOCIAL CHANGE. AFR CULTURE ECO/UNDEV KIN NEIGH SEX...GEOG QU TREND CHARTS BIBLIOG 19/20. PAGE 163 H3254
MARRIAGE SECT SOC EDU/PROP

B62
WHITING K.R.,THE SOVIET UNION TODAY: A CONCISE HANDBOOK. USSR ELITES AGRI INDUS POL/PAR FORCES DIPLOM EDU/PROP LEAD...GEOG TREND 19/20. PAGE 168 H3354
NAT/G ATTIT MARXISM POLICY

B62
ZIESEL K.,DAS VERLORENE GEWISSEN. GERMANY/W NAT/G VOL/ASSN EDU/PROP PRESS SUPEGO...POLICY 20. PAGE 173 H3455
MORAL PWR ORD/FREE RESPECT

B62
ZINKIN T.,REPORTING INDIA. INDIA PAKISTAN WOR+45 SOCIETY SECT FORCES EDU/PROP CROWD DISCRIM NAT/LISM MARXISM...POLICY 20. PAGE 173 H3457
STRATA COLONIAL BAL/PWR CONTROL

L62
NOLTE E.,"ZUR PHANOMENOLOGIE DES FASCHIMUS." EUR+WWI GERMANY ITALY TURKEY INTELL NAT/G CHIEF CONSULT FORCES CREATE DOMIN EDU/PROP COERCE WAR CHOOSE DRIVE FASCISM...PSY CONCPT MYTH GEN/METH LEAGUE/NAT NAZI 20. PAGE 118 H2367
ATTIT PWR

S62
ANSPRENGER F.,"NATIONALISM, COMMUNISM, AND THE UNCOMMITTED NATIONS: AMERICAN PROFILES." FUT ISLAM CULTURE SOCIETY ECO/UNDEV NAT/G POL/PAR PLAN ECO/TAC EDU/PROP COERCE CHOOSE ALL/VALS MARXISM SOCISM...SOC CONCPT BIOG TREND 20. PAGE 7 H0142
AFR COM NAT/LISM

S62
CROAN M.,"POLYCENTRISM: COMMUNIST INTERNATIONAL RELATIONS." ASIA STRUCT INT/ORG NAT/G POL/PAR CONSULT PLAN DOMIN EDU/PROP COERCE ATTIT RIGID/FLEX SOCISM...POLICY CONCPT TREND CON/ANAL GEN/LAWS MARX/KARL. PAGE 35 H0703
COM CREATE DIPLOM NAT/LISM

S62
FESLER J.W.,"FRENCH FIELD ADMINISTRATION: THE BEGINNINGS." CHRIST-17C CULTURE SOCIETY STRATA NAT/G ECO/TAC DOMIN EDU/PROP LEGIT ADJUD COERCE ATTIT ALL/VALS...TIME/SEQ CON/ANAL GEN/METH VAL/FREE 13/15. PAGE 49 H0988
EX/STRUC FRANCE

S62
GUETZKOW H.,"THE POTENTIAL OF CASE STUDY IN ANALYZING INTERNATIONAL CONFLICT." EUR+WWI FUT GERMANY INTELL SOCIETY STRUCT INT/ORG LOC/G NAT/G CONSULT CREATE PLAN CHOOSE ATTIT RIGID/FLEX ...POLICY SAAR 20. PAGE 62 H1246
EDU/PROP METH/CNCPT COERCE FRANCE

S62
HYDE D.,"COMMUNISM IN LATIN AMERICA." L/A+17C ECO/DEV NAT/G SECT EDU/PROP ATTIT ALL/VALS MARXISM ...SOC CONCPT TOT/POP COLD/WAR OAS 20. PAGE 76 H1515
COM POL/PAR REV

S62
IOVTCHOUK M.T.,"ON SOME THEORETICAL PRINCIPLES AND METHODS OF SOCIOLOGICAL INVESTIGATIONS (IN RUSSIAN)." FUT USA+45 STRATA R+D NAT/G POL/PAR TOP/EX ACT/RES PLAN ECO/TAC EDU/PROP ROUTINE ATTIT RIGID/FLEX MARXISM SOCISM...MARXIST METH/CNCPT OBS TREND NAT/COMP GEN/LAWS 20. PAGE 78 H1564
COM ECO/DEV CAP/ISM USSR

S62
KOLARZ W.,"THE IMPACT OF COMMUNISM ON WEST AFRICA." AFR FUT SOCIETY INT/ORG NAT/G CREATE PLAN DOMIN EDU/PROP COERCE NAT/LISM ATTIT RIGID/FLEX SOCISM ...POLICY CONCPT TREND MARX/KARL 20. PAGE 88 H1751
COM POL/PAR COLONIAL

S62
LANGER W.L.,"FAREWELL TO EMPIRE." EUR+WWI MOD/EUR NAT/G DIPLOM EDU/PROP COLONIAL ATTIT ORD/FREE PWR SOVEREIGN WEALTH...CONCPT TIME/SEQ GEN/LAWS TOT/POP VAL/FREE CMN/WLTH 20. PAGE 91 H1810
DOMIN ECO/TAC NAT/LISM

S62
MBOYA T.,"RELATIONS BETWEEN THE PRESS AND GOVERNMENT IN AFRICA." AFR DIPLOM EDU/PROP NAT/LISM ORD/FREE SOVEREIGN 20. PAGE 106 H2115
PRESS GP/REL ATTIT NAT/G

S62
MU FU-SHENG,"THE WILTING OF THE HUNDRED FLOWERS: FREE THOUGHT IN CHINA TODAY." ASIA CHINA/COM CULTURE FAM NAT/G EDU/PROP REV TOTALISM ATTIT PERSON RESPECT...GEOG INT UNPLAN/INT COLD/WAR 20. PAGE 114 H2278
INTELL ELITES

S62
PASSIN H.,"THE SOURCES OF PROTEST IN JAPAN." CULTURE SOCIETY EDU/PROP COERCE NAT/LISM DISPL DRIVE PWR RESPECT...POLICY SOC TREND 20 CHINJAP. PAGE 124 H2473
ASIA ATTIT REV

S62
PISTRAK L.,"SOVIET VIEWS ON AFRICA." AFR COM FUT ISLAM USSR INTELL STRUCT KIN POL/PAR PLAN EDU/PROP RIGID/FLEX PWR MARXISM...TIME/SEQ WORK TOT/POP 20. PAGE 126 H2516
NAT/G ATTIT SOCISM

S62
SARKISYANZ E.,"NATIONALISM, CAPITALISM, AND THE UNCOMMITED NATIONS: MARXISM AND ASIAN CULTURAL TRADITIONS." ASIA BURMA CHINA/COM COM CULTURE SOCIETY NAT/G POL/PAR PLAN DOMIN EDU/PROP COLONIAL COERCE ATTIT RIGID/FLEX...CONCPT TREND MARX/KARL 20 TIBET BUDDHISM. PAGE 138 H2755
S/ASIA SECT NAT/LISM CAP/ISM

S62
STRACHEY J.,"COMMUNIST INTENTIONS." ASIA USSR YUGOSLAVIA INT/ORG NAT/G FORCES DOMIN EDU/PROP COERCE NUC/PWR NAT/LISM PEACE RIGID/FLEX PWR MARXISM...CONCPT MYTH OBS TIME/SEQ TREND COLD/WAR TOT/POP 20. PAGE 150 H2992
COM ATTIT WAR

C62
BACON F.,"OF SEDITIONS AND TROUBLES" (1625) IN F. BACON, ESSAYS." INDUS MARKET CHIEF ECO/TAC EDU/PROP CONTROL LEAD PEACE WEALTH 17 MACHIAVELL. PAGE 9 H0191
REV ORD/FREE NAT/G GEN/LAWS

B63
BARNETT A.D.,COMMUNIST STRATEGIES IN ASIA: A COMPARATIVE ANALYSIS OF GOVERNMENTS AND PARTIES. COM FUT S/ASIA CULTURE SOCIETY STRATA NAT/G DELIB/GP ACT/RES ECO/TAC EDU/PROP COERCE CHOOSE ATTIT RIGID/FLEX ORD/FREE PWR SKILL...SIMUL VAL/FREE 20. PAGE 11 H0223
ASIA POL/PAR DIPLOM USSR

B63
BERLIN I.,KARL MARX, HIS LIFE AND ENVIRONMENT (3RD ED.). MOD/EUR USSR INTELL EDU/PROP PARTIC REV ATTIT 19 MARX/KARL. PAGE 15 H0307
BIOG PERSON MARXISM CONCPT

B63
BRZEZINSKI Z.K.,AFRICA AND THE COMMUNIST WORLD. AFR ASIA COM CULTURE SOCIETY INT/ORG DELIB/GP ACT/RES ECO/TAC COERCE ORD/FREE PWR WEALTH...STAT TOT/POP VAL/FREE 20. PAGE 23 H0461
ATTIT EDU/PROP DIPLOM USSR

B63
CARTER G.M.,FIVE AFRICAN STATES: RESPONSES TO DIVERSITY. CONSTN CULTURE STRATA LEGIS PLAN ECO/TAC DOMIN EDU/PROP CT/SYS EXEC CHOOSE ATTIT HEALTH ORD/FREE PWR...TIME/SEQ TOT/POP VAL/FREE. PAGE 27 H0547
AFR SOCIETY

B63
CREMEANS C.,THE ARABS AND THE WORLD: NASSER'S ARAB NATIONALIST POLICY. FUT ISLAM UAR USA+45 SOCIETY STRATA NAT/G POL/PAR PLAN DIPLOM EDU/PROP LEGIT DRIVE ALL/VALS...INT TIME/SEQ CHARTS 20 NASSER/G. PAGE 35 H0700
TOP/EX ATTIT REGION NAT/LISM

B63
CRUICKSHANK M.,CHURCH AND STATE IN ENGLISH EDUCATION 1870 TO PRESENT. UK LEGIS TAX GIVE DOMIN LEGIT ORD/FREE 19/20 CHURCH/STA. PAGE 36 H0715
NAT/G SECT EDU/PROP GP/REL

B63
DE VRIES E.,SOCIAL ASPECTS OF ECONOMIC DEVELOPMENT IN LATIN AMERICA. CULTURE SOCIETY STRATA FINAN INDUS INT/ORG DELIB/GP ACT/RES ECO/TAC EDU/PROP ADMIN ATTIT SUPEGO HEALTH KNOWL ORD/FREE...SOC STAT TREND ANTHOL TOT/POP VAL/FREE. PAGE 39 H0777
L/A+17C ECO/UNDEV

B63
DEUTSCH K.W.,THE NERVES OF GOVERNMENT. NAT/G CREATE EDU/PROP CONTROL LEAD PWR...CONCPT GEN/LAWS 20. PAGE 40 H0799
DECISION GAME SIMUL OP/RES

B63
DRIVER H.E.,ETHNOGRAPHY AND ACCULTURATION OF THE CHICHIMECA-JONAZ OF NORTHEAST MEXICO. ECO/UNDEV AGRI FAM KIN EDU/PROP MARRIAGE HEALTH...GEOG INT CHARTS WORSHIP 18/20 MEXIC/AMER. PAGE 42 H0848
CULTURE HABITAT STRUCT GP/REL

B63
ELWIN V.,A NEW DEAL FOR TRIBAL INDIA. INDIA AGRI COM/IND INDUS KIN TEC/DEV TAX EDU/PROP OWN HEALTH 20. PAGE 46 H0912
ECO/UNDEV CULTURE CONSTN SOC/WK

B63
FABER K.,DIE NATIONALISTISCHE PUBLIZISTIK DEUTSCHLANDS VON 1866 BIS 1871 (2 VOLS.). EUR+WWI GERMANY DIPLOM EDU/PROP 19. PAGE 48 H0957
BIBLIOG/A NAT/G NAT/LISM POL/PAR

B63
FALL B.,THE TWO VIETNAMS. CULTURE SOCIETY ECO/UNDEV NAT/G TOP/EX ACT/RES PLAN ECO/TAC DOMIN EDU/PROP COERCE ATTIT DRIVE PERSON ORD/FREE PWR...SOC TIME/SEQ COLD/WAR 20. PAGE 48 H0965
S/ASIA BIOG VIETNAM

B63
GAMBLE S.D.,NORTH CHINA VILLAGES: SOCIAL, POLITICAL, AND ECONOMIC ACTIVITIES BEFORE 1933. ASIA CULTURE STRUCT FAM DOMIN EDU/PROP WORSHIP 20. PAGE 55 H1093
MUNIC AGRI LEAD FINAN

B63
GEERTZ C.,OLD SOCIETIES AND NEW STATES: THE QUEST FOR MODERNITY IN ASIA AND AFRICA. AFR ASIA LAW CULTURE SECT EDU/PROP REV...GOV/COMP NAT/COMP 20. PAGE 55 H1107
ECO/UNDEV TEC/DEV NAT/LISM SOVEREIGN

B63
GERSCHENKRON A.,THE STABILITY OF DICTATORSHIPS. NAT/G EDU/PROP TASK ATTIT PERSON...POLICY PSY SOC METH 19/20. PAGE 56 H1116
TOTALISM CONCPT CONTROL ORD/FREE

B63
GLUCKMAN M.,ORDER AND REBELLION IN TRIBAL AFRICA. EUR+WWI LAW CULTURE STRATA KIN MUNIC DELIB/GP ACT/RES DOMIN EDU/PROP LEGIT ADMIN COERCE CHOOSE ATTIT PERSON ORD/FREE PWR...SOC CHARTS GEN/LAWS TOT/POP VAL/FREE. PAGE 57 H1147
AFR SOCIETY

B63
GRIMOND J.,THE LIBERAL CHALLENGE. UK SOCIETY INDUS POL/PAR LEGIS PLAN CAP/ISM DIPLOM EDU/PROP GOV/REL CONSERVE 20 PARLIAMENT REFORMERS. PAGE 61 H1227
NAT/G NEW/LIB ECO/DEV POLICY

B63
HOLLANDER P.,THE NEW MAN AND HIS ENEMIES: A STUDY OF THE STALINIST CONCEPTIONS OF GOOD AND EVIL PERSONIFIED (DOCTORAL THESIS). USSR SOCIETY ECO/DEV NAT/G EDU/PROP WRITING...SOC STERTYP BIBLIOG 20 STALIN/J. PAGE 73 H1455
CONTROL ATTIT TOTALISM MARXISM

B63
HUNTER G.,EDUCATION FOR A DEVELOPING REGION: A STUDY IN EAST AFRICA. AFR TANZANIA UGANDA NAT/G TEC/DEV INGP/REL ADJUST LITERACY ATTIT 20 AFRICA/E. PAGE 75 H1501
EDU/PROP POLICY ECO/UNDEV EFFICIENCY

B63
JAIRAZBHOY R.A.,FOREIGN INFLUENCE IN ANCIENT INDIA. INDIA ELITES SECT DIPLOM EDU/PROP COLONIAL REGION GP/REL...ART/METH LING WORSHIP +/14 GRECO/ROMN MESOPOTAM PERSIA PARTH/SASS. PAGE 79 H1587
CULTURE SOCIETY COERCE DOMIN

B63
KAPP W.K.,HINDU CULTURE: ECONOMIC DEVELOPMENT AND ECONOMIC PLANNING IN INDIA. INDIA S/ASIA CULTURE ECO/TAC EDU/PROP ADMIN ALL/VALS...POLICY MGT TIME/SEQ VAL/FREE 20. PAGE 83 H1660
SECT ECO/UNDEV

B63
KHADDURI M.,MODERN LIBYA: A STUDY IN POLITICAL DEVELOPMENT. EUR+WWI ISLAM LIBYA ELITES INT/ORG POL/PAR FORCES DIPLOM FOR/AID DOMIN EDU/PROP LEGIT NAT/LISM DRIVE RIGID/FLEX SKILL...CONCPT TIME/SEQ TREND 20. PAGE 85 H1704
NAT/G STRUCT

B63
KURZMAN D.,SUBVERSION OF THE INNOCENTS: PATTERNS OF COMMUNIST PENETRATION OF AFRICA, THE MIDDLE EAST AND AFRICA. AFR ASIA ISLAM S/ASIA CULTURE NAT/G FORCES PLAN EDU/PROP ADMIN ATTIT...CONCPT INT UNPLAN/INT TIME/SEQ. PAGE 89 H1785
COM COERCE

B63
LAMB B.P.,INDIA: A WORLD IN TRANSITION. INDIA ECO/UNDEV SECT EDU/PROP COLONIAL HABITAT ORD/FREE ...GEOG CHARTS BIBLIOG SOC/INTEG 20. PAGE 90 H1799
POL/PAR NAT/G DIPLOM STRATA

B63
LYON P.,NEUTRALISM. ECO/UNDEV EDU/PROP COLONIAL ALL/IDEOS...IDEA/COMP 20 COLD/WAR UN. PAGE 99 H1985
NAT/COMP NAT/LISM DIPLOM NEUTRAL

B63
MCPHEE W.N.,FORMAL THEORIES OF MASS BEHAVIOR. CULTURE STRUCT DOMIN EDU/PROP CHOOSE...MATH 20. PAGE 108 H2149
SOC METH CONCPT ATTIT

B63
NKRUMAH K.,AFRICA MUST UNITE. AFR FUT GHANA CONSTN CULTURE SOCIETY NAT/G POL/PAR DELIB/GP TOP/EX PLAN DOMIN EDU/PROP ATTIT DRIVE...TIME/SEQ CHARTS TOT/POP 20. PAGE 118 H2364
CONCPT GEN/LAWS REGION

B63
PAUW B.A.,THE SECOND GENERATION. SOUTH/AFR INDUS FAM LABOR SECT EDU/PROP MARRIAGE ATTIT...SOC 20. PAGE 124 H2478
KIN CULTURE STRUCT SOCIETY

B63
QUAISON-SACKEY A.,AFRICA UNBOUND: REFLECTIONS OF AN AFRICAN STATESMAN. ISLAM CULTURE INTELL INT/ORG POL/PAR TOP/EX DOMIN EDU/PROP LEGIT ATTIT PERSON ...CONCPT OBS TIME/SEQ CHARTS STERTYP 20 UN. PAGE 129 H2571
AFR BIOG

B63
RUITENBEER H.M.,THE DILEMMA OF ORGANIZATIONAL SOCIETY. CULTURE ECO/DEV MUNIC SECT TEC/DEV EDU/PROP NAT/LISM ORD/FREE...NAT/COMP 20 RIESMAN/D WHYTE/WF MERTON/R MEAD/MARG JASPERS/K. PAGE 136 H2716
PERSON ROLE ADMIN WORKER

B63
SETON-WATSON H.,THE NEW IMPERIALISM. COM EUR+WWI MOD/EUR ECO/UNDEV NAT/G FORCES DIPLOM DOMIN EDU/PROP LEGIT COLONIAL EXEC COERCE GP/REL RACE/REL DISCRIM ATTIT...TIME/SEQ 20. PAGE 142 H2833
ECO/TAC RUSSIA USSR

B63
SHANNON R.T.,GLADSTONE AND THE BULGARIAN AGITATION OF 1876. BULGARIA TURKEY UK DIPLOM COERCE REV ATTIT 19 GLADSTON/W DISRAELI/B. PAGE 142 H2841
EDU/PROP NAT/G PWR CONSEN

B63
SILONE I.,THE SCHOOL FOR DICTATORS. EUR+WWI GERMANY ITALY SOCIETY NAT/G CHIEF EX/STRUC ATTIT MORAL PWR ...HIST/WRIT 20. PAGE 144 H2876
TOTALISM EDU/PROP ORD/FREE FASCISM

B63
SKLAR R.L.,NIGERIAN POLITICAL PARTIES: POWER IN AN EMERGENT AFRICAN NATION. AFR EUR+WWI CULTURE STRATA NAT/G DELIB/GP EX/STRUC LEGIS DOMIN EDU/PROP ROUTINE CHOOSE ATTIT PERCEPT ORD/FREE PWR...SOC CONCPT OBS TOT/POP VAL/FREE. PAGE 145 H2898
POL/PAR SOCIETY NAT/LISM NIGERIA

B63
STEVENS G.G.,EGYPT YESTERDAY AND TODAY. CONSTN ECO/UNDEV AGRI INDUS NAT/G POL/PAR FORCES ECO/TAC EDU/PROP COERCE WAR NAT/LISM DRIVE ALL/VALS ...TIME/SEQ WORK SUEZ 20. PAGE 149 H2983
ISLAM TOP/EX REV UAR

B63
TOUVAL S.,SOMALI NATIONALISM: INTERNATIONAL POLITICS AND THE DRIVE FOR UNITY IN THE HORN OF AFRICA. AFR CULTURE PROVS LEGIS EDU/PROP REGION COERCE ATTIT...MYTH UNPLAN/INT TIME/SEQ SOMALI VAL/FREE 20. PAGE 156 H3118
SOCIETY EXEC NAT/LISM

B63
TUCKER R.C.,THE SOVIET POLITICAL MIND. COM INTELL NAT/G TOP/EX EDU/PROP ADMIN COERCE TOTALISM ATTIT PWR MARXISM...PSY MYTH HYPO/EXP 20. PAGE 157 H3136
STRUCT RIGID/FLEX ELITES USSR

B63
ULAM A.B.,THE NEW FACE OF SOVIET TOTALITARIANISM. FUT INTELL NAT/G POL/PAR EX/STRUC TOP/EX DIPLOM ECO/TAC DOMIN EDU/PROP LEGIT COERCE ATTIT RIGID/FLEX...OBS HIST/WRIT TREND TOT/POP VAL/FREE COLD/WAR. PAGE 158 H3150
COM PWR TOTALISM USSR

B63
VIARD R.,LA FIN DE L'EMPIRE COLONIAL FRANCAIS. AFR FUT S/ASIA ECO/UNDEV NAT/G CONSULT PLAN ECO/TAC EDU/PROP REGION NAT/LISM ALL/VALS...CONCPT TIME/SEQ TREND VAL/FREE 20. PAGE 162 H3248
VOL/ASSN COLONIAL FRANCE

B63
VON DER MEHDEN F.R.,RELIGION AND NATIONALISM IN SOUTHEAST ASIA. BURMA PHILIPPINE S/ASIA INTELL SOCIETY DOMIN EDU/PROP LEGIT ATTIT MORAL ORD/FREE ...SOC CENSUS HIST/WRIT TOT/POP VAL/FREE 20 WORSHIP LONDON. PAGE 163 H3265
SECT CULTURE NAT/LISM

B63
ZARTMAN I.W.,GOVERNMENT AND POLITICS IN NORTHERN AFRICA. AFR ALGERIA ISLAM LIBYA MOROCCO UAR ELITES SOCIETY PLAN ECO/TAC DOMIN EDU/PROP LEGIT ATTIT ...GEOG CONCPT TIME/SEQ 20 TUNIS. PAGE 172 H3448
CULTURE DRIVE NAT/LISM

L63
CORWIN A.F.,"CONTEMPORARY MEXICAN ATTITUDES TOWARD POPULATION, POVERTY, AND PUBLIC OPINION." L/A+17C CULTURE SOCIETY ACT/RES ECO/TAC EDU/PROP PERSON HEALTH KNOWL...GEOG PHIL/SCI STAT OBS INT SAMP MEXIC/AMER VAL/FREE 20. PAGE 34 H0672
ATTIT QU

L63
NASH M.,"PSYCHO-CULTURAL FACTORS IN ASIAN ECONOMIC GROWTH." ASIA ISLAM S/ASIA CULTURE ECO/UNDEV DELIB/GP EDU/PROP COERCE ATTIT PERSON HEALTH KNOWL ORD/FREE...PSY SOC STAT TREND ANTHOL VAL/FREE 20. PAGE 116 H2313
SOCIETY ECO/TAC

L63
ROSE R.,"COMPARATIVE STUDIES IN POLITICAL FINANCE: A SYMPOSIUM." ASIA EUR+WWI S/ASIA LAW CULTURE DELIB/GP LEGIS ACT/RES ECO/TAC EDU/PROP CHOOSE ATTIT RIGID/FLEX SUPEGO PWR SKILL WEALTH...STAT ANTHOL VAL/FREE. PAGE 134 H2674
FINAN POL/PAR

L63
ZARTMAN I.W.,"THE SAHARA--BRIDGE OR BARRIER." ISLAM CULTURE SOCIETY NAT/G DELIB/GP DOMIN EDU/PROP LEGIT ATTIT...HIST/WRIT TIME/SEQ CHARTS TOT/POP VAL/FREE 20. PAGE 172 H3447
INT/ORG PWR NAT/LISM

S63
ARASTEH R.,"THE ROLE OF INTELLECTUALS IN ADMINISTRATIVE DEVELOPMENT AND SOCIAL CHANGE IN MODERN IRAN." ISLAM CULTURE NAT/G CONSULT ACT/RES EDU/PROP EXEC ATTIT BIO/SOC PERCEPT SUPEGO ALL/VALS ...POLICY MGT PSY SOC CONCPT 20. PAGE 8 H0157
INTELL ADMIN IRAN

S63
BECHHOEFER B.G.,"SOVIET ATTITUDE TOWARD DISARMAMENT." COM USSR NAT/G ACT/RES TEC/DEV NUC/PWR ATTIT DISPL RIGID/FLEX PWR...METH/CNCPT TREND GEN/LAWS COLD/WAR 20. PAGE 13 H0252
FORCES EDU/PROP ARMS/CONT

S63
DEUTSCHMANN P.J.,"THE MASS MEDIA IN AN UNDERDEVELOPED VILLAGE." L/A+17C EDU/PROP PERCEPT KNOWL ORD/FREE...SOC INT VAL/FREE 20. PAGE 40 H0809
COM/IND CULTURE

S63
DUDLEY B.J.,"THE NOMINATION OF PARLIAMENTARY CANDIDATES IN NORTHERN NIGERIA." AFR CONSTN CULTURE ELITES STRATA DELIB/GP LEGIS DOMIN EDU/PROP COERCE ATTIT SUPEGO PWR...STAT VAL/FREE 20. PAGE 43 H0854
POL/PAR CHOOSE NIGERIA

S63
HALPERN A.M.,"THE EMERGENCE OF AN ASIAN COMMUNIST BLOC." ASIA CHINA/COM COM FUT KOREA/N S/ASIA VIETNAM/N STRATA NAT/G DELIB/GP FORCES TOP/EX PLAN BAL/PWR COERCE DETER PWR COLD/WAR WORK 20. PAGE 65 H1295
POL/PAR EDU/PROP DIPLOM

S63
HARRIS R.L.,"A COMPARATIVE ANALYSIS OF THE ADMINISTRATIVE SYSTEMS OF CANADA AND CEYLON." S/ASIA CULTURE SOCIETY STRATA TOP/EX ACT/RES DOMIN EDU/PROP LEGIT COERCE ATTIT SUPEGO ALL/VALS...MGT CHARTS GEN/LAWS VAL/FREE 20. PAGE 67 H1343
DELIB/GP EX/STRUC CANADA CEYLON

S63
HARRIS R.L.,"COMMUNISM AND ASIA: ILLUSIONS AND MISCONCEPTIONS." ASIA COM FUT S/ASIA ECO/UNDEV AGRI NAT/G POL/PAR EX/STRUC EDU/PROP COERCE ATTIT MARXISM COLD/WAR TOT/POP 20. PAGE 67 H1344
PWR GUERRILLA

S63
HOSKINS H.L.,"ARAB SOCIALISM IN THE UAR." ISLAM USSR AGRI INDUS NAT/G TOP/EX CREATE DIPLOM EDU/PROP DRIVE KNOWL PWR SOCISM...POLICY CONCPT TREND SUEZ 20. PAGE 74 H1478
ECO/DEV PLAN UAR

S63
HUREWITZ J.C.,"LEBANESE DEMOCRACY IN ITS INTERNATIONAL SETTING." FRANCE ISLAM UK LOC/G NAT/G SECT DOMIN EDU/PROP EXEC ATTIT PWR...TIME/SEQ 20. PAGE 75 H1507
STRUCT LEBANON

S63
LEE J.M.,"PARLIAMENT IN REPUBLICAN GHANA." AFR CONSTN CULTURE SOCIETY STRATA POL/PAR DELIB/GP TOP/EX DOMIN EDU/PROP LEGIT COERCE CHOOSE ATTIT ALL/VALS...CONCPT STAT TIME/SEQ VAL/FREE 20. PAGE 93 H1857
LEGIS GHANA

S63
LOPEZIBOR J.,"L'EUROPE, FORME DE VIE." CHRIST-17C EUR+WWI FUT MOD/EUR SOCIETY INT/ORG SECT EDU/PROP ATTIT RIGID/FLEX ALL/VALS...POLICY HUM SOC TIME/SEQ TREND GEN/LAWS. PAGE 98 H1966
NAT/G CULTURE

S63
MAZRUI A.A.,"ON THE CONCEPT 'WE ARE ALL AFRICANS'." AFR CULTURE KIN LOC/G NAT/G DOMIN EDU/PROP LEGIT ATTIT PERCEPT PERSON KNOWL ORD/FREE...TIME/SEQ TOT/POP 20. PAGE 106 H2110
PROVS INT/ORG NAT/LISM

S63
MORISON D.,"AFRICAN STUDIES IN THE SOVIET UNION." AFR COM CULTURE INTELL REGION ATTIT KNOWL...HUM TREND 20. PAGE 113 H2258
EDU/PROP USSR

S63
NICHOLAS W.,"VILLAGE FACTIONS AND POLITICAL PARTIES IN RURAL WEST BENGAL." S/ASIA CULTURE STRATA FACE/GP KIN MUNIC DELIB/GP LEGIS DOMIN EDU/PROP COERCE CHOOSE ATTIT ALL/VALS...STAT TOT/POP VAL/FREE 20. PAGE 117 H2348
NEIGH POL/PAR

S63
RINTELEN F.,"L'HOMME EUROPEEN." EUR+WWI FUT CULTURE INTELL SECT EDU/PROP ATTIT ALL/VALS...HUM SOC METH/CNCPT TREND GEN/LAWS 20 WORSHIP. PAGE 132 H2631
SOCIETY PERSON

S63
ROUGEMONT D.,"LES NOUVELLES CHANCES DE L'EUROPE." EUR+WWI FUT ECO/DEV INT/ORG NAT/G ACT/RES PLAN TEC/DEV EDU/PROP ADMIN COLONIAL FEDERAL ATTIT PWR SKILL...TREND 20. PAGE 135 H2696
ECO/UNDEV PERCEPT

S63
SOEMARDJORN S.,"SOME SOCIAL AND CULTURAL IMPLICATIONS OF INDONESIA'S PLANNED AND UNPLANNED DEVELOPMENT." EUR+WWI FUT MOD/EUR S/ASIA CONSTN SOCIETY DELIB/GP ACT/RES PLAN ECO/TAC EDU/PROP COERCE ATTIT ALL/VALS...TIME/SEQ 20. PAGE 146 H2927
ECO/UNDEV CULTURE INDONESIA

S63
TANG P.S.H.,"SINO-SOVIET TENSIONS." ASIA CHINA/COM COM CUBA KOREA/N VIETNAM/N NAT/G VOL/ASSN DELIB/GP PEACE PERCEPT PWR...METH/CNCPT MYTH RECORD TREND GEN/LAWS 20. PAGE 152 H3041
ACT/RES EDU/PROP REV

S63
TILMAN R.O.,"MALAYSIA: THE PROBLEMS OF FEDERATION." ISLAM S/ASIA CONSTN PROVS SECT DELIB/GP DOMIN EDU/PROP LEGIT EXEC COERCE CHOOSE ATTIT HEALTH ORD/FREE PWR...STAT TOT/POP VAL/FREE 20. PAGE 155 H3097
NAT/G CULTURE MALAYSIA

S63
WELLS H.,"THE OAS AND THE DOMINICAN ELECTIONS." L/A+17C INT/ORG NAT/G POL/PAR TEC/DEV ECO/TAC EDU/PROP PERCEPT...TIME/SEQ OAS TOT/POP 20. PAGE 166 H3332
CONSULT CHOOSE DOMIN/REP

C63
HSU F.L.,"COHESION AND DIVISION IN THE AMERICAN WORLD" HSU FL. CLAN, CASTE, AND CLUB." CULTURE EDU/PROP CONFER SANCTION PERSON...PSY GP/COMP. PAGE 74 H1484
PERS/REL AGE/Y ADJUST VOL/ASSN

N63
LIBRARY HUNGARIAN ACADEMY SCI,HUNGARIAN PUBLICATIONS ON ASIA AND AFRICA, 1950-1962: A SELECTED BIBLIOGRAPHY (PAMPHLET). AFR ASIA HUNGARY S/ASIA ECO/UNDEV NAT/G EDU/PROP ATTIT 20 UNESCO. PAGE 96 H1922
BIBLIOG REGION DIPLOM WRITING

B64
AFRO ASIAN SOLIDARITY AGAINST IMPERIALISM. AFR ISLAM S/ASIA ECO/UNDEV NAT/G POL/PAR TOP/EX PRESS ...INT ANTHOL 20 CHOU/ENLAI. PAGE 2 H0043
MARXISM DIPLOM EDU/PROP CHIEF

B64
ANDREWS D.H.,LATIN AMERICA: A BIBLIOGRAPHY OF PAPERBACK BOOKS. SECT INT/TRADE EDU/PROP WAR GOV/REL ADJUST NAT/LISM ATTIT...ART/METH LING BIOG 20. PAGE 7 H0138
BIBLIOG L/A+17C CULTURE NAT/G

B64
CAUTE D.,COMMUNISM AND THE FRENCH INTELLECTUALS, 1914-1960. COM EUR+WWI MOD/EUR NAT/G PERF/ART PROF/ORG CREATE EDU/PROP ATTIT PERSON KNOWL MARXISM ...SOC TIME/SEQ MARX/KARL 20 MALRAUX/A GIDE/A SARTRE/J. PAGE 28 H0563
POL/PAR INTELL

B64
CLUBB O.E. JR.,TWENTIETH CENTURY CHINA. ASIA CHINA/COM INTELL NAT/G POL/PAR VOL/ASSN ACT/RES EDU/PROP COERCE REV PWR...TIME/SEQ 20. PAGE 30
TOP/EX DRIVE

H0608

B64
CURTIN P.D.,THE IMAGE OF AFRICA: BRITISH IDEAS AND ACTION, 1780-1850. MOD/EUR SOCIETY FORCES ACT/RES DOMIN EDU/PROP COERCE ATTIT PERCEPT RIGID/FLEX SUPEGO HEALTH KNOWL MORAL ORD/FREE WEALTH...CONCPT WORK VAL/FREE. PAGE 36 H0726
AFR CULTURE UK DIPLOM

B64
FREISEN J.,STAAT UND KATHOLISCHE KIRCHE IN DEN DEUTSCHEN BUNDESSTAATEN (2 VOLS.). GERMANY LAW FAM NAT/G EDU/PROP GP/REL MARRIAGE WEALTH 19/20 CHURCH/STA. PAGE 53 H1056
SECT CATHISM JURID PROVS

B64
FRIEDLAND W.H.,AFRICAN SOCIALISM. ECO/UNDEV MARKET LABOR NAT/G POL/PAR PLAN CAP/ISM ECO/TAC EDU/PROP CHOOSE ATTIT DRIVE PWR WEALTH...POLICY CONCPT RECORD STERTYP 20. PAGE 53 H1063
AFR SOCISM

B64
GRIFFITH W.E.,THE SINO-SOVIET RIFT. ASIA CHINA/COM COM CUBA USSR YUGOSLAVIA NAT/G POL/PAR VOL/ASSN DELIB/GP FORCES TOP/EX DIPLOM EDU/PROP DRIVE PERSON PWR...TREND 20 TREATY. PAGE 61 H1224
ATTIT TIME/SEQ BAL/PWR SOCISM

B64
HALPERIN S.W.,MUSSOLINI AND ITALIAN FASCISM. ITALY NAT/G POL/PAR SECT ECO/TAC LEAD PWR SOCISM...POLICY 20 MUSSOLIN/B. PAGE 64 H1294
FASCISM NAT/LISM EDU/PROP CHIEF

B64
HAMILTON W.B.,THE TRANSFER OF INSTITUTIONS. CANADA INDIA UK LAW AGRI LABOR SECT COLONIAL 18/20. PAGE 65 H1301
NAT/COMP ECO/UNDEV EDU/PROP CULTURE

B64
HARBISON F.H.,EDUCATION, MANPOWER, AND ECONOMIC GROWTH. WOR+45 ECO/DEV ECO/UNDEV ACADEM LABOR SCHOOL WORKER UTIL...IDEA/COMP NAT/COMP. PAGE 66 H1326
PLAN TEC/DEV EDU/PROP SKILL

B64
HEIMSATH C.H.,INDIAN NATIONALISM AND HINDU SOCIAL REFORM. S/ASIA LAW CULTURE SOCIETY STRATA PROVS VOL/ASSN DELIB/GP LEGIS TOP/EX DOMIN EDU/PROP LEGIT ATTIT ALL/VALS...POLICY SOC TIME/SEQ STERTYP VAL/FREE 19/20. PAGE 69 H1385
SECT NAT/G

B64
HUXLEY M.,FAREWILL TO EDEN. SOCIETY ACT/RES EDU/PROP HEALTH...SOC AUD/VIS. PAGE 76 H1513
ECO/UNDEV SECT CULTURE ADJUST

B64
INTL CONF ON POPULATION,POPULATION DYNAMICS: INTERNATIONAL ACTION AND TRAINING PROGRAMS. INDIA KOREA L/A+17C TAIWAN USA+45 WOR+45 FAM PLAN CONFER ...NEW/IDEA ANTHOL 20 CHINJAP BIRTH/CON. PAGE 78 H1561
NAT/COMP CONTROL ATTIT EDU/PROP

B64
JOHNSON A.F.,BIBLIOGRAPHY OF GHANA: 1930-1961. GHANA LAW AGRI INDUS NAT/G INT/TRADE EDU/PROP HEALTH...GEOG AUD/VIS CHARTS 20. PAGE 81 H1618
BIBLIOG/A CULTURE SOC

B64
KELLER J.W.,GERMANY, THE WALL AND BERLIN. EUR+WWI ECO/DEV NAT/G VOL/ASSN FORCES PLAN ECO/TAC EDU/PROP COERCE...POLICY CONCPT INT TREND COLD/WAR BER/BLOC 20 BERLIN. PAGE 84 H1685
ATTIT ALL/VALS DIPLOM GERMANY

B64
LATORRE A.,UNIVERSIDAD Y SOCIEDAD. SPAIN EDU/PROP LEAD GP/REL PERS/REL ATTIT KNOWL. PAGE 92 H1837
ACADEM CULTURE ROLE INTELL

B64
MEAD M.,CONTINUITIES IN CULTURAL EVOLUTION. FACE/GP KIN ACT/RES EDU/PROP GP/REL INGP/REL DRIVE HEREDITY ROLE...TIME/SEQ TREND METH SOC/INTEG 20. PAGE 108 H2153
CULTURE SOC PERS/REL

B64
MELADY T.,FACES OF AFRICA. AFR FUT ISLAM NAT/G POL/PAR SCHOOL DELIB/GP PLAN ECO/TAC EDU/PROP ATTIT ALL/VALS...CHARTS TOT/POP VAL/FREE 20. PAGE 108 H2168
ECO/UNDEV TREND NAT/LISM

B64
MOUMOUNI A.,L'EDUCATION EN AFRIQUE. UNIV CULTURE ELITES INTELL EDU/PROP ADMIN COLONIAL...LING TREND BIBLIOG 20. PAGE 114 H2271
SCHOOL AFR PROB/SOLV

B64
PERKINS D.,THE AMERICAN DEMOCRACY: ITS RISE TO POWER. ASIA USSR LAW CULTURE FINAN EDU/PROP COLONIAL CHOOSE...POLICY CHARTS BIBLIOG WORSHIP PRESIDENT 15/20 NEGRO. PAGE 125 H2492
LOC/G ECO/TAC WAR DIPLOM

B64
PIKE F.B.,THE CONFLICT BETWEEN CHURCH AND STATE IN LATIN AMERICA. L/A+17C CULTURE SOCIETY STRATA DOMIN EDU/PROP LEGIT COERCE ATTIT ORD/FREE PWR WEALTH ...CONCPT TIME/SEQ TREND VAL/FREE. PAGE 125 H2510
SECT NAT/G

B64
RAISON T.,WHY CONSERVATIVE? UK FORCES DIPLOM ECO/TAC GIVE EDU/PROP ORD/FREE WEALTH LAISSEZ ...GOV/COMP 20 TORY/PARTY CONSRV/PAR. PAGE 129 H2583
PLURISM CONSERVE POL/PAR NAT/G

B64
ROSENAU J.N.,INTERNATIONAL ASPECTS OF CIVIL STRIFE. CHINA/COM CUBA EUR+WWI USA+45 USSR BAL/PWR EDU/PROP NEUTRAL COERCE MORAL...NAT/COMP 20 COLD/WAR UN. PAGE 134 H2676
POLICY DIPLOM REV WAR

B64
SANDEE J.,EUROPE'S FUTURE CONSUMPTION. EUR+WWI FUT EDU/PROP...IDEA/COMP NAT/COMP ANTHOL 20 EUROPE. PAGE 137 H2750
MARKET ECO/DEV PREDICT PRICE

B64
SKINNER E.P.,THE MOSSI OF UPPER VOLTA: THE POLITICAL DEVELOPMENT OF A SUDANESE PEOPLE. AFR LAW AGRI FAM KIN POL/PAR PROVS SECT DELIB/GP EX/STRUC FORCES TOP/EX DOMIN EDU/PROP LEGIT CT/SYS COERCE CHOOSE ORD/FREE PWR WEALTH...SOC MYTH VAL/FREE. PAGE 145 H2897
CULTURE OBS UPPER/VOLT

B64
TAWNEY R.H.,EQUALITY. UK CULTURE STRATA ECO/TAC EDU/PROP REPRESENT OWN NEW/LIB...MAJORIT WELF/ST SOC 20. PAGE 153 H3051
WEALTH STRUCT ELITES POPULISM

B64
TEPASKE J.J.,EXPLOSIVE FORCES IN LATIN AMERICA. CULTURE INTELL ECO/UNDEV INT/ORG NAT/G SECT FORCES ECO/TAC EDU/PROP PWR WEALTH SOC. PAGE 153 H3063
L/A+17C RIGID/FLEX FOR/AID USSR

B64
TIERNEY B.,THE CRISIS OF CHURCH AND STATE 1050-1300. DOMIN EDU/PROP CONTROL PWR CONSERVE 11/14. PAGE 155 H3092
SECT NAT/G GP/REL

B64
TODD W.B.,A BIBLIOGRAPHY OF EDMUND BURKE. MOD/EUR UK NAT/G EDU/PROP ATTIT...HUM 18 BURKE/EDM. PAGE 156 H3110
BIBLIOG/A PHIL/SCI WRITING CONCPT

B64
UNESCO,WORLD COMMUNICATIONS: PRESS, RADIO, TELEVISION, FILM (4TH ED.). WOR+45 DIPLOM TV PEACE ...NAT/COMP SOC/INTEG 20 FILM. PAGE 158 H3163
COM/IND EDU/PROP PRESS TEC/DEV

B64
UTECHIN S.V.,RUSSIAN POLITICAL THOUGHT: A CONCISE HISTORY. RUSSIA USSR INTELL STRATA POL/PAR SECT LEGIS EDU/PROP REV WAR MARXISM...ANARCH BIBLIOG 9/20 REFORMERS SLAVS. PAGE 161 H3218
IDEA/COMP ATTIT ALL/IDEOS NAT/G

B64
WARD R.E.,POLITICAL MODERNIZATION IN JAPAN AND TURKEY. ASIA ISLAM S/ASIA CONSTN CULTURE STRATA COM/IND POL/PAR FORCES ACT/RES ECO/TAC DOMIN EDU/PROP LEGIT ADMIN CHOOSE ATTIT ALL/VALS...STAT TIME/SEQ VAL/FREE CHINJAP. PAGE 165 H3307
SOCIETY TURKEY

B64
WRAITH R.,CORRUPTION IN DEVELOPING COUNTRIES. NIGERIA UK LAW ELITES STRATA INDUS LOC/G NAT/G SECT FORCES EDU/PROP ADMIN PWR WEALTH 18/20. PAGE 171 H3414
ECO/UNDEV CRIME SANCTION ATTIT

B64
WRIGHT G.,RURAL REVOLUTION IN FRANCE: THE PEASANTRY IN THE TWENTIETH CENTURY. EUR+WWI MOD/EUR LAW CULTURE AGRI POL/PAR DELIB/GP LEGIS ECO/TAC EDU/PROP COERCE CHOOSE ATTIT RIGID/FLEX HEALTH ...STAT CENSUS CHARTS VAL/FREE 20. PAGE 171 H3419
PWR STRATA FRANCE REV

L64
BERELSON B.,"SAMPLE SURVEYS AND POPULATION CONTROL." ASIA FUT ISLAM L/A+17C CULTURE SOCIETY FAM NAT/G CONSULT PLAN EDU/PROP ATTIT DRIVE ALL/VALS...POLICY RELATIV HEAL PSY SOC CONCPT METH/CNCPT OBS OBS/ENVIR TOT/POP. PAGE 15 H0297
BIO/SOC SAMP

L64
FINDLATER R.,"US." EUR+WWI GERMANY USSR SOCIETY FACE/GP EDU/PROP PERCEPT PERSON ALL/VALS...PSY SOC CONCPT SELF/OBS SAMP TREND 20. PAGE 50 H1001
CULTURE ATTIT UK

L64
MACKINTOSH J.P.,"NIGERIA'S EXTERNAL AFFAIRS." UK CULTURE ECO/UNDEV NAT/G VOL/ASSN EDU/PROP LEGIT ADMIN ATTIT ORD/FREE PWR 20. PAGE 100 H2002
AFR DIPLOM NIGERIA

L64
SYMONDS R.,"REFLECTIONS IN LOCALISATION." AFR S/ASIA UK STRATA INT/ORG NAT/G SCHOOL EDU/PROP LEGIT KNOWL ORD/FREE PWR RESPECT CMN/WLTH 20. PAGE 151 H3023
ADMIN MGT COLONIAL

S64
ADAMS R.,"POLITICS AND SOCIAL ANTHROPOLOGY IN SPANISH AMERICA." FUT CULTURE SOCIETY NAT/G PROF/ORG EDU/PROP ATTIT RIGID/FLEX ALL/VALS ...POLICY GEOG METH/CNCPT MYTH TREND VAL/FREE 20. PAGE 3 H0065
L/A+17C SOC

S64
BARIETY J.,"LA POLITIQUE EXTERIEURE ALLEMANDE DANS L'HIVER 1939-1940." COM FINLAND GERMANY ISLAM ITALY USSR NAT/G FORCES ECO/TAC DOMIN EDU/PROP COERCE WAR PWR WEALTH...HIST/WRIT NAZI TOT/POP VAL/FREE 20. PAGE 11 H0216
EUR+WWI DIPLOM

S64
CATTELL D.T.,"SOVIET POLICIES IN LATIN AMERICA." COM CUBA L/A+17C USSR SOCIETY NAT/G POL/PAR FORCES CREATE ECO/TAC EDU/PROP REGION REV RIGID/FLEX ...GEN/LAWS COLD/WAR 20. PAGE 28 H0560
DRIVE PWR

S64
DE GAULLE C.,"FRENCH WORLD VIEW." AFR ASIA CHINA/COM EUR+WWI ISLAM ECO/UNDEV INT/ORG NAT/G VOL/ASSN ACT/RES DIPLOM ECO/TAC EDU/PROP ATTIT DRIVE WEALTH 20. PAGE 37 H0751
TOP/EX PWR FOR/AID FRANCE

S64
GARMARNIKOW M.,"INFLUENCE-BUYING IN WEST AFRICA." COM FUT USSR INTELL NAT/G PLAN TEC/DEV ECO/TAC DOMIN EDU/PROP REGION NAT/LISM ATTIT DRIVE ALL/VALS SOVEREIGN...POLICY PSY SOC CONCPT TREND STERTYP WORK COLD/WAR 20. PAGE 55 H1102
AFR ECO/UNDEV FOR/AID SOCISM

S64
GRUNER E.,"PRENSA, PARTIDOS POLITICOS, Y GRUPOS DE PRESION EN SUIZA." EUR+WWI MOD/EUR NAT/G EDU/PROP LEGIT PRESS ATTIT KNOWL ORD/FREE...CONCPT STAT CON/ANAL CHARTS 20. PAGE 62 H1241
POL/PAR SWITZERLND

S64
HIRAI N.,"SHINTO AND INTERNATIONAL PROBLEMS." SOCIETY NAT/G PLAN EDU/PROP RACE/REL PEACE ATTIT PERCEPT LOVE MORAL...HUM MYTH RECORD SAMP TREND STERTYP TOT/POP 20 UN CHINJAP SHINTO. PAGE 71 H1423
ASIA SECT

S64
JOHNSON K.F.,"CAUSAL FACTORS IN LATIN AMERICAN POLITICAL INSTABILITY." CULTURE NAT/G VOL/ASSN EX/STRUC FORCES EDU/PROP LEGIT ADMIN COERCE REV ATTIT KNOWL PWR...STYLE RECORD CHARTS WORK 20. PAGE 81 H1624
L/A+17C PERCEPT ELITES

S64
KOVNER M.,"THE SINO-SOVIET DISPUTE: COMMUNISM AT THE CROSSROADS." ASIA CHINA/COM COM USSR ECO/UNDEV NAT/G TOP/EX CREATE BAL/PWR DOMIN EDU/PROP PWR ...CONCPT COMECON 20. PAGE 88 H1760
ATTIT TREND

S64
LANGER P.F.,"JAPAN'S RELATIONS WITH CHINA." ASIA CHINA/COM KOREA S/ASIA ECO/DEV NAT/G POL/PAR EDU/PROP ATTIT ALL/VALS...METH/CNCPT TIME/SEQ TREND 20 CHINJAP. PAGE 91 H1808
RIGID/FLEX ECO/TAC

S64
LANGERHANS H.,"NEHRU'S BITTERNESS." FUT INDIA S/ASIA CONSTN CULTURE ECO/UNDEV ECO/TAC DOMIN EDU/PROP ATTIT PERCEPT PERSON...POLICY 20 NEHRU/J. PAGE 91 H1811
ECO/DEV BIOG

S64
LERNER W.,"THE HISTORICAL ORIGINS OF THE SOVIET DOCTRINE OF PEACEFUL COEXISTENCE." COM USSR INT/ORG NAT/G VOL/ASSN PLAN PEACE ATTIT RIGID/FLEX PWR MARXISM...TIME/SEQ COLD/WAR 20. PAGE 95 H1891
EDU/PROP DIPLOM

S64
LEWIS B.,"THE QUEST FOR FREEDOM--A SAD STORY OF THE MIDDLE EAST." ISLAM ISRAEL LEBANON TURKEY CULTURE NAT/G SECT LEGIS TOP/EX DOMIN EDU/PROP LEGIT ORD/FREE PWR RESPECT...POLICY TIME/SEQ VAL/FREE 20. PAGE 96 H1911
CONSTN ATTIT NAT/LISM

S64
LEWIS R.,"OPINION SURVEYING IN KOREA." ASIA FUT KOREA LEGIS EDU/PROP EXEC ALL/VALS...POLICY CONCPT MYTH TESTS CON/ANAL GEN/METH TOT/POP VAL/FREE 20. PAGE 96 H1915
NAT/G QU

S64
MERKL P.H.,"EUROPEAN ASSEMBLY PARTIES AND NATIONAL DELEGATIONS." INT/ORG DELIB/GP DOMIN EDU/PROP LEGIT CHOOSE PWR...STAT VAL/FREE 20. PAGE 109 H2180
EUR+WWI POL/PAR REGION

S64
MOZINGO D.P.,"CHINA'S RELATIONS WITH HER ASIAN NEIGHBORS." ASIA CHINA/COM S/ASIA VIETNAM NAT/G DELIB/GP FORCES CREATE DOMIN EDU/PROP REV RIGID/FLEX PWR...TIME/SEQ GEN/LAWS COLD/WAR 20. PAGE 114 H2277
VOL/ASSN POLICY DIPLOM

S64
NASH M.,"SOCIAL PREREQUISITES TO ECONOMIC GROWTH IN LATIN AMERICA AND SOUTHEAST ASIA." L/A+17C S/ASIA CULTURE SOCIETY ECO/UNDEV AGRI INDUS NAT/G PLAN TEC/DEV EDU/PROP ROUTINE ALL/VALS...POLICY RELATIV SOC NAT/COMP WORK TOT/POP 20. PAGE 116 H2314
ECO/DEV PERCEPT

S64
NEEDHAM T.,"SCIENCE AND SOCIETY IN EAST AND WEST." INTELL STRATA R+D LOC/G NAT/G PROVS CONSULT ACT/RES CREATE PLAN TEC/DEV EDU/PROP ADMIN ATTIT ALL/VALS ...POLICY RELATIV MGT CONCPT NEW/IDEA TIME/SEQ WORK WORK. PAGE 116 H2327
ASIA STRUCT

S64
POWELL R.L.,"COMMUNIST CHINA'S MILITARY POTENTIAL." ASIA CHINA/COM NAT/G EX/STRUC EDU/PROP COERCE GUERRILLA NUC/PWR WAR...RECORD CON/ANAL 20. PAGE 128 H2551
FORCES PWR

S64
PRELOT M.,"LA INFLUENCIA POLITICA Y ELECTORAL DE LA PRENSA EN LA FRANCIA ACTUAL." EUR+WWI SOCIETY NAT/G POL/PAR PROF/ORG PRESS ATTIT PWR...CONCPT 20. PAGE 128 H2556
EDU/PROP FRANCE

S64
REISS I.,"LE DECLENCHEMENT DE LA PREMIERE GUERRE MONDIALE." GERMANY RUSSIA NAT/G FORCES DOMIN EDU/PROP COERCE RIGID/FLEX PWR SOVEREIGN...RELATIV HIST/WRIT TOT/POP AUST/HUNG SERBIA 20. PAGE 131 H2612
MOD/EUR BAL/PWR DIPLOM WAR

S64
RUDOLPH L.I.,"GENERALS AND POLITICIANS IN INDIA." INDIA S/ASIA CULTURE STRATA NAT/G LEGIS TOP/EX EDU/PROP ATTIT ORD/FREE PWR RESPECT SKILL...POLICY BIOG TIME/SEQ STERTYP VAL/FREE 20. PAGE 136 H2713
FORCES COERCE

B65
ACHTERBERG E.,BERLINER HOCHFINANZ - KAISER, FURSTEN, MILLIONARE UM 1900. GERMANY NAT/G EDU/PROP PERSON...MGT 19/20. PAGE 3 H0060
FINAN MUNIC BIOG ECO/TAC

B65
AIR UNIVERSITY LIBRARY,LATIN AMERICA, SELECTED REFERENCES. ECO/UNDEV FORCES EDU/PROP MARXISM 20 OAS. PAGE 4 H0084
BIBLIOG L/A+17C NAT/G DIPLOM

B65
ARENSBERG C.M.,CULTURE AND COMMUNITY. UNIV FACE/GP ACT/RES EDU/PROP LEAD REGION GP/REL PERS/REL HABITAT ALL/VALS...SOC CONCPT 20. PAGE 8 H0162
SOCIETY CULTURE NEIGH NEW/IDEA

B65
BENTWICH J.S.,EDUCATION IN ISRAEL. ISRAEL CULTURE STRATA PROB/SOLV TEC/DEV ADJUST ALL/VALS 20 JEWS. PAGE 15 H0293
SECT EDU/PROP ACADEM SCHOOL

B65
BETTISON D.G.,THE PAPUA-GUINEA ELECTIONS 1964. S/ASIA CONSTN POL/PAR EDU/PROP PARTIC SUFF CENTRAL CONSEN...OBS CHARTS BIBLIOG 20. PAGE 16 H0324
NAT/G LEGIS CHOOSE REPRESENT

B65
BORTOLI G.,SOCIOLOGIE DU REFERENDUM DANS LA FRANCE MODERNE. FRANCE CONSTN EDU/PROP SUFF ATTIT ORD/FREE ...POLICY DECISION CHARTS BIBLIOG 20 DEGAULLE/C. PAGE 19 H0379
LEGIS SOCIETY PWR NAT/G

B65
BRAMSTED E.K.,GOEBBELS AND NATIONAL SOCIALIST PROPAGANDA, 1925-1945. EUR+WWI GERMANY UK USSR NAT/G FORCES WAR FASCISM...TIME/SEQ 20 GOEBBELS/J NAZI. PAGE 20 H0403
EDU/PROP PSY COM/IND

B65
BRIDGMAN J.,GERMAN AFRICA: A SELECT ANNOTATED BIBLIOGRAPHY. AFR AGRI DIPLOM REPAR WAR FASCISM 20. PAGE 21 H0414
BIBLIOG/A COLONIAL NAT/G EDU/PROP

B65
CENTRAL GAZETTEERS UNIT,THE GAZETTEER OF INDIA (VOL. I). INDIA SOCIETY STRATA PLAN EDU/PROP NAT/LISM ORD/FREE WEALTH...GEOG LING CHARTS SOC/INTEG 20. PAGE 28 H0568
PRESS CULTURE SECT STRUCT

B65
CHARNAY J.P.,LE SUFFRAGE POLITIQUE EN FRANCE; ELECTIONS PARLEMENTAIRES, ELECTION PRESIDENTIELLE, REFERENDUMS. FRANCE CONSTN CHIEF DELIB/GP ECO/TAC EDU/PROP CRIME INGP/REL MORAL ORD/FREE PWR CATHISM 20 PARLIAMENT PRESIDENT. PAGE 29 H0584
CHOOSE SUFF NAT/G LEGIS

B65
CHENG C.-Y.,SCIENTIFIC AND ENGINEERING MANPOWER IN COMMUNIST CHINA, 1949-1963. CHINA/COM USSR ELITES ECO/DEV R+D ACADEM LABOR NAT/G EDU/PROP CONTROL UTIL...POLICY BIBLIOG 20. PAGE 29 H0588
WORKER CONSULT MARXISM BIOG

B65
COWAN L.G.,EDUCATION AND NATION-BUILDING IN AFRICA. AFR CULTURE ECO/UNDEV POL/PAR ACT/RES LEAD SOVEREIGN...METH/COMP ANTHOL BIBLIOG 20. PAGE 34 H0684
EDU/PROP COLONIAL ACADEM NAT/LISM

B65
CRAMER J.F.,CONTEMPORARY EDUCATION: A COMPARATIVE STUDY OF NATIONAL SYSTEMS (2ND ED.). CHINA/COM EUR+WWI INDIA USA+45 FINAN PROB/SOLV ADMIN CONTROL ATTIT...IDEA/COMP METH/COMP 20 CHINJAP. PAGE 35 H0697
EDU/PROP NAT/COMP SCHOOL ACADEM

B65
DOLCI D.,A NEW WORLD IN THE MAKING. GHANA SENEGAL USSR YUGOSLAVIA CULTURE INT/ORG PLAN EDU/PROP GP/REL PEACE MORAL...GEOG SOC 20 COLD/WAR. PAGE 42 H0834
SOCIETY ALL/VALS DRIVE PERSON

B65
GUERIN D.,SUR LE FASCISME: FASCISME ET GRAND CAPITAL (VOL. II). GERMANY ITALY SOCIETY STRATA AGRI WORKER 20. PAGE 62 H1245
FASCISM NAT/G TOTALISM EDU/PROP

B65
HARBISON F.,MANPOWER AND EDUCATION. AFR CHINA/COM IRAN L/A+17C S/ASIA TEC/DEV ADJUST OPTIMAL SKILL ...ANTHOL 20. PAGE 66 H1325
ECO/UNDEV EDU/PROP WORKER NAT/COMP

B65
JACKSON G.,THE SPANISH REPUBLIC AND THE CIVIL WAR, 1931-1939. EUR+WWI INTELL STRUCT COM/IND NAT/G
ATTIT GUERRILLA

POL/PAR LEGIS EDU/PROP EXEC COERCE NAT/LISM DRIVE PWR...INT TIME/SEQ TOT/POP 20. PAGE 79 H1574 — SPAIN

B65
JACOB H.,POLITICS IN THE AMERICAN STATES; A COMPARATIVE ANALYSIS. USA+45 POL/PAR CHIEF LEGIS TAX EDU/PROP CONTROL CT/SYS LOBBY PARTIC...DECISION CHARTS 20. PAGE 79 H1578 — PROVS GOV/COMP PWR

B65
KOUSOULAS D.G.,REVOLUTION AND DEFEAT; THE STORY OF THE GREEK COMMUNIST PARTY. GREECE INT/ORG EX/STRUC DIPLOM FOR/AID EDU/PROP PARL/PROC ADJUST ATTIT 20 COM/PARTY. PAGE 88 H1759 — REV MARXISM POL/PAR ORD/FREE

B65
OBUKAR C.,THE MODERN AFRICAN. AGRI INDUS WORKER CAP/ISM EDU/PROP PARTIC RACE/REL NAT/LISM ALL/VALS MARXISM...SOC IDEA/COMP 20. PAGE 120 H2393 — AFR ECO/UNDEV CULTURE SOVEREIGN

B65
OECD,MEDITERRANEAN REGIONAL PROJECT: TURKEY; EDUCATION AND DEVELOPMENT. FUT TURKEY SOCIETY STRATA FINAN NAT/G PROF/ORG PLAN PROB/SOLV ADMIN COST...STAT CHARTS 20 OECD. PAGE 120 H2399 — EDU/PROP ACADEM SCHOOL ECO/UNDEV

B65
OECD,THE MEDITERRANEAN REGIONAL PROJECT: ITALY; EDUCATION AND DEVELOPMENT. ITALY SOCIETY STRATA FINAN NAT/G PROF/ORG WORKER PLAN PROB/SOLV ADMIN ...STAT CHARTS METH 20 OECD. PAGE 120 H2400 — SCHOOL EDU/PROP ECO/UNDEV ACADEM

B65
OECD,THE MEDITERRANEAN REGIONAL PROJECT: GREECE; EDUCATION AND DEVELOPMENT. FUT GREECE SOCIETY AGRI FINAN NAT/G PROF/ORG WORKER PLAN PROB/SOLV ADMIN DEMAND ATTIT 20 OECD. PAGE 120 H2401 — EDU/PROP SCHOOL ACADEM ECO/UNDEV

B65
OECD,THE MEDITERRANEAN REGIONAL PROJECT: SPAIN; EDUCATION AND DEVELOPMENT. FUT SPAIN STRATA FINAN NAT/G WORKER PLAN PROB/SOLV ADMIN COST...POLICY STAT CHARTS 20 OECD. PAGE 120 H2402 — ECO/UNDEV EDU/PROP ACADEM SCHOOL

B65
OGILVY-WEBB M.,THE GOVERNMENT EXPLAINS: A STUDY OF THE INFORMATION SERVICES. UK DELIB/GP LEGIS WORKER BUDGET DIPLOM 20. PAGE 121 H2409 — EDU/PROP ATTIT NAT/G ADMIN

B65
ORG FOR ECO COOP AND DEVEL,THE MEDITERRANEAN REGIONAL PROJECT: AN EXPERIMENT IN PLANNING BY SIX COUNTRIES. FUT GREECE SPAIN TURKEY YUGOSLAVIA SOCIETY FINAN NAT/G PROF/ORG EDU/PROP ADMIN REGION COST...POLICY STAT CHARTS 20 OECD. PAGE 121 H2427 — PLAN ECO/UNDEV ACADEM SCHOOL

B65
POBEDONOSTSEV K.P.,REFLECTIONS OF A RUSSIAN STATESMAN. RUSSIA LAW ELITES EDU/PROP PRESS ADJUD MARRIAGE ATTIT PWR...MAJORIT TRADIT 19 CHURCH/STA. PAGE 127 H2531 — TOTALISM POLICY CONSTN NAT/G

B65
QURESHI I.H.,THE STRUGGLE FOR PAKISTAN. INDIA PAKISTAN UK CULTURE LEGIS DIPLOM EDU/PROP COLONIAL ATTIT SOVEREIGN 19/20 MUSLIM. PAGE 129 H2576 — GP/REL RACE/REL WAR SECT

B65
ROSENBERG A.,DEMOCRACY AND SOCIALISM. COM EUR+WWI FRANCE MOD/EUR STRUCT INT/ORG NAT/G POL/PAR TOP/EX EDU/PROP COERCE PERSON PWR FASCISM MARXISM...CONCPT TIME/SEQ MARX/KARL 19/20. PAGE 134 H2677 — ATTIT

B65
SABLE M.H.,MASTER DIRECTORY FOR LATIN AMERICA. AGRI COM/IND FINAN R+D ACADEM LABOR NAT/G POL/PAR VOL/ASSN INT/TRADE EDU/PROP 20. PAGE 136 H2728 — INDEX L/A+17C INT/ORG DIPLOM

B65
SCALAPINO R.A.,THE COMMUNIST REVOLUTION IN ASIA* TACTICS, GOALS, AND ACHIEVEMENTS. INDIA INTELL POL/PAR FORCES DOMIN EDU/PROP LEGIT COERCE REV ATTIT CHINJAP. PAGE 138 H2763 — ASIA S/ASIA MARXISM NAT/COMP

B65
SCHULER E.A.,THE PAKISTAN ACADEMIES FOR RURAL DEVELOPMENT COMILLA AND PESHAWAR 1959-1964. PAKISTAN S/ASIA SOCIETY STRUCT AGRI NAT/G TEC/DEV EDU/PROP 20. PAGE 140 H2801 — BIBLIOG PLAN ECO/TAC ECO/UNDEV

B65
SHRIMALI K.L.,EDUCATION IN CHANGING INDIA. INDIA CULTURE DIPLOM FOR/AID GP/REL RACE/REL ATTIT SOC/INTEG 20 UNESCO CMN/WLTH. PAGE 143 H2866 — EDU/PROP PROF/ORG ACADEM

B65
US DEPARTMENT OF DEFENSE,US SECURITY ARMS CONTROL, AND DISARMAMENT 1961-1965 (PAMPHLET). CHINA/COM COM GERMANY/W ISRAEL SPACE USA+45 USSR WOR+45 FORCES EDU/PROP DETER EQUILIB PEACE ALL/VALS...GOV/COMP 20 NATO. PAGE 159 H3183 — BIBLIOG/A ARMS/CONT NUC/PWR DIPLOM

B65
VERMOT-GAUCHY M.,L'EDUCATION NATIONALE DANS LA FRANCE DE 1975. FRANCE FUT CULTURE ELITES R+D SCHOOL PLAN EDU/PROP EFFICIENCY...POLICY PREDICT CHARTS INDEX 20. PAGE 162 H3245 — ACADEM CREATE TREND INTELL

B65
VON STACKELBERG K.,ALLE KRETER LUGEN VORURTEILE UBER MENSCHEN UND VOLKER. DIPLOM DOMIN RUMOR NAT/LISM PERSON KNOWL...SOC QU BIBLIOG 20. PAGE 164 H3277 — NAT/COMP ATTIT EDU/PROP SAMP

S65
"FURTHER READING." INDIA NAT/G ADMIN 20. PAGE 2 H0045 — BIBLIOG EDU/PROP SCHOOL ACADEM

S65
GOLDMAN M.I.,"A BALANCE SHEET OF SOVIET FOREIGN AID." USA+45 ECO/UNDEV BAL/PWR ECO/TAC RENT GIVE EDU/PROP CONTROL COST PROFIT GEN/METH. PAGE 58 H1158 — USSR FOR/AID NAT/COMP EFFICIENCY

S65
ROGGER H.,"EAST GERMANY: STABLE OR IMMOBILE." COM EUR+WWI GERMANY/E NAT/G INT/TRADE DOMIN EDU/PROP COERCE TOTALISM COLD/WAR 20. PAGE 133 H2659 — TOP/EX RIGID/FLEX GERMANY

S65
SPAAK P.H.,"THE SEARCH FOR CONSENSUS: A NEW EFFORT TO BUILD EUROPE." FRANCE GERMANY ECO/DEV NAT/G CONSULT FORCES PLAN EDU/PROP REGION CONSEN ATTIT ...SOC METH/CNCPT OBS TREND EEC NATO WORK 20. PAGE 147 H2941 — EUR+WWI INT/ORG

S65
STAAR R.F.,"RETROGRESSION IN POLAND." COM USSR AGRI INDUS NAT/G CREATE EDU/PROP TOTALISM RIGID/FLEX ORD/FREE PWR SOCISM...RECORD CHARTS 20. PAGE 148 H2965 — TOP/EX ECO/TAC POLAND

S65
THOMAS F.C. JR.,"THE PEACE CORPS IN MOROCCO." CULTURE MUNIC PROVS CREATE ROUTINE TASK ADJUST STRANGE...OBS PEACE/CORP. PAGE 154 H3077 — MOROCCO FRANCE FOR/AID EDU/PROP

S65
TRISKA J.F.,"SOVIET-AMERICAN RELATIONS* A MULTIPLE SYMMETRY MODEL." USA+45 USSR ACADEM ACT/RES EDU/PROP COERCE PERCEPT...NET/THEORY CHARTS NAT/COMP GEN/LAWS COLD/WAR. PAGE 157 H3132 — SIMUL EQUILIB DIPLOM

C65
BORTOLI G.,"SOCIOLOGIE DU REFERENDUM DANS LA FRANCE MODERNE." FRANCE CONSTN NAT/G EDU/PROP SUFF ATTIT ORD/FREE...POLICY DECISION SOC CHARTS 20. PAGE 19 H0378 — BIBLIOG LEGIS SOCIETY PWR

C65
COLEMAN J.S.,"EDUCATION AND POLITICAL DEVELOPMENT." COM CULTURE INTELL STRUCT SCHOOL PERSON SOVEREIGN ...POLICY ANTHOL BIBLIOG/A METH 20. PAGE 31 H0629 — ECO/UNDEV NAT/LISM EDU/PROP TEC/DEV

C65
NEUMANN S.,"PERMANENT REVOLUTION: TOTALITARIANISM IN THE AGE OF INTERNA TIONAL CIVIL WAR (2ND ED.)" EUR+WWI ELITES POL/PAR DOMIN EDU/PROP LEAD CROWD REPRESENT...MAJORIT GOV/COMP BIBLIOG 20. PAGE 117 H2340 — TOTALISM REV FASCISM STRUCT

B66
BARRETT J.,THAT BETTER COUNTRY: RELIGIOUS ASPECT OF LIFE IN EASTERN AUSTRALIA, 1835-1850. LAW ECO/UNDEV SCHOOL TEC/DEV EDU/PROP CONTROL HABITAT MORAL WORSHIP 19 AUSTRAL CHURCH/STA. PAGE 11 H0229 — SECT CULTURE GOV/REL

B66
BERELSON B.,READER IN PUBLIC OPINION AND COMMUNICATION (2ND ED.). UNIV NAT/G PRESS GP/REL PERS/REL PERCEPT RIGID/FLEX...MAJORIT QUANT METH/COMP ANTHOL BIBLIOG 20. PAGE 15 H0298 — EDU/PROP ATTIT CONCPT COM/IND

B66
BRACKMAN A.C.,SOUTHEAST ASIA'S SECOND FRONT: THE POWER STRUGGLE IN THE MALAY ARCHIPELAGO. CHINA/COM INDONESIA MALAYSIA ECO/UNDEV INT/ORG NAT/G FORCES DIPLOM EDU/PROP REGION COERCE GUERRILLA AUTHORIT POPULISM...MAJORIT 20 KENNEDY/JF SEATO. PAGE 20 H0396 — S/ASIA MARXISM REV

B66
BUKHARIN N.,THE ABC OF COMMUNISM: A POPULAR EXPLANATION OF THE PROGRAM OF THE COMMUNIST PARTY OF RUSSIA. USSR STRATA SECT FORCES WORKER CAP/ISM RECEIVE EDU/PROP NAT/LISM TOTALISM 20. PAGE 23 H0468 — MARXISM CONCPT POLICY REV

B66
FAGEN R.R.,POLITICS AND COMMUNICATION. WOR+45 ECO/DEV NAT/G CONTROL ATTIT 20. PAGE 48 H0958 — COM/IND GOV/COMP PWR EDU/PROP

B66
FINER S.E.,ANONYMOUS EMPIRE: STUDY OF THE LOBBY IN GREAT BRITAIN. UK CONSTN LABOR POL/PAR SECT DOMIN EDU/PROP PRESS CHOOSE...CONCPT CHARTS 20 PARLIAMENT. PAGE 50 H1004 — LOBBY NAT/G LEGIS PWR

B66
HANSON J.W.,EDUCATION AND THE DEVELOPMENT OF NATIONS. DIPLOM TASK ADJUST EFFICIENCY...POLICY ANTHOL 20. PAGE 66 H1322 — ECO/UNDEV EDU/PROP NAT/G PLAN

B66
HERMANN F.G.,DER KAMPF GEGEN RELIGION UND KIRCHE IN DER SOWJETISCHEN BESATZUNGSZONE DEUTSCHLANDS. GERMANY/E EDU/PROP ATTIT PERSON MORAL MARXISM 20 LENIN/VI STALIN/J KHRUSH/N. PAGE 70 H1400 — SECT ORD/FREE GP/REL NAT/G

B66
HOWE R.W.,BLACK AFRICA: FROM PRE-HISTORY TO THE EVE OF THE COLONIAL ERA. ECO/UNDEV KIN PROVS SECT INT/TRADE EDU/PROP COLONIAL...BIBLIOG WORSHIP. PAGE 74 H1482
AFR CULTURE SOC

B66
KAZAMIAS A.M.,EDUCATION AND QUEST FOR MODERNITY IN TURKEY. ISLAM SOCIETY SECT NAT/LISM ATTIT ORD/FREE SOVEREIGN TURKS. PAGE 84 H1672
NAT/G EDU/PROP STRATA CULTURE

B66
KEITH G.,THE FADING COLOUR BAR. AFR CENTRL/AFR UK ZAMBIA CULTURE SCHOOL EDU/PROP PERS/REL DISCRIM AGE ...AUD/VIS NAT/COMP SOC/INTEG 20 NEGRO. PAGE 84 H1682
RACE/REL STRUCT ATTIT NAT/G

B66
MAC DONALD H.M.,THE INTELLECTUAL IN POLITICS. GERMANY PERU SWEDEN UK USSR NAT/G CONSULT PLAN EDU/PROP TASK INGP/REL EFFICIENCY RATIONAL ALL/VALS 20. PAGE 99 H1987
ALL/IDEOS INTELL POL/PAR PARTIC

B66
MACFARQUHAR R.,CHINA UNDER MAO: POLITICS TAKES COMMAND. CHINA/COM COM AGRI INDUS CHIEF FORCES DIPLOM INT/TRADE EDU/PROP TASK REV ADJUST...ANTHOL 20 MAO. PAGE 100 H1992
ECO/UNDEV TEC/DEV ECO/TAC ADMIN

B66
MAICHEL K.,CATALOG OF SOVIET AND RUSSIAN NEWSPAPERS AT THE HOOVER INSTITUTION OF WAR, REVOLUTION AND PEACE. USSR NAT/G EDU/PROP LEAD REV WAR PEACE ATTIT 19/20. PAGE 101 H2017
BIBLIOG/A PRESS COM MARXISM

B66
O'NEILL R.J.,THE GERMAN ARMY AND THE NAZI PARTY, 1933-1939. GERMANY ELITES NAT/G EDU/PROP CONTROL LEAD COERCE WAR...POLICY INT TIME/SEQ BIBLIOG 20 HITLER/A NAZI. PAGE 120 H2391
CIVMIL/REL FORCES FASCISM POL/PAR

B66
OECD DEVELOPMENT CENTRE,CATALOGUE OF SOCIAL AND ECONOMIC DEVELOPMENT INSTITUTES AND PROGRAMMES* RESEARCH. ACT/RES PLAN TEC/DEV EDU/PROP...SOC GP/COMP NAT/COMP. PAGE 120 H2403
ECO/UNDEV ECO/DEV R+D ACADEM

B66
RAEFF M.,ORIGINS OF THE RUSSIAN INTELLIGENTSIA: THE EIGHTEENTH-CENTURY NOBILITY. RUSSIA FAM NAT/G EDU/PROP ADMIN PERS/REL ATTIT...HUM BIOG 18. PAGE 129 H2580
INTELL ELITES STRATA CONSERVE

B66
SAINDERICHIN P.,HISTORIE SECRETE D'UNE ELECTION, DECEMBER 5-19, 1965. FRANCE NAT/G DELIB/GP LEGIS PLAN EDU/PROP TV SOCISM...MARXIST 20 DEGAULLE/C. PAGE 137 H2731
CHOOSE CHIEF PROB/SOLV POL/PAR

B66
SCHATTEN F.,COMMUNISM IN AFRICA. AFR GHANA GUINEA MALI CULTURE ECO/UNDEV LABOR SECT ECO/TAC EDU/PROP REV 20. PAGE 139 H2774
COLONIAL NAT/LISM MARXISM DIPLOM

B66
SYMONDS R.,THE BRITISH AND THEIR SUCCESSORS. AFR CEYLON INDIA UK SCHOOL FORCES EDU/PROP ADMIN PARTIC ...NAT/COMP BIBLIOG 20 AFRICA/W AFRICA/E. PAGE 151 H3024
NAT/G ECO/UNDEV POLICY COLONIAL

B66
US DEPARTMENT OF STATE,RESEARCH ON AFRICA (EXTERNAL RESEARCH LIST NO 5-25). LAW CULTURE ECO/UNDEV POL/PAR DIPLOM EDU/PROP LEAD REGION MARXISM...GEOG LING WORSHIP 20. PAGE 159 H3188
BIBLIOG/A ASIA S/ASIA NAT/G

B66
US DEPARTMENT OF STATE,RESEARCH ON THE AMERICAN REPUBLICS (EXTERNAL RESEARCH LIST NO 6-25). CULTURE SOCIETY POL/PAR DIPLOM EDU/PROP MARXISM WORSHIP 20 OAS. PAGE 159 H3189
BIBLIOG/A L/A+17C REGION NAT/G

B66
US DEPARTMENT OF STATE,RESEARCH ON THE MIDDLE EAST (EXTERNAL RESEARCH LIST NO 4-25). GREECE ISRAEL SYRIA UAR YEMEN CULTURE SOCIETY POL/PAR SECT DIPLOM EDU/PROP WAR NAT/LISM...GEOG GOV/COMP 20. PAGE 160 H3190
BIBLIOG/A ISLAM NAT/G REGION

B66
US DEPARTMENT OF STATE,RESEARCH ON THE USSR AND EASTERN EUROPE (EXTERNAL RESEARCH LIST NO 1-25). USSR LAW CULTURE SOCIETY NAT/G TEC/DEV DIPLOM EDU/PROP REGION...GEOG LING. PAGE 160 H3191
BIBLIOG/A EUR+WWI COM MARXISM

B66
US DEPARTMENT OF STATE,RESEARCH ON WESTERN EUROPE, GREAT BRITAIN, AND CANADA (EXTERNAL RESEARCH LIST NO 3-25). CANADA GERMANY/W UK LAW CULTURE NAT/G POL/PAR FORCES EDU/PROP REGION MARXISM...GEOG SOC WORSHIP 20 CMN/WLTH. PAGE 160 H3192
BIBLIOG/A EUR+WWI DIPLOM

B66
WANG Y.C.,CHINESE INTELLECTUALS AND THE WEST 1872-1949. ASIA ELITES LEAD STRANGE ROLE MARXISM ...CHARTS 19/20. PAGE 165 H3301
INTELL EDU/PROP CULTURE SOCIETY

S66
HAIGH G.,"FIELD TRAINING IN HUMAN RELATIONS FOR THE PEACE CORPS." CONSULT CREATE EDU/PROP ADMIN TASK GP/REL ATTIT PERSON...PSY OBS SOC/EXP PEACE/CORP. PAGE 64 H1276
CULTURE PERS/REL FOR/AID ADJUST

S66
TURKEVICH J.,"SOVIET SCIENCE APPRAISED." USA+45 R+D ACADEM FORCES DIPLOM EDU/PROP WAR EFFICIENCY PEACE SKILL OBS. PAGE 157 H3137
USSR TEC/DEV NAT/COMP ATTIT

B67
BARNETT A.D.,CADRES, BUREAUCRACY, AND POLITICAL POWER IN COMMUNIST CHINA. CHINA/COM ELITES LOC/G NAT/G INGP/REL...SOC INT DICTIONARY 20. PAGE 11 H0224
GOV/REL STRUCT MARXISM EDU/PROP

B67
COWLES M.,PERSPECTIVES IN THE EDUCATION OF DISADVANTAGED CHILDREN. CULTURE OP/RES PLAN PERS/REL ADJUST HABITAT PERCEPT KNOWL WEALTH ...SOC/WK IDEA/COMP ANTHOL 20. PAGE 34 H0686
EDU/PROP AGE/C TEC/DEV SCHOOL

B67
DENISON E.F.,WHY GROWTH RATES DIFFER; POSTWAR EXPERIENCE IN NINE WESTERN COUNTRIES. WOR+45 FINAN WORKER TEC/DEV EDU/PROP PRICE PRODUC WEALTH ...ECOMETRIC STAT CHARTS BIBLIOG. PAGE 40 H0791
METH NAT/COMP ECO/DEV ECO/TAC

B67
KAROL K.S.,CHINA, THE OTHER COMMUNISM (TRANS. BY TOM BAISTOW). CHINA/COM CULTURE INDUS FORCES DIPLOM EDU/PROP CONTROL EXEC NUC/PWR ATTIT...SOC CHARTS 20. PAGE 83 H1663
NAT/G POL/PAR MARXISM INGP/REL

B67
LAMBERT W.E.,CHILDREN'S VIEWS OF FOREIGN PEOPLES: A CROSS-NATIONAL STUDY. UNIV CULTURE EDU/PROP RACE/REL ATTIT PERCEPT ROLE...STAT STAND/INT CHARTS GP/COMP NAT/COMP. PAGE 90 H1802
AGE/C STRANGE GP/REL STERTYP

B67
MCLAUGHLIN M.R.,RELIGIOUS EDUCATION AND THE STATE: DEMOCRACY FINDS A WAY. CANADA EUR+WWI GP/REL POPULISM...CATH NAT/COMP 20 AUSTRAL. PAGE 107 H2141
SECT NAT/G EDU/PROP POLICY

B67
MEHDI M.T.,PEACE IN THE MIDDLE EAST. ISRAEL SOCIETY NAT/G PLAN EDU/PROP NAT/LISM DRIVE...IDEA/COMP 20 JEWS. PAGE 108 H2160
ISLAM DIPLOM GP/REL COERCE

B67
MICKIEWICZ E.P.,SOVIET POLITICAL SCHOOLS: THE COMMUNIST PARTY ADULT INSTRUCTION SYSTEM. COM USSR INTELL SCHOOL WORKER CREATE PRESS ADMIN CONTROL ATTIT KNOWL...PROG/TEAC SOC/INTEG 20 COM/PARTY. PAGE 110 H2200
NAT/G EDU/PROP AGE/A MARXISM

B67
PIKE F.B.,FREEDOM AND REFORM IN LATIN AMERICA. BRAZIL URUGUAY CONSTN CULTURE SECT DIPLOM EDU/PROP PARTIC DRIVE ALL/VALS CATHISM...GEOG ANTHOL BIBLIOG REFORMERS BOLIV. PAGE 126 H2511
L/A+17C ORD/FREE ECO/UNDEV REV

B67
POMEROY W.J.,HALF A CENTURY OF SOCIALISM. USSR LAW AGRI INDUS NAT/G CREATE DIPLOM EDU/PROP PERSON ORD/FREE WEALTH...POLICY TREND 20. PAGE 127 H2541
SOCISM MARXISM COM SOCIETY

B67
RIESMAN D.,CONVERSATIONS IN JAPAN: MODERNIZATION, POLITICS, AND CULTURE. CHINA/COM STRATA STRUCT ECO/DEV INDUS ACADEM EDU/PROP...ART/METH SOC MODAL INT IDEA/COMP SOC/INTEG 20 CHINJAP HIROSHIMA. PAGE 131 H2629
CULTURE SOCIETY ASIA

B67
RUDMAN H.C.,THE SCHOOL AND STATE IN THE USSR. COM USSR ACADEM LABOR LOC/G PUB/INST EDU/PROP GP/REL ROLE...POLICY DECISION MGT CHARTS 20. PAGE 136 H2712
SCHOOL ADMIN NAT/G POL/PAR

L67
EGBERT D.D.,"THE IDEA OF 'AVANT-GARDE' IN ART AND POLITICS." USSR CULTURE INTELL POL/PAR CREATE EDU/PROP CONTROL REV ANOMIE DRIVE ROLE...IDEA/COMP 20. PAGE 45 H0895
ART/METH COM ATTIT

L67
EINAUDI L.,"ANNOTATED BIBLIOGRAPHY OF LATIN AMERICAN MILITARY JOURNALS" LAW TEC/DEV DOMIN EDU/PROP COERCE WAR CIVMIL/REL 20. PAGE 45 H0899
BIBLIOG/A NAT/G FORCES L/A+17C

L67
GALTUNG J.,"ON THE EFFECTS OF INTERNATIONAL ECONOMIC SANCTIONS, WITH EXAMPLES FROM THE CASE OF RHODESIA." NAT/G DIPLOM EDU/PROP ADJUST EFFICIENCY ATTIT MORAL...OBS CHARTS 20. PAGE 55 H1091
SANCTION ECO/TAC INT/TRADE ECO/UNDEV

L67
GLAZER M.,"LAS ACTITUDES Y ACTIVIDADES POLITICAS DE LOS ESTUDIANTES DE LA UNIVERSIDAD DE CHILE." CHILE NAT/G POL/PAR EDU/PROP LOBBY ATTIT 20. PAGE 57 H1141
ACADEM AGE/Y PARTIC ELITES

L67
GRAUBARD S.R.,"TOWARD THE YEAR 2000: WORK IN PROGRESS." FUT ACADEM SECT DELIB/GP DIPLOM EDU/PROP AGE/Y PERSON ROLE...PSY ANTHOL. PAGE 60 H1199
PREDICT PROB/SOLV SOCIETY CULTURE

L67
LATIN AMERICAN STUDIES ASSN,"RESEARCH ON EDUCATION IN LATIN AMERICA." L/A+17C NAT/G HABITAT...GOV/COMP
EDU/PROP SCHOOL

ANTHOL 20. PAGE 92 H1836 ACADEM R+D

L67
PICKERING J.F.,"RECRUITMENT TO THE ADMINISTRATIVE CLASS, 1960-1964: PART 2" UK STRATA NAT/G WORKER ...STAT CHARTS 20. PAGE 125 H2505 PERS/COMP ADMIN KNO/TEST EDU/PROP

L67
UNESCO,"APARTHEID." SOUTH/AFR STRUCT KIN SCHOOL SECT WORKER DOMIN EDU/PROP REGION RACE/REL ISOLAT 20. PAGE 158 H3164 DISCRIM CULTURE COERCE COLONIAL

S67
ALGER C.F.,"INTERNATIONALIZING COLLEGES AND UNIVERSITIES." WOR+45...NAT/COMP SIMUL. PAGE 5 H0104 DIPLOM EDU/PROP ACADEM GP/REL

S67
ALPANDER G.G.,"ENTREPRENEURS AND PRIVATE ENTERPRISE IN TURKEY." TURKEY INDUS PROC/MFG EDU/PROP ATTIT DRIVE WEALTH...GEOG MGT SOC STAT TREND CHARTS 20. PAGE 6 H0114 ECO/UNDEV LG/CO NAT/G POLICY

S67
BASOV V.,"THE DEVELOPMENT OF PUBLIC EDUCATION AND THE BUDGET." USSR NAT/G CONTROL REV COST AGE...STAT 20. PAGE 12 H0235 BUDGET GIVE EDU/PROP SCHOOL

S67
BHATNAGAR J.K.,"THE VALUES AND ATTITUDES OF SOME INDIAN AND BRITISH STUDENTS." INDIA UK ECO/UNDEV LEGIT COLONIAL GP/REL SOVEREIGN...QU 20. PAGE 16 H0328 NAT/COMP ATTIT EDU/PROP ACADEM

S67
CAMERON R.,"SOME LESSONS OF HISTORY FOR DEVELOPING NATIONS." WOR+45 WOR-45 FINAN NAT/G WORKER EDU/PROP PARTIC ROLE...DECISION METH/COMP 18/20. PAGE 25 H0511 ECO/UNDEV NAT/COMP POLICY CONCPT

S67
EPSTEIN E.H.,"NATIONAL IDENTITY AND THE LANGUAGE ISSUE IN PUERTO RICO." PUERT/RICO CULTURE STRUCT NAT/G PROB/SOLV SKILL...JURID STAT METH/COMP 20. PAGE 47 H0931 EDU/PROP SCHOOL LING NAT/LISM

S67
GLOBERSON A.,"SOCIAL GROWTH IN THE DEVELOPING COUNTRIES." CULTURE SOCIETY CONSULT PROB/SOLV SOC. PAGE 57 H1144 ECO/UNDEV FOR/AID EDU/PROP PLAN

S67
HAMMOND R.J.,"RACE ATTITUDES AND POLICIES IN PORTUGUESE AFRICA IN THE NINETEENTH AND TWENTIETH CENTURIES." AFR PORTUGAL NAT/G SECT EDU/PROP COLONIAL ATTIT RIGID/FLEX SEX MORAL RESPECT 19/20 NEGRO. PAGE 65 H1309 POLICY RACE/REL DISCRIM SOCIETY

S67
KNOWLES A.F.,"NOTES ON A CANADIAN MASS MEDIA POLICY." CANADA TV CONTROL ROLE...METH/COMP 20. PAGE 87 H1735 EDU/PROP COM/IND NAT/G POLICY

S67
KROLL M.,"POLITICAL LEADERSHIP AND ADMINISTRATIVE COMMUNICATIONS IN NEW NATION STATES* CASE STUDY OF TRINIDAD AND TOBAGO." L/A+17C TRINIDAD INTELL OP/RES DOMIN COLONIAL LEAD GP/REL CENTRAL EFFICIENCY...DECISION OBS METH/COMP 20. PAGE 89 H1774 NAT/G ADMIN EDU/PROP CONTROL

S67
LANE J.P.,"FUNCTIONS OF MASS MEDIA IN BRAZIL'S 1964 CRISIS." BRAZIL NAT/G FORCES TOP/EX PRESS TV ATTIT PWR...METH/CNCPT 20. PAGE 90 H1807 CIVMIL/REL REV COM/IND EDU/PROP

S67
LEVI W.,"THE ELITIST NATURE OF NEW ASIA'S FOREIGN POLICY." CULTURE ECO/UNDEV NAT/G PROB/SOLV EDU/PROP COLONIAL CONTROL REGION NAT/LISM...NAT/COMP 20. PAGE 95 H1898 POLICY ELITES DIPLOM CREATE

S67
NEUBAUER D.E.,"SOME CONDITIONS OF DEMOCRACY." ECO/DEV COM/IND DIST/IND POL/PAR EDU/PROP REPRESENT ...SOC STAT NAT/COMP 20. PAGE 117 H2331 NAT/G CHOOSE MAJORIT ECO/UNDEV

S67
PONOMARYOV B.,"THE OCTOBER REVOLUTION - BEGINNING OF THE EPOCH OF SOCIALISM AND COMMUNISM." COM FUT USSR WOR+45 SOCIETY STRATA CHIEF CREATE DIPLOM ECO/TAC EDU/PROP SOCISM...NAT/COMP 20. PAGE 127 H2542 MARXIST WORKER INT/ORG POLICY

S67
POWELL D.,"THE EFFECTIVENESS OF SOVIET ANTI-RELIGIOUS PROPAGANDA." USSR NAT/G DOMIN LEGIT NAT/LISM 20. PAGE 127 H2549 EDU/PROP ATTIT SECT CONTROL

S67
READ J.S.,"CENSORED." UGANDA CONSTN INTELL SOCIETY NAT/G DIPLOM PRESS WRITING ADJUD ADMIN COLONIAL RISK...IDEA/COMP 20. PAGE 130 H2602 EDU/PROP AFR CREATE

S67
RENFIELD R.L.,"A POLICY FOR VIETNAM." COM VIETNAM NAT/G POL/PAR VOL/ASSN CHIEF DIPLOM EDU/PROP DETER REPRESENT ATTIT ORD/FREE 20. PAGE 131 H2615 WAR POLICY PLAN COERCE

S67
ROCHET W.,"THE OCTOBER REVOLUTION AND THE STRUGGLE OF THE FRENCH COMMUNISTS." COM FRANCE ELITES SOCIETY STRATA ECO/TAC EDU/PROP GP/REL WEALTH ...MARXIST IDEA/COMP NAT/COMP 20. PAGE 133 H2654 SOCISM CHOOSE METH/COMP NAT/G

S67
SHIGEO N.,"THE GREAT CULTURAL REVOLUTION." ASIA ECO/UNDEV AGRI NAT/G CHIEF ECO/TAC EDU/PROP CONTROL LEAD PWR 20 MAO. PAGE 143 H2860 CREATE REV CULTURE POL/PAR

S67
SLOAN P.,"FIFTY YEARS OF SOVIET RULE." USSR INDUS EDU/PROP EFFICIENCY PRODUC HEALTH KNOWL MORAL WEALTH MARXISM...POLICY 20. PAGE 145 H2900 CREATE NAT/G PLAN INSPECT

S67
SMITH J.E.,"THE RED PRUSSIANISM OF THE GERMAN DEMOCRATIC REPUBLIC." GERMANY/E INTELL NAT/G SECT CHIEF...PREDICT TIME/SEQ 20. PAGE 146 H2913 MARXISM NAT/LISM GOV/COMP EDU/PROP

S67
SZALAY L.B.,"SOVIET DOMESTIC PROPAGANDA AND LIBERALIZATION." COM USSR SOCIETY COM/IND NAT/G POL/PAR EX/STRUC TEC/DEV LEAD ATTIT ROLE MARXISM ...METH/COMP 20. PAGE 151 H3026 EDU/PROP TOTALISM PERSON PERCEPT

S67
TANTER R.,"A THEORY OF REVOLUTION." ASIA CUBA L/A+17C S/ASIA SOCIETY NAT/G ADJUST...CONCPT CHARTS. PAGE 152 H3046 REV ECO/UNDEV EDU/PROP METH/COMP

C67
GEHLEN M.P.,"THE POLITICS OF COEXISTENCE: SOVIET METHODS AND MOTIVES." COM USSR NAT/G INT/TRADE EDU/PROP ARMS/CONT DETER KNOWL...CHARTS IDEA/COMP 20 COLD/WAR. PAGE 55 H1108 BIBLIOG PEACE DIPLOM MARXISM

S68
CHAPMAN A.R.,"THE CIVIL WAR IN NIGERIA." AFR NIGERIA NAT/G PLAN ECO/TAC EDU/PROP COERCE WAR GOV/REL INGP/REL ORD/FREE PWR WEALTH SOC/INTEG 20 BIAFRA. PAGE 29 H0579 REV RACE/REL

S68
SHAPIRO J.P.,"SOVIET HISTORIOGRAPHY AND THE MOSCOW TRIALS: AFTER THIRTY YEARS." USSR NAT/G LEGIT PRESS CONTROL LEAD ATTIT MARXISM...NEW/IDEA METH 20 TROTSKY/L STALIN/J KHRUSH/N. PAGE 142 H2843 HIST/WRIT EDU/PROP SANCTION ADJUD

S68
VERAX,"L'EUROPE ET LA FRANCE SUR LA SELLETTE." FRANCE UK NAT/G CHIEF DIPLOM EDU/PROP GP/REL 20 EEC DEGAULLE/C. PAGE 162 H3242 INT/TRADE INT/ORG POLICY ECO/TAC

B82
MACDONALD D.,AFRICANA; OR, THE HEART OF HEATHEN AFRICA, VOL. II: MISSION LIFE. SOCIETY STRATA KIN CREATE EDU/PROP ADMIN COERCE LITERACY HEALTH...MYTH WORSHIP 19 LIVNGSTN/D MISSION NEGRO. PAGE 100 H1990 SECT AFR CULTURE ORD/FREE

B85
TAINE H.A.,THE FRENCH REVOLUTION (3 VOLS.) (TRANS. BY J. DURAND). FRANCE MOD/EUR SOCIETY STRATA POL/PAR ECO/TAC DOMIN EDU/PROP GP/REL PWR ...GOV/COMP IDEA/COMP 18. PAGE 152 H3036 REV NAT/G EX/STRUC LEAD

EDUARDO O.D.C. H0890

EDUCATION....SEE EDU/PROP

EDUCATIONAL INSTITUTIONS....SEE ACADEM, SCHOOL

EDWARDS A.C. H0891

EDWARDS C.D. H0892

EDWARDS L.P. H0893

EEC....EUROPEAN ECONOMIC COMMUNITY; SEE ALSO VOL/ASSN, INT/ORG

NCO
CARRINGTON C.E.,THE COMMONWEALTH IN AFRICA (PAMPHLET). UK STRUCT NAT/G COLONIAL REPRESENT GOV/REL RACE/REL NAT/LISM...MAJORIT 20 EEC NEGRO COLD/WAR. PAGE 27 H0540 ECO/UNDEV AFR DIPLOM PLAN

B57
ARON R.,L'UNIFICATION ECONOMIQUE DE L'EUROPE. EUR+WWI SWITZERLND UK INT/ORG NAT/G REGION NAT/LISM ORD/FREE PWR...CONCPT METH/CNCPT OBS TREND STERTYP GEN/LAWS EEC 20. PAGE 8 H0168 VOL/ASSN ECO/TAC

B58
HAAS E.B.,THE UNITING OF EUROPE. EUR+WWI INT/ORG NAT/G POL/PAR TOP/EX ECO/TAC EDU/PROP LEGIT FEDERAL NAT/LISM DRIVE RIGID/FLEX ORD/FREE PWR PLURISM ...POLICY CONCPT INT GEN/LAWS ECSC EEC 20. PAGE 63 VOL/ASSN ECO/DEV

H1264

B59
LEITES N.,ON THE GAME OF POLITICS IN FRANCE. ALGERIA FRANCE CONSTN SECT VOL/ASSN ECO/TAC INT/TRADE PARL/PROC WAR SOCISM 20 DEGAULLE/C EEC. PAGE 94 H1871 — POL/PAR NAT/G LEGIS IDEA/COMP

L59
MURPHY J.C.,"SOME IMPLICATIONS OF EUROPE'S COMMON MARKET. IN (COOK P, ECONOMIC DEVELOPMENT AND INTERNATIONAL TRADE,." EUR+WWI ECO/DEV DIST/IND INDUS NAT/G PLAN ECO/TAC INT/TRADE WEALTH...STAT TREND OEEC TOT/POP 20 EEC. PAGE 115 H2298 — MARKET INT/ORG REGION

B60
THE ECONOMIST (LONDON),THE COMMONWEALTH AND EUROPE. EUR+WWI WOR+45 AGRI FINAN INCOME...STAT CENSUS CHARTS CMN/WLTH EEC. PAGE 153 H3067 — INT/TRADE INDUS INT/ORG NAT/COMP

B61
BELOFF M.,NEW DIMENSIONS IN FOREIGN POLICY: A STUDY IN BRITISH ADMINISTRATION. UK NAT/G ATTIT RIGID/FLEX ORD/FREE...GEN/LAWS EUR+WWI CMN/WLTH EEC 20. PAGE 14 H0271 — INT/ORG DIPLOM

S61
RAY J.,"THE EUROPEAN FREE-TRADE ASSOCIATION AND ITS IMPACT ON INDIA'S TRADE." EUR+WWI FRANCE GERMANY INDIA S/ASIA UK NAT/G VOL/ASSN PLAN INT/TRADE ROUTINE WEALTH...STAT CHARTS CMN/WLTH EEC OEEC 20 EFTA. PAGE 130 H2600 — ECO/DEV ECO/TAC

B62
FRIEDMANN W.,METHODS AND POLICIES OF PRINCIPAL DONOR COUNTRIES IN PUBLIC INTERNATIONAL DEVELOPMENT FINANCING: PRELIMINARY APPRAISAL. FRANCE GERMANY/W UK USA+45 USSR WOR+45 FINAN TEC/DEV CAP/ISM DIPLOM ECO/TAC ATTIT 20 EEC. PAGE 53 H1066 — INT/ORG FOR/AID NAT/COMP ADMIN

B62
HENDERSON W.O.,THE GENESIS OF THE COMMON MARKET. EUR+WWI FRANCE MOD/EUR UK SEA COM/IND EXTR/IND COLONIAL DISCRIM...TIME/SEQ CHARTS BIBLIOG 18/20 EEC TREATY. PAGE 70 H1395 — ECO/DEV INT/TRADE DIPLOM

B62
MEADE J.E.,CASE STUDIES IN EUROPEAN ECONOMIC UNION. BELGIUM EUR+WWI LUXEMBOURG NAT/G INT/TRADE REGION ROUTINE WEALTH...METH/CNCPT STAT CHARTS ECSC TOT/POP OEEC EEC 20. PAGE 108 H2154 — INT/ORG ECO/TAC

B62
ROBINSON A.D.,DUTCH ORGANIZED AGRICULTURE IN INTERNATIONAL POLITICS, 1945-1960. EUR+WWI NETHERLAND STRUCT ECO/DEV NAT/G VOL/ASSN CONSULT DELIB/GP PLAN TEC/DEV INT/TRADE EDU/PROP ATTIT RIGID/FLEX ALL/VALS...NEW/IDEA TREND EEC 20. PAGE 132 H2648 — AGRI INT/ORG

S62
THOMPSON D.,"THE UNITED KINGDOM AND THE TREATY OF ROME." EUR+WWI INT/ORG NAT/G DELIB/GP LEGIS INT/TRADE RIGID/FLEX...CONCPT EEC PARLIAMENT CMN/WLTH 20. PAGE 154 H3079 — ADJUD JURID

B63
KLEIMAN R.,ATLANTIC CRISIS; AMERICAN DIPLOMACY CONFRONTS A RESURGENT EUROPE. EUR+WWI USA+45 ECO/DEV AGRI NAT/G CHIEF FORCES PLAN LEAD ATTIT ...CONCPT 20 NATO KENNEDY/JF DEGAULLE/C EEC JOHNSON/LB. PAGE 87 H1731 — DIPLOM REGION POLICY

B63
MAYNE R.,THE COMMUNITY OF EUROPE. UK CONSTN NAT/G CONSULT DELIB/GP CREATE PLAN ECO/TAC LEGIT ADMIN ROUTINE ORD/FREE PWR WEALTH...CONCPT TIME/SEQ EEC EURATOM 20. PAGE 105 H2107 — EUR+WWI INT/ORG REGION

S63
APPERT K.,"BERECHTIGE VORBEHALTE DER SCHWEIZERISCHEN ZUR INTEGRATION." EUR+WWI UK MARKET SERV/IND NAT/G PLAN RIGID/FLEX OEEC 20 EEC. PAGE 7 H0146 — FINAN ATTIT SWITZERLND

S63
LERNER D.,"WILL EUROPEAN UNION BRING ABOUT MERGED NATIONAL GOALS." EUR+WWI FRANCE GERMANY UK ECO/DEV NAT/G VOL/ASSN DELIB/GP BAL/PWR ECO/TAC NAT/LISM EEC 20 DEGAULLE/C. PAGE 95 H1889 — ATTIT STERTYP ELITES REGION

S63
MONROE A.D.,"BRITAIN AND THE EUROPEAN COMMUNITY." EUR+WWI FRANCE NAT/G DELIB/GP TOP/EX ECO/TAC DOMIN PWR...POLICY RECORD GEN/LAWS EEC EFTA 20 EFTA CMN/WLTH. PAGE 112 H2241 — VOL/ASSN ATTIT UK

B64
RAMAZANI R.K.,THE MIDDLE EAST AND THE EUROPEAN COMMON MARKET. EUR+WWI ISLAM ECO/DEV EXTR/IND MARKET PROC/MFG INT/ORG NAT/G TEC/DEV ECO/TAC REGION DRIVE WEALTH...STAT CHARTS EEC TOT/POP 20. PAGE 129 H2587 — ECO/UNDEV ATTIT INT/TRADE

S64
SALVADORI M.,"EL CAPITALISMO EN LA EUROPA DE LA POSGUERRA." INT/ORG NAT/G POL/PAR PLAN ECO/TAC ATTIT ORD/FREE WEALTH...HIST/WRIT COLD/WAR EEC 20. PAGE 137 H2743 — EUR+WWI ECO/DEV CAP/ISM

B65
CALLEO D.P.,EUROPE'S FUTURE: THE GRAND ALTERNATIVES. UK INT/ORG DIPLOM PWR SOVEREIGN ...CONCPT IDEA/COMP NAT/COMP BIBLIOG 20 EEC EUROPE DEGAULLE/C NATO. PAGE 25 H0506 — FUT EUR+WWI FEDERAL NAT/LISM

B65
CARTER G.M.,POLITICS IN EUROPE. EUR+WWI FRANCE GERMANY/W UK USSR LAW CONSTN POL/PAR VOL/ASSN PRESS LOBBY PWR...ANTHOL SOC/INTEG EEC. PAGE 27 H0548 — GOV/COMP OP/RES ECO/DEV

B65
NYE J.S. JR.,PAN-AFRICANISM AND EAST AFRICAN INTEGRATION. TANZANIA UGANDA STRUCT ECO/UNDEV NAT/G DIPLOM FEDERAL NAT/LISM...STAT SOC/EXP BIBLIOG EEC OAU. PAGE 119 H2382 — REGION ATTIT GEN/LAWS AFR

S65
HAYTER T.,"FRENCH AID TO AFRICA* ITS SCOPE AND ACHIEVEMENTS." CULTURE ECO/TAC INT/TRADE ADMIN REGION CENTRAL FEDERAL LOVE PWR SOVEREIGN EEC. PAGE 68 H1370 — AFR FRANCE FOR/AID COLONIAL

S65
KINDLEBERGER C.P.,"MASS MIGRATION, THEN AND NOW." LAW ECO/DEV ECO/UNDEV INDUS LABOR INT/TRADE FEEDBACK REGION RIGID/FLEX...SOC NAT/COMP EEC. PAGE 86 H1714 — EUR+WWI USA-45 WORKER IDEA/COMP

S65
SPAAK P.H.,"THE SEARCH FOR CONSENSUS: A NEW EFFORT TO BUILD EUROPE." FRANCE GERMANY ECO/DEV NAT/G CONSULT FORCES PLAN EDU/PROP REGION CONSEN ATTIT ...SOC METH/CNCPT OBS TREND EEC NATO WORK 20. PAGE 147 H2941 — EUR+WWI INT/ORG

B66
EDWARDS C.D.,TRADE REGULATIONS OVERSEAS. IRELAND NEW/ZEALND SOUTH/AFR NAT/G CAP/ISM TARIFFS CONTROL ...POLICY JURID 20 EEC CHINJAP. PAGE 45 H0892 — INT/TRADE DIPLOM INT/LAW ECO/TAC

B66
HAY P.,FEDERALISM AND SUPRANATIONAL ORGANIZATIONS: PATTERNS FOR NEW LEGAL STRUCTURES. EUR+WWI LAW NAT/G VOL/ASSN DIPLOM PWR...NAT/COMP TREATY EEC. PAGE 68 H1364 — SOVEREIGN FEDERAL INT/ORG INT/LAW

S66
FELD W.,"NATIONAL ECONOMIC INTEREST GROUPS AND POLICY FORMATION IN THE EEC." NAT/G POL/PAR REGION CENTRAL SOVEREIGN...INT NET/THEORY EEC. PAGE 49 H0985 — LOBBY ELITES DECISION

B67
MAZRUI A.A.,THE ANGLO-AFRICAN COMMONWEALTH; POLITICAL FRICTION AND CULTURAL FUSION. AFR INT/ORG VOL/ASSN CHIEF GP/REL INGP/REL RACE/REL NAT/LISM 20 CMN/WLTH EEC. PAGE 106 H2111 — COLONIAL SOVEREIGN DIPLOM CULTURE

L67
KELLEHER G.W.,"THE COMMON MARKET ANTITRUST LAWS: THE FIRST TEN YEARS." EUR+WWI INDUS PRICE ADJUD AGREE CONTROL PROFIT...POLICY 20 EEC. PAGE 84 H1684 — INT/ORG INT/TRADE MARKET NAT/G

L67
WAELBROECK M.,"THE APPLICATION OF EEC LAW BY NATIONAL COURTS." EUR+WWI INT/ORG CT/SYS...JURID EEC TREATY. PAGE 164 H3284 — INT/LAW NAT/G LAW PROB/SOLV

S67
NUGENT J.B.,"ECONOMIC THOUGHT, INVESTMENT CRITERIA, AND DEVELOPMENT STRATEGIES IN GREECE* A POSTWAR SURVEY." GREECE AGRI INDUS INT/ORG NAT/G OP/RES DEMAND OPTIMAL PRODUC WEALTH 20 EEC. PAGE 119 H2379 — ECO/UNDEV PLAN FINAN

L68
CURRENT HISTORY,"DE GAULLE'S FRANCE." FRANCE MOD/EUR WOR+45 INDUS MARKET INT/ORG BUDGET DIPLOM AUTHORIT DRIVE...GOV/COMP IDEA/COMP 20 DEGAULLE/C EEC. PAGE 36 H0723 — INT/TRADE PERSON LEAD NAT/LISM

S68
LUKASZEWSKI J.,"WESTERN INTEGRATION AND THE PEOPLE'S DEMOCRACIES." USSR ELITES ECO/DEV NAT/G VOL/ASSN INT/TRADE AGREE REV FEDERAL WEALTH SOCISM ...NAT/COMP SOC/INTEG 20 EEC. PAGE 99 H1977 — DIPLOM INT/ORG COM REGION

S68
VERAX,"L'EUROPE ET LA FRANCE SUR LA SELLETTE." FRANCE UK NAT/G CHIEF DIPLOM EDU/PROP GP/REL 20 EEC DEGAULLE/C. PAGE 162 H3242 — INT/TRADE INT/ORG POLICY ECO/TAC

EFFECTIVENESS....SEE EFFICIENCY, PRODUC

EFFICIENCY....EFFECTIVENESS

N19
GRIFFITH W.,THE PUBLIC SERVICE (PAMPHLET). UK LAW LOC/G NAT/G PARTIC CHOOSE DRIVE ROLE SKILL...CHARTS 20 CIVIL/SERV. PAGE 61 H1222 — ADMIN EFFICIENCY EDU/PROP GOV/REL

N19
WILSON T.,FINANCIAL ASSISTANCE WITH REGIONAL DEVELOPMENT (PAMPHLET). CANADA INDUS NAT/G PLAN TAX CONTROL COST EFFICIENCY...POLICY CHARTS 20. PAGE 169 H3382 — FINAN ECO/TAC REGION GOV/REL

B30
CANAWAY A.P.,THE FAILURE OF FEDERALISM IN AUSTRALIA. UK PROB/SOLV ADMIN EFFICIENCY ATTIT ...POLICY NAT/COMP 20 AUSTRAL. PAGE 26 H0518 — FEDERAL NAT/G CONSTN

OP/RES

S32
BEARD C.A.,"REPRESENTATIVE GOVERNMENT IN EVOLUTION" WOR-45 AGRI TEC/DEV DOMIN EFFICIENCY ORD/FREE CONSERVE...TIME/SEQ GOV/COMP IDEA/COMP GRECO/ROMN. PAGE 12 H0248
REPRESENT POPULISM NAT/G PWR

B43
CONOVER H.F.,SOVIET RUSSIA: SELECTED LIST OF REFERENCES. USSR CULTURE INDUS NAT/G TOP/EX TEC/DEV BUDGET WAR CIVMIL/REL EFFICIENCY MARXISM 20. PAGE 32 H0644
BIBLIOG ECO/DEV COM DIPLOM

B45
CONOVER H.F.,ITALY: ECONOMICS, POLITICS AND MILITARY AFFAIRS, 1940-1945. ITALY ELITES NAT/G POL/PAR EX/STRUC TOP/EX DIPLOM DOMIN CONTROL COERCE WAR CIVMIL/REL EFFICIENCY 20. PAGE 32 H0646
BIBLIOG TOTALISM FORCES

B48
ROSENFARB J.,FREEDOM AND THE ADMINISTRATIVE STATE. NAT/G ROUTINE EFFICIENCY PRODUC RATIONAL UTIL ...TECHNIC WELF/ST MGT 20 BUREAUCRCY. PAGE 134 H2680
ECO/DEV INDUS PLAN WEALTH

B52
LOPEZ-AMO A.,LA MONARQUIA DE LA REFORMA SOCIAL. MOD/EUR SPAIN CONSTN NAT/G TASK EFFICIENCY CONSERVE ...ANARCH TRADIT SOC CONCPT IDEA/COMP 19/20. PAGE 98 H1967
MARXISM REV LEGIT ORD/FREE

B53
FLORENCE P.S.,THE LOGIC OF BRITISH AND AMERICAN INDUSTRY; A REALISTIC ANALYSIS OF ECONOMIC STRUCTURE AND GOVERNMENT. UK USA+45 USA-45 FINAN LABOR CAP/ISM INGP/REL EFFICIENCY...MGT CONCPT STAT CHARTS METH 20. PAGE 51 H1028
INDUS ECO/DEV NAT/G NAT/COMP

B53
SQUIRES J.D.,BRITISH PROPAGANDA AT HOME AND IN THE UNITED STATES FROM 1914 TO 1917. UK NAT/G PROB/SOLV DOMIN PRESS EFFICIENCY...PSY PREDICT 20 WWI INTERVENT PSY/WAR. PAGE 148 H2960
EDU/PROP CONTROL WAR DIPLOM

N53
VITO F.,"RECENT DEVELOPMENTS IN THE THEORY OF DEMOCRATIC ADMIN" INTL POL SCI ASS'N CONFERENCE ON PUBLIC ADMINISTRATION... FRANCE ITALY UK REPRESENT EFFICIENCY NEW/LIB SOCISM...WELF/ST 20. PAGE 163 H3257
GOV/COMP CONTROL EX/STRUC

B54
BUTZ O.,GERMANY: DILEMMA FOR AMERICAN POLICY. GERMANY USA+45 USA-45 USSR WOR+45 INT/ORG FORCES NUC/PWR EFFICIENCY PEACE PWR...GOV/COMP 20 COLD/WAR. PAGE 25 H0501
DIPLOM NAT/G WAR POLICY

B55
GALLOWAY G.B.,CONGRESS AND PARLIAMENT: THEIR ORGANIZATION AND OPERATION IN THE US AND THE UK: PLANNING PAMPHLET NO. 93. POL/PAR EX/STRUC DEBATE CONTROL LEAD ROUTINE EFFICIENCY PWR...POLICY CONGRESS PARLIAMENT. PAGE 54 H1089
DELIB/GP LEGIS PARL/PROC GOV/COMP

B55
WHEARE K.C.,GOVERNMENT BY COMMITTEE; AN ESSAY ON THE BRITISH CONSTITUTION. UK NAT/G LEGIS INSPECT CONFER ADJUD ADMIN CONTROL TASK EFFICIENCY ROLE POPULISM 20. PAGE 167 H3337
DELIB/GP CONSTN LEAD GP/COMP

S56
ALMOND G.A.,"COMPARATIVE POLITICAL SYSTEMS" (BMR)" WOR+45 WOR-45 PROB/SOLV DIPLOM EFFICIENCY ...PHIL/SCI SOC METH 17/20. PAGE 5 H0111
GOV/COMP CONCPT ALL/IDEOS NAT/COMP

S57
HODGETTS J.E.,"THE CIVIL SERVICE AND POLICY FORMATION." CANADA NAT/G EX/STRUC ROUTINE GOV/REL 20. PAGE 72 H1443
ADMIN DECISION EFFICIENCY POLICY

B58
SCOTT D.J.R.,RUSSIAN POLITICAL INSTITUTIONS. RUSSIA USSR CONSTN AGRI DELIB/GP PLAN EDU/PROP CONTROL CHOOSE EFFICIENCY ATTIT MARXISM...BIBLIOG/A 13/20. PAGE 141 H2813
NAT/G POL/PAR ADMIN DECISION

B59
HANSON A.H.,THE STRUCTURE AND CONTROL OF STATE ENTERPRISES IN TURKEY. TURKEY LAW ADMIN GOV/REL EFFICIENCY...CHARTS 20. PAGE 66 H1319
NAT/G LG/CO OWN CONTROL

B59
SISSON C.H.,THE SPIRIT OF BRITISH ADMINISTRATION AND SOME EUROPEAN COMPARISONS. FRANCE GERMANY/W SWEDEN UK LAW EX/STRUC INGP/REL EFFICIENCY ORD/FREE ...DECISION 20. PAGE 144 H2890
GOV/COMP ADMIN ELITES ATTIT

S59
MENDELSON W.,"JUDICIAL REVIEW AND PARTY POLITICS" (BMR)" UK USA+45 USA-45 NAT/G LEGIS PROB/SOLV EDU/PROP ADJUD EFFICIENCY...POLICY NAT/COMP 19/20 AUSTRAL SUPREME/CT. PAGE 109 H2171
CT/SYS POL/PAR BAL/PWR JURID

B60
BHAMBHRI C.P.,PARLIAMENTARY CONTROL OVER STATE ENTERPRISE IN INDIA. INDIA DELIB/GP ADMIN CONTROL INGP/REL EFFICIENCY 20 PARLIAMENT. PAGE 16 H0327
NAT/G OWN INDUS PARL/PROC

B60
KERSELL J.E.,PARLIAMENTARY SUPERVISION OF DELEGATED LEGISLATION. UK EFFICIENCY PWR...POLICY CHARTS BIBLIOG METH 20 PARLIAMENT. PAGE 85 H1699
LEGIS CONTROL NAT/G EX/STRUC

B60
NEALE A.D.,THE FLOW OF RESOURCES FROM RICH TO POOR. WOR+45 ECO/DEV ECO/UNDEV FINAN INDUS NAT/G PLAN EFFICIENCY WEALTH...POLICY NAT/COMP 20 RESOURCE/N. PAGE 116 H2325
FOR/AID DIPLOM METH/CNCPT

B60
PICKLES D.,THE FIFTH FRENCH REPUBLIC. ALGERIA FRANCE CHOOSE GOV/REL ATTIT CONSERVE...CHARTS 20 DEGAULLE/C. PAGE 125 H2506
CONSTN ADJUD NAT/G EFFICIENCY

B60
ROBINSON E.A.G.,ECONOMIC CONSEQUENCES OF THE SIZE OF NATIONS. AGRI INDUS DELIB/GP FOR/AID ADMIN EFFICIENCY...METH/COMP 20. PAGE 132 H2649
CONCPT INT/ORG NAT/COMP

B61
HUNT E.F.,SOCIAL SCIENCE. DIPLOM ECO/TAC ROUTINE GP/REL DEMAND DISCRIM EFFICIENCY HABITAT ALL/IDEOS ...SOC T 20. PAGE 75 H1497
CULTURE ADJUST STRATA ROLE

B61
NARAIN J.P.,SWARAJ FOR THE PEOPLE. INDIA CONSTN LOC/G MUNIC POL/PAR CHOOSE REPRESENT EFFICIENCY ATTIT PWR SOVEREIGN 20. PAGE 116 H2311
NAT/G ORD/FREE EDU/PROP EX/STRUC

B61
NARASIMHAN V.K.,THE PRESS, THE PUBLIC AND THE ADMINISTRATION (PAMPHLET). INDIA COM/IND CONTROL REPRESENT GOV/REL EFFICIENCY...ANTHOL 20. PAGE 116 H2312
NAT/G ADMIN PRESS NEW/LIB

B61
NOVE A.,THE SOVIET ECONOMY. USSR ECO/DEV FINAN NAT/G ECO/TAC PRICE ADMIN EFFICIENCY MARXISM ...TREND BIBLIOG 20. PAGE 119 H2378
PLAN PRODUC POLICY

B61
ROSE D.L.,THE VIETNAMESE CIVIL SERVICE. VIETNAM CONSULT DELIB/GP GIVE PAY EDU/PROP COLONIAL GOV/REL UTIL...CHARTS 20. PAGE 134 H2672
ADMIN EFFICIENCY STAT NAT/G

B62
HANSON A.H.,MANAGERIAL PROBLEMS IN PUBLIC ENTERPRISE. INDIA DELIB/GP GP/REL INGP/REL EFFICIENCY 20 PARLIAMENT. PAGE 66 H1320
MGT NAT/G INDUS PROB/SOLV

B62
KARNJAHAPRAKORN C.,MUNICIPAL GOVERNMENT IN THAILAND AS AN INSTITUTION AND PROCESS OF SELF-GOVERNMENT. THAILAND CULTURE FINAN EX/STRUC LEGIS PLAN CONTROL GOV/REL EFFICIENCY ATTIT...POLICY 20. PAGE 83 H1662
LOC/G MUNIC ORD/FREE ADMIN

B62
MARTINS A.F.,REVOLUCAO BRANCA NO CAMPO. L/A+17C SERV/IND DEMAND EFFICIENCY PRODUC...POLICY METH/COMP. PAGE 104 H2070
AGRI ECO/UNDEV TEC/DEV NAT/COMP

B63
COLUMBIA U SCHOOL OF LAW,PUBLIC INTERNATIONAL DEVELOPMENT FINANCING IN SENEGAL. SENEGAL FINAN DELIB/GP GIVE EFFICIENCY...CHARTS GOV/COMP ANTHOL 20. PAGE 32 H0636
FOR/AID PLAN RECEIVE ECO/UNDEV

B63
DUE J.F.,STATE SALES TAX ADMINISTRATION. OP/RES BUDGET PAY ADMIN EXEC ROUTINE COST EFFICIENCY PROFIT...CHARTS METH/COMP 20. PAGE 43 H0855
PROVS TAX STAT GOV/COMP

B63
FRIED R.C.,THE ITALIAN PREFECTS. ITALY STRATA ECO/DEV NAT/LISM ALL/IDEOS...TREND CHARTS METH/COMP BIBLIOG 17/20 PREFECT. PAGE 53 H1061
ADMIN NAT/G EFFICIENCY

B63
HUNTER G.,EDUCATION FOR A DEVELOPING REGION; A STUDY IN EAST AFRICA. AFR TANZANIA UGANDA NAT/G TEC/DEV INGP/REL ADJUST LITERACY ATTIT 20 AFRICA/E. PAGE 75 H1501
EDU/PROP POLICY ECO/UNDEV EFFICIENCY

B63
LETHBRIDGE H.J.,THE PEASANT AND THE COMMUNES. CHINA/COM COM USSR NEIGH PROB/SOLV ADJUST EFFICIENCY...POLICY METH/COMP NAT/COMP 20. PAGE 95 H1894
MARXISM ECO/TAC AGRI WORKER

B63
STIFEL L.D.,THE TEXTILE INDUSTRY - A CASE STUDY OF INDUSTRIAL DEVELOPMENT IN THE PHILIPPINES (PAPER). PHILIPPINE WORKER CAP/ISM INT/TRADE TARIFFS RECEIVE PRICE ADMIN COST EFFICIENCY WEALTH...BIBLIOG 20. PAGE 149 H2986
S/ASIA ECO/UNDEV PROC/MFG NAT/G

B63
US ATOMIC ENERGY COMMISSION,ATOMIC ENERGY IN THE SOVIET UNION: TRIP REPORT OF THE US ATOMIC ENERGY DELEGATION, MAY 1933. USSR R+D NAT/G CONSULT CREATE DIPLOM ADMIN ROUTINE EFFICIENCY PRODUC KNOWL SKILL ...NAT/COMP 20 AEC TRAVEL TREATY. PAGE 159 H3176
METH/COMP OP/RES TEC/DEV NUC/PWR

B63
VON BECKERATH E.,PROBLEME DER NORMATIVEN OKONOMIK UND DER WIRTSCHAFTSPOLITISCHEN BERATUNG. GERMANY UK ELITES CAP/ISM EFFICIENCY...CONCPT GOV/COMP
ECO/TAC DELIB/GP ECO/DEV

IDEA/COMP 20. PAGE 163 H3264 — CONSULT

S63
NYE J.,"TANGANYIKA'S SELF-HELP." TANZANIA NAT/G GIVE COST EFFICIENCY NAT/LISM 20. PAGE 119 H2381 — ECO/TAC POL/PAR ECO/UNDEV WORKER

B64
BERNDT R.M.,THE WORLD OF THE FIRST AUSTRALIANS. S/ASIA ECO/UNDEV WORKER PROB/SOLV EFFICIENCY ROLE ...SOC MYTH WORSHIP AUSTRAL ABORIGINES. PAGE 16 H0311 — CULTURE KIN STRUCT DRIVE

B64
COONDOO R.,THE DIVISION OF POWERS IN THE INDIAN CONSTITUTION. INDIA ECO/UNDEV FINAN TEC/DEV WAR CENTRAL EFFICIENCY NAT/LISM PWR WEALTH NEW/LIB ...BIBLIOG 18/20. PAGE 33 H0659 — CONSTN LEGIS WELF/ST GOV/COMP

B64
GOODNOW H.F.,THE CIVIL SERVICE OF PAKISTAN: BUREAUCRACY IN A NEW NATION. INDIA PAKISTAN S/ASIA ECO/UNDEV PROVS CHIEF PARTIC CHOOSE EFFICIENCY PWR ...BIBLIOG 20. PAGE 59 H1173 — ADMIN GOV/REL LAW NAT/G

B64
HAAR C.M.,LAW AND LAND: ANGLO-AMERICAN PLANNING PRACTICE. UK USA+45 NAT/G TEC/DEV BUDGET CT/SYS INGP/REL EFFICIENCY OWN...JURID 20. PAGE 63 H1263 — LAW PLAN MUNIC NAT/COMP

B64
LEBRUN J.,BIBLIOGRAPHIE DE LA FERTILITE DES SOLS ET ELEMENTS DE SOCIOLOGIE RURALE EN AFRIQUE AU SUD DU SAHARA. AFR PLAN TEC/DEV EFFICIENCY PRODUC...GEOG SOC NAT/COMP 20. PAGE 93 H1850 — BIBLIOG/A ECO/UNDEV HABITAT AGRI

B64
RAPHAEL M.,PENSIONS AND PUBLIC SERVANTS. UK NAT/G PLAN INGP/REL COST EFFICIENCY ATTIT...POLICY 17/20 CIVIL/SERV. PAGE 130 H2593 — RECEIVE ADMIN INCOME AGE/O

B64
RIDLEY F.,PUBLIC ADMINISTRATION IN FRANCE. FRANCE UK EX/STRUC CONTROL PARTIC EFFICIENCY 20. PAGE 131 H2625 — ADMIN REPRESENT GOV/COMP PWR

B64
THAILAND NATIONAL ECO DEV,THE NATIONAL ECONOMIC DEVELOPMENT PLAN: 1961-66: SECOND PHASE 1964-66. THAILAND AGRI FINAN BUDGET EFFICIENCY INCOME...STAT CHARTS 20. PAGE 153 H3065 — ECO/UNDEV ECO/TAC PLAN NAT/G

B64
TILMAN R.O.,BUREAUCRATIC TRANSITION IN MALAYA. MALAYSIA S/ASIA UK NAT/G EX/STRUC DIPLOM...CHARTS BIBLIOG 20. PAGE 155 H3098 — ADMIN COLONIAL SOVEREIGN EFFICIENCY

B64
US HOUSE COMM BANKING-CURR,INTERNATIONAL DEVELOPMENT ASSOCIATION ACT AMENDMENT. CHINA/COM USA+45 USSR FINAN FORCES LEGIS DIPLOM CONFER EFFICIENCY...CHARTS GOV/COMP 20 PRESIDENT CONGRESS INTL/DEV. PAGE 160 H3196 — BAL/PAY FOR/AID RECORD ECO/TAC

B65
EASTON D.,A SYSTEM ANALYSIS OF POLITICAL LIFE. UNIV STRUCT NAT/G FEEDBACK PARTIC PERS/REL EFFICIENCY ...TREND CHARTS METH/COMP 20. PAGE 44 H0881 — SIMUL POLICY GEN/METH

B65
FOSTER P.,EDUCATION AND SOCIAL CHANGE IN GHANA. GHANA CULTURE STRUCT ECO/UNDEV TEC/DEV REGION EFFICIENCY LITERACY ALL/VALS SOVEREIGN...STAT METH/COMP 19/20 GOLD/COAST. PAGE 52 H1043 — SCHOOL CREATE SOCIETY

B65
HAEFELE E.T.,GOVERNMENT CONTROLS ON TRANSPORT. AFR RHODESIA TANZANIA DIPLOM ECO/TAC TARIFFS PRICE ADJUD CONTROL REGION EFFICIENCY...POLICY 20 CONGO. PAGE 64 H1274 — ECO/UNDEV DIST/IND FINAN NAT/G

B65
HYMES D.,THE USE OF COMPUTERS IN ANTHROPOLOGY. CULTURE PROF/ORG CONSULT CREATE EFFICIENCY PERCEPT ...CLASSIF LING CON/ANAL COMPUT/IR METH/COMP ANTHOL 20. PAGE 76 H1517 — METH COMPUTER TEC/DEV SOC

B65
INST INTL DES CIVILISATION DIF,THE CONSTITUTIONS AND ADMINISTRATIVE INSTITUTIONS OF THE NEW STATES. AFR ISLAM S/ASIA NAT/G POL/PAR DELIB/GP EX/STRUC CONFER EFFICIENCY NAT/LISM...JURID SOC 20. PAGE 77 H1535 — CONSTN ADMIN ADJUD ECO/UNDEV

B65
O'BRIEN F.,CRISIS IN WORLD COMMUNISM* MARXISM IN SEARCH OF EFFICIENCY. COM ECO/DEV PLAN INT/TRADE WAR ADJUST PEACE...STAT TIME/SEQ GOV/COMP NAT/COMP COLD/WAR. PAGE 119 H2384 — MARXISM USSR DRIVE EFFICIENCY

B65
UN,SPACE ACTIVITIES AND RESOURCES: REVIEW OF UNITED NATION'S NATIONAL AND INTERNATIONAL PROGRAMS. INT/ORG LABOR PLAN TEC/DEV DIPLOM EFFICIENCY HEALTH ...GOV/COMP 20 UN. PAGE 158 H3155 — SPACE NUC/PWR FOR/AID PEACE

B65
VERMOT-GAUCHY M.,L'EDUCATION NATIONALE DANS LA FRANCE DE 1975. FRANCE FUT CULTURE ELITES R+D SCHOOL PLAN EDU/PROP EFFICIENCY...POLICY PREDICT — ACADEM CREATE TREND

CHARTS INDEX 20. PAGE 162 H3245 — INTELL

S65
GOLDMAN M.I.,"A BALANCE SHEET OF SOVIET FOREIGN AID." USA+45 ECO/UNDEV BAL/PWR ECO/TAC RENT GIVE EDU/PROP CONTROL COST PROFIT GEN/METH. PAGE 58 H1158 — USSR FOR/AID NAT/COMP EFFICIENCY

B66
FRANK E.,LAWMAKERS IN A CHANGING WORLD. FRANCE UK USSR WOR+45 PARTIC EFFICIENCY ROLE ALL/IDEOS ...CHARTS ANTHOL PARLIAMENT 20 UN COLD/WAR. PAGE 52 H1049 — GOV/COMP LEGIS NAT/G DIPLOM

B66
FRIED R.C.,COMPARATIVE POLITICAL INSTITUTIONS. USSR EX/STRUC FORCES LEGIS JUDGE CONTROL REPRESENT ALL/IDEOS 20 CONGRESS BUREAUCRCY. PAGE 53 H1062 — NAT/G PWR EFFICIENCY GOV/COMP

B66
GARCON M.,LETTRE OUVERTE A LA JUSTICE. FRANCE NAT/G PROB/SOLV PAY EFFICIENCY MORAL 20. PAGE 55 H1100 — ORD/FREE ADJUD CT/SYS

B66
HANSON J.W.,EDUCATION AND THE DEVELOPMENT OF NATIONS. DIPLOM TASK ADJUST EFFICIENCY...POLICY ANTHOL 20. PAGE 66 H1322 — ECO/UNDEV EDU/PROP NAT/G PLAN

B66
HOYT E.C.,NATIONAL POLICY AND INTERNATIONAL LAW* CASE STUDIES FROM AMERICAN CANAL POLICY* MONOGRAPH NO. 1 -- 1966-1967. PANAMA UK ELITES BAL/PWR EFFICIENCY...CLASSIF NAT/COMP SOC/EXP COLOMB TREATY. PAGE 74 H1483 — INT/LAW USA-45 DIPLOM PWR

B66
KUZNETS S.,MODERN ECONOMIC GROWTH. WOR+45 WOR-45 ECO/DEV ECO/UNDEV AGRI FINAN INDUS TEC/DEV EFFICIENCY INCOME...NAT/COMP 19/20. PAGE 89 H1786 — TIME/SEQ WEALTH PRODUC

B66
MAC DONALD H.M.,THE INTELLECTUAL IN POLITICS. GERMANY PERU SWEDEN UK USSR NAT/G CONSULT PLAN EDU/PROP TASK INGP/REL EFFICIENCY RATIONAL ALL/VALS 20. PAGE 99 H1987 — ALL/IDEOS INTELL POL/PAR PARTIC

B66
SHARMA B.M.,THE REPUBLIC OF INDIA; CONSTITUTION AND GOVERNMENT. INDIA POL/PAR LEGIS EFFICIENCY ...TIME/SEQ GOV/COMP 20. PAGE 142 H2846 — PROVS NAT/G CONSTN

B66
WILLNER A.R.,THE NEOTRADITIONAL ACCOMMODATION TO POLITICAL INDEPENDENCE* THE CASE OF INDONESIA * RESEARCH MONOGRAPH NO. 26. CULTURE ECO/UNDEV CREATE PROB/SOLV FOR/AID LEGIT COLONIAL EFFICIENCY NAT/LISM ALL/VALS SOC. PAGE 168 H3371 — INDONESIA CONSERVE ELITES ADMIN

L66
"FEDERAL, STATE AND LOCAL GOVERNMENT PUBLICATIONS." ACADEM LOC/G NAT/G PROVS SCHOOL EFFICIENCY ...PHIL/SCI ANTHOL. PAGE 143 H2854 — BIBLIOG OP/RES METH

S66
FLEMING W.G.,"AUTHORITY, EFFICIENCY, AND ROLE STRESS: PROBLEMS IN THE DEVELOPMENT OF EAST AFRICAN BUREAUCRACIES." AFR UGANDA STRUCT PROB/SOLV ROUTINE INGP/REL ROLE...MGT SOC GP/COMP GOV/COMP 20 TANGANYIKA AFRICA/E. PAGE 51 H1024 — DOMIN EFFICIENCY COLONIAL ADMIN

S66
TURKEVICH J.,"SOVIET SCIENCE APPRAISED." USA+45 R+D ACADEM FORCES DIPLOM EDU/PROP WAR EFFICIENCY PEACE SKILL OBS. PAGE 157 H3137 — USSR TEC/DEV NAT/COMP ATTIT

B67
AMERICAN FRIENDS SERVICE COMM,IN PLACE OF WAR. NAT/G ACT/RES DIPLOM ADMIN NUC/PWR EFFICIENCY ...POLICY 20. PAGE 6 H0122 — PEACE PACIFISM WAR DETER

B67
GILL R.T.,ECONOMIC DEVELOPMENT: PAST AND PRESENT (2ND ED.). ASIA INDIA USA+45 USA-45 WOR+45 WOR-45 DEMAND EFFICIENCY NAT/LISM WEALTH...GOV/COMP METH/COMP 18/20. PAGE 56 H1127 — ECO/DEV ECO/UNDEV PLAN PROB/SOLV

B67
HODGKINSON R.G.,THE ORIGINS OF THE NATIONAL HEALTH SERVICE: THE MEDICAL SERVICES OF THE NEW POOR LAW, 1834-1871. UK INDUS MUNIC WORKER PROB/SOLV EFFICIENCY ATTIT HEALTH WEALTH SOCISM...JURID SOC/WK 19/20. PAGE 72 H1445 — HEAL NAT/G POLICY LAW

B67
KENNETT L.,THE FRENCH ARMIES IN THE SEVEN YEARS' WAR. FRANCE NAT/G CONTROL LEAD WAR CIVMIL/REL EFFICIENCY ATTIT PWR SKILL CONSERVE 18. PAGE 85 H1690 — FORCES CHIEF METH/COMP

B67
MOORE J.R.,THE ECONOMIC IMPACT OF THE TVA. AGRI INDUS PLAN BARGAIN CONTROL REGION GOV/REL DEMAND EFFICIENCY SOCISM 20 TVA. PAGE 112 H2249 — ECO/UNDEV ECO/DEV NAT/G CREATE

B67
PAPANEK G.F.,PAKISTAN'S DEVELOPMENT: SOCIAL GOALS AND PRIVATE INCENTIVES. PAKISTAN INDUS NAT/G PROB/SOLV CONTROL EFFICIENCY SOCISM...CHARTS 20. PAGE 123 H2463 — ECO/UNDEV PLAN CAP/ISM ECO/TAC

B67
POSNER M.V.,ITALIAN PUBLIC ENTERPRISE. ITALY ECO/DEV FINAN INDUS CREATE ECO/TAC ADMIN CONTROL EFFICIENCY PRODUC...TREND CHARTS 20. PAGE 127 H2545
NAT/G PLAN CAP/ISM SOCISM

B67
THOMPSON E.T.,PERSPECTIVES ON THE SOUTH: AGENDA FOR RESEARCH. CULTURE ECO/UNDEV SECT GP/REL EFFICIENCY ALL/VALS...HUM SOC CONCPT LING 20 NEGRO. PAGE 154 H3080
PROB/SOLV IDEA/COMP REGION ACT/RES

B67
VENKATESWARAN R.J.,CABINET GOVERNMENT IN INDIA. INDIA UK SOCIETY OP/RES COLONIAL LEAD EFFICIENCY ORD/FREE 20. PAGE 162 H3241
DELIB/GP ADMIN CONSTN NAT/G

B67
ZALESKI E.,PLANNING REFORMS IN THE SOVIET UNION 1962-1966. COM USSR NAT/G CONFER CONTROL EFFICIENCY MARXISM...POLICY DECISION 20. PAGE 172 H3446
ECO/DEV PLAN ADMIN CENTRAL

L67
GALTUNG J.,"ON THE EFFECTS OF INTERNATIONAL ECONOMIC SANCTIONS, WITH EXAMPLES FROM THE CASE OF RHODESIA." NAT/G DIPLOM EDU/PROP ADJUST EFFICIENCY ATTIT MORAL...OBS CHARTS 20. PAGE 55 H1091
SANCTION ECO/TAC INT/TRADE ECO/UNDEV

L67
RUTH J.M.,"THE ADMINISTRATION OF WATER RESOURCES IN GUATEMALA." GUATEMALA L/A+17C DIST/IND LOC/G NAT/G EX/STRUC ADMIN GOV/REL DEMAND EQUILIB WEALTH...GEOG MGT 20. PAGE 136 H2723
EFFICIENCY ECO/UNDEV PLAN ACT/RES

S67
AKE C.,"POLITICAL INTEGRATION AND POLITICAL STABILITY." ELITES POL/PAR LEAD ADJUST EFFICIENCY ATTIT AUTHORIT DRIVE...CONCPT 20. PAGE 4 H0088
CULTURE NAT/G CONTROL GP/REL

S67
BERLINER J.S.,"RUSSIA'S BUREAUCRATS - WHY THEY'RE REACTIONARY." USSR NAT/G OP/RES PROB/SOLV TEC/DEV CONTROL SANCTION EFFICIENCY DRIVE PERSON...TECHNIC SOC 20. PAGE 15 H0308
CREATE ADMIN INDUS PRODUC

S67
BRANCO R.,"LAND REFORM* THE ANSWER TO LATIN AMERICA'S AGRICULTURAL DEVELOPMENT?" L/A+17C NAT/G PLAN TEC/DEV BUDGET RENT EFFICIENCY 20. PAGE 20 H0404
ECO/UNDEV AGRI TAX OWN

S67
CARR E.H.,"REVOLUTION FROM ABOVE." USSR STRATA FINAN INDUS NAT/G DOMIN LEAD GP/REL INGP/REL OWN PRODUC PWR 20 STALIN/J. PAGE 27 H0538
AGRI POLICY COM EFFICIENCY

S67
COLLINS B.A.,"SOME NOTES ON PUBLIC SERVICE COMMISSIONS IN THE COMMONWEALTH CARIBBEAN." JAMAICA L/A+17C TRINIDAD UK NAT/G OP/RES DOMIN SENIOR COLONIAL CONTROL INGP/REL CENTRAL EFFICIENCY PWR ...DECISION 20. PAGE 31 H0631
ADMIN EX/STRUC ECO/UNDEV CHOOSE

S67
DOERN G.B.,"THE ROYAL COMMISSIONS IN THE GENERAL POLICY PROCESS AND IN FEDERAL-PROVINCIAL RELATIONS." CANADA CONSTN ACADEM PROVS CONSULT DELIB/GP LEGIS ACT/RES PROB/SOLV CONFER CONTROL EFFICIENCY...METH/COMP 20 SENATE ROYAL/COMM. PAGE 42 H0832
R+D EX/STRUC GOV/REL NAT/G

S67
ELLISON H.J.,"THE SOCIALIST REVOLUTIONARIES." USSR ECO/UNDEV NAT/G INGP/REL EFFICIENCY ATTIT PWR MARXISM...CONCPT IDEA/COMP 20 SOC/REVPAR. PAGE 46 H0911
POL/PAR REV AGRI

S67
GRANT C.H.,"RURAL LOCAL GOVERNMENT IN GUYANA AND BRITISH HONDURAS." GUYANA HONDURAS L/A+17C AGRI NAT/G EX/STRUC ACT/RES REGION GOV/REL EFFICIENCY ORD/FREE 20. PAGE 60 H1196
ECO/UNDEV LOC/G ADMIN MUNIC

S67
JOINER C.A.,"THE UBIQUITY OF THE ADMINISTRATIVE ROLE IN COUNTERINSURGENC. VIETNAM/S SOCIETY STRUCT NAT/G GP/REL EFFICIENCY 20. PAGE 81 H1627
ADMIN POLICY REV ATTIT

S67
KROLL M.,"POLITICAL LEADERSHIP AND ADMINISTRATIVE COMMUNICATIONS IN NEW NATION STATES* CASE STUDY OF TRINIDAD AND TOBAGO." L/A+17C TRINIDAD INTELL OP/RES DOMIN COLONIAL LEAD GP/REL CENTRAL EFFICIENCY...DECISION OBS METH/COMP 20. PAGE 89 H1774
NAT/G ADMIN EDU/PROP CONTROL

S67
LEVCIK B.,"WAGES AND EMPLOYMENT PROBLEMS IN THE NEW SYSTEM OF PLANNED MANAGEMENT IN CZECHOSLOVAKIA." CZECHOSLVK EUR+WWI NAT/G OP/RES PLAN ADMIN ROUTINE INGP/REL CENTRAL EFFICIENCY PRODUC DECISION. PAGE 95 H1895
MARXISM WORKER MGT PAY

S67
MALLORY J.R.,"THE MINISTER'S OFFICE STAFF* AN UNREFORMED PART OF PUBLIC SERVICE." CONSTN ELITES STRATA NAT/G PROB/SOLV TASK CHOOSE PERS/REL EFFICIENCY...DECISION 20. PAGE 102 H2033
CANADA ADMIN EX/STRUC STRUCT

S67
MOZINGO D.,"CONTAINMENT IN ASIA RECONSIDERED." NAT/G DIPLOM REV PEACE ORD/FREE 20. PAGE 114 H2275
ATTIT CONTROL NAT/LISM EFFICIENCY

S67
RICHMAN B.M.,"CAPITALISTS & MANAGERS IN COMMUNIST CHINA." ASIA CHINA/COM ECO/UNDEV NAT/G CONSULT EX/STRUC PLAN EFFICIENCY PRODUC WEALTH MARXISM ...MGT CHARTS 20. PAGE 131 H2623
CAP/ISM INDUS

S67
SALYZYN V.,"FEDERAL-PROVINCIAL TAX SHARING SCHEMES." CANADA LOC/G PROB/SOLV TEC/DEV BUDGET GOV/REL EFFICIENCY 20. PAGE 137 H2746
PROVS TAX MUNIC NAT/G

S67
SEIDLER G.L.,"MARXIST LEGAL THOUGHT IN POLAND." POLAND SOCIETY R+D LOC/G NAT/G ACT/RES ADJUD CT/SYS SUPEGO PWR...SOC TREND 20 MARX/KARL. PAGE 141 H2822
MARXISM LAW CONCPT EFFICIENCY

S67
SINGH B.,"ITALIAN EXPERIENCE IN REGIONAL ECONOMIC DEVELOPMENT AND LESSONS FOR OTHER COUNTRIES." EUR+WWI ITALY INDUS NAT/G ACT/RES REGION GP/REL EFFICIENCY EQUILIB PRODUC WEALTH. PAGE 144 H2884
ECO/UNDEV PLAN ECO/TAC CONTROL

S67
SLOAN P.,"FIFTY YEARS OF SOVIET RULE." USSR INDUS EDU/PROP EFFICIENCY PRODUC HEALTH KNOWL MORAL WEALTH MARXISM...POLICY 20. PAGE 145 H2900
CREATE NAT/G PLAN INSPECT

S67
SNELLEN I.T.,"APARTHEID* CHECKS AND CHANGES." SOUTH/AFR NAT/G PROB/SOLV COLONIAL REGION TASK GP/REL RACE/REL EFFICIENCY PRIVIL ORD/FREE 20. PAGE 146 H2923
DISCRIM NAT/LISM EQUILIB CONTROL

S67
SPITTMANN I.,"EAST GERMANY: THE SWINGING PENDULUM." COM GERMANY/E NAT/G EFFICIENCY MARXISM 20. PAGE 148 H2952
PRODUC POL/PAR WEALTH ATTIT

S67
TATU M.,"URSS: LES FLOTTEMENTS DE LA DIRECTION COLLEGIALE." UAR USSR CHIEF LEAD INGP/REL EFFICIENCY...DECISION TREND 20 MID/EAST. PAGE 152 H3047
POLICY NAT/G EX/STRUC DIPLOM

S67
TIVEY L.,"THE POLITICAL CONSEQUENCES OF ECONOMIC PLANNING." UK CONSTN INDUS ACT/RES ADMIN CONTROL LOBBY REPRESENT EFFICIENCY SUPEGO SOVEREIGN ...DECISION 20. PAGE 155 H3108
PLAN POLICY NAT/G

EFTA....EUROPEAN FREE TRADE ASSOCIATION

S61
RAY J.,"THE EUROPEAN FREE-TRADE ASSOCIATION AND ITS IMPACT ON INDIA'S TRADE." EUR+WWI FRANCE GERMANY INDIA S/ASIA UK NAT/G VOL/ASSN PLAN INT/TRADE ROUTINE WEALTH...STAT CHARTS CMN/WLTH EEC OEEC 20 EFTA. PAGE 130 H2600
ECO/DEV ECO/TAC

S63
MONROE A.D.,"BRITAIN AND THE EUROPEAN COMMUNITY." EUR+WWI FRANCE NAT/G DELIB/GP TOP/EX ECO/TAC DOMIN PWR...POLICY RECORD GEN/LAWS EEC EFTA 20 EFTA CMN/WLTH. PAGE 112 H2241
VOL/ASSN ATTIT UK

S63
MONROE A.D.,"BRITAIN AND THE EUROPEAN COMMUNITY." EUR+WWI FRANCE NAT/G DELIB/GP TOP/EX ECO/TAC DOMIN PWR...POLICY RECORD GEN/LAWS EEC EFTA 20 EFTA CMN/WLTH. PAGE 112 H2241
VOL/ASSN ATTIT UK

B65
EUROPEAN FREE TRADE ASSN,REGIONAL DEVELOPMENT POLICIES IN EFTA. ECO/UNDEV INT/ORG PLAN REGION ...POLICY GEOG EFTA. PAGE 48 H0950
EUR+WWI ECO/DEV NAT/COMP INT/TRADE

EGBERT D.D. H0894,H0895

EGGAN F. H0896

EGYPT....SEE ALSO ISLAM, UAR, EGYPT/ANC

EGYPT/ANC....ANCIENT EGYPT

N
BURY J.B.,THE CAMBRIDGE ANCIENT HISTORY (12 VOLS.). MEDIT-7 DIPLOM COLONIAL WAR...HUM EGYPT/ANC ROME/EMP BABYLONIA GREECE/ANC. PAGE 25 H0495
BIBLIOG/A SOCIETY CULTURE NAT/G

B59
MURDOCK G.P.,AFRICA: ITS PEOPLES AND THEIR CULTURE HISTORY. AFR CULTURE AGRI LOC/G INGP/REL HABITAT ...GEOG SOC LING CHARTS BIBLIOG 20 NEGRO EGYPT/ANC. PAGE 115 H2293
SOCIETY ECO/TAC GP/COMP KIN

B66
IBRAHIM-HILMY,THE LITERATURE OF EGYPT AND THE SOUDAN: FROM THE EARLIEST TIMES TO THE YEAR 1885
BIBLIOG CULTURE

INCLUSIVE (2 VOLS.). MEDIT-7 SUDAN UAR LAW SOCIETY SECT ATTIT EGYPT/ANC. PAGE 76 H1520 — ISLAM NAT/G

EHRMANN H.W. H0897

EIB....EUROPEAN INVESTMENT BANK

EICH H. H0898

EICHMANN/A....ADOLF EICHMANN

EINAUDI L. H0899

EINSTEIN/A....ALBERT EINSTEIN

EISENSTADT S.N. H0900,H0901

EISNHWR/DD....PRESIDENT DWIGHT DAVID EISENHOWER

EISTER A.W. H0902

EL/SALVADR....EL SALVADOR; SEE ALSO L/A+17C

B47
DE NOIA J.,GUIDE TO OFFICIAL PUBLICATIONS OF THE OTHER AMERICAN REPUBLICS: EL SALVADOR. EL/SALVADR LAW LEGIS EDU/PROP CT/SYS 20. PAGE 38 H0764 — BIBLIOG/A CONSTN NAT/G ADMIN

B60
FLORES R.H.,CATALOGO DE TESIS DOCTORALES DE LAS FACULTADES DE LA UNIVERSIDAD DE EL SALVADOR. EL/SALVADR LAW DIPLOM ADMIN LEAD GOV/REL...SOC 19/20. PAGE 52 H1030 — BIBLIOG ACADEM L/A+17C NAT/G

S67
GRIEB K.J.,"THE UNITED STATES AND THE CENTRAL AMERICAN CONFEDERATION." COSTA/RICA EL/SALVADR GUATEMALA HONDURAS L/A+17C NICARAGUA NAT/G FORCES CONFER AGREE EXEC ARMS/CONT REV WAR PEACE ATTIT 20. PAGE 60 H1212 — INT/ORG DIPLOM POLICY REGION

ELAHI K.N. H0903

ELAZAR D.J. H0904

ELDRIDGE H.T. H0905

ELECT/COLL....ELECTORAL COLLEGE

ELECTIONS....SEE CHOOSE

ELECTORAL COLLEGE....SEE ELECT/COLL

ELIA O.H. H0942

ELIAS T.O. H0906

ELITES....POWER-DOMINANT GROUPINGS OF A SOCIETY

B00
HOBSON J.A.,THE WAR IN SOUTH AFRICA: ITS CAUSES AND EFFECTS. NETHERLAND SOUTH/AFR UK ELITES AGRI EXTR/IND POL/PAR DIPLOM PRESS RACE/REL ATTIT ORD/FREE SOVEREIGN...INT 19 NEGRO. PAGE 72 H1439 — WAR DOMIN POLICY NAT/G

B14
OPPENHEIMER F.,THE STATE. FUT SOCIETY STRATA STRUCT WORKER CAP/ISM WAR GP/REL SOCISM...SOC NAT/COMP SOC/INTEG. PAGE 121 H2424 — ELITES OWN DOMIN NAT/G

B16
TREITSCHKE H.,POLITICS. UNIV SOCIETY STRATA NAT/G EX/STRUC LEGIS DOMIN EDU/PROP ATTIT PWR RESPECT ...CONCPT TIME/SEQ GEN/LAWS TOT/POP 20. PAGE 157 H3129 — EXEC ELITES GERMANY

N19
ADMINISTRATIVE STAFF COLLEGE,THE ACCOUNTABILITY OF GOVERNMENT DEPARTMENTS (PAMPHLET) (REV. ED.). UK CONSTN FINAN NAT/G CONSULT ADMIN INGP/REL CONSEN PRIVIL 20 PARLIAMENT. PAGE 3 H0070 — PARL/PROC ELITES SANCTION PROB/SOLV

N19
MAO TSE-TUNG,ON SOME IMPORTANT PROBLEMS OF THE PARTY'S PRESENT POLICY. CHINA/COM CONSTN ELITES INTELL AGRI DOMIN EDU/PROP REV REPRESENT GP/REL OWN PEACE ORD/FREE 20 COM/PARTY. PAGE 102 H2044 — POLICY NAT/G CHIEF LEGIT

N19
SENGHOR L.S.,AFRICAN SOCIALISM (PAMPHLET). AFR FRANCE MALI USSR ELITES ECO/UNDEV NAT/G DIPLOM DOMIN EDU/PROP ATTIT 20 NEGRO. PAGE 141 H2827 — SOCISM MARXISM ORD/FREE NAT/LISM

B22
FICHTE J.G.,ADDRESSES TO THE GERMAN NATION. GERMANY PRUSSIA ELITES NAT/G SECT CREATE INT/TRADE HEREDITY ...ART/METH LING 19 FRANK/PARL. PAGE 50 H0989 — NAT/LISM CULTURE EDU/PROP REGION

B23
FRANK T.,A HISTORY OF ROME. MEDIT-7 INTELL SOCIETY LOC/G NAT/G POL/PAR FORCES LEGIS DOMIN LEGIT ALL/VALS...POLICY CONCPT TIME/SEQ GEN/LAWS ROM/EMP ROM/EMP. PAGE 53 H1050 — EXEC STRUCT ELITES

B30
BYNKERSHOEK C.,QUAESTIONUM JURIS PUBLICI LIBRI DUO. CHRIST-17C MOD/EUR CONSTN ELITES SOCIETY NAT/G PROVS EX/STRUC FORCES TOP/EX BAL/PWR DIPLOM ATTIT MORAL...TRADIT CONCPT. PAGE 25 H0502 — INT/ORG LAW NAT/LISM INT/LAW

B30
MASON E.S.,THE PARIS COMMUNE: AN EPISODE IN THE HISTORY OF THE SOCIALIST MOVEMENT. FRANCE MOD/EUR ELITES SOCIETY STRATA ECO/DEV WORKER EDU/PROP CHOOSE INGP/REL SOCISM 19 MARX/KARL PARIS. PAGE 104 H2085 — NAT/G REV MARXISM

S31
HEINBERG J.G.,"THE PERSONNEL OF FRENCH CABINETS, 1871-1930." FRANCE STRATA CHIEF CHOOSE REPRESENT MAJORITY...STAT QU CENSUS TREND CHARTS PERS/COMP 19/20 CHAMBR/DEP. PAGE 69 H1386 — ELITES NAT/G DELIB/GP TOP/EX

B32
MCKISACK M.,THE PARLIAMENTARY REPRESENTATION OF THE ENGLISH BOROUGHS DURING THE MIDDLE AGES. UK CONSTN CULTURE ELITES EX/STRUC TAX PAY ADJUD PARL/PROC APPORT FEDERAL...POLICY 13/15 PARLIAMENT. PAGE 107 H2139 — NAT/G MUNIC LEGIS CHOOSE

B34
STALIN J.,PROBLEMS OF LENINISM. USSR STRATA INDUS LOC/G POL/PAR ECO/TAC CONTROL TOTALISM PWR SOCISM LENIN/VI STALIN/J. PAGE 148 H2968 — MARXISM REV ELITES NAT/G

B35
LASKI H.J.,THE STATE IN THEORY AND PRACTICE. ELITES ECO/TAC REPRESENT ORD/FREE PWR WEALTH POPULISM ...GOV/COMP GEN/LAWS 19/20. PAGE 92 H1829 — CAP/ISM COERCE NAT/G FASCISM

B35
PARETO V.,THE MIND AND SOCIETY (4 VOLS.). ELITES SECT ECO/TAC COERCE PERSON ORD/FREE PWR SOVEREIGN FASCISM POPULISM...TRADIT 19/20. PAGE 123 H2465 — GEN/LAWS SOC PSY

B35
TAKEUCHI T.,WAR AND DIPLOMACY IN THE JAPANESE EMPIRE. ASIA ELITES STRATA NAT/G SECT LEGIS ACT/RES PLAN LEGIT PARL/PROC ROUTINE WAR...MGT BIOG CHINJAP TOT/POP 19/20 CHINJAP. PAGE 152 H3038 — EXEC STRUCT

B36
LAPRADE W.T.,PUBLIC OPINION AND POLITICS IN EIGHTEENTH CENTURY ENGLAND. UK CULTURE POL/PAR CHIEF TOP/EX LEAD REV NAT/LISM PWR 18 PROTESTANT PROTESTANT CHURCH/STA. PAGE 91 H1815 — POLICY ELITES ATTIT TIME/SEQ

B38
COUPLAND R.,EAST AFRICA AND ITS INVADERS. AFR ISLAM STRATA SECT FORCES DIPLOM TRIBUTE CONTROL DISCRIM NAT/LISM 19 AFRICA/E EUROPE MISSION. PAGE 34 H0680 — CULTURE ELITES COLONIAL MARKET

B38
DAVIES E.,"NATIONAL" CAPITALISM: THE GOVERNMENT'S RECORD AS PROTECTOR OF PRIVATE MONOPOLY. UK ELITES SOCIETY STRATA POL/PAR WORKER PROB/SOLV CONTROL SOCISM 20 MONOPOLY LABOR/PAR CHAMBRLN/N. PAGE 37 H0747 — CAP/ISM NAT/G INDUS POLICY

B38
DEL TORO J.,A BIBLIOGRAPHY OF THE COLLECTIVE BIOGRAPHY OF SPANISH AMERICA. ELITES NAT/G WRITING LEAD PERSON 19/20. PAGE 39 H0786 — BIBLIOG/A L/A+17C BIOG

B38
IIZAWA S.,POLITICS AND POLITICAL PARTIES IN JAPAN. ELITES VOL/ASSN CHOOSE SUFF CIVMIL/REL GP/REL 19/20 CHINJAP. PAGE 76 H1522 — POL/PAR REPRESENT FORCES NAT/G

C39
BURKE E.,"ON THE REFORM OF THE REPRESENTATION IN THE HOUSE OF COMMONS" (1782) IN COLLECTED WORKS (VOL. 5)" UK ELITES STRATA NAT/G REPRESENT ORD/FREE PWR POPULISM...POLICY NEW/IDEA GEN/LAWS 18 BURKE/EDM. PAGE 24 H0486 — TRADIT CONSTN PARL/PROC LEGIS

S40
FAHS C.B.,"POLITICAL GROUPS IN THE JAPANESE HOUSE OF PEERS." ELITES NAT/G ADMIN GP/REL...TREND CHINJAP. PAGE 48 H0961 — ROUTINE POL/PAR LEGIS

B41
PALMER R.R.,TWELVE WHO RULED. MOD/EUR ELITES STRUCT NAT/G POL/PAR DELIB/GP DOMIN ATTIT SUPEGO PWR ...POLICY CONCPT 18. PAGE 123 H2453 — TOP/EX BIOG REV FRANCE

B42
FEFFERO G.,THE PRINCIPLES OF POWER (TRANS. BY T. JAECKEL). MOD/EUR CONSTN NAT/G CHIEF CONTROL REV WAR ORD/FREE CONSERVE FASCISM POPULISM...GEN/LAWS 18/20 EUROPE. PAGE 49 H0980 — PWR LEGIT TRADIT ELITES

B42
FORTESCU J.,IN PRAISE OF ENGLISH LAW (1464) (TRANS. BY S.B. CHRIMES). UK ELITES CHIEF FORCES CT/SYS COERCE CRIME GOV/REL ILLEGIT...JURID GOV/COMP GEN/LAWS 15. PAGE 52 H1040 — LAW CONSTN LEGIS ORD/FREE

B43
GRIERSON P.,BOOKS ON SOVIET RUSSIA 1917-42: A BIBLIOGRAPHY AND A GUIDE TO READING. USSR CULTURE ELITES NAT/G PLAN DIPLOM REV...GEOG 20. PAGE 61 H1213
BIBLIOG/A COM MARXISM LEAD

C43
BENTHAM J.,"ON THE LIBERTY OF THE PRESS, AND PUBLIC DISCUSSION" IN J. BOWRING, ED., THE WORKS OF JEREMY BENTHAM." SPAIN UK LAW ELITES NAT/G LEGIS INSPECT LEGIT WRITING CONTROL PRIVIL TOTALISM AUTHORIT ...TRADIT 19 FREE/SPEE. PAGE 15 H0290
ORD/FREE PRESS CONFER CONSERVE

B44
BERDYAEV N.,SLAVERY AND FREEDOM. NAT/G REV WAR NAT/LISM OWN AUTHORIT SEX CONSERVE SOCISM...TRADIT PHIL/SCI CIVIL/LIB. PAGE 15 H0295
ORD/FREE PERSON ELITES SOCIETY

B45
CONOVER H.F.,ITALY: ECONOMICS, POLITICS AND MILITARY AFFAIRS, 1940-1945. ITALY ELITES NAT/G POL/PAR EX/STRUC TOP/EX DIPLOM DOMIN CONTROL COERCE WAR CIVMIL/REL EFFICIENCY 20. PAGE 32 H0646
BIBLIOG TOTALISM FORCES

B48
TOWSTER J.,POLITICAL POWER IN THE USSR: 1917-1947. USSR CONSTN CULTURE ELITES CREATE PLAN COERCE CENTRAL ATTIT RIGID/FLEX ORD/FREE...BIBLIOG SOC/INTEG 20 LENIN/VI STALIN/J. PAGE 156 H3122
EX/STRUC NAT/G MARXISM PWR

S48
ALEXANDER L.,"WAR CRIMES, THEIR SOCIAL-PSYCHOLOGICAL ASPECTS." EUR+WWI GERMANY LAW CULTURE ELITES KIN POL/PAR PUB/INST FORCES DOMIN EDU/PROP COERCE CRIME ATTIT SUPEGO HEALTH MORAL PWR FASCISM ...PSY OBS TREND GEN/LAWS NAZI 20. PAGE 5 H0100
DRIVE WAR

B49
ROGERS C.B.,THE SPIRIT OF REVOLUTION IN 1789: A STUDY OF PUBLIC OPINION ...AT THE BEGINNING OF THE FRENCH REVOLUTION. FRANCE CULTURE ELITES EDU/PROP COERCE CROWD...BIBLIOG 18 MUSIC. PAGE 133 H2658
ATTIT POPULISM REV CREATE

B49
VIERECK P.,CONSERVATISM REVISITED: THE REVOLT AGAINST REVOLT 1815-1949. EUR+WWI ELITES NAT/G FORCES PARTIC GOV/REL NAT/LISM...MAJORIT CONCPT GOV/COMP METTRNCH/K. PAGE 163 H3251
CONSERVE MARXISM REALPOL

B51
BISSAINTHE M.,DICTIONNAIRE DE BIBLIOGRAPHIE HAITIENNE. HAITI ELITES AGRI LEGIS DIPLOM INT/TRADE WRITING ORD/FREE CATHISM...ART/METH GEOG 19/20 NEGRO TREATY. PAGE 17 H0347
BIBLIOG L/A+17C SOCIETY NAT/G

B51
MARX K.,THE EIGHTEENTH BRUMAIRE OF LOUIS BONAPARTE (1852). FRANCE STRATA FINAN INDUS LABOR CHIEF FORCES WORKER CAP/ISM ECO/TAC PARL/PROC ORD/FREE ...MARXIST 19. PAGE 104 H2080
REV MARXISM ELITES NAT/G

B52
GURLAND A.R.L.,POLITICAL SCIENCE IN WESTERN GERMANY: THOUGHTS AND WRITINGS, 1950-1952 (PAMPHLET). EUR+WWI GERMANY/W ELITES SOCIETY NAT/G NAT/LISM TOTALISM 20. PAGE 63 H1253
BIBLIOG/A DIPLOM CIVMIL/REL FASCISM

B52
ISAACS H.R.,AFRICA: NEW CRISES IN THE MAKING (PAMPHLET). EUR+WWI USA+45 ELITES ECO/UNDEV WAR DISCRIM NAT/LISM ATTIT...POLICY NEW/IDEA CHARTS GOV/COMP 20 NEGRO COLD/WAR. PAGE 78 H1570
COLONIAL AFR RACE/REL ORD/FREE

B52
THOM J.M.,GUIDE TO RESEARCH MATERIAL IN POLITICAL SCIENCE (PAMPHLET). ELITES LOC/G MUNIC NAT/G LEGIS DIPLOM ADJUD CIVMIL/REL GOV/REL PWR MGT. PAGE 154 H3074
BIBLIOG/A KNOWL

B53
LEITES N.,A STUDY OF BOLSHEVISM. WOR+45 WOR-45 ELITES SOCIETY INT/ORG NAT/G EX/STRUC EDU/PROP EXEC ROUTINE ATTIT MORAL MARXISM...CONCPT OBS VAL/FREE 20. PAGE 94 H1869
COM POL/PAR USSR TOTALISM

B53
LEITES N.,A STUDY OF BOLSHEVISM. ELITES STRATA INT/ORG LOC/G POL/PAR WORKER EDU/PROP REV TOTALISM UTOPIA PWR...CONCPT 20 BOLSHEVISM. PAGE 94 H1870
MARXISM PLAN COM

B54
HAMSON C.J.,EXECUTIVE DISCRETION AND JUDICIAL CONTROL; AN ASPECT OF THE FRENCH CONSEIL D'ETAT. EUR+WWI FRANCE MOD/EUR UK NAT/G EX/STRUC PARTIC CONSERVE...JURID BIBLIOG/A 18/20 SUPREME/CT. PAGE 65 H1310
ELITES ADJUD NAT/COMP

B54
HAZARD B.H. JR.,KOREAN STUDIES GUIDE. KOREA CONSTN CULTURE AGRI FAM SECT CREATE WAR NAT/LISM HABITAT PWR...CHARTS 14/20. PAGE 68 H1371
BIBLIOG/A ELITES GP/REL

B55
COLE G.D.H.,STUDIES IN CLASS STRUCTURE. UK NAT/G WORKER TEC/DEV EDU/PROP...CLASSIF CHARTS 20. PAGE 31 H0623
STRUCT STRATA ELITES CONCPT

B55
HEYDTE A F.,SOZIOLOGIE DER DEUTSCHEN PARTEIEN. GERMANY/W CONSTN ELITES CHOOSE 20. PAGE 70 H1412
POL/PAR SOC STRUCT NAT/G

B55
SMITH G.,A CONSTITUTIONAL AND LEGAL HISTORY OF ENGLAND. UK ELITES NAT/G LEGIS ADJUD OWN HABITAT POPULISM...JURID 20 ENGLSH/LAW. PAGE 145 H2909
CONSTN PARTIC LAW CT/SYS

B55
TAN C.C.,THE BOXER CATASTROPHE. ASIA UK USSR ELITES POL/PAR VOL/ASSN FORCES PROB/SOLV DIPLOM ADMIN COLONIAL NAT/LISM PEACE TREATY 19/20 BOXER/REBL. PAGE 152 H3040
REV NAT/G WAR

S56
KHAMA T.,"POLITICAL CHANGE IN AFRICAN SOCIETY." CONSTN SOCIETY LOC/G NAT/G POL/PAR EX/STRUC LEGIS LEGIT ADMIN CHOOSE REPRESENT NAT/LISM MORAL ORD/FREE PWR...CONCPT OBS TREND GEN/METH CMN/WLTH 17/20. PAGE 85 H1706
AFR ELITES

C56
NEUMANN S.,"MODERN POLITICAL PARTIES: APPROACHES TO COMPARATIVE POLITIC. FRANCE UK EX/STRUC DOMIN ADMIN LEAD REPRESENT TOTALISM ATTIT...POLICY TREND METH/COMP ANTHOL BIBLIOG/A 20 CMN/WLTH. PAGE 117 H2338
POL/PAR GOV/COMP ELITES MAJORIT

B57
CHANDRA S.,PARTIES AND POLITICS AT THE MUGHAL COURT: 1707-1740. INDIA CULTURE EX/STRUC CREATE PLAN PWR...BIBLIOG/A 18. PAGE 29 H0574
POL/PAR ELITES NAT/G

B57
HERNANDEZ-ARREGU J.,IMPERIALISMO Y CULTURA (LA POLITICA EN LA INTELIGENCIA ARGENTINA). L/A+17C CULTURE ELITES WRITING COLONIAL CROWD ATTIT FASCISM MARXISM SOCISM...BIOG IDEA/COMP 20 ARGEN PERON/JUAN COM/PARTY. PAGE 70 H1403
INTELL CREATE ART/METH HUM

B57
KOENTJARANINGRAT R.,A PRELIMINARY DESCRIPTION OF THE JAVANESE KINSHIP SYSTEM. INDONESIA STRATA FAM INGP/REL ADJUST MARRIAGE AGE/C AGE/Y AGE/A PERSON ...OBS CHARTS DICTIONARY 20 JAVA. PAGE 87 H1736
KIN STRUCT ELITES CULTURE

B57
LAQUER W.Z.,COMMUNISM AND NATIONALISM IN THE MIDDLE EAST. ELITES INTELL STRATA NAT/G POL/PAR SECT VOL/ASSN TOP/EX DOMIN LEGIT REGION COERCE ATTIT PERSON PWR...CONCPT HIST/WRIT TIME/SEQ TREND GEN/LAWS VAL/FREE. PAGE 91 H1817
ISLAM NAT/LISM

B57
MENDIETTA Y NUNE L.,THEORIE DES GROUPEMENT SOCIAUX SUIVI D'UNE ETUDE SUR LE DROIT SOCIAL. ELITES FAM KIN NAT/G PROB/SOLV CROWD ISOLAT ATTIT PERSON ...JURID CONCPT SOC/INTEG. PAGE 109 H2174
SOC STRATA STRUCT DISCRIM

S57
HAILEY,"TOMORROW IN AFRICA." CONSTN SOCIETY LOC/G NAT/G DOMIN ADJUD ADMIN GP/REL DISCRIM NAT/LISM ATTIT MORAL ORD/FREE...PSY SOC CONCPT OBS RECORD TREND GEN/LAWS CMN/WLTH 20. PAGE 64 H1277
AFR PERSON ELITES RACE/REL

C57
WITTFOGEL K.A.,"ORIENTAL DESPOTISM: A COMPARATIVE STUDY OF TOTAL POWER." ASIA CULTURE STRATA NAT/G LEAD OWN ORD/FREE PWR...CONCPT TREND BIBLIOG 20. PAGE 170 H3393
TOTALISM HABITAT DOMIN ELITES

B58
HSU U.T.,THE INVISIBLE CONFLICT. ASIA USSR ELITES NAT/G CONTROL LEAD COERCE REV WAR NAT/LISM ORD/FREE PWR 20 COM/PARTY ESPIONAGE. PAGE 74 H1485
MARXISM POL/PAR EDU/PROP FORCES

B58
JOHNSON J.J.,POLITICAL CHANGE IN LATIN AMERICA: THE EMERGENCE OF THE MIDDLE SECTORS. INTELL STRATA STRUCT ECO/UNDEV MUNIC TEC/DEV LEAD REV...DECISION TREND GOV/COMP BIBLIOG/A 20. PAGE 81 H1621
L/A+17C ELITES GP/REL DOMIN

B58
OGILVIE C.,THE KING'S GOVERNMENT AND THE COMMON LAW, 1471-1641. UK STRUCT NAT/G CHIEF LEGIS WORKER BAL/PWR GP/REL AUTHORIT 15/17 COMMON/LAW. PAGE 120 H2408
CONSTN ELITES DOMIN

B58
PAYNO M.,LA REFORMA SOCIAL EN ESPANA Y MEXICO. SPAIN ECO/TAC TAX LOBBY COERCE REV OWN CATHISM 19/20 MEXIC/AMER. PAGE 124 H2479
SECT NAT/G LAW ELITES

B58
SCHOEPS H.J.,KONSERVATIVE ERNEUERUNG IDEEN ZUR DEUTSCHEN POLITIK. GERMANY ELITES SOCIETY ACADEM CHOOSE SOCISM 19/20. PAGE 140 H2796
POL/PAR IDEA/COMP CONSERVE NAT/G

B58
SYME R.,COLONIAL ELITES: ROME, SPAIN, AND THE AMERICAS. CHRIST-17C MOD/EUR SPAIN UK USA-45 CULTURE NAT/G CHIEF TOP/EX...GOV/COMP IDEA/COMP NAT/COMP ROM/EMP GIBBON/EDW TOYNBEE/A. PAGE 151 H3022
COLONIAL ELITES DOMIN

S58
EULAV H.,"HD LASSWELL'S DEVELOPMENTAL ANALYSIS." FUT CULTURE TOP/EX PLAN CHOOSE SUPEGO PWR...TREND HYPO/EXP SIMUL GEN/METH VAL/FREE 20 LASSWELL/H. PAGE 47 H0948
CONCPT NEW/IDEA ELITES

S58
GARCEAU O.,"INTEREST GROUP THEORY IN POLITICAL
GP/COMP

RESEARCH." ELITES NAT/G PLAN LEAD REPRESENT INGP/REL POLICY. PAGE 55 H1098
GP/REL LOBBY PLURISM

S58
GUSFIELD J.R.,"EQUALITARIANISM AND BUREAUCRATIC RECRUITMENT." UK USA+45 USA-45 EX/STRUC 19/20. PAGE 63 H1257
GOV/COMP REPRESENT TOP/EX ELITES

S58
MAIR L.P.,"REPRESENTATIVE LOCAL GOVERNMENT AS A PROBLEM IN SOCIAL CHANGE." ECO/UNDEV KIN LOC/G NAT/G SCHOOL JUDGE ADMIN ROUTINE REPRESENT RIGID/FLEX RESPECT...CONCPT STERTYP CMN/WLTH 20. PAGE 101 H2025
AFR PWR ELITES

B59
EAENZA L.,COMMUNISMO E CATTOLICESIMO IN UNA PARROCHIA DI CAMPAGNA. ITALY CULTURE ELITES ECO/DEV AGRI KIN POL/PAR DOMIN LEGIT RIGID/FLEX...DECISION OBS IDEA/COMP 20 COM/PARTY CHURCH/STA. PAGE 44 H0878
ATTIT CATHISM NEIGH MARXISM

B59
GOLDWIN R.A.,READINGS IN RUSSIAN FOREIGN POLICY. HUNGARY USSR YUGOSLAVIA ELITES INT/ORG NAT/G REV WAR NAT/LISM PERSON SOCISM...CHARTS 20 MAPS BOLSHEVISM. PAGE 58 H1160
COM MARXISM DIPLOM POLICY

B59
SISSON C.H.,THE SPIRIT OF BRITISH ADMINISTRATION AND SOME EUROPEAN COMPARISONS. FRANCE GERMANY/W SWEDEN UK LAW EX/STRUC INGP/REL EFFICIENCY ORD/FREE ...DECISION 20. PAGE 144 H2890
GOV/COMP ADMIN ELITES ATTIT

B59
SVALASTOGA K.,PRESTIGE, CLASS, AND MOBILITY. DENMARK UK EDU/PROP INCOME WEALTH...SOC SAMP 20. PAGE 151 H3010
NAT/COMP STRATA STRUCT ELITES

B59
THOMAS D.H.,GUIDE TO THE DIPLOMATIC ARCHIVES OF WESTERN EUROPE. EUR+WWI ELITES INT/ORG NAT/G BAL/PWR INT/TRADE PEACE. PAGE 154 H3076
BIBLIOG DIPLOM CONFER

C59
EASTON D.,"POLITICAL ANTHROPOLOGY" IN BIENNIAL REVIEW OF ANTHROPOLOGY" UNIV LAW CULTURE ELITES SOCIETY CREATE...PSY CONCPT GP/COMP GEN/METH 20. PAGE 44 H0880
SOC BIBLIOG/A NEW/IDEA

C59
KORNHAUSER W.,"THE POLITICS OF MASS SOCIETY." COM CULTURE ELITES INTELL STRATA POL/PAR ATTIT...SOC CHARTS GEN/LAWS BIBLIOG 20. PAGE 88 H1757
CROWD PLURISM CONSTN SOCIETY

B60
BEATTIE J.,BUNYORO, AN AFRICAN KINGDOM. UGANDA STRATA INGP/REL PERS/REL...SOC BIBLIOG 19/20. PAGE 13 H0250
CULTURE ELITES SECT KIN

B60
FURNIA A.H.,THE DIPLOMACY OF APPEASEMENT: ANGLO-FRENCH RELATIONS AND THE PRELUDE TO WORLD WAR II 1931-1938. FRANCE GERMANY UK ELITES NAT/G DELIB/GP FORCES WAR PEACE RIGID/FLEX 20. PAGE 54 H1077
DIPLOM BAL/PWR COERCE

B60
KOHN H.,PAN-SLAVISM: ITS HISTORY AND IDEOLOGY. COM CZECHOSLVK EUR+WWI MOD/EUR USSR YUGOSLAVIA CULTURE ELITES INTELL KIN NAT/G EDU/PROP DRIVE SOVEREIGN ...HUM PHIL/SCI MYTH HIST/WRIT 19/20. PAGE 87 H1745
ATTIT CONCPT NAT/LISM

B60
MC CLELLAN G.S.,INDIA. CHINA/COM INDIA CONSTN ELITES STRATA AGRI POL/PAR FOR/AID ARMS/CONT REV MARXISM...CENSUS BIBLIOG 20 COLD/WAR GANDHI/M NEHRU/J. PAGE 106 H2117
DIPLOM NAT/G SOCIETY ECO/UNDEV

B60
MORRIS I.,NATIONALISM AND THE RIGHT WING IN JAPAN: A STUDY OF POST WAR TRENDS. ASIA ELITES NAT/G DELIB/GP FORCES TOP/EX CHOOSE ATTIT...INT GEN/LAWS CONGRESS 20 CHINJAP. PAGE 113 H2262
POL/PAR TREND NAT/LISM

B60
PINTO F.B.M.,ENRIQUECIMENTO ILICITO NO EXERCICIO DE CARGOS PUBLICOS. BRAZIL L/A+17C USA+45 ELITES TRIBUTE CONTROL INGP/REL ORD/FREE PWR...NAT/COMP 20. PAGE 126 H2513
ADMIN NAT/G CRIME LAW

B60
SOUTH AFRICAN CONGRESS OF DEM,FACE THE FUTURE. SOUTH/AFR ELITES LEGIS ADMIN REGION COERCE PEACE ATTIT 20. PAGE 147 H2938
RACE/REL DISCRIM CONSTN NAT/G

S60
SHILS E.,"THE INTELLECTUALS IN THE POLITICAL DEVELOPMENT OF THE NEW STATES." AFR ASIA S/ASIA ELITES LOC/G NAT/G CONSULT EX/STRUC CREATE PLAN ECO/TAC DOMIN LEGIT DRIVE PWR...TRADIT CONCPT STERTYP GEN/LAWS 20. PAGE 143 H2861
POL/PAR INTELL NAT/LISM

S60
TURNER R.H.,"SPONSORED AND CONTEST MOBILITY IN THE SCHOOL SYSTEM." UK USA+45 ELITES STRATA ACADEM FACE/GP EDU/PROP CONTROL INGP/REL ADJUST ATTIT PERSON...METH/COMP 20. PAGE 157 H3142
AGE/Y NAT/COMP SCHOOL STRUCT

B61
ALSTON P.L.,STATE EDUCATION AND SOCIAL CHANGE IN THE RUSSIAN EMPIRE 1871-1914 (PAPER). RUSSIA ELITES PROF/ORG EDU/PROP CONTROL PRIVIL AGE/Y...BIBLIOG 19/20. PAGE 6 H0115
SCHOOL SOCIETY NAT/G GP/REL

B61
AYLMER G.,THE KING'S SERVANTS. UK ELITES CHIEF PAY CT/SYS WEALTH 17 CROMWELL/O CHARLES/I. PAGE 9 H0187
ADMIN ROUTINE EX/STRUC NAT/G

B61
CARNELL F.,THE POLITICS OF THE NEW STATES: A SELECT ANNOTATED BIBLIOGRAPHY WITH SPECIAL REFERENCE TO THE COMMONWEALTH. CONSTN ELITES LABOR NAT/G POL/PAR EX/STRUC DIPLOM ADJUD ADMIN...GOV/COMP 20 COMMONWLTH. PAGE 27 H0534
BIBLIOG/A AFR ASIA COLONIAL

B61
DELEFORTRIE-SOU N.,LES DIRIGEANTS DE L'INDUSTRIE FRANCAISE. FRANCE CULTURE ELITES PROB/SOLV ...DECISION STAT CHARTS 20. PAGE 39 H0789
INDUS STRATA TOP/EX LEAD

B61
DIA M.,THE AFRICAN NATIONS AND WORLD SOLIDARITY. ISLAM CULTURE ELITES ECO/DEV ECO/UNDEV INT/ORG NAT/G PLAN ECO/TAC INT/TRADE EDU/PROP NAT/LISM ATTIT DRIVE ORD/FREE WEALTH...SOCIALIST CONCPT CON/ANAL GEN/LAWS TOT/POP 20. PAGE 41 H0817
AFR REGION SOCISM

B61
EMMET C.,THE VANISHING SWASTIKA. GERMANY/W ELITES CRIME WAR...SAMP 20. PAGE 46 H0922
FASCISM ATTIT AGE/Y NAT/G

B61
MARVICK D.,POLITICAL DECISION-MAKERS. INTELL STRATA NAT/G POL/PAR EX/STRUC LEGIS DOMIN EDU/PROP ATTIT PERSON PWR...PSY STAT OBS CONT/OBS STAND/INT UNPLAN/INT TIME/SEQ CHARTS STERTYP VAL/FREE. PAGE 104 H2073
TOP/EX BIOG ELITES

B61
MONAS S.,THE THIRD SECTION: POLICE AND SOCIETY IN RUSSIA UNDER NICHOLAS I. MOD/EUR RUSSIA ELITES STRUCT NAT/G EX/STRUC ADMIN CONTROL PWR CONSERVE ...DECISION 19 NICHOLAS/I. PAGE 112 H2238
ORD/FREE COM FORCES COERCE

B61
SCHWARTZ H.,THE RED PHOENIX: RUSSIA SINCE WORLD WAR II. USA+45 WOR+45 ELITES POL/PAR TEC/DEV ECO/TAC MARXISM. PAGE 140 H2810
DIPLOM NAT/G ECO/DEV

S61
DOGAN M.,"LES OFFICIERS DANS LA CARRIERE POLITIQUE DE MARECHAL MACMAHON AU GENERAL DE GAULLE." EUR+WWI FRANCE MOD/EUR ELITES STRATA POL/PAR LEGIT ATTIT ALL/VALS...SOC CONCPT 19/20. PAGE 42 H0833
PROF/ORG FORCES NAT/G DELIB/GP

S61
VALLET R.,"IRAN: KEY TO THE MIDDLE EAST." COM IRAQ ISLAM KUWAIT LEBANON SAUDI/ARAB TURKEY ELITES SOCIETY INDUS PROC/MFG POL/PAR TOP/EX PLAN BAL/PWR DIPLOM ECO/TAC ALL/VALS...TREND CENTO 20. PAGE 161 H3224
NAT/G ECO/UNDEV IRAN

B62
ANDREWS W.G.,FRENCH POLITICS AND ALGERIA: THE PROCESS OF POLICY FORMATION 1954-1962. ALGERIA FRANCE CONSTN ELITES POL/PAR CHIEF DELIB/GP LEGIS DIPLOM PRESS CHOOSE 20. PAGE 7 H0140
GOV/COMP EXEC COLONIAL

B62
BELL D.,THE END OF IDEOLOGY (REV. ED.). USA+45 USA-45 ELITES STRATA LABOR CREATE CRIME PWR MARXISM ...PHIL/SCI METH/COMP 20 EUROPE. PAGE 13 H0265
CROWD CAP/ISM SOCISM IDEA/COMP

B62
CALVOCORESSI P.,WORLD ORDER AND NEW STATES: PROBLEMS OF KEEPING THE PEACE. AFR EUR+WWI S/ASIA ELITES NAT/G ECO/TAC FOR/AID EDU/PROP COERCE ATTIT DRIVE ALL/VALS...GEN/LAWS COLD/WAR 20 UN. PAGE 25 H0509
INT/ORG PEACE

B62
DAVAR F.C.,IRAN AND INDIA THROUGH THE AGES. INDIA IRAN ELITES SECT CREATE ORD/FREE...LING BIBLIOG. PAGE 37 H0743
NAT/COMP DIPLOM CULTURE

B62
ESCUELA SUPERIOR DE ADMIN PUBL,INFORME DEL SEMINARIO SOBRE SERVICIO CIVIL O CARRERA ADMINISTRATIVA. L/A+17C ELITES STRATA CONFER CONTROL GOV/REL INGP/REL SUPEGO 20 CENTRAL/AM CIVIL/SERV. PAGE 47 H0939
ADMIN NAT/G PROB/SOLV ATTIT

B62
FEIT E.,SOUTH AFRICA, THE DYNAMICS OF THE AFRICAN NATIONAL CONGRESS. AFR SOUTH/AFR LAW INTELL STRATA KIN NAT/G POL/PAR ECO/TAC DOMIN RISK COERCE 20 NEGRO. PAGE 49 H0984
RACE/REL ELITES CONTROL STRUCT

B62
FINER S.E.,THE MAN ON HORSEBACK: ROLE OF THE MILITARY IN POLITICS. UNIV LAW CONSTN ELITES SOCIETY POL/PAR BAL/PWR CHIEF EDU/PROP LEGIT COERCE GUERRILLA REV WAR WEAPON DRIVE SUPEGO ORD/FREE PWR RESPECT...POLICY CONCPT GEN/METH. PAGE 50 H1003
NAT/G FORCES TOTALISM

B62
KINDERSLEY R.,THE FIRST RUSSIAN REVISIONISTS. COM USSR LAW ELITES INTELL NAT/G LEGIS ECO/TAC EDU/PROP CONTROL LEAD GP/REL SOCISM 19/20 MARX/KARL BOLSHEVISM. PAGE 86 H1712
CONSTN MARXISM POPULISM BIOG

B62
MANSUR F.,PROCESS OF INDEPENDENCE. GHANA INDIA INDONESIA PAKISTAN CONSTN ELITES INTELL STRUCT ACADEM NAT/G REV PWR 20. PAGE 102 H2043
NAT/COMP POL/PAR SOVEREIGN COLONIAL

B62
MELADY T.,THE WHITE MAN'S FUTURE IN BLACK AFRICA. FUT CULTURE SOCIETY NAT/G POL/PAR PLAN ECO/TAC DOMIN EDU/PROP LEGIT COLONIAL RACE/REL ATTIT DRIVE ALL/VALS...PSY SOC CONCPT TIME/SEQ TOT/POP VAL/FREE 20. PAGE 108 H2167
AFR STRATA ELITES

B62
NOBECOURT R.G.,LES SECRETS DE LA PROPAGANDE EN FRANCE OCCUPEE. FRANCE ELITES NAT/G DIPLOM GP/REL NAT/LISM TOTALISM ORD/FREE 20 VICHY VICHY. PAGE 118 H2365
METH/COMP EDU/PROP WAR CONTROL

B62
SCALAPINO R.A.,PARTIES AND POLITICS IN CONTEMPORARY JAPAN. EX/STRUC DIPLOM CHOOSE NAT/LISM ATTIT ...POLICY 20 CHINJAP. PAGE 138 H2762
POL/PAR PARL/PROC ELITES DECISION

B62
SELOSOEMARDJAN O.,SOCIAL CHANGES IN JOGJAKARTA. INDONESIA NETHERLAND ELITES STRATA STRUCT FAM POL/PAR CREATE DIPLOM INT/TRADE EDU/PROP ADMIN GOV/REL...SOC 20 JAVA CHINJAP. PAGE 141 H2825
ECO/UNDEV CULTURE REV COLONIAL

B62
WHITING K.R.,THE SOVIET UNION TODAY: A CONCISE HANDBOOK. USSR ELITES AGRI INDUS POL/PAR FORCES DIPLOM EDU/PROP LEAD...GEOG TREND 19/20. PAGE 168 H3354
NAT/G ATTIT MARXISM POLICY

L62
COHEN R.,"POWER IN COMPLEX SOCIETIES IN AFRICA." AFR KIN MUNIC POL/PAR DELIB/GP DOMIN ROUTINE ATTIT ALL/VALS...SOC STAT OBS INT QU CHARTS ANTHOL 20. PAGE 31 H0617
CULTURE STRATA ELITES

S62
BELL W.,"EQUALITY AND ATTITUDES OF ELITES IN JAMAICA" L/A+17C STRATA PWR WEALTH...SOC QU TREND. PAGE 13 H0266
ELITES FUT SOCIETY CULTURE

S62
MU FU-SHENG,"THE WILTING OF THE HUNDRED FLOWERS: FREE THOUGHT IN CHINA TODAY." ASIA CHINA/COM CULTURE FAM NAT/G EDU/PROP REV TOTALISM ATTIT PERSON RESPECT...GEOG INT UNPLAN/INT COLD/WAR 20. PAGE 114 H2278
INTELL ELITES

C62
BACON F.,"OF EMPIRE" (1612) IN F. BACON, ESSAYS." ELITES NAT/G PROB/SOLV DIPLOM ADMIN CONTROL WEALTH 16/17 KING. PAGE 9 H0190
PWR CHIEF DOMIN GEN/LAWS

B63
BLONDEL J.,VOTERS, PARTIES, AND LEADERS. UK ELITES LOC/G NAT/G PROVS ACT/RES DOMIN REPRESENT GP/REL INGP/REL...SOC BIBLIOG 20. PAGE 18 H0358
POL/PAR STRATA LEGIS ADMIN

B63
BORKENAU F.,THE SPANISH COCKPIT. SPAIN ELITES STRATA POL/PAR ACT/RES CROWD WAR GP/REL INGP/REL ...SOC NAT/COMP 20. PAGE 19 H0377
REV CONSERVE SOCISM FORCES

B63
CROSS C.,THE FASCISTS IN BRITAIN. UK ELITES LABOR NAT/G DOMIN PARTIC DISCRIM TOTALISM ATTIT...STERTYP 20. PAGE 35 H0708
POL/PAR FASCISM RACE/REL LEAD

B63
FARMER B.H.,CEYLON: A DIVIDED NATION. CEYLON INDIA NETHERLAND PORTUGAL UK ELITES POL/PAR COLONIAL ...SOC MYTH CHARTS GOV/COMP WORSHIP 20. PAGE 49 H0972
DOMIN ORD/FREE ECO/UNDEV POLICY

B63
FLECHTHEIM O.K.,DOKUMENTE ZUR PARTEIPOLITISCHEN ENTWICKLUNG IN DEUTSCHLAND SEIT 1945 (2 VOLS.). EUR+WWI GERMANY/W...CONCPT ANTHOL 20. PAGE 51 H1023
POL/PAR ELITES NAT/G TIME/SEQ

B63
FRANKEL J.,THE MAKING OF FOREIGN POLICY: AN ANALYSIS OF DECISION-MAKING. CHINA/COM EUR+WWI USA+45 ELITES INTELL FORCES LEGIS PLAN ATTIT ALL/VALS MORAL CONSERVE...GOV/COMP 20 PRESIDENT UN TREATY. PAGE 53 H1051
POLICY DECISION PROB/SOLV DIPLOM

B63
GEERTZ C.,PEDDLERS AND PRINCES: SOCIAL DEVELOPMENT AND ECONOMIC CHANGE IN TWO INDONESIAN TOWNS. S/ASIA CULTURE SOCIETY STRATA FACE/GP MUNIC CREATE TEC/DEV ECO/TAC ORD/FREE WEALTH...OBS INT CENSUS CHARTS WORK TOT/POP VAL/FREE 20. PAGE 55 H1106
ECO/UNDEV SOC ELITES INDONESIA

B63
HAMM H.,ALBANIA - CHINA'S BEACHHEAD IN EUROPE. ALBANIA CHINA/COM USSR YUGOSLAVIA ELITES SOCIETY POL/PAR DELIB/GP FORCES ECO/TAC COERCE ISOLAT PEACE MARXISM...IDEA/COMP 20 MAO. PAGE 65 H1304
DIPLOM REV NAT/G POLICY

B63
HARTLEY A.,A STATE OF ENGLAND. UK ELITES SOCIETY ACADEM NAT/G SCHOOL INGP/REL CONSEN ORD/FREE NEW/LIB...POLICY 20. PAGE 67 H1349
DIPLOM ATTIT INTELL ECO/DEV

B63
JAIRAZBHOY R.A.,FOREIGN INFLUENCE IN ANCIENT INDIA. INDIA ELITES SECT DIPLOM EDU/PROP COLONIAL REGION GP/REL...ART/METH LING WORSHIP +/14 GRECO/ROMN MESOPOTAM PERSIA PARTH/SASS. PAGE 79 H1587
CULTURE SOCIETY COERCE DOMIN

B63
KAHIN G.M.,MAJOR GOVERNMENTS OF ASIA (2ND ED.). ASIA INDIA INDONESIA PAKISTAN S/ASIA DIPLOM...SOC 20 CHINJAP. PAGE 83 H1650
GOV/COMP POL/PAR ELITES

B63
KHADDURI M.,MODERN LIBYA: A STUDY IN POLITICAL DEVELOPMENT. EUR+WWI ISLAM LIBYA ELITES INT/ORG POL/PAR FORCES DIPLOM FOR/AID DOMIN EDU/PROP LEGIT NAT/LISM DRIVE RIGID/FLEX SKILL...CONCPT TIME/SEQ TREND 20. PAGE 85 H1704
NAT/G STRUCT

B63
MAC MILLAN W.M.,BANTU, BOER, AND BRITON: THE MAKING OF THE SOUTH AFRICAN NATIVE PROBLEM. SOUTH/AFR UK LAW KIN NAT/G SECT LEGIS COLONIAL ISOLAT ATTIT ...BIOG 18/20 BANTU NEGRO PHILIP/J MISSION. PAGE 100 H1989
AFR RACE/REL ELITES

B63
MENZEL J.M.,THE CHINESE CIVIL SERVICE: CAREER OPEN TO TALENT? ASIA ROUTINE INGP/REL DISCRIM ATTIT ROLE KNOWL ANTHOL. PAGE 109 H2177
ADMIN NAT/G DECISION ELITES

B63
MONTAGUE J.B. JR.,CLASS AND NATIONALITY; ENGLISH AND AMERICAN STUDIES. UK USA+45 ELITES STRUCT WORKER ATTIT PWR...SOC CHARTS SOC/EXP 20. PAGE 112 H2243
STRATA NAT/LISM PERSON NAT/COMP

B63
PELLING H.M.,A HISTORY OF BRITISH TRADE UNIONISM. UK ELITES ECO/DEV POL/PAR GP/REL PWR NEW/LIB 19/20. PAGE 124 H2485
LABOR VOL/ASSN NAT/G

B63
SPRING D.,THE ENGLISH LANDED ESTATE IN THE NINETEENTH CENTURY: ITS ADMINISTRATION. UK ELITES STRUCT AGRI NAT/G GP/REL OWN PWR WEALTH...BIBLIOG 19 HOUSE/LORD. PAGE 148 H2954
STRATA PERS/REL MGT

B63
THOMPSON F.M.L.,ENGLISH LANDED SOCIETY IN THE NINETEENTH CENTURY. UK STRUCT MUNIC NAT/G CONTROL WAR GP/REL OWN WEALTH...BIBLIOG 18/20. PAGE 154 H3081
STRATA PWR ELITES GOV/REL

B63
THORBURN H.G.,PARTY POLITICS IN CANADA. CANADA ELITES STRUCT INDUS PWR 20. PAGE 154 H3086
POL/PAR CONCPT NAT/G PROVS

B63
TUCKER R.C.,THE SOVIET POLITICAL MIND. COM INTELL NAT/G TOP/EX EDU/PROP ADMIN COERCE TOTALISM ATTIT PWR MARXISM...PSY MYTH HYPO/EXP 20. PAGE 157 H3136
STRUCT RIGID/FLEX ELITES USSR

B63
VON BECKERATH E.,PROBLEME DER NORMATIVEN OKONOMIK UND DER WIRTSCHAFTSPOLITISCHEN BERATUNG. GERMANY UK ELITES CAP/ISM EFFICIENCY...CONCPT GOV/COMP IDEA/COMP 20. PAGE 163 H3264
ECO/TAC DELIB/GP ECO/DEV CONSULT

B63
WAGLEY C.,INTRODUCTION TO BRAZIL. BRAZIL L/A+17C FAM KIN SCHOOL SECT ATTIT WEALTH...GEOG SOC. PAGE 164 H3286
ECO/UNDEV ELITES HABITAT STRATA

B63
WEINER M.,POLITICAL CHANGE IN SOUTH ASIA. CEYLON INDIA PAKISTAN S/ASIA CULTURE ELITES ECO/UNDEV EX/STRUC ADMIN CONTROL CHOOSE CONSERVE...GOV/COMP ANTHOL 20. PAGE 166 H3328
NAT/G CONSTN TEC/DEV

B63
WODDIS J.,AFRICA, THE WAY AHEAD. AFR FUT ELITES POL/PAR CAP/ISM DIPLOM DOMIN RACE/REL ATTIT ORD/FREE SOVEREIGN SOCISM 20 PANAF/FREE. PAGE 170 H3394
REV COLONIAL ECO/UNDEV NAT/G

B63
ZARTMAN I.W.,GOVERNMENT AND POLITICS IN NORTHERN AFRICA. AFR ALGERIA ISLAM LIBYA MOROCCO UAR ELITES SOCIETY PLAN ECO/TAC DOMIN EDU/PROP LEGIT ATTIT ...GEOG CONCPT TIME/SEQ 20 TUNIS. PAGE 172 H3448
CULTURE DRIVE NAT/LISM

S63
BANFIELD J.,"FEDERATION IN EAST-AFRICA." AFR UGANDA ELITES INT/ORG NAT/G VOL/ASSN LEGIS ECO/TAC FEDERAL ATTIT SOVEREIGN TOT/POP 20 TANGANYIKA. PAGE 10 H0210
EX/STRUC PWR REGION

S63
DUDLEY B.J.,"THE NOMINATION OF PARLIAMENTARY CANDIDATES IN NORTHERN NIGERIA." AFR CONSTN CULTURE
POL/PAR CHOOSE

ELITES STRATA DELIB/GP LEGIS DOMIN EDU/PROP COERCE ATTIT SUPEGO PWR...STAT VAL/FREE 20. PAGE 43 H0854
NIGERIA

S63
EMERI C.,"LES FORCES POLITIQUES AU PARLEMENT" EUR+WWI FRANCE ELITES DELIB/GP TOP/EX LEGIT ATTIT ...SOC 20 PARLIAMENT. PAGE 46 H0917
POL/PAR LEGIS PWR NAT/G

S63
LERNER D.,"WILL EUROPEAN UNION BRING ABOUT MERGED NATIONAL GOALS." EUR+WWI FRANCE GERMANY UK ECO/DEV NAT/G VOL/ASSN DELIB/GP BAL/PWR ECO/TAC NAT/LISM EEC 20 DEGAULLE/C. PAGE 95 H1889
ATTIT STERTYP ELITES REGION

S63
RUSTOW D.A.,"THE MILITARY IN MIDDLE EASTERN SOCIETY AND POLITICS." FUT ISLAM CONSTN SOCIETY FACE/GP NAT/G POL/PAR PROF/ORG CONSULT DOMIN ADMIN EXEC REGION COERCE NAT/LISM ATTIT DRIVE PERSON ORD/FREE PWR...POLICY CONCPT OBS STERTYP 20. PAGE 136 H2721
FORCES ELITES

B64
DOOLIN D.J.,COMMUNIST CHINA: THE POLITICS OF STUDENT OPPOSITION. CHINA/COM ELITES STRATA ACADEM NAT/G WRITING CT/SYS LEAD PARTIC COERCE TOTALISM 20. PAGE 42 H0838
MARXISM DEBATE AGE/Y PWR

B64
GUTTERIDGE W.,MILITARY INSTITUTIONS AND POWER IN THE NEW STATES. WOR+45 INT/ORG FOR/AID NEUTRAL REV CIVMIL/REL ATTIT ROLE...GOV/COMP 20. PAGE 63 H1258
FORCES DIPLOM ECO/UNDEV ELITES

B64
HILL C.R.,BANTUSTANS: THE FRAGMENTATION OF SOUTH AFRICA. AFR SOUTH/AFR ELITES SOCIETY KIN CONTROL DISCRIM ANOMIE ATTIT...POLICY CHARTS GOV/COMP 20 NEGRO BANTUSTANS TRANSKEI NATAL. PAGE 71 H1416
RACE/REL CULTURE LOC/G ORD/FREE

B64
HOROWITZ I.L.,REVOLUTION IN BRAZIL. BRAZIL L/A+17C ELITES STRATA NAT/G BAL/PWR PARTIC ATTIT 20. PAGE 74 H1473
ECO/UNDEV DIPLOM POLICY ORD/FREE

B64
IMAZ J.L.,LOS QUE MANDAN. INDUS LABOR NAT/G POL/PAR PROVS SECT CHIEF TOP/EX CONTROL 20 ARGEN. PAGE 76 H1524
LEAD FORCES ELITES ATTIT

B64
MOUMOUNI A.,L'EDUCATION EN AFRIQUE. UNIV CULTURE ELITES INTELL EDU/PROP ADMIN COLONIAL...LING TREND BIBLIOG 20. PAGE 114 H2271
SCHOOL AFR PROB/SOLV

B64
REMAK J.,THE GENTLE CRITIC: THEODOR FONTANE AND GERMAN POLITICS, 1848-1898. GERMANY PRUSSIA CULTURE ELITES BAL/PWR DIPLOM WRITING GOV/REL...HUM BIOG 19 BISMARCK/O JUNKER FONTANE/T. PAGE 131 H2614
PERSON SOCIETY WORKER CHIEF

B64
SINAI I.R.,THE CHALLENGE OF MODERNISATION* THE WEST'S IMPACT ON THE NON-WESTERN WORLD. EUR+WWI CULTURE ELITES SECT CONSERVE SOCISM...GP/COMP IDEA/COMP NAT/COMP GEN/LAWS. PAGE 144 H2881
ASIA S/ASIA ECO/UNDEV CREATE

B64
TAWNEY R.H.,EQUALITY. UK CULTURE STRATA ECO/TAC EDU/PROP REPRESENT OWN NEW/LIB...MAJORIT WELF/ST SOC 20. PAGE 153 H3051
WEALTH STRUCT ELITES POPULISM

B64
WRAITH R.,CORRUPTION IN DEVELOPING COUNTRIES. NIGERIA UK LAW ELITES STRATA INDUS LOC/G NAT/G SECT FORCES EDU/PROP ADMIN PWR WEALTH 18/20. PAGE 171 H3414
ECO/UNDEV CRIME SANCTION ATTIT

S64
CLIGNET R.,"POTENTIAL ELITES IN GHANA AND THE IVORY COAST: A PRELIMINARY SURVEY." AFR CULTURE ELITES STRATA KIN NAT/G SECT DOMIN EXEC ORD/FREE RESPECT SKILL...POLICY RELATIV GP/COMP NAT/COMP 20. PAGE 30 H0605
PWR LEGIT IVORY/CST GHANA

S64
JOHNSON K.F.,"CAUSAL FACTORS IN LATIN AMERICAN POLITICAL INSTABILITY." CULTURE NAT/G VOL/ASSN EX/STRUC FORCES EDU/PROP LEGIT ADMIN COERCE REV ATTIT KNOWL PWR...STYLE RECORD CHARTS WORK 20. PAGE 81 H1624
L/A+17C PERCEPT ELITES

S64
MARTELLI G.,"PORTUGAL AND THE UNITED NATIONS." AFR EUR+WWI ELITES INT/ORG NAT/G PROVS PLAN DIPLOM ECO/TAC DOMIN COLONIAL RIGID/FLEX MORAL ORD/FREE PWR WEALTH...MYTH UN 20. PAGE 103 H2060
ATTIT PORTUGAL

S64
RAMAZANI R.K.,"CHURCH AND STATE IN MODERNIZING SOCIETY: THE CASE OF IRAN." ISLAM CULTURE ORD/FREE PWR...TIME/SEQ VAL/FREE 17/20. PAGE 129 H2586
SECT NAT/G ELITES IRAN

S64
SOLOVEYTCHIK G.,"BOOKS ON RUSSIA." USSR ELITES NAT/G PERF/ART REV GOV/REL MARXISM...AUD/VIS 20. PAGE 147 H2929
BIBLIOG/A COM CULTURE

S64
SWEARER H.R.,"AFTER KHRUSHCHEV: WHAT NEXT." COM FUT USSR CONSTN ELITES NAT/G POL/PAR CHIEF DELIB/GP LEGIS DOMIN LEAD...RECORD TREND STERTYP GEN/METH 20. PAGE 151 H3016
EX/STRUC PWR

B65
CANTRIL H.,THE PATTERN OF HUMAN CONCERNS. ELITES ECO/DEV ECO/UNDEV...STAT CHARTS METH 20. PAGE 26 H0524
ATTIT ALL/VALS NAT/COMP CULTURE

B65
CHANDA A.,FEDERALISM IN INDIA. INDIA UK ELITES FINAN NAT/G POL/PAR EX/STRUC LEGIS DIPLOM TAX GOV/REL POPULISM...POLICY 20. PAGE 28 H0572
CONSTN CENTRAL FEDERAL

B65
CHEN T.H.,THE CHINESE COMMUNIST REGIME: A DOCUMENTARY STUDY (2 VOLS.). CHINA/COM LAW CONSTN ELITES ECO/UNDEV LEGIS ECO/TAC ADMIN CONTROL PWR ...SOC 20. PAGE 29 H0587
MARXISM POL/PAR NAT/G

B65
CHENG C.-Y.,SCIENTIFIC AND ENGINEERING MANPOWER IN COMMUNIST CHINA, 1949-1963. CHINA/COM USSR ELITES ECO/DEV R+D ACADEM LABOR NAT/G EDU/PROP CONTROL UTIL...POLICY BIBLIOG 20. PAGE 29 H0588
WORKER CONSULT MARXISM BIOG

B65
FILIPINIANA BOOK GUILD,THE COLONIZATION AND CONQUEST OF THE PHILIPPINES BY SPAIN. PHILIPPINE SPAIN ELITES AGRI KIN CHIEF DOMIN CONTROL ATTIT PWR ...ANTHOL WORSHIP 16. PAGE 50 H1000
COLONIAL COERCE CULTURE WAR

B65
FREY F.W.,THE TURKISH POLITICAL ELITE. TURKEY CULTURE INTELL NAT/G EX/STRUC CHOOSE ATTIT PWR ...METH/CNCPT CHARTS WORSHIP 20. PAGE 53 H1059
ELITES SOCIETY POL/PAR

B65
GOPAL S.,BRITISH POLICY IN INDIA 1858-1905. INDIA UK ELITES CHIEF DELIB/GP ECO/TAC GP/REL DISCRIM ATTIT...IDEA/COMP NAT/COMP PERS/COMP BIBLIOG/A 19/20. PAGE 59 H1176
COLONIAL ADMIN POL/PAR ECO/UNDEV

B65
GWYN R.J.,THE SHAPE OF SCANDAL: A STUDY OF A GOVERNMENT IN CRISIS. CANADA LEGIS ADJUD CT/SYS SANCTION CMN/WLTH 20 PEARSON/L. PAGE 63 H1260
ELITES NAT/G CRIME

B65
HAPGOOD D.,AFRICA: FROM INDEPENDENCE TO TOMARROW. AFR GUINEA SENEGAL CULTURE ELITES ECO/UNDEV AGRI SCHOOL FOR/AID COLONIAL MARXISM...TREND 20. PAGE 66 H1323
ECO/TAC SOCIETY NAT/G

B65
LEWIS W.A.,POLITICS IN WEST AFRICA. AFR BAL/PWR DIPLOM REPRESENT...POLICY 20. PAGE 96 H1916
POL/PAR ELITES NAT/G ECO/UNDEV

B65
MOORE C.H.,TUNISIA SINCE INDEPENDENCE. ELITES LOC/G POL/PAR ADMIN COLONIAL CONTROL EXEC GOV/REL TOTALISM MARXISM...INT 20 TUNIS. PAGE 112 H2248
NAT/G EX/STRUC SOCISM

B65
POBEDONOSTSEV K.P.,REFLECTIONS OF A RUSSIAN STATESMAN. RUSSIA LAW ELITES EDU/PROP PRESS ADJUD MARRIAGE ATTIT PWR...MAJORIT TRADIT 19 CHURCH/STA. PAGE 127 H2531
TOTALISM POLICY CONSTN NAT/G

B65
RUBINSTEIN A.Z.,THE CHALLENGE OF POLITICS: IDEAS AND ISSUES (2ND ED.). UNIV ELITES SOCIETY EX/STRUC BAL/PWR PARL/PROC AUTHORIT...DECISION ANTHOL 20. PAGE 136 H2709
NAT/G DIPLOM GP/REL ORD/FREE

B65
SVALASTOGA K.,SOCIAL DIFFERENTIATION. CULTURE ELITES SOCIETY MARRIAGE...CONCPT SIMUL. PAGE 151 H3011
SOC STRATA STRUCT GP/REL

B65
TINGSTEN H.,THE PROBLEM OF DEMOCRACY. ELITES SOCIETY STRATA NAT/G CONSEN TOTALISM WELF/ST. PAGE 155 H3101
IDEA/COMP GOV/COMP POPULISM SOCISM

B65
VAN DEN BERGHE P.L.,AFRICA: SOCIAL PROBLEMS OF CHANGE AND CONFLICT. ELITES STRATA ECO/UNDEV KIN MUNIC DIPLOM GP/REL RACE/REL NAT/LISM...ANTHOL BIBLIOG 20. PAGE 161 H3228
SOC CULTURE AFR STRUCT

B65
VERMOT-GAUCHY M.,L'EDUCATION NATIONALE DANS LA FRANCE DE 1975. FRANCE FUT CULTURE ELITES R+D SCHOOL PLAN EDU/PROP EFFICIENCY...POLICY PREDICT CHARTS INDEX 20. PAGE 162 H3245
ACADEM CREATE TREND INTELL

L65
SCHAFFER B.B.,"THE CONCEPT OF PREPARATION* SOME QUESTIONS ABOUT THE TRANSFER OF SYSTEMS OF GOVERNMENT." AFR ASIA CANADA ELITES NAT/G POL/PAR COLONIAL RIGID/FLEX IDEA/COMP. PAGE 138 H2769
ECO/UNDEV UK RECORD

S65
GORDON M.,"THE SETTING FOR EUROPEAN ARMS CONTROLS* POLITICAL AND STRATEGIC CHOICES OF EUROPEAN ELITES." FRANCE GERMANY UK USA+45 USSR ARMS/CONT DETER ATTIT ORD/FREE...SAMP NAT/COMP NATO. PAGE 59 H1179
REC/INT ELITES RISK WAR

S65
LAULICHT J.,"PUBLIC OPINION AND FOREIGN POLICY
DIPLOM

DECISIONS." CANADA ELITES NAT/G FOR/AID LEAD NUC/PWR PERCEPT...INT QU CHARTS UN COLD/WAR. PAGE 92 H1839 — ATTIT CON/ANAL SAMP

S65
TABORSKY E.,"CHANGE IN CZECHOSLOVAKIA." COM USSR ELITES INTELL AGRI INDUS NAT/G DELIB/GP EX/STRUC ECO/TAC TOTALISM ATTIT RIGID/FLEX SOCISM...MGT CONCPT TREND 20. PAGE 152 H3031 — ECO/DEV PLAN CZECHOSLVK

S65
WOLF C. JR.,"THE POLITICAL EFFECTS OF SOME MILITARY PROGRAMS* SOME INDICATIONS FROM LATIN AMERICA." ELITES STRATA BUDGET FOR/AID WEAPON ATTIT PERCEPT PWR...REGRESS SYS/QU CHARTS NAT/COMP. PAGE 170 H3397 — L/A+17C FORCES CIVMIL/REL PROBABIL

C65
NEUMANN S.,"PERMANENT REVOLUTION: TOTALITARIANISM IN THE AGE OF INTERNA TIONAL CIVIL WAR (2ND ED.)" EUR+WWI ELITES POL/PAR DOMIN EDU/PROP LEAD CROWD REPRESENT...MAJORIT GOV/COMP BIBLIOG 20. PAGE 117 H2340 — TOTALISM REV FASCISM STRUCT

B66
AFRIFA A.A.,THE GHANA COUP. AFR GHANA ELITES NAT/G DIPLOM DOMIN 20 NKRUMAH/K. PAGE 4 H0076 — TOP/EX REV FORCES POL/PAR

B66
ASHRAF A.,THE CITY GOVERNMENT OF CALCUTTA: A STUDY OF INERTIA. INDIA ELITES INDUS NAT/G EX/STRUC ACT/RES PLAN PROB/SOLV LEAD HABITAT...BIBLIOG 20 CALCUTTA. PAGE 9 H0175 — LOC/G MUNIC ADMIN ECO/UNDEV

B66
BRAIBANTI R.,ASIAN BUREAUCRATIC SYSTEMS EMERGENT FROM THE BRITISH IMPERIAL TRADITION. BURMA CEYLON INDIA PAKISTAN UK ELITES ECO/UNDEV NAT/G...MGT SOC CHARTS ANTHOL 19/20. PAGE 20 H0401 — GOV/COMP COLONIAL ADMIN S/ASIA

B66
DODGE D.,AFRICAN POLITICS IN PERSPECTIVE. ELITES POL/PAR PROB/SOLV LEAD...POLICY 20 THIRD/WRLD. PAGE 41 H0831 — AFR NAT/G COLONIAL SOVEREIGN

B66
HAMILTON W.B.,A DECADE OF THE COMMONWEALTH, 1955-1964. UK LAW ELITES FINAN FOR/AID CONFER COLONIAL PWR...GEOG CHARTS ANTHOL 20 CMN/WLTH UN. PAGE 65 H1302 — INT/ORG INGP/REL DIPLOM NAT/G

B66
HINTON W.,FANSHEN: A DOCUMENTARY OF REVOLUTION IN A CHINESE VILLAGE. ASIA ELITES MUNIC NAT/G POL/PAR SECT WORKER LEAD WAR PRIVIL PWR 20 MAO. PAGE 71 H1422 — MARXISM REV NEIGH OWN

B66
HOYT E.C.,NATIONAL POLICY AND INTERNATIONAL LAW* CASE STUDIES FROM AMERICAN CANAL POLICY* MONOGRAPH NO. 1 -- 1966-1967. PANAMA UK ELITES BAL/PWR EFFICIENCY...CLASSIF NAT/COMP SOC/EXP COLOMB TREATY. PAGE 74 H1483 — INT/LAW USA-45 DIPLOM PWR

B66
KEAY E.A.,THE NATIVE AND CUSTOMARY COURTS OF NIGERIA. NIGERIA CONSTN ELITES NAT/G TOP/EX PARTIC REGION...DECISION JURID 19/20. PAGE 84 H1673 — AFR ADJUD LAW

B66
KOMIYA R.,POSTWAR ECONOMIC GROWTH IN JAPAN. ELITES NAT/G EX/STRUC TEC/DEV BUDGET DIPLOM CONTROL BAL/PAY PRODUC...BIBLIOG 20 CHINJAP. PAGE 88 H1754 — ECO/DEV POLICY PLAN ADJUST

B66
LOVEDAY P.,PARLIAMENT FACTIONS AND PARTIES: THE FIRST THIRTY YEARS OF RESPONSIBLE GOVERNMENT IN NEW SOUTH WALES, 1856-1889. PROVS LEAD PARL/PROC PARTIC GP/REL INGP/REL MAJORITY PWR...GP/COMP 19 AUSTRAL. PAGE 99 H1970 — POL/PAR ELITES NAT/G LEGIS

B66
MASUR G.,NATIONALISM IN LATIN AMERICA* DIVERSITY AND UNITY. CHRIST-17C PRE/AMER ELITES ECO/UNDEV CREATE DIPLOM INT/TRADE COLONIAL REV SOVEREIGN SOC. PAGE 105 H2089 — L/A+17C NAT/LISM CULTURE

B66
MATTHEWS R.,AFRICAN POWDER KEG: REVOLT AND DISSENT IN SIX EMERGENT NATIONS. AFR ALGERIA DAHOMEY GABON GHANA MALAWI GAMBLE LEAD PARTIC REV DRIVE...BIOG TREND GOV/COMP 20. PAGE 105 H2098 — ELITES ECO/UNDEV TOP/EX CONTROL

B66
O'NEILL R.J.,THE GERMAN ARMY AND THE NAZI PARTY, 1933-1939. GERMANY ELITES NAT/G EDU/PROP CONTROL LEAD COERCE WAR...POLICY INT TIME/SEQ BIBLIOG 20 HITLER/A NAZI. PAGE 120 H2391 — CIVMIL/REL FORCES FASCISM POL/PAR

B66
POLE J.R.,POLITICAL REPRESENTATION IN ENGLAND AND THE ORIGINS OF THE AMERICAN REPUBLIC. UK USA-45 CONSTN ELITES NAT/G POL/PAR LEGIS PARL/PROC ...MAJORIT 17/19. PAGE 127 H2534 — REPRESENT GOV/COMP

B66
RAEFF M.,ORIGINS OF THE RUSSIAN INTELLIGENTSIA: THE EIGHTEENTH-CENTURY NOBILITY. RUSSIA FAM NAT/G EDU/PROP ADMIN PERS/REL ATTIT...HUM BIOG 18. PAGE 129 H2580 — INTELL ELITES STRATA CONSERVE

B66
SILBERMAN B.S.,MODERN JAPANESE LEADERSHIP; TRANSITION AND CHANGE. NAT/G POL/PAR CHIEF ADMIN REPRESENT GP/REL ADJUST RIGID/FLEX...SOC METH/COMP ANTHOL 19/20 CHINJAP CHRISTIAN. PAGE 144 H2873 — LEAD CULTURE ELITES MUNIC

B66
SKILLING H.G.,THE GOVERNMENTS OF COMMUNIST EAST EUROPE. COM EUR+WWI ELITES FORCES DIPLOM ECO/TAC CONTROL HABITAT SOCISM...DECISION BIBLIOG 20 EUROPE/E COM/PARTY. PAGE 145 H2895 — MARXISM NAT/COMP GP/COMP DOMIN

B66
WANG Y.C.,CHINESE INTELLECTUALS AND THE WEST 1872-1949. ASIA ELITES LEAD STRANGE ROLE MARXISM ...CHARTS 19/20. PAGE 165 H3301 — INTELL EDU/PROP CULTURE SOCIETY

B66
WILLNER A.R.,THE NEOTRADITIONAL ACCOMMODATION TO POLITICAL INDEPENDENCE* THE CASE OF INDONESIA * RESEARCH MONOGRAPH NO. 26. CULTURE ECO/UNDEV CREATE PROB/SOLV FOR/AID LEGIT COLONIAL EFFICIENCY NAT/LISM ALL/VALS SOC. PAGE 168 H3371 — INDONESIA CONSERVE ELITES ADMIN

L66
LEMARCHAND R.,"SOCIAL CHANGE AND POLITICAL MODERNISATION IN BURUNDI." AFR BURUNDI STRATA CHIEF EX/STRUC RIGID/FLEX PWR...SOC 20. PAGE 94 H1874 — NAT/G STRUCT ELITES CONSERVE

L66
MCAUSLAN J.P.W.,"CONSTITUTIONAL INNOVATION AND POLITICAL STABILITY IN TANZANIA: A PRELIMINARY ASSESSMENT." AFR TANZANIA ELITES CHIEF EX/STRUC RIGID/FLEX PWR 20 PRESIDENT BUREAUCRCY. PAGE 106 H2122 — CONSTN NAT/G EXEC POL/PAR

S66
"RESEARCH WORK 1965-1966." NEW/ZEALND ELITES ACADEM LOC/G MUNIC POL/PAR PROVS DIPLOM COLONIAL...SOC 20 AUSTRAL. PAGE 2 H0047 — BIBLIOG NAT/G CULTURE S/ASIA

S66
FELD W.,"NATIONAL ECONOMIC INTEREST GROUPS AND POLICY FORMATION IN THE EEC." NAT/G POL/PAR REGION CENTRAL SOVEREIGN...INT NET/THEORY EEC. PAGE 49 H0985 — LOBBY ELITES DECISION

S66
LODGE G.C.,"REVOLUTION IN LATIN AMERICA." USA+45 ELITES INDUS LABOR PROF/ORG SECT TEC/DEV CAP/ISM SKILL MARXISM...POLICY NAT/COMP. PAGE 98 H1950 — ATTIT REV L/A+17C IDEA/COMP

S66
MALENBAUM W.,"GOVERNMENT, ENTREPRENEURSHIP, AND ECONOMIC GROWTH IN POOR LANDS." ELITES ECO/UNDEV INDUS CREATE DRIVE. PAGE 101 H2028 — ECO/TAC PLAN CONSERVE NAT/G

S66
MERRITT R.L.,"SELECTED ARTICLES AND DOCUMENTS ON COMPARATIVE GOVERNMENT AND CROSS-NATIONAL RESEARCH." AFR ASIA EUR+WWI L/A+17C MOD/EUR ELITES R+D ACT/RES DIPLOM PWR...SOC CONCPT 18/20. PAGE 109 H2185 — BIBLIOG GOV/COMP NAT/G GOV/REL

S66
ROTHCHILD D.,"THE LIMITS OF FEDERALISM: AN EXAMINATION OF POLITICAL INSTITUTIONAL TRANSFER IN AFRICA." AFR CONSTN CULTURE ELITES ECO/UNDEV KIN PROB/SOLV ADMIN ORD/FREE PWR...POLICY 20. PAGE 135 H2695 — FEDERAL NAT/G NAT/LISM COLONIAL

S66
STRAYER J.R.,"PROBLEMS OF DICTATORSHIP* THE RUSSIAN EXPERIENCE." ASIA MOD/EUR ELITES STRATA POL/PAR CREATE NAT/LISM MARXISM...GOV/COMP NAT/COMP. PAGE 150 H2997 — NAT/G GEN/LAWS USSR TOTALISM

B67
ALBINSKI H.S.,EUROPEAN POLITICAL PROCESSES: ESSAYS AND READINGS. EUR+WWI FRANCE GERMANY MOD/EUR UK ELITES POL/PAR PWR...CHARTS ANTHOL 18/20. PAGE 5 H0094 — NAT/COMP POLICY IDEA/COMP

B67
BARNETT A.D.,CADRES, BUREAUCRACY, AND POLITICAL POWER IN COMMUNIST CHINA. CHINA/COM ELITES LOC/G NAT/G INGP/REL...SOC INT DICTIONARY 20. PAGE 11 H0224 — GOV/REL STRUCT MARXISM EDU/PROP

B67
DEUTSCH K.W.,FRANCE, GERMANY AND THE WESTERN ALLIANCE. FRANCE GERMANY/W INT/ORG ARMS/CONT NAT/LISM SOVEREIGN...INT NAT/COMP 20. PAGE 40 H0801 — ELITES ATTIT DIPLOM POLICY

B67
DIX R.H.,COLOMBIA: THE POLITICAL DIMENSIONS OF CHANGE. ELITES POL/PAR DOMIN REV...AUD/VIS 20 COLOMB. PAGE 41 H0828 — L/A+17C NAT/G TEC/DEV LEAD

B67
FALL B.B.,HO CHI MINH ON REVOLUTION: SELECTED WRITINGS, 1920-66. COM VIETNAM ELITES NAT/G COERCE GUERRILLA RACE/REL MARXISM...MARXIST ANTHOL 20. PAGE 48 H0968 — REV COLONIAL ECO/UNDEV S/ASIA

B67
FANON F.,TOWARD THE AFRICAN REVOLUTION. AFR FRANCE — COLONIAL

CULTURE ELITES LEAD REV GP/REL ORD/FREE SOVEREIGN 20. PAGE 49 H0969
DOMIN ECO/UNDEV RACE/REL

B67
KOLKOWICZ R.,THE SOVIET MILITARY AND THE COMMUNIST PARTY. COM USSR ELITES NAT/G CREATE CIVMIL/REL GP/REL...TREND BIBLIOG/A 20 COM/PARTY. PAGE 88 H1753
MARXISM CONSTN FORCES POL/PAR

B67
MENARD O.D.,THE ARMY AND THE FIFTH REPUBLIC. ALGERIA FRANCE VIETNAM ELITES STRATA COLONIAL CONTROL LOBBY WAR CIVMIL/REL ROLE PWR...POLICY 20 DEGAULLE/C. PAGE 108 H2169
FORCES ATTIT NAT/G

B67
MUNGER E.S.,AFRIKANER AND AFRICAN NATIONALISM: SOUTH AFRICAN PARALLELS AND PARAMETERS. SOUTH/AFR WOR+45 CULTURE ELITES STRUCT NAT/G PROB/SOLV DOMIN CONTROL PERS/REL NAT/LISM...SOC 20. PAGE 115 H2289
AFR RACE/REL

B67
NYERERE J.K.,FREEDOM AND UNITY/UHURU NA UMOJA: A SELECTION FROM WRITINGS AND SPEECHES, 1952-65. TANZANIA ELITES ECO/UNDEV INT/ORG NAT/G CREATE DIPLOM COLONIAL REGION RACE/REL...ANTHOL 20. PAGE 119 H2383
SOVEREIGN AFR TREND ORD/FREE

B67
PATAI R.,GOLDEN RIVER TO GOLDEN ROAD: SOCIETY, CULTURE, AND CHANGE IN THE MIDDLE EAST (2ND ED.). ELITES FAM KIN TEC/DEV MARRIAGE NAT/LISM SEX ORD/FREE...TREND GP/COMP WORSHIP 20. PAGE 124 H2476
CULTURE SOCIETY ISLAM STRUCT

L67
GLAZER M.,"LAS ACTITUDES Y ACTIVIDADES POLITICAS DE LOS ESTUDIANTES DE LA UNIVERSIDAD DE CHILE." CHILE NAT/G POL/PAR EDU/PROP LOBBY ATTIT 20. PAGE 57 H1141
ACADEM AGE/Y PARTIC ELITES

L67
VAN DER KROEF J.M.,"INDONESIA: THE BATTLE OF THE 'OLD' AND THE 'NEW ORDER'." INDONESIA ISLAM ELITES POL/PAR DOMIN INGP/REL NAT/LISM PWR...IDEA/COMP 20. PAGE 161 H3229
FORCES MARXISM NAT/G BAL/PWR

S67
AKE C.,"POLITICAL INTEGRATION AND POLITICAL STABILITY." ELITES POL/PAR LEAD ADJUST EFFICIENCY ATTIT AUTHORIT DRIVE...CONCPT 20. PAGE 4 H0088
CULTURE NAT/G CONTROL GP/REL

S67
BUTTINGER J.,"VIETNAM* FRAUD OF THE 'OTHER WAR'." VIETNAM/S ELITES STRUCT AGRI NAT/G FOR/AID RENT TREND. PAGE 25 H0499
PLAN WEALTH REV ECO/UNDEV

S67
CHIU S.M.,"CHINA'S MILITARY POSTURE." CHINA/COM ELITES NAT/G POL/PAR TEC/DEV ECO/TAC DOMIN CONTROL LEAD REV MARXISM 20 MAO. PAGE 30 H0595
FORCES CIVMIL/REL NUC/PWR DIPLOM

S67
LEVI W.,"THE ELITIST NATURE OF NEW ASIA'S FOREIGN POLICY." CULTURE ECO/UNDEV NAT/G PROB/SOLV EDU/PROP COLONIAL CONTROL REGION NAT/LISM...NAT/COMP 20. PAGE 95 H1898
POLICY ELITES DIPLOM CREATE

S67
MALLORY J.R.,"THE MINISTER'S OFFICE STAFF* AN UNREFORMED PART OF PUBLIC SERVICE." CONSTN ELITES STRATA NAT/G PROB/SOLV TASK CHOOSE PERS/REL EFFICIENCY...DECISION 20. PAGE 102 H2033
CANADA ADMIN EX/STRUC STRUCT

S67
PAI G.A.,"TAXATION AND PLANNING IN INDIA: A BIRDS-EYE VIEW." INDIA ELITES NAT/G LEGIS BUDGET CONTROL LOBBY INCOME...STAT CHARTS 20. PAGE 122 H2443
TAX PLAN WEALTH STRATA

S67
RAMA C.M.,"PASADO Y PRESENTE DE LA RELIGION EN AMERICA LATINA." L/A+17C ELITES SOCIETY STRATA MARXISM...STAT WORSHIP PROTESTANT. PAGE 129 H2585
SECT CATHISM STRUCT NAT/COMP

S67
ROCHET W.,"THE OCTOBER REVOLUTION AND THE STRUGGLE OF THE FRENCH COMMUNISTS." COM FRANCE ELITES SOCIETY STRATA ECO/TAC EDU/PROP GP/REL WEALTH ...MARXIST IDEA/COMP NAT/COMP 20. PAGE 133 H2654
SOCISM CHOOSE METH/COMP NAT/G

S67
SUBRAMANIAM V.,"REPRESENTATIVE BUREAUCRACY: A REASSESSMENT." USA+45 ELITES LOC/G NAT/G ADMIN GOV/REL PRIVIL DRIVE ROLE...POLICY CENSUS 20 CIVIL/SERV BUREAUCRCY. PAGE 150 H3006
STRATA GP/REL MGT GOV/COMP

S67
SUNG C.H.,"POLITICAL DIAGNOSIS OF KOREAN SOCIETY* A SURVEY OF MILITARY AND CIVILIAN VALUES." KOREA/S ECO/UNDEV NAT/G CIVMIL/REL...QU SAMP GP/COMP. PAGE 151 H3009
ELITES FORCES ATTIT ORD/FREE

S67
THIEN T.T.,"VIETNAM: A CASE OF SOCIAL ALIENATION." VIETNAM AGRI FORCES FOR/AID ADMIN REPRESENT INGP/REL PWR 19/20. PAGE 154 H3071
NAT/G ELITES WORKER STRANGE

S67
ULC O.,"CLASS STRUGGLE AND SOCIALIST JUSTICE: THE CASE OF CZECHOSLOVAKIA." COM CZECHOSLVK LAW CONSTN ELITES STRUCT NAT/G CRIME GP/REL MARXISM 20. PAGE 158 H3151
TOTALISM CT/SYS ADJUD STRATA

S67
VON LAUE T.H.,"WESTERNIZATION, REVOLUTION AND THE SEARCH FOR A BASIS OF AUTHORITY - RUSSIA IN 1917." USSR ELITES INTELL ECO/UNDEV NAT/G WORKER ECO/TAC TAX ADMIN LEAD AUTHORIT 20 LENIN/VI. PAGE 164 H3274
MARXISM REV COM DOMIN

S68
KANET R.E.,"RECENT SOVIET REASSESSMENT OF DEVELOPMENTS IN THE THIRD WORLD." ALGERIA GHANA INDONESIA USSR WOR+45 CONSTN ELITES INTELL STRUCT DOMIN CONTROL REV PWR MARXISM...IDEA/COMP METH 20 THIRD/WRLD. PAGE 83 H1653
DIPLOM NEUTRAL NAT/G NAT/COMP

S68
LAWRIE G.,"WHAT WILL CHANGE SOUTH AFRICA?" AFR SOUTH/AFR ELITES DOMIN CONTROL REPRESENT...TIME/SEQ TREND 20. PAGE 93 H1848
RACE/REL DIPLOM NAT/G POLICY

S68
LUKASZEWSKI J.,"WESTERN INTEGRATION AND THE PEOPLE'S DEMOCRACIES." USSR ELITES ECO/DEV NAT/G VOL/ASSN INT/TRADE AGREE REV FEDERAL WEALTH SOCISM ...NAT/COMP SOC/INTEG 20 EEC. PAGE 99 H1977
DIPLOM INT/ORG COM REGION

B75
MAINE H.S.,LECTURES ON THE EARLY HISTORY OF INSTITUTIONS. IRELAND UK CONSTN ELITES STRUCT FAM KIN CHIEF LEGIS CT/SYS OWN SOVEREIGN...CONCPT 16 BENTHAM/J BREHON ROMAN/LAW. PAGE 101 H2021
CULTURE LAW INGP/REL

C80
ARNOLD M.,"DEMOCRACY" IN MIXED ESSAYS (2ND ED.)" UK SOCIETY STRUCT...CONCPT METH/COMP 19. PAGE 8 H0166
NAT/G MAJORIT EX/STRUC ELITES

C80
ARNOLD M.,"EQUALITY" IN MIXED ESSAYS." MOD/EUR UK ELITES STRATA NAT/G...CONCPT IDEA/COMP NAT/COMP SOC/INTEG 19. PAGE 8 H0167
ORD/FREE UTOPIA SOCIETY STRUCT

N80
MILL J.S.,"AN ESSAY ON GOVERNMENT" (PAMPHLET). ELITES NAT/G CHIEF OWN ORD/FREE PWR WEALTH GEN/LAWS. PAGE 110 H2207
CONSTN POPULISM REPRESENT UTIL

B84
ENGELS F.,THE ORIGIN OF THE FAMILY, PRIVATE PROPERTY, AND THE STATE (TRANS. BY E. UNTERMANN). UNIV ELITES SOCIETY CAP/ISM ECO/TAC MARRIAGE ORD/FREE POPULISM...MARXIST SOC ENGELS. PAGE 46 H0926
FAM OWN WEALTH SOCISM

B96
LOWELL A.L.,GOVERNMENTS AND PARTIES IN CONTINENTAL EUROPE, VOL. II. AUSTRIA GERMANY HUNGARY MOD/EUR SWITZERLND SOCIETY EX/STRUC LEGIS DIPLOM AGREE LEAD PARL/PROC PWR...POLICY 19. PAGE 99 H1974
POL/PAR NAT/G GOV/REL ELITES

B96
MARX K.,REVOLUTION AND COUNTER-REVOLUTION. GERMANY CONSTN ELITES INDUS NAT/G DIPLOM ECO/TAC WEALTH. PAGE 104 H2083
MARXIST REV PWR STRATA

ELIZABTH/I....ELIZABETH I OF ENGLAND

B57
KANTOROWICZ E.,THE KING'S TWO BODIES; A STUDY IN MEDIEVAL POLITICAL THEOLOGY. UK LAW CONSTN NAT/G CT/SYS...ART/METH HUM CONCPT MYTH TIME/SEQ BIBLIOG 4/17 ELIZABTH/I POPE CHURCH/STA. PAGE 83 H1657
JURID SECT CHIEF SOVEREIGN

ELKIN A.B. H0907

ELKIN A.P. H0908

ELKIN/AP....A.P. ELKIN

B65
BERNDT R.M.,ABORIGINAL MAN IN AUSTRALIA. LAW DOMIN ADMIN COLONIAL MARRIAGE HABITAT ORD/FREE...LING CHARTS ANTHOL BIBLIOG WORSHIP 20 AUSTRAL ABORIGINES MUSIC ELKIN/AP. PAGE 16 H0312
SOC CULTURE SOCIETY STRUCT

ELLIOT J.H. H0909

ELLIS A.B. H0910

ELLISON H.J. H0911

ELWIN V. H0912

EMBREE A.T. H0913,H0914

EMBREE J.F. H0915

EMDEN C.S. H0916

EMERGENCY....SEE DECISION

EMERI C. H0917

EMERSON R. H0918,H0919,H2439

EMERY E. H0920

EMME E.M. H0921

EMMET C. H0922

EMMET D.M. H0923

EMPLOYMENT....SEE WORKER

ENG/CIV/WR....ENGLISH CIVIL WAR

ENGELENBURG F.V. H0433

ENGELS F. H0924,H0925,H0926,H2078,H2081

ENGELS/F....FRIEDRICH ENGELS

B45
VENABLE V.,HUMAN NATURE: THE MARXIAN VIEW. UNIV STRATA CAP/ISM REV GP/REL PERS/REL PRODUC KNOWL ...PHIL/SCI CONCPT IDEA/COMP 19 MARX/KARL ENGELS/F. PAGE 162 H3240 — PERSON MARXISM WORKER UTOPIA

B59
LIPSET S.M.,SOCIAL MOBILITY IN INDUSTRIAL SOCIETY. EUR+WWI USA+45 USSR STRUCT INDUS WRITING GP/REL INGP/REL DRIVE...SOC CHARTS NAT/COMP SOC/INTEG 20 MARX/KARL ENGELS/F. PAGE 97 H1940 — STRATA ECO/DEV SOCIETY

B61
LEVIN L.A.,BIBLIOGRAFIIA BIBLIOGRAFII PROIZVEDENII K. MARKSA, F. ENGELSA, V.I. LENINA. COM USSR NAT/G POL/PAR WORKER LEAD REV ATTIT...POLICY IDEA/COMP 20 MARX/KARL LENIN/VI ENGELS. PAGE 95 H1899 — BIBLIOG/A MARXISM MARXIST CONCPT

B62
EBENSTEIN W.,TWO WAYS OF LIFE. USA+45 CULTURE ECO/DEV PLAN EDU/PROP CONTROL ORD/FREE...GOV/COMP IDEA/COMP T 20 MARX/KARL ENGELS/F LENIN/VI LOCKE/JOHN MILL/JS. PAGE 44 H0885 — MARXISM POPULISM ECO/TAC DIPLOM

B84
ENGELS F.,THE ORIGIN OF THE FAMILY, PRIVATE PROPERTY, AND THE STATE (TRANS. BY E. UNTERMANN). UNIV ELITES SOCIETY CAP/ISM ECO/TAC MARRIAGE ORD/FREE POPULISM...MARXIST SOC ENGELS. PAGE 46 H0926 — FAM OWN WEALTH SOCISM

ENGLAND, BANK OF....SEE BANK/ENGL

ENGLAND....SEE UK, ALSO APPROPRIATE TIME/SPACE/CULTURE INDEX

B75
NEWMAN J.H.,A LETTER ADDRESSED TO THE DUKE OF NORFOLK ON THE OCCASION OF MR. GLADSTONE'S RECENT EXPOSTULATION. NAT/G SECT CHIEF LEGIS CONTROL LEAD GP/REL SUPEGO SOC/INTEG WORSHIP 19 ENGLAND. PAGE 117 H2346 — POLICY DOMIN SOVEREIGN CATHISM

ENGLISH H.E. H0412

ENGLISH CIVIL WAR....SEE ENG/CIV/WR

ENGLSH/LAW....ENGLISH LAW

B10
MCILWAIN C.H.,THE HIGH COURT OF PARLIAMENT AND ITS SUPREMACY B1910 1878 408. UK EX/STRUC PARL/PROC GOV/REL INGP/REL PRIVIL 12/20 PARLIAMENT ENGLSH/LAW. PAGE 107 H2132 — LAW LEGIS CONSTN NAT/G

B24
HOLDSWORTH W.S.,A HISTORY OF ENGLISH LAW; THE COMMON LAW AND ITS RIVALS (VOL. IV). UK SEA AGRI CHIEF ADJUD CONTROL CRIME GOV/REL...INT/LAW JURID NAT/COMP 16/17 PARLIAMENT COMMON/LAW CANON/LAW ENGLSH/LAW. PAGE 72 H1449 — LAW LEGIS CT/SYS CONSTN

B32
LUNT D.C.,THE ROAD TO THE LAW. UK USA-45 LEGIS EDU/PROP OWN ORD/FREE...DECISION TIME/SEQ NAT/COMP 16/20 AUSTRAL ENGLSH/LAW COMMON/LAW. PAGE 99 H1980 — ADJUD LAW JURID CT/SYS

B35
RAM J.,THE SCIENCE OF LEGAL JUDGMENT: A TREATISE... UK CONSTN NAT/G LEGIS CREATE PROB/SOLV AGREE CT/SYS ...INT/LAW CONCPT 19 ENGLSH/LAW CANON/LAW CIVIL/LAW CTS/WESTM. PAGE 129 H2584 — LAW JURID EX/STRUC ADJUD

B38
HOLDSWORTH W.S.,A HISTORY OF ENGLISH LAW; THE CENTURIES OF SETTLEMENT AND REFORM (VOL. XI). UK CONSTN NAT/G EX/STRUC DIPLOM ADJUD CT/SYS LEAD CRIME ATTIT...INT/LAW JURID 18 CMN/WLTH PARLIAMENT ENGLSH/LAW. PAGE 73 H1452 — LAW COLONIAL LEGIS PARL/PROC

B49
DENNING A.,FREEDOM UNDER THE LAW. MOD/EUR UK LAW SOCIETY CHIEF EX/STRUC LEGIS ADJUD CT/SYS PERS/REL PERSON 17/20 ENGLSH/LAW. PAGE 40 H0793 — ORD/FREE JURID NAT/G

B50
WADE E.C.S.,CONSTITUTIONAL LAW; AN OUTLINE OF THE LAW AND PRACTICE OF THE CONSTITUTION. UK LEGIS DOMIN ADMIN GP/REL 16/20 CMN/WLTH PARLIAMENT ENGLSH/LAW. PAGE 164 H3283 — CONSTN NAT/G PARL/PROC LAW

B54
SCHWARTZ B.,FRENCH ADMINISTRATIVE LAW AND THE COMMON-LAW WORLD. FRANCE CULTURE LOC/G NAT/G PROVS DELIB/GP EX/STRUC LEGIS PROB/SOLV CT/SYS EXEC GOV/REL...IDEA/COMP ENGLSH/LAW. PAGE 140 H2808 — JURID LAW METH/COMP ADJUD

B55
SMITH G.,A CONSTITUTIONAL AND LEGAL HISTORY OF ENGLAND. UK ELITES NAT/G LEGIS ADJUD OWN HABITAT POPULISM...JURID 20 ENGLSH/LAW. PAGE 145 H2909 — CONSTN PARTIC LAW CT/SYS

B59
GINSBURG M.,LAW AND OPINION IN ENGLAND. UK CULTURE KIN LABOR LEGIS EDU/PROP ADMIN CT/SYS CRIME OWN HEALTH...ANTHOL 20 ENGLSH/LAW. PAGE 56 H1132 — JURID POLICY ECO/TAC

B59
SQUIBB G.D.,THE HIGH COURT OF CHIVALRY. UK NAT/G FORCES ADJUD WAR 14/20 PARLIAMENT ENGLSH/LAW. PAGE 148 H2959 — CT/SYS PARL/PROC JURID

B64
NEWARK F.H.,NOTES ON IRISH LEGAL HISTORY (2ND ED.). IRELAND UK PARL/PROC ORD/FREE SOVEREIGN 12/20 ENGLSH/LAW. PAGE 117 H2344 — CT/SYS JURID ADJUD NAT/G

B66
KASUNMU A.B.,NIGERIAN FAMILY LAW. NIGERIA KIN LEGIT ILLEGIT MARRIAGE AGE DRIVE HABITAT ALL/VALS...JURID IDEA/COMP T 20 ENGLSH/LAW. PAGE 83 H1667 — FAM LAW CULTURE AFR

ENKE S. H0927,H0928

ENLIGHTNMT....THE ENLIGHTENMENT

N19
HARTUNG F.,ENLIGHTENED DESPOTISM (PAMPHLET). ORD/FREE SOVEREIGN CONSERVE...PHIL/SCI FREDERICK ENLIGHTNMT. PAGE 67 H1350 — NAT/G CHIEF CONCPT PWR

S68
HOOK S.,"THE ENLIGHTENMENT AND MARXISM." CULTURE SOCIETY RATIONAL ORD/FREE PLURISM SOCISM...CONCPT HIST/WRIT 18/19 MARX/KARL HEGEL/GWF ENLIGHTNMT. PAGE 73 H1462 — IDEA/COMP MARXISM OBJECTIVE

ENNIS T.E. H0929

ENSOR R.C.K. H0930

ENTREPRENEURSHIP....SEE OWN, INDUS, CAP/ISM

ENVY....SEE WEALTH, LOVE, AND VALUES INDEX

EPIST....EPISTEMOLOGY, SOCIOLOGY OF KNOWLEDGE

N
INTERNATIONAL BIBLIOGRAPHIE DER DEUTSCHEN ZEITSCHRIFTENLITERATUR. EUR+WWI GERMANY MOD/EUR ECO/DEV POL/PAR LEAD WAR NAT/LISM ATTIT...EPIST PHIL/SCI 19/20. PAGE 1 H0004 — BIBLIOG/A NAT/G PERSON CULTURE

B38
JESSOP T.E.,A BIBLIOGRAPHY OF DAVID HUME AND OF SCOTTISH PHILOSOPHY FROM FRANCIS HUTCHESON TO LORD BALFOUR. UK INTELL NAT/G ATTIT...CONCPT 17/20 HUME/D CMN/WLTH. PAGE 81 H1615 — BIBLIOG EPIST PERCEPT BIOG

S38
LUNDBERG G.A.,"THE CONCEPT OF LAW IN THE SOCIAL SCIENCES"(BMR)" CULTURE INTELL SOCIETY STRUCT CREATE...NEW/IDEA 20. PAGE 99 H1978 — EPIST GEN/LAWS CONCPT PHIL/SCI

S39
LASSWELL H.D.,"PERSON, PERSONALITY, GROUP, CULTURE" (BMR)" UNIV CREATE EDU/PROP...EPIST CONCPT LING METH. PAGE 92 H1833 — PERSON GP/REL CULTURE PERS/REL

S40
GURVITCH G.,"MAJOR PROBLEMS OF THE SOCIOLOGY OF LAW." CULTURE SANCTION KNOWL MORAL...POLICY EPIST JURID WORSHIP. PAGE 63 H1255 — SOC LAW PHIL/SCI

S57
DEXTER L.A.,"A SOCIAL THEORY OF MENTAL DEFICIENCY." CULTURE PUB/INST PROB/SOLV CRIME PERS/REL STRANGE PERSON SUPEGO SKILL...EPIST SOC/WK HYPO/EXP. PAGE 41 H0814 — SOC PSY HEALTH ROLE

C60
BOGARDUS E.S.,"THE DEVELOPMENT OF SOCIAL THOUGHT." SOCIETY PERSON KNOWL...EPIST CONCPT BIBLIOG T. — INTELL CULTURE

PAGE 18 H0365 IDEA/COMP GP/COMP

B62
HUCKER C.O.,CHINA: A CRITICAL BIBLIOGRAPHY (PAMPHLET). ASIA STRUCT AGRI FINAN INDUS HABITAT MARXISM...EPIST HUM. PAGE 74 H1487 BIBLIOG/A CULTURE INTELL SOCIETY

B64
COBBAN A.,ROUSSEAU AND THE MODERN STATE (2ND ED.). FRANCE PROB/SOLV NAT/LISM UTOPIA PERSON MORAL ...EPIST PHIL/SCI SOC IDEA/COMP 18 ROUSSEAU/J BURKE/EDM HOBBES/T HUME/D. PAGE 30 H0612 GEN/LAWS INGP/REL NAT/G ORD/FREE

B64
NORTHROP F.S.,CROSS-CULTURAL UNDERSTANDING: EPISTEMOLOGY IN ANTHROPOLOGY. BURMA GREECE THAILAND HABITAT PERCEPT PERSON...PHIL/SCI SOC METH 20 MEXIC/AMER CHINJAP. PAGE 119 H2375 EPIST PSY CULTURE CONCPT

B66
SOROKIN P.A.,SOCIOLOGICAL THEORIES OF TODAY. SOCIETY STRUCT FAM SECT GP/REL ADJUST...PHIL/SCI PSY TREND METH/COMP 20. PAGE 147 H2935 SOC CULTURE METH/CNCPT EPIST

EPISTEMOLOGY....SEE EPIST

EPSTEIN E.H. H0931

EPSTEIN F.T. H0932,H0933

EPSTEIN L.D. H0934,H0935,H0936

EPTA....EXPANDED PROGRAM OF TECHNICAL ASSISTANCE

EQUILIB....EQUILIBRIUM; SEE ALSO BAL/PWR

B27
BELLOC H.,THE SERVILE STATE (1912) (3RD ED.). PRUSSIA UK CULTURE STRATA INDUS NAT/G ECO/TAC CONTROL LEAD SUFF DISCRIM EQUILIB ORD/FREE WEALTH 20. PAGE 13 H0269 WORKER CAP/ISM DOMIN CATH

B38
LAWLEY F.E.,THE GROWTH OF COLLECTIVE ECONOMY VOL. 2: INTERNATIONAL. WOR-45 AGRI INDUS EQUILIB OPTIMAL OWN WEALTH...NAT/COMP 19/20 NAZI NEW/DEAL MONOPOLY. PAGE 92 H1845 ECO/TAC SOCISM NAT/LISM CONTROL

S46
TANNENBAUM F.,"THE BALANCE OF POWER IN SOCIETY." UNIV STRUCT FAM NAT/G SECT PERS/REL EQUILIB UTOPIA DRIVE ALL/IDEOS...OLD/LIB CONCPT. PAGE 152 H3044 SOCIETY ALL/VALS GP/REL PEACE

C50
ROUSSEAU J.J.,"A DISCOURSE ON POLITICAL ECONOMY" (1755) IN THE SOCIAL CONTRACT AND DISCOURSES." UNIV SOCIETY STRATA STRUCT CONSEN EQUILIB HAPPINESS UTOPIA HEALTH WEALTH...POLICY WELF/ST. PAGE 135 H2699 NAT/G ECO/TAC TAX GEN/LAWS

B58
GLUCKMAN M.,ANALYSIS OF A SOCIAL SITUATION IN MODERN ZULULAND. AFR PERS/REL ADJUST DISCRIM EQUILIB NAT/LISM...SOC RECORD AUD/VIS 20 ZULULAND. PAGE 57 H1146 CULTURE RACE/REL STRUCT GP/REL

S59
LEYS C.,"MODELS, THEORIES, AND THE THEORY OF POLITICAL PARTIES" CANADA LIECHTENST UK LOC/G NAT/G PARTIC REPRESENT GP/REL CONSEN EQUILIB MAJORITY ...NEW/IDEA MATH CHARTS 20. PAGE 96 H1919 POL/PAR CHOOSE METH/CNCPT SIMUL

B61
GANGULI B.N.,ECONOMIC INTEGRATION. FINAN LABOR CAP/ISM DIPLOM WEALTH...NAT/COMP 20. PAGE 55 H1096 ECO/TAC METH/CNCPT EQUILIB ECO/UNDEV

B64
HERSKOVITS M.J.,ECONOMIC TRANSITION IN AFRICA. FUT INT/ORG NAT/G WORKER PROB/SOLV TEC/DEV INT/TRADE EQUILIB INCOME...ANTHOL 20. PAGE 70 H1408 AFR ECO/UNDEV PLAN ADMIN

B65
US DEPARTMENT OF DEFENSE,US SECURITY ARMS CONTROL, AND DISARMAMENT 1961-1965 (PAMPHLET). CHINA/COM COM GERMANY/W ISRAEL SPACE USA+45 USSR WOR+45 FORCES EDU/PROP DETER EQUILIB PEACE ALL/VALS...GOV/COMP 20 NATO. PAGE 159 H3183 BIBLIOG/A ARMS/CONT NUC/PWR DIPLOM

S65
TRISKA J.F.,"SOVIET-AMERICAN RELATIONS* A MULTIPLE SYMMETRY MODEL." USA+45 USSR ACADEM ACT/RES EDU/PROP COERCE PERCEPT...NET/THEORY CHARTS NAT/COMP GEN/LAWS COLD/WAR. PAGE 157 H3132 SIMUL EQUILIB DIPLOM

B66
FOX K.A.,THE THEORY OF QUANTITATIVE ECONOMIC POLICY WITH APPLICATIONS TO ECONOMIC GROWTH AND STABILIZATION. ECO/DEV AGRI NAT/G PLAN ADMIN RISK ...DECISION IDEA/COMP SIMUL T. PAGE 52 H1045 ECO/TAC ECOMETRIC EQUILIB GEN/LAWS

B67
NESS G.D.,BUREAUCRACY AND RURAL DEVELOPMENT IN MALAYSIA. MALAYSIA UK SOCIETY FINAN INDUS WORKER TEC/DEV ECO/TAC COLONIAL EQUILIB ORD/FREE...STAT CHARTS 20. PAGE 117 H2330 ECO/UNDEV PLAN NAT/G ADMIN

B67
WARD L.,LESTER WARD AND THE WELFARE STATE. SOCIETY NAT/G CREATE RECEIVE EQUILIB UTOPIA HABITAT HEREDITY PERSON...POLICY SOC BIOG 19/20 WARD/LEST. PAGE 165 H3303 ALL/VALS NEW/IDEA WELF/ST CONCPT

L67
RUTH J.M.,"THE ADMINISTRATION OF WATER RESOURCES IN GUATEMALA." GUATEMALA L/A+17C DIST/IND LOC/G NAT/G EX/STRUC ADMIN GOV/REL DEMAND EQUILIB WEALTH...GEOG MGT 20. PAGE 136 H2723 EFFICIENCY ECO/UNDEV PLAN ACT/RES

L67
SEGAL A.,"THE INTEGRATION OF DEVELOPING COUNTRIES: SOME THOUGHTS ON EAST AFRICA AND CENTRAL AMERICA." AFR L/A+17C INT/ORG NAT/G VOL/ASSN FOR/AID INT/TRADE EQUILIB NAT/LISM PWR 20. PAGE 141 H2820 ECO/UNDEV DIPLOM REGION

L67
WRIGHT W.R.,"FOREIGN-OWNED RAILWAYS IN ARGENTINA: A CASE STUDY OF ECONOMIC NATIONALISM." L/A+17C UK ECO/UNDEV SERV/IND LG/CO NAT/G TEC/DEV BAL/PWR EQUILIB ARGEN. PAGE 171 H3423 NAT/LISM CAP/ISM ECO/TAC COLONIAL

S67
DIAMANT A.,"EUROPEAN MODELS OF BUREAUCRACY AND DEVELOPMENT." EX/STRUC PLAN ADMIN CONTROL ROUTINE GOV/REL CENTRAL...DECISION TIME/SEQ CHARTS. PAGE 41 H0818 NAT/G EQUILIB ACT/RES NAT/COMP

S67
ROOT W.,"REPORT FROM PARIS - DE GAULLE: WHICH WAY TO THE FUTURE?" CANADA FRANCE ISLAM UK INT/ORG CHIEF CREATE AGREE CONTROL ARMS/CONT NUC/PWR EQUILIB PEACE PWR 20 DEGAULLE/C NATO. PAGE 134 H2670 POLICY DIPLOM NAT/G BAL/PWR

S67
SINGH B.,"ITALIAN EXPERIENCE IN REGIONAL ECONOMIC DEVELOPMENT AND LESSONS FOR OTHER COUNTRIES." EUR+WWI ITALY INDUS NAT/G ACT/RES REGION GP/REL EFFICIENCY EQUILIB PRODUC WEALTH. PAGE 144 H2884 ECO/UNDEV PLAN ECO/TAC CONTROL

S67
SNELLEN I.T.,"APARTHEID* CHECKS AND CHANGES." SOUTH/AFR NAT/G PROB/SOLV COLONIAL REGION TASK GP/REL RACE/REL EFFICIENCY PRIVIL ORD/FREE 20. PAGE 146 H2923 DISCRIM NAT/LISM EQUILIB CONTROL

S68
GUZZARDI W.,"THE DECLINE OF THE STERLING CLUB." UK WOR+45 NAT/G PLAN DIPLOM INT/TRADE AGREE CONSEN EQUILIB SOVEREIGN...POLICY NEW/IDEA 20 COMMONWLTH GOLD/STAND. PAGE 63 H1259 FINAN ECO/TAC WEALTH NAT/COMP

B76
TAINE H.A.,THE ANCIENT REGIME. FRANCE STRATA FORCES PARTIC EQUILIB WEALTH CONSERVE POPULISM...GOV/COMP SOC/INTEG 18/19. PAGE 152 H3035 NAT/G GOV/REL TAX REV

ERASMUS C.J. H0937

ERDEMLI....ERDEMLI, TURKEY

ERDMAN H.L. H0938

ESCUELA SUPERIOR DE ADMIN PUBL H0939

ESMEIN A. H0940

ESPIONAGE....ESPIONAGE

B37
THOMPSON J.W.,SECRET DIPLOMACY: A RECORD OF ESPIONAGE AND DOUBLE-DEALING: 1500-1815. CHRIST-17C MOD/EUR NAT/G WRITING RISK MORAL...ANTHOL BIBLIOG 16/19 ESPIONAGE. PAGE 154 H3084 DIPLOM CRIME

B58
HSU U.T.,THE INVISIBLE CONFLICT. ASIA USSR ELITES NAT/G CONTROL LEAD COERCE REV WAR NAT/LISM ORD/FREE PWR 20 COM/PARTY ESPIONAGE. PAGE 74 H1485 MARXISM POL/PAR EDU/PROP FORCES

ESTEBAN J.C. H0941

ESTEVEZ A. H0942

ESTIMATION....SEE COST

ESTONIA....SEE ALSO USSR

B58
KURL S.,ESTONIA: A SELECTED BIBLIOGRAPHY. USSR ESTONIA LAW INTELL SECT...ART/METH GEOG HUM SOC 20. BIBLIOG CULTURE

PAGE 89 H1784 NAT/G

ESTRANGEMENT....SEE STRANGE

ETHIC....PERSONAL ETHICS

ETHIOPIA....SEE ALSO AFR

B39
HILL R.L.,A BIBLIOGRAPHY OF THE ANGLO-EGYPTIAN SUDAN FROM THE EARLIEST TIMES TO 1937. AFR ETHIOPIA SUDAN UAR LAW COM/IND SECT RACE/REL...GEOG HEAL SOC LING 19/20 NEGRO. PAGE 71 H1417
BIBLIOG CULTURE NAT/COMP GP/COMP

B55
INTERNATIONAL AFRICAN INST,ETHNOGRAPHIC SURVEY OF AFRICA: NORTH EASTERN AFRICA (VOLUMES 1-2, 1955-56). AFR ETHIOPIA CULTURE ECO/UNDEV KIN GOV/REL ATTIT HEREDITY...GEOG CHARTS BIBLIOG WORSHIP 20. PAGE 77 H1545
STRUCT ECO/TAC INGP/REL HABITAT

L65
MATTHEWS D.G.,"A CURRENT BIBLIOGRAPHY ON ETHIOPIAN AFFAIRS: A SELECT BIBLIOGRAPHY FROM 1950-1964." ETHIOPIA LAW CULTURE ECO/UNDEV INDUS LABOR SECT FORCES DIPLOM CIVMIL/REL RACE/REL...LING STAT 20. PAGE 105 H2093
BIBLIOG/A ADMIN POL/PAR NAT/G

S66
MATTHEWS D.G.,"ETHIOPIAN OUTLINE: A BIBLIOGRAPHIC RESEARCH GUIDE." ETHIOPIA LAW STRUCT ECO/UNDEV AGRI LABOR SECT CHIEF DELIB/GP EX/STRUC ADMIN...LING ORG/CHARTS 20. PAGE 105 H2095
BIBLIOG NAT/G DIPLOM POL/PAR

L68
CURRENT HISTORY,"AFRICA, 1968." ETHIOPIA GHANA NIGERIA SOUTH/AFR CULTURE ECO/UNDEV KIN SECT CHIEF EX/STRUC WAR WEAPON CHOOSE CIVMIL/REL...GOV/COMP 20 AFRICA/E. PAGE 36 H0724
RACE/REL NAT/LISM FORCES AFR

ETHNICITY....SEE RACE/REL, CULTURE

ETIQUET....ETIQUETTE, STYLING, FASHION, MANNERS

B06
SUMNER W.G.,FOLKWAYS: STUDY OF THE SOCIOLOGICAL IMPORTANCE OF USAGES, MANNERS, CUSTOMS, MORES, AND MORALS. STRUCT KIN ETIQUET ROUTINE MURDER MARRIAGE PEACE SEX ALL/VALS WEALTH BIBLIOG. PAGE 150 H3008
CULTURE SOC SANCTION MORAL

B35
DE TOCQUEVILLE A.,DEMOCRACY IN AMERICA (4 VOLS.) (TRANS. BY HENRY REEVE). CONSTN STRUCT LOC/G NAT/G POL/PAR PROVS ETIQUET CT/SYS MAJORITY ATTIT 18/19. PAGE 39 H0772
POPULISM MAJORIT ORD/FREE SOCIETY

B58
SALETORE B.A.,INDIA'S DIPLOMATIC RELATIONS WITH THE WEST. GREECE INDIA CULTURE ETIQUET...IDEA/COMP 3 ROM/EMP PERSIA. PAGE 137 H2739
DIPLOM CONCPT INT/TRADE

B60
SALETORE B.A.,INDIA'S DIPLOMATIC RELATIONS WITH THE EAST. ASIA CEYLON INDIA NEPAL S/ASIA CULTURE 7/14 PERSIA. PAGE 137 H2740
DIPLOM NAT/COMP ETIQUET

B65
KLEIN J.,SAMPLES FROM ENGLISH CULTURES (2 VOLS.). UK STRATA FAM NEIGH WORKER ETIQUET ISOLAT AGE/C AGE/A HABITAT RIGID/FLEX...NET/THEORY CHARTS 20. PAGE 87 H1732
CULTURE INGP/REL ATTIT SOC

ETSCHMANN R. H0943

ETTINGHAUSEN R. H0944

ETZIONI A. H0945,H0946

EUCKEN W. H0947

EUGENICS....SEE BIO/SOC+GEOG

EUGENIE....EMPRESS EUGENIE (FRANCE)

EULAU H. H0948

EURATOM....EUROPEAN ATOMIC ENERGY COMMUNITY

B63
MAYNE R.,THE COMMUNITY OF EUROPE. UK CONSTN NAT/G CONSULT DELIB/GP CREATE PLAN ECO/TAC LEGIT ADMIN ROUTINE ORD/FREE PWR WEALTH...CONCPT TIME/SEQ EEC EURATOM 20. PAGE 105 H2107
EUR+WWI INT/ORG REGION

EURCOALSTL....EUROPEAN COAL AND STEEL COMMUNITY; SEE ALSO VOL/ASSN, INT/ORG

EURCT/JUST....EUROPEAN COURT OF JUSTICE

EUROPA PUBLICATIONS LIMITED H0949

EUROPE....SEE MOD/EUR

B19
DE MAN H.,THE REMAKING OF A MIND. EUR+WWI NAT/G ECO/TAC REGION ORD/FREE SOCISM...BIOG 20 WWI EUROPE. PAGE 38 H0762
PSY WAR SELF/OBS PARTIC

N19
POUND R.,ORGANIZATION OF THE COURTS (PAMPHLET). MOD/EUR UK USA-45 ADJUD PWR...GOV/COMP 10/20 EUROPE. PAGE 127 H2546
CT/SYS JURID STRUCT ADMIN

B23
GRANT C.F.,STUDIES IN NORTH AFRICA. ALGERIA MOROCCO ROMAN/EMP CULTURE STRUCT NAT/G DIPLOM WAR ...NAT/COMP TUNIS EUROPE. PAGE 60 H1195
ISLAM SECT DOMIN COLONIAL

B23
WILLOUGHBY W.C.,RACE PROBLEMS IN THE NEW AFRICA: A STUDY OF THE RELATION OF BANTU AND BRITONS IN THOSE PARTS OF BANTU AFRICA... AFR STRUCT SECT DOMIN EDU/PROP GP/REL ATTIT WORSHIP 20 BANTU EUROPE MISSION CHRISTIAN. PAGE 168 H3372
KIN COLONIAL RACE/REL CULTURE

B38
COUPLAND R.,EAST AFRICA AND ITS INVADERS. AFR ISLAM STRATA SECT FORCES DIPLOM TRIBUTE CONTROL DISCRIM NAT/LISM 19 AFRICA/E EUROPE MISSION. PAGE 34 H0680
CULTURE ELITES COLONIAL MARKET

B39
MARQUAND H.A.,ORGANIZED LABOUR IN FOUR CONTINENTS. EUR+WWI USA-45 INDUS NAT/G PAY GP/REL TOTALISM ATTIT WEALTH ALL/IDEOS...TREND NAT/COMP 20 ILO AFL/CIO EUROPE CHINJAP MEXIC/AMER. PAGE 103 H2055
LABOR WORKER CONCPT ANTHOL

B42
FEFFERO G.,THE PRINCIPLES OF POWER (TRANS. BY T. JAECKEL). MOD/EUR CONSTN NAT/G CHIEF CONTROL REV WAR ORD/FREE CONSERVE FASCISM POPULISM...GEN/LAWS 18/20 EUROPE. PAGE 49 H0980
PWR LEGIT TRADIT ELITES

B47
MCILWAIN C.H.,CONSTITUTIONALISM: ANCIENT AND MODERN. USA+45 ROMAN/EMP LAW CHIEF LEGIS CT/SYS GP/REL ORD/FREE SOVEREIGN...POLICY TIME/SEQ ROMAN/REP EUROPE. PAGE 107 H2135
CONSTN NAT/G PARL/PROC GOV/COMP

S49
BOUSCAREN A.T.,"THE EUROPEAN CHRISTIAN DEMOCRATS" EUR+WWI NAT/G LEGIS 19/20 CHRIS/DEM EUROPE. PAGE 19 H0387
REPRESENT POL/PAR

B50
DUCLOS P.,L'EVOLUTION DES RAPPORTS POLITIQUES DEPUIS 1750 (LIBERTE, INTEGRATION, UNITE). LAW INT/ORG FEDERAL TOTALISM ATTIT PWR...MAJORIT BIBLIOG 18/20 PARLIAMENT EUROPE. PAGE 43 H0852
ORD/FREE DIPLOM NAT/G GOV/COMP

B54
FRIEDMAN W.,THE PUBLIC CORPORATION: A COMPARATIVE SYMPOSIUM (UNIVERSITY OF TORONTO SCHOOL OF LAW COMPARATIVE LAW SERIES, VOL. I). SWEDEN USA+45 INDUS INT/ORG NAT/G REGION CENTRAL FEDERAL...POLICY JURID IDEA/COMP NAT/COMP ANTHOL 20 COMMONWLTH MONOPOLY EUROPE. PAGE 53 H1065
LAW SOCISM LG/CO OWN

B59
EMME E.M.,THE IMPACT OF AIR POWER - NATIONAL SECURITY AND WORLD POLITICS. USA+45 USSR FORCES DIPLOM WEAPON PEACE TOTALISM...POLICY NAT/COMP 20 EUROPE. PAGE 46 H0921
DETER AIR WAR ORD/FREE

B60
ALBRECHT-CARRIE R.,FRANCE, EUROPE AND THE TWO WORLD WARS. EUR+WWI FRANCE GERMANY MOD/EUR UK ECO/DEV NAT/G FORCES BAL/PWR DOMIN ARMS/CONT PEACE PWR 20 TREATY EUROPE. PAGE 5 H0096
DIPLOM WAR

B62
BELL D.,THE END OF IDEOLOGY (REV. ED.). USA+45 USA-45 ELITES STRATA LABOR CREATE CRIME PWR MARXISM ...PHIL/SCI METH/COMP 20 EUROPE. PAGE 13 H0265
CROWD CAP/ISM SOCISM IDEA/COMP

B64
FROMM E.,MARX'S CONCEPT OF MAN. LABOR OWN PERSON ...HUM IDEA/COMP GEN/LAWS 17 MARX/KARL EUROPE SPINOZA/B GOETHE/J HEGEL/GWF. PAGE 54 H1072
INGP/REL CONCPT MARXISM SOCISM

B64
SANDEE J.,EUROPE'S FUTURE CONSUMPTION. EUR+WWI FUT EDU/PROP...IDEA/COMP NAT/COMP ANTHOL 20 EUROPE. PAGE 137 H2750
MARKET ECO/DEV PREDICT PRICE

S64
KANOUTE P.,"AFRICAN SOCIALISM." AFR CONSTN NAT/G COLONIAL ORD/FREE...GOV/COMP METH/COMP 20 EUROPE. PAGE 83 H1655
SOCISM CULTURE STRUCT IDEA/COMP

B65
CALLEO D.P.,EUROPE'S FUTURE: THE GRAND ALTERNATIVES. UK INT/ORG DIPLOM PWR SOVEREIGN ...CONCPT IDEA/COMP NAT/COMP BIBLIOG 20 EEC EUROPE DEGAULLE/C NATO. PAGE 25 H0506
FUT EUR+WWI FEDERAL NAT/LISM

B65
MEYER F.S.,THE AFRICAN NETTLE. SOUTH/AFR NAT/LISM SOVEREIGN...ANTHOL 20 EUROPE. PAGE 110 H2191
AFR COLONIAL RACE/REL ECO/UNDEV

B66
FUCHS W.P.,STAAT UND KIRCHE IM WANDEL DER JAHRHUNDERTE. EUR+WWI MOD/EUR UK REV...JURID CONCPT 4/20 EUROPE CHRISTIAN CHURCH/STA. PAGE 54 H1074
SECT NAT/G ORD/FREE GP/REL

EUROPE/E....EASTERN EUROPE (ALL EUROPEAN COMMUNIST NATIONS)

B61
BURKS R.V.,THE DYNAMICS OF COMMUNISM IN EASTERN EUROPE. COM YUGOSLAVIA POL/PAR RACE/REL ISOLAT ...CORREL CON/ANAL CHARTS GP/COMP DICTIONARY 20 EUROPE/E SLAV/MACED. PAGE 24 H0489
MARXISM STRUCT WORKER REPRESENT

L63
BOLGAR V.,"THE PUBLIC INTEREST: A JURISPRUDENTIAL AND COMPARATIVE OVERVIEW OF SYMPOSIUM ON FUNDAMENTAL CONCEPTS OF PUBLIC LAW" COM FRANCE GERMANY SWITZERLND LAW ADJUD ADMIN AGREE LAISSEZ ...JURID GEN/LAWS 20 EUROPE/E. PAGE 18 H0369
CONCPT ORD/FREE CONTROL NAT/COMP

B64
GRIFFITH W.E.,COMMUNISM IN EUROPE (2 VOLS.). CZECHOSLVK USSR WOR+45 WOR-45 YUGOSLAVIA INGP/REL MARXISM SOCISM...ANTHOL 20 EUROPE/E. PAGE 61 H1225
COM POL/PAR DIPLOM GOV/COMP

B64
KIS T.I.,LES PAYS DE L'EUROPE DE L'EST: LEURS RAPPORTS MUTUELS ET LE PROBLEME DE LEUR INTEGRATION DANS L'ORBITE DE L'USSR. EUR+WWI RUSSIA USSR INT/ORG NAT/G REV ATTIT...JURID SOC BIBLIOG WARSAW/P COMECON EUROPE/E. PAGE 86 H1727
DIPLOM COM MARXISM REGION

B66
SKILLING H.G.,THE GOVERNMENTS OF COMMUNIST EAST EUROPE. COM EUR+WWI ELITES FORCES DIPLOM ECO/TAC CONTROL HABITAT SOCISM...DECISION BIBLIOG 20 EUROPE/E COM/PARTY. PAGE 145 H2895
MARXISM NAT/COMP GP/COMP DOMIN

EUROPE/W....WESTERN EUROPE (NON-COMMUNIST EUROPE, EXCLUDING GREECE, TURKEY, SCANDINAVIA, AND THE BRITISH ISLES)

N19
HACKETT J.,ECONOMIC PLANNING IN FRANCE; ITS RELATION TO THE POLICIES OF THE DEVELOPED COUNTRIES OF WESTERN EUROPE (PAMPHLET). EUR+WWI FRANCE ECO/DEV PROB/SOLV CONTROL...POLICY 20 EUROPE/W. PAGE 63 H1270
ECO/TAC NAT/G PLAN INSPECT

B47
ISAAC J.,ECONOMICS OF MIGRATION. MOD/EUR CULTURE STRATA STRUCT NAT/G COLONIAL WEALTH...OLD/LIB TREND TIME 19/20 EUROPE/W MIGRATION. PAGE 78 H1569
HABITAT SOC GEOG

B59
BLOOMFIELD L.P.,WESTERN EUROPE AND THE UN - TRENDS AND PROSPECTS. EUR+WWI BAL/PWR DIPLOM ECO/TAC COLONIAL ATTIT PWR...POLICY 20 UN EUROPE/W. PAGE 18 H0359
INT/ORG TREND FUT NAT/G

B66
MARTIN L.W.,DIPLOMACY IN MODERN EUROPEAN HISTORY. EUR+WWI MOD/EUR INT/ORG NAT/G EX/STRUC ROUTINE WAR PEACE TOTALISM PWR 15/20 COLD/WAR EUROPE/W. PAGE 103 H2064
DIPLOM POLICY

EUROPEAN ATOMIC ENERGY COMMUNITY....SEE EURATOM

EUROPEAN COAL AND STEEL COMMUNITY....SEE EURCOALSTL

EUROPEAN CONVENTION ON HUMAN RIGHTS....SEE ECHR

EUROPEAN COURT OF JUSTICE....SEE EURCT/JUST

EUROPEAN ECONOMIC COMMUNITY....SEE EEC

EUROPEAN FREE TRADE ASSOCIATION....SEE EFTA

EUROPEAN INVESTMENT BANK....SEE EIB

EUROPEAN FREE TRADE ASSN H0950

EUSDEN J.D. H0951

EUSTOW D.A. H3307

EVANS R.H. H0952

EVANS-PRITCHARD E.E. H0953,H0954,H1039

EVERS/MED....MEDGAR EVERS

EX POST FACTO LAWS....SEE EXPOSTFACT

EX/IM/BANK....EXPORT-IMPORT BANK

EX/STRUC....EXECUTIVE ESTABLISHMENTS

N
INSTITUTE OF HISPANIC STUDIES,HISPANIC AMERICAN REPORT. EUR+WWI SPAIN LAW CONSTN ECO/UNDEV POL/PAR EX/STRUC LEGIS LEAD...HUM SOC 20. PAGE 77 H1538
BIBLIOG/A L/A+17C NAT/G DIPLOM

B03
GRIFFIN A.P.C.,LIST OF BOOKS ON THE CABINETS OF ENGLAND AND AMERICA (PAMPHLET). MOD/EUR UK USA-45 CONSTN NAT/G CONSULT EX/STRUC 19/20. PAGE 61 H1216
BIBLIOG/A GOV/COMP ADMIN DELIB/GP

B08
THE GOVERNMENT OF SOUTH AFRICA (VOL. II). SOUTH/AFR STRATA EXTR/IND EX/STRUC TOP/EX BUDGET ADJUD ADMIN CT/SYS PRODUC...CORREL CENSUS 19 RAILROAD CIVIL/SERV POSTAL/SYS. PAGE 2 H0030
CONSTN FINAN LEGIS NAT/G

B10
MCILWAIN C.H.,THE HIGH COURT OF PARLIAMENT AND ITS SUPREMACY B1910 1878 408. UK EX/STRUC PARL/PROC GOV/REL INGP/REL PRIVIL 12/20 PARLIAMENT ENGLSH/LAW. PAGE 107 H2132
LAW LEGIS CONSTN NAT/G

B10
TEMPERLEY H.W.V.,SENATES AND UPPER CHAMBERS; THEIR USE AND FUNCTION IN THE MODERN STATE... UK WOR-45 CONSTN NAT/G POL/PAR PROVS SECT COLONIAL LEAD CHOOSE REPRESENT PWR...BIBLIOG 19/20 PARLIAMENT SENATE CMN/WLTH HOUSE/LORD. PAGE 153 H3059
PARL/PROC NAT/COMP LEGIS EX/STRUC

B12
HARIOU M.,LA SOUVERAINTE NATIONALE. EX/STRUC FORCES LEGIS CHOOSE PWR JURID. PAGE 66 H1331
SOVEREIGN CONCPT NAT/G REPRESENT

B16
TREITSCHKE H.,POLITICS. UNIV SOCIETY STRATA NAT/G EX/STRUC LEGIS DOMIN EDU/PROP ATTIT PWR RESPECT ...CONCPT TIME/SEQ GEN/LAWS TOT/POP 20. PAGE 157 H3129
EXEC ELITES GERMANY

B17
HARLOW R.V.,THE HISTORY OF LEGISLATIVE METHODS IN THE PERIOD BEFORE 1825. USA-45 EX/STRUC ADMIN COLONIAL LEAD PARL/PROC ROUTINE...GP/COMP GOV/COMP HOUSE/REP. PAGE 66 H1333
LEGIS DELIB/GP PROVS POL/PAR

B18
WILSON W.,THE STATE: ELEMENTS OF HISTORICAL AND PRACTICAL POLITICS. FRANCE GERMANY ITALY UK USSR CONSTN EX/STRUC LEGIS CT/SYS WAR PWR...POLICY GOV/COMP 20. PAGE 169 H3385
NAT/G JURID CONCPT NAT/COMP

B18
YUKIO O.,THE VOICE OF JAPANESE DEMOCRACY, AN ESSAY ON CONSTITUTIONAL LOYALTY (TRANS BY J. E. BECKER). ASIA POL/PAR DELIB/GP EX/STRUC RIGID/FLEX ORD/FREE PWR...POLICY JURID METH/COMP 19/20 CHINJAP. PAGE 172 H3443
CONSTN MAJORIT CHOOSE NAT/G

B19
NATHAN M.,THE SOUTH AFRICAN COMMONWEALTH: CONSTITUTION, PROBLEMS, SOCIAL CONDITIONS. SOUTH/AFR UK CULTURE INDUS EX/STRUC LEGIS BUDGET EDU/PROP ADMIN CT/SYS GP/REL RACE/REL...LING 19/20 CMN/WLTH. PAGE 116 H2317
CONSTN NAT/G POL/PAR SOCIETY

N19
CANADA CIVIL SERV COMM,THE ANALYSIS OF ORGANIZATION IN THE GOVERNMENT OF CANADA (PAMPHLET). CANADA CONSTN EX/STRUC LEGIS TOP/EX CREATE PLAN CONTROL GP/REL 20. PAGE 26 H0517
NAT/G MGT ADMIN DELIB/GP

N19
FIKS M.,PUBLIC ADMINISTRATION IN ISRAEL (PAMPHLET). ISRAEL SCHOOL EX/STRUC BUDGET PAY INGP/REL ...DECISION 20 CIVIL/SERV. PAGE 50 H0999
EDU/PROP NAT/G ADMIN WORKER

N19
PROVISIONS SECTION OAU,ORGANIZATION OF AFRICAN UNITY: BASIC DOCUMENTS AND RESOLUTIONS (PAMPHLET). AFR CULTURE ECO/UNDEV DIPLOM ECO/TAC EDU/PROP COLONIAL ARMS/CONT NUC/PWR RACE/REL DISCRIM NAT/LISM 20 UN OAU. PAGE 128 H2564
CONSTN EX/STRUC SOVEREIGN INT/ORG

C20
BLACHLY F.F.,"THE GOVERNMENT AND ADMINISTRATION OF GERMANY." GERMANY CONSTN LOC/G PROVS DELIB/GP EX/STRUC FORCES LEGIS TOP/EX CT/SYS...BIBLIOG/A 19/20. PAGE 17 H0348
NAT/G GOV/REL ADMIN PHIL/SCI

B21
STUART G.H.,FRENCH FOREIGN POLICY. CONSTN INT/ORG NAT/G POL/PAR EX/STRUC FORCES PLAN ECO/TAC DOMIN EDU/PROP ADJUD COERCE ATTIT DRIVE RIGID/FLEX ALL/VALS...POLICY OBS RECORD BIOG TIME/SEQ TREND.
MOD/EUR DIPLOM FRANCE

PAGE 150 H3000

B26

POLLARD A.F.,THE EVOLUTION OF PARLIAMENT. UK CONSTN POL/PAR EX/STRUC GOV/REL INGP/REL PRIVIL RIGID/FLEX ...TIME/SEQ 11/20 CMN/WLTH PARLIAMENT. PAGE 127 H2536 LEGIS PARL/PROC NAT/G

B27

GOOCH G.P.,ENGLISH DEMOCRATIC IDEAS IN THE SEVENTEENTH CENTURY (2ND ED.). UK LAW SECT FORCES DIPLOM LEAD PARL/PROC REV ATTIT AUTHORIT...ANARCH CONCPT 17 PARLIAMENT CMN/WLTH REFORMERS. PAGE 58 H1167 IDEA/COMP MAJORIT EX/STRUC CONSERVE

B27

HOCART A.M.,KINGSHIP. UNIV CULTURE EX/STRUC TRIBUTE ROUTINE CHOOSE ROLE SOVEREIGN RITUAL 20 KING. PAGE 72 H1441 CHIEF MYTH IDEA/COMP

B27

WILLOUGHBY W.F.,PRINCIPLES OF PUBLIC ADMINISTRATION WITH SPECIAL REFERENCE TO THE NATIONAL AND STATE GOVERNMENTS OF THE UNITED STATES. FINAN PROVS CHIEF CONSULT LEGIS CREATE BUDGET EXEC ROUTINE GOV/REL CENTRAL...MGT 20 BUR/BUDGET CONGRESS PRESIDENT. PAGE 169 H3373 NAT/G EX/STRUC OP/RES ADMIN

B30

BURLAMAQUI J.J.,PRINCIPLES OF NATURAL AND POLITIC LAW (2 VOLS.) (1747-51). EX/STRUC LEGIS AGREE CT/SYS CHOOSE ROLE SOVEREIGN 18 NATURL/LAW. PAGE 24 H0490 LAW NAT/G ORD/FREE CONCPT

B30

BYNKERSHOEK C.,QUAESTIONUM JURIS PUBLICI LIBRI DUO. CHRIST-17C MOD/EUR CONSTN ELITES SOCIETY NAT/G PROVS EX/STRUC FORCES TOP/EX BAL/PWR DIPLOM ATTIT MORAL...TRADIT CONCPT. PAGE 25 H0502 INT/ORG LAW NAT/LISM INT/LAW

B31

DEKAT A.D.A.,COLONIAL POLICY. S/ASIA CULTURE EX/STRUC ECO/TAC DOMIN ADMIN COLONIAL ROUTINE SOVEREIGN WEALTH...POLICY MGT RECORD KNO/TEST SAMP. PAGE 39 H0785 DRIVE PWR INDONESIA NETHERLAND

B31

KIRKPATRICK F.A.,A HISTORY OF THE ARGENTINE REPUBLIC. SPAIN UK CONSTN SOCIETY ECO/UNDEV EX/STRUC DIPLOM FOR/AID LEAD WAR ATTIT...BIOG CHARTS 16/20 ARGEN SAN/MARTIN. PAGE 86 H1724 NAT/G L/A+17C COLONIAL

B32

CARDINALL AW,A BIBLIOGRAPHY OF THE GOLD COAST. AFR UK NAT/G EX/STRUC ATTIT...POLICY 19/20. PAGE 26 H0527 BIBLIOG ADMIN COLONIAL DIPLOM

B32

CHILDS J.B.,THE MEMORIAS OF THE REPUBLICS OF CENTRAL AMERICA AND OF THE ANTILLES. L/A+17C 19/20 CENTRAL/AM. PAGE 29 H0592 BIBLIOG GOV/REL NAT/G EX/STRUC

B32

GREAT BRIT COMM MINISTERS PWR,REPORT. UK LAW CONSTN CONSULT LEGIS PARL/PROC SANCTION SOVEREIGN ...DECISION JURID 20 PARLIAMENT. PAGE 60 H1201 EX/STRUC NAT/G PWR CONTROL

B32

MCKISACK M.,THE PARLIAMENTARY REPRESENTATION OF THE ENGLISH BOROUGHS DURING THE MIDDLE AGES. UK CONSTN CULTURE ELITES EX/STRUC TAX PAY ADJUD PARL/PROC APPORT FEDERAL...POLICY 13/15 PARLIAMENT. PAGE 107 H2139 NAT/G MUNIC LEGIS CHOOSE

B33

ENSOR R.C.K.,COURTS AND JUDGES IN FRANCE, GERMANY, AND ENGLAND. FRANCE GERMANY UK LAW PROB/SOLV ADMIN ROUTINE CRIME ROLE...METH/COMP 20 CIVIL/LAW. PAGE 46 H0930 CT/SYS EX/STRUC ADJUD NAT/COMP

B34

RIDLEY C.E.,THE CITY-MANAGER PROFESSION. CHIEF PLAN ADMIN CONTROL ROUTINE CHOOSE...TECHNIC CHARTS GOV/COMP BIBLIOG 20. PAGE 131 H2624 MUNIC EX/STRUC LOC/G EXEC

B35

RAM J.,THE SCIENCE OF LEGAL JUDGMENT: A TREATISE... UK CONSTN NAT/G LEGIS CREATE PROB/SOLV AGREE CT/SYS ...INT/LAW CONCPT 19 ENGLSH/LAW CANON/LAW CIVIL/LAW CTS/WESTM. PAGE 129 H2584 LAW JURID EX/STRUC ADJUD

B36

RAPPARD W.E.,THE GOVERNMENT OF SWITZERLAND. SWITZERLND INT/ORG POL/PAR EX/STRUC DIPLOM NEUTRAL PARL/PROC REGION WAR HABITAT SOVEREIGN...NAT/COMP SOC/INTEG 20 LEAGUE/NAT WWI. PAGE 130 H2594 CONSTN NAT/G CULTURE FEDERAL

B38

FIELD G.L.,THE SYNDICAL AND CORPORATIVE INSTITUTIONS OF ITALIAN FASCISM. ITALY CONSTN STRATA LABOR EX/STRUC TOP/EX ADJUD ADMIN LEAD TOTALISM AUTHORIT...MGT 20 MUSSOLIN/B. PAGE 50 H0991 FASCISM INDUS NAT/G WORKER

B38

HOLDSWORTH W.S.,A HISTORY OF ENGLISH LAW; THE CENTURIES OF SETTLEMENT AND REFORM (VOL. X). INDIA UK CONSTN NAT/G CHIEF LEGIS ADMIN COLONIAL CT/SYS CHOOSE ORD/FREE PWR...JURID 18 PARLIAMENT COMMONWLTH COMMON/LAW. PAGE 72 H1451 LAW LOC/G EX/STRUC ADJUD

B38

HOLDSWORTH W.S.,A HISTORY OF ENGLISH LAW; THE CENTURIES OF SETTLEMENT AND REFORM (VOL. XI). UK CONSTN NAT/G EX/STRUC DIPLOM ADJUD CT/SYS LEAD CRIME ATTIT...INT/LAW JURID 18 CMN/WLTH PARLIAMENT ENGLSH/LAW. PAGE 73 H1452 LAW COLONIAL LEGIS PARL/PROC

B39

SIEYES E.J.,LES DISCOURS DE SIEYES DANS LES DEBATS CONSTITUTIONNELS DE L'AN III (2 ET 18 THERMIDOR). FRANCE LAW NAT/G PROB/SOLV BAL/PWR GOV/REL 18 JURY. PAGE 144 H2871 CONSTN ADJUD LEGIS EX/STRUC

B41

CHILDS J.B.,COLOMBIAN GOVERNMENT PUBLICATIONS (PAMPHLET). L/A+17C SOCIETY 19/20 COLOMB. PAGE 30 H0593 BIBLIOG GOV/REL NAT/G EX/STRUC

B41

CHILDS J.B.,A GUIDE TO THE OFFICIAL PUBLICATIONS OF THE OTHER AMERICAN REPUBLICS: ARGENTINA. CHIEF DIPLOM GOV/REL...BIBLIOG 18/19 ARGEN. PAGE 30 H0594 NAT/G EX/STRUC METH/CNCPT LEGIS

S41

DENNERY E.,"DEMOCRACY AND THE FRENCH ARMY." FRANCE NAT/G EX/STRUC LEAD REV ROLE 18/20. PAGE 40 H0792 FORCES POPULISM STRATA CIVMIL/REL

B42

NEUMANN S.,PERMANENT REVOLUTION: THE TOTAL STATE IN A WORLD AT WAR. COM EUR+WWI GERMANY USSR EX/STRUC DIPLOM CONTROL COERCE REPRESENT MARXISM...SOC GOV/COMP BIBLIOG 20 HITLER/A STALIN/J. PAGE 117 H2337 FASCISM TOTALISM DOMIN EDU/PROP

B42

SINGTON D.,THE GOEBBELS EXPERIMENT. GERMANY MOD/EUR NAT/G EX/STRUC FORCES CONTROL ROUTINE WAR TOTALISM PWR...ART/METH HUM 20 NAZI GOEBBELS/J. PAGE 144 H2886 FASCISM EDU/PROP ATTIT COM/IND

S43

PRICE D.K.,"THE PARLIAMENTARY AND PRESIDENTIAL SYSTEMS" (BMR)" USA-45 NAT/G EX/STRUC PARL/PROC GOV/REL PWR 20 PRESIDENT CONGRESS PARLIAMENT. PAGE 128 H2561 LEGIS REPRESENT ADMIN GOV/COMP

B44

BARKER E.,THE DEVELOPMENT OF PUBLIC SERVICES IN WESTERN WUROPE: 1660-1930. FRANCE GERMANY UK SCHOOL CONTROL REPRESENT ROLE...WELF/ST 17/20. PAGE 11 H0219 GOV/COMP ADMIN EX/STRUC

B45

CONOVER H.F.,THE GOVERNMENTS OF THE MAJOR FOREIGN POWERS: A BIBLIOGRAPHY. FRANCE GERMANY ITALY UK USSR CONSTN LOC/G POL/PAR EX/STRUC FORCES ADMIN CT/SYS CIVMIL/REL TOTALISM...POLICY 19/20. PAGE 32 H0645 BIBLIOG NAT/G DIPLOM

B45

CONOVER H.F.,ITALY: ECONOMICS, POLITICS AND MILITARY AFFAIRS, 1940-1945. ITALY ELITES NAT/G POL/PAR EX/STRUC TOP/EX DIPLOM DOMIN CONTROL COERCE WAR CIVMIL/REL EFFICIENCY 20. PAGE 32 H0646 BIBLIOG TOTALISM FORCES

B46

DAVIES E.,NATIONAL ENTERPRISE: THE DEVELOPMENT OF THE PUBLIC CORPORATION. UK LG/CO EX/STRUC WORKER PROB/SOLV COST ATTIT SOCISM 20. PAGE 37 H0748 ADMIN NAT/G CONTROL INDUS

B47

MARX F.M.,THE PRESIDENT AND HIS STAFF SERVICES PUBLIC ADMINISTRATION SERVICES NUMBER 98 (PAMPHLET). FINAN ADMIN CT/SYS REPRESENT PWR 20 PRESIDENT. PAGE 104 H2075 CONSTN CHIEF NAT/G EX/STRUC

B48

ROSSITER C.L.,CONSTITUTIONAL DICTATORSHIP; CRISIS GOVERNMENT IN THE MODERN DEMOCRACIES. FRANCE GERMANY UK USA-45 WOR-45 EX/STRUC BAL/PWR CONTROL COERCE WAR CENTRAL ORD/FREE...DECISION 19/20. PAGE 134 H2688 NAT/G AUTHORIT CONSTN TOTALISM

B48

TOWSTER J.,POLITICAL POWER IN THE USSR: 1917-1947. USSR CONSTN CULTURE ELITES CREATE PLAN COERCE CENTRAL ATTIT RIGID/FLEX ORD/FREE...BIBLIOG SOC/INTEG 20 LENIN/VI STALIN/J. PAGE 156 H3122 EX/STRUC NAT/G MARXISM PWR

B49

DENNING A.,FREEDOM UNDER THE LAW. MOD/EUR UK LAW SOCIETY CHIEF EX/STRUC LEGIS ADJUD CT/SYS PERS/REL PERSON 17/20 ENGLSH/LAW. PAGE 40 H0793 ORD/FREE JURID NAT/G

B49

MCLEAN J.M.,THE PUBLIC SERVICE AND UNIVERSITY EDUCATION. UK USA-45 DELIB/GP EX/STRUC TOP/EX ADMIN ...GOV/COMP METH/COMP NAT/COMP ANTHOL 20. PAGE 107 H2142 ACADEM NAT/G EXEC EDU/PROP

B49

SCHWARTZ B.,LAW AND THE EXECUTIVE IN BRITAIN: A COMPARATIVE STUDY. UK USA+45 LAW EX/STRUC PWR ...GOV/COMP 20. PAGE 140 H2807 ADMIN EXEC CONTROL REPRESENT

L49

BRECHT A.,"THE NEW GERMAN CONSTITUTION." GERMANY/W NAT/G CHIEF EX/STRUC LEGIS PROB/SOLV ADMIN CONSTN DIPLOM

REPRESENT TOTALISM ORD/FREE PLURISM...MAJORIT CHARTS 20. PAGE 20 H0409
SOVEREIGN FEDERAL

B50

MCHENRY D.E.,THE THIRD FORCE IN CANADA: THE COOPERATIVE COMMONWEALTH FEDERATION, 1932-1948. CANADA EX/STRUC LEGIS REPRESENT 20 LABOR/PAR. PAGE 107 H2131
POL/PAR ADMIN CHOOSE POLICY

B51

CHRISTENSEN A.N.,THE EVOLUTION OF LATIN AMERICAN GOVERNMENT: A BOOK OF READINGS. ECO/UNDEV INDUS LOC/G POL/PAR EX/STRUC LEGIS FOR/AID CT/SYS ...SOC/WK 20 SOUTH/AMER. PAGE 30 H0599
NAT/G CONSTN DIPLOM L/A+17C

B51

LEONARD L.L.,INTERNATIONAL ORGANIZATION. WOR+45 WOR-45 EX/STRUC FORCES LEGIS ECO/TAC INT/TRADE COLONIAL ARMS/CONT...SOC/WK GOV/COMP BIBLIOG. PAGE 94 H1884
NAT/G DIPLOM INT/ORG DELIB/GP

B52

APPADORAI A.,THE SUBSTANCE OF POLITICS (6TH ED.). EX/STRUC LEGIS DIPLOM CT/SYS CHOOSE FASCISM MARXISM SOCISM...BIBLIOG T. PAGE 7 H0145
PHIL/SCI NAT/G

B53

APPLEBY P.H.,PUBLIC ADMINISTRATION IN INDIA: REPORT OF A SURVEY. INDIA LOC/G OP/RES ATTIT ORD/FREE 20. PAGE 7 H0147
ADMIN NAT/G EX/STRUC GOV/REL

B53

LEITES N.,A STUDY OF BOLSHEVISM. WOR+45 WOR-45 ELITES SOCIETY INT/ORG NAT/G EX/STRUC EDU/PROP EXEC ROUTINE ATTIT MORAL MARXISM...CONCPT OBS VAL/FREE 20. PAGE 94 H1869
COM POL/PAR USSR TOTALISM

B53

WAGLEY C.,AMAZON TOWN: A STUDY OF MAN IN THE TROPICS. BRAZIL L/A+17C STRATA STRUCT ECO/UNDEV AGRI EX/STRUC RACE/REL DISCRIM HABITAT WEALTH...OBS SOC/EXP 20. PAGE 164 H3285
SOC NEIGH CULTURE INGP/REL

N53

VITO F.,"RECENT DEVELOPMENTS IN THE THEORY OF DEMOCRATIC ADMIN" INTL POL SCI ASS'N CONFERENCE ON PUBLIC ADMINISTRATION... FRANCE ITALY UK REPRESENT EFFICIENCY NEW/LIB SOCISM...WELF/ST 20. PAGE 163 H3257
GOV/COMP CONTROL EX/STRUC

B54

HAMSON C.J.,EXECUTIVE DISCRETION AND JUDICIAL CONTROL; AN ASPECT OF THE FRENCH CONSEIL D'ETAT. EUR+WWI FRANCE MOD/EUR UK NAT/G EX/STRUC PARTIC CONSERVE...JURID BIBLIOG/A 18/20 SUPREME/CT. PAGE 65 H1310
ELITES ADJUD NAT/COMP

B54

MATTHEWS D.R.,THE SOCIAL BACKGROUND OF POLITICAL DECISION-MAKERS. CULTURE SOCIETY STRATA FAM EX/STRUC LEAD ATTIT BIO/SOC DRIVE PERSON ALL/VALS HIST/WRIT. PAGE 105 H2097
DECISION BIOG SOC

B54

MORRISON H.,GOVERNMENT AND PARLIAMENT. UK NAT/G PARLIAMENT. PAGE 113 H2266
GOV/REL EX/STRUC LEGIS PARL/PROC

B54

SCHWARTZ B.,FRENCH ADMINISTRATIVE LAW AND THE COMMON-LAW WORLD. FRANCE CULTURE LOC/G NAT/G PROVS DELIB/GP EX/STRUC LEGIS PROB/SOLV CT/SYS EXEC GOV/REL...IDEA/COMP ENGLSH/LAW. PAGE 140 H2808
JURID LAW METH/COMP ADJUD

S54

COLE T.,"LESSONS FROM RECENT EUROPEAN EXPERIENCE." EUR+WWI EX/STRUC 20. PAGE 31 H0626
GOV/COMP ADMIN REPRESENT

B55

DE ARAGAO J.G.,LA JURIDICTION ADMINISTRATIVE AU BRESIL. BRAZIL ADJUD COLONIAL CT/SYS REV FEDERAL ORD/FREE...BIBLIOG 19/20. PAGE 37 H0749
EX/STRUC ADMIN NAT/G

B55

GALLOWAY G.B.,CONGRESS AND PARLIAMENT: THEIR ORGANIZATION AND OPERATION IN THE US AND THE UK: PLANNING PAMPHLET NO. 93. POL/PAR EX/STRUC DEBATE CONTROL LEAD ROUTINE EFFICIENCY PWR...POLICY CONGRESS PARLIAMENT. PAGE 54 H1089
DELIB/GP LEGIS PARL/PROC GOV/COMP

B55

MAZZINI J.,THE DUTIES OF MAN. MOD/EUR LAW SOCIETY FAM NAT/G POL/PAR SECT VOL/ASSN EX/STRUC ACT/RES CREATE REV PEACE ATTIT ALL/VALS...GEN/LAWS WORK 19. PAGE 106 H2113
SUPEGO CONCPT NAT/LISM

B55

RUSTOW D.A.,THE POLITICS OF COMPROMISE. SWEDEN LABOR EX/STRUC LEGIS PLAN REPRESENT SOCISM...SOC 19/20. PAGE 136 H2720
POL/PAR NAT/G POLICY ECO/TAC

C55

GRASSMUCK G.L.,"A MANUAL OF LEBANESE ADMINISTRATION." LEBANON PLAN...CHARTS BIBLIOG/A 20. PAGE 60 H1198
ADMIN NAT/G ISLAM EX/STRUC

S56

KHAMA T.,"POLITICAL CHANGE IN AFRICAN SOCIETY." CONSTN SOCIETY LOC/G NAT/G POL/PAR EX/STRUC LEGIS LEGIT ADMIN CHOOSE REPRESENT NAT/LISM MORAL ORD/FREE PWR...CONCPT OBS TREND GEN/METH CMN/WLTH 17/20. PAGE 85 H1706
AFR ELITES

C56

FALL B.B.,"THE VIET-MINH REGIME." VIETNAM LAW ECO/UNDEV POL/PAR FORCES DOMIN WAR ATTIT MARXISM ...BIOG PREDICT BIBLIOG/A 20. PAGE 48 H0967
NAT/G ADMIN EX/STRUC LEAD

C56

NEUMANN S.,"MODERN POLITICAL PARTIES: APPROACHES TO COMPARATIVE POLITIC. FRANCE UK EX/STRUC DOMIN ADMIN LEAD REPRESENT TOTALISM ATTIT...POLICY TREND METH/COMP ANTHOL BIBLIOG/A 20 CMN/WLTH. PAGE 117 H2338
POL/PAR GOV/COMP ELITES MAJORIT

B57

CHANDRA S.,PARTIES AND POLITICS AT THE MUGHAL COURT: 1707-1740. INDIA CULTURE EX/STRUC CREATE PLAN PWR...BIBLIOG/A 18. PAGE 29 H0574
POL/PAR ELITES NAT/G

B57

SCARROW H.A.,THE HIGHER PUBLIC SERVICE OF THE COMMONWEALTH OF AUSTRALIA. LAW SENIOR LOBBY ROLE 20 AUSTRAL CIVIL/SERV COMMONWLTH. PAGE 138 H2766
ADMIN NAT/G EX/STRUC GOV/COMP

S57

HODGETTS J.E.,"THE CIVIL SERVICE AND POLICY FORMATION." CANADA NAT/G EX/STRUC ROUTINE GOV/REL 20. PAGE 72 H1443
ADMIN DECISION EFFICIENCY POLICY

C57

MORRIS-JONES W.H.,"PARLIAMENT IN INDIA." INDIA CONSTN LEGIS CONFER COLONIAL CHOOSE PRIVIL ATTIT ...GOV/COMP BIBLIOG 20. PAGE 113 H2264
PARL/PROC EX/STRUC NAT/G POL/PAR

B58

BRADY A.,DEMOCRACY IN THE DOMINIONS (3RD ED.). CANADA NEW/ZEALND SOUTH/AFR WOR+45 LAW EX/STRUC DOMIN COLONIAL PARL/PROC REPRESENT RACE/REL NAT/LISM WEALTH 20 AUSTRAL CMN/WLTH. PAGE 20 H0399
GOV/COMP POL/PAR POPULISM NAT/G

B58

CAMPBELL P.,FRENCH ELECTORAL SYSTEMS AND ELECTIONS SINCE 1789 (2ND ED.). FRANCE NAT/G EX/STRUC PWR ...CHARTS 18/20. PAGE 26 H0516
REPRESENT CHOOSE POL/PAR SUFF

B58

LAHBABI M.,LE GOUVERNEMENT MAROCAIN A L'AUBE DU XXE SIECLE. FRANCE MOROCCO CHIEF EX/STRUC LEGIS ORD/FREE PWR...JURID BIBLIOG 19/20. PAGE 90 H1797
NAT/G COLONIAL SOVEREIGN

B58

SHARMA M.P.,PUBLIC ADMINISTRATION IN THEORY AND PRACTICE. INDIA UK USA+45 USA-45 EX/STRUC ADJUD ...POLICY CONCPT NAT/COMP 20. PAGE 142 H2847
MGT ADMIN DELIB/GP JURID

B58

STRONG C.F.,MODERN POLITICAL CONSTITUTIONS. LAW CHIEF DELIB/GP EX/STRUC LEGIS ADJUD CHOOSE FEDERAL POPULISM...CONCPT BIBLIOG 20 UN. PAGE 150 H2998
CONSTN IDEA/COMP NAT/G

S58

ELKIN A.B.,"OEEC-ITS STRUCTURE AND POWERS." EUR+WWI CONSTN INDUS INT/ORG NAT/G VOL/ASSN DELIB/GP ACT/RES PLAN ORD/FREE WEALTH...CHARTS ORG/CHARTS OEEC 20. PAGE 45 H0907
ECO/DEV EX/STRUC

S58

GUSFIELD J.R.,"EQUALITARIANISM AND BUREAUCRATIC RECRUITMENT." UK USA+45 USA-45 EX/STRUC 19/20. PAGE 63 H1257
GOV/COMP REPRESENT TOP/EX ELITES

C58

GOLAY J.F.,"THE FOUNDING OF THE FEDERAL REPUBLIC OF GERMANY." GERMANY/W CONSTN EX/STRUC DIPLOM ADMIN CHOOSE...DECISION BIBLIOG 20. PAGE 58 H1155
FEDERAL NAT/G PARL/PROC POL/PAR

B59

SISSON C.H.,THE SPIRIT OF BRITISH ADMINISTRATION AND SOME EUROPEAN COMPARISONS. FRANCE GERMANY/W SWEDEN UK LAW EX/STRUC INGP/REL EFFICIENCY ORD/FREE ...DECISION 20. PAGE 144 H2890
GOV/COMP ADMIN ELITES ATTIT

S59

DUNCAN O.D.,"CULTURAL, BEHAVIORAL, AND ECOLOGICAL PERSPECTIVES IN THE STUDY OF SOCIAL ORGANIZATION" (BMR)" UNIV STRATA EX/STRUC PROB/SOLV ADMIN ATTIT SOC/INTEG 20 BUREAUCRCY. PAGE 43 H0862
CULTURE METH/COMP SOCIETY HABITAT

S59

GABLE R.W.,"CULTURE AND ADMINISTRATION IN IRAN." IRAN EXEC PARTIC REPRESENT PWR. PAGE 54 H1085
ADMIN CULTURE EX/STRUC INGP/REL

S59

PRESTHUS R.V.,"BEHAVIOR AND BUREAUCRACY IN MANY CULTURES." EXEC INGP/REL 20. PAGE 128 H2558
ADMIN EX/STRUC GOV/COMP METH/CNCPT

B60

ALMOND G.A.,THE POLITICS OF THE DEVELOPING AREAS. AFR ISLAM L/A+17C S/ASIA SOCIETY ECO/UNDEV NAT/G ADMIN PERCEPT KNOWL SOVEREIGN...CONCPT GEN/LAWS 20. PAGE 6 H0112
EX/STRUC ATTIT NAT/LISM

B60
AYEARST M.,THE BRITISH WEST INDIES: THE SEARCH FOR SELF-GOVERNMENT. FUT WEST/IND LOC/G POL/PAR EX/STRUC LEGIS CHOOSE FEDERAL...NAT/COMP BIBLIOG 17/20. PAGE 9 H0186 — CONSTN COLONIAL REPRESENT NAT/G

B60
KERSELL J.E.,PARLIAMENTARY SUPERVISION OF DELEGATED LEGISLATION. UK EFFICIENCY PWR...POLICY CHARTS BIBLIOG METH 20 PARLIAMENT. PAGE 85 H1699 — LEGIS CONTROL NAT/G EX/STRUC

S60
BRZEZINSKI Z.K.,"PATTERNS AND LIMITS OF THE SINO-SOVIET DISPUTE." ASIA CHINA/COM COM FUT STRATA NAT/G EX/STRUC FORCES BAL/PWR DIPLOM ECO/TAC DOMIN EDU/PROP ADMIN COERCE WAR ATTIT RIGID/FLEX ...GEN/LAWS VAL/FREE 20. PAGE 23 H0459 — POL/PAR PWR REV USSR

S60
SHILS E.,"THE INTELLECTUALS IN THE POLITICAL DEVELOPMENT OF THE NEW STATES." AFR ASIA S/ASIA ELITES LOC/G NAT/G CONSULT EX/STRUC CREATE PLAN ECO/TAC DOMIN LEGIT DRIVE PWR...TRADIT CONCPT STERTYP GEN/LAWS 20. PAGE 143 H2861 — POL/PAR INTELL NAT/LISM

B61
AYLMER G.,THE KING'S SERVANTS. UK ELITES CHIEF PAY CT/SYS WEALTH 17 CROMWELL/O CHARLES/I. PAGE 9 H0187 — ADMIN ROUTINE EX/STRUC NAT/G

B61
CARNELL F.,THE POLITICS OF THE NEW STATES: A SELECT ANNOTATED BIBLIOGRAPHY WITH SPECIAL REFERENCE TO THE COMMONWEALTH. CONSTN ELITES LABOR NAT/G POL/PAR EX/STRUC DIPLOM ADJUD ADMIN...GOV/COMP 20 COMMONWLTH. PAGE 27 H0534 — BIBLIOG/A AFR ASIA COLONIAL

B61
DRAGNICH A.N.,MAJOR EUROPEAN GOVERNMENTS. FRANCE GERMANY/W UK USSR LOC/G EX/STRUC CT/SYS PARL/PROC ATTIT MARXISM...JURID MGT NAT/COMP 19/20. PAGE 42 H0846 — NAT/G LEGIS CONSTN POL/PAR

B61
KEE R.,REFUGEE WORLD. AUSTRIA EUR+WWI GERMANY NEIGH EX/STRUC WORKER PROB/SOLV ECO/TAC RENT EDU/PROP INGP/REL COST LITERACY HABITAT 20 MIGRATION. PAGE 84 H1676 — NAT/G GIVE WEALTH STRANGE

B61
MARVICK D.,POLITICAL DECISION-MAKERS. INTELL STRATA NAT/G POL/PAR EX/STRUC LEGIS DOMIN EDU/PROP ATTIT PERSON PWR...PSY STAT OBS CONT/OBS STAND/INT UNPLAN/INT TIME/SEQ CHARTS STERTYP VAL/FREE. PAGE 104 H2073 — TOP/EX BIOG ELITES

B61
MONAS S.,THE THIRD SECTION: POLICE AND SOCIETY IN RUSSIA UNDER NICHOLAS I. MOD/EUR RUSSIA ELITES STRUCT NAT/G EX/STRUC ADMIN CONTROL PWR CONSERVE ...DECISION 19 NICHOLAS/I. PAGE 112 H2238 — ORD/FREE COM FORCES COERCE

B61
NARAIN J.P.,SWARAJ FOR THE PEOPLE. INDIA CONSTN LOC/G MUNIC POL/PAR CHOOSE REPRESENT EFFICIENCY ATTIT PWR SOVEREIGN 20. PAGE 116 H2311 — NAT/G ORD/FREE EDU/PROP EX/STRUC

B61
RAO K.V.,PARLIAMENTARY DEMOCRACY OF INDIA. INDIA EX/STRUC TOP/EX COLONIAL CT/SYS PARL/PROC ORD/FREE ...POLICY CONCPT TREND 20 PARLIAMENT. PAGE 130 H2592 — CONSTN ADJUD NAT/G FEDERAL

B62
ANDREWS W.G.,EUROPEAN POLITICAL INSTITUTIONS. FRANCE GERMANY UK USSR TOP/EX LEAD PARL/PROC CHOOSE 20. PAGE 7 H0139 — NAT/COMP POL/PAR EX/STRUC LEGIS

B62
BROWN B.E.,NEW DIRECTIONS IN COMPARATIVE POLITICS. AUSTRIA FRANCE GERMANY UK WOR+45 EX/STRUC LEGIS ORD/FREE 20. PAGE 22 H0439 — NAT/COMP METH POL/PAR FORCES

B62
BROWN L.C.,LATIN AMERICA, A BIBLIOGRAPHY. EX/STRUC ADMIN LEAD ATTIT...POLICY 20. PAGE 22 H0445 — BIBLIOG L/A+17C DIPLOM NAT/G

B62
CARTER G.M.,THE GOVERNMENT OF THE SOVIET UNION. USSR CULTURE LOC/G DIPLOM ECO/TAC ADJUD CT/SYS LEAD WEALTH...CHARTS T 20 COM/PARTY. PAGE 27 H0546 — NAT/G MARXISM POL/PAR EX/STRUC

B62
INAYATULLAH,BUREAUCRACY AND DEVELOPMENT IN PAKISTAN. PAKISTAN ECO/UNDEV EDU/PROP CONFER ...ANTHOL DICTIONARY 20 BUREAUCRCY. PAGE 76 H1526 — EX/STRUC ADMIN NAT/G LOC/G

B62
JACKSON W.A.D.,RUSSO-CHINESE BORDERLANDS. ASIA COM USSR NAT/G PROVS EX/STRUC FORCES DOMIN COERCE PEACE ATTIT PWR SOVEREIGN WEALTH...CONCPT TREND CHARTS STERTYP VAL/FREE. PAGE 79 H1576 — GEOG DIPLOM RUSSIA

B62
JAIN R.S.,THE GROWTH AND DEVELOPMENT OF GOVERNOR-GENERAL'S EXECUTIVE COUNCIL 1858-1919. INDIA UK CONSTN EX/STRUC LEGIS ADJUD ADMIN INGP/REL ATTIT 19/20. PAGE 79 H1585 — NAT/G DELIB/GP CHIEF CONSULT

B62
KARNJAHAPRAKORN C.,MUNICIPAL GOVERNMENT IN THAILAND AS AN INSTITUTION AND PROCESS OF SELF-GOVERNMENT. THAILAND CULTURE FINAN EX/STRUC LEGIS PLAN CONTROL GOV/REL EFFICIENCY ATTIT...POLICY 20. PAGE 83 H1662 — LOC/G MUNIC ORD/FREE ADMIN

B62
NEW ZEALAND COMM OF ST SERVICE,THE STATE SERVICES IN NEW ZEALAND. NEW/ZEALND CONSULT EX/STRUC ACT/RES ...BIBLIOG 20. PAGE 117 H2343 — ADMIN WORKER TEC/DEV NAT/G

B62
PHILLIPS O.H.,CONSTITUTIONAL AND ADMINISTRATIVE LAW (3RD ED.). UK INT/ORG LOC/G CHIEF EX/STRUC LEGIS BAL/PWR ADJUD COLONIAL CT/SYS PWR...CHARTS 20. PAGE 125 H2503 — JURID ADMIN CONSTN NAT/G

B62
SCALAPINO R.A.,PARTIES AND POLITICS IN CONTEMPORARY JAPAN. EX/STRUC DIPLOM CHOOSE NAT/LISM ATTIT ...POLICY 20 CHINJAP. PAGE 138 H2762 — POL/PAR PARL/PROC ELITES DECISION

B62
THIERRY S.S.,LE VATICAN SECRET. CHRIST-17C EUR+WWI MOD/EUR VATICAN NAT/G SECT DELIB/GP DOMIN LEGIT SOVEREIGN. PAGE 154 H3072 — ADMIN EX/STRUC CATHISM DECISION

S62
FESLER J.W.,"FRENCH FIELD ADMINISTRATION: THE BEGINNINGS." CHRIST-17C CULTURE SOCIETY STRATA NAT/G ECO/TAC DOMIN EDU/PROP LEGIT ADJUD COERCE ATTIT ALL/VALS...TIME/SEQ CON/ANAL GEN/METH VAL/FREE 13/15. PAGE 49 H0988 — EX/STRUC FRANCE

B63
ADRIAN C.R.,GOVERNING OVER FIFTY STATES AND THEIR COMMUNITIES. USA+45 CONSTN FINAN MUNIC NAT/G POL/PAR EX/STRUC LEGIS ADMIN CONTROL CT/SYS ...CHARTS 20. PAGE 4 H0073 — PROVS LOC/G GOV/REL GOV/COMP

B63
BADI J.,THE GOVERNMENT OF THE STATE OF ISRAEL: A CRITICAL ACCOUNT OF ITS PARLIAMENT, EXECUTIVE, AND JUDICIARY. ISRAEL ECO/DEV CHIEF DELIB/GP LEGIS DIPLOM CT/SYS INGP/REL PEACE ORD/FREE...BIBLIOG 20 PARLIAMENT ARABS MIGRATION. PAGE 10 H0193 — NAT/G CONSTN EX/STRUC POL/PAR

B63
GOURNAY B.,PUBLIC ADMINISTRATION. FRANCE LAW CONSTN AGRI FINAN LABOR SCHOOL EX/STRUC CHOOSE...MGT METH/COMP 20. PAGE 59 H1189 — BIBLIOG/A ADMIN NAT/G LOC/G

B63
MILLER W.J.,THE MEANING OF COMMUNISM. USSR SOCIETY ECO/DEV EX/STRUC WORKER TEC/DEV ADMIN TOTALISM ...POLICY CONCPT CHARTS BIBLIOG T 20 COLD/WAR LENIN/VI STALIN/J. PAGE 111 H2215 — MARXISM TRADIT DIPLOM NAT/G

B63
RICHARDSON H.G.,THE ADMINISTRATION OF IRELAND 1172-1377. IRELAND CONSTN EX/STRUC LEGIS JUDGE CT/SYS PARL/PROC...CHARTS BIBLIOG 12/14. PAGE 131 H2621 — ADMIN NAT/G PWR

B63
SCHECHTMAN J.B.,THE REFUGEE IN THE WORLD: DISPLACEMENT AND INTEGRATION. AFR ASIA EUR+WWI ISLAM L/A+17C S/ASIA CULTURE STRATA LOC/G EX/STRUC PLAN ECO/TAC ROUTINE...CONCPT TIME/SEQ VAL/FREE 20. PAGE 139 H2779 — INT/ORG SOC

B63
SILONE I.,THE SCHOOL FOR DICTATORS. EUR+WWI GERMANY ITALY SOCIETY NAT/G CHIEF EX/STRUC ATTIT MORAL PWR ...HIST/WRIT 20. PAGE 144 H2876 — TOTALISM EDU/PROP ORD/FREE FASCISM

B63
SKLAR R.L.,NIGERIAN POLITICAL PARTIES: POWER IN AN EMERGENT AFRICAN NATION. AFR EUR+WWI CULTURE STRATA NAT/G DELIB/GP EX/STRUC LEGIS DOMIN EDU/PROP ROUTINE CHOOSE ATTIT PERCEPT ORD/FREE PWR...SOC CONCPT OBS TOT/POP VAL/FREE. PAGE 145 H2898 — POL/PAR SOCIETY NAT/LISM NIGERIA

B63
ULAM A.B.,THE NEW FACE OF SOVIET TOTALITARIANISM. FUT INTELL NAT/G POL/PAR EX/STRUC TOP/EX DIPLOM ECO/TAC DOMIN EDU/PROP LEGIT COERCE ATTIT RIGID/FLEX...OBS HIST/WRIT TREND TOT/POP VAL/FREE COLD/WAR. PAGE 158 H3150 — COM PWR TOTALISM USSR

B63
WEINER M.,POLITICAL CHANGE IN SOUTH ASIA. CEYLON INDIA PAKISTAN S/ASIA CULTURE ELITES ECO/UNDEV EX/STRUC ADMIN CONTROL CHOOSE CONSERVE...GOV/COMP ANTHOL 20. PAGE 166 H3328 — NAT/G CONSTN TEC/DEV

S63
ANTHON C.G.,"THE END OF THE ADENAUER ERA." EUR+WWI GERMANY/W CONSTN EX/STRUC CREATE DIPLOM LEGIT ATTIT PERSON ALL/VALS...RECORD 20 ADENAUER/K. PAGE 7 H0144 — NAT/G TOP/EX BAL/PWR GERMANY

S63
BANFIELD J.,"FEDERATION IN EAST-AFRICA." AFR UGANDA ELITES INT/ORG NAT/G VOL/ASSN LEGIS ECO/TAC FEDERAL — EX/STRUC PWR

ATTIT SOVEREIGN TOT/POP 20 TANGANYIKA. PAGE 10 H0210 REGION
S63

HARRIS R.L.,"A COMPARATIVE ANALYSIS OF THE ADMINISTRATIVE SYSTEMS OF CANADA AND CEYLON." S/ASIA CULTURE SOCIETY STRATA TOP/EX ACT/RES DOMIN EDU/PROP LEGIT COERCE ATTIT SUPEGO ALL/VALS...MGT CHARTS GEN/LAWS VAL/FREE 20. PAGE 67 H1343 DELIB/GP EX/STRUC CANADA CEYLON
S63

HARRIS R.L.,"COMMUNISM AND ASIA: ILLUSIONS AND MISCONCEPTIONS." ASIA COM FUT S/ASIA ECO/UNDEV AGRI NAT/G POL/PAR EX/STRUC EDU/PROP COERCE ATTIT MARXISM COLD/WAR TOT/POP 20. PAGE 67 H1344 PWR GUERRILLA
S63

LAMBERT D.,"LA TRANSPOSITION DU REGIME PRESIDENTIEL HORS DES ETATSUNIS; LE CAS DE L'AMERIQUE LATINE." NAT/G EX/STRUC LEGIS PARL/PROC PWR 18/20 PRESIDENT CENTRAL/AM SOUTH/AMER. PAGE 90 H1800 DELIB/GP CHIEF L/A+17C GOV/REL
B64

AGGARWALA R.C.,CONSTITUTIONAL HISTORY OF INDIA AND NATIONAL MOVEMENT INCLUDING COMPARATIVE STUDY OF MODERN INDIA CONSTITUTION. INDIA S/ASIA SECT VOL/ASSN EX/STRUC LEGIS COERCE REV INGP/REL ORD/FREE...SOC BIBLIOG 18/20 CMN/WLTH. PAGE 4 H0077 CONSTN COLONIAL DOMIN NAT/G
B64

BINDER L.,THE IDEOLOGICAL REVOLUTION IN THE MIDDLE EAST. ISLAM STRUCT INT/ORG KIN SECT EX/STRUC TOP/EX PLAN ATTIT DRIVE RIGID/FLEX PWR...MYTH TOT/POP 20. PAGE 17 H0338 POL/PAR NAT/G NAT/LISM
B64

CAPLOW T.,PRINCIPLES OF ORGANIZATION. UNIV CULTURE STRUCT CREATE INGP/REL UTOPIA...GEN/LAWS TIME. PAGE 26 H0526 VOL/ASSN CONCPT SIMUL EX/STRUC
B64

DE SMITH S.A.,THE NEW COMMONWEALTH AND ITS CONSTITUTIONS. AFR CYPRUS PAKISTAN S/ASIA INT/ORG NAT/G LEGIS LEGIT RIGID/FLEX PWR...CONCPT TIME/SEQ CMN/WLTH 20. PAGE 38 H0770 EX/STRUC CONSTN SOVEREIGN
B64

FAINSOD M.,HOW RUSSIA IS RULED (REV. ED.). RUSSIA USSR AGRI PROC/MFG LABOR POL/PAR EX/STRUC CONTROL PWR...POLICY BIBLIOG 19/20 KHRUSH/N COM/PARTY. PAGE 48 H0963 NAT/G REV MARXISM
B64

HOLDSWORTH W.S.,A HISTORY OF ENGLISH LAW; THE CENTURIES OF DEVELOPMENT AND REFORM (VOL. XIV). UK CONSTN LOC/G NAT/G POL/PAR CHIEF EX/STRUC ADJUD COLONIAL ATTIT...INT/LAW JURID 18/19 TORY/PARTY COMMONWLTH WHIG/PARTY COMMON/LAW. PAGE 73 H1453 LAW LEGIS LEAD CT/SYS
B64

JUCKER-FLEETWOOD E.,MONEY AND FINANCE IN AFRICA. ISLAM ECO/UNDEV SERV/IND NAT/G EX/STRUC PLAN ECO/TAC ROUTINE WEALTH...MGT TOT/POP 20. PAGE 82 H1639 AFR FINAN
B64

KARIEL H.S.,IN SEARCH OF AUTHORITY: TWENTIETH-CENTURY POLITICAL THOUGHT. WOR+45 WOR-45 NAT/G EX/STRUC TOTALISM DRIVE PWR...MGT PHIL/SCI GEN/LAWS 19/20 NIETZSCH/F FREUD/S WEBER/MAX NIEBUHR/R MARITAIN/J. PAGE 83 H1661 CONSTN CONCPT ORD/FREE IDEA/COMP
B64

O'HEARN P.J.T.,PEACE, ORDER AND GOOD GOVERNMENT; A NEW CONSTITUTION FOR CANADA. CANADA EX/STRUC LEGIS CT/SYS PARL/PROC...BIBLIOG 20. PAGE 120 H2388 NAT/G CONSTN LAW CREATE
B64

RIDLEY F.,PUBLIC ADMINISTRATION IN FRANCE. FRANCE UK EX/STRUC CONTROL PARTIC EFFICIENCY 20. PAGE 131 H2625 ADMIN REPRESENT GOV/COMP PWR
B64

RIES J.C.,THE MANAGEMENT OF DEFENSE: ORGANIZATION AND CONTROL OF THE US ARMED SERVICES. PROF/ORG DELIB/GP EX/STRUC LEGIS GOV/REL PERS/REL CENTRAL RATIONAL PWR...POLICY TREND GOV/COMP BIBLIOG. PAGE 131 H2626 FORCES ACT/RES DECISION CONTROL
B64

SINGER M.R.,THE EMERGING ELITE: A STUDY OF POLITICAL LEADERSHIP IN CEYLON. S/ASIA ECO/UNDEV AGRI KIN NAT/G SECT EX/STRUC LEGIT ATTIT PWR RESPECT...SOC STAT CHARTS 20. PAGE 144 H2883 TOP/EX STRATA NAT/LISM CEYLON
B64

SKINNER E.P.,THE MOSSI OF UPPER VOLTA: THE POLITICAL DEVELOPMENT OF A SUDANESE PEOPLE. AFR LAW AGRI FAM KIN POL/PAR PROVS SECT DELIB/GP EX/STRUC FORCES TOP/EX DOMIN EDU/PROP LEGIT CT/SYS COERCE CHOOSE ORD/FREE PWR WEALTH...SOC MYTH VAL/FREE. PAGE 145 H2897 CULTURE OBS UPPER/VOLT
B64

TILMAN R.O.,BUREAUCRATIC TRANSITION IN MALAYA. MALAYSIA S/ASIA UK NAT/G EX/STRUC DIPLOM...CHARTS BIBLIOG 20. PAGE 155 H3098 ADMIN COLONIAL SOVEREIGN EFFICIENCY
B64

VECCHIO G.D.,L'ETAT ET LE DROIT. ITALY CONSTN EX/STRUC LEGIS DIPLOM CT/SYS...JURID 20 UN. PAGE 162 H3238 NAT/G SOVEREIGN CONCPT INT/LAW
B64

VON STEIN L.J.,THE HISTORY OF THE SOCIAL MOVEMENT IN FRANCE, 1789-1850 (TRANS. BY K. MENGELBERG). COM FRANCE MOD/EUR NAT/G EX/STRUC INGP/REL ALL/IDEOS CONSERVE MARXISM...SOC BIBLIOG 18/19. PAGE 164 H3278 REV STRATA
B64

WHEARE K.C.,FEDERAL GOVERNMENT (4TH ED.). WOR+45 WOR-45 POL/PAR LEGIS BAL/PWR CT/SYS...POLICY JURID CONCPT GOV/COMP 17/20. PAGE 167 H3339 FEDERAL CONSTN EX/STRUC NAT/COMP
B64

ZOLLSCHAN G.K.,EXPLORATIONS IN SOCIAL CHANGE. SOCIETY STRATA STRUCT ECO/UNDEV EX/STRUC...PSY ANTHOL 20. PAGE 173 H3463 ORD/FREE SIMUL CONCPT CULTURE
S64

GROSS J.A.,"WHITEHALL AND THE COMMONWEALTH." EUR+WWI MOD/EUR INT/ORG NAT/G CONSULT DELIB/GP LEGIS DOMIN ADMIN COLONIAL ROUTINE PWR CMN/WLTH 19/20. PAGE 62 H1233 EX/STRUC ATTIT TREND
S64

JOHNSON K.F.,"CAUSAL FACTORS IN LATIN AMERICAN POLITICAL INSTABILITY." CULTURE NAT/G VOL/ASSN EX/STRUC FORCES EDU/PROP LEGIT ADMIN COERCE REV ATTIT KNOWL PWR...STYLE RECORD CHARTS WORK 20. PAGE 81 H1624 L/A+17C PERCEPT ELITES
S64

POWELL R.L.,"COMMUNIST CHINA'S MILITARY POTENTIAL." ASIA CHINA/COM NAT/G EX/STRUC EDU/PROP COERCE GUERRILLA NUC/PWR WAR...RECORD CON/ANAL 20. PAGE 128 H2551 FORCES PWR
S64

SWEARER H.R.,"AFTER KHRUSHCHEV: WHAT NEXT." COM FUT USSR CONSTN ELITES NAT/G POL/PAR CHIEF DELIB/GP LEGIS DOMIN LEAD...RECORD TREND STERTYP GEN/METH 20. PAGE 151 H3016 EX/STRUC PWR
B65

ALTON T.P.,POLISH NATIONAL INCOME AND PRODUCT IN 1954, 1955, AND 1956. POLAND FINAN EX/STRUC ECO/TAC PRICE COST WEALTH 20. PAGE 6 H0117 COM INDUS NAT/G ECO/DEV
B65

CHANDA A.,FEDERALISM IN INDIA. INDIA UK ELITES FINAN NAT/G POL/PAR EX/STRUC LEGIS DIPLOM TAX GOV/REL POPULISM...POLICY 20. PAGE 28 H0572 CONSTN CENTRAL FEDERAL
B65

FREY F.W.,THE TURKISH POLITICAL ELITE. TURKEY CULTURE INTELL NAT/G EX/STRUC CHOOSE ATTIT PWR ...METH/CNCPT CHARTS WORSHIP 20. PAGE 53 H1059 ELITES SOCIETY POL/PAR
B65

GOLEMBIEWSKI R.T.,MEN, MANAGEMENT, AND MORALITY; TOWARD A NEW ORGANIZATIONAL ETHIC. CONSTN EX/STRUC CREATE ADMIN CONTROL INGP/REL PERSON SUPEGO MORAL PWR...GOV/COMP METH/COMP 20 BUREAUCRCY. PAGE 58 H1161 LG/CO MGT PROB/SOLV
B65

GREGG J.L.,POLITICAL PARTIES AND PARTY SYSTEMS IN GUATEMALA, 1944-1963. GUATEMALA L/A+17C EX/STRUC FORCES CREATE CONTROL REV CHOOSE PWR...TREND IDEA/COMP 20. PAGE 60 H1209 LEAD POL/PAR NAT/G CHIEF
B65

HANSER C.J.,GUIDE TO DECISION: ROYAL COMMISSION. UK INTELL EXTR/IND SCHOOL PROB/SOLV EXEC ROUTINE CHOOSE GOV/REL GP/REL HEALTH...CHARTS 20. PAGE 66 H1318 NAT/G DELIB/GP EX/STRUC PWR
B65

INST INTL DES CIVILISATION DIF,THE CONSTITUTIONS AND ADMINISTRATIVE INSTITUTIONS OF THE NEW STATES. AFR ISLAM S/ASIA NAT/G POL/PAR DELIB/GP EX/STRUC CONFER EFFICIENCY NAT/LISM...JURID SOC 20. PAGE 77 H1535 CONSTN ADMIN ADJUD ECO/UNDEV
B65

INT. BANK RECONSTR. DEVELOP.,ECONOMIC DEVELOPMENT OF KUWAIT. ISLAM KUWAIT AGRI FINAN MARKET EX/STRUC TEC/DEV ECO/TAC ADMIN WEALTH...OBS CON/ANAL CHARTS 20. PAGE 77 H1541 INDUS NAT/G
B65

JONAS E.,DIE VOLKSKONSERVATIVEN 1928-1933. GERMANY EX/STRUC...CONCPT TIME/SEQ 20 HITLER/A. PAGE 82 H1628 POL/PAR NAT/G GP/REL
B65

KOUSOULAS D.G.,REVOLUTION AND DEFEAT; THE STORY OF THE GREEK COMMUNIST PARTY. GREECE INT/ORG EX/STRUC DIPLOM FOR/AID EDU/PROP PARL/PROC ADJUST ATTIT 20 COM/PARTY. PAGE 88 H1759 REV MARXISM POL/PAR ORD/FREE
B65

MCSHERRY J.E.,RUSSIA AND THE UNITED STATES UNDER EISENHOWER, KHRUSHCHEV, AND KENNEDY. USSR EX/STRUC TOP/EX PRESS WAR...POLICY TREND 20. PAGE 108 H2150 DIPLOM CHIEF NAT/G PEACE
B65

MONTESQUIEU C DE S.,CONSIDERATIONS ON THE CAUSES OF NAT/G

THE GREATNESS OF THE ROMANS AND THEIR DECLINE (1748 TRANS. BY D. LOWENTHAL). ROMAN/EMP SECT CHIEF EX/STRUC FORCES LEGIS DOMIN WAR POPULISM...POLICY REALPOL ROME/ANC. PAGE 112 H2244 PWR COLONIAL MORAL

B65
MOORE C.H.,TUNISIA SINCE INDEPENDENCE. ELITES LOC/G POL/PAR ADMIN COLONIAL CONTROL EXEC GOV/REL TOTALISM MARXISM...INT 20 TUNIS. PAGE 112 H2248 NAT/G EX/STRUC SOCISM

B65
NORDEN A.,WAR AND NAZI CRIMINALS IN WEST GERMANY: STATE, ECONOMY, ADMINISTRATION, ARMY, JUSTICE, SCIENCE. GERMANY GERMANY/W MOD/EUR ECO/DEV ACADEM EX/STRUC FORCES DOMIN ADMIN CT/SYS...POLICY MAJORIT PACIFIST 20. PAGE 119 H2370 FASCIST WAR NAT/G TOP/EX

B65
ONUOHA B.,THE ELEMENTS OF AFRICAN SOCIALISM. AFR FINAN SECT TEC/DEV FOR/AID GP/REL OWN LAISSEZ MARXISM...CONCPT BIBLIOG 20. PAGE 121 H2419 SOCISM ECO/UNDEV NAT/G EX/STRUC

B65
PANJABI K.L.,THE CIVIL SERVANT IN INDIA. INDIA UK NAT/G CONSULT EX/STRUC REGION GP/REL RACE/REL 20. PAGE 123 H2462 ADMIN WORKER BIOG COLONIAL

B65
PEASLEE A.J.,CONSTITUTIONS OF NATIONS* THIRD REVISED EDITION (VOLUME I* AFRICA). LAW EX/STRUC LEGIS TOP/EX LEGIT CT/SYS ROUTINE ORD/FREE PWR SOVEREIGN...CON/ANAL CHARTS. PAGE 124 H2481 AFR CHOOSE CONSTN NAT/G

B65
PYLEE M.V.,CONSTITUTIONAL GOVERNMENT IN INDIA (2ND REV. ED.). INDIA POL/PAR EX/STRUC DIPLOM COLONIAL CT/SYS PARL/PROC PRIVIL...JURID 16/20. PAGE 128 H2569 CONSTN NAT/G PROVS FEDERAL

B65
ROTBERG R.I.,A POLITICAL HISTORY OF TROPICAL AFRICA. EX/STRUC DIPLOM INT/TRADE DOMIN ADMIN RACE/REL NAT/LISM PWR SOVEREIGN...GEOG TIME/SEQ BIBLIOG 1/20. PAGE 135 H2692 AFR CULTURE COLONIAL

B65
RUBINSTEIN A.Z.,THE CHALLENGE OF POLITICS: IDEAS AND ISSUES (2ND ED.). UNIV ELITES SOCIETY EX/STRUC BAL/PWR PARL/PROC AUTHORIT...DECISION ANTHOL 20. PAGE 136 H2709 NAT/G DIPLOM GP/REL ORD/FREE

B65
WARD W.E.,GOVERNMENT IN WEST AFRICA. WOR+45 POL/PAR EX/STRUC PLAN PARTIC GP/REL SOVEREIGN 20 AFRICA/W. PAGE 165 H3308 GOV/COMP CONSTN COLONIAL ECO/UNDEV

L65
LASSWELL H.D.,"THE POLICY SCIENCES OF DEVELOPMENT." CULTURE SOCIETY EX/STRUC CREATE ADMIN ATTIT KNOWL ...SOC CONCPT SIMUL GEN/METH. PAGE 92 H1835 PWR METH/CNCPT DIPLOM

S65
ASHFORD D.E.,"BUREAUCRATS AND CITIZENS." MOROCCO PAKISTAN PARTIC 20 TUNIS. PAGE 9 H0172 GOV/COMP ADMIN EX/STRUC ROLE

S65
RUBINSTEIN A.Z.,"YUGOSLAVIA'S OPENING SOCIETY." COM USSR INTELL NAT/G LEGIS TOP/EX LEGIT CT/SYS RIGID/FLEX ALL/VALS SOCISM...HUM TIME/SEQ TREND 20. PAGE 135 H2708 CONSTN EX/STRUC YUGOSLAVIA

S65
TABORSKY E.,"CHANGE IN CZECHOSLOVAKIA." COM USSR ELITES INTELL AGRI INDUS NAT/G DELIB/GP EX/STRUC ECO/TAC TOTALISM ATTIT RIGID/FLEX SOCISM...MGT CONCPT TREND 20. PAGE 152 H3031 ECO/DEV PLAN CZECHOSLVK

B66
ADAMS J.C.,THE GOVERNMENT OF REPUBLICAN ITALY (2ND ED.). ITALY LOC/G POL/PAR DELIB/GP LEGIS WORKER ADMIN CT/SYS FASCISM...CHARTS BIBLIOG 20 PARLIAMENT. PAGE 3 H0064 NAT/G CHOOSE EX/STRUC CONSTN

B66
ASHRAF A.,THE CITY GOVERNMENT OF CALCUTTA: A STUDY OF INERTIA. INDIA ELITES INDUS NAT/G EX/STRUC ACT/RES PLAN PROB/SOLV LEAD HABITAT...BIBLIOG 20 CALCUTTA. PAGE 9 H0175 LOC/G MUNIC ADMIN ECO/UNDEV

B66
BHALERAO C.N.,PUBLIC SERVICE COMMISSIONS OF INDIA: A STUDY. INDIA SERV/IND EX/STRUC ROUTINE CHOOSE GOV/REL INGP/REL...KNO/TEST EXHIBIT 20. PAGE 16 H0326 NAT/G OP/RES LOC/G ADMIN

B66
CHAPMAN B.,THE PROFESSION OF GOVERNMENT: THE PUBLIC SERVICE IN EUROPE. CONSTN NAT/G POL/PAR EX/STRUC LEGIS TOP/EX PROB/SOLV DEBATE EXEC PARL/PROC PARTIC 20. PAGE 29 H0581 BIBLIOG ADMIN EUR+WWI GOV/COMP

B66
FRIED R.C.,COMPARATIVE POLITICAL INSTITUTIONS. USSR EX/STRUC FORCES LEGIS JUDGE CONTROL REPRESENT ALL/IDEOS 20 CONGRESS BUREAUCRCY. PAGE 53 H1062 NAT/G PWR EFFICIENCY GOV/COMP

B66
GHOSH P.K.,THE CONSTITUTION OF INDIA: HOW IT HAS BEEN FRAMED. INDIA LOC/G DELIB/GP EX/STRUC PROB/SOLV BUDGET INT/TRADE CT/SYS CHOOSE...LING 20. PAGE 56 H1121 CONSTN NAT/G LEGIS FEDERAL

B66
HACKETT J.,L'ECONOMIE BRITANNIQUE: PROBLEMES ET PERSPECTIVES. FRANCE UK LABOR MUNIC NAT/G EX/STRUC PROB/SOLV BAL/PAY INCOME RIGID/FLEX...MGT PHIL/SCI CHARTS 20. PAGE 63 H1271 ECO/DEV FINAN ECO/TAC PLAN

B66
HIDAYATULLAH M.,DEMOCRACY IN INDIA AND THE JUDICIAL PROCESS. INDIA EX/STRUC LEGIS LEAD GOV/REL ATTIT ORD/FREE...MAJORIT CONCPT 20 NEHRU/J. PAGE 71 H1415 NAT/G CT/SYS CONSTN JURID

B66
HOLDSWORTH W.S.,A HISTORY OF ENGLISH LAW; THE CENTURIES OF SETTLEMENT AND REFORM (VOL. XVI). UK LOC/G NAT/G EX/STRUC LEGIS CT/SYS LEAD ATTIT ...POLICY DECISION JURID IDEA/COMP 18 PARLIAMENT. PAGE 73 H1454 BIOG PERSON PROF/ORG LAW

B66
HOLT R.T.,THE POLITICAL BASIS OF ECONOMIC DEVELOPMENT. STRATA STRUCT NAT/G DIPLOM ADMIN...SOC NAT/COMP BIBLIOG 20. PAGE 73 H1458 ECO/TAC GOV/COMP CONSTN EX/STRUC

B66
INTERPARLIAMENTARY UNION,PARLIAMENTS: COMPARATIVE STUDY ON STRUCTURE AND FUNCTIONING OF REPRESENTATIVE INSTITUTIONS IN FIFTY-FIVE COUNTRIES. WOR+45 POL/PAR DELIB/GP BUDGET ADMIN CONTROL CHOOSE. PAGE 78 H1560 PARL/PROC LEGIS GOV/COMP EX/STRUC

B66
JOHNSON N.,PARLIAMENT AND ADMINISTRATION: THE ESTIMATES COMMITTEE 1945-65. FUT UK NAT/G EX/STRUC PLAN BUDGET ORD/FREE...T 20 PARLIAMENT HOUSE/CMNS. PAGE 81 H1625 LEGIS ADMIN FINAN DELIB/GP

B66
KIRDAR U.,THE STRUCTURE OF UNITED NATIONS ECONOMIC AID TO UNDERDEVELOPED COUNTRIES. AGRI FINAN INDUS NAT/G EX/STRUC PLAN GIVE TASK...POLICY 20 UN. PAGE 86 H1721 INT/ORG FOR/AID ECO/UNDEV ADMIN

B66
KOMIYA R.,POSTWAR ECONOMIC GROWTH IN JAPAN. ELITES NAT/G EX/STRUC TEC/DEV BUDGET DIPLOM CONTROL BAL/PAY PRODUC...BIBLIOG 20 CHINJAP. PAGE 88 H1754 ECO/DEV POLICY PLAN ADJUST

B66
MARTIN L.W.,DIPLOMACY IN MODERN EUROPEAN HISTORY. EUR+WWI MOD/EUR INT/ORG NAT/G EX/STRUC ROUTINE WAR PEACE TOTALISM PWR 15/20 COLD/WAR EUROPE/W. PAGE 103 H2064 DIPLOM POLICY

B66
NEUMANN R.G.,THE GOVERNMENT OF THE GERMAN FEDERAL REPUBLIC. EUR+WWI GERMANY/W LOC/G EX/STRUC LEGIS CT/SYS INGP/REL PWR...BIBLIOG 20 ADENAUER/K. PAGE 117 H2336 NAT/G POL/PAR DIPLOM CONSTN

B66
US DEPARTMENT OF THE ARMY,COMMUNIST CHINA: A STRATEGIC SURVEY: A BIBLIOGRAPHY (PAMPHLET NO. 20-67). CHINA/COM COM INDIA USSR NAT/G POL/PAR EX/STRUC FORCES NUC/PWR REV ATTIT...POLICY GEOG CHARTS. PAGE 160 H3194 BIBLIOG/A MARXISM S/ASIA DIPLOM

B66
WUEST J.J.,NEW SOURCE BOOK IN MAJOR EUROPEAN GOVERNMENTS. CHRIST-17C EUR+WWI FRANCE GERMANY ITALY MOD/EUR UK USSR LOC/G POL/PAR CHIEF EX/STRUC CHOOSE CONSERVE MARXISM...JURID T 13/20. PAGE 171 H3425 NAT/G CONSTN LEGIS

L66
LEMARCHAND R.,"SOCIAL CHANGE AND POLITICAL MODERNISATION IN BURUNDI." AFR BURUNDI STRATA CHIEF EX/STRUC RIGID/FLEX PWR...SOC 20. PAGE 94 H1874 NAT/G STRUCT ELITES CONSERVE

L66
MCAUSLAN J.P.W.,"CONSTITUTIONAL INNOVATION AND POLITICAL STABILITY IN TANZANIA: A PRELIMINARY ASSESSMENT." AFR TANZANIA ELITES CHIEF EX/STRUC RIGID/FLEX PWR 20 PRESIDENT BUREAUCRCY. PAGE 106 H2122 CONSTN NAT/G EXEC POL/PAR

S66
KAPIL R.L.,"ON THE CONFLICT POTENTIAL OF INHERITED BOUNDARIES IN AFRICA." MOD/EUR MOROCCO UAR EX/STRUC DIPLOM LEGIT REGION ADJUST...RECORD NAT/COMP GEN/LAWS. PAGE 83 H1658 AFR COLONIAL PREDICT GEOG

S66
MATTHEWS D.G.,"ETHIOPIAN OUTLINE: A BIBLIOGRAPHIC RESEARCH GUIDE." ETHIOPIA LAW STRUCT ECO/UNDEV AGRI LABOR SECT CHIEF DELIB/GP EX/STRUC ADMIN...LING ORG/CHARTS 20. PAGE 105 H2095 BIBLIOG NAT/G DIPLOM POL/PAR

B67
BROWN L.N.,FRENCH ADMINISTRATIVE LAW. FRANCE UK CONSTN NAT/G LEGIS DOMIN CONTROL EXEC PARL/PROC PWR ...JURID METH/COMP GEN/METH. PAGE 22 H0447 EX/STRUC LAW IDEA/COMP CT/SYS

B67
BRZEZINSKI Z.K.,IDEOLOGY AND POWER IN SOVIET POLITICS. USSR NAT/G POL/PAR PWR...GEN/LAWS 19/20. PAGE 23 H0462 DIPLOM EX/STRUC MARXISM

B67
BRZEZINSKI Z.K.,THE SOVIET BLOC: UNITY AND CONFLICT (2ND ED., REV., ENLARGED). COM POLAND USSR INTELL CHIEF EX/STRUC CONTROL EXEC GOV/REL PWR MARXISM ...TREND IDEA/COMP 20 LENIN/VI MARX/KARL STALIN/J. PAGE 23 H0463
NAT/G DIPLOM

B67
JOUVENEL B D.E.,THE ART OF CONJECTURE. FUT CONSULT EX/STRUC CHOOSE GOV/REL ALL/VALS. PAGE 82 H1638
PREDICT DELIB/GP PLAN NAT/G

B67
MACRIDIS R.C.,FOREIGN POLICY IN WORLD POLITICS (3RD ED.). EX/STRUC BAL/PWR COLONIAL NAT/LISM SKILL SOVEREIGN WEALTH...CONCPT TIME/SEQ ANTHOL 20 COLD/WAR. PAGE 101 H2011
DIPLOM POLICY NAT/G IDEA/COMP

B67
MILNE R.S.,GOVERNMENT AND POLITICS IN MALAYSIA. INDONESIA MALAYSIA LOC/G EX/STRUC FORCES DIPLOM GP/REL 20 SINGAPORE. PAGE 111 H2217
NAT/G LEGIS ADMIN

B67
PYE L.W.,SOUTHEAST ASIA'S POLITICAL SYSTEMS. ASIA S/ASIA STRUCT ECO/UNDEV EX/STRUC CAP/ISM DIPLOM ALL/IDEOS...TREND CHARTS. PAGE 128 H2568
NAT/G POL/PAR GOV/COMP

L67
RUTH J.M.,"THE ADMINISTRATION OF WATER RESOURCES IN GUATEMALA." GUATEMALA L/A+17C DIST/IND LOC/G NAT/G EX/STRUC ADMIN GOV/REL DEMAND EQUILIB WEALTH...GEOG MGT 20. PAGE 136 H2723
EFFICIENCY ECO/UNDEV PLAN ACT/RES

L67
WILBER L.A.,"THE GOVERNMENTAL STRUCTURE OF MISSISSIPPI: ITS STRENGTHS AND WEAKNESSES." AGRI LOC/G SCHOOL EX/STRUC LEGIS TOP/EX BUDGET CT/SYS APPORT RACE/REL...GOV/COMP 20 MISSISSIPP. PAGE 168 H3359
CONSTN PROVS STAT CON/ANAL

S67
ABDEL-MALEK A.,"THE CRISIS IN NASSER'S EGYPT." ISLAM UAR STRUCT POL/PAR EX/STRUC CREATE PLAN WAR ATTIT ORD/FREE PWR...POLICY DECISION 20. PAGE 3 H0054
FORCES LEAD PROB/SOLV NAT/G

S67
ALEXANDER A.,"CANADA'S PARLIAMENTARY SECRETARIES: THEIR POLITICAL AND CONSTITUTIONAL POSITION." CANADA UK NAT/G POL/PAR GOV/REL...GOV/COMP 20. PAGE 5 H0099
CONSTN ADMIN EX/STRUC DELIB/GP

S67
ANDERSON L.G.,"ADMINISTERING A GOVERNMENT SOCIAL SERVICE" NEW/ZEALND EX/STRUC TASK ROLE 20. PAGE 6 H0129
ADMIN NAT/G DELIB/GP SOC/WK

S67
COLLINS B.A.,"SOME NOTES ON PUBLIC SERVICE COMMISSIONS IN THE COMMONWEALTH CARIBBEAN." JAMAICA L/A+17C TRINIDAD UK NAT/G OP/RES DOMIN SENIOR COLONIAL CONTROL INGP/REL CENTRAL EFFICIENCY PWR ...DECISION 20. PAGE 31 H0631
ADMIN EX/STRUC ECO/UNDEV CHOOSE

S67
DIAMANT A.,"EUROPEAN MODELS OF BUREAUCRACY AND DEVELOPMENT." EX/STRUC PLAN ADMIN CONTROL ROUTINE GOV/REL CENTRAL...DECISION TIME/SEQ CHARTS. PAGE 41 H0818
NAT/G EQUILIB ACT/RES NAT/COMP

S67
DOERN G.B.,"THE ROYAL COMMISSIONS IN THE GENERAL POLICY PROCESS AND IN FEDERAL-PROVINCIAL RELATIONS." CANADA CONSTN ACADEM PROVS CONSULT DELIB/GP LEGIS ACT/RES PROB/SOLV CONFER CONTROL EFFICIENCY...METH/COMP 20 SENATE ROYAL/COMM. PAGE 42 H0832
R+D EX/STRUC GOV/REL NAT/G

S67
GRANT C.H.,"RURAL LOCAL GOVERNMENT IN GUYANA AND BRITISH HONDURAS." GUYANA HONDURAS L/A+17C AGRI NAT/G EX/STRUC ACT/RES REGION GOV/REL EFFICIENCY ORD/FREE 20. PAGE 60 H1196
ECO/UNDEV LOC/G ADMIN MUNIC

S67
HARNON E.,"CRIMINAL PROCEDURE IN ISRAEL - SOME COMPARATIVE ASPECTS." ISRAEL USA+45 CLIENT EX/STRUC LEGIS...JURID NAT/COMP 20. PAGE 67 H1336
ADJUD CONSTN CT/SYS CRIME

S67
IDENBURG P.J.,"POLITICAL STRUCTURAL DEVELOPMENT IN TROPICAL AFRICA." UK ECO/UNDEV KIN POL/PAR CHIEF EX/STRUC CREATE COLONIAL CONTROL REPRESENT RACE/REL ...MAJORIT TREND 20. PAGE 76 H1521
AFR CONSTN NAT/G GOV/COMP

S67
INDER S.,"AFTER THE CORONATION." CONSTN ECO/UNDEV EX/STRUC LEGIS INT/TRADE CONTROL SOVEREIGN ...TIME/SEQ 20 TONGA COMMONWLTH INAUGURATE. PAGE 76 H1527
CHIEF NAT/G POLICY

S67
LALL B.G.,"GAPS IN THE ABM DEBATE." NAT/G DIPLOM DETER CIVMIL/REL 20. PAGE 90 H1798
NUC/PWR ARMS/CONT EX/STRUC FORCES

S67
MALLORY J.R.,"THE MINISTER'S OFFICE STAFF* AN UNREFORMED PART OF PUBLIC SERVICE." CONSTN ELITES STRATA NAT/G PROB/SOLV TASK CHOOSE PERS/REL EFFICIENCY...DECISION 20. PAGE 102 H2033
CANADA ADMIN EX/STRUC STRUCT

S67
PAK H.,"CHINA'S MILITIA AND MAO TSE-TUNG'S 'PEOPLE'S WAR'." CHINA/COM SOCIETY POL/PAR EX/STRUC PROB/SOLV PARTIC COERCE WAR CIVMIL/REL ATTIT DRIVE MARXISM...METH/COMP 20 MAO. PAGE 122 H2447
FORCES NAT/G WORKER CHIEF

S67
RAUM O.,"THE MODERN LEADERSHIP GROUP AMONG THE SOUTH AFRICAN XHOSA." SOUTH/AFR SOCIETY SECT EX/STRUC REPRESENT GP/REL INGP/REL PERSON ...METH/COMP 17/20 XHOSA NEGRO. PAGE 130 H2596
RACE/REL KIN LEAD CULTURE

S67
RICHMAN B.M.,"CAPITALISTS & MANAGERS IN COMMUNIST CHINA." ASIA CHINA/COM ECO/UNDEV NAT/G CONSULT EX/STRUC PLAN EFFICIENCY PRODUC WEALTH MARXISM ...MGT CHARTS 20. PAGE 131 H2623
CAP/ISM INDUS

S67
ROTBERG R.I.,"COLONIALISM AND AFTER: THE POLITICAL LITERATURE OF CENTRAL AFRICA - A BIBLIOGRAPHIC ESSAY." AFR CHIEF EX/STRUC REV INGP/REL RACE/REL SOVEREIGN 20. PAGE 135 H2693
BIBLIOG/A COLONIAL DIPLOM NAT/G

S67
SZALAY L.B.,"SOVIET DOMESTIC PROPAGANDA AND LIBERALIZATION." COM USSR SOCIETY COM/IND NAT/G POL/PAR EX/STRUC TEC/DEV LEAD ATTIT ROLE MARXISM ...METH/COMP 20. PAGE 151 H3026
EDU/PROP TOTALISM PERSON PERCEPT

S67
TATU M.,"URSS: LES FLOTTEMENTS DE LA DIRECTION COLLEGIALE." UAR USSR CHIEF LEAD INGP/REL EFFICIENCY...DECISION TREND 20 MID/EAST. PAGE 152 H3047
POLICY NAT/G EX/STRUC DIPLOM

L68
CURRENT HISTORY,"AFRICA, 1968." ETHIOPIA GHANA NIGERIA SOUTH/AFR CULTURE ECO/UNDEV KIN SECT CHIEF EX/STRUC WAR WEAPON CHOOSE CIVMIL/REL...GOV/COMP 20 AFRICA/E. PAGE 36 H0724
RACE/REL NAT/LISM FORCES AFR

C80
ARNOLD M.,"DEMOCRACY" IN MIXED ESSAYS (2ND ED.)" UK SOCIETY STRUCT...CONCPT METH/COMP 19. PAGE 8 H0166
NAT/G MAJORIT EX/STRUC ELITES

B83
AMOS S.,THE SCIENCE OF POLITICS. MOD/EUR CONSTN LOC/G NAT/G EX/STRUC LEGIS DIPLOM...METH/COMP 19/20. PAGE 6 H0124
NEW/IDEA PHIL/SCI CONCPT

B85
TAINE H.A.,THE FRENCH REVOLUTION (3 VOLS.) (TRANS. BY J. DURAND). FRANCE MOD/EUR SOCIETY STRATA POL/PAR ECO/TAC DOMIN EDU/PROP GP/REL PWR ...GOV/COMP IDEA/COMP 18. PAGE 152 H3036
REV NAT/G EX/STRUC LEAD

B87
ADAMS J.,A DEFENSE OF THE CONSTITUTIONS OF GOVERNMENT OF THE UNITED STATES OF AMERICA. USA-45 STRATA CHIEF EX/STRUC LEGIS CT/SYS CONSERVE POPULISM...CONCPT CON/ANAL GOV/COMP. PAGE 3 H0063
CONSTN BAL/PWR PWR NAT/G

B87
KINNEAR J.B.,PRINCIPLES OF CIVIL GOVERNMENT. MOD/EUR USA-45 CONSTN LOC/G EX/STRUC ADMIN PARL/PROC RACE/REL...CONCPT 18/19. PAGE 86 H1718
POL/PAR NAT/G GOV/COMP REPRESENT

B96
ESMEIN A.,ELEMENTS DE DROIT CONSTITUTIONNEL. FRANCE UK CHIEF EX/STRUC LEGIS ADJUD CT/SYS PARL/PROC REV GOV/REL ORD/FREE...JURID METH/COMP 18/19. PAGE 47 H0940
LAW CONSTN NAT/G CONCPT

B96
LOWELL A.L.,GOVERNMENTS AND PARTIES IN CONTINENTAL EUROPE (VOL. I). MOD/EUR LOC/G NAT/G SECT CHIEF LEGIS PARL/PROC GOV/REL...POLICY 19. PAGE 99 H1973
POL/PAR GOV/COMP CONSTN EX/STRUC

B96
LOWELL A.L.,GOVERNMENTS AND PARTIES IN CONTINENTAL EUROPE, VOL. II. AUSTRIA GERMANY HUNGARY MOD/EUR SWITZERLND SOCIETY EX/STRUC LEGIS DIPLOM AGREE LEAD PARL/PROC PWR...POLICY 19. PAGE 99 H1974
POL/PAR NAT/G GOV/REL ELITES

EXEC....EXECUTIVE PROCESS

B00
DE JOMINI A.H.,THE ART OF WAR. MOD/EUR NAT/G BAL/PWR DIPLOM DOMIN EXEC ROUTINE COERCE DRIVE PWR SKILL...POLICY CONCPT CHARTS STERTYP 19. PAGE 38 H0755
PLAN FORCES WAR WEAPON

B11
PHILLIPSON C.,THE INTERNATIONAL LAW AND CUSTOM OF ANCIENT GREECE AND ROME. MEDIT-7 UNIV INTELL SOCIETY STRUCT NAT/G LEGIS EXEC PERSON...CONCPT OBS CON/ANAL ROM/EMP. PAGE 125 H2504
INT/ORG LAW INT/LAW

B16
TREITSCHKE H.,POLITICS. UNIV SOCIETY STRATA NAT/G EX/STRUC LEGIS DOMIN EDU/PROP ATTIT PWR RESPECT ...CONCPT TIME/SEQ GEN/LAWS TOT/POP 20. PAGE 157 H3129
EXEC ELITES GERMANY

N17
BURKE E.,THOUGHTS ON THE CAUSE OF THE PRESENT
ORD/FREE

DISCONTENTS (PAMPHLET). MOD/EUR UK CONSTN CHIEF LEGIS DOMIN CONTROL EXEC REPRESENT POPULISM ...TRADIT NEW/IDEA METH/COMP 18 BURKE/EDM. PAGE 24 H0484
REV PARL/PROC NAT/G

N19
OPERATIONS AND POLICY RESEARCH,PERU ELECTION MEMORANDA (PAMPHLET). L/A+17C PERU POL/PAR LEGIS EXEC APPORT REPRESENT 20. PAGE 121 H2421
CHOOSE CONSTN SUFF NAT/G

N19
TREVELYAN G.M.,THE TWO-PARTY SYSTEM IN ENGLISH POLITICAL HISTORY (PAMPHLET). UK CHIEF LEGIS COLONIAL EXEC REV CHOOSE 17/19. PAGE 157 H3131
PARL/PROC POL/PAR NAT/G PWR

B23
FRANK T.,A HISTORY OF ROME. MEDIT-7 INTELL SOCIETY LOC/G NAT/G POL/PAR FORCES LEGIS DOMIN LEGIT ALL/VALS...POLICY CONCPT TIME/SEQ GEN/LAWS ROM/EMP ROM/EMP. PAGE 53 H1050
EXEC STRUCT ELITES

B24
BAGEHOT W.,THE ENGLISH CONSTITUTION AND OTHER POLITICAL ESSAYS. UK DELIB/GP BAL/PWR ADMIN CONTROL EXEC ROUTINE CONSERVE...METH PARLIAMENT 19/20. PAGE 10 H0197
NAT/G STRUCT CONCPT

B27
WILLOUGHBY W.F.,PRINCIPLES OF PUBLIC ADMINISTRATION WITH SPECIAL REFERENCE TO THE NATIONAL AND STATE GOVERNMENTS OF THE UNITED STATES. FINAN PROVS CHIEF CONSULT LEGIS CREATE BUDGET EXEC ROUTINE GOV/REL CENTRAL...MGT 20 BUR/BUDGET CONGRESS PRESIDENT. PAGE 169 H3373
NAT/G EX/STRUC OP/RES ADMIN

B34
RIDLEY C.E.,THE CITY-MANAGER PROFESSION. CHIEF PLAN ADMIN CONTROL ROUTINE CHOOSE...TECHNIC CHARTS GOV/COMP BIBLIOG 20. PAGE 131 H2624
MUNIC EX/STRUC LOC/G EXEC

B35
TAKEUCHI T.,WAR AND DIPLOMACY IN THE JAPANESE EMPIRE. ASIA ELITES STRATA NAT/G SECT LEGIS ACT/RES PLAN LEGIT PARL/PROC ROUTINE WAR...MGT BIOG CHINJAP TOT/POP 19/20 CHINJAP. PAGE 152 H3038
EXEC STRUCT

C39
REISCHAUER R.,"JAPAN'S GOVERNMENT--POLITICS." CONSTN STRATA POL/PAR FORCES LEGIS DIPLOM ADMIN EXEC CENTRAL...POLICY BIBLIOG 20 CHINJAP. PAGE 131 H2610
NAT/G S/ASIA CONCPT ROUTINE

B40
KER A.M.,MEXICAN GOVERNMENT PUBLICATIONS: A GUIDE TO THE MORE IMPORTANT PUBLICATIONS OF THE GOVERNMENT OF MEXICO, 1821-1936. CHIEF ADJUD 19/20 MEXIC/AMER. PAGE 85 H1693
BIBLIOG NAT/G EXEC LEGIS

B49
MCLEAN J.M.,THE PUBLIC SERVICE AND UNIVERSITY EDUCATION. UK USA-45 DELIB/GP EX/STRUC TOP/EX ADMIN ...GOV/COMP METH/COMP NAT/COMP ANTHOL 20. PAGE 107 H2142
ACADEM NAT/G EXEC EDU/PROP

B49
SCHWARTZ B.,LAW AND THE EXECUTIVE IN BRITAIN: A COMPARATIVE STUDY. UK USA+45 LAW EX/STRUC PWR ...GOV/COMP 20. PAGE 140 H2807
ADMIN EXEC CONTROL REPRESENT

B50
TRAGER F.N.,MARXISM IN SOUTHEAST ASIA. BURMA INDONESIA THAILAND VIETNAM CULTURE SOCIETY NAT/G VOL/ASSN EXEC ROUTINE COERCE ATTIT RIGID/FLEX PWR ...METH/CNCPT TIME/SEQ STERTYP GEN/LAWS MARX/KARL VAL/FREE COLD/WAR NAM 20. PAGE 156 H3126
S/ASIA POL/PAR REV

B52
ULAM A.B.,TITOISM AND THE COMINFORM. USSR WOR+45 STRUCT INT/ORG NAT/G ACT/RES PLAN EXEC ATTIT DRIVE ALL/VALS...CONCPT OBS VAL/FREE 20 COMINTERN TITO/MARSH. PAGE 157 H3149
COM POL/PAR TOTALISM YUGOSLAVIA

B53
LEITES N.,A STUDY OF BOLSHEVISM. WOR+45 WOR-45 ELITES SOCIETY INT/ORG NAT/G EX/STRUC EDU/PROP EXEC ROUTINE ATTIT MORAL MARXISM...CONCPT OBS VAL/FREE 20. PAGE 94 H1869
COM POL/PAR USSR TOTALISM

B54
SCHWARTZ B.,FRENCH ADMINISTRATIVE LAW AND THE COMMON-LAW WORLD. FRANCE CULTURE LOC/G NAT/G PROVS DELIB/GP EX/STRUC LEGIS PROB/SOLV CT/SYS EXEC GOV/REL...IDEA/COMP ENGLSH/LAW. PAGE 140 H2808
JURID LAW METH/COMP ADJUD

L54
FRIEDRICH C.J.,"TOTALITARIANISM." COM EUR+WWI NAT/G POL/PAR SECT FORCES PLAN ECO/TAC DOMIN EDU/PROP EXEC COERCE REV ORD/FREE PWR...SOC CONCPT NAZI 20. PAGE 53 H1067
ATTIT TOTALISM

L54
FURNISS E.S.,"WEAKNESSES IN FRENCH FOREIGN POLICY-MAKING." EUR+WWI LEGIS LEGIT EXEC ATTIT RIGID/FLEX ORD/FREE...SOC CONCPT METH/CNCPT OBS 20. PAGE 54 H1078
NAT/G STRUCT DIPLOM FRANCE

B55
ALFIERI D.,DICTATORS FACE TO FACE. NAT/G TOP/EX DIPLOM EXEC COERCE ORD/FREE FASCISM...POLICY OBS 20 HITLER/A MUSSOLIN/B. PAGE 5 H0103
WAR CHIEF TOTALISM PERS/REL

B56
JENNINGS W.I.,THE APPROACH TO SELF-GOVERNMENT. CEYLON INDIA PAKISTAN S/ASIA UK SOCIETY POL/PAR DELIB/GP LEGIS ECO/TAC EDU/PROP ADMIN EXEC CHOOSE ATTIT ALL/VALS...JURID CONCPT GEN/METH TOT/POP 20. PAGE 81 H1610
NAT/G CONSTN COLONIAL

B58
KINTNER W.R.,ORGANIZING FOR CONFLICT: A PROPOSAL. USSR STRUCT NAT/G LEGIS ADMIN EXEC PEACE ORD/FREE PWR...CONCPT OBS TREND NAT/COMP VAL/FREE COLD/WAR 20. PAGE 86 H1719
USA+45 PLAN DIPLOM

B58
LAQUER W.Z.,THE MIDDLE EAST IN TRANSITION. COM USSR ECO/UNDEV NAT/G VOL/ASSN EDU/PROP EXEC ATTIT DRIVE PWR MARXISM COLD/WAR TOT/POP 20. PAGE 91 H1818
ISLAM TREND NAT/LISM

B58
WILMERDING L. JR.,THE ELECTORAL COLLEGE. CONSTN NAT/G POL/PAR DELIB/GP LEGIS PROB/SOLV CONFER EXEC LEAD APPORT REPRESENT. PAGE 169 H3377
CHOOSE DECISION ACT/RES

B59
LAQUER W.Z.,THE SOVIET UNION AND THE MIDDLE EAST. COM UAR USSR ECO/UNDEV NAT/G VOL/ASSN ECO/TAC EDU/PROP COLONIAL EXEC PWR...TIME/SEQ TREND COLD/WAR 20. PAGE 91 H1819
ISLAM DRIVE FOR/AID NAT/LISM

B59
PARK R.L.,LEADERSHIP AND POLITICAL INSTITUTIONS IN INDIA. S/ASIA CULTURE ECO/UNDEV LOC/G MUNIC PROVS LEGIS PLAN ADMIN LEAD ORD/FREE WEALTH...GEOG SOC BIOG TOT/POP VAL/FREE 20. PAGE 123 H2468
NAT/G EXEC INDIA

B59
SANCHEZ A.L.,EL CONCEPTO DEL ESTADO EN EL PENSAMIENTO ESPANOL DEL SIGLO XVI. SPAIN LEGIS JUDGE BAL/PWR LEGIT EXEC WAR PWR...MAJORIT 16. PAGE 137 H2747
NAT/G PHIL/SCI LAW SOVEREIGN

S59
GABLE R.W.,"CULTURE AND ADMINISTRATION IN IRAN." IRAN EXEC PARTIC REPRESENT PWR. PAGE 54 H1085
ADMIN CULTURE EX/STRUC INGP/REL

S59
PRESTHUS R.V.,"BEHAVIOR AND BUREAUCRACY IN MANY CULTURES." EXEC INGP/REL 20. PAGE 128 H2558
ADMIN EX/STRUC GOV/COMP METH/CNCPT

B60
ALBI F.,TRATADO DE LOS MODOS DE GESTION DE LAS CORPORACIONES LOCALES. SPAIN FINAN NAT/G BUDGET CONTROL EXEC ROUTINE GOV/REL ORD/FREE SOVEREIGN ...MGT 20. PAGE 5 H0092
LOC/G LAW ADMIN MUNIC

L60
KAPLAN M.A.,"COMMUNIST COUP IN CZECHOSLOVAKIA." COM EUR+WWI INTELL LABOR LOC/G NAT/G POL/PAR FORCES EDU/PROP EXEC MARXISM...TIME/SEQ HYPO/EXP 20. PAGE 83 H1659
STRUCT COERCE CZECHOSLVK

B61
BULLOCK A.,HITLER: A STUDY IN TYRANNY. EUR+WWI GERMANY SOCIETY STRUCT NAT/G POL/PAR FORCES CREATE DOMIN EDU/PROP EXEC COERCE WAR NAT/LISM DISPL DRIVE PERSON PWR...PSY NAZI 20 HITLER/A. PAGE 23 H0470
ATTIT BIOG TOTALISM

B61
MILIBAND R.,PARLIAMENTARY SOCIALISM. EUR+WWI UK EXEC LEAD PARL/PROC GP/REL...POLICY 20 PARLIAMENT LABOR/PAR. PAGE 110 H2203
POL/PAR NAT/G PWR SOCISM

B61
MOLLAU G.,INTERNATIONAL COMMUNISM AND WORLD REVOLUTION: HISTORY AND METHODS. RUSSIA USSR INT/ORG NAT/G POL/PAR VOL/ASSN FORCES BAL/PWR DIPLOM EXEC REGION WAR ATTIT PWR MARXISM...CONCPT TIME/SEQ COLD/WAR 19/20. PAGE 112 H2237
COM REV

B61
MUNGER E.S.,AFRICAN FIELD REPORTS 1952-1961. SOUTH/AFR SOCIETY ECO/UNDEV NAT/G POL/PAR COLONIAL EXEC PARL/PROC GUERRILLA RACE/REL ALL/IDEOS...SOC AUD/VIS 20. PAGE 114 H2288
AFR DISCRIM RECORD

B61
PANIKKAR K.M.,REVOLUTION IN AFRICA. AFR GUINEA ECO/UNDEV POL/PAR DIPLOM COLONIAL EXEC LEAD SOVEREIGN...CHARTS 20. PAGE 123 H2461
NAT/LISM NAT/G CHIEF

S61
BRZEZINSKI Z.K.,"THE ORGANIZATION OF THE COMMUNIST CAMP." COM CZECHOSLVK COM/IND NAT/G DELIB/GP INT/TRADE DOMIN EDU/PROP EXEC ROUTINE COERCE ATTIT PWR...MGT CONCPT TIME/SEQ CHARTS VAL/FREE 20 TREATY. PAGE 23 H0460
VOL/ASSN DIPLOM USSR

B62
ANDREWS W.G.,FRENCH POLITICS AND ALGERIA: THE PROCESS OF POLICY FORMATION 1954-1962. ALGERIA FRANCE CONSTN ELITES POL/PAR CHIEF DELIB/GP LEGIS DIPLOM PRESS CHOOSE 20. PAGE 7 H0140
GOV/COMP EXEC COLONIAL

B62
BRETTON H.L.,POWER AND STABILITY IN NIGERIA: THE POLITICS OF DECOLONIZATION. AFR CONSTN INTELL ECO/UNDEV COM/IND KIN NAT/G POL/PAR PROVS VOL/ASSN LEGIS DOMIN EDU/PROP LEGIT EXEC ROUTINE CHOOSE
CULTURE OBS NIGERIA

NAT/LISM ATTIT PERCEPT ALL/VALS. PAGE 20 H0411

B62
CARTER G.M.,AFRICAN ONE-PARTY STATES. ISLAM IVORY/CST LIBERIA CONSTN CULTURE SOCIETY POL/PAR PLAN DOMIN EDU/PROP EXEC REGION CHOOSE ATTIT ALL/VALS...CONCPT TIME/SEQ CHARTS VAL/FREE 20 TANGANYIKA. PAGE 27 H0545
AFR NAT/LISM

L62
CORET A.,"L'INDEPENDANCE DU SAMOA OCCIDENTAL." S/ASIA LAW INT/ORG EXEC ALL/VALS SAMOA UN 20. PAGE 33 H0668
NAT G STRUCT SOVEREIGN

S62
MURACCIOLE L.,"LES CONSTITUTIONS DES ETATS AFRICAINS D'EXPRESSION FRANCAISE: LA CONSTITUTION DU 16 AVRIL 1962 DE LA REPUBLIQUE DU" AFR CHAD CHIEF LEGIS LEGIT COLONIAL EXEC ROUTINE ORD/FREE SOVEREIGN...SOC CONCPT 20. PAGE 115 H2291
NAT/G CONSTN

B63
CARTER G.M.,FIVE AFRICAN STATES: RESPONSES TO DIVERSITY. CONSTN CULTURE STRATA LEGIS PLAN ECO/TAC DOMIN EDU/PROP CT/SYS EXEC CHOOSE ATTIT HEALTH ORD/FREE PWR...TIME/SEQ TOT/POP VAL/FREE. PAGE 27 H0547
AFR SOCIETY

B63
DUE J.F.,STATE SALES TAX ADMINISTRATION. OP/RES BUDGET PAY ADMIN EXEC ROUTINE COST EFFICIENCY PROFIT...CHARTS METH/COMP 20. PAGE 43 H0855
PROVS TAX STAT GOV/COMP

B63
ISSAWI C.,EGYPT IN REVOLUTION: AN ECONOMIC ANALYSIS. ISLAM STRUCT ECO/UNDEV AGRI FINAN INDUS PLAN EXEC REV NAT/LISM ATTIT RIGID/FLEX WEALTH SOCISM...STAT WORK 20. PAGE 79 H1573
NAT/G UAR

B63
KOGAN N.,THE POLITICS OF ITALIAN FOREIGN POLICY. EUR+WWI LEGIS DOMIN LEGIT EXEC PWR RESPECT SKILL ...POLICY DECISION HUM SOC METH/CNCPT OBS INT CHARTS 20. PAGE 87 H1737
NAT/G ROUTINE DIPLOM ITALY

B63
SETON-WATSON H.,THE NEW IMPERIALISM. COM EUR+WWI MOD/EUR ECO/UNDEV NAT/G FORCES DIPLOM DOMIN EDU/PROP LEGIT COLONIAL EXEC COERCE GP/REL RACE/REL DISCRIM ATTIT...TIME/SEQ 20. PAGE 142 H2833
ECO/TAC RUSSIA USSR

B63
TOUVAL S.,SOMALI NATIONALISM: INTERNATIONAL POLITICS AND THE DRIVE FOR UNITY IN THE HORN OF AFRICA. AFR CULTURE PROVS LEGIS EDU/PROP REGION COERCE ATTIT...MYTH UNPLAN/INT TIME/SEQ SOMALI VAL/FREE 20. PAGE 156 H3118
SOCIETY EXEC NAT/LISM

S63
ARASTEH R.,"THE ROLE OF INTELLECTUALS IN ADMINISTRATIVE DEVELOPMENT AND SOCIAL CHANGE IN MODERN IRAN." ISLAM CULTURE NAT/G CONSULT ACT/RES EDU/PROP EXEC ATTIT BIO/SOC PERCEPT SUPEGO ALL/VALS ...POLICY MGT PSY SOC CONCPT 20. PAGE 8 H0157
INTELL ADMIN IRAN

S63
HUREWITZ J.C.,"LEBANESE DEMOCRACY IN ITS INTERNATIONAL SETTING." FRANCE ISLAM UK LOC/G NAT/G SECT DOMIN EDU/PROP EXEC ATTIT PWR...TIME/SEQ 20. PAGE 75 H1507
STRUCT LEBANON

S63
RUSTOW D.A.,"THE MILITARY IN MIDDLE EASTERN SOCIETY AND POLITICS." FUT ISLAM CONSTN SOCIETY FACE/GP NAT/G POL/PAR PROF/ORG CONSULT DOMIN ADMIN EXEC REGION COERCE NAT/LISM ATTIT DRIVE PERSON ORD/FREE PWR...POLICY CONCPT OBS STERTYP 20. PAGE 136 H2721
FORCES ELITES

S63
TILMAN R.O.,"MALAYSIA: THE PROBLEMS OF FEDERATION." ISLAM S/ASIA CONSTN PROVS SECT DELIB/GP DOMIN EDU/PROP LEGIT EXEC COERCE CHOOSE ATTIT HEALTH ORD/FREE PWR...STAT TOT/POP VAL/FREE 20. PAGE 155 H3097
NAT/G CULTURE MALAYSIA

B64
LI C.M.,INDUSTRIAL DEVELOPMENT IN COMMUNIST CHINA. CHINA/COM ECO/DEV ECO/UNDEV AGRI FINAN INDUS MARKET LABOR NAT/G ECO/TAC INT/TRADE EXEC ALL/VALS ...POLICY RELATIV TREND WORK TOT/POP VAL/FREE 20. PAGE 96 H1921
ASIA TEC/DEV

B64
MINAR D.W.,IDEAS AND POLITICS: THE AMERICAN EXPERIENCE. SECT CHIEF LEGIS CREATE ADJUD EXEC REV PWR...PHIL/SCI CONCPT IDEA/COMP 18/20 HAMILTON/A JEFFERSN/T DECLAR/IND JACKSON/A PRESIDENT. PAGE 111 H2220
CONSTN NAT/G FEDERAL

B64
PHILLIPS C.S.,THE DEVELOPMENT OF NIGERIAN FOREIGN POLICY. AFR CONSTN CULTURE STRATA NAT/G LEGIS DOMIN LEGIT EXEC...RELATIV SOC TIME/SEQ TREND TOT/POP 20. PAGE 125 H2502
CHOOSE POLICY DIPLOM NIGERIA

B64
PIPES R.,THE FORMATION OF THE SOVIET UNION. EUR+WWI MOD/EUR STRUCT ECO/UNDEV NAT/G LEGIS DOMIN LEGIT CT/SYS EXEC COERCE ALL/VALS...POLICY RELATIV HIST/WRIT TIME/SEQ TOT/POP 19/20. PAGE 126 H2514
COM USSR RUSSIA

B64
RESHETAR J.S. JR.,A CONCISE HISTORY OF THE COMMUNIST PARTY OF THE SOVIET UNION (REV. ED.). COM USSR NAT/G EXEC 19/20 LENIN/VI STALIN/J KHRUSH/N. PAGE 131 H2618
CHIEF POL/PAR MARXISM PWR

B64
STRONG C.F.,HISTORY OF MODERN POLITICAL CONSTITUTIONS. STRUCT INT/ORG NAT/G LEGIS TEC/DEV DIPLOM INT/TRADE CT/SYS EXEC...METH/COMP T 12/20 UN. PAGE 150 H2999
CONSTN CONCPT

S64
CLIGNET R.,"POTENTIAL ELITES IN GHANA AND THE IVORY COAST: A PRELIMINARY SURVEY." AFR CULTURE ELITES STRATA KIN NAT/G SECT DOMIN EXEC ORD/FREE RESPECT SKILL...POLICY RELATIV GP/COMP NAT/COMP 20. PAGE 30 H0605
PWR LEGIT IVORY/CST GHANA

S64
LEWIS R.,"OPINION SURVEYING IN KOREA." ASIA FUT KOREA LEGIS EDU/PROP EXEC ALL/VALS...POLICY CONCPT MYTH TESTS CON/ANAL GEN/METH TOT/POP VAL/FREE 20. PAGE 96 H1915
NAT/G QU

S64
SCHEFFLER H.W.,"THE GENESIS AND REPRESSION OF CONFLICT: CHOISEUL ISLAND." S/ASIA LOC/G NAT/G FORCES LEGIS DIPLOM DOMIN LEGIT EXEC CHOOSE ATTIT RESPECT SKILL...POLICY JURID OBS TREND GEN/METH 20. PAGE 139 H2781
PWR COERCE WAR

B65
HANSER C.J.,GUIDE TO DECISION: ROYAL COMMISSION. UK INTELL EXTR/IND SCHOOL PROB/SOLV EXEC ROUTINE CHOOSE GOV/REL GP/REL HEALTH...CHARTS 20. PAGE 66 H1318
NAT/G DELIB/GP EX/STRUC PWR

B65
JACKSON G.,THE SPANISH REPUBLIC AND THE CIVIL WAR, 1931-1939. EUR+WWI INTELL STRUCT COM/IND NAT/G POL/PAR LEGIS EDU/PROP EXEC COERCE NAT/LISM DRIVE PWR...INT TIME/SEQ TOT/POP 20. PAGE 79 H1574
ATTIT GUERRILLA SPAIN

B65
MCWHINNEY E.,JUDICIAL REVIEW IN THE ENGLISH-SPEAKING WORLD (3RD ED.). CANADA UK WOR+45 LEGIS CONTROL EXEC PARTIC...JURID 20 AUSTRAL. PAGE 108 H2151
GOV/COMP CT/SYS ADJUD CONSTN

B65
MOORE C.H.,TUNISIA SINCE INDEPENDENCE. ELITES LOC/G POL/PAR ADMIN COLONIAL CONTROL EXEC GOV/REL TOTALISM MARXISM...INT 20 TUNIS. PAGE 112 H2248
NAT/G EX/STRUC SOCISM

S65
HUGHES T.L.,"SCHOLARS AND FOREIGN POLICY* VARIETIES OF RESEARCH EXPERIENCE." COM/IND DIPLOM ADMIN EXEC ROUTINE...MGT OBS CONGRESS PRESIDENT CAMELOT. PAGE 75 H1491
ACT/RES ACADEM CONTROL NAT/G

B66
CHAPMAN B.,THE PROFESSION OF GOVERNMENT: THE PUBLIC SERVICE IN EUROPE. CONSTN NAT/G POL/PAR EX/STRUC LEGIS TOP/EX PROB/SOLV DEBATE EXEC PARL/PROC PARTIC 20. PAGE 29 H0581
BIBLIOG ADMIN EUR+WWI GOV/COMP

B66
LEROY P.,L'ORGANIZATION CONSTITUTIONNELLE ET LES CRISES. FRANCE NAT/G ADJUD CONTROL PARL/PROC WAR ...POLICY BIBLIOG 20. PAGE 95 H1892
CONSTN PWR EXEC LEGIS

B66
ROSS A.M.,INDUSTRIAL RELATIONS AND ECONOMIC DEVELOPMENT. POL/PAR LEGIS WORKER BARGAIN PRICE EXEC LOBBY INCOME PWR...DECISION ANTHOL BIBLIOG 20. PAGE 134 H2686
ECO/UNDEV LABOR NAT/G GP/REL

L66
MCAUSLAN J.P.W.,"CONSTITUTIONAL INNOVATION AND POLITICAL STABILITY IN TANZANIA: A PRELIMINARY ASSESSMENT." AFR TANZANIA ELITES CHIEF EX/STRUC RIGID/FLEX PWR 20 PRESIDENT BUREAUCRCY. PAGE 106 H2122
CONSTN NAT/G EXEC POL/PAR

S66
CRANMER-BYNG J.L.,"THE CHINESE ATTITUDE TOWARDS EXTERNAL RELATIONS." ASIA CHINA/COM EXEC NAT/LISM MARXISM...POLICY 20. PAGE 35 H0699
ATTIT DIPLOM NAT/G

B67
BROWN L.N.,FRENCH ADMINISTRATIVE LAW. FRANCE UK CONSTN NAT/G LEGIS DOMIN CONTROL EXEC PARL/PROC PWR ...JURID METH/COMP GEN/METH. PAGE 22 H0447
EX/STRUC LAW IDEA/COMP CT/SYS

B67
BRZEZINSKI Z.K.,THE SOVIET BLOC: UNITY AND CONFLICT (2ND ED., REV., ENLARGED). COM POLAND USSR INTELL CHIEF EX/STRUC CONTROL EXEC GOV/REL PWR MARXISM ...TREND IDEA/COMP 20 LENIN/VI MARX/KARL STALIN/J. PAGE 23 H0463
NAT/G DIPLOM

B67
GALBRAITH J.K.,THE NEW INDUSTRIAL STATE. INDUS LABOR LG/CO NAT/G POL/PAR SCHOOL OP/RES CAP/ISM EXEC TREND. PAGE 54 H1087
TEC/DEV ECO/DEV SOCIETY MARKET

B67
HILSMAN R.,TO MOVE A NATION: THE POLITICS OF FOREIGN POLICY IN THE ADMINISTRATION OF JOHN F. KENNEDY. CHINA/COM COM USSR VIETNAM NAT/G DELIB/GP FORCES PLAN PROB/SOLV BAL/PWR COLONIAL EXEC REV PWR 20 KENNEDY/JF PRESIDENT. PAGE 71 H1418
CHIEF DIPLOM

B67
KAROL K.S.,CHINA, THE OTHER COMMUNISM (TRANS. BY TOM BAISTOW). CHINA/COM CULTURE INDUS FORCES DIPLOM EDU/PROP CONTROL EXEC NUC/PWR ATTIT...SOC CHARTS 20. PAGE 83 H1663
NAT/G POL/PAR MARXISM INGP/REL

B67
WARREN S.,THE AMERICAN PRESIDENT. POL/PAR FORCES LEGIS DIPLOM ECO/TAC ADMIN EXEC PWR...ANTHOL 18/20 ROOSEVLT/F KENNEDY/JF JOHNSON/LB TRUMAN/HS WILSON/W. PAGE 165 H3312
CHIEF LEAD NAT/G CONSTN

S67
ADOKO A.,"THE CONSTITUTION OF UGANDA." AFR UGANDA LOC/G CHIEF FORCES LEGIS ADJUD EXEC CHOOSE NAT/LISM ...IDEA/COMP 20. PAGE 4 H0072
NAT/G CONSTN ORD/FREE LAW

S67
BRADLEY A.W.,"CONSTITUTION-MAKING IN UGANDA." UGANDA LAW CHIEF DELIB/GP LEGIS ADMIN EXEC PARL/PROC RACE/REL ORD/FREE...GOV/COMP 20. PAGE 20 H0397
NAT/G CREATE CONSTN FEDERAL

S67
CROCKETT D.G.,"THE MP AND HIS CONSTITUENTS." UK POL/PAR...DECISION 20. PAGE 35 H0706
EXEC NAT/G PERS/REL REPRESENT

S67
GRIEB K.J.,"THE UNITED STATES AND THE CENTRAL AMERICAN CONFEDERATION." COSTA/RICA EL/SALVADR GUATEMALA HONDURAS L/A+17C NICARAGUA NAT/G FORCES CONFER AGREE EXEC ARMS/CONT REV WAR PEACE ATTIT 20. PAGE 60 H1212
INT/ORG DIPLOM POLICY REGION

B91
SIDGWICK H.,THE ELEMENTS OF POLITICS. LOC/G NAT/G LEGIS DIPLOM ADJUD CONTROL EXEC PARL/PROC REPRESENT GOV/REL SOVEREIGN ALL/IDEOS 19 MILL/JS BENTHAM/J. PAGE 143 H2868
POLICY LAW CONCPT

EXECUTIVE....SEE TOP/EX

EXECUTIVE ESTABLISHMENTS....SEE EX/STRUC

EXECUTIVE PROCESS....SEE EXEC

EXHIBIT....DISPLAY

EXPECTATIONS....SEE PROBABIL, SUPEGO, PREDICT

EXPERIMENTATION....SEE EXPERIMENTATION INDEX, P. XIV

EXPOSTFACT....EX POST FACTO LAWS

EXPROPRIAT....EXPROPRIATION

EXTR/IND....EXTRACTIVE INDUSTRY (FISHING, LUMBERING, ETC.)

B00
HOBSON J.A.,THE WAR IN SOUTH AFRICA: ITS CAUSES AND EFFECTS. NETHERLAND SOUTH/AFR UK ELITES AGRI EXTR/IND POL/PAR DIPLOM PRESS RACE/REL ATTIT ORD/FREE SOVEREIGN...INT 19 NEGRO. PAGE 72 H1439
WAR DOMIN POLICY NAT/G

B08
THE GOVERNMENT OF SOUTH AFRICA (VOL. II). SOUTH/AFR STRATA EXTR/IND EX/STRUC TOP/EX BUDGET ADJUD ADMIN CT/SYS PRODUC...CORREL CENSUS 19 RAILROAD CIVIL/SERV POSTAL/SYS. PAGE 2 H0030
CONSTN FINAN LEGIS NAT/G

B10
MENDELSSOHN S.,SOUTH AFRICAN BIBLIOGRAPHY (2 VOLS.). SOUTH/AFR EXTR/IND LABOR SECT DIPLOM INT/TRADE COLONIAL RACE/REL DISCRIM...GEOG 20. PAGE 109 H2172
BIBLIOG/A AFR NAT/G NAT/LISM

B12
BRUNHES J.,LA GEOGRAPHIE HUMAINE: ESSAI DE CLASSIFICATION POSITIVE PRINCIPES ET EXEMPLES (2ND ED.). UNIV SEA AGRI EXTR/IND DRIVE...SOC CHARTS 20. PAGE 23 H0454
GEOG HABITAT CULTURE

B16
CALVERT A.F.,SOUTHWEST AFRICA 1884-1914 (2ND ED.). GERMANY EXTR/IND NAT/G FORCES...GEOG AUD/VIS CHARTS 19/20 RESOURCE/N AFRICA/SW. PAGE 25 H0508
COLONIAL ECO/UNDEV AFR

N19
SALKEVER L.R.,SUB-SAHARA AFRICA (PAMPHLET). AFR USSR EXTR/IND NAT/G SCHOOL DIPLOM COLONIAL WEALTH ...GEOG CHARTS 16/20. PAGE 137 H2742
ECO/UNDEV TEC/DEV TASK INT/TRADE

B27
WEBER M.,GENERAL ECONOMIC HISTORY. CHRIST-17C MOD/EUR STRUCT AGRI EXTR/IND FINAN INDUS MARKET FAM MUNIC NAT/G PROF/ORG SECT ECO/TAC 8/20. PAGE 166 H3319
ECO/DEV CAP/ISM

B40
MEEK C.K.,EUROPE AND WEST AFRICA. AFR EUR+WWI EXTR/IND DIPLOM INT/TRADE EDU/PROP GP/REL...SOC 20. PAGE 108 H2158
CULTURE TEC/DEV ECO/UNDEV COLONIAL

B42
CONOVER H.F.,THE NETHERLANDS EAST INDIES: A SELECTED LIST OF REFERENCES. ECO/UNDEV AGRI EXTR/IND LABOR SCHOOL SECT INT/TRADE COLONIAL HEALTH...GEOG 19/20. PAGE 32 H0642
BIBLIOG S/ASIA CULTURE

B48
WHITE C.L.,HUMAN GEOGRAPHY: AN ECOLOGICAL STUDY OF GEOGRAPHY. UNIV SEA CULTURE AGRI EXTR/IND RACE/REL PRODUC...CHARTS HYPO/EXP SIMUL GEN/LAWS T. PAGE 167 H3345
SOC HABITAT GEOG SOCIETY

B55
JONES T.B.,A BIBLIOGRAPHY ON SOUTH AMERICAN ECONOMIC AFFAIRS: ARTICLES IN NINETEENTH CENTURY PERIODICALS (PAMPHLET). AGRI COM/IND DIST/IND EXTR/IND FINAN INDUS LABOR NAT/G 19. PAGE 82 H1634
BIBLIOG ECO/UNDEV L/A+17C TEC/DEV

B55
RESHETAR J.S.,PROBLEMS OF ANALYZING AND PREDICTING SOVIET BEHAVIOR. USSR CULTURE ECO/DEV AGRI DIST/IND EXTR/IND PROC/MFG NAT/G SECT TOP/EX ACT/RES ADMIN PWR WEALTH...SOC METH TOT/POP VAL/FREE 20. PAGE 131 H2617
COM ATTIT

B57
CENTRAL ASIAN RESEARCH CENTRE,BIBLIOGRAPHY OF RECENT SOVIET SOURCE MATERIAL ON SOVIET CENTRAL ASIA AND THE BORDERLANDS. AFGHANISTN INDIA PAKISTAN UAR USSR ECO/UNDEV AGRI EXTR/IND INDUS ACADEM ADMIN ...HEAL HUM LING CON/ANAL 20. PAGE 28 H0567
BIBLIOG/A COM CULTURE NAT/G

B57
PALACIOS A.L.,PETROLEO, MONOPOLIOS, Y LATIFUNDIOS. L/A+17C EXTR/IND NAT/G TEC/DEV ECO/TAC CONTROL PRODUC 20 ARGEN MONOPOLY RESOURCE/N. PAGE 123 H2448
ECO/UNDEV NAT/LISM INDUS AGRI

B60
COUGHLIN R.,DOUBLE IDENTITY: THE CHINESE AND MODERN THAILAND. CHINA/COM S/ASIA THAILAND ECO/UNDEV EXTR/IND FINAN INDUS KIN MUNIC NAT/G PROF/ORG SCHOOL SECT ATTIT DRIVE...CONCPT OBS 20. PAGE 34 H0676
ASIA FAM CULTURE

B60
LISTER L.,EUROPE'S COAL AND STEEL COMMUNITY. FRANCE GERMANY STRUCT ECO/DEV EXTR/IND INDUS MARKET NAT/G DELIB/GP ECO/TAC INT/TRADE EDU/PROP ATTIT RIGID/FLEX ORD/FREE PWR WEALTH...CONCPT STAT TIME/SEQ CHARTS ECSC 20. PAGE 97 H1941
EUR+WWI INT/ORG REGION

S60
RIVKIN A.,"AFRICAN ECONOMIC DEVELOPMENT: ADVANCED TECHNOLOGY AND THE STAGES OF GROWTH." CULTURE ECO/UNDEV AGRI COM/IND EXTR/IND PLAN ECO/TAC ATTIT DRIVE RIGID/FLEX SKILL WEALTH...MGT SOC GEN/LAWS WORK TOT/POP 20. PAGE 132 H2634
AFR TEC/DEV FOR/AID

B61
LAHAYE R.,LES ENTREPRISES PUBLIQUES AU MAROC. FRANCE MOROCCO LAW DIST/IND EXTR/IND FINAN CONSULT PLAN TEC/DEV ADMIN AGREE CONTROL OWN...POLICY 20. PAGE 90 H1796
NAT/G INDUS ECO/UNDEV ECO/TAC

B61
SCHNAPPER B.,LA POLITIQUE ET LE COMMERCE FRANCAIS DANS LE GOLFE DE GUINEE DE 1838 A 1871. FRANCE GUINEA UK SEA EXTR/IND NAT/G DELIB/GP LEGIS ADMIN ORD/FREE...POLICY GEOG CENSUS CHARTS BIBLIOG 19. PAGE 139 H2791
COLONIAL INT/TRADE DOMIN AFR

B62
HENDERSON W.O.,THE GENESIS OF THE COMMON MARKET. EUR+WWI FRANCE MOD/EUR UK SEA COM/IND EXTR/IND COLONIAL DISCRIM...TIME/SEQ CHARTS BIBLIOG 18/20 EEC TREATY. PAGE 70 H1395
ECO/DEV INT/TRADE DIPLOM

B63
FURTADO C.,THE ECONOMIC GROWTH OF BRAZIL: A SURVEY FROM COLONIAL TO MODERN TIMES. L/A+17C AGRI DIST/IND EXTR/IND INDUS WORKER COLONIAL RACE/REL OWN GOV/COMP. PAGE 54 H1082
ECO/UNDEV TEC/DEV LABOR DOMIN

B64
MCCALL D.F.,AFRICA IN TIME PERSPECTIVE. AFR EXTR/IND KIN SECT CREATE PERS/REL HABITAT...GEOG METH/CNCPT LING BIBLIOG/A TIME 20. PAGE 106 H2124
HIST/WRIT OBS/ENVIR CULTURE

B64
RAMAZANI R.K.,THE MIDDLE EAST AND THE EUROPEAN COMMON MARKET. EUR+WWI ISLAM ECO/DEV EXTR/IND MARKET PROC/MFG INT/ORG NAT/G TEC/DEV ECO/TAC REGION DRIVE WEALTH...STAT CHARTS EEC TOT/POP 20. PAGE 129 H2587
ECO/UNDEV ATTIT INT/TRADE

B64
WITHERELL J.W.,OFFICIAL PUBLICATIONS OF FRENCH EQUATORIAL AFRICA, FRENCH CAMEROONS, AND TOGO, 1946-1958 (PAMPHLET). CAMEROON CHAD FRANCE GABON TOGO LAW ECO/UNDEV EXTR/IND INT/TRADE...GEOG HEAL 20. PAGE 169 H3392
BIBLIOG/A AFR NAT/G ADMIN

S64
ZARTMAN I.W.,"LES RELATIONS ENTRE LA FRANCE ET L'ALGERIA DEPUIS LES ACCORDS D'EVIAN." EUR+WWI FUT ISLAM CULTURE AGRI EXTR/IND FINAN INDUS POL/PAR DIPLOM ECO/TAC FOR/AID PEACE ATTIT DRIVE ALL/VALS ...TIME/SEQ VAL/FREE 20. PAGE 172 H3450
ECO/UNDEV ALGERIA FRANCE

B65
BARRY E.E.,NATIONALISATION IN BRITISH POLITICS: THE HISTORICAL BACKGROUND. UK AGRI DIST/IND EXTR/IND LABOR LG/CO ATTIT CONSERVE SOCISM 19/20 LABOR/PAR. PAGE 12 H0231
NAT/G OWN INDUS POL/PAR

B65
HANSER C.J.,GUIDE TO DECISION: ROYAL COMMISSION. UK INTELL EXTR/IND SCHOOL PROB/SOLV EXEC ROUTINE CHOOSE GOV/REL GP/REL HEALTH...CHARTS 20. PAGE 66 H1318 — NAT/G DELIB/GP EX/STRUC PWR

B65
POLK W.R.,THE UNITED STATES AND THE ARAB WORLD. USA+45 ECO/UNDEV EXTR/IND SECT WAR NAT/LISM ATTIT ...NAT/COMP COLD/WAR. PAGE 127 H2535 — ISLAM REGION CULTURE DIPLOM

B66
LAVEN P.,RENAISSANCE ITALY: 1464-1534. ITALY AGRI EXTR/IND FINAN MUNIC INT/TRADE DRIVE...CATH GEOG CHARTS BIBLIOG/A 15. PAGE 92 H1841 — CULTURE HUM TEC/DEV KNOWL

S67
JENCKS C.E.,"SOCIAL STATUS OF COAL MINERS IN BRITAIN SINCE NATIONALIZATION." UK STRATA STRUCT LABOR RECEIVE GP/REL INCOME OWN ATTIT HABITAT...MGT T 20. PAGE 80 H1600 — EXTR/IND WORKER CONTROL NAT/G

S67
SANCHEZ J.D.,"DESARROLLO ECONOMICO Y FUTURO DE COLOMBIA." L/A+17C AGRI EXTR/IND FINAN INDUS MARKET INT/TRADE CONTROL...STAT TREND COLOMB. PAGE 137 H2748 — ECO/UNDEV FUT NAT/G ECO/TAC

C89
PLAYFAIR R.L.,"A BIBLIOGRAPHY OF ALGERIA." ALGERIA CULTURE ECO/UNDEV DIST/IND EXTR/IND FINAN SECT CRIME 16/19. PAGE 126 H2525 — BIBLIOG/A ISLAM GEOG

B99
KINGSLEY M.H.,WEST AFRICAN STUDIES. GHANA NIGERIA SIER/LEONE LAW EXTR/IND SECT DIPLOM INT/TRADE DOMIN RACE/REL OWN HEALTH...SOC 19. PAGE 86 H1717 — AFR HEREDITY COLONIAL CULTURE

EXTRACTIVE INDUSTRY....SEE EXTR/IND

EYBERS G.W. H0955

EZELL P.H. H0957

F

FAA....U.S. FEDERAL AVIATION AGENCY

FABER K. H0957

FABIAN....FABIANS: MEMBERS AND/OR SUPPORTERS OF FABIAN SOCIETY

FACE/GP....ACQUAINTANCE GROUP

B27
MCCOWN A.C.,THE CONGRESSIONAL CONFERENCE COMMITTEE. FACE/GP CONTROL. PAGE 106 H2128 — DELIB/GP GOV/COMP LEGIS CONFER

S60
TURNER R.H.,"SPONSORED AND CONTEST MOBILITY IN THE SCHOOL SYSTEM." UK USA+45 ELITES STRATA ACADEM FACE/GP EDU/PROP CONTROL INGP/REL ADJUST ATTIT PERSON...METH/COMP 20. PAGE 157 H3142 — AGE/Y NAT/COMP SCHOOL STRUCT

B61
BERKOWITZ L.,AGGRESSION: AS A SOCIAL PSYCHOLOGICAL ANALYSIS. UNIV CULTURE FACE/GP FAM KIN NEIGH EDU/PROP DISPL DRIVE HEALTH LOVE ORD/FREE...PSY SOC CONCPT OBS TREND. PAGE 15 H0305 — SOCIETY COERCE WAR

B61
VON MERING O.,A GRAMMAR OF HUMAN VALUES. WOR+45 CULTURE FACE/GP NEIGH CREATE EDU/PROP LEGIT ATTIT DRIVE PERSON ORD/FREE...PSY SOC METH/CNCPT OBS RECORD INT REC/INT STAND/INT QU CHARTS VAL/FREE. PAGE 164 H3275 — SOCIETY MORAL

B63
GEERTZ C.,PEDDLERS AND PRINCES: SOCIAL DEVELOPMENT AND ECONOMIC CHANGE IN TWO INDONESIAN TOWNS. S/ASIA CULTURE SOCIETY STRATA FACE/GP MUNIC CREATE TEC/DEV ECO/TAC ORD/FREE WEALTH...OBS INT CENSUS CHARTS WORK TOT/POP VAL/FREE 20. PAGE 55 H1106 — ECO/UNDEV SOC ELITES INDONESIA

S63
NICHOLAS W.,"VILLAGE FACTIONS AND POLITICAL PARTIES IN RURAL WEST BENGAL." S/ASIA CULTURE STRATA FACE/GP KIN MUNIC DELIB/GP LEGIS DOMIN EDU/PROP COERCE CHOOSE ATTIT ALL/VALS...STAT TOT/POP VAL/FREE 20. PAGE 117 H2348 — NEIGH POL/PAR

S63
RUSTOW D.A.,"THE MILITARY IN MIDDLE EASTERN SOCIETY AND POLITICS." FUT ISLAM CONSTN SOCIETY FACE/GP NAT/G POL/PAR PROF/ORG CONSULT DOMIN ADMIN EXEC REGION COERCE NAT/LISM ATTIT DRIVE PERSON ORD/FREE PWR...POLICY CONCPT OBS STERTYP 20. PAGE 136 H2721 — FORCES ELITES

B64
COLLINS B.E.,A SOCIAL PSYCHOLOGY OF GROUP PROCESSES FOR DECISION-MAKING. PROB/SOLV ROUTINE...SOC CHARTS HYPO/EXP. PAGE 32 H0632 — FACE/GP DECISION NAT/G INDUS

B64
MEAD M.,CONTINUITIES IN CULTURAL EVOLUTION. FACE/GP KIN ACT/RES EDU/PROP GP/REL INGP/REL DRIVE HEREDITY ROLE...TIME/SEQ TREND METH SOC/INTEG 20. PAGE 108 H2153 — CULTURE SOC PERS/REL

L64
FINDLATER R.,"US." EUR+WWI GERMANY USSR SOCIETY FACE/GP EDU/PROP PERCEPT PERSON ALL/VALS...PSY SOC CONCPT SELF/OBS SAMP TREND 20. PAGE 50 H1001 — CULTURE ATTIT UK

B65
ARENSBERG C.M.,CULTURE AND COMMUNITY. UNIV FACE/GP ACT/RES EDU/PROP LEAD REGION GP/REL PERS/REL HABITAT ALL/VALS...SOC CONCPT 20. PAGE 8 H0162 — SOCIETY CULTURE NEIGH NEW/IDEA

B67
POLSKY N.,HUSTLERS, BEATS, AND OTHERS. FACE/GP PRESS CRIME ADJUST ANOMIE DRIVE WEALTH...PSY SOC 20. PAGE 127 H2540 — CULTURE CRIMLGY NEW/IDEA STRUCT

FACTION....FACTION

FACTOR ANALYSIS....SEE CON/ANAL

FAGEN R.R. H0958

FAGG J.E. H0959

FAGUET E. H0960

FAHS C.B. H0961,H0962

FAINSOD M. H0963

FAIR T.J.D. H1206

FAIR/LABOR....FAIR LABOR STANDARD ACT

FAIRNESS, JUSTICE....SEE VALUES INDEX

FALANGE....FALANGE PARTY (SPAIN)

FALKENBERG J. H0964

FALKLAND/I....FALKLAND ISLANDS

FALL B.B. H0965,H0966,H0967,H0968

FAM....FAMILY

N
HERSKOVITS M.V.,CULTURAL ANTHROPOLOGY. UNIV SOCIETY STRUCT FAM...AUD/VIS BIBLIOG. PAGE 70 H1410 — CULTURE SOC INGP/REL GEOG

N
KRADER L.,SOCIAL ORGANIZATION OF THE MONGOL-TURKIC PASTORAL NOMADS. SOCIETY FAM KIN NEIGH GP/REL MARRIAGE 16/20 MONGOLIA TURKIC MIGRATION. PAGE 88 H1763 — BIO/SOC HABITAT CULTURE STRUCT

N
PRESSE UNIVERSITAIRES,ANNEE SOCIOLOGIQUE. EUR+WWI FRANCE MOD/EUR FAM ACT/RES WAR INGP/REL PERS/REL CONSEN DRIVE MORAL...CON/ANAL 19/20. PAGE 128 H2557 — BIBLIOG SOC CULTURE SOCIETY

B00
MAINE H.S.,ANCIENT LAW. MEDIT-7 CULTURE SOCIETY KIN SECT LEGIS LEGIT ROUTINE...JURID HIST/WRIT CON/ANAL TOT/POP VAL/FREE. PAGE 101 H2020 — FAM LAW

B05
PHILIPPINE ISLANDS BUREAU SCI,ETHNOLOGICAL SURVEY: THE BONTOC IGOROT. ECO/UNDEV AGRI FAM MARRIAGE HEALTH WEALTH...LING OBS AUD/VIS CHARTS WORSHIP 20 LUZON BONTOC. PAGE 125 H2500 — CULTURE INGP/REL KIN STRUCT

B09
JUSTINIAN,THE DIGEST (DIGESTA CORPUS JURIS CIVILIS) (2 VOLS.) (TRANS. BY C. H. MONRO). ROMAN/EMP LAW FAM LOC/G LEGIS EDU/PROP CONTROL MARRIAGE OWN ROLE CIVIL/LAW. PAGE 82 H1645 — JURID CT/SYS NAT/G STRATA

B18
BARRES M.,THE FAITH OF FRANCE (TRANS. BY ELISABETH MARBURY). FRANCE FAM MUNIC NEIGH POL/PAR SECT ALL/VALS 20. PAGE 11 H0227 — TRADIT CULTURE WAR GP/REL

N19
TEMPLE W.,AN ESSAY UPON THE ORIGINAL AND NATURE OF GOVERNMENT (PAMPHLET). CHRIST-17C UK FAM LOC/G LEGIT ORD/FREE CONSERVE 17. PAGE 153 H3060 — NAT/G CONCPT PWR SOCIETY

B24
WALKER F.D.,AFRICA AND HER PEOPLES. ISLAM STRUCT FAM SECT EDU/PROP INGP/REL RACE/REL HABITAT...GEOG SOC IDEA/COMP WORSHIP 20 NEGRO. PAGE 164 H3292 — CULTURE AFR GP/COMP KIN

B26
MALINOWSKI B.,CRIME AND CUSTOM IN SAVAGE SOCIETY. SOCIETY FAM SECT LEGIT SANCTION MARRIAGE MYSTISM ...PSY SOC 19/20 MELANESIA CANON/LAW. PAGE 102 H2030
LAW CULTURE CRIME ADJUD

B27
WEBER M.,GENERAL ECONOMIC HISTORY. CHRIST-17C MOD/EUR STRUCT AGRI EXTR/IND FINAN INDUS MARKET FAM MUNIC NAT/G PROF/ORG SECT ECO/TAC 8/20. PAGE 166 H3319
ECO/DEV CAP/ISM

B31
MACIVER R.M.,SOCIETY: ITS STRUCTURE AND CHANGES. CULTURE STRATA FAM CROWD HABITAT ORD/FREE...PSY SOC CONCPT BIBLIOG 20. PAGE 100 H1998
STRUCT SOCIETY PERSON DRIVE

B34
BENEDICT R.,PATTERNS OF CULTURE. S/ASIA FAM KIN PERSON RESPECT...CONCPT SELF/OBS. PAGE 14 H0278
CULTURE SOC

B35
AQUINAS T.,ON THE GOVERNANCE OF RULERS (1265-66). UNIV SOCIETY STRATA FAM HABITAT PERSON ALL/VALS PWR SOVEREIGN CONSERVE...POLICY BIBLE. PAGE 8 H0155
CATH NAT/G CHIEF SUPEGO

B35
MORE T.,UTOPIA (1516) (TRANS. BY R. ROBYNSON). LAW CULTURE SOCIETY STRUCT FAM SECT EDU/PROP WAR OWN UTIL KNOWL WEALTH 16. PAGE 113 H2253
UTOPIA NAT/G ECO/TAC GEN/LAWS

B39
AKIGA,AKIGA'S STORY: THE TIV TRIBE AS SEEN BY ONE OF ITS MEMBERS. NIGERIA LAW STRUCT ECO/UNDEV FAM LEAD GP/REL MARRIAGE...LING WORSHIP 20. PAGE 4 H0089
KIN SECT SOC CULTURE

B39
ENGELS F.,HERRN EUGEN DUHRING'S REVOLUTION IN SCIENCE (1878). CULTURE STRATA STRUCT FAM SECT ECO/TAC REV WAR SOCISM...MARXIST 19. PAGE 46 H0925
PWR SOCIETY WEALTH GEN/LAWS

B40
TONNIES F.,FUNDAMENTAL CONCEPTS OF SOCIOLOGY (1887) (TRANS. BY C. LOOMIS). LAW STRATA STRUCT FAM MUNIC NAT/G DOMIN LEGIT SANCTION COERCE CRIME PERSON 19. PAGE 156 H3115
CULTURE SOCIETY GEN/LAWS SOC

B41
KEESING F.M.,THE SOUTH SEAS IN THE MODERN WORLD. INDONESIA STRUCT FAM SECT EDU/PROP LEAD INCOME WEALTH...HEAL SOC 20. PAGE 84 H1678
CULTURE ECO/UNDEV GOV/COMP DIPLOM

B42
BARNES H.E.,SOCIAL INSTITUTIONS IN AN ERA OF WORLD UPHEAVAL. INDUS FAM NAT/G PERF/ART SECT AUTOMAT PERSON MORAL...PREDICT 20. PAGE 11 H0221
SOCIETY CULTURE TECHRACY TREND

B42
HEGEL G.W.F.,PHILOSOPHY OF RIGHT. UNIV FAM SECT CHIEF AGREE WAR MARRIAGE OWN ORD/FREE...POLICY CONCPT. PAGE 69 H1383
NAT/G LAW RATIONAL

B42
REDFIELD R.,THE FOLK CULTURE OF YUCATAN. STRATA FAM KIN MUNIC SECT DISCRIM ISOLAT ANOMIE HEALTH ...BIBLIOG 20 MEXIC/AMER. PAGE 130 H2605
CULTURE NEIGH GP/COMP SOCIETY

B45
LASKER B.,ASIA ON THE MOVE. ASIA BURMA S/ASIA THAILAND USSR ECO/UNDEV FAM KIN WAR NAT/LISM ATTIT ...GEOG CENSUS TREND AUSTRAL 20. PAGE 91 H1826
CULTURE RIGID/FLEX

B45
WARNER W.L.,THE SOCIAL SYSTEM OF AMERICAN ETHNIC GROUPS. STRATA FAM EDU/PROP ATTIT HABITAT RESPECT CLASSIF. PAGE 165 H3309
CULTURE VOL/ASSN SECT GP/COMP

S46
TANNENBAUM F.,"THE BALANCE OF POWER IN SOCIETY." UNIV STRUCT FAM NAT/G SECT PERS/REL EQUILIB UTOPIA DRIVE ALL/IDEOS...OLD/LIB CONCPT. PAGE 152 H3044
SOCIETY ALL/VALS GP/REL PEACE

B47
GITLOW A.L.,ECONOMICS OF THE MOUNT HAGEN TRIBES, NEW GUINEA. S/ASIA STRUCT AGRI FAM...GEOG MYTH 20 NEW/GUINEA. PAGE 57 H1137
HABITAT ECO/UNDEV CULTURE KIN

B48
EDUARDO O.D.C.,THE NEGRO IN NORTHERN BRAZIL: A STUDY IN ACCULTURATION. BRAZIL ECO/UNDEV FAM SECT PAY REGION HABITAT CATHISM MYSTISM...GEOG OBS SOC/INTEG WORSHIP 20 NEGRO MARANHAO. PAGE 44 H0890
CULTURE ADJUST GP/REL

B49
SARGENT S.S.,CULTURE AND PERSONALITY. FUT UNIV SOCIETY FAM KIN NEIGH BIO/SOC DRIVE PERCEPT RIGID/FLEX LOVE RESPECT...PSY SOC CONCPT OBS TIME/SEQ TREND CON/ANAL CHARTS HYPO/EXP SIMUL TOT/POP. PAGE 138 H2754
CULTURE PERSON

B50
IRION F.C.,PUBLIC OPINION AND PROPAGANDA. STRUCT COM/IND FAM SECT COERCE 20 FILM. PAGE 78 H1568
EDU/PROP ATTIT NAT/G PRESS

B50
ROHEIM G.,PSYCHOANALYSIS AND ANTHROPOLOGY. UNIV FAM PERS/REL ATTIT HABITAT...SOC OBS WORSHIP. PAGE 133 H2663
PSY BIOG CULTURE PERSON

B52
KROEBER A.L.,THE NATURE OF CULTURE. UNIV STRATA FAM KIN SECT...PSY GP/COMP 16/20 INDIAN/AM. PAGE 89 H1771
CULTURE SOCIETY CONCPT STRUCT

B53
MURPHY G.,IN THE MINDS OF MEN: THE STUDY OF HUMAN BEHAVIOR AND SOCIAL TENSIONS IN INDIA. FUT S/ASIA FAM INT/ORG NAT/G DIPLOM EDU/PROP GP/REL ATTIT RIGID/FLEX ALL/VALS...SOC QU UNESCO 20. PAGE 115 H2297
SECT STRATA INDIA

B54
HAZARD B.H. JR.,KOREAN STUDIES GUIDE. KOREA CONSTN CULTURE AGRI FAM SECT CREATE WAR NAT/LISM HABITAT PWR...CHARTS 14/20. PAGE 68 H1371
BIBLIOG/A ELITES GP/REL

B54
MATTHEWS D.R.,THE SOCIAL BACKGROUND OF POLITICAL DECISION-MAKERS. CULTURE SOCIETY STRATA FAM EX/STRUC LEAD ATTIT BIO/SOC DRIVE PERSON ALL/VALS HIST/WRIT. PAGE 105 H2097
DECISION BIOG SOC

C54
GUINS G.C.,"SOVIET LAW AND SOVIET SOCIETY." COM USSR STRATA FAM NAT/G WORKER DOMIN RACE/REL ...BIBLIOG 20. PAGE 62 H1249
LAW STRUCT PLAN

B55
APTER D.E.,THE GOLD COAST IN TRANSITION. FUT CONSTN CULTURE SOCIETY ECO/UNDEV FAM KIN LOC/G NAT/G POL/PAR LEGIS TOP/EX EDU/PROP LEGIT ADMIN ATTIT PERSON PWR...CONCPT STAT INT CENSUS TOT/POP VAL/FREE. PAGE 7 H0149
AFR SOVEREIGN

B55
KHADDURI M.,LAW IN THE MIDDLE EAST. LAW CONSTN ACADEM FAM EDU/PROP CT/SYS SANCTION CRIME...INT/LAW GOV/COMP ANTHOL 6/20 MID/EAST. PAGE 85 H1703
ADJUD JURID ISLAM

B55
MAZZINI J.,THE DUTIES OF MAN. MOD/EUR LAW SOCIETY FAM NAT/G POL/PAR SECT VOL/ASSN EX/STRUC ACT/RES CREATE REV PEACE ATTIT ALL/VALS...GEN/LAWS WORK 19. PAGE 106 H2113
SUPEGO CONCPT NAT/LISM

B55
RODNICK D.,THE NORWEGIANS: A STUDY IN NATIONAL CULTURE. NORWAY FAM INGP/REL PERS/REL AGE...PSY SOC SELF/OBS WORSHIP 20. PAGE 133 H2655
CULTURE INT RECORD ATTIT

B55
WRONG D.H.,AMERICAN AND CANADIAN VIEWPOINTS. CANADA USA+45 CONSTN STRATA FAM SECT WORKER ECO/TAC EDU/PROP ADJUD MARRIAGE...IDEA/COMP 20. PAGE 171 H3424
DIPLOM ATTIT NAT/COMP CULTURE

S55
GOODENOUGH W.H.,"A PROBLEM IN MALAYO-POLYNESIAN SOCIAL ORGANIZATION" (BMR)" MALAYSIA S/ASIA CULTURE AGRI PROB/SOLV OWN HABITAT...SOC 20 20 POLYNESIA. PAGE 58 H1170
KIN STRUCT FAM ECO/UNDEV

C55
SANTAYANA G.,"REASON IN SOCIETY" IN G. SANTAYANA, THE LIFE OF REASON." INDUS FAM NAT/G WAR GP/REL HAPPINESS PRODUC LOVE WEALTH CONSERVE POPULISM CONCPT. PAGE 138 H2752
RATIONAL SOCIETY CULTURE ATTIT

B56
BECKER H.,MAN IN RECIPROCITY: INTRODUCTORY LECTURES ON CULTURE, SOCIETY, AND PERSONALITY. LAW FAM SECT REGION GP/REL ADJUST ATTIT PERSON...BIBLIOG 20. PAGE 13 H0253
CULTURE STRUCT SOC PSY

B56
GLUCKMAN M.,CUSTOM AND CONFLICT IN AFRICA. AFR FAM KIN NAT/G DOMIN DISCRIM DRIVE MORAL PWR...SOC BIBLIOG WORSHIP 20. PAGE 57 H1145
CULTURE CREATE PERS/REL GP/COMP

B56
INTERNATIONAL AFRICAN INST,ETHNOGRAPHIC SURVEY OF AFRICA; WESTERN AFRICA: PAGAN PEOPLES OF CENTRAL AREA OF NORTHERN NIGERIA (VOL. XII). NIGERIA FAM KIN SECT ECO/TAC GOV/REL GP/REL ATTIT...LING CHARTS 20. PAGE 77 H1548
STRUCT INGP/REL HABITAT CULTURE

B56
MANNONI D.O.,PROSPERO AND CALIBAN: THE PSYCHOLOGY OF COLONIZATION. AFR EUR+WWI FAM KIN MUNIC SECT DOMIN ADMIN ATTIT DRIVE LOVE PWR RESPECT...PSY SOC CONCPT MYTH OBS DEEP/INT BIOG GEN/METH MALAGASY 20. PAGE 102 H2040
CULTURE COLONIAL

B56
SHAPIRO H.L.,MAN, CULTURE, AND SOCIETY. STRUCT FAM SECT GP/REL INGP/REL...ART/METH GEOG PSY LING ANTHOL BIBLIOG. PAGE 142 H2842
CULTURE PERSON SOC

B57
IKE N.,JAPANESE POLITICS. INTELL STRUCT AGRI INDUS FAM KIN LABOR PRESS CHOOSE ATTIT...DECISION BIBLIOG 19/20 CHINJAP. PAGE 76 H1523
NAT/G ADMIN POL/PAR CULTURE

B57
INTERNATIONAL AFRICAN INST,ETHNOGRAPHIC SURVEY OF AFRICA: WESTERN AFRICA: THE WOLOF OF SENEGAMBIA. AFR SENEGAL CULTURE ECO/UNDEV FAM KIN REGION ...CHARTS GP/COMP BIBLIOG WORSHIP 20. PAGE 78 H1551
STRUCT GEOG HABITAT INGP/REL

B57
KOENTJARANINGRAT R.,A PRELIMINARY DESCRIPTION OF THE JAVANESE KINSHIP SYSTEM. INDONESIA STRATA FAM INGP/REL ADJUST MARRIAGE AGE/C AGE/Y AGE/A PERSON ...OBS CHARTS DICTIONARY 20 JAVA. PAGE 87 H1736
KIN STRUCT ELITES CULTURE

B57
MENDIETTA Y NUNE L.,THEORIE DES GROUPEMENT SOCIAUX SUIVI D'UNE ETUDE SUR LE DROIT SOCIAL. ELITES FAM KIN NAT/G PROB/SOLV CROWD ISOLAT ATTIT PERSON ...JURID CONCPT SOC/INTEG. PAGE 109 H2174
SOC STRATA STRUCT DISCRIM

B57
PIDDINGTON R.,AN INTRODUCTION TO SOCIAL ANTHROPOLOGY (VOL. II). SOCIETY STRUCT FAM INGP/REL ...OBS CHARTS. PAGE 125 H2507
CULTURE SOC TEC/DEV GEOG

B58
MATOS J.,LAS ACTUALES COMMUNIDADES DE INDIGENAS: HUAROCHIRI EN 1955. PERU FAM NAT/G SECT EDU/PROP ADJUD GP/REL INGP/REL 20 INDIAN/AM. PAGE 105 H2091
STRUCT NEIGH KIN ECO/UNDEV

B58
MEHNERT K.,DER SOWJETMENSCH. USSR NAT/G SECT EDU/PROP TOTALISM ORD/FREE 20. PAGE 108 H2161
SOCIETY ATTIT PERSON FAM

B58
ORNES G.E.,TRUJILLO: LITTLE CAESAR OF THE CARIBBEAN. DOMIN/REP FAM NAT/G FORCES BUDGET CRIME REV PERSON 20 TRUJILLO/R. PAGE 122 H2429
BIOG PWR TOTALISM CHIEF

B58
SCOTT J.P.,AGGRESSION. CULTURE FAM SCHOOL ATTIT DISPL HEALTH...SOC CONCPT NEW/IDEA CHARTS LAB/EXP. PAGE 141 H2814
DRIVE PSY WAR

B58
STUBEL H.,THE MEWU FANTZU. CHINA/COM INDIA EDU/PROP ADJUD CRIME GP/REL OWN...OBS 20 TIBET. PAGE 150 H3001
CULTURE STRUCT SECT FAM

B58
WARNER W.L.,A BLACK CIVILIZATION - A SOCIAL STUDY OF AN AUSTRALIAN TRIBE. SOCIETY FAM MARRIAGE...PSY SOC MYTH CHARTS 20 AUSTRAL MAPS MURNGIN RITUAL. PAGE 165 H3310
CULTURE KIN STRUCT DEATH

B58
WIGGIN L.M.,THE FACTION OF COUSINS: A POLITICAL ACCOUNT OF THE GRENVILLES, 1733-1763. UK STRUCT KIN NAT/G INGP/REL...CONCPT BIOG BIBLIOG/A 18 GRENVILLES. PAGE 168 H3357
FAM POL/PAR PWR

C58
BLANCHARD W.,"THAILAND." THAILAND CULTURE AGRI FINAN INDUS FAM LABOR INT/TRADE ATTIT...GEOG HEAL SOC BIBLIOG 20. PAGE 18 H0354
NAT/G DIPLOM ECO/UNDEV S/ASIA

B59
LEE D.,FREEDOM AND CULTURE. WOR+45 WOR-45 FAM HABITAT PERSON LOVE MORAL...PSY SOC OBS NAT/COMP WORSHIP 20. PAGE 93 H1856
CULTURE SOCIETY CONCPT INGP/REL

B59
SHARMA R.S.,ASPECTS OF POLITICAL IDEAS AND INSTITUTIONS IN ANCIENT INDIA. INDIA SOCIETY STRUCT FAM VOL/ASSN TAX DOMIN...CONCPT HIST/WRIT 7. PAGE 142 H2848
CULTURE JURID DELIB/GP SECT

B59
VORSPAN A.,JUSTICE AND JUDAISM. FAM DIPLOM ECO/TAC EDU/PROP CRIME RACE/REL MARRIAGE ANOMIE ATTIT ORD/FREE...POLICY 20 UN. PAGE 164 H3279
SECT CULTURE ACT/RES GP/REL

S59
LYNN D.B.,"THE EFFECTS OF FATHER-ABSENCE ON NORWEGIAN BOYS AND GIRLS." NORWAY CULTURE PERS/REL ADJUST DISPL LOVE...PSY CORREL STAT INT CON/ANAL CHARTS SOC/INTEG 20. PAGE 99 H1983
SOC FAM AGE/C ANOMIE

B60
BURRIDGE K.,MAMBU: A MELANESIAN MILLENNIUM. ECO/UNDEV PROC/MFG FAM KIN CHIEF COLONIAL COERCE GP/REL DRIVE WEALTH WORSHIP 20 NEW/GUINEA. PAGE 25 H0494
S/ASIA SECT CULTURE MYTH

B60
COUGHLIN R.,DOUBLE IDENTITY: THE CHINESE AND MODERN THAILAND. CHINA/COM S/ASIA THAILAND ECO/UNDEV EXTR/IND FINAN INDUS KIN MUNIC NAT/G PROF/ORG SCHOOL SECT ATTIT DRIVE...CONCPT OBS 20. PAGE 34 H0676
ASIA FAM CULTURE

B60
HAMADY S.,TEMPERAMENT AND CHARACTER OF THE ARABS. FAM NAT/G SECT DIPLOM NAT/LISM...POLICY 20 ARABS. PAGE 65 H1299
NAT/COMP PERSON CULTURE ISLAM

B60
HUGHES C.C.,PEOPLE OF COVE AND WOODLOT: COMMUNITIES FROM THE VIEWPOINT OF SOCIAL PSYCHIATRY. CULTURE FAM PROVS HABITAT...PSY QU SAMP/SIZ CHARTS BIBLIOG 20. PAGE 74 H1489
GEOG SOCIETY STRUCT HEALTH

B60
JOHNSON H.M.,SOCIOLOGY: A SYSTEMATIC INTRODUCTION. MARKET FAM LABOR POL/PAR CHOOSE DISCRIM MARRIAGE ALL/IDEOS...BIBLIOG T WORSHIP. PAGE 81 H1620
SOC SOCIETY CULTURE GEN/LAWS

B60
RUDD J.,TABOO, A STUDY OF MALAGASY CUSTOMS AND BELIEFS. MADAGASCAR LAW FAM CONTROL CRIME PERSON ...CONCPT 20. PAGE 173 H3466
CULTURE DOMIN SECT SANCTION

S60
EMERSON R.,"THE EROSION OF DEMOCRACY." AFR FUT LAW CULTURE INTELL SOCIETY ECO/UNDEV FAM LOC/G NAT/G FORCES PLAN TEC/DEV ECO/TAC ADMIN CT/SYS ATTIT ORD/FREE PWR...SOCIALIST SOC CONCPT STAND/INT TIME/SEQ WORK 20. PAGE 46 H0918
S/ASIA POL/PAR

S60
JAFFEE A.J.,"POPULATION TRENDS AND CONTROLS IN UNDERDEVELOPED COUNTRIES." AFR FUT ISLAM L/A+17C S/ASIA CULTURE R+D FAM ACT/RES PLAN EDU/PROP BIO/SOC RIGID/FLEX HEALTH...SOC STAT OBS CHARTS 20. PAGE 79 H1582
ECO/UNDEV GEOG

S60
LEVINE R.A.,"THE INTERNALIZATION OF POLITICAL VALUES IN STATELESS SOCIETIES." AFR FAM KIN LOC/G PROVS JUDGE PERSON RIGID/FLEX...DECISION SOC TIME/SEQ 20. PAGE 95 H1904
CULTURE ATTIT

C60
FITZSIMMONS T.,"USSR: ITS PEOPLE, ITS SOCIETY, ITS CULTURE." USSR FAM SECT DIPLOM EDU/PROP ADMIN RACE/REL ATTIT...POLICY CHARTS BIBLIOG 20. PAGE 51 H1021
CULTURE STRUCT SOCIETY COM

B61
BERKOWITZ L.,AGGRESSION: AS A SOCIAL PSYCHOLOGICAL ANALYSIS. UNIV CULTURE FACE/GP FAM KIN NEIGH EDU/PROP DISPL DRIVE HEALTH LOVE ORD/FREE...PSY SOC CONCPT OBS TREND. PAGE 15 H0305
SOCIETY COERCE WAR

B61
BLAKE J.,FAMILY STRUCTURE IN JAMAICA. JAMAICA CULTURE SOCIETY ACT/RES CONTROL MARRIAGE AGE ...POLICY SOC BIBLIOG 20. PAGE 18 H0351
FAM SEX STRUCT ATTIT

B61
SOUTHALL A.,SOCIAL CHANGE IN MODERN AFRICA. CULTURE STRATA ECO/UNDEV AGRI FAM KIN MUNIC GP/REL INGP/REL MARRIAGE...GEOG ANTHOL 20. PAGE 147 H2940
AFR TREND SOCIETY SOC

L61
EZELLPH,"THE HISPANIC AGRICULTURATION OF THE GILA RIVER PIMAS." FAM TEC/DEV PERS/REL ADJUST...GEOG MYTH CHARTS BIBLIOG WORSHIP 17/20. PAGE 48 H0956
CULTURE SOC AGRI DRIVE

L61
LEVINE R.A.,"THE ANTHROPOLOGY OF CONFLICT." FUT CULTURE INTELL FAM INT/ORG LG/CO SML/CO ATTIT KNOWL ...METH/CNCPT VAL/FREE 20. PAGE 95 H1905
SOCIETY ACT/RES

B62
BERGER M.,THE ARAB WORLD TODAY. CULTURE FAM INT/ORG NAT/G SECT FORCES ECO/TAC NAT/LISM HABITAT...CHARTS BIBLIOG 20 ARABS. PAGE 15 H0301
ISLAM PERSON STRUCT SOCIETY

B62
BERNOT R.M.,EXCESS AND RESTRAINT: SOCIAL CONTROL AMONG GUINEA MOUNTAIN PEOPLE. CULTURE FAM KIN CT/SYS COERCE WAR PERS/REL MARRIAGE HABITAT SEX ...MYTH 20 NEW/GUINEA. PAGE 16 H0314
SOCIETY CONTROL STRUCT ADJUST

B62
EDWARDS A.C.,THE OVIMBUNDU UNDER TWO SOVEREIGNTIES. CULTURE STRUCT FAM MARRIAGE HABITAT...SOC 19/20 OVIMBUNDU. PAGE 45 H0891
KIN NEIGH SOCIETY CONTROL

B62
FALKENBERG J.,KIN AND TOTEM; GROUP RELATIONS OF AUSTRALIAN ABORIGINES IN THE PORT KEATS DISTRICT. SOCIETY STRATA STRUCT GP/REL PERS/REL MARRIAGE AGE ATTIT SEX...SOC STAT CHARTS AUSTRAL ABORIGINES. PAGE 48 H0964
KIN INGP/REL CULTURE FAM

B62
HO PING-TI,THE LADDER OF SUCCESS IN IMPERIAL CHINA: ASPECTS OF SOCIAL MOBILITY, 1368-1911. INTELL STRATA FAM KIN MUNIC NAT/G PROVS SCHOOL DELIB/GP DOMIN EDU/PROP ADMIN ROUTINE PERSON ALL/VALS...SOC STAT BIOG HIST/WRIT TIME/SEQ VAL/FREE. PAGE 71 H1431
ASIA CULTURE

B62
KEESING F.M.,THE ETHNOHISTORY OF NORTHERN LUZON. PHILIPPINE ECO/UNDEV FAM SECT CHIEF REGION GP/REL HABITAT...GEOG LING BIBLIOG WORSHIP 20. PAGE 84 H1680
CULTURE SOC KIN

B62
MALINOWSKI B.,SEX, CULTURE, AND MYTH. UNIV SOCIETY
MYTH

FAM PERS/REL MARRIAGE RATIONAL HABITAT PERSON SUPEGO MORAL WORSHIP 20. PAGE 102 H2032 — SECT SEX CULTURE

B62
MEHNERT K.,SOVIET MAN AND HIS WORLD. COM USSR INTELL FAM WORKER PLAN EDU/PROP REV PRODUC MARXISM ...SOC TREND SOC/INTEG 20 LENIN/VI STALIN/J KHRUSH/N. PAGE 108 H2162 — SOCIETY CULTURE ECO/DEV

B62
PASTOR R.S.,A STATEMENT OF THE LAWS OF PARAGUAY IN MATTERS AFFECTING BUSINESS (2ND ED.). PARAGUAY INDUS FAM LABOR LG/CO NAT/G LEGIS TAX CONTROL MARRIAGE 20. PAGE 124 H2474 — FINAN ECO/UNDEV LAW CONSTN

B62
ROSENZWEIG F.,HEGEL UND DER STAAT. GERMANY SOCIETY FAM POL/PAR NAT/LISM...BIOG 19. PAGE 134 H2682 — JURID NAT/G CONCPT PHIL/SCI

B62
RUDY Z.,ETHNOSOZIOLOGIE SOWJETISCHER VOLKER. USSR SOCIETY STRUCT FAM SECT GP/REL ATTIT...SOC SOC/INTEG 20. PAGE 136 H2714 — MYTH CULTURE KIN

B62
SELOSOEMARDJAN O.,SOCIAL CHANGES IN JOGJAKARTA. INDONESIA NETHERLAND ELITES STRATA STRUCT FAM POL/PAR CREATE DIPLOM INT/TRADE EDU/PROP ADMIN GOV/REL...SOC 20 JAVA CHINJAP. PAGE 141 H2825 — ECO/UNDEV CULTURE REV COLONIAL

B62
SMITH M.G.,KINSHIP AND COMMUNITY IN CARRIACOU. WEST/IND STRATA AGRI FAM SECT WORKER MARRIAGE OWN HEREDITY WEALTH...SOC 18/20. PAGE 146 H2915 — CULTURE HABITAT KIN STRUCT

B62
YOUNG G.,THE HILL TRIBES OF NORTHERN THAILAND. S/ASIA THAILAND FAM KIN LOC/G GP/REL HABITAT...GEOG LING OBS 20. PAGE 172 H3438 — CULTURE STRUCT ECO/UNDEV SECT

S62
MU FU-SHENG,"THE WILTING OF THE HUNDRED FLOWERS: FREE THOUGHT IN CHINA TODAY." ASIA CHINA/COM CULTURE FAM NAT/G EDU/PROP REV TOTALISM ATTIT PERSON RESPECT...GEOG INT UNPLAN/INT COLD/WAR 20. PAGE 114 H2278 — INTELL ELITES

B63
AZEVEDO T.,SOCIAL CHANGE IN BRAZIL. BRAZIL ECO/DEV COM/IND FAM NAT/G SECT GP/REL PERS/REL...CONCPT WORSHIP 20. PAGE 9 H0188 — TEC/DEV STRUCT SOC CULTURE

B63
BOHANNAN P.,SOCIAL ANTHROPOLOGY. ECO/DEV GP/REL DEMAND MARRIAGE HABITAT...CHARTS GP/COMP BIBLIOG T WORSHIP 20. PAGE 18 H0366 — SOC STRUCT FAM CULTURE

B63
DRIVER H.E.,ETHNOGRAPHY AND ACCULTURATION OF THE CHICHIMECA-JONAZ OF NORTHEAST MEXICO. ECO/UNDEV AGRI FAM KIN EDU/PROP MARRIAGE HEALTH...GEOG INT CHARTS WORSHIP 18/20 MEXIC/AMER. PAGE 42 H0848 — CULTURE HABITAT STRUCT GP/REL

B63
GAMBLE S.D.,NORTH CHINA VILLAGES: SOCIAL, POLITICAL, AND ECONOMIC ACTIVITIES BEFORE 1933. ASIA CULTURE STRUCT FAM DOMIN EDU/PROP WORSHIP 20. PAGE 55 H1093 — MUNIC AGRI LEAD FINAN

B63
GOODE W.J.,WORLD REVOLUTION AND FAMILY PATTERNS. AFR CHINA/COM INDIA UAR CREATE ADJUST ATTIT SEX ...SOC 20 CHINJAP. PAGE 58 H1169 — FAM NAT/COMP CULTURE MARRIAGE

B63
MAIR L.,NEW NATIONS. AFR FAM MUNIC SECT DOMIN CHOOSE NAT/LISM ORD/FREE...SOC 19/20. PAGE 101 H2022 — COLONIAL CULTURE TEC/DEV ECO/UNDEV

B63
MARTINDALE D.,COMMUNITY, CHARACTER AND CIVILIZATION: STUDIES IN SOCIAL BEHAVIORISM. INTELL FAM NEIGH VOL/ASSN GP/REL NAT/LISM ATTIT PERSON ...CONCPT GP/COMP 20 BEHAVIORSM. PAGE 103 H2066 — SOC METH/COMP CULTURE STRUCT

B63
PAUW B.A.,THE SECOND GENERATION. SOUTH/AFR INDUS FAM LABOR SECT EDU/PROP MARRIAGE ATTIT...SOC 20. PAGE 124 H2478 — KIN CULTURE STRUCT SOCIETY

B63
WAGLEY C.,INTRODUCTION TO BRAZIL. BRAZIL L/A+17C FAM KIN SCHOOL SECT ATTIT WEALTH...GEOG SOC. PAGE 164 H3286 — ECO/UNDEV ELITES HABITAT STRATA

S63
ROBINSON W.C.,"URBANIZATION AND FERTILITY: THE NON-WESTERN EXPERIENCE (BMR)" DEATH MARRIAGE AGE/C BIO/SOC...STAT CENSUS CON/ANAL CHARTS NAT/COMP 20 THIRD/WRLD. PAGE 133 H2651 — GEOG MUNIC FAM ECO/UNDEV

B64
BEARDSLEY R.K.,STUDIES ON ECONOMIC LIFE IN JAPAN (OCCASIONAL PAPERS NO. 8). INDUS FAM HABITAT...GEOG GOV/COMP 20 CHINJAP. PAGE 12 H0249 — WEALTH PRESS PRODUC INCOME

B64
BEATTIE J.,OTHER CULTURES. UNIV LAW FAM POL/PAR SECT ADJUD OWN ALL/VALS WEALTH...SOC NAT/COMP SOC/INTEG 20. PAGE 13 H0251 — METH/CNCPT CULTURE STRUCT

B64
ELKIN A.P.,THE AUSTRALIAN ABORIGINES - HOW TO UNDERSTAND THEM (4TH ED.). FAM NEIGH DEATH MARRIAGE ATTIT BIO/SOC HABITAT...PSY SOC MYTH WORSHIP AUSTRAL ABORIGINES. PAGE 45 H0908 — CULTURE STRUCT SOCIETY KIN

B64
FREISEN J.,STAAT UND KATHOLISCHE KIRCHE IN DEN DEUTSCHEN BUNDESSTAATEN (2 VOLS.). GERMANY LAW FAM NAT/G EDU/PROP GP/REL MARRIAGE WEALTH 19/20 CHURCH/STA. PAGE 53 H1056 — SECT CATHISM JURID PROVS

B64
HALPERN J.M.,GOVERNMENT, POLITICS, AND SOCIAL STRUCTURE IN LAOS. LAOS CULTURE SOCIETY STRATA STRUCT FAM DIPLOM DOMIN MARXISM...INT GOV/COMP WORSHIP SOC/INTEG 20. PAGE 65 H1297 — NAT/G SOC LOC/G

B64
INTL CONF ON POPULATION,POPULATION DYNAMICS: INTERNATIONAL ACTION AND TRAINING PROGRAMS. INDIA KOREA L/A+17C TAIWAN USA+45 WOR+45 FAM PLAN CONFER ...NEW/IDEA ANTHOL 20 CHINJAP BIRTH/CON. PAGE 78 H1561 — NAT/COMP CONTROL ATTIT EDU/PROP

B64
LIENHARDT G.,SOCIAL ANTHROPOLOGY. SOCIETY FAM KIN ...CONCPT METH. PAGE 97 H1928 — SOC HABITAT HEREDITY CULTURE

B64
MORGAN L.H.,ANCIENT SOCIETY (1877). SOCIETY FAM OWN ...INT QU GEN/LAWS SOC/INTEG. PAGE 113 H2255 — KIN MARRIAGE CULTURE

B64
ON CULTURE AND SOCIAL CHANGE. FAM NAT/G ACT/RES ECO/TAC RACE/REL...PSY TIME/SEQ TREND IDEA/COMP METH/COMP ANTHOL BIBLIOG 20. PAGE 120 H2406 — CULTURE TEC/DEV STRUCT CREATE

B64
SAKAI R.K.,STUDIES ON ASIA, 1964. ASIA CHINA/COM ISRAEL MALAYSIA S/ASIA USA+45 USSR ECO/UNDEV FAM POL/PAR SECT CONSULT NAT/LISM...POLICY SOC 20 CHINJAP. PAGE 137 H2736 — PWR DIPLOM

B64
SCHNITGER F.M.,FORGOTTEN KINGDOMS IN SUMATRA. FAM SECT LEISURE HABITAT...OBS AUD/VIS WORSHIP 20 SUMATRA. PAGE 140 H2793 — CULTURE AFR SOCIETY STRUCT

B64
SKINNER E.P.,THE MOSSI OF UPPER VOLTA: THE POLITICAL DEVELOPMENT OF A SUDANESE PEOPLE. AFR LAW AGRI FAM KIN POL/PAR PROVS SECT DELIB/GP EX/STRUC FORCES TOP/EX DOMIN EDU/PROP LEGIT CT/SYS COERCE CHOOSE ORD/FREE PWR WEALTH...SOC MYTH VAL/FREE. PAGE 145 H2897 — CULTURE OBS UPPER/VOLT

B64
THORNBURG M.W.,PEOPLE AND POLICY IN THE MIDDLE EAST. ISLAM ECO/UNDEV FAM KIN MUNIC NAT/G NEIGH POL/PAR SECT DELIB/GP LEGIS PLAN ECO/TAC DOMIN ADMIN ATTIT HEALTH RESPECT...SOC CONCPT METH/CNCPT OBS TIME/SEQ TOT/POP VAL/FREE. PAGE 154 H3088 — TEC/DEV CULTURE

L64
BERELSON B.,"SAMPLE SURVEYS AND POPULATION CONTROL." ASIA FUT ISLAM L/A+17C CULTURE SOCIETY FAM NAT/G CONSULT PLAN EDU/PROP ATTIT DRIVE ALL/VALS...POLICY RELATIV HEAL PSY SOC CONCPT METH/CNCPT OBS OBS/ENVIR TOT/POP. PAGE 15 H0297 — BIO/SOC SAMP

S64
TOUVAL S.,"THE SOMALI REPUBLIC." AFR ISLAM SOMALIA FAM KIN NAT/G CREATE FOR/AID LEGIT ATTIT ALL/VALS ...RECORD TREND 20. PAGE 156 H3119 — ECO/UNDEV RIGID/FLEX

B65
BOISSEVAIN J.,SAINTS AND FIREWORKS: RELIGION AND POLITICS IN RURAL MALTA. MALTA STRUCT FAM NEIGH POL/PAR REPRESENT INGP/REL CENTRAL...CHARTS BIBLIOG 20. PAGE 18 H0368 — GP/REL NAT/G SECT MUNIC

B65
GIBBS S.L.,PEOPLES OF AFRICA. AFR INGP/REL HABITAT ...GEOG ANTHOL 20. PAGE 56 H1122 — CULTURE AGRI FAM KIN

B65
GOULD J.,PENGUIN SURVEY OF THE SOCIAL SCIENCES* 1965. CULTURE SOCIETY R+D FAM KIN MUNIC ACT/RES DIPLOM SKILL. PAGE 59 H1186 — SOC PHIL/SCI USSR UK

B65
KLEIN J.,SAMPLES FROM ENGLISH CULTURES (2 VOLS.). UK STRATA FAM NEIGH WORKER ETIQUET ISOLAT AGE/C AGE/A HABITAT RIGID/FLEX...NET/THEORY CHARTS 20. PAGE 87 H1732 — CULTURE INGP/REL ATTIT SOC

B65
KUNSTADTER P.,THE LUA (LAWA) OF NORTHERN THAILAND: — STRUCT

ASPECTS OF SOCIAL STRUCTURE, AGRICULTURE, AND RELIGION. THAILAND AGRI FAM KIN INGP/REL ISOLAT MARRIAGE HEALTH WORSHIP 20 BUDDHISM LUA. PAGE 89 H1780 — ECO/UNDEV CULTURE

B65
LAMBIRI I.,SOCIAL CHANGE IN A GREEK COUNTRY TOWN. GREECE FAM PROB/SOLV ROUTINE TASK LEISURE INGP/REL CONSEN ORD/FREE...SOC INT QU CHARTS 20. PAGE 90 H1803 — INDUS WORKER CULTURE NEIGH

B65
LAWRENCE P.,GODS, GHOSTS, AND MEN IN MELANESIA: SOME RELIGIONS OF AUSTRALIAN NEW GUINEA AND THE NEW HEBRIDES. SOCIETY ECO/UNDEV FAM GP/REL INGP/REL HABITAT PERSON...GEOG SOC ANTHOL BIBLIOG WORSHIP 20 NEW/GUINEA. PAGE 92 H1847 — MYTH S/ASIA SECT CULTURE

B65
MAIR L.,AN INTRODUCTION TO SOCIAL ANTHROPOLOGY. LAW STRATA FINAN FAM KIN SECT INT/TRADE RACE/REL ADJUST PRODUC...T 20. PAGE 101 H2023 — SOC STRUCT CULTURE SOCIETY

B65
RENNER K.,MENSCH UND GESELLSCHAFT - GRUNDRISS EINER SOZIOLOGIE (2ND ED.). STRATA FAM LABOR PROF/ORG WAR ...JURID CLASSIF 20. PAGE 131 H2616 — SOC STRUCT NAT/G SOCIETY

B65
SPENCER P.,THE SAMBURU: A STUDY OF GERONTOCRACY IN A NOMADIC TRIBE. AFR SOCIETY ECO/UNDEV AGRI FAM NEIGH SECT GP/REL MARRIAGE WORSHIP 20 SAMBURU. PAGE 147 H2945 — KIN STRUCT AGE/O CULTURE

B65
SWIFT M.G.,MALAY PEASANT SOCIETY IN JELEBU. MALAYSIA FAM INT/TRADE ADJUD OWN WEALTH...SOC WORSHIP 20. PAGE 151 H3020 — STRUCT ECO/UNDEV CULTURE SOCIETY

B66
HAHN C.H.L.,THE NATIVE TRIBES OF SOUTH WEST AFRICA. LAW FAM SECT HABITAT SKILL...SOC AUD/VIS WORSHIP RITUAL 20 AFRICA/SW. PAGE 64 H1275 — CULTURE SOCIETY STRUCT AFR

B66
KASUNMU A.B.,NIGERIAN FAMILY LAW. NIGERIA KIN LEGIT ILLEGIT MARRIAGE AGE DRIVE HABITAT ALL/VALS...JURID IDEA/COMP T 20 ENGLSH/LAW. PAGE 83 H1667 — FAM LAW CULTURE AFR

B66
LEYBURN J.G.,THE HAITIAN PEOPLE (REV. ED.). HAITI SOCIETY FAM SECT DOMIN COLONIAL MARRIAGE...SOC CHARTS BIBLIOG/A 18/10. PAGE 96 H1917 — STRUCT STRATA INGP/REL CULTURE

B66
RAEFF M.,ORIGINS OF THE RUSSIAN INTELLIGENTSIA: THE EIGHTEENTH-CENTURY NOBILITY. RUSSIA FAM NAT/G EDU/PROP ADMIN PERS/REL ATTIT...HUM BIOG 18. PAGE 129 H2580 — INTELL ELITES STRATA CONSERVE

B66
SOROKIN P.A.,SOCIOLOGICAL THEORIES OF TODAY. SOCIETY STRUCT FAM SECT GP/REL ADJUST...PHIL/SCI PSY TREND METH/COMP 20. PAGE 147 H2935 — SOC CULTURE METH/CNCPT EPIST

B66
TSURUMI K.,ADULT SOCIALIZATION AND SOCIAL CHANGE: JAPAN BEFORE AND AFTER DEFEAT IN WORLD WAR II. FAM DEATH SUPEGO...PSY SOC 20 CHINJAP. PAGE 157 H3133 — SOCIETY AGE/A WAR PERSON

B67
DALTON G.,TRIBAL AND PEASANT ECONOMIES. SOCIETY FINAN FAM INT/TRADE RATION ADJUST WEALTH...CHARTS ANTHOL BIBLIOG T. PAGE 37 H0738 — SOC ECO/UNDEV NAT/COMP

B67
PATAI R.,GOLDEN RIVER TO GOLDEN ROAD: SOCIETY, CULTURE, AND CHANGE IN THE MIDDLE EAST (2ND ED.). ELITES FAM KIN TEC/DEV MARRIAGE NAT/LISM SEX ORD/FREE...TREND GP/COMP WORSHIP 20. PAGE 124 H2476 — CULTURE SOCIETY ISLAM STRUCT

S67
HOPE M.,"THE RELUCTANT WAY: SELF-IMMOLATION IN VIETNAM." VIETNAM SOCIETY FAM KIN SECT DRIVE ALL/VALS...TRADIT OBS INT 20. PAGE 73 H1465 — CULTURE SUICIDE IDEA/COMP ATTIT

S67
SCOTT J.W.,"SOURCES OF SOCIAL CHANGE IN COMMUNITY, FAMILY, AND FERTILITY IN A PUERTO RICAN TOWN." PUERT/RICO CULTURE STRUCT ECO/UNDEV INDUS PERS/REL ROLE...SOC STAND/INT. PAGE 141 H2815 — FAM MARRIAGE LITERACY ATTIT

B75
MAINE H.S.,LECTURES ON THE EARLY HISTORY OF INSTITUTIONS. IRELAND UK CONSTN ELITES STRUCT FAM KIN CHIEF LEGIS CT/SYS OWN SOVEREIGN...CONCPT 16 BENTHAM/J BREHON ROMAN/LAW. PAGE 101 H2021 — CULTURE LAW INGP/REL

B84
ENGELS F.,THE ORIGIN OF THE FAMILY, PRIVATE PROPERTY, AND THE STATE (TRANS. BY E. UNTERMANN). UNIV ELITES SOCIETY CAP/ISM ECO/TAC MARRIAGE ORD/FREE POPULISM...MARXIST SOC ENGELS. PAGE 46 H0926 — FAM OWN WEALTH SOCISM

B90
TAINE H.A.,MODERN REGIME (2 VOLS.). FRANCE FAM REV CENTRAL MARRIAGE PWR...TREND 19 NAPOLEON/B. PAGE 152 H3037 — STRUCT NAT/G OLD/LIB MORAL

FAMILY....SEE FAM

FAMINE....SEE AGRI, HEALTH

FANON F. H0969,H0970

FAO....FOOD AND AGRICULTURE ORGANIZATION; SEE ALSO UN, INT/ORG

FARIES J.C. H0971

FARM/BUR....FARM BUREAU

FARMER B.H. H0972

FARMING....SEE AGRI

FARRELL R.B. H0973

FARWELL G. H0974

FASCISM....FASCISM; SEE ALSO TOTALISM, FASCIST

N19
WEBB L.C.,CHURCH AND STATE IN ITALY: 1947-1957 (PAMPHLET). GERMANY ITALY CONSTN POL/PAR AGREE CONTROL PARTIC CHOOSE ATTIT ORD/FREE FASCISM MARXISM 20 CHURCH/STA MARITAIN/J SALO. PAGE 166 H3316 — SECT CATHISM NAT/G GP/REL

C28
SCHNEIDER H.W.,"MAKING THE FASCIST STATE." ITALY CULTURE LABOR DIPLOM REV WAR NAT/LISM TOTALISM ATTIT DRIVE SOCISM...BIBLIOG PARLIAMENT 20. PAGE 140 H2792 — FASCISM POLICY POL/PAR

B35
LASKI H.J.,THE STATE IN THEORY AND PRACTICE. ELITES ECO/TAC REPRESENT ORD/FREE PWR WEALTH POPULISM ...GOV/COMP GEN/LAWS 19/20. PAGE 92 H1829 — CAP/ISM COERCE NAT/G FASCISM

B35
PARETO V.,THE MIND AND SOCIETY (4 VOLS.). ELITES SECT ECO/TAC COERCE PERSON ORD/FREE PWR SOVEREIGN FASCISM POPULISM...TRADIT 19/20. PAGE 123 H2465 — GEN/LAWS SOC PSY

B36
SMITH T.V.,THE PROMISE OF AMERICAN POLITICS. USA-45 WOR-45 LAW CONSTN STRATA PARTIC FASCISM LAISSEZ MARXISM...MAJORIT METH/COMP 18/20 JEFFERSN/T LOCKE/JOHN BENTHAM/J. PAGE 146 H2920 — CONCPT ORD/FREE IDEA/COMP NAT/COMP

B37
BORGESE G.A.,GOLIATH: THE MARCH OF FASCISM. GERMANY ITALY LAW POL/PAR SECT DIPLOM SOCISM...JURID MYTH 20 DANTE MACHIAVELL MUSSOLIN/B. PAGE 19 H0375 — POLICY NAT/LISM FASCISM NAT/G

B38
FIELD G.L.,THE SYNDICAL AND CORPORATIVE INSTITUTIONS OF ITALIAN FASCISM. ITALY CONSTN STRATA LABOR EX/STRUC TOP/EX ADJUD ADMIN LEAD TOTALISM AUTHORIT...MGT 20 MUSSOLIN/B. PAGE 50 H0991 — FASCISM INDUS NAT/G WORKER

B38
HEIMANN E.,COMMUNISM, FASCISM, OR DEMOCRACY? WOR-45 CONSTN SOCIETY STRATA AGRI CAP/ISM MORAL ORD/FREE ...MAJORIT METH/COMP NAT/COMP 19/20. PAGE 69 H1384 — SOCISM MARXISM FASCISM PLURISM

B38
REICH N.,LABOR RELATIONS IN REPUBLICAN GERMANY. GERMANY CONSTN ECO/DEV INDUS NAT/G ADMIN CONTROL GP/REL FASCISM POPULISM 20 WEIMAR/REP. PAGE 130 H2609 — WORKER MGT LABOR BARGAIN

B39
BENES E.,DEMOCRACY TODAY AND TOMORROW. EUR+WWI SOCIETY ECO/DEV DELIB/GP ECO/TAC REGION ATTIT PWR FASCISM...CONCPT LEAGUE/NAT 20. PAGE 14 H0281 — NAT/G LEGIT NAT/LISM

B39
COBBAN A.,DICTATORSHIP: ITS HISTORY AND THEORY. EUR+WWI MOD/EUR SOCIETY STRUCT NAT/G TEC/DEV LEAD NAT/LISM SOVEREIGN...IDEA/COMP 14/20. PAGE 30 H0610 — TOTALISM FASCISM CONCPT

B39
KOHN H.,REVOLUTIONS AND DICTATORSHIPS. COM EUR+WWI ISLAM MOD/EUR NAT/G CHIEF FORCES WAR CIVMIL/REL PWR MARXISM 18/20. PAGE 87 H1739 — NAT/LISM TOTALISM REV FASCISM

B39
OAKESHOTT M.,THE SOCIAL AND POLITICAL DOCTRINES OF CONTEMPORARY EUROPE. EUR+WWI RATIONAL CATHISM FASCISM MARXISM POPULISM...POLICY ANTHOL 20 NAZI. PAGE 120 H2392 — IDEA/COMP GOV/COMP ALL/IDEOS NAT/G

B39
SCHOCKEL E.,DAS POLITISCHE PLAKAT. EUR+WWI GERMANY NAT/G PWR FASCISM EXHIBIT. PAGE 140 H2794 — EDU/PROP ATTIT

DOMIN
POL/PAR

S39
COLE G.D.H.,"NAZI ECONOMICS: HOW DO THEY MANAGE IT?" GERMANY FORCES WORKER BUDGET INT/TRADE ROUTINE COERCE WAR 20 HITLER/A NAZI. PAGE 31 H0622
FASCISM ECO/TAC ATTIT PLAN

B40
HUNTER R.,REVOLUTION: WHY, HOW, WHEN? NAT/G ECO/TAC EDU/PROP COERCE ORD/FREE FASCISM POPULISM SOCISM 18/20 HITLER/A LENIN/VI. PAGE 75 H1502
REV METH/COMP LEAD CONSTN

B40
LEDERER E.,STATE OF THE MASSES. GERMANY ITALY SOCIETY NAT/G ECO/TAC EDU/PROP LEAD TOTALISM ...SOCIALIST PSY 20. PAGE 93 H1852
CROWD FASCISM AUTHORIT PERSON

B41
HITLER A.,MEIN KAMPF (UNABR. ENG. VERSION) (1925). GERMANY CONSTN TEC/DEV RACE/REL NAT/LISM TOTALISM SOVEREIGN...BIOG 20 HITLER/A TREATY. PAGE 71 H1429
EDU/PROP WAR PLAN FASCISM

B42
BAYNES N.H.,INTELLECTUAL LIBERTY AND TOTALITARIAN CLAIMS. EUR+WWI GERMANY ITALY INTELL POL/PAR CIVMIL/REL NAT/LISM SOCISM CONCPT. PAGE 12 H0245
KNOWL FASCISM EDU/PROP ACADEM

B42
FEFFERO G.,THE PRINCIPLES OF POWER (TRANS. BY T. JAECKEL). MOD/EUR CONSTN NAT/G CHIEF CONTROL REV WAR ORD/FREE CONSERVE FASCISM POPULISM...GEN/LAWS 18/20 EUROPE. PAGE 49 H0980
PWR LEGIT TRADIT ELITES

B42
NEUBURGER O.,OFFICIAL PUBLICATIONS OF PRESENT-DAY GERMANY: GOVERNMENT, CORPORATE ORGANIZATIONS, AND NATIONAL SOCIALIST PARTY. GERMANY CONSTN COM/IND POL/PAR EDU/PROP PRESS 20 NAZI. PAGE 117 H2332
BIBLIOG/A FASCISM NAT/G ADMIN

B42
NEUMANN S.,PERMANENT REVOLUTION: THE TOTAL STATE IN A WORLD AT WAR. COM EUR+WWI GERMANY USSR EX/STRUC DIPLOM CONTROL COERCE REPRESENT MARXISM...SOC GOV/COMP BIBLIOG 20 HITLER/A STALIN/J. PAGE 117 H2337
FASCISM TOTALISM DOMIN EDU/PROP

B42
SINGTON D.,THE GOEBBELS EXPERIMENT. GERMANY MOD/EUR NAT/G EX/STRUC FORCES CONTROL ROUTINE WAR TOTALISM PWR...ART/METH HUM 20 NAZI GOEBBELS/J. PAGE 144 H2886
FASCISM EDU/PROP ATTIT COM/IND

B43
SERENI A.P.,THE ITALIAN CONCEPTION OF INTERNATIONAL LAW. EUR+WWI MOD/EUR INT/ORG NAT/G DOMIN COERCE ORD/FREE FASCISM...OBS/ENVIR TREND 20. PAGE 141 H2829
LAW TIME/SEQ INT/LAW ITALY

B44
GYORGY A.,GEOPOLITICS: THE NEW GERMAN SCIENCE. EUR+WWI GERMANY STRATA NAT/G PROVS DOMIN EDU/PROP ATTIT DRIVE FASCISM...GEOG NAZI 20. PAGE 63 H1261
PWR LEGIT WAR

B44
KRIS E.,GERMAN RADIO PROPAGANDA: REPORT ON HOME BROADCASTS DURING THE WAR. EUR+WWI GERMANY CULTURE CONSULT PROB/SOLV FEEDBACK TASK INGP/REL DRIVE PWR FASCISM...CON/ANAL METH/COMP 20. PAGE 89 H1768
EDU/PROP DOMIN ACT/RES ATTIT

B46
BLUM L.,FOR ALL MANKIND (TRANS. BY W. PICKLES). FRANCE GERMANY USSR LAW SOCIETY STRUCT POL/PAR WORKER DIPLOM DOMIN CHOOSE ORD/FREE FASCISM 20. PAGE 18 H0361
POPULISM SOCIALIST NAT/G WAR

B46
CASSIRER E.,THE MYTH OF THE STATE. WOR-45 SOCIETY RACE/REL RATIONAL PWR FASCISM...PHIL/SCI PSY LING TREND HEGEL/GWF MACHIAVELL. PAGE 28 H0557
MYTH CONCPT NAT/G IDEA/COMP

S48
ALEXANDER L.,"WAR CRIMES, THEIR SOCIAL-PSYCHOLOGICAL ASPECTS." EUR+WWI GERMANY LAW CULTURE ELITES KIN POL/PAR PUB/INST FORCES DOMIN EDU/PROP COERCE CRIME ATTIT SUPEGO HEALTH MORAL PWR FASCISM ...PSY OBS TREND GEN/LAWS NAZI 20. PAGE 5 H0100
DRIVE WAR

C49
SCHAPIRO J.S.,"LIBERALISM AND THE CHALLENGE OF FASCISM." FRANCE UK STRATA PERSON...CONCPT BIOG IDEA/COMP BIBLIOG 18/20. PAGE 139 H2771
FASCISM LAISSEZ ATTIT

B50
ALBRECHT-CARRIE R.,ITALY FROM NAPOLEON TO MUSSOLINI. GERMANY ITALY SPAIN SOCIETY ECO/DEV POL/PAR LEGIS AGREE CONTROL WAR NAT/LISM TOTALISM PWR SOCISM...SOC 19/20 TREATY. PAGE 5 H0095
FASCISM NAT/G

S51
GOULD J.,"THE KOMSOMOL AND THE HITLER JUGEND." COM EUR+WWI GERMANY SOCIETY NAT/G POL/PAR SCHOOL TOTALISM DRIVE PERCEPT KNOWL FASCISM...SOC NAZI TOT/POP 20. PAGE 59 H1185
EDU/PROP CON/ANAL SOCISM

B52
APPADORAI A.,THE SUBSTANCE OF POLITICS (6TH ED.). EX/STRUC LEGIS DIPLOM CT/SYS CHOOSE FASCISM MARXISM SOCISM...BIBLIOG T. PAGE 7 H0145
PHIL/SCI NAT/G

B52
GURLAND A.R.L.,POLITICAL SCIENCE IN WESTERN GERMANY: THOUGHTS AND WRITINGS, 1950-1952 (PAMPHLET). EUR+WWI GERMANY/W ELITES SOCIETY NAT/G NAT/LISM TOTALISM 20. PAGE 63 H1253
BIBLIOG/A DIPLOM CIVMIL/REL FASCISM

B54
FRIEDRICH C.J.,TOTALITARIAN DICTATORSHIP AND AUTOCRACY. COM EUR+WWI GERMANY ITALY USSR INTELL ECO/DEV NAT/G POL/PAR FORCES TOP/EX ECO/TAC EDU/PROP LEGIT COERCE ATTIT ORD/FREE PWR FASCISM ...CONCPT TIME/SEQ GEN/LAWS NAZI 20. PAGE 53 H1068
SOCIETY DOMIN TOTALISM

B54
SALVEMINI G.,PRELUDE TO WORLD WAR II. ITALY MOD/EUR INT/ORG BAL/PWR EDU/PROP CONTROL TOTALISM...TREND NAT/COMP BIBLIOG 19 HITLER/A LEAGUE/NAT MUSSOLIN/B. PAGE 137 H2745
WAR FASCISM LEAD PWR

B55
ALFIERI D.,DICTATORS FACE TO FACE. NAT/G TOP/EX DIPLOM EXEC COERCE ORD/FREE FASCISM...POLICY OBS 20 HITLER/A MUSSOLIN/B. PAGE 5 H0103
WAR CHIEF TOTALISM PERS/REL

B55
KOHN H.,NATIONALISM: ITS MEANING AND HISTORY. GP/REL INGP/REL ATTIT...CONCPT NAT/COMP 16/20 MACHIAVELL. PAGE 87 H1743
NAT/LISM DIPLOM FASCISM REV

B55
VERGNAUD P.,L'IDEE DE LA NATIONALITE ET DE LA LIBRE DISPOSITION DES PEUPLES DANS SES RAPPORTS AVEC L'IDEE DE L'ETAT. STRATA NAT/G EDU/PROP RACE/REL AUTHORIT FASCISM MARXISM MYTH. PAGE 162 H3243
NAT/LISM DISCRIM ORD/FREE

B56
DE JONG L.,THE GERMAN FIFTH COLUMN IN THE SECOND WORLD WAR. EUR+WWI GERMANY NAT/G DIPLOM ATTIT FASCISM...MYTH 20 NAZI. PAGE 38 H0756
EDU/PROP WAR RUMOR

B57
HALLGARTEN G.W.,DAMONEN ODER RETTER. ASIA L/A+17C CAP/ISM ATTIT MARXISM SOCISM...NAT/COMP. PAGE 64 H1289
TOTALISM FASCISM COERCE DOMIN

B57
HERNANDEZ-ARREGU J.,IMPERIALISMO Y CULTURA (LA POLITICA EN LA INTELIGENCIA ARGENTINA). L/A+17C CULTURE ELITES WRITING COLONIAL CROWD ATTIT FASCISM MARXISM SOCISM...BIOG IDEA/COMP 20 ARGEN PERON/JUAN COM/PARTY. PAGE 70 H1403
INTELL CREATE ART/METH HUM

B59
INTERNATIONAL PRESS INSTITUTE,THE PRESS IN AUTHORITARIAN COUNTRIES. COM PORTUGAL SPAIN UAR USSR NAT/G DOMIN LEGIT ORD/FREE FASCISM SOCISM 20. PAGE 78 H1559
PRESS CONTROL TOTALISM EDU/PROP

B59
SCHORN H.,DER RICHTER IM DRITTEN REICH; GESCHICHTE UND DOKUMENTE. GERMANY NAT/G LEGIT CT/SYS INGP/REL MORAL ORD/FREE RESPECT...JURID GP/COMP 20. PAGE 140 H2798
ADJUD JUDGE FASCISM

B59
SZLUC T.,TWILIGHT OF THE TYRANTS. BRAZIL L/A+17C PERU VENEZUELA NAT/G FORCES CONTROL PERSON MORAL ORD/FREE PWR...CONCPT 20 ARGEN COLOMB. PAGE 151 H3028
TOTALISM CHIEF REV FASCISM

B60
JEMOLO A.C.,CHURCH AND STATE IN ITALY 1850-1950 (TRANS. BY DAVID MOORE). ITALY CONSTN STRATA WAR FASCISM SOCISM...TIME/SEQ 19/20 CHURCH/STA CHRIS/DEM. PAGE 80 H1599
GP/REL NAT/G CATHISM POL/PAR

B60
LOMBARDO TOLEDANO V,EL NEONAZISMO; SUS CHARACTERISTICAS Y PELIGROS. GERMANY/W POL/PAR COLONIAL LEAD LOBBY ATTIT 20 NAZI. PAGE 98 H1956
NAT/G FASCISM POLICY DIPLOM

B60
MATTHIAS E.,DAS ENDE DER PARTEIEN 1933. GERMANY NAT/G COERCE CHOOSE ORD/FREE PWR 20. PAGE 105 H2100
FASCISM POL/PAR DOMIN ATTIT

S60
CASSINELLI C.,"TOTALITARIANISM, IDEOLOGY AND PROPAGANDA." EUR+WWI CULTURE SOCIETY NAT/G DOMIN COERCE ORD/FREE FASCISM MARXISM...MARXIST CONCPT STERTYP GEN/LAWS TOT/POP 20. PAGE 28 H0554
ATTIT EDU/PROP TOTALISM

B61
EMMET C.,THE VANISHING SWASTIKA. GERMANY/W ELITES CRIME WAR...SAMP 20. PAGE 46 H0922
FASCISM ATTIT AGE/Y NAT/G

L62
NOLTE E.,"ZUR PHANOMENOLOGIE DES FASCHIMUS." EUR+WWI GERMANY ITALY TURKEY INTELL NAT/G CHIEF CONSULT FORCES CREATE DOMIN EDU/PROP COERCE WAR CHOOSE DRIVE FASCISM...PSY CONCPT MYTH GEN/METH LEAGUE/NAT NAZI 20. PAGE 118 H2367
ATTIT PWR

B63
CONZE W.,DIE DEUTSCHE NATION. GERMANY NAT/G POL/PAR WAR ORD/FREE...TREND 8/20 NAZI. PAGE 33 H0657
NAT/LISM FASCISM ATTIT

SOCIETY

B63
CROSS C.,THE FASCISTS IN BRITAIN. UK ELITES LABOR NAT/G DOMIN PARTIC DISCRIM TOTALISM ATTIT...STERTYP 20. PAGE 35 H0708
POL/PAR FASCISM RACE/REL LEAD

B63
EICH H.,THE UNLOVED GERMANS. EUR+WWI GERMANY PERS/REL RACE/REL DISCRIM HABITAT SUPEGO FASCISM ...PSY SOC AUD/VIS 19/20 JEWS. PAGE 45 H0898
STERTYP PERSON CULTURE ATTIT

B63
JACOB H.,GERMAN ADMINISTRATION SINCE BISMARCK: CENTRAL AUTHORITY VERSUS LOCAL AUTONOMY. GERMANY GERMANY/W LAW POL/PAR CONTROL CENTRAL TOTALISM FASCISM...MAJORIT DECISION STAT CHARTS GOV/COMP 19/20 BISMARCK/O HITLER/A WEIMAR/REP. PAGE 79 H1577
ADMIN NAT/G LOC/G POLICY

B63
SILONE I.,THE SCHOOL FOR DICTATORS. EUR+WWI GERMANY ITALY SOCIETY NAT/G CHIEF EX/STRUC ATTIT MORAL PWR ...HIST/WRIT 20. PAGE 144 H2876
TOTALISM EDU/PROP ORD/FREE FASCISM

B64
HALE O.J.,THE CAPTIVE PRESS IN THE THIRD REICH. GERMANY CULTURE LG/CO NAT/G POL/PAR PLAN DOMIN TASK CENTRAL OWN TOTALISM PWR...BIBLIOG 20 HITLER/A NAZI AMMAN/MAX. PAGE 64 H1283
COM/IND PRESS CONTROL FASCISM

B64
HALPERIN S.W.,MUSSOLINI AND ITALIAN FASCISM. ITALY NAT/G POL/PAR SECT ECO/TAC LEAD PWR SOCISM...POLICY 20 MUSSOLIN/B. PAGE 64 H1294
FASCISM NAT/LISM EDU/PROP CHIEF

B64
WHEELER-BENNETT J.W.,THE NEMESIS OF POWER (2ND ED.). EUR+WWI GERMANY TOP/EX TEC/DEV ADMIN WAR PERS/REL RIGID/FLEX ROLE ORD/FREE PWR FASCISM 20 HITLER/A. PAGE 167 H3342
FORCES NAT/G GP/REL STRUCT

B65
ALLEN W.S.,THE NAZI SEIZURE OF POWER. GERMANY NAT/G CHIEF LEAD COERCE CHOOSE REPRESENT GOV/REL AUTHORIT ...DECISION 20 HITLER/A NAZI. PAGE 5 H0106
MUNIC FASCISM TOTALISM LOC/G

B65
BRAMSTED E.K.,GOEBBELS AND NATIONAL SOCIALIST PROPAGANDA, 1925-1945. EUR+WWI GERMANY UK USSR NAT/G FORCES WAR FASCISM...TIME/SEQ 20 GOEBBELS/J NAZI. PAGE 20 H0403
EDU/PROP PSY COM/IND

B65
BRIDGMAN J.,GERMAN AFRICA: A SELECT ANNOTATED BIBLIOGRAPHY. AFR AGRI DIPLOM REPAR WAR FASCISM 20. PAGE 21 H0414
BIBLIOG/A COLONIAL NAT/G EDU/PROP

B65
COX R.H.,THE STATE IN INTERNATIONAL RELATIONS. INT/ORG DIPLOM REV WAR PEACE MARXISM...CONCPT GOV/COMP. PAGE 34 H0690
SOVEREIGN NAT/G FASCISM ORD/FREE

B65
GUERIN D.,SUR LE FASCISME: FASCISME ET GRAND CAPITAL (VOL. II). GERMANY ITALY SOCIETY STRATA AGRI WORKER 20. PAGE 62 H1245
FASCISM NAT/G TOTALISM EDU/PROP

B65
HAMIL H.M.,DICTATORSHIP IN SPANISH AMERICA. NAT/G COERCE MORAL ORD/FREE...POLICY PSY SOC ANTHOL 18/20. PAGE 65 H1300
TOTALISM CHIEF L/A+17C FASCISM

B65
HART B.H.L.,THE MEMOIRS OF CAPTAIN LIDDELL HART (VOL. I). UK NAT/G PLAN TEC/DEV DIPLOM ADMIN WEAPON GOV/REL PERS/REL ATTIT PWR FASCISM...POLICY 20. PAGE 67 H1348
FORCES BIOG LEAD WAR

B65
ROSENBERG A.,DEMOCRACY AND SOCIALISM. COM EUR+WWI FRANCE MOD/EUR STRUCT INT/ORG NAT/G POL/PAR TOP/EX EDU/PROP COERCE PERSON PWR FASCISM MARXISM...CONCPT TIME/SEQ MARX/KARL 19/20. PAGE 134 H2677
ATTIT

B65
SALVADORI M.,ITALY. AUSTRIA FRANCE GERMANY ITALY SPAIN CULTURE NAT/G POL/PAR DIPLOM WAR FASCISM LAISSEZ MARXISM...TIME/SEQ CHARTS BIBLIOG/A. PAGE 137 H2744
NAT/LISM CATHISM SOCIETY

B65
STERN F.,THE POLITICS OF CULTURAL DESPAIR. EUR+WWI GERMANY POL/PAR SECT RACE/REL STRANGE TOTALISM ...ART/METH MYTH BIBLIOG 20 JEWS. PAGE 149 H2980
CULTURE ATTIT NAT/LISM FASCISM

C65
NEUMANN S.,"PERMANENT REVOLUTION: TOTALITARIANISM IN THE AGE OF INTERNA TIONAL CIVIL WAR (2ND ED.)" EUR+WWI ELITES POL/PAR DOMIN EDU/PROP LEAD CROWD REPRESENT...MAJORIT GOV/COMP BIBLIOG 20. PAGE 117 H2340
TOTALISM REV FASCISM STRUCT

B66
ADAMS J.C.,THE GOVERNMENT OF REPUBLICAN ITALY (2ND ED.). ITALY LOC/G POL/PAR DELIB/GP LEGIS WORKER ADMIN CT/SYS FASCISM...CHARTS BIBLIOG 20 PARLIAMENT. PAGE 3 H0064
NAT/G CHOOSE EX/STRUC CONSTN

B66
COLE G.D.H.,THE MEANING OF MARXISM. USSR WOR+45 STRATA STRUCT NAT/G WORKER COST FASCISM...IDEA/COMP 20. PAGE 31 H0625
MARXISM CONCPT HIST/WRIT CAP/ISM

B66
NOLTE E.,THREE FACES OF FASCISM. FRANCE GERMANY DOMIN LEGIT COERCE CROWD REV WAR GP/REL RACE/REL SOVEREIGN...GOV/COMP IDEA/COMP 19/20 HITLER/A MUSSOLIN/B MARX/KARL. PAGE 118 H2368
FASCISM TOTALISM NAT/G POL/PAR

B66
O'NEILL R.J.,THE GERMAN ARMY AND THE NAZI PARTY, 1933-1939. GERMANY ELITES NAT/G EDU/PROP CONTROL LEAD COERCE WAR...POLICY INT TIME/SEQ BIBLIOG 20 HITLER/A NAZI. PAGE 120 H2391
CIVMIL/REL FORCES FASCISM POL/PAR

B66
RICHERT F.,DIE NATIONALE WELLE. GERMANY GERMANY/W PARL/PROC ORD/FREE FASCISM...TREND 19/20. PAGE 131 H2622
POL/PAR ATTIT NAT/LISM NAT/G

B66
RISTIC D.N.,YUGOSLAVIA'S REVOLUTION OF 1941. EUR+WWI YUGOSLAVIA NAT/G WAR ORD/FREE...RECORD BIBLIOG 20 HITLER/A TREATY. PAGE 132 H2633
REV ATTIT FASCISM DIPLOM

B66
ROSNER J.,DER FASCHISMUS. AUSTRIA GERMANY ITALY STRATA NAT/G POL/PAR COERCE RACE/REL TOTALISM ATTIT AUTHORIT...IDEA/COMP 20 NAZI ANTI/SEMIT. PAGE 134 H2684
NAT/LISM FASCISM ORD/FREE WAR

B66
THORNTON M.J.,NAZISM, 1918-1945. GERMANY INT/ORG DIPLOM REV PEACE FASCISM...CONCPT 20 HITLER/A WEIMAR/REP NAZI. PAGE 155 H3089
TOTALISM POL/PAR NAT/G WAR

B67
DAVIDSON E.,THE TRIAL OF THE GERMANS* NUREMBERG* 1946-48. EUR+WWI GERMANY CULTURE NAT/G LEAD PERSON HEALTH...CRIMLGY PSY SOC BIOG JEWS. PAGE 37 H0745
FASCISM ADJUD TOTALISM WAR

S67
LAQUEUR W.,"BONN IS NOT WEIMAR* REFLECTIONS ON THE RADICAL RIGHT IN GER MANY." CULTURE LOC/G NAT/G PARTIC CHOOSE. PAGE 91 H1822
GERMANY/W FASCISM NAT/LISM

S67
SAVER W.,"NATIONAL SOCIALISM: TOTALITARIANISM OR FASCISM?" GERMANY STRUCT POL/PAR PROB/SOLV MARXISM ...SOC CONCPT HIST/WRIT IDEA/COMP 20 HITLER/A COLD/WAR. PAGE 138 H2760
SOCISM NAT/G TOTALISM FASCISM

FASCIST....FASCIST

N19
BARRES M.,"THE WAR AND THE SPIRIT OF YOUTH" (PAMPHLET). FRANCE FORCES DOMIN LEAD DEATH AGE/Y ATTIT RESPECT...FASCIST 20 WWI. PAGE 11 H0228
WAR NAT/LISM CULTURE MYSTIC

B50
US DEPARTMENT OF STATE,DOCUMENTS ON GERMAN FOREIGN POLICY, 1918-1945 (13 VOLS.). EUR+WWI GERMANY NAT/G PLAN DIPLOM DOMIN EDU/PROP CONTROL NAT/LISM ...ANTHOL 20. PAGE 159 H3186
BIBLIOG/A WAR POLICY FASCIST

B54
GERMANY FOREIGN MINISTRY,DOCUMENTS ON GERMAN FOREIGN POLICY 1918-1945, SERIES C (1933-1937) VOLS. I-V. GERMANY MOD/EUR FORCES PLAN ECO/TAC ...FASCIST CHARTS ANTHOL 20. PAGE 56 H1115
NAT/G DIPLOM POLICY

B65
NORDEN A.,WAR AND NAZI CRIMINALS IN WEST GERMANY: STATE, ECONOMY, ADMINISTRATION, ARMY, JUSTICE, SCIENCE. GERMANY GERMANY/W MOD/EUR ECO/DEV ACADEM EX/STRUC FORCES DOMIN ADMIN CT/SYS...POLICY MAJORIT PACIFIST 20. PAGE 119 H2370
FASCIST WAR NAT/G TOP/EX

S67
CATTELL D.T.,"A NEO-MARXIST THEORY OF COMPARATIVE ANALYSIS." USSR STRATA INSPECT DOMIN CONTROL COERCE OWN TOTALISM PWR...FASCIST HYPO/EXP METH 20. PAGE 28 H0561
GOV/COMP MARXISM SIMUL CLASSIF

FASHION....SEE ETIQUET, MODAL

FATHER/DIV....FATHER DIVINE AND HIS FOLLOWERS

FATOUROS A.A. H0975

FAUST J.J. H0976

FAWCETT J.E.S. H0977

FAY S.B. H0978

FAYERWEATHER J. H0979

FBI....U.S. FEDERAL BUREAU OF INVESTIGATION

B66
HOEVELER H.J.,INTERNATIONALE BEKAMPFUNG DES VERBRECHENS. AUSTRIA SWITZERLND WOR+45 INT/ORG CONTROL BIO/SOC...METH/COMP NAT/COMP 20 MAFIA SCOT/YARD FBI. PAGE 72 H1446
CRIMLGY CRIME DIPLOM INT/LAW

FCC....U.S. FEDERAL COMMUNICATIONS COMMISSION

FDA....U.S. FOOD AND DRUG ADMINISTRATION

FDR....FRANKLIN D. ROOSEVELT

FEARS....SEE ANOMIE

FECHNER/GT....GUSTAV THEODOR FECHNER

FED/OPNMKT....FEDERAL OPEN MARKET COMMITTEE

FED/RESERV....U.S. FEDERAL RESERVE SYSTEM (INCLUDES FEDERAL RESERVE BANK)

FEDERAL AVIATION AGENCY....SEE FAA

FEDERAL BUREAU OF INVESTIGATION....SEE FBI

FEDERAL COMMUNICATIONS COMMISSION....SEE FCC

FEDERAL COUNCIL FOR SCIENCE + TECHNOLOGY....SEE FEDSCI/TEC

FEDERAL HOUSING ADMINISTRATION...SEE FHA

FEDERAL RESERVE SYSTEM....SEE FED/RESERV

FEDERAL TRADE COMMISSION....SEE FTC

FEDERAL....FEDERALISM

N19
FREEMAN H.A.,COERCION OF STATES IN FEDERAL UNIONS (PAMPHLET). WOR-45 DIPLOM CONTROL COERCE PEACE ORD/FREE...GOV/COMP METH/COMP NAT/COMP PACIFIST 20. PAGE 53 H1055
FEDERAL WAR INT/ORG PACIFISM

B30
CANAWAY A.P.,THE FAILURE OF FEDERALISM IN AUSTRALIA. UK PROB/SOLV ADMIN EFFICIENCY ATTIT ...POLICY NAT/COMP 20 AUSTRAL. PAGE 26 H0518
FEDERAL NAT/G CONSTN OP/RES

C31
MOGI S.,"THE PROBLEM OF FEDERALISM: A STUDY IN THE HISTORY OF POLITICAL THEORY." CONSTN COLONIAL NAT/LISM SOVEREIGN LAISSEZ PLURISM 18/20. PAGE 112 H2235
FEDERAL CONCPT NAT/G

B32
MCKISACK M.,THE PARLIAMENTARY REPRESENTATION OF THE ENGLISH BOROUGHS DURING THE MIDDLE AGES. UK CONSTN CULTURE ELITES EX/STRUC TAX PAY ADJUD PARL/PROC APPORT FEDERAL...POLICY 13/15 PARLIAMENT. PAGE 107 H2139
NAT/G MUNIC LEGIS CHOOSE

B36
RAPPARD W.E.,THE GOVERNMENT OF SWITZERLAND. SWITZERLND INT/ORG POL/PAR EX/STRUC DIPLOM NEUTRAL PARL/PROC REGION WAR HABITAT SOVEREIGN...NAT/COMP SOC/INTEG 20 LEAGUE/NAT WWI. PAGE 130 H2594
CONSTN NAT/G CULTURE FEDERAL

L49
BRECHT A.,"THE NEW GERMAN CONSTITUTION." GERMANY/W NAT/G CHIEF EX/STRUC LEGIS PROB/SOLV ADMIN REPRESENT TOTALISM ORD/FREE PLURISM...MAJORIT CHARTS 20. PAGE 20 H0409
CONSTN DIPLOM SOVEREIGN FEDERAL

S49
STEINMETZ H.,"THE PROBLEMS OF THE LANDRAT: A STUDY OF COUNTY GOVERNMENT IN THE US ZONE OF GERMANY." GERMANY/W USA+45 INDUS PLAN DIPLOM EDU/PROP CONTROL WAR GOV/REL FEDERAL WEALTH PLURISM...GOV/COMP 20 LANDRAT. PAGE 149 H2977
LOC/G COLONIAL MGT TOP/EX

B50
DUCLOS P.,L'EVOLUTION DES RAPPORTS POLITIQUES DEPUIS 1750 (LIBERTE, INTEGRATION, UNITE). LAW INT/ORG FEDERAL TOTALISM ATTIT PWR...MAJORIT BIBLIOG 18/20 PARLIAMENT EUROPE. PAGE 43 H0852
ORD/FREE DIPLOM NAT/G GOV/COMP

B50
KANN R.A.,THE MULTINATIONAL EMPIRE (2 VOLS.). AUSTRIA CZECHOSLVK GERMANY HUNGARY CULTURE NAT/G POL/PAR PROVS REGION REV FEDERAL...GEOG TREND CHARTS IDEA/COMP NAT/COMP 19/20. PAGE 83 H1654
NAT/LISM MOD/EUR

B53
MAXIMOFF G.P.,THE POLITICAL PHILOSOPHY OF BAKUNIN: SCIENTIFIC ANARCHISM. STRUCT INGP/REL FEDERAL MARXISM...ANARCH BIOG 19 BAKUNIN. PAGE 105 H2104
SOCIETY PHIL/SCI NAT/G IDEA/COMP

B54
FRIEDMAN W.,THE PUBLIC CORPORATION: A COMPARATIVE SYMPOSIUM (UNIVERSITY OF TORONTO SCHOOL OF LAW COMPARATIVE LAW SERIES, VOL. I). SWEDEN USA+45 INDUS INT/ORG NAT/G REGION CENTRAL FEDERAL...POLICY JURID IDEA/COMP NAT/COMP ANTHOL 20 COMMONWLTH MONOPOLY EUROPE. PAGE 53 H1065
LAW SOCISM LG/CO OWN

B55
DE ARAGAO J.G.,LA JURIDICTION ADMINISTRATIVE AU BRESIL. BRAZIL ADJUD COLONIAL CT/SYS REV FEDERAL ORD/FREE...BIBLIOG 19/20. PAGE 37 H0749
EX/STRUC ADMIN NAT/G

B56
DOUGLAS W.O.,WE THE JUDGES. INDIA USA+45 USA-45 LAW NAT/G SECT LEGIS PRESS CRIME FEDERAL ORD/FREE ...POLICY GOV/COMP 19/20 WARRN/EARL MARSHALL/J SUPREME/CT. PAGE 42 H0841
ADJUD CT/SYS CONSTN GOV/REL

B56
PADMORE G.,PAN-AFRICANISM OR COMMUNISM. AFR FUT NIGERIA INTELL NAT/G COLONIAL FEDERAL ATTIT DRIVE PWR RESPECT WEALTH MARXISM...CONCPT AUD/VIS STERTYP 20. PAGE 122 H2440
POL/PAR NAT/LISM

B57
KOHN H.,AMERICAN NATIONALISM. EUR+WWI USA+45 USA-45 COLONIAL REGION 18/20. PAGE 87 H1744
NAT/LISM NAT/COMP FEDERAL DIPLOM

B57
LONG H.A.,USURPERS - FOES OF FREE MAN. LAW NAT/G CHIEF LEGIS DOMIN ADJUD REPRESENT GOV/REL ORD/FREE LAISSEZ POPULISM...POLICY 18/20 SUPREME/CT ROOSEVLT/F CONGRESS CON/INTERP. PAGE 98 H1961
CT/SYS CENTRAL FEDERAL CONSTN

B58
CARTER G.M.,TRANSITION IN AFRICA; STUDIES IN POLITICAL ADAPTATION. AFR CENTRL/AFR GHANA NIGERIA CONSTN LOC/G POL/PAR ADMIN GP/REL FEDERAL...MAJORIT BIBLIOG 20. PAGE 27 H0543
NAT/COMP PWR CONTROL NAT/G

B58
HAAS E.B.,THE UNITING OF EUROPE. EUR+WWI INT/ORG NAT/G POL/PAR TOP/EX ECO/TAC EDU/PROP LEGIT FEDERAL NAT/LISM DRIVE RIGID/FLEX ORD/FREE PWR PLURISM ...POLICY CONCPT INT GEN/LAWS ECSC EEC 20. PAGE 63 H1264
VOL/ASSN ECO/DEV

B58
LOWER A.R.M.,EVOLVING CANADIAN FEDERALISM. CANADA WEST/IND CONSTN PROB/SOLV COLONIAL REGION NAT/LISM ...ANTHOL 20. PAGE 99 H1976
FEDERAL NAT/G DIPLOM RACE/REL

B58
STRONG C.F.,MODERN POLITICAL CONSTITUTIONS. LAW CHIEF DELIB/GP EX/STRUC LEGIS ADJUD CHOOSE FEDERAL POPULISM...CONCPT BIBLIOG 20 UN. PAGE 150 H2998
CONSTN IDEA/COMP NAT/G

C58
GOLAY J.F.,"THE FOUNDING OF THE FEDERAL REPUBLIC OF GERMANY." GERMANY/W CONSTN EX/STRUC DIPLOM ADMIN CHOOSE...DECISION BIBLIOG 20. PAGE 58 H1155
FEDERAL NAT/G PARL/PROC POL/PAR

B59
MILLER A.S.,PRIVATE GOVERNMENTS AND THE CONSTITUTION (PAMPHLET). LAW LABOR NAT/G ROLE PWR PLURISM...POLICY DECISION. PAGE 111 H2211
FEDERAL CONSTN VOL/ASSN CONSEN

B60
AYEARST M.,THE BRITISH WEST INDIES: THE SEARCH FOR SELF-GOVERNMENT. FUT WEST/IND LOC/G POL/PAR EX/STRUC LEGIS CHOOSE FEDERAL...NAT/COMP BIBLIOG 17/20. PAGE 9 H0186
CONSTN COLONIAL REPRESENT NAT/G

B60
JHA C.,INDIAN GOVERNMENT AND POLITICS. INDIA SERV/IND POL/PAR PROVS LEGIS CT/SYS CHOOSE GOV/REL FEDERAL 20. PAGE 81 H1616
NAT/G PARL/PROC CONSTN ADJUST

B60
LASKIN B.,CANADIAN CONSTITUTIONAL LAW: TEXT AND NOTES ON DISTRIBUTION OF LEGISLATIVE POWER (2ND ED.). CANADA LOC/G ECO/TAC TAX CONTROL CT/SYS CRIME FEDERAL PWR...JURID 20 PARLIAMENT. PAGE 92 H1832
CONSTN NAT/G LAW LEGIS

B61
AIYAR S.P.,FEDERALISM AND SOCIAL CHANGE. CANADA CULTURE STRUCT PLAN PROB/SOLV TEC/DEV ECO/TAC ORD/FREE...TIME/SEQ 18/20 AUSTRAL. PAGE 4 H0085
FEDERAL NAT/G CENTRAL GOV/COMP

B61
BIEBUYCK D.,CONGO TRIBES AND PARTIES. AFR CONGO/BRAZ CONSTN NAT/G COLONIAL CHOOSE FEDERAL 20 CONGO/LEOP. PAGE 17 H0333
KIN POL/PAR GP/REL SOVEREIGN

B61
BREWIS T.N.,CANADIAN ECONOMIC POLICY. CANADA BUDGET CAP/ISM INT/TRADE RATION TARIFFS TAX PRICE CONTROL ROUTINE FEDERAL INCOME PRODUC 20 GOLD/STAND. PAGE 20 H0412
ECO/DEV ECO/TAC NAT/G PLAN

B61
RAO K.V.,PARLIAMENTARY DEMOCRACY OF INDIA. INDIA EX/STRUC TOP/EX COLONIAL CT/SYS PARL/PROC ORD/FREE ...POLICY CONCPT TREND 20 PARLIAMENT. PAGE 130 H2592
CONSTN ADJUD NAT/G FEDERAL

B62
AMERICAN SOCIETY AFR CULTURE,PAN-AFRICANISM RECONSIDERED. AFR SOCIETY STRUCT SCHOOL CAP/ISM EDU/PROP...ART/METH NEW/IDEA PREDICT ANTHOL 20 PANAF/FREE NEGRO. PAGE 6 H0123
DIPLOM FEDERAL NAT/LISM CULTURE

B62
INSTITUTE OF PUBLIC ADMIN,A SHORT HISTORY OF THE PUBLIC SERVICE IN IRELAND. IRELAND UK DIST/IND INGP/REL FEDERAL 13/20 CIVIL/SERV. PAGE 77 H1539
ADMIN WORKER GOV/REL NAT/G

B62
LEGUM C.,PAN-AFRICANISM: A SHORT POLITICAL GUIDE. ISLAM CULTURE INTELL ECO/DEV NAT/G POL/PAR DELIB/GP PLAN EDU/PROP FEDERAL NAT/LISM ATTIT DRIVE PERSON ...RECORD TIME/SEQ CHARTS STERTYP 20. PAGE 93 H1861
AFR CONCPT

B62
TILMAN R.O.,THE NIGERIAN POLITICAL SXENE. NIGERIA DIPLOM COLONIAL PARTIC...POLICY SOC OBS PREDICT ANTHOL 20. PAGE 155 H3096
NAT/G AFR ECO/UNDEV FEDERAL

S62
SPRINGER H.W.,"FEDERATION IN THE CARIBBEAN: AN ATTEMPT THAT FAILED." L/A+17C ECO/UNDEV INT/ORG POL/PAR PROVS LEGIS CREATE PLAN LEGIT ADMIN FEDERAL ATTIT DRIVE PERSON ORD/FREE PWR...POLICY GEOG PSY CONCPT OBS CARIBBEAN CMN/WLTH 20. PAGE 148 H2955
VOL/ASSN NAT/G REGION

B63
FRITZ H.E.,THE MOVEMENT FOR INDIAN ASSIMILATION, 1860-1890. SECT FORCES GP/REL RACE/REL DISCRIM FEDERAL CATHISM...BIBLIOG 19 INDIAN/AM PROTESTANT GRANT/US. PAGE 54 H1071
CULTURE NAT/G ECO/TAC ATTIT

B63
LEONARD T.J.,THE FEDERAL SYSTEM OF INDIA. INDIA MUNIC NAT/G PROVS ADMIN SOVEREIGN...IDEA/COMP 20. PAGE 94 H1885
FEDERAL MGT NAT/COMP METH/COMP

B63
LIVINGSTON W.S.,FEDERALISM IN THE COMMONWEALTH - A BIBLIOGRAPHICAL COMMENTARY. CANADA INDIA PAKISTAN UK STRUCT LOC/G NAT/G POL/PAR...NAT/COMP 20 AUSTRAL. PAGE 97 H1943
BIBLIOG JURID FEDERAL CONSTN

B63
WILCOX W.A.,PAKISTAN; THE CONSOLIDATION OF A NATION. INDIA PAKISTAN CONSTN SECT PROB/SOLV COLONIAL PARTIC GP/REL FEDERAL...POLICY 19/20. PAGE 168 H3361
NAT/LISM ECO/UNDEV DIPLOM STRUCT

S63
BANFIELD J.,"FEDERATION IN EAST-AFRICA." AFR UGANDA ELITES INT/ORG NAT/G VOL/ASSN LEGIS ECO/TAC FEDERAL ATTIT SOVEREIGN TOT/POP 20 TANGANYIKA. PAGE 10 H0210
EX/STRUC PWR REGION

S63
ROUGEMONT D.,"LES NOUVELLES CHANCES DE L'EUROPE." EUR+WWI FUT ECO/DEV INT/ORG NAT/G ACT/RES PLAN TEC/DEV EDU/PROP ADMIN COLONIAL FEDERAL ATTIT PWR SKILL...TREND 20. PAGE 135 H2696
ECO/UNDEV PERCEPT

B64
CURRIE D.P.,FEDERALISM AND THE NEW NATIONS OF AFRICA. CANADA USA+45 INT/TRADE TAX GP/REL ...NAT/COMP SOC/INTEG 20. PAGE 36 H0725
FEDERAL AFR ECO/UNDEV INT/LAW

B64
FRANCK T.M.,EAST AFRICAN UNITY THROUGH LAW. MALAWI TANZANIA UGANDA UK ZAMBIA CONSTN INT/ORG NAT/G ADMIN ROUTINE TASK NAT/LISM ATTIT SOVEREIGN ...RECORD IDEA/COMP NAT/COMP. PAGE 52 H1048
AFR FEDERAL REGION INT/LAW

B64
GROVES H.E.,THE CONSTITUTION OF MALAYSIA. MALAYSIA POL/PAR CHIEF CONSULT DELIB/GP CT/SYS PARL/PROC CHOOSE FEDERAL ORD/FREE 20. PAGE 62 H1238
CONSTN NAT/G LAW

B64
MINAR D.W.,IDEAS AND POLITICS: THE AMERICAN EXPERIENCE. SECT CHIEF LEGIS CREATE ADJUD EXEC REV PWR...PHIL/SCI CONCPT IDEA/COMP 18/20 HAMILTON/A JEFFERSN/T DECLAR/IND JACKSON/A PRESIDENT. PAGE 111 H2220
CONSTN NAT/G FEDERAL

B64
WHEARE K.C.,FEDERAL GOVERNMENT (4TH ED.). WOR+45 WOR-45 POL/PAR LEGIS BAL/PWR CT/SYS...POLICY JURID CONCPT GOV/COMP 17/20. PAGE 167 H3339
FEDERAL CONSTN EX/STRUC NAT/COMP

S64
GIROD R.,"LE SYSTEME DES PARTIS EN SUISSE." CONSTN LOC/G DELIB/GP FEDERAL ALL/VALS. PAGE 57 H1136
POL/PAR LEGIS NAT/G PARL/PROC

B65
BROWNSON O.A.,THE AMERICAN REPUBLIC. NAT/G PROVS WAR GOV/REL PRIVIL ORD/FREE PWR ALL/IDEOS CONSERVE ...CONCPT 19 CIVIL/WAR. PAGE 22 H0452
CONSTN FEDERAL SOVEREIGN

B65
CALLEO D.P.,EUROPE'S FUTURE: THE GRAND ALTERNATIVES. UK INT/ORG DIPLOM PWR SOVEREIGN ...CONCPT IDEA/COMP NAT/COMP BIBLIOG 20 EEC EUROPE DEGAULLE/C NATO. PAGE 25 H0506
FUT EUR+WWI FEDERAL NAT/LISM

B65
CHANDA A.,FEDERALISM IN INDIA. INDIA UK ELITES FINAN NAT/G POL/PAR EX/STRUC LEGIS DIPLOM TAX GOV/REL POPULISM...POLICY 20. PAGE 28 H0572
CONSTN CENTRAL FEDERAL

B65
HALEVY E.,THE ERA OF TYRANNIES (TRANS. BY R. K. WEBB). FRANCE MOD/EUR UK ECO/DEV LABOR NAT/G BAL/PWR FEDERAL ALL/VALS...OLD/LIB TREND 18/20 SAINTSIMON. PAGE 64 H1285
SOCISM CONCPT UTOPIA ORD/FREE

B65
MERKL P.H.,GERMANY: YESTERDAY AND TOMORROW. GERMANY POL/PAR PLAN DIPLOM LEAD FEDERAL 19/20. PAGE 109 H2181
NAT/G FUT

B65
NYE J.S. JR.,PAN-AFRICANISM AND EAST AFRICAN INTEGRATION. TANZANIA UGANDA STRUCT ECO/UNDEV NAT/G DIPLOM FEDERAL NAT/LISM...STAT SOC/EXP BIBLIOG EEC OAU. PAGE 119 H2382
REGION ATTIT GEN/LAWS AFR

B65
PYLEE M.V.,CONSTITUTIONAL GOVERNMENT IN INDIA (2ND REV. ED.). INDIA POL/PAR EX/STRUC DIPLOM COLONIAL CT/SYS PARL/PROC PRIVIL...JURID 16/20. PAGE 128 H2569
CONSTN NAT/G PROVS FEDERAL

B65
SHARMA S.A.,PARLIAMENTARY GOVERNMENT IN INDIA. INDIA FINAN LOC/G PROVS DELIB/GP PLAN ADMIN CT/SYS FEDERAL...JURID 20. PAGE 142 H2849
NAT/G CONSTN PARL/PROC LEGIS

S65
HAYTER T.,"FRENCH AID TO AFRICA* ITS SCOPE AND ACHIEVEMENTS." CULTURE ECO/TAC INT/TRADE ADMIN REGION CENTRAL FEDERAL LOVE PWR SOVEREIGN EEC. PAGE 68 H1370
AFR FRANCE FOR/AID COLONIAL

S65
STAROBIN J.R.,"COMMUNISM IN WESTERN EUROPE." FRANCE GERMANY ITALY USA+45 USSR ECO/DEV FEDERAL PEACE ATTIT DRIVE PWR TREND. PAGE 149 H2972
MARXISM EUR+WWI POL/PAR NAT/COMP

B66
DE TOCQUEVILLE A,DEMOCRACY IN AMERICA (1834-1840) (2 VOLS. IN I; TRANS. BY G. LAWRENCE). FRANCE CULTURE STRATA POL/PAR CT/SYS REPRESENT FEDERAL ORD/FREE SOVEREIGN...MAJORIT TREND GEN/LAWS 18/19. PAGE 39 H0773
POPULISM USA-45 CONSTN NAT/COMP

B66
DIAMOND S.,THE TRANSFORMATION OF EAST AFRICA. NAT/G SCHOOL CREATE PROB/SOLV COLONIAL REGION RACE/REL FEDERAL...SOC ANTHOL WORSHIP 20 AFRICA/E. PAGE 41 H0819
CULTURE AFR TEC/DEV INDUS

B66
GHOSH P.K.,THE CONSTITUTION OF INDIA: HOW IT HAS BEEN FRAMED. INDIA LOC/G DELIB/GP EX/STRUC PROB/SOLV BUDGET INT/TRADE CT/SYS CHOOSE...LING 20. PAGE 56 H1121
CONSTN NAT/G LEGIS FEDERAL

B66
HAY P.,FEDERALISM AND SUPRANATIONAL ORGANIZATIONS: PATTERNS FOR NEW LEGAL STRUCTURES. EUR+WWI LAW NAT/G VOL/ASSN DIPLOM PWR...NAT/COMP TREATY EEC. PAGE 68 H1364
SOVEREIGN FEDERAL INT/ORG INT/LAW

B66
RAY A.,INTER-GOVERNMENTAL RELATIONS IN INDIA: A STUDY OF INDIAN FEDERALISM. CANADA INDIA SWITZERLND USA+45 USSR ADMIN GOV/REL...NAT/COMP BIBLIOG. PAGE 130 H2599
CONSTN FEDERAL SOVEREIGN NAT/G

B66
SASTRI K.V.S.,FEDERAL-STATE FISCAL RELATIONS IN INDIA: A STUDY OF THE FINANCE COMMISSION AND TECHNIQUES OF FINANCIAL ADJUSTMENT. INDIA PROVS DELIB/GP GOV/REL FEDERAL...MATH CHARTS 20. PAGE 138 H2756
TAX BUDGET FINAN NAT/G

S66
ROTHCHILD D.,"THE LIMITS OF FEDERALISM: AN EXAMINATION OF POLITICAL INSTITUTIONAL TRANSFER IN AFRICA." AFR CONSTN CULTURE ELITES ECO/UNDEV KIN PROB/SOLV ADMIN ORD/FREE PWR...POLICY 20. PAGE 135 H2695
FEDERAL NAT/G NAT/LISM COLONIAL

B67
ARIKPO O.,THE DEVELOPMENT OF MODERN NIGERIA. AFR NIGERIA SOCIETY ECO/UNDEV KIN ADMIN FEDERAL NAT/LISM ORD/FREE WEALTH...POLICY GEOG BIBLIOG 19/20. PAGE 8 H0163
NAT/G CULTURE CONSTN COLONIAL

L67
BERNSTEIN T.P.,"LEADERSHIP AND MASS MOBILIZATION IN THE SOVIET AND CHINESE COLLECTIVISATION CAMPAIGNS OF 1929-30, 1955-56: COMPARISON." CHINA/COM USSR WORKER CONTROL COERCE PRODUC ATTIT...NAT/COMP 20. PAGE 16 H0317
FEDERAL PLAN AGRI NAT/G

S67
BRADLEY A.W.,"CONSTITUTION-MAKING IN UGANDA." UGANDA LAW CHIEF DELIB/GP LEGIS ADMIN EXEC PARL/PROC RACE/REL ORD/FREE...GOV/COMP 20. PAGE 20 H0397
NAT/G CREATE CONSTN FEDERAL

S67
HANSON A.H.,"INDIA AFTER THE ELECTIONS." INDIA ECO/UNDEV LEGIS TEC/DEV FOR/AID GP/REL FEDERAL ATTIT 20. PAGE 66 H1321
NAT/G POL/PAR REGION CENTRAL

S67
HOFMANN W.,"THE PUBLIC INTEREST PRESSURE GROUP: THE CASE OF THE DEUTSCHE STADTETAG." GERMANY GERMANY/W CONSTN STRUCT NAT/G CENTRAL FEDERAL PWR...TIME/SEQ 20. PAGE 72 H1447
LOC/G VOL/ASSN LOBBY ADMIN

S67
KASFIR N.,"THE UGANDA CONSTITUENT ASSEMBLY DEBATE." UGANDA REPRESENT FEDERAL ORD/FREE POPULISM...POLICY DECISION 20. PAGE 83 H1665 CONSTN CONFER LAW NAT/G

S67
MAYANJA A.,"THE GOVERNMENT'S PROPOSALS ON THE NEW CONSTITUTION." AFR UGANDA LAW CHIEF LEGIS ADJUD REPRESENT FEDERAL PWR 20. PAGE 105 H2105 CONSTN CONFER ORD/FREE NAT/G

S67
SPINELLI A.,"EUROPEAN UNION IN THE RESISTANCE." NAT/G BAL/PWR DIPLOM CONFER REGION TOTALISM ORD/FREE POLICY. PAGE 147 H2948 NAT/LISM FEDERAL EUR+WWI INT/ORG

S68
BURGESS J.W.,"VON HOLST'S PUBLIC LAW OF THE UNITED STATES" USA-45 LAW GOV/REL...GOV/COMP IDEA/COMP 19. PAGE 24 H0480 CONSTN FEDERAL NAT/G JURID

S68
LUKASZEWSKI J.,"WESTERN INTEGRATION AND THE PEOPLE'S DEMOCRACIES." USSR ELITES ECO/DEV NAT/G VOL/ASSN INT/TRADE AGREE REV FEDERAL WEALTH SOCISM ...NAT/COMP SOC/INTEG 20 EEC. PAGE 99 H1977 DIPLOM INT/ORG COM REGION

B85
BLISS P.,OF SOVEREIGNTY. NAT/G PROVS GOV/REL PRIVIL ORD/FREE PWR CONSERVE...CONCPT 19. PAGE 18 H0356 CONSTN SOVEREIGN FEDERAL

FEDERALIST....FEDERALIST PARTY (ALL NATIONS)

FEDSCI/TEC....FEDERAL COUNCIL FOR SCIENCE AND TECHNOLOGY

FEEDBACK....FEEDBACK PHENOMENA

B44
KRIS E.,GERMAN RADIO PROPAGANDA: REPORT ON HOME BROADCASTS DURING THE WAR. EUR+WWI GERMANY CULTURE CONSULT PROB/SOLV FEEDBACK TASK INGP/REL DRIVE PWR FASCISM...CON/ANAL METH/COMP 20. PAGE 89 H1768 EDU/PROP DOMIN ACT/RES ATTIT

B53
MEAD M.,CULTURAL PATTERNS AND TECHNICAL CHANGE. BURMA GREECE NIGERIA ECO/UNDEV AGRI INDUS SCHOOL SECT CREATE FEEDBACK HABITAT...PSY METH/COMP BIBLIOG 20 UN. PAGE 108 H2152 HEALTH TEC/DEV CULTURE ADJUST

B58
STEINBERG C.S.,THE MASS COMMUNICATORS: PUBLIC RELATIONS, PUBLIC OPINION, AND MASS MEDIA. CULTURE CONSULT ACT/RES FEEDBACK DISPL WEALTH 20. PAGE 149 H2975 EDU/PROP ATTIT COM/IND PERCEPT

B59
BARRON R.,PARTIES AND POLITICS IN MODERN FRANCE. FRANCE LOC/G DELIB/GP LEGIS TOP/EX EDU/PROP LEGIT TV FEEDBACK 20. PAGE 12 H0230 POL/PAR ALL/IDEOS CHOOSE PARTIC

B61
DOOB L.W.,COMMUNICATION IN AFRICA: A SEARCH FOR BOUNDARIES. CULTURE SOCIETY EDU/PROP WRITING INGP/REL DRIVE ORD/FREE...ART/METH SOC LING BIBLIOG 20. PAGE 42 H0837 AFR FEEDBACK PERCEPT PERS/REL

B65
EASTON D.,A SYSTEM ANALYSIS OF POLITICAL LIFE. UNIV STRUCT NAT/G FEEDBACK PARTIC PERS/REL EFFICIENCY ...TREND CHARTS METH/COMP 20. PAGE 44 H0881 SIMUL POLICY GEN/METH

B65
ROWAT D.C.,THE OMBUDSMAN: CITIZEN'S DEFENDER. DENMARK FINLAND NEW/ZEALND NORWAY SWEDEN CONSULT PROB/SOLV FEEDBACK PARTIC GP/REL...SOC CONCPT NEW/IDEA METH/COMP ANTHOL BIBLIOG 20. PAGE 135 H2701 INSPECT CONSTN NAT/G ADMIN

S65
KINDLEBERGER C.P.,"MASS MIGRATION, THEN AND NOW." LAW ECO/DEV ECO/UNDEV INDUS LABOR INT/TRADE FEEDBACK REGION RIGID/FLEX...SOC NAT/COMP EEC. PAGE 86 H1714 EUR+WWI USA-45 WORKER IDEA/COMP

FEFFERO G. H0980

FEIBLEMAN J. H0981

FEINE H.E. H0982

FEIS H. H0983

FEIT E. H0984

FELD W. H0985

FELDMAN A.S. H2250

FEMALE/SEX....FEMALE SEX

B37
TINGSTEN H.,POLITICAL BEHAVIOR. EUR+WWI STRATA NAT/G POL/PAR ACT/RES AGE...TREND CHARTS 20 FEMALE/SEX. PAGE 155 H3100 CHOOSE ATTIT PARTIC

B40
ZWEIG F.,THE WORKER IN AN AFFLUENT SOCIETY: FAMILY LIFE AND INDUSTRY. UK STRATA LG/CO ECO/TAC LEISURE INGP/REL HAPPINESS HEALTH...PSY SOC/WK INT CHARTS WORSHIP 20 FEMALE/SEX. PAGE 173 H3465 MARRIAGE ATTIT FINAN CULTURE

B55
DUVERGER M.,THE POLITICAL ROLE OF WOMEN. FRANCE GERMANY/W NORWAY YUGOSLAVIA STRATA LOBBY AGE ATTIT ROLE...STAT SAMP CHARTS METH/COMP NAT/COMP HYPO/EXP FEMALE/SEX. PAGE 44 H0875 SEX LEAD PARTIC CHOOSE

S67
NEALE R.S.,"WORKING CLASS WOMEN AND WOMEN'S SUFFRAGE." UK LAW CONSTN LABOR NAT/G DELIB/GP LEGIS WORKER PAY PARTIC CHOOSE 19 FEMALE/SEX. PAGE 116 H2326 STRATA SEX SUFF DISCRIM

FEPC....FAIR EMPLOYMENT PRACTICES COMMISSION

FERNEUIL T. H0986

FERRERO G. H0987

FESLER J.W. H0988

FEUDALISM....FEUDALISM

FHA....U.S. FEDERAL HOUSING ADMINISTRATION

FICHTE J.G. H0989

FICHTE/JG....JOHANN GOTTLIEB FICHTE

FICTIONS....SEE MYTH

FIELD G.C. H0990

FIELD G.L. H0991

FIELD H. H0992

FIELD M.G. H0993

FIELD/S....STEVEN FIELD

FIELDHOUSE D.K. H0994

FIFIELD R.H. H0995,H0996

FIGANIERE J.C. H0997

FIGGIS J.N. H0998

FIJI

B61
WEST F.J.,POLITICAL ADVANCEMENT IN THE SOUTH PACIFIC. CONSTN CULTURE POL/PAR LEGIS DOMIN ADMIN CHOOSE SOVEREIGN VAL/FREE 20 FIJI TAHITI SAMOA. PAGE 167 H3335 S/ASIA LOC/G COLONIAL

FIKS M. H0999

FILIPINIANA BOOK GUILD H1000

FILLMORE/M....PRESIDENT MILLARD FILLMORE

FILM....FILM AND CINEMA

B50
IRION F.C.,PUBLIC OPINION AND PROPAGANDA. STRUCT COM/IND FAM SECT COERCE 20 FILM. PAGE 78 H1568 EDU/PROP ATTIT NAT/G PRESS

B64
UNESCO,WORLD COMMUNICATIONS: PRESS, RADIO, TELEVISION, FILM (4TH ED.). WOR+45 DIPLOM TV PEACE ...NAT/COMP SOC/INTEG 20 FILM. PAGE 158 H3163 COM/IND EDU/PROP PRESS TEC/DEV

FINAN....FINANCIAL SERVICE, BANKS, INSURANCE SYSTEMS, SECURITIES, EXCHANGES

N
ACAD RUMANIAN SCI DOC CTR,RUMANIAN SCIENTIFIC ABSTRACTS: SOCIAL SCIENCES. ROMANIA FINAN HABITAT ...ART/METH GEOG HUM JURID PSY 20. PAGE 3 H0059 BIBLIOG/A CULTURE LING LAW

N
CANADIAN GOVERNMENT PUBLICATIONS (1955-). CANADA AGRI FINAN LABOR FORCES INT/TRADE HEALTH...JURID 20 PARLIAMENT. PAGE 1 H0003 BIBLIOG/A NAT/G DIPLOM INT/ORG

N
THE STATESMAN'S YEARBOOK; STATISTICAL AND HISTORICAL ANNUAL OF THE STATES OF THE WORLD. NAT/COMP GOV/COMP

WOR+45 WOR-45 COM/IND FINAN INDUS SECT FORCES STAT
TEC/DEV EDU/PROP...GEOG BIBLIOG 19/20. PAGE 1 H0023 CONSTN

N
THE MIDDLE EAST AND NORTH AFRICA. AFR ISLAM CULTURE INDEX
ECO/UNDEV AGRI NAT/G TEC/DEV FOR/AID INT/TRADE INDUS
EDU/PROP...CHARTS 20. PAGE 2 H0026 FINAN
STAT

N
THE MIDDLE EAST. CULTURE...BIOG BIBLIOG. PAGE 2 ISLAM
H0028 INDUS
FINAN

N
EUROPA PUBLICATIONS LIMITED,THE EUROPA YEAR BOOK. BIBLIOG
CONSTN FINAN INDUS POL/PAR DIPLOM TV CT/SYS...STAT NAT/G
BIOG CHARTS WORSHIP 20. PAGE 47 H0949 PRESS
INT/ORG

N
INTERNATIONAL CENTRE AFRICAN,BULLETIN OF BIBLIOG/A
INFORMATION ON THESES AND STUDIES IN PROGRESS OR ACT/RES
PROPOSED. LAW CULTURE FINAN INDUS LABOR TEC/DEV ACADEM
EDU/PROP...GEOG SOC NAT/COMP 20. PAGE 78 H1554 INTELL

N
KYRIAK T.E.,CHINA: A BIBLIOGRAPHY. ASIA CHINA/COM BIBLIOG/A
AGRI FINAN INDUS NAT/G INT/TRADE PRESS...SOC 20. MARXISM
PAGE 90 H1789 TOP/EX
POL/PAR

B03
FORTESCUE G.K.,SUBJECT INDEX OF THE MODERN WORKS BIBLIOG
ADDED TO THE LIBRARY OF THE BRITISH MUSEUM IN THE INDEX
YEARS 1881-1900 (3 VOLS.). UK LAW CONSTN FINAN WRITING
NAT/G FORCES INT/TRADE COLONIAL 19. PAGE 52 H1041

B04
GRIFFIN A.P.C.,LIST OF REFERENCES ON BUDGETS OF BIBLIOG/A
FOREIGN COUNTRIES (PAMPHLET). MOD/EUR FINAN MARKET BUDGET
TAX...MGT STAT 19/20. PAGE 61 H1218 NAT/G

B08
THE GOVERNMENT OF SOUTH AFRICA (VOL. II). SOUTH/AFR CONSTN
STRATA EXTR/IND EX/STRUC TOP/EX BUDGET ADJUD ADMIN FINAN
CT/SYS PRODUC...CORREL CENSUS 19 RAILROAD LEGIS
CIVIL/SERV POSTAL/SYS. PAGE 2 H0030 NAT/G

B12
POLLOCK F.,THE GENIUS OF THE COMMON LAW. CHRIST-17C LAW
UK FINAN CHIEF ACT/RES ADMIN GP/REL ATTIT SOCISM CULTURE
...ANARCH JURID. PAGE 127 H2537 CREATE

B17
VEBLEN T.B.,AN INQUIRY INTO THE NATURE OF PEACE AND PEACE
THE TERMS OF ITS PERPETUATION. UNIV STRATA FINAN DIPLOM
EDU/PROP PRICE COST DISCRIM NAT/LISM MORAL ORD/FREE WAR
PACIFIST 20 WORLDUNITY. PAGE 162 H3237 NAT/G

N19
ADMINISTRATIVE STAFF COLLEGE,THE ACCOUNTABILITY OF PARL/PROC
GOVERNMENT DEPARTMENTS (PAMPHLET) (REV. ED.). UK ELITES
CONSTN FINAN NAT/G CONSULT ADMIN INGP/REL CONSEN SANCTION
PRIVIL 20 PARLIAMENT. PAGE 3 H0070 PROB/SOLV

N19
ANDERSON J.,THE ORGANIZATION OF ECONOMIC STUDIES IN ECO/TAC
RELATION TO THE PROBLEMS OF GOVERNMENT (PAMPHLET). ACT/RES
UK FINAN INDUS DELIB/GP PLAN PROB/SOLV ADMIN 20. NAT/G
PAGE 6 H0128 CENTRAL

N19
HABERLER G.,A SURVEY OF INTERNATIONAL TRADE THEORY INT/TRADE
(PAMPHLET). FINAN NAT/G COST INCOME 18/20 MONEY BAL/PAY
HUME/D MARSHALL/A. PAGE 63 H1267 GEN/LAWS
POLICY

N19
STEUBER F.A.,THE CONTRIBUTION OF SWITZERLAND TO THE FOR/AID
ECONOMIC AND SOCIAL DEVELOPMENT OF LOW-INCOME ECO/UNDEV
COUNTRIES (PAMPHLET). SWITZERLND FINAN NAT/G PLAN
VOL/ASSN INT/TRADE DRIVE...CHARTS 20. PAGE 149 DIPLOM
H2982

N19
WILSON T.,FINANCIAL ASSISTANCE WITH REGIONAL FINAN
DEVELOPMENT (PAMPHLET). CANADA INDUS NAT/G PLAN TAX ECO/TAC
CONTROL COST EFFICIENCY...POLICY CHARTS 20. REGION
PAGE 169 H3382 GOV/REL

B22
URE P.N.,THE ORIGIN OF TYRANNY. MEDIT-7 FINAN INDUS AUTHORIT
CHIEF FORCES ECO/TAC WEALTH. PAGE 159 H3174 PWR
NAT/G
MARKET

B26
FORTESCUE J.,THE GOVERNANCE OF ENGLAND (1471-76). CONSERVE
UK LAW FINAN SECT LEGIS PROB/SOLV TAX DOMIN ADMIN CONSTN
GP/REL COST ORD/FREE PWR 14/15. PAGE 52 H1042 CHIEF
NAT/G

B26
MCPHEE A.,THE ECONOMIC REVOLUTION IN BRITISH WEST ECO/UNDEV
AFRICA. AFR UK CULTURE DIST/IND FINAN INDUS PLAN INT/TRADE
GP/REL RACE/REL 20 AFRICA/W. PAGE 107 H2148 COLONIAL
GEOG

B27
SMITH E.W.,THE GOLDEN STOOL: SOME ASPECTS OF THE COLONIAL
CONFLICT OF CULTURES IN AFRICA. AFR FINAN INDUS CULTURE
SECT INT/TRADE COERCE CHOOSE RACE/REL ATTIT...GEOG GP/REL
LING 20 NEGRO. PAGE 145 H2907 EDU/PROP

B27
WEBER M.,GENERAL ECONOMIC HISTORY. CHRIST-17C ECO/DEV
MOD/EUR STRUCT AGRI EXTR/IND FINAN INDUS MARKET FAM CAP/ISM
MUNIC NAT/G PROF/ORG SECT ECO/TAC 8/20. PAGE 166
H3319

B27
WILLOUGHBY W.F.,PRINCIPLES OF PUBLIC ADMINISTRATION NAT/G
WITH SPECIAL REFERENCE TO THE NATIONAL AND STATE EX/STRUC
GOVERNMENTS OF THE UNITED STATES. FINAN PROVS CHIEF OP/RES
CONSULT LEGIS CREATE BUDGET EXEC ROUTINE GOV/REL ADMIN
CENTRAL...MGT 20 BUR/BUDGET CONGRESS PRESIDENT.
PAGE 169 H3373

B29
LEITZ F.,DIE PUBLIZITAT DER AKTIENGESELLSCHAFT. LG/CO
BELGIUM FRANCE GERMANY UK FINAN PRESS GP/REL PROFIT JURID
KNOWL 20. PAGE 94 H1872 ECO/TAC
NAT/COMP

B29
ROBERTS S.H.,HISTORY OF FRENCH COLONIAL POLICY. AFR INT/ORG
ASIA L/A+17C S/ASIA CULTURE ECO/DEV ECO/UNDEV FINAN ACT/RES
NAT/G PLAN ECO/TAC DOMIN ROUTINE SOVEREIGN...OBS FRANCE
HIST/WRIT TREND CHARTS VAL/FREE 19/20. PAGE 132 COLONIAL
H2642

B33
FERRERO G.,PEACE AND WAR (TRANS. BY BERTHA WAR
PRITCHARD). CULTURE FINAN SECT ATTIT SUPEGO MORAL PEACE
ORD/FREE CONSERVE POPULISM SOCISM POLICY. PAGE 49 DIPLOM
H0987 PROB/SOLV

B33
MOSS W.,POLITICAL PARTIES IN THE IRISH FREE STATE. POL/PAR
IRELAND UK LAW FINAN LABOR DELIB/GP TOP/EX TARIFFS NAT/G
EDU/PROP...CHARTS GP/COMP 20. PAGE 113 H2269 CHOOSE
POLICY

B35
DOUGLASS H.P.,THE PROTESTANT CHURCH AS A SOCIAL SECT
INSTITUTION. CULTURE FINAN NEIGH PROF/ORG OP/RES PARTIC
ADMIN...POLICY SOC/WK STAT BIBLIOG. PAGE 42 H0843 INGP/REL
GP/REL

B37
HAMILTON W.H.,THE POWER TO GOVERN. ECO/DEV FINAN LING
INDUS ECO/TAC INT/TRADE TARIFFS TAX CONTROL CT/SYS CONSTN
WAR COST PWR 18/20 SUPREME/CT. PAGE 65 H1303 NAT/G
POLICY

B37
VON HAYEK F.A.,MONETARY NATIONALISM AND ECO/TAC
INTERNATIONAL STABILITY. WOR-45 ECO/DEV NAT/G FINAN
PROB/SOLV INT/TRADE...POLICY CONCPT METH/COMP DIPLOM
NAT/COMP 20. PAGE 163 H3271 NAT/LISM

B40
CONOVER H.F.,JAPAN-ECONOMIC DEVELOPMENT AND FOREIGN BIBLIOG
POLICY, A SELECTED LIST OF REFERENCES (PAMPHLET). ASIA
CULTURE FINAN INDUS NAT/G FORCES INT/TRADE WAR ECO/DEV
...SOC TREND 20 CHINJAP. PAGE 32 H0640 DIPLOM

B40
MCHENRY D.E.,HIS MAJESTY'S OPPOSITION: STRUCTURE POL/PAR
AND PROBLEMS OF THE BRITISH LABOUR PARTY 1931-1938. MGT
UK FINAN LABOR LOC/G DELIB/GP LEGIS EDU/PROP LEAD NAT/G
PARTIC CHOOSE GP/REL SOCISM...TREND 20 LABOR/PAR. POLICY
PAGE 107 H2130

B40
ZWEIG F.,THE WORKER IN AN AFFLUENT SOCIETY: FAMILY MARRIAGE
LIFE AND INDUSTRY. UK STRATA LG/CO ECO/TAC LEISURE ATTIT
INGP/REL HAPPINESS HEALTH...PSY SOC/WK INT CHARTS FINAN
WORSHIP 20 FEMALE/SEX. PAGE 173 H3465 CULTURE

C40
FAHS C.B.,"GOVERNMENT IN JAPAN." FINAN FORCES LEGIS ASIA
TOP/EX BUDGET INT/TRADE EDU/PROP SOVEREIGN DIPLOM
...CON/ANAL BIBLIOG/A 20 CHINJAP. PAGE 48 H0962 NAT/G
ADMIN

B41
STATIST REICHSAMTE,BIBLIOGRAPHIE DER STAATS- UND BIBLIOG
WIRSCHAFTSWISSENSCHAFTEN. EUR+WWI GERMANY FINAN ECO/DEV
ADMIN. PAGE 149 H2974 NAT/G
POLICY

B43
BROWN A.D.,GREECE: SELECTED LIST OF REFERENCES. BIBLIOG/A
GREECE ECO/UNDEV AGRI FINAN INDUS LABOR SECT WAR
TEC/DEV INT/TRADE LEAD...SOC 20. PAGE 22 H0438 DIPLOM
NAT/G

B46
ALLEN J.S.,WORLD MONOPOLY AND PEACE. GERMANY UK CAP/ISM
USSR FINAN INDUS LG/CO DOMIN CONTROL PEACE PWR DIPLOM
WEALTH SOCISM...NAT/COMP 20 MONOPOLY. PAGE 5 H0105 WAR
COLONIAL

S46
SILBERNER E.,"THE PROBLEM OF WAR IN NINETEENTH ATTIT
CENTURY ECONOMIC THOUGHT." EUR+WWI MOD/EUR UNIV LAW ECO/TAC
ECO/DEV ECO/UNDEV FINAN INDUS MARKET INT/ORG NAT/G WAR
CONSULT FORCES...CONCPT GEN/LAWS GEN/METH 19.
PAGE 144 H2875

B47
DE NOIA J.,GUIDE TO OFFICIAL PUBLICATIONS OF OTHER BIBLIOG/A
AMERICAN REPUBLICS: ECUADOR (VOL. IX). ECUADOR LAW CONSTN
FINAN LEGIS BUDGET CT/SYS 19/20. PAGE 38 H0763 NAT/G
EDU/PROP

B47
ENKE S.,INTERNATIONAL ECONOMICS. UK USA+45 USSR INT/ORG BAL/PWR BARGAIN CAP/ISM BAL/PAY...NAT/COMP 20 TREATY. PAGE 46 H0927
INT/TRADE FINAN TARIFFS ECO/TAC

B47
MARX F.M.,THE PRESIDENT AND HIS STAFF SERVICES PUBLIC ADMINISTRATION SERVICES NUMBER 98 (PAMPHLET). FINAN ADMIN CT/SYS REPRESENT PWR 20 PRESIDENT. PAGE 104 H2075
CONSTN CHIEF NAT/G EX/STRUC

B47
NEUBURGER O.,GUIDE TO OFFICIAL PUBLICATIONS OF THE OTHER AMERICAN REPUBLICS: HAITI (VOL. XII). HAITI LAW FINAN LEGIS PRESS...JURID 20. PAGE 117 H2334
BIBLIOG/A CONSTN NAT/G EDU/PROP

B48
HARRIS G.M.,COMPARATIVE LOCAL GOVERNMENT. FINAN CHOOSE ALL/VALS. PAGE 67 H1339
PARTIC GOV/REL LOC/G GOV/COMP

B48
MINISTERE FINANCES ET ECO,BULLETIN BIBLIOGRAPHIQUE. AFR EUR+WWI FRANCE CULTURE STRUCT FINAN NAT/G ACT/RES INT/TRADE ADMIN REGION PRODUC STAT. PAGE 111 H2224
BIBLIOG/A ECO/UNDEV TEC/DEV COLONIAL

B48
NEUBURGER O.,GUIDE TO OFFICIAL PUBLICATIONS OF THE OTHER AMERICAN REPUBLICS: VENEZUELA (VOL. XIX). VENEZUELA FINAN LEGIS PLAN BUDGET DIPLOM CT/SYS PARL/PROC 19/20. PAGE 117 H2335
BIBLIOG/A NAT/G CONSTN LAW

B51
MARX K.,THE EIGHTEENTH BRUMAIRE OF LOUIS BONAPARTE (1852). FRANCE STRATA FINAN INDUS LABOR CHIEF FORCES WORKER CAP/ISM ECO/TAC PARL/PROC ORD/FREE ...MARXIST 19. PAGE 104 H2080
REV MARXISM ELITES NAT/G

C52
HUME D.,"OF TAXES" IN D. HUME, POLITICAL DISCOURSES (1752)" UK NAT/G COST INCOME LAISSEZ...GEN/LAWS 18. PAGE 75 H1493
TAX FINAN WEALTH POLICY

B53
FLORENCE P.S.,THE LOGIC OF BRITISH AND AMERICAN INDUSTRY; A REALISTIC ANALYSIS OF ECONOMIC STRUCTURE AND GOVERNMENT. UK USA+45 USA-45 FINAN LABOR CAP/ISM INGP/REL EFFICIENCY...MGT CONCPT STAT CHARTS METH 20. PAGE 51 H1028
INDUS ECO/DEV NAT/G NAT/COMP

B53
STOUT H.M.,BRITISH GOVERNMENT. UK FINAN LOC/G POL/PAR DELIB/GP DIPLOM ADMIN COLONIAL CHOOSE ORD/FREE...JURID BIBLIOG 20 COMMONWLTH. PAGE 150 H2990
NAT/G PARL/PROC CONSTN NEW/LIB

B54
BINANI G.D.,INDIA AT A GLANCE (REV. ED.). INDIA COM/IND FINAN INDUS LABOR PROVS SCHOOL PLAN DIPLOM INT/TRADE ADMIN...JURID 20. PAGE 17 H0335
INDEX CON/ANAL NAT/G ECO/UNDEV

B54
CAMPANELLA T.,A DISCOURSE TOUCHING THE SPANISH MONARCHY... (1640). SPAIN UNIV SEA STRATA FINAN SECT FORCES SUPEGO LOVE ORD/FREE...CONCPT 17. PAGE 26 H0514
CONSERVE CHIEF NAT/G DIPLOM

B54
GATZKE H.W.,STRESEMANN AND THE REARMAMENT OF GERMANY. EUR+WWI GERMANY USSR FINAN NAT/G ECO/TAC ATTIT...BIOG METH 20 STRESEMN/G. PAGE 55 H1105
FORCES INDUS PWR

B55
FLECHTHEIM O.K.,DIE DEUTSCHEN PARTEIEN SEIT 1945. GERMANY/W CONSTN STRUCT FINAN ATTIT 20. PAGE 51 H1022
POL/PAR NAT/G GP/COMP

B55
FOGARTY M.P.,ECONOMIC CONTROL. FUT UK ECO/DEV FINAN CONSULT INT/TRADE...CHARTS BIBLIOG/A 20. PAGE 52 H1033
ECO/TAC NAT/G CONTROL PROB/SOLV

B55
JONES T.B.,A BIBLIOGRAPHY ON SOUTH AMERICAN ECONOMIC AFFAIRS: ARTICLES IN NINETEENTH CENTURY PERIODICALS (PAMPHLET). AGRI COM/IND DIST/IND EXTR/IND FINAN INDUS LABOR NAT/G 19. PAGE 82 H1634
BIBLIOG ECO/UNDEV L/A+17C TEC/DEV

B55
SERRANO MOSCOSO E.,A STATEMENT OF THE LAWS OF ECUADOR IN MATTERS AFFECTING BUSINESS (2ND ED.). ECUADOR INDUS LABOR LG/CO NAT/G LEGIS TAX CONTROL MARRIAGE 20. PAGE 141 H2830
FINAN ECO/UNDEV LAW CONSTN

B55
UN ECONOMIC COMN ASIA & FAR E,ECONOMIC SURVEY OF ASIA AND THE FAR EAST, 1954. AFGHANISTN CEYLON INDIA PHILIPPINE S/ASIA ECO/DEV FINAN INDUS INT/TRADE PRODUC WEALTH...STAT CHARTS 20 CHINJAP. PAGE 158 H3158
ECO/UNDEV PRICE NAT/COMP ASIA

B55
WOYTINSKY W.S.,WORLD COMMERCE AND GOVERNMENTS: TRENDS AND OUTLOOK. WOR+45 FINAN POL/PAR DIPLOM ECO/TAC FOR/AID DOMIN WAR CHOOSE...CHARTS BIBLIOG 20 LEAGUE/NAT UN ILO. PAGE 171 H3413
INT/TRADE DIST/IND NAT/COMP NAT/G

B57
BARAN P.A.,THE POLITICAL ECONOMY OF GROWTH. MOD/EUR USA+45 USA-45 TEC/DEV TAX SOCISM...MGT CONCPT GOV/COMP. PAGE 11 H0213
CAP/ISM CONTROL ECO/UNDEV FINAN

B57
HAMMOND B.,BANKS AND POLITICS IN AMERICA FROM THE REVOLUTION TO THE CIVIL WAR. CANADA USA-45 STRATA ...NAT/COMP 18/19. PAGE 65 H1306
FINAN PWR POL/PAR NAT/G

B57
SHEIKH N.A.,SOME ASPECTS OF THE CONSTITUTION AND THE ECONOMICS OF ISLAM. PAKISTAN CULTURE AGRI FINAN LABOR NAT/G SECT INT/TRADE 20 MUSLIM. PAGE 143 H2855
ISLAM POLICY ECO/TAC CONSTN

B58
AVRAMOVIC D.,POSTWAR GROWTH IN INTERNATIONAL INDEBTEDNESS. WOR+45 AGRI INDUS CAP/ISM PRICE INCOME...NAT/COMP 20 GOLD/STAND SILVER. PAGE 9 H0184
INT/TRADE FINAN COST BAL/PAY

B58
INTERNATIONAL ECONOMIC ASSN,ECONOMICS OF INTERNATIONAL MIGRATION. WOR+45 WOR-45 ECO/UNDEV FINAN NAT/G REGION...NAT/COMP METH 20. PAGE 78 H1556
CENSUS GEOG DIPLOM ECO/TAC

B58
JACOBSSON P.,SOME MONETARY PROBLEMS, INTERNATIONAL AND NATIONAL. WOR+45 WOR-45 ECO/DEV FORCES WORKER PROB/SOLV DIPLOM INT/TRADE...ANTHOL 20. PAGE 79 H1580
FINAN PLAN ECO/TAC NAT/COMP

B58
MCIVOR R.C.,CANADIAN MONETARY, BANKING, AND FISCAL DEVELOPMENT. CANADA INDUS LG/CO NAT/G SML/CO CONTROL WAR...GEN/LAWS BIBLIOG 17/20. PAGE 107 H2137
ECO/TAC FINAN ECO/DEV WEALTH

B58
SHAW S.J.,THE FINANCIAL AND ADMINISTRATIVE ORGANIZATION AND DEVELOPMENT OF OTTOMAN EGYPT 1517-1798. UAR LOC/G FORCES BUDGET INT/TRADE TAX EATING INCOME WEALTH...CHARTS BIBLIOG 16/18 OTTOMAN NAPOLEON/B. PAGE 143 H2853
FINAN ADMIN GOV/REL CULTURE

S58
LOCKWOOD W.W.,"THE SOCIALISTIC SOCIETY: INDIA AND JAPAN." INDIA ECO/DEV ECO/UNDEV INDUS NAT/G CONTROL LEAD PRODUC WEALTH 20 CHINJAP. PAGE 98 H1948
ECO/TAC NAT/COMP FINAN SOCISM

C58
BLANCHARD W.,"THAILAND." THAILAND CULTURE AGRI FINAN INDUS FAM LABOR INT/TRADE ATTIT...GEOG HEAL SOC BIBLIOG 20. PAGE 18 H0354
NAT/G DIPLOM ECO/UNDEV S/ASIA

B59
CONOVER H.F.,NIGERIAN OFFICIAL PUBLICATIONS, 1869-1959: A GUIDE. NIGER CONSTN FINAN ACADEM SCHOOL FORCES PRESS ADMIN COLONIAL...HIST/WRIT 19/20. PAGE 33 H0650
BIBLIOG NAT/G CON/ANAL

B59
CUCCORESE H.J.,HISTORIA DE LA CONVERSION DEL PAPEL MONEDA EN BUENOS AIRES, 1861-1867. LAW LOC/G NAT/G ATTIT...POLICY BIBLIOG 19 ARGEN BUENOS/AIR GOLD/STAND. PAGE 36 H0717
FINAN PLAN LEGIS

B59
EPSTEIN F.T.,EAST GERMANY: A SELECTED BIBLIOGRAPHY (PAMPHLET). COM GERMANY/E LAW AGRI FINAN INDUS LABOR POL/PAR EDU/PROP ADMIN AGE/Y 20. PAGE 47 H0932
BIBLIOG/A INTELL MARXISM NAT/G

B59
ETSCHMANN R.,DIE WAHRUNGS- UND DEVISENPOLITIK DES OSTBLOCKS UND IHRE AUSWIRKUNGEN AUF DIE WIRTSCHAFTSBEZIEHUNGEN ZWISCHEN OST U WEST. BULGARIA CZECHOSLVK HUNGARY POLAND USSR MARKET NAT/G PLAN DIPLOM...NAT/COMP 20. PAGE 47 H0943
ECO/TAC FINAN POLICY INT/TRADE

B59
GUDIN E.,INFLACAO (2ND ED.). INDUS NAT/G PLAN ECO/TAC CONTROL COST 20. PAGE 62 H1243
ECO/UNDEV INT/TRADE BAL/PAY FINAN

B60
ALBI F.,TRATADO DE LOS MODOS DE GESTION DE LAS CORPORACIONES LOCALES. SPAIN FINAN NAT/G BUDGET CONTROL EXEC ROUTINE GOV/REL ORD/FREE SOVEREIGN ...MGT 20. PAGE 5 H0092
LOC/G LAW ADMIN MUNIC

B60
BAYER H.,WIRTSCHAFTSPROGNOSE UND WIRTSCHAFTSGESTALTUNG. GERMANY NETHERLAND MARKET PLAN CAP/ISM DEBATE...NAT/COMP 20. PAGE 12 H0242
ECO/DEV ECO/UNDEV FINAN POLICY

B60
BOMBACH G.,STABILE PREISE IN WACHSENDER WIRTSCHAFT: DAS INFLATIONSPROBLEM. BARGAIN CAP/ISM PRICE COST ...NAT/COMP 20 GOLD/STAND. PAGE 19 H0371
ECO/UNDEV PLAN FINAN ECO/TAC

B60
CONOVER H.F.,OFFICIAL PUBLICATIONS OF SOMALILAND, 1941-1959: A GUIDE. SOMALIA AGRI FINAN INT/ORG SCHOOL INT/TRADE PRESS CONFER COLONIAL PARL/PROC 20
BIBLIOG NAT/G CON/ANAL

CONGRESS. PAGE 33 H0652

B60
COUGHLIN R.,DOUBLE IDENTITY: THE CHINESE AND MODERN THAILAND. CHINA/COM S/ASIA THAILAND ECO/UNDEV EXTR/IND FINAN INDUS KIN MUNIC NAT/G PROF/ORG SCHOOL SECT ATTIT DRIVE...CONCPT OBS 20. PAGE 34 H0676
ASIA FAM CULTURE

B60
EASTON S.C.,THE TWILIGHT OF EUROPEAN COLONIALISM. AFR S/ASIA CONSTN SOCIETY STRUCT ECO/UNDEV INDUS NAT/G FORCES ECO/TAC COLONIAL CT/SYS ATTIT KNOWL ORD/FREE PWR...SOCIALIST TIME/SEQ TREND CON/ANAL 20. PAGE 44 H0882
FINAN ADMIN

B60
KENEN P.B.,BRITISH MONETARY POLICY AND THE BALANCE OF PAYMENTS 1951-57. UK PLAN BUDGET ECO/TAC INT/TRADE PAY PRICE COST ATTIT 20. PAGE 84 H1687
BAL/PAY PROB/SOLV FINAN NAT/G

B60
NEALE A.D.,THE FLOW OF RESOURCES FROM RICH TO POOR. WOR+45 ECO/DEV ECO/UNDEV FINAN INDUS NAT/G PLAN EFFICIENCY WEALTH...POLICY NAT/COMP 20 RESOURCE/N. PAGE 116 H2325
FOR/AID DIPLOM METH/CNCPT

B60
PRASAD B.,THE ORIGINS OF PROVINCIAL AUTONOMY. INDIA UK FINAN LOC/G FORCES LEGIS CONTROL CT/SYS PWR ...JURID 19/20. PAGE 128 H2554
CENTRAL PROVS COLONIAL NAT/G

B60
ROBERTSON D.,THE CONTROL OF INDUSTRY. UK MARKET LABOR WORKER PRICE CONTROL GP/REL COST DEMAND ORD/FREE WEALTH NEW/LIB SOCISM 20. PAGE 132 H2646
INDUS FINAN NAT/G ECO/DEV

B60
STOLPER W.F.,GERMANY BETWEEN EAST AND WEST: THE ECONOMICS OF COMPETITIVE COEXISTENCE. FUT GERMANY/E GERMANY/W WOR+45 FINAN POL/PAR BUDGET ECO/TAC FOR/AID INT/TRADE...STAT CHARTS METH/COMP 20 COLD/WAR. PAGE 150 H2989
ECO/DEV DIPLOM GOV/COMP BAL/PWR

B60
THE ECONOMIST (LONDON),THE COMMONWEALTH AND EUROPE. EUR+WWI WOR+45 AGRI FINAN INCOME...STAT CENSUS CHARTS CMN/WLTH EEC. PAGE 153 H3067
INT/TRADE INDUS INT/ORG NAT/COMP

B60
WORLEY P.,ASIA TODAY (REV. ED.) (PAMPHLET). COM ECO/UNDEV AGRI FINAN INDUS POL/PAR FOR/AID ADMIN MARXISM 20. PAGE 170 H3411
BIBLIOG/A ASIA DIPLOM NAT/G

S60
"THE EMERGING COMMON MARKETS IN LATIN AMERICA." FUT L/A+17C STRATA DIST/IND INDUS LABOR NAT/G LEGIS ECO/TAC ADMIN RIGID/FLEX HEALTH...NEW/IDEA TIME/SEQ OAS 20. PAGE 2 H0038
FINAN ECO/UNDEV INT/TRADE

S60
FRANKEL S.H.,"ECONOMIC ASPECTS OF POLITICAL INDEPENDENCE IN AFRICA." AFR FUT SOCIETY ECO/UNDEV COM/IND FINAN LEGIS PLAN TEC/DEV CAP/ISM ECO/TAC INT/TRADE ADMIN ATTIT DRIVE RIGID/FLEX PWR WEALTH ...MGT NEW/IDEA MATH TIME/SEQ VAL/FREE 20. PAGE 53 H1052
NAT/G FOR/AID

B61
ESTEBAN J.C.,IMPERIALISMO Y DESARROLLO ECONOMICO. L/A+17C FINAN INDUS NAT/G ECO/TAC CONTROL ROLE. PAGE 47 H0941
ECO/UNDEV NAT/LISM DIPLOM BAL/PAY

B61
ESTEVEZ A.,ASPECTOS ECONOMICO-FINANCIEROS DE LA CAMPANA SANMARITANA. L/A+17C SPAIN FINAN COLONIAL LEAD ROLE ORD/FREE WEALTH 19 SOUTH/AMER SAN/MARTIN. PAGE 47 H0942
ECO/UNDEV REV BUDGET NAT/G

B61
GANGULI B.N.,ECONOMIC INTEGRATION. FINAN LABOR CAP/ISM DIPLOM WEALTH...NAT/COMP 20. PAGE 55 H1096
ECO/TAC METH/CNCPT EQUILIB ECO/UNDEV

B61
HALPERIN S.,THE POLITICAL WORLD OF AMERICAN ZIONISM. ISRAEL FINAN LABOR VOL/ASSN GIVE LOBBY REPRESENT GP/REL ATTIT POLICY. PAGE 64 H1293
CULTURE SECT EDU/PROP DELIB/GP

B61
HAUSER M.,DIE URSACHEN DER FRANZOSISCHEN INFLATION IN DEN JAHREN 1946-1952. FRANCE INDUS NAT/G BUDGET DIPLOM ECO/TAC FOR/AID COST MONEY 20 GOLD/STAND. PAGE 68 H1357
ECO/DEV FINAN PRICE

B61
INTL UNION LOCAL AUTHORITIES,METROPOLIS. WOR+45 DIST/IND FINAN GIVE EDU/PROP CRIME COST HEALTH WEALTH 20. PAGE 78 H1563
MUNIC GOV/COMP LOC/G BIBLIOG

B61
LAHAYE R.,LES ENTREPRISES PUBLIQUES AU MAROC. FRANCE MOROCCO LAW DIST/IND EXTR/IND FINAN CONSULT PLAN TEC/DEV ADMIN AGREE CONTROL OWN...POLICY 20. PAGE 90 H1796
NAT/G INDUS ECO/UNDEV ECO/TAC

B61
MARX K.,THE COMMUNIST MANIFESTO. IN (MENDEL A. ESSENTIAL WORKS OF MARXISM, NEW YORK: BANTAM. FUT MOD/EUR CULTURE ECO/DEV ECO/UNDEV AGRI FINAN INDUS MARKET PROC/MFG LABOR MUNIC POL/PAR CONSULT FORCES CREATE PLAN ADMIN ATTIT DRIVE RIGID/FLEX ORD/FREE PWR RESPECT MARX/KARL WORK. PAGE 104 H2081
COM NEW/IDEA CAP/ISM REV

B61
MIT CENTER INTERNATIONAL STU,OFFICIAL SERIAL PUBLICATIONS RELATING TO ECONOMIC DEVELOPMENT IN AFRICA SOUTH OF THE SAHARA. AFR SOCIETY AGRI FINAN INDUS LG/CO ADMIN 20. PAGE 111 H2228
BIBLIOG ECO/UNDEV ECO/TAC NAT/G

B61
NATIONAL BANK OF LIBYA,INFLATION IN LIBYA (PAMPHLET). LIBYA SOCIETY NAT/G PLAN INT/TRADE ...STAT CHARTS 20 GOLD/STAND. PAGE 116 H2318
ECO/TAC ECO/UNDEV FINAN BUDGET

B61
NOVE A.,THE SOVIET ECONOMY. USSR ECO/DEV FINAN NAT/G ECO/TAC PRICE ADMIN EFFICIENCY MARXISM ...TREND BIBLIOG 20. PAGE 119 H2378
PLAN PRODUC POLICY

B61
OECD,STATISTICS OF BALANCE OF PAYMENTS 1950-61. WOR+45 FINAN ECO/TAC INT/TRADE DEMAND WEALTH...STAT NAT/COMP 20 OEEC OECD. PAGE 120 H2396
BAL/PAY ECO/DEV INT/ORG CHARTS

B61
PANIKKAR K.M.,THE VOICE OF FREEDOM: SELECTED SPEECHES OF PANDIT MOTILAL NEHRU. INDIA UK CONSTN FINAN FORCES LEGIS DIPLOM TAX COLONIAL...POLICY MAJORIT ANTHOL 20 NEHRU/PM. PAGE 123 H2460
NAT/LISM ORD/FREE CHIEF NAT/G

B61
SAKAI R.K.,STUDIES ON ASIA, 1961. ASIA BURMA INDIA S/ASIA FINAN ECO/TAC NAT/LISM SOCISM...POLICY ANTHOL 19/20 CHINJAP. PAGE 137 H2734
ECO/UNDEV SECT

B61
SANTHANAM K.,DEMOCRATIC PLANNING. INDIA AGRI FINAN LEGIS DIPLOM PARL/PROC ORD/FREE 20. PAGE 138 H2753
PLAN NAT/G CONSTN POLICY

B61
STANLEY C.J.,LATE CH'ING FINANCE: HU KUANG-YUNG AS AN INNOVATOR. ASIA NAT/G FORCES BUDGET TAX WAR GOV/REL COST...POLICY BIOG CHARTS BIBLIOG 19. PAGE 148 H2969
FINAN ECO/TAC CIVMIL/REL ADMIN

B61
VEIT O.,GRUNDRISS DER WAHRUNGSPOLITIK. FRANCE GERMANY USSR DIPLOM INT/TRADE...NAT/COMP 19/20 GOLD/STAND SILVER. PAGE 162 H3239
FINAN POLICY ECO/TAC CAP/ISM

B62
FATOUROS A.A.,GOVERNMENT GUARANTEES TO FOREIGN INVESTORS. WOR+45 ECO/UNDEV INDUS WORKER ADJUD ...NAT/COMP BIBLIOG TREATY. PAGE 49 H0975
NAT/G FINAN INT/TRADE ECO/DEV

B62
FRIEDMANN W.,METHODS AND POLICIES OF PRINCIPAL DONOR COUNTRIES IN PUBLIC INTERNATIONAL DEVELOPMENT FINANCING: PRELIMINARY APPRAISAL. FRANCE GERMANY/W UK USA+45 USSR WOR+45 FINAN TEC/DEV CAP/ISM DIPLOM ECO/TAC ATTIT 20 EEC. PAGE 53 H1066
INT/ORG FOR/AID NAT/COMP ADMIN

B62
GROVE J.W.,GOVERNMENT AND INDUSTRY IN BRITAIN. UK FINAN LOC/G CONSULT DELIB/GP INT/TRADE ADMIN CONTROL...BIBLIOG 20. PAGE 62 H1237
ECO/TAC INDUS NAT/G GP/REL

B62
HUCKER C.O.,CHINA: A CRITICAL BIBLIOGRAPHY (PAMPHLET). ASIA STRUCT AGRI FINAN INDUS HABITAT MARXISM...EPIST HUM. PAGE 74 H1487
BIBLIOG/A CULTURE INTELL SOCIETY

B62
KARNJAHAPRAKORN C.,MUNICIPAL GOVERNMENT IN THAILAND AS AN INSTITUTION AND PROCESS OF SELF-GOVERNMENT. THAILAND CULTURE FINAN EX/STRUC LEGIS PLAN CONTROL GOV/REL EFFICIENCY ATTIT...POLICY 20. PAGE 83 H1662
LOC/G MUNIC ORD/FREE ADMIN

B62
MICHAELY M.,CONCENTRATION IN INTERNATIONAL TRADE. ECO/DEV ECO/UNDEV PRICE INCOME...CHARTS NAT/COMP 20. PAGE 110 H2197
INT/TRADE MARKET FINAN GEOG

B62
MITCHELL B.R.,ABSTRACT OF BRITISH HISTORICAL STATISTICS. UK FINAN NAT/G 12/20. PAGE 111 H2229
BIBLIOG STAT INDEX ECO/DEV

B62
MOUSSA P.,THE UNDERPRIVILEGED NATIONS. FINAN INT/ORG PLAN PROB/SOLV CAP/ISM GIVE TASK WEALTH ...POLICY SOC 20. PAGE 114 H2273
ECO/UNDEV NAT/G DIPLOM FOR/AID

B62
PASTOR R.S.,A STATEMENT OF THE LAWS OF PARAGUAY IN MATTERS AFFECTING BUSINESS (2ND ED.). PARAGUAY INDUS FAM LABOR LG/CO NAT/G LEGIS TAX CONTROL MARRIAGE 20. PAGE 124 H2474
FINAN ECO/UNDEV LAW CONSTN

B62
PHELPS E.S.,THE GOAL OF ECONOMIC GROWTH: SOURCES, COSTS, BENEFITS. USA+45 USSR FINAN TAX CONTROL DEMAND WEALTH...POLICY NAT/COMP ANTHOL BIBLIOG 20. PAGE 125 H2499
ECO/TAC ECO/DEV NAT/G FUT

L62
MURACCIOLE L.,"LA BANQUE CENTRALE DES ETATS DE L'AFRIQUE DE L'OUEST." AFR LAW ECO/UNDEV INT/ORG NAT/G CONSULT ECO/TAC ROUTINE...CHARTS 20. PAGE 115 H2292
ISLAM FINAN INT/TRADE

B63
BRITISH AID. UK AGRI DIST/IND INDUS SCHOOL TEC/DEV INT/TRADE COLONIAL DEMAND...TREND CHARTS 20. PAGE 2 H0041
FOR/AID ECO/UNDEV NAT/G FINAN

B63
ADRIAN C.R.,GOVERNING OVER FIFTY STATES AND THEIR COMMUNITIES. USA+45 CONSTN FINAN MUNIC NAT/G POL/PAR EX/STRUC LEGIS ADMIN CONTROL CT/SYS ...CHARTS 20. PAGE 4 H0073
PROVS LOC/G GOV/REL GOV/COMP

B63
AHN L.A.,FUNFZIG JAHRE ZWISCHEN INFLATION UND DEFLATION. GERMANY DIPLOM PRICE...CONCPT 20 GOLD/STAND. PAGE 4 H0081
FINAN CAP/ISM NAT/COMP ECO/TAC

B63
BANERJI A.K.,INDIA'S BALANCE OF PAYMENTS. INDIA NAT/G PRICE BAL/PAY COST INCOME 20. PAGE 10 H0208
INT/TRADE DIPLOM FINAN BUDGET

B63
CHOU S.H.,THE CHINESE INFLATION 1937-1949. ASIA SOCIETY POL/PAR FOR/AID INT/TRADE BAL/PAY WEALTH MARXISM...STAT CHARTS 20 COM/PARTY GOLD/STAND. PAGE 30 H0597
FINAN ECO/TAC BUDGET NAT/G

B63
COLUMBIA U SCHOOL OF LAW,PUBLIC INTERNATIONAL DEVELOPMENT FINANCING IN SENEGAL. SENEGAL FINAN DELIB/GP GIVE EFFICIENCY...CHARTS GOV/COMP ANTHOL 20. PAGE 32 H0636
FOR/AID PLAN RECEIVE ECO/UNDEV

B63
DE VRIES E.,SOCIAL ASPECTS OF ECONOMIC DEVELOPMENT IN LATIN AMERICA. CULTURE SOCIETY STRATA FINAN INDUS INT/ORG DELIB/GP ACT/RES ECO/TAC EDU/PROP ADMIN ATTIT SUPEGO HEALTH KNOWL ORD/FREE...SOC STAT TREND ANTHOL TOT/POP VAL/FREE. PAGE 39 H0777
L/A+17C ECO/UNDEV

B63
GAMBLE S.D.,NORTH CHINA VILLAGES: SOCIAL, POLITICAL, AND ECONOMIC ACTIVITIES BEFORE 1933. ASIA CULTURE STRUCT FAM DOMIN EDU/PROP WORSHIP 20. PAGE 55 H1093
MUNIC AGRI LEAD FINAN

B63
GLADE W.P. JR.,THE POLITICAL ECONOMY OF MEXICO. FUT L/A+17C CULTURE SOCIETY AGRI INDUS DELIB/GP ACT/RES ECO/TAC ATTIT HEALTH ORD/FREE...STAT TIME/SEQ TREND MEXIC/AMER TOT/POP VAL/FREE 20. PAGE 57 H1138
FINAN ECO/UNDEV

B63
GOURNAY B.,PUBLIC ADMINISTRATION. FRANCE LAW CONSTN AGRI FINAN LABOR SCHOOL EX/STRUC CHOOSE...MGT METH/COMP 20. PAGE 59 H1189
BIBLIOG/A ADMIN NAT/G LOC/G

B63
GUIMARAES A.P.,INFLACAO E MONOPOLIO NO BRASIL. BRAZIL FINAN NAT/G PLAN PAY...METH/COMP 20. PAGE 62 H1248
ECO/UNDEV PRICE INT/TRADE BAL/PAY

B63
HAQ M.,THE STRATEGY OF ECONOMIC PLANNING. PAKISTAN AGRI FINAN INDUS NAT/G FOR/AID TAX CONTROL REGION PRODUC...POLICY CHARTS 20. PAGE 66 H1324
ECO/TAC ECO/UNDEV PLAN PROB/SOLV

B63
ISSAWI C.,EGYPT IN REVOLUTION: AN ECONOMIC ANALYSIS. ISLAM STRUCT ECO/UNDEV AGRI FINAN INDUS PLAN EXEC REV NAT/LISM ATTIT RIGID/FLEX WEALTH SOCISM...STAT WORK 20. PAGE 79 H1573
NAT/G UAR

B63
OECD,FOOD AID: ITS ROLE IN ECONOMIC DEVELOPMENT. FINAN NAT/G PLAN DIPLOM GIVE TASK WEALTH ...METH/COMP METH 20. PAGE 120 H2397
ECO/UNDEV FOR/AID INT/ORG POLICY

B63
UAR MINISTRY OF CULTURE,A BIBLIOGRAPHICAL LIST OF ARABIAN PENINSULA. ISLAM SAUDI/ARAB YEMEN FINAN NAT/G DIPLOM 19/20. PAGE 157 H3147
BIBLIOG GEOG INDUS SECT

B63
UN SECRETARY GENERAL,PLANNING FOR ECONOMIC DEVELOPMENT. ECO/UNDEV FINAN BUDGET INT/TRADE TARIFFS TAX ADMIN 20 UN. PAGE 158 H3159
PLAN ECO/TAC MGT NAT/COMP

L63
ROSE R.,"COMPARATIVE STUDIES IN POLITICAL FINANCE: A SYMPOSIUM." ASIA EUR+WWI S/ASIA LAW CULTURE DELIB/GP LEGIS ACT/RES ECO/TAC EDU/PROP CHOOSE ATTIT RIGID/FLEX SUPEGO PWR SKILL WEALTH...STAT ANTHOL VAL/FREE. PAGE 134 H2674
FINAN POL/PAR

S63
APPERT K.,"BERECHTIGE VORBEHALTE DER SCHWEIZERISCHEN ZUR INTEGRATION." EUR+WWI UK MARKET SERV/IND NAT/G PLAN RIGID/FLEX OEEC 20 EEC. PAGE 7 H0146
FINAN ATTIT SWITZERLND

N63
LEDERER W.,THE BALANCE ON FOREIGN TRANSACTIONS: PROBLEMS OF DEFINITION AND MEASUREMENT (PAMPHLET). USA+45 BUDGET DIPLOM ECO/TAC PRICE GOV/REL...POLICY STAT NAT/COMP METH 20. PAGE 93 H1853
FINAN BAL/PAY INT/TRADE ECO/DEV

B64
AVASTHI A.,ASPECTS OF ADMINISTRATION. INDIA UK USA+45 FINAN ACADEM DELIB/GP LEGIS RECEIVE PARL/PROC PRIVIL...NAT/COMP 20. PAGE 9 H0183
MGT ADMIN SOC/WK ORD/FREE

B64
BALOGH T.,THE ECONOMIC IMPACT OF MONETARY AND COMMERCIAL INSTITUTIONS OF A EUROPEAN ORIGIN IN AFRICA. AFR UAR INDUS FOR/AID COLONIAL CONTROL ...NAT/COMP 20. PAGE 10 H0205
TEC/DEV FINAN ECO/UNDEV ECO/TAC

B64
BROWN C.V.,GOVERNMENT AND BANKING IN WESTERN NIGERIA. AFR NIGERIA GOV/REL GP/REL...POLICY 20. PAGE 22 H0440
ADMIN ECO/UNDEV FINAN NAT/G

B64
BROWN W.M.,THE EXTERNAL LIQUIDITY OF AN ADVANCED COUNTRY. CANADA FRANCE GERMANY/W SWEDEN UK USA+45 ECO/DEV DIPLOM PRICE...CONCPT STAT NAT/COMP 20. PAGE 22 H0451
FINAN INT/TRADE COST INCOME

B64
COONDOO R.,THE DIVISION OF POWERS IN THE INDIAN CONSTITUTION. INDIA ECO/UNDEV FINAN TEC/DEV WAR CENTRAL EFFICIENCY NAT/LISM PWR WEALTH NEW/LIB ...BIBLIOG 18/20. PAGE 33 H0659
CONSTN LEGIS WELF/ST GOV/COMP

B64
GESELLSCHAFT RECHTSVERGLEICH,BIBLIOGRAPHIE DES DEUTSCHEN RECHTS (BIBLIOGRAPHY OF GERMAN LAW, TRANS. BY COURTLAND PETERSON). GERMANY FINAN INDUS LABOR SECT FORCES CT/SYS PARL/PROC CRIME...INT/LAW SOC NAT/COMP 20. PAGE 56 H1117
BIBLIOG/A JURID CONSTN ADMIN

B64
HAZLEWOOD A.,THE ECONOMICS OF DEVELOPMENT: AN ANNOTATED LIST OF BOOKS AND ARTICLES PUBLISHED 1958-1962. AGRI FINAN INDUS LABOR NAT/G DIPLOM INT/TRADE INCOME...MGT 20. PAGE 69 H1374
BIBLIOG/A ECO/UNDEV TEC/DEV

B64
JUCKER-FLEETWOOD E.,MONEY AND FINANCE IN AFRICA. ISLAM ECO/UNDEV SERV/IND NAT/G EX/STRUC PLAN ECO/TAC ROUTINE WEALTH...MGT TOT/POP 20. PAGE 82 H1639
AFR FINAN

B64
KALDOR N.,ESSAYS ON ECONOMIC POLICY (VOL. II). CHILE GERMANY INDIA FINAN...GOV/COMP METH/COMP 20 KEYNES/JM. PAGE 83 H1651
BAL/PAY INT/TRADE METH/CNCPT ECO/UNDEV

B64
LI C.M.,INDUSTRIAL DEVELOPMENT IN COMMUNIST CHINA. CHINA/COM ECO/DEV ECO/UNDEV AGRI FINAN INDUS MARKET LABOR NAT/G ECO/TAC INT/TRADE EXEC ALL/VALS ...POLICY RELATIV TREND WORK TOT/POP VAL/FREE 20. PAGE 96 H1921
ASIA TEC/DEV

B64
PERKINS D.,THE AMERICAN DEMOCRACY: ITS RISE TO POWER. ASIA USSR LAW CULTURE FINAN EDU/PROP COLONIAL CHOOSE...POLICY CHARTS BIBLIOG WORSHIP PRESIDENT 15/20 NEGRO. PAGE 125 H2492
LOC/G ECO/TAC WAR DIPLOM

B64
PINNICK A.W.,COUNTRY PLANNERS IN ACTION. UK FINAN SERV/IND NAT/G CONSULT DELIB/GP PRICE CONTROL ROUTINE LEISURE AGE/C...GEOG 20 URBAN/RNWL. PAGE 126 H2512
MUNIC PLAN INDUS ATTIT

B64
SZLADITS C.,BIBLIOGRAPHY ON FOREIGN AND COMPARATIVE LAW: BOOKS AND ARTICLES IN ENGLISH (SUPPLEMENT 1962). FINAN INDUS JUDGE LICENSE ADMIN CT/SYS PARL/PROC OWN...INT/LAW CLASSIF METH/COMP NAT/COMP 20. PAGE 151 H3027
BIBLIOG/A JURID ADJUD LAW

B64
THAILAND NATIONAL ECO DEV,THE NATIONAL ECONOMIC DEVELOPMENT PLAN: 1961-66: SECOND PHASE 1964-66. THAILAND AGRI FINAN BUDGET EFFICIENCY INCOME...STAT CHARTS 20. PAGE 153 H3065
ECO/UNDEV ECO/TAC PLAN NAT/G

B64
URQUIDI V.L.,THE CHALLENGE OF DEVELOPMENT IN LATIN AMERICA. L/A+17C FINAN INT/ORG TEC/DEV DIPLOM INT/TRADE PRICE REGION PRODUC...CHARTS 20. PAGE 159 H3175
ECO/UNDEV ECO/TAC NAT/G TREND

B64
US HOUSE COMM BANKING-CURR,INTERNATIONAL DEVELOPMENT ASSOCIATION ACT AMENDMENT. CHINA/COM USA+45 USSR FINAN FORCES LEGIS DIPLOM CONFER EFFICIENCY...CHARTS GOV/COMP 20 PRESIDENT CONGRESS INTL/DEV. PAGE 160 H3196
BAL/PAY FOR/AID RECORD ECO/TAC

B64
WERNETTE J.P.,GOVERNMENT AND BUSINESS. LABOR CAP/ISM ECO/TAC INT/TRADE TAX ADMIN AUTOMAT NUC/PWR CIVMIL/REL DEMAND...MGT 20 MONOPOLY. PAGE 167 H3333 NAT/G FINAN ECO/DEV CONTROL

B64
WILSON T.,POLICIES FOR REGIONAL DEVELOPMENT. CANADA UK FINAN INDUS NAT/G BUDGET TAX GIVE COST ...NAT/COMP 20. PAGE 169 H3383 REGION PLAN ECO/DEV ECO/TAC

S64
ZARTMAN I.W.,"LES RELATIONS ENTRE LA FRANCE ET L'ALGERIA DEPUIS LES ACCORDS D'EVIAN." EUR+WWI FUT ISLAM CULTURE AGRI EXTR/IND FINAN INDUS POL/PAR DIPLOM ECO/TAC FOR/AID PEACE ATTIT DRIVE ALL/VALS ...TIME/SEQ VAL/FREE 20. PAGE 172 H3450 ECO/UNDEV ALGERIA FRANCE

B65
ACHTERBERG E.,BERLINER HOCHFINANZ - KAISER, FURSTEN, MILLIONARE UM 1900. GERMANY NAT/G EDU/PROP PERSON...MGT 19/20. PAGE 3 H0060 FINAN MUNIC BIOG ECO/TAC

B65
ADU A.L.,THE CIVIL SERVICE IN NEW AFRICAN STATES. AFR GHANA FINAN SOVEREIGN...POLICY 20 CIVIL/SERV AFRICA/E AFRICA/W. PAGE 4 H0074 ECO/UNDEV ADMIN COLONIAL NAT/G

B65
ALTON T.P.,POLISH NATIONAL INCOME AND PRODUCT IN 1954, 1955, AND 1956. POLAND FINAN EX/STRUC ECO/TAC PRICE COST WEALTH 20. PAGE 6 H0117 COM INDUS NAT/G ECO/DEV

B65
CAMPBELL G.A.,THE CIVIL SERVICE IN BRITAIN (2ND ED.). UK DELIB/GP FORCES WORKER CREATE PLAN ...POLICY AUD/VIS 19/20 CIVIL/SERV. PAGE 26 H0515 ADMIN LEGIS NAT/G FINAN

B65
CHANDA A.,FEDERALISM IN INDIA. INDIA UK ELITES FINAN NAT/G POL/PAR EX/STRUC LEGIS DIPLOM TAX GOV/REL POPULISM...POLICY 20. PAGE 28 H0572 CONSTN CENTRAL FEDERAL

B65
CRAMER J.F.,CONTEMPORARY EDUCATION: A COMPARATIVE STUDY OF NATIONAL SYSTEMS (2ND ED.). CHINA/COM EUR+WWI INDIA USA+45 FINAN PROB/SOLV ADMIN CONTROL ATTIT...IDEA/COMP METH/COMP 20 CHINJAP. PAGE 35 H0697 EDU/PROP NAT/COMP SCHOOL ACADEM

B65
GRIMAL H.,HISTOIRE DU COMMONWEALTH BRITANNIQUE. UK FINAN DOMIN ATTIT ORD/FREE...T 15/20 CMN/WLTH. PAGE 61 H1226 NAT/G COLONIAL DIPLOM INT/TRADE

B65
HAEFELE E.T.,GOVERNMENT CONTROLS ON TRANSPORT. AFR RHODESIA TANZANIA DIPLOM ECO/TAC TARIFFS PRICE ADJUD CONTROL REGION EFFICIENCY...POLICY 20 CONGO. PAGE 64 H1274 ECO/UNDEV DIST/IND FINAN NAT/G

B65
HLA MYINT U.,THE ECONOMICS OF THE DEVELOPING COUNTRIES. USA+45 WOR+45 AGRI FINAN NAT/G INT/TRADE ...CLASSIF CENSUS TREND NAT/COMP SIMUL GEN/LAWS. PAGE 71 H1430 ECO/UNDEV FOR/AID GEOG

B65
IANNI O.,ESTADO E CAPITALISMO. L/A+17C FINAN TEC/DEV ECO/TAC ORD/FREE WEALTH POLICY. PAGE 76 H1518 ECO/UNDEV STRUCT INDUS NAT/G

B65
INT. BANK RECONSTR. DEVELOP.,ECONOMIC DEVELOPMENT OF KUWAIT. ISLAM KUWAIT AGRI FINAN MARKET EX/STRUC TEC/DEV ECO/TAC ADMIN WEALTH...OBS CON/ANAL CHARTS 20. PAGE 77 H1541 INDUS NAT/G

B65
MAIR L.,AN INTRODUCTION TO SOCIAL ANTHROPOLOGY. LAW STRATA FINAN FAM KIN SECT INT/TRADE RACE/REL ADJUST PRODUC...T 20. PAGE 101 H2023 SOC STRUCT CULTURE SOCIETY

B65
MEAGHER R.F.,PUBLIC INTERNATIONAL DEVELOPMENT FINANCING IN SUDAN. SUDAN FINAN DELIB/GP GIVE ...CHARTS GOV/COMP 20. PAGE 108 H2155 FOR/AID PLAN RECEIVE ECO/UNDEV

B65
OECD,MEDITERRANEAN REGIONAL PROJECT: TURKEY; EDUCATION AND DEVELOPMENT. FUT TURKEY SOCIETY STRATA FINAN NAT/G PROF/ORG PLAN PROB/SOLV ADMIN COST...STAT CHARTS 20 OECD. PAGE 120 H2399 EDU/PROP ACADEM SCHOOL ECO/UNDEV

B65
OECD,THE MEDITERRANEAN REGIONAL PROJECT: ITALY; EDUCATION AND DEVELOPMENT. ITALY SOCIETY STRATA FINAN NAT/G PROF/ORG WORKER PLAN PROB/SOLV ADMIN ...STAT CHARTS METH 20 OECD. PAGE 120 H2400 SCHOOL EDU/PROP ECO/UNDEV ACADEM

B65
OECD,THE MEDITERRANEAN REGIONAL PROJECT: GREECE; EDUCATION AND DEVELOPMENT. FUT GREECE SOCIETY AGRI FINAN NAT/G PROF/ORG WORKER PLAN PROB/SOLV ADMIN DEMAND ATTIT 20 OECD. PAGE 120 H2401 EDU/PROP SCHOOL ACADEM ECO/UNDEV

B65
OECD,THE MEDITERRANEAN REGIONAL PROJECT: SPAIN; EDUCATION AND DEVELOPMENT. FUT SPAIN STRATA FINAN NAT/G WORKER PLAN PROB/SOLV ADMIN COST...POLICY STAT CHARTS 20 OECD. PAGE 120 H2402 ECO/UNDEV EDU/PROP ACADEM SCHOOL

B65
ONUOHA B.,THE ELEMENTS OF AFRICAN SOCIALISM. AFR FINAN SECT TEC/DEV FOR/AID GP/REL OWN LAISSEZ MARXISM...CONCPT BIBLIOG 20. PAGE 121 H2419 SOCISM ECO/UNDEV NAT/G EX/STRUC

B65
ORG FOR ECO COOP AND DEVEL,THE MEDITERRANEAN REGIONAL PROJECT: AN EXPERIMENT IN PLANNING BY SIX COUNTRIES. FUT GREECE SPAIN TURKEY YUGOSLAVIA SOCIETY FINAN NAT/G PROF/ORG EDU/PROP ADMIN REGION COST...POLICY STAT CHARTS 20 OECD. PAGE 121 H2427 PLAN ECO/UNDEV ACADEM SCHOOL

B65
PROEHL P.O.,FOREIGN ENTERPRISE IN NIGERIA. NIGERIA FINAN LABOR NAT/G TAX 20. PAGE 128 H2562 ECO/UNDEV ECO/TAC JURID CAP/ISM

B65
SABLE M.H.,MASTER DIRECTORY FOR LATIN AMERICA. AGRI COM/IND FINAN R+D ACADEM LABOR NAT/G POL/PAR VOL/ASSN INT/TRADE EDU/PROP 20. PAGE 136 H2728 INDEX L/A+17C INT/ORG DIPLOM

B65
SHARMA S.A.,PARLIAMENTARY GOVERNMENT IN INDIA. INDIA FINAN LOC/G PROVS DELIB/GP PLAN ADMIN CT/SYS FEDERAL...JURID 20. PAGE 142 H2849 NAT/G CONSTN PARL/PROC LEGIS

B65
SHEPHERD W.G.,ECONOMIC PERFORMANCE UNDER PUBLIC OWNERSHIP: BRITISH FUEL AND POWER. UK BUDGET GP/REL ...METH/CNCPT CHARTS BIBLIOG 20. PAGE 143 H2858 PROC/MFG NAT/G OWN FINAN

B65
TEW B.,WEALTH AND INCOME. UK BUDGET INT/TRADE PRICE BAL/PAY DEMAND...CHARTS GOV/COMP 20 AUSTRAL. PAGE 153 H3064 FINAN ECO/DEV WEALTH INCOME

B65
WURFEL S.W.,FOREIGN ENTERPRISE IN COLOMBIA. FINAN LABOR NAT/G ECO/TAC TAX REGION 20 COLOMB. PAGE 171 H3429 ECO/UNDEV INT/TRADE JURID CAP/ISM

B65
YOUNG A.N.,CHINA'S WARTIME FINANCE AND INFLATION. ASIA AGRI INDUS NAT/G ECO/TAC CONFER PRICE WAR COST 20. PAGE 172 H3437 FINAN FOR/AID TAX BUDGET

L65
MATTHEWS D.G.,"A CURRENT BIBLIOGRAPHY ON SUDANESE AFFAIRS; A SELECT BIBLIOGRAPHY FROM 1960-1964." SUDAN LAW CULTURE AGRI FINAN INDUS LABOR POL/PAR TEC/DEV FOR/AID RACE/REL LITERACY...LING 20. PAGE 105 H2094 BIBLIOG ECO/UNDEV NAT/G DIPLOM

L65
WIONCZEK M.,"LATIN AMERICA FREE TRADE ASSOCIATION." AGRI DIST/IND FINAN INDUS INT/ORG LABOR NAT/G TEC/DEV ECO/TAC HEALTH SKILL WEALTH...POLICY RELATIV MGT LAFTA 20. PAGE 169 H3390 L/A+17C MARKET REGION

B66
AGGARWALA R.N.,FINANCIAL COMMITTEES OF THE INDIAN PARLIAMENT: A STUDY IN PARLIAMENTARY CONTROL OVER PUBLIC EXPENDITURE. INDIA FINAN NAT/G ROLE...CHARTS METH/COMP METH 20 PARLIAMENT. PAGE 4 H0078 PARL/PROC BUDGET CONTROL DELIB/GP

B66
AMER ENTERPRISE INST PUB POL,SIGNIFICANT ISSUES IN ECONOMIC AID TO DEVELOPING COUNTRIES. FINAN INT/ORG NAT/G PLAN PROB/SOLV GIVE TASK WEALTH...DECISION 20. PAGE 6 H0119 ECO/UNDEV FOR/AID DIPLOM POLICY

B66
BIRKHEAD G.S.,ADMINISTRATIVE PROBLEMS IN PAKISTAN. PAKISTAN AGRI FINAN INDUS LG/CO ECO/TAC CONTROL PWR ...CHARTS ANTHOL 20. PAGE 17 H0340 ADMIN NAT/G ORD/FREE ECO/UNDEV

B66
DUNCOMBE H.S.,COUNTY GOVERNMENT IN AMERICA. USA+45 FINAN MUNIC ADMIN ROUTINE GOV/REL...GOV/COMP 20. PAGE 43 H0863 LOC/G PROVS CT/SYS TOP/EX

B66
GUNN G.E.,THE POLITICAL HISTORY OF NEWFOUNDLAND 1832-1864. CANADA FINAN LEGIS CHOOSE REPRESENT ...CHARTS 19. PAGE 62 H1252 POL/PAR NAT/G CONSTN

B66
HACKETT J.,L'ECONOMIE BRITANNIQUE: PROBLEMES ET PERSPECTIVES. FRANCE UK LABOR MUNIC NAT/G EX/STRUC PROB/SOLV BAL/PAY INCOME RIGID/FLEX...MGT PHIL/SCI CHARTS 20. PAGE 63 H1271 ECO/DEV FINAN ECO/TAC PLAN

B66
HAMILTON W.B.,A DECADE OF THE COMMONWEALTH, 1955-1964. UK LAW ELITES FINAN FOR/AID CONFER COLONIAL PWR...GEOG CHARTS ANTHOL 20 CMN/WLTH UN. PAGE 65 H1302 INT/ORG INGP/REL DIPLOM NAT/G

B66
JOHNSON N.,PARLIAMENT AND ADMINISTRATION: THE ESTIMATES COMMITTEE 1945-65. FUT UK NAT/G EX/STRUC PLAN BUDGET ORD/FREE...T 20 PARLIAMENT HOUSE/CMNS. PAGE 81 H1625
LEGIS ADMIN FINAN DELIB/GP

B66
KIRDAR U.,THE STRUCTURE OF UNITED NATIONS ECONOMIC AID TO UNDERDEVELOPED COUNTRIES. AGRI FINAN INDUS NAT/G EX/STRUC PLAN GIVE TASK...POLICY 20 UN. PAGE 86 H1721
INT/ORG FOR/AID ECO/UNDEV ADMIN

B66
KUZNETS S.,MODERN ECONOMIC GROWTH. WOR+45 WOR-45 ECO/DEV ECO/UNDEV AGRI FINAN INDUS TEC/DEV EFFICIENCY INCOME...NAT/COMP 19/20. PAGE 89 H1786
TIME/SEQ WEALTH PRODUC

B66
LAVEN P.,RENAISSANCE ITALY: 1464-1534. ITALY AGRI EXTR/IND FINAN MUNIC INT/TRADE DRIVE...CATH GEOG CHARTS BIBLIOG/A 15. PAGE 92 H1841
CULTURE HUM TEC/DEV KNOWL

B66
MADAN G.R.,ECONOMIC THINKING IN INDIA. INDIA ECO/UNDEV AGRI FINAN INDUS LABOR PLAN CAP/ISM INT/TRADE MARXISM SOCISM...POLICY 1/20. PAGE 101 H2013
ECO/TAC PHIL/SCI NAT/G POL/PAR

B66
MASON E.S.,ECONOMIC DEVELOPMENT IN INDIA AND PAKISTAN. INDIA PAKISTAN AGRI FINAN PLAN BUDGET INT/TRADE WEALTH...POLICY STAT TREND CHARTS 20. PAGE 104 H2086
NAT/COMP ECO/UNDEV ECO/TAC FOR/AID

B66
PLATE H.,PARTEIFINANZIERUNG UND GRUNDESETZ. GERMANY NAT/G PLAN GIVE PAY INCOME WEALTH...JURID 20. PAGE 126 H2522
POL/PAR CONSTN FINAN

B66
SASTRI K.V.S.,FEDERAL-STATE FISCAL RELATIONS IN INDIA: A STUDY OF THE FINANCE COMMISSION AND TECHNIQUES OF FINANCIAL ADJUSTMENT. INDIA PROVS DELIB/GP GOV/REL FEDERAL...MATH CHARTS 20. PAGE 138 H2756
TAX BUDGET FINAN NAT/G

B66
SMITH H.E.,READINGS IN ECONOMIC DEVELOPMENT AND ADMINISTRATION IN TANZANIA. TANZANIA FINAN INDUS LABOR NAT/G PLAN PROB/SOLV INT/TRADE COLONIAL REGION...ANTHOL BIBLIOG 20 AFRICA/E. PAGE 146 H2910
TEC/DEV ADMIN GOV/REL

B66
TYSON G.,NEHRU: THE YEARS OF POWER. INDIA UK STRATA ECO/UNDEV FINAN SECT TASK WAR ORD/FREE MARXISM ...POLICY BIBLIOG 20 NEHRU/J. PAGE 157 H3145
CHIEF PWR DIPLOM NAT/G

B66
YEAGER L.B.,INTERNATIONAL MONETARY RELATIONS: THEORY, HISTORY, AND POLICY. WOR+45 WOR-45 INT/TRADE BAL/PAY...NAT/COMP 18/20 MONEY. PAGE 172 H3435
FINAN DIPLOM ECO/TAC IDEA/COMP

B66
ZINKIN T.,CHALLENGES IN INDIA. INDIA PAKISTAN LAW AGRI FINAN INDUS TOP/EX TEC/DEV CONTROL ROUTINE ORD/FREE PWR 20 NEHRU/J SHASTRI/LB CIVIL/SERV. PAGE 173 H3458
NAT/G ECO/TAC POLICY ADMIN

B67
CAMERON R.,BANKING IN THE EARLY STAGES OF INDUSTRIALIZATION: A STUDY IN ECONOMIC COMPARATIVE HISTORY. FRANCE GERMANY UK USSR...CHARTS IDEA/COMP NAT/COMP 18/20 CHINJAP. PAGE 26 H0512
FINAN INDUS GOV/COMP

B67
DALTON G.,TRIBAL AND PEASANT ECONOMIES. SOCIETY FINAN FAM INT/TRADE RATION ADJUST WEALTH...CHARTS ANTHOL BIBLIOG T. PAGE 37 H0738
SOC ECO/UNDEV NAT/COMP

B67
DENISON E.F.,WHY GROWTH RATES DIFFER; POSTWAR EXPERIENCE IN NINE WESTERN COUNTRIES. WOR+45 FINAN WORKER TEC/DEV EDU/PROP PRICE PRODUC WEALTH ...ECOMETRIC STAT CHARTS BIBLIOG. PAGE 40 H0791
METH NAT/COMP ECO/DEV ECO/TAC

B67
DICKSON P.G.M.,THE FINANCIAL REVOLUTION IN ENGLAND. UK NAT/G TEC/DEV ADMIN GOV/REL...SOC METH/CNCPT CHARTS GP/COMP BIBLIOG 17/18. PAGE 41 H0823
ECO/DEV FINAN CAP/ISM MGT

B67
FIELD M.G.,SOVIET SOCIALIZED MEDICINE. USSR FINAN R+D PROB/SOLV ADMIN SOCISM...MGT SOC CONCPT 20. PAGE 50 H0993
PUB/INST HEALTH NAT/G MARXISM

B67
HAWTREY R.,INCOMES AND MONEY. EUR+WWI FUT UK LABOR WORKER INT/TRADE TAX PAY BAL/PAY COST WEALTH 20. PAGE 68 H1363
FINAN NAT/G POLICY ECO/DEV

B67
JAIN R.K.,MANAGEMENT OF STATE ENTERPRISES. INDIA SOCIETY FINAN WORKER BUDGET ADMIN CONTROL OWN 20. PAGE 79 H1584
NAT/G SOCISM INDUS MGT

B67
KONCZACKI Z.A.,PUBLIC FINANCE AND ECONOMIC DEVELOPMENT OF NATAL 1893-1910. TAX ADMIN COLONIAL ...STAT CHARTS BIBLIOG 19/20 NATAL. PAGE 88 H1755
ECO/TAC FINAN NAT/G ECO/UNDEV

B67
LEVY J.-P.,THE ECONOMIC LIFE OF THE ANCIENT WORLD. CULTURE SOCIETY INT/TRADE COLONIAL WEALTH ...BIBLIOG. PAGE 95 H1906
ECO/TAC ECO/UNDEV FINAN MEDIT-7

B67
LYON B.,MEDIEVAL FINANCE. CHRIST-17C...SOC 11/12. PAGE 99 H1984
FINAN METH/COMP ECO/TAC NAT/COMP

B67
NESS G.D.,BUREAUCRACY AND RURAL DEVELOPMENT IN MALAYSIA. MALAYSIA UK SOCIETY FINAN INDUS WORKER TEC/DEV ECO/TAC COLONIAL EQUILIB ORD/FREE...STAT CHARTS 20. PAGE 117 H2330
ECO/UNDEV PLAN NAT/G ADMIN

B67
POSNER M.V.,ITALIAN PUBLIC ENTERPRISE. ITALY ECO/DEV FINAN INDUS CREATE ECO/TAC ADMIN CONTROL EFFICIENCY PRODUC...TREND CHARTS 20. PAGE 127 H2545
NAT/G PLAN CAP/ISM SOCISM

B67
ROSENTHAL A.H.,THE SOCIAL PROGRAMS OF SWEDEN. SWEDEN USA+45 FINAN NAT/G PLAN PROB/SOLV INSPECT ORD/FREE...POLICY HEAL SOC CHARTS NAT/COMP 20. PAGE 134 H2681
GIVE SOC/WK WEALTH METH/COMP

B67
RUEFF J.,BALANCE OF PAYMENTS. WOR+45 FINAN TEC/DEV DIPLOM TARIFFS PRICE CONTROL...POLICY CONCPT IDEA/COMP. PAGE 136 H2715
INT/TRADE BAL/PAY ECO/TAC NAT/COMP

B67
YAMAMURA K.,ECONOMIC POLICY IN POSTWAR JAPAN. ASIA FINAN POL/PAR DIPLOM LEAD NAT/LISM ATTIT NEW/LIB POPULISM 20 CHINJAP. PAGE 171 H3432
ECO/DEV POLICY NAT/G TEC/DEV

L67
LARKIN E.,"ECONOMIC GROWTH, CAPITAL INVESTMENT, AND THE ROMAN CATHOLIC CHURCH IN NINETEENTH-CENTURY IRELAND." IRELAND AGRI DIST/IND NAT/G GIVE OWN CATHISM...CHARTS 19. PAGE 91 H1823
FINAN SECT WEALTH ECO/UNDEV

L67
ROTH A.R.,"CAPITAL-MARKET DEVELOPMENT IN ISRAEL AND BRAZIL: TWO EXAMPLES OF THE ROLE OF LAW IN DEVELOPMENT." BRAZIL ISRAEL L/A+17C INDUS MARKET ECO/TAC FOR/AID INT/TRADE CONTROL BAL/PAY 20. PAGE 135 H2694
LAW ECO/UNDEV NAT/COMP FINAN

S67
BAER W.,"THE INFLATION CONTROVERSY IN LATIN AMERICA: SURVEY." L/A+17C ECO/UNDEV AGRI FINAN INDUS PLAN PROB/SOLV TEC/DEV...BIBLIOG/A 20. PAGE 10 H0194
NAT/G BAL/PAY ECO/TAC BUDGET

S67
BOSHER J.F.,"GOVERNMENT AND PRIVATE INTERESTS IN NEW FRANCE." CANADA FRANCE INDUS LG/CO SML/CO CAP/ISM INT/TRADE COLONIAL GP/REL...HIST/WRIT 17/18. PAGE 19 H0381
NAT/G FINAN ADMIN CONTROL

S67
CAMERON R.,"SOME LESSONS OF HISTORY FOR DEVELOPING NATIONS." WOR+45 WOR-45 FINAN NAT/G WORKER EDU/PROP PARTIC ROLE...DECISION METH/COMP 18/20. PAGE 25 H0511
ECO/UNDEV NAT/COMP POLICY CONCPT

S67
CARR E.H.,"REVOLUTION FROM ABOVE." USSR STRATA FINAN INDUS NAT/G DOMIN LEAD GP/REL INGP/REL OWN PRODUC PWR 20 STALIN/J. PAGE 27 H0538
AGRI POLICY COM EFFICIENCY

S67
DESHPANDE A.M.,"FEDERAL-STATE FISCAL RELATIONS IN INDIA" (REVIEW ARTICLE)" GERMANY USSR DELIB/GP PLAN BUDGET ECO/TAC INCOME 20 SOC/DEMPAR SOC/REVPAR. PAGE 40 H0795
FINAN NAT/G GOV/REL TAX

S67
HASSAN M.F.,"THE SECOND FOUR-YEAR PLAN OF VENEZUELA." L/A+17C VENEZUELA AGRI INDUS NAT/G PLAN RATION CONTROL HABITAT...MATH STAT 20. PAGE 67 H1352
ECO/UNDEV FINAN BUDGET PROB/SOLV

S67
NUGENT J.B.,"ECONOMIC THOUGHT, INVESTMENT CRITERIA, AND DEVELOPMENT STRATEGIES IN GREECE* A POSTWAR SURVEY." GREECE AGRI INDUS INT/ORG NAT/G OP/RES DEMAND OPTIMAL PRODUC WEALTH 20 EEC. PAGE 119 H2379
ECO/UNDEV PLAN FINAN

S67
SANCHEZ J.D.,"DESARROLLO ECONOMICO Y FUTURO DE COLOMBIA." L/A+17C AGRI EXTR/IND FINAN INDUS MARKET INT/TRADE CONTROL...STAT TREND COLOMB. PAGE 137 H2748
ECO/UNDEV FUT NAT/G ECO/TAC

S67
SCOVILLE W.J.,"GOVERNMENT REGULATION AND GROWTH IN THE FRENCH PAPER INDUSTRY DURING THE EIGHTEENTH CENTURY." FRANCE MOD/EUR FINAN CAP/ISM TAX ADMIN CONTROL PRIVIL LAISSEZ...POLICY 18. PAGE 141 H2818
NAT/G PROC/MFG ECO/DEV INGP/REL

S67
WHITE W.L.,"THE TREASURY BOARD AND PARLIAMENT." CANADA CONSTN CONSULT LEGIS LEAD PARL/PROC GP/REL
FINAN DELIB/GP

...DECISION 20. PAGE 167 H3351 NAT/G ADMIN

S68
GUZZARDI W.,"THE DECLINE OF THE STERLING CLUB." UK WOR+45 NAT/G PLAN DIPLOM INT/TRADE AGREE CONSEN EQUILIB SOVEREIGN...POLICY NEW/IDEA 20 COMMONWLTH GOLD/STAND. PAGE 63 H1259 FINAN ECO/TAC WEALTH NAT/COMP

S68
LAPIERRE J.W.,"TRADITION ET MODERNITE A MADAGASCAR." ISLAM MADAGASCAR AGRI FINAN KIN NAT/G CREATE OP/RES GP/REL INGP/REL ATTIT CONSERVE...PSY 20. PAGE 91 H1813 ECO/UNDEV FOR/AID CULTURE TEC/DEV

B82
CUNNINGHAM W.,THE GROWTH OF ENGLISH INDUSTRY AND COMMERCE. FUT UK FINAN NAT/G CAP/ISM...POLICY 20 MERCANTLST CHRISTIAN POPE. PAGE 36 H0721 INDUS INT/TRADE SML/CO CONSERVE

C89
PLAYFAIR R.L.,"A BIBLIOGRAPHY OF ALGERIA." ALGERIA CULTURE ECO/UNDEV DIST/IND EXTR/IND FINAN SECT CRIME 16/19. PAGE 126 H2525 BIBLIOG/A ISLAM GEOG

B96
DE VATTEL E.,THE LAW OF NATIONS. AGRI FINAN CHIEF DIPLOM INT/TRADE AGREE OWN ALL/VALS MORAL ORD/FREE SOVEREIGN...GEN/LAWS 18 NATURL/LAW WOLFF/C. PAGE 39 H0774 LAW CONCPT NAT/G INT/LAW

FINANCE....SEE FINAN

FINCH/D....DANIEL FINCH

FINCH/ER....E.R. FINCH

FINDLATER R. H1001

FINE ARTS....SEE ART/METH

FINER H. H1002

FINER S.E. H1003,H1004

FINLAND....SEE ALSO APPROPRIATE TIME/SPACE/CULTURE INDEX

B56
VON HARPE W.,DIE SOWJETUNION FINNLAND UND SKANDANAVIEN, 1945-1955. EUR+WWI FINLAND GERMANY USSR WAR INGP/REL ORD/FREE SOVEREIGN MARXISM ...POLICY GOV/COMP BIBLIOG 20 STALIN/J. PAGE 163 H3270 DIPLOM COM NEUTRAL BAL/PWR

B59
FOX A.,THE POWER OF SMALL STATES: DIPLOMACY IN WORLD WAR TWO. EUR+WWI FINLAND NORWAY SPAIN SWEDEN TURKEY NAT/G TOP/EX DIPLOM PWR...HIST/WRIT 20. PAGE 52 H1044 CONCPT STERTYP BAL/PWR

B61
JAKOBSON M.,THE DIPLOMACY OF THE WINTER WAR. EUR+WWI FINLAND GERMANY USSR INT/ORG NAT/G PEACE TOTALISM PWR...POLICY CONCPT 20 TREATY. PAGE 79 H1588 WAR ORD/FREE DIPLOM

B62
KASTARI P.,LA PRESIDENCE DE LA REPUBLIQUE EN FINLANDE. FINLAND CONSTN NAT/G POL/PAR LEGIS LEGIT ATTIT...JURID CONCPT 20 PRESIDENT. PAGE 83 H1666 PARL/PROC CHIEF PWR DECISION

B64
ANDREN N.,GOVERNMENT AND POLITICS IN THE NORDIC COUNTRIES: DENMARK, FINLAND, ICELAND, NORWAY, SWEDEN. DENMARK FINLAND ICELAND NORWAY SWEDEN POL/PAR CHIEF LEGIS ADMIN REGION REPRESENT ATTIT CONSERVE...CHARTS BIBLIOG/A 20. PAGE 7 H0137 CONSTN NAT/G CULTURE GOV/COMP

B64
HALLER W.,DER SCHWEDISCHE JUSTITIEOMBUDSMAN. DENMARK FINLAND NORWAY SWEDEN LEGIS ADJUD CONTROL PERSON ORD/FREE...NAT/COMP 20 OMBUDSMAN. PAGE 64 H1288 JURID PARL/PROC ADMIN CHIEF

S64
BARIETY J.,"LA POLITIQUE EXTERIEURE ALLEMANDE DANS L'HIVER 1939-1940." COM FINLAND GERMANY ISLAM ITALY USSR NAT/G FORCES ECO/TAC DOMIN EDU/PROP COERCE WAR PWR WEALTH...HIST/WRIT NAZI TOT/POP VAL/FREE 20. PAGE 11 H0216 EUR+WWI DIPLOM

B65
ROWAT D.C.,THE OMBUDSMAN: CITIZEN'S DEFENDER. DENMARK FINLAND NEW/ZEALND NORWAY SWEDEN CONSULT PROB/SOLV FEEDBACK PARTIC GP/REL...SOC CONCPT NEW/IDEA METH/COMP ANTHOL BIBLIOG 20. PAGE 135 H2701 INSPECT CONSTN NAT/G ADMIN

B65
UPTON A.F.,FINLAND IN CRISIS 1940-1941. NAT/G FORCES DIPLOM COERCE...DECISION GEOG. PAGE 159 H3173 FINLAND GERMANY USSR WAR

B65
WUORINEN J.H.,SCANDINAVIA. DENMARK FINLAND ICELAND NORWAY SWEDEN SOCIETY AGRI INDUS DELIB/GP DIPLOM INT/TRADE NEUTRAL...GEOG CHARTS BIBLIOG TREATY. PAGE 171 H3428 NAT/G POL/PAR TREND POLICY

C65
WUORINEN J.H.,"SCANDINAVIA." DENMARK FINLAND ICELAND NORWAY SWEDEN SOCIETY AGRI POL/PAR DELIB/GP DIPLOM INT/TRADE NEUTRAL WAR...CHARTS TREATY 20. PAGE 171 H3427 BIBLIOG NAT/G POLICY

B67
ANDERSON S.V.,THE NORDIC COUNCIL: A STUDY OF SCANDINAVIAN REGIONALISM. DENMARK FINLAND ICELAND NORWAY SWEDEN MARKET NAT/G VOL/ASSN CONSULT PARL/PROC ATTIT...TIME/SEQ BIBLIOG 20. PAGE 7 H0134 INT/ORG REGION DIPLOM LEGIS

FINLAY D.J. H1005

FINLEY D.D. H3132

FIRM....SEE INDUS

FIRST R. H1006

FIRTH R. H0953,H1007,H1008,H1009

FISCAL POLICY....SEE BUDGET

FISCHER L. H1010,H1011

FISCHER-GALATI S.A. H1012

FISHEL L.H. H1013

FISHER M. H1014

FISHER S.N. H3063

FISHING INDUSTRY....SEE EXTR/IND

FISK E.K. H1015

FITZGERALD C.P. H1016,H1017,H1018

FITZGIBBON R.H. H1019,H1020

FITZSIMMONS T. H1021

FLANDERS....FLANDERS

FLECHTHEIM O.K. H1022,H1023

FLEMING R.W. H0888

FLEMING W.G. H1024

FLETCHER-COOKE J. H1025

FLINT J.E. H1026

FLOREN LOZANO L. H1027

FLORENCE P.S. H1028,H1029

FLORENCE....MEDIEVAL AND RENAISSANCE

FLORES R.H. H1030

FLORES X. H1031

FLORIDA....FLORIDA

FLOURNOY F. H1032

FLYNN H.M. H2742

FLYNN/BOSS....BOSS FLYNN

FNMA....FEDERAL NATIONAL MORTGAGE ASSOCIATION

FOCH/F....FERDINAND FOCH

FOGARTY M.P. H1033

FOLKLORE....SEE MYTH

FONER P.S. H2445

FONTANE/T....THEODORE FONTANE

B64
REMAK J.,THE GENTLE CRITIC: THEODOR FONTANE AND GERMAN POLITICS, 1848-1898. GERMANY PRUSSIA CULTURE ELITES BAL/PWR DIPLOM WRITING GOV/REL...HUM BIOG 19 BISMARCK/O JUNKER FONTANE/T. PAGE 131 H2614 PERSON SOCIETY WORKER CHIEF

FOOD....SEE AGRI, ALSO EATING

FOOD/PEACE....OFFICE OF FOOD FOR PEACE

FOR/AID....FOREIGN AID

N
BULLETIN ANALYTIQUE DE DOCUMENTATION POLITIQUE, ECONOMIQUE, ET SOCIAL CONTEMPORAIRE. FRANCE WOR+45 SOCIETY ECO/DEV ECO/UNDEV INT/ORG LOC/G PROB/SOLV FOR/AID LEAD REGION SOC. PAGE 1 H0002
BIBLIOG/A DIPLOM NAT/COMP NAT/G

N
THE MIDDLE EAST AND NORTH AFRICA. AFR ISLAM CULTURE ECO/UNDEV AGRI NAT/G TEC/DEV FOR/AID INT/TRADE EDU/PROP...CHARTS 20. PAGE 2 H0026
INDEX INDUS FINAN STAT

N
AFRICAN BIBLIOGRAPHIC CENTER,A CURRENT BIBLIOGRAPHY ON AFRICAN AFFAIRS. LAW CULTURE ECO/UNDEV LABOR SECT DIPLOM FOR/AID COLONIAL NAT/LISM...LING 20. PAGE 4 H0075
BIBLIOG/A AFR NAT/G REGION

N
MINISTRY OF OVERSEAS DEVELOPME,TECHNICAL CO-OPERATION -- A BIBLIOGRAPHY. UK LAW SOCIETY DIPLOM ECO/TAC FOR/AID...STAT 20 CMN/WLTH. PAGE 111 H2225
BIBLIOG TEC/DEV ECO/DEV NAT/G

N
US DEPARTMENT OF STATE,BIBLIOGRAPHY (PAMPHLETS). AGRI INDUS INT/ORG FOR/AID EDU/PROP WAR MARXISM ...SOC GOV/COMP METH/COMP 20. PAGE 159 H3184
BIBLIOG DIPLOM ECO/DEV NAT/G

N19
STEUBER F.A.,THE CONTRIBUTION OF SWITZERLAND TO THE ECONOMIC AND SOCIAL DEVELOPMENT OF LOW-INCOME COUNTRIES (PAMPHLET). SWITZERLND FINAN NAT/G VOL/ASSN INT/TRADE DRIVE...CHARTS 20. PAGE 149 H2982
FOR/AID ECO/UNDEV PLAN DIPLOM

B31
KIRKPATRICK F.A.,A HISTORY OF THE ARGENTINE REPUBLIC. SPAIN UK CONSTN SOCIETY ECO/UNDEV EX/STRUC DIPLOM FOR/AID LEAD WAR ATTIT...BIOG CHARTS 16/20 ARGEN SAN/MARTIN. PAGE 86 H1724
NAT/G L/A+17C COLONIAL

B48
PELCOVITS N.A.,OLD CHINA HANDS AND THE FOREIGN OFFICE. ASIA BURMA UK ECO/UNDEV NAT/G ECO/TAC FOR/AID TARIFFS DOMIN COLONIAL GOV/REL SOVEREIGN 19 HONG/KONG TREATY. PAGE 124 H2483
INT/TRADE ATTIT DIPLOM

B50
CORNELL U DEPT ASIAN STUDIES,SOUTHEAST ASIA PROGRAM DATA PAPER. BURMA CAMBODIA INDONESIA MALAYSIA VIETNAM SOCIETY STRUCT NAT/G SECT DIPLOM FOR/AID PWR WEALTH...SOC 20. PAGE 33 H0670
BIBLIOG/A CULTURE S/ASIA ECO/UNDEV

B51
CHRISTENSEN A.N.,THE EVOLUTION OF LATIN AMERICAN GOVERNMENT: A BOOK OF READINGS. ECO/UNDEV INDUS LOC/G POL/PAR EX/STRUC LEGIS FOR/AID CT/SYS ...SOC/WK 20 SOUTH/AMER. PAGE 30 H0599
NAT/G CONSTN DIPLOM L/A+17C

B54
EPSTEIN L.D.,BRITAIN - UNEASY ALLY. KOREA UK USA+45 NAT/G POL/PAR ECO/TAC FOR/AID INT/TRADE WAR LABOR/PAR CONSRV/PAR. PAGE 47 H0934
DIPLOM ATTIT POLICY NAT/COMP

B55
WOYTINSKY W.S.,WORLD COMMERCE AND GOVERNMENTS: TRENDS AND OUTLOOK. WOR+45 FINAN POL/PAR DIPLOM ECO/TAC FOR/AID DOMIN WAR CHOOSE...CHARTS BIBLIOG 20 LEAGUE/NAT UN ILO. PAGE 171 H3413
INT/TRADE DIST/IND NAT/COMP NAT/G

B56
ROBERTS H.L.,RUSSIA AND AMERICA. CHINA/COM S/ASIA USSR FORCES TEC/DEV FOR/AID NUC/PWR ALL/IDEOS ...MAJORIT TREND NAT/COMP 20 COLD/WAR UN NATO. PAGE 132 H2641
DIPLOM INT/ORG BAL/PWR TOTALISM

N56
US HOUSE COMM FOREIGN AFFAIRS,REPORT OF THE SPECIAL STUDY MISSION TO AFRICA, SOUTH AND EAST OF THE SAHARA (PAMPHLET). AFR SOUTH/AFR USA+45 STRUCT INT/TRADE PARL/PROC NAT/LISM ATTIT ALL/VALS HEALTH ...POLICY 20 CONGRESS. PAGE 160 H3197
FOR/AID COLONIAL ECO/UNDEV DIPLOM

B57
DEAN V.M.,THE NATURE OF THE NON-WESTERN WORLD. AFR ASIA L/A+17C S/ASIA CULTURE SOCIETY STRATA ECO/DEV DIPLOM ECO/TAC FOR/AID ATTIT DRIVE ALL/VALS ...RELATIV SOC CONCPT TIME/SEQ TREND TOT/POP 20. PAGE 39 H0778
ECO/UNDEV STERTYP NAT/LISM

B57
US SENATE SPEC COMM FOR AID,COMPILATION OF STUDIES AND SURVEYS. AFR ASIA L/A+17C USA+45 ECO/UNDEV AGRI INT/ORG CONSULT TEC/DEV CONFER TOTALISM...NAT/COMP 20 CONGRESS. PAGE 161 H3216
FOR/AID DIPLOM ORD/FREE DELIB/GP

B57
US SENATE SPEC COMM FOR AID,HEARINGS BEFORE THE SPECIAL COMMITTEE TO STUDY THE FOREIGN AID PROGRAM. USA+45 USSR ECO/UNDEV INT/ORG FORCES WEAPON TOTALISM ATTIT SUPEGO...NAT/COMP CONGRESS. PAGE 161 H3217
FOR/AID DIPLOM ORD/FREE TEC/DEV

B58
HANCE W.A.,AFRICAN ECONOMIC DEVELOPMENT. AGRI DIST/IND INDUS R+D ACT/RES PLAN CAP/ISM FOR/AID ...GOV/COMP BIBLIOG 20. PAGE 65 H1312
AFR ECO/UNDEV PROB/SOLV TEC/DEV

B59
LAQUER W.Z.,THE SOVIET UNION AND THE MIDDLE EAST. COM UAR USSR ECO/UNDEV NAT/G VOL/ASSN ECO/TAC EDU/PROP COLONIAL EXEC PWR...TIME/SEQ TREND COLD/WAR 20. PAGE 91 H1819
ISLAM DRIVE FOR/AID NAT/LISM

B59
VINACKE H.M.,A HISTORY OF THE FAR EAST IN MODERN TIMES (6TH ED.). KOREA S/ASIA USSR CONSTN CULTURE STRATA ECO/UNDEV NAT/G CHIEF FOR/AID INT/TRADE GP/REL...SOC NAT/COMP 19/20 CHINJAP. PAGE 163 H3255
STRUCT ASIA

B60
MC CLELLAN G.S.,INDIA. CHINA/COM INDIA CONSTN ELITES STRATA AGRI POL/PAR FOR/AID ARMS/CONT REV MARXISM...CENSUS BIBLIOG 20 COLD/WAR GANDHI/M NEHRU/J. PAGE 106 H2117
DIPLOM NAT/G SOCIETY ECO/UNDEV

B60
NEALE A.D.,THE FLOW OF RESOURCES FROM RICH TO POOR. WOR+45 ECO/DEV ECO/UNDEV FINAN INDUS NAT/G PLAN EFFICIENCY WEALTH...POLICY NAT/COMP 20 RESOURCE/N. PAGE 116 H2325
FOR/AID DIPLOM METH/CNCPT

B60
ROBINSON E.A.G.,ECONOMIC CONSEQUENCES OF THE SIZE OF NATIONS. AGRI INDUS DELIB/GP FOR/AID ADMIN EFFICIENCY...METH/COMP 20. PAGE 132 H2649
CONCPT INT/ORG NAT/COMP

B60
STOLPER W.F.,GERMANY BETWEEN EAST AND WEST: THE ECONOMICS OF COMPETITIVE COEXISTENCE. FUT GERMANY/E GERMANY/W WOR+45 FINAN POL/PAR BUDGET ECO/TAC FOR/AID INT/TRADE...STAT CHARTS METH/COMP 20 COLD/WAR. PAGE 150 H2989
ECO/DEV DIPLOM GOV/COMP BAL/PWR

B60
THEOBOLD R.,THE NEW NATIONS OF WEST AFRICA. GHANA NIGERIA CULTURE INT/ORG ECO/TAC FOR/AID COLONIAL RACE/REL POPULISM...ANTHOL BIBLIOG 20 UN. PAGE 153 H3068
AFR SOVEREIGN ECO/UNDEV DIPLOM

B60
WOLF C.,FOREIGN AID: THEORY AND PRACTICE IN SOUTHERN ASIA. CEYLON INDONESIA PHILIPPINE S/ASIA CULTURE STRATA ECO/UNDEV PLAN EDU/PROP ATTIT ...METH/CNCPT MATH QUANT STAT CONT/OBS TIME/SEQ SIMUL TOT/POP 20. PAGE 170 H3396
ACT/RES ECO/TAC FOR/AID

B60
WORLEY P.,ASIA TODAY (REV. ED.) (PAMPHLET). COM ECO/UNDEV AGRI FINAN INDUS POL/PAR FOR/AID ADMIN MARXISM 20. PAGE 170 H3411
BIBLIOG/A ASIA DIPLOM NAT/G

S60
FRANKEL S.H.,"ECONOMIC ASPECTS OF POLITICAL INDEPENDENCE IN AFRICA." AFR FUT SOCIETY ECO/UNDEV COM/IND FINAN LEGIS PLAN TEC/DEV CAP/ISM ECO/TAC INT/TRADE ADMIN ATTIT DRIVE RIGID/FLEX PWR WEALTH ...MGT NEW/IDEA MATH TIME/SEQ VAL/FREE 20. PAGE 53 H1052
NAT/G FOR/AID

S60
KEYFITZ N.,"WESTERN PERSPECTIVES AND ASIAN PROBLEMS." ASIA EUR+WWI S/ASIA SOCIETY FOR/AID ...POLICY SOC CONCPT STERTYP WORK TOT/POP 20. PAGE 85 H1701
CULTURE ATTIT

S60
RIVKIN A.,"AFRICAN ECONOMIC DEVELOPMENT: ADVANCED TECHNOLOGY AND THE STAGES OF GROWTH." CULTURE ECO/UNDEV AGRI COM/IND EXTR/IND PLAN ECO/TAC ATTIT DRIVE RIGID/FLEX SKILL WEALTH...MGT SOC GEN/LAWS WORK TOT/POP 20. PAGE 132 H2634
AFR TEC/DEV FOR/AID

S60
SPIRO H.J.,"NEW CONSTITUTIONAL FORMS IN AFRICA." FUT CULTURE SOCIETY ECO/UNDEV NAT/G POL/PAR VOL/ASSN EDU/PROP ATTIT DRIVE ORD/FREE PWR RESPECT ...POLICY CONCPT OBS TREND CON/ANAL STERTYP GEN/LAWS VAL/FREE. PAGE 148 H2950
AFR CONSTN FOR/AID NAT/LISM

B61
BONNEFOUS M.,EUROPE ET TIERS MONDE. EUR+WWI SOCIETY INT/ORG NAT/G VOL/ASSN ACT/RES TEC/DEV CAP/ISM ECO/TAC ATTIT ORD/FREE SOVEREIGN...POLICY CONCPT TREND 20. PAGE 19 H0373
AFR ECO/UNDEV FOR/AID INT/TRADE

B61
HAUSER M.,DIE URSACHEN DER FRANZOSISCHEN INFLATION IN DEN JAHREN 1946-1952. FRANCE INDUS NAT/G BUDGET DIPLOM ECO/TAC FOR/AID COST MONEY 20 GOLD/STAND. PAGE 68 H1357
ECO/DEV FINAN PRICE

B61
MILLIKAW M.F.,THE EMERGING NATIONS: THEIR GROWTH AND UNITED STATES POLICY. FUT USA+45 WOR+45 WOR-45 NAT/G PLAN TEC/DEV BAL/PWR GOV/REL PEACE ORD/FREE 20. PAGE 111 H2216
ECO/UNDEV POLICY DIPLOM FOR/AID

B62
CALVOCORESSI P.,WORLD ORDER AND NEW STATES: PROBLEMS OF KEEPING THE PEACE. AFR EUR+WWI S/ASIA ELITES NAT/G ECO/TAC FOR/AID EDU/PROP COERCE ATTIT DRIVE ALL/VALS...GEN/LAWS COLD/WAR 20 UN. PAGE 25 H0509
INT/ORG PEACE

B62
FRIEDMANN W.,METHODS AND POLICIES OF PRINCIPAL DONOR COUNTRIES IN PUBLIC INTERNATIONAL DEVELOPMENT FINANCING: PRELIMINARY APPRAISAL. FRANCE GERMANY/W UK USA+45 USSR WOR+45 FINAN TEC/DEV CAP/ISM DIPLOM ECO/TAC ATTIT 20 EEC. PAGE 53 H1066
INT/ORG FOR/AID NAT/COMP ADMIN

B62
GUENA Y.,HISTORIQUE DE LA COMMUNAUTE. FUT ECO/UNDEV NAT/G PLAN EDU/PROP COLONIAL REGION NAT/LISM ALL/VALS SOVEREIGN...CONCPT OBS CHARTS 20. PAGE 62 H1244
AFR VOL/ASSN FOR/AID FRANCE

B62
MOUSSA P.,THE UNDERPRIVILEGED NATIONS. FINAN INT/ORG PLAN PROB/SOLV CAP/ISM GIVE TASK WEALTH ...POLICY SOC 20. PAGE 114 H2273
ECO/UNDEV NAT/G DIPLOM FOR/AID

B63
BRITISH AID. UK AGRI DIST/IND INDUS SCHOOL TEC/DEV INT/TRADE COLONIAL DEMAND...TREND CHARTS 20. PAGE 2 H0041
FOR/AID ECO/UNDEV NAT/G FINAN

B63
BROEKMEIJER M.W.,DEVELOPING COUNTRIES AND NATO. USSR FORCES DIPLOM NUC/PWR WAR PEACE TOTALISM 20 NATO. PAGE 21 H0427
ECO/UNDEV FOR/AID ORD/FREE NAT/G

B63
CHOU S.H.,THE CHINESE INFLATION 1937-1949. ASIA SOCIETY POL/PAR FOR/AID INT/TRADE BAL/PAY WEALTH MARXISM...STAT CHARTS 20 COM/PARTY GOLD/STAND. PAGE 30 H0597
FINAN ECO/TAC BUDGET NAT/G

B63
COLUMBIA U SCHOOL OF LAW,PUBLIC INTERNATIONAL DEVELOPMENT FINANCING IN SENEGAL. SENEGAL FINAN DELIB/GP GIVE EFFICIENCY...CHARTS GOV/COMP ANTHOL 20. PAGE 32 H0636
FOR/AID PLAN RECEIVE ECO/UNDEV

B63
GONZALEZ PEDRERO E.,ANATOMIA DE UN CONFLICTO. WOR+45 ECO/DEV ECO/UNDEV ECO/TAC FOR/AID CONTROL ARMS/CONT GOV/REL...NAT/COMP 20 COLD/WAR. PAGE 58 H1166
DIPLOM DETER BAL/PWR

B63
HAQ M.,THE STRATEGY OF ECONOMIC PLANNING. PAKISTAN AGRI FINAN INDUS NAT/G FOR/AID TAX CONTROL REGION PRODUC...POLICY CHARTS 20. PAGE 66 H1324
ECO/TAC ECO/UNDEV PLAN PROB/SOLV

B63
KHADDURI M.,MODERN LIBYA: A STUDY IN POLITICAL DEVELOPMENT. EUR+WWI ISLAM LIBYA ELITES INT/ORG POL/PAR FORCES DIPLOM FOR/AID DOMIN EDU/PROP LEGIT NAT/LISM DRIVE RIGID/FLEX SKILL...CONCPT TIME/SEQ TREND 20. PAGE 85 H1704
NAT/G STRUCT

B63
OECD,FOOD AID: ITS ROLE IN ECONOMIC DEVELOPMENT. FINAN NAT/G PLAN DIPLOM GIVE TASK WEALTH ...METH/COMP METH 20. PAGE 120 H2397
ECO/UNDEV FOR/AID INT/ORG POLICY

S63
HINDLEY D.,"FOREIGN AID TO INDONESIA AND ITS POLITICAL IMPLICATIONS." INDONESIA POL/PAR ATTIT SOVEREIGN...CHARTS 20. PAGE 71 H1421
FOR/AID NAT/G WEALTH ECO/TAC

S63
LIGOT M.,"LA COOPERATION MILITAIRE DANS LES ACCORDS, PASSES ENTRE LA FRANCE ET LES ETATS AFRICAINS ET MALGACHE D'EXPRESSION." ECO/UNDEV INT/ORG NAT/G VOL/ASSN...CONCPT TIME/SEQ 20. PAGE 97 H1931
AFR FORCES FOR/AID FRANCE

S63
MBOYA T.,"AFRICAN SOCIALISM." ECO/UNDEV INT/ORG DIPLOM FOR/AID INT/TRADE REGION GP/REL ATTIT ORD/FREE EACM. PAGE 106 H2116
AFR SOCISM CULTURE NAT/LISM

B64
BALOGH T.,THE ECONOMIC IMPACT OF MONETARY AND COMMERCIAL INSTITUTIONS OF A EUROPEAN ORIGIN IN AFRICA. AFR UAR INDUS FOR/AID COLONIAL CONTROL ...NAT/COMP 20. PAGE 10 H0205
TEC/DEV FINAN ECO/UNDEV ECO/TAC

B64
FALL B.,STREET WITHOUT JOY. FRANCE USA+45 DIPLOM ECO/TAC FOR/AID GUERRILLA REV WEAPON...TREND 20. PAGE 48 H0966
WAR S/ASIA FORCES COERCE

B64
GUTTERIDGE W.,MILITARY INSTITUTIONS AND POWER IN THE NEW STATES. WOR+45 INT/ORG FOR/AID NEUTRAL REV CIVMIL/REL ATTIT ROLE...GOV/COMP 20. PAGE 63 H1258
FORCES DIPLOM ECO/UNDEV ELITES

B64
LEWIN P.,THE FOREIGN TRADE OF COMMUNIST CHINA* ITS IMPACT ON THE FREE WORLD. AFR EUR+WWI L/A+17C S/ASIA ECO/UNDEV CREATE FOR/AID...STAT NET/THEORY TREND CHARTS. PAGE 96 H1910
ASIA INT/TRADE NAT/COMP USSR

B64
LIEVWEN E.,GENERALS VS PRESIDENTS: WEOMILITARISM IN LATIN AMERICA. L/A+17C FORCES DIPLOM FOR/AID LEAD
CIVMIL/REL REV

...NAT/COMP 20 PRESIDENT. PAGE 97 H1929
CONSERVE ORD/FREE

B64
MAIER J.,POLITICS OF CHANGE IN LATIN AMERICA. BRAZIL L/A+17C STRATA INT/ORG NAT/G POL/PAR FOR/AID REV 20. PAGE 101 H2019
SOCIETY NAT/LISM DIPLOM REGION

B64
MAUD J.,AID FOR DEVELOPING COUNTRIES. COM EUR+WWI UK INT/TRADE ORD/FREE...GOV/COMP 20. PAGE 105 H2101
FOR/AID DIPLOM ECO/TAC ECO/UNDEV

B64
MILIBAND R.,THE SOCIALIST REGISTER: 1964. GERMANY/W ITALY UK LABOR POL/PAR ECO/TAC FOR/AID NUC/PWR ...POLICY SOCIALIST IDEA/COMP 20 MAO NASSER/G. PAGE 110 H2204
MARXISM SOCISM CAP/ISM PROB/SOLV

B64
OECD,DEVELOPMENT ASSISTANCE EFFORTS - POLICIES OF THE MEMBERS. AGRI INDUS BUDGET...GEOG NAT/COMP 20 OECD. PAGE 120 H2398
INT/ORG FOR/AID ECO/UNDEV TEC/DEV

B64
ROBERTS HL,FOREIGN AFFAIRS BIBLIOGRAPHY, 1952-1962. ECO/DEV SECT PLAN FOR/AID INT/TRADE ARMS/CONT NAT/LISM ATTIT...INT/LAW GOV/COMP IDEA/COMP 20. PAGE 132 H2643
BIBLIOG/A DIPLOM INT/ORG WAR

B64
TEPASKE J.J.,EXPLOSIVE FORCES IN LATIN AMERICA. CULTURE INTELL ECO/UNDEV INT/ORG NAT/G SECT FORCES ECO/TAC EDU/PROP PWR WEALTH SOC. PAGE 153 H3063
L/A+17C RIGID/FLEX FOR/AID USSR

B64
US HOUSE COMM BANKING-CURR,INTERNATIONAL DEVELOPMENT ASSOCIATION ACT AMENDMENT. CHINA/COM USA+45 USSR FINAN FORCES LEGIS DIPLOM CONFER EFFICIENCY...CHARTS GOV/COMP 20 PRESIDENT CONGRESS INTL/DEV. PAGE 160 H3196
BAL/PAY FOR/AID RECORD ECO/TAC

S64
DE GAULLE C.,"FRENCH WORLD VIEW." AFR ASIA CHINA/COM EUR+WWI ISLAM ECO/UNDEV INT/ORG NAT/G VOL/ASSN ACT/RES DIPLOM ECO/TAC EDU/PROP ATTIT DRIVE WEALTH 20. PAGE 37 H0751
TOP/EX PWR FOR/AID FRANCE

S64
GARMARNIKOW M.,"INFLUENCE-BUYING IN WEST AFRICA." COM FUT USSR INTELL NAT/G PLAN TEC/DEV ECO/TAC DOMIN EDU/PROP REGION NAT/LISM ATTIT DRIVE ALL/VALS SOVEREIGN...POLICY PSY SOC CONCPT TREND STERTYP WORK COLD/WAR 20. PAGE 55 H1102
AFR ECO/UNDEV FOR/AID SOCISM

S64
TOUVAL S.,"THE SOMALI REPUBLIC." AFR ISLAM SOMALIA FAM KIN NAT/G CREATE FOR/AID LEGIT ATTIT ALL/VALS ...RECORD TREND 20. PAGE 156 H3119
ECO/UNDEV RIGID/FLEX

S64
ZARTMAN I.W.,"LES RELATIONS ENTRE LA FRANCE ET L'ALGERIA DEPUIS LES ACCORDS D'EVIAN." EUR+WWI FUT ISLAM CULTURE AGRI EXTR/IND FINAN INDUS POL/PAR DIPLOM ECO/TAC FOR/AID PEACE ATTIT DRIVE ALL/VALS ...TIME/SEQ VAL/FREE 20. PAGE 172 H3450
ECO/UNDEV ALGERIA FRANCE

B65
HAPGOOD D.,AFRICA: FROM INDEPENDENCE TO TOMARROW. AFR GUINEA SENEGAL CULTURE ELITES ECO/UNDEV AGRI SCHOOL FOR/AID COLONIAL MARXISM...TREND 20. PAGE 66 H1323
ECO/TAC SOCIETY NAT/G

B65
HLA MYINT U.,THE ECONOMICS OF THE DEVELOPING COUNTRIES. USA+45 WOR+45 AGRI FINAN NAT/G INT/TRADE ...CLASSIF CENSUS TREND NAT/COMP SIMUL GEN/LAWS. PAGE 71 H1430
ECO/UNDEV FOR/AID GEOG

B65
KOUSOULAS D.G.,REVOLUTION AND DEFEAT; THE STORY OF THE GREEK COMMUNIST PARTY. GREECE INT/ORG EX/STRUC DIPLOM FOR/AID EDU/PROP PARL/PROC ADJUST ATTIT 20 COM/PARTY. PAGE 88 H1759
REV MARXISM POL/PAR ORD/FREE

B65
MEAGHER R.F.,PUBLIC INTERNATIONAL DEVELOPMENT FINANCING IN SUDAN. SUDAN FINAN DELIB/GP GIVE ...CHARTS GOV/COMP 20. PAGE 108 H2155
FOR/AID PLAN RECEIVE ECO/UNDEV

B65
MEIER R.L.,DEVELOPMENTAL PLANNING. PUERT/RICO INDUS PUB/INST SCHOOL CREATE ECO/TAC FOR/AID...NAT/COMP 20. PAGE 108 H2165
PLAN ECO/UNDEV GOV/COMP TEC/DEV

B65
ONSLOW C.,ASIAN ECONOMIC DEVELOPMENT. BURMA CEYLON INDIA MALAYSIA PAKISTAN S/ASIA AGRI INDUS MARKET PROB/SOLV CAP/ISM FOR/AID INT/TRADE DEMAND WEALTH ...POLICY ANTHOL 20. PAGE 121 H2418
ECO/UNDEV ECO/TAC PLAN NAT/G

B65
ONUOHA B.,THE ELEMENTS OF AFRICAN SOCIALISM. AFR FINAN SECT TEC/DEV FOR/AID GP/REL OWN LAISSEZ MARXISM...CONCPT BIBLIOG 20. PAGE 121 H2419
SOCISM ECO/UNDEV NAT/G EX/STRUC

B65
SHRIMALI K.L.,EDUCATION IN CHANGING INDIA. INDIA
EDU/PROP

CULTURE DIPLOM FOR/AID GP/REL RACE/REL ATTIT PROF/ORG
SOC/INTEG 20 UNESCO CMN/WLTH. PAGE 143 H2866 ACADEM

B65
UN,SPACE ACTIVITIES AND RESOURCES: REVIEW OF UNITED SPACE
NATION'S NATIONAL AND INTERNATIONAL PROGRAMS. NUC/PWR
INT/ORG LABOR PLAN TEC/DEV DIPLOM EFFICIENCY HEALTH FOR/AID
...GOV/COMP 20 UN. PAGE 158 H3155 PEACE

B65
YOUNG A.N.,CHINA'S WARTIME FINANCE AND INFLATION. FINAN
ASIA AGRI INDUS NAT/G ECO/TAC CONFER PRICE WAR COST FOR/AID
20. PAGE 172 H3437 TAX
BUDGET

L65
MATTHEWS D.G.,"A CURRENT BIBLIOGRAPHY ON SUDANESE BIBLIOG
AFFAIRS: A SELECT BIBLIOGRAPHY FROM 1960-1964." ECO/UNDEV
SUDAN LAW CULTURE AGRI FINAN INDUS LABOR POL/PAR NAT/G
TEC/DEV FOR/AID RACE/REL LITERACY...LING 20. DIPLOM
PAGE 105 H2094

S65
GOLDMAN M.I.,"A BALANCE SHEET OF SOVIET FOREIGN USSR
AID." USA+45 ECO/UNDEV BAL/PWR ECO/TAC RENT GIVE FOR/AID
EDU/PROP CONTROL COST PROFIT GEN/METH. PAGE 58 NAT/COMP
H1158 EFFICIENCY

S65
HAYTER T.,"FRENCH AID TO AFRICA* ITS SCOPE AND AFR
ACHIEVEMENTS." CULTURE ECO/TAC INT/TRADE ADMIN FRANCE
REGION CENTRAL FEDERAL LOVE PWR SOVEREIGN EEC. FOR/AID
PAGE 68 H1370 COLONIAL

S65
LAULICHT J.,"PUBLIC OPINION AND FOREIGN POLICY DIPLOM
DECISIONS." CANADA ELITES NAT/G FOR/AID LEAD ATTIT
NUC/PWR PERCEPT...INT QU CHARTS UN COLD/WAR. CON/ANAL
PAGE 92 H1839 SAMP

S65
POWELL J.D.,"MILITARY ASSISTANCE AND MILITARISM IN L/A+17C
LATIN AMERICA." USA+45 INT/ORG NAT/G CONTROL REGION FORCES
PRODUC WEALTH...CLASSIF STAT NAT/COMP CONGRESS. FOR/AID
PAGE 128 H2550 PWR

S65
THOMAS F.C. JR.,"THE PEACE CORPS IN MOROCCO." MOROCCO
CULTURE MUNIC PROVS CREATE ROUTINE TASK ADJUST FRANCE
STRANGE...OBS PEACE/CORP. PAGE 154 H3077 FOR/AID
EDU/PROP

S65
WHITE J.,"WEST GERMAN AID TO DEVELOPING COUNTRIES." GERMANY
INT/ORG OP/RES GIVE CENTRAL ATTIT DRIVE...STAT FOR/AID
NAT/COMP COLD/WAR. PAGE 167 H3348 ECO/UNDEV
CAP/ISM

S65
WOLF C. JR.,"THE POLITICAL EFFECTS OF SOME MILITARY L/A+17C
PROGRAMS* SOME INDICATIONS FROM LATIN AMERICA." FORCES
ELITES STRATA BUDGET FOR/AID WEAPON ATTIT PERCEPT CIVMIL/REL
PWR...REGRESS SYS/QU CHARTS NAT/COMP. PAGE 170 PROBABIL
H3397

B66
AMER ENTERPRISE INST PUB POL,SIGNIFICANT ISSUES IN ECO/UNDEV
ECONOMIC AID TO DEVELOPING COUNTRIES. FINAN INT/ORG FOR/AID
NAT/G PLAN PROB/SOLV GIVE TASK WEALTH...DECISION DIPLOM
20. PAGE 6 H0119 POLICY

B66
HAMILTON W.B.,A DECADE OF THE COMMONWEALTH, INT/ORG
1955-1964. UK LAW ELITES FINAN FOR/AID CONFER INGP/REL
COLONIAL PWR...GEOG CHARTS ANTHOL 20 CMN/WLTH UN. DIPLOM
PAGE 65 H1302 NAT/G

B66
KIRDAR U.,THE STRUCTURE OF UNITED NATIONS ECONOMIC INT/ORG
AID TO UNDERDEVELOPED COUNTRIES. AGRI FINAN INDUS FOR/AID
NAT/G EX/STRUC PLAN GIVE TASK...POLICY 20 UN. ECO/UNDEV
PAGE 86 H1721 ADMIN

B66
LEONTIEF W.,ESSAYS IN ECONOMICS. ECO/UNDEV INDUS CONCPT
NAT/G CAP/ISM FOR/AID AUTOMAT MARXISM...ECOMETRIC METH/CNCPT
CHARTS ANTHOL METH 20 KEYNES/JM. PAGE 94 H1886 METH/COMP

B66
MASON E.S.,ECONOMIC DEVELOPMENT IN INDIA AND NAT/COMP
PAKISTAN. INDIA PAKISTAN AGRI FINAN PLAN BUDGET ECO/UNDEV
INT/TRADE WEALTH...POLICY STAT TREND CHARTS 20. ECO/TAC
PAGE 104 H2086 FOR/AID

B66
SOBEL L.A.,SOUTH VIETNAM: US-COMMUNIST WAR
CONFRONTATION IN SOUTHEAST ASIA 1961-65. VIETNAM TIME/SEQ
FOR/AID CROWD DETER REV PEACE...GEOG 20 INTERVENT FORCES
DIEM COLD/WAR. PAGE 146 H2926 NAT/G

B66
US DEPARTMENT OF THE ARMY,SOUTH ASIA: A STRATEGIC BIBLIOG/A
SURVEY (PAMPHLET NO. 550-3). AFGHANISTN INDIA NEPAL S/ASIA
PAKISTAN ECO/UNDEV INT/ORG POL/PAR FORCES FOR/AID DIPLOM
INT/TRADE LEAD WAR...POLICY SOC TREND 20. PAGE 160 NAT/G
H3195

B66
WILLNER A.R.,THE NEOTRADITIONAL ACCOMMODATION TO INDONESIA
POLITICAL INDEPENDENCE* THE CASE OF INDONESIA * CONSERVE
RESEARCH MONOGRAPH NO. 26. CULTURE ECO/UNDEV CREATE ELITES
PROB/SOLV FOR/AID LEGIT COLONIAL EFFICIENCY ADMIN
NAT/LISM ALL/VALS SOC. PAGE 168 H3371

S66
GILBERT S.P.,"WARS OF LIBERATION AND SOVIET USSR
MILITARY AID POLICY." ASIA INDIA INDONESIA UAR FOR/AID
USA+45 STRATA WAR PERCEPT MARXISM...STAT NAT/COMP. WEAPON
PAGE 56 H1124 DRIVE

S66
HAIGH G.,"FIELD TRAINING IN HUMAN RELATIONS FOR THE CULTURE
PEACE CORPS." CONSULT CREATE EDU/PROP ADMIN TASK PERS/REL
GP/REL ATTIT PERSON...PSY OBS SOC/EXP PEACE/CORP. FOR/AID
PAGE 64 H1276 ADJUST

B67
BURR R.N.,OUR TROUBLED HEMISPHERE: PERSPECTIVES ON DIPLOM
UNITED STATES-LATIN AMERICAN RELATIONS. L/A+17C NAT/COMP
USA+45 USA-45 INT/ORG FOR/AID COLONIAL PWR 19/20 NAT/G
OAS. PAGE 25 H0493 POLICY

B67
OVERSEAS DEVELOPMENT INSTIT,EFFECTIVE AID. WOR+45 FOR/AID
INT/ORG TEC/DEV DIPLOM INT/TRADE ADMIN. PAGE 122 ECO/UNDEV
H2434 ECO/TAC
NAT/COMP

B67
PLISCHKE E.,CONDUCT OF AMERICAN DIPLOMACY (3RD REV. DIPLOM
ED.). INT/ORG NAT/G PROB/SOLV FOR/AID...CHARTS RATIONAL
BIBLIOG T 20 DEPT/STATE. PAGE 126 H2529 PLAN

L67
ROTH A.R.,"CAPITAL-MARKET DEVELOPMENT IN ISRAEL AND LAW
BRAZIL: TWO EXAMPLES OF THE ROLE OF LAW IN ECO/UNDEV
DEVELOPMENT." BRAZIL ISRAEL L/A+17C INDUS MARKET NAT/COMP
ECO/TAC FOR/AID INT/TRADE CONTROL BAL/PAY 20. FINAN
PAGE 135 H2694

L67
SEGAL A.,"THE INTEGRATION OF DEVELOPING COUNTRIES: ECO/UNDEV
SOME THOUGHTS ON EAST AFRICA AND CENTRAL AMERICA." DIPLOM
AFR L/A+17C INT/ORG NAT/G VOL/ASSN FOR/AID REGION
INT/TRADE EQUILIB NAT/LISM PWR 20. PAGE 141 H2820

S67
BUTTINGER J.,"VIETNAM* FRAUD OF THE 'OTHER WAR'." PLAN
VIETNAM/S ELITES STRUCT AGRI NAT/G FOR/AID RENT WEALTH
TREND. PAGE 25 H0499 REV
ECO/UNDEV

S67
FINLAY D.J.,"THE GHANA COUP...ONE YEAR LATER." REV
GHANA FORCES FOR/AID PRESS CONTROL CIVMIL/REL NAT/G
NAT/LISM AUTHORIT PWR...PREDICT 20. PAGE 50 H1005 ATTIT
ECO/UNDEV

S67
GLOBERSON A.,"SOCIAL GROWTH IN THE DEVELOPING ECO/UNDEV
COUNTRIES." CULTURE SOCIETY CONSULT PROB/SOLV SOC. FOR/AID
PAGE 57 H1144 EDU/PROP
PLAN

S67
GRUNDY K.W.,"AFRICA IN THE WORLD ARENA." ECO/UNDEV AFR
BAL/PWR FOR/AID NEUTRAL REV NAT/LISM GOV/COMP. DIPLOM
PAGE 62 H1240 INT/ORG
COLONIAL

S67
HANSON A.H.,"INDIA AFTER THE ELECTIONS." INDIA NAT/G
ECO/UNDEV LEGIS TEC/DEV FOR/AID GP/REL FEDERAL POL/PAR
ATTIT 20. PAGE 66 H1321 REGION
CENTRAL

S67
JAIN G.,"INDIA REJECTS THE POWER RACE* REALISM INDIA
ABOUT NUCLEAR WEAPONS." FORCES PROB/SOLV FOR/AID CHINA/COM
ARMS/CONT COST PWR...GOV/COMP 20. PAGE 79 H1583 NUC/PWR
DIPLOM

S67
PLUMPTRE A.F.W.,"PERSPECTIVE ON OUR AID TO OTHERS." FOR/AID
CANADA CREATE 20. PAGE 127 H2530 DIPLOM
NAT/G
PLAN

S67
ROSE S.,"ASIAN NATIONALISM* THE SECOND STAGE." ASIA NAT/LISM
COM ECO/UNDEV NAT/G PROB/SOLV DIPLOM FOR/AID DOMIN S/ASIA
NEUTRAL REGION TASK...METH/COMP 20. PAGE 134 H2675 BAL/PWR
COLONIAL

S67
THIEN T.T.,"VIETNAM: A CASE OF SOCIAL ALIENATION." NAT/G
VIETNAM AGRI FORCES FOR/AID ADMIN REPRESENT ELITES
INGP/REL PWR 19/20. PAGE 154 H3071 WORKER
STRANGE

N67
US HOUSE COMM SCI ASTRONAUT,GOVERNMENT, SCIENCE, NAT/G
AND INTERNATIONAL POLICY (PAMPHLET). INDIA POLICY
NETHERLAND ECO/DEV ECO/UNDEV R+D ACADEM PLAN DIPLOM CREATE
FOR/AID CONFER...PREDICT 20 CHINJAP. PAGE 160 H3198 TEC/DEV

S68
LAPIERRE J.W.,"TRADITION ET MODERNITE A ECO/UNDEV
MADAGASCAR." ISLAM MADAGASCAR AGRI FINAN KIN NAT/G FOR/AID
CREATE OP/RES GP/REL INGP/REL ATTIT CONSERVE...PSY CULTURE
20. PAGE 91 H1813 TEC/DEV

FORBES A.H. H1034

FORCE AND VIOLENCE....SEE COERCE

FORCES....ARMED FORCES AND POLICE

B
DEUTSCHE BIBLIOTH FRANKF A M,DEUTSCHE BIBLIOGRAPHIE. EUR+WWI GERMANY ECO/DEV FORCES DIPLOM LEAD...POLICY PHIL/SCI SOC 20. PAGE 40 H0802 BIBLIOG LAW ADMIN NAT/G

N
CANADIAN GOVERNMENT PUBLICATIONS (1955-). CANADA AGRI FINAN LABOR FORCES INT/TRADE HEALTH...JURID 20 PARLIAMENT. PAGE 1 H0003 BIBLIOG/A NAT/G DIPLOM INT/ORG

N
INDIA: A REFERENCE ANNUAL. INDIA CULTURE COM/IND R+D FORCES PLAN RECEIVE EDU/PROP HEALTH...STAT CHARTS BIBLIOG 20. PAGE 1 H0017 CONSTN LABOR INT/ORG

N
THE STATESMAN'S YEARBOOK; STATISTICAL AND HISTORICAL ANNUAL OF THE STATES OF THE WORLD. WOR+45 WOR-45 COM/IND FINAN INDUS SECT FORCES TEC/DEV EDU/PROP...GEOG BIBLIOG 19/20. PAGE 1 H0023 NAT/COMP GOV/COMP STAT CONSTN

B00
DE JOMINI A.H.,THE ART OF WAR. MOD/EUR NAT/G BAL/PWR DIPLOM DOMIN EXEC ROUTINE COERCE DRIVE PWR SKILL...POLICY CONCPT CHARTS STERTYP 19. PAGE 38 H0755 PLAN FORCES WAR WEAPON

B00
OMAN C.,A HISTORY OF THE ART OF WAR: THE MIDDLE AGES FROM THE FOURTH TO THE FOURTEENTH CENTURY. CHRIST-17C MEDIT-7 CULTURE SOCIETY INT/ORG ROUTINE PERSON...CONT/OBS HIST/WRIT CHARTS VAL/FREE. PAGE 121 H2417 FORCES SKILL WAR

B00
VOLPICELLI Z.,RUSSIA ON THE PACIFIC AND THE SIBERIAN RAILWAY. MOD/EUR ECO/UNDEV INT/ORG FORCES PLAN DOMIN COLONIAL ROUTINE ATTIT ALL/VALS...OBS HIST/WRIT TIME/SEQ TREND CON/ANAL AUD/VIS CHARTS 18/19. PAGE 163 H3261 NAT/G ACT/RES RUSSIA

B02
SEELEY J.R.,THE EXPANSION OF ENGLAND. MOD/EUR S/ASIA UK CULTURE NAT/G FORCES PLAN DOMIN EDU/PROP COLONIAL ROUTINE ATTIT ALL/VALS SOVEREIGN...CONCPT HIST/WRIT PARLIAMENT 18 CMN/WLTH. PAGE 141 H2819 INT/ORG ACT/RES CAP/ISM INDIA

B03
FORTESCUE G.K.,SUBJECT INDEX OF THE MODERN WORKS ADDED TO THE LIBRARY OF THE BRITISH MUSEUM IN THE YEARS 1881-1900 (3 VOLS.). UK LAW CONSTN FINAN NAT/G FORCES INT/TRADE COLONIAL 19. PAGE 52 H1041 BIBLIOG INDEX WRITING

B05
MACHIAVELLI N.,THE ART OF WAR. CHRIST-17C TOP/EX DRIVE ORD/FREE PWR SKILL...MGT CHARTS. PAGE 100 H1993 NAT/G FORCES WAR ITALY

B12
HARIOU M.,LA SOUVERAINTE NATIONALE. EX/STRUC FORCES LEGIS CHOOSE PWR JURID. PAGE 66 H1331 SOVEREIGN CONCPT NAT/G REPRESENT

B12
SONOLET L.,L'AFRIQUE OCCIDENTALE FRANCAISE. FRANCE AGRI INDUS NAT/G SECT FORCES INT/TRADE EDU/PROP RACE/REL HEALTH ORD/FREE...CHARTS 19/20 NEGRO AFRICA/W. PAGE 147 H2933 DOMIN ADMIN COLONIAL AFR

B14
BERHARDI F.,GERMANY AND THE NEXT WAR. MOD/EUR NAT/G SCHOOL FORCES ACT/RES DOMIN EDU/PROP SUPEGO PWR ...TIME/SEQ STERTYP TOT/POP 20 WWI. PAGE 15 H0304 DRIVE COERCE WAR GERMANY

B14
BERNHARDI F.,ON THE WAR OF TODAY. MOD/EUR INT/ORG NAT/G TOP/EX PWR CHARTS. PAGE 16 H0313 FORCES SKILL WAR

B14
CRAIG J.,ELEMENTS OF POLITICAL SCIENCE (3 VOLS.). CONSTN AGRI INDUS SCHOOL FORCES TAX CT/SYS SUFF MORAL WEALTH...CONCPT 19 CIVIL/LIB. PAGE 35 H0696 PHIL/SCI NAT/G ORD/FREE

B16
CALVERT A.F.,SOUTHWEST AFRICA 1884-1914 (2ND ED.). GERMANY EXTR/IND NAT/G FORCES...GEOG AUD/VIS CHARTS 19/20 RESOURCE/N AFRICA/SW. PAGE 25 H0508 COLONIAL ECO/UNDEV AFR

B17
BARRES M.,THE UNDYING SPIRIT OF FRANCE (TRANS. BY M. CORWIN). FRANCE DOMIN LEAD DEATH ATTIT RESPECT ...NAT/COMP 20 WWI. PAGE 11 H0226 NAT/LISM FORCES WAR CULTURE

N19
BARRES M.,"THE WAR AND THE SPIRIT OF YOUTH" (PAMPHLET). FRANCE FORCES DOMIN LEAD DEATH AGE/Y ATTIT RESPECT...FASCIST 20 WWI. PAGE 11 H0228 WAR NAT/LISM CULTURE MYSTIC

N19
BENTHAM J.,A PLAN FOR AN UNIVERSAL AND PERPETUAL PEACE (1838) (PAMPHLET). NAT/G FORCES BAL/PWR INT/TRADE ADMIN AGREE CT/SYS ARMS/CONT SOVEREIGN WEALTH GEN/LAWS. PAGE 14 H0288 INT/ORG INT/LAW PEACE COLONIAL

N19
BRIMMELL G.H.,COMMUNISM IN SOUTHEAST ASIA (PAMPHLET). BURMA CAMBODIA COM INDIA INDONESIA LAOS MOD/EUR NAT/G POL/PAR FORCES CAP/ISM CONTROL WEALTH ...MYTH 20. PAGE 21 H0420 MARXISM S/ASIA REV ECO/UNDEV

N19
GOODMAN G.K.,IMPERIAL JAPAN AND ASIA: A REASSESSMENT (PAMPHLET). ASIA S/ASIA ECO/DEV FORCES LEAD WAR NAT/LISM ATTIT...DECISION CONCPT BIBLIOG 19/20 CHINJAP. PAGE 59 H1172 DIPLOM NAT/G POLICY COLONIAL

N19
SOUTH AFRICA COMMISSION ON FUT,INTERIM AND FINAL REPORTS ON FUTURE FORM OF GOVERNMENT IN THE SOUTH-WEST AFRICAN PROTECTORATE (PAMPHLET). SOUTH/AFR NAT/G FORCES CONFER COLONIAL CONTROL 20 AFRICA/SW. PAGE 147 H2936 CONSTN REPRESENT ADMIN PROB/SOLV

C20
BLACHLY F.F.,"THE GOVERNMENT AND ADMINISTRATION OF GERMANY." GERMANY CONSTN LOC/G PROVS DELIB/GP EX/STRUC FORCES LEGIS TOP/EX CT/SYS...BIBLIOG/A 19/20. PAGE 17 H0348 NAT/G GOV/REL ADMIN PHIL/SCI

B21
KREY A.C.,THE FIRST CRUSADE. CHRIST-17C SOCIETY STRATA NAT/G SECT FORCES WORKER WRITING LEAD ATTIT ...CHARTS 11 CHRISTIAN CRUSADES. PAGE 88 H1767 WAR CATH DIPLOM PARTIC

B21
STUART G.H.,FRENCH FOREIGN POLICY. CONSTN INT/ORG NAT/G POL/PAR EX/STRUC FORCES PLAN ECO/TAC DOMIN EDU/PROP ADJUD COERCE ATTIT DRIVE RIGID/FLEX ALL/VALS...POLICY OBS RECORD BIOG TIME/SEQ TREND. PAGE 150 H3000 MOD/EUR DIPLOM FRANCE

B22
URE P.N.,THE ORIGIN OF TYRANNY. MEDIT-7 FINAN INDUS CHIEF FORCES ECO/TAC WEALTH. PAGE 159 H3174 AUTHORIT PWR NAT/G MARKET

B23
FRANK T.,A HISTORY OF ROME. MEDIT-7 INTELL SOCIETY LOC/G NAT/G POL/PAR FORCES LEGIS DOMIN LEGIT ALL/VALS...POLICY CONCPT TIME/SEQ GEN/LAWS ROM/EMP ROM/EMP. PAGE 53 H1050 EXEC STRUCT ELITES

B27
FLOURNOY F.,PARLIAMENT AND WAR. MOD/EUR UK NAT/G FORCES LEGIS TOP/EX DIPLOM LEGIT DEBATE ATTIT RIGID/FLEX PWR...DECISION TIME/SEQ PARLIAMENT 19/20. PAGE 52 H1032 COERCE WAR

B27
GOOCH G.P.,ENGLISH DEMOCRATIC IDEAS IN THE SEVENTEENTH CENTURY (2ND ED.). UK LAW SECT FORCES DIPLOM LEAD PARL/PROC REV ATTIT AUTHORIT...ANARCH CONCPT 17 PARLIAMENT CMN/WLTH REFORMERS. PAGE 58 H1167 IDEA/COMP MAJORIT EX/STRUC CONSERVE

B28
CORBETT P.E.,CANADA AND WORLD POLITICS. LAW CULTURE SOCIETY STRUCT MARKET INT/ORG FORCES ACT/RES PLAN ECO/TAC LEGIT ORD/FREE PWR RESPECT...SOC CONCPT TIME/SEQ TREND CMN/WLTH 20 LEAGUE/NAT. PAGE 33 H0662 NAT/G CANADA

B29
DAVIE M.R.,THE EVOLUTION OF WAR. CULTURE KIN COERCE WAR ATTIT DRIVE...PSY SOC TIME/SEQ TREND GEN/LAWS. PAGE 37 H0746 FORCES STERTYP

B29
LANGER W.L.,THE FRANCO-RUSSIAN ALLIANCE: 1890-1894. FRANCE MOD/EUR UK USSR NAT/G CHIEF FORCES BAL/PWR AGREE WAR PEACE PWR...TIME/SEQ TREATY 19 BISMARCK/O. PAGE 91 H1809 DIPLOM

B30
BYNKERSHOEK C.,QUAESTIONUM JURIS PUBLICI LIBRI DUO. CHRIST-17C MOD/EUR CONSTN ELITES SOCIETY NAT/G PROVS EX/STRUC FORCES TOP/EX BAL/PWR DIPLOM ATTIT MORAL...TRADIT CONCPT. PAGE 25 H0502 INT/ORG LAW NAT/LISM INT/LAW

B31
DUFFIELD M.,KING LEGION. NAT/G PROVS SECT LEGIS EDU/PROP PRESS GP/REL AGE/Y MARXISM POLICY. PAGE 43 H0856 SUPEGO FORCES VOL/ASSN LOBBY

B32
BLUM L.,PEACE AND DISARMAMENT (TRANS. BY A. WERTH). NAT/G FORCES WORKER DIPLOM AGREE WAR ATTIT AUTHORIT ORD/FREE. PAGE 18 H0360 SOCIALIST PEACE INT/ORG ARMS/CONT

B32
MARRARO H.R.,AMERICAN OPINION ON THE UNIFICATION OF ITALY. ITALY FORCES DIPLOM SOVEREIGN CATHISM CONSERVE...CONCPT NAT/COMP BIBLIOG 19. PAGE 103 H2056 ORD/FREE NAT/LISM REV CONSTN

B35
GORER G.,AFRICA DANCES: A BOOK ABOUT WEST AFRICAN NEGROES. STRUCT LOC/G SECT FORCES TAX ADMIN COLONIAL...ART/METH MYTH WORSHIP 20 NEGRO AFRICA/W CHRISTIAN RITUAL. PAGE 59 H1181 AFR ATTIT CULTURE SOCIETY

B37
BOURNE H.E.,THE WORLD WAR: A LIST OF THE MORE IMPORTANT BOOKS PUBLISHED BEFORE 1937 (PAMPHLET). EUR+WWI NAT/G DIPLOM ATTIT SOC. PAGE 19 H0386 BIBLIOG/A WAR FORCES PLAN

B37
CARLYLE T.,THE FRENCH REVOLUTION (2 VOLS.). FRANCE CONSTN NAT/G FORCES COERCE MURDER PEACE MORAL POPULISM...TIME/SEQ IDEA/COMP GEN/LAWS 18. PAGE 26 H0532
REV CHIEF TRADIT

B37
UNION OF SOUTH AFRICA,REPORT CONCERNING ADMINISTRATION OF SOUTH WEST AFRICA (6 VOLS.). SOUTH/AFR INDUS PUB/INST FORCES LEGIS BUDGET DIPLOM EDU/PROP ADJUD CT/SYS...GEOG CHARTS 20 AFRICA/SW LEAGUE/NAT. PAGE 158 H3166
NAT/G ADMIN COLONIAL CONSTN

B38
COUPLAND R.,EAST AFRICA AND ITS INVADERS. AFR ISLAM STRATA SECT FORCES DIPLOM TRIBUTE CONTROL DISCRIM NAT/LISM 19 AFRICA/E EUROPE MISSION. PAGE 34 H0680
CULTURE ELITES COLONIAL MARKET

B38
IIZAWA S.,POLITICS AND POLITICAL PARTIES IN JAPAN. ELITES VOL/ASSN CHOOSE SUFF CIVMIL/REL GP/REL 19/20 CHINJAP. PAGE 76 H1522
POL/PAR REPRESENT FORCES NAT/G

B38
RAWLINSON H.G.,INDIA: A SHORT CULTURAL HISTORY. INDIA LAW STRATA FORCES INT/TRADE ADMIN COLONIAL PERSON...GEOG HUM BIBLIOG WORSHIP 20. PAGE 130 H2598
CULTURE SECT MYTH ART/METH

B38
SAINT-PIERRE C.I.,SCHEME FOR LASTING PEACE (TRANS. BY H. BELLOT). INDUS NAT/G CHIEF FORCES INT/TRADE CT/SYS WAR PWR SOVEREIGN WEALTH...POLICY 18. PAGE 137 H2732
INT/ORG PEACE AGREE INT/LAW

B39
HITLER A.,MEIN KAMPF. EUR+WWI FUT MOD/EUR STRUCT INT/ORG LABOR NAT/G POL/PAR FORCES CREATE PLAN BAL/PWR DIPLOM ECO/TAC DOMIN EDU/PROP ADMIN COERCE ATTIT...SOCIALIST BIOG TREND NAZI. PAGE 71 H1428
PWR NEW/IDEA WAR

B39
KOHN H.,REVOLUTIONS AND DICTATORSHIPS. COM EUR+WWI ISLAM MOD/EUR NAT/G CHIEF FORCES WAR CIVMIL/REL PWR MARXISM 18/20. PAGE 87 H1739
NAT/LISM TOTALISM REV FASCISM

B39
TAGGART F.J.,ROME AND CHINA. MEDIT-7 INT/ORG NAT/G FORCES LEGIS TOP/EX PLAN PWR SOVEREIGN...CHARTS TOT/POP ROM/EMP. PAGE 152 H3034
ASIA WAR

S39
COLE G.D.H.,"NAZI ECONOMICS: HOW DO THEY MANAGE IT?" GERMANY FORCES WORKER BUDGET INT/TRADE ROUTINE COERCE WAR 20 HITLER/A NAZI. PAGE 31 H0622
FASCISM ECO/TAC ATTIT PLAN

C39
REISCHAUER R.,"JAPAN'S GOVERNMENT--POLITICS." CONSTN STRATA POL/PAR FORCES LEGIS DIPLOM ADMIN EXEC CENTRAL...POLICY BIBLIOG 20 CHINJAP. PAGE 131 H2610
NAT/G S/ASIA CONCPT ROUTINE

B40
CONOVER H.F.,JAPAN-ECONOMIC DEVELOPMENT AND FOREIGN POLICY, A SELECTED LIST OF REFERENCES (PAMPHLET). CULTURE FINAN INDUS NAT/G FORCES INT/TRADE WAR ...SOC TREND 20 CHINJAP. PAGE 32 H0640
BIBLIOG ASIA ECO/DEV DIPLOM

C40
FAHS C.B.,"GOVERNMENT IN JAPAN." FINAN FORCES LEGIS TOP/EX BUDGET INT/TRADE EDU/PROP SOVEREIGN ...CON/ANAL BIBLIOG/A 20 CHINJAP. PAGE 48 H0962
ASIA DIPLOM NAT/G ADMIN

B41
HAUSHOFER K.,WEHR-GEOPOLITIK. EUR+WWI GERMANY MOD/EUR NAT/G ACT/RES BAL/PWR PWR...STAT TIME/SEQ CHARTS NAZI 20. PAGE 68 H1361
FORCES GEOG WAR

S41
ABEL T.,"THE ELEMENT OF DECISION IN THE PATTERN OF WAR." EUR+WWI FUT NAT/G TOP/EX DIPLOM ROUTINE COERCE DISPL PERCEPT PWR...SOC METH/CNCPT HIST/WRIT TREND GEN/LAWS 20. PAGE 3 H0055
TEC/DEV FORCES WAR

S41
DENNERY E.,"DEMOCRACY AND THE FRENCH ARMY." FRANCE NAT/G EX/STRUC LEAD REV ROLE 18/20. PAGE 40 H0792
FORCES POPULISM STRATA CIVMIL/REL

B42
CONOVER H.F.,FRENCH COLONIES IN AFRICA: A LIST OF REFERENCES. ALGERIA FRANCE MOROCCO SOMALIA SUDAN CULTURE AGRI LOC/G SECT FORCES DIPLOM INT/TRADE NAT/LISM HEALTH...CON/ANAL 20. PAGE 32 H0641
BIBLIOG AFR ECO/UNDEV COLONIAL

B42
CONOVER H.F.,NEW ZEALAND: A SELECTED LIST OF REFERENCES (PAMPHLET). NEW/ZEALND ECO/UNDEV AGRI INDUS LABOR NAT/G SCHOOL FORCES DIPLOM COLONIAL WAR ...HUM 20. PAGE 32 H0643
BIBLIOG/A S/ASIA CULTURE

B42
FORTESCU J.,IN PRAISE OF ENGLISH LAW (1464) (TRANS. BY S.B. CHRIMES). UK ELITES CHIEF FORCES CT/SYS COERCE CRIME GOV/REL ILLEGIT...JURID GOV/COMP GEN/LAWS 15. PAGE 52 H1040
LAW CONSTN LEGIS ORD/FREE

B42
SINGTON D.,THE GOEBBELS EXPERIMENT. GERMANY MOD/EUR NAT/G EX/STRUC FORCES CONTROL ROUTINE WAR TOTALISM PWR...ART/METH HUM 20 NAZI GOEBBELS/J. PAGE 144 H2886
FASCISM EDU/PROP ATTIT COM/IND

B43
EARLE E.M.,MAKERS OF MODERN STRATEGY: MILITARY THOUGHT FROM MACHIAVELLI TO HITLER. EUR+WWI MOD/EUR NAT/G ACT/RES BAL/PWR DOMIN COERCE ATTIT DRIVE RIGID/FLEX ALL/VALS...METH/CNCPT BIOG 16/20. PAGE 44 H0879
PLAN FORCES WAR

B45
CONOVER H.F.,THE GOVERNMENTS OF THE MAJOR FOREIGN POWERS: A BIBLIOGRAPHY. FRANCE GERMANY ITALY UK USSR CONSTN LOC/G POL/PAR EX/STRUC FORCES ADMIN CT/SYS CIVMIL/REL TOTALISM...POLICY 19/20. PAGE 32 H0645
BIBLIOG NAT/G DIPLOM

B45
CONOVER H.F.,ITALY: ECONOMICS, POLITICS AND MILITARY AFFAIRS, 1940-1945. ITALY ELITES NAT/G POL/PAR EX/STRUC TOP/EX DIPLOM DOMIN CONTROL COERCE WAR CIVMIL/REL EFFICIENCY 20. PAGE 32 H0646
BIBLIOG TOTALISM FORCES

B45
CONOVER H.F.,THE NAZI STATE: WAR CRIMES AND WAR CRIMINALS. GERMANY CULTURE NAT/G SECT FORCES DIPLOM INT/TRADE EDU/PROP...INT/LAW BIOG HIST/WRIT TIME/SEQ 20. PAGE 32 H0647
BIBLIOG WAR CRIME

B46
NICOLSON H.,THE CONGRESS OF VIENNA. MOD/EUR NAT/G FORCES BAL/PWR DOMIN LEGIT COERCE PERSON PWR ...RECORD TIME/SEQ STERTYP 19 CONG/VIENN. PAGE 118 H2353
CONCPT POLICY DIPLOM

S46
SILBERNER E.,"THE PROBLEM OF WAR IN NINETEENTH CENTURY ECONOMIC THOUGHT." EUR+WWI MOD/EUR UNIV LAW ECO/DEV ECO/UNDEV FINAN INDUS MARKET INT/ORG NAT/G CONSULT FORCES...CONCPT GEN/LAWS GEN/METH 19. PAGE 144 H2875
ATTIT ECO/TAC WAR

B48
GRIFFITH E.S.,RESEARCH IN POLITICAL SCIENCE: THE WORK OF PANELS OF RESEARCH COMMITTEE, APSA. WOR+45 WOR-45 COM/IND R+D FORCES ACT/RES WAR...GOV/COMP ANTHOL 20. PAGE 61 H1220
BIBLIOG PHIL/SCI DIPLOM JURID

L48
SHILS E.A.,"COHESION AND DISINTEGRATION IN THE WEHRMACHT IN WORLD WAR II." GERMANY STRUCT DOMIN WAR INGP/REL ISOLAT NAT/LISM ATTIT AUTHORIT SUPEGO RESPECT...PSY CON/ANAL 20 NAZI. PAGE 143 H2862
EDU/PROP DRIVE PERS/REL FORCES

S48
ALEXANDER L.,"WAR CRIMES, THEIR SOCIAL-PSYCHOLOGICAL ASPECTS." EUR+WWI GERMANY LAW CULTURE ELITES KIN POL/PAR PUB/INST FORCES DOMIN EDU/PROP COERCE CRIME ATTIT SUPEGO HEALTH MORAL PWR FASCISM ...PSY OBS TREND GEN/LAWS NAZI 20. PAGE 5 H0100
DRIVE WAR

B49
VIERECK P.,CONSERVATISM REVISITED: THE REVOLT AGAINST REVOLT 1815-1949. EUR+WWI ELITES NAT/G FORCES PARTIC GOV/REL NAT/LISM...MAJORIT CONCPT GOV/COMP METTRNCH/K. PAGE 163 H3251
CONSERVE MARXISM REALPOL

C49
YANAGA C.,"JAPAN SINCE PERRY." S/ASIA CULTURE ECO/DEV FORCES WAR 19/20 CHINJAP. PAGE 172 H3433
DIPLOM POL/PAR CIVMIL/REL NAT/LISM

B50
BERMAN H.J.,JUSTICE IN RUSSIA; AN INTERPRETATION OF SOVIET LAW. USSR LAW STRUCT LABOR FORCES AGREE GP/REL ORD/FREE SOCISM...TIME/SEQ 20. PAGE 15 H0309
JURID ADJUD MARXISM COERCE

B50
GATZKE H.W.,GERMANY'S DRIVE TO THE WEST. BELGIUM GERMANY MOD/EUR AGRI INDUS POL/PAR FORCES DOMIN AGREE CONTROL REGION COERCE 20 TREATY WWI. PAGE 55 H1104
WAR POLICY NAT/G DIPLOM

B50
JONES H.D.,KOREA, AN ANNOTATED BIBLIOGRAPHY OF PUBLICATIONS IN WESTERN LANGUAGES. KOREA CULTURE MUNIC SECT FORCES DIPLOM HEALTH WEALTH...ART/METH GEOG SOC LING 20. PAGE 82 H1632
BIBLIOG/A ASIA NAT/G ECO/UNDEV

B50
MACHIAVELLI N.,THE DISCOURSES (1516). NAT/G SECT FORCES DOMIN LEGIT CONTROL LEAD COERCE TOTALISM ORD/FREE. PAGE 100 H1995
PWR GEN/LAWS CHIEF

B50
WILBUR C.M.,CHINESE SOURCES ON THE HISTORY OF THE CHINESE COMMUNIST MOVEMENT (PAMPHLET). CHINA/COM ECO/UNDEV PROVS FORCES WAR...PHIL/SCI 20. PAGE 168 H3360
BIBLIOG/A MARXISM REV NAT/G

B51
LEONARD L.L.,INTERNATIONAL ORGANIZATION. WOR+45 WOR-45 EX/STRUC FORCES LEGIS ECO/TAC INT/TRADE COLONIAL ARMS/CONT...SOC/WK GOV/COMP BIBLIOG. PAGE 94 H1884
NAT/G DIPLOM INT/ORG DELIB/GP

B51
MARX K.,THE EIGHTEENTH BRUMAIRE OF LOUIS BONAPARTE (1852). FRANCE STRATA FINAN INDUS LABOR CHIEF FORCES WORKER CAP/ISM ECO/TAC PARL/PROC ORD/FREE ...MARXIST 19. PAGE 104 H2080
REV MARXISM ELITES NAT/G

B51
WEBSTER C.,THE FOREIGN POLICY OF PALMERSTON - 1830 TO 1841. MOD/EUR UK LAW CONSTN INTELL SOCIETY STRUCT NAT/G FORCES TOP/EX CREATE BAL/PWR PWR 19. PAGE 166 H3323
ADMIN PERSON DIPLOM

B52
SPENCER F.A.,WAR AND POSTWAR GREECE: AN ANALYSIS BASED ON GREEK WRITINGS. GREECE SOCIETY NAT/G POL/PAR FORCES CREATE DIPLOM LEAD MARXISM...SOC 20. PAGE 147 H2943
BIBLIOG/A WAR REV

B53
HUNTER E.,BRAIN-WASHING IN RED CHINA. ASIA CHINA/COM CULTURE SOCIETY FORCES WAR TOTALISM ATTIT BIO/SOC DISPL DRIVE PERSON SUPEGO KNOWL ORD/FREE ...INT REC/INT COLD/WAR 20. PAGE 75 H1499
EDU/PROP COERCE

B53
SHIRATO I.,JAPANESE SOURCES ON THE HISTORY OF THE CHINESE COMMUNIST MOVEMENT (PAMPHLET). CHINA/COM USSR CONSTRUC NAT/G POL/PAR FORCES DIPLOM DOMIN EDU/PROP CONTROL WAR TOTALISM SOCISM 20. PAGE 143 H2863
BIBLIOG/A MARXISM ECO/UNDEV

B54
BUTZ O.,GERMANY: DILEMMA FOR AMERICAN POLICY. GERMANY USA+45 USA-45 USSR WOR+45 INT/ORG FORCES NUC/PWR EFFICIENCY PEACE PWR...GOV/COMP 20 COLD/WAR. PAGE 25 H0501
DIPLOM NAT/G WAR POLICY

B54
CAMPANELLA T.,A DISCOURSE TOUCHING THE SPANISH MONARCHY... (1640). SPAIN UNIV SEA STRATA FINAN SECT FORCES SUPEGO LOVE ORD/FREE...CONCPT 17. PAGE 26 H0514
CONSERVE CHIEF NAT/G DIPLOM

B54
FRIEDRICH C.J.,TOTALITARIAN DICTATORSHIP AND AUTOCRACY. COM EUR+WWI GERMANY ITALY USSR INTELL ECO/DEV NAT/G POL/PAR FORCES TOP/EX ECO/TAC EDU/PROP LEGIT COERCE ATTIT ORD/FREE PWR FASCISM ...CONCPT TIME/SEQ GEN/LAWS NAZI 20. PAGE 53 H1068
SOCIETY DOMIN TOTALISM

B54
GATZKE H.W.,STRESEMANN AND THE REARMAMENT OF GERMANY. EUR+WWI GERMANY USSR FINAN NAT/G ECO/TAC ATTIT...BIOG METH 20 STRESEMN/G. PAGE 55 H1105
FORCES INDUS PWR

B54
GERMANY FOREIGN MINISTRY,DOCUMENTS ON GERMAN FOREIGN POLICY 1918-1945, SERIES C (1933-1937) VOLS. I-V. GERMANY MOD/EUR FORCES PLAN ECO/TAC ...FASCIST CHARTS ANTHOL 20. PAGE 56 H1115
NAT/G DIPLOM POLICY

L54
FRIEDRICH C.J.,"TOTALITARIANISM." COM EUR+WWI NAT/G POL/PAR SECT FORCES PLAN ECO/TAC DOMIN EDU/PROP EXEC COERCE REV ORD/FREE PWR...SOC CONCPT NAZI 20. PAGE 53 H1067
ATTIT TOTALISM

B55
CRAIG G.A.,THE POLITICS OF THE PRUSSIAN ARMY 1640-1945. CHRIST-17C EUR+WWI MOD/EUR PRUSSIA STRUCT DIPLOM ADMIN REV WAR...SOC BIBLIOG 17/20. PAGE 35 H0694
FORCES NAT/G ROLE CHIEF

B55
KHADDURI M.,WAR AND PEACE IN THE LAW OF ISLAM. CONSTN CULTURE SOCIETY STRATA NAT/G PROVS SECT FORCES TOP/EX CREATE DOMIN EDU/PROP ADJUD COERCE ATTIT RIGID/FLEX ALL/VALS...CONCPT TIME/SEQ TOT/POP VAL/FREE. PAGE 85 H1702
ISLAM JURID PEACE WAR

B55
KOHN H.,THE MIND OF MODERN RUSSIA. COM MOD/EUR USSR SOCIETY NAT/G SECT FORCES TOP/EX COERCE TOTALISM DRIVE RIGID/FLEX PWR SOVEREIGN...CONCPT TIME/SEQ WORK. PAGE 87 H1742
INTELL GEN/LAWS SOCISM RUSSIA

B55
TAN C.C.,THE BOXER CATASTROPHE. ASIA UK USSR ELITES POL/PAR VOL/ASSN FORCES PROB/SOLV DIPLOM ADMIN COLONIAL NAT/LISM PEACE TREATY 19/20 BOXER/REBL. PAGE 152 H3040
REV NAT/G WAR

B55
VIGON J.,TEORIA DEL MILITARISMO. NAT/G DIPLOM COLONIAL COERCE GUERRILLA CIVMIL/REL NAT/LISM MORAL ALL/IDEOS PACIFISM 18/20. PAGE 163 H3253
FORCES PHIL/SCI WAR POLICY

S55
GLADSTONE A.E.,"THE POSSIBILITY OF PREDICTING REACTIONS TO INTERNATIONAL EVENTS." UNIV SOCIETY NAT/G FORCES CREATE EDU/PROP COERCE WAR ATTIT PERSON KNOWL PWR SKILL...METH/CNCPT NEW/IDEA ORG/CHARTS. PAGE 57 H1139
PHIL/SCI CONCPT

B56
CARRIL B.,PROBLEMAS DE LA REVOLUCION Y LA DEMOCRACIA. CONSTN FORCES DOMIN CONTROL TOTALISM PWR 20. PAGE 27 H0539
REV ORD/FREE LEGIT NAT/G

B56
ROBERTS H.L.,RUSSIA AND AMERICA. CHINA/COM S/ASIA USSR FORCES TEC/DEV FOR/AID NUC/PWR ALL/IDEOS ...MAJORIT TREND NAT/COMP 20 COLD/WAR UN NATO. PAGE 132 H2641
DIPLOM INT/ORG BAL/PWR TOTALISM

B56
SMEDLEY A.,THE GREAT ROAD: THE LIFE AND TIMES OF CHU TEH. ASIA USSR NAT/G POL/PAR DIPLOM COERCE GUERRILLA CIVMIL/REL NAT/LISM PERSON SKILL MARXISM ...BIOG 20 CHINJAP MAO. PAGE 145 H2903
REV WAR FORCES

B56
WHITAKER A.P.,ARGENTINE UPHEAVAL. STRUCT FORCES DIPLOM COERCE PWR 20 ARGEN. PAGE 167 H3343
REV POL/PAR STRATA NAT/G

B56
WILSON P.,GOVERNMENT AND POLITICS OF INDIA AND PAKISTAN: 1885-1955; A BIBLIOGRAPHY OF WORKS IN WESTERN LANGUAGES. INDIA PAKISTAN CONSTN LOC/G POL/PAR FORCES DIPLOM ADMIN WAR CHOOSE...BIOG CON/ANAL 19/20. PAGE 169 H3380
BIBLIOG COLONIAL NAT/G S/ASIA

C56
FALL B.B.,"THE VIET-MINH REGIME." VIETNAM LAW ECO/UNDEV POL/PAR FORCES DOMIN WAR ATTIT MARXISM ...BIOG PREDICT BIBLIOG/A 20. PAGE 48 H0967
NAT/G ADMIN EX/STRUC LEAD

B57
BUNDESMIN FUR VERTRIEBENE,DIE VERTREIBUNG DER DEUTSCHEN BEVOLKERUNG AUS DER TSCHECHOSLOWAKEI. CZECHOSLVK GERMANY NAT/G FORCES MURDER WAR INGP/REL ATTIT 20 MIGRATION. PAGE 24 H0474
GP/REL DOMIN COERCE DISCRIM

B57
NEUMARK S.D.,ECONOMIC INFLUENCES ON THE SOUTH AFRICAN FRONTIER, 1652-1836. SOUTH/AFR SEA AGRI NAT/G FORCES WORKER DIPLOM INT/TRADE PRICE DEMAND PRODUC...STAT CHARTS 17/19 FRONTIER. PAGE 117 H2341
COLONIAL ECO/UNDEV ECO/TAC MARKET

B57
REISS J.,GEORGE KENNANS POLITIK DER EINDAMMUNG. USSR NAT/G FORCES TOTALISM ATTIT ORD/FREE...POLICY 20 NATO TRUMAN/HS MARSHL/PLN KENNAN/G. PAGE 131 H2613
DIPLOM DETER PEACE

B57
US SENATE SPEC COMM FOR AID,HEARINGS BEFORE THE SPECIAL COMMITTEE TO STUDY THE FOREIGN AID PROGRAM. USA+45 USSR ECO/UNDEV INT/ORG FORCES WEAPON TOTALISM ATTIT SUPEGO...NAT/COMP CONGRESS. PAGE 161 H3217
FOR/AID DIPLOM ORD/FREE TEC/DEV

B58
CRAIG G.A.,FROM BISMARCK TO ADENAUER: ASPECTS OF GERMAN STATECRAFT. GERMANY INTELL FORCES ECO/TAC CONFER COERCE WAR GP/REL ORD/FREE PWR CONSERVE 19/20 BISMARCK/O ADENAUER/K. PAGE 35 H0695
DIPLOM LEAD NAT/G

B58
GARTHOFF R.L.,SOVIET STRATEGY IN THE NUCLEAR AGE. FUT USSR R+D INT/ORG NAT/G ACT/RES TEC/DEV DOMIN DETER WAR ATTIT PWR...RELATIV METH/CNCPT SELF/OBS TREND CON/ANAL STERTYP GEN/LAWS 20. PAGE 55 H1103
COM FORCES BAL/PWR NUC/PWR

B58
HSU U.T.,THE INVISIBLE CONFLICT. ASIA USSR ELITES NAT/G CONTROL LEAD COERCE REV WAR NAT/LISM ORD/FREE PWR 20 COM/PARTY ESPIONAGE. PAGE 74 H1485
MARXISM POL/PAR EDU/PROP FORCES

B58
INDIAN COUNCIL WORLD AFFAIRS,DEFENCE AND SECURITY IN THE INDIAN OCEAN AREA. INDIA S/ASIA CULTURE CONSULT DELIB/GP FORCES PROB/SOLV DIPLOM INT/TRADE 20 CMN/WLTH. PAGE 77 H1531
GEOG HABITAT ECO/UNDEV ORD/FREE

B58
JACOBSSON P.,SOME MONETARY PROBLEMS, INTERNATIONAL AND NATIONAL. WOR+45 WOR-45 ECO/DEV FORCES WORKER PROB/SOLV DIPLOM INT/TRADE...ANTHOL 20. PAGE 79 H1580
FINAN PLAN ECO/TAC NAT/COMP

B58
ORNES G.E.,TRUJILLO: LITTLE CAESAR OF THE CARIBBEAN. DOMIN/REP FAM NAT/G FORCES BUDGET CRIME REV PERSON 20 TRUJILLO/R. PAGE 122 H2429
BIOG PWR TOTALISM CHIEF

B58
SHAW S.J.,THE FINANCIAL AND ADMINISTRATIVE ORGANIZATION AND DEVELOPMENT OF OTTOMAN EGYPT 1517-1798. UAR LOC/G FORCES BUDGET INT/TRADE TAX EATING INCOME WEALTH...CHARTS BIBLIOG 16/18 OTTOMAN NAPOLEON/B. PAGE 143 H2853
FINAN ADMIN GOV/REL CULTURE

B59
CONOVER H.F.,NIGERIAN OFFICIAL PUBLICATIONS, 1869-1959: A GUIDE. NIGER CONSTN FINAN ACADEM SCHOOL FORCES PRESS ADMIN COLONIAL...HIST/WRIT 19/20. PAGE 33 H0650
BIBLIOG NAT/G CON/ANAL

B59
EMME E.M.,THE IMPACT OF AIR POWER - NATIONAL SECURITY AND WORLD POLITICS. USA+45 USSR FORCES DIPLOM WEAPON PEACE TOTALISM...POLICY NAT/COMP 20 EUROPE. PAGE 46 H0921
DETER AIR WAR ORD/FREE

B59
MATHER F.C.,PUBLIC ORDER IN THE AGE OF THE CHARTISTS. UK CULTURE ADJUD CONTROL. PAGE 105 H2090
ORD/FREE FORCES COERCE CIVMIL/REL

B59
SQUIBB G.D.,THE HIGH COURT OF CHIVALRY. UK NAT/G FORCES ADJUD WAR 14/20 PARLIAMENT ENGLSH/LAW. PAGE 148 H2959
CT/SYS PARL/PROC JURID

B59
STERNBERG F.,THE MILITARY AND INDUSTRIAL REVOLUTION
DIPLOM

OF OUR TIME. USA+45 USSR WOR+45 WORKER COMPUTER PLAN TEC/DEV NUC/PWR GP/REL...POLICY NAT/COMP 20. PAGE 149 H2981
FORCES INDUS CIVMIL/REL

B59

SZLUC T.,TWILIGHT OF THE TYRANTS. BRAZIL L/A+17C PERU VENEZUELA NAT/G FORCES CONTROL PERSON MORAL ORD/FREE PWR...CONCPT 20 ARGEN COLOMB. PAGE 151 H3028
TOTALISM CHIEF REV FASCISM

B59

VITTACHIT,EMERGENCY '58. CEYLON UK STRUCT NAT/G FORCES ADJUD CRIME REV NAT/LISM 20. PAGE 163 H3258
RACE/REL DISCRIM DIPLOM SOVEREIGN

S59

SILBERMAN L.,"CHANGE AND CONFLICT IN THE HORN OF AFRICA." EUR+WWI ITALY UK CULTURE FORCES ECO/TAC ADJUD COLONIAL ATTIT ORD/FREE PWR...DECISION METH/CNCPT HIST/WRIT SOMALI 20. PAGE 144 H2874
AFR TIME/SEQ

B60

ALBRECHT-CARRIE R.,FRANCE, EUROPE AND THE TWO WORLD WARS. EUR+WWI FRANCE GERMANY MOD/EUR UK ECO/DEV NAT/G FORCES BAL/PWR DOMIN ARMS/CONT PEACE PWR 20 TREATY EUROPE. PAGE 5 H0096
DIPLOM WAR

B60

EASTON S.C.,THE TWILIGHT OF EUROPEAN COLONIALISM. AFR S/ASIA CONSTN SOCIETY STRUCT ECO/UNDEV INDUS NAT/G FORCES ECO/TAC COLONIAL CT/SYS ATTIT KNOWL ORD/FREE PWR...SOCIALIST TIME/SEQ TREND CON/ANAL 20. PAGE 44 H0882
FINAN ADMIN

B60

FURNIA A.H.,THE DIPLOMACY OF APPEASEMENT: ANGLO-FRENCH RELATIONS AND THE PRELUDE TO WORLD WAR II 1931-1938. FRANCE GERMANY UK ELITES NAT/G DELIB/GP FORCES WAR PEACE RIGID/FLEX 20. PAGE 54 H1077
DIPLOM BAL/PWR COERCE

B60

MCCLOSKY H.,THE SOVIET DICTATORSHIP. FUT CONSTN CULTURE INTELL SOCIETY POL/PAR SECT VOL/ASSN FORCES PLAN TEC/DEV DOMIN EDU/PROP COERCE PWR MARXISM ...POLICY CONCPT MYTH STERTYP 20. PAGE 106 H2127
COM NAT/G TOTALISM USSR

B60

MINIFIE J.M.,PEACEMAKER OR POWDER-MONKEY. CANADA INT/ORG NAT/G FORCES LEAD WAR...PREDICT 20. PAGE 111 H2222
DIPLOM POLICY NEUTRAL PEACE

B60

MORAES F.,THE REVOLT IN TIBET. ASIA CHINA/COM INDIA CULTURE CONTROL COERCE WAR TOTALISM...POLICY SOC WORSHIP 20 TIBET INTERVENT. PAGE 113 H2252
COLONIAL FORCES DIPLOM ORD/FREE

B60

MORRIS I.,NATIONALISM AND THE RIGHT WING IN JAPAN: A STUDY OF POST WAR TRENDS. ASIA ELITES NAT/G DELIB/GP FORCES TOP/EX CHOOSE ATTIT...INT GEN/LAWS CONGRESS 20 CHINJAP. PAGE 113 H2262
POL/PAR TREND NAT/LISM

B60

PRASAD B.,THE ORIGINS OF PROVINCIAL AUTONOMY. INDIA UK FINAN LOC/G FORCES LEGIS CONTROL CT/SYS PWR ...JURID 19/20. PAGE 128 H2554
CENTRAL PROVS COLONIAL NAT/G

B60

SHIRER W.L.,THE RISE AND FALL OF THE THIRD REICH: A HISTORY OF NAZI GERMANY. EUR+WWI CULTURE ECO/DEV INDUS NAT/G POL/PAR FORCES PLAN TEC/DEV ECO/TAC COERCE ATTIT DRIVE PERSON PWR...MYSTIC PSY SOC MYTH STAT CHARTS EXHIBIT WORK VAL/FREE. PAGE 143 H2864
STRUCT GERMANY TOTALISM

B60

THORD-GRAY I.,GRINGO REBEL. L/A+17C NAT/G CONTROL LEAD ATTIT...OBS 20 MEXIC/AMER. PAGE 154 H3087
REV FORCES CIVMIL/REL ORD/FREE

L60

KAPLAN M.A.,"COMMUNIST COUP IN CZECHOSLOVAKIA." COM EUR+WWI INTELL LABOR LOC/G NAT/G POL/PAR FORCES EDU/PROP EXEC MARXISM...TIME/SEQ HYPO/EXP 20. PAGE 83 H1659
STRUCT COERCE CZECHOSLVK

S60

BRZEZINSKI Z.K.,"PATTERNS AND LIMITS OF THE SINO-SOVIET DISPUTE." ASIA CHINA/COM COM FUT STRATA NAT/G EX/STRUC FORCES BAL/PWR DIPLOM ECO/TAC DOMIN EDU/PROP ADMIN COERCE WAR ATTIT RIGID/FLEX ...GEN/LAWS VAL/FREE 20. PAGE 23 H0459
POL/PAR PWR REV USSR

S60

CROZIER B.,"FRANCE AND ALGERIA." ALGERIA EUR+WWI FRANCE FUT ISLAM ECO/UNDEV NEIGH CONSULT DELIB/GP ECO/TAC COLONIAL COERCE ATTIT...SOC INT CON/ANAL 20. PAGE 36 H0713
NAT/G FORCES GUERRILLA NAT/LISM

S60

EMERSON R.,"THE EROSION OF DEMOCRACY." AFR FUT LAW CULTURE INTELL SOCIETY ECO/UNDEV FAM LOC/G NAT/G FORCES PLAN TEC/DEV ECO/TAC ADMIN CT/SYS ATTIT ORD/FREE PWR...SOCIALIST SOC CONCPT STAND/INT TIME/SEQ WORK 20. PAGE 46 H0918
S/ASIA POL/PAR

S60

GINSBURGS G.,"PEKING-LHASA-NEW DELHI." CHINA/COM FUT INDIA S/ASIA KIN NAT/G PROVS SECT FORCES BAL/PWR ECO/TAC DOMIN EDU/PROP LEGIT ADMIN REGION GUERRILLA PWR...TREND TIBET 20. PAGE 57 H1134
ASIA COERCE DIPLOM

S60

GRIMSHAW A.D.,"URBAN RACIAL VIOLENCE IN THE UNITED STATES: CHANGING ECOLOGICAL CONSIDERATIONS." STRUCT MUNIC FORCES PARTIC DISCRIM ATTIT HABITAT ...IDEA/COMP 20 NEGRO. PAGE 61 H1228
CROWD RACE/REL GOV/COMP NEIGH

S60

HOWARD M.,"BRITAIN'S DEFENSE: COMMITMENTS AND CAPABILITIES." EUR+WWI ECO/DEV NAT/G FORCES LEGIS PLAN DETER ORD/FREE WEALTH...POLICY CONCPT TIME/SEQ GEN/METH 20. PAGE 74 H1481
FUT PWR DIPLOM UK

S60

KELLEY G.A.,"THE POLITICAL BACKGROUND OF THE FRENCH A-BOMB." EUR+WWI USSR FORCES TOP/EX TEC/DEV NUC/PWR ATTIT PWR...CONCPT OBS/ENVIR TREND 20. PAGE 84 H1686
NAT/G RESPECT NAT/LISM FRANCE

S60

MAGATHAN W.,"SOME BASES OF WEST GERMAN MILITARY POLICY." EUR+WWI FUT INT/ORG TOP/EX ECO/TAC DOMIN DRIVE ORD/FREE PWR...TRADIT GEOG OBS TREND. PAGE 101 H2015
NAT/G FORCES GERMANY

S60

PERLMANN H.,"UPHEAVAL IN TURKEY." EUR+WWI ISLAM NAT/G FORCES TOP/EX LEGIT COERCE CHOOSE DRIVE ORD/FREE PWR...TIME/SEQ TOT/POP 20. PAGE 125 H2494
CONSTN TURKEY

S60

WYCKOFF T.,"THE ROLE OF THE MILITARY IN LATIN AMERICAN POLITICS." L/A+17C CONSTN CULTURE ECO/UNDEV POL/PAR FORCES LEGIS TOP/EX LEGIT GUERRILLA REV CHOOSE ORD/FREE PWR...TIME/SEQ VAL/FREE 20. PAGE 171 H3430
NAT/G COERCE TOTALISM

C60

WRIGGINS W.H.,"CEYLON: DILEMMAS OF A NEW NATION." ASIA CEYLON CONSTN STRUCT POL/PAR SECT FORCES DIPLOM GOV/REL NAT/LISM...CHARTS BIBLIOG 20. PAGE 171 H3417
PROB/SOLV NAT/G ECO/UNDEV

B61

BULLOCK A.,HITLER: A STUDY IN TYRANNY. EUR+WWI GERMANY SOCIETY STRUCT NAT/G POL/PAR FORCES CREATE DOMIN EDU/PROP EXEC COERCE WAR NAT/LISM DISPL DRIVE PERSON PWR...PSY NAZI 20 HITLER/A. PAGE 23 H0470
ATTIT BIOG TOTALISM

B61

DALLIN D.J.,SOVIET FOREIGN POLICY AFTER STALIN. ASIA CHINA/COM EUR+WWI GERMANY IRAN UK YUGOSLAVIA INT/ORG NAT/G VOL/ASSN FORCES TOP/EX BAL/PWR DOMIN EDU/PROP COERCE ATTIT PWR 20. PAGE 37 H0737
COM DIPLOM USSR

B61

DONNISON F.S.V.,CIVIL AFFAIRS AND MILITARY GOVERNMENT NORTH-WEST EUROPE 1944-1946. EUR+WWI FRANCE GERMANY UK USSR LOC/G PROVS PLAN PROB/SOLV BAL/PWR ECO/TAC CONTROL PWR...CHARTS 20. PAGE 42 H0836
NAT/G WAR FORCES CIVMIL/REL

B61

FULLER J.F.C.,THE CONDUCT OF WAR, 1789-1961. FRANCE RUSSIA SOCIETY NAT/G FORCES PROB/SOLV AGREE NUC/PWR WEAPON PEACE...SOC 18/20 TREATY COLD/WAR. PAGE 54 H1076
WAR POLICY REV ROLE

B61

GUEVARA E.,GUERRILLA WARFARE. L/A+17C ECO/UNDEV NAT/G POL/PAR VOL/ASSN PLAN DOMIN REV DRIVE PWR WEALTH...NEW/IDEA RECORD BIOG COLD/WAR MARX/KARL OAS 20. PAGE 62 H1247
FORCES COERCE GUERRILLA CUBA

B61

GUIZOT F.P.G.,HISTORY OF THE ORIGIN OF REPRESENTATIVE GOVERNMENT IN EUROPE. CHRIST-17C FRANCE MOD/EUR SPAIN UK LAW CHIEF FORCES POPULISM ...MAJORIT TIME/SEQ GOV/COMP NAT/COMP 4/19 PARLIAMENT. PAGE 62 H1250
LEGIS REPRESENT CONSTN NAT/G

B61

HARDT J.P.,THE COLD WAR ECONOMIC GAP. USA+45 USSR ECO/DEV FORCES INT/TRADE NUC/PWR PWR 20 COLD/WAR. PAGE 66 H1328
DIPLOM ECO/TAC NAT/COMP POLICY

B61

MARX K.,THE COMMUNIST MANIFESTO. IN (MENDEL A. ESSENTIAL WORKS OF MARXISM, NEW YORK: BANTAM. FUT MOD/EUR CULTURE ECO/DEV ECO/UNDEV AGRI FINAN INDUS MARKET PROC/MFG LABOR MUNIC POL/PAR CONSULT FORCES CREATE PLAN ADMIN ATTIT DRIVE RIGID/FLEX ORD/FREE PWR RESPECT MARX/KARL WORK. PAGE 104 H2081
COM NEW/IDEA CAP/ISM REV

B61

MOLLAU G.,INTERNATIONAL COMMUNISM AND WORLD REVOLUTION: HISTORY AND METHODS. RUSSIA USSR INT/ORG NAT/G POL/PAR VOL/ASSN FORCES BAL/PWR DIPLOM EXEC REGION WAR ATTIT PWR MARXISM...CONCPT TIME/SEQ COLD/WAR 19/20. PAGE 112 H2237
COM REV

B61

MONAS S.,THE THIRD SECTION: POLICE AND SOCIETY IN RUSSIA UNDER NICHOLAS I. MOD/EUR RUSSIA ELITES STRUCT NAT/G EX/STRUC ADMIN CONTROL PWR CONSERVE ...DECISION 19 NICHOLAS/I. PAGE 112 H2238
ORD/FREE COM FORCES COERCE

B61

PANIKKAR K.M.,THE VOICE OF FREEDOM: SELECTED SPEECHES OF PANDIT MOTILAL NEHRU. INDIA UK CONSTN FINAN FORCES LEGIS DIPLOM TAX COLONIAL...POLICY MAJORIT ANTHOL 20 NEHRU/PM. PAGE 123 H2460
NAT/LISM ORD/FREE CHIEF NAT/G

B61
SOKOL A.E.,SEAPOWER IN THE NUCLEAR AGE. USA+45 USSR DIST/IND FORCES INT/TRADE DETER WAR...POLICY NAT/COMP BIBLIOG COLD/WAR. PAGE 146 H2928
SEA PWR WEAPON NUC/PWR

B61
STAHL W.,EDUCATION FOR DEMOCRACY IN WEST GERMANY: ACHIEVEMENT SHORTCOMINGS - PROSPECTS. GERMANY/W SOCIETY NAT/G FORCES PLAN PROB/SOLV PRESS ALL/VALS ...POLICY MAJORIT CONCPT ANTHOL 20. PAGE 148 H2967
EDU/PROP POPULISM AGE/Y ADJUST

B61
STANLEY C.J.,LATE CH'ING FINANCE: HU KUANG-YUNG AS AN INNOVATOR. ASIA NAT/G FORCES BUDGET TAX WAR GOV/REL COST...POLICY BIOG CHARTS BIBLIOG 19. PAGE 148 H2969
FINAN ECO/TAC CIVMIL/REL ADMIN

S61
DOGAN M.,"LES OFFICIERS DANS LA CARRIERE POLITIQUE DE MARECHAL MACMAHON AU GENERAL DE GAULLE." EUR+WWI FRANCE MOD/EUR ELITES STRATA POL/PAR LEGIT ATTIT ALL/VALS...SOC CONCPT 19/20. PAGE 42 H0833
PROF/ORG FORCES NAT/G DELIB/GP

S61
SCHELLING T.C.,"NUCLEAR STRATEGY IN EUROPE." COM EUR+WWI USSR NAT/G FORCES NUC/PWR DRIVE ORD/FREE PWR...DECISION CONCPT OBS TREND HYPO/EXP 20. PAGE 139 H2784
FUT COERCE ARMS/CONT WAR

S61
TANHAM B.K.,"COMMUNIST REVOLUTIONARY WARFARE: THE VIETMINH IN INDOCHINA." EUR+WWI S/ASIA VIETNAM NAT/G EDU/PROP LEGIT GUERRILLA ATTIT PWR...CONCPT GEN/LAWS 20. PAGE 152 H3042
FORCES ECO/TAC WAR FRANCE

B62
ABOSCH H.,THE MENACE OF THE MIRACLE: GERMANY FROM HITLER TO ADENAUER. EUR+WWI GERMANY/W CULTURE FORCES PRESS NUC/PWR WAR CHOOSE 20 HITLER/A ADENAUER/K. PAGE 3 H0057
DIPLOM PEACE POLICY

B62
BERGER M.,THE ARAB WORLD TODAY. CULTURE FAM INT/ORG NAT/G SECT FORCES ECO/TAC NAT/LISM HABITAT...CHARTS BIBLIOG 20 ARABS. PAGE 15 H0301
ISLAM PERSON STRUCT SOCIETY

B62
BROWN B.E.,NEW DIRECTIONS IN COMPARATIVE POLITICS. AUSTRIA FRANCE GERMANY UK WOR+45 EX/STRUC LEGIS ORD/FREE 20. PAGE 22 H0439
NAT/COMP METH POL/PAR FORCES

B62
FINER S.E.,THE MAN ON HORSEBACK: ROLE OF THE MILITARY IN POLITICS. UNIV LAW CONSTN ELITES SOCIETY POL/PAR BAL/PWR DOMIN EDU/PROP LEGIT COERCE GUERRILLA REV WAR WEAPON DRIVE SUPEGO ORD/FREE PWR RESPECT...POLICY CONCPT GEN/METH. PAGE 50 H1003
NAT/G FORCES TOTALISM

B62
GOURE L.,CIVIL DEFENSE IN THE SOVIET UNION. COM USA+45 USSR MUNIC NAT/G DETER ATTIT MARXISM ...NAT/COMP 20 CIV/DEFENS. PAGE 59 H1188
PLAN FORCES WAR COERCE

B62
INSTITUTE FOR STUDY OF USSR,YOUTH IN FERMENT. INTELL NAT/G PERF/ART POL/PAR SCHOOL VOL/ASSN FORCES EDU/PROP ATTIT DRIVE PERCEPT HEALTH KNOWL MORAL ORD/FREE RESPECT...SOC OBS HIST/WRIT VAL/FREE. PAGE 77 H1537
COM CULTURE USSR

B62
JACKSON W.A.D.,RUSSO-CHINESE BORDERLANDS. ASIA COM USSR NAT/G PROVS EX/STRUC FORCES DOMIN COERCE PEACE ATTIT PWR SOVEREIGN WEALTH...CONCPT TREND CHARTS STERTYP VAL/FREE. PAGE 79 H1576
GEOG DIPLOM RUSSIA

B62
JOHNSON J.J.,THE ROLE OF THE MILITARY IN UNDERDEVELOPED COUNTRIES. AFR BURMA INDONESIA ISLAM ISRAEL L/A+17C S/ASIA THAILAND CULTURE ECO/UNDEV KIN PROVS CONSULT ACT/RES COERCE REV DRIVE RIGID/FLEX ORD/FREE...RECORD ANTHOL 20. PAGE 81 H1622
FORCES CONCPT

B62
MORGENSTERN O.,STRATEGIE - HEUTE (2ND ED.). USA+45 USSR ECO/DEV DELIB/GP WAR PEACE ORD/FREE...GOV/COMP NAT/COMP 20 COLD/WAR NATO. PAGE 113 H2256
NUC/PWR DIPLOM FORCES TEC/DEV

B62
US DEPARTMENT OF THE ARMY,GUIDE TO JAPANESE MONOGRAPHS AND JAPANESE STUDIES ON MANCHURIA: 1945-1960. CHINA/COM NAT/G DIPLOM LEAD COERCE WAR ...CHARTS 19/20 CHINJAP. PAGE 160 H3193
BIBLIOG/A FORCES ASIA S/ASIA

B62
VALERIANO N.D.,COUNTER-GUERRILLA OPERATIONS: THE PHILLIPINE EXPERIENCE. NAT/G CONSULT ACT/RES PLAN COERCE GUERRILLA ATTIT ORD/FREE PWR SKILL...GEOG NEW/IDEA TIME/SEQ CHARTS 20. PAGE 161 H3221
S/ASIA FORCES PHILIPPINE

B62
WHITING K.R.,THE SOVIET UNION TODAY: A CONCISE HANDBOOK. USSR ELITES AGRI INDUS POL/PAR FORCES DIPLOM EDU/PROP LEAD...GEOG TREND 19/20. PAGE 168 H3354
NAT/G ATTIT MARXISM POLICY

B62
ZINKIN T.,REPORTING INDIA. INDIA PAKISTAN WOR+45 SOCIETY SECT FORCES EDU/PROP CROWD DISCRIM NAT/LISM MARXISM...POLICY 20. PAGE 173 H3457
STRATA COLONIAL BAL/PWR CONTROL

L62
NOLTE E.,"ZUR PHANOMENOLOGIE DES FASCHIMUS." EUR+WWI GERMANY ITALY TURKEY INTELL NAT/G CHIEF CONSULT FORCES CREATE DOMIN EDU/PROP COERCE WAR CHOOSE DRIVE FASCISM...PSY CONCPT MYTH GEN/METH LEAGUE/NAT NAZI 20. PAGE 118 H2367
ATTIT PWR

S62
MARTIN L.W.,"THE MARKET FOR STRATEGIC IDEAS IN BRITAIN: THE 'SANDYS ERA'" UK ARMS/CONT WAR GOV/REL OPTIMAL...POLICY DECISION GOV/COMP COLD/WAR CMN/WLTH. PAGE 103 H2063
DIPLOM COERCE FORCES PWR

S62
STRACHEY J.,"COMMUNIST INTENTIONS." ASIA USSR YUGOSLAVIA INT/ORG NAT/G FORCES DOMIN EDU/PROP COERCE NUC/PWR NAT/LISM PEACE RIGID/FLEX PWR MARXISM...CONCPT MYTH OBS TIME/SEQ TREND COLD/WAR TOT/POP 20. PAGE 150 H2992
COM ATTIT WAR

B63
ATTIA G.E.D.,LES FORCES ARMEES DES NATIONS UNIES EN COREE ET AU MOYENORIENT. KOREA CONSTN NAT/G DELIB/GP LEGIS PWR...IDEA/COMP NAT/COMP BIBLIOG UN SUEZ. PAGE 9 H0177
FORCES INT/LAW

B63
BERGSON A.,ECONOMIC TRENDS IN THE SOVIET UNION. USSR ECO/UNDEV AGRI NAT/G FORCES PLAN TEC/DEV INT/TRADE BAL/PAY...POLICY ANTHOL 20. PAGE 15 H0302
ECO/DEV NAT/COMP INDUS LABOR

B63
BORKENAU F.,THE SPANISH COCKPIT. SPAIN ELITES STRATA POL/PAR ACT/RES CROWD WAR GP/REL INGP/REL ...SOC NAT/COMP 20. PAGE 19 H0377
REV CONSERVE SOCISM FORCES

B63
BROEKMEIJER M.W.,DEVELOPING COUNTRIES AND NATO. USSR FORCES DIPLOM NUC/PWR WAR PEACE TOTALISM 20 NATO. PAGE 21 H0427
ECO/UNDEV FOR/AID ORD/FREE NAT/G

B63
ELLIOT J.H.,THE REVOLT OF THE CATALANS. SPAIN LOC/G PROVS FORCES DIPLOM TASK WAR GOV/REL INGP/REL ...POLICY 17 OLIVARES. PAGE 45 H0909
REV NAT/G TOP/EX DOMIN

B63
FRANKEL J.,THE MAKING OF FOREIGN POLICY: AN ANALYSIS OF DECISION-MAKING. CHINA/COM EUR+WWI USA+45 ELITES INTELL FORCES LEGIS PLAN ATTIT ALL/VALS MORAL CONSERVE...GOV/COMP 20 PRESIDENT UN TREATY. PAGE 53 H1051
POLICY DECISION PROB/SOLV DIPLOM

B63
FRITZ H.E.,THE MOVEMENT FOR INDIAN ASSIMILATION, 1860-1890. SECT FORCES GP/REL RACE/REL DISCRIM FEDERAL CATHISM...BIBLIOG 19 INDIAN/AM PROTESTANT GRANT/US. PAGE 54 H1071
CULTURE NAT/G ECO/TAC ATTIT

B63
HAMM H.,ALBANIA - CHINA'S BEACHHEAD IN EUROPE. ALBANIA CHINA/COM USSR YUGOSLAVIA ELITES SOCIETY POL/PAR DELIB/GP FORCES ECO/TAC COERCE ISOLAT PEACE MARXISM...IDEA/COMP 20 MAO. PAGE 65 H1304
DIPLOM REV NAT/G POLICY

B63
KHADDURI M.,MODERN LIBYA: A STUDY IN POLITICAL DEVELOPMENT. EUR+WWI ISLAM LIBYA ELITES INT/ORG POL/PAR FORCES DIPLOM FOR/AID DOMIN EDU/PROP LEGIT NAT/LISM DRIVE RIGID/FLEX SKILL...CONCPT TIME/SEQ TREND 20. PAGE 85 H1704
NAT/G STRUCT

B63
KLEIMAN R.,ATLANTIC CRISIS; AMERICAN DIPLOMACY CONFRONTS A RESURGENT EUROPE. EUR+WWI USA+45 ECO/DEV AGRI NAT/G CHIEF FORCES PLAN LEAD ATTIT ...CONCPT 20 NATO KENNEDY/JF DEGAULLE/C EEC JOHNSON/LB. PAGE 87 H1731
DIPLOM REGION POLICY

B63
KURZMAN D.,SUBVERSION OF THE INNOCENTS: PATTERNS OF COMMUNIST PENETRATION OF AFRICA, THE MIDDLE EAST AND AFRICA. AFR ASIA ISLAM S/ASIA CULTURE NAT/G FORCES PLAN EDU/PROP ADMIN ATTIT...CONCPT INT UNPLAN/INT TIME/SEQ. PAGE 89 H1785
COM COERCE

B63
LARSON A.,A WARLESS WORLD. FUT CULTURE NAT/G VOL/ASSN FORCES CREATE DOMIN PEACE ALL/VALS...HUM STERTYP 20. PAGE 91 H1824
SOCIETY CONCPT ARMS/CONT

B63
PRICE A.G.,THE WESTERN INVASIONS OF THE PACIFIC AND ITS CONTINENTS. ASIA PRE/AMER S/ASIA ECO/UNDEV KIN NAT/G SECT FORCES DOMIN HEALTH...SOC 16/20. PAGE 128 H2560
COLONIAL CULTURE GEOG HABITAT

B63
SETON-WATSON H.,THE NEW IMPERIALISM. COM EUR+WWI MOD/EUR ECO/UNDEV NAT/G FORCES DIPLOM DOMIN EDU/PROP LEGIT COLONIAL EXEC COERCE GP/REL RACE/REL DISCRIM ATTIT...TIME/SEQ 20. PAGE 142 H2833
ECO/TAC RUSSIA USSR

B63
SINGH H.L.,PROBLEMS AND OLICIES OF THE BRITISH IN INDIA, 1885-1898. INDIA K NAT/G FORCES LEGIS
COLONIAL PWR

PROB/SOLV CONTROL RACE/REL ADJUST DISCRIM NAT/LISM RIGID/FLEX...MGT 19 CIVIL/SERV. PAGE 144 H2885
POLICY ADMIN

B63
STEVENS G.G.,EGYPT YESTERDAY AND TODAY. CONSTN ECO/UNDEV AGRI INDUS NAT/G POL/PAR FORCES ECO/TAC EDU/PROP COERCE WAR NAT/LISM DRIVE ALL/VALS ...TIME/SEQ WORK SUEZ 20. PAGE 149 H2983
ISLAM TOP/EX REV UAR

B63
STIRNIMANN H.,NGUNI UND GNONI: EINE KULTURGESCHICHTLICHE STUDIE (ACTA ETHNOLOGICA ET LINGUISTICA, NUMBER 6). AFR MALAWI SOUTH/AFR FORCES HABITAT...RECORD CHARTS BIBLIOG WORSHIP 19/20 NATAL. PAGE 149 H2987
CULTURE GP/COMP SOCIETY

B63
SWEARER H.R.,CONTEMPORARY COMMUNISM: THEORY AND PRACTICE. COM USSR SOCIETY ECO/DEV POL/PAR FORCES PLAN ADMIN LEAD NAT/LISM...POLICY ANTHOL 20 LENIN/VI COM/PARTY. PAGE 151 H3015
MARXISM CONCPT DIPLOM NAT/G

B63
THUCYDIDES,THE PELOPONESIAN WARS. MEDIT-7 CULTURE INT/ORG NAT/G FORCES TOP/EX PLAN ROUTINE PWR ...CONCPT. PAGE 155 H3091
ATTIT COERCE WAR

L63
FREUND G.,"ADENAUER AND THE FUTURE OF GERMANY." EUR+WWI FUT GERMANY/W FORCES LEGIT ADMIN ROUTINE ATTIT DRIVE PERSON PWR...POLICY TIME/SEQ TREND VAL/FREE 20 ADENAUER/K. PAGE 53 H1058
NAT/G BIOG DIPLOM GERMANY

S63
BECHHOEFER B.G.,"SOVIET ATTITUDE TOWARD DISARMAMENT." COM USSR NAT/G ACT/RES TEC/DEV NUC/PWR ATTIT DISPL RIGID/FLEX PWR...METH/CNCPT TREND GEN/LAWS COLD/WAR 20. PAGE 13 H0252
FORCES EDU/PROP ARMS/CONT

S63
DUTT V.P.,"CHINA: JEALOUS NEIGHBOR." ASIA CHINA/COM INDIA S/ASIA NAT/G TOP/EX DOMIN COERCE REV ATTIT ...POLICY COLD/WAR 20. PAGE 44 H0874
FORCES PWR DIPLOM

S63
GLUCKMAN M.,"CIVIL WAR AND THEORIES OF POWER IN BAROTSE-LAND: AFRICAN AND MEDIEVAL ANALOGIES." AFR CHRIST-17C LAW CONSTN CULTURE STRATA KIN DELIB/GP FORCES DOMIN LEGIT COERCE PERCEPT ORD/FREE...SOC INT TIME/SEQ GEN/LAWS VAL/FREE. PAGE 57 H1148
TOP/EX PWR WAR

S63
HALPERN A.M.,"THE EMERGENCE OF AN ASIAN COMMUNIST BLOC." ASIA CHINA/COM COM FUT KOREA/N S/ASIA VIETNAM/N STRATA NAT/G DELIB/GP FORCES TOP/EX PLAN BAL/PWR COERCE DETER PWR COLD/WAR WORK 20. PAGE 65 H1295
POL/PAR EDU/PROP DIPLOM

S63
LIGOT M.,"LA COOPERATION MILITAIRE DANS LES ACCORDS, PASSES ENTRE LA FRANCE ET LES ETATS AFRICAINS ET MALGACHE D'EXPRESSION." ECO/UNDEV INT/ORG NAT/G VOL/ASSN...CONCPT TIME/SEQ 20. PAGE 97 H1931
AFR FORCES FOR/AID FRANCE

S63
RUSTOW D.A.,"THE MILITARY IN MIDDLE EASTERN SOCIETY AND POLITICS." FUT ISLAM CONSTN SOCIETY FACE/GP NAT/G POL/PAR PROF/ORG CONSULT DOMIN ADMIN EXEC REGION COERCE NAT/LISM ATTIT DRIVE PERSON ORD/FREE PWR...POLICY CONCPT OBS STERTYP 20. PAGE 136 H2721
FORCES ELITES

S63
STAAR R.F.,"HOW STRONG IS THE SOVIET BLOC." COM USSR ECO/DEV NAT/G DELIB/GP ECO/TAC RIGID/FLEX ...CONCPT RECORD CHARTS 20. PAGE 148 H2964
FORCES MYTH TOTALISM

C63
ATTIA G.E.O.,"LES FORCES ARMEES DES NATIONS UNIES EN COREE ET AU MOYENORIENT." KOREA CONSTN DELIB/GP LEGIS PWR...IDEA/COMP NAT/COMP BIBLIOG UN SUEZ. PAGE 9 H0178
FORCES NAT/G INT/LAW

B64
BELL C.,THE DEBATABLE ALLIANCE. COM UK USA+45 NAT/G FORCES PLAN BAL/PWR NUC/PWR WAR ATTIT...GOV/COMP 20. PAGE 13 H0263
DIPLOM PWR PEACE POLICY

B64
BROWN N.,NUCLEAR WAR* THE IMPENDING STRATEGIC DEADLOCK. USA+45 USSR TEC/DEV BUDGET RISK ARMS/CONT NUC/PWR WEAPON COST BIO/SOC...GEOG IDEA/COMP NAT/COMP GAME NATO WARSAW/P. PAGE 22 H0448
FORCES OP/RES WAR GEN/LAWS

B64
BRZEZINSKI Z.,POLITICAL POWER: USA/USSR. USA+45 USSR AGRI POL/PAR FORCES CREATE CHOOSE ATTIT ORD/FREE PWR MARXISM...MYTH 20 KENNEDY/JF. PAGE 23 H0457
NAT/G NAT/COMP POLICY LEAD

B64
BUNTING B.P.,THE RISE OF THE SOUTH AFRICAN REICH. SOUTH/AFR INT/ORG NAT/G FORCES DIPLOM CONTROL WAR TOTALISM ATTIT...GOV/COMP 19/20. PAGE 24 H0477
RACE/REL DISCRIM NAT/LISM TREND

B64
CURTIN P.D.,THE IMAGE OF AFRICA: BRITISH IDEAS AND ACTION, 1780-1850. MOD/EUR SOCIETY FORCES ACT/RES DOMIN EDU/PROP COERCE ATTIT PERCEPT RIGID/FLEX SUPEGO HEALTH KNOWL MORAL ORD/FREE WEALTH...CONCPT WORK VAL/FREE. PAGE 36 H0726
AFR CULTURE UK DIPLOM

B64
FALL B.,STREET WITHOUT JOY. FRANCE USA+45 DIPLOM ECO/TAC FOR/AID GUERRILLA REV WEAPON...TREND 20. PAGE 48 H0966
WAR S/ASIA FORCES COERCE

B64
GESELLSCHAFT RECHTSVERGLEICH,BIBLIOGRAPHIE DES DEUTSCHEN RECHTS (BIBLIOGRAPHY OF GERMAN LAW, TRANS. BY COURTLAND PETERSON). GERMANY FINAN INDUS LABOR SECT FORCES CT/SYS PARL/PROC CRIME...INT/LAW SOC NAT/COMP 20. PAGE 56 H1117
BIBLIOG/A JURID CONSTN ADMIN

B64
GREEN M.M.,IBO VILLAGE AFFAIRS. AFR FORCES PERS/REL ADJUST ISOLAT ATTIT HABITAT PERSON ALL/VALS...JURID RECORD SOC/INTEG 20 IBO. PAGE 60 H1207
MUNIC CULTURE ECO/UNDEV SOC

B64
GRIFFITH W.E.,THE SINO-SOVIET RIFT. ASIA CHINA/COM COM CUBA USSR YUGOSLAVIA NAT/G POL/PAR VOL/ASSN DELIB/GP FORCES TOP/EX DIPLOM EDU/PROP DRIVE PERSON PWR...TREND 20 TREATY. PAGE 61 H1224
ATTIT TIME/SEQ BAL/PWR SOCISM

B64
GUTTERIDGE W.,MILITARY INSTITUTIONS AND POWER IN THE NEW STATES. WOR+45 INT/ORG FOR/AID NEUTRAL REV CIVMIL/REL ATTIT ROLE...GOV/COMP 20. PAGE 63 H1258
FORCES DIPLOM ECO/UNDEV ELITES

B64
IMAZ J.L.,LOS QUE MANDAN. INDUS LABOR NAT/G POL/PAR PROVS SECT CHIEF TOP/EX CONTROL 20 ARGEN. PAGE 76 H1524
LEAD FORCES ELITES ATTIT

B64
JOHNSON J.J.,CONTINUITY AND CHANGE IN LATIN AMERICA. L/A+17C INTELL FORCES WORKER CIVMIL/REL CHINJAP. PAGE 81 H1623
ANTHOL CULTURE STRATA GP/COMP

B64
KELLER J.W.,GERMANY, THE WALL AND BERLIN. EUR+WWI ECO/DEV NAT/G VOL/ASSN FORCES PLAN ECO/TAC EDU/PROP COERCE...POLICY CONCPT INT TREND COLD/WAR BER/BLOC 20 BERLIN. PAGE 84 H1685
ATTIT ALL/VALS DIPLOM GERMANY

B64
KITCHEN H.,A HANDBOOK OF AFRICAN AFFAIRS. ECO/UNDEV CREATE DIPLOM COLONIAL RACE/REL...ART/METH GEOG CHARTS 20. PAGE 87 H1729
AFR NAT/G INT/ORG FORCES

B64
LIEVWEN E.,GENERALS VS PRESIDENTS: WEOMILITARISM IN LATIN AMERICA. L/A+17C FORCES DIPLOM FOR/AID LEAD ...NAT/COMP 20 PRESIDENT. PAGE 97 H1929
CIVMIL/REL REV CONSERVE ORD/FREE

B64
MORRIS J.,THE PRESENCE OF SPAIN. SPAIN MUNIC NAT/G FORCES ATTIT CATHISM...AUD/VIS 16/20. PAGE 113 H2263
CULTURE HABITAT SOCIETY GEOG

B64
PITTMAN J.,PEACEFUL COEXISTENCE. USSR NAT/G NUC/PWR WAR ATTIT 20. PAGE 126 H2518
DIPLOM PEACE POLICY FORCES

B64
RAISON T.,WHY CONSERVATIVE? UK FORCES DIPLOM ECO/TAC GIVE EDU/PROP ORD/FREE WEALTH LAISSEZ ...GOV/COMP 20 TORY/PARTY CONSRV/PAR. PAGE 129 H2583
PLURISM CONSERVE POL/PAR NAT/G

B64
RIES J.C.,THE MANAGEMENT OF DEFENSE: ORGANIZATION AND CONTROL OF THE US ARMED SERVICES. PROF/ORG DELIB/GP EX/STRUC LEGIS GOV/REL PERS/REL CENTRAL RATIONAL PWR...POLICY TREND GOV/COMP BIBLIOG. PAGE 131 H2626
FORCES ACT/RES DECISION CONTROL

B64
SKINNER E.P.,THE MOSSI OF UPPER VOLTA: THE POLITICAL DEVELOPMENT OF A SUDANESE PEOPLE. AFR LAW AGRI FAM KIN POL/PAR PROVS SECT DELIB/GP EX/STRUC FORCES TOP/EX DOMIN EDU/PROP LEGIT CT/SYS COERCE CHOOSE ORD/FREE PWR WEALTH...SOC MYTH VAL/FREE. PAGE 145 H2897
CULTURE OBS UPPER/VOLT

B64
TEPASKE J.J.,EXPLOSIVE FORCES IN LATIN AMERICA. CULTURE INTELL ECO/UNDEV INT/ORG NAT/G SECT FORCES ECO/TAC EDU/PROP PWR WEALTH SOC. PAGE 153 H3063
L/A+17C RIGID/FLEX FOR/AID USSR

B64
US HOUSE COMM BANKING-CURR,INTERNATIONAL DEVELOPMENT ASSOCIATION ACT AMENDMENT. CHINA/COM USA+45 USSR FINAN FORCES LEGIS DIPLOM CONFER EFFICIENCY...CHARTS GOV/COMP 20 PRESIDENT CONGRESS INTL/DEV. PAGE 160 H3196
BAL/PAY FOR/AID RECORD ECO/TAC

B64
WALDMAN E.,THE GOOSE STEP IS VERBOTEN: THE GERMAN ARMY TODAY. GERMANY/W LAW CONSTN LEGIS PROB/SOLV DOMIN CONTROL CIVMIL/REL GOV/REL INGP/REL ATTIT ...DEEP/QU 20. PAGE 164 H3289
SOC FORCES NAT/G

B64
WARD R.E.,POLITICAL MODERNIZATION IN JAPAN AND TURKEY. ASIA ISLAM S/ASIA CONSTN CULTURE STRATA COM/IND POL/PAR FORCES ACT/RES ECO/TAC DOMIN EDU/PROP LEGIT ADMIN CHOOSE ATTIT ALL/VALS...STAT TIME/SEQ VAL/FREE CHINJAP. PAGE 165 H3307 SOCIETY TURKEY

B64
WHEELER-BENNETT J.W.,THE NEMESIS OF POWER (2ND ED.). EUR+WWI GERMANY TOP/EX TEC/DEV ADMIN WAR PERS/REL RIGID/FLEX ROLE ORD/FREE PWR FASCISM 20 HITLER/A. PAGE 167 H3342 FORCES NAT/G GP/REL STRUCT

B64
WHITE D.S.,SEEDS OF DISCORD. EUR+WWI FRANCE NAT/G VOL/ASSN FORCES DIPLOM DOMIN NAT/LISM DISPL RIGID/FLEX PWR...RECORD INT BIOG 20 DEGAULLE/C ROOSEVLT/F CHURCHLL/W HULL. PAGE 167 H3347 TOP/EX ATTIT

B64
WILCOX W.A.,INDIA, PAKISTAN AND THE RISE OF CHINA. ASIA BURMA CEYLON CHINA/COM INDIA PAKISTAN S/ASIA NAT/G VOL/ASSN FORCES TOP/EX ACT/RES DOMIN REGION RIGID/FLEX ORD/FREE...POLICY GEN/LAWS COLD/WAR 20. PAGE 168 H3362 CULTURE ATTIT DIPLOM

B64
WRAITH R.,CORRUPTION IN DEVELOPING COUNTRIES. NIGERIA UK LAW ELITES STRATA INDUS LOC/G NAT/G SECT FORCES EDU/PROP ADMIN PWR WEALTH 18/20. PAGE 171 H3414 ECO/UNDEV CRIME SANCTION ATTIT

B64
ZARTMAN I.W.,MOROCCO: PROBLEMS OF NEW POWER. ISLAM CULTURE ECO/UNDEV AGRI POL/PAR SCHOOL FORCES ADMIN ...CONCPT STAT INT CENSUS TIME/SEQ CHARTS WORK VAL/FREE 20. PAGE 172 H3449 CHOOSE MOROCCO DELIB/GP DECISION

L64
ROTBERG R.,"THE FEDERATION MOVEMENT IN BRITISH EAST AND CENTRAL AFRICA." AFR RHODESIA UGANDA ECO/UNDEV NAT/G POL/PAR FORCES DOMIN LEGIT ADMIN COERCE ATTIT ...CONCPT TREND 20 TANGANYIKA. PAGE 135 H2691 VOL/ASSN PWR REGION

S64
BARIETY J.,"LA POLITIQUE EXTERIEURE ALLEMANDE DANS L'HIVER 1939-1940." COM FINLAND GERMANY ISLAM ITALY USSR NAT/G FORCES ECO/TAC DOMIN EDU/PROP COERCE WAR PWR WEALTH...HIST/WRIT NAZI TOT/POP VAL/FREE 20. PAGE 11 H0216 EUR+WWI DIPLOM

S64
CATTELL D.T.,"SOVIET POLICIES IN LATIN AMERICA." COM CUBA L/A+17C USSR SOCIETY NAT/G POL/PAR FORCES CREATE ECO/TAC EDU/PROP REGION REV RIGID/FLEX ...GEN/LAWS COLD/WAR 20. PAGE 28 H0560 DRIVE PWR

S64
ENNIS T.E.,"VIETNAM: LAND WITHOUT LAUGHTER." S/ASIA VIETNAM VIETNAM/S INTELL SOCIETY SECT FORCES DIPLOM LEGIT COERCE WAR ATTIT RIGID/FLEX ORD/FREE COLD/WAR 20. PAGE 46 H0929 NAT/G TOP/EX GUERRILLA

S64
GOLDBERG A.,"THE MILITARY ORIGINS OF THE BRITISH NUCLEAR DETERRENT." EUR+WWI ECO/DEV NAT/G PLAN NUC/PWR ATTIT PWR...DECISION HIST/WRIT COLD/WAR 20. PAGE 58 H1156 FORCES CONCPT DETER UK

S64
JOHNSON K.F.,"CAUSAL FACTORS IN LATIN AMERICAN POLITICAL INSTABILITY." CULTURE NAT/G VOL/ASSN EX/STRUC FORCES EDU/PROP LEGIT ADMIN COERCE REV ATTIT KNOWL PWR...STYLE RECORD CHARTS WORK 20. PAGE 81 H1624 L/A+17C PERCEPT ELITES

S64
LOW D.A.,"LION RAMPANT." EUR+WWI MOD/EUR S/ASIA ECO/UNDEV NAT/G FORCES TEC/DEV ECO/TAC LEGIT ADMIN COLONIAL COERCE ORD/FREE RESPECT 19/20. PAGE 99 H1972 AFR DOMIN DIPLOM UK

S64
MOZINGO D.P.,"CHINA'S RELATIONS WITH HER ASIAN NEIGHBORS." ASIA CHINA/COM S/ASIA VIETNAM NAT/G DELIB/GP FORCES CREATE DOMIN EDU/PROP REV RIGID/FLEX PWR...TIME/SEQ GEN/LAWS COLD/WAR 20. PAGE 114 H2277 VOL/ASSN POLICY DIPLOM

S64
POWELL R.L.,"COMMUNIST CHINA'S MILITARY POTENTIAL." ASIA CHINA/COM NAT/G EX/STRUC EDU/PROP COERCE GUERRILLA NUC/PWR WAR...RECORD CON/ANAL 20. PAGE 128 H2551 FORCES PWR

S64
REISS I.,"LE DECLENCHEMENT DE LA PREMIERE GUERRE MONDIALE." GERMANY RUSSIA NAT/G FORCES DOMIN EDU/PROP COERCE RIGID/FLEX PWR SOVEREIGN...RELATIV HIST/WRIT TOT/POP AUST/HUNG SERBIA 20. PAGE 131 H2612 MOD/EUR BAL/PWR DIPLOM WAR

S64
RUDOLPH L.I.,"GENERALS AND POLITICIANS IN INDIA." INDIA S/ASIA CULTURE STRATA NAT/G LEGIS TOP/EX EDU/PROP ATTIT ORD/FREE PWR RESPECT SKILL...POLICY BIOG TIME/SEQ STERTYP VAL/FREE 20. PAGE 136 H2713 FORCES COERCE

S64
SAAB H.,"THE ARAB SEARCH FOR A FEDERAL UNION." SOCIETY INT/ORG NAT/G DELIB/GP FORCES ACT/RES TEC/DEV ECO/TAC DOMIN LEGIT REGION ROUTINE ATTIT DRIVE RIGID/FLEX ALL/VALS...SOC CONCPT NEW/IDEA TIME/SEQ TREND. PAGE 136 H2726 ISLAM PLAN

S64
SCHEFFLER H.W.,"THE GENESIS AND REPRESSION OF CONFLICT: CHOISEUL ISLAND." S/ASIA LOC/G NAT/G FORCES LEGIS DIPLOM DOMIN LEGIT EXEC CHOOSE ATTIT RESPECT SKILL...POLICY JURID OBS TREND GEN/METH 20. PAGE 139 H2781 PWR COERCE WAR

S64
VANDENBOSCH A.,"POWER BALANCE IN INDONESIA." S/ASIA USSR NAT/G TOP/EX BAL/PWR DOMIN NEUTRAL ORD/FREE PWR...POLICY TIME/SEQ GEN/LAWS 20 SUKARNO/A. PAGE 162 H3233 FORCES TREND DIPLOM INDONESIA

B65
ADENAUER K.,MEMOIRS 1945-53. EUR+WWI GERMANY/W ECO/DEV CHIEF FORCES ECO/TAC WAR GOV/REL PWR SOVEREIGN 20 NATO ADENAUER/K. PAGE 3 H0068 BIOG DIPLOM NAT/G PERS/REL

B65
ADENAUER K.,MEINE ERINNERUNGEN, 1945-53 (VOL. I), 1953-55 (VOL. II). EUR+WWI GERMANY CHIEF FORCES PROB/SOLV DIPLOM ARMS/CONT INGP/REL PEACE SOVEREIGN ...OBS/ENVIR RECORD 20. PAGE 3 H0069 NAT/G BIOG SELF/OBS

B65
AIR UNIVERSITY LIBRARY,LATIN AMERICA, SELECTED REFERENCES. ECO/UNDEV FORCES EDU/PROP MARXISM 20 OAS. PAGE 4 H0084 BIBLIOG L/A+17C NAT/G DIPLOM

B65
BRAMSTED E.K.,GOEBBELS AND NATIONAL SOCIALIST PROPAGANDA, 1925-1945. EUR+WWI GERMANY UK USSR NAT/G FORCES WAR FASCISM...TIME/SEQ 20 GOEBBELS/J NAZI. PAGE 20 H0403 EDU/PROP PSY COM/IND

B65
CAMPBELL G.A.,THE CIVIL SERVICE IN BRITAIN (2ND ED.). UK DELIB/GP FORCES WORKER CREATE PLAN ...POLICY AUD/VIS 19/20 CIVIL/SERV. PAGE 26 H0515 ADMIN LEGIS NAT/G FINAN

B65
FAUST J.J.,A REVOLUCAO DEVORA SEUS PRESIDENTES. BRAZIL NAT/G POL/PAR LEAD CHOOSE CIVMIL/REL ORD/FREE 20 PRESIDENT. PAGE 49 H0976 PARTIC REV FORCES GP/REL

B65
GRAHAM G.S.,THE POLITICS OF NAVAL SUPREMACY; STUDIES IN BRITISH MARITIME ASCENDANCY. UK SEA NAT/G BAL/PWR LEAD WAR WEAPON PEACE...POLICY 18/19 COMMONWLTH. PAGE 60 H1191 FORCES PWR COLONIAL DIPLOM

B65
GREGG J.L.,POLITICAL PARTIES AND PARTY SYSTEMS IN GUATEMALA, 1944-1963. GUATEMALA L/A+17C EX/STRUC FORCES CREATE CONTROL REV CHOOSE PWR...TREND IDEA/COMP 20. PAGE 60 H1209 LEAD POL/PAR NAT/G CHIEF

B65
GRETTON P.,MARITIME STRATEGY - A STUDY OF DEFENSE PROBLEMS. ASIA UK USSR DIPLOM COERCE DETER NUC/PWR WEAPON...CONCPT NAT/COMP 20. PAGE 60 H1211 FORCES PLAN WAR SEA

B65
HALPERIN M.H.,COMMUNIST CHINA AND ARMS CONTROL. CHINA/COM FUT USA+45 CULTURE FORCES TEC/DEV ECO/TAC WAR PEACE ORD/FREE MARXISM 20 COLD/WAR. PAGE 64 H1292 ATTIT POLICY ARMS/CONT NUC/PWR

B65
HART B.H.L.,THE MEMOIRS OF CAPTAIN LIDDELL HART (VOL. I). UK NAT/G PLAN TEC/DEV DIPLOM ADMIN WEAPON GOV/REL PERS/REL ATTIT PWR FASCISM...POLICY 20. PAGE 67 H1348 FORCES BIOG LEAD WAR

B65
MONTESQUIEU C DE S.,CONSIDERATIONS ON THE CAUSES OF THE GREATNESS OF THE ROMANS AND THEIR DECLINE (1748 TRANS. BY D. LOWENTHAL). ROMAN/EMP SECT CHIEF EX/STRUC FORCES LEGIS DOMIN WAR POPULISM...POLICY REALPOL ROME/ANC. PAGE 112 H2244 NAT/G PWR COLONIAL MORAL

B65
NORDEN A.,WAR AND NAZI CRIMINALS IN WEST GERMANY: STATE, ECONOMY, ADMINISTRATION, ARMY, JUSTICE, SCIENCE. GERMANY GERMANY/W MOD/EUR ECO/DEV ACADEM EX/STRUC FORCES DOMIN ADMIN CT/SYS...POLICY MAJORIT PACIFIST 20. PAGE 119 H2370 FASCIST WAR NAT/G TOP/EX

B65
O'BRIEN W.V.,THE NEW NATIONS IN INTERNATIONAL LAW AND DIPLOMACY* THE YEAR BOOK OF WORLD POLITY* VOLUME III. USA+45 ECO/UNDEV INT/ORG FORCES DIPLOM COLONIAL NEUTRAL REV NAT/LISM ATTIT RESPECT. PAGE 119 H2385 INT/LAW CULTURE SOVEREIGN ANTHOL

B65
SCALAPINO R.A.,THE COMMUNIST REVOLUTION IN ASIA* TACTICS, GOALS, AND ACHIEVEMENTS. INDIA INTELL POL/PAR FORCES DOMIN EDU/PROP LEGIT COERCE REV ATTIT CHINJAP. PAGE 138 H2763 ASIA S/ASIA MARXISM NAT/COMP

B65
SLATER J.,A REVALUATION OF COLLECTIVE SECURITY* THE OAS IN ACTION. L/A+17C USA+45 NAT/G ADMIN COERCE ORD/FREE PWR...GOV/COMP IDEA/COMP GEN/LAWS OAS. PAGE 145 H2899 REGION INT/ORG FORCES

B65
TILLY C.,MEASURING POLITICAL UPHEAVAL* RESEARCH MONOGRAPH NO. 19. FRANCE INDUS NAT/G FORCES WORKER ...GEOG RECORD EXHIBIT GEN/METH BIBLIOG INDEX. PAGE 155 H3095
CLASSIF QUANT COERCE REV

B65
UPTON A.F.,FINLAND IN CRISIS 1940-1941. NAT/G FORCES DIPLOM COERCE...DECISION GEOG. PAGE 159 H3173
FINLAND GERMANY USSR WAR

B65
US DEPARTMENT OF DEFENSE,US SECURITY ARMS CONTROL, AND DISARMAMENT 1961-1965 (PAMPHLET). CHINA/COM COM GERMANY/W ISRAEL SPACE USA+45 USSR WOR+45 FORCES EDU/PROP DETER EQUILIB PEACE ALL/VALS...GOV/COMP 20 NATO. PAGE 159 H3183
BIBLIOG/A ARMS/CONT NUC/PWR DIPLOM

L65
MATTHEWS D.G.,"A CURRENT BIBLIOGRAPHY ON ETHIOPIAN AFFAIRS: A SELECT BIBLIOGRAPHY FROM 1950-1964." ETHIOPIA LAW CULTURE ECO/UNDEV INDUS LABOR SECT FORCES DIPLOM CIVMIL/REL RACE/REL...LING STAT 20. PAGE 105 H2093
BIBLIOG/A ADMIN POL/PAR NAT/G

S65
GRIFFITH S.B.,"COMMUNIST CHINA'S CAPACITY TO MAKE WAR." CHINA/COM COM NAT/G TOP/EX PLAN DOMIN COERCE NUC/PWR ATTIT RESPECT SKILL...CONCPT MYTH TIME/SEQ TREND COLD/WAR 20. PAGE 61 H1221
FORCES PWR WEAPON ASIA

S65
MCALISTER L.N.,"CHANGING CONCEPTS OF THE ROLE OF THE MILITARY IN LATIN AMERICA." CULTURE NAT/G CREATE REGION NAT/LISM ATTIT SOVEREIGN...NAT/COMP GEN/LAWS. PAGE 106 H2120
L/A+17C FORCES IDEA/COMP PWR

S65
PLANK J.N.,"THE CARIBBEAN* INTERVENTION, WHEN AND HOW." CUBA GUATEMALA HAITI PANAMA USA+45 VENEZUELA FORCES PROB/SOLV RISK COERCE...NAT/COMP OAS TIME. PAGE 126 H2521
SOVEREIGN MARXISM REV

S65
POWELL J.D.,"MILITARY ASSISTANCE AND MILITARISM IN LATIN AMERICA." USA+45 INT/ORG NAT/G CONTROL REGION PRODUC WEALTH...CLASSIF STAT NAT/COMP CONGRESS. PAGE 128 H2550
L/A+17C FORCES FOR/AID PWR

S65
SANDERS R.,"MASS SUPPORT AND COMMUNIST INSURRECTION." GREECE MALAYSIA PHILIPPINE VIETNAM STRUCT ECO/UNDEV POL/PAR FORCES CREATE REV ...GP/COMP IDEA/COMP. PAGE 138 H2751
GUERRILLA MARXISM GOV/COMP

S65
SPAAK P.H.,"THE SEARCH FOR CONSENSUS: A NEW EFFORT TO BUILD EUROPE." FRANCE GERMANY ECO/DEV NAT/G CONSULT FORCES PLAN EDU/PROP REGION CONSEN ATTIT ...SOC METH/CNCPT OBS TREND EEC NATO WORK 20. PAGE 147 H2941
EUR+WWI INT/ORG

S65
WOHLSTETTER R.,"CUBA AND PEARL HARBOR* HINDSIGHT AND FORESIGHT." USSR FORCES OP/RES TEC/DEV ATTIT PERCEPT...DECISION IDEA/COMP NAT/COMP STERTYP TIME. PAGE 170 H3395
CUBA RISK WAR ACT/RES

S65
WOLF C. JR.,"THE POLITICAL EFFECTS OF SOME MILITARY PROGRAMS* SOME INDICATIONS FROM LATIN AMERICA." ELITES STRATA BUDGET FOR/AID WEAPON ATTIT PERCEPT PWR...REGRESS SYS/QU CHARTS NAT/COMP. PAGE 170 H3397
L/A+17C FORCES CIVMIL/REL PROBABIL

S65
WRIGHT Q.,"THE ESCALATION OF INTERNATIONAL CONFLICTS." WOR+45 WOR-45 FORCES DIPLOM RISK COST ATTIT ALL/VALS...INT/LAW QUANT STAT NAT/COMP. PAGE 171 H3422
WAR PERCEPT PREDICT MATH

B66
AFRIFA A.A.,THE GHANA COUP. AFR GHANA ELITES NAT/G DIPLOM DOMIN 20 NKRUMAH/K. PAGE 4 H0076
TOP/EX REV FORCES POL/PAR

B66
BIRMINGHAM D.,TRADE AND CONFLICT IN ANGOLA. PORTUGAL CULTURE FORCES DIPLOM GP/REL PROFIT HABITAT NAT/COMP. PAGE 17 H0341
WAR INT/TRADE ECO/UNDEV COLONIAL

B66
BRACKMAN A.C.,SOUTHEAST ASIA'S SECOND FRONT: THE POWER STRUGGLE IN THE MALAY ARCHIPELAGO. CHINA/COM INDONESIA MALAYSIA ECO/UNDEV INT/ORG NAT/G FORCES DIPLOM EDU/PROP REGION COERCE GUERRILLA AUTHORIT POPULISM...MAJORIT 20 KENNEDY/JF SEATO. PAGE 20 H0396
S/ASIA MARXISM REV

B66
BRECHER M.,SUCCESSION IN INDIA. INDIA USA+45 CONSTN AGRI POL/PAR PROVS SECT DELIB/GP FORCES PROB/SOLV ECO/TAC PWR...LING 20 CONGRESS NEHRU/J. PAGE 20 H0408
CHIEF DECISION CHOOSE

B66
BUKHARIN N.,THE ABC OF COMMUNISM: A POPULAR EXPLANATION OF THE PROGRAM OF THE COMMUNIST PARTY OF RUSSIA. USSR STRATA SECT FORCES WORKER CAP/ISM RECEIVE EDU/PROP NAT/LISM TOTALISM 20. PAGE 23 H0468
MARXISM CONCPT POLICY REV

B66
COEDES G.,THE MAKING OF SOUTH EAST ASIA. BURMA CAMBODIA LAOS S/ASIA THAILAND VIETNAM REV WAR CIVMIL/REL...GEOG 6/13. PAGE 31 H0614
CULTURE FORCES DOMIN

B66
DAENIKER G.,STRATEGIE DES KLEIN STAATS. SWITZERLND ACT/RES CREATE DIPLOM NEUTRAL DETER WAR WEAPON PWR SOVEREIGN...IDEA/COMP 20 COLD/WAR. PAGE 36 H0730
NUC/PWR PLAN FORCES NAT/G

B66
DALLIN A.,POLITICS IN THE SOVIET UNION: 7 CASES. COM USSR LAW POL/PAR CHIEF FORCES WRITING CONTROL PARL/PROC CIVMIL/REL TOTALISM...ANTHOL 20 KHRUSH/N STALIN/J CASEBOOK COM/PARTY. PAGE 37 H0736
MARXISM DOMIN ORD/FREE GOV/REL

B66
DEUTSCHER I.,STALIN: A POLITICAL BIOGRAPHY. EUR+WWI USSR POL/PAR FORCES DIPLOM ADMIN LEAD REV WAR TOTALISM PERSON 20 STALIN/J ROOSEVLT/F LENIN/VI HITLER/A. PAGE 40 H0807
BIOG MARXISM TOP/EX PWR

B66
ELLIS A.B.,THE EWE-SPEAKING PEOPLES OF THE SLAVE COAST OF WEST AFRICA. AFR FORCES ADJUST...LING RECORD GP/COMP WORSHIP 20 AFRICA/W DEITY. PAGE 45 H0910
MYTH CULTURE HABITAT

B66
EMBREE A.T.,ASIA: A GUIDE TO BASIC BOOKS (PAMPHLET). ECO/UNDEV SECT FORCES DIPLOM ALL/IDEOS ...SOC 20. PAGE 46 H0914
BIBLIOG/A ASIA S/ASIA NAT/G

B66
EPSTEIN F.T.,THE AMERICAN BIBLIOGRAPHY OF RUSSIAN AND EAST EUROPEAN STUDIES FOR 1964. USSR LOC/G NAT/G POL/PAR FORCES ADMIN ARMS/CONT...JURID CONCPT 20 UN. PAGE 47 H0933
BIBLIOG COM MARXISM DIPLOM

B66
FRIED R.C.,COMPARATIVE POLITICAL INSTITUTIONS. USSR EX/STRUC FORCES LEGIS JUDGE CONTROL REPRESENT ALL/IDEOS 20 CONGRESS BUREAUCRCY. PAGE 53 H1062
NAT/G PWR EFFICIENCY GOV/COMP

B66
GERARD-LIBOIS J.,KATANGA SECESSION. INT/ORG FORCES DIPLOM ADMIN CONTROL WAR CHOOSE PWR...CHARTS 20 KATANGA TSHOMBE/M UN. PAGE 56 H1114
NAT/G REGION ORD/FREE REV

B66
GORDON B.K.,THE DIMENSIONS OF CONFLICT IN SOUTHEAST ASIA. S/ASIA FORCES ADJUD REGION...CHARTS 20. PAGE 59 H1177
DIPLOM NAT/COMP INT/ORG VOL/ASSN

B66
GRAHAM I.C.C.,PUBLICATIONS OF THE SOCIAL SCIENCE DEPARTMENT, THE RAND CORPORATION, 1948-1966. USSR WOR+45 NAT/G ARMS/CONT DETER WAR NAT/LISM...SOC GOV/COMP. PAGE 60 H1192
BIBLIOG DIPLOM NUC/PWR FORCES

B66
KEYES J.G.,A BIBLIOGRAPHY OF WESTERN LANGUAGE PUBLICATIONS CONCERNING NORTH VIETNAM IN THE CORNELL LIBRARY. VIETNAM/N NAT/G FORCES TEC/DEV DIPLOM LEAD RACE/REL...GEOG SOC 20. PAGE 85 H1700
BIBLIOG/A CULTURE ECO/UNDEV S/ASIA

B66
MACFARQUHAR R.,CHINA UNDER MAO: POLITICS TAKES COMMAND. CHINA/COM COM AGRI INDUS CHIEF FORCES DIPLOM INT/TRADE EDU/PROP TASK REV ADJUST...ANTHOL 20 MAO. PAGE 100 H1992
ECO/UNDEV TEC/DEV ECO/TAC ADMIN

B66
NIEDERGANG M.,LA REVOLUTION DE SAINT-DOMINGUE. DOMIN/REP INT/ORG NAT/G CONTROL LEAD GP/REL ORD/FREE MARXISM 20. PAGE 118 H2361
REV FORCES DIPLOM

B66
O'NEILL R.J.,THE GERMAN ARMY AND THE NAZI PARTY, 1933-1939. GERMANY ELITES NAT/G EDU/PROP CONTROL LEAD COERCE WAR...POLICY INT TIME/SEQ BIBLIOG 20 HITLER/A NAZI. PAGE 120 H2391
CIVMIL/REL FORCES FASCISM POL/PAR

B66
SKILLING H.G.,THE GOVERNMENTS OF COMMUNIST EAST EUROPE. COM EUR+WWI ELITES FORCES DIPLOM ECO/TAC CONTROL HABITAT SOCISM...DECISION BIBLIOG 20 EUROPE/E COM/PARTY. PAGE 145 H2895
MARXISM NAT/COMP GP/COMP DOMIN

B66
SOBEL L.A.,SOUTH VIETNAM: US-COMMUNIST CONFRONTATION IN SOUTHEAST ASIA 1961-65. VIETNAM FOR/AID CROWD DETER REV PEACE...GEOG 20 INTERVENT DIEM COLD/WAR. PAGE 146 H2926
WAR TIME/SEQ FORCES NAT/G

B66
SPEARS E.L.,TWO MEN WHO SAVED FRANCE: PETAIN AND DE GAULLE. FRANCE CONSTN FORCES DIPLOM WAR PERSON 20 WWI PETAIN/HP DEGAULLE/C. PAGE 147 H2942
BIOG LEAD CHIEF NAT/G

B66
SYMONDS R.,THE BRITISH AND THEIR SUCCESSORS. AFR CEYLON INDIA UK SCHOOL FORCES EDU/PROP ADMIN PARTIC ...NAT/COMP BIBLIOG 20 AFRICA/W AFRICA/E. PAGE 151 H3024
NAT/G ECO/UNDEV POLICY COLONIAL

B66
US DEPARTMENT OF STATE,RESEARCH ON WESTERN EUROPE,
BIBLIOG/A

GREAT BRITAIN, AND CANADA (EXTERNAL RESEARCH LIST NO 3-25). CANADA GERMANY/W UK LAW CULTURE NAT/G POL/PAR FORCES EDU/PROP REGION MARXISM...GEOG SOC WORSHIP 20 CMN/WLTH. PAGE 160 H3192 EUR+WWI DIPLOM

B66
US DEPARTMENT OF THE ARMY,COMMUNIST CHINA: A STRATEGIC SURVEY: A BIBLIOGRAPHY (PAMPHLET NO. 20-67). CHINA/COM COM INDIA USSR NAT/G POL/PAR EX/STRUC FORCES NUC/PWR REV ATTIT...POLICY GEOG CHARTS. PAGE 160 H3194 BIBLIOG/A MARXISM S/ASIA DIPLOM

B66
US DEPARTMENT OF THE ARMY,SOUTH ASIA: A STRATEGIC SURVEY (PAMPHLET NO. 550-3). AFGHANISTN INDIA NEPAL PAKISTAN ECO/UNDEV INT/ORG POL/PAR FORCES FOR/AID INT/TRADE LEAD WAR...POLICY SOC TREND 20. PAGE 160 H3195 BIBLIOG/A S/ASIA DIPLOM NAT/G

B66
WHEELER G.,THE PEOPLES OF SOVIET CENTRAL ASIA: A BACKGROUND BOOK. ISLAM USSR STRATA STRUCT FORCES REV WAR HABITAT 7/20. PAGE 167 H3341 COLONIAL DOMIN CULTURE ADJUST

B66
ZABLOCKI C.J.,SINO-SOVIET RIVALRY. AFR ASIA CHINA/COM CUBA EUR+WWI L/A+17C USA+45 USSR WOR+45 POL/PAR FORCES COERCE NUC/PWR...GOV/COMP IDEA/COMP 20 MAO KHRUSH/N. PAGE 172 H3444 DIPLOM MARXISM COM

S66
BENOIT J.,"WORLD DEFENSE EXPENDITURES." WOR+45 WEAPON COST PRODUC. PAGE 14 H0284 FORCES STAT NAT/COMP BUDGET

S66
BLANC N.,"SPAIN: LEARNING THROUGH STRUGGLE" SPAIN STRATA STRUCT SECT FORCES PROB/SOLV AGE/Y ATTIT ORD/FREE PWR WEALTH MARXISM SOCISM 19/20 FRANCO/F SUCCESSION. PAGE 18 H0352 NAT/G FUT SOCIALIST TOTALISM

S66
COWAN L.G.,"THE MILITARY AND AFRICAN POLITICS." AFR FUT NAT/G POL/PAR PARTIC REV 20. PAGE 34 H0685 CIVMIL/REL FORCES PWR LEAD

S66
MCLANE C.B.,"SOVIET DOCTRINE AND THE MILITARY COUPS IN AFRICA." ALGERIA GHANA COLONIAL NAT/LISM RIGID/FLEX SOVEREIGN MARXISM...DECISION NAT/COMP. PAGE 107 H2140 USSR ATTIT AFR FORCES

S66
SCHOENBRON D.,"VIETNAM* THE CASE FOR EXTRICATION." NAT/G FORCES PROB/SOLV DIPLOM COLONIAL CONTROL COERCE...CONCPT 20. PAGE 140 H2795 VIETNAM WAR GUERRILLA

S66
TURKEVICH J.,"SOVIET SCIENCE APPRAISED." USA+45 R+D ACADEM FORCES DIPLOM EDU/PROP WAR EFFICIENCY PEACE SKILL OBS. PAGE 157 H3137 USSR TEC/DEV NAT/COMP ATTIT

B67
ANDERSON O.,A LIBERAL STATE AT WAR. MOD/EUR UK LAW CULTURE STRUCT ECO/DEV NAT/G DIPLOM PARL/PROC GP/REL ALL/VALS...CONCPT 19. PAGE 7 H0131 WAR FORCES

B67
BAIN C.A.,VIETNAM: THE ROOTS OF CONFLICT. FRANCE S/ASIA USSR VIETNAM POL/PAR SECT FORCES COLONIAL NAT/LISM PEACE ORD/FREE MARXISM...GEOG CHARTS 4/20. PAGE 10 H0202 NAT/G WAR CULTURE

B67
BANKWITZ P.C.,MAXINE WEYGAND AND CIVIL-MILITARY RELATIONS IN MODERN FRANCE. FRANCE LEAD WAR PWR ...INT BIBLIOG 20. PAGE 11 H0212 CIVMIL/REL FORCES NAT/G TOP/EX

B67
BURNHAM J.,THE WAR WE ARE IN, THE LAST DECADE AND THE NEXT. ASIA COM EUR+WWI S/ASIA WOR+45 ECO/UNDEV INT/ORG FORCES WAR...OLD/LIB TREND 20 COLD/WAR. PAGE 25 H0492 POLICY NAT/G DIPLOM NAT/COMP

B67
FAY S.B.,THE ORIGINS OF THE WORLD WAR (2ND REV. ED. 2 VOLS.). NAT/G FORCES DIPLOM CONFER LEAD PEACE ...REALPOL GOV/COMP 19/20. PAGE 49 H0978 MOD/EUR WAR REGION INT/ORG

B67
HILSMAN R.,TO MOVE A NATION: THE POLITICS OF FOREIGN POLICY IN THE ADMINISTRATION OF JOHN F. KENNEDY. CHINA/COM COM USSR VIETNAM NAT/G DELIB/GP FORCES PLAN PROB/SOLV BAL/PWR COLONIAL EXEC REV PWR 20 KENNEDY/JF PRESIDENT. PAGE 71 H1418 CHIEF DIPLOM

B67
KAROL K.S.,CHINA, THE OTHER COMMUNISM (TRANS. BY TOM BAISTOW). CHINA/COM CULTURE INDUS FORCES DIPLOM EDU/PROP CONTROL EXEC NUC/PWR ATTIT...SOC CHARTS 20. PAGE 83 H1663 NAT/G POL/PAR MARXISM INGP/REL

B67
KENNETT L.,THE FRENCH ARMIES IN THE SEVEN YEARS' WAR. FRANCE NAT/G CONTROL LEAD WAR CIVMIL/REL EFFICIENCY ATTIT PWR SKILL CONSERVE 18. PAGE 85 H1690 FORCES CHIEF METH/COMP

B67
KOLKOWICZ R.,THE SOVIET MILITARY AND THE COMMUNIST PARTY. COM USSR ELITES NAT/G CREATE CIVMIL/REL GP/REL...TREND BIBLIOG/A 20 COM/PARTY. PAGE 88 H1753 MARXISM CONSTN FORCES POL/PAR

B67
LENG S.C.,JUSTICE IN COMMUNIST CHINA: A SURVEY OF THE JUDICIAL SYSTEM OF THE CHINESE PEOPLE'S REPUBLIC. CHINA/COM LAW CONSTN LOC/G NAT/G PROF/ORG CONSULT FORCES ADMIN CRIME ORD/FREE...BIBLIOG 20 MAO. PAGE 94 H1877 CT/SYS ADJUD JURID MARXISM

B67
MCCLINTOCK R.,THE MEANING OF LIMITED WAR. FUT WOR+45 NAT/G FORCES GUERRILLA REV...POLICY SAMP/SIZ TREND NAT/COMP 45 COLD/WAR. PAGE 106 H2126 WAR NUC/PWR BAL/PWR DIPLOM

B67
MENARD O.D.,THE ARMY AND THE FIFTH REPUBLIC. ALGERIA FRANCE VIETNAM ELITES STRATA COLONIAL CONTROL LOBBY WAR CIVMIL/REL ROLE PWR...POLICY 20 DEGAULLE/C. PAGE 108 H2169 FORCES ATTIT NAT/G

B67
MILNE R.S.,GOVERNMENT AND POLITICS IN MALAYSIA. INDONESIA MALAYSIA LOC/G EX/STRUC FORCES DIPLOM GP/REL 20 SINGAPORE. PAGE 111 H2217 NAT/G LEGIS ADMIN

B67
PLANK J.,CUBA AND THE UNITED STATES: LONG RANGE PERSPECTIVES. CUBA L/A+17C USSR ECO/UNDEV NAT/G FORCES ECO/TAC INT/TRADE AGREE REV...PREDICT TREND ANTHOL 20 CASTRO/F COLD/WAR OAS. PAGE 126 H2520 DIPLOM

B67
POGANY A.H.,POLITICAL SCIENCE AND INTERNATIONAL RELATIONS, BOOKS RECOMMENDED FOR AMERICAN CATHOLIC COLLEGE LIBRARIES. INT/ORG LOC/G NAT/G FORCES BAL/PWR ECO/TAC NUC/PWR...CATH INT/LAW TREATY 20. PAGE 127 H2532 BIBLIOG DIPLOM

B67
REES D.,THE AGE OF CONTAINMENT. WOR+45 FORCES ARMS/CONT ATTIT PWR...CONCPT TREND METH/COMP BIBLIOG/A 20. PAGE 130 H2608 DIPLOM NUC/PWR MARXISM GOV/COMP

B67
RUSTOW D.A.,A WORLD OF NATIONS; PROBLEMS OF POLITICAL MODERNIZATION. CONSTN NAT/G POL/PAR FORCES DIPLOM LEAD AUTHORIT...CHARTS IDEA/COMP 20. PAGE 136 H2722 PROB/SOLV ECO/UNDEV CONCPT NAT/COMP

B67
WARREN S.,THE AMERICAN PRESIDENT. POL/PAR FORCES LEGIS DIPLOM ECO/TAC ADMIN EXEC PWR...ANTHOL 18/20 ROOSEVLT/F KENNEDY/JF JOHNSON/LB TRUMAN/HS WILSON/W. PAGE 165 H3312 CHIEF LEAD NAT/G CONSTN

B67
WIENER F.B.,CIVILIANS UNDER MILITARY JUSTICE; THE BRITISH PRACTICE SINCE 1689 ESPECIALLY IN NORTH AMERICA. UK USA-45 LAW CONSTN CRIME REV...DECISION CHARTS NAT/COMP BIBLIOG 17/20. PAGE 168 H3356 CT/SYS FORCES ADJUD

L67
EINAUDI L.,"ANNOTATED BIBLIOGRAPHY OF LATIN AMERICAN MILITARY JOURNALS" LAW TEC/DEV DOMIN EDU/PROP COERCE WAR CIVMIL/REL 20. PAGE 45 H0899 BIBLIOG/A NAT/G FORCES L/A+17C

L67
VAN DER KROEF J.M.,"INDONESIA: THE BATTLE OF THE 'OLD' AND THE 'NEW ORDER'." INDONESIA ISLAM ELITES POL/PAR DOMIN INGP/REL NAT/LISM PWR...IDEA/COMP 20. PAGE 161 H3229 FORCES MARXISM NAT/G BAL/PWR

S67
ABDEL-MALEK A.,"THE CRISIS IN NASSER'S EGYPT." ISLAM UAR STRUCT POL/PAR EX/STRUC CREATE PLAN WAR ATTIT ORD/FREE PWR...POLICY DECISION 20. PAGE 3 H0054 FORCES LEAD PROB/SOLV NAT/G

S67
ADOKO A.,"THE CONSTITUTION OF UGANDA." AFR UGANDA LOC/G CHIEF FORCES LEGIS ADJUD EXEC CHOOSE NAT/LISM ...IDEA/COMP 20. PAGE 4 H0072 NAT/G CONSTN ORD/FREE LAW

S67
BELGION M.,"THE CASE FOR REHABILITATING MARSHAL PETAIN." EUR+WWI FRANCE NAT/G DIPLOM ATTIT PERSON MORAL PETAIN/HP. PAGE 13 H0262 WAR FORCES LEAD

S67
BEVEL D.N.,"JOURNEY TO NORTH VIETNAM." VIETNAM/N CONSTN NAT/G FORCES PROB/SOLV DEATH CIVMIL/REL PEACE MORAL...ANTHOL 20 NEGRO. PAGE 16 H0325 ATTIT DIPLOM ORD/FREE WAR

S67
CHIU S.M.,"CHINA'S MILITARY POSTURE." CHINA/COM ELITES NAT/G POL/PAR TEC/DEV ECO/TAC DOMIN CONTROL LEAD REV MARXISM 20 MAO. PAGE 30 H0595 FORCES CIVMIL/REL NUC/PWR DIPLOM

S67
FINLAY D.J.,"THE GHANA COUP...ONE YEAR LATER." GHANA FORCES FOR/AID PRESS CONTROL CIVMIL/REL NAT/LISM AUTHORIT PWR...PREDICT 20. PAGE 50 H1005 REV NAT/G ATTIT ECO/UNDEV

S67
GONZALEZ M.P.,"CUBA, UNA REVOLUCION EN MARCHA." CUBA L/A+17C USA+45 VIETNAM ECO/UNDEV FORCES DIPLOM DOMIN...POLICY MARXIST NAT/COMP CASTRO/F. PAGE 58 H1163
REV NAT/G COLONIAL SOVEREIGN

S67
GRIEB K.J.,"THE UNITED STATES AND THE CENTRAL AMERICAN CONFEDERATION." COSTA/RICA EL/SALVADR GUATEMALA HONDURAS L/A+17C NICARAGUA NAT/G FORCES CONFER AGREE EXEC ARMS/CONT REV WAR PEACE ATTIT 20. PAGE 60 H1212
INT/ORG DIPLOM POLICY REGION

S67
HALPERN B.,"THE ORIGINS OF THE CRISIS." ISLAM ISRAEL INT/ORG FORCES WEAPON PEACE ORD/FREE TREATY 20 UN. PAGE 65 H1296
WAR NAT/G DIPLOM

S67
HARBRON J.D.,"UNIFICATION IN CANADA: FAIT ACCOMPLI" CANADA STRATA NAT/G DELIB/GP BUDGET GP/REL 20 NAVY. PAGE 66 H1327
INGP/REL FORCES PLAN ATTIT

S67
JAIN G.,"INDIA REJECTS THE POWER RACE* REALISM ABOUT NUCLEAR WEAPONS." FORCES PROB/SOLV FOR/AID ARMS/CONT COST PWR...GOV/COMP 20. PAGE 79 H1583
INDIA CHINA/COM NUC/PWR DIPLOM

S67
LALL B.G.,"GAPS IN THE ABM DEBATE." NAT/G DIPLOM DETER CIVMIL/REL 20. PAGE 90 H1798
NUC/PWR ARMS/CONT EX/STRUC FORCES

S67
LANE J.P.,"FUNCTIONS OF MASS MEDIA IN BRAZIL'S 1964 CRISIS." BRAZIL NAT/G FORCES TOP/EX PRESS TV ATTIT PWR...METH/CNCPT 20. PAGE 90 H1807
CIVMIL/REL REV COM/IND EDU/PROP

S67
LOFCHIE M.F.,"OKELLO'S REVOLUTION." TANZANIA NAT/G POL/PAR FORCES PLAN CONTROL 20. PAGE 98 H1954
AFR REV LEAD CHIEF

S67
MENDL W.,"FRENCH ATTITUDES ON DISARMAMENT." FRANCE CULTURE CHIEF FORCES DIPLOM LEAD WAR...TIME/SEQ 20 DEGAULLE/C. PAGE 109 H2175
NUC/PWR WEAPON ARMS/CONT POLICY

S67
OOSTEN F.,"SUDVIETNAM IM JAHR VOR DER ENTSCHEIDUNG." VIETNAM/S VIETNAM/N NAT/G DIPLOM COERCE CHOOSE 20. PAGE 121 H2420
FORCES WAR WEAPON ATTIT

S67
PAK H.,"CHINA'S MILITIA AND MAO TSE-TUNG'S 'PEOPLE'S WAR'." CHINA/COM SOCIETY POL/PAR EX/STRUC PROB/SOLV PARTIC COERCE WAR CIVMIL/REL ATTIT DRIVE MARXISM...METH/COMP 20 MAO. PAGE 122 H2447
FORCES NAT/G WORKER CHIEF

S67
SUNG C.H.,"POLITICAL DIAGNOSIS OF KOREAN SOCIETY* A SURVEY OF MILITARY AND CIVILIAN VALUES." KOREA/S ECO/UNDEV NAT/G CIVMIL/REL...QU SAMP GP/COMP. PAGE 151 H3009
ELITES FORCES ATTIT ORD/FREE

S67
SYRKIN M.,"THE RIGHT TO BE ORDINARY." ISLAM ISRAEL NAT/G COERCE NAT/LISM RIGID/FLEX 20. PAGE 151 H3025
SOVEREIGN WAR FORCES DIPLOM

S67
THIEN T.T.,"VIETNAM: A CASE OF SOCIAL ALIENATION." VIETNAM AGRI FORCES FOR/AID ADMIN REPRESENT INGP/REL PWR 19/20. PAGE 154 H3071
NAT/G ELITES WORKER STRANGE

S67
VINCENT S.,"SHOULD BIAFRA SURVIVE?" NIGERIA ECO/UNDEV CHIEF FORCES ECO/TAC GP/REL DISCRIM PEACE ORD/FREE SOC/INTEG 20 BIAFRA IBO. PAGE 163 H3256
AFR REV REGION NAT/G

L68
CURRENT HISTORY,"AFRICA, 1968." ETHIOPIA GHANA NIGERIA SOUTH/AFR CULTURE ECO/UNDEV KIN SECT CHIEF EX/STRUC WAR WEAPON CHOOSE CIVMIL/REL...GOV/COMP 20 AFRICA/E. PAGE 36 H0724
RACE/REL NAT/LISM FORCES AFR

S68
DOUGLAS-HOME C.,"A MISTAKEN POLICY IN ADEN." YEMEN CULTURE ECO/UNDEV INDUS FORCES WORKER DIPLOM ECO/TAC CONTROL 20 ADEN. PAGE 42 H0842
SOVEREIGN COLONIAL POLICY REGION

B76
TAINE H.A.,THE ANCIENT REGIME. FRANCE STRATA FORCES PARTIC EQUILIB WEALTH CONSERVE POPULISM...GOV/COMP SOC/INTEG 18/19. PAGE 152 H3035
NAT/G GOV/REL TAX REV

B86
MAS LATRIE L.,RELATIONS ET COMMERCE DE L'AFRIQUE SEPTENTRIONALE OU MAGREB AVEC LES NATIONS CHRETIENNES AU MOYEN AGE. CULTURE CHIEF FORCES WAR ...SOC CENSUS TREATY 10/16. PAGE 104 H2084
ISLAM SECT DIPLOM INT/TRADE

C93
PLAYFAIR R.L.,"A BIBLIOGRAPHY OF MOROCCO." MOROCCO CULTURE AGRI FORCES DIPLOM WAR HEALTH...GEOG JURID SOC CHARTS. PAGE 126 H2526
BIBLIOG ISLAM MEDIT-7

FORD P. H1035

FORD FOUNDATION....SEE FORD/FOUND

FORD/FOUND....FORD FOUNDATION

FORDE C.D. H1036

FORDE L.D. H1037

FOREIGN AID....SEE FOR/AID

FOREIGN TRADE....SEE INT/TRADE

FOREIGNREL....UNITED STATES SENATE COMMITTEE ON FOREIGN RELATIONS

FORGN/SERV....FOREIGN SERVICE

FORM W.H. H1038

FORMOSA....FORMOSA, PRE-1949; FOR POST-1949, SEE TAIWAN; SEE ALSO ASIA, CHINA

FORTES M. H1039

FORTESCU J. H1040

FORTESCUE G.K. H1041

FORTESCUE J. H1042

FORTRAN....FORTRAN - COMPUTER LANGUAGE

FOSTER P. H0605,H1043

FOSTER/G....G. FOSTER

FOURIE L. H1275

FOURIER/FM....FRANCOIS MARIE CHARLES FOURIER

FOX A. H1044

FOX K.A. H1045

FOX/CJ....CHARLES J. FOX

FOX/INDIAN....FOX INDIANS

FPC....U.S. FEDERAL POWER COMMISSION

FRANCE....SEE ALSO APPROPRIATE TIME/SPACE/CULTURE INDEX

N
BULLETIN ANALYTIQUE DE DOCUMENTATION POLITIQUE, ECONOMIQUE, ET SOCIAL CONTEMPORAIRE. FRANCE WOR+45 SOCIETY ECO/DEV ECO/UNDEV INT/ORG LOC/G PROB/SOLV FOR/AID LEAD REGION SOC. PAGE 1 H0002
BIBLIOG/A DIPLOM NAT/COMP NAT/G

N
REVUE FRANCAISE DE SCIENCE POLITIQUE. FRANCE UK ...BIBLIOG/A 20. PAGE 1 H0021
NAT/G DIPLOM CONCPT ROUTINE

N
CARIBBEAN COMMISSION,CURRENT CARIBBEAN BIBLIOGRAPHY. FRANCE NETHERLAND UK CULTURE ECO/UNDEV PRESS LEAD ATTIT...GEOG SOC 20. PAGE 26 H0530
BIBLIOG NAT/G L/A+17C DIPLOM

N
MINISTERE DE L'EDUC NATIONALE,CATALOGUE DES THESES DE DOCTORAT SOUTENNES DEVANT LES UNIVERSITAIRES FRANCAISES. FRANCE LAW DIPLOM ADMIN...HUM SOC 20. PAGE 111 H2223
BIBLIOG ACADEM KNOWL NAT/G

N
PRESSE UNIVERSITAIRES,ANNEE SOCIOLOGIQUE. EUR+WWI FRANCE MOD/EUR FAM ACT/RES WAR INGP/REL PERS/REL CONSEN DRIVE MORAL...CON/ANAL 19/20. PAGE 128 H2557
BIBLIOG SOC CULTURE SOCIETY

B00
BENEDETTI V.,STUDIES IN DIPLOMACY. BELGIUM FRANCE GERMANY MOD/EUR CONSTN NAT/G CONSULT TOP/EX DOMIN EDU/PROP COERCE ATTIT...CONCPT INT BIOG TREND 19. PAGE 14 H0276
PWR GEN/LAWS DIPLOM

B00
MOCKLER-FERRYMAN A.,BRITISH WEST AFRICA. FRANCE GERMANY NIGER SIER/LEONE UK CULTURE DIPLOM WAR RACE/REL PRODUC PROFIT WEALTH...POLICY PREDICT 19. PAGE 112 H2232
AFR COLONIAL INT/TRADE CAP/ISM

B02
JELLINEK G.,LA DECLARATION DES DROITS DE L'HOMME ET
ORD/FREE

DU CITOYEN (1895) (TRANSLATED FROM GERMAN BY G. FARDIS). FRANCE GERMANY USA-45 NAT/G SECT LEGIS 18. PAGE 80 H1598
CONCPT REV

B03
FAGUET E.,LE LIBERALISME. FRANCE PRESS ADJUD ADMIN DISCRIM CONSERVE SOCISM...TRADIT SOC LING WORSHIP PARLIAMENT. PAGE 48 H0960
ORD/FREE EDU/PROP NAT/G LAW

B09
LOBINGIER C.S.,THE PEOPLE'S LAW OR POPULAR PARTICIPATION IN LAW-MAKING. FRANCE SWITZERLND UK LOC/G NAT/G PROVS LEGIS SUFF MAJORITY PWR POPULISM ...GOV/COMP BIBLIOG 19. PAGE 97 H1945
CONSTN LAW PARTIC

B12
SONOLET L.,L'AFRIQUE OCCIDENTALE FRANCAISE. FRANCE AGRI INDUS NAT/G SECT FORCES INT/TRADE EDU/PROP RACE/REL HEALTH ORD/FREE...CHARTS 19/20 NEGRO AFRICA/W. PAGE 147 H2933
DOMIN ADMIN COLONIAL AFR

B13
SIEGFRIED A.,TABLEAU POLITIQUE DE LA FRANCE DE L'OUEST SOUS LA TROISIEME REPUBLIQUE. FRANCE STRATA STRUCT NAT/G POL/PAR PROVS REGION GOV/REL ATTIT PWR ...TREND TIME 19. PAGE 143 H2869
SOC GEOG SOCIETY

B14
LEVINE L.,SYNDICALISM IN FRANCE (2ND ED.). FRANCE LAW SOCIETY ECO/DEV NAT/G ECO/TAC LEAD ATTIT ...POLICY CONCPT STAT BIBLIOG 18/20 REFORMERS. PAGE 95 H1902
LABOR INDUS SOCISM REV

B17
BARRES M.,THE UNDYING SPIRIT OF FRANCE (TRANS. BY M. CORWIN). FRANCE DOMIN LEAD DEATH ATTIT RESPECT ...NAT/COMP 20 WWI. PAGE 11 H0226
NAT/LISM FORCES WAR CULTURE

B17
DE MAISTRE J.,DU PAPE (1817). FRANCE LAW SOCIETY SECT DOMIN REV HAPPINESS PWR SOVEREIGN 18/19 PROTESTANT. PAGE 38 H0761
CATH CHIEF LEGIT NAT/G

N17
BURKE E.,THOUGHTS ON THE PROSPECT OF A REGICIDE PEACE (PAMPHLET). FRANCE UK SECT DOMIN MURDER PEACE ORD/FREE SOVEREIGN POPULISM...POLICY GOV/COMP IDEA/COMP 18 JACOBINISM COEXIST. PAGE 24 H0483
REV CHIEF NAT/G DIPLOM

B18
BARRES M.,THE FAITH OF FRANCE (TRANS. BY ELISABETH MARBURY). FRANCE FAM MUNIC NEIGH POL/PAR SECT ALL/VALS 20. PAGE 11 H0227
TRADIT CULTURE WAR GP/REL

B18
WILSON W.,THE STATE: ELEMENTS OF HISTORICAL AND PRACTICAL POLITICS. FRANCE GERMANY ITALY UK USSR CONSTN EX/STRUC LEGIS CT/SYS WAR PWR...POLICY GOV/COMP 20. PAGE 169 H3385
NAT/G JURID CONCPT NAT/COMP

N19
BARRES M.,"THE WAR AND THE SPIRIT OF YOUTH" (PAMPHLET). FRANCE FORCES DOMIN LEAD DEATH AGE/Y ATTIT RESPECT...FASCIST 20 WWI. PAGE 11 H0228
WAR NAT/LISM CULTURE MYSTIC

N19
COUTROT A.,THE FIGHT OVER THE 1959 PRIVATE EDUCATION LAW IN FRANCE (PAMPHLET). FRANCE NAT/G SECT GIVE EDU/PROP GP/REL ATTIT RIGID/FLEX ORD/FREE 20 CHURCH/STA. PAGE 34 H0681
SCHOOL PARL/PROC CATHISM LAW

N19
HACKETT J.,ECONOMIC PLANNING IN FRANCE; ITS RELATION TO THE POLICIES OF THE DEVELOPED COUNTRIES OF WESTERN EUROPE (PAMPHLET). EUR+WWI FRANCE ECO/DEV PROB/SOLV CONTROL...POLICY 20 EUROPE/W. PAGE 63 H1270
ECO/TAC NAT/G PLAN INSPECT

N19
HANNA A.J.,EUROPEAN RULE IN AFRICA (PAMPHLET). BELGIUM FRANCE MOD/EUR UK WOR+45 WOR-45 ECO/UNDEV NAT/G PARTIC SOVEREIGN...NAT/COMP 19/20. PAGE 66 H1314
DIPLOM COLONIAL AFR NAT/LISM

N19
SENGHOR L.S.,AFRICAN SOCIALISM (PAMPHLET). AFR FRANCE MALI USSR ELITES ECO/UNDEV NAT/G DIPLOM DOMIN EDU/PROP ATTIT 20 NEGRO. PAGE 141 H2827
SOCISM MARXISM ORD/FREE NAT/LISM

B21
STUART G.H.,FRENCH FOREIGN POLICY. CONSTN INT/ORG NAT/G POL/PAR EX/STRUC FORCES PLAN ECO/TAC DOMIN EDU/PROP ADJUD COERCE ATTIT DRIVE RIGID/FLEX ALL/VALS...POLICY OBS RECORD BIOG TIME/SEQ TREND. PAGE 150 H3000
MOD/EUR DIPLOM FRANCE

B22
TONNIES F.,KRITIK DER OFFENTLICHEN MEINUNG. FRANCE UK CULTURE COM/IND DOMIN PRESS RUMOR ROLE NAT/COMP. PAGE 156 H3114
SOCIETY SOC ATTIT

B23
KADEN E.H.,DER POLITISCHE CHARAKTER DER FRANZOSISCHEN KULTURPROPAGANDA AM RHEIN. FRANCE MOD/EUR DOMIN PRESS...GEOG METH/COMP 20. PAGE 82 H1648
EDU/PROP ATTIT DIPLOM NAT/G

B25
MAURRAS C.,ENQUETE SUR LA MONARCHIE (1909). FRANCE CONTROL REPRESENT DISCRIM HEREDITY PWR CONSERVE 20 BUREAUCRCY. PAGE 105 H2103
TRADIT AUTHORIT NAT/G CHIEF

B27
QUERARD J.M.,LA FRANCE LITTERAIRE (12 VOLS.). FRANCE CULTURE...HUM SOC 16/19. PAGE 129 H2573
BIBLIOG/A BIOG ART/METH

B29
LANGER W.L.,THE FRANCO-RUSSIAN ALLIANCE: 1890-1894. FRANCE MOD/EUR UK USSR NAT/G CHIEF FORCES BAL/PWR AGREE WAR PEACE PWR...TIME/SEQ TREATY 19 BISMARCK/O. PAGE 91 H1809
DIPLOM

B29
LEITZ F.,DIE PUBLIZITAT DER AKTIENGESELLSCHAFT. BELGIUM FRANCE GERMANY UK FINAN PRESS GP/REL PROFIT KNOWL 20. PAGE 94 H1872
LG/CO JURID ECO/TAC NAT/COMP

B29
ROBERTS S.H.,HISTORY OF FRENCH COLONIAL POLICY. AFR ASIA L/A+17C S/ASIA CULTURE ECO/DEV ECO/UNDEV FINAN NAT/G PLAN ECO/TAC DOMIN ROUTINE SOVEREIGN...OBS HIST/WRIT TREND CHARTS VAL/FREE 19/20. PAGE 132 H2642
INT/ORG ACT/RES FRANCE COLONIAL

B30
MASON E.S.,THE PARIS COMMUNE: AN EPISODE IN THE HISTORY OF THE SOCIALIST MOVEMENT. FRANCE MOD/EUR ELITES SOCIETY STRATA ECO/DEV WORKER EDU/PROP CHOOSE INGP/REL SOCISM 19 MARX/KARL PARIS. PAGE 104 H2085
NAT/G REV MARXISM

B31
CROOK W.H.,THE GENERAL STRIKE: A STUDY OF LABOR'S TRAGIC WEAPON IN THEORY AND PRACTICE. BELGIUM FRANCE SWEDEN UK WOR-45 PROB/SOLV ECO/TAC DOMIN PWR ...POLICY TIME/SEQ NAT/COMP GEN/LAWS 19/20 STRIKE. PAGE 35 H0707
LABOR WORKER LG/CO BARGAIN

B31
LORWIN L.L.,ADVISORY ECONOMIC COUNCILS. EUR+WWI FRANCE GERMANY PROB/SOLV INGP/REL...CLASSIF GP/COMP. PAGE 99 H1968
CONSULT DELIB/GP ECO/TAC NAT/G

S31
HEINBERG J.G.,"THE PERSONNEL OF FRENCH CABINETS, 1871-1930." FRANCE STRATA CHIEF CHOOSE REPRESENT MAJORITY...STAT QU CENSUS TREND CHARTS PERS/COMP 19/20 CHAMBR/DEP. PAGE 69 H1386
ELITES NAT/G DELIB/GP TOP/EX

B32
THIBAUDET A.,LES IDEES POLITIQUES DE LA FRANCE. FRANCE NAT/G SECT PRESS REV NAT/LISM PEACE ATTIT ...PSY 19/20 JACOBINISM JAURES/JL. PAGE 154 H3070
IDEA/COMP ALL/IDEOS CATHISM

B33
DAHLIN E.,FRENCH AND GERMAN PUBLIC OPINION ON DECLARED WAR AIMS 1914-1918. BELGIUM FRANCE GERMANY NAT/G POL/PAR DIPLOM COERCE REV WAR PEACE 20 WWI WILSON/W. PAGE 37 H0733
ATTIT EDU/PROP DOMIN NAT/COMP

B33
ENSOR R.C.K.,COURTS AND JUDGES IN FRANCE, GERMANY, AND ENGLAND. FRANCE GERMANY UK LAW PROB/SOLV ADMIN ROUTINE CRIME ROLE...METH/COMP 20 CIVIL/LAW. PAGE 46 H0930
CT/SYS EX/STRUC ADJUD NAT/COMP

C33
MURET C.T.,"FRENCH ROYALIST DOCTRINES SINCE THE REVOLUTION." FRANCE CONSTN NAT/G SECT ADMIN LEAD SOVEREIGN...POLICY BIOG IDEA/COMP BIBLIOG 18/20. PAGE 115 H2295
POL/PAR ATTIT INTELL CONSERVE

B34
DE CENIVAL P.,BIBLIOGRAPHIE MAROCAINE: 1923-1933. FRANCE MOROCCO SECT ADMIN LEAD GP/REL ATTIT...LING 20. PAGE 37 H0750
BIBLIOG/A ISLAM NAT/G COLONIAL

B34
MARX K.,THE CLASS STRUGGLES IN FRANCE. FRANCE INDUS WORKER CONSERVE...TREND GEN/LAWS 19. PAGE 104 H2077
MARXIST STRATA REV INT/TRADE

B36
BOYCE A.N.,EUROPE AND SOUTH AFRICA. FRANCE GERMANY ITALY SOUTH/AFR UK INDUS NAT/G CONTROL REV WAR NAT/LISM...CONCPT HIST/WRIT 20. PAGE 20 H0392
COLONIAL GOV/COMP NAT/COMP DIPLOM

B37
CARLYLE T.,THE FRENCH REVOLUTION (2 VOLS.). FRANCE CONSTN NAT/G FORCES COERCE MURDER PEACE MORAL POPULISM...TIME/SEQ IDEA/COMP GEN/LAWS 18. PAGE 26 H0532
REV CHIEF TRADIT

B39
ANDERSON W.,LOCAL GOVERNMENT IN EUROPE. FRANCE GERMANY ITALY UK USSR MUNIC PROVS ADMIN GOV/REL CENTRAL SOVEREIGN 20. PAGE 7 H0136
GOV/COMP NAT/COMP LOC/G CONSTN

B39
SIEYES E.J.,LES DISCOURS DE SIEYES DANS LES DEBATS CONSTITUTIONNELS DE L'AN III (2 ET 18 THERMIDOR). FRANCE LAW NAT/G PROB/SOLV BAL/PWR GOV/REL 18 JURY. PAGE 144 H2871
CONSTN ADJUD LEGIS EX/STRUC

B40
BROGAN D.W.,THE DEVELOPMENT OF MODERN FRANCE
MOD/EUR

(1870-1939). FRANCE GERMANY UK USSR CONSTN CHIEF LEGIS DIPLOM AGREE COLONIAL WAR NAT/LISM PEACE SOCISM 19/20 TREATY. PAGE 21 H0428
NAT/G

B40
WANDERSCHECK H.,FRANKREICHS PROPAGANDA GEGEN DEUTSCHLAND. FRANCE GERMANY MOD/EUR UK NAT/G DIPLOM WAR 20 JEWS. PAGE 165 H3300
EDU/PROP ATTIT DOMIN PRESS

B40
WOLFERS A.,BRITAIN AND FRANCE BETWEEN TWO WORLD WARS. FRANCE UK INT/ORG NAT/G PLAN BARGAIN ECO/TAC AGREE ISOLAT ALL/IDEOS...DECISION GEOG 20 TREATY VERSAILLES INTERVENT. PAGE 170 H3402
DIPLOM WAR POLICY

B41
BAUMANN G.,GRUNDLAGEN UND PRAXIS DER INTERNATIONALEN PROPAGANDA. FRANCE GERMANY UK CULTURE COM/IND PRESS PWR...PSY METH/COMP 20. PAGE 12 H0241
EDU/PROP DOMIN ATTIT DIPLOM

B41
PALMER R.R.,TWELVE WHO RULED. MOD/EUR ELITES STRUCT NAT/G POL/PAR DELIB/GP DOMIN ATTIT SUPEGO PWR ...POLICY CONCPT 18. PAGE 123 H2453
TOP/EX BIOG REV FRANCE

S41
DENNERY E.,"DEMOCRACY AND THE FRENCH ARMY." FRANCE NAT/G EX/STRUC LEAD REV ROLE 18/20. PAGE 40 H0792
FORCES POPULISM STRATA CIVMIL/REL

B42
CONOVER H.F.,FRENCH COLONIES IN AFRICA: A LIST OF REFERENCES. ALGERIA FRANCE MOROCCO SOMALIA SUDAN CULTURE AGRI LOC/G SECT FORCES DIPLOM INT/TRADE NAT/LISM HEALTH...CON/ANAL 20. PAGE 32 H0641
BIBLIOG AFR ECO/UNDEV COLONIAL

B42
CRAIG A.,ABOVE ALL LIBERTIES. FRANCE UK USA-45 LAW CONSTN CULTURE INTELL NAT/G SECT JUDGE...IDEA/COMP BIBLIOG 18/20. PAGE 35 H0692
ORD/FREE MORAL WRITING EDU/PROP

C42
CRAIG A.,"ABOVE ALL LIBERTIES." FRANCE UK LAW CULTURE INTELL SECT ORD/FREE 18/20. PAGE 35 H0693
BIBLIOG/A EDU/PROP WRITING MORAL

B44
BARKER E.,THE DEVELOPMENT OF PUBLIC SERVICES IN WESTERN WUROPE: 1660-1930. FRANCE GERMANY UK SCHOOL CONTROL REPRESENT ROLE...WELF/ST 17/20. PAGE 11 H0219
GOV/COMP ADMIN EX/STRUC

B44
SUAREZ F.,A TREATISE ON LAWS AND GOD THE LAWGIVER (1612) IN SELECTIONS FROM THREE WORKS, VOL. II. FRANCE ITALY UK CULTURE NAT/G SECT CHIEF LEGIS DOMIN LEGIT CT/SYS ORD/FREE PWR WORSHIP 16/17. PAGE 150 H3004
LAW JURID GEN/LAWS CATH

C44
VAN VALKENBURG S.,"ELEMENTS OF POLITICAL GEOGRAPHY." FRANCE COM/IND INDUS NAT/G SECT RACE/REL...LING TREND GEN/LAWS BIBLIOG 20. PAGE 162 H3232
GEOG DIPLOM COLONIAL

B45
CONOVER H.F.,THE GOVERNMENTS OF THE MAJOR FOREIGN POWERS: A BIBLIOGRAPHY. FRANCE GERMANY ITALY UK USSR CONSTN LOC/G POL/PAR EX/STRUC FORCES ADMIN CT/SYS CIVMIL/REL TOTALISM...POLICY 19/20. PAGE 32 H0645
BIBLIOG NAT/G DIPLOM

B45
HARVARD WIDENER LIBRARY,INDOCHINA: A SELECTED LIST OF REFERENCES. CAMBODIA FRANCE S/ASIA VIETNAM COLONIAL...POLICY 19/20. PAGE 67 H1351
BIBLIOG/A ACADEM DIPLOM NAT/G

B46
BLUM L.,FOR ALL MANKIND (TRANS. BY W. PICKLES). FRANCE GERMANY USSR LAW SOCIETY STRUCT POL/PAR WORKER DIPLOM DOMIN CHOOSE ORD/FREE FASCISM 20. PAGE 18 H0361
POPULISM SOCIALIST NAT/G WAR

B47
CROCKER W.R.,ON GOVERNING COLONIES: BEING AN OUTLINE OF THE REAL ISSUES AND A COMPARISON OF THE BRITISH, FRENCH, AND BELGIAN... AFR BELGIUM FRANCE UK CULTURE SOVEREIGN...OBS 20. PAGE 35 H0705
COLONIAL POLICY GOV/COMP ADMIN

B48
MINISTERE FINANCES ET ECO,BULLETIN BIBLIOGRAPHIQUE. AFR EUR+WWI FRANCE CULTURE STRUCT FINAN NAT/G ACT/RES INT/TRADE ADMIN REGION PRODUC STAT. PAGE 111 H2224
BIBLIOG/A ECO/UNDEV TEC/DEV COLONIAL

B48
ROSSITER C.L.,CONSTITUTIONAL DICTATORSHIP; CRISIS GOVERNMENT IN THE MODERN DEMOCRACIES. FRANCE GERMANY UK USA-45 WOR-45 EX/STRUC BAL/PWR CONTROL COERCE WAR CENTRAL ORD/FREE...DECISION 19/20. PAGE 134 H2688
NAT/G AUTHORIT CONSTN TOTALISM

B48
WRIGHT G.,THE RESHAPING OF FRENCH DEMOCRACY. FRANCE NAT/G POL/PAR SECT LEAD CHOOSE GP/REL INGP/REL MARXISM SOCISM...CHARTS BIBLIOG 20 DEGAULLE/C. PAGE 171 H3418
CONSTN POPULISM CREATE LEGIS

B49
ROGERS C.B.,THE SPIRIT OF REVOLUTION IN 1789: A STUDY OF PUBLIC OPINION ...AT THE BEGINNING OF THE FRENCH REVOLUTION. FRANCE CULTURE ELITES EDU/PROP COERCE CROWD...BIBLIOG 18 MUSIC. PAGE 133 H2658
ATTIT POPULISM REV CREATE

B49
SAUVY A.,LE POUVOIR ET L'OPINION. FRANCE STRATA NAT/G PERCEPT...POLICY PSY 20. PAGE 138 H2758
EDU/PROP MYTH PARTIC ATTIT

C49
SCHAPIRO J.S.,"LIBERALISM AND THE CHALLENGE OF FASCISM." FRANCE UK STRATA PERSON...CONCPT BIOG IDEA/COMP BIBLIOG 18/20. PAGE 139 H2771
FASCISM LAISSEZ ATTIT

B51
MARX K.,THE EIGHTEENTH BRUMAIRE OF LOUIS BONAPARTE (1852). FRANCE STRATA FINAN INDUS LABOR CHIEF FORCES WORKER CAP/ISM ECO/TAC PARL/PROC ORD/FREE ...MARXIST 19. PAGE 104 H2080
REV MARXISM ELITES NAT/G

B52
JULIEN C.A.,L'AFRIQUE DU NORD EN MARCHE: NATIONALISMES MUSULMANS ET SOUVERAINETE FRANCAISE (2ND ED). AFR ALGERIA FRANCE ISLAM MOROCCO NAT/G CONTROL ORD/FREE...POLICY 19/20 TUNIS MUSLIM. PAGE 82 H1641
NAT/LISM COERCE DOMIN COLONIAL

B52
SKALWEIT S.,FRANKREICH UND FRIEDRICH DER GROSSE. FRANCE GERMANY PRUSSIA NAT/G DOMIN WAR 18 FREDERICK. PAGE 145 H2893
ATTIT EDU/PROP DIPLOM SOC

S52
MUEHLMANN W.E.,"L'IDEE NATIONALE ALLEMANDE ET L'IDEE NATIONALE FRANCAISE." EUR+WWI MOD/EUR SOCIETY KIN NAT/G PWR RESPECT...SOC CONCPT TIME/SEQ GEN/LAWS 19/20. PAGE 114 H2279
CULTURE ATTIT FRANCE GERMANY

S52
SABINE G.H.,"THE TWO DEMOCRATIC TRADITIONS" (BMR)" FRANCE UK USA-45 NAT/G CONTROL CHOOSE ALL/IDEOS ...PHIL/SCI CONCPT IDEA/COMP 20. PAGE 136 H2727
ORD/FREE POPULISM INGP/REL NAT/COMP

S53
ROGOFF N.,"SOCIAL STRATIFICATION IN FRANCE AND IN THE UNITED STATES" (BMR)" FRANCE USA+45 WORKER ADJUST PERSON...SOC 20. PAGE 133 H2662
STRUCT STRATA ATTIT NAT/COMP

N53
VITO F.,"RECENT DEVELOPMENTS IN THE THEORY OF DEMOCRATIC ADMIN" INTL POL SCI ASS'N CONFERENCE ON PUBLIC ADMINISTRATION... FRANCE ITALY UK REPRESENT EFFICIENCY NEW/LIB SOCISM...WELF/ST 20. PAGE 163 H3257
GOV/COMP CONTROL EX/STRUC

B54
HAMSON C.J.,EXECUTIVE DISCRETION AND JUDICIAL CONTROL; AN ASPECT OF THE FRENCH CONSEIL D'ETAT. EUR+WWI FRANCE MOD/EUR UK NAT/G EX/STRUC PARTIC CONSERVE...JURID BIBLIOG/A 18/20 SUPREME/CT. PAGE 65 H1310
ELITES ADJUD NAT/COMP

B54
SCHWARTZ B.,FRENCH ADMINISTRATIVE LAW AND THE COMMON-LAW WORLD. FRANCE CULTURE LOC/G NAT/G PROVS DELIB/GP EX/STRUC LEGIS PROB/SOLV CT/SYS EXEC GOV/REL...IDEA/COMP ENGLSH/LAW. PAGE 140 H2808
JURID LAW METH/COMP ADJUD

L54
FURNISS E.S.,"WEAKNESSES IN FRENCH FOREIGN POLICY-MAKING." EUR+WWI LEGIS LEGIT EXEC ATTIT RIGID/FLEX ORD/FREE...SOC CONCPT METH/CNCPT OBS 20. PAGE 54 H1078
NAT/G STRUCT DIPLOM FRANCE

C54
DE GRAZIA A.,"THE COMPARATIVE SURVEY OF EUROPEAN-AMERICAN POLITICAL BEHAV IOR; A RESEARCH PROSPECTUS (PAPER)" EUR+WWI FRANCE GERMANY SPAIN UK USA+45 WOR+45 STRATA POL/PAR DIPLOM EDU/PROP COLONIAL LEAD WAR NAT/LISM CONCPT. PAGE 37 H0752
BIBLIOG R+D METH NAT/COMP

B55
CHARMATZ J.P.,COMPARATIVE STUDIES IN COMMUNITY PROPERTY LAW. FRANCE USA+45...JURID GOV/COMP ANTHOL 20. PAGE 29 H0583
MARRIAGE LAW OWN MUNIC

B55
DUVERGER M.,THE POLITICAL ROLE OF WOMEN. FRANCE GERMANY/W NORWAY YUGOSLAVIA STRATA LOBBY AGE ATTIT ROLE...STAT SAMP CHARTS METH/COMP NAT/COMP HYPO/EXP FEMALE/SEX. PAGE 44 H0875
SEX LEAD PARTIC CHOOSE

B55
ROWE C.,VOLTAIRE AND THE STATE. FRANCE MOD/EUR BAL/PWR CONTROL TASK SUPEGO ORD/FREE PWR...CONCPT 18 VOLTAIRE. PAGE 135 H2702
NAT/G DIPLOM NAT/LISM ATTIT

B55
SHAFER B.C.,NATIONALISM: MYTH AND REALITY. FRANCE UK USA+45 USA-45 CULTURE SOCIETY STRUCT ECO/DEV WAR PWR...NAT/COMP BIBLIOG 18/20. PAGE 142 H2837
NAT/LISM MYTH NAT/G CONCPT

C56
NEUMANN S.,"MODERN POLITICAL PARTIES: APPROACHES TO COMPARATIVE POLITIC. FRANCE UK EX/STRUC DOMIN ADMIN
POL/PAR GOV/COMP

LEAD REPRESENT TOTALISM ATTIT...POLICY TREND ELITES
METH/COMP ANTHOL BIBLIOG/A 20 CMN/WLTH. PAGE 117 MAJORIT
H2338

B57
ARON R.,THE OPIUM OF THE INTELLECTUALS (TRANS. BY INTELL
TERENCE KILMARTIN). FRANCE USSR WOR+45 CULTURE UTOPIA
POL/PAR PLAN DOMIN EDU/PROP REV ATTIT ORD/FREE MYTH
...IDEA/COMP METH/COMP NAT/COMP 20 COM/PARTY. MARXISM
PAGE 8 H0169

B57
BUCK P.W.,CONTOL OF FOREIGN RELATIONS IN MODERN NAT/G
NATIONS. FRANCE L/A+17C NETHERLAND USSR WOR+45 PWR
INT/ORG TOP/EX BAL/PWR DOMIN EDU/PROP COERCE PEACE DIPLOM
ATTIT...CONCPT TREND 20 CMN/WLTH. PAGE 23 H0465

B57
MEINECKE F.,MACHIAVELLISM. CHRIST-17C FRANCE NAT/LISM
GERMANY ITALY MOD/EUR BAL/PWR PARL/PROC TOTALISM NAT/G
...PHIL/SCI 15/20 MACHIAVELL. PAGE 108 H2166 PWR

S57
LEWIS E.G.,"PARLIAMENTARY CONTROL OF NATIONALIZED PWR
INDUSTRY IN FRANCE." FRANCE NAT/G DELIB/GP ACT/RES LEGIS
PLAN PROB/SOLV ECO/TAC DOMIN CENTRAL. PAGE 96 H1914 INDUS
CONTROL

B58
ARON R.,SOCIOLOGIE DES SOCIETES INDUSTRIELLES: TOTALISM
ESQUISSE D'UNE THEORIE DES REGIMES POLITIQUES. INDUS
FRANCE SOCIETY NAT/G PROB/SOLV ATTIT RIGID/FLEX CONSTN
MARXISM POPULISM...POLICY SOC T 20 MARX/KARL GOV/COMP
TOCQUEVILL. PAGE 8 H0170

B58
BUISSON L.,POTESTAS UND CARITAS. FRANCE GERMANY UK GP/REL
ORD/FREE...JURID IDEA/COMP NAT/COMP 12/16 POPE PWR
CHURCH/STA. PAGE 23 H0467 CATHISM
NAT/G

B58
CAMPBELL P.,FRENCH ELECTORAL SYSTEMS AND ELECTIONS REPRESENT
SINCE 1789 (2ND ED.). FRANCE NAT/G EX/STRUC PWR CHOOSE
...CHARTS 18/20. PAGE 26 H0516 POL/PAR
SUFF

B58
COWAN L.G.,LOCAL GOVERNMENT IN WEST AFRICA. AFR LOC/G
FRANCE UK CULTURE KIN POL/PAR CHIEF LEGIS CREATE COLONIAL
ADMIN PARTIC GOV/REL GP/REL...METH/COMP 20. PAGE 34 SOVEREIGN
H0682 REPRESENT

B58
DUCLOUX L.,FROM BLACKMAIL TO TREASON. FRANCE PLAN COERCE
DIPLOM EDU/PROP PRESS RUMOR NAT/LISM...CRIMLGY 20. CRIME
PAGE 43 H0853 NAT/G
PWR

B58
GURVITCH G.,TRAITE DE SOCIOLOGIE (2 VOLS.). FRANCE ANTHOL
CULTURE INDUS GP/REL INGP/REL...PSY BIBLIOG 20. SOC
PAGE 63 H1256 METH/COMP
METH/CNCPT

B58
LAHBABI M.,LE GOUVERNEMENT MAROCAIN A L'AUBE DU XXE NAT/G
SIECLE. FRANCE MOROCCO CHIEF EX/STRUC LEGIS COLONIAL
ORD/FREE PWR...JURID BIBLIOG 19/20. PAGE 90 H1797 SOVEREIGN

B58
LEPOINTE G.,ELEMENTS DE BIBLIOGRAPHIE SUR BIBLIOG
L'HISTOIRE DES INSTITUTIONS ET DES FAITS SOCIAUX, LAW
987-1875. FRANCE SOCIETY NAT/G PROVS SECT
...PHIL/SCI 19/20. PAGE 94 H1887

B58
TILLION G.,ALGERIA: THE REALITIES. ALGERIA FRANCE ECO/UNDEV
ISLAM CULTURE STRATA PROB/SOLV DOMIN REV NAT/LISM SOC
WEALTH MARXISM...GEOG 20. PAGE 155 H3094 COLONIAL
DIPLOM

S58
SCHUMM S.,"INTEREST REPRESENTATION IN FRANCE AND LOBBY
GERMANY." EUR+WWI FRANCE GERMANY INSPECT PARL/PROC DELIB/GP
REPRESENT 20 WEIMAR/REP. PAGE 140 H2803 NAT/G

B59
BARRON R.,PARTIES AND POLITICS IN MODERN FRANCE. POL/PAR
FRANCE LOC/G DELIB/GP LEGIS TOP/EX EDU/PROP LEGIT ALL/IDEOS
TV FEEDBACK 20. PAGE 12 H0230 CHOOSE
PARTIC

B59
DEHIO L.,GERMANY AND WORLD POLITICS IN THE DIPLOM
TWENTIETH CENTURY. EUR+WWI FRANCE GERMANY MOD/EUR WAR
UK USSR NAT/G CHIEF BAL/PWR DOMIN COLONIAL CONTROL NAT/LISM
LEAD...IDEA/COMP 20 VERSAILLES. PAGE 39 H0783 SOVEREIGN

B59
LEITES N.,ON THE GAME OF POLITICS IN FRANCE. POL/PAR
ALGERIA FRANCE CONSTN SECT VOL/ASSN ECO/TAC NAT/G
INT/TRADE PARL/PROC WAR SOCISM 20 DEGAULLE/C EEC. LEGIS
PAGE 94 H1871 IDEA/COMP

B59
MAIER H.,REVOLUTION UND KIRCHE. FRANCE MOD/EUR SECT NAT/G
REV ORD/FREE...IDEA/COMP 18/19. PAGE 101 H2018 CATHISM
ATTIT
POL/PAR

B59
SENGHOR L.S.,RAPPORT SUR LA DOCTRINE ET LA ATTIT
PROGRAMME DU PART I. FRANCE MALI CONSTN POL/PAR NAT/G
PLAN CHOOSE OWN ORD/FREE MARXISM...SOCIALIST 20 AFR
NEGRO. PAGE 141 H2828 SOCISM

B59
SISSON C.H.,THE SPIRIT OF BRITISH ADMINISTRATION GOV/COMP
AND SOME EUROPEAN COMPARISONS. FRANCE GERMANY/W ADMIN
SWEDEN UK LAW EX/STRUC INGP/REL EFFICIENCY ORD/FREE ELITES
...DECISION 20. PAGE 144 H2890 ATTIT

S59
CHAPMAN B.,"THE FRENCH CONSEIL D'ETAT." FRANCE ADMIN
NAT/G CONSULT OP/RES PROB/SOLV PWR...OBS 20. LAW
PAGE 29 H0580 CT/SYS
LEGIS

C59
COLLINS I.,"THE GOVERNMENT AND THE NEWSPAPER PRESS PRESS
IN FRANCE, 1814-1881. FRANCE LAW ADMIN CT/SYS ORD/FREE
...CON/ANAL BIBLIOG 19. PAGE 32 H0634 NAT/G
EDU/PROP

B60
ALBRECHT-CARRIE R.,FRANCE, EUROPE AND THE TWO WORLD DIPLOM
WARS. EUR+WWI FRANCE GERMANY MOD/EUR UK ECO/DEV WAR
NAT/G FORCES BAL/PWR DOMIN ARMS/CONT PEACE PWR 20
TREATY EUROPE. PAGE 5 H0096

B60
CASTBERG F.,FREEDOM OF SPEECH IN THE WEST. FRANCE ORD/FREE
GERMANY USA+45 USA-45 LAW CONSTN CHIEF PRESS SANCTION
DISCRIM...CONCPT 18/20. PAGE 28 H0558 ADJUD
NAT/COMP

B60
FURNIA A.H.,THE DIPLOMACY OF APPEASEMENT: ANGLO- DIPLOM
FRENCH RELATIONS AND THE PRELUDE TO WORLD WAR II BAL/PWR
1931-1938. FRANCE GERMANY UK ELITES NAT/G DELIB/GP COERCE
FORCES WAR PEACE RIGID/FLEX 20. PAGE 54 H1077

B60
FURNISS E.S.,FRANCE, TROUBLED ALLY. EUR+WWI FUT NAT/G
CULTURE SOCIETY BAL/PWR ADMIN ATTIT DRIVE PWR FRANCE
...TREND TOT/POP 20 DEGAULLE/C. PAGE 54 H1079

B60
LISTER L.,EUROPE'S COAL AND STEEL COMMUNITY. FRANCE EUR+WWI
GERMANY STRUCT ECO/DEV EXTR/IND INDUS MARKET NAT/G INT/ORG
DELIB/GP ECO/TAC INT/TRADE EDU/PROP ATTIT REGION
RIGID/FLEX ORD/FREE PWR WEALTH...CONCPT STAT
TIME/SEQ CHARTS ECSC 20. PAGE 97 H1941

B60
MACRIDIS R.C.,THE DE GAULLE REPUBLIC: QUEST FOR TOP/EX
UNITY. EUR+WWI NAT/G POL/PAR LEGIS LEGIT NAT/LISM STRUCT
ATTIT RIGID/FLEX ORD/FREE PWR...JURID CONCPT FRANCE
TIME/SEQ 20 DEGAULLE/C. PAGE 100 H2009

B60
MEYRIAT J.,LA SCIENCE POLITIQUE EN FRANCE, BIBLIOG/A
1945-1958; BIBLIOGRAPHIES FRANCAISES DE SCIENCES NAT/G
SOCIALES (VOL. I). EUR+WWI FRANCE POL/PAR DIPLOM CONCPT
ADMIN CHOOSE ATTIT...IDEA/COMP METH/COMP NAT/COMP PHIL/SCI
20. PAGE 110 H2193

B60
MINER H.M.,OASIS AND CASBAH: ALGERIAN CULTURE AND GP/COMP
PERSONALITY IN CHANGE. ALGERIA FRANCE SOCIETY MUNIC PERSON
COLONIAL ATTIT...INT PROJ/TEST CHARTS 20. PAGE 111 CULTURE
H2221 ADJUST

B60
PETERSON W.C.,THE WELFARE STATE IN FRANCE. EUR+WWI NEW/LIB
FRANCE FUT STRATA PROB/SOLV TAX GIVE RECEIVE INCOME ECO/TAC
ORD/FREE PWR...CHARTS 20. PAGE 125 H2496 WEALTH
NAT/G

B60
PICKLES D.,THE FIFTH FRENCH REPUBLIC. ALGERIA CONSTN
FRANCE CHOOSE GOV/REL ATTIT CONSERVE...CHARTS 20 ADJUD
DEGAULLE/C. PAGE 125 H2506 NAT/G
EFFICIENCY

S60
BERG E.J.,"ECONOMIC BASIS OF POLITICAL CHOICE IN AFR
FRENCH WEST AFRICA." FRANCE ECO/UNDEV AGRI INDUS ECO/TAC
NAT/G PLAN LEGIT COLONIAL REGION ATTIT PWR WEALTH
...CONCPT 20. PAGE 15 H0299

S60
CROZIER B.,"FRANCE AND ALGERIA." ALGERIA EUR+WWI NAT/G
FRANCE FUT ISLAM ECO/UNDEV NEIGH CONSULT DELIB/GP FORCES
ECO/TAC COLONIAL COERCE ATTIT...SOC INT CON/ANAL GUERRILLA
20. PAGE 36 H0713 NAT/LISM

S60
KELLEY G.A.,"THE POLITICAL BACKGROUND OF THE FRENCH NAT/G
A-BOMB." EUR+WWI USSR FORCES TOP/EX TEC/DEV NUC/PWR RESPECT
ATTIT PWR...CONCPT OBS/ENVIR TREND 20. PAGE 84 NAT/LISM
H1686 FRANCE

B61
ANSPRENGER F.,POLITIK IM SCHWARZEN AFRIKA. FRANCE AFR
NAT/G DIPLOM REGION REV NAT/LISM...CHARTS BIBLIOG COLONIAL
19/20. PAGE 7 H0141 SOVEREIGN

B61
BEDFORD S.,THE FACES OF JUSTICE: A TRAVELLER'S CT/SYS
REPORT. AUSTRIA FRANCE GERMANY/W SWITZERLND UK UNIV ORD/FREE
WOR+45 WOR-45 CULTURE PARTIC GOV/REL MORAL...JURID PERSON
OBS GOV/COMP 20. PAGE 13 H0257 LAW

B61
BURDEAU G.,O PODER EXECUTIVO NA FRANCA. EUR+WWI TOP/EX
FRANCE CONSTN DELIB/GP LEGIT ADMIN ATTIT ALL/VALS POL/PAR
CONCPT. PAGE 24 H0478 NAT/G
LEGIS

B61
CATHERINE R.,LE FONCTIONNAIRE FRANCAIS. FRANCE NAT/G INGP/REL ATTIT MORAL ORD/FREE...T CIVIL/SERV. PAGE 28 H0559
ADMIN GP/REL LEAD SUPEGO

B61
DELEFORTRIE-SOU N.,LES DIRIGEANTS DE L'INDUSTRIE FRANCAISE. FRANCE CULTURE ELITES PROB/SOLV ...DECISION STAT CHARTS 20. PAGE 39 H0789
INDUS STRATA TOP/EX LEAD

B61
DONNISON F.S.V.,CIVIL AFFAIRS AND MILITARY GOVERNMENT NORTH-WEST EUROPE 1944-1946. EUR+WWI FRANCE GERMANY UK USSR LOC/G PROVS PLAN PROB/SOLV BAL/PWR ECO/TAC CONTROL PWR...CHARTS 20. PAGE 42 H0836
NAT/G WAR FORCES CIVMIL/REL

B61
DRAGNICH A.N.,MAJOR EUROPEAN GOVERNMENTS. FRANCE GERMANY/W UK USSR LOC/G EX/STRUC CT/SYS PARL/PROC ATTIT MARXISM...JURID MGT NAT/COMP 19/20. PAGE 42 H0846
NAT/G LEGIS CONSTN POL/PAR

B61
FULLER J.F.C.,THE CONDUCT OF WAR, 1789-1961. FRANCE RUSSIA SOCIETY NAT/G FORCES PROB/SOLV AGREE NUC/PWR WEAPON PEACE...SOC 18/20 TREATY COLD/WAR. PAGE 54 H1076
WAR POLICY REV ROLE

B61
GUIZOT F.P.G.,HISTORY OF THE ORIGIN OF REPRESENTATIVE GOVERNMENT IN EUROPE. CHRIST-17C FRANCE MOD/EUR SPAIN UK LAW CHIEF FORCES POPULISM ...MAJORIT TIME/SEQ GOV/COMP NAT/COMP 4/19 PARLIAMENT. PAGE 62 H1250
LEGIS REPRESENT CONSTN NAT/G

B61
HAUSER M.,DIE URSACHEN DER FRANZOSISCHEN INFLATION IN DEN JAHREN 1946-1952. FRANCE INDUS NAT/G BUDGET DIPLOM ECO/TAC FOR/AID COST MONEY 20 GOLD/STAND. PAGE 68 H1357
ECO/DEV FINAN PRICE

B61
LA DOCUMENTATION FRANCAISE,L'AFRIQUE A TRAVERS LES PUBLICATIONS DE LA DOCUMENTATION FRANCAISE; BIBLIOGRAPHIE 1945-1961 (PAMPHLET). FRANCE 20. PAGE 90 H1791
BIBLIOG AFR COLONIAL NAT/G

B61
LA PONCE J.A.,THE GOVERNMENT OF THE FIFTH REPUBLIC: FRENCH POLITICAL PARTIES AND THE CONSTITUTION. ALGERIA FRANCE LAW NAT/G DELIB/GP LEGIS ECO/TAC MARXISM SOCISM...CHARTS BIBLIOG/A 20 DEGAULLE/C. PAGE 90 H1794
PWR POL/PAR CONSTN CHIEF

B61
LAHAYE R.,LES ENTREPRISES PUBLIQUES AU MAROC. FRANCE MOROCCO LAW DIST/IND EXTR/IND FINAN CONSULT PLAN TEC/DEV ADMIN AGREE CONTROL OWN...POLICY 20. PAGE 90 H1796
NAT/G INDUS ECO/UNDEV ECO/TAC

B61
SCHNAPPER B.,LA POLITIQUE ET LE COMMERCE FRANCAIS DANS LE GOLFE DE GUINEE DE 1838 A 1871. FRANCE GUINEA UK SEA EXTR/IND NAT/G DELIB/GP LEGIS ADMIN ORD/FREE...POLICY GEOG CENSUS CHARTS BIBLIOG 19. PAGE 139 H2791
COLONIAL INT/TRADE DOMIN AFR

B61
VEIT O.,GRUNDRISS DER WAHRUNGSPOLITIK. FRANCE GERMANY USSR DIPLOM INT/TRADE...NAT/COMP 19/20 GOLD/STAND SILVER. PAGE 162 H3239
FINAN POLICY ECO/TAC CAP/ISM

S61
DOGAN M.,"LES OFFICIERS DANS LA CARRIERE POLITIQUE DE MARECHAL MACMAHON AU GENERAL DE GAULLE." EUR+WWI FRANCE MOD/EUR ELITES STRATA POL/PAR LEGIT ATTIT ALL/VALS...SOC CONCPT 19/20. PAGE 42 H0833
PROF/ORG FORCES NAT/G DELIB/GP

S61
EHRMANN H.W.,"FRENCH BUREAUCRACY AND ORGANIZED INTERESTS" (BMR)" FRANCE NAT/G DELIB/GP ROUTINE ...INT 20 BUREAUCRCY CIVIL/SERV. PAGE 45 H0897
ADMIN DECISION PLURISM LOBBY

S61
RAY J.,"THE EUROPEAN FREE-TRADE ASSOCIATION AND ITS IMPACT ON INDIA'S TRADE." EUR+WWI FRANCE GERMANY INDIA S/ASIA UK NAT/G VOL/ASSN PLAN INT/TRADE ROUTINE WEALTH...STAT CHARTS CMN/WLTH EEC OEEC 20 EFTA. PAGE 130 H2600
ECO/DEV ECO/TAC

S61
TANHAM B.K.,"COMMUNIST REVOLUTIONARY WARFARE: THE VIETMINH IN INDOCHINA." EUR+WWI S/ASIA VIETNAM NAT/G EDU/PROP LEGIT GUERRILLA ATTIT PWR...CONCPT GEN/LAWS 20. PAGE 152 H3042
FORCES ECO/TAC WAR FRANCE

C61
LAPONCE J.A.,"THE GOVERNMENT OF THE FIFTH REPUBLIC." FRANCE CHIEF LEGIS PARL/PROC CHOOSE ...CHARTS GP/COMP IDEA/COMP BIBLIOG/A 20. PAGE 91 H1814
POL/PAR NAT/G CONSTN DOMIN

B62
ANDREWS W.G.,EUROPEAN POLITICAL INSTITUTIONS. FRANCE GERMANY UK USSR TOP/EX LEAD PARL/PROC CHOOSE 20. PAGE 7 H0139
NAT/COMP POL/PAR EX/STRUC LEGIS

B62
ANDREWS W.G.,FRENCH POLITICS AND ALGERIA: THE PROCESS OF POLICY FORMATION 1954-1962. ALGERIA FRANCE CONSTN ELITES POL/PAR CHIEF DELIB/GP LEGIS DIPLOM PRESS CHOOSE 20. PAGE 7 H0140
GOV/COMP EXEC COLONIAL

B62
ARNE S.,LE PRESIDENT DU CONSEIL DES MINISTRES SOUS LA IV REPUBLIQUE. EUR+WWI FRANCE LEGIT PWR...BIOG CHARTS. PAGE 8 H0165
DELIB/GP POL/PAR NAT/G LEGIS

B62
BROWN B.E.,NEW DIRECTIONS IN COMPARATIVE POLITICS. AUSTRIA FRANCE GERMANY UK WOR+45 EX/STRUC LEGIS ORD/FREE 20. PAGE 22 H0439
NAT/COMP METH POL/PAR FORCES

B62
DEHIO L.,THE PRECARIOUS BALANCE: FOUR CENTURIES OF THE EUROPEAN POWER STRUGGLE. FRANCE GERMANY SPAIN NAT/G DOMIN PWR...GOV/COMP 8/20. PAGE 39 H0784
BAL/PWR WAR DIPLOM COERCE

B62
DUROSELLE J.B.,LES NOUVEAUX ETATS DANS LES RELATIONS INTERNATIONALES. AFR CHINA/COM FRANCE MOROCCO S/ASIA USSR ECO/UNDEV INT/ORG PLAN ECO/TAC EDU/PROP ATTIT DRIVE...TREND TOT/POP TUNIS 20. PAGE 44 H0872
NAT/G CONSTN DIPLOM

B62
FRIEDMANN W.,METHODS AND POLICIES OF PRINCIPAL DONOR COUNTRIES IN PUBLIC INTERNATIONAL DEVELOPMENT FINANCING: PRELIMINARY APPRAISAL. FRANCE GERMANY/W UK USA+45 USSR WOR+45 FINAN TEC/DEV CAP/ISM DIPLOM ECO/TAC ATTIT 20 EEC. PAGE 53 H1066
INT/ORG FOR/AID NAT/COMP ADMIN

B62
GUENA Y.,HISTORIQUE DE LA COMMUNAUTE. FUT ECO/UNDEV NAT/G PLAN EDU/PROP COLONIAL REGION NAT/LISM ALL/VALS SOVEREIGN...CONCPT OBS CHARTS 20. PAGE 62 H1244
AFR VOL/ASSN FOR/AID FRANCE

B62
HENDERSON W.O.,THE GENESIS OF THE COMMON MARKET. EUR+WWI FRANCE MOD/EUR UK SEA COM/IND EXTR/IND COLONIAL DISCRIM...TIME/SEQ CHARTS BIBLIOG 18/20 EEC TREATY. PAGE 70 H1395
ECO/DEV INT/TRADE DIPLOM

B62
HUNKIN P.,ENSEIGNEMENT ET POLITIQUE EN FRANCE ET EN ANGLETERRE. FRANCE UK CONSTN ACADEM SECT CHIEF DELIB/GP PROB/SOLV CONTROL REV ORD/FREE CONSERVE ...BIBLIOG 18/20. PAGE 75 H1496
EDU/PROP LEGIS IDEA/COMP NAT/G

B62
NOBECOURT R.G.,LES SECRETS DE LA PROPAGANDE EN FRANCE OCCUPEE. FRANCE ELITES NAT/G DIPLOM GP/REL NAT/LISM TOTALISM ORD/FREE 20 VICHY VICHY. PAGE 118 H2365
METH/COMP EDU/PROP WAR CONTROL

B62
OLLE-LAPRUNE J.,LA STABILITE DES MINISTRES SOUS LA TROISIEME REPUBLIQUE, 1879-1940. FRANCE CONSTN POL/PAR LEAD WAR INGP/REL RIGID/FLEX PWR...POLICY CHARTS 19/20. PAGE 121 H2415
LEGIS NAT/G ADMIN PERSON

B62
UMENDRAS H.,LES SOCIETESRFRANCAISES; BIBLIOGRAPHIES FRANCAISES DE SCIENCE SOCIALES (VOL. III). FRANCE SECT WORKER 20. PAGE 158 H3154
BIBLIOG/A AGRI MUNIC CULTURE

L62
ORDONNEAU P.,"LES PROBLEMES POSES PAR L'INDEPENDANCE DES NOUVEAUX ETATS AFRICAINS ET MALGACHE SUR LE PLAN DU CONTENTIEUX." FRANCE ISLAM MADAGASCAR LAW STRATA ECO/UNDEV NAT/G LEGIS LEGIT ...JURID TIME/SEQ 20. PAGE 121 H2425
AFR ADJUD COLONIAL SOVEREIGN

S62
FESLER J.W.,"FRENCH FIELD ADMINISTRATION: THE BEGINNINGS." CHRIST-17C CULTURE SOCIETY STRATA NAT/G ECO/TAC DOMIN EDU/PROP LEGIT ADJUD COERCE ATTIT ALL/VALS...TIME/SEQ CON/ANAL GEN/METH VAL/FREE 13/15. PAGE 49 H0988
EX/STRUC FRANCE

S62
GUETZKOW H.,"THE POTENTIAL OF CASE STUDY IN ANALYZING INTERNATIONAL CONFLICT." EUR+WWI FUT GERMANY INTELL SOCIETY STRUCT INT/ORG LOC/G NAT/G CONSULT CREATE PLAN CHOOSE ATTIT RIGID/FLEX ...POLICY SAAR 20. PAGE 62 H1246
EDU/PROP METH/CNCPT COERCE FRANCE

S62
PIQUEMAL M.,"LES PROBLEMES DES UNIONS D'ETATS EN AFRIQUE NOIRE." FRANCE SOCIETY INT/ORG NAT/G DELIB/GP PLAN LEGIT ADMIN COLONIAL ROUTINE ATTIT ORD/FREE PWR...GEOG METH/CNCPT 20. PAGE 126 H2515
AFR ECO/UNDEV REGION

S62
VIGNES D.,"L'AUTORITE DES TRAITES INTERNATIONAUX EN DROIT INTERNE." EUR+WWI UNIV LAW CONSTN INTELL NAT/G POL/PAR DIPLOM ATTIT PERCEPT ALL/VALS ...POLICY INT/LAW JURID CONCPT TIME/SEQ 20 TREATY. PAGE 163 H3252
STRUCT LEGIT FRANCE

B63
BROGAN D.W.,POLITICAL PATTERNS IN TODAY'S WORLD. FRANCE USA+45 USSR WOR+45 CONSTN STRUCT PLAN DIPLOM ADMIN LEAD ROLE SUPEGO...PHIL/SCI 20. PAGE 21 H0429
NAT/COMP NEW/LIB COM TOTALISM

B63
GARDINIER D.E.,CAMEROON: UNITED NATIONS CHALLENGE TO FRENCH POLICY. AFR CAMEROON FRANCE NAT/G LEGIS CONTROL SOVEREIGN 20 UN. PAGE 55 H1101
DIPLOM POLICY INT/ORG COLONIAL

B63
GOURNAY B.,PUBLIC ADMINISTRATION. FRANCE LAW CONSTN AGRI FINAN LABOR SCHOOL EX/STRUC CHOOSE...MGT METH/COMP 20. PAGE 59 H1189
BIBLIOG/A ADMIN NAT/G LOC/G

B63
KRAEHE E.,METTERNICH'S GERMAN POLICY: THE CONTEST WITH NAPOLEON, 1799-1814, VOL. 1. FRANCE MOD/EUR NAT/G CONSULT TOP/EX PLAN BAL/PWR DOMIN COERCE ATTIT DRIVE PERCEPT PERSON SKILL...CONCPT RECORD TIME/SEQ TREND 18/19. PAGE 88 H1764
BIOG GERMANY DIPLOM

B63
MONGER G.W.,THE END OF ISOLATION. FRANCE MOD/EUR RUSSIA UK NAT/G LEGIS TOP/EX GOV/REL PWR 20 TREATY CHINJAP. PAGE 112 H2239
DIPLOM POLICY WAR

B63
OLSON M. JR.,THE ECONOMICS OF WARTIME SHORTAGE. FRANCE GERMANY MOD/EUR UK AGRI PROB/SOLV ADMIN DEMAND WEALTH...POLICY OLD/LIB 17/20. PAGE 121 H2416
WAR ADJUST ECO/TAC NAT/COMP

B63
VIARD R.,LA FIN DE L'EMPIRE COLONIAL FRANCAIS. AFR FUT S/ASIA ECO/UNDEV NAT/G CONSULT PLAN ECO/TAC EDU/PROP REGION NAT/LISM ALL/VALS...CONCPT TIME/SEQ TREND VAL/FREE 20. PAGE 162 H3248
VOL/ASSN COLONIAL FRANCE

L63
BOLGAR V.,"THE PUBLIC INTEREST: A JURISPRUDENTIAL AND COMPARATIVE OVERVIEW OF SYMPOSIUM ON FUNDAMENTAL CONCEPTS OF PUBLIC LAW" COM FRANCE GERMANY SWITZERLND LAW ADJUD ADMIN AGREE LAISSEZ ...JURID GEN/LAWS 20 EUROPE/E. PAGE 18 H0369
CONCPT ORD/FREE CONTROL NAT/COMP

S63
EMERI C.,"LES FORCES POLITIQUES AU PARLEMENT" EUR+WWI FRANCE ELITES DELIB/GP TOP/EX LEGIT ATTIT ...SOC 20 PARLIAMENT. PAGE 46 H0917
POL/PAR LEGIS PWR NAT/G

S63
GROSSER A.,"FRANCE AND GERMANY IN THE ATLANTIC COMMUNITY." INT/ORG NAT/G TOP/EX DIPLOM REGION PEACE ATTIT ORD/FREE PWR...CONCPT RECORD TIME/SEQ GEN/LAWS VAL/FREE COLD/WAR 20. PAGE 62 H1234
EUR+WWI VOL/ASSN FRANCE GERMANY

S63
HUREWITZ J.C.,"LEBANESE DEMOCRACY IN ITS INTERNATIONAL SETTING." FRANCE ISLAM UK LOC/G NAT/G SECT DOMIN EDU/PROP EXEC ATTIT PWR...TIME/SEQ 20. PAGE 75 H1507
STRUCT LEBANON

S63
LERNER D.,"WILL EUROPEAN UNION BRING ABOUT MERGED NATIONAL GOALS." EUR+WWI FRANCE GERMANY UK ECO/DEV NAT/G VOL/ASSN DELIB/GP BAL/PWR ECO/TAC NAT/LISM EEC 20 DEGAULLE/C. PAGE 95 H1889
ATTIT STERTYP ELITES REGION

S63
LIGOT M.,"LA COOPERATION MILITAIRE DANS LES ACCORDS, PASSES ENTRE LA FRANCE ET LES ETATS AFRICAINS ET MALGACHE D'EXPRESSION." ECO/UNDEV INT/ORG NAT/G VOL/ASSN...CONCPT TIME/SEQ 20. PAGE 97 H1931
AFR FORCES FOR/AID FRANCE

S63
MONROE A.D.,"BRITAIN AND THE EUROPEAN COMMUNITY." EUR+WWI FRANCE NAT/G DELIB/GP TOP/EX ECO/TAC DOMIN PWR...POLICY RECORD GEN/LAWS EEC EFTA 20 EFTA CMN/WLTH. PAGE 112 H2241
VOL/ASSN ATTIT UK

B64
BAUCHET P.,ECONOMIC PLANNING. FRANCE STRATA LG/CO CAP/ISM ADMIN PARL/PROC DEMAND OPTIMAL ATTIT PWR SOCISM...POLICY CHARTS 20. PAGE 12 H0238
ECO/DEV NAT/G PLAN ECO/TAC

B64
BERRINGTON H.,HOW NATIONS ARE GOVERNED. FRANCE WOR+45 ECO/UNDEV INT/ORG POL/PAR CHOOSE TOTALISM KNOWL...MAJORIT T 20 UN COMMONWLTH THIRD/WRLD. PAGE 16 H0320
NAT/G GOV/COMP ECO/DEV CONSTN

B64
BROWN W.M.,THE EXTERNAL LIQUIDITY OF AN ADVANCED COUNTRY. CANADA FRANCE GERMANY/W SWEDEN UK USA+45 ECO/DEV DIPLOM PRICE...CONCPT STAT NAT/COMP 20. PAGE 22 H0451
FINAN INT/TRADE COST INCOME

B64
COBBAN A.,ROUSSEAU AND THE MODERN STATE (2ND ED.). FRANCE PROB/SOLV NAT/LISM UTOPIA PERSON MORAL ...EPIST PHIL/SCI SOC IDEA/COMP 18 ROUSSEAU/J BURKE/EDM HOBBES/T HUME/D. PAGE 30 H0612
GEN/LAWS INGP/REL NAT/G ORD/FREE

B64
FALL B.,STREET WITHOUT JOY. FRANCE USA+45 DIPLOM ECO/TAC FOR/AID GUERRILLA REV WEAPON...TREND 20. PAGE 48 H0966
WAR S/ASIA FORCES COERCE

B64
HELMREICH E.,A FREE CHURCH IN A FREE STATE? FRANCE GERMANY ITALY SECT LEAD PWR CATHISM...POLICY ANTHOL WORSHIP 19/20 CHURCH/STA. PAGE 69 H1389
GP/REL NAT/G

B64
MARTINET G.,MARXISM OF OUR TIME: OR THE CONTRADICTIONS OF SOCIALISM. FRANCE NAT/G OPTIMAL RIGID/FLEX SOCISM...IDEA/COMP 20. PAGE 103 H2067
MARXISM MARXIST PROB/SOLV CREATE

B64
MORGENTHAU R.S.,POLITICAL PARTIES IN FRENCH-SPEAKING WEST AFRICA. AFR FRANCE GUINEA IVORY/CST MALI SENEGAL CONSTN LEGIS CREATE PLAN LOBBY PARTIC GP/REL...POLICY BIBLIOG 20. PAGE 113 H2257
POL/PAR NAT/G SOVEREIGN COLONIAL

B64
QUIGG P.W.,AFRICA: A FOREIGN AFFAIRS READER. AFR FRANCE PORTUGAL UK DIPLOM LEAD PARL/PROC MARXISM ...MAJORIT METH/CNCPT GOV/COMP IDEA/COMP ANTHOL 19/20. PAGE 129 H2575
COLONIAL SOVEREIGN NAT/LISM RACE/REL

B64
RIDLEY F.,PUBLIC ADMINISTRATION IN FRANCE. FRANCE UK EX/STRUC CONTROL PARTIC EFFICIENCY 20. PAGE 131 H2625
ADMIN REPRESENT GOV/COMP PWR

B64
VON STEIN L.J.,THE HISTORY OF THE SOCIAL MOVEMENT IN FRANCE, 1789-1850 (TRANS. BY K. MENGELBERG). COM FRANCE MOD/EUR NAT/G EX/STRUC INGP/REL ALL/IDEOS CONSERVE MARXISM...SOC BIBLIOG 18/19. PAGE 164 H3278
REV STRATA

B64
WHITE D.S.,SEEDS OF DISCORD. EUR+WWI FRANCE NAT/G VOL/ASSN FORCES DIPLOM DOMIN NAT/LISM DISPL RIGID/FLEX PWR...RECORD INT BIOG 20 DEGAULLE/C ROOSEVLT/F CHURCHLL/W HULL. PAGE 167 H3347
TOP/EX ATTIT

B64
WITHERELL J.W.,OFFICIAL PUBLICATIONS OF FRENCH EQUATORIAL AFRICA, FRENCH CAMEROONS, AND TOGO, 1946-1958 (PAMPHLET). CAMEROON CHAD FRANCE GABON TOGO LAW ECO/UNDEV EXTR/IND INT/TRADE...GEOG HEAL 20. PAGE 169 H3392
BIBLIOG/A AFR NAT/G ADMIN

B64
WRIGHT G.,RURAL REVOLUTION IN FRANCE: THE PEASANTRY IN THE TWENTIETH CENTURY. EUR+WWI MOD/EUR LAW CULTURE AGRI POL/PAR DELIB/GP LEGIS ECO/TAC EDU/PROP COERCE CHOOSE ATTIT RIGID/FLEX HEALTH ...STAT CENSUS CHARTS VAL/FREE 20. PAGE 171 H3419
PWR STRATA FRANCE REV

S64
DE GAULLE C.,"FRENCH WORLD VIEW." AFR ASIA CHINA/COM EUR+WWI ISLAM ECO/UNDEV INT/ORG NAT/G VOL/ASSN ACT/RES DIPLOM ECO/TAC EDU/PROP ATTIT DRIVE WEALTH 20. PAGE 37 H0751
TOP/EX PWR FOR/AID FRANCE

S64
PRELOT M.,"LA INFLUENCIA POLITICA Y ELECTORAL DE LA PRENSA EN LA FRANCIA ACTUAL." EUR+WWI SOCIETY NAT/G POL/PAR PROF/ORG PRESS ATTIT PWR...CONCPT 20. PAGE 128 H2556
EDU/PROP FRANCE

S64
ZARTMAN I.W.,"LES RELATIONS ENTRE LA FRANCE ET L'ALGERIA DEPUIS LES ACCORDS D'EVIAN." EUR+WWI FUT ISLAM CULTURE AGRI EXTR/IND FINAN INDUS POL/PAR DIPLOM ECO/TAC FOR/AID PEACE ATTIT DRIVE ALL/VALS ...TIME/SEQ VAL/FREE 20. PAGE 172 H3450
ECO/UNDEV ALGERIA FRANCE

B65
BORTOLI G.,SOCIOLOGIE DU REFERENDUM DANS LA FRANCE MODERNE. FRANCE CONSTN EDU/PROP SUFF ATTIT ORD/FREE ...POLICY DECISION CHARTS BIBLIOG 20 DEGAULLE/C. PAGE 19 H0379
LEGIS SOCIETY PWR NAT/G

B65
CARTER G.M.,POLITICS IN EUROPE. EUR+WWI FRANCE GERMANY/W UK USSR LAW CONSTN POL/PAR VOL/ASSN PRESS LOBBY PWR...ANTHOL SOC/INTEG EEC. PAGE 27 H0548
GOV/COMP OP/RES ECO/DEV

B65
CHARNAY J.P.,LE SUFFRAGE POLITIQUE EN FRANCE; ELECTIONS PARLEMENTAIRES, ELECTION PRESIDENTIELLE, REFERENDUMS. FRANCE CONSTN CHIEF DELIB/GP ECO/TAC EDU/PROP CRIME INGP/REL MORAL ORD/FREE PWR CATHISM 20 PARLIAMENT PRESIDENT. PAGE 29 H0584
CHOOSE SUFF NAT/G LEGIS

B65
GODECHOT J.,FRANCE AND THE ATLANTIC REVOLUTION OF THE EIGHTEENTH CENTURY 1770-1799. FRANCE CULTURE SOCIETY...GEOG 18. PAGE 57 H1150
MOD/EUR NAT/G REV ECO/UNDEV

B65
HALEVY E.,THE ERA OF TYRANNIES (TRANS. BY R. K. WEBB). FRANCE MOD/EUR UK ECO/DEV LABOR NAT/G BAL/PWR FEDERAL ALL/VALS...OLD/LIB TREND 18/20 SAINTSIMON. PAGE 64 H1285
SOCISM CONCPT UTOPIA ORD/FREE

B65
O'CONNELL M.R.,IRISH POLITICS AND SOCIAL CONFLICT IN THE AGE OF THE AMERICAN REVOLUTION. FRANCE IRELAND MOD/EUR STRATA SECT LEGIS DIPLOM INT/TRADE DOMIN REV WAR...BIBLIOG 18 PARLIAMENT. PAGE 119 H2387
CATHISM ATTIT NAT/G DELIB/GP

B65
ROSENBERG A.,DEMOCRACY AND SOCIALISM. COM EUR+WWI FRANCE MOD/EUR STRUCT INT/ORG NAT/G POL/PAR TOP/EX EDU/PROP COERCE PERSON PWR FASCISM MARXISM...CONCPT TIME/SEQ MARX/KARL 19/20. PAGE 134 H2677
ATTIT

B65
SALVADORI M.,ITALY. AUSTRIA FRANCE GERMANY ITALY SPAIN CULTURE NAT/G POL/PAR DIPLOM WAR FASCISM LAISSEZ MARXISM...TIME/SEQ CHARTS BIBLIOG/A. PAGE 137 H2744
NAT/LISM CATHISM SOCIETY

B65
TILLY C.,MEASURING POLITICAL UPHEAVAL* RESEARCH MONOGRAPH NO. 19. FRANCE INDUS NAT/G FORCES WORKER ...GEOG RECORD EXHIBIT GEN/METH BIBLIOG INDEX. PAGE 155 H3095
CLASSIF QUANT COERCE REV

B65
VERMOT-GAUCHY M.,L'EDUCATION NATIONALE DANS LA FRANCE DE 1975. FRANCE FUT CULTURE ELITES R+D SCHOOL PLAN EDU/PROP EFFICIENCY...POLICY PREDICT CHARTS INDEX 20. PAGE 162 H3245
ACADEM CREATE TREND INTELL

S65
CAIRNS J.C.,"FRANCE, DECEMBER 1965: END OF THE ELECTIVE MONARACHY" EUR+WWI FRANCE FUT CONSTN SOCIETY CHIEF BAL/PWR ATTIT ALL/IDEOS 20 DEGAULLE/C PRESIDENT. PAGE 25 H0505
CHOOSE NAT/G POL/PAR PWR

S65
GORDON M.,"THE SETTING FOR EUROPEAN ARMS CONTROLS* POLITICAL AND STRATEGIC CHOICES OF EUROPEAN ELITES." FRANCE GERMANY UK USA+45 USSR ARMS/CONT DETER ATTIT ORD/FREE...SAMP NAT/COMP NATO. PAGE 59 H1179
REC/INT ELITES RISK WAR

S65
HAYTER T.,"FRENCH AID TO AFRICA* ITS SCOPE AND ACHIEVEMENTS." CULTURE ECO/TAC INT/TRADE ADMIN REGION CENTRAL FEDERAL LOVE PWR SOVEREIGN EEC. PAGE 68 H1370
AFR FRANCE FOR/AID COLONIAL

S65
SPAAK P.H.,"THE SEARCH FOR CONSENSUS: A NEW EFFORT TO BUILD EUROPE." FRANCE GERMANY ECO/DEV NAT/G CONSULT FORCES PLAN EDU/PROP REGION CONSEN ATTIT ...SOC METH/CNCPT OBS TREND EEC NATO WORK 20. PAGE 147 H2941
EUR+WWI INT/ORG

S65
STAROBIN J.R.,"COMMUNISM IN WESTERN EUROPE." FRANCE GERMANY ITALY USA+45 USSR ECO/DEV FEDERAL PEACE ATTIT DRIVE PWR TREND. PAGE 149 H2972
MARXISM EUR+WWI POL/PAR NAT/COMP

S65
THOMAS F.C. JR.,"THE PEACE CORPS IN MOROCCO." CULTURE MUNIC PROVS CREATE ROUTINE TASK ADJUST STRANGE...OBS PEACE/CORP. PAGE 154 H3077
MOROCCO FRANCE FOR/AID EDU/PROP

C65
BORTOLI G.,"SOCIOLOGIE DU REFERENDUM DANS LA FRANCE MODERNE." FRANCE CONSTN NAT/G EDU/PROP SUFF ATTIT ORD/FREE...POLICY DECISION SOC CHARTS 20. PAGE 19 H0378
BIBLIOG LEGIS SOCIETY PWR

B66
CADY J.F.,THAILAND, BURMA, LAOS AND CAMBODIA. FRANCE UK CULTURE NAT/G DOMIN GP/REL RACE/REL HABITAT...GEOG TREND CHINJAP BUDDHISM. PAGE 25 H0504
S/ASIA COLONIAL REGION SECT

B66
DE TOCQUEVILLE A,DEMOCRACY IN AMERICA (1834-1840) (2 VOLS. IN I; TRANS. BY G. LAWRENCE). FRANCE CULTURE STRATA POL/PAR CT/SYS REPRESENT FEDERAL ORD/FREE SOVEREIGN...MAJORIT TREND GEN/LAWS 18/19. PAGE 39 H0773
POPULISM USA-45 CONSTN NAT/COMP

B66
FRANK E.,LAWMAKERS IN A CHANGING WORLD. FRANCE UK USSR WOR+45 PARTIC EFFICIENCY ROLE ALL/IDEOS ...CHARTS ANTHOL PARLIAMENT 20 UN COLD/WAR. PAGE 52 H1049
GOV/COMP LEGIS NAT/G DIPLOM

B66
GARCON M.,LETTRE OUVERTE A LA JUSTICE. FRANCE NAT/G PROB/SOLV PAY EFFICIENCY MORAL 20. PAGE 55 H1100
ORD/FREE ADJUD CT/SYS

B66
HACKETT J.,L'ECONOMIE BRITANNIQUE: PROBLEMES ET PERSPECTIVES. FRANCE UK LABOR MUNIC NAT/G EX/STRUC PROB/SOLV BAL/PAY INCOME RIGID/FLEX...MGT PHIL/SCI CHARTS 20. PAGE 63 H1271
ECO/DEV FINAN ECO/TAC PLAN

B66
LEROY P.,L'ORGANIZATION CONSTITUTIONNELLE ET LES CRISES. FRANCE NAT/G ADJUD CONTROL PARL/PROC WAR ...POLICY BIBLIOG 20. PAGE 95 H1892
CONSTN PWR EXEC LEGIS

B66
NOLTE E.,THREE FACES OF FASCISM. FRANCE GERMANY DOMIN LEGIT COERCE CROWD REV WAR GP/REL RACE/REL SOVEREIGN...GOV/COMP IDEA/COMP 19/20 HITLER/A MUSSOLIN/B MARX/KARL. PAGE 118 H2368
FASCISM TOTALISM NAT/G POL/PAR

B66
PAN S.,VIETNAM CRISIS. ASIA FRANCE USA+45 USA-45 VIETNAM CULTURE SOCIETY INT/ORG ECO/TAC AGREE CONTROL WAR MARXISM 20. PAGE 123 H2454
ECO/UNDEV POLICY DIPLOM NAT/COMP

B66
SAINDERICHIN P.,HISTORIE SECRETE D'UNE ELECTION, DECEMBER 5-19, 1965. FRANCE NAT/G DELIB/GP LEGIS PLAN EDU/PROP TV SOCISM...MARXIST 20 DEGAULLE/C. PAGE 137 H2731
CHOOSE CHIEF PROB/SOLV POL/PAR

B66
SPEARS E.L.,TWO MEN WHO SAVED FRANCE: PETAIN AND DE GAULLE. FRANCE CONSTN FORCES DIPLOM WAR PERSON 20 WWI PETAIN/HP DEGAULLE/C. PAGE 147 H2942
BIOG LEAD CHIEF NAT/G

B66
WUEST J.J.,NEW SOURCE BOOK IN MAJOR EUROPEAN GOVERNMENTS. CHRIST-17C EUR+WWI FRANCE GERMANY ITALY MOD/EUR UK USSR LOC/G POL/PAR CHIEF EX/STRUC CHOOSE CONSERVE MARXISM...JURID T 13/20. PAGE 171 H3425
NAT/G CONSTN LEGIS

B67
ALBINSKI H.S.,EUROPEAN POLITICAL PROCESSES: ESSAYS AND READINGS. EUR+WWI FRANCE GERMANY MOD/EUR UK ELITES POL/PAR PWR...CHARTS ANTHOL 18/20. PAGE 5 H0094
NAT/COMP POLICY IDEA/COMP

B67
BAIN C.A.,VIETNAM: THE ROOTS OF CONFLICT. FRANCE S/ASIA USSR VIETNAM POL/PAR SECT FORCES COLONIAL NAT/LISM PEACE ORD/FREE MARXISM...GEOG CHARTS 4/20. PAGE 10 H0202
NAT/G WAR CULTURE

B67
BANKWITZ P.C.,MAXINE WEYGAND AND CIVIL-MILITARY RELATIONS IN MODERN FRANCE. FRANCE LEAD WAR PWR ...INT BIBLIOG 20. PAGE 11 H0212
CIVMIL/REL FORCES NAT/G TOP/EX

B67
BROWN L.N.,FRENCH ADMINISTRATIVE LAW. FRANCE UK CONSTN NAT/G LEGIS DOMIN CONTROL EXEC PARL/PROC PWR ...JURID METH/COMP GEN/METH. PAGE 22 H0447
EX/STRUC LAW IDEA/COMP CT/SYS

B67
BUNN R.F.,POLITICS AND CIVIL LIBERTIES IN EUROPE: FOUR CASE STUDIES. FRANCE GERMANY/W UK USSR NAT/G PRESS CRIME CROWD PRIVIL ATTIT 20. PAGE 24 H0476
ORD/FREE CONSTN NAT/COMP LAW

B67
CAMERON R.,BANKING IN THE EARLY STAGES OF INDUSTRIALIZATION: A STUDY IN ECONOMIC COMPARATIVE HISTORY. FRANCE GERMANY UK USSR...CHARTS IDEA/COMP NAT/COMP 18/20 CHINJAP. PAGE 26 H0512
FINAN INDUS GOV/COMP

B67
COLLINS R.O.,EGYPT AND THE SUDAN. COM FRANCE ISLAM SUDAN UAR UK SOCIETY NAT/G COLONIAL NAT/LISM...GEOG SOC LING TREND SOC/INTEG 7/20 SUEZ. PAGE 32 H0635
AGRI CULTURE ECO/UNDEV

B67
CORDIER A.W.,COLUMBIA ESSAYS IN INTERNATIONAL AFFAIRS. ASIA CHINA/COM FRANCE S/ASIA SPAIN UAR ECO/UNDEV LOC/G ECO/TAC GUERRILLA PWR...BIOG ANTHOL 18/20 MAU/MAU. PAGE 33 H0663
NAT/G DIPLOM MARXISM POLICY

B67
DEUTSCH K.W.,FRANCE, GERMANY AND THE WESTERN ALLIANCE. FRANCE GERMANY/W INT/ORG ARMS/CONT NAT/LISM SOVEREIGN...INT NAT/COMP 20. PAGE 40 H0801
ELITES ATTIT DIPLOM POLICY

B67
FANON F.,TOWARD THE AFRICAN REVOLUTION. AFR FRANCE CULTURE ELITES LEAD REV GP/REL ORD/FREE SOVEREIGN 20. PAGE 49 H0969
COLONIAL DOMIN ECO/UNDEV RACE/REL

B67
KENNETT L.,THE FRENCH ARMIES IN THE SEVEN YEARS' WAR. FRANCE NAT/G CONTROL LEAD WAR CIVMIL/REL EFFICIENCY ATTIT PWR SKILL CONSERVE 18. PAGE 85 H1690
FORCES CHIEF METH/COMP

B67
MENARD O.D.,THE ARMY AND THE FIFTH REPUBLIC. ALGERIA FRANCE VIETNAM ELITES STRATA COLONIAL CONTROL LOBBY WAR CIVMIL/REL ROLE PWR...POLICY 20 DEGAULLE/C. PAGE 108 H2169
FORCES ATTIT NAT/G

B67
WALTZ K.N.,FOREIGN POLICY AND DEMOCRATIC POLITICS: THE AMERICAN AND BRITISH EXPERIENCE. FRANCE UK USA+45 PARL/PROC GOV/REL CONSERVE...DECISION 20. PAGE 165 H3298
POLICY DIPLOM NAT/G GOV/COMP

L67
"A PROPOS DES INCITATIONS FINANCIERES AUX GROUPEMENTS DES COMMUNES: ESSAI D'INTERPRETATION." FRANCE NAT/G LEGIS ADMIN GOV/REL CENTRAL 20. PAGE 3 H0051
LOC/G ECO/TAC APPORT ADJUD

S67
BELGION M.,"THE CASE FOR REHABILITATING MARSHAL PETAIN." EUR+WWI FRANCE NAT/G DIPLOM ATTIT PERSON MORAL PETAIN/HP. PAGE 13 H0262
WAR FORCES LEAD

S67
BOSHER J.F.,"GOVERNMENT AND PRIVATE INTERESTS IN NEW FRANCE." CANADA FRANCE INDUS LG/CO SML/CO CAP/ISM INT/TRADE COLONIAL GP/REL...HIST/WRIT 17/18. PAGE 19 H0381
NAT/G FINAN ADMIN CONTROL

S67
CARIAS B.,"EL CONTROL DE LAS EMPRESAS PUBLICAS POR GRUPOS DE INTERESES DE LA COMUNIDAD." FRANCE UK VENEZUELA INDUS NAT/G CONTROL OWN PWR...DECISION NAT/COMP 20. PAGE 26 H0529
WORKER REPRESENT MGT SOCISM

S67
LEGRES A.,"LES FONCTIONS D'UN PARLEMENT MODERNE." FRANCE DEBATE PARL/PROC SANCTION ATTIT PWR 20 PARLIAMENT. PAGE 93 H1860 — NAT/G LAW LEGIS CHOOSE

S67
MATTHEWS R.O.,"THE SUEZ CANAL DISPUTE* A CASE STUDY IN PEACEFUL SETTLEMENT." FRANCE ISRAEL UAR UK NAT/G CONTROL LEAD COERCE WAR NAT/LISM ROLE ORD/FREE PWR ...INT/LAW UN 20. PAGE 105 H2099 — PEACE DIPLOM ADJUD

S67
MENDL W.,"FRENCH ATTITUDES ON DISARMAMENT." FRANCE CULTURE CHIEF FORCES DIPLOM LEAD WAR...TIME/SEQ 20 DEGAULLE/C. PAGE 109 H2175 — NUC/PWR WEAPON ARMS/CONT POLICY

S67
ROCHET W.,"THE OCTOBER REVOLUTION AND THE STRUGGLE OF THE FRENCH COMMUNISTS." COM FRANCE ELITES SOCIETY STRATA ECO/TAC EDU/PROP GP/REL WEALTH ...MARXIST IDEA/COMP NAT/COMP 20. PAGE 133 H2654 — SOCISM CHOOSE METH/COMP NAT/G

S67
ROOT W.,"REPORT FROM PARIS - DE GAULLE: WHICH WAY TO THE FUTURE?" CANADA FRANCE ISLAM UK INT/ORG CHIEF CREATE AGREE CONTROL ARMS/CONT NUC/PWR EQUILIB PEACE PWR 20 DEGAULLE/C NATO. PAGE 134 H2670 — POLICY DIPLOM NAT/G BAL/PWR

S67
SCOVILLE W.J.,"GOVERNMENT REGULATION AND GROWTH IN THE FRENCH PAPER INDUSTRY DURING THE EIGHTEENTH CENTURY." FRANCE MOD/EUR FINAN CAP/ISM TAX ADMIN CONTROL PRIVIL LAISSEZ...POLICY 18. PAGE 141 H2818 — NAT/G PROC/MFG ECO/DEV INGP/REL

S67
STRAFFORD P.,"FRENCH ELECTIONS." FRANCE NAT/G CHIEF LEGIS BAL/PWR ECO/TAC PARL/PROC PARTIC ATTIT 20. PAGE 150 H2993 — POL/PAR SOCISM CENTRAL MARXISM

S67
WILLIAMS P.M.,"THE FRENCH GENERAL ELECTION OF MARCH 1967." FRANCE INDUS WORKER NAT/LISM PWR SOCISM 20. PAGE 168 H3368 — POL/PAR NAT/G ATTIT CHOOSE

B68
PROUDHON J.P.,IDEE GENERALE DE LA REVOLUTION AU XIXE SIECLE (1851). FRANCE UNIV NAT/G CREATE AGREE UTOPIA ORD/FREE...ANARCH 19. PAGE 128 H2563 — REV SOCIETY WORKER LABOR

L68
CURRENT HISTORY,"DE GAULLE'S FRANCE." FRANCE MOD/EUR WOR+45 INDUS MARKET INT/ORG BUDGET DIPLOM AUTHORIT DRIVE...GOV/COMP IDEA/COMP 20 DEGAULLE/C EEC. PAGE 36 H0723 — INT/TRADE PERSON LEAD NAT/LISM

S68
VERAX,"L'EUROPE ET LA FRANCE SUR LA SELLETTE." FRANCE UK NAT/G CHIEF DIPLOM EDU/PROP GP/REL 20 EEC DEGAULLE/C. PAGE 162 H3242 — INT/TRADE INT/ORG POLICY ECO/TAC

B76
TAINE H.A.,THE ANCIENT REGIME. FRANCE STRATA FORCES PARTIC EQUILIB WEALTH CONSERVE POPULISM...GOV/COMP SOC/INTEG 18/19. PAGE 152 H3035 — NAT/G GOV/REL TAX REV

B85
TAINE H.A.,THE FRENCH REVOLUTION (3 VOLS.) (TRANS. BY J. DURAND). FRANCE MOD/EUR SOCIETY STRATA POL/PAR ECO/TAC DOMIN EDU/PROP GP/REL PWR ...GOV/COMP IDEA/COMP 18. PAGE 152 H3036 — REV NAT/G EX/STRUC LEAD

B89
FERNEUIL T.,LES PRINCIPES DE 1789 ET LA SCIENCE SOCIALE. FRANCE NAT/G REV ATTIT...CONCPT TREND IDEA/COMP 18/19. PAGE 49 H0986 — CONSTN POLICY LAW

B90
BURKE E.,REFLECTIONS ON THE REVOLUTION IN FRANCE. FRANCE UK NAT/G DOMIN LEGIT PEACE PWR SOVEREIGN CONSERVE...POLICY GEN/LAWS 18. PAGE 24 H0487 — REV ORD/FREE CHIEF TRADIT

B90
TAINE H.A.,MODERN REGIME (2 VOLS.). FRANCE FAM REV CENTRAL MARRIAGE PWR...TREND 19 NAPOLEON/B. PAGE 152 H3037 — STRUCT NAT/G OLD/LIB MORAL

B91
PAINE T.,RIGHTS OF MAN. FRANCE MOD/EUR CONSTN NAT/G CHIEF DOMIN LEGIT SOVEREIGN...MAJORIT IDEA/COMP 18 BURKE/EDM CIVIL/LIB. PAGE 122 H2446 — GEN/LAWS ORD/FREE REV AGREE

B94
BENOIST C.,LA POLITIQUE. FRANCE LAW SOCIETY STRUCT POL/PAR PARL/PROC GP/REL ATTIT PWR 19/20. PAGE 14 H0283 — NAT/G REPRESENT ORD/FREE

B96
ESMEIN A.,ELEMENTS DE DROIT CONSTITUTIONNEL. FRANCE UK CHIEF EX/STRUC LEGIS ADJUD CT/SYS PARL/PROC REV GOV/REL ORD/FREE...JURID METH/COMP 18/19. PAGE 47 H0940 — LAW CONSTN NAT/G CONCPT

FRANCHISE....FRANCHISE

FRANCIS M.J. H1046

FRANCIS R.G. H1047

FRANCK T.M. H1048

FRANCO/F....FRANCISCO FRANCO

S66
BLANC N.,"SPAIN: LEARNING THROUGH STRUGGLE" SPAIN STRATA STRUCT SECT FORCES PROB/SOLV AGE/Y ATTIT ORD/FREE PWR WEALTH MARXISM SOCISM 19/20 FRANCO/F SUCCESSION. PAGE 18 H0352 — NAT/G FUT SOCIALIST TOTALISM

FRANK E. H1049

FRANK T. H1050

FRANK/PARL....FRANKFURT PARLIAMENT

B22
FICHTE J.G.,ADDRESSES TO THE GERMAN NATION. GERMANY PRUSSIA ELITES NAT/G SECT CREATE INT/TRADE HEREDITY ...ART/METH LING 19 FRANK/PARL. PAGE 50 H0989 — NAT/LISM CULTURE EDU/PROP REGION

FRANKEL J. H1051

FRANKEL S.H. H1052

FRANKFUR/F....FELIX FRANKFURTER

FRANKFURT PARLIAMENT....SEE FRANK/PARL

FRANKLIN/B....BENJAMIN FRANKLIN

FRANZ G. H1053,H1054

FREDERICK....FREDERICK THE GREAT

N19
HARTUNG F.,ENLIGHTENED DESPOTISM (PAMPHLET). ORD/FREE SOVEREIGN CONSERVE...PHIL/SCI FREDERICK ENLIGHTNMT. PAGE 67 H1350 — NAT/G CHIEF CONCPT PWR

B52
SKALWEIT S.,FRANKREICH UND FRIEDRICH DER GROSSE. FRANCE GERMANY PRUSSIA NAT/G DOMIN WAR 18 FREDERICK. PAGE 145 H2893 — ATTIT EDU/PROP DIPLOM SOC

FREDRKSBRG....FREDERICKSBURG, VIRGINIA

FREE/SOIL....FREE-SOIL DEBATE (U.S.)

FREE/SPEE....FREE SPEECH MOVEMENT; SEE ALSO AMEND/I

C43
BENTHAM J.,"ON THE LIBERTY OF THE PRESS, AND PUBLIC DISCUSSION" IN J. BOWRING, ED., THE WORKS OF JEREMY BENTHAM." SPAIN UK LAW ELITES NAT/G LEGIS INSPECT LEGIT WRITING CONTROL PRIVIL TOTALISM AUTHORIT ...TRADIT 19 FREE/SPEE. PAGE 15 H0290 — ORD/FREE PRESS CONFER CONSERVE

FREEDOM....SEE ORD/FREE

FREEDOM/HS....FREEDOM HOUSE

FREEMAN H.A. H1055

FREISEN J. H1056

FRELIMO....MOZAMBIQUE LIBERATION FRONT

FRENCH D.S. H1057

FRENCH/CAN....FRENCH CANADA

FREUD/S....SIGMUND FREUD

B39
MARITAIN J.,SCHOLASTICISM AND POLITICS. CONSTN SOCIETY NAT/G INGP/REL PERSON CATHISM POPULISM 19/20 FREUD/S SCHOLASTIC CHURCH/STA CHRISTIAN. PAGE 103 H2050 — SECT GEN/LAWS ORD/FREE

B60
MANIS J.G.,MAN AND SOCIETY. STRATA LEAD INGP/REL PERS/REL ATTIT PWR...PSY ANTHOL T SOC/INTEG MARX/KARL MILL/JS FREUD/S CHURCHLL/W SPENCER/H RUSSELL/B. PAGE 102 H2036 — SOC SOCIETY STRUCT CULTURE

DETER WAR ATTIT PWR...RELATIV METH/CNCPT SELF/OBS BAL/PWR
TREND CON/ANAL STERTYP GEN/LAWS 20. PAGE 55 H1103 NUC/PWR

S58
EULAV H.,"HD LASSWELL'S DEVELOPMENTAL ANALYSIS." CONCPT
FUT CULTURE TOP/EX PLAN CHOOSE SUPEGO PWR...TREND NEW/IDEA
HYPO/EXP SIMUL GEN/METH VAL/FREE 20 LASSWELL/H. ELITES
PAGE 47 H0948

B59
BLOOMFIELD L.P.,WESTERN EUROPE AND THE UN - TRENDS INT/ORG
AND PROSPECTS. EUR+WWI BAL/PWR DIPLOM ECO/TAC TREND
COLONIAL ATTIT PWR...POLICY 20 UN EUROPE/W. PAGE 18 FUT
H0359 NAT/G

B59
VERNEY D.V.,PUBLIC ENTERPRISE IN SWEDEN. FUT SWEDEN ECO/DEV
UK INDUS POL/PAR LEGIS PROB/SOLV CAP/ISM INT/TRADE POLICY
CONTROL SOCISM...MGT CONCPT NAT/COMP 20 SOCDEM/PAR LG/CO
CIVIL/SERV. PAGE 162 H3246 NAT/G

S59
JENKS C.W.,"THE CHALLENGE OF UNIVERSALITY." FUT INT/ORG
UNIV CONSTN CULTURE CONSULT CREATE PLAN LEGIT ATTIT LAW
MORAL ORD/FREE RESPECT...MAJORIT JURID 20. PAGE 80 PEACE
H1602 INT/LAW

S59
PLAZA G.,"FOR A REGIONAL MARKET IN LATIN AMERICA." MARKET
FUT L/A+17C CULTURE INDUS NAT/G ECO/TAC INT/TRADE INT/ORG
ATTIT WEALTH...NEW/IDEA TREND OAS 20. PAGE 126 REGION
H2527

B60
AYEARST M.,THE BRITISH WEST INDIES: THE SEARCH FOR CONSTN
SELF-GOVERNMENT. FUT WEST/IND LOC/G POL/PAR COLONIAL
EX/STRUC LEGIS CHOOSE FEDERAL...NAT/COMP BIBLIOG REPRESENT
17/20. PAGE 9 H0186 NAT/G

B60
CARTER G.M.,INDEPENDENCE FOR AFRICA. AFR FUT NAT/G
SOCIETY STRATA ECO/DEV POL/PAR DELIB/GP PLAN DOMIN PWR
EDU/PROP COLONIAL REGION ATTIT DRIVE SOVEREIGN NAT/LISM
...RECORD INT TIME/SEQ CHARTS 20. PAGE 27 H0544

B60
FURNISS E.S.,FRANCE, TROUBLED ALLY. EUR+WWI FUT NAT/G
CULTURE SOCIETY BAL/PWR ADMIN ATTIT DRIVE PWR FRANCE
...TREND TOT/POP 20 DEGAULLE/C. PAGE 54 H1079

B60
MCCLOSKY H.,THE SOVIET DICTATORSHIP. FUT CONSTN COM
CULTURE INTELL SOCIETY POL/PAR SECT VOL/ASSN FORCES NAT/G
PLAN TEC/DEV DOMIN EDU/PROP COERCE PWR MARXISM TOTALISM
...POLICY CONCPT MYTH STERTYP 20. PAGE 106 H2127 USSR

B60
PETERSON W.C.,THE WELFARE STATE IN FRANCE. EUR+WWI NEW/LIB
FRANCE FUT STRATA PROB/SOLV TAX GIVE RECEIVE INCOME ECO/TAC
ORD/FREE PWR...CHARTS 20. PAGE 125 H2496 WEALTH
NAT/G

B60
STOLPER W.F.,GERMANY BETWEEN EAST AND WEST: THE ECO/DEV
ECONOMICS OF COMPETITIVE COEXISTENCE. FUT GERMANY/E DIPLOM
GERMANY/W WOR+45 FINAN POL/PAR BUDGET ECO/TAC GOV/COMP
FOR/AID INT/TRADE...STAT CHARTS METH/COMP 20 BAL/PWR
COLD/WAR. PAGE 150 H2989

S60
"THE EMERGING COMMON MARKETS IN LATIN AMERICA." FUT FINAN
L/A+17C STRATA DIST/IND INDUS LABOR NAT/G LEGIS ECO/UNDEV
ECO/TAC ADMIN RIGID/FLEX HEALTH...NEW/IDEA TIME/SEQ INT/TRADE
OAS 20. PAGE 2 H0038

S60
ARENDT H.,"SOCIETY AND CULTURE." FUT CULTURE INTELL SOCIETY
STRATA EDU/PROP ATTIT PERSON KNOWL...ART/METH HUM CREATE
20. PAGE 8 H0161

S60
BRZEZINSKI Z.K.,"PATTERNS AND LIMITS OF THE SINO- POL/PAR
SOVIET DISPUTE." ASIA CHINA/COM COM FUT STRATA PWR
NAT/G EX/STRUC FORCES BAL/PWR DIPLOM ECO/TAC DOMIN REV
EDU/PROP ADMIN COERCE WAR ATTIT RIGID/FLEX USSR
...GEN/LAWS VAL/FREE 20. PAGE 23 H0459

S60
CROZIER B.,"FRANCE AND ALGERIA." ALGERIA EUR+WWI NAT/G
FRANCE FUT ISLAM ECO/UNDEV NEIGH CONSULT DELIB/GP FORCES
ECO/TAC COLONIAL COERCE ATTIT...SOC INT CON/ANAL GUERRILLA
20. PAGE 36 H0713 NAT/LISM

S60
EMERSON R.,"THE EROSION OF DEMOCRACY." AFR FUT LAW S/ASIA
CULTURE INTELL SOCIETY ECO/UNDEV FAM LOC/G NAT/G POL/PAR
FORCES PLAN TEC/DEV ECO/TAC ADMIN CT/SYS ATTIT
ORD/FREE PWR...SOCIALIST SOC CONCPT STAND/INT
TIME/SEQ WORK 20. PAGE 46 H0918

S60
FITZGIBBON R.H.,"DICTATORSHIP AND DEMOCRACY IN L/A+17C
LATIN AMERICA." FUT ECO/DEV ECO/UNDEV INT/ORG LOC/G ACT/RES
NAT/G TOP/EX PLAN TEC/DEV ECO/TAC CHOOSE ATTIT INT/TRADE
DRIVE PERSON ALL/VALS OAS TOT/POP 20. PAGE 51 H1019

S60
FRANKEL S.H.,"ECONOMIC ASPECTS OF POLITICAL NAT/G
INDEPENDENCE IN AFRICA." AFR FUT SOCIETY ECO/UNDEV FOR/AID
COM/IND FINAN LEGIS PLAN TEC/DEV CAP/ISM ECO/TAC
INT/TRADE ADMIN ATTIT DRIVE RIGID/FLEX PWR WEALTH
...MGT NEW/IDEA MATH TIME/SEQ VAL/FREE 20. PAGE 53
H1052

S60
GINSBURGS G.,"PEKING-LHASA-NEW DELHI." CHINA/COM ASIA
FUT INDIA S/ASIA KIN NAT/G PROVS SECT FORCES COERCE
BAL/PWR ECO/TAC DOMIN EDU/PROP LEGIT ADMIN REGION DIPLOM
GUERRILLA PWR...TREND TIBET 20. PAGE 57 H1134

S60
HOWARD M.,"BRITAIN'S DEFENSE: COMMITMENTS AND FUT
CAPABILITIES." EUR+WWI ECO/DEV NAT/G FORCES LEGIS PWR
PLAN DETER ORD/FREE WEALTH...POLICY CONCPT TIME/SEQ DIPLOM
GEN/METH 20. PAGE 74 H1481 UK

S60
JAFFEE A.J.,"POPULATION TRENDS AND CONTROLS IN ECO/UNDEV
UNDERDEVELOPED COUNTRIES." AFR FUT ISLAM L/A+17C GEOG
S/ASIA CULTURE R+D FAM ACT/RES PLAN EDU/PROP
BIO/SOC RIGID/FLEX HEALTH...SOC STAT OBS CHARTS 20.
PAGE 79 H1582

S60
MAGATHAN W.,"SOME BASES OF WEST GERMAN MILITARY NAT/G
POLICY." EUR+WWI FUT INT/ORG TOP/EX ECO/TAC DOMIN FORCES
DRIVE ORD/FREE PWR...TRADIT GEOG OBS TREND. GERMANY
PAGE 101 H2015

S60
NORTH R.C.,"THE NEW EXPANSIONISM." ASIA CHINA/COM ATTIT
FUT INDIA CULTURE SOCIETY NAT/G TOP/EX DOMIN COERCE DRIVE
PWR MARXISM...CONCPT TIME/SEQ TREND GEN/LAWS NAT/LISM
COLD/WAR 20 MAO. PAGE 119 H2372

S60
NORTH R.C.,"DIE DISKREPANZ ZWISCHEN REALITAT UND SOCIETY
WUNSCHBILD ALS INNENPOLITISCHER FAKTOR." ASIA ECO/TAC
CHINA/COM COM FUT ECO/UNDEV NAT/G PLAN DOMIN ADMIN
COERCE PERCEPT...SOC MYTH GEN/METH WORK TOT/POP 20.
PAGE 119 H2373

S60
NORTHEDGE F.S.,"BRITISH FOREIGN POLICY AND THE POL/PAR
PARTY SYSTEM." EUR+WWI FUT INT/ORG NAT/G EDU/PROP CHOOSE
ATTIT PWR...POLICY CONCPT MYTH TIME/SEQ TREND 20 DIPLOM
UN. PAGE 119 H2374 UK

S60
SPIRO H.J.,"NEW CONSTITUTIONAL FORMS IN AFRICA." AFR
FUT CULTURE SOCIETY ECO/UNDEV NAT/G POL/PAR CONSTN
VOL/ASSN EDU/PROP ATTIT DRIVE ORD/FREE PWR RESPECT FOR/AID
...POLICY CONCPT OBS TREND CON/ANAL STERTYP NAT/LISM
GEN/LAWS VAL/FREE. PAGE 148 H2950

B61
CASSINELLI C.W.,THE POLITICS OF FREEDOM. FUT UNIV MAJORIT
LAW POL/PAR CHOOSE ORD/FREE...POLICY CONCPT MYTH NAT/G
BIBLIOG. PAGE 28 H0555 PARL/PROC
PARTIC

B61
DUFFY J.,AFRICA SPEAKS. GHANA TOGO CULTURE AFR
ECO/UNDEV PROB/SOLV COLONIAL NEUTRAL DISCRIM NAT/G
NAT/LISM SOVEREIGN ALL/IDEOS...CONCPT ANTHOL FUT
SOC/INTEG 20 NEGRO THIRD/WRLD. PAGE 43 H0857 STRUCT

B61
GOULD S.H.,SCIENCES IN COMMUNIST CHINA. CHINA/COM ASIA
FUT INDUS NAT/G TOTALISM...RECORD TOT/POP 20. TEC/DEV
PAGE 59 H1187

B61
KISSINGER H.A.,THE NECESSITY FOR CHOICE. FUT USA+45 TOP/EX
ECO/UNDEV NAT/G PLAN BAL/PWR ECO/TAC ARMS/CONT TREND
DETER NUC/PWR ATTIT...POLICY CONCPT RECORD GEN/LAWS DIPLOM
COLD/WAR 20. PAGE 87 H1728

B61
LETHBRIDGE H.J.,CHINA'S URBAN COMMUNES. CHINA/COM MUNIC
FUT ECO/UNDEV DIPLOM EDU/PROP DEMAND INCOME MARXISM CONTROL
...POLICY 20. PAGE 95 H1893 ECO/TAC
NAT/G

B61
MARX K.,THE COMMUNIST MANIFESTO. IN (MENDEL A. COM
ESSENTIAL WORKS OF MARXISM, NEW YORK: BANTAM. FUT NEW/IDEA
MOD/EUR CULTURE ECO/DEV ECO/UNDEV AGRI FINAN INDUS CAP/ISM
MARKET PROC/MFG LABOR MUNIC POL/PAR CONSULT FORCES REV
CREATE PLAN ADMIN ATTIT DRIVE RIGID/FLEX ORD/FREE
PWR RESPECT MARX/KARL WORK. PAGE 104 H2081

B61
MERRIAM A.,CONGO: BACKGROUND OF CONFLICT. AFR FUT CHOOSE
KIN MUNIC NAT/G POL/PAR PROVS DELIB/GP PLAN DOMIN GUERRILLA
COERCE ATTIT...TIME/SEQ CHARTS CONGO 20. PAGE 109
H2182

B61
MILLIKAW M.F.,THE EMERGING NATIONS: THEIR GROWTH ECO/UNDEV
AND UNITED STATES POLICY. FUT USA+45 WOR+45 WOR-45 POLICY
NAT/G PLAN TEC/DEV BAL/PWR GOV/REL PEACE ORD/FREE DIPLOM
20. PAGE 111 H2216 FOR/AID

B61
SPOONER F.P.,SOUTH AFRICAN PREDICAMENT. FUT ECO/DEV
SOUTH/AFR INDUS POL/PAR RACE/REL INCOME...CHARTS 20 DISCRIM
NEGRO. PAGE 148 H2953 ECO/TAC
POLICY

B61
STARK H.,SOCIAL AND ECONOMIC FRONTIERS IN LATIN L/A+17C
AMERICA (2ND ED.). CUBA FUT CULTURE AGRI INDUS SOCIETY
ECO/TAC PRODUC ATTIT MARXISM...NAT/COMP BIBLIOG T DIPLOM
20. PAGE 149 H2971 ECO/UNDEV

L61
LEVINE R.A.,"THE ANTHROPOLOGY OF CONFLICT." FUT SOCIETY

CULTURE INTELL FAM INT/ORG LG/CO SML/CO ATTIT KNOWL ACT/RES ...METH/CNCPT VAL/FREE 20. PAGE 95 H1905

S61
SCHELLING T.C.,"NUCLEAR STRATEGY IN EUROPE." COM EUR+WWI USSR NAT/G FORCES NUC/PWR DRIVE ORD/FREE PWR...DECISION CONCPT OBS TREND HYPO/EXP 20. PAGE 139 H2784 FUT COERCE ARMS/CONT WAR

B62
BARNETT A.D.,COMMUNIST CHINA IN PERSPECTIVE. CHINA/COM FUT CULTURE ECO/UNDEV TEC/DEV CONTROL 20. PAGE 11 H0222 REV MARXISM TREND PLAN

B62
BAULIN J.,THE ARAB ROLE IN AFRICA. AFR ALGERIA FUT ISLAM MOROCCO UAR COLONIAL NEUTRAL REV...SOC 20 TUNIS BOURGUIBA. PAGE 12 H0240 NAT/LISM DIPLOM NAT/G SECT

B62
BRUMBERG A.,RUSSIA UNDER KHRUSHCHEV. FUT USSR SOCIETY ECO/DEV AGRI PERF/ART WORKER PWR...SOC ANTHOL 20 KHRUSH/N. PAGE 22 H0453 COM MARXISM NAT/G CHIEF

B62
GUENA Y.,HISTORIQUE DE LA COMMUNAUTE. FUT ECO/UNDEV NAT/G PLAN EDU/PROP COLONIAL REGION NAT/LISM ALL/VALS SOVEREIGN...CONCPT OBS CHARTS 20. PAGE 62 H1244 AFR VOL/ASSN FOR/AID FRANCE

B62
HATCH J.,AFRICA TODAY-AND TOMORROW: AN OUTLINE OF BASIC FACTS AND MAJOR PROBLEMS. AFR FUT ISLAM STRATA ECO/UNDEV INT/ORG NAT/G POL/PAR DELIB/GP TOP/EX EDU/PROP LEGIT CHOOSE ATTIT...TIME/SEQ TOT/POP COLD/WAR 20. PAGE 67 H1353 PLAN CONSTN NAT/LISM

B62
LAQUEUR W.,THE FUTURE OF COMMUNIST SOCIETY. CHINA/COM USSR LAW ECO/DEV NAT/G POL/PAR PLAN PROB/SOLV DIPLOM LEAD...POLICY CONCPT IDEA/COMP ANTHOL 20. PAGE 91 H1820 MARXISM COM FUT SOCIETY

B62
MELADY T.,THE WHITE MAN'S FUTURE IN BLACK AFRICA. FUT CULTURE SOCIETY NAT/G POL/PAR PLAN ECO/TAC DOMIN EDU/PROP LEGIT COLONIAL RACE/REL ATTIT DRIVE ALL/VALS...PSY SOC CONCPT TIME/SEQ TOT/POP VAL/FREE 20. PAGE 108 H2167 AFR STRATA ELITES

B62
PHELPS E.S.,THE GOAL OF ECONOMIC GROWTH: SOURCES, COSTS, BENEFITS. USA+45 USSR FINAN TAX CONTROL DEMAND WEALTH...POLICY NAT/COMP ANTHOL BIBLIOG 20. PAGE 125 H2499 ECO/TAC ECO/DEV NAT/G FUT

B62
WOODS H.D.,LABOUR POLICY AND LABOUR ECONOMICS IN CANADA. CANADA FUT NAT/G VOL/ASSN WORKER BARGAIN ECO/TAC PAY CONFER GP/REL 20. PAGE 170 H3409 LABOR POLICY INDUS ECO/DEV

S62
ANSPRENGER F.,"NATIONALISM, COMMUNISM, AND THE UNCOMMITTED NATIONS: AMERICAN PROFILES." FUT ISLAM CULTURE SOCIETY ECO/UNDEV NAT/G POL/PAR PLAN ECO/TAC EDU/PROP COERCE CHOOSE ALL/VALS MARXISM SOCISM...SOC CONCPT BIOG TREND 20. PAGE 7 H0142 AFR COM NAT/LISM

S62
BELL W.,"EQUALITY AND ATTITUDES OF ELITES IN JAMAICA" L/A+17C STRATA PWR WEALTH...SOC QU TREND. PAGE 13 H0266 ELITES FUT SOCIETY CULTURE

S62
CORET A.,"LE STATUT DE L'ILE CHRISTMAS DE L'OCEAN INDIEN." FUT S/ASIA ECO/DEV ECO/UNDEV VOL/ASSN DELIB/GP PLAN...RELATIV OBS TIME/SEQ TREND AUSTRAL 20. PAGE 33 H0667 NAT/G INT/ORG NEW/ZEALND

S62
GUETZKOW H.,"THE POTENTIAL OF CASE STUDY IN ANALYZING INTERNATIONAL CONFLICT." EUR+WWI FUT GERMANY INTELL SOCIETY STRUCT INT/ORG LOC/G NAT/G CONSULT CREATE PLAN CHOOSE ATTIT RIGID/FLEX ...POLICY SAAR 20. PAGE 62 H1246 EDU/PROP METH/CNCPT COERCE FRANCE

S62
IOVTCHOUK M.T.,"ON SOME THEORETICAL PRINCIPLES AND METHODS OF SOCIOLOGICAL INVESTIGATIONS (IN RUSSIAN)." FUT USA+45 STRATA R+D NAT/G POL/PAR TOP/EX ACT/RES PLAN ECO/TAC EDU/PROP ROUTINE ATTIT RIGID/FLEX MARXISM SOCISM...MARXIST METH/CNCPT OBS TREND NAT/COMP GEN/LAWS 20. PAGE 78 H1564 COM ECO/DEV CAP/ISM USSR

S62
KOLARZ W.,"THE IMPACT OF COMMUNISM ON WEST AFRICA." AFR FUT SOCIETY INT/ORG NAT/G CREATE PLAN DOMIN EDU/PROP COERCE NAT/LISM ATTIT RIGID/FLEX SOCISM ...POLICY CONCPT TREND MARX/KARL 20. PAGE 88 H1751 COM POL/PAR COLONIAL

S62
PISTRAK L.,"SOVIET VIEWS ON AFRICA." AFR COM FUT ISLAM USSR INTELL STRUCT KIN POL/PAR PLAN EDU/PROP RIGID/FLEX PWR MARXISM...TIME/SEQ WORK TOT/POP 20. PAGE 126 H2516 NAT/G ATTIT SOCISM

S62
SHATTEN F.,"POLYCENTRISM: AFRICA: NATIONALISM AND COMMUNISM." ASIA COM FUT ISLAM CULTURE SOCIETY ECO/UNDEV NAT/G PLAN DOMIN COLONIAL COERCE CHOOSE RIGID/FLEX ALL/VALS MARXISM...CONCPT TREND 20. PAGE 143 H2852 AFR ATTIT NAT/LISM SOCISM

B63
BARNETT A.D.,COMMUNIST STRATEGIES IN ASIA: A COMPARATIVE ANALYSIS OF GOVERNMENTS AND PARTIES. COM FUT S/ASIA CULTURE SOCIETY STRATA NAT/G DELIB/GP ACT/RES ECO/TAC EDU/PROP COERCE CHOOSE ATTIT RIGID/FLEX ORD/FREE PWR SKILL...SIMUL VAL/FREE 20. PAGE 11 H0223 ASIA POL/PAR DIPLOM USSR

B63
CREMEANS C.,THE ARABS AND THE WORLD: NASSER'S ARAB NATIONALIST POLICY. FUT ISLAM UAR USA+45 SOCIETY STRATA NAT/G POL/PAR PLAN DIPLOM EDU/PROP LEGIT DRIVE ALL/VALS...INT TIME/SEQ CHARTS 20 NASSER/G. PAGE 35 H0700 TOP/EX ATTIT REGION NAT/LISM

B63
GLADE W.P. JR.,THE POLITICAL ECONOMY OF MEXICO. FUT L/A+17C CULTURE SOCIETY AGRI INDUS DELIB/GP ACT/RES ECO/TAC ATTIT HEALTH ORD/FREE...STAT TIME/SEQ TREND MEXIC/AMER TOT/POP VAL/FREE 20. PAGE 57 H1138 FINAN ECO/UNDEV

B63
LARSON A.,A WARLESS WORLD. FUT CULTURE NAT/G VOL/ASSN FORCES CREATE DOMIN PEACE ALL/VALS...HUM STERTYP 20. PAGE 91 H1824 SOCIETY CONCPT ARMS/CONT

B63
NKRUMAH K.,AFRICA MUST UNITE. AFR FUT GHANA CONSTN CULTURE SOCIETY NAT/G POL/PAR DELIB/GP TOP/EX PLAN DOMIN EDU/PROP ATTIT DRIVE...TIME/SEQ CHARTS TOT/POP 20. PAGE 118 H2364 CONCPT GEN/LAWS REGION

B63
ULAM A.B.,THE NEW FACE OF SOVIET TOTALITARIANISM. FUT INTELL NAT/G POL/PAR EX/STRUC TOP/EX DIPLOM ECO/TAC DOMIN EDU/PROP LEGIT COERCE ATTIT RIGID/FLEX...OBS HIST/WRIT TREND TOT/POP VAL/FREE COLD/WAR. PAGE 158 H3150 COM PWR TOTALISM USSR

B63
VIARD R.,LA FIN DE L'EMPIRE COLONIAL FRANCAIS. AFR FUT S/ASIA ECO/UNDEV NAT/G CONSULT PLAN ECO/TAC EDU/PROP REGION NAT/LISM ALL/VALS...CONCPT TIME/SEQ TREND VAL/FREE 20. PAGE 162 H3248 VOL/ASSN COLONIAL FRANCE

B63
WODDIS J.,AFRICA, THE WAY AHEAD. AFR FUT ELITES POL/PAR CAP/ISM DIPLOM DOMIN RACE/REL ATTIT ORD/FREE SOVEREIGN SOCISM 20 PANAF/FREE. PAGE 170 H3394 REV COLONIAL ECO/UNDEV NAT/G

L63
FREUND G.,"ADENAUER AND THE FUTURE OF GERMANY." EUR+WWI FUT GERMANY/W FORCES LEGIT ADMIN ROUTINE ATTIT DRIVE PERSON PWR...POLICY TIME/SEQ TREND VAL/FREE 20 ADENAUER/K. PAGE 53 H1058 NAT/G BIOG DIPLOM GERMANY

L63
MICHAEL F.,"KHRUSHCHEV'S DISLOYAL OPPOSITION: STRUCTURAL CHANGE AND POWER STRUGGLE IN COMMUNIST BLOC." ASIA CHINA/COM FUT NAT/G POL/PAR CONSULT PLAN DOMIN ATTIT...POLICY CONCPT TREND MARX/KARL 20 KHRUSH/N. PAGE 110 H2195 COM STRUCT NAT/LISM USSR

S63
HALPERN A.M.,"THE EMERGENCE OF AN ASIAN COMMUNIST BLOC." ASIA CHINA/COM COM FUT KOREA/N S/ASIA VIETNAM/N STRATA NAT/G DELIB/GP FORCES TOP/EX PLAN BAL/PWR COERCE DETER PWR COLD/WAR WORK 20. PAGE 65 H1295 POL/PAR EDU/PROP DIPLOM

S63
HARRIS R.L.,"COMMUNISM AND ASIA: ILLUSIONS AND MISCONCEPTIONS." ASIA COM FUT S/ASIA ECO/UNDEV AGRI NAT/G POL/PAR EX/STRUC EDU/PROP COERCE ATTIT MARXISM COLD/WAR TOT/POP 20. PAGE 67 H1344 PWR GUERRILLA

S63
LOPEZIBOR J.,"L'EUROPE, FORME DE VIE." CHRIST-17C EUR+WWI FUT MOD/EUR SOCIETY INT/ORG SECT EDU/PROP ATTIT RIGID/FLEX ALL/VALS...POLICY HUM SOC TIME/SEQ TREND GEN/LAWS. PAGE 98 H1966 NAT/G CULTURE

S63
RINTELEN F.,"L'HOMME EUROPEEN." EUR+WWI FUT CULTURE INTELL SECT EDU/PROP ATTIT ALL/VALS...HUM SOC METH/CNCPT TREND GEN/LAWS 20 WORSHIP. PAGE 132 H2631 SOCIETY PERSON

S63
ROUGEMONT D.,"LES NOUVELLES CHANCES DE L'EUROPE." EUR+WWI FUT ECO/DEV INT/ORG NAT/G ACT/RES PLAN TEC/DEV EDU/PROP ADMIN COLONIAL FEDERAL ATTIT PWR SKILL...TREND 20. PAGE 135 H2696 ECO/UNDEV PERCEPT

S63
RUSTOW D.A.,"THE MILITARY IN MIDDLE EASTERN SOCIETY AND POLITICS." FUT ISLAM CONSTN SOCIETY FACE/GP NAT/G POL/PAR PROF/ORG CONSULT DOMIN ADMIN EXEC REGION COERCE NAT/LISM ATTIT DRIVE PERSON ORD/FREE PWR...POLICY CONCPT OBS STERTYP 20. PAGE 136 H2721 FORCES ELITES

S63
SOEMARDJORN S.,"SOME SOCIAL AND CULTURAL IMPLICATIONS OF INDONESIA'S PLANNED AND UNPLANNED DEVELOPMENT." EUR+WWI FUT MOD/EUR S/ASIA CONSTN SOCIETY DELIB/GP ACT/RES PLAN ECO/TAC EDU/PROP COERCE ATTIT ALL/VALS...TIME/SEQ 20. PAGE 146 H2927 ECO/UNDEV CULTURE INDONESIA

B64
HERSKOVITS M.J.,ECONOMIC TRANSITION IN AFRICA. FUT INT/ORG NAT/G WORKER PROB/SOLV TEC/DEV INT/TRADE EQUILIB INCOME...ANTHOL 20. PAGE 70 H1408
AFR ECO/UNDEV PLAN ADMIN

B64
LATOURETTE K.S.,CHINA. ASIA CHINA/COM FUT USSR ECO/UNDEV ECO/TAC WAR 19/20. PAGE 92 H1838
MARXISM NAT/G POLICY DIPLOM

B64
MELADY T.,FACES OF AFRICA. AFR FUT ISLAM NAT/G POL/PAR SCHOOL DELIB/GP PLAN ECO/TAC EDU/PROP ATTIT ALL/VALS...CHARTS TOT/POP VAL/FREE 20. PAGE 108 H2168
ECO/UNDEV TREND NAT/LISM

B64
SANDEE J.,EUROPE'S FUTURE CONSUMPTION. EUR+WWI FUT EDU/PROP...IDEA/COMP NAT/COMP ANTHOL 20 EUROPE. PAGE 137 H2750
MARKET ECO/DEV PREDICT PRICE

B64
WAINHOUSE D.W.,REMNANTS OF EMPIRE: THE UNITED NATIONS AND THE END OF COLONIALISM. FUT PORTUGAL WOR+45 NAT/G CONSULT DOMIN LEGIT ADMIN ROUTINE ATTIT ORD/FREE...POLICY JURID RECORD INT TIME/SEQ UN CMN/WLTH 20. PAGE 164 H3287
INT/ORG TREND COLONIAL

L64
BERELSON B.,"SAMPLE SURVEYS AND POPULATION CONTROL." ASIA FUT ISLAM L/A+17C CULTURE SOCIETY FAM NAT/G CONSULT PLAN EDU/PROP ATTIT DRIVE ALL/VALS...POLICY RELATIV HEAL PSY SOC CONCPT METH/CNCPT OBS OBS/ENVIR TOT/POP. PAGE 15 H0297
BIO/SOC SAMP

S64
ADAMS R.,"POLITICS AND SOCIAL ANTHROPOLOGY IN SPANISH AMERICA." FUT CULTURE SOCIETY NAT/G PROF/ORG EDU/PROP ATTIT RIGID/FLEX ALL/VALS ...POLICY GEOG METH/CNCPT MYTH TREND VAL/FREE 20. PAGE 3 H0065
L/A+17C SOC

S64
GARMARNIKOW M.,"INFLUENCE-BUYING IN WEST AFRICA." COM FUT USSR INTELL NAT/G PLAN TEC/DEV ECO/TAC DOMIN EDU/PROP REGION NAT/LISM ATTIT DRIVE ALL/VALS SOVEREIGN...POLICY PSY SOC CONCPT TREND STERTYP WORK COLD/WAR 20. PAGE 55 H1102
AFR ECO/UNDEV FOR/AID SOCISM

S64
LANGERHANS H.,"NEHRU'S BITTERNESS." FUT INDIA S/ASIA CONSTN CULTURE ECO/UNDEV ECO/TAC DOMIN EDU/PROP ATTIT PERCEPT PERSON...POLICY 20 NEHRU/J. PAGE 91 H1811
ECO/DEV BIOG

S64
LEWIS R.,"OPINION SURVEYING IN KOREA." ASIA FUT KOREA LEGIS EDU/PROP EXEC ALL/VALS...POLICY CONCPT MYTH TESTS CON/ANAL GEN/METH TOT/POP VAL/FREE 20. PAGE 96 H1915
NAT/G QU

S64
SWEARER H.R.,"AFTER KHRUSHCHEV: WHAT NEXT." COM FUT USSR CONSTN ELITES NAT/G POL/PAR CHIEF DELIB/GP LEGIS DOMIN LEAD...RECORD TREND STERTYP GEN/METH 20. PAGE 151 H3016
EX/STRUC PWR

S64
ZARTMAN I.W.,"LES RELATIONS ENTRE LA FRANCE ET L'ALGERIA DEPUIS LES ACCORDS D'EVIAN." EUR+WWI FUT ISLAM CULTURE AGRI EXTR/IND FINAN INDUS POL/PAR DIPLOM ECO/TAC FOR/AID PEACE ATTIT DRIVE ALL/VALS ...TIME/SEQ VAL/FREE 20. PAGE 172 H3450
ECO/UNDEV ALGERIA FRANCE

B65
CALLEO D.P.,EUROPE'S FUTURE: THE GRAND ALTERNATIVES. UK INT/ORG DIPLOM PWR SOVEREIGN ...CONCPT IDEA/COMP NAT/COMP BIBLIOG 20 EEC EUROPE DEGAULLE/C NATO. PAGE 25 H0506
FUT EUR+WWI FEDERAL NAT/LISM

B65
HALPERIN M.H.,COMMUNIST CHINA AND ARMS CONTROL. CHINA/COM FUT USA+45 CULTURE FORCES TEC/DEV ECO/TAC WAR PEACE ORD/FREE MARXISM 20 COLD/WAR. PAGE 64 H1292
ATTIT POLICY ARMS/CONT NUC/PWR

B65
MERKL P.H.,GERMANY: YESTERDAY AND TOMORROW. GERMANY POL/PAR PLAN DIPLOM LEAD FEDERAL 19/20. PAGE 109 H2181
NAT/G FUT

B65
OECD,MEDITERRANEAN REGIONAL PROJECT: TURKEY; EDUCATION AND DEVELOPMENT. FUT TURKEY SOCIETY STRATA FINAN NAT/G PROF/ORG PLAN PROB/SOLV ADMIN COST...STAT CHARTS 20 OECD. PAGE 120 H2399
EDU/PROP ACADEM SCHOOL ECO/UNDEV

B65
OECD,THE MEDITERRANEAN REGIONAL PROJECT: GREECE; EDUCATION AND DEVELOPMENT. FUT GREECE SOCIETY AGRI FINAN NAT/G PROF/ORG WORKER PLAN PROB/SOLV ADMIN DEMAND ATTIT 20 OECD. PAGE 120 H2401
EDU/PROP SCHOOL ACADEM ECO/UNDEV

B65
OECD,THE MEDITERRANEAN REGIONAL PROJECT: SPAIN; EDUCATION AND DEVELOPMENT. FUT SPAIN STRATA FINAN NAT/G WORKER PLAN PROB/SOLV ADMIN COST...POLICY STAT CHARTS 20 OECD. PAGE 120 H2402
ECO/UNDEV EDU/PROP ACADEM SCHOOL

B65
ORG FOR ECO COOP AND DEVEL,THE MEDITERRANEAN REGIONAL PROJECT: AN EXPERIMENT IN PLANNING BY SIX COUNTRIES. FUT GREECE SPAIN TURKEY YUGOSLAVIA SOCIETY FINAN NAT/G PROF/ORG EDU/PROP ADMIN REGION COST...POLICY STAT CHARTS 20 OECD. PAGE 121 H2427
PLAN ECO/UNDEV ACADEM SCHOOL

B65
VERMOT-GAUCHY M.,L'EDUCATION NATIONALE DANS LA FRANCE DE 1975. FRANCE FUT CULTURE ELITES R+D SCHOOL PLAN EDU/PROP EFFICIENCY...POLICY PREDICT CHARTS INDEX 20. PAGE 162 H3245
ACADEM CREATE TREND INTELL

S65
CAIRNS J.C.,"FRANCE, DECEMBER 1965: END OF THE ELECTIVE MONARACHY" EUR+WWI FRANCE FUT CONSTN SOCIETY CHIEF BAL/PWR ATTIT ALL/IDEOS 20 DEGAULLE/C PRESIDENT. PAGE 25 H0505
CHOOSE NAT/G POL/PAR PWR

B66
IOWA STATE U CTR AGRI AND ECO.RESEARCH AND EDUCATION FOR REGIONAL AND AREA DEVELOPMENT. FUT LAW CULTURE R+D LOC/G PLAN KNOWL...POLICY CHARTS ANTHOL 20. PAGE 78 H1565
REGION ACT/RES ECO/TAC INDUS

B66
JOHNSON N.,PARLIAMENT AND ADMINISTRATION: THE ESTIMATES COMMITTEE 1945-65. FUT UK NAT/G EX/STRUC PLAN BUDGET ORD/FREE...T 20 PARLIAMENT HOUSE/CMNS. PAGE 81 H1625
LEGIS ADMIN FINAN DELIB/GP

B66
KAUNDA K.,ZAMBIA: INDEPENDENCE AND BEYOND: THE SPEECHES OF KENNETH KAUNDA. AFR FUT ZAMBIA SOCIETY ECO/UNDEV NAT/G PROB/SOLV ECO/TAC ADMIN RACE/REL SOVEREIGN 20. PAGE 84 H1670
ORD/FREE COLONIAL CONSTN LEAD

B66
THOMPSON J.H.,MODERNIZATION OF THE ARAB WORLD. FUT ISRAEL STRUCT ECO/UNDEV DIPLOM INGP/REL ATTIT ...CENSUS ANTHOL 20 ARABS. PAGE 154 H3082
ADJUST ISLAM PROB/SOLV NAT/COMP

B66
UN ECONOMIC AND SOCIAL COUNCIL,WORLD POPULATION PROSPECTS AS ASSESSED IN 1963. FUT WOR+45 DEATH AGE ...TREND CHARTS UN. PAGE 158 H3157
PREDICT CENSUS GEOG NAT/COMP

L66
KRENZ F.E.,"THE REFUGEE AS A SUBJECT OF INTERNATIONAL LAW." FUT LAW NAT/G CREATE ADJUD ISOLAT STRANGE...RECORD UN. PAGE 88 H1766
INT/LAW DISCRIM NEW/IDEA

S66
ADAMS T.W.,"THE FIRST REPUBLIC OF CYPRUS: A REVIEW OF AN UNWORKABLE CONSTITUTION." CYPRUS FUT PLAN NAT/LISM POPULISM 20. PAGE 3 H0067
CONSTN NAT/G PROB/SOLV

S66
BLANC N.,"SPAIN: LEARNING THROUGH STRUGGLE" SPAIN STRATA STRUCT SECT FORCES PROB/SOLV AGE/Y ATTIT ORD/FREE PWR WEALTH MARXISM SOCISM 19/20 FRANCO/F SUCCESSION. PAGE 18 H0352
NAT/G FUT SOCIALIST TOTALISM

S66
COWAN L.G.,"THE MILITARY AND AFRICAN POLITICS." AFR FUT NAT/G POL/PAR PARTIC REV 20. PAGE 34 H0685
CIVMIL/REL FORCES PWR LEAD

B67
HAWTREY R.,INCOMES AND MONEY. EUR+WWI FUT UK LABOR WORKER INT/TRADE TAX PAY BAL/PAY COST WEALTH 20. PAGE 68 H1363
FINAN NAT/G POLICY ECO/DEV

B67
JOUVENEL B D.E.,THE ART OF CONJECTURE. FUT CONSULT EX/STRUC CHOOSE GOV/REL ALL/VALS. PAGE 82 H1638
PREDICT DELIB/GP PLAN NAT/G

B67
MCCLINTOCK R.,THE MEANING OF LIMITED WAR. FUT WOR+45 NAT/G FORCES GUERRILLA REV...POLICY SAMP/SIZ TREND NAT/COMP 45 COLD/WAR. PAGE 106 H2126
WAR NUC/PWR BAL/PWR DIPLOM

B67
ROSENBLUTH G.,THE CANADIAN ECONOMY AND DISARMAMENT. CANADA FUT ECO/DEV INDUS R+D DELIB/GP DIPLOM ECO/TAC CIVMIL/REL PEACE...POLICY BIBLIOG PACIFIST 20. PAGE 134 H2679
ARMS/CONT STAT PLAN NAT/G

B67
WISEMAN H.V.,BRITAIN AND THE COMMONWEALTH. EUR+WWI FUT UK ECO/DEV POL/PAR TEC/DEV INT/TRADE LEAD ROLE SOVEREIGN...SOC TREND 20 CMN/WLTH. PAGE 169 H3391
INT/ORG DIPLOM NAT/G NAT/COMP

L67
GRAUBARD S.R.,"TOWARD THE YEAR 2000: WORK IN PROGRESS." FUT ACADEM SECT DELIB/GP DIPLOM EDU/PROP AGE/Y PERSON ROLE...PSY ANTHOL. PAGE 60 H1199
PREDICT PROB/SOLV SOCIETY CULTURE

L67
ISRAEL J.,"THE RED GUARDS IN HISTORICAL PERSPECTIVE: CONTINUITY AND CHANGE IN THE CHINESE YOUTH MOVEMENT." CHINA/COM FUT POL/PAR CONTROL REV GP/REL 20. PAGE 79 H1572
AGE/Y LOBBY MARXISM NAT/G

S67
GOODSELL J.N.,"BALAGUER'S DOMINICAN REPUBLIC." DOMIN/REP FUT L/A+17C POL/PAR PROB/SOLV ECO/TAC 20. PAGE 59 H1174
ECO/UNDEV CHIEF POLICY

NAT/G

S67
GRAHAM R.,"BRAZIL'S DILEMMA." BRAZIL FUT L/A+17C NAT/G CHIEF PROB/SOLV ECO/TAC PWR 20. PAGE 60 H1193
ECO/UNDEV CONSTN POL/PAR POLICY

S67
HEBAL J.J.,"APPROACHES TO REGIONAL AND METROPOLITAN GOVERNMENTS IN THE UNITED STATES AND CANADA." CANADA FUT USA+45 MUNIC...TREND 20. PAGE 69 H1380
ADMIN REGION LOC/G NAT/COMP

S67
PERKINS D.H.,"ECONOMIC GROWTH IN CHINA AND THE CULTURAL REVOLUTION(1960APRIL 1967)" CHINA/COM FUT AGRI INDUS PLAN LEAD MARXISM...CHARTS 20 MAO. PAGE 125 H2493
ECO/TAC CULTURE REV ECO/UNDEV

S67
PONOMARYOV B.,"THE OCTOBER REVOLUTION - BEGINNING OF THE EPOCH OF SOCIALISM AND COMMUNISM." COM FUT USSR WOR+45 SOCIETY STRATA CHIEF CREATE DIPLOM ECO/TAC EDU/PROP SOCISM...NAT/COMP 20. PAGE 127 H2542
MARXIST WORKER INT/ORG POLICY

S67
SANCHEZ J.D.,"DESARROLLO ECONOMICO Y FUTURO DE COLOMBIA." L/A+17C AGRI EXTR/IND FINAN INDUS MARKET INT/TRADE CONTROL...STAT TREND COLOMB. PAGE 137 H2748
ECO/UNDEV FUT NAT/G ECO/TAC

S67
WILLIAMS F.R.A.,"FUNDAMENTAL RIGHTS AND THE PROSPECT FOR DEMOCRACY IN NIGERIA." FUT NIGERIA SOCIETY ECO/UNDEV LEGIS ADJUD CHOOSE 20. PAGE 168 H3366
CONSTN LAW ORD/FREE NAT/G

S68
DEUTSCHER I.,"GERMANY AND MARXISM." FUT GERMANY/W NAT/G...MARXIST TREND 20. PAGE 40 H0808
SOCISM ORD/FREE POPULISM POL/PAR

B82
CUNNINGHAM W.,THE GROWTH OF ENGLISH INDUSTRY AND COMMERCE. FUT UK FINAN NAT/G CAP/ISM...POLICY 20 MERCANTLST CHRISTIAN POPE. PAGE 36 H0721
INDUS INT/TRADE SML/CO CONSERVE

FUTURE....SEE FUT

FYFE H. H1084

G

GABLE R.W. H1085

GABON....SEE ALSO AFR

B64
WITHERELL J.W.,OFFICIAL PUBLICATIONS OF FRENCH EQUATORIAL AFRICA, FRENCH CAMEROONS, AND TOGO, 1946-1958 (PAMPHLET). CAMEROON CHAD FRANCE GABON TOGO LAW ECO/UNDEV EXTR/IND INT/TRADE...GEOG HEAL 20. PAGE 169 H3392
BIBLIOG/A AFR NAT/G ADMIN

B66
MATTHEWS R.,AFRICAN POWDER KEG: REVOLT AND DISSENT IN SIX EMERGENT NATIONS. AFR ALGERIA DAHOMEY GABON GHANA MALAWI GAMBLE LEAD PARTIC REV DRIVE...BIOG TREND GOV/COMP 20. PAGE 105 H2098
ELITES ECO/UNDEV TOP/EX CONTROL

B66
WEINSTEIN B.,GABON: NATION-BUILDING ON THE OGOOUE. AFR GABON WOR+45 CULTURE SOCIETY PLAN DIPLOM COLONIAL INGP/REL ANOMIE HABITAT SUPEGO 20. PAGE 166 H3329
ECO/UNDEV GP/REL LEAD NAT/G

GAJENDRAGADKAR P.B. H1086

GALBRAITH J.K. H1087

GALBRAITH, JOHN KENNETH....SEE GALBRTH/JK

GALBRTH/JK....JOHN KENNETH GALBRAITH

GALENSON W. H1088

GALLOWAY G.B. H1089

GALTUNG J. H1090,H1091

GAMARNIKOW M. H1092

GAMBIA....SEE ALSO AFR

B63
WALKER A.A.,OFFICIAL PUBLICATIONS OF SIERRA LEONE AND GAMBIA. GAMBIA SIER/LEONE UK LAW CONSTN LEGIS PLAN BUDGET DIPLOM...SOC SAMP CON/ANAL 20. PAGE 164 H3290
BIBLIOG NAT/G COLONIAL ADMIN

GAMBLE S.D. H1093

GAMBLE....SPECULATION ON AN UNCERTAIN EVENT

B66
MATTHEWS R.,AFRICAN POWDER KEG: REVOLT AND DISSENT IN SIX EMERGENT NATIONS. AFR ALGERIA DAHOMEY GABON GHANA MALAWI GAMBLE LEAD PARTIC REV DRIVE...BIOG TREND GOV/COMP 20. PAGE 105 H2098
ELITES ECO/UNDEV TOP/EX CONTROL

GAMBLING....SEE RISK, GAMBLE

GAME....GAME THEORY AND DECISION THEORY IN MODELS

B55
BAILEY S.K.,RESEARCH FRONTIERS IN POLITICS AND GOVERNMENT. CONSTN LEGIS ADMIN REV CHOOSE...CONCPT IDEA/COMP GAME ANTHOL 20. PAGE 10 H0201
R+D METH NAT/G

B63
DEUTSCH K.W.,THE NERVES OF GOVERNMENT. NAT/G CREATE EDU/PROP CONTROL LEAD PWR...CONCPT GEN/LAWS 20. PAGE 40 H0799
DECISION GAME SIMUL OP/RES

B64
BROWN N.,NUCLEAR WAR* THE IMPENDING STRATEGIC DEADLOCK. USA+45 USSR TEC/DEV BUDGET RISK ARMS/CONT NUC/PWR WEAPON COST BIO/SOC...GEOG IDEA/COMP NAT/COMP GAME NATO WARSAW/P. PAGE 22 H0448
FORCES OP/RES WAR GEN/LAWS

GAMER R.E. H1094

GANDHI/I....MME. INDIRA GANDHI

GANDHI/M....MAHATMA GANDHI

B30
HULL W.I.,INDIA'S POLITICAL CRISIS. INDIA UK INT/ORG LABOR SECT DELIB/GP LEGIS DIPLOM NEUTRAL REGION CROWD GOV/REL MAJORITY ATTIT 20 NEHRU/J GANDHI/M COMMONWLTH. PAGE 75 H1492
ORD/FREE NAT/G COLONIAL NAT/LISM

B53
BROWN D.M.,THE WHITE UMBRELLA: INDIAN POLITICAL THOUGHT FROM MANU TO GANDHI. INDIA LAW NAT/G SECT WRITING NAT/LISM...ANTHOL BIBLIOG 20 HINDU GANDHI/M MANU. PAGE 22 H0442
CONCPT DOMIN CONSERVE

B59
MADHOK B.,POLITICAL TRENDS IN INDIA. INDIA PAKISTAN UK STRATA ECO/UNDEV POL/PAR LEGIS CAP/ISM DIPLOM COLONIAL CHOOSE MARXISM...SOC TREND 20 GANDHI/M NEHRU/J. PAGE 101 H2014
GEOG NAT/G

B60
MC CLELLAN G.S.,INDIA. CHINA/COM INDIA CONSTN ELITES STRATA AGRI POL/PAR FOR/AID ARMS/CONT REV MARXISM...CENSUS BIBLIOG 20 COLD/WAR GANDHI/M NEHRU/J. PAGE 106 H2117
DIPLOM NAT/G SOCIETY ECO/UNDEV

B61
CHAKRABARTI A.,NEHRU: HIS DEMOCRACY AND INDIA. ASIA INDIA UK CONSTN ECO/UNDEV SECT DIPLOM COLONIAL PEACE WEALTH...BIBLIOG 20 CONGRESS NEHRU/J GANDHI/M. PAGE 28 H0570
ORD/FREE STRATA NAT/G CHIEF

GANGAL S.C. H1095

GANGULI B.N. H1096

GANJI M. H1097

GAO....THE EMPIRE OF GAO

GARCEAU O. H1098

GARCIA E. H1099

GARCON M. H1100

GARDINIER D.E. H1101

GARFIELD/J....PRESIDENT JAMES A. GARFIELD

GARIBALD/G....GUISEPPE GARIBALDI

GAMARNIKOW M. H1102

GARNER J.F. H0447

GARTHOFF R.L. H1103

GARY....GARY, INDIANA

GAS/NATURL....GAS, NATURAL

GATT....GENERAL AGREEMENT ON TARIFFS AND TRADE; SEE ALSO VOL/ASSN, INT/ORG

GATZKE H.W. H1104,H1105

GEARY....GEARY ACT

GEERTZ C. H1106,H1107

GEHLEN M.P. H1108

GELLHORN W. H1109

GEN/DYNMCS....GENERAL DYNAMICS CORPORATION

GEN/ELCTRC....GENERAL ELECTRIC CO.

GEN/LAWS....SYSTEMS AND APPROACHES BASED ON SUBSTANTIVE RELATIONS

GEN/METH....SYSTEMS BASED ON METHODOLGY

GEN/MOTORS....GENERAL MOTORS CORPORATION

GENACCOUNT....GENERAL ACCOUNTING OFFICE

GENERAL ACCOUNTING OFFICE....SEE GENACCOUNT

GENERAL AND COMPLETE DISARMAMENT....SEE ARMS/CONT

GENERAL ASSEMBLY....SEE UN+LEGIS

GENERAL DYNAMICS CORPORATION....SEE GEN/DYNMCS

GENERAL ELECTRIC COMPANY....SEE GEN/ELCTRC

GENERAL MOTORS CORPORATION....SEE GEN/MOTORS

GENEVA/CON....GENEVA CONFERENCES (ANY OR ALL)

B66
WEINSTEIN F.B.,VIETNAM'S UNHELD ELECTIONS: THE FAILURE TO CARRY OUT THE 1956 REUNIFICATION ELECTIONS... (MONOGRAPH). VIETNAM/S VIETNAM/N LEGIT CONFER ADJUD WAR PEACE 20 TREATY GENEVA/CON UNIFICA. PAGE 166 H3330
AGREE NAT/G CHOOSE DIPLOM

GENTILE G. H1111

GEOG....DEMOGRAPHY AND GEOGRAPHY

N
ACAD RUMANIAN SCI DOC CTR,RUMANIAN SCIENTIFIC ABSTRACTS: SOCIAL SCIENCES. ROMANIA FINAN HABITAT ...ART/METH GEOG HUM JURID PSY 20. PAGE 3 H0059
BIBLIOG/A CULTURE LING LAW

N
HERSKOVITS M.V.,CULTURAL ANTHROPOLOGY. UNIV SOCIETY STRUCT FAM...AUD/VIS BIBLIOG. PAGE 70 H1410
CULTURE SOC INGP/REL GEOG

N
THE STATESMAN'S YEARBOOK; STATISTICAL AND HISTORICAL ANNUAL OF THE STATES OF THE WORLD. WOR+45 WOR-45 COM/IND FINAN INDUS SECT FORCES TEC/DEV EDU/PROP...GEOG BIBLIOG 19/20. PAGE 1 H0023
NAT/COMP GOV/COMP STAT CONSTN

N
CARIBBEAN COMMISSION,CURRENT CARIBBEAN BIBLIOGRAPHY. FRANCE NETHERLAND UK CULTURE ECO/UNDEV PRESS LEAD ATTIT...GEOG SOC 20. PAGE 26 H0530
BIBLIOG NAT/G L/A+17C DIPLOM

N
CORDIER H.,BIBLIOTECA SINICA. SOCIETY STRUCT SECT DIPLOM COLONIAL...GEOG SOC CON/ANAL. PAGE 33 H0664
BIBLIOG/A NAT/G CULTURE ASIA

N
INTERNATIONAL CENTRE AFRICAN,BULLETIN OF INFORMATION ON THESES AND STUDIES IN PROGRESS OR PROPOSED. LAW CULTURE FINAN INDUS LABOR TEC/DEV EDU/PROP...GEOG SOC NAT/COMP 20. PAGE 78 H1554
BIBLIOG/A ACT/RES ACADEM INTELL

N
US LIBRARY OF CONGRESS,SOUTHERN ASIA ACCESSIONS LIST. BURMA CEYLON INDIA NEPAL PAKISTAN S/ASIA THAILAND AGRI INDUS SCHOOL WORKER...ART/METH GEOG HEAL PHIL/SCI LING 20. PAGE 160 H3201
BIBLIOG/A SOCIETY CULTURE ECO/UNDEV

B01
GRIFFIN A.P.C.,A LIST OF BOOKS ON THE DANISH WEST INDIES (PAMPHLET). L/A+17C WEST/IND CULTURE LOC/G ...GEOG MGT 18/20. PAGE 61 H1214
BIBLIOG/A SOCIETY COLONIAL ADMIN

B01
GRIFFIN A.P.C.,A LIST OF BOOKS ON PORTO RICO. PUERT/RICO CULTURE LOC/G...GEOG MGT 19/20. PAGE 61 H1215
BIBLIOG/A SOCIETY COLONIAL ADMIN

B10
MENDELSSOHN S.,SOUTH AFRICAN BIBLIOGRAPHY (2 VOLS.). SOUTH/AFR EXTR/IND LABOR SECT DIPLOM INT/TRADE COLONIAL RACE/REL DISCRIM...GEOG 20. PAGE 109 H2172
BIBLIOG/A AFR NAT/G NAT/LISM

B10
MENDELSSOHN S.,MENDELSSOHN'S SOUTH AFRICA BIBLIOGRAPHY (VOL. I). SOUTH/AFR RACE/REL...GEOG JURID 19/20. PAGE 109 H2173
BIBLIOG/A CULTURE

B12
BRUNHES J.,LA GEOGRAPHIE HUMAINE: ESSAI DE CLASSIFICATION POSITIVE PRINCIPES ET EXEMPLES (2ND ED.). UNIV SEA AGRI EXTR/IND DRIVE...SOC CHARTS 20. PAGE 23 H0454
GEOG HABITAT CULTURE

B12
CORDIER H.,BIBLIOTHECA INDOSINICA: DICTIONAIRE BIBLIOGRAPHIQUE DES OUVRAGES RELATIFS A LA PENINSULE INDOCHINOISE. BURMA LAOS MALAYSIA S/ASIA THAILAND VIETNAM SECT...LING 20. PAGE 33 H0665
BIBLIOG/A GEOG NAT/G

B13
SIEGFRIED A.,TABLEAU POLITIQUE DE LA FRANCE DE L'OUEST SOUS LA TROISIEME REPUBLIQUE. FRANCE STRATA STRUCT NAT/G POL/PAR PROVS REGION GOV/REL ATTIT PWR ...TREND TIME 19. PAGE 143 H2869
SOC GEOG SOCIETY

B16
CALVERT A.F.,SOUTHWEST AFRICA 1884-1914 (2ND ED.). GERMANY EXTR/IND NAT/G FORCES...GEOG AUD/VIS CHARTS 19/20 RESOURCE/N AFRICA/SW. PAGE 25 H0508
COLONIAL ECO/UNDEV AFR

B18
CVIJIC J.,THE BALKAN PENINSULA. MOD/EUR COERCE ...SOC CHARTS GP/COMP NAT/COMP 20 BALKANS MAPS. PAGE 36 H0729
GEOG HABITAT GOV/COMP CULTURE

N19
SALKEVER L.R.,SUB-SAHARA AFRICA (PAMPHLET). AFR USSR EXTR/IND NAT/G SCHOOL DIPLOM COLONIAL WEALTH ...GEOG CHARTS 16/20. PAGE 137 H2742
ECO/UNDEV TEC/DEV TASK INT/TRADE

B22
HUNTINGTON E.,CIVILIZATION AND CLIMATE (2ND ED.). UNIV WORKER...SOC CHARTS. PAGE 75 H1503
GEOG HABITAT CULTURE

B23
KADEN E.H.,DER POLITISCHE CHARAKTER DER FRANZOSISCHEN KULTURPROPAGANDA AM RHEIN. FRANCE MOD/EUR DOMIN PRESS...GEOG METH/COMP 20. PAGE 82 H1648
EDU/PROP ATTIT DIPLOM NAT/G

B24
WALKER F.D.,AFRICA AND HER PEOPLES. ISLAM STRUCT FAM SECT EDU/PROP INGP/REL RACE/REL HABITAT...GEOG SOC IDEA/COMP WORSHIP 20 NEGRO. PAGE 164 H3292
CULTURE AFR GP/COMP KIN

B26
MCPHEE A.,THE ECONOMIC REVOLUTION IN BRITISH WEST AFRICA. AFR UK CULTURE DIST/IND FINAN INDUS PLAN GP/REL RACE/REL 20 AFRICA/W. PAGE 107 H2148
ECO/UNDEV INT/TRADE COLONIAL GEOG

B27
SMITH E.W.,THE GOLDEN STOOL: SOME ASPECTS OF THE CONFLICT OF CULTURES IN AFRICA. AFR FINAN INDUS SECT INT/TRADE COERCE CHOOSE RACE/REL ATTIT...GEOG LING 20 NEGRO. PAGE 145 H2907
COLONIAL CULTURE GP/REL EDU/PROP

B29
DE REPARAZ G.,GEOGRAFIA Y POLITICA. CHILE SPAIN USSR NAT/G DIPLOM REV MARXISM...POLICY 19/20. PAGE 38 H0768
GEOG MOD/EUR

B29
PRATT I.A.,MODERN EGYPT: A LIST OF REFERENCES TO MATERIAL IN THE NEW YORK PUBLIC LIBRARY. UAR ECO/UNDEV...GEOG JURID SOC LING 20. PAGE 128 H2555
BIBLIOG ISLAM DIPLOM NAT/G

B31
BONAR J.,THEORIES OF POPULATION FROM RALEIGH TO ARTHUR YOUNG. CHRIST-17C MOD/EUR CULTURE SOCIETY R+D CREATE ATTIT PERCEPT RIGID/FLEX...OLD/LIB CONCPT NEW/IDEA TIME/SEQ IDEA/COMP STERTYP GEN/LAWS. PAGE 19 H0372
GEOG BIOG

B31
HENNIG P.,GEOPOLITIK (2ND ED.). CULTURE MUNIC COLONIAL...CENSUS CHARTS 20. PAGE 70 H1398
GEOG HABITAT CREATE NEIGH

B32
BRYCE J.,THE HOLY ROMAN EMPIRE. GERMANY ITALY MOD/EUR CULTURE SOCIETY STRUCT INT/ORG NAT/G SECT DIPLOM DOMIN WAR SUPEGO ALL/VALS SOVEREIGN...GEOG SOC TIME/SEQ CHARTS STERTYP. PAGE 23 H0456
CHRIST-17C NAT/LISM

B36
CULVER D.C.,METHODOLOGY OF SOCIAL SCIENCE RESEARCH: A BIBLIOGRAPHY. LAW CULTURE...CRIMLGY GEOG STAT OBS INT QU HIST/WRIT CHARTS 20. PAGE 36 H0719
BIBLIOG/A METH SOC

B37
UNION OF SOUTH AFRICA,REPORT CONCERNING ADMINISTRATION OF SOUTH WEST AFRICA (6 VOLS.). SOUTH/AFR INDUS PUB/INST FORCES LEGIS BUDGET DIPLOM EDU/PROP ADJUD CT/SYS...GEOG CHARTS 20 AFRICA/SW LEAGUE/NAT. PAGE 158 H3166
NAT/G ADMIN COLONIAL CONSTN

B38
CARVALHO C.M.,GEOGRAPHIA HUMANA; POLITICA E ECONOMICA (3RD ED.). BRAZIL CULTURE AGRI INDUS DIPLOM COLONIAL GP/REL RACE/REL...LING 20 RESOURCE/N. PAGE 27 H0551
GEOG HABITAT

B38
RAWLINSON H.G.,INDIA: A SHORT CULTURAL HISTORY. INDIA LAW STRATA FORCES INT/TRADE ADMIN COLONIAL PERSON...GEOG HUM BIBLIOG WORSHIP 20. PAGE 130 H2598
CULTURE SECT MYTH ART/METH

B39
HILL R.L.,A BIBLIOGRAPHY OF THE ANGLO-EGYPTIAN SUDAN FROM THE EARLIEST TIMES TO 1937. AFR ETHIOPIA SUDAN UAR LAW COM/IND SECT RACE/REL...GEOG HEAL SOC LING 19/20 NEGRO. PAGE 71 H1417
BIBLIOG CULTURE NAT/COMP GP/COMP

B39
KERNER R.J.,NORTHEAST ASIA: A SELECTED BIBLIOGRAPHY (2 VOLS.). KOREA RUSSIA NAT/G DIPLOM...GEOG 19/20 CHINJAP. PAGE 85 H1696
BIBLIOG ASIA SOCIETY CULTURE

B40
BROWN A.D.,PANAMA CANAL AND PANAMA CANAL ZONE: A SELECTED LIST OF REFERENCES. PANAMA NAT/G SCHOOL DIPLOM HEALTH...GEOG SOC 20 CANAL/ZONE. PAGE 22 H0436
BIBLIOG/A ECO/UNDEV

B40
WOLFERS A.,BRITAIN AND FRANCE BETWEEN TWO WORLD WARS. FRANCE UK INT/ORG NAT/G PLAN BARGAIN ECO/TAC AGREE ISOLAT ALL/IDEOS...DECISION GEOG 20 TREATY VERSAILLES INTERVENT. PAGE 170 H3402
DIPLOM WAR POLICY

B41
GRISMER R.,A NEW BIBLIOGRAPHY OF THE LITERATURES OF SPAIN AND SPANISH AMERICA. CHRIST-17C MOD/EUR PRE/AMER SPAIN CULTURE DIPLOM EDU/PROP...ART/METH GEOG HUM PHIL/SCI 20. PAGE 61 H1229
BIBLIOG LAW NAT/G ECO/UNDEV

B41
HAUSHOFER K.,WEHR-GEOPOLITIK. EUR+WWI GERMANY MOD/EUR NAT/G ACT/RES BAL/PWR PWR...STAT TIME/SEQ CHARTS NAZI 20. PAGE 68 H1361
FORCES GEOG WAR

B42
BLANCHARD L.R.,MARTINIQUE: A SELECTED LIST OF REFERENCES (PAMPHLET). WEST/IND AGRI LOC/G SCHOOL ...ART/METH GEOG JURID CHARTS 20. PAGE 18 H0353
BIBLIOG/A SOCIETY CULTURE COLONIAL

B42
CONOVER H.F.,THE NETHERLANDS EAST INDIES: A SELECTED LIST OF REFERENCES. ECO/UNDEV AGRI EXTR/IND LABOR SCHOOL SECT INT/TRADE COLONIAL HEALTH...GEOG 19/20. PAGE 32 H0642
BIBLIOG S/ASIA CULTURE

S42
TISDALE H.,"THE PROCESS OF URBANIZATION" (BMR)" UNIV CULTURE...CENSUS GEN/LAWS. PAGE 155 H3106
MUNIC GEOG CONCPT TEC/DEV

B43
BROWN A.D.,BRITISH POSSESSIONS IN THE CARIBBEAN AREA: A SELECTED LIST OF REFERENCES. UK NAT/G DIPLOM...GEOG 20 CARIBBEAN. PAGE 22 H0437
BIBLIOG COLONIAL ECO/UNDEV L/A+17C

B43
GRIERSON P.,BOOKS ON SOVIET RUSSIA 1917-42: A BIBLIOGRAPHY AND A GUIDE TO READING. USSR CULTURE ELITES NAT/G PLAN DIPLOM REV...GEOG 20. PAGE 61 H1213
BIBLIOG/A COM MARXISM LEAD

B43
JONES C.K.,A BIBLIOGRAPHY OF LATIN AMERICAN BIBLIOGRAPHIES (2ND ED.). CULTURE ALL/VALS...POLICY GEOG HUM SOC LING BIOG TREND 20. PAGE 82 H1629
BIBLIOG/A L/A+17C HIST/WRIT

B44
FULLER G.H.,TURKEY: A SELECTED LIST OF REFERENCES. ISLAM TURKEY CULTURE ECO/UNDEV AGRI DIPLOM NAT/LISM CONSERVE...GEOG HUM INT/LAW SOC 7/20 MAPS. PAGE 54 H1075
BIBLIOG/A ALL/VALS

B44
GYORGY A.,GEOPOLITICS: THE NEW GERMAN SCIENCE. EUR+WWI GERMANY STRATA NAT/G PROVS DOMIN EDU/PROP ATTIT DRIVE FASCISM...GEOG NAZI 20. PAGE 63 H1261
PWR LEGIT WAR

B44
SHELBY C.,LATIN AMERICAN PERIODICALS CURRENTLY RECEIVED IN THE LIBRARY OF CONGRESS AND IN LIBRARY OF DEPARTMENT OF AGRICULTURE. SOCIETY AGRI INDUS LABOR POL/PAR INT/TRADE...GEOG SOC 20. PAGE 143 H2856
BIBLIOG ECO/UNDEV CULTURE L/A+17C

C44
VAN VALKENBURG S.,"ELEMENTS OF POLITICAL GEOGRAPHY." FRANCE COM/IND INDUS NAT/G SECT RACE/REL...LING TREND GEN/LAWS BIBLIOG 20. PAGE 162 H3232
GEOG DIPLOM COLONIAL

B45
HUNTINGTON E.,MAINSPRINGS OF CIVILIZATION. UNIV CULTURE SOCIETY BIO/SOC PERSON KNOWL SKILL...PSY RECORD HIST/WRIT TREND CHARTS TOT/POP. PAGE 75 H1504
SOC GEOG

B45
LASKER B.,ASIA ON THE MOVE. ASIA BURMA S/ASIA THAILAND USSR ECO/UNDEV FAM KIN WAR NAT/LISM ATTIT ...GEOG CENSUS TREND AUSTRAL 20. PAGE 91 H1826
CULTURE RIGID/FLEX

B45
MCBRYDE F.W.,CULTURAL AND HISTORICAL GEOGRAPHY OF SOUTHWEST GUATEMALA. GUATEMALA AGRI KIN PERSON ...GEOG AUD/VIS CHARTS 20. PAGE 106 H2123
HABITAT ISOLAT CULTURE ECO/UNDEV

B45
PERAZA SARAUSA F.,BIBLIOGRAFIAS CUBANAS. CUBA CULTURE ECO/UNDEV AGRI EDU/PROP PRESS CIVMIL/REL ...POLICY GEOG PHIL/SCI BIOG 19/20. PAGE 125 H2489
BIBLIOG/A L/A+17C NAT/G DIPLOM

B45
US LIBRARY OF CONGRESS,NETHERLANDS EAST INDIES. INDONESIA LAW CULTURE AGRI INDUS SCHOOL COLONIAL HEALTH...GEOG JURID SOC 19/20 NETH/IND. PAGE 160 H3205
BIBLIOG/A S/ASIA NAT/G

B45
WOOLBERT R.G.,FOREIGN AFFAIRS BIBLIOGRAPHY, 1932-1942. INT/ORG SECT INT/TRADE COLONIAL RACE/REL NAT/LISM...GEOG INT/LAW GOV/COMP IDEA/COMP 20. PAGE 170 H3410
BIBLIOG/A DIPLOM WAR

N46
HOBBS C.C.,SOUTHEAST ASIA, 1935-45: A SELECTED LIST OF REFERENCE BOOKS (PAMPHLET). S/ASIA AGRI INDUS NAT/G SECT DIPLOM WAR...ART/METH GEOG SOC LING 20. PAGE 72 H1435
BIBLIOG/A CULTURE HABITAT

B47
BEHAR D.,BIBLIOGRAFIA HISPANOAMERICANA. LIBROS ANTIGUOS Y MODERNOS REFERENTES A AMERICA Y ESPANA. PORTUGAL SPAIN CONSTN NAT/G SECT CREATE REV WAR GOV/REL...ART/METH GEOG PHIL/SCI LING 20 ARGEN. PAGE 13 H0260
BIBLIOG L/A+17C CULTURE

B47
GITLOW A.L.,ECONOMICS OF THE MOUNT HAGEN TRIBES, NEW GUINEA. S/ASIA STRUCT AGRI FAM...GEOG MYTH 20 NEW/GUINEA. PAGE 57 H1137
HABITAT ECO/UNDEV CULTURE KIN

B47
ISAAC J.,ECONOMICS OF MIGRATION. MOD/EUR CULTURE STRATA STRUCT NAT/G COLONIAL WEALTH...OLD/LIB TREND TIME 19/20 EUROPE/W MIGRATION. PAGE 78 H1569
HABITAT SOC GEOG

B48
EDUARDO O.D.C.,THE NEGRO IN NORTHERN BRAZIL: A STUDY IN ACCULTURATION. BRAZIL ECO/UNDEV FAM SECT PAY REGION HABITAT CATHISM MYSTISM...GEOG OBS SOC/INTEG WORSHIP 20 NEGRO MARANHAO. PAGE 44 H0890
CULTURE ADJUST GP/REL

B48
FLOREN LOZANO L.,BIBLIOGRAFIA DE LA BIBLIOGRAFIA DOMINICANA. DOMIN/REP NAT/G DIPLOM EDU/PROP CIVMIL/REL...POLICY ART/METH GEOG PHIL/SCI HIST/WRIT 20. PAGE 51 H1027
BIBLIOG/A BIOG L/A+17C CULTURE

B48
FURNIVAL J.,COLONIAL POLICY AND PRACTICE A COMPARATIVE STUDY OF BURMA, AND NETHERLANDS INDIA. BURMA INDONESIA S/ASIA...GEOG OBS GOV/COMP METH/COMP 20. PAGE 54 H1080
COLONIAL NAT/LISM WEALTH SOVEREIGN

B48
TOYNBEE A.J.,CIVILIZATION ON TRIAL. FUT WOR-45 NAT/G CREATE CAP/ISM DIPLOM NUC/PWR CHOOSE MARXISM ...GEOG CONCPT WORSHIP. PAGE 156 H3125
SOCIETY TIME/SEQ NAT/COMP

B48
WHITE C.L.,HUMAN GEOGRAPHY: AN ECOLOGICAL STUDY OF GEOGRAPHY. UNIV SEA CULTURE AGRI EXTR/IND RACE/REL PRODUC...CHARTS HYPO/EXP SIMUL GEN/LAWS T. PAGE 167 H3345
SOC HABITAT GEOG SOCIETY

B48
YAKOBSON S.,FIVE HUNDRED RUSSIAN WORKS FOR COLLEGE LIBRARIES (PAMPHLET). MOD/EUR USSR MARXISM SOCISM ...ART/METH GEOG HUM JURID SOC 13/20. PAGE 171 H3431
BIBLIOG NAT/G CULTURE COM

B49
PELZER K.J.,SELECTED BIBLIOGRAPHY ON THE GEOGRAPHY OF SOUTHEAST ASIA (3 VOLS., 1949-1956). PHILIPPINE CULTURE...SOC 20 MALAYA. PAGE 124 H2486
BIBLIOG S/ASIA GEOG

B49
UNSTEAD J.F.,A WORLD SURVEY FROM THE HUMAN ASPECT. AGRI INDUS...SOC CENSUS CHARTS 20 MAPS MIGRATION. PAGE 159 H3172
CULTURE HABITAT GEOG ATTIT

B49
US DEPARTMENT OF STATE,SOVIET BIBLIOGRAPHY (PAMPHLET). CHINA/COM COM USSR LAW AGRI INT/ORG ECO/TAC EDU/PROP...POLICY GEOG 20. PAGE 159 H3185
BIBLIOG/A MARXISM CULTURE DIPLOM

S49
MACKENZIE R.D.,"ECOLOGY, HUMAN." UNIV CULTURE ECO/DEV ECO/UNDEV ATTIT...POLICY GEOG PSY CONCPT METH/CNCPT CONT/OBS TREND GEN/LAWS. PAGE 100 H2001
SOCIETY BIO/SOC

B50
CONOVER H.F.,INTRODUCTION TO EUROPE: A SELECTIVE GUIDE TO BACKGROUND READING. COM EUR+WWI NAT/G KNOWL...ART/METH GEOG SOC. PAGE 32 H0648
BIBLIOG/A MOD/EUR HIST/WRIT

B50
EMBREE J.F.,BIBLIOGRAPHY OF THE PEOPLES AND CULTURES OF MAINLAND SOUTHEAST ASIA. CAMBODIA LAOS THAILAND VIETNAM LAW...GEOG HUM SOC MYTH LING CHARTS WORSHIP 20. PAGE 46 H0915
BIBLIOG/A CULTURE S/ASIA

B50
HARLEY G.W.,MASKS AS AGENTS OF SOCIAL CONTROL IN NORTHEAST LIBERIA. AFR LIBERIA LAW CULTURE ADJUST CONSEN MORAL...GEOG SOC WORSHIP 20. PAGE 66 H1332
CONTROL ECO/UNDEV SECT

CHIEF

B50
HOBBS C.C.,INDOCHINA, A BIBLIOGRAPHY OF THE LAND AND PEOPLE. VIETNAM CULTURE AGRI INDUS NAT/G SECT ...ART/METH GEOG SOC LING 20. PAGE 72 H1436
BIBLIOG/A S/ASIA COLONIAL ECO/UNDEV

B50
JONES H.D.,KOREA, AN ANNOTATED BIBLIOGRAPHY OF PUBLICATIONS IN WESTERN LANGUAGES. KOREA CULTURE MUNIC SECT FORCES DIPLOM HEALTH WEALTH...ART/METH GEOG SOC LING 20. PAGE 82 H1632
BIBLIOG/A ASIA NAT/G ECO/UNDEV

B50
KANN R.A.,THE MULTINATIONAL EMPIRE (2 VOLS.). AUSTRIA CZECHOSLVK GERMANY HUNGARY CULTURE NAT/G POL/PAR PROVS REGION REV FEDERAL...GEOG TREND CHARTS IDEA/COMP NAT/COMP 19/20. PAGE 83 H1654
NAT/LISM MOD/EUR

C50
STOKES W.S.,"HONDURAS: AN AREA STUDY IN GOVERNMENT." HONDURAS NAT/G POL/PAR COLONIAL CT/SYS ROUTINE CHOOSE REPRESENT...GEOG RECORD BIBLIOG 19/20. PAGE 149 H2988
CONSTN LAW L/A+17C ADMIN

B51
BISSAINTHE M.,DICTIONNAIRE DE BIBLIOGRAPHIE HAITIENNE. HAITI ELITES AGRI LEGIS DIPLOM INT/TRADE WRITING ORD/FREE CATHISM...ART/METH GEOG 19/20 NEGRO TREATY. PAGE 17 H0347
BIBLIOG L/A+17C SOCIETY NAT/G

B51
GHANI A.R.,PAKISTAN: A SELECT BIBLIOGRAPHY. PAKISTAN S/ASIA CULTURE...GEOG 20. PAGE 56 H1120
BIBLIOG AGRI INDUS

B51
INTERNATIONAL AFRICAN INST,ETHNOGRAPHIC SURVEY OF AFRICA: WEST CENTRAL AFRICA (VOLS. I-III, 1951-1953). AFR RHODESIA CULTURE ECO/UNDEV HEREDITY ...GEOG SOC CHARTS BIBLIOG WORSHIP 20 CONGO/LEOP. PAGE 77 H1543
STRUCT KIN INGP/REL HABITAT

C51
BEST H.,"THE SOVIET STATE AND ITS INCEPTION." USSR CULTURE INDUS DIPLOM WEALTH...GEOG SOC BIBLIOG 20. PAGE 16 H0322
COM GEN/METH REV MARXISM

B52
ETTINGHAUSEN R.,SELECTED AND ANNOTATED BIBLIOGRAPHY OF BOOKS AND PERIODICALS IN WESTERN LANGUAGES DEALING WITH NEAR AND MIDDLE EAST. LAW CULTURE SECT ...ART/METH GEOG SOC. PAGE 47 H0944
BIBLIOG/A ISLAM MEDIT-7

B52
FORDE L.D.,HABITAT, ECONOMY AND SOCIETY. AFR L/A+17C S/ASIA STRUCT AGRI INGP/REL...GEOG OBS BIBLIOG 20. PAGE 52 H1037
SOC HABITAT CULTURE ECO/UNDEV

B52
INTERNATIONAL AFRICAN INST,ETHNOGRAPHIC SURVEY OF AFRICA: SOUTHERN AFRICA (VOLS. I-III, 1952-1954). AFR SOUTH/AFR CULTURE ECO/UNDEV GOV/REL HEREDITY ...GEOG SOC CHARTS BIBLIOG WORSHIP 20. PAGE 77 H1544
STRUCT KIN INGP/REL HABITAT

B52
LEBON J.H.C.,AN INTRODUCTION TO HUMAN GEOGRAPHY. CULTURE...GEOG SOC CONCPT CENSUS CHARTS 20 MIGRATION. PAGE 93 H1849
HABITAT GP/REL SOCIETY

B53
PIERCE R.A.,RUSSIAN CENTRAL ASIA, 1867-1917: A SELECTED BIBLIOGRAPHY (PAMPHLET). USSR LAW CULTURE NAT/G EDU/PROP WAR...GEOG SOC 19/20. PAGE 125 H2508
BIBLIOG COLONIAL ADMIN COM

B54
GIRALSO JARAMLLO G.,BIBLIOGRAFIA DE BIBLIOGRAFIAS COLOMBIANAS. L/A+17C ACADEM SECT CREATE EDU/PROP ...ART/METH GEOG LING TREND 20 COLOMB. PAGE 57 H1135
BIBLIOG/A CULTURE PHIL/SCI ECO/UNDEV

B54
CHECKLIST OF ARCHIVES IN THE JAPANESE MINISTRY OF FOREIGN AFFAIRS....GEOG SOC METH 19/20 CHINJAP. PAGE 161 H3219
BIBLIOG/A NAT/G ASIA

B54
WILLIAMSON H.F.,ECONOMIC DEVELOPMENT - PRINCIPLES AND PATTERNS. INDIA KOREA CULTURE ECO/DEV ECO/UNDEV TEC/DEV...CENSUS NAT/COMP 20 CHINJAP MEXIC/AMER RESOURCE/N. PAGE 168 H3369
ECO/TAC GEOG LABOR

B55
INTERNATIONAL AFRICAN INST,ETHNOGRAPHIC SURVEY OF AFRICA: NORTH EASTERN AFRICA (VOLUMES 1-2, 1955-56). AFR ETHIOPIA CULTURE ECO/UNDEV KIN GOV/REL ATTIT HEREDITY...GEOG CHARTS BIBLIOG WORSHIP 20. PAGE 77 H1545
STRUCT ECO/TAC INGP/REL HABITAT

B55
INTERNATIONAL AFRICAN INST,ETHNOGRAPHIC SURVEY OF AFRICA: WESTERN AFRICA: PEOPLES OF THE NIGER-BENUE CONFLUENCE. AFR NIGER CULTURE ECO/UNDEV KIN GOV/REL GP/REL ATTIT HEREDITY...CHARTS BIBLIOG WORSHIP 20. PAGE 77 H1546
STRUCT GEOG HABITAT INGP/REL

B55
NAMIER L.,PERSONALITIES AND POWERS. EUR+WWI MOD/EUR NAT/G POL/PAR TOP/EX EDU/PROP KNOWL...GEOG 17/20. PAGE 115 H2308
TIME/SEQ DIPLOM UK

B55
THOMPSON V.,MINORITY PROBLEMS IN SOUTHEAST ASIA. CAMBODIA CHINA/COM LAOS S/ASIA KIN NAT/G SECT PROB/SOLV EDU/PROP REGION GP/REL RACE/REL MARXISM ...SOC 20 BUDDHISM UN. PAGE 154 H3085
INGP/REL GEOG DIPLOM STRUCT

B55
UN ECONOMIC AND SOCIAL COUNCIL,ANALYTICAL BIBLIOGRAPHY OF INTERNATIONAL MIGRATION STATISTICS, SELECTED COUNTRIES, 1925-1950. STRATA...CLASSIF CENSUS NAT/COMP 20. PAGE 158 H3156
BIBLIOG STAT GEOG HABITAT

B56
BRITISH BORNEO RESEARCH PROJ,BIBLIOGRAPHY OF BRITISH BORNEO (PAMPHLET). UK COM/IND NAT/G EDU/PROP...GEOG 20. PAGE 21 H0421
BIBLIOG/A SOC

B56
SHAPIRO H.L.,MAN, CULTURE, AND SOCIETY. STRUCT FAM SECT GP/REL INGP/REL...ART/METH GEOG PSY LING ANTHOL BIBLIOG. PAGE 142 H2842
CULTURE PERSON SOC

B56
TRAGER F.N.,ANNOTATED BIBLIOGRAPHY OF BURMA. BURMA STRUCT NAT/G...GEOG JURID MGT SOC 20. PAGE 156 H3127
BIBLIOG/A S/ASIA CULTURE SOCIETY

B56
WILBER D.N.,ANNOTATED BIBLIOGRAPHY OF AFGHANISTAN. AFGHANISTN...ART/METH GEOG HUM SOC CON/ANAL 19/20. PAGE 168 H3358
BIBLIOG/A SOCIETY NAT/G ASIA

B56
WOLFF R.L.,THE BALKANS IN OUR TIME. ALBANIA FUT MOD/EUR USSR YUGOSLAVIA CULTURE INT/ORG SECT DIPLOM EDU/PROP COERCE WAR ORD/FREE...CHARTS 4/20 BALKANS COMINFORM. PAGE 170 H3403
GEOG COM

B57
ALEXANDER L.M.,WORLD POLITICAL PATTERNS. NAT/G PROVS CAP/ISM DIPLOM COLONIAL NAT/LISM...POLICY GEOG CHARTS METH/COMP NAT/COMP 20. PAGE 5 H0101
CONTROL METH GOV/COMP

B57
BOUSTEDT O.,REGIONALE STRUKTUR- UND WIRTSCHAFTSFORSCHUNG. WOR+45 WOR-45 MUNIC PROVS STAT. PAGE 19 H0388
GEOG CONCPT NAT/COMP

B57
BYRNES R.F.,BIBLIOGRAPHY OF AMERICAN PUBLICATIONS ON EAST CENTRAL EUROPE, 1945-1957 (VOL. XXII). SECT DIPLOM EDU/PROP RACE/REL...ART/METH GEOG JURID SOC LING 20 JEWS. PAGE 25 H0503
BIBLIOG/A COM MARXISM NAT/G

B57
HIRSCH F.E.,EUROPE TODAY; A BIBLIOGRAPHY (2ND ED.). EUR+WWI MOD/EUR NAT/G WAR 20. PAGE 71 H1424
BIBLIOG/A GEOG DIPLOM

B57
INTERNATIONAL AFRICAN INST,ETHNOGRAPHIC SURVEY OF AFRICA: WESTERN AFRICA: THE BENIN KINGDOM. AFR NIGERIA CULTURE ECO/UNDEV KIN ECO/TAC GOV/REL AGE ATTIT HEREDITY...CHARTS BIBLIOG WORSHIP 20. PAGE 77 H1550
STRUCT INGP/REL GEOG HABITAT

B57
INTERNATIONAL AFRICAN INST,ETHNOGRAPHIC SURVEY OF AFRICA: WESTERN AFRICA: THE WOLOF OF SENEGAMBIA. AFR SENEGAL CULTURE ECO/UNDEV FAM KIN REGION ...CHARTS GP/COMP BIBLIOG WORSHIP 20. PAGE 78 H1551
STRUCT GEOG HABITAT INGP/REL

B57
PIDDINGTON R.,AN INTRODUCTION TO SOCIAL ANTHROPOLOGY (VOL. II). SOCIETY STRUCT FAM INGP/REL ...OBS CHARTS. PAGE 125 H2507
CULTURE SOC TEC/DEV GEOG

S57
SPROUT H.,"ENVIRONMENTAL FACTORS IN THE STUDY OF INTERNATIONAL POLITICS." UNIV SOCIETY ECO/DEV NAT/G DELIB/GP TOP/EX ROUTINE ATTIT PERCEPT...POLICY GEOG CONCPT MYTH TIME/SEQ. PAGE 148 H2957
DECISION GEN/LAWS DIPLOM

B58
BRIGGS L.C.,THE LIVING RACES OF THE SAHARA. STRATA AGRI KIN INT/TRADE HABITAT...GEOG AUD/VIS CHARTS BIBLIOG 20 SAHARA MIGRATION. PAGE 21 H0417
STRUCT SOCIETY SOC CULTURE

B58
HAYCRAFT J.,BABEL IN SPAIN. SPAIN ATTIT...RELATIV 20. PAGE 68 H1367
CULTURE PERSON BIOG GEOG

B58
INDIAN COUNCIL WORLD AFFAIRS,DEFENCE AND SECURITY IN THE INDIAN OCEAN AREA. INDIA S/ASIA CULTURE CONSULT DELIB/GP FORCES PROB/SOLV DIPLOM INT/TRADE 20 CMN/WLTH. PAGE 77 H1531
GEOG HABITAT ECO/UNDEV ORD/FREE

B58
INTERNATIONAL ECONOMIC ASSN,ECONOMICS OF INTERNATIONAL MIGRATION. WOR+45 WOR-45 ECO/UNDEV FINAN NAT/G REGION...NAT/COMP METH 20. PAGE 78 H1556
CENSUS GEOG DIPLOM ECO/TAC

B58
KURL S.,ESTONIA: A SELECTED BIBLIOGRAPHY. USSR ESTONIA LAW INTELL SECT...ART/METH GEOG HUM SOC 20. PAGE 89 H1784
BIBLIOG CULTURE NAT/G

B58
MACRO E.,BIBLIOGRAPHY OF THE ARABIAN PENINSULA (PAMPHLET). KUWAIT SAUDI/ARAB YEMEN COLONIAL...GEOG 19/20. PAGE 101 H2012
BIBLIOG ISLAM CULTURE NAT/G

B58
MASON J.B.,THAILAND BIBLIOGRAPHY. S/ASIA THAILAND CULTURE EDU/PROP ADMIN...GEOG SOC LING 20. PAGE 104 H2087
BIBLIOG/A ECO/UNDEV DIPLOM NAT/G

B58
TILLION G.,ALGERIA: THE REALITIES. ALGERIA FRANCE ISLAM CULTURE STRATA PROB/SOLV DOMIN REV NAT/LISM WEALTH MARXISM...GEOG 20. PAGE 155 H3094
ECO/UNDEV SOC COLONIAL DIPLOM

B58
VON FURER-HAIMEN E.,AN ANTHROPOLOGICAL BIBLIOGRAPHY OF SOUTH ASIA (VOL. I). STRATA STRUCT KIN SECT ACT/RES CREATE HABITAT...GEOG OBS 19/20. PAGE 163 H3267
BIBLIOG/A CULTURE S/ASIA SOC

B58
YUAN TUNG-LI,CHINA IN WESTERN LITERATURE. SECT DIPLOM...ART/METH GEOG JURID SOC BIOG CON/ANAL. PAGE 172 H3441
BIBLIOG ASIA CULTURE HUM

C58
BLANCHARD W.,"THAILAND." THAILAND CULTURE AGRI FINAN INDUS FAM LABOR INT/TRADE ATTIT...GEOG HEAL SOC BIBLIOG 20. PAGE 18 H0354
NAT/G DIPLOM ECO/UNDEV S/ASIA

C58
GINSBURG N.,"MALAYA." MALAYSIA PROB/SOLV REGION NAT/LISM KNOWL WEALTH...GEOG SOC CHARTS BIBLIOG 20. PAGE 57 H1133
COM/IND ECO/UNDEV CULTURE NAT/G

B59
DUNHAM H.W.,SOCIOLOGICAL THEORY AND MENTAL DISORDER. UNIV SOCIETY STRATA HABITAT PERSON...GEOG CHARTS SOC/EXP TIME. PAGE 43 H0864
HEALTH SOC PSY CULTURE

B59
ELDRIDGE H.T.,THE MATERIALS OF DEMOGRAPHY: A SELECTED AND ANNOTATED BIBLIOGRAPHY. R+D DEATH ...SAMP METH/COMP NAT/COMP 20. PAGE 45 H0905
BIBLIOG/A GEOG STAT TREND

B59
GOLDSCHMIDT W.,UNDERSTANDING HUMAN SOCIETY. SOCIETY CREATE ATTIT...GEOG PHIL/SCI CONCPT GP/COMP. PAGE 58 H1159
CULTURE STRUCT TEC/DEV PERSON

B59
HEMMERLE J.,SUDETENDEUTSCHE BIBLIOGRAPHIE 1949-1953. CZECHOSLVK GERMANY SOCIETY STRUCT SECT ...GEOG JURID 20. PAGE 69 H1391
BIBLIOG PROVS GP/REL CULTURE

B59
KITTLER G.D.,EQUATORIAL AFRICA: THE NEW WORLD OF TOMORROW. CENTRL/AFR INDUS KIN SECT CHIEF EDU/PROP CHOOSE HEALTH...GEOG WORSHIP 20. PAGE 87 H1730
RACE/REL AFR ECO/UNDEV CULTURE

B59
MADHOK B.,POLITICAL TRENDS IN INDIA. INDIA PAKISTAN UK STRATA ECO/UNDEV POL/PAR LEGIS CAP/ISM DIPLOM COLONIAL CHOOSE MARXISM...SOC TREND 20 GANDHI/M NEHRU/J. PAGE 101 H2014
GEOG NAT/G

B59
MURDOCK G.P.,AFRICA: ITS PEOPLES AND THEIR CULTURE HISTORY. AFR CULTURE AGRI LOC/G INGP/REL HABITAT ...GEOG SOC LING CHARTS BIBLIOG 20 NEGRO EGYPT/ANC. PAGE 115 H2293
SOCIETY ECO/TAC GP/COMP KIN

B59
PARK R.L.,LEADERSHIP AND POLITICAL INSTITUTIONS IN INDIA. S/ASIA CULTURE ECO/UNDEV LOC/G MUNIC PROVS LEGIS PLAN ADMIN LEAD ORD/FREE WEALTH...GEOG SOC BIOG TOT/POP VAL/FREE 20. PAGE 123 H2468
NAT/G EXEC INDIA

B59
ROCHE J.,LA COLONISATION ALLEMANDE ET LE RIO GRANDE DO SUL. BRAZIL L/A+17C NAT/G PROVS INGP/REL RACE/REL DISCRIM HABITAT...GEOG SOC/INTEG 19/20 MIGRATION. PAGE 133 H2652
ECO/UNDEV GP/REL ATTIT

B60
BRIGGS L.C.,TRIBES OF THE SAHARA. AFR MOROCCO STRATA AGRI GP/REL HEALTH...GEOG SOC MYTH LING BIBLIOG 13/20 ARABS. PAGE 21 H0418
CULTURE HABITAT KIN SELF/OBS

B60
GONZALEZ NAVARRO M.,LA COLONIZACION EN MEXICO, 1877-1910. AGRI NAT/G PLAN PROB/SOLV INCOME ...POLICY JURID CENSUS 19/20 MEXIC/AMER MIGRATION. PAGE 58 H1164
ECO/UNDEV GEOG HABITAT COLONIAL

B60
HALBWACHS M.,POPULATION AND SOCIETY: INTRODUCTION TO SOCIAL MORPHOLOGY (TRANS. BY DUNCAN AND PFAUTZ). CULTURE SOCIETY AGRI INDUS HABITAT...CONCPT 20. PAGE 64 H1281
BIO/SOC GEOG NEIGH GP/COMP

B60
HUGHES C.C.,PEOPLE OF COVE AND WOODLOT; COMMUNITIES FROM THE VIEWPOINT OF SOCIAL PSYCHIATRY. CULTURE FAM PROVS HABITAT...PSY QU SAMP/SIZ CHARTS BIBLIOG 20. PAGE 74 H1489
GEOG SOCIETY STRUCT HEALTH

B60
INTERNATIONAL AFRICAN INST,ETHNOGRAPHIC SURVEY OF AFRICA: WESTERN AFRICA: PEOPLES OF THE MIDDLE NIGER REGION, NORTHERN NIGERIA. AFR NIGER CULTURE ECO/UNDEV KIN NEIGH GOV/REL GP/REL ATTIT HEREDITY ...CHARTS BIBLIOG WORSHIP 20. PAGE 78 H1552
STRUCT GEOG HABITAT INGP/REL

B60
KEPHART C.,RACES OF MAN. GP/REL HABITAT...LING SOC/INTEG 20 MIGRATION MISCEGEN. PAGE 85 H1692
CULTURE RACE/REL HEREDITY GEOG

B60
LEYDER J.,BIBLIOGRAPHIE DE L'ENSEIGNEMENT SUPERIEUR ET DE LA RECHERCHE SCIENTIFIQUE EN AFRIQUE INTERTROPICALE (2 VOLS.). AFR CULTURE ECO/UNDEV AGRI PLAN EDU/PROP ADMIN COLONIAL...GEOG SOC/INTEG 20 NEGRO. PAGE 96 H1918
BIBLIOG/A ACT/RES ACADEM R+D

B60
PANIKKAR K.M.,THE STATE AND THE CITIZEN (2ND ED.). INDIA DOMIN ATTIT SUPEGO ORD/FREE WEALTH...GEOG CONCPT GP/COMP 20. PAGE 123 H2459
TEC/DEV POL/PAR NAT/G EDU/PROP

B60
VON KOENIGSWALD H.,SIE SUCHEN ZUFLUCHT. GERMANY/E NAT/G PLAN ECO/TAC SOCISM...GEOG CENSUS 20 BERLIN. PAGE 164 H3273
GP/REL COERCE DOMIN PERSON

B60
WILLIAMS L.E.,OVERSEAS CHINESE NATIONALISM: THE GENESIS OF THE PAN-CHINESE MOVEMENT IN INDONESIA, 1900-1916. ASIA COM INDONESIA AGRI INT/ORG LOC/G DIPLOM EDU/PROP HABITAT PWR POPULISM...GEOG LING CENSUS 20. PAGE 168 H3367
NAT/LISM GP/REL DECISION NAT/G

S60
COOK R.C.,"THE WORLD'S GREAT CITIES: EVOLUTION OR DEVOLUTION?" WOR+45 WOR-45 ECO/DEV ECO/UNDEV ACT/RES PROB/SOLV...GEOG TREND CHARTS NAT/COMP BIBLIOG 20. PAGE 33 H0658
MUNIC HABITAT PLAN CENSUS

S60
JAFFEE A.J.,"POPULATION TRENDS AND CONTROLS IN UNDERDEVELOPED COUNTRIES." AFR FUT ISLAM L/A+17C S/ASIA CULTURE R+D FAM ACT/RES PLAN EDU/PROP BIO/SOC RIGID/FLEX HEALTH...SOC STAT OBS CHARTS 20. PAGE 79 H1582
ECO/UNDEV GEOG

S60
MAGATHAN W.,"SOME BASES OF WEST GERMAN MILITARY POLICY." EUR+WWI FUT INT/ORG TOP/EX ECO/TAC DOMIN DRIVE ORD/FREE PWR...TRADIT GEOG OBS TREND. PAGE 101 H2015
NAT/G FORCES GERMANY

N60
RHODESIA-NYASA NATL ARCHIVES,A SELECT BIBLIOGRAPHY OF RECENT PUBLICATIONS CONCERNING THE FEDERATION OF RHODESIA AND NYASALAND (PAMPHLET). MALAWI RHODESIA LAW CULTURE STRUCT ECO/UNDEV LEGIS...GEOG 20. PAGE 131 H2620
BIBLIOG ADMIN ORD/FREE NAT/G

B61
APTER D.E.,THE POLITICAL KINGDOM IN UGANDA. UGANDA CULTURE ECO/UNDEV AGRI KIN SECT TOP/EX REGION ATTIT HABITAT CONSERVE...GEOG AUD/VIS 20. PAGE 8 H0153
NAT/LISM POL/PAR COLONIAL ECO/TAC

B61
INDIAN NATIONAL CONGRESS,SOUVENIR, 66TH SESSION. INDIA S/ASIA CONSTN CULTURE LEGIS CREATE TEC/DEV LEAD TASK...GEOG CHARTS 20. PAGE 77 H1533
CONFER PLAN NAT/G POLICY

B61
KEREKES T.,THE ARAB MIDDLE EAST AND MUSLIM AFRICA. ISLAM SOCIETY ECO/UNDEV SECT VOL/ASSN TOP/EX REGION ATTIT PWR...GEOG CONCPT TIME/SEQ GEN/LAWS 20. PAGE 85 H1694
NAT/G TREND NAT/LISM

B61
SCHECHTMAN J.B.,ON WINGS OF EAGLES: THE PLIGHT, EXODUS, AND HOMECOMING OF ORIENTAL JEWRY. ASIA ISLAM ISRAEL VOL/ASSN DIPLOM CONTROL ORD/FREE ...GEOG WORSHIP SOC/INTEG 20 JEWS ARABS MIGRATION. PAGE 139 H2777
CULTURE HABITAT KIN SECT

B61
SCHIEDER T.,DOCUMENTS ON THE EXPULSION OF THE GERMANS FROM EASTERN-CENTRAL-EUROPE (VOL. II/III). COM EUR+WWI GERMANY HUNGARY ROMANIA USSR DIPLOM RACE/REL 20 MIGRATION. PAGE 139 H2785
GEOG CULTURE

B61
SCHNAPPER B.,LA POLITIQUE ET LE COMMERCE FRANCAIS DANS LE GOLFE DE GUINEE DE 1838 A 1871. FRANCE GUINEA UK SEA EXTR/IND NAT/G DELIB/GP LEGIS ADMIN ORD/FREE...POLICY GEOG CENSUS CHARTS BIBLIOG 19. PAGE 139 H2791
COLONIAL INT/TRADE DOMIN AFR

B61
SOUTHALL A.,SOCIAL CHANGE IN MODERN AFRICA. CULTURE STRATA ECO/UNDEV AGRI FAM KIN MUNIC GP/REL INGP/REL MARRIAGE...GEOG ANTHOL 20. PAGE 147 H2940
AFR TREND SOCIETY

SOC

B61
TURNBULL C.M.,THE FOREST PEOPLE. EATING GP/REL INGP/REL RACE/REL ISOLAT HABITAT HEREDITY...GEOG SOC LING DICTIONARY WORSHIP 20 CONGO NEGRO BA/MBUTI. PAGE 157 H3138
AFR CULTURE KIN RECORD

B61
UAR MINISTRY OF CULTURE,A BIBLIOGRAPHICAL LIST OF TUNISIA. ISLAM CULTURE NAT/G EDU/PROP COLONIAL ...GEOG 19/20 TUNIS. PAGE 157 H3146
BIBLIOG DIPLOM SECT

B61
ZIMMERMAN I.,A GUIDE TO CURRENT LATIN AMERICAN PERIODICALS: HUMANITIES AND SOCIAL SCIENCES. LABOR SECT EDU/PROP...GEOG HUM SOC LING STAT NAT/COMP 20. PAGE 173 H3456
BIBLIOG/A DIPLOM L/A+17C PHIL/SCI

L61
EZELLPH,"THE HISPANIC AGRICULTURATION OF THE GILA RIVER PIMAS." FAM TEC/DEV PERS/REL ADJUST...GEOG MYTH CHARTS BIBLIOG WORSHIP 17/20. PAGE 48 H0956
CULTURE SOC AGRI DRIVE

S61
LIEBERSON S.,"THE IMPACT OF RESIDENTIAL SEGREGATION ON ETHNIC ASSIMILATION" (BMR)" CULTURE MUNIC GP/REL RACE/REL DISCRIM...GEOG STAT CON/ANAL CHARTS SOC/INTEG 20 MIGRATION. PAGE 96 H1926
HABITAT ISOLAT NEIGH

S61
TOMASIC D.,"POLITICAL LEADERSHIP IN CONTEMPORARY POLAND." COM EUR+WWI GERMANY NAT/G POL/PAR SECT DELIB/GP PLAN ECO/TAC DOMIN EDU/PROP PWR MARXISM ...MARXIST GEOG MGT CONCPT TIME/SEQ STERTYP 20. PAGE 156 H3111
SOCIETY ROUTINE USSR POLAND

B62
DEBUYST F.,LAS CLASES SOCIALES EN AMERICA LATINA. L/A+17C SOCIETY STRUCT WORKER EDU/PROP RACE/REL ATTIT HABITAT ROLE...GEOG SOC NAT/COMP SOC/INTEG 20. PAGE 39 H0780
STRATA GP/REL WEALTH

B62
GREEN L.P.,DEVELOPMENT IN AFRICA. AFR CENTRL/AFR GHANA RHODESIA SOUTH/AFR AGRI PROC/MFG INT/TRADE DEMAND NAT/LISM PRODUC WEALTH...GEOG METH/CNCPT CHARTS BIBLIOG 20. PAGE 60 H1206
CULTURE ECO/UNDEV GOV/REL TREND

B62
JACKSON W.A.D.,RUSSO-CHINESE BORDERLANDS. ASIA COM USSR NAT/G PROVS EX/STRUC FORCES DOMIN COERCE PEACE ATTIT PWR SOVEREIGN WEALTH...CONCPT TREND CHARTS STERTYP VAL/FREE. PAGE 79 H1576
GEOG DIPLOM RUSSIA

B62
KEESING F.M.,THE ETHNOHISTORY OF NORTHERN LUZON. PHILIPPINE ECO/UNDEV FAM SECT CHIEF REGION GP/REL HABITAT...GEOG LING BIBLIOG WORSHIP 20. PAGE 84 H1680
CULTURE SOC KIN

B62
KENNEDY R.,BIBLIOGRAPHY OF INDONESIAN PEOPLES AND CULTURES (2ND REV. ED.). INDONESIA STRUCT ECO/UNDEV SCHOOL EDU/PROP COLONIAL...GEOG SOC LING NAT/COMP 20. PAGE 85 H1689
BIBLIOG S/ASIA CULTURE KIN

B62
KIDDER F.E.,THESES ON PAN AMERICAN TOPICS. LAW CULTURE NAT/G SECT DIPLOM HEALTH...ART/METH GEOG SOC 13/20. PAGE 86 H1709
BIBLIOG CHRIST-17C L/A+17C SOCIETY

B62
LOWENSTEIN A.K.,BRUTAL MANDATE: A JOURNEY TO SOUTH WEST AFRICA. CULTURE INT/ORG NAT/G DIPLOM...GEOG 20 UN AFRICA/SW. PAGE 99 H1975
AFR POLICY RACE/REL PROB/SOLV

B62
MANNING H.T.,THE REVOLT OF FRENCH CANADA 1800-1835. CANADA UK CULTURE GOV/REL RACE/REL...BIBLIOG 19. PAGE 102 H2039
NAT/LISM COLONIAL GEOG

B62
MEGGITT M.J.,DESERT PEOPLE. ECO/UNDEV KIN CREATE PROB/SOLV CONTROL DRIVE ROLE...GEOG SOC MYTH CHARTS BIBLIOG 20 AUSTRAL. PAGE 108 H2159
ADJUST CULTURE INGP/REL HABITAT

B62
MICHAELY M.,CONCENTRATION IN INTERNATIONAL TRADE. ECO/DEV ECO/UNDEV PRICE INCOME...CHARTS NAT/COMP 20. PAGE 110 H2197
INT/TRADE MARKET FINAN GEOG

B62
PAIKERT G.C.,THE GERMAN EXODUS. EUR+WWI GERMANY/W LAW CULTURE SOCIETY STRUCT INDUS NAT/LISM RESPECT SOVEREIGN...CHARTS BIBLIOG SOC/INTEG 20 MIGRATION. PAGE 122 H2444
INGP/REL STRANGE GEOG GP/REL

B62
SCHECHTMAN J.B.,POSTWAR POPULATION TRANSFERS IN EUROPE: 1945-1955. COM CZECHOSLVK GERMANY POLAND USSR CULTURE SOCIETY PROB/SOLV AGREE NAT/LISM...SOC STAT TREND CHARTS METH/COMP 20 MIGRATION. PAGE 139 H2778
GEOG CENSUS EUR+WWI HABITAT

B62
STARCKE V.,DENMARK IN WORLD HISTORY. DENMARK AGRI KIN WAR...BIBLIOG T 20. PAGE 149 H2970
GEOG CULTURE SOC

B62
UNECA LIBRARY,NEW ACQUISITIONS IN THE UNECA LIBRARY. LAW NAT/G PLAN PROB/SOLV TEC/DEV ADMIN REGION...GEOG SOC 20 UN. PAGE 158 H3161
BIBLIOG AFR ECO/UNDEV INT/ORG

B62
US LIBRARY OF CONGRESS,A LIST OF AMERICAN DOCTORAL DISSERTATIONS ON AFRICA. SOCIETY SECT DIPLOM EDU/PROP ADMIN...GEOG 19/20. PAGE 161 H3212
BIBLIOG AFR ACADEM CULTURE

B62
VALERIANO N.D.,COUNTER-GUERRILLA OPERATIONS: THE PHILLIPINE EXPERIENCE. NAT/G CONSULT ACT/RES PLAN COERCE GUERRILLA ATTIT ORD/FREE PWR SKILL...GEOG NEW/IDEA TIME/SEQ CHARTS 20. PAGE 161 H3221
S/ASIA FORCES PHILIPPINE

B62
VILAKAZI A.,ZULU TRANSFORMATIONS: A STUDY OF THE DYNAMICS OF SOCIAL CHANGE. AFR CULTURE ECO/UNDEV KIN NEIGH SEX...GEOG QU TREND CHARTS BIBLIOG 19/20. PAGE 163 H3254
MARRIAGE SECT SOC EDU/PROP

B62
WHITING K.R.,THE SOVIET UNION TODAY: A CONCISE HANDBOOK. USSR ELITES AGRI INDUS POL/PAR FORCES DIPLOM EDU/PROP LEAD...GEOG TREND 19/20. PAGE 168 H3354
NAT/G ATTIT MARXISM POLICY

B62
YOUNG G.,THE HILL TRIBES OF NORTHERN THAILAND. S/ASIA THAILAND FAM KIN LOC/G GP/REL HABITAT...GEOG LING OBS 20. PAGE 172 H3438
CULTURE STRUCT ECO/UNDEV SECT

S62
MU FU-SHENG,"THE WILTING OF THE HUNDRED FLOWERS: FREE THOUGHT IN CHINA TODAY." ASIA CHINA/COM CULTURE FAM NAT/G EDU/PROP REV TOTALISM ATTIT PERSON RESPECT...GEOG INT UNPLAN/INT COLD/WAR 20. PAGE 114 H2278
INTELL ELITES

S62
PIQUEMAL M.,"LES PROBLEMES DES UNIONS D'ETATS EN AFRIQUE NOIRE." FRANCE SOCIETY INT/ORG NAT/G DELIB/GP PLAN LEGIT ADMIN COLONIAL ROUTINE ATTIT ORD/FREE PWR...GEOG METH/CNCPT 20. PAGE 126 H2515
AFR ECO/UNDEV REGION

S62
SPRINGER H.W.,"FEDERATION IN THE CARIBBEAN: AN ATTEMPT THAT FAILED." L/A+17C ECO/UNDEV INT/ORG POL/PAR PROVS LEGIS CREATE PLAN LEGIT ADMIN FEDERAL ATTIT DRIVE PERSON ORD/FREE PWR...POLICY GEOG PSY CONCPT OBS CARIBBEAN CMN/WLTH 20. PAGE 148 H2955
VOL/ASSN NAT/G REGION

B63
CONFERENCE ABORIGINAL STUDIES,AUSTRALIAN ABORIGINAL STUDIES. ECO/UNDEV INT/TRADE COLONIAL ADJUST HABITAT HEREDITY...GEOG PSY LING SOC/EXP ANTHOL WORSHIP 20 AUSTRAL ABORIGINES. PAGE 32 H0638
SOC SOCIETY CULTURE STRUCT

B63
CONOVER H.F.,AFRICA SOUTH OF THE SAHARA. CULTURE SECT TEC/DEV...ART/METH GEOG SOC. PAGE 33 H0654
BIBLIOG/A AFR CON/ANAL

B63
DRIVER H.E.,ETHNOGRAPHY AND ACCULTURATION OF THE CHICHIMECA-JONAZ OF NORTHEAST MEXICO. ECO/UNDEV AGRI FAM KIN EDU/PROP MARRIAGE HEALTH...GEOG INT CHARTS WORSHIP 18/20 MEXIC/AMER. PAGE 42 H0848
CULTURE HABITAT STRUCT GP/REL

B63
FISCHER-GALATI S.A.,RUMANIA; A BIBLIOGRAPHIC GUIDE (PAMPHLET). ROMANIA INTELL ECO/DEV LABOR SECT WEALTH...GEOG SOC/WK LING 20. PAGE 51 H1012
BIBLIOG/A NAT/G COM LAW

B63
JELAVICH C.,THE BALKANS IN TRANSITION: ESSAYS ON THE DEVELOPMENT OF BALKAN LIFE AND POLITICS SINCE THE EIGHTEENTH CENTURY. COM GREECE TURKEY ECO/UNDEV NAT/G SECT ATTIT...GEOG SOC CONCPT TIME/SEQ ANTHOL 18/20. PAGE 80 H1596
CULTURE RIGID/FLEX

B63
JUNOD V.,HANDBOOK OF AFRICA. AFR ISLAM CONSTN SOCIETY NAT/G POL/PAR...GEOG SOC STAT CHARTS WORK 20. PAGE 82 H1642
ECO/UNDEV REGION

B63
LAMB B.P.,INDIA: A WORLD IN TRANSITION. INDIA ECO/UNDEV SECT EDU/PROP COLONIAL HABITAT ORD/FREE ...GEOG CHARTS BIBLIOG SOC/INTEG 20. PAGE 90 H1799
POL/PAR NAT/G DIPLOM STRATA

B63
LEVIN M.G.,ETHNIC ORIGINS OF THE PEOPLES OF NORTHEASTERN ASIA. CONSTN LEGIS...STAT CENSUS CHARTS 20 TEXAS MAPS. PAGE 95 H1901
HEREDITY HABITAT CULTURE GEOG

B63
O'LEARY T.J.,ETHNOGRAPHIC BIBLIOGRAPHY OF SOUTH AMERICA. SOCIETY KIN...GEOG 19/20 SOUTH/AMER. PAGE 120 H2389
SOC CULTURE L/A+17C BIBLIOG

B63
OTERO L.M.,HONDURAS. HONDURAS SPAIN STRUCT SECT COLONIAL REV WAR ATTIT PWR...GEOG WORSHIP 16/20. PAGE 122 H2432
NAT/G SOCIETY NAT/LISM ECO/UNDEV

B63
PRICE A.G.,THE WESTERN INVASIONS OF THE PACIFIC AND ITS CONTINENTS. ASIA PRE/AMER S/ASIA ECO/UNDEV KIN NAT/G SECT FORCES DOMIN HEALTH...SOC 16/20. PAGE 128 H2560
COLONIAL CULTURE GEOG HABITAT

B63
STUCKI C.W.,AMERICAN DOCTORAL DISSERTATIONS ON ASIA 1933-62 (A PAPER). PREHIST INDUS NAT/G GOV/REL ALL/IDEOS...ART/METH GEOG SOC LING 20. PAGE 150 H3002
BIBLIOG ASIA SOCIETY S/ASIA

B63
UAR MINISTRY OF CULTURE,A BIBLIOGRAPHICAL LIST OF ARABIAN PENINSULA. ISLAM SAUDI/ARAB YEMEN FINAN NAT/G DIPLOM 19/20. PAGE 157 H3147
BIBLIOG GEOG INDUS SECT

B63
WAGLEY C.,INTRODUCTION TO BRAZIL. BRAZIL L/A+17C FAM KIN SCHOOL SECT ATTIT WEALTH...GEOG SOC. PAGE 164 H3286
ECO/UNDEV ELITES HABITAT STRATA

B63
ZARTMAN I.W.,GOVERNMENT AND POLITICS IN NORTHERN AFRICA. AFR ALGERIA ISLAM LIBYA MOROCCO UAR ELITES SOCIETY PLAN ECO/TAC DOMIN EDU/PROP LEGIT ATTIT ...GEOG CONCPT TIME/SEQ 20 TUNIS. PAGE 172 H3448
CULTURE DRIVE NAT/LISM

L63
CORWIN A.F.,"CONTEMPORARY MEXICAN ATTITUDES TOWARD POPULATION, POVERTY, AND PUBLIC OPINION." L/A+17C CULTURE SOCIETY ACT/RES ECO/TAC EDU/PROP PERSON HEALTH KNOWL...GEOG PHIL/SCI STAT OBS INT SAMP MEXIC/AMER VAL/FREE 20. PAGE 34 H0672
ATTIT QU

S63
ROBINSON W.C.,"URBANIZATION AND FERTILITY: THE NON-WESTERN EXPERIENCE (BMR)" DEATH MARRIAGE AGE/C BIO/SOC...STAT CENSUS CON/ANAL CHARTS NAT/COMP 20 THIRD/WRLD. PAGE 133 H2651
GEOG MUNIC FAM ECO/UNDEV

S63
WEISSBERG G.,"MAPS AS EVIDENCE IN INTERNATIONAL BOUNDARY DISPUTES: A REAPPRAISAL." CHINA/COM EUR+WWI INDIA MOD/EUR S/ASIA INT/ORG NAT/G LEGIT PERCEPT...JURID CHARTS 20. PAGE 166 H3331
LAW GEOG SOVEREIGN

B64
BEARDSLEY R.K.,STUDIES ON ECONOMIC LIFE IN JAPAN (OCCASIONAL PAPERS NO. 8). INDUS FAM HABITAT...GEOG GOV/COMP 20 CHINJAP. PAGE 12 H0249
WEALTH PRESS PRODUC INCOME

B64
BROWN N.,NUCLEAR WAR* THE IMPENDING STRATEGIC DEADLOCK. USA+45 USSR TEC/DEV BUDGET RISK ARMS/CONT NUC/PWR WEAPON COST BIO/SOC...GEOG IDEA/COMP NAT/COMP GAME NATO WARSAW/P. PAGE 22 H0448
FORCES OP/RES WAR GEN/LAWS

B64
CULLINGWORTH J.B.,TOWN AND COUNTRY PLANNING IN ENGLAND AND WALES. UK LAW SOCIETY CONSULT ACT/RES ADMIN ROUTINE LEISURE INGP/REL ADJUST PWR...GEOG 20 OPEN/SPACE URBAN/RNWL. PAGE 36 H0718
MUNIC PLAN NAT/G PROB/SOLV

B64
FLORENCE P.S.,ECONOMICS AND SOCIOLOGY OF INDUSTRY; A REALISTIC ANALYSIS OF DEVELOPMENT. ECO/UNDEV LG/CO NAT/G PLAN...GEOG MGT BIBLIOG 20. PAGE 51 H1029
INDUS SOC ADMIN

B64
JOHNSON A.F.,BIBLIOGRAPHY OF GHANA: 1930-1961. GHANA LAW AGRI INDUS NAT/G INT/TRADE EDU/PROP HEALTH...GEOG AUD/VIS CHARTS 20. PAGE 81 H1618
BIBLIOG/A CULTURE SOC

B64
KITCHEN H.,A HANDBOOK OF AFRICAN AFFAIRS. ECO/UNDEV CREATE DIPLOM COLONIAL RACE/REL...ART/METH GEOG CHARTS 20. PAGE 87 H1729
AFR NAT/G INT/ORG FORCES

B64
LEBRUN J.,BIBLIOGRAPHIE DE LA FERTILITE DES SOLS ET ELEMENTS DE SOCIOLOGIE RURALE EN AFRIQUE AU SUD DU SAHARA. AFR PLAN TEC/DEV EFFICIENCY PRODUC...GEOG SOC NAT/COMP 20. PAGE 93 H1850
BIBLIOG/A ECO/UNDEV HABITAT AGRI

B64
MCCALL D.F.,AFRICA IN TIME PERSPECTIVE. AFR EXTR/IND KIN SECT CREATE PERS/REL HABITAT...GEOG METH/CNCPT LING BIBLIOG/A TIME 20. PAGE 106 H2124
HIST/WRIT OBS/ENVIR CULTURE

B64
MORRIS J.,THE PRESENCE OF SPAIN. SPAIN MUNIC NAT/G FORCES ATTIT CATHISM...AUD/VIS 16/20. PAGE 113 H2263
CULTURE. HABITAT SOCIETY GEOG

B64
OECD,DEVELOPMENT ASSISTANCE EFFORTS - POLICIES OF THE MEMBERS. AGRI INDUS BUDGET...GEOG NAT/COMP 20 OECD. PAGE 120 H2398
INT/ORG FOR/AID ECO/UNDEV TEC/DEV

B64
OECD SEMINAR REGIONAL DEV,REGIONAL DEVELOPMENT IN ISRAEL. ISRAEL STRUCT ECO/UNDEV NAT/G REGION...GEOG 20. PAGE 120 H2404
ADMIN PROVS PLAN METH/COMP

B64
PINNICK A.W.,COUNTRY PLANNERS IN ACTION. UK FINAN SERV/IND NAT/G CONSULT DELIB/GP PRICE CONTROL ROUTINE LEISURE AGE/C...GEOG 20 URBAN/RNWL. PAGE 126 H2512
MUNIC PLAN INDUS ATTIT

B64
RUSSET B.M.,WORLD HANDBOOK OF POLITICAL AND SOCIAL INDICATORS. WOR+45 COM/IND ADMIN WEALTH...GEOG 20. PAGE 136 H2719
DIPLOM STAT NAT/G NAT/COMP

B64
VON FURER-HAIMEN E.,AN ANTHROPOLOGICAL BIBLIOGRAPHY OF SOUTH ASIA (VOL. II). STRATA STRUCT KIN SECT ACT/RES CREATE HABITAT...GEOG OBS 20. PAGE 163 H3268
BIBLIOG/A CULTURE S/ASIA SOC

B64
WITHERELL J.W.,OFFICIAL PUBLICATIONS OF FRENCH EQUATORIAL AFRICA, FRENCH CAMEROONS, AND TOGO, 1946-1958 (PAMPHLET). CAMEROON CHAD FRANCE GABON TOGO LAW ECO/UNDEV EXTR/IND INT/TRADE...GEOG HEAL 20. PAGE 169 H3392
BIBLIOG/A AFR NAT/G ADMIN

S64
ADAMS R.,"POLITICS AND SOCIAL ANTHROPOLOGY IN SPANISH AMERICA." FUT CULTURE SOCIETY NAT/G PROF/ORG EDU/PROP ATTIT RIGID/FLEX ALL/VALS ...POLICY GEOG METH/CNCPT MYTH TREND VAL/FREE 20. PAGE 3 H0065
L/A+17C SOC

S64
SMYTHE H.H.,"NEHRU AND INDIAN FOREIGN POLICY." S/ASIA ECO/UNDEV NAT/G POL/PAR CONSULT PLAN DIPLOM NEUTRAL COERCE ATTIT DRIVE PERSON MORAL ORD/FREE RESPECT...GEOG CONCPT TIME/SEQ TREND GEN/LAWS 20 NEHRU/J. PAGE 146 H2922
TOP/EX BIOG INDIA

B65
APPLEMAN P.,THE SILENT EXPLOSION. WOR+45 ECO/DEV ECO/UNDEV PLAN HEALTH ALL/IDEOS CATHISM...POLICY STAT RECORD GP/COMP IDEA/COMP NAT/COMP 20 BIRTH/CON COM/PARTY. PAGE 7 H0148
GEOG CENSUS AGRI BIO/SOC

B65
BLITZ L.F.,THE POLITICS AND ADMINISTRATION OF NIGERIAN GOVERNMENT. NIGER CULTURE LOC/G LEGIS DIPLOM COLONIAL CT/SYS SOVEREIGN...GEOG SOC ANTHOL 20. PAGE 18 H0357
NAT/G GOV/REL POL/PAR

B65
CAMERON W.J.,NEW ZEALAND. NEW/ZEALND S/ASIA DIPLOM INT/TRADE WRITING COLONIAL PARL/PROC...GEOG CMN/WLTH. PAGE 26 H0513
SOCIETY GP/REL STRUCT

B65
CENTRAL GAZETTEERS UNIT,THE GAZETTEER OF INDIA (VOL. I). INDIA SOCIETY STRATA PLAN EDU/PROP NAT/LISM ORD/FREE WEALTH...GEOG LING CHARTS SOC/INTEG 20. PAGE 28 H0568
PRESS CULTURE SECT STRUCT

B65
DOLCI D.,A NEW WORLD IN THE MAKING. GHANA SENEGAL USSR YUGOSLAVIA CULTURE INT/ORG PLAN EDU/PROP GP/REL PEACE MORAL...GEOG SOC 20 COLD/WAR. PAGE 42 H0834
SOCIETY ALL/VALS DRIVE PERSON

B65
EUROPEAN FREE TRADE ASSN,REGIONAL DEVELOPMENT POLICIES IN EFTA. ECO/UNDEV INT/ORG PLAN REGION ...POLICY GEOG EFTA. PAGE 48 H0950
EUR+WWI ECO/DEV NAT/COMP INT/TRADE

B65
GIBBS S.L.,PEOPLES OF AFRICA. AFR INGP/REL HABITAT ...GEOG ANTHOL 20. PAGE 56 H1122
CULTURE AGRI FAM KIN

B65
GODECHOT J.,FRANCE AND THE ATLANTIC REVOLUTION OF THE EIGHTEENTH CENTURY 1770-1799. FRANCE CULTURE SOCIETY...GEOG 18. PAGE 57 H1150
MOD/EUR NAT/G REV ECO/UNDEV

B65
HAUSER P.M.,THE STUDY OF URBANIZATION. S/ASIA ECO/DEV ECO/UNDEV NEIGH ACT/RES GEOG. PAGE 68 H1359
CULTURE MUNIC SOC

B65
HERRICK B.H.,URBAN MIGRATION AND ECONOMIC DEVELOPMENT IN CHILE. CHILE AGRI INDUS LABOR NAT/G CENTRAL PRODUC...STAT SAMP CHARTS BIBLIOG/A 20 MIGRATION. PAGE 70 H1404
HABITAT GEOG MUNIC ECO/UNDEV

B65
HLA MYINT U.,THE ECONOMICS OF THE DEVELOPING COUNTRIES. USA+45 WOR+45 AGRI FINAN NAT/G INT/TRADE ...CLASSIF CENSUS TREND NAT/COMP SIMUL GEN/LAWS. PAGE 71 H1430
ECO/UNDEV FOR/AID GEOG

B65
KUPER H.,URBANIZATION AND MIGRATION IN WEST AFRICA. UPPER/VOLT CULTURE ECO/UNDEV WORKER REGION GOV/REL ...LING ANTHOL SOC/INTEG 20 AFRICA/W OSHOGBO MOSSI MIGRATION. PAGE 89 H1781
AFR HABITAT MUNIC GEOG

B65
LAWRENCE P.,GODS, GHOSTS, AND MEN IN MELANESIA: SOME RELIGIONS OF AUSTRALIAN NEW GUINEA AND THE NEW HEBRIDES. SOCIETY ECO/UNDEV FAM GP/REL INGP/REL HABITAT PERSON...GEOG SOC ANTHOL BIBLIOG WORSHIP 20 NEW/GUINEA. PAGE 92 H1847
MYTH S/ASIA SECT CULTURE

B65
ROTBERG R.I.,A POLITICAL HISTORY OF TROPICAL AFRICA. EX/STRUC DIPLOM INT/TRADE DOMIN ADMIN RACE/REL NAT/LISM PWR SOVEREIGN...GEOG TIME/SEQ BIBLIOG 1/20. PAGE 135 H2692
AFR CULTURE COLONIAL

B65
SAUVAGET J.,INTRODUCTION TO THE HISTORY OF THE MIDDLE EAST (A BIBLIOGRAPHICAL GUIDE). LAW CULTURE GEOG. PAGE 138 H2757
BIBLIOG/A ISLAM GOV/COMP

B65
TILLY C.,MEASURING POLITICAL UPHEAVAL* RESEARCH MONOGRAPH NO. 19. FRANCE INDUS NAT/G FORCES WORKER ...GEOG RECORD EXHIBIT GEN/METH BIBLIOG INDEX. PAGE 155 H3095
CLASSIF QUANT COERCE REV

B65
UPTON A.F.,FINLAND IN CRISIS 1940-1941. NAT/G FORCES DIPLOM COERCE...DECISION GEOG. PAGE 159 H3173
FINLAND GERMANY USSR WAR

B65
WINT G.,ASIA: A HANDBOOK. ASIA COM INDIA USSR CULTURE INTELL NAT/G...GEOG STAT CENSUS NAT/COMP WORSHIP 20 TREATY CHINJAP. PAGE 169 H3387
DIPLOM SOC

B65
WUORINEN J.H.,SCANDINAVIA. DENMARK FINLAND ICELAND NORWAY SWEDEN SOCIETY AGRI INDUS DELIB/GP DIPLOM INT/TRADE NEUTRAL...GEOG CHARTS BIBLIOG TREATY. PAGE 171 H3428
NAT/G POL/PAR TREND POLICY

B66
BROWN R.T.,TRANSPORT AND THE ECONOMIC INTEGRATION OF SOUTH AMERICA. L/A+17C ECO/UNDEV NAT/G OP/RES DIPLOM INT/TRADE REGION WEALTH...ECOMETRIC GEOG STAT LAFTA TIME. PAGE 22 H0449
MARKET DIST/IND SIMUL

B66
CADY J.F.,THAILAND, BURMA, LAOS AND CAMBODIA. FRANCE UK CULTURE NAT/G DOMIN GP/REL RACE/REL HABITAT...GEOG TREND CHINJAP BUDDHISM. PAGE 25 H0504
S/ASIA COLONIAL REGION SECT

B66
COEDES G.,THE MAKING OF SOUTH EAST ASIA. BURMA CAMBODIA LAOS S/ASIA THAILAND VIETNAM REV WAR CIVMIL/REL...GEOG 6/13. PAGE 31 H0614
CULTURE FORCES DOMIN

B66
CROWDER M.,A SHORT HISTORY OF NIGERIA. AFR NIGERIA UK ECO/UNDEV CHIEF INT/TRADE RACE/REL NAT/LISM ORD/FREE...GEOG SOC CHARTS BIBLIOG 14/20. PAGE 36 H0711
COLONIAL NAT/G CULTURE

B66
DARLING M.,APPRENTICE TO POWER INDIA 1904-1908. INDIA LEAD GP/REL PERSON...GEOG 20. PAGE 37 H0742
OBS SOCIETY ADMIN NAT/G

B66
HAMILTON W.B.,A DECADE OF THE COMMONWEALTH, 1955-1964. UK LAW ELITES FINAN FOR/AID CONFER COLONIAL PWR...GEOG CHARTS ANTHOL 20 CMN/WLTH UN. PAGE 65 H1302
INT/ORG INGP/REL DIPLOM NAT/G

B66
HOPKINS J.F.K.,ARABIC PERIODICAL LITERATURE, 1961. ISLAM LAW CULTURE SECT...GEOG HEAL PHIL/SCI PSY SOC 20. PAGE 73 H1466
BIBLIOG/A NAT/LISM TEC/DEV INDUS

B66
KEYES J.G.,A BIBLIOGRAPHY OF WESTERN LANGUAGE PUBLICATIONS CONCERNING NORTH VIETNAM IN THE CORNELL LIBRARY. VIETNAM/N NAT/G FORCES TEC/DEV DIPLOM LEAD RACE/REL...GEOG SOC 20. PAGE 85 H1700
BIBLIOG/A CULTURE ECO/UNDEV S/ASIA

B66
KIRKLAND E.C.,A BIBLIOGRAPHY OF SOUTH ASIAN FOLKLORE. WRITING HABITAT ALL/VALS MYSTISM ...ART/METH GEOG PSY SOC MYTH WORSHIP 13/20. PAGE 86 H1723
BIBLIOG S/ASIA CULTURE CREATE

B66
LAVEN P.,RENAISSANCE ITALY: 1464-1534. ITALY AGRI EXTR/IND FINAN MUNIC INT/TRADE DRIVE...CATH GEOG CHARTS BIBLIOG/A 15. PAGE 92 H1841
CULTURE HUM TEC/DEV KNOWL

B66
MILONE P.D.,URBAN AREAS IN INDONESIA. INDONESIA LABOR NAT/G COLONIAL GP/REL...CENSUS CHARTS 17/20. PAGE 111 H2218
MUNIC GEOG STRUCT SOCIETY

B66
ODEGARD P.H.,POLITICAL POWER AND SOCIAL CHANGE. UNIV NAT/G CREATE ALL/IDEOS...POLICY GEOG SOC CENSUS TREND. PAGE 120 H2394
PWR TEC/DEV IDEA/COMP

B66
SOBEL L.A.,SOUTH VIETNAM: US-COMMUNIST CONFRONTATION IN SOUTHEAST ASIA 1961-65. VIETNAM FOR/AID CROWD DETER REV PEACE...GEOG 20 INTERVENT DIEM COLD/WAR. PAGE 146 H2926
WAR TIME/SEQ FORCES NAT/G

B66
UN ECONOMIC AND SOCIAL COUNCIL,WORLD POPULATION PROSPECTS AS ASSESSED IN 1963. FUT WOR+45 DEATH AGE ...TREND CHARTS UN. PAGE 158 H3157
PREDICT CENSUS GEOG NAT/COMP

B66
US DEPARTMENT OF STATE,RESEARCH ON AFRICA (EXTERNAL RESEARCH LIST NO 5-25). LAW CULTURE ECO/UNDEV POL/PAR DIPLOM EDU/PROP LEAD REGION MARXISM...GEOG LING WORSHIP 20. PAGE 159 H3188
BIBLIOG/A ASIA S/ASIA NAT/G

B66
US DEPARTMENT OF STATE,RESEARCH ON THE MIDDLE EAST (EXTERNAL RESEARCH LIST NO 4-25). GREECE ISRAEL SYRIA UAR YEMEN CULTURE SOCIETY POL/PAR SECT DIPLOM EDU/PROP WAR NAT/LISM...GEOG GOV/COMP 20. PAGE 160 H3190
BIBLIOG/A ISLAM NAT/G REGION

B66
US DEPARTMENT OF STATE,RESEARCH ON THE USSR AND EASTERN EUROPE (EXTERNAL RESEARCH LIST NO 1-25). USSR LAW CULTURE SOCIETY NAT/G TEC/DEV DIPLOM EDU/PROP REGION...GEOG LING. PAGE 160 H3191
BIBLIOG/A EUR+WWI COM MARXISM

B66
US DEPARTMENT OF STATE,RESEARCH ON WESTERN EUROPE, GREAT BRITAIN, AND CANADA (EXTERNAL RESEARCH LIST NO 3-25). CANADA GERMANY/W UK LAW CULTURE NAT/G POL/PAR FORCES EDU/PROP REGION MARXISM...GEOG SOC WORSHIP 20 CMN/WLTH. PAGE 160 H3192
BIBLIOG/A EUR+WWI DIPLOM

B66
US DEPARTMENT OF THE ARMY,COMMUNIST CHINA: A STRATEGIC SURVEY: A BIBLIOGRAPHY (PAMPHLET NO. 20-67). CHINA/COM COM INDIA USSR NAT/G POL/PAR EX/STRUC FORCES NUC/PWR REV ATTIT...POLICY GEOG CHARTS. PAGE 160 H3194
BIBLIOG/A MARXISM S/ASIA DIPLOM

B66
VOGT E.Z.,PEOPLE OF RIMROCK. STRATA STRUCT KIN SECT GP/REL HABITAT ALL/VALS...GEOG INT QU 20 TEXAS NAVAHO MORMON SPAN/AMER ZUNI. PAGE 163 H3260
CULTURE GP/COMP SOC SOCIETY

S66
"FURTHER READING." INDIA LOC/G NAT/G PLAN ADMIN WEALTH...GEOG SOC CONCPT CENSUS 20. PAGE 2 H0049
BIBLIOG ECO/UNDEV TEC/DEV PROVS

S66
DETTER I.,"THE PROBLEM OF UNEQUAL TREATIES." CONSTN NAT/G LEGIS COLONIAL COERCE PWR...GEOG UN TIME TREATY. PAGE 40 H0796
SOVEREIGN DOMIN INT/LAW ECO/UNDEV

S66
KAPIL R.L.,"ON THE CONFLICT POTENTIAL OF INHERITED BOUNDARIES IN AFRICA." MOD/EUR MOROCCO UAR EX/STRUC DIPLOM LEGIT REGION ADJUST...RECORD NAT/COMP GEN/LAWS. PAGE 83 H1658
AFR COLONIAL PREDICT GEOG

S66
TOUVAL S.,"AFRICA'S FRONTIERS* REACTIONS TO A COLONIAL LEGACY." L/A+17C CONFER ADJUD COLONIAL APPORT CONSEN NAT/LISM RESPECT...RECORD NAT/COMP. PAGE 156 H3120
AFR GEOG SOVEREIGN WAR

N66
HISPANIC LUSO-BRAZILIAN COUN,LATIN AMERICA; AN INTRODUCTION TO MODERN BOOKS IN ENGLISH CONCERNING THE COUNTRIES OF LATIN AMERICA (2ND ED., PAMPH). CULTURE GOV/REL GEOG. PAGE 71 H1425
BIBLIOG/A ECO/UNDEV NAT/G L/A+17C

B67
ALBA V.,THE MEXICANS; THE MAKING OF A NATION. SOCIETY ECO/UNDEV AGRI INDUS SECT STRANGE ATTIT ...GEOG 20 MEXIC/AMER. PAGE 4 H0091
CONSTN NAT/G CULTURE ANOMIE

B67
ALLWORTH E.,CENTRAL ASIA: A CENTURY OF RUSSIAN RULE. USSR INTELL SOCIETY AGRI INDUS COLONIAL REV WAR NAT/LISM...ART/METH GEOG LING 19/20. PAGE 5 H0108
ASIA CULTURE NAT/G

B67
ARIKPO O.,THE DEVELOPMENT OF MODERN NIGERIA. AFR NIGERIA SOCIETY ECO/UNDEV KIN ADMIN FEDERAL NAT/LISM ORD/FREE WEALTH...POLICY GEOG BIBLIOG 19/20. PAGE 8 H0163
NAT/G CULTURE CONSTN COLONIAL

B67
BAIN C.A.,VIETNAM: THE ROOTS OF CONFLICT. FRANCE S/ASIA USSR VIETNAM POL/PAR SECT FORCES COLONIAL NAT/LISM PEACE ORD/FREE MARXISM...GEOG CHARTS 4/20. PAGE 10 H0202
NAT/G WAR CULTURE

B67
CHANDRASEKHAR S.,ASIA'S POPULATION PROBLEMS. ASIA ECO/UNDEV PLAN AGE/C...OBS CHARTS BIBLIOG 18/20 AUSTRAL. PAGE 29 H0575
PROB/SOLV NAT/COMP GEOG TREND

B67
COLLINS R.O.,EGYPT AND THE SUDAN. COM FRANCE ISLAM SUDAN UAR UK SOCIETY NAT/G COLONIAL NAT/LISM...GEOG SOC LING TREND SOC/INTEG 7/20 SUEZ. PAGE 32 H0635
AGRI CULTURE ECO/UNDEV

B67
FISHER M.,PROVINCES AND PROVINCIAL CAPITALS OF THE WORLD. WOR+45 PROVS REGION. PAGE 51 H1014
GEOG NAT/G NAT/COMP STAT

B67
PENDLE G.,PARAGUAY: A RIVERSIDE NATION (3RD ED.). PARAGUAY CHIEF ISOLAT...HUM CHARTS BIBLIOG 16/20. PAGE 124 H2487
CULTURE GEOG ECO/UNDEV

B67
PIKE F.B.,FREEDOM AND REFORM IN LATIN AMERICA. L/A+17C
BRAZIL URUGUAY CONSTN CULTURE SECT DIPLOM EDU/PROP ORD/FREE
PARTIC DRIVE ALL/VALS CATHISM...GEOG ANTHOL BIBLIOG ECO/UNDEV
REFORMERS BOLIV. PAGE 126 H2511 REV

B67
ROWLAND J.,A HISTORY OF SINO-INDIAN RELATIONS; DIPLOM
HOSTILE CO-EXISTENCE. ASIA CHINA/COM INDIA NAT/G CENSUS
NUC/PWR PWR WEALTH...GEOG BIBLIOG 13/20 COLD/WAR. IDEA/COMP
PAGE 135 H2704

B67
THOMAN R.S.,GEOGRAPHY OF INTERNATIONAL TRADE. INT/TRADE
WOR+45 ECO/DEV ECO/UNDEV INT/ORG LG/CO PLAN BAL/PAY GEOG
...STAT CHARTS NAT/COMP 20. PAGE 154 H3075 ECO/TAC
DIPLOM

L67
HOSHII I.,"JAPAN'S STAKE IN ASIA." ASIA S/ASIA DIPLOM
CAP/ISM ECO/TAC ROLE...GEOG 20 CHINJAP. PAGE 74 REGION
H1477 NAT/G
INT/ORG

L67
RUTH J.M.,"THE ADMINISTRATION OF WATER RESOURCES IN EFFICIENCY
GUATEMALA." GUATEMALA L/A+17C DIST/IND LOC/G NAT/G ECO/UNDEV
EX/STRUC ADMIN GOV/REL DEMAND EQUILIB WEALTH...GEOG PLAN
MGT 20. PAGE 136 H2723 ACT/RES

S67
"PROTEST AGAINST SOVIET INDUSTRIALIZATION ILLS IN INDUS
LITHUANIA* A MEMORANDUM." USSR LITHUANIA NAT/G COLONIAL
PROVS COST GEOG. PAGE 2 H0050 NAT/LISM
PLAN

S67
ALPANDER G.G.,"ENTREPRENEURS AND PRIVATE ENTERPRISE ECO/UNDEV
IN TURKEY." TURKEY INDUS PROC/MFG EDU/PROP ATTIT LG/CO
DRIVE WEALTH...GEOG MGT SOC STAT TREND CHARTS 20. NAT/G
PAGE 6 H0114 POLICY

S67
GREGORY R.,"THE MINISTER'S LINE: OR, THE M4 COMES DECISION
TO BERKSHIRE. PART I." UK CONSTN DIST/IND LEGIS CONSTRUC
TOP/EX PLAN ADJUD...GEOG 20. PAGE 60 H1210 NAT/G
DELIB/GP

S67
KRISTOF L.K.D.,"THE STATE-IDEA, THE NATIONAL IDEA GEOG
AND THE IMAGE OF THE FATHERLAND." CONSTN CULTURE CONCPT
INTELL SOCIETY WORKER TASK DRIVE HABITAT...MYTH NAT/G
GOV/COMP IDEA/COMP. PAGE 89 H1769 PERCEPT

S67
THEROUX P.,"HATING THE ASIANS." TANZANIA UGANDA AFR
CONSTN INDUS NAT/G POL/PAR WORKER ECO/TAC HABITAT RACE/REL
LOVE...POLICY GEOG 20 MIGRATION. PAGE 154 H3069 SOVEREIGN
ATTIT

S68
LAVRIN J.,"THE TWO WORLDS." RUSSIA USSR SOCIETY NAT/COMP
STRUCT NAT/G DIPLOM ATTIT PERSON MARXISM...GEOG SOC NAT/LISM
IDEA/COMP PERS/COMP 18/20. PAGE 92 H1842 CULTURE

B82
RATZEL F.,ANTHROPO-GEOGRAPHIE. SEA AGRI NEIGH. GEOG
PAGE 130 H2595 CULTURE
HABITAT

B89
ASHBEE H.S.,A BIBLIOGRAPHY OF TUNISIA FROM THE BIBLIOG
EARLIEST TIMES TO THE END OF 1888. AGRI ADMIN COLONIAL
...GEOG TUNIS. PAGE 8 H0171 CULTURE
NAT/G

C89
PLAYFAIR R.L.,"A BIBLIOGRAPHY OF ALGERIA." ALGERIA BIBLIOG/A
CULTURE ECO/UNDEV DIST/IND EXTR/IND FINAN SECT ISLAM
CRIME 16/19. PAGE 126 H2525 GEOG

C93
PLAYFAIR R.L.,"A BIBLIOGRAPHY OF MOROCCO." MOROCCO BIBLIOG
CULTURE AGRI FORCES DIPLOM WAR HEALTH...GEOG JURID ISLAM
SOC CHARTS. PAGE 126 H2526 MEDIT-7

B99
RIPLEY W.Z.,A SELECTED BIBLIOGRAPHY OF THE BIBLIOG/A
ANTHROPOLOGY AND ETHNOLOGY OF EUROPE. SOCIETY MOD/EUR
STRATA STRUCT KIN SECT VOL/ASSN GP/REL INGP/REL SOC
HABITAT...GEOG 19. PAGE 132 H2632 CULTURE

GEOGRAPHY....SEE GEOG

GEOPOLITIC....GEOPOLITICS

GEOPOLITICS....SEE GEOG+POL, GEOPOLITIC

GEORGE M. H1113

GEORGE/DL....DAVID LLOYD GEORGE

GEORGE/III....GEORGE THE THIRD OF ENGLAND

GEORGIA....GEORGIA

GER/CONFED....GERMAN CONFEDERATION

GERARD-LIBOIS J. H1114

GERMAN CONFEDERATION....SEE GER/CONFED

GERMAN/AM....GERMAN-AMERICANS

GERMANS/PA....GERMANS IN PENNSYLVANIA

B57
REAMAN G.E.,THE TRAIL OF THE BLACK WALNUT. CANADA STRANGE
AGRI COLONIAL...CHARTS BIBLIOG 18 GERMANS/PA. SECT
PAGE 130 H2604 CULTURE

GERMANY....GERMANY IN GENERAL; SEE ALSO APPROPRIATE TIME/
SPACE/CULTURE INDEX

B
DEUTSCHE BIBLIOTH FRANKF A M,DEUTSCHE BIBLIOG
BIBLIOGRAPHIE. EUR+WWI GERMANY ECO/DEV FORCES LAW
DIPLOM LEAD...POLICY PHIL/SCI SOC 20. PAGE 40 H0802 ADMIN
NAT/G

N
INTERNATIONAL BIBLIOGRAPHIE DER DEUTSCHEN BIBLIOG/A
ZEITSCHRIFTENLITERATUR. EUR+WWI GERMANY MOD/EUR NAT/G
ECO/DEV POL/PAR LEAD WAR NAT/LISM ATTIT...EPIST PERSON
PHIL/SCI 19/20. PAGE 1 H0004 CULTURE

N
NEUE POLITISCHE LITERATUR. AFR ASIA EUR+WWI GERMANY BIBLIOG
RUSSIA SOCIETY ECO/DEV ECO/UNDEV PLAN PROB/SOLV DIPLOM
LEAD MARXISM...PHIL/SCI CONCPT 20. PAGE 1 H0008 COM
NAT/G

N
DEUTSCHE BUCHEREI,DEUTSCHE NATIONALBIBLIOGRAPHIE. BIBLIOG
GERMANY ECO/DEV DIPLOM AGE/Y ATTIT...PHIL/SCI SOC NAT/G
20. PAGE 40 H0803 LEAD
POLICY

N
DEUTSCHE BUCHEREI,JAHRESVERZEICHNIS DES DEUTSCHEN BIBLIOG
SCHRIFTUMS. AUSTRIA EUR+WWI GERMANY SWITZERLND LAW WRITING
LOC/G DIPLOM ADMIN...MGT SOC 19/20. PAGE 40 H0804 NAT/G

N
DEUTSCHE BUCHEREI,DEUTSCHES BUCHERVERZEICHNIS. BIBLIOG
GERMANY LAW CULTURE POL/PAR ADMIN LEAD ATTIT PERSON NAT/G
...SOC 20. PAGE 40 H0805 DIPLOM
ECO/DEV

B00
BENEDETTI V.,STUDIES IN DIPLOMACY. BELGIUM FRANCE PWR
GERMANY MOD/EUR CONSTN NAT/G CONSULT TOP/EX DOMIN GEN/LAWS
EDU/PROP COERCE ATTIT...CONCPT INT BIOG TREND 19. DIPLOM
PAGE 14 H0276

B00
MOCKLER-FERRYMAN A.,BRITISH WEST AFRICA. FRANCE AFR
GERMANY NIGER SIER/LEONE UK CULTURE DIPLOM WAR COLONIAL
RACE/REL PRODUC PROFIT WEALTH...POLICY PREDICT 19. INT/TRADE
PAGE 112 H2232 CAP/ISM

B02
JELLINEK G.,LA DECLARATION DES DROITS DE L'HOMME ET ORD/FREE
DU CITOYEN (1895) (TRANSLATED FROM GERMAN BY G. CONCPT
FARDIS). FRANCE GERMANY USA-45 NAT/G SECT LEGIS 18. REV
PAGE 80 H1598

B08
NIRRNHEIM O.,DAS ERSTE JAHR DES MINISTERIUMS CHIEF
BISMARCK UND DIE OEFFENTLICHE MEINUNG (HEIDELBERGER PRESS
ABHANDLUNGEN. 20. HEFT). GERMANY MOD/EUR LEGIS NAT/G
DIPLOM EDU/PROP INGP/REL...BIOG GOV/COMP IDEA/COMP ATTIT
BIBLIOG 19 BISMARCK/O. PAGE 118 H2363

C09
SCHAPIRO J.S.,"SOCIAL REFORM AND THE REFORMATION." ORD/FREE
CHRIST-17C GERMANY LAW CONSTN LG/CO NAT/G WORKER SECT
PROB/SOLV CT/SYS REV...BIBLIOG 16. PAGE 138 H2770 ECO/TAC
BIOG

B12
HEINSIUS W.,ALLGEMEINES BUCHER-LEXICON ODER BIBLIOG
VOLLSTANDIGES ALPHABETISCHES VERZEICHNIS ALLER VON POLICY
1700 BIS ZU ENDE...(1892). GERMANY PERF/ART...HUM ATTIT
SOC 18/19. PAGE 69 H1387 NAT/G

B13
DIE REKLAME IHRE KUNST UND WISSENSCHAFT. GERMANY EDU/PROP
POLAND SWITZERLND USA+45 TEC/DEV CAP/ISM DEMAND MARKET
...ART/METH EXHIBIT METH/COMP ANTHOL 20. PAGE 135 NAT/COMP
H2707 ATTIT

B14
BERHARDI F.,GERMANY AND THE NEXT WAR. MOD/EUR NAT/G DRIVE
SCHOOL FORCES ACT/RES DOMIN EDU/PROP SUPEGO PWR COERCE
...TIME/SEQ STERTYP TOT/POP 20 WWI. PAGE 15 H0304 WAR
GERMANY

B15
VEBLEN T.,IMPERIAL GERMANY AND THE INDUSTRIAL ECO/DEV
REVOLUTION. GERMANY MOD/EUR UK USA-45 NAT/G TEC/DEV INDUS
CAP/ISM...MAJORIT NAT/COMP 19/20 CHINJAP. PAGE 162 TECHNIC
H3236 BAL/PWR

B16
CALVERT A.F.,SOUTHWEST AFRICA 1884-1914 (2ND ED.). COLONIAL
GERMANY EXTR/IND NAT/G FORCES...GEOG AUD/VIS CHARTS ECO/UNDEV
19/20 RESOURCE/N AFRICA/SW. PAGE 25 H0508 AFR

B16
TREITSCHKE H.,POLITICS. UNIV SOCIETY STRATA NAT/G EXEC
EX/STRUC LEGIS DOMIN EDU/PROP ATTIT PWR RESPECT ELITES
...CONCPT TIME/SEQ GEN/LAWS TOT/POP 20. PAGE 157 GERMANY
H3129

B18
WILSON W.,THE STATE: ELEMENTS OF HISTORICAL AND PRACTICAL POLITICS. FRANCE GERMANY ITALY UK USSR CONSTN EX/STRUC LEGIS CT/SYS WAR PWR...POLICY GOV/COMP 20. PAGE 169 H3385
NAT/G JURID CONCPT NAT/COMP

N19
WEBB L.C.,CHURCH AND STATE IN ITALY: 1947-1957 (PAMPHLET). GERMANY ITALY CONSTN POL/PAR AGREE CONTROL PARTIC CHOOSE ATTIT ORD/FREE FASCISM MARXISM 20 CHURCH/STA MARITAIN/J SALO. PAGE 166 H3316
SECT CATHISM NAT/G GP/REL

C20
BLACHLY F.F.,"THE GOVERNMENT AND ADMINISTRATION OF GERMANY." GERMANY CONSTN LOC/G PROVS DELIB/GP EX/STRUC FORCES LEGIS TOP/EX CT/SYS...BIBLIOG/A 19/20. PAGE 17 H0348
NAT/G GOV/REL ADMIN PHIL/SCI

B21
BERGSTRASSER L.,GESCHICHTE DER POLITISCHEN PARTEIEN. GERMANY MOD/EUR NAT/G PRESS PWR ...TIME/SEQ 17/20. PAGE 15 H0303
POL/PAR LAISSEZ CONSERVE

B22
FICHTE J.G.,ADDRESSES TO THE GERMAN NATION. GERMANY PRUSSIA ELITES NAT/G SECT CREATE INT/TRADE HEREDITY ...ART/METH LING 19 FRANK/PARL. PAGE 50 H0989
NAT/LISM CULTURE EDU/PROP REGION

B23
FINER H.,REPRESENTATIVE GOVERNMENT AND A PARLIAMENT OF INDUSTRY. A STUDY OF THE GERMAN FEDERAL ECONOMIC COUNCIL. GERMANY UK CONSTN INDUS PARL/PROC ...NAT/COMP 20. PAGE 50 H1002
DELIB/GP ECO/TAC WAR REV

B27
ENGELS F.,THE PEASANT WAR IN GERMANY (1850). GERMANY MOD/EUR AGRI WORKER LEAD COERCE INGP/REL ...TREND 16/19. PAGE 46 H0924
WAR STRATA REV MARXIST

B29
LEITZ F.,DIE PUBLIZITAT DER AKTIENGESELLSCHAFT. BELGIUM FRANCE GERMANY UK FINAN PRESS GP/REL PROFIT KNOWL 20. PAGE 94 H1872
LG/CO JURID ECO/TAC NAT/COMP

B31
LORWIN L.L.,ADVISORY ECONOMIC COUNCILS. EUR+WWI FRANCE GERMANY PROB/SOLV INGP/REL...CLASSIF GP/COMP. PAGE 99 H1968
CONSULT DELIB/GP ECO/TAC NAT/G

B32
BRYCE J.,THE HOLY ROMAN EMPIRE. GERMANY ITALY MOD/EUR CULTURE SOCIETY STRUCT INT/ORG NAT/G SECT DIPLOM DOMIN WAR SUPEGO ALL/VALS SOVEREIGN...GEOG SOC TIME/SEQ CHARTS STERTYP. PAGE 23 H0456
CHRIST-17C NAT/LISM

B33
DAHLIN E.,FRENCH AND GERMAN PUBLIC OPINION ON DECLARED WAR AIMS 1914-1918. BELGIUM FRANCE GERMANY NAT/G POL/PAR DIPLOM COERCE REV WAR PEACE 20 WWI WILSON/W. PAGE 37 H0733
ATTIT EDU/PROP DOMIN NAT/COMP

B33
ENSOR R.C.K.,COURTS AND JUDGES IN FRANCE, GERMANY, AND ENGLAND. FRANCE GERMANY UK LAW PROB/SOLV ADMIN ROUTINE CRIME ROLE...METH/COMP 20 CIVIL/LAW. PAGE 46 H0930
CT/SYS EX/STRUC ADJUD NAT/COMP

B34
LOVELL R.I.,THE STRUGGLE FOR SOUTH AFRICA, 1875-1899. GERMANY RHODESIA SOUTH/AFR UK NAT/G ECO/TAC HABITAT WEALTH...POLICY 19. PAGE 99 H1971
COLONIAL DIPLOM WAR GP/REL

B35
MARRIOTT J.A.,DICTATORSHIP AND DEMOCRACY. GERMANY GREECE UK CHIEF DIPLOM DOMIN LEGIT PEACE ORD/FREE CONSERVE...TREND ROME HITLER/A. PAGE 103 H2057
TOTALISM POPULISM PLURIST NAT/G

B36
BOYCE A.N.,EUROPE AND SOUTH AFRICA. FRANCE GERMANY ITALY SOUTH/AFR UK INDUS NAT/G CONTROL REV WAR NAT/LISM...CONCPT HIST/WRIT 20. PAGE 20 H0392
COLONIAL GOV/COMP NAT/COMP DIPLOM

B36
WANDERSCHECK H.,WELTKRIEG UND PROPAGANDA. GERMANY MOD/EUR UK COM/IND NAT/G DOMIN PRESS ATTIT...POLICY 20 HITLER/A. PAGE 165 H3299
EDU/PROP PSY WAR KNOWL

B37
BORGESE G.A.,GOLIATH: THE MARCH OF FASCISM. GERMANY ITALY LAW POL/PAR SECT DIPLOM SOCISM...JURID MYTH 20 DANTE MACHIAVELL MUSSOLIN/B. PAGE 19 H0375
POLICY NAT/LISM FASCISM NAT/G

B38
REICH N.,LABOR RELATIONS IN REPUBLICAN GERMANY. GERMANY CONSTN ECO/DEV INDUS NAT/G ADMIN CONTROL GP/REL FASCISM POPULISM 20 WEIMAR/REP. PAGE 130 H2609
WORKER MGT LABOR BARGAIN

B39
ANDERSON P.R.,THE BACKGROUND OF ANTI-ENGLISH FEELING IN GERMANY, 1890-1902. GERMANY MOD/EUR UK NAT/G POL/PAR TOP/EX WAR...IDEA/COMP 19/20. PAGE 7 H0132
DIPLOM EDU/PROP ATTIT COLONIAL

B39
ANDERSON W.,LOCAL GOVERNMENT IN EUROPE. FRANCE GERMANY ITALY UK USSR MUNIC PROVS ADMIN GOV/REL CENTRAL SOVEREIGN 20. PAGE 7 H0136
GOV/COMP NAT/COMP LOC/G CONSTN

B39
BENES E.,INTERNATIONAL SECURITY. GERMANY UK NAT/G DELIB/GP PLAN BAL/PWR ATTIT ORD/FREE PWR LEAGUE/NAT 20 TREATY. PAGE 14 H0280
EUR+WWI INT/ORG WAR

B39
CARR E.H.,PROPAGANDA IN INTERNATIONAL POLITICS (PAMPHLET). EUR+WWI GERMANY MOD/EUR NAT/G AGREE WAR MORAL...POLICY 20 TREATY. PAGE 27 H0536
DIPLOM EDU/PROP CONTROL ATTIT

B39
SCHOCKEL E.,DAS POLITISCHE PLAKAT. EUR+WWI GERMANY NAT/G PWR FASCISM EXHIBIT. PAGE 140 H2794
EDU/PROP ATTIT DOMIN POL/PAR

S39
COLE G.D.H.,"NAZI ECONOMICS: HOW DO THEY MANAGE IT?" GERMANY FORCES WORKER BUDGET INT/TRADE ROUTINE COERCE WAR 20 HITLER/A NAZI. PAGE 31 H0622
FASCISM ECO/TAC ATTIT PLAN

B40
BROGAN D.W.,THE DEVELOPMENT OF MODERN FRANCE (1870-1939). FRANCE GERMANY UK USSR CONSTN CHIEF LEGIS DIPLOM AGREE COLONIAL WAR NAT/LISM PEACE SOCISM 19/20 TREATY. PAGE 21 H0428
MOD/EUR NAT/G

B40
LEDERER E.,STATE OF THE MASSES. GERMANY ITALY SOCIETY NAT/G ECO/TAC EDU/PROP LEAD TOTALISM ...SOCIALIST PSY 20. PAGE 93 H1852
CROWD FASCISM AUTHORIT PERSON

B40
WANDERSCHECK H.,FRANKREICHS PROPAGANDA GEGEN DEUTSCHLAND. FRANCE GERMANY MOD/EUR UK NAT/G DIPLOM WAR 20 JEWS. PAGE 165 H3300
EDU/PROP ATTIT DOMIN PRESS

B40
WUNDERLICH F.,LABOR UNDER GERMAN DEMOCRACY, ARBITRATION 1918-1933. GERMANY NAT/G PAY REPAR ADJUD CT/SYS GP/REL...MAJORIT 20. PAGE 171 H3426
LABOR WORKER INDUS BARGAIN

B41
BAUMANN G.,GRUNDLAGEN UND PRAXIS DER INTERNATIONALEN PROPAGANDA. FRANCE GERMANY UK CULTURE COM/IND PRESS PWR...PSY METH/COMP 20. PAGE 12 H0241
EDU/PROP DOMIN ATTIT DIPLOM

B41
CROTHERS G.D.,THE GERMAN ELECTIONS OF 1907. GERMANY NAT/G EDU/PROP COLONIAL ATTIT. PAGE 35 H0709
CHOOSE PARL/PROC NAT/LISM POL/PAR

B41
HAUSHOFER K.,WEHR-GEOPOLITIK. EUR+WWI GERMANY MOD/EUR NAT/G ACT/RES BAL/PWR PWR...STAT TIME/SEQ CHARTS NAZI 20. PAGE 68 H1361
FORCES GEOG WAR

B41
HITLER A.,MEIN KAMPF (UNABR. ENG. VERSION) (1925). GERMANY CONSTN TEC/DEV RACE/REL NAT/LISM TOTALISM SOVEREIGN...BIOG 20 HITLER/A TREATY. PAGE 71 H1429
EDU/PROP WAR PLAN FASCISM

B41
STATIST REICHSAMTE,BIBLIOGRAPHIE DER STAATS- UND WIRSCHAFTSWISSENSCHAFTEN. EUR+WWI GERMANY FINAN ADMIN. PAGE 149 H2974
BIBLIOG ECO/DEV NAT/G POLICY

B42
BAYNES N.H.,INTELLECTUAL LIBERTY AND TOTALITARIAN CLAIMS. EUR+WWI GERMANY ITALY INTELL POL/PAR CIVMIL/REL NAT/LISM SOCISM CONCPT. PAGE 12 H0245
KNOWL FASCISM EDU/PROP ACADEM

B42
NEUBURGER O.,OFFICIAL PUBLICATIONS OF PRESENT-DAY GERMANY: GOVERNMENT, CORPORATE ORGANIZATIONS, AND NATIONAL SOCIALIST PARTY. GERMANY CONSTN COM/IND POL/PAR EDU/PROP PRESS 20 NAZI. PAGE 117 H2332
BIBLIOG/A FASCISM NAT/G ADMIN

B42
NEUMANN S.,PERMANENT REVOLUTION: THE TOTAL STATE IN A WORLD AT WAR. COM EUR+WWI GERMANY USSR EX/STRUC DIPLOM CONTROL COERCE REPRESENT MARXISM...SOC GOV/COMP BIBLIOG 20 HITLER/A STALIN/J. PAGE 117 H2337
FASCISM TOTALISM DOMIN EDU/PROP

B42
PAGINSKY P.,GERMAN WORKS RELATING TO AMERICA, 1493-1800; A LIST COMPILED FROM THE COLLECTIONS OF THE NEW YORK PUBLIC LIBRARY. GERMANY PRE/AMER CULTURE COLONIAL ATTIT...POLICY SOC 15/19. PAGE 122 H2442
BIBLIOG/A NAT/G L/A+17C DIPLOM

B42
SINGTON D.,THE GOEBBELS EXPERIMENT. GERMANY MOD/EUR NAT/G EX/STRUC FORCES CONTROL ROUTINE WAR TOTALISM PWR...ART/METH HUM 20 NAZI GOEBBELS/J. PAGE 144 H2886
FASCISM EDU/PROP ATTIT COM/IND

B43
LENIN V.I.,LEFT WING COMMUNISM: AN INFANTILE DISORDER (1920). GERMANY MOD/EUR USSR STRUCT CHIEF DOMIN EDU/PROP LEGIT LEAD REPRESENT POPULISM ...METH/COMP 19 LENIN/VI COM/PARTY MENSHEVIK. PAGE 94 H1879
COM MARXISM NAT/G REV

B44
BARKER E.,THE DEVELOPMENT OF PUBLIC SERVICES IN WESTERN WUROPE: 1660-1930. FRANCE GERMANY UK SCHOOL CONTROL REPRESENT ROLE...WELF/ST 17/20. PAGE 11 H0219
GOV/COMP ADMIN EX/STRUC

B44
GYORGY A.,GEOPOLITICS: THE NEW GERMAN SCIENCE. EUR+WWI GERMANY STRATA NAT/G PROVS DOMIN EDU/PROP ATTIT DRIVE FASCISM...GEOG NAZI 20. PAGE 63 H1261
PWR LEGIT WAR

B44
KRIS E.,GERMAN RADIO PROPAGANDA: REPORT ON HOME BROADCASTS DURING THE WAR. EUR+WWI GERMANY CULTURE CONSULT PROB/SOLV FEEDBACK TASK INGP/REL DRIVE PWR FASCISM...CON/ANAL METH/COMP 20. PAGE 89 H1768
EDU/PROP DOMIN ACT/RES ATTIT

B45
CONOVER H.F.,THE GOVERNMENTS OF THE MAJOR FOREIGN POWERS: A BIBLIOGRAPHY. FRANCE GERMANY ITALY UK USSR CONSTN LOC/G POL/PAR EX/STRUC FORCES ADMIN CT/SYS CIVMIL/REL TOTALISM...POLICY 19/20. PAGE 32 H0645
BIBLIOG NAT/G DIPLOM

B45
CONOVER H.F.,THE NAZI STATE: WAR CRIMES AND WAR CRIMINALS. GERMANY CULTURE NAT/G SECT FORCES DIPLOM INT/TRADE EDU/PROP...INT/LAW BIOG HIST/WRIT TIME/SEQ 20. PAGE 32 H0647
BIBLIOG WAR CRIME

B45
DITTMANN,DAS POLITISCHE DEUTSCHLAND VOR HITLER. GERMANY LOC/G PROVS...CHARTS GP/COMP 20. PAGE 41 H0827
POL/PAR NAT/G PARTIC

B46
ALLEN J.S.,WORLD MONOPOLY AND PEACE. GERMANY UK USSR FINAN INDUS LG/CO DOMIN CONTROL PEACE PWR WEALTH SOCISM...NAT/COMP 20 MONOPOLY. PAGE 5 H0105
CAP/ISM DIPLOM WAR COLONIAL

B46
BLUM L.,FOR ALL MANKIND (TRANS. BY W. PICKLES). FRANCE GERMANY USSR LAW SOCIETY STRUCT POL/PAR WORKER DIPLOM DOMIN CHOOSE ORD/FREE FASCISM 20. PAGE 18 H0361
POPULISM SOCIALIST NAT/G WAR

B47
BOWEN R.H.,GERMAN THEORIES OF THE CORPORATIVE STATE, WITH SPECIAL REFERENCES TO THE PERIOD 1870-1919. GERMANY INDUS LG/CO CATHISM SOCISM...SOC 18/20. PAGE 19 H0389
IDEA/COMP CENTRAL NAT/G POLICY

B48
ROSSITER C.L.,CONSTITUTIONAL DICTATORSHIP; CRISIS GOVERNMENT IN THE MODERN DEMOCRACIES. FRANCE GERMANY UK USA-45 WOR-45 EX/STRUC BAL/PWR CONTROL COERCE WAR CENTRAL ORD/FREE...DECISION 19/20. PAGE 134 H2688
NAT/G AUTHORIT CONSTN TOTALISM

L48
SHILS E.A.,"COHESION AND DISINTEGRATION IN THE WEHRMACHT IN WORLD WAR II." GERMANY STRUCT DOMIN WAR INGP/REL ISOLAT NAT/LISM ATTIT AUTHORIT SUPEGO RESPECT...PSY CON/ANAL 20 NAZI. PAGE 143 H2862
EDU/PROP DRIVE PERS/REL FORCES

S48
ALEXANDER L.,"WAR CRIMES, THEIR SOCIAL-PSYCHOLOGICAL ASPECTS." EUR+WWI GERMANY LAW CULTURE ELITES KIN POL/PAR PUB/INST FORCES DOMIN EDU/PROP COERCE CRIME ATTIT SUPEGO HEALTH MORAL PWR FASCISM ...PSY OBS TREND GEN/LAWS NAZI 20. PAGE 5 H0100
DRIVE WAR

B50
ALBRECHT-CARRIE R.,ITALY FROM NAPOLEON TO MUSSOLINI. GERMANY ITALY SPAIN SOCIETY ECO/DEV POL/PAR LEGIS AGREE CONTROL WAR NAT/LISM TOTALISM PWR SOCISM...SOC 19/20 TREATY. PAGE 5 H0095
FASCISM NAT/G

B50
GATZKE H.W.,GERMANY'S DRIVE TO THE WEST. BELGIUM GERMANY MOD/EUR AGRI INDUS POL/PAR FORCES DOMIN AGREE CONTROL REGION COERCE 20 TREATY WWI. PAGE 55 H1104
WAR POLICY NAT/G DIPLOM

B50
GOFF F.R.,FIFTEENTH CENTURY BOOKS IN THE LIBRARY OF CONGRESS. CHRIST-17C GERMANY ITALY CULTURE INTELL SECT CREATE...PHIL/SCI CONCPT CLASSIF BIOG TIME/SEQ 15. PAGE 58 H1153
BIBLIOG KNOWL HUM

B50
KANN R.A.,THE MULTINATIONAL EMPIRE (2 VOLS.). AUSTRIA CZECHOSLVK GERMANY HUNGARY CULTURE NAT/G POL/PAR PROVS REGION REV FEDERAL...GEOG TREND CHARTS IDEA/COMP NAT/COMP 19/20. PAGE 83 H1654
NAT/LISM MOD/EUR

B50
US DEPARTMENT OF STATE,DOCUMENTS ON GERMAN FOREIGN POLICY, 1918-1945 (13 VOLS.). EUR+WWI GERMANY NAT/G PLAN DIPLOM DOMIN EDU/PROP CONTROL NAT/LISM ...ANTHOL 20. PAGE 159 H3186
BIBLIOG/A WAR POLICY FASCIST

B51
BORKENAU F.,EUROPEAN COMMUNISM. COM EUR+WWI GERMANY SPAIN USSR INT/ORG PLAN REV WAR ATTIT 20 STALIN/J HITLER/A. PAGE 19 H0376
MARXISM POLICY DIPLOM

NAT/G

B51
EUCKEN W.,THIS UNSUCCESSFUL AGE. GERMANY NAT/G WORKER TEC/DEV ECO/TAC ORD/FREE 20. PAGE 47 H0947
ECO/DEV PLAN LAISSEZ NEW/LIB

S51
GOULD J.,"THE KOMSOMOL AND THE HITLER JUGEND." COM EUR+WWI GERMANY SOCIETY NAT/G POL/PAR SCHOOL TOTALISM DRIVE PERCEPT KNOWL FASCISM...SOC NAZI TOT/POP 20. PAGE 59 H1185
EDU/PROP CON/ANAL SOCISM

B52
SKALWEIT S.,FRANKREICH UND FRIEDRICH DER GROSSE. FRANCE GERMANY PRUSSIA NAT/G DOMIN WAR 18 FREDERICK. PAGE 145 H2893
ATTIT EDU/PROP DIPLOM SOC

S52
MUEHLMANN W.E.,"L'IDEE NATIONALE ALLEMANDE ET L'IDEE NATIONALE FRANCAISE." EUR+WWI MOD/EUR SOCIETY KIN NAT/G PWR RESPECT...SOC CONCPT TIME/SEQ GEN/LAWS 19/20. PAGE 114 H2279
CULTURE ATTIT FRANCE GERMANY

B53
BARZEL R.,DIE DEUTSCHEN PARTEIEN. GERMANY MARXISM SOCISM...CONCPT IDEA/COMP 19/20 SOC/DEMPAR CHRIS/DEM. PAGE 12 H0232
POL/PAR NAT/G LAISSEZ

B53
BUCHHEIM K.,GESCHICHTE DER CHRISTLICHEN PARTEIEN IN DEUTSCHLAND. GERMANY CREATE ATTIT SUPEGO ORD/FREE ...TIME/SEQ IDEA/COMP 19/20 CHRIS/DEM. PAGE 23 H0464
POL/PAR NAT/G

C53
DORWART R.A.,"THE ADMINISTRATIVE REFORMS OF FREDRICK WILLIAM I OF PRUSSIA. GERMANY MOD/EUR CHIEF CONTROL PWR...BIBLIOG 16/18. PAGE 42 H0839
ADMIN NAT/G CENTRAL GOV/REL

B54
BUTZ O.,GERMANY: DILEMMA FOR AMERICAN POLICY. GERMANY USA+45 USA-45 USSR WOR+45 INT/ORG FORCES NUC/PWR EFFICIENCY PEACE PWR...GOV/COMP 20 COLD/WAR. PAGE 25 H0501
DIPLOM NAT/G WAR POLICY

B54
FRIEDRICH C.J.,TOTALITARIAN DICTATORSHIP AND AUTOCRACY. COM EUR+WWI GERMANY ITALY USSR INTELL ECO/DEV NAT/G POL/PAR FORCES TOP/EX ECO/TAC EDU/PROP LEGIT COERCE ATTIT ORD/FREE PWR FASCISM ...CONCPT TIME/SEQ GEN/LAWS NAZI 20. PAGE 53 H1068
SOCIETY DOMIN TOTALISM

B54
GATZKE H.W.,STRESEMANN AND THE REARMAMENT OF GERMANY. EUR+WWI GERMANY USSR FINAN NAT/G ECO/TAC ATTIT...BIOG METH 20 STRESEMN/G. PAGE 55 H1105
FORCES INDUS PWR

B54
GERMANY FOREIGN MINISTRY,DOCUMENTS ON GERMAN FOREIGN POLICY 1918-1945, SERIES C (1933-1937) VOLS. I-V. GERMANY MOD/EUR FORCES PLAN ECO/TAC ...FASCIST CHARTS ANTHOL 20. PAGE 56 H1115
NAT/G DIPLOM POLICY

B54
TOTOK W.,HANDBUCH DER BIBLIOGRAPHISCHEN NACHSCHLAGEWERKE. GERMANY LAW CULTURE ADMIN...SOC 20. PAGE 156 H3117
BIBLIOG/A NAT/G DIPLOM POLICY

C54
DE GRAZIA A.,"THE COMPARATIVE SURVEY OF EUROPEAN-AMERICAN POLITICAL BEHAV IOR; A RESEARCH PROSPECTUS (PAPER)" EUR+WWI FRANCE GERMANY SPAIN UK USA+45 WOR+45 STRATA POL/PAR DIPLOM EDU/PROP COLONIAL LEAD WAR NAT/LISM CONCPT. PAGE 37 H0752
BIBLIOG R+D METH NAT/COMP

B55
BRACHER K.D.,DIE AUFLOSUNG DER WEIMARER REPUBLIK. EUR+WWI GERMANY...TIME/SEQ 20. PAGE 20 H0395
TOTALISM NAT/G POL/PAR PARL/PROC

B55
FRANZ G.,KULTURKAMPF. AUSTRIA GERMANY PRUSSIA SWITZERLND POL/PAR DIPLOM GP/REL ATTIT ORD/FREE 18/19 CHURCH/STA. PAGE 53 H1053
NAT/LISM CATHISM NAT/G REV

B56
DE JONG L.,THE GERMAN FIFTH COLUMN IN THE SECOND WORLD WAR. EUR+WWI GERMANY NAT/G DIPLOM ATTIT FASCISM...MYTH 20 NAZI. PAGE 38 H0756
EDU/PROP WAR RUMOR

B56
VON BECKERATH E.,HANDWORTERBUCH DER SOCIALWISSENSCHAFTEN (II VOLS.). EUR+WWI GERMANY POL/PAR WORKER DIPLOM LEAD CHOOSE SUFF WEALTH...SOC 20. PAGE 163 H3263
BIBLIOG INT/TRADE NAT/G ECO/DEV

B56
VON HARPE W.,DIE SOWJETUNION FINNLAND UND SKANDANAVIEN, 1945-1955. EUR+WWI FINLAND GERMANY USSR WAR INGP/REL ORD/FREE SOVEREIGN MARXISM ...POLICY GOV/COMP BIBLIOG 20 STALIN/J. PAGE 163 H3270
DIPLOM COM NEUTRAL BAL/PWR

B57
BUNDESMIN FUR VERTRIEBENE,DIE VERTREIBUNG DER DEUTSCHEN BEVOLKERUNG AUS DER TSCHECHOSLOWAKEI. CZECHOSLVK GERMANY NAT/G FORCES MURDER WAR INGP/REL ATTIT 20 MIGRATION. PAGE 24 H0474
GP/REL DOMIN COERCE DISCRIM

B57
MEINECKE F.,MACHIAVELLISM. CHRIST-17C FRANCE GERMANY ITALY MOD/EUR BAL/PWR PARL/PROC TOTALISM ...PHIL/SCI 15/20 MACHIAVELL. PAGE 108 H2166 NAT/LISM NAT/G PWR

B58
BUISSON L.,POTESTAS UND CARITAS. FRANCE GERMANY UK ORD/FREE...JURID IDEA/COMP NAT/COMP 12/16 POPE CHURCH/STA. PAGE 23 H0467 GP/REL PWR CATHISM NAT/G

B58
CRAIG G.A.,FROM BISMARCK TO ADENAUER: ASPECTS OF GERMAN STATECRAFT. GERMANY INTELL FORCES ECO/TAC CONFER COERCE WAR GP/REL ORD/FREE PWR CONSERVE 19/20 BISMARCK/O ADENAUER/K. PAGE 35 H0695 DIPLOM LEAD NAT/G

B58
SCHOEPS H.J.,KONSERVATIVE ERNEUERUNG IDEEN ZUR DEUTSCHEN POLITIK. GERMANY ELITES SOCIETY ACADEM CHOOSE SOCISM 19/20. PAGE 140 H2796 POL/PAR IDEA/COMP CONSERVE NAT/G

S58
SCHUMM S.,"INTEREST REPRESENTATION IN FRANCE AND GERMANY." EUR+WWI FRANCE GERMANY INSPECT PARL/PROC REPRESENT 20 WEIMAR/REP. PAGE 140 H2803 LOBBY DELIB/GP NAT/G

B59
DEHIO L.,GERMANY AND WORLD POLITICS IN THE TWENTIETH CENTURY. EUR+WWI FRANCE GERMANY MOD/EUR UK USSR NAT/G CHIEF BAL/PWR DOMIN COLONIAL CONTROL LEAD...IDEA/COMP 20 VERSAILLES. PAGE 39 H0783 DIPLOM WAR NAT/LISM SOVEREIGN

B59
HEMMERLE J.,SUDETENDEUTSCHE BIBLIOGRAPHIE 1949-1953. CZECHOSLVK GERMANY SOCIETY STRUCT SECT ...GEOG JURID 20. PAGE 69 H1391 BIBLIOG PROVS GP/REL CULTURE

B59
SCHORN H.,DER RICHTER IM DRITTEN REICH; GESCHICHTE UND DOKUMENTE. GERMANY NAT/G LEGIT CT/SYS INGP/REL MORAL ORD/FREE RESPECT...JURID GP/COMP 20. PAGE 140 H2798 ADJUD JUDGE FASCISM

S59
WARBURG J.P.,"THE CENTRAL EUROPEAN CRISIS: A PROPOSAL FOR WESTERN INITIATIVE." EUR+WWI INT/ORG NAT/G LEGIT DETER WAR...CONCPT BER/BLOC UN 20. PAGE 165 H3302 PLAN GERMANY

B60
ALBRECHT-CARRIE R.,FRANCE, EUROPE AND THE TWO WORLD WARS. EUR+WWI FRANCE GERMANY MOD/EUR UK ECO/DEV NAT/G FORCES BAL/PWR DOMIN ARMS/CONT PEACE PWR 20 TREATY EUROPE. PAGE 5 H0096 DIPLOM WAR

B60
BAYER H.,WIRTSCHAFTSPROGNOSE UND WIRTSCHAFTSGESTALTUNG. GERMANY NETHERLAND MARKET PLAN CAP/ISM DEBATE...NAT/COMP 20. PAGE 12 H0242 ECO/DEV ECO/UNDEV FINAN POLICY

B60
CASTBERG F.,FREEDOM OF SPEECH IN THE WEST. FRANCE GERMANY USA+45 USA-45 LAW CONSTN CHIEF PRESS DISCRIM...CONCPT 18/20. PAGE 28 H0558 ORD/FREE SANCTION ADJUD NAT/COMP

B60
FURNIA A.H.,THE DIPLOMACY OF APPEASEMENT: ANGLO-FRENCH RELATIONS AND THE PRELUDE TO WORLD WAR II 1931-1938. FRANCE GERMANY UK ELITES NAT/G DELIB/GP FORCES WAR PEACE RIGID/FLEX 20. PAGE 54 H1077 DIPLOM BAL/PWR COERCE

B60
JAECKH A.,WELTSAAT; ERLEBTES UND ERSTREBTES. GERMANY WOR+45 WOR-45 PLAN WAR...POLICY OBS/ENVIR NAT/COMP PERS/COMP 20. PAGE 79 H1581 BIOG NAT/G SELF/OBS DIPLOM

B60
LISTER L.,EUROPE'S COAL AND STEEL COMMUNITY. FRANCE GERMANY STRUCT ECO/DEV EXTR/IND INDUS MARKET NAT/G DELIB/GP ECO/TAC INT/TRADE EDU/PROP ATTIT RIGID/FLEX ORD/FREE PWR WEALTH...CONCPT STAT TIME/SEQ CHARTS ECSC 20. PAGE 97 H1941 EUR+WWI INT/ORG REGION

B60
MATTHIAS E.,DAS ENDE DER PARTEIEN 1933. GERMANY NAT/G COERCE CHOOSE ORD/FREE PWR 20. PAGE 105 H2100 FASCISM POL/PAR DOMIN ATTIT

B60
SHIRER W.L.,THE RISE AND FALL OF THE THIRD REICH: A HISTORY OF NAZI GERMANY. EUR+WWI CULTURE ECO/DEV INDUS NAT/G POL/PAR FORCES PLAN TEC/DEV ECO/TAC COERCE ATTIT DRIVE PERSON PWR...MYSTIC PSY SOC MYTH STAT CHARTS EXHIBIT WORK VAL/FREE. PAGE 143 H2864 STRUCT GERMANY TOTALISM

B60
THE AFRICA 1960 COMMITTEE,MANDATE IN TRUST; THE PROBLEM OF SOUTH WEST AFRICA. GERMANY STRUCT REGION SANCTION CHOOSE DISCRIM...INT/LAW 20 AFRICA/SW UN LEAGUE/NAT TRUST/TERR. PAGE 153 H3066 NAT/G DIPLOM COLONIAL RACE/REL

S60
MAGATHAN W.,"SOME BASES OF WEST GERMAN MILITARY POLICY." EUR+WWI FUT INT/ORG TOP/EX ECO/TAC DOMIN DRIVE ORD/FREE PWR...TRADIT GEOG OBS TREND. PAGE 101 H2015 NAT/G FORCES GERMANY

S60
TAUBER K.,"ASPECTS OF NATIONALIST-COMMUNIST COLLABORATION IN POSTWAR GERMANY." COM EUR+WWI USSR NAT/G VOL/ASSN ATTIT DRIVE PWR...TIME/SEQ COLD/WAR TOT/POP 20. PAGE 152 H3049 POL/PAR EDU/PROP GERMANY

B61
BULLOCK A.,HITLER: A STUDY IN TYRANNY. EUR+WWI GERMANY SOCIETY STRUCT NAT/G POL/PAR FORCES CREATE DOMIN EDU/PROP EXEC COERCE WAR NAT/LISM DISPL DRIVE PERSON PWR...PSY NAZI 20 HITLER/A. PAGE 23 H0470 ATTIT BIOG TOTALISM

B61
DALLIN D.J.,SOVIET FOREIGN POLICY AFTER STALIN. ASIA CHINA/COM EUR+WWI GERMANY IRAN UK YUGOSLAVIA INT/ORG NAT/G VOL/ASSN FORCES TOP/EX BAL/PWR DOMIN EDU/PROP COERCE ATTIT PWR 20. PAGE 37 H0737 COM DIPLOM USSR

B61
DONNISON F.S.V.,CIVIL AFFAIRS AND MILITARY GOVERNMENT NORTH-WEST EUROPE 1944-1946. EUR+WWI FRANCE GERMANY UK USSR LOC/G PROVS PLAN PROB/SOLV BAL/PWR ECO/TAC CONTROL PWR...CHARTS 20. PAGE 42 H0836 NAT/G WAR FORCES CIVMIL/REL

B61
JAKOBSON M.,THE DIPLOMACY OF THE WINTER WAR. EUR+WWI FINLAND GERMANY USSR INT/ORG NAT/G PEACE TOTALISM PWR...POLICY CONCPT 20 TREATY. PAGE 79 H1588 WAR ORD/FREE DIPLOM

B61
KEE R.,REFUGEE WORLD. AUSTRIA EUR+WWI GERMANY NEIGH EX/STRUC WORKER PROB/SOLV ECO/TAC RENT EDU/PROP INGP/REL COST LITERACY HABITAT 20 MIGRATION. PAGE 84 H1676 NAT/G GIVE WEALTH STRANGE

B61
LICHTHEIM G.,MARXISM. GERMANY SOCIETY WORKER CAP/ISM ECO/TAC NAT/LISM POPULISM...TIME/SEQ GOV/COMP NAT/COMP 18/20 COM/PARTY. PAGE 96 H1924 MARXISM SOCISM IDEA/COMP CULTURE

B61
NIPPERDEY T.,DIE ORGANISATION DER DEUTSCHEN PARTEIEN VOR 1918. GERMANY CONSTN STRUCT TEC/DEV CHOOSE ADJUST ATTIT...CONCPT TIME/SEQ 19/20. PAGE 118 H2362 POL/PAR PARL/PROC NAT/G

B61
SCHIEDER T.,DOCUMENTS ON THE EXPULSION OF THE GERMANS FROM EASTERN-CENTRAL-EUROPE (VOL. II/III). COM EUR+WWI GERMANY HUNGARY ROMANIA USSR DIPLOM RACE/REL 20 MIGRATION. PAGE 139 H2785 GEOG CULTURE

B61
TREVE W.,DEUTSCHE PARTEIPROGRAMME 1861-1961. GERMANY GERMANY/W DELIB/GP CONFER CHOOSE REPRESENT 19/20. PAGE 157 H3130 POL/PAR NAT/G LEGIS PARL/PROC

B61
VEIT O.,GRUNDRISS DER WAHRUNGSPOLITIK. FRANCE GERMANY USSR DIPLOM INT/TRADE...NAT/COMP 19/20 GOLD/STAND SILVER. PAGE 162 H3239 FINAN POLICY ECO/TAC CAP/ISM

S61
RAY J.,"THE EUROPEAN FREE-TRADE ASSOCIATION AND ITS IMPACT ON INDIA'S TRADE." EUR+WWI FRANCE GERMANY INDIA S/ASIA UK NAT/G VOL/ASSN PLAN INT/TRADE ROUTINE WEALTH...STAT CHARTS CMN/WLTH EEC OEEC 20 EFTA. PAGE 130 H2600 ECO/DEV ECO/TAC

S61
TOMASIC D.,"POLITICAL LEADERSHIP IN CONTEMPORARY POLAND." COM EUR+WWI GERMANY NAT/G POL/PAR SECT DELIB/GP PLAN ECO/TAC DOMIN EDU/PROP PWR MARXISM ...MARXIST GEOG MGT CONCPT TIME/SEQ STERTYP 20. PAGE 156 H3111 SOCIETY ROUTINE USSR POLAND

B62
ANDREWS W.G.,EUROPEAN POLITICAL INSTITUTIONS. FRANCE GERMANY UK USSR TOP/EX LEAD PARL/PROC CHOOSE 20. PAGE 7 H0139 NAT/COMP POL/PAR EX/STRUC LEGIS

B62
BROWN B.E.,NEW DIRECTIONS IN COMPARATIVE POLITICS. AUSTRIA FRANCE GERMANY UK WOR+45 EX/STRUC LEGIS ORD/FREE 20. PAGE 22 H0439 NAT/COMP METH POL/PAR FORCES

B62
DEHIO L.,THE PRECARIOUS BALANCE: FOUR CENTURIES OF THE EUROPEAN POWER STRUGGLE. FRANCE GERMANY SPAIN NAT/G DOMIN PWR...GOV/COMP 8/20. PAGE 39 H0784 BAL/PWR WAR DIPLOM COERCE

B62
HACHMANN R.,VOLKER ZWISCHEN GERMANEN UND KELTEN. GERMANY CULTURE STRUCT MUNIC...ART/METH CHARTS MAPS. PAGE 63 H1269 LING SOC KIN GP/REL

B62
ROSENZWEIG F.,HEGEL UND DER STAAT. GERMANY SOCIETY FAM POL/PAR NAT/LISM...BIOG 19. PAGE 134 H2682 JURID NAT/G CONCPT PHIL/SCI

B62
SCHECHTMAN J.B.,POSTWAR POPULATION TRANSFERS IN EUROPE: 1945-1955. COM CZECHOSLVK GERMANY POLAND GEOG CENSUS

USSR CULTURE SOCIETY PROB/SOLV AGREE NAT/LISM...SOC EUR+WWI
STAT TREND CHARTS METH/COMP 20 MIGRATION. PAGE 139 HABITAT
H2778

B62
SCHMIDT-VOLKMAR E.,DER KULTURKAMPF IN DEUTSCHLAND POL/PAR
1871-1890. GERMANY PRUSSIA SOCIETY STRUCT SECT CATHISM
DIPLOM GP/REL NAT/LISM 19 CHURCH/STA BISMARCK/O. ATTIT
PAGE 139 H2789 NAT/G

B62
WEHLER H.V.,SOZIALDEMOKRATIE UND NATIONALSTAAT. NAT/LISM
GERMANY POLAND USSR CULTURE SOCIETY STRUCT NAT/G SOVEREIGN
POL/PAR DIPLOM ORD/FREE 19/20. PAGE 166 H3325 GP/REL
ATTIT

L62
NOLTE E.,"ZUR PHANOMENOLOGIE DES FASCHIMUS." ATTIT
EUR+WWI GERMANY ITALY TURKEY INTELL NAT/G CHIEF PWR
CONSULT FORCES CREATE DOMIN EDU/PROP COERCE WAR
CHOOSE DRIVE FASCISM...PSY CONCPT MYTH GEN/METH
LEAGUE/NAT NAZI 20. PAGE 118 H2367

S62
GUETZKOW H.,"THE POTENTIAL OF CASE STUDY IN EDU/PROP
ANALYZING INTERNATIONAL CONFLICT." EUR+WWI FUT METH/CNCPT
GERMANY INTELL SOCIETY STRUCT INT/ORG LOC/G NAT/G COERCE
CONSULT CREATE PLAN CHOOSE ATTIT RIGID/FLEX FRANCE
...POLICY SAAR 20. PAGE 62 H1246

B63
AHN L.A.,FUNFZIG JAHRE ZWISCHEN INFLATION UND FINAN
DEFLATION. GERMANY DIPLOM PRICE...CONCPT 20 CAP/ISM
GOLD/STAND. PAGE 4 H0081 NAT/COMP
ECO/TAC

B63
CONZE W.,DIE DEUTSCHE NATION. GERMANY NAT/G POL/PAR NAT/LISM
WAR ORD/FREE...TREND 8/20 NAZI. PAGE 33 H0657 FASCISM
ATTIT
SOCIETY

B63
EICH H.,THE UNLOVED GERMANS. EUR+WWI GERMANY STERTYP
PERS/REL RACE/REL DISCRIM HABITAT SUPEGO FASCISM PERSON
...PSY SOC AUD/VIS 19/20 JEWS. PAGE 45 H0898 CULTURE
ATTIT

B63
FABER K.,DIE NATIONALISTISCHE PUBLIZISTIK BIBLIOG/A
DEUTSCHLANDS VON 1866 BIS 1871 (2 VOLS.). EUR+WWI NAT/G
GERMANY DIPLOM EDU/PROP 19. PAGE 48 H0957 NAT/LISM
POL/PAR

B63
FRANZ G.,TEILUNG UND WIEDERVEREINIGUNG. GERMANY DIPLOM
IRELAND ITALY NETHERLAND POLAND CULTURE BAL/PWR WAR
CHOOSE NAT/LISM ORD/FREE SOVEREIGN 19/20. PAGE 53 NAT/COMP
H1054 ATTIT

B63
JACOB H.,GERMAN ADMINISTRATION SINCE BISMARCK: ADMIN
CENTRAL AUTHORITY VERSUS LOCAL AUTONOMY. GERMANY NAT/G
GERMANY/W LAW POL/PAR CONTROL CENTRAL TOTALISM LOC/G
FASCISM...MAJORIT DECISION STAT CHARTS GOV/COMP POLICY
19/20 BISMARCK/O HITLER/A WEIMAR/REP. PAGE 79 H1577

B63
KRAEHE E.,METTERNICH'S GERMAN POLICY: THE CONTEST BIOG
WITH NAPOLEON, 1799-1814, VOL. 1. FRANCE MOD/EUR GERMANY
NAT/G CONSULT TOP/EX PLAN BAL/PWR DOMIN COERCE DIPLOM
ATTIT DRIVE PERCEPT PERSON SKILL...CONCPT RECORD
TIME/SEQ TREND 18/19. PAGE 88 H1764

B63
OLSON M. JR.,THE ECONOMICS OF WARTIME SHORTAGE. WAR
FRANCE GERMANY MOD/EUR UK AGRI PROB/SOLV ADMIN ADJUST
DEMAND WEALTH...POLICY OLD/LIB 17/20. PAGE 121 ECO/TAC
H2416 NAT/COMP

B63
SILONE I.,THE SCHOOL FOR DICTATORS. EUR+WWI GERMANY TOTALISM
ITALY SOCIETY NAT/G CHIEF EX/STRUC ATTIT MORAL PWR EDU/PROP
...HIST/WRIT 20. PAGE 144 H2876 ORD/FREE
FASCISM

B63
VALJAVEC F.,AUSGEWAHLTE AUFSATZE. GERMANY HUNGARY SOCIETY
STRUCT ATTIT...CONCPT IDEA/COMP 18/20 BALKANS. CULTURE
PAGE 161 H3223 GP/REL
NAT/LISM

B63
VON BECKERATH E.,PROBLEME DER NORMATIVEN OKONOMIK ECO/TAC
UND DER WIRTSCHAFTSPOLITISCHEN BERATUNG. GERMANY UK DELIB/GP
ELITES CAP/ISM EFFICIENCY...CONCPT GOV/COMP ECO/DEV
IDEA/COMP 20. PAGE 163 H3264 CONSULT

L63
BOLGAR V.,"THE PUBLIC INTEREST: A JURISPRUDENTIAL CONCPT
AND COMPARATIVE OVERVIEW OF SYMPOSIUM ON ORD/FREE
FUNDAMENTAL CONCEPTS OF PUBLIC LAW" COM FRANCE CONTROL
GERMANY SWITZERLND LAW ADJUD ADMIN AGREE LAISSEZ NAT/COMP
...JURID GEN/LAWS 20 EUROPE/E. PAGE 18 H0369

L63
FREUND G.,"ADENAUER AND THE FUTURE OF GERMANY." NAT/G
EUR+WWI FUT GERMANY/W FORCES LEGIT ADMIN ROUTINE BIOG
ATTIT DRIVE PERSON PWR...POLICY TIME/SEQ TREND DIPLOM
VAL/FREE 20 ADENAUER/K. PAGE 53 H1058 GERMANY

S63
ANTHON C.G.,"THE END OF THE ADENAUER ERA." EUR+WWI NAT/G
GERMANY/W CONSTN EX/STRUC CREATE DIPLOM LEGIT ATTIT TOP/EX
PERSON ALL/VALS...RECORD 20 ADENAUER/K. PAGE 7 BAL/PWR
H0144 GERMANY

S63
GROSSER A.,"FRANCE AND GERMANY IN THE ATLANTIC EUR+WWI
COMMUNITY." INT/ORG NAT/G TOP/EX DIPLOM REGION VOL/ASSN
PEACE ATTIT ORD/FREE PWR...CONCPT RECORD TIME/SEQ FRANCE
GEN/LAWS VAL/FREE COLD/WAR 20. PAGE 62 H1234 GERMANY

S63
KOHN H.,"GERMANY IN WORLD POLITICS." EUR+WWI ACT/RES
GERMANY GERMANY/W USSR NAT/G POL/PAR TOP/EX ATTIT ORD/FREE
...CONCPT TREND GEN/LAWS 20 NATO ADENAUER/K. BAL/PWR
PAGE 87 H1746

S63
LERNER D.,"WILL EUROPEAN UNION BRING ABOUT MERGED ATTIT
NATIONAL GOALS." EUR+WWI FRANCE GERMANY UK ECO/DEV STERTYP
NAT/G VOL/ASSN DELIB/GP BAL/PWR ECO/TAC NAT/LISM ELITES
EEC 20 DEGAULLE/C. PAGE 95 H1889 REGION

B64
FREISEN J.,STAAT UND KATHOLISCHE KIRCHE IN DEN SECT
DEUTSCHEN BUNDESSTAATEN (2 VOLS.). GERMANY LAW FAM CATHISM
NAT/G EDU/PROP GP/REL MARRIAGE WEALTH 19/20 JURID
CHURCH/STA. PAGE 53 H1056 PROVS

B64
GESELLSCHAFT RECHTSVERGLEICH,BIBLIOGRAPHIE DES BIBLIOG/A
DEUTSCHEN RECHTS (BIBLIOGRAPHY OF GERMAN LAW, JURID
TRANS. BY COURTLAND PETERSON). GERMANY FINAN INDUS CONSTN
LABOR SECT FORCES CT/SYS PARL/PROC CRIME...INT/LAW ADMIN
SOC NAT/COMP 20. PAGE 56 H1117

B64
HALE O.J.,THE CAPTIVE PRESS IN THE THIRD REICH. COM/IND
GERMANY CULTURE LG/CO NAT/G POL/PAR PLAN DOMIN TASK PRESS
CENTRAL OWN TOTALISM PWR...BIBLIOG 20 HITLER/A NAZI CONTROL
AMMAN/MAX. PAGE 64 H1283 FASCISM

B64
HELMREICH E.,A FREE CHURCH IN A FREE STATE? FRANCE GP/REL
GERMANY ITALY SECT LEAD PWR CATHISM...POLICY ANTHOL NAT/G
WORSHIP 19/20 CHURCH/STA. PAGE 69 H1389

B64
KALDOR N.,ESSAYS ON ECONOMIC POLICY (VOL. II). BAL/PAY
CHILE GERMANY INDIA FINAN...GOV/COMP METH/COMP 20 INT/TRADE
KEYNES/JM. PAGE 83 H1651 METH/CNCPT
ECO/UNDEV

B64
KELLER J.W.,GERMANY, THE WALL AND BERLIN. EUR+WWI ATTIT
ECO/DEV NAT/G VOL/ASSN FORCES PLAN ECO/TAC EDU/PROP ALL/VALS
COERCE...POLICY CONCPT INT TREND COLD/WAR BER/BLOC DIPLOM
20 BERLIN. PAGE 84 H1685 GERMANY

B64
REMAK J.,THE GENTLE CRITIC: THEODOR FONTANE AND PERSON
GERMAN POLITICS, 1848-1898. GERMANY PRUSSIA CULTURE SOCIETY
ELITES BAL/PWR DIPLOM WRITING GOV/REL...HUM BIOG 19 WORKER
BISMARCK/O JUNKER FONTANE/T. PAGE 131 H2614 CHIEF

B64
WHEELER-BENNETT J.W.,THE NEMESIS OF POWER (2ND FORCES
ED.). EUR+WWI GERMANY TOP/EX TEC/DEV ADMIN WAR NAT/G
PERS/REL RIGID/FLEX ROLE ORD/FREE PWR FASCISM 20 GP/REL
HITLER/A. PAGE 167 H3342 STRUCT

L64
FINDLATER R.,"US." EUR+WWI GERMANY USSR SOCIETY CULTURE
FACE/GP EDU/PROP PERCEPT PERSON ALL/VALS...PSY SOC ATTIT
CONCPT SELF/OBS SAMP TREND 20. PAGE 50 H1001 UK

S64
BARIETY J.,"LA POLITIQUE EXTERIEURE ALLEMANDE DANS EUR+WWI
L'HIVER 1939-1940." COM FINLAND GERMANY ISLAM ITALY DIPLOM
USSR NAT/G FORCES ECO/TAC DOMIN EDU/PROP COERCE WAR
PWR WEALTH...HIST/WRIT NAZI TOT/POP VAL/FREE 20.
PAGE 11 H0216

S64
REISS I.,"LE DECLENCHEMENT DE LA PREMIERE GUERRE MOD/EUR
MONDIALE." GERMANY RUSSIA NAT/G FORCES DOMIN BAL/PWR
EDU/PROP COERCE RIGID/FLEX PWR SOVEREIGN...RELATIV DIPLOM
HIST/WRIT TOT/POP AUST/HUNG SERBIA 20. PAGE 131 WAR
H2612

B65
ACHTERBERG E.,BERLINER HOCHFINANZ - KAISER, FINAN
FURSTEN, MILLIONARE UM 1900. GERMANY NAT/G EDU/PROP MUNIC
PERSON...MGT 19/20. PAGE 3 H0060 BIOG
ECO/TAC

B65
ADENAUER K.,MEINE ERINNERUNGEN, 1945-53 (VOL. I), NAT/G
1953-55 (VOL. II). EUR+WWI GERMANY CHIEF FORCES BIOG
PROB/SOLV DIPLOM ARMS/CONT INGP/REL PEACE SOVEREIGN SELF/OBS
...OBS/ENVIR RECORD 20. PAGE 3 H0069

B65
ALLEN W.S.,THE NAZI SEIZURE OF POWER. GERMANY NAT/G MUNIC
CHIEF LEAD COERCE CHOOSE REPRESENT GOV/REL AUTHORIT FASCISM
...DECISION 20 HITLER/A NAZI. PAGE 5 H0106 TOTALISM
LOC/G

B65
BRAMSTED E.K.,GOEBBELS AND NATIONAL SOCIALIST EDU/PROP
PROPAGANDA, 1925-1945. EUR+WWI GERMANY UK USSR PSY
NAT/G FORCES WAR FASCISM...TIME/SEQ 20 GOEBBELS/J COM/IND
NAZI. PAGE 20 H0403

B65
EDELMAN M.,THE POLITICS OF WAGE-PRICE DECISIONS. GOV/COMP
GERMANY ITALY NETHERLAND UK INDUS LABOR POL/PAR CONTROL

PROB/SOLV BARGAIN PRICE ROUTINE BAL/PAY COST DEMAND 20. PAGE 44 H0888 ECO/TAC PLAN

B65
EDINGER L.J.,KURT SCHUMACHER: A STUDY IN PERSONALITY AND POLITICAL BEHAVIOR. EUR+WWI GERMANY NAT/G DRIVE ROLE PWR SOCISM...BIBLIOG 20 SOC/DEMPAR SCHUMCHR/K. PAGE 44 H0889 TOP/EX LEAD PERSON BIOG

B65
GILG P.,DIE ERNEUERUNG DES DEMOKRATISCHEN DENKENS IM WILHELMINISCHEN DEUTSCHLAND. GERMANY PARL/PROC CHOOSE REPRESENT...CONCPT 19/20 BISMARCK/O WILHELM/II. PAGE 56 H1126 POL/PAR ORD/FREE NAT/G

B65
GOETHE J.W.,GOETHE UBER DIE DEUTSCHEN. GERMANY CULTURE...NAT/COMP 18/19 GOETHE/J. PAGE 58 H1152 ATTIT PERSON SOCIETY

B65
GUERIN D.,SUR LE FASCISME: FASCISME ET GRAND CAPITAL (VOL. II). GERMANY ITALY SOCIETY STRATA AGRI WORKER 20. PAGE 62 H1245 FASCISM NAT/G TOTALISM EDU/PROP

B65
HERBST J.,THE GERMAN HISTORICAL SCHOOL IN AMERICAN SCHOLARSHIP; A STUDY IN THE TRANSFER OF CULTURE. GERMANY USA+45 INTELL SOCIETY ACADEM PLAN ATTIT IDEA/COMP. PAGE 70 H1399 CULTURE NAT/COMP HIST/WRIT

B65
JONAS E.,DIE VOLKSKONSERVATIVEN 1928-1933. GERMANY EX/STRUC...CONCPT TIME/SEQ 20 HITLER/A. PAGE 82 H1628 POL/PAR NAT/G GP/REL

B65
MERKL P.H.,GERMANY: YESTERDAY AND TOMORROW. GERMANY POL/PAR PLAN DIPLOM LEAD FEDERAL 19/20. PAGE 109 H2181 NAT/G FUT

B65
NORDEN A.,WAR AND NAZI CRIMINALS IN WEST GERMANY: STATE, ECONOMY, ADMINISTRATION, ARMY, JUSTICE, SCIENCE. GERMANY GERMANY/W MOD/EUR ECO/DEV ACADEM EX/STRUC FORCES DOMIN ADMIN CT/SYS...POLICY MAJORIT PACIFIST 20. PAGE 119 H2370 FASCIST WAR NAT/G TOP/EX

B65
SALVADORI M.,ITALY. AUSTRIA FRANCE GERMANY ITALY SPAIN CULTURE NAT/G POL/PAR DIPLOM WAR FASCISM LAISSEZ MARXISM...TIME/SEQ CHARTS BIBLIOG/A. PAGE 137 H2744 NAT/LISM CATHISM SOCIETY

B65
STERN F.,THE POLITICS OF CULTURAL DESPAIR. EUR+WWI GERMANY POL/PAR SECT RACE/REL STRANGE TOTALISM ...ART/METH MYTH BIBLIOG 20 JEWS. PAGE 149 H2980 CULTURE ATTIT NAT/LISM FASCISM

B65
UPTON A.F.,FINLAND IN CRISIS 1940-1941. NAT/G FORCES DIPLOM COERCE...DECISION GEOG. PAGE 159 H3173 FINLAND GERMANY USSR WAR

B65
ZIOCK H.,SIND DIE DEUTSCHEN WIRKLICH SO? GERMANY SOCIETY...NAT/COMP ANTHOL 19/20. PAGE 173 H3460 PERSON ATTIT CULTURE STRUCT

S65
GORDON M.,"THE SETTING FOR EUROPEAN ARMS CONTROLS* POLITICAL AND STRATEGIC CHOICES OF EUROPEAN ELITES." FRANCE GERMANY UK USA+45 USSR ARMS/CONT DETER ATTIT ORD/FREE...SAMP NAT/COMP NATO. PAGE 59 H1179 REC/INT ELITES RISK WAR

S65
ROGGER H.,"EAST GERMANY: STABLE OR IMMOBILE." COM EUR+WWI GERMANY/E NAT/G INT/TRADE DOMIN EDU/PROP COERCE TOTALISM COLD/WAR 20. PAGE 133 H2659 TOP/EX RIGID/FLEX GERMANY

S65
SPAAK P.H.,"THE SEARCH FOR CONSENSUS: A NEW EFFORT TO BUILD EUROPE." FRANCE GERMANY ECO/DEV NAT/G CONSULT FORCES PLAN EDU/PROP REGION CONSEN ATTIT ...SOC METH/CNCPT OBS TREND EEC NATO WORK 20. PAGE 147 H2941 EUR+WWI INT/ORG

S65
STAROBIN J.R.,"COMMUNISM IN WESTERN EUROPE." FRANCE GERMANY ITALY USA+45 USSR ECO/DEV FEDERAL PEACE ATTIT DRIVE PWR TREND. PAGE 149 H2972 MARXISM EUR+WWI POL/PAR NAT/COMP

S65
WHITE J.,"WEST GERMAN AID TO DEVELOPING COUNTRIES." INT/ORG OP/RES GIVE CENTRAL ATTIT DRIVE...STAT NAT/COMP COLD/WAR. PAGE 167 H3348 GERMANY FOR/AID ECO/UNDEV CAP/ISM

B66
DYCK H.V.,WEIMAR GERMANY AND SOVIET RUSSIA 1926-1933. EUR+WWI GERMANY UK USSR ECO/TAC INT/TRADE NEUTRAL WAR ATTIT 20 WEIMAR/REP TREATY. PAGE 44 H0877 DIPLOM GOV/REL POLICY

B66
HATTICH M.,NATIONALBEWUSSTSEIN UND STAATSBEWUSSTSEIN IN DER PLURALISTISCHEN GESELLSCHAFT. GERMANY GP/REL ATTIT SOVEREIGN SOC/INTEG 20. PAGE 68 H1356 NAT/G NAT/LISM SOCIETY OBJECTIVE

B66
HENKYS R.,DEUTSCHLAND UND DIE OSTLICHEN NACHBARN. GERMANY POLAND NAT/G POL/PAR INGP/REL ATTIT 20 MIGRATION. PAGE 70 H1396 GP/REL JURID INT/LAW DIPLOM

B66
MAC DONALD H.M.,THE INTELLECTUAL IN POLITICS. GERMANY PERU SWEDEN UK USSR NAT/G CONSULT PLAN EDU/PROP TASK INGP/REL EFFICIENCY RATIONAL ALL/VALS 20. PAGE 99 H1987 ALL/IDEOS INTELL POL/PAR PARTIC

B66
NOLTE E.,THREE FACES OF FASCISM. FRANCE GERMANY DOMIN LEGIT COERCE CROWD REV WAR GP/REL RACE/REL SOVEREIGN...GOV/COMP IDEA/COMP 19/20 HITLER/A MUSSOLIN/B MARX/KARL. PAGE 118 H2368 FASCISM TOTALISM NAT/G POL/PAR

B66
O'NEILL R.J.,THE GERMAN ARMY AND THE NAZI PARTY, 1933-1939. GERMANY ELITES NAT/G EDU/PROP CONTROL LEAD COERCE WAR...POLICY INT TIME/SEQ BIBLIOG 20 HITLER/A NAZI. PAGE 120 H2391 CIVMIL/REL FORCES FASCISM POL/PAR

B66
PLATE H.,PARTEIFINANZIERUNG UND GRUNDESETZ. GERMANY NAT/G PLAN GIVE PAY INCOME WEALTH...JURID 20. PAGE 126 H2522 POL/PAR CONSTN FINAN

B66
RICHERT F.,DIE NATIONALE WELLE. GERMANY GERMANY/W PARL/PROC ORD/FREE FASCISM...TREND 19/20. PAGE 131 H2622 POL/PAR ATTIT NAT/LISM NAT/G

B66
ROSNER J.,DER FASCHISMUS. AUSTRIA GERMANY ITALY STRATA NAT/G POL/PAR COERCE RACE/REL TOTALISM ATTIT AUTHORIT...IDEA/COMP 20 NAZI ANTI/SEMIT. PAGE 134 H2684 NAT/LISM FASCISM ORD/FREE WAR

B66
THORNTON M.J.,NAZISM, 1918-1945. GERMANY INT/ORG DIPLOM REV PEACE FASCISM...CONCPT 20 HITLER/A WEIMAR/REP NAZI. PAGE 155 H3089 TOTALISM POL/PAR NAT/G WAR

B66
TORMIN W.,GESCHICHTE DER DEUTSCHEN PARTEIEN SEIT 1848. GERMANY CHOOSE PWR...CONCPT 19/20 WEIMAR/REP. PAGE 156 H3116 POL/PAR CONSTN NAT/G TOTALISM

B66
WUEST J.J.,NEW SOURCE BOOK IN MAJOR EUROPEAN GOVERNMENTS. CHRIST-17C EUR+WWI FRANCE GERMANY ITALY MOD/EUR UK USSR LOC/G POL/PAR CHIEF EX/STRUC CHOOSE CONSERVE MARXISM...JURID T 13/20. PAGE 171 H3425 NAT/G CONSTN LEGIS

B67
ALBINSKI H.S.,EUROPEAN POLITICAL PROCESSES: ESSAYS AND READINGS. EUR+WWI FRANCE GERMANY MOD/EUR UK ELITES POL/PAR PWR...CHARTS ANTHOL 18/20. PAGE 5 H0094 NAT/COMP POLICY IDEA/COMP

B67
BROMKE A.,POLAND'S POLITICS: IDEALISM VS. REALISM. COM GERMANY POLAND RUSSIA USSR POL/PAR CATHISM ...BIBLIOG 19/20. PAGE 21 H0431 NAT/G DIPLOM MARXISM

B67
CAMERON R.,BANKING IN THE EARLY STAGES OF INDUSTRIALIZATION: A STUDY IN ECONOMIC COMPARATIVE HISTORY. FRANCE GERMANY UK USSR...CHARTS IDEA/COMP NAT/COMP 18/20 CHINJAP. PAGE 26 H0512 FINAN INDUS GOV/COMP

B67
DAVIDSON E.,THE TRIAL OF THE GERMANS* NUREMBERG* 1946-48. EUR+WWI GERMANY CULTURE NAT/G LEAD PERSON HEALTH...CRIMLGY PSY SOC BIOG JEWS. PAGE 37 H0745 FASCISM ADJUD TOTALISM WAR

B67
GIFFORD P.,BRITAIN AND GERMANY IN AFRICA. AFR GERMANY UK ECO/UNDEV LEAD WAR NAT/LISM ATTIT ...POLICY HIST/WRIT METH/COMP ANTHOL BIBLIOG 19/20 WWI. PAGE 56 H1123 COLONIAL ADMIN DIPLOM NAT/COMP

B67
PLANCK C.R.,THE CHANGING STATUS OF GERMAN REUNIFICATION IN WESTERN DIPLOMACY, 1955-1966. GERMANY DELIB/GP PLAN PEACE...TREND 20 KENNEDY/JF DEGAULLE/C. PAGE 126 H2519 NAT/G DIPLOM CENTRAL

B67
RYDER A.J.,THE GERMAN REVOLUTION OF 1918; A STUDY OF GERMAN SOCIALISM IN WAR AND REVOLT. GERMANY NAT/G POL/PAR GP/REL...BIBLIOG 20. PAGE 136 H2724 SOCISM WAR REV INGP/REL

B67
SCHUTZ W.W.,RETHINKING GERMAN POLICY; NEW APPROACHES TO REUNIFICATION. GERMANY USSR PLAN CONFER...POLICY 20. PAGE 140 H2806 REGION NAT/G DIPLOM PROB/SOLV

B67
VALI F.A.,THE QUEST FOR A UNITED GERMANY. GERMANY PROB/SOLV DIPLOM ADJUST...BIBLIOG 20. PAGE 161 H3222 NAT/G ATTIT PLAN CENTRAL

S67
DESHPANDE A.M.,"FEDERAL-STATE FISCAL RELATIONS IN FINAN

INDIA" (REVIEW ARTICLE)" GERMANY USSR DELIB/GP PLAN BUDGET ECO/TAC INCOME 20 SOC/DEMPAR SOC/REVPAR. PAGE 40 H0795
NAT/G GOV/REL TAX

S67
HOFMANN W.,"THE PUBLIC INTEREST PRESSURE GROUP: THE CASE OF THE DEUTSCHE STADTETAG." GERMANY GERMANY/W CONSTN STRUCT NAT/G CENTRAL FEDERAL PWR...TIME/SEQ 20. PAGE 72 H1447
LOC/G VOL/ASSN LOBBY ADMIN

S67
KROGER K.,"ZUR ENTWICKLUNG DER STAATSZWECKLEHRE IM 19 JAHRHUNDERT." GERMANY RATIONAL ATTIT...IDEA/COMP 19. PAGE 89 H1773
CONCPT NAT/G JURID OBJECTIVE

S67
SAVER W.,"NATIONAL SOCIALISM: TOTALITARIANISM OR FASCISM?" GERMANY STRUCT POL/PAR PROB/SOLV MARXISM ...SOC CONCPT HIST/WRIT IDEA/COMP 20 HITLER/A COLD/WAR. PAGE 138 H2760
SOCISM NAT/G TOTALISM FASCISM

S67
WILPERT C.,"A LOOK IN THE MIRROR AND OVER THE WALL." GERMANY POL/PAR...KNO/TEST COLD/WAR. PAGE 169 H3378
NAT/G PLAN DIPLOM ATTIT

B85
BLUNTSCHLI J.K.,THE THEORY OF THE STATE. GERMANY CONSTN INGP/REL NAT/LISM PERSON SOVEREIGN CONSERVE ...SOC. PAGE 18 H0362
CONCPT LEGIS NAT/G

B96
LOWELL A.L.,GOVERNMENTS AND PARTIES IN CONTINENTAL EUROPE, VOL. II. AUSTRIA GERMANY HUNGARY MOD/EUR SWITZERLND SOCIETY EX/STRUC LEGIS DIPLOM AGREE LEAD PARL/PROC PWR...POLICY 19. PAGE 99 H1974
POL/PAR NAT/G GOV/REL ELITES

B96
MARX K.,REVOLUTION AND COUNTER-REVOLUTION. GERMANY CONSTN ELITES INDUS NAT/G DIPLOM ECO/TAC WEALTH. PAGE 104 H2083
MARXIST REV PWR STRATA

GERMANY FOREIGN MINISTRY H1115

GERMANY/E....EAST GERMANY; SEE ALSO COM

B18
KERNER R.J.,SLAVIC EUROPE: A SELECTED BIBLIOGRAPHY IN THE WESTERN EUROPEAN LANGUAGES. BULGARIA CZECHOSLVK GERMANY/E POLAND RUSSIA YUGOSLAVIA NAT/G DIPLOM MARXISM...LING 19/20. PAGE 85 H1695
BIBLIOG SOCIETY CULTURE COM

B59
BUNDESMIN FUR VERTRIEBENE,ZEITTAFEL DER VORGESCHICHTE UND DES ABLAUFS DER VERTREIBUNG SOWIE DER UNTERBRINGUNG UND EINGLIEDERUNG DER (2 VOLS.). GERMANY/E GERMANY/W NAT/G PROVS PROB/SOLV DIPLOM PARL/PROC ATTIT...BIBLIOG SOC/INTEG 20 MIGRATION PARLIAMENT. PAGE 24 H0475
JURID GP/REL INT/LAW

B59
EPSTEIN F.T.,EAST GERMANY: A SELECTED BIBLIOGRAPHY (PAMPHLET). COM GERMANY/E LAW AGRI FINAN INDUS LABOR POL/PAR EDU/PROP ADMIN AGE/Y 20. PAGE 47 H0932
BIBLIOG/A INTELL MARXISM NAT/G

B60
STOLPER W.F.,GERMANY BETWEEN EAST AND WEST: THE ECONOMICS OF COMPETITIVE COEXISTENCE. FUT GERMANY/E GERMANY/W WOR+45 FINAN POL/PAR BUDGET ECO/TAC FOR/AID INT/TRADE...STAT CHARTS METH/COMP 20 COLD/WAR. PAGE 150 H2989
ECO/DEV DIPLOM GOV/COMP BAL/PWR

B60
VON KOENIGSWALD H.,SIE SUCHEN ZUFLUCHT. GERMANY/E NAT/G PLAN ECO/TAC SOCISM...GEOG CENSUS 20 BERLIN. PAGE 164 H3273
GP/REL COERCE DOMIN PERSON

S65
ROGGER H.,"EAST GERMANY: STABLE OR IMMOBILE." COM EUR+WWI GERMANY/E NAT/G INT/TRADE DOMIN EDU/PROP COERCE TOTALISM COLD/WAR 20. PAGE 133 H2659
TOP/EX RIGID/FLEX GERMANY

B66
HERMANN F.G.,DER KAMPF GEGEN RELIGION UND KIRCHE IN DER SOWJETISCHEN BESATZUNGSZONE DEUTSCHLANDS. GERMANY/E EDU/PROP ATTIT PERSON MORAL MARXISM 20 LENIN/VI STALIN/J KHRUSH/N. PAGE 70 H1400
SECT ORD/FREE GP/REL NAT/G

S67
SMITH J.E.,"THE GERMAN DEMOCRATIC REPUBLIC AND THE WEST." GERMANY/E ECO/DEV NAT/G PROB/SOLV CONTROL REV TOTALISM...GOV/COMP 20. PAGE 146 H2911
DIPLOM PWR MARXISM

S67
SMITH J.E.,"RED PRUSSIANISM OF THE GERMAN DEMOCRATIC REPUBLIC." GERMANY/E INTELL TOP/EX WORKER PLAN DIPLOM PRODUC ATTIT WEALTH MARXISM. PAGE 146 H2912
NAT/G TOTALISM INDUS NAT/LISM

S67
SMITH J.E.,"THE RED PRUSSIANISM OF THE GERMAN DEMOCRATIC REPUBLIC." GERMANY/E INTELL NAT/G SECT CHIEF...PREDICT TIME/SEQ 20. PAGE 146 H2913
MARXISM NAT/LISM GOV/COMP EDU/PROP

S67
SPITTMANN I.,"EAST GERMANY: THE SWINGING PENDULUM." COM GERMANY/E NAT/G EFFICIENCY MARXISM 20. PAGE 148 H2952
PRODUC POL/PAR WEALTH ATTIT

GERMANY/W....WEST GERMANY

L49
BRECHT A.,"THE NEW GERMAN CONSTITUTION." GERMANY/W NAT/G CHIEF EX/STRUC LEGIS PROB/SOLV ADMIN REPRESENT TOTALISM ORD/FREE PLURISM...MAJORIT CHARTS 20. PAGE 20 H0409
CONSTN DIPLOM SOVEREIGN FEDERAL

S49
STEINMETZ H.,"THE PROBLEMS OF THE LANDRAT: A STUDY OF COUNTY GOVERNMENT IN THE US ZONE OF GERMANY." GERMANY/W USA+45 INDUS PLAN DIPLOM EDU/PROP CONTROL WAR GOV/REL FEDERAL WEALTH PLURISM...GOV/COMP 20 LANDRAT. PAGE 149 H2977
LOC/G COLONIAL MGT TOP/EX

B51
MEYER E.W.,POLITICAL PARTIES IN WESTERN GERMANY (PAMPHLET). GERMANY/W MUNIC NAT/G GOV/REL ALL/IDEOS 20 UNIFICA BERLIN. PAGE 109 H2190
POL/PAR LOBBY CHOOSE CONSTN

N51
MEYER E.W.,POLITICAL PARTIES IN WESTERN GERMANY (PAMPHLET). EUR+WWI GERMANY/W PRESS LEAD CHOOSE REPRESENT ATTIT 20. PAGE 109 H2189
BIBLIOG POL/PAR NAT/G VOL/ASSN

B52
GURLAND A.R.L.,POLITICAL SCIENCE IN WESTERN GERMANY: THOUGHTS AND WRITINGS, 1950-1952 (PAMPHLET). EUR+WWI GERMANY/W ELITES SOCIETY NAT/G NAT/LISM TOTALISM 20. PAGE 63 H1253
BIBLIOG/A DIPLOM CIVMIL/REL FASCISM

B55
DUVERGER M.,THE POLITICAL ROLE OF WOMEN. FRANCE GERMANY/W NORWAY YUGOSLAVIA STRATA LOBBY AGE ATTIT ROLE...STAT SAMP CHARTS METH/COMP NAT/COMP HYPO/EXP FEMALE/SEX. PAGE 44 H0875
SEX LEAD PARTIC CHOOSE

B55
FLECHTHEIM O.K.,DIE DEUTSCHEN PARTEIEN SEIT 1945. GERMANY/W CONSTN STRUCT FINAN ATTIT 20. PAGE 51 H1022
POL/PAR NAT/G GP/COMP

B55
HEYDTE A F.,SOZIOLOGIE DER DEUTSCHEN PARTEIEN. GERMANY/W CONSTN ELITES CHOOSE 20. PAGE 70 H1412
POL/PAR SOC STRUCT NAT/G

B55
POLLOCK J.K.,GERMAN DEMOCRACY AT WORK. GERMANY/W LOC/G NAT/G DIPLOM PARL/PROC...OBS IDEA/COMP 20. PAGE 127 H2539
PARTIC POL/PAR CHOOSE EDU/PROP

C58
GOLAY J.F.,"THE FOUNDING OF THE FEDERAL REPUBLIC OF GERMANY." GERMANY/W CONSTN EX/STRUC DIPLOM ADMIN CHOOSE...DECISION BIBLIOG 20. PAGE 58 H1155
FEDERAL NAT/G PARL/PROC POL/PAR

B59
BUNDESMIN FUR VERTRIEBENE,ZEITTAFEL DER VORGESCHICHTE UND DES ABLAUFS DER VERTREIBUNG SOWIE DER UNTERBRINGUNG UND EINGLIEDERUNG DER (2 VOLS.). GERMANY/E GERMANY/W NAT/G PROVS PROB/SOLV DIPLOM PARL/PROC ATTIT...BIBLIOG SOC/INTEG 20 MIGRATION PARLIAMENT. PAGE 24 H0475
JURID GP/REL INT/LAW

B59
LEMBERG E.,DIE VERTRIEBENEN IN WESTDEUTSCHLAND (3 VOLS.). GERMANY/W CULTURE STRUCT AGRI PROVS ADMIN ...JURID 20 MIGRATION. PAGE 94 H1875
GP/REL INGP/REL SOCIETY

B59
SISSON C.H.,THE SPIRIT OF BRITISH ADMINISTRATION AND SOME EUROPEAN COMPARISONS. FRANCE GERMANY/W SWEDEN UK LAW EX/STRUC INGP/REL EFFICIENCY ORD/FREE ...DECISION 20. PAGE 144 H2890
GOV/COMP ADMIN ELITES ATTIT

B60
LOMBARDO TOLEDANO V,EL NEONAZISMO; SUS CHARACTERISTICAS Y PELIGROS. GERMANY/W POL/PAR COLONIAL LEAD LOBBY ATTIT 20 NAZI. PAGE 98 H1956
NAT/G FASCISM POLICY DIPLOM

B60
STOLPER W.F.,GERMANY BETWEEN EAST AND WEST: THE ECONOMICS OF COMPETITIVE COEXISTENCE. FUT GERMANY/E GERMANY/W WOR+45 FINAN POL/PAR BUDGET ECO/TAC FOR/AID INT/TRADE...STAT CHARTS METH/COMP 20 COLD/WAR. PAGE 150 H2989
ECO/DEV DIPLOM GOV/COMP BAL/PWR

B61
BEDFORD S.,THE FACES OF JUSTICE: A TRAVELLER'S REPORT. AUSTRIA FRANCE GERMANY/W SWITZERLND UK UNIV WOR+45 WOR-45 CULTURE PARTIC GOV/REL MORAL...JURID OBS GOV/COMP 20. PAGE 13 H0257
CT/SYS ORD/FREE PERSON LAW

B61
DRAGNICH A.N.,MAJOR EUROPEAN GOVERNMENTS. FRANCE GERMANY/W UK USSR LOC/G EX/STRUC CT/SYS PARL/PROC ATTIT MARXISM...JURID MGT NAT/COMP 19/20. PAGE 42 H0846
NAT/G LEGIS CONSTN POL/PAR

B61
EMMET C.,THE VANISHING SWASTIKA. GERMANY/W ELITES CRIME WAR...SAMP 20. PAGE 46 H0922
FASCISM ATTIT AGE/Y

NAT/G

B61
PECKERT J.,DIE GROSSEN UND DIE KLEINEN MAECHTE. COM GERMANY/W ECO/DEV ECO/UNDEV NAT/G WAR RACE/REL PEACE...POLICY GP/COMP GOV/COMP 20 COLD/WAR. PAGE 124 H2482
DIPLOM ECO/TAC BAL/PWR

B61
STAHL W.,EDUCATION FOR DEMOCRACY IN WEST GERMANY: ACHIEVEMENT SHORTCOMINGS - PROSPECTS. GERMANY/W SOCIETY NAT/G FORCES PLAN PROB/SOLV PRESS ALL/VALS ...POLICY MAJORIT CONCPT ANTHOL 20. PAGE 148 H2967
EDU/PROP POPULISM AGE/Y ADJUST

B61
TREVE W.,DEUTSCHE PARTEIPROGRAMME 1861-1961. GERMANY GERMANY/W DELIB/GP CONFER CHOOSE REPRESENT 19/20. PAGE 157 H3130
POL/PAR NAT/G LEGIS PARL/PROC

S61
LOEWENBERG G.,"PARLIAMENTARISM IN WESTERN GERMANY: THE FUNCTIONING OF THE BUNDESTAG" (BMR)" GERMANY/W NAT/G POL/PAR CHIEF LEAD 20 PARLIAMENT. PAGE 98 H1952
LEGIS CHOOSE CONSTN PARL/PROC

B62
ABOSCH H.,THE MENACE OF THE MIRACLE: GERMANY FROM HITLER TO ADENAUER. EUR+WWI GERMANY/W CULTURE FORCES PRESS NUC/PWR WAR CHOOSE 20 HITLER/A ADENAUER/K. PAGE 3 H0057
DIPLOM PEACE POLICY

B62
FRIEDMANN W.,METHODS AND POLICIES OF PRINCIPAL DONOR COUNTRIES IN PUBLIC INTERNATIONAL DEVELOPMENT FINANCING: PRELIMINARY APPRAISAL. FRANCE GERMANY/W UK USA+45 USSR WOR+45 FINAN TEC/DEV CAP/ISM DIPLOM ECO/TAC ATTIT 20 EEC. PAGE 53 H1066
INT/ORG FOR/AID NAT/COMP ADMIN

B62
PAIKERT G.C.,THE GERMAN EXODUS. EUR+WWI GERMANY/W LAW CULTURE SOCIETY STRUCT INDUS NAT/LISM RESPECT SOVEREIGN...CHARTS BIBLIOG SOC/INTEG 20 MIGRATION. PAGE 122 H2444
INGP/REL STRANGE GEOG GP/REL

B62
ZIESEL K.,DAS VERLORENE GEWISSEN. GERMANY/W NAT/G VOL/ASSN EDU/PROP PRESS SUPEGO...POLICY 20. PAGE 173 H3455
MORAL PWR ORD/FREE RESPECT

B63
ALMOND G.A.,THE CIVIC CULTURE: POLITICAL ATTITUDES AND DEMOCRACY IN FIVE NATIONS. GERMANY/W ITALY UK USA+45 SOCIETY STRUCT PARTIC...SOC DEEP/INT SAMP 20 MEXIC/AMER. PAGE 6 H0113
POPULISM CULTURE NAT/COMP ATTIT

B63
FLECHTHEIM O.K.,DOKUMENTE ZUR PARTEIPOLITISCHEN ENTWICKLUNG IN DEUTSCHLAND SEIT 1945 (2 VOLS.). EUR+WWI GERMANY/W...CONCPT ANTHOL 20. PAGE 51 H1023
POL/PAR ELITES NAT/G TIME/SEQ

B63
JACOB H.,GERMAN ADMINISTRATION SINCE BISMARCK: CENTRAL AUTHORITY VERSUS LOCAL AUTONOMY. GERMANY GERMANY/W LAW POL/PAR CONTROL CENTRAL TOTALISM FASCISM...MAJORIT DECISION STAT CHARTS GOV/COMP 19/20 BISMARCK/O HITLER/A WEIMAR/REP. PAGE 79 H1577
ADMIN NAT/G LOC/G POLICY

B63
MERKL P.H.,THE ORIGIN OF THE WEST GERMAN REPUBLIC. GERMANY/W WOR+45 POL/PAR DIPLOM LEAD LOBBY REPRESENT GP/REL NAT/LISM 20. PAGE 109 H2179
CONSTN PARL/PROC CONTROL BAL/PWR

L63
FREUND G.,"ADENAUER AND THE FUTURE OF GERMANY." EUR+WWI FUT GERMANY/W FORCES LEGIT ADMIN ROUTINE ATTIT DRIVE PERSON PWR...POLICY TIME/SEQ TREND VAL/FREE 20 ADENAUER/K. PAGE 53 H1058
NAT/G BIOG DIPLOM GERMANY

S63
ANTHON C.G.,"THE END OF THE ADENAUER ERA." EUR+WWI GERMANY/W CONSTN EX/STRUC CREATE DIPLOM LEGIT ATTIT PERSON ALL/VALS...RECORD 20 ADENAUER/K. PAGE 7 H0144
NAT/G TOP/EX BAL/PWR GERMANY

S63
KOHN H.,"GERMANY IN WORLD POLITICS." EUR+WWI GERMANY GERMANY/W USSR NAT/G POL/PAR TOP/EX ATTIT ...CONCPT TREND GEN/LAWS 20 NATO ADENAUER/K. PAGE 87 H1746
ACT/RES ORD/FREE BAL/PWR

B64
BROWN W.M.,THE EXTERNAL LIQUIDITY OF AN ADVANCED COUNTRY. CANADA FRANCE GERMANY/W SWEDEN UK USA+45 ECO/DEV DIPLOM PRICE...CONCPT STAT NAT/COMP 20. PAGE 22 H0451
FINAN INT/TRADE COST INCOME

B64
GROSSER A.,THE FEDERAL REPUBLIC OF GERMANY: A CONCISE HISTORY. GERMANY/W STRUCT MORAL ORD/FREE POPULISM SOCISM...SOC CONCPT 20. PAGE 62 H1235
NAT/G POL/PAR CHOOSE DIPLOM

B64
KAACK H.,DIE PARTEIEN IN DER VERFASSUNGSWIRKLICHKEIT DER BUNDESREPUBLIK. GERMANY/W ADMIN PARL/PROC CHOOSE...JURID 20. PAGE 82 H1646
POL/PAR PROVS NAT/G

B64
MILIBAND R.,THE SOCIALIST REGISTER: 1964. GERMANY/W ITALY UK LABOR POL/PAR ECO/TAC FOR/AID NUC/PWR ...POLICY SOCIALIST IDEA/COMP 20 MAO NASSER/G. PAGE 110 H2204
MARXISM SOCISM CAP/ISM PROB/SOLV

B64
WALDMAN E.,THE GOOSE STEP IS VERBOTEN: THE GERMAN ARMY TODAY. GERMANY/W LAW CONSTN LEGIS PROB/SOLV DOMIN CONTROL CIVMIL/REL GOV/REL INGP/REL ATTIT ...DEEP/QU 20. PAGE 164 H3289
SOC FORCES NAT/G

B65
ADENAUER K.,MEMOIRS 1945-53. EUR+WWI GERMANY/W ECO/DEV CHIEF FORCES ECO/TAC WAR GOV/REL PWR SOVEREIGN 20 NATO ADENAUER/K. PAGE 3 H0068
BIOG DIPLOM NAT/G PERS/REL

B65
CARTER G.M.,POLITICS IN EUROPE. EUR+WWI FRANCE GERMANY/W UK USSR LAW CONSTN POL/PAR VOL/ASSN PRESS LOBBY PWR...ANTHOL SOC/INTEG EEC. PAGE 27 H0548
GOV/COMP OP/RES ECO/DEV

B65
NORDEN A.,WAR AND NAZI CRIMINALS IN WEST GERMANY: STATE, ECONOMY, ADMINISTRATION, ARMY, JUSTICE, SCIENCE. GERMANY GERMANY/W MOD/EUR ECO/DEV ACADEM EX/STRUC FORCES DOMIN ADMIN CT/SYS...POLICY MAJORIT PACIFIST 20. PAGE 119 H2370
FASCIST WAR NAT/G TOP/EX

B65
US DEPARTMENT OF DEFENSE,US SECURITY ARMS CONTROL, AND DISARMAMENT 1961-1965 (PAMPHLET). CHINA/COM COM GERMANY/W ISRAEL SPACE USA+45 USSR WOR+45 FORCES EDU/PROP DETER EQUILIB PEACE ALL/VALS...GOV/COMP 20 NATO. PAGE 159 H3183
BIBLIOG/A ARMS/CONT NUC/PWR DIPLOM

S65
PLISCHKE E.,"INTEGRATING BERLIN AND THE FEDERAL REPUBLIC OF GERMANY." EUR+WWI GERMANY/W LEGIS TEC/DEV DOMIN ORD/FREE PWR...JURID 20 BERLIN. PAGE 126 H2528
DIPLOM NAT/G MUNIC

B66
DEUTSCHE INST ZEITGESCHICHTE,DIE WESTDEUTSCHEN PARTEIEN: 1945-1965. GERMANY/W CHOOSE PWR ...TIME/SEQ 20. PAGE 40 H0806
POL/PAR CONCPT NAT/G PROVS

B66
NEUMANN R.G.,THE GOVERNMENT OF THE GERMAN FEDERAL REPUBLIC. EUR+WWI GERMANY/W LOC/G EX/STRUC LEGIS CT/SYS INGP/REL PWR...BIBLIOG 20 ADENAUER/K. PAGE 117 H2336
NAT/G POL/PAR DIPLOM CONSTN

B66
RICHERT F.,DIE NATIONALE WELLE. GERMANY GERMANY/W PARL/PROC ORD/FREE FASCISM...TREND 19/20. PAGE 131 H2622
POL/PAR ATTIT NAT/LISM NAT/G

B66
US DEPARTMENT OF STATE,RESEARCH ON WESTERN EUROPE, GREAT BRITAIN, AND CANADA (EXTERNAL RESEARCH LIST NO 3-25). CANADA GERMANY/W UK LAW CULTURE NAT/G POL/PAR FORCES EDU/PROP REGION MARXISM...GEOG SOC WORSHIP 20 CMN/WLTH. PAGE 160 H3192
BIBLIOG/A EUR+WWI DIPLOM

B67
BUNN R.F.,POLITICS AND CIVIL LIBERTIES IN EUROPE: FOUR CASE STUDIES. FRANCE GERMANY/W UK USSR NAT/G PRESS CRIME CROWD PRIVIL ATTIT 20. PAGE 24 H0476
ORD/FREE CONSTN NAT/COMP LAW

B67
DEUTSCH K.W.,FRANCE, GERMANY AND THE WESTERN ALLIANCE. FRANCE GERMANY/W INT/ORG ARMS/CONT NAT/LISM SOVEREIGN...INT NAT/COMP 20. PAGE 40 H0801
ELITES ATTIT DIPLOM POLICY

B67
HANRIEDER W.F.,WEST GERMAN FOREIGN POLICY 1949-1963: INTERNATIONAL PRESSURE AND DOMESTIC RESPONSE. EUR+WWI GERMANY/W POL/PAR LOBBY CONSEN 20. PAGE 66 H1316
DIPLOM POLICY NAT/G ATTIT

S67
BAIKALOV A.,"EMERGENCY LEGISLATION IN WEST GERMANY." GERMANY/W LABOR NAT/G POL/PAR SANCTION ...MARXIST 20. PAGE 10 H0199
LAW TOTALISM LEGIS PARL/PROC

S67
HOFMANN W.,"THE PUBLIC INTEREST PRESSURE GROUP: THE CASE OF THE DEUTSCHE STADTETAG." GERMANY GERMANY/W CONSTN STRUCT NAT/G CENTRAL FEDERAL PWR...TIME/SEQ 20. PAGE 72 H1447
LOC/G VOL/ASSN LOBBY ADMIN

S67
LAQUEUR W.,"BONN IS NOT WEIMAR* REFLECTIONS ON THE RADICAL RIGHT IN GER MANY." CULTURE LOC/G NAT/G PARTIC CHOOSE. PAGE 91 H1822
GERMANY/W FASCISM NAT/LISM

S67
SHELDON C.H.,"PUBLIC OPINION AND HIGH COURTS: COMMUNIST PARTY CASES IN FOUR CONSTITUTIONAL SYSTEMS." CANADA GERMANY/W WOR+45 POL/PAR MARXISM ...METH/COMP NAT/COMP 20 AUSTRAL. PAGE 143 H2857
ATTIT CT/SYS CONSTN DECISION

S67
SOMMER T.,"BONN CHANGES COURSE." GERMANY/W NAT/G POL/PAR PROB/SOLV NAT/LISM 20 NATO BERLIN/BLO. PAGE 147 H2932
DIPLOM BAL/PWR INT/ORG

S67
YEFROMEV A.,"THE TRUE FACE OF THE WEST GERMAN NATIONAL-DEMOCRATS." GERMANY/W NAT/G DOMIN LEAD SANCTION WAR ATTIT PERSON...MARXIST 20. PAGE 172
POL/PAR TOTALISM PARL/PROC

H3436 — DIPLOM

S68
DEUTSCHER I.,"GERMANY AND MARXISM." FUT GERMANY/W NAT/G...MARXIST TREND 20. PAGE 40 H0808
SOCISM ORD/FREE POPULISM POL/PAR

GERSCHENKRON A. H1116

GESELLSCHAFT RECHTSVERGLEICH H1117

GETTYSBURG....BATTLE OF GETTYSBURG

GEWIRTH A. H1118

GHAI D.P. H1119

GHAI Y.P. H2122

GHANA....SEE ALSO AFR

N
BROCKWAY A.F.,AFRICAN SOCIALISM. EUR+WWI GHANA ISLAM UAR ECO/UNDEV CAP/ISM INT/TRADE COLONIAL COERCE GOV/REL DISCRIM 20 NEGRO NKRUMAH/K NASSER/G. PAGE 21 H0423
AFR SOCISM MARXISM

B58
CARTER G.M.,TRANSITION IN AFRICA; STUDIES IN POLITICAL ADAPTATION. AFR CENTRL/AFR GHANA NIGERIA CONSTN LOC/G POL/PAR ADMIN GP/REL FEDERAL...MAJORIT BIBLIOG 20. PAGE 27 H0543
NAT/COMP PWR CONTROL NAT/G

B59
WRAITH R.E.,EAST AFRICAN CITIZEN. AFR GHANA UK AGRI INDUS LOC/G POL/PAR PROB/SOLV CONTROL REGION REPRESENT NAT/LISM PWR...OBS 20 AFRICA/E AFRICA/W. PAGE 171 H3415
ECO/UNDEV RACE/REL NAT/G NAT/COMP

B60
JEFFRIES C.,TRANSFER OF POWER: PROBLEMS OF THE PASSAGE TO SELFGOVERNMENT. CEYLON GHANA MALAYSIA NIGERIA UK INT/ORG CONSULT DELIB/GP LEGIS DIPLOM CONFER PARL/PROC 20. PAGE 80 H1595
SOVEREIGN COLONIAL ORD/FREE NAT/G

B60
PITCHER G.M.,BIBLIOGRAPHY OF GHANA. AFR GHANA NAT/G 20. PAGE 126 H2517
BIBLIOG/A SOC

B60
THEOBOLD R.,THE NEW NATIONS OF WEST AFRICA. GHANA NIGERIA CULTURE INT/ORG ECO/TAC FOR/AID COLONIAL RACE/REL POPULISM...ANTHOL BIBLIOG 20 UN. PAGE 153 H3068
AFR SOVEREIGN ECO/UNDEV DIPLOM

S60
APTER D.E.,"THE ROLE OF TRADITIONALISM IN THE POLITICAL MODERNIZATION OF GHANA AND UGANDA" (BMR)" AFR GHANA UGANDA CULTURE NAT/G POL/PAR NAT/LISM ...CON/ANAL 20. PAGE 8 H0152
CONSERVE ADMIN GOV/COMP PROB/SOLV

B61
DUFFY J.,AFRICA SPEAKS. GHANA TOGO CULTURE ECO/UNDEV PROB/SOLV COLONIAL NEUTRAL DISCRIM NAT/LISM SOVEREIGN ALL/IDEOS...CONCPT ANTHOL SOC/INTEG 20 NEGRO THIRD/WRLD. PAGE 43 H0857
AFR NAT/G FUT STRUCT

B62
ABRAHAM W.E.,THE MIND OF AFRICA. AFR SOCIETY STRATA KIN ECO/TAC DOMIN EDU/PROP LEGIT COERCE ATTIT ALL/VALS...MAJORIT SOC OBS HIST/WRIT TIME/SEQ TREND TOT/POP 20. PAGE 3 H0058
CULTURE SIMUL GHANA

B62
GREEN L.P.,DEVELOPMENT IN AFRICA. AFR CENTRL/AFR GHANA RHODESIA SOUTH/AFR AGRI PROC/MFG INT/TRADE DEMAND NAT/LISM PRODUC WEALTH...GEOG METH/CNCPT CHARTS BIBLIOG 20. PAGE 60 H1206
CULTURE ECO/UNDEV GOV/REL TREND

B62
MANSUR F.,PROCESS OF INDEPENDENCE. GHANA INDIA INDONESIA PAKISTAN CONSTN ELITES INTELL STRUCT ACADEM NAT/G REV PWR 20. PAGE 102 H2043
NAT/COMP POL/PAR SOVEREIGN COLONIAL

B63
NKRUMAH K.,AFRICA MUST UNITE. AFR FUT GHANA CONSTN CULTURE SOCIETY NAT/G POL/PAR DELIB/GP TOP/EX PLAN DOMIN EDU/PROP ATTIT DRIVE...TIME/SEQ CHARTS TOT/POP 20. PAGE 118 H2364
CONCPT GEN/LAWS REGION

S63
LEE J.M.,"PARLIAMENT IN REPUBLICAN GHANA." AFR CONSTN CULTURE SOCIETY STRATA POL/PAR DELIB/GP TOP/EX DOMIN EDU/PROP LEGIT COERCE CHOOSE ATTIT ALL/VALS...CONCPT STAT TIME/SEQ VAL/FREE 20. PAGE 93 H1857
LEGIS GHANA

B64
JOHNSON A.F.,BIBLIOGRAPHY OF GHANA: 1930-1961. GHANA LAW AGRI INDUS NAT/G INT/TRADE EDU/PROP HEALTH...GEOG AUD/VIS CHARTS 20. PAGE 81 H1618
BIBLIOG/A CULTURE SOC

S64
CLIGNET R.,"POTENTIAL ELITES IN GHANA AND THE IVORY COAST: A PRELIMINARY SURVEY." AFR CULTURE ELITES STRATA KIN NAT/G SECT DOMIN EXEC ORD/FREE RESPECT SKILL...POLICY RELATIV GP/COMP NAT/COMP 20. PAGE 30 H0605
PWR LEGIT IVORY/CST GHANA

B65
ADU A.L.,THE CIVIL SERVICE IN NEW AFRICAN STATES. AFR GHANA FINAN SOVEREIGN...POLICY 20 CIVIL/SERV AFRICA/E AFRICA/W. PAGE 4 H0074
ECO/UNDEV ADMIN COLONIAL NAT/G

B65
DOLCI D.,A NEW WORLD IN THE MAKING. GHANA SENEGAL USSR YUGOSLAVIA CULTURE INT/ORG PLAN EDU/PROP GP/REL PEACE MORAL...GEOG SOC 20 COLD/WAR. PAGE 42 H0834
SOCIETY ALL/VALS DRIVE PERSON

B65
FOSTER P.,EDUCATION AND SOCIAL CHANGE IN GHANA. GHANA CULTURE STRUCT ECO/UNDEV TEC/DEV REGION EFFICIENCY LITERACY ALL/VALS SOVEREIGN...STAT METH/COMP 19/20 GOLD/COAST. PAGE 52 H1043
SCHOOL CREATE SOCIETY

B66
AFRIFA A.A.,THE GHANA COUP. AFR GHANA ELITES NAT/G DIPLOM DOMIN 20 NKRUMAH/K. PAGE 4 H0076
TOP/EX REV FORCES POL/PAR

B66
BIRMINGHAM W.,A STUDY OF CONTEMPORARY GHANA VOL I: THE ECONOMY OF GHANA. AFR GHANA PLAN...POLICY STAT CHARTS ANTHOL BIBLIOG 20. PAGE 17 H0342
ECO/UNDEV ECO/TAC NAT/G PRODUC

B66
FLINT J.E.,NIGERIA AND GHANA. AFR GHANA NIGERIA UK NAT/G DOMIN DISCRIM...CHARTS BIBLIOG/A 15/20 NEGRO MAPS. PAGE 51 H1026
CULTURE COLONIAL NAT/LISM

B66
MATTHEWS R.,AFRICAN POWDER KEG: REVOLT AND DISSENT IN SIX EMERGENT NATIONS. AFR ALGERIA DAHOMEY GABON GHANA MALAWI GAMBLE LEAD PARTIC REV DRIVE...BIOG TREND GOV/COMP 20. PAGE 105 H2098
ELITES ECO/UNDEV TOP/EX CONTROL

B66
SCHATTEN F.,COMMUNISM IN AFRICA. AFR GHANA GUINEA MALI CULTURE ECO/UNDEV LABOR SECT ECO/TAC EDU/PROP REV 20. PAGE 139 H2774
COLONIAL NAT/LISM MARXISM DIPLOM

B66
ZOLBERG A.R.,CREATING POLITICAL ORDER. AFR CONGO/BRAZ GHANA NIGER KIN NAT/G DOMIN COLONIAL REGION CENTRAL NAT/LISM ATTIT PWR 20 CONGO/LEOP. PAGE 173 H3462
SOVEREIGN ORD/FREE CONSTN POL/PAR

S66
MCLANE C.B.,"SOVIET DOCTRINE AND THE MILITARY COUPS IN AFRICA." ALGERIA GHANA COLONIAL NAT/LISM RIGID/FLEX SOVEREIGN MARXISM...DECISION NAT/COMP. PAGE 107 H2140
USSR ATTIT AFR FORCES

S67
FINLAY D.J.,"THE GHANA COUP...ONE YEAR LATER." GHANA FORCES FOR/AID PRESS CONTROL CIVMIL/REL NAT/LISM AUTHORIT PWR...PREDICT 20. PAGE 50 H1005
REV NAT/G ATTIT ECO/UNDEV

L68
CURRENT HISTORY,"AFRICA, 1968." ETHIOPIA GHANA NIGERIA SOUTH/AFR CULTURE ECO/UNDEV KIN SECT CHIEF EX/STRUC WAR WEAPON CHOOSE CIVMIL/REL...GOV/COMP 20 AFRICA/E. PAGE 36 H0724
RACE/REL NAT/LISM FORCES AFR

S68
KANET R.E.,"RECENT SOVIET REASSESSMENT OF DEVELOPMENTS IN THE THIRD WORLD." ALGERIA GHANA INDONESIA USSR WOR+45 CONSTN ELITES INTELL STRUCT DOMIN CONTROL REV PWR MARXISM...IDEA/COMP METH 20 THIRD/WRLD. PAGE 83 H1653
DIPLOM NEUTRAL NAT/G NAT/COMP

B99
KINGSLEY M.H.,WEST AFRICAN STUDIES. GHANA NIGERIA SIER/LEONE LAW EXTR/IND SECT DIPLOM INT/TRADE DOMIN RACE/REL OWN HEALTH...SOC 19. PAGE 86 H1717
AFR HEREDITY COLONIAL CULTURE

GHANI A.R. H1120

GHOSH P.K. H1121

GIBBON/EDW....EDWARD GIBBON

B58
SYME R.,COLONIAL ELITES: ROME, SPAIN, AND THE AMERICAS. CHRIST-17C MOD/EUR SPAIN UK USA-45 CULTURE NAT/G CHIEF TOP/EX...GOV/COMP IDEA/COMP NAT/COMP ROM/EMP GIBBON/EDW TOYNBEE/A. PAGE 151 H3022
COLONIAL ELITES DOMIN

GIBBS S.L. H1122

GIBRALTAR....SEE UK

GIDE/A....ANDRE GIDE

B64
CAUTE D.,COMMUNISM AND THE FRENCH INTELLECTUALS, 1914-1960. COM EUR+WWI MOD/EUR NAT/G PERF/ART PROF/ORG CREATE EDU/PROP ATTIT PERSON KNOWL MARXISM ...SOC TIME/SEQ MARX/KARL 20 MALRAUX/A GIDE/A SARTRE/J. PAGE 28 H0563
POL/PAR INTELL

GIERSCH H. H3264

GIFFORD P. H1123

GILBERT F. H0879

GILBERT S.P. H1124

GILG P. H1126

GILL R.T. H1127

GILLIN J.P. H1128

GILLY A. H1129

GILMORE M.P. H1130

GINIEWSKI P. H1131

GINSBURG M. H1132

GINSBURG N. H1133

GINSBURGS G. H1134

GIRALDO JARAMILLO G. H1135

GIROD R. H1136

GITLOW A.L. H1137

GIVE....GIVING, PHILANTHROPY

N19
COUTROT A.,THE FIGHT OVER THE 1959 PRIVATE EDUCATION LAW IN FRANCE (PAMPHLET). FRANCE NAT/G SECT GIVE EDU/PROP GP/REL ATTIT RIGID/FLEX ORD/FREE 20 CHURCH/STA. PAGE 34 H0681
SCHOOL PARL/PROC CATHISM LAW

B60
PETERSON W.C.,THE WELFARE STATE IN FRANCE. EUR+WWI FRANCE FUT STRATA PROB/SOLV TAX GIVE RECEIVE INCOME ORD/FREE PWR...CHARTS 20. PAGE 125 H2496
NEW/LIB ECO/TAC WEALTH NAT/G

B61
HALPERIN S.,THE POLITICAL WORLD OF AMERICAN ZIONISM. ISRAEL FINAN LABOR VOL/ASSN GIVE LOBBY REPRESENT GP/REL ATTIT POLICY. PAGE 64 H1293
CULTURE SECT EDU/PROP DELIB/GP

B61
INTL UNION LOCAL AUTHORITIES,METROPOLIS. WOR+45 DIST/IND FINAN GIVE EDU/PROP CRIME COST HEALTH WEALTH 20. PAGE 78 H1563
MUNIC GOV/COMP LOC/G BIBLIOG

B61
KEE R.,REFUGEE WORLD. AUSTRIA EUR+WWI GERMANY NEIGH EX/STRUC WORKER PROB/SOLV ECO/TAC RENT EDU/PROP INGP/REL COST LITERACY HABITAT 20 MIGRATION. PAGE 84 H1676
NAT/G GIVE WEALTH STRANGE

B61
ROSE D.L.,THE VIETNAMESE CIVIL SERVICE. VIETNAM CONSULT DELIB/GP GIVE PAY EDU/PROP COLONIAL GOV/REL UTIL...CHARTS 20. PAGE 134 H2672
ADMIN EFFICIENCY STAT NAT/G

B62
HANAK H.,GREAT BRITAIN AND AUSTRIA-HUNGARY DURING THE FIRST WORLD WAR: A STUDY IN THE FORMATION OF PUBLIC OPINION. CZECHOSLVK UK NAT/G GIVE DOMIN EDU/PROP CONSERVE...BIBLIOG 20 AUST/HUNG WWI. PAGE 65 H1311
WAR DIPLOM ATTIT PRESS

B62
MOUSSA P.,THE UNDERPRIVILEGED NATIONS. FINAN INT/ORG PLAN PROB/SOLV CAP/ISM GIVE TASK WEALTH ...POLICY SOC 20. PAGE 114 H2273
ECO/UNDEV NAT/G DIPLOM FOR/AID

B63
COLUMBIA U SCHOOL OF LAW,PUBLIC INTERNATIONAL DEVELOPMENT FINANCING IN SENEGAL. SENEGAL FINAN DELIB/GP GIVE EFFICIENCY...CHARTS GOV/COMP ANTHOL 20. PAGE 32 H0636
FOR/AID PLAN RECEIVE ECO/UNDEV

B63
CRUICKSHANK M.,CHURCH AND STATE IN ENGLISH EDUCATION 1870 TO PRESENT. UK LEGIS TAX GIVE DOMIN LEGIT ORD/FREE 19/20 CHURCH/STA. PAGE 36 H0715
NAT/G SECT EDU/PROP GP/REL

B63
OECD,FOOD AID: ITS ROLE IN ECONOMIC DEVELOPMENT. FINAN NAT/G PLAN DIPLOM GIVE TASK WEALTH ...METH/COMP METH 20. PAGE 120 H2397
ECO/UNDEV FOR/AID INT/ORG POLICY

S63
NYE J.,"TANGANYIKA'S SELF-HELP." TANZANIA NAT/G GIVE COST EFFICIENCY NAT/LISM 20. PAGE 119 H2381
ECO/TAC POL/PAR ECO/UNDEV WORKER

B64
RAISON T.,WHY CONSERVATIVE? UK FORCES DIPLOM ECO/TAC GIVE EDU/PROP ORD/FREE WEALTH LAISSEZ ...GOV/COMP 20 TORY/PARTY CONSRV/PAR. PAGE 129 H2583
PLURISM CONSERVE POL/PAR NAT/G

B64
WILSON T.,POLICIES FOR REGIONAL DEVELOPMENT. CANADA UK FINAN INDUS NAT/G BUDGET TAX GIVE COST ...NAT/COMP 20. PAGE 169 H3383
REGION PLAN ECO/DEV ECO/TAC

B65
MEAGHER R.F.,PUBLIC INTERNATIONAL DEVELOPMENT FINANCING IN SUDAN. SUDAN FINAN DELIB/GP GIVE ...CHARTS GOV/COMP 20. PAGE 108 H2155
FOR/AID PLAN RECEIVE ECO/UNDEV

S65
GOLDMAN M.I.,"A BALANCE SHEET OF SOVIET FOREIGN AID." USA+45 ECO/UNDEV BAL/PWR ECO/TAC RENT GIVE EDU/PROP CONTROL COST PROFIT GEN/METH. PAGE 58 H1158
USSR FOR/AID NAT/COMP EFFICIENCY

S65
WHITE J.,"WEST GERMAN AID TO DEVELOPING COUNTRIES." INT/ORG OP/RES GIVE CENTRAL ATTIT DRIVE...STAT NAT/COMP COLD/WAR. PAGE 167 H3348
GERMANY FOR/AID ECO/UNDEV CAP/ISM

B66
AMER ENTERPRISE INST PUB POL,SIGNIFICANT ISSUES IN ECONOMIC AID TO DEVELOPING COUNTRIES. FINAN INT/ORG NAT/G PLAN PROB/SOLV GIVE TASK WEALTH...DECISION 20. PAGE 6 H0119
ECO/UNDEV FOR/AID DIPLOM POLICY

B66
GLAZER M.,THE FEDERAL GOVERNMENT AND THE UNIVERSITY. CHILE PROB/SOLV DIPLOM GIVE ADMIN WAR ...POLICY SOC 20. PAGE 57 H1140
BIBLIOG/A NAT/G PLAN ACADEM

B66
KIRDAR U.,THE STRUCTURE OF UNITED NATIONS ECONOMIC AID TO UNDERDEVELOPED COUNTRIES. AGRI FINAN INDUS NAT/G EX/STRUC PLAN GIVE TASK...POLICY 20 UN. PAGE 86 H1721
INT/ORG FOR/AID ECO/UNDEV ADMIN

B66
KIRKENDALL R.S.,SOCIAL SCIENTISTS AND FARM POLITICS IN THE AGE OF ROOSEVELT. ACADEM PLAN ECO/TAC GIVE ADMIN CONTROL PRODUC...SOC 20 NEW/DEAL ROOSEVLT/F BURAGR/ECO. PAGE 86 H1722
AGRI INTELL POLICY NAT/G

B66
PLATE H.,PARTEIFINANZIERUNG UND GRUNDESETZ. GERMANY NAT/G PLAN GIVE PAY INCOME WEALTH...JURID 20. PAGE 126 H2522
POL/PAR CONSTN FINAN

B67
ROSENTHAL A.H.,THE SOCIAL PROGRAMS OF SWEDEN. SWEDEN USA+45 FINAN NAT/G PLAN PROB/SOLV INSPECT ORD/FREE...POLICY HEAL SOC CHARTS NAT/COMP 20. PAGE 134 H2681
GIVE SOC/WK WEALTH METH/COMP

L67
LARKIN E.,"ECONOMIC GROWTH, CAPITAL INVESTMENT, AND THE ROMAN CATHOLIC CHURCH IN NINETEENTH-CENTURY IRELAND." IRELAND AGRI DIST/IND NAT/G GIVE OWN CATHISM...CHARTS 19. PAGE 91 H1823
FINAN SECT WEALTH ECO/UNDEV

S67
BASOV V.,"THE DEVELOPMENT OF PUBLIC EDUCATION AND THE BUDGET." USSR NAT/G CONTROL REV COST AGE...STAT 20. PAGE 12 H0235
BUDGET GIVE EDU/PROP SCHOOL

S67
BELLER I.,"ECONOMIC POLICY AND THE DEMANDS OF LABOR." PLAN TAX GIVE PRICE WAR COST PRODUC WEALTH. PAGE 13 H0268
NAT/G ECO/TAC SOC/WK INCOME

S67
SHARKANSKY I.,"ECONOMIC AND POLITICAL CORRELATES OF STATE GOVERNMENT EXPENDITURE: GENERAL TENDENCIES AND DEVIANT CASES." USA+45 LOC/G NAT/G TAX GIVE INCOME...CENSUS CHARTS. PAGE 142 H2845
PROVS BUDGET GOV/COMP

GLADE W.P. H1138

GLADSTON/W....WILLIAM GLADSTONE

B63
SHANNON R.T.,GLADSTONE AND THE BULGARIAN AGITATION OF 1876. BULGARIA TURKEY UK DIPLOM COERCE REV ATTIT 19 GLADSTON/W DISRAELI/B. PAGE 142 H2841
EDU/PROP NAT/G PWR CONSEN

GLADSTONE A.E. H1139

GLAZER M. H1140,H1141

GLEASON J.H. H1142

GLEICHER D.B. H0239

GLENN N.D. H1143

GLOBERSON A. H1144

GLUCKMAN M. H1145,H1146,H1147,H1148,H1149

GMP/REG....GOOD MANUFACTURING PRACTICE REGULATIONS

GOD AND GODS....SEE DEITY

GODECHOT J. H1150

GODWIN W. H1151

GOEBBELS/J....JOSEPH GOEBBELS

B42
SINGTON D.,THE GOEBBELS EXPERIMENT. GERMANY MOD/EUR NAT/G EX/STRUC FORCES CONTROL ROUTINE WAR TOTALISM PWR...ART/METH HUM 20 NAZI GOEBBELS/J. PAGE 144 H2886
FASCISM EDU/PROP ATTIT COM/IND

B65
BRAMSTED E.K.,GOEBBELS AND NATIONAL SOCIALIST PROPAGANDA, 1925-1945. EUR+WWI GERMANY UK USSR NAT/G FORCES WAR FASCISM...TIME/SEQ 20 GOEBBELS/J NAZI. PAGE 20 H0403
EDU/PROP PSY COM/IND

GOETHE J.W. H1152

GOETHE/J....JOHANN WOLFGANG VON GOETHE

B64
FROMM E.,MARX'S CONCEPT OF MAN. LABOR OWN PERSON ...HUM IDEA/COMP GEN/LAWS 17 MARX/KARL EUROPE SPINOZA/B GOETHE/J HEGEL/GWF. PAGE 54 H1072
INGP/REL CONCPT MARXISM SOCISM

B65
GOETHE J.W.,GOETHE UBER DIE DEUTSCHEN. GERMANY CULTURE...NAT/COMP 18/19 GOETHE/J. PAGE 58 H1152
ATTIT PERSON SOCIETY

GOFF F.R. H1153

GOFFMAN E. H1154

GOLAY J.F. H1155

GOLD....GOLD

GOLD/COAST....GOLD COAST (PRE-GHANA)

B65
FOSTER P.,EDUCATION AND SOCIAL CHANGE IN GHANA. GHANA CULTURE STRUCT ECO/UNDEV TEC/DEV REGION EFFICIENCY LITERACY ALL/VALS SOVEREIGN...STAT METH/COMP 19/20 GOLD/COAST. PAGE 52 H1043
SCHOOL CREATE SOCIETY

GOLD/STAND....GOLD STANDARD

B58
AVRAMOVIC D.,POSTWAR GROWTH IN INTERNATIONAL INDEBTEDNESS. WOR+45 AGRI INDUS CAP/ISM PRICE INCOME...NAT/COMP 20 GOLD/STAND SILVER. PAGE 9 H0184
INT/TRADE FINAN COST BAL/PAY

B59
CUCCORESE H.J.,HISTORIA DE LA CONVERSION DEL PAPEL MONEDA EN BUENOS AIRES, 1861-1867. LAW LOC/G NAT/G ATTIT...POLICY BIBLIOG 19 ARGEN BUENOS/AIR GOLD/STAND. PAGE 36 H0717
FINAN PLAN LEGIS

B60
BOMBACH G.,STABILE PREISE IN WACHSENDER WIRTSCHAFT: DAS INFLATIONSPROBLEM. BARGAIN CAP/ISM PRICE COST ...NAT/COMP 20 GOLD/STAND. PAGE 19 H0371
ECO/UNDEV PLAN FINAN ECO/TAC

B61
BREWIS T.N.,CANADIAN ECONOMIC POLICY. CANADA BUDGET CAP/ISM INT/TRADE RATION TARIFFS TAX PRICE CONTROL ROUTINE FEDERAL INCOME PRODUC 20 GOLD/STAND. PAGE 20 H0412
ECO/DEV ECO/TAC NAT/G PLAN

B61
HAUSER M.,DIE URSACHEN DER FRANZOSISCHEN INFLATION IN DEN JAHREN 1946-1952. FRANCE INDUS NAT/G BUDGET DIPLOM ECO/TAC FOR/AID COST MONEY 20 GOLD/STAND. PAGE 68 H1357
ECO/DEV FINAN PRICE

B61
NATIONAL BANK OF LIBYA,INFLATION IN LIBYA (PAMPHLET). LIBYA SOCIETY NAT/G PLAN INT/TRADE ...STAT CHARTS 20 GOLD/STAND. PAGE 116 H2318
ECO/TAC ECO/UNDEV FINAN BUDGET

B61
VEIT O.,GRUNDRISS DER WAHRUNGSPOLITIK. FRANCE GERMANY USSR DIPLOM INT/TRADE...NAT/COMP 19/20 GOLD/STAND SILVER. PAGE 162 H3239
FINAN POLICY ECO/TAC CAP/ISM

B63
AHN L.A.,FUNFZIG JAHRE ZWISCHEN INFLATION UND DEFLATION. GERMANY DIPLOM PRICE...CONCPT 20 GOLD/STAND. PAGE 4 H0081
FINAN CAP/ISM NAT/COMP ECO/TAC

B63
CHOU S.H.,THE CHINESE INFLATION 1937-1949. ASIA SOCIETY POL/PAR FOR/AID INT/TRADE BAL/PAY WEALTH MARXISM...STAT CHARTS 20 COM/PARTY GOLD/STAND. PAGE 30 H0597
FINAN ECO/TAC BUDGET NAT/G

B64
MORGAN H.W.,AMERICAN SOCIALISM 1900-1960. USA+45 USA-45 INTELL AGRI LABOR WORKER BARGAIN ECO/TAC GP/REL RACE/REL 20 NEGRO MIGRATION GOLD/STAND. PAGE 113 H2254
SOCISM POL/PAR ECO/DEV STRATA

S68
GUZZARDI W.,"THE DECLINE OF THE STERLING CLUB." UK WOR+45 NAT/G PLAN DIPLOM INT/TRADE AGREE CONSEN EQUILIB SOVEREIGN...POLICY NEW/IDEA 20 COMMONWLTH GOLD/STAND. PAGE 63 H1259
FINAN ECO/TAC WEALTH NAT/COMP

GOLDBERG A. H1156

GOLDEY D.B. H3368

GOLDHAMMER H. H0899

GOLDMAN M.I. H1157,H1158

GOLDMAN/E....ERIC GOLDMAN

GOLDRICH D. H0079

GOLDSCHMIDT W. H1159

GOLDWATR/B....BARRY GOLDWATER

GOLDWIN R.A. H1160

GOLEMBIEWSKI R.T. H1161

GOMILLN/CG....C.G. GOMILLION

GONZALEZ M.P. H1163

GONZALEZ NAVARRO M. H1164

GONZALEZ PALENCIA A H1165

GONZALEZ PEDRERO E. H1166

GOOCH G.P. H1167

GOOD E.M. H1168

GOOD MANUFACTURING PRACTICE REGULATIONS....SEE GMP/REG

GOODE W.J. H1169

GOODENOUGH W.H. H1170

GOODHART A.L. H1454

GOODMAN E. H1171

GOODMAN G.K. H1172

GOODNOW H.F. H1173

GOODRICH L. H2437

GOODSELL J.N. H1174

GOODWIN C.D.W. H1302

GOPAL R. H1175

GOPAL S. H1176

GORDON B.K. H1177

GORDON L. H1178

GORDON M. H1179

GORDON M.S. H1180

GORDON/K....K. GORDON

GORDON/W....WILLIAM GORDON

GORER G. H1181,H1182

GORWALA A.D. H1183

GOSNELL H.F. H1184

GOUGH J.W. H1947

GOULD J. H1185,H1186

GOULD S.H. H1187

GOURE L. H1188

GOURNAY B. H1189

GOV/COMP....COMPARISON OF GOVERNMENTS

GOV/REL....RELATIONS BETWEEN GOVERNMENTS

N
BROCKWAY A.F.,AFRICAN SOCIALISM. EUR+WWI GHANA ISLAM UAR ECO/UNDEV CAP/ISM INT/TRADE COLONIAL COERCE GOV/REL DISCRIM 20 NEGRO NKRUMAH/K NASSER/G. PAGE 21 H0423
AFR SOCISM MARXISM

N
UNIVERSITY OF FLORIDA LIBRARY,DOORS TO LATIN AMERICA; RECENT BOOKS AND PAMPHLETS. CONSTN CULTURE SOCIETY ECO/UNDEV COLONIAL LEAD GOV/REL NAT/LISM ATTIT...HUM SOC 20. PAGE 159 H3170
BIBLIOG/A L/A+17C DIPLOM NAT/G

N
MIDDLE EAST JOURNAL. CULTURE SECT DIPLOM LEAD GOV/REL ATTIT...POLICY PHIL/SCI SOC LING BIOG 20. PAGE 1 H0007
BIBLIOG ISLAM NAT/G ECO/UNDEV

N
CHINA QUARTERLY. COM AGRI INDUS ACADEM POL/PAR INT/TRADE CONFER GOV/REL...TIME/SEQ CON/ANAL INDEX 20. PAGE 1 H0014
BIBLIOG/A ASIA DIPLOM POLICY

N
NEUE POLITISCHE LITERATUR; BERICHTE UBER DAS INTERNATIONALE SCHRIFTTUM ZUR POLITIK. WOR+45 LAW CONSTN POL/PAR ADMIN LEAD GOV/REL...POLICY IDEA/COMP. PAGE 2 H0027
BIBLIOG/A DIPLOM NAT/G NAT/COMP

N
AVTOREFERATY DISSERTATSII. USSR INTELL ACADEM NAT/G DIPLOM GOV/REL KNOWL CONCPT. PAGE 2 H0029
BIBLIOG MARXISM MARXIST COM

N
"PROLOG",DIGEST OF THE SOVIET UKRANIAN PRESS. USSR LAW AGRI INDUS PROVS SCHOOL DIPLOM GOV/REL ATTIT ...HUM LING 20. PAGE 3 H0053
BIBLIOG/A NAT/G PRESS COM

NCO
CARRINGTON C.E.,THE COMMONWEALTH IN AFRICA (PAMPHLET). UK STRUCT NAT/G COLONIAL REPRESENT GOV/REL RACE/REL NAT/LISM...MAJORIT 20 EEC NEGRO COLD/WAR. PAGE 27 H0540
ECO/UNDEV AFR DIPLOM PLAN

B10
MCILWAIN C.H.,THE HIGH COURT OF PARLIAMENT AND ITS SUPREMACY B1910 1878 408. UK EX/STRUC PARL/PROC GOV/REL INGP/REL PRIVIL 12/20 PARLIAMENT ENGLSH/LAW. PAGE 107 H2132
LAW LEGIS CONSTN NAT/G

B13
SIEGFRIED A.,TABLEAU POLITIQUE DE LA FRANCE DE L'OUEST SOUS LA TROISIEME REPUBLIQUE. FRANCE STRATA STRUCT NAT/G POL/PAR PROVS REGION GOV/REL ATTIT PWR ...TREND TIME 19. PAGE 143 H2869
SOC GEOG SOCIETY

N19
GORWALA A.D.,THE ADMINISTRATIVE JUNGLE (PAMPHLET). INDIA NAT/G LEGIS ECO/TAC CONTROL GOV/REL ...METH/COMP 20. PAGE 59 H1183
ADMIN POLICY PLAN ECO/UNDEV

N19
GRIFFITH W.,THE PUBLIC SERVICE (PAMPHLET). UK LAW LOC/G NAT/G PARTIC CHOOSE DRIVE ROLE SKILL...CHARTS 20 CIVIL/SERV. PAGE 61 H1222
ADMIN EFFICIENCY EDU/PROP GOV/REL

N19
WILSON T.,FINANCIAL ASSISTANCE WITH REGIONAL DEVELOPMENT (PAMPHLET). CANADA INDUS NAT/G PLAN TAX CONTROL COST EFFICIENCY...POLICY CHARTS 20. PAGE 169 H3382
FINAN ECO/TAC REGION GOV/REL

C20
BLACHLY F.F.,"THE GOVERNMENT AND ADMINISTRATION OF GERMANY." GERMANY CONSTN LOC/G PROVS DELIB/GP EX/STRUC FORCES LEGIS TOP/EX CT/SYS...BIBLIOG/A 19/20. PAGE 17 H0348
NAT/G GOV/REL ADMIN PHIL/SCI

B24
HOLDSWORTH W.S.,A HISTORY OF ENGLISH LAW; THE COMMON LAW AND ITS RIVALS (VOL. IV). UK SEA AGRI CHIEF ADJUD CONTROL CRIME GOV/REL...INT/LAW JURID NAT/COMP 16/17 PARLIAMENT COMMON/LAW CANON/LAW ENGLSH/LAW. PAGE 72 H1449
LAW LEGIS CT/SYS CONSTN

B25
WILLIAMS B.,THE SELBORNE MEMORANDUM. AFR FUT SOUTH/AFR UK NAT/G BUDGET DIPLOM REGION GOV/REL SOVEREIGN...POLICY CHARTS 20 UNIFICA SELBORNE/W. PAGE 168 H3365
COLONIAL PROVS

B26
POLLARD A.F.,THE EVOLUTION OF PARLIAMENT. UK CONSTN POL/PAR EX/STRUC GOV/REL INGP/REL PRIVIL RIGID/FLEX ...TIME/SEQ 11/20 CMN/WLTH PARLIAMENT. PAGE 127 H2536
LEGIS PARL/PROC NAT/G

B27
WILLOUGHBY W.F.,PRINCIPLES OF PUBLIC ADMINISTRATION WITH SPECIAL REFERENCE TO THE NATIONAL AND STATE GOVERNMENTS OF THE UNITED STATES. FINAN PROVS CHIEF CONSULT LEGIS CREATE BUDGET EXEC ROUTINE GOV/REL CENTRAL...MGT 20 BUR/BUDGET CONGRESS PRESIDENT. PAGE 169 H3373
NAT/G EX/STRUC OP/RES ADMIN

B30
HULL W.I.,INDIA'S POLITICAL CRISIS. INDIA UK INT/ORG LABOR SECT DELIB/GP LEGIS DIPLOM NEUTRAL REGION CROWD GOV/REL MAJORITY ATTIT 20 NEHRU/J GANDHI/M COMMONWLTH. PAGE 75 H1492
ORD/FREE NAT/G COLONIAL NAT/LISM

B30
SMUTS J.C.,AFRICA AND SOME WORLD PROBLEMS. RHODESIA SOUTH/AFR CULTURE ECO/UNDEV INDUS INT/ORG SECT PROB/SOLV REGION GOV/REL DISCRIM ATTIT 19/20 LEAGUE/NAT LIVNGSTN/D NEGRO. PAGE 146 H2921
LEGIS AFR COLONIAL RACE/REL

B32
CHILDS J.B.,THE MEMORIAS OF THE REPUBLICS OF CENTRAL AMERICA AND OF THE ANTILLES. L/A+17C 19/20 CENTRAL/AM. PAGE 29 H0592
BIBLIOG GOV/REL NAT/G EX/STRUC

B32
NIEBUHR R.,MORAL MAN AND IMMORAL SOCIETY* A STUDY IN ETHICS AND POLITICS. UNIV CULTURE SOCIETY STRUCT DIPLOM GOV/REL GP/REL PERS/REL...TREND IDEA/COMP. PAGE 118 H2357
MORAL PWR

B39
ANDERSON W.,LOCAL GOVERNMENT IN EUROPE. FRANCE GERMANY ITALY UK USSR MUNIC PROVS ADMIN GOV/REL CENTRAL SOVEREIGN 20. PAGE 7 H0136
GOV/COMP NAT/COMP LOC/G CONSTN

B39
SIEYES E.J.,LES DISCOURS DE SIEYES DANS LES DEBATS CONSTITUTIONNELS DE L'AN III (2 ET 18 THERMIDOR). FRANCE LAW NAT/G PROB/SOLV BAL/PWR GOV/REL 18 JURY. PAGE 144 H2871
CONSTN ADJUD LEGIS EX/STRUC

B41
CHILDS J.B.,COLOMBIAN GOVERNMENT PUBLICATIONS (PAMPHLET). L/A+17C SOCIETY 19/20 COLOMB. PAGE 30 H0593
BIBLIOG GOV/REL NAT/G EX/STRUC

B41
CHILDS J.B.,A GUIDE TO THE OFFICIAL PUBLICATIONS OF THE OTHER AMERICAN REPUBLICS: ARGENTINA. CHIEF DIPLOM GOV/REL...BIBLIOG 18/19 ARGEN. PAGE 30 H0594
NAT/G EX/STRUC METH/CNCPT LEGIS

B41
COHEN E.W.,THE GROWTH OF THE BRITISH CIVIL SERVICE 1780-1939. UK NAT/G SENIOR ROUTINE GOV/REL...MGT METH/COMP BIBLIOG 18/20. PAGE 31 H0616
OP/RES TIME/SEQ CENTRAL ADMIN

B41
GILMORE M.P.,ARGUMENT FROM ROMAN LAW IN POLITICAL THOUGHT, 1200-1600. INTELL LICENSE CONTROL CT/SYS GOV/REL PRIVIL PWR...IDEA/COMP BIBLIOG 13/16. PAGE 56 H1130
JURID LAW CONCPT NAT/G

B42
FORTESCU J.,IN PRAISE OF ENGLISH LAW (1464) (TRANS. BY S.B. CHRIMES). UK ELITES CHIEF FORCES CT/SYS COERCE CRIME GOV/REL ILLEGIT...JURID GOV/COMP GEN/LAWS 15. PAGE 52 H1040
LAW CONSTN LEGIS ORD/FREE

S43
PRICE D.K.,"THE PARLIAMENTARY AND PRESIDENTIAL SYSTEMS" (BMR)" USA-45 NAT/G EX/STRUC PARL/PROC GOV/REL PWR 20 PRESIDENT CONGRESS PARLIAMENT. PAGE 128 H2561
LEGIS REPRESENT ADMIN GOV/COMP

B47
BEHAR D.,BIBLIOGRAFIA HISPANOAMERICANA. LIBROS ANTIGUOS Y MODERNOS REFERENTES A AMERICA Y ESPANA. PORTUGAL SPAIN CONSTN NAT/G SECT CREATE REV WAR GOV/REL...ART/METH GEOG PHIL/SCI LING 20 ARGEN. PAGE 13 H0260
BIBLIOG L/A+17C CULTURE

B48
HARRIS G.M.,COMPARATIVE LOCAL GOVERNMENT. FINAN CHOOSE ALL/VALS. PAGE 67 H1339
PARTIC GOV/REL LOC/G GOV/COMP

B48
PELCOVITS N.A.,OLD CHINA HANDS AND THE FOREIGN OFFICE. ASIA BURMA UK ECO/UNDEV NAT/G ECO/TAC FOR/AID TARIFFS DOMIN COLONIAL GOV/REL SOVEREIGN 19 HONG/KONG TREATY. PAGE 124 H2483
INT/TRADE ATTIT DIPLOM

B49
GRODZINS M.,AMERICANS BETRAYED: POLITICS AND THE JAPANESE EXPANSION. PROVS COERCE CHOOSE GOV/REL GP/REL INGP/REL ATTIT ORD/FREE...DECISION CHARTS 20 NISEI. PAGE 61 H1230
DISCRIM POLICY NAT/G WAR

B49
HEADLAM-MORLEY,BIBLIOGRAPHY IN POLITICS FOR THE HONOUR SCHOOL OF PHILOSOPHY, POLITICS AND ECONOMICS (PAMPHLET). UK CONSTN LABOR MUNIC DIPLOM ADMIN 19/20. PAGE 69 H1375
BIBLIOG NAT/G PHIL/SCI GOV/REL

B49
VIERECK P.,CONSERVATISM REVISITED: THE REVOLT AGAINST REVOLT 1815-1949. EUR+WWI ELITES NAT/G
CONSERVE MARXISM

FORCES PARTIC GOV/REL NAT/LISM...MAJORIT CONCPT GOV/COMP METTRNCH/K. PAGE 163 H3251
REALPOL

S49
STEINMETZ H.,"THE PROBLEMS OF THE LANDRAT: A STUDY OF COUNTY GOVERNMENT IN THE US ZONE OF GERMANY." GERMANY/W USA+45 INDUS PLAN DIPLOM EDU/PROP CONTROL WAR GOV/REL FEDERAL WEALTH PLURISM...GOV/COMP 20 LANDRAT. PAGE 149 H2977
LOC/G COLONIAL MGT TOP/EX

B51
CATALOGO GENERAL DE LA LIBRERIA ESPANOLA E HISPANOAMERICANA 1901-1930; AUTORES (5 VOLS., 1932-1951). SPAIN COLONIAL GOV/REL...SOC 20. PAGE 2 H0036
BIBLIOG L/A+17C DIPLOM NAT/G

B51
MEYER E.W.,POLITICAL PARTIES IN WESTERN GERMANY (PAMPHLET). GERMANY/W MUNIC NAT/G GOV/REL ALL/IDEOS 20 UNIFICA BERLIN. PAGE 109 H2190
POL/PAR LOBBY CHOOSE CONSTN

B52
INTERNATIONAL AFRICAN INST,ETHNOGRAPHIC SURVEY OF AFRICA: SOUTHERN AFRICA (VOLS. I-III, 1952-1954). AFR SOUTH/AFR CULTURE ECO/UNDEV GOV/REL HEREDITY ...GEOG SOC CHARTS BIBLIOG WORSHIP 20. PAGE 77 H1544
STRUCT KIN INGP/REL HABITAT

B52
THOM J.M.,GUIDE TO RESEARCH MATERIAL IN POLITICAL SCIENCE (PAMPHLET). ELITES LOC/G MUNIC NAT/G LEGIS DIPLOM ADJUD CIVMIL/REL GOV/REL PWR MGT. PAGE 154 H3074
BIBLIOG/A KNOWL

B53
APPLEBY P.H.,PUBLIC ADMINISTRATION IN INDIA: REPORT OF A SURVEY. INDIA LOC/G OP/RES ATTIT ORD/FREE 20. PAGE 7 H0147
ADMIN NAT/G EX/STRUC GOV/REL

C53
DORWART R.A.,"THE ADMINISTRATIVE REFORMS OF FREDRICK WILLIAM I OF PRUSSIA. GERMANY MOD/EUR CHIEF CONTROL PWR...BIBLIOG 16/18. PAGE 42 H0839
ADMIN NAT/G CENTRAL GOV/REL

B54
LEWIS E.,MEDIEVAL POLITICAL IDEAS. LAW CULTURE SOCIETY ECO/UNDEV NAT/G SECT GOV/REL ATTIT ...BIBLIOG/A T 11/15. PAGE 96 H1913
CHRIST-17C IDEA/COMP INTELL CONCPT

B54
MORRISON H.,GOVERNMENT AND PARLIAMENT. UK NAT/G PARLIAMENT. PAGE 113 H2266
GOV/REL EX/STRUC LEGIS PARL/PROC

B54
SCHWARTZ B.,FRENCH ADMINISTRATIVE LAW AND THE COMMON-LAW WORLD. FRANCE CULTURE LOC/G NAT/G PROVS DELIB/GP EX/STRUC LEGIS PROB/SOLV CT/SYS EXEC GOV/REL...IDEA/COMP ENGLSH/LAW. PAGE 140 H2808
JURID LAW METH/COMP ADJUD

B55
INTERNATIONAL AFRICAN INST,ETHNOGRAPHIC SURVEY OF AFRICA: NORTH EASTERN AFRICA (VOLUMES 1-2, 1955-56). AFR ETHIOPIA CULTURE ECO/UNDEV KIN GOV/REL ATTIT HEREDITY...GEOG CHARTS BIBLIOG WORSHIP 20. PAGE 77 H1545
STRUCT ECO/TAC INGP/REL HABITAT

B55
INTERNATIONAL AFRICAN INST,ETHNOGRAPHIC SURVEY OF AFRICA: WESTERN AFRICA: PEOPLES OF THE NIGER-BENUE CONFLUENCE. AFR NIGER CULTURE ECO/UNDEV KIN GOV/REL GP/REL ATTIT HEREDITY...CHARTS BIBLIOG WORSHIP 20. PAGE 77 H1546
STRUCT GEOG HABITAT INGP/REL

B55
MID-EUROPEAN LAW PROJECT,CHURCH AND STATE BEHIND THE IRON CURTAIN. COM CZECHOSLVK HUNGARY POLAND USSR CULTURE SECT EDU/PROP GOV/REL CATHISM...CHARTS ANTHOL BIBLIOG WORSHIP 20 CHURCH/STA. PAGE 110 H2202
LAW MARXISM POLICY

C55
APTER D.E.,"THE GOLD COAST IN TRANSITION." AFR CONSTN LOC/G LEGIS DIPLOM COLONIAL CONTROL GOV/REL ...CHARTS BIBLIOG 20 CMN/WLTH. PAGE 7 H0150
ORD/FREE REPRESENT PARL/PROC NAT/G

B56
DOUGLAS W.O.,WE THE JUDGES. INDIA USA+45 USA-45 LAW NAT/G SECT LEGIS PRESS CRIME FEDERAL ORD/FREE ...POLICY GOV/COMP 19/20 WARRN/EARL MARSHALL/J SUPREME/CT. PAGE 42 H0841
ADJUD CT/SYS CONSTN GOV/REL

B56
INTERNATIONAL AFRICAN INST,ETHNOGRAPHIC SURVEY OF AFRICA; WESTERN AFRICA: PAGAN PEOPLES OF CENTRAL AREA OF NORTHERN NIGERIA (VOL. XII). NIGERIA FAM KIN SECT ECO/TAC GOV/REL GP/REL ATTIT...LING CHARTS 20. PAGE 77 H1548
STRUCT INGP/REL HABITAT CULTURE

B57
INTERNATIONAL AFRICAN INST,ETHNOGRAPHIC SURVEY OF AFRICA: WESTERN AFRICA: THE BENIN KINGDOM. AFR NIGERIA CULTURE ECO/UNDEV KIN ECO/TAC GOV/REL AGE ATTIT HEREDITY...CHARTS BIBLIOG WORSHIP 20. PAGE 77 H1550
STRUCT INGP/REL GEOG HABITAT

B57
LONG H.A.,USURPERS - FOES OF FREE MAN. LAW NAT/G
CT/SYS

CHIEF LEGIS DOMIN ADJUD REPRESENT GOV/REL ORD/FREE LAISSEZ POPULISM...POLICY 18/20 SUPREME/CT ROOSEVLT/F CONGRESS CON/INTERP. PAGE 98 H1961
CENTRAL FEDERAL CONSTN

S57
HODGETTS J.E.,"THE CIVIL SERVICE AND POLICY FORMATION." CANADA NAT/G EX/STRUC ROUTINE GOV/REL 20. PAGE 72 H1443
ADMIN DECISION EFFICIENCY POLICY

B58
COWAN L.G.,LOCAL GOVERNMENT IN WEST AFRICA. AFR FRANCE UK CULTURE KIN POL/PAR CHIEF LEGIS CREATE ADMIN PARTIC GOV/REL GP/REL...METH/COMP 20. PAGE 34 H0682
LOC/G COLONIAL SOVEREIGN REPRESENT

B58
INDIA (REPUBLIC) PARLIAMENT,CLASSIFIED LIST OF PUBLIC UNDERTAKINGS AND OTHER BODIES IN INDIA. INDIA ACADEM LG/CO CONSULT LEGIT CONFER GOV/REL 20. PAGE 76 H1528
NAT/G LEGIS LICENSE PROF/ORG

B58
MECRENSKY E.,SCIENTIFIC MANPOWER IN EUROPE. WOR+45 EDU/PROP GOV/REL SKILL...TECHNIC PHIL/SCI INT CHARTS BIBLIOG 20. PAGE 108 H2157
ECO/TAC TEC/DEV METH/COMP NAT/COMP

B58
PAN AMERICAN UNION,REPERTORIO DE PUBLICACIONES PERIODICAS ACTUALES LATINO-AMERICANAS. CULTURE ECO/UNDEV ADMIN LEAD GOV/REL 20 OAS. PAGE 123 H2455
BIBLIOG L/A+17C NAT/G DIPLOM

B58
SHAW S.J.,THE FINANCIAL AND ADMINISTRATIVE ORGANIZATION AND DEVELOPMENT OF OTTOMAN EGYPT 1517-1798. UAR LOC/G FORCES BUDGET INT/TRADE TAX EATING INCOME WEALTH...CHARTS BIBLIOG 16/18 OTTOMAN NAPOLEON/B. PAGE 143 H2853
FINAN ADMIN GOV/REL CULTURE

B58
STRAUSZ-HUPE R.,THE IDEA OF COLONIALISM. WOR+45 WOR-45 BAL/PWR GOV/REL...POLICY CLASSIF TIME/SEQ GOV/COMP ANTHOL 20 UN. PAGE 150 H2996
IDEA/COMP COLONIAL CONTROL CONCPT

B59
HANSON A.H.,THE STRUCTURE AND CONTROL OF STATE ENTERPRISES IN TURKEY. TURKEY LAW ADMIN GOV/REL EFFICIENCY...CHARTS 20. PAGE 66 H1319
NAT/G LG/CO OWN CONTROL

B59
HENDERSON G.P.,REFERENCE MANUAL OF DIRECTORIES (16 VOLS.). MUNIC PROVS GOV/REL 20. PAGE 70 H1394
BIBLIOG/A NAT/COMP NAT/G INDUS

B59
MARTZ J.D.,CENTRAL AMERICA: THE CRISIS AND THE CHALLENGE. L/A+17C POL/PAR CHIEF CHOOSE SOVEREIGN ...BIOG TREND BIBLIOG 20 CENTRAL/AM. PAGE 104 H2071
NAT/G GOV/REL DIPLOM GOV/COMP

B59
ROSOLIO D.,TEN YEARS OF THE CIVIL SERVICE IN ISRAEL (1948-1958) (PAMPHLET). ISRAEL NAT/G RECEIVE 20. PAGE 134 H2685
ADMIN WORKER GOV/REL PAY

B60
ALBI F.,TRATADO DE LOS MODOS DE GESTION DE LAS CORPORACIONES LOCALES. SPAIN FINAN NAT/G BUDGET CONTROL EXEC ROUTINE GOV/REL ORD/FREE SOVEREIGN ...MGT 20. PAGE 5 H0092
LOC/G LAW ADMIN MUNIC

B60
FLORES R.H.,CATALOGO DE TESIS DOCTORALES DE LAS FACULTADES DE LA UNIVERSIDAD DE EL SALVADOR. EL/SALVADR LAW DIPLOM ADMIN LEAD GOV/REL...SOC 19/20. PAGE 52 H1030
BIBLIOG ACADEM L/A+17C NAT/G

B60
INTERNATIONAL AFRICAN INST,ETHNOGRAPHIC SURVEY OF AFRICA: WESTERN AFRICA: PEOPLES OF THE MIDDLE NIGER REGION, NORTHERN NIGERIA. AFR NIGER CULTURE ECO/UNDEV KIN NEIGH GOV/REL GP/REL ATTIT HEREDITY ...CHARTS BIBLIOG WORSHIP 20. PAGE 78 H1552
STRUCT GEOG HABITAT INGP/REL

B60
JHA C.,INDIAN GOVERNMENT AND POLITICS. INDIA SERV/IND POL/PAR PROVS LEGIS CT/SYS CHOOSE GOV/REL FEDERAL 20. PAGE 81 H1616
NAT/G PARL/PROC CONSTN ADJUST

B60
PICKLES D.,THE FIFTH FRENCH REPUBLIC. ALGERIA FRANCE CHOOSE GOV/REL ATTIT CONSERVE...CHARTS 20 DEGAULLE/C. PAGE 125 H2506
CONSTN ADJUD NAT/G EFFICIENCY

B60
SCHEIBER H.N.,THE WILSON ADMINISTRATION AND CIVIL LIBERTIES 1917-1921. LAW GOV/REL ATTIT 20 WILSON/W CIVIL/LIB. PAGE 139 H2782
ORD/FREE WAR NAT/G CONTROL

C60
SMITH T.E.,"ELECTIONS IN DEVELOPING COUNTRIES: A STUDY OF ELECTORAL PROCEDURES USED IN TOPICAL AFRICA, SOUTH-EAST ASIA..." AFR S/ASIA UK ROUTINE GOV/REL RACE/REL...GOV/COMP BIBLIOG 20. PAGE 146 H2918
ECO/UNDEV CHOOSE REPRESENT ADMIN

C60
WRIGGINS W.H.,"CEYLON: DILEMMAS OF A NEW NATION." ASIA CEYLON CONSTN STRUCT POL/PAR SECT FORCES DIPLOM GOV/REL NAT/LISM...CHARTS BIBLIOG 20. PAGE 171 H3417
PROB/SOLV NAT/G ECO/UNDEV

B61
BEDFORD S.,THE FACES OF JUSTICE: A TRAVELLER'S REPORT. AUSTRIA FRANCE GERMANY/W SWITZERLND UK UNIV WOR+45 WOR-45 CULTURE PARTIC GOV/REL MORAL...JURID OBS GOV/COMP 20. PAGE 13 H0257
CT/SYS ORD/FREE PERSON LAW

B61
CONQUEST R.,POWER AND POLICY IN THE USSR. USSR NAT/G POL/PAR DIPLOM MARXISM 20. PAGE 33 H0655
COM HIST/WRIT GOV/REL PWR

B61
GARCIA E.,LA ADMINISTRACION ESPANOLA. SPAIN GOV/REL ...CONCPT METH/COMP 20. PAGE 55 H1099
ADMIN NAT/G LOC/G DECISION

B61
HARE T.,A TREATISE ON THE ELECTION OF REPRESENTATIVES, PARLIAMENTARY AND MUNICIPAL. UK CONSTN NAT/G PARL/PROC CHOOSE ATTIT...MAJORIT 18/19 PARLIAMENT. PAGE 66 H1330
LEGIS GOV/REL CONSEN REPRESENT

B61
HICKS U.K.,DEVELOPMENT FROM BELOW. UK INDUS ADMIN COLONIAL ROUTINE GOV/REL...POLICY METH/CNCPT CHARTS 19/20 CMN/WLTH. PAGE 71 H1414
ECO/UNDEV LOC/G GOV/COMP METH/COMP

B61
MILLIKAW M.F.,THE EMERGING NATIONS: THEIR GROWTH AND UNITED STATES POLICY. FUT USA+45 WOR+45 WOR-45 NAT/G PLAN TEC/DEV BAL/PWR GOV/REL PEACE ORD/FREE 20. PAGE 111 H2216
ECO/UNDEV POLICY DIPLOM FOR/AID

B61
NARASIMHAN V.K.,THE PRESS, THE PUBLIC AND THE ADMINISTRATION (PAMPHLET). INDIA COM/IND CONTROL REPRESENT GOV/REL EFFICIENCY...ANTHOL 20. PAGE 116 H2312
NAT/G ADMIN PRESS NEW/LIB

B61
ROSE D.L.,THE VIETNAMESE CIVIL SERVICE. VIETNAM CONSULT DELIB/GP GIVE PAY EDU/PROP COLONIAL GOV/REL UTIL...CHARTS 20. PAGE 134 H2672
ADMIN EFFICIENCY STAT NAT/G

B61
STANLEY C.J.,LATE CH'ING FINANCE: HU KUANG-YUNG AS AN INNOVATOR. ASIA NAT/G FORCES BUDGET TAX WAR GOV/REL COST...POLICY BIOG CHARTS BIBLIOG 19. PAGE 148 H2969
FINAN ECO/TAC CIVMIL/REL ADMIN

B62
CARY J.,THE CASE FOR AFRICAN FREEDOM AND OTHER WRITINGS ON AFRICA. AFR UK INDUS LOC/G NAT/G SECT INT/TRADE EDU/PROP GOV/REL RACE/REL ORD/FREE ...CONCPT ANTHOL 19/20. PAGE 27 H0552
NAT/LISM COLONIAL TREND ECO/UNDEV

B62
ESCUELA SUPERIOR DE ADMIN PUBL,INFORME DEL SEMINARIO SOBRE SERVICIO CIVIL O CARRERA ADMINISTRATIVA. L/A+17C ELITES STRATA CONFER CONTROL GOV/REL INGP/REL SUPEGO 20 CENTRAL/AM CIVIL/SERV. PAGE 47 H0939
ADMIN NAT/G PROB/SOLV ATTIT

B62
GREEN L.P.,DEVELOPMENT IN AFRICA. AFR CENTRL/AFR GHANA RHODESIA SOUTH/AFR AGRI PROC/MFG INT/TRADE DEMAND NAT/LISM PRODUC WEALTH...GEOG METH/CNCPT CHARTS BIBLIOG 20. PAGE 60 H1206
CULTURE ECO/UNDEV GOV/REL TREND

B62
INSTITUTE OF PUBLIC ADMIN,A SHORT HISTORY OF THE PUBLIC SERVICE IN IRELAND. IRELAND UK DIST/IND INGP/REL FEDERAL 13/20 CIVIL/SERV. PAGE 77 H1539
ADMIN WORKER GOV/REL NAT/G

B62
KARNJAHAPRAKORN C.,MUNICIPAL GOVERNMENT IN THAILAND AS AN INSTITUTION AND PROCESS OF SELF-GOVERNMENT. THAILAND CULTURE FINAN EX/STRUC LEGIS PLAN CONTROL GOV/REL EFFICIENCY ATTIT...POLICY 20. PAGE 83 H1662
LOC/G MUNIC ORD/FREE ADMIN

B62
MANNING H.T.,THE REVOLT OF FRENCH CANADA 1800-1835. CANADA UK CULTURE GOV/REL RACE/REL...BIBLIOG 19. PAGE 102 H2039
NAT/LISM COLONIAL GEOG

B62
STATE AND LOCAL GOVERNMENT. MUNIC NAT/G NEIGH PRESS CONTROL CHOOSE REPRESENT...BIBLIOG 20. PAGE 104 H2076
PROVS LOC/G GOV/REL PWR

B62
SELOSOEMARDJAN O.,SOCIAL CHANGES IN JOGJAKARTA. INDONESIA NETHERLAND ELITES STRATA STRUCT FAM POL/PAR CREATE DIPLOM INT/TRADE EDU/PROP ADMIN GOV/REL...SOC 20 JAVA CHINJAP. PAGE 141 H2825
ECO/UNDEV CULTURE REV COLONIAL

S62
MARTIN L.W.,"THE MARKET FOR STRATEGIC IDEAS IN BRITAIN: THE 'SANDYS ERA'" UK ARMS/CONT WAR GOV/REL OPTIMAL...POLICY DECISION GOV/COMP COLD/WAR CMN/WLTH. PAGE 103 H2063
DIPLOM COERCE FORCES PWR

B63
ADRIAN C.R.,GOVERNING OVER FIFTY STATES AND THEIR COMMUNITIES. USA+45 CONSTN FINAN MUNIC NAT/G POL/PAR EX/STRUC LEGIS ADMIN CONTROL CT/SYS ...CHARTS 20. PAGE 4 H0073
PROVS LOC/G GOV/REL GOV/COMP

B63
BIALEK R.W.,CATHOLIC POLITICS: A HISTORY BASED ON ECUADOR. ECUADOR SPAIN CULTURE STRUCT CONTROL REV PWR...BIBLIOG WORSHIP 18/20. PAGE 16 H0329
COLONIAL CATHISM GOV/REL HABITAT

B63
DALAND R.T.,PERSPECTIVES OF BRAZILIAN PUBLIC ADMINISTRATION (VOL. I). BRAZIL LAW ECO/UNDEV SCHOOL CHIEF TEC/DEV CONFER CONTROL GP/REL ATTIT ROLE PWR...ANTHOL 20. PAGE 37 H0735
ADMIN NAT/G PLAN GOV/REL

B63
ELLIOT J.H.,THE REVOLT OF THE CATALANS. SPAIN LOC/G PROVS FORCES DIPLOM TASK WAR GOV/REL INGP/REL ...POLICY 17 OLIVARES. PAGE 45 H0909
REV NAT/G TOP/EX DOMIN

B63
GONZALEZ PEDRERO E.,ANATOMIA DE UN CONFLICTO. WOR+45 ECO/DEV ECO/UNDEV ECO/TAC FOR/AID CONTROL ARMS/CONT GOV/REL...NAT/COMP 20 COLD/WAR. PAGE 58 H1166
DIPLOM DETER BAL/PWR

B63
GRIMOND J.,THE LIBERAL CHALLENGE. UK SOCIETY INDUS POL/PAR LEGIS PLAN CAP/ISM DIPLOM EDU/PROP GOV/REL CONSERVE 20 PARLIAMENT REFORMERS. PAGE 61 H1227
NAT/G NEW/LIB ECO/DEV POLICY

B63
MONGER G.W.,THE END OF ISOLATION. FRANCE MOD/EUR RUSSIA UK NAT/G LEGIS TOP/EX GOV/REL PWR 20 TREATY CHINJAP. PAGE 112 H2239
DIPLOM POLICY WAR

B63
SHANKS M.,THE LESSONS OF PUBLIC ENTERPRISE. UK LEGIS WORKER ECO/TAC ADMIN PARL/PROC GOV/REL ATTIT ...POLICY MGT METH/COMP NAT/COMP ANTHOL 20 PARLIAMENT. PAGE 142 H2840
SOCISM OWN NAT/G INDUS

B63
STUCKI C.W.,AMERICAN DOCTORAL DISSERTATIONS ON ASIA 1933-62 (A PAPER). PREHIST INDUS NAT/G GOV/REL ALL/IDEOS...ART/METH GEOG SOC LING 20. PAGE 150 H3002
BIBLIOG ASIA SOCIETY S/ASIA

B63
THOMPSON F.M.L.,ENGLISH LANDED SOCIETY IN THE NINETEENTH CENTURY. UK STRUCT MUNIC NAT/G CONTROL WAR GP/REL OWN WEALTH...BIBLIOG 18/20. PAGE 154 H3081
STRATA PWR ELITES GOV/REL

S63
LAMBERT D.,"LA TRANSPOSITION DU REGIME PRESIDENTIEL HORS DES ETATSUNIS; LE CAS DE L'AMERIQUE LATINE." NAT/G EX/STRUC LEGIS PARL/PROC PWR 18/20 PRESIDENT CENTRAL/AM SOUTH/AMER. PAGE 90 H1800
DELIB/GP CHIEF L/A+17C GOV/REL

N63
LEDERER W.,THE BALANCE ON FOREIGN TRANSACTIONS: PROBLEMS OF DEFINITION AND MEASUREMENT (PAMPHLET). USA+45 BUDGET DIPLOM ECO/TAC PRICE GOV/REL...POLICY STAT NAT/COMP METH 20. PAGE 93 H1853
FINAN BAL/PAY INT/TRADE ECO/DEV

B64
ANDREWS D.H.,LATIN AMERICA: A BIBLIOGRAPHY OF PAPERBACK BOOKS. SECT INT/TRADE EDU/PROP WAR GOV/REL ADJUST NAT/LISM ATTIT...ART/METH LING BIOG 20. PAGE 7 H0138
BIBLIOG L/A+17C CULTURE NAT/G

B64
BENDIX R.,NATION-BUILDING AND CITIZENSHIP: STUDIES OF OUR CHANGING SOCIAL ORDER. WOR+45 CULTURE LOC/G GOV/REL INGP/REL ORD/FREE PWR 20. PAGE 14 H0275
PARTIC NAT/COMP ADMIN AUTHORIT

B64
BROWN C.V.,GOVERNMENT AND BANKING IN WESTERN NIGERIA. AFR NIGERIA GOV/REL GP/REL...POLICY 20. PAGE 22 H0440
ADMIN ECO/UNDEV FINAN NAT/G

B64
GOODNOW H.F.,THE CIVIL SERVICE OF PAKISTAN: BUREAUCRACY IN A NEW NATION. INDIA PAKISTAN S/ASIA ECO/UNDEV PROVS CHIEF PARTIC CHOOSE EFFICIENCY PWR ...BIBLIOG 20. PAGE 59 H1173
ADMIN GOV/REL LAW NAT/G

B64
INDIAN COMM PREVENTION CORRUPT,REPORT, 1964. INDIA NAT/G GOV/REL ATTIT ORD/FREE...CRIMLGY METH 20. PAGE 76 H1530
CRIME ADMIN LEGIS LOC/G

B64
LIGGETT E.,BRITISH POLITICAL ISSUES: VOLUME 1. UK LAW CONSTN LOC/G NAT/G ADJUD 20. PAGE 97 H1930
POL/PAR GOV/REL CT/SYS DIPLOM

B64
NICOL D.,AFRICA - A SUBJECTIVE VIEW. AFR INT/ORG PLAN ADMIN COLONIAL PARL/PROC PARTIC REGION GOV/REL LITERACY ATTIT...BIBLIOG 20 CIVIL/SERV. PAGE 118 H2350
NAT/G LEAD CULTURE ACADEM

B64
REMAK J.,THE GENTLE CRITIC: THEODOR FONTANE AND
PERSON

GERMAN POLITICS, 1848-1898. GERMANY PRUSSIA CULTURE SOCIETY
ELITES BAL/PWR DIPLOM WRITING GOV/REL...HUM BIOG 19 WORKER
BISMARCK/O JUNKER FONTANE/T. PAGE 131 H2614 CHIEF

B64
RIES J.C.,THE MANAGEMENT OF DEFENSE: ORGANIZATION FORCES
AND CONTROL OF THE US ARMED SERVICES. PROF/ORG ACT/RES
DELIB/GP EX/STRUC LEGIS GOV/REL PERS/REL CENTRAL DECISION
RATIONAL PWR...POLICY TREND GOV/COMP BIBLIOG. CONTROL
PAGE 131 H2626

B64
WALDMAN E.,THE GOOSE STEP IS VERBOTEN: THE GERMAN SOC
ARMY TODAY. GERMANY/W LAW CONSTN LEGIS PROB/SOLV FORCES
DOMIN CONTROL CIVMIL/REL GOV/REL INGP/REL ATTIT NAT/G
...DEEP/QU 20. PAGE 164 H3289

S64
HORECKY P.L.,"LIBRARY OF CONGRESS PUBLICATIONS IN BIBLIOG/A
AID OF USSR AND EAST EUROPEAN RESEARCH." BULGARIA COM
CZECHOSLVK POLAND USSR YUGOSLAVIA NAT/G POL/PAR MARXISM
DIPLOM ADMIN GOV/REL...CLASSIF 20. PAGE 73 H1468

S64
SOLOVEYTCHIK G.,"BOOKS ON RUSSIA." USSR ELITES BIBLIOG/A
NAT/G PERF/ART REV GOV/REL MARXISM...AUD/VIS 20. COM
PAGE 147 H2929 CULTURE

S64
UNRUH J.M.,"SCIENTIFIC INPUTS TO LEGISLATIVE CREATE
DECISION-MAKING (SUPPLEMENT)" USA+45 ACADEM NAT/G DECISION
PROVS GOV/REL GOV/COMP. PAGE 159 H3171 LEGIS
PARTIC

B65
ADENAUER K.,MEMOIRS 1945-53. EUR+WWI GERMANY/W BIOG
ECO/DEV CHIEF FORCES ECO/TAC WAR GOV/REL PWR DIPLOM
SOVEREIGN 20 NATO ADENAUER/K. PAGE 3 H0068 NAT/G
PERS/REL

B65
ALLEN W.S.,THE NAZI SEIZURE OF POWER. GERMANY NAT/G MUNIC
CHIEF LEAD COERCE CHOOSE REPRESENT GOV/REL AUTHORIT FASCISM
...DECISION 20 HITLER/A NAZI. PAGE 5 H0106 TOTALISM
LOC/G

B65
BLITZ L.F.,THE POLITICS AND ADMINISTRATION OF NAT/G
NIGERIAN GOVERNMENT. NIGER CULTURE LOC/G LEGIS GOV/REL
DIPLOM COLONIAL CT/SYS SOVEREIGN...GEOG SOC ANTHOL POL/PAR
20. PAGE 18 H0357

B65
BROWNSON O.A.,THE AMERICAN REPUBLIC. NAT/G PROVS CONSTN
WAR GOV/REL PRIVIL ORD/FREE PWR ALL/IDEOS CONSERVE FEDERAL
...CONCPT 19 CIVIL/WAR. PAGE 22 H0452 SOVEREIGN

B65
CHANDA A.,FEDERALISM IN INDIA. INDIA UK ELITES CONSTN
FINAN NAT/G POL/PAR EX/STRUC LEGIS DIPLOM TAX CENTRAL
GOV/REL POPULISM...POLICY 20. PAGE 28 H0572 FEDERAL

B65
DUGGAR G.S.,RENEWAL OF TOWN AND VILLAGE I: A WORLD- MUNIC
WIDE SURVEY OF LOCAL GOVERNMENT EXPERIENCE. WOR+45 NEIGH
CONSTRUC INDUS CREATE BUDGET REGION GOV/REL...QU PLAN
NAT/COMP 20 URBAN/RNWL. PAGE 43 H0859 ADMIN

B65
GEORGE M.,THE WARPED VISION. EUR+WWI UK NAT/G LEAD
POL/PAR LEGIS PARL/PROC SANCTION COERCE WAR GOV/REL ATTIT
PEACE RESPECT 20 CONSRV/PAR. PAGE 56 H1113 DIPLOM
POLICY

B65
HANSER C.J.,GUIDE TO DECISION: ROYAL COMMISSION. UK NAT/G
INTELL EXTR/IND SCHOOL PROB/SOLV EXEC ROUTINE DELIB/GP
CHOOSE GOV/REL GP/REL HEALTH...CHARTS 20. PAGE 66 EX/STRUC
H1318 PWR

B65
HART B.H.L.,THE MEMOIRS OF CAPTAIN LIDDELL HART FORCES
(VOL. I). UK NAT/G PLAN TEC/DEV DIPLOM ADMIN WEAPON BIOG
GOV/REL PERS/REL ATTIT PWR FASCISM...POLICY 20. LEAD
PAGE 67 H1348 WAR

B65
KUPER H.,URBANIZATION AND MIGRATION IN WEST AFRICA. AFR
UPPER/VOLT CULTURE ECO/UNDEV WORKER REGION GOV/REL HABITAT
...LING ANTHOL SOC/INTEG 20 AFRICA/W OSHOGBO MOSSI MUNIC
MIGRATION. PAGE 89 H1781 GEOG

B65
MOORE C.H.,TUNISIA SINCE INDEPENDENCE. ELITES LOC/G NAT/G
POL/PAR ADMIN COLONIAL CONTROL EXEC GOV/REL EX/STRUC
TOTALISM MARXISM...INT 20 TUNIS. PAGE 112 H2248 SOCISM

B65
NAMIER L.B.,THE STRUCTURE OF POLITICS AT THE PARL/PROC
ACCESSION OF GEORGE III. UK LOC/G TOP/EX COLONIAL LEGIS
LEAD PARTIC REV CHOOSE REPRESENT GOV/REL PERSON NAT/G
SOVEREIGN...GOV/COMP 18 PARLIAMENT. PAGE 115 H2309 POL/PAR

S65
"FURTHER READING." INDIA ADMIN COLONIAL WAR GOV/REL BIBLIOG
ATTIT 20. PAGE 2 H0046 DIPLOM
NAT/G
POLICY

S65
GANGAL S.C.,"SURVEY OF RECENT RESEARCH: INDIA AND BIBLIOG
THE COMMONWEALTH" INDIA UK NAT/G INT/TRADE PARTIC POLICY
GOV/REL ROLE 20 CMN/WLTH. PAGE 55 H1095 REGION
DIPLOM

N65
MOTE M.E.,SOVIET LOCAL AND REPUBLIC ELECTIONS. COM CHOOSE
USSR NAT/G PLAN PARTIC GOV/REL TOTALISM PWR ADMIN
...CHARTS 20. PAGE 114 H2270 CONTROL
LOC/G

B66
BARRETT J.,THAT BETTER COUNTRY: RELIGIOUS ASPECT OF SECT
LIFE IN EASTERN AUSTRALIA, 1835-1850. LAW ECO/UNDEV CULTURE
SCHOOL TEC/DEV EDU/PROP CONTROL HABITAT MORAL GOV/REL
WORSHIP 19 AUSTRAL CHURCH/STA. PAGE 11 H0229

B66
BHALERAO C.N.,PUBLIC SERVICE COMMISSIONS OF INDIA: NAT/G
A STUDY. INDIA SERV/IND EX/STRUC ROUTINE CHOOSE OP/RES
GOV/REL INGP/REL...KNO/TEST EXHIBIT 20. PAGE 16 LOC/G
H0326 ADMIN

B66
DALLIN A.,POLITICS IN THE SOVIET UNION: 7 CASES. MARXISM
COM USSR LAW POL/PAR CHIEF FORCES WRITING CONTROL DOMIN
PARL/PROC CIVMIL/REL TOTALISM...ANTHOL 20 KHRUSH/N ORD/FREE
STALIN/J CASEBOOK COM/PARTY. PAGE 37 H0736 GOV/REL

B66
DUNCOMBE H.S.,COUNTY GOVERNMENT IN AMERICA. USA+45 LOC/G
FINAN MUNIC ADMIN ROUTINE GOV/REL...GOV/COMP 20. PROVS
PAGE 43 H0863 CT/SYS
TOP/EX

B66
DYCK H.V.,WEIMAR GERMANY AND SOVIET RUSSIA DIPLOM
1926-1933. EUR+WWI GERMANY UK USSR ECO/TAC GOV/REL
INT/TRADE NEUTRAL WAR ATTIT 20 WEIMAR/REP TREATY. POLICY
PAGE 44 H0877

B66
FARRELL R.B.,APPROACHES TO COMPARATIVE AND DIPLOM
INTERNATIONAL POLITICS. RUSSIA SOCIETY ACADEM NAT/COMP
GOV/REL GP/REL...METH/CNCPT NET/THEORY GOV/COMP NAT/G
HYPO/EXP SOC/EXP GEN/METH ANTHOL. PAGE 49 H0973

B66
HARMON R.B.,SOURCES AND PROBLEMS OF BIBLIOGRAPHY IN BIBLIOG
POLITICAL SCIENCE (PAMPHLET). INT/ORG LOC/G MUNIC DIPLOM
POL/PAR ADMIN GOV/REL ALL/IDEOS...JURID MGT CONCPT INT/LAW
19/20. PAGE 67 H1335 NAT/G

B66
HIDAYATULLAH M.,DEMOCRACY IN INDIA AND THE JUDICIAL NAT/G
PROCESS. INDIA EX/STRUC LEGIS LEAD GOV/REL ATTIT CT/SYS
ORD/FREE...MAJORIT CONCPT 20 NEHRU/J. PAGE 71 H1415 CONSTN
JURID

B66
RAY A.,INTER-GOVERNMENTAL RELATIONS IN INDIA: A CONSTN
STUDY OF INDIAN FEDERALISM. CANADA INDIA SWITZERLND FEDERAL
USA+45 USSR ADMIN GOV/REL...NAT/COMP BIBLIOG. SOVEREIGN
PAGE 130 H2599 NAT/G

B66
SASTRI K.V.S.,FEDERAL-STATE FISCAL RELATIONS IN TAX
INDIA: A STUDY OF THE FINANCE COMMISSION AND BUDGET
TECHNIQUES OF FINANCIAL ADJUSTMENT. INDIA PROVS FINAN
DELIB/GP GOV/REL FEDERAL...MATH CHARTS 20. PAGE 138 NAT/G
H2756

B66
SMITH H.E.,READINGS IN ECONOMIC DEVELOPMENT AND TEC/DEV
ADMINISTRATION IN TANZANIA. TANZANIA FINAN INDUS ADMIN
LABOR NAT/G PLAN PROB/SOLV INT/TRADE COLONIAL GOV/REL
REGION...ANTHOL BIBLIOG 20 AFRICA/E. PAGE 146 H2910

B66
THIESENHUSEN W.C.,CHILE'S EXPERIMENTS IN AGRARIAN AGRI
REFORM. CHILE STRUCT NAT/G ACT/RES ECO/TAC GOV/REL ECO/UNDEV
COST SOCISM...TREND CHARTS SOC/EXP 20. PAGE 154 SOC
H3073 TEC/DEV

S66
MATTHEWS D.G.,"PRELUDE-COUP D'ETAT-MILITARY BIBLIOG
GOVERNMENT: A BIBLIOGRAPHICAL AND RESEARCH GUIDE TO NAT/G
NIGERIAN POL AND GOVT, JAN, 1965-66." AFR NIGER LAW ADMIN
CONSTN POL/PAR LEGIS CIVMIL/REL GOV/REL...STAT 20. CHOOSE
PAGE 105 H2096

S66
MERRITT R.L.,"SELECTED ARTICLES AND DOCUMENTS ON BIBLIOG
COMPARATIVE GOVERNMENT AND CROSS-NATIONAL GOV/COMP
RESEARCH." AFR ASIA EUR+WWI L/A+17C MOD/EUR ELITES NAT/G
R+D ACT/RES DIPLOM PWR...SOC CONCPT 18/20. PAGE 109 GOV/REL
H2185

N66
HISPANIC LUSO-BRAZILIAN COUN,LATIN AMERICA; AN BIBLIOG/A
INTRODUCTION TO MODERN BOOKS IN ENGLISH CONCERNING ECO/UNDEV
THE COUNTRIES OF LATIN AMERICA (2ND ED., PAMPH). NAT/G
CULTURE GOV/REL GEOG. PAGE 71 H1425 L/A+17C

B67
BARNETT A.D.,CADRES, BUREAUCRACY, AND POLITICAL GOV/REL
POWER IN COMMUNIST CHINA. CHINA/COM ELITES LOC/G STRUCT
NAT/G INGP/REL...SOC INT DICTIONARY 20. PAGE 11 MARXISM
H0224 EDU/PROP

B67
BRZEZINSKI Z.K.,THE SOVIET BLOC: UNITY AND CONFLICT NAT/G
(2ND ED., REV., ENLARGED). COM POLAND USSR INTELL DIPLOM
CHIEF EX/STRUC CONTROL EXEC GOV/REL PWR MARXISM
...TREND IDEA/COMP 20 LENIN/VI MARX/KARL STALIN/J.
PAGE 23 H0463

B67
CARTER G.M.,SOUTH AFRICA'S TRANSKEI: THE POLITICS STRATA

OF DOMESTIC COLONIALISM. SOUTH/AFR ECO/UNDEV AGRI NAT/G PROVS PLAN DOMIN REPRESENT ADJUST DISCRIM ...OBS BIBLIOG 20 BANTUSTANS TRANSKEI. PAGE 27 H0550
GOV/REL COLONIAL POLICY

B67
DICKSON P.G.M.,THE FINANCIAL REVOLUTION IN ENGLAND. UK NAT/G TEC/DEV ADMIN GOV/REL...SOC METH/CNCPT CHARTS GP/COMP BIBLIOG 17/18. PAGE 41 H0823
ECO/DEV FINAN CAP/ISM MGT

B67
JOUVENEL B D.E.,THE ART OF CONJECTURE. FUT CONSULT EX/STRUC CHOOSE GOV/REL ALL/VALS. PAGE 82 H1638
PREDICT DELIB/GP PLAN NAT/G

B67
MOORE J.R.,THE ECONOMIC IMPACT OF THE TVA. AGRI INDUS PLAN BARGAIN CONTROL REGION GOV/REL DEMAND EFFICIENCY SOCISM 20 TVA. PAGE 112 H2249
ECO/UNDEV ECO/DEV NAT/G CREATE

B67
WALTZ K.N.,FOREIGN POLICY AND DEMOCRATIC POLITICS: THE AMERICAN AND BRITISH EXPERIENCE. FRANCE UK USA+45 PARL/PROC GOV/REL CONSERVE...DECISION 20. PAGE 165 H3298
POLICY DIPLOM NAT/G GOV/COMP

B67
WOODRUFF W.,IMPACT OF WESTERN MAN. ECO/DEV INDUS CREATE PLAN PROB/SOLV COLONIAL GOV/REL...CHARTS GOV/COMP BIBLIOG 18/20. PAGE 170 H3407
EUR+WWI MOD/EUR CAP/ISM

L67
"A PROPOS DES INCITATIONS FINANCIERES AUX GROUPEMENTS DES COMMUNES: ESSAI D'INTERPRETATION." FRANCE NAT/G LEGIS ADMIN GOV/REL CENTRAL 20. PAGE 3 H0051
LOC/G ECO/TAC APPORT ADJUD

L67
RUTH J.M.,"THE ADMINISTRATION OF WATER RESOURCES IN GUATEMALA." GUATEMALA L/A+17C DIST/IND LOC/G NAT/G EX/STRUC ADMIN GOV/REL DEMAND EQUILIB WEALTH...GEOG MGT 20. PAGE 136 H2723
EFFICIENCY ECO/UNDEV PLAN ACT/RES

S67
ALEXANDER A.,"CANADA'S PARLIAMENTARY SECRETARIES: THEIR POLITICAL AND CONSTITUTIONAL POSITION." CANADA UK NAT/G POL/PAR GOV/REL...GOV/COMP 20. PAGE 5 H0099
CONSTN ADMIN EX/STRUC DELIB/GP

S67
BEFU H.,"THE POLITICAL RELATION OF THE VILLAGE TO THE STATE." NAT/G DOMIN GOV/REL GP/REL MGT. PAGE 13 H0259
GOV/COMP NAT/LISM KIN MUNIC

S67
DANA MONTANO S.M.,"APLICACIONES CONCRETAS DE LAS RESOLUCIONES Y RECOMENDACIONES DE LAS CONFERENCIAS INTERAMERICANAS DE ABOGADOS" L/A+17C NAT/G PROVS GOV/REL PERCEPT 20 ARGEN. PAGE 37 H0739
JURID CT/SYS ORD/FREE BAL/PWR

S67
DESHPANDE A.M.,"FEDERAL-STATE FISCAL RELATIONS IN INDIA" (REVIEW ARTICLE)" GERMANY USSR DELIB/GP PLAN BUDGET ECO/TAC INCOME 20 SOC/DEMPAR SOC/REVPAR. PAGE 40 H0795
FINAN NAT/G GOV/REL TAX

S67
DIAMANT A.,"EUROPEAN MODELS OF BUREAUCRACY AND DEVELOPMENT." EX/STRUC PLAN ADMIN CONTROL ROUTINE GOV/REL CENTRAL...DECISION TIME/SEQ CHARTS. PAGE 41 H0818
NAT/G EQUILIB ACT/RES NAT/COMP

S67
DOERN G.B.,"THE ROYAL COMMISSIONS IN THE GENERAL POLICY PROCESS AND IN FEDERAL-PROVINCIAL RELATIONS." CANADA CONSTN ACADEM PROVS CONSULT DELIB/GP LEGIS ACT/RES PROB/SOLV CONFER CONTROL EFFICIENCY...METH/COMP 20 SENATE ROYAL/COMM. PAGE 42 H0832
R+D EX/STRUC GOV/REL NAT/G

S67
DRYDEN S.,"LOCAL GOVERNMENT IN TANZANIA PART II" TANZANIA LAW NAT/G POL/PAR CONTROL PARTIC REPRESENT ...DECISION 20. PAGE 42 H0850
LOC/G GOV/REL ADMIN STRUCT

S67
GRANT C.H.,"RURAL LOCAL GOVERNMENT IN GUYANA AND BRITISH HONDURAS." GUYANA HONDURAS L/A+17C AGRI NAT/G EX/STRUC ACT/RES REGION GOV/REL EFFICIENCY ORD/FREE 20. PAGE 60 H1196
ECO/UNDEV LOC/G ADMIN MUNIC

S67
MITCHELL W.C.,"THE SHAPE OF POLITICAL THEORY TO COME: FROM POLITICAL SOCIOLOGY TO POLITICAL ECONOMY." ACADEM NAT/G BUDGET TAX LEGIT LOBBY GOV/REL INGP/REL...SOC NEW/IDEA TREND CHARTS 20 MONEY. PAGE 112 H2231
ECO/TAC GEN/LAWS

S67
NIEBUHR R.,"THE ETHICS OF WAR AND PEACE IN THE NUCLEAR AGE." VIETNAM INTELL CONFER CONTROL WAR GOV/REL PERS/REL ORD/FREE...POLICY INT GOV/COMP NAT/COMP 20 UN. PAGE 118 H2360
MORAL PEACE NUC/PWR DIPLOM

S67
SALYZYN V.,"FEDERAL-PROVINCIAL TAX SHARING SCHEMES." CANADA LOC/G PROB/SOLV TEC/DEV BUDGET GOV/REL EFFICIENCY 20. PAGE 137 H2746
PROVS TAX MUNIC NAT/G

S67
SAVELYEV N.,"MONOPOLY DRIVE IN INDIA." INDIA INDUS NAT/G INT/TRADE NEUTRAL SANCTION GOV/REL CONSERVE ...MARXIST 20. PAGE 138 H2759
ECO/UNDEV POL/PAR ECO/TAC CONTROL

S67
SUBRAMANIAM V.,"REPRESENTATIVE BUREAUCRACY: A REASSESSMENT." USA+45 ELITES LOC/G NAT/G ADMIN GOV/REL PRIVIL DRIVE ROLE...POLICY CENSUS 20 CIVIL/SERV BUREAUCRCY. PAGE 150 H3006
STRATA GP/REL MGT GOV/COMP

S68
BURGESS J.W.,"VON HOLST'S PUBLIC LAW OF THE UNITED STATES" USA-45 LAW GOV/REL...GOV/COMP IDEA/COMP 19. PAGE 24 H0480
CONSTN FEDERAL NAT/G JURID

S68
CHAPMAN A.R.,"THE CIVIL WAR IN NIGERIA." AFR NIGERIA NAT/G PLAN ECO/TAC EDU/PROP COERCE WAR GOV/REL INGP/REL ORD/FREE PWR WEALTH SOC/INTEG 20 BIAFRA. PAGE 29 H0579
REV RACE/REL

B76
TAINE H.A.,THE ANCIENT REGIME. FRANCE STRATA FORCES PARTIC EQUILIB WEALTH CONSERVE POPULISM...GOV/COMP SOC/INTEG 18/19. PAGE 152 H3035
NAT/G GOV/REL TAX REV

B85
BLISS P.,OF SOVEREIGNTY. NAT/G PROVS GOV/REL PRIVIL ORD/FREE PWR CONSERVE...CONCPT 19. PAGE 18 H0356
CONSTN SOVEREIGN FEDERAL

L86
BURGESS J.W.,"THE RECENT CONSTITUTIONAL CRISIS IN NORWAY" MOD/EUR NORWAY SWEDEN LOC/G NAT/G CHIEF BAL/PWR NAT/LISM ORD/FREE 19. PAGE 24 H0481
CONSTN SOVEREIGN GOV/REL

B91
SIDGWICK H.,THE ELEMENTS OF POLITICS. LOC/G NAT/G LEGIS DIPLOM ADJUD CONTROL EXEC PARL/PROC REPRESENT GOV/REL SOVEREIGN ALL/IDEOS 19 MILL/JS BENTHAM/J. PAGE 143 H2868
POLICY LAW CONCPT

B96
ESMEIN A.,ELEMENTS DE DROIT CONSTITUTIONNEL. FRANCE UK CHIEF EX/STRUC LEGIS ADJUD CT/SYS PARL/PROC REV GOV/REL ORD/FREE...JURID METH/COMP 18/19. PAGE 47 H0940
LAW CONSTN NAT/G CONCPT

B96
LOWELL A.L.,GOVERNMENTS AND PARTIES IN CONTINENTAL EUROPE (VOL. I). MOD/EUR LOC/G NAT/G SECT CHIEF LEGIS PARL/PROC GOV/REL...POLICY 19. PAGE 99 H1973
POL/PAR GOV/COMP CONSTN EX/STRUC

B96
LOWELL A.L.,GOVERNMENTS AND PARTIES IN CONTINENTAL EUROPE, VOL. II. AUSTRIA GERMANY HUNGARY MOD/EUR SWITZERLND SOCIETY EX/STRUC LEGIS DIPLOM AGREE LEAD PARL/PROC PWR...POLICY 19. PAGE 99 H1974
POL/PAR NAT/G GOV/REL ELITES

GOVERNMENT....SEE LOC/G

GOVERNOR....GOVERNOR; SEE ALSO PROVS, CHIEF, LEAD

B57
SCHLESINGER J.A.,HOW THEY BECAME GOVERNOR; A STUDY OF COMPARATIVE STATE POLITICS, 1870-1950. USA+45 USA-45 LAW POL/PAR LEGIS EDU/PROP REGION...STAT TREND CHARTS TIME 19/20 GOVERNOR. PAGE 139 H2788
PROVS CHIEF GOV/COMP CHOOSE

GP/COMP....COMPARISON OF GROUPS

B17
HARLOW R.V.,THE HISTORY OF LEGISLATIVE METHODS IN THE PERIOD BEFORE 1825. USA-45 EX/STRUC ADMIN COLONIAL LEAD PARL/PROC ROUTINE...GP/COMP GOV/COMP HOUSE/REP. PAGE 66 H1333
LEGIS DELIB/GP PROVS POL/PAR

B18
CVIJIC J.,THE BALKAN PENINSULA. MOD/EUR COERCE ...SOC CHARTS GP/COMP NAT/COMP 20 BALKANS MAPS. PAGE 36 H0729
GEOG HABITAT GOV/COMP CULTURE

B23
LEES-SMITH H.B.,SECOND CHAMBERS IN THEORY AND PRACTICE. IRELAND NORWAY SOUTH/AFR UK LAW POL/PAR LEGIS CONTROL 20 CMN/WLTH. PAGE 93 H1858
PARL/PROC DELIB/GP REPRESENT GP/COMP

B24
WALKER F.D.,AFRICA AND HER PEOPLES. ISLAM STRUCT FAM SECT EDU/PROP INGP/REL RACE/REL HABITAT...GEOG SOC IDEA/COMP WORSHIP 20 NEGRO. PAGE 164 H3292
CULTURE AFR GP/COMP KIN

B31
KROEBER A.L.,SOURCE BOOK IN ANTHROPOLOGY. PREHIST SECT RACE/REL...LING GP/COMP ANTHOL. PAGE 89 H1770
SOC HEREDITY CULTURE ALL/VALS

B31
LORWIN L.L.,ADVISORY ECONOMIC COUNCILS. EUR+WWI FRANCE GERMANY PROB/SOLV INGP/REL...CLASSIF GP/COMP. PAGE 99 H1968
CONSULT DELIB/GP ECO/TAC NAT/G

B33
MOSS W.,POLITICAL PARTIES IN THE IRISH FREE STATE. IRELAND UK LAW FINAN LABOR DELIB/GP TOP/EX TARIFFS EDU/PROP...CHARTS GP/COMP 20. PAGE 113 H2269 POL/PAR NAT/G CHOOSE POLICY

B39
HILL R.L.,A BIBLIOGRAPHY OF THE ANGLO-EGYPTIAN SUDAN FROM THE EARLIEST TIMES TO 1937. AFR ETHIOPIA SUDAN UAR LAW COM/IND SECT RACE/REL...GEOG HEAL SOC LING 19/20 NEGRO. PAGE 71 H1417 BIBLIOG CULTURE NAT/COMP GP/COMP

B42
REDFIELD R.,THE FOLK CULTURE OF YUCATAN. STRATA FAM KIN MUNIC SECT DISCRIM ISOLAT ANOMIE HEALTH ...BIBLIOG 20 MEXIC/AMER. PAGE 130 H2605 CULTURE NEIGH GP/COMP SOCIETY

B45
DITTMANN,DAS POLITISCHE DEUTSCHLAND VOR HITLER. GERMANY LOC/G PROVS...CHARTS GP/COMP 20. PAGE 41 H0827 POL/PAR NAT/G PARTIC

B45
WARNER W.L.,THE SOCIAL SYSTEM OF AMERICAN ETHNIC GROUPS. STRATA FAM EDU/PROP ATTIT HABITAT RESPECT CLASSIF. PAGE 165 H3309 CULTURE VOL/ASSN SECT GP/COMP

B46
BIRKET-SMITH K.A.J.,GESCHICHTE DER KULTUR (3RD ED., TRANS. BY HANS DIETSCHY). KIN...GP/COMP SOC/INTEG. PAGE 17 H0339 CULTURE SOC CONCPT

B52
BAILEY S.D.,THE BRITISH PARTY SYSTEM. UK LEGIS ...POLICY GP/COMP ANTHOL 11/20. PAGE 10 H0200 POL/PAR LOC/G NAT/G DELIB/GP

B52
KROEBER A.L.,THE NATURE OF CULTURE. UNIV STRATA FAM KIN SECT...PSY GP/COMP 16/20 INDIAN/AM. PAGE 89 H1771 CULTURE SOCIETY CONCPT STRUCT

B52
UNESCO,DOCUMENTATION IN THE SOCIAL SCIENCES. CULTURE...GP/COMP METH 20 UNESCO. PAGE 158 H3162 BIBLIOG SOC

B53
COBLENTZ S.A.,FROM ARROW TO ATOM BOMB: THE PSYCHOLOGICAL HISTORY OF WAR. PREHIST CULTURE CROWD PEACE DRIVE MORAL PWR...GP/COMP IDEA/COMP. PAGE 31 H0613 WAR PSY SOCIETY

B55
FLECHTHEIM O.K.,DIE DEUTSCHEN PARTEIEN SEIT 1945. GERMANY/W CONSTN STRUCT FINAN ATTIT 20. PAGE 51 H1022 POL/PAR NAT/G GP/COMP

B55
WHEARE K.C.,GOVERNMENT BY COMMITTEE; AN ESSAY ON THE BRITISH CONSTITUTION. UK NAT/G LEGIS INSPECT CONFER ADJUD ADMIN CONTROL TASK EFFICIENCY ROLE POPULISM 20. PAGE 167 H3337 DELIB/GP CONSTN LEAD GP/COMP

B56
GLUCKMAN M.,CUSTOM AND CONFLICT IN AFRICA. AFR FAM KIN NAT/G DOMIN DISCRIM DRIVE MORAL PWR...SOC BIBLIOG WORSHIP 20. PAGE 57 H1145 CULTURE CREATE PERS/REL GP/COMP

S56
EPSTEIN L.D.,"COHESION OF BRITISH PARLIAMENTARY PARTIES." UK STRUCT ADMIN ROUTINE INGP/REL PWR ...GP/COMP PARLIAMENT. PAGE 47 H0935 NAT/G PARL/PROC POL/PAR

B57
INTERNATIONAL AFRICAN INST,ETHNOGRAPHIC SURVEY OF AFRICA: WESTERN AFRICA: THE WOLOF OF SENEGAMBIA. AFR SENEGAL CULTURE ECO/UNDEV FAM KIN REGION ...CHARTS GP/COMP BIBLIOG WORSHIP 20. PAGE 78 H1551 STRUCT GEOG HABITAT INGP/REL

B58
BAGBY P.,CULTURE AND HISTORY....PHIL/SCI CONCPT LING LOG IDEA/COMP GEN/LAWS BIBLIOG 20. PAGE 10 H0196 HIST/WRIT CULTURE GP/COMP NAT/COMP

S58
GARCEAU O.,"INTEREST GROUP THEORY IN POLITICAL RESEARCH." ELITES NAT/G PLAN LEAD REPRESENT INGP/REL POLICY. PAGE 55 H1098 GP/COMP GP/REL LOBBY PLURISM

B59
GOLDSCHMIDT W.,UNDERSTANDING HUMAN SOCIETY. SOCIETY CREATE ATTIT...GEOG PHIL/SCI CONCPT GP/COMP. PAGE 58 H1159 CULTURE STRUCT TEC/DEV PERSON

B59
MURDOCK G.P.,AFRICA: ITS PEOPLES AND THEIR CULTURE HISTORY. AFR CULTURE AGRI LOC/G INGP/REL HABITAT ...GEOG SOC LING CHARTS BIBLIOG 20 NEGRO EGYPT/ANC. PAGE 115 H2293 SOCIETY ECO/TAC GP/COMP KIN

B59
SCHORN H.,DER RICHTER IM DRITTEN REICH; GESCHICHTE UND DOKUMENTE. GERMANY NAT/G LEGIT CT/SYS INGP/REL MORAL ORD/FREE RESPECT...JURID GP/COMP 20. PAGE 140 H2798 ADJUD JUDGE FASCISM

C59
EASTON D.,"POLITICAL ANTHROPOLOGY" IN BIENNIAL REVIEW OF ANTHROPOLOGY" UNIV LAW CULTURE ELITES SOCIETY CREATE...PSY CONCPT GP/COMP GEN/METH 20. PAGE 44 H0880 SOC BIBLIOG/A NEW/IDEA

B60
HALBWACHS M.,POPULATION AND SOCIETY: INTRODUCTION TO SOCIAL MORPHOLOGY (TRANS. BY DUNCAN AND PFAUTZ). CULTURE SOCIETY AGRI INDUS HABITAT...CONCPT 20. PAGE 64 H1281 BIO/SOC GEOG NEIGH GP/COMP

B60
LA PONCE J.A.,THE PROTECTION OF MINORITIES. WOR+45 WOR-45 NAT/G POL/PAR SUFF...INT/LAW CLASSIF GP/COMP GOV/COMP BIBLIOG 17/20 CIVIL/LIB CIV/RIGHTS. PAGE 90 H1793 INGP/REL DOMIN SOCIETY RACE/REL

B60
MINER H.M.,OASIS AND CASBAH: ALGERIAN CULTURE AND PERSONALITY IN CHANGE. ALGERIA FRANCE SOCIETY MUNIC COLONIAL ATTIT...INT PROJ/TEST CHARTS 20. PAGE 111 H2221 GP/COMP PERSON CULTURE ADJUST

B60
PANIKKAR K.M.,THE STATE AND THE CITIZEN (2ND ED.). INDIA DOMIN ATTIT SUPEGO ORD/FREE WEALTH...GEOG CONCPT GP/COMP 20. PAGE 123 H2459 TEC/DEV POL/PAR NAT/G EDU/PROP

B60
ZENKOVSKY S.A.,PAN-TURKISM AND ISLAM IN RUSSIA. ASIA RUSSIA USSR CULTURE POL/PAR DOMIN REV GP/REL MARXISM...LING GP/COMP BIBLIOG 19/20 TURKIC. PAGE 173 H3454 SECT NAT/LISM COM ISLAM

L60
ROKKAN S.,"NORWAY AND THE UNITED STATES OF AMERICA." NORWAY CHOOSE...SOC STAND/INT SAMP CHARTS GP/COMP METH/COMP 20. PAGE 133 H2665 STRUCT NAT/G PARTIC REPRESENT

C60
BOGARDUS E.S.,"THE DEVELOPMENT OF SOCIAL THOUGHT." SOCIETY PERSON KNOWL...EPIST CONCPT BIBLIOG T. PAGE 18 H0365 INTELL CULTURE IDEA/COMP GP/COMP

B61
BURKS R.V.,THE DYNAMICS OF COMMUNISM IN EASTERN EUROPE. COM YUGOSLAVIA POL/PAR RACE/REL ISOLAT ...CORREL CON/ANAL CHARTS GP/COMP DICTIONARY 20 EUROPE/E SLAV/MACED. PAGE 24 H0489 MARXISM STRUCT WORKER REPRESENT

B61
FIELD H.,ANCIENT AND MODERN MAN IN SOUTHWESTERN ASIA: II. CULTURE SOCIETY...CLASSIF MATH GP/COMP NAT/COMP 20. PAGE 50 H0992 STAT CHARTS PHIL/SCI RECORD

B61
FIRTH R.,ELEMENTS OF SOCIAL ORGANIZATION (3RD ED.). STRATA STRUCT ECO/UNDEV NEIGH CHIEF INGP/REL ATTIT MORAL...PHIL/SCI GP/COMP WORSHIP SOC/INTEG 20. PAGE 50 H1009 SOC CULTURE SOCIETY KIN

B61
PATAI R.,CULTURES IN CONFLICT; AN INQUIRY INTO THE SOCIO-CULTURAL PROBLEMS OF ISRAEL AND HER NEIGHBORS (2ND REV. ED.). ISLAM ISRAEL SOCIETY STRUCT DIPLOM GP/REL ALL/VALS...SOC 20 JEWS ARABS. PAGE 124 H2475 NAT/COMP CULTURE GP/COMP ATTIT

B61
PECKERT J.,DIE GROSSEN UND DIE KLEINEN MAECHTE. COM GERMANY/W ECO/DEV ECO/UNDEV NAT/G WAR RACE/REL PEACE...POLICY GP/COMP GOV/COMP 20 COLD/WAR. PAGE 124 H2482 DIPLOM ECO/TAC BAL/PWR

S61
MACRIDIS R.C.,"INTEREST GROUPS IN COMPARATIVE ANALYSIS." CULTURE OP/RES LOBBY REPRESENT GP/REL AUTHORIT ORD/FREE PWR...POLICY DECISION METH/CNCPT CLASSIF. PAGE 101 H2010 GP/COMP CONCPT PLURISM

S61
TUCKER R.C.,"TOWARDS A COMPARATIVE POLITICS OF MOVEMENT-REGIMES" (BMR)" USSR CONSTN NAT/G CREATE PROB/SOLV DIPLOM DOMIN REV...GP/COMP IDEA/COMP METH 20 STALIN/J BOLSHEVISM. PAGE 157 H3135 MARXISM POLICY GEN/LAWS PWR

C61
LAPONCE J.A.,"THE GOVERNMENT OF THE FIFTH REPUBLIC." FRANCE CHIEF LEGIS PARL/PROC CHOOSE ...CHARTS GP/COMP IDEA/COMP BIBLIOG/A 20. PAGE 91 H1814 POL/PAR NAT/G CONSTN DOMIN

B63
BOHANNAN P.,SOCIAL ANTHROPOLOGY. ECO/DEV GP/REL DEMAND MARRIAGE HABITAT...CHARTS GP/COMP BIBLIOG T WORSHIP 20. PAGE 18 H0366 SOC STRUCT FAM CULTURE

B63
LEIGHTON D.C.,THE CHARACTER OF DANGER (VOL. III). SOCIETY STRUCT STRANGE ANOMIE...SOC STAT CHARTS GP/COMP SOC/EXP SOC/INTEG 20 NOVA/SCOT. PAGE 94 H1868 HEALTH PSY CULTURE

B63
MAJUMDAR O.N.,AN INTRODUCTION TO SOCIAL ANTHROPOLOGY. INDIA LAW STRATA ECO/UNDEV KIN DEMAND MARRIAGE...GP/COMP BIBLIOG T WORSHIP 20. PAGE 101 H2026 SOC CULTURE STRUCT GP/REL

B63
MARTINDALE D.,COMMUNITY, CHARACTER AND CIVILIZATION: STUDIES IN SOCIAL BEHAVIORISM. INTELL SOC METH/COMP

FAM NEIGH VOL/ASSN GP/REL NAT/LISM ATTIT PERSON ...CONCPT GP/COMP 20 BEHAVIORSM. PAGE 103 H2066 CULTURE STRUCT

B63
SCHELER M.,SCHRIFTEN ZUR SOZIOLOGIE UND WELTANSCHAUUNGSLEHRE (GESAMMELTE WERKE, BAND 6; 2ND ED.). SECT ALL/IDEOS...SOC CONCPT GP/COMP NAT/COMP 20. PAGE 139 H2783 SOCIETY IDEA/COMP PHIL/SCI

B63
STIRNIMANN H.,NGUNI UND GNONI; EINE KULTURGESCHICHTLICHE STUDIE (ACTA ETHNOLOGICA ET LINGUISTICA, NUMBER 6). AFR MALAWI SOUTH/AFR FORCES HABITAT...RECORD CHARTS BIBLIOG WORSHIP 19/20 NATAL. PAGE 149 H2987 CULTURE GP/COMP SOCIETY

C63
HSU F.L.,"COHESION AND DIVISION IN THE AMERICAN WORLD" HSU FL. CLAN, CASTE, AND CLUB." CULTURE EDU/PROP CONFER SANCTION PERSON...PSY GP/COMP. PAGE 74 H1484 PERS/REL AGE/Y ADJUST VOL/ASSN

B64
JOHNSON J.J.,CONTINUITY AND CHANGE IN LATIN AMERICA. L/A+17C INTELL FORCES WORKER CIVMIL/REL CHINJAP. PAGE 81 H1623 ANTHOL CULTURE STRATA GP/COMP

B64
MARTINEZ J.R.,THREE CASES OF COMMUNISM: CUBA, BRAZIL, AND MEXICO. BRAZIL CUBA L/A+17C CONSTN NAT/G DIPLOM ECO/TAC GP/REL INGP/REL...GP/COMP BIBLIOG 20 MEXIC/AMER COM/PARTY. PAGE 103 H2068 MARXISM BIOG REV NAT/COMP

B64
SINAI I.R.,THE CHALLENGE OF MODERNISATION* THE WEST'S IMPACT ON THE NON-WESTERN WORLD. EUR+WWI CULTURE ELITES SECT CONSERVE SOCISM...GP/COMP IDEA/COMP NAT/COMP GEN/LAWS. PAGE 144 H2881 ASIA S/ASIA ECO/UNDEV CREATE

S64
CLIGNET R.,"POTENTIAL ELITES IN GHANA AND THE IVORY COAST: A PRELIMINARY SURVEY." AFR CULTURE ELITES STRATA KIN NAT/G SECT DOMIN EXEC ORD/FREE RESPECT SKILL...POLICY RELATIV GP/COMP NAT/COMP 20. PAGE 30 H0605 PWR LEGIT IVORY/CST GHANA

B65
APPLEMAN P.,THE SILENT EXPLOSION. WOR+45 ECO/DEV ECO/UNDEV PLAN HEALTH ALL/IDEOS CATHISM...POLICY STAT RECORD GP/COMP IDEA/COMP NAT/COMP 20 BIRTH/CON COM/PARTY. PAGE 7 H0148 GEOG CENSUS AGRI BIO/SOC

B65
MURDOCK G.P.,CULTURE AND SOCIETY. SOCIETY STRATA STRUCT SECT CREATE CONTROL ORD/FREE...GP/COMP ANTHOL 20. PAGE 115 H2294 CULTURE PHIL/SCI METH IDEA/COMP

B65
SLOTKIN J.S.,READINGS IN EARLY ANTHROPOLOGY. INTELL SECT CREATE ATTIT KNOWL...HUM PHIL/SCI PSY LING 1/18. PAGE 145 H2902 SOC CULTURE GP/COMP

S65
SANDERS R.,"MASS SUPPORT AND COMMUNIST INSURRECTION." GREECE MALAYSIA PHILIPPINE VIETNAM STRUCT ECO/UNDEV POL/PAR FORCES CREATE REV ...GP/COMP IDEA/COMP. PAGE 138 H2751 GUERRILLA MARXISM GOV/COMP

B66
BEER S.H.,BRITISH POLITICS IN THE COLLECTIVIST AGE. UK NAT/G CONTROL CHOOSE GP/REL ATTIT PWR PLURISM ...MAJORIT WELF/ST 16/20. PAGE 13 H0258 POL/PAR SOCISM TRADIT GP/COMP

B66
ELLIS A.B.,THE EWE-SPEAKING PEOPLES OF THE SLAVE COAST OF WEST AFRICA. AFR FORCES ADJUST...LING RECORD GP/COMP WORSHIP 20 AFRICA/W DEITY. PAGE 45 H0910 MYTH CULTURE HABITAT

B66
LOVEDAY P.,PARLIAMENT FACTIONS AND PARTIES: THE FIRST THIRTY YEARS OF RESPONSIBLE GOVERNMENT IN NEW SOUTH WALES, 1856-1889. PROVS LEAD PARL/PROC PARTIC GP/REL INGP/REL MAJORITY PWR...GP/COMP 19 AUSTRAL. PAGE 99 H1970 POL/PAR ELITES NAT/G LEGIS

B66
MERRITT R.L.,COMPARING NATIONS* THE USE OF QUANTITATIVE DATA IN CROSSNATIONAL RESEARCH. ACADEM DIPLOM GP/REL...PHIL/SCI STAT TREND GP/COMP PERS/COMP GEN/METH ANTHOL BIBLIOG INDEX. PAGE 109 H2184 NAT/COMP MATH COMPUT/IR QUANT

B66
OECD DEVELOPMENT CENTRE,CATALOGUE OF SOCIAL AND ECONOMIC DEVELOPMENT INSTITUTES AND PROGRAMMES* RESEARCH. ACT/RES PLAN TEC/DEV EDU/PROP...SOC GP/COMP NAT/COMP. PAGE 120 H2403 ECO/UNDEV ECO/DEV R+D ACADEM

B66
SKILLING H.G.,THE GOVERNMENTS OF COMMUNIST EAST EUROPE. COM EUR+WWI ELITES FORCES DIPLOM ECO/TAC CONTROL HABITAT SOCISM...DECISION BIBLIOG 20 EUROPE/E COM/PARTY. PAGE 145 H2895 MARXISM NAT/COMP GP/COMP DOMIN

B66
SWARTZ M.J.,POLITICAL ANTHROPOLOGY. WOR+45 POL/PAR ACT/RES REV GP/REL DRIVE...SOC CONCPT TIME/SEQ GP/COMP ANTHOL WORSHIP 20. PAGE 151 H3013 PARTIC RIGID/FLEX LOC/G CREATE

B66
VOGT E.Z.,PEOPLE OF RIMROCK. STRATA STRUCT KIN SECT GP/REL HABITAT ALL/VALS...GEOG INT QU 20 TEXAS NAVAHO MORMON SPAN/AMER ZUNI. PAGE 163 H3260 CULTURE GP/COMP SOC SOCIETY

S66
FLEMING W.G.,"AUTHORITY, EFFICIENCY, AND ROLE STRESS: PROBLEMS IN THE DEVELOPMENT OF EAST AFRICAN BUREAUCRACIES." AFR UGANDA STRUCT PROB/SOLV ROUTINE INGP/REL ROLE...MGT SOC GP/COMP GOV/COMP 20 TANGANYIKA AFRICA/E. PAGE 51 H1024 DOMIN EFFICIENCY COLONIAL ADMIN

B67
DICKSON P.G.M.,THE FINANCIAL REVOLUTION IN ENGLAND. UK NAT/G TEC/DEV ADMIN GOV/REL...SOC METH/CNCPT CHARTS GP/COMP BIBLIOG 17/18. PAGE 41 H0823 ECO/DEV FINAN CAP/ISM MGT

B67
ERDMAN H.L.,THE SWATANTRA PARTY AND INDIAN CONSERVATISM. INDIA S/ASIA SOCIETY STRATA LOC/G NAT/G LEAD PARTIC GP/REL ATTIT...CONCPT GP/COMP BIBLIOG 20 SWATANTRA. PAGE 47 H0938 POL/PAR CONSERVE CHOOSE POLICY

B67
LAMBERT W.E.,CHILDREN'S VIEWS OF FOREIGN PEOPLES: A CROSS-NATIONAL STUDY. UNIV CULTURE EDU/PROP RACE/REL ATTIT PERCEPT ROLE...STAT STAND/INT CHARTS GP/COMP NAT/COMP. PAGE 90 H1802 AGE/C STRANGE GP/REL STERTYP

B67
PATAI R.,GOLDEN RIVER TO GOLDEN ROAD: SOCIETY, CULTURE, AND CHANGE IN THE MIDDLE EAST (2ND ED.). ELITES FAM KIN TEC/DEV MARRIAGE NAT/LISM SEX ORD/FREE...TREND GP/COMP WORSHIP 20. PAGE 124 H2476 CULTURE SOCIETY ISLAM STRUCT

L67
GOOD E.M.,"CAPITAL PUNISHMENT AND ITS ALTERNATIVES IN ANCIENT NEAR EASTERN LAW." SOCIETY SECT INGP/REL CONSEN ATTIT SEX MORAL...CRIMLGY GP/COMP. PAGE 58 H1168 MEDIT-7 LAW JURID CULTURE

S67
BASKIN D.B.,"NATIONALITY DOCTRINE AND ANTI-SEMITISM IN THE USSR." USSR CULTURE STRATA ISOLAT MAJORITY ATTIT RIGID/FLEX RESPECT...GP/COMP JEWS. PAGE 12 H0234 NAT/LISM MARXISM GP/REL DISCRIM

S67
LEHMBRUCH G.,"WAHLREFORM UND POLITISCHES SYSTEM." NETHERLAND NAT/G LEGIS PARL/PROC...SOC 20. PAGE 93 H1864 CHOOSE POL/PAR METH/CNCPT GP/COMP

S67
SUNG C.H.,"POLITICAL DIAGNOSIS OF KOREAN SOCIETY* A SURVEY OF MILITARY AND CIVILIAN VALUES." KOREA/S ECO/UNDEV NAT/G CIVMIL/REL...QU SAMP GP/COMP. PAGE 151 H3009 ELITES FORCES ATTIT ORD/FREE

S67
WRAITH R.E.,"ADMINISTRATIVE CHANGE IN THE NEW AFRICA." AFR LG/CO ADJUD INGP/REL PWR...RECORD GP/COMP 20. PAGE 171 H3416 ADMIN NAT/G LOC/G ECO/UNDEV

S68
MILLAR T.B.,"THE COMMONWEALTH AND THE UN." UK DIPLOM TARIFFS AGREE COLONIAL CONTROL SOVEREIGN WEALTH...GP/COMP GOV/COMP 20 CMN/WLTH UN. PAGE 111 H2210 INT/ORG POLICY TREND ECO/TAC

GP/REL....RELATIONS AMONG GROUPS

N
KRADER L.,SOCIAL ORGANIZATION OF THE MONGOL-TURKIC PASTORAL NOMADS. SOCIETY FAM KIN NEIGH GP/REL MARRIAGE 16/20 MONGOLIA TURKIC MIGRATION. PAGE 88 H1763 BIO/SOC HABITAT CULTURE STRUCT

N
NORTHWESTERN UNIVERSITY LIB,JOINT ACQUISITIONS LIST OF AFRICANA. AFR SOCIETY STRUCT EDU/PROP COLONIAL GP/REL RACE/REL NAT/LISM SOVEREIGN...SOC 20. PAGE 119 H2377 BIBLIOG CULTURE ECO/UNDEV INDUS

N
US CONSOLATE GENERAL HONG KONG,REVIEW OF THE HONG KONG CHINESE PRESS. ECO/UNDEV LOC/G NAT/G PLAN DIPLOM EDU/PROP LEAD GP/REL MARXISM...POLICY INDEX 20. PAGE 159 H3178 BIBLIOG/A ASIA PRESS ATTIT

N
US LIBRARY OF CONGRESS,ACCESSIONS LIST - INDIA. INDIA CULTURE AGRI LOC/G POL/PAR PLAN PROB/SOLV TEC/DEV DIPLOM EDU/PROP LEAD GP/REL ATTIT 20. PAGE 160 H3199 BIBLIOG S/ASIA ECO/UNDEV NAT/G

N
US LIBRARY OF CONGRESS,ACCESSIONS LIST -- ISRAEL. ISRAEL CULTURE ECO/UNDEV POL/PAR PLAN PROB/SOLV TEC/DEV DIPLOM EDU/PROP LEAD WAR ATTIT 20 JEWS. PAGE 160 H3200 BIBLIOG ISLAM NAT/G GP/REL

B12
POLLOCK F.,THE GENIUS OF THE COMMON LAW. CHRIST-17C UK FINAN CHIEF ACT/RES ADMIN GP/REL ATTIT SOCISM ...ANARCH JURID. PAGE 127 H2537 LAW CULTURE CREATE

B14
OPPENHEIMER F.,THE STATE. FUT SOCIETY STRATA STRUCT WORKER CAP/ISM WAR GP/REL SOCISM...SOC NAT/COMP ELITES OWN

SOC/INTEG. PAGE 121 H2424 DOMIN NAT/G B17

DOS SANTOS M.,BIBLIOGRAPHIA GERAL, A DESCRIPCAO BIBLIOGRAFICA DE LIVROS TANTO DE AUTORES PORTUGUEZES COMO BRASILEIROS... BRAZIL PORTUGAL NAT/G LEAD GP/REL 15/20. PAGE 42 H0840 BIBLIOG/A L/A+17C DIPLOM COLONIAL B18

BARRES M.,THE FAITH OF FRANCE (TRANS. BY ELISABETH MARBURY). FRANCE FAM MUNIC NEIGH POL/PAR SECT ALL/VALS 20. PAGE 11 H0227 TRADIT CULTURE WAR GP/REL B19

NATHAN M.,THE SOUTH AFRICAN COMMONWEALTH: CONSTITUTION, PROBLEMS, SOCIAL CONDITIONS. SOUTH/AFR UK CULTURE INDUS EX/STRUC LEGIS BUDGET EDU/PROP ADMIN CT/SYS GP/REL RACE/REL...LING 19/20 CMN/WLTH. PAGE 116 H2317 CONSTN NAT/G POL/PAR SOCIETY N19

CANADA CIVIL SERV COMM,THE ANALYSIS OF ORGANIZATION IN THE GOVERNMENT OF CANADA (PAMPHLET). CANADA CONSTN EX/STRUC LEGIS TOP/EX CREATE PLAN CONTROL GP/REL 20. PAGE 26 H0517 NAT/G MGT ADMIN DELIB/GP N19

COUTROT A.,THE FIGHT OVER THE 1959 PRIVATE EDUCATION LAW IN FRANCE (PAMPHLET). FRANCE NAT/G SECT GIVE EDU/PROP GP/REL ATTIT RIGID/FLEX ORD/FREE 20 CHURCH/STA. PAGE 34 H0681 SCHOOL PARL/PROC CATHISM LAW N19

MAO TSE-TUNG,ON SOME IMPORTANT PROBLEMS OF THE PARTY'S PRESENT POLICY. CHINA/COM CONSTN ELITES INTELL AGRI DOMIN EDU/PROP REV REPRESENT GP/REL OWN PEACE ORD/FREE 20 COM/PARTY. PAGE 102 H2044 POLICY NAT/G CHIEF LEGIT N19

WEBB L.C.,CHURCH AND STATE IN ITALY: 1947-1957 (PAMPHLET). GERMANY ITALY CONSTN POL/PAR AGREE CONTROL PARTIC CHOOSE ATTIT ORD/FREE FASCISM MARXISM 20 CHURCH/STA MARITAIN/J SALO. PAGE 166 H3316 SECT CATHISM NAT/G GP/REL B20

MACIVER R.M.,COMMUNITY: A SOCIOLOGICAL STUDY; BEING AN ATTEMPT TO SET OUT THE FUNDAMENTAL LAWS OF SOCIAL LIFE. UNIV STRUCT NAT/G CONTROL WAR BIO/SOC ...PSY SOC CONCPT GEN/LAWS. PAGE 100 H1996 REGION SOCIETY GP/REL B20

WEBB S.,INDUSTRIAL DEMOCRACY. UK PARTIC GP/REL ...SOC OBS RECORD CHARTS 18/20. PAGE 166 H3317 LABOR NAT/G VOL/ASSN MAJORIT B21

WALLAS G.,HUMAN NATURE IN POLITICS (3RD ED.). UNIV NAT/G LEAD CHOOSE REPRESENT GP/REL NAT/LISM RATIONAL BIO/SOC HEREDITY ALL/VALS MAJORIT. PAGE 165 H3293 PSY DRIVE PERSON B22

OGBURN W.F.,SOCIAL CHANGE WITH RESPECT TO CULTURE AND ORIGINAL NATURE. ACT/RES OP/RES CRIME GP/REL ANOMIE BIO/SOC PWR...PSY SOC TIME/SEQ METH SOC/INTEG. PAGE 120 H2405 CULTURE CREATE TEC/DEV B23

ROBERT H.M.,PARLIAMENTARY LAW. POL/PAR LEGIS PARTIC CHOOSE REPRESENT GP/REL. PAGE 132 H2640 PARL/PROC DELIB/GP NAT/G JURID B23

WILLOUGHBY W.C.,RACE PROBLEMS IN THE NEW AFRICA: A STUDY OF THE RELATION OF BANTU AND BRITONS IN THOSE PARTS OF BANTU AFRICA... AFR STRUCT SECT DOMIN EDU/PROP GP/REL ATTIT WORSHIP 20 BANTU EUROPE MISSION CHRISTIAN. PAGE 168 H3372 KIN COLONIAL RACE/REL CULTURE B24

SHIROKOGOROFF S.M.,ETHNICAL UNIT AND MILIEU. GP/REL ...PHIL/SCI SOC MATH METH. PAGE 143 H2865 IDEA/COMP HABITAT CULTURE SOCIETY B26

FORTESCUE J.,THE GOVERNANCE OF ENGLAND (1471-76). UK LAW FINAN SECT LEGIS PROB/SOLV TAX DOMIN ADMIN GP/REL COST ORD/FREE PWR 14/15. PAGE 52 H1042 CONSERVE CONSTN CHIEF NAT/G B26

MCPHEE A.,THE ECONOMIC REVOLUTION IN BRITISH WEST AFRICA. AFR UK CULTURE DIST/IND FINAN INDUS PLAN GP/REL RACE/REL 20 AFRICA/W. PAGE 107 H2148 ECO/UNDEV INT/TRADE COLONIAL GEOG B27

JOHN OF SALISBURY,THE STATESMAN'S BOOK (1159) (TRANS. BY J. DICKINSON). DOMIN GP/REL MORAL ORD/FREE PWR CONSERVE...CATH CONCPT 12. PAGE 81 H1617 NAT/G SECT CHIEF LAW B27

PANIKKAR K.M.,INDIAN STATES AND THE GOVERNMENT OF INDIA. INDIA UK CONSTN CONTROL TASK GP/REL SOVEREIGN WEALTH...TREND BIBLIOG 19. PAGE 123 H2457 GOV/COMP COLONIAL BAL/PWR PROVS B27

SMITH E.W.,THE GOLDEN STOOL: SOME ASPECTS OF THE CONFLICT OF CULTURES IN AFRICA. AFR FINAN INDUS SECT INT/TRADE COERCE CHOOSE RACE/REL ATTIT...GEOG LING 20 NEGRO. PAGE 145 H2907 COLONIAL CULTURE GP/REL EDU/PROP B28

FYFE H.,THE BRITISH LIBERAL PARTY. UK SECT ADMIN LEAD CHOOSE GP/REL PWR SOCISM...MAJORIT TIME/SEQ 19/20 LIB/PARTY CONSRV/PAR. PAGE 54 H1084 POL/PAR NAT/G REPRESENT POPULISM B29

LEITZ F.,DIE PUBLIZITAT DER AKTIENGESELLSCHAFT. BELGIUM FRANCE GERMANY UK FINAN PRESS GP/REL PROFIT KNOWL 20. PAGE 94 H1872 LG/CO JURID ECO/TAC NAT/COMP B31

DUFFIELD M.,KING LEGION. NAT/G PROVS SECT LEGIS EDU/PROP PRESS GP/REL AGE/Y MARXISM POLICY. PAGE 43 H0856 SUPEGO FORCES VOL/ASSN LOBBY B32

CATALOGUE OF BOOKS, MANSUCRIPTS, ETC. IN THE CARIBBEANA SECTION OF THE N.M. WILLIAMS MEMORIAL ETHNOLOGICAL COLLECTION. JAMAICA WEST/IND GP/REL ATTIT SOC. PAGE 2 H0031 BIBLIOG L/A+17C CULTURE SOCIETY B32

NIEBUHR R.,MORAL MAN AND IMMORAL SOCIETY* A STUDY IN ETHICS AND POLITICS. UNIV CULTURE SOCIETY STRUCT DIPLOM GOV/REL GP/REL PERS/REL...TREND IDEA/COMP. PAGE 118 H2357 MORAL PWR B33

BERDYAYEV N.,CHRISTIANITY AND CLASS WAR. UNIV SOCIETY WORKER CREATE PROB/SOLV ATTIT PERSON ORD/FREE...CONCPT CHRISTIAN. PAGE 15 H0296 SECT MARXISM STRATA GP/REL B33

PUBLIC OPINION AND WORLD POLITICS. UNIV LAW CULTURE NAT/G PRESS REV GP/REL...MAJORIT METH/COMP ANTHOL 20. PAGE 171 H3420 DIPLOM EDU/PROP ATTIT MAJORITY B34

DE CENIVAL P.,BIBLIOGRAPHIE MAROCAINE: 1923-1933. FRANCE MOROCCO SECT ADMIN LEAD GP/REL ATTIT...LING 20. PAGE 37 H0750 BIBLIOG/A ISLAM NAT/G COLONIAL B34

LOVELL R.I.,THE STRUGGLE FOR SOUTH AFRICA, 1875-1899. GERMANY RHODESIA SOUTH/AFR UK NAT/G ECO/TAC HABITAT WEALTH...POLICY 19. PAGE 99 H1971 COLONIAL DIPLOM WAR GP/REL C34

BENEDICT R.,"RITUAL" IN ERA SELIGMAN, ENCYCLOPEDIA OF THE SOCIAL SCIENCES." GP/REL...SOC STYLE IDEA/COMP WORSHIP. PAGE 14 H0279 CULTURE ROUTINE ROLE STRUCT B35

DOUGLASS H.P.,THE PROTESTANT CHURCH AS A SOCIAL INSTITUTION. CULTURE FINAN NEIGH PROF/ORG OP/RES ADMIN...POLICY SOC/WK STAT BIBLIOG. PAGE 42 H0843 SECT PARTIC INGP/REL GP/REL B38

CARVALHO C.M.,GEOGRAPHIA HUMANA; POLITICA E ECONOMICA (3RD ED.). BRAZIL CULTURE AGRI INDUS DIPLOM COLONIAL GP/REL RACE/REL...LING 20 RESOURCE/N. PAGE 27 H0551 GEOG HABITAT B38

IIZAWA S.,POLITICS AND POLITICAL PARTIES IN JAPAN. ELITES VOL/ASSN CHOOSE SUFF CIVMIL/REL GP/REL 19/20 CHINJAP. PAGE 76 H1522 POL/PAR REPRESENT FORCES NAT/G B38

REICH N.,LABOR RELATIONS IN REPUBLICAN GERMANY. GERMANY CONSTN ECO/DEV INDUS NAT/G ADMIN CONTROL GP/REL FASCISM POPULISM 20 WEIMAR/REP. PAGE 130 H2609 WORKER MGT LABOR BARGAIN B39

AKIGA,AKIGA'S STORY: THE TIV TRIBE AS SEEN BY ONE OF ITS MEMBERS. NIGERIA LAW STRUCT ECO/UNDEV FAM LEAD GP/REL MARRIAGE...LING WORSHIP 20. PAGE 4 H0089 KIN SECT SOC CULTURE B39

JENNINGS W.I.,PARLIAMENT. UK POL/PAR OP/RES BUDGET LEAD CHOOSE GP/REL...MGT 20 PARLIAMENT HOUSE/LORD HOUSE/CMNS. PAGE 80 H1609 PARL/PROC LEGIS CONSTN NAT/G B39

MARQUAND H.A.,ORGANIZED LABOUR IN FOUR CONTINENTS. EUR+WWI USA-45 INDUS NAT/G PAY GP/REL TOTALISM ATTIT WEALTH ALL/IDEOS...TREND NAT/COMP 20 ILO AFL/CIO EUROPE CHINJAP MEXIC/AMER. PAGE 103 H2055 LABOR WORKER CONCPT ANTHOL S39

LASSWELL H.D.,"PERSON, PERSONALITY, GROUP, CULTURE" (BMR)" UNIV CREATE EDU/PROP...EPIST CONCPT LING METH. PAGE 92 H1833 PERSON GP/REL CULTURE PERS/REL

B40
MCHENRY D.E.,HIS MAJESTY'S OPPOSITION: STRUCTURE AND PROBLEMS OF THE BRITISH LABOUR PARTY 1931-1938. UK FINAN LABOR LOC/G DELIB/GP LEGIS EDU/PROP LEAD PARTIC CHOOSE GP/REL SOCISM...TREND 20 LABOR/PAR. PAGE 107 H2130
POL/PAR MGT NAT/G POLICY

B40
MEEK C.K.,EUROPE AND WEST AFRICA. AFR EUR+WWI EXTR/IND DIPLOM INT/TRADE EDU/PROP GP/REL...SOC 20. PAGE 108 H2158
CULTURE TEC/DEV ECO/UNDEV COLONIAL

B40
WUNDERLICH F.,LABOR UNDER GERMAN DEMOCRACY, ARBITRATION 1918-1933. GERMANY NAT/G PAY REPAR ADJUD CT/SYS GP/REL...MAJORIT 20. PAGE 171 H3426
LABOR WORKER INDUS BARGAIN

S40
FAHS C.B.,"POLITICAL GROUPS IN THE JAPANESE HOUSE OF PEERS." ELITES NAT/G ADMIN GP/REL...TREND CHINJAP. PAGE 48 H0961
ROUTINE POL/PAR LEGIS

B42
ROBBINS J.J.,THE GOVERNMENT OF LABOR RELATIONS IN SWEDEN. SWEDEN LAW CONSTN ADJUD CT/SYS GP/REL ...JURID 20. PAGE 132 H2638
NAT/G BARGAIN LABOR INDUS

B44
KOHN H.,THE IDEA OF NATIONALISM. UNIV SOCIETY KIN CREATE REGION CENTRAL SOVEREIGN. PAGE 87 H1740
NAT/LISM CONCPT NAT/G GP/REL

B45
VENABLE V.,HUMAN NATURE: THE MARXIAN VIEW. UNIV STRATA CAP/ISM REV GP/REL PERS/REL PRODUC KNOWL ...PHIL/SCI CONCPT IDEA/COMP 19 MARX/KARL ENGELS/F. PAGE 162 H3240
PERSON MARXISM WORKER UTOPIA

B46
GODWIN W.,ENQUIRY CONCERNING POLITICAL JUSTICE AND ITS INFLUENCE ON MORALS AND HAPPINESS (1793). UNIV SOCIETY NAT/G GP/REL INGP/REL HAPPINESS ALL/VALS CONCPT. PAGE 58 H1151
MORAL PERSON ORD/FREE

S46
DE GRE G.,"FREEDOM AND SOCIAL STRUCTURE" (BMR)" UNIV SOCIETY DOMIN CONTROL TOTALISM PLURISM...SOC CHARTS. PAGE 38 H0753
ORD/FREE STRUCT CONCPT GP/REL

S46
TANNENBAUM F.,"THE BALANCE OF POWER IN SOCIETY." UNIV STRUCT FAM NAT/G SECT PERS/REL EQUILIB UTOPIA DRIVE ALL/IDEOS...OLD/LIB CONCPT. PAGE 152 H3044
SOCIETY ALL/VALS GP/REL PEACE

B47
MCILWAIN C.H.,CONSTITUTIONALISM: ANCIENT AND MODERN. USA+45 ROMAN/EMP LAW CHIEF LEGIS CT/SYS GP/REL ORD/FREE SOVEREIGN...POLICY TIME/SEQ ROMAN/REP EUROPE. PAGE 107 H2135
CONSTN NAT/G PARL/PROC GOV/COMP

B47
NIEBUHR R.,THE CHILDREN OF LIGHT AND THE CHILDREN OF DARKNESS: A VINDICATION OF DEMOCRACY AND CRITIQUE OF TRADITIONAL DEFENSE. UNIV STRUCT NAT/G SECT INGP/REL OWN PEACE ORD/FREE MARXISM ...IDEA/COMP GEN/LAWS 20 CHRISTIAN. PAGE 118 H2358
POPULISM DIPLOM NEIGH GP/REL

N47
CANNON J.P.,AMERICAN STALINISM AND ANTI-STALINISM (PAMPHLET). NAT/G WORKER DOMIN EDU/PROP REV GP/REL ...MARXIST CONCPT 20 STALIN/J TROTSKY/L. PAGE 26 H0521
LABOR MARXISM CAP/ISM POL/PAR

B48
EDUARDO O.D.C.,THE NEGRO IN NORTHERN BRAZIL: A STUDY IN ACCULTURATION. BRAZIL ECO/UNDEV FAM SECT PAY REGION HABITAT CATHISM MYSTISM...GEOG OBS SOC/INTEG WORSHIP 20 NEGRO MARANHAO. PAGE 44 H0890
CULTURE ADJUST GP/REL

B48
WOLFE B.D.,THREE WHO MADE A REVOLUTION. USSR CONSTN NAT/G CAP/ISM EDU/PROP CONTROL WAR GP/REL INGP/REL PERS/REL ROLE 20 STALIN/J LENIN/VI TROTSKY/L BOLSHEVISM. PAGE 170 H3398
BIOG REV LEAD MARXISM

B48
WRIGHT G.,THE RESHAPING OF FRENCH DEMOCRACY. FRANCE NAT/G POL/PAR SECT LEAD CHOOSE GP/REL INGP/REL MARXISM SOCISM...CHARTS BIBLIOG 20 DEGAULLE/C. PAGE 171 H3418
CONSTN POPULISM CREATE LEGIS

B49
GRODZINS M.,AMERICANS BETRAYED: POLITICS AND THE JAPANESE EXPANSION. PROVS COERCE CHOOSE GOV/REL GP/REL INGP/REL ATTIT ORD/FREE...DECISION CHARTS 20 NISEI. PAGE 61 H1230
DISCRIM POLICY NAT/G WAR

B49
HOLLERAN M.P.,CHURCH AND STATE IN GUATEMALA. GUATEMALA LAW STRUCT CATHISM...SOC SOC/INTEG 17/20 CHURCH/STA. PAGE 73 H1456
SECT NAT/G GP/REL CULTURE

B49
SCHONS D.,BOOK CENSORSHIP IN NEW SPAIN (NEW WORLD STUDIES, BOOK II). SPAIN LAW CULTURE INSPECT ADJUD CT/SYS SANCTION GP/REL ORD/FREE 14/17. PAGE 140 H2797
CHRIST-17C EDU/PROP CONTROL PRESS

L49
LOEWENSTEIN K.,"THE PRESIDENCY OUTSIDE THE UNITED STATES: A STUDY IN COMPARATIVE POLITICAL INSTITUTIONS." WOR-45 LEGIS GP/REL...POLICY 18/20. PAGE 98 H1953
CHIEF CONSTN GOV/COMP NAT/G

B50
BERMAN H.J.,JUSTICE IN RUSSIA; AN INTERPRETATION OF SOVIET LAW. USSR LAW STRUCT LABOR FORCES AGREE GP/REL ORD/FREE SOCISM...TIME/SEQ 20. PAGE 15 H0309
JURID ADJUD MARXISM COERCE

B50
LYONS F.S.L.,THE IRISH PARLIAMENTARY PARTY, 1890-1910: STUDIES IN IRISH HISTORY (VOL. 4). IRELAND DELIB/GP LEGIS PAY EDU/PROP ADMIN GP/REL ATTIT...BIBLIOG 19/20 PARLIAMENT PARNELL/CS DIRECT/NAT. PAGE 99 H1986
POL/PAR CHOOSE NAT/G POLICY

B50
WADE E.C.S.,CONSTITUTIONAL LAW; AN OUTLINE OF THE LAW AND PRACTICE OF THE CONSTITUTION. UK LEGIS DOMIN ADMIN GP/REL 16/20 CMN/WLTH PARLIAMENT ENGLSH/LAW. PAGE 164 H3283
CONSTN NAT/G PARL/PROC LAW

C50
NUMELIN R.,"THE BEGINNINGS OF DIPLOMACY." INT/TRADE WAR GP/REL PEACE STRANGE ATTIT...INT/LAW CONCPT BIBLIOG. PAGE 119 H2380
DIPLOM KIN CULTURE LAW

B51
BERNATZIK H.A.,THE SPIRITS OF THE YELLOW LEAVES. BURMA LAOS S/ASIA THAILAND VIETNAM SOCIETY AGRI COLONIAL LEISURE GP/REL PERS/REL ISOLAT AGE HABITAT SEX WORSHIP 20. PAGE 16 H0310
SOC KIN ECO/UNDEV CULTURE

B51
CARRINGTON C.E.,THE LIQUIDATION OF THE BRITISH EMPIRE. AFR NAT/G INT/TRADE COLONIAL RACE/REL ATTIT ORD/FREE...POLICY NAT/COMP 20 CMN/WLTH. PAGE 27 H0541
SOVEREIGN NAT/LISM DIPLOM GP/REL

B52
CALLOT E.,LA SOCIETE ET SON ENVIRONNEMENT: ESSAI SUR LES PRINCIPES DES SCIENCES SOCIALES. GP/REL ADJUST CONSEN ISOLAT HABITAT PERCEPT PERSON ...BIBLIOG SOC/INTEG 20. PAGE 25 H0507
SOCIETY PHIL/SCI CULTURE

B52
LEBON J.H.C.,AN INTRODUCTION TO HUMAN GEOGRAPHY. CULTURE...GEOG SOC CONCPT CENSUS CHARTS 20 MIGRATION. PAGE 93 H1849
HABITAT GP/REL SOCIETY

B52
SPICER E.H.,HUMAN PROBLEMS IN TECHNOLOGICAL CHANGE. ECO/UNDEV AGRI INDUS NAT/G ACT/RES LEAD GP/REL INGP/REL ROLE...INT METH 20 CASEBOOK. PAGE 147 H2947
TEC/DEV CULTURE STRUCT OP/RES

B52
US LIBRARY OF CONGRESS,INTRODUCTION TO AFRICA; A SELECTIVE GUIDE TO BACKGROUND READING. ECO/UNDEV COLONIAL GP/REL...SOC 19/20. PAGE 160 H3208
BIBLIOG/A AFR CULTURE NAT/G

C52
HUME D.,"IDEA OF A PERFECT COMMONWEALTH" IN D. HUME, POLITICAL DISCOURSES (1752)" UK NAT/G DOMIN GP/REL CONSERVE...POLICY CONCPT GEN/LAWS 18 MORE/THOM PLATO. PAGE 75 H1494
CONSTN CHIEF SOCIETY GOV/COMP

B53
CURTISS J.S.,THE RUSSIAN CHURCH AND THE SOVIET STATE 1917-1950. COM USSR CONTROL LEAD REV MARXISM ...POLICY BIBLIOG 20 CHURCH/STA ORTHO/RUSS. PAGE 36 H0728
GP/REL NAT/G SECT PWR

B53
DAVIDSON B.,THE NEW WEST AFRICA: PROBLEMS OF INDEPENDENCE. UK AGRI TEC/DEV DIPLOM GP/REL RACE/REL SOVEREIGN...ANTHOL 20 AFRICA/W. PAGE 37 H0744
AFR COLONIAL ECO/UNDEV NAT/G

B53
MARITAIN J.,L'HOMME ET L'ETAT. SECT DIPLOM GP/REL PEACE ORD/FREE...IDEA/COMP 17/20 CHURCH/STA NATURL/LAW. PAGE 103 H2052
CONCPT NAT/G SOVEREIGN COERCE

B53
MURPHY G.,IN THE MINDS OF MEN: THE STUDY OF HUMAN BEHAVIOR AND SOCIAL TENSIONS IN INDIA. FUT S/ASIA FAM INT/ORG NAT/G DIPLOM EDU/PROP GP/REL ATTIT RIGID/FLEX ALL/VALS...SOC QU UNESCO 20. PAGE 115 H2297
SECT STRATA INDIA

L53
DEUTSCH K.W.,"THE GROWTH OF NATIONS: SOME RECURRENT PATTERNS OF POLITICAL AND SOCIAL INTEGRATION" (BMR)" UNIV CULTURE SOCIETY ECO/DEV ECO/UNDEV NAT/G CREATE GP/REL...CONCPT GEN/LAWS SOC/INTEG 11/20. PAGE 40 H0797
TREND NAT/LISM ORD/FREE

C53
BULNER-THOMAS I.,"THE PARTY SYSTEM IN GREAT BRITAIN." UK CONSTN SECT PRESS CONFER GP/REL ATTIT ...POLICY TREND BIBLIOG 19/20 PARLIAMENT. PAGE 23 H0473
NAT/G POL/PAR ADMIN ROUTINE

C53
KRACKE E.A. JR.,"CIVIL SERVICE IN EARLY SUNG CHINA, 960-1067." ASIA GP/REL...BIBLIOG/A 10/11. PAGE 88 H1762
ADMIN NAT/G WORKER

CONTROL
B54

FORDE C.D.,AFRICAN WORLDS. AFR CULTURE ROUTINE GP/REL PERS/REL ATTIT DRIVE ALL/VALS...OBS ANTHOL WORSHIP 20. PAGE 52 H1036 SOCIETY KIN SOC
B54

HAZARD B.H. JR.,KOREAN STUDIES GUIDE. KOREA CONSTN CULTURE AGRI FAM SECT CREATE WAR NAT/LISM HABITAT PWR...CHARTS 14/20. PAGE 68 H1371 BIBLIOG/A ELITES GP/REL
B54

MALINOWSKI B.,MAGIC, SCIENCE AND RELIGION. AGRI KIN GP/REL ALL/VALS...MYTH OBS RECORD IDEA/COMP WORSHIP 20 NEW/GUINEA. PAGE 102 H2031 CULTURE ATTIT SOC
B54

PARRINDER G.,AFRICAN TRADITIONAL RELIGION. AFR SOCIETY EDU/PROP GP/REL PWR...SOC CONCPT IDEA/COMP WORSHIP 20 DEITY. PAGE 124 H2469 SECT MYTH ATTIT CULTURE
B54

SPROTT W.J.H.,SCIENCE AND SOCIAL ACTION. STRUCT ACT/RES CRIME GP/REL INGP/REL ANOMIE...PSY SOC/INTEG 19/20. PAGE 148 H2956 SOC CULTURE PHIL/SCI
B54

TITIEV M.,THE SCIENCE OF MAN. LAW STRATA KIN GP/REL PERS/REL HABITAT HEREDITY KNOWL...LING CHARTS BIBLIOG WORSHIP. PAGE 155 H3107 SOC PSY CULTURE
B55

FRANZ G.,KULTURKAMPF. AUSTRIA GERMANY PRUSSIA SWITZERLND POL/PAR DIPLOM GP/REL ATTIT ORD/FREE 18/19 CHURCH/STA. PAGE 53 H1053 NAT/LISM CATHISM NAT/G REV
B55

INTERNATIONAL AFRICAN INST,ETHNOGRAPHIC SURVEY OF AFRICA: WESTERN AFRICA: PEOPLES OF THE NIGER-BENUE CONFLUENCE. AFR NIGER CULTURE ECO/UNDEV KIN GOV/REL GP/REL ATTIT HEREDITY...CHARTS BIBLIOG WORSHIP 20. PAGE 77 H1546 STRUCT GEOG HABITAT INGP/REL
B55

KOHN H.,NATIONALISM: ITS MEANING AND HISTORY. GP/REL INGP/REL ATTIT...CONCPT NAT/COMP 16/20 MACHIAVELL. PAGE 87 H1743 NAT/LISM DIPLOM FASCISM REV
B55

KRUSE H.,DAS STAATSANGEHORIGKEITSRECHT DER ARABISCHEN STAATEN. ISLAM JORDAN LIBYA SYRIA UAR NAT/G SECT RACE/REL...INT/LAW 6/20 TREATY. PAGE 89 H1779 JURID NAT/LISM DIPLOM GP/REL
B55

SHUMSKY A.,THE CLASH OF CULTURES IN ISRAEL: A PROBLEM FOR EDUCATION. ISRAEL CULTURE INTELL NAT/G ACT/RES DISCRIM AGE/Y...BIBLIOG 20 JEWS. PAGE 143 H2867 GP/REL EDU/PROP SCHOOL AGE/C
B55

STEWARD J.H.,THEORY OF CULTURE CHANGE; THE METHODOLOGY OF MULTILINEAR EVOLUTION. SOCIETY KIN SECT GP/REL INGP/REL...BIBLIOG SOC/INTEG 20. PAGE 149 H2984 CULTURE CONCPT METH/COMP HABITAT
B55

THOMPSON V.,MINORITY PROBLEMS IN SOUTHEAST ASIA. CAMBODIA CHINA/COM LAOS S/ASIA KIN NAT/G SECT PROB/SOLV EDU/PROP REGION GP/REL RACE/REL MARXISM ...SOC 20 BUDDHISM UN. PAGE 154 H3085 INGP/REL GEOG DIPLOM STRUCT
C55

SANTAYANA G.,"REASON IN SOCIETY" IN G. SANTAYANA, THE LIFE OF REASON." INDUS FAM NAT/G WAR GP/REL HAPPINESS PRODUC LOVE WEALTH CONSERVE POPULISM CONCPT. PAGE 138 H2752 RATIONAL SOCIETY CULTURE ATTIT
B56

BECKER H.,MAN IN RECIPROCITY: INTRODUCTORY LECTURES ON CULTURE, SOCIETY, AND PERSONALITY. LAW FAM SECT REGION GP/REL ADJUST ATTIT PERSON...BIBLIOG 20. PAGE 13 H0253 CULTURE STRUCT SOC PSY
B56

CENTRAL AFRICAN ARCHIVES,A GUIDE TO THE PUBLIC RECORDS OF SOUTHERN RHODESIA UNDER THE REGIME OF THE BRITISH SOUTH AFRICA COMPANY, 1890-1923. UK STRUCT NAT/G WRITING GP/REL 19/20. PAGE 28 H0566 BIBLIOG/A COLONIAL ADMIN AFR
B56

HERNANDEZ URBINA A.,LOS PARTIDOS Y LA CRISIS DEL APRA. PERU NAT/G LEAD LOBBY CHOOSE SOCISM...POLICY DECISION 20 COM/PARTY APRA CONGRESS. PAGE 70 H1402 POL/PAR PARTIC PARL/PROC GP/REL
B56

INTERNATIONAL AFRICAN INST,ETHNOGRAPHIC SURVEY OF AFRICA; WESTERN AFRICA: PAGAN PEOPLES OF CENTRAL AREA OF NORTHERN NIGERIA (VOL. XII). NIGERIA FAM KIN SECT ECO/TAC GOV/REL GP/REL ATTIT...LING CHARTS 20. PAGE 77 H1548 STRUCT INGP/REL HABITAT CULTURE
B56

KALLEN H.M.,CULTURAL PLURALISM AND THE AMERICAN IDEA. RACE/REL ADJUST PERSON ORD/FREE LAISSEZ ...PLURIST GEN/LAWS ANTHOL. PAGE 83 H1652 PLURISM CULTURE GP/REL SECT
B56

SHAPIRO H.L.,MAN, CULTURE, AND SOCIETY. STRUCT FAM SECT GP/REL INGP/REL...ART/METH GEOG PSY LING CULTURE PERSON

ANTHOL BIBLIOG. PAGE 142 H2842 SOC
B56

SPINKA M.,THE CHURCH IN SOVIET RUSSIA. USSR CONTROL LEAD TASK COERCE 20. PAGE 147 H2949 GP/REL NAT/G SECT PWR
B56

VIANNA F.J.,EVOLUCAO DE POVO BRASILEIRO (4TH ED.). BRAZIL TEC/DEV COLONIAL GP/REL ATTIT SOVEREIGN ...SOC SOC/INTEG 15/20. PAGE 162 H3247 STRUCT RACE/REL NAT/G
B57

BUNDESMIN FUR VERTRIEBENE,DIE VERTREIBUNG DER DEUTSCHEN BEVOLKERUNG AUS DER TSCHECHOSLOWAKEI. CZECHOSLVK GERMANY NAT/G FORCES MURDER WAR INGP/REL ATTIT 20 MIGRATION. PAGE 24 H0474 GP/REL DOMIN COERCE DISCRIM
B57

PARK A.G.,BOLSHEVISM IN TURKESTAN 1917-1927. COM RUSSIA USSR CULTURE AGRI SECT DOMIN GP/REL INGP/REL NAT/LISM...BIBLIOG 20 TURKESTAN. PAGE 123 H2467 REV POLICY MARXISM ISLAM
B57

ROSS R.,THE FABRIC OF SOCIETY. STRATA GP/REL PERSON ...CONCPT METH T 20. PAGE 134 H2687 SOC PHIL/SCI CULTURE STRUCT
B57

TAYLOR J.V.,CHRISTIANITY AND POLITICS IN AFRICA. AFR CONTROL PARTIC GP/REL RACE/REL ATTIT...POLICY BIBLIOG/A WORSHIP 20. PAGE 153 H3055 SECT NAT/G NAT/LISM
S57

COSER L.A.,"SOCIAL CONFLICT AND THE THEORY OF SOCIAL CHANGE." EUR+WWI CULTURE TEC/DEV PRODUC RIGID/FLEX SOC. PAGE 34 H0673 GP/REL ROLE SOCIETY ORD/FREE
S57

HAILEY,"TOMORROW IN AFRICA." CONSTN SOCIETY LOC/G NAT/G DOMIN ADJUD ADMIN GP/REL DISCRIM NAT/LISM ATTIT MORAL ORD/FREE...PSY SOC CONCPT OBS RECORD TREND GEN/LAWS CMN/WLTH 20. PAGE 64 H1277 AFR PERSON ELITES RACE/REL
B58

ALMAGRO BASCH M.,ORIGEN Y FORMACION DEL PUEBLO HISPANO. PREHIST SPAIN REGION WAR RACE/REL HABITAT ORD/FREE...SOC SOC/INTEG 20. PAGE 5 H0109 CULTURE GP/REL ADJUST
B58

BUISSON L.,POTESTAS UND CARITAS. FRANCE GERMANY UK ORD/FREE...JURID IDEA/COMP NAT/COMP 12/16 POPE CHURCH/STA. PAGE 23 H0467 GP/REL PWR CATHISM NAT/G
B58

CARTER G.M.,TRANSITION IN AFRICA; STUDIES IN POLITICAL ADAPTATION. AFR CENTRL/AFR GHANA NIGERIA CONSTN LOC/G POL/PAR ADMIN GP/REL FEDERAL...MAJORIT BIBLIOG 20. PAGE 27 H0543 NAT/COMP PWR CONTROL NAT/G
B58

COWAN L.G.,LOCAL GOVERNMENT IN WEST AFRICA. AFR FRANCE UK CULTURE KIN POL/PAR CHIEF LEGIS CREATE ADMIN PARTIC GOV/REL GP/REL...METH/COMP 20. PAGE 34 H0682 LOC/G COLONIAL SOVEREIGN REPRESENT
B58

CRAIG G.A.,FROM BISMARCK TO ADENAUER: ASPECTS OF GERMAN STATECRAFT. GERMANY INTELL FORCES ECO/TAC CONFER COERCE WAR GP/REL ORD/FREE PWR CONSERVE 19/20 BISMARCK/O ADENAUER/K. PAGE 35 H0695 DIPLOM LEAD NAT/G
B58

CUNNINGHAM W.B.,COMPULSORY CONCILIATION AND COLLECTIVE BARGAINING. CANADA NAT/G LEGIS ADJUD CT/SYS GP/REL...MGT 20 NEW/BRUNS STRIKE CASEBOOK. PAGE 36 H0722 POLICY BARGAIN LABOR INDUS
B58

DUNAYEVSKAYA R.,MARXISM AND FREEDOM: FROM 1776 UNTIL TODAY. COM USSR WORKER CAP/ISM DOMIN REV GP/REL TOTALISM ALL/VALS...MYTH BIOG IDEA/COMP 18/20 MARX/KARL LENIN/VI STALIN/J. PAGE 43 H0861 MARXISM CONCPT ORD/FREE
B58

DWARKADAS R.,ROLE OF HIGHER CIVIL SERVICE IN INDIA. INDIA ECO/UNDEV LEGIS PROB/SOLV GP/REL PERS/REL ...POLICY WELF/ST DECISION ORG/CHARTS BIBLIOG 20 CIVIL/SERV INTRVN/ECO. PAGE 44 H0876 ADMIN NAT/G ROLE PLAN
B58

EUSDEN J.D.,PURITANS, LAWYERS, AND POLITICS IN EARLY SEVENTEENTH-CENTURY ENGLAND. UK CT/SYS PARL/PROC RATIONAL PWR SOVEREIGN...IDEA/COMP BIBLIOG 17 PURITAN COMMON/LAW. PAGE 48 H0951 GP/REL SECT NAT/G LAW
B58

FLORES X.,LA TRADICION CATOLICA Y EL FUTURO POLITICO DE ESPANA (PAMPHLET). SPAIN NAT/G ACT/RES LEAD GP/REL CATHISM 20 CHRISTIAN CHURCH/STA. PAGE 52 H1031 SECT POL/PAR ATTIT ORD/FREE
B58

GLUCKMAN M.,ANALYSIS OF A SOCIAL SITUATION IN MODERN ZULULAND. AFR PERS/REL ADJUST DISCRIM EQUILIB NAT/LISM...SOC RECORD AUD/VIS 20 ZULULAND. PAGE 57 H1146 CULTURE RACE/REL STRUCT GP/REL
B58

GURVITCH G.,TRAITE DE SOCIOLOGIE (2 VOLS.). FRANCE CULTURE INDUS GP/REL INGP/REL...PSY BIBLIOG 20. ANTHOL SOC

PAGE 63 H1256 METH/COMP METH/CNCPT

B58
HANSARD SOCIETY PARL GOVT,WHAT ARE THE PROBLEMS OF PARLIAMENTARY GOVERNMENT IN WEST AFRICA? PROB/SOLV DIPLOM GP/REL 20 PARLIAMENT AFRICA/W. PAGE 66 H1317 PARL/PROC POL/PAR AFR NAT/G

B58
HENLE P.,LANGUAGE, THOUGHT AND CULTURE. CULTURE GP/REL PERCEPT...PSY TREND ANTHOL 20. PAGE 70 H1397 LING RATIONAL CONCPT SOC

B58
HERRMANN K.,DAS STAATSDENKEN BEI LEIBNIZ. GP/REL ATTIT ORD/FREE...CONCPT IDEA/COMP 17 LEIBNITZ/G CHURCH/STA. PAGE 70 H1406 NAT/G JURID SECT EDU/PROP

B58
JOHNSON J.J.,POLITICAL CHANGE IN LATIN AMERICA: THE EMERGENCE OF THE MIDDLE SECTORS. INTELL STRATA STRUCT ECO/UNDEV MUNIC TEC/DEV LEAD REV...DECISION TREND GOV/COMP BIBLIOG/A 20. PAGE 81 H1621 L/A+17C ELITES GP/REL DOMIN

B58
MATOS J.,LAS ACTUALES COMMUNIDADES DE INDIGENAS: HUAROCHIRI EN 1955. PERU FAM NAT/G SECT EDU/PROP ADJUD GP/REL INGP/REL 20 INDIAN/AM. PAGE 105 H2091 STRUCT NEIGH KIN ECO/UNDEV

B58
OGILVIE C.,THE KING'S GOVERNMENT AND THE COMMON LAW, 1471-1641. UK STRUCT NAT/G CHIEF LEGIS WORKER BAL/PWR GP/REL AUTHORIT 15/17 COMMON/LAW. PAGE 120 H2408 CONSTN ELITES DOMIN

B58
PALMER E.E.,"POLITICAL MAN" IN E. PALMER, PROBLEMS IN DEMOCRATIC CITIZENSHIP. LOC/G NAT/G LEGIS PRESS CHOOSE REPRESENT GP/REL...DECISION SOC IDEA/COMP ANTHOL 20. PAGE 123 H2449 PARTIC POL/PAR EDU/PROP MAJORIT

B58
STUBEL H.,THE MEWU FANTZU. CHINA/COM INDIA EDU/PROP ADJUD CRIME GP/REL OWN...OBS 20 TIBET. PAGE 150 H3001 CULTURE STRUCT SECT FAM

B58
WOODS H.D.,PATTERNS OF INDUSTRIAL DISPUTE SETTLEMENT IN FIVE CANADIAN INDUSTRIES. CANADA USA+45 CONSULT ADJUD GP/REL...JURID GOV/COMP METH/COMP ANTHOL 20. PAGE 170 H3408 BARGAIN INDUS LABOR NAT/G

S58
GARCEAU O.,"INTEREST GROUP THEORY IN POLITICAL RESEARCH." ELITES NAT/G PLAN LEAD REPRESENT INGP/REL POLICY. PAGE 55 H1098 GP/COMP GP/REL LOBBY PLURISM

B59
BRIGGS A.,CHARTIST STUDIES. UK LAW NAT/G WORKER EDU/PROP COERCE SUFF GP/REL ATTIT...ANTHOL 19. PAGE 21 H0416 INDUS STRATA LABOR POLICY

B59
BROSE O.J.,CHURCH AND PARLIAMENT: THE RESHAPING OF THE CHURCH OF ENGLAND 1828-1860. UK SOCIETY TEC/DEV ATTIT LAISSEZ...BIBLIOG 19 CHURCH/STA. PAGE 22 H0434 SECT LEGIS GP/REL NAT/G

B59
BUNDESMIN FUR VERTRIEBENE,ZEITTAFEL DER VORGESCHICHTE UND DES ABLAUFS DER VERTREIBUNG SOWIE DER UNTERBRINGUNG UND EINGLIEDERUNG DER (2 VOLS.). GERMANY/E GERMANY/W NAT/G PROVS PROB/SOLV DIPLOM PARL/PROC ATTIT...BIBLIOG SOC/INTEG 20 MIGRATION PARLIAMENT. PAGE 24 H0475 JURID GP/REL INT/LAW

B59
DAHRENDORF R.,CLASS AND CLASS CONFLICT IN INDUSTRIAL SOCIETY. LABOR NAT/G COERCE ROLE PLURISM ...POLICY MGT CONCPT CLASSIF. PAGE 37 H0734 VOL/ASSN STRUCT SOC GP/REL

B59
GOPAL R.,INDIAN MUSLIMS: A POLITICAL HISTORY (1858-1947). INDIA ISLAM PAKISTAN NAT/G SECT LEGIS LEAD COERCE WAR REPRESENT ISOLAT ORD/FREE 19/20 HINDU MUSLIM. PAGE 59 H1175 COLONIAL GP/REL POL/PAR REGION

B59
HEMMERLE J.,SUDETENDEUTSCHE BIBLIOGRAPHIE 1949-1953. CZECHOSLVK GERMANY SOCIETY STRUCT SECT ...GEOG JURID 20. PAGE 69 H1391 BIBLIOG PROVS GP/REL CULTURE

B59
HOBSBAWM E.J.,PRIMITIVE REBELS; STUDIES IN ARCHAIC FORMS OF SOCIAL MOVEMENT IN THE 19TH AND 20TH CENTURIES. ITALY SPAIN CULTURE VOL/ASSN RISK CROWD GP/REL INGP/REL ISOLAT TOTALISM...PSY SOC 18/20. PAGE 72 H1438 SOCIETY CRIME REV GUERRILLA

B59
JENNINGS W.I.,CABINET GOVERNMENT (3RD ED.). UK POL/PAR CHIEF BUDGET ADMIN CHOOSE GP/REL 20. PAGE 81 H1612 DELIB/GP NAT/G CONSTN OP/RES

B59
KIRCHHEIMER O.,GEGENWARTSPROBLEME DER ASYLGEWAHRUNG. DOMIN GP/REL ATTIT...NAT/COMP 20. PAGE 86 H1720 DIPLOM INT/LAW JURID ORD/FREE

B59
LEMBERG E.,DIE VERTRIEBENEN IN WESTDEUTSCHLAND (3 VOLS.). GERMANY/W CULTURE STRUCT AGRI PROVS ADMIN ...JURID 20 MIGRATION. PAGE 94 H1875 GP/REL INGP/REL SOCIETY

B59
LIPSET S.M.,SOCIAL MOBILITY IN INDUSTRIAL SOCIETY. EUR+WWI USA+45 USSR STRUCT INDUS WRITING GP/REL INGP/REL DRIVE...SOC CHARTS NAT/COMP SOC/INTEG 20 MARX/KARL ENGELS/F. PAGE 97 H1940 STRATA ECO/DEV SOCIETY

B59
MAC MILLAN W.M.,THE ROAD TO SELF-RULE. SOUTH/AFR UK CULTURE SOCIETY AGRI LABOR NAT/G INT/TRADE CONTROL GP/REL...SOC 19/20. PAGE 100 H1988 AFR COLONIAL SOVEREIGN POLICY

B59
OVERSTREET G.D.,COMMUNISM IN INDIA. INDIA S/ASIA CONSTN INT/ORG LEAD GP/REL...CHARTS BIBLIOG 20. PAGE 122 H2435 MARXISM NAT/LISM POL/PAR WAR

B59
ROCHE J.,LA COLONISATION ALLEMANDE ET LE RIO GRANDE DO SUL. BRAZIL L/A+17C NAT/G PROVS INGP/REL RACE/REL DISCRIM HABITAT...GEOG SOC/INTEG 19/20 MIGRATION. PAGE 133 H2652 ECO/UNDEV GP/REL ATTIT

B59
SISSONS C.B.,CHURCH AND STATE IN CANADIAN EDUCATION: AN HISTORICAL STUDY. CANADA ACADEM NAT/G SCHOOL LEGIS REGION MAJORITY...MAJORIT WORSHIP 18/20 CHURCH/STA. PAGE 145 H2891 SECT EDU/PROP PROVS GP/REL

B59
STERNBERG F.,THE MILITARY AND INDUSTRIAL REVOLUTION OF OUR TIME. USA+45 USSR WOR+45 WORKER COMPUTER PLAN TEC/DEV NUC/PWR GP/REL...POLICY NAT/COMP 20. PAGE 149 H2981 DIPLOM FORCES INDUS CIVMIL/REL

B59
VINACKE H.M.,A HISTORY OF THE FAR EAST IN MODERN TIMES (6TH ED.). KOREA S/ASIA USSR CONSTN CULTURE STRATA ECO/UNDEV NAT/G CHIEF FOR/AID INT/TRADE GP/REL...SOC NAT/COMP 19/20 CHINJAP. PAGE 163 H3255 STRUCT ASIA

B59
VORSPAN A.,JUSTICE AND JUDAISM. FAM DIPLOM ECO/TAC EDU/PROP CRIME RACE/REL MARRIAGE ANOMIE ATTIT ORD/FREE...POLICY 20 UN. PAGE 164 H3279 SECT CULTURE ACT/RES GP/REL

S59
LEYS C.,"MODELS, THEORIES, AND THE THEORY OF POLITICAL PARTIES" CANADA LIECHTENST UK LOC/G NAT/G PARTIC REPRESENT GP/REL CONSEN EQUILIB MAJORITY ...NEW/IDEA MATH CHARTS 20. PAGE 96 H1919 POL/PAR CHOOSE METH/CNCPT SIMUL

B60
BRIGGS L.C.,TRIBES OF THE SAHARA. AFR MOROCCO STRATA AGRI GP/REL HEALTH...GEOG SOC MYTH LING BIBLIOG 13/20 ARABS. PAGE 21 H0418 CULTURE HABITAT KIN SELF/OBS

B60
BURRIDGE K.,MAMBU: A MELANESIAN MILLENNIUM. ECO/UNDEV PROC/MFG FAM KIN CHIEF COLONIAL COERCE GP/REL DRIVE WEALTH WORSHIP 20 NEW/GUINEA. PAGE 25 H0494 S/ASIA SECT CULTURE MYTH

B60
CHATTERJI S.K.,AFRICANISM: THE AFRICAN PERSONALITY. KIN NAT/G SECT CREATE DIPLOM COLONIAL GP/REL ATTIT ORD/FREE...LING WORSHIP 20. PAGE 29 H0585 PERSON NAT/LISM AFR CULTURE

B60
HARRISON S.S.,INDIA: THE MOST DANGEROUS DECADES. INDIA CONSTN STRATA POL/PAR SECT PLAN ADMIN CHOOSE GP/REL TOTALISM MARXISM...LING 20 NEHRU/J. PAGE 67 H1347 CULTURE ECO/UNDEV PROB/SOLV REGION

B60
INTERNATIONAL AFRICAN INST,ETHNOGRAPHIC SURVEY OF AFRICA: WESTERN AFRICA: PEOPLES OF THE MIDDLE NIGER REGION, NORTHERN NIGERIA. AFR NIGER CULTURE ECO/UNDEV KIN NEIGH GOV/REL GP/REL ATTIT HEREDITY ...CHARTS BIBLIOG WORSHIP 20. PAGE 78 H1552 STRUCT GEOG HABITAT INGP/REL

B60
JEMOLO A.C.,CHURCH AND STATE IN ITALY 1850-1950 (TRANS. BY DAVID MOORE). ITALY CONSTN STRATA WAR FASCISM SOCISM...TIME/SEQ 19/20 CHURCH/STA CHRIS/DEM. PAGE 80 H1599 GP/REL NAT/G CATHISM POL/PAR

B60
KEPHART C.,RACES OF MAN. GP/REL HABITAT...LING SOC/INTEG 20 MIGRATION MISCEGEN. PAGE 85 H1692 CULTURE RACE/REL HEREDITY GEOG

B60
MACFARQUHAR R.,THE HUNDRED FLOWERS. ASIA NAT/G WORKER GP/REL ORD/FREE MARXISM 20 MAO. PAGE 100 H1991 DEBATE PRESS POL/PAR ATTIT

B60
MOCTEZUMA A.P.,EL CONFLICTO RELIGIOSO DE 1926 (2ND ED.). L/A+17C LAW NAT/G LOBBY COERCE GP/REL ATTIT ...POLICY 20 MEXIC/AMER CHURCH/STA. PAGE 112 H2233 SECT ORD/FREE DISCRIM REV

B60
OTTENBERG S.,CULTURES AND SOCIETIES OF AFRICA. AFR KIN TEC/DEV GP/REL MARRIAGE ATTIT HABITAT HEREDITY ...ANTHOL BIBLIOG T WORSHIP 20. PAGE 122 H2433 SOCIETY INGP/REL STRUCT CULTURE

B60
ROBERTSON D.,THE CONTROL OF INDUSTRY. UK MARKET LABOR WORKER PRICE CONTROL GP/REL COST DEMAND ORD/FREE WEALTH NEW/LIB SOCISM 20. PAGE 132 H2646 INDUS FINAN NAT/G ECO/DEV

B60
ROSKAM K.L.,APARTHEID AND DISCRIMINATION. SOUTH/AFR SOCIETY STRUCT NAT/G POL/PAR GP/REL ISOLAT ...BIBLIOG 20. PAGE 134 H2683 DISCRIM RACE/REL CULTURE POLICY

B60
VON KOENIGSWALD H.,SIE SUCHEN ZUFLUCHT. GERMANY/E NAT/G PLAN ECO/TAC SOCISM...GEOG CENSUS 20 BERLIN. PAGE 164 H3273 GP/REL COERCE DOMIN PERSON

B60
WILLIAMS L.E.,OVERSEAS CHINESE NATIONALISM: THE GENESIS OF THE PAN-CHINESE MOVEMENT IN INDONESIA, 1900-1916. ASIA COM INDONESIA AGRI INT/ORG LOC/G DIPLOM EDU/PROP HABITAT PWR POPULISM...GEOG LING CENSUS 20. PAGE 168 H3367 NAT/LISM GP/REL DECISION NAT/G

B60
ZENKOVSKY S.A.,PAN-TURKISM AND ISLAM IN RUSSIA. ASIA RUSSIA USSR CULTURE POL/PAR DOMIN REV GP/REL MARXISM...LING GP/COMP BIBLIOG 19/20 TURKIC. PAGE 173 H3454 SECT NAT/LISM COM ISLAM

S60
BANFIELD E.C.,"THE POLITICAL IMPLICATIONS OF METROPOLITAN GROWTH" (BMR)" UK USA+45 LOC/G PROB/SOLV ADMIN GP/REL...METH/COMP NAT/COMP 20. PAGE 10 H0209 TASK MUNIC GOV/COMP CENSUS

S60
BERREMAN G.D.,"CASTE IN INDIA AND THE UNITED STATES" (BMR)" INDIA USA+45 CULTURE SOCIETY STRUCT SECT GP/REL DISCRIM HEREDITY...SOC STERTYP 20 NEGRO HINDU. PAGE 16 H0318 STRATA RACE/REL NAT/COMP ATTIT

S60
TAYLOR M.G.,"THE ROLE OF THE MEDICAL PROFESSION IN THE FORMULATION AND EXECUTION OF PUBLIC POLICY" (BMR)" CANADA NAT/G CONSULT ADMIN REPRESENT GP/REL ROLE SOVEREIGN...DECISION 20 CMA. PAGE 153 H3056 PROF/ORG HEALTH LOBBY POLICY

S60
TIRYAKIAN E.A.,"APARTHEID AND POLITICS IN SOUTH AFRICA." SOUTH/AFR CULTURE STRATA ECO/DEV NAT/G POL/PAR ROUTINE CHOOSE GP/REL RACE/REL DISCRIM ATTIT ALL/VALS...CONCPT OBS TIME/SEQ VAL/FREE 20. PAGE 155 H3105 AFR DIPLOM

B61
ACOSTA SAIGNES M.,ESTUDIOS DE ETNOLOGIA ANTIGUA DE VENEZUELA (2ND ED.). PRE/AMER VENEZUELA...ART/METH SOC BIBLIOG INDIAN/AM. PAGE 3 H0061 CULTURE STRUCT GP/REL HABITAT

B61
ALSTON P.L.,STATE EDUCATION AND SOCIAL CHANGE IN THE RUSSIAN EMPIRE 1871-1914 (PAPER). RUSSIA ELITES PROF/ORG EDU/PROP CONTROL PRIVIL AGE/Y...BIBLIOG 19/20. PAGE 6 H0115 SCHOOL SOCIETY NAT/G GP/REL

B61
ATTLEE C.R.,EMPIRE INTO COMMONWEALTH. AFR ASIA CANADA UK NAT/G WAR NAT/LISM ATTIT...POLICY 20 AUSTRAL. PAGE 9 H0179 DIPLOM GP/REL COLONIAL SOVEREIGN

B61
BIEBUYCK D.,CONGO TRIBES AND PARTIES. AFR CONGO/BRAZ CONSTN NAT/G COLONIAL CHOOSE FEDERAL 20 CONGO/LEOP. PAGE 17 H0333 KIN POL/PAR GP/REL SOVEREIGN

B61
BINDER L.,RELIGION AND POLITICS IN PAKISTAN. ISLAM PAKISTAN NAT/G SECT LEGIS CREATE CHOOSE GP/REL ...MAJORIT TRADIT 20. PAGE 17 H0336 CONSTN CONFER NAT/LISM POL/PAR

B61
BOURDIEU P.,THE ALGERIANS (TRANS. BY A.C. ROSS; REV. ED.). ALGERIA ISLAM CULTURE MUNIC CAP/ISM COLONIAL GP/REL ORD/FREE SOVEREIGN 20. PAGE 19 H0385 SOCIETY STRUCT ATTIT WAR

B61
BROUGHTON M.,PRESS AND POLITICS OF SOUTH AFRICA. SOUTH/AFR NAT/G COLONIAL GP/REL ADJUST 20. PAGE 22 H0435 NAT/LISM PRESS PWR CULTURE

B61
CARROTHERS A.W.R.,LABOR ARBITRATION IN CANADA. CANADA LAW NAT/G CONSULT LEGIS WORKER ADJUD ADMIN CT/SYS 20. PAGE 27 H0542 LABOR MGT GP/REL

BARGAIN
B61
CATHERINE R.,LE FONCTIONNAIRE FRANCAIS. FRANCE NAT/G INGP/REL ATTIT MORAL ORD/FREE...T CIVIL/SERV. PAGE 28 H0559 ADMIN GP/REL LEAD SUPEGO

B61
FREYRE G.,THE PORTUGUESE AND THE TROPICS. L/A+17C PORTUGAL SOCIETY PERF/ART ADMIN TASK GP/REL ...ART/METH CONCPT SOC/INTEG 20. PAGE 53 H1060 COLONIAL METH PLAN CULTURE

B61
HALPERIN S.,THE POLITICAL WORLD OF AMERICAN ZIONISM. ISRAEL FINAN LABOR VOL/ASSN GIVE LOBBY REPRESENT GP/REL ATTIT POLICY. PAGE 64 H1293 CULTURE SECT EDU/PROP DELIB/GP

B61
HUNT E.F.,SOCIAL SCIENCE. DIPLOM ECO/TAC ROUTINE GP/REL DEMAND DISCRIM EFFICIENCY HABITAT ALL/IDEOS ...SOC T 20. PAGE 75 H1497 CULTURE ADJUST STRATA ROLE

B61
KHALIQUZZAMAN C.,PATHWAY TO PAKISTAN. INDIA PAKISTAN UK SECT LEGIS CHOOSE RACE/REL ATTIT ORD/FREE 20 MUSLIM. PAGE 85 H1705 GP/REL NAT/G COLONIAL SOVEREIGN

B61
KHAN A.W.,INDIA WINS FREEDOM: THE OTHER SIDE. INDIA PAKISTAN CULTURE LEGIS DIPLOM PARL/PROC REV WAR NAT/LISM 20. PAGE 85 H1707 SOVEREIGN GP/REL RACE/REL ORD/FREE

B61
MILIBAND R.,PARLIAMENTARY SOCIALISM. EUR+WWI UK EXEC LEAD PARL/PROC GP/REL...POLICY 20 PARLIAMENT LABOR/PAR. PAGE 110 H2203 POL/PAR NAT/G PWR SOCISM

B61
PATAI R.,CULTURES IN CONFLICT; AN INQUIRY INTO THE SOCIO-CULTURAL PROBLEMS OF ISRAEL AND HER NEIGHBORS (2ND REV. ED.). ISLAM ISRAEL SOCIETY STRUCT DIPLOM GP/REL ALL/VALS...SOC 20 JEWS ARABS. PAGE 124 H2475 NAT/COMP CULTURE GP/COMP ATTIT

B61
RAHNER H.,KIRCHE UND STAAT IM FRUHEN CHRISTENTUM. INGP/REL ORD/FREE PWR CATHISM...JURID 1/9 CHURCH/STA CHRISTIAN. PAGE 129 H2582 NAT/G SECT ATTIT GP/REL

B61
SHARMA T.R.,THE WORKING OF STATE ENTERPRISES IN INDIA. INDIA DELIB/GP LEGIS WORKER BUDGET PRICE CONTROL GP/REL OWN ATTIT...MGT CHARTS 20. PAGE 142 H2851 NAT/G INDUS ADMIN SOCISM

B61
SOUTHALL A.,SOCIAL CHANGE IN MODERN AFRICA. CULTURE STRATA ECO/UNDEV AGRI FAM KIN MUNIC GP/REL INGP/REL MARRIAGE...GEOG ANTHOL 20. PAGE 147 H2940 AFR TREND SOCIETY SOC

B61
TURNBULL C.M.,THE FOREST PEOPLE. EATING GP/REL INGP/REL RACE/REL ISOLAT HABITAT HEREDITY...GEOG SOC LING DICTIONARY WORSHIP 20 CONGO NEGRO BA/MBUTI. PAGE 157 H3138 AFR CULTURE KIN RECORD

B61
VON EICKSTEDT E.,TURKEN, KURDEN UND IRANER SEIT DEM ALTERTUM. IRAN TURKEY GP/REL BIO/SOC HABITAT...PSY 20 PERSIA. PAGE 163 H3266 CULTURE SOC SOCIETY STRUCT

B61
WARD R.E.,JAPANESE POLITICAL SCIENCE: A GUIDE TO JAPANESE REFERENCE AND RESEARCH MATERIALS (2ND ED.). LAW CONSTN STRATA NAT/G POL/PAR DELIB/GP LEGIS ADMIN CHOOSE GP/REL...INT/LAW 19/20 CHINJAP. PAGE 165 H3306 BIBLIOG/A PHIL/SCI

L61
KAUPER P.G.,"CHURCH AND STATE: COOPERATIVE SEPARATISM." NAT/G LEGIS OP/RES TAX EDU/PROP GP/REL TREND. PAGE 84 H1671 SECT CONSTN LAW POLICY

S61
HOSELITZ B.F.,"ECONOMIC DEVELOPMENT AND POLITICAL STABILITY IN INDIA" INDIA NAT/G GP/REL...POLICY 20. PAGE 74 H1475 ECO/UNDEV GEN/LAWS PROB/SOLV

S61
LIEBERSON S.,"THE IMPACT OF RESIDENTIAL SEGREGATION ON ETHNIC ASSIMILATION" (BMR)" CULTURE MUNIC GP/REL RACE/REL DISCRIM...GEOG STAT CON/ANAL CHARTS SOC/INTEG 20 MIGRATION. PAGE 96 H1926 HABITAT ISOLAT NEIGH

S61
MACRIDIS R.C.,"INTEREST GROUPS IN COMPARATIVE ANALYSIS." CULTURE OP/RES LOBBY REPRESENT GP/REL AUTHORIT ORD/FREE PWR...POLICY DECISION METH/CNCPT CLASSIF. PAGE 101 H2010 GP/COMP CONCPT PLURISM

S61
SCHECHTMAN J.B.,"MINORITIES IN THE MIDDLE EAST." ISLAM INTELL SOCIETY STRATA KIN NAT/G VOL/ASSN EDU/PROP REGION GP/REL DISCRIM ATTIT BIO/SOC DISPL PERSON ALL/VALS...PSY SOC OBS SAMP GEN/LAWS 20. SECT CULTURE RACE/REL

PAGE 139 H2776

B62
BINDER L.,IRAN: POLITICAL DEVELOPMENT IN A CHANGING SOCIETY. IRAN OP/RES REV GP/REL CENTRAL RATIONAL PWR...PHIL/SCI NAT/COMP GEN/LAWS 20. PAGE 17 H0337 LEGIT NAT/G ADMIN STRUCT

B62
DEBUYST F.,LAS CLASES SOCIALES EN AMERICA LATINA. L/A+17C SOCIETY STRUCT WORKER EDU/PROP RACE/REL ATTIT HABITAT ROLE...GEOG SOC NAT/COMP SOC/INTEG 20. PAGE 39 H0780 STRATA GP/REL WEALTH

B62
FALKENBERG J.,KIN AND TOTEM; GROUP RELATIONS OF AUSTRALIAN ABORIGINES IN THE PORT KEATS DISTRICT. SOCIETY STRATA STRUCT GP/REL PERS/REL MARRIAGE AGE ATTIT SEX...SOC STAT CHARTS AUSTRAL ABORIGINES. PAGE 48 H0964 KIN INGP/REL CULTURE FAM

B62
GALENSON W.,LABOR IN DEVELOPING COUNTRIES. BRAZIL INDONESIA ISRAEL PAKISTAN TURKEY AGRI INDUS WORKER PAY PRICE GP/REL WEALTH...MGT CHARTS METH/COMP NAT/COMP 20. PAGE 54 H1088 LABOR ECO/UNDEV BARGAIN POL/PAR

B62
GROVE J.W.,GOVERNMENT AND INDUSTRY IN BRITAIN. UK FINAN LOC/G CONSULT DELIB/GP INT/TRADE ADMIN CONTROL...BIBLIOG 20. PAGE 62 H1237 ECO/TAC INDUS NAT/G GP/REL

B62
HACHMANN R.,VOLKER ZWISCHEN GERMANEN UND KELTEN. GERMANY CULTURE STRUCT MUNIC...ART/METH CHARTS MAPS. PAGE 63 H1269 LING SOC KIN GP/REL

B62
HAIM S.G.,ARAB NATIONALISM. ISLAM CONSTN GP/REL ...ANTHOL BIBLIOG JEWS 20 MID/EAST ARABS. PAGE 64 H1279 NAT/LISM REV SECT DIPLOM

B62
HANSON A.H.,MANAGERIAL PROBLEMS IN PUBLIC ENTERPRISE. INDIA DELIB/GP GP/REL INGP/REL EFFICIENCY 20 PARLIAMENT. PAGE 66 H1320 MGT NAT/G INDUS PROB/SOLV

B62
JENNINGS I.,PARTY POLITICS: THE STUFF OF POLITICS (VOL.III). UK NAT/G SECT CHIEF INT/TRADE RECEIVE COLONIAL GP/REL NAT/LISM ORD/FREE SOCISM 19/20 CHURCH/STA WHIG/PARTY. PAGE 80 H1607 POL/PAR CONSTN PWR ALL/IDEOS

B62
KEESING F.M.,THE ETHNOHISTORY OF NORTHERN LUZON. PHILIPPINE ECO/UNDEV FAM SECT CHIEF REGION GP/REL HABITAT...GEOG LING BIBLIOG WORSHIP 20. PAGE 84 H1680 CULTURE SOC KIN

B62
KINDERSLEY R.,THE FIRST RUSSIAN REVISIONISTS. COM USSR LAW ELITES INTELL NAT/G LEGIS ECO/TAC EDU/PROP CONTROL LEAD GP/REL SOCISM 19/20 MARX/KARL BOLSHEVISM. PAGE 86 H1712 CONSTN MARXISM POPULISM BIOG

B62
MARTINDALE D.,SOCIAL LIFE AND CULTURAL CHANGE. GP/REL...PHIL/SCI SOC CONCPT. PAGE 103 H2065 INTELL CULTURE ORD/FREE STRUCT

B62
NOBECOURT R.G.,LES SECRETS DE LA PROPAGANDE EN FRANCE OCCUPEE. FRANCE ELITES NAT/G DIPLOM GP/REL NAT/LISM TOTALISM ORD/FREE 20 VICHY VICHY. PAGE 118 H2365 METH/COMP EDU/PROP WAR CONTROL

B62
PAIKERT G.C.,THE GERMAN EXODUS. EUR+WWI GERMANY/W LAW CULTURE SOCIETY STRUCT INDUS NAT/LISM RESPECT SOVEREIGN...CHARTS BIBLIOG SOC/INTEG 20 MIGRATION. PAGE 122 H2444 INGP/REL STRANGE GEOG GP/REL

B62
ROUSSEAU J.J.,THE SOCIAL CONTRACT. LAW CONSTN CHIEF DOMIN REPRESENT GP/REL ORD/FREE POPULISM...MAJORIT GOV/COMP 18. PAGE 135 H2700 GEN/LAWS AGREE REV

B62
RUDY Z.,ETHNOSOZIOLOGIE SOWJETISCHER VOLKER. USSR SOCIETY STRUCT FAM SECT GP/REL ATTIT...SOC SOC/INTEG 20. PAGE 136 H2714 MYTH CULTURE KIN

B62
SCHIEDER T.,THE STATE AND SOCIETY IN OUR TIMES (TRANS. BY C.A.M. SYM). SOCIETY NAT/G POL/PAR REV GP/REL ALL/IDEOS 19/20. PAGE 139 H2786 STRUCT PWR HIST/WRIT

B62
SCHMIDT-VOLKMAR E.,DER KULTURKAMPF IN DEUTSCHLAND 1871-1890. GERMANY PRUSSIA SOCIETY STRUCT SECT DIPLOM GP/REL NAT/LISM 19 CHURCH/STA BISMARCK/O. PAGE 139 H2789 POL/PAR CATHISM ATTIT NAT/G

B62
TATZ C.M.,SHADOW AND SUBSTANCE IN SOUTH AFRICA. SOUTH/AFR AGRI NAT/G POL/PAR DOMIN GP/REL ATTIT PWR 20. PAGE 152 H3048 RACE/REL REPRESENT DISCRIM LEGIS

B62
TYSKEVIC S.,DIE EINHEIT DER KIRCHE UND BYZANZ (TRANS. BY F.K. LIESNER). ROMAN/EMP ADJUD GP/REL 1/17 CHRISTIAN BYZANTINE. PAGE 157 H3144 SECT NAT/G CATHISM ATTIT

B62
WEHLER H.V.,SOZIALDEMOKRATIE UND NATIONALSTAAT. GERMANY POLAND USSR CULTURE SOCIETY STRUCT NAT/G POL/PAR DIPLOM ORD/FREE 19/20. PAGE 166 H3325 NAT/LISM SOVEREIGN GP/REL ATTIT

B62
WOODS H.D.,LABOUR POLICY AND LABOUR ECONOMICS IN CANADA. CANADA FUT NAT/G VOL/ASSN WORKER BARGAIN ECO/TAC PAY CONFER GP/REL 20. PAGE 170 H3409 LABOR POLICY INDUS ECO/DEV

B62
YOUNG G.,THE HILL TRIBES OF NORTHERN THAILAND. S/ASIA THAILAND FAM KIN LOC/G GP/REL HABITAT...GEOG LING OBS 20. PAGE 172 H3438 CULTURE STRUCT ECO/UNDEV SECT

S62
MBOYA T.,"RELATIONS BETWEEN THE PRESS AND GOVERNMENT IN AFRICA." AFR DIPLOM EDU/PROP NAT/LISM ORD/FREE SOVEREIGN 20. PAGE 106 H2115 PRESS GP/REL ATTIT NAT/G

B63
AZEVEDO T.,SOCIAL CHANGE IN BRAZIL. BRAZIL ECO/DEV COM/IND FAM NAT/G SECT GP/REL PERS/REL...CONCPT WORSHIP 20. PAGE 9 H0188 TEC/DEV STRUCT SOC CULTURE

B63
BELFRAGE C.,THE MAN AT THE DOOR WITH THE GUN. CUBA L/A+17C NAT/G LEAD PARTIC GP/REL PWR...POLICY 20 CASTRO/F. PAGE 13 H0261 REGION ECO/UNDEV STRUCT ATTIT

B63
BERREMAN G.D.,HINDUS OF THE HIMALAYAS. INDIA STRATA STRUCT KIN MUNIC 20 HINDU. PAGE 16 H0319 CULTURE SECT GP/REL ECO/UNDEV

B63
BLONDEL J.,VOTERS, PARTIES, AND LEADERS. UK ELITES LOC/G NAT/G PROVS ACT/RES DOMIN REPRESENT GP/REL INGP/REL...SOC BIBLIOG 20. PAGE 18 H0358 POL/PAR STRATA LEGIS ADMIN

B63
BOHANNAN P.,SOCIAL ANTHROPOLOGY. ECO/DEV GP/REL DEMAND MARRIAGE HABITAT...CHARTS GP/COMP BIBLIOG T WORSHIP 20. PAGE 18 H0366 SOC STRUCT FAM CULTURE

B63
BORKENAU F.,THE SPANISH COCKPIT. SPAIN ELITES STRATA POL/PAR ACT/RES CROWD WAR GP/REL INGP/REL ...SOC NAT/COMP 20. PAGE 19 H0377 REV CONSERVE SOCISM FORCES

B63
CRUICKSHANK M.,CHURCH AND STATE IN ENGLISH EDUCATION 1870 TO PRESENT. UK LEGIS TAX GIVE DOMIN LEGIT ORD/FREE 19/20 CHURCH/STA. PAGE 36 H0715 NAT/G SECT EDU/PROP GP/REL

B63
DALAND R.T.,PERSPECTIVES OF BRAZILIAN PUBLIC ADMINISTRATION (VOL. I). BRAZIL LAW ECO/UNDEV SCHOOL CHIEF TEC/DEV CONFER CONTROL GP/REL ATTIT ROLE PWR...ANTHOL 20. PAGE 37 H0735 ADMIN NAT/G PLAN GOV/REL

B63
DE JOUVENEL B.,THE PURE THEORY OF POLITICS. NAT/G DIPLOM CONTROL GP/REL PERS/REL PERSON PWR OBJECTIVE CONCPT. PAGE 38 H0758 GEN/LAWS SOCIETY METH/CNCPT

B63
DRIVER H.E.,ETHNOGRAPHY AND ACCULTURATION OF THE CHICHIMECA-JONAZ OF NORTHEAST MEXICO. ECO/UNDEV AGRI FAM KIN EDU/PROP MARRIAGE HEALTH...GEOG INT CHARTS WORSHIP 18/20 MEXIC/AMER. PAGE 42 H0848 CULTURE HABITAT STRUCT GP/REL

B63
FRITZ H.E.,THE MOVEMENT FOR INDIAN ASSIMILATION, 1860-1890. SECT FORCES GP/REL RACE/REL DISCRIM FEDERAL CATHISM...BIBLIOG 19 INDIAN/AM PROTESTANT GRANT/US. PAGE 54 H1071 CULTURE NAT/G ECO/TAC ATTIT

B63
JAIRAZBHOY R.A.,FOREIGN INFLUENCE IN ANCIENT INDIA. INDIA ELITES SECT DIPLOM EDU/PROP COLONIAL REGION GP/REL...ART/METH LING WORSHIP +/14 GRECO/ROMN MESOPOTAM PERSIA PARTH/SASS. PAGE 79 H1587 CULTURE SOCIETY COERCE DOMIN

B63
JENNINGS W.I.,DEMOCRACY IN AFRICA. UK CULTURE STRUCT ECO/UNDEV DIPLOM COLONIAL GP/REL ADJUST NAT/LISM ORD/FREE...GOV/COMP 20 THIRD/WRLD. PAGE 81 H1613 PROB/SOLV AFR CONSTN POPULISM

B63
LEWIN J.,POLITICS AND LAW IN SOUTH AFRICA. SOUTH/AFR UK POL/PAR BAL/PWR ECO/TAC COLONIAL CONTROL GP/REL DISCRIM PWR 20 NEGRO. PAGE 96 H1909 NAT/LISM POLICY LAW RACE/REL

B63
MAJUMDAR O.N.,AN INTRODUCTION TO SOCIAL ANTHROPOLOGY. INDIA LAW STRATA ECO/UNDEV KIN DEMAND MARRIAGE...GP/COMP BIBLIOG T WORSHIP 20. PAGE 101 SOC CULTURE STRUCT

H2026 GP/REL

B63

MARTINDALE D.,COMMUNITY, CHARACTER AND CIVILIZATION: STUDIES IN SOCIAL BEHAVIORISM. INTELL FAM NEIGH VOL/ASSN GP/REL NAT/LISM ATTIT PERSON ...CONCPT GP/COMP 20 BEHAVIORSM. PAGE 103 H2066 SOC METH/COMP CULTURE STRUCT

B63

MERKL P.H.,THE ORIGIN OF THE WEST GERMAN REPUBLIC. GERMANY/W WOR+45 POL/PAR DIPLOM LEAD LOBBY REPRESENT GP/REL NAT/LISM 20. PAGE 109 H2179 CONSTN PARL/PROC CONTROL BAL/PWR

B63

PELLING H.M.,A HISTORY OF BRITISH TRADE UNIONISM. UK ELITES ECO/DEV POL/PAR GP/REL PWR NEW/LIB 19/20. PAGE 124 H2485 LABOR VOL/ASSN NAT/G

B63

SELF P.,THE STATE AND THE FARMER. UK ECO/DEV MARKET WORKER PRICE CONTROL GP/REL...WELF/ST 20 DEPT/AGRI. PAGE 141 H2823 AGRI NAT/G ADMIN VOL/ASSN

B63

SETON-WATSON H.,THE NEW IMPERIALISM. COM EUR+WWI MOD/EUR ECO/UNDEV NAT/G FORCES DIPLOM DOMIN EDU/PROP LEGIT COLONIAL EXEC COERCE GP/REL RACE/REL DISCRIM ATTIT...TIME/SEQ 20. PAGE 142 H2833 ECO/TAC RUSSIA USSR

B63

SPRING D.,THE ENGLISH LANDED ESTATE IN THE NINETEENTH CENTURY: ITS ADMINISTRATION. UK ELITES STRUCT AGRI NAT/G GP/REL OWN PWR WEALTH...BIBLIOG 19 HOUSE/LORD. PAGE 148 H2954 STRATA PERS/REL MGT

B63

THOMPSON F.M.L.,ENGLISH LANDED SOCIETY IN THE NINETEENTH CENTURY. UK STRUCT MUNIC NAT/G CONTROL WAR GP/REL OWN WEALTH...BIBLIOG 18/20. PAGE 154 H3081 STRATA PWR ELITES GOV/REL

B63

VALJAVEC F.,AUSGEWAHLTE AUFSATZE. GERMANY HUNGARY STRUCT ATTIT...CONCPT IDEA/COMP 18/20 BALKANS. PAGE 161 H3223 SOCIETY CULTURE GP/REL NAT/LISM

B63

WILCOX W.A.,PAKISTAN; THE CONSOLIDATION OF A NATION. INDIA PAKISTAN CONSTN SECT PROB/SOLV COLONIAL PARTIC GP/REL FEDERAL...POLICY 19/20. PAGE 168 H3361 NAT/LISM ECO/UNDEV DIPLOM STRUCT

S63

MBOYA T.,"AFRICAN SOCIALISM." ECO/UNDEV INT/ORG DIPLOM FOR/AID INT/TRADE REGION GP/REL ATTIT ORD/FREE EACM. PAGE 106 H2116 AFR SOCISM CULTURE NAT/LISM

S63

TANNER R.,"WHO GOES HOME?" CULTURE GP/REL SOC/INTEG 20 TANGANYIKA MIGRATION. PAGE 152 H3045 ADMIN COLONIAL NAT/G NAT/LISM

S63

ZOLBERG A.R.,"MASS PARTIES AND NATIONAL INTEGRATION: THE CASE OF THE IVORY COAST" (BMR)" AFR IVORY/CST CONSTN VOL/ASSN DIPLOM LEAD GP/REL INGP/REL 20. PAGE 173 H3461 POL/PAR ECO/UNDEV NAT/G ADJUST

C63

BECKHAM R.S.,"A BASIC LIST OF BOOKS AND PERIODICALS FOR COLLEGE LIBRARIES." UNIV GP/REL...PSY SOC. PAGE 13 H0255 BIBLIOG SOCIETY CULTURE KNOWL

B64

AKZIN B.,STATE AND NATION. UNIV ECO/UNDEV DIPLOM RACE/REL NAT/LISM ATTIT PLURISM...CONCPT IDEA/COMP 20. PAGE 4 H0090 GP/REL NAT/G KIN

B64

BROWN C.V.,GOVERNMENT AND BANKING IN WESTERN NIGERIA. AFR NIGERIA GOV/REL GP/REL...POLICY 20. PAGE 22 H0440 ADMIN ECO/UNDEV FINAN NAT/G

B64

CURRIE D.P.,FEDERALISM AND THE NEW NATIONS OF AFRICA. CANADA USA+45 INT/TRADE TAX GP/REL ...NAT/COMP SOC/INTEG 20. PAGE 36 H0725 FEDERAL AFR ECO/UNDEV INT/LAW

B64

FREISEN J.,STAAT UND KATHOLISCHE KIRCHE IN DEN DEUTSCHEN BUNDESSTAATEN (2 VOLS.). GERMANY LAW FAM NAT/G EDU/PROP GP/REL MARRIAGE WEALTH 19/20 CHURCH/STA. PAGE 53 H1056 SECT CATHISM JURID PROVS

B64

HARRIS M.,THE NATURE OF CULTURAL THINGS. GP/REL PERS/REL DRIVE HABITAT PERSON ROLE...PHIL/SCI PSY SOC CHARTS BIBLIOG 20. PAGE 67 H1341 CULTURE OBS CLASSIF NEW/IDEA

B64

HELMREICH E.,A FREE CHURCH IN A FREE STATE? FRANCE GERMANY ITALY SECT LEAD PWR CATHISM...POLICY ANTHOL WORSHIP 19/20 CHURCH/STA. PAGE 69 H1389 GP/REL NAT/G

B64

LATORRE A.,UNIVERSIDAD Y SOCIEDAD. SPAIN EDU/PROP LEAD GP/REL PERS/REL ATTIT KNOWL. PAGE 92 H1837 ACADEM CULTURE ROLE INTELL

B64

LAWRENCE P.,ROAD BELONG CARGO: A STUDY OF CARGO MOVEMENT IN SOUTHERN MADANG DISTRICT, NEW GUINEA. S/ASIA CULTURE ECO/UNDEV PROC/MFG KIN CHIEF COLONIAL COERCE GP/REL DRIVE WEALTH WORSHIP 20 NEW/GUINEA. PAGE 92 H1846 SOC SECT ALL/VALS MYTH

B64

LEMARCHAND R.,POLITICAL AWAKENING IN THE BELGIAN CONGO. ECO/UNDEV VOL/ASSN DOMIN CHOOSE GP/REL INGP/REL DISCRIM ORD/FREE PWR...CHARTS 20 CONGO ARABS. PAGE 94 H1873 NAT/LISM COLONIAL POL/PAR RACE/REL

B64

MARTINEZ J.R.,THREE CASES OF COMMUNISM: CUBA, BRAZIL, AND MEXICO. BRAZIL CUBA L/A+17C CONSTN NAT/G DIPLOM ECO/TAC GP/REL INGP/REL...GP/COMP BIBLIOG 20 MEXIC/AMER COM/PARTY. PAGE 103 H2068 MARXISM BIOG REV NAT/COMP

B64

MEAD M.,CONTINUITIES IN CULTURAL EVOLUTION. FACE/GP KIN ACT/RES EDU/PROP GP/REL INGP/REL DRIVE HEREDITY ROLE...TIME/SEQ TREND METH SOC/INTEG 20. PAGE 108 H2153 CULTURE SOC PERS/REL

B64

MORGAN H.W.,AMERICAN SOCIALISM 1900-1960. USA+45 USA-45 INTELL AGRI LABOR WORKER BARGAIN ECO/TAC GP/REL RACE/REL 20 NEGRO MIGRATION GOLD/STAND. PAGE 113 H2254 SOCISM POL/PAR ECO/DEV STRATA

B64

MORGENTHAU R.S.,POLITICAL PARTIES IN FRENCH-SPEAKING WEST AFRICA. AFR FRANCE GUINEA IVORY/CST MALI SENEGAL CONSTN LEGIS CREATE PLAN LOBBY PARTIC GP/REL...POLICY BIBLIOG 20. PAGE 113 H2257 POL/PAR NAT/G SOVEREIGN COLONIAL

B64

MUSEUM FUR VOLKERKUNDE WIEN,ZENTRALAMERIKA MEXIKO VOLKER UND KULTUREN. COSTA/RICA GUATEMALA L/A+17C PANAMA SECT WAR GP/REL SOVEREIGN...ART/METH 20 CENTRAL/AM MEXIC/AMER. PAGE 115 H2300 SOCIETY STRUCT CULTURE AGRI

B64

SANCHEZ J.M.,REFORM AND REACTION. SPAIN STRATA NAT/LISM TOTALISM 20. PAGE 137 H2749 NAT/G SECT GP/REL REV

B64

TIERNEY B.,THE CRISIS OF CHURCH AND STATE 1050-1300. DOMIN EDU/PROP CONTROL PWR CONSERVE 11/14. PAGE 155 H3092 SECT NAT/G GP/REL

B64

WALLBANK T.W.,DOCUMENTS ON MODERN AFRICA. NAT/G COLONIAL GP/REL ATTIT PWR...BIBLIOG 19/20. PAGE 165 H3294 AFR NAT/LISM ECO/UNDEV DIPLOM

B64

WHEELER-BENNETT J.W.,THE NEMESIS OF POWER (2ND ED.). EUR+WWI GERMANY TOP/EX TEC/DEV ADMIN WAR PERS/REL RIGID/FLEX ROLE ORD/FREE PWR FASCISM 20 HITLER/A. PAGE 167 H3342 FORCES NAT/G GP/REL STRUCT

S64

"FURTHER READING." INDIA PAKISTAN SECT WAR PEACE ATTIT...POLICY 20. PAGE 2 H0044 BIBLIOG GP/REL DIPLOM NAT/G

C64

HARRIS M.,"THE NATURE OF CULTURAL THINGS." GP/REL DRIVE HABITAT PERSON ROLE...PHIL/SCI 20. PAGE 67 H1340 BIBLIOG CULTURE PSY SOC

C64

SCOTT R.E.,"MEXICAN GOVERNMENT IN TRANSITION (REV ED)" CULTURE STRUCT POL/PAR CHIEF ADMIN LOBBY REV CHOOSE GP/REL DRIVE...BIBLIOG METH 20 MEXIC/AMER. PAGE 141 H2816 NAT/G L/A+17C ROUTINE CONSTN

B65

ARENSBERG C.M.,CULTURE AND COMMUNITY. UNIV FACE/GP ACT/RES EDU/PROP LEAD REGION GP/REL PERS/REL HABITAT ALL/VALS...SOC CONCPT 20. PAGE 8 H0162 SOCIETY CULTURE NEIGH NEW/IDEA

B65

BETEILLE A.,CASTE, CLASS, AND POWER. INDIA MUNIC SECT REGION GP/REL PERS/REL ATTIT HABITAT RIGID/FLEX...SOC 20. PAGE 16 H0323 STRATA CULTURE PWR STRUCT

B65

BOISSEVAIN J.,SAINTS AND FIREWORKS: RELIGION AND POLITICS IN RURAL MALTA. MALTA STRUCT FAM NEIGH POL/PAR REPRESENT INGP/REL CENTRAL...CHARTS BIBLIOG 20. PAGE 18 H0368 GP/REL NAT/G SECT MUNIC

B65

BRASS P.R.,FACTIONAL POLITICS IN AN INDIAN STATE: THE CONGRESS PARTY IN UTTAR PRADESH. INDIA UK CONSTN CULTURE ECO/UNDEV LOC/G DOMIN COLONIAL CROWD GP/REL ADJUST CENTRAL RIGID/FLEX SOVEREIGN 20 UTTAR/PRAD CONGRESS/P. PAGE 20 H0406 POL/PAR PROVS LEGIS CHOOSE

B65

BURLING R.,HILL FARMS AND PADI FIELDS. BURMA S/ASIA THAILAND VIETNAM AGRI NEIGH SECT GP/REL NAT/LISM SOCIETY STRUCT

ORD/FREE 20 MID/EAST MIGRATION. PAGE 24 H0491 CULTURE SOVEREIGN

B65
CAMERON W.J.,NEW ZEALAND. NEW/ZEALND S/ASIA DIPLOM INT/TRADE WRITING COLONIAL PARL/PROC...GEOG CMN/WLTH. PAGE 26 H0513 SOCIETY GP/REL STRUCT

B65
CONRING E.,KIRCHE UND STAAT NACH DER LEHRE DER NIEDERLANDISCHEN CALVINISTEN IN DER ERSTEN HALFTE DES 17. JAHRHUNDERTS. NETHERLAND GP/REL...CONCPT 17 CHURCH/STA. PAGE 33 H0656 SECT JURID NAT/G ORD/FREE

B65
DOLCI D.,A NEW WORLD IN THE MAKING. GHANA SENEGAL USSR YUGOSLAVIA CULTURE INT/ORG PLAN EDU/PROP GP/REL PEACE MORAL...GEOG SOC 20 COLD/WAR. PAGE 42 H0834 SOCIETY ALL/VALS DRIVE PERSON

B65
FAUST J.J.,A REVOLUCAO DEVORA SEUS PRESIDENTES. BRAZIL NAT/G POL/PAR LEAD CHOOSE CIVMIL/REL ORD/FREE 20 PRESIDENT. PAGE 49 H0976 PARTIC REV FORCES GP/REL

B65
FORM W.H.,INDUSTRIAL RELATIONS AND SOCIAL CHANGE IN LATIN AMERICA. L/A+17C AGRI LABOR NAT/G PLAN PROB/SOLV DIPLOM...MGT SOC ANTHOL BIBLIOG/A METH 20. PAGE 52 H1038 INDUS GP/REL NAT/COMP ECO/UNDEV

B65
GEWIRTH A.,POLITICAL PHILOSOPHY. UNIV SOCIETY NAT/G GP/REL INGP/REL CONSEN PWR...IDEA/COMP GEN/LAWS 17/19 HOBBES/T LOCKE/JOHN MARX/KARL MILL/JS ROUSSEAU/J. PAGE 56 H1118 ORD/FREE SOVEREIGN PHIL/SCI

B65
GHAI D.P.,PORTRAIT OF A MINORITY: ASIANS IN EAST AFRICA. S/ASIA TANZANIA UGANDA COLONIAL...SOC OBS PREDICT ANTHOL 20. PAGE 56 H1119 RACE/REL GP/REL CULTURE AFR

B65
GOPAL S.,BRITISH POLICY IN INDIA 1858-1905. INDIA UK ELITES CHIEF DELIB/GP ECO/TAC GP/REL DISCRIM ATTIT...IDEA/COMP NAT/COMP PERS/COMP BIBLIOG/A 19/20. PAGE 59 H1176 COLONIAL ADMIN POL/PAR ECO/UNDEV

B65
HADWIGER D.F.,PRESSURES AND PROTEST. NAT/G LEGIS PLAN LEAD PARTIC ROUTINE ATTIT POLICY. PAGE 63 H1273 AGRI GP/REL LOBBY CHOOSE

B65
HANSER C.J.,GUIDE TO DECISION: ROYAL COMMISSION. UK INTELL EXTR/IND SCHOOL PROB/SOLV EXEC ROUTINE CHOOSE GOV/REL GP/REL HEALTH...CHARTS 20. PAGE 66 H1318 NAT/G DELIB/GP EX/STRUC PWR

B65
HORNE A.J.,THE COMMONWEALTH TODAY. AFR ASIA CANADA UK STRUCT ECO/UNDEV NAT/G SECT GP/REL 20 AUSTRAL CMN/WLTH. PAGE 73 H1470 BIBLIOG/A SOCIETY CULTURE

B65
JOHNSON P.,KHRUSHCHEV AND THE ARTS: POLITICS OF SOVIET CULTURE, 1962-1964. COM USSR NAT/G PERF/ART CONFER DEBATE GP/REL PERS/REL UTIL ATTIT DRIVE 20 KHRUSH/N. PAGE 81 H1626 CULTURE MARXISM POLICY CHIEF

B65
JONAS E.,DIE VOLKSKONSERVATIVEN 1928-1933. GERMANY EX/STRUC...CONCPT TIME/SEQ 20 HITLER/A. PAGE 82 H1628 POL/PAR NAT/G GP/REL

B65
KAAS L.,DIE GEISTLICHE GERICHTSBARKEIT DER KATHOLISCHEN KIRCHE IN PREUSSEN (2 VOLS.). PRUSSIA CONSTN NAT/G PROVS SECT ADJUD ADMIN ATTIT 16/20. PAGE 82 H1647 JURID CATHISM GP/REL CT/SYS

B65
LAWRENCE P.,GODS, GHOSTS, AND MEN IN MELANESIA: SOME RELIGIONS OF AUSTRALIAN NEW GUINEA AND THE NEW HEBRIDES. SOCIETY ECO/UNDEV FAM GP/REL INGP/REL HABITAT PERSON...GEOG SOC ANTHOL BIBLIOG WORSHIP 20 NEW/GUINEA. PAGE 92 H1847 MYTH S/ASIA SECT CULTURE

B65
MEHROTRA S.R.,INDIA AND THE COMMONWEALTH 1885-1929. INDIA UK INT/ORG VOL/ASSN GP/REL ATTIT...POLICY BIBLIOG 19/20 CMN/WLTH. PAGE 108 H2163 DIPLOM NAT/G POL/PAR NAT/LISM

B65
ONUOHA B.,THE ELEMENTS OF AFRICAN SOCIALISM. AFR FINAN SECT TEC/DEV FOR/AID GP/REL OWN LAISSEZ MARXISM...CONCPT BIBLIOG 20. PAGE 121 H2419 SOCISM ECO/UNDEV NAT/G EX/STRUC

B65
PANJABI K.L.,THE CIVIL SERVANT IN INDIA. INDIA UK NAT/G CONSULT EX/STRUC REGION GP/REL RACE/REL 20. PAGE 123 H2462 ADMIN WORKER BIOG COLONIAL

B65
PARRIS H.W.,GOVERNMENT AND THE RAILWAYS IN NINETEENTH-CENTURY BRITAIN. UK DELIB/GP CONTROL LEAD CENTRAL 19 RAILROAD. PAGE 124 H2470 DIST/IND NAT/G PLAN GP/REL

B65
PELLING H.,A SHORT HISTORY OF THE LABOUR PARTY (2ND ED.). UK NAT/G CHIEF PARL/PROC GP/REL INGP/REL 20 LABOR/PAR PARLIAMENT WILSON/H. PAGE 124 H2484 POL/PAR NEW/LIB LEAD LABOR

B65
QURESHI I.H.,THE STRUGGLE FOR PAKISTAN. INDIA PAKISTAN UK CULTURE LEGIS DIPLOM EDU/PROP COLONIAL ATTIT SOVEREIGN 19/20 MUSLIM. PAGE 129 H2576 GP/REL RACE/REL WAR SECT

B65
ROWAT D.C.,THE OMBUDSMAN: CITIZEN'S DEFENDER. DENMARK FINLAND NEW/ZEALND NORWAY SWEDEN CONSULT PROB/SOLV FEEDBACK PARTIC GP/REL...SOC CONCPT NEW/IDEA METH/COMP ANTHOL BIBLIOG 20. PAGE 135 H2701 INSPECT CONSTN NAT/G ADMIN

B65
RUBINSTEIN A.Z.,THE CHALLENGE OF POLITICS: IDEAS AND ISSUES (2ND ED.). UNIV ELITES SOCIETY EX/STRUC BAL/PWR PARL/PROC AUTHORIT...DECISION ANTHOL 20. PAGE 136 H2709 NAT/G DIPLOM GP/REL ORD/FREE

B65
SHEPHERD W.G.,ECONOMIC PERFORMANCE UNDER PUBLIC OWNERSHIP: BRITISH FUEL AND POWER. UK BUDGET GP/REL ...METH/CNCPT CHARTS BIBLIOG 20. PAGE 143 H2858 PROC/MFG NAT/G OWN FINAN

B65
SHRIMALI K.L.,EDUCATION IN CHANGING INDIA. INDIA CULTURE DIPLOM FOR/AID GP/REL RACE/REL ATTIT SOC/INTEG 20 UNESCO CMN/WLTH. PAGE 143 H2866 EDU/PROP PROF/ORG ACADEM

B65
SPENCER P.,THE SAMBURU: A STUDY OF GERONTOCRACY IN A NOMADIC TRIBE. AFR SOCIETY ECO/UNDEV AGRI FAM NEIGH SECT GP/REL MARRIAGE WORSHIP 20 SAMBURU. PAGE 147 H2945 KIN STRUCT AGE/O CULTURE

B65
SVALASTOGA K.,SOCIAL DIFFERENTIATION. CULTURE ELITES SOCIETY MARRIAGE...CONCPT SIMUL. PAGE 151 H3011 SOC STRATA STRUCT GP/REL

B65
VAN DEN BERGHE P.L.,AFRICA: SOCIAL PROBLEMS OF CHANGE AND CONFLICT. ELITES STRATA ECO/UNDEV KIN MUNIC DIPLOM GP/REL RACE/REL NAT/LISM...ANTHOL BIBLIOG 20. PAGE 161 H3228 SOC CULTURE AFR STRUCT

B65
WARD W.E.,GOVERNMENT IN WEST AFRICA. WOR+45 POL/PAR EX/STRUC PLAN PARTIC GP/REL SOVEREIGN 20 AFRICA/W. PAGE 165 H3308 GOV/COMP CONSTN COLONIAL ECO/UNDEV

B65
WOLPERT S.,INDIA. INDIA UK ECO/UNDEV DIPLOM GP/REL WEALTH 20 NEHRU/J. PAGE 170 H3405 CULTURE COLONIAL NAT/LISM SECT

L65
HOUN F.S.,"THE COMMUNIST MONOLITH VERSUS THE CHINESE TRADITION." CULTURE INTELL SOCIETY STRUCT DOMIN GP/REL ORD/FREE CONSERVE PLURISM...GOV/COMP WORSHIP. PAGE 74 H1479 ASIA MARXISM TOTALISM

S65
KEE W.S.,"CENTRAL CITY EXPENDITURES AND METROPOLITAN AREAS." PLAN BUDGET ECO/TAC TAX GP/REL WEALTH...CHARTS 20. PAGE 84 H1677 LOC/G MUNIC GOV/COMP NEIGH

B66
BECKER J.,BESSARABIEN UND SEIN DEUTSCHTUM. ROMANIA USSR STRUCT INDUS PROF/ORG SECT GP/REL INGP/REL 15/20 BESSARABIA. PAGE 13 H0254 PROVS CULTURE SOCIETY

B66
BEER S.H.,BRITISH POLITICS IN THE COLLECTIVIST AGE. UK NAT/G CONTROL CHOOSE GP/REL ATTIT PWR PLURISM ...MAJORIT WELF/ST 16/20. PAGE 13 H0258 POL/PAR SOCISM TRADIT GP/COMP

B66
BERELSON B.,READER IN PUBLIC OPINION AND COMMUNICATION (2ND ED.). UNIV NAT/G PRESS GP/REL PERS/REL PERCEPT RIGID/FLEX...MAJORIT QUANT METH/COMP ANTHOL BIBLIOG 20. PAGE 15 H0298 EDU/PROP ATTIT CONCPT COM/IND

B66
BIRMINGHAM D.,TRADE AND CONFLICT IN ANGOLA. PORTUGAL CULTURE FORCES DIPLOM GP/REL PROFIT HABITAT NAT/COMP. PAGE 17 H0341 WAR INT/TRADE ECO/UNDEV COLONIAL

B66
BUTLER D.E.,THE BRITISH GENERAL ELECTION OF 1966. UK LOC/G NAT/G OP/RES CONFER CHOOSE MAJORITY ATTIT ...CHARTS TIME 20. PAGE 25 H0498 POL/PAR REPRESENT GP/REL PERS/REL

B66
CADY J.F.,THAILAND, BURMA, LAOS AND CAMBODIA. FRANCE UK CULTURE NAT/G DOMIN GP/REL RACE/REL HABITAT...GEOG TREND CHINJAP BUDDHISM. PAGE 25 H0504 S/ASIA COLONIAL REGION SECT

B66
CHANG,THE PARTY AND THE NATIONAL QUESTION IN CHINA GP/REL

(TRANS. BY GEORGE MOSELEY). CHINA/COM CULTURE CONTROL NAT/LISM...CHARTS BIBLIOG/A 20. PAGE 29 H0576
REGION ISOLAT MARXISM

B66
COLEMAN-NORTON P.R.,ROMAN STATE AND CHRISTIAN CHURCH: A COLLECTION OF LEGAL DOCUMENTS TO A.D. 535 (3 VOLS.). CHRIST-17C ROMAN/EMP...ANTHOL DICTIONARY 6 CHRISTIAN CHURCH/STA. PAGE 31 H0630
GP/REL NAT/G SECT LAW

B66
DARLING M.,APPRENTICE TO POWER INDIA 1904-1908. INDIA LEAD GP/REL PERSON...GEOG 20. PAGE 37 H0742
OBS SOCIETY ADMIN NAT/G

B66
DEXTER N.C.,GUIDE TO CONTEMPORARY POLITICS. EUR+WWI UK PARL/PROC GP/REL KNOWL...POLICY MAJORIT IDEA/COMP 20. PAGE 41 H0815
POL/PAR CONCPT NAT/G

B66
FARRELL R.B.,APPROACHES TO COMPARATIVE AND INTERNATIONAL POLITICS. RUSSIA SOCIETY ACADEM GOV/REL GP/REL...METH/CNCPT NET/THEORY GOV/COMP HYPO/EXP SOC/EXP GEN/METH ANTHOL. PAGE 49 H0973
DIPLOM NAT/COMP NAT/G

B66
FEINE H.E.,REICH UND KIRCHE. CHRIST-17C MOD/EUR ROMAN/EMP LAW CHOOSE ATTIT 10/19 CHURCH/STA ROMAN/LAW. PAGE 49 H0982
JURID SECT NAT/G GP/REL

B66
FUCHS W.P.,STAAT UND KIRCHE IM WANDEL DER JAHRHUNDERTE. EUR+WWI MOD/EUR UK REV...JURID CONCPT 4/20 EUROPE CHRISTIAN CHURCH/STA. PAGE 54 H1074
SECT NAT/G ORD/FREE GP/REL

B66
HATTICH M.,NATIONALBEWUSSTSEIN UND STAATSBEWUSSTSEIN IN DER PLURALISTISCHEN GESELLSCHAFT. GERMANY GP/REL ATTIT SOVEREIGN SOC/INTEG 20. PAGE 68 H1356
NAT/G NAT/LISM SOCIETY OBJECTIVE

B66
HENKYS R.,DEUTSCHLAND UND DIE OSTLICHEN NACHBARN. GERMANY POLAND NAT/G POL/PAR INGP/REL ATTIT 20 MIGRATION. PAGE 70 H1396
GP/REL JURID INT/LAW DIPLOM

B66
HERMANN F.G.,DER KAMPF GEGEN RELIGION UND KIRCHE IN DER SOWJETISCHEN BESATZUNGSZONE DEUTSCHLANDS. GERMANY/E EDU/PROP ATTIT PERSON MORAL MARXISM 20 LENIN/VI STALIN/J KHRUSH/N. PAGE 70 H1400
SECT ORD/FREE GP/REL NAT/G

B66
LEIGH M.B.,CHECK LIST OF HOLDINGS ON BORNEO IN THE CORNELL UNIVERSITY LIBRARIES (PAMPHLET). BORNEO MALAYSIA LAW CONSTN GP/REL SOC. PAGE 93 H1866
BIBLIOG S/ASIA DIPLOM NAT/G

B66
LOVEDAY P.,PARLIAMENT FACTIONS AND PARTIES: THE FIRST THIRTY YEARS OF RESPONSIBLE GOVERNMENT IN NEW SOUTH WALES, 1856-1889. PROVS LEAD PARL/PROC PARTIC GP/REL INGP/REL MAJORITY PWR...GP/COMP 19 AUSTRAL. PAGE 99 H1970
POL/PAR ELITES NAT/G LEGIS

B66
MERRITT R.L.,COMPARING NATIONS* THE USE OF QUANTITATIVE DATA IN CROSSNATIONAL RESEARCH. ACADEM DIPLOM GP/REL...PHIL/SCI STAT TREND GP/COMP PERS/COMP GEN/METH ANTHOL BIBLIOG INDEX. PAGE 109 H2184
NAT/COMP MATH COMPUT/IR QUANT

B66
MILONE P.D.,URBAN AREAS IN INDONESIA. INDONESIA LABOR NAT/G COLONIAL GP/REL...CENSUS CHARTS 17/20. PAGE 111 H2218
MUNIC GEOG STRUCT SOCIETY

B66
NIEDERGANG M.,LA REVOLUTION DE SAINT-DOMINGUE. DOMIN/REP INT/ORG NAT/G CONTROL LEAD GP/REL ORD/FREE MARXISM 20. PAGE 118 H2361
REV FORCES DIPLOM

B66
NOLTE E.,THREE FACES OF FASCISM. FRANCE GERMANY DOMIN LEGIT COERCE CROWD REV WAR GP/REL RACE/REL SOVEREIGN...GOV/COMP IDEA/COMP 19/20 HITLER/A MUSSOLIN/B MARX/KARL. PAGE 118 H2368
FASCISM TOTALISM NAT/G POL/PAR

B66
O'NEILL C.E.,CHURCH AND STATE IN FRENCH COLONIAL LOUISIANA: POLICY AND POLITICS TO 1732. PROVS VOL/ASSN DELIB/GP ADJUD ADMIN GP/REL ATTIT DRIVE ...POLICY BIBLIOG 17/18 LOUISIANA CHURCH/STA. PAGE 120 H2390
COLONIAL NAT/G SECT PWR

B66
RIZK C.,LE REGIME POLITIQUE LIBANAIS. ISLAM LEBANON STRUCT POL/PAR SECT LOBBY GP/REL 20 ARABS MUSLIM CHRISTIAN. PAGE 132 H2637
ECO/UNDEV NAT/G CULTURE

B66
ROSS A.M.,INDUSTRIAL RELATIONS AND ECONOMIC DEVELOPMENT. POL/PAR LEGIS WORKER BARGAIN PRICE EXEC LOBBY INCOME PWR...DECISION ANTHOL BIBLIOG 20. PAGE 134 H2686
ECO/UNDEV LABOR NAT/G GP/REL

B66
SETTON K.M.,GREAT PROBLEMS IN EUROPEAN CIVILIZATION. CHRIST-17C EUR+WWI MOD/EUR SECT GP/REL ALL/VALS ORD/FREE ALL/IDEOS...TREND ANTHOL T CHRISTIAN RENAISSAN PROTESTANT. PAGE 142 H2835
CULTURE CONCPT IDEA/COMP

B66
SILBERMAN B.S.,MODERN JAPANESE LEADERSHIP; TRANSITION AND CHANGE. NAT/G POL/PAR CHIEF ADMIN REPRESENT GP/REL ADJUST RIGID/FLEX...SOC METH/COMP ANTHOL 19/20 CHINJAP CHRISTIAN. PAGE 144 H2873
LEAD CULTURE ELITES MUNIC

B66
SOROKIN P.A.,SOCIOLOGICAL THEORIES OF TODAY. SOCIETY STRUCT FAM SECT GP/REL ADJUST...PHIL/SCI PSY TREND METH/COMP 20. PAGE 147 H2935
SOC CULTURE METH/CNCPT EPIST

B66
SWARTZ M.J.,POLITICAL ANTHROPOLOGY. WOR+45 POL/PAR ACT/RES REV GP/REL DRIVE...SOC CONCPT TIME/SEQ GP/COMP ANTHOL WORSHIP 20. PAGE 151 H3013
PARTIC RIGID/FLEX LOC/G CREATE

B66
TIVEY L.J.,NATIONALISATION IN BRITISH INDUSTRY. UK LEGIS PARL/PROC GP/REL OWN ATTIT SOCISM 20. PAGE 156 H3109
NAT/G INDUS CONTROL LG/CO

B66
VOGT E.Z.,PEOPLE OF RIMROCK. STRATA STRUCT KIN SECT GP/REL HABITAT ALL/VALS...GEOG INT QU 20 TEXAS NAVAHO MORMON SPAN/AMER ZUNI. PAGE 163 H3260
CULTURE GP/COMP SOC SOCIETY

B66
WEBER J.,EOTVOS UND DIE UNGARISCHE NATIONALITATENFRAGE. HUNGARY CULTURE SOCIETY REV ORD/FREE SOVEREIGN...BIOG 19. PAGE 166 H3318
NAT/LISM GP/REL ATTIT CONCPT

B66
WEINSTEIN B.,GABON: NATION-BUILDING ON THE OGOOUE. AFR GABON WOR+45 CULTURE SOCIETY PLAN DIPLOM COLONIAL INGP/REL ANOMIE HABITAT SUPEGO 20. PAGE 166 H3329
ECO/UNDEV GP/REL LEAD NAT/G

S66
HAIGH G.,"FIELD TRAINING IN HUMAN RELATIONS FOR THE PEACE CORPS." CONSULT CREATE EDU/PROP ADMIN TASK GP/REL ATTIT PERSON...PSY OBS SOC/EXP PEACE/CORP. PAGE 64 H1276
CULTURE PERS/REL FOR/AID ADJUST

S66
MANSERGH N.,"THE PARTITION OF INDIA IN RETROSPECT." INDIA PAKISTAN S/ASIA UK DIPLOM COLONIAL GP/REL PWR 20. PAGE 102 H2042
NAT/G PARL/PROC POLICY POL/PAR

B67
ANDERSON O.,A LIBERAL STATE AT WAR. MOD/EUR UK LAW CULTURE STRUCT ECO/DEV NAT/G DIPLOM PARL/PROC GP/REL ALL/VALS...CONCPT 19. PAGE 7 H0131
WAR FORCES

B67
BADGLEY R.F.,DOCTORS' STRIKE; MEDICAL CARE AND CONFLICT IN SASKATCHEWAN. CANADA NAT/G PROF/ORG GP/REL ADJUST ATTIT...HEAL SOC 20. PAGE 10 H0192
HEALTH PLAN LABOR BARGAIN

B67
CURTIN P.D.,AFRICA REMEMBERED. NIGERIA SENEGAL CULTURE DIPLOM INT/TRADE GP/REL RACE/REL...RECORD ANTHOL 18/19 NEGRO. PAGE 36 H0727
DOMIN ORD/FREE AFR DISCRIM

B67
ERDMAN H.L.,THE SWATANTRA PARTY AND INDIAN CONSERVATISM. INDIA S/ASIA SOCIETY STRATA LOC/G NAT/G LEAD PARTIC GP/REL ATTIT...CONCPT GP/COMP BIBLIOG 20 SWATANTRA. PAGE 47 H0938
POL/PAR CONSERVE CHOOSE POLICY

B67
FANON F.,TOWARD THE AFRICAN REVOLUTION. AFR FRANCE CULTURE ELITES LEAD REV GP/REL ORD/FREE SOVEREIGN 20. PAGE 49 H0969
COLONIAL DOMIN ECO/UNDEV RACE/REL

B67
HUTCHINS F.G.,THE ILLUSION OF PERMANENCE: BRITISH IMPERIALISM IN INDIA. INDIA UK CULTURE STRUCT NAT/G REV GP/REL RACE/REL ADJUST DISCRIM ATTIT MORAL PWR SOC/INTEG 18/20. PAGE 75 H1509
COLONIAL CONTROL SOVEREIGN CONSERVE

B67
KOLKOWICZ R.,THE SOVIET MILITARY AND THE COMMUNIST PARTY. COM USSR ELITES NAT/G CREATE CIVMIL/REL GP/REL...TREND BIBLIOG/A 20 COM/PARTY. PAGE 88 H1753
MARXISM CONSTN FORCES POL/PAR

B67
LAMBERT W.E.,CHILDREN'S VIEWS OF FOREIGN PEOPLES: A CROSS-NATIONAL STUDY. UNIV CULTURE EDU/PROP RACE/REL ATTIT PERCEPT ROLE...STAT STAND/INT CHARTS GP/COMP NAT/COMP. PAGE 90 H1802
AGE/C STRANGE GP/REL STERTYP

B67
MAZRUI A.A.,THE ANGLO-AFRICAN COMMONWEALTH; POLITICAL FRICTION AND CULTURAL FUSION. AFR INT/ORG VOL/ASSN CHIEF GP/REL INGP/REL RACE/REL NAT/LISM 20 CMN/WLTH EEC. PAGE 106 H2111
COLONIAL SOVEREIGN DIPLOM CULTURE

B67
MCLAUGHLIN M.R.,RELIGIOUS EDUCATION AND THE STATE: DEMOCRACY FINDS A WAY. CANADA EUR+WWI GP/REL POPULISM...CATH NAT/COMP 20 AUSTRAL. PAGE 107 H2141
SECT NAT/G EDU/PROP POLICY

B67
MEHDI M.T.,PEACE IN THE MIDDLE EAST. ISRAEL SOCIETY NAT/G PLAN EDU/PROP NAT/LISM DRIVE...IDEA/COMP 20 JEWS. PAGE 108 H2160
ISLAM DIPLOM GP/REL COERCE

B67
MILNE R.S.,GOVERNMENT AND POLITICS IN MALAYSIA. INDONESIA MALAYSIA LOC/G EX/STRUC FORCES DIPLOM GP/REL 20 SINGAPORE. PAGE 111 H2217
NAT/G LEGIS ADMIN

B67
RAE D.,THE POLITICAL CONSEQUENCES OF ELECTORAL LAWS. EUR+WWI ICELAND ISRAEL NEW/ZEALND UK USA+45 ADJUD APPORT GP/REL MAJORITY...MATH STAT CENSUS CHARTS BIBLIOG 20 AUSTRAL. PAGE 129 H2579
POL/PAR CHOOSE NAT/COMP REPRESENT

B67
RUDMAN H.C.,THE SCHOOL AND STATE IN THE USSR. COM USSR ACADEM LABOR LOC/G PUB/INST EDU/PROP GP/REL ROLE...POLICY DECISION MGT CHARTS 20. PAGE 136 H2712
SCHOOL ADMIN NAT/G POL/PAR

B67
RYDER A.J.,THE GERMAN REVOLUTION OF 1918; A STUDY OF GERMAN SOCIALISM IN WAR AND REVOLT. GERMANY NAT/G POL/PAR GP/REL...BIBLIOG 20. PAGE 136 H2724
SOCISM WAR REV INGP/REL

B67
SCHWARTZ M.A.,PUBLIC OPINION AND CANADIAN IDENTITY. CANADA SOCIETY LOC/G DIPLOM ADMIN LEAD REGION GP/REL SAMP. PAGE 141 H2812
ATTIT NAT/G NAT/LISM POL/PAR

B67
THOMAS P.,DOWN THESE MEAN STREETS. GP/REL RACE/REL ADJUST...SOC SELF/OBS 20. PAGE 154 H3078
DISCRIM KIN CULTURE BIOG

B67
THOMPSON E.T.,PERSPECTIVES ON THE SOUTH: AGENDA FOR RESEARCH. CULTURE ECO/UNDEV SECT GP/REL EFFICIENCY ALL/VALS...HUM SOC CONCPT LING 20 NEGRO. PAGE 154 H3080
PROB/SOLV IDEA/COMP REGION ACT/RES

B67
WINTER E.H.,CONTEMPORARY CHANGE IN TRADITIONAL SOCIETIES: VOLUME I INTRODUCTION AND AFRICAN TRIBES. NIGERIA AGRI LOC/G NAT/G CREATE DOMIN COLONIAL CONTROL GP/REL PWR SOVEREIGN...SOC OBS 20 TANGANYIKA. PAGE 169 H3389
SOCIETY AFR CONSERVE KIN

L67
ISRAEL J.,"THE RED GUARDS IN HISTORICAL PERSPECTIVE: CONTINUITY AND CHANGE IN THE CHINESE YOUTH MOVEMENT." CHINA/COM FUT POL/PAR CONTROL REV GP/REL 20. PAGE 79 H1572
AGE/Y LOBBY MARXISM NAT/G

S67
AKE C.,"POLITICAL INTEGRATION AND POLITICAL STABILITY." ELITES POL/PAR LEAD ADJUST EFFICIENCY ATTIT AUTHORIT DRIVE...CONCPT 20. PAGE 4 H0088
CULTURE NAT/G CONTROL GP/REL

S67
ALBINSKI H.S.,"POLITICS AND BICULTURISM IN CANADA: THE FLAG DEBATE." CANADA SOCIETY NAT/G PROVS DELIB/GP DEBATE REGION SOVEREIGN PLURISM...POLICY SOC/INTEG 20. PAGE 5 H0093
NAT/LISM GP/REL POL/PAR CULTURE

S67
ALGER C.F.,"INTERNATIONALIZING COLLEGES AND UNIVERSITIES." WOR+45...NAT/COMP SIMUL. PAGE 5 H0104
DIPLOM EDU/PROP ACADEM GP/REL

S67
ALTBACH P.,"STUDENT POLITICS." GP/REL ATTIT ROLE PWR 20. PAGE 6 H0116
INTELL PARTIC UTIL NAT/G

S67
AMERASINGHE C.F.,"SOME LEGAL PROBLEMS OF STATE TRADING IN SOUTHEAST ASIA." PROB/SOLV ADJUD CONTROL CT/SYS GP/REL 20. PAGE 6 H0120
INT/TRADE NAT/G INT/LAW PRIVIL

S67
BASKIN D.B.,"NATIONALITY DOCTRINE AND ANTI-SEMITISM IN THE USSR." USSR CULTURE STRATA ISOLAT MAJORITY ATTIT RIGID/FLEX RESPECT...GP/COMP JEWS. PAGE 12 H0234
NAT/LISM MARXISM GP/REL DISCRIM

S67
BEFU H.,"THE POLITICAL RELATION OF THE VILLAGE TO THE STATE." NAT/G DOMIN GOV/REL GP/REL MGT. PAGE 13 H0259
GOV/COMP NAT/LISM KIN MUNIC

S67
BHATNAGAR J.K.,"THE VALUES AND ATTITUDES OF SOME INDIAN AND BRITISH STUDENTS." INDIA UK ECO/UNDEV LEGIT COLONIAL GP/REL SOVEREIGN...QU 20. PAGE 16 H0328
NAT/COMP ATTIT EDU/PROP ACADEM

S67
BOSHER J.F.,"GOVERNMENT AND PRIVATE INTERESTS IN NEW FRANCE." CANADA FRANCE INDUS LG/CO SML/CO CAP/ISM INT/TRADE COLONIAL GP/REL...HIST/WRIT 17/18. PAGE 19 H0381
NAT/G FINAN ADMIN CONTROL

S67
BULLOUGH B.,"ALIENATION IN THE GHETTO." CULTURE NEIGH GP/REL INGP/REL ATTIT...PSY SOC SAMP. PAGE 23 H0471
DISCRIM ANOMIE ADJUST

S67
CARR E.H.,"REVOLUTION FROM ABOVE." USSR STRATA FINAN INDUS NAT/G DOMIN LEAD GP/REL INGP/REL OWN PRODUC PWR 20 STALIN/J. PAGE 27 H0538
AGRI POLICY COM EFFICIENCY

S67
DERRICK P.,"THE WHITE PAPER ON INCOMES." EUR+WWI UK LAW LABOR NAT/G PLAN PROB/SOLV GP/REL...GOV/COMP PARLIAMENT. PAGE 40 H0794
INCOME POL/PAR POLICY

S67
FLETCHER-COOKE J.,"THE EMERGING AFRICAN STATE." AFR GP/REL NAT/LISM. PAGE 51 H1025
ECO/UNDEV NAT/COMP DIPLOM ATTIT

S67
FUSARO A.,"THE EFFECT OF PROPORTIONAL REPRESENTATION ON VOTING IN THE AUSTRALIAN SENATE." S/ASIA CONSTN POL/PAR CONTROL GP/REL PWR...CHARTS 20 AUSTRAL HOUSE/REP SENATE. PAGE 54 H1083
LEGIS CHOOSE REPRESENT NAT/G

S67
GLENN N.D.,"RURAL-URBAN DIFFERENCES IN REPORTED ATTITUDES AND BEHAVIOR" STRATA GP/REL CONSEN HABITAT RIGID/FLEX SAMP. PAGE 57 H1143
CULTURE ATTIT KIN CHARTS

S67
HANSON A.H.,"INDIA AFTER THE ELECTIONS." INDIA ECO/UNDEV LEGIS TEC/DEV FOR/AID GP/REL FEDERAL ATTIT 20. PAGE 66 H1321
NAT/G POL/PAR REGION CENTRAL

S67
HARBRON J.D.,"UNIFICATION IN CANADA: FAIT ACCOMPLI" CANADA STRATA NAT/G DELIB/GP BUDGET GP/REL 20 NAVY. PAGE 66 H1327
INGP/REL FORCES PLAN ATTIT

S67
JENCKS C.E.,"SOCIAL STATUS OF COAL MINERS IN BRITAIN SINCE NATIONALIZATION." UK STRATA STRUCT LABOR RECEIVE GP/REL INCOME OWN ATTIT HABITAT...MGT T 20. PAGE 80 H1600
EXTR/IND WORKER CONTROL NAT/G

S67
JOINER C.A.,"THE UBIQUITY OF THE ADMINISTRATIVE ROLE IN COUNTERINSURGENC. VIETNAM/S SOCIETY STRUCT NAT/G GP/REL EFFICIENCY 20. PAGE 81 H1627
ADMIN POLICY REV ATTIT

S67
KROLL M.,"POLITICAL LEADERSHIP AND ADMINISTRATIVE COMMUNICATIONS IN NEW NATION STATES* CASE STUDY OF TRINIDAD AND TOBAGO." L/A+17C TRINIDAD INTELL OP/RES DOMIN COLONIAL LEAD GP/REL CENTRAL EFFICIENCY...DECISION OBS METH/COMP 20. PAGE 89 H1774
NAT/G ADMIN EDU/PROP CONTROL

S67
MAIR L.,"BUSOGA LOCAL GOVERNMENT" AFR UGANDA UK CONSTN GP/REL...GOV/COMP METH/COMP 20. PAGE 101 H2024
LOC/G COLONIAL LAW ATTIT

S67
MURVAR V.,"MAX WEBER'S CONCEPT OF HEIROCRACY: A STUDY IN THE TYPOLOGY OF CHURCH-STATE RELATIONS" UNIV INGP/REL ATTIT PLURISM...SOC CONCPT 20 WEBER/MAX. PAGE 115 H2299
SECT NAT/G GP/REL STRUCT

S67
RAUM O.,"THE MODERN LEADERSHIP GROUP AMONG THE SOUTH AFRICAN XHOSA." SOUTH/AFR SOCIETY SECT EX/STRUC REPRESENT GP/REL INGP/REL PERSON ...METH/COMP 17/20 XHOSA NEGRO. PAGE 130 H2596
RACE/REL KIN LEAD CULTURE

S67
ROCHET W.,"THE OCTOBER REVOLUTION AND THE STRUGGLE OF THE FRENCH COMMUNISTS." COM FRANCE ELITES SOCIETY STRATA ECO/TAC EDU/PROP GP/REL WEALTH ...MARXIST IDEA/COMP NAT/COMP 20. PAGE 133 H2654
SOCISM CHOOSE METH/COMP NAT/G

S67
SINGH B.,"ITALIAN EXPERIENCE IN REGIONAL ECONOMIC DEVELOPMENT AND LESSONS FOR OTHER COUNTRIES." EUR+WWI ITALY INDUS NAT/G ACT/RES REGION GP/REL EFFICIENCY EQUILIB PRODUC WEALTH. PAGE 144 H2884
ECO/UNDEV PLAN ECO/TAC CONTROL

S67
SNELLEN I.T.,"APARTHEID* CHECKS AND CHANGES." SOUTH/AFR NAT/G PROB/SOLV COLONIAL REGION TASK GP/REL RACE/REL EFFICIENCY PRIVIL ORD/FREE 20. PAGE 146 H2923
DISCRIM NAT/LISM EQUILIB CONTROL

S67
SOLT L.F.,"PURITANISM, CAPITALISM, DEMOCRACY, AND THE NEW SCIENCE." NAT/G GP/REL CONSERVE...IDEA/COMP GEN/LAWS. PAGE 147 H2931
SECT CAP/ISM RATIONAL POPULISM

S67
SUBRAMANIAM V.,"REPRESENTATIVE BUREAUCRACY: A REASSESSMENT." USA+45 ELITES LOC/G NAT/G ADMIN GOV/REL PRIVIL DRIVE ROLE...POLICY CENSUS 20 CIVIL/SERV BUREAUCRCY. PAGE 150 H3006
STRATA GP/REL MGT GOV/COMP

S67
TIKHOMIROV I.A.,"DIVISION OF POWERS OR DIVISION OF LABOR?" USSR NAT/G DELIB/GP ADJUD GP/REL MARXISM SOCISM 20. PAGE 155 H3093 BAL/PWR WORKER STRATA ADMIN

S67
ULC O.,"CLASS STRUGGLE AND SOCIALIST JUSTICE: THE CASE OF CZECHOSLOVAKIA." COM CZECHOSLVK LAW CONSTN ELITES STRUCT NAT/G CRIME GP/REL MARXISM 20. PAGE 158 H3151 TOTALISM CT/SYS ADJUD STRATA

S67
VINCENT S.,"SHOULD BIAFRA SURVIVE?" NIGERIA ECO/UNDEV CHIEF FORCES ECO/TAC GP/REL DISCRIM PEACE ORD/FREE SOC/INTEG 20 BIAFRA IBO. PAGE 163 H3256 AFR REV REGION NAT/G

S67
WHITE J.W.,"MASS MOVEMENTS AND DEMOCRACY: SOKAGAKKAI IN JAPANESE POLITICS." NAT/G GP/REL ALL/VALS ORD/FREE WORSHIP 20 CHINJAP. PAGE 167 H3349 SECT PWR ATTIT POL/PAR

S67
WHITE W.L.,"THE TREASURY BOARD AND PARLIAMENT." CANADA CONSTN CONSULT LEGIS LEAD PARL/PROC GP/REL ...DECISION 20. PAGE 167 H3351 FINAN DELIB/GP NAT/G ADMIN

S68
BOSSCHERE G D.E.,"A L'EST DU NOUVEAU." CZECHOSLVK HUNGARY POLAND ROMANIA YUGOSLAVIA AGRI CREATE ECO/TAC COERCE GP/REL ATTIT MARXISM SOCISM 20. PAGE 19 H0382 ORD/FREE COM NAT/G DIPLOM

S68
LAPIERRE J.W.,"TRADITION ET MODERNITE A MADAGASCAR." ISLAM MADAGASCAR AGRI FINAN KIN NAT/G CREATE OP/RES GP/REL INGP/REL ATTIT CONSERVE...PSY 20. PAGE 91 H1813 ECO/UNDEV FOR/AID CULTURE TEC/DEV

S68
VERAX,"L'EUROPE ET LA FRANCE SUR LA SELLETTE." FRANCE UK NAT/G CHIEF DIPLOM EDU/PROP GP/REL 20 EEC DEGAULLE/C. PAGE 162 H3242 INT/TRADE INT/ORG POLICY ECO/TAC

B70
BOSSUET J.B.,"POLITIQUE TIREE DE L'ECRITURE SAINTE" (1679-1709) IN J.B. BOSSUET, OEVRES DE BOSSUET. NAT/G GP/REL AUTHORIT HEREDITY PERSON ALL/VALS SOVEREIGN 18 BIBLE DEITY CHRISTIAN. PAGE 19 H0383 TRADIT CHIEF SECT CONCPT

B75
NEWMAN J.H.,A LETTER ADDRESSED TO THE DUKE OF NORFOLK ON THE OCCASION OF MR. GLADSTONE'S RECENT EXPOSTULATION. NAT/G SECT CHIEF LEGIS CONTROL LEAD GP/REL SUPEGO SOC/INTEG WORSHIP 19 ENGLAND. PAGE 117 H2346 POLICY DOMIN SOVEREIGN CATHISM

B79
BRODERICK G.C.,POLITICAL STUDIES. IRELAND UK ROMAN/EMP LAW ACADEM LOC/G NAT/G DIPLOM PARL/PROC SUFF GP/REL LAISSEZ...ANTHOL. PAGE 21 H0424 CONSTN COLONIAL

B85
TAINE H.A.,THE FRENCH REVOLUTION (3 VOLS.) (TRANS. BY J. DURAND). FRANCE MOD/EUR SOCIETY STRATA POL/PAR ECO/TAC DOMIN EDU/PROP GP/REL PWR ...GOV/COMP IDEA/COMP 18. PAGE 152 H3036 REV NAT/G EX/STRUC LEAD

B94
BENOIST C.,LA POLITIQUE. FRANCE LAW SOCIETY STRUCT POL/PAR PARL/PROC GP/REL ATTIT PWR 19/20. PAGE 14 H0283 NAT/G REPRESENT ORD/FREE

B97
JENKS E.J.,LAW AND POLITICS IN THE MIDDLE AGES. CHRIST-17C CULTURE STRUCT KIN NAT/G SECT CT/SYS GP/REL...CLASSIF CHARTS IDEA/COMP BIBLIOG 8/16. PAGE 80 H1603 LAW SOCIETY ADJUST

B98
FORTES M.,AFRICAN POLITICAL SYSTEMS. ECO/UNDEV KIN LOC/G NEIGH POL/PAR SECT LEAD GP/REL ORD/FREE...SOC 20 NEGRO. PAGE 52 H1039 AFR CULTURE STRUCT

B99
RIPLEY W.Z.,A SELECTED BIBLIOGRAPHY OF THE ANTHROPOLOGY AND ETHNOLOGY OF EUROPE. SOCIETY STRATA STRUCT KIN SECT VOL/ASSN GP/REL INGP/REL HABITAT...GEOG 19. PAGE 132 H2632 BIBLIOG/A MOD/EUR SOC CULTURE

GRAFT....SEE TRIBUTE

GRAHAM B.D. H1190

GRAHAM G.S. H1191

GRAHAM I.C.C. H1192

GRAHAM R. H1193

GRAMPP W.D. H1194

GRAND/JURY....GRAND JURIES

GRANGE....GRANGE AND GRANGERS

GRANIER J.A. H1629

GRANT C.F. H1195

GRANT C.H. H1196

GRANT/US....PRESIDENT ULYSSES S. GRANT

B63
FRITZ H.E.,THE MOVEMENT FOR INDIAN ASSIMILATION, 1860-1890. SECT FORCES GP/REL RACE/REL DISCRIM FEDERAL CATHISM...BIBLIOG 19 INDIAN/AM PROTESTANT GRANT/US. PAGE 54 H1071 CULTURE NAT/G ECO/TAC ATTIT

GRANTS....SEE GIVE+FOR/AID

GRASES P. H1197

GRASSMUCK G.L. H1198

GRAUBARD S.R. H1199

GRAYSON H. H1200

GREAT BRITAIN....SEE UK

GREAT BRIT COMM MINISTERS PWR H1201

GREAT BRITAIN CENTRAL OFF INF H1202

GREAT/SOC....GREAT SOCIETY

GREAVES H.R. H1203

GREBLER L. H1205

GRECO/ROMN....GRECO-ROMAN CIVILIZATION

S32
BEARD C.A.,"REPRESENTATIVE GOVERNMENT IN EVOLUTION" WOR-45 AGRI TEC/DEV DOMIN EFFICIENCY ORD/FREE CONSERVE...TIME/SEQ GOV/COMP IDEA/COMP GRECO/ROMN. PAGE 12 H0248 REPRESENT POPULISM NAT/G PWR

B63
JAIRAZBHOY R.A.,FOREIGN INFLUENCE IN ANCIENT INDIA. INDIA ELITES SECT DIPLOM EDU/PROP COLONIAL REGION GP/REL...ART/METH LING WORSHIP +/14 GRECO/ROMN MESOPOTAM PERSIA PARTH/SASS. PAGE 79 H1587 CULTURE SOCIETY COERCE DOMIN

GREECE....MODERN GREECE

B35
MARRIOTT J.A.,DICTATORSHIP AND DEMOCRACY. GERMANY GREECE UK CHIEF DIPLOM DOMIN LEGIT PEACE ORD/FREE CONSERVE...TREND ROME HITLER/A. PAGE 103 H2057 TOTALISM POPULISM PLURIST NAT/G

B43
BROWN A.D.,GREECE: SELECTED LIST OF REFERENCES. GREECE ECO/UNDEV AGRI FINAN INDUS LABOR SECT TEC/DEV INT/TRADE LEAD...SOC 20. PAGE 22 H0438 BIBLIOG/A WAR DIPLOM NAT/G

B49
WORMUTH F.D.,THE ORIGINS OF MODERN CONSTITUTIONALISM. GREECE UK LEGIS CREATE TEC/DEV BAL/PWR DOMIN ADJUD REV WAR PWR...JURID ROMAN/REP CROMWELL/O. PAGE 170 H3412 NAT/G CONSTN LAW

B52
SPENCER F.A.,WAR AND POSTWAR GREECE: AN ANALYSIS BASED ON GREEK WRITINGS. GREECE SOCIETY NAT/G POL/PAR FORCES CREATE DIPLOM LEAD MARXISM...SOC 20. PAGE 147 H2943 BIBLIOG/A WAR REV

B53
MEAD M.,CULTURAL PATTERNS AND TECHNICAL CHANGE. BURMA GREECE NIGERIA ECO/UNDEV AGRI INDUS SCHOOL SECT CREATE FEEDBACK HABITAT...PSY METH/COMP BIBLIOG 20 UN. PAGE 108 H2152 HEALTH TEC/DEV CULTURE ADJUST

B55
POHLENZ M.,GRIECHISCHE FREIHEIT. GREECE DIPLOM WAR SUPEGO PWR RESPECT...IDEA/COMP. PAGE 127 H2533 ORD/FREE CONCPT JURID NAT/G

B55
TOYNBEE A.,THE REALIGNMENT OF EUROPE. COM GREECE ITALY NAT/G BAL/PWR ECO/TAC EDU/PROP REV SOVEREIGN ...SOC TIME/SEQ TREND COLD/WAR 20. PAGE 156 H3123 EUR+WWI PLAN USSR

B57
VON HIPPEL E.,GESCHICHTE DER STAATSPHILOSOPHIE (2 VOLS.). ASIA GREECE INDIA PRE/AMER UAR NAT/LISM ORD/FREE MARXISM. PAGE 164 H3272 CULTURE CONCPT NAT/G

B58
SALETORE B.A.,INDIA'S DIPLOMATIC RELATIONS WITH THE WEST. GREECE INDIA CULTURE ETIQUET...IDEA/COMP 3 ROM/EMP PERSIA. PAGE 137 H2739 DIPLOM CONCPT INT/TRADE

B60
BARBU Z.,PROBLEMS OF HISTORICAL PSYCHOLOGY. GREECE MEDIT-7 UK CULTURE TEC/DEV ADJUST RATIONAL ATTIT PERSON PSY

PERCEPT...METH/CNCPT NEW/IDEA TIME/SEQ GEN/METH. PAGE 11 H0214 — HIST/WRIT IDEA/COMP

N61
PLATO,APOLOGY" IN PLATO, THE COLLECTED DIALOGUES, ED. BY E. HAMILTON AND H. CAIRNS (TRANS. BY H. TREDENNICK). GREECE SOCIETY NAT/G...CONCPT GEN/LAWS SOCRATES. PAGE 126 H2523 — DEATH CT/SYS ATTIT MORAL

B63
JELAVICH C.,THE BALKANS IN TRANSITION: ESSAYS ON THE DEVELOPMENT OF BALKAN LIFE AND POLITICS SINCE THE EIGHTEENTH CENTURY. COM GREECE TURKEY ECO/UNDEV NAT/G SECT ATTIT...GEOG SOC CONCPT TIME/SEQ ANTHOL 18/20. PAGE 80 H1596 — CULTURE RIGID/FLEX

B64
NORTHROP F.S.,CROSS-CULTURAL UNDERSTANDING: EPISTEMOLOGY IN ANTHROPOLOGY. BURMA GREECE THAILAND HABITAT PERCEPT PERSON...PHIL/SCI SOC METH 20 MEXIC/AMER CHINJAP. PAGE 119 H2375 — EPIST PSY CULTURE CONCPT

B65
JELAVICH C.,THE BALKANS. ALBANIA BULGARIA GREECE ROMANIA YUGOSLAVIA ECO/UNDEV WAR SOVEREIGN MARXISM 6/20. PAGE 80 H1597 — NAT/LISM NAT/G

B65
KOUSOULAS D.G.,REVOLUTION AND DEFEAT; THE STORY OF THE GREEK COMMUNIST PARTY. GREECE INT/ORG EX/STRUC DIPLOM FOR/AID EDU/PROP PARL/PROC ADJUST ATTIT 20 COM/PARTY. PAGE 88 H1759 — REV MARXISM POL/PAR ORD/FREE

B65
LAMBIRI I.,SOCIAL CHANGE IN A GREEK COUNTRY TOWN. GREECE FAM PROB/SOLV ROUTINE TASK LEISURE INGP/REL CONSEN ORD/FREE...SOC INT QU CHARTS 20. PAGE 90 H1803 — INDUS WORKER CULTURE NEIGH

B65
OECD,THE MEDITERRANEAN REGIONAL PROJECT: GREECE; EDUCATION AND DEVELOPMENT. FUT GREECE SOCIETY AGRI FINAN NAT/G PROF/ORG WORKER PLAN PROB/SOLV ADMIN DEMAND ATTIT 20 OECD. PAGE 120 H2401 — EDU/PROP SCHOOL ACADEM ECO/UNDEV

B65
ORG FOR ECO COOP AND DEVEL,THE MEDITERRANEAN REGIONAL PROJECT: AN EXPERIMENT IN PLANNING BY SIX COUNTRIES. FUT GREECE SPAIN TURKEY YUGOSLAVIA SOCIETY FINAN NAT/G PROF/ORG EDU/PROP ADMIN REGION COST...POLICY STAT CHARTS 20 OECD. PAGE 121 H2427 — PLAN ECO/UNDEV ACADEM SCHOOL

S65
SANDERS R.,"MASS SUPPORT AND COMMUNIST INSURRECTION." GREECE MALAYSIA PHILIPPINE VIETNAM STRUCT ECO/UNDEV POL/PAR FORCES CREATE REV ...GP/COMP IDEA/COMP. PAGE 138 H2751 — GUERRILLA MARXISM GOV/COMP

B66
US DEPARTMENT OF STATE,RESEARCH ON THE MIDDLE EAST (EXTERNAL RESEARCH LIST NO 4-25). GREECE ISRAEL SYRIA UAR YEMEN CULTURE SOCIETY POL/PAR SECT DIPLOM EDU/PROP WAR NAT/LISM...GEOG GOV/COMP 20. PAGE 160 H3190 — BIBLIOG/A ISLAM NAT/G REGION

S67
ANTHEM T.,"CYPRUS* WHAT NOW?" CYPRUS GREECE TURKEY NAT/G BUDGET MAJORITY 20 NATO. PAGE 7 H0143 — DIPLOM COERCE INT/TRADE ADJUD

S67
NUGENT J.B.,"ECONOMIC THOUGHT, INVESTMENT CRITERIA, AND DEVELOPMENT STRATEGIES IN GREECE* A POSTWAR SURVEY." GREECE AGRI INDUS INT/ORG NAT/G OP/RES DEMAND OPTIMAL PRODUC WEALTH 20 EEC. PAGE 119 H2379 — ECO/UNDEV PLAN FINAN

B95
HAMMOND B.E.,THE POLITICAL INSTITUTIONS OF THE ANCIENT GREEKS. GREECE MUNIC PROVS COERCE WAR ORD/FREE ARISTOTLE. PAGE 65 H1307 — GOV/COMP NAT/G IDEA/COMP CONCPT

GREECE/ANC....ANCIENT GREECE

N
BURY J.B.,THE CAMBRIDGE ANCIENT HISTORY (12 VOLS.). MEDIT-7 DIPLOM COLONIAL WAR...HUM EGYPT/ANC ROME/EMP BABYLONIA GREECE/ANC. PAGE 25 H0495 — BIBLIOG/A SOCIETY CULTURE NAT/G

GREEN L.P. H1206

GREEN M.M. H1207

GREEN T.H. H1208

GREEN/TH....T.H. GREEN

B28
BARKER E.,POLITICAL THOUGHT IN ENGLAND: FROM HERBERT SPENCER TO THE PRESENT DAY. UK ALL/IDEOS ...PHIL/SCI 19/20 SPENCER/H GREEN/TH BENTHAM/J MAITLAND/F. PAGE 11 H0217 — INTELL GEN/LAWS IDEA/COMP

GREENBACK....GREENBACK PARTY

GREENWICH VILLAGE....SEE GRNWCH/VIL

GREENWICH....GREENWICH, ENGLAND

GREGG J.L. H1209

GREGG P.M. H0211

GREGORY R. H1210

GRENADA....GRENADA (WEST INDIES)

GRENVILLES....GRENVILLES - ENGLISH FAMILY; SEE ALSO UK

B58
WIGGIN L.M.,THE FACTION OF COUSINS: A POLITICAL ACCOUNT OF THE GRENVILLES, 1733-1763. UK STRUCT KIN NAT/G INGP/REL...CONCPT BIOG BIBLIOG/A 18 GRENVILLES. PAGE 168 H3357 — FAM POL/PAR PWR

GRESHAM-YANG TREATY....SEE GRESHMYANG

GRESHAM'S LAW....SEE GRESHM/LAW

GRESHM/LAW....GRESHAM'S LAW

GRESHMYANG....GRESHAM-YANG TREATY

GRETTON P. H1211

GRIEB K.J. H1212

GRIERSON P. H1213

GRIFFIN A.P.C. H1214,H1215,H1216,H1217,H1218,H1219

GRIFFITH E.S. H1220

GRIFFITH S.B. H1221

GRIFFITH W. H1222,H1223

GRIFFITH W.E. H1224,H1225

GRIMAL H. H1226

GRIMOND J. H1227

GRIMSHAW A.D. H1228

GRISMER R. H1229

GRNWCH/VIL....GREENWICH VILLAGE

GRODZINS M. H1230

GROGAN V. H1231

GROSS B.M. H1232

GROSS J.A. H1233

GROSS NATIONAL PRODUCT....WEALTH+ECO+PRODUC

GROSSER A. H1234,H1235

GROSSMAN G. H1236

GROUP RELATIONS....SEE GP/REL

GROVE J.W. H1237

GROVES H.E. H1238

GROWTH....SEE CREATE,CREATE+ECO/UNDEV

GRUNDY K.W. H1239,H1240

GRUNER E. H1241

GRZYBOWSKI K. H1242

GSOVSKI V. H2870

GUAM....GUAM

GUATEMALA....SEE ALSO L/A+17C

B45
MCBRYDE F.W.,CULTURAL AND HISTORICAL GEOGRAPHY OF SOUTHWEST GUATEMALA. GUATEMALA AGRI KIN PERSON ...GEOG AUD/VIS CHARTS 20. PAGE 106 H2123 — HABITAT ISOLAT CULTURE ECO/UNDEV

B49
HOLLERAN M.P.,CHURCH AND STATE IN GUATEMALA. GUATEMALA LAW STRUCT CATHISM...SOC SOC/INTEG 17/20 — SECT NAT/G

CHURCH/STA. PAGE 73 H1456
GP/REL CULTURE

B59
CORDONA G.D.,INDICE BIBLIOGRAFICO GUATEMALTECO 1958. GUATEMALA...SOC 20. PAGE 33 H0666
BIBLIOG NAT/G LOC/G L/A+17C

B64
MUSEUM FUR VOLKERKUNDE WIEN,ZENTRALAMERIKA MEXIKO VOLKER UND KULTUREN. COSTA/RICA GUATEMALA L/A+17C PANAMA SECT WAR GP/REL SOVEREIGN...ART/METH 20 CENTRAL/AM MEXIC/AMER. PAGE 115 H2300
SOCIETY STRUCT CULTURE AGRI

B65
GREGG J.L.,POLITICAL PARTIES AND PARTY SYSTEMS IN GUATEMALA, 1944-1963. GUATEMALA L/A+17C EX/STRUC FORCES CREATE CONTROL REV CHOOSE PWR...TREND IDEA/COMP 20. PAGE 60 H1209
LEAD POL/PAR NAT/G CHIEF

B65
RODRIGUEZ M.,CENTRAL AMERICA. COSTA/RICA GUATEMALA L/A+17C NICARAGUA DIPLOM COLONIAL REGION NAT/LISM ALL/IDEOS SOCISM...MAJORIT TIME/SEQ BIBLIOG 19/20. PAGE 133 H2656
CULTURE NAT/COMP NAT/G ECO/UNDEV

S65
PLANK J.N.,"THE CARIBBEAN* INTERVENTION, WHEN AND HOW." CUBA GUATEMALA HAITI PANAMA USA+45 VENEZUELA FORCES PROB/SOLV RISK COERCE...NAT/COMP OAS TIME. PAGE 126 H2521
SOVEREIGN MARXISM REV

B67
NASH M.,MACHINE AGE MAYA. GUATEMALA L/A+17C STRUCT AGRI WORKER CREATE INCOME ATTIT RIGID/FLEX ROLE ...IDEA/COMP SOC/EXP WORSHIP 20 INDIAN/AM. PAGE 116 H2315
INDUS CULTURE SOC MUNIC

L67
RUTH J.M.,"THE ADMINISTRATION OF WATER RESOURCES IN GUATEMALA." GUATEMALA L/A+17C DIST/IND LOC/G NAT/G EX/STRUC ADMIN GOV/REL DEMAND EQUILIB WEALTH...GEOG MGT 20. PAGE 136 H2723
EFFICIENCY ECO/UNDEV PLAN ACT/RES

S67
GRIEB K.J.,"THE UNITED STATES AND THE CENTRAL AMERICAN CONFEDERATION." COSTA/RICA EL/SALVADR GUATEMALA HONDURAS L/A+17C NICARAGUA NAT/G FORCES CONFER AGREE EXEC ARMS/CONT REV WAR PEACE ATTIT 20. PAGE 60 H1212
INT/ORG DIPLOM POLICY REGION

S67
PETRAS J.,"GUERRILLA MOVEMENTS IN LATIN AMERICA - I." GUATEMALA PERU VENEZUELA NAT/G COLONIAL LEAD ATTIT PWR...TIME/SEQ METH/COMP 20 COLOMB. PAGE 125 H2497
GUERRILLA REV L/A+17C MARXISM

GUDIN E. H1243

GUEMES/M....MARTIN GUEMES

GUENA Y. H1244

GUERIN D. H1245

GUERRILLA....GUERRILLA WARFARE

N
PEKING REVIEW. CHINA/COM CULTURE AGRI INDUS DIPLOM EDU/PROP GUERRILLA ATTIT MARXISM...BIBLIOG 20. PAGE 1 H0009
MARXIST NAT/G POL/PAR PRESS

B27
EDWARDS L.P.,THE NATURAL HISTORY OF REVOLUTION. UNIV NAT/G VOL/ASSN COERCE DRIVE WEALTH...TREND GEN/LAWS. PAGE 45 H0893
PWR GUERRILLA REV

B45
CLAGETT H.L.,COMMUNIST CHINA: RUTHLESS ENEMY OR PAPER TIGER (PAMPHLET). CHINA/COM ECO/UNDEV AGRI INDUS NAT/G POL/PAR ECO/TAC INT/TRADE GUERRILLA ATTIT...CHARTS NAT/COMP ORG/CHARTS 20. PAGE 30 H0602
BIBLIOG/A MARXISM DIPLOM COERCE

B55
VIGON J.,TEORIA DEL MILITARISMO. NAT/G DIPLOM COLONIAL COERCE GUERRILLA CIVMIL/REL NAT/LISM MORAL ALL/IDEOS PACIFISM 18/20. PAGE 163 H3253
FORCES PHIL/SCI WAR POLICY

B56
HATCH J.C.,NEW FROM AFRICA. AFR FUT UK NAT/G GUERRILLA ATTIT ORD/FREE PWR...AUD/VIS CHARTS 20. PAGE 68 H1354
NAT/LISM COLONIAL RACE/REL

B56
SMEDLEY A.,THE GREAT ROAD: THE LIFE AND TIMES OF CHU TEH. ASIA USSR NAT/G POL/PAR DIPLOM COERCE GUERRILLA CIVMIL/REL NAT/LISM PERSON SKILL MARXISM ...BIOG 20 CHINJAP MAO. PAGE 145 H2903
REV WAR FORCES

B59
HOBSBAWM E.J.,PRIMITIVE REBELS; STUDIES IN ARCHAIC FORMS OF SOCIAL MOVEMENT IN THE 19TH AND 20TH CENTURIES. ITALY SPAIN CULTURE VOL/ASSN RISK CROWD GP/REL INGP/REL ISOLAT TOTALISM...PSY SOC 18/20. PAGE 72 H1438
SOCIETY CRIME REV GUERRILLA

S60
CROZIER B.,"FRANCE AND ALGERIA." ALGERIA EUR+WWI FRANCE FUT ISLAM ECO/UNDEV NEIGH CONSULT DELIB/GP ECO/TAC COLONIAL COERCE ATTIT...SOC INT CON/ANAL 20. PAGE 36 H0713
NAT/G FORCES GUERRILLA NAT/LISM

S60
GINSBURGS G.,"PEKING-LHASA-NEW DELHI." CHINA/COM FUT INDIA S/ASIA KIN NAT/G PROVS SECT FORCES BAL/PWR ECO/TAC DOMIN EDU/PROP LEGIT ADMIN REGION GUERRILLA PWR...TREND TIBET 20. PAGE 57 H1134
ASIA COERCE DIPLOM

S60
WYCKOFF T.,"THE ROLE OF THE MILITARY IN LATIN AMERICAN POLITICS." L/A+17C CONSTN CULTURE ECO/UNDEV POL/PAR FORCES LEGIS TOP/EX LEGIT GUERRILLA REV CHOOSE ORD/FREE PWR...TIME/SEQ VAL/FREE 20. PAGE 171 H3430
NAT/G COERCE TOTALISM

B61
GUEVARA E.,GUERRILLA WARFARE. L/A+17C ECO/UNDEV NAT/G POL/PAR VOL/ASSN PLAN DOMIN REV DRIVE PWR WEALTH...NEW/IDEA RECORD BIOG COLD/WAR MARX/KARL OAS 20. PAGE 62 H1247
FORCES COERCE GUERRILLA CUBA

B61
MERRIAM A.,CONGO: BACKGROUND OF CONFLICT. AFR FUT KIN MUNIC NAT/G POL/PAR PROVS DELIB/GP PLAN DOMIN COERCE ATTIT...TIME/SEQ CHARTS CONGO 20. PAGE 109 H2182
CHOOSE GUERRILLA

B61
MUNGER E.S.,AFRICAN FIELD REPORTS 1952-1961. SOUTH/AFR SOCIETY ECO/UNDEV NAT/G POL/PAR COLONIAL EXEC PARL/PROC GUERRILLA RACE/REL ALL/IDEOS...SOC AUD/VIS 20. PAGE 114 H2288
AFR DISCRIM RECORD

B61
SETON-WATSON H.,FROM LENIN TO KHRUSHCHEV: THE HISTORY OF WORLD COMMUNISM. ASIA COM EUR+WWI ISLAM S/ASIA ECO/DEV ECO/UNDEV NAT/G POL/PAR DIPLOM ECO/TAC EDU/PROP COERCE GUERRILLA ATTIT DRIVE WORK TOT/POP NAZI 20. PAGE 141 H2832
PWR REV USSR

S61
TANHAM B.K.,"COMMUNIST REVOLUTIONARY WARFARE: THE VIETMINH IN INDOCHINA." EUR+WWI S/ASIA VIETNAM NAT/G EDU/PROP LEGIT GUERRILLA ATTIT PWR...CONCPT GEN/LAWS 20. PAGE 152 H3042
FORCES ECO/TAC WAR FRANCE

B62
FINER S.E.,THE MAN ON HORSEBACK: ROLE OF THE MILITARY IN POLITICS. UNIV LAW CONSTN ELITES SOCIETY POL/PAR BAL/PWR DOMIN EDU/PROP LEGIT COERCE GUERRILLA REV WAR WEAPON DRIVE SUPEGO ORD/FREE PWR RESPECT...POLICY CONCPT GEN/METH. PAGE 50 H1003
NAT/G FORCES TOTALISM

B62
HAY S.N.,SOUTHEAST ASIAN HISTORY: A BIBLIOGRAPHICAL GUIDE. STRATA KIN NAT/G REGION GUERRILLA REV WAR ADJUST HABITAT PERCEPT ALL/IDEOS...CHARTS 5/20. PAGE 68 H1365
BIBLIOG/A S/ASIA CULTURE

B62
VALERIANO N.D.,COUNTER-GUERRILLA OPERATIONS: THE PHILLIPINE EXPERIENCE. NAT/G CONSULT ACT/RES PLAN COERCE GUERRILLA ATTIT ORD/FREE PWR SKILL...GEOG NEW/IDEA TIME/SEQ CHARTS 20. PAGE 161 H3221
S/ASIA FORCES PHILIPPINE

S63
HARRIS R.L.,"COMMUNISM AND ASIA: ILLUSIONS AND MISCONCEPTIONS." ASIA COM FUT S/ASIA ECO/UNDEV AGRI NAT/G POL/PAR EX/STRUC EDU/PROP COERCE ATTIT MARXISM COLD/WAR TOT/POP 20. PAGE 67 H1344
PWR GUERRILLA

B64
FALL B.,STREET WITHOUT JOY. FRANCE USA+45 DIPLOM ECO/TAC FOR/AID GUERRILLA REV WEAPON...TREND 20. PAGE 48 H0966
WAR S/ASIA FORCES COERCE

S64
ENNIS T.E.,"VIETNAM: LAND WITHOUT LAUGHTER." S/ASIA VIETNAM VIETNAM/S INTELL SOCIETY SECT FORCES DIPLOM LEGIT COERCE WAR ATTIT RIGID/FLEX ORD/FREE COLD/WAR 20. PAGE 46 H0929
NAT/G TOP/EX GUERRILLA

S64
POWELL R.L.,"COMMUNIST CHINA'S MILITARY POTENTIAL." ASIA CHINA/COM NAT/G EX/STRUC EDU/PROP COERCE GUERRILLA NUC/PWR WAR...RECORD CON/ANAL 20. PAGE 128 H2551
FORCES PWR

S64
TINKER H.,"POLITICS IN SOUTHEAST ASIA." INT/ORG NAT/G CREATE PLAN TEC/DEV GUERRILLA KNOWL ORD/FREE COLD/WAR. PAGE 155 H3103
S/ASIA ACT/RES REGION

B65
JACKSON G.,THE SPANISH REPUBLIC AND THE CIVIL WAR, 1931-1939. EUR+WWI INTELL STRUCT COM/IND NAT/G POL/PAR LEGIS EDU/PROP EXEC COERCE NAT/LISM DRIVE PWR...INT TIME/SEQ TOT/POP 20. PAGE 79 H1574
ATTIT GUERRILLA SPAIN

S65
SANDERS R.,"MASS SUPPORT AND COMMUNIST INSURRECTION." GREECE MALAYSIA PHILIPPINE VIETNAM STRUCT ECO/UNDEV POL/PAR FORCES CREATE REV ...GP/COMP IDEA/COMP. PAGE 138 H2751
GUERRILLA MARXISM GOV/COMP

B66
BARNETT D.L.,MAU MAU FROM WITHIN. AFR UK POL/PAR LEAD GUERRILLA AUTHORIT ORD/FREE...SOC BIOG 20 NEGRO MAU/MAU. PAGE 11 H0225
REV CULTURE NAT/G

B66
BRACKMAN A.C.,SOUTHEAST ASIA'S SECOND FRONT: THE
S/ASIA

POWER STRUGGLE IN THE MALAY ARCHIPELAGO. CHINA/COM INDONESIA MALAYSIA ECO/UNDEV INT/ORG NAT/G FORCES DIPLOM EDU/PROP REGION COERCE GUERRILLA AUTHORIT POPULISM...MAJORIT 20 KENNEDY/JF SEATO. PAGE 20 H0396 — MARXISM REV

B66
SCHRAM S.,MAO TSE-TUNG. ASIA CHINA/COM CONTROL REGION ATTIT...POLICY IDEA/COMP 20 MAO. PAGE 140 H2799 — BIOG MARXISM TOP/EX GUERRILLA

S66
SCHOENBRON D.,"VIETNAM* THE CASE FOR EXTRICATION." NAT/G FORCES PROB/SOLV DIPLOM COLONIAL CONTROL COERCE...CONCPT 20. PAGE 140 H2795 — VIETNAM WAR GUERRILLA

B67
CORDIER A.W.,COLUMBIA ESSAYS IN INTERNATIONAL AFFAIRS. ASIA CHINA/COM FRANCE S/ASIA SPAIN UAR ECO/UNDEV LOC/G ECO/TAC GUERRILLA PWR...BIOG ANTHOL 18/20 MAU/MAU. PAGE 33 H0663 — NAT/G DIPLOM MARXISM POLICY

B67
FALL B.B.,HO CHI MINH ON REVOLUTION: SELECTED WRITINGS, 1920-66. COM VIETNAM ELITES NAT/G COERCE GUERRILLA RACE/REL MARXISM...MARXIST ANTHOL 20. PAGE 48 H0968 — REV COLONIAL ECO/UNDEV S/ASIA

B67
MCCLINTOCK R.,THE MEANING OF LIMITED WAR. FUT WOR+45 NAT/G FORCES GUERRILLA REV...POLICY SAMP/SIZ TREND NAT/COMP 45 COLD/WAR. PAGE 106 H2126 — WAR NUC/PWR BAL/PWR DIPLOM

B67
SALISBURY H.E.,BEHIND THE LINES - HANOI. VIETNAM/N NAT/G GUERRILLA CIVMIL/REL NAT/LISM KNOWL 20. PAGE 137 H2741 — WAR PROB/SOLV DIPLOM OBS

S67
PETRAS J.,"GUERRILLA MOVEMENTS IN LATIN AMERICA - I." GUATEMALA PERU VENEZUELA NAT/G COLONIAL LEAD ATTIT PWR...TIME/SEQ METH/COMP 20 COLOMB. PAGE 125 H2497 — GUERRILLA REV L/A+17C MARXISM

GUETZKOW H. H0632,H1246

GUEVARA E. H1247

GUEVARA/E....ERNESTO GUEVARA

GUIANA/BR....BRITISH GUIANA; SEE ALSO GUYANA

GUIANA/FR....FRENCH GUIANA

GUILDS....SEE PROF/ORG

GUIMARAES A.P. H1248

GUINEA....SEE ALSO AFR

B61
PANIKKAR K.M.,REVOLUTION IN AFRICA. AFR GUINEA ECO/UNDEV POL/PAR DIPLOM COLONIAL EXEC LEAD SOVEREIGN...CHARTS 20. PAGE 123 H2461 — NAT/LISM NAT/G CHIEF

B61
SCHNAPPER B.,LA POLITIQUE ET LE COMMERCE FRANCAIS DANS LE GOLFE DE GUINEE DE 1838 A 1871. FRANCE GUINEA UK SEA EXTR/IND NAT/G DELIB/GP LEGIS ADMIN ORD/FREE...POLICY GEOG CENSUS CHARTS BIBLIOG 19. PAGE 139 H2791 — COLONIAL INT/TRADE DOMIN AFR

B62
DILLING A.R.,ABORIGINE CULTURE HISTORY - A SURVEY OF PUBLICATIONS 1954-1957. GUINEA...SOC CHARTS NAT/COMP BIBLIOG/A AUSTRAL ABORIGINES. PAGE 41 H0825 — S/ASIA HIST/WRIT CULTURE KIN

B64
ALDEFER H.F.,A BIBLIOGRAPHY OF AFRICAN GOVERNMENT: 1950-1964. ALGERIA GUINEA LIBERIA UAR ECO/UNDEV POL/PAR LEGIS COLONIAL LEAD PARL/PROC NAT/LISM 20. PAGE 5 H0098 — BIBLIOG AFR LOC/G NAT/G

B64
MORGENTHAU R.S.,POLITICAL PARTIES IN FRENCH-SPEAKING WEST AFRICA. AFR FRANCE GUINEA IVORY/CST MALI SENEGAL CONSTN LEGIS CREATE PLAN LOBBY PARTIC GP/REL...POLICY BIBLIOG 20. PAGE 113 H2257 — POL/PAR NAT/G SOVEREIGN COLONIAL

B65
HAPGOOD D.,AFRICA: FROM INDEPENDENCE TO TOMARROW. AFR GUINEA SENEGAL CULTURE ELITES ECO/UNDEV AGRI SCHOOL FOR/AID COLONIAL MARXISM...TREND 20. PAGE 66 H1323 — ECO/TAC SOCIETY NAT/G

B66
SCHATTEN F.,COMMUNISM IN AFRICA. AFR GHANA GUINEA MALI CULTURE ECO/UNDEV LABOR SECT ECO/TAC EDU/PROP REV 20. PAGE 139 H2774 — COLONIAL NAT/LISM MARXISM DIPLOM

GUINS G.C. H1249

GUIZOT F.P.G. H1250

GUJARAT....GUJARAT (STATE OF INDIA)

GUMPLOWICZ L. H1251

GUNN G.E. H1252

GURLAND A.R.L. H1253

GURR T. H1254

GURVITCH G. H1255,H1256

GUSFIELD J.R. H1257

GUTTERIDGE W. H1258

GUTTMAN/L....LOUIS GUTTMAN (AND GUTTMAN SCALE)

GUYANA....GUYANA; SEE ALSO GUIANA/BR, L/A+17C

S67
GRANT C.H.,"RURAL LOCAL GOVERNMENT IN GUYANA AND BRITISH HONDURAS." GUYANA HONDURAS L/A+17C AGRI NAT/G EX/STRUC ACT/RES REGION GOV/REL EFFICIENCY ORD/FREE 20. PAGE 60 H1196 — ECO/UNDEV LOC/G ADMIN MUNIC

GUZZARDI W. H1259

GWYN R.J. H1260

GYORGY A. H1261

H

HAAR C.M. H1263

HAAS E.B. H1264,H1265,H1266

HABERLER G. H1267

HABERMAS J. H1268

HABITAT....ECOLOGY

N
ACAD RUMANIAN SCI DOC CTR,RUMANIAN SCIENTIFIC ABSTRACTS: SOCIAL SCIENCES. ROMANIA FINAN HABITAT ...ART/METH GEOG HUM JURID PSY 20. PAGE 3 H0059 — BIBLIOG/A CULTURE LING LAW

N
KRADER L.,SOCIAL ORGANIZATION OF THE MONGOL-TURKIC PASTORAL NOMADS. SOCIETY FAM KIN NEIGH GP/REL MARRIAGE 16/20 MONGOLIA TURKIC MIGRATION. PAGE 88 H1763 — BIO/SOC HABITAT CULTURE STRUCT

B04
REED W.A.,ETHNOLOGICAL SURVEY PUBLICATIONS (VOL. II). PHILIPPINE STRUCT INDUS SECT DEATH LEISURE HABITAT...AUD/VIS CHARTS WORSHIP 20 NABOLOI NEGRITO BATAK. PAGE 130 H2607 — CULTURE SOCIETY SOC OBS

B12
BRUNHES J.,LA GEOGRAPHIE HUMAINE: ESSAI DE CLASSIFICATION POSITIVE PRINCIPES ET EXEMPLES (2ND ED.). UNIV SEA AGRI EXTR/IND DRIVE...SOC CHARTS 20. PAGE 23 H0454 — GEOG HABITAT CULTURE

B18
CVIJIC J.,THE BALKAN PENINSULA. MOD/EUR COERCE ...SOC CHARTS GP/COMP NAT/COMP 20 BALKANS MAPS. PAGE 36 H0729 — GEOG HABITAT GOV/COMP CULTURE

B22
HUNTINGTON E.,CIVILIZATION AND CLIMATE (2ND ED.). UNIV WORKER...SOC CHARTS. PAGE 75 H1503 — GEOG HABITAT CULTURE

B24
SHIROKOGOROFF S.M.,ETHNICAL UNIT AND MILIEU. GP/REL ...PHIL/SCI SOC MATH METH. PAGE 143 H2865 — IDEA/COMP HABITAT CULTURE SOCIETY

B24
WALKER F.D.,AFRICA AND HER PEOPLES. ISLAM STRUCT FAM SECT EDU/PROP INGP/REL RACE/REL HABITAT...GEOG SOC IDEA/COMP WORSHIP 20 NEGRO. PAGE 164 H3292 — CULTURE AFR GP/COMP KIN

B31
HENNIG P.,GEOPOLITIK (2ND ED.). CULTURE MUNIC COLONIAL...CENSUS CHARTS 20. PAGE 70 H1398 — GEOG HABITAT CREATE NEIGH

B31
MACIVER R.M.,SOCIETY: ITS STRUCTURE AND CHANGES. CULTURE STRATA FAM CROWD HABITAT ORD/FREE...PSY SOC CONCPT BIBLIOG 20. PAGE 100 H1998 — STRUCT SOCIETY PERSON DRIVE

B34
LOVELL R.I.,THE STRUGGLE FOR SOUTH AFRICA, 1875-1899. GERMANY RHODESIA SOUTH/AFR UK NAT/G — COLONIAL DIPLOM

ECO/TAC HABITAT WEALTH...POLICY 19. PAGE 99 H1971 WAR GP/REL

B35
AQUINAS T.,ON THE GOVERNANCE OF RULERS (1265-66). UNIV SOCIETY STRATA FAM HABITAT PERSON ALL/VALS PWR SOVEREIGN CONSERVE...POLICY BIBLE. PAGE 8 H0155 CATH NAT/G CHIEF SUPEGO

B36
RAPPARD W.E.,THE GOVERNMENT OF SWITZERLAND. SWITZERLND INT/ORG POL/PAR EX/STRUC DIPLOM NEUTRAL PARL/PROC REGION WAR HABITAT SOVEREIGN...NAT/COMP SOC/INTEG 20 LEAGUE/NAT WWI. PAGE 130 H2594 CONSTN NAT/G CULTURE FEDERAL

B38
CARVALHO C.M.,GEOGRAPHIA HUMANA; POLITICA E ECONOMICA (3RD ED.). BRAZIL CULTURE AGRI INDUS DIPLOM COLONIAL GP/REL RACE/REL...LING 20 RESOURCE/N. PAGE 27 H0551 GEOG HABITAT

B45
MCBRYDE F.W.,CULTURAL AND HISTORICAL GEOGRAPHY OF SOUTHWEST GUATEMALA. GUATEMALA AGRI KIN PERSON ...GEOG AUD/VIS CHARTS 20. PAGE 106 H2123 HABITAT ISOLAT CULTURE ECO/UNDEV

B45
WARNER W.L.,THE SOCIAL SYSTEM OF AMERICAN ETHNIC GROUPS. STRATA FAM EDU/PROP ATTIT HABITAT RESPECT CLASSIF. PAGE 165 H3309 CULTURE VOL/ASSN SECT GP/COMP

N46
HOBBS C.C.,SOUTHEAST ASIA, 1935-45: A SELECTED LIST OF REFERENCE BOOKS (PAMPHLET). S/ASIA AGRI INDUS NAT/G SECT DIPLOM WAR...ART/METH GEOG SOC LING 20. PAGE 72 H1435 BIBLIOG/A CULTURE HABITAT

B47
GITLOW A.L.,ECONOMICS OF THE MOUNT HAGEN TRIBES, NEW GUINEA. S/ASIA STRUCT AGRI FAM...GEOG MYTH 20 NEW/GUINEA. PAGE 57 H1137 HABITAT ECO/UNDEV CULTURE KIN

B47
HERSKOVITS M.U.,MAN AND HIS WORK. UNIV SECT TEC/DEV PARTIC...PHIL/SCI LING AUD/VIS BIBLIOG. PAGE 70 H1409 SOC CULTURE INGP/REL HABITAT

B47
ISAAC J.,ECONOMICS OF MIGRATION. MOD/EUR CULTURE STRATA STRUCT NAT/G COLONIAL WEALTH...OLD/LIB TREND TIME 19/20 EUROPE/W MIGRATION. PAGE 78 H1569 HABITAT SOC GEOG

B48
EDUARDO O.D.C.,THE NEGRO IN NORTHERN BRAZIL: A STUDY IN ACCULTURATION. BRAZIL ECO/UNDEV FAM SECT PAY REGION HABITAT CATHISM MYSTISM...GEOG OBS SOC/INTEG WORSHIP 20 NEGRO MARANHAO. PAGE 44 H0890 CULTURE ADJUST GP/REL

B48
WHITE C.L.,HUMAN GEOGRAPHY: AN ECOLOGICAL STUDY OF GEOGRAPHY. UNIV SEA CULTURE AGRI EXTR/IND RACE/REL PRODUC...CHARTS HYPO/EXP SIMUL GEN/LAWS T. PAGE 167 H3345 SOC HABITAT GEOG SOCIETY

B49
UNSTEAD J.F.,A WORLD SURVEY FROM THE HUMAN ASPECT. AGRI INDUS...SOC CENSUS CHARTS 20 MAPS MIGRATION. PAGE 159 H3172 CULTURE HABITAT GEOG ATTIT

B50
ROHEIM G.,PSYCHOANALYSIS AND ANTHROPOLOGY. UNIV FAM PERS/REL ATTIT HABITAT...SOC OBS WORSHIP. PAGE 133 H2663 PSY BIOG CULTURE PERSON

B51
BERNATZIK H.A.,THE SPIRITS OF THE YELLOW LEAVES. BURMA LAOS S/ASIA THAILAND VIETNAM SOCIETY AGRI COLONIAL LEISURE GP/REL PERS/REL ISOLAT AGE HABITAT SEX WORSHIP 20. PAGE 16 H0310 SOC KIN ECO/UNDEV CULTURE

B51
INTERNATIONAL AFRICAN INST,ETHNOGRAPHIC SURVEY OF AFRICA: WEST CENTRAL AFRICA (VOLS. I-III, 1951-1953). AFR RHODESIA CULTURE ECO/UNDEV HEREDITY ...GEOG SOC CHARTS BIBLIOG WORSHIP 20 CONGO/LEOP. PAGE 77 H1543 STRUCT KIN INGP/REL HABITAT

B51
YOUNG T.C.,NEAR EASTERN CULTURE AND SOCIETY. ISLAM ECO/UNDEV SECT WRITING ATTIT HABITAT ORD/FREE 20. PAGE 172 H3439 CULTURE STRUCT REGION DIPLOM

B52
CALLOT E.,LA SOCIETE ET SON ENVIRONNEMENT: ESSAI SUR LES PRINCIPES DES SCIENCES SOCIALES. GP/REL ADJUST CONSEN ISOLAT HABITAT PERCEPT PERSON ...BIBLIOG SOC/INTEG 20. PAGE 25 H0507 SOCIETY PHIL/SCI CULTURE

B52
FORDE L.D.,HABITAT, ECONOMY AND SOCIETY. AFR L/A+17C S/ASIA STRUCT AGRI INGP/REL...GEOG OBS BIBLIOG 20. PAGE 52 H1037 SOC HABITAT CULTURE ECO/UNDEV

B52
INTERNATIONAL AFRICAN INST,ETHNOGRAPHIC SURVEY OF AFRICA: SOUTHERN AFRICA (VOLS. I-III, 1952-1954). AFR SOUTH/AFR CULTURE ECO/UNDEV GOV/REL HEREDITY ...GEOG SOC CHARTS BIBLIOG WORSHIP 20. PAGE 77 H1544 STRUCT KIN INGP/REL HABITAT

B52
LEBON J.H.C.,AN INTRODUCTION TO HUMAN GEOGRAPHY. CULTURE...GEOG SOC CONCPT CENSUS CHARTS 20 MIGRATION. PAGE 93 H1849 HABITAT GP/REL SOCIETY

B52
MONTAGU A.,MAN'S MOST DANGEROUS MYTH: THE FALLACY OF RACE. LAW PROB/SOLV WAR HABITAT POPULISM...PSY CONCPT CHARTS BIBLIOG NEGRO JEWS. PAGE 112 H2242 DISCRIM MYTH CULTURE RACE/REL

S52
EISENSTADT S.N.,"THE PROCESS OF ABSORPTION OF NEW IMMIGRANTS IN ISRAEL" (BMR)" ISRAEL CULTURE SCHOOL WORKER PARTIC DRIVE ORD/FREE...STAT OBS INT CHARTS SOC/INTEG 20 JEWS. PAGE 45 H0900 HABITAT ATTIT SAMP

B53
MEAD M.,CULTURAL PATTERNS AND TECHNICAL CHANGE. BURMA GREECE NIGERIA ECO/UNDEV AGRI INDUS SCHOOL SECT CREATE FEEDBACK HABITAT...PSY METH/COMP BIBLIOG 20 UN. PAGE 108 H2152 HEALTH TEC/DEV CULTURE ADJUST

B53
WAGLEY C.,AMAZON TOWN: A STUDY OF MAN IN THE TROPICS. BRAZIL L/A+17C STRATA STRUCT ECO/UNDEV AGRI EX/STRUC RACE/REL DISCRIM HABITAT WEALTH...OBS SOC/EXP 20. PAGE 164 H3285 SOC NEIGH CULTURE INGP/REL

B54
HAZARD B.H. JR.,KOREAN STUDIES GUIDE. KOREA CONSTN CULTURE AGRI FAM SECT CREATE WAR NAT/LISM HABITAT PWR...CHARTS 14/20. PAGE 68 H1371 BIBLIOG/A ELITES GP/REL

B54
TITIEV M.,THE SCIENCE OF MAN. LAW STRATA KIN GP/REL PERS/REL HABITAT HEREDITY KNOWL...LING CHARTS BIBLIOG WORSHIP. PAGE 155 H3107 SOC PSY CULTURE

B55
INTERNATIONAL AFRICAN INST,ETHNOGRAPHIC SURVEY OF AFRICA: NORTH EASTERN AFRICA (VOLUMES 1-2, 1955-56). AFR ETHIOPIA CULTURE ECO/UNDEV KIN GOV/REL ATTIT HEREDITY...GEOG CHARTS BIBLIOG WORSHIP 20. PAGE 77 H1545 STRUCT ECO/TAC INGP/REL HABITAT

B55
INTERNATIONAL AFRICAN INST,ETHNOGRAPHIC SURVEY OF AFRICA: WESTERN AFRICA: PEOPLES OF THE NIGER-BENUE CONFLUENCE. AFR NIGER CULTURE ECO/UNDEV KIN GOV/REL GP/REL ATTIT HEREDITY...CHARTS BIBLIOG WORSHIP 20. PAGE 77 H1546 STRUCT GEOG HABITAT INGP/REL

B55
LIPSCOMB J.F.,WHITE AFRICANS. SOCIETY STRUCT AGRI ECO/TAC ADJUD COLONIAL COERCE PERS/REL ADJUST. PAGE 97 H1937 RACE/REL HABITAT ECO/UNDEV ORD/FREE

B55
SMITH G.,A CONSTITUTIONAL AND LEGAL HISTORY OF ENGLAND. UK ELITES NAT/G LEGIS ADJUD OWN HABITAT POPULISM...JURID 20 ENGLSH/LAW. PAGE 145 H2909 CONSTN PARTIC LAW CT/SYS

B55
STEWARD J.H.,THEORY OF CULTURE CHANGE; THE METHODOLOGY OF MULTILINEAR EVOLUTION. SOCIETY KIN SECT GP/REL INGP/REL...BIBLIOG SOC/INTEG 20. PAGE 149 H2984 CULTURE CONCPT METH/COMP HABITAT

B55
UN ECONOMIC AND SOCIAL COUNCIL,ANALYTICAL BIBLIOGRAPHY OF INTERNATIONAL MIGRATION STATISTICS, SELECTED COUNTRIES, 1925-1950. STRATA...CLASSIF CENSUS NAT/COMP 20. PAGE 158 H3156 BIBLIOG STAT GEOG HABITAT

S55
GOODENOUGH W.H.,"A PROBLEM IN MALAYO-POLYNESIAN SOCIAL ORGANIZATION" (BMR)" MALAYSIA S/ASIA CULTURE AGRI PROB/SOLV OWN HABITAT...SOC 20 20 POLYNESIA. PAGE 58 H1170 KIN STRUCT FAM ECO/UNDEV

C55
STEWARD J.H.,"THE CONCEPT AND METHOD OF CULTURAL ECOLOGY" IN T.H. STEWARD'S THEORY OF CULTURAL CHANGE." SOCIETY INGP/REL...CONCPT CON/ANAL METH/COMP 20. PAGE 149 H2985 HABITAT CULTURE CREATE ADJUST

B56
DEUTSCH K.W.,AN INTERDISCIPLINARY BIBLIOGRAPHY ON NATIONALISM, 1935-1953. CULTURE SOCIETY SECT ATTIT HABITAT HEREDITY PERCEPT ROLE WEALTH...METH/CNCPT LING 20. PAGE 40 H0798 BIBLIOG/A NAT/LISM COLONIAL ADJUST

B56
DRIVER H.E.,AN INTEGRATION OF FUNCTIONAL, EVOLUTIONARY AND HISTORICAL THEORY BY MEANS OF CORRELATIONS. INGP/REL BIO/SOC HABITAT...PHIL/SCI GEN/LAWS. PAGE 42 H0847 CULTURE METH SOC CORREL

B56
INTERNATIONAL AFRICAN INST,SELECT ANNOTATED BIBLIOGRAPHY OF TROPICAL AFRICA. NAT/G EDU/PROP ADMIN HEALTH. PAGE 77 H1547 BIBLIOG/A AFR SOC HABITAT

B56
INTERNATIONAL AFRICAN INST,ETHNOGRAPHIC SURVEY OF AFRICA; WESTERN AFRICA: PAGAN PEOPLES OF CENTRAL AREA OF NORTHERN NIGERIA (VOL. XII). NIGERIA FAM KIN SECT ECO/TAC GOV/REL GP/REL ATTIT...LING CHARTS STRUCT INGP/REL HABITAT CULTURE

20. PAGE 77 H1548

B56

LEVIN M.G.,THE PEOPLES OF SIBERIA. PREHIST ECO/UNDEV KIN SECT HABITAT...CLASSIF AUD/VIS WORSHIP 20 SIBERIA. PAGE 95 H1900
CULTURE SOCIETY ASIA

B56

MUMFORD L.,THE TRANSFORMATIONS OF MAN. UNIV CULTURE INGP/REL HABITAT HEREDITY ALL/VALS ORD/FREE...MYTH TIME/SEQ TREND WORSHIP. PAGE 114 H2287
IDEA/COMP PERSON CONCPT

B56

READ M.,EDUCATION AND SOCIAL CHANGE IN TROPICAL AREAS. AFR L/A+17C SOCIETY LITERACY PERCEPT PERSON WEALTH...HEAL PHIL/SCI SOC 20. PAGE 130 H2603
EDU/PROP HABITAT DRIVE CULTURE

B57

INTERNATIONAL AFRICAN INST,ETHNOGRAPHIC SURVEY OF AFRICA: WESTERN AFRICA: THE BENIN KINGDOM. AFR NIGERIA CULTURE ECO/UNDEV KIN ECO/TAC GOV/REL AGE ATTIT HEREDITY...CHARTS BIBLIOG WORSHIP 20. PAGE 77 H1550
STRUCT INGP/REL GEOG HABITAT

B57

INTERNATIONAL AFRICAN INST,ETHNOGRAPHIC SURVEY OF AFRICA: WESTERN AFRICA: THE WOLOF OF SENEGAMBIA. AFR SENEGAL CULTURE ECO/UNDEV FAM KIN REGION ...CHARTS GP/COMP BIBLIOG WORSHIP 20. PAGE 78 H1551
STRUCT GEOG HABITAT INGP/REL

C57

WITTFOGEL K.A.,"ORIENTAL DESPOTISM: A COMPARATIVE STUDY OF TOTAL POWER." ASIA CULTURE STRATA NAT/G LEAD OWN ORD/FREE PWR...CONCPT TREND BIBLIOG 20. PAGE 170 H3393
TOTALISM HABITAT DOMIN ELITES

B58

ALMAGRO BASCH M.,ORIGEN Y FORMACION DEL PUEBLO HISPANO. PREHIST SPAIN REGION WAR RACE/REL HABITAT ORD/FREE...SOC SOC/INTEG 20. PAGE 5 H0109
CULTURE GP/REL ADJUST

B58

BRIGGS L.C.,THE LIVING RACES OF THE SAHARA. STRATA AGRI KIN INT/TRADE HABITAT...GEOG AUD/VIS CHARTS BIBLIOG 20 SAHARA MIGRATION. PAGE 21 H0417
STRUCT SOCIETY SOC CULTURE

B58

CROWE S.,THE LANDSCAPE OF POWER. UK CULTURE SERV/IND NAT/G CONSULT PARTIC NUC/PWR LEISURE...SOC EXHIBIT 20. PAGE 36 H0712
HABITAT TEC/DEV PLAN CONTROL

B58

INDIAN COUNCIL WORLD AFFAIRS,DEFENCE AND SECURITY IN THE INDIAN OCEAN AREA. INDIA S/ASIA CULTURE CONSULT DELIB/GP FORCES PROB/SOLV DIPLOM INT/TRADE 20 CMN/WLTH. PAGE 77 H1531
GEOG HABITAT ECO/UNDEV ORD/FREE

B58

VON FURER-HAIMEN E.,AN ANTHROPOLOGICAL BIBLIOGRAPHY OF SOUTH ASIA (VOL. I). STRATA STRUCT KIN SECT ACT/RES CREATE HABITAT...GEOG OBS 19/20. PAGE 163 H3267
BIBLIOG/A CULTURE S/ASIA SOC

B59

DUNHAM H.W.,SOCIOLOGICAL THEORY AND MENTAL DISORDER. UNIV SOCIETY STRATA HABITAT PERSON...GEOG CHARTS SOC/EXP TIME. PAGE 43 H0864
HEALTH SOC PSY CULTURE

B59

HONINGMAN J.J.,THE WORLD OF MAN. CHRIST-17C MEDIT-7 PRE/AMER PREHIST CREATE INGP/REL BIO/SOC HABITAT ...PSY SOC BIBLIOG. PAGE 73 H1460
CULTURE METH PERSON STRUCT

B59

LEE D.,FREEDOM AND CULTURE. WOR+45 WOR-45 FAM HABITAT PERSON LOVE MORAL...PSY SOC OBS NAT/COMP WORSHIP 20. PAGE 93 H1856
CULTURE SOCIETY CONCPT INGP/REL

B59

LEIGHTON A.H.,MY NAME IS LEGION; FOUNDATIONS FOR A THEORY OF MAN IN RELATION TO CULTURE (VOL. I). CULTURE STRANGE ANOMIE...SOC CONCPT METH/CNCPT CHARTS BIBLIOG METH 20 NOVA/SCOT. PAGE 93 H1867
HEALTH PSY SOCIETY HABITAT

B59

MURDOCK G.P.,AFRICA: ITS PEOPLES AND THEIR CULTURE HISTORY. AFR CULTURE AGRI LOC/G INGP/REL HABITAT ...GEOG SOC LING CHARTS BIBLIOG 20 NEGRO EGYPT/ANC. PAGE 115 H2293
SOCIETY ECO/TAC GP/COMP KIN

B59

ROCHE J.,LA COLONISATION ALLEMANDE ET LE RIO GRANDE DO SUL. BRAZIL L/A+17C NAT/G PROVS INGP/REL RACE/REL DISCRIM HABITAT...GEOG SOC/INTEG 19/20 MIGRATION. PAGE 133 H2652
ECO/UNDEV GP/REL ATTIT

S59

DUNCAN O.D.,"CULTURAL, BEHAVIORAL, AND ECOLOGICAL PERSPECTIVES IN THE STUDY OF SOCIAL ORGANIZATION" (BMR)" UNIV STRATA EX/STRUC PROB/SOLV ADMIN ATTIT SOC/INTEG 20 BUREAUCRCY. PAGE 43 H0862
CULTURE METH/COMP SOCIETY HABITAT

B60

BRIGGS L.C.,TRIBES OF THE SAHARA. AFR MOROCCO STRATA AGRI GP/REL HEALTH...GEOG SOC MYTH LING BIBLIOG 13/20 ARABS. PAGE 21 H0418
CULTURE HABITAT KIN SELF/OBS

B60

GONZALEZ NAVARRO M.,LA COLONIZACION EN MEXICO, 1877-1910. AGRI NAT/G PLAN PROB/SOLV INCOME ...POLICY JURID CENSUS 19/20 MEXIC/AMER MIGRATION. PAGE 58 H1164
ECO/UNDEV GEOG HABITAT COLONIAL

B60

HALBWACHS M.,POPULATION AND SOCIETY: INTRODUCTION TO SOCIAL MORPHOLOGY (TRANS. BY DUNCAN AND PFAUTZ). CULTURE SOCIETY AGRI INDUS HABITAT...CONCPT 20. PAGE 64 H1281
BIO/SOC GEOG NEIGH GP/COMP

B60

HUGHES C.C.,PEOPLE OF COVE AND WOODLOT; COMMUNITIES FROM THE VIEWPOINT OF SOCIAL PSYCHIATRY. CULTURE FAM PROVS HABITAT...PSY QU SAMP/SIZ CHARTS BIBLIOG 20. PAGE 74 H1489
GEOG SOCIETY STRUCT HEALTH

B60

INTERNATIONAL AFRICAN INST,ETHNOGRAPHIC SURVEY OF AFRICA: WESTERN AFRICA: PEOPLES OF THE MIDDLE NIGER REGION, NORTHERN NIGERIA. AFR NIGER CULTURE ECO/UNDEV KIN NEIGH GOV/REL GP/REL ATTIT HEREDITY ...CHARTS BIBLIOG WORSHIP 20. PAGE 78 H1552
STRUCT GEOG HABITAT INGP/REL

B60

KEPHART C.,RACES OF MAN. GP/REL HABITAT...LING SOC/INTEG 20 MIGRATION MISCEGEN. PAGE 85 H1692
CULTURE RACE/REL HEREDITY GEOG

B60

OTTENBERG S.,CULTURES AND SOCIETIES OF AFRICA. AFR KIN TEC/DEV GP/REL MARRIAGE ATTIT HABITAT HEREDITY ...ANTHOL BIBLIOG T WORSHIP 20. PAGE 122 H2433
SOCIETY INGP/REL STRUCT CULTURE

B60

SAHLINS M.D.,EVOLUTION AND CULTURE. CREATE...MYTH METH/COMP BIBLIOG 20. PAGE 137 H2730
CULTURE NEW/IDEA CONCPT HABITAT

B60

SLOTKIN J.S.,FROM FIELD TO FACTORY; NEW INDUSTRIAL EMPLOYEES. HABITAT...MGT NEW/IDEA NAT/COMP BIBLIOG SOC/INTEG 20. PAGE 145 H2901
INDUS LABOR CULTURE WORKER

B60

WILLIAMS L.E.,OVERSEAS CHINESE NATIONALISM: THE GENESIS OF THE PAN-CHINESE MOVEMENT IN INDONESIA, 1900-1916. ASIA COM INDONESIA AGRI INT/ORG LOC/G DIPLOM EDU/PROP HABITAT PWR POPULISM...GEOG LING CENSUS 20. PAGE 168 H3367
NAT/LISM GP/REL DECISION NAT/G

S60

COOK R.C.,"THE WORLD'S GREAT CITIES: EVOLUTION OR DEVOLUTION?" WOR+45 WOR-45 ECO/DEV ECO/UNDEV ACT/RES PROB/SOLV...GEOG TREND CHARTS NAT/COMP BIBLIOG 20. PAGE 33 H0658
MUNIC HABITAT PLAN CENSUS

S60

GRIMSHAW A.D.,"URBAN RACIAL VIOLENCE IN THE UNITED STATES: CHANGING ECOLOGICAL CONSIDERATIONS." STRUCT MUNIC FORCES PARTIC DISCRIM ATTIT HABITAT ...IDEA/COMP 20 NEGRO. PAGE 61 H1228
CROWD RACE/REL GOV/COMP NEIGH

B61

ACOSTA SAIGNES M.,ESTUDIOS DE ETNOLOGIA ANTIGUA DE VENEZUELA (2ND ED.). PRE/AMER VENEZUELA...ART/METH SOC BIBLIOG INDIAN/AM. PAGE 3 H0061
CULTURE STRUCT GP/REL HABITAT

B61

APTER D.E.,THE POLITICAL KINGDOM IN UGANDA. UGANDA CULTURE ECO/UNDEV AGRI KIN SECT TOP/EX REGION ATTIT HABITAT CONSERVE...GEOG AUD/VIS 20. PAGE 8 H0153
NAT/LISM POL/PAR COLONIAL ECO/TAC

B61

HOLDSWORTH M.,SOVIET AFRICAN STUDIES 1918-1959. USSR ACADEM NAT/G DIPLOM REGION KNOWL 20. PAGE 72 H1448
BIBLIOG/A AFR HABITAT NAT/COMP

B61

HUNT E.F.,SOCIAL SCIENCE. DIPLOM ECO/TAC ROUTINE GP/REL DEMAND DISCRIM EFFICIENCY HABITAT ALL/IDEOS ...SOC T 20. PAGE 75 H1497
CULTURE ADJUST STRATA ROLE

B61

KEE R.,REFUGEE WORLD. AUSTRIA EUR+WWI GERMANY NEIGH EX/STRUC WORKER PROB/SOLV ECO/TAC RENT EDU/PROP INGP/REL COST LITERACY HABITAT 20 MIGRATION. PAGE 84 H1676
NAT/G GIVE WEALTH STRANGE

B61

SCHECHTMAN J.B.,ON WINGS OF EAGLES: THE PLIGHT, EXODUS, AND HOMECOMING OF ORIENTAL JEWRY. ASIA ISLAM ISRAEL VOL/ASSN DIPLOM CONTROL ORD/FREE ...GEOG WORSHIP SOC/INTEG 20 JEWS ARABS MIGRATION. PAGE 139 H2777
CULTURE HABITAT KIN SECT

B61

TURNBULL C.M.,THE FOREST PEOPLE. EATING GP/REL INGP/REL RACE/REL ISOLAT HABITAT HEREDITY...GEOG SOC LING DICTIONARY WORSHIP 20 CONGO NEGRO BA/MBUTI. PAGE 157 H3138
AFR CULTURE KIN RECORD

B61

VON EICKSTEDT E.,TURKEN, KURDEN UND IRANER SEIT DEM ALTERTUM. IRAN TURKEY GP/REL BIO/SOC HABITAT...PSY 20 PERSIA. PAGE 163 H3266
CULTURE SOC SOCIETY STRUCT

S61
LIEBERSON S.,"THE IMPACT OF RESIDENTIAL SEGREGATION ON ETHNIC ASSIMILATION" (BMR)" CULTURE MUNIC GP/REL RACE/REL DISCRIM...GEOG STAT CON/ANAL CHARTS SOC/INTEG 20 MIGRATION. PAGE 96 H1926
HABITAT ISOLAT NEIGH

B62
BERGER M.,THE ARAB WORLD TODAY. CULTURE FAM INT/ORG NAT/G SECT FORCES ECO/TAC NAT/LISM HABITAT...CHARTS BIBLIOG 20 ARABS. PAGE 15 H0301
ISLAM PERSON STRUCT SOCIETY

B62
BERNOT R.M.,EXCESS AND RESTRAINT: SOCIAL CONTROL AMONG GUINEA MOUNTAIN PEOPLE. CULTURE FAM KIN CT/SYS COERCE WAR PERS/REL MARRIAGE HABITAT SEX ...MYTH 20 NEW/GUINEA. PAGE 16 H0314
SOCIETY CONTROL STRUCT ADJUST

B62
DEBUYST F.,LAS CLASES SOCIALES EN AMERICA LATINA. L/A+17C SOCIETY STRUCT WORKER EDU/PROP RACE/REL ATTIT HABITAT ROLE...GEOG SOC NAT/COMP SOC/INTEG 20. PAGE 39 H0780
STRATA GP/REL WEALTH

B62
EDWARDS A.C.,THE OVIMBUNDU UNDER TWO SOVEREIGNTIES. CULTURE STRUCT FAM MARRIAGE HABITAT...SOC 19/20 OVIMBUNDU. PAGE 45 H0891
KIN NEIGH SOCIETY CONTROL

B62
EVANS-PRITCHARD E.E.,ESSAYS IN SOCIAL ANTHROPOLOGY. AFR KIN REGION INGP/REL DRIVE HABITAT...OBS METH 20 ZANDE. PAGE 48 H0954
SOCIETY CULTURE SOC STRUCT

B62
HAY S.N.,SOUTHEAST ASIAN HISTORY: A BIBLIOGRAPHICAL GUIDE. STRATA KIN NAT/G REGION GUERRILLA REV WAR ADJUST HABITAT PERCEPT ALL/IDEOS...CHARTS 5/20. PAGE 68 H1365
BIBLIOG/A S/ASIA CULTURE

B62
HUCKER C.O.,CHINA: A CRITICAL BIBLIOGRAPHY (PAMPHLET). ASIA STRUCT AGRI FINAN INDUS HABITAT MARXISM...EPIST HUM. PAGE 74 H1487
BIBLIOG/A CULTURE INTELL SOCIETY

B62
KEESING F.M.,THE ETHNOHISTORY OF NORTHERN LUZON. PHILIPPINE ECO/UNDEV FAM SECT CHIEF REGION GP/REL HABITAT...GEOG LING BIBLIOG WORSHIP 20. PAGE 84 H1680
CULTURE SOC KIN

B62
KOSAMBI D.D.,MYTH AND REALITY. INDIA AGRI KIN SECT HABITAT...SOC 20. PAGE 88 H1758
CULTURE SOCIETY MYTH ATTIT

B62
MALINOWSKI B.,SEX, CULTURE, AND MYTH. UNIV SOCIETY FAM PERS/REL MARRIAGE RATIONAL HABITAT PERSON SUPEGO MORAL WORSHIP 20. PAGE 102 H2032
MYTH SECT SEX CULTURE

B62
MEGGITT M.J.,DESERT PEOPLE. ECO/UNDEV KIN CREATE PROB/SOLV CONTROL DRIVE ROLE...GEOG SOC MYTH CHARTS BIBLIOG 20 AUSTRAL. PAGE 108 H2159
ADJUST CULTURE INGP/REL HABITAT

B62
MICHAEL H.N.,STUDIES IN SIBERIAN ETHNOGENESIS. USSR KIN...ART/METH SOC 20 SIBERIA. PAGE 110 H2196
HABITAT HEREDITY CULTURE LING

B62
SCHECHTMAN J.B.,POSTWAR POPULATION TRANSFERS IN EUROPE: 1945-1955. COM CZECHOSLVK GERMANY POLAND USSR CULTURE SOCIETY PROB/SOLV AGREE NAT/LISM...SOC STAT TREND CHARTS METH/COMP 20 MIGRATION. PAGE 139 H2778
GEOG CENSUS EUR+WWI HABITAT

B62
SMITH M.G.,KINSHIP AND COMMUNITY IN CARRIACOU. WEST/IND STRATA AGRI FAM SECT WORKER MARRIAGE OWN HEREDITY WEALTH...SOC 18/20. PAGE 146 H2915
CULTURE HABITAT KIN STRUCT

B62
YOUNG G.,THE HILL TRIBES OF NORTHERN THAILAND. S/ASIA THAILAND FAM KIN LOC/G GP/REL HABITAT...GEOG LING OBS 20. PAGE 172 H3438
CULTURE STRUCT ECO/UNDEV SECT

B63
BIALEK R.W.,CATHOLIC POLITICS: A HISTORY BASED ON ECUADOR. ECUADOR SPAIN CULTURE STRUCT CONTROL REV PWR...BIBLIOG WORSHIP 18/20. PAGE 16 H0329
COLONIAL CATHISM GOV/REL HABITAT

B63
BOHANNAN P.,SOCIAL ANTHROPOLOGY. ECO/DEV GP/REL DEMAND MARRIAGE HABITAT...CHARTS GP/COMP BIBLIOG T WORSHIP 20. PAGE 18 H0366
SOC STRUCT FAM CULTURE

B63
CONFERENCE ABORIGINAL STUDIES,AUSTRALIAN ABORIGINAL STUDIES. ECO/UNDEV INT/TRADE COLONIAL ADJUST HABITAT HEREDITY...GEOG PSY LING SOC/EXP ANTHOL WORSHIP 20 AUSTRAL ABORIGINES. PAGE 32 H0638
SOC SOCIETY CULTURE STRUCT

B63
DRIVER H.E.,ETHNOGRAPHY AND ACCULTURATION OF THE CHICHIMECA-JONAZ OF NORTHEAST MEXICO. ECO/UNDEV AGRI FAM KIN EDU/PROP MARRIAGE HEALTH...GEOG INT CHARTS WORSHIP 18/20 MEXIC/AMER. PAGE 42 H0848
CULTURE HABITAT STRUCT GP/REL

B63
EICH H.,THE UNLOVED GERMANS. EUR+WWI GERMANY PERS/REL RACE/REL DISCRIM HABITAT SUPEGO FASCISM ...PSY SOC AUD/VIS 19/20 JEWS. PAGE 45 H0898
STERTYP PERSON CULTURE ATTIT

B63
ENKE S.,ECONOMICS FOR DEVELOPMENT. AGRI TEC/DEV CAP/ISM DIPLOM ECO/TAC TAX ATTIT DRIVE HABITAT WEALTH...GOV/COMP BIBLIOG 20. PAGE 46 H0928
ECO/UNDEV PHIL/SCI CON/ANAL

B63
KROEBER A.L.,ANTHROPOLOGY: BIOLOGY AND RACE. UNIV CULTURE HABITAT...PSY 20. PAGE 89 H1772
SOC PHIL/SCI RACE/REL INGP/REL

B63
LAMB B.P.,INDIA: A WORLD IN TRANSITION. INDIA ECO/UNDEV SECT EDU/PROP COLONIAL HABITAT ORD/FREE ...GEOG CHARTS BIBLIOG SOC/INTEG 20. PAGE 90 H1799
POL/PAR NAT/G DIPLOM STRATA

B63
LEVIN M.G.,ETHNIC ORIGINS OF THE PEOPLES OF NORTHEASTERN ASIA. CONSTN LEGIS...STAT CENSUS CHARTS 20 TEXAS MAPS. PAGE 95 H1901
HEREDITY HABITAT CULTURE GEOG

B63
LOOMIE A.J.,THE SPANISH ELIZABETHANS: THE ENGLISH EXILES AT THE COURT OF PHILIP II. SPAIN UK WAR INGP/REL DRIVE HABITAT CATHISM...BIOG 16/17 MIGRATION. PAGE 98 H1962
NAT/G STRANGE POLICY DIPLOM

B63
PRICE A.G.,THE WESTERN INVASIONS OF THE PACIFIC AND ITS CONTINENTS. ASIA PRE/AMER S/ASIA ECO/UNDEV KIN NAT/G SECT FORCES DOMIN HEALTH...SOC 16/20. PAGE 128 H2560
COLONIAL CULTURE GEOG HABITAT

B63
REYNOLDS B.,MAGIC, DIVINATION AND WITCHCRAFT AMONG THE BAROTSE OF NORTHERN RHODESIA. RHODESIA CULTURE KIN CREATE LEGIT PARTIC DEATH DREAM STRANGE HABITAT PERSON...AUD/VIS WORSHIP 20. PAGE 131 H2619
AFR SOC MYTH SECT

B63
STIRNIMANN H.,NGUNI UND GNONI; EINE KULTURGESCHICHTLICHE STUDIE (ACTA ETHNOLOGICA ET LINGUISTICA, NUMBER 6). AFR MALAWI SOUTH/AFR FORCES HABITAT...RECORD CHARTS BIBLIOG WORSHIP 19/20 NATAL. PAGE 149 H2987
CULTURE GP/COMP SOCIETY

B63
TINDALE N.B.,ABORIGINAL AUSTRALIANS. KIN CREATE ROLE...SOC MYTH TREND 20 AUSTRAL ABORIGINES MIGRATION. PAGE 155 H3099
CULTURE DRIVE ECO/UNDEV HABITAT

B63
WAGLEY C.,INTRODUCTION TO BRAZIL. BRAZIL L/A+17C FAM KIN SCHOOL SECT ATTIT WEALTH...GEOG SOC. PAGE 164 H3286
ECO/UNDEV ELITES HABITAT STRATA

B64
BEARDSLEY R.K.,STUDIES ON ECONOMIC LIFE IN JAPAN (OCCASIONAL PAPERS NO. 8). INDUS FAM HABITAT...GEOG GOV/COMP 20 CHINJAP. PAGE 12 H0249
WEALTH PRESS PRODUC INCOME

B64
COUNT E.W.,FACT AND THEORY IN SOCIAL SCIENCE. UNIV HABITAT...BIOG TREND CHARTS ANTHOL BIBLIOG. PAGE 34 H0679
STRUCT SOC CULTURE ADJUST

B64
ELKIN A.P.,THE AUSTRALIAN ABORIGINES - HOW TO UNDERSTAND THEM (4TH ED.). FAM NEIGH DEATH MARRIAGE ATTIT BIO/SOC HABITAT...PSY SOC MYTH WORSHIP AUSTRAL ABORIGINES. PAGE 45 H0908
CULTURE STRUCT SOCIETY KIN

B64
GREEN M.M.,IBO VILLAGE AFFAIRS. AFR FORCES PERS/REL ADJUST ISOLAT ATTIT HABITAT PERSON ALL/VALS...JURID RECORD SOC/INTEG 20 IBO. PAGE 60 H1207
MUNIC CULTURE ECO/UNDEV SOC

B64
HARRIS M.,THE NATURE OF CULTURAL THINGS. GP/REL PERS/REL DRIVE HABITAT PERSON ROLE...PHIL/SCI PSY SOC CHARTS BIBLIOG 20. PAGE 67 H1341
CULTURE OBS CLASSIF NEW/IDEA

B64
KIDD K.E.,BRIEF BIBLIOGRAPHY OF ONTARIO ANTHROPOLOGY (PAMPHLET). CANADA PREHIST HABITAT ...MYTH WORSHIP. PAGE 86 H1708
BIBLIOG SOC LING CULTURE

B64
LEBRUN J.,BIBLIOGRAPHIE DE LA FERTILITE DES SOLS ET ELEMENTS DE SOCIOLOGIE RURALE EN AFRIQUE AU SUD DU SAHARA. AFR PLAN TEC/DEV EFFICIENCY PRODUC...GEOG SOC NAT/COMP 20. PAGE 93 H1850
BIBLIOG/A ECO/UNDEV HABITAT AGRI

B64
LIENHARDT G.,SOCIAL ANTHROPOLOGY. SOCIETY FAM KIN ...CONCPT METH. PAGE 97 H1928
SOC HABITAT HEREDITY CULTURE

B64
MCCALL D.F.,AFRICA IN TIME PERSPECTIVE. AFR EXTR/IND KIN SECT CREATE PERS/REL HABITAT...GEOG METH/CNCPT LING BIBLIOG/A TIME 20. PAGE 106 H2124
HIST/WRIT OBS/ENVIR CULTURE

B64
MORRIS J.,THE PRESENCE OF SPAIN. SPAIN MUNIC NAT/G FORCES ATTIT CATHISM...AUD/VIS 16/20. PAGE 113 H2263
CULTURE HABITAT SOCIETY GEOG

B64
NORTHROP F.S.,CROSS-CULTURAL UNDERSTANDING: EPISTEMOLOGY IN ANTHROPOLOGY. BURMA GREECE THAILAND HABITAT PERCEPT PERSON...PHIL/SCI SOC METH 20 MEXIC/AMER CHINJAP. PAGE 119 H2375
EPIST PSY CULTURE CONCPT

B64
SCHNITGER F.M.,FORGOTTEN KINGDOMS IN SUMATRA. FAM SECT LEISURE HABITAT...OBS AUD/VIS WORSHIP 20 SUMATRA. PAGE 140 H2793
CULTURE AFR SOCIETY STRUCT

B64
VON FURER-HAIMEN E.,AN ANTHROPOLOGICAL BIBLIOGRAPHY OF SOUTH ASIA (VOL. II). STRATA STRUCT KIN SECT ACT/RES CREATE HABITAT...GEOG OBS 20. PAGE 163 H3268
BIBLIOG/A CULTURE S/ASIA SOC

C64
HARRIS M.,"THE NATURE OF CULTURAL THINGS." GP/REL DRIVE HABITAT PERSON ROLE...PHIL/SCI 20. PAGE 67 H1340
BIBLIOG CULTURE PSY SOC

B65
ARENSBERG C.M.,CULTURE AND COMMUNITY. UNIV FACE/GP ACT/RES EDU/PROP LEAD REGION GP/REL PERS/REL HABITAT ALL/VALS...SOC CONCPT 20. PAGE 8 H0162
SOCIETY CULTURE NEIGH NEW/IDEA

B65
BERNDT R.M.,ABORIGINAL MAN IN AUSTRALIA. LAW DOMIN ADMIN COLONIAL MARRIAGE HABITAT ORD/FREE...LING CHARTS ANTHOL BIBLIOG WORSHIP 20 AUSTRAL ABORIGINES MUSIC ELKIN/AP. PAGE 16 H0312
SOC CULTURE SOCIETY STRUCT

B65
BETEILLE A.,CASTE, CLASS, AND POWER. INDIA MUNIC SECT REGION GP/REL PERS/REL ATTIT HABITAT RIGID/FLEX...SOC 20. PAGE 16 H0323
STRATA CULTURE PWR STRUCT

B65
GIBBS S.L.,PEOPLES OF AFRICA. AFR INGP/REL HABITAT ...GEOG ANTHOL 20. PAGE 56 H1122
CULTURE AGRI FAM KIN

B65
HERRICK B.H.,URBAN MIGRATION AND ECONOMIC DEVELOPMENT IN CHILE. CHILE AGRI INDUS LABOR NAT/G CENTRAL PRODUC...STAT SAMP CHARTS BIBLIOG/A 20 MIGRATION. PAGE 70 H1404
HABITAT GEOG MUNIC ECO/UNDEV

B65
KLEIN J.,SAMPLES FROM ENGLISH CULTURES (2 VOLS.). UK STRATA FAM NEIGH WORKER ETIQUET ISOLAT AGE/C AGE/A HABITAT RIGID/FLEX...NET/THEORY CHARTS 20. PAGE 87 H1732
CULTURE INGP/REL ATTIT SOC

B65
KUPER H.,URBANIZATION AND MIGRATION IN WEST AFRICA. UPPER/VOLT CULTURE ECO/UNDEV WORKER REGION GOV/REL ...LING ANTHOL SOC/INTEG 20 AFRICA/W OSHOGBO MOSSI MIGRATION. PAGE 89 H1781
AFR HABITAT MUNIC GEOG

B65
LAWRENCE P.,GODS, GHOSTS, AND MEN IN MELANESIA: SOME RELIGIONS OF AUSTRALIAN NEW GUINEA AND THE NEW HEBRIDES. SOCIETY ECO/UNDEV FAM GP/REL INGP/REL HABITAT PERSON...GEOG SOC ANTHOL BIBLIOG WORSHIP 20 NEW/GUINEA. PAGE 92 H1847
MYTH S/ASIA SECT CULTURE

B66
AHMED Z.,DUSK AND DAWN IN VILLAGE INDIA. INDIA S/ASIA UK CULTURE SOCIETY NAT/G DOMIN COLONIAL HABITAT SOVEREIGN...SOC DICTIONARY 20. PAGE 4 H0080
NEIGH ECO/UNDEV AGRI ADJUST

B66
ASHRAF A.,THE CITY GOVERNMENT OF CALCUTTA: A STUDY OF INERTIA. INDIA ELITES INDUS NAT/G EX/STRUC ACT/RES PLAN PROB/SOLV LEAD HABITAT...BIBLIOG 20 CALCUTTA. PAGE 9 H0175
LOC/G MUNIC ADMIN ECO/UNDEV

B66
BARRETT J.,THAT BETTER COUNTRY: RELIGIOUS ASPECT OF LIFE IN EASTERN AUSTRALIA, 1835-1850. LAW ECO/UNDEV SCHOOL TEC/DEV EDU/PROP CONTROL HABITAT MORAL WORSHIP 19 AUSTRAL CHURCH/STA. PAGE 11 H0229
SECT CULTURE GOV/REL

B66
BASDEN G.T.,NIGER IBOS. NIGERIA STRUCT SECT CHIEF COLONIAL HABITAT...POLICY SOC MYTH OBS WORSHIP 20 IBO. PAGE 12 H0233
CULTURE AFR SOCIETY

B66
BIRMINGHAM D.,TRADE AND CONFLICT IN ANGOLA. PORTUGAL CULTURE FORCES DIPLOM GP/REL PROFIT HABITAT NAT/COMP. PAGE 17 H0341
WAR INT/TRADE ECO/UNDEV COLONIAL

B66
BRAIBANTI R.,RESEARCH ON THE BUREAUCRACY OF PAKISTAN. PAKISTAN LAW CULTURE INTELL ACADEM LOC/G SECT PRESS CT/SYS...LING CHARTS 20 BUREAUCRCY. PAGE 20 H0402
HABITAT NAT/G ADMIN CONSTN

B66
CADY J.F.,THAILAND, BURMA, LAOS AND CAMBODIA. FRANCE UK CULTURE NAT/G DOMIN GP/REL RACE/REL HABITAT...GEOG TREND CHINJAP BUDDHISM. PAGE 25 H0504
S/ASIA COLONIAL REGION SECT

B66
ELLIS A.B.,THE EWE-SPEAKING PEOPLES OF THE SLAVE COAST OF WEST AFRICA. AFR FORCES ADJUST...LING RECORD GP/COMP WORSHIP 20 AFRICA/W DEITY. PAGE 45 H0910
MYTH CULTURE HABITAT

B66
FIELDHOUSE D.K.,THE COLONIAL EMPIRES: A COMPARATIVE SURVEY FROM THE 18TH CENTURY. UK WOR-45 REV HABITAT 17/18. PAGE 50 H0994
NAT/COMP COLONIAL NAT/G DOMIN

B66
HAHN C.H.L.,THE NATIVE TRIBES OF SOUTH WEST AFRICA. LAW FAM SECT HABITAT SKILL...SOC AUD/VIS WORSHIP RITUAL 20 AFRICA/SW. PAGE 64 H1275
CULTURE SOCIETY STRUCT AFR

B66
KASUNMU A.B.,NIGERIAN FAMILY LAW. NIGERIA KIN LEGIT ILLEGIT MARRIAGE AGE DRIVE HABITAT ALL/VALS...JURID IDEA/COMP T 20 ENGLSH/LAW. PAGE 83 H1667
FAM LAW CULTURE AFR

B66
KIRKLAND E.C.,A BIBLIOGRAPHY OF SOUTH ASIAN FOLKLORE. WRITING HABITAT ALL/VALS MYSTISM ...ART/METH GEOG PSY SOC MYTH WORSHIP 13/20. PAGE 86 H1723
BIBLIOG S/ASIA CULTURE CREATE

B66
NEVITT A.A.,THE ECONOMIC PROBLEMS OF HOUSING. WOR+45 ECO/DEV ECO/UNDEV ACT/RES PROB/SOLV ECO/TAC RENT...OBS CHARTS 20. PAGE 117 H2342
HABITAT PROC/MFG DELIB/GP NAT/COMP

B66
RADIN P.,THE METHOD AND THEORY OF ETHNOLOGY. CULTURE STRUCT BIO/SOC HABITAT...HUM OBS/ENVIR METH/COMP GEN/LAWS 20 HUMANISM. PAGE 129 H2578
PHIL/SCI SOC METH SOCIETY

B66
SKILLING H.G.,THE GOVERNMENTS OF COMMUNIST EAST EUROPE. COM EUR+WWI ELITES FORCES DIPLOM ECO/TAC CONTROL HABITAT SOCISM...DECISION BIBLIOG 20 EUROPE/E COM/PARTY. PAGE 145 H2895
MARXISM NAT/COMP GP/COMP DOMIN

B66
VOGT E.Z.,PEOPLE OF RIMROCK. STRATA STRUCT KIN SECT GP/REL HABITAT ALL/VALS...GEOG INT QU 20 TEXAS NAVAHO MORMON SPAN/AMER ZUNI. PAGE 163 H3260
CULTURE GP/COMP SOC SOCIETY

B66
WEINSTEIN B.,GABON: NATION-BUILDING ON THE OGOOUE. AFR GABON WOR+45 CULTURE SOCIETY PLAN DIPLOM COLONIAL INGP/REL ANOMIE HABITAT SUPEGO 20. PAGE 166 H3329
ECO/UNDEV GP/REL LEAD NAT/G

B66
WHEELER G.,THE PEOPLES OF SOVIET CENTRAL ASIA: A BACKGROUND BOOK. ISLAM USSR STRATA STRUCT FORCES REV WAR HABITAT 7/20. PAGE 167 H3341
COLONIAL DOMIN CULTURE ADJUST

B67
COWLES M.,PERSPECTIVES IN THE EDUCATION OF DISADVANTAGED CHILDREN. CULTURE OP/RES PLAN PERS/REL ADJUST HABITAT PERCEPT KNOWL WEALTH ...SOC/WK IDEA/COMP ANTHOL 20. PAGE 34 H0686
EDU/PROP AGE/C TEC/DEV SCHOOL

B67
FANON F.,BLACK SKIN, WHITE MASKS: THE EXPERIENCES OF A BLACK MAN IN A WHITE WORLD. CULTURE COLONIAL HAPPINESS ISOLAT STRANGE ATTIT HABITAT RIGID/FLEX SEX...BIOG STERTYP SOC/INTEG 20 NEGRO. PAGE 49 H0970
DISCRIM PERS/REL RACE/REL PSY

B67
GROSS B.M.,ACTION UNDER PLANNING: THE GUIDANCE OF ECONOMIC DEVELOPMENT. STRUCT R+D NAT/G ACT/RES HABITAT...DECISION 20. PAGE 62 H1232
ECO/UNDEV PLAN ADMIN MGT

B67
WARD L.,LESTER WARD AND THE WELFARE STATE. SOCIETY NAT/G CREATE RECEIVE EQUILIB UTOPIA HABITAT HEREDITY PERSON...POLICY SOC BIOG 19/20 WARD/LEST. PAGE 165 H3303
ALL/VALS NEW/IDEA WELF/ST CONCPT

L67
CRIBBET J.E.,"SOME REFLECTIONS ON THE LAW OF LAND - A VIEW FROM SCANDINAVIA." DENMARK NETHERLAND NORWAY SWEDEN INDUS MUNIC NEIGH RACE/REL ATTIT HABITAT ...IDEA/COMP 20. PAGE 35 H0701
LAW PLAN CONTROL NAT/G

L67
LATIN AMERICAN STUDIES ASSN,"RESEARCH ON EDUCATION
EDU/PROP

IN LATIN AMERICA." L/A+17C NAT/G HABITAT...GOV/COMP ANTHOL 20. PAGE 92 H1836 SCHOOL ACADEM R+D

S67
CRITTENDEN J.,"DIMENSIONS OF MODERNIZATION IN THE AMERICAN STATES." USA+45 STRUCT MUNIC PROB/SOLV CONTROL LITERACY HABITAT...CONCPT METH/CNCPT CORREL CONT/OBS CENSUS 20. PAGE 35 H0702 PROVS GOV/COMP STAT ECO/DEV

S67
GLENN N.D.,"RURAL-URBAN DIFFERENCES IN REPORTED ATTITUDES AND BEHAVIOR" STRATA GP/REL CONSEN HABITAT RIGID/FLEX SAMP. PAGE 57 H1143 CULTURE ATTIT KIN CHARTS

S67
HASSAN M.F.,"THE SECOND FOUR-YEAR PLAN OF VENEZUELA." L/A+17C VENEZUELA AGRI INDUS NAT/G PLAN RATION CONTROL HABITAT...MATH STAT 20. PAGE 67 H1352 ECO/UNDEV FINAN BUDGET PROB/SOLV

S67
JENCKS C.E.,"SOCIAL STATUS OF COAL MINERS IN BRITAIN SINCE NATIONALIZATION." UK STRATA STRUCT LABOR RECEIVE GP/REL INCOME OWN ATTIT HABITAT...MGT T 20. PAGE 80 H1600 EXTR/IND WORKER CONTROL NAT/G

S67
KRISTOF L.K.D.,"THE STATE-IDEA, THE NATIONAL IDEA AND THE IMAGE OF THE FATHERLAND." CONSTN CULTURE INTELL SOCIETY WORKER TASK DRIVE HABITAT...MYTH GOV/COMP IDEA/COMP. PAGE 89 H1769 GEOG CONCPT NAT/G PERCEPT

S67
THEROUX P.,"HATING THE ASIANS." TANZANIA UGANDA CONSTN INDUS NAT/G POL/PAR WORKER ECO/TAC HABITAT LOVE...POLICY GEOG 20 MIGRATION. PAGE 154 H3069 AFR RACE/REL SOVEREIGN ATTIT

B82
RATZEL F.,ANTHROPO-GEOGRAPHIE. SEA AGRI NEIGH. PAGE 130 H2595 GEOG CULTURE HABITAT

B99
DU BOIS W.E.B.,THE PHILADELPHIA NEGRO: A SOCIAL STUDY. CULTURE STRATA KIN CRIME SUFF ADJUST DISCRIM ISOLAT HABITAT HEREDITY ALL/VALS SOC/INTEG 17/19 NEGRO PHILADELPH. PAGE 42 H0851 INGP/REL RACE/REL SOC CENSUS

B99
RIPLEY W.Z.,A SELECTED BIBLIOGRAPHY OF THE ANTHROPOLOGY AND ETHNOLOGY OF EUROPE. SOCIETY STRATA STRUCT KIN SECT VOL/ASSN GP/REL INGP/REL HABITAT...GEOG 19. PAGE 132 H2632 BIBLIOG/A MOD/EUR SOC CULTURE

HACHMANN R. H1269

HACKETT A.M. H1271

HACKETT J. H1270,H1271

HADDAD J.A. H1272

HADWIGER D.F. H1273

HAEFELE E.T. H1274

HAGUE/F....FRANK HAGUE

HAHN C.H.L. H1275

HAIGH G. H1276

HAILEY L. H1277,H1278

HAIM S.G. H1279

HAITI....SEE ALSO L/A+17C

B47
NEUBURGER O.,GUIDE TO OFFICIAL PUBLICATIONS OF THE OTHER AMERICAN REPUBLICS: HAITI (VOL. XII). HAITI LAW FINAN LEGIS PRESS...JURID 20. PAGE 117 H2334 BIBLIOG/A CONSTN NAT/G EDU/PROP

B51
BISSAINTHE M.,DICTIONNAIRE DE BIBLIOGRAPHIE HAITIENNE. HAITI ELITES AGRI LEGIS DIPLOM INT/TRADE WRITING ORD/FREE CATHISM...ART/METH GEOG 19/20 NEGRO TREATY. PAGE 17 H0347 BIBLIOG L/A+17C SOCIETY NAT/G

B65
FAGG J.E.,CUBA, HAITI, AND THE DOMINICAN REPUBLIC. CUBA DOMIN/REP HAITI L/A+17C NAT/G DIPLOM ECO/TAC DOMIN CHOOSE AUTHORIT ROLE SOVEREIGN POPULISM 17/20. PAGE 48 H0959 COLONIAL ECO/UNDEV REV GOV/COMP

S65
PLANK J.N.,"THE CARIBBEAN* INTERVENTION, WHEN AND HOW." CUBA GUATEMALA HAITI PANAMA USA+45 VENEZUELA FORCES PROB/SOLV RISK COERCE...NAT/COMP OAS TIME. PAGE 126 H2521 SOVEREIGN MARXISM REV

B66
LEYBURN J.G.,THE HAITIAN PEOPLE (REV. ED.). HAITI SOCIETY FAM SECT DOMIN COLONIAL MARRIAGE...SOC CHARTS BIBLIOG/A 18/10. PAGE 96 H1917 STRUCT STRATA INGP/REL CULTURE

HAJDA J. H1280

HAKLUYT/R....RICHARD HAKLUYT

B38
DUNHAM W.H. JR.,COMPLAINT AND REFORM IN ENGLAND 1436-1714. UK LAW ACADEM NAT/G POL/PAR SCHOOL PRESS COLONIAL PARL/PROC MORAL...SOC/WK ANTHOL 15/18 HAKLUYT/R COWPER/W. PAGE 43 H0865 ATTIT SOCIETY SECT

HALBWACHS M. H1281

HALDANE R.B. H1282

HALE O.J. H1283

HALEVY E. H1284,H1285,H1286

HALL R.C. H1287

HALLECK/C....CHARLES HALLECK

HALLER W. H1288

HALLGARTEN G.W. H1289

HALLOWELL J.H. H1290

HALPERIN M.H. H1291,H1292

HALPERIN S. H1293

HALPERIN S.W. H1294

HALPERN A.M. H1295

HALPERN B. H1296,H1297

HALSEY A.H. H1298

HAMADY S. H1299

HAMBLIN R.L. H2925

HAMBURG....HAMBURG, GERMANY

HAMIL H.M. H1300

HAMILTON W.B. H1301,H1302

HAMILTON W.H. H1303

HAMILTON/A....ALEXANDER HAMILTON

B64
MINAR D.W.,IDEAS AND POLITICS: THE AMERICAN EXPERIENCE. SECT CHIEF LEGIS CREATE ADJUD EXEC REV PWR...PHIL/SCI CONCPT IDEA/COMP 18/20 HAMILTON/A JEFFERSN/T DECLAR/IND JACKSON/A PRESIDENT. PAGE 111 H2220 CONSTN NAT/G FEDERAL

HAMM H. H1304

HAMMARSK/D....DAG HAMMARSKJOLD

HAMMARSKJOLD, DAG....SEE HAMMARSK/D

HAMMER E.J. H1305

HAMMOND B. H1306

HAMMOND B.E. H1307

HAMMOND M. H1308

HAMMOND R.J. H1309

HAMSON C.J. H1310

HANAK H. H1311

HANBURY H.G. H1454

HANCE W.A. H1312
HANG T. H1262
HANKE L. H1313

HANNA A.J. H1314

HANNA J.L. H1315

HANNA W.J. H1315

HANNA/MARK....MARK HANNA

HANRIEDER W.F. H1316

HANSARD SOCIETY PARL GOVT H1317

HANSER C.J. H1318

HANSON A.H. H1319,H1320,H1321

HANSON J.W. H1322

HAPGOOD D. H1323

HAPPINESS.... HAPPINESS AS A CONDITION (UNHAPPINESS)

B10
MILL J.S.,UTILITARIANISM, LIBERTY, AND REPRESENTATIVE GOVERNMENT. CONTROL PERCEPT PERSON MORAL...CONCPT GEN/LAWS. PAGE 110 H2205 — HAPPINESS ORD/FREE REPRESENT NAT/G

B13
KROPOTKIN P.,THE CONQUEST OF BREAD. SOCIETY STRATA AGRI INDUS WORKER REV HAPPINESS INCOME PRODUC HEALTH MORAL ORD/FREE. PAGE 89 H1775 — ANARCH SOCIALIST OWN AGREE

B17
DE MAISTRE J.,DU PAPE (1817). FRANCE LAW SOCIETY SECT DOMIN REV HAPPINESS PWR SOVEREIGN 18/19 PROTESTANT. PAGE 38 H0761 — CATH CHIEF LEGIT NAT/G

B37
HORNEY K.,THE NEUROTIC PERSONALITY OF OUR TIME. SOCIETY PERS/REL ADJUST HAPPINESS ANOMIE ATTIT DRIVE SEX LOVE PWR CONCPT. PAGE 74 H1472 — PSY PERSON STRANGE CULTURE

B40
ZWEIG F.,THE WORKER IN AN AFFLUENT SOCIETY: FAMILY LIFE AND INDUSTRY. UK STRATA LG/CO ECO/TAC LEISURE INGP/REL HAPPINESS HEALTH...PSY SOC/WK INT CHARTS WORSHIP 20 FEMALE/SEX. PAGE 173 H3465 — MARRIAGE ATTIT FINAN CULTURE

B46
GODWIN W.,ENQUIRY CONCERNING POLITICAL JUSTICE AND ITS INFLUENCE ON MORALS AND HAPPINESS (1793). UNIV SOCIETY NAT/G GP/REL INGP/REL HAPPINESS ALL/VALS CONCPT. PAGE 58 H1151 — MORAL PERSON ORD/FREE

C50
ROUSSEAU J.J.,"DISCOURSE ON THE ORIGIN OF INEQUALITY" (1755) IN THE SOCIAL CONTRACT AND DISCOURSES." UNIV NAT/G PLAN BAL/PWR HAPPINESS UTOPIA BIO/SOC HEREDITY MORAL...WELF/ST CONCPT. PAGE 135 H2698 — SOCIETY STRUCT PERSON GEN/LAWS

C50
ROUSSEAU J.J.,"A DISCOURSE ON POLITICAL ECONOMY" (1755) IN THE SOCIAL CONTRACT AND DISCOURSES." UNIV SOCIETY STRATA STRUCT CONSEN EQUILIB HAPPINESS UTOPIA HEALTH WEALTH...POLICY WELF/ST. PAGE 135 H2699 — NAT/G ECO/TAC TAX GEN/LAWS

B55
FRIEDMAN G.,INDUSTRIAL SOCIETY: THE EMERGENCE OF THE HUMAN PROBLEMS OF AUTOMATION. UNIV CULTURE ECO/DEV TEC/DEV INGP/REL HAPPINESS RATIONAL UTOPIA ROLE...HUM SOC TIME/SEQ 20. PAGE 53 H1064 — AUTOMAT ADJUST ALL/VALS CONCPT

C55
SANTAYANA G.,"REASON IN SOCIETY" IN G. SANTAYANA, THE LIFE OF REASON." INDUS FAM NAT/G WAR GP/REL HAPPINESS PRODUC LOVE WEALTH CONSERVE POPULISM CONCPT. PAGE 138 H2752 — RATIONAL SOCIETY CULTURE ATTIT

B61
COBBAN A.,ROUSSEAU AND THE MODERN STATE. SOCIETY DOMIN INGP/REL HAPPINESS ALL/VALS...CON/ANAL 18/20 ROUSSEAU/J. PAGE 30 H0611 — ORD/FREE ROLE NAT/G POLICY

B62
WALSTON H.,AGRICULTURE UNDER COMMUNISM. CHINA/COM COM PROB/SOLV HAPPINESS RIGID/FLEX...POLICY METH/COMP 20. PAGE 165 H3295 — AGRI MARXISM PLAN CREATE

B64
PARANJAPE H.K.,THE FLIGHT OF TECHNICAL PERSONNEL IN PUBLIC UNDERTAKINGS. INDIA PAY DEMAND HAPPINESS ORD/FREE...MGT QU 20 MIGRATION. PAGE 123 H2464 — ADMIN NAT/G WORKER PLAN

B67
FANON F.,BLACK SKIN, WHITE MASKS: THE EXPERIENCES OF A BLACK MAN IN A WHITE WORLD. CULTURE COLONIAL HAPPINESS ISOLAT STRANGE ATTIT HABITAT RIGID/FLEX SEX...BIOG STERTYP SOC/INTEG 20 NEGRO. PAGE 49 H0970 — DISCRIM PERS/REL RACE/REL PSY

B91
BENTHAM J.,A FRAGMENT ON GOVERNMENT (1776). CONSTN MUNIC NAT/G SECT AGREE HAPPINESS UTIL MORAL ORD/FREE...JURID CONCPT. PAGE 15 H0292 — SOVEREIGN LAW DOMIN

HAPSBURG....HAPSBURG MONARCHY

HAPTHEKER....HAPTHEKER THEORY

HAQ M. H1324

HARBISON F.H. H1325,H1326

HARBRON J.D. H1327

HARDING J.S. H1868

HARDING/WG....PRESIDENT WARREN G. HARDING

HARDT J.P. H1328

HARDY M.J.L. H1329

HARE T. H1330

HARGIS/BJ....BILLY JAMES HARGIS

HARIOU M. H1331

HARLAN/JM....JOHN MARSHALL HARLAN

HARLEM....HARLEM

HARLEY G.W. H1332

HARLOW R.V. H1333

HARMON R.B. H1334,H1335

HARNON E. H1336

HAROOTUNIAN H.D. H2873

HARPER S.N. H1337

HARRIMAN/A....AVERILL HARRIMAN

HARRINGTON M. H1338

HARRIS G.M. H1339

HARRIS M. H1340,H1341,H1342

HARRIS R.L. H1343,H1344,H1345

HARRISN/WH....PRESIDENT WILLIAM HENRY HARRISON

HARRISON B. H1346

HARRISON S.S. H1347

HARRISON/B....PRESIDENT BENJAMIN HARRISON

HART B.H.L. H1348

HARTLEY A. H1349

HARTUNG F. H1350

HARVARD WIDENER LIBRARY H1351

HARVARD/U....HARVARD UNIVERSITY

HARWITZ M. H1408

HASSAN M.F. H1352

HATCH J.C. H1533,H1534

HATCHER/R....RICHARD HATCHER

HATRED....SEE LOVE

HATTERSLEY A.F. H1355

HATTICH M. H1356

HAUSER M. H1357

HAUSER O. H1358

HAUSER P. H1359

HAUSER R. H1360

HAUSHOFER K. H1361

HAVIGHURST R.J. H1362

HAWAII....HAWAII

HAWTREY R. H1363

HAY P. H1364

HAY S.N. H1365

HAYAKAWA S.I. H1366

HAYCRAFT J. H1367

HAYEK/V....FRIEDRICH AUGUST VON HAYEK

HAYES/RB....PRESIDENT RUTHERFORD B. HAYES

HAYTER T. H1370

HAZARD B.H. H1371

HAZARD H.W. H2996

HAZARD J.N. H1372,H1373

HAZLEWOOD A. H1374

HEAD/START....THE "HEAD START" PROGRAM

HEADLAM-MORLEY H1375

HEADY F. H1376

HEAL....HEALTH SCIENCES

N
AUSTRALIAN NATIONAL RES COUN,AUSTRALIAN SOCIAL SCIENCE ABSTRACTS. NEW/ZEALND CULTURE SOCIETY LOC/G CT/SYS PARL/PROC...HEAL JURID PSY SOC 20 AUSTRAL. PAGE 9 H0181
BIBLIOG/A POLICY NAT/G ADMIN

N
AUSTRALIAN PUBLIC AFFAIRS INFORMATION SERVICE. LAW ...HEAL HUM MGT SOC CON/ANAL 20 AUSTRAL. PAGE 1 H0011
BIBLIOG NAT/G CULTURE DIPLOM

N
US LIBRARY OF CONGRESS,SOUTHERN ASIA ACCESSIONS LIST. BURMA CEYLON INDIA NEPAL PAKISTAN S/ASIA THAILAND AGRI INDUS SCHOOL WORKER...ART/METH GEOG HEAL PHIL/SCI LING 20. PAGE 160 H3201
BIBLIOG/A SOCIETY CULTURE ECO/UNDEV

B39
HILL R.L.,A BIBLIOGRAPHY OF THE ANGLO-EGYPTIAN SUDAN FROM THE EARLIEST TIMES TO 1937. AFR ETHIOPIA SUDAN UAR LAW COM/IND SECT RACE/REL...GEOG HEAL SOC LING 19/20 NEGRO. PAGE 71 H1417
BIBLIOG CULTURE NAT/COMP GP/COMP

B41
KEESING F.M.,THE SOUTH SEAS IN THE MODERN WORLD. INDONESIA STRUCT FAM SECT EDU/PROP LEAD INCOME WEALTH...HEAL SOC 20. PAGE 84 H1678
CULTURE ECO/UNDEV GOV/COMP DIPLOM

B56
READ M.,EDUCATION AND SOCIAL CHANGE IN TROPICAL AREAS. AFR L/A+17C SOCIETY LITERACY PERCEPT PERSON WEALTH...HEAL PHIL/SCI SOC 20. PAGE 130 H2603
EDU/PROP HABITAT DRIVE CULTURE

B57
CENTRAL ASIAN RESEARCH CENTRE,BIBLIOGRAPHY OF RECENT SOVIET SOURCE MATERIAL ON SOVIET CENTRAL ASIA AND THE BORDERLANDS. AFGHANISTN INDIA PAKISTAN UAR USSR ECO/UNDEV AGRI EXTR/IND INDUS ACADEM ADMIN ...HEAL HUM LING CON/ANAL 20. PAGE 28 H0567
BIBLIOG/A COM CULTURE NAT/G

B57
PLAYFAIR G.,THE OFFENDERS: THE CASE AGAINST LEGAL VENGEANCE. UNIV LAW SOCIETY NAT/G PROB/SOLV DEATH PERSON ORD/FREE...HEAL INT/LAW BIBLIOG 20 REFORMERS. PAGE 126 H2524
CRIME TEC/DEV SANCTION CT/SYS

C58
BLANCHARD W.,"THAILAND." THAILAND CULTURE AGRI FINAN INDUS FAM LABOR INT/TRADE ATTIT...GEOG HEAL SOC BIBLIOG 20. PAGE 18 H0354
NAT/G DIPLOM ECO/UNDEV S/ASIA

B64
WITHERELL J.W.,OFFICIAL PUBLICATIONS OF FRENCH EQUATORIAL AFRICA, FRENCH CAMEROONS, AND TOGO, 1946-1958 (PAMPHLET). CAMEROON CHAD FRANCE GABON TOGO LAW ECO/UNDEV EXTR/IND INT/TRADE...GEOG HEAL 20. PAGE 169 H3392
BIBLIOG/A AFR NAT/G ADMIN

L64
BERELSON B.,"SAMPLE SURVEYS AND POPULATION CONTROL." ASIA FUT ISLAM L/A+17C CULTURE SOCIETY FAM NAT/G CONSULT PLAN EDU/PROP ATTIT DRIVE ALL/VALS...POLICY RELATIV HEAL PSY SOC CONCPT METH/CNCPT OBS OBS/ENVIR TOT/POP. PAGE 15 H0297
BIO/SOC SAMP

B66
HOPKINS J.F.K.,ARABIC PERIODICAL LITERATURE, 1961. ISLAM LAW CULTURE SECT...GEOG HEAL PHIL/SCI PSY SOC 20. PAGE 73 H1466
BIBLIOG/A NAT/LISM TEC/DEV INDUS

B67
BADGLEY R.F.,DOCTORS' STRIKE; MEDICAL CARE AND CONFLICT IN SASKATCHEWAN. CANADA NAT/G PROF/ORG GP/REL ADJUST ATTIT...HEAL SOC 20. PAGE 10 H0192
HEALTH PLAN LABOR BARGAIN

B67
HODGKINSON R.G.,THE ORIGINS OF THE NATIONAL HEALTH SERVICE: THE MEDICAL SERVICES OF THE NEW POOR LAW, 1834-1871. UK INDUS MUNIC WORKER PROB/SOLV EFFICIENCY ATTIT HEALTH WEALTH SOCISM...JURID SOC/WK 19/20. PAGE 72 H1445
HEAL NAT/G POLICY LAW

B67
ROSENTHAL A.H.,THE SOCIAL PROGRAMS OF SWEDEN. SWEDEN USA+45 FINAN NAT/G PLAN PROB/SOLV INSPECT ORD/FREE...POLICY HEAL SOC CHARTS NAT/COMP 20. PAGE 134 H2681
GIVE SOC/WK WEALTH METH/COMP

S67
MARWICK A.,"THE LABOUR PARTY AND THE WELFARE STATE IN BRITAIN, 19001948." UK SOCIETY STRUCT ECO/DEV WORKER CREATE PRICE CHOOSE WEALTH NEW/LIB SOCISM ...POLICY HEAL 20 PARLIAMENT LABOR/PAR. PAGE 104 H2074
POL/PAR RECEIVE LEGIS NAT/G

HEALEY/D....DOROTHY HEALEY

HEALTH....WELL-BEING, BODILY AND PSYCHIC INTEGRITY

N
CANADIAN GOVERNMENT PUBLICATIONS (1955-). CANADA AGRI FINAN LABOR FORCES INT/TRADE HEALTH...JURID 20 PARLIAMENT. PAGE 1 H0003
BIBLIOG/A NAT/G DIPLOM INT/ORG

N
INDIA: A REFERENCE ANNUAL. INDIA CULTURE COM/IND R+D FORCES PLAN RECEIVE EDU/PROP HEALTH...STAT CHARTS BIBLIOG 20. PAGE 1 H0017
CONSTN LABOR INT/ORG

N
HOOVER INSTITUTION,UNITED STATES AND CANADIAN PUBLICATIONS ON AFRICA. CULTURE ECO/UNDEV AGRI TEC/DEV EDU/PROP COLONIAL RACE/REL NAT/LISM ATTIT HEALTH...SOC SOC/WK 20. PAGE 73 H1464
BIBLIOG DIPLOM NAT/G AFR

B05
PHILIPPINE ISLANDS BUREAU SCI,ETHNOLOGICAL SURVEY: THE BONTOC IGOROT. ECO/UNDEV AGRI FAM MARRIAGE HEALTH WEALTH...LING OBS AUD/VIS CHARTS WORSHIP 20 LUZON BONTOC. PAGE 125 H2500
CULTURE INGP/REL KIN STRUCT

B12
SONOLET L.,L'AFRIQUE OCCIDENTALE FRANCAISE. FRANCE AGRI INDUS NAT/G SECT FORCES INT/TRADE EDU/PROP RACE/REL HEALTH ORD/FREE...CHARTS 19/20 NEGRO AFRICA/W. PAGE 147 H2933
DOMIN ADMIN COLONIAL AFR

B13
KROPOTKIN P.,THE CONQUEST OF BREAD. SOCIETY STRATA AGRI INDUS WORKER REV HAPPINESS INCOME PRODUC HEALTH MORAL ORD/FREE. PAGE 89 H1775
ANARCH SOCIALIST OWN AGREE

B40
BROWN A.D.,PANAMA CANAL AND PANAMA CANAL ZONE: A SELECTED LIST OF REFERENCES. PANAMA NAT/G SCHOOL DIPLOM HEALTH...GEOG SOC 20 CANAL/ZONE. PAGE 22 H0436
BIBLIOG/A ECO/UNDEV

B40
ZWEIG F.,THE WORKER IN AN AFFLUENT SOCIETY: FAMILY LIFE AND INDUSTRY. UK STRATA LG/CO ECO/TAC LEISURE INGP/REL HAPPINESS HEALTH...PSY SOC/WK INT CHARTS WORSHIP 20 FEMALE/SEX. PAGE 173 H3465
MARRIAGE ATTIT FINAN CULTURE

B42
CONOVER H.F.,FRENCH COLONIES IN AFRICA: A LIST OF REFERENCES. ALGERIA FRANCE MOROCCO SOMALIA SUDAN CULTURE AGRI LOC/G SECT FORCES DIPLOM INT/TRADE NAT/LISM HEALTH...CON/ANAL 20. PAGE 32 H0641
BIBLIOG AFR ECO/UNDEV COLONIAL

B42
CONOVER H.F.,THE NETHERLANDS EAST INDIES: A SELECTED LIST OF REFERENCES. ECO/UNDEV AGRI EXTR/IND LABOR SCHOOL SECT INT/TRADE COLONIAL HEALTH...GEOG 19/20. PAGE 32 H0642
BIBLIOG S/ASIA CULTURE

B42
REDFIELD R.,THE FOLK CULTURE OF YUCATAN. STRATA FAM KIN MUNIC SECT DISCRIM ISOLAT ANOMIE HEALTH ...BIBLIOG 20 MEXIC/AMER. PAGE 130 H2605
CULTURE NEIGH GP/COMP SOCIETY

B45
US LIBRARY OF CONGRESS,NETHERLANDS EAST INDIES. INDONESIA LAW CULTURE AGRI INDUS SCHOOL COLONIAL HEALTH...GEOG JURID SOC 19/20 NETH/IND. PAGE 160 H3205
BIBLIOG/A S/ASIA NAT/G

S48
ALEXANDER L.,"WAR CRIMES, THEIR SOCIAL-PSYCHOLOGICAL ASPECTS." EUR+WWI GERMANY LAW CULTURE ELITES KIN POL/PAR PUB/INST FORCES DOMIN EDU/PROP COERCE CRIME ATTIT SUPEGO HEALTH MORAL PWR FASCISM
DRIVE WAR

...PSY OBS TREND GEN/LAWS NAZI 20. PAGE 5 H0100

B50
JONES H.D.,KOREA, AN ANNOTATED BIBLIOGRAPHY OF PUBLICATIONS IN WESTERN LANGUAGES. KOREA CULTURE MUNIC SECT FORCES DIPLOM HEALTH WEALTH...ART/METH GEOG SOC LING 20. PAGE 82 H1632
BIBLIOG/A ASIA NAT/G ECO/UNDEV

C50
ROUSSEAU J.J.,"A DISCOURSE ON POLITICAL ECONOMY" (1755) IN THE SOCIAL CONTRACT AND DISCOURSES." UNIV SOCIETY STRATA STRUCT CONSEN EQUILIB HAPPINESS UTOPIA HEALTH WEALTH...POLICY WELF/ST. PAGE 135 H2699
NAT/G ECO/TAC TAX GEN/LAWS

B52
ROBBINS L.,THE THEORY OF ECONOMIC POLICY IN ENGLISH CLASSICAL POLITICAL ECONOMY. UK ECO/DEV WORKER PLAN CAP/ISM EDU/PROP CONTROL INCOME OWN HEALTH SOCISM ...POLICY 17/19. PAGE 132 H2639
ECO/TAC ORD/FREE IDEA/COMP NAT/G

B53
MEAD M.,CULTURAL PATTERNS AND TECHNICAL CHANGE. BURMA GREECE NIGERIA ECO/UNDEV AGRI INDUS SCHOOL SECT CREATE FEEDBACK HABITAT...PSY METH/COMP BIBLIOG 20 UN. PAGE 108 H2152
HEALTH TEC/DEV CULTURE ADJUST

B53
MEYER P.,THE JEWS IN THE SOVIET SATELLITES. CZECHOSLVK POLAND SOCIETY STRATA NAT/G BAL/PWR ECO/TAC EDU/PROP LEGIT ADMIN COERCE ATTIT DISPL PERCEPT HEALTH PWR RESPECT WEALTH...METH/CNCPT JEWS VAL/FREE NAZI 20. PAGE 110 H2192
COM SECT TOTALISM USSR

B53
NELSON G.R.,FREEDOM AND WELFARE: SOCIAL PATTERNS IN THE NORTHERN COUNTRIES OF EUROPE. EUR+WWI ECO/DEV NAT/G EDU/PROP LEGIT HEALTH ORD/FREE SKILL WEALTH ...STAT AUD/VIS SCANDINAV WORK TOT/POP 20. PAGE 116 H2329
PLAN ECO/TAC

B56
INTERNATIONAL AFRICAN INST,SELECT ANNOTATED BIBLIOGRAPHY OF TROPICAL AFRICA. NAT/G EDU/PROP ADMIN HEALTH. PAGE 77 H1547
BIBLIOG/A AFR SOC HABITAT

N56
US HOUSE COMM FOREIGN AFFAIRS,REPORT OF THE SPECIAL STUDY MISSION TO AFRICA, SOUTH AND EAST OF THE SAHARA (PAMPHLET). AFR SOUTH/AFR USA+45 STRUCT INT/TRADE PARL/PROC NAT/LISM ATTIT ALL/VALS HEALTH ...POLICY 20 CONGRESS. PAGE 160 H3197
FOR/AID COLONIAL ECO/UNDEV DIPLOM

B57
LOOMIS C.P.,RURAL SOCIOLOGY. CULTURE KIN NAT/G SECT VOL/ASSN ACT/RES EDU/PROP HEALTH. PAGE 98 H1963
SOC AGRI METH T

S57
DEXTER L.A.,"A SOCIAL THEORY OF MENTAL DEFICIENCY." CULTURE PUB/INST PROB/SOLV CRIME PERS/REL STRANGE PERSON SUPEGO SKILL...EPIST SOC/WK HYPO/EXP. PAGE 41 H0814
SOC PSY HEALTH ROLE

B58
SCOTT J.P.,AGGRESSION. CULTURE FAM SCHOOL ATTIT DISPL HEALTH...SOC CONCPT NEW/IDEA CHARTS LAB/EXP. PAGE 141 H2814
DRIVE PSY WAR

B59
DUNHAM H.W.,SOCIOLOGICAL THEORY AND MENTAL DISORDER. UNIV SOCIETY STRATA HABITAT PERSON...GEOG CHARTS SOC/EXP TIME. PAGE 43 H0864
HEALTH SOC PSY CULTURE

B59
GINSBURG M.,LAW AND OPINION IN ENGLAND. UK CULTURE KIN LABOR LEGIS EDU/PROP ADMIN CT/SYS CRIME OWN HEALTH...ANTHOL 20 ENGLSH/LAW. PAGE 56 H1132
JURID POLICY ECO/TAC

B59
KITTLER G.D.,EQUATORIAL AFRICA: THE NEW WORLD OF TOMORROW. CENTRL/AFR INDUS KIN SECT CHIEF EDU/PROP CHOOSE HEALTH...GEOG WORSHIP 20. PAGE 87 H1730
RACE/REL AFR ECO/UNDEV CULTURE

B59
LEIGHTON A.H.,MY NAME IS LEGION; FOUNDATIONS FOR A THEORY OF MAN IN RELATION TO CULTURE (VOL. I). CULTURE STRANGE ANOMIE...SOC CONCPT METH/CNCPT CHARTS BIBLIOG METH 20 NOVA/SCOT. PAGE 93 H1867
HEALTH PSY SOCIETY HABITAT

S59
MCNEIL E.B.,"PSYCHOLOGY AND AGGRESSION." CULTURE SOCIETY ACT/RES DISPL PERSON HEALTH. PAGE 107 H2146
DRIVE PSY

B60
BRIGGS L.C.,TRIBES OF THE SAHARA. AFR MOROCCO STRATA AGRI GP/REL HEALTH...GEOG SOC MYTH LING BIBLIOG 13/20 ARABS. PAGE 21 H0418
CULTURE HABITAT KIN SELF/OBS

B60
HUGHES C.C.,PEOPLE OF COVE AND WOODLOT; COMMUNITIES FROM THE VIEWPOINT OF SOCIAL PSYCHIATRY. CULTURE FAM PROVS HABITAT...PSY QU SAMP/SIZ CHARTS BIBLIOG 20. PAGE 74 H1489
GEOG SOCIETY STRUCT HEALTH

S60
"THE EMERGING COMMON MARKETS IN LATIN AMERICA." FUT L/A+17C STRATA DIST/IND INDUS LABOR NAT/G LEGIS ECO/TAC ADMIN RIGID/FLEX HEALTH...NEW/IDEA TIME/SEQ OAS 20. PAGE 2 H0038
FINAN ECO/UNDEV INT/TRADE

S60
JAFFEE A.J.,"POPULATION TRENDS AND CONTROLS IN UNDERDEVELOPED COUNTRIES." AFR FUT ISLAM L/A+17C S/ASIA CULTURE R+D FAM ACT/RES PLAN EDU/PROP BIO/SOC RIGID/FLEX HEALTH...SOC STAT OBS CHARTS 20. PAGE 79 H1582
ECO/UNDEV GEOG

S60
TAYLOR M.G.,"THE ROLE OF THE MEDICAL PROFESSION IN THE FORMULATION AND EXECUTION OF PUBLIC POLICY" (BMR)" CANADA NAT/G CONSULT ADMIN REPRESENT GP/REL ROLE SOVEREIGN...DECISION 20 CMA. PAGE 153 H3056
PROF/ORG HEALTH LOBBY POLICY

B61
BERKOWITZ L.,AGGRESSION: AS A SOCIAL PSYCHOLOGICAL ANALYSIS. UNIV CULTURE FACE/GP FAM KIN NEIGH EDU/PROP DISPL DRIVE HEALTH LOVE ORD/FREE...PSY SOC CONCPT OBS TREND. PAGE 15 H0305
SOCIETY COERCE WAR

B61
INTL UNION LOCAL AUTHORITIES,METROPOLIS. WOR+45 DIST/IND FINAN GIVE EDU/PROP CRIME COST HEALTH WEALTH 20. PAGE 78 H1563
MUNIC GOV/COMP LOC/G BIBLIOG

B62
INSTITUTE FOR STUDY OF USSR,YOUTH IN FERMENT. INTELL NAT/G PERF/ART POL/PAR SCHOOL VOL/ASSN FORCES EDU/PROP ATTIT DRIVE PERCEPT HEALTH KNOWL MORAL ORD/FREE RESPECT...SOC OBS HIST/WRIT VAL/FREE. PAGE 77 H1537
COM CULTURE USSR

B62
KIDDER F.E.,THESES ON PAN AMERICAN TOPICS. LAW CULTURE NAT/G SECT DIPLOM HEALTH...ART/METH GEOG SOC 13/20. PAGE 86 H1709
BIBLIOG CHRIST-17C L/A+17C SOCIETY

B63
CARTER G.M.,FIVE AFRICAN STATES: RESPONSES TO DIVERSITY. CONSTN CULTURE STRATA LEGIS PLAN ECO/TAC DOMIN EDU/PROP CT/SYS EXEC CHOOSE ATTIT HEALTH ORD/FREE PWR...TIME/SEQ TOT/POP VAL/FREE. PAGE 27 H0547
AFR SOCIETY

B63
DE VRIES E.,SOCIAL ASPECTS OF ECONOMIC DEVELOPMENT IN LATIN AMERICA. CULTURE SOCIETY STRATA FINAN INDUS INT/ORG DELIB/GP ACT/RES ECO/TAC EDU/PROP ADMIN ATTIT SUPEGO HEALTH KNOWL ORD/FREE...SOC STAT TREND ANTHOL TOT/POP VAL/FREE. PAGE 39 H0777
L/A+17C ECO/UNDEV

B63
DRIVER H.E.,ETHNOGRAPHY AND ACCULTURATION OF THE CHICHIMECA-JONAZ OF NORTHEAST MEXICO. ECO/UNDEV AGRI FAM KIN EDU/PROP MARRIAGE HEALTH...GEOG INT CHARTS WORSHIP 18/20 MEXIC/AMER. PAGE 42 H0848
CULTURE HABITAT STRUCT GP/REL

B63
ELWIN V.,A NEW DEAL FOR TRIBAL INDIA. INDIA AGRI COM/IND INDUS KIN TEC/DEV TAX EDU/PROP OWN HEALTH 20. PAGE 46 H0912
ECO/UNDEV CULTURE CONSTN SOC/WK

B63
GLADE W.P. JR.,THE POLITICAL ECONOMY OF MEXICO. FUT L/A+17C CULTURE SOCIETY AGRI INDUS DELIB/GP ACT/RES ECO/TAC ATTIT HEALTH ORD/FREE...STAT TIME/SEQ TREND MEXIC/AMER TOT/POP VAL/FREE 20. PAGE 57 H1138
FINAN ECO/UNDEV

B63
LEIGHTON D.C.,THE CHARACTER OF DANGER (VOL. III). SOCIETY STRUCT STRANGE ANOMIE...SOC STAT CHARTS GP/COMP SOC/EXP SOC/INTEG 20 NOVA/SCOT. PAGE 94 H1868
HEALTH PSY CULTURE

B63
PRICE A.G.,THE WESTERN INVASIONS OF THE PACIFIC AND ITS CONTINENTS. ASIA PRE/AMER S/ASIA ECO/UNDEV KIN NAT/G SECT FORCES DOMIN HEALTH...SOC 16/20. PAGE 128 H2560
COLONIAL CULTURE GEOG HABITAT

L63
CORWIN A.F.,"CONTEMPORARY MEXICAN ATTITUDES TOWARD POPULATION, POVERTY, AND PUBLIC OPINION." L/A+17C CULTURE SOCIETY ACT/RES ECO/TAC EDU/PROP PERSON HEALTH KNOWL...GEOG PHIL/SCI STAT OBS INT SAMP MEXIC/AMER VAL/FREE 20. PAGE 34 H0672
ATTIT QU

L63
JAY R.,"RELIGION AND POLITICS IN RURAL CENTRAL JAVA." S/ASIA SOCIETY NEIGH SECT PERSON HEALTH MORAL...SOC UNPLAN/INT TIME/SEQ JAVA VAL/FREE 20 WORSHIP. PAGE 80 H1594
CULTURE OBS

L63
NASH M.,"PSYCHO-CULTURAL FACTORS IN ASIAN ECONOMIC GROWTH." ASIA ISLAM S/ASIA CULTURE ECO/UNDEV DELIB/GP EDU/PROP COERCE ATTIT PERSON HEALTH KNOWL ORD/FREE...PSY SOC STAT TREND ANTHOL VAL/FREE 20. PAGE 116 H2313
SOCIETY ECO/TAC

S63
TILMAN R.O.,"MALAYSIA: THE PROBLEMS OF FEDERATION." ISLAM S/ASIA CONSTN PROVS SECT DELIB/GP DOMIN EDU/PROP LEGIT EXEC COERCE CHOOSE ATTIT HEALTH ORD/FREE PWR...STAT TOT/POP VAL/FREE 20. PAGE 155 H3097
NAT/G CULTURE MALAYSIA

B64
CURTIN P.D.,THE IMAGE OF AFRICA: BRITISH IDEAS AND ACTION, 1780-1850. MOD/EUR SOCIETY FORCES ACT/RES DOMIN EDU/PROP COERCE ATTIT PERCEPT RIGID/FLEX
AFR CULTURE UK

SUPEGO HEALTH KNOWL MORAL ORD/FREE WEALTH...CONCPT WORK VAL/FREE. PAGE 36 H0726 DIPLOM

B64
DEL VAYO J.A.,CHINA TRIUMPHS. CHINA/COM CULTURE DIPLOM HEALTH 20. PAGE 39 H0787 MARXISM CREATE ORD/FREE POLICY

B64
HUXLEY M.,FAREWILL TO EDEN. SOCIETY ACT/RES EDU/PROP HEALTH...SOC AUD/VIS. PAGE 76 H1513 ECO/UNDEV SECT CULTURE ADJUST

B64
JOHNSON A.F.,BIBLIOGRAPHY OF GHANA: 1930-1961. GHANA LAW AGRI INDUS NAT/G INT/TRADE EDU/PROP HEALTH...GEOG AUD/VIS CHARTS 20. PAGE 81 H1618 BIBLIOG/A CULTURE SOC

B64
THORNBURG M.W.,PEOPLE AND POLICY IN THE MIDDLE EAST. ISLAM ECO/UNDEV FAM KIN MUNIC NAT/G NEIGH POL/PAR SECT DELIB/GP LEGIS PLAN ECO/TAC DOMIN ADMIN ATTIT HEALTH RESPECT...SOC CONCPT METH/CNCPT OBS TIME/SEQ TOT/POP VAL/FREE. PAGE 154 H3088 TEC/DEV CULTURE

B64
WRIGHT G.,RURAL REVOLUTION IN FRANCE: THE PEASANTRY IN THE TWENTIETH CENTURY. EUR+WWI MOD/EUR LAW CULTURE AGRI POL/PAR DELIB/GP LEGIS ECO/TAC EDU/PROP COERCE CHOOSE ATTIT RIGID/FLEX HEALTH ...STAT CENSUS CHARTS VAL/FREE 20. PAGE 171 H3419 PWR STRATA FRANCE REV

S64
LEVI W.,"INDIAN NEUTRALISM RECONSIDERED." ASIA CHINA/COM S/ASIA SOCIETY NAT/G ACT/RES LEGIT NEUTRAL COERCE ATTIT DRIVE PERCEPT RIGID/FLEX HEALTH LOVE PWR...DECISION RECORD TREND STERTYP 20. PAGE 95 H1896 ORD/FREE CONCPT INDIA

B65
APPLEMAN P.,THE SILENT EXPLOSION. WOR+45 ECO/DEV ECO/UNDEV PLAN HEALTH ALL/IDEOS CATHISM...POLICY STAT RECORD GP/COMP IDEA/COMP NAT/COMP 20 BIRTH/CON COM/PARTY. PAGE 7 H0148 GEOG CENSUS AGRI BIO/SOC

B65
HANSER C.J.,GUIDE TO DECISION: ROYAL COMMISSION. UK INTELL EXTR/IND SCHOOL PROB/SOLV EXEC ROUTINE CHOOSE GOV/REL GP/REL HEALTH...CHARTS 20. PAGE 66 H1318 NAT/G DELIB/GP EX/STRUC PWR

B65
KUNSTADTER P.,THE LUA (LAWA) OF NORTHERN THAILAND: ASPECTS OF SOCIAL STRUCTURE, AGRICULTURE, AND RELIGION. THAILAND AGRI FAM KIN INGP/REL ISOLAT MARRIAGE HEALTH WORSHIP 20 BUDDHISM LUA. PAGE 89 H1780 STRUCT ECO/UNDEV CULTURE

B65
UN,SPACE ACTIVITIES AND RESOURCES: REVIEW OF UNITED NATION'S NATIONAL AND INTERNATIONAL PROGRAMS. INT/ORG LABOR PLAN TEC/DEV DIPLOM EFFICIENCY HEALTH ...GOV/COMP 20 UN. PAGE 158 H3155 SPACE NUC/PWR FOR/AID PEACE

L65
WIONCZEK M.,"LATIN AMERICA FREE TRADE ASSOCIATION." AGRI DIST/IND FINAN INDUS INT/ORG LABOR NAT/G TEC/DEV ECO/TAC HEALTH SKILL WEALTH...POLICY RELATIV MGT LAFTA 20. PAGE 169 H3390 L/A+17C MARKET REGION

S66
QUESTER G.H.,"ON THE IDENTIFICATION OF REAL AND PRETENDED COMMUNIST MILITARY DOCTRINE." ASIA USSR DETER WAR ATTIT DRIVE HEALTH TIME/SEQ. PAGE 129 H2574 RATIONAL PERCEPT NUC/PWR NAT/COMP

B67
BADGLEY R.F.,DOCTORS' STRIKE; MEDICAL CARE AND CONFLICT IN SASKATCHEWAN. CANADA NAT/G PROF/ORG GP/REL ADJUST ATTIT...HEAL SOC 20. PAGE 10 H0192 HEALTH PLAN LABOR BARGAIN

B67
DAVIDSON E.,THE TRIAL OF THE GERMANS* NUREMBERG* 1946-48. EUR+WWI GERMANY CULTURE NAT/G LEAD PERSON HEALTH...CRIMLGY PSY SOC BIOG JEWS. PAGE 37 H0745 FASCISM ADJUD TOTALISM WAR

B67
FIELD M.G.,SOVIET SOCIALIZED MEDICINE. USSR FINAN R+D PROB/SOLV ADMIN SOCISM...MGT SOC CONCPT 20. PAGE 50 H0993 PUB/INST HEALTH NAT/G MARXISM

B67
HODGKINSON R.G.,THE ORIGINS OF THE NATIONAL HEALTH SERVICE: THE MEDICAL SERVICES OF THE NEW POOR LAW, 1834-1871. UK INDUS MUNIC WORKER PROB/SOLV EFFICIENCY ATTIT HEALTH WEALTH SOCISM...JURID SOC/WK 19/20. PAGE 72 H1445 HEAL NAT/G POLICY LAW

S67
SLOAN P.,"FIFTY YEARS OF SOVIET RULE." USSR INDUS EDU/PROP EFFICIENCY PRODUC HEALTH KNOWL MORAL WEALTH MARXISM...POLICY 20. PAGE 145 H2900 CREATE NAT/G PLAN INSPECT

B82
MACDONALD D.,AFRICANA; OR, THE HEART OF HEATHEN AFRICA, VOL. II: MISSION LIFE. SOCIETY STRATA KIN CREATE EDU/PROP ADMIN COERCE LITERACY HEALTH...MYTH WORSHIP 19 LIVNGSTN/D MISSION NEGRO. PAGE 100 H1990 SECT AFR CULTURE ORD/FREE

C93
PLAYFAIR R.L.,"A BIBLIOGRAPHY OF MOROCCO." MOROCCO CULTURE AGRI FORCES DIPLOM WAR HEALTH...GEOG JURID SOC CHARTS. PAGE 126 H2526 BIBLIOG ISLAM MEDIT-7

B99
KINGSLEY M.H.,WEST AFRICAN STUDIES. GHANA NIGERIA SIER/LEONE LAW EXTR/IND SECT DIPLOM INT/TRADE DOMIN RACE/REL OWN HEALTH...SOC 19. PAGE 86 H1717 AFR HEREDITY COLONIAL CULTURE

HEAPHEY J. H1377

HEASMAN D.J. H1378

HEATH D.B. H1379

HEBAL J.J. H1380

HECKSCHER G. H1382

HEGEL G.W.F. H1383

HEGEL/G....GEORG WILHELM FRIEDRICH HEGEL

B45
CROCE B.,POLITICS AND MORALS. UNIV NAT/G ECO/TAC ORD/FREE MARXISM POPULISM SOCISM...REALPOL 15/20 HEGEL/GWF ROUSSEAU/J. PAGE 35 H0704 MORAL GEN/LAWS IDEA/COMP

B46
CASSIRER E.,THE MYTH OF THE STATE. WOR-45 SOCIETY RACE/REL RATIONAL PWR FASCISM...PHIL/SCI PSY LING TREND HEGEL/GWF MACHIAVELL. PAGE 28 H0557 MYTH CONCPT NAT/G IDEA/COMP

B63
STRAUSS L.,HISTORY OF POLITICAL PHILOSOPHY. LAW SOCIETY CAP/ISM MARXISM 19 AQUINAS/T BACON/F HEGEL/GWF MILL/JS NIETZSCH/F. PAGE 150 H2995 IDEA/COMP PHIL/SCI ANTHOL

B64
FROMM E.,MARX'S CONCEPT OF MAN. LABOR OWN PERSON ...HUM IDEA/COMP GEN/LAWS 17 MARX/KARL EUROPE SPINOZA/B GOETHE/J HEGEL/GWF. PAGE 54 H1072 INGP/REL CONCPT MARXISM SOCISM

S68
HOOK S.,"THE ENLIGHTENMENT AND MARXISM." CULTURE SOCIETY RATIONAL ORD/FREE PLURISM SOCISM...CONCPT HIST/WRIT 18/19 MARX/KARL HEGEL/GWF ENLIGHTNMT. PAGE 73 H1462 IDEA/COMP MARXISM OBJECTIVE

HEIDENHEIMER A. H2674

HEILBRNR/R....ROBERT HEILBRONER

HEIMANN E. H1384

HEIMSATH C.H. H1385

HEINBERG J.G. H1386

HEINSIUS W. H1387

HELANDER S. H1388

HELLMAN F.S. H0438

HELMREICH E.C. H1389,H1390

HEMMERLE J. H1391

HEMPSTONE S. H1392

HENDEL S. H1393

HENDERSON G.P. H1394

HENDERSON W.O. H1395

HENKYS R. H1396

HENLE P. H1397

HENNIG P. H1398

HERBST J. H1399

HERDER/J....JOHANN GOTTFRIED VON HERDER

HEREDITY....GENETIC INFLUENCES ON PERSONALITY DEVELOPMENT AND SOCIAL GROWTH

B21
WALLAS G.,HUMAN NATURE IN POLITICS (3RD ED.). UNIV NAT/G LEAD CHOOSE REPRESENT GP/REL NAT/LISM PSY DRIVE

RATIONAL BIO/SOC HEREDITY ALL/VALS MAJORIT. PAGE 165 H3293 — PERSON

B22
FICHTE J.G.,ADDRESSES TO THE GERMAN NATION. GERMANY PRUSSIA ELITES NAT/G SECT CREATE INT/TRADE HEREDITY ...ART/METH LING 19 FRANK/PARL. PAGE 50 H0989 — NAT/LISM CULTURE EDU/PROP REGION

B25
MAURRAS C.,ENQUETE SUR LA MONARCHIE (1909). FRANCE CONTROL REPRESENT DISCRIM HEREDITY PWR CONSERVE 20 BUREAUCRCY. PAGE 105 H2103 — TRADIT AUTHORIT NAT/G CHIEF

B31
KROEBER A.L.,SOURCE BOOK IN ANTHROPOLOGY. PREHIST SECT RACE/REL...LING GP/COMP ANTHOL. PAGE 89 H1770 — SOC HEREDITY CULTURE ALL/VALS

B47
LOCKE J.,TWO TREATISES OF GOVERNMENT (1690). UK LAW SOCIETY LEGIS LEGIT AGREE REV OWN HEREDITY MORAL CONSERVE...POLICY MAJORIT 17 WILLIAM/3 NATURL/LAW. PAGE 97 H1946 — CONCPT ORD/FREE NAT/G CONSEN

C50
ROUSSEAU J.J.,"DISCOURSE ON THE ORIGIN OF INEQUALITY" (1755) IN THE SOCIAL CONTRACT AND DISCOURSES." UNIV NAT/G PLAN BAL/PWR HAPPINESS UTOPIA BIO/SOC HEREDITY MORAL...WELF/ST CONCPT. PAGE 135 H2698 — SOCIETY STRUCT PERSON GEN/LAWS

B51
INTERNATIONAL AFRICAN INST,ETHNOGRAPHIC SURVEY OF AFRICA: WEST CENTRAL AFRICA (VOLS. I-III, 1951-1953). AFR RHODESIA CULTURE ECO/UNDEV HEREDITY ...GEOG SOC CHARTS BIBLIOG WORSHIP 20 CONGO/LEOP. PAGE 77 H1543 — STRUCT KIN INGP/REL HABITAT

B52
INTERNATIONAL AFRICAN INST,ETHNOGRAPHIC SURVEY OF AFRICA: SOUTHERN AFRICA (VOLS. I-III, 1952-1954). AFR SOUTH/AFR CULTURE ECO/UNDEV GOV/REL HEREDITY ...GEOG SOC CHARTS BIBLIOG WORSHIP 20. PAGE 77 H1544 — STRUCT KIN INGP/REL HABITAT

B54
TITIEV M.,THE SCIENCE OF MAN. LAW STRATA KIN GP/REL PERS/REL HABITAT HEREDITY KNOWL...LING CHARTS BIBLIOG WORSHIP. PAGE 155 H3107 — SOC PSY CULTURE

B55
INTERNATIONAL AFRICAN INST,ETHNOGRAPHIC SURVEY OF AFRICA: NORTH EASTERN AFRICA (VOLUMES 1-2, 1955-56). AFR ETHIOPIA CULTURE ECO/UNDEV KIN GOV/REL ATTIT HEREDITY...GEOG CHARTS BIBLIOG WORSHIP 20. PAGE 77 H1545 — STRUCT ECO/TAC INGP/REL HABITAT

B55
INTERNATIONAL AFRICAN INST,ETHNOGRAPHIC SURVEY OF AFRICA: WESTERN AFRICA: PEOPLES OF THE NIGER-BENUE CONFLUENCE. AFR NIGER CULTURE ECO/UNDEV KIN GOV/REL GP/REL ATTIT HEREDITY...CHARTS BIBLIOG WORSHIP 20. PAGE 77 H1546 — STRUCT GEOG HABITAT INGP/REL

B56
DEUTSCH K.W.,AN INTERDISCIPLINARY BIBLIOGRAPHY ON NATIONALISM, 1935-1953. CULTURE SOCIETY SECT ATTIT HABITAT HEREDITY PERCEPT ROLE WEALTH...METH/CNCPT LING 20. PAGE 40 H0798 — BIBLIOG/A NAT/LISM COLONIAL ADJUST

B56
MUMFORD L.,THE TRANSFORMATIONS OF MAN. UNIV CULTURE INGP/REL HABITAT HEREDITY ALL/VALS ORD/FREE...MYTH TIME/SEQ TREND WORSHIP. PAGE 114 H2287 — IDEA/COMP PERSON CONCPT

B57
INTERNATIONAL AFRICAN INST,ETHNOGRAPHIC SURVEY OF AFRICA: WESTERN AFRICA: THE BENIN KINGDOM. AFR NIGERIA CULTURE ECO/UNDEV KIN ECO/TAC GOV/REL AGE ATTIT HEREDITY...CHARTS BIBLIOG WORSHIP 20. PAGE 77 H1550 — STRUCT INGP/REL GEOG HABITAT

B60
INTERNATIONAL AFRICAN INST,ETHNOGRAPHIC SURVEY OF AFRICA: WESTERN AFRICA: PEOPLES OF THE MIDDLE NIGER REGION, NORTHERN NIGERIA. AFR NIGER CULTURE ECO/UNDEV KIN NEIGH GOV/REL GP/REL ATTIT HEREDITY ...CHARTS BIBLIOG WORSHIP 20. PAGE 78 H1552 — STRUCT GEOG HABITAT INGP/REL

B60
KEPHART C.,RACES OF MAN. GP/REL HABITAT...LING SOC/INTEG 20 MIGRATION MISCEGEN. PAGE 85 H1692 — CULTURE RACE/REL HEREDITY GEOG

B60
OTTENBERG S.,CULTURES AND SOCIETIES OF AFRICA. AFR KIN TEC/DEV GP/REL MARRIAGE ATTIT HABITAT HEREDITY ...ANTHOL BIBLIOG T WORSHIP 20. PAGE 122 H2433 — SOCIETY INGP/REL STRUCT CULTURE

S60
BERREMAN G.D.,"CASTE IN INDIA AND THE UNITED STATES" (BMR)" INDIA USA+45 CULTURE SOCIETY STRUCT SECT GP/REL DISCRIM HEREDITY...SOC STERTYP 20 NEGRO HINDU. PAGE 16 H0318 — STRATA RACE/REL NAT/COMP ATTIT

B61
TURNBULL C.M.,THE FOREST PEOPLE. EATING GP/REL INGP/REL RACE/REL ISOLAT HABITAT HEREDITY...GEOG SOC LING DICTIONARY WORSHIP 20 CONGO NEGRO BA/MBUTI. PAGE 157 H3138 — AFR CULTURE KIN RECORD

B62
MICHAEL H.N.,STUDIES IN SIBERIAN ETHNOGENESIS. USSR KIN...ART/METH SOC 20 SIBERIA. PAGE 110 H2196 — HABITAT HEREDITY CULTURE LING

B62
SMITH M.G.,KINSHIP AND COMMUNITY IN CARRIACOU. WEST/IND STRATA AGRI FAM SECT WORKER MARRIAGE OWN HEREDITY WEALTH...SOC 18/20. PAGE 146 H2915 — CULTURE HABITAT KIN STRUCT

B63
CONFERENCE ABORIGINAL STUDIES,AUSTRALIAN ABORIGINAL STUDIES. ECO/UNDEV INT/TRADE COLONIAL ADJUST HABITAT HEREDITY...GEOG PSY LING SOC/EXP ANTHOL WORSHIP 20 AUSTRAL ABORIGINES. PAGE 32 H0638 — SOC SOCIETY CULTURE STRUCT

B63
LEVIN M.G.,ETHNIC ORIGINS OF THE PEOPLES OF NORTHEASTERN ASIA. CONSTN LEGIS...STAT CENSUS CHARTS 20 TEXAS MAPS. PAGE 95 H1901 — HEREDITY HABITAT CULTURE GEOG

B64
LIENHARDT G.,SOCIAL ANTHROPOLOGY. SOCIETY FAM KIN ...CONCPT METH. PAGE 97 H1928 — SOC HABITAT HEREDITY CULTURE

B64
MEAD M.,CONTINUITIES IN CULTURAL EVOLUTION. FACE/GP KIN ACT/RES EDU/PROP GP/REL INGP/REL DRIVE HEREDITY ROLE...TIME/SEQ TREND METH SOC/INTEG 20. PAGE 108 H2153 — CULTURE SOC PERS/REL

B67
WARD L.,LESTER WARD AND THE WELFARE STATE. SOCIETY NAT/G CREATE RECEIVE EQUILIB UTOPIA HABITAT HEREDITY PERSON...POLICY SOC BIOG 19/20 WARD/LEST. PAGE 165 H3303 — ALL/VALS NEW/IDEA WELF/ST CONCPT

B70
BOSSUET J.B.,"POLITIQUE TIREE DE L'ECRITURE SAINTE" (1679-1709) IN J.B. BOSSUET, OEVRES DE BOSSUET. NAT/G GP/REL AUTHORIT HEREDITY PERSON ALL/VALS SOVEREIGN 18 BIBLE DEITY CHRISTIAN. PAGE 19 H0383 — TRADIT CHIEF SECT CONCPT

B99
DU BOIS W.E.B.,THE PHILADELPHIA NEGRO: A SOCIAL STUDY. CULTURE STRATA KIN CRIME SUFF ADJUST DISCRIM ISOLAT HABITAT HEREDITY ALL/VALS SOC/INTEG 17/19 NEGRO PHILADELPH. PAGE 42 H0851 — INGP/REL RACE/REL SOC CENSUS

B99
KINGSLEY M.H.,WEST AFRICAN STUDIES. GHANA NIGERIA SIER/LEONE LAW EXTR/IND SECT DIPLOM INT/TRADE DOMIN RACE/REL OWN HEALTH...SOC 19. PAGE 86 H1717 — AFR HEREDITY COLONIAL CULTURE

HERESY....HERESY

HERMANN F.G. H1400

HERMANS F.A. H1401

HERNANDEZ URBINA A. H1402

HERNANDEZ-ARREGU J. H1403

HERRICK B.H. H1404

HERRICK M.D. H1405

HERRMANN K. H1406

HERSKOVITS M.J. H1407,H1408,H1409,H1410

HERZ J.H. H0549

HESS A.G. H1411

HEYDTE A F. H1412

HEYMANN F.G. H1413

HICKS U.K. H1414

HIDAYATULLAH M. H1415

HIESTAND/F....FRED J. HIESTAND

HIGGINS/G....GODFREY HIGGINS

HIGHWAY PLANNING AND DEVELOPMENT....SEE HIGHWAY

HIGHWAY....HIGHWAY PLANNING AND DEVELOPMENT

HILL C.R. H1416

HILL R.L. H1417

HILLMON T.J. H0138

HILSMAN R. H1418

HIMMELFARB G. H1419

HINDEN R. H1420

HINDLEY D. H1421

HINDU....HINDUISM AND HINDU PEOPLE

B48
COX O.C.,CASTE, CLASS, AND RACE. INDIA WOR+45 WOR-45 SECT TEC/DEV MARRIAGE ROLE MARXISM...MAJORIT NAT/COMP SOC/INTEG 20 NEGRO HINDU. PAGE 34 H0688
RACE/REL STRUCT STRATA DISCRIM

B53
BROWN D.M.,THE WHITE UMBRELLA: INDIAN POLITICAL THOUGHT FROM MANU TO GANDHI. INDIA LAW NAT/G SECT WRITING NAT/LISM...ANTHOL BIBLIOG 20 HINDU GANDHI/M MANU. PAGE 22 H0442
CONCPT DOMIN CONSERVE

B57
NARAIN D.,HINDU CHARACTER (A FEW GLIMPSES). INDIA DIPLOM SUICIDE PERS/REL ATTIT...PSY NAT/COMP PERS/COMP BIBLIOG WORSHIP 20 HINDU. PAGE 116 H2310
PERSON STERTYP SUPEGO SECT

B59
GOPAL R.,INDIAN MUSLIMS: A POLITICAL HISTORY (1858-1947). INDIA ISLAM PAKISTAN NAT/G SECT LEGIS LEAD COERCE WAR REPRESENT ISOLAT ORD/FREE 19/20 HINDU MUSLIM. PAGE 59 H1175
COLONIAL GP/REL POL/PAR REGION

S60
BERREMAN G.D.,"CASTE IN INDIA AND THE UNITED STATES" (BMR)" INDIA USA+45 CULTURE SOCIETY STRUCT SECT GP/REL DISCRIM HEREDITY...SOC STERTYP 20 NEGRO HINDU. PAGE 16 H0318
STRATA RACE/REL NAT/COMP ATTIT

B61
BROWN D.M.,THE NATIONALIST MOVEMENT. INDIA CULTURE STRATA REV MORAL ORD/FREE...BIBLIOG 20 HINDU. PAGE 22 H0443
NAT/LISM LEAD CHIEF POL/PAR

B63
BERREMAN G.D.,HINDUS OF THE HIMALAYAS. INDIA STRATA STRUCT KIN MUNIC 20 HINDU. PAGE 16 H0319
CULTURE SECT GP/REL ECO/UNDEV

B65
GAJENDRAGADKAR P.B.,LAW, LIBERTY AND SOCIAL JUSTICE. INDIA CONSTN NAT/G SECT PLAN ECO/TAC PRESS POPULISM...SOC METH/COMP 20 HINDU. PAGE 54 H1086
ORD/FREE LAW ADJUD JURID

HINTON W. H1422

HIRAI N. H1423

HIROMITSU K. H2962

HIROSHIMA.... NUC/PWR, PLAN, PROB/SOLV, CONSULT

B67
RIESMAN D.,CONVERSATIONS IN JAPAN: MODERNIZATION, POLITICS, AND CULTURE. CHINA/COM STRATA STRUCT ECO/DEV INDUS ACADEM EDU/PROP...ART/METH SOC MODAL INT IDEA/COMP SOC/INTEG 20 CHINJAP HIROSHIMA. PAGE 131 H2629
CULTURE SOCIETY ASIA

HIRSCH F.E. H1424

HIRSCH W. H3463

HISPANIC LUSO-BRAZILIAN COUN H1425

HISPANIC SOCIETY OF AMERICA H1426

HISS/ALGER....ALGER HISS

HIST....HISTORY, INCLUDING CURRENT EVENTS

HIST/WRIT....HISTORIOGRAPHY

B00
MAINE H.S.,ANCIENT LAW. MEDIT-7 CULTURE SOCIETY KIN SECT LEGIS LEGIT ROUTINE...JURID HIST/WRIT CON/ANAL TOT/POP VAL/FREE. PAGE 101 H2020
FAM LAW

B00
OMAN C.,A HISTORY OF THE ART OF WAR: THE MIDDLE AGES FROM THE FOURTH TO THE FOURTEENTH CENTURY. CHRIST-17C MEDIT-7 CULTURE SOCIETY INT/ORG ROUTINE PERSON...CONT/OBS HIST/WRIT CHARTS VAL/FREE. PAGE 121 H2417
FORCES SKILL WAR

B00
VOLPICELLI Z.,RUSSIA ON THE PACIFIC AND THE SIBERIAN RAILWAY. MOD/EUR ECO/UNDEV INT/ORG FORCES PLAN DOMIN COLONIAL ROUTINE ATTIT ALL/VALS...OBS HIST/WRIT TIME/SEQ TREND CON/ANAL AUD/VIS CHARTS 18/19. PAGE 163 H3261
NAT/G ACT/RES RUSSIA

B02
SEELEY J.R.,THE EXPANSION OF ENGLAND. MOD/EUR S/ASIA UK CULTURE NAT/G FORCES PLAN DOMIN EDU/PROP COLONIAL ROUTINE ATTIT ALL/VALS SOVEREIGN...CONCPT HIST/WRIT PARLIAMENT 18 CMN/WLTH. PAGE 141 H2819
INT/ORG ACT/RES CAP/ISM INDIA

B28
HOLDSWORTH W.S.,THE HISTORIANS OF ANGLO-AMERICAN LAW. UK USA-45 INTELL LEGIS RESPECT...BIOG NAT/COMP 17/20 COMMON/LAW. PAGE 72 H1450
HIST/WRIT LAW JURID

B29
ROBERTS S.H.,HISTORY OF FRENCH COLONIAL POLICY. AFR ASIA L/A+17C S/ASIA CULTURE ECO/DEV ECO/UNDEV FINAN NAT/G PLAN ECO/TAC DOMIN ROUTINE SOVEREIGN...OBS HIST/WRIT TREND CHARTS VAL/FREE 19/20. PAGE 132 H2642
INT/ORG ACT/RES FRANCE COLONIAL

B36
BOYCE A.N.,EUROPE AND SOUTH AFRICA. FRANCE GERMANY ITALY SOUTH/AFR UK INDUS NAT/G CONTROL REV WAR NAT/LISM...CONCPT HIST/WRIT 20. PAGE 20 H0392
COLONIAL GOV/COMP NAT/COMP DIPLOM

B36
CULVER D.C.,METHODOLOGY OF SOCIAL SCIENCE RESEARCH: A BIBLIOGRAPHY. LAW CULTURE...CRIMLGY GEOG STAT OBS INT QU HIST/WRIT CHARTS 20. PAGE 36 H0719
BIBLIOG/A METH SOC

S41
ABEL T.,"THE ELEMENT OF DECISION IN THE PATTERN OF WAR." EUR+WWI FUT NAT/G TOP/EX DIPLOM ROUTINE COERCE DISPL PERCEPT PWR...SOC METH/CNCPT HIST/WRIT TREND GEN/LAWS 20. PAGE 3 H0055
TEC/DEV FORCES WAR

B43
JONES C.K.,A BIBLIOGRAPHY OF LATIN AMERICAN BIBLIOGRAPHIES (2ND ED.). CULTURE ALL/VALS...POLICY GEOG HUM SOC LING BIOG TREND 20. PAGE 82 H1629
BIBLIOG/A L/A+17C HIST/WRIT

B45
CONOVER H.F.,THE NAZI STATE: WAR CRIMES AND WAR CRIMINALS. GERMANY CULTURE NAT/G SECT FORCES DIPLOM INT/TRADE EDU/PROP...INT/LAW BIOG HIST/WRIT TIME/SEQ 20. PAGE 32 H0647
BIBLIOG WAR CRIME

B45
HUNTINGTON E.,MAINSPRINGS OF CIVILIZATION. UNIV CULTURE SOCIETY BIO/SOC PERSON KNOWL SKILL...PSY RECORD HIST/WRIT TREND CHARTS TOT/POP. PAGE 75 H1504
SOC GEOG

B47
JURJI E.J.,THE GREAT RELIGIONS OF THE MODERN WORLD. CULTURE INTELL SOCIETY INT/ORG CONSULT CHOOSE ATTIT DRIVE PERSON RIGID/FLEX...HUM CONCPT OBS BIOG HIST/WRIT TREND GEN/LAWS 20 WORSHIP. PAGE 82 H1643
UNIV SECT

B48
FLOREN LOZANO L.,BIBLIOGRAFIA DE LA BIBLIOGRAFIA DOMINICANA. DOMIN/REP NAT/G DIPLOM EDU/PROP CIVMIL/REL...POLICY ART/METH GEOG PHIL/SCI HIST/WRIT 20. PAGE 51 H1027
BIBLIOG/A BIOG L/A+17C CULTURE

B50
CONOVER H.F.,INTRODUCTION TO EUROPE: A SELECTIVE GUIDE TO BACKGROUND READING. COM EUR+WWI NAT/G KNOWL...ART/METH GEOG SOC. PAGE 32 H0648
BIBLIOG/A MOD/EUR HIST/WRIT

B50
MACIVER R.M.,GREAT EXPRESSIONS OF HUMAN RIGHTS. LAW CONSTN CULTURE INTELL SOCIETY R+D INT/ORG ATTIT DRIVE...JURID OBS HIST/WRIT GEN/LAWS. PAGE 100 H1999
UNIV CONCPT

B51
MORLEY C.,GUIDE TO RESEARCH IN RUSSIAN HISTORY. USSR MARXISM...BIOG HIST/WRIT ANTHOL DICTIONARY. PAGE 113 H2259
BIBLIOG/A R+D NAT/G COM

B53
LENZ F.,DIE BEWEGUNGEN DER GROSSEN MACHTE. USA+45 USA-45 USSR SOCIETY STRATA STRUCT NAT/G PERSON MARXISM...CONCPT IDEA/COMP NAT/COMP 18/20. PAGE 94 H1883
BAL/PWR TREND DIPLOM HIST/WRIT

B54
MATTHEWS D.R.,THE SOCIAL BACKGROUND OF POLITICAL DECISION-MAKERS. CULTURE SOCIETY STRATA FAM EX/STRUC LEAD ATTIT BIO/SOC DRIVE PERSON ALL/VALS HIST/WRIT. PAGE 105 H2097
DECISION BIOG SOC

B55
MAYO H.B.,DEMOCRACY AND MARXISM. COM USSR STRATA NAT/G WORKER ECO/TAC REV MORAL...PHIL/SCI HIST/WRIT IDEA/COMP WORSHIP 20 MARX/KARL LENIN/VI STALIN/J TROTSKY/L. PAGE 105 H2108
MARXISM CAP/ISM

B57
LAQUER W.Z.,COMMUNISM AND NATIONALISM IN THE MIDDLE EAST. ELITES INTELL STRATA NAT/G POL/PAR SECT VOL/ASSN TOP/EX DOMIN LEGIT REGION COERCE ATTIT PERSON PWR...CONCPT HIST/WRIT TIME/SEQ TREND GEN/LAWS VAL/FREE. PAGE 91 H1817
ISLAM NAT/LISM

B58
BAGBY P.,CULTURE AND HISTORY....PHIL/SCI CONCPT LING LOG IDEA/COMP GEN/LAWS BIBLIOG 20. PAGE 10 H0196
HIST/WRIT CULTURE GP/COMP

NAT/COMP

C58
MORRALL J.B.,"POLITICAL THOUGHT IN MEDIEVAL TIMES." CHRIST-17C
LAW NAT/G SECT DOMIN ATTIT PWR...BIOG HIST/WRIT CONCPT
BIBLIOG. PAGE 113 H2260

B59
CONOVER H.F.,NIGERIAN OFFICIAL PUBLICATIONS, BIBLIOG
1869-1959: A GUIDE. NIGER CONSTN FINAN ACADEM NAT/G
SCHOOL FORCES PRESS ADMIN COLONIAL...HIST/WRIT CON/ANAL
19/20. PAGE 33 H0650

B59
FOX A.,THE POWER OF SMALL STATES: DIPLOMACY IN CONCPT
WORLD WAR TWO. EUR+WWI FINLAND NORWAY SPAIN SWEDEN STERTYP
TURKEY NAT/G TOP/EX DIPLOM PWR...HIST/WRIT 20. BAL/PWR
PAGE 52 H1044

B59
SHARMA R.S.,ASPECTS OF POLITICAL IDEAS AND CULTURE
INSTITUTIONS IN ANCIENT INDIA. INDIA SOCIETY STRUCT JURID
FAM VOL/ASSN TAX DOMIN...CONCPT HIST/WRIT 7. DELIB/GP
PAGE 142 H2848 SECT

S59
LABEDZ L.,"IDEOLOGY: THE FOURTH STAGE." COM USSR CONCPT
NAT/G TOP/EX LEGIT ATTIT PWR MARXISM...METH/CNCPT GEN/LAWS
HIST/WRIT STERTYP TOT/POP 20. PAGE 90 H1795

S59
SILBERMAN L.,"CHANGE AND CONFLICT IN THE HORN OF AFR
AFRICA." EUR+WWI ITALY UK CULTURE FORCES ECO/TAC TIME/SEQ
ADJUD COLONIAL ATTIT ORD/FREE PWR...DECISION
METH/CNCPT HIST/WRIT SOMALI 20. PAGE 144 H2874

B60
BARBU Z.,PROBLEMS OF HISTORICAL PSYCHOLOGY. GREECE PERSON
MEDIT-7 UK CULTURE TEC/DEV ADJUST RATIONAL ATTIT PSY
PERCEPT...METH/CNCPT NEW/IDEA TIME/SEQ GEN/METH. HIST/WRIT
PAGE 11 H0214 IDEA/COMP

B60
KOHN H.,PAN-SLAVISM: ITS HISTORY AND IDEOLOGY. COM ATTIT
CZECHOSLVK EUR+WWI MOD/EUR USSR YUGOSLAVIA CULTURE CONCPT
ELITES INTELL KIN NAT/G EDU/PROP DRIVE SOVEREIGN NAT/LISM
...HUM PHIL/SCI MYTH HIST/WRIT 19/20. PAGE 87 H1745

B61
CONQUEST R.,POWER AND POLICY IN THE USSR. USSR COM
NAT/G POL/PAR DIPLOM MARXISM 20. PAGE 33 H0655 HIST/WRIT
GOV/REL
PWR

B62
ABRAHAM W.E.,THE MIND OF AFRICA. AFR SOCIETY STRATA CULTURE
KIN ECO/TAC DOMIN EDU/PROP LEGIT COERCE ATTIT SIMUL
ALL/VALS...MAJORIT SOC OBS HIST/WRIT TIME/SEQ TREND GHANA
TOT/POP 20. PAGE 3 H0058

B62
DILLING A.R.,ABORIGINE CULTURE HISTORY - A SURVEY S/ASIA
OF PUBLICATIONS 1954-1957. GUINEA...SOC CHARTS HIST/WRIT
NAT/COMP BIBLIOG/A AUSTRAL ABORIGINES. PAGE 41 CULTURE
H0825 KIN

B62
HO PING-TI,THE LADDER OF SUCCESS IN IMPERIAL CHINA: ASIA
ASPECTS OF SOCIAL MOBILITY, 1368-1911. INTELL CULTURE
STRATA FAM KIN MUNIC NAT/G PROVS SCHOOL DELIB/GP
DOMIN EDU/PROP ADMIN ROUTINE PERSON ALL/VALS...SOC
STAT BIOG HIST/WRIT TIME/SEQ VAL/FREE. PAGE 71
H1431

B62
INSTITUTE FOR STUDY OF USSR,YOUTH IN FERMENT. COM
INTELL NAT/G PERF/ART POL/PAR SCHOOL VOL/ASSN CULTURE
FORCES EDU/PROP ATTIT DRIVE PERCEPT HEALTH KNOWL USSR
MORAL ORD/FREE RESPECT...SOC OBS HIST/WRIT
VAL/FREE. PAGE 77 H1537

B62
SCHIEDER T.,THE STATE AND SOCIETY IN OUR TIMES STRUCT
(TRANS. BY C.A.M. SYM). SOCIETY NAT/G POL/PAR REV PWR
GP/REL ALL/IDEOS 19/20. PAGE 139 H2786 HIST/WRIT

S62
DUNN S.D.,"DIRECTED CULTURE CHANGE IN THE SOVIET COM
UNION: SOME SOVIET STUDIES." SOCIETY ORD/FREE...SOC CULTURE
HIST/WRIT VAL/FREE 20. PAGE 43 H0866 USSR

B63
SILONE I.,THE SCHOOL FOR DICTATORS. EUR+WWI GERMANY TOTALISM
ITALY SOCIETY NAT/G CHIEF EX/STRUC ATTIT MORAL PWR EDU/PROP
...HIST/WRIT 20. PAGE 144 H2876 ORD/FREE
FASCISM

B63
ULAM A.B.,THE NEW FACE OF SOVIET TOTALITARIANISM. COM
FUT INTELL NAT/G POL/PAR EX/STRUC TOP/EX DIPLOM PWR
ECO/TAC DOMIN EDU/PROP LEGIT COERCE ATTIT TOTALISM
RIGID/FLEX...OBS HIST/WRIT TREND TOT/POP VAL/FREE USSR
COLD/WAR. PAGE 158 H3150

B63
VON DER MEHDEN F.R.,RELIGION AND NATIONALISM IN SECT
SOUTHEAST ASIA. BURMA PHILIPPINE S/ASIA INTELL CULTURE
SOCIETY DOMIN EDU/PROP LEGIT ATTIT MORAL ORD/FREE NAT/LISM
...SOC CENSUS HIST/WRIT TOT/POP VAL/FREE 20 WORSHIP
LONDON. PAGE 163 H3265

L63
ZARTMAN I.W.,"THE SAHARA--BRIDGE OR BARRIER." ISLAM INT/ORG
CULTURE SOCIETY NAT/G DELIB/GP DOMIN EDU/PROP LEGIT PWR
ATTIT...HIST/WRIT TIME/SEQ CHARTS TOT/POP VAL/FREE NAT/LISM
20. PAGE 172 H3447

B64
MCCALL D.F.,AFRICA IN TIME PERSPECTIVE. AFR HIST/WRIT
EXTR/IND KIN SECT CREATE PERS/REL HABITAT...GEOG OBS/ENVIR
METH/CNCPT LING BIBLIOG/A TIME 20. PAGE 106 H2124 CULTURE

B64
PIPES R.,THE FORMATION OF THE SOVIET UNION. EUR+WWI COM
MOD/EUR STRUCT ECO/UNDEV NAT/G LEGIS DOMIN LEGIT USSR
CT/SYS EXEC COERCE ALL/VALS...POLICY RELATIV RUSSIA
HIST/WRIT TIME/SEQ TOT/POP 19/20. PAGE 126 H2514

S64
BARIETY J.,"LA POLITIQUE EXTERIEURE ALLEMANDE DANS EUR+WWI
L'HIVER 1939-1940." COM FINLAND GERMANY ISLAM ITALY DIPLOM
USSR NAT/G FORCES ECO/TAC DOMIN EDU/PROP COERCE WAR
PWR WEALTH...HIST/WRIT NAZI TOT/POP VAL/FREE 20.
PAGE 11 H0216

S64
CROUZET F.,"WARS, BLOCKADE, AND ECONOMIC CHANGE IN MOD/EUR
EUROPE, 1792-1815." UK INDUS NAT/G TEC/DEV ECO/TAC MARKET
WEALTH...POLICY RELATIV HIST/WRIT TIME/SEQ 18/19.
PAGE 35 H0710

S64
GOLDBERG A.,"THE MILITARY ORIGINS OF THE BRITISH FORCES
NUCLEAR DETERRENT." EUR+WWI ECO/DEV NAT/G PLAN CONCPT
NUC/PWR ATTIT PWR...DECISION HIST/WRIT COLD/WAR 20. DETER
PAGE 58 H1156 UK

S64
REISS I.,"LE DECLENCHEMENT DE LA PREMIERE GUERRE MOD/EUR
MONDIALE." GERMANY RUSSIA NAT/G FORCES DOMIN BAL/PWR
EDU/PROP COERCE RIGID/FLEX PWR SOVEREIGN...RELATIV DIPLOM
HIST/WRIT TOT/POP AUST/HUNG SERBIA 20. PAGE 131 WAR
H2612

S64
SALVADORI M.,"EL CAPITALISMO EN LA EUROPA DE LA EUR+WWI
POSGUERRA." INT/ORG NAT/G POL/PAR PLAN ECO/TAC ECO/DEV
ATTIT ORD/FREE WEALTH...HIST/WRIT COLD/WAR EEC 20. CAP/ISM
PAGE 137 H2743

S64
TOYNBEE A.,"BRITAIN AND THE ARABS: THE NEED FOR A ISLAM
NEW START." NAT/G CREATE COLONIAL ATTIT RIGID/FLEX ECO/TAC
MORAL PWR...POLICY HIST/WRIT 20. PAGE 156 H3124 DIPLOM
UK

B65
CHANDLER M.J.,A GUIDE TO RECORDS IN BARBADOS. BIBLIOG
WEST/IND PUB/INST SCHOOL SECT...HIST/WRIT 20. LOC/G
PAGE 28 H0573 L/A+17C
NAT/G

B65
HERBST J.,THE GERMAN HISTORICAL SCHOOL IN AMERICAN CULTURE
SCHOLARSHIP; A STUDY IN THE TRANSFER OF CULTURE. NAT/COMP
GERMANY USA+45 INTELL SOCIETY ACADEM PLAN ATTIT HIST/WRIT
IDEA/COMP. PAGE 70 H1399

S65
WATT D.C.,"RESTRICTIONS ON RESEARCH* THE FIFTY-YEAR UK
RULE AND BRITISH FOREIGN POLICY." ACADEM PERCEPT USA+45
...HIST/WRIT NAT/COMP TIME. PAGE 166 H3315 DIPLOM

B66
COLE G.D.H.,THE MEANING OF MARXISM. USSR WOR+45 MARXISM
STRATA STRUCT NAT/G WORKER COST FASCISM...IDEA/COMP CONCPT
20. PAGE 31 H0625 HIST/WRIT
CAP/ISM

B66
WINKS R.W.,THE HISTORIOGRAPHY OF THE BRITISH HIST/WRIT
EMPIRE-COMMONWEALTH. CANADA INDIA PAKISTAN UK TREND
CULTURE SOCIETY STRUCT POL/PAR...CONCPT NAT/COMP 20 IDEA/COMP
AUSTRAL. PAGE 169 H3386 METH/COMP

B67
GIFFORD P.,BRITAIN AND GERMANY IN AFRICA. AFR COLONIAL
GERMANY UK ECO/UNDEV LEAD WAR NAT/LISM ATTIT ADMIN
...POLICY HIST/WRIT METH/COMP ANTHOL BIBLIOG 19/20 DIPLOM
WWI. PAGE 56 H1123 NAT/COMP

B67
LAQUER W.,THE FATE OF THE REVOLUTION: REV
INTERPRETATIONS OF SOVIET HISTORY. RUSSIA NAT/G KNOWL
MARXISM...BIBLIOG 20 STALIN/J. PAGE 91 H1816 HIST/WRIT
IDEA/COMP

S67
BOSHER J.F.,"GOVERNMENT AND PRIVATE INTERESTS IN NAT/G
NEW FRANCE." CANADA FRANCE INDUS LG/CO SML/CO FINAN
CAP/ISM INT/TRADE COLONIAL GP/REL...HIST/WRIT ADMIN
17/18. PAGE 19 H0381 CONTROL

S67
SAVER W.,"NATIONAL SOCIALISM: TOTALITARIANISM OR SOCISM
FASCISM?" GERMANY STRUCT POL/PAR PROB/SOLV MARXISM NAT/G
...SOC CONCPT HIST/WRIT IDEA/COMP 20 HITLER/A TOTALISM
COLD/WAR. PAGE 138 H2760 FASCISM

S68
HOOK S.,"THE ENLIGHTENMENT AND MARXISM." CULTURE IDEA/COMP
SOCIETY RATIONAL ORD/FREE PLURISM SOCISM...CONCPT MARXISM
HIST/WRIT 18/19 MARX/KARL HEGEL/GWF ENLIGHTNMT. OBJECTIVE
PAGE 73 H1462

S68
SHAPIRO J.P.,"SOVIET HISTORIOGRAPHY AND THE MOSCOW HIST/WRIT
TRIALS: AFTER THIRTY YEARS." USSR NAT/G LEGIT PRESS EDU/PROP
CONTROL LEAD ATTIT MARXISM...NEW/IDEA METH 20 SANCTION
TROTSKY/L STALIN/J KHRUSH/N. PAGE 142 H2843 ADJUD

HISTORICAL RESEARCH INSTITUTE H1427

HITLER A. H1428,H1429

HITLER/A....ADOLF HITLER

B35
MARRIOTT J.A.,DICTATORSHIP AND DEMOCRACY. GERMANY GREECE UK CHIEF DIPLOM DOMIN LEGIT PEACE ORD/FREE CONSERVE...TREND ROME HITLER/A. PAGE 103 H2057 — TOTALISM POPULISM PLURIST NAT/G

B36
WANDERSCHECK H.,WELTKRIEG UND PROPAGANDA. GERMANY MOD/EUR UK COM/IND NAT/G DOMIN PRESS ATTIT...POLICY 20 HITLER/A. PAGE 165 H3299 — EDU/PROP PSY WAR KNOWL

S39
COLE G.D.H.,"NAZI ECONOMICS: HOW DO THEY MANAGE IT?" GERMANY FORCES WORKER BUDGET INT/TRADE ROUTINE COERCE WAR 20 HITLER/A NAZI. PAGE 31 H0622 — FASCISM ECO/TAC ATTIT PLAN

B40
HUNTER R.,REVOLUTION: WHY, HOW, WHEN? NAT/G ECO/TAC EDU/PROP COERCE ORD/FREE FASCISM POPULISM SOCISM 18/20 HITLER/A LENIN/VI. PAGE 75 H1502 — REV METH/COMP LEAD CONSTN

B41
HITLER A.,MEIN KAMPF (UNABR. ENG. VERSION) (1925). GERMANY CONSTN TEC/DEV RACE/REL NAT/LISM TOTALISM SOVEREIGN...BIOG 20 HITLER/A TREATY. PAGE 71 H1429 — EDU/PROP WAR PLAN FASCISM

B42
NEUMANN S.,PERMANENT REVOLUTION: THE TOTAL STATE IN A WORLD AT WAR. COM EUR+WWI GERMANY USSR EX/STRUC DIPLOM CONTROL COERCE REPRESENT MARXISM...SOC GOV/COMP BIBLIOG 20 HITLER/A STALIN/J. PAGE 117 H2337 — FASCISM TOTALISM DOMIN EDU/PROP

B51
BORKENAU F.,EUROPEAN COMMUNISM. COM EUR+WWI GERMANY SPAIN USSR INT/ORG PLAN REV WAR ATTIT 20 STALIN/J HITLER/A. PAGE 19 H0376 — MARXISM POLICY DIPLOM NAT/G

B54
SALVEMINI G.,PRELUDE TO WORLD WAR II. ITALY MOD/EUR INT/ORG BAL/PWR EDU/PROP CONTROL TOTALISM...TREND NAT/COMP BIBLIOG 19 HITLER/A LEAGUE/NAT MUSSOLIN/B. PAGE 137 H2745 — WAR FASCISM LEAD PWR

B55
ALFIERI D.,DICTATORS FACE TO FACE. NAT/G TOP/EX DIPLOM EXEC COERCE ORD/FREE FASCISM...POLICY OBS 20 HITLER/A MUSSOLIN/B. PAGE 5 H0103 — WAR CHIEF TOTALISM PERS/REL

B59
LANDAUER C.,EUROPEAN SOCIALISM (2 VOLS.). COM EUR+WWI MOD/EUR INTELL INDUS REV WAR...MAJORIT IDEA/COMP BIBLIOG 19/20 HITLER/A. PAGE 90 H1805 — SOCISM NAT/COMP LABOR MARXISM

B61
BULLOCK A.,HITLER: A STUDY IN TYRANNY. EUR+WWI GERMANY SOCIETY STRUCT NAT/G POL/PAR FORCES CREATE DOMIN EDU/PROP EXEC COERCE WAR NAT/LISM DISPL DRIVE PERSON PWR...PSY NAZI 20 HITLER/A. PAGE 23 H0470 — ATTIT BIOG TOTALISM

B62
ABOSCH H.,THE MENACE OF THE MIRACLE: GERMANY FROM HITLER TO ADENAUER. EUR+WWI GERMANY/W CULTURE FORCES PRESS NUC/PWR WAR CHOOSE 20 HITLER/A ADENAUER/K. PAGE 3 H0057 — DIPLOM PEACE POLICY

B63
JACOB H.,GERMAN ADMINISTRATION SINCE BISMARCK: CENTRAL AUTHORITY VERSUS LOCAL AUTONOMY. GERMANY GERMANY/W LAW POL/PAR CONTROL CENTRAL TOTALISM FASCISM...MAJORIT DECISION STAT CHARTS GOV/COMP 19/20 BISMARCK/O HITLER/A WEIMAR/REP. PAGE 79 H1577 — ADMIN NAT/G LOC/G POLICY

B64
HALE O.J.,THE CAPTIVE PRESS IN THE THIRD REICH. GERMANY CULTURE LG/CO NAT/G POL/PAR PLAN DOMIN TASK CENTRAL OWN TOTALISM PWR...BIBLIOG 20 HITLER/A NAZI AMMAN/MAX. PAGE 64 H1283 — COM/IND PRESS CONTROL FASCISM

B64
WHEELER-BENNETT J.W.,THE NEMESIS OF POWER (2ND ED.). EUR+WWI GERMANY TOP/EX TEC/DEV ADMIN WAR PERS/REL RIGID/FLEX ROLE ORD/FREE PWR FASCISM 20 HITLER/A. PAGE 167 H3342 — FORCES NAT/G GP/REL STRUCT

B65
ALLEN W.S.,THE NAZI SEIZURE OF POWER. GERMANY NAT/G CHIEF LEAD COERCE CHOOSE REPRESENT GOV/REL AUTHORIT ...DECISION 20 HITLER/A NAZI. PAGE 5 H0106 — MUNIC FASCISM TOTALISM LOC/G

B65
JONAS E.,DIE VOLKSKONSERVATIVEN 1928-1933. GERMANY EX/STRUC...CONCPT TIME/SEQ 20 HITLER/A. PAGE 82 H1628 — POL/PAR NAT/G GP/REL

B66
DEUTSCHER I.,STALIN: A POLITICAL BIOGRAPHY. EUR+WWI USSR POL/PAR FORCES DIPLOM ADMIN LEAD REV WAR TOTALISM PERSON 20 STALIN/J ROOSEVLT/F LENIN/VI HITLER/A. PAGE 40 H0807 — BIOG MARXISM TOP/EX PWR

B66
NOLTE E.,THREE FACES OF FASCISM. FRANCE GERMANY DOMIN LEGIT COERCE CROWD REV WAR GP/REL RACE/REL SOVEREIGN...GOV/COMP IDEA/COMP 19/20 HITLER/A MUSSOLIN/B MARX/KARL. PAGE 118 H2368 — FASCISM TOTALISM NAT/G POL/PAR

B66
O'NEILL R.J.,THE GERMAN ARMY AND THE NAZI PARTY, 1933-1939. GERMANY ELITES NAT/G EDU/PROP CONTROL LEAD COERCE WAR...POLICY INT TIME/SEQ BIBLIOG 20 HITLER/A NAZI. PAGE 120 H2391 — CIVMIL/REL FORCES FASCISM POL/PAR

B66
RISTIC D.N.,YUGOSLAVIA'S REVOLUTION OF 1941. EUR+WWI YUGOSLAVIA NAT/G WAR ORD/FREE...RECORD BIBLIOG 20 HITLER/A TREATY. PAGE 132 H2633 — REV ATTIT FASCISM DIPLOM

B66
THORNTON M.J.,NAZISM, 1918-1945. GERMANY INT/ORG DIPLOM REV PEACE FASCISM...CONCPT 20 HITLER/A WEIMAR/REP NAZI. PAGE 155 H3089 — TOTALISM POL/PAR NAT/G WAR

S67
SAVER W.,"NATIONAL SOCIALISM: TOTALITARIANISM OR FASCISM?" GERMANY STRUCT POL/PAR PROB/SOLV MARXISM ...SOC CONCPT HIST/WRIT IDEA/COMP 20 HITLER/A COLD/WAR. PAGE 138 H2760 — SOCISM NAT/G TOTALISM FASCISM

HLA MYINT U. H1430

HO PING-TI H1431

HO/CHI/MIN....HO CHI MINH

HOBBES T. H1432,H1433,H1434

HOBBES/T....THOMAS HOBBES

B50
HALLOWELL J.H.,MAIN CURRENTS IN MODERN POLITICAL THOUGHT. CONSTN SECT LEGIS...MAJORIT CONCPT 17/20 MARX/KARL MILL/JS HOBBES/T LENIN/VI. PAGE 64 H1290 — IDEA/COMP POPULISM SOCISM

B64
COBBAN A.,ROUSSEAU AND THE MODERN STATE (2ND ED.). FRANCE PROB/SOLV NAT/LISM UTOPIA PERSON MORAL ...EPIST PHIL/SCI SOC IDEA/COMP 18 ROUSSEAU/J BURKE/EDM HOBBES/T HUME/D. PAGE 30 H0612 — GEN/LAWS INGP/REL NAT/G ORD/FREE

B64
GUMPLOWICZ L.,RECHTSSTAAT UND SOZIALISMUS. STRATA ORD/FREE SOVEREIGN MARXISM...IDEA/COMP 16/20 KANT/I HOBBES/T. PAGE 62 H1251 — JURID NAT/G SOCISM CONCPT

B65
GEWIRTH A.,POLITICAL PHILOSOPHY. UNIV SOCIETY NAT/G GP/REL INGP/REL CONSEN PWR...IDEA/COMP GEN/LAWS 17/19 HOBBES/T LOCKE/JOHN MARX/KARL MILL/JS ROUSSEAU/J. PAGE 56 H1118 — ORD/FREE SOVEREIGN PHIL/SCI

HOBBS C.C. H1435,H1436,H1437

HOBSBAWM E.J. H1438

HOBSON J.A. H1439,H1440

HOC V.V. H2672

HOCART A.M. H1441

HOCKING W.E. H1442

HODGETTS J.E. H1443

HODGKIN T. H1444

HODGKINSON R.G. H1445

HOEVELER H.J. H1446

HOFFA/J....JAMES HOFFA

HOFMANN W. H1447

HOLDSWORTH M. H1448

HOLDSWORTH W.S. H1449,H1450,H1451,H1452,H1453,H1454

HOLIFLD/C....CHET HOLIFIELD

HOLLAND....SEE NETHERLAND

HOLLANDER P. H1455

HOLLERAN M.P. H1456

HOLLERMAN L. H1457

HOLMES/OW....OLIVER WENDELL HOLMES

HOLMES/OWJ....OLIVER WENDELL HOLMES, JR.

HOLSTI/KJ....K.J. HOLSTI

HOLT R.T. H1458

HOMEOSTASIS....SEE FEEDBACK

HOMER....HOMER

HOMEST/ACT....HOMESTEAD ACT OF 1862

HOMESTEAD ACT OF 1862....SEE HOMEST/ACT

HOMICIDE....SEE MURDER

HOMOSEXUAL....HOMOSEXUALITY; SEE ALSO BIO/SOC, CRIME, SEX

HOMOSEXUALITY....SEE BIO/SOC, SEX, CRIME, HOMOSEXUAL

HONDURAS....SEE ALSO L/A+17C

B43
DURON J.F.,REPERTORIO BIBLIOGRAFICO HONDURENO. HONDURAS WRITING. PAGE 44 H0871
BIBLIOG NAT/G L/A+17C

B47
NEUBURGER O.,GUIDE TO OFFICIAL PUBLICATIONS OF OTHER AMERICAN REPUBLICS: HONDURAS (VOL. XIII). HONDURAS LAW LEGIS ADMIN CT/SYS...JURID 19/20. PAGE 117 H2333
BIBLIOG/A NAT/G EDU/PROP CONSTN

C50
STOKES W.S.,"HONDURAS: AN AREA STUDY IN GOVERNMENT." HONDURAS NAT/G POL/PAR COLONIAL CT/SYS ROUTINE CHOOSE REPRESENT...GEOG RECORD BIBLIOG 19/20. PAGE 149 H2988
CONSTN LAW L/A+17C ADMIN

B63
OTERO L.M.,HONDURAS. HONDURAS SPAIN STRUCT SECT COLONIAL REV WAR ATTIT PWR...GEOG WORSHIP 16/20. PAGE 122 H2432
NAT/G SOCIETY NAT/LISM ECO/UNDEV

B65
HONDURAS CONSEJO NAC DE ECO,PLAN NACIONAL DE DESARROLLO ECONOMICO Y SOCIAL DE HONDURAS 1965-69. HONDURAS AGRI INDUS BAL/PAY INCOME 20. PAGE 73 H1459
ECO/UNDEV NAT/G PLAN POLICY

S67
GRANT C.H.,"RURAL LOCAL GOVERNMENT IN GUYANA AND BRITISH HONDURAS." GUYANA HONDURAS L/A+17C AGRI NAT/G EX/STRUC ACT/RES REGION GOV/REL EFFICIENCY ORD/FREE 20. PAGE 60 H1196
ECO/UNDEV LOC/G ADMIN MUNIC

S67
GRIEB K.J.,"THE UNITED STATES AND THE CENTRAL AMERICAN CONFEDERATION." COSTA/RICA EL/SALVADR GUATEMALA HONDURAS L/A+17C NICARAGUA NAT/G FORCES CONFER AGREE EXEC ARMS/CONT REV WAR PEACE ATTIT 20. PAGE 60 H1212
INT/ORG DIPLOM POLICY REGION

HONDURAS CONSEJO NAC DE ECO H1459

HONG/KONG....HONG KONG

B48
PELCOVITS N.A.,OLD CHINA HANDS AND THE FOREIGN OFFICE. ASIA BURMA UK ECO/UNDEV NAT/G ECO/TAC FOR/AID TARIFFS DOMIN COLONIAL GOV/REL SOVEREIGN 19 HONG/KONG TREATY. PAGE 124 H2483
INT/TRADE ATTIT DIPLOM

B65
HESS A.G.,CHASING THE DRAGON: A REPORT ON DRUG ADDICTION IN HONG KONG. ASIA CULTURE PROB/SOLV TRIBUTE...POLICY PSY SOC CLASSIF STAT 17/20 HONG/KONG. PAGE 70 H1411
BIO/SOC CRIME SOCIETY LAW

HONINGMAN J.J. H1460

HOOK S. H1461,H1462

HOOKER R. H1463

HOOVER INSTITUTION H1464

HOOVER/H....HERBERT HOOVER

HOPE M. H1465

HOPI....HOPI INDIANS

HOPKINS J.F.K. H1466

HOPKINS/H....HARRY HOPKINS

HOPKINSON T. H1467

HORECKY P.L. H1468

HORN O.B. H1469

HORNE A.J. H1470

HORNE D. H1471

HORNEY K. H1472

HOROWITZ I.L. H1473

HOSELITZ B.F. H1474,H1475,H1476

HOSHII I. H1477

HOSKINS H.L. H1478

HOSPITALS....SEE PUB/INST

HOUN F.S. H1479

HOUN F.W. H1480

HOUSE COMMITTEE ON SCIENCE AND ASTRONAUTICS....SEE HS/SCIASTR

HOUSE OF REPRESENTATIVES....SEE HOUSE/REP

HOUSE RULES COMMITTEE....SEE RULES/COMM, HOUSE/REP

HOUSE UNAMERICAN ACTIVITIES COMMITTEE....SEE HUAC

HOUSE/CMNS....HOUSE OF COMMONS (ALL NATIONS)

S38
HALL R.C.,"REPRESENTATION OF BIG BUSINESS IN THE HOUSE OF COMMONS." UK ECO/DEV INDUS PROF/ORG LEGIS CAP/ISM ECO/TAC LAISSEZ...POLICY OLD/LIB PLURIST MGT 20 HOUSE/CMNS. PAGE 64 H1287
LOBBY NAT/G

B39
JENNINGS W.I.,PARLIAMENT. UK POL/PAR OP/RES BUDGET LEAD CHOOSE GP/REL...MGT 20 PARLIAMENT HOUSE/LORD HOUSE/CMNS. PAGE 80 H1609
PARL/PROC LEGIS CONSTN NAT/G

B39
MCILWAIN C.H.,CONSTITUTIONALISM AND THE CHANGING WORLD. UK USA-45 LEGIS PRIVIL AUTHORIT SOVEREIGN ...GOV/COMP 15/20 MAGNA/CART HOUSE/CMNS. PAGE 107 H2133
CONSTN POLICY JURID

B66
JOHNSON N.,PARLIAMENT AND ADMINISTRATION: THE ESTIMATES COMMITTEE 1945-65. FUT UK NAT/G EX/STRUC PLAN BUDGET ORD/FREE...T 20 PARLIAMENT HOUSE/CMNS. PAGE 81 H1625
LEGIS ADMIN FINAN DELIB/GP

B66
LONDON DAILY TELEGRAPH,ELECTION '66: GALLUP ANALYSIS OF THE VOTING RESULTS. UK LEGIS COMPUTER ATTIT...QU SAMP CHARTS 20 LABOR/PAR HOUSE/CMNS. PAGE 98 H1959
STAT CHOOSE REPRESENT POL/PAR

HOUSE/LORD....HOUSE OF LORDS (ALL NATIONS)

B10
TEMPERLEY H.W.V.,SENATES AND UPPER CHAMBERS; THEIR USE AND FUNCTION IN THE MODERN STATE... UK WOR-45 CONSTN NAT/G POL/PAR PROVS SECT COLONIAL LEAD CHOOSE REPRESENT PWR...BIBLIOG 19/20 PARLIAMENT SENATE CMN/WLTH HOUSE/LORD. PAGE 153 H3059
PARL/PROC NAT/COMP LEGIS EX/STRUC

B39
JENNINGS W.I.,PARLIAMENT. UK POL/PAR OP/RES BUDGET LEAD CHOOSE GP/REL...MGT 20 PARLIAMENT HOUSE/LORD HOUSE/CMNS. PAGE 80 H1609
PARL/PROC LEGIS CONSTN NAT/G

B63
SPRING D.,THE ENGLISH LANDED ESTATE IN THE NINETEENTH CENTURY: ITS ADMINISTRATION. UK ELITES STRUCT AGRI NAT/G GP/REL OWN PWR WEALTH...BIBLIOG 19 HOUSE/LORD. PAGE 148 H2954
STRATA PERS/REL MGT

HOUSE/REP....HOUSE OF REPRESENTATIVES (ALL NATIONS) SEE ALSO CONGRESS, LEGIS

B17
HARLOW R.V.,THE HISTORY OF LEGISLATIVE METHODS IN THE PERIOD BEFORE 1825. USA-45 EX/STRUC ADMIN COLONIAL LEAD PARL/PROC ROUTINE...GP/COMP GOV/COMP HOUSE/REP. PAGE 66 H1333
LEGIS DELIB/GP PROVS POL/PAR

S67
FUSARO A.,"THE EFFECT OF PROPORTIONAL REPRESENTATION ON VOTING IN THE AUSTRALIAN SENATE." S/ASIA CONSTN POL/PAR CONTROL GP/REL PWR...CHARTS 20 AUSTRAL HOUSE/REP SENATE. PAGE 54 H1083
LEGIS CHOOSE REPRESENT NAT/G

HOUSTON....HOUSTON, TEXAS

HOWARD M. H1481

HOWE R.W. H1482

HOYT E.C. H1483

HS/SCIASTR....HOUSE COMMITTEE ON SCIENCE AND ASTRONAUTICS

HSU F.L.K. H1484

HSU U.T. H1485

HU/FENG....HU FENG

HUBERMAN L. H1486

HUCKER C.O. H1487

HUGHES A.J. H1488

HUGHES C.A. H0324

HUGHES C.C. H1489

HUGHES E.C. H1490

HUGHES T.L. H1491

HUKS....HUKS (PHILIPPINES)

HULL W.I. H1492

HULL....CORDELL HULL

B64
WHITE D.S.,SEEDS OF DISCORD. EUR+WWI FRANCE NAT/G VOL/ASSN FORCES DIPLOM DOMIN NAT/LISM DISPL RIGID/FLEX PWR...RECORD INT BIOG 20 DEGAULLE/C ROOSEVLT/F CHURCHLL/W HULL. PAGE 167 H3347 — TOP/EX ATTIT

HUM....METHODS OF HUMANITIES, LITERARY ANALYSIS

N
ACAD RUMANIAN SCI DOC CTR,RUMANIAN SCIENTIFIC ABSTRACTS: SOCIAL SCIENCES. ROMANIA FINAN HABITAT ...ART/METH GEOG HUM JURID PSY 20. PAGE 3 H0059 — BIBLIOG/A CULTURE LING LAW

N
BIBLIOTECH NACIONAL,CATALOGO BREVE DE LA BIBLIOTECA AMERICANA DE JT MEDINA (2 VOLS.). CHILE NAT/G PERSON HUM. PAGE 16 H0330 — BIBLIOG/A CHARTS L/A+17C

N
UNIVERSITY OF FLORIDA LIBRARY,DOORS TO LATIN AMERICA; RECENT BOOKS AND PAMPHLETS. CONSTN CULTURE SOCIETY ECO/UNDEV COLONIAL LEAD GOV/REL NAT/LISM ATTIT...HUM SOC 20. PAGE 159 H3170 — BIBLIOG/A L/A+17C DIPLOM NAT/G

N
AUSTRALIAN PUBLIC AFFAIRS INFORMATION SERVICE. LAW ...HEAL HUM MGT SOC CON/ANAL 20 AUSTRAL. PAGE 1 H0011 — BIBLIOG NAT/G CULTURE DIPLOM

N
BIBLIOGRAPHIE DE LA PHILOSOPHIE. LAW CULTURE SECT EDU/PROP MORAL...HUM METH/CNCPT 20. PAGE 1 H0012 — BIBLIOG/A PHIL/SCI CONCPT LOG

N
PUBLISHERS' CIRCULAR, THE OFFICIAL ORGAN OF THE PUBLISHERS' ASSOCIATION OF GREAT BRITAIN AND IRELAND. EUR+WWI MOD/EUR UK LAW PROB/SOLV DIPLOM COLONIAL ATTIT...HUM 19/20 CMN/WLTH. PAGE 1 H0019 — BIBLIOG NAT/G WRITING LEAD

N
PUBLISHERS' TRADE LIST ANNUAL. LAW POL/PAR ADMIN PERSON ALL/IDEOS...HUM SOC 19/20. PAGE 1 H0020 — BIBLIOG NAT/G DIPLOM POLICY

N
"PROLOG",DIGEST OF THE SOVIET UKRANIAN PRESS. USSR LAW AGRI INDUS PROVS SCHOOL DIPLOM GOV/REL ATTIT ...HUM LING 20. PAGE 3 H0053 — BIBLIOG/A NAT/G PRESS COM

N
BURY J.B.,THE CAMBRIDGE ANCIENT HISTORY (12 VOLS.). MEDIT-7 DIPLOM COLONIAL WAR...HUM EGYPT/ANC ROME/EMP BABYLONIA GREECE/ANC. PAGE 25 H0495 — BIBLIOG/A SOCIETY CULTURE NAT/G

N
INADA S.,INTRODUCTION TO SCIENTIFIC WORKS IN HUMANITIES AND SOCIAL SCIENCES PUBLISHED IN JAPAN. LAW CULTURE ACADEM EDU/PROP...ART/METH HUM 20 CHINJAP. PAGE 76 H1525 — BIBLIOG/A NAT/G SOC S/ASIA

N
INSTITUTE OF HISPANIC STUDIES,HISPANIC AMERICAN REPORT. EUR+WWI SPAIN LAW CONSTN ECO/UNDEV POL/PAR EX/STRUC LEGIS LEAD...HUM SOC 20. PAGE 77 H1538 — BIBLIOG/A L/A+17C NAT/G DIPLOM

N
MINISTERE DE L'EDUC NATIONALE,CATALOGUE DES THESES DE DOCTORAT SOUTENNES DEVANT LES UNIVERSITAIRES FRANCAISES. FRANCE LAW DIPLOM ADMIN...HUM SOC 20. PAGE 111 H2223 — BIBLIOG ACADEM KNOWL NAT/G

B12
HEINSIUS W.,ALLGEMEINES BUCHER-LEXICON ODER VOLLSTANDIGES ALPHABETISCHES VERZEICHNIS ALLER VON 1700 BIS ZU ENDE...(1892). GERMANY PERF/ART...HUM SOC 18/19. PAGE 69 H1387 — BIBLIOG POLICY ATTIT NAT/G

N13
H T.,GRUNDZUGE DES CHINESISCHEN VOLKSCHARACTERS. ASIA CULTURE SOCIETY...HUM 19/20. PAGE 63 H1262 — ATTIT PERSON ART/METH LING

B27
QUERARD J.M.,LA FRANCE LITTERAIRE (12 VOLS.). FRANCE CULTURE...HUM SOC 16/19. PAGE 129 H2573 — BIBLIOG/A BIOG ART/METH

B34
SMITH P.,A HISTORY OF MODERN CULTURE (2 VOLS.). NAT/G...HUM SOC TREND. PAGE 146 H2916 — BIBLIOG CULTURE CONCPT

B37
BERDYAEV N.,THE ORIGIN OF RUSSIAN COMMUNISM. MOD/EUR RUSSIA USSR INTELL SECT REV...ANARCH HUM 19/20 ORTHO/RUSS COM/PARTY CHRISTIAN. PAGE 15 H0294 — MARXISM NAT/LISM CULTURE ATTIT

B38
RAWLINSON H.G.,INDIA: A SHORT CULTURAL HISTORY. INDIA LAW STRATA FORCES INT/TRADE ADMIN COLONIAL PERSON...GEOG HUM BIBLIOG WORSHIP 20. PAGE 130 H2598 — CULTURE SECT MYTH ART/METH

B40
THE GUIDE TO CATHOLIC LITERATURE, 1888-1940. ALL/VALS...POLICY MYSTIC HUM PHIL/SCI 19/20. PAGE 2 H0032 — BIBLIOG/A CATHISM DIPLOM CULTURE

B41
GRISMER R.,A NEW BIBLIOGRAPHY OF THE LITERATURES OF SPAIN AND SPANISH AMERICA. CHRIST-17C MOD/EUR PRE/AMER SPAIN CULTURE DIPLOM EDU/PROP...ART/METH GEOG HUM PHIL/SCI 20. PAGE 61 H1229 — BIBLIOG LAW NAT/G ECO/UNDEV

B42
CONOVER H.F.,NEW ZEALAND: A SELECTED LIST OF REFERENCES (PAMPHLET). NEW/ZEALND ECO/UNDEV AGRI INDUS LABOR NAT/G SCHOOL FORCES DIPLOM COLONIAL WAR ...HUM 20. PAGE 32 H0643 — BIBLIOG/A S/ASIA CULTURE

B42
SINGTON D.,THE GOEBBELS EXPERIMENT. GERMANY MOD/EUR NAT/G EX/STRUC FORCES CONTROL ROUTINE WAR TOTALISM PWR...ART/METH HUM 20 NAZI GOEBBELS/J. PAGE 144 H2886 — FASCISM EDU/PROP ATTIT COM/IND

B43
JONES C.K.,A BIBLIOGRAPHY OF LATIN AMERICAN BIBLIOGRAPHIES (2ND ED.). CULTURE ALL/VALS...POLICY GEOG HUM SOC LING BIOG TREND 20. PAGE 82 H1629 — BIBLIOG/A L/A+17C HIST/WRIT

B44
CASSIRER E.,AN ESSAY ON MAN: AN INTRODUCTION TO A PHILOSOPHY OF HUMAN CULTURE. UNIV SECT CREATE EDU/PROP ATTIT KNOWL...HUM CONCPT MYTH TOT/POP. PAGE 28 H0556 — CULTURE SOC

B44
FULLER G.H.,TURKEY: A SELECTED LIST OF REFERENCES. ISLAM TURKEY CULTURE ECO/UNDEV AGRI DIPLOM NAT/LISM CONSERVE...GEOG HUM INT/LAW SOC 7/20 MAPS. PAGE 54 H1075 — BIBLIOG/A ALL/VALS

B44
US LIBRARY OF CONGRESS,RUSSIA: A CHECK LIST PRELIMINARY TO A BASIC BIBLIOGRAPHY OF MATERIALS IN THE RUSSIAN LANGUAGE. COM USSR CULTURE EDU/PROP MARXISM...ART/METH HUM LING 19/20. PAGE 160 H3204 — BIBLIOG LAW SECT

B47
JURJI E.J.,THE GREAT RELIGIONS OF THE MODERN WORLD. CULTURE INTELL SOCIETY INT/ORG CONSULT CHOOSE ATTIT DRIVE PERSON RIGID/FLEX...HUM CONCPT OBS BIOG HIST/WRIT TREND GEN/LAWS 20 WORSHIP. PAGE 82 H1643 — UNIV SECT

B48
YAKOBSON S.,FIVE HUNDRED RUSSIAN WORKS FOR COLLEGE LIBRARIES (PAMPHLET). MOD/EUR USSR MARXISM SOCISM ...ART/METH GEOG HUM JURID SOC 13/20. PAGE 171 H3431 — BIBLIOG NAT/G CULTURE COM

B50
CANTRIL H.,TENSIONS THAT CAUSE WAR. UNIV CULTURE R+D CREATE EDU/PROP DRIVE PERSON KNOWL ORD/FREE ...HUM PSY SOC OBS CENSUS TREND CON/ANAL SOC/EXP SIMUL GEN/METH ANTHOL COLD/WAR TOT/POP. PAGE 26 H0523 — SOCIETY PHIL/SCI PEACE

B50
COUNCIL BRITISH NATIONAL BIB,BRITISH NATIONAL BIBLIOGRAPHY. UK AGRI CONSTRUC PERF/ART POL/PAR SECT CREATE INT/TRADE LEAD...HUM JURID PHIL/SCI 20. PAGE 34 H0677 — BIBLIOG/A NAT/G TEC/DEV DIPLOM

B50
EMBREE J.F.,BIBLIOGRAPHY OF THE PEOPLES AND CULTURES OF MAINLAND SOUTHEAST ASIA. CAMBODIA LAOS — BIBLIOG/A CULTURE

THAILAND VIETNAM LAW...GEOG HUM SOC MYTH LING CHARTS WORSHIP 20. PAGE 46 H0915 S/ASIA

B50
GOFF F.R.,FIFTEENTH CENTURY BOOKS IN THE LIBRARY OF CONGRESS. CHRIST-17C GERMANY ITALY CULTURE INTELL SECT CREATE...PHIL/SCI CONCPT CLASSIF BIOG TIME/SEQ 15. PAGE 58 H1153 BIBLIOG KNOWL HUM

B51
HUXLEY J.,FREEDOM AND CULTURE. UNIV LAW SOCIETY R+D ACADEM SCHOOL CREATE SANCTION ATTIT KNOWL...HUM ANTHOL 20. PAGE 76 H1512 CULTURE ORD/FREE PHIL/SCI IDEA/COMP

B51
WABEKE B.H.,A GUIDE TO DUTCH BIBLIOGRAPHIES. BELGIUM INDONESIA NETHERLAND DIPLOM INT/TRADE WAR NAT/LISM KNOWL...ART/METH HUM JURID CON/ANAL 14/20. PAGE 164 H3282 BIBLIOG/A NAT/G CULTURE COLONIAL

B52
LEYS W.,ETHICS FOR POLICY DECISIONS. INTELL NAT/G CONSULT PLAN DOMIN EDU/PROP LEGIT COERCE KNOWL MORAL PWR...HUM GEN/LAWS. PAGE 96 H1920 ACT/RES POLICY

S54
ALBRECT M.C.,"THE RELATIONSHIP OF LITERATURE AND SOCIETY." STRATA STRUCT DIPLOM...POLICY SOC/INTEG. PAGE 5 H0097 HUM CULTURE WRITING NAT/COMP

B55
FRIEDMAN G.,INDUSTRIAL SOCIETY: THE EMERGENCE OF THE HUMAN PROBLEMS OF AUTOMATION. UNIV CULTURE ECO/DEV TEC/DEV INGP/REL HAPPINESS RATIONAL UTOPIA ROLE...HUM SOC TIME/SEQ 20. PAGE 53 H1064 AUTOMAT ADJUST ALL/VALS CONCPT

B56
WILBER D.N.,ANNOTATED BIBLIOGRAPHY OF AFGHANISTAN. AFGHANISTN...ART/METH GEOG HUM SOC CON/ANAL 19/20. PAGE 168 H3358 BIBLIOG/A SOCIETY NAT/G ASIA

B57
CENTRAL ASIAN RESEARCH CENTRE,BIBLIOGRAPHY OF RECENT SOVIET SOURCE MATERIAL ON SOVIET CENTRAL ASIA AND THE BORDERLANDS. AFGHANISTN INDIA PAKISTAN UAR USSR ECO/UNDEV AGRI EXTR/IND INDUS ACADEM ADMIN ...HEAL HUM LING CON/ANAL 20. PAGE 28 H0567 BIBLIOG/A COM CULTURE NAT/G

B57
HERNANDEZ-ARREGU J.,IMPERIALISMO Y CULTURA (LA POLITICA EN LA INTELIGENCIA ARGENTINA). L/A+17C CULTURE ELITES WRITING COLONIAL CROWD ATTIT FASCISM MARXISM SOCISM...BIOG IDEA/COMP 20 ARGEN PERON/JUAN COM/PARTY. PAGE 70 H1403 INTELL CREATE ART/METH HUM

B57
KANTOROWICZ E.,THE KING'S TWO BODIES; A STUDY IN MEDIEVAL POLITICAL THEOLOGY. UK LAW CONSTN NAT/G CT/SYS...ART/METH HUM CONCPT MYTH TIME/SEQ BIBLIOG 4/17 ELIZABTH/I POPE CHURCH/STA. PAGE 83 H1657 JURID SECT CHIEF SOVEREIGN

B58
KURL S.,ESTONIA: A SELECTED BIBLIOGRAPHY. USSR ESTONIA LAW INTELL SECT...ART/METH GEOG HUM SOC 20. PAGE 89 H1784 BIBLIOG CULTURE NAT/G

B58
YUAN TUNG-LI,CHINA IN WESTERN LITERATURE. SECT DIPLOM...ART/METH GEOG JURID SOC BIOG CON/ANAL. PAGE 172 H3441 BIBLIOG ASIA CULTURE HUM

B60
KOHN H.,PAN-SLAVISM: ITS HISTORY AND IDEOLOGY. COM CZECHOSLVK EUR+WWI MOD/EUR USSR YUGOSLAVIA CULTURE ELITES INTELL KIN NAT/G EDU/PROP DRIVE SOVEREIGN ...HUM PHIL/SCI MYTH HIST/WRIT 19/20. PAGE 87 H1745 ATTIT CONCPT NAT/LISM

B60
MORRISON C.,THE POWERS THAT BE. NAT/G SUPEGO ...POLICY CONCPT IDEA/COMP WORSHIP 20 BIBLE. PAGE 113 H2265 HUM ORD/FREE

B60
NAKAMURA H.,THE WAYS OF THINKING OF EASTERN PEOPLES. ASIA INDIA PERSON...HUM SOC LING LOG WORSHIP CHINJAP. PAGE 115 H2305 CULTURE SECT ATTIT

S60
ARENDT H.,"SOCIETY AND CULTURE." FUT CULTURE INTELL STRATA EDU/PROP ATTIT PERSON KNOWL...ART/METH HUM 20. PAGE 8 H0161 SOCIETY CREATE

B61
BEARCE G.D.,BRITISH ATTITUDES TOWARDS INDIA 1784-1858. INDIA S/ASIA UK SECT ECO/TAC...POLICY HUM 18/19. PAGE 12 H0246 COLONIAL ATTIT ALL/IDEOS NAT/G

B61
FIRTH R.,HISTORY AND TRADITIONS OF TIKOPIA. S/ASIA KIN SECT RUMOR WAR...MYTH WORSHIP 20 POLYNESIA. PAGE 50 H1008 CULTURE STRUCT HUM

B61
TACHAKKYO K.,BIBLIOGRAPHY OF KOREAN STUDIES: A BIBLIOGRAPHICAL GUIDE TO KOREAN PUBLICATIONS ON KOREAN STUDIES APPEARING 1945-1958. KOREA LAW...HUM JURID PHIL/SCI LING 19/20. PAGE 152 H3033 BIBLIOG/A SOCIETY CULTURE WAR

B61
YUAN TUNG-LI,A GUIDE TO DOCTORAL DISSERTATIONS BY CHINESE STUDENTS IN AMERICA, 1905-1960. ASIA CULTURE SOCIETY ECO/UNDEV NAT/G PROB/SOLV DIPLOM LEAD ATTIT...HUM SOC STAT 20. PAGE 172 H3442 BIBLIOG ACADEM ACT/RES OP/RES

B61
ZIMMERMAN I.,A GUIDE TO CURRENT LATIN AMERICAN PERIODICALS: HUMANITIES AND SOCIAL SCIENCES. LABOR SECT EDU/PROP...GEOG HUM SOC LING STAT NAT/COMP 20. PAGE 173 H3456 BIBLIOG/A DIPLOM L/A+17C PHIL/SCI

S61
RANDALL F.B.,"COMMUNISM IN THE HIGH ANDES." L/A+17C PERU USSR SOCIETY PLAN EDU/PROP TOTALISM ATTIT RIGID/FLEX PWR WEALTH...HUM CONCPT GEN/LAWS 20 BOLIV EQUADOR. PAGE 129 H2589 CULTURE DRIVE

B62
HUCKER C.O.,CHINA: A CRITICAL BIBLIOGRAPHY (PAMPHLET). ASIA STRUCT AGRI FINAN INDUS HABITAT MARXISM...EPIST HUM. PAGE 74 H1487 BIBLIOG/A CULTURE INTELL SOCIETY

B62
SILBERMAN B.S.,JAPAN AND KOREA; A CRITICAL BIBLIOGRAPHY. KOREA LAW STRATA STRUCT AGRI INDUS NAT/G POL/PAR SECT...HUM LING IDEA/COMP 5/20 CHINJAP. PAGE 144 H2872 BIBLIOG/A CULTURE S/ASIA

B63
KOGAN N.,THE POLITICS OF ITALIAN FOREIGN POLICY. EUR+WWI LEGIS DOMIN LEGIT EXEC PWR RESPECT SKILL ...POLICY DECISION HUM SOC METH/CNCPT OBS INT CHARTS 20. PAGE 87 H1737 NAT/G ROUTINE DIPLOM ITALY

B63
LARSON A.,A WARLESS WORLD. FUT CULTURE NAT/G VOL/ASSN FORCES CREATE DOMIN PEACE ALL/VALS...HUM STERTYP 20. PAGE 91 H1824 SOCIETY CONCPT ARMS/CONT

S63
LOPEZIBOR J.,"L'EUROPE, FORME DE VIE." CHRIST-17C EUR+WWI FUT MOD/EUR SOCIETY INT/ORG SECT EDU/PROP ATTIT RIGID/FLEX ALL/VALS...POLICY HUM SOC TIME/SEQ TREND GEN/LAWS. PAGE 98 H1966 NAT/G CULTURE

S63
MORISON D.,"AFRICAN STUDIES IN THE SOVIET UNION." AFR COM CULTURE INTELL REGION ATTIT KNOWL...HUM TREND 20. PAGE 113 H2258 EDU/PROP USSR

S63
RINTELEN F.,"L'HOMME EUROPEEN." EUR+WWI FUT CULTURE INTELL SECT EDU/PROP ATTIT ALL/VALS...HUM SOC METH/CNCPT TREND GEN/LAWS 20 WORSHIP. PAGE 132 H2631 SOCIETY PERSON

B64
BERNSTEIN H.,A BOOKSHELF ON BRAZIL. BRAZIL ADMIN COLONIAL...HUM JURID SOC 20. PAGE 16 H0315 BIBLIOG/A NAT/G L/A+17C ECO/UNDEV

B64
FROMM E.,MARX'S CONCEPT OF MAN. LABOR OWN PERSON ...HUM IDEA/COMP GEN/LAWS 17 MARX/KARL EUROPE SPINOZA/B GOETHE/J HEGEL/GWF. PAGE 54 H1072 INGP/REL CONCPT MARXISM SOCISM

B64
REMAK J.,THE GENTLE CRITIC: THEODOR FONTANE AND GERMAN POLITICS, 1848-1898. GERMANY PRUSSIA CULTURE ELITES BAL/PWR DIPLOM WRITING GOV/REL...HUM BIOG 19 BISMARCK/O JUNKER FONTANE/T. PAGE 131 H2614 PERSON SOCIETY WORKER CHIEF

B64
TODD W.B.,A BIBLIOGRAPHY OF EDMUND BURKE. MOD/EUR UK NAT/G EDU/PROP ATTIT...HUM 18 BURKE/EDM. PAGE 156 H3110 BIBLIOG/A PHIL/SCI WRITING CONCPT

B64
TURNER M.C.,LIBROS EN VENTA EN HISPANOAMERICA Y ESPANA. SPAIN LAW CONSTN CULTURE ADMIN LEAD...HUM SOC 20. PAGE 157 H3141 BIBLIOG L/A+17C NAT/G DIPLOM

B64
VON GRUNEBAUM G.E.,MODERN ISLAM: THE SEARCH FOR CULTURAL IDENTITY. ACADEM NEIGH WRITING NAT/LISM ...HUM CONCPT 19/20 MUSLIM MID/EAST ARABS. PAGE 163 H3269 ISLAM CULTURE CREATE SECT

S64
HIRAI N.,"SHINTO AND INTERNATIONAL PROBLEMS." SOCIETY NAT/G PLAN EDU/PROP RACE/REL PEACE ATTIT PERCEPT LOVE MORAL...HUM MYTH RECORD SAMP TREND STERTYP TOT/POP 20 UN CHINJAP SHINTO. PAGE 71 H1423 ASIA SECT

S64
IRELE A.,"A DEFENSE OF NEGRITUDE." AFR NAT/LISM ...HUM 20 NEGRO. PAGE 78 H1566 CONCPT CULTURE NAT/COMP KIN

B65
SLOTKIN J.S.,READINGS IN EARLY ANTHROPOLOGY. INTELL SECT CREATE ATTIT KNOWL...HUM PHIL/SCI PSY LING 1/18. PAGE 145 H2902 SOC CULTURE GP/COMP

S65
RUBINSTEIN A.Z.,"YUGOSLAVIA'S OPENING SOCIETY." COM USSR INTELL NAT/G LEGIS TOP/EX LEGIT CT/SYS RIGID/FLEX ALL/VALS SOCISM...HUM TIME/SEQ TREND 20. PAGE 135 H2708 CONSTN EX/STRUC YUGOSLAVIA

B66
HANKE L.,HANDBOOK OF LATIN AMERICAN STUDIES. BIBLIOG/A

ECO/UNDEV ADMIN LEAD...HUM SOC 20. PAGE 65 H1313 L/A+17C INDEX NAT/G

B66
LAVEN P.,RENAISSANCE ITALY: 1464-1534. ITALY AGRI EXTR/IND FINAN MUNIC INT/TRADE DRIVE...CATH GEOG CHARTS BIBLIOG/A 15. PAGE 92 H1841 CULTURE HUM TEC/DEV KNOWL

B66
RADIN P.,THE METHOD AND THEORY OF ETHNOLOGY. CULTURE STRUCT BIO/SOC HABITAT...HUM OBS/ENVIR METH/COMP GEN/LAWS 20 HUMANISM. PAGE 129 H2578 PHIL/SCI SOC METH SOCIETY

B66
RAEFF M.,ORIGINS OF THE RUSSIAN INTELLIGENTSIA: THE EIGHTEENTH-CENTURY NOBILITY. RUSSIA FAM NAT/G EDU/PROP ADMIN PERS/REL ATTIT...HUM BIOG 18. PAGE 129 H2580 INTELL ELITES STRATA CONSERVE

B67
PENDLE G.,PARAGUAY: A RIVERSIDE NATION (3RD ED.). PARAGUAY CHIEF ISOLAT...HUM CHARTS BIBLIOG 16/20. PAGE 124 H2487 CULTURE GEOG ECO/UNDEV

B67
THOMPSON E.T.,PERSPECTIVES ON THE SOUTH: AGENDA FOR RESEARCH. CULTURE ECO/UNDEV SECT GP/REL EFFICIENCY ALL/VALS...HUM SOC CONCPT LING 20 NEGRO. PAGE 154 H3080 PROB/SOLV IDEA/COMP REGION ACT/RES

HUM/RIGHTS....HUMAN RIGHTS, DECLARATIONS OF HUMAN RIGHTS, AND HUMAN RIGHTS COMMISSIONS (OFFICIAL ORGANIZATIONS)

HUMAN DEVELOPMENTAL CHANGE....SEE DEVELOPMNT

HUMAN NATURE....SEE PERSON

HUMAN RELATIONS....SEE RELATIONS INDEX

HUMAN RIGHTS, DECLARATIONS OF HUMAN RIGHTS, AND HUMAN RIGHTS COMMISSIONS (OFFICIAL ORGANIZATIONS)....SEE HUM/RIGHTS

HUMANISM....HUMANISM AND HUMANISTS

B36
MARITAIN J.,FREEDOM IN THE MODERN WORLD. CONSTN NAT/G SECT CAP/ISM MARXISM SOCISM...GOV/COMP IDEA/COMP 19/20 HUMANISM CHRISTIAN. PAGE 102 H2049 GEN/LAWS POLICY ORD/FREE

B66
RADIN P.,THE METHOD AND THEORY OF ETHNOLOGY. CULTURE STRUCT BIO/SOC HABITAT...HUM OBS/ENVIR METH/COMP GEN/LAWS 20 HUMANISM. PAGE 129 H2578 PHIL/SCI SOC METH SOCIETY

HUMANITARIANISM....SEE HUMANISM

HUMANITIES....SEE HUM

HUME D. H1493,H1494

HUME/D....DAVID HUME

N19
HABERLER G.,A SURVEY OF INTERNATIONAL TRADE THEORY (PAMPHLET). FINAN NAT/G COST INCOME 18/20 MONEY HUME/D MARSHALL/A. PAGE 63 H1267 INT/TRADE BAL/PAY GEN/LAWS POLICY

B38
JESSOP T.E.,A BIBLIOGRAPHY OF DAVID HUME AND OF SCOTTISH PHILOSOPHY FROM FRANCIS HUTCHESON TO LORD BALFOUR. UK INTELL NAT/G ATTIT...CONCPT 17/20 HUME/D CMN/WLTH. PAGE 81 H1615 BIBLIOG EPIST PERCEPT BIOG

B64
COBBAN A.,ROUSSEAU AND THE MODERN STATE (2ND ED.). FRANCE PROB/SOLV NAT/LISM UTOPIA PERSON MORAL ...EPIST PHIL/SCI SOC IDEA/COMP 18 ROUSSEAU/J BURKE/EDM HOBBES/T HUME/D. PAGE 30 H0612 GEN/LAWS INGP/REL NAT/G ORD/FREE

HUMPHREY/H....HUBERT HORATIO HUMPHREY

HUMPHREYS R.A. H1495

HUNGARY....SEE ALSO COM

N19
TABORSKY E.,CONFORMITY UNDER COMMUNISM (PAMPHLET). CZECHOSLVK HUNGARY POLAND SCHOOL DOMIN PRESS ...TREND GOV/COMP 20. PAGE 152 H3030 COM CONTROL EDU/PROP NAT/G

B50
KANN R.A.,THE MULTINATIONAL EMPIRE (2 VOLS.). AUSTRIA CZECHOSLVK GERMANY HUNGARY CULTURE NAT/G POL/PAR PROVS REGION REV FEDERAL...GEOG TREND CHARTS IDEA/COMP NAT/COMP 19/20. PAGE 83 H1654 NAT/LISM MOD/EUR

B55
MID-EUROPEAN LAW PROJECT,CHURCH AND STATE BEHIND THE IRON CURTAIN. COM CZECHOSLVK HUNGARY POLAND USSR CULTURE SECT EDU/PROP GOV/REL CATHISM...CHARTS ANTHOL BIBLIOG WORSHIP 20 CHURCH/STA. PAGE 110 H2202 LAW MARXISM POLICY

B59
ETSCHMANN R.,DIE WAHRUNGS- UND DEVISENPOLITIK DES OSTBLOCKS UND IHRE AUSWIRKUNGEN AUF DIE WIRTSCHAFTSBEZIEHUNGEN ZWISCHEN OST U WEST. BULGARIA CZECHOSLVK HUNGARY POLAND USSR MARKET NAT/G PLAN DIPLOM...NAT/COMP 20. PAGE 47 H0943 ECO/TAC FINAN POLICY INT/TRADE

B59
GOLDWIN R.A.,READINGS IN RUSSIAN FOREIGN POLICY. HUNGARY USSR YUGOSLAVIA ELITES INT/ORG NAT/G REV WAR NAT/LISM PERSON SOCISM...CHARTS 20 MAPS BOLSHEVISM. PAGE 58 H1160 COM MARXISM DIPLOM POLICY

B60
SZTARAY Z.,BIBLIOGRAPHY ON HUNGARY. HUNGARY MOD/EUR CULTURE INDUS SECT DIPLOM REV...ART/METH SOC LING 18/20. PAGE 151 H3029 BIBLIOG NAT/G COM MARXISM

B61
SCHIEDER T.,DOCUMENTS ON THE EXPULSION OF THE GERMANS FROM EASTERN-CENTRAL-EUROPE (VOL. II/III). COM EUR+WWI GERMANY HUNGARY ROMANIA USSR DIPLOM RACE/REL 20 MIGRATION. PAGE 139 H2785 GEOG CULTURE

B63
VALJAVEC F.,AUSGEWAHLTE AUFSATZE. GERMANY HUNGARY STRUCT ATTIT...CONCPT IDEA/COMP 18/20 BALKANS. PAGE 161 H3223 SOCIETY CULTURE GP/REL NAT/LISM

N63
LIBRARY HUNGARIAN ACADEMY SCI,HUNGARIAN PUBLICATIONS ON ASIA AND AFRICA, 1950-1962: A SELECTED BIBLIOGRAPHY (PAMPHLET). AFR ASIA HUNGARY S/ASIA ECO/UNDEV NAT/G EDU/PROP ATTIT 20 UNESCO. PAGE 96 H1922 BIBLIOG REGION DIPLOM WRITING

S64
MARES V.E.,"EAST EUROPE'S SECOND CHANCE." COM EUR+WWI HUNGARY ROMANIA USSR YUGOSLAVIA ECO/UNDEV NAT/G TOP/EX CREATE PLAN TEC/DEV REGION NAT/LISM RIGID/FLEX PWR...CONCPT STAT COMECON 20. PAGE 102 H2047 VOL/ASSN ECO/TAC

S65
HELMREICH E.C.,"KADAR'S HUNGARY." COM EUR+WWI HUNGARY USSR INTELL ECO/DEV AGRI INT/ORG TOP/EX DOMIN ALL/VALS WORK COLD/WAR 20. PAGE 69 H1390 NAT/G RIGID/FLEX TOTALISM

B66
BROWN J.F.,THE NEW EASTERN EUROPE. ALBANIA BULGARIA HUNGARY POLAND ROMANIA CULTURE AGRI POL/PAR WAR NAT/LISM MARXISM...CHARTS BIBLIOG 20. PAGE 22 H0444 DIPLOM COM NAT/G ECO/UNDEV

B66
SPULBER N.,THE STATE AND ECONOMIC DEVELOPMENT IN EASTERN EUROPE. BULGARIA COM CZECHOSLVK HUNGARY POLAND YUGOSLAVIA CULTURE PLAN CAP/ISM INT/TRADE CONTROL...POLICY CHARTS METH/COMP BIBLIOG/A 19/20. PAGE 148 H2958 ECO/DEV ECO/UNDEV NAT/G TOTALISM

B66
WEBER J.,EOTVOS UND DIE UNGARISCHE NATIONALITATENFRAGE. HUNGARY CULTURE SOCIETY REV ORD/FREE SOVEREIGN...BIOG 19. PAGE 166 H3318 NAT/LISM GP/REL ATTIT CONCPT

B67
NATIONAL SCIENCE FOUNDATION,DIRECTORY OF SELECTED RESEARCH INSTITUTES IN EASTERN EUROPE. BULGARIA CZECHOSLVK HUNGARY POLAND ROMANIA INTELL ACADEM NAT/G ACT/RES 20. PAGE 116 H2323 INDEX R+D COM PHIL/SCI

S68
BOSSCHERE G D.E.,"A L'EST DU NOUVEAU." CZECHOSLVK HUNGARY POLAND ROMANIA YUGOSLAVIA AGRI CREATE ECO/TAC COERCE GP/REL ATTIT MARXISM SOCISM 20. PAGE 19 H0382 ORD/FREE COM NAT/G DIPLOM

B96
LOWELL A.L.,GOVERNMENTS AND PARTIES IN CONTINENTAL EUROPE, VOL. II. AUSTRIA GERMANY HUNGARY MOD/EUR SWITZERLND SOCIETY EX/STRUC LEGIS DIPLOM AGREE LEAD PARL/PROC PWR...POLICY 19. PAGE 99 H1974 POL/PAR NAT/G GOV/REL ELITES

HUNKIN P. H1496

HUNT E.F. H1497

HUNT G.L. H1498

HUNTER E. H1499

HUNTER G. H1500,H1501

HUNTER R. H1502

HUNTINGTON E. H1503,H1504

HUNTINGTON S.P. H0457,H1505,H1506

HUNTNGTN/S....SAMUEL P. HUNTINGTON

HUNTON/P....PHILIP HUNTON

HUREWITZ J.C. H1507

HURLEY/PJ....PATRICK J. HURLEY

HURST C. H1508

HUSSEIN....KING HUSSEIN I, KING OF JORDAN

HUSSEY E.R. H2158

HUTCHINS F.G. H1509

HUTCHINS/R....ROBERT HUTCHINS

HUTTON J. H1510

HUXLEY J. H1511,H1512

HUXLEY M. H1513

HUXLEY T.H. H1514

HYDE D. H1515,H1516

HYMES D. H1517

HYPO/EXP....INTELLECTUAL CONSTRUCTS

B48
WHITE C.L.,HUMAN GEOGRAPHY: AN ECOLOGICAL STUDY OF GEOGRAPHY. UNIV SEA CULTURE AGRI EXTR/IND RACE/REL PRODUC...CHARTS HYPO/EXP SIMUL GEN/LAWS T. PAGE 167 H3345 — SOC HABITAT GEOG SOCIETY

B49
SARGENT S.S.,CULTURE AND PERSONALITY. FUT UNIV SOCIETY FAM KIN NEIGH BIO/SOC DRIVE PERCEPT RIGID/FLEX LOVE RESPECT...PSY SOC CONCPT OBS TIME/SEQ TREND CON/ANAL CHARTS HYPO/EXP SIMUL TOT/POP. PAGE 138 H2754 — CULTURE PERSON

S49
DEXTER L.A.,"A DIALOGUE ON THE SOCIAL PSYCHOLOGY OF COLONIALISM AND ON CERTAIN PUERTO RICAN PROFESSIONAL PERSONALITY PATTERNS." L/A+17C PUERT/RICO STRATA STRUCT DOMIN ISOLAT DRIVE ...NAT/COMP PERS/COMP HYPO/EXP 20 JEWS NEGRO. PAGE 41 H0813 — COLONIAL SOC PSY PERSON

B55
DUVERGER M.,THE POLITICAL ROLE OF WOMEN. FRANCE GERMANY/W NORWAY YUGOSLAVIA STRATA LOBBY AGE ATTIT ROLE...STAT SAMP CHARTS METH/COMP NAT/COMP HYPO/EXP FEMALE/SEX. PAGE 44 H0875 — SEX LEAD PARTIC CHOOSE

S57
DEXTER L.A.,"A SOCIAL THEORY OF MENTAL DEFICIENCY." CULTURE PUB/INST PROB/SOLV CRIME PERS/REL STRANGE PERSON SUPEGO SKILL...EPIST SOC/WK HYPO/EXP. PAGE 41 H0814 — SOC PSY HEALTH ROLE

S57
MARCH J.C.,"PARTY LEGISLATIVE REPRESENTATION AS A FUNCTION OF ELECTION RESULTS." DRIVE...PROBABIL REGRESS STYLE CHARTS HYPO/EXP SIMUL. PAGE 102 H2046 — REPRESENT GOV/COMP LEGIS CHOOSE

S58
EULAV H.,"HD LASSWELL'S DEVELOPMENTAL ANALYSIS." FUT CULTURE TOP/EX PLAN CHOOSE SUPEGO PWR...TREND HYPO/EXP SIMUL GEN/METH VAL/FREE 20 LASSWELL/H. PAGE 47 H0948 — CONCPT NEW/IDEA ELITES

S59
LEVINE R.A.,"ANTI-EUROPEAN VIOLENCE IN AFRICA: A COMPARATIVE ANALYSIS." AFR CULTURE NAT/G DIPLOM EDU/PROP COLONIAL REGION COERCE ATTIT PWR...PSY CONCPT TIME/SEQ TREND HYPO/EXP SOC/EXP STERTYP GEN/METH COLD/WAR 20. PAGE 95 H1903 — DRIVE ORD/FREE REV

L60
KAPLAN M.A.,"COMMUNIST COUP IN CZECHOSLOVAKIA." COM EUR+WWI INTELL LABOR LOC/G NAT/G POL/PAR FORCES EDU/PROP EXEC MARXISM...TIME/SEQ HYPO/EXP 20. PAGE 83 H1659 — STRUCT COERCE CZECHOSLVK

S61
SCHELLING T.C.,"NUCLEAR STRATEGY IN EUROPE." COM EUR+WWI USSR NAT/G FORCES NUC/PWR DRIVE ORD/FREE PWR...DECISION CONCPT OBS TREND HYPO/EXP 20. PAGE 139 H2784 — FUT COERCE ARMS/CONT WAR

B63
TUCKER R.C.,THE SOVIET POLITICAL MIND. COM INTELL NAT/G TOP/EX EDU/PROP ADMIN COERCE TOTALISM ATTIT PWR MARXISM...PSY MYTH HYPO/EXP 20. PAGE 157 H3136 — STRUCT RIGID/FLEX ELITES USSR

B64
COLLINS B.E.,A SOCIAL PSYCHOLOGY OF GROUP PROCESSES FOR DECISION-MAKING. PROB/SOLV ROUTINE...SOC CHARTS HYPO/EXP. PAGE 32 H0632 — FACE/GP DECISION NAT/G INDUS

B66
FARRELL R.B.,APPROACHES TO COMPARATIVE AND INTERNATIONAL POLITICS. RUSSIA SOCIETY ACADEM GOV/REL GP/REL...METH/CNCPT NET/THEORY GOV/COMP HYPO/EXP SOC/EXP GEN/METH ANTHOL. PAGE 49 H0973 — DIPLOM NAT/COMP NAT/G

B66
GURR T.,NEW ERROR-COMPENSATED MEASURES FOR COMPARING NATIONS* SOME CORRELATES OF CIVIL VIOLENCE. WOR+45 SOCIETY REV ISOLAT...PHIL/SCI SOC QUANT TESTS SAMP/SIZ HYPO/EXP. PAGE 63 H1254 — NAT/COMP INDEX COERCE NEW/IDEA

B66
LENSKI G.E.,POWER AND PRIVILEGE: A THEORY OF SOCIAL STRATIFICATION. SWEDEN UK UNIV USSR CULTURE ECO/UNDEV PRIVIL PWR...PHIL/SCI CONCPT CHARTS IDEA/COMP HYPO/EXP METH MARX/KARL. PAGE 94 H1882 — SOC STRATA STRUCT SOCIETY

S66
GALTUNG J.,"EAST-WEST INTERACTION PATTERNS." DIPLOM INT/TRADE...NET/THEORY CON/ANAL CHARTS NAT/COMP INDEX NATO COLD/WAR UN WARSAW/P. PAGE 55 H1090 — STAT HYPO/EXP

S67
CATTELL D.T.,"A NEO-MARXIST THEORY OF COMPARATIVE ANALYSIS." USSR STRATA INSPECT DOMIN CONTROL COERCE OWN TOTALISM PWR...FASCIST HYPO/EXP METH 20. PAGE 28 H0561 — GOV/COMP MARXISM SIMUL CLASSIF

HYPOTHETICAL EXPERIMENTS....SEE HYPO/EXP

IADB....INTER-ASIAN DEVELOPMENT BANK

IAEA....INTERNATIONAL ATOMIC ENERGY AGENCY

IANNI O. H1518

IBERO-AMERICAN INSTITUTES H1519

IBO....IBO TRIBE

B64
GREEN M.M.,IBO VILLAGE AFFAIRS. AFR FORCES PERS/REL ADJUST ISOLAT ATTIT HABITAT PERSON ALL/VALS...JURID RECORD SOC/INTEG 20 IBO. PAGE 60 H1207 — MUNIC CULTURE ECO/UNDEV SOC

B66
BASDEN G.T.,NIGER IBOS. NIGERIA STRUCT SECT CHIEF COLONIAL HABITAT...POLICY SOC MYTH OBS WORSHIP 20 IBO. PAGE 12 H0233 — CULTURE AFR SOCIETY

S67
VINCENT S.,"SHOULD BIAFRA SURVIVE?" NIGERIA ECO/UNDEV CHIEF FORCES ECO/TAC GP/REL DISCRIM PEACE ORD/FREE SOC/INTEG 20 BIAFRA IBO. PAGE 163 H3256 — AFR REV REGION NAT/G

IBRAHIM-HILMY H1520

IBRD....INTERNATIONAL BANK FOR RECONSTRUCTION AND DEVELOPMENT

ICA....INTERNATIONAL COOPERATION ADMINISTRATION

ICC....U.S. INTERSTATE COMMERCE COMMISSION

ICELAND....ICELAND

B01
BRYCE J.,STUDIES IN HISTORY AND JURISPRUDENCE (2 VOLS.). ICELAND SOUTH/AFR UK LAW PROB/SOLV SOVEREIGN...PHIL/SCI NAT/COMP ROME/ANC ROMAN/LAW. PAGE 23 H0455 — IDEA/COMP CONSTN JURID

B53
ORFIELD L.B.,THE GROWTH OF SCANDINAVIAN LAW. DENMARK ICELAND NORWAY SWEDEN LAW DIPLOM...BIBLIOG 9/20. PAGE 121 H2426 — JURID CT/SYS NAT/G

B64
ANDREN N.,GOVERNMENT AND POLITICS IN THE NORDIC COUNTRIES: DENMARK, FINLAND, ICELAND, NORWAY, SWEDEN. DENMARK FINLAND ICELAND NORWAY SWEDEN POL/PAR CHIEF LEGIS ADMIN REGION REPRESENT ATTIT CONSERVE...CHARTS BIBLIOG/A 20. PAGE 7 H0137 — CONSTN NAT/G CULTURE GOV/COMP

B65
WUORINEN J.H.,SCANDINAVIA. DENMARK FINLAND ICELAND NORWAY SWEDEN SOCIETY AGRI INDUS DELIB/GP DIPLOM INT/TRADE NEUTRAL...GEOG CHARTS BIBLIOG TREATY. PAGE 171 H3428 — NAT/G POL/PAR TREND POLICY

C65
WUORINEN J.H.,"SCANDINAVIA." DENMARK FINLAND ICELAND NORWAY SWEDEN SOCIETY AGRI POL/PAR DELIB/GP DIPLOM INT/TRADE NEUTRAL WAR...CHARTS TREATY 20. PAGE 171 H3427 — BIBLIOG NAT/G POLICY

B67
ANDERSON S.V.,THE NORDIC COUNCIL: A STUDY OF SCANDINAVIAN REGIONALISM. DENMARK FINLAND ICELAND NORWAY SWEDEN MARKET NAT/G VOL/ASSN CONSULT PARL/PROC ATTIT...TIME/SEQ BIBLIOG 20. PAGE 7 H0134 — INT/ORG REGION DIPLOM LEGIS

B67
RAE D.,THE POLITICAL CONSEQUENCES OF ELECTORAL LAWS. EUR+WWI ICELAND ISRAEL NEW/ZEALND UK USA+45 ADJUD APPORT GP/REL MAJORITY...MATH STAT CENSUS CHARTS BIBLIOG 20 AUSTRAL. PAGE 129 H2579 — POL/PAR CHOOSE NAT/COMP REPRESENT

ICJ....INTERNATIONAL COURT OF JUSTICE; SEE ALSO WORLD/CT

ICSU....INTERNATIONAL COUNCIL OF SCIENTIFIC UNIONS

IDA....INTERNATIONAL DEVELOPMENT ASSOCIATION

IDAHO....IDAHO

IDEA/COMP....COMPARISON OF IDEAS

N
NEUE POLITISCHE LITERATUR; BERICHTE UBER DAS INTERNATIONALE SCHRIFTTUM ZUR POLITIK. WOR+45 LAW CONSTN POL/PAR ADMIN LEAD GOV/REL...POLICY IDEA/COMP. PAGE 2 H0027
BIBLIOG/A DIPLOM NAT/G NAT/COMP

B01
BRYCE J.,STUDIES IN HISTORY AND JURISPRUDENCE (2 VOLS.). ICELAND SOUTH/AFR UK LAW PROB/SOLV SOVEREIGN...PHIL/SCI NAT/COMP ROME/ANC ROMAN/LAW. PAGE 23 H0455
IDEA/COMP CONSTN JURID

B08
NIRRNHEIM O.,DAS ERSTE JAHR DES MINISTERIUMS BISMARCK UND DIE OEFFENTLICHE MEINUNG (HEIDELBERGER ABHANDLUNGEN, 20. HEFT). GERMANY MOD/EUR LEGIS DIPLOM EDU/PROP INGP/REL...BIOG GOV/COMP IDEA/COMP BIBLIOG 19 BISMARCK/O. PAGE 118 H2363
CHIEF PRESS NAT/G ATTIT

B11
HUXLEY T.H.,METHOD AND RESULTS: ESSAYS. EDU/PROP REPRESENT OWN PERSON PWR WEALTH...PSY IDEA/COMP GEN/LAWS. PAGE 76 H1514
ORD/FREE NAT/G POPULISM PLURIST

N17
BURKE E.,THOUGHTS ON THE PROSPECT OF A REGICIDE PEACE (PAMPHLET). FRANCE UK SECT DOMIN MURDER PEACE ORD/FREE SOVEREIGN POPULISM...POLICY GOV/COMP IDEA/COMP 18 JACOBINISM COEXIST. PAGE 24 H0483
REV CHIEF NAT/G DIPLOM

B20
BOSANQUET B.,THE PHILOSOPHICAL THEORY OF THE STATE (3RD ED.). SECT LEGIS EDU/PROP ORD/FREE...POLICY SOC GOV/COMP IDEA/COMP NAT/COMP. PAGE 19 H0380
GEN/LAWS CONSTN NAT/G

C20
DUNNING W.A.,"A HISTORY OF POLITICAL THINKERS FROM ROUSSEAU TO SPENCER." NAT/G REV NAT/LISM UTIL CONSERVE MARXISM POPULISM...JURID BIBLIOG 18/19. PAGE 43 H0868
IDEA/COMP PHIL/SCI CONCPT GEN/LAWS

B22
KRABBE H.,THE MODERN IDEA OF THE STATE. LAW CHIEF DIPLOM DOMIN ADMIN REPRESENT CENTRAL ORD/FREE ...NEW/IDEA GOV/COMP IDEA/COMP. PAGE 88 H1761
SOVEREIGN CONSTN PHIL/SCI

B23
POUND R.,INTERPRETATIONS OF LEGAL HISTORY. CULTURE ...PHIL/SCI NEW/IDEA CLASSIF SIMUL GEN/LAWS 19/20. PAGE 127 H2547
LAW IDEA/COMP JURID

B24
SHIROKOGOROFF S.M.,ETHNICAL UNIT AND MILIEU. GP/REL ...PHIL/SCI SOC MATH METH. PAGE 143 H2865
IDEA/COMP HABITAT CULTURE SOCIETY

B24
WALKER F.D.,AFRICA AND HER PEOPLES. ISLAM STRUCT FAM SECT EDU/PROP INGP/REL RACE/REL HABITAT...GEOG SOC IDEA/COMP WORSHIP 20 NEGRO. PAGE 164 H3292
CULTURE AFR GP/COMP KIN

B26
MCIVER R.M.,THE MODERN STATE. UNIV LAW AUTHORIT SOVEREIGN IDEA/COMP. PAGE 107 H2136
GEN/LAWS CONSTN NAT/G PWR

B26
SMITH T.V.,THE DEMOCRATIC WAY OF LIFE. UNIV SOCIETY NAT/G WORKER TASK CHOOSE ALL/VALS...IDEA/COMP WORSHIP. PAGE 146 H2919
MAJORIT CONCPT ORD/FREE LEAD

B27
GOOCH G.P.,ENGLISH DEMOCRATIC IDEAS IN THE SEVENTEENTH CENTURY (2ND ED.). UK LAW SECT FORCES DIPLOM LEAD PARL/PROC REV ATTIT AUTHORIT...ANARCH CONCPT 17 PARLIAMENT CMN/WLTH REFORMERS. PAGE 58 H1167
IDEA/COMP MAJORIT EX/STRUC CONSERVE

B27
HOCART A.M.,KINGSHIP. UNIV CULTURE EX/STRUC TRIBUTE ROUTINE CHOOSE ROLE SOVEREIGN RITUAL 20 KING. PAGE 72 H1441
CHIEF MYTH IDEA/COMP

B28
BARKER E.,POLITICAL THOUGHT IN ENGLAND: FROM HERBERT SPENCER TO THE PRESENT DAY. UK ALL/IDEOS ...PHIL/SCI 19/20 SPENCER/H GREEN/TH BENTHAM/J MAITLAND/F. PAGE 11 H0217
INTELL GEN/LAWS IDEA/COMP

C28
WARD P.W.,"SOVEREIGNTY: A STUDY OF A CONTEMPORARY POLITICAL NOTION." CONSTN NAT/G DIPLOM REPRESENT PLURISM...IDEA/COMP BIBLIOG. PAGE 165 H3304
SOVEREIGN CONCPT NAT/LISM

B29
STURZO L.,THE INTERNATIONAL COMMUNITY AND THE RIGHT OF WAR (TRANS. BY BARBARA BARCLAY CARTER). CULTURE CREATE PROB/SOLV DIPLOM ADJUD CONTROL PEACE PERSON ORD/FREE...INT/LAW IDEA/COMP PACIFIST 20 LEAGUE/NAT. PAGE 150 H3003
INT/ORG PLAN WAR CONCPT

B31
BONAR J.,THEORIES OF POPULATION FROM RALEIGH TO ARTHUR YOUNG. CHRIST-17C MOD/EUR CULTURE SOCIETY R+D CREATE ATTIT PERCEPT RIGID/FLEX...OLD/LIB CONCPT NEW/IDEA TIME/SEQ IDEA/COMP STERTYP GEN/LAWS. PAGE 19 H0372
GEOG BIOG

B32
NIEBUHR R.,MORAL MAN AND IMMORAL SOCIETY* A STUDY IN ETHICS AND POLITICS. UNIV CULTURE SOCIETY STRUCT DIPLOM GOV/REL GP/REL PERS/REL...TREND IDEA/COMP. PAGE 118 H2357
MORAL PWR

B32
THIBAUDET A.,LES IDEES POLITIQUES DE LA FRANCE. FRANCE NAT/G SECT PRESS REV NAT/LISM PEACE ATTIT ...PSY 19/20 JACOBINISM JAURES/JL. PAGE 154 H3070
IDEA/COMP ALL/IDEOS CATHISM

S32
BEARD C.A.,"THE TEUTONIC ORIGINS OF REPRESENTATIVE GOVERNMENT" UK ROMAN/EMP TAX COERCE PWR IDEA/COMP. PAGE 12 H0247
REPRESENT NAT/G

S32
BEARD C.A.,"REPRESENTATIVE GOVERNMENT IN EVOLUTION" WOR-45 AGRI TEC/DEV DOMIN EFFICIENCY ORD/FREE CONSERVE...TIME/SEQ GOV/COMP IDEA/COMP GRECO/ROMN. PAGE 12 H0248
REPRESENT POPULISM NAT/G PWR

C33
MURET C.T.,"FRENCH ROYALIST DOCTRINES SINCE THE REVOLUTION." FRANCE CONSTN NAT/G SECT ADMIN LEAD SOVEREIGN...POLICY BIOG IDEA/COMP BIBLIOG 18/20. PAGE 115 H2295
POL/PAR ATTIT INTELL CONSERVE

B34
LIPPMANN W.,THE METHOD OF FREEDOM. SOCIETY INDUS LABOR LOBBY WAR REPRESENT...POLICY IDEA/COMP METH/COMP 19/20. PAGE 97 H1936
CONCPT MAJORIT NAT/G

C34
BENEDICT R.,"RITUAL" IN ERA SELIGMAN, ENCYCLOPEDIA OF THE SOCIAL SCIENCES." GP/REL...SOC STYLE IDEA/COMP WORSHIP. PAGE 14 H0279
CULTURE ROUTINE ROLE STRUCT

S35
RADCLIFFE-BROWN A.R.,"ON THE CONCEPT OF FUNCTION IN SOCIAL SCIENCE" (BMR)" UNIV CULTURE INTELL ...METH/CNCPT IDEA/COMP 20. PAGE 129 H2577
STRUCT SOCIETY CONCPT GEN/LAWS

B36
MARITAIN J.,FREEDOM IN THE MODERN WORLD. CONSTN NAT/G SECT CAP/ISM MARXISM SOCISM...GOV/COMP IDEA/COMP 19/20 HUMANISM CHRISTIAN. PAGE 102 H2049
GEN/LAWS POLICY ORD/FREE

B36
PREVITE-ORTON C.W.,THE CAMBRIDGE MEDIEVAL HISTORY (8 VOLS.). CHRIST-17C NAT/G PROB/SOLV TEC/DEV LEAD ...POLICY CONCPT WORSHIP. PAGE 128 H2559
BIBLIOG IDEA/COMP TREND

B36
SMITH T.V.,THE PROMISE OF AMERICAN POLITICS. USA-45 WOR-45 LAW CONSTN STRATA PARTIC FASCISM LAISSEZ MARXISM...MAJORIT METH/COMP 18/20 JEFFERSN/T LOCKE/JOHN BENTHAM/J. PAGE 146 H2920
CONCPT ORD/FREE IDEA/COMP NAT/COMP

B37
CARLYLE T.,THE FRENCH REVOLUTION (2 VOLS.). FRANCE CONSTN NAT/G FORCES COERCE MURDER PEACE MORAL POPULISM...TIME/SEQ IDEA/COMP GEN/LAWS 18. PAGE 26 H0532
REV CHIEF TRADIT

B38
POUND R.,THE FORMATIVE ERA OF AMERICAN LAW. CULTURE NAT/G PROVS LEGIS ADJUD CT/SYS PERSON SOVEREIGN ...POLICY IDEA/COMP GEN/LAWS 18/19. PAGE 127 H2548
CONSTN LAW CREATE JURID

B39
ANDERSON P.R.,THE BACKGROUND OF ANTI-ENGLISH FEELING IN GERMANY, 1890-1902. GERMANY MOD/EUR UK NAT/G POL/PAR TOP/EX WAR...IDEA/COMP 19/20. PAGE 7 H0132
DIPLOM EDU/PROP ATTIT COLONIAL

B39
COBBAN A.,DICTATORSHIP: ITS HISTORY AND THEORY. EUR+WWI MOD/EUR SOCIETY STRUCT NAT/G TEC/DEV LEAD NAT/LISM SOVEREIGN...IDEA/COMP 14/20. PAGE 30 H0610
TOTALISM FASCISM CONCPT

B39
OAKESHOTT M.,THE SOCIAL AND POLITICAL DOCTRINES OF CONTEMPORARY EUROPE. EUR+WWI RATIONAL CATHISM FASCISM MARXISM POPULISM...POLICY ANTHOL 20 NAZI. PAGE 120 H2392
IDEA/COMP GOV/COMP ALL/IDEOS NAT/G

B40
MANNHEIM K.,MAN AND SOCIETY IN AN AGE OF RECONSTRUCTION. MOD/EUR CULTURE ECO/DEV PLAN TEC/DEV PERSON LAISSEZ NEW/LIB...NEW/IDEA IDEA/COMP BIBLIOG 19/20. PAGE 102 H2038
CONCPT ATTIT SOCIETY TOTALISM

B41
GILMORE M.P.,ARGUMENT FROM ROMAN LAW IN POLITICAL THOUGHT, 1200-1600. INTELL LICENSE CONTROL CT/SYS GOV/REL PRIVIL PWR...IDEA/COMP BIBLIOG 13/16. PAGE 56 H1130
JURID LAW CONCPT NAT/G

B41
GREEN T.H.,PRINCIPLES OF PUBLIC ADMINISTRATION. UNIV CONSTN VOL/ASSN INGP/REL MORAL ORD/FREE ...GOV/COMP IDEA/COMP GEN/LAWS 20. PAGE 60 H1208
POLICY LAISSEZ MAJORIT

C41
WASSERMAN L.,"HANDBOOK OF POLITICAL "ISMS" CAP/ISM REPRESENT TOTALISM MARXISM NEW/LIB SOCISM...MAJORIT BIBLIOG 20. PAGE 166 H3313
IDEA/COMP PHIL/SCI OWN NAT/G

B42
CRAIG A.,ABOVE ALL LIBERTIES. FRANCE UK USA-45 LAW CONSTN CULTURE INTELL NAT/G SECT JUDGE...IDEA/COMP BIBLIOG 18/20. PAGE 35 H0692
ORD/FREE MORAL WRITING EDU/PROP

B43
LENIN V.I.,STATE AND REVOLUTION. USSR CAP/ISM ...ANARCH MARXIST PHIL/SCI IDEA/COMP 20. PAGE 94 H1878
SOCIETY NAT/G REV MARXISM

B43
MC DOWELL R.B.,IRISH PUBLIC OPINION, 1750-1800. IRELAND CONSTN VOL/ASSN WORKER ORD/FREE CATHISM CONSERVE...POLICY IDEA/COMP BIBLIOG 18/ PARLIAMENT. PAGE 106 H2118
ATTIT NAT/G DIPLOM REV

B45
CROCE B.,POLITICS AND MORALS. UNIV NAT/G ECO/TAC ORD/FREE MARXISM POPULISM SOCISM...REALPOL 15/20 HEGEL/GWF ROUSSEAU/J. PAGE 35 H0704
MORAL GEN/LAWS IDEA/COMP

B45
VENABLE V.,HUMAN NATURE: THE MARXIAN VIEW. UNIV STRATA CAP/ISM REV GP/REL PERS/REL PRODUC KNOWL ...PHIL/SCI CONCPT IDEA/COMP 19 MARX/KARL ENGELS/F. PAGE 162 H3240
PERSON MARXISM WORKER UTOPIA

B45
WOOLBERT R.G.,FOREIGN AFFAIRS BIBLIOGRAPHY, 1932-1942. INT/ORG SECT INT/TRADE COLONIAL RACE/REL NAT/LISM...GEOG INT/LAW GOV/COMP IDEA/COMP 20. PAGE 170 H3410
BIBLIOG/A DIPLOM WAR

B46
CASSIRER E.,THE MYTH OF THE STATE. WOR-45 SOCIETY RACE/REL RATIONAL PWR FASCISM...PHIL/SCI PSY LING TREND HEGEL/GWF MACHIAVELL. PAGE 28 H0557
MYTH CONCPT NAT/G IDEA/COMP

B47
BOWEN R.H.,GERMAN THEORIES OF THE CORPORATIVE STATE, WITH SPECIAL REFERENCES TO THE PERIOD 1870-1919. GERMANY INDUS LG/CO CATHISM SOCISM...SOC 18/20. PAGE 19 H0389
IDEA/COMP CENTRAL NAT/G POLICY

B47
BOWLE J.,WESTERN POLITICAL THOUGHT: AN HISTORICAL INTRODUCTION FROM THE ORIGINS TO ROUSSEAU. CONSTN NAT/G SECT CREATE RATIONAL ORD/FREE...SOC BIBLIOG/A. PAGE 19 H0391
ATTIT IDEA/COMP PHIL/SCI

B47
NIEBUHR R.,THE CHILDREN OF LIGHT AND THE CHILDREN OF DARKNESS: A VINDICATION OF DEMOCRACY AND CRITIQUE OF TRADITIONAL DEFENSE. UNIV STRUCT NAT/G SECT INGP/REL OWN PEACE ORD/FREE MARXISM ...IDEA/COMP GEN/LAWS 20 CHRISTIAN. PAGE 118 H2358
POPULISM DIPLOM NEIGH GP/REL

C49
SCHAPIRO J.S.,"LIBERALISM AND THE CHALLENGE OF FASCISM." FRANCE UK STRATA PERSON...CONCPT BIOG IDEA/COMP BIBLIOG 18/20. PAGE 139 H2771
FASCISM LAISSEZ ATTIT

B50
CARR E.H.,STUDIES IN REVOLUTION. CREATE WAR PERSON ALL/IDEOS MARXISM SOCISM...PHIL/SCI METH/COMP ANTHOL 18/20 SAINTSIMON MARX/KARL PROUDHON/P LASSALLE/F PLEKHNV/GV. PAGE 27 H0537
REV IDEA/COMP COERCE BIOG

B50
HALLOWELL J.H.,MAIN CURRENTS IN MODERN POLITICAL THOUGHT. CONSTN SECT LEGIS...MAJORIT CONCPT 17/20 MARX/KARL MILL/JS HOBBES/T LENIN/VI. PAGE 64 H1290
IDEA/COMP POPULISM SOCISM

B50
KANN R.A.,THE MULTINATIONAL EMPIRE (2 VOLS.). AUSTRIA CZECHOSLVK GERMANY HUNGARY CULTURE NAT/G POL/PAR PROVS REGION REV FEDERAL...GEOG TREND CHARTS IDEA/COMP NAT/COMP 19/20. PAGE 83 H1654
NAT/LISM MOD/EUR

B50
SCHUMPETER J.A.,CAPITALISM, SOCIALISM, AND DEMOCRACY (3RD ED.). USA-45 USSR WOR+45 WOR-45 INTELL ECO/DEV ECO/UNDEV ECO/TAC WAR PRODUC ORD/FREE...MGT SOC 20 MARX/KARL. PAGE 140 H2804
SOCIALIST CAP/ISM MARXISM IDEA/COMP

B50
SMITH E.W.,AFRICAN IDEAS OF GOD. ATTIT...CONCPT MYTH IDEA/COMP ANTHOL BIBLIOG. PAGE 145 H2908
SOC AFR CULTURE SECT

B51
HUXLEY J.,FREEDOM AND CULTURE. UNIV LAW SOCIETY R+D ACADEM SCHOOL CREATE SANCTION ATTIT KNOWL...HUM ANTHOL 20. PAGE 76 H1512
CULTURE ORD/FREE PHIL/SCI IDEA/COMP

B52
KOHN H.,PROPHETS AND PEOPLES: STUDIES IN NINETEENTH CENTURY NATIONALISM. MOD/EUR...IDEA/COMP 19. PAGE 87 H1741
CONCPT NAT/LISM SOVEREIGN

B52
LOPEZ-AMO A.,LA MONARQUIA DE LA REFORMA SOCIAL. MOD/EUR SPAIN CONSTN NAT/G TASK EFFICIENCY CONSERVE ...ANARCH TRADIT SOC CONCPT IDEA/COMP 19/20. PAGE 98 H1967
MARXISM REV LEGIT ORD/FREE

B52
ROBBINS L.,THE THEORY OF ECONOMIC POLICY IN ENGLISH CLASSICAL POLITICAL ECONOMY. UK ECO/DEV WORKER PLAN CAP/ISM EDU/PROP CONTROL INCOME OWN HEALTH SOCISM ...POLICY 17/19. PAGE 132 H2639
ECO/TAC ORD/FREE IDEA/COMP NAT/G

S52
MCDOUGAL M.S.,"THE COMPARATIVE STUDY OF LAW FOR POLICY PURPOSES." FUT NAT/G POL/PAR CONSULT ADJUD PWR SOVEREIGN...METH/CNCPT IDEA/COMP SIMUL 20. PAGE 106 H2129
PLAN JURID NAT/LISM

S52
SABINE G.H.,"THE TWO DEMOCRATIC TRADITIONS" (BMR)" FRANCE UK USA-45 NAT/G CONTROL CHOOSE ALL/IDEOS ...PHIL/SCI CONCPT IDEA/COMP 20. PAGE 136 H2727
ORD/FREE POPULISM INGP/REL NAT/COMP

C52
EBENSTEIN W.,"INTRODUCTION TO POLITICAL PHILOSOPHY." COM CONSTN INTELL CONTROL PERSON NEW/LIB SOCISM...PSY GEN/LAWS BIBLIOG/A. PAGE 44 H0883
ALL/IDEOS PHIL/SCI IDEA/COMP NAT/G

B53
BARZEL R.,DIE DEUTSCHEN PARTEIEN. GERMANY MARXISM SOCISM...CONCPT IDEA/COMP 19/20 SOC/DEMPAR CHRIS/DEM. PAGE 12 H0232
POL/PAR NAT/G LAISSEZ

B53
BIDNEY D.,THEORETICAL ANTHROPOLOGY. DRIVE ROLE ORD/FREE...CONCPT METH/CNCPT MYTH CLASSIF OBS IDEA/COMP METH/COMP BIBLIOG METH 20. PAGE 17 H0331
CULTURE SOC PSY PHIL/SCI

B53
BUCHHEIM K.,GESCHICHTE DER CHRISTLICHEN PARTEIEN IN DEUTSCHLAND. GERMANY CREATE ATTIT SUPEGO ORD/FREE ...TIME/SEQ IDEA/COMP 19/20 CHRIS/DEM. PAGE 23 H0464
POL/PAR NAT/G

B53
COBLENTZ S.A.,FROM ARROW TO ATOM BOMB: THE PSYCHOLOGICAL HISTORY OF WAR. PREHIST CULTURE CROWD PEACE DRIVE MORAL PWR...GP/COMP IDEA/COMP. PAGE 31 H0613
WAR PSY SOCIETY

B53
LENZ F.,DIE BEWEGUNGEN DER GROSSEN MACHTE. USA+45 USA-45 USSR SOCIETY STRATA STRUCT NAT/G PERSON MARXISM...CONCPT IDEA/COMP NAT/COMP 18/20. PAGE 94 H1883
BAL/PWR TREND DIPLOM HIST/WRIT

B53
MARITAIN J.,L'HOMME ET L'ETAT. SECT DIPLOM GP/REL PEACE ORD/FREE...IDEA/COMP 17/20 CHURCH/STA NATURL/LAW. PAGE 103 H2052
CONCPT NAT/G SOVEREIGN COERCE

B53
MAXIMOFF G.P.,THE POLITICAL PHILOSOPHY OF BAKUNIN: SCIENTIFIC ANARCHISM. STRUCT INGP/REL FEDERAL MARXISM...ANARCH BIOG 19 BAKUNIN. PAGE 105 H2104
SOCIETY PHIL/SCI NAT/G IDEA/COMP

S53
ARENDT H.,"IDEOLOGY AND TERROR: A NOVEL FORM OF GOVERNMENT." WOR-45 DOMIN STRANGE ATTIT SUPEGO MARXISM...GOV/COMP IDEA/COMP 20 NAZI. PAGE 8 H0160
TOTALISM ANOMIE ALL/IDEOS SOCIETY

B54
FRIEDMAN W.,THE PUBLIC CORPORATION: A COMPARATIVE SYMPOSIUM (UNIVERSITY OF TORONTO SCHOOL OF LAW COMPARATIVE LAW SERIES, VOL. I). SWEDEN USA+45 INDUS INT/ORG NAT/G REGION CENTRAL FEDERAL...POLICY JURID IDEA/COMP NAT/COMP ANTHOL 20 COMMONWLTH MONOPOLY EUROPE. PAGE 53 H1065
LAW SOCISM LG/CO OWN

B54
LEWIS E.,MEDIEVAL POLITICAL IDEAS. LAW CULTURE SOCIETY ECO/UNDEV NAT/G SECT GOV/REL ATTIT ...BIBLIOG/A T 11/15. PAGE 96 H1913
CHRIST-17C IDEA/COMP INTELL CONCPT

B54
MALINOWSKI B.,MAGIC, SCIENCE AND RELIGION. AGRI KIN GP/REL ALL/VALS...MYTH OBS RECORD IDEA/COMP WORSHIP 20 NEW/GUINEA. PAGE 102 H2031
CULTURE ATTIT SOC

B54
PARRINDER G.,AFRICAN TRADITIONAL RELIGION. AFR SOCIETY EDU/PROP GP/REL PWR...SOC CONCPT IDEA/COMP WORSHIP 20 DEITY. PAGE 124 H2469
SECT MYTH ATTIT CULTURE

B54
SCHWARTZ B.,FRENCH ADMINISTRATIVE LAW AND THE COMMON-LAW WORLD. FRANCE CULTURE LOC/G NAT/G PROVS DELIB/GP EX/STRUC LEGIS PROB/SOLV CT/SYS EXEC GOV/REL...IDEA/COMP ENGLSH/LAW. PAGE 140 H2808
JURID LAW METH/COMP ADJUD

B55
BAILEY S.K.,RESEARCH FRONTIERS IN POLITICS AND GOVERNMENT. CONSTN LEGIS ADMIN REV CHOOSE...CONCPT IDEA/COMP GAME ANTHOL 20. PAGE 10 H0201
R+D METH NAT/G

B55
MAYO H.B.,DEMOCRACY AND MARXISM. COM USSR STRATA NAT/G WORKER ECO/TAC REV MORAL...PHIL/SCI HIST/WRIT IDEA/COMP WORSHIP 20 MARX/KARL LENIN/VI STALIN/J TROTSKY/L. PAGE 105 H2108
MARXISM CAP/ISM

POHLENZ M.,GRIECHISCHE FREIHEIT. GREECE DIPLOM WAR SUPEGO PWR RESPECT...IDEA/COMP. PAGE 127 H2533 — B55 ORD/FREE CONCPT JURID NAT/G

POLLOCK J.K.,GERMAN DEMOCRACY AT WORK. GERMANY/W LOC/G NAT/G DIPLOM PARL/PROC...OBS IDEA/COMP 20. PAGE 127 H2539 — B55 PARTIC POL/PAR CHOOSE EDU/PROP

WRONG D.H.,AMERICAN AND CANADIAN VIEWPOINTS. CANADA USA+45 CONSTN STRATA FAM SECT WORKER ECO/TAC EDU/PROP ADJUD MARRIAGE...IDEA/COMP 20. PAGE 171 H3424 — B55 DIPLOM ATTIT NAT/COMP CULTURE

BENN S.I.,"THE USES OF 'SOVEREIGNTY'." UNIV NAT/G LEGIS DIPLOM COERCE...METH/CNCPT GEN/LAWS. PAGE 14 H0282 — S55 SOVEREIGN IDEA/COMP CONCPT PWR

FIELD G.C.,POLITICAL THEORY. POL/PAR REPRESENT MORAL SOVEREIGN...JURID IDEA/COMP. PAGE 50 H0990 — B56 CONCPT NAT/G ORD/FREE DIPLOM

MUMFORD L.,THE TRANSFORMATIONS OF MAN. UNIV CULTURE INGP/REL HABITAT HEREDITY ALL/VALS ORD/FREE...MYTH TIME/SEQ TREND WORSHIP. PAGE 114 H2287 — B56 IDEA/COMP PERSON CONCPT

RIESENBERG P.N.,INALIENABILITY OF SOVEREIGNTY IN MEDIEVAL POLITICAL THOUGHT. CHRIST-17C INTELL NAT/G SECT CHIEF LEGIS SANCTION AUTHORIT ORD/FREE CONSERVE...IDEA/COMP BIBLIOG 12/16. PAGE 131 H2627 — B56 SOVEREIGN ATTIT

WEBER M.,WIRTSCHAFT UND GESELLSCHAFT (2ND VOL.). STRUCT NAT/G POL/PAR LEAD PWR OBJECTIVE IDEA/COMP. PAGE 166 H3321 — B56 LEGIT JURID SOC

AMERICAN COUNCIL LEARNED SOC,GOVERNMENT UNDER LAW AND THE INDIVIDUAL. ASIA ISLAM USSR NAT/G...POLICY SOC NAT/COMP 20. PAGE 6 H0121 — B57 SOCIETY ORD/FREE CONCPT IDEA/COMP

ARON R.,THE OPIUM OF THE INTELLECTUALS (TRANS. BY TERENCE KILMARTIN). FRANCE USSR WOR+45 CULTURE POL/PAR PLAN DOMIN EDU/PROP REV ATTIT ORD/FREE ...IDEA/COMP METH/COMP NAT/COMP 20 COM/PARTY. PAGE 8 H0169 — B57 INTELL UTOPIA MYTH MARXISM

HERNANDEZ-ARREGU J.,IMPERIALISMO Y CULTURA (LA POLITICA EN LA INTELIGENCIA ARGENTINA). L/A+17C CULTURE ELITES WRITING COLONIAL CROWD ATTIT FASCISM MARXISM SOCISM...BIOG IDEA/COMP 20 ARGEN PERON/JUAN COM/PARTY. PAGE 70 H1403 — B57 INTELL CREATE ART/METH HUM

LOUCKS W.N.,COMPARATIVE ECONOMIC SYSTEMS (5TH ED.). COM UK USSR INDUS POL/PAR PLAN CAP/ISM TOTALISM MARXISM...PHIL/SCI BIBLIOG 19/20. PAGE 99 H1969 — B57 NAT/COMP IDEA/COMP SOCISM

BENDIX R.,"POLITICAL SOCIOLOGY." CULTURE INTELL LABOR POL/PAR SECT LEGIS EDU/PROP ADMIN CHOOSE CIVMIL/REL ATTIT...IDEA/COMP 20. PAGE 14 H0274 — L57 BIBLIOG/A ACT/RES SOC

BAGBY P.,CULTURE AND HISTORY....PHIL/SCI CONCPT LING LOG IDEA/COMP GEN/LAWS BIBLIOG 20. PAGE 10 H0196 — B58 HIST/WRIT CULTURE GP/COMP NAT/COMP

BUISSON L.,POTESTAS UND CARITAS. FRANCE GERMANY UK ORD/FREE...JURID IDEA/COMP NAT/COMP 12/16 POPE CHURCH/STA. PAGE 23 H0467 — B58 GP/REL PWR CATHISM NAT/G

CHANG H.,WITHIN THE FOUR SEAS. ASIA WAR MORAL MARXISM...IDEA/COMP NAT/COMP 20 CONFUCIUS. PAGE 29 H0577 — B58 PEACE DIPLOM KNOWL CULTURE

DUNAYEVSKAYA R.,MARXISM AND FREEDOM: FROM 1776 UNTIL TODAY. COM USSR WORKER CAP/ISM DOMIN REV GP/REL TOTALISM ALL/VALS...MYTH BIOG IDEA/COMP 18/20 MARX/KARL LENIN/VI STALIN/J. PAGE 43 H0861 — B58 MARXISM CONCPT ORD/FREE

EUSDEN J.D.,PURITANS, LAWYERS, AND POLITICS IN EARLY SEVENTEENTH-CENTURY ENGLAND. UK CT/SYS PARL/PROC RATIONAL PWR SOVEREIGN...IDEA/COMP BIBLIOG 17 PURITAN COMMON/LAW. PAGE 48 H0951 — B58 GP/REL SECT NAT/G LAW

GREAVES H.R.,THE FOUNDATIONS OF POLITICAL THEORY. WAR ATTIT SUPEGO ORD/FREE...IDEA/COMP SOC/INTEG. PAGE 60 H1203 — B58 CONCPT MORAL PERSON

HERRMANN K.,DAS STAATSDENKEN BEI LEIBNIZ. GP/REL ATTIT ORD/FREE...CONCPT IDEA/COMP 17 LEIBNITZ/G CHURCH/STA. PAGE 70 H1406 — B58 NAT/G JURID SECT

EDU/PROP

PALMER E.E.,"POLITICAL MAN" IN E. PALMER, PROBLEMS IN DEMOCRATIC CITIZENSHIP. LOC/G NAT/G LEGIS PRESS CHOOSE REPRESENT GP/REL...DECISION SOC IDEA/COMP ANTHOL 20. PAGE 123 H2449 — B58 PARTIC POL/PAR EDU/PROP MAJORIT

PALMER E.E.,THE COMMUNIST CHALLENGE. COM USA+45 USA-45 ECO/DEV ECO/UNDEV NEUTRAL ORD/FREE POPULISM ...CONCPT NAT/COMP ANTHOL 19/20 LENIN/VI STALIN/J MAO MARX/KARL COM/PARTY. PAGE 123 H2450 — B58 MARXISM DIPLOM IDEA/COMP POLICY

SALETORE B.A.,INDIA'S DIPLOMATIC RELATIONS WITH THE WEST. GREECE INDIA CULTURE ETIQUET...IDEA/COMP 3 ROM/EMP PERSIA. PAGE 137 H2739 — B58 DIPLOM CONCPT INT/TRADE

SCHOEPS H.J.,KONSERVATIVE ERNEUERUNG IDEEN ZUR DEUTSCHEN POLITIK. GERMANY ELITES SOCIETY ACADEM CHOOSE SOCISM 19/20. PAGE 140 H2796 — B58 POL/PAR IDEA/COMP CONSERVE NAT/G

STRAUSZ-HUPE R.,THE IDEA OF COLONIALISM. WOR+45 WOR-45 BAL/PWR GOV/REL...POLICY CLASSIF TIME/SEQ GOV/COMP ANTHOL 20 UN. PAGE 150 H2996 — B58 IDEA/COMP COLONIAL CONTROL CONCPT

STRONG C.F.,MODERN POLITICAL CONSTITUTIONS. LAW CHIEF DELIB/GP EX/STRUC LEGIS ADJUD CHOOSE FEDERAL POPULISM...CONCPT BIBLIOG 20 UN. PAGE 150 H2998 — B58 CONSTN IDEA/COMP NAT/G

SYME R.,COLONIAL ELITES: ROME, SPAIN, AND THE AMERICAS. CHRIST-17C MOD/EUR SPAIN UK USA-45 CULTURE NAT/G CHIEF TOP/EX...GOV/COMP IDEA/COMP NAT/COMP ROM/EMP GIBBON/EDW TOYNBEE/A. PAGE 151 H3022 — B58 COLONIAL ELITES DOMIN

BELL D.,"TEN THEORIES IN SEARCH OF REALITY: THE PREDICTION OF SOVIET BEHAVIOR IN THE SOCIAL SCIENCES" (BMR)" COM USSR...POLICY SOC METH/COMP 20. PAGE 13 H0264 — L58 MARXISM PREDICT IDEA/COMP

DEHIO L.,GERMANY AND WORLD POLITICS IN THE TWENTIETH CENTURY. EUR+WWI FRANCE GERMANY MOD/EUR UK USSR NAT/G CHIEF BAL/PWR DOMIN COLONIAL CONTROL LEAD...IDEA/COMP 20 VERSAILLES. PAGE 39 H0783 — B59 DIPLOM WAR NAT/LISM SOVEREIGN

EAENZA L.,COMMUNISMO E CATTOLICESIMO IN UNA PARROCHIA DI CAMPAGNA. ITALY CULTURE ELITES ECO/DEV AGRI KIN POL/PAR DOMIN LEGIT RIGID/FLEX...DECISION OBS IDEA/COMP 20 COM/PARTY CHURCH/STA. PAGE 44 H0878 — B59 ATTIT CATHISM NEIGH MARXISM

LANDAUER C.,EUROPEAN SOCIALISM (2 VOLS.). COM EUR+WWI MOD/EUR INTELL INDUS REV WAR...MAJORIT IDEA/COMP BIBLIOG 19/20 HITLER/A. PAGE 90 H1805 — B59 SOCISM NAT/COMP LABOR MARXISM

LEITES N.,ON THE GAME OF POLITICS IN FRANCE. ALGERIA FRANCE CONSTN SECT VOL/ASSN ECO/TAC INT/TRADE PARL/PROC WAR SOCISM 20 DEGAULLE/C EEC. PAGE 94 H1871 — B59 POL/PAR NAT/G LEGIS IDEA/COMP

MAIER H.,REVOLUTION UND KIRCHE. FRANCE MOD/EUR SECT REV ORD/FREE...IDEA/COMP 18/19. PAGE 101 H2018 — B59 NAT/G CATHISM ATTIT POL/PAR

WARNER W.L.,THE LIVING AND THE DEAD: A STUDY OF SYMBOLIC LIFE OF AMERICANS. INTELL KIN DEATH ALL/VALS ALL/IDEOS...CONCPT MYTH LING OBS/ENVIR CHARTS BIBLIOG WORSHIP 18/20. PAGE 165 H3311 — B59 CULTURE SOC TIME/SEQ IDEA/COMP

WILDNER H.,DIE TECHNIK DER DIPLOMATIE. TOP/EX ROLE ORD/FREE...INT/LAW JURID IDEA/COMP NAT/COMP 20. PAGE 168 H3364 — B59 DIPLOM POLICY DELIB/GP NAT/G

BANERJEE D.N.,OUR FUNDAMENTAL RIGHTS: THEIR NATURE AND EXTENT (AS JUDICIALLY DETERMINED). INDIA UK CULTURE STRATA NAT/G WORKER EDU/PROP CONTROL DISCRIM OWN...IDEA/COMP WORSHIP 20 REFORMERS COMMONWLTH. PAGE 10 H0207 — B60 CONSTN ORD/FREE LEGIS POLICY

BARBU Z.,PROBLEMS OF HISTORICAL PSYCHOLOGY. GREECE MEDIT-7 UK CULTURE TEC/DEV ADJUST RATIONAL ATTIT PERCEPT...METH/CNCPT NEW/IDEA TIME/SEQ GEN/METH. PAGE 11 H0214 — B60 PERSON PSY HIST/WRIT IDEA/COMP

GRAMPP W.D.,THE MANCHESTER SCHOOL OF ECONOMICS. UK LAW ECO/DEV COERCE ATTIT ORD/FREE LAISSEZ ...PHIL/SCI IDEA/COMP 19/20 MANCHESTER CORN/LAWS. PAGE 60 H1194 — B60 ECO/TAC VOL/ASSN LOBBY NAT/G

HAYEK F.A.,THE CONSTITUTION OF LIBERTY. UNIV LAW CONSTN WORKER TAX EDU/PROP ADMIN CT/SYS COERCE DISCRIM...IDEA/COMP 20. PAGE 68 H1369 — B60 ORD/FREE CHOOSE NAT/G

CONCPT

B60
MAYO H.B.,AN INTRODUCTION TO DEMOCRATIC THEORY. ORD/FREE...POLICY TIME/SEQ GOV/COMP STERTYP. PAGE 105 H2109 — POPULISM CONCPT IDEA/COMP

B60
MEYRIAT J.,LA SCIENCE POLITIQUE EN FRANCE, 1945-1958; BIBLIOGRAPHIES FRANCAISES DE SCIENCES SOCIALES (VOL. I). EUR+WWI FRANCE POL/PAR DIPLOM ADMIN CHOOSE ATTIT...IDEA/COMP METH/COMP NAT/COMP 20. PAGE 110 H2193 — BIBLIOG/A NAT/G CONCPT PHIL/SCI

B60
MORRISON C.,THE POWERS THAT BE. NAT/G SUPEGO ...POLICY CONCPT IDEA/COMP WORSHIP 20 BIBLE. PAGE 113 H2265 — HUM ORD/FREE

S60
GRIMSHAW A.D.,"URBAN RACIAL VIOLENCE IN THE UNITED STATES: CHANGING ECOLOGICAL CONSIDERATIONS." STRUCT MUNIC FORCES PARTIC DISCRIM ATTIT HABITAT ...IDEA/COMP 20 NEGRO. PAGE 61 H1228 — CROWD RACE/REL GOV/COMP NEIGH

C60
BOGARDUS E.S.,"THE DEVELOPMENT OF SOCIAL THOUGHT." SOCIETY PERSON KNOWL...EPIST CONCPT BIBLIOG T. PAGE 18 H0365 — INTELL CULTURE IDEA/COMP GP/COMP

C60
COX R.H.,"LOCKE ON WAR AND PEACE." UK DIPLOM DOMIN PWR...BIOG IDEA/COMP BIBLIOG 18. PAGE 34 H0689 — CONCPT NAT/G PEACE WAR

C60
EBENSTEIN W.,"MODERN POLITICAL THOUGHT (2ND ED.)" NAT/G CAP/ISM NAT/LISM PERSON ORD/FREE PWR ALL/IDEOS NEW/LIB SOCISM...TRADIT PSY BIBLIOG/A 18/20. PAGE 44 H0884 — IDEA/COMP PHIL/SCI CONCPT GEN/LAWS

C60
HOSELITZ B.,"THE ROLE OF CITIES IN THE ECONOMIC GROWTH OF UNDERDEVELOPED COUNTRIES" IN "SOCIOLOGICAL ASPECTS OF ECONOMIC GROWTH"(BMR). CULTURE LOC/G ACT/RES...SOC IDEA/COMP METH/COMP METH 14/20 REDFIELD/R. PAGE 74 H1474 — METH/CNCPT MUNIC TEC/DEV ECO/UNDEV

B61
JUSTICE,THE CITIZEN AND THE ADMINISTRATION: THE REDRESS OF GRIEVANCES (PAMPHLET). EUR+WWI UK LAW CONSTN STRATA NAT/G CT/SYS PARTIC COERCE...NEW/IDEA IDEA/COMP 20 OMBUDSMAN. PAGE 82 H1644 — INGP/REL CONSULT ADJUD REPRESENT

B61
LENIN V.I.,WHAT IS TO BE DONE? (1902). RUSSIA LABOR NAT/G POL/PAR WORKER CAP/ISM ECO/TAC ADMIN PARTIC ...MARXIST IDEA/COMP GEN/LAWS 19/20. PAGE 94 H1881 — EDU/PROP PRESS MARXISM METH/COMP

B61
LEVIN L.A.,BIBLIOGRAFIIA BIBLIOGRAFII PROIZVEDENII K. MARKSA, F. ENGELSA, V.I. LENINA. COM USSR NAT/G POL/PAR WORKER LEAD REV ATTIT...POLICY IDEA/COMP 20 MARX/KARL LENIN/VI ENGELS. PAGE 95 H1899 — BIBLIOG/A MARXISM MARXIST CONCPT

B61
LICHTHEIM G.,MARXISM. GERMANY SOCIETY WORKER CAP/ISM ECO/TAC NAT/LISM POPULISM...TIME/SEQ GOV/COMP NAT/COMP 18/20 COM/PARTY. PAGE 96 H1924 — MARXISM SOCISM IDEA/COMP CULTURE

B61
NEWMAN R.P.,RECOGNITION OF COMMUNIST CHINA? A STUDY IN ARGUMENT. CHINA/COM NAT/G PROB/SOLV RATIONAL ...INT/LAW LOG IDEA/COMP BIBLIOG 20. PAGE 117 H2347 — MARXISM ATTIT DIPLOM POLICY

B61
ULLMAN W.,PRINCIPLES OF GOVERNMENT AND POLITICS IN THE MIDDLE AGES. LAW CONSTN DOMIN EDU/PROP LEGIT TOTALISM SOVEREIGN POPULISM...POLICY GOV/COMP IDEA/COMP 12/16 POPE KING CHURCH/STA. PAGE 158 H3152 — SECT CHIEF NAT/G LEGIS

S61
TUCKER R.C.,"TOWARDS A COMPARATIVE POLITICS OF MOVEMENT-REGIMES" (BMR)" USSR CONSTN NAT/G CREATE PROB/SOLV DIPLOM DOMIN REV...GP/COMP IDEA/COMP METH 20 STALIN/J BOLSHEVISM. PAGE 157 H3135 — MARXISM POLICY GEN/LAWS PWR

C61
LAPONCE J.A.,"THE GOVERNMENT OF THE FIFTH REPUBLIC." FRANCE CHIEF LEGIS PARL/PROC CHOOSE ...CHARTS GP/COMP IDEA/COMP BIBLIOG/A 20. PAGE 91 H1814 — POL/PAR NAT/G CONSTN DOMIN

B62
BELL D.,THE END OF IDEOLOGY (REV. ED.). USA+45 USA-45 ELITES STRATA LABOR CREATE CRIME PWR MARXISM ...PHIL/SCI METH/COMP 20 EUROPE. PAGE 13 H0265 — CROWD CAP/ISM SOCISM IDEA/COMP

B62
EBENSTEIN W.,TWO WAYS OF LIFE. USA+45 CULTURE ECO/DEV PLAN EDU/PROP CONTROL ORD/FREE...GOV/COMP IDEA/COMP T 20 MARX/KARL ENGELS/F LENIN/VI LOCKE/JOHN MILL/JS. PAGE 44 H0885 — MARXISM POPULISM ECO/TAC DIPLOM

B62
FRYKLUND R.,100 MILLION LIVES: MAXIMUM SURVIVAL IN A NUCLEAR WAR. USA+45 USSR CONTROL WEAPON ...IDEA/COMP NAT/COMP 20. PAGE 54 H1073 — NUC/PWR WAR PLAN

DETER

B62
GANJI M.,INTERNATIONAL PROTECTION OF HUMAN RIGHTS. WOR+45 CONSTN INT/TRADE CT/SYS SANCTION CRIME WAR RACE/REL...CHARTS IDEA/COMP NAT/COMP BIBLIOG 20 TREATY NEGRO LEAGUE/NAT UN CIVIL/LIB. PAGE 55 H1097 — ORD/FREE DISCRIM LEGIS DELIB/GP

B62
HOOK S.,THE PARADOXES OF FREEDOM. UNIV CONSTN INTELL LEGIS CONTROL REV CHOOSE SUPEGO...POLICY JURID IDEA/COMP 19/20 CIV/RIGHTS. PAGE 73 H1461 — CONCPT MAJORIT ORD/FREE ALL/VALS

B62
HUNKIN P.,ENSEIGNEMENT ET POLITIQUE EN FRANCE ET EN ANGLETERRE. FRANCE UK CONSTN ACADEM SECT CHIEF DELIB/GP PROB/SOLV CONTROL REV ORD/FREE CONSERVE ...BIBLIOG 18/20. PAGE 75 H1496 — EDU/PROP LEGIS IDEA/COMP NAT/G

B62
LAQUEUR W.,THE FUTURE OF COMMUNIST SOCIETY. CHINA/COM USSR LAW ECO/DEV NAT/G POL/PAR PLAN PROB/SOLV DIPLOM LEAD...POLICY CONCPT IDEA/COMP ANTHOL 20. PAGE 91 H1820 — MARXISM COM FUT SOCIETY

B62
LITT T.,FREIHEIT UND LEBENS ORDNUNG. COM NAT/G ATTIT KNOWL...POLICY 20. PAGE 97 H1942 — ORD/FREE MARXISM CONCPT IDEA/COMP

B62
MACPHERSON C.B.,THE POLITICAL THEORY OF POSSESSIVE INDIVIDUALISM. UK MARKET NAT/G PERS/REL RATIONAL ...IDEA/COMP 17/19 LOCKE/JOHN. PAGE 100 H2006 — PHIL/SCI OWN

B62
MILLER J.D.B.,THE NATURE OF POLITICS. NAT/G DOMIN LEGIT LEAD...CONCPT METH. PAGE 111 H2213 — METH/COMP IDEA/COMP PHIL/SCI

B62
RANNEY A.,THE DOCTRINE OF RESPONSIBLE PARTY GOVERNMENT. USA+45 USA-45 CONSTN PLAN CHOOSE ...MAJORIT GOV/COMP IDEA/COMP 20. PAGE 130 H2591 — POL/PAR POLICY REPRESENT NAT/G

B62
SILBERMAN B.S.,JAPAN AND KOREA; A CRITICAL BIBLIOGRAPHY. KOREA LAW STRATA STRUCT AGRI INDUS NAT/G POL/PAR SECT...HUM LING IDEA/COMP 5/20 CHINJAP. PAGE 144 H2872 — BIBLIOG/A CULTURE S/ASIA

B63
ATTIA G.E.D.,LES FORCES ARMEES DES NATIONS UNIES EN COREE ET AU MOYENORIENT. KOREA CONSTN NAT/G DELIB/GP LEGIS PWR...IDEA/COMP NAT/COMP BIBLIOG UN SUEZ. PAGE 9 H0177 — FORCES INT/LAW

B63
BROOKES E.H.,POWER, LAW, RIGHT, AND LOVE: A STUDY IN POLITICAL VALUES. SOUTH/AFR NAT/G PERSON ...CONCPT IDEA/COMP 20. PAGE 21 H0432 — PWR ORD/FREE JURID LOVE

B63
CRANKSHAW E.,THE NEW COLD WAR: MOSCOW V. PEKIN. CHINA/COM USSR INTELL POL/PAR DELIB/GP CAP/ISM COERCE REV NAT/LISM TOTALISM DRIVE...POLICY IDEA/COMP 20 KHRUSH/N. PAGE 35 H0698 — ATTIT DIPLOM NAT/COMP MARXISM

B63
HAMM H.,ALBANIA - CHINA'S BEACHHEAD IN EUROPE. ALBANIA CHINA/COM USSR YUGOSLAVIA ELITES SOCIETY POL/PAR DELIB/GP FORCES ECO/TAC COERCE ISOLAT PEACE MARXISM...IDEA/COMP 20 MAO. PAGE 65 H1304 — DIPLOM REV NAT/G POLICY

B63
KATEB G.,UTOPIA AND ITS ENEMIES. CULTURE STRATA ECO/DEV INDUS REV MORAL...PSY IDEA/COMP 19/20. PAGE 84 H1668 — UTOPIA SOCIETY PHIL/SCI PEACE

B63
LEONARD T.J.,THE FEDERAL SYSTEM OF INDIA. INDIA MUNIC NAT/G PROVS ADMIN SOVEREIGN...IDEA/COMP 20. PAGE 94 H1885 — FEDERAL MGT NAT/COMP METH/COMP

B63
LERNER R.,MEDIEVAL POLITICAL PHILOSOPHY. ISLAM MORAL PWR CATHISM...CATH CONCPT OBS IDEA/COMP ANTHOL 9/15 JEWS CHRISTIAN BACON/R AQUINAS/T. PAGE 95 H1890 — KNOWL PHIL/SCI

B63
LYON P.,NEUTRALISM. ECO/UNDEV EDU/PROP COLONIAL ALL/IDEOS...IDEA/COMP 20 COLD/WAR UN. PAGE 99 H1985 — NAT/COMP NAT/LISM DIPLOM NEUTRAL

B63
MCNEAL R.H.,THE BOLSHEVIK TRADITION: LENIN, STALIN, KHRUSHCHEV. USSR NAT/G SUPEGO CONSERVE...IDEA/COMP GEN/LAWS 20 LENIN/VI STALIN/J KHRUSH/N. PAGE 107 H2145 — INTELL BIOG PERS/COMP

B63
NALBANDIAN L.,THE ARMENIAN REVOLUTIONARY MOVEMENT. MOD/EUR RUSSIA...IDEA/COMP NAT/COMP BIBLIOG 19 ARMENIA OTTOMAN. PAGE 115 H2306 — NAT/LISM REV POL/PAR ORD/FREE

B63
NOMAD M.,POLITICAL HERETICS: FROM PLATO TO MAO TSE- — SOCIETY

TUNG. UNIV INGP/REL...SOC IDEA/COMP. PAGE 119 H2369 UTOPIA ALL/IDEOS CONCPT

B63
SCHELER M.,SCHRIFTEN ZUR SOZIOLOGIE UND WELTANSCHAUUNGSLEHRE (GESAMMELTE WERKE, BAND 6; 2ND ED.). SECT ALL/IDEOS...SOC CONCPT GP/COMP NAT/COMP 20. PAGE 139 H2783 SOCIETY IDEA/COMP PHIL/SCI

B63
STRAUSS L.,HISTORY OF POLITICAL PHILOSOPHY. LAW SOCIETY CAP/ISM MARXISM 19 AQUINAS/T BACON/F HEGEL/GWF MILL/JS NIETZSCH/F. PAGE 150 H2995 IDEA/COMP PHIL/SCI ANTHOL

B63
VALJAVEC F.,AUSGEWAHLTE AUFSATZE. GERMANY HUNGARY STRUCT ATTIT...CONCPT IDEA/COMP 18/20 BALKANS. PAGE 161 H3223 SOCIETY CULTURE GP/REL NAT/LISM

B63
VON BECKERATH E.,PROBLEME DER NORMATIVEN OKONOMIK UND DER WIRTSCHAFTSPOLITISCHEN BERATUNG. GERMANY UK ELITES CAP/ISM EFFICIENCY...CONCPT GOV/COMP IDEA/COMP 20. PAGE 163 H3264 ECO/TAC DELIB/GP ECO/DEV CONSULT

S63
ROGIN M.,"ROUSSEAU IN AFRICA." AFR MARXISM POPULISM SOCISM 20 ROUSSEAU/J. PAGE 133 H2661 IDEA/COMP CULTURE CONSTN ORD/FREE

C63
ATTIA G.E.O.,"LES FORCES ARMEES DES NATIONS UNIES EN COREE ET AU MOYENORIENT." KOREA CONSTN DELIB/GP LEGIS PWR...IDEA/COMP NAT/COMP BIBLIOG UN SUEZ. PAGE 9 H0178 FORCES NAT/G INT/LAW

B64
AKZIN B.,STATE AND NATION. UNIV ECO/UNDEV DIPLOM RACE/REL NAT/LISM ATTIT PLURISM...CONCPT IDEA/COMP 20. PAGE 4 H0090 GP/REL NAT/G KIN

B64
BROWN N.,NUCLEAR WAR* THE IMPENDING STRATEGIC DEADLOCK. USA+45 USSR TEC/DEV BUDGET RISK ARMS/CONT NUC/PWR WEAPON COST BIO/SOC...GEOG IDEA/COMP NAT/COMP GAME NATO WARSAW/P. PAGE 22 H0448 FORCES OP/RES WAR GEN/LAWS

B64
COBBAN A.,ROUSSEAU AND THE MODERN STATE (2ND ED.). FRANCE PROB/SOLV NAT/LISM UTOPIA PERSON MORAL ...EPIST PHIL/SCI SOC IDEA/COMP 18 ROUSSEAU/J BURKE/EDM HOBBES/T HUME/D. PAGE 30 H0612 GEN/LAWS INGP/REL NAT/G ORD/FREE

B64
FRANCK T.M.,EAST AFRICAN UNITY THROUGH LAW. MALAWI TANZANIA UGANDA UK ZAMBIA CONSTN INT/ORG NAT/G ADMIN ROUTINE TASK NAT/LISM ATTIT SOVEREIGN ...RECORD IDEA/COMP NAT/COMP. PAGE 52 H1048 AFR FEDERAL REGION INT/LAW

B64
FROMM E.,MARX'S CONCEPT OF MAN. LABOR OWN PERSON ...HUM IDEA/COMP GEN/LAWS 17 MARX/KARL EUROPE SPINOZA/B GOETHE/J HEGEL/GWF. PAGE 54 H1072 INGP/REL CONCPT MARXISM SOCISM

B64
GLUCKMANN M.,CLOSED SYSTEMS AND OPEN MINDS: THE LIMITS OF NAIVETY IN SOCIAL ANTHROPOLOGY. AFR INDIA MUNIC...IDEA/COMP METH/COMP ANTHOL. PAGE 57 H1149 CULTURE OBS SOC

B64
GUMPLOWICZ L.,RECHTSSTAAT UND SOZIALISMUS. STRATA ORD/FREE SOVEREIGN MARXISM...IDEA/COMP 16/20 KANT/I HOBBES/T. PAGE 62 H1251 JURID NAT/G SOCISM CONCPT

B64
HARBISON F.H.,EDUCATION, MANPOWER, AND ECONOMIC GROWTH. WOR+45 ECO/DEV ECO/UNDEV ACADEM LABOR SCHOOL WORKER UTIL...IDEA/COMP NAT/COMP. PAGE 66 H1326 PLAN TEC/DEV EDU/PROP SKILL

B64
KARIEL H.S.,IN SEARCH OF AUTHORITY: TWENTIETH-CENTURY POLITICAL THOUGHT. WOR+45 WOR-45 NAT/G EX/STRUC TOTALISM DRIVE PWR...MGT PHIL/SCI GEN/LAWS 19/20 NIETZSCH/F FREUD/S WEBER/MAX NIEBUHR/R MARITAIN/J. PAGE 83 H1661 CONSTN CONCPT ORD/FREE IDEA/COMP

B64
KOLARZ W.,BOOKS ON COMMUNISM. USSR WOR+45 CULTURE NAT/G POL/PAR DIPLOM LEAD...CONCPT GOV/COMP IDEA/COMP. PAGE 88 H1752 BIBLIOG/A SOCIETY COM MARXISM

B64
KRUEGER H.,ALLGEMEINE STAATSLEHRE. WOR+45 CONSTN SECT CHOOSE INGP/REL PWR NEW/LIB...JURID CLASSIF IDEA/COMP. PAGE 89 H1777 NAT/G GOV/COMP SOCIETY

B64
LAPENNA I.,STATE AND LAW: SOVIET AND YUGOSLAV THEORY. USSR YUGOSLAVIA STRATA STRUCT NAT/G DOMIN COERCE MARXISM...GOV/COMP IDEA/COMP 20. PAGE 91 H1812 JURID COM LAW SOVEREIGN

B64
MARTINET G.,MARXISM OF OUR TIME: OR THE CONTRADICTIONS OF SOCIALISM. FRANCE NAT/G OPTIMAL RIGID/FLEX SOCISM...IDEA/COMP 20. PAGE 103 H2067 MARXISM MARXIST PROB/SOLV CREATE

B64
MILIBAND R.,THE SOCIALIST REGISTER: 1964. GERMANY/W ITALY UK LABOR POL/PAR ECO/TAC FOR/AID NUC/PWR ...POLICY SOCIALIST IDEA/COMP 20 MAO NASSER/G. PAGE 110 H2204 MARXISM SOCISM CAP/ISM PROB/SOLV

B64
MINAR D.W.,IDEAS AND POLITICS: THE AMERICAN EXPERIENCE. SECT CHIEF LEGIS CREATE ADJUD EXEC REV PWR...PHIL/SCI CONCPT IDEA/COMP 18/20 HAMILTON/A JEFFERSN/T DECLAR/IND JACKSON/A PRESIDENT. PAGE 111 H2220 CONSTN NAT/G FEDERAL

B64
ON CULTURE AND SOCIAL CHANGE. FAM NAT/G ACT/RES ECO/TAC RACE/REL...PSY TIME/SEQ TREND IDEA/COMP METH/COMP ANTHOL BIBLIOG 20. PAGE 120 H2406 CULTURE TEC/DEV STRUCT CREATE

B64
QUIGG P.W.,AFRICA: A FOREIGN AFFAIRS READER. AFR FRANCE PORTUGAL UK DIPLOM LEAD PARL/PROC MARXISM ...MAJORIT METH/CNCPT GOV/COMP IDEA/COMP ANTHOL 19/20. PAGE 129 H2575 COLONIAL SOVEREIGN NAT/LISM RACE/REL

B64
ROBERTS HL,FOREIGN AFFAIRS BIBLIOGRAPHY, 1952-1962. ECO/DEV SECT PLAN FOR/AID INT/TRADE ARMS/CONT NAT/LISM ATTIT...INT/LAW GOV/COMP IDEA/COMP 20. PAGE 132 H2643 BIBLIOG/A DIPLOM INT/ORG WAR

B64
SANDEE J.,EUROPE'S FUTURE CONSUMPTION. EUR+WWI FUT EDU/PROP...IDEA/COMP NAT/COMP ANTHOL 20 EUROPE. PAGE 137 H2750 MARKET ECO/DEV PREDICT PRICE

B64
SINAI I.R.,THE CHALLENGE OF MODERNISATION* THE WEST'S IMPACT ON THE NON-WESTERN WORLD. EUR+WWI CULTURE ELITES SECT CONSERVE SOCISM...GP/COMP IDEA/COMP NAT/COMP GEN/LAWS. PAGE 144 H2881 ASIA S/ASIA ECO/UNDEV CREATE

B64
UTECHIN S.V.,RUSSIAN POLITICAL THOUGHT: A CONCISE HISTORY. RUSSIA USSR INTELL STRATA POL/PAR SECT LEGIS EDU/PROP REV WAR MARXISM...ANARCH BIBLIOG 9/20 REFORMERS SLAVS. PAGE 161 H3218 IDEA/COMP ATTIT ALL/IDEOS NAT/G

S64
KANOUTE P.,"AFRICAN SOCIALISM." AFR CONSTN NAT/G COLONIAL ORD/FREE...GOV/COMP METH/COMP 20 EUROPE. PAGE 83 H1655 SOCISM CULTURE STRUCT IDEA/COMP

C64
GOLDMAN M.I.,"COMPARATIVE ECONOMIC SYSTEMS: A READER." COM ECO/UNDEV NAT/G BUDGET CAP/ISM ADMIN TOTALISM MARXISM SOCISM...MGT ANTHOL BIBLIOG 19/20. PAGE 58 H1157 NAT/COMP CONTROL IDEA/COMP

B65
APPLEMAN P.,THE SILENT EXPLOSION. WOR+45 ECO/DEV ECO/UNDEV PLAN HEALTH ALL/IDEOS CATHISM...POLICY STAT RECORD GP/COMP IDEA/COMP NAT/COMP 20 BIRTH/CON COM/PARTY. PAGE 7 H0148 GEOG CENSUS AGRI BIO/SOC

B65
CALLEO D.P.,EUROPE'S FUTURE: THE GRAND ALTERNATIVES. UK INT/ORG DIPLOM PWR SOVEREIGN ...CONCPT IDEA/COMP NAT/COMP BIBLIOG 20 EEC EUROPE DEGAULLE/C NATO. PAGE 25 H0506 FUT EUR+WWI FEDERAL NAT/LISM

B65
CRAMER J.F.,CONTEMPORARY EDUCATION: A COMPARATIVE STUDY OF NATIONAL SYSTEMS (2ND ED.). CHINA/COM EUR+WWI INDIA USA+45 FINAN PROB/SOLV ADMIN CONTROL ATTIT...IDEA/COMP METH/COMP 20 CHINJAP. PAGE 35 H0697 EDU/PROP NAT/COMP SCHOOL ACADEM

B65
DURKHEIM E.,THE ELEMENTARY FORMS OF THE RELIGIOUS LIFE. KIN PARTIC MORAL...PSY MYTH OBS IDEA/COMP METH WORSHIP 19/20. PAGE 43 H0870 SOC CULTURE CONCPT

B65
GEWIRTH A.,POLITICAL PHILOSOPHY. UNIV SOCIETY NAT/G GP/REL INGP/REL CONSEN PWR...IDEA/COMP GEN/LAWS 17/19 HOBBES/T LOCKE/JOHN MARX/KARL MILL/JS ROUSSEAU/J. PAGE 56 H1118 ORD/FREE SOVEREIGN PHIL/SCI

B65
GOPAL S.,BRITISH POLICY IN INDIA 1858-1905. INDIA UK ELITES CHIEF DELIB/GP ECO/TAC GP/REL DISCRIM ATTIT...IDEA/COMP NAT/COMP PERS/COMP BIBLIOG/A 19/20. PAGE 59 H1176 COLONIAL ADMIN POL/PAR ECO/UNDEV

B65
GREGG J.L.,POLITICAL PARTIES AND PARTY SYSTEMS IN GUATEMALA, 1944-1963. GUATEMALA L/A+17C EX/STRUC FORCES CREATE CONTROL REV CHOOSE PWR...TREND IDEA/COMP 20. PAGE 60 H1209 LEAD POL/PAR NAT/G CHIEF

B65
HALEVY E.,THE ERA OF TYRANNIES (TRANS. BY R. K. WEBB). WOR-45 ECO/DEV PROB/SOLV CONTROL COERCE REV WAR TOTALISM 20. PAGE 64 H1286 SOCISM IDEA/COMP DOMIN

B65
HERBST J.,THE GERMAN HISTORICAL SCHOOL IN AMERICAN SCHOLARSHIP; A STUDY IN THE TRANSFER OF CULTURE. GERMANY USA+45 INTELL SOCIETY ACADEM PLAN ATTIT IDEA/COMP. PAGE 70 H1399 CULTURE NAT/COMP HIST/WRIT

B65
HUNT G.L.,CALVINISM AND THE POLITICAL ORDER. NAT/G LEAD...POLICY IDEA/COMP ANTHOL WORSHIP 20. PAGE 75 H1498 — SECT CONCPT

B65
LARUS J.,COMPARATIVE WORLD POLITICS. ASIA INDIA WOR+45 WOR-45 BAL/PWR WAR PEACE RATIONAL MORAL PWR ...REALPOL INT/LAW MUSLIM. PAGE 91 H1825 — GOV/COMP IDEA/COMP DIPLOM NAT/COMP

B65
MURDOCK G.P.,CULTURE AND SOCIETY. SOCIETY STRATA STRUCT SECT CREATE CONTROL ORD/FREE...GP/COMP ANTHOL 20. PAGE 115 H2294 — CULTURE PHIL/SCI METH IDEA/COMP

B65
OBUKAR C.,THE MODERN AFRICAN. AGRI INDUS WORKER CAP/ISM EDU/PROP PARTIC RACE/REL NAT/LISM ALL/VALS MARXISM...SOC IDEA/COMP 20. PAGE 120 H2393 — AFR ECO/UNDEV CULTURE SOVEREIGN

B65
SLATER J.,A REVALUATION OF COLLECTIVE SECURITY* THE OAS IN ACTION. L/A+17C USA+45 NAT/G ADMIN COERCE ORD/FREE PWR...GOV/COMP IDEA/COMP GEN/LAWS OAS. PAGE 145 H2899 — REGION INT/ORG FORCES

B65
TINGSTEN H.,THE PROBLEM OF DEMOCRACY. ELITES SOCIETY STRATA NAT/G CONSEN TOTALISM WELF/ST. PAGE 155 H3101 — IDEA/COMP GOV/COMP POPULISM SOCISM

B65
ULLMANN W.,A HISTORY OF POLITICAL THOUGHT: THE MIDDLE AGES. CHRIST-17C LOC/G NAT/G CENTRAL PWR ...PHIL/SCI LOG BIBLIOG 6/15. PAGE 158 H3153 — IDEA/COMP SOVEREIGN SECT LAW

B65
WHITEMAN M.M.,DIGEST OF INTERNATIONAL LAW* VOLUME 5, DEPARTMENT OF STATE PUBLICATION 7873. USA+45 WOR+45 OP/RES...CONCPT CLASSIF RECORD IDEA/COMP. PAGE 167 H3353 — INT/LAW NAT/G NAT/COMP

L65
SCHAFFER B.B.,"THE CONCEPT OF PREPARATION* SOME QUESTIONS ABOUT THE TRANSFER OF SYSTEMS OF GOVERNMENT." AFR ASIA CANADA ELITES NAT/G POL/PAR COLONIAL RIGID/FLEX IDEA/COMP. PAGE 138 H2769 — ECO/UNDEV UK RECORD

S65
BIRNBAUM K.,"SWEDEN'S NUCLEAR POLICY." WOR+45 POL/PAR CREATE TEC/DEV NEUTRAL RISK WAR ORD/FREE ...DECISION IDEA/COMP NAT/COMP TIME. PAGE 17 H0343 — SWEDEN NUC/PWR DIPLOM ARMS/CONT

S65
KINDLEBERGER C.P.,"MASS MIGRATION, THEN AND NOW." LAW ECO/DEV ECO/UNDEV INDUS LABOR INT/TRADE FEEDBACK REGION RIGID/FLEX...SOC NAT/COMP EEC. PAGE 86 H1714 — EUR+WWI USA-45 WORKER IDEA/COMP

S65
LEVI W.,"THE CONCEPT OF INTEGRATION IN RESEARCH ON PEACE." NAT/G VOL/ASSN DIPLOM TASK ADJUST NAT/LISM PEACE DRIVE LOVE...PSY NET/THEORY GEN/LAWS. PAGE 95 H1897 — CONCPT IDEA/COMP INT/ORG CENTRAL

S65
MARK M.,"MUST WE FIGHT SOCIAL REVOLUTIONS OF THE LEFT?" L/A+17C USA+45 ECO/UNDEV DIPLOM ADJUST PERCEPT...IDEA/COMP NAT/COMP. PAGE 103 H2053 — NAT/LISM REV MARXISM CREATE

S65
MCALISTER L.N.,"CHANGING CONCEPTS OF THE ROLE OF THE MILITARY IN LATIN AMERICA." CULTURE NAT/G CREATE REGION NAT/LISM ATTIT SOVEREIGN...NAT/COMP GEN/LAWS. PAGE 106 H2120 — L/A+17C FORCES IDEA/COMP PWR

S65
SANDERS R.,"MASS SUPPORT AND COMMUNIST INSURRECTION." GREECE MALAYSIA PHILIPPINE VIETNAM STRUCT ECO/UNDEV POL/PAR FORCES CREATE REV ...GP/COMP IDEA/COMP. PAGE 138 H2751 — GUERRILLA MARXISM GOV/COMP

S65
WOHLSTETTER R.,"CUBA AND PEARL HARBOR* HINDSIGHT AND FORESIGHT." USSR FORCES OP/RES TEC/DEV ATTIT PERCEPT...DECISION IDEA/COMP NAT/COMP STERTYP TIME. PAGE 170 H3395 — CUBA RISK WAR ACT/RES

C65
STERN F.,"THE POLITICS OF CULTURAL DESPAIR." NAT/LISM...IDEA/COMP BIBLIOG 19/20. PAGE 149 H2979 — CULTURE PHIL/SCI CONSERVE TOTALISM

B66
AIYAR S.P.,PERSPECTIVES ON THE WELFARE STATE. INDIA S/ASIA UK CONSTN ECO/UNDEV NAT/G INGP/REL CENTRAL NAT/LISM ATTIT...CONCPT ANTHOL BIBLIOG 20. PAGE 4 H0087 — NEW/LIB WELF/ST IDEA/COMP ADJUST

B66
ANDERSON S.V.,CANADIAN OMBUDSMAN PROPOSALS. CANADA LEGIS DEBATE PARL/PROC...MAJORIT JURID TIME/SEQ IDEA/COMP 20 OMBUDSMAN PARLIAMENT. PAGE 7 H0133 — NAT/G CREATE ADMIN POL/PAR

B66
BESSON W.,DIE GROSSEN MACHTE - STRUKTURFRAGEN DER GEGENWARTIGEN WELTPOLITIK. ASIA USSR WOR+45 ATTIT ...IDEA/COMP 20 KENNEDY/JF. PAGE 16 H0321 — NAT/COMP DIPLOM STRUCT

B66
CAPELL A.,STUDIES IN SOCIO-LINGUISTICS. CULTURE ADJUST...CLASSIF IDEA/COMP SOC/EXP BIBLIOG 20. PAGE 26 H0525 — LING SOC PHIL/SCI CORREL

B66
COLE G.D.H.,THE MEANING OF MARXISM. USSR WOR+45 STRATA STRUCT NAT/G WORKER COST FASCISM...IDEA/COMP 20. PAGE 31 H0625 — MARXISM CONCPT HIST/WRIT CAP/ISM

B66
DAENIKER G.,STRATEGIE DES KLEIN STAATS. SWITZERLND ACT/RES CREATE DIPLOM NEUTRAL DETER WAR WEAPON PWR SOVEREIGN...IDEA/COMP 20 COLD/WAR. PAGE 36 H0730 — NUC/PWR PLAN FORCES NAT/G

B66
DEXTER N.C.,GUIDE TO CONTEMPORARY POLITICS. EUR+WWI UK PARL/PROC GP/REL KNOWL...POLICY MAJORIT IDEA/COMP 20. PAGE 41 H0815 — POL/PAR CONCPT NAT/G

B66
FOX K.A.,THE THEORY OF QUANTITATIVE ECONOMIC POLICY WITH APPLICATIONS TO ECONOMIC GROWTH AND STABILIZATION. ECO/DEV AGRI NAT/G PLAN ADMIN RISK ...DECISION IDEA/COMP SIMUL T. PAGE 52 H1045 — ECO/TAC ECOMETRIC EQUILIB GEN/LAWS

B66
FRIEDRICH C.J.,REVOLUTION: NOMOS VIII. NAT/G SOCISM ...OBS TREND IDEA/COMP ANTHOL 18/20. PAGE 54 H1070 — REV MARXISM CONCPT DIPLOM

B66
HOLDSWORTH W.S.,A HISTORY OF ENGLISH LAW; THE CENTURIES OF SETTLEMENT AND REFORM (VOL. XVI). UK LOC/G NAT/G EX/STRUC LEGIS CT/SYS LEAD ATTIT ...POLICY DECISION JURID IDEA/COMP 18 PARLIAMENT. PAGE 73 H1454 — BIOG PERSON PROF/ORG LAW

B66
KASUNMU A.B.,NIGERIAN FAMILY LAW. NIGERIA KIN LEGIT ILLEGIT MARRIAGE AGE DRIVE HABITAT ALL/VALS...JURID IDEA/COMP T 20 ENGLSH/LAW. PAGE 83 H1667 — FAM LAW CULTURE AFR

B66
LENSKI G.E.,POWER AND PRIVILEGE: A THEORY OF SOCIAL STRATIFICATION. SWEDEN UK UNIV USSR CULTURE ECO/UNDEV PRIVIL PWR...PHIL/SCI CONCPT CHARTS IDEA/COMP HYPO/EXP METH MARX/KARL. PAGE 94 H1882 — SOC STRATA STRUCT SOCIETY

B66
NOLTE E.,THREE FACES OF FASCISM. FRANCE GERMANY DOMIN LEGIT COERCE CROWD REV WAR GP/REL RACE/REL SOVEREIGN...GOV/COMP IDEA/COMP 19/20 HITLER/A MUSSOLIN/B MARX/KARL. PAGE 118 H2368 — FASCISM TOTALISM NAT/G POL/PAR

B66
ODEGARD P.H.,POLITICAL POWER AND SOCIAL CHANGE. UNIV NAT/G CREATE ALL/IDEOS...POLICY GEOG SOC CENSUS TREND. PAGE 120 H2394 — PWR TEC/DEV IDEA/COMP

B66
RINGHOFER K.,STRUKTURPROBLEME DES RECHTES. AUSTRIA ATTIT ORD/FREE...IDEA/COMP 20. PAGE 132 H2630 — JURID PROVS NAT/G NAT/LISM

B66
ROGGER H.,THE EUROPEAN RIGHT. EUR+WWI CONSERVE ...ANTHOL BIBLIOG 20. PAGE 133 H2660 — NAT/COMP POL/PAR IDEA/COMP TRADIT

B66
ROSNER J.,DER FASCHISMUS. AUSTRIA GERMANY ITALY STRATA NAT/G POL/PAR COERCE RACE/REL TOTALISM ATTIT AUTHORIT...IDEA/COMP 20 NAZI ANTI/SEMIT. PAGE 134 H2684 — NAT/LISM FASCISM ORD/FREE WAR

B66
SCHRAM S.,MAO TSE-TUNG. ASIA CHINA/COM CONTROL REGION ATTIT...POLICY IDEA/COMP 20 MAO. PAGE 140 H2799 — BIOG MARXISM TOP/EX GUERRILLA

B66
SETTON K.M.,GREAT PROBLEMS IN EUROPEAN CIVILIZATION. CHRIST-17C EUR+WWI MOD/EUR SECT GP/REL ALL/VALS ORD/FREE ALL/IDEOS...TREND ANTHOL T CHRISTIAN RENAISSAN PROTESTANT. PAGE 142 H2835 — CULTURE CONCPT IDEA/COMP

B66
WINKS R.W.,THE HISTORIOGRAPHY OF THE BRITISH EMPIRE-COMMONWEALTH. CANADA INDIA PAKISTAN UK CULTURE SOCIETY STRUCT POL/PAR...CONCPT NAT/COMP 20 AUSTRAL. PAGE 169 H3386 — HIST/WRIT TREND IDEA/COMP METH/COMP

B66
YEAGER L.B.,INTERNATIONAL MONETARY RELATIONS: THEORY, HISTORY, AND POLICY. WOR+45 WOR-45 INT/TRADE BAL/PAY...NAT/COMP 18/20 MONEY. PAGE 172 H3435 — FINAN DIPLOM ECO/TAC IDEA/COMP

B66
ZABLOCKI C.J.,SINO-SOVIET RIVALRY. AFR ASIA CHINA/COM CUBA EUR+WWI L/A+17C USA+45 USSR WOR+45 POL/PAR FORCES COERCE NUC/PWR...GOV/COMP IDEA/COMP 20 MAO KHRUSH/N. PAGE 172 H3444 — DIPLOM MARXISM COM

S66
GRUNDY K.W.,"RECENT CONTRIBUTIONS TO THE STUDY OF AFRICAN POLITICAL THOUGHT." DIPLOM NAT/LISM ALL/IDEOS...NEW/IDEA GOV/COMP 20. PAGE 62 H1239 BIBLIOG/A AFR ATTIT IDEA/COMP

S66
LODGE G.C.,"REVOLUTION IN LATIN AMERICA." USA+45 ELITES INDUS LABOR PROF/ORG SECT TEC/DEV CAP/ISM SKILL MARXISM...POLICY NAT/COMP. PAGE 98 H1950 ATTIT REV L/A+17C IDEA/COMP

S66
MCLENNAN B.N.,"EVOLUTION OF CONCEPTS OF REPRESENTATION IN INDONESIA" INDONESIA...CONCPT IDEA/COMP METH 20. PAGE 107 H2143 REPRESENT NAT/G POPULISM PWR

C66
DEUTSCH K.W.,"NATIONALISM AND SOCIAL COMMUNICATION." CULTURE INGP/REL ATTIT PWR...PSY SOC CONCPT LING IDEA/COMP 20. PAGE 40 H0800 BIBLIOG NAT/LISM GEN/LAWS

B67
ALBINSKI H.S.,EUROPEAN POLITICAL PROCESSES: ESSAYS AND READINGS. EUR+WWI FRANCE GERMANY MOD/EUR UK ELITES POL/PAR PWR...CHARTS ANTHOL 18/20. PAGE 5 H0094 NAT/COMP POLICY IDEA/COMP

B67
BROWN L.N.,FRENCH ADMINISTRATIVE LAW. FRANCE UK CONSTN NAT/G LEGIS DOMIN CONTROL EXEC PARL/PROC PWR ...JURID METH/COMP GEN/METH. PAGE 22 H0447 EX/STRUC LAW IDEA/COMP CT/SYS

B67
BRZEZINSKI Z.K.,THE SOVIET BLOC: UNITY AND CONFLICT (2ND ED., REV., ENLARGED). COM POLAND USSR INTELL CHIEF EX/STRUC CONTROL EXEC GOV/REL PWR MARXISM ...TREND IDEA/COMP 20 LENIN/VI MARX/KARL STALIN/J. PAGE 23 H0463 NAT/G DIPLOM

B67
CAMERON R.,BANKING IN THE EARLY STAGES OF INDUSTRIALIZATION: A STUDY IN ECONOMIC COMPARATIVE HISTORY. FRANCE GERMANY UK USSR...CHARTS IDEA/COMP NAT/COMP 18/20 CHINJAP. PAGE 26 H0512 FINAN INDUS GOV/COMP

B67
CANTOR N.F.,THE ENGLISH TRADITION* TWENTIETH-CENTURY VIEWS OF ENGLISH HISTORY (2VOLS.). UK STRATA NAT/G SECT WAR...POLICY GOV/COMP IDEA/COMP ANTHOL T PARLIAMENT CMN/WLTH. PAGE 26 H0522 CT/SYS LAW POL/PAR

B67
CHILCOTE R.H.,PORTUGUESE AFRICA. PORTUGAL CULTURE SOCIETY ECO/UNDEV DOMIN NAT/LISM...TREND IDEA/COMP NAT/COMP BIBLIOG 15/20. PAGE 29 H0589 AFR COLONIAL ORD/FREE PROB/SOLV

B67
COWLES M.,PERSPECTIVES IN THE EDUCATION OF DISADVANTAGED CHILDREN. CULTURE OP/RES PLAN PERS/REL ADJUST HABITAT PERCEPT KNOWL WEALTH ...SOC/WK IDEA/COMP ANTHOL 20. PAGE 34 H0686 EDU/PROP AGE/C TEC/DEV SCHOOL

B67
LAQUER W.,THE FATE OF THE REVOLUTION: INTERPRETATIONS OF SOVIET HISTORY. RUSSIA NAT/G MARXISM...BIBLIOG 20 STALIN/J. PAGE 91 H1816 REV KNOWL HIST/WRIT IDEA/COMP

B67
MACRIDIS R.C.,FOREIGN POLICY IN WORLD POLITICS (3RD ED.). EX/STRUC BAL/PWR COLONIAL NAT/LISM SKILL SOVEREIGN WEALTH...CONCPT TIME/SEQ ANTHOL 20 COLD/WAR. PAGE 101 H2011 DIPLOM POLICY NAT/G IDEA/COMP

B67
MEHDI M.T.,PEACE IN THE MIDDLE EAST. ISRAEL SOCIETY NAT/G PLAN EDU/PROP NAT/LISM DRIVE...IDEA/COMP 20 JEWS. PAGE 108 H2160 ISLAM DIPLOM GP/REL COERCE

B67
NASH M.,MACHINE AGE MAYA. GUATEMALA L/A+17C STRUCT AGRI WORKER CREATE INCOME ATTIT RIGID/FLEX ROLE ...IDEA/COMP SOC/EXP WORSHIP 20 INDIAN/AM. PAGE 116 H2315 INDUS CULTURE SOC MUNIC

B67
RIESMAN D.,CONVERSATIONS IN JAPAN: MODERNIZATION, POLITICS, AND CULTURE. CHINA/COM STRATA STRUCT ECO/DEV INDUS ACADEM EDU/PROP...ART/METH SOC MODAL INT IDEA/COMP SOC/INTEG 20 CHINJAP HIROSHIMA. PAGE 131 H2629 CULTURE SOCIETY ASIA

B67
ROWLAND J.,A HISTORY OF SINO-INDIAN RELATIONS; HOSTILE CO-EXISTENCE. ASIA CHINA/COM INDIA NAT/G NUC/PWR PWR WEALTH...GEOG BIBLIOG 13/20 COLD/WAR. PAGE 135 H2704 DIPLOM CENSUS IDEA/COMP

B67
RUEFF J.,BALANCE OF PAYMENTS. WOR+45 FINAN TEC/DEV DIPLOM TARIFFS PRICE CONTROL...POLICY CONCPT IDEA/COMP. PAGE 136 H2715 INT/TRADE BAL/PAY ECO/TAC NAT/COMP

B67
RUSTOW D.A.,A WORLD OF NATIONS; PROBLEMS OF POLITICAL MODERNIZATION. CONSTN NAT/G POL/PAR FORCES DIPLOM LEAD AUTHORIT...CHARTS IDEA/COMP 20. PAGE 136 H2722 PROB/SOLV ECO/UNDEV CONCPT NAT/COMP

B67
SETON-WATSON H.,THE RUSSIAN EMPIRE, 1801-1917. COM RUSSIA STRATA ECO/DEV AGRI INDUS POL/PAR DIPLOM NAT/LISM MARXISM...IDEA/COMP BIBLIOG 19/20 MARX/KARL. PAGE 142 H2834 SOCIETY NAT/G LEAD POLICY

B67
SHAFFER H.G.,THE COMMUNIST WORLD: MARXIST AND NON-MARXIST VIEWS. WOR+45 SOCIETY DIPLOM ECO/TAC CONTROL SOCISM...MARXIST ANTHOL BIBLIOG/A 20. PAGE 142 H2838 MARXISM NAT/COMP IDEA/COMP COM

B67
THOMPSON E.T.,PERSPECTIVES ON THE SOUTH: AGENDA FOR RESEARCH. CULTURE ECO/UNDEV SECT GP/REL EFFICIENCY ALL/VALS...HUM SOC CONCPT LING 20 NEGRO. PAGE 154 H3080 PROB/SOLV IDEA/COMP REGION ACT/RES

B67
TOMPKINS S.R.,THE TRIUMPH OF BOLSHEVISM: REVOLUTION OR REACTION? USSR WORKER PRESS WEALTH MARXISM POPULISM...BIOG TREND IDEA/COMP BIBLIOG 19/20 LENIN/VI. PAGE 156 H3113 REV NAT/G POL/PAR NAT/LISM

B67
UNIVERSAL REFERENCE SYSTEM,COMPARATIVE GOVERNMENT AND CULTURES (VOLUME X). WOR+45 WOR-45 NAT/G POL/PAR ATTIT...CON/ANAL COMPUT/IR IDEA/COMP GEN/METH. PAGE 158 H3168 BIBLIOG/A GOV/COMP CULTURE NAT/COMP

L67
CRIBBET J.E.,"SOME REFLECTIONS ON THE LAW OF LAND - A VIEW FROM SCANDINAVIA." DENMARK NETHERLAND NORWAY SWEDEN INDUS MUNIC NEIGH RACE/REL ATTIT HABITAT ...IDEA/COMP 20. PAGE 35 H0701 LAW PLAN CONTROL NAT/G

L67
EGBERT D.D.,"THE IDEA OF 'AVANT-GARDE' IN ART AND POLITICS." USSR CULTURE INTELL POL/PAR CREATE EDU/PROP CONTROL REV ANOMIE DRIVE ROLE...IDEA/COMP 20. PAGE 45 H0895 ART/METH COM ATTIT

L67
VAN DER KROEF J.M.,"INDONESIA: THE BATTLE OF THE 'OLD' AND THE 'NEW ORDER'." INDONESIA ISLAM ELITES POL/PAR DOMIN INGP/REL NAT/LISM PWR...IDEA/COMP 20. PAGE 161 H3229 FORCES MARXISM NAT/G BAL/PWR

S67
ADOKO A.,"THE CONSTITUTION OF UGANDA." AFR UGANDA LOC/G CHIEF FORCES LEGIS ADJUD EXEC CHOOSE NAT/LISM ...IDEA/COMP 20. PAGE 4 H0072 NAT/G CONSTN ORD/FREE LAW

S67
COHEN R.,"ANTHROPOLOGY AND POLITICAL SCIENCE: COURTSHIP OR MARRIAGE?" CULTURE STRATA STRUCT MUNIC REGION UTOPIA...NEW/IDEA TREND IDEA/COMP METH/COMP 20. PAGE 31 H0618 SOC INGP/REL AFR

S67
ELLISON H.J.,"THE SOCIALIST REVOLUTIONARIES." USSR ECO/UNDEV NAT/G INGP/REL EFFICIENCY ATTIT PWR MARXISM...CONCPT IDEA/COMP 20 SOC/REVPAR. PAGE 46 H0911 POL/PAR REV AGRI

S67
FRANCIS M.J.,"THE US PRESS AND CASTRO: A STUDY IN DECLINING RELATIONS." COM DIPLOM WAR TOTALISM ATTIT SOCISM...POLICY IDEA/COMP 20. PAGE 52 H1046 PRESS LEAD REV NAT/G

S67
GAMARNIKOW M.,"THE NEW ROLE OF PRIVATE ENTERPRISE." ECO/DEV INDUS NAT/G SML/CO CREATE PROB/SOLV MARXISM ...POLICY TREND IDEA/COMP 20. PAGE 55 H1092 ECO/TAC ATTIT CAP/ISM COM

S67
HOPE M.,"THE RELUCTANT WAY: SELF-IMMOLATION IN VIETNAM." VIETNAM SOCIETY FAM KIN SECT DRIVE ALL/VALS...TRADIT OBS INT 20. PAGE 73 H1465 CULTURE SUICIDE IDEA/COMP ATTIT

S67
KINGSBURY E.C.,"LAW AS COMPACT: ANCIENT ISRAEL'S CONTRIBUTION TO THE UNDERSTANDING OF LAW." ISRAEL MEDIT-7 CULTURE KIN KNOWL...JURID CONCPT TREND IDEA/COMP METH/COMP WORSHIP JEWS DEITY. PAGE 86 H1716 LAW AGREE CONSTN INGP/REL

S67
KRISTOF L.K.D.,"THE STATE-IDEA, THE NATIONAL IDEA AND THE IMAGE OF THE FATHERLAND." CONSTN CULTURE INTELL SOCIETY WORKER TASK DRIVE HABITAT...MYTH GOV/COMP IDEA/COMP. PAGE 89 H1769 GEOG CONCPT NAT/G PERCEPT

S67
KROGER K.,"ZUR ENTWICKLUNG DER STAATSZWECKLEHRE IM 19 JAHRHUNDERT." GERMANY RATIONAL ATTIT...IDEA/COMP 19. PAGE 89 H1773 CONCPT NAT/G JURID OBJECTIVE

S67
LICHFIELD N.,"THE EVALUATION OF CAPITAL INVESTMENT PROJECTS IN TOWN CENTRE REDEVELOPMENT." UK CONSTRUC MUNIC CONSULT COST...METH/CNCPT IDEA/COMP 20. PAGE 96 H1923 PLAN ECO/TAC NAT/G DECISION

S67
READ J.S.,"CENSORED." UGANDA CONSTN INTELL SOCIETY NAT/G DIPLOM PRESS WRITING ADJUD ADMIN COLONIAL RISK...IDEA/COMP 20. PAGE 130 H2602 EDU/PROP AFR CREATE

POLICY

B41
KEESING F.M.,THE SOUTH SEAS IN THE MODERN WORLD. INDONESIA STRUCT FAM SECT EDU/PROP LEAD INCOME WEALTH...HEAL SOC 20. PAGE 84 H1678
CULTURE ECO/UNDEV GOV/COMP DIPLOM

B52
ROBBINS L.,THE THEORY OF ECONOMIC POLICY IN ENGLISH CLASSICAL POLITICAL ECONOMY. UK ECO/DEV WORKER PLAN CAP/ISM EDU/PROP CONTROL INCOME OWN HEALTH SOCISM ...POLICY 17/19. PAGE 132 H2639
ECO/TAC ORD/FREE IDEA/COMP NAT/G

C52
HUME D.,"OF TAXES" IN D. HUME, POLITICAL DISCOURSES (1752)" UK NAT/G COST INCOME LAISSEZ...GEN/LAWS 18. PAGE 75 H1493
TAX FINAN WEALTH POLICY

B58
AVRAMOVIC D.,POSTWAR GROWTH IN INTERNATIONAL INDEBTEDNESS. WOR+45 AGRI INDUS CAP/ISM PRICE INCOME...NAT/COMP 20 GOLD/STAND SILVER. PAGE 9 H0184
INT/TRADE FINAN COST BAL/PAY

B58
SHAW S.J.,THE FINANCIAL AND ADMINISTRATIVE ORGANIZATION AND DEVELOPMENT OF OTTOMAN EGYPT 1517-1798. UAR LOC/G FORCES BUDGET INT/TRADE TAX EATING INCOME WEALTH...CHARTS BIBLIOG 16/18 OTTOMAN NAPOLEON/B. PAGE 143 H2853
FINAN ADMIN GOV/REL CULTURE

B59
SVALASTOGA K.,PRESTIGE, CLASS, AND MOBILITY. DENMARK UK EDU/PROP INCOME WEALTH...SOC SAMP 20. PAGE 151 H3010
NAT/COMP STRATA STRUCT ELITES

B60
GONZALEZ NAVARRO M.,LA COLONIZACION EN MEXICO, 1877-1910. AGRI NAT/G PLAN PROB/SOLV INCOME ...POLICY JURID CENSUS 19/20 MEXIC/AMER MIGRATION. PAGE 58 H1164
ECO/UNDEV GEOG HABITAT COLONIAL

B60
PETERSON W.C.,THE WELFARE STATE IN FRANCE. EUR+WWI FRANCE FUT STRATA PROB/SOLV TAX GIVE RECEIVE INCOME ORD/FREE PWR...CHARTS 20. PAGE 125 H2496
NEW/LIB ECO/TAC WEALTH NAT/G

B60
ROY N.C.,THE CIVIL SERVICE IN INDIA. INDIA POL/PAR ECO/TAC INCOME...JURID MGT 20 CIVIL/SERV. PAGE 135 H2705
ADMIN NAT/G DELIB/GP CONFER

B60
THE ECONOMIST (LONDON),THE COMMONWEALTH AND EUROPE. EUR+WWI WOR+45 AGRI FINAN INCOME...STAT CENSUS CHARTS CMN/WLTH EEC. PAGE 153 H3067
INT/TRADE INDUS INT/ORG NAT/COMP

B61
BREWIS T.N.,CANADIAN ECONOMIC POLICY. CANADA BUDGET CAP/ISM INT/TRADE RATION TARIFFS TAX PRICE CONTROL ROUTINE FEDERAL INCOME PRODUC 20 GOLD/STAND. PAGE 20 H0412
ECO/DEV ECO/TAC NAT/G PLAN

B61
LETHBRIDGE H.J.,CHINA'S URBAN COMMUNES. CHINA/COM FUT ECO/UNDEV DIPLOM EDU/PROP DEMAND INCOME MARXISM ...POLICY 20. PAGE 95 H1893
MUNIC CONTROL ECO/TAC NAT/G

B61
SPOONER F.P.,SOUTH AFRICAN PREDICAMENT. FUT SOUTH/AFR INDUS POL/PAR RACE/REL INCOME...CHARTS 20 NEGRO. PAGE 148 H2953
ECO/DEV DISCRIM ECO/TAC POLICY

B62
HARRINGTON M.,THE OTHER AMERICA: POVERTY IN THE UNITED STATES. WORKER CREATE REPRESENT RACE/REL AGE/O DRIVE POLICY. PAGE 67 H1338
WEALTH WELF/ST INCOME CULTURE

B62
MICHAELY M.,CONCENTRATION IN INTERNATIONAL TRADE. ECO/DEV ECO/UNDEV PRICE INCOME...CHARTS NAT/COMP 20. PAGE 110 H2197
INT/TRADE MARKET FINAN GEOG

B63
BANERJI A.K.,INDIA'S BALANCE OF PAYMENTS. INDIA NAT/G PRICE BAL/PAY COST INCOME 20. PAGE 10 H0208
INT/TRADE DIPLOM FINAN BUDGET

B63
GORDON M.S.,THE ECONOMICS OF WELFARE POLICIES. INDUS LOC/G NAT/G LEGIS WORKER INCOME AGE/O SKILL WEALTH...METH/COMP NAT/COMP 20. PAGE 59 H1180
METH/CNCPT ECO/TAC POLICY

B63
INTERNATIONAL ASSOCIATION RES,AFRICAN STUDIES IN INCOME AND WEALTH. AFR NAT/G PROB/SOLV DEMAND INCOME...ECOMETRIC METH/COMP 20. PAGE 78 H1553
WEALTH PLAN ECO/UNDEV BUDGET

B64
BEARDSLEY R.K.,STUDIES ON ECONOMIC LIFE IN JAPAN (OCCASIONAL PAPERS NO. 8). INDUS FAM HABITAT...GEOG GOV/COMP 20 CHINJAP. PAGE 12 H0249
WEALTH PRESS PRODUC INCOME

B64
BROWN W.M.,THE EXTERNAL LIQUIDITY OF AN ADVANCED COUNTRY. CANADA FRANCE GERMANY/W SWEDEN UK USA+45 ECO/DEV DIPLOM PRICE...CONCPT STAT NAT/COMP 20. PAGE 22 H0451
FINAN INT/TRADE COST INCOME

B64
HAZLEWOOD A.,THE ECONOMICS OF DEVELOPMENT: AN ANNOTATED LIST OF BOOKS AND ARTICLES PUBLISHED 1958-1962. AGRI FINAN INDUS LABOR NAT/G DIPLOM INT/TRADE INCOME...MGT 20. PAGE 69 H1374
BIBLIOG/A ECO/UNDEV TEC/DEV

B64
HERSKOVITS M.J.,ECONOMIC TRANSITION IN AFRICA. FUT INT/ORG NAT/G WORKER PROB/SOLV TEC/DEV INT/TRADE EQUILIB INCOME...ANTHOL 20. PAGE 70 H1408
AFR ECO/UNDEV PLAN ADMIN

B64
INTERNATIONAL LABOUR OFFICE,EMPLOYMENT AND ECONOMIC GROWTH. ECO/DEV ECO/UNDEV NAT/G PLAN DIPLOM INT/TRADE CONTROL INCOME PRODUC WEALTH...STAT NAT/COMP 20 ILO. PAGE 78 H1558
WORKER METH/COMP ECO/TAC OPTIMAL

B64
RAPHAEL M.,PENSIONS AND PUBLIC SERVANTS. UK NAT/G PLAN INGP/REL COST EFFICIENCY ATTIT...POLICY 17/20 CIVIL/SERV. PAGE 130 H2593
RECEIVE ADMIN INCOME AGE/O

B64
THAILAND NATIONAL ECO DEV,THE NATIONAL ECONOMIC DEVELOPMENT PLAN: 1961-66: SECOND PHASE 1964-66. THAILAND AGRI FINAN BUDGET EFFICIENCY INCOME...STAT CHARTS 20. PAGE 153 H3065
ECO/UNDEV ECO/TAC PLAN NAT/G

B65
HONDURAS CONSEJO NAC DE ECO,PLAN NACIONAL DE DESARROLLO ECONOMICO Y SOCIAL DE HONDURAS 1965-69. HONDURAS AGRI INDUS BAL/PAY INCOME 20. PAGE 73 H1459
ECO/UNDEV NAT/G PLAN POLICY

B65
TEW B.,WEALTH AND INCOME. UK BUDGET INT/TRADE PRICE BAL/PAY DEMAND...CHARTS GOV/COMP 20 AUSTRAL. PAGE 153 H3064
FINAN ECO/DEV WEALTH INCOME

S65
VAN DEN BERG M.,"SOME METHODOLOGICAL ASPECTS OF SOUTH AFRICA'S FIRST E.D.P." SOUTH/AFR NAT/G CREATE TEC/DEV CAP/ISM INCOME PRODUC...CON/ANAL CHARTS 20. PAGE 161 H3226
ECO/DEV PLAN METH STAT

B66
HACKETT J.,L'ECONOMIE BRITANNIQUE: PROBLEMES ET PERSPECTIVES. FRANCE UK LABOR MUNIC NAT/G EX/STRUC PROB/SOLV BAL/PAY INCOME RIGID/FLEX...MGT PHIL/SCI CHARTS 20. PAGE 63 H1271
ECO/DEV FINAN ECO/TAC PLAN

B66
KUZNETS S.,MODERN ECONOMIC GROWTH. WOR+45 WOR-45 ECO/DEV ECO/UNDEV AGRI FINAN INDUS TEC/DEV EFFICIENCY INCOME...NAT/COMP 19/20. PAGE 89 H1786
TIME/SEQ WEALTH PRODUC

B66
PLATE H.,PARTEIFINANZIERUNG UND GRUNDESETZ. GERMANY NAT/G PLAN GIVE PAY INCOME WEALTH...JURID 20. PAGE 126 H2522
POL/PAR CONSTN FINAN

B66
ROSS A.M.,INDUSTRIAL RELATIONS AND ECONOMIC DEVELOPMENT. POL/PAR LEGIS WORKER BARGAIN PRICE EXEC LOBBY INCOME PWR...DECISION ANTHOL BIBLIOG 20. PAGE 134 H2686
ECO/UNDEV LABOR NAT/G GP/REL

B67
NASH M.,MACHINE AGE MAYA. GUATEMALA L/A+17C STRUCT AGRI WORKER CREATE INCOME ATTIT RIGID/FLEX ROLE ...IDEA/COMP SOC/EXP WORSHIP 20 INDIAN/AM. PAGE 116 H2315
INDUS CULTURE SOC MUNIC

S67
ADNITT F.W.,"THE RISE OF ENGLISH RADICALISM -- PART 2." UK NAT/G WORKER INCOME WEALTH...BIOG 19 PARLIAMENT. PAGE 4 H0071
LEGIS LOBBY

S67
BELLER I.,"ECONOMIC POLICY AND THE DEMANDS OF LABOR." PLAN TAX GIVE PRICE WAR COST PRODUC WEALTH. PAGE 13 H0268
NAT/G ECO/TAC SOC/WK INCOME

S67
DENISON E.F.,"SOURCES OF GROWTH IN NINE WESTERN COUNTRIES." WORKER TEC/DEV COST PRODUC...TREND NAT/COMP. PAGE 39 H0790
INCOME NAT/G EUR+WWI ECO/DEV

S67
DERRICK P.,"THE WHITE PAPER ON INCOMES." EUR+WWI UK LAW LABOR NAT/G PLAN PROB/SOLV GP/REL...GOV/COMP PARLIAMENT. PAGE 40 H0794
INCOME POL/PAR POLICY

S67
DESHPANDE A.M.,"FEDERAL-STATE FISCAL RELATIONS IN INDIA" (REVIEW ARTICLE)" GERMANY USSR DELIB/GP PLAN BUDGET ECO/TAC INCOME 20 SOC/DEMPAR SOC/REVPAR. PAGE 40 H0795
FINAN NAT/G GOV/REL TAX

S67
JENCKS C.E.,"SOCIAL STATUS OF COAL MINERS IN BRITAIN SINCE NATIONALIZATION." UK STRATA STRUCT LABOR RECEIVE GP/REL INCOME OWN ATTIT HABITAT...MGT T 20. PAGE 80 H1600
EXTR/IND WORKER CONTROL NAT/G

S67
PAI G.A.,"TAXATION AND PLANNING IN INDIA: A BIRDS-EYE VIEW." INDIA ELITES NAT/G LEGIS BUDGET CONTROL LOBBY INCOME...STAT CHARTS 20. PAGE 122 H2443
TAX PLAN WEALTH STRATA

S67
SCHACHTER G.,"REGIONAL DEVELOPMENT IN THE ITALIAN DUAL ECONOMY" ITALY AGRI INDUS MARKET WORKER ECO/TAC CONTROL INCOME PRODUC 20. PAGE 138 H2767
REGION ECO/UNDEV NAT/G PROB/SOLV

S67
SHARKANSKY I.,"ECONOMIC AND POLITICAL CORRELATES OF STATE GOVERNMENT EXPENDITURE: GENERAL TENDENCIES AND DEVIANT CASES." USA+45 LOC/G NAT/G TAX GIVE INCOME...CENSUS CHARTS. PAGE 142 H2845
PROVS BUDGET GOV/COMP

B91
MILL J.S.,SOCIALISM (1859). MOD/EUR AGRI INDUS NAT/G REV INCOME PRODUC ORD/FREE POPULISM SOCISM ...GOV/COMP METH/COMP 19. PAGE 110 H2209
WEALTH SOCIALIST ECO/TAC OWN

B95
SELIGMAN E.R.A.,ESSAYS IN TAXATION. NEW/ZEALND PRUSSIA UK USA-45 MARKET LOC/G CREATE PRICE CONTROL INCOME OWN WEALTH...GOV/COMP METH/COMP 19. PAGE 141 H2824
TAX TARIFFS INDUS NAT/G

L95
BELSHAW C.S.,"IN SEARCH OF WEALTH; STUDY OF EMERGENCE OF COMMERCIAL OPERA TIONS IN MELANESIAN SOCIETY OF SOUTHEASTERN PAPUA." S/ASIA CULTURE KIN ECO/TAC DEMAND INCOME 20 MELANESIA PAPUA. PAGE 14 H0272
INT/TRADE ECO/UNDEV METH/COMP SOCIETY

INCOMPETENCE....SEE SKILL

IND/WRK/AF....INDUSTRIAL AND WORKERS' COMMERCIAL UNION OF AFRICA

INDER S. H1527

INDEX....INDEX SYSTEM

N
CHINA QUARTERLY. COM AGRI INDUS ACADEM POL/PAR INT/TRADE CONFER GOV/REL...TIME/SEQ CON/ANAL INDEX 20. PAGE 1 H0014
BIBLIOG/A ASIA DIPLOM POLICY

N
LONDON TIMES OFFICIAL INDEX. UK LAW ECO/DEV NAT/G DIPLOM LEAD ATTIT 20. PAGE 1 H0018
BIBLIOG INDEX PRESS WRITING

N
THE MIDDLE EAST AND NORTH AFRICA. AFR ISLAM CULTURE ECO/UNDEV AGRI NAT/G TEC/DEV FOR/AID INT/TRADE EDU/PROP...CHARTS 20. PAGE 2 H0026
INDEX INDUS FINAN STAT

N
US CONSOLATE GENERAL HONG KONG,REVIEW OF THE HONG KONG CHINESE PRESS. ECO/UNDEV LOC/G NAT/G PLAN DIPLOM EDU/PROP LEAD GP/REL MARXISM...POLICY INDEX 20. PAGE 159 H3178
BIBLIOG/A ASIA PRESS ATTIT

N
US CONSULATE GENERAL HONG KONG,CURRENT BACKGROUND. CHINA/COM ECO/UNDEV LOC/G NAT/G PLAN DIPLOM EDU/PROP LEAD REV ATTIT...POLICY INDEX 20. PAGE 159 H3179
BIBLIOG/A MARXIST ASIA PRESS

N
US CONSULATE GENERAL HONG KONG,EXTRACTS FROM CHINA MAINLAND MAGAZINES. ASIA CHINA/COM ECO/UNDEV NAT/G CHIEF LEAD ATTIT...MARXIST INDEX 20. PAGE 159 H3180
BIBLIOG MARXISM PRESS

N
US CONSULATE GENERAL HONG KONG,SURVEY OF CHINA MAINLAND PRESS. CHINA/COM ECO/UNDEV LOC/G NAT/G PLAN DIPLOM EDU/PROP LEAD REV ATTIT...POLICY INDEX 20. PAGE 159 H3181
BIBLIOG/A MARXIST ASIA PRESS

N
US CONSULATE GENERAL HONG KONG,US CONSULATE GENERAL, HONG KONG, PRESS SUMMARIES. CHINA/COM ECO/UNDEV LOC/G NAT/G PLAN DIPLOM EDU/PROP LEAD REV ATTIT...POLICY INDEX 20. PAGE 159 H3182
BIBLIOG/A MARXIST ASIA PRESS

B03
FORTESCUE G.K.,SUBJECT INDEX OF THE MODERN WORKS ADDED TO THE LIBRARY OF THE BRITISH MUSEUM IN THE YEARS 1881-1900 (3 VOLS.). UK LAW CONSTN FINAN NAT/G FORCES INT/TRADE COLONIAL 19. PAGE 52 H1041
BIBLIOG INDEX WRITING

B28
LODGE H.C.,THE HISTORY OF NATIONS (25 VOLS.). UNIV LEAD...ANTHOL BIBLIOG INDEX. PAGE 98 H1951
DIPLOM SOCIETY NAT/G

B50
TENG S.,AN ANNOTATED BIBLIOGRAPHY OF SELECTED CHINESE REFERENCE WORKS (REV. ED.). CULTURE ECO/UNDEV LEAD MARXISM...LING INDEX 3/20. PAGE 153 H3062
BIBLIOG/A ASIA NAT/G

B54
BINANI G.D.,INDIA AT A GLANCE (REV. ED.). INDIA COM/IND FINAN INDUS LABOR PROVS SCHOOL PLAN DIPLOM INT/TRADE ADMIN...JURID 20. PAGE 17 H0335
INDEX CON/ANAL NAT/G ECO/UNDEV

L60
HAAS E.B.,"CONSENSUS FORMATION IN THE COUNCIL OF EUROPE." EUR+WWI NAT/G DELIB/GP DIPLOM REGION CHOOSE PWR SOVEREIGN...RELATIV NEW/IDEA QUANT CHARTS INDEX TOT/POP OEEC 20 COUNCL/EUR. PAGE 63 H1265
POL/PAR INT/ORG STAT

B62
MITCHELL B.R.,ABSTRACT OF BRITISH HISTORICAL STATISTICS. UK FINAN NAT/G 12/20. PAGE 111 H2229
BIBLIOG STAT INDEX ECO/DEV

B62
YU LIEN YEN CHIU,INDEX TO THE CLASSIFIED FILES ON COMMUNIST CHINA. CHINA/COM CULTURE ECO/UNDEV CIVMIL/REL PWR WEALTH MARXISM...PSY SOC METH 20. PAGE 172 H3440
BIBLIOG INDEX COM

B64
HERRICK M.D.,CATALOG OF AFRICAN GOVERNMENT DOCUMENTS AND AFRICAN AREA INDEX (2ND REV. ED.) ....SOC INDEX METH 20. PAGE 70 H1405
BIBLIOG ECO/UNDEV AFR NAT/G

B65
CHAO K.,THE RATE AND PATTERN OF INDUSTRIAL GROWTH IN COMMUNIST CHINA. CHINA/COM ECO/UNDEV TEC/DEV PRICE...NAT/COMP BIBLIOG 20. PAGE 29 H0578
INDUS INDEX STAT PRODUC

B65
NATIONAL REFERRAL CENTER SCI,A DIRECTORY OF INFORMATION RESOURCES IN THE UNITED STATES; SOCIAL SCIENCES. USA+45 PROF/ORG...PSY SOC 20. PAGE 116 H2322
INDEX R+D ACADEM ACT/RES

B65
SABLE M.H.,MASTER DIRECTORY FOR LATIN AMERICA. AGRI COM/IND FINAN R+D ACADEM LABOR NAT/G POL/PAR VOL/ASSN INT/TRADE EDU/PROP 20. PAGE 136 H2728
INDEX L/A+17C INT/ORG DIPLOM

B65
TILLY C.,MEASURING POLITICAL UPHEAVAL* RESEARCH MONOGRAPH NO. 19. FRANCE INDUS NAT/G FORCES WORKER ...GEOG RECORD EXHIBIT GEN/METH BIBLIOG INDEX. PAGE 155 H3095
CLASSIF QUANT COERCE REV

B65
VERMOT-GAUCHY M.,L'EDUCATION NATIONALE DANS LA FRANCE DE 1975. FRANCE FUT CULTURE ELITES R+D SCHOOL PLAN EDU/PROP EFFICIENCY...POLICY PREDICT CHARTS INDEX 20. PAGE 162 H3245
ACADEM CREATE TREND INTELL

B66
GURR T.,NEW ERROR-COMPENSATED MEASURES FOR COMPARING NATIONS* SOME CORRELATES OF CIVIL VIOLENCE. WOR+45 SOCIETY REV ISOLAT...PHIL/SCI SOC QUANT TESTS SAMP/SIZ HYPO/EXP. PAGE 63 H1254
NAT/COMP INDEX COERCE NEW/IDEA

B66
HANKE L.,HANDBOOK OF LATIN AMERICAN STUDIES. ECO/UNDEV ADMIN LEAD...HUM SOC 20. PAGE 65 H1313
BIBLIOG/A L/A+17C INDEX NAT/G

B66
INDIA PUBLICATIONS BRANCH,CATALOGUE OF GOVERNMENT OF INDIA CIVIL PUBLICATIONS. INDIA...INDEX 20. PAGE 76 H1529
BIBLIOG NAT/G WRITING

B66
MERRITT R.L.,COMPARING NATIONS* THE USE OF QUANTITATIVE DATA IN CROSSNATIONAL RESEARCH. ACADEM DIPLOM GP/REL...PHIL/SCI STAT TREND GP/COMP PERS/COMP GEN/METH ANTHOL BIBLIOG INDEX. PAGE 109 H2184
NAT/COMP MATH COMPUT/IR QUANT

S66
GALTUNG J.,"EAST-WEST INTERACTION PATTERNS." DIPLOM INT/TRADE...NET/THEORY CON/ANAL CHARTS NAT/COMP INDEX NATO COLD/WAR UN WARSAW/P. PAGE 55 H1090
STAT HYPO/EXP

B67
NATIONAL SCIENCE FOUNDATION,DIRECTORY OF SELECTED RESEARCH INSTITUTES IN EASTERN EUROPE. BULGARIA CZECHOSLVK HUNGARY POLAND ROMANIA INTELL ACADEM NAT/G ACT/RES 20. PAGE 116 H2323
INDEX R+D COM PHIL/SCI

INDIA....SEE ALSO S/ASIA

N
INDIA: A REFERENCE ANNUAL. INDIA CULTURE COM/IND R+D FORCES PLAN RECEIVE EDU/PROP HEALTH...STAT CHARTS BIBLIOG 20. PAGE 1 H0017
CONSTN LABOR INT/ORG

N
SEMINAR: THE MONTHLY SYMPOSIUM. INDIA ACT/RES TEC/DEV DIPLOM ATTIT...BIBLIOG 20. PAGE 1 H0022
NAT/G ECO/UNDEV SOVEREIGN POLICY

N
US LIBRARY OF CONGRESS,ACCESSIONS LIST - INDIA. INDIA CULTURE AGRI LOC/G POL/PAR PLAN PROB/SOLV TEC/DEV DIPLOM EDU/PROP LEAD GP/REL ATTIT 20. PAGE 160 H3199
BIBLIOG S/ASIA ECO/UNDEV NAT/G

N
US LIBRARY OF CONGRESS,SOUTHERN ASIA ACCESSIONS LIST. BURMA CEYLON INDIA NEPAL PAKISTAN S/ASIA THAILAND AGRI INDUS SCHOOL WORKER...ART/METH GEOG HEAL PHIL/SCI LING 20. PAGE 160 H3201 BIBLIOG/A SOCIETY CULTURE ECO/UNDEV

B02
SEELEY J.R.,THE EXPANSION OF ENGLAND. MOD/EUR S/ASIA UK CULTURE NAT/G FORCES PLAN DOMIN EDU/PROP COLONIAL ROUTINE ATTIT ALL/VALS SOVEREIGN...CONCPT HIST/WRIT PARLIAMENT 18 CMN/WLTH. PAGE 141 H2819 INT/ORG ACT/RES CAP/ISM INDIA

N19
BRIMMELL G.H.,COMMUNISM IN SOUTHEAST ASIA (PAMPHLET). BURMA CAMBODIA COM INDIA INDONESIA LAOS MOD/EUR NAT/G POL/PAR FORCES CAP/ISM CONTROL WEALTH ...MYTH 20. PAGE 21 H0420 MARXISM S/ASIA REV ECO/UNDEV

N19
GORWALA A.D.,THE ADMINISTRATIVE JUNGLE (PAMPHLET). INDIA NAT/G LEGIS ECO/TAC CONTROL GOV/REL ...METH/COMP 20. PAGE 59 H1183 ADMIN POLICY PLAN ECO/UNDEV

B27
PANIKKAR K.M.,INDIAN STATES AND THE GOVERNMENT OF INDIA. INDIA UK CONSTN CONTROL TASK GP/REL SOVEREIGN WEALTH...TREND BIBLIOG 19. PAGE 123 H2457 GOV/COMP COLONIAL BAL/PWR PROVS

B30
HULL W.I.,INDIA'S POLITICAL CRISIS. INDIA UK INT/ORG LABOR SECT DELIB/GP LEGIS DIPLOM NEUTRAL REGION CROWD GOV/REL MAJORITY ATTIT 20 NEHRU/J GANDHI/M COMMONWLTH. PAGE 75 H1492 ORD/FREE NAT/G COLONIAL NAT/LISM

B38
HOLDSWORTH W.S.,A HISTORY OF ENGLISH LAW; THE CENTURIES OF SETTLEMENT AND REFORM (VOL. X). INDIA UK CONSTN NAT/G CHIEF LEGIS ADMIN COLONIAL CT/SYS CHOOSE ORD/FREE PWR...JURID 18 PARLIAMENT COMMONWLTH COMMON/LAW. PAGE 72 H1451 LAW LOC/G EX/STRUC ADJUD

B38
RAWLINSON H.G.,INDIA: A SHORT CULTURAL HISTORY. INDIA LAW STRATA FORCES INT/TRADE ADMIN COLONIAL PERSON...GEOG HUM BIBLIOG WORSHIP 20. PAGE 130 H2598 CULTURE SECT MYTH ART/METH

B39
FURNIVALL J.S.,NETHERLANDS INDIA. INDIA NETHERLAND CULTURE INDUS NAT/G DIPLOM ADMIN WEALTH...POLICY CHARTS 17/20. PAGE 54 H1081 COLONIAL ECO/UNDEV SOVEREIGN PLURISM

B42
JOSHI P.S.,THE TYRANNY OF COLOUR. INDIA SOUTH/AFR UK ECO/UNDEV NAT/G POL/PAR DIPLOM ECO/TAC WAR ...POLICY 19/20. PAGE 82 H1637 COLONIAL DISCRIM RACE/REL

N45
INDIA QUARTERLY, A JOURNAL OF INTERNATIONAL AFFAIRS. INDIA LAW CONSTN ECO/UNDEV INT/ORG POL/PAR COLONIAL LEAD PARL/PROC WAR ATTIT...SOC 20 CMN/WLTH. PAGE 2 H0033 BIBLIOG/A S/ASIA DIPLOM NAT/G

B48
COX O.C.,CASTE, CLASS, AND RACE. INDIA WOR+45 WOR-45 SECT TEC/DEV MARRIAGE ROLE MARXISM...MAJORIT NAT/COMP SOC/INTEG 20 NEGRO HINDU. PAGE 34 H0688 RACE/REL STRUCT STRATA DISCRIM

B51
JENNINGS I.,THE COMMONWEALTH IN ASIA. CEYLON INDIA PAKISTAN CULTURE STRATA NAT/G LEGIS DIPLOM COLONIAL ATTIT...DECISION 20 CMN/WLTH. PAGE 80 H1604 CONSTN INT/ORG POLICY PLAN

B51
JENNINGS S.I.,THE COMMONWEALTH IN ASIA. CEYLON INDIA PAKISTAN S/ASIA UK CONSTN CULTURE SOCIETY STRATA STRUCT NAT/G POL/PAR EDU/PROP LEAD WAR 20 CMN/WLTH. PAGE 80 H1608 NAT/LISM REGION COLONIAL DIPLOM

B53
APPLEBY P.H.,PUBLIC ADMINISTRATION IN INDIA: REPORT OF A SURVEY. INDIA LOC/G OP/RES ATTIT ORD/FREE 20. PAGE 7 H0147 ADMIN NAT/G EX/STRUC GOV/REL

B53
BROWN D.M.,THE WHITE UMBRELLA: INDIAN POLITICAL THOUGHT FROM MANU TO GANDHI. INDIA LAW NAT/G SECT WRITING NAT/LISM...ANTHOL BIBLIOG 20 HINDU GANDHI/M MANU. PAGE 22 H0442 CONCPT DOMIN CONSERVE

B53
MURPHY G.,IN THE MINDS OF MEN: THE STUDY OF HUMAN BEHAVIOR AND SOCIAL TENSIONS IN INDIA. FUT S/ASIA FAM INT/ORG NAT/G DIPLOM EDU/PROP GP/REL ATTIT RIGID/FLEX ALL/VALS...SOC QU UNESCO 20. PAGE 115 H2297 SECT STRATA INDIA

B54
BINANI G.D.,INDIA AT A GLANCE (REV. ED.). INDIA COM/IND FINAN INDUS LABOR PROVS SCHOOL PLAN DIPLOM INT/TRADE ADMIN...JURID 20. PAGE 17 H0335 INDEX CON/ANAL NAT/G ECO/UNDEV

B54
WILLIAMSON H.F.,ECONOMIC DEVELOPMENT - PRINCIPLES AND PATTERNS. INDIA KOREA CULTURE ECO/DEV ECO/UNDEV TEC/DEV...CENSUS NAT/COMP 20 CHINJAP MEXIC/AMER RESOURCE/N. PAGE 168 H3369 ECO/TAC GEOG LABOR

B55
UN ECONOMIC COMN ASIA & FAR E,ECONOMIC SURVEY OF ASIA AND THE FAR EAST, 1954. AFGHANISTN CEYLON INDIA PHILIPPINE S/ASIA ECO/DEV FINAN INDUS INT/TRADE PRODUC WEALTH...STAT CHARTS 20 CHINJAP. PAGE 158 H3158 ECO/UNDEV PRICE NAT/COMP ASIA

B56
DOUGLAS W.O.,WE THE JUDGES. INDIA USA+45 USA-45 LAW NAT/G SECT LEGIS PRESS CRIME FEDERAL ORD/FREE ...POLICY GOV/COMP 19/20 WARRN/EARL MARSHALL/J SUPREME/CT. PAGE 42 H0841 ADJUD CT/SYS CONSTN GOV/REL

B56
JENNINGS W.I.,THE APPROACH TO SELF-GOVERNMENT. CEYLON INDIA PAKISTAN S/ASIA UK SOCIETY POL/PAR DELIB/GP LEGIS ECO/TAC EDU/PROP ADMIN EXEC CHOOSE ATTIT ALL/VALS...JURID CONCPT GEN/METH TOT/POP 20. PAGE 81 H1610 NAT/G CONSTN COLONIAL

B56
WILSON P.,GOVERNMENT AND POLITICS OF INDIA AND PAKISTAN: 1885-1955; A BIBLIOGRAPHY OF WORKS IN WESTERN LANGUAGES. INDIA PAKISTAN CONSTN LOC/G POL/PAR FORCES DIPLOM ADMIN WAR CHOOSE...BIOG CON/ANAL 19/20. PAGE 169 H3380 BIBLIOG COLONIAL NAT/G S/ASIA

B57
CENTRAL ASIAN RESEARCH CENTRE,BIBLIOGRAPHY OF RECENT SOVIET SOURCE MATERIAL ON SOVIET CENTRAL ASIA AND THE BORDERLANDS. AFGHANISTN INDIA PAKISTAN UAR USSR ECO/UNDEV AGRI EXTR/IND INDUS ACADEM ADMIN ...HEAL HUM LING CON/ANAL 20. PAGE 28 H0567 BIBLIOG/A COM CULTURE NAT/G

B57
CHANDRA S.,PARTIES AND POLITICS AT THE MUGHAL COURT: 1707-1740. INDIA CULTURE EX/STRUC CREATE PLAN PWR...BIBLIOG/A 18. PAGE 29 H0574 POL/PAR ELITES NAT/G

B57
KENNEDY M.D.,A SHORT HISTORY OF COMMUNISM IN ASIA. ASIA BURMA INDIA S/ASIA THAILAND NAT/G POL/PAR LEAD REV WAR MARXISM SOCISM...POLICY 20 CHINJAP. PAGE 85 H1688 DIPLOM NAT/LISM TOTALISM COERCE

B57
NARAIN D.,HINDU CHARACTER (A FEW GLIMPSES). INDIA DIPLOM SUICIDE PERS/REL ATTIT...PSY NAT/COMP PERS/COMP BIBLIOG WORSHIP 20 HINDU. PAGE 116 H2310 PERSON STERTYP SUPEGO SECT

B57
POPLAI S.L.,NATIONAL POLITICS AND 1957 ELECTIONS IN INDIA. INDIA BARGAIN PARL/PROC CONSEN NAT/LISM PWR WEALTH 20. PAGE 127 H2543 POL/PAR CHOOSE POLICY NAT/G

B57
VON HIPPEL E.,GESCHICHTE DER STAATSPHILOSOPHIE (2 VOLS.). ASIA GREECE INDIA PRE/AMER UAR NAT/LISM ORD/FREE MARXISM. PAGE 164 H3272 CULTURE CONCPT NAT/G

B57
WILSON P.,SOUTH ASIA; A SELECTED BIBLIOGRAPHY ON INDIA, PAKISTAN, CEYLON (PAMPHLET). CEYLON INDIA PAKISTAN LAW ECO/UNDEV PLAN DIPLOM 20. PAGE 169 H3381 BIBLIOG S/ASIA CULTURE NAT/G

C57
MORRIS-JONES W.H.,"PARLIAMENT IN INDIA." INDIA CONSTN LEGIS CONFER COLONIAL CHOOSE PRIVIL ATTIT ...GOV/COMP BIBLIOG 20. PAGE 113 H2264 PARL/PROC EX/STRUC NAT/G POL/PAR

N57
JENNINGS W.I.,NATIONALISM, COLONIALISM, AND NEUTRALISM (PAMPHLET). ASIA INDIA S/ASIA UK INTELL ACADEM POL/PAR 20. PAGE 81 H1611 NAT/LISM COLONIAL NEUTRAL ATTIT

B58
LIST OF PUBLICATIONS (PERIODICAL OR AD HOC) ISSUED BY VARIOUS MINISTRIES OF THE GOVERNMENT OF INDIA (3RD ED.). INDIA ECO/UNDEV PLAN...POLICY MGT 20. PAGE 2 H0037 BIBLIOG NAT/G ADMIN

B58
DWARKADAS R.,ROLE OF HIGHER CIVIL SERVICE IN INDIA. INDIA ECO/UNDEV LEGIS PROB/SOLV GP/REL PERS/REL ...POLICY WELF/ST DECISION ORG/CHARTS BIBLIOG 20 CIVIL/SERV INTRVN/ECO. PAGE 44 H0876 ADMIN NAT/G ROLE PLAN

B58
INDIA (REPUBLIC) PARLIAMENT,CLASSIFIED LIST OF PUBLIC UNDERTAKINGS AND OTHER BODIES IN INDIA. INDIA ACADEM LG/CO CONSULT LEGIT CONFER GOV/REL 20. PAGE 76 H1528 NAT/G LEGIS LICENSE PROF/ORG

B58
INDIAN COUNCIL WORLD AFFAIRS,DEFENCE AND SECURITY IN THE INDIAN OCEAN AREA. INDIA S/ASIA CULTURE CONSULT DELIB/GP FORCES PROB/SOLV DIPLOM INT/TRADE 20 CMN/WLTH. PAGE 77 H1531 GEOG HABITAT ECO/UNDEV ORD/FREE

B58
SALETORE B.A.,INDIA'S DIPLOMATIC RELATIONS WITH THE WEST. GREECE INDIA CULTURE ETIQUET...IDEA/COMP 3 ROM/EMP PERSIA. PAGE 137 H2739 DIPLOM CONCPT INT/TRADE

B58
SHARMA M.P.,PUBLIC ADMINISTRATION IN THEORY AND PRACTICE. INDIA UK USA+45 USA-45 EX/STRUC ADJUD ...POLICY CONCPT NAT/COMP 20. PAGE 142 H2847 MGT ADMIN DELIB/GP JURID

B58
STUBEL H.,THE MEWU FANTZU. CHINA/COM INDIA EDU/PROP ADJUD CRIME GP/REL OWN...OBS 20 TIBET. PAGE 150 H3001
CULTURE STRUCT SECT FAM

S58
LOCKWOOD W.W.,"THE SOCIALISTIC SOCIETY: INDIA AND JAPAN." INDIA ECO/DEV ECO/UNDEV INDUS NAT/G CONTROL LEAD PRODUC WEALTH 20 CHINJAP. PAGE 98 H1948
ECO/TAC NAT/COMP FINAN SOCISM

B59
GOPAL R.,INDIAN MUSLIMS: A POLITICAL HISTORY (1858-1947). INDIA ISLAM PAKISTAN NAT/G SECT LEGIS LEAD COERCE WAR REPRESENT ISOLAT ORD/FREE 19/20 HINDU MUSLIM. PAGE 59 H1175
COLONIAL GP/REL POL/PAR REGION

B59
MADHOK B.,POLITICAL TRENDS IN INDIA. INDIA PAKISTAN UK STRATA ECO/UNDEV POL/PAR LEGIS CAP/ISM DIPLOM COLONIAL CHOOSE MARXISM...SOC TREND 20 GANDHI/M NEHRU/J. PAGE 101 H2014
GEOG NAT/G

B59
OVERSTREET G.D.,COMMUNISM IN INDIA. INDIA S/ASIA CONSTN INT/ORG LEAD GP/REL...CHARTS BIBLIOG 20. PAGE 122 H2435
MARXISM NAT/LISM POL/PAR WAR

B59
PARK R.L.,LEADERSHIP AND POLITICAL INSTITUTIONS IN INDIA. S/ASIA CULTURE ECO/UNDEV LOC/G MUNIC PROVS LEGIS PLAN ADMIN LEAD ORD/FREE WEALTH...GEOG SOC BIOG TOT/POP VAL/FREE 20. PAGE 123 H2468
NAT/G EXEC INDIA

B59
SHARMA R.S.,ASPECTS OF POLITICAL IDEAS AND INSTITUTIONS IN ANCIENT INDIA. INDIA SOCIETY STRUCT FAM VOL/ASSN TAX DOMIN...CONCPT HIST/WRIT 7. PAGE 142 H2848
CULTURE JURID DELIB/GP SECT

B60
BANERJEE D.N.,OUR FUNDAMENTAL RIGHTS: THEIR NATURE AND EXTENT (AS JUDICIALLY DETERMINED). INDIA UK CULTURE STRATA NAT/G WORKER EDU/PROP CONTROL DISCRIM OWN...IDEA/COMP WORSHIP 20 REFORMERS COMMONWLTH. PAGE 10 H0207
CONSTN ORD/FREE LEGIS POLICY

B60
BHAMBHRI C.P.,PARLIAMENTARY CONTROL OVER STATE ENTERPRISE IN INDIA. INDIA DELIB/GP ADMIN CONTROL INGP/REL EFFICIENCY 20 PARLIAMENT. PAGE 16 H0327
NAT/G OWN INDUS PARL/PROC

B60
HARRISON S.S.,INDIA: THE MOST DANGEROUS DECADES. INDIA CONSTN STRATA POL/PAR SECT PLAN ADMIN CHOOSE GP/REL TOTALISM MARXISM...LING 20 NEHRU/J. PAGE 67 H1347
CULTURE ECO/UNDEV PROB/SOLV REGION

B60
JHA C.,INDIAN GOVERNMENT AND POLITICS. INDIA SERV/IND POL/PAR PROVS LEGIS CT/SYS CHOOSE GOV/REL FEDERAL 20. PAGE 81 H1616
NAT/G PARL/PROC CONSTN ADJUST

B60
MC CLELLAN G.S.,INDIA. CHINA/COM INDIA CONSTN ELITES STRATA AGRI POL/PAR FOR/AID ARMS/CONT REV MARXISM...CENSUS BIBLIOG 20 COLD/WAR GANDHI/M NEHRU/J. PAGE 106 H2117
DIPLOM NAT/G SOCIETY ECO/UNDEV

B60
MORAES F.,THE REVOLT IN TIBET. ASIA CHINA/COM INDIA CULTURE CONTROL COERCE WAR TOTALISM...POLICY SOC WORSHIP 20 TIBET INTERVENT. PAGE 113 H2252
COLONIAL FORCES DIPLOM ORD/FREE

B60
NAKAMURA H.,THE WAYS OF THINKING OF EASTERN PEOPLES. ASIA INDIA PERSON...HUM SOC LING LOG WORSHIP CHINJAP. PAGE 115 H2305
CULTURE SECT ATTIT

B60
PANIKKAR K.M.,THE STATE AND THE CITIZEN (2ND ED.). INDIA DOMIN ATTIT SUPEGO ORD/FREE WEALTH...GEOG CONCPT GP/COMP 20. PAGE 123 H2459
TEC/DEV POL/PAR NAT/G EDU/PROP

B60
PRASAD B.,THE ORIGINS OF PROVINCIAL AUTONOMY. INDIA UK FINAN LOC/G FORCES LEGIS CONTROL CT/SYS PWR ...JURID 19/20. PAGE 128 H2554
CENTRAL PROVS COLONIAL NAT/G

B60
ROY N.C.,THE CIVIL SERVICE IN INDIA. INDIA POL/PAR ECO/TAC INCOME...JURID MGT 20 CIVIL/SERV. PAGE 135 H2705
ADMIN NAT/G DELIB/GP CONFER

B60
SALETORE B.A.,INDIA'S DIPLOMATIC RELATIONS WITH THE EAST. ASIA CEYLON INDIA NEPAL S/ASIA CULTURE 7/14 PERSIA. PAGE 137 H2740
DIPLOM NAT/COMP ETIQUET

S60
BERREMAN G.D.,"CASTE IN INDIA AND THE UNITED STATES" (BMR)" INDIA USA+45 CULTURE SOCIETY STRUCT SECT GP/REL DISCRIM HEREDITY...SOC STERTYP 20 NEGRO HINDU. PAGE 16 H0318
STRATA RACE/REL NAT/COMP ATTIT

S60
GINSBURGS G.,"PEKING-LHASA-NEW DELHI." CHINA/COM FUT INDIA S/ASIA KIN NAT/G PROVS SECT FORCES BAL/PWR ECO/TAC DOMIN EDU/PROP LEGIT ADMIN REGION GUERRILLA PWR...TREND TIBET 20. PAGE 57 H1134
ASIA COERCE DIPLOM

S60
NORTH R.C.,"THE NEW EXPANSIONISM." ASIA CHINA/COM FUT INDIA CULTURE SOCIETY NAT/G TOP/EX DOMIN COERCE PWR MARXISM...CONCPT TIME/SEQ TREND GEN/LAWS COLD/WAR 20 MAO. PAGE 119 H2372
ATTIT DRIVE NAT/LISM

B61
BEARCE G.D.,BRITISH ATTITUDES TOWARDS INDIA 1784-1858. INDIA S/ASIA UK SECT ECO/TAC...POLICY HUM 18/19. PAGE 12 H0246
COLONIAL ATTIT ALL/IDEOS NAT/G

B61
BROWN D.M.,THE NATIONALIST MOVEMENT. INDIA CULTURE STRATA REV MORAL ORD/FREE...BIBLIOG 20 HINDU. PAGE 22 H0443
NAT/LISM LEAD CHIEF POL/PAR

B61
CHAKRABARTI A.,NEHRU: HIS DEMOCRACY AND INDIA. ASIA INDIA UK CONSTN ECO/UNDEV SECT DIPLOM COLONIAL PEACE WEALTH...BIBLIOG 20 CONGRESS NEHRU/J GANDHI/M. PAGE 28 H0570
ORD/FREE STRATA NAT/G CHIEF

B61
COHN B.S.,DEVELOPMENT AND IMPACT OF BRITISH ADMINISTRATION IN INDIA: A BIBLIOGRAPHIC ESSAY. INDIA UK ECO/UNDEV NAT/G DOMIN...POLICY MGT SOC 19/20. PAGE 31 H0619
BIBLIOG/A COLONIAL S/ASIA ADMIN

B61
HISTORICAL RESEARCH INSTITUTE,A SHORT BIBLIOGRAPHY OF INDO-MUSLIM HISTORY. INDIA S/ASIA DIPLOM EDU/PROP COLONIAL LEAD NAT/LISM ATTIT...BIOG 19/20. PAGE 71 H1427
BIBLIOG NAT/G SECT POL/PAR

B61
INDIAN NATIONAL CONGRESS,SOUVENIR, 66TH SESSION. INDIA S/ASIA CONSTN CULTURE LEGIS CREATE TEC/DEV LEAD TASK...GEOG CHARTS 20. PAGE 77 H1533
CONFER PLAN NAT/G POLICY

B61
KHALIQUZZAMAN C.,PATHWAY TO PAKISTAN. INDIA PAKISTAN UK SECT LEGIS CHOOSE RACE/REL ATTIT ORD/FREE 20 MUSLIM. PAGE 85 H1705
GP/REL NAT/G COLONIAL SOVEREIGN

B61
KHAN A.W.,INDIA WINS FREEDOM: THE OTHER SIDE. INDIA PAKISTAN CULTURE LEGIS DIPLOM PARL/PROC REV WAR NAT/LISM 20. PAGE 85 H1707
SOVEREIGN GP/REL RACE/REL ORD/FREE

B61
NARAIN J.P.,SWARAJ FOR THE PEOPLE. INDIA CONSTN LOC/G MUNIC POL/PAR CHOOSE REPRESENT EFFICIENCY ATTIT PWR SOVEREIGN 20. PAGE 116 H2311
NAT/G ORD/FREE EDU/PROP EX/STRUC

B61
NARASIMHAN V.K.,THE PRESS, THE PUBLIC AND THE ADMINISTRATION (PAMPHLET). INDIA COM/IND CONTROL REPRESENT GOV/REL EFFICIENCY...ANTHOL 20. PAGE 116 H2312
NAT/G ADMIN PRESS NEW/LIB

B61
PALMER N.D.,THE INDIAN POLITICAL SYSTEM. INDIA ECO/UNDEV SECT CHIEF COLONIAL CHOOSE ALL/IDEOS SOCISM...CHARTS BIBLIOG/A 20. PAGE 123 H2452
NAT/LISM POL/PAR NAT/G DIPLOM

B61
PANIKKAR K.M.,THE VOICE OF FREEDOM: SELECTED SPEECHES OF PANDIT MOTILAL NEHRU. INDIA UK CONSTN FINAN FORCES LEGIS DIPLOM TAX COLONIAL...POLICY MAJORIT ANTHOL 20 NEHRU/PM. PAGE 123 H2460
NAT/LISM ORD/FREE CHIEF NAT/G

B61
RAO K.V.,PARLIAMENTARY DEMOCRACY OF INDIA. INDIA EX/STRUC TOP/EX COLONIAL CT/SYS PARL/PROC ORD/FREE ...POLICY CONCPT TREND 20 PARLIAMENT. PAGE 130 H2592
CONSTN ADJUD NAT/G FEDERAL

B61
SAKAI R.K.,STUDIES ON ASIA, 1961. ASIA BURMA INDIA S/ASIA FINAN ECO/TAC NAT/LISM SOCISM...POLICY ANTHOL 19/20 CHINJAP. PAGE 137 H2734
ECO/UNDEV SECT

B61
SANTHANAM K.,DEMOCRATIC PLANNING. INDIA AGRI FINAN LEGIS DIPLOM PARL/PROC ORD/FREE 20. PAGE 138 H2753
PLAN NAT/G CONSTN POLICY

B61
SEMINAR REPRESENTATIVE GOVT,AFRO-ASIAN ATTITUDES: SEMINAR ON REPRESENTATIVE GOVERNMENTSPUBLIC LIBERTIES IN STATES OF ASIA AND AFRICA, RHODES, 1958. AFR ASIA BURMA INDIA ISLAM UAR VIETNAM/S SOCIETY POL/PAR CHIEF EDU/PROP PRESS PERSON ...POLICY INT 20 TUNIS. PAGE 141 H2826
CHOOSE ATTIT NAT/COMP ORD/FREE

B61
SHARMA T.R.,THE WORKING OF STATE ENTERPRISES IN INDIA. INDIA DELIB/GP LEGIS WORKER BUDGET PRICE CONTROL GP/REL OWN ATTIT...MGT CHARTS 20. PAGE 142 H2851
NAT/G INDUS ADMIN SOCISM

S61
HOSELITZ B.F.,"ECONOMIC DEVELOPMENT AND POLITICAL
ECO/UNDEV

STABILITY IN INDIA" INDIA NAT/G GP/REL...POLICY 20. PAGE 74 H1475 — GEN/LAWS PROB/SOLV

S61
RAY J.,"THE EUROPEAN FREE-TRADE ASSOCIATION AND ITS IMPACT ON INDIA'S TRADE." EUR+WWI FRANCE GERMANY INDIA S/ASIA UK NAT/G VOL/ASSN PLAN INT/TRADE ROUTINE WEALTH...STAT CHARTS CMN/WLTH EEC OEEC 20 EFTA. PAGE 130 H2600 — ECO/DEV ECO/TAC

B62
BROWN S.D.,STUDIES ON ASIA, 1962. ASIA BURMA INDIA ISLAM ISRAEL S/ASIA ECO/UNDEV POL/PAR SECT ECO/TAC ...ANTHOL 20 CHINJAP. PAGE 22 H0450 — PWR PARL/PROC

B62
CHAKRAVARTI P.C.,INDIA'S CHINA POLICY. ASIA CHINA/COM S/ASIA CULTURE NAT/G TOP/EX ACT/RES EDU/PROP DRIVE ALL/VALS...MYTH 20. PAGE 28 H0571 — RIGID/FLEX TREND INDIA

B62
DAVAR F.C.,IRAN AND INDIA THROUGH THE AGES. INDIA IRAN ELITES SECT CREATE ORD/FREE...LING BIBLIOG. PAGE 37 H0743 — NAT/COMP DIPLOM CULTURE

B62
HANSON A.H.,MANAGERIAL PROBLEMS IN PUBLIC ENTERPRISE. INDIA DELIB/GP GP/REL INGP/REL EFFICIENCY 20 PARLIAMENT. PAGE 66 H1320 — MGT NAT/G INDUS PROB/SOLV

B62
JAIN R.S.,THE GROWTH AND DEVELOPMENT OF GOVERNOR-GENERAL'S EXECUTIVE COUNCIL 1858-1919. INDIA UK CONSTN EX/STRUC LEGIS ADJUD ADMIN INGP/REL ATTIT 19/20. PAGE 79 H1585 — NAT/G DELIB/GP CHIEF CONSULT

B62
KAGZI M.C.,THE INDIAN ADMINISTRATIVE LAW. INDIA LG/CO CONTROL CT/SYS...CONCPT 20. PAGE 83 H1649 — JURID ADJUD DELIB/GP NAT/G

B62
KOSAMBI D.D.,MYTH AND REALITY. INDIA AGRI KIN SECT HABITAT...SOC 20. PAGE 88 H1758 — CULTURE SOCIETY MYTH ATTIT

B62
MANSUR F.,PROCESS OF INDEPENDENCE. GHANA INDIA INDONESIA PAKISTAN CONSTN ELITES INTELL STRUCT ACADEM NAT/G REV PWR 20. PAGE 102 H2043 — NAT/COMP POL/PAR SOVEREIGN COLONIAL

B62
MODELSKI G.,SEATO-SIX STUDIES. ASIA CHINA/COM INDIA S/ASIA INT/ORG NAT/G ECO/TAC DETER ATTIT ORD/FREE PWR...TIME/SEQ COLD/WAR TOT/POP 20 SEATO. PAGE 112 H2234 — MARKET ECO/UNDEV INT/TRADE

B62
TINKER H.,INDIA AND PAKISTAN. INDIA PAKISTAN NAT/G POL/PAR...OLD/LIB TRADIT TREND CHARTS BIBLIOG 20. PAGE 155 H3102 — ORD/FREE STRATA REPRESENT AUTHORIT

B62
ZINKIN T.,REPORTING INDIA. INDIA PAKISTAN WOR+45 SOCIETY SECT FORCES EDU/PROP CROWD DISCRIM NAT/LISM MARXISM...POLICY 20. PAGE 173 H3457 — STRATA COLONIAL BAL/PWR CONTROL

B63
BANERJI A.K.,INDIA'S BALANCE OF PAYMENTS. INDIA NAT/G PRICE BAL/PAY COST INCOME 20. PAGE 10 H0208 — INT/TRADE DIPLOM FINAN BUDGET

B63
BERREMAN G.D.,HINDUS OF THE HIMALAYAS. INDIA STRATA STRUCT KIN MUNIC 20 HINDU. PAGE 16 H0319 — CULTURE SECT GP/REL ECO/UNDEV

B63
ELWIN V.,A NEW DEAL FOR TRIBAL INDIA. INDIA AGRI COM/IND INDUS KIN TEC/DEV TAX EDU/PROP OWN HEALTH 20. PAGE 46 H0912 — ECO/UNDEV CULTURE CONSTN SOC/WK

B63
FARMER B.H.,CEYLON: A DIVIDED NATION. CEYLON INDIA NETHERLAND PORTUGAL UK ELITES POL/PAR COLONIAL ...SOC MYTH CHARTS GOV/COMP WORSHIP 20. PAGE 49 H0972 — DOMIN ORD/FREE ECO/UNDEV POLICY

B63
GOODE W.J.,WORLD REVOLUTION AND FAMILY PATTERNS. AFR CHINA/COM INDIA UAR CREATE ADJUST ATTIT SEX ...SOC 20 CHINJAP. PAGE 58 H1169 — FAM NAT/COMP CULTURE MARRIAGE

B63
INDIAN INSTITUTE PUBLIC ADMIN,CASES IN INDIAN ADMINISTRATION. INDIA AGRI NAT/G PROB/SOLV TEC/DEV ECO/TAC ADMIN...ANTHOL METH 20. PAGE 77 H1532 — DECISION PLAN MGT ECO/UNDEV

B63
JAIRAZBHOY R.A.,FOREIGN INFLUENCE IN ANCIENT INDIA. INDIA ELITES SECT DIPLOM EDU/PROP COLONIAL REGION GP/REL...ART/METH LING WORSHIP +/14 GRECO/ROMN MESOPOTAM PERSIA PARTH/SASS. PAGE 79 H1587 — CULTURE SOCIETY COERCE DOMIN

B63
KAHIN G.M.,MAJOR GOVERNMENTS OF ASIA (2ND ED.). ASIA INDIA INDONESIA PAKISTAN S/ASIA DIPLOM...SOC 20 CHINJAP. PAGE 83 H1650 — GOV/COMP POL/PAR ELITES

B63
KAPP W.K.,HINDU CULTURE: ECONOMIC DEVELOPMENT AND ECONOMIC PLANNING IN INDIA. INDIA S/ASIA CULTURE ECO/TAC EDU/PROP ADMIN ALL/VALS...POLICY MGT TIME/SEQ VAL/FREE 20. PAGE 83 H1660 — SECT ECO/UNDEV

B63
LAMB B.P.,INDIA: A WORLD IN TRANSITION. INDIA ECO/UNDEV SECT EDU/PROP COLONIAL HABITAT ORD/FREE ...GEOG CHARTS BIBLIOG SOC/INTEG 20. PAGE 90 H1799 — POL/PAR NAT/G DIPLOM STRATA

B63
LEONARD T.J.,THE FEDERAL SYSTEM OF INDIA. INDIA MUNIC NAT/G PROVS ADMIN SOVEREIGN...IDEA/COMP 20. PAGE 94 H1885 — FEDERAL MGT NAT/COMP METH/COMP

B63
LIVINGSTON W.S.,FEDERALISM IN THE COMMONWEALTH - A BIBLIOGRAPHICAL COMMENTARY. CANADA INDIA PAKISTAN UK STRUCT LOC/G NAT/G POL/PAR...NAT/COMP 20 AUSTRAL. PAGE 97 H1943 — BIBLIOG JURID FEDERAL CONSTN

B63
MAJUMDAR O.N.,AN INTRODUCTION TO SOCIAL ANTHROPOLOGY. INDIA LAW STRATA ECO/UNDEV KIN DEMAND MARRIAGE...GP/COMP BIBLIOG T WORSHIP 20. PAGE 101 H2026 — SOC CULTURE STRUCT GP/REL

B63
SAKAI R.K.,STUDIES ON ASIA, 1963. ASIA INDIA ISRAEL S/ASIA USA+45 PERF/ART POL/PAR SECT REGION NAT/LISM ...SOC LING TREND ANTHOL 19/20 CHINJAP. PAGE 137 H2735 — PWR CULTURE

B63
SINGH H.L.,PROBLEMS AND POLICIES OF THE BRITISH IN INDIA, 1885-1898. INDIA UK NAT/G FORCES LEGIS PROB/SOLV CONTROL RACE/REL ADJUST DISCRIM NAT/LISM RIGID/FLEX...MGT 19 CIVIL/SERV. PAGE 144 H2885 — COLONIAL PWR POLICY ADMIN

B63
WEINER M.,POLITICAL CHANGE IN SOUTH ASIA. CEYLON INDIA PAKISTAN S/ASIA CULTURE ELITES ECO/UNDEV EX/STRUC ADMIN CONTROL CHOOSE CONSERVE...GOV/COMP ANTHOL 20. PAGE 166 H3328 — NAT/G CONSTN TEC/DEV

B63
WILCOX W.A.,PAKISTAN; THE CONSOLIDATION OF A NATION. INDIA PAKISTAN CONSTN SECT PROB/SOLV COLONIAL PARTIC GP/REL FEDERAL...POLICY 19/20. PAGE 168 H3361 — NAT/LISM ECO/UNDEV DIPLOM STRUCT

S63
DUTT V.P.,"CHINA: JEALOUS NEIGHBOR." ASIA CHINA/COM INDIA S/ASIA NAT/G TOP/EX DOMIN COERCE REV ATTIT ...POLICY COLD/WAR 20. PAGE 44 H0874 — FORCES PWR DIPLOM

S63
WEISSBERG G.,"MAPS AS EVIDENCE IN INTERNATIONAL BOUNDARY DISPUTES: A REAPPRAISAL." CHINA/COM EUR+WWI INDIA MOD/EUR S/ASIA INT/ORG NAT/G LEGIT PERCEPT...JURID CHARTS 20. PAGE 166 H3331 — LAW GEOG SOVEREIGN

B64
AGGARWALA R.C.,CONSTITUTIONAL HISTORY OF INDIA AND NATIONAL MOVEMENT INCLUDING COMPARATIVE STUDY OF MODERN INDIA CONSTITUTION. INDIA S/ASIA SECT VOL/ASSN EX/STRUC LEGIS COERCE REV INGP/REL ORD/FREE...SOC BIBLIOG 18/20 CMN/WLTH. PAGE 4 H0077 — CONSTN COLONIAL DOMIN NAT/G

B64
AVASTHI A.,ASPECTS OF ADMINISTRATION. INDIA UK USA+45 FINAN ACADEM DELIB/GP LEGIS RECEIVE PARL/PROC PRIVIL...NAT/COMP 20. PAGE 9 H0183 — MGT ADMIN SOC/WK ORD/FREE

B64
COONDOO R.,THE DIVISION OF POWERS IN THE INDIAN CONSTITUTION. INDIA ECO/UNDEV FINAN TEC/DEV WAR CENTRAL EFFICIENCY NAT/LISM PWR WEALTH NEW/LIB ...BIBLIOG 18/20. PAGE 33 H0659 — CONSTN LEGIS WELF/ST GOV/COMP

B64
GLUCKMANN M.,CLOSED SYSTEMS AND OPEN MINDS: THE LIMITS OF NAIVETY IN SOCIAL ANTHROPOLOGY. AFR INDIA MUNIC...IDEA/COMP METH/COMP ANTHOL. PAGE 57 H1149 — CULTURE OBS SOC

B64
GOODNOW H.F.,THE CIVIL SERVICE OF PAKISTAN: BUREAUCRACY IN A NEW NATION. INDIA PAKISTAN S/ASIA ECO/UNDEV PROVS CHIEF PARTIC CHOOSE EFFICIENCY PWR ...BIBLIOG 20. PAGE 59 H1173 — ADMIN GOV/REL LAW NAT/G

B64
HAMILTON W.B.,THE TRANSFER OF INSTITUTIONS. CANADA INDIA UK LAW AGRI LABOR SECT COLONIAL 18/20. PAGE 65 H1301 — NAT/COMP ECO/UNDEV EDU/PROP CULTURE

B64
INDIAN COMM PREVENTION CORRUPT,REPORT, 1964. INDIA NAT/G GOV/REL ATTIT ORD/FREE...CRIMLGY METH 20. PAGE 76 H1530 — CRIME ADMIN LEGIS LOC/G

B64
INTL CONF ON POPULATION,POPULATION DYNAMICS: INTERNATIONAL ACTION AND TRAINING PROGRAMS. INDIA — NAT/COMP CONTROL

KOREA L/A+17C TAIWAN USA+45 WOR+45 FAM PLAN CONFER ...NEW/IDEA ANTHOL 20 CHINJAP BIRTH/CON. PAGE 78 H1561 ATTIT EDU/PROP

B64
KALDOR N.,ESSAYS ON ECONOMIC POLICY (VOL. II). CHILE GERMANY INDIA FINAN...GOV/COMP METH/COMP 20 KEYNES/JM. PAGE 83 H1651 BAL/PAY INT/TRADE METH/CNCPT ECO/UNDEV

B64
MAHAR J.M.,INDIA: A CRITICAL BIBLIOGRAPHY. INDIA PAKISTAN CULTURE ECO/UNDEV LOC/G POL/PAR SECT PROB/SOLV DIPLOM ADMIN COLONIAL PARL/PROC ATTIT 20. PAGE 101 H2016 BIBLIOG/A S/ASIA NAT/G LEAD

B64
PARANJAPE H.K.,THE FLIGHT OF TECHNICAL PERSONNEL IN PUBLIC UNDERTAKINGS. INDIA PAY DEMAND HAPPINESS ORD/FREE...MGT QU 20 MIGRATION. PAGE 123 H2464 ADMIN NAT/G WORKER PLAN

B64
RAGHAVAN M.D.,INDIA IN CEYLONESE HISTORY, SOCIETY AND CULTURE. CEYLON INDIA S/ASIA LAW SOCIETY INT/TRADE ATTIT...ART/METH JURID SOC LING 20. PAGE 129 H2581 DIPLOM CULTURE SECT STRUCT

B64
TAYLOR E.,RICHER BY ASIA. S/ASIA CULTURE VOL/ASSN ACT/RES ATTIT DISPL PERSON ALL/VALS...INT/LAW MYTH SELF/OBS 20. PAGE 153 H3054 SOCIETY RIGID/FLEX INDIA

B64
TINKER H.,BALLOT BOX AND BAYONET - PEOPLE AND GOVERNMENT IN EMERGENT ASIAN COUNTRIES. CEYLON INDIA INDONESIA PHILIPPINE POL/PAR ADMIN COLONIAL LEAD PARL/PROC CHOOSE CONSEN ORD/FREE SOVEREIGN PLURISM...GOV/COMP THIRD/WRLD. PAGE 155 H3104 MYTH S/ASIA NAT/COMP NAT/LISM

B64
WILCOX W.A.,INDIA, PAKISTAN AND THE RISE OF CHINA. ASIA BURMA CEYLON CHINA/COM INDIA PAKISTAN S/ASIA NAT/G VOL/ASSN FORCES TOP/EX ACT/RES DOMIN REGION RIGID/FLEX ORD/FREE...POLICY GEN/LAWS COLD/WAR 20. PAGE 168 H3362 CULTURE ATTIT DIPLOM

S64
"FURTHER READING." INDIA ATTIT...POLICY 20 NEHRU/J. PAGE 2 H0042 BIBLIOG S/ASIA CHIEF NAT/G

S64
"FURTHER READING." INDIA PAKISTAN SECT WAR PEACE ATTIT...POLICY 20. PAGE 2 H0044 BIBLIOG GP/REL DIPLOM NAT/G

S64
BRADLEY C.P.,"THE FORMATION OF MALAYSIA." INDIA S/ASIA POL/PAR VOL/ASSN TOP/EX LEGIT RACE/REL ORD/FREE 20. PAGE 20 H0398 NAT/G CREATE COLONIAL MALAYSIA

S64
LANGERHANS H.,"NEHRU'S BITTERNESS." FUT INDIA S/ASIA CONSTN CULTURE ECO/UNDEV ECO/TAC DOMIN EDU/PROP ATTIT PERCEPT PERSON...POLICY 20 NEHRU/J. PAGE 91 H1811 ECO/DEV BIOG

S64
LEVI W.,"INDIAN NEUTRALISM RECONSIDERED." ASIA CHINA/COM S/ASIA SOCIETY NAT/G ACT/RES LEGIT NEUTRAL COERCE ATTIT DRIVE PERCEPT RIGID/FLEX HEALTH LOVE PWR...DECISION RECORD TREND STERTYP 20. PAGE 95 H1896 ORD/FREE CONCPT INDIA

S64
RUDOLPH L.I.,"GENERALS AND POLITICIANS IN INDIA." INDIA S/ASIA CULTURE STRATA NAT/G LEGIS TOP/EX EDU/PROP ATTIT ORD/FREE PWR RESPECT SKILL...POLICY BIOG TIME/SEQ STERTYP VAL/FREE 20. PAGE 136 H2713 FORCES COERCE

S64
SMYTHE H.H.,"NEHRU AND INDIAN FOREIGN POLICY." S/ASIA ECO/UNDEV NAT/G POL/PAR CONSULT PLAN DIPLOM NEUTRAL COERCE ATTIT DRIVE PERSON MORAL ORD/FREE RESPECT...GEOG CONCPT TIME/SEQ TREND GEN/LAWS 20 NEHRU/J. PAGE 146 H2922 TOP/EX BIOG INDIA

B65
AIYAR S.P.,STUDIES IN INDIAN DEMOCRACY. INDIA STRATA ECO/UNDEV LABOR POL/PAR LEGIS DIPLOM LOBBY REGION CHOOSE ATTIT SOCISM...ANTHOL 20. PAGE 4 H0086 ORD/FREE REPRESENT ADMIN NAT/G

B65
BETEILLE A.,CASTE, CLASS, AND POWER. INDIA MUNIC SECT REGION GP/REL PERS/REL ATTIT HABITAT RIGID/FLEX...SOC 20. PAGE 16 H0323 STRATA CULTURE PWR STRUCT

B65
BRASS P.R.,FACTIONAL POLITICS IN AN INDIAN STATE: THE CONGRESS PARTY IN UTTAR PRADESH. INDIA UK CONSTN CULTURE ECO/UNDEV LOC/G DOMIN COLONIAL CROWD GP/REL ADJUST CENTRAL RIGID/FLEX SOVEREIGN 20 UTTAR/PRAD CONGRESS/P. PAGE 20 H0406 POL/PAR PROVS LEGIS CHOOSE

B65
CENTRAL GAZETTEERS UNIT,THE GAZETTEER OF INDIA (VOL. I). INDIA SOCIETY STRATA PLAN EDU/PROP NAT/LISM ORD/FREE WEALTH...GEOG LING CHARTS SOC/INTEG 20. PAGE 28 H0568 PRESS CULTURE SECT STRUCT

B65
CHANDA A.,FEDERALISM IN INDIA. INDIA UK ELITES FINAN NAT/G POL/PAR EX/STRUC LEGIS DIPLOM TAX GOV/REL POPULISM...POLICY 20. PAGE 28 H0572 CONSTN CENTRAL FEDERAL

B65
CRABB C.V. JR.,THE ELEPHANTS AND THE GRASS* A STUDY OF NONALIGNMENT. AFR ASIA INDIA S/ASIA USA+45 USSR BAL/PWR NEUTRAL ATTIT...TREND NAT/COMP COLD/WAR. PAGE 34 H0691 ECO/UNDEV DIPLOM CONCPT

B65
CRAMER J.F.,CONTEMPORARY EDUCATION: A COMPARATIVE STUDY OF NATIONAL SYSTEMS (2ND ED.). CHINA/COM EUR+WWI INDIA USA+45 FINAN PROB/SOLV ADMIN CONTROL ATTIT...IDEA/COMP METH/COMP 20 CHINJAP. PAGE 35 H0697 EDU/PROP NAT/COMP SCHOOL ACADEM

B65
GAJENDRAGADKAR P.B.,LAW, LIBERTY AND SOCIAL JUSTICE. INDIA CONSTN NAT/G SECT PLAN ECO/TAC PRESS POPULISM...SOC METH/COMP 20 HINDU. PAGE 54 H1086 ORD/FREE LAW ADJUD JURID

B65
GOPAL S.,BRITISH POLICY IN INDIA 1858-1905. INDIA UK ELITES CHIEF DELIB/GP ECO/TAC GP/REL DISCRIM ATTIT...IDEA/COMP NAT/COMP PERS/COMP BIBLIOG/A 19/20. PAGE 59 H1176 COLONIAL ADMIN POL/PAR ECO/UNDEV

B65
JAIN S.C.,THE STATE AND AGRICULTURE. INDIA S/ASIA ECO/UNDEV PROB/SOLV CAP/ISM MARXISM SOCISM 20. PAGE 79 H1586 NAT/G POLICY AGRI ECO/TAC

B65
JANSEN M.B.,CHANGING JAPANESE ATTITUDES TOWARD MODERNIZATION. ASIA CHINA/COM S/ASIA INTELL SOCIETY KIN NAT/G SECT PERCEPT RIGID/FLEX...SOC CONCPT TIME/SEQ TREND TOT/POP 19/20 CHINJAP. PAGE 80 H1591 TEC/DEV ATTIT INDIA

B65
LARUS J.,COMPARATIVE WORLD POLITICS. ASIA INDIA WOR+45 WOR-45 BAL/PWR WAR PEACE RATIONAL MORAL PWR ...REALPOL INT/LAW MUSLIM. PAGE 91 H1825 GOV/COMP IDEA/COMP DIPLOM NAT/COMP

B65
MEHROTRA S.R.,INDIA AND THE COMMONWEALTH 1885-1929. INDIA UK INT/ORG VOL/ASSN GP/REL ATTIT...POLICY BIBLIOG 19/20 CMN/WLTH. PAGE 108 H2163 DIPLOM NAT/G POL/PAR NAT/LISM

B65
MENON K.P.S.,MANY WORLDS. INDIA BAL/PWR CAP/ISM COLONIAL REV ORD/FREE PWR MARXISM...POLICY 20 COLD/WAR. PAGE 109 H2176 BIOG DIPLOM NAT/G

B65
ONSLOW C.,ASIAN ECONOMIC DEVELOPMENT. BURMA CEYLON INDIA MALAYSIA PAKISTAN S/ASIA AGRI INDUS MARKET PROB/SOLV CAP/ISM FOR/AID INT/TRADE DEMAND WEALTH ...POLICY ANTHOL 20. PAGE 121 H2418 ECO/UNDEV ECO/TAC PLAN NAT/G

B65
PANJABI K.L.,THE CIVIL SERVANT IN INDIA. INDIA UK NAT/G CONSULT EX/STRUC REGION GP/REL RACE/REL 20. PAGE 123 H2462 ADMIN WORKER BIOG COLONIAL

B65
PYLEE M.V.,CONSTITUTIONAL GOVERNMENT IN INDIA (2ND REV. ED.). INDIA POL/PAR EX/STRUC DIPLOM COLONIAL CT/SYS PARL/PROC PRIVIL...JURID 16/20. PAGE 128 H2569 CONSTN NAT/G PROVS FEDERAL

B65
QURESHI I.H.,THE STRUGGLE FOR PAKISTAN. INDIA PAKISTAN UK CULTURE LEGIS DIPLOM EDU/PROP COLONIAL ATTIT SOVEREIGN 19/20 MUSLIM. PAGE 129 H2576 GP/REL RACE/REL WAR SECT

B65
SAKAI R.K.,STUDIES ON ASIA, 1965. INDIA KOREA S/ASIA USA+45 CONSTN KIN SECT PARTIC SUFF NAT/LISM ...POLICY SOC 19/20 CHINJAP. PAGE 137 H2737 PARL/PROC ASIA

B65
SCALAPINO R.A.,THE COMMUNIST REVOLUTION IN ASIA* TACTICS, GOALS, AND ACHIEVEMENTS. INDIA INTELL POL/PAR FORCES DOMIN EDU/PROP LEGIT COERCE REV ATTIT CHINJAP. PAGE 138 H2763 ASIA S/ASIA MARXISM NAT/COMP

B65
SHARMA S.A.,PARLIAMENTARY GOVERNMENT IN INDIA. INDIA FINAN LOC/G PROVS DELIB/GP PLAN ADMIN CT/SYS FEDERAL...JURID 20. PAGE 142 H2849 NAT/G CONSTN PARL/PROC LEGIS

B65
SHRIMALI K.L.,EDUCATION IN CHANGING INDIA. INDIA CULTURE DIPLOM FOR/AID GP/REL RACE/REL ATTIT SOC/INTEG 20 UNESCO CMN/WLTH. PAGE 143 H2866 EDU/PROP PROF/ORG ACADEM

B65
SIRISKAR V.M.,POLITICAL BEHAVIOR IN INDIA. INDIA SOCIETY MUNIC NAT/G PROVS ACT/RES SUFF...OBS CHARTS 20 POONA. PAGE 144 H2889 CHOOSE POL/PAR PWR ATTIT

B65
WINT G.,ASIA: A HANDBOOK. ASIA COM INDIA USSR CULTURE INTELL NAT/G...GEOG STAT CENSUS NAT/COMP DIPLOM SOC

WORSHIP 20 TREATY CHINJAP. PAGE 169 H3387

B65
WOLPERT S.,INDIA. INDIA UK ECO/UNDEV DIPLOM GP/REL WEALTH 20 NEHRU/J. PAGE 170 H3405 CULTURE COLONIAL NAT/LISM SECT

L65
SHARMA S.P.,"THE INDIA-CHINA BORDER DISPUTE: AN INDIAN PERSPECTIVE." ASIA CHINA/COM S/ASIA NAT/G LEGIT CT/SYS NAT/LISM DRIVE MORAL ORD/FREE PWR 20. PAGE 142 H2850 LAW ATTIT SOVEREIGN INDIA

S65
"FURTHER READING." INDIA NAT/G ADMIN 20. PAGE 2 H0045 BIBLIOG EDU/PROP SCHOOL ACADEM

S65
"FURTHER READING." INDIA ADMIN COLONIAL WAR GOV/REL ATTIT 20. PAGE 2 H0046 BIBLIOG DIPLOM NAT/G POLICY

S65
GANGAL S.C.,"SURVEY OF RECENT RESEARCH: INDIA AND THE COMMONWEALTH" INDIA UK NAT/G INT/TRADE PARTIC GOV/REL ROLE 20 CMN/WLTH. PAGE 55 H1095 BIBLIOG POLICY REGION DIPLOM

S65
PRABHAKAR P.,"SURVEY OF RESEARCH AND SOURCE MATERIALS; THE SINO-INDIAN BORDER DISPUTE." CHINA/COM INDIA LAW NAT/G PLAN BAL/PWR WAR...POLICY 20 COLD/WAR. PAGE 128 H2553 BIBLIOG ASIA S/ASIA DIPLOM

B66
AGGARWALA R.N.,FINANCIAL COMMITTEES OF THE INDIAN PARLIAMENT: A STUDY IN PARLIAMENTARY CONTROL OVER PUBLIC EXPENDITURE. INDIA FINAN NAT/G ROLE...CHARTS METH/COMP METH 20 PARLIAMENT. PAGE 4 H0078 PARL/PROC BUDGET CONTROL DELIB/GP

B66
AHMED Z.,DUSK AND DAWN IN VILLAGE INDIA. INDIA S/ASIA UK CULTURE SOCIETY NAT/G DOMIN COLONIAL HABITAT SOVEREIGN...SOC DICTIONARY 20. PAGE 4 H0080 NEIGH ECO/UNDEV AGRI ADJUST

B66
AIYAR S.P.,PERSPECTIVES ON THE WELFARE STATE. INDIA S/ASIA UK CONSTN ECO/UNDEV NAT/G INGP/REL CENTRAL NAT/LISM ATTIT...CONCPT ANTHOL BIBLIOG 20. PAGE 4 H0087 NEW/LIB WELF/ST IDEA/COMP ADJUST

B66
ASHRAF A.,THE CITY GOVERNMENT OF CALCUTTA: A STUDY OF INERTIA. INDIA ELITES INDUS NAT/G EX/STRUC ACT/RES PLAN PROB/SOLV LEAD HABITAT...BIBLIOG 20 CALCUTTA. PAGE 9 H0175 LOC/G MUNIC ADMIN ECO/UNDEV

B66
BHALERAO C.N.,PUBLIC SERVICE COMMISSIONS OF INDIA: A STUDY. INDIA SERV/IND EX/STRUC ROUTINE CHOOSE GOV/REL INGP/REL...KNO/TEST EXHIBIT 20. PAGE 16 H0326 NAT/G OP/RES LOC/G ADMIN

B66
BRAIBANTI R.,ASIAN BUREAUCRATIC SYSTEMS EMERGENT FROM THE BRITISH IMPERIAL TRADITION. BURMA CEYLON INDIA PAKISTAN UK ELITES ECO/UNDEV NAT/G...MGT SOC CHARTS ANTHOL 19/20. PAGE 20 H0401 GOV/COMP COLONIAL ADMIN S/ASIA

B66
BRECHER M.,SUCCESSION IN INDIA. INDIA USA+45 CONSTN AGRI POL/PAR PROVS SECT DELIB/GP FORCES PROB/SOLV ECO/TAC PWR...LING 20 CONGRESS NEHRU/J. PAGE 20 H0408 CHIEF DECISION CHOOSE

B66
DARLING M.,APPRENTICE TO POWER INDIA 1904-1908. INDIA LEAD GP/REL PERSON...GEOG 20. PAGE 37 H0742 OBS SOCIETY ADMIN NAT/G

B66
GHOSH P.K.,THE CONSTITUTION OF INDIA: HOW IT HAS BEEN FRAMED. INDIA LOC/G DELIB/GP EX/STRUC PROB/SOLV BUDGET INT/TRADE CT/SYS CHOOSE...LING 20. PAGE 56 H1121 CONSTN NAT/G LEGIS FEDERAL

B66
HIDAYATULLAH M.,DEMOCRACY IN INDIA AND THE JUDICIAL PROCESS. INDIA EX/STRUC LEGIS LEAD GOV/REL ATTIT ORD/FREE...MAJORIT CONCPT 20 NEHRU/J. PAGE 71 H1415 NAT/G CT/SYS CONSTN JURID

B66
INDIA PUBLICATIONS BRANCH,CATALOGUE OF GOVERNMENT OF INDIA CIVIL PUBLICATIONS. INDIA...INDEX 20. PAGE 76 H1529 BIBLIOG NAT/G WRITING

B66
KOH S.J.,STAGES OF INDUSTRIAL DEVELOPMENT IN ASIA. ASIA INDIA KOREA STRATA STRUCT NAT/G INT/TRADE ...CHARTS 19/20 CHINJAP. PAGE 87 H1738 INDUS ECO/UNDEV ECO/DEV LABOR

B66
MADAN G.R.,ECONOMIC THINKING IN INDIA. INDIA ECO/UNDEV AGRI FINAN INDUS LABOR PLAN CAP/ISM INT/TRADE MARXISM SOCISM...POLICY 1/20. PAGE 101 H2013 ECO/TAC PHIL/SCI NAT/G POL/PAR

B66
MASON E.S.,ECONOMIC DEVELOPMENT IN INDIA AND PAKISTAN. INDIA PAKISTAN AGRI FINAN PLAN BUDGET INT/TRADE WEALTH...POLICY STAT TREND CHARTS 20. PAGE 104 H2086 NAT/COMP ECO/UNDEV ECO/TAC FOR/AID

B66
NAMBOODIRIPAD E.M.,ECONOMICS AND POLITICS OF INDIA'S SOCIALIST PATTERN. INDIA STRATA AGRI INDUS NAT/G PRICE ORD/FREE SOVEREIGN 20. PAGE 115 H2307 ECO/UNDEV PLAN SOCISM CAP/ISM

B66
RAY A.,INTER-GOVERNMENTAL RELATIONS IN INDIA: A STUDY OF INDIAN FEDERALISM. CANADA INDIA SWITZERLND USA+45 USSR ADMIN GOV/REL...NAT/COMP BIBLIOG. PAGE 130 H2599 CONSTN FEDERAL SOVEREIGN NAT/G

B66
SAKAI R.K.,STUDIES ON ASIA, 1966. CEYLON INDIA USA-45 INDUS POL/PAR DIPLOM ECO/TAC MARXISM ...POLICY 19/20 CHINJAP. PAGE 137 H2738 SECT ECO/UNDEV

B66
SASTRI K.V.S.,FEDERAL-STATE FISCAL RELATIONS IN INDIA: A STUDY OF THE FINANCE COMMISSION AND TECHNIQUES OF FINANCIAL ADJUSTMENT. INDIA PROVS DELIB/GP GOV/REL FEDERAL...MATH CHARTS 20. PAGE 138 H2756 TAX BUDGET FINAN NAT/G

B66
SHARMA B.M.,THE REPUBLIC OF INDIA; CONSTITUTION AND GOVERNMENT. INDIA POL/PAR LEGIS EFFICIENCY ...TIME/SEQ GOV/COMP 20. PAGE 142 H2846 PROVS NAT/G CONSTN

B66
SRINIVAS M.N.,SOCIAL CHANGE IN MODERN INDIA. INDIA CULTURE SOCIETY STRUCT SECT TEC/DEV...METH/CNCPT SELF/OBS WORSHIP 20. PAGE 148 H2961 ORD/FREE STRATA SOC ECO/UNDEV

B66
SYMONDS R.,THE BRITISH AND THEIR SUCCESSORS. AFR CEYLON INDIA UK SCHOOL FORCES EDU/PROP ADMIN PARTIC ...NAT/COMP BIBLIOG 20 AFRICA/W AFRICA/E. PAGE 151 H3024 NAT/G ECO/UNDEV POLICY COLONIAL

B66
TYSON G.,NEHRU: THE YEARS OF POWER. INDIA UK STRATA ECO/UNDEV FINAN SECT TASK WAR ORD/FREE MARXISM ...POLICY BIBLIOG 20 NEHRU/J. PAGE 157 H3145 CHIEF PWR DIPLOM NAT/G

B66
US DEPARTMENT OF THE ARMY,COMMUNIST CHINA: A STRATEGIC SURVEY: A BIBLIOGRAPHY (PAMPHLET NO. 20-67). CHINA/COM COM INDIA USSR NAT/G POL/PAR EX/STRUC FORCES NUC/PWR REV ATTIT...POLICY GEOG CHARTS. PAGE 160 H3194 BIBLIOG/A MARXISM S/ASIA DIPLOM

B66
US DEPARTMENT OF THE ARMY,SOUTH ASIA: A STRATEGIC SURVEY (PAMPHLET NO. 550-3). AFGHANISTN INDIA NEPAL PAKISTAN ECO/UNDEV INT/ORG POL/PAR FORCES FOR/AID INT/TRADE LEAD WAR...POLICY SOC TREND 20. PAGE 160 H3195 BIBLIOG/A S/ASIA DIPLOM NAT/G

B66
WINKS R.W.,THE HISTORIOGRAPHY OF THE BRITISH EMPIRE-COMMONWEALTH. CANADA INDIA PAKISTAN UK CULTURE SOCIETY STRUCT POL/PAR...CONCPT NAT/COMP 20 AUSTRAL. PAGE 169 H3386 HIST/WRIT TREND IDEA/COMP METH/COMP

B66
ZINKIN T.,CHALLENGES IN INDIA. INDIA PAKISTAN LAW AGRI FINAN INDUS TOP/EX TEC/DEV CONTROL ROUTINE ORD/FREE PWR 20 NEHRU/J SHASTRI/LB CIVIL/SERV. PAGE 173 H3458 NAT/G ECO/TAC POLICY ADMIN

S66
"FURTHER READING." INDIA LEAD ATTIT...CONCPT 20. PAGE 2 H0048 BIBLIOG NAT/G DIPLOM POLICY

S66
"FURTHER READING." INDIA LOC/G NAT/G PLAN ADMIN WEALTH...GEOG SOC CONCPT CENSUS 20. PAGE 2 H0049 BIBLIOG ECO/UNDEV TEC/DEV PROVS

S66
GILBERT S.P.,"WARS OF LIBERATION AND SOVIET MILITARY AID POLICY." ASIA INDIA INDONESIA UAR USA+45 STRATA WAR PERCEPT MARXISM...STAT NAT/COMP. PAGE 56 H1124 USSR FOR/AID WEAPON DRIVE

S66
MANSERGH N.,"THE PARTITION OF INDIA IN RETROSPECT." INDIA PAKISTAN S/ASIA UK DIPLOM COLONIAL GP/REL PWR 20. PAGE 102 H2042 NAT/G PARL/PROC POLICY POL/PAR

B67
ERDMAN H.L.,THE SWATANTRA PARTY AND INDIAN CONSERVATISM. INDIA S/ASIA SOCIETY STRATA LOC/G NAT/G LEAD PARTIC GP/REL ATTIT...CONCPT GP/COMP BIBLIOG 20 SWATANTRA. PAGE 47 H0938 POL/PAR CONSERVE CHOOSE POLICY

B67
GILL R.T.,ECONOMIC DEVELOPMENT: PAST AND PRESENT (2ND ED.). ASIA INDIA USA+45 USA-45 WOR+45 WOR-45 DEMAND EFFICIENCY NAT/LISM WEALTH...GOV/COMP METH/COMP 18/20. PAGE 56 H1127 ECO/DEV ECO/UNDEV PLAN PROB/SOLV

B67
HUTCHINS F.G.,THE ILLUSION OF PERMANENCE: BRITISH IMPERIALISM IN INDIA. INDIA UK CULTURE STRUCT NAT/G REV GP/REL RACE/REL ADJUST DISCRIM ATTIT MORAL PWR SOC/INTEG 18/20. PAGE 75 H1509
COLONIAL CONTROL SOVEREIGN CONSERVE

B67
JAIN R.K.,MANAGEMENT OF STATE ENTERPRISES. INDIA SOCIETY FINAN WORKER BUDGET ADMIN CONTROL OWN 20. PAGE 79 H1584
NAT/G SOCISM INDUS MGT

B67
ROWLAND J.,A HISTORY OF SINO-INDIAN RELATIONS; HOSTILE CO-EXISTENCE. ASIA CHINA/COM INDIA NAT/G NUC/PWR PWR WEALTH...GEOG BIBLIOG 13/20 COLD/WAR. PAGE 135 H2704
DIPLOM CENSUS IDEA/COMP

B67
VENKATESWARAN R.J.,CABINET GOVERNMENT IN INDIA. INDIA UK SOCIETY OP/RES COLONIAL LEAD EFFICIENCY ORD/FREE 20. PAGE 162 H3241
DELIB/GP ADMIN CONSTN NAT/G

L67
TAMBIAH S.J.,"THE POLITICS OF LANGUAGE IN INDIA AND CEYLON." CEYLON INDIA NAT/G DOMIN ADMIN...SOC 20. PAGE 152 H3039
POL/PAR LING NAT/LISM REGION

S67
BHATNAGAR J.K.,"THE VALUES AND ATTITUDES OF SOME INDIAN AND BRITISH STUDENTS." INDIA UK ECO/UNDEV LEGIT COLONIAL GP/REL SOVEREIGN...QU 20. PAGE 16 H0328
NAT/COMP ATTIT EDU/PROP ACADEM

S67
HANSON A.H.,"INDIA AFTER THE ELECTIONS." INDIA ECO/UNDEV LEGIS TEC/DEV FOR/AID GP/REL FEDERAL ATTIT 20. PAGE 66 H1321
NAT/G POL/PAR REGION CENTRAL

S67
JAIN G.,"INDIA REJECTS THE POWER RACE* REALISM ABOUT NUCLEAR WEAPONS." FORCES PROB/SOLV FOR/AID ARMS/CONT COST PWR...GOV/COMP 20. PAGE 79 H1583
INDIA CHINA/COM NUC/PWR DIPLOM

S67
PAI G.A.,"TAXATION AND PLANNING IN INDIA: A BIRDS-EYE VIEW." INDIA ELITES NAT/G LEGIS BUDGET CONTROL LOBBY INCOME...STAT CHARTS 20. PAGE 122 H2443
TAX PLAN WEALTH STRATA

S67
SAVELYEV N.,"MONOPOLY DRIVE IN INDIA." INDIA INDUS NAT/G INT/TRADE NEUTRAL SANCTION GOV/REL CONSERVE ...MARXIST 20. PAGE 138 H2759
ECO/UNDEV POL/PAR ECO/TAC CONTROL

S67
SIPPEL D.,"INDIENS UNSICHERE ZUKUNFT." INDIA CULTURE ACADEM POL/PAR LEGIS COLONIAL CHOOSE SOVEREIGN...JURID 20. PAGE 144 H2888
SOCIETY STRUCT ECO/UNDEV NAT/G

N67
US HOUSE COMM SCI ASTRONAUT,GOVERNMENT, SCIENCE, AND INTERNATIONAL POLICY (PAMPHLET). INDIA NETHERLAND ECO/DEV ECO/UNDEV R+D ACADEM PLAN DIPLOM FOR/AID CONFER...PREDICT 20 CHINJAP. PAGE 160 H3198
NAT/G POLICY CREATE TEC/DEV

INDIA (REPUBLIC) PARLIAMENT H1528

INDIA PUBLICATIONS BRANCH H1529

INDIAN COMM PREVENTION CORRUPT H1530

INDIAN COUNCIL WORLD AFFAIRS H1531

INDIAN INSTITUTE PUBLIC ADMIN H1532

INDIAN NATIONAL CONGRESS H1533

INDIAN/AM....AMERICAN INDIANS

B17
DE VICTORIA F.,DE INDIS ET DE JURE BELLI (1557) IN F. DE VICTORIA, DE INDIS ET DE JURE BELLI REFLECTIONES. UNIV NAT/G SECT CHIEF PARTIC COERCE PEACE MORAL...POLICY 16 INDIAN/AM CHRISTIAN CONSCN/OBJ. PAGE 39 H0775
WAR INT/LAW OWN

B33
TANNENBAUM F.,PEACE BY REVOLUTION. ECO/UNDEV AGRI SECT WORKER DIPLOM EDU/PROP DISCRIM OWN WEALTH POPULISM 17/20 MEXIC/AMER INDIAN/AM. PAGE 152 H3043
CULTURE COLONIAL RACE/REL REV

C41
KLUCKHOHN C.,"PATTERNING AS EXEMPLIFIED IN NAVAHO CULTURE" IN EDWARD SAPIR, LANGUAGE, CULTURE, AND PERSONALITY (BMR)" KIN PERS/REL ATTIT PERSON...SOC CONCPT METH/CNCPT LING OBS/ENVIR CON/ANAL BIBLIOG SOC/INTEG 20 NAVAHO INDIAN/AM SAPIR/EDW. PAGE 87 H1733
CULTURE INGP/REL STRUCT

B52
KROEBER A.L.,THE NATURE OF CULTURE. UNIV STRATA FAM KIN SECT...PSY GP/COMP 16/20 INDIAN/AM. PAGE 89 H1771
CULTURE SOCIETY CONCPT STRUCT

B58
MATOS J.,LAS ACTUALES COMMUNIDADES DE INDIGENAS: HUAROCHIRI EN 1955. PERU FAM NAT/G SECT EDU/PROP ADJUD GP/REL INGP/REL 20 INDIAN/AM. PAGE 105 H2091
STRUCT NEIGH KIN ECO/UNDEV

B61
ACOSTA SAIGNES M.,ESTUDIOS DE ETNOLOGIA ANTIGUA DE VENEZUELA (2ND ED.). PRE/AMER VENEZUELA...ART/METH SOC BIBLIOG INDIAN/AM. PAGE 3 H0061
CULTURE STRUCT GP/REL HABITAT

B61
MARTINEZ RIOS J.,BIBLIOGRAFIA ANTROPOLOGICA Y SOCIOLOGICA DEL ESTADO DE OAXACA. WRITING...LING 12/20 INDIAN/AM MEXIC/AMER. PAGE 103 H2069
BIBLIOG SOC PROVS CULTURE

B63
FRITZ H.E.,THE MOVEMENT FOR INDIAN ASSIMILATION, 1860-1890. SECT FORCES GP/REL RACE/REL DISCRIM FEDERAL CATHISM...BIBLIOG 19 INDIAN/AM PROTESTANT GRANT/US. PAGE 54 H1071
CULTURE NAT/G ECO/TAC ATTIT

B64
BEDERMAN S.H.,THE ETHNOLOGICAL CONTRIBUTIONS OF JOHN LEDYARD (PAMPHLET). ASIA PRE/AMER S/ASIA...SOC 18 LEDYARD/J KAMCHATKA TAHITI TARTARS INDIAN/AM. PAGE 13 H0256
CULTURE BIOG METH/CNCPT STRUCT

B64
HARRIS M.,PATTERNS OF RACE IN THE AMERICAS. BRAZIL L/A+17C STRATA ECO/UNDEV AGRI KIN MUNIC SECT COLONIAL RACE/REL...SOC SOC/INTEG 17/20 NEGRO INDIAN/AM. PAGE 67 H1342
STRUCT PRE/AMER CULTURE SOCIETY

B67
NASH M.,MACHINE AGE MAYA. GUATEMALA L/A+17C STRUCT AGRI WORKER CREATE INCOME ATTIT RIGID/FLEX ROLE ...IDEA/COMP SOC/EXP WORSHIP 20 INDIAN/AM. PAGE 116 H2315
INDUS CULTURE SOC MUNIC

S67
MALAN V.D.,"THE SILENT VILLAGE." KIN MUNIC NEIGH CHOOSE ISOLAT ROLE...SOC INDIAN/AM. PAGE 101 H2027
CULTURE STRUCT PREDICT

INDIANA....INDIANA

INDICATOR....NUMERICAL INDICES AND INDICATORS

INDIVIDUAL....SEE PERSON

INDOCTRINATION....SEE EDU/PROP

INDONESIA....SEE ALSO S/ASIA

N
KYRIAK T.E.,ASIAN DEVELOPMENTS: A BIBLIOGRAPHY. INDONESIA KOREA/N VIETNAM/N CULTURE SOCIETY ECO/UNDEV NAT/G DIPLOM...SOC TREND 20 MONGOLIA. PAGE 90 H1788
BIBLIOG/A ALL/IDEOS S/ASIA ASIA

N19
BRIMMELL G.H.,COMMUNISM IN SOUTHEAST ASIA (PAMPHLET). BURMA CAMBODIA COM INDIA INDONESIA LAOS MOD/EUR NAT/G POL/PAR FORCES CAP/ISM CONTROL WEALTH ...MYTH 20. PAGE 21 H0420
MARXISM S/ASIA REV ECO/UNDEV

B31
DEKAT A.D.A.,COLONIAL POLICY. S/ASIA CULTURE EX/STRUC ECO/TAC DOMIN ADMIN COLONIAL ROUTINE SOVEREIGN WEALTH...POLICY MGT RECORD KNO/TEST SAMP. PAGE 39 H0785
DRIVE PWR INDONESIA NETHERLAND

B41
KEESING F.M.,THE SOUTH SEAS IN THE MODERN WORLD. INDONESIA STRUCT FAM SECT EDU/PROP LEAD INCOME WEALTH...HEAL SOC 20. PAGE 84 H1678
CULTURE ECO/UNDEV GOV/COMP DIPLOM

B45
US LIBRARY OF CONGRESS,NETHERLANDS EAST INDIES. INDONESIA LAW CULTURE AGRI INDUS SCHOOL COLONIAL HEALTH...GEOG JURID SOC 19/20 NETH/IND. PAGE 160 H3205
BIBLIOG/A S/ASIA NAT/G

B48
FURNIVAL J.,COLONIAL POLICY AND PRACTICE A COMPARATIVE STUDY OF BURMA, AND NETHERLANDS INDIA. BURMA INDONESIA S/ASIA...GEOG OBS GOV/COMP METH/COMP 20. PAGE 54 H1080
COLONIAL NAT/LISM WEALTH SOVEREIGN

B50
CORNELL U DEPT ASIAN STUDIES,SOUTHEAST ASIA PROGRAM DATA PAPER. BURMA CAMBODIA INDONESIA MALAYSIA VIETNAM SOCIETY STRUCT NAT/G SECT DIPLOM FOR/AID PWR WEALTH...SOC 20. PAGE 33 H0670
BIBLIOG/A CULTURE S/ASIA ECO/UNDEV

B50
TRAGER F.N.,MARXISM IN SOUTHEAST ASIA. BURMA INDONESIA THAILAND VIETNAM CULTURE SOCIETY NAT/G VOL/ASSN EXEC ROUTINE COERCE ATTIT RIGID/FLEX PWR ...METH/CNCPT TIME/SEQ STERTYP GEN/LAWS MARX/KARL VAL/FREE COLD/WAR NAM 20. PAGE 156 H3126
S/ASIA POL/PAR REV

B51
WABEKE B.H.,A GUIDE TO DUTCH BIBLIOGRAPHIES. BELGIUM INDONESIA NETHERLAND DIPLOM INT/TRADE WAR
BIBLIOG/A NAT/G

NAT/LISM KNOWL...ART/METH HUM JURID CON/ANAL 14/20. PAGE 164 H3282
CULTURE COLONIAL

B53
MIT CENTER INTERNATIONAL STU,BIBLIOGRAPHY OF THE ECONOMIC AND POLITICAL DEVELOPMENT OF INDONESIA. INDONESIA STRUCT NAT/G COLONIAL LEAD...STAT 20. PAGE 111 H2226
BIBLIOG ECO/UNDEV TEC/DEV S/ASIA

B57
KOENTJARANINGRAT R.,A PRELIMINARY DESCRIPTION OF THE JAVANESE KINSHIP SYSTEM. INDONESIA STRATA FAM INGP/REL ADJUST MARRIAGE AGE/C AGE/Y AGE/A PERSON ...OBS CHARTS DICTIONARY 20 JAVA. PAGE 87 H1736
KIN STRUCT ELITES CULTURE

B60
WILLIAMS L.E.,OVERSEAS CHINESE NATIONALISM: THE GENESIS OF THE PAN-CHINESE MOVEMENT IN INDONESIA, 1900-1916. ASIA COM INDONESIA AGRI INT/ORG LOC/G DIPLOM EDU/PROP HABITAT PWR POPULISM...GEOG LING CENSUS 20. PAGE 168 H3367
NAT/LISM GP/REL DECISION NAT/G

B60
WOLF C.,FOREIGN AID: THEORY AND PRACTICE IN SOUTHERN ASIA. CEYLON INDONESIA PHILIPPINE S/ASIA CULTURE STRATA ECO/UNDEV PLAN EDU/PROP ATTIT ...METH/CNCPT MATH QUANT STAT CONT/OBS TIME/SEQ SIMUL TOT/POP 20. PAGE 170 H3396
ACT/RES ECO/TAC FOR/AID

B62
GALENSON W.,LABOR IN DEVELOPING COUNTRIES. BRAZIL INDONESIA ISRAEL PAKISTAN TURKEY AGRI INDUS WORKER PAY PRICE GP/REL WEALTH...MGT CHARTS METH/COMP NAT/COMP 20. PAGE 54 H1088
LABOR ECO/UNDEV BARGAIN POL/PAR

B62
JOHNSON J.J.,THE ROLE OF THE MILITARY IN UNDERDEVELOPED COUNTRIES. AFR BURMA INDONESIA ISLAM ISRAEL L/A+17C S/ASIA THAILAND CULTURE ECO/UNDEV KIN PROVS CONSULT ACT/RES COERCE REV DRIVE RIGID/FLEX ORD/FREE...RECORD ANTHOL 20. PAGE 81 H1622
FORCES CONCPT

B62
KENNEDY R.,BIBLIOGRAPHY OF INDONESIAN PEOPLES AND CULTURES (2ND REV. ED.). INDONESIA STRUCT ECO/UNDEV SCHOOL EDU/PROP COLONIAL...GEOG SOC LING NAT/COMP 20. PAGE 85 H1689
BIBLIOG S/ASIA CULTURE KIN

B62
MANSUR F.,PROCESS OF INDEPENDENCE. GHANA INDIA INDONESIA PAKISTAN CONSTN ELITES INTELL STRUCT ACADEM NAT/G REV PWR 20. PAGE 102 H2043
NAT/COMP POL/PAR SOVEREIGN COLONIAL

B62
SELOSOEMARDJAN O.,SOCIAL CHANGES IN JOGJAKARTA. INDONESIA NETHERLAND ELITES STRATA STRUCT FAM POL/PAR CREATE DIPLOM INT/TRADE EDU/PROP ADMIN GOV/REL...SOC 20 JAVA CHINJAP. PAGE 141 H2825
ECO/UNDEV CULTURE REV COLONIAL

B63
GEERTZ C.,PEDDLERS AND PRINCES: SOCIAL DEVELOPMENT AND ECONOMIC CHANGE IN TWO INDONESIAN TOWNS. S/ASIA CULTURE SOCIETY STRATA FACE/GP MUNIC CREATE TEC/DEV ECO/TAC ORD/FREE WEALTH...OBS INT CENSUS CHARTS WORK TOT/POP VAL/FREE 20. PAGE 55 H1106
ECO/UNDEV SOC ELITES INDONESIA

B63
KAHIN G.M.,MAJOR GOVERNMENTS OF ASIA (2ND ED.). ASIA INDIA INDONESIA PAKISTAN S/ASIA DIPLOM...SOC 20 CHINJAP. PAGE 83 H1650
GOV/COMP POL/PAR ELITES

S63
HINDLEY D.,"FOREIGN AID TO INDONESIA AND ITS POLITICAL IMPLICATIONS." INDONESIA POL/PAR ATTIT SOVEREIGN...CHARTS 20. PAGE 71 H1421
FOR/AID NAT/G WEALTH ECO/TAC

S63
SOEMARDJORN S.,"SOME SOCIAL AND CULTURAL IMPLICATIONS OF INDONESIA'S PLANNED AND UNPLANNED DEVELOPMENT." EUR+WWI FUT MOD/EUR S/ASIA CONSTN SOCIETY DELIB/GP ACT/RES PLAN ECO/TAC EDU/PROP COERCE ATTIT ALL/VALS...TIME/SEQ 20. PAGE 146 H2927
ECO/UNDEV CULTURE INDONESIA

B64
HOBBS C.C.,SOUTHEAST ASIA: AN ANNOTATED BIBLIOGRAPHY OF SELECTED REFERENCES IN WESTERN LANGUAGES (REV. ED.). CAMBODIA INDONESIA LAOS THAILAND VIETNAM CONSTN NAT/G...SOC WORSHIP 20. PAGE 72 H1437
BIBLIOG/A S/ASIA CULTURE SOCIETY

B64
TINKER H.,BALLOT BOX AND BAYONET - PEOPLE AND GOVERNMENT IN EMERGENT ASIAN COUNTRIES. CEYLON INDIA INDONESIA PHILIPPINE POL/PAR ADMIN COLONIAL LEAD PARL/PROC CHOOSE CONSEN ORD/FREE SOVEREIGN PLURISM...GOV/COMP THIRD/WRLD. PAGE 155 H3104
MYTH S/ASIA NAT/COMP NAT/LISM

B64
WERTHEIM W.F.,EAST-WEST PARALLELS. INDONESIA S/ASIA NAT/G SECT...TIME/SEQ METH REFORMERS S/EASTASIA. PAGE 167 H3334
SOC ECO/UNDEV CULTURE NAT/LISM

S64
VANDENBOSCH A.,"POWER BALANCE IN INDONESIA." S/ASIA USSR NAT/G TOP/EX BAL/PWR DOMIN NEUTRAL ORD/FREE PWR...POLICY TIME/SEQ GEN/LAWS 20 SUKARNO/A. PAGE 162 H3233
FORCES TREND DIPLOM INDONESIA

B66
BRACKMAN A.C.,SOUTHEAST ASIA'S SECOND FRONT: THE POWER STRUGGLE IN THE MALAY ARCHIPELAGO. CHINA/COM INDONESIA MALAYSIA ECO/UNDEV INT/ORG NAT/G FORCES DIPLOM EDU/PROP REGION COERCE GUERRILLA AUTHORIT POPULISM...MAJORIT 20 KENNEDY/JF SEATO. PAGE 20 H0396
S/ASIA MARXISM REV

B66
MILONE P.D.,URBAN AREAS IN INDONESIA. INDONESIA LABOR NAT/G COLONIAL GP/REL...CENSUS CHARTS 17/20. PAGE 111 H2218
MUNIC GEOG STRUCT SOCIETY

B66
WILLNER A.R.,THE NEOTRADITIONAL ACCOMMODATION TO POLITICAL INDEPENDENCE* THE CASE OF INDONESIA * RESEARCH MONOGRAPH NO. 26. CULTURE ECO/UNDEV CREATE PROB/SOLV FOR/AID LEGIT COLONIAL EFFICIENCY NAT/LISM ALL/VALS SOC. PAGE 168 H3371
INDONESIA CONSERVE ELITES ADMIN

S66
GILBERT S.P.,"WARS OF LIBERATION AND SOVIET MILITARY AID POLICY." ASIA INDIA INDONESIA UAR USA+45 STRATA WAR PERCEPT MARXISM...STAT NAT/COMP. PAGE 56 H1124
USSR FOR/AID WEAPON DRIVE

S66
MCLENNAN B.N.,"EVOLUTION OF CONCEPTS OF REPRESENTATION IN INDONESIA" INDONESIA...CONCPT IDEA/COMP METH 20. PAGE 107 H2143
REPRESENT NAT/G POPULISM PWR

B67
MILNE R.S.,GOVERNMENT AND POLITICS IN MALAYSIA. INDONESIA MALAYSIA LOC/G EX/STRUC FORCES DIPLOM GP/REL 20 SINGAPORE. PAGE 111 H2217
NAT/G LEGIS ADMIN

L67
VAN DER KROEF J.M.,"INDONESIA: THE BATTLE OF THE 'OLD' AND THE 'NEW ORDER'." INDONESIA ISLAM ELITES POL/PAR DOMIN INGP/REL NAT/LISM PWR...IDEA/COMP 20. PAGE 161 H3229
FORCES MARXISM NAT/G BAL/PWR

S67
MOZINGO D.,"CHINA AND INDONESIA." CHINA/COM INDONESIA POL/PAR 20. PAGE 114 H2276
MARXISM CONTROL DIPLOM NAT/G

S67
SULLIVAN J.H.,"THE PRESS AND POLITICS IN INDONESIA." INDONESIA NAT/G WRITING REV...TREND GOV/COMP 20. PAGE 150 H3007
CIVMIL/REL KNOWL TOTALISM

S68
KANET R.E.,"RECENT SOVIET REASSESSMENT OF DEVELOPMENTS IN THE THIRD WORLD." ALGERIA GHANA INDONESIA USSR WOR+45 CONSTN ELITES INTELL STRUCT DOMIN CONTROL REV PWR MARXISM...IDEA/COMP METH 20 THIRD/WRLD. PAGE 83 H1653
DIPLOM NEUTRAL NAT/G NAT/COMP

INDUS....ALL OR MOST INDUSTRY; SEE ALSO SPECIFIC INDUSTRIES, INSTITUTIONAL INDEX, PART C, P. XII

N
PEKING REVIEW. CHINA/COM CULTURE AGRI INDUS DIPLOM EDU/PROP GUERRILLA ATTIT MARXISM...BIBLIOG 20. PAGE 1 H0009
MARXIST NAT/G POL/PAR PRESS

N
CHINA QUARTERLY. COM AGRI INDUS ACADEM POL/PAR INT/TRADE CONFER GOV/REL...TIME/SEQ CON/ANAL INDEX 20. PAGE 1 H0014
BIBLIOG/A ASIA DIPLOM POLICY

N
THE STATESMAN'S YEARBOOK; STATISTICAL AND HISTORICAL ANNUAL OF THE STATES OF THE WORLD. WOR+45 WOR-45 COM/IND FINAN INDUS SECT FORCES TEC/DEV EDU/PROP...GEOG BIBLIOG 19/20. PAGE 1 H0023
NAT/COMP GOV/COMP STAT CONSTN

N
THE MIDDLE EAST AND NORTH AFRICA. AFR ISLAM CULTURE ECO/UNDEV AGRI NAT/G TEC/DEV FOR/AID INT/TRADE EDU/PROP...CHARTS 20. PAGE 2 H0026
INDEX INDUS FINAN STAT

N
THE MIDDLE EAST. CULTURE...BIOG BIBLIOG. PAGE 2 H0028
ISLAM INDUS FINAN

N
"PROLOG",DIGEST OF THE SOVIET UKRANIAN PRESS. USSR LAW AGRI INDUS PROVS SCHOOL DIPLOM GOV/REL ATTIT ...HUM LING 20. PAGE 3 H0053
BIBLIOG/A NAT/G PRESS COM

N
EUROPA PUBLICATIONS LIMITED,THE EUROPA YEAR BOOK. CONSTN FINAN INDUS POL/PAR DIPLOM TV CT/SYS...STAT BIOG CHARTS WORSHIP 20. PAGE 47 H0949
BIBLIOG NAT/G PRESS INT/ORG

N
INTERNATIONAL CENTRE AFRICAN,BULLETIN OF INFORMATION ON THESES AND STUDIES IN PROGRESS OR PROPOSED. LAW CULTURE FINAN INDUS LABOR TEC/DEV EDU/PROP...GEOG SOC NAT/COMP 20. PAGE 78 H1554
BIBLIOG/A ACT/RES ACADEM INTELL

N
KYRIAK T.E.,CHINA: A BIBLIOGRAPHY. ASIA CHINA/COM AGRI FINAN INDUS NAT/G INT/TRADE PRESS...SOC 20.
BIBLIOG/A MARXISM

PAGE 90 H1789 TOP/EX POL/PAR
N

NORTHWESTERN UNIVERSITY LIB,JOINT ACQUISITIONS LIST OF AFRICANA. AFR SOCIETY STRUCT EDU/PROP COLONIAL GP/REL RACE/REL NAT/LISM SOVEREIGN...SOC 20. PAGE 119 H2377 BIBLIOG CULTURE ECO/UNDEV INDUS
N

US DEPARTMENT OF STATE,BIBLIOGRAPHY (PAMPHLETS). AGRI INDUS INT/ORG FOR/AID EDU/PROP WAR MARXISM ...SOC GOV/COMP METH/COMP 20. PAGE 159 H3184 BIBLIOG DIPLOM ECO/DEV NAT/G
N

US LIBRARY OF CONGRESS,SOUTHERN ASIA ACCESSIONS LIST. BURMA CEYLON INDIA NEPAL PAKISTAN S/ASIA THAILAND AGRI INDUS SCHOOL WORKER...ART/METH GEOG HEAL PHIL/SCI LING 20. PAGE 160 H3201 BIBLIOG/A SOCIETY CULTURE ECO/UNDEV
B04

REED W.A.,ETHNOLOGICAL SURVEY PUBLICATIONS (VOL. II). PHILIPPINE STRUCT INDUS SECT DEATH LEISURE HABITAT...AUD/VIS CHARTS WORSHIP 20 NABOLOI NEGRITO BATAK. PAGE 130 H2607 CULTURE SOCIETY SOC OBS
B08

LLOYD H.D.,THE SWISS DEMOCRACY. SWITZERLND INDUS NAT/G WORKER CHOOSE OWN ORD/FREE SOCISM...PLURIST 19/20 MONOPOLY. PAGE 97 H1944 NAT/COMP GOV/COMP REPRESENT POPULISM
B12

HOBSON J.A.,THE EVOLUTION OF MODERN CAPITALISM. MOD/EUR UK STRATA ECO/DEV INDUS INCOME UTIL WEALTH ...SOC GEN/LAWS 7/20. PAGE 72 H1440 CAP/ISM WORKER TEC/DEV TIME/SEQ
B12

SONOLET L.,L'AFRIQUE OCCIDENTALE FRANCAISE. FRANCE AGRI INDUS NAT/G SECT FORCES INT/TRADE EDU/PROP RACE/REL HEALTH ORD/FREE...CHARTS 19/20 NEGRO AFRICA/W. PAGE 147 H2933 DOMIN ADMIN COLONIAL AFR
B13

KROPOTKIN P.,THE CONQUEST OF BREAD. SOCIETY STRATA AGRI INDUS WORKER REV HAPPINESS INCOME PRODUC HEALTH MORAL ORD/FREE. PAGE 89 H1775 ANARCH SOCIALIST OWN AGREE
B14

CRAIG J.,ELEMENTS OF POLITICAL SCIENCE (3 VOLS.). CONSTN AGRI INDUS SCHOOL FORCES TAX CT/SYS SUFF MORAL WEALTH...CONCPT 19 CIVIL/LIB. PAGE 35 H0696 PHIL/SCI NAT/G ORD/FREE
B14

LEVINE L.,SYNDICALISM IN FRANCE (2ND ED.). FRANCE LAW SOCIETY ECO/DEV NAT/G ECO/TAC LEAD ATTIT ...POLICY CONCPT STAT BIBLIOG 18/20 REFORMERS. PAGE 95 H1902 LABOR INDUS SOCISM REV
B15

VEBLEN T.,IMPERIAL GERMANY AND THE INDUSTRIAL REVOLUTION. GERMANY MOD/EUR UK USA-45 NAT/G TEC/DEV CAP/ISM...MAJORIT NAT/COMP 19/20 CHINJAP. PAGE 162 H3236 ECO/DEV INDUS TECHNIC BAL/PWR
B19

NATHAN M.,THE SOUTH AFRICAN COMMONWEALTH: CONSTITUTION, PROBLEMS, SOCIAL CONDITIONS. SOUTH/AFR UK CULTURE INDUS EX/STRUC LEGIS BUDGET EDU/PROP ADMIN CT/SYS GP/REL RACE/REL...LING 19/20 CMN/WLTH. PAGE 116 H2317 CONSTN NAT/G POL/PAR SOCIETY
N19

ANDERSON J.,THE ORGANIZATION OF ECONOMIC STUDIES IN RELATION TO THE PROBLEMS OF GOVERNMENT (PAMPHLET). UK FINAN INDUS DELIB/GP PLAN PROB/SOLV ADMIN 20. PAGE 6 H0128 ECO/TAC ACT/RES NAT/G CENTRAL
N19

BUSINESS ECONOMISTS' GROUP,INCOME POLICIES (PAMPHLET). UK INDUS LABOR TOP/EX PAY COST PRODUC ...ECOMETRIC GOV/COMP SIMUL ANTHOL 20. PAGE 25 H0497 INCOME WORKER WEALTH POLICY
N19

INTERNATIONAL LABOUR OFFICE,EMPLOYMENT, UNEMPLOYMENT AND LABOUR FORCE STATISTICS (PAMPHLET). EUR+WWI STRATA AGRI INDUS NAT/G PROB/SOLV PAY AGE SEX...SAMP NAT/COMP METH 20 ILO. PAGE 78 H1557 WORKER LABOR STAT ECO/DEV
N19

WILSON T.,FINANCIAL ASSISTANCE WITH REGIONAL DEVELOPMENT (PAMPHLET). CANADA INDUS NAT/G PLAN TAX CONTROL COST EFFICIENCY...POLICY CHARTS 20. PAGE 169 H3382 FINAN ECO/TAC REGION GOV/REL
B20

MALTHUS T.R.,PRINCIPLES OF POLITICAL ECONOMY. UK AGRI INDUS MARKET NAT/G DIPLOM PRICE CONTROL BAL/PAY COST OWN PWR LAISSEZ 18/19. PAGE 102 H2034 GEN/LAWS DEMAND WEALTH
B22

URE P.N.,THE ORIGIN OF TYRANNY. MEDIT-7 FINAN INDUS CHIEF FORCES ECO/TAC WEALTH. PAGE 159 H3174 AUTHORIT PWR NAT/G MARKET
B23

FINER H.,REPRESENTATIVE GOVERNMENT AND A PARLIAMENT OF INDUSTRY. A STUDY OF THE GERMAN FEDERAL ECONOMIC COUNCIL. GERMANY UK CONSTN INDUS PARL/PROC ...NAT/COMP 20. PAGE 50 H1002 DELIB/GP ECO/TAC WAR REV
B26

MCPHEE A.,THE ECONOMIC REVOLUTION IN BRITISH WEST AFRICA. AFR UK CULTURE DIST/IND FINAN INDUS PLAN GP/REL RACE/REL 20 AFRICA/W. PAGE 107 H2148 ECO/UNDEV INT/TRADE COLONIAL GEOG
B26

TAWNEY R.H.,RELIGION AND THE RISE OF CAPITALISM. UK CULTURE NAT/G TEC/DEV OWN LAISSEZ...POLICY SOC TIME/SEQ 16/19. PAGE 153 H3050 SECT WEALTH INDUS CAP/ISM
B27

BELLOC H.,THE SERVILE STATE (1912) (3RD ED.). PRUSSIA UK CULTURE STRATA INDUS NAT/G ECO/TAC CONTROL LEAD SUFF DISCRIM EQUILIB ORD/FREE WEALTH 20. PAGE 13 H0269 WORKER CAP/ISM DOMIN CATH
B27

SMITH E.W.,THE GOLDEN STOOL: SOME ASPECTS OF THE CONFLICT OF CULTURES IN AFRICA. AFR FINAN INDUS SECT INT/TRADE COERCE CHOOSE RACE/REL ATTIT...GEOG LING 20 NEGRO. PAGE 145 H2907 COLONIAL CULTURE GP/REL EDU/PROP
B27

WEBER M.,GENERAL ECONOMIC HISTORY. CHRIST-17C MOD/EUR STRUCT AGRI EXTR/IND FINAN INDUS MARKET FAM MUNIC NAT/G PROF/ORG SECT ECO/TAC 8/20. PAGE 166 H3319 ECO/DEV CAP/ISM
B30

SMUTS J.C.,AFRICA AND SOME WORLD PROBLEMS. RHODESIA SOUTH/AFR CULTURE ECO/UNDEV INDUS INT/ORG SECT PROB/SOLV REGION GOV/REL DISCRIM ATTIT 19/20 LEAGUE/NAT LIVNGSTN/D NEGRO. PAGE 146 H2921 LEGIS AFR COLONIAL RACE/REL
B33

MANNHEIM E.,DIE TRAGER DER OFFENTLICHEN MEINUNG. ADJUST ATTIT...PSY 19/20. PAGE 102 H2037 SOC CULTURE CONCPT INDUS
B34

LIPPMANN W.,THE METHOD OF FREEDOM. SOCIETY INDUS LABOR LOBBY WAR REPRESENT...POLICY IDEA/COMP METH/COMP 19/20. PAGE 97 H1936 CONCPT MAJORIT NAT/G
B34

MARX K.,THE CLASS STRUGGLES IN FRANCE. FRANCE INDUS WORKER CONSERVE...TREND GEN/LAWS 19. PAGE 104 H2077 MARXIST STRATA REV INT/TRADE
B34

STALIN J.,PROBLEMS OF LENINISM. USSR STRATA INDUS LOC/G POL/PAR ECO/TAC CONTROL TOTALISM PWR SOCISM LENIN/VI STALIN/J. PAGE 148 H2968 MARXISM REV ELITES NAT/G
B35

NORDSKOG J.E.,SOCIAL REFORM IN NORWAY. NORWAY INDUS NAT/G POL/PAR LEGIS ADJUD...SOC BIBLIOG SOC/INTEG 20. PAGE 119 H2371 LABOR ADJUST
B36

BOYCE A.N.,EUROPE AND SOUTH AFRICA. FRANCE GERMANY ITALY SOUTH/AFR UK INDUS NAT/G CONTROL REV WAR NAT/LISM...CONCPT HIST/WRIT 20. PAGE 20 H0392 COLONIAL GOV/COMP NAT/COMP DIPLOM
B37

HAMILTON W.H.,THE POWER TO GOVERN. ECO/DEV FINAN INDUS ECO/TAC INT/TRADE TARIFFS TAX CONTROL CT/SYS WAR COST PWR 18/20 SUPREME/CT. PAGE 65 H1303 LING CONSTN NAT/G POLICY
B37

PARSONS T.,THE STRUCTURE OF SOCIAL ACTION. UNIV INTELL SOCIETY INDUS MARKET ECO/TAC ROUTINE CHOOSE ALL/VALS...CONCPT OBS BIOG TREND GEN/LAWS 20. PAGE 124 H2471 CULTURE ATTIT CAP/ISM
B37

UNION OF SOUTH AFRICA,REPORT CONCERNING ADMINISTRATION OF SOUTH WEST AFRICA (6 VOLS.). SOUTH/AFR INDUS PUB/INST FORCES LEGIS BUDGET DIPLOM EDU/PROP ADJUD CT/SYS...GEOG CHARTS 20 AFRICA/SW LEAGUE/NAT. PAGE 158 H3166 NAT/G ADMIN COLONIAL CONSTN
B38

CARVALHO C.M.,GEOGRAPHIA HUMANA; POLITICA E ECONOMICA (3RD ED.). BRAZIL CULTURE AGRI INDUS DIPLOM COLONIAL GP/REL RACE/REL...LING 20 RESOURCE/N. PAGE 27 H0551 GEOG HABITAT
B38

DAVIES E.,"NATIONAL" CAPITALISM: THE GOVERNMENT'S RECORD AS PROTECTOR OF PRIVATE MONOPOLY. UK ELITES SOCIETY STRATA POL/PAR WORKER PROB/SOLV CONTROL SOCISM 20 MONOPOLY LABOR/PAR CHAMBRLN/N. PAGE 37 H0747 CAP/ISM NAT/G INDUS POLICY
B38

FIELD G.L.,THE SYNDICAL AND CORPORATIVE INSTITUTIONS OF ITALIAN FASCISM. ITALY CONSTN STRATA LABOR EX/STRUC TOP/EX ADJUD ADMIN LEAD TOTALISM AUTHORIT...MGT 20 MUSSOLIN/B. PAGE 50 H0991 FASCISM INDUS NAT/G WORKER
B38

LAWLEY F.E.,THE GROWTH OF COLLECTIVE ECONOMY VOL. 1: NATIONAL. EUR+WWI AGRI INDUS NAT/G BARGAIN CAP/ISM ECO/TAC WAR OPTIMAL WEALTH...GOV/COMP SOCISM PRICE CONTROL

METH/COMP 19/20 MONOPOLY. PAGE 92 H1844 OWN

B38
LAWLEY F.E.,THE GROWTH OF COLLECTIVE ECONOMY VOL. 2: INTERNATIONAL. WOR-45 AGRI INDUS EQUILIB OPTIMAL OWN WEALTH...NAT/COMP 19/20 NAZI NEW/DEAL MONOPOLY. PAGE 92 H1845 ECO/TAC SOCISM NAT/LISM CONTROL

B38
REICH N.,LABOR RELATIONS IN REPUBLICAN GERMANY. GERMANY CONSTN ECO/DEV INDUS NAT/G ADMIN CONTROL GP/REL FASCISM POPULISM 20 WEIMAR/REP. PAGE 130 H2609 WORKER MGT LABOR BARGAIN

B38
SAINT-PIERRE C.I.,SCHEME FOR LASTING PEACE (TRANS. BY H. BELLOT). INDUS NAT/G CHIEF FORCES INT/TRADE CT/SYS WAR PWR SOVEREIGN WEALTH...POLICY 18. PAGE 137 H2732 INT/ORG PEACE AGREE INT/LAW

S38
HALL R.C.,"REPRESENTATION OF BIG BUSINESS IN THE HOUSE OF COMMONS." UK ECO/DEV INDUS PROF/ORG LEGIS CAP/ISM ECO/TAC LAISSEZ...POLICY OLD/LIB PLURIST MGT 20 HOUSE/CMNS. PAGE 64 H1287 LOBBY NAT/G

B39
BARNES H.E.,SOCIETY IN TRANSITION: PROBLEMS OF A CHANGING ERA. USA-45 INDUS MUNIC PUB/INST EDU/PROP CRIME RACE/REL...SOC MYTH NAT/COMP. PAGE 11 H0220 SOCIETY CULTURE TECHRACY TEC/DEV

B39
FURNIVALL J.S.,NETHERLANDS INDIA. INDIA NETHERLAND CULTURE INDUS NAT/G DIPLOM ADMIN WEALTH...POLICY CHARTS 17/20. PAGE 54 H1081 COLONIAL ECO/UNDEV SOVEREIGN PLURISM

B39
MARQUAND H.A.,ORGANIZED LABOUR IN FOUR CONTINENTS. EUR+WWI USA-45 INDUS NAT/G PAY GP/REL TOTALISM ATTIT WEALTH ALL/IDEOS...TREND NAT/COMP 20 ILO AFL/CIO EUROPE CHINJAP MEXIC/AMER. PAGE 103 H2055 LABOR WORKER CONCPT ANTHOL

B39
VAN BILJON F.J.,STATE INTERFERENCE IN SOUTH AFRICA. SOUTH/AFR ECO/UNDEV AGRI INDUS WORKER RATION WEALTH ...JURID 20. PAGE 161 H3225 ECO/TAC POLICY INT/TRADE NAT/G

S39
HECKSCHER G.,"GROUP ORGANIZATION IN SWEDEN." SWEDEN STRATA ECO/DEV AGRI INDUS LABOR NAT/G PROF/ORG ECO/TAC CENTRAL SOCISM...MGT 19/20. PAGE 69 H1382 LAISSEZ SOC

B40
CONOVER H.F.,JAPAN-ECONOMIC DEVELOPMENT AND FOREIGN POLICY, A SELECTED LIST OF REFERENCES (PAMPHLET). CULTURE FINAN INDUS NAT/G FORCES INT/TRADE WAR ...SOC TREND 20 CHINJAP. PAGE 32 H0640 BIBLIOG ASIA ECO/DEV DIPLOM

B40
HERSKOVITS M.J.,THE ECONOMIC LIFE OF PRIMITIVE PEOPLES. INDUS OP/RES PLAN PROB/SOLV...BIBLIOG METH 20. PAGE 70 H1407 CULTURE ECO/TAC ECO/UNDEV PRODUC

B40
WUNDERLICH F.,LABOR UNDER GERMAN DEMOCRACY, ARBITRATION 1918-1933. GERMANY NAT/G PAY REPAR ADJUD CT/SYS GP/REL...MAJORIT 20. PAGE 171 H3426 LABOR WORKER INDUS BARGAIN

B42
BARNES H.E.,SOCIAL INSTITUTIONS IN AN ERA OF WORLD UPHEAVAL. INDUS FAM NAT/G PERF/ART SECT AUTOMAT PERSON MORAL...PREDICT 20. PAGE 11 H0221 SOCIETY CULTURE TECHRACY TREND

B42
CONOVER H.F.,NEW ZEALAND: A SELECTED LIST OF REFERENCES (PAMPHLET). NEW/ZEALND ECO/UNDEV AGRI INDUS LABOR NAT/G SCHOOL FORCES DIPLOM COLONIAL WAR ...HUM 20. PAGE 32 H0643 BIBLIOG/A S/ASIA CULTURE

B42
ROBBINS J.J.,THE GOVERNMENT OF LABOR RELATIONS IN SWEDEN. SWEDEN LAW CONSTN ADJUD CT/SYS GP/REL ...JURID 20. PAGE 132 H2638 NAT/G BARGAIN LABOR INDUS

B43
BROWN A.D.,GREECE: SELECTED LIST OF REFERENCES. GREECE ECO/UNDEV AGRI FINAN INDUS LABOR SECT TEC/DEV INT/TRADE LEAD...SOC 20. PAGE 22 H0438 BIBLIOG/A WAR DIPLOM NAT/G

B43
CONOVER H.F.,SOVIET RUSSIA: SELECTED LIST OF REFERENCES. USSR CULTURE INDUS NAT/G TOP/EX TEC/DEV BUDGET WAR CIVMIL/REL EFFICIENCY MARXISM 20. PAGE 32 H0644 BIBLIOG ECO/DEV COM DIPLOM

B43
US LIBRARY OF CONGRESS,BRITISH MALAYA AND BRITISH NORTH BORNEO. BORNEO MALAYSIA CONSTN AGRI COM/IND INDUS EDU/PROP 19/20. PAGE 160 H3203 BIBLIOG CULTURE

B44
SHELBY C.,LATIN AMERICAN PERIODICALS CURRENTLY RECEIVED IN THE LIBRARY OF CONGRESS AND IN LIBRARY OF DEPARTMENT OF AGRICULTURE. SOCIETY AGRI INDUS LABOR POL/PAR INT/TRADE...GEOG SOC 20. PAGE 143 H2856 BIBLIOG ECO/UNDEV CULTURE L/A+17C

C44
VAN VALKENBURG S.,"ELEMENTS OF POLITICAL GEOGRAPHY." FRANCE COM/IND INDUS NAT/G SECT RACE/REL...LING TREND GEN/LAWS BIBLIOG 20. PAGE 162 H3232 GEOG DIPLOM COLONIAL

B45
CLAGETT H.L.,COMMUNIST CHINA: RUTHLESS ENEMY OR PAPER TIGER (PAMPHLET). CHINA/COM ECO/UNDEV AGRI INDUS NAT/G POL/PAR ECO/TAC INT/TRADE GUERRILLA ATTIT...CHARTS NAT/COMP ORG/CHARTS 20. PAGE 30 H0602 BIBLIOG/A MARXISM DIPLOM COERCE

B45
US LIBRARY OF CONGRESS,NETHERLANDS EAST INDIES. INDONESIA LAW CULTURE AGRI INDUS SCHOOL COLONIAL HEALTH...GEOG JURID SOC 19/20 NETH/IND. PAGE 160 H3205 BIBLIOG/A S/ASIA NAT/G

B46
ALLEN J.S.,WORLD MONOPOLY AND PEACE. GERMANY UK USSR FINAN INDUS LG/CO DOMIN CONTROL PEACE PWR WEALTH SOCISM...NAT/COMP 20 MONOPOLY. PAGE 5 H0105 CAP/ISM DIPLOM WAR COLONIAL

B46
DAVIES E.,NATIONAL ENTERPRISE: THE DEVELOPMENT OF THE PUBLIC CORPORATION. UK LG/CO EX/STRUC WORKER PROB/SOLV COST ATTIT SOCISM 20. PAGE 37 H0748 ADMIN NAT/G CONTROL INDUS

S46
SILBERNER E.,"THE PROBLEM OF WAR IN NINETEENTH CENTURY ECONOMIC THOUGHT." EUR+WWI MOD/EUR UNIV LAW ECO/DEV ECO/UNDEV FINAN INDUS MARKET INT/ORG NAT/G CONSULT FORCES...CONCPT GEN/LAWS GEN/METH 19. PAGE 144 H2875 ATTIT ECO/TAC WAR

N46
HOBBS C.C.,SOUTHEAST ASIA, 1935-45: A SELECTED LIST OF REFERENCE BOOKS (PAMPHLET). S/ASIA AGRI INDUS NAT/G SECT DIPLOM WAR...ART/METH GEOG SOC LING 20. PAGE 72 H1435 BIBLIOG/A CULTURE HABITAT

B47
BOWEN R.H.,GERMAN THEORIES OF THE CORPORATIVE STATE, WITH SPECIAL REFERENCES TO THE PERIOD 1870-1919. GERMANY INDUS LG/CO CATHISM SOCISM...SOC 18/20. PAGE 19 H0389 IDEA/COMP CENTRAL NAT/G POLICY

B48
LASKI H.S.,THE AMERICAN DEMOCRACY. CULTURE INDUS SECT WORKER DIPLOM EDU/PROP REPRESENT RACE/REL ORD/FREE PWR...NAT/COMP 18/20. PAGE 92 H1831 NAT/G LOC/G USA-45 POPULISM

B48
ROSENFARB J.,FREEDOM AND THE ADMINISTRATIVE STATE. NAT/G ROUTINE EFFICIENCY PRODUC RATIONAL UTIL ...TECHNIC WELF/ST MGT 20 BUREAUCRCY. PAGE 134 H2680 ECO/DEV INDUS PLAN WEALTH

B49
UNSTEAD J.F.,A WORLD SURVEY FROM THE HUMAN ASPECT. AGRI INDUS...SOC CENSUS CHARTS 20 MAPS MIGRATION. PAGE 159 H3172 CULTURE HABITAT GEOG ATTIT

S49
STEINMETZ H.,"THE PROBLEMS OF THE LANDRAT: A STUDY OF COUNTY GOVERNMENT IN THE US ZONE OF GERMANY." GERMANY/W USA+45 INDUS PLAN DIPLOM EDU/PROP CONTROL WAR GOV/REL FEDERAL WEALTH PLURISM...GOV/COMP 20 LANDRAT. PAGE 149 H2977 LOC/G COLONIAL MGT TOP/EX

B50
GATZKE H.W.,GERMANY'S DRIVE TO THE WEST. BELGIUM GERMANY MOD/EUR AGRI INDUS POL/PAR FORCES DOMIN AGREE CONTROL REGION COERCE 20 TREATY WWI. PAGE 55 H1104 WAR POLICY NAT/G DIPLOM

B50
HOBBS C.C.,INDOCHINA, A BIBLIOGRAPHY OF THE LAND AND PEOPLE. VIETNAM CULTURE AGRI INDUS NAT/G SECT ...ART/METH GEOG SOC LING 20. PAGE 72 H1436 BIBLIOG/A S/ASIA COLONIAL ECO/UNDEV

B51
CHRISTENSEN A.N.,THE EVOLUTION OF LATIN AMERICAN GOVERNMENT: A BOOK OF READINGS. ECO/UNDEV INDUS LOC/G POL/PAR EX/STRUC LEGIS FOR/AID CT/SYS ...SOC/WK 20 SOUTH/AMER. PAGE 30 H0599 NAT/G CONSTN DIPLOM L/A+17C

B51
GHANI A.R.,PAKISTAN: A SELECT BIBLIOGRAPHY. PAKISTAN S/ASIA CULTURE...GEOG 20. PAGE 56 H1120 BIBLIOG AGRI INDUS

B51
MARX K.,THE EIGHTEENTH BRUMAIRE OF LOUIS BONAPARTE (1852). FRANCE STRATA FINAN INDUS LABOR CHIEF FORCES WORKER CAP/ISM ECO/TAC PARL/PROC ORD/FREE ...MARXIST 19. PAGE 104 H2080 REV MARXISM ELITES NAT/G

C51
BEST H.,"THE SOVIET STATE AND ITS INCEPTION." USSR CULTURE INDUS DIPLOM WEALTH...GEOG SOC BIBLIOG 20. PAGE 16 H0322 COM GEN/METH REV MARXISM

B52
SPICER E.H.,HUMAN PROBLEMS IN TECHNOLOGICAL CHANGE. ECO/UNDEV AGRI INDUS NAT/G ACT/RES LEAD GP/REL INGP/REL ROLE...INT METH 20 CASEBOOK. PAGE 147 TEC/DEV CULTURE STRUCT

H2947 OP/RES

C52
LEWIS B.W.,"BRITISH PLANNING AND NATIONALIZATION." UK INDUS SERV/IND LABOR NAT/G OP/RES TEC/DEV TAX WEALTH...CHARTS BIBLIOG 20. PAGE 96 H1912 NEW/LIB ECO/DEV POL/PAR PLAN

B53
FLORENCE P.S.,THE LOGIC OF BRITISH AND AMERICAN INDUSTRY; A REALISTIC ANALYSIS OF ECONOMIC STRUCTURE AND GOVERNMENT. UK USA+45 USA-45 FINAN LABOR CAP/ISM INGP/REL EFFICIENCY...MGT CONCPT STAT CHARTS METH 20. PAGE 51 H1028 INDUS ECO/DEV NAT/G NAT/COMP

B53
MEAD M.,CULTURAL PATTERNS AND TECHNICAL CHANGE. BURMA GREECE NIGERIA ECO/UNDEV AGRI INDUS SCHOOL SECT CREATE FEEDBACK HABITAT...PSY METH/COMP BIBLIOG 20 UN. PAGE 108 H2152 HEALTH TEC/DEV CULTURE ADJUST

B54
BINANI G.D.,INDIA AT A GLANCE (REV. ED.). INDIA COM/IND FINAN INDUS LABOR PROVS SCHOOL PLAN DIPLOM INT/TRADE ADMIN...JURID 20. PAGE 17 H0335 INDEX CON/ANAL NAT/G ECO/UNDEV

B54
FRIEDMAN W.,THE PUBLIC CORPORATION: A COMPARATIVE SYMPOSIUM (UNIVERSITY OF TORONTO SCHOOL OF LAW COMPARATIVE LAW SERIES, VOL. I). SWEDEN USA+45 INDUS INT/ORG NAT/G REGION CENTRAL FEDERAL...POLICY JURID IDEA/COMP NAT/COMP ANTHOL 20 COMMONWLTH MONOPOLY EUROPE. PAGE 53 H1065 LAW SOCISM LG/CO OWN

B54
GATZKE H.W.,STRESEMANN AND THE REARMAMENT OF GERMANY. EUR+WWI GERMANY USSR FINAN NAT/G ECO/TAC ATTIT...BIOG METH 20 STRESEMN/G. PAGE 55 H1105 FORCES INDUS PWR

B54
MOSK S.A.,INDUSTRIAL REVOLUTION IN MEXICO. MARKET LABOR CREATE CAP/ISM ADMIN ATTIT SOCISM...POLICY 20 MEXIC/AMER. PAGE 113 H2268 INDUS TEC/DEV ECO/UNDEV NAT/G

B54
US LIBRARY OF CONGRESS,RESEARCH AND INFORMATION ON AFRICA: CONTINUING SOURCES. ISLAM ECO/UNDEV AGRI INDUS R+D ACADEM NAT/G INT/TRADE...SOC 20. PAGE 161 H3210 BIBLIOG/A AFR PRESS COM/IND

B55
JONES T.B.,A BIBLIOGRAPHY ON SOUTH AMERICAN ECONOMIC AFFAIRS: ARTICLES IN NINETEENTH CENTURY PERIODICALS (PAMPHLET). AGRI COM/IND DIST/IND EXTR/IND FINAN INDUS LABOR NAT/G 19. PAGE 82 H1634 BIBLIOG ECO/UNDEV L/A+17C TEC/DEV

B55
SERRANO MOSCOSO E.,A STATEMENT OF THE LAWS OF ECUADOR IN MATTERS AFFECTING BUSINESS (2ND ED.). ECUADOR INDUS LABOR LG/CO NAT/G LEGIS TAX CONTROL MARRIAGE 20. PAGE 141 H2830 FINAN ECO/UNDEV LAW CONSTN

B55
UN ECONOMIC COMN ASIA & FAR E,ECONOMIC SURVEY OF ASIA AND THE FAR EAST, 1954. AFGHANISTN CEYLON INDIA PHILIPPINE S/ASIA ECO/DEV FINAN INDUS INT/TRADE PRODUC WEALTH...STAT CHARTS 20 CHINJAP. PAGE 158 H3158 ECO/UNDEV PRICE NAT/COMP ASIA

C55
SANTAYANA G.,"REASON IN SOCIETY" IN G. SANTAYANA, THE LIFE OF REASON." INDUS FAM NAT/G WAR GP/REL HAPPINESS PRODUC LOVE WEALTH CONSERVE POPULISM CONCPT. PAGE 138 H2752 RATIONAL SOCIETY CULTURE ATTIT

B56
INTERNATIONAL AFRICAN INST,SOCIAL IMPLICATIONS OF INDUSTRIALIZATION AND URBANIZATION IN AFRICA SOUTH OF THE SAHARA. SOUTH/AFR INDUS LABOR MUNIC WORKER TEC/DEV...SOC OBS TREND ANTHOL 20. PAGE 77 H1549 AFR ECO/UNDEV ADJUST CULTURE

S56
GORDON L.,"THE ORGANIZATION FOR EUROPEAN ECONOMIC COOPERATION." EUR+WWI INDUS INT/ORG NAT/G CONSULT DELIB/GP ACT/RES CREATE PLAN TEC/DEV EDU/PROP LEGIT WEALTH OEEC 20. PAGE 59 H1178 VOL/ASSN ECO/DEV

B57
CENTRAL ASIAN RESEARCH CENTRE,BIBLIOGRAPHY OF RECENT SOVIET SOURCE MATERIAL ON SOVIET CENTRAL ASIA AND THE BORDERLANDS. AFGHANISTN INDIA PAKISTAN UAR USSR ECO/UNDEV AGRI EXTR/IND INDUS ACADEM ADMIN ...HEAL HUM LING CON/ANAL 20. PAGE 28 H0567 BIBLIOG/A COM CULTURE NAT/G

B57
IKE N.,JAPANESE POLITICS. INTELL STRUCT AGRI INDUS FAM KIN LABOR PRESS CHOOSE ATTIT...DECISION BIBLIOG 19/20 CHINJAP. PAGE 76 H1523 NAT/G ADMIN POL/PAR CULTURE

B57
LOUCKS W.N.,COMPARATIVE ECONOMIC SYSTEMS (5TH ED.). COM UK USSR INDUS POL/PAR PLAN CAP/ISM TOTALISM MARXISM...PHIL/SCI BIBLIOG 19/20. PAGE 99 H1969 NAT/COMP IDEA/COMP SOCISM

B57
PALACIOS A.L.,PETROLEO, MONOPOLIOS, Y LATIFUNDIOS. L/A+17C EXTR/IND NAT/G TEC/DEV ECO/TAC CONTROL PRODUC 20 ARGEN MONOPOLY RESOURCE/N. PAGE 123 H2448 ECO/UNDEV NAT/LISM INDUS AGRI

S57
LEWIS E.G.,"PARLIAMENTARY CONTROL OF NATIONALIZED INDUSTRY IN FRANCE." FRANCE NAT/G DELIB/GP ACT/RES PLAN PROB/SOLV ECO/TAC DOMIN CENTRAL. PAGE 96 H1914 PWR LEGIS INDUS CONTROL

B58
ARON R.,SOCIOLOGIE DES SOCIETES INDUSTRIELLES: ESQUISSE D'UNE THEORIE DES REGIMES POLITIQUES. FRANCE SOCIETY NAT/G PROB/SOLV ATTIT RIGID/FLEX MARXISM POPULISM...POLICY SOC T 20 MARX/KARL TOCQUEVILL. PAGE 8 H0170 TOTALISM INDUS CONSTN GOV/COMP

B58
AVRAMOVIC D.,POSTWAR GROWTH IN INTERNATIONAL INDEBTEDNESS. WOR+45 AGRI INDUS CAP/ISM PRICE INCOME...NAT/COMP 20 GOLD/STAND SILVER. PAGE 9 H0184 INT/TRADE FINAN COST BAL/PAY

B58
CUNNINGHAM W.B.,COMPULSORY CONCILIATION AND COLLECTIVE BARGAINING. CANADA NAT/G LEGIS ADJUD CT/SYS GP/REL...MGT 20 NEW/BRUNS STRIKE CASEBOOK. PAGE 36 H0722 POLICY BARGAIN LABOR INDUS

B58
GURVITCH G.,TRAITE DE SOCIOLOGIE (2 VOLS.). FRANCE CULTURE INDUS GP/REL INGP/REL...PSY BIBLIOG 20. PAGE 63 H1256 ANTHOL SOC METH/COMP METH/CNCPT

B58
HANCE W.A.,AFRICAN ECONOMIC DEVELOPMENT. AGRI DIST/IND INDUS R+D ACT/RES PLAN CAP/ISM FOR/AID ...GOV/COMP BIBLIOG 20. PAGE 65 H1312 AFR ECO/UNDEV PROB/SOLV TEC/DEV

B58
MCIVOR R.C.,CANADIAN MONETARY, BANKING, AND FISCAL DEVELOPMENT. CANADA INDUS LG/CO NAT/G SML/CO CONTROL WAR...GEN/LAWS BIBLIOG 17/20. PAGE 107 H2137 ECO/TAC FINAN ECO/DEV WEALTH

B58
WOODS H.D.,PATTERNS OF INDUSTRIAL DISPUTE SETTLEMENT IN FIVE CANADIAN INDUSTRIES. CANADA USA+45 CONSULT ADJUD GP/REL...JURID GOV/COMP METH/COMP ANTHOL 20. PAGE 170 H3408 BARGAIN INDUS LABOR NAT/G

S58
ELKIN A.B.,"OEEC-ITS STRUCTURE AND POWERS." EUR+WWI CONSTN INDUS INT/ORG NAT/G VOL/ASSN DELIB/GP ACT/RES PLAN ORD/FREE WEALTH...CHARTS ORG/CHARTS OEEC 20. PAGE 45 H0907 ECO/DEV EX/STRUC

S58
LOCKWOOD W.W.,"THE SOCIALISTIC SOCIETY: INDIA AND JAPAN." INDIA ECO/DEV ECO/UNDEV INDUS NAT/G CONTROL LEAD PRODUC WEALTH 20 CHINJAP. PAGE 98 H1948 ECO/TAC NAT/COMP FINAN SOCISM

C58
BLANCHARD W.,"THAILAND." THAILAND CULTURE AGRI FINAN INDUS FAM LABOR INT/TRADE ATTIT...GEOG HEAL SOC BIBLIOG 20. PAGE 18 H0354 NAT/G DIPLOM ECO/UNDEV S/ASIA

B59
BRIGGS A.,CHARTIST STUDIES. UK LAW NAT/G WORKER EDU/PROP COERCE SUFF GP/REL ATTIT...ANTHOL 19. PAGE 21 H0416 INDUS STRATA LABOR POLICY

B59
CARPENTER G.W.,THE WAY IN AFRICA. AFR INDUS MUNIC DIPLOM DOMIN EDU/PROP COERCE DISCRIM NAT/LISM ORD/FREE 20 NEGRO CHRISTIAN. PAGE 27 H0535 CULTURE SECT ECO/UNDEV COLONIAL

B59
EPSTEIN F.T.,EAST GERMANY: A SELECTED BIBLIOGRAPHY (PAMPHLET). COM GERMANY/E LAW AGRI FINAN INDUS LABOR POL/PAR EDU/PROP ADMIN AGE/Y 20. PAGE 47 H0932 BIBLIOG/A INTELL MARXISM NAT/G

B59
GUDIN E.,INFLACAO (2ND ED.). INDUS NAT/G PLAN ECO/TAC CONTROL COST 20. PAGE 62 H1243 ECO/UNDEV INT/TRADE BAL/PAY FINAN

B59
HENDERSON G.P.,REFERENCE MANUAL OF DIRECTORIES (16 VOLS.). MUNIC PROVS GOV/REL 20. PAGE 70 H1394 BIBLIOG/A NAT/COMP NAT/G INDUS

B59
JENKINS C.,POWER AT THE TOP: A CRITICAL SURVEY OF THE NATIONALIZED INDUSTRIES. UK POL/PAR CONTROL ...WELF/ST CHARTS 20 LABOR/PAR. PAGE 80 H1601 NAT/G OWN INDUS NEW/LIB

B59
KELF-COHEN R.,NATIONALISATION IN BRITAIN: THE END OF DOGMA. EUR+WWI UK NAT/G POL/PAR WORKER ECO/TAC PARL/PROC WEALTH SOCISM...GOV/COMP 20. PAGE 84 H1683 NEW/LIB ECO/DEV INDUS OWN

B59
KITTLER G.D.,EQUATORIAL AFRICA: THE NEW WORLD OF TOMORROW. CENTRL/AFR INDUS KIN SECT CHIEF EDU/PROP CHOOSE HEALTH...GEOG WORSHIP 20. PAGE 87 H1730 RACE/REL AFR ECO/UNDEV CULTURE

B59
LANDAUER C.,EUROPEAN SOCIALISM (2 VOLS.). COM SOCISM

EUR+WWI MOD/EUR INTELL INDUS REV WAR...MAJORIT IDEA/COMP BIBLIOG 19/20 HITLER/A. PAGE 90 H1805
NAT/COMP LABOR MARXISM

B59

LIPSET S.M.,SOCIAL MOBILITY IN INDUSTRIAL SOCIETY. EUR+WWI USA+45 USSR STRUCT INDUS WRITING GP/REL INGP/REL DRIVE...SOC CHARTS NAT/COMP SOC/INTEG 20 MARX/KARL ENGELS/F. PAGE 97 H1940
STRATA ECO/DEV SOCIETY

B59

MEYER A.J.,MIDDLE EASTERN CAPITALISM: NINE ESSAYS. ISLAM CULTURE ECO/UNDEV INDUS MARKET NAT/G PLAN ATTIT RIGID/FLEX...STAT OBS TREND GEN/LAWS. PAGE 109 H2188
TEC/DEV ECO/TAC ANTHOL

B59

STERNBERG F.,THE MILITARY AND INDUSTRIAL REVOLUTION OF OUR TIME. USA+45 USSR WOR+45 WORKER COMPUTER PLAN TEC/DEV NUC/PWR GP/REL...POLICY NAT/COMP 20. PAGE 149 H2981
DIPLOM FORCES INDUS CIVMIL/REL

B59

VERNEY D.V.,PUBLIC ENTERPRISE IN SWEDEN. FUT SWEDEN UK INDUS POL/PAR LEGIS PROB/SOLV CAP/ISM INT/TRADE CONTROL SOCISM...MGT CONCPT NAT/COMP 20 SOCDEM/PAR CIVIL/SERV. PAGE 162 H3246
ECO/DEV POLICY LG/CO NAT/G

B59

WRAITH R.E.,EAST AFRICAN CITIZEN. AFR GHANA UK AGRI INDUS LOC/G POL/PAR PROB/SOLV CONTROL REGION REPRESENT NAT/LISM PWR...OBS 20 AFRICA/E AFRICA/W. PAGE 171 H3415
ECO/UNDEV RACE/REL NAT/G NAT/COMP

L59

MURPHY J.C.,"SOME IMPLICATIONS OF EUROPE'S COMMON MARKET. IN (COOK P. ECONOMIC DEVELOPMENT AND INTERNATIONAL TRADE.," EUR+WWI ECO/DEV DIST/IND INDUS NAT/G PLAN ECO/TAC INT/TRADE WEALTH...STAT TREND OEEC TOT/POP 20 EEC. PAGE 115 H2298
MARKET INT/ORG REGION

S59

PLAZA G.,"FOR A REGIONAL MARKET IN LATIN AMERICA." FUT L/A+17C CULTURE INDUS NAT/G ECO/TAC INT/TRADE ATTIT WEALTH...NEW/IDEA TREND OAS 20. PAGE 126 H2527
MARKET INT/ORG REGION

S59

ZAUBERMAN A.,"SOVIET BLOC ECONOMIC INTEGRATION." COM CULTURE INTELL ECO/DEV INDUS TOP/EX ACT/RES PLAN ECO/TAC INT/TRADE ROUTINE CHOOSE ATTIT ...TIME/SEQ 20. PAGE 172 H3452
MARKET INT/ORG USSR TOTALISM

B60

BHAMBHRI C.P.,PARLIAMENTARY CONTROL OVER STATE ENTERPRISE IN INDIA. INDIA DELIB/GP ADMIN CONTROL INGP/REL EFFICIENCY 20 PARLIAMENT. PAGE 16 H0327
NAT/G OWN INDUS PARL/PROC

B60

COUGHLIN R.,DOUBLE IDENTITY: THE CHINESE AND MODERN THAILAND. CHINA/COM S/ASIA THAILAND ECO/UNDEV EXTR/IND FINAN INDUS KIN MUNIC NAT/G PROF/ORG SCHOOL SECT ATTIT DRIVE...CONCPT OBS 20. PAGE 34 H0676
ASIA FAM CULTURE

B60

EASTON S.C.,THE TWILIGHT OF EUROPEAN COLONIALISM. AFR S/ASIA CONSTN SOCIETY STRUCT ECO/UNDEV INDUS NAT/G FORCES ECO/TAC COLONIAL CT/SYS ATTIT KNOWL ORD/FREE PWR...SOCIALIST TIME/SEQ TREND CON/ANAL 20. PAGE 44 H0882
FINAN ADMIN

B60

HALBWACHS M.,POPULATION AND SOCIETY: INTRODUCTION TO SOCIAL MORPHOLOGY (TRANS. BY DUNCAN AND PFAUTZ). CULTURE SOCIETY AGRI INDUS HABITAT...CONCPT 20. PAGE 64 H1281
BIO/SOC GEOG NEIGH GP/COMP

B60

KERR C.,INDUSTRIALISM AND INDUSTRIAL MAN. CULTURE SOCIETY ECO/UNDEV NAT/G ADMIN PRODUC WEALTH ...PREDICT TREND NAT/COMP 19/20. PAGE 85 H1697
WORKER MGT ECO/DEV INDUS

B60

LISTER L.,EUROPE'S COAL AND STEEL COMMUNITY. FRANCE GERMANY STRUCT ECO/DEV EXTR/IND INDUS MARKET NAT/G DELIB/GP ECO/TAC INT/TRADE EDU/PROP ATTIT RIGID/FLEX ORD/FREE PWR WEALTH...CONCPT STAT TIME/SEQ CHARTS ECSC 20. PAGE 97 H1941
EUR+WWI INT/ORG REGION

B60

MOORE W.E.,LABOR COMMITMENT AND SOCIAL CHANGE IN DEVELOPING AREAS. SOCIETY STRATA ECO/UNDEV MARKET VOL/ASSN WORKER AUTHORIT SKILL...MGT NAT/COMP SOC/INTEG 20. PAGE 113 H2250
LABOR ORD/FREE ATTIT INDUS

B60

NEALE A.D.,THE FLOW OF RESOURCES FROM RICH TO POOR. WOR+45 ECO/DEV ECO/UNDEV FINAN INDUS NAT/G PLAN EFFICIENCY WEALTH...POLICY NAT/COMP 20 RESOURCE/N. PAGE 116 H2325
FOR/AID DIPLOM METH/CNCPT

B60

PIERCE R.A.,RUSSIAN CENTRAL ASIA, 1867-1917. ASIA RUSSIA CULTURE AGRI INDUS EDU/PROP REV NAT/LISM ...CHARTS BIBLIOG 19/20 BOLSHEVISM INTERVENT. PAGE 125 H2509
COLONIAL DOMIN ADMIN ECO/UNDEV

B60

ROBERTSON D.,THE CONTROL OF INDUSTRY. UK MARKET LABOR WORKER PRICE CONTROL GP/REL COST DEMAND ORD/FREE WEALTH NEW/LIB SOCISM 20. PAGE 132 H2646
INDUS FINAN NAT/G ECO/DEV

B60

ROBINSON E.A.G.,ECONOMIC CONSEQUENCES OF THE SIZE OF NATIONS. AGRI INDUS DELIB/GP FOR/AID ADMIN EFFICIENCY...METH/COMP 20. PAGE 132 H2649
CONCPT INT/ORG NAT/COMP

B60

SHIRER W.L.,THE RISE AND FALL OF THE THIRD REICH: A HISTORY OF NAZI GERMANY. EUR+WWI CULTURE ECO/DEV INDUS NAT/G POL/PAR FORCES PLAN TEC/DEV ECO/TAC COERCE ATTIT DRIVE PERSON PWR...MYSTIC PSY SOC MYTH STAT CHARTS EXHIBIT WORK VAL/FREE. PAGE 143 H2864
STRUCT GERMANY TOTALISM

B60

SLOTKIN J.S.,FROM FIELD TO FACTORY; NEW INDUSTRIAL EMPLOYEES. HABITAT...MGT NEW/IDEA NAT/COMP BIBLIOG SOC/INTEG 20. PAGE 145 H2901
INDUS LABOR CULTURE WORKER

B60

SZTARAY Z.,BIBLIOGRAPHY ON HUNGARY. HUNGARY MOD/EUR CULTURE INDUS SECT DIPLOM REV...ART/METH SOC LING 18/20. PAGE 151 H3029
BIBLIOG NAT/G COM MARXISM

B60

THE ECONOMIST (LONDON),THE COMMONWEALTH AND EUROPE. EUR+WWI WOR+45 AGRI FINAN INCOME...STAT CENSUS CHARTS CMN/WLTH EEC. PAGE 153 H3067
INT/TRADE INDUS INT/ORG NAT/COMP

B60

WEINER H.E.,BRITISH LABOR AND PUBLIC OWNERSHIP. UK SERV/IND LG/CO WORKER CONTROL OWN 20. PAGE 166 H3327
LABOR NAT/G INDUS ATTIT

B60

WORLEY P.,ASIA TODAY (REV. ED.) (PAMPHLET). COM ECO/UNDEV AGRI FINAN INDUS POL/PAR FOR/AID ADMIN MARXISM 20. PAGE 170 H3411
BIBLIOG/A ASIA DIPLOM NAT/G

S60

"THE EMERGING COMMON MARKETS IN LATIN AMERICA." FUT L/A+17C STRATA DIST/IND INDUS LABOR NAT/G LEGIS ECO/TAC ADMIN RIGID/FLEX HEALTH...NEW/IDEA TIME/SEQ OAS 20. PAGE 2 H0038
FINAN ECO/UNDEV INT/TRADE

S60

BERG E.J.,"ECONOMIC BASIS OF POLITICAL CHOICE IN FRENCH WEST AFRICA." FRANCE ECO/UNDEV AGRI INDUS NAT/G PLAN LEGIT COLONIAL REGION ATTIT PWR WEALTH ...CONCPT 20. PAGE 15 H0299
AFR ECO/TAC

C60

HAZARD J.N.,"THE SOVIET SYSTEM OF GOVERNMENT." USSR SOCIETY INDUS NAT/G POL/PAR DIPLOM CT/SYS...JURID CHARTS BIBLIOG/A 20. PAGE 69 H1373
COM NAT/COMP STRUCT ADMIN

B61

DELEFORTRIE-SOU N.,LES DIRIGEANTS DE L'INDUSTRIE FRANCAISE. FRANCE CULTURE ELITES PROB/SOLV ...DECISION STAT CHARTS 20. PAGE 39 H0789
INDUS STRATA TOP/EX LEAD

B61

ESTEBAN J.C.,IMPERIALISMO Y DESARROLLO ECONOMICO. L/A+17C FINAN INDUS NAT/G ECO/TAC CONTROL ROLE. PAGE 47 H0941
ECO/UNDEV NAT/LISM DIPLOM BAL/PAY

B61

GOULD S.H.,SCIENCES IN COMMUNIST CHINA. CHINA/COM FUT INDUS NAT/G TOTALISM...RECORD TOT/POP 20. PAGE 59 H1187
ASIA TEC/DEV

B61

HAUSER M.,DIE URSACHEN DER FRANZOSISCHEN INFLATION IN DEN JAHREN 1946-1952. FRANCE INDUS NAT/G BUDGET DIPLOM ECO/TAC FOR/AID COST MONEY 20 GOLD/STAND. PAGE 68 H1357
ECO/DEV FINAN PRICE

B61

HEMPSTONE S.,THE NEW AFRICA. AGRI INDUS KIN NAT/G COLONIAL MARXISM...SOC INT TREND NAT/COMP BIBLIOG/A 20. PAGE 69 H1392
AFR ORD/FREE PERSON CULTURE

B61

HICKS U.K.,DEVELOPMENT FROM BELOW. UK INDUS ADMIN COLONIAL ROUTINE GOV/REL...POLICY METH/CNCPT CHARTS 19/20 CMN/WLTH. PAGE 71 H1414
ECO/UNDEV LOC/G GOV/COMP METH/COMP

B61

LAHAYE R.,LES ENTREPRISES PUBLIQUES AU MAROC. FRANCE MOROCCO LAW DIST/IND EXTR/IND FINAN CONSULT PLAN TEC/DEV ADMIN AGREE CONTROL OWN...POLICY 20. PAGE 90 H1796
NAT/G INDUS ECO/UNDEV ECO/TAC

B61

LUZ N.V.,A LUTA PELA INDUSTRIALIZACAO DO BRAZIL. BRAZIL L/A+17C AGRI NAT/G TEC/DEV COLONIAL 19/20. PAGE 99 H1981
ECO/UNDEV INDUS NAT/LISM POLICY

B61

MARX K.,THE COMMUNIST MANIFESTO. IN (MENDEL A. ESSENTIAL WORKS OF MARXISM, NEW YORK: BANTAM. FUT MOD/EUR CULTURE ECO/DEV ECO/UNDEV AGRI FINAN INDUS MARKET PROC/MFG LABOR MUNIC POL/PAR CONSULT FORCES CREATE PLAN ADMIN ATTIT DRIVE RIGID/FLEX ORD/FREE
COM NEW/IDEA CAP/ISM REV

PWR RESPECT MARX/KARL WORK. PAGE 104 H2081

B61
MIT CENTER INTERNATIONAL STU,OFFICIAL SERIAL PUBLICATIONS RELATING TO ECONOMIC DEVELOPMENT IN AFRICA SOUTH OF THE SAHARA. AFR SOCIETY AGRI FINAN INDUS LG/CO ADMIN 20. PAGE 111 H2228 BIBLIOG ECO/UNDEV ECO/TAC NAT/G

B61
SHARMA T.R.,THE WORKING OF STATE ENTERPRISES IN INDIA. INDIA DELIB/GP LEGIS WORKER BUDGET PRICE CONTROL GP/REL OWN ATTIT...MGT CHARTS 20. PAGE 142 H2851 NAT/G INDUS ADMIN SOCISM

B61
SPOONER F.P.,SOUTH AFRICAN PREDICAMENT. FUT SOUTH/AFR INDUS POL/PAR RACE/REL INCOME...CHARTS 20 NEGRO. PAGE 148 H2953 ECO/DEV DISCRIM ECO/TAC POLICY

B61
STARK H.,SOCIAL AND ECONOMIC FRONTIERS IN LATIN AMERICA (2ND ED.). CUBA FUT CULTURE AGRI INDUS ECO/TAC PRODUC ATTIT MARXISM...NAT/COMP BIBLIOG T 20. PAGE 149 H2971 L/A+17C SOCIETY DIPLOM ECO/UNDEV

S61
PADELFORD N.J.,"POLITICS AND THE FUTURE OF ECOSOC." AFR S/ASIA ECO/UNDEV INDUS NAT/G DELIB/GP ACT/RES ORD/FREE WEALTH...CONCPT CHARTS UN 20 ECOSOC. PAGE 122 H2438 INT/ORG TEC/DEV

S61
VALLET R.,"IRAN: KEY TO THE MIDDLE EAST." COM IRAQ ISLAM KUWAIT LEBANON SAUDI/ARAB TURKEY ELITES SOCIETY INDUS PROC/MFG POL/PAR TOP/EX PLAN BAL/PWR DIPLOM ECO/TAC ALL/VALS...TREND CENTO 20. PAGE 161 H3224 NAT/G ECO/UNDEV IRAN

B62
CARY J.,THE CASE FOR AFRICAN FREEDOM AND OTHER WRITINGS ON AFRICA. AFR UK INDUS LOC/G NAT/G SECT INT/TRADE EDU/PROP GOV/REL RACE/REL ORD/FREE ...CONCPT ANTHOL 19/20. PAGE 27 H0552 NAT/LISM COLONIAL TREND ECO/UNDEV

B62
FATOUROS A.A.,GOVERNMENT GUARANTEES TO FOREIGN INVESTORS. WOR+45 ECO/UNDEV INDUS WORKER ADJUD ...NAT/COMP BIBLIOG TREATY. PAGE 49 H0975 NAT/G FINAN INT/TRADE ECO/DEV

B62
GALENSON W.,LABOR IN DEVELOPING COUNTRIES. BRAZIL INDONESIA ISRAEL PAKISTAN TURKEY AGRI INDUS WORKER PAY PRICE GP/REL WEALTH...MGT CHARTS METH/COMP NAT/COMP 20. PAGE 54 H1088 LABOR ECO/UNDEV BARGAIN POL/PAR

B62
GROVE J.W.,GOVERNMENT AND INDUSTRY IN BRITAIN. UK FINAN LOC/G CONSULT DELIB/GP INT/TRADE ADMIN CONTROL...BIBLIOG 20. PAGE 62 H1237 ECO/TAC INDUS NAT/G GP/REL

B62
HANSON A.H.,MANAGERIAL PROBLEMS IN PUBLIC ENTERPRISE. INDIA DELIB/GP GP/REL INGP/REL EFFICIENCY 20 PARLIAMENT. PAGE 66 H1320 MGT NAT/G INDUS PROB/SOLV

B62
HUCKER C.O.,CHINA: A CRITICAL BIBLIOGRAPHY (PAMPHLET). ASIA STRUCT AGRI FINAN INDUS HABITAT MARXISM...EPIST HUM. PAGE 74 H1487 BIBLIOG/A CULTURE INTELL SOCIETY

B62
HUNTER G.,THE NEW SOCIETIES OF TROPICAL AFRICA. CULTURE INDUS KIN MUNIC WORKER INT/TRADE EDU/PROP ORD/FREE...INT TREND 20. PAGE 75 H1500 AFR GOV/COMP ECO/UNDEV SOCIETY

B62
PAIKERT G.C.,THE GERMAN EXODUS. EUR+WWI GERMANY/W LAW CULTURE SOCIETY STRUCT INDUS NAT/LISM RESPECT SOVEREIGN...CHARTS BIBLIOG SOC/INTEG 20 MIGRATION. PAGE 122 H2444 INGP/REL STRANGE GEOG GP/REL

B62
PASTOR R.S.,A STATEMENT OF THE LAWS OF PARAGUAY IN MATTERS AFFECTING BUSINESS (2ND ED.). PARAGUAY INDUS FAM LABOR LG/CO NAT/G LEGIS TAX CONTROL MARRIAGE 20. PAGE 124 H2474 FINAN ECO/UNDEV LAW CONSTN

B62
SILBERMAN B.S.,JAPAN AND KOREA; A CRITICAL BIBLIOGRAPHY. KOREA LAW STRATA STRUCT AGRI INDUS NAT/G POL/PAR SECT...HUM LING IDEA/COMP 5/20 CHINJAP. PAGE 144 H2872 BIBLIOG/A CULTURE S/ASIA

B62
TAYLOR D.,THE BRITISH IN AFRICA. UK CULTURE ECO/UNDEV INDUS DIPLOM INT/TRADE ADMIN WAR RACE/REL ORD/FREE SOVEREIGN...POLICY BIBLIOG 15/20 CMN/WLTH. PAGE 153 H3053 AFR COLONIAL DOMIN

B62
WHITING K.R.,THE SOVIET UNION TODAY: A CONCISE HANDBOOK. USSR ELITES AGRI INDUS POL/PAR FORCES DIPLOM EDU/PROP LEAD...GEOG TREND 19/20. PAGE 168 H3354 NAT/G ATTIT MARXISM POLICY

B62
WOODS H.D.,LABOUR POLICY AND LABOUR ECONOMICS IN CANADA. CANADA FUT NAT/G VOL/ASSN WORKER BARGAIN ECO/TAC PAY CONFER GP/REL 20. PAGE 170 H3409 LABOR POLICY INDUS

ECO/DEV

C62
BACON F.,"OF SEDITIONS AND TROUBLES" (1625) IN F. BACON, ESSAYS." INDUS MARKET CHIEF ECO/TAC EDU/PROP CONTROL LEAD PEACE WEALTH 17 MACHIAVELL. PAGE 9 H0191 REV ORD/FREE NAT/G GEN/LAWS

B63
BRITISH AID. UK AGRI DIST/IND INDUS SCHOOL TEC/DEV INT/TRADE COLONIAL DEMAND...TREND CHARTS 20. PAGE 2 H0041 FOR/AID ECO/UNDEV NAT/G FINAN

B63
BERGSON A.,ECONOMIC TRENDS IN THE SOVIET UNION. USSR ECO/UNDEV AGRI NAT/G FORCES PLAN TEC/DEV INT/TRADE BAL/PAY...POLICY ANTHOL 20. PAGE 15 H0302 ECO/DEV NAT/COMP INDUS LABOR

B63
DE VRIES E.,SOCIAL ASPECTS OF ECONOMIC DEVELOPMENT IN LATIN AMERICA. CULTURE SOCIETY STRATA FINAN INDUS INT/ORG DELIB/GP ACT/RES ECO/TAC EDU/PROP ADMIN ATTIT SUPEGO HEALTH KNOWL ORD/FREE...SOC STAT TREND ANTHOL TOT/POP VAL/FREE. PAGE 39 H0777 L/A+17C ECO/UNDEV

B63
ELWIN V.,A NEW DEAL FOR TRIBAL INDIA. INDIA AGRI COM/IND INDUS KIN TEC/DEV TAX EDU/PROP OWN HEALTH 20. PAGE 46 H0912 ECO/UNDEV CULTURE CONSTN SOC/WK

B63
FURTADO C.,THE ECONOMIC GROWTH OF BRAZIL: A SURVEY FROM COLONIAL TO MODERN TIMES. L/A+17C AGRI DIST/IND EXTR/IND INDUS WORKER COLONIAL RACE/REL OWN GOV/COMP. PAGE 54 H1082 ECO/UNDEV TEC/DEV LABOR DOMIN

B63
GLADE W.P. JR.,THE POLITICAL ECONOMY OF MEXICO. FUT L/A+17C CULTURE SOCIETY AGRI INDUS DELIB/GP ACT/RES ECO/TAC ATTIT HEALTH ORD/FREE...STAT TIME/SEQ TREND MEXIC/AMER TOT/POP VAL/FREE 20. PAGE 57 H1138 FINAN ECO/UNDEV

B63
GORDON M.S.,THE ECONOMICS OF WELFARE POLICIES. INDUS LOC/G NAT/G LEGIS WORKER INCOME AGE/O SKILL WEALTH...METH/COMP NAT/COMP 20. PAGE 59 H1180 METH/CNCPT ECO/TAC POLICY

B63
GRIMOND J.,THE LIBERAL CHALLENGE. UK SOCIETY INDUS POL/PAR LEGIS PLAN CAP/ISM DIPLOM EDU/PROP GOV/REL CONSERVE 20 PARLIAMENT REFORMERS. PAGE 61 H1227 NAT/G NEW/LIB ECO/DEV POLICY

B63
HAQ M.,THE STRATEGY OF ECONOMIC PLANNING. PAKISTAN AGRI FINAN INDUS NAT/G FOR/AID TAX CONTROL REGION PRODUC...POLICY CHARTS 20. PAGE 66 H1324 ECO/TAC ECO/UNDEV PLAN PROB/SOLV

B63
ISSAWI C.,EGYPT IN REVOLUTION: AN ECONOMIC ANALYSIS. ISLAM STRUCT ECO/UNDEV AGRI FINAN INDUS PLAN EXEC REV NAT/LISM ATTIT RIGID/FLEX WEALTH SOCISM...STAT WORK 20. PAGE 79 H1573 NAT/G UAR

B63
KATEB G.,UTOPIA AND ITS ENEMIES. CULTURE STRATA ECO/DEV INDUS REV MORAL...PSY IDEA/COMP 19/20. PAGE 84 H1668 UTOPIA SOCIETY PHIL/SCI PEACE

B63
MARX K.,THE POVERTY OF PHILOSOPHY (1847). SOCIETY STRATA INDUS WORKER OWN UTOPIA SOCISM...GEN/LAWS MARX/KARL. PAGE 104 H2082 MARXIST PRODUC

B63
PAUW B.A.,THE SECOND GENERATION. SOUTH/AFR INDUS FAM LABOR SECT EDU/PROP MARRIAGE ATTIT...SOC 20. PAGE 124 H2478 KIN CULTURE STRUCT SOCIETY

B63
SHANKS M.,THE LESSONS OF PUBLIC ENTERPRISE. UK LEGIS WORKER ECO/TAC ADMIN PARL/PROC GOV/REL ATTIT ...POLICY MGT METH/COMP NAT/COMP ANTHOL 20 PARLIAMENT. PAGE 142 H2840 SOCISM OWN NAT/G INDUS

B63
STEVENS G.G.,EGYPT YESTERDAY AND TODAY. CONSTN ECO/UNDEV AGRI INDUS NAT/G POL/PAR FORCES ECO/TAC EDU/PROP COERCE WAR NAT/LISM DRIVE ALL/VALS ...TIME/SEQ WORK SUEZ 20. PAGE 149 H2983 ISLAM TOP/EX REV UAR

B63
STUCKI C.W.,AMERICAN DOCTORAL DISSERTATIONS ON ASIA 1933-62 (A PAPER). PREHIST INDUS NAT/G GOV/REL ALL/IDEOS...ART/METH GEOG SOC LING 20. PAGE 150 H3002 BIBLIOG ASIA SOCIETY S/ASIA

B63
THORBURN H.G.,PARTY POLITICS IN CANADA. CANADA ELITES STRUCT INDUS PWR 20. PAGE 154 H3086 POL/PAR CONCPT NAT/G PROVS

B63
UAR MINISTRY OF CULTURE,A BIBLIOGRAPHICAL LIST OF ARABIAN PENINSULA. ISLAM SAUDI/ARAB YEMEN FINAN NAT/G DIPLOM 19/20. PAGE 157 H3147 BIBLIOG GEOG INDUS SECT

S63

HOSKINS H.L.,"ARAB SOCIALISM IN THE UAR." ISLAM USSR AGRI INDUS NAT/G TOP/EX CREATE DIPLOM EDU/PROP DRIVE KNOWL PWR SOCISM...POLICY CONCPT TREND SUEZ 20. PAGE 74 H1478
ECO/DEV PLAN UAR

B64

BALOGH T.,THE ECONOMIC IMPACT OF MONETARY AND COMMERCIAL INSTITUTIONS OF A EUROPEAN ORIGIN IN AFRICA. AFR UAR INDUS FOR/AID COLONIAL CONTROL ...NAT/COMP 20. PAGE 10 H0205
TEC/DEV FINAN ECO/UNDEV ECO/TAC

B64

BEARDSLEY R.K.,STUDIES ON ECONOMIC LIFE IN JAPAN (OCCASIONAL PAPERS NO. 8). INDUS FAM HABITAT...GEOG GOV/COMP 20 CHINJAP. PAGE 12 H0249
WEALTH PRESS PRODUC INCOME

B64

BRIGHT J.R.,RESEARCH, DEVELOPMENT AND TECHNOLOGICAL INNOVATION. CULTURE R+D CREATE PLAN PROB/SOLV AUTOMAT RISK PERSON...DECISION CONCPT PREDICT BIBLIOG. PAGE 21 H0419
TEC/DEV NEW/IDEA INDUS MGT

B64

COLLINS B.E.,A SOCIAL PSYCHOLOGY OF GROUP PROCESSES FOR DECISION-MAKING. PROB/SOLV ROUTINE...SOC CHARTS HYPO/EXP. PAGE 32 H0632
FACE/GP DECISION NAT/G INDUS

B64

COWAN L.G.,THE DILEMMAS OF AFRICAN INDEPENDENCE. AFR INDUS NAT/G SECT DIPLOM ECO/TAC REGION MARXISM ...CHARTS BIBLIOG 20 MAPS. PAGE 34 H0683
ORD/FREE COLONIAL REV ECO/UNDEV

B64

FLORENCE P.S.,ECONOMICS AND SOCIOLOGY OF INDUSTRY; A REALISTIC ANALYSIS OF DEVELOPMENT. ECO/UNDEV LG/CO NAT/G PLAN...GEOG MGT BIBLIOG 20. PAGE 51 H1029
INDUS SOC ADMIN

B64

GESELLSCHAFT RECHTSVERGLEICH,BIBLIOGRAPHIE DES DEUTSCHEN RECHTS (BIBLIOGRAPHY OF GERMAN LAW, TRANS. BY COURTLAND PETERSON). GERMANY FINAN INDUS LABOR SECT FORCES CT/SYS PARL/PROC CRIME...INT/LAW SOC NAT/COMP 20. PAGE 56 H1117
BIBLIOG/A JURID CONSTN ADMIN

B64

GILLY A.,INSIDE THE CUBAN REVOLUTION. CUBA AGRI INDUS LABOR CREATE DIPLOM...METH/COMP 20. PAGE 56 H1129
REV PLAN MARXISM ECO/UNDEV

B64

HAZLEWOOD A.,THE ECONOMICS OF DEVELOPMENT: AN ANNOTATED LIST OF BOOKS AND ARTICLES PUBLISHED 1958-1962. AGRI FINAN INDUS LABOR NAT/G DIPLOM INT/TRADE INCOME...MGT 20. PAGE 69 H1374
BIBLIOG/A ECO/UNDEV TEC/DEV

B64

IMAZ J.L.,LOS QUE MANDAN. INDUS LABOR NAT/G POL/PAR PROVS SECT CHIEF TOP/EX CONTROL 20 ARGEN. PAGE 76 H1524
LEAD FORCES ELITES ATTIT

B64

JOHNSON A.F.,BIBLIOGRAPHY OF GHANA: 1930-1961. GHANA LAW AGRI INDUS NAT/G INT/TRADE EDU/PROP HEALTH...GEOG AUD/VIS CHARTS 20. PAGE 81 H1618
BIBLIOG/A CULTURE SOC

B64

LI C.M.,INDUSTRIAL DEVELOPMENT IN COMMUNIST CHINA. CHINA/COM ECO/DEV ECO/UNDEV AGRI FINAN INDUS MARKET LABOR NAT/G ECO/TAC INT/TRADE EXEC ALL/VALS ...POLICY RELATIV TREND WORK TOT/POP VAL/FREE 20. PAGE 96 H1921
ASIA TEC/DEV

B64

OECD,DEVELOPMENT ASSISTANCE EFFORTS - POLICIES OF THE MEMBERS. AGRI INDUS BUDGET...GEOG NAT/COMP 20 OECD. PAGE 120 H2398
INT/ORG FOR/AID ECO/UNDEV TEC/DEV

B64

PINNICK A.W.,COUNTRY PLANNERS IN ACTION. UK FINAN SERV/IND NAT/G CONSULT DELIB/GP PRICE CONTROL ROUTINE LEISURE AGE/C...GEOG 20 URBAN/RNWL. PAGE 126 H2512
MUNIC PLAN INDUS ATTIT

B64

POWELSON J.P.,LATIN AMERICA: TODAY'S ECONOMIC AND SOCIAL REVOLUTION. L/A+17C INTELL SOCIETY STRUCT AGRI INDUS NAT/G DIPLOM ECO/TAC REV...POLICY 20. PAGE 128 H2552
ECO/UNDEV WEALTH ADJUST PLAN

B64

SOLOW R.M.,THE NATURE AND SOURCES OF UNEMPLOYMENT IN THE UNITED STATES (PAMPHLET). USA+45 INDUS LABOR TEC/DEV ECO/TAC SKILL WEALTH...TREND NAT/COMP 20. PAGE 147 H2930
ECO/DEV WORKER STAT PRODUC

B64

SZLADITS C.,BIBLIOGRAPHY ON FOREIGN AND COMPARATIVE LAW: BOOKS AND ARTICLES IN ENGLISH (SUPPLEMENT 1962). FINAN INDUS JUDGE LICENSE ADMIN CT/SYS PARL/PROC OWN...INT/LAW CLASSIF METH/COMP NAT/COMP 20. PAGE 151 H3027
BIBLIOG/A JURID ADJUD LAW

B64

THORNTON T.P.,THE THIRD WORLD IN SOVIET PERSPECTIVE: STUDIES BY SOVIET WRITERS ON THE DEVELOPING AREAS. AFR L/A+17C S/ASIA STRATA AGRI INDUS MARKET NAT/G POL/PAR ECO/TAC COLONIAL PERCEPT PWR WEALTH...MARXIST STAT CHARTS WORK MARX/KARL 20. PAGE 155 H3090
ECO/UNDEV ACT/RES USSR DIPLOM

B64

WILSON T.,POLICIES FOR REGIONAL DEVELOPMENT. CANADA UK FINAN INDUS NAT/G BUDGET TAX GIVE COST ...NAT/COMP 20. PAGE 169 H3383
REGION PLAN ECO/DEV ECO/TAC

B64

WRAITH R.,CORRUPTION IN DEVELOPING COUNTRIES. NIGERIA UK LAW ELITES STRATA INDUS LOC/G NAT/G SECT FORCES EDU/PROP ADMIN PWR WEALTH 18/20. PAGE 171 H3414
ECO/UNDEV CRIME SANCTION ATTIT

S64

CLIFFE L.,"TANGANYIKA'S TWO YEARS OF INDEPENDENCE." AFR INDUS MARKET NAT/G POL/PAR DELIB/GP CREATE ECO/TAC LEGIT DRIVE ALL/VALS...METH/CNCPT RECORD 20 TANGANYIKA. PAGE 30 H0604
ECO/UNDEV PLAN

S64

CROUZET F.,"WARS, BLOCKADE, AND ECONOMIC CHANGE IN EUROPE, 1792-1815." UK INDUS NAT/G TEC/DEV ECO/TAC WEALTH...POLICY RELATIV HIST/WRIT TIME/SEQ 18/19. PAGE 35 H0710
MOD/EUR MARKET

S64

NASH M.,"SOCIAL PREREQUISITES TO ECONOMIC GROWTH IN LATIN AMERICA AND SOUTHEAST ASIA." L/A+17C S/ASIA CULTURE SOCIETY ECO/UNDEV AGRI INDUS NAT/G PLAN TEC/DEV EDU/PROP ROUTINE ALL/VALS...POLICY RELATIV SOC NAT/COMP WORK TOT/POP 20. PAGE 116 H2314
ECO/DEV PERCEPT

S64

ZARTMAN I.W.,"LES RELATIONS ENTRE LA FRANCE ET L'ALGERIA DEPUIS LES ACCORDS D'EVIAN." EUR+WWI FUT ISLAM CULTURE AGRI EXTR/IND FINAN INDUS POL/PAR DIPLOM ECO/TAC FOR/AID PEACE ATTIT DRIVE ALL/VALS ...TIME/SEQ VAL/FREE 20. PAGE 172 H3450
ECO/UNDEV ALGERIA FRANCE

N64

KENYA MINISTRY ECO PLAN DEV,AFRICAN SOCIALISM AND ITS APPLICATION TO PLANNING IN KENYA (PAMPHLET). AFR AGRI INDUS WORKER TAX COLONIAL WEALTH 20. PAGE 85 H1691
NAT/G SOCISM PLAN ECO/UNDEV

B65

ALTON T.P.,POLISH NATIONAL INCOME AND PRODUCT IN 1954, 1955, AND 1956. POLAND FINAN EX/STRUC ECO/TAC PRICE COST WEALTH 20. PAGE 6 H0117
COM INDUS NAT/G ECO/DEV

B65

BARRY E.E.,NATIONALISATION IN BRITISH POLITICS: THE HISTORICAL BACKGROUND. UK AGRI DIST/IND EXTR/IND LABOR LG/CO ATTIT CONSERVE SOCISM 19/20 LABOR/PAR. PAGE 12 H0231
NAT/G OWN INDUS POL/PAR

B65

CHAO K.,THE RATE AND PATTERN OF INDUSTRIAL GROWTH IN COMMUNIST CHINA. CHINA/COM ECO/UNDEV TEC/DEV PRICE...NAT/COMP BIBLIOG 20. PAGE 29 H0578
INDUS INDEX STAT PRODUC

B65

COLLINS H.,KARL MARX AND THE BRITISH LABOR MOVEMENT, YEARS OF THE FIRST INTERNATIONAL. EUR+WWI MOD/EUR UK STRATA INDUS NAT/G POL/PAR SOCISM ...CONCPT 19/20 MARX/KARL. PAGE 32 H0633
MARXISM LABOR INT/ORG WORKER

B65

DUGGAR G.S.,RENEWAL OF TOWN AND VILLAGE I: A WORLD-WIDE SURVEY OF LOCAL GOVERNMENT EXPERIENCE. WOR+45 CONSTRUC INDUS CREATE BUDGET REGION GOV/REL...QU NAT/COMP 20 URBAN/RNWL. PAGE 43 H0859
MUNIC NEIGH PLAN ADMIN

B65

EDELMAN M.,THE POLITICS OF WAGE-PRICE DECISIONS. GERMANY ITALY NETHERLAND UK INDUS LABOR POL/PAR PROB/SOLV BARGAIN PRICE ROUTINE BAL/PAY COST DEMAND 20. PAGE 44 H0888
GOV/COMP CONTROL ECO/TAC PLAN

B65

FORM W.H.,INDUSTRIAL RELATIONS AND SOCIAL CHANGE IN LATIN AMERICA. L/A+17C AGRI LABOR NAT/G PLAN PROB/SOLV DIPLOM...MGT SOC ANTHOL BIBLIOG/A METH 20. PAGE 52 H1038
INDUS GP/REL NAT/COMP ECO/UNDEV

B65

GINIEWSKI P.,THE TWO FACES OF APARTHEID. AFR SOUTH/AFR STRATA AGRI INDUS COLONIAL PARTIC SOVEREIGN...CONCPT GOV/COMP NAT/COMP 19/20 NEGRO. PAGE 56 H1131
DISCRIM NAT/G RACE/REL STRUCT

B65

HAVIGHURST R.J.,SOCIETY AND EDUCATION IN BRAZIL. BRAZIL PORTUGAL ECO/UNDEV INDUS NAT/G CREATE INSPECT COLONIAL ADJUST DEMAND LITERACY...CENSUS TREND CHARTS 16/20. PAGE 68 H1362
SCHOOL ACADEM ACT/RES CULTURE

B65

HERRICK B.H.,URBAN MIGRATION AND ECONOMIC DEVELOPMENT IN CHILE. CHILE AGRI INDUS LABOR NAT/G CENTRAL PRODUC...STAT SAMP CHARTS BIBLIOG/A 20 MIGRATION. PAGE 70 H1404
HABITAT GEOG MUNIC ECO/UNDEV

B65

HONDURAS CONSEJO NAC DE ECO,PLAN NACIONAL DE DESARROLLO ECONOMICO Y SOCIAL DE HONDURAS 1965-69. HONDURAS AGRI INDUS BAL/PAY INCOME 20. PAGE 73 H1459
ECO/UNDEV NAT/G PLAN POLICY

B65
HOSELITZ B.F.,ECONOMICS AND THE IDEA OF MANKIND. UNIV ECO/DEV ECO/UNDEV DIST/IND INDUS INT/ORG NAT/G ACT/RES ECO/TAC WEALTH...CONCPT STAT. PAGE 74 H1476
CREATE INT/TRADE

B65
IANNI O.,ESTADO E CAPITALISMO. L/A+17C FINAN TEC/DEV ECO/TAC ORD/FREE WEALTH POLICY. PAGE 76 H1518
ECO/UNDEV STRUCT INDUS NAT/G

B65
INT. BANK RECONSTR. DEVELOP.,ECONOMIC DEVELOPMENT OF KUWAIT. ISLAM KUWAIT AGRI FINAN MARKET EX/STRUC TEC/DEV ECO/TAC ADMIN WEALTH...OBS CON/ANAL CHARTS 20. PAGE 77 H1541
INDUS NAT/G

B65
LAMBIRI I.,SOCIAL CHANGE IN A GREEK COUNTRY TOWN. GREECE FAM PROB/SOLV ROUTINE TASK LEISURE INGP/REL CONSEN ORD/FREE...SOC INT QU CHARTS 20. PAGE 90 H1803
INDUS WORKER CULTURE NEIGH

B65
THE STATE AND ECONOMIC ENTERPRISE IN JAPAN; ESSAYS IN THE POLITICAL ECONOMY OF GROWTH. AGRI INDUS DRIVE POPULISM...CHARTS NAT/COMP ANTHOL 19/20 CHINJAP. PAGE 98 H1949
ECO/UNDEV ECO/DEV CAP/ISM ECO/TAC

B65
MEIER R.L.,DEVELOPMENTAL PLANNING. PUERT/RICO INDUS PUB/INST SCHOOL CREATE ECO/TAC FOR/AID...NAT/COMP 20. PAGE 108 H2165
PLAN ECO/UNDEV GOV/COMP TEC/DEV

B65
MOORE W.E.,THE IMPACT OF INDUSTRY. CULTURE STRUCT ORD/FREE...TREND 20. PAGE 113 H2251
INDUS MGT TEC/DEV ECO/UNDEV

B65
OBUKAR C.,THE MODERN AFRICAN. AGRI INDUS WORKER CAP/ISM EDU/PROP PARTIC RACE/REL NAT/LISM ALL/VALS MARXISM...SOC IDEA/COMP 20. PAGE 120 H2393
AFR ECO/UNDEV CULTURE SOVEREIGN

B65
ONSLOW C.,ASIAN ECONOMIC DEVELOPMENT. BURMA CEYLON INDIA MALAYSIA PAKISTAN S/ASIA AGRI INDUS MARKET PROB/SOLV CAP/ISM FOR/AID INT/TRADE DEMAND WEALTH ...POLICY ANTHOL 20. PAGE 121 H2418
ECO/UNDEV ECO/TAC PLAN NAT/G

B65
ORGANSKI A.F.K.,THE STAGES OF POLITICAL DEVELOPMENT. STRATA AGRI INDUS NAT/G POL/PAR COLONIAL PWR WEALTH...CLASSIF TIME/SEQ. PAGE 121 H2428
ECO/DEV ECO/UNDEV GEN/LAWS CREATE

B65
RANDALL F.B.,STALIN'S RUSSIA. USSR STRUCT AGRI NAT/G PLAN DIPLOM WAR TOTALISM MARXISM...BIBLIOG/A 19/20 STALIN/J. PAGE 129 H2590
BIOG INDUS ECO/DEV

B65
TILLY C.,MEASURING POLITICAL UPHEAVAL* RESEARCH MONOGRAPH NO. 19. FRANCE INDUS NAT/G FORCES WORKER ...GEOG RECORD EXHIBIT GEN/METH BIBLIOG INDEX. PAGE 155 H3095
CLASSIF QUANT COERCE REV

B65
WUORINEN J.H.,SCANDINAVIA. DENMARK FINLAND ICELAND NORWAY SWEDEN SOCIETY AGRI INDUS DELIB/GP DIPLOM INT/TRADE NEUTRAL...GEOG CHARTS BIBLIOG TREATY. PAGE 171 H3428
NAT/G POL/PAR TREND POLICY

B65
YOUNG A.N.,CHINA'S WARTIME FINANCE AND INFLATION. ASIA AGRI INDUS NAT/G ECO/TAC CONFER PRICE WAR COST 20. PAGE 172 H3437
FINAN FOR/AID TAX BUDGET

L65
MATTHEWS D.G.,"A CURRENT BIBLIOGRAPHY ON ETHIOPIAN AFFAIRS: A SELECT BIBLIOGRAPHY FROM 1950-1964." ETHIOPIA LAW CULTURE ECO/UNDEV INDUS LABOR SECT FORCES DIPLOM CIVMIL/REL RACE/REL...LING STAT 20. PAGE 105 H2093
BIBLIOG/A ADMIN POL/PAR NAT/G

L65
MATTHEWS D.G.,"A CURRENT BIBLIOGRAPHY ON SUDANESE AFFAIRS; A SELECT BIBLIOGRAPHY FROM 1960-1964." SUDAN LAW CULTURE AGRI FINAN INDUS LABOR POL/PAR TEC/DEV FOR/AID RACE/REL LITERACY...LING 20. PAGE 105 H2094
BIBLIOG ECO/UNDEV NAT/G DIPLOM

L65
WIONCZEK M.,"LATIN AMERICA FREE TRADE ASSOCIATION." AGRI DIST/IND FINAN INDUS INT/ORG LABOR NAT/G TEC/DEV ECO/TAC HEALTH SKILL WEALTH...POLICY RELATIV MGT LAFTA 20. PAGE 169 H3390
L/A+17C MARKET REGION

S65
KINDLEBERGER C.P.,"MASS MIGRATION, THEN AND NOW." LAW ECO/DEV ECO/UNDEV INDUS LABOR INT/TRADE FEEDBACK REGION RIGID/FLEX...SOC NAT/COMP EEC. PAGE 86 H1714
EUR+WWI USA-45 WORKER IDEA/COMP

S65
STAAR R.F.,"RETROGRESSION IN POLAND." COM USSR AGRI INDUS NAT/G CREATE EDU/PROP TOTALISM RIGID/FLEX ORD/FREE PWR SOCISM...RECORD CHARTS 20. PAGE 148 H2965
TOP/EX ECO/TAC POLAND

S65
TABORSKY E.,"CHANGE IN CZECHOSLOVAKIA." COM USSR ELITES INTELL AGRI INDUS NAT/G DELIB/GP EX/STRUC ECO/TAC TOTALISM ATTIT RIGID/FLEX SOCISM...MGT CONCPT TREND 20. PAGE 152 H3031
ECO/DEV PLAN CZECHOSLVK

S65
TENDLER J.D.,"TECHNOLOGY AND ECONOMIC DEVELOPMENT* THE CASE OF HYDRO VS THERMAL POWER." CONSTRUC DIST/IND CREATE TEC/DEV INT/TRADE CENTRAL PWR SKILL WEALTH...MGT NAT/COMP ARGEN. PAGE 153 H3061
BRAZIL INDUS ECO/UNDEV

B66
ASHRAF A.,THE CITY GOVERNMENT OF CALCUTTA: A STUDY OF INERTIA. INDIA ELITES INDUS NAT/G EX/STRUC ACT/RES PLAN PROB/SOLV LEAD HABITAT...BIBLIOG 20 CALCUTTA. PAGE 9 H0175
LOC/G MUNIC ADMIN ECO/UNDEV

B66
BECKER J.,BESSARABIEN UND SEIN DEUTSCHTUM. ROMANIA USSR STRUCT INDUS PROF/ORG SECT GP/REL INGP/REL 15/20 BESSARABIA. PAGE 13 H0254
PROVS CULTURE SOCIETY

B66
BIRKHEAD G.S.,ADMINISTRATIVE PROBLEMS IN PAKISTAN. PAKISTAN AGRI FINAN INDUS LG/CO ECO/TAC CONTROL PWR ...CHARTS ANTHOL 20. PAGE 17 H0340
ADMIN NAT/G ORD/FREE ECO/UNDEV

B66
BRODERSEN A.,THE SOVIET WORKER: LABOR AND GOVERNMENT IN SOVIET SOCIETY. USSR STRUCT INDUS LABOR PLAN PAY INGP/REL PRODUC...POLICY GEN/LAWS BIBLIOG 20 STALIN/J LENIN/VI BOLSHEVISM KHRUSH/N. PAGE 21 H0425
WORKER ROLE NAT/G MARXISM

B66
BROWN L.C.,STATE AND SOCIETY IN INDEPENDENT NORTH AFRICA. ALGERIA LIBYA MOROCCO AGRI INDUS INT/ORG POL/PAR SECT PLAN DIPLOM COLONIAL...LING NAT/COMP ANTHOL BIBLIOG 20 TUNIS MUSLIM. PAGE 22 H0446
NAT/G SOCIETY CULTURE ECO/UNDEV

B66
DIAMOND S.,THE TRANSFORMATION OF EAST AFRICA. NAT/G SCHOOL CREATE PROB/SOLV COLONIAL REGION RACE/REL FEDERAL...SOC ANTHOL WORSHIP 20 AFRICA/E. PAGE 41 H0819
CULTURE AFR TEC/DEV INDUS

B66
DOBB M.,SOVIET ECONOMIC DEVELOPMENT SINCE 1917. USSR ECO/DEV ECO/UNDEV LABOR NAT/G TEC/DEV ECO/TAC ROUTINE PRODUC MARXISM 20. PAGE 41 H0829
PLAN INDUS WORKER

B66
HARRISON B.,SOUTH-EAST ASIA: A SHORT HISTORY (3RD ED.). ECO/UNDEV INDUS NAT/G SECT BAL/PWR NAT/LISM ...SOC 15/20 S/EASTASIA. PAGE 67 H1346
COLONIAL S/ASIA CULTURE

B66
HOPKINS J.F.K.,ARABIC PERIODICAL LITERATURE, 1961. ISLAM LAW CULTURE SECT...GEOG HEAL PHIL/SCI PSY SOC 20. PAGE 73 H1466
BIBLIOG/A NAT/LISM TEC/DEV INDUS

B66
IOWA STATE U CTR AGRI AND ECO.RESEARCH AND EDUCATION FOR REGIONAL AND AREA DEVELOPMENT. FUT LAW CULTURE R+D LOC/G PLAN KNOWL...POLICY CHARTS ANTHOL 20. PAGE 78 H1565
REGION ACT/RES ECO/TAC INDUS

B66
KIRDAR U.,THE STRUCTURE OF UNITED NATIONS ECONOMIC AID TO UNDERDEVELOPED COUNTRIES. AGRI FINAN INDUS NAT/G EX/STRUC PLAN GIVE TASK...POLICY 20 UN. PAGE 86 H1721
INT/ORG FOR/AID ECO/UNDEV ADMIN

B66
KOH S.J.,STAGES OF INDUSTRIAL DEVELOPMENT IN ASIA. ASIA INDIA KOREA STRATA STRUCT NAT/G INT/TRADE ...CHARTS 19/20 CHINJAP. PAGE 87 H1738
INDUS ECO/UNDEV ECO/DEV LABOR

B66
KUZNETS S.,MODERN ECONOMIC GROWTH. WOR+45 WOR-45 ECO/DEV ECO/UNDEV AGRI FINAN INDUS TEC/DEV EFFICIENCY INCOME...NAT/COMP 19/20. PAGE 89 H1786
TIME/SEQ WEALTH PRODUC

B66
LEONTIEF W.,ESSAYS IN ECONOMICS. ECO/UNDEV INDUS NAT/G CAP/ISM FOR/AID AUTOMAT MARXISM...ECOMETRIC CHARTS ANTHOL METH 20 KEYNES/JM. PAGE 94 H1886
CONCPT METH/CNCPT METH/COMP

B66
MACFARQUHAR R.,CHINA UNDER MAO: POLITICS TAKES COMMAND. CHINA/COM COM AGRI INDUS CHIEF FORCES DIPLOM INT/TRADE EDU/PROP TASK REV ADJUST...ANTHOL 20 MAO. PAGE 100 H1992
ECO/UNDEV TEC/DEV ECO/TAC ADMIN

B66
MADAN G.R.,ECONOMIC THINKING IN INDIA. INDIA ECO/UNDEV AGRI FINAN INDUS LABOR PLAN CAP/ISM INT/TRADE MARXISM SOCISM...POLICY 1/20. PAGE 101 H2013
ECO/TAC PHIL/SCI NAT/G POL/PAR

B66
NAMBOODIRIPAD E.M.,ECONOMICS AND POLITICS OF INDIA'S SOCIALIST PATTERN. INDIA STRATA AGRI INDUS NAT/G PRICE ORD/FREE SOVEREIGN 20. PAGE 115 H2307
ECO/UNDEV PLAN SOCISM CAP/ISM

B66
OWEN G.,INDUSTRY IN THE UNITED STATES. UK USA+45 NAT/G WEALTH...DECISION NAT/COMP 20. PAGE 122 H2436
METH/COMP INDUS MGT PROB/SOLV

ORD/FREE
B60
PIERCE R.A.,RUSSIAN CENTRAL ASIA, 1867-1917. ASIA RUSSIA CULTURE AGRI INDUS EDU/PROP REV NAT/LISM ...CHARTS BIBLIOG 19/20 BOLSHEVISM INTERVENT. PAGE 125 H2509 — COLONIAL DOMIN ADMIN ECO/UNDEV
B61
ROIG E.,MARTI, ANTIIMPERIALISTA. CUBA L/A+17C DIPLOM DOMIN COLONIAL CONTROL LEAD PWR SOVEREIGN ...PHIL/SCI 19 MARTI/JOSE INTERVENT. PAGE 133 H2664 — PERSON NAT/LISM ECO/UNDEV ORD/FREE
B66
SOBEL L.A.,SOUTH VIETNAM: US-COMMUNIST CONFRONTATION IN SOUTHEAST ASIA 1961-65. VIETNAM FOR/AID CROWD DETER REV PEACE...GEOG 20 INTERVENT DIEM COLD/WAR. PAGE 146 H2926 — WAR TIME/SEQ FORCES NAT/G

INTERVIEWING....SEE INT, REC/INT

INTERVIEWS....SEE INTERVIEWS INDEX, P. XIV

INTGOV/REL....ADVISORY COMMISSION ON INTERGOVERNMENTAL RELATIONS

INTL CONF ON POPULATION H1561

INTL CONF ON WORLD POLITICS-5 H1562

INTL UNION LOCAL AUTHORITIES H1563

INTL/DEV....INTERNATIONAL DEVELOPMENT ASSOCIATION

B64
US HOUSE COMM BANKING-CURR,INTERNATIONAL DEVELOPMENT ASSOCIATION ACT AMENDMENT. CHINA/COM USA+45 USSR FINAN FORCES LEGIS DIPLOM CONFER EFFICIENCY...CHARTS GOV/COMP 20 PRESIDENT CONGRESS INTL/DEV. PAGE 160 H3196 — BAL/PAY FOR/AID RECORD ECO/TAC

INTL/ECON....INTERNATIONAL ECONOMIC ASSOCIATION

INTL/FINAN....INTERNATIONAL FINANCE CORPORATION

INTRAGROUP RELATIONS....SEE INGP/REL

INTRVN/ECO....INTERVENTION (ECONOMIC) - PHILOSOPHY OF GOVERNMENTAL INTERFERENCE IN DOMESTIC ECONOMIC AFFAIRS

B58
DWARKADAS R.,ROLE OF HIGHER CIVIL SERVICE IN INDIA. INDIA ECO/UNDEV LEGIS PROB/SOLV GP/REL PERS/REL ...POLICY WELF/ST DECISION ORG/CHARTS BIBLIOG 20 CIVIL/SERV INTRVN/ECO. PAGE 44 H0876 — ADMIN NAT/G ROLE PLAN

INTST/CRIM....U.S. INTERSTATE COMMISSION ON CRIME

INVENTION....SEE CREATE

INVESTMENT....SEE FINAN

IOVTCHOUK M.T. H1564

IOWA....IOWA

IOWA STATE U CTR AGRI AND ECO H1565

IRAN....SEE ALSO ISLAM

B58
LERNER D.,THE PASSING OF TRADITIONAL SOCIETY: MODERNIZING THE MIDDLE EAST. IRAN ISLAM LEBANON SYRIA TURKEY UAR CULTURE INTELL STRATA KIN NAT/G NEIGH SECT EDU/PROP ATTIT PERSON...MYTH OBS 20. PAGE 95 H1888 — ECO/UNDEV RIGID/FLEX
S59
GABLE R.W.,"CULTURE AND ADMINISTRATION IN IRAN." IRAN EXEC PARTIC REPRESENT PWR. PAGE 54 H1085 — ADMIN CULTURE EX/STRUC INGP/REL
B61
DALLIN D.J.,SOVIET FOREIGN POLICY AFTER STALIN. ASIA CHINA/COM EUR+WWI GERMANY IRAN UK YUGOSLAVIA INT/ORG NAT/G VOL/ASSN FORCES TOP/EX BAL/PWR DOMIN EDU/PROP COERCE ATTIT PWR 20. PAGE 37 H0737 — COM DIPLOM USSR
B61
VON EICKSTEDT E.,TURKEN, KURDEN UND IRANER SEIT DEM ALTERTUM. IRAN TURKEY GP/REL BIO/SOC HABITAT...PSY 20 PERSIA. PAGE 163 H3266 — CULTURE SOC SOCIETY STRUCT
S61
VALLET R.,"IRAN: KEY TO THE MIDDLE EAST." COM IRAQ ISLAM KUWAIT LEBANON SAUDI/ARAB TURKEY ELITES SOCIETY INDUS PROC/MFG POL/PAR TOP/EX PLAN BAL/PWR DIPLOM ECO/TAC ALL/VALS...TREND CENTO 20. PAGE 161 H3224 — NAT/G ECO/UNDEV IRAN
B62
BINDER L.,IRAN: POLITICAL DEVELOPMENT IN A CHANGING SOCIETY. IRAN OP/RES REV GP/REL CENTRAL RATIONAL PWR...PHIL/SCI NAT/COMP GEN/LAWS 20. PAGE 17 H0337 — LEGIT NAT/G ADMIN STRUCT
B62
DAVAR F.C.,IRAN AND INDIA THROUGH THE AGES. INDIA IRAN ELITES SECT CREATE ORD/FREE...LING BIBLIOG. PAGE 37 H0743 — NAT/COMP DIPLOM CULTURE
S63
ARASTEH R.,"THE ROLE OF INTELLECTUALS IN ADMINISTRATIVE DEVELOPMENT AND SOCIAL CHANGE IN MODERN IRAN." ISLAM CULTURE NAT/G CONSULT ACT/RES EDU/PROP EXEC ATTIT BIO/SOC PERCEPT SUPEGO ALL/VALS ...POLICY MGT PSY SOC CONCPT 20. PAGE 8 H0157 — INTELL ADMIN IRAN
S63
BILL J.A.,"THE SOCIAL AND ECONOMIC FOUNDATIONS OF POWER IN CONTEMPORARY IRAN." ISLAM CULTURE NAT/G ECO/TAC DOMIN COERCE ATTIT PWR WEALTH...TREND VAL/FREE 20. PAGE 17 H0334 — SOCIETY STRATA IRAN
B64
WICKENS G.M.,PERSIA IN ISLAMIC TIMES: A PRACTICAL BIBLIOGRAPHY OF ITS HISTORY, CULTURE AND LANGUAGE (PAMPHLET). IRAN ISLAM SECT. PAGE 168 H3355 — BIBLIOG CULTURE LING
S64
RAMAZANI R.K.,"CHURCH AND STATE IN MODERNIZING SOCIETY: THE CASE OF IRAN." ISLAM CULTURE ORD/FREE PWR...TIME/SEQ VAL/FREE 17/20. PAGE 129 H2586 — SECT NAT/G ELITES IRAN
B65
BAYNE E.A.,FOUR WAYS OF POLITICS: STATE AND NATION IN ITALY, SOMALIA, ISRAEL, AND IRAN. IRAN ISRAEL ITALY SOMALIA LEAD CHOOSE MAJORITY GOV/COMP. PAGE 12 H0244 — ECO/UNDEV NAT/G DECISION TOP/EX
B65
HARBISON F.,MANPOWER AND EDUCATION. AFR CHINA/COM IRAN L/A+17C S/ASIA TEC/DEV ADJUST OPTIMAL SKILL ...ANTHOL 20. PAGE 66 H1325 — ECO/UNDEV EDU/PROP WORKER NAT/COMP

IRAQ....SEE ALSO ISLAM

S61
VALLET R.,"IRAN: KEY TO THE MIDDLE EAST." COM IRAQ ISLAM KUWAIT LEBANON SAUDI/ARAB TURKEY ELITES SOCIETY INDUS PROC/MFG POL/PAR TOP/EX PLAN BAL/PWR DIPLOM ECO/TAC ALL/VALS...TREND CENTO 20. PAGE 161 H3224 — NAT/G ECO/UNDEV IRAN

IRELAND....SEE ALSO UK

N17
BURKE E.,LETTER TO SIR HERCULES LANGRISHE (PAMPHLET). IRELAND UK NAT/G CHIEF DIPLOM DOMIN PARL/PROC COERCE ORD/FREE SOVEREIGN POPULISM ...TRADIT 18 BURKE/EDM. PAGE 24 H0485 — POLICY COLONIAL SECT
B23
LEES-SMITH H.B.,SECOND CHAMBERS IN THEORY AND PRACTICE. IRELAND NORWAY SOUTH/AFR UK LAW POL/PAR LEGIS CONTROL 20 CMN/WLTH. PAGE 93 H1858 — PARL/PROC DELIB/GP REPRESENT GP/COMP
B33
MOSS W.,POLITICAL PARTIES IN THE IRISH FREE STATE. IRELAND UK LAW FINAN LABOR DELIB/GP TOP/EX TARIFFS EDU/PROP...CHARTS GP/COMP 20. PAGE 113 H2269 — POL/PAR NAT/G CHOOSE POLICY
B36
CLARKE M.V.,MEDIEVAL REPRESENTATION AND CONSENT. IRELAND UK REPRESENT SUFF. PAGE 30 H0603 — PARL/PROC LEGIS NAT/G
S40
BROMAGE A.W.,"THE VOCATIONAL SENATE IN IRELAND" EUR+WWI IRELAND. PAGE 21 H0430 — PWR NAT/G REPRESENT LEGIS
B43
MC DOWELL R.B.,IRISH PUBLIC OPINION, 1750-1800. IRELAND CONSTN VOL/ASSN WORKER ORD/FREE CATHISM CONSERVE...POLICY IDEA/COMP BIBLIOG 18/ PARLIAMENT. PAGE 106 H2118 — ATTIT NAT/G DIPLOM REV
B50
LYONS F.S.L.,THE IRISH PARLIAMENTARY PARTY, 1890-1910: STUDIES IN IRISH HISTORY (VOL. 4). IRELAND DELIB/GP LEGIS PAY EDU/PROP ADMIN GP/REL ATTIT...BIBLIOG 19/20 PARLIAMENT PARNELL/CS DIRECT/NAT. PAGE 99 H1986 — POL/PAR CHOOSE NAT/G POLICY
B57
DONALDSON A.G.,SOME COMPARATIVE ASPECTS OF IRISH LAW. IRELAND NAT/G DIPLOM ADMIN CT/SYS LEAD ATTIT SOVEREIGN...JURID BIBLIOG/A 12/20 CMN/WLTH. PAGE 42 H0835 — CONSTN LAW NAT/COMP INT/LAW
B62
GROGAN V.,ADMINISTRATIVE TRIBUNALS IN THE PUBLIC SERVICE. IRELAND UK NAT/G CONTROL CT/SYS...JURID GOV/COMP 20. PAGE 61 H1231 — ADMIN LAW ADJUD DELIB/GP

S67
BOSHER J.F.,"GOVERNMENT AND PRIVATE INTERESTS IN NEW FRANCE." CANADA FRANCE INDUS LG/CO SML/CO CAP/ISM INT/TRADE COLONIAL GP/REL...HIST/WRIT 17/18. PAGE 19 H0381
NAT/G FINAN ADMIN CONTROL

S67
CARIAS B.,"EL CONTROL DE LAS EMPRESAS PUBLICAS POR GRUPOS DE INTERESES DE LA COMUNIDAD." FRANCE UK VENEZUELA INDUS NAT/G CONTROL OWN PWR...DECISION NAT/COMP 20. PAGE 26 H0529
WORKER REPRESENT MGT SOCISM

S67
CARR E.H.,"REVOLUTION FROM ABOVE." USSR STRATA FINAN INDUS NAT/G DOMIN LEAD GP/REL INGP/REL OWN PRODUC PWR 20 STALIN/J. PAGE 27 H0538
AGRI POLICY COM EFFICIENCY

S67
CHU-YUAN CHENG,"THE CULTURAL REVOLUTION AND CHINA'S ECONOMY." CHINA/COM AGRI DIST/IND INDUS MARKET NAT/G WORKER PLAN INT/TRADE DOMIN DEMAND PRODUC ...CHARTS 20 MAO. PAGE 30 H0600
ECO/DEV ECO/TAC REV SOCISM

S67
DEWHURST A.,"THE WAGE MOVEMENT IN CANADA." CANADA AGRI NAT/G PARTIC COST PRODUC PROFIT 20. PAGE 41 H0811
WORKER MARXIST INDUS LABOR

S67
GAMARNIKOW M.,"THE NEW ROLE OF PRIVATE ENTERPRISE." ECO/DEV INDUS NAT/G SML/CO CREATE PROB/SOLV MARXISM ...POLICY TREND IDEA/COMP 20. PAGE 55 H1092
ECO/TAC ATTIT CAP/ISM COM

S67
HASSAN M.F.,"THE SECOND FOUR-YEAR PLAN OF VENEZUELA." L/A+17C VENEZUELA AGRI INDUS NAT/G PLAN RATION CONTROL HABITAT...MATH STAT 20. PAGE 67 H1352
ECO/UNDEV FINAN BUDGET PROB/SOLV

S67
NUGENT J.B.,"ECONOMIC THOUGHT, INVESTMENT CRITERIA, AND DEVELOPMENT STRATEGIES IN GREECE* A POSTWAR SURVEY." GREECE AGRI INDUS INT/ORG NAT/G OP/RES DEMAND OPTIMAL PRODUC WEALTH 20 EEC. PAGE 119 H2379
ECO/UNDEV PLAN FINAN

S67
PERKINS D.H.,"ECONOMIC GROWTH IN CHINA AND THE CULTURAL REVOLUTION(1960APRIL 1967)" CHINA/COM FUT AGRI INDUS PLAN LEAD MARXISM...CHARTS 20 MAO. PAGE 125 H2493
ECO/TAC CULTURE REV ECO/UNDEV

S67
RICHMAN B.M.,"CAPITALISTS & MANAGERS IN COMMUNIST CHINA." ASIA CHINA/COM ECO/UNDEV NAT/G CONSULT EX/STRUC PLAN EFFICIENCY PRODUC WEALTH MARXISM ...MGT CHARTS 20. PAGE 131 H2623
CAP/ISM INDUS

S67
SANCHEZ J.D.,"DESARROLLO ECONOMICO Y FUTURO DE COLOMBIA." L/A+17C AGRI EXTR/IND FINAN INDUS MARKET INT/TRADE CONTROL...STAT TREND COLOMB. PAGE 137 H2748
ECO/UNDEV FUT NAT/G ECO/TAC

S67
SAVELYEV N.,"MONOPOLY DRIVE IN INDIA." INDIA INDUS NAT/G INT/TRADE NEUTRAL SANCTION GOV/REL CONSERVE ...MARXIST 20. PAGE 138 H2759
ECO/UNDEV POL/PAR ECO/TAC CONTROL

S67
SCHACHTER G.,"REGIONAL DEVELOPMENT IN THE ITALIAN DUAL ECONOMY" ITALY AGRI INDUS MARKET WORKER ECO/TAC CONTROL INCOME PRODUC 20. PAGE 138 H2767
REGION ECO/UNDEV NAT/G PROB/SOLV

S67
SCOTT J.W.,"SOURCES OF SOCIAL CHANGE IN COMMUNITY, FAMILY, AND FERTILITY IN A PUERTO RICAN TOWN." PUERT/RICO CULTURE STRUCT ECO/UNDEV INDUS PERS/REL ROLE...SOC STAND/INT. PAGE 141 H2815
FAM MARRIAGE LITERACY ATTIT

S67
SINGH B.,"ITALIAN EXPERIENCE IN REGIONAL ECONOMIC DEVELOPMENT AND LESSONS FOR OTHER COUNTRIES." EUR+WWI ITALY INDUS NAT/G ACT/RES REGION GP/REL EFFICIENCY EQUILIB PRODUC WEALTH. PAGE 144 H2884
ECO/UNDEV PLAN ECO/TAC CONTROL

S67
SLOAN P.,"FIFTY YEARS OF SOVIET RULE." USSR INDUS EDU/PROP EFFICIENCY PRODUC HEALTH KNOWL MORAL WEALTH MARXISM...POLICY 20. PAGE 145 H2900
CREATE NAT/G PLAN INSPECT

S67
SMITH J.E.,"RED PRUSSIANISM OF THE GERMAN DEMOCRATIC REPUBLIC." GERMANY/E INTELL TOP/EX WORKER PLAN DIPLOM PRODUC ATTIT WEALTH MARXISM. PAGE 146 H2912
NAT/G TOTALISM INDUS NAT/LISM

S67
SOARES G.,"SOCIO-ECONOMIC VARIABLES AND VOTING FOR THE RADICAL LEFT: CHILE 1952." CHILE INDUS NAT/G WORKER ADJUST STRANGE ANOMIE WEALTH...METH/CNCPT CORREL 20. PAGE 146 H2925
STRATA POL/PAR CHOOSE STAT

S67
TAYLOR P.B. JR.,"PROGRESS IN VENEZUELA." L/A+17C VENEZUELA AGRI INDUS LG/CO NAT/G SML/CO CHOOSE ...POLICY 20. PAGE 153 H3057
ECO/UNDEV ECO/TAC POL/PAR ORD/FREE

S67
THEROUX P.,"HATING THE ASIANS." TANZANIA UGANDA CONSTN INDUS NAT/G POL/PAR WORKER ECO/TAC HABITAT LOVE...POLICY GEOG 20 MIGRATION. PAGE 154 H3069
AFR RACE/REL SOVEREIGN ATTIT

S67
TIVEY L.,"THE POLITICAL CONSEQUENCES OF ECONOMIC PLANNING." UK CONSTN INDUS ACT/RES ADMIN CONTROL LOBBY REPRESENT EFFICIENCY SUPEGO SOVEREIGN ...DECISION 20. PAGE 155 H3108
PLAN POLICY NAT/G

S67
WILLIAMS P.M.,"THE FRENCH GENERAL ELECTION OF MARCH 1967." FRANCE INDUS WORKER NAT/LISM PWR SOCISM 20. PAGE 168 H3368
POL/PAR NAT/G ATTIT CHOOSE

L68
CURRENT HISTORY,"DE GAULLE'S FRANCE." FRANCE MOD/EUR WOR+45 INDUS MARKET INT/ORG BUDGET DIPLOM AUTHORIT DRIVE...GOV/COMP IDEA/COMP 20 DEGAULLE/C EEC. PAGE 36 H0723
INT/TRADE PERSON LEAD NAT/LISM

S68
DOUGLAS-HOME C.,"A MISTAKEN POLICY IN ADEN." YEMEN CULTURE ECO/UNDEV INDUS FORCES WORKER DIPLOM ECO/TAC CONTROL 20 ADEN. PAGE 42 H0842
SOVEREIGN COLONIAL POLICY REGION

B76
SMITH A.,THE WEALTH OF NATIONS. UK STRUCT WORKER DIPLOM ECO/TAC OPTIMAL DRIVE PERSON ORD/FREE ...OLD/LIB GEN/LAWS 17/18. PAGE 145 H2905
WEALTH PRODUC INDUS LAISSEZ

B82
CUNNINGHAM W.,THE GROWTH OF ENGLISH INDUSTRY AND COMMERCE. FUT UK FINAN NAT/G CAP/ISM...POLICY 20 MERCANTLST CHRISTIAN POPE. PAGE 36 H0721
INDUS INT/TRADE SML/CO CONSERVE

B91
MILL J.S.,SOCIALISM (1859). MOD/EUR AGRI INDUS NAT/G REV INCOME PRODUC ORD/FREE POPULISM SOCISM ...GOV/COMP METH/COMP 19. PAGE 110 H2209
WEALTH SOCIALIST ECO/TAC OWN

B95
SELIGMAN E.R.A.,ESSAYS IN TAXATION. NEW/ZEALND PRUSSIA UK USA-45 MARKET LOC/G CREATE PRICE CONTROL INCOME OWN WEALTH...GOV/COMP METH/COMP 19. PAGE 141 H2824
TAX TARIFFS INDUS NAT/G

B96
MARX K.,REVOLUTION AND COUNTER-REVOLUTION. GERMANY CONSTN ELITES INDUS NAT/G DIPLOM ECO/TAC WEALTH. PAGE 104 H2083
MARXIST REV PWR STRATA

B96
SCHMOLLER G.,THE MERCANTILE SYSTEM AND ITS HISTORICAL SIGNIFICANCE: ILLUSTRATED CHIEFLY FROM PRUSSIAN HISTORY (TRANS.). PRUSSIA CULTURE INDUS KIN MUNIC NAT/G PROVS OP/RES ECO/TAC INT/TRADE SUPEGO PWR WEALTH 19 MERCANTLST. PAGE 139 H2790
GEN/METH INGP/REL CONCPT

INDUS/REV....INDUSTRIAL REVOLUTION

INDUSTRIAL RELATIONS....SEE LABOR, MGT, INDUS

INDUSTRIALIZATION....SEE ECO/DEV, ECO/UNDEV

INDUSTRY....SEE INDUS

INDUSTRY, COMMUNICATION....SEE COM/IND

INDUSTRY, CONSTRUCTION....SEE CONSTRUC

INDUSTRY, EXTRACTIVE....SEE EXTR/IND

INDUSTRY, MANUFACTURING....SEE PROC/MFG

INDUSTRY, PROCESSING....SEE PROC/MFG

INDUSTRY, SERVICE....SEE SERV/IND

INDUSTRY, TRANSPORTATION....SEE DIST/IND

INDUSTRY, WAREHOUSING....SEE DIST/IND

INFLATION....INFLATION

INFLUENCING....SEE MORE SPECIFIC FORMS, E.G., DOMIN, PWR, WEALTH, EDU/PROP, SKILL, CHANGE, LOBBY

INGHAM K. H1534

INGP/REL....INTRAGROUP RELATIONS

N
HERSKOVITS M.V.,CULTURAL ANTHROPOLOGY. UNIV SOCIETY STRUCT FAM...AUD/VIS BIBLIOG. PAGE 70 H1410
CULTURE SOC

INGP/REL
GEOG

N
CIVIL SERVICE JOURNAL. PARTIC INGP/REL PERS/REL ...MGT BIBLIOG/A 20. PAGE 1 H0015
ADMIN NAT/G SERV/IND WORKER

N
PRESSE UNIVERSITAIRES,ANNEE SOCIOLOGIQUE. EUR+WWI FRANCE MOD/EUR FAM ACT/RES WAR INGP/REL PERS/REL CONSEN DRIVE MORAL...CON/ANAL 19/20. PAGE 128 H2557
BIBLIOG SOC CULTURE SOCIETY

B05
PHILIPPINE ISLANDS BUREAU SCI,ETHNOLOGICAL SURVEY: THE BONTOC IGOROT. ECO/UNDEV AGRI FAM MARRIAGE HEALTH WEALTH...LING OBS AUD/VIS CHARTS WORSHIP 20 LUZON BONTOC. PAGE 125 H2500
CULTURE INGP/REL KIN STRUCT

B08
NIRRNHEIM O.,DAS ERSTE JAHR DES MINISTERIUMS BISMARCK UND DIE OEFFENTLICHE MEINUNG (HEIDELBERGER ABHANDLUNGEN, 20. HEFT). GERMANY MOD/EUR LEGIS DIPLOM EDU/PROP INGP/REL...BIOG GOV/COMP IDEA/COMP BIBLIOG 19 BISMARCK/O. PAGE 118 H2363
CHIEF PRESS NAT/G ATTIT

B10
MCILWAIN C.H.,THE HIGH COURT OF PARLIAMENT AND ITS SUPREMACY B1910 1878 408. UK EX/STRUC PARL/PROC GOV/REL INGP/REL PRIVIL 12/20 PARLIAMENT ENGLSH/LAW. PAGE 107 H2132
LAW LEGIS CONSTN NAT/G

N19
ADMINISTRATIVE STAFF COLLEGE,THE ACCOUNTABILITY OF GOVERNMENT DEPARTMENTS (PAMPHLET) (REV. ED.). UK CONSTN FINAN NAT/G CONSULT ADMIN INGP/REL CONSEN PRIVIL 20 PARLIAMENT. PAGE 3 H0070
PARL/PROC ELITES SANCTION PROB/SOLV

N19
FIKS M.,PUBLIC ADMINISTRATION IN ISRAEL (PAMPHLET). ISRAEL SCHOOL EX/STRUC BUDGET PAY INGP/REL ...DECISION 20 CIVIL/SERV. PAGE 50 H0999
EDU/PROP NAT/G ADMIN WORKER

B24
WALKER F.D.,AFRICA AND HER PEOPLES. ISLAM STRUCT FAM SECT EDU/PROP INGP/REL RACE/REL HABITAT...GEOG SOC IDEA/COMP WORSHIP 20 NEGRO. PAGE 164 H3292
CULTURE AFR GP/COMP KIN

B26
POLLARD A.F.,THE EVOLUTION OF PARLIAMENT. UK CONSTN POL/PAR EX/STRUC GOV/REL INGP/REL PRIVIL RIGID/FLEX ...TIME/SEQ 11/20 CMN/WLTH PARLIAMENT. PAGE 127 H2536
LEGIS PARL/PROC NAT/G

B27
ENGELS F.,THE PEASANT WAR IN GERMANY (1850). GERMANY MOD/EUR AGRI WORKER LEAD COERCE INGP/REL ...TREND 16/19. PAGE 46 H0924
WAR STRATA REV MARXIST

B30
MASON E.S.,THE PARIS COMMUNE: AN EPISODE IN THE HISTORY OF THE SOCIALIST MOVEMENT. FRANCE MOD/EUR ELITES SOCIETY STRATA ECO/DEV WORKER EDU/PROP CHOOSE INGP/REL SOCISM 19 MARX/KARL PARIS. PAGE 104 H2085
NAT/G REV MARXISM

B30
WILLOUGHBY W.W.,THE ETHICAL BASIS OF POLITICAL AUTHORITY. NAT/G LEGIS PARL/PROC INGP/REL UTOPIA ORD/FREE 16/20. PAGE 169 H3374
MORAL POLICY CONSTN

B31
LORWIN L.L.,ADVISORY ECONOMIC COUNCILS. EUR+WWI FRANCE GERMANY PROB/SOLV INGP/REL...CLASSIF GP/COMP. PAGE 99 H1968
CONSULT DELIB/GP ECO/TAC NAT/G

B34
GONZALEZ PALENCIA A,ESTUDIO HISTORICO SOBRE LA CENSURA GUBERNATIVA EN ESPANA 1800-1833. NAT/G COERCE INGP/REL ATTIT AUTHORIT KNOWL...POLICY JURID 19. PAGE 58 H1165
LEGIT EDU/PROP PRESS CONTROL

B35
DOUGLASS H.P.,THE PROTESTANT CHURCH AS A SOCIAL INSTITUTION. CULTURE FINAN NEIGH PROF/ORG OP/RES ADMIN...POLICY SOC/WK STAT BIBLIOG. PAGE 42 H0843
SECT PARTIC INGP/REL GP/REL

B39
MARITAIN J.,SCHOLASTICISM AND POLITICS. CONSTN SOCIETY NAT/G INGP/REL PERSON CATHISM POPULISM 19/20 FREUD/S SCHOLASTIC CHURCH/STA CHRISTIAN. PAGE 103 H2050
SECT GEN/LAWS ORD/FREE

B39
MILLER P.,THE NEW ENGLAND MIND: THE SEVENTEENTH CENTURY. CULTURE DOMIN WRITING INGP/REL CONSEN MAJORITY PERCEPT KNOWL MORAL...CONCPT LING WORSHIP 17 NEW/ENGLND PROTESTANT. PAGE 111 H2214
SECT REGION SOC ATTIT

B40
ZWEIG F.,THE WORKER IN AN AFFLUENT SOCIETY: FAMILY LIFE AND INDUSTRY. UK STRATA LG/CO ECO/TAC LEISURE INGP/REL HAPPINESS HEALTH...PSY SOC/WK INT CHARTS WORSHIP 20 FEMALE/SEX. PAGE 173 H3465
MARRIAGE ATTIT FINAN CULTURE

B41
GREEN T.H.,PRINCIPLES OF PUBLIC ADMINISTRATION. UNIV CONSTN VOL/ASSN INGP/REL MORAL ORD/FREE ...GOV/COMP IDEA/COMP GEN/LAWS 20. PAGE 60 H1208
POLICY LAISSEZ MAJORIT

C41
KLUCKHOHN C.,"PATTERNING AS EXEMPLIFIED IN NAVAHO CULTURE" IN EDWARD SAPIR, LANGUAGE, CULTURE, AND PERSONALITY (BMR)" KIN PERS/REL ATTIT PERSON...SOC CONCPT METH/CNCPT LING OBS/ENVIR CON/ANAL BIBLIOG SOC/INTEG 20 NAVAHO INDIAN/AM SAPIR/EDW. PAGE 87 H1733
CULTURE INGP/REL STRUCT

B43
MARITAIN J.,THE RIGHTS OF MAN AND NATURAL LAW. CONSTN NAT/G DOMIN LEGIT INGP/REL TOTALISM MORAL POPULISM WORSHIP 19/20 CIVIL/LIB CHURCH/STA NATURL/LAW. PAGE 103 H2051
PLURIST ORD/FREE GEN/LAWS

B44
KRIS E.,GERMAN RADIO PROPAGANDA: REPORT ON HOME BROADCASTS DURING THE WAR. EUR+WWI GERMANY CULTURE CONSULT PROB/SOLV FEEDBACK TASK INGP/REL DRIVE PWR FASCISM...CON/ANAL METH/COMP 20. PAGE 89 H1768
EDU/PROP DOMIN ACT/RES ATTIT

B46
GODWIN W.,ENQUIRY CONCERNING POLITICAL JUSTICE AND ITS INFLUENCE ON MORALS AND HAPPINESS (1793). UNIV SOCIETY NAT/G GP/REL INGP/REL HAPPINESS ALL/VALS CONCPT. PAGE 58 H1151
MORAL PERSON ORD/FREE

B47
HERSKOVITS M.U.,MAN AND HIS WORK. UNIV SECT TEC/DEV PARTIC...PHIL/SCI LING AUD/VIS BIBLIOG. PAGE 70 H1409
SOC CULTURE INGP/REL HABITAT

B47
NIEBUHR R.,THE CHILDREN OF LIGHT AND THE CHILDREN OF DARKNESS: A VINDICATION OF DEMOCRACY AND CRITIQUE OF TRADITIONAL DEFENSE. UNIV STRUCT NAT/G SECT INGP/REL OWN PEACE ORD/FREE MARXISM ...IDEA/COMP GEN/LAWS 20 CHRISTIAN. PAGE 118 H2358
POPULISM DIPLOM NEIGH GP/REL

B48
LAUTERBACH A.,ECONOMIC SECURITY AND INDIVIDUAL FREEDOM: CAN WE HAVE BOTH? COM EUR+WWI MOD/EUR UNIV WOR+45 CAP/ISM TOTALISM ALL/VALS...GOV/COMP BIBLIOG 20. PAGE 92 H1840
ORD/FREE ECO/DEV DECISION INGP/REL

B48
WOLFE B.D.,THREE WHO MADE A REVOLUTION. USSR CONSTN NAT/G CAP/ISM EDU/PROP CONTROL WAR GP/REL INGP/REL PERS/REL ROLE 20 STALIN/J LENIN/VI TROTSKY/L BOLSHEVISM. PAGE 170 H3398
BIOG REV LEAD MARXISM

B48
WRIGHT G.,THE RESHAPING OF FRENCH DEMOCRACY. FRANCE NAT/G POL/PAR SECT LEAD CHOOSE GP/REL INGP/REL MARXISM SOCISM...CHARTS BIBLIOG 20 DEGAULLE/C. PAGE 171 H3418
CONSTN POPULISM CREATE LEGIS

L48
SHILS E.A.,"COHESION AND DISINTEGRATION IN THE WEHRMACHT IN WORLD WAR II." GERMANY STRUCT DOMIN WAR INGP/REL ISOLAT NAT/LISM ATTIT AUTHORIT SUPEGO RESPECT...PSY CON/ANAL 20 NAZI. PAGE 143 H2862
EDU/PROP DRIVE PERS/REL FORCES

B49
GRODZINS M.,AMERICANS BETRAYED: POLITICS AND THE JAPANESE EXPANSION. PROVS COERCE CHOOSE GOV/REL GP/REL INGP/REL ATTIT ORD/FREE...DECISION CHARTS 20 NISEI. PAGE 61 H1230
DISCRIM POLICY NAT/G WAR

B51
INTERNATIONAL AFRICAN INST,ETHNOGRAPHIC SURVEY OF AFRICA: WEST CENTRAL AFRICA (VOLS. I-III, 1951-1953). AFR RHODESIA CULTURE ECO/UNDEV HEREDITY ...GEOG SOC CHARTS BIBLIOG WORSHIP 20 CONGO/LEOP. PAGE 77 H1543
STRUCT KIN INGP/REL HABITAT

B52
FORDE L.D.,HABITAT, ECONOMY AND SOCIETY. AFR L/A+17C S/ASIA STRUCT AGRI INGP/REL...GEOG OBS BIBLIOG 20. PAGE 52 H1037
SOC HABITAT CULTURE ECO/UNDEV

B52
INTERNATIONAL AFRICAN INST,ETHNOGRAPHIC SURVEY OF AFRICA: SOUTHERN AFRICA (VOLS. I-III, 1952-1954). AFR SOUTH/AFR CULTURE ECO/UNDEV GOV/REL HEREDITY ...GEOG SOC CHARTS BIBLIOG WORSHIP 20. PAGE 77 H1544
STRUCT KIN INGP/REL HABITAT

B52
SPICER E.H.,HUMAN PROBLEMS IN TECHNOLOGICAL CHANGE. ECO/UNDEV AGRI INDUS NAT/G ACT/RES LEAD GP/REL INGP/REL ROLE...INT METH 20 CASEBOOK. PAGE 147 H2947
TEC/DEV CULTURE STRUCT OP/RES

S52
SABINE G.H.,"THE TWO DEMOCRATIC TRADITIONS" (BMR)" FRANCE UK USA-45 NAT/G CONTROL CHOOSE ALL/IDEOS ...PHIL/SCI CONCPT IDEA/COMP 20. PAGE 136 H2727
ORD/FREE POPULISM INGP/REL NAT/COMP

B53
FLORENCE P.S.,THE LOGIC OF BRITISH AND AMERICAN INDUSTRY; A REALISTIC ANALYSIS OF ECONOMIC STRUCTURE AND GOVERNMENT. UK USA+45 USA-45 FINAN LABOR CAP/ISM INGP/REL EFFICIENCY...MGT CONCPT STAT CHARTS METH 20. PAGE 51 H1028
INDUS ECO/DEV NAT/G NAT/COMP

B53
MAXIMOFF G.P.,THE POLITICAL PHILOSOPHY OF BAKUNIN: SCIENTIFIC ANARCHISM. STRUCT INGP/REL FEDERAL MARXISM...ANARCH BIOG 19 BAKUNIN. PAGE 105 H2104
SOCIETY PHIL/SCI NAT/G

IDEA/COMP

B53
WAGLEY C.,AMAZON TOWN: A STUDY OF MAN IN THE TROPICS. BRAZIL L/A+17C STRATA STRUCT ECO/UNDEV AGRI EX/STRUC RACE/REL DISCRIM HABITAT WEALTH...OBS SOC/EXP 20. PAGE 164 H3285
SOC NEIGH CULTURE INGP/REL

B54
BERGER M.,FREEDOM AND CONTROL IN MODERN SOCIETY. LABOR NAT/G VOL/ASSN AUTHORIT DRIVE PLURISM ...METH/CNCPT CLASSIF. PAGE 15 H0300
ORD/FREE CONTROL INGP/REL

B54
SPROTT W.J.H.,SCIENCE AND SOCIAL ACTION. STRUCT ACT/RES CRIME GP/REL INGP/REL ANOMIE...PSY SOC/INTEG 19/20. PAGE 148 H2956
SOC CULTURE PHIL/SCI

B55
FRIEDMAN G.,INDUSTRIAL SOCIETY: THE EMERGENCE OF THE HUMAN PROBLEMS OF AUTOMATION. UNIV CULTURE ECO/DEV TEC/DEV INGP/REL HAPPINESS RATIONAL UTOPIA ROLE...HUM SOC TIME/SEQ 20. PAGE 53 H1064
AUTOMAT ADJUST ALL/VALS CONCPT

B55
INTERNATIONAL AFRICAN INST,ETHNOGRAPHIC SURVEY OF AFRICA: NORTH EASTERN AFRICA (VOLUMES 1-2, 1955-56). AFR ETHIOPIA CULTURE ECO/UNDEV KIN GOV/REL ATTIT HEREDITY...GEOG CHARTS BIBLIOG WORSHIP 20. PAGE 77 H1545
STRUCT ECO/TAC INGP/REL HABITAT

B55
INTERNATIONAL AFRICAN INST,ETHNOGRAPHIC SURVEY OF AFRICA: WESTERN AFRICA: PEOPLES OF THE NIGER-BENUE CONFLUENCE. AFR NIGER CULTURE ECO/UNDEV KIN GOV/REL GP/REL ATTIT HEREDITY...CHARTS BIBLIOG WORSHIP 20. PAGE 77 H1546
STRUCT GEOG HABITAT INGP/REL

B55
KOHN H.,NATIONALISM: ITS MEANING AND HISTORY. GP/REL INGP/REL ATTIT...CONCPT NAT/COMP 16/20 MACHIAVELL. PAGE 87 H1743
NAT/LISM DIPLOM FASCISM REV

B55
RODNICK D.,THE NORWEGIANS: A STUDY IN NATIONAL CULTURE. NORWAY FAM INGP/REL PERS/REL AGE...PSY SOC SELF/OBS WORSHIP 20. PAGE 133 H2655
CULTURE INT RECORD ATTIT

B55
STEWARD J.H.,THEORY OF CULTURE CHANGE; THE METHODOLOGY OF MULTILINEAR EVOLUTION. SOCIETY KIN SECT GP/REL INGP/REL...BIBLIOG SOC/INTEG 20. PAGE 149 H2984
CULTURE CONCPT METH/COMP HABITAT

B55
THOMPSON V.,MINORITY PROBLEMS IN SOUTHEAST ASIA. CAMBODIA CHINA/COM LAOS S/ASIA KIN NAT/G SECT PROB/SOLV EDU/PROP REGION GP/REL RACE/REL MARXISM ...SOC 20 BUDDHISM UN. PAGE 154 H3085
INGP/REL GEOG DIPLOM STRUCT

S55
DE SMITH S.A.,"CONSTITUTIONAL MONARCHY IN BURGANDA." AFR UGANDA UK STRUCT CHIEF REGION INGP/REL ADJUST NAT/LISM SOVEREIGN CONSERVE ...POLICY 19/20 BURGANDA. PAGE 38 H0769
NAT/G DIPLOM CONSTN COLONIAL

C55
STEWARD J.H.,"THE CONCEPT AND METHOD OF CULTURAL ECOLOGY" IN T.H. STEWARD'S THEORY OF CULTURAL CHANGE." SOCIETY INGP/REL...CONCPT CON/ANAL METH/COMP 20. PAGE 149 H2985
HABITAT CULTURE CREATE ADJUST

B56
DRIVER H.E.,AN INTEGRATION OF FUNCTIONAL, EVOLUTIONARY AND HISTORICAL THEORY BY MEANS OF CORRELATIONS. INGP/REL BIO/SOC HABITAT...PHIL/SCI GEN/LAWS. PAGE 42 H0847
CULTURE METH SOC CORREL

B56
GOFFMAN E.,THE PRESENTATION OF SELF IN EVERYDAY LIFE. CULTURE INGP/REL ATTIT DRIVE...SOC OBS RECORD 20. PAGE 58 H1154
PERS/COMP PERSON PERCEPT ROLE

B56
INTERNATIONAL AFRICAN INST,ETHNOGRAPHIC SURVEY OF AFRICA; WESTERN AFRICA: PAGAN PEOPLES OF CENTRAL AREA OF NORTHERN NIGERIA (VOL. XII). NIGERIA FAM KIN SECT ECO/TAC GOV/REL GP/REL ATTIT...LING CHARTS 20. PAGE 77 H1548
STRUCT INGP/REL HABITAT CULTURE

B56
MUMFORD L.,THE TRANSFORMATIONS OF MAN. UNIV CULTURE INGP/REL HABITAT HEREDITY ALL/VALS ORD/FREE...MYTH TIME/SEQ TREND WORSHIP. PAGE 114 H2287
IDEA/COMP PERSON CONCPT

B56
SHAPIRO H.L.,MAN, CULTURE, AND SOCIETY. STRUCT FAM SECT GP/REL INGP/REL...ART/METH GEOG PSY LING ANTHOL BIBLIOG. PAGE 142 H2842
CULTURE PERSON SOC

B56
SYKES G.M.,CRIME AND SOCIETY. LAW STRATA STRUCT ACT/RES ROUTINE ANOMIE WEALTH...POLICY SOC/INTEG 20. PAGE 151 H3021
CRIMLGY CRIME CULTURE INGP/REL

B56
VON HARPE W.,DIE SOWJETUNION FINNLAND UND SKANDANAVIEN, 1945-1955. EUR+WWI FINLAND GERMANY USSR WAR INGP/REL ORD/FREE SOVEREIGN MARXISM ...POLICY GOV/COMP BIBLIOG 20 STALIN/J. PAGE 163 H3270
DIPLOM COM NEUTRAL BAL/PWR

S56
BLAU P.M.,"SOCIAL MOBILITY AND INTERPERSONAL RELATIONS" (BMR)" UNIV CULTURE STRUCT WORKER ANOMIE ...SOC SOC/INTEG 19/20. PAGE 18 H0355
INGP/REL PERS/REL ORD/FREE STRATA

S56
EPSTEIN L.D.,"COHESION OF BRITISH PARLIAMENTARY PARTIES." UK STRUCT ADMIN ROUTINE INGP/REL PWR ...GP/COMP PARLIAMENT. PAGE 47 H0935
NAT/G PARL/PROC POL/PAR

B57
BUNDESMIN FUR VERTRIEBENE,DIE VERTREIBUNG DER DEUTSCHEN BEVOLKERUNG AUS DER TSCHECHOSLOWAKEI. CZECHOSLVK GERMANY NAT/G FORCES MURDER WAR INGP/REL ATTIT 20 MIGRATION. PAGE 24 H0474
GP/REL DOMIN COERCE DISCRIM

B57
INTERNATIONAL AFRICAN INST,ETHNOGRAPHIC SURVEY OF AFRICA: WESTERN AFRICA: THE BENIN KINGDOM. AFR NIGERIA CULTURE ECO/UNDEV KIN ECO/TAC GOV/REL AGE ATTIT HEREDITY...CHARTS BIBLIOG WORSHIP 20. PAGE 77 H1550
STRUCT INGP/REL GEOG HABITAT

B57
INTERNATIONAL AFRICAN INST,ETHNOGRAPHIC SURVEY OF AFRICA: WESTERN AFRICA: THE WOLOF OF SENEGAMBIA. AFR SENEGAL CULTURE ECO/UNDEV FAM KIN REGION ...CHARTS GP/COMP BIBLIOG WORSHIP 20. PAGE 78 H1551
STRUCT GEOG HABITAT INGP/REL

B57
KOENTJARANINGRAT R.,A PRELIMINARY DESCRIPTION OF THE JAVANESE KINSHIP SYSTEM. INDONESIA STRATA FAM INGP/REL ADJUST MARRIAGE AGE/C AGE/Y AGE/A PERSON ...OBS CHARTS DICTIONARY 20 JAVA. PAGE 87 H1736
KIN STRUCT ELITES CULTURE

B57
PARK A.G.,BOLSHEVISM IN TURKESTAN 1917-1927. COM RUSSIA USSR CULTURE AGRI SECT DOMIN GP/REL INGP/REL NAT/LISM...BIBLIOG 20 TURKESTAN. PAGE 123 H2467
REV POLICY MARXISM ISLAM

B57
PIDDINGTON R.,AN INTRODUCTION TO SOCIAL ANTHROPOLOGY (VOL. II). SOCIETY STRUCT FAM INGP/REL ...OBS CHARTS. PAGE 125 H2507
CULTURE SOC TEC/DEV GEOG

B58
GURVITCH G.,TRAITE DE SOCIOLOGIE (2 VOLS.). FRANCE CULTURE INDUS GP/REL INGP/REL...PSY BIBLIOG 20. PAGE 63 H1256
ANTHOL SOC METH/COMP METH/CNCPT

B58
MATOS J.,LAS ACTUALES COMMUNIDADES DE INDIGENAS: HUAROCHIRI EN 1955. PERU FAM NAT/G SECT EDU/PROP ADJUD GP/REL INGP/REL 20 INDIAN/AM. PAGE 105 H2091
STRUCT NEIGH KIN ECO/UNDEV

B58
WIGGIN L.M.,THE FACTION OF COUSINS: A POLITICAL ACCOUNT OF THE GRENVILLES, 1733-1763. UK STRUCT KIN NAT/G INGP/REL...CONCPT BIOG BIBLIOG/A 18 GRENVILLES. PAGE 168 H3357
FAM POL/PAR PWR

S58
GARCEAU O.,"INTEREST GROUP THEORY IN POLITICAL RESEARCH." ELITES NAT/G PLAN LEAD REPRESENT INGP/REL POLICY. PAGE 55 H1098
GP/COMP GP/REL LOBBY PLURISM

C58
WILDING N.,"AN ENCYCLOPEDIA OF PARLIAMENT." UK LAW CONSTN CHIEF PROB/SOLV DIPLOM DEBATE WAR INGP/REL PRIVIL...BIBLIOG DICTIONARY 13/20 CMN/WLTH PARLIAMENT. PAGE 168 H3363
PARL/PROC POL/PAR NAT/G ADMIN

B59
CHODOROV F.,THE RISE AND FALL OF SOCIETY. NAT/G CONTROL ORD/FREE...TIME/SEQ 20. PAGE 30 H0596
SOC INGP/REL ECO/DEV ATTIT

B59
HOBSBAWM E.J.,PRIMITIVE REBELS; STUDIES IN ARCHAIC FORMS OF SOCIAL MOVEMENT IN THE 19TH AND 20TH CENTURIES. ITALY SPAIN CULTURE VOL/ASSN RISK CROWD GP/REL INGP/REL ISOLAT TOTALISM...PSY SOC 18/20. PAGE 72 H1438
SOCIETY CRIME REV GUERRILLA

B59
HONINGMAN J.J.,THE WORLD OF MAN. CHRIST-17C MEDIT-7 PRE/AMER PREHIST CREATE INGP/REL BIO/SOC HABITAT ...PSY SOC BIBLIOG. PAGE 73 H1460
CULTURE METH PERSON STRUCT

B59
LEE D.,FREEDOM AND CULTURE. WOR+45 WOR-45 FAM HABITAT PERSON LOVE MORAL...PSY SOC OBS NAT/COMP WORSHIP 20. PAGE 93 H1856
CULTURE SOCIETY CONCPT INGP/REL

B59
LEMBERG E.,DIE VERTRIEBENEN IN WESTDEUTSCHLAND (3 VOLS.). GERMANY/W CULTURE STRUCT AGRI PROVS ADMIN ...JURID 20 MIGRATION. PAGE 94 H1875
GP/REL INGP/REL SOCIETY

B59
LIPSET S.M.,SOCIAL MOBILITY IN INDUSTRIAL SOCIETY. EUR+WWI USA+45 USSR STRUCT INDUS WRITING GP/REL INGP/REL DRIVE...SOC CHARTS NAT/COMP SOC/INTEG 20 MARX/KARL ENGELS/F. PAGE 97 H1940
STRATA ECO/DEV SOCIETY

B59
MURDOCK G.P.,AFRICA: ITS PEOPLES AND THEIR CULTURE HISTORY. AFR CULTURE AGRI LOC/G INGP/REL HABITAT ...GEOG SOC LING CHARTS BIBLIOG 20 NEGRO EGYPT/ANC. PAGE 115 H2293
SOCIETY ECO/TAC GP/COMP KIN

B59
ROCHE J.,LA COLONISATION ALLEMANDE ET LE RIO GRANDE DO SUL. BRAZIL L/A+17C NAT/G PROVS INGP/REL RACE/REL DISCRIM HABITAT...GEOG SOC/INTEG 19/20 MIGRATION. PAGE 133 H2652
ECO/UNDEV GP/REL ATTIT

B59
SCHORN H.,DER RICHTER IM DRITTEN REICH; GESCHICHTE UND DOKUMENTE. GERMANY NAT/G LEGIT CT/SYS INGP/REL MORAL ORD/FREE RESPECT...JURID GP/COMP 20. PAGE 140 H2798
ADJUD JUDGE FASCISM

B59
SISSON C.H.,THE SPIRIT OF BRITISH ADMINISTRATION AND SOME EUROPEAN COMPARISONS. FRANCE GERMANY/W SWEDEN UK LAW EX/STRUC INGP/REL EFFICIENCY ORD/FREE ...DECISION 20. PAGE 144 H2890
GOV/COMP ADMIN ELITES ATTIT

S59
GABLE R.W.,"CULTURE AND ADMINISTRATION IN IRAN." IRAN EXEC PARTIC REPRESENT PWR. PAGE 54 H1085
ADMIN CULTURE EX/STRUC INGP/REL

S59
PRESTHUS R.V.,"BEHAVIOR AND BUREAUCRACY IN MANY CULTURES." EXEC INGP/REL 20. PAGE 128 H2558
ADMIN EX/STRUC GOV/COMP METH/CNCPT

B60
BEATTIE J.,BUNYORO, AN AFRICAN KINGDOM. UGANDA STRATA INGP/REL PERS/REL...SOC BIBLIOG 19/20. PAGE 13 H0250
CULTURE ELITES SECT KIN

B60
BHAMBHRI C.P.,PARLIAMENTARY CONTROL OVER STATE ENTERPRISE IN INDIA. INDIA DELIB/GP ADMIN CONTROL INGP/REL EFFICIENCY 20 PARLIAMENT. PAGE 16 H0327
NAT/G OWN INDUS PARL/PROC

B60
INTERNATIONAL AFRICAN INST,ETHNOGRAPHIC SURVEY OF AFRICA: WESTERN AFRICA: PEOPLES OF THE MIDDLE NIGER REGION, NORTHERN NIGERIA. AFR NIGER CULTURE ECO/UNDEV KIN NEIGH GOV/REL GP/REL ATTIT HEREDITY ...CHARTS BIBLIOG WORSHIP 20. PAGE 78 H1552
STRUCT GEOG HABITAT INGP/REL

B60
LA PONCE J.A.,THE PROTECTION OF MINORITIES. WOR+45 WOR-45 NAT/G POL/PAR SUFF...INT/LAW CLASSIF GP/COMP GOV/COMP BIBLIOG 17/20 CIVIL/LIB CIV/RIGHTS. PAGE 90 H1793
INGP/REL DOMIN SOCIETY RACE/REL

B60
MANIS J.G.,MAN AND SOCIETY. STRATA LEAD INGP/REL PERS/REL ATTIT PWR...PSY ANTHOL T SOC/INTEG MARX/KARL MILL/JS FREUD/S CHURCHLL/W SPENCER/H RUSSELL/B. PAGE 102 H2036
SOC SOCIETY STRUCT CULTURE

B60
OTTENBERG S.,CULTURES AND SOCIETIES OF AFRICA. AFR KIN TEC/DEV GP/REL MARRIAGE ATTIT HABITAT HEREDITY ...ANTHOL BIBLIOG T WORSHIP 20. PAGE 122 H2433
SOCIETY INGP/REL STRUCT CULTURE

B60
PINTO F.B.M.,ENRIQUECIMENTO ILICITO NO EXERCICIO DE CARGOS PUBLICOS. BRAZIL L/A+17C USA+45 ELITES TRIBUTE CONTROL INGP/REL ORD/FREE PWR...NAT/COMP 20. PAGE 126 H2513
ADMIN NAT/G CRIME LAW

S60
TURNER R.H.,"SPONSORED AND CONTEST MOBILITY IN THE SCHOOL SYSTEM." UK USA+45 ELITES STRATA ACADEM FACE/GP EDU/PROP CONTROL INGP/REL ADJUST ATTIT PERSON...METH/COMP 20. PAGE 157 H3142
AGE/Y NAT/COMP SCHOOL STRUCT

S60
WOLFINGER R.E.,"REPUTATION AND REALITY IN THE STUDY OF COMMUNITY POWER." STRUCT PROB/SOLV INGP/REL ATTIT OBJECTIVE...SOC METH/CNCPT PERS/COMP. PAGE 170 H3404
CULTURE MUNIC DOMIN PWR

B61
CATHERINE R.,LE FONCTIONNAIRE FRANCAIS. FRANCE NAT/G INGP/REL ATTIT MORAL ORD/FREE...T CIVIL/SERV. PAGE 28 H0559
ADMIN GP/REL LEAD SUPEGO

B61
COBBAN A.,ROUSSEAU AND THE MODERN STATE. SOCIETY DOMIN INGP/REL HAPPINESS ALL/VALS...CON/ANAL 18/20 ROUSSEAU/J. PAGE 30 H0611
ORD/FREE ROLE NAT/G POLICY

B61
DOOB L.W.,COMMUNICATION IN AFRICA: A SEARCH FOR BOUNDARIES. CULTURE SOCIETY EDU/PROP WRITING INGP/REL DRIVE ORD/FREE...ART/METH SOC LING BIBLIOG 20. PAGE 42 H0837
AFR FEEDBACK PERCEPT PERS/REL

B61
FIRTH R.,ELEMENTS OF SOCIAL ORGANIZATION (3RD ED.). STRATA STRUCT ECO/UNDEV NEIGH CHIEF INGP/REL ATTIT MORAL...PHIL/SCI GP/COMP WORSHIP SOC/INTEG 20. PAGE 50 H1009
SOC CULTURE SOCIETY KIN

B61
JUSTICE,THE CITIZEN AND THE ADMINISTRATION: THE REDRESS OF GRIEVANCES (PAMPHLET). EUR+WWI UK LAW CONSTN STRATA NAT/G CT/SYS PARTIC COERCE...NEW/IDEA IDEA/COMP 20 OMBUDSMAN. PAGE 82 H1644
INGP/REL CONSULT ADJUD REPRESENT

B61
KEE R.,REFUGEE WORLD. AUSTRIA EUR+WWI GERMANY NEIGH EX/STRUC WORKER PROB/SOLV ECO/TAC RENT EDU/PROP INGP/REL COST LITERACY HABITAT 20 MIGRATION. PAGE 84 H1676
NAT/G GIVE WEALTH STRANGE

B61
RAHNER H.,KIRCHE UND STAAT IM FRUHEN CHRISTENTUM. INGP/REL ORD/FREE PWR CATHISM...JURID 1/9 CHURCH/STA CHRISTIAN. PAGE 129 H2582
NAT/G SECT ATTIT GP/REL

B61
SHIELS W.E.,KING AND CHURCH: THE RISE AND FALL OF THE PATRONATO REAL. SPAIN INGP/REL...CONCPT WORSHIP 16/19 CHURCH/STA MISSION. PAGE 143 H2859
SECT NAT/G CHIEF POLICY

B61
SOUTHALL A.,SOCIAL CHANGE IN MODERN AFRICA. CULTURE STRATA ECO/UNDEV AGRI FAM KIN MUNIC GP/REL INGP/REL MARRIAGE...GEOG ANTHOL 20. PAGE 147 H2940
AFR TREND SOCIETY SOC

B61
TURNBULL C.M.,THE FOREST PEOPLE. EATING GP/REL INGP/REL RACE/REL ISOLAT HABITAT HEREDITY...GEOG SOC LING DICTIONARY WORSHIP 20 CONGO NEGRO BA/MBUTI. PAGE 157 H3138
AFR CULTURE KIN RECORD

B62
ESCUELA SUPERIOR DE ADMIN PUBL,INFORME DEL SEMINARIO SOBRE SERVICIO CIVIL O CARRERA ADMINISTRATIVA. L/A+17C ELITES STRATA CONFER CONTROL GOV/REL INGP/REL SUPEGO 20 CENTRAL/AM CIVIL/SERV. PAGE 47 H0939
ADMIN NAT/G PROB/SOLV ATTIT

B62
EVANS-PRITCHARD E.E.,ESSAYS IN SOCIAL ANTHROPOLOGY. AFR KIN REGION INGP/REL DRIVE HABITAT...OBS METH 20 ZANDE. PAGE 48 H0954
SOCIETY CULTURE SOC STRUCT

B62
FALKENBERG J.,KIN AND TOTEM; GROUP RELATIONS OF AUSTRALIAN ABORIGINES IN THE PORT KEATS DISTRICT. SOCIETY STRATA STRUCT GP/REL PERS/REL MARRIAGE AGE ATTIT SEX...SOC STAT CHARTS AUSTRAL ABORIGINES. PAGE 48 H0964
KIN INGP/REL CULTURE FAM

B62
HANSON A.H.,MANAGERIAL PROBLEMS IN PUBLIC ENTERPRISE. INDIA DELIB/GP GP/REL INGP/REL EFFICIENCY 20 PARLIAMENT. PAGE 66 H1320
MGT NAT/G INDUS PROB/SOLV

B62
INSTITUTE OF PUBLIC ADMIN,A SHORT HISTORY OF THE PUBLIC SERVICE IN IRELAND. IRELAND UK DIST/IND INGP/REL FEDERAL 13/20 CIVIL/SERV. PAGE 77 H1539
ADMIN WORKER GOV/REL NAT/G

B62
JAIN R.S.,THE GROWTH AND DEVELOPMENT OF GOVERNOR-GENERAL'S EXECUTIVE COUNCIL 1858-1919. INDIA UK CONSTN EX/STRUC LEGIS ADJUD ADMIN INGP/REL ATTIT 19/20. PAGE 79 H1585
NAT/G DELIB/GP CHIEF CONSULT

B62
KRECH D.,INDIVIDUAL IN SOCIETY; A TEXTBOOK OF SOCIAL PSYCHOLOGY. UNIV CULTURE LEAD INGP/REL ATTIT DRIVE PERCEPT ROLE...PHIL/SCI BIBLIOG T. PAGE 88 H1765
PSY SOC SOCIETY PERS/REL

B62
MEGGITT M.J.,DESERT PEOPLE. ECO/UNDEV KIN CREATE PROB/SOLV CONTROL DRIVE ROLE...GEOG SOC MYTH CHARTS BIBLIOG 20 AUSTRAL. PAGE 108 H2159
ADJUST CULTURE INGP/REL HABITAT

B62
OLLE-LAPRUNE J.,LA STABILITE DES MINISTRES SOUS LA TROISIEME REPUBLIQUE, 1879-1940. FRANCE CONSTN POL/PAR LEAD WAR INGP/REL RIGID/FLEX PWR...POLICY CHARTS 19/20. PAGE 121 H2415
LEGIS NAT/G ADMIN PERSON

B62
PAIKERT G.C.,THE GERMAN EXODUS. EUR+WWI GERMANY/W LAW CULTURE SOCIETY STRUCT INDUS NAT/LISM RESPECT SOVEREIGN...CHARTS BIBLIOG SOC/INTEG 20 MIGRATION. PAGE 122 H2444
INGP/REL STRANGE GEOG GP/REL

B63
BADI J.,THE GOVERNMENT OF THE STATE OF ISRAEL: A CRITICAL ACCOUNT OF ITS PARLIAMENT, EXECUTIVE, AND JUDICIARY. ISRAEL ECO/DEV CHIEF DELIB/GP LEGIS DIPLOM CT/SYS INGP/REL PEACE ORD/FREE...BIBLIOG 20 PARLIAMENT ARABS MIGRATION. PAGE 10 H0193
NAT/G CONSTN EX/STRUC POL/PAR

B63
BLONDEL J.,VOTERS, PARTIES, AND LEADERS. UK ELITES LOC/G NAT/G PROVS ACT/RES DOMIN REPRESENT GP/REL INGP/REL...SOC BIBLIOG 20. PAGE 18 H0358
POL/PAR STRATA LEGIS ADMIN

B63
BORKENAU F.,THE SPANISH COCKPIT. SPAIN ELITES STRATA POL/PAR ACT/RES CROWD WAR GP/REL INGP/REL
REV CONSERVE

...SOC NAT/COMP 20. PAGE 19 H0377 — SOCISM FORCES

B63
ELLIOT J.H.,THE REVOLT OF THE CATALANS. SPAIN LOC/G PROVS FORCES DIPLOM TASK WAR GOV/REL INGP/REL ...POLICY 17 OLIVARES. PAGE 45 H0909 — REV NAT/G TOP/EX DOMIN

B63
FRIEDRICH C.J.,MAN AND HIS GOVERNMENT: AN EMPIRICAL THEORY OF POLITICS. UNIV LOC/G NAT/G ADJUD REV INGP/REL DISCRIM PWR BIBLIOG. PAGE 53 H1069 — PERSON ORD/FREE PARTIC CONTROL

B63
HARTLEY A.,A STATE OF ENGLAND. UK ELITES SOCIETY ACADEM NAT/G SCHOOL INGP/REL CONSEN ORD/FREE NEW/LIB...POLICY 20. PAGE 67 H1349 — DIPLOM ATTIT INTELL ECO/DEV

B63
HUNTER G.,EDUCATION FOR A DEVELOPING REGION; A STUDY IN EAST AFRICA. AFR TANZANIA UGANDA NAT/G TEC/DEV INGP/REL ADJUST LITERACY ATTIT 20 AFRICA/E. PAGE 75 H1501 — EDU/PROP POLICY ECO/UNDEV EFFICIENCY

B63
KROEBER A.L.,ANTHROPOLOGY: BIOLOGY AND RACE. UNIV CULTURE HABITAT...PSY 20. PAGE 89 H1772 — SOC PHIL/SCI RACE/REL INGP/REL

B63
LOOMIE A.J.,THE SPANISH ELIZABETHANS: THE ENGLISH EXILES AT THE COURT OF PHILIP II. SPAIN UK WAR INGP/REL DRIVE HABITAT CATHISM...BIOG 16/17 MIGRATION. PAGE 98 H1962 — NAT/G STRANGE POLICY DIPLOM

B63
MENZEL J.M.,THE CHINESE CIVIL SERVICE: CAREER OPEN TO TALENT? ASIA ROUTINE INGP/REL DISCRIM ATTIT ROLE KNOWL ANTHOL. PAGE 109 H2177 — ADMIN NAT/G DECISION ELITES

B63
NOMAD M.,POLITICAL HERETICS: FROM PLATO TO MAO TSE-TUNG. UNIV INGP/REL...SOC IDEA/COMP. PAGE 119 H2369 — SOCIETY UTOPIA ALL/IDEOS CONCPT

S63
ZOLBERG A.R.,"MASS PARTIES AND NATIONAL INTEGRATION: THE CASE OF THE IVORY COAST" (BMR)" AFR IVORY/CST CONSTN VOL/ASSN DIPLOM LEAD GP/REL INGP/REL 20. PAGE 173 H3461 — POL/PAR ECO/UNDEV NAT/G ADJUST

B64
AGGARWALA R.C.,CONSTITUTIONAL HISTORY OF INDIA AND NATIONAL MOVEMENT INCLUDING COMPARATIVE STUDY OF MODERN INDIA CONSTITUTION. INDIA S/ASIA SECT VOL/ASSN EX/STRUC LEGIS COERCE REV INGP/REL ORD/FREE...SOC BIBLIOG 18/20 CMN/WLTH. PAGE 4 H0077 — CONSTN COLONIAL DOMIN NAT/G

B64
BENDIX R.,NATION-BUILDING AND CITIZENSHIP: STUDIES OF OUR CHANGING SOCIAL ORDER. WOR+45 CULTURE LOC/G GOV/REL INGP/REL ORD/FREE PWR 20. PAGE 14 H0275 — PARTIC NAT/COMP ADMIN AUTHORIT

B64
CAPLOW T.,PRINCIPLES OF ORGANIZATION. UNIV CULTURE STRUCT CREATE INGP/REL UTOPIA...GEN/LAWS TIME. PAGE 26 H0526 — VOL/ASSN CONCPT SIMUL EX/STRUC

B64
COBBAN A.,ROUSSEAU AND THE MODERN STATE (2ND ED.). FRANCE PROB/SOLV NAT/LISM UTOPIA PERSON MORAL ...EPIST PHIL/SCI SOC IDEA/COMP 18 ROUSSEAU/J BURKE/EDM HOBBES/T HUME/D. PAGE 30 H0612 — GEN/LAWS INGP/REL NAT/G ORD/FREE

B64
CULLINGWORTH J.B.,TOWN AND COUNTRY PLANNING IN ENGLAND AND WALES. UK LAW SOCIETY CONSULT ACT/RES ADMIN ROUTINE LEISURE INGP/REL ADJUST PWR...GEOG 20 OPEN/SPACE URBAN/RNWL. PAGE 36 H0718 — MUNIC PLAN NAT/G PROB/SOLV

B64
FROMM E.,MARX'S CONCEPT OF MAN. LABOR OWN PERSON ...HUM IDEA/COMP GEN/LAWS 17 MARX/KARL EUROPE SPINOZA/B GOETHE/J HEGEL/GWF. PAGE 54 H1072 — INGP/REL CONCPT MARXISM SOCISM

B64
GREAT BRITAIN CENTRAL OFF INF,CONSTITUTIONAL DEVELOPMENT IN THE COMMONWEALTH. VOL/ASSN PLAN DIPLOM COLONIAL INGP/REL NAT/LISM ORD/FREE PWR 17/20 CMN/WLTH. PAGE 60 H1202 — REGION CONSTN NAT/G SOVEREIGN

B64
GRIFFITH W.E.,COMMUNISM IN EUROPE (2 VOLS.). CZECHOSLVK USSR WOR+45 WOR-45 YUGOSLAVIA INGP/REL MARXISM SOCISM...ANTHOL 20 EUROPE/E. PAGE 61 H1225 — COM POL/PAR DIPLOM GOV/COMP

B64
HAAR C.M.,LAW AND LAND: ANGLO-AMERICAN PLANNING PRACTICE. UK USA+45 NAT/G TEC/DEV BUDGET CT/SYS INGP/REL EFFICIENCY OWN...JURID 20. PAGE 63 H1263 — LAW PLAN MUNIC NAT/COMP

B64
KRUEGER H.,ALLGEMEINE STAATSLEHRE. WOR+45 CONSTN SECT CHOOSE INGP/REL PWR NEW/LIB...JURID CLASSIF IDEA/COMP. PAGE 89 H1777 — NAT/G GOV/COMP SOCIETY

B64
LEMARCHAND R.,POLITICAL AWAKENING IN THE BELGIAN CONGO. ECO/UNDEV VOL/ASSN DOMIN CHOOSE GP/REL INGP/REL DISCRIM ORD/FREE PWR...CHARTS 20 CONGO ARABS. PAGE 94 H1873 — NAT/LISM COLONIAL POL/PAR RACE/REL

B64
MARTINEZ J.R.,THREE CASES OF COMMUNISM: CUBA, BRAZIL, AND MEXICO. BRAZIL CUBA L/A+17C CONSTN NAT/G DIPLOM ECO/TAC GP/REL INGP/REL...GP/COMP BIBLIOG 20 MEXIC/AMER COM/PARTY. PAGE 103 H2068 — MARXISM BIOG REV NAT/COMP

B64
MEAD M.,CONTINUITIES IN CULTURAL EVOLUTION. FACE/GP KIN ACT/RES EDU/PROP GP/REL INGP/REL DRIVE HEREDITY ROLE...TIME/SEQ TREND METH SOC/INTEG 20. PAGE 108 H2153 — CULTURE SOC PERS/REL

B64
RAPHAEL M.,PENSIONS AND PUBLIC SERVANTS. UK NAT/G PLAN INGP/REL COST EFFICIENCY ATTIT...POLICY 17/20 CIVIL/SERV. PAGE 130 H2593 — RECEIVE ADMIN INCOME AGE/O

B64
VALEN H.,POLITICAL PARTIES IN NORWAY. NORWAY ACADEM PARTIC ROUTINE INGP/REL KNOWL...QU 20. PAGE 161 H3220 — LOC/G POL/PAR PERSON

B64
VON STEIN L.J.,THE HISTORY OF THE SOCIAL MOVEMENT IN FRANCE, 1789-1850 (TRANS. BY K. MENGELBERG). COM FRANCE MOD/EUR NAT/G EX/STRUC INGP/REL ALL/IDEOS CONSERVE MARXISM...SOC BIBLIOG 18/19. PAGE 164 H3278 — REV STRATA

B64
WALDMAN E.,THE GOOSE STEP IS VERBOTEN: THE GERMAN ARMY TODAY. GERMANY/W LAW CONSTN LEGIS PROB/SOLV DOMIN CONTROL CIVMIL/REL GOV/REL INGP/REL ATTIT ...DEEP/QU 20. PAGE 164 H3289 — SOC FORCES NAT/G

S64
COLEMAN J.S.,"COLLECTIVE DECISIONS." CULTURE ATTIT PERCEPT PWR SOC. PAGE 31 H0628 — DECISION INGP/REL PERSON METH/COMP

B65
ADENAUER K.,MEINE ERINNERUNGEN, 1945-53 (VOL. I), 1953-55 (VOL. II). EUR+WWI GERMANY CHIEF FORCES PROB/SOLV DIPLOM ARMS/CONT INGP/REL PEACE SOVEREIGN ...OBS/ENVIR RECORD 20. PAGE 3 H0069 — NAT/G BIOG SELF/OBS

B65
BOISSEVAIN J.,SAINTS AND FIREWORKS: RELIGION AND POLITICS IN RURAL MALTA. MALTA STRUCT FAM NEIGH POL/PAR REPRESENT INGP/REL CENTRAL...CHARTS BIBLIOG 20. PAGE 18 H0368 — GP/REL NAT/G SECT MUNIC

B65
CHARNAY J.P.,LE SUFFRAGE POLITIQUE EN FRANCE; ELECTIONS PARLEMENTAIRES, ELECTION PRESIDENTIELLE, REFERENDUMS. FRANCE CONSTN CHIEF DELIB/GP ECO/TAC EDU/PROP CRIME INGP/REL MORAL ORD/FREE PWR CATHISM 20 PARLIAMENT PRESIDENT. PAGE 29 H0584 — CHOOSE SUFF NAT/G LEGIS

B65
GEWIRTH A.,POLITICAL PHILOSOPHY. UNIV SOCIETY NAT/G GP/REL INGP/REL CONSEN PWR...IDEA/COMP GEN/LAWS 17/19 HOBBES/T LOCKE/JOHN MARX/KARL MILL/JS ROUSSEAU/J. PAGE 56 H1118 — ORD/FREE SOVEREIGN PHIL/SCI

B65
GIBBS S.L.,PEOPLES OF AFRICA. AFR INGP/REL HABITAT ...GEOG ANTHOL 20. PAGE 56 H1122 — CULTURE AGRI FAM KIN

B65
GOLEMBIEWSKI R.T.,MEN, MANAGEMENT, AND MORALITY; TOWARD A NEW ORGANIZATIONAL ETHIC. CONSTN EX/STRUC CREATE ADMIN CONTROL INGP/REL PERSON SUPEGO MORAL PWR...GOV/COMP METH/COMP 20 BUREAUCRCY. PAGE 58 H1161 — LG/CO MGT PROB/SOLV

B65
KLEIN J.,SAMPLES FROM ENGLISH CULTURES (2 VOLS.). UK STRATA FAM NEIGH WORKER ETIQUET ISOLAT AGE/C AGE/A HABITAT RIGID/FLEX...NET/THEORY CHARTS 20. PAGE 87 H1732 — CULTURE INGP/REL ATTIT SOC

B65
KUNSTADTER P.,THE LUA (LAWA) OF NORTHERN THAILAND: ASPECTS OF SOCIAL STRUCTURE, AGRICULTURE, AND RELIGION. THAILAND AGRI FAM KIN INGP/REL ISOLAT MARRIAGE HEALTH WORSHIP 20 BUDDHISM LUA. PAGE 89 H1780 — STRUCT ECO/UNDEV CULTURE

B65
LAMBIRI I.,SOCIAL CHANGE IN A GREEK COUNTRY TOWN. GREECE FAM PROB/SOLV ROUTINE TASK LEISURE INGP/REL CONSEN ORD/FREE...SOC INT QU CHARTS 20. PAGE 90 H1803 — INDUS WORKER CULTURE NEIGH

B65
LAWRENCE P.,GODS, GHOSTS, AND MEN IN MELANESIA: SOME RELIGIONS OF AUSTRALIAN NEW GUINEA AND THE NEW HEBRIDES. SOCIETY ECO/UNDEV FAM GP/REL INGP/REL HABITAT PERSON...GEOG SOC ANTHOL BIBLIOG WORSHIP 20 NEW/GUINEA. PAGE 92 H1847 — MYTH S/ASIA SECT CULTURE

B65
PELLING H.,A SHORT HISTORY OF THE LABOUR PARTY (2ND ED.). UK NAT/G CHIEF PARL/PROC GP/REL INGP/REL 20 LABOR/PAR PARLIAMENT WILSON/H. PAGE 124 H2484 POL/PAR NEW/LIB LEAD LABOR

B65
WILLIAMSON J.A.,GREAT BRITAIN AND THE COMMONWEALTH. UK DOMIN COLONIAL INGP/REL...POLICY 18/20 CMN/WLTH. PAGE 168 H3370 NAT/G DIPLOM INT/ORG SOVEREIGN

B66
AIYAR S.P.,PERSPECTIVES ON THE WELFARE STATE. INDIA S/ASIA UK CONSTN ECO/UNDEV NAT/G INGP/REL CENTRAL NAT/LISM ATTIT...CONCPT ANTHOL BIBLIOG 20. PAGE 4 H0087 NEW/LIB WELF/ST IDEA/COMP ADJUST

B66
BECKER J.,BESSARABIEN UND SEIN DEUTSCHTUM. ROMANIA USSR STRUCT INDUS PROF/ORG SECT GP/REL INGP/REL 15/20 BESSARABIA. PAGE 13 H0254 PROVS CULTURE SOCIETY

B66
BHALERAO C.N.,PUBLIC SERVICE COMMISSIONS OF INDIA: A STUDY. INDIA SERV/IND EX/STRUC ROUTINE CHOOSE GOV/REL INGP/REL...KNO/TEST EXHIBIT 20. PAGE 16 H0326 NAT/G OP/RES LOC/G ADMIN

B66
BRODERSEN A.,THE SOVIET WORKER: LABOR AND GOVERNMENT IN SOVIET SOCIETY. USSR STRUCT INDUS LABOR PLAN PAY INGP/REL PRODUC...POLICY GEN/LAWS BIBLIOG 20 STALIN/J LENIN/VI BOLSHEVISM KHRUSH/N. PAGE 21 H0425 WORKER ROLE NAT/G MARXISM

B66
HAMILTON W.B.,A DECADE OF THE COMMONWEALTH, 1955-1964. UK LAW ELITES FINAN FOR/AID CONFER COLONIAL PWR...GEOG CHARTS ANTHOL 20 CMN/WLTH UN. PAGE 65 H1302 INT/ORG INGP/REL DIPLOM NAT/G

B66
HENKYS R.,DEUTSCHLAND UND DIE OSTLICHEN NACHBARN. GERMANY POLAND NAT/G POL/PAR INGP/REL ATTIT 20 MIGRATION. PAGE 70 H1396 GP/REL JURID INT/LAW DIPLOM

B66
LEYBURN J.G.,THE HAITIAN PEOPLE (REV. ED.). HAITI SOCIETY FAM SECT DOMIN COLONIAL MARRIAGE...SOC CHARTS BIBLIOG/A 18/10. PAGE 96 H1917 STRUCT STRATA INGP/REL CULTURE

B66
LOVEDAY P.,PARLIAMENT FACTIONS AND PARTIES: THE FIRST THIRTY YEARS OF RESPONSIBLE GOVERNMENT IN NEW SOUTH WALES, 1856-1889. PROVS LEAD PARL/PROC PARTIC GP/REL INGP/REL MAJORITY PWR...GP/COMP 19 AUSTRAL. PAGE 99 H1970 POL/PAR ELITES NAT/G LEGIS

B66
MAC DONALD H.M.,THE INTELLECTUAL IN POLITICS. GERMANY PERU SWEDEN UK USSR NAT/G CONSULT PLAN EDU/PROP TASK INGP/REL EFFICIENCY RATIONAL ALL/VALS 20. PAGE 99 H1987 ALL/IDEOS INTELL POL/PAR PARTIC

B66
NEUMANN R.G.,THE GOVERNMENT OF THE GERMAN FEDERAL REPUBLIC. EUR+WWI GERMANY/W LOC/G EX/STRUC LEGIS CT/SYS INGP/REL PWR...BIBLIOG 20 ADENAUER/K. PAGE 117 H2336 NAT/G POL/PAR DIPLOM CONSTN

B66
THOMPSON J.H.,MODERNIZATION OF THE ARAB WORLD. FUT ISRAEL STRUCT ECO/UNDEV DIPLOM INGP/REL ATTIT ...CENSUS ANTHOL 20 ARABS. PAGE 154 H3082 ADJUST ISLAM PROB/SOLV NAT/COMP

B66
WEINSTEIN B.,GABON: NATION-BUILDING ON THE OGOOUE. AFR GABON WOR+45 CULTURE SOCIETY PLAN DIPLOM COLONIAL INGP/REL ANOMIE HABITAT SUPEGO 20. PAGE 166 H3329 ECO/UNDEV GP/REL LEAD NAT/G

S66
FLEMING W.G.,"AUTHORITY, EFFICIENCY, AND ROLE STRESS: PROBLEMS IN THE DEVELOPMENT OF EAST AFRICAN BUREAUCRACIES." AFR UGANDA STRUCT PROB/SOLV ROUTINE INGP/REL ROLE...MGT SOC GP/COMP GOV/COMP 20 TANGANYIKA AFRICA/E. PAGE 51 H1024 DOMIN EFFICIENCY COLONIAL ADMIN

C66
DEUTSCH K.W.,"NATIONALISM AND SOCIAL COMMUNICATION." CULTURE INGP/REL ATTIT PWR...PSY SOC CONCPT LING IDEA/COMP 20. PAGE 40 H0800 BIBLIOG NAT/LISM GEN/LAWS

B67
BARNETT A.D.,CADRES, BUREAUCRACY, AND POLITICAL POWER IN COMMUNIST CHINA. CHINA/COM ELITES LOC/G NAT/G INGP/REL...SOC INT DICTIONARY 20. PAGE 11 H0224 GOV/REL STRUCT MARXISM EDU/PROP

B67
BODENHEIMER E.,TREATISE ON JUSTICE. INT/ORG NAT/G PUB/INST ACT/RES RISK CRIME INGP/REL DISCRIM DRIVE LAISSEZ 20. PAGE 18 H0363 ALL/VALS STRUCT JURID CONCPT

B67
GELLHORN W.,OMBUDSMEN AND OTHERS: CITIZENS' PROTECTORS IN NINE COUNTRIES. WOR+45 LAW CONSTN LEGIS INSPECT ADJUD ADMIN CONTROL CT/SYS CHOOSE PERS/REL...STAT CHARTS 20. PAGE 55 H1109 NAT/COMP REPRESENT INGP/REL PROB/SOLV

B67
KAROL K.S.,CHINA, THE OTHER COMMUNISM (TRANS. BY TOM BAISTOW). CHINA/COM CULTURE INDUS FORCES DIPLOM EDU/PROP CONTROL EXEC NUC/PWR ATTIT...SOC CHARTS 20. PAGE 83 H1663 NAT/G POL/PAR MARXISM INGP/REL

B67
KING M.L. JR.,WHERE DO WE GO FROM HERE: CHAOS OR COMMUNITY? MUNIC NAT/G PARTIC INGP/REL ALL/VALS ...POLICY CONCPT BIOG 20. PAGE 86 H1715 RACE/REL DISCRIM STRUCT PWR

B67
KORNBERG A.,CANADIAN LEGISLATIVE BEHAVIOR: A STUDY OF THE 25TH PARLIAMENT. CANADA NAT/G POL/PAR PARL/PROC CHOOSE INGP/REL ADJUST ANOMIE RIGID/FLEX ...SOC STAND/INT CHARTS SOC/EXP 20 PARLIAMENT. PAGE 88 H1756 ATTIT LEGIS ROLE

B67
MAZRUI A.A.,THE ANGLO-AFRICAN COMMONWEALTH; POLITICAL FRICTION AND CULTURAL FUSION. AFR INT/ORG VOL/ASSN CHIEF GP/REL INGP/REL RACE/REL NAT/LISM 20 CMN/WLTH EEC. PAGE 106 H2111 COLONIAL SOVEREIGN DIPLOM CULTURE

B67
RYDER A.J.,THE GERMAN REVOLUTION OF 1918; A STUDY OF GERMAN SOCIALISM IN WAR AND REVOLT. GERMANY NAT/G POL/PAR GP/REL...BIBLIOG 20. PAGE 136 H2724 SOCISM WAR REV INGP/REL

L67
GOOD E.M.,"CAPITAL PUNISHMENT AND ITS ALTERNATIVES IN ANCIENT NEAR EASTERN LAW." SOCIETY SECT INGP/REL CONSEN ATTIT SEX MORAL...CRIMLGY GP/COMP. PAGE 58 H1168 MEDIT-7 LAW JURID CULTURE

L67
VAN DER KROEF J.M.,"INDONESIA: THE BATTLE OF THE 'OLD' AND THE 'NEW ORDER'." INDONESIA ISLAM ELITES POL/PAR DOMIN INGP/REL NAT/LISM PWR...IDEA/COMP 20. PAGE 161 H3229 FORCES MARXISM NAT/G BAL/PWR

S67
BULLOUGH B.,"ALIENATION IN THE GHETTO." CULTURE NEIGH GP/REL INGP/REL ATTIT...PSY SOC SAMP. PAGE 23 H0471 DISCRIM ANOMIE ADJUST

S67
CARR E.H.,"REVOLUTION FROM ABOVE." USSR STRATA FINAN INDUS NAT/G DOMIN LEAD GP/REL INGP/REL OWN PRODUC PWR 20 STALIN/J. PAGE 27 H0538 AGRI POLICY COM EFFICIENCY

S67
COHEN R.,"ANTHROPOLOGY AND POLITICAL SCIENCE: COURTSHIP OR MARRIAGE?" CULTURE STRATA STRUCT MUNIC REGION UTOPIA...NEW/IDEA TREND IDEA/COMP METH/COMP 20. PAGE 31 H0618 SOC INGP/REL AFR

S67
COLLINS B.A.,"SOME NOTES ON PUBLIC SERVICE COMMISSIONS IN THE COMMONWEALTH CARIBBEAN." JAMAICA L/A+17C TRINIDAD UK NAT/G OP/RES DOMIN SENIOR COLONIAL CONTROL INGP/REL CENTRAL EFFICIENCY PWR ...DECISION 20. PAGE 31 H0631 ADMIN EX/STRUC ECO/UNDEV CHOOSE

S67
EGBERT D.D.,"POLITICS AND ART IN COMMUNIST BULGARIA" BULGARIA COM USSR CULTURE DIPLOM INGP/REL TOTALISM...TREND 20. PAGE 45 H0894 CREATE ART/METH CONTROL MARXISM

S67
ELLISON H.J.,"THE SOCIALIST REVOLUTIONARIES." USSR ECO/UNDEV NAT/G INGP/REL EFFICIENCY ATTIT PWR MARXISM...CONCPT IDEA/COMP 20 SOC/REVPAR. PAGE 46 H0911 POL/PAR REV AGRI

S67
HARBRON J.D.,"UNIFICATION IN CANADA: FAIT ACCOMPLI" CANADA STRATA NAT/G DELIB/GP BUDGET GP/REL 20 NAVY. PAGE 66 H1327 INGP/REL FORCES PLAN ATTIT

S67
KINGSBURY E.C.,"LAW AS COMPACT: ANCIENT ISRAEL'S CONTRIBUTION TO THE UNDERSTANDING OF LAW." ISRAEL MEDIT-7 CULTURE KIN KNOWL...JURID CONCPT TREND IDEA/COMP METH/COMP WORSHIP JEWS DEITY. PAGE 86 H1716 LAW AGREE CONSTN INGP/REL

S67
LEVCIK B.,"WAGES AND EMPLOYMENT PROBLEMS IN THE NEW SYSTEM OF PLANNED MANAGEMENT IN CZECHOSLOVAKIA." CZECHOSLVK EUR+WWI NAT/G OP/RES PLAN ADMIN ROUTINE INGP/REL CENTRAL EFFICIENCY PRODUC DECISION. PAGE 95 H1895 MARXISM WORKER MGT PAY

S67
MITCHELL W.C.,"THE SHAPE OF POLITICAL THEORY TO COME: FROM POLITICAL SOCIOLOGY TO POLITICAL ECONOMY." ACADEM NAT/G BUDGET TAX LEGIT LOBBY GOV/REL INGP/REL...SOC NEW/IDEA TREND CHARTS 20 MONEY. PAGE 112 H2231 ECO/TAC GEN/LAWS

S67
MURVAR V.,"MAX WEBER'S CONCEPT OF HEIROCRACY: A STUDY IN THE TYPOLOGY OF CHURCH-STATE RELATIONS" UNIV INGP/REL ATTIT PLURISM...SOC CONCPT 20 WEBER/MAX. PAGE 115 H2299 SECT NAT/G GP/REL STRUCT

S67
RAUM O.,"THE MODERN LEADERSHIP GROUP AMONG THE RACE/REL

SOUTH AFRICAN XHOSA." SOUTH/AFR SOCIETY SECT EX/STRUC REPRESENT GP/REL INGP/REL PERSON ...METH/COMP 17/20 XHOSA NEGRO. PAGE 130 H2596 — KIN LEAD CULTURE

S67
ROTBERG R.I.,"COLONIALISM AND AFTER: THE POLITICAL LITERATURE OF CENTRAL AFRICA - A BIBLIOGRAPHIC ESSAY." AFR CHIEF EX/STRUC REV INGP/REL RACE/REL SOVEREIGN 20. PAGE 135 H2693 — BIBLIOG/A COLONIAL DIPLOM NAT/G

S67
SCOVILLE W.J.,"GOVERNMENT REGULATION AND GROWTH IN THE FRENCH PAPER INDUSTRY DURING THE EIGHTEENTH CENTURY." FRANCE MOD/EUR FINAN CAP/ISM TAX ADMIN CONTROL PRIVIL LAISSEZ...POLICY 18. PAGE 141 H2818 — NAT/G PROC/MFG ECO/DEV INGP/REL

S67
TATU M.,"URSS: LES FLOTTEMENTS DE LA DIRECTION COLLEGIALE." UAR USSR CHIEF LEAD INGP/REL EFFICIENCY...DECISION TREND 20 MID/EAST. PAGE 152 H3047 — POLICY NAT/G EX/STRUC DIPLOM

S67
THIEN T.T.,"VIETNAM: A CASE OF SOCIAL ALIENATION." VIETNAM AGRI FORCES FOR/AID ADMIN REPRESENT INGP/REL PWR 19/20. PAGE 154 H3071 — NAT/G ELITES WORKER STRANGE

S67
WRAITH R.E.,"ADMINISTRATIVE CHANGE IN THE NEW AFRICA." AFR LG/CO ADJUD INGP/REL PWR...RECORD GP/COMP 20. PAGE 171 H3416 — ADMIN NAT/G LOC/G ECO/UNDEV

S68
CHAPMAN A.R.,"THE CIVIL WAR IN NIGERIA." AFR NIGERIA NAT/G PLAN ECO/TAC EDU/PROP COERCE WAR GOV/REL INGP/REL ORD/FREE PWR WEALTH SOC/INTEG 20 BIAFRA. PAGE 29 H0579 — REV RACE/REL

S68
LAPIERRE J.W.,"TRADITION ET MODERNITE A MADAGASCAR." ISLAM MADAGASCAR AGRI FINAN KIN NAT/G CREATE OP/RES GP/REL INGP/REL ATTIT CONSERVE...PSY 20. PAGE 91 H1813 — ECO/UNDEV FOR/AID CULTURE TEC/DEV

B75
MAINE H.S.,LECTURES ON THE EARLY HISTORY OF INSTITUTIONS. IRELAND UK CONSTN ELITES STRUCT FAM KIN CHIEF LEGIS CT/SYS OWN SOVEREIGN...CONCPT 16 BENTHAM/J BREHON ROMAN/LAW. PAGE 101 H2021 — CULTURE LAW INGP/REL

B85
BLUNTSCHLI J.K.,THE THEORY OF THE STATE. GERMANY CONSTN INGP/REL NAT/LISM PERSON SOVEREIGN CONSERVE ...SOC. PAGE 18 H0362 — CONCPT LEGIS NAT/G

B96
SCHMOLLER G.,THE MERCANTILE SYSTEM AND ITS HISTORICAL SIGNIFICANCE: ILLUSTRATED CHIEFLY FROM PRUSSIAN HISTORY (TRANS.). PRUSSIA CULTURE INDUS KIN MUNIC NAT/G PROVS OP/RES ECO/TAC INT/TRADE SUPEGO PWR WEALTH 19 MERCANTLST. PAGE 139 H2790 — GEN/METH INGP/REL CONCPT

B99
DU BOIS W.E.B.,THE PHILADELPHIA NEGRO: A SOCIAL STUDY. CULTURE STRATA KIN CRIME SUFF ADJUST DISCRIM ISOLAT HABITAT HEREDITY ALL/VALS SOC/INTEG 17/19 NEGRO PHILADELPH. PAGE 42 H0851 — INGP/REL RACE/REL SOC CENSUS

B99
RIPLEY W.Z.,A SELECTED BIBLIOGRAPHY OF THE ANTHROPOLOGY AND ETHNOLOGY OF EUROPE. SOCIETY STRATA STRUCT KIN SECT VOL/ASSN GP/REL INGP/REL HABITAT...GEOG 19. PAGE 132 H2632 — BIBLIOG/A MOD/EUR SOC CULTURE

INNIS/H....HAROLD ADAMS INNIS

INNOVATION....SEE CREATE

INONU/I....ISMET INONU

INSPECT....EXAMINING FOR QUALITY, OUTPUT, LEGALITY

N19
HACKETT J.,ECONOMIC PLANNING IN FRANCE; ITS RELATION TO THE POLICIES OF THE DEVELOPED COUNTRIES OF WESTERN EUROPE (PAMPHLET). EUR+WWI FRANCE ECO/DEV PROB/SOLV CONTROL...POLICY 20 EUROPE/W. PAGE 63 H1270 — ECO/TAC NAT/G PLAN INSPECT

L34
GOSNELL H.F.,"BRITISH ROYAL COMMISSIONS OF INQUIRY" UK CONSTN LEGIS PRESS ADMIN PARL/PROC...DECISION 20 PARLIAMENT. PAGE 59 H1184 — DELIB/GP INSPECT POLICY NAT/G

B37
CLOKIE H.M.,ROYAL COMMISSIONS OF INQUIRY; THE SIGNIFICANCE OF INVESTIGATIONS IN BRITISH POLITICS. UK POL/PAR CONFER ROUTINE...POLICY DECISION TIME/SEQ 16/20. PAGE 30 H0607 — NAT/G DELIB/GP INSPECT

B40
MCILWAIN C.H.,CONSTITUTIONALISM, ANCIENT AND MODERN. CHRIST-17C MOD/EUR NAT/G CHIEF PROB/SOLV INSPECT AUTHORIT ORD/FREE PWR...TIME/SEQ ROMAN/REP. PAGE 107 H2134 — CONSTN GEN/LAWS LAW

C43
BENTHAM J.,"ON THE LIBERTY OF THE PRESS, AND PUBLIC DISCUSSION" IN J. BOWRING, ED., THE WORKS OF JEREMY BENTHAM." SPAIN UK LAW ELITES NAT/G LEGIS INSPECT LEGIT WRITING CONTROL PRIVIL TOTALISM AUTHORIT ...TRADIT 19 FREE/SPEE. PAGE 15 H0290 — ORD/FREE PRESS CONFER CONSERVE

B49
SCHONS D.,BOOK CENSORSHIP IN NEW SPAIN (NEW WORLD STUDIES, BOOK II). SPAIN LAW CULTURE INSPECT ADJUD CT/SYS SANCTION GP/REL ORD/FREE 14/17. PAGE 140 H2797 — CHRIST-17C EDU/PROP CONTROL PRESS

B55
WHEARE K.C.,GOVERNMENT BY COMMITTEE; AN ESSAY ON THE BRITISH CONSTITUTION. UK NAT/G LEGIS INSPECT CONFER ADJUD ADMIN CONTROL TASK EFFICIENCY ROLE POPULISM 20. PAGE 167 H3337 — DELIB/GP CONSTN LEAD GP/COMP

S58
SCHUMM S.,"INTEREST REPRESENTATION IN FRANCE AND GERMANY." EUR+WWI FRANCE GERMANY INSPECT PARL/PROC REPRESENT 20 WEIMAR/REP. PAGE 140 H2803 — LOBBY DELIB/GP NAT/G

B64
MARSH D.C.,THE FUTURE OF THE WELFARE STATE. UK CONSTN NAT/G POL/PAR...POLICY WELF/ST 20. PAGE 103 H2058 — NEW/LIB ADMIN CONCPT INSPECT

B65
HAVIGHURST R.J.,SOCIETY AND EDUCATION IN BRAZIL. BRAZIL PORTUGAL ECO/UNDEV INDUS NAT/G CREATE INSPECT COLONIAL ADJUST DEMAND LITERACY...CENSUS TREND CHARTS 16/20. PAGE 68 H1362 — SCHOOL ACADEM ACT/RES CULTURE

B65
ROWAT D.C.,THE OMBUDSMAN: CITIZEN'S DEFENDER. DENMARK FINLAND NEW/ZEALND NORWAY SWEDEN CONSULT PROB/SOLV FEEDBACK PARTIC GP/REL...SOC CONCPT NEW/IDEA METH/COMP ANTHOL BIBLIOG 20. PAGE 135 H2701 — INSPECT CONSTN NAT/G ADMIN

B67
GELLHORN W.,OMBUDSMEN AND OTHERS: CITIZENS' PROTECTORS IN NINE COUNTRIES. WOR+45 LAW CONSTN LEGIS INSPECT ADJUD ADMIN CONTROL CT/SYS CHOOSE PERS/REL...STAT CHARTS 20. PAGE 55 H1109 — NAT/COMP REPRESENT INGP/REL PROB/SOLV

B67
ROSENTHAL A.H.,THE SOCIAL PROGRAMS OF SWEDEN. SWEDEN USA+45 FINAN NAT/G PLAN PROB/SOLV INSPECT ORD/FREE...POLICY HEAL SOC CHARTS NAT/COMP 20. PAGE 134 H2681 — GIVE SOC/WK WEALTH METH/COMP

S67
CATTELL D.T.,"A NEO-MARXIST THEORY OF COMPARATIVE ANALYSIS." USSR STRATA INSPECT DOMIN CONTROL COERCE OWN TOTALISM PWR...FASCIST HYPO/EXP METH 20. PAGE 28 H0561 — GOV/COMP MARXISM SIMUL CLASSIF

S67
SLOAN P.,"FIFTY YEARS OF SOVIET RULE." USSR INDUS EDU/PROP EFFICIENCY PRODUC HEALTH KNOWL MORAL WEALTH MARXISM...POLICY 20. PAGE 145 H2900 — CREATE NAT/G PLAN INSPECT

B99
BROOKS S.,BRITAIN AND THE BOERS. AFR SOUTH/AFR UK CULTURE INSPECT LEGIT...INT/LAW 19/20 BOER/WAR. PAGE 22 H0433 — WAR DIPLOM NAT/G

INST INTL DES CIVILISATION DIF H1535

INSTITUTE COMP STUDY POL SYS H1536

INSTITUTE FOR STUDY OF USSR H1537

INSTITUTE OF HISPANIC STUDIES H1538

INSTITUTE OF PUBLIC ADMIN H1539

INSTITUTE POLITISCHE WISSEN H1540

INSTITUTION, EDUCATIONAL....SEE SCHOOL, ACADEM

INSTITUTION, MENTAL....SEE PUB/INST

INSTITUTION, RELIGIOUS....SEE SECT

INSTITUTIONS....SEE DESCRIPTORS IN INSTITUTIONAL INDEX (TOPICAL INDEX, NO. 2)

INSURANCE....SEE FINAN, SERV/IND

INSURRECTION....SEE REV

INT....INTERVIEW; SEE ALSO INTERVIEWS INDEX, P. XIV

B00
BENEDETTI V.,STUDIES IN DIPLOMACY. BELGIUM FRANCE GERMANY MOD/EUR CONSTN NAT/G CONSULT TOP/EX DOMIN EDU/PROP COERCE ATTIT...CONCPT INT BIOG TREND 19. PAGE 14 H0276 — PWR GEN/LAWS DIPLOM

B00
HOBSON J.A.,THE WAR IN SOUTH AFRICA: ITS CAUSES AND EFFECTS. NETHERLAND SOUTH/AFR UK ELITES AGRI EXTR/IND POL/PAR DIPLOM PRESS RACE/REL ATTIT ORD/FREE SOVEREIGN...INT 19 NEGRO. PAGE 72 H1439 — WAR DOMIN POLICY NAT/G

B36
CULVER D.C.,METHODOLOGY OF SOCIAL SCIENCE RESEARCH: A BIBLIOGRAPHY. LAW CULTURE...CRIMLGY GEOG STAT OBS INT QU HIST/WRIT CHARTS 20. PAGE 36 H0719
BIBLIOG/A METH SOC

B40
ZWEIG F.,THE WORKER IN AN AFFLUENT SOCIETY: FAMILY LIFE AND INDUSTRY. UK STRATA LG/CO ECO/TAC LEISURE INGP/REL HAPPINESS HEALTH...PSY SOC/WK INT CHARTS WORSHIP 20 FEMALE/SEX. PAGE 173 H3465
MARRIAGE ATTIT FINAN CULTURE

B52
SPICER E.H.,HUMAN PROBLEMS IN TECHNOLOGICAL CHANGE. ECO/UNDEV AGRI INDUS NAT/G ACT/RES LEAD GP/REL INGP/REL ROLE...INT METH 20 CASEBOOK. PAGE 147 H2947
TEC/DEV CULTURE STRUCT OP/RES

S52
EISENSTADT S.N.,"THE PROCESS OF ABSORPTION OF NEW IMMIGRANTS IN ISRAEL" (BMR)" ISRAEL CULTURE SCHOOL WORKER PARTIC DRIVE ORD/FREE...STAT OBS INT CHARTS SOC/INTEG 20 JEWS. PAGE 45 H0900
HABITAT ATTIT SAMP

B53
HUNTER E.,BRAIN-WASHING IN RED CHINA. ASIA CHINA/COM CULTURE SOCIETY FORCES WAR TOTALISM ATTIT BIO/SOC DISPL DRIVE PERSON SUPEGO KNOWL ORD/FREE ...INT REC/INT COLD/WAR 20. PAGE 75 H1499
EDU/PROP COERCE

S53
BAUER R.A.,"WORD-OF-MOUTH COMMUNICATION IN THE SOVIET UNION." COM INTELL SOCIETY LABOR ATTIT KNOWL ...INT QU SAMP CHARTS 20. PAGE 12 H0239
CULTURE USSR

B55
APTER D.E.,THE GOLD COAST IN TRANSITION. FUT CONSTN CULTURE SOCIETY ECO/UNDEV FAM KIN LOC/G NAT/G POL/PAR LEGIS TOP/EX EDU/PROP LEGIT ADMIN ATTIT PERSON PWR...CONCPT STAT INT CENSUS TOT/POP VAL/FREE. PAGE 7 H0149
AFR SOVEREIGN

B55
RODNICK D.,THE NORWEGIANS: A STUDY IN NATIONAL CULTURE. NORWAY FAM INGP/REL PERS/REL AGE...PSY SOC SELF/OBS WORSHIP 20. PAGE 133 H2655
CULTURE INT RECORD ATTIT

B58
COLEMAN J.S.,NIGERIA: BACKGROUND TO NATIONALISM. AFR SOCIETY ECO/DEV KIN LOC/G POL/PAR TEC/DEV DOMIN ADMIN DRIVE PWR RESPECT...TRADIT SOC INT SAMP TIME/SEQ 20. PAGE 31 H0627
NAT/G NAT/LISM NIGERIA

B58
HAAS E.B.,THE UNITING OF EUROPE. EUR+WWI INT/ORG NAT/G POL/PAR TOP/EX ECO/TAC EDU/PROP LEGIT FEDERAL NAT/LISM DRIVE RIGID/FLEX ORD/FREE PWR PLURISM ...POLICY CONCPT INT GEN/LAWS ECSC EEC 20. PAGE 63 H1264
VOL/ASSN ECO/DEV

B58
MECRENSKY E.,SCIENTIFIC MANPOWER IN EUROPE. WOR+45 EDU/PROP GOV/REL SKILL...TECHNIC PHIL/SCI INT CHARTS BIBLIOG 20. PAGE 108 H2157
ECO/TAC TEC/DEV METH/COMP NAT/COMP

S59
LYNN D.B.,"THE EFFECTS OF FATHER-ABSENCE ON NORWEGIAN BOYS AND GIRLS." NORWAY CULTURE PERS/REL ADJUST DISPL LOVE...PSY CORREL STAT INT CON/ANAL CHARTS SOC/INTEG 20. PAGE 99 H1983
SOC FAM AGE/C ANOMIE

B60
CARTER G.M.,INDEPENDENCE FOR AFRICA. AFR FUT SOCIETY STRATA ECO/DEV POL/PAR DELIB/GP PLAN DOMIN EDU/PROP COLONIAL REGION ATTIT DRIVE SOVEREIGN ...RECORD INT TIME/SEQ CHARTS 20. PAGE 27 H0544
NAT/G PWR NAT/LISM

B60
MINER H.M.,OASIS AND CASBAH: ALGERIAN CULTURE AND PERSONALITY IN CHANGE. ALGERIA FRANCE SOCIETY MUNIC COLONIAL ATTIT...INT PROJ/TEST CHARTS 20. PAGE 111 H2221
GP/COMP PERSON CULTURE ADJUST

B60
MORRIS I.,NATIONALISM AND THE RIGHT WING IN JAPAN: A STUDY OF POST WAR TRENDS. ASIA ELITES NAT/G DELIB/GP FORCES TOP/EX CHOOSE ATTIT...INT GEN/LAWS CONGRESS 20 CHINJAP. PAGE 113 H2262
POL/PAR TREND NAT/LISM

S60
CROZIER B.,"FRANCE AND ALGERIA." ALGERIA EUR+WWI FRANCE FUT ISLAM ECO/UNDEV NEIGH CONSULT DELIB/GP ECO/TAC COLONIAL COERCE ATTIT...SOC INT CON/ANAL 20. PAGE 36 H0713
NAT/G FORCES GUERRILLA NAT/LISM

B61
HEMPSTONE S.,THE NEW AFRICA. AGRI INDUS KIN NAT/G COLONIAL MARXISM...SOC INT TREND NAT/COMP BIBLIOG/A 20. PAGE 69 H1392
AFR ORD/FREE PERSON CULTURE

B61
SEMINAR REPRESENTATIVE GOVT,AFRO-ASIAN ATTITUDES: SEMINAR ON REPRESENTATIVE GOVERNMENTSPUBLIC LIBERTIES IN STATES OF ASIA AND AFRICA, RHODES, 1958. AFR ASIA BURMA INDIA ISLAM UAR VIETNAM/S SOCIETY POL/PAR CHIEF EDU/PROP PRESS PERSON ...POLICY INT 20 TUNIS. PAGE 141 H2826
CHOOSE ATTIT NAT/COMP ORD/FREE

B61
VON MERING O.,A GRAMMAR OF HUMAN VALUES. WOR+45 CULTURE FACE/GP NEIGH CREATE EDU/PROP LEGIT ATTIT DRIVE PERSON ORD/FREE...PSY SOC METH/CNCPT OBS RECORD INT REC/INT STAND/INT QU CHARTS VAL/FREE. PAGE 164 H3275
SOCIETY MORAL

S61
EHRMANN H.W.,"FRENCH BUREAUCRACY AND ORGANIZED INTERESTS" (BMR)" FRANCE NAT/G DELIB/GP ROUTINE ...INT 20 BUREAUCRCY CIVIL/SERV. PAGE 45 H0897
ADMIN DECISION PLURISM LOBBY

B62
HUNTER G.,THE NEW SOCIETIES OF TROPICAL AFRICA. CULTURE INDUS KIN MUNIC WORKER INT/TRADE EDU/PROP ORD/FREE...INT TREND 20. PAGE 75 H1500
AFR GOV/COMP ECO/UNDEV SOCIETY

L62
COHEN R.,"POWER IN COMPLEX SOCIETIES IN AFRICA." AFR KIN MUNIC POL/PAR DELIB/GP DOMIN ROUTINE ATTIT ALL/VALS...SOC STAT OBS INT QU CHARTS ANTHOL 20. PAGE 31 H0617
CULTURE STRATA ELITES

S62
MU FU-SHENG,"THE WILTING OF THE HUNDRED FLOWERS: FREE THOUGHT IN CHINA TODAY." ASIA CHINA/COM CULTURE FAM NAT/G EDU/PROP REV TOTALISM ATTIT PERSON RESPECT...GEOG INT UNPLAN/INT COLD/WAR 20. PAGE 114 H2278
INTELL ELITES

B63
CREMEANS C.,THE ARABS AND THE WORLD: NASSER'S ARAB NATIONALIST POLICY. FUT ISLAM UAR USA+45 SOCIETY STRATA NAT/G POL/PAR PLAN DIPLOM EDU/PROP LEGIT DRIVE ALL/VALS...INT TIME/SEQ CHARTS 20 NASSER/G. PAGE 35 H0700
TOP/EX ATTIT REGION NAT/LISM

B63
DRIVER H.E.,ETHNOGRAPHY AND ACCULTURATION OF THE CHICHIMECA-JONAZ OF NORTHEAST MEXICO. ECO/UNDEV AGRI FAM KIN EDU/PROP MARRIAGE HEALTH...GEOG INT CHARTS WORSHIP 18/20 MEXIC/AMER. PAGE 42 H0848
CULTURE HABITAT STRUCT GP/REL

B63
GEERTZ C.,PEDDLERS AND PRINCES: SOCIAL DEVELOPMENT AND ECONOMIC CHANGE IN TWO INDONESIAN TOWNS. S/ASIA CULTURE SOCIETY STRATA FACE/GP MUNIC CREATE TEC/DEV ECO/TAC ORD/FREE WEALTH...OBS INT CENSUS CHARTS WORK TOT/POP VAL/FREE 20. PAGE 55 H1106
ECO/UNDEV SOC ELITES INDONESIA

B63
KOGAN N.,THE POLITICS OF ITALIAN FOREIGN POLICY. EUR+WWI LEGIS DOMIN LEGIT EXEC PWR RESPECT SKILL ...POLICY DECISION HUM SOC METH/CNCPT OBS INT CHARTS 20. PAGE 87 H1737
NAT/G ROUTINE DIPLOM ITALY

B63
KURZMAN D.,SUBVERSION OF THE INNOCENTS: PATTERNS OF COMMUNIST PENETRATION OF AFRICA, THE MIDDLE EAST AND AFRICA. AFR ASIA ISLAM S/ASIA CULTURE NAT/G FORCES PLAN EDU/PROP ADMIN ATTIT...CONCPT INT UNPLAN/INT TIME/SEQ. PAGE 89 H1785
COM COERCE

L63
CORWIN A.F.,"CONTEMPORARY MEXICAN ATTITUDES TOWARD POPULATION, POVERTY, AND PUBLIC OPINION." L/A+17C CULTURE SOCIETY ACT/RES ECO/TAC EDU/PROP PERSON HEALTH KNOWL...GEOG PHIL/SCI STAT OBS INT SAMP MEXIC/AMER VAL/FREE 20. PAGE 34 H0672
ATTIT QU

S63
DEUTSCHMANN P.J.,"THE MASS MEDIA IN AN UNDERDEVELOPED VILLAGE." L/A+17C EDU/PROP PERCEPT KNOWL ORD/FREE...SOC INT VAL/FREE 20. PAGE 40 H0809
COM/IND CULTURE

S63
GLUCKMAN M.,"CIVIL WAR AND THEORIES OF POWER IN BAROTSE-LAND: AFRICAN AND MEDIEVAL ANALOGIES." AFR CHRIST-17C LAW CONSTN CULTURE STRATA KIN DELIB/GP FORCES DOMIN LEGIT COERCE PERCEPT ORD/FREE...SOC INT TIME/SEQ GEN/LAWS VAL/FREE. PAGE 57 H1148
TOP/EX PWR WAR

B64
AFRO ASIAN SOLIDARITY AGAINST IMPERIALISM. AFR ISLAM S/ASIA ECO/UNDEV NAT/G POL/PAR TOP/EX PRESS ...INT ANTHOL 20 CHOU/ENLAI. PAGE 2 H0043
MARXISM DIPLOM EDU/PROP CHIEF

B64
HALPERN J.M.,GOVERNMENT, POLITICS, AND SOCIAL STRUCTURE IN LAOS. LAOS CULTURE SOCIETY STRATA STRUCT FAM DIPLOM DOMIN MARXISM...INT GOV/COMP WORSHIP SOC/INTEG 20. PAGE 65 H1297
NAT/G SOC LOC/G

B64
KELLER J.W.,GERMANY, THE WALL AND BERLIN. EUR+WWI ECO/DEV NAT/G VOL/ASSN FORCES PLAN ECO/TAC EDU/PROP COERCE...POLICY CONCPT INT TREND COLD/WAR BER/BLOC 20 BERLIN. PAGE 84 H1685
ATTIT ALL/VALS DIPLOM GERMANY

B64
MORGAN L.H.,ANCIENT SOCIETY (1877). SOCIETY FAM OWN ...INT QU GEN/LAWS SOC/INTEG. PAGE 113 H2255
KIN MARRIAGE CULTURE

B64
WAINHOUSE D.W.,REMNANTS OF EMPIRE: THE UNITED NATIONS AND THE END OF COLONIALISM. FUT PORTUGAL WOR+45 NAT/G CONSULT DOMIN LEGIT ADMIN ROUTINE ATTIT ORD/FREE...POLICY JURID RECORD INT TIME/SEQ UN CMN/WLTH 20. PAGE 164 H3287
INT/ORG TREND COLONIAL

B64
WHITE D.S.,SEEDS OF DISCORD. EUR+WWI FRANCE NAT/G VOL/ASSN FORCES DIPLOM DOMIN NAT/LISM DISPL RIGID/FLEX PWR...RECORD INT BIOG 20 DEGAULLE/C
TOP/EX ATTIT

ROOSEVLT/F CHURCHLL/W HULL. PAGE 167 H3347

B64
ZARTMAN I.W.,MOROCCO: PROBLEMS OF NEW POWER. ISLAM CULTURE ECO/UNDEV AGRI POL/PAR SCHOOL FORCES ADMIN ...CONCPT STAT INT CENSUS TIME/SEQ CHARTS WORK VAL/FREE 20. PAGE 172 H3449 — CHOOSE MOROCCO DELIB/GP DECISION

B65
JACKSON G.,THE SPANISH REPUBLIC AND THE CIVIL WAR, 1931-1939. EUR+WWI INTELL STRUCT COM/IND NAT/G POL/PAR LEGIS EDU/PROP EXEC COERCE NAT/LISM DRIVE PWR...INT TIME/SEQ TOT/POP 20. PAGE 79 H1574 — ATTIT GUERRILLA SPAIN

B65
LAMBIRI I.,SOCIAL CHANGE IN A GREEK COUNTRY TOWN. GREECE FAM PROB/SOLV ROUTINE TASK LEISURE INGP/REL CONSEN ORD/FREE...SOC INT QU CHARTS 20. PAGE 90 H1803 — INDUS WORKER CULTURE NEIGH

B65
MOORE C.H.,TUNISIA SINCE INDEPENDENCE. ELITES LOC/G POL/PAR ADMIN COLONIAL CONTROL EXEC GOV/REL TOTALISM MARXISM...INT 20 TUNIS. PAGE 112 H2248 — NAT/G EX/STRUC SOCISM

S65
LAULICHT J.,"PUBLIC OPINION AND FOREIGN POLICY DECISIONS." CANADA ELITES NAT/G FOR/AID LEAD NUC/PWR PERCEPT...INT QU CHARTS UN COLD/WAR. PAGE 92 H1839 — DIPLOM ATTIT CON/ANAL SAMP

B66
O'NEILL R.J.,THE GERMAN ARMY AND THE NAZI PARTY, 1933-1939. GERMANY ELITES NAT/G EDU/PROP CONTROL LEAD COERCE WAR...POLICY INT TIME/SEQ BIBLIOG 20 HITLER/A NAZI. PAGE 120 H2391 — CIVMIL/REL FORCES FASCISM POL/PAR

B66
VOGT E.Z.,PEOPLE OF RIMROCK. STRATA STRUCT KIN SECT GP/REL HABITAT ALL/VALS...GEOG INT QU 20 TEXAS NAVAHO MORMON SPAN/AMER ZUNI. PAGE 163 H3260 — CULTURE GP/COMP SOC SOCIETY

S66
FELD W.,"NATIONAL ECONOMIC INTEREST GROUPS AND POLICY FORMATION IN THE EEC." NAT/G POL/PAR REGION CENTRAL SOVEREIGN...INT NET/THEORY EEC. PAGE 49 H0985 — LOBBY ELITES DECISION

B67
BANKWITZ P.C.,MAXINE WEYGAND AND CIVIL-MILITARY RELATIONS IN MODERN FRANCE. FRANCE LEAD WAR PWR ...INT BIBLIOG 20. PAGE 11 H0212 — CIVMIL/REL FORCES NAT/G TOP/EX

B67
BARNETT A.D.,CADRES, BUREAUCRACY, AND POLITICAL POWER IN COMMUNIST CHINA. CHINA/COM ELITES LOC/G NAT/G INGP/REL...SOC INT DICTIONARY 20. PAGE 11 H0224 — GOV/REL STRUCT MARXISM EDU/PROP

B67
DEUTSCH K.W.,FRANCE, GERMANY AND THE WESTERN ALLIANCE. FRANCE GERMANY/W INT/ORG ARMS/CONT NAT/LISM SOVEREIGN...INT NAT/COMP 20. PAGE 40 H0801 — ELITES ATTIT DIPLOM POLICY

B67
RIESMAN D.,CONVERSATIONS IN JAPAN: MODERNIZATION, POLITICS, AND CULTURE. CHINA/COM STRATA STRUCT ECO/DEV INDUS ACADEM EDU/PROP...ART/METH SOC MODAL INT IDEA/COMP SOC/INTEG 20 CHINJAP HIROSHIMA. PAGE 131 H2629 — CULTURE SOCIETY ASIA

B67
SHAKABPA T.W.D.,TIBET: A POLITICAL HISTORY. CHINA/COM UK CHIEF LEAD...INT BIBLIOG 20 TIBET. PAGE 142 H2839 — DIPLOM SECT NAT/G

S67
HOPE M.,"THE RELUCTANT WAY: SELF-IMMOLATION IN VIETNAM." VIETNAM SOCIETY FAM KIN SECT DRIVE ALL/VALS...TRADIT OBS INT 20. PAGE 73 H1465 — CULTURE SUICIDE IDEA/COMP ATTIT

S67
NIEBUHR R.,"THE ETHICS OF WAR AND PEACE IN THE NUCLEAR AGE." VIETNAM INTELL CONFER CONTROL WAR GOV/REL PERS/REL ORD/FREE...POLICY INT GOV/COMP NAT/COMP 20 UN. PAGE 118 H2360 — MORAL PEACE NUC/PWR DIPLOM

INT. BANK RECONSTR. DEVELOP. H1541

INT/AM/DEV....INTER-AMERICAN DEVELOPMENT BANK

INT/AVIATN....INTERNATIONAL CIVIL AVIATION ORGANIZATION

INT/LAW....INTERNATIONAL LAW

N
AMERICAN POLITICAL SCIENCE REVIEW. USA+45 USA-45 WOR+45 WOR-45 INT/ORG ADMIN...INT/LAW PHIL/SCI CONCPT METH 20 UN. PAGE 1 H0001 — BIBLIOG/A DIPLOM NAT/G GOV/COMP

B11
PHILLIPSON C.,THE INTERNATIONAL LAW AND CUSTOM OF ANCIENT GREECE AND ROME. MEDIT-7 UNIV INTELL SOCIETY STRUCT NAT/G LEGIS EXEC PERSON...CONCPT OBS CON/ANAL ROM/EMP. PAGE 125 H2504 — INT/ORG LAW INT/LAW

B16
PUFENDORF S.,LAW OF NATURE AND OF NATIONS (ABRIDGED). UNIV LAW NAT/G DIPLOM AGREE WAR PERSON ALL/VALS PWR...POLICY 18 DEITY NATURL/LAW. PAGE 128 H2565 — CONCPT INT/LAW SECT MORAL

B17
DE VICTORIA F.,DE INDIS ET DE JURE BELLI (1557) IN F. DE VICTORIA, DE INDIS ET DE JURE BELLI REFLECTIONES. UNIV NAT/G SECT CHIEF PARTIC COERCE PEACE MORAL...POLICY 16 INDIAN/AM CHRISTIAN CONSCN/OBJ. PAGE 39 H0775 — WAR INT/LAW OWN

N19
BENTHAM J.,A PLAN FOR AN UNIVERSAL AND PERPETUAL PEACE (1838) (PAMPHLET). NAT/G FORCES BAL/PWR INT/TRADE ADMIN AGREE CT/SYS ARMS/CONT SOVEREIGN WEALTH GEN/LAWS. PAGE 14 H0288 — INT/ORG INT/LAW PEACE COLONIAL

B21
BALFOUR A.J.,ESSAYS SPECULATIVE AND POLITICAL. SEA CULTURE CREATE WAR NAT/LISM PEACE LOVE...ART/METH INT/LAW CONCPT ANTHOL 20 JEWS. PAGE 10 H0204 — PHIL/SCI SOCIETY DIPLOM

B24
HOLDSWORTH W.S.,A HISTORY OF ENGLISH LAW; THE COMMON LAW AND ITS RIVALS (VOL. IV). UK SEA AGRI CHIEF ADJUD CONTROL CRIME GOV/REL...INT/LAW JURID NAT/COMP 16/17 PARLIAMENT COMMON/LAW CANON/LAW ENGLSH/LAW. PAGE 72 H1449 — LAW LEGIS CT/SYS CONSTN

B29
STURZO L.,THE INTERNATIONAL COMMUNITY AND THE RIGHT OF WAR (TRANS. BY BARBARA BARCLAY CARTER). CULTURE CREATE PROB/SOLV DIPLOM ADJUD CONTROL PEACE PERSON ORD/FREE...INT/LAW IDEA/COMP PACIFIST 20 LEAGUE/NAT. PAGE 150 H3003 — INT/ORG PLAN WAR CONCPT

B30
BYNKERSHOEK C.,QUAESTIONUM JURIS PUBLICI LIBRI DUO. CHRIST-17C MOD/EUR CONSTN ELITES SOCIETY NAT/G PROVS EX/STRUC FORCES TOP/EX BAL/PWR DIPLOM ATTIT MORAL...TRADIT CONCPT. PAGE 25 H0502 — INT/ORG LAW NAT/LISM INT/LAW

B35
RAM J.,THE SCIENCE OF LEGAL JUDGMENT: A TREATISE... UK CONSTN NAT/G LEGIS CREATE PROB/SOLV AGREE CT/SYS ...INT/LAW CONCPT 19 ENGLSH/LAW CANON/LAW CIVIL/LAW CTS/WESTM. PAGE 129 H2584 — LAW JURID EX/STRUC ADJUD

B38
HOLDSWORTH W.S.,A HISTORY OF ENGLISH LAW; THE CENTURIES OF SETTLEMENT AND REFORM (VOL. XI). UK CONSTN NAT/G EX/STRUC DIPLOM ADJUD CT/SYS LEAD CRIME ATTIT...INT/LAW JURID 18 CMN/WLTH PARLIAMENT ENGLSH/LAW. PAGE 73 H1452 — LAW COLONIAL LEGIS PARL/PROC

B38
MCNAIR A.D.,THE LAW OF TREATIES: BRITISH PRACTICE AND OPINIONS. UK CREATE DIPLOM LEGIT WRITING ADJUD WAR...INT/LAW JURID TREATY. PAGE 107 H2144 — AGREE LAW CT/SYS NAT/G

B38
SAINT-PIERRE C.I.,SCHEME FOR LASTING PEACE (TRANS. BY H. BELLOT). INDUS NAT/G CHIEF FORCES INT/TRADE CT/SYS WAR PWR SOVEREIGN WEALTH...POLICY 18. PAGE 137 H2732 — INT/ORG PEACE AGREE INT/LAW

B43
SERENI A.P.,THE ITALIAN CONCEPTION OF INTERNATIONAL LAW. EUR+WWI MOD/EUR INT/ORG NAT/G DOMIN COERCE ORD/FREE FASCISM...OBS/ENVIR TREND 20. PAGE 141 H2829 — LAW TIME/SEQ INT/LAW ITALY

C43
BENTHAM J.,"PRINCIPLES OF INTERNATIONAL LAW" IN J. BOWRING, ED., THE WORKS OF JEREMY BENTHAM." UNIV NAT/G PLAN PROB/SOLV DIPLOM CONTROL SANCTION MORAL ORD/FREE PWR SOVEREIGN 19. PAGE 15 H0291 — INT/LAW JURID WAR PEACE

B44
FULLER G.H.,TURKEY: A SELECTED LIST OF REFERENCES. ISLAM TURKEY CULTURE ECO/UNDEV AGRI DIPLOM NAT/LISM CONSERVE...GEOG HUM INT/LAW SOC 7/20 MAPS. PAGE 54 H1075 — BIBLIOG/A ALL/VALS

C44
SUAREZ F.,"ON WAR" (1621) IN SELECTIONS FROM THREE WORKS, VOL. I." NAT/G SECT CHIEF DIPLOM LEGIT MORAL PWR...POLICY INT/LAW 17. PAGE 150 H3005 — WAR REV ORD/FREE CATH

B45
CONOVER H.F.,THE NAZI STATE: WAR CRIMES AND WAR CRIMINALS. GERMANY CULTURE NAT/G SECT FORCES DIPLOM INT/TRADE EDU/PROP...INT/LAW BIOG HIST/WRIT TIME/SEQ 20. PAGE 32 H0647 — BIBLIOG WAR CRIME

B45
WOOLBERT R.G.,FOREIGN AFFAIRS BIBLIOGRAPHY, 1932-1942. INT/ORG SECT INT/TRADE COLONIAL RACE/REL NAT/LISM...GEOG INT/LAW GOV/COMP IDEA/COMP 20. PAGE 170 H3410 — BIBLIOG/A DIPLOM WAR

C50
NUMELIN R.,"THE BEGINNINGS OF DIPLOMACY." INT/TRADE WAR GP/REL PEACE STRANGE ATTIT...INT/LAW CONCPT BIBLIOG. PAGE 119 H2380 — DIPLOM KIN CULTURE LAW

B53
KANTOR H.,A BIBLIOGRAPHY OF UNPUBLISHED DOCTORAL DISSERTATIONS AND MASTERS' THESES DEALING WITH GOVTS, POL, INT REL OF LAT AM. L/A+17C INT/ORG POL/PAR ACT/RES OP/RES CONFER ATTIT...INT/LAW — BIBLIOG ACADEM DIPLOM NAT/G

PHIL/SCI 20. PAGE 83 H1656

B55
KHADDURI M.,LAW IN THE MIDDLE EAST. LAW CONSTN ACADEM FAM EDU/PROP CT/SYS SANCTION CRIME...INT/LAW GOV/COMP ANTHOL 6/20 MID/EAST. PAGE 85 H1703
ADJUD JURID ISLAM

B55
KRUSE H.,DAS STAATSANGEHORIGKEITSRECHT DER ARABISCHEN STAATEN. ISLAM JORDAN LIBYA SYRIA UAR NAT/G SECT RACE/REL...INT/LAW 6/20 TREATY. PAGE 89 H1779
JURID NAT/LISM DIPLOM GP/REL

B55
SVARLIEN O.,AN INTRODUCTION TO THE LAW OF NATIONS. SEA AIR INT/ORG NAT/G CHIEF ADMIN AGREE WAR PRIVIL ORD/FREE SOVEREIGN...BIBLIOG 16/20. PAGE 151 H3012
INT/LAW DIPLOM

B56
WATT D.C.,BRITAIN AND THE SUEZ CANAL. COM UAR UK ...INT/LAW 20 SUEZ TREATY. PAGE 166 H3314
DIPLOM INT/TRADE DIST/IND NAT/G

B57
DONALDSON A.G.,SOME COMPARATIVE ASPECTS OF IRISH LAW. IRELAND NAT/G DIPLOM ADMIN CT/SYS LEAD ATTIT SOVEREIGN...JURID BIBLIOG/A 12/20 CMN/WLTH. PAGE 42 H0835
CONSTN LAW NAT/COMP INT/LAW

B57
PLAYFAIR G.,THE OFFENDERS: THE CASE AGAINST LEGAL VENGEANCE. UNIV LAW SOCIETY NAT/G PROB/SOLV DEATH PERSON ORD/FREE...HEAL INT/LAW BIBLIOG 20 REFORMERS. PAGE 126 H2524
CRIME TEC/DEV SANCTION CT/SYS

B58
BRIERLY J.L.,THE BASIS OF OBLIGATION IN INTERNATIONAL LAW, AND OTHER PAPERS. WOR+45 WOR-45 LEGIS...JURID CONCPT NAT/COMP ANTHOL 20. PAGE 21 H0415
INT/LAW DIPLOM ADJUD SOVEREIGN

B59
BUNDESMIN FUR VERTRIEBENE,ZEITTAFEL DER VORGESCHICHTE UND DES ABLAUFS DER VERTREIBUNG SOWIE DER UNTERBRINGUNG UND EINGLIEDERUNG DER (2 VOLS.). GERMANY/E GERMANY/W NAT/G PROVS PROB/SOLV DIPLOM PARL/PROC ATTIT...BIBLIOG SOC/INTEG 20 MIGRATION PARLIAMENT. PAGE 24 H0475
JURID GP/REL INT/LAW

B59
KIRCHHEIMER O.,GEGENWARTSPROBLEME DER ASYLGEWAHRUNG. DOMIN GP/REL ATTIT...NAT/COMP 20. PAGE 86 H1720
DIPLOM INT/LAW JURID ORD/FREE

B59
PANAMERICAN UNION,PUBLICATIONS: PAU AND OFFICIAL RECORDS OF THE OAS, IN ENGLISH, SPANISH, PORTUGUESE, AND FRENCH, 1958-59. NAT/G ATTIT...SOC 20 OAS. PAGE 123 H2456
BIBLIOG L/A+17C INT/LAW DIPLOM

B59
WILDNER H.,DIE TECHNIK DER DIPLOMATIE. TOP/EX ROLE ORD/FREE...INT/LAW JURID IDEA/COMP NAT/COMP 20. PAGE 168 H3364
DIPLOM POLICY DELIB/GP NAT/G

S59
JENKS C.W.,"THE CHALLENGE OF UNIVERSALITY." FUT UNIV CONSTN CULTURE CONSULT CREATE PLAN LEGIT ATTIT MORAL ORD/FREE RESPECT...MAJORIT JURID 20. PAGE 80 H1602
INT/ORG LAW PEACE INT/LAW

B60
LA PONCE J.A.,THE PROTECTION OF MINORITIES. WOR+45 WOR-45 NAT/G POL/PAR SUFF...INT/LAW CLASSIF GP/COMP GOV/COMP BIBLIOG 17/20 CIVIL/LIB CIV/RIGHTS. PAGE 90 H1793
INGP/REL DOMIN SOCIETY RACE/REL

B60
THE AFRICA 1960 COMMITTEE,MANDATE IN TRUST; THE PROBLEM OF SOUTH WEST AFRICA. GERMANY STRUCT REGION SANCTION CHOOSE DISCRIM...INT/LAW 20 AFRICA/SW UN LEAGUE/NAT TRUST/TERR. PAGE 153 H3066
NAT/G DIPLOM COLONIAL RACE/REL

B61
NEWMAN R.P.,RECOGNITION OF COMMUNIST CHINA? A STUDY IN ARGUMENT. CHINA/COM NAT/G PROB/SOLV RATIONAL ...INT/LAW LOG IDEA/COMP BIBLIOG 20. PAGE 117 H2347
MARXISM ATTIT DIPLOM POLICY

B61
WARD R.E.,JAPANESE POLITICAL SCIENCE: A GUIDE TO JAPANESE REFERENCE AND RESEARCH MATERIALS (2ND ED.). LAW CONSTN STRATA NAT/G POL/PAR DELIB/GP LEGIS ADMIN CHOOSE GP/REL...INT/LAW 19/20 CHINJAP. PAGE 165 H3306
BIBLIOG/A PHIL/SCI

S62
MONNIER J.P.,"LA SUCCESSION D'ETATS EN MATIERE DE RESPONSABILITE INTERNATIONALE." UNIV CONSTN INTELL SOCIETY ADJUD ROUTINE PERCEPT SUPEGO...GEN/LAWS TOT/POP 20. PAGE 112 H2240
NAT/G JURID INT/LAW

S62
MOUSKHELY M.,"LA NAISSANCE DES ETATS EN DROIT INTERNATIONAL PUBLIC." UNIV SOCIETY INT/ORG VOL/ASSN LEGIT ATTIT RIGID/FLEX...JURID TIME/SEQ 20. PAGE 114 H2272
NAT/G STRUCT INT/LAW

S62
VIGNES D.,"L'AUTORITE DES TRAITES INTERNATIONAUX EN DROIT INTERNE." EUR+WWI UNIV LAW CONSTN INTELL NAT/G POL/PAR DIPLOM ATTIT PERCEPT ALL/VALS ...POLICY INT/LAW JURID CONCPT TIME/SEQ 20 TREATY. PAGE 163 H3252
STRUCT LEGIT FRANCE

B63
ATTIA G.E.D.,LES FORCES ARMEES DES NATIONS UNIES EN COREE ET AU MOYENORIENT. KOREA CONSTN NAT/G DELIB/GP LEGIS PWR...IDEA/COMP NAT/COMP BIBLIOG UN SUEZ. PAGE 9 H0177
FORCES INT/LAW

B63
FAWCETT J.E.S.,THE BRITISH COMMONWEALTH IN INTERNATIONAL LAW. LAW INT/ORG NAT/G VOL/ASSN OP/RES DIPLOM ADJUD CENTRAL CONSEN...NET/THEORY CMN/WLTH TREATY. PAGE 49 H0977
INT/LAW STRUCT COLONIAL

B63
PEREZ ORTIZ R.,ANUARIO BIBLIOGRAFICO COLOMBIANO, 1961. AGRI...INT/LAW JURID SOC LING 20 COLOMB. PAGE 125 H2491
BIBLIOG L/A+17C NAT/G

C63
ATTIA G.E.O.,"LES FORCES ARMEES DES NATIONS UNIES EN COREE ET AU MOYENORIENT." KOREA CONSTN DELIB/GP LEGIS PWR...IDEA/COMP NAT/COMP BIBLIOG UN SUEZ. PAGE 9 H0178
FORCES NAT/G INT/LAW

B64
CURRIE D.P.,FEDERALISM AND THE NEW NATIONS OF AFRICA. CANADA USA+45 INT/TRADE TAX GP/REL ...NAT/COMP SOC/INTEG 20. PAGE 36 H0725
FEDERAL AFR ECO/UNDEV INT/LAW

B64
FRANCK T.M.,EAST AFRICAN UNITY THROUGH LAW. MALAWI TANZANIA UGANDA UK ZAMBIA CONSTN INT/ORG NAT/G ADMIN ROUTINE TASK NAT/LISM ATTIT SOVEREIGN ...RECORD IDEA/COMP NAT/COMP. PAGE 52 H1048
AFR FEDERAL REGION INT/LAW

B64
GESELLSCHAFT RECHTSVERGLEICH,BIBLIOGRAPHIE DES DEUTSCHEN RECHTS (BIBLIOGRAPHY OF GERMAN LAW, TRANS. BY COURTLAND PETERSON). GERMANY FINAN INDUS LABOR SECT FORCES CT/SYS PARL/PROC CRIME...INT/LAW SOC NAT/COMP 20. PAGE 56 H1117
BIBLIOG/A JURID CONSTN ADMIN

B64
HOLDSWORTH W.S.,A HISTORY OF ENGLISH LAW; THE CENTURIES OF DEVELOPMENT AND REFORM (VOL. XIV). UK CONSTN LOC/G NAT/G POL/PAR CHIEF EX/STRUC ADJUD COLONIAL ATTIT...INT/LAW JURID 18/19 TORY/PARTY COMMONWLTH WHIG/PARTY COMMON/LAW. PAGE 73 H1453
LAW LEGIS LEAD CT/SYS

B64
ROBERTS HL,FOREIGN AFFAIRS BIBLIOGRAPHY, 1952-1962. ECO/DEV SECT PLAN FOR/AID INT/TRADE ARMS/CONT NAT/LISM ATTIT...INT/LAW GOV/COMP IDEA/COMP 20. PAGE 132 H2643
BIBLIOG/A DIPLOM INT/ORG WAR

B64
SEGAL R.,SANCTIONS AGAINST SOUTH AFRICA. AFR SOUTH/AFR NAT/G INT/TRADE RACE/REL PEACE PWR ...INT/LAW ANTHOL 20 UN. PAGE 141 H2821
SANCTION DISCRIM ECO/TAC POLICY

B64
SZLADITS C.,BIBLIOGRAPHY ON FOREIGN AND COMPARATIVE LAW: BOOKS AND ARTICLES IN ENGLISH (SUPPLEMENT 1962). FINAN INDUS JUDGE LICENSE ADMIN CT/SYS PARL/PROC OWN...INT/LAW CLASSIF METH/COMP NAT/COMP 20. PAGE 151 H3027
BIBLIOG/A JURID ADJUD LAW

B64
TAYLOR E.,RICHER BY ASIA. S/ASIA CULTURE VOL/ASSN ACT/RES ATTIT DISPL PERSON ALL/VALS...INT/LAW MYTH SELF/OBS 20. PAGE 153 H3054
SOCIETY RIGID/FLEX INDIA

B64
VECCHIO G.D.,L'ETAT ET LE DROIT. ITALY CONSTN EX/STRUC LEGIS DIPLOM CT/SYS...JURID 20 UN. PAGE 162 H3238
NAT/G SOVEREIGN CONCPT INT/LAW

B65
LARUS J.,COMPARATIVE WORLD POLITICS. ASIA INDIA WOR+45 WOR-45 BAL/PWR WAR PEACE RATIONAL MORAL PWR ...REALPOL INT/LAW MUSLIM. PAGE 91 H1825
GOV/COMP IDEA/COMP DIPLOM NAT/COMP

B65
O'BRIEN W.V.,THE NEW NATIONS IN INTERNATIONAL LAW AND DIPLOMACY* THE YEAR BOOK OF WORLD POLITY* VOLUME III. USA+45 ECO/UNDEV INT/ORG FORCES DIPLOM COLONIAL NEUTRAL REV NAT/LISM ATTIT RESPECT. PAGE 119 H2385
INT/LAW CULTURE SOVEREIGN ANTHOL

B65
WHITEMAN M.M.,DIGEST OF INTERNATIONAL LAW* VOLUME 5. DEPARTMENT OF STATE PUBLICATION 7873. USA+45 WOR+45 OP/RES...CONCPT CLASSIF RECORD IDEA/COMP. PAGE 167 H3353
INT/LAW NAT/G NAT/COMP

S65
WRIGHT Q.,"THE ESCALATION OF INTERNATIONAL CONFLICTS." WOR+45 WOR-45 FORCES DIPLOM RISK COST ATTIT ALL/VALS...INT/LAW QUANT STAT NAT/COMP. PAGE 171 H3422
WAR PERCEPT PREDICT MATH

B66
EDWARDS C.D.,TRADE REGULATIONS OVERSEAS. IRELAND NEW/ZEALND SOUTH/AFR NAT/G CAP/ISM TARIFFS CONTROL ...POLICY JURID 20 EEC CHINJAP. PAGE 45 H0892
INT/TRADE DIPLOM INT/LAW ECO/TAC

B66
HARMON R.B.,SOURCES AND PROBLEMS OF BIBLIOGRAPHY IN
BIBLIOG

POLITICAL SCIENCE (PAMPHLET). INT/ORG LOC/G MUNIC POL/PAR ADMIN GOV/REL ALL/IDEOS...JURID MGT CONCPT 19/20. PAGE 67 H1335 — DIPLOM INT/LAW NAT/G

B66
HAY P.,FEDERALISM AND SUPRANATIONAL ORGANIZATIONS: PATTERNS FOR NEW LEGAL STRUCTURES. EUR+WWI LAW NAT/G VOL/ASSN DIPLOM PWR...NAT/COMP TREATY EEC. PAGE 68 H1364 — SOVEREIGN FEDERAL INT/ORG INT/LAW

B66
HENKYS R.,DEUTSCHLAND UND DIE OSTLICHEN NACHBARN. GERMANY POLAND NAT/G POL/PAR INGP/REL ATTIT 20 MIGRATION. PAGE 70 H1396 — GP/REL JURID INT/LAW DIPLOM

B66
HOEVELER H.J.,INTERNATIONALE BEKAMPFUNG DES VERBRECHENS. AUSTRIA SWITZERLND WOR+45 INT/ORG CONTROL BIO/SOC...METH/COMP NAT/COMP 20 MAFIA SCOT/YARD FBI. PAGE 72 H1446 — CRIMLGY CRIME DIPLOM INT/LAW

B66
HOYT E.C.,NATIONAL POLICY AND INTERNATIONAL LAW* CASE STUDIES FROM AMERICAN CANAL POLICY* MONOGRAPH NO. 1 -- 1966-1967. PANAMA UK ELITES BAL/PWR EFFICIENCY...CLASSIF NAT/COMP SOC/EXP COLOMB TREATY. PAGE 74 H1483 — INT/LAW USA-45 DIPLOM PWR

B66
MCKAY V.,AFRICAN DIPLOMACY STUDIES IN THE DETERMINANTS OF FOREIGN POLICY. AFR SOUTH/AFR CULTURE NEUTRAL REGION SOVEREIGN...INT/LAW GOV/COMP ANTHOL 20. PAGE 107 H2138 — ECO/UNDEV RACE/REL CIVMIL/REL DIPLOM

B66
MERILLAT H.C.L.,LEGAL ADVISERS AND INTERNATIONAL ORGANIZATIONS. LAW NAT/G CONSULT OP/RES ADJUD SANCTION TASK CONSEN ORG/CHARTS. PAGE 109 H2178 — INT/ORG INT/LAW CREATE OBS

L66
KRENZ F.E.,"THE REFUGEE AS A SUBJECT OF INTERNATIONAL LAW." FUT LAW NAT/G CREATE ADJUD ISOLAT STRANGE...RECORD UN. PAGE 88 H1766 — INT/LAW DISCRIM NEW/IDEA

L66
SEYLER W.C.,"DOCTORAL DISSERTATIONS IN POLITICAL SCIENCE IN UNIVERSITIES OF THE UNITED STATES AND CANADA." INT/ORG LOC/G ADMIN...INT/LAW MGT GOV/COMP. PAGE 142 H2836 — BIBLIOG LAW NAT/G

S66
DETTER I.,"THE PROBLEM OF UNEQUAL TREATIES." CONSTN NAT/G LEGIS COLONIAL COERCE PWR...GEOG UN TIME TREATY. PAGE 40 H0796 — SOVEREIGN DOMIN INT/LAW ECO/UNDEV

B67
POGANY A.H.,POLITICAL SCIENCE AND INTERNATIONAL RELATIONS, BOOKS RECOMMENDED FOR AMERICAN CATHOLIC COLLEGE LIBRARIES. INT/ORG LOC/G NAT/G FORCES BAL/PWR ECO/TAC NUC/PWR...CATH INT/LAW TREATY 20. PAGE 127 H2532 — BIBLIOG DIPLOM

B67
RAMUNDO B.A.,PEACEFUL COEXISTENCE: INTERNATIONAL LAW IN THE BUILDING OF COMMUNISM. USSR INT/ORG DIPLOM COLONIAL ARMS/CONT ROLE SOVEREIGN...POLICY METH/COMP NAT/COMP BIBLIOG. PAGE 129 H2588 — INT/LAW PEACE MARXISM METH/CNCPT

L67
WAELBROECK M.,"THE APPLICATION OF EEC LAW BY NATIONAL COURTS." EUR+WWI INT/ORG CT/SYS...JURID EEC TREATY. PAGE 164 H3284 — INT/LAW NAT/G LAW PROB/SOLV

S67
AMERASINGHE C.F.,"SOME LEGAL PROBLEMS OF STATE TRADING IN SOUTHEAST ASIA." PROB/SOLV ADJUD CONTROL CT/SYS GP/REL 20. PAGE 6 H0120 — INT/TRADE NAT/G INT/LAW PRIVIL

S67
CUMMINS L.,"THE FORMULATION OF THE "PLATT" AMENDMENT." CUBA L/A+17C NAT/G DELIB/GP CONFER ...POLICY 20. PAGE 36 H0720 — DIPLOM INT/LAW LEGIS

S67
MATTHEWS R.O.,"THE SUEZ CANAL DISPUTE* A CASE STUDY IN PEACEFUL SETTLEMENT." FRANCE ISRAEL UAR UK NAT/G CONTROL LEAD COERCE WAR NAT/LISM ROLE ORD/FREE PWR ...INT/LAW UN 20. PAGE 105 H2099 — PEACE DIPLOM ADJUD

B96
DE VATTEL E.,THE LAW OF NATIONS. AGRI FINAN CHIEF DIPLOM INT/TRADE AGREE OWN ALL/VALS MORAL ORD/FREE SOVEREIGN...GEN/LAWS 18 NATURL/LAW WOLFF/C. PAGE 39 H0774 — LAW CONCPT NAT/G INT/LAW

B99
BROOKS S.,BRITAIN AND THE BOERS. AFR SOUTH/AFR UK CULTURE INSPECT LEGIT...INT/LAW 19/20 BOER/WAR. PAGE 22 H0433 — WAR DIPLOM NAT/G

INT/ORG....INTERNATIONAL ORGANIZATIONS; SEE ALSO VOL/ASSN AND APPROPRIATE ORGANIZATION

N
AMERICAN POLITICAL SCIENCE REVIEW. USA+45 USA-45 WOR+45 WOR-45 INT/ORG ADMIN...INT/LAW PHIL/SCI CONCPT METH 20 UN. PAGE 1 H0001 — BIBLIOG/A DIPLOM NAT/G GOV/COMP

N
BULLETIN ANALYTIQUE DE DOCUMENTATION POLITIQUE, ECONOMIQUE, ET SOCIAL CONTEMPORAIRE. FRANCE WOR+45 SOCIETY ECO/DEV ECO/UNDEV INT/ORG LOC/G PROB/SOLV FOR/AID LEAD REGION SOC. PAGE 1 H0002 — BIBLIOG/A DIPLOM NAT/COMP NAT/G

N
CANADIAN GOVERNMENT PUBLICATIONS (1955-). CANADA AGRI FINAN LABOR FORCES INT/TRADE HEALTH...JURID 20 PARLIAMENT. PAGE 1 H0003 — BIBLIOG/A NAT/G DIPLOM INT/ORG

N
INDIA: A REFERENCE ANNUAL. INDIA CULTURE COM/IND R+D FORCES PLAN RECEIVE EDU/PROP HEALTH...STAT CHARTS BIBLIOG 20. PAGE 1 H0017 — CONSTN LABOR INT/ORG

N
ASIA FOUNDATION,LIBRARY NOTES. LAW CONSTN CULTURE SOCIETY ECO/UNDEV INT/ORG NAT/G COLONIAL LEAD REGION NAT/LISM ATTIT 20 UN. PAGE 9 H0176 — BIBLIOG/A ASIA S/ASIA DIPLOM

N
EUROPA PUBLICATIONS LIMITED,THE EUROPA YEAR BOOK. CONSTN FINAN INDUS POL/PAR DIPLOM TV CT/SYS...STAT BIOG CHARTS WORSHIP 20. PAGE 47 H0949 — BIBLIOG NAT/G PRESS INT/ORG

N
US DEPARTMENT OF STATE,BIBLIOGRAPHY (PAMPHLETS). AGRI INDUS INT/ORG FOR/AID EDU/PROP WAR MARXISM ...SOC GOV/COMP METH/COMP 20. PAGE 159 H3184 — BIBLIOG DIPLOM ECO/DEV NAT/G

B00
OMAN C.,A HISTORY OF THE ART OF WAR: THE MIDDLE AGES FROM THE FOURTH TO THE FOURTEENTH CENTURY. CHRIST-17C MEDIT-7 CULTURE SOCIETY INT/ORG ROUTINE PERSON...CONT/OBS HIST/WRIT CHARTS VAL/FREE. PAGE 121 H2417 — FORCES SKILL WAR

B00
VOLPICELLI Z.,RUSSIA ON THE PACIFIC AND THE SIBERIAN RAILWAY. MOD/EUR ECO/UNDEV INT/ORG FORCES PLAN DOMIN COLONIAL ROUTINE ATTIT ALL/VALS...OBS HIST/WRIT TIME/SEQ TREND CON/ANAL AUD/VIS CHARTS 18/19. PAGE 163 H3261 — NAT/G ACT/RES RUSSIA

B02
SEELEY J.R.,THE EXPANSION OF ENGLAND. MOD/EUR S/ASIA UK CULTURE NAT/G FORCES PLAN DOMIN EDU/PROP COLONIAL ROUTINE ATTIT ALL/VALS SOVEREIGN...CONCPT HIST/WRIT PARLIAMENT 18 CMN/WLTH. PAGE 141 H2819 — INT/ORG ACT/RES CAP/ISM INDIA

B11
PHILLIPSON C.,THE INTERNATIONAL LAW AND CUSTOM OF ANCIENT GREECE AND ROME. MEDIT-7 UNIV INTELL SOCIETY STRUCT NAT/G LEGIS EXEC PERSON...CONCPT OBS CON/ANAL ROM/EMP. PAGE 125 H2504 — INT/ORG LAW INT/LAW

B14
BERNHARDI F.,ON THE WAR OF TODAY. MOD/EUR INT/ORG NAT/G TOP/EX PWR CHARTS. PAGE 16 H0313 — FORCES SKILL WAR

B15
FARIES J.C.,THE RISE OF INTERNATIONALISM. ASIA MOD/EUR NAT/G VOL/ASSN DELIB/GP BAL/PWR EDU/PROP ARMS/CONT RIGID/FLEX TREND. PAGE 49 H0971 — INT/ORG DIPLOM PEACE

B19
ROUSSEAU J.J.,A LASTING PEACE. INT/ORG NAT/G CHIEF DIPLOM DETER WAR POLICY. PAGE 135 H2697 — PLAN PEACE UTIL

N19
BENTHAM J.,A PLAN FOR AN UNIVERSAL AND PERPETUAL PEACE (1838) (PAMPHLET). NAT/G FORCES BAL/PWR INT/TRADE ADMIN AGREE CT/SYS ARMS/CONT SOVEREIGN WEALTH GEN/LAWS. PAGE 14 H0288 — INT/ORG INT/LAW PEACE COLONIAL

N19
FREEMAN H.A.,COERCION OF STATES IN FEDERAL UNIONS (PAMPHLET). WOR-45 DIPLOM CONTROL COERCE PEACE ORD/FREE...GOV/COMP METH/COMP NAT/COMP PACIFIST 20. PAGE 53 H1055 — FEDERAL WAR INT/ORG PACIFISM

N19
PROVISIONS SECTION OAU,ORGANIZATION OF AFRICAN UNITY: BASIC DOCUMENTS AND RESOLUTIONS (PAMPHLET). AFR CULTURE ECO/UNDEV DIPLOM ECO/TAC EDU/PROP COLONIAL ARMS/CONT NUC/PWR RACE/REL DISCRIM NAT/LISM 20 UN OAU. PAGE 128 H2564 — CONSTN EX/STRUC SOVEREIGN INT/ORG

B20
HALDANE R.B.,BEFORE THE WAR. MOD/EUR SOCIETY INT/ORG NAT/G DELIB/GP PLAN DOMIN EDU/PROP LEGIT ADMIN COERCE ATTIT DRIVE MORAL ORD/FREE PWR...SOC CONCPT SELF/OBS RECORD BIOG TIME/SEQ. PAGE 64 H1282 — POLICY DIPLOM UK

B21
STUART G.H.,FRENCH FOREIGN POLICY. CONSTN INT/ORG NAT/G POL/PAR EX/STRUC FORCES PLAN ECO/TAC DOMIN EDU/PROP ADJUD COERCE ATTIT DRIVE RIGID/FLEX ALL/VALS...POLICY OBS RECORD BIOG TIME/SEQ TREND. PAGE 150 H3000 — MOD/EUR DIPLOM FRANCE

B28
CORBETT P.E.,CANADA AND WORLD POLITICS. LAW CULTURE SOCIETY STRUCT MARKET INT/ORG FORCES ACT/RES PLAN ECO/TAC LEGIT ORD/FREE PWR RESPECT...SOC CONCPT TIME/SEQ TREND CMN/WLTH 20 LEAGUE/NAT. PAGE 33 H0662 — NAT/G CANADA

B28
HURST C.,GREAT BRITAIN AND THE DOMINIONS. EUR+WWI CULTURE ECO/DEV INT/ORG NAT/G DIPLOM ECO/TAC COLONIAL ATTIT PWR SOVEREIGN...TIME/SEQ GEN/LAWS TOT/POP VAL/FREE 20 CMN/WLTH. PAGE 75 H1508 — VOL/ASSN DOMIN UK

B29
ROBERTS S.H.,HISTORY OF FRENCH COLONIAL POLICY. AFR ASIA L/A+17C S/ASIA CULTURE ECO/DEV ECO/UNDEV FINAN NAT/G PLAN ECO/TAC DOMIN ROUTINE SOVEREIGN...OBS HIST/WRIT TREND CHARTS VAL/FREE 19/20. PAGE 132 H2642 — INT/ORG ACT/RES FRANCE COLONIAL

B29
STURZO L.,THE INTERNATIONAL COMMUNITY AND THE RIGHT OF WAR (TRANS. BY BARBARA BARCLAY CARTER). CULTURE CREATE PROB/SOLV DIPLOM ADJUD CONTROL PEACE PERSON ORD/FREE...INT/LAW IDEA/COMP PACIFIST 20 LEAGUE/NAT. PAGE 150 H3003 — INT/ORG PLAN WAR CONCPT

B30
BYNKERSHOEK C.,QUAESTIONUM JURIS PUBLICI LIBRI DUO. CHRIST-17C MOD/EUR CONSTN ELITES SOCIETY NAT/G PROVS EX/STRUC FORCES TOP/EX BAL/PWR DIPLOM ATTIT MORAL...TRADIT CONCPT. PAGE 25 H0502 — INT/ORG LAW NAT/LISM INT/LAW

B30
HULL W.I.,INDIA'S POLITICAL CRISIS. INDIA UK INT/ORG LABOR SECT DELIB/GP LEGIS DIPLOM NEUTRAL REGION CROWD GOV/REL MAJORITY ATTIT 20 NEHRU/J GANDHI/M COMMONWLTH. PAGE 75 H1492 — ORD/FREE NAT/G COLONIAL NAT/LISM

B30
SMUTS J.C.,AFRICA AND SOME WORLD PROBLEMS. RHODESIA SOUTH/AFR CULTURE ECO/UNDEV INDUS INT/ORG SECT PROB/SOLV REGION GOV/REL DISCRIM ATTIT 19/20 LEAGUE/NAT LIVNGSTN/D NEGRO. PAGE 146 H2921 — LEGIS AFR COLONIAL RACE/REL

B32
BLUM L.,PEACE AND DISARMAMENT (TRANS. BY A. WERTH). NAT/G FORCES WORKER DIPLOM AGREE WAR ATTIT AUTHORIT ORD/FREE. PAGE 18 H0360 — SOCIALIST PEACE INT/ORG ARMS/CONT

B32
BRYCE J.,THE HOLY ROMAN EMPIRE. GERMANY ITALY MOD/EUR CULTURE SOCIETY STRUCT INT/ORG NAT/G SECT DIPLOM DOMIN WAR SUPEGO ALL/VALS SOVEREIGN...GEOG SOC TIME/SEQ CHARTS STERTYP. PAGE 23 H0456 — CHRIST-17C NAT/LISM

B36
RAPPARD W.E.,THE GOVERNMENT OF SWITZERLAND. SWITZERLND INT/ORG POL/PAR EX/STRUC DIPLOM NEUTRAL PARL/PROC REGION WAR HABITAT SOVEREIGN...NAT/COMP SOC/INTEG 20 LEAGUE/NAT WWI. PAGE 130 H2594 — CONSTN NAT/G CULTURE FEDERAL

B38
SAINT-PIERRE C.I.,SCHEME FOR LASTING PEACE (TRANS. BY H. BELLOT). INDUS NAT/G CHIEF FORCES INT/TRADE CT/SYS WAR PWR SOVEREIGN WEALTH...POLICY 18. PAGE 137 H2732 — INT/ORG PEACE AGREE INT/LAW

B39
BENES E.,INTERNATIONAL SECURITY. GERMANY UK NAT/G DELIB/GP PLAN BAL/PWR ATTIT ORD/FREE PWR LEAGUE/NAT 20 TREATY. PAGE 14 H0280 — EUR+WWI INT/ORG WAR

B39
HITLER A.,MEIN KAMPF. EUR+WWI FUT MOD/EUR STRUCT INT/ORG LABOR NAT/G POL/PAR FORCES CREATE PLAN BAL/PWR DIPLOM ECO/TAC DOMIN EDU/PROP ADMIN COERCE ATTIT...SOCIALIST BIOG TREND NAZI. PAGE 71 H1428 — PWR NEW/IDEA WAR

B39
TAGGART F.J.,ROME AND CHINA. MEDIT-7 INT/ORG NAT/G FORCES LEGIS TOP/EX PLAN PWR SOVEREIGN...CHARTS TOT/POP ROM/EMP. PAGE 152 H3034 — ASIA WAR

B40
WOLFERS A.,BRITAIN AND FRANCE BETWEEN TWO WORLD WARS. FRANCE UK INT/ORG NAT/G PLAN BARGAIN ECO/TAC AGREE ISOLAT ALL/IDEOS...DECISION GEOG 20 TREATY VERSAILLES INTERVENT. PAGE 170 H3402 — DIPLOM WAR POLICY

B43
SERENI A.P.,THE ITALIAN CONCEPTION OF INTERNATIONAL LAW. EUR+WWI MOD/EUR INT/ORG NAT/G DOMIN COERCE ORD/FREE FASCISM...OBS/ENVIR TREND 20. PAGE 141 H2829 — LAW TIME/SEQ INT/LAW ITALY

N45
INDIA QUARTERLY, A JOURNAL OF INTERNATIONAL AFFAIRS. INDIA LAW CONSTN ECO/UNDEV INT/ORG POL/PAR COLONIAL LEAD PARL/PROC WAR ATTIT...SOC 20 CMN/WLTH. PAGE 2 H0033 — BIBLIOG/A S/ASIA DIPLOM NAT/G

B45
WOOLBERT R.G.,FOREIGN AFFAIRS BIBLIOGRAPHY, 1932-1942. INT/ORG SECT INT/TRADE COLONIAL RACE/REL NAT/LISM...GEOG INT/LAW GOV/COMP IDEA/COMP 20. PAGE 170 H3410 — BIBLIOG/A DIPLOM WAR

S46
SILBERNER E.,"THE PROBLEM OF WAR IN NINETEENTH CENTURY ECONOMIC THOUGHT." EUR+WWI MOD/EUR UNIV LAW ECO/DEV ECO/UNDEV FINAN INDUS MARKET INT/ORG NAT/G CONSULT FORCES...CONCPT GEN/LAWS GEN/METH 19. PAGE 144 H2875 — ATTIT ECO/TAC WAR

B47
ENKE S.,INTERNATIONAL ECONOMICS. UK USA+45 USSR INT/ORG BAL/PWR BARGAIN CAP/ISM BAL/PAY...NAT/COMP 20 TREATY. PAGE 46 H0927 — INT/TRADE FINAN TARIFFS ECO/TAC

B47
JURJI E.J.,THE GREAT RELIGIONS OF THE MODERN WORLD. CULTURE INTELL SOCIETY INT/ORG CONSULT CHOOSE ATTIT DRIVE PERSON RIGID/FLEX...HUM CONCPT OBS BIOG HIST/WRIT TREND GEN/LAWS 20 WORSHIP. PAGE 82 H1643 — UNIV SECT

B48
JONES H.D.,UNESCO: A SELECTED LIST OF REFERENCES. CULTURE CREATE PEACE ATTIT DRIVE 20 UNESCO UN. PAGE 82 H1631 — BIBLIOG/A INT/ORG DIPLOM EDU/PROP

B49
SINGER K.,THE IDEA OF CONFLICT. UNIV INTELL INT/ORG NAT/G PLAN ROUTINE ATTIT DRIVE ALL/VALS...POLICY CONCPT TIME/SEQ. PAGE 144 H2882 — ACT/RES SOC

B49
US DEPARTMENT OF STATE,SOVIET BIBLIOGRAPHY (PAMPHLET). CHINA/COM COM USSR LAW AGRI INT/ORG ECO/TAC EDU/PROP...POLICY GEOG 20. PAGE 159 H3185 — BIBLIOG/A MARXISM CULTURE DIPLOM

B50
DUCLOS P.,L'EVOLUTION DES RAPPORTS POLITIQUES DEPUIS 1750 (LIBERTE, INTEGRATION, UNITE). LAW INT/ORG FEDERAL TOTALISM ATTIT PWR...MAJORIT BIBLIOG 18/20 PARLIAMENT EUROPE. PAGE 43 H0852 — ORD/FREE DIPLOM NAT/G GOV/COMP

B50
MACIVER R.M.,GREAT EXPRESSIONS OF HUMAN RIGHTS. LAW CONSTN CULTURE INTELL SOCIETY R+D INT/ORG ATTIT DRIVE...JURID OBS HIST/WRIT GEN/LAWS. PAGE 100 H1999 — UNIV CONCPT

B51
BORKENAU F.,EUROPEAN COMMUNISM. COM EUR+WWI GERMANY SPAIN USSR INT/ORG PLAN REV WAR ATTIT 20 STALIN/J HITLER/A. PAGE 19 H0376 — MARXISM POLICY DIPLOM NAT/G

B51
JENNINGS I.,THE COMMONWEALTH IN ASIA. CEYLON INDIA PAKISTAN CULTURE STRATA NAT/G LEGIS DIPLOM COLONIAL ATTIT...DECISION 20 CMN/WLTH. PAGE 80 H1604 — CONSTN INT/ORG POLICY PLAN

B51
LEONARD L.L.,INTERNATIONAL ORGANIZATION. WOR+45 WOR-45 EX/STRUC FORCES LEGIS ECO/TAC INT/TRADE COLONIAL ARMS/CONT...SOC/WK GOV/COMP BIBLIOG. PAGE 94 H1884 — NAT/G DIPLOM INT/ORG DELIB/GP

B52
ULAM A.B.,TITOISM AND THE COMINFORM. USSR WOR+45 STRUCT INT/ORG NAT/G ACT/RES PLAN EXEC ATTIT DRIVE ALL/VALS...CONCPT OBS VAL/FREE 20 COMINTERN TITO/MARSH. PAGE 157 H3149 — COM POL/PAR TOTALISM YUGOSLAVIA

B52
WALTERS F.P.,A HISTORY OF THE LEAGUE OF NATIONS. EUR+WWI CONSTN NAT/G LEGIS TOP/EX ACT/RES PLAN EDU/PROP LEGIT ROUTINE ATTIT...TREND LEAGUE/NAT 20 CHINJAP. PAGE 165 H3297 — INT/ORG TIME/SEQ NAT/LISM

C52
FIFIELD R.H.,"WOODROW WILSON AND THE FAR EAST." ASIA CHIEF DELIB/GP BAL/PWR CONFER COLONIAL ARMS/CONT WAR...TIME/SEQ NAT/COMP 19/20 WILSON/W LEAGUE/NAT. PAGE 50 H0995 — BIBLIOG DIPLOM INT/ORG

N52
COORDINATING COMM DOC SOC SCI,INTERNATIONAL REPERTORY OF SOCIAL SCIENCE DOCUMENTATION CENTERS (PAMPHLET). ACT/RES OP/RES WRITING KNOWL...CON/ANAL METH. PAGE 33 H0661 — BIBLIOG/A R+D NAT/G INT/ORG

B53
KANTOR H.,A BIBLIOGRAPHY OF UNPUBLISHED DOCTORAL DISSERTATIONS AND MASTERS' THESES DEALING WITH GOVTS, POL, INT REL OF LAT AM. L/A+17C INT/ORG POL/PAR ACT/RES OP/RES CONFER ATTIT...INT/LAW PHIL/SCI 20. PAGE 83 H1656 — BIBLIOG ACADEM DIPLOM NAT/G

B53
LEITES N.,A STUDY OF BOLSHEVISM. WOR+45 WOR-45 ELITES SOCIETY INT/ORG NAT/G EX/STRUC EDU/PROP EXEC ROUTINE ATTIT MORAL MARXISM...CONCPT OBS VAL/FREE 20. PAGE 94 H1869 — COM POL/PAR USSR TOTALISM

B53
LEITES N.,A STUDY OF BOLSHEVISM. ELITES STRATA INT/ORG LOC/G POL/PAR WORKER EDU/PROP REV TOTALISM UTOPIA PWR...CONCPT 20 BOLSHEVISM. PAGE 94 H1870 — MARXISM PLAN COM

B53
MURPHY G.,IN THE MINDS OF MEN: THE STUDY OF HUMAN BEHAVIOR AND SOCIAL TENSIONS IN INDIA. FUT S/ASIA FAM INT/ORG NAT/G DIPLOM EDU/PROP GP/REL ATTIT RIGID/FLEX ALL/VALS...SOC QU UNESCO 20. PAGE 115 H2297 — SECT STRATA INDIA

B54
BUTZ O.,GERMANY: DILEMMA FOR AMERICAN POLICY. GERMANY USA+45 USA-45 USSR WOR+45 INT/ORG FORCES NUC/PWR EFFICIENCY PEACE PWR...GOV/COMP 20 COLD/WAR. PAGE 25 H0501 — DIPLOM NAT/G WAR POLICY

B54
FRIEDMAN W.,THE PUBLIC CORPORATION: A COMPARATIVE SYMPOSIUM (UNIVERSITY OF TORONTO SCHOOL OF LAW COMPARATIVE LAW SERIES, VOL. I). SWEDEN USA+45 INDUS INT/ORG NAT/G REGION CENTRAL FEDERAL...POLICY JURID IDEA/COMP NAT/COMP ANTHOL 20 COMMONWLTH — LAW SOCISM LG/CO OWN

MONOPOLY EUROPE. PAGE 53 H1065

B54
SALVEMINI G.,PRELUDE TO WORLD WAR II. ITALY MOD/EUR INT/ORG BAL/PWR EDU/PROP CONTROL TOTALISM...TREND NAT/COMP BIBLIOG 19 HITLER/A LEAGUE/NAT MUSSOLIN/B. PAGE 137 H2745 WAR FASCISM LEAD PWR

S54
DODD S.C.,"THE SCIENTIFIC MEASUREMENT OF FITNESS FOR SELF-GOVERNMENT." FUT CONSTN ECO/UNDEV INT/ORG PLAN PWR...CONCPT QUANT CON/ANAL SOC/EXP UN LEAGUE/NAT 20. PAGE 41 H0830 NAT/G STAT SOVEREIGN

B55
INSTITUTE POLITISCHE WISSEN,POLITISCHE LITERATUR (3 VOLS.). INT/ORG LEAD WAR PEACE...CONCPT TREND NAT/COMP 20. PAGE 77 H1540 BIBLIOG/A NAT/G DIPLOM POLICY

B55
SVARLIEN O.,AN INTRODUCTION TO THE LAW OF NATIONS. SEA AIR INT/ORG NAT/G CHIEF ADMIN AGREE WAR PRIVIL ORD/FREE SOVEREIGN...BIBLIOG 16/20. PAGE 151 H3012 INT/LAW DIPLOM

L55
ROSTOW W.W.,"RUSSIA AND CHINA UNDER COMMUNISM." CHINA/COM USSR INTELL STRUCT INT/ORG NAT/G POL/PAR TOP/EX ACT/RES PLAN ADMIN ATTIT ALL/VALS MARXISM ...CONCPT OBS TIME/SEQ TREND GOV/COMP VAL/FREE 20. PAGE 134 H2689 COM ASIA

B56
ROBERTS H.L.,RUSSIA AND AMERICA. CHINA/COM S/ASIA USSR FORCES TEC/DEV FOR/AID NUC/PWR ALL/IDEOS ...MAJORIT TREND NAT/COMP 20 COLD/WAR UN NATO. PAGE 132 H2641 DIPLOM INT/ORG BAL/PWR TOTALISM

B56
WOLFF R.L.,THE BALKANS IN OUR TIME. ALBANIA FUT MOD/EUR USSR YUGOSLAVIA CULTURE INT/ORG SECT DIPLOM EDU/PROP COERCE WAR ORD/FREE...CHARTS 4/20 BALKANS COMINFORM. PAGE 170 H3403 GEOG COM

S56
GORDON L.,"THE ORGANIZATION FOR EUROPEAN ECONOMIC COOPERATION." EUR+WWI INDUS INT/ORG NAT/G CONSULT DELIB/GP ACT/RES CREATE PLAN TEC/DEV EDU/PROP LEGIT WEALTH OEEC 20. PAGE 59 H1178 VOL/ASSN ECO/DEV

B57
ARON R.,L'UNIFICATION ECONOMIQUE DE L'EUROPE. EUR+WWI SWITZERLND UK INT/ORG NAT/G REGION NAT/LISM ORD/FREE PWR...CONCPT METH/CNCPT OBS TREND STERTYP GEN/LAWS EEC 20. PAGE 8 H0168 VOL/ASSN ECO/TAC

B57
BUCK P.W.,CONTOL OF FOREIGN RELATIONS IN MODERN NATIONS. FRANCE L/A+17C NETHERLAND USSR WOR+45 INT/ORG TOP/EX BAL/PWR DOMIN EDU/PROP COERCE PEACE ATTIT...CONCPT TREND 20 CMN/WLTH. PAGE 23 H0465 NAT/G PWR DIPLOM

B57
CARIBBEAN COMMISSION,A CATALOGUE OF CARIBBEAN COMMISSION PUBLICATIONS (PAMPHLET). WEST/IND CULTURE ECO/UNDEV LOC/G DIPLOM SOC. PAGE 26 H0531 BIBLIOG L/A+17C INT/ORG NAT/G

B57
CONOVER H.F.,NORTH AND NORTHEAST AFRICA; A SELECTED ANNOTATED LIST OF WRITINGS. ALGERIA MOROCCO SUDAN UAR CULTURE INT/ORG PROB/SOLV ADJUD NAT/LISM PWR WEALTH...SOC 20 UN. PAGE 32 H0649 BIBLIOG/A DIPLOM AFR ECO/UNDEV

B57
PALMER N.D.,INTERNATIONAL RELATIONS. WOR+45 INT/ORG NAT/G ECO/TAC EDU/PROP COLONIAL WAR PWR SOVEREIGN ...POLICY T 20 TREATY. PAGE 123 H2451 DIPLOM BAL/PWR NAT/COMP

B57
US SENATE SPEC COMM FOR AID,COMPILATION OF STUDIES AND SURVEYS. AFR ASIA L/A+17C USA+45 ECO/UNDEV AGRI INT/ORG CONSULT TEC/DEV CONFER TOTALISM...NAT/COMP 20 CONGRESS. PAGE 161 H3216 FOR/AID DIPLOM ORD/FREE DELIB/GP

B57
US SENATE SPEC COMM FOR AID,HEARINGS BEFORE THE SPECIAL COMMITTEE TO STUDY THE FOREIGN AID PROGRAM. USA+45 USSR ECO/UNDEV INT/ORG FORCES WEAPON TOTALISM ATTIT SUPEGO...NAT/COMP CONGRESS. PAGE 161 H3217 FOR/AID DIPLOM ORD/FREE TEC/DEV

B58
GARTHOFF R.L.,SOVIET STRATEGY IN THE NUCLEAR AGE. FUT USSR R+D INT/ORG NAT/G ACT/RES TEC/DEV DOMIN DETER WAR ATTIT PWR...RELATIV METH/CNCPT SELF/OBS TREND CON/ANAL STERTYP GEN/LAWS 20. PAGE 55 H1103 COM FORCES BAL/PWR NUC/PWR

B58
HAAS E.B.,THE UNITING OF EUROPE. EUR+WWI INT/ORG NAT/G POL/PAR TOP/EX ECO/TAC EDU/PROP LEGIT FEDERAL NAT/LISM DRIVE RIGID/FLEX ORD/FREE PWR PLURISM ...POLICY CONCPT INT GEN/LAWS ECSC EEC 20. PAGE 63 H1264 VOL/ASSN ECO/DEV

S58
ELKIN A.B.,"OEEC-ITS STRUCTURE AND POWERS." EUR+WWI CONSTN INDUS INT/ORG NAT/G VOL/ASSN DELIB/GP ACT/RES PLAN ORD/FREE WEALTH...CHARTS ORG/CHARTS OEEC 20. PAGE 45 H0907 ECO/DEV EX/STRUC

S58
STAAR R.F.,"ELECTIONS IN COMMUNIST POLAND." EUR+WWI SOCIETY INT/ORG NAT/G POL/PAR LEGIS ACT/RES ECO/TAC EDU/PROP ADJUD ADMIN ROUTINE COERCE TOTALISM ATTIT ORD/FREE PWR 20. PAGE 148 H2963 COM CHOOSE POLAND

C58
FIFIELD R.H.,"THE DIPLOMACY OF SOUTHEAST ASIA: 1945-1958." INT/ORG NAT/G COLONIAL REGION...CHARTS BIBLIOG 20 UN. PAGE 50 H0996 S/ASIA DIPLOM NAT/LISM

B59
BLOOMFIELD L.P.,WESTERN EUROPE AND THE UN - TRENDS AND PROSPECTS. EUR+WWI BAL/PWR DIPLOM ECO/TAC COLONIAL ATTIT PWR...POLICY 20 UN EUROPE/W. PAGE 18 H0359 INT/ORG TREND FUT NAT/G

B59
GOLDWIN R.A.,READINGS IN RUSSIAN FOREIGN POLICY. HUNGARY USSR YUGOSLAVIA ELITES INT/ORG NAT/G REV WAR NAT/LISM PERSON SOCISM...CHARTS 20 MAPS BOLSHEVISM. PAGE 58 H1160 COM MARXISM DIPLOM POLICY

B59
OVERSTREET G.D.,COMMUNISM IN INDIA. INDIA S/ASIA CONSTN INT/ORG LEAD GP/REL...CHARTS BIBLIOG 20. PAGE 122 H2435 MARXISM NAT/LISM POL/PAR WAR

B59
THOMAS D.H.,GUIDE TO THE DIPLOMATIC ARCHIVES OF WESTERN EUROPE. EUR+WWI ELITES INT/ORG NAT/G BAL/PWR INT/TRADE PEACE. PAGE 154 H3076 BIBLIOG DIPLOM CONFER

L59
MURPHY J.C.,"SOME IMPLICATIONS OF EUROPE'S COMMON MARKET. IN (COOK P, ECONOMIC DEVELOPMENT AND INTERNATIONAL TRADE.." EUR+WWI ECO/DEV DIST/IND INDUS NAT/G PLAN ECO/TAC INT/TRADE WEALTH...STAT TREND OEEC TOT/POP 20 EEC. PAGE 115 H2298 MARKET INT/ORG REGION

S59
JENKS C.W.,"THE CHALLENGE OF UNIVERSALITY." FUT UNIV CONSTN CULTURE CONSULT CREATE PLAN LEGIT ATTIT MORAL ORD/FREE RESPECT...MAJORIT JURID 20. PAGE 80 H1602 INT/ORG LAW PEACE INT/LAW

S59
PLAZA G.,"FOR A REGIONAL MARKET IN LATIN AMERICA." FUT L/A+17C CULTURE INDUS NAT/G ECO/TAC INT/TRADE ATTIT WEALTH...NEW/IDEA TREND OAS 20. PAGE 126 H2527 MARKET INT/ORG REGION

S59
WARBURG J.P.,"THE CENTRAL EUROPEAN CRISIS: A PROPOSAL FOR WESTERN INITIATIVE." EUR+WWI INT/ORG NAT/G LEGIT DETER WAR...CONCPT BER/BLOC UN 20. PAGE 165 H3302 PLAN GERMANY

S59
ZAUBERMAN A.,"SOVIET BLOC ECONOMIC INTEGRATION." COM CULTURE INTELL ECO/DEV INDUS TOP/EX ACT/RES PLAN ECO/TAC INT/TRADE ROUTINE CHOOSE ATTIT ...TIME/SEQ 20. PAGE 172 H3452 MARKET INT/ORG USSR TOTALISM

B60
CONOVER H.F.,OFFICIAL PUBLICATIONS OF SOMALILAND, 1941-1959: A GUIDE. SOMALIA AGRI FINAN INT/ORG SCHOOL INT/TRADE PRESS CONFER COLONIAL PARL/PROC 20 CONGRESS. PAGE 33 H0652 BIBLIOG NAT/G CON/ANAL

B60
FISCHER L.,THE SOVIETS IN WORLD AFFAIRS. CHINA/COM COM EUR+WWI USSR INT/ORG CONFER LEAD ARMS/CONT REV PWR...CHARTS 20 TREATY VERSAILLES. PAGE 51 H1010 DIPLOM NAT/G POLICY MARXISM

B60
JEFFRIES C.,TRANSFER OF POWER: PROBLEMS OF THE PASSAGE TO SELFGOVERNMENT. CEYLON GHANA MALAYSIA NIGERIA UK INT/ORG CONSULT DELIB/GP LEGIS DIPLOM CONFER PARL/PROC 20. PAGE 80 H1595 SOVEREIGN COLONIAL ORD/FREE NAT/G

B60
LINDSAY K.,EUROPEAN ASSEMBLIES: THE EXPERIMENTAL PERIOD 1949-1959. EUR+WWI ECO/DEV NAT/G POL/PAR LEGIS TOP/EX ACT/RES PLAN ECO/TAC DOMIN LEGIT ROUTINE ATTIT DRIVE ORD/FREE PWR SKILL...SOC CONCPT TREND CHARTS GEN/LAWS VAL/FREE. PAGE 97 H1932 VOL/ASSN INT/ORG REGION

B60
LISTER L.,EUROPE'S COAL AND STEEL COMMUNITY. FRANCE GERMANY STRUCT ECO/DEV EXTR/IND INDUS MARKET NAT/G DELIB/GP ECO/TAC INT/TRADE EDU/PROP ATTIT RIGID/FLEX ORD/FREE PWR WEALTH...CONCPT STAT TIME/SEQ CHARTS ECSC 20. PAGE 97 H1941 EUR+WWI INT/ORG REGION

B60
MINIFIE J.M.,PEACEMAKER OR POWDER-MONKEY. CANADA INT/ORG NAT/G FORCES LEAD WAR...PREDICT 20. PAGE 111 H2222 DIPLOM POLICY NEUTRAL PEACE

B60
ROBINSON E.A.G.,ECONOMIC CONSEQUENCES OF THE SIZE OF NATIONS. AGRI INDUS DELIB/GP FOR/AID ADMIN EFFICIENCY...METH/COMP 20. PAGE 132 H2649 CONCPT INT/ORG NAT/COMP

B60
SCANLON D.G.,INTERNATIONAL EDUCATION: A DOCUMENTARY HISTORY. ADMIN CONTROL ATTIT PERCEPT...BIOG ANTHOL METH 20. PAGE 138 H2765 EDU/PROP INT/ORG NAT/COMP DIPLOM

B60
THE ECONOMIST (LONDON),THE COMMONWEALTH AND EUROPE. EUR+WWI WOR+45 AGRI FINAN INCOME...STAT CENSUS CHARTS CMN/WLTH EEC. PAGE 153 H3067 INT/TRADE INDUS INT/ORG NAT/COMP

B60
THEOBOLD R.,THE NEW NATIONS OF WEST AFRICA. GHANA NIGERIA CULTURE INT/ORG ECO/TAC FOR/AID COLONIAL RACE/REL POPULISM...ANTHOL BIBLIOG 20 UN. PAGE 153 H3068
AFR SOVEREIGN ECO/UNDEV DIPLOM

B60
WILLIAMS L.E.,OVERSEAS CHINESE NATIONALISM: THE GENESIS OF THE PAN-CHINESE MOVEMENT IN INDONESIA, 1900-1916. ASIA COM INDONESIA AGRI INT/ORG LOC/G DIPLOM EDU/PROP HABITAT PWR POPULISM...GEOG LING CENSUS 20. PAGE 168 H3367
NAT/LISM GP/REL DECISION NAT/G

L60
HAAS E.B.,"CONSENSUS FORMATION IN THE COUNCIL OF EUROPE." EUR+WWI NAT/G DELIB/GP DIPLOM REGION CHOOSE PWR SOVEREIGN...RELATIV NEW/IDEA QUANT CHARTS INDEX TOT/POP OEEC 20 COUNCL/EUR. PAGE 63 H1265
POL/PAR INT/ORG STAT

S60
FITZGIBBON R.H.,"DICTATORSHIP AND DEMOCRACY IN LATIN AMERICA." FUT ECO/DEV ECO/UNDEV INT/ORG LOC/G NAT/G TOP/EX PLAN TEC/DEV ECO/TAC CHOOSE ATTIT DRIVE PERSON ALL/VALS OAS TOT/POP 20. PAGE 51 H1019
L/A+17C ACT/RES INT/TRADE

S60
MAGATHAN W.,"SOME BASES OF WEST GERMAN MILITARY POLICY." EUR+WWI FUT INT/ORG TOP/EX ECO/TAC DOMIN DRIVE ORD/FREE PWR...TRADIT GEOG OBS TREND. PAGE 101 H2015
NAT/G FORCES GERMANY

S60
NORTHEDGE F.S.,"BRITISH FOREIGN POLICY AND THE PARTY SYSTEM." EUR+WWI FUT INT/ORG NAT/G EDU/PROP ATTIT PWR...POLICY CONCPT MYTH TIME/SEQ TREND 20 UN. PAGE 119 H2374
POL/PAR CHOOSE DIPLOM UK

B61
BELOFF M.,NEW DIMENSIONS IN FOREIGN POLICY: A STUDY IN BRITISH ADMINISTRATION. UK NAT/G ATTIT RIGID/FLEX ORD/FREE...GEN/LAWS EUR+WWI CMN/WLTH EEC 20. PAGE 14 H0271
INT/ORG DIPLOM

B61
BISHOP D.G.,THE ADMINISTRATION OF BRITISH FOREIGN RELATIONS. EUR+WWI MOD/EUR INT/ORG NAT/G POL/PAR DELIB/GP LEGIS TOP/EX ECO/TAC DOMIN EDU/PROP ADMIN COERCE 20. PAGE 17 H0344
ROUTINE PWR DIPLOM UK

B61
BONNEFOUS M.,EUROPE ET TIERS MONDE. EUR+WWI SOCIETY INT/ORG NAT/G VOL/ASSN ACT/RES TEC/DEV CAP/ISM ECO/TAC ATTIT ORD/FREE SOVEREIGN...POLICY CONCPT TREND 20. PAGE 19 H0373
AFR ECO/UNDEV FOR/AID INT/TRADE

B61
DALLIN D.J.,SOVIET FOREIGN POLICY AFTER STALIN. ASIA CHINA/COM EUR+WWI GERMANY IRAN UK YUGOSLAVIA INT/ORG NAT/G VOL/ASSN FORCES TOP/EX BAL/PWR DOMIN EDU/PROP COERCE ATTIT PWR 20. PAGE 37 H0737
COM DIPLOM USSR

B61
DIA M.,THE AFRICAN NATIONS AND WORLD SOLIDARITY. ISLAM CULTURE ELITES ECO/DEV ECO/UNDEV INT/ORG NAT/G PLAN ECO/TAC INT/TRADE EDU/PROP NAT/LISM ATTIT DRIVE ORD/FREE WEALTH...SOCIALIST CONCPT CON/ANAL GEN/LAWS TOT/POP 20. PAGE 41 H0817
AFR REGION SOCISM

B61
JAKOBSON M.,THE DIPLOMACY OF THE WINTER WAR. EUR+WWI FINLAND GERMANY USSR INT/ORG NAT/G PEACE TOTALISM PWR...POLICY CONCPT 20 TREATY. PAGE 79 H1588
WAR ORD/FREE DIPLOM

B61
MOLLAU G.,INTERNATIONAL COMMUNISM AND WORLD REVOLUTION: HISTORY AND METHODS. RUSSIA USSR INT/ORG NAT/G POL/PAR VOL/ASSN FORCES BAL/PWR DIPLOM EXEC REGION WAR ATTIT PWR MARXISM...CONCPT TIME/SEQ COLD/WAR 19/20. PAGE 112 H2237
COM REV

B61
NICOLSON H.G.,THE OLD DIPLOMACY AND THE NEW. NAT/G PLAN PROB/SOLV...METH 20. PAGE 118 H2355
DIPLOM POLICY INT/ORG

B61
OECD,STATISTICS OF BALANCE OF PAYMENTS 1950-61. WOR+45 FINAN ECO/TAC INT/TRADE DEMAND WEALTH...STAT NAT/COMP 20 OEEC OECD. PAGE 120 H2396
BAL/PAY ECO/DEV INT/ORG CHARTS

B61
ROBERTSON A.H.,THE LAW OF INTERNATIONAL INSTITUTIONS IN EUROPE. EUR+WWI MOD/EUR INT/ORG NAT/G VOL/ASSN DELIB/GP...JURID TIME/SEQ TOT/POP 20 TREATY. PAGE 132 H2644
RIGID/FLEX ORD/FREE

L61
LEVINE R.A.,"THE ANTHROPOLOGY OF CONFLICT." FUT CULTURE INTELL FAM INT/ORG LG/CO SML/CO ATTIT KNOWL ...METH/CNCPT VAL/FREE 20. PAGE 95 H1905
SOCIETY ACT/RES

S61
MILLER E.,"LEGAL ASPECTS OF UN ACTION IN THE CONGO." AFR CULTURE ADMIN PEACE DRIVE RIGID/FLEX ORD/FREE...WELF/ST JURID OBS UN CONGO 20. PAGE 111 H2212
INT/ORG LEGIT

S61
PADELFORD N.J.,"POLITICS AND THE FUTURE OF ECOSOC." AFR S/ASIA ECO/UNDEV INDUS NAT/G DELIB/GP ACT/RES ORD/FREE WEALTH...CONCPT CHARTS UN 20 ECOSOC. PAGE 122 H2438
INT/ORG TEC/DEV

S61
SCHAPIRO L.,"SOVIET GOVERNMENT TODAY." COM EUR+WWI INT/ORG POL/PAR VOL/ASSN ACT/RES PLAN PERCEPT ...CONCPT TREND TOT/POP VAL/FREE 20. PAGE 139 H2773
NAT/G TOTALISM USSR

S61
ZAGORIA D.S.,"THE FUTURE OF SINO-SOVIET RELATIONS." CHINA/COM INT/ORG NAT/G POL/PAR VOL/ASSN ACT/RES PLAN PERSON...METH/CNCPT TIME/SEQ TOT/POP VAL/FREE 20 MAO KHRUSH/N. PAGE 172 H3445
ASIA COM TOTALISM USSR

B62
BERGER M.,THE ARAB WORLD TODAY. CULTURE FAM INT/ORG NAT/G SECT FORCES ECO/TAC NAT/LISM HABITAT...CHARTS BIBLIOG 20 ARABS. PAGE 15 H0301
ISLAM PERSON STRUCT SOCIETY

B62
CALVOCORESSI P.,WORLD ORDER AND NEW STATES: PROBLEMS OF KEEPING THE PEACE. AFR EUR+WWI S/ASIA ELITES NAT/G ECO/TAC FOR/AID EDU/PROP COERCE ATTIT DRIVE ALL/VALS...GEN/LAWS COLD/WAR 20 UN. PAGE 25 H0509
INT/ORG PEACE

B62
COUNCIL ON WORLD TENSIONS,RESTLESS NATIONS. WOR+45 STRUCT INT/ORG NAT/G PLAN ECO/TAC...NAT/COMP ANTHOL 20. PAGE 34 H0678
ECO/UNDEV POLICY DIPLOM TASK

B62
DUROSELLE J.B.,LES NOUVEAUX ETATS DANS LES RELATIONS INTERNATIONALES. AFR CHINA/COM FRANCE MOROCCO S/ASIA USSR ECO/UNDEV INT/ORG PLAN ECO/TAC EDU/PROP ATTIT DRIVE...TREND TOT/POP TUNIS 20. PAGE 44 H0872
NAT/G CONSTN DIPLOM

B62
DUTOIT B.,LA NEUTRALITE SUISSE A L'HEURE EUROPEENNE. EUR+WWI MOD/EUR INT/ORG NAT/G VOL/ASSN PLAN BAL/PWR LEGIT NEUTRAL REGION PEACE ORD/FREE SOVEREIGN...CONCPT OBS TIME/SEQ TREND STERTYP VAL/FREE LEAGUE/NAT UN 20. PAGE 44 H0873
ATTIT DIPLOM SWITZERLND

B62
FRIEDMANN W.,METHODS AND POLICIES OF PRINCIPAL DONOR COUNTRIES IN PUBLIC INTERNATIONAL DEVELOPMENT FINANCING: PRELIMINARY APPRAISAL. FRANCE GERMANY/W UK USA+45 USSR WOR+45 FINAN TEC/DEV CAP/ISM DIPLOM ECO/TAC ATTIT 20 EEC. PAGE 53 H1066
INT/ORG FOR/AID NAT/COMP ADMIN

B62
HATCH J.,AFRICA TODAY-AND TOMORROW: AN OUTLINE OF BASIC FACTS AND MAJOR PROBLEMS. AFR FUT ISLAM STRATA ECO/UNDEV INT/ORG NAT/G POL/PAR DELIB/GP TOP/EX EDU/PROP LEGIT CHOOSE ATTIT...TIME/SEQ TOT/POP COLD/WAR 20. PAGE 67 H1353
PLAN CONSTN NAT/LISM

B62
LAQUEUR W.,POLYCENTRISM. CHINA/COM COM USSR WOR+45 INT/ORG NAT/G ECO/TAC DOMIN LEAD ATTIT PWR SOVEREIGN...ANTHOL 20. PAGE 91 H1821
MARXISM DIPLOM BAL/PWR POLICY

B62
LOWENSTEIN A.K.,BRUTAL MANDATE: A JOURNEY TO SOUTH WEST AFRICA. CULTURE INT/ORG NAT/G DIPLOM...GEOG 20 UN AFRICA/SW. PAGE 99 H1975
AFR POLICY RACE/REL PROB/SOLV

B62
MEADE J.E.,CASE STUDIES IN EUROPEAN ECONOMIC UNION. BELGIUM EUR+WWI LUXEMBOURG NAT/G INT/TRADE REGION ROUTINE WEALTH...METH/CNCPT STAT CHARTS ECSC TOT/POP OEEC EEC 20. PAGE 108 H2154
INT/ORG ECO/TAC

B62
MODELSKI G.,SEATO-SIX STUDIES. ASIA CHINA/COM INDIA S/ASIA INT/ORG NAT/G ECO/TAC DETER ATTIT ORD/FREE PWR...TIME/SEQ COLD/WAR TOT/POP 20 SEATO. PAGE 112 H2234
MARKET ECO/UNDEV INT/TRADE

B62
MOUSSA P.,THE UNDERPRIVILEGED NATIONS. FINAN INT/ORG PLAN PROB/SOLV CAP/ISM GIVE TASK WEALTH ...POLICY SOC 20. PAGE 114 H2273
ECO/UNDEV NAT/G DIPLOM FOR/AID

B62
PHILLIPS O.H.,CONSTITUTIONAL AND ADMINISTRATIVE LAW (3RD ED.). UK INT/ORG LOC/G CHIEF EX/STRUC LEGIS BAL/PWR ADJUD COLONIAL CT/SYS PWR...CHARTS 20. PAGE 125 H2503
JURID ADMIN CONSTN NAT/G

B62
ROBINSON A.D.,DUTCH ORGANIZED AGRICULTURE IN INTERNATIONAL POLITICS, 1945-1960. EUR+WWI NETHERLAND STRUCT ECO/DEV NAT/G VOL/ASSN CONSULT DELIB/GP PLAN TEC/DEV INT/TRADE EDU/PROP ATTIT RIGID/FLEX ALL/VALS...NEW/IDEA TREND EEC 20. PAGE 132 H2648
AGRI INT/ORG

B62
UNECA LIBRARY,BOOKS ON AFRICA IN THE UNECA LIBRARY. WOR+45 AGRI INT/ORG NAT/G PLAN WRITING REGION...SOC STAT UN. PAGE 158 H3160
BIBLIOG AFR ECO/UNDEV TEC/DEV

B62
UNECA LIBRARY,NEW ACQUISITIONS IN THE UNECA LIBRARY. LAW NAT/G PLAN PROB/SOLV TEC/DEV ADMIN REGION...GEOG SOC 20 UN. PAGE 158 H3161
BIBLIOG AFR ECO/UNDEV

INT/ORG

CORET A.,"L'INDEPENDANCE DU SAMOA OCCIDENTAL." S/ASIA LAW INT/ORG EXEC ALL/VALS SAMOA UN 20. PAGE 33 H0668
NAT/G STRUCT SOVEREIGN L62

MURACCIOLE L.,"LA BANQUE CENTRALE DES ETATS DE L'AFRIQUE DE L'OUEST." AFR LAW ECO/UNDEV INT/ORG NAT/G CONSULT ECO/TAC ROUTINE...CHARTS 20. PAGE 115 H2292
ISLAM FINAN INT/TRADE L62

CORET A.,"LE STATUT DE L'ILE CHRISTMAS DE L'OCEAN INDIEN." FUT S/ASIA ECO/DEV ECO/UNDEV VOL/ASSN DELIB/GP PLAN...RELATIV OBS TIME/SEQ TREND AUSTRAL 20. PAGE 33 H0667
NAT/G INT/ORG NEW/ZEALND S62

CROAN M.,"POLYCENTRISM: COMMUNIST INTERNATIONAL RELATIONS." ASIA STRUCT INT/ORG NAT/G POL/PAR CONSULT PLAN DOMIN EDU/PROP COERCE ATTIT RIGID/FLEX SOCISM...POLICY CONCPT TREND CON/ANAL GEN/LAWS MARX/KARL. PAGE 35 H0703
COM CREATE DIPLOM NAT/LISM S62

GUETZKOW H.,"THE POTENTIAL OF CASE STUDY IN ANALYZING INTERNATIONAL CONFLICT." EUR+WWI FUT GERMANY INTELL SOCIETY STRUCT INT/ORG LOC/G NAT/G CONSULT CREATE PLAN CHOOSE ATTIT RIGID/FLEX ...POLICY SAAR 20. PAGE 62 H1246
EDU/PROP METH/CNCPT COERCE FRANCE S62

KOLARZ W.,"THE IMPACT OF COMMUNISM ON WEST AFRICA." AFR FUT SOCIETY INT/ORG NAT/G CREATE PLAN DOMIN EDU/PROP COERCE NAT/LISM ATTIT RIGID/FLEX SOCISM ...POLICY CONCPT TREND MARX/KARL 20. PAGE 88 H1751
COM POL/PAR COLONIAL S62

LONDON K.,"SINO-SOVIET RELATIONS IN THE CONTEXT OF THE 'WORLD SOCIALIST SYSTEM'." ASIA CHINA/COM COM USSR INT/ORG NAT/G TOP/EX BAL/PWR DIPLOM DOMIN ATTIT PERCEPT RIGID/FLEX PWR MARXISM...METH/CNCPT TREND 20. PAGE 98 H1957
DELIB/GP CONCPT SOCISM S62

MARIAS J.,"A PROGRAM FOR EUROPE." EUR+WWI INT/ORG NAT/G PLAN DIPLOM DOMIN PWR...STERTYP TOT/POP 20. PAGE 102 H2048
VOL/ASSN CREATE REGION S62

MOUSKHELY M.,"LA NAISSANCE DES ETATS EN DROIT INTERNATIONAL PUBLIC." UNIV SOCIETY INT/ORG VOL/ASSN LEGIT ATTIT RIGID/FLEX...JURID TIME/SEQ 20. PAGE 114 H2272
NAT/G STRUCT INT/LAW S62

PIQUEMAL M.,"LES PROBLEMES DES UNIONS D'ETATS EN AFRIQUE NOIRE." FRANCE SOCIETY INT/ORG NAT/G DELIB/GP PLAN LEGIT ADMIN COLONIAL ROUTINE ATTIT ORD/FREE PWR...GEOG METH/CNCPT 20. PAGE 126 H2515
AFR ECO/UNDEV REGION S62

RAZAFIMBAHINY J.,"L'ORGANISATION AFRICAINE ET MALGACHE DE COOPERATION ECONOMIQUE." AFR ISLAM MADAGASCAR NAT/G ACT/RES ECO/TAC ALL/VALS ...TIME/SEQ 20. PAGE 130 H2601
INT/ORG ECO/UNDEV S62

SPRINGER H.W.,"FEDERATION IN THE CARIBBEAN: AN ATTEMPT THAT FAILED." L/A+17C ECO/UNDEV INT/ORG POL/PAR PROVS LEGIS CREATE PLAN LEGIT ADMIN FEDERAL ATTIT DRIVE PERSON ORD/FREE PWR...POLICY GEOG PSY CONCPT OBS CARIBBEAN CMN/WLTH 20. PAGE 148 H2955
VOL/ASSN NAT/G REGION S62

STRACHEY J.,"COMMUNIST INTENTIONS." ASIA USSR YUGOSLAVIA INT/ORG NAT/G FORCES DOMIN EDU/PROP COERCE NUC/PWR NAT/LISM PEACE RIGID/FLEX PWR MARXISM...CONCPT MYTH OBS TIME/SEQ TREND COLD/WAR TOT/POP 20. PAGE 150 H2992
COM ATTIT WAR S62

THOMPSON D.,"THE UNITED KINGDOM AND THE TREATY OF ROME." EUR+WWI INT/ORG NAT/G DELIB/GP LEGIS INT/TRADE RIGID/FLEX...CONCPT EEC PARLIAMENT CMN/WLTH 20. PAGE 154 H3079
ADJUD JURID S62

BRECHER M.,THE NEW STATES OF ASIA. ASIA S/ASIA INT/ORG BAL/PWR COLONIAL NEUTRAL ORD/FREE PWR 20 UN. PAGE 20 H0407
NAT/G ECO/UNDEV DIPLOM POLICY B63

BRZEZINSKI Z.K.,AFRICA AND THE COMMUNIST WORLD. AFR ASIA COM CULTURE SOCIETY INT/ORG DELIB/GP ACT/RES ECO/TAC COERCE ORD/FREE PWR WEALTH...STAT TOT/POP VAL/FREE 20. PAGE 23 H0461
ATTIT EDU/PROP DIPLOM USSR B63

COMISION DE HISTORIO,GUIA DE LOS DOCUMENTOS MICROFOTOGRAFIADOS POR LA UNIDAD MOVIL DE LA UNESCO. SOCIETY ECO/UNDEV INT/ORG ADMIN...SOC 20 UNESCO. PAGE 32 H0637
BIBLIOG NAT/G L/A+17C DIPLOM B63

DE VRIES E.,SOCIAL ASPECTS OF ECONOMIC DEVELOPMENT IN LATIN AMERICA. CULTURE SOCIETY STRATA FINAN INDUS INT/ORG DELIB/GP ACT/RES ECO/TAC EDU/PROP ADMIN ATTIT SUPEGO HEALTH KNOWL ORD/FREE...SOC STAT TREND ANTHOL TOT/POP VAL/FREE. PAGE 39 H0777
L/A+17C ECO/UNDEV B63

FAWCETT J.E.S.,THE BRITISH COMMONWEALTH IN INTERNATIONAL LAW. LAW INT/ORG NAT/G VOL/ASSN OP/RES DIPLOM ADJUD CENTRAL CONSEN...NET/THEORY CMN/WLTH TREATY. PAGE 49 H0977
INT/LAW STRUCT COLONIAL B63

FIRST R.,SOUTH WEST AFRICA. SOUTH/AFR INT/ORG KIN NAT/G WORKER COLONIAL WAR...POLICY 20 UN TRUST/TERR AFRICA/SW. PAGE 50 H1006
DISCRIM ORD/FREE RACE/REL CONTROL B63

GARDINIER D.E.,CAMEROON: UNITED NATIONS CHALLENGE TO FRENCH POLICY. AFR CAMEROON FRANCE NAT/G LEGIS CONTROL SOVEREIGN 20 UN. PAGE 55 H1101
DIPLOM POLICY INT/ORG COLONIAL B63

HAILEY L.,THE REPUBLIC OF SOUTH AFRICA AND THE HIGH COMMISSION TERRITORIES. AFR SOUTH/AFR UK INT/ORG NAT/G PROVS RACE/REL SOVEREIGN...CHARTS 19/20 COMMONWLTH. PAGE 64 H1278
COLONIAL DIPLOM ATTIT B63

KHADDURI M.,MODERN LIBYA: A STUDY IN POLITICAL DEVELOPMENT. EUR+WWI ISLAM LIBYA ELITES INT/ORG POL/PAR FORCES DIPLOM FOR/AID DOMIN EDU/PROP LEGIT NAT/LISM DRIVE RIGID/FLEX SKILL...CONCPT TIME/SEQ TREND 20. PAGE 85 H1704
NAT/G STRUCT B63

MAYNE R.,THE COMMUNITY OF EUROPE. UK CONSTN NAT/G CONSULT DELIB/GP CREATE PLAN ECO/TAC LEGIT ADMIN ROUTINE ORD/FREE PWR WEALTH...CONCPT TIME/SEQ EEC EURATOM 20. PAGE 105 H2107
EUR+WWI INT/ORG REGION B63

NICOLSON H.,DIPLOMACY (3RD ED.). INT/ORG NAT/G CONSULT DELIB/GP CONFER 19/20 LEAGUE/NAT UN. PAGE 118 H2354
DIPLOM CONCPT NAT/COMP B63

OECD,FOOD AID: ITS ROLE IN ECONOMIC DEVELOPMENT. FINAN NAT/G PLAN DIPLOM GIVE TASK WEALTH ...METH/COMP METH 20. PAGE 120 H2397
ECO/UNDEV FOR/AID INT/ORG POLICY B63

QUAISON-SACKEY A.,AFRICA UNBOUND: REFLECTIONS OF AN AFRICAN STATESMAN. ISLAM CULTURE INTELL INT/ORG POL/PAR TOP/EX DOMIN EDU/PROP LEGIT ATTIT PERSON ...CONCPT OBS TIME/SEQ CHARTS STERTYP 20 UN. PAGE 129 H2571
AFR BIOG B63

RIVKIN A.,THE AFRICAN PRESENCE IN WORLD AFFAIRS. ECO/UNDEV AGRI INT/ORG LOC/G NAT/LISM...OBS PREDICT GOV/COMP 20. PAGE 132 H2635
AFR NAT/G DIPLOM BAL/PWR B63

ROBERTSON A.H.,HUMAN RIGHTS IN EUROPE. CONSTN SOCIETY INT/ORG NAT/G VOL/ASSN DELIB/GP ACT/RES PLAN ADJUD REGION ROUTINE ATTIT LOVE ORD/FREE RESPECT...JURID SOC CONCPT SOC/EXP UN 20. PAGE 132 H2645
EUR+WWI PERSON B63

SCHECHTMAN J.B.,THE REFUGEE IN THE WORLD: DISPLACEMENT AND INTEGRATION. AFR ASIA EUR+WWI ISLAM L/A+17C S/ASIA CULTURE STRATA LOC/G EX/STRUC PLAN ECO/TAC ROUTINE...CONCPT TIME/SEQ VAL/FREE 20. PAGE 139 H2779
INT/ORG SOC B63

THUCYDIDES,THE PELOPONESIAN WARS. MEDIT-7 CULTURE INT/ORG NAT/G FORCES TOP/EX PLAN ROUTINE PWR ...CONCPT. PAGE 155 H3091
ATTIT COERCE WAR L63

ZARTMAN I.W.,"THE SAHARA--BRIDGE OR BARRIER." ISLAM CULTURE SOCIETY NAT/G DELIB/GP DOMIN EDU/PROP LEGIT ATTIT...HIST/WRIT TIME/SEQ CHARTS TOT/POP VAL/FREE 20. PAGE 172 H3447
INT/ORG PWR NAT/LISM S63

BANFIELD J.,"FEDERATION IN EAST-AFRICA." AFR UGANDA ELITES INT/ORG NAT/G VOL/ASSN LEGIS ECO/TAC FEDERAL ATTIT SOVEREIGN TOT/POP 20 TANGANYIKA. PAGE 10 H0210
EX/STRUC PWR REGION S63

GROSSER A.,"FRANCE AND GERMANY IN THE ATLANTIC COMMUNITY." INT/ORG NAT/G TOP/EX DIPLOM REGION PEACE ATTIT ORD/FREE PWR...CONCPT RECORD TIME/SEQ GEN/LAWS VAL/FREE COLD/WAR 20. PAGE 62 H1234
EUR+WWI VOL/ASSN FRANCE GERMANY S63

LIGOT M.,"LA COOPERATION MILITAIRE DANS LES ACCORDS, PASSES ENTRE LA FRANCE ET LES ETATS AFRICAINS ET MALGACHE D'EXPRESSION." ECO/UNDEV INT/ORG NAT/G VOL/ASSN...CONCPT TIME/SEQ 20. PAGE 97 H1931
AFR FORCES FOR/AID FRANCE S63

LOPEZIBOR J.,"L'EUROPE, FORME DE VIE." CHRIST-17C EUR+WWI FUT MOD/EUR SOCIETY INT/ORG SECT EDU/PROP ATTIT RIGID/FLEX ALL/VALS...POLICY HUM SOC TIME/SEQ TREND GEN/LAWS. PAGE 98 H1966
NAT/G CULTURE S63

MAZRUI A.A.,"ON THE CONCEPT 'WE ARE ALL AFRICANS'." AFR CULTURE KIN LOC/G NAT/G DOMIN EDU/PROP LEGIT
PROVS INT/ORG

ATTIT PERCEPT PERSON KNOWL ORD/FREE...TIME/SEQ TOT/POP 20. PAGE 106 H2110 NAT/LISM

S63
MBOYA T.,"AFRICAN SOCIALISM." ECO/UNDEV INT/ORG DIPLOM FOR/AID INT/TRADE REGION GP/REL ATTIT ORD/FREE EACM. PAGE 106 H2116 AFR SOCISM CULTURE NAT/LISM

S63
ROUGEMONT D.,"LES NOUVELLES CHANCES DE L'EUROPE." EUR+WWI FUT ECO/DEV INT/ORG NAT/G ACT/RES PLAN TEC/DEV EDU/PROP ADMIN COLONIAL FEDERAL ATTIT PWR SKILL...TREND 20. PAGE 135 H2696 ECO/UNDEV PERCEPT

S63
WEISSBERG G.,"MAPS AS EVIDENCE IN INTERNATIONAL BOUNDARY DISPUTES: A REAPPRAISAL." CHINA/COM EUR+WWI INDIA MOD/EUR S/ASIA INT/ORG NAT/G LEGIT PERCEPT...JURID CHARTS 20. PAGE 166 H3331 LAW GEOG SOVEREIGN

S63
WELLS H.,"THE OAS AND THE DOMINICAN ELECTIONS." L/A+17C INT/ORG NAT/G POL/PAR TEC/DEV ECO/TAC EDU/PROP PERCEPT...TIME/SEQ OAS TOT/POP 20. PAGE 166 H3332 CONSULT CHOOSE DOMIN/REP

B64
BERRINGTON H.,HOW NATIONS ARE GOVERNED. FRANCE WOR+45 ECO/UNDEV INT/ORG POL/PAR CHOOSE TOTALISM KNOWL...MAJORIT T 20 UN COMMONWLTH THIRD/WRLD. PAGE 16 H0320 NAT/G GOV/COMP ECO/DEV CONSTN

B64
BINDER L.,THE IDEOLOGICAL REVOLUTION IN THE MIDDLE EAST. ISLAM STRUCT INT/ORG KIN SECT EX/STRUC TOP/EX PLAN ATTIT DRIVE RIGID/FLEX PWR...MYTH TOT/POP 20. PAGE 17 H0338 POL/PAR NAT/G NAT/LISM

B64
BUNTING B.P.,THE RISE OF THE SOUTH AFRICAN REICH. SOUTH/AFR INT/ORG NAT/G FORCES DIPLOM CONTROL WAR TOTALISM ATTIT...GOV/COMP 19/20. PAGE 24 H0477 RACE/REL DISCRIM NAT/LISM TREND

B64
DE SMITH S.A.,THE NEW COMMONWEALTH AND ITS CONSTITUTIONS. AFR CYPRUS PAKISTAN S/ASIA INT/ORG NAT/G LEGIS LEGIT RIGID/FLEX PWR...CONCPT TIME/SEQ CMN/WLTH 20. PAGE 38 H0770 EX/STRUC CONSTN SOVEREIGN

B64
FRANCK T.M.,EAST AFRICAN UNITY THROUGH LAW. MALAWI TANZANIA UGANDA UK ZAMBIA CONSTN INT/ORG NAT/G ADMIN ROUTINE TASK NAT/LISM ATTIT SOVEREIGN ...RECORD IDEA/COMP NAT/COMP. PAGE 52 H1048 AFR FEDERAL REGION INT/LAW

B64
GUTTERIDGE W.,MILITARY INSTITUTIONS AND POWER IN THE NEW STATES. WOR+45 INT/ORG FOR/AID NEUTRAL REV CIVMIL/REL ATTIT ROLE...GOV/COMP 20. PAGE 63 H1258 FORCES DIPLOM ECO/UNDEV ELITES

B64
HERSKOVITS M.J.,ECONOMIC TRANSITION IN AFRICA. FUT INT/ORG NAT/G WORKER PROB/SOLV TEC/DEV INT/TRADE EQUILIB INCOME...ANTHOL 20. PAGE 70 H1408 AFR ECO/UNDEV PLAN ADMIN

B64
KIS T.I.,LES PAYS DE L'EUROPE DE L'EST: LEURS RAPPORTS MUTUELS ET LE PROBLEME DE LEUR INTEGRATION DANS L'ORBITE DE L'USSR. EUR+WWI RUSSIA USSR INT/ORG NAT/G REV ATTIT...JURID SOC BIBLIOG WARSAW/P COMECON EUROPE/E. PAGE 86 H1727 DIPLOM COM MARXISM REGION

B64
KITCHEN H.,A HANDBOOK OF AFRICAN AFFAIRS. ECO/UNDEV CREATE DIPLOM COLONIAL RACE/REL...ART/METH GEOG CHARTS 20. PAGE 87 H1729 AFR NAT/G INT/ORG FORCES

B64
MAIER J.,POLITICS OF CHANGE IN LATIN AMERICA. BRAZIL L/A+17C STRATA INT/ORG NAT/G POL/PAR FOR/AID REV 20. PAGE 101 H2019 SOCIETY NAT/LISM DIPLOM REGION

B64
NICOL D.,AFRICA - A SUBJECTIVE VIEW. AFR INT/ORG PLAN ADMIN COLONIAL PARL/PROC PARTIC REGION GOV/REL LITERACY ATTIT...BIBLIOG 20 CIVIL/SERV. PAGE 118 H2350 NAT/G LEAD CULTURE ACADEM

B64
OECD,DEVELOPMENT ASSISTANCE EFFORTS - POLICIES OF THE MEMBERS. AGRI INDUS BUDGET...GEOG NAT/COMP 20 OECD. PAGE 120 H2398 INT/ORG FOR/AID ECO/UNDEV TEC/DEV

B64
RAMAZANI R.K.,THE MIDDLE EAST AND THE EUROPEAN COMMON MARKET. EUR+WWI ISLAM ECO/DEV EXTR/IND MARKET PROC/MFG INT/ORG NAT/G TEC/DEV ECO/TAC REGION DRIVE WEALTH...STAT CHARTS EEC TOT/POP 20. PAGE 129 H2587 ECO/UNDEV ATTIT INT/TRADE

B64
ROBERTS HL,FOREIGN AFFAIRS BIBLIOGRAPHY, 1952-1962. ECO/DEV SECT PLAN FOR/AID INT/TRADE ARMS/CONT NAT/LISM ATTIT...INT/LAW GOV/COMP IDEA/COMP 20. PAGE 132 H2643 BIBLIOG/A DIPLOM INT/ORG WAR

B64
STRONG C.F.,HISTORY OF MODERN POLITICAL CONSTITUTIONS. STRUCT INT/ORG NAT/G LEGIS TEC/DEV DIPLOM INT/TRADE CT/SYS EXEC...METH/COMP T 12/20 UN. PAGE 150 H2999 CONSTN CONCPT

B64
TEPASKE J.J.,EXPLOSIVE FORCES IN LATIN AMERICA. CULTURE INTELL ECO/UNDEV INT/ORG NAT/G SECT FORCES ECO/TAC EDU/PROP PWR WEALTH SOC. PAGE 153 H3063 L/A+17C RIGID/FLEX FOR/AID USSR

B64
URQUIDI V.L.,THE CHALLENGE OF DEVELOPMENT IN LATIN AMERICA. L/A+17C FINAN INT/ORG TEC/DEV DIPLOM INT/TRADE PRICE REGION PRODUC...CHARTS 20. PAGE 159 H3175 ECO/UNDEV ECO/TAC NAT/G TREND

B64
WAINHOUSE D.W.,REMNANTS OF EMPIRE: THE UNITED NATIONS AND THE END OF COLONIALISM. FUT PORTUGAL WOR+45 NAT/G CONSULT DOMIN LEGIT ADMIN ROUTINE ATTIT ORD/FREE...POLICY JURID RECORD INT TIME/SEQ UN CMN/WLTH 20. PAGE 164 H3287 INT/ORG TREND COLONIAL

L64
HAAS E.B.,"ECONOMICS AND DIFFERENTIAL PATTERNS OF POLITICAL INTEGRATION: PROJECTIONS ABOUT UNITY IN LATIN AMERICA." SOCIETY NAT/G DELIB/GP ACT/RES CREATE PLAN ECO/TAC REGION ROUTINE ATTIT DRIVE PWR WEALTH...CONCPT TREND CHARTS LAFTA 20. PAGE 63 H1266 L/A+17C INT/ORG MARKET

L64
SYMONDS R.,"REFLECTIONS IN LOCALISATION." AFR S/ASIA UK STRATA INT/ORG NAT/G SCHOOL EDU/PROP LEGIT KNOWL ORD/FREE PWR RESPECT CMN/WLTH 20. PAGE 151 H3023 ADMIN MGT COLONIAL

S64
DE GAULLE C.,"FRENCH WORLD VIEW." AFR ASIA CHINA/COM EUR+WWI ISLAM ECO/UNDEV INT/ORG NAT/G VOL/ASSN ACT/RES DIPLOM ECO/TAC EDU/PROP ATTIT DRIVE WEALTH 20. PAGE 37 H0751 TOP/EX PWR FOR/AID FRANCE

S64
GROSS J.A.,"WHITEHALL AND THE COMMONWEALTH." EUR+WWI MOD/EUR INT/ORG NAT/G CONSULT DELIB/GP LEGIS DOMIN ADMIN COLONIAL ROUTINE PWR CMN/WLTH 19/20. PAGE 62 H1233 EX/STRUC ATTIT TREND

S64
LERNER W.,"THE HISTORICAL ORIGINS OF THE SOVIET DOCTRINE OF PEACEFUL COEXISTENCE." COM USSR INT/ORG NAT/G VOL/ASSN PLAN PEACE ATTIT RIGID/FLEX PWR MARXISM...TIME/SEQ COLD/WAR 20. PAGE 95 H1891 EDU/PROP DIPLOM

S64
MARTELLI G.,"PORTUGAL AND THE UNITED NATIONS." AFR EUR+WWI ELITES INT/ORG NAT/G PROVS PLAN DIPLOM ECO/TAC DOMIN COLONIAL RIGID/FLEX MORAL ORD/FREE PWR WEALTH...MYTH UN 20. PAGE 103 H2060 ATTIT PORTUGAL

S64
MERKL P.H.,"EUROPEAN ASSEMBLY PARTIES AND NATIONAL DELEGATIONS." INT/ORG DELIB/GP DOMIN EDU/PROP LEGIT CHOOSE PWR...STAT VAL/FREE 20. PAGE 109 H2180 EUR+WWI POL/PAR REGION

S64
SAAB H.,"THE ARAB SEARCH FOR A FEDERAL UNION." SOCIETY INT/ORG NAT/G DELIB/GP FORCES ACT/RES TEC/DEV ECO/TAC DOMIN LEGIT REGION ROUTINE ATTIT DRIVE RIGID/FLEX ALL/VALS...SOC CONCPT NEW/IDEA TIME/SEQ TREND. PAGE 136 H2726 ISLAM PLAN

S64
SALVADORI M.,"EL CAPITALISMO EN LA EUROPA DE LA POSGUERRA." INT/ORG NAT/G POL/PAR PLAN ECO/TAC ATTIT ORD/FREE WEALTH...HIST/WRIT COLD/WAR EEC 20. PAGE 137 H2743 EUR+WWI ECO/DEV CAP/ISM

S64
TINKER H.,"POLITICS IN SOUTHEAST ASIA." INT/ORG NAT/G CREATE PLAN TEC/DEV GUERRILLA KNOWL ORD/FREE COLD/WAR. PAGE 155 H3103 S/ASIA ACT/RES REGION

B65
ALEXANDER R.J.,ORGANIZED LABOR IN LATIN AMERICA. L/A+17C INT/ORG LEGIS WORKER TEC/DEV BARGAIN INT/TRADE REV...NAT/COMP BIBLIOG 20. PAGE 5 H0102 LABOR POL/PAR ECO/UNDEV POLICY

B65
BROCK C.,A GUIDE TO LIBRARY RESOURCES FOR POLITICAL SCIENCE STUDENTS AT THE UNIVERSITY OF NORTH CAROLINA (PAMPHLET). USA+45 WOR+45 PROVS ATTIT MARXISM...POLICY NAT/COMP UN. PAGE 21 H0422 BIBLIOG/A DIPLOM NAT/G INT/ORG

B65
CALLEO D.P.,EUROPE'S FUTURE: THE GRAND ALTERNATIVES. UK INT/ORG DIPLOM PWR SOVEREIGN ...CONCPT IDEA/COMP NAT/COMP BIBLIOG 20 EEC EUROPE DEGAULLE/C NATO. PAGE 25 H0506 FUT EUR+WWI FEDERAL NAT/LISM

B65
COLLINS H.,KARL MARX AND THE BRITISH LABOR MOVEMENT, YEARS OF THE FIRST INTERNATIONAL. EUR+WWI MOD/EUR UK STRATA INDUS NAT/G POL/PAR SOCISM ...CONCPT 19/20 MARX/KARL. PAGE 32 H0633 MARXISM LABOR INT/ORG WORKER

B65
COX R.H.,THE STATE IN INTERNATIONAL RELATIONS. INT/ORG DIPLOM REV WAR PEACE MARXISM...CONCPT GOV/COMP. PAGE 34 H0690 SOVEREIGN NAT/G FASCISM ORD/FREE

B65
DOLCI D.,A NEW WORLD IN THE MAKING. GHANA SENEGAL USSR YUGOSLAVIA CULTURE INT/ORG PLAN EDU/PROP GP/REL PEACE MORAL...GEOG SOC 20 COLD/WAR. PAGE 42 H0834
SOCIETY ALL/VALS DRIVE PERSON

B65
EUROPEAN FREE TRADE ASSN,REGIONAL DEVELOPMENT POLICIES IN EFTA. ECO/UNDEV INT/ORG PLAN REGION ...POLICY GEOG EFTA. PAGE 48 H0950
EUR+WWI ECO/DEV NAT/COMP INT/TRADE

B65
HARMON R.B.,POLITICAL SCIENCE: A BIBLIOGRAPHICAL GUIDE TO THE LITERATURE. WOR+45 WOR-45 R+D INT/ORG LOC/G NAT/G DIPLOM ADMIN...CONCPT METH. PAGE 67 H1334
BIBLIOG POL/PAR LAW GOV/COMP

B65
HOSELITZ B.F.,ECONOMICS AND THE IDEA OF MANKIND. UNIV ECO/DEV ECO/UNDEV DIST/IND INDUS INT/ORG NAT/G ACT/RES ECO/TAC WEALTH...CONCPT STAT. PAGE 74 H1476
CREATE INT/TRADE

B65
KOUSOULAS D.G.,REVOLUTION AND DEFEAT; THE STORY OF THE GREEK COMMUNIST PARTY. GREECE INT/ORG EX/STRUC DIPLOM FOR/AID EDU/PROP PARL/PROC ADJUST ATTIT 20 COM/PARTY. PAGE 88 H1759
REV MARXISM POL/PAR ORD/FREE

B65
MEHROTRA S.R.,INDIA AND THE COMMONWEALTH 1885-1929. INDIA UK INT/ORG VOL/ASSN GP/REL ATTIT...POLICY BIBLIOG 19/20 CMN/WLTH. PAGE 108 H2163
DIPLOM NAT/G POL/PAR NAT/LISM

B65
O'BRIEN W.V.,THE NEW NATIONS IN INTERNATIONAL LAW AND DIPLOMACY* THE YEAR BOOK OF WORLD POLITY* VOLUME III. USA+45 ECO/UNDEV INT/ORG FORCES DIPLOM COLONIAL NEUTRAL REV NAT/LISM ATTIT RESPECT. PAGE 119 H2385
INT/LAW CULTURE SOVEREIGN ANTHOL

B65
PADELFORD N.,THE UNITED NATIONS IN THE BALANCE* ACCOMPLISHMENTS AND PROSPECTS. NAT/G VOL/ASSN DIPLOM ADMIN COLONIAL CT/SYS REGION WAR ORD/FREE ...ANTHOL UN. PAGE 122 H2437
INT/ORG CONTROL

B65
ROSENBERG A.,DEMOCRACY AND SOCIALISM. COM EUR+WWI FRANCE MOD/EUR STRUCT INT/ORG NAT/G POL/PAR TOP/EX EDU/PROP COERCE PERSON PWR FASCISM MARXISM...CONCPT TIME/SEQ MARX/KARL 19/20. PAGE 134 H2677
ATTIT

B65
SABLE M.H.,MASTER DIRECTORY FOR LATIN AMERICA. AGRI COM/IND FINAN R+D ACADEM LABOR NAT/G POL/PAR VOL/ASSN INT/TRADE EDU/PROP 20. PAGE 136 H2728
INDEX L/A+17C INT/ORG DIPLOM

B65
SLATER J.,A REVALUATION OF COLLECTIVE SECURITY* THE OAS IN ACTION. L/A+17C USA+45 NAT/G ADMIN COERCE ORD/FREE PWR...GOV/COMP IDEA/COMP GEN/LAWS OAS. PAGE 145 H2899
REGION INT/ORG FORCES

B65
UN,SPACE ACTIVITIES AND RESOURCES: REVIEW OF UNITED NATION'S NATIONAL AND INTERNATIONAL PROGRAMS. INT/ORG LABOR PLAN TEC/DEV DIPLOM EFFICIENCY HEALTH ...GOV/COMP 20 UN. PAGE 158 H3155
SPACE NUC/PWR FOR/AID PEACE

B65
WILLIAMSON J.A.,GREAT BRITAIN AND THE COMMONWEALTH. UK DOMIN COLONIAL INGP/REL...POLICY 18/20 CMN/WLTH. PAGE 168 H3370
NAT/G DIPLOM INT/ORG SOVEREIGN

L65
WIONCZEK M.,"LATIN AMERICA FREE TRADE ASSOCIATION." AGRI DIST/IND FINAN INDUS INT/ORG LABOR NAT/G TEC/DEV ECO/TAC HEALTH SKILL WEALTH...POLICY RELATIV MGT LAFTA 20. PAGE 169 H3390
L/A+17C MARKET REGION

S65
HELMREICH E.C.,"KADAR'S HUNGARY." COM EUR+WWI HUNGARY USSR INTELL ECO/DEV AGRI INT/ORG TOP/EX DOMIN ALL/VALS WORK COLD/WAR 20. PAGE 69 H1390
NAT/G RIGID/FLEX TOTALISM

S65
LEVI W.,"THE CONCEPT OF INTEGRATION IN RESEARCH ON PEACE." NAT/G VOL/ASSN DIPLOM TASK ADJUST NAT/LISM PEACE DRIVE LOVE...PSY NET/THEORY GEN/LAWS. PAGE 95 H1897
CONCPT IDEA/COMP INT/ORG CENTRAL

S65
POWELL J.D.,"MILITARY ASSISTANCE AND MILITARISM IN LATIN AMERICA." USA+45 INT/ORG NAT/G CONTROL REGION PRODUC WEALTH...CLASSIF STAT NAT/COMP CONGRESS. PAGE 128 H2550
L/A+17C FORCES FOR/AID PWR

S65
SPAAK P.H.,"THE SEARCH FOR CONSENSUS: A NEW EFFORT TO BUILD EUROPE." FRANCE GERMANY ECO/DEV NAT/G CONSULT FORCES PLAN EDU/PROP REGION CONSEN ATTIT ...SOC METH/CNCPT OBS TREND EEC NATO WORK 20. PAGE 147 H2941
EUR+WWI INT/ORG

S65
WHITE J.,"WEST GERMAN AID TO DEVELOPING COUNTRIES." INT/ORG OP/RES GIVE CENTRAL ATTIT DRIVE...STAT NAT/COMP COLD/WAR. PAGE 167 H3348
GERMANY FOR/AID ECO/UNDEV CAP/ISM

B66
AMER ENTERPRISE INST PUB POL,SIGNIFICANT ISSUES IN ECONOMIC AID TO DEVELOPING COUNTRIES. FINAN INT/ORG NAT/G PLAN PROB/SOLV GIVE TASK WEALTH...DECISION 20. PAGE 6 H0119
ECO/UNDEV FOR/AID DIPLOM POLICY

B66
BRACKMAN A.C.,SOUTHEAST ASIA'S SECOND FRONT: THE POWER STRUGGLE IN THE MALAY ARCHIPELAGO. CHINA/COM INDONESIA MALAYSIA ECO/UNDEV INT/ORG NAT/G FORCES DIPLOM EDU/PROP REGION COERCE GUERRILLA AUTHORIT POPULISM...MAJORIT 20 KENNEDY/JF SEATO. PAGE 20 H0396
S/ASIA MARXISM REV

B66
BROWN L.C.,STATE AND SOCIETY IN INDEPENDENT NORTH AFRICA. ALGERIA LIBYA MOROCCO AGRI INDUS INT/ORG POL/PAR SECT PLAN DIPLOM COLONIAL...LING NAT/COMP ANTHOL BIBLIOG 20 TUNIS MUSLIM. PAGE 22 H0446
NAT/G SOCIETY CULTURE ECO/UNDEV

B66
DOUMA J.,BIBLIOGRAPHY ON THE INTERNATIONAL COURT INCLUDING THE PERMANENT COURT, 1918-1964. WOR+45 WOR-45 DELIB/GP WAR PRIVIL...JURID NAT/COMP 20 UN LEAGUE/NAT. PAGE 42 H0844
BIBLIOG/A INT/ORG CT/SYS DIPLOM

B66
GERARD-LIBOIS J.,KATANGA SECESSION. INT/ORG FORCES DIPLOM ADMIN CONTROL WAR CHOOSE PWR...CHARTS 20 KATANGA TSHOMBE/M UN. PAGE 56 H1114
NAT/G REGION ORD/FREE REV

B66
GORDON B.K.,THE DIMENSIONS OF CONFLICT IN SOUTHEAST ASIA. S/ASIA FORCES ADJUD REGION...CHARTS 20. PAGE 59 H1177
DIPLOM NAT/COMP INT/ORG VOL/ASSN

B66
HAMILTON W.B.,A DECADE OF THE COMMONWEALTH, 1955-1964. UK LAW ELITES FINAN FOR/AID CONFER COLONIAL PWR...GEOG CHARTS ANTHOL 20 CMN/WLTH UN. PAGE 65 H1302
INT/ORG INGP/REL DIPLOM NAT/G

B66
HARMON R.B.,SOURCES AND PROBLEMS OF BIBLIOGRAPHY IN POLITICAL SCIENCE (PAMPHLET). INT/ORG LOC/G MUNIC POL/PAR ADMIN GOV/REL ALL/IDEOS...JURID MGT CONCPT 19/20. PAGE 67 H1335
BIBLIOG DIPLOM INT/LAW NAT/G

B66
HAY P.,FEDERALISM AND SUPRANATIONAL ORGANIZATIONS: PATTERNS FOR NEW LEGAL STRUCTURES. EUR+WWI LAW NAT/G VOL/ASSN DIPLOM PWR...NAT/COMP TREATY EEC. PAGE 68 H1364
SOVEREIGN FEDERAL INT/ORG INT/LAW

B66
HOEVELER H.J.,INTERNATIONALE BEKAMPFUNG DES VERBRECHENS. AUSTRIA SWITZERLND WOR+45 INT/ORG CONTROL BIO/SOC...METH/COMP NAT/COMP 20 MAFIA SCOT/YARD FBI. PAGE 72 H1446
CRIMLGY CRIME DIPLOM INT/LAW

B66
JACKSON G.D.,COMINTERN AND PEASANT IN EAST EUROPE 1919-1930. BULGARIA COM CZECHOSLVK EUR+WWI POLAND ROMANIA YUGOSLAVIA STRATA AGRI VOL/ASSN DIPLOM CONTROL CROWD WEALTH...POLICY NAT/COMP 20. PAGE 79 H1575
MARXISM ECO/UNDEV WORKER INT/ORG

B66
KIRDAR U.,THE STRUCTURE OF UNITED NATIONS ECONOMIC AID TO UNDERDEVELOPED COUNTRIES. AGRI FINAN INDUS NAT/G EX/STRUC PLAN GIVE TASK...POLICY 20 UN. PAGE 86 H1721
INT/ORG FOR/AID ECO/UNDEV ADMIN

B66
MARTIN L.W.,DIPLOMACY IN MODERN EUROPEAN HISTORY. EUR+WWI MOD/EUR INT/ORG NAT/G EX/STRUC ROUTINE WAR PEACE TOTALISM PWR 15/20 COLD/WAR EUROPE/W. PAGE 103 H2064
DIPLOM POLICY

B66
MERILLAT H.C.L.,LEGAL ADVISERS AND INTERNATIONAL ORGANIZATIONS. LAW NAT/G CONSULT OP/RES ADJUD SANCTION TASK CONSEN ORG/CHARTS. PAGE 109 H2178
INT/ORG INT/LAW CREATE OBS

B66
NIEDERGANG M.,LA REVOLUTION DE SAINT-DOMINGUE. DOMIN/REP INT/ORG NAT/G CONTROL LEAD GP/REL ORD/FREE MARXISM 20. PAGE 118 H2361
REV FORCES DIPLOM

B66
PAN S.,VIETNAM CRISIS. ASIA FRANCE USA+45 USA-45 VIETNAM CULTURE SOCIETY INT/ORG ECO/TAC AGREE CONTROL WAR MARXISM 20. PAGE 123 H2454
ECO/UNDEV POLICY DIPLOM NAT/COMP

B66
THOMPSON J.M.,RUSSIA, BOLSHEVISM, AND THE VERSAILLES PEACE. RUSSIA USSR INT/ORG NAT/G DELIB/GP AGREE REV WAR PWR 20 TREATY VERSAILLES BOLSHEVISM. PAGE 154 H3083
DIPLOM PEACE MARXISM

B66
THORNTON M.J.,NAZISM, 1918-1945. GERMANY INT/ORG DIPLOM REV PEACE FASCISM...CONCPT 20 HITLER/A WEIMAR/REP NAZI. PAGE 155 H3089
TOTALISM POL/PAR NAT/G WAR

B66
US DEPARTMENT OF THE ARMY,SOUTH ASIA: A STRATEGIC SURVEY (PAMPHLET NO. 550-3). AFGHANISTN INDIA NEPAL PAKISTAN ECO/UNDEV INT/ORG POL/PAR FORCES FOR/AID
BIBLIOG/A S/ASIA DIPLOM

INT/TRADE LEAD WAR...POLICY SOC TREND 20. PAGE 160 H3195 NAT/G

L66
SEYLER W.C.,"DOCTORAL DISSERTATIONS IN POLITICAL SCIENCE IN UNIVERSITIES OF THE UNITED STATES AND CANADA." INT/ORG LOC/G ADMIN...INT/LAW MGT GOV/COMP. PAGE 142 H2836 BIBLIOG LAW NAT/G

B67
ANDERSON S.V.,THE NORDIC COUNCIL: A STUDY OF SCANDINAVIAN REGIONALISM. DENMARK FINLAND ICELAND NORWAY SWEDEN MARKET NAT/G VOL/ASSN CONSULT PARL/PROC ATTIT...TIME/SEQ BIBLIOG 20. PAGE 7 H0134 INT/ORG REGION DIPLOM LEGIS

B67
BODENHEIMER E.,TREATISE ON JUSTICE. INT/ORG NAT/G PUB/INST ACT/RES RISK CRIME INGP/REL DISCRIM DRIVE LAISSEZ 20. PAGE 18 H0363 ALL/VALS STRUCT JURID CONCPT

B67
BURNHAM J.,THE WAR WE ARE IN, THE LAST DECADE AND THE NEXT. ASIA COM EUR+WWI S/ASIA WOR+45 ECO/UNDEV INT/ORG FORCES WAR...OLD/LIB TREND 20 COLD/WAR. PAGE 25 H0492 POLICY NAT/G DIPLOM NAT/COMP

B67
BURR R.N.,OUR TROUBLED HEMISPHERE: PERSPECTIVES ON UNITED STATES-LATIN AMERICAN RELATIONS. L/A+17C USA+45 USA-45 INT/ORG FOR/AID COLONIAL PWR 19/20 OAS. PAGE 25 H0493 DIPLOM NAT/COMP NAT/G POLICY

B67
DEUTSCH K.W.,FRANCE, GERMANY AND THE WESTERN ALLIANCE. FRANCE GERMANY/W INT/ORG ARMS/CONT NAT/LISM SOVEREIGN...INT NAT/COMP 20. PAGE 40 H0801 ELITES ATTIT DIPLOM POLICY

B67
FAY S.B.,THE ORIGINS OF THE WORLD WAR (2ND REV. ED. 2 VOLS.). NAT/G FORCES DIPLOM CONFER LEAD PEACE ...REALPOL GOV/COMP 19/20. PAGE 49 H0978 MOD/EUR WAR REGION INT/ORG

B67
MAZRUI A.A.,THE ANGLO-AFRICAN COMMONWEALTH; POLITICAL FRICTION AND CULTURAL FUSION. AFR INT/ORG VOL/ASSN CHIEF GP/REL INGP/REL RACE/REL NAT/LISM 20 CMN/WLTH EEC. PAGE 106 H2111 COLONIAL SOVEREIGN DIPLOM CULTURE

B67
NYERERE J.K.,FREEDOM AND UNITY/UHURU NA UMOJA: A SELECTION FROM WRITINGS AND SPEECHES, 1952-65. TANZANIA ELITES ECO/UNDEV INT/ORG NAT/G CREATE DIPLOM COLONIAL REGION RACE/REL...ANTHOL 20. PAGE 119 H2383 SOVEREIGN AFR TREND ORD/FREE

B67
OVERSEAS DEVELOPMENT INSTIT,EFFECTIVE AID. WOR+45 INT/ORG TEC/DEV DIPLOM INT/TRADE ADMIN. PAGE 122 H2434 FOR/AID ECO/UNDEV ECO/TAC NAT/COMP

B67
PLISCHKE E.,CONDUCT OF AMERICAN DIPLOMACY (3RD REV. ED.). INT/ORG NAT/G PROB/SOLV FOR/AID...CHARTS BIBLIOG T 20 DEPT/STATE. PAGE 126 H2529 DIPLOM RATIONAL PLAN

B67
POGANY A.H.,POLITICAL SCIENCE AND INTERNATIONAL RELATIONS, BOOKS RECOMMENDED FOR AMERICAN CATHOLIC COLLEGE LIBRARIES. INT/ORG LOC/G NAT/G FORCES BAL/PWR ECO/TAC NUC/PWR...CATH INT/LAW TREATY 20. PAGE 127 H2532 BIBLIOG DIPLOM

B67
RAMUNDO B.A.,PEACEFUL COEXISTENCE: INTERNATIONAL LAW IN THE BUILDING OF COMMUNISM. USSR INT/ORG DIPLOM COLONIAL ARMS/CONT ROLE SOVEREIGN...POLICY METH/COMP NAT/COMP BIBLIOG. PAGE 129 H2588 INT/LAW PEACE MARXISM METH/CNCPT

B67
THOMAN R.S.,GEOGRAPHY OF INTERNATIONAL TRADE. WOR+45 ECO/DEV ECO/UNDEV INT/ORG LG/CO PLAN BAL/PAY ...STAT CHARTS NAT/COMP 20. PAGE 154 H3075 INT/TRADE GEOG ECO/TAC DIPLOM

B67
UNESCO,PRINCIPLES AND PROBLEMS OF NATIONAL SCIENCE POLICIES. WOR+45 ECO/DEV ECO/UNDEV R+D INT/ORG PROB/SOLV CONFER...PHIL/SCI CHARTS 20 UNESCO UN. PAGE 158 H3165 NAT/COMP POLICY TEC/DEV CREATE

B67
WISEMAN H.V.,BRITAIN AND THE COMMONWEALTH. EUR+WWI FUT UK ECO/DEV POL/PAR TEC/DEV INT/TRADE LEAD ROLE SOVEREIGN...SOC TREND 20 CMN/WLTH. PAGE 169 H3391 INT/ORG DIPLOM NAT/G NAT/COMP

L67
HOSHII I.,"JAPAN'S STAKE IN ASIA." ASIA S/ASIA CAP/ISM ECO/TAC ROLE...GEOG 20 CHINJAP. PAGE 74 H1477 DIPLOM REGION NAT/G INT/ORG

L67
KELLEHER G.W.,"THE COMMON MARKET ANTITRUST LAWS: THE FIRST TEN YEARS." EUR+WWI INDUS PRICE ADJUD AGREE CONTROL PROFIT...POLICY 20 EEC. PAGE 84 H1684 INT/ORG INT/TRADE MARKET NAT/G

L67
MCALLISTER J.T. JR.,"THE POSSIBILITIES FOR DIPLOMACY IN SOUTHEAST ASIA." LAOS VIETNAM INT/ORG NAT/G PROVS BAL/PWR DOMIN AGREE COLONIAL WAR PWR 17/20 TREATY. PAGE 106 H2121 DIPLOM S/ASIA

L67
SEGAL A.,"THE INTEGRATION OF DEVELOPING COUNTRIES: SOME THOUGHTS ON EAST AFRICA AND CENTRAL AMERICA." AFR L/A+17C INT/ORG NAT/G VOL/ASSN FOR/AID INT/TRADE EQUILIB NAT/LISM PWR 20. PAGE 141 H2820 ECO/UNDEV DIPLOM REGION

L67
WAELBROECK M.,"THE APPLICATION OF EEC LAW BY NATIONAL COURTS." EUR+WWI INT/ORG CT/SYS...JURID EEC TREATY. PAGE 164 H3284 INT/LAW NAT/G LAW PROB/SOLV

S67
FRENCH D.S.,"DOES THE U.S. EXPLOIT THE DEVELOPING NATIONS?" INT/ORG NAT/G CAP/ISM BAL/PAY WEALTH POLICY. PAGE 53 H1057 ECO/UNDEV INT/TRADE ECO/TAC COLONIAL

S67
GRIEB K.J.,"THE UNITED STATES AND THE CENTRAL AMERICAN CONFEDERATION." COSTA/RICA EL/SALVADR GUATEMALA HONDURAS L/A+17C NICARAGUA NAT/G FORCES CONFER AGREE EXEC ARMS/CONT REV WAR PEACE ATTIT 20. PAGE 60 H1212 INT/ORG DIPLOM POLICY REGION

S67
GRUNDY K.W.,"AFRICA IN THE WORLD ARENA." ECO/UNDEV BAL/PWR FOR/AID NEUTRAL REV NAT/LISM GOV/COMP. PAGE 62 H1240 AFR DIPLOM INT/ORG COLONIAL

S67
HALPERN B.,"THE ORIGINS OF THE CRISIS." ISLAM ISRAEL INT/ORG FORCES WEAPON PEACE ORD/FREE TREATY 20 UN. PAGE 65 H1296 WAR NAT/G DIPLOM

S67
NUGENT J.B.,"ECONOMIC THOUGHT, INVESTMENT CRITERIA, AND DEVELOPMENT STRATEGIES IN GREECE* A POSTWAR SURVEY." GREECE AGRI INDUS INT/ORG NAT/G OP/RES DEMAND OPTIMAL PRODUC WEALTH 20 EEC. PAGE 119 H2379 ECO/UNDEV PLAN FINAN

S67
PONOMARYOV B.,"THE OCTOBER REVOLUTION - BEGINNING OF THE EPOCH OF SOCIALISM AND COMMUNISM." COM FUT USSR WOR+45 SOCIETY STRATA CHIEF CREATE DIPLOM ECO/TAC EDU/PROP SOCISM...NAT/COMP 20. PAGE 127 H2542 MARXIST WORKER INT/ORG POLICY

S67
ROOT W.,"REPORT FROM PARIS - DE GAULLE: WHICH WAY TO THE FUTURE?" CANADA FRANCE ISLAM UK INT/ORG CHIEF CREATE AGREE CONTROL ARMS/CONT NUC/PWR EQUILIB PEACE PWR 20 DEGAULLE/C NATO. PAGE 134 H2670 POLICY DIPLOM NAT/G BAL/PWR

S67
SOMMER T.,"BONN CHANGES COURSE." GERMANY/W NAT/G POL/PAR PROB/SOLV NAT/LISM 20 NATO BERLIN/BLO. PAGE 147 H2932 DIPLOM BAL/PWR INT/ORG

S67
SPINELLI A.,"EUROPEAN UNION IN THE RESISTANCE." NAT/G BAL/PWR DIPLOM CONFER REGION TOTALISM ORD/FREE POLICY. PAGE 147 H2948 NAT/LISM FEDERAL EUR+WWI INT/ORG

L68
CURRENT HISTORY,"DE GAULLE'S FRANCE." FRANCE MOD/EUR WOR+45 INDUS MARKET INT/ORG BUDGET DIPLOM AUTHORIT DRIVE...GOV/COMP IDEA/COMP 20 DEGAULLE/C EEC. PAGE 36 H0723 INT/TRADE PERSON LEAD NAT/LISM

S68
DUGARD J.,"THE REVOCATION OF THE MANDATE FOR SOUTH WEST AFRICA." SOUTH/AFR WOR+45 STRATA NAT/G DELIB/GP DIPLOM ADJUD SANCTION CHOOSE RACE/REL ...POLICY NAT/COMP 20 AFRICA/SW UN TRUST/TERR LEAGUE/NAT. PAGE 43 H0858 AFR INT/ORG DISCRIM COLONIAL

S68
LUKASZEWSKI J.,"WESTERN INTEGRATION AND THE PEOPLE'S DEMOCRACIES." USSR ELITES ECO/DEV NAT/G VOL/ASSN INT/TRADE AGREE REV FEDERAL WEALTH SOCISM ...NAT/COMP SOC/INTEG 20 EEC. PAGE 99 H1977 DIPLOM INT/ORG COM REGION

S68
MILLAR T.B.,"THE COMMONWEALTH AND THE UN." UK DIPLOM TARIFFS AGREE COLONIAL CONTROL SOVEREIGN WEALTH...GP/COMP GOV/COMP 20 CMN/WLTH UN. PAGE 111 H2210 INT/ORG POLICY TREND ECO/TAC

S68
VERAX,"L'EUROPE ET LA FRANCE SUR LA SELLETTE." FRANCE UK NAT/G CHIEF DIPLOM EDU/PROP GP/REL 20 EEC DEGAULLE/C. PAGE 162 H3242 INT/TRADE INT/ORG POLICY ECO/TAC

INT/REL....INTERNATIONAL RELATIONS

INT/TRADE....INTERNATIONAL TRADE

N
BROCKWAY A.F.,AFRICAN SOCIALISM. EUR+WWI GHANA ISLAM UAR ECO/UNDEV CAP/ISM INT/TRADE COLONIAL COERCE GOV/REL DISCRIM 20 NEGRO NKRUMAH/K NASSER/G. PAGE 21 H0423 AFR SOCISM MARXISM

N
CANADIAN GOVERNMENT PUBLICATIONS (1955-). CANADA BIBLIOG/A

AGRI FINAN LABOR FORCES INT/TRADE HEALTH...JURID 20 PARLIAMENT. PAGE 1 H0003
NAT/G DIPLOM INT/ORG
N

CHINA QUARTERLY. COM AGRI INDUS ACADEM POL/PAR INT/TRADE CONFER GOV/REL...TIME/SEQ CON/ANAL INDEX 20. PAGE 1 H0014
BIBLIOG/A ASIA DIPLOM POLICY
N

THE MIDDLE EAST AND NORTH AFRICA. AFR ISLAM CULTURE ECO/UNDEV AGRI NAT/G TEC/DEV FOR/AID INT/TRADE EDU/PROP...CHARTS 20. PAGE 2 H0026
INDEX INDUS FINAN STAT
N

KYRIAK T.E.,CHINA: A BIBLIOGRAPHY. ASIA CHINA/COM AGRI FINAN INDUS NAT/G INT/TRADE PRESS...SOC 20. PAGE 90 H1789
BIBLIOG/A MARXISM TOP/EX POL/PAR
B00

MOCKLER-FERRYMAN A.,BRITISH WEST AFRICA. FRANCE GERMANY NIGER SIER/LEONE UK CULTURE DIPLOM WAR RACE/REL PRODUC PROFIT WEALTH...POLICY PREDICT 19. PAGE 112 H2232
AFR COLONIAL INT/TRADE CAP/ISM
B03

FORTESCUE G.K.,SUBJECT INDEX OF THE MODERN WORKS ADDED TO THE LIBRARY OF THE BRITISH MUSEUM IN THE YEARS 1881-1900 (3 VOLS.). UK LAW CONSTN FINAN NAT/G FORCES INT/TRADE COLONIAL 19. PAGE 52 H1041
BIBLIOG INDEX WRITING
B10

MENDELSSOHN S.,SOUTH AFRICAN BIBLIOGRAPHY (2 VOLS.). SOUTH/AFR EXTR/IND LABOR SECT DIPLOM INT/TRADE COLONIAL RACE/REL DISCRIM...GEOG 20. PAGE 109 H2172
BIBLIOG/A AFR NAT/G NAT/LISM
B12

SONOLET L.,L'AFRIQUE OCCIDENTALE FRANCAISE. FRANCE AGRI INDUS NAT/G SECT FORCES INT/TRADE EDU/PROP RACE/REL HEALTH ORD/FREE...CHARTS 19/20 NEGRO AFRICA/W. PAGE 147 H2933
DOMIN ADMIN COLONIAL AFR
N19

BENTHAM J.,A PLAN FOR AN UNIVERSAL AND PERPETUAL PEACE (1838) (PAMPHLET). NAT/G FORCES BAL/PWR INT/TRADE ADMIN AGREE CT/SYS ARMS/CONT SOVEREIGN WEALTH GEN/LAWS. PAGE 14 H0288
INT/ORG INT/LAW PEACE COLONIAL
N19

HABERLER G.,A SURVEY OF INTERNATIONAL TRADE THEORY (PAMPHLET). FINAN NAT/G COST INCOME 18/20 MONEY HUME/D MARSHALL/A. PAGE 63 H1267
INT/TRADE BAL/PAY GEN/LAWS POLICY
N19

SALKEVER L.R.,SUB-SAHARA AFRICA (PAMPHLET). AFR USSR EXTR/IND NAT/G SCHOOL DIPLOM COLONIAL WEALTH ...GEOG CHARTS 16/20. PAGE 137 H2742
ECO/UNDEV TEC/DEV TASK INT/TRADE
N19

STEUBER F.A.,THE CONTRIBUTION OF SWITZERLAND TO THE ECONOMIC AND SOCIAL DEVELOPMENT OF LOW-INCOME COUNTRIES (PAMPHLET). SWITZERLND FINAN NAT/G VOL/ASSN INT/TRADE DRIVE...CHARTS 20. PAGE 149 H2982
FOR/AID ECO/UNDEV PLAN DIPLOM
B20

COX H.,ECONOMIC LIBERTY. UNIV LAW INT/TRADE RATION TARIFFS RACE/REL SOCISM POLICY. PAGE 34 H0687
NAT/G ORD/FREE ECO/TAC PERSON
B22

FICHTE J.G.,ADDRESSES TO THE GERMAN NATION. GERMANY PRUSSIA ELITES NAT/G SECT CREATE INT/TRADE HEREDITY ...ART/METH LING 19 FRANK/PARL. PAGE 50 H0989
NAT/LISM CULTURE EDU/PROP REGION
B26

MCPHEE A.,THE ECONOMIC REVOLUTION IN BRITISH WEST AFRICA. AFR UK CULTURE DIST/IND FINAN INDUS PLAN GP/REL RACE/REL 20 AFRICA/W. PAGE 107 H2148
ECO/UNDEV INT/TRADE COLONIAL GEOG
B27

SMITH E.W.,THE GOLDEN STOOL: SOME ASPECTS OF THE CONFLICT OF CULTURES IN AFRICA. AFR FINAN INDUS SECT INT/TRADE COERCE CHOOSE RACE/REL ATTIT...GEOG LING 20 NEGRO. PAGE 145 H2907
COLONIAL CULTURE GP/REL EDU/PROP
B34

MARX K.,THE CLASS STRUGGLES IN FRANCE. FRANCE INDUS WORKER CONSERVE...TREND GEN/LAWS 19. PAGE 104 H2077
MARXIST STRATA REV INT/TRADE
B37

HAMILTON W.H.,THE POWER TO GOVERN. ECO/DEV FINAN INDUS ECO/TAC INT/TRADE TARIFFS TAX CONTROL CT/SYS WAR COST PWR 18/20 SUPREME/CT. PAGE 65 H1303
LING CONSTN NAT/G POLICY
B37

MARX K.,THE CIVIL WAR IN THE UNITED STATES. USA-45 WORKER DIPLOM INT/TRADE DOMIN RACE/REL ATTIT ...TREND 19. PAGE 104 H2078
WAR REV MARXIST ORD/FREE
B37

VON HAYEK F.A.,MONETARY NATIONALISM AND INTERNATIONAL STABILITY. WOR-45 ECO/DEV NAT/G PROB/SOLV INT/TRADE...POLICY CONCPT METH/COMP NAT/COMP 20. PAGE 163 H3271
ECO/TAC FINAN DIPLOM NAT/LISM
B38

HARPER S.N.,THE GOVERNMENT OF THE SOVIET UNION. COM USSR LAW CONSTN ECO/DEV PLAN TEC/DEV DIPLOM INT/TRADE ADMIN REV NAT/LISM...POLICY 20. PAGE 67 H1337
MARXISM NAT/G LEAD POL/PAR
B38

RAWLINSON H.G.,INDIA: A SHORT CULTURAL HISTORY. INDIA LAW STRATA FORCES INT/TRADE ADMIN COLONIAL PERSON...GEOG HUM BIBLIOG WORSHIP 20. PAGE 130 H2598
CULTURE SECT MYTH ART/METH
B38

SAINT-PIERRE C.I.,SCHEME FOR LASTING PEACE (TRANS. BY H. BELLOT). INDUS NAT/G CHIEF FORCES INT/TRADE CT/SYS WAR PWR SOVEREIGN WEALTH...POLICY 18. PAGE 137 H2732
INT/ORG PEACE AGREE INT/LAW
B39

VAN BILJON F.J.,STATE INTERFERENCE IN SOUTH AFRICA. SOUTH/AFR ECO/UNDEV AGRI INDUS WORKER RATION WEALTH ...JURID 20. PAGE 161 H3225
ECO/TAC POLICY INT/TRADE NAT/G
S39

COLE G.D.H.,"NAZI ECONOMICS: HOW DO THEY MANAGE IT?" GERMANY FORCES WORKER BUDGET INT/TRADE ROUTINE COERCE WAR 20 HITLER/A NAZI. PAGE 31 H0622
FASCISM ECO/TAC ATTIT PLAN
B40

CONOVER H.F.,JAPAN-ECONOMIC DEVELOPMENT AND FOREIGN POLICY, A SELECTED LIST OF REFERENCES (PAMPHLET). CULTURE FINAN INDUS NAT/G FORCES INT/TRADE WAR ...SOC TREND 20 CHINJAP. PAGE 32 H0640
BIBLIOG ASIA ECO/DEV DIPLOM
B40

MEEK C.K.,EUROPE AND WEST AFRICA. AFR EUR+WWI EXTR/IND DIPLOM INT/TRADE EDU/PROP GP/REL...SOC 20. PAGE 108 H2158
CULTURE TEC/DEV ECO/UNDEV COLONIAL
C40

FAHS C.B.,"GOVERNMENT IN JAPAN." FINAN FORCES LEGIS TOP/EX BUDGET INT/TRADE EDU/PROP SOVEREIGN ...CON/ANAL BIBLIOG/A 20 CHINJAP. PAGE 48 H0962
ASIA DIPLOM NAT/G ADMIN
B42

CONOVER H.F.,FRENCH COLONIES IN AFRICA: A LIST OF REFERENCES. ALGERIA FRANCE MOROCCO SOMALIA SUDAN CULTURE AGRI LOC/G SECT FORCES DIPLOM INT/TRADE NAT/LISM HEALTH...CON/ANAL 20. PAGE 32 H0641
BIBLIOG AFR ECO/UNDEV COLONIAL
B42

CONOVER H.F.,THE NETHERLANDS EAST INDIES: A SELECTED LIST OF REFERENCES. ECO/UNDEV AGRI EXTR/IND LABOR SCHOOL SECT INT/TRADE COLONIAL HEALTH...GEOG 19/20. PAGE 32 H0642
BIBLIOG S/ASIA CULTURE
B43

BROWN A.D.,GREECE: SELECTED LIST OF REFERENCES. GREECE ECO/UNDEV AGRI FINAN INDUS LABOR SECT TEC/DEV INT/TRADE LEAD...SOC 20. PAGE 22 H0438
BIBLIOG/A WAR DIPLOM NAT/G
B44

SHELBY C.,LATIN AMERICAN PERIODICALS CURRENTLY RECEIVED IN THE LIBRARY OF CONGRESS AND IN LIBRARY OF DEPARTMENT OF AGRICULTURE. SOCIETY AGRI INDUS LABOR POL/PAR INT/TRADE...GEOG SOC 20. PAGE 143 H2856
BIBLIOG ECO/UNDEV CULTURE L/A+17C
B45

CLAGETT H.L.,COMMUNIST CHINA: RUTHLESS ENEMY OR PAPER TIGER (PAMPHLET). CHINA/COM ECO/UNDEV AGRI INDUS NAT/G POL/PAR ECO/TAC INT/TRADE GUERRILLA ATTIT...CHARTS NAT/COMP ORG/CHARTS 20. PAGE 30 H0602
BIBLIOG/A MARXISM DIPLOM COERCE
B45

CONOVER H.F.,THE NAZI STATE: WAR CRIMES AND WAR CRIMINALS. GERMANY CULTURE NAT/G SECT FORCES DIPLOM INT/TRADE EDU/PROP...INT/LAW BIOG HIST/WRIT TIME/SEQ 20. PAGE 32 H0647
BIBLIOG WAR CRIME
B45

WOOLBERT R.G.,FOREIGN AFFAIRS BIBLIOGRAPHY, 1932-1942. INT/ORG SECT INT/TRADE COLONIAL RACE/REL NAT/LISM...GEOG INT/LAW GOV/COMP IDEA/COMP 20. PAGE 170 H3410
BIBLIOG/A DIPLOM WAR
B47

ENKE S.,INTERNATIONAL ECONOMICS. UK USA+45 USSR INT/ORG BAL/PWR BARGAIN CAP/ISM BAL/PAY...NAT/COMP 20 TREATY. PAGE 46 H0927
INT/TRADE FINAN TARIFFS ECO/TAC
B48

CLYDE P.H.,THE FAR EAST: A HISTORY OF THE IMPACT OF THE WEST ON EASTERN ASIA. CHINA/COM CULTURE INT/TRADE DOMIN COLONIAL WAR PWR...CHARTS BIBLIOG 19/20 CHINJAP. PAGE 30 H0609
DIPLOM ASIA
B48

MINISTERE FINANCES ET ECO,BULLETIN BIBLIOGRAPHIQUE. AFR EUR+WWI FRANCE CULTURE STRUCT FINAN NAT/G ACT/RES INT/TRADE ADMIN REGION PRODUC STAT. PAGE 111 H2224
BIBLIOG/A ECO/UNDEV TEC/DEV COLONIAL

B48
PELCOVITS N.A.,OLD CHINA HANDS AND THE FOREIGN OFFICE. ASIA BURMA UK ECO/UNDEV NAT/G ECO/TAC FOR/AID TARIFFS DOMIN COLONIAL GOV/REL SOVEREIGN 19 HONG/KONG TREATY. PAGE 124 H2483
INT/TRADE ATTIT DIPLOM

B49
HINDEN R.,EMPIRE AND AFTER. UK POL/PAR BAL/PWR DIPLOM INT/TRADE WAR NAT/LISM PWR 17/20. PAGE 71 H1420
NAT/G COLONIAL ATTIT POLICY

B50
COUNCIL BRITISH NATIONAL BIB,BRITISH NATIONAL BIBLIOGRAPHY. UK AGRI CONSTRUC PERF/ART POL/PAR SECT CREATE INT/TRADE LEAD...HUM JURID PHIL/SCI 20. PAGE 34 H0677
BIBLIOG/A NAT/G TEC/DEV DIPLOM

B50
FITZGERALD C.P.,CHINA, A SHORT CULTURAL HISTORY. ASIA DIPLOM INT/TRADE...ART/METH SOC MANCHU/DYN. PAGE 51 H1016
NAT/G SOCIETY

C50
NUMELIN R.,"THE BEGINNINGS OF DIPLOMACY." INT/TRADE WAR GP/REL PEACE STRANGE ATTIT...INT/LAW CONCPT BIBLIOG. PAGE 119 H2380
DIPLOM KIN CULTURE LAW

B51
BISSAINTHE M.,DICTIONNAIRE DE BIBLIOGRAPHIE HAITIENNE. HAITI ELITES AGRI LEGIS DIPLOM INT/TRADE WRITING ORD/FREE CATHISM...ART/METH GEOG 19/20 NEGRO TREATY. PAGE 17 H0347
BIBLIOG L/A+17C SOCIETY NAT/G

B51
CARRINGTON C.E.,THE LIQUIDATION OF THE BRITISH EMPIRE. AFR NAT/G INT/TRADE COLONIAL RACE/REL ATTIT ORD/FREE...POLICY NAT/COMP 20 CMN/WLTH. PAGE 27 H0541
SOVEREIGN NAT/LISM DIPLOM GP/REL

B51
LEONARD L.L.,INTERNATIONAL ORGANIZATION. WOR+45 WOR-45 EX/STRUC FORCES LEGIS ECO/TAC INT/TRADE COLONIAL ARMS/CONT...SOC/WK GOV/COMP BIBLIOG. PAGE 94 H1884
NAT/G DIPLOM INT/ORG DELIB/GP

B51
WABEKE B.H.,A GUIDE TO DUTCH BIBLIOGRAPHIES. BELGIUM INDONESIA NETHERLAND DIPLOM INT/TRADE WAR NAT/LISM KNOWL...ART/METH HUM JURID CON/ANAL 14/20. PAGE 164 H3282
BIBLIOG/A NAT/G CULTURE COLONIAL

B54
BINANI G.D.,INDIA AT A GLANCE (REV. ED.). INDIA COM/IND FINAN INDUS LABOR PROVS SCHOOL PLAN DIPLOM INT/TRADE ADMIN...JURID 20. PAGE 17 H0335
INDEX CON/ANAL NAT/G ECO/UNDEV

B54
EPSTEIN L.D.,BRITAIN - UNEASY ALLY. KOREA UK USA+45 NAT/G POL/PAR ECO/TAC FOR/AID INT/TRADE WAR LABOR/PAR CONSRV/PAR. PAGE 47 H0934
DIPLOM ATTIT POLICY NAT/COMP

B54
US LIBRARY OF CONGRESS,RESEARCH AND INFORMATION ON AFRICA: CONTINUING SOURCES. ISLAM ECO/UNDEV AGRI INDUS R+D ACADEM NAT/G INT/TRADE...SOC 20. PAGE 161 H3210
BIBLIOG/A AFR PRESS COM/IND

B55
FOGARTY M.P.,ECONOMIC CONTROL. FUT UK ECO/DEV FINAN CONSULT INT/TRADE...CHARTS BIBLIOG/A 20. PAGE 52 H1033
ECO/TAC NAT/G CONTROL PROB/SOLV

B55
UN ECONOMIC COMN ASIA & FAR E,ECONOMIC SURVEY OF ASIA AND THE FAR EAST, 1954. AFGHANISTN CEYLON INDIA PHILIPPINE S/ASIA ECO/DEV FINAN INDUS INT/TRADE PRODUC WEALTH...STAT CHARTS 20 CHINJAP. PAGE 158 H3158
ECO/UNDEV PRICE NAT/COMP ASIA

B55
WOYTINSKY W.S.,WORLD COMMERCE AND GOVERNMENTS: TRENDS AND OUTLOOK. WOR+45 FINAN POL/PAR DIPLOM ECO/TAC FOR/AID DOMIN WAR CHOOSE...CHARTS BIBLIOG 20 LEAGUE/NAT UN ILO. PAGE 171 H3413
INT/TRADE DIST/IND NAT/COMP NAT/G

B56
VON BECKERATH E.,HANDWORTERBUCH DER SOCIALWISSENSCHAFTEN (II VOLS.). EUR+WWI GERMANY POL/PAR WORKER DIPLOM LEAD CHOOSE SUFF WEALTH...SOC 20. PAGE 163 H3263
BIBLIOG INT/TRADE NAT/G ECO/DEV

B56
WATT D.C.,BRITAIN AND THE SUEZ CANAL. COM UAR UK ...INT/LAW 20 SUEZ TREATY. PAGE 166 H3314
DIPLOM INT/TRADE DIST/IND NAT/G

N56
US HOUSE COMM FOREIGN AFFAIRS,REPORT OF THE SPECIAL STUDY MISSION TO AFRICA, SOUTH AND EAST OF THE SAHARA (PAMPHLET). AFR SOUTH/AFR USA+45 STRUCT INT/TRADE PARL/PROC NAT/LISM ATTIT ALL/VALS HEALTH ...POLICY 20 CONGRESS. PAGE 160 H3197
FOR/AID COLONIAL ECO/UNDEV DIPLOM

B57
NEUMARK S.D.,ECONOMIC INFLUENCES ON THE SOUTH AFRICAN FRONTIER, 1652-1836. SOUTH/AFR SEA AGRI NAT/G FORCES WORKER DIPLOM INT/TRADE PRICE DEMAND PRODUC...STAT CHARTS 17/19 FRONTIER. PAGE 117 H2341
COLONIAL ECO/UNDEV ECO/TAC MARKET

B57
SHEIKH N.A.,SOME ASPECTS OF THE CONSTITUTION AND THE ECONOMICS OF ISLAM. PAKISTAN CULTURE AGRI FINAN LABOR NAT/G SECT INT/TRADE 20 MUSLIM. PAGE 143 H2855
ISLAM POLICY ECO/TAC CONSTN

B58
AVRAMOVIC D.,POSTWAR GROWTH IN INTERNATIONAL INDEBTEDNESS. WOR+45 AGRI INDUS CAP/ISM PRICE INCOME...NAT/COMP 20 GOLD/STAND SILVER. PAGE 9 H0184
INT/TRADE FINAN COST BAL/PAY

B58
BRIGGS L.C.,THE LIVING RACES OF THE SAHARA. STRATA AGRI KIN INT/TRADE HABITAT...GEOG AUD/VIS CHARTS BIBLIOG 20 SAHARA MIGRATION. PAGE 21 H0417
STRUCT SOCIETY SOC CULTURE

B58
INDIAN COUNCIL WORLD AFFAIRS,DEFENCE AND SECURITY IN THE INDIAN OCEAN AREA. INDIA S/ASIA CULTURE CONSULT DELIB/GP FORCES PROB/SOLV DIPLOM INT/TRADE 20 CMN/WLTH. PAGE 77 H1531
GEOG HABITAT ECO/UNDEV ORD/FREE

B58
JACOBSSON P.,SOME MONETARY PROBLEMS, INTERNATIONAL AND NATIONAL. WOR+45 WOR-45 ECO/DEV FORCES WORKER PROB/SOLV DIPLOM INT/TRADE...ANTHOL 20. PAGE 79 H1580
FINAN PLAN ECO/TAC NAT/COMP

B58
SALETORE B.A.,INDIA'S DIPLOMATIC RELATIONS WITH THE WEST. GREECE INDIA CULTURE ETIQUET...IDEA/COMP 3 ROM/EMP PERSIA. PAGE 137 H2739
DIPLOM CONCPT INT/TRADE

B58
SHAW S.J.,THE FINANCIAL AND ADMINISTRATIVE ORGANIZATION AND DEVELOPMENT OF OTTOMAN EGYPT 1517-1798. UAR LOC/G FORCES BUDGET INT/TRADE TAX EATING INCOME WEALTH...CHARTS BIBLIOG 16/18 OTTOMAN NAPOLEON/B. PAGE 143 H2853
FINAN ADMIN GOV/REL CULTURE

C58
BLANCHARD W.,"THAILAND." THAILAND CULTURE AGRI FINAN INDUS FAM LABOR INT/TRADE ATTIT...GEOG HEAL SOC BIBLIOG 20. PAGE 18 H0354
NAT/G DIPLOM ECO/UNDEV S/ASIA

B59
ETSCHMANN R.,DIE WAHRUNGS- UND DEVISENPOLITIK DES OSTBLOCKS UND IHRE AUSWIRKUNGEN AUF DIE WIRTSCHAFTSBEZIEHUNGEN ZWISCHEN OST U WEST. BULGARIA CZECHOSLVK HUNGARY POLAND USSR MARKET NAT/G PLAN DIPLOM...NAT/COMP 20. PAGE 47 H0943
ECO/TAC FINAN POLICY INT/TRADE

B59
FAYERWEATHER J.,THE EXECUTIVE OVERSEAS: ADMINISTRATIVE ATTITUDES AND RELATIONSHIPS IN A FOREIGN CULTURE. USA+45 WOR+45 CULTURE LG/CO SML/CO ATTIT...MGT PERS/COMP 20 MEXIC/AMER. PAGE 49 H0979
INT/TRADE TOP/EX NAT/COMP PERS/REL

B59
GUDIN E.,INFLACAO (2ND ED.). INDUS NAT/G PLAN ECO/TAC CONTROL COST 20. PAGE 62 H1243
ECO/UNDEV INT/TRADE BAL/PAY FINAN

B59
LEITES N.,ON THE GAME OF POLITICS IN FRANCE. ALGERIA FRANCE CONSTN SECT VOL/ASSN ECO/TAC INT/TRADE PARL/PROC WAR SOCISM 20 DEGAULLE/C EEC. PAGE 94 H1871
POL/PAR NAT/G LEGIS IDEA/COMP

B59
MAC MILLAN W.M.,THE ROAD TO SELF-RULE. SOUTH/AFR UK CULTURE SOCIETY AGRI LABOR NAT/G INT/TRADE CONTROL GP/REL...SOC 19/20. PAGE 100 H1988
AFR COLONIAL SOVEREIGN POLICY

B59
THOMAS D.H.,GUIDE TO THE DIPLOMATIC ARCHIVES OF WESTERN EUROPE. EUR+WWI ELITES INT/ORG NAT/G BAL/PWR INT/TRADE PEACE. PAGE 154 H3076
BIBLIOG DIPLOM CONFER

B59
VERNEY D.V.,PUBLIC ENTERPRISE IN SWEDEN. FUT SWEDEN UK INDUS POL/PAR LEGIS PROB/SOLV CAP/ISM INT/TRADE CONTROL SOCISM...MGT CONCPT NAT/COMP 20 SOCDEM/PAR CIVIL/SERV. PAGE 162 H3246
ECO/DEV POLICY LG/CO NAT/G

B59
VINACKE H.M.,A HISTORY OF THE FAR EAST IN MODERN TIMES (6TH ED.). KOREA S/ASIA USSR CONSTN CULTURE STRATA ECO/UNDEV NAT/G CHIEF FOR/AID INT/TRADE GP/REL...SOC NAT/COMP 19/20 CHINJAP. PAGE 163 H3255
STRUCT ASIA

L59
MURPHY J.C.,"SOME IMPLICATIONS OF EUROPE'S COMMON MARKET. IN (COOK P, ECONOMIC DEVELOPMENT AND INTERNATIONAL TRADE,." EUR+WWI ECO/DEV DIST/IND INDUS NAT/G PLAN ECO/TAC INT/TRADE WEALTH...STAT TREND OEEC TOT/POP 20 EEC. PAGE 115 H2298
MARKET INT/ORG REGION

S59
PLAZA G.,"FOR A REGIONAL MARKET IN LATIN AMERICA." FUT L/A+17C CULTURE INDUS NAT/G ECO/TAC INT/TRADE ATTIT WEALTH...NEW/IDEA TREND OAS 20. PAGE 126 H2527
MARKET INT/ORG REGION

S59
ZAUBERMAN A.,"SOVIET BLOC ECONOMIC INTEGRATION." COM CULTURE INTELL ECO/DEV INDUS TOP/EX ACT/RES PLAN ECO/TAC INT/TRADE ROUTINE CHOOSE ATTIT ...TIME/SEQ 20. PAGE 172 H3452
MARKET INT/ORG USSR TOTALISM

B60
CONOVER H.F.,OFFICIAL PUBLICATIONS OF SOMALILAND, 1941-1959: A GUIDE. SOMALIA AGRI FINAN INT/ORG SCHOOL INT/TRADE PRESS CONFER COLONIAL PARL/PROC 20 CONGRESS. PAGE 33 H0652
BIBLIOG NAT/G CON/ANAL

B60
DIA M.,REFLEXIONS SUR L'ECONOMIE DE L'AFRIQUE NOIRE (REV. ED.). CULTURE ECO/UNDEV CREATE TEC/DEV DIPLOM INT/TRADE OPTIMAL ATTIT...POLICY 20. PAGE 41 H0816
AFR ECO/TAC SOCISM PLAN

B60
KENEN P.B.,BRITISH MONETARY POLICY AND THE BALANCE OF PAYMENTS 1951-57. UK PLAN BUDGET ECO/TAC INT/TRADE PAY PRICE COST ATTIT 20. PAGE 84 H1687
BAL/PAY PROB/SOLV FINAN NAT/G

B60
LISTER L.,EUROPE'S COAL AND STEEL COMMUNITY. FRANCE GERMANY STRUCT ECO/DEV EXTR/IND INDUS MARKET NAT/G DELIB/GP ECO/TAC INT/TRADE EDU/PROP ATTIT RIGID/FLEX ORD/FREE PWR WEALTH...CONCPT STAT TIME/SEQ CHARTS ECSC 20. PAGE 97 H1941
EUR+WWI INT/ORG REGION

B60
STOLPER W.F.,GERMANY BETWEEN EAST AND WEST: THE ECONOMICS OF COMPETITIVE COEXISTENCE. FUT GERMANY/E GERMANY/W WOR+45 FINAN POL/PAR BUDGET ECO/TAC FOR/AID INT/TRADE...STAT CHARTS METH/COMP 20 COLD/WAR. PAGE 150 H2989
ECO/DEV DIPLOM GOV/COMP BAL/PWR

B60
STRACHEY J.,THE END OF EMPIRE. UK WOR+45 WOR-45 DIPLOM INT/TRADE DOMIN ADJUST ORD/FREE WEALTH ...SOCIALIST GOV/COMP TIME COMMONWLTH. PAGE 150 H2991
COLONIAL ECO/DEV BAL/PWR LAISSEZ

B60
THE ECONOMIST (LONDON),THE COMMONWEALTH AND EUROPE. EUR+WWI WOR+45 AGRI FINAN INCOME...STAT CENSUS CHARTS CMN/WLTH EEC. PAGE 153 H3067
INT/TRADE INDUS INT/ORG NAT/COMP

S60
"THE EMERGING COMMON MARKETS IN LATIN AMERICA." FUT L/A+17C STRATA DIST/IND INDUS LABOR NAT/G LEGIS ECO/TAC ADMIN RIGID/FLEX HEALTH...NEW/IDEA TIME/SEQ OAS 20. PAGE 2 H0038
FINAN ECO/UNDEV INT/TRADE

S60
FITZGIBBON R.H.,"DICTATORSHIP AND DEMOCRACY IN LATIN AMERICA." FUT ECO/DEV ECO/UNDEV INT/ORG LOC/G NAT/G TOP/EX PLAN TEC/DEV ECO/TAC CHOOSE ATTIT DRIVE PERSON ALL/VALS OAS TOT/POP 20. PAGE 51 H1019
L/A+17C ACT/RES INT/TRADE

S60
FRANKEL S.H.,"ECONOMIC ASPECTS OF POLITICAL INDEPENDENCE IN AFRICA." AFR FUT SOCIETY ECO/UNDEV COM/IND FINAN LEGIS PLAN TEC/DEV CAP/ISM ECO/TAC INT/TRADE ADMIN ATTIT DRIVE RIGID/FLEX PWR WEALTH ...MGT NEW/IDEA MATH TIME/SEQ VAL/FREE 20. PAGE 53 H1052
NAT/G FOR/AID

B61
BONNEFOUS M.,EUROPE ET TIERS MONDE. EUR+WWI SOCIETY INT/ORG NAT/G VOL/ASSN ACT/RES TEC/DEV CAP/ISM ECO/TAC ATTIT ORD/FREE SOVEREIGN...POLICY CONCPT TREND 20. PAGE 19 H0373
AFR ECO/UNDEV FOR/AID INT/TRADE

B61
BREWIS T.N.,CANADIAN ECONOMIC POLICY. CANADA BUDGET CAP/ISM INT/TRADE RATION TARIFFS TAX PRICE CONTROL ROUTINE FEDERAL INCOME PRODUC 20 GOLD/STAND. PAGE 20 H0412
ECO/DEV ECO/TAC NAT/G PLAN

B61
DIA M.,THE AFRICAN NATIONS AND WORLD SOLIDARITY. ISLAM CULTURE ELITES ECO/DEV ECO/UNDEV INT/ORG NAT/G PLAN ECO/TAC INT/TRADE EDU/PROP NAT/LISM ATTIT DRIVE ORD/FREE WEALTH...SOCIALIST CONCPT CON/ANAL GEN/LAWS TOT/POP 20. PAGE 41 H0817
AFR REGION SOCISM

B61
HARDT J.P.,THE COLD WAR ECONOMIC GAP. USA+45 USSR ECO/DEV FORCES INT/TRADE NUC/PWR PWR 20 COLD/WAR. PAGE 66 H1328
DIPLOM ECO/TAC NAT/COMP POLICY

B61
NATIONAL BANK OF LIBYA,INFLATION IN LIBYA (PAMPHLET). LIBYA SOCIETY NAT/G PLAN INT/TRADE ...STAT CHARTS 20 GOLD/STAND. PAGE 116 H2318
ECO/TAC ECO/UNDEV FINAN BUDGET

B61
OECD,STATISTICS OF BALANCE OF PAYMENTS 1950-61. WOR+45 FINAN ECO/TAC INT/TRADE DEMAND WEALTH...STAT NAT/COMP 20 OEEC OECD. PAGE 120 H2396
BAL/PAY ECO/DEV INT/ORG CHARTS

B61
SCHNAPPER B.,LA POLITIQUE ET LE COMMERCE FRANCAIS DANS LE GOLFE DE GUINEE DE 1838 A 1871. FRANCE GUINEA UK SEA EXTR/IND NAT/G DELIB/GP LEGIS ADMIN ORD/FREE...POLICY GEOG CENSUS CHARTS BIBLIOG 19. PAGE 139 H2791
COLONIAL INT/TRADE DOMIN AFR

B61
SOKOL A.E.,SEAPOWER IN THE NUCLEAR AGE. USA+45 USSR DIST/IND FORCES INT/TRADE DETER WAR...POLICY NAT/COMP BIBLIOG COLD/WAR. PAGE 146 H2928
SEA PWR WEAPON NUC/PWR

B61
VEIT O.,GRUNDRISS DER WAHRUNGSPOLITIK. FRANCE GERMANY USSR DIPLOM INT/TRADE...NAT/COMP 19/20 GOLD/STAND SILVER. PAGE 162 H3239
FINAN POLICY ECO/TAC CAP/ISM

S61
BRZEZINSKI Z.K.,"THE ORGANIZATION OF THE COMMUNIST CAMP." COM CZECHOSLVK COM/IND NAT/G DELIB/GP INT/TRADE DOMIN EDU/PROP EXEC ROUTINE COERCE ATTIT PWR...MGT CONCPT TIME/SEQ CHARTS VAL/FREE 20 TREATY. PAGE 23 H0460
VOL/ASSN DIPLOM USSR

S61
RAY J.,"THE EUROPEAN FREE-TRADE ASSOCIATION AND ITS IMPACT ON INDIA'S TRADE." EUR+WWI FRANCE GERMANY INDIA S/ASIA UK NAT/G VOL/ASSN PLAN INT/TRADE ROUTINE WEALTH...STAT CHARTS CMN/WLTH EEC OEEC 20 EFTA. PAGE 130 H2600
ECO/DEV ECO/TAC

B62
CARY J.,THE CASE FOR AFRICAN FREEDOM AND OTHER WRITINGS ON AFRICA. AFR UK INDUS LOC/G NAT/G SECT INT/TRADE EDU/PROP GOV/REL RACE/REL ORD/FREE ...CONCPT ANTHOL 19/20. PAGE 27 H0552
NAT/LISM COLONIAL TREND ECO/UNDEV

B62
FATOUROS A.A.,GOVERNMENT GUARANTEES TO FOREIGN INVESTORS. WOR+45 ECO/UNDEV INDUS WORKER ADJUD ...NAT/COMP BIBLIOG TREATY. PAGE 49 H0975
NAT/G FINAN INT/TRADE ECO/DEV

B62
GANJI M.,INTERNATIONAL PROTECTION OF HUMAN RIGHTS. WOR+45 CONSTN INT/TRADE CT/SYS SANCTION CRIME WAR RACE/REL...CHARTS IDEA/COMP NAT/COMP BIBLIOG 20 TREATY NEGRO LEAGUE/NAT UN CIVIL/LIB. PAGE 55 H1097
ORD/FREE DISCRIM LEGIS DELIB/GP

B62
GREEN L.P.,DEVELOPMENT IN AFRICA. AFR CENTRL/AFR GHANA RHODESIA SOUTH/AFR AGRI PROC/MFG INT/TRADE DEMAND NAT/LISM PRODUC WEALTH...GEOG METH/CNCPT CHARTS BIBLIOG 20. PAGE 60 H1206
CULTURE ECO/UNDEV GOV/REL TREND

B62
GROVE J.W.,GOVERNMENT AND INDUSTRY IN BRITAIN. UK FINAN LOC/G CONSULT DELIB/GP INT/TRADE ADMIN CONTROL...BIBLIOG 20. PAGE 62 H1237
ECO/TAC INDUS NAT/G GP/REL

B62
HENDERSON W.O.,THE GENESIS OF THE COMMON MARKET. EUR+WWI FRANCE MOD/EUR UK SEA COM/IND EXTR/IND COLONIAL DISCRIM...TIME/SEQ CHARTS BIBLIOG 18/20 EEC TREATY. PAGE 70 H1395
ECO/DEV INT/TRADE DIPLOM

B62
HUNTER G.,THE NEW SOCIETIES OF TROPICAL AFRICA. CULTURE INDUS KIN MUNIC WORKER INT/TRADE EDU/PROP ORD/FREE...INT TREND 20. PAGE 75 H1500
AFR GOV/COMP ECO/UNDEV SOCIETY

B62
JENNINGS I.,PARTY POLITICS: THE STUFF OF POLITICS (VOL.III). UK NAT/G SECT CHIEF INT/TRADE RECEIVE COLONIAL GP/REL NAT/LISM ORD/FREE SOCISM 19/20 CHURCH/STA WHIG/PARTY. PAGE 80 H1607
POL/PAR CONSTN PWR ALL/IDEOS

B62
KINDLEBERGER C.P.,FOREIGN TRADE AND THE NATIONAL ECONOMY. WOR+45 ECO/DEV ECO/UNDEV ECO/TAC COST DEMAND 20. PAGE 86 H1713
INT/TRADE GOV/COMP BAL/PAY POLICY

B62
MEADE J.E.,CASE STUDIES IN EUROPEAN ECONOMIC UNION. BELGIUM EUR+WWI LUXEMBOURG NAT/G INT/TRADE REGION ROUTINE WEALTH...METH/CNCPT STAT CHARTS ECSC TOT/POP OEEC EEC 20. PAGE 108 H2154
INT/ORG ECO/TAC

B62
MICHAELY M.,CONCENTRATION IN INTERNATIONAL TRADE. ECO/DEV ECO/UNDEV PRICE INCOME...CHARTS NAT/COMP 20. PAGE 110 H2197
INT/TRADE MARKET FINAN GEOG

B62
MODELSKI G.,SEATO-SIX STUDIES. ASIA CHINA/COM INDIA S/ASIA INT/ORG NAT/G ECO/TAC DETER ATTIT ORD/FREE PWR...TIME/SEQ COLD/WAR TOT/POP 20 SEATO. PAGE 112 H2234
MARKET ECO/UNDEV INT/TRADE

B62
ROBINSON A.D.,DUTCH ORGANIZED AGRICULTURE IN INTERNATIONAL POLITICS, 1945-1960. EUR+WWI NETHERLAND STRUCT ECO/DEV NAT/G VOL/ASSN CONSULT DELIB/GP PLAN TEC/DEV INT/TRADE EDU/PROP ATTIT RIGID/FLEX ALL/VALS...NEW/IDEA TREND EEC 20. PAGE 132 H2648
AGRI INT/ORG

B62
SELOSOEMARDJAN O.,SOCIAL CHANGES IN JOGJAKARTA. INDONESIA NETHERLAND ELITES STRATA STRUCT FAM POL/PAR CREATE DIPLOM INT/TRADE EDU/PROP ADMIN GOV/REL...SOC 20 JAVA CHINJAP. PAGE 141 H2825
ECO/UNDEV CULTURE REV COLONIAL

B62
TAYLOR D.,THE BRITISH IN AFRICA. UK CULTURE ECO/UNDEV INDUS DIPLOM INT/TRADE ADMIN WAR RACE/REL ORD/FREE SOVEREIGN...POLICY BIBLIOG 15/20 CMN/WLTH. PAGE 153 H3053
AFR COLONIAL DOMIN

L62
MURACCIOLE L.,"LA BANQUE CENTRALE DES ETATS DE
ISLAM

L'AFRIQUE DE L'OUEST." AFR LAW ECO/UNDEV INT/ORG NAT/G CONSULT ECO/TAC ROUTINE...CHARTS 20. PAGE 115 H2292 — FINAN INT/TRADE

S62

THOMPSON D.,"THE UNITED KINGDOM AND THE TREATY OF ROME." EUR+WWI INT/ORG NAT/G DELIB/GP LEGIS INT/TRADE RIGID/FLEX...CONCPT EEC PARLIAMENT CMN/WLTH 20. PAGE 154 H3079 — ADJUD JURID

B63

BRITISH AID. UK AGRI DIST/IND INDUS SCHOOL TEC/DEV INT/TRADE COLONIAL DEMAND...TREND CHARTS 20. PAGE 2 H0041 — FOR/AID ECO/UNDEV NAT/G FINAN

B63

BANERJI A.K.,INDIA'S BALANCE OF PAYMENTS. INDIA NAT/G PRICE BAL/PAY COST INCOME 20. PAGE 10 H0208 — INT/TRADE DIPLOM FINAN BUDGET

B63

BERGSON A.,ECONOMIC TRENDS IN THE SOVIET UNION. USSR ECO/UNDEV AGRI NAT/G FORCES PLAN TEC/DEV INT/TRADE BAL/PAY...POLICY ANTHOL 20. PAGE 15 H0302 — ECO/DEV NAT/COMP INDUS LABOR

B63

CHOU S.H.,THE CHINESE INFLATION 1937-1949. ASIA SOCIETY POL/PAR FOR/AID INT/TRADE BAL/PAY WEALTH MARXISM...STAT CHARTS 20 COM/PARTY GOLD/STAND. PAGE 30 H0597 — FINAN ECO/TAC BUDGET NAT/G

B63

CONFERENCE ABORIGINAL STUDIES,AUSTRALIAN ABORIGINAL STUDIES. ECO/UNDEV INT/TRADE COLONIAL ADJUST HABITAT HEREDITY...GEOG PSY LING SOC/EXP ANTHOL WORSHIP 20 AUSTRAL ABORIGINES. PAGE 32 H0638 — SOC SOCIETY CULTURE STRUCT

B63

GUIMARAES A.P.,INFLACAO E MONOPOLIO NO BRASIL. BRAZIL FINAN NAT/G PLAN PAY...METH/COMP 20. PAGE 62 H1248 — ECO/UNDEV PRICE INT/TRADE BAL/PAY

B63

MOSELY P.E.,THE SOVIET UNION, 1922-1962: A FOREIGN AFFAIRS READER. ASIA POLAND USSR CULTURE INTELL AGRI POL/PAR WORKER INT/TRADE DOMIN WAR NAT/LISM MARXISM SOCISM 20 KHRUSH/N. PAGE 113 H2267 — PWR POLICY DIPLOM

B63

STIFEL L.D.,THE TEXTILE INDUSTRY - A CASE STUDY OF INDUSTRIAL DEVELOPMENT IN THE PHILIPPINES (PAPER). PHILIPPINE WORKER CAP/ISM INT/TRADE TARIFFS RECEIVE PRICE ADMIN COST EFFICIENCY WEALTH...BIBLIOG 20. PAGE 149 H2986 — S/ASIA ECO/UNDEV PROC/MFG NAT/G

B63

UN SECRETARY GENERAL,PLANNING FOR ECONOMIC DEVELOPMENT. ECO/UNDEV FINAN BUDGET INT/TRADE TARIFFS TAX ADMIN 20 UN. PAGE 158 H3159 — PLAN ECO/TAC MGT NAT/COMP

S63

MBOYA T.,"AFRICAN SOCIALISM." ECO/UNDEV INT/ORG DIPLOM FOR/AID INT/TRADE REGION GP/REL ATTIT ORD/FREE EACM. PAGE 106 H2116 — AFR SOCISM CULTURE NAT/LISM

N63

LEDERER W.,THE BALANCE ON FOREIGN TRANSACTIONS: PROBLEMS OF DEFINITION AND MEASUREMENT (PAMPHLET). USA+45 BUDGET DIPLOM ECO/TAC PRICE GOV/REL...POLICY STAT NAT/COMP METH 20. PAGE 93 H1853 — FINAN BAL/PAY INT/TRADE ECO/DEV

B64

ALVIM J.C.,A REVOLUCAO SEM RUMO. BRAZIL NAT/G BAL/PWR DIPLOM INT/TRADE PARTIC WEALTH...POLICY SOC SOC/INTEG 20. PAGE 6 H0118 — REV CIVMIL/REL ECO/UNDEV ORD/FREE

B64

ANDREWS D.H.,LATIN AMERICA: A BIBLIOGRAPHY OF PAPERBACK BOOKS. SECT INT/TRADE EDU/PROP WAR GOV/REL ADJUST NAT/LISM ATTIT...ART/METH LING BIOG 20. PAGE 7 H0138 — BIBLIOG L/A+17C CULTURE NAT/G

B64

BROWN W.M.,THE EXTERNAL LIQUIDITY OF AN ADVANCED COUNTRY. CANADA FRANCE GERMANY/W SWEDEN UK USA+45 ECO/DEV DIPLOM PRICE...CONCPT STAT NAT/COMP 20. PAGE 22 H0451 — FINAN INT/TRADE COST INCOME

B64

CURRIE D.P.,FEDERALISM AND THE NEW NATIONS OF AFRICA. CANADA USA+45 INT/TRADE TAX GP/REL ...NAT/COMP SOC/INTEG 20. PAGE 36 H0725 — FEDERAL AFR ECO/UNDEV INT/LAW

B64

HAZLEWOOD A.,THE ECONOMICS OF DEVELOPMENT: AN ANNOTATED LIST OF BOOKS AND ARTICLES PUBLISHED 1958-1962. AGRI FINAN INDUS LABOR NAT/G DIPLOM INT/TRADE INCOME...MGT 20. PAGE 69 H1374 — BIBLIOG/A ECO/UNDEV TEC/DEV

B64

HERSKOVITS M.J.,ECONOMIC TRANSITION IN AFRICA. FUT INT/ORG NAT/G WORKER PROB/SOLV TEC/DEV INT/TRADE EQUILIB INCOME...ANTHOL 20. PAGE 70 H1408 — AFR ECO/UNDEV PLAN ADMIN

B64

INTERNATIONAL LABOUR OFFICE,EMPLOYMENT AND ECONOMIC GROWTH. ECO/DEV ECO/UNDEV NAT/G PLAN DIPLOM INT/TRADE CONTROL INCOME PRODUC WEALTH...STAT NAT/COMP 20 ILO. PAGE 78 H1558 — WORKER METH/COMP ECO/TAC OPTIMAL

B64

JOHNSON A.F.,BIBLIOGRAPHY OF GHANA: 1930-1961. GHANA LAW AGRI INDUS NAT/G INT/TRADE EDU/PROP HEALTH...GEOG AUD/VIS CHARTS 20. PAGE 81 H1618 — BIBLIOG/A CULTURE SOC

B64

KALDOR N.,ESSAYS ON ECONOMIC POLICY (VOL. II). CHILE GERMANY INDIA FINAN...GOV/COMP METH/COMP 20 KEYNES/JM. PAGE 83 H1651 — BAL/PAY INT/TRADE METH/CNCPT ECO/UNDEV

B64

LEWIN P.,THE FOREIGN TRADE OF COMMUNIST CHINA* ITS IMPACT ON THE FREE WORLD. AFR EUR+WWI L/A+17C S/ASIA ECO/UNDEV CREATE FOR/AID...STAT NET/THEORY TREND CHARTS. PAGE 96 H1910 — ASIA INT/TRADE NAT/COMP USSR

B64

LI C.M.,INDUSTRIAL DEVELOPMENT IN COMMUNIST CHINA. CHINA/COM ECO/DEV ECO/UNDEV AGRI FINAN INDUS MARKET LABOR NAT/G ECO/TAC INT/TRADE EXEC ALL/VALS ...POLICY RELATIV TREND WORK TOT/POP VAL/FREE 20. PAGE 96 H1921 — ASIA TEC/DEV

B64

MAUD J.,AID FOR DEVELOPING COUNTRIES. COM EUR+WWI UK INT/TRADE ORD/FREE...GOV/COMP 20. PAGE 105 H2101 — FOR/AID DIPLOM ECO/TAC ECO/UNDEV

B64

RAGHAVAN M.D.,INDIA IN CEYLONESE HISTORY, SOCIETY AND CULTURE. CEYLON INDIA S/ASIA LAW SOCIETY INT/TRADE ATTIT...ART/METH JURID SOC LING 20. PAGE 129 H2581 — DIPLOM CULTURE SECT STRUCT

B64

RAMAZANI R.K.,THE MIDDLE EAST AND THE EUROPEAN COMMON MARKET. EUR+WWI ISLAM ECO/DEV EXTR/IND MARKET PROC/MFG INT/ORG NAT/G TEC/DEV ECO/TAC REGION DRIVE WEALTH...STAT CHARTS EEC TOT/POP 20. PAGE 129 H2587 — ECO/UNDEV ATTIT INT/TRADE

B64

ROBERTS HL,FOREIGN AFFAIRS BIBLIOGRAPHY, 1952-1962. ECO/DEV SECT PLAN FOR/AID INT/TRADE ARMS/CONT NAT/LISM ATTIT...INT/LAW GOV/COMP IDEA/COMP 20. PAGE 132 H2643 — BIBLIOG/A DIPLOM INT/ORG WAR

B64

SEGAL R.,SANCTIONS AGAINST SOUTH AFRICA. AFR SOUTH/AFR NAT/G INT/TRADE RACE/REL PEACE PWR ...INT/LAW ANTHOL 20 UN. PAGE 141 H2821 — SANCTION DISCRIM ECO/TAC POLICY

B64

STRONG C.F.,HISTORY OF MODERN POLITICAL CONSTITUTIONS. STRUCT INT/ORG NAT/G LEGIS TEC/DEV DIPLOM INT/TRADE CT/SYS EXEC...METH/COMP T 12/20 UN. PAGE 150 H2999 — CONSTN CONCPT

B64

URQUIDI V.L.,THE CHALLENGE OF DEVELOPMENT IN LATIN AMERICA. L/A+17C FINAN INT/ORG TEC/DEV DIPLOM INT/TRADE PRICE REGION PRODUC...CHARTS 20. PAGE 159 H3175 — ECO/UNDEV ECO/TAC NAT/G TREND

B64

WERNETTE J.P.,GOVERNMENT AND BUSINESS. LABOR CAP/ISM ECO/TAC INT/TRADE TAX ADMIN AUTOMAT NUC/PWR CIVMIL/REL DEMAND...MGT 20 MONOPOLY. PAGE 167 H3333 — NAT/G FINAN ECO/DEV CONTROL

B64

WITHERELL J.W.,OFFICIAL PUBLICATIONS OF FRENCH EQUATORIAL AFRICA, FRENCH CAMEROONS, AND TOGO, 1946-1958 (PAMPHLET). CAMEROON CHAD FRANCE GABON TOGO LAW ECO/UNDEV EXTR/IND INT/TRADE...GEOG HEAL 20. PAGE 169 H3392 — BIBLIOG/A AFR NAT/G ADMIN

B65

ALEXANDER R.J.,ORGANIZED LABOR IN LATIN AMERICA. L/A+17C INT/ORG LEGIS WORKER TEC/DEV BARGAIN INT/TRADE REV...NAT/COMP BIBLIOG 20. PAGE 5 H0102 — LABOR POL/PAR ECO/UNDEV POLICY

B65

CAMERON W.J.,NEW ZEALAND. NEW/ZEALND S/ASIA DIPLOM INT/TRADE WRITING COLONIAL PARL/PROC...GEOG CMN/WLTH. PAGE 26 H0513 — SOCIETY GP/REL STRUCT

B65

EUROPEAN FREE TRADE ASSN,REGIONAL DEVELOPMENT POLICIES IN EFTA. ECO/UNDEV INT/ORG PLAN REGION ...POLICY GEOG EFTA. PAGE 48 H0950 — EUR+WWI ECO/DEV NAT/COMP INT/TRADE

B65

GRIMAL H.,HISTOIRE DU COMMONWEALTH BRITANNIQUE. UK FINAN DOMIN ATTIT ORD/FREE...T 15/20 CMN/WLTH. PAGE 61 H1226 — NAT/G COLONIAL DIPLOM INT/TRADE

B65

HLA MYINT U.,THE ECONOMICS OF THE DEVELOPING COUNTRIES. USA+45 WOR+45 AGRI FINAN NAT/G INT/TRADE ...CLASSIF CENSUS TREND NAT/COMP SIMUL GEN/LAWS. PAGE 71 H1430 — ECO/UNDEV FOR/AID GEOG

B65

HOSELITZ B.F.,ECONOMICS AND THE IDEA OF MANKIND. — CREATE

UNIV ECO/DEV ECO/UNDEV DIST/IND INDUS INT/ORG NAT/G ACT/RES ECO/TAC WEALTH...CONCPT STAT. PAGE 74 H1476 — INT/TRADE

B65
MAIR L.,AN INTRODUCTION TO SOCIAL ANTHROPOLOGY. LAW STRATA FINAN FAM KIN SECT INT/TRADE RACE/REL ADJUST PRODUC...T 20. PAGE 101 H2023 — SOC STRUCT CULTURE SOCIETY

B65
NEWBURY C.W.,BRITISH POLICY TOWARDS WEST AFRICA: SELECT DOCUMENTS 1786-1874. AFR UK INT/TRADE DOMIN ADMIN COLONIAL CT/SYS COERCE ORD/FREE...BIBLIOG/A 18/19. PAGE 117 H2345 — DIPLOM POLICY NAT/G WRITING

B65
O'BRIEN F.,CRISIS IN WORLD COMMUNISM* MARXISM IN SEARCH OF EFFICIENCY. COM ECO/DEV PLAN INT/TRADE WAR ADJUST PEACE...STAT TIME/SEQ GOV/COMP NAT/COMP COLD/WAR. PAGE 119 H2384 — MARXISM USSR DRIVE EFFICIENCY

B65
O'CONNELL M.R.,IRISH POLITICS AND SOCIAL CONFLICT IN THE AGE OF THE AMERICAN REVOLUTION. FRANCE IRELAND MOD/EUR STRATA SECT LEGIS DIPLOM INT/TRADE DOMIN REV WAR...BIBLIOG 18 PARLIAMENT. PAGE 119 H2387 — CATHISM ATTIT NAT/G DELIB/GP

B65
ONSLOW C.,ASIAN ECONOMIC DEVELOPMENT. BURMA CEYLON INDIA MALAYSIA PAKISTAN S/ASIA AGRI INDUS MARKET PROB/SOLV CAP/ISM FOR/AID INT/TRADE DEMAND WEALTH ...POLICY ANTHOL 20. PAGE 121 H2418 — ECO/UNDEV ECO/TAC PLAN NAT/G

B65
ROTBERG R.I.,A POLITICAL HISTORY OF TROPICAL AFRICA. EX/STRUC DIPLOM INT/TRADE DOMIN ADMIN RACE/REL NAT/LISM PWR SOVEREIGN...GEOG TIME/SEQ BIBLIOG 1/20. PAGE 135 H2692 — AFR CULTURE COLONIAL

B65
SABLE M.H.,MASTER DIRECTORY FOR LATIN AMERICA. AGRI COM/IND FINAN R+D ACADEM LABOR NAT/G POL/PAR VOL/ASSN INT/TRADE EDU/PROP 20. PAGE 136 H2728 — INDEX L/A+17C INT/ORG DIPLOM

B65
SWIFT M.G.,MALAY PEASANT SOCIETY IN JELEBU. MALAYSIA FAM INT/TRADE ADJUD OWN WEALTH...SOC WORSHIP 20. PAGE 151 H3020 — STRUCT ECO/UNDEV CULTURE SOCIETY

B65
TEW B.,WEALTH AND INCOME. UK BUDGET INT/TRADE PRICE BAL/PAY DEMAND...CHARTS GOV/COMP 20 AUSTRAL. PAGE 153 H3064 — FINAN ECO/DEV WEALTH INCOME

B65
WUORINEN J.H.,SCANDINAVIA. DENMARK FINLAND ICELAND NORWAY SWEDEN SOCIETY AGRI INDUS DELIB/GP DIPLOM INT/TRADE NEUTRAL...GEOG CHARTS BIBLIOG TREATY. PAGE 171 H3428 — NAT/G POL/PAR TREND POLICY

B65
WURFEL S.W.,FOREIGN ENTERPRISE IN COLOMBIA. FINAN LABOR NAT/G ECO/TAC TAX REGION 20 COLOMB. PAGE 171 H3429 — ECO/UNDEV INT/TRADE JURID CAP/ISM

S65
GANGAL S.C.,"SURVEY OF RECENT RESEARCH: INDIA AND THE COMMONWEALTH" INDIA UK NAT/G INT/TRADE PARTIC GOV/REL ROLE 20 CMN/WLTH. PAGE 55 H1095 — BIBLIOG POLICY REGION DIPLOM

S65
HAYTER T.,"FRENCH AID TO AFRICA* ITS SCOPE AND ACHIEVEMENTS." CULTURE ECO/TAC INT/TRADE ADMIN REGION CENTRAL FEDERAL LOVE PWR SOVEREIGN EEC. PAGE 68 H1370 — AFR FRANCE FOR/AID COLONIAL

S65
KINDLEBERGER C.P.,"MASS MIGRATION, THEN AND NOW." LAW ECO/DEV ECO/UNDEV INDUS LABOR INT/TRADE FEEDBACK REGION RIGID/FLEX...SOC NAT/COMP EEC. PAGE 86 H1714 — EUR+WWI USA-45 WORKER IDEA/COMP

S65
ROGGER H.,"EAST GERMANY: STABLE OR IMMOBILE." COM EUR+WWI GERMANY/E NAT/G INT/TRADE DOMIN EDU/PROP COERCE TOTALISM COLD/WAR 20. PAGE 133 H2659 — TOP/EX RIGID/FLEX GERMANY

S65
TENDLER J.D.,"TECHNOLOGY AND ECONOMIC DEVELOPMENT* THE CASE OF HYDRO VS THERMAL POWER." CONSTRUC DIST/IND CREATE TEC/DEV INT/TRADE CENTRAL PWR SKILL WEALTH...MGT NAT/COMP ARGEN. PAGE 153 H3061 — BRAZIL INDUS ECO/UNDEV

C65
WUORINEN J.H.,"SCANDINAVIA." DENMARK FINLAND ICELAND NORWAY SWEDEN SOCIETY AGRI POL/PAR DELIB/GP DIPLOM INT/TRADE NEUTRAL WAR...CHARTS TREATY 20. PAGE 171 H3427 — BIBLIOG NAT/G POLIC\

B66
BIRMINGHAM D.,TRADE AND CONFLICT IN ANGOLA. PORTUGAL CULTURE FORCES DIPLOM GP/REL PROFIT HABITAT NAT/COMP. PAGE 17 H0341 — WAR INT/TRADE ECO/UNDEV COLONIAL

B66
BROWN R.T.,TRANSPORT AND THE ECONOMIC INTEGRATION OF SOUTH AMERICA. L/A+17C ECO/UNDEV NAT/G OP/RES DIPLOM INT/TRADE REGION WEALTH...ECOMETRIC GEOG STAT LAFTA TIME. PAGE 22 H0449 — MARKET DIST/IND SIMUL

B66
CROWDER M.,A SHORT HISTORY OF NIGERIA. AFR NIGERIA UK ECO/UNDEV CHIEF INT/TRADE RACE/REL NAT/LISM ORD/FREE...GEOG SOC CHARTS BIBLIOG 14/20. PAGE 36 H0711 — COLONIAL NAT/G CULTURE

B66
DYCK H.V.,WEIMAR GERMANY AND SOVIET RUSSIA 1926-1933. EUR+WWI GERMANY UK USSR ECO/TAC INT/TRADE NEUTRAL WAR ATTIT 20 WEIMAR/REP TREATY. PAGE 44 H0877 — DIPLOM GOV/REL POLICY

B66
EDWARDS C.D.,TRADE REGULATIONS OVERSEAS. IRELAND NEW/ZEALND SOUTH/AFR NAT/G CAP/ISM TARIFFS CONTROL ...POLICY JURID 20 EEC CHINJAP. PAGE 45 H0892 — INT/TRADE DIPLOM INT/LAW ECO/TAC

B66
FISK E.K.,NEW GUINEA ON THE THRESHOLD; ASPECTS OF SOCIAL, POLITICAL, AND ECONOMIC DEVELOPMENT. AGRI NAT/G INT/TRADE ADMIN ADJUST LITERACY ROLE...CHARTS ANTHOL 20 NEW/GUINEA. PAGE 51 H1015 — ECO/UNDEV SOCIETY

B66
FITZGERALD C.P.,A CONCISE HISTORY OF EAST ASIA. ASIA KOREA S/ASIA INT/TRADE REGION MARXISM 20 CHINJAP. PAGE 51 H1017 — ECO/UNDEV COLONIAL CULTURE

B66
FITZGERALD C.P.,THE BIRTH OF COMMUNIST CHINA (2ND ED.). ASIA CHINA/COM STRUCT BAL/PWR DIPLOM ECO/TAC INT/TRADE WEALTH 20. PAGE 51 H1018 — REV MARXISM ECO/UNDEV

B66
GHOSH P.K.,THE CONSTITUTION OF INDIA: HOW IT HAS BEEN FRAMED. INDIA LOC/G DELIB/GP EX/STRUC PROB/SOLV BUDGET INT/TRADE CT/SYS CHOOSE...LING 20. PAGE 56 H1121 — CONSTN NAT/G LEGIS FEDERAL

B66
HOWE R.W.,BLACK AFRICA: FROM PRE-HISTORY TO THE EVE OF THE COLONIAL ERA. ECO/UNDEV KIN PROVS SECT INT/TRADE EDU/PROP COLONIAL...BIBLIOG WORSHIP. PAGE 74 H1482 — AFR CULTURE SOC

B66
KOH S.J.,STAGES OF INDUSTRIAL DEVELOPMENT IN ASIA. ASIA INDIA KOREA STRATA STRUCT NAT/G INT/TRADE ...CHARTS 19/20 CHINJAP. PAGE 87 H1738 — INDUS ECO/UNDEV ECO/DEV LABOR

B66
LAVEN P.,RENAISSANCE ITALY: 1464-1534. ITALY AGRI EXTR/IND FINAN MUNIC INT/TRADE DRIVE...CATH GEOG CHARTS BIBLIOG/A 15. PAGE 92 H1841 — CULTURE HUM TEC/DEV KNOWL

B66
MACFARQUHAR R.,CHINA UNDER MAO: POLITICS TAKES COMMAND. CHINA/COM COM AGRI INDUS CHIEF FORCES DIPLOM INT/TRADE EDU/PROP TASK REV ADJUST...ANTHOL 20 MAO. PAGE 100 H1992 — ECO/UNDEV TEC/DEV ECO/TAC ADMIN

B66
MADAN G.R.,ECONOMIC THINKING IN INDIA. INDIA ECO/UNDEV AGRI FINAN INDUS LABOR PLAN CAP/ISM INT/TRADE MARXISM SOCISM...POLICY 1/20. PAGE 101 H2013 — ECO/TAC PHIL/SCI NAT/G POL/PAR

B66
MASON E.S.,ECONOMIC DEVELOPMENT IN INDIA AND PAKISTAN. INDIA PAKISTAN AGRI FINAN PLAN BUDGET INT/TRADE WEALTH...POLICY STAT TREND CHARTS 20. PAGE 104 H2086 — NAT/COMP ECO/UNDEV ECO/TAC FOR/AID

B66
MASUR G.,NATIONALISM IN LATIN AMERICA* DIVERSITY AND UNITY. CHRIST-17C PRE/AMER ELITES ECO/UNDEV CREATE DIPLOM INT/TRADE COLONIAL REV SOVEREIGN SOC. PAGE 105 H2089 — L/A+17C NAT/LISM CULTURE

B66
SMITH H.E.,READINGS IN ECONOMIC DEVELOPMENT AND ADMINISTRATION IN TANZANIA. TANZANIA FINAN INDUS LABOR NAT/G PLAN PROB/SOLV INT/TRADE COLONIAL REGION...ANTHOL BIBLIOG 20 AFRICA/E. PAGE 146 H2910 — TEC/DEV ADMIN GOV/REL

B66
SPULBER N.,THE STATE AND ECONOMIC DEVELOPMENT IN EASTERN EUROPE. BULGARIA COM CZECHOSLVK HUNGARY POLAND YUGOSLAVIA CULTURE PLAN CAP/ISM INT/TRADE CONTROL...POLICY CHARTS METH/COMP BIBLIOG/A 19/20. PAGE 148 H2958 — ECO/DEV ECO/UNDEV NAT/G TOTALISM

B66
US DEPARTMENT OF THE ARMY,SOUTH ASIA: A STRATEGIC SURVEY (PAMPHLET NO. 550-3). AFGHANISTN INDIA NEPAL PAKISTAN ECO/UNDEV INT/ORG POL/PAR FORCES FOR/AID INT/TRADE LEAD WAR...POLICY SOC TREND 20. PAGE 160 H3195 — BIBLIOG/A S/ASIA DIPLOM NAT/G

B66
YEAGER L.B.,INTERNATIONAL MONETARY RELATIONS: THEORY, HISTORY, AND POLICY. WOR+45 WOR-45 INT/TRADE BAL/PAY...NAT/COMP 18/20 MONEY. PAGE 172 H3435 — FINAN DIPLOM ECO/TAC IDEA/COMP

S66
GALTUNG J.,"EAST-WEST INTERACTION PATTERNS." DIPLOM INT/TRADE...NET/THEORY CON/ANAL CHARTS NAT/COMP INDEX NATO COLD/WAR UN WARSAW/P. PAGE 55 H1090 — STAT HYPO/EXP

B67
CURTIN P.D.,AFRICA REMEMBERED. NIGERIA SENEGAL CULTURE DIPLOM INT/TRADE GP/REL RACE/REL...RECORD ANTHOL 18/19 NEGRO. PAGE 36 H0727
DOMIN ORD/FREE AFR DISCRIM

B67
DALTON G.,TRIBAL AND PEASANT ECONOMIES. SOCIETY FINAN FAM INT/TRADE RATION ADJUST WEALTH...CHARTS ANTHOL BIBLIOG T. PAGE 37 H0738
SOC ECO/UNDEV NAT/COMP

B67
DILLARD D.,ECONOMIC DEVELOPMENT OF THE NORTH ATLANTIC COMMUNITY. EUR+WWI MOD/EUR USA+45 USA-45 ECO/UNDEV LABOR CAP/ISM WAR BAL/PAY...NAT/COMP 15/20. PAGE 41 H0824
ECO/DEV INT/TRADE INDUS DIPLOM

B67
HAWTREY R.,INCOMES AND MONEY. EUR+WWI FUT UK LABOR WORKER INT/TRADE TAX PAY BAL/PAY COST WEALTH 20. PAGE 68 H1363
FINAN NAT/G POLICY ECO/DEV

B67
HOLLERMAN L.,JAPAN'S DEPENDENCE ON THE WORLD ECONOMY. INDUS MARKET LABOR NAT/G DIPLOM 20 CHINJAP. PAGE 73 H1457
PLAN ECO/DEV ECO/TAC INT/TRADE

B67
LEVY J.-.P.,THE ECONOMIC LIFE OF THE ANCIENT WORLD. CULTURE SOCIETY INT/TRADE COLONIAL WEALTH ...BIBLIOG. PAGE 95 H1906
ECO/TAC ECO/UNDEV FINAN MEDIT-7

B67
MORRIS A.J.A.,PARLIAMENTARY DEMOCRACY IN THE NINETEENTH CENTURY. UK INDUS LOC/G NAT/G POL/PAR CONSULT LEGIS INT/TRADE ADMIN CHOOSE SUFF SOVEREIGN 19 PARLIAMENT. PAGE 113 H2261
TIME/SEQ CONSTN PARL/PROC POPULISM

B67
OVERSEAS DEVELOPMENT INSTIT,EFFECTIVE AID. WOR+45 INT/ORG TEC/DEV DIPLOM INT/TRADE ADMIN. PAGE 122 H2434
FOR/AID ECO/UNDEV ECO/TAC NAT/COMP

B67
PLANK J.,CUBA AND THE UNITED STATES: LONG RANGE PERSPECTIVES. CUBA L/A+17C USSR ECO/UNDEV NAT/G FORCES ECO/TAC INT/TRADE AGREE REV...PREDICT TREND ANTHOL 20 CASTRO/F COLD/WAR OAS. PAGE 126 H2520
DIPLOM

B67
RUEFF J.,BALANCE OF PAYMENTS. WOR+45 FINAN TEC/DEV DIPLOM TARIFFS PRICE CONTROL...POLICY CONCPT IDEA/COMP. PAGE 136 H2715
INT/TRADE BAL/PAY ECO/TAC NAT/COMP

B67
THOMAN R.S.,GEOGRAPHY OF INTERNATIONAL TRADE. WOR+45 ECO/DEV ECO/UNDEV INT/ORG LG/CO PLAN BAL/PAY ...STAT CHARTS NAT/COMP 20. PAGE 154 H3075
INT/TRADE GEOG ECO/TAC DIPLOM

B67
WISEMAN H.V.,BRITAIN AND THE COMMONWEALTH. EUR+WWI FUT UK ECO/DEV POL/PAR TEC/DEV INT/TRADE LEAD ROLE SOVEREIGN...SOC TREND 20 CMN/WLTH. PAGE 169 H3391
INT/ORG DIPLOM NAT/G NAT/COMP

L67
GALTUNG J.,"ON THE EFFECTS OF INTERNATIONAL ECONOMIC SANCTIONS, WITH EXAMPLES FROM THE CASE OF RHODESIA." NAT/G DIPLOM EDU/PROP ADJUST EFFICIENCY ATTIT MORAL...OBS CHARTS 20. PAGE 55 H1091
SANCTION ECO/TAC INT/TRADE ECO/UNDEV

L67
KELLEHER G.W.,"THE COMMON MARKET ANTITRUST LAWS: THE FIRST TEN YEARS." EUR+WWI INDUS PRICE ADJUD AGREE CONTROL PROFIT...POLICY 20 EEC. PAGE 84 H1684
INT/ORG INT/TRADE MARKET NAT/G

L67
ROTH A.R.,"CAPITAL-MARKET DEVELOPMENT IN ISRAEL AND BRAZIL: TWO EXAMPLES OF THE ROLE OF LAW IN DEVELOPMENT." BRAZIL ISRAEL L/A+17C INDUS MARKET ECO/TAC FOR/AID INT/TRADE CONTROL BAL/PAY 20. PAGE 135 H2694
LAW ECO/UNDEV NAT/COMP FINAN

L67
SEGAL A.,"THE INTEGRATION OF DEVELOPING COUNTRIES: SOME THOUGHTS ON EAST AFRICA AND CENTRAL AMERICA." AFR L/A+17C INT/ORG NAT/G VOL/ASSN FOR/AID INT/TRADE EQUILIB NAT/LISM PWR 20. PAGE 141 H2820
ECO/UNDEV DIPLOM REGION

S67
AMERASINGHE C.F.,"SOME LEGAL PROBLEMS OF STATE TRADING IN SOUTHEAST ASIA." PROB/SOLV ADJUD CONTROL CT/SYS GP/REL 20. PAGE 6 H0120
INT/TRADE NAT/G INT/LAW PRIVIL

S67
ANTHEM T.,"CYPRUS* WHAT NOW?" CYPRUS GREECE TURKEY NAT/G BUDGET MAJORITY 20 NATO. PAGE 7 H0143
DIPLOM COERCE INT/TRADE ADJUD

S67
BOSHER J.F.,"GOVERNMENT AND PRIVATE INTERESTS IN NEW FRANCE." CANADA FRANCE INDUS LG/CO SML/CO CAP/ISM INT/TRADE COLONIAL GP/REL...HIST/WRIT 17/18. PAGE 19 H0381
NAT/G FINAN ADMIN CONTROL

S67
CHU-YUAN CHENG,"THE CULTURAL REVOLUTION AND CHINA'S ECONOMY." CHINA/COM AGRI DIST/IND INDUS MARKET NAT/G WORKER PLAN INT/TRADE DOMIN DEMAND PRODUC ...CHARTS 20 MAO. PAGE 30 H0600
ECO/DEV ECO/TAC REV SOCISM

S67
FRENCH D.S.,"DOES THE U.S. EXPLOIT THE DEVELOPING NATIONS?" INT/ORG NAT/G CAP/ISM BAL/PAY WEALTH POLICY. PAGE 53 H1057
ECO/UNDEV INT/TRADE ECO/TAC COLONIAL

S67
INDER S.,"AFTER THE CORONATION." CONSTN ECO/UNDEV EX/STRUC LEGIS INT/TRADE CONTROL SOVEREIGN ...TIME/SEQ 20 TONGA COMMONWLTH INAUGURATE. PAGE 76 H1527
CHIEF NAT/G POLICY

S67
SANCHEZ J.D.,"DESARROLLO ECONOMICO Y FUTURO DE COLOMBIA." L/A+17C AGRI EXTR/IND FINAN INDUS MARKET INT/TRADE CONTROL...STAT TREND COLOMB. PAGE 137 H2748
ECO/UNDEV FUT NAT/G ECO/TAC

S67
SAVELYEV N.,"MONOPOLY DRIVE IN INDIA." INDIA INDUS NAT/G INT/TRADE NEUTRAL SANCTION GOV/REL CONSERVE ...MARXIST 20. PAGE 138 H2759
ECO/UNDEV POL/PAR ECO/TAC CONTROL

C67
GEHLEN M.P.,"THE POLITICS OF COEXISTENCE: SOVIET METHODS AND MOTIVES." COM USSR NAT/G INT/TRADE EDU/PROP ARMS/CONT DETER KNOWL...CHARTS IDEA/COMP 20 COLD/WAR. PAGE 55 H1108
BIBLIOG PEACE DIPLOM MARXISM

L68
CURRENT HISTORY,"DE GAULLE'S FRANCE." FRANCE MOD/EUR WOR+45 INDUS MARKET INT/ORG BUDGET DIPLOM AUTHORIT DRIVE...GOV/COMP IDEA/COMP 20 DEGAULLE/C EEC. PAGE 36 H0723
INT/TRADE PERSON LEAD NAT/LISM

S68
GUZZARDI W.,"THE DECLINE OF THE STERLING CLUB." UK WOR+45 NAT/G PLAN DIPLOM INT/TRADE AGREE CONSEN EQUILIB SOVEREIGN...POLICY NEW/IDEA 20 COMMONWLTH GOLD/STAND. PAGE 63 H1259
FINAN ECO/TAC WEALTH NAT/COMP

S68
LUKASZEWSKI J.,"WESTERN INTEGRATION AND THE PEOPLE'S DEMOCRACIES." USSR ELITES ECO/DEV NAT/G VOL/ASSN INT/TRADE AGREE REV FEDERAL WEALTH SOCISM ...NAT/COMP SOC/INTEG 20 EEC. PAGE 99 H1977
DIPLOM INT/ORG COM REGION

S68
VERAX,"L'EUROPE ET LA FRANCE SUR LA SELLETTE." FRANCE UK NAT/G CHIEF DIPLOM EDU/PROP GP/REL 20 EEC DEGAULLE/C. PAGE 162 H3242
INT/TRADE INT/ORG POLICY ECO/TAC

B82
CUNNINGHAM W.,THE GROWTH OF ENGLISH INDUSTRY AND COMMERCE. FUT UK FINAN NAT/G CAP/ISM...POLICY 20 MERCANTLST CHRISTIAN POPE. PAGE 36 H0721
INDUS INT/TRADE SML/CO CONSERVE

B86
MAS LATRIE L.,RELATIONS ET COMMERCE DE L'AFRIQUE SEPTENTRIONALE OU MAGREB AVEC LES NATIONS CHRETIENNES AU MOYEN AGE. CULTURE CHIEF FORCES WAR ...SOC CENSUS TREATY 10/16. PAGE 104 H2084
ISLAM SECT DIPLOM INT/TRADE

L95
BELSHAW C.S.,"IN SEARCH OF WEALTH; STUDY OF EMERGENCE OF COMMERCIAL OPERA TIONS IN MELANESIAN SOCIETY OF SOUTHEASTERN PAPUA." S/ASIA CULTURE KIN ECO/TAC DEMAND INCOME 20 MELANESIA PAPUA. PAGE 14 H0272
INT/TRADE ECO/UNDEV METH/COMP SOCIETY

B96
DE VATTEL E.,THE LAW OF NATIONS. AGRI FINAN CHIEF DIPLOM INT/TRADE AGREE OWN ALL/VALS MORAL ORD/FREE SOVEREIGN...GEN/LAWS 18 NATURL/LAW WOLFF/C. PAGE 39 H0774
LAW CONCPT NAT/G INT/LAW

B96
SCHMOLLER G.,THE MERCANTILE SYSTEM AND ITS HISTORICAL SIGNIFICANCE: ILLUSTRATED CHIEFLY FROM PRUSSIAN HISTORY (TRANS.). PRUSSIA CULTURE INDUS KIN MUNIC NAT/G PROVS OP/RES ECO/TAC INT/TRADE SUPEGO PWR WEALTH 19 MERCANTLST. PAGE 139 H2790
GEN/METH INGP/REL CONCPT

B99
KINGSLEY M.H.,WEST AFRICAN STUDIES. GHANA NIGERIA SIER/LEONE LAW EXTR/IND SECT DIPLOM INT/TRADE DOMIN RACE/REL OWN HEALTH...SOC 19. PAGE 86 H1717
AFR HEREDITY COLONIAL CULTURE

INTEGRATION....SEE NEGRO, SOUTH/US, RACE/REL, SOC/INTEG, CIV/RIGHTS, DISCRIM, ISOLAT, SCHOOL, STRANGE

INTEGRATION, POLITICAL+ECONOMIC....SEE REGION+INT/ORG+ VOL/ASSN+CENTRAL

INTELL....INTELLIGENTSIA

N
AVTOREFERATY DISSERTATSII. USSR INTELL ACADEM NAT/G DIPLOM GOV/REL KNOWL CONCPT. PAGE 2 H0029
BIBLIOG MARXISM MARXIST COM

N
INTERNATIONAL CENTRE AFRICAN,BULLETIN OF INFORMATION ON THESES AND STUDIES IN PROGRESS OR PROPOSED. LAW CULTURE FINAN INDUS LABOR TEC/DEV EDU/PROP...GEOG SOC NAT/COMP 20. PAGE 78 H1554 BIBLIOG/A ACT/RES ACADEM INTELL

B11
PHILLIPSON C.,THE INTERNATIONAL LAW AND CUSTOM OF ANCIENT GREECE AND ROME. MEDIT-7 UNIV INTELL SOCIETY STRUCT NAT/G LEGIS EXEC PERSON...CONCPT OBS CON/ANAL ROM/EMP. PAGE 125 H2504 INT/ORG LAW INT/LAW

N19
MAO TSE-TUNG,ON SOME IMPORTANT PROBLEMS OF THE PARTY'S PRESENT POLICY. CHINA/COM CONSTN ELITES INTELL AGRI DOMIN EDU/PROP REV REPRESENT GP/REL OWN PEACE ORD/FREE 20 COM/PARTY. PAGE 102 H2044 POLICY NAT/G CHIEF LEGIT

B23
FRANK T.,A HISTORY OF ROME. MEDIT-7 INTELL SOCIETY LOC/G NAT/G POL/PAR FORCES LEGIS DOMIN LEGIT ALL/VALS...POLICY CONCPT TIME/SEQ GEN/LAWS ROM/EMP ROM/EMP. PAGE 53 H1050 EXEC STRUCT ELITES

B26
HOCKING W.E.,PRESENT STATUS OF THE PHILOSOPHY OF LAW AND OF RIGHTS. UNIV CULTURE INTELL SOCIETY NAT/G CREATE LEGIT SANCTION ALL/VALS SOC/INTEG 18/20. PAGE 72 H1442 JURID PHIL/SCI ORD/FREE

B28
BARKER E.,POLITICAL THOUGHT IN ENGLAND: FROM HERBERT SPENCER TO THE PRESENT DAY. UK ALL/IDEOS ...PHIL/SCI 19/20 SPENCER/H GREEN/TH BENTHAM/J MAITLAND/F. PAGE 11 H0217 INTELL GEN/LAWS IDEA/COMP

B28
HOLDSWORTH W.S.,THE HISTORIANS OF ANGLO-AMERICAN LAW. UK USA-45 INTELL LEGIS RESPECT...BIOG NAT/COMP 17/20 COMMON/LAW. PAGE 72 H1450 HIST/WRIT LAW JURID

C33
MURET C.T.,"FRENCH ROYALIST DOCTRINES SINCE THE REVOLUTION." FRANCE CONSTN NAT/G SECT ADMIN LEAD SOVEREIGN...POLICY BIOG IDEA/COMP BIBLIOG 18/20. PAGE 115 H2295 POL/PAR ATTIT INTELL CONSERVE

S35
RADCLIFFE-BROWN A.R.,"ON THE CONCEPT OF FUNCTION IN SOCIAL SCIENCE" (BMR)" UNIV CULTURE INTELL ...METH/CNCPT IDEA/COMP 20. PAGE 129 H2577 STRUCT SOCIETY CONCPT GEN/LAWS

B37
BERDYAEV N.,THE ORIGIN OF RUSSIAN COMMUNISM. MOD/EUR RUSSIA USSR INTELL SECT REV...ANARCH HUM 19/20 ORTHO/RUSS COM/PARTY CHRISTIAN. PAGE 15 H0294 MARXISM NAT/LISM CULTURE ATTIT

B37
PARSONS T.,THE STRUCTURE OF SOCIAL ACTION. UNIV INTELL SOCIETY INDUS MARKET ECO/TAC ROUTINE CHOOSE ALL/VALS...CONCPT OBS BIOG TREND GEN/LAWS 20. PAGE 124 H2471 CULTURE ATTIT CAP/ISM

B38
JESSOP T.E.,A BIBLIOGRAPHY OF DAVID HUME AND OF SCOTTISH PHILOSOPHY FROM FRANCIS HUTCHESON TO LORD BALFOUR. UK INTELL NAT/G ATTIT...CONCPT 17/20 HUME/D CMN/WLTH. PAGE 81 H1615 BIBLIOG EPIST PERCEPT BIOG

S38
LUNDBERG G.A.,"THE CONCEPT OF LAW IN THE SOCIAL SCIENCES"(BMR)" CULTURE INTELL SOCIETY STRUCT CREATE...NEW/IDEA 20. PAGE 99 H1978 EPIST GEN/LAWS CONCPT PHIL/SCI

B39
DEWEY J.,FREEDOM AND CULTURE. FUT CONSTN CULTURE INTELL NAT/G CONSULT PLAN CHOOSE ATTIT...CONCPT GEN/METH 20. PAGE 40 H0810 SOCIETY CREATE

B41
GILMORE M.P.,ARGUMENT FROM ROMAN LAW IN POLITICAL THOUGHT, 1200-1600. INTELL LICENSE CONTROL CT/SYS GOV/REL PRIVIL PWR...IDEA/COMP BIBLIOG 13/16. PAGE 56 H1130 JURID LAW CONCPT NAT/G

B41
HAYAKAWA S.I.,LANGUAGE IN ACTION. CULTURE INTELL SOCIETY KNOWL...METH/CNCPT LING LOG RECORD STERTYP GEN/METH TOT/POP 20. PAGE 68 H1366 EDU/PROP SOC

B42
BAYNES N.H.,INTELLECTUAL LIBERTY AND TOTALITARIAN CLAIMS. EUR+WWI GERMANY ITALY INTELL POL/PAR CIVMIL/REL NAT/LISM SOCISM CONCPT. PAGE 12 H0245 KNOWL FASCISM EDU/PROP ACADEM

B42
CRAIG A.,ABOVE ALL LIBERTIES. FRANCE UK USA-45 LAW CONSTN CULTURE INTELL NAT/G SECT JUDGE...IDEA/COMP BIBLIOG 18/20. PAGE 35 H0692 ORD/FREE MORAL WRITING EDU/PROP

C42
CRAIG A.,"ABOVE ALL LIBERTIES." FRANCE UK LAW CULTURE INTELL SECT ORD/FREE 18/20. PAGE 35 H0693 BIBLIOG/A EDU/PROP WRITING MORAL

B47
JURJI E.J.,THE GREAT RELIGIONS OF THE MODERN WORLD. CULTURE INTELL SOCIETY INT/ORG CONSULT CHOOSE ATTIT DRIVE PERSON RIGID/FLEX...HUM CONCPT OBS BIOG HIST/WRIT TREND GEN/LAWS 20 WORSHIP. PAGE 82 H1643 UNIV SECT

B49
SINGER K.,THE IDEA OF CONFLICT. UNIV INTELL INT/ORG NAT/G PLAN ROUTINE ATTIT DRIVE ALL/VALS...POLICY CONCPT TIME/SEQ. PAGE 144 H2882 ACT/RES SOC

B50
GOFF F.R.,FIFTEENTH CENTURY BOOKS IN THE LIBRARY OF CONGRESS. CHRIST-17C GERMANY ITALY CULTURE INTELL SECT CREATE...PHIL/SCI CONCPT CLASSIF BIOG TIME/SEQ 15. PAGE 58 H1153 BIBLIOG KNOWL HUM

B50
MACIVER R.M.,GREAT EXPRESSIONS OF HUMAN RIGHTS. LAW CONSTN CULTURE INTELL SOCIETY R+D INT/ORG ATTIT DRIVE...JURID OBS HIST/WRIT GEN/LAWS. PAGE 100 H1999 UNIV CONCPT

B50
ORTON W.A.,THE ECONOMIC ROLE OF THE STATE. INTELL ECO/UNDEV PLAN CONTROL PWR SOVEREIGN...POLICY 17/20. PAGE 122 H2431 ECO/DEV NAT/G ECO/TAC ORD/FREE

B50
SCHUMPETER J.A.,CAPITALISM, SOCIALISM, AND DEMOCRACY (3RD ED.). USA-45 USSR WOR+45 WOR-45 INTELL ECO/DEV ECO/UNDEV ECO/TAC WAR PRODUC ORD/FREE...MGT SOC 20 MARX/KARL. PAGE 140 H2804 SOCIALIST CAP/ISM MARXISM IDEA/COMP

B51
LOOS W.A.,RELIGIOUS FAITH AND WORLD CULTURE. INTELL SOCIETY SECT EDU/PROP ROUTINE ATTIT PERSON ALL/VALS MORAL...CONCPT GEN/LAWS VAL/FREE. PAGE 98 H1964 UNIV CULTURE PEACE

B51
WEBSTER C.,THE FOREIGN POLICY OF PALMERSTON - 1830 TO 1841. MOD/EUR UK LAW CONSTN INTELL SOCIETY STRUCT NAT/G FORCES TOP/EX CREATE BAL/PWR PWR 19. PAGE 166 H3323 ADMIN PERSON DIPLOM

S51
MACRAE D.G.,"THE BOLSHEVIK IDEOLOGY; THE INTELLECTUAL AND EMOTIONAL FACTORS IN COMMUNIST AFFILIATION" (BMR)" COM LEAD REV ATTIT ORD/FREE ...SOC CON/ANAL 20 BOLSHEVISM. PAGE 100 H2008 MARXISM INTELL PHIL/SCI SECT

C51
HAMMOND M.,"CITY-STATE AND WORLD STATE." CONSTN INTELL LOC/G LEGIT CENTRAL RATIONAL BIBLIOG. PAGE 65 H1308 NAT/G ATTIT REGION MEDIT-7

B52
BENTHAM A.,HANDBOOK OF POLITICAL FALLACIES. FUT MOD/EUR LAW INTELL LOC/G MUNIC NAT/G DELIB/GP LEGIS CREATE EDU/PROP CT/SYS ATTIT RIGID/FLEX KNOWL PWR ...RELATIV PSY SOC CONCPT SELF/OBS TREND STERTYP TOT/POP. PAGE 14 H0286 POL/PAR

B52
LEYS W.,ETHICS FOR POLICY DECISIONS. INTELL NAT/G CONSULT PLAN DOMIN EDU/PROP LEGIT COERCE KNOWL MORAL PWR...HUM GEN/LAWS. PAGE 96 H1920 ACT/RES POLICY

B52
SCHATTSCHNEIDER E.E.,A GUIDE TO THE STUDY OF PUBLIC AFFAIRS. LAW LOC/G NAT/G LEGIS BUDGET PRESS ADMIN LOBBY...JURID CHARTS 20. PAGE 139 H2775 ACT/RES INTELL ACADEM METH/COMP

S52
KECSKEMETI P.,"THE 'POLICY SCIENCES': ASPIRATION AND OUTLOOK." UNIV CULTURE INTELL SOCIETY STRUCT EDU/PROP ATTIT PERCEPT RIGID/FLEX KNOWL...PHIL/SCI METH/CNCPT OBS 20. PAGE 84 H1674 CREATE NEW/IDEA

C52
EBENSTEIN W.,"INTRODUCTION TO POLITICAL PHILOSOPHY." COM CONSTN INTELL CONTROL PERSON NEW/LIB SOCISM...PSY GEN/LAWS BIBLIOG/A. PAGE 44 H0883 ALL/IDEOS PHIL/SCI IDEA/COMP NAT/G

S53
BAUER R.A.,"WORD-OF-MOUTH COMMUNICATION IN THE SOVIET UNION." COM INTELL SOCIETY LABOR ATTIT KNOWL ...INT QU SAMP CHARTS 20. PAGE 12 H0239 CULTURE USSR

B54
FRIEDRICH C.J.,TOTALITARIAN DICTATORSHIP AND AUTOCRACY. COM EUR+WWI GERMANY ITALY USSR INTELL ECO/DEV NAT/G POL/PAR FORCES TOP/EX ECO/TAC EDU/PROP LEGIT COERCE ATTIT ORD/FREE PWR FASCISM ...CONCPT TIME/SEQ GEN/LAWS NAZI 20. PAGE 53 H1068 SOCIETY DOMIN TOTALISM

B54
LENIN V.I.,SELECTED WORKS (12 VOLS.). USSR INTELL SOCIETY STRATA STRUCT NAT/G POL/PAR WORKER CAP/ISM REV WAR...MARXIST PHIL/SCI 20 MARX/KARL LENIN/VI. PAGE 94 H1880 COM MARXISM

B54
LEWIS E.,MEDIEVAL POLITICAL IDEAS. LAW CULTURE SOCIETY ECO/UNDEV NAT/G SECT GOV/REL ATTIT ...BIBLIOG/A T 11/15. PAGE 96 H1913 CHRIST-17C IDEA/COMP INTELL CONCPT

B54
SCHRAMM W.,THE PROCESS AND EFFECTS OF MASS COMMUNICATION. CULTURE INTELL SOCIETY COM/IND DRIVE PERCEPT PERSON RIGID/FLEX KNOWL...PSY SOC CONCPT CHARTS. PAGE 140 H2800 ATTIT EDU/PROP

S54
MIT CENTER INTERNATIONAL STU,"A PLAN OF RESEARCH IN R+D

INTERNATIONAL COMMUNICATION: A REPORT." UNIV CULTURE INTELL SOCIETY ACT/RES ALL/VALS...CONCPT METH/CNCPT. PAGE 111 H2227 — STYLE

B55
KOHN H.,THE MIND OF MODERN RUSSIA. COM MOD/EUR USSR SOCIETY NAT/G SECT FORCES TOP/EX COERCE TOTALISM DRIVE RIGID/FLEX PWR SOVEREIGN...CONCPT TIME/SEQ WORK. PAGE 87 H1742 — INTELL GEN/LAWS SOCISM RUSSIA

B55
SHUMSKY A.,THE CLASH OF CULTURES IN ISRAEL: A PROBLEM FOR EDUCATION. ISRAEL CULTURE INTELL NAT/G ACT/RES DISCRIM AGE/Y...BIBLIOG 20 JEWS. PAGE 143 H2867 — GP/REL EDU/PROP SCHOOL AGE/C

L55
ROSTOW W.W.,"RUSSIA AND CHINA UNDER COMMUNISM." CHINA/COM USSR INTELL STRUCT INT/ORG NAT/G POL/PAR TOP/EX ACT/RES PLAN ADMIN ATTIT ALL/VALS MARXISM ...CONCPT OBS TIME/SEQ TREND GOV/COMP VAL/FREE 20. PAGE 134 H2689 — COM ASIA

B56
PADMORE G.,PAN-AFRICANISM OR COMMUNISM. AFR FUT NIGERIA INTELL NAT/G COLONIAL FEDERAL ATTIT DRIVE PWR RESPECT WEALTH MARXISM...CONCPT AUD/VIS STERTYP 20. PAGE 122 H2440 — POL/PAR NAT/LISM

B56
RIESENBERG P.N.,INALIENABILITY OF SOVEREIGNTY IN MEDIEVAL POLITICAL THOUGHT. CHRIST-17C INTELL NAT/G SECT CHIEF LEGIS SANCTION AUTHORIT ORD/FREE CONSERVE...IDEA/COMP BIBLIOG 12/16. PAGE 131 H2627 — SOVEREIGN ATTIT

B56
VUCINICH A.,THE SOVIET ACADEMY OF SCIENCES. USSR STRUCT ACADEM NAT/G EDU/PROP ADMIN LEAD ROLE ...BIBLIOG 20 ACADEM/SCI. PAGE 164 H3280 — PHIL/SCI CREATE INTELL PROF/ORG

B57
ARON R.,THE OPIUM OF THE INTELLECTUALS (TRANS. BY TERENCE KILMARTIN). FRANCE USSR WOR+45 CULTURE POL/PAR PLAN DOMIN EDU/PROP REV ATTIT ORD/FREE ...IDEA/COMP METH/COMP NAT/COMP 20 COM/PARTY. PAGE 8 H0169 — INTELL UTOPIA MYTH MARXISM

B57
BULLOCK A.,THE LIBERAL TRADITION FROM FOX TO KEYNES. UK CULTURE INTELL CREATE WRITING COLONIAL PERS/REL ATTIT ORD/FREE...POLICY OLD/LIB TRADIT CONCPT 18/20 CHURCHLL/W MILL/JS KEYNES/JM ASQUITH/HH. PAGE 23 H0469 — ANTHOL DEBATE LAISSEZ

B57
HERNANDEZ-ARREGU J.,IMPERIALISMO Y CULTURA (LA POLITICA EN LA INTELIGENCIA ARGENTINA). L/A+17C CULTURE ELITES WRITING COLONIAL CROWD ATTIT FASCISM MARXISM SOCISM...BIOG IDEA/COMP 20 ARGEN PERON/JUAN COM/PARTY. PAGE 70 H1403 — INTELL CREATE ART/METH HUM

B57
IKE N.,JAPANESE POLITICS. INTELL STRUCT AGRI INDUS FAM KIN LABOR PRESS CHOOSE ATTIT...DECISION BIBLIOG 19/20 CHINJAP. PAGE 76 H1523 — NAT/G ADMIN POL/PAR CULTURE

B57
LAQUER W.Z.,COMMUNISM AND NATIONALISM IN THE MIDDLE EAST. ELITES INTELL STRATA NAT/G POL/PAR SECT VOL/ASSN TOP/EX DOMIN LEGIT REGION COERCE ATTIT PERSON PWR...CONCPT HIST/WRIT TIME/SEQ TREND GEN/LAWS VAL/FREE. PAGE 91 H1817 — ISLAM NAT/LISM

L57
BENDIX R.,"POLITICAL SOCIOLOGY." CULTURE INTELL LABOR POL/PAR SECT LEGIS EDU/PROP ADMIN CHOOSE CIVMIL/REL ATTIT...IDEA/COMP 20. PAGE 14 H0274 — BIBLIOG/A ACT/RES SOC

N57
JENNINGS W.I.,NATIONALISM, COLONIALISM, AND NEUTRALISM (PAMPHLET). ASIA INDIA S/ASIA UK INTELL ACADEM POL/PAR 20. PAGE 81 H1611 — NAT/LISM COLONIAL NEUTRAL ATTIT

B58
CRAIG G.A.,FROM BISMARCK TO ADENAUER: ASPECTS OF GERMAN STATECRAFT. GERMANY INTELL FORCES ECO/TAC CONFER COERCE WAR GP/REL ORD/FREE PWR CONSERVE 19/20 BISMARCK/O ADENAUER/K. PAGE 35 H0695 — DIPLOM LEAD NAT/G

B58
JOHNSON J.J.,POLITICAL CHANGE IN LATIN AMERICA: THE EMERGENCE OF THE MIDDLE SECTORS. INTELL STRATA STRUCT ECO/UNDEV MUNIC TEC/DEV LEAD REV...DECISION TREND GOV/COMP BIBLIOG/A 20. PAGE 81 H1621 — L/A+17C ELITES GP/REL DOMIN

B58
KURL S.,ESTONIA: A SELECTED BIBLIOGRAPHY. USSR ESTONIA LAW INTELL SECT...ART/METH GEOG HUM SOC 20. PAGE 89 H1784 — BIBLIOG CULTURE NAT/G

B58
LERNER D.,THE PASSING OF TRADITIONAL SOCIETY: MODERNIZING THE MIDDLE EAST. IRAN ISLAM LEBANON SYRIA TURKEY UAR CULTURE INTELL STRATA KIN NAT/G NEIGH SECT EDU/PROP ATTIT PERSON...MYTH OBS 20. PAGE 95 H1888 — ECO/UNDEV RIGID/FLEX

B59
EPSTEIN F.T.,EAST GERMANY: A SELECTED BIBLIOGRAPHY (PAMPHLET). COM GERMANY/E LAW AGRI FINAN INDUS LABOR POL/PAR EDU/PROP ADMIN AGE/Y 20. PAGE 47 H0932 — BIBLIOG/A INTELL MARXISM NAT/G

B59
ISRAEL J.,THE CHINESE STUDENT MOVEMENT, 1927-1937; A BIBLIOGRAPHICAL ESSAY BASED ON THE RESOURCES OF THE HOOVER INSTITUTION. ASIA INTELL NAT/G EDU/PROP 20. PAGE 79 H1571 — BIBLIOG/A ACADEM ATTIT

B59
JACOBS N.,CULTURE FOR THE MILLIONS? INTELL SOCIETY NAT/G...POLICY SOC OBS ANTHOL 20. PAGE 79 H1579 — CULTURE COM/IND PERF/ART CONCPT

B59
LANDAUER C.,EUROPEAN SOCIALISM (2 VOLS.). COM EUR+WWI MOD/EUR INTELL INDUS REV WAR...MAJORIT IDEA/COMP BIBLIOG 19/20 HITLER/A. PAGE 90 H1805 — SOCISM NAT/COMP LABOR MARXISM

B59
WARNER W.L.,THE LIVING AND THE DEAD: A STUDY OF SYMBOLIC LIFE OF AMERICANS. INTELL KIN DEATH ALL/VALS ALL/IDEOS...CONCPT MYTH LING OBS/ENVIR CHARTS BIBLIOG WORSHIP 18/20. PAGE 165 H3311 — CULTURE SOC TIME/SEQ IDEA/COMP

L59
JANIS I.L.,"DECISIONAL CONFLICT: A THEORETICAL ANALYSIS." INTELL NAT/G POL/PAR DELIB/GP LEGIS TOP/EX PLAN...DECISION CONGRESS NAZI 20 WWI. PAGE 80 H1590 — ACT/RES PSY DIPLOM

S59
ZAUBERMAN A.,"SOVIET BLOC ECONOMIC INTEGRATION." COM CULTURE INTELL ECO/DEV INDUS TOP/EX ACT/RES PLAN ECO/TAC INT/TRADE ROUTINE CHOOSE ATTIT ...TIME/SEQ 20. PAGE 172 H3452 — MARKET INT/ORG USSR TOTALISM

C59
KORNHAUSER W.,"THE POLITICS OF MASS SOCIETY." COM CULTURE ELITES INTELL STRATA POL/PAR ATTIT...SOC CHARTS GEN/LAWS BIBLIOG 20. PAGE 88 H1757 — CROWD PLURISM CONSTN SOCIETY

B60
KOHN H.,PAN-SLAVISM: ITS HISTORY AND IDEOLOGY. COM CZECHOSLVK EUR+WWI MOD/EUR USSR YUGOSLAVIA CULTURE ELITES INTELL KIN NAT/G EDU/PROP DRIVE SOVEREIGN ...HUM PHIL/SCI MYTH HIST/WRIT 19/20. PAGE 87 H1745 — ATTIT CONCPT NAT/LISM

B60
MCCLOSKY H.,THE SOVIET DICTATORSHIP. FUT CONSTN CULTURE INTELL SOCIETY POL/PAR SECT VOL/ASSN FORCES PLAN TEC/DEV DOMIN EDU/PROP COERCE PWR MARXISM ...POLICY CONCPT MYTH STERTYP 20. PAGE 106 H2127 — COM NAT/G TOTALISM USSR

B60
SCHAPIRO L.,THE COMMUNIST PARTY OF THE SOVIET UNION. COM LAW SOCIETY STRATA STRUCT ECO/DEV LABOR NAT/G POL/PAR CREATE DOMIN EDU/PROP COERCE TOTALISM MARXISM...POLICY CONCPT MYTH TIME/SEQ WORK TOT/POP 20 LENIN/VI STALIN/J. PAGE 139 H2772 — INTELL PWR USSR

L60
KAPLAN M.A.,"COMMUNIST COUP IN CZECHOSLOVAKIA." COM EUR+WWI INTELL LABOR LOC/G NAT/G POL/PAR FORCES EDU/PROP EXEC MARXISM...TIME/SEQ HYPO/EXP 20. PAGE 83 H1659 — STRUCT COERCE CZECHOSLVK

S60
ARENDT H.,"SOCIETY AND CULTURE." FUT CULTURE INTELL STRATA EDU/PROP ATTIT PERSON KNOWL...ART/METH HUM 20. PAGE 8 H0161 — SOCIETY CREATE

S60
EMERSON R.,"THE EROSION OF DEMOCRACY." AFR FUT LAW CULTURE INTELL SOCIETY ECO/UNDEV FAM LOC/G NAT/G FORCES PLAN TEC/DEV ECO/TAC ADMIN CT/SYS ATTIT ORD/FREE PWR...SOCIALIST SOC CONCPT STAND/INT TIME/SEQ WORK 20. PAGE 46 H0918 — S/ASIA POL/PAR

S60
MURPHEY R.,"ECONOMIC CONFLICTS IN SOUTH ASIA." ASIA CULTURE INTELL ECO/TAC REGION ATTIT DRIVE KNOWL ...METH/CNCPT TIME/SEQ STERTYP TOT/POP VAL/FREE 20. PAGE 115 H2296 — S/ASIA ECO/UNDEV

S60
SHILS E.,"THE INTELLECTUALS IN THE POLITICAL DEVELOPMENT OF THE NEW STATES." AFR ASIA S/ASIA ELITES LOC/G NAT/G CONSULT EX/STRUC CREATE PLAN ECO/TAC DOMIN LEGIT DRIVE PWR...TRADIT CONCPT STERTYP GEN/LAWS 20. PAGE 143 H2861 — POL/PAR INTELL NAT/LISM

C60
BOGARDUS E.S.,"THE DEVELOPMENT OF SOCIAL THOUGHT." SOCIETY PERSON KNOWL...EPIST CONCPT BIBLIOG T. PAGE 18 H0365 — INTELL CULTURE IDEA/COMP GP/COMP

B61
LUNDBERG G.A.,CAN SCIENCE SAVE US. UNIV CULTURE INTELL SOCIETY ECO/DEV R+D PLAN EDU/PROP ROUTINE CHOOSE ATTIT PERCEPT ALL/VALS...TREND 20. PAGE 99 H1979 — ACT/RES CONCPT TOTALISM

B61
MARVICK D.,POLITICAL DECISION-MAKERS. INTELL STRATA NAT/G POL/PAR EX/STRUC LEGIS DOMIN EDU/PROP ATTIT PERSON PWR...PSY STAT OBS CONT/OBS STAND/INT UNPLAN/INT TIME/SEQ CHARTS STERTYP VAL/FREE. PAGE 104 H2073 — TOP/EX BIOG ELITES

B61
PAZ O.,THE LABYRINTH OF SOLITUDE; LIFE AND THOUGHT — CULTURE

IN MEXICO (TRANS. BY LYSANDER KEMP). INTELL COLONIAL REV...PSY SOC TIME/SEQ 16/20 MEXIC/AMER. PAGE 124 H2480 — PERSON PERS/REL SOCIETY

B61
SAFRAN M.,EGYPT IN SEARCH OF POLITICAL COMMUNITY: AN ANALYSIS OF THE INTELLECTUAL AND POLITICAL EVOLUTION OF EGYPT, 1804-1952. ISLAM NAT/G SECT EDU/PROP COERCE ATTIT DRIVE KNOWL PWR...TIME/SEQ 20. PAGE 137 H2729 — INTELL NAT/LISM UAR

L61
LEVINE R.A.,"THE ANTHROPOLOGY OF CONFLICT." FUT CULTURE INTELL FAM INT/ORG LG/CO SML/CO ATTIT KNOWL ...METH/CNCPT VAL/FREE 20. PAGE 95 H1905 — SOCIETY ACT/RES

S61
SCHECHTMAN J.B.,"MINORITIES IN THE MIDDLE EAST." ISLAM INTELL SOCIETY STRATA KIN NAT/G VOL/ASSN EDU/PROP REGION GP/REL DISCRIM ATTIT BIO/SOC DISPL PERSON ALL/VALS...PSY SOC OBS SAMP GEN/LAWS 20. PAGE 139 H2776 — SECT CULTURE RACE/REL

B62
BRETTON H.L.,POWER AND STABILITY IN NIGERIA: THE POLITICS OF DECOLONIZATION. AFR CONSTN INTELL ECO/UNDEV COM/IND KIN NAT/G POL/PAR PROVS VOL/ASSN LEGIS DOMIN EDU/PROP LEGIT EXEC ROUTINE CHOOSE NAT/LISM ATTIT PERCEPT ALL/VALS. PAGE 20 H0411 — CULTURE OBS NIGERIA

B62
FEIT E.,SOUTH AFRICA, THE DYNAMICS OF THE AFRICAN NATIONAL CONGRESS. AFR SOUTH/AFR LAW INTELL STRATA KIN NAT/G POL/PAR ECO/TAC DOMIN RISK COERCE 20 NEGRO. PAGE 49 H0984 — RACE/REL ELITES CONTROL STRUCT

B62
HO PING-TI,THE LADDER OF SUCCESS IN IMPERIAL CHINA: ASPECTS OF SOCIAL MOBILITY, 1368-1911. INTELL STRATA FAM KIN MUNIC NAT/G PROVS SCHOOL DELIB/GP DOMIN EDU/PROP ADMIN ROUTINE PERSON ALL/VALS...SOC STAT BIOG HIST/WRIT TIME/SEQ VAL/FREE. PAGE 71 H1431 — ASIA CULTURE

B62
HOOK S.,THE PARADOXES OF FREEDOM. UNIV CONSTN INTELL LEGIS CONTROL REV CHOOSE SUPEGO...POLICY JURID IDEA/COMP 19/20 CIV/RIGHTS. PAGE 73 H1461 — CONCPT MAJORIT ORD/FREE ALL/VALS

B62
HUCKER C.O.,CHINA: A CRITICAL BIBLIOGRAPHY (PAMPHLET). ASIA STRUCT AGRI FINAN INDUS HABITAT MARXISM...EPIST HUM. PAGE 74 H1487 — BIBLIOG/A CULTURE INTELL SOCIETY

B62
INSTITUTE FOR STUDY OF USSR,YOUTH IN FERMENT. INTELL NAT/G PERF/ART POL/PAR SCHOOL VOL/ASSN FORCES EDU/PROP ATTIT DRIVE PERCEPT HEALTH KNOWL MORAL ORD/FREE RESPECT...SOC OBS HIST/WRIT VAL/FREE. PAGE 77 H1537 — COM CULTURE USSR

B62
KINDERSLEY R.,THE FIRST RUSSIAN REVISIONISTS. COM USSR LAW ELITES INTELL NAT/G LEGIS ECO/TAC EDU/PROP CONTROL LEAD GP/REL SOCISM 19/20 MARX/KARL BOLSHEVISM. PAGE 86 H1712 — CONSTN MARXISM POPULISM BIOG

B62
LEGUM C.,PAN-AFRICANISM: A SHORT POLITICAL GUIDE. ISLAM CULTURE INTELL ECO/DEV NAT/G POL/PAR DELIB/GP PLAN EDU/PROP FEDERAL NAT/LISM ATTIT DRIVE PERSON ...RECORD TIME/SEQ CHARTS STERTYP 20. PAGE 93 H1861 — AFR CONCPT

B62
MANSUR F.,PROCESS OF INDEPENDENCE. GHANA INDIA INDONESIA PAKISTAN CONSTN ELITES INTELL STRUCT ACADEM NAT/G REV PWR 20. PAGE 102 H2043 — NAT/COMP POL/PAR SOVEREIGN COLONIAL

B62
MARTINDALE D.,SOCIAL LIFE AND CULTURAL CHANGE. GP/REL...PHIL/SCI SOC CONCPT. PAGE 103 H2065 — INTELL CULTURE ORD/FREE STRUCT

B62
MEHNERT K.,SOVIET MAN AND HIS WORLD. COM USSR INTELL FAM WORKER PLAN EDU/PROP REV PRODUC MARXISM ...SOC TREND SOC/INTEG 20 LENIN/VI STALIN/J KHRUSH/N. PAGE 108 H2162 — SOCIETY CULTURE ECO/DEV

L62
NOLTE E.,"ZUR PHANOMENOLOGIE DES FASCHIMUS." EUR+WWI GERMANY ITALY TURKEY INTELL NAT/G CHIEF CONSULT FORCES CREATE DOMIN EDU/PROP COERCE WAR CHOOSE DRIVE FASCISM...PSY CONCPT MYTH GEN/METH LEAGUE/NAT NAZI 20. PAGE 118 H2367 — ATTIT PWR

S62
GUETZKOW H.,"THE POTENTIAL OF CASE STUDY IN ANALYZING INTERNATIONAL CONFLICT." EUR+WWI FUT GERMANY INTELL SOCIETY STRUCT INT/ORG LOC/G NAT/G CONSULT CREATE PLAN CHOOSE ATTIT RIGID/FLEX ...POLICY SAAR 20. PAGE 62 H1246 — EDU/PROP METH/CNCPT COERCE FRANCE

S62
MONNIER J.P.,"LA SUCCESSION D'ETATS EN MATIERE DE RESPONSABILITE INTERNATIONALE." UNIV CONSTN INTELL SOCIETY ADJUD ROUTINE PERCEPT SUPEGO...GEN/LAWS TOT/POP 20. PAGE 112 H2240 — NAT/G JURID INT/LAW

S62
MU FU-SHENG,"THE WILTING OF THE HUNDRED FLOWERS: FREE THOUGHT IN CHINA TODAY." ASIA CHINA/COM CULTURE FAM NAT/G EDU/PROP REV TOTALISM ATTIT PERSON RESPECT...GEOG INT UNPLAN/INT COLD/WAR 20. PAGE 114 H2278 — INTELL ELITES

S62
PISTRAK L.,"SOVIET VIEWS ON AFRICA." AFR COM FUT ISLAM USSR INTELL STRUCT KIN POL/PAR PLAN EDU/PROP RIGID/FLEX PWR MARXISM...TIME/SEQ WORK TOT/POP 20. PAGE 126 H2516 — NAT/G ATTIT SOCISM

S62
VIGNES D.,"L'AUTORITE DES TRAITES INTERNATIONAUX EN DROIT INTERNE." EUR+WWI UNIV LAW CONSTN INTELL NAT/G POL/PAR DIPLOM ATTIT PERCEPT ALL/VALS ...POLICY INT/LAW JURID CONCPT TIME/SEQ 20 TREATY. PAGE 163 H3252 — STRUCT LEGIT FRANCE

S62
WALTER E.,"VERS UNE CLASSIFICATION SCIENTIFIQUE DE LA SOCIOLOGIA." UNIV CULTURE INTELL SOCIETY R+D ACT/RES LEGIT ROUTINE ATTIT KNOWL...JURID MGT TREND GEN/LAWS 20. PAGE 165 H3296 — PLAN CONCPT

B63
BERLIN I.,KARL MARX, HIS LIFE AND ENVIRONMENT (3RD ED.). MOD/EUR USSR INTELL EDU/PROP PARTIC REV ATTIT 19 MARX/KARL. PAGE 15 H0307 — BIOG PERSON MARXISM CONCPT

B63
CRANKSHAW E.,THE NEW COLD WAR: MOSCOW V. PEKIN. CHINA/COM USSR INTELL POL/PAR DELIB/GP CAP/ISM COERCE REV NAT/LISM TOTALISM DRIVE...POLICY IDEA/COMP 20 KHRUSH/N. PAGE 35 H0698 — ATTIT DIPLOM NAT/COMP MARXISM

B63
FISCHER-GALATI S.A.,RUMANIA; A BIBLIOGRAPHIC GUIDE (PAMPHLET). ROMANIA INTELL ECO/DEV LABOR SECT WEALTH...GEOG SOC/WK LING 20. PAGE 51 H1012 — BIBLIOG/A NAT/G COM LAW

B63
FRANKEL J.,THE MAKING OF FOREIGN POLICY: AN ANALYSIS OF DECISION-MAKING. CHINA/COM EUR+WWI USA+45 ELITES INTELL FORCES LEGIS PLAN ATTIT ALL/VALS MORAL CONSERVE...GOV/COMP 20 PRESIDENT UN TREATY. PAGE 53 H1051 — POLICY DECISION PROB/SOLV DIPLOM

B63
HARTLEY A.,A STATE OF ENGLAND. UK ELITES SOCIETY ACADEM NAT/G SCHOOL INGP/REL CONSEN ORD/FREE NEW/LIB...POLICY 20. PAGE 67 H1349 — DIPLOM ATTIT INTELL ECO/DEV

B63
MARTINDALE D.,COMMUNITY, CHARACTER AND CIVILIZATION: STUDIES IN SOCIAL BEHAVIORISM. INTELL FAM NEIGH VOL/ASSN GP/REL NAT/LISM ATTIT PERSON ...CONCPT GP/COMP 20 BEHAVIORSM. PAGE 103 H2066 — SOC METH/COMP CULTURE STRUCT

B63
MCNEAL R.H.,THE BOLSHEVIK TRADITION: LENIN, STALIN, KHRUSHCHEV. USSR NAT/G SUPEGO CONSERVE...IDEA/COMP GEN/LAWS 20 LENIN/VI STALIN/J KHRUSH/N. PAGE 107 H2145 — INTELL BIOG PERS/COMP

B63
MOSELY P.E.,THE SOVIET UNION, 1922-1962: A FOREIGN AFFAIRS READER. ASIA POLAND USSR CULTURE INTELL AGRI POL/PAR WORKER INT/TRADE DOMIN WAR NAT/LISM MARXISM SOCISM 20 KHRUSH/N. PAGE 113 H2267 — PWR POLICY DIPLOM

B63
QUAISON-SACKEY A.,AFRICA UNBOUND: REFLECTIONS OF AN AFRICAN STATESMAN. ISLAM CULTURE INTELL INT/ORG POL/PAR TOP/EX DOMIN EDU/PROP LEGIT ATTIT PERSON ...CONCPT OBS TIME/SEQ CHARTS STERTYP 20 UN. PAGE 129 H2571 — AFR BIOG

B63
TUCKER R.C.,THE SOVIET POLITICAL MIND. COM INTELL NAT/G TOP/EX EDU/PROP ADMIN COERCE TOTALISM ATTIT PWR MARXISM...PSY MYTH HYPO/EXP 20. PAGE 157 H3136 — STRUCT RIGID/FLEX ELITES USSR

B63
ULAM A.B.,THE NEW FACE OF SOVIET TOTALITARIANISM. FUT INTELL NAT/G POL/PAR EX/STRUC TOP/EX DIPLOM ECO/TAC DOMIN EDU/PROP LEGIT COERCE ATTIT RIGID/FLEX...OBS HIST/WRIT TREND TOT/POP VAL/FREE COLD/WAR. PAGE 158 H3150 — COM PWR TOTALISM USSR

B63
VON DER MEHDEN F.R.,RELIGION AND NATIONALISM IN SOUTHEAST ASIA. BURMA PHILIPPINE S/ASIA INTELL SOCIETY DOMIN EDU/PROP LEGIT ATTIT MORAL ORD/FREE ...SOC CENSUS HIST/WRIT TOT/POP VAL/FREE 20 WORSHIP LONDON. PAGE 163 H3265 — SECT CULTURE NAT/LISM

S63
ARASTEH R.,"THE ROLE OF INTELLECTUALS IN ADMINISTRATIVE DEVELOPMENT AND SOCIAL CHANGE IN MODERN IRAN." ISLAM CULTURE NAT/G CONSULT ACT/RES EDU/PROP EXEC ATTIT BIO/SOC PERCEPT SUPEGO ALL/VALS ...POLICY MGT PSY SOC CONCPT 20. PAGE 8 H0157 — INTELL ADMIN IRAN

S63
MORISON D.,"AFRICAN STUDIES IN THE SOVIET UNION." AFR COM CULTURE INTELL REGION ATTIT KNOWL...HUM TREND 20. PAGE 113 H2258 — EDU/PROP USSR

S63
RINTELEN F.,"L'HOMME EUROPEEN." EUR+WWI FUT CULTURE INTELL SECT EDU/PROP ATTIT ALL/VALS...HUM SOC METH/CNCPT TREND GEN/LAWS 20 WORSHIP. PAGE 132 H2631
SOCIETY PERSON

B64
BERNSTEIN H.,VENEZUELA AND COLOMBIA. L/A+17C VENEZUELA INTELL COLONIAL ATTIT 20 COLOMB. PAGE 16 H0316
CULTURE NAT/LISM LEAD

B64
CAUTE D.,COMMUNISM AND THE FRENCH INTELLECTUALS, 1914-1960. COM EUR+WWI MOD/EUR NAT/G PERF/ART PROF/ORG CREATE EDU/PROP ATTIT PERSON KNOWL MARXISM ...SOC TIME/SEQ MARX/KARL 20 MALRAUX/A GIDE/A SARTRE/J. PAGE 28 H0563
POL/PAR INTELL

B64
CLUBB O.E. JR.,TWENTIETH CENTURY CHINA. ASIA CHINA/COM INTELL NAT/G POL/PAR VOL/ASSN ACT/RES EDU/PROP COERCE REV PWR...TIME/SEQ 20. PAGE 30 H0608
TOP/EX DRIVE

B64
JOHNSON J.J.,CONTINUITY AND CHANGE IN LATIN AMERICA. L/A+17C INTELL FORCES WORKER CIVMIL/REL CHINJAP. PAGE 81 H1623
ANTHOL CULTURE STRATA GP/COMP

B64
LATORRE A.,UNIVERSIDAD Y SOCIEDAD. SPAIN EDU/PROP LEAD GP/REL PERS/REL ATTIT KNOWL. PAGE 92 H1837
ACADEM CULTURE ROLE INTELL

B64
MORGAN H.W.,AMERICAN SOCIALISM 1900-1960. USA+45 USA-45 INTELL AGRI LABOR WORKER BARGAIN ECO/TAC GP/REL RACE/REL 20 NEGRO MIGRATION GOLD/STAND. PAGE 113 H2254
SOCISM POL/PAR ECO/DEV STRATA

B64
MOUMOUNI A.,L'EDUCATION EN AFRIQUE. UNIV CULTURE ELITES INTELL EDU/PROP ADMIN COLONIAL...LING TREND BIBLIOG 20. PAGE 114 H2271
SCHOOL AFR PROB/SOLV

B64
POWELSON J.P.,LATIN AMERICA: TODAY'S ECONOMIC AND SOCIAL REVOLUTION. L/A+17C INTELL SOCIETY STRUCT AGRI INDUS NAT/G DIPLOM ECO/TAC REV...POLICY 20. PAGE 128 H2552
ECO/UNDEV WEALTH ADJUST PLAN

B64
TEPASKE J.J.,EXPLOSIVE FORCES IN LATIN AMERICA. CULTURE INTELL ECO/UNDEV INT/ORG NAT/G SECT FORCES ECO/TAC EDU/PROP PWR WEALTH SOC. PAGE 153 H3063
L/A+17C RIGID/FLEX FOR/AID USSR

B64
UTECHIN S.V.,RUSSIAN POLITICAL THOUGHT: A CONCISE HISTORY. RUSSIA USSR INTELL STRATA POL/PAR SECT LEGIS EDU/PROP REV WAR MARXISM...ANARCH BIBLIOG 9/20 REFORMERS SLAVS. PAGE 161 H3218
IDEA/COMP ATTIT ALL/IDEOS NAT/G

S64
BENSON M.,"SOUTH AFRICA AND WORLD OPINION." AFR SOUTH/AFR INTELL SOCIETY TOP/EX ECO/TAC DOMIN COERCE DISCRIM ATTIT PWR WEALTH...POLICY RECORD 20. PAGE 14 H0285
NAT/G RIGID/FLEX RACE/REL

S64
ENNIS T.E.,"VIETNAM: LAND WITHOUT LAUGHTER." S/ASIA VIETNAM VIETNAM/S INTELL SOCIETY SECT FORCES DIPLOM LEGIT COERCE WAR ATTIT RIGID/FLEX ORD/FREE COLD/WAR 20. PAGE 46 H0929
NAT/G TOP/EX GUERRILLA

S64
GARMARNIKOW M.,"INFLUENCE-BUYING IN WEST AFRICA." COM FUT USSR INTELL NAT/G PLAN TEC/DEV ECO/TAC DOMIN EDU/PROP REGION NAT/LISM ATTIT DRIVE ALL/VALS SOVEREIGN...POLICY PSY SOC CONCPT TREND STERTYP WORK COLD/WAR 20. PAGE 55 H1102
AFR ECO/UNDEV FOR/AID SOCISM

S64
NEEDHAM T.,"SCIENCE AND SOCIETY IN EAST AND WEST." INTELL STRATA R+D LOC/G NAT/G PROVS CONSULT ACT/RES CREATE PLAN TEC/DEV EDU/PROP ADMIN ATTIT ALL/VALS ...POLICY RELATIV MGT CONCPT NEW/IDEA TIME/SEQ WORK WORK. PAGE 116 H2327
ASIA STRUCT

B65
ADAM T.R.,GOVERNMENT AND POLITICS IN AFRICA SOUTH OF THE SAHARA. AFR EUR+WWI CONSTN CULTURE INTELL POL/PAR TOP/EX LEGIT REGION DRIVE...OBS TREND CMN/WLTH 20. PAGE 3 H0062
NAT/G TIME/SEQ RACE/REL COLONIAL

B65
FREY F.W.,THE TURKISH POLITICAL ELITE. TURKEY CULTURE INTELL NAT/G EX/STRUC CHOOSE ATTIT PWR ...METH/CNCPT CHARTS WORSHIP 20. PAGE 53 H1059
ELITES SOCIETY POL/PAR

B65
HANSER C.J.,GUIDE TO DECISION: ROYAL COMMISSION. UK INTELL EXTR/IND SCHOOL PROB/SOLV EXEC ROUTINE CHOOSE GOV/REL GP/REL HEALTH...CHARTS 20. PAGE 66 H1318
NAT/G DELIB/GP EX/STRUC PWR

B65
HERBST J.,THE GERMAN HISTORICAL SCHOOL IN AMERICAN SCHOLARSHIP; A STUDY IN THE TRANSFER OF CULTURE. GERMANY USA+45 INTELL SOCIETY ACADEM PLAN ATTIT IDEA/COMP. PAGE 70 H1399
CULTURE NAT/COMP HIST/WRIT

B65
JACKSON G.,THE SPANISH REPUBLIC AND THE CIVIL WAR, 1931-1939. EUR+WWI INTELL STRUCT COM/IND NAT/G POL/PAR LEGIS EDU/PROP EXEC COERCE NAT/LISM DRIVE PWR...INT TIME/SEQ TOT/POP 20. PAGE 79 H1574
ATTIT GUERRILLA SPAIN

B65
JANSEN M.B.,CHANGING JAPANESE ATTITUDES TOWARD MODERNIZATION. ASIA CHINA/COM S/ASIA INTELL SOCIETY KIN NAT/G SECT PERCEPT RIGID/FLEX...SOC CONCPT TIME/SEQ TREND TOT/POP 19/20 CHINJAP. PAGE 80 H1591
TEC/DEV ATTIT INDIA

B65
KUPER L.,AN AFRICAN BOURGEOISIE. SOUTH/AFR LAW INTELL NAT/G POL/PAR VOL/ASSN DISCRIM...POLICY 20. PAGE 89 H1783
RACE/REL SOC STRUCT

B65
PUNDEEF M.V.,BULGARIA; A BIBLIOGRAPHIC GUIDE. BULGARIA LAW CULTURE INTELL ECO/DEV LEAD MARXISM 20. PAGE 128 H2566
BIBLIOG/A NAT/G COM SOCISM

B65
SCALAPINO R.A.,THE COMMUNIST REVOLUTION IN ASIA* TACTICS, GOALS, AND ACHIEVEMENTS. INDIA INTELL POL/PAR FORCES DOMIN EDU/PROP LEGIT COERCE REV ATTIT CHINJAP. PAGE 138 H2763
ASIA S/ASIA MARXISM NAT/COMP

B65
SLOTKIN J.S.,READINGS IN EARLY ANTHROPOLOGY. INTELL SECT CREATE ATTIT KNOWL...HUM PHIL/SCI PSY LING 1/18. PAGE 145 H2902
SOC CULTURE GP/COMP

B65
VERMOT-GAUCHY M.,L'EDUCATION NATIONALE DANS LA FRANCE DE 1975. FRANCE FUT CULTURE ELITES R+D SCHOOL PLAN EDU/PROP EFFICIENCY...POLICY PREDICT CHARTS INDEX 20. PAGE 162 H3245
ACADEM CREATE TREND INTELL

B65
WINT G.,ASIA: A HANDBOOK. ASIA COM INDIA USSR CULTURE INTELL NAT/G...GEOG STAT CENSUS NAT/COMP WORSHIP 20 TREATY CHINJAP. PAGE 169 H3387
DIPLOM SOC

L65
HOUN F.S.,"THE COMMUNIST MONOLITH VERSUS THE CHINESE TRADITION." CULTURE INTELL SOCIETY STRUCT DOMIN GP/REL ORD/FREE CONSERVE PLURISM...GOV/COMP WORSHIP. PAGE 74 H1479
ASIA MARXISM TOTALISM

S65
HELMREICH E.C.,"KADAR'S HUNGARY." COM EUR+WWI HUNGARY USSR INTELL ECO/DEV AGRI INT/ORG TOP/EX DOMIN ALL/VALS WORK COLD/WAR 20. PAGE 69 H1390
NAT/G RIGID/FLEX TOTALISM

S65
RUBINSTEIN A.Z.,"YUGOSLAVIA'S OPENING SOCIETY." COM USSR INTELL NAT/G LEGIS TOP/EX LEGIT CT/SYS RIGID/FLEX ALL/VALS SOCISM...HUM TIME/SEQ TREND 20. PAGE 135 H2708
CONSTN EX/STRUC YUGOSLAVIA

S65
TABORSKY E.,"CHANGE IN CZECHOSLOVAKIA." COM USSR ELITES INTELL AGRI INDUS NAT/G DELIB/GP EX/STRUC ECO/TAC TOTALISM ATTIT RIGID/FLEX SOCISM...MGT CONCPT TREND 20. PAGE 152 H3031
ECO/DEV PLAN CZECHOSLVK

C65
COLEMAN J.S.,"EDUCATION AND POLITICAL DEVELOPMENT." COM CULTURE INTELL STRUCT SCHOOL PERSON SOVEREIGN ...POLICY ANTHOL BIBLIOG/A METH 20. PAGE 31 H0629
ECO/UNDEV NAT/LISM EDU/PROP TEC/DEV

B66
BRAIBANTI R.,RESEARCH ON THE BUREAUCRACY OF PAKISTAN. PAKISTAN LAW CULTURE INTELL ACADEM LOC/G SECT PRESS CT/SYS...LING CHARTS 20 BUREAUCRCY. PAGE 20 H0402
HABITAT NAT/G ADMIN CONSTN

B66
DE VORE B.B.,LAND AND LIBERTY; A HISTORY OF THE MEXICAN REVOLUTION. CONSTN INTELL NAT/G CONTROL LEAD CHOOSE TOTALISM AUTHORIT...BIBLIOG 19/20 MEXIC/AMER DIAZ/P LIB/PARTY MAGON/F MADERO/F. PAGE 39 H0776
REV CHIEF POL/PAR

B66
KIRKENDALL R.S.,SOCIAL SCIENTISTS AND FARM POLITICS IN THE AGE OF ROOSEVELT. ACADEM PLAN ECO/TAC GIVE ADMIN CONTROL PRODUC...SOC 20 NEW/DEAL ROOSEVLT/F BURAGR/ECO. PAGE 86 H1722
AGRI INTELL POLICY NAT/G

B66
LEIBLER I.,SOVIET JEWRY AND HUMAN RIGHTS. USSR INTELL NAT/G DOMIN ATTIT 20 AUSTRAL JEWS. PAGE 93 H1865
DISCRIM RACE/REL MARXISM POL/PAR

B66
MAC DONALD H.M.,THE INTELLECTUAL IN POLITICS. GERMANY PERU SWEDEN UK USSR NAT/G CONSULT PLAN EDU/PROP TASK INGP/REL EFFICIENCY RATIONAL ALL/VALS 20. PAGE 99 H1987
ALL/IDEOS INTELL POL/PAR PARTIC

B66
RAEFF M.,ORIGINS OF THE RUSSIAN INTELLIGENTSIA: THE EIGHTEENTH-CENTURY NOBILITY. RUSSIA FAM NAT/G EDU/PROP ADMIN PERS/REL ATTIT...HUM BIOG 18. PAGE 129 H2580
INTELL ELITES STRATA CONSERVE

B66
ROOS H.,A HISTORY OF MODERN POLAND FROM THE FOUNDATION OF THE STATE IN THE FIRST WORLD WAR TO THE PRESENT DAY. EUR+WWI POLAND INTELL SOCIETY
NAT/G WAR DIPLOM

ECO/TAC LEAD REV ATTIT ORD/FREE MARXISM...BIBLIOG 20 WWI PARTITION. PAGE 133 H2669

B66
WANG Y.C.,CHINESE INTELLECTUALS AND THE WEST 1872-1949. ASIA ELITES LEAD STRANGE ROLE MARXISM ...CHARTS 19/20. PAGE 165 H3301 — INTELL EDU/PROP CULTURE SOCIETY

B67
ALLWORTH E.,CENTRAL ASIA: A CENTURY OF RUSSIAN RULE. USSR INTELL SOCIETY AGRI INDUS COLONIAL REV WAR NAT/LISM...ART/METH GEOG LING 19/20. PAGE 5 H0108 — ASIA CULTURE NAT/G

B67
BRZEZINSKI Z.K.,THE SOVIET BLOC: UNITY AND CONFLICT (2ND ED., REV., ENLARGED). COM POLAND USSR INTELL CHIEF EX/STRUC CONTROL EXEC GOV/REL PWR MARXISM ...TREND IDEA/COMP 20 LENIN/VI MARX/KARL STALIN/J. PAGE 23 H0463 — NAT/G DIPLOM

B67
MICKIEWICZ E.P.,SOVIET POLITICAL SCHOOLS: THE COMMUNIST PARTY ADULT INSTRUCTION SYSTEM. COM USSR INTELL SCHOOL WORKER CREATE PRESS ADMIN CONTROL ATTIT KNOWL...PROG/TEAC SOC/INTEG 20 COM/PARTY. PAGE 110 H2200 — NAT/G EDU/PROP AGE/A MARXISM

B67
NATIONAL SCIENCE FOUNDATION,DIRECTORY OF SELECTED RESEARCH INSTITUTES IN EASTERN EUROPE. BULGARIA CZECHOSLVK HUNGARY POLAND ROMANIA INTELL ACADEM NAT/G ACT/RES 20. PAGE 116 H2323 — INDEX R+D COM PHIL/SCI

L67
EGBERT D.D.,"THE IDEA OF 'AVANT-GARDE' IN ART AND POLITICS." USSR CULTURE INTELL POL/PAR CREATE EDU/PROP CONTROL REV ANOMIE DRIVE ROLE...IDEA/COMP 20. PAGE 45 H0895 — ART/METH COM ATTIT

L67
TABORSKY E.,"THE COMMUNIST PARTIES OF THE 'THIRD WORLD' IN SOVIET STRATEGY." AFR ASIA L/A+17C USSR INTELL NAT/G WORKER PLAN CONTROL LEAD PARTIC REV ...GOV/COMP 20 COM/PARTY THIRD/WRLD. PAGE 152 H3032 — POL/PAR MARXISM ECO/UNDEV DIPLOM

S67
ADAMS R.N.,"ETHICS AND THE SOCIAL ANTHROPOLOGIST IN LATIN AMERICA." USA+45 INTELL PROB/SOLV ECO/TAC LEAD...DECISION SOC NAT/COMP PERS/COMP. PAGE 3 H0066 — L/A+17C POLICY ECO/UNDEV CONSULT

S67
ALTBACH P.,"STUDENT POLITICS." GP/REL ATTIT ROLE PWR 20. PAGE 6 H0116 — INTELL PARTIC UTIL NAT/G

S67
KRISTOF L.K.D.,"THE STATE-IDEA, THE NATIONAL IDEA AND THE IMAGE OF THE FATHERLAND." CONSTN CULTURE INTELL SOCIETY WORKER TASK DRIVE HABITAT...MYTH GOV/COMP IDEA/COMP. PAGE 89 H1769 — GEOG CONCPT NAT/G PERCEPT

S67
KROLL M.,"POLITICAL LEADERSHIP AND ADMINISTRATIVE COMMUNICATIONS IN NEW NATION STATES* CASE STUDY OF TRINIDAD AND TOBAGO." L/A+17C TRINIDAD INTELL OP/RES DOMIN COLONIAL LEAD GP/REL CENTRAL EFFICIENCY...DECISION OBS METH/COMP 20. PAGE 89 H1774 — NAT/G ADMIN EDU/PROP CONTROL

S67
MCCLEERY W.,"AN INTERVIEW WITH J. DOUGLAS BROWN ON THE 'WAY' OF VIETNAM" COM VIETNAM INTELL ECO/DEV ACADEM NAT/G COERCE PERSON SUPEGO ORD/FREE 20. PAGE 106 H2125 — ATTIT WAR COLONIAL MARXISM

S67
NIEBUHR R.,"THE ETHICS OF WAR AND PEACE IN THE NUCLEAR AGE." VIETNAM INTELL CONFER CONTROL WAR GOV/REL PERS/REL ORD/FREE...POLICY INT GOV/COMP NAT/COMP 20 UN. PAGE 118 H2360 — MORAL PEACE NUC/PWR DIPLOM

S67
READ J.S.,"CENSORED." UGANDA CONSTN INTELL SOCIETY NAT/G DIPLOM PRESS WRITING ADJUD ADMIN COLONIAL RISK...IDEA/COMP 20. PAGE 130 H2602 — EDU/PROP AFR CREATE

S67
SMITH J.E.,"RED PRUSSIANISM OF THE GERMAN DEMOCRATIC REPUBLIC." GERMANY/E INTELL TOP/EX WORKER PLAN DIPLOM PRODUC ATTIT WEALTH MARXISM. PAGE 146 H2912 — NAT/G TOTALISM INDUS NAT/LISM

S67
SMITH J.E.,"THE RED PRUSSIANISM OF THE GERMAN DEMOCRATIC REPUBLIC." GERMANY/E INTELL NAT/G SECT CHIEF...PREDICT TIME/SEQ 20. PAGE 146 H2913 — MARXISM NAT/LISM GOV/COMP EDU/PROP

S67
VON LAUE T.H.,"WESTERNIZATION, REVOLUTION AND THE SEARCH FOR A BASIS OF AUTHORITY - RUSSIA IN 1917." USSR ELITES INTELL ECO/UNDEV NAT/G WORKER ECO/TAC TAX ADMIN LEAD AUTHORIT 20 LENIN/VI. PAGE 164 H3274 — MARXISM REV COM DOMIN

S68
KANET R.E.,"RECENT SOVIET REASSESSMENT OF DEVELOPMENTS IN THE THIRD WORLD." ALGERIA GHANA INDONESIA USSR WOR+45 CONSTN ELITES INTELL STRUCT DOMIN CONTROL REV PWR MARXISM...IDEA/COMP METH 20 THIRD/WRLD. PAGE 83 H1653 — DIPLOM NEUTRAL NAT/G NAT/COMP

INTELLIGENCE, MILITARY....SEE ACT/RES+FORCES+KNOWL

INTELLIGENTSIA....SEE INTELL

INTERAMERICAN CULTURAL COUN H1542

INTEREST....INTEREST

INTER-ASIAN DEVELOPMENT BANK....SEE IADB

INTERNAL REVENUE SERVICE....SEE IRS

INTERNAL WARFARE....SEE REV

INTERNATIONAL AFRICAN INST H1543,H1544,H1545,H1546,H1547,H1548, H1549,H1550,H1551,H1552

INTERNATIONAL ASSOCIATION RES H1553

INTERNATIONAL CTR. AFRICAN DOC.H1554

INTERNATIONAL COMN JURISTS H1555

INTERNATIONAL ECONOMIC ASSN H1556

INTERNATIONAL LABOUR OFFICE H1557,H1558

INTERNATIONAL PRESS INSTITUTE H1559

INTERNATIONAL ATOMIC ENERGY AGENCY....SEE IAEA

INTERNATIONAL BANK FOR RECONSTRUCT. AND DEV....SEE IBRD

INTERNATIONAL CIVIL AVIATION ORGANIZATION....SEE INT/AVIATN

INTERNATIONAL COOPERATION ADMINISTRATION....SEE ICA

INTERNATIONAL COUNCIL OF SCIENTIFIC UNIONS....SEE ICSU

INTERNATIONAL COURT OF JUSTICE....SEE ICJ

INTERNATIONAL DEVELOPMENT ASSOCIATION....SEE INTL/DEV

INTERNATIONAL ECONOMIC ASSOCIATION....SEE INTL/ECON

INTERNATIONAL FINANCE CORPORATION....SEE INTL/FINAN

INTERNATIONAL GEOPHYSICAL YEAR....SEE IGY

INTERNATIONAL INTEGRATION....SEE INT/ORG, INT/REL

INTERNATIONAL LABOR ORGANIZATION....SEE ILO

INTERNATIONAL LAW....SEE INT/LAW

INTERNATIONAL MONETARY FUND....SEE IMF

INTERNATIONAL ORGANIZATIONS....SEE INT/ORG

INTERNATIONAL RELATIONS....SEE INT/REL

INTERNATIONAL SYSTEMS....SEE NET/THEORY+INT/REL+WOR+45

INTERNATIONAL TELECOMMUNICATIONS UNION....SEE ITU

INTERNATIONAL TRADE....SEE INT/TRADE

INTERNATIONAL WORKERS OF THE WORLD....SEE IWW

INTERPARLIAMENTARY UNION H1560

INTERSTATE COMMERCE COMMISSION....SEE ICC

INTERSTATE COMMISSION ON CRIME....SEE INTST/CRIM

INTERVENT....INTERVENTIONISM (MILITARY, POLITICAL, AND/OR ECONOMIC INTERFERENCE BY A SOVEREIGN STATE OR AN INTERNATIONAL AGENCY IN THE AFFAIRS OF ANOTHER SOVEREIGN STATE)

B40
WOLFERS A.,BRITAIN AND FRANCE BETWEEN TWO WORLD WARS. FRANCE UK INT/ORG NAT/G PLAN BARGAIN ECO/TAC AGREE ISOLAT ALL/IDEOS...DECISION GEOG 20 TREATY VERSAILLES INTERVENT. PAGE 170 H3402 — DIPLOM WAR POLICY

B53
SQUIRES J.D.,BRITISH PROPAGANDA AT HOME AND IN THE UNITED STATES FROM 1914 TO 1917. UK NAT/G PROB/SOLV DOMIN PRESS EFFICIENCY...PSY PREDICT 20 WWI INTERVENT PSY/WAR. PAGE 148 H2960 — EDU/PROP CONTROL WAR DIPLOM

B60
MORAES F.,THE REVOLT IN TIBET. ASIA CHINA/COM INDIA CULTURE CONTROL COERCE WAR TOTALISM...POLICY SOC WORSHIP 20 TIBET INTERVENT. PAGE 113 H2252 — COLONIAL FORCES DIPLOM

ORD/FREE
B60
PIERCE R.A.,RUSSIAN CENTRAL ASIA, 1867-1917. ASIA RUSSIA CULTURE AGRI INDUS EDU/PROP REV NAT/LISM ...CHARTS BIBLIOG 19/20 BOLSHEVISM INTERVENT. PAGE 125 H2509 — COLONIAL DOMIN ADMIN ECO/UNDEV
B61
ROIG E.,MARTI, ANTIIMPERIALISTA. CUBA L/A+17C DIPLOM DOMIN COLONIAL CONTROL LEAD PWR SOVEREIGN ...PHIL/SCI 19 MARTI/JOSE INTERVENT. PAGE 133 H2664 — PERSON NAT/LISM ECO/UNDEV ORD/FREE
B66
SOBEL L.A.,SOUTH VIETNAM: US-COMMUNIST CONFRONTATION IN SOUTHEAST ASIA 1961-65. VIETNAM FOR/AID CROWD DETER REV PEACE...GEOG 20 INTERVENT DIEM COLD/WAR. PAGE 146 H2926 — WAR TIME/SEQ FORCES NAT/G

INTERVIEWING....SEE INT, REC/INT

INTERVIEWS....SEE INTERVIEWS INDEX, P. XIV

INTGOV/REL....ADVISORY COMMISSION ON INTERGOVERNMENTAL RELATIONS

INTL CONF ON POPULATION H1561

INTL CONF ON WORLD POLITICS-5 H1562

INTL UNION LOCAL AUTHORITIES H1563

INTL/DEV....INTERNATIONAL DEVELOPMENT ASSOCIATION

B64
US HOUSE COMM BANKING-CURR,INTERNATIONAL DEVELOPMENT ASSOCIATION ACT AMENDMENT. CHINA/COM USA+45 USSR FINAN FORCES LEGIS DIPLOM CONFER EFFICIENCY...CHARTS GOV/COMP 20 PRESIDENT CONGRESS INTL/DEV. PAGE 160 H3196 — BAL/PAY FOR/AID RECORD ECO/TAC

INTL/ECON....INTERNATIONAL ECONOMIC ASSOCIATION

INTL/FINAN....INTERNATIONAL FINANCE CORPORATION

INTRAGROUP RELATIONS....SEE INGP/REL

INTRVN/ECO....INTERVENTION (ECONOMIC) - PHILOSOPHY OF GOVERNMENTAL INTERFERENCE IN DOMESTIC ECONOMIC AFFAIRS

B58
DWARKADAS R.,ROLE OF HIGHER CIVIL SERVICE IN INDIA. INDIA ECO/UNDEV LEGIS PROB/SOLV GP/REL PERS/REL ...POLICY WELF/ST DECISION ORG/CHARTS BIBLIOG 20 CIVIL/SERV INTRVN/ECO. PAGE 44 H0876 — ADMIN NAT/G ROLE PLAN

INTST/CRIM....U.S. INTERSTATE COMMISSION ON CRIME

INVENTION....SEE CREATE

INVESTMENT....SEE FINAN

IOVTCHOUK M.T. H1564

IOWA....IOWA

IOWA STATE U CTR AGRI AND ECO H1565

IRAN....SEE ALSO ISLAM

B58
LERNER D.,THE PASSING OF TRADITIONAL SOCIETY: MODERNIZING THE MIDDLE EAST. IRAN ISLAM LEBANON SYRIA TURKEY UAR CULTURE INTELL STRATA KIN NAT/G NEIGH SECT EDU/PROP ATTIT PERSON...MYTH OBS 20. PAGE 95 H1888 — ECO/UNDEV RIGID/FLEX
S59
GABLE R.W.,"CULTURE AND ADMINISTRATION IN IRAN." IRAN EXEC PARTIC REPRESENT PWR. PAGE 54 H1085 — ADMIN CULTURE EX/STRUC INGP/REL
B61
DALLIN D.J.,SOVIET FOREIGN POLICY AFTER STALIN. ASIA CHINA/COM EUR+WWI GERMANY IRAN UK YUGOSLAVIA INT/ORG NAT/G VOL/ASSN FORCES TOP/EX BAL/PWR DOMIN EDU/PROP COERCE ATTIT PWR 20. PAGE 37 H0737 — COM DIPLOM USSR
B61
VON EICKSTEDT E.,TURKEN, KURDEN UND IRANER SEIT DEM ALTERTUM. IRAN TURKEY GP/REL BIO/SOC HABITAT...PSY 20 PERSIA. PAGE 163 H3266 — CULTURE SOC SOCIETY STRUCT
S61
VALLET R.,"IRAN: KEY TO THE MIDDLE EAST." COM IRAQ ISLAM KUWAIT LEBANON SAUDI/ARAB TURKEY ELITES SOCIETY INDUS PROC/MFG POL/PAR TOP/EX PLAN BAL/PWR DIPLOM ECO/TAC ALL/VALS...TREND CENTO 20. PAGE 161 H3224 — NAT/G ECO/UNDEV IRAN
B62
BINDER L.,IRAN: POLITICAL DEVELOPMENT IN A CHANGING SOCIETY. IRAN OP/RES REV GP/REL CENTRAL RATIONAL PWR...PHIL/SCI NAT/COMP GEN/LAWS 20. PAGE 17 H0337 — LEGIT NAT/G ADMIN STRUCT
B62
DAVAR F.C.,IRAN AND INDIA THROUGH THE AGES. INDIA IRAN ELITES SECT CREATE ORD/FREE...LING BIBLIOG. PAGE 37 H0743 — NAT/COMP DIPLOM CULTURE
S63
ARASTEH R.,"THE ROLE OF INTELLECTUALS IN ADMINISTRATIVE DEVELOPMENT AND SOCIAL CHANGE IN MODERN IRAN." ISLAM CULTURE NAT/G CONSULT ACT/RES EDU/PROP EXEC ATTIT BIO/SOC PERCEPT SUPEGO ALL/VALS ...POLICY MGT PSY SOC CONCPT 20. PAGE 8 H0157 — INTELL ADMIN IRAN
S63
BILL J.A.,"THE SOCIAL AND ECONOMIC FOUNDATIONS OF POWER IN CONTEMPORARY IRAN." ISLAM CULTURE NAT/G ECO/TAC DOMIN COERCE ATTIT PWR WEALTH...TREND VAL/FREE 20. PAGE 17 H0334 — SOCIETY STRATA IRAN
B64
WICKENS G.M.,PERSIA IN ISLAMIC TIMES: A PRACTICAL BIBLIOGRAPHY OF ITS HISTORY, CULTURE AND LANGUAGE (PAMPHLET). IRAN ISLAM SECT. PAGE 168 H3355 — BIBLIOG CULTURE LING
S64
RAMAZANI R.K.,"CHURCH AND STATE IN MODERNIZING SOCIETY: THE CASE OF IRAN." ISLAM CULTURE ORD/FREE PWR...TIME/SEQ VAL/FREE 17/20. PAGE 129 H2586 — SECT NAT/G ELITES IRAN
B65
BAYNE E.A.,FOUR WAYS OF POLITICS: STATE AND NATION IN ITALY, SOMALIA, ISRAEL, AND IRAN. IRAN ISRAEL ITALY SOMALIA LEAD CHOOSE MAJORITY GOV/COMP. PAGE 12 H0244 — ECO/UNDEV NAT/G DECISION TOP/EX
B65
HARBISON F.,MANPOWER AND EDUCATION. AFR CHINA/COM IRAN L/A+17C S/ASIA TEC/DEV ADJUST OPTIMAL SKILL ...ANTHOL 20. PAGE 66 H1325 — ECO/UNDEV EDU/PROP WORKER NAT/COMP

IRAQ....SEE ALSO ISLAM

S61
VALLET R.,"IRAN: KEY TO THE MIDDLE EAST." COM IRAQ ISLAM KUWAIT LEBANON SAUDI/ARAB TURKEY ELITES SOCIETY INDUS PROC/MFG POL/PAR TOP/EX PLAN BAL/PWR DIPLOM ECO/TAC ALL/VALS...TREND CENTO 20. PAGE 161 H3224 — NAT/G ECO/UNDEV IRAN

IRELAND....SEE ALSO UK

N17
BURKE E.,LETTER TO SIR HERCULES LANGRISHE (PAMPHLET). IRELAND UK NAT/G CHIEF DIPLOM DOMIN PARL/PROC COERCE ORD/FREE SOVEREIGN POPULISM ...TRADIT 18 BURKE/EDM. PAGE 24 H0485 — POLICY COLONIAL SECT
B23
LEES-SMITH H.B.,SECOND CHAMBERS IN THEORY AND PRACTICE. IRELAND NORWAY SOUTH/AFR UK LAW POL/PAR LEGIS CONTROL 20 CMN/WLTH. PAGE 93 H1858 — PARL/PROC DELIB/GP REPRESENT GP/COMP
B33
MOSS W.,POLITICAL PARTIES IN THE IRISH FREE STATE. IRELAND UK LAW FINAN LABOR DELIB/GP TOP/EX TARIFFS EDU/PROP...CHARTS GP/COMP 20. PAGE 113 H2269 — POL/PAR NAT/G CHOOSE POLICY
B36
CLARKE M.V.,MEDIEVAL REPRESENTATION AND CONSENT. IRELAND UK REPRESENT SUFF. PAGE 30 H0603 — PARL/PROC LEGIS NAT/G
S40
BROMAGE A.W.,"THE VOCATIONAL SENATE IN IRELAND" EUR+WWI IRELAND. PAGE 21 H0430 — PWR NAT/G REPRESENT LEGIS
B43
MC DOWELL R.B.,IRISH PUBLIC OPINION, 1750-1800. IRELAND CONSTN VOL/ASSN WORKER ORD/FREE CATHISM CONSERVE...POLICY IDEA/COMP BIBLIOG 18/ PARLIAMENT. PAGE 106 H2118 — ATTIT NAT/G DIPLOM REV
B50
LYONS F.S.L.,THE IRISH PARLIAMENTARY PARTY, 1890-1910: STUDIES IN IRISH HISTORY (VOL. 4). IRELAND DELIB/GP LEGIS PAY EDU/PROP ADMIN GP/REL ATTIT...BIBLIOG 19/20 PARLIAMENT PARNELL/CS DIRECT/NAT. PAGE 99 H1986 — POL/PAR CHOOSE NAT/G POLICY
B57
DONALDSON A.G.,SOME COMPARATIVE ASPECTS OF IRISH LAW. IRELAND NAT/G DIPLOM ADMIN CT/SYS LEAD ATTIT SOVEREIGN...JURID BIBLIOG/A 12/20 CMN/WLTH. PAGE 42 H0835 — CONSTN LAW NAT/COMP INT/LAW
B62
GROGAN V.,ADMINISTRATIVE TRIBUNALS IN THE PUBLIC SERVICE. IRELAND UK NAT/G CONTROL CT/SYS...JURID GOV/COMP 20. PAGE 61 H1231 — ADMIN LAW ADJUD DELIB/GP

B62
INSTITUTE OF PUBLIC ADMIN,A SHORT HISTORY OF THE PUBLIC SERVICE IN IRELAND. IRELAND UK DIST/IND INGP/REL FEDERAL 13/20 CIVIL/SERV. PAGE 77 H1539
ADMIN WORKER GOV/REL NAT/G

B63
FRANZ G.,TEILUNG UND WIEDERVEREINIGUNG. GERMANY IRELAND ITALY NETHERLAND POLAND CULTURE BAL/PWR CHOOSE NAT/LISM ORD/FREE SOVEREIGN 19/20. PAGE 53 H1054
DIPLOM WAR NAT/COMP ATTIT

B63
RICHARDSON H.G.,THE ADMINISTRATION OF IRELAND 1172-1377. IRELAND CONSTN EX/STRUC LEGIS JUDGE CT/SYS PARL/PROC...CHARTS BIBLIOG 12/14. PAGE 131 H2621
ADMIN NAT/G PWR

B64
NEWARK F.H.,NOTES ON IRISH LEGAL HISTORY (2ND ED.). IRELAND UK PARL/PROC ORD/FREE SOVEREIGN 12/20 ENGLSH/LAW. PAGE 117 H2344
CT/SYS JURID ADJUD NAT/G

B65
O'CONNELL M.R.,IRISH POLITICS AND SOCIAL CONFLICT IN THE AGE OF THE AMERICAN REVOLUTION. FRANCE IRELAND MOD/EUR STRATA SECT LEGIS DIPLOM INT/TRADE DOMIN REV WAR...BIBLIOG 18 PARLIAMENT. PAGE 119 H2387
CATHISM ATTIT NAT/G DELIB/GP

B66
EDWARDS C.D.,TRADE REGULATIONS OVERSEAS. IRELAND NEW/ZEALND SOUTH/AFR NAT/G CAP/ISM TARIFFS CONTROL ...POLICY JURID 20 EEC CHINJAP. PAGE 45 H0892
INT/TRADE DIPLOM INT/LAW ECO/TAC

L67
LARKIN E.,"ECONOMIC GROWTH, CAPITAL INVESTMENT, AND THE ROMAN CATHOLIC CHURCH IN NINETEENTH-CENTURY IRELAND." IRELAND AGRI DIST/IND NAT/G GIVE OWN CATHISM...CHARTS 19. PAGE 91 H1823
FINAN SECT WEALTH ECO/UNDEV

B75
MAINE H.S.,LECTURES ON THE EARLY HISTORY OF INSTITUTIONS. IRELAND UK CONSTN ELITES STRUCT FAM KIN CHIEF LEGIS CT/SYS OWN SOVEREIGN...CONCPT 16 BENTHAM/J BREHON ROMAN/LAW. PAGE 101 H2021
CULTURE LAW INGP/REL

B79
BRODERICK G.C.,POLITICAL STUDIES. IRELAND UK ROMAN/EMP LAW ACADEM LOC/G NAT/G DIPLOM PARL/PROC SUFF GP/REL LAISSEZ...ANTHOL. PAGE 21 H0424
CONSTN COLONIAL

IRELE A. H1566

IRGUN....IRGUN - PALESTINE REVOLUTIONARY ORGANIZATION

IRIKURA J.K. H1567

IRION F.C. H1568

IRISH/AMER....IRISH AMERICANS

IRS....U.S. INTERNAL REVENUE SERVICE

ISAAC J. H1569

ISAACS H.R. H1570

ISLAM....ISLAMIC WORLD; SEE ALSO APPROPRIATE NATIONS

N
BROCKWAY A.F.,AFRICAN SOCIALISM. EUR+WWI GHANA ISLAM UAR ECO/UNDEV CAP/ISM INT/TRADE COLONIAL COERCE GOV/REL DISCRIM 20 NEGRO NKRUMAH/K NASSER/G. PAGE 21 H0423
AFR SOCISM MARXISM

N
MIDDLE EAST JOURNAL. CULTURE SECT DIPLOM LEAD GOV/REL ATTIT...POLICY PHIL/SCI SOC LING BIOG 20. PAGE 1 H0007
BIBLIOG ISLAM NAT/G ECO/UNDEV

N
THE MIDDLE EAST AND NORTH AFRICA. AFR ISLAM CULTURE ECO/UNDEV AGRI NAT/G TEC/DEV FOR/AID INT/TRADE EDU/PROP...CHARTS 20. PAGE 2 H0026
INDEX INDUS FINAN STAT

N
THE MIDDLE EAST. CULTURE...BIOG BIBLIOG. PAGE 2 H0028
ISLAM INDUS FINAN

N
MIDDLE EAST INSTITUTE,CURRENT RESEARCH ON THE MIDDLE EAST....PHIL/SCI PSY SOC LING 20. PAGE 110 H2201
BIBLIOG R+D ISLAM NAT/G

N
US LIBRARY OF CONGRESS,ACCESSIONS LIST -- ISRAEL. ISRAEL CULTURE ECO/UNDEV POL/PAR PLAN PROB/SOLV TEC/DEV DIPLOM EDU/PROP LEAD WAR ATTIT 20 JEWS. PAGE 160 H3200
BIBLIOG ISLAM NAT/G GP/REL

B23
GRANT C.F.,STUDIES IN NORTH AFRICA. ALGERIA MOROCCO ROMAN/EMP CULTURE STRUCT NAT/G DIPLOM WAR ...NAT/COMP TUNIS EUROPE. PAGE 60 H1195
ISLAM SECT DOMIN COLONIAL

B24
WALKER F.D.,AFRICA AND HER PEOPLES. ISLAM STRUCT FAM SECT EDU/PROP INGP/REL RACE/REL HABITAT...GEOG SOC IDEA/COMP WORSHIP 20 NEGRO. PAGE 164 H3292
CULTURE AFR GP/COMP KIN

B29
PRATT I.A.,MODERN EGYPT: A LIST OF REFERENCES TO MATERIAL IN THE NEW YORK PUBLIC LIBRARY. UAR ECO/UNDEV...GEOG JURID SOC LING 20. PAGE 128 H2555
BIBLIOG ISLAM DIPLOM NAT/G

B34
DE CENIVAL P.,BIBLIOGRAPHIE MAROCAINE: 1923-1933. FRANCE MOROCCO SECT ADMIN LEAD GP/REL ATTIT...LING 20. PAGE 37 H0750
BIBLIOG/A ISLAM NAT/G COLONIAL

B38
COUPLAND R.,EAST AFRICA AND ITS INVADERS. AFR ISLAM STRATA SECT FORCES DIPLOM TRIBUTE CONTROL DISCRIM NAT/LISM 19 AFRICA/E EUROPE MISSION. PAGE 34 H0680
CULTURE ELITES COLONIAL MARKET

B39
KOHN H.,REVOLUTIONS AND DICTATORSHIPS. COM EUR+WWI ISLAM MOD/EUR NAT/G CHIEF FORCES WAR CIVMIL/REL PWR MARXISM 18/20. PAGE 87 H1739
NAT/LISM TOTALISM REV FASCISM

B44
FULLER G.H.,TURKEY: A SELECTED LIST OF REFERENCES. ISLAM TURKEY CULTURE ECO/UNDEV AGRI DIPLOM NAT/LISM CONSERVE...GEOG HUM INT/LAW SOC 7/20 MAPS. PAGE 54 H1075
BIBLIOG/A ALL/VALS

B48
MAUGHAM R.,NORTH AFRICAN NOTEBOOK. ALGERIA ISLAM LIBYA MOROCCO STRUCT ECO/UNDEV COLONIAL...SOC OBS AUD/VIS NAT/COMP WORSHIP 20 TUNIS. PAGE 105 H2102
SOCIETY RECORD NAT/LISM

B51
YOUNG T.C.,NEAR EASTERN CULTURE AND SOCIETY. ISLAM ECO/UNDEV SECT WRITING ATTIT HABITAT ORD/FREE 20. PAGE 172 H3439
CULTURE STRUCT REGION DIPLOM

S51
NORTHROP F.S.C.,"ASIAN MENTALITY AND UNITED STATES FOREIGN POLICY." ASIA ISLAM USA+45 CULTURE SOCIETY SECT EDU/PROP LEGIT COERCE DRIVE MORAL ORD/FREE ...POLICY RELATIV TOT/POP 20. PAGE 119 H2376
S/ASIA ATTIT DIPLOM

B52
ETTINGHAUSEN R.,SELECTED AND ANNOTATED BIBLIOGRAPHY OF BOOKS AND PERIODICALS IN WESTERN LANGUAGES DEALING WITH NEAR AND MIDDLE EAST. LAW CULTURE SECT ...ART/METH GEOG SOC. PAGE 47 H0944
BIBLIOG/A ISLAM MEDIT-7

B52
JULIEN C.A.,L'AFRIQUE DU NORD EN MARCHE: NATIONALISMES MUSULMANS ET SOUVERAINETE FRANCAISE (2ND ED). AFR ALGERIA FRANCE ISLAM MOROCCO NAT/G CONTROL ORD/FREE...POLICY 19/20 TUNIS MUSLIM. PAGE 82 H1641
NAT/LISM COERCE DOMIN COLONIAL

B52
US LIBRARY OF CONGRESS,EGYPT AND THE ANGLO-EGYPTIAN SUDAN: A SELECTIVE GUIDE TO BACKGROUND READING (PAMPHLET). SUDAN UAR UK DIPLOM...POLICY 20. PAGE 160 H3209
BIBLIOG/A COLONIAL ISLAM NAT/G

B54
US LIBRARY OF CONGRESS,RESEARCH AND INFORMATION ON AFRICA: CONTINUING SOURCES. ISLAM ECO/UNDEV AGRI INDUS R+D ACADEM NAT/G INT/TRADE...SOC 20. PAGE 161 H3210
BIBLIOG/A AFR PRESS COM/IND

C54
LANDAU J.M.,"PARLIAMENTS AND PARTIES IN EGYPT." UAR NAT/G SECT CONSULT LEGIS TOP/EX PROB/SOLV ADMIN COLONIAL...GEN/LAWS BIBLIOG 19/20. PAGE 90 H1804
ISLAM NAT/LISM PARL/PROC POL/PAR

B55
BENEDICT B.,A SHORT ANNOTATED BIBLIOGRAPHY RELATING TO THE SOCIOLOGY OF MUSLIM PEOPLES. NAT/G...SOC 20. PAGE 14 H0277
BIBLIOG/A ISLAM SECT CULTURE

B55
KHADDURI M.,WAR AND PEACE IN THE LAW OF ISLAM. CONSTN CULTURE SOCIETY STRATA NAT/G PROVS SECT FORCES TOP/EX CREATE DOMIN EDU/PROP ADJUD COERCE ATTIT RIGID/FLEX ALL/VALS...CONCPT TIME/SEQ TOT/POP VAL/FREE. PAGE 85 H1702
ISLAM JURID PEACE WAR

B55
KHADDURI M.,LAW IN THE MIDDLE EAST. LAW CONSTN ACADEM FAM EDU/PROP CT/SYS SANCTION CRIME...INT/LAW GOV/COMP ANTHOL 6/20 MID/EAST. PAGE 85 H1703
ADJUD JURID ISLAM

B55
KRUSE H.,DAS STAATSANGEHORIGKEITSRECHT DER ARABISCHEN STAATEN. ISLAM JORDAN LIBYA SYRIA UAR NAT/G SECT RACE/REL...INT/LAW 6/20 TREATY. PAGE 89 H1779
JURID NAT/LISM DIPLOM GP/REL

C55
GRASSMUCK G.L.,"A MANUAL OF LEBANESE ADMINISTRATION." LEBANON PLAN...CHARTS BIBLIOG/A 20. PAGE 60 H1198
ADMIN NAT/G ISLAM

EX/STRUC
B57

AMERICAN COUNCIL LEARNED SOC,GOVERNMENT UNDER LAW AND THE INDIVIDUAL. ASIA ISLAM USSR NAT/G...POLICY SOC NAT/COMP 20. PAGE 6 H0121 — SOCIETY ORD/FREE CONCPT IDEA/COMP
B57

LAQUER W.Z.,COMMUNISM AND NATIONALISM IN THE MIDDLE EAST. ELITES INTELL STRATA NAT/G POL/PAR SECT VOL/ASSN TOP/EX DOMIN LEGIT REGION COERCE ATTIT PERSON PWR...CONCPT HIST/WRIT TIME/SEQ TREND GEN/LAWS VAL/FREE. PAGE 91 H1817 — ISLAM NAT/LISM
B57

MOYER K.E.,FROM IRAN TO MORROCCO; FROM TURKEY TO THE SUDAN: A SELECTED AND ANNOTATED BIBLIOGRAPHY OF NORTH AFRICA AND NEAR EAST... ISLAM DIPLOM EDU/PROP 20. PAGE 114 H2274 — BIBLIOG/A ECO/UNDEV SECT NAT/G
B57

PARK A.G.,BOLSHEVISM IN TURKESTAN 1917-1927. COM RUSSIA USSR CULTURE AGRI SECT DOMIN GP/REL INGP/REL NAT/LISM...BIBLIOG 20 TURKESTAN. PAGE 123 H2467 — REV POLICY MARXISM ISLAM
B57

SHEIKH N.A.,SOME ASPECTS OF THE CONSTITUTION AND THE ECONOMICS OF ISLAM. PAKISTAN CULTURE AGRI FINAN LABOR NAT/G SECT INT/TRADE 20 MUSLIM. PAGE 143 H2855 — ISLAM POLICY ECO/TAC CONSTN
B58

LAQUER W.Z.,THE MIDDLE EAST IN TRANSITION. COM USSR ECO/UNDEV NAT/G VOL/ASSN EDU/PROP EXEC ATTIT DRIVE PWR MARXISM COLD/WAR TOT/POP 20. PAGE 91 H1818 — ISLAM TREND NAT/LISM
B58

LERNER D.,THE PASSING OF TRADITIONAL SOCIETY: MODERNIZING THE MIDDLE EAST. IRAN ISLAM LEBANON SYRIA TURKEY UAR CULTURE INTELL STRATA KIN NAT/G NEIGH SECT EDU/PROP ATTIT PERSON...MYTH OBS 20. PAGE 95 H1888 — ECO/UNDEV RIGID/FLEX
B58

MACRO E.,BIBLIOGRAPHY OF THE ARABIAN PENINSULA (PAMPHLET). KUWAIT SAUDI/ARAB YEMEN COLONIAL...GEOG 19/20. PAGE 101 H2012 — BIBLIOG ISLAM CULTURE NAT/G
B58

TILLION G.,ALGERIA: THE REALITIES. ALGERIA FRANCE ISLAM CULTURE STRATA PROB/SOLV DOMIN REV NAT/LISM WEALTH MARXISM...GEOG 20. PAGE 155 H3094 — ECO/UNDEV SOC COLONIAL DIPLOM
S58

PYE L.W.,"THE NON-WESTERN POLITICAL PROCESS" (BMR)" AFR ASIA ISLAM S/ASIA DIPLOM ADMIN LEAD LOBBY ROUTINE CONSEN...DECISION 20. PAGE 128 H2567 — CULTURE POL/PAR NAT/G LOC/G
B59

BOLTON A.R.,SOVIET MIDDLE EAST STUDIES: AN ANALYSIS AND BIBLIOGRAPHY. ISLAM JORDAN UAR USSR NAT/G SOC. PAGE 18 H0370 — BIBLIOG NAT/COMP ECO/UNDEV
B59

GOPAL R.,INDIAN MUSLIMS: A POLITICAL HISTORY (1858-1947). INDIA ISLAM PAKISTAN NAT/G SECT LEGIS LEAD COERCE WAR REPRESENT ISOLAT ORD/FREE 19/20 HINDU MUSLIM. PAGE 59 H1175 — COLONIAL GP/REL POL/PAR REGION
B59

LAQUER W.Z.,THE SOVIET UNION AND THE MIDDLE EAST. COM UAR USSR ECO/UNDEV NAT/G VOL/ASSN ECO/TAC EDU/PROP COLONIAL EXEC PWR...TIME/SEQ TREND COLD/WAR 20. PAGE 91 H1819 — ISLAM DRIVE FOR/AID NAT/LISM
B59

MEYER A.J.,MIDDLE EASTERN CAPITALISM: NINE ESSAYS. ISLAM CULTURE ECO/UNDEV INDUS MARKET NAT/G PLAN ATTIT RIGID/FLEX...STAT OBS TREND GEN/LAWS. PAGE 109 H2188 — TEC/DEV ECO/TAC ANTHOL
B60

ALMOND G.A.,THE POLITICS OF THE DEVELOPING AREAS. AFR ISLAM L/A+17C S/ASIA SOCIETY ECO/UNDEV NAT/G ADMIN PERCEPT KNOWL SOVEREIGN...CONCPT GEN/LAWS 20. PAGE 6 H0112 — EX/STRUC ATTIT NAT/LISM
B60

AUSTRUY J.,STRUCTURE ECONOMIQUE ET CIVILISATION: L'EGYPTE ET LE DESTIN ECONOMIQUE DE L'ISLAM. ISLAM UAR CREATE OP/RES ECO/TAC...SOC BIBLIOG 20 MUSLIM. PAGE 9 H0182 — ECO/UNDEV CULTURE STRUCT
B60

HAMADY S.,TEMPERAMENT AND CHARACTER OF THE ARABS. FAM NAT/G SECT DIPLOM NAT/LISM...POLICY 20 ARABS. PAGE 65 H1299 — NAT/COMP PERSON CULTURE ISLAM
B60

ZENKOVSKY S.A.,PAN-TURKISM AND ISLAM IN RUSSIA. ASIA RUSSIA USSR CULTURE POL/PAR DOMIN REV GP/REL MARXISM...LING GP/COMP BIBLIOG 19/20 TURKIC. PAGE 173 H3454 — SECT NAT/LISM COM ISLAM
S60

CROZIER B.,"FRANCE AND ALGERIA." ALGERIA EUR+WWI FRANCE FUT ISLAM ECO/UNDEV NEIGH CONSULT DELIB/GP ECO/TAC COLONIAL COERCE ATTIT...SOC INT CON/ANAL 20. PAGE 36 H0713 — NAT/G FORCES GUERRILLA NAT/LISM
S60

JAFFEE A.J.,"POPULATION TRENDS AND CONTROLS IN UNDERDEVELOPED COUNTRIES." AFR FUT ISLAM L/A+17C S/ASIA CULTURE R+D FAM ACT/RES PLAN EDU/PROP BIO/SOC RIGID/FLEX HEALTH...SOC STAT OBS CHARTS 20. PAGE 79 H1582 — ECO/UNDEV GEOG
S60

PERLMANN H.,"UPHEAVAL IN TURKEY." EUR+WWI ISLAM NAT/G FORCES TOP/EX LEGIT COERCE CHOOSE DRIVE ORD/FREE PWR...TIME/SEQ TOT/POP 20. PAGE 125 H2494 — CONSTN TURKEY
B61

BINDER L.,RELIGION AND POLITICS IN PAKISTAN. ISLAM PAKISTAN NAT/G SECT LEGIS CREATE CHOOSE GP/REL ...MAJORIT TRADIT 20. PAGE 17 H0336 — CONSTN CONFER NAT/LISM POL/PAR
B61

BOURDIEU P.,THE ALGERIANS (TRANS. BY A.C. ROSS; REV. ED.). ALGERIA ISLAM CULTURE MUNIC CAP/ISM COLONIAL GP/REL ORD/FREE SOVEREIGN 20. PAGE 19 H0385 — SOCIETY STRUCT ATTIT WAR
B61

DIA M.,THE AFRICAN NATIONS AND WORLD SOLIDARITY. ISLAM CULTURE ELITES ECO/DEV ECO/UNDEV INT/ORG NAT/G PLAN ECO/TAC INT/TRADE EDU/PROP NAT/LISM ATTIT DRIVE ORD/FREE WEALTH...SOCIALIST CONCPT CON/ANAL GEN/LAWS TOT/POP 20. PAGE 41 H0817 — AFR REGION SOCISM
B61

KEREKES T.,THE ARAB MIDDLE EAST AND MUSLIM AFRICA. ISLAM SOCIETY ECO/UNDEV SECT VOL/ASSN TOP/EX REGION ATTIT PWR...GEOG CONCPT TIME/SEQ GEN/LAWS 20. PAGE 85 H1694 — NAT/G TREND NAT/LISM
B61

PATAI R.,CULTURES IN CONFLICT; AN INQUIRY INTO THE SOCIO-CULTURAL PROBLEMS OF ISRAEL AND HER NEIGHBORS (2ND REV. ED.). ISLAM ISRAEL SOCIETY STRUCT DIPLOM GP/REL ALL/VALS...SOC 20 JEWS ARABS. PAGE 124 H2475 — NAT/COMP CULTURE GP/COMP ATTIT
B61

SAFRAN M.,EGYPT IN SEARCH OF POLITICAL COMMUNITY: AN ANALYSIS OF THE INTELLECTUAL AND POLITICAL EVOLUTION OF EGYPT, 1804-1952. ISLAM NAT/G SECT EDU/PROP COERCE ATTIT DRIVE KNOWL PWR...TIME/SEQ 20. PAGE 137 H2729 — INTELL NAT/LISM UAR
B61

SCHECHTMAN J.B.,ON WINGS OF EAGLES: THE PLIGHT, EXODUS, AND HOMECOMING OF ORIENTAL JEWRY. ASIA ISLAM ISRAEL VOL/ASSN DIPLOM CONTROL ORD/FREE ...GEOG WORSHIP SOC/INTEG 20 JEWS ARABS MIGRATION. PAGE 139 H2777 — CULTURE HABITAT KIN SECT
B61

SEMINAR REPRESENTATIVE GOVT,AFRO-ASIAN ATTITUDES: SEMINAR ON REPRESENTATIVE GOVERNMENTSPUBLIC LIBERTIES IN STATES OF ASIA AND AFRICA, RHODES, 1958. AFR ASIA BURMA INDIA ISLAM UAR VIETNAM/S SOCIETY POL/PAR CHIEF EDU/PROP PRESS PERSON ...POLICY INT 20 TUNIS. PAGE 141 H2826 — CHOOSE ATTIT NAT/COMP ORD/FREE
B61

SETON-WATSON H.,FROM LENIN TO KHRUSHCHEV: THE HISTORY OF WORLD COMMUNISM. ASIA COM EUR+WWI ISLAM S/ASIA ECO/DEV ECO/UNDEV NAT/G POL/PAR DIPLOM ECO/TAC EDU/PROP COERCE GUERRILLA ATTIT DRIVE WORK TOT/POP NAZI 20. PAGE 141 H2832 — PWR REV USSR
B61

UAR MINISTRY OF CULTURE,A BIBLIOGRAPHICAL LIST OF TUNISIA. ISLAM CULTURE NAT/G EDU/PROP COLONIAL ...GEOG 19/20 TUNIS. PAGE 157 H3146 — BIBLIOG DIPLOM SECT
S61

SCHECHTMAN J.B.,"MINORITIES IN THE MIDDLE EAST." ISLAM INTELL SOCIETY STRATA KIN NAT/G VOL/ASSN EDU/PROP REGION GP/REL DISCRIM ATTIT BIO/SOC DISPL PERSON ALL/VALS...PSY SOC OBS SAMP GEN/LAWS 20. PAGE 139 H2776 — SECT CULTURE RACE/REL
S61

VALLET R.,"IRAN: KEY TO THE MIDDLE EAST." COM IRAQ ISLAM KUWAIT LEBANON SAUDI/ARAB TURKEY ELITES SOCIETY INDUS PROC/MFG POL/PAR TOP/EX PLAN BAL/PWR DIPLOM ECO/TAC ALL/VALS...TREND CENTO 20. PAGE 161 H3224 — NAT/G ECO/UNDEV IRAN
B62

BAULIN J.,THE ARAB ROLE IN AFRICA. AFR ALGERIA FUT ISLAM MOROCCO UAR COLONIAL NEUTRAL REV...SOC 20 TUNIS BOURGUIBA. PAGE 12 H0240 — NAT/LISM DIPLOM NAT/G SECT
B62

BERGER M.,THE ARAB WORLD TODAY. CULTURE FAM INT/ORG NAT/G SECT FORCES ECO/TAC NAT/LISM HABITAT...CHARTS BIBLIOG 20 ARABS. PAGE 15 H0301 — ISLAM PERSON STRUCT SOCIETY
B62

BROWN S.D.,STUDIES ON ASIA, 1962. ASIA BURMA INDIA ISLAM ISRAEL S/ASIA ECO/UNDEV POL/PAR SECT ECO/TAC ...ANTHOL 20 CHINJAP. PAGE 22 H0450 — PWR PARL/PROC
B62

CARTER G.M.,AFRICAN ONE-PARTY STATES. ISLAM IVORY/CST LIBERIA CONSTN CULTURE SOCIETY POL/PAR PLAN DOMIN EDU/PROP EXEC REGION CHOOSE ATTIT ALL/VALS...CONCPT TIME/SEQ CHARTS VAL/FREE 20 — AFR NAT/LISM

TANGANYIKA. PAGE 27 H0545

B62
HAIM S.G.,ARAB NATIONALISM. ISLAM CONSTN GP/REL ...ANTHOL BIBLIOG JEWS 20 MID/EAST ARABS. PAGE 64 H1279 — NAT/LISM REV SECT DIPLOM

B62
HATCH J.,AFRICA TODAY-AND TOMORROW: AN OUTLINE OF BASIC FACTS AND MAJOR PROBLEMS. AFR FUT ISLAM STRATA ECO/UNDEV INT/ORG NAT/G POL/PAR DELIB/GP TOP/EX EDU/PROP LEGIT CHOOSE ATTIT...TIME/SEQ TOT/POP COLD/WAR 20. PAGE 67 H1353 — PLAN CONSTN NAT/LISM

B62
JOHNSON J.J.,THE ROLE OF THE MILITARY IN UNDERDEVELOPED COUNTRIES. AFR BURMA INDONESIA ISLAM ISRAEL L/A+17C S/ASIA THAILAND CULTURE ECO/UNDEV KIN PROVS CONSULT ACT/RES COERCE REV DRIVE RIGID/FLEX ORD/FREE...RECORD ANTHOL 20. PAGE 81 H1622 — FORCES CONCPT

B62
LEGUM C.,PAN-AFRICANISM: A SHORT POLITICAL GUIDE. ISLAM CULTURE INTELL ECO/DEV NAT/G POL/PAR DELIB/GP PLAN EDU/PROP FEDERAL NAT/LISM ATTIT DRIVE PERSON ...RECORD TIME/SEQ CHARTS STERTYP 20. PAGE 93 H1861 — AFR CONCPT

L62
MURACCIOLE L.,"LA BANQUE CENTRALE DES ETATS DE L'AFRIQUE DE L'OUEST." AFR LAW ECO/UNDEV INT/ORG NAT/G CONSULT ECO/TAC ROUTINE...CHARTS 20. PAGE 115 H2292 — ISLAM FINAN INT/TRADE

L62
ORDONNEAU P.,"LES PROBLEMES POSES PAR L'INDEPENDANCE DES NOUVEAUX ETATS AFRICAINS ET MALGACHE SUR LE PLAN DU CONTENTIEUX." FRANCE ISLAM MADAGASCAR LAW STRATA ECO/UNDEV NAT/G LEGIS LEGIT ...JURID TIME/SEQ 20. PAGE 121 H2425 — AFR ADJUD COLONIAL SOVEREIGN

S62
ANSPRENGER F.,"NATIONALISM, COMMUNISM, AND THE UNCOMMITTED NATIONS: AMERICAN PROFILES." FUT ISLAM CULTURE SOCIETY ECO/UNDEV NAT/G POL/PAR PLAN ECO/TAC EDU/PROP COERCE CHOOSE ALL/VALS MARXISM SOCISM...SOC CONCPT BIOG TREND 20. PAGE 7 H0142 — AFR COM NAT/LISM

S62
PISTRAK L.,"SOVIET VIEWS ON AFRICA." AFR COM FUT ISLAM USSR INTELL STRUCT KIN POL/PAR PLAN EDU/PROP RIGID/FLEX PWR MARXISM...TIME/SEQ WORK TOT/POP 20. PAGE 126 H2516 — NAT/G ATTIT SOCISM

S62
RAZAFIMBAHINY J.,"L'ORGANISATION AFRICAINE ET MALGACHE DE COOPERATION ECONOMIQUE." AFR ISLAM MADAGASCAR NAT/G ACT/RES ECO/TAC ALL/VALS ...TIME/SEQ 20. PAGE 130 H2601 — INT/ORG ECO/UNDEV

S62
SHATTEN F.,"POLYCENTRISM: AFRICA: NATIONALISM AND COMMUNISM." ASIA COM FUT ISLAM CULTURE SOCIETY ECO/UNDEV NAT/G PLAN DOMIN COLONIAL COERCE CHOOSE RIGID/FLEX ALL/VALS MARXISM...CONCPT TREND 20. PAGE 143 H2852 — AFR ATTIT NAT/LISM SOCISM

B63
CREMEANS C.,THE ARABS AND THE WORLD: NASSER'S ARAB NATIONALIST POLICY. FUT ISLAM UAR USA+45 SOCIETY STRATA NAT/G POL/PAR PLAN DIPLOM EDU/PROP LEGIT DRIVE ALL/VALS...INT TIME/SEQ CHARTS 20 NASSER/G. PAGE 35 H0700 — TOP/EX ATTIT REGION NAT/LISM

B63
HALPERIN M.H.,THE POLITICS OF SOCIAL CHANGE IN THE MIDDLE EAST AND NORTH AFRICA. ISLAM CULTURE ACT/RES REV ATTIT PERCEPT KNOWL...METH/CNCPT OBS TIME/SEQ GEN/METH TOT/POP VAL/FREE 20. PAGE 64 H1291 — SOC TREND

B63
HARDY M.J.L.,BLOOD FEUDS AND THE PAYMENT OF BLOOD MONEY IN THE MIDDLE EAST. ISLAM SOCIETY SECT REGION SANCTION COERCE DEATH MURDER 7/20 ARABS. PAGE 66 H1329 — KIN TRIBUTE LAW CULTURE

B63
ISSAWI C.,EGYPT IN REVOLUTION: AN ECONOMIC ANALYSIS. ISLAM STRUCT ECO/UNDEV AGRI FINAN INDUS PLAN EXEC REV NAT/LISM ATTIT RIGID/FLEX WEALTH SOCISM...STAT WORK 20. PAGE 79 H1573 — NAT/G UAR

B63
JUNOD V.,HANDBOOK OF AFRICA. AFR ISLAM CONSTN SOCIETY NAT/G POL/PAR...GEOG SOC STAT CHARTS WORK 20. PAGE 82 H1642 — ECO/UNDEV REGION

B63
KHADDURI M.,MODERN LIBYA: A STUDY IN POLITICAL DEVELOPMENT. EUR+WWI ISLAM LIBYA ELITES INT/ORG POL/PAR FORCES DIPLOM FOR/AID DOMIN EDU/PROP LEGIT NAT/LISM DRIVE RIGID/FLEX SKILL...CONCPT TIME/SEQ TREND 20. PAGE 85 H1704 — NAT/G STRUCT

B63
KURZMAN D.,SUBVERSION OF THE INNOCENTS: PATTERNS OF COMMUNIST PENETRATION OF AFRICA, THE MIDDLE EAST AND AFRICA. AFR ASIA ISLAM S/ASIA CULTURE NAT/G FORCES PLAN EDU/PROP ADMIN ATTIT...CONCPT INT UNPLAN/INT TIME/SEQ. PAGE 89 H1785 — COM COERCE

B63
LERNER R.,MEDIEVAL POLITICAL PHILOSOPHY. ISLAM MORAL PWR CATHISM...CATH CONCPT OBS IDEA/COMP ANTHOL 9/15 JEWS CHRISTIAN BACON/R AQUINAS/T. PAGE 95 H1890 — KNOWL PHIL/SCI

B63
QUAISON-SACKEY A.,AFRICA UNBOUND: REFLECTIONS OF AN AFRICAN STATESMAN. ISLAM CULTURE INTELL INT/ORG POL/PAR TOP/EX DOMIN EDU/PROP LEGIT ATTIT PERSON ...CONCPT OBS TIME/SEQ CHARTS STERTYP 20 UN. PAGE 129 H2571 — AFR BIOG

B63
SCHECHTMAN J.B.,THE REFUGEE IN THE WORLD: DISPLACEMENT AND INTEGRATION. AFR ASIA EUR+WWI ISLAM L/A+17C S/ASIA CULTURE STRATA LOC/G EX/STRUC PLAN ECO/TAC ROUTINE...CONCPT TIME/SEQ VAL/FREE 20. PAGE 139 H2779 — INT/ORG SOC

B63
STEVENS G.G.,EGYPT YESTERDAY AND TODAY. CONSTN ECO/UNDEV AGRI INDUS NAT/G POL/PAR FORCES ECO/TAC EDU/PROP COERCE WAR NAT/LISM DRIVE ALL/VALS ...TIME/SEQ WORK SUEZ 20. PAGE 149 H2983 — ISLAM TOP/EX REV UAR

B63
UAR MINISTRY OF CULTURE,A BIBLIOGRAPHICAL LIST OF ARABIAN PENINSULA. ISLAM SAUDI/ARAB YEMEN FINAN NAT/G DIPLOM 19/20. PAGE 157 H3147 — BIBLIOG GEOG INDUS SECT

B63
ZARTMAN I.W.,GOVERNMENT AND POLITICS IN NORTHERN AFRICA. AFR ALGERIA ISLAM LIBYA MOROCCO UAR ELITES SOCIETY PLAN ECO/TAC DOMIN EDU/PROP LEGIT ATTIT ...GEOG CONCPT TIME/SEQ 20 TUNIS. PAGE 172 H3448 — CULTURE DRIVE NAT/LISM

L63
NASH M.,"PSYCHO-CULTURAL FACTORS IN ASIAN ECONOMIC GROWTH." ASIA ISLAM S/ASIA CULTURE ECO/UNDEV DELIB/GP EDU/PROP COERCE ATTIT PERSON HEALTH KNOWL ORD/FREE...PSY SOC STAT TREND ANTHOL VAL/FREE 20. PAGE 116 H2313 — SOCIETY ECO/TAC

L63
ZARTMAN I.W.,"THE SAHARA--BRIDGE OR BARRIER." ISLAM CULTURE SOCIETY NAT/G DELIB/GP DOMIN EDU/PROP LEGIT ATTIT...HIST/WRIT TIME/SEQ CHARTS TOT/POP VAL/FREE 20. PAGE 172 H3447 — INT/ORG PWR NAT/LISM

S63
ARASTEH R.,"THE ROLE OF INTELLECTUALS IN ADMINISTRATIVE DEVELOPMENT AND SOCIAL CHANGE IN MODERN IRAN." ISLAM CULTURE NAT/G CONSULT ACT/RES EDU/PROP EXEC ATTIT BIO/SOC PERCEPT SUPEGO ALL/VALS ...POLICY MGT PSY SOC CONCPT 20. PAGE 8 H0157 — INTELL ADMIN IRAN

S63
BILL J.A.,"THE SOCIAL AND ECONOMIC FOUNDATIONS OF POWER IN CONTEMPORARY IRAN." ISLAM CULTURE NAT/G ECO/TAC DOMIN COERCE ATTIT PWR WEALTH...TREND VAL/FREE 20. PAGE 17 H0334 — SOCIETY STRATA IRAN

S63
HOSKINS H.L.,"ARAB SOCIALISM IN THE UAR." ISLAM USSR AGRI INDUS NAT/G TOP/EX CREATE DIPLOM EDU/PROP DRIVE KNOWL PWR SOCISM...POLICY CONCPT TREND SUEZ 20. PAGE 74 H1478 — ECO/DEV PLAN UAR

S63
HUREWITZ J.C.,"LEBANESE DEMOCRACY IN ITS INTERNATIONAL SETTING." FRANCE ISLAM UK LOC/G NAT/G SECT DOMIN EDU/PROP EXEC ATTIT PWR...TIME/SEQ 20. PAGE 75 H1507 — STRUCT LEBANON

S63
RUSTOW D.A.,"THE MILITARY IN MIDDLE EASTERN SOCIETY AND POLITICS." FUT ISLAM CONSTN SOCIETY FACE/GP NAT/G POL/PAR PROF/ORG CONSULT DOMIN ADMIN EXEC REGION COERCE NAT/LISM ATTIT DRIVE PERSON ORD/FREE PWR...POLICY CONCPT OBS STERTYP 20. PAGE 136 H2721 — FORCES ELITES

S63
TILMAN R.O.,"MALAYSIA: THE PROBLEMS OF FEDERATION." ISLAM S/ASIA CONSTN PROVS SECT DELIB/GP DOMIN EDU/PROP LEGIT EXEC COERCE CHOOSE ATTIT HEALTH ORD/FREE PWR...STAT TOT/POP VAL/FREE 20. PAGE 155 H3097 — NAT/G CULTURE MALAYSIA

B64
AFRO ASIAN SOLIDARITY AGAINST IMPERIALISM. AFR ISLAM S/ASIA ECO/UNDEV NAT/G POL/PAR TOP/EX PRESS ...INT ANTHOL 20 CHOU/ENLAI. PAGE 2 H0043 — MARXISM DIPLOM EDU/PROP CHIEF

B64
BINDER L.,THE IDEOLOGICAL REVOLUTION IN THE MIDDLE EAST. ISLAM STRUCT INT/ORG KIN SECT EX/STRUC TOP/EX PLAN ATTIT DRIVE RIGID/FLEX PWR...MYTH TOT/POP 20. PAGE 17 H0338 — POL/PAR NAT/G NAT/LISM

B64
JUCKER-FLEETWOOD E.,MONEY AND FINANCE IN AFRICA. ISLAM ECO/UNDEV SERV/IND NAT/G EX/STRUC PLAN ECO/TAC ROUTINE WEALTH...MGT TOT/POP 20. PAGE 82 H1639 — AFR FINAN

B64
MELADY T.,FACES OF AFRICA. AFR FUT ISLAM NAT/G POL/PAR SCHOOL DELIB/GP PLAN ECO/TAC EDU/PROP ATTIT ALL/VALS...CHARTS TOT/POP VAL/FREE 20. PAGE 108 H2168 — ECO/UNDEV TREND NAT/LISM

B64
RAMAZANI R.K.,THE MIDDLE EAST AND THE EUROPEAN — ECO/UNDEV

COMMON MARKET. EUR+WWI ISLAM ECO/DEV EXTR/IND MARKET PROC/MFG INT/ORG NAT/G TEC/DEV ECO/TAC REGION DRIVE WEALTH...STAT CHARTS EEC TOT/POP 20. PAGE 129 H2587
ATTIT INT/TRADE

B64
THORNBURG M.W.,PEOPLE AND POLICY IN THE MIDDLE EAST. ISLAM ECO/UNDEV FAM KIN MUNIC NAT/G NEIGH POL/PAR SECT DELIB/GP LEGIS PLAN ECO/TAC DOMIN ADMIN ATTIT HEALTH RESPECT...SOC CONCPT METH/CNCPT OBS TIME/SEQ TOT/POP VAL/FREE. PAGE 154 H3088
TEC/DEV CULTURE

B64
VON GRUNEBAUM G.E.,MODERN ISLAM: THE SEARCH FOR CULTURAL IDENTITY. ACADEM NEIGH WRITING NAT/LISM ...HUM CONCPT 19/20 MUSLIM MID/EAST ARABS. PAGE 163 H3269
ISLAM CULTURE CREATE SECT

B64
WARD R.E.,POLITICAL MODERNIZATION IN JAPAN AND TURKEY. ASIA ISLAM S/ASIA CONSTN CULTURE STRATA COM/IND POL/PAR FORCES ACT/RES ECO/TAC DOMIN EDU/PROP LEGIT ADMIN CHOOSE ATTIT ALL/VALS...STAT TIME/SEQ VAL/FREE CHINJAP. PAGE 165 H3307
SOCIETY TURKEY

B64
WICKENS G.M.,PERSIA IN ISLAMIC TIMES: A PRACTICAL BIBLIOGRAPHY OF ITS HISTORY, CULTURE AND LANGUAGE (PAMPHLET). IRAN ISLAM SECT. PAGE 168 H3355
BIBLIOG CULTURE LING

B64
ZARTMAN I.W.,MOROCCO: PROBLEMS OF NEW POWER. ISLAM CULTURE ECO/UNDEV AGRI POL/PAR SCHOOL FORCES ADMIN ...CONCPT STAT INT CENSUS TIME/SEQ CHARTS WORK VAL/FREE 20. PAGE 172 H3449
CHOOSE MOROCCO DELIB/GP DECISION

L64
BERELSON B.,"SAMPLE SURVEYS AND POPULATION CONTROL." ASIA FUT ISLAM L/A+17C CULTURE SOCIETY FAM NAT/G CONSULT PLAN EDU/PROP ATTIT DRIVE ALL/VALS...POLICY RELATIV HEAL PSY SOC CONCPT METH/CNCPT OBS OBS/ENVIR TOT/POP. PAGE 15 H0297
BIO/SOC SAMP

S64
BARIETY J.,"LA POLITIQUE EXTERIEURE ALLEMANDE DANS L'HIVER 1939-1940." COM FINLAND GERMANY ISLAM ITALY USSR NAT/G FORCES ECO/TAC DOMIN EDU/PROP COERCE WAR PWR WEALTH...HIST/WRIT NAZI TOT/POP VAL/FREE 20. PAGE 11 H0216
EUR+WWI DIPLOM

S64
DE GAULLE C.,"FRENCH WORLD VIEW." AFR ASIA CHINA/COM EUR+WWI ISLAM ECO/UNDEV INT/ORG NAT/G VOL/ASSN ACT/RES DIPLOM ECO/TAC EDU/PROP ATTIT DRIVE WEALTH 20. PAGE 37 H0751
TOP/EX PWR FOR/AID FRANCE

S64
EISTER A.W.,"PERSPECTIVE ON FUNCTIONS OF RELIGION IN A DEVELOPING COUNTRY: ISLAM IN PAKISTAN." ISLAM CULTURE MUNIC ACT/RES CREATE PROB/SOLV TEC/DEV WORSHIP. PAGE 45 H0902
ATTIT SECT ECO/DEV

S64
LEWIS B.,"THE QUEST FOR FREEDOM--A SAD STORY OF THE MIDDLE EAST." ISLAM ISRAEL LEBANON TURKEY CULTURE NAT/G SECT LEGIS TOP/EX DOMIN EDU/PROP LEGIT ORD/FREE PWR RESPECT...POLICY TIME/SEQ VAL/FREE 20. PAGE 96 H1911
CONSTN ATTIT NAT/LISM

S64
RAMAZANI R.K.,"CHURCH AND STATE IN MODERNIZING SOCIETY: THE CASE OF IRAN." ISLAM CULTURE ORD/FREE PWR...TIME/SEQ VAL/FREE 17/20. PAGE 129 H2586
SECT NAT/G ELITES IRAN

S64
SAAB H.,"THE ARAB SEARCH FOR A FEDERAL UNION." SOCIETY INT/ORG NAT/G DELIB/GP FORCES ACT/RES TEC/DEV ECO/TAC DOMIN LEGIT REGION ROUTINE ATTIT DRIVE RIGID/FLEX ALL/VALS...SOC CONCPT NEW/IDEA TIME/SEQ TREND. PAGE 136 H2726
ISLAM PLAN

S64
SAYEED K.,"PATHAN REGIONALISM." ISLAM PAKISTAN S/ASIA CULTURE SOCIETY NAT/G NEIGH DIPLOM LEGIT COERCE CHOOSE ATTIT DISPL PERCEPT ALL/VALS SOVEREIGN...POLICY RELATIV SOC TIME/SEQ TOT/POP 20. PAGE 138 H2761
SECT NAT/LISM REGION

S64
TOUVAL S.,"THE SOMALI REPUBLIC." AFR ISLAM SOMALIA FAM KIN NAT/G CREATE FOR/AID LEGIT ATTIT ALL/VALS ...RECORD TREND 20. PAGE 156 H3119
ECO/UNDEV RIGID/FLEX

S64
TOYNBEE A.,"BRITAIN AND THE ARABS: THE NEED FOR A NEW START." NAT/G CREATE COLONIAL ATTIT RIGID/FLEX MORAL PWR...POLICY HIST/WRIT 20. PAGE 156 H3124
ISLAM ECO/TAC DIPLOM UK

S64
ZARTMAN I.W.,"LES RELATIONS ENTRE LA FRANCE ET L'ALGERIA DEPUIS LES ACCORDS D'EVIAN." EUR+WWI FUT ISLAM CULTURE AGRI EXTR/IND FINAN INDUS POL/PAR DIPLOM ECO/TAC FOR/AID PEACE ATTIT DRIVE ALL/VALS ...TIME/SEQ VAL/FREE 20. PAGE 172 H3450
ECO/UNDEV ALGERIA FRANCE

B65
INST INTL DES CIVILISATION DIF,THE CONSTITUTIONS AND ADMINISTRATIVE INSTITUTIONS OF THE NEW STATES. AFR ISLAM S/ASIA NAT/G POL/PAR DELIB/GP EX/STRUC CONFER EFFICIENCY NAT/LISM...JURID SOC 20. PAGE 77 H1535
CONSTN ADMIN ADJUD ECO/UNDEV

B65
INT. BANK RECONSTR. DEVELOP.,ECONOMIC DEVELOPMENT OF KUWAIT. ISLAM KUWAIT AGRI FINAN MARKET EX/STRUC TEC/DEV ECO/TAC ADMIN WEALTH...OBS CON/ANAL CHARTS 20. PAGE 77 H1541
INDUS NAT/G

B65
POLK W.R.,THE UNITED STATES AND THE ARAB WORLD. USA+45 ECO/UNDEV EXTR/IND SECT WAR NAT/LISM ATTIT ...NAT/COMP COLD/WAR. PAGE 127 H2535
ISLAM REGION CULTURE DIPLOM

B65
RIVLIN B.,THE CONTEMPORARY MIDDLE EAST* TRADITION AND INNOVATION. CULTURE SOCIETY ECO/UNDEV NAT/G TREND. PAGE 132 H2636
ANTHOL ISLAM NAT/LISM DIPLOM

B65
SAUVAGET J.,INTRODUCTION TO THE HISTORY OF THE MIDDLE EAST (A BIBLIOGRAPHICAL GUIDE). LAW CULTURE GEOG. PAGE 138 H2757
BIBLIOG/A ISLAM GOV/COMP

B65
TUTSCH H.E.,FACETS OF ARAB NATIONALISM. ISLAM ISRAEL CULTURE STRUCT SECT RIGID/FLEX ORD/FREE MARXISM SOCISM 20. PAGE 157 H3143
ECO/UNDEV NAT/LISM TEC/DEV SOCIETY

B65
VON RENESSE E.A.,UNVOLLENDETE DEMOKRATIEN. AFR ISLAM S/ASIA SOCIETY ACT/RES COLONIAL...JURID CHARTS BIBLIOG METH 13/20. PAGE 164 H3276
ECO/UNDEV NAT/COMP SOVEREIGN

B66
HOPKINS J.F.K.,ARABIC PERIODICAL LITERATURE, 1961. ISLAM LAW CULTURE SECT...GEOG HEAL PHIL/SCI PSY SOC 20. PAGE 73 H1466
BIBLIOG/A NAT/LISM TEC/DEV INDUS

B66
IBRAHIM-HILMY,THE LITERATURE OF EGYPT AND THE SOUDAN: FROM THE EARLIEST TIMES TO THE YEAR 1885 INCLUSIVE (2 VOLS.). MEDIT-7 SUDAN UAR LAW SOCIETY SECT ATTIT EGYPT/ANC. PAGE 76 H1520
BIBLIOG CULTURE ISLAM NAT/G

B66
KAZAMIAS A.M.,EDUCATION AND QUEST FOR MODERNITY IN TURKEY. ISLAM SOCIETY SECT NAT/LISM ATTIT ORD/FREE SOVEREIGN TURKS. PAGE 84 H1672
NAT/G EDU/PROP STRATA CULTURE

B66
KERR M.H.,ISLAMIC REFORM: THE POLITICAL AND LEGAL THEORIES OF MUHAMMAD 'ABDUH AND RASHID RIDA. NAT/G SECT LEAD SOVEREIGN CONSERVE...JURID BIBLIOG WORSHIP 20. PAGE 85 H1698
LAW CONCPT ISLAM

B66
RIZK C.,LE REGIME POLITIQUE LIBANAIS. ISLAM LEBANON STRUCT POL/PAR SECT LOBBY GP/REL 20 ARABS MUSLIM CHRISTIAN. PAGE 132 H2637
ECO/UNDEV NAT/G CULTURE

B66
THOMPSON J.H.,MODERNIZATION OF THE ARAB WORLD. FUT ISRAEL STRUCT ECO/UNDEV DIPLOM INGP/REL ATTIT ...CENSUS ANTHOL 20 ARABS. PAGE 154 H3082
ADJUST ISLAM PROB/SOLV NAT/COMP

B66
US DEPARTMENT OF STATE,RESEARCH ON THE MIDDLE EAST (EXTERNAL RESEARCH LIST NO 4-25). GREECE ISRAEL SYRIA UAR YEMEN CULTURE SOCIETY POL/PAR SECT DIPLOM EDU/PROP WAR NAT/LISM...GEOG GOV/COMP 20. PAGE 160 H3190
BIBLIOG/A ISLAM NAT/G REGION

B66
WHEELER G.,THE PEOPLES OF SOVIET CENTRAL ASIA: A BACKGROUND BOOK. ISLAM USSR STRATA STRUCT FORCES REV WAR HABITAT 7/20. PAGE 167 H3341
COLONIAL DOMIN CULTURE ADJUST

B66
ZEINE Z.N.,THE EMERGENCE OF ARAB NATIONALISM (REV. ED.). TURKEY UK NAT/G SECT TEC/DEV LEAD REV WAR AGE/Y ROLE ORD/FREE...TRADIT CHARTS BIBLIOG 20 ARABS OTTOMAN. PAGE 173 H3453
ISLAM NAT/LISM DIPLOM

B67
COLLINS R.O.,EGYPT AND THE SUDAN. COM FRANCE ISLAM SUDAN UAR UK SOCIETY NAT/G COLONIAL NAT/LISM...GEOG SOC LING TREND SOC/INTEG 7/20 SUEZ. PAGE 32 H0635
AGRI CULTURE ECO/UNDEV

B67
MEHDI M.T.,PEACE IN THE MIDDLE EAST. ISRAEL SOCIETY NAT/G PLAN EDU/PROP NAT/LISM DRIVE...IDEA/COMP 20 JEWS. PAGE 108 H2160
ISLAM DIPLOM GP/REL COERCE

B67
OLIVER R.,AFRICA SINCE 1800. AFR ISLAM CULTURE ECO/UNDEV SECT DOMIN RACE/REL DISCRIM SOVEREIGN 19/20. PAGE 121 H2414
DIPLOM COLONIAL REGION

B67
PATAI R.,GOLDEN RIVER TO GOLDEN ROAD: SOCIETY, CULTURE, AND CHANGE IN THE MIDDLE EAST (2ND ED.). ELITES FAM KIN TEC/DEV MARRIAGE NAT/LISM SEX ORD/FREE...TREND GP/COMP WORSHIP 20. PAGE 124 H2476
CULTURE SOCIETY ISLAM STRUCT

L67
VAN DER KROEF J.M.,"INDONESIA: THE BATTLE OF THE 'OLD' AND THE 'NEW ORDER'." INDONESIA ISLAM ELITES POL/PAR DOMIN INGP/REL NAT/LISM PWR...IDEA/COMP 20. PAGE 161 H3229
FORCES MARXISM NAT/G BAL/PWR

S67
ABDEL-MALEK A.,"THE CRISIS IN NASSER'S EGYPT." ISLAM UAR STRUCT POL/PAR EX/STRUC CREATE PLAN WAR ATTIT ORD/FREE PWR...POLICY DECISION 20. PAGE 3 H0054
FORCES LEAD PROB/SOLV NAT/G

S67
HALPERN B.,"THE ORIGINS OF THE CRISIS." ISLAM ISRAEL INT/ORG FORCES WEAPON PEACE ORD/FREE TREATY 20 UN. PAGE 65 H1296
WAR NAT/G DIPLOM

S67
KYLE K.,"BACKGROUND TO THE CRISIS" ISLAM ISRAEL UAR UK USSR NAT/G PROB/SOLV LEGIT CONTROL REGION STRANGE MORAL 20 JEWS. PAGE 89 H1787
DIPLOM POLICY SOVEREIGN COERCE

S67
NAHUMI M.,"THE POWERS IN THE MIDDLE EAST CONFLICT." ISLAM ISRAEL JORDAN UAR NAT/G PEACE ATTIT 20 JEWS. PAGE 115 H2304
DIPLOM WAR NAT/LISM

S67
ROOT W.,"REPORT FROM PARIS - DE GAULLE: WHICH WAY TO THE FUTURE?" CANADA FRANCE ISLAM UK INT/ORG CHIEF CREATE AGREE CONTROL ARMS/CONT NUC/PWR EQUILIB PEACE PWR 20 DEGAULLE/C NATO. PAGE 134 H2670
POLICY DIPLOM NAT/G BAL/PWR

S67
SYRKIN M.,"THE RIGHT TO BE ORDINARY." ISLAM ISRAEL NAT/G COERCE NAT/LISM RIGID/FLEX 20. PAGE 151 H3025
SOVEREIGN WAR FORCES DIPLOM

S67
ZARTMAN I.W.," NAT/G POL/PAR VOL/ASSN NAT/LISM ORD/FREE PWR...CONCPT NAT/COMP ORG/CHARTS OAU MAGHREB. PAGE 172 H3451
AFR ISLAM DIPLOM REGION

S68
LAPIERRE J.W.,"TRADITION ET MODERNITE A MADAGASCAR." ISLAM MADAGASCAR AGRI FINAN KIN NAT/G CREATE OP/RES GP/REL INGP/REL ATTIT CONSERVE...PSY 20. PAGE 91 H1813
ECO/UNDEV FOR/AID CULTURE TEC/DEV

B86
MAS LATRIE L.,RELATIONS ET COMMERCE DE L'AFRIQUE SEPTENTRIONALE OU MAGREB AVEC LES NATIONS CHRETIENNES AU MOYEN AGE. CULTURE CHIEF FORCES WAR ...SOC CENSUS TREATY 10/16. PAGE 104 H2084
ISLAM SECT DIPLOM INT/TRADE

C89
PLAYFAIR R.L.,"A BIBLIOGRAPHY OF ALGERIA." ALGERIA CULTURE ECO/UNDEV DIST/IND EXTR/IND FINAN SECT CRIME 16/19. PAGE 126 H2525
BIBLIOG/A ISLAM GEOG

B93
ROYAL GEOGRAPHIC SOCIETY,BIBLIOGRAPHY OF BARBARY STATES (4 SUPPLEMENTARY PAPERS). ALGERIA LIBYA MOROCCO SOCIETY STRUCT DIPLOM LEAD 14/19 TUNIS. PAGE 135 H2706
BIBLIOG ISLAM NAT/G COLONIAL

C93
PLAYFAIR R.L.,"A BIBLIOGRAPHY OF MOROCCO." MOROCCO CULTURE AGRI FORCES DIPLOM WAR HEALTH...GEOG JURID SOC CHARTS. PAGE 126 H2526
BIBLIOG ISLAM MEDIT-7

ISOLAT....ISOLATION AND COMMUNITY, CONDITIONS OF HIGH GROUP SEGREGATION

N
US LIBRARY OF CONGRESS,EAST EUROPEAN ACCESSIONS INDEX. NAT/G ISOLAT ATTIT KNOWL...POLICY 20. PAGE 160 H3202
BIBLIOG COM MARXIST DIPLOM

B30
OLDMAN J.H.,WHITE AND BLACK IN AFRICA. AFR STRUCT COLONIAL PARTIC DISCRIM ISOLAT PRIVIL 20 SMUTS/JAN NEGRO WHITE/SUP. PAGE 121 H2412
SOVEREIGN ORD/FREE RACE/REL NAT/G

B40
WOLFERS A.,BRITAIN AND FRANCE BETWEEN TWO WORLD WARS. FRANCE UK INT/ORG NAT/G PLAN BARGAIN ECO/TAC AGREE ISOLAT ALL/IDEOS...DECISION GEOG 20 TREATY VERSAILLES INTERVENT. PAGE 170 H3402
DIPLOM WAR POLICY

B42
REDFIELD R.,THE FOLK CULTURE OF YUCATAN. STRATA FAM KIN MUNIC SECT DISCRIM ISOLAT ANOMIE HEALTH ...BIBLIOG 20 MEXIC/AMER. PAGE 130 H2605
CULTURE NEIGH GP/COMP SOCIETY

B45
MCBRYDE F.W.,CULTURAL AND HISTORICAL GEOGRAPHY OF SOUTHWEST GUATEMALA. GUATEMALA AGRI KIN PERSON ...GEOG AUD/VIS CHARTS 20. PAGE 106 H2123
HABITAT ISOLAT CULTURE ECO/UNDEV

L48
SHILS E.A.,"COHESION AND DISINTEGRATION IN THE WEHRMACHT IN WORLD WAR II." GERMANY STRUCT DOMIN WAR INGP/REL ISOLAT NAT/LISM ATTIT AUTHORIT SUPEGO RESPECT...PSY CON/ANAL 20 NAZI. PAGE 143 H2862
EDU/PROP DRIVE PERS/REL FORCES

B49
GORER G.,THE PEOPLE OF GREAT RUSSIA: A PSYCHOLOGICAL STUDY. RUSSIA USSR NAT/G DIPLOM LEAD AGE/C ANOMIE ATTIT DRIVE...POLICY 20. PAGE 59 H1182
ISOLAT PERSON PSY SOCIETY

S49
DEXTER L.A.,"A DIALOGUE ON THE SOCIAL PSYCHOLOGY OF COLONIALISM AND ON CERTAIN PUERTO RICAN PROFESSIONAL PERSONALITY PATTERNS." L/A+17C PUERT/RICO STRATA STRUCT DOMIN ISOLAT DRIVE ...NAT/COMP PERS/COMP HYPO/EXP 20 JEWS NEGRO. PAGE 41 H0813
COLONIAL SOC PSY PERSON

B51
BERNATZIK H.A.,THE SPIRITS OF THE YELLOW LEAVES. BURMA LAOS S/ASIA THAILAND VIETNAM SOCIETY AGRI COLONIAL LEISURE GP/REL PERS/REL ISOLAT AGE HABITAT SEX WORSHIP 20. PAGE 16 H0310
SOC KIN ECO/UNDEV CULTURE

B52
CALLOT E.,LA SOCIETE ET SON ENVIRONNEMENT: ESSAI SUR LES PRINCIPES DES SCIENCES SOCIALES. GP/REL ADJUST CONSEN ISOLAT HABITAT PERCEPT PERSON ...BIBLIOG SOC/INTEG 20. PAGE 25 H0507
SOCIETY PHIL/SCI CULTURE

B54
KOLARZ W.,THE PEOPLES OF THE SOVIET FAR EAST. RUSSIA USSR STRUCT LEAD ISOLAT NAT/LISM...CHARTS 20. PAGE 88 H1750
COLONIAL RACE/REL ADJUST CULTURE

B57
MENDIETTA Y NUNE L.,THEORIE DES GROUPEMENT SOCIAUX SUIVI D'UNE ETUDE SUR LE DROIT SOCIAL. ELITES FAM KIN NAT/G PROB/SOLV CROWD ISOLAT ATTIT PERSON ...JURID CONCPT SOC/INTEG. PAGE 109 H2174
SOC STRATA STRUCT DISCRIM

B59
GOPAL R.,INDIAN MUSLIMS: A POLITICAL HISTORY (1858-1947). INDIA ISLAM PAKISTAN NAT/G SECT LEGIS LEAD COERCE WAR REPRESENT ISOLAT ORD/FREE 19/20 HINDU MUSLIM. PAGE 59 H1175
COLONIAL GP/REL POL/PAR REGION

B59
HOBSBAWM E.J.,PRIMITIVE REBELS; STUDIES IN ARCHAIC FORMS OF SOCIAL MOVEMENT IN THE 19TH AND 20TH CENTURIES. ITALY SPAIN CULTURE VOL/ASSN RISK CROWD GP/REL INGP/REL ISOLAT TOTALISM...PSY SOC 18/20. PAGE 72 H1438
SOCIETY CRIME REV GUERRILLA

B60
ROSKAM K.L.,APARTHEID AND DISCRIMINATION. SOUTH/AFR SOCIETY STRUCT NAT/G POL/PAR GP/REL ISOLAT ...BIBLIOG 20. PAGE 134 H2683
DISCRIM RACE/REL CULTURE POLICY

B61
BURKS R.V.,THE DYNAMICS OF COMMUNISM IN EASTERN EUROPE. COM YUGOSLAVIA POL/PAR RACE/REL ISOLAT ...CORREL CON/ANAL CHARTS GP/COMP DICTIONARY 20 EUROPE/E SLAV/MACED. PAGE 24 H0489
MARXISM STRUCT WORKER REPRESENT

B61
TURNBULL C.M.,THE FOREST PEOPLE. EATING GP/REL INGP/REL RACE/REL ISOLAT HABITAT HEREDITY...GEOG SOC LING DICTIONARY WORSHIP 20 CONGO NEGRO BA/MBUTI. PAGE 157 H3138
AFR CULTURE KIN RECORD

S61
LIEBERSON S.,"THE IMPACT OF RESIDENTIAL SEGREGATION ON ETHNIC ASSIMILATION" (BMR)" CULTURE MUNIC GP/REL RACE/REL DISCRIM...GEOG STAT CON/ANAL CHARTS SOC/INTEG 20 MIGRATION. PAGE 96 H1926
HABITAT ISOLAT NEIGH

B62
TURNBULL C.M.,THE LONELY AFRICAN. AFR MUNIC SECT ANOMIE ALL/VALS...DECISION 20. PAGE 157 H3139
CULTURE ISOLAT KIN TRADIT

B63
HAMM H.,ALBANIA - CHINA'S BEACHHEAD IN EUROPE. ALBANIA CHINA/COM USSR YUGOSLAVIA ELITES SOCIETY POL/PAR DELIB/GP FORCES ECO/TAC COERCE ISOLAT PEACE MARXISM...IDEA/COMP 20 MAO. PAGE 65 H1304
DIPLOM REV NAT/G POLICY

B63
MAC MILLAN W.M.,BANTU, BOER, AND BRITON: THE MAKING OF THE SOUTH AFRICAN NATIVE PROBLEM. SOUTH/AFR UK LAW KIN NAT/G SECT LEGIS COLONIAL ISOLAT ATTIT ...BIOG 18/20 BANTU NEGRO PHILIP/J MISSION. PAGE 100 H1989
AFR RACE/REL ELITES

B64
GREEN M.M.,IBO VILLAGE AFFAIRS. AFR FORCES PERS/REL ADJUST ISOLAT ATTIT HABITAT PERSON ALL/VALS...JURID RECORD SOC/INTEG 20 IBO. PAGE 60 H1207
MUNIC CULTURE ECO/UNDEV SOC

B65
KLEIN J.,SAMPLES FROM ENGLISH CULTURES (2 VOLS.). UK STRATA FAM NEIGH WORKER ETIQUET ISOLAT AGE/C AGE/A HABITAT RIGID/FLEX...NET/THEORY CHARTS 20. PAGE 87 H1732
CULTURE INGP/REL ATTIT SOC

B65
KUNSTADTER P.,THE LUA (LAWA) OF NORTHERN THAILAND: ASPECTS OF SOCIAL STRUCTURE, AGRICULTURE, AND RELIGION. THAILAND AGRI FAM KIN INGP/REL ISOLAT MARRIAGE HEALTH WORSHIP 20 BUDDHISM LUA. PAGE 89 H1780
STRUCT ECO/UNDEV CULTURE

B66
CHANG,THE PARTY AND THE NATIONAL QUESTION IN CHINA (TRANS. BY GEORGE MOSELEY). CHINA/COM CULTURE CONTROL NAT/LISM...CHARTS BIBLIOG/A 20. PAGE 29 H0576
GP/REL REGION ISOLAT MARXISM

B66
GURR T.,NEW ERROR-COMPENSATED MEASURES FOR NAT/COMP
COMPARING NATIONS* SOME CORRELATES OF CIVIL INDEX
VIOLENCE. WOR+45 SOCIETY REV ISOLAT...PHIL/SCI SOC COERCE
QUANT TESTS SAMP/SIZ HYPO/EXP. PAGE 63 H1254 NEW/IDEA

L66
KRENZ F.E.,"THE REFUGEE AS A SUBJECT OF INT/LAW
INTERNATIONAL LAW." FUT LAW NAT/G CREATE ADJUD DISCRIM
ISOLAT STRANGE...RECORD UN. PAGE 88 H1766 NEW/IDEA

B67
FANON F.,BLACK SKIN, WHITE MASKS: THE EXPERIENCES DISCRIM
OF A BLACK MAN IN A WHITE WORLD. CULTURE COLONIAL PERS/REL
HAPPINESS ISOLAT STRANGE ATTIT HABITAT RIGID/FLEX RACE/REL
SEX...BIOG STERTYP SOC/INTEG 20 NEGRO. PAGE 49 PSY
H0970

B67
PENDLE G.,PARAGUAY: A RIVERSIDE NATION (3RD ED.). CULTURE
PARAGUAY CHIEF ISOLAT...HUM CHARTS BIBLIOG 16/20. GEOG
PAGE 124 H2487 ECO/UNDEV

L67
UNESCO,"APARTHEID." SOUTH/AFR STRUCT KIN SCHOOL DISCRIM
SECT WORKER DOMIN EDU/PROP REGION RACE/REL ISOLAT CULTURE
20. PAGE 158 H3164 COERCE
COLONIAL

S67
BASKIN D.B.,"NATIONALITY DOCTRINE AND ANTI-SEMITISM NAT/LISM
IN THE USSR." USSR CULTURE STRATA ISOLAT MAJORITY MARXISM
ATTIT RIGID/FLEX RESPECT...GP/COMP JEWS. PAGE 12 GP/REL
H0234 DISCRIM

S67
MALAN V.D.,"THE SILENT VILLAGE." KIN MUNIC NEIGH CULTURE
CHOOSE ISOLAT ROLE...SOC INDIAN/AM. PAGE 101 H2027 STRUCT
PREDICT

B99
DU BOIS W.E.B.,THE PHILADELPHIA NEGRO: A SOCIAL INGP/REL
STUDY. CULTURE STRATA KIN CRIME SUFF ADJUST DISCRIM RACE/REL
ISOLAT HABITAT HEREDITY ALL/VALS SOC/INTEG 17/19 SOC
NEGRO PHILADELPH. PAGE 42 H0851 CENSUS

ISOLATION....SEE ISOLAT

ISRAEL J. H1571,H1572

ISRAEL....SEE ALSO JEWS, ISLAM

N
US LIBRARY OF CONGRESS,ACCESSIONS LIST -- ISRAEL. BIBLIOG
ISRAEL CULTURE ECO/UNDEV POL/PAR PLAN PROB/SOLV ISLAM
TEC/DEV DIPLOM EDU/PROP LEAD WAR ATTIT 20 JEWS. NAT/G
PAGE 160 H3200 GP/REL

N19
FIKS M.,PUBLIC ADMINISTRATION IN ISRAEL (PAMPHLET). EDU/PROP
ISRAEL SCHOOL EX/STRUC BUDGET PAY INGP/REL NAT/G
...DECISION 20 CIVIL/SERV. PAGE 50 H0999 ADMIN
WORKER

S52
EISENSTADT S.N.,"THE PROCESS OF ABSORPTION OF NEW HABITAT
IMMIGRANTS IN ISRAEL" (BMR)" ISRAEL CULTURE SCHOOL ATTIT
WORKER PARTIC DRIVE ORD/FREE...STAT OBS INT CHARTS SAMP
SOC/INTEG 20 JEWS. PAGE 45 H0900

B55
SHUMSKY A.,THE CLASH OF CULTURES IN ISRAEL: A GP/REL
PROBLEM FOR EDUCATION. ISRAEL CULTURE INTELL NAT/G EDU/PROP
ACT/RES DISCRIM AGE/Y...BIBLIOG 20 JEWS. PAGE 143 SCHOOL
H2867 AGE/C

B59
ROSOLIO D.,TEN YEARS OF THE CIVIL SERVICE IN ISRAEL ADMIN
(1948-1958) (PAMPHLET). ISRAEL NAT/G RECEIVE 20. WORKER
PAGE 134 H2685 GOV/REL
PAY

B61
HALPERIN S.,THE POLITICAL WORLD OF AMERICAN CULTURE
ZIONISM. ISRAEL FINAN LABOR VOL/ASSN GIVE LOBBY SECT
REPRESENT GP/REL ATTIT POLICY. PAGE 64 H1293 EDU/PROP
DELIB/GP

B61
PATAI R.,CULTURES IN CONFLICT; AN INQUIRY INTO THE NAT/COMP
SOCIO-CULTURAL PROBLEMS OF ISRAEL AND HER NEIGHBORS CULTURE
(2ND REV. ED.). ISLAM ISRAEL SOCIETY STRUCT DIPLOM GP/COMP
GP/REL ALL/VALS...SOC 20 JEWS ARABS. PAGE 124 H2475 ATTIT

B61
SCHECHTMAN J.B.,ON WINGS OF EAGLES: THE PLIGHT, CULTURE
EXODUS, AND HOMECOMING OF ORIENTAL JEWRY. ASIA HABITAT
ISLAM ISRAEL VOL/ASSN DIPLOM CONTROL ORD/FREE KIN
...GEOG WORSHIP SOC/INTEG 20 JEWS ARABS MIGRATION. SECT
PAGE 139 H2777

B62
BROWN S.D.,STUDIES ON ASIA, 1962. ASIA BURMA INDIA PWR
ISLAM ISRAEL S/ASIA ECO/UNDEV POL/PAR SECT ECO/TAC PARL/PROC
...ANTHOL 20 CHINJAP. PAGE 22 H0450

B62
GALENSON W.,LABOR IN DEVELOPING COUNTRIES. BRAZIL LABOR
INDONESIA ISRAEL PAKISTAN TURKEY AGRI INDUS WORKER ECO/UNDEV
PAY PRICE GP/REL WEALTH...MGT CHARTS METH/COMP BARGAIN
NAT/COMP 20. PAGE 54 H1088 POL/PAR

B62
JOHNSON J.J.,THE ROLE OF THE MILITARY IN FORCES
UNDERDEVELOPED COUNTRIES. AFR BURMA INDONESIA ISLAM CONCPT
ISRAEL L/A+17C S/ASIA THAILAND CULTURE ECO/UNDEV
KIN PROVS CONSULT ACT/RES COERCE REV DRIVE
RIGID/FLEX ORD/FREE...RECORD ANTHOL 20. PAGE 81
H1622

B63
ARAZI A.,LE SYSTEME ELECTORAL ISRAELIEN. ISRAEL LEGIS
NAT/G ADMIN ALL/VALS PARLIAMENT. PAGE 8 H0158 CHOOSE
POL/PAR

B63
BADI J.,THE GOVERNMENT OF THE STATE OF ISRAEL: A NAT/G
CRITICAL ACCOUNT OF ITS PARLIAMENT, EXECUTIVE, AND CONSTN
JUDICIARY. ISRAEL ECO/DEV CHIEF DELIB/GP LEGIS EX/STRUC
DIPLOM CT/SYS INGP/REL PEACE ORD/FREE...BIBLIOG 20 POL/PAR
PARLIAMENT ARABS MIGRATION. PAGE 10 H0193

B63
SAKAI R.K.,STUDIES ON ASIA, 1963. ASIA INDIA ISRAEL PWR
S/ASIA USA+45 PERF/ART POL/PAR SECT REGION NAT/LISM CULTURE
...SOC LING TREND ANTHOL 19/20 CHINJAP. PAGE 137
H2735

B64
OECD SEMINAR REGIONAL DEV,REGIONAL DEVELOPMENT IN ADMIN
ISRAEL. ISRAEL STRUCT ECO/UNDEV NAT/G REGION...GEOG PROVS
20. PAGE 120 H2404 PLAN
METH/COMP

B64
SAKAI R.K.,STUDIES ON ASIA, 1964. ASIA CHINA/COM PWR
ISRAEL MALAYSIA S/ASIA USA+45 USSR ECO/UNDEV FAM DIPLOM
POL/PAR SECT CONSULT NAT/LISM...POLICY SOC 20
CHINJAP. PAGE 137 H2736

S64
LEWIS B.,"THE QUEST FOR FREEDOM--A SAD STORY OF THE CONSTN
MIDDLE EAST." ISLAM ISRAEL LEBANON TURKEY CULTURE ATTIT
NAT/G SECT LEGIS TOP/EX DOMIN EDU/PROP LEGIT NAT/LISM
ORD/FREE PWR RESPECT...POLICY TIME/SEQ VAL/FREE 20.
PAGE 96 H1911

B65
BAYNE E.A.,FOUR WAYS OF POLITICS: STATE AND NATION ECO/UNDEV
IN ITALY, SOMALIA, ISRAEL, AND IRAN. IRAN ISRAEL NAT/G
ITALY SOMALIA LEAD CHOOSE MAJORITY GOV/COMP. DECISION
PAGE 12 H0244 TOP/EX

B65
BENTWICH J.S.,EDUCATION IN ISRAEL. ISRAEL CULTURE SECT
STRATA PROB/SOLV TEC/DEV ADJUST ALL/VALS 20 JEWS. EDU/PROP
PAGE 15 H0293 ACADEM
SCHOOL

B65
TUTSCH H.E.,FACETS OF ARAB NATIONALISM. ISLAM ECO/UNDEV
ISRAEL CULTURE STRUCT SECT RIGID/FLEX ORD/FREE NAT/LISM
MARXISM SOCISM 20. PAGE 157 H3143 TEC/DEV
SOCIETY

B65
US DEPARTMENT OF DEFENSE,US SECURITY ARMS CONTROL, BIBLIOG/A
AND DISARMAMENT 1961-1965 (PAMPHLET). CHINA/COM COM ARMS/CONT
GERMANY/W ISRAEL SPACE USA+45 USSR WOR+45 FORCES NUC/PWR
EDU/PROP DETER EQUILIB PEACE ALL/VALS...GOV/COMP 20 DIPLOM
NATO. PAGE 159 H3183

B66
THOMPSON J.H.,MODERNIZATION OF THE ARAB WORLD. FUT ADJUST
ISRAEL STRUCT ECO/UNDEV DIPLOM INGP/REL ATTIT ISLAM
...CENSUS ANTHOL 20 ARABS. PAGE 154 H3082 PROB/SOLV
NAT/COMP

B66
US DEPARTMENT OF STATE,RESEARCH ON THE MIDDLE EAST BIBLIOG/A
(EXTERNAL RESEARCH LIST NO 4-25). GREECE ISRAEL ISLAM
SYRIA UAR YEMEN CULTURE SOCIETY POL/PAR SECT DIPLOM NAT/G
EDU/PROP WAR NAT/LISM...GEOG GOV/COMP 20. PAGE 160 REGION
H3190

B67
MEHDI M.T.,PEACE IN THE MIDDLE EAST. ISRAEL SOCIETY ISLAM
NAT/G PLAN EDU/PROP NAT/LISM DRIVE...IDEA/COMP 20 DIPLOM
JEWS. PAGE 108 H2160 GP/REL
COERCE

B67
RAE D.,THE POLITICAL CONSEQUENCES OF ELECTORAL POL/PAR
LAWS. EUR+WWI ICELAND ISRAEL NEW/ZEALND UK USA+45 CHOOSE
ADJUD APPORT GP/REL MAJORITY...MATH STAT CENSUS NAT/COMP
CHARTS BIBLIOG 20 AUSTRAL. PAGE 129 H2579 REPRESENT

L67
ROTH A.R.,"CAPITAL-MARKET DEVELOPMENT IN ISRAEL AND LAW
BRAZIL: TWO EXAMPLES OF THE ROLE OF LAW IN ECO/UNDEV
DEVELOPMENT." BRAZIL ISRAEL L/A+17C INDUS MARKET NAT/COMP
ECO/TAC FOR/AID INT/TRADE CONTROL BAL/PAY 20. FINAN
PAGE 135 H2694

S67
HALPERN B.,"THE ORIGINS OF THE CRISIS." ISLAM WAR
ISRAEL INT/ORG FORCES WEAPON PEACE ORD/FREE TREATY NAT/G
20 UN. PAGE 65 H1296 DIPLOM

S67
HARNON E.,"CRIMINAL PROCEDURE IN ISRAEL - SOME ADJUD
COMPARATIVE ASPECTS." ISRAEL USA+45 CLIENT EX/STRUC CONSTN
LEGIS...JURID NAT/COMP 20. PAGE 67 H1336 CT/SYS
CRIME

S67
KINGSBURY E.C.,"LAW AS COMPACT: ANCIENT ISRAEL'S CONTRIBUTION TO THE UNDERSTANDING OF LAW." ISRAEL MEDIT-7 CULTURE KIN KNOWL...JURID CONCPT TREND IDEA/COMP METH/COMP WORSHIP JEWS DEITY. PAGE 86 H1716
LAW AGREE CONSTN INGP/REL

S67
KYLE K.,"BACKGROUND TO THE CRISIS" ISLAM ISRAEL UAR UK USSR NAT/G PROB/SOLV LEGIT CONTROL REGION STRANGE MORAL 20 JEWS. PAGE 89 H1787
DIPLOM POLICY SOVEREIGN COERCE

S67
MATTHEWS R.O.,"THE SUEZ CANAL DISPUTE* A CASE STUDY IN PEACEFUL SETTLEMENT." FRANCE ISRAEL UAR UK NAT/G CONTROL LEAD COERCE WAR NAT/LISM ROLE ORD/FREE PWR ...INT/LAW UN 20. PAGE 105 H2099
PEACE DIPLOM ADJUD

S67
NAHUMI M.,"THE POWERS IN THE MIDDLE EAST CONFLICT." ISLAM ISRAEL JORDAN UAR NAT/G PEACE ATTIT 20 JEWS. PAGE 115 H2304
DIPLOM WAR NAT/LISM

S67
SYRKIN M.,"THE RIGHT TO BE ORDINARY." ISLAM ISRAEL NAT/G COERCE NAT/LISM RIGID/FLEX 20. PAGE 151 H3025
SOVEREIGN WAR FORCES DIPLOM

ISSAWI C. H1573

ISSUES (CURRENT SUBJECTS OF DISCOURSE)....SEE CONCPT, POLICY

ITAL/AMER....ITALIAN-AMERICANS

ITALY....SEE ALSO APPROPRIATE TIME/SPACE/CULTURE INDEX

B04
DANTE ALIGHIERI,DE MONARCHIA (CA .1310). CHRIST-17C ITALY DOMIN LEGIT ATTIT PWR...CATH CONCPT TIME/SEQ. PAGE 37 H0741
SECT NAT/G SOVEREIGN

B05
MACHIAVELLI N.,THE ART OF WAR. CHRIST-17C TOP/EX DRIVE ORD/FREE PWR SKILL...MGT CHARTS. PAGE 100 H1993
NAT/G FORCES WAR ITALY

B18
WILSON W.,THE STATE: ELEMENTS OF HISTORICAL AND PRACTICAL POLITICS. FRANCE GERMANY ITALY UK USSR CONSTN EX/STRUC LEGIS CT/SYS WAR PWR...POLICY GOV/COMP 20. PAGE 169 H3385
NAT/G JURID CONCPT NAT/COMP

N19
WEBB L.C.,CHURCH AND STATE IN ITALY: 1947-1957 (PAMPHLET). GERMANY ITALY CONSTN POL/PAR AGREE CONTROL PARTIC CHOOSE ATTIT ORD/FREE FASCISM MARXISM 20 CHURCH/STA MARITAIN/J SALO. PAGE 166 H3316
SECT CATHISM NAT/G GP/REL

C28
SCHNEIDER H.W.,"MAKING THE FASCIST STATE." ITALY CULTURE LABOR DIPLOM REV WAR NAT/LISM TOTALISM ATTIT DRIVE SOCISM...BIBLIOG PARLIAMENT 20. PAGE 140 H2792
FASCISM POLICY POL/PAR

B32
BRYCE J.,THE HOLY ROMAN EMPIRE. GERMANY ITALY MOD/EUR CULTURE SOCIETY STRUCT INT/ORG NAT/G SECT DIPLOM DOMIN WAR SUPEGO ALL/VALS SOVEREIGN...GEOG SOC TIME/SEQ CHARTS STERTYP. PAGE 23 H0456
CHRIST-17C NAT/LISM

B32
MARRARO H.R.,AMERICAN OPINION ON THE UNIFICATION OF ITALY. ITALY FORCES DIPLOM SOVEREIGN CATHISM CONSERVE...CONCPT NAT/COMP BIBLIOG 19. PAGE 103 H2056
ORD/FREE NAT/LISM REV CONSTN

B36
BATTAGLIA F.,LINEAMENTI DI STORIA DELLE DOCTRINE POLITICHE CON APPENDICI BIBLIOGRAFICHE. ITALY PROB/SOLV LEAD 20. PAGE 12 H0237
BIBLIOG PHIL/SCI CONCPT NAT/G

B36
BOYCE A.N.,EUROPE AND SOUTH AFRICA. FRANCE GERMANY ITALY SOUTH/AFR UK INDUS NAT/G CONTROL REV WAR NAT/LISM...CONCPT HIST/WRIT 20. PAGE 20 H0392
COLONIAL GOV/COMP NAT/COMP DIPLOM

C36
MAZZINI J.,"FROM THE COUNCIL TO GOD" (1870) IN J. MAZZINI, ESSAYS." ITALY NAT/G EDU/PROP PARTIC ORD/FREE PWR SOVEREIGN 19 POPE CHRISTIAN DEITY. PAGE 106 H2112
CATHISM DOMIN NAT/LISM SUPEGO

B37
BORGESE G.A.,GOLIATH: THE MARCH OF FASCISM. GERMANY ITALY LAW POL/PAR SECT DIPLOM SOCISM...JURID MYTH 20 DANTE MACHIAVELL MUSSOLIN/B. PAGE 19 H0375
POLICY NAT/LISM FASCISM NAT/G

B38
FIELD G.L.,THE SYNDICAL AND CORPORATIVE INSTITUTIONS OF ITALIAN FASCISM. ITALY CONSTN STRATA LABOR EX/STRUC TOP/EX ADJUD ADMIN LEAD TOTALISM AUTHORIT...MGT 20 MUSSOLIN/B. PAGE 50 H0991
FASCISM INDUS NAT/G WORKER

B39
ANDERSON W.,LOCAL GOVERNMENT IN EUROPE. FRANCE GERMANY ITALY UK USSR MUNIC PROVS ADMIN GOV/REL CENTRAL SOVEREIGN 20. PAGE 7 H0136
GOV/COMP NAT/COMP LOC/G CONSTN

B40
LEDERER E.,STATE OF THE MASSES. GERMANY ITALY SOCIETY NAT/G ECO/TAC EDU/PROP LEAD TOTALISM ...SOCIALIST PSY 20. PAGE 93 H1852
CROWD FASCISM AUTHORIT PERSON

B42
BAYNES N.H.,INTELLECTUAL LIBERTY AND TOTALITARIAN CLAIMS. EUR+WWI GERMANY ITALY INTELL POL/PAR CIVMIL/REL NAT/LISM SOCISM CONCPT. PAGE 12 H0245
KNOWL FASCISM EDU/PROP ACADEM

B43
SERENI A.P.,THE ITALIAN CONCEPTION OF INTERNATIONAL LAW. EUR+WWI MOD/EUR INT/ORG NAT/G DOMIN COERCE ORD/FREE FASCISM...OBS/ENVIR TREND 20. PAGE 141 H2829
LAW TIME/SEQ INT/LAW ITALY

B44
SUAREZ F.,A TREATISE ON LAWS AND GOD THE LAWGIVER (1612) IN SELECTIONS FROM THREE WORKS, VOL. II. FRANCE ITALY UK CULTURE NAT/G SECT CHIEF LEGIS DOMIN LEGIT CT/SYS ORD/FREE PWR WORSHIP 16/17. PAGE 150 H3004
LAW JURID GEN/LAWS CATH

B45
CONOVER H.F.,THE GOVERNMENTS OF THE MAJOR FOREIGN POWERS: A BIBLIOGRAPHY. FRANCE GERMANY ITALY UK USSR CONSTN LOC/G POL/PAR EX/STRUC FORCES ADMIN CT/SYS CIVMIL/REL TOTALISM...POLICY 19/20. PAGE 32 H0645
BIBLIOG NAT/G DIPLOM

B45
CONOVER H.F.,ITALY: ECONOMICS, POLITICS AND MILITARY AFFAIRS, 1940-1945. ITALY ELITES NAT/G POL/PAR EX/STRUC TOP/EX DIPLOM DOMIN CONTROL COERCE WAR CIVMIL/REL EFFICIENCY 20. PAGE 32 H0646
BIBLIOG TOTALISM FORCES

B49
BOZZA T.,SCRITTORI POLITICI ITALIANI DAL 1550 AL 1650. CHRIST-17C ITALY DIPLOM DOMIN 16/17. PAGE 20 H0394
BIBLIOG/A NAT/G CONCPT WRITING

B50
ALBRECHT-CARRIE R.,ITALY FROM NAPOLEON TO MUSSOLINI. GERMANY ITALY SPAIN SOCIETY ECO/DEV POL/PAR LEGIS AGREE CONTROL WAR NAT/LISM TOTALISM PWR SOCISM...SOC 19/20 TREATY. PAGE 5 H0095
FASCISM NAT/G

B50
GOFF F.R.,FIFTEENTH CENTURY BOOKS IN THE LIBRARY OF CONGRESS. CHRIST-17C GERMANY ITALY CULTURE INTELL SECT CREATE...PHIL/SCI CONCPT CLASSIF BIOG TIME/SEQ 15. PAGE 58 H1153
BIBLIOG KNOWL HUM

N53
VITO F.,"RECENT DEVELOPMENTS IN THE THEORY OF DEMOCRATIC ADMIN" INTL POL SCI ASS'N CONFERENCE ON PUBLIC ADMINISTRATION... FRANCE ITALY UK REPRESENT EFFICIENCY NEW/LIB SOCISM...WELF/ST 20. PAGE 163 H3257
GOV/COMP CONTROL EX/STRUC

B54
FRIEDRICH C.J.,TOTALITARIAN DICTATORSHIP AND AUTOCRACY. COM EUR+WWI GERMANY ITALY USSR INTELL ECO/DEV NAT/G POL/PAR FORCES TOP/EX ECO/TAC EDU/PROP LEGIT COERCE ATTIT ORD/FREE PWR FASCISM ...CONCPT TIME/SEQ GEN/LAWS NAZI 20. PAGE 53 H1068
SOCIETY DOMIN TOTALISM

B54
SALVEMINI G.,PRELUDE TO WORLD WAR II. ITALY MOD/EUR INT/ORG BAL/PWR EDU/PROP CONTROL TOTALISM...TREND NAT/COMP BIBLIOG 19 HITLER/A LEAGUE/NAT MUSSOLIN/B. PAGE 137 H2745
WAR FASCISM LEAD PWR

B55
TOYNBEE A.,THE REALIGNMENT OF EUROPE. COM GREECE ITALY NAT/G BAL/PWR ECO/TAC EDU/PROP REV SOVEREIGN ...SOC TIME/SEQ TREND COLD/WAR 20. PAGE 156 H3123
EUR+WWI PLAN USSR

B57
MEINECKE F.,MACHIAVELLISM. CHRIST-17C FRANCE GERMANY ITALY MOD/EUR BAL/PWR PARL/PROC TOTALISM ...PHIL/SCI 15/20 MACHIAVELL. PAGE 108 H2166
NAT/LISM NAT/G PWR

B59
EAENZA L.,COMMUNISMO E CATTOLICESIMO IN UNA PARROCHIA DI CAMPAGNA. ITALY CULTURE ELITES ECO/DEV AGRI KIN POL/PAR DOMIN LEGIT RIGID/FLEX...DECISION OBS IDEA/COMP 20 COM/PARTY CHURCH/STA. PAGE 44 H0878
ATTIT CATHISM NEIGH MARXISM

B59
HOBSBAWM E.J.,PRIMITIVE REBELS; STUDIES IN ARCHAIC FORMS OF SOCIAL MOVEMENT IN THE 19TH AND 20TH CENTURIES. ITALY SPAIN CULTURE VOL/ASSN RISK CROWD GP/REL INGP/REL ISOLAT TOTALISM...PSY SOC 18/20. PAGE 72 H1438
SOCIETY CRIME REV GUERRILLA

S59
SILBERMAN L.,"CHANGE AND CONFLICT IN THE HORN OF AFRICA." EUR+WWI ITALY UK CULTURE FORCES ECO/TAC ADJUD COLONIAL ATTIT ORD/FREE PWR...DECISION METH/CNCPT HIST/WRIT SOMALI 20. PAGE 144 H2874
AFR TIME/SEQ

B60
JEMOLO A.C.,CHURCH AND STATE IN ITALY 1850-1950
GP/REL

(TRANS. BY DAVID MOORE). ITALY CONSTN STRATA WAR FASCISM SOCISM...TIME/SEQ 19/20 CHURCH/STA CHRIS/DEM. PAGE 80 H1599 — NAT/G CATHISM POL/PAR

L62
NOLTE E.,"ZUR PHANOMENOLOGIE DES FASCHIMUS." EUR+WWI GERMANY ITALY TURKEY INTELL NAT/G CHIEF CONSULT FORCES CREATE DOMIN EDU/PROP COERCE WAR CHOOSE DRIVE FASCISM...PSY CONCPT MYTH GEN/METH LEAGUE/NAT NAZI 20. PAGE 118 H2367 — ATTIT PWR

B63
ALMOND G.A.,THE CIVIC CULTURE: POLITICAL ATTITUDES AND DEMOCRACY IN FIVE NATIONS. GERMANY/W ITALY UK USA+45 SOCIETY STRUCT PARTIC...SOC DEEP/INT SAMP 20 MEXIC/AMER. PAGE 6 H0113 — POPULISM CULTURE NAT/COMP ATTIT

B63
FRANZ G.,TEILUNG UND WIEDERVEREINIGUNG. GERMANY IRELAND ITALY NETHERLAND POLAND CULTURE BAL/PWR CHOOSE NAT/LISM ORD/FREE SOVEREIGN 19/20. PAGE 53 H1054 — DIPLOM WAR NAT/COMP ATTIT

B63
FRIED R.C.,THE ITALIAN PREFECTS. ITALY STRATA ECO/DEV NAT/LISM ALL/IDEOS...TREND CHARTS METH/COMP BIBLIOG 17/20 PREFECT. PAGE 53 H1061 — ADMIN NAT/G EFFICIENCY

B63
KOGAN N.,THE POLITICS OF ITALIAN FOREIGN POLICY. EUR+WWI LEGIS DOMIN LEGIT EXEC PWR RESPECT SKILL ...POLICY DECISION HUM SOC METH/CNCPT OBS INT CHARTS 20. PAGE 87 H1737 — NAT/G ROUTINE DIPLOM ITALY

B63
SILONE I.,THE SCHOOL FOR DICTATORS. EUR+WWI GERMANY ITALY SOCIETY NAT/G CHIEF EX/STRUC ATTIT MORAL PWR ...HIST/WRIT 20. PAGE 144 H2876 — TOTALISM EDU/PROP ORD/FREE FASCISM

B64
HALPERIN S.W.,MUSSOLINI AND ITALIAN FASCISM. ITALY NAT/G POL/PAR SECT ECO/TAC LEAD PWR SOCISM...POLICY 20 MUSSOLIN/B. PAGE 64 H1294 — FASCISM NAT/LISM EDU/PROP CHIEF

B64
HELMREICH E.,A FREE CHURCH IN A FREE STATE? FRANCE GERMANY ITALY SECT LEAD PWR CATHISM...POLICY ANTHOL WORSHIP 19/20 CHURCH/STA. PAGE 69 H1389 — GP/REL NAT/G

B64
MILIBAND R.,THE SOCIALIST REGISTER: 1964. GERMANY/W ITALY UK LABOR POL/PAR ECO/TAC FOR/AID NUC/PWR ...POLICY SOCIALIST IDEA/COMP 20 MAO NASSER/G. PAGE 110 H2204 — MARXISM SOCISM CAP/ISM PROB/SOLV

B64
VECCHIO G.D.,L'ETAT ET LE DROIT. ITALY CONSTN EX/STRUC LEGIS DIPLOM CT/SYS...JURID 20 UN. PAGE 162 H3238 — NAT/G SOVEREIGN CONCPT INT/LAW

S64
BARIETY J.,"LA POLITIQUE EXTERIEURE ALLEMANDE DANS L'HIVER 1939-1940." COM FINLAND GERMANY ISLAM ITALY USSR NAT/G FORCES ECO/TAC DOMIN EDU/PROP COERCE WAR PWR WEALTH...HIST/WRIT NAZI TOT/POP VAL/FREE 20. PAGE 11 H0216 — EUR+WWI DIPLOM

B65
BAYNE E.A.,FOUR WAYS OF POLITICS: STATE AND NATION IN ITALY, SOMALIA, ISRAEL, AND IRAN. IRAN ISRAEL ITALY SOMALIA LEAD CHOOSE MAJORITY GOV/COMP. PAGE 12 H0244 — ECO/UNDEV NAT/G DECISION TOP/EX

B65
EDELMAN M.,THE POLITICS OF WAGE-PRICE DECISIONS. GERMANY ITALY NETHERLAND UK INDUS LABOR POL/PAR PROB/SOLV BARGAIN PRICE ROUTINE BAL/PAY COST DEMAND 20. PAGE 44 H0888 — GOV/COMP CONTROL ECO/TAC PLAN

B65
GUERIN D.,SUR LE FASCISME: FASCISME ET GRAND CAPITAL (VOL. II). GERMANY ITALY SOCIETY STRATA AGRI WORKER 20. PAGE 62 H1245 — FASCISM NAT/G TOTALISM EDU/PROP

B65
OECD,THE MEDITERRANEAN REGIONAL PROJECT: ITALY; EDUCATION AND DEVELOPMENT. ITALY SOCIETY STRATA FINAN NAT/G PROF/ORG WORKER PLAN PROB/SOLV ADMIN ...STAT CHARTS METH 20 OECD. PAGE 120 H2400 — SCHOOL EDU/PROP ECO/UNDEV ACADEM

B65
SALVADORI M.,ITALY. AUSTRIA FRANCE GERMANY ITALY SPAIN CULTURE NAT/G POL/PAR DIPLOM WAR FASCISM LAISSEZ MARXISM...TIME/SEQ CHARTS BIBLIOG/A. PAGE 137 H2744 — NAT/LISM CATHISM SOCIETY

S65
STAROBIN J.R.,"COMMUNISM IN WESTERN EUROPE." FRANCE GERMANY ITALY USA+45 USSR ECO/DEV FEDERAL PEACE ATTIT DRIVE PWR TREND. PAGE 149 H2972 — MARXISM EUR+WWI POL/PAR NAT/COMP

B66
ADAMS J.C.,THE GOVERNMENT OF REPUBLICAN ITALY (2ND ED.). ITALY LOC/G POL/PAR DELIB/GP LEGIS WORKER ADMIN CT/SYS FASCISM...CHARTS BIBLIOG 20 PARLIAMENT. PAGE 3 H0064 — NAT/G CHOOSE EX/STRUC CONSTN

B66
LAVEN P.,RENAISSANCE ITALY: 1464-1534. ITALY AGRI EXTR/IND FINAN MUNIC INT/TRADE DRIVE...CATH GEOG CHARTS BIBLIOG/A 15. PAGE 92 H1841 — CULTURE HUM TEC/DEV KNOWL

B66
ROSNER J.,DER FASCHISMUS. AUSTRIA GERMANY ITALY STRATA NAT/G POL/PAR COERCE RACE/REL TOTALISM ATTIT AUTHORIT...IDEA/COMP 20 NAZI ANTI/SEMIT. PAGE 134 H2684 — NAT/LISM FASCISM ORD/FREE WAR

B66
WUEST J.J.,NEW SOURCE BOOK IN MAJOR EUROPEAN GOVERNMENTS. CHRIST-17C EUR+WWI FRANCE GERMANY ITALY MOD/EUR UK USSR LOC/G POL/PAR CHIEF EX/STRUC CHOOSE CONSERVE MARXISM...JURID T 13/20. PAGE 171 H3425 — NAT/G CONSTN LEGIS

B67
EVANS R.H.,COEXISTENCE: COMMUNISM AND ITS PRACTICE IN BOLOGNA, 1945-1965. ITALY CAP/ISM ADMIN CHOOSE PEACE ORD/FREE...SOC STAT DEEP/INT SAMP CHARTS BIBLIOG 20. PAGE 48 H0952 — MARXISM CULTURE MUNIC POL/PAR

B67
POSNER M.V.,ITALIAN PUBLIC ENTERPRISE. ITALY ECO/DEV FINAN INDUS CREATE ECO/TAC ADMIN CONTROL EFFICIENCY PRODUC...TREND CHARTS 20. PAGE 127 H2545 — NAT/G PLAN CAP/ISM SOCISM

S67
SCHACHTER G.,"REGIONAL DEVELOPMENT IN THE ITALIAN DUAL ECONOMY" ITALY AGRI INDUS MARKET WORKER ECO/TAC CONTROL INCOME PRODUC 20. PAGE 138 H2767 — REGION ECO/UNDEV NAT/G PROB/SOLV

S67
SINGH B.,"ITALIAN EXPERIENCE IN REGIONAL ECONOMIC DEVELOPMENT AND LESSONS FOR OTHER COUNTRIES." EUR+WWI ITALY INDUS NAT/G ACT/RES REGION GP/REL EFFICIENCY EQUILIB PRODUC WEALTH. PAGE 144 H2884 — ECO/UNDEV PLAN ECO/TAC CONTROL

ITO....INTERNATIONAL TRADE ORGANIZATION

ITU....INTERNATIONAL TELECOMMUNICATIONS UNION

IVORY COAST....SEE IVORY/CST

IVORY/CST....IVORY COAST; SEE ALSO AFR

B60
CONOVER H.F.,OFFICIAL PUBLICATIONS OF FRENCH WEST AFRICA, 1946-1958. DAHOMEY IVORY/CST NIGER SENEGAL UPPER/VOLT CONSTN AGRI PRESS...CON/ANAL 20. PAGE 33 H0651 — BIBLIOG COLONIAL NAT/G AFR

B62
CARTER G.M.,AFRICAN ONE-PARTY STATES. ISLAM IVORY/CST LIBERIA CONSTN CULTURE SOCIETY POL/PAR PLAN DOMIN EDU/PROP EXEC REGION CHOOSE ATTIT ALL/VALS...CONCPT TIME/SEQ CHARTS VAL/FREE 20 TANGANYIKA. PAGE 27 H0545 — AFR NAT/LISM

S63
ZOLBERG A.R.,"MASS PARTIES AND NATIONAL INTEGRATION: THE CASE OF THE IVORY COAST" (BMR)" AFR IVORY/CST CONSTN VOL/ASSN DIPLOM LEAD GP/REL INGP/REL 20. PAGE 173 H3461 — POL/PAR ECO/UNDEV NAT/G ADJUST

B64
MORGENTHAU R.S.,POLITICAL PARTIES IN FRENCH-SPEAKING WEST AFRICA. AFR FRANCE GUINEA IVORY/CST MALI SENEGAL CONSTN LEGIS CREATE PLAN LOBBY PARTIC GP/REL...POLICY BIBLIOG 20. PAGE 113 H2257 — POL/PAR NAT/G SOVEREIGN COLONIAL

S64
CLIGNET R.,"POTENTIAL ELITES IN GHANA AND THE IVORY COAST: A PRELIMINARY SURVEY." AFR CULTURE ELITES STRATA KIN NAT/G SECT DOMIN EXEC ORD/FREE RESPECT SKILL...POLICY RELATIV GP/COMP NAT/COMP 20. PAGE 30 H0605 — PWR LEGIT IVORY/CST GHANA

IWW....INTERNATIONAL WORKERS OF THE WORLD

J

JACKSON G. H1574

JACKSON G.D. H1575

JACKSON W.A.D. H1576

JACKSON W.R. H0582

JACKSON/A....PRESIDENT ANDREW JACKSON

B64
MINAR D.W.,IDEAS AND POLITICS: THE AMERICAN EXPERIENCE. SECT CHIEF LEGIS CREATE ADJUD EXEC REV PWR...PHIL/SCI CONCPT IDEA/COMP 18/20 HAMILTON/A JEFFERSN/T DECLAR/IND JACKSON/A PRESIDENT. PAGE 111 H2220 — CONSTN NAT/G FEDERAL

JACKSON/RH....R.H. JACKSON

JACOB H. H1577,H1578

JACOBINISM....JACOBINISM: FRENCH DEMOCRATIC REVOLUTIONARY DOCTRINE, 1789

N17
BURKE E.,THOUGHTS ON THE PROSPECT OF A REGICIDE PEACE (PAMPHLET). FRANCE UK SECT DOMIN MURDER PEACE ORD/FREE SOVEREIGN POPULISM...POLICY GOV/COMP IDEA/COMP 18 JACOBINISM COEXIST. PAGE 24 H0483 — REV CHIEF NAT/G DIPLOM

B32
THIBAUDET A.,LES IDEES POLITIQUES DE LA FRANCE. FRANCE NAT/G SECT PRESS REV NAT/LISM PEACE ATTIT ...PSY 19/20 JACOBINISM JAURES/JL. PAGE 154 H3070 — IDEA/COMP ALL/IDEOS CATHISM

JACOBS N. H1579

JACOBSSON P. H1580

JAECKH A. H1581

JAFFA/HU....H.U. JAFFA

JAFFEE A.J. H1582

JAIN G. H1583

JAIN R.K. H1584

JAIN R.S. H1585

JAIN S.C. H1586

JAIRAZBHOY R.A. H1587

JAKARTA....JAKARTA, INDONESIA

JAKOBSON M. H1588

JAMAICA....SEE ALSO L/A+17C

B32
CATALOGUE OF BOOKS, MANSUCRIPTS, ETC. IN THE CARIBBEANA SECTION OF THE N.M. WILLIAMS MEMORIAL ETHNOLOGICAL COLLECTION. JAMAICA WEST/IND GP/REL ATTIT SOC. PAGE 2 H0031 — BIBLIOG L/A+17C CULTURE SOCIETY

B61
BLAKE J.,FAMILY STRUCTURE IN JAMAICA. JAMAICA CULTURE SOCIETY ACT/RES CONTROL MARRIAGE AGE ...POLICY SOC BIBLIOG 20. PAGE 18 H0351 — FAM SEX STRUCT ATTIT

B64
BELL W.,JAMAICAN LEADERS: POLITICAL ATTITUDES IN A NEW NATION. JAMAICA STRUCT ACT/RES CREATE PROB/SOLV DIPLOM COLONIAL LEAD...QU 20. PAGE 13 H0267 — NAT/LISM ATTIT DRIVE SOVEREIGN

S67
COLLINS B.A.,"SOME NOTES ON PUBLIC SERVICE COMMISSIONS IN THE COMMONWEALTH CARIBBEAN." JAMAICA L/A+17C TRINIDAD UK NAT/G OP/RES DOMIN SENIOR COLONIAL CONTROL INGP/REL CENTRAL EFFICIENCY PWR ...DECISION 20. PAGE 31 H0631 — ADMIN EX/STRUC ECO/UNDEV CHOOSE

JANET/P....PIERRE JANET

JANICKE M. H1589

JANIS I.L. H1590

JANOWITZ M. H0298,H2862

JANSEN M.B. H1591

JAPAN....SEE ALSO ASIA

JAPANESE AMERICANS....SEE NISEI

JARMO....JARMO, A PRE- OR EARLY HISTORIC SOCIETY

JARVIE I.C. H1592

JASNY H. H1593

JASPERS/K....KARL JASPERS

B63
RUITENBEER H.M.,THE DILEMMA OF ORGANIZATIONAL SOCIETY. CULTURE ECO/DEV MUNIC SECT TEC/DEV EDU/PROP NAT/LISM ORD/FREE...NAT/COMP 20 RIESMAN/D WHYTE/WF MERTON/R MEAD/MARG JASPERS/K. PAGE 136 H2716 — PERSON ROLE ADMIN WORKER

JAT....A POLITICAL SYSTEM OF INDIA

JAURES/JL....JEAN LEON JAURES (FRENCH SOCIALIST 1859-1914)

B32
THIBAUDET A.,LES IDEES POLITIQUES DE LA FRANCE. FRANCE NAT/G SECT PRESS REV NAT/LISM PEACE ATTIT ...PSY 19/20 JACOBINISM JAURES/JL. PAGE 154 H3070 — IDEA/COMP ALL/IDEOS CATHISM

JAVA....JAVA, INDONESIA; SEE ALSO INDONESIA

B57
KOENTJARANINGRAT R.,A PRELIMINARY DESCRIPTION OF THE JAVANESE KINSHIP SYSTEM. INDONESIA STRATA FAM INGP/REL ADJUST MARRIAGE AGE/C AGE/Y AGE/A PERSON ...OBS CHARTS DICTIONARY 20 JAVA. PAGE 87 H1736 — KIN STRUCT ELITES CULTURE

B62
SELOSOEMARDJAN O.,SOCIAL CHANGES IN JOGJAKARTA. INDONESIA NETHERLAND ELITES STRATA STRUCT FAM POL/PAR CREATE DIPLOM INT/TRADE EDU/PROP ADMIN GOV/REL...SOC 20 JAVA CHINJAP. PAGE 141 H2825 — ECO/UNDEV CULTURE REV COLONIAL

L63
JAY R.,"RELIGION AND POLITICS IN RURAL CENTRAL JAVA." S/ASIA SOCIETY NEIGH SECT PERSON HEALTH MORAL...SOC UNPLAN/INT TIME/SEQ JAVA VAL/FREE 20 WORSHIP. PAGE 80 H1594 — CULTURE OBS

JAY R. H1594

JEFFERSN/T....PRESIDENT THOMAS JEFFERSON

B36
SMITH T.V.,THE PROMISE OF AMERICAN POLITICS. USA-45 WOR-45 LAW CONSTN STRATA PARTIC FASCISM LAISSEZ MARXISM...MAJORIT METH/COMP 18/20 JEFFERSN/T LOCKE/JOHN BENTHAM/J. PAGE 146 H2920 — CONCPT ORD/FREE IDEA/COMP NAT/COMP

B64
MINAR D.W.,IDEAS AND POLITICS: THE AMERICAN EXPERIENCE. SECT CHIEF LEGIS CREATE ADJUD EXEC REV PWR...PHIL/SCI CONCPT IDEA/COMP 18/20 HAMILTON/A JEFFERSN/T DECLAR/IND JACKSON/A PRESIDENT. PAGE 111 H2220 — CONSTN NAT/G FEDERAL

JEFFRIES C. H1595

JEHOVA/WIT....JEHOVAHOS WITNESSES

B64
KAUFMANN R.,MILLENARISME ET ACCULTURATION. SOCIETY DOMIN COLONIAL NAT/LISM ATTIT...SOC BIBLIOG 20 JEHOVA/WIT SEVENTHDAY. PAGE 84 H1669 — AFR SECT MYTH CULTURE

JELAVICH B. H1596,H1597

JELAVICH C. H1596,H1597

JELLINEK G. H1598

JEMOLO A.C. H1599

JENCKS C.E. H1600

JENCKS/C....C. JENCKS

JENKINS C. H1601

JENKS C.W. H1602

JENKS E.J. H1603

JENNINGS W.I. H1604,H1605,H1606,H1607,H1608,H1609,H1610,H1611, H1612,H1613

JENSEN L. H1614

JESSOP T.E. H1615

JEWS....JEWS, JUDAISM

N
US LIBRARY OF CONGRESS,ACCESSIONS LIST -- ISRAEL. ISRAEL CULTURE ECO/UNDEV POL/PAR PLAN PROB/SOLV TEC/DEV DIPLOM EDU/PROP LEAD WAR ATTIT 20 JEWS. PAGE 160 H3200 — BIBLIOG ISLAM NAT/G GP/REL

B21
BALFOUR A.J.,ESSAYS SPECULATIVE AND POLITICAL. SEA CULTURE CREATE WAR NAT/LISM PEACE LOVE...ART/METH INT/LAW CONCPT ANTHOL 20 JEWS. PAGE 10 H0204 — PHIL/SCI SOCIETY DIPLOM

B40
WANDERSCHECK H.,FRANKREICHS PROPAGANDA GEGEN DEUTSCHLAND. FRANCE GERMANY MOD/EUR UK NAT/G DIPLOM WAR 20 JEWS. PAGE 165 H3300 — EDU/PROP ATTIT DOMIN PRESS

S49
DEXTER L.A.,"A DIALOGUE ON THE SOCIAL PSYCHOLOGY OF COLONIALISM AND ON CERTAIN PUERTO RICAN PROFESSIONAL PERSONALITY PATTERNS." L/A+17C PUERT/RICO STRATA STRUCT DOMIN ISOLAT DRIVE ...NAT/COMP PERS/COMP HYPO/EXP 20 JEWS NEGRO. PAGE 41 H0813 — COLONIAL SOC PSY PERSON

JUCKER-FLEETWOOD E. H1639

JUDD P. H1640

JUDGE....JUDGES; SEE ALSO ADJUD

B07
BENTHAM J.,AN INTRODUCTION TO THE PRINCIPLES OF LAW
MORALS AND LEGISLATION. UNIV CONSTN CULTURE SOCIETY GEN/LAWS
NAT/G CONSULT LEGIS JUDGE ADJUD CT/SYS...JURID
CONCPT NEW/IDEA. PAGE 14 H0287

B42
CRAIG A.,ABOVE ALL LIBERTIES. FRANCE UK USA-45 LAW ORD/FREE
CONSTN CULTURE INTELL NAT/G SECT JUDGE...IDEA/COMP MORAL
BIBLIOG 18/20. PAGE 35 H0692 WRITING
EDU/PROP

S58
MAIR L.P.,"REPRESENTATIVE LOCAL GOVERNMENT AS A AFR
PROBLEM IN SOCIAL CHANGE." ECO/UNDEV KIN LOC/G PWR
NAT/G SCHOOL JUDGE ADMIN ROUTINE REPRESENT ELITES
RIGID/FLEX RESPECT...CONCPT STERTYP CMN/WLTH 20.
PAGE 101 H2025

B59
PAULSEN M.G.,LEGAL INSTITUTIONS TODAY AND TOMORROW. JURID
UK USA+45 NAT/G PROF/ORG PROVS ADMIN PARL/PROC ADJUD
ORD/FREE NAT/COMP. PAGE 124 H2477 JUDGE
LEGIS

B59
SANCHEZ A.L.,EL CONCEPTO DEL ESTADO EN EL NAT/G
PENSAMIENTO ESPANOL DEL SIGLO XVI. SPAIN LEGIS PHIL/SCI
JUDGE BAL/PWR LEGIT EXEC WAR PWR...MAJORIT 16. LAW
PAGE 137 H2747 SOVEREIGN

B59
SCHORN H.,DER RICHTER IM DRITTEN REICH; GESCHICHTE ADJUD
UND DOKUMENTE. GERMANY NAT/G LEGIT CT/SYS INGP/REL JUDGE
MORAL ORD/FREE RESPECT...JURID GP/COMP 20. PAGE 140 FASCISM
H2798

S60
LEVINE R.A.,"THE INTERNALIZATION OF POLITICAL CULTURE
VALUES IN STATELESS SOCIETIES." AFR FAM KIN LOC/G ATTIT
PROVS JUDGE PERSON RIGID/FLEX...DECISION SOC
TIME/SEQ 20. PAGE 95 H1904

B61
BAYITCH S.A.,LATIN AMERICA: A BIBLIOGRAPHICAL BIBLIOG
GUIDE. LAW CONSTN LEGIS JUDGE ADJUD CT/SYS 20. L/A+17C
PAGE 12 H0243 NAT/G
JURID

B63
RICHARDSON H.G.,THE ADMINISTRATION OF IRELAND ADMIN
1172-1377. IRELAND CONSTN EX/STRUC LEGIS JUDGE NAT/G
CT/SYS PARL/PROC...CHARTS BIBLIOG 12/14. PAGE 131 PWR
H2621

B64
SZLADITS C.,BIBLIOGRAPHY ON FOREIGN AND COMPARATIVE BIBLIOG/A
LAW: BOOKS AND ARTICLES IN ENGLISH (SUPPLEMENT JURID
1962). FINAN INDUS JUDGE LICENSE ADMIN CT/SYS ADJUD
PARL/PROC OWN...INT/LAW CLASSIF METH/COMP NAT/COMP LAW
20. PAGE 151 H3027

B66
ARCHER P.,FREEDOM AT STAKE. UK LAW NAT/G LEGIS ORD/FREE
JUDGE CRIME MORAL...CONCPT 20 CIVIL/LIB. PAGE 8 NAT/COMP
H0159 POLICY

B66
FRIED R.C.,COMPARATIVE POLITICAL INSTITUTIONS. USSR NAT/G
EX/STRUC FORCES LEGIS JUDGE CONTROL REPRESENT PWR
ALL/IDEOS 20 CONGRESS BUREAUCRCY. PAGE 53 H1062 EFFICIENCY
GOV/COMP

JUDICIAL PROCESS....SEE ADJUD

JUGOSLAVIA....SEE YUGOSLAVIA

JULIEN C.A. H1641

JUNKER ....JUNKER: REACTIONARY PRUSSIAN ARISTOCRACY

B64
REMAK J.,THE GENTLE CRITIC: THEODOR FONTANE AND PERSON
GERMAN POLITICS, 1848-1898. GERMANY PRUSSIA CULTURE SOCIETY
ELITES BAL/PWR DIPLOM WRITING GOV/REL...HUM BIOG 19 WORKER
BISMARCK/O JUNKER FONTANE/T. PAGE 131 H2614 CHIEF

JUNOD V. H1642
JUNZ A.J. H0052
JURID....LAW

N
ACAD RUMANIAN SCI DOC CTR,RUMANIAN SCIENTIFIC BIBLIOG/A
ABSTRACTS: SOCIAL SCIENCES. ROMANIA FINAN HABITAT CULTURE
...ART/METH GEOG HUM JURID PSY 20. PAGE 3 H0059 LING
LAW

N
AUSTRALIAN NATIONAL RES COUN,AUSTRALIAN SOCIAL BIBLIOG/A
SCIENCE ABSTRACTS. NEW/ZEALND CULTURE SOCIETY LOC/G POLICY
CT/SYS PARL/PROC...HEAL JURID PSY SOC 20 AUSTRAL. NAT/G
PAGE 9 H0181 ADMIN

N
CANADIAN GOVERNMENT PUBLICATIONS (1955-). CANADA BIBLIOG/A
AGRI FINAN LABOR FORCES INT/TRADE HEALTH...JURID 20 NAT/G
PARLIAMENT. PAGE 1 H0003 DIPLOM
INT/ORG

B00
MAINE H.S.,ANCIENT LAW. MEDIT-7 CULTURE SOCIETY KIN FAM
SECT LEGIS LEGIT ROUTINE...JURID HIST/WRIT CON/ANAL LAW
TOT/POP VAL/FREE. PAGE 101 H2020

B01
BRYCE J.,STUDIES IN HISTORY AND JURISPRUDENCE (2 IDEA/COMP
VOLS.). ICELAND SOUTH/AFR UK LAW PROB/SOLV CONSTN
SOVEREIGN...PHIL/SCI NAT/COMP ROME/ANC ROMAN/LAW. JURID
PAGE 23 H0455

B05
GRIFFIN A.P.C.,LIST OF BOOKS ON RAILROADS IN BIBLIOG/A
FOREIGN COUNTRIES. MOD/EUR ECO/DEV NAT/G CONTROL SERV/IND
SOCISM...JURID 19/20 RAILROAD. PAGE 61 H1219 ADMIN
DIST/IND

B07
BENTHAM J.,AN INTRODUCTION TO THE PRINCIPLES OF LAW
MORALS AND LEGISLATION. UNIV CONSTN CULTURE SOCIETY GEN/LAWS
NAT/G CONSULT LEGIS JUDGE ADJUD CT/SYS...JURID
CONCPT NEW/IDEA. PAGE 14 H0287

B09
JUSTINIAN,THE DIGEST (DIGESTA CORPUS JURIS CIVILIS) JURID
(2 VOLS.) (TRANS. BY C. H. MONRO). ROMAN/EMP LAW CT/SYS
FAM LOC/G LEGIS EDU/PROP CONTROL MARRIAGE OWN ROLE NAT/G
CIVIL/LAW. PAGE 82 H1645 STRATA

B10
MENDELSSOHN S.,MENDELSSOHN'S SOUTH AFRICA BIBLIOG/A
BIBLIOGRAPHY (VOL. I). SOUTH/AFR RACE/REL...GEOG CULTURE
JURID 19/20. PAGE 109 H2173

B12
HARIOU M.,LA SOUVERAINTE NATIONALE. EX/STRUC FORCES SOVEREIGN
LEGIS CHOOSE PWR JURID. PAGE 66 H1331 CONCPT
NAT/G
REPRESENT

B12
POLLOCK F.,THE GENIUS OF THE COMMON LAW. CHRIST-17C LAW
UK FINAN CHIEF ACT/RES ADMIN GP/REL ATTIT SOCISM CULTURE
...ANARCH JURID. PAGE 127 H2537 CREATE

B18
EYBERS G.W.,SELECT CONSTITUTIONAL DOCUMENTS CONSTN
ILLUSTRATING SOUTH AFRICAN HISTORY 1795-1910. LAW
SOUTH/AFR LOC/G LEGIS CT/SYS...JURID ANTHOL 18/20 NAT/G
NATAL CAPE/HOPE ORANGE/STA. PAGE 48 H0955 COLONIAL

B18
WILSON W.,THE STATE: ELEMENTS OF HISTORICAL AND NAT/G
PRACTICAL POLITICS. FRANCE GERMANY ITALY UK USSR JURID
CONSTN EX/STRUC LEGIS CT/SYS WAR PWR...POLICY CONCPT
GOV/COMP 20. PAGE 169 H3385 NAT/COMP

B18
YUKIO O.,THE VOICE OF JAPANESE DEMOCRACY, AN ESSAY CONSTN
ON CONSTITUTIONAL LOYALTY (TRANS BY J. E. BECKER). MAJORIT
ASIA POL/PAR DELIB/GP EX/STRUC RIGID/FLEX ORD/FREE CHOOSE
PWR...POLICY JURID METH/COMP 19/20 CHINJAP. NAT/G
PAGE 172 H3443

N19
POUND R.,ORGANIZATION OF THE COURTS (PAMPHLET). CT/SYS
MOD/EUR UK USA-45 ADJUD PWR...GOV/COMP 10/20 JURID
EUROPE. PAGE 127 H2546 STRUCT
ADMIN

C20
DUNNING W.A.,"A HISTORY OF POLITICAL THINKERS FROM IDEA/COMP
ROUSSEAU TO SPENCER." NAT/G REV NAT/LISM UTIL PHIL/SCI
CONSERVE MARXISM POPULISM...JURID BIBLIOG 18/19. CONCPT
PAGE 43 H0868 GEN/LAWS

B23
POUND R.,INTERPRETATIONS OF LEGAL HISTORY. CULTURE LAW
...PHIL/SCI NEW/IDEA CLASSIF SIMUL GEN/LAWS 19/20. IDEA/COMP
PAGE 127 H2547 JURID

B23
ROBERT H.M.,PARLIAMENTARY LAW. POL/PAR LEGIS PARTIC PARL/PROC
CHOOSE REPRESENT GP/REL. PAGE 132 H2640 DELIB/GP
NAT/G
JURID

B24
HOLDSWORTH W.S.,A HISTORY OF ENGLISH LAW; THE LAW
COMMON LAW AND ITS RIVALS (VOL. IV). UK SEA AGRI LEGIS
CHIEF ADJUD CONTROL CRIME GOV/REL...INT/LAW JURID CT/SYS
NAT/COMP 16/17 PARLIAMENT COMMON/LAW CANON/LAW CONSTN
ENGLSH/LAW. PAGE 72 H1449

B26
HOCKING W.E.,PRESENT STATUS OF THE PHILOSOPHY OF JURID
LAW AND OF RIGHTS. UNIV CULTURE INTELL SOCIETY PHIL/SCI
NAT/G CREATE LEGIT SANCTION ALL/VALS SOC/INTEG ORD/FREE
18/20. PAGE 72 H1442

B26
MACIVER R.M.,THE MODERN STATE. POL/PAR ORD/FREE NAT/G
TIME/SEQ. PAGE 100 H1997 CONCPT
JURID
SOVEREIGN

B28
HOLDSWORTH W.S.,THE HISTORIANS OF ANGLO-AMERICAN LAW. UK USA-45 INTELL LEGIS RESPECT...BIOG NAT/COMP 17/20 COMMON/LAW. PAGE 72 H1450
HIST/WRIT LAW JURID

B28
YANG KUNG-SUN,THE BOOK OF LORD SHANG. LAW ECO/UNDEV LOC/G NAT/G NEIGH PLAN ECO/TAC LEGIT ATTIT SKILL ...CONCPT CON/ANAL WORK TOT/POP. PAGE 172 H3434
ASIA JURID

B29
LEITZ F.,DIE PUBLIZITAT DER AKTIENGESELLSCHAFT. BELGIUM FRANCE GERMANY UK FINAN PRESS GP/REL PROFIT KNOWL 20. PAGE 94 H1872
LG/CO JURID ECO/TAC NAT/COMP

B29
PRATT I.A.,MODERN EGYPT: A LIST OF REFERENCES TO MATERIAL IN THE NEW YORK PUBLIC LIBRARY. UAR ECO/UNDEV...GEOG JURID SOC LING 20. PAGE 128 H2555
BIBLIOG ISLAM DIPLOM NAT/G

B30
BENTHAM J.,THE RATIONALE OF PUNISHMENT. UK LAW LOC/G NAT/G LEGIS CONTROL...JURID GEN/LAWS COURT/SYS 19. PAGE 14 H0289
CRIME SANCTION COERCE ORD/FREE

B32
GREAT BRIT COMM MINISTERS PWR,REPORT. UK LAW CONSTN CONSULT LEGIS PARL/PROC SANCTION SOVEREIGN ...DECISION JURID 20 PARLIAMENT. PAGE 60 H1201
EX/STRUC NAT/G PWR CONTROL

B32
LUNT D.C.,THE ROAD TO THE LAW. UK USA-45 LEGIS EDU/PROP OWN ORD/FREE...DECISION TIME/SEQ NAT/COMP 16/20 AUSTRAL ENGLSH/LAW COMMON/LAW. PAGE 99 H1980
ADJUD LAW JURID CT/SYS

B34
GONZALEZ PALENCIA A,ESTUDIO HISTORICO SOBRE LA CENSURA GUBERNATIVA EN ESPANA 1800-1833. NAT/G COERCE INGP/REL ATTIT AUTHORIT KNOWL...POLICY JURID 19. PAGE 58 H1165
LEGIT EDU/PROP PRESS CONTROL

B35
RAM J.,THE SCIENCE OF LEGAL JUDGMENT: A TREATISE... UK CONSTN NAT/G LEGIS CREATE PROB/SOLV AGREE CT/SYS ...INT/LAW CONCPT 19 ENGLSH/LAW CANON/LAW CIVIL/LAW CTS/WESTM. PAGE 129 H2584
LAW JURID EX/STRUC ADJUD

B36
VICO G.B.,DIRITTO UNIVERSALE (1722) (VOL. 2, PARTS 1,2, AND 3, OF G.B. VICO, OPERE). UNIV DIPLOM AGREE WAR OWN KNOWL ORD/FREE SOVEREIGN DEITY. PAGE 162 H3249
JURID SECT CONCPT NAT/G

B37
BORGESE G.A.,GOLIATH: THE MARCH OF FASCISM. GERMANY ITALY LAW POL/PAR SECT DIPLOM SOCISM...JURID MYTH 20 DANTE MACHIAVELL MUSSOLIN/B. PAGE 19 H0375
POLICY NAT/LISM FASCISM NAT/G

B38
HOLDSWORTH W.S.,A HISTORY OF ENGLISH LAW; THE CENTURIES OF SETTLEMENT AND REFORM (VOL. X). INDIA UK CONSTN NAT/G CHIEF LEGIS ADMIN COLONIAL CT/SYS CHOOSE ORD/FREE PWR...JURID 18 PARLIAMENT COMMONWLTH COMMON/LAW. PAGE 72 H1451
LAW LOC/G EX/STRUC ADJUD

B38
HOLDSWORTH W.S.,A HISTORY OF ENGLISH LAW; THE CENTURIES OF SETTLEMENT AND REFORM (VOL. XI). UK CONSTN NAT/G EX/STRUC DIPLOM ADJUD CT/SYS LEAD CRIME ATTIT...INT/LAW JURID 18 CMN/WLTH PARLIAMENT ENGLSH/LAW. PAGE 73 H1452
LAW COLONIAL LEGIS PARL/PROC

B38
MCNAIR A.D.,THE LAW OF TREATIES: BRITISH PRACTICE AND OPINIONS. UK CREATE DIPLOM LEGIT WRITING ADJUD WAR...INT/LAW JURID TREATY. PAGE 107 H2144
AGREE LAW CT/SYS NAT/G

B38
POUND R.,THE FORMATIVE ERA OF AMERICAN LAW. CULTURE NAT/G PROVS LEGIS ADJUD CT/SYS PERSON SOVEREIGN ...POLICY IDEA/COMP GEN/LAWS 18/19. PAGE 127 H2548
CONSTN LAW CREATE JURID

B39
MCILWAIN C.H.,CONSTITUTIONALISM AND THE CHANGING WORLD. UK USA-45 LEGIS PRIVIL AUTHORIT SOVEREIGN ...GOV/COMP 15/20 MAGNA/CART HOUSE/CMNS. PAGE 107 H2133
CONSTN POLICY JURID

B39
VAN BILJON F.J.,STATE INTERFERENCE IN SOUTH AFRICA. SOUTH/AFR ECO/UNDEV AGRI INDUS WORKER RATION WEALTH ...JURID 20. PAGE 161 H3225
ECO/TAC POLICY INT/TRADE NAT/G

S40
GURVITCH G.,"MAJOR PROBLEMS OF THE SOCIOLOGY OF LAW." CULTURE SANCTION KNOWL MORAL...POLICY EPIST JURID WORSHIP. PAGE 63 H1255
SOC LAW PHIL/SCI

B41
GILMORE M.P.,ARGUMENT FROM ROMAN LAW IN POLITICAL THOUGHT, 1200-1600. INTELL LICENSE CONTROL CT/SYS GOV/REL PRIVIL PWR...IDEA/COMP BIBLIOG 13/16. PAGE 56 H1130
JURID LAW CONCPT NAT/G

B42
BLANCHARD L.R.,MARTINIQUE: A SELECTED LIST OF REFERENCES (PAMPHLET). WEST/IND AGRI LOC/G SCHOOL ...ART/METH GEOG JURID CHARTS 20. PAGE 18 H0353
BIBLIOG/A SOCIETY CULTURE COLONIAL

B42
FORTESCU J.,IN PRAISE OF ENGLISH LAW (1464) (TRANS. BY S.B. CHRIMES). UK ELITES CHIEF FORCES CT/SYS COERCE CRIME GOV/REL ILLEGIT...JURID GOV/COMP GEN/LAWS 15. PAGE 52 H1040
LAW CONSTN LEGIS ORD/FREE

B42
ROBBINS J.J.,THE GOVERNMENT OF LABOR RELATIONS IN SWEDEN. SWEDEN LAW CONSTN ADJUD CT/SYS GP/REL ...JURID 20. PAGE 132 H2638
NAT/G BARGAIN LABOR INDUS

C43
BENTHAM J.,"PRINCIPLES OF INTERNATIONAL LAW" IN J. BOWRING, ED., THE WORKS OF JEREMY BENTHAM." UNIV NAT/G PLAN PROB/SOLV DIPLOM CONTROL SANCTION MORAL ORD/FREE PWR SOVEREIGN 19. PAGE 15 H0291
INT/LAW JURID WAR PEACE

B44
SUAREZ F.,A TREATISE ON LAWS AND GOD THE LAWGIVER (1612) IN SELECTIONS FROM THREE WORKS, VOL. II. FRANCE ITALY UK CULTURE NAT/G SECT CHIEF LEGIS DOMIN LEGIT CT/SYS ORD/FREE PWR WORSHIP 16/17. PAGE 150 H3004
LAW JURID GEN/LAWS CATH

B45
US LIBRARY OF CONGRESS,NETHERLANDS EAST INDIES. INDONESIA LAW CULTURE AGRI INDUS SCHOOL COLONIAL HEALTH...GEOG JURID SOC 19/20 NETH/IND. PAGE 160 H3205
BIBLIOG/A S/ASIA NAT/G

B47
DE NOIA J.,GUIDE TO OFFICIAL PUBLICATIONS OF THE OTHER AMERICAN REPUBLICS: NICARAGUA (VOL. XIV). NICARAGUA LAW LEGIS ADMIN CT/SYS...JURID 19/20. PAGE 38 H0765
BIBLIOG/A EDU/PROP NAT/G CONSTN

B47
NEUBURGER O.,GUIDE TO OFFICIAL PUBLICATIONS OF OTHER AMERICAN REPUBLICS: HONDURAS (VOL. XIII). HONDURAS LAW LEGIS ADMIN CT/SYS...JURID 19/20. PAGE 117 H2333
BIBLIOG/A NAT/G EDU/PROP CONSTN

B47
NEUBURGER O.,GUIDE TO OFFICIAL PUBLICATIONS OF THE OTHER AMERICAN REPUBLICS: HAITI (VOL. XII). HAITI LAW FINAN LEGIS PRESS...JURID 20. PAGE 117 H2334
BIBLIOG/A CONSTN NAT/G EDU/PROP

B48
DE NOIA J.,GUIDE TO OFFICIAL PUBLICATIONS OF OTHER AMERICAN REPUBLICS: PERU (VOL. XVII). PERU LAW LEGIS ADMIN CT/SYS...JURID 19/20. PAGE 38 H0767
BIBLIOG/A CONSTN NAT/G EDU/PROP

B48
GRIFFITH E.S.,RESEARCH IN POLITICAL SCIENCE: THE WORK OF PANELS OF RESEARCH COMMITTEE, APSA. WOR+45 WOR-45 COM/IND R+D FORCES ACT/RES WAR...GOV/COMP ANTHOL 20. PAGE 61 H1220
BIBLIOG PHIL/SCI DIPLOM JURID

B48
YAKOBSON S.,FIVE HUNDRED RUSSIAN WORKS FOR COLLEGE LIBRARIES (PAMPHLET). MOD/EUR USSR MARXISM SOCISM ...ART/METH GEOG HUM JURID SOC 13/20. PAGE 171 H3431
BIBLIOG NAT/G CULTURE COM

B49
DENNING A.,FREEDOM UNDER THE LAW. MOD/EUR UK LAW SOCIETY CHIEF EX/STRUC LEGIS ADJUD CT/SYS PERS/REL PERSON 17/20 ENGLSH/LAW. PAGE 40 H0793
ORD/FREE JURID NAT/G

B49
HAUSER R.,AUTORITAT UND MACHT. SOCIETY SECT PWR CATHISM...JURID CONCPT 16/20 PROTESTANT LUTHER/M CALVIN/J CHURCH/STA. PAGE 68 H1360
SOVEREIGN NAT/G LEGIT

B49
WORMUTH F.D.,THE ORIGINS OF MODERN CONSTITUTIONALISM. GREECE UK LEGIS CREATE TEC/DEV BAL/PWR DOMIN ADJUD REV WAR PWR...JURID ROMAN/REP CROMWELL/O. PAGE 170 H3412
NAT/G CONSTN LAW

B50
BERMAN H.J.,JUSTICE IN RUSSIA; AN INTERPRETATION OF SOVIET LAW. USSR LAW STRUCT LABOR FORCES AGREE GP/REL ORD/FREE SOCISM...TIME/SEQ 20. PAGE 15 H0309
JURID ADJUD MARXISM COERCE

B50
COUNCIL BRITISH NATIONAL BIB,BRITISH NATIONAL BIBLIOGRAPHY. UK AGRI CONSTRUC PERF/ART POL/PAR SECT CREATE INT/TRADE LEAD...HUM JURID PHIL/SCI 20. PAGE 34 H0677
BIBLIOG/A NAT/G TEC/DEV DIPLOM

B50
HOOKER R.,OF THE LAWS OF ECCLESIASTICAL POLITY (1594) (ABR. BY J. S. MARSHALL). UK UNIV CHIEF PARTIC MORAL...JURID GEN/LAWS WORSHIP 16. PAGE 73 H1463
SECT CONCPT LAW NAT/G

B50
MACIVER R.M.,GREAT EXPRESSIONS OF HUMAN RIGHTS. LAW CONSTN CULTURE INTELL SOCIETY R+D INT/ORG ATTIT DRIVE...JURID OBS HIST/WRIT GEN/LAWS. PAGE 100 H1999
UNIV CONCPT

B51
WABEKE B.H.,A GUIDE TO DUTCH BIBLIOGRAPHIES. BELGIUM INDONESIA NETHERLAND DIPLOM INT/TRADE WAR NAT/LISM KNOWL...ART/METH HUM JURID CON/ANAL 14/20.
BIBLIOG/A NAT/G CULTURE

PAGE 164 H3282 COLONIAL

B52
SCHATTSCHNEIDER E.E.,A GUIDE TO THE STUDY OF PUBLIC AFFAIRS. LAW LOC/G NAT/G LEGIS BUDGET PRESS ADMIN LOBBY...JURID CHARTS 20. PAGE 139 H2775 ACT/RES INTELL ACADEM METH/COMP

S52
MCDOUGAL M.S.,"THE COMPARATIVE STUDY OF LAW FOR POLICY PURPOSES." FUT NAT/G POL/PAR CONSULT ADJUD PWR SOVEREIGN...METH/CNCPT IDEA/COMP SIMUL 20. PAGE 106 H2129 PLAN JURID NAT/LISM

B53
ORFIELD L.B.,THE GROWTH OF SCANDINAVIAN LAW. DENMARK ICELAND NORWAY SWEDEN LAW DIPLOM...BIBLIOG 9/20. PAGE 121 H2426 JURID CT/SYS NAT/G

B53
STOUT H.M.,BRITISH GOVERNMENT. UK FINAN LOC/G POL/PAR DELIB/GP DIPLOM ADMIN COLONIAL CHOOSE ORD/FREE...JURID BIBLIOG 20 COMMONWLTH. PAGE 150 H2990 NAT/G PARL/PROC CONSTN NEW/LIB

B54
BINANI G.D.,INDIA AT A GLANCE (REV. ED.). INDIA COM/IND FINAN INDUS LABOR PROVS SCHOOL PLAN DIPLOM INT/TRADE ADMIN...JURID 20. PAGE 17 H0335 INDEX CON/ANAL NAT/G ECO/UNDEV

B54
FRIEDMAN W.,THE PUBLIC CORPORATION: A COMPARATIVE SYMPOSIUM (UNIVERSITY OF TORONTO SCHOOL OF LAW COMPARATIVE LAW SERIES, VOL. I). SWEDEN USA+45 INDUS INT/ORG NAT/G REGION CENTRAL FEDERAL...POLICY JURID IDEA/COMP NAT/COMP ANTHOL 20 COMMONWLTH MONOPOLY EUROPE. PAGE 53 H1065 LAW SOCISM LG/CO OWN

B54
HAMSON C.J.,EXECUTIVE DISCRETION AND JUDICIAL CONTROL; AN ASPECT OF THE FRENCH CONSEIL D'ETAT. EUR+WWI FRANCE MOD/EUR UK NAT/G EX/STRUC PARTIC CONSERVE...JURID BIBLIOG/A 18/20 SUPREME/CT. PAGE 65 H1310 ELITES ADJUD NAT/COMP

B54
SCHWARTZ B.,FRENCH ADMINISTRATIVE LAW AND THE COMMON-LAW WORLD. FRANCE CULTURE LOC/G NAT/G PROVS DELIB/GP EX/STRUC LEGIS PROB/SOLV CT/SYS EXEC GOV/REL...IDEA/COMP ENGLSH/LAW. PAGE 140 H2808 JURID LAW METH/COMP ADJUD

B55
CHARMATZ J.P.,COMPARATIVE STUDIES IN COMMUNITY PROPERTY LAW. FRANCE USA+45...JURID GOV/COMP ANTHOL 20. PAGE 29 H0583 MARRIAGE LAW OWN MUNIC

B55
KHADDURI M.,WAR AND PEACE IN THE LAW OF ISLAM. CONSTN CULTURE SOCIETY STRATA NAT/G PROVS SECT FORCES TOP/EX CREATE DOMIN EDU/PROP ADJUD COERCE ATTIT RIGID/FLEX ALL/VALS...CONCPT TIME/SEQ TOT/POP VAL/FREE. PAGE 85 H1702 ISLAM JURID PEACE WAR

B55
KHADDURI M.,LAW IN THE MIDDLE EAST. LAW CONSTN ACADEM FAM EDU/PROP CT/SYS SANCTION CRIME...INT/LAW GOV/COMP ANTHOL 6/20 MID/EAST. PAGE 85 H1703 ADJUD JURID ISLAM

B55
KRUSE H.,DAS STAATSANGEHORIGKEITSRECHT DER ARABISCHEN STAATEN. ISLAM JORDAN LIBYA SYRIA UAR NAT/G SECT RACE/REL...INT/LAW 6/20 TREATY. PAGE 89 H1779 JURID NAT/LISM DIPLOM GP/REL

B55
MOHL R.V.,DIE GESCHICHTE UND LITERATUR DER STAATSWISSENSCHAFTEN (3 VOLS.). LAW NAT/G...JURID METH/COMP METH. PAGE 112 H2236 PHIL/SCI MOD/EUR

B55
POHLENZ M.,GRIECHISCHE FREIHEIT. GREECE DIPLOM WAR SUPEGO PWR RESPECT...IDEA/COMP. PAGE 127 H2533 ORD/FREE CONCPT JURID NAT/G

B55
SMITH G.,A CONSTITUTIONAL AND LEGAL HISTORY OF ENGLAND. UK ELITES NAT/G LEGIS ADJUD OWN HABITAT POPULISM...JURID 20 ENGLSH/LAW. PAGE 145 H2909 CONSTN PARTIC LAW CT/SYS

B56
FIELD G.C.,POLITICAL THEORY. POL/PAR REPRESENT MORAL SOVEREIGN...JURID IDEA/COMP. PAGE 50 H0990 CONCPT NAT/G ORD/FREE DIPLOM

B56
JENNINGS W.I.,THE APPROACH TO SELF-GOVERNMENT. CEYLON INDIA PAKISTAN S/ASIA UK SOCIETY POL/PAR DELIB/GP LEGIS ECO/TAC EDU/PROP ADMIN EXEC CHOOSE ATTIT ALL/VALS...JURID CONCPT GEN/METH TOT/POP 20. PAGE 81 H1610 NAT/G CONSTN COLONIAL

B56
TRAGER F.N.,ANNOTATED BIBLIOGRAPHY OF BURMA. BURMA STRUCT NAT/G...GEOG JURID MGT SOC 20. PAGE 156 H3127 BIBLIOG/A S/ASIA CULTURE SOCIETY

B56
WEBER M.,STAATSSOZIOLOGIE. STRUCT LEGIT ADMIN PARL/PROC SUPEGO CONSERVE JURID. PAGE 166 H3320 SOC NAT/G POL/PAR LEAD

B56
WEBER M.,WIRTSCHAFT UND GESELLSCHAFT (2ND VOL.). STRUCT NAT/G POL/PAR LEAD PWR OBJECTIVE IDEA/COMP. PAGE 166 H3321 LEGIT JURID SOC

B57
BYRNES R.F.,BIBLIOGRAPHY OF AMERICAN PUBLICATIONS ON EAST CENTRAL EUROPE, 1945-1957 (VOL. XXII). SECT DIPLOM EDU/PROP RACE/REL...ART/METH GEOG JURID SOC LING 20 JEWS. PAGE 25 H0503 BIBLIOG/A COM MARXISM NAT/G

B57
DONALDSON A.G.,SOME COMPARATIVE ASPECTS OF IRISH LAW. IRELAND NAT/G DIPLOM ADMIN CT/SYS LEAD ATTIT SOVEREIGN...JURID BIBLIOG/A 12/20 CMN/WLTH. PAGE 42 H0835 CONSTN LAW NAT/COMP INT/LAW

B57
KANTOROWICZ E.,THE KING'S TWO BODIES; A STUDY IN MEDIEVAL POLITICAL THEOLOGY. UK LAW CONSTN NAT/G CT/SYS...ART/METH HUM CONCPT MYTH TIME/SEQ BIBLIOG 4/17 ELIZABTH/I POPE CHURCH/STA. PAGE 83 H1657 JURID SECT CHIEF SOVEREIGN

B57
MENDIETTA Y NUNE L.,THEORIE DES GROUPEMENT SOCIAUX SUIVI D'UNE ETUDE SUR LE DROIT SOCIAL. ELITES FAM KIN NAT/G PROB/SOLV CROWD ISOLAT ATTIT PERSON ...JURID CONCPT SOC/INTEG. PAGE 109 H2174 SOC STRATA STRUCT DISCRIM

B58
BRIERLY J.L.,THE BASIS OF OBLIGATION IN INTERNATIONAL LAW, AND OTHER PAPERS. WOR+45 WOR-45 LEGIS...JURID CONCPT NAT/COMP ANTHOL 20. PAGE 21 H0415 INT/LAW DIPLOM ADJUD SOVEREIGN

B58
BUISSON L.,POTESTAS UND CARITAS. FRANCE GERMANY UK ORD/FREE...JURID IDEA/COMP NAT/COMP 12/16 POPE CHURCH/STA. PAGE 23 H0467 GP/REL PWR CATHISM NAT/G

B58
HERRMANN K.,DAS STAATSDENKEN BEI LEIBNIZ. GP/REL ATTIT ORD/FREE...CONCPT IDEA/COMP 17 LEIBNITZ/G CHURCH/STA. PAGE 70 H1406 NAT/G JURID SECT EDU/PROP

B58
LAHBABI M.,LE GOUVERNEMENT MAROCAIN A L'AUBE DU XXE SIECLE. FRANCE MOROCCO CHIEF EX/STRUC LEGIS ORD/FREE PWR...JURID BIBLIOG 19/20. PAGE 90 H1797 NAT/G COLONIAL SOVEREIGN

B58
SHARMA M.P.,PUBLIC ADMINISTRATION IN THEORY AND PRACTICE. INDIA UK USA+45 USA-45 EX/STRUC ADJUD ...POLICY CONCPT NAT/COMP 20. PAGE 142 H2847 MGT ADMIN DELIB/GP JURID

B58
WOODS H.D.,PATTERNS OF INDUSTRIAL DISPUTE SETTLEMENT IN FIVE CANADIAN INDUSTRIES. CANADA USA+45 CONSULT ADJUD GP/REL...JURID GOV/COMP METH/COMP ANTHOL 20. PAGE 170 H3408 BARGAIN INDUS LABOR NAT/G

B58
YUAN TUNG-LI,CHINA IN WESTERN LITERATURE. SECT DIPLOM...ART/METH GEOG JURID SOC BIOG CON/ANAL. PAGE 172 H3441 BIBLIOG ASIA CULTURE HUM

B59
BUNDESMIN FUR VERTRIEBENE,ZEITTAFEL DER VORGESCHICHTE UND DES ABLAUFS DER VERTREIBUNG SOWIE DER UNTERBRINGUNG UND EINGLIEDERUNG DER (2 VOLS.). GERMANY/E GERMANY/W NAT/G PROVS PROB/SOLV DIPLOM PARL/PROC ATTIT...BIBLIOG SOC/INTEG 20 MIGRATION PARLIAMENT. PAGE 24 H0475 JURID GP/REL INT/LAW

B59
GINSBURG M.,LAW AND OPINION IN ENGLAND. UK CULTURE KIN LABOR LEGIS EDU/PROP ADMIN CT/SYS CRIME OWN HEALTH...ANTHOL 20 ENGLSH/LAW. PAGE 56 H1132 JURID POLICY ECO/TAC

B59
HEMMERLE J.,SUDETENDEUTSCHE BIBLIOGRAPHIE 1949-1953. CZECHOSLVK GERMANY SOCIETY STRUCT SECT ...GEOG JURID 20. PAGE 69 H1391 BIBLIOG PROVS GP/REL CULTURE

B59
KIRCHHEIMER O.,GEGENWARTSPROBLEME DER ASYLGEWAHRUNG. DOMIN GP/REL ATTIT...NAT/COMP 20. PAGE 86 H1720 DIPLOM INT/LAW JURID ORD/FREE

B59
LEMBERG E.,DIE VERTRIEBENEN IN WESTDEUTSCHLAND (3 VOLS.). GERMANY/W CULTURE STRUCT AGRI PROVS ADMIN ...JURID 20 MIGRATION. PAGE 94 H1875 GP/REL INGP/REL SOCIETY

B59
PAULSEN M.G.,LEGAL INSTITUTIONS TODAY AND TOMORROW. UK USA+45 NAT/G PROF/ORG PROVS ADMIN PARL/PROC ORD/FREE NAT/COMP. PAGE 124 H2477 JURID ADJUD JUDGE LEGIS

B59
SCHORN H.,DER RICHTER IM DRITTEN REICH; GESCHICHTE UND DOKUMENTE. GERMANY NAT/G LEGIT CT/SYS INGP/REL MORAL ORD/FREE RESPECT...JURID GP/COMP 20. PAGE 140 H2798 ADJUD JUDGE FASCISM

B59
SHARMA R.S.,ASPECTS OF POLITICAL IDEAS AND INSTITUTIONS IN ANCIENT INDIA. INDIA SOCIETY STRUCT FAM VOL/ASSN TAX DOMIN...CONCPT HIST/WRIT 7. PAGE 142 H2848
CULTURE JURID DELIB/GP SECT

B59
SQUIBB G.D.,THE HIGH COURT OF CHIVALRY. UK NAT/G FORCES ADJUD WAR 14/20 PARLIAMENT ENGLSH/LAW. PAGE 148 H2959
CT/SYS PARL/PROC JURID

B59
WILDNER H.,DIE TECHNIK DER DIPLOMATIE. TOP/EX ROLE ORD/FREE...INT/LAW JURID IDEA/COMP NAT/COMP 20. PAGE 168 H3364
DIPLOM POLICY DELIB/GP NAT/G

S59
JENKS C.W.,"THE CHALLENGE OF UNIVERSALITY." FUT UNIV CONSTN CULTURE CONSULT CREATE PLAN LEGIT ATTIT MORAL ORD/FREE RESPECT...MAJORIT JURID 20. PAGE 80 H1602
INT/ORG LAW PEACE INT/LAW

S59
MENDELSON W.,"JUDICIAL REVIEW AND PARTY POLITICS" (BMR)" UK USA+45 USA-45 NAT/G LEGIS PROB/SOLV EDU/PROP ADJUD EFFICIENCY...POLICY NAT/COMP 19/20 AUSTRAL SUPREME/CT. PAGE 109 H2171
CT/SYS POL/PAR BAL/PWR JURID

B60
BREDVOLD L.I.,THE PHILOSOPHY OF EDMUND BURKE. POL/PAR PARL/PROC REPRESENT CONSERVE...JURID 18 BURKE/EDM. PAGE 20 H0410
PHIL/SCI NAT/G CONCPT

B60
GENTILE G.,GENESIS AND STRUCTURE OF SOCIETY (TRANS. BY H.S. HARRIS). NAT/G SECT ATTIT SUPEGO...JURID 20. PAGE 56 H1111
SOCIETY STRUCT PERSON

B60
GONZALEZ NAVARRO M.,LA COLONIZACION EN MEXICO, 1877-1910. AGRI NAT/G PLAN PROB/SOLV INCOME ...POLICY JURID CENSUS 19/20 MEXIC/AMER MIGRATION. PAGE 58 H1164
ECO/UNDEV GEOG HABITAT COLONIAL

B60
LASKIN B.,CANADIAN CONSTITUTIONAL LAW: TEXT AND NOTES ON DISTRIBUTION OF LEGISLATIVE POWER (2ND ED.). CANADA LOC/G ECO/TAC TAX CONTROL CT/SYS CRIME FEDERAL PWR...JURID 20 PARLIAMENT. PAGE 92 H1832
CONSTN NAT/G LAW LEGIS

B60
MACRIDIS R.C.,THE DE GAULLE REPUBLIC: QUEST FOR UNITY. EUR+WWI NAT/G POL/PAR LEGIS LEGIT NAT/LISM ATTIT RIGID/FLEX ORD/FREE PWR...JURID CONCPT TIME/SEQ 20 DEGAULLE/C. PAGE 100 H2009
TOP/EX STRUCT FRANCE

B60
PRASAD B.,THE ORIGINS OF PROVINCIAL AUTONOMY. INDIA UK FINAN LOC/G FORCES LEGIS CONTROL CT/SYS PWR ...JURID 19/20. PAGE 128 H2554
CENTRAL PROVS COLONIAL NAT/G

B60
ROY N.C.,THE CIVIL SERVICE IN INDIA. INDIA POL/PAR ECO/TAC INCOME...JURID MGT 20 CIVIL/SERV. PAGE 135 H2705
ADMIN NAT/G DELIB/GP CONFER

B60
US LIBRARY OF CONGRESS,INDEX TO LATIN AMERICAN LEGISLATION: 1950-1960 (2 VOLS.). NAT/G DELIB/GP ADMIN PARL/PROC 20. PAGE 161 H3211
BIBLIOG/A LEGIS L/A+17C JURID

C60
HAZARD J.N.,"SETTLING DISPUTES IN SOVIET SOCIETY: THE FORMATIVE YEARS OF LEGAL INSTITUTIONS." USSR NAT/G PROF/ORG PROB/SOLV CONTROL CT/SYS ROUTINE REV CENTRAL...JURID BIBLIOG 20. PAGE 68 H1372
ADJUD LAW COM POLICY

C60
HAZARD J.N.,"THE SOVIET SYSTEM OF GOVERNMENT." USSR SOCIETY INDUS NAT/G POL/PAR DIPLOM CT/SYS...JURID CHARTS BIBLIOG/A 20. PAGE 69 H1373
COM NAT/COMP STRUCT ADMIN

B61
BAYITCH S.A.,LATIN AMERICA: A BIBLIOGRAPHICAL GUIDE. LAW CONSTN LEGIS JUDGE ADJUD CT/SYS 20. PAGE 12 H0243
BIBLIOG L/A+17C NAT/G JURID

B61
BEDFORD S.,THE FACES OF JUSTICE: A TRAVELLER'S REPORT. AUSTRIA FRANCE GERMANY/W SWITZERLND UK UNIV WOR+45 WOR-45 CULTURE PARTIC GOV/REL MORAL...JURID OBS GOV/COMP 20. PAGE 13 H0257
CT/SYS ORD/FREE PERSON LAW

B61
DRAGNICH A.N.,MAJOR EUROPEAN GOVERNMENTS. FRANCE GERMANY/W UK USSR LOC/G EX/STRUC CT/SYS PARL/PROC ATTIT MARXISM...JURID MGT NAT/COMP 19/20. PAGE 42 H0846
NAT/G LEGIS CONSTN POL/PAR

B61
JONES R.,AFRICA BIBLIOGRAPHY SERIES: SOUTH EAST CENTRAL AFRICA AND MADAGASCAR. AFR MADAGASCAR RHODESIA SECT BIO/SOC...JURID NAT/COMP 20. PAGE 82 H1633
BIBLIOG/A SOC CULTURE LING

B61
RAHNER H.,KIRCHE UND STAAT IM FRUHEN CHRISTENTUM. INGP/REL ORD/FREE PWR CATHISM...JURID 1/9 CHURCH/STA CHRISTIAN. PAGE 129 H2582
NAT/G SECT ATTIT

GP/REL

B61
ROBERTSON A.H.,THE LAW OF INTERNATIONAL INSTITUTIONS IN EUROPE. EUR+WWI MOD/EUR INT/ORG NAT/G VOL/ASSN DELIB/GP...JURID TIME/SEQ TOT/POP 20 TREATY. PAGE 132 H2644
RIGID/FLEX ORD/FREE

B61
ROCHE J.P.,COURTS AND RIGHTS: THE AMERICAN JUDICIARY IN ACTION (2ND ED.). UK USA+45 USA-45 STRUCT TEC/DEV SANCTION PERS/REL RACE/REL ORD/FREE ...METH/CNCPT GOV/COMP METH/COMP T 13/20. PAGE 133 H2653
JURID CT/SYS NAT/G PROVS

B61
TACHAKKYO K.,BIBLIOGRAPHY OF KOREAN STUDIES: A BIBLIOGRAPHICAL GUIDE TO KOREAN PUBLICATIONS ON KOREAN STUDIES APPEARING 1945-1958. KOREA LAW...HUM JURID PHIL/SCI LING 19/20. PAGE 152 H3033
BIBLIOG/A SOCIETY CULTURE WAR

S61
MILLER E.,"LEGAL ASPECTS OF UN ACTION IN THE CONGO." AFR CULTURE ADMIN PEACE DRIVE RIGID/FLEX ORD/FREE...WELF/ST JURID OBS UN CONGO 20. PAGE 111 H2212
INT/ORG LEGIT

B62
GROGAN V.,ADMINISTRATIVE TRIBUNALS IN THE PUBLIC SERVICE. IRELAND UK NAT/G CONTROL CT/SYS...JURID GOV/COMP 20. PAGE 61 H1231
ADMIN LAW ADJUD DELIB/GP

B62
GRZYBOWSKI K.,SOVIET LEGAL INSTITUTIONS. USA+45 USSR ECO/DEV NAT/G EDU/PROP CONTROL CT/SYS CRIME OWN ATTIT PWR SOCISM...NAT/COMP 20. PAGE 62 H1242
ADJUD LAW JURID

B62
HOOK S.,THE PARADOXES OF FREEDOM. UNIV CONSTN INTELL LEGIS CONTROL REV CHOOSE SUPEGO...POLICY JURID IDEA/COMP 19/20 CIV/RIGHTS. PAGE 73 H1461
CONCPT MAJORIT ORD/FREE ALL/VALS

B62
KAGZI M.C.,THE INDIAN ADMINISTRATIVE LAW. INDIA LG/CO CONTROL CT/SYS...CONCPT 20. PAGE 83 H1649
JURID ADJUD DELIB/GP NAT/G

B62
KASTARI P.,LA PRESIDENCE DE LA REPUBLIQUE EN FINLANDE. FINLAND CONSTN NAT/G POL/PAR LEGIS LEGIT ATTIT...JURID CONCPT 20 PRESIDENT. PAGE 83 H1666
PARL/PROC CHIEF PWR DECISION

B62
PHILLIPS O.H.,CONSTITUTIONAL AND ADMINISTRATIVE LAW (3RD ED.). UK INT/ORG LOC/G CHIEF EX/STRUC LEGIS BAL/PWR ADJUD COLONIAL CT/SYS PWR...CHARTS 20. PAGE 125 H2503
JURID ADMIN CONSTN NAT/G

B62
ROSENZWEIG F.,HEGEL UND DER STAAT. GERMANY SOCIETY FAM POL/PAR NAT/LISM...BIOG 19. PAGE 134 H2682
JURID NAT/G CONCPT PHIL/SCI

B62
SWAYZE H.,POLITICAL CONTROL OF LITERATURE IN THE USSR, 1946-1959. USSR NAT/G CREATE LICENSE...JURID 20. PAGE 151 H3014
MARXISM WRITING CONTROL DOMIN

L62
ORDONNEAU P.,"LES PROBLEMES POSES PAR L'INDEPENDANCE DES NOUVEAUX ETATS AFRICAINS ET MALGACHE SUR LE PLAN DU CONTENTIEUX." FRANCE ISLAM MADAGASCAR LAW STRATA ECO/UNDEV NAT/G LEGIS LEGIT ...JURID TIME/SEQ 20. PAGE 121 H2425
AFR ADJUD COLONIAL SOVEREIGN

S62
MONNIER J.P.,"LA SUCCESSION D'ETATS EN MATIERE DE RESPONSABILITE INTERNATIONALE." UNIV CONSTN INTELL SOCIETY ADJUD ROUTINE PERCEPT SUPEGO...GEN/LAWS TOT/POP 20. PAGE 112 H2240
NAT/G JURID INT/LAW

S62
MOUSKHELY M.,"LA NAISSANCE DES ETATS EN DROIT INTERNATIONAL PUBLIC." UNIV SOCIETY INT/ORG VOL/ASSN LEGIT ATTIT RIGID/FLEX...JURID TIME/SEQ 20. PAGE 114 H2272
NAT/G STRUCT INT/LAW

S62
THOMPSON D.,"THE UNITED KINGDOM AND THE TREATY OF ROME." EUR+WWI INT/ORG NAT/G DELIB/GP LEGIS INT/TRADE RIGID/FLEX...CONCPT EEC PARLIAMENT CMN/WLTH 20. PAGE 154 H3079
ADJUD JURID

S62
VIGNES D.,"L'AUTORITE DES TRAITES INTERNATIONAUX EN DROIT INTERNE." EUR+WWI UNIV LAW CONSTN INTELL NAT/G POL/PAR DIPLOM ATTIT PERCEPT ALL/VALS ...POLICY INT/LAW JURID CONCPT TIME/SEQ 20 TREATY. PAGE 163 H3252
STRUCT LEGIT FRANCE

S62
WALTER E.,"VERS UNE CLASSIFICATION SCIENTIFIQUE DE LA SOCIOLOGIA." UNIV CULTURE INTELL SOCIETY R+D ACT/RES LEGIT ROUTINE ATTIT KNOWL...JURID MGT TREND GEN/LAWS 20. PAGE 165 H3296
PLAN CONCPT

B63
BROOKES E.H.,POWER, LAW, RIGHT, AND LOVE: A STUDY IN POLITICAL VALUES. SOUTH/AFR NAT/G PERSON
PWR ORD/FREE

...CONCPT IDEA/COMP 20. PAGE 21 H0432 JURID LOVE

B63
DECOTTIGNIES R.,LES NATIONALITES AFRICAINES. AFR NAT/G PROB/SOLV DIPLOM COLONIAL ORD/FREE...CHARTS GOV/COMP 20. PAGE 39 H0781 NAT/LISM JURID LEGIS LAW

B63
EDDY J.P.,JUSTICE OF THE PEACE. UK LAW CONSTN CULTURE 14/20 COMMON/LAW. PAGE 44 H0887 CRIME JURID CT/SYS ADJUD

B63
LAVROFF D.-G.,LES LIBERTES PUBLIQUES EN UNION SOVIETIQUE (REV. ED.). USSR NAT/G WORKER SANCTION CRIME MARXISM NEW/LIB...JURID BIBLIOG WORSHIP 20. PAGE 92 H1843 ORD/FREE LAW ATTIT COM

B63
LIVINGSTON W.S.,FEDERALISM IN THE COMMONWEALTH - A BIBLIOGRAPHICAL COMMENTARY. CANADA INDIA PAKISTAN UK STRUCT LOC/G NAT/G POL/PAR...NAT/COMP 20 AUSTRAL. PAGE 97 H1943 BIBLIOG JURID FEDERAL CONSTN

B63
PEREZ ORTIZ R.,ANUARIO BIBLIOGRAFICO COLOMBIANO, 1961. AGRI...INT/LAW JURID SOC LING 20 COLOMB. PAGE 125 H2491 BIBLIOG L/A+17C NAT/G

B63
ROBERTSON A.H.,HUMAN RIGHTS IN EUROPE. CONSTN SOCIETY INT/ORG NAT/G VOL/ASSN DELIB/GP ACT/RES PLAN ADJUD REGION ROUTINE ATTIT LOVE ORD/FREE RESPECT...JURID SOC CONCPT SOC/EXP UN 20. PAGE 132 H2645 EUR+WWI PERSON

B63
WHEARE K.C.,LEGISLATURES. POL/PAR DELIB/GP WAR PEACE CONCPT. PAGE 167 H3338 LEGIS PARL/PROC JURID GOV/COMP

L63
BOLGAR V.,"THE PUBLIC INTEREST: A JURISPRUDENTIAL AND COMPARATIVE OVERVIEW OF SYMPOSIUM ON FUNDAMENTAL CONCEPTS OF PUBLIC LAW" COM FRANCE GERMANY SWITZERLND LAW ADJUD ADMIN AGREE LAISSEZ ...JURID GEN/LAWS 20 EUROPE/E. PAGE 18 H0369 CONCPT ORD/FREE CONTROL NAT/COMP

S63
WEISSBERG G.,"MAPS AS EVIDENCE IN INTERNATIONAL BOUNDARY DISPUTES: A REAPPRAISAL." CHINA/COM EUR+WWI INDIA MOD/EUR S/ASIA INT/ORG NAT/G LEGIT PERCEPT...JURID CHARTS 20. PAGE 166 H3331 LAW GEOG SOVEREIGN

B64
BERNSTEIN H.,A BOOKSHELF ON BRAZIL. BRAZIL ADMIN COLONIAL...HUM JURID SOC 20. PAGE 16 H0315 BIBLIOG/A NAT/G L/A+17C ECO/UNDEV

B64
FORBES A.H.,CURRENT RESEARCH IN BRITISH STUDIES. UK CONSTN CULTURE POL/PAR SECT DIPLOM ADMIN...JURID BIOG WORSHIP 20. PAGE 52 H1034 BIBLIOG PERSON NAT/G PARL/PROC

B64
FREISEN J.,STAAT UND KATHOLISCHE KIRCHE IN DEN DEUTSCHEN BUNDESSTAATEN (2 VOLS.). GERMANY LAW FAM NAT/G EDU/PROP GP/REL MARRIAGE WEALTH 19/20 CHURCH/STA. PAGE 53 H1056 SECT CATHISM JURID PROVS

B64
GESELLSCHAFT RECHTSVERGLEICH,BIBLIOGRAPHIE DES DEUTSCHEN RECHTS (BIBLIOGRAPHY OF GERMAN LAW. TRANS. BY COURTLAND PETERSON). GERMANY FINAN INDUS LABOR SECT FORCES CT/SYS PARL/PROC CRIME...INT/LAW SOC NAT/COMP 20. PAGE 56 H1117 BIBLIOG/A JURID CONSTN ADMIN

B64
GREEN M.M.,IBO VILLAGE AFFAIRS. AFR FORCES PERS/REL ADJUST ISOLAT ATTIT HABITAT PERSON ALL/VALS...JURID RECORD SOC/INTEG 20 IBO. PAGE 60 H1207 MUNIC CULTURE ECO/UNDEV SOC

B64
GUMPLOWICZ L.,RECHTSSTAAT UND SOZIALISMUS. STRATA ORD/FREE SOVEREIGN MARXISM...IDEA/COMP 16/20 KANT/I HOBBES/T. PAGE 62 H1251 JURID NAT/G SOCISM CONCPT

B64
HAAR C.M.,LAW AND LAND: ANGLO-AMERICAN PLANNING PRACTICE. UK USA+45 NAT/G TEC/DEV BUDGET CT/SYS INGP/REL EFFICIENCY OWN...JURID 20. PAGE 63 H1263 LAW PLAN MUNIC NAT/COMP

B64
HALLER W.,DER SCHWEDISCHE JUSTITIEOMBUDSMAN. DENMARK FINLAND NORWAY SWEDEN LEGIS ADJUD CONTROL PERSON ORD/FREE...NAT/COMP 20 OMBUDSMAN. PAGE 64 H1288 JURID PARL/PROC ADMIN CHIEF

B64
HOLDSWORTH W.S.,A HISTORY OF ENGLISH LAW; THE CENTURIES OF DEVELOPMENT AND REFORM (VOL. XIV). UK CONSTN LOC/G NAT/G POL/PAR CHIEF EX/STRUC ADJUD COLONIAL ATTIT...INT/LAW JURID 18/19 TORY/PARTY COMMONWLTH WHIG/PARTY COMMON/LAW. PAGE 73 H1453 LAW LEGIS LEAD CT/SYS

B64
HOPKINSON T.,SOUTH AFRICA. SOUTH/AFR UK NAT/G POL/PAR LEGIS ECO/TAC PARL/PROC WAR...JURID AUD/VIS 19/20. PAGE 73 H1467 SOCIETY RACE/REL DISCRIM

B64
KAACK H.,DIE PARTEIEN IN DER VERFASSUNGSWIRKLICHKEIT DER BUNDESREPUBLIK. GERMANY/W ADMIN PARL/PROC CHOOSE...JURID 20. PAGE 82 H1646 POL/PAR PROVS NAT/G

B64
KIS T.I.,LES PAYS DE L'EUROPE DE L'EST: LEURS RAPPORTS MUTUELS ET LE PROBLEME DE LEUR INTEGRATION DANS L'ORBITE DE L'USSR. EUR+WWI RUSSIA USSR INT/ORG NAT/G REV ATTIT...JURID SOC BIBLIOG WARSAW/P COMECON EUROPE/E. PAGE 86 H1727 DIPLOM COM MARXISM REGION

B64
KRUEGER H.,ALLGEMEINE STAATSLEHRE. WOR+45 CONSTN SECT CHOOSE INGP/REL PWR NEW/LIB...JURID CLASSIF IDEA/COMP. PAGE 89 H1777 NAT/G GOV/COMP SOCIETY

B64
LAPENNA I.,STATE AND LAW: SOVIET AND YUGOSLAV THEORY. USSR YUGOSLAVIA STRATA STRUCT NAT/G DOMIN COERCE MARXISM...GOV/COMP IDEA/COMP 20. PAGE 91 H1812 JURID COM LAW SOVEREIGN

B64
LEDERMAN W.R.,THE COURTS AND THE CANDIAN CONSTITUTION. CANADA PARL/PROC...POLICY JURID GOV/COMP ANTHOL 19/20 SUPREME/CT PARLIAMENT. PAGE 93 H1854 CONSTN CT/SYS LEGIS LAW

B64
NATIONAL BOOK LEAGUE,THE COMMONWEALTH IN BOOKS: AN ANNOTATED LIST. CANADA UK LOC/G SECT ADMIN...SOC BIOG 20 CMN/WLTH. PAGE 116 H2320 BIBLIOG/A JURID NAT/G

B64
NEWARK F.H.,NOTES ON IRISH LEGAL HISTORY (2ND ED.). IRELAND UK PARL/PROC ORD/FREE SOVEREIGN 12/20 ENGLSH/LAW. PAGE 117 H2344 CT/SYS JURID ADJUD NAT/G

B64
RAGHAVAN M.D.,INDIA IN CEYLONESE HISTORY, SOCIETY AND CULTURE. CEYLON INDIA S/ASIA LAW SOCIETY INT/TRADE ATTIT...ART/METH JURID SOC LING 20. PAGE 129 H2581 DIPLOM CULTURE SECT STRUCT

B64
SIEKANOWICZ P.,LEGAL SOURCES AND BIBLIOGRAPHY OF POLAND. COM POLAND CONSTN NAT/G PARL/PROC SANCTION CRIME MARXISM 16/20. PAGE 143 H2870 BIBLIOG ADJUD LAW JURID

B64
SZLADITS C.,BIBLIOGRAPHY ON FOREIGN AND COMPARATIVE LAW: BOOKS AND ARTICLES IN ENGLISH (SUPPLEMENT 1962). FINAN INDUS JUDGE LICENSE ADMIN CT/SYS PARL/PROC OWN...INT/LAW CLASSIF METH/COMP NAT/COMP 20. PAGE 151 H3027 BIBLIOG/A JURID ADJUD LAW

B64
VECCHIO G.D.,L'ETAT ET LE DROIT. ITALY CONSTN EX/STRUC LEGIS DIPLOM CT/SYS...JURID 20 UN. PAGE 162 H3238 NAT/G SOVEREIGN CONCPT INT/LAW

B64
WAINHOUSE D.W.,REMNANTS OF EMPIRE: THE UNITED NATIONS AND THE END OF COLONIALISM. FUT PORTUGAL WOR+45 NAT/G CONSULT DOMIN LEGIT ADMIN ROUTINE ATTIT ORD/FREE...POLICY JURID RECORD INT TIME/SEQ UN CMN/WLTH 20. PAGE 164 H3287 INT/ORG TREND COLONIAL

B64
WHEARE K.C.,FEDERAL GOVERNMENT (4TH ED.). WOR+45 WOR-45 POL/PAR LEGIS BAL/PWR CT/SYS...POLICY JURID CONCPT GOV/COMP 17/20. PAGE 167 H3339 FEDERAL CONSTN EX/STRUC NAT/COMP

S64
SCHEFFLER H.W.,"THE GENESIS AND REPRESSION OF CONFLICT: CHOISEUL ISLAND." S/ASIA LOC/G NAT/G FORCES LEGIS DIPLOM DOMIN LEGIT EXEC CHOOSE ATTIT RESPECT SKILL...POLICY JURID OBS TREND GEN/METH 20. PAGE 139 H2781 PWR COERCE WAR

B65
CONRING E.,KIRCHE UND STAAT NACH DER LEHRE DER NIEDERLANDISCHEN CALVINISTEN IN DER ERSTEN HALFTE DES 17. JAHRHUNDERTS. NETHERLAND GP/REL...CONCPT 17 CHURCH/STA. PAGE 33 H0656 SECT JURID NAT/G ORD/FREE

B65
GAJENDRAGADKAR P.B.,LAW, LIBERTY AND SOCIAL JUSTICE. INDIA CONSTN NAT/G SECT PLAN ECO/TAC PRESS POPULISM...SOC METH/COMP 20 HINDU. PAGE 54 H1086 ORD/FREE LAW ADJUD JURID

B65
INST INTL DES CIVILISATION DIF,THE CONSTITUTIONS AND ADMINISTRATIVE INSTITUTIONS OF THE NEW STATES. AFR ISLAM S/ASIA NAT/G POL/PAR DELIB/GP EX/STRUC CONFER EFFICIENCY NAT/LISM...JURID SOC 20. PAGE 77 H1535 CONSTN ADMIN ADJUD ECO/UNDEV

B65
KAAS L.,DIE GEISTLICHE GERICHTSBARKEIT DER KATHOLISCHEN KIRCHE IN PREUSSEN (2 VOLS.). PRUSSIA CONSTN NAT/G PROVS SECT ADJUD ADMIN ATTIT 16/20. JURID CATHISM GP/REL

PAGE 82 H1647 — CT/SYS

B65
MCWHINNEY E.,JUDICIAL REVIEW IN THE ENGLISH-SPEAKING WORLD (3RD ED.). CANADA UK WOR+45 LEGIS CONTROL EXEC PARTIC...JURID 20 AUSTRAL. PAGE 108 H2151 — GOV/COMP CT/SYS ADJUD CONSTN

B65
PROEHL P.O.,FOREIGN ENTERPRISE IN NIGERIA. NIGERIA FINAN LABOR NAT/G TAX 20. PAGE 128 H2562 — ECO/UNDEV ECO/TAC JURID CAP/ISM

B65
PYLEE M.V.,CONSTITUTIONAL GOVERNMENT IN INDIA (2ND REV. ED.). INDIA POL/PAR EX/STRUC DIPLOM COLONIAL CT/SYS PARL/PROC PRIVIL...JURID 16/20. PAGE 128 H2569 — CONSTN NAT/G PROVS FEDERAL

B65
RENNER K.,MENSCH UND GESELLSCHAFT - GRUNDRISS EINER SOZIOLOGIE (2ND ED.). STRATA FAM LABOR PROF/ORG WAR ...JURID CLASSIF 20. PAGE 131 H2616 — SOC STRUCT NAT/G SOCIETY

B65
SHARMA S.A.,PARLIAMENTARY GOVERNMENT IN INDIA. INDIA FINAN LOC/G PROVS DELIB/GP PLAN ADMIN CT/SYS FEDERAL...JURID 20. PAGE 142 H2849 — NAT/G CONSTN PARL/PROC LEGIS

B65
STEINER K.,LOCAL GOVERNMENT IN JAPAN. CONSTN CULTURE NAT/G ADMIN CHOOSE...SOC STAT 20 CHINJAP. PAGE 149 H2976 — LOC/G SOCIETY JURID ORD/FREE

B65
VON RENESSE E.A.,UNVOLLENDETE DEMOKRATIEN. AFR ISLAM S/ASIA SOCIETY ACT/RES COLONIAL...JURID CHARTS BIBLIOG METH 13/20. PAGE 164 H3276 — ECO/UNDEV NAT/COMP SOVEREIGN

B65
WURFEL S.W.,FOREIGN ENTERPRISE IN COLOMBIA. FINAN LABOR NAT/G ECO/TAC TAX REGION 20 COLOMB. PAGE 171 H3429 — ECO/UNDEV INT/TRADE JURID CAP/ISM

S65
PLISCHKE E.,"INTEGRATING BERLIN AND THE FEDERAL REPUBLIC OF GERMANY." EUR+WWI GERMANY/W LEGIS TEC/DEV DOMIN ORD/FREE PWR...JURID 20 BERLIN. PAGE 126 H2528 — DIPLOM NAT/G MUNIC

B66
ANDERSON S.V.,CANADIAN OMBUDSMAN PROPOSALS. CANADA LEGIS DEBATE PARL/PROC...MAJORIT JURID TIME/SEQ IDEA/COMP 20 OMBUDSMAN PARLIAMENT. PAGE 7 H0133 — NAT/G CREATE ADMIN POL/PAR

B66
DOUMA J.,BIBLIOGRAPHY ON THE INTERNATIONAL COURT INCLUDING THE PERMANENT COURT, 1918-1964. WOR+45 WOR-45 DELIB/GP WAR PRIVIL...JURID NAT/COMP 20 UN LEAGUE/NAT. PAGE 42 H0844 — BIBLIOG/A INT/ORG CT/SYS DIPLOM

B66
EDWARDS C.D.,TRADE REGULATIONS OVERSEAS. IRELAND NEW/ZEALND SOUTH/AFR NAT/G CAP/ISM TARIFFS CONTROL ...POLICY JURID 20 EEC CHINJAP. PAGE 45 H0892 — INT/TRADE DIPLOM INT/LAW ECO/TAC

B66
EPSTEIN F.T.,THE AMERICAN BIBLIOGRAPHY OF RUSSIAN AND EAST EUROPEAN STUDIES FOR 1964. USSR LOC/G NAT/G POL/PAR FORCES ADMIN ARMS/CONT...JURID CONCPT 20 UN. PAGE 47 H0933 — BIBLIOG COM MARXISM DIPLOM

B66
FEINE H.E.,REICH UND KIRCHE. CHRIST-17C MOD/EUR ROMAN/EMP LAW CHOOSE ATTIT 10/19 CHURCH/STA ROMAN/LAW. PAGE 49 H0982 — JURID SECT NAT/G GP/REL

B66
FUCHS W.P.,STAAT UND KIRCHE IM WANDEL DER JAHRHUNDERTE. EUR+WWI MOD/EUR UK REV...JURID CONCPT 4/20 EUROPE CHRISTIAN CHURCH/STA. PAGE 54 H1074 — SECT NAT/G ORD/FREE GP/REL

B66
HARMON R.B.,SOURCES AND PROBLEMS OF BIBLIOGRAPHY IN POLITICAL SCIENCE (PAMPHLET). INT/ORG LOC/G MUNIC POL/PAR ADMIN GOV/REL ALL/IDEOS...JURID MGT CONCPT 19/20. PAGE 67 H1335 — BIBLIOG DIPLOM INT/LAW NAT/G

B66
HENKYS R.,DEUTSCHLAND UND DIE OSTLICHEN NACHBARN. GERMANY POLAND NAT/G POL/PAR INGP/REL ATTIT 20 MIGRATION. PAGE 70 H1396 — GP/REL JURID INT/LAW DIPLOM

B66
HIDAYATULLAH M.,DEMOCRACY IN INDIA AND THE JUDICIAL PROCESS. INDIA EX/STRUC LEGIS LEAD GOV/REL ATTIT ORD/FREE...MAJORIT CONCPT 20 NEHRU/J. PAGE 71 H1415 — NAT/G CT/SYS CONSTN JURID

B66
HOLDSWORTH W.S.,A HISTORY OF ENGLISH LAW; THE CENTURIES OF SETTLEMENT AND REFORM (VOL. XVI). UK LOC/G NAT/G EX/STRUC LEGIS CT/SYS LEAD ATTIT ...POLICY DECISION JURID IDEA/COMP 18 PARLIAMENT. PAGE 73 H1454 — BIOG PERSON PROF/ORG LAW

B66
INSTITUTE COMP STUDY POL SYS,DOMINICAN REPUBLIC ELECTION FACT BOOK. DOMIN/REP LAW LEGIS REPRESENT ...JURID CHARTS 20. PAGE 77 H1536 — SUFF CHOOSE POL/PAR NAT/G

B66
JONES D.H.,AFRICA BIBLIOGRAPHY SERIES: EAST AFRICA. AFR UGANDA SECT BIO/SOC...JURID NAT/COMP 20. PAGE 82 H1630 — BIBLIOG/A SOC CULTURE LING

B66
KASUNMU A.B.,NIGERIAN FAMILY LAW. NIGERIA KIN LEGIT ILLEGIT MARRIAGE AGE DRIVE HABITAT ALL/VALS...JURID IDEA/COMP T 20 ENGLSH/LAW. PAGE 83 H1667 — FAM LAW CULTURE AFR

B66
KEAY E.A.,THE NATIVE AND CUSTOMARY COURTS OF NIGERIA. NIGERIA CONSTN ELITES NAT/G TOP/EX PARTIC REGION...DECISION JURID 19/20. PAGE 84 H1673 — AFR ADJUD LAW

B66
KERR M.H.,ISLAMIC REFORM: THE POLITICAL AND LEGAL THEORIES OF MUHAMMAD 'ABDUH AND RASHID RIDA. NAT/G SECT LEAD SOVEREIGN CONSERVE...JURID BIBLIOG WORSHIP 20. PAGE 85 H1698 — LAW CONCPT ISLAM

B66
PLATE H.,PARTEIFINANZIERUNG UND GRUNDESETZ. GERMANY NAT/G PLAN GIVE PAY INCOME WEALTH...JURID 20. PAGE 126 H2522 — POL/PAR CONSTN FINAN

B66
RINGHOFER K.,STRUKTURPROBLEME DES RECHTES. AUSTRIA ATTIT ORD/FREE...IDEA/COMP 20. PAGE 132 H2630 — JURID PROVS NAT/G NAT/LISM

B66
WUEST J.J.,NEW SOURCE BOOK IN MAJOR EUROPEAN GOVERNMENTS. CHRIST-17C EUR+WWI FRANCE GERMANY ITALY MOD/EUR UK USSR LOC/G POL/PAR CHIEF EX/STRUC CHOOSE CONSERVE MARXISM...JURID T 13/20. PAGE 171 H3425 — NAT/G CONSTN LEGIS

B67
BODENHEIMER E.,TREATISE ON JUSTICE. INT/ORG NAT/G PUB/INST ACT/RES RISK CRIME INGP/REL DISCRIM DRIVE LAISSEZ 20. PAGE 18 H0363 — ALL/VALS STRUCT JURID CONCPT

B67
BOHANNAN P.,LAW AND WARFARE. CULTURE CT/SYS COERCE REV PEACE...JURID SOC CONCPT ANTHOL 20. PAGE 18 H0367 — METH/COMP ADJUD WAR LAW

B67
BROWN L.N.,FRENCH ADMINISTRATIVE LAW. FRANCE UK CONSTN NAT/G LEGIS DOMIN CONTROL EXEC PARL/PROC PWR ...JURID METH/COMP GEN/METH. PAGE 22 H0447 — EX/STRUC LAW IDEA/COMP CT/SYS

B67
HODGKINSON R.G.,THE ORIGINS OF THE NATIONAL HEALTH SERVICE: THE MEDICAL SERVICES OF THE NEW POOR LAW, 1834-1871. UK INDUS MUNIC WORKER PROB/SOLV EFFICIENCY ATTIT HEALTH WEALTH SOCISM...JURID SOC/WK 19/20. PAGE 72 H1445 — HEAL NAT/G POLICY LAW

B67
LENG S.C.,JUSTICE IN COMMUNIST CHINA: A SURVEY OF THE JUDICIAL SYSTEM OF THE CHINESE PEOPLE'S REPUBLIC. CHINA/COM LAW CONSTN LOC/G NAT/G PROF/ORG CONSULT FORCES ADMIN CRIME ORD/FREE...BIBLIOG 20 MAO. PAGE 94 H1877 — CT/SYS ADJUD JURID MARXISM

B67
ROELOFS H.M.,THE LANGUAGE OF MODERN POLITICS: AN INTRODUCTION TO THE STUDY OF GOVERNMENT. DIPLOM ADMIN MARXISM NEW/LIB...JURID CONCPT METH/COMP T 20. PAGE 133 H2657 — LEAD NAT/COMP PERS/REL NAT/G

B67
SCHWARTZ B.,THE ROOTS OF FREEDOM: A CONSTITUTIONAL HISTORY OF ENGLAND. UK LAW POL/PAR DELIB/GP LEGIS REV REPRESENT...JURID BIBLIOG/A 13/20. PAGE 140 H2809 — CONSTN PARL/PROC NAT/G

L67
GOOD E.M.,"CAPITAL PUNISHMENT AND ITS ALTERNATIVES IN ANCIENT NEAR EASTERN LAW." SOCIETY SECT INGP/REL CONSEN ATTIT SEX MORAL...CRIMLGY GP/COMP. PAGE 58 H1168 — MEDIT-7 LAW JURID CULTURE

L67
WAELBROECK M.,"THE APPLICATION OF EEC LAW BY NATIONAL COURTS." EUR+WWI INT/ORG CT/SYS...JURID EEC TREATY. PAGE 164 H3284 — INT/LAW NAT/G LAW PROB/SOLV

S67
DANA MONTANO S.M.,"APLICACIONES CONCRETAS DE LAS RESOLUCIONES Y RECOMENDACIONES DE LAS CONFERENCIAS INTERAMERICANAS DE ABOGADOS" L/A+17C NAT/G PROVS GOV/REL PERCEPT 20 ARGEN. PAGE 37 H0739 — JURID CT/SYS ORD/FREE BAL/PWR

S67
EPSTEIN E.H.,"NATIONAL IDENTITY AND THE LANGUAGE ISSUE IN PUERTO RICO." PUERT/RICO CULTURE STRUCT NAT/G PROB/SOLV SKILL...JURID STAT METH/COMP 20. PAGE 47 H0931 — EDU/PROP SCHOOL LING NAT/LISM

S67
HARNON E.,"CRIMINAL PROCEDURE IN ISRAEL - SOME COMPARATIVE ASPECTS." ISRAEL USA+45 CLIENT EX/STRUC LEGIS...JURID NAT/COMP 20. PAGE 67 H1336 — ADJUD CONSTN CT/SYS CRIME

S67
KINGSBURY E.C.,"LAW AS COMPACT: ANCIENT ISRAEL'S CONTRIBUTION TO THE UNDERSTANDING OF LAW." ISRAEL MEDIT-7 CULTURE KIN KNOWL...JURID CONCPT TREND IDEA/COMP METH/COMP WORSHIP JEWS DEITY. PAGE 86 H1716 — LAW AGREE CONSTN INGP/REL

S67
KROGER K.,"ZUR ENTWICKLUNG DER STAATSZWECKLEHRE IM 19 JAHRHUNDERT." GERMANY RATIONAL ATTIT...IDEA/COMP 19. PAGE 89 H1773 — CONCPT NAT/G JURID OBJECTIVE

S67
SIPPEL D.,"INDIENS UNSICHERE ZUKUNFT." INDIA CULTURE ACADEM POL/PAR LEGIS COLONIAL CHOOSE SOVEREIGN...JURID 20. PAGE 144 H2888 — SOCIETY STRUCT ECO/UNDEV NAT/G

S68
BURGESS J.W.,"VON HOLST'S PUBLIC LAW OF THE UNITED STATES" USA-45 LAW GOV/REL...GOV/COMP IDEA/COMP 19. PAGE 24 H0480 — CONSTN FEDERAL NAT/G JURID

B91
BENTHAM J.,A FRAGMENT ON GOVERNMENT (1776). CONSTN MUNIC NAT/G SECT AGREE HAPPINESS UTIL MORAL ORD/FREE...JURID CONCPT. PAGE 15 H0292 — SOVEREIGN LAW DOMIN

C93
PLAYFAIR R.L.,"A BIBLIOGRAPHY OF MOROCCO." MOROCCO CULTURE AGRI FORCES DIPLOM WAR HEALTH...GEOG JURID SOC CHARTS. PAGE 126 H2526 — BIBLIOG ISLAM MEDIT-7

B96
ESMEIN A.,ELEMENTS DE DROIT CONSTITUTIONNEL. FRANCE UK CHIEF EX/STRUC LEGIS ADJUD CT/SYS PARL/PROC REV GOV/REL ORD/FREE...JURID METH/COMP 18/19. PAGE 47 H0940 — LAW CONSTN NAT/G CONCPT

B98
POLLOCK F.,THE HISTORY OF ENGLISH LAW BEFORE THE TIME OF EDWARD I (2 VOLS, 2ND ED.). UK CULTURE LOC/G LEGIS LICENSE AGREE CONTROL CT/SYS SANCTION CRIME...TIME/SEQ 13 COMMON/LAW CANON/LAW. PAGE 127 H2538 — LAW ADJUD JURID

JURISPRUDENCE....SEE LAW

JURJI E.J. H1643

JURY....JURIES AND JURY BEHAVIOR; SEE ALSO DELIB/GP, ADJUD

B39
SIEYES E.J.,LES DISCOURS DE SIEYES DANS LES DEBATS CONSTITUTIONNELS DE L'AN III (2 ET 18 THERMIDOR). FRANCE LAW NAT/G PROB/SOLV BAL/PWR GOV/REL 18 JURY. PAGE 144 H2871 — CONSTN ADJUD LEGIS EX/STRUC

JUSTICE (SOCIETY) H1644

JUSTICE DEPARTMENT....SEE DEPT/JUST

JUSTINIAN H1645

K

KAACK H. H1646

KAAS L. H1647

KADALIE/C....CLEMENTS KADALIE

KADEN E.H. H1648

KAGZI M.C. H1649

KAHIN G.M. H1650

KAISR/ALUM....KAISER ALUMINUM

KALDOR N. H1651

KALLEN H.M. H1652

KAMCHATKA....KAMCHATKA, U.S.S.R.

B64
BEDERMAN S.H.,THE ETHNOLOGICAL CONTRIBUTIONS OF JOHN LEDYARD (PAMPHLET). ASIA PRE/AMER S/ASIA...SOC 18 LEDYARD/J KAMCHATKA TAHITI TARTARS INDIAN/AM. PAGE 13 H0256 — CULTURE BIOG METH/CNCPT STRUCT

KANET R.E. H1653

KANN R.A. H1654

KANOUTE P. H1655

KANSAS....KANSAS

KANT/I....IMMANUEL KANT

B64
GUMPLOWICZ L.,RECHTSSTAAT UND SOZIALISMUS. STRATA ORD/FREE SOVEREIGN MARXISM...IDEA/COMP 16/20 KANT/I HOBBES/T. PAGE 62 H1251 — JURID NAT/G SOCISM CONCPT

KANTOR H. H1656

KANTOROWICZ E. H1657

KAPIL R.L. H1658

KAPINGAMAR....KAPINGAMARANGI

KAPLAN M.A. H1659

KAPP W.K. H1660

KARIEL H.S. H1661

KARIS T. H0550

KARNJAHAPRAKORN C. H1662

KAROL K.S. H1663

KARPAT K.H. H1664

KASFIR N. H1665

KASHMIR....SEE ALSO S/ASIA

KASTARI P. H1666

KASUNMU A.B. H1667

KATANGA....SEE ALSO AFR

B66
GERARD-LIBOIS J.,KATANGA SECESSION. INT/ORG FORCES DIPLOM ADMIN CONTROL WAR CHOOSE PWR...CHARTS 20 KATANGA TSHOMBE/M UN. PAGE 56 H1114 — NAT/G REGION ORD/FREE REV

KATEB G. H1668

KATZ D. H3220

KAUFMANN R. H1669

KAUNDA K. H1670

KAUNDA/K....KENNETH KAUNDA, PRESIDENT OF ZAMBIA

KAUPER P.G. H1671

KAZAMIAS A.M. H1672

KEARNEY R.N. H1343

KEAY E.A. H1673

KECSKEMETI P. H1674

KEDOURIE E. H1675

KEE R. H1676

KEE W.S. H1677

KEESING F.M. H1678,H1679,H1680

KEFAUVER/E....ESTES KEFAUVER

KEIL S. H1681

KEITA/M....MOBIDO KEITA

KEITH G. H1682

KEL/BRIAND....KELLOGG BRIAND PEACE PACT

KELF-COHEN R. H1683

KELLEHER G.W. H1684

KELLER J.W. H1685

KELLEY G.A. H1686

KELSEN/H....HANS KELSEN

KENEN P.B. H1687

KENJI M. H2962

KENNAN/G....GEORGE KENNAN

B57
REISS J.,GEORGE KENNANS POLITIK DER EINDAMMUNG. USSR NAT/G FORCES TOTALISM ATTIT ORD/FREE...POLICY 20 NATO TRUMAN/HS MARSHL/PLN KENNAN/G. PAGE 131 H2613 — DIPLOM DETER PEACE

KENNEDY M.D. H1688

KENNEDY R. H1689

KENNEDY/JF....PRESIDENT JOHN F. KENNEDY

B63
KLEIMAN R.,ATLANTIC CRISIS: AMERICAN DIPLOMACY CONFRONTS A RESURGENT EUROPE. EUR+WWI USA+45 ECO/DEV AGRI NAT/G CHIEF FORCES PLAN LEAD ATTIT ...CONCPT 20 NATO KENNEDY/JF DEGAULLE/C EEC JOHNSON/LB. PAGE 87 H1731 — DIPLOM REGION POLICY

B64
BRZEZINSKI Z.,POLITICAL POWER: USA/USSR. USA+45 USSR AGRI POL/PAR FORCES CREATE CHOOSE ATTIT ORD/FREE PWR MARXISM...MYTH 20 KENNEDY/JF. PAGE 23 H0457 — NAT/G NAT/COMP POLICY LEAD

B66
BESSON W.,DIE GROSSEN MACHTE - STRUKTURFRAGEN DER GEGENWARTIGEN WELTPOLITIK. ASIA USSR WOR+45 ATTIT ...IDEA/COMP 20 KENNEDY/JF. PAGE 16 H0321 — NAT/COMP DIPLOM STRUCT

B66
BRACKMAN A.C.,SOUTHEAST ASIA'S SECOND FRONT: THE POWER STRUGGLE IN THE MALAY ARCHIPELAGO. CHINA/COM INDONESIA MALAYSIA ECO/UNDEV INT/ORG NAT/G FORCES DIPLOM EDU/PROP REGION COERCE GUERRILLA AUTHORIT POPULISM...MAJORIT 20 KENNEDY/JF SEATO. PAGE 20 H0396 — S/ASIA MARXISM REV

B67
HILSMAN R.,TO MOVE A NATION: THE POLITICS OF FOREIGN POLICY IN THE ADMINISTRATION OF JOHN F. KENNEDY. CHINA/COM COM USSR VIETNAM NAT/G DELIB/GP FORCES PLAN PROB/SOLV BAL/PWR COLONIAL EXEC REV PWR 20 KENNEDY/JF PRESIDENT. PAGE 71 H1418 — CHIEF DIPLOM

B67
PLANCK C.R.,THE CHANGING STATUS OF GERMAN REUNIFICATION IN WESTERN DIPLOMACY, 1955-1966. GERMANY DELIB/GP PLAN PEACE...TREND 20 KENNEDY/JF DEGAULLE/C. PAGE 126 H2519 — NAT/G DIPLOM CENTRAL

B67
WARREN S.,THE AMERICAN PRESIDENT. POL/PAR FORCES LEGIS DIPLOM ECO/TAC ADMIN EXEC PWR...ANTHOL 18/20 ROOSEVLT/F KENNEDY/JF JOHNSON/LB TRUMAN/HS WILSON/W. PAGE 165 H3312 — CHIEF LEAD NAT/G CONSTN

KENNEDY/RF....ROBERT F. KENNEDY

KENNETT L. H1690

KENTUCKY....KENTUCKY

KENYA....KENYA

KENYA MINISTRY ECO PLAN DEV H1691

KENYATTA....JOMO KENYATTA

B67
ODINGA O.,NOT YET UHURU. NAT/G POL/PAR PROB/SOLV COERCE REV WAR PERS/REL PERSON ORD/FREE...POLICY 20 ODINGA/O KENYATTA. PAGE 120 H2395 — ATTIT BIOG LEAD AFR

KENYON W.A. H1708

KEPHART C. H1692

KER A.M. H1693

KEREKES T. H1694

KERNER R.J. H1695,H1696

KERR C. H1697

KERR M.H. H1698

KERSELL J.E. H1699

KEYES J.G. H1700

KEYFITZ N. H1701

KEYNES/G....GEOFFREY KEYNES

KEYNES/JM....JOHN MAYNARD KEYNES

B57
BULLOCK A.,THE LIBERAL TRADITION FROM FOX TO KEYNES. UK CULTURE INTELL CREATE WRITING COLONIAL PERS/REL ATTIT ORD/FREE...POLICY OLD/LIB TRADIT CONCPT 18/20 CHURCHLL/W MILL/JS KEYNES/JM ASQUITH/HH. PAGE 23 H0469 — ANTHOL DEBATE LAISSEZ

B64
KALDOR N.,ESSAYS ON ECONOMIC POLICY (VOL. II). CHILE GERMANY INDIA FINAN...GOV/COMP METH/COMP 20 KEYNES/JM. PAGE 83 H1651 — BAL/PAY INT/TRADE METH/CNCPT ECO/UNDEV

B66
LEONTIEF W.,ESSAYS IN ECONOMICS. ECO/UNDEV INDUS NAT/G CAP/ISM FOR/AID AUTOMAT MARXISM...ECOMETRIC CHARTS ANTHOL METH 20 KEYNES/JM. PAGE 94 H1886 — CONCPT METH/CNCPT METH/COMP

KHADDURI M. H1702,H1703,H1704

KHALIQUZZAMAN C. H1705

KHAMA T. H1706

KHAN A.W. H1707

KHASAS....KHASAS (ANCIENT COMMUNITY)

KHRUSH/N....NIKITA KHRUSHCHEV

S60
WOLFE T.W.,"KHRUSHCHEV'S DISARMAMENT STRATEGY." COM NAT/G TOP/EX PLAN BAL/PWR DIPLOM ARMS/CONT COERCE ATTIT...POLICY CONCPT RECORD TREND CON/ANAL COLD/WAR 20 KHRUSH/N. PAGE 170 H3401 — PWR GEN/LAWS USSR

S61
ZAGORIA D.S.,"THE FUTURE OF SINO-SOVIET RELATIONS." CHINA/COM INT/ORG NAT/G POL/PAR VOL/ASSN ACT/RES PLAN PERSON...METH/CNCPT TIME/SEQ TOT/POP VAL/FREE 20 MAO KHRUSH/N. PAGE 172 H3445 — ASIA COM TOTALISM USSR

B62
BAFFREY S.A.,THE RED MYTH: A HISTORY OF COMMUNISM FROM MARX TO KHRUSHCHEV. USSR NAT/G CHIEF CAP/ISM DIPLOM EDU/PROP REV WAR PEACE TOTALISM...POLICY 20 STALIN/J KHRUSH/N. PAGE 10 H0195 — CONCPT MARXISM TV

B62
BRUMBERG A.,RUSSIA UNDER KHRUSHCHEV. FUT USSR SOCIETY ECO/DEV AGRI PERF/ART WORKER PWR...SOC ANTHOL 20 KHRUSH/N. PAGE 22 H0453 — COM MARXISM NAT/G CHIEF

B62
MEHNERT K.,SOVIET MAN AND HIS WORLD. COM USSR INTELL FAM WORKER PLAN EDU/PROP REV PRODUC MARXISM ...SOC TREND SOC/INTEG 20 LENIN/VI STALIN/J KHRUSH/N. PAGE 108 H2162 — SOCIETY CULTURE ECO/DEV

B63
CRANKSHAW E.,THE NEW COLD WAR: MOSCOW V. PEKIN. CHINA/COM USSR INTELL POL/PAR DELIB/GP CAP/ISM COERCE REV NAT/LISM TOTALISM DRIVE...POLICY IDEA/COMP 20 KHRUSH/N. PAGE 35 H0698 — ATTIT DIPLOM NAT/COMP MARXISM

B63
MCNEAL R.H.,THE BOLSHEVIK TRADITION: LENIN, STALIN, KHRUSHCHEV. USSR NAT/G SUPEGO CONSERVE...IDEA/COMP GEN/LAWS 20 LENIN/VI STALIN/J KHRUSH/N. PAGE 107 H2145 — INTELL BIOG PERS/COMP

B63
MOSELY P.E.,THE SOVIET UNION, 1922-1962: A FOREIGN AFFAIRS READER. ASIA POLAND USSR CULTURE INTELL AGRI POL/PAR WORKER INT/TRADE DOMIN WAR NAT/LISM MARXISM SOCISM 20 KHRUSH/N. PAGE 113 H2267 — PWR POLICY DIPLOM

L63
MICHAEL F.,"KHRUSHCHEV'S DISLOYAL OPPOSITION: STRUCTURAL CHANGE AND POWER STRUGGLE IN COMMUNIST BLOC." ASIA CHINA/COM FUT NAT/G POL/PAR CONSULT PLAN DOMIN ATTIT...POLICY CONCPT TREND MARX/KARL 20 KHRUSH/N. PAGE 110 H2195 — COM STRUCT NAT/LISM USSR

B64
FAINSOD M.,HOW RUSSIA IS RULED (REV. ED.). RUSSIA USSR AGRI PROC/MFG LABOR POL/PAR EX/STRUC CONTROL PWR...POLICY BIBLIOG 19/20 KHRUSH/N COM/PARTY. PAGE 48 H0963 — NAT/G REV MARXISM

B64
RESHETAR J.S. JR.,A CONCISE HISTORY OF THE COMMUNIST PARTY OF THE SOVIET UNION (REV. ED.). COM USSR NAT/G EXEC 19/20 LENIN/VI STALIN/J KHRUSH/N. PAGE 131 H2618 — CHIEF POL/PAR MARXISM PWR

B65
JASNY H.,KHRUSHCHEV'S CROP POLICY. USSR ECO/DEV PLAN MARXISM...STAT 20 KHRUSH/N RESOURCE/N. PAGE 80 H1593 — AGRI NAT/G POLICY ECO/TAC

B65
JOHNSON P.,KHRUSHCHEV AND THE ARTS: POLITICS OF SOVIET CULTURE, 1962-1964. COM USSR NAT/G PERF/ART — CULTURE MARXISM

CONFER DEBATE GP/REL PERS/REL UTIL ATTIT DRIVE 20 KHRUSH/N. PAGE 81 H1626
POLICY CHIEF

B66
BRODERSEN A.,THE SOVIET WORKER: LABOR AND GOVERNMENT IN SOVIET SOCIETY. USSR STRUCT INDUS LABOR PLAN PAY INGP/REL PRODUC...POLICY GEN/LAWS BIBLIOG 20 STALIN/J LENIN/VI BOLSHEVISM KHRUSH/N. PAGE 21 H0425
WORKER ROLE NAT/G MARXISM

B66
DALLIN A.,POLITICS IN THE SOVIET UNION: 7 CASES. COM USSR LAW POL/PAR CHIEF FORCES WRITING CONTROL PARL/PROC CIVMIL/REL TOTALISM...ANTHOL 20 KHRUSH/N STALIN/J CASEBOOK COM/PARTY. PAGE 37 H0736
MARXISM DOMIN ORD/FREE GOV/REL

B66
HERMANN F.G.,DER KAMPF GEGEN RELIGION UND KIRCHE IN DER SOWJETISCHEN BESATZUNGSZONE DEUTSCHLANDS. GERMANY/E EDU/PROP ATTIT PERSON MORAL MARXISM 20 LENIN/VI STALIN/J KHRUSH/N. PAGE 70 H1400
SECT ORD/FREE GP/REL NAT/G

B66
SWEARINGEN A.R.,SOVIET AND CHINESE COMMUNIST POWER IN THE WORLD TODAY. COM USA+45 ECO/UNDEV CREATE LEAD WAR ADJUST...TREND NAT/COMP ANTHOL COLD/WAR KHRUSH/N. PAGE 151 H3017
USSR ASIA DIPLOM ATTIT

B66
ZABLOCKI C.J.,SINO-SOVIET RIVALRY. AFR ASIA CHINA/COM CUBA EUR+WWI L/A+17C USA+45 USSR WOR+45 POL/PAR FORCES COERCE NUC/PWR...GOV/COMP IDEA/COMP 20 MAO KHRUSH/N. PAGE 172 H3444
DIPLOM MARXISM COM

S67
CATTELL D.T.,"THE FIFTIETH ANNIVERSARY: A SOVIET WATERSHED?" USSR CONSTN ECO/DEV NAT/G LEAD TOTALISM 20 KHRUSH/N. PAGE 28 H0562
MARXISM CHIEF POLICY ADJUST

S68
SHAPIRO J.P.,"SOVIET HISTORIOGRAPHY AND THE MOSCOW TRIALS: AFTER THIRTY YEARS." USSR NAT/G LEGIT PRESS CONTROL LEAD ATTIT MARXISM...NEW/IDEA METH 20 TROTSKY/L STALIN/J KHRUSH/N. PAGE 142 H2843
HIST/WRIT EDU/PROP SANCTION ADJUD

KIDD K.E. H1708

KIDDER F.E. H1709

KIERKE/S....SOREN KIERKEGAARD

KILSON M.L. H1710

KIM/IL-SON....IL-SON KIM

KIMBALL S.T. H0162

KIN....KINSHIP (EXCEPT NUCLEAR FAMILY)

N
KRADER L.,SOCIAL ORGANIZATION OF THE MONGOL-TURKIC PASTORAL NOMADS. SOCIETY FAM KIN NEIGH GP/REL MARRIAGE 16/20 MONGOLIA TURKIC MIGRATION. PAGE 88 H1763
BIO/SOC HABITAT CULTURE STRUCT

B00
MAINE H.S.,ANCIENT LAW. MEDIT-7 CULTURE SOCIETY KIN SECT LEGIS LEGIT ROUTINE...JURID HIST/WRIT CON/ANAL TOT/POP VAL/FREE. PAGE 101 H2020
FAM LAW

B05
PHILIPPINE ISLANDS BUREAU SCI,ETHNOLOGICAL SURVEY: THE BONTOC IGOROT. ECO/UNDEV AGRI FAM MARRIAGE HEALTH WEALTH...LING OBS AUD/VIS CHARTS WORSHIP 20 LUZON BONTOC. PAGE 125 H2500
CULTURE INGP/REL KIN STRUCT

B06
SUMNER W.G.,FOLKWAYS: STUDY OF THE SOCIOLOGICAL IMPORTANCE OF USAGES, MANNERS, CUSTOMS, MORES, AND MORALS. STRUCT KIN ETIQUET ROUTINE MURDER MARRIAGE PEACE SEX ALL/VALS WEALTH BIBLIOG. PAGE 150 H3008
CULTURE SOC SANCTION MORAL

B23
WILLOUGHBY W.C.,RACE PROBLEMS IN THE NEW AFRICA: A STUDY OF THE RELATION OF BANTU AND BRITONS IN THOSE PARTS OF BANTU AFRICA... AFR STRUCT SECT DOMIN EDU/PROP GP/REL ATTIT WORSHIP 20 BANTU EUROPE MISSION CHRISTIAN. PAGE 168 H3372
KIN COLONIAL RACE/REL CULTURE

B24
WALKER F.D.,AFRICA AND HER PEOPLES. ISLAM STRUCT FAM SECT EDU/PROP INGP/REL RACE/REL HABITAT...GEOG SOC IDEA/COMP WORSHIP 20 NEGRO. PAGE 164 H3292
CULTURE AFR GP/COMP KIN

B28
BUELL R.,THE NATIVE PROBLEM IN AFRICA. KIN LABOR LOC/G ECO/TAC ROUTINE ORD/FREE...REC/INT KNO/TEST CENSUS TREND CHARTS SOC/EXP STERTYP 20. PAGE 23 H0466
AFR CULTURE

B29
DAVIE M.R.,THE EVOLUTION OF WAR. CULTURE KIN COERCE WAR ATTIT DRIVE...PSY SOC TIME/SEQ TREND GEN/LAWS. PAGE 37 H0746
FORCES STERTYP

B34
BENEDICT R.,PATTERNS OF CULTURE. S/ASIA FAM KIN PERSON RESPECT...CONCPT SELF/OBS. PAGE 14 H0278
CULTURE SOC

B39
AKIGA,AKIGA'S STORY: THE TIV TRIBE AS SEEN BY ONE OF ITS MEMBERS. NIGERIA LAW STRUCT ECO/UNDEV FAM LEAD GP/REL MARRIAGE...LING WORSHIP 20. PAGE 4 H0089
KIN SECT SOC CULTURE

C41
KLUCKHOHN C.,"PATTERNING AS EXEMPLIFIED IN NAVAHO CULTURE" IN EDWARD SAPIR, LANGUAGE, CULTURE, AND PERSONALITY (BMR)" KIN PERS/REL ATTIT PERSON...SOC CONCPT METH/CNCPT LING OBS/ENVIR CON/ANAL BIBLIOG SOC/INTEG 20 NAVAHO INDIAN/AM SAPIR/EDW. PAGE 87 H1733
CULTURE INGP/REL STRUCT

B42
REDFIELD R.,THE FOLK CULTURE OF YUCATAN. STRATA FAM KIN MUNIC SECT DISCRIM ISOLAT ANOMIE HEALTH ...BIBLIOG 20 MEXIC/AMER. PAGE 130 H2605
CULTURE NEIGH GP/COMP SOCIETY

B44
KOHN H.,THE IDEA OF NATIONALISM. UNIV SOCIETY KIN CREATE REGION CENTRAL SOVEREIGN. PAGE 87 H1740
NAT/LISM CONCPT NAT/G GP/REL

B45
LASKER B.,ASIA ON THE MOVE. ASIA BURMA S/ASIA THAILAND USSR ECO/UNDEV FAM KIN WAR NAT/LISM ATTIT ...GEOG CENSUS TREND AUSTRAL 20. PAGE 91 H1826
CULTURE RIGID/FLEX

B45
MCBRYDE F.W.,CULTURAL AND HISTORICAL GEOGRAPHY OF SOUTHWEST GUATEMALA. GUATEMALA AGRI KIN PERSON ...GEOG AUD/VIS CHARTS 20. PAGE 106 H2123
HABITAT ISOLAT CULTURE ECO/UNDEV

B46
BIRKET-SMITH K.A.J.,GESCHICHTE DER KULTUR (3RD ED., TRANS. BY HANS DIETSCHY). KIN...GP/COMP SOC/INTEG. PAGE 17 H0339
CULTURE SOC CONCPT

B47
GITLOW A.L.,ECONOMICS OF THE MOUNT HAGEN TRIBES, NEW GUINEA. S/ASIA STRUCT AGRI FAM...GEOG MYTH 20 NEW/GUINEA. PAGE 57 H1137
HABITAT ECO/UNDEV CULTURE KIN

S48
ALEXANDER L.,"WAR CRIMES, THEIR SOCIAL-PSYCHOLOGICAL ASPECTS." EUR+WWI GERMANY LAW CULTURE ELITES KIN POL/PAR PUB/INST FORCES DOMIN EDU/PROP COERCE CRIME ATTIT SUPEGO HEALTH MORAL PWR FASCISM ...PSY OBS TREND GEN/LAWS NAZI 20. PAGE 5 H0100
DRIVE WAR

B49
SARGENT S.S.,CULTURE AND PERSONALITY. FUT UNIV SOCIETY FAM KIN NEIGH BIO/SOC DRIVE PERCEPT RIGID/FLEX LOVE RESPECT...PSY SOC CONCPT OBS TIME/SEQ TREND CON/ANAL CHARTS HYPO/EXP SIMUL TOT/POP. PAGE 138 H2754
CULTURE PERSON

C50
NUMELIN R.,"THE BEGINNINGS OF DIPLOMACY." INT/TRADE WAR GP/REL PEACE STRANGE ATTIT...INT/LAW CONCPT BIBLIOG. PAGE 119 H2380
DIPLOM KIN CULTURE LAW

B51
BERNATZIK H.A.,THE SPIRITS OF THE YELLOW LEAVES. BURMA LAOS S/ASIA THAILAND VIETNAM SOCIETY AGRI COLONIAL LEISURE GP/REL PERS/REL ISOLAT AGE HABITAT SEX WORSHIP 20. PAGE 16 H0310
SOC KIN ECO/UNDEV CULTURE

B51
INTERNATIONAL AFRICAN INST,ETHNOGRAPHIC SURVEY OF AFRICA: WEST CENTRAL AFRICA (VOLS. I-III, 1951-1953). AFR RHODESIA CULTURE ECO/UNDEV HEREDITY ...GEOG SOC CHARTS BIBLIOG WORSHIP 20 CONGO/LEOP. PAGE 77 H1543
STRUCT KIN INGP/REL HABITAT

B52
INTERNATIONAL AFRICAN INST,ETHNOGRAPHIC SURVEY OF AFRICA: SOUTHERN AFRICA (VOLS. I-III, 1952-1954). AFR SOUTH/AFR CULTURE ECO/UNDEV GOV/REL HEREDITY ...GEOG SOC CHARTS BIBLIOG WORSHIP 20. PAGE 77 H1544
STRUCT KIN INGP/REL HABITAT

B52
KOLARZ W.,RUSSIA AND HER COLONIES. COM RUSSIA LAW CULTURE ECO/DEV KIN LOC/G SECT TEC/DEV ECO/TAC EDU/PROP REGION COERCE ATTIT PWR SOVEREIGN...SOC TIME/SEQ CON/ANAL VAL/FREE 19/20. PAGE 88 H1749
NAT/G DOMIN USSR COLONIAL

B52
KROEBER A.L.,THE NATURE OF CULTURE. UNIV STRATA FAM KIN SECT...PSY GP/COMP 16/20 INDIAN/AM. PAGE 89 H1771
CULTURE SOCIETY CONCPT STRUCT

S52
MUEHLMANN W.E.,"L'IDEE NATIONALE ALLEMANDE ET L'IDEE NATIONALE FRANCAISE." EUR+WWI MOD/EUR SOCIETY KIN NAT/G PWR RESPECT...SOC CONCPT TIME/SEQ GEN/LAWS 19/20. PAGE 114 H2279
CULTURE ATTIT FRANCE GERMANY

B54
FORDE C.D.,AFRICAN WORLDS. AFR CULTURE ROUTINE GP/REL PERS/REL ATTIT DRIVE ALL/VALS...OBS ANTHOL WORSHIP 20. PAGE 52 H1036
SOCIETY KIN SOC

B54
MALINOWSKI B.,MAGIC, SCIENCE AND RELIGION. AGRI KIN GP/REL ALL/VALS...MYTH OBS RECORD IDEA/COMP WORSHIP
CULTURE ATTIT

20 NEW/GUINEA. PAGE 102 H2031 SOC

B54
TITIEV M.,THE SCIENCE OF MAN. LAW STRATA KIN GP/REL PERS/REL HABITAT HEREDITY KNOWL...LING CHARTS BIBLIOG WORSHIP. PAGE 155 H3107 SOC PSY CULTURE

S54
BALANDIER G.,"SOCIOLOGIE DE LA COLONISATION ET RELATIONS ENTRE SOCIETES GLOBALES." AFR SOCIETY ECO/UNDEV KIN DOMIN EDU/PROP RIGID/FLEX PWR...PSY CONCPT TREND TOT/POP. PAGE 10 H0203 CULTURE SOC COLONIAL

B55
APTER D.E.,THE GOLD COAST IN TRANSITION. FUT CONSTN CULTURE SOCIETY ECO/UNDEV FAM KIN LOC/G NAT/G POL/PAR LEGIS TOP/EX EDU/PROP LEGIT ADMIN ATTIT PERSON PWR...CONCPT STAT INT CENSUS TOT/POP VAL/FREE. PAGE 7 H0149 AFR SOVEREIGN

B55
INTERNATIONAL AFRICAN INST,ETHNOGRAPHIC SURVEY OF AFRICA: NORTH EASTERN AFRICA (VOLUMES 1-2, 1955-56). AFR ETHIOPIA CULTURE ECO/UNDEV KIN GOV/REL ATTIT HEREDITY...GEOG CHARTS BIBLIOG WORSHIP 20. PAGE 77 H1545 STRUCT ECO/TAC INGP/REL HABITAT

B55
INTERNATIONAL AFRICAN INST,ETHNOGRAPHIC SURVEY OF AFRICA: WESTERN AFRICA: PEOPLES OF THE NIGER-BENUE CONFLUENCE. AFR NIGER CULTURE ECO/UNDEV KIN GOV/REL GP/REL ATTIT HEREDITY...CHARTS BIBLIOG WORSHIP 20. PAGE 77 H1546 STRUCT GEOG HABITAT INGP/REL

B55
STEWARD J.H.,THEORY OF CULTURE CHANGE; THE METHODOLOGY OF MULTILINEAR EVOLUTION. SOCIETY KIN SECT GP/REL INGP/REL...BIBLIOG SOC/INTEG 20. PAGE 149 H2984 CULTURE CONCPT METH/COMP HABITAT

B55
THOMPSON V.,MINORITY PROBLEMS IN SOUTHEAST ASIA. CAMBODIA CHINA/COM LAOS S/ASIA KIN NAT/G SECT PROB/SOLV EDU/PROP REGION GP/REL RACE/REL MARXISM ...SOC 20 BUDDHISM UN. PAGE 154 H3085 INGP/REL GEOG DIPLOM STRUCT

S55
GOODENOUGH W.H.,"A PROBLEM IN MALAYO-POLYNESIAN SOCIAL ORGANIZATION" (BMR)" MALAYSIA S/ASIA CULTURE AGRI PROB/SOLV OWN HABITAT...SOC 20 20 POLYNESIA. PAGE 58 H1170 KIN STRUCT FAM ECO/UNDEV

C55
OLIVER D.L.,"A LEADER IN ACTION," IN D. A. OLIVER, SOLOMON ISLAND SOCIETY." S/ASIA SOCIETY STRUCT CONTROL TASK PWR...OBS/ENVIR WORSHIP 20. PAGE 121 H2413 LEAD RESPECT CULTURE KIN

B56
EVANS-PRITCHARD E.E.,THE INSTITUTIONS OF PRIMITIVE SOCIETY. LAW SOCIETY KIN ACT/RES CREATE ALL/VALS ...ART/METH SOC METH/CNCPT WORSHIP 20. PAGE 48 H0953 STRUCT PHIL/SCI CULTURE CONCPT

B56
GLUCKMAN M.,CUSTOM AND CONFLICT IN AFRICA. AFR FAM KIN NAT/G DOMIN DISCRIM DRIVE MORAL PWR...SOC BIBLIOG WORSHIP 20. PAGE 57 H1145 CULTURE CREATE PERS/REL GP/COMP

B56
INTERNATIONAL AFRICAN INST,ETHNOGRAPHIC SURVEY OF AFRICA; WESTERN AFRICA: PAGAN PEOPLES OF CENTRAL AREA OF NORTHERN NIGERIA (VOL. XII). NIGERIA FAM KIN SECT ECO/TAC GOV/REL GP/REL ATTIT...LING CHARTS 20. PAGE 77 H1548 STRUCT INGP/REL HABITAT CULTURE

B56
LEVIN M.G.,THE PEOPLES OF SIBERIA. PREHIST ECO/UNDEV KIN SECT HABITAT...CLASSIF AUD/VIS WORSHIP 20 SIBERIA. PAGE 95 H1900 CULTURE SOCIETY ASIA

B56
MANNONI D.O.,PROSPERO AND CALIBAN: THE PSYCHOLOGY OF COLONIZATION. AFR EUR+WWI FAM KIN MUNIC SECT DOMIN ADMIN ATTIT DRIVE LOVE PWR RESPECT...PSY SOC CONCPT MYTH OBS DEEP/INT BIOG GEN/METH MALAGASY 20. PAGE 102 H2040 CULTURE COLONIAL

B57
IKE N.,JAPANESE POLITICS. INTELL STRUCT AGRI INDUS FAM KIN LABOR PRESS CHOOSE ATTIT...DECISION BIBLIOG 19/20 CHINJAP. PAGE 76 H1523 NAT/G ADMIN POL/PAR CULTURE

B57
INTERNATIONAL AFRICAN INST,ETHNOGRAPHIC SURVEY OF AFRICA: WESTERN AFRICA: THE BENIN KINGDOM. AFR NIGERIA CULTURE ECO/UNDEV KIN ECO/TAC GOV/REL AGE ATTIT HEREDITY...CHARTS BIBLIOG WORSHIP 20. PAGE 77 H1550 STRUCT INGP/REL GEOG HABITAT

B57
INTERNATIONAL AFRICAN INST,ETHNOGRAPHIC SURVEY OF AFRICA: WESTERN AFRICA: THE WOLOF OF SENEGAMBIA. AFR SENEGAL CULTURE ECO/UNDEV FAM KIN REGION ...CHARTS GP/COMP BIBLIOG WORSHIP 20. PAGE 78 H1551 STRUCT GEOG HABITAT INGP/REL

B57
KOENTJARANINGRAT R.,A PRELIMINARY DESCRIPTION OF THE JAVANESE KINSHIP SYSTEM. INDONESIA STRATA FAM INGP/REL ADJUST MARRIAGE AGE/C AGE/Y AGE/A PERSON ...OBS CHARTS DICTIONARY 20 JAVA. PAGE 87 H1736 KIN STRUCT ELITES CULTURE

B57
LOOMIS C.P.,RURAL SOCIOLOGY. CULTURE KIN NAT/G SECT VOL/ASSN ACT/RES EDU/PROP HEALTH. PAGE 98 H1963 SOC AGRI METH T

B57
MENDIETTA Y NUNE L.,THEORIE DES GROUPEMENT SOCIAUX SUIVI D'UNE ETUDE SUR LE DROIT SOCIAL. ELITES FAM KIN NAT/G PROB/SOLV CROWD ISOLAT ATTIT PERSON ...JURID CONCPT SOC/INTEG. PAGE 109 H2174 SOC STRATA STRUCT DISCRIM

S57
KILSON M.L.,"LAND AND POLITICS IN KENYA: AN ANALYSIS OF AFRICAN POLITICS IN A PLURAL SOCIETY." FUT LAW CULTURE KIN NAT/G ECO/TAC DOMIN REV NAT/LISM ORD/FREE PWR RESPECT SOVEREIGN WEALTH ...SOC OBS TREND WORK VAL/FREE CMN/WLTH 20. PAGE 86 H1710 AFR ECO/UNDEV

B58
BRIGGS L.C.,THE LIVING RACES OF THE SAHARA. STRATA AGRI KIN INT/TRADE HABITAT...GEOG AUD/VIS CHARTS BIBLIOG 20 SAHARA MIGRATION. PAGE 21 H0417 STRUCT SOCIETY SOC CULTURE

B58
COLEMAN J.S.,NIGERIA: BACKGROUND TO NATIONALISM. AFR SOCIETY ECO/DEV KIN LOC/G POL/PAR TEC/DEV DOMIN ADMIN DRIVE PWR RESPECT...TRADIT SOC INT SAMP TIME/SEQ 20. PAGE 31 H0627 NAT/G NAT/LISM NIGERIA

B58
COWAN L.G.,LOCAL GOVERNMENT IN WEST AFRICA. AFR FRANCE UK CULTURE KIN POL/PAR CHIEF LEGIS CREATE ADMIN PARTIC GOV/REL GP/REL...METH/COMP 20. PAGE 34 H0682 LOC/G COLONIAL SOVEREIGN REPRESENT

B58
LERNER D.,THE PASSING OF TRADITIONAL SOCIETY: MODERNIZING THE MIDDLE EAST. IRAN ISLAM LEBANON SYRIA TURKEY UAR CULTURE INTELL STRATA KIN NAT/G NEIGH SECT EDU/PROP ATTIT PERSON...MYTH OBS 20. PAGE 95 H1888 ECO/UNDEV RIGID/FLEX

B58
MATOS J.,LAS ACTUALES COMMUNIDADES DE INDIGENAS: HUAROCHIRI EN 1955. PERU FAM NAT/G SECT EDU/PROP ADJUD GP/REL INGP/REL 20 INDIAN/AM. PAGE 105 H2091 STRUCT NEIGH KIN ECO/UNDEV

B58
VON FURER-HAIMEN E.,AN ANTHROPOLOGICAL BIBLIOGRAPHY OF SOUTH ASIA (VOL. I). STRATA STRUCT KIN SECT ACT/RES CREATE HABITAT...GEOG OBS 19/20. PAGE 163 H3267 BIBLIOG/A CULTURE S/ASIA SOC

B58
WARNER W.L.,A BLACK CIVILIZATION - A SOCIAL STUDY OF AN AUSTRALIAN TRIBE. SOCIETY FAM MARRIAGE...PSY SOC MYTH CHARTS 20 AUSTRAL MAPS MURNGIN RITUAL. PAGE 165 H3310 CULTURE KIN STRUCT DEATH

B58
WIGGIN L.M.,THE FACTION OF COUSINS: A POLITICAL ACCOUNT OF THE GRENVILLES, 1733-1763. UK STRUCT KIN NAT/G INGP/REL...CONCPT BIOG BIBLIOG/A 18 GRENVILLES. PAGE 168 H3357 FAM POL/PAR PWR

S58
MAIR L.P.,"REPRESENTATIVE LOCAL GOVERNMENT AS A PROBLEM IN SOCIAL CHANGE." ECO/UNDEV KIN LOC/G NAT/G SCHOOL JUDGE ADMIN ROUTINE REPRESENT RIGID/FLEX RESPECT...CONCPT STERTYP CMN/WLTH 20. PAGE 101 H2025 AFR PWR ELITES

B59
EAENZA L.,COMMUNISMO E CATTOLICESIMO IN UNA PARROCHIA DI CAMPAGNA. ITALY CULTURE ELITES ECO/DEV AGRI KIN POL/PAR DOMIN LEGIT RIGID/FLEX...DECISION OBS IDEA/COMP 20 COM/PARTY CHURCH/STA. PAGE 44 H0878 ATTIT CATHISM NEIGH MARXISM

B59
GINSBURG M.,LAW AND OPINION IN ENGLAND. UK CULTURE KIN LABOR LEGIS EDU/PROP ADMIN CT/SYS CRIME OWN HEALTH...ANTHOL 20 ENGLSH/LAW. PAGE 56 H1132 JURID POLICY ECO/TAC

B59
KITTLER G.D.,EQUATORIAL AFRICA: THE NEW WORLD OF TOMORROW. CENTRL/AFR INDUS KIN SECT CHIEF EDU/PROP CHOOSE HEALTH...GEOG WORSHIP 20. PAGE 87 H1730 RACE/REL AFR ECO/UNDEV CULTURE

B59
MURDOCK G.P.,AFRICA: ITS PEOPLES AND THEIR CULTURE HISTORY. AFR CULTURE AGRI LOC/G INGP/REL HABITAT ...GEOG SOC LING CHARTS BIBLIOG 20 NEGRO EGYPT/ANC. PAGE 115 H2293 SOCIETY ECO/TAC GP/COMP KIN

B59
PANIKKAR K.M.,THE AFRO-ASIAN STATES AND THEIR PROBLEMS. COM CULTURE KIN POL/PAR SECT DIPLOM EDU/PROP COLONIAL SOVEREIGN...TECHNIC GOV/COMP 20. PAGE 123 H2458 AFR S/ASIA ECO/UNDEV

B59
WARNER W.L.,THE LIVING AND THE DEAD: A STUDY OF SYMBOLIC LIFE OF AMERICANS. INTELL KIN DEATH ALL/VALS ALL/IDEOS...CONCPT MYTH LING OBS/ENVIR CHARTS BIBLIOG WORSHIP 18/20. PAGE 165 H3311 CULTURE SOC TIME/SEQ IDEA/COMP

B60
BEATTIE J.,BUNYORO, AN AFRICAN KINGDOM. UGANDA CULTURE

STRATA INGP/REL PERS/REL...SOC BIBLIOG 19/20. PAGE 13 H0250 ELITES SECT KIN

B60
BRIGGS L.C.,TRIBES OF THE SAHARA. AFR MOROCCO STRATA AGRI GP/REL HEALTH...GEOG SOC MYTH LING BIBLIOG 13/20 ARABS. PAGE 21 H0418 CULTURE HABITAT KIN SELF/OBS

B60
BURRIDGE K.,MAMBU: A MELANESIAN MILLENNIUM. ECO/UNDEV PROC/MFG FAM KIN CHIEF COLONIAL COERCE GP/REL DRIVE WEALTH WORSHIP 20 NEW/GUINEA. PAGE 25 H0494 S/ASIA SECT CULTURE MYTH

B60
CHATTERJI S.K.,AFRICANISM: THE AFRICAN PERSONALITY. KIN NAT/G SECT CREATE DIPLOM COLONIAL GP/REL ATTIT ORD/FREE...LING WORSHIP 20. PAGE 29 H0585 PERSON NAT/LISM AFR CULTURE

B60
COUGHLIN R.,DOUBLE IDENTITY: THE CHINESE AND MODERN THAILAND. CHINA/COM S/ASIA THAILAND ECO/UNDEV EXTR/IND FINAN INDUS KIN MUNIC NAT/G PROF/ORG SCHOOL SECT ATTIT DRIVE...CONCPT OBS 20. PAGE 34 H0676 ASIA FAM CULTURE

B60
INTERNATIONAL AFRICAN INST,ETHNOGRAPHIC SURVEY OF AFRICA: WESTERN AFRICA: PEOPLES OF THE MIDDLE NIGER REGION, NORTHERN NIGERIA. AFR NIGER CULTURE ECO/UNDEV KIN NEIGH GOV/REL GP/REL ATTIT HEREDITY ...CHARTS BIBLIOG WORSHIP 20. PAGE 78 H1552 STRUCT GEOG HABITAT INGP/REL

B60
KOHN H.,PAN-SLAVISM: ITS HISTORY AND IDEOLOGY. COM CZECHOSLVK EUR+WWI MOD/EUR USSR YUGOSLAVIA CULTURE ELITES INTELL KIN NAT/G EDU/PROP DRIVE SOVEREIGN ...HUM PHIL/SCI MYTH HIST/WRIT 19/20. PAGE 87 H1745 ATTIT CONCPT NAT/LISM

B60
OTTENBERG S.,CULTURES AND SOCIETIES OF AFRICA. AFR KIN TEC/DEV GP/REL MARRIAGE ATTIT HABITAT HEREDITY ...ANTHOL BIBLIOG T WORSHIP 20. PAGE 122 H2433 SOCIETY INGP/REL STRUCT CULTURE

B60
SMITH M.G.,GOVERNMENT IN ZAZZAU 1800-1950. NIGERIA UK CULTURE SOCIETY LOC/G ADMIN COLONIAL ...METH/CNCPT NEW/IDEA METH 19/20. PAGE 146 H2914 REGION CONSTN KIN ECO/UNDEV

S60
GINSBURGS G.,"PEKING-LHASA-NEW DELHI." CHINA/COM FUT INDIA S/ASIA KIN NAT/G PROVS SECT FORCES BAL/PWR ECO/TAC DOMIN EDU/PROP LEGIT ADMIN REGION GUERRILLA PWR...TREND TIBET 20. PAGE 57 H1134 ASIA COERCE DIPLOM

S60
LEVINE R.A.,"THE INTERNALIZATION OF POLITICAL VALUES IN STATELESS SOCIETIES." AFR FAM KIN LOC/G PROVS JUDGE PERSON RIGID/FLEX...DECISION SOC TIME/SEQ 20. PAGE 95 H1904 CULTURE ATTIT

B61
APTER D.E.,THE POLITICAL KINGDOM IN UGANDA. UGANDA CULTURE ECO/UNDEV AGRI KIN SECT TOP/EX REGION ATTIT HABITAT CONSERVE...GEOG AUD/VIS 20. PAGE 8 H0153 NAT/LISM POL/PAR COLONIAL ECO/TAC

B61
BERKOWITZ L.,AGGRESSION: AS A SOCIAL PSYCHOLOGICAL ANALYSIS. UNIV CULTURE FACE/GP FAM KIN NEIGH EDU/PROP DISPL DRIVE HEALTH LOVE ORD/FREE...PSY SOC CONCPT OBS TREND. PAGE 15 H0305 SOCIETY COERCE WAR

B61
BIEBUYCK D.,CONGO TRIBES AND PARTIES. AFR CONGO/BRAZ CONSTN NAT/G COLONIAL CHOOSE FEDERAL 20 CONGO/LEOP. PAGE 17 H0333 KIN POL/PAR GP/REL SOVEREIGN

B61
FIRTH R.,HISTORY AND TRADITIONS OF TIKOPIA. S/ASIA KIN SECT RUMOR WAR...MYTH WORSHIP 20 POLYNESIA. PAGE 50 H1008 CULTURE STRUCT HUM

B61
FIRTH R.,ELEMENTS OF SOCIAL ORGANIZATION (3RD ED.). STRATA STRUCT ECO/UNDEV NEIGH CHIEF INGP/REL ATTIT MORAL...PHIL/SCI GP/COMP WORSHIP SOC/INTEG 20. PAGE 50 H1009 SOC CULTURE SOCIETY KIN

B61
HEMPSTONE S.,THE NEW AFRICA. AGRI INDUS KIN NAT/G COLONIAL MARXISM...SOC INT TREND NAT/COMP BIBLIOG/A 20. PAGE 69 H1392 AFR ORD/FREE PERSON CULTURE

B61
MERRIAM A.,CONGO: BACKGROUND OF CONFLICT. AFR FUT KIN MUNIC NAT/G POL/PAR PROVS DELIB/GP PLAN DOMIN COERCE ATTIT...TIME/SEQ CHARTS CONGO 20. PAGE 109 H2182 CHOOSE GUERRILLA

B61
SCHECHTMAN J.B.,ON WINGS OF EAGLES: THE PLIGHT, EXODUS, AND HOMECOMING OF ORIENTAL JEWRY. ASIA ISLAM ISRAEL VOL/ASSN DIPLOM CONTROL ORD/FREE ...GEOG WORSHIP SOC/INTEG 20 JEWS ARABS MIGRATION. PAGE 139 H2777 CULTURE HABITAT KIN SECT

B61
SOUTHALL A.,SOCIAL CHANGE IN MODERN AFRICA. CULTURE STRATA ECO/UNDEV AGRI FAM KIN MUNIC GP/REL INGP/REL MARRIAGE...GEOG ANTHOL 20. PAGE 147 H2940 AFR TREND SOCIETY SOC

B61
TURNBULL C.M.,THE FOREST PEOPLE. EATING GP/REL INGP/REL RACE/REL ISOLAT HABITAT HEREDITY...GEOG SOC LING DICTIONARY WORSHIP 20 CONGO NEGRO BA/MBUTI. PAGE 157 H3138 AFR CULTURE KIN RECORD

S61
SCHECHTMAN J.B.,"MINORITIES IN THE MIDDLE EAST." ISLAM INTELL SOCIETY STRATA KIN NAT/G VOL/ASSN EDU/PROP REGION GP/REL DISCRIM ATTIT BIO/SOC DISPL PERSON ALL/VALS...PSY SOC OBS SAMP GEN/LAWS 20. PAGE 139 H2776 SECT CULTURE RACE/REL

B62
ABRAHAM W.E.,THE MIND OF AFRICA. AFR SOCIETY STRATA KIN ECO/TAC DOMIN EDU/PROP LEGIT COERCE ATTIT ALL/VALS...MAJORIT SOC OBS HIST/WRIT TIME/SEQ TREND TOT/POP 20. PAGE 3 H0058 CULTURE SIMUL GHANA

B62
BERNOT R.M.,EXCESS AND RESTRAINT: SOCIAL CONTROL AMONG GUINEA MOUNTAIN PEOPLE. CULTURE FAM KIN CT/SYS COERCE WAR PERS/REL MARRIAGE HABITAT SEX ...MYTH 20 NEW/GUINEA. PAGE 16 H0314 SOCIETY CONTROL STRUCT ADJUST

B62
BRETTON H.L.,POWER AND STABILITY IN NIGERIA: THE POLITICS OF DECOLONIZATION. AFR CONSTN INTELL ECO/UNDEV COM/IND KIN NAT/G POL/PAR PROVS VOL/ASSN LEGIS DOMIN EDU/PROP LEGIT EXEC ROUTINE CHOOSE NAT/LISM ATTIT PERCEPT ALL/VALS. PAGE 20 H0411 CULTURE OBS NIGERIA

B62
BUSIA K.A.,THE CHALLENGE OF AFRICA. CULTURE KIN MUNIC NAT/G POL/PAR SCHOOL DELIB/GP PLAN ECO/TAC DOMIN EDU/PROP TOTALISM ATTIT PERSON ALL/VALS SOVEREIGN...SOC CONCPT STERTYP TOT/POP VAL/FREE 20. PAGE 25 H0496 AFR ECO/UNDEV NAT/LISM

B62
DILLING A.R.,ABORIGINE CULTURE HISTORY - A SURVEY OF PUBLICATIONS 1954-1957. GUINEA...SOC CHARTS NAT/COMP BIBLIOG/A AUSTRAL ABORIGINES. PAGE 41 H0825 S/ASIA HIST/WRIT CULTURE KIN

B62
EDWARDS A.C.,THE OVIMBUNDU UNDER TWO SOVEREIGNTIES. CULTURE STRUCT FAM MARRIAGE HABITAT...SOC 19/20 OVIMBUNDU. PAGE 45 H0891 KIN NEIGH SOCIETY CONTROL

B62
EVANS-PRITCHARD E.E.,ESSAYS IN SOCIAL ANTHROPOLOGY. AFR KIN REGION INGP/REL DRIVE HABITAT...OBS METH 20 ZANDE. PAGE 48 H0954 SOCIETY CULTURE SOC STRUCT

B62
FALKENBERG J.,KIN AND TOTEM; GROUP RELATIONS OF AUSTRALIAN ABORIGINES IN THE PORT KEATS DISTRICT. SOCIETY STRATA STRUCT GP/REL PERS/REL MARRIAGE AGE ATTIT SEX...SOC STAT CHARTS AUSTRAL ABORIGINES. PAGE 48 H0964 KIN INGP/REL CULTURE FAM

B62
FEIT E.,SOUTH AFRICA, THE DYNAMICS OF THE AFRICAN NATIONAL CONGRESS. AFR SOUTH/AFR LAW INTELL STRATA KIN NAT/G POL/PAR ECO/TAC DOMIN RISK COERCE 20 NEGRO. PAGE 49 H0984 RACE/REL ELITES CONTROL STRUCT

B62
HACHMANN R.,VOLKER ZWISCHEN GERMANEN UND KELTEN. GERMANY CULTURE STRUCT MUNIC...ART/METH CHARTS MAPS. PAGE 63 H1269 LING SOC KIN GP/REL

B62
HAY S.N.,SOUTHEAST ASIAN HISTORY: A BIBLIOGRAPHICAL GUIDE. STRATA KIN NAT/G REGION GUERRILLA REV WAR ADJUST HABITAT PERCEPT ALL/IDEOS...CHARTS 5/20. PAGE 68 H1365 BIBLIOG/A S/ASIA CULTURE

B62
HO PING-TI,THE LADDER OF SUCCESS IN IMPERIAL CHINA: ASPECTS OF SOCIAL MOBILITY, 1368-1911. INTELL STRATA FAM KIN MUNIC NAT/G PROVS SCHOOL DELIB/GP DOMIN EDU/PROP ADMIN ROUTINE PERSON ALL/VALS...SOC STAT BIOG HIST/WRIT TIME/SEQ VAL/FREE. PAGE 71 H1431 ASIA CULTURE

B62
HUNTER G.,THE NEW SOCIETIES OF TROPICAL AFRICA. CULTURE INDUS KIN MUNIC WORKER INT/TRADE EDU/PROP ORD/FREE...INT TREND 20. PAGE 75 H1500 AFR GOV/COMP ECO/UNDEV SOCIETY

B62
JOHNSON J.J.,THE ROLE OF THE MILITARY IN UNDERDEVELOPED COUNTRIES. AFR BURMA INDONESIA ISLAM ISRAEL L/A+17C S/ASIA THAILAND CULTURE ECO/UNDEV KIN PROVS CONSULT ACT/RES COERCE REV DRIVE RIGID/FLEX ORD/FREE...RECORD ANTHOL 20. PAGE 81 H1622 FORCES CONCPT

B62
KEESING F.M.,THE ETHNOHISTORY OF NORTHERN LUZON. PHILIPPINE ECO/UNDEV FAM SECT CHIEF REGION GP/REL CULTURE SOC

HABITAT...GEOG LING BIBLIOG WORSHIP 20. PAGE 84 H1680 — KIN

B62
KENNEDY R.,BIBLIOGRAPHY OF INDONESIAN PEOPLES AND CULTURES (2ND REV. ED.). INDONESIA STRUCT ECO/UNDEV SCHOOL EDU/PROP COLONIAL...GEOG SOC LING NAT/COMP 20. PAGE 85 H1689 — BIBLIOG S/ASIA CULTURE KIN

B62
KOSAMBI D.D.,MYTH AND REALITY. INDIA AGRI KIN SECT HABITAT...SOC 20. PAGE 88 H1758 — CULTURE SOCIETY MYTH ATTIT

B62
MEGGITT M.J.,DESERT PEOPLE. ECO/UNDEV KIN CREATE PROB/SOLV CONTROL DRIVE ROLE...GEOG SOC MYTH CHARTS BIBLIOG 20 AUSTRAL. PAGE 108 H2159 — ADJUST CULTURE INGP/REL HABITAT

B62
MICHAEL H.N.,STUDIES IN SIBERIAN ETHNOGENESIS. USSR KIN...ART/METH SOC 20 SIBERIA. PAGE 110 H2196 — HABITAT HEREDITY CULTURE LING

B62
RUDY Z.,ETHNOSOZIOLOGIE SOWJETISCHER VOLKER. USSR SOCIETY STRUCT FAM SECT GP/REL ATTIT...SOC SOC/INTEG 20. PAGE 136 H2714 — MYTH CULTURE KIN

B62
SMITH M.G.,KINSHIP AND COMMUNITY IN CARRIACOU. WEST/IND STRATA AGRI FAM SECT WORKER MARRIAGE OWN HEREDITY WEALTH...SOC 18/20. PAGE 146 H2915 — CULTURE HABITAT KIN STRUCT

B62
STARCKE V.,DENMARK IN WORLD HISTORY. DENMARK AGRI KIN WAR...BIBLIOG T 20. PAGE 149 H2970 — GEOG CULTURE SOC

B62
TURNBULL C.M.,THE LONELY AFRICAN. AFR MUNIC SECT ANOMIE ALL/VALS...DECISION 20. PAGE 157 H3139 — CULTURE ISOLAT KIN TRADIT

B62
VILAKAZI A.,ZULU TRANSFORMATIONS: A STUDY OF THE DYNAMICS OF SOCIAL CHANGE. AFR CULTURE ECO/UNDEV KIN NEIGH SEX...GEOG QU TREND CHARTS BIBLIOG 19/20. PAGE 163 H3254 — MARRIAGE SECT SOC EDU/PROP

B62
YOUNG G.,THE HILL TRIBES OF NORTHERN THAILAND. S/ASIA THAILAND FAM KIN LOC/G GP/REL HABITAT...GEOG LING OBS 20. PAGE 172 H3438 — CULTURE STRUCT ECO/UNDEV SECT

L62
COHEN R.,"POWER IN COMPLEX SOCIETIES IN AFRICA." AFR KIN MUNIC POL/PAR DELIB/GP DOMIN ROUTINE ATTIT ALL/VALS...SOC STAT OBS INT QU CHARTS ANTHOL 20. PAGE 31 H0617 — CULTURE STRATA ELITES

S62
PISTRAK L.,"SOVIET VIEWS ON AFRICA." AFR COM FUT ISLAM USSR INTELL STRUCT KIN POL/PAR PLAN EDU/PROP RIGID/FLEX PWR MARXISM...TIME/SEQ WORK TOT/POP 20. PAGE 126 H2516 — NAT/G ATTIT SOCISM

B63
BERREMAN G.D.,HINDUS OF THE HIMALAYAS. INDIA STRATA STRUCT KIN MUNIC 20 HINDU. PAGE 16 H0319 — CULTURE SECT GP/REL ECO/UNDEV

B63
DRIVER H.E.,ETHNOGRAPHY AND ACCULTURATION OF THE CHICHIMECA-JONAZ OF NORTHEAST MEXICO. ECO/UNDEV AGRI FAM KIN EDU/PROP MARRIAGE HEALTH...GEOG INT CHARTS WORSHIP 18/20 MEXIC/AMER. PAGE 42 H0848 — CULTURE HABITAT STRUCT GP/REL

B63
ELWIN V.,A NEW DEAL FOR TRIBAL INDIA. INDIA AGRI COM/IND INDUS KIN TEC/DEV TAX EDU/PROP OWN HEALTH 20. PAGE 46 H0912 — ECO/UNDEV CULTURE CONSTN SOC/WK

B63
FIRST R.,SOUTH WEST AFRICA. SOUTH/AFR INT/ORG KIN NAT/G WORKER COLONIAL WAR...POLICY 20 UN TRUST/TERR AFRICA/SW. PAGE 50 H1006 — DISCRIM ORD/FREE RACE/REL CONTROL

B63
GLUCKMAN M.,ORDER AND REBELLION IN TRIBAL AFRICA. EUR+WWI LAW CULTURE STRATA KIN MUNIC DELIB/GP ACT/RES DOMIN EDU/PROP LEGIT ADMIN COERCE CHOOSE ATTIT PERSON ORD/FREE PWR...SOC CHARTS GEN/LAWS TOT/POP VAL/FREE. PAGE 57 H1147 — AFR SOCIETY

B63
HARDY M.J.L.,BLOOD FEUDS AND THE PAYMENT OF BLOOD MONEY IN THE MIDDLE EAST. ISLAM SOCIETY SECT REGION SANCTION COERCE DEATH MURDER 7/20 ARABS. PAGE 66 H1329 — KIN TRIBUTE LAW CULTURE

B63
JUDD P.,AFRICAN INDEPENDENCE: THE EXPLODING EMERGENCE OF THE NEW AFRICAN NATIONS. AFR UK LAW CONSTN CULTURE KIN DIPLOM ATTIT...CHARTS BIBLIOG 20 UN DEGAULLE/C NEGRO THIRD/WRLD. PAGE 82 H1640 — ORD/FREE POLICY DOMIN LOC/G

B63
MAC MILLAN W.M.,BANTU, BOER, AND BRITON: THE MAKING OF THE SOUTH AFRICAN NATIVE PROBLEM. SOUTH/AFR UK LAW KIN NAT/G SECT LEGIS COLONIAL ISOLAT ATTIT ...BIOG 18/20 BANTU NEGRO PHILIP/J MISSION. PAGE 100 H1989 — AFR RACE/REL ELITES

B63
MAJUMDAR O.N.,AN INTRODUCTION TO SOCIAL ANTHROPOLOGY. INDIA LAW STRATA ECO/UNDEV KIN DEMAND MARRIAGE...GP/COMP BIBLIOG T WORSHIP 20. PAGE 101 H2026 — SOC CULTURE STRUCT GP/REL

B63
O'LEARY T.J.,ETHNOGRAPHIC BIBLIOGRAPHY OF SOUTH AMERICA. SOCIETY KIN...GEOG 19/20 SOUTH/AMER. PAGE 120 H2389 — SOC CULTURE L/A+17C BIBLIOG

B63
PAUW B.A.,THE SECOND GENERATION. SOUTH/AFR INDUS FAM LABOR SECT EDU/PROP MARRIAGE ATTIT...SOC 20. PAGE 124 H2478 — KIN CULTURE STRUCT SOCIETY

B63
PRICE A.G.,THE WESTERN INVASIONS OF THE PACIFIC AND ITS CONTINENTS. ASIA PRE/AMER S/ASIA ECO/UNDEV KIN NAT/G SECT FORCES DOMIN HEALTH...SOC 16/20. PAGE 128 H2560 — COLONIAL CULTURE GEOG HABITAT

B63
REYNOLDS B.,MAGIC, DIVINATION AND WITCHCRAFT AMONG THE BAROTSE OF NORTHERN RHODESIA. RHODESIA CULTURE KIN CREATE LEGIT PARTIC DEATH DREAM STRANGE HABITAT PERSON...AUD/VIS WORSHIP 20. PAGE 131 H2619 — AFR SOC MYTH SECT

B63
SINOR D.,INTRODUCTION A L'ETUDE DE L'EURASIE CENTRALE. ASIA CULTURE KIN. PAGE 144 H2887 — BIBLIOG SOC LING

B63
TINDALE N.B.,ABORIGINAL AUSTRALIANS. KIN CREATE ROLE...SOC MYTH TREND 20 AUSTRAL ABORIGINES MIGRATION. PAGE 155 H3099 — CULTURE DRIVE ECO/UNDEV HABITAT

B63
WAGLEY C.,INTRODUCTION TO BRAZIL. BRAZIL L/A+17C FAM KIN SCHOOL SECT ATTIT WEALTH...GEOG SOC. PAGE 164 H3286 — ECO/UNDEV ELITES HABITAT STRATA

S63
GLUCKMAN M.,"CIVIL WAR AND THEORIES OF POWER IN BAROTSE-LAND: AFRICAN AND MEDIEVAL ANALOGIES." AFR CHRIST-17C LAW CONSTN CULTURE STRATA KIN DELIB/GP FORCES DOMIN LEGIT COERCE PERCEPT ORD/FREE...SOC INT TIME/SEQ GEN/LAWS VAL/FREE. PAGE 57 H1148 — TOP/EX PWR WAR

S63
MAZRUI A.A.,"ON THE CONCEPT 'WE ARE ALL AFRICANS'." AFR CULTURE KIN LOC/G NAT/G DOMIN EDU/PROP LEGIT ATTIT PERCEPT PERSON KNOWL ORD/FREE...TIME/SEQ TOT/POP 20. PAGE 106 H2110 — PROVS INT/ORG NAT/LISM

S63
NICHOLAS W.,"VILLAGE FACTIONS AND POLITICAL PARTIES IN RURAL WEST BENGAL." S/ASIA CULTURE STRATA FACE/GP KIN MUNIC DELIB/GP LEGIS DOMIN EDU/PROP COERCE CHOOSE ATTIT ALL/VALS...STAT TOT/POP VAL/FREE 20. PAGE 117 H2348 — NEIGH POL/PAR

B64
AKZIN B.,STATE AND NATION. UNIV ECO/UNDEV DIPLOM RACE/REL NAT/LISM ATTIT PLURISM...CONCPT IDEA/COMP 20. PAGE 4 H0090 — GP/REL NAT/G KIN

B64
BERNDT R.M.,THE WORLD OF THE FIRST AUSTRALIANS. S/ASIA ECO/UNDEV WORKER PROB/SOLV EFFICIENCY ROLE ...SOC MYTH WORSHIP AUSTRAL ABORIGINES. PAGE 16 H0311 — CULTURE KIN STRUCT DRIVE

B64
BINDER L.,THE IDEOLOGICAL REVOLUTION IN THE MIDDLE EAST. ISLAM STRUCT INT/ORG KIN SECT EX/STRUC TOP/EX PLAN ATTIT DRIVE RIGID/FLEX PWR...MYTH TOT/POP 20. PAGE 17 H0338 — POL/PAR NAT/G NAT/LISM

B64
BURKE F.G.,AFRICA'S QUEST FOR ORDER. AFR CULTURE KIN MUNIC NAT/G DIPLOM COLONIAL REV DISCRIM NAT/LISM AGE/Y 20. PAGE 24 H0488 — ORD/FREE CONSEN RACE/REL LEAD

B64
ELKIN A.P.,THE AUSTRALIAN ABORIGINES - HOW TO UNDERSTAND THEM (4TH ED.). FAM NEIGH DEATH MARRIAGE ATTIT BIO/SOC HABITAT...PSY SOC MYTH WORSHIP AUSTRAL ABORIGINES. PAGE 45 H0908 — CULTURE STRUCT SOCIETY KIN

B64
HARRIS M.,PATTERNS OF RACE IN THE AMERICAS. BRAZIL L/A+17C STRATA ECO/UNDEV AGRI KIN MUNIC SECT COLONIAL RACE/REL...SOC SOC/INTEG 17/20 NEGRO INDIAN/AM. PAGE 67 H1342 — STRUCT PRE/AMER CULTURE SOCIETY

B64
HILL C.R.,BANTUSTANS: THE FRAGMENTATION OF SOUTH AFRICA. AFR SOUTH/AFR ELITES SOCIETY KIN CONTROL DISCRIM ANOMIE ATTIT...POLICY CHARTS GOV/COMP 20 NEGRO BANTUSTANS TRANSKEI NATAL. PAGE 71 H1416 — RACE/REL CULTURE LOC/G ORD/FREE

B64
LAWRENCE P.,ROAD BELONG CARGO: A STUDY OF CARGO MOVEMENT IN SOUTHERN MADANG DISTRICT, NEW GUINEA. S/ASIA CULTURE ECO/UNDEV PROC/MFG KIN CHIEF COLONIAL COERCE GP/REL DRIVE WEALTH WORSHIP 20 NEW/GUINEA. PAGE 92 H1846
SOC SECT ALL/VALS MYTH

B64
LIENHARDT G.,SOCIAL ANTHROPOLOGY. SOCIETY FAM KIN ...CONCPT METH. PAGE 97 H1928
SOC HABITAT HEREDITY CULTURE

B64
MCCALL D.F.,AFRICA IN TIME PERSPECTIVE. AFR EXTR/IND KIN SECT CREATE PERS/REL HABITAT...GEOG METH/CNCPT LING BIBLIOG/A TIME 20. PAGE 106 H2124
HIST/WRIT OBS/ENVIR CULTURE

B64
MEAD M.,CONTINUITIES IN CULTURAL EVOLUTION. FACE/GP KIN ACT/RES EDU/PROP GP/REL INGP/REL DRIVE HEREDITY ROLE...TIME/SEQ TREND METH SOC/INTEG 20. PAGE 108 H2153
CULTURE SOC PERS/REL

B64
MORGAN L.H.,ANCIENT SOCIETY (1877). SOCIETY FAM OWN ...INT QU GEN/LAWS SOC/INTEG. PAGE 113 H2255
KIN MARRIAGE CULTURE

B64
SINGER M.R.,THE EMERGING ELITE: A STUDY OF POLITICAL LEADERSHIP IN CEYLON. S/ASIA ECO/UNDEV AGRI KIN NAT/G SECT EX/STRUC LEGIT ATTIT PWR RESPECT...SOC STAT CHARTS 20. PAGE 144 H2883
TOP/EX STRATA NAT/LISM CEYLON

B64
SKINNER E.P.,THE MOSSI OF UPPER VOLTA: THE POLITICAL DEVELOPMENT OF A SUDANESE PEOPLE. AFR LAW AGRI FAM KIN POL/PAR PROVS SECT DELIB/GP EX/STRUC FORCES TOP/EX DOMIN EDU/PROP LEGIT CT/SYS COERCE CHOOSE ORD/FREE PWR WEALTH...SOC MYTH VAL/FREE. PAGE 145 H2897
CULTURE OBS UPPER/VOLT

B64
THORNBURG M.W.,PEOPLE AND POLICY IN THE MIDDLE EAST. ISLAM ECO/UNDEV FAM KIN MUNIC NAT/G NEIGH POL/PAR SECT DELIB/GP LEGIS PLAN ECO/TAC DOMIN ADMIN ATTIT HEALTH RESPECT...SOC CONCPT METH/CNCPT OBS TIME/SEQ TOT/POP VAL/FREE. PAGE 154 H3088
TEC/DEV CULTURE

B64
VON FURER-HAIMEN E.,AN ANTHROPOLOGICAL BIBLIOGRAPHY OF SOUTH ASIA (VOL. II). STRATA STRUCT KIN SECT ACT/RES CREATE HABITAT...GEOG OBS 20. PAGE 163 H3268
BIBLIOG/A CULTURE S/ASIA SOC

S64
CLIGNET R.,"POTENTIAL ELITES IN GHANA AND THE IVORY COAST: A PRELIMINARY SURVEY." AFR CULTURE ELITES STRATA KIN NAT/G SECT DOMIN EXEC ORD/FREE RESPECT SKILL...POLICY RELATIV GP/COMP NAT/COMP 20. PAGE 30 H0605
PWR LEGIT IVORY/CST GHANA

S64
IRELE A.,"A DEFENSE OF NEGRITUDE." AFR NAT/LISM ...HUM 20 NEGRO. PAGE 78 H1566
CONCPT CULTURE NAT/COMP KIN

S64
TOUVAL S.,"THE SOMALI REPUBLIC." AFR ISLAM SOMALIA FAM KIN NAT/G CREATE FOR/AID LEGIT ATTIT ALL/VALS ...RECORD TREND 20. PAGE 156 H3119
ECO/UNDEV RIGID/FLEX

B65
DURKHEIM E.,THE ELEMENTARY FORMS OF THE RELIGIOUS LIFE. KIN PARTIC MORAL...PSY MYTH OBS IDEA/COMP METH WORSHIP 19/20. PAGE 43 H0870
SOC CULTURE CONCPT

B65
FILIPINIANA BOOK GUILD,THE COLONIZATION AND CONQUEST OF THE PHILIPPINES BY SPAIN. PHILIPPINE SPAIN ELITES AGRI KIN CHIEF DOMIN CONTROL ATTIT PWR ...ANTHOL WORSHIP 16. PAGE 50 H1000
COLONIAL COERCE CULTURE WAR

B65
GIBBS S.L.,PEOPLES OF AFRICA. AFR INGP/REL HABITAT ...GEOG ANTHOL 20. PAGE 56 H1122
CULTURE AGRI FAM KIN

B65
GOULD J.,PENGUIN SURVEY OF THE SOCIAL SCIENCES* 1965. CULTURE SOCIETY R+D FAM KIN MUNIC ACT/RES DIPLOM SKILL. PAGE 59 H1186
SOC PHIL/SCI USSR UK

B65
JANSEN M.B.,CHANGING JAPANESE ATTITUDES TOWARD MODERNIZATION. ASIA CHINA/COM S/ASIA INTELL SOCIETY KIN NAT/G SECT PERCEPT RIGID/FLEX...SOC CONCPT TIME/SEQ TREND TOT/POP 19/20 CHINJAP. PAGE 80 H1591
TEC/DEV ATTIT INDIA

B65
KUNSTADTER P.,THE LUA (LAWA) OF NORTHERN THAILAND: ASPECTS OF SOCIAL STRUCTURE, AGRICULTURE, AND RELIGION. THAILAND AGRI FAM KIN INGP/REL ISOLAT MARRIAGE HEALTH WORSHIP 20 BUDDHISM LUA. PAGE 89 H1780
STRUCT ECO/UNDEV CULTURE

B65
MAIR L.,AN INTRODUCTION TO SOCIAL ANTHROPOLOGY. LAW STRATA FINAN FAM KIN SECT INT/TRADE RACE/REL ADJUST PRODUC...T 20. PAGE 101 H2023
SOC STRUCT CULTURE

SOCIETY

B65
SAKAI R.K.,STUDIES ON ASIA, 1965. INDIA KOREA S/ASIA USA+45 CONSTN KIN SECT PARTIC SUFF NAT/LISM ...POLICY SOC 19/20 CHINJAP. PAGE 137 H2737
PARL/PROC ASIA

B65
SPENCER P.,THE SAMBURU: A STUDY OF GERONTOCRACY IN A NOMADIC TRIBE. AFR SOCIETY ECO/UNDEV AGRI FAM NEIGH SECT GP/REL MARRIAGE WORSHIP 20 SAMBURU. PAGE 147 H2945
KIN STRUCT AGE/O CULTURE

B65
VAN DEN BERGHE P.L.,AFRICA: SOCIAL PROBLEMS OF CHANGE AND CONFLICT. ELITES STRATA ECO/UNDEV KIN MUNIC DIPLOM GP/REL RACE/REL NAT/LISM...ANTHOL BIBLIOG 20. PAGE 161 H3228
SOC CULTURE AFR STRUCT

B66
HOWE R.W.,BLACK AFRICA: FROM PRE-HISTORY TO THE EVE OF THE COLONIAL ERA. ECO/UNDEV KIN PROVS SECT INT/TRADE EDU/PROP COLONIAL...BIBLIOG WORSHIP. PAGE 74 H1482
AFR CULTURE SOC

B66
KASUNMU A.B.,NIGERIAN FAMILY LAW. NIGERIA KIN LEGIT ILLEGIT MARRIAGE AGE DRIVE HABITAT ALL/VALS...JURID IDEA/COMP T 20 ENGLSH/LAW. PAGE 83 H1667
FAM LAW CULTURE AFR

B66
VOGT E.Z.,PEOPLE OF RIMROCK. STRATA STRUCT KIN SECT GP/REL HABITAT ALL/VALS...GEOG INT QU 20 TEXAS NAVAHO MORMON SPAN/AMER ZUNI. PAGE 163 H3260
CULTURE GP/COMP SOC SOCIETY

B66
ZOLBERG A.R.,CREATING POLITICAL ORDER. AFR CONGO/BRAZ GHANA NIGER KIN NAT/G DOMIN COLONIAL REGION CENTRAL NAT/LISM ATTIT PWR 20 CONGO/LEOP. PAGE 173 H3462
SOVEREIGN ORD/FREE CONSTN POL/PAR

S66
ROTHCHILD D.,"THE LIMITS OF FEDERALISM: AN EXAMINATION OF POLITICAL INSTITUTIONAL TRANSFER IN AFRICA." AFR CONSTN CULTURE ELITES ECO/UNDEV KIN PROB/SOLV ADMIN ORD/FREE PWR...POLICY 20. PAGE 135 H2695
FEDERAL NAT/G NAT/LISM COLONIAL

B67
ARIKPO O.,THE DEVELOPMENT OF MODERN NIGERIA. AFR NIGERIA SOCIETY ECO/UNDEV KIN ADMIN FEDERAL NAT/LISM ORD/FREE WEALTH...POLICY GEOG BIBLIOG 19/20. PAGE 8 H0163
NAT/G CULTURE CONSTN COLONIAL

B67
PATAI R.,GOLDEN RIVER TO GOLDEN ROAD: SOCIETY, CULTURE, AND CHANGE IN THE MIDDLE EAST (2ND ED.). ELITES FAM KIN TEC/DEV MARRIAGE NAT/LISM SEX ORD/FREE...TREND GP/COMP WORSHIP 20. PAGE 124 H2476
CULTURE SOCIETY ISLAM STRUCT

B67
THOMAS P.,DOWN THESE MEAN STREETS. GP/REL RACE/REL ADJUST...SOC SELF/OBS 20. PAGE 154 H3078
DISCRIM KIN CULTURE BIOG

B67
WINTER E.H.,CONTEMPORARY CHANGE IN TRADITIONAL SOCIETIES: VOLUME I INTRODUCTION AND AFRICAN TRIBES. NIGERIA AGRI LOC/G NAT/G CREATE DOMIN COLONIAL CONTROL GP/REL PWR SOVEREIGN...SOC OBS 20 TANGANYIKA. PAGE 169 H3389
SOCIETY AFR CONSERVE KIN

L67
UNESCO,"APARTHEID." SOUTH/AFR STRUCT KIN SCHOOL SECT WORKER DOMIN EDU/PROP REGION RACE/REL ISOLAT 20. PAGE 158 H3164
DISCRIM CULTURE COERCE COLONIAL

S67
BEFU H.,"THE POLITICAL RELATION OF THE VILLAGE TO THE STATE." NAT/G DOMIN GOV/REL GP/REL MGT. PAGE 13 H0259
GOV/COMP NAT/LISM KIN MUNIC

S67
GLENN N.D.,"RURAL-URBAN DIFFERENCES IN REPORTED ATTITUDES AND BEHAVIOR" STRATA GP/REL CONSEN HABITAT RIGID/FLEX SAMP. PAGE 57 H1143
CULTURE ATTIT KIN CHARTS

S67
HOPE M.,"THE RELUCTANT WAY: SELF-IMMOLATION IN VIETNAM." VIETNAM SOCIETY FAM KIN SECT DRIVE ALL/VALS...TRADIT OBS INT 20. PAGE 73 H1465
CULTURE SUICIDE IDEA/COMP ATTIT

S67
IDENBURG P.J.,"POLITICAL STRUCTURAL DEVELOPMENT IN TROPICAL AFRICA." UK ECO/UNDEV KIN POL/PAR CHIEF EX/STRUC CREATE COLONIAL CONTROL REPRESENT RACE/REL ...MAJORIT TREND 20. PAGE 76 H1521
AFR CONSTN NAT/G GOV/COMP

S67
KINGSBURY E.C.,"LAW AS COMPACT: ANCIENT ISRAEL'S CONTRIBUTION TO THE UNDERSTANDING OF LAW." ISRAEL MEDIT-7 CULTURE KIN KNOWL...JURID CONCPT TREND IDEA/COMP METH/COMP WORSHIP JEWS DEITY. PAGE 86 H1716
LAW AGREE CONSTN INGP/REL

S67
MALAN V.D.,"THE SILENT VILLAGE." KIN MUNIC NEIGH CHOOSE ISOLAT ROLE...SOC INDIAN/AM. PAGE 101 H2027
CULTURE STRUCT

PREDICT
S67
RAUM O.,"THE MODERN LEADERSHIP GROUP AMONG THE SOUTH AFRICAN XHOSA." SOUTH/AFR SOCIETY SECT EX/STRUC REPRESENT GP/REL INGP/REL PERSON ...METH/COMP 17/20 XHOSA NEGRO. PAGE 130 H2596 RACE/REL KIN LEAD CULTURE
L68
CURRENT HISTORY,"AFRICA, 1968." ETHIOPIA GHANA NIGERIA SOUTH/AFR CULTURE ECO/UNDEV KIN SECT CHIEF EX/STRUC WAR WEAPON CHOOSE CIVMIL/REL...GOV/COMP 20 AFRICA/E. PAGE 36 H0724 RACE/REL NAT/LISM FORCES AFR
S68
LAPIERRE J.W.,"TRADITION ET MODERNITE A MADAGASCAR." ISLAM MADAGASCAR AGRI FINAN KIN NAT/G CREATE OP/RES GP/REL INGP/REL ATTIT CONSERVE...PSY 20. PAGE 91 H1813 ECO/UNDEV FOR/AID CULTURE TEC/DEV
B75
MAINE H.S.,LECTURES ON THE EARLY HISTORY OF INSTITUTIONS. IRELAND UK CONSTN ELITES STRUCT FAM KIN CHIEF LEGIS CT/SYS OWN SOVEREIGN...CONCPT 16 BENTHAM/J BREHON ROMAN/LAW. PAGE 101 H2021 CULTURE LAW INGP/REL
B82
MACDONALD D.,AFRICANA; OR, THE HEART OF HEATHEN AFRICA, VOL. II: MISSION LIFE. SOCIETY STRATA KIN CREATE EDU/PROP ADMIN COERCE LITERACY HEALTH...MYTH WORSHIP 19 LIVNGSTN/D MISSION NEGRO. PAGE 100 H1990 SECT AFR CULTURE ORD/FREE
L95
BELSHAW C.S.,"IN SEARCH OF WEALTH; STUDY OF EMERGENCE OF COMMERCIAL OPERA TIONS IN MELANESIAN SOCIETY OF SOUTHEASTERN PAPUA." S/ASIA CULTURE KIN ECO/TAC DEMAND INCOME 20 MELANESIA PAPUA. PAGE 14 H0272 INT/TRADE ECO/UNDEV METH/COMP SOCIETY
B96
SCHMOLLER G.,THE MERCANTILE SYSTEM AND ITS HISTORICAL SIGNIFICANCE: ILLUSTRATED CHIEFLY FROM PRUSSIAN HISTORY (TRANS.). PRUSSIA CULTURE INDUS KIN MUNIC NAT/G PROVS OP/RES ECO/TAC INT/TRADE SUPEGO PWR WEALTH 19 MERCANTLST. PAGE 139 H2790 GEN/METH INGP/REL CONCPT
B97
JENKS E.J.,LAW AND POLITICS IN THE MIDDLE AGES. CHRIST-17C CULTURE STRUCT KIN NAT/G SECT CT/SYS GP/REL...CLASSIF CHARTS IDEA/COMP BIBLIOG 8/16. PAGE 80 H1603 LAW SOCIETY ADJUST
B98
FORTES M.,AFRICAN POLITICAL SYSTEMS. ECO/UNDEV KIN LOC/G NEIGH POL/PAR SECT LEAD GP/REL ORD/FREE...SOC 20 NEGRO. PAGE 52 H1039 AFR CULTURE STRUCT
B99
DU BOIS W.E.B.,THE PHILADELPHIA NEGRO: A SOCIAL STUDY. CULTURE STRATA KIN CRIME SUFF ADJUST DISCRIM ISOLAT HABITAT HEREDITY ALL/VALS SOC/INTEG 17/19 NEGRO PHILADELPH. PAGE 42 H0851 INGP/REL RACE/REL SOC CENSUS
B99
RIPLEY W.Z.,A SELECTED BIBLIOGRAPHY OF THE ANTHROPOLOGY AND ETHNOLOGY OF EUROPE. SOCIETY STRATA STRUCT KIN SECT VOL/ASSN GP/REL INGP/REL HABITAT...GEOG 19. PAGE 132 H2632 BIBLIOG/A MOD/EUR SOC CULTURE

KINDERSLEY R. H1712

KINDLEBERGER C.P. H1713,H1714

KING A. H0498

KING M.L. H1715

KING....KING AND KINGSHIP; SEE ALSO CHIEF, CONSERVE, TRADIT

B27
HOCART A.M.,KINGSHIP. UNIV CULTURE EX/STRUC TRIBUTE ROUTINE CHOOSE ROLE SOVEREIGN RITUAL 20 KING. PAGE 72 H1441 CHIEF MYTH IDEA/COMP
B61
ULLMAN W.,PRINCIPLES OF GOVERNMENT AND POLITICS IN THE MIDDLE AGES. LAW CONSTN DOMIN EDU/PROP LEGIT TOTALISM SOVEREIGN POPULISM...POLICY GOV/COMP IDEA/COMP 12/16 POPE KING CHURCH/STA. PAGE 158 H3152 SECT CHIEF NAT/G LEGIS
C62
BACON F.,"OF EMPIRE" (1612) IN F. BACON, ESSAYS." ELITES NAT/G PROB/SOLV DIPLOM ADMIN CONTROL WEALTH 16/17 KING. PAGE 9 H0190 PWR CHIEF DOMIN GEN/LAWS

KING/MAR/L....REVEREND MARTIN LUTHER KING

KINGSBURY E.C. H1716

KINGSLEY M.H. H1717

KINNEAR J.B. H1718

KINSEY/A....ALFRED KINSEY

KINTNER W.R. H1719

KIPLING/R....RUDYARD KIPLING

KIRCHHEIMER O. H1720

KIRDAR U. H1721

KIRK/GRAY....GRAYSON KIRK

KIRKENDALL R.S. H1722

KIRKLAND E.C. H1723

KIRKPATRICK F.A. H1724

KIRKWOOD K. H1725

KIRPICEVA I.K. H1726

KIS T.I. H1727

KISSINGER H.A. H1728

KITCHEN H. H1729

KITTLER G.D. H1730

KKK....KU KLUX KLAN

KLEIMAN R. H1731

KLEIN J. H1732

KLINEBERG O. H1802

KLUCKHN/C....CLYDE KLUCKHOHN

KLUCKHOHN C. H1733

KNO/TEST....TESTS FOR FACTUAL KNOWLEDGE

B28
BUELL R.,THE NATIVE PROBLEM IN AFRICA. KIN LABOR LOC/G ECO/TAC ROUTINE ORD/FREE...REC/INT KNO/TEST CENSUS TREND CHARTS SOC/EXP STERTYP 20. PAGE 23 H0466 AFR CULTURE
B31
DEKAT A.D.A.,COLONIAL POLICY. S/ASIA CULTURE EX/STRUC ECO/TAC DOMIN ADMIN COLONIAL ROUTINE SOVEREIGN WEALTH...POLICY MGT RECORD KNO/TEST SAMP. PAGE 39 H0785 DRIVE PWR INDONESIA NETHERLAND
B66
BHALERAO C.N.,PUBLIC SERVICE COMMISSIONS OF INDIA: A STUDY. INDIA SERV/IND EX/STRUC ROUTINE CHOOSE GOV/REL INGP/REL...KNO/TEST EXHIBIT 20. PAGE 16 H0326 NAT/G OP/RES LOC/G ADMIN
L67
PICKERING J.F.,"RECRUITMENT TO THE ADMINISTRATIVE CLASS, 1960-1964: PART 2" UK STRATA NAT/G WORKER ...STAT CHARTS 20. PAGE 125 H2505 PERS/COMP ADMIN KNO/TEST EDU/PROP
S67
WILPERT C.,"A LOOK IN THE MIRROR AND OVER THE WALL." GERMANY POL/PAR...KNO/TEST COLD/WAR. PAGE 169 H3378 NAT/G PLAN DIPLOM ATTIT

KNORR K.E. H1734

KNOWL....ENLIGHTENMENT, KNOWLEDGE

N
AVTOREFERATY DISSERTATSII. USSR INTELL ACADEM NAT/G DIPLOM GOV/REL KNOWL CONCPT. PAGE 2 H0029 BIBLIOG MARXISM MARXIST COM
N
MINISTERE DE L'EDUC NATIONALE,CATALOGUE DES THESES DE DOCTORAT SOUTENNES DEVANT LES UNIVERSITAIRES FRANCAISES. FRANCE LAW DIPLOM ADMIN...HUM SOC 20. PAGE 111 H2223 BIBLIOG ACADEM KNOWL NAT/G
N
US LIBRARY OF CONGRESS,EAST EUROPEAN ACCESSIONS INDEX. NAT/G ISOLAT ATTIT KNOWL...POLICY 20. PAGE 160 H3202 BIBLIOG COM MARXIST DIPLOM
B27
CHILDS J.B.,AN ACCOUNT OF GOVERNMENT DOCUMENT BIBLIOGRAPHY IN THE UNITED STATES AND ELSEWHERE (A PAPER). LOC/G PRESS CENTRAL KNOWL...METH 19/20 LEAGUE/NAT. PAGE 29 H0590 BIBLIOG/A CON/ANAL NAT/G
B29
LEITZ F.,DIE PUBLIZITAT DER AKTIENGESELLSCHAFT. BELGIUM FRANCE GERMANY UK FINAN PRESS GP/REL PROFIT KNOWL 20. PAGE 94 H1872 LG/CO JURID ECO/TAC NAT/COMP

B34
GONZALEZ PALENCIA A,ESTUDIO HISTORICO SOBRE LA CENSURA GUBERNATIVA EN ESPANA 1800-1833. NAT/G COERCE INGP/REL ATTIT AUTHORIT KNOWL...POLICY JURID 19. PAGE 58 H1165
LEGIT EDU/PROP PRESS CONTROL

B35
MORE T.,UTOPIA (1516) (TRANS. BY R. ROBYNSON). LAW CULTURE SOCIETY STRUCT FAM SECT EDU/PROP WAR OWN UTIL KNOWL WEALTH 16. PAGE 113 H2253
UTOPIA NAT/G ECO/TAC GEN/LAWS

B36
VICO G.B.,DIRITTO UNIVERSALE (1722) (VOL. 2, PARTS 1,2, AND 3, OF G.B. VICO, OPERE). UNIV DIPLOM AGREE WAR OWN KNOWL ORD/FREE SOVEREIGN DEITY. PAGE 162 H3249
JURID SECT CONCPT NAT/G

B36
WANDERSCHECK H.,WELTKRIEG UND PROPAGANDA. GERMANY MOD/EUR UK COM/IND NAT/G DOMIN PRESS ATTIT...POLICY 20 HITLER/A. PAGE 165 H3299
EDU/PROP PSY WAR KNOWL

B39
MILLER P.,THE NEW ENGLAND MIND: THE SEVENTEENTH CENTURY. CULTURE DOMIN WRITING INGP/REL CONSEN MAJORITY PERCEPT KNOWL MORAL...CONCPT LING WORSHIP 17 NEW/ENGLND PROTESTANT. PAGE 111 H2214
SECT REGION SOC ATTIT

S40
GURVITCH G.,"MAJOR PROBLEMS OF THE SOCIOLOGY OF LAW." CULTURE SANCTION KNOWL MORAL...POLICY EPIST JURID WORSHIP. PAGE 63 H1255
SOC LAW PHIL/SCI

B41
HAYAKAWA S.I.,LANGUAGE IN ACTION. CULTURE INTELL SOCIETY KNOWL...METH/CNCPT LING LOG RECORD STERTYP GEN/METH TOT/POP 20. PAGE 68 H1366
EDU/PROP SOC

B42
BAYNES N.H.,INTELLECTUAL LIBERTY AND TOTALITARIAN CLAIMS. EUR+WWI GERMANY ITALY INTELL POL/PAR CIVMIL/REL NAT/LISM SOCISM CONCPT. PAGE 12 H0245
KNOWL FASCISM EDU/PROP ACADEM

B44
CASSIRER E.,AN ESSAY ON MAN: AN INTRODUCTION TO A PHILOSOPHY OF HUMAN CULTURE. UNIV SECT CREATE EDU/PROP ATTIT KNOWL...HUM CONCPT MYTH TOT/POP. PAGE 28 H0556
CULTURE SOC

B45
HUNTINGTON E.,MAINSPRINGS OF CIVILIZATION. UNIV CULTURE SOCIETY BIO/SOC PERSON KNOWL SKILL...PSY RECORD HIST/WRIT TREND CHARTS TOT/POP. PAGE 75 H1504
SOC GEOG

B45
VENABLE V.,HUMAN NATURE: THE MARXIAN VIEW. UNIV STRATA CAP/ISM REV GP/REL PERS/REL PRODUC KNOWL ...PHIL/SCI CONCPT IDEA/COMP 19 MARX/KARL ENGELS/F. PAGE 162 H3240
PERSON MARXISM WORKER UTOPIA

C45
PAINE T.,"THE AGE OF REASON IN T. PAINE, THE COMPLETE WRITINGS OF THOMAS PAINE (VOL. 1) (1794-95)" CULTURE ACT/RES DOMIN UTOPIA ATTIT PERCEPT WORSHIP. PAGE 122 H2445
SECT KNOWL PHIL/SCI ORD/FREE

B50
CANTRIL H.,TENSIONS THAT CAUSE WAR. UNIV CULTURE R+D CREATE EDU/PROP DRIVE PERSON KNOWL ORD/FREE ...HUM PSY SOC OBS CENSUS TREND CON/ANAL SOC/EXP SIMUL GEN/METH ANTHOL COLD/WAR TOT/POP. PAGE 26 H0523
SOCIETY PHIL/SCI PEACE

B50
CONOVER H.F.,INTRODUCTION TO EUROPE: A SELECTIVE GUIDE TO BACKGROUND READING. COM EUR+WWI NAT/G KNOWL...ART/METH GEOG SOC. PAGE 32 H0648
BIBLIOG/A MOD/EUR HIST/WRIT

B50
GOFF F.R.,FIFTEENTH CENTURY BOOKS IN THE LIBRARY OF CONGRESS. CHRIST-17C GERMANY ITALY CULTURE INTELL SECT CREATE...PHIL/SCI CONCPT CLASSIF BIOG TIME/SEQ 15. PAGE 58 H1153
BIBLIOG KNOWL HUM

B51
HUXLEY J.,FREEDOM AND CULTURE. UNIV LAW SOCIETY R+D ACADEM SCHOOL CREATE SANCTION ATTIT KNOWL...HUM ANTHOL 20. PAGE 76 H1512
CULTURE ORD/FREE PHIL/SCI IDEA/COMP

B51
WABEKE B.H.,A GUIDE TO DUTCH BIBLIOGRAPHIES. BELGIUM INDONESIA NETHERLAND DIPLOM INT/TRADE WAR NAT/LISM KNOWL...ART/METH HUM JURID CON/ANAL 14/20. PAGE 164 H3282
BIBLIOG/A NAT/G CULTURE COLONIAL

S51
GOULD J.,"THE KOMSOMOL AND THE HITLER JUGEND." COM EUR+WWI GERMANY SOCIETY NAT/G POL/PAR SCHOOL TOTALISM DRIVE PERCEPT KNOWL FASCISM...SOC NAZI TOT/POP 20. PAGE 59 H1185
EDU/PROP CON/ANAL SOCISM

B52
BENTHAM A.,HANDBOOK OF POLITICAL FALLACIES. FUT MOD/EUR LAW INTELL LOC/G MUNIC NAT/G DELIB/GP LEGIS CREATE EDU/PROP CT/SYS ATTIT RIGID/FLEX KNOWL PWR ...RELATIV PSY SOC CONCPT SELF/OBS TREND STERTYP TOT/POP. PAGE 14 H0286
POL/PAR

B52
LEVY M.,THE STRUCTURE OF SOCIETY. CULTURE STRATA DRIVE KNOWL...PSY CONCPT METH/CNCPT NEW/IDEA STYLE GEN/LAWS. PAGE 95 H1907
SOCIETY SOC

B52
LEYS W.,ETHICS FOR POLICY DECISIONS. INTELL NAT/G CONSULT PLAN DOMIN EDU/PROP LEGIT COERCE KNOWL MORAL PWR...HUM GEN/LAWS. PAGE 96 H1920
ACT/RES POLICY

B52
THOM J.M.,GUIDE TO RESEARCH MATERIAL IN POLITICAL SCIENCE (PAMPHLET). ELITES LOC/G MUNIC NAT/G LEGIS DIPLOM ADJUD CIVMIL/REL GOV/REL PWR MGT. PAGE 154 H3074
BIBLIOG/A KNOWL

S52
KECSKEMETI P.,"THE 'POLICY SCIENCES': ASPIRATION AND OUTLOOK." UNIV CULTURE INTELL SOCIETY STRUCT EDU/PROP ATTIT PERCEPT RIGID/FLEX KNOWL...PHIL/SCI METH/CNCPT OBS 20. PAGE 84 H1674
CREATE NEW/IDEA

N52
COORDINATING COMM DOC SOC SCI,INTERNATIONAL REPERTORY OF SOCIAL SCIENCE DOCUMENTATION CENTERS (PAMPHLET). ACT/RES OP/RES WRITING KNOWL...CON/ANAL METH. PAGE 33 H0661
BIBLIOG/A R+D NAT/G INT/ORG

B53
HUNTER E.,BRAIN-WASHING IN RED CHINA. ASIA CHINA/COM CULTURE SOCIETY FORCES WAR TOTALISM ATTIT BIO/SOC DISPL DRIVE PERSON SUPEGO KNOWL ORD/FREE ...INT REC/INT COLD/WAR 20. PAGE 75 H1499
EDU/PROP COERCE

S53
BAUER R.A.,"WORD-OF-MOUTH COMMUNICATION IN THE SOVIET UNION." COM INTELL SOCIETY LABOR ATTIT KNOWL ...INT QU SAMP CHARTS 20. PAGE 12 H0239
CULTURE USSR

B54
SCHRAMM W.,THE PROCESS AND EFFECTS OF MASS COMMUNICATION. CULTURE INTELL SOCIETY COM/IND DRIVE PERCEPT PERSON RIGID/FLEX KNOWL...PSY SOC CONCPT CHARTS. PAGE 140 H2800
ATTIT EDU/PROP

B54
TITIEV M.,THE SCIENCE OF MAN. LAW STRATA KIN GP/REL PERS/REL HABITAT HEREDITY KNOWL...LING CHARTS BIBLIOG WORSHIP. PAGE 155 H3107
SOC PSY CULTURE

B55
NAMIER L.,PERSONALITIES AND POWERS. EUR+WWI MOD/EUR NAT/G POL/PAR TOP/EX EDU/PROP KNOWL...GEOG 17/20. PAGE 115 H2308
TIME/SEQ DIPLOM UK

S55
GLADSTONE A.E.,"THE POSSIBILITY OF PREDICTING REACTIONS TO INTERNATIONAL EVENTS." UNIV SOCIETY NAT/G FORCES CREATE EDU/PROP COERCE WAR ATTIT PERSON KNOWL PWR SKILL...METH/CNCPT NEW/IDEA ORG/CHARTS. PAGE 57 H1139
PHIL/SCI CONCPT

B56
MYERS F.M.,THE WARFARE OF DEMOCRATIC IDEALS. SECT KNOWL MORAL CATHISM...TRADIT CONCPT 20. PAGE 115 H2302
POPULISM CHOOSE REPRESENT PERCEPT

B58
CHANG H.,WITHIN THE FOUR SEAS. ASIA WAR MORAL MARXISM...IDEA/COMP NAT/COMP 20 CONFUCIUS. PAGE 29 H0577
PEACE DIPLOM KNOWL CULTURE

C58
GINSBURG N.,"MALAYA." MALAYSIA PROB/SOLV REGION NAT/LISM KNOWL WEALTH...GEOG SOC CHARTS BIBLIOG 20. PAGE 57 H1133
COM/IND ECO/UNDEV CULTURE NAT/G

B60
ALMOND G.A.,THE POLITICS OF THE DEVELOPING AREAS. AFR ISLAM L/A+17C S/ASIA SOCIETY ECO/UNDEV NAT/G ADMIN PERCEPT KNOWL SOVEREIGN...CONCPT GEN/LAWS 20. PAGE 6 H0112
EX/STRUC ATTIT NAT/LISM

B60
EASTON S.C.,THE TWILIGHT OF EUROPEAN COLONIALISM. AFR S/ASIA CONSTN SOCIETY STRUCT ECO/UNDEV INDUS NAT/G FORCES ECO/TAC COLONIAL CT/SYS ATTIT KNOWL ORD/FREE PWR...SOCIALIST TIME/SEQ TREND CON/ANAL 20. PAGE 44 H0882
FINAN ADMIN

S60
ARENDT H.,"SOCIETY AND CULTURE." FUT CULTURE INTELL STRATA EDU/PROP ATTIT PERSON KNOWL...ART/METH HUM 20. PAGE 8 H0161
SOCIETY CREATE

S60
MURPHEY R.,"ECONOMIC CONFLICTS IN SOUTH ASIA." ASIA CULTURE INTELL ECO/TAC REGION ATTIT DRIVE KNOWL ...METH/CNCPT TIME/SEQ STERTYP TOT/POP VAL/FREE 20. PAGE 115 H2296
S/ASIA ECO/UNDEV

C60
BOGARDUS E.S.,"THE DEVELOPMENT OF SOCIAL THOUGHT." SOCIETY PERSON KNOWL...EPIST CONCPT BIBLIOG T. PAGE 18 H0365
INTELL CULTURE IDEA/COMP GP/COMP

B61
HOLDSWORTH M.,SOVIET AFRICAN STUDIES 1918-1959. USSR ACADEM NAT/G DIPLOM REGION KNOWL 20. PAGE 72 H1448
BIBLIOG/A AFR HABITAT NAT/COMP

B61
SAFRAN M.,EGYPT IN SEARCH OF POLITICAL COMMUNITY:
INTELL

AN ANALYSIS OF THE INTELLECTUAL AND POLITICAL EVOLUTION OF EGYPT, 1804-1952. ISLAM NAT/G SECT EDU/PROP COERCE ATTIT DRIVE KNOWL PWR...TIME/SEQ 20. PAGE 137 H2729
NAT/LISM UAR

L61
LEVINE R.A.,"THE ANTHROPOLOGY OF CONFLICT." FUT CULTURE INTELL FAM INT/ORG LG/CO SML/CO ATTIT KNOWL ...METH/CNCPT VAL/FREE 20. PAGE 95 H1905
SOCIETY ACT/RES

S61
FITZGIBBON R.H.,"MEASUREMENT OF LATIN AMERICAN POLITICAL CHANGE." L/A+17C CONSTN CULTURE SOCIETY ECO/UNDEV NAT/G POL/PAR PUB/INST ACT/RES EDU/PROP PERCEPT KNOWL ORD/FREE SOVEREIGN...METH/CNCPT TREND OAS 20. PAGE 51 H1020
CHOOSE ATTIT

B62
INSTITUTE FOR STUDY OF USSR,YOUTH IN FERMENT. INTELL NAT/G PERF/ART POL/PAR SCHOOL VOL/ASSN FORCES EDU/PROP ATTIT DRIVE PERCEPT HEALTH KNOWL MORAL ORD/FREE RESPECT...SOC OBS HIST/WRIT VAL/FREE. PAGE 77 H1537
COM CULTURE USSR

B62
KRUGLAK T.E.,THE TWO FACES OF TASS. COM COM/IND NAT/G ACT/RES PLAN PRESS PERCEPT PERSON KNOWL 20. PAGE 89 H1778
PUB/INST EDU/PROP USSR

B62
LITT T.,FREIHEIT UND LEBENS ORDNUNG. COM NAT/G ATTIT KNOWL...POLICY 20. PAGE 97 H1942
ORD/FREE MARXISM CONCPT IDEA/COMP

B62
MEIER R.L.,A COMMUNICATIONS THEORY OF URBAN GROWTH. CULTURE ECO/DEV COMPUTER BUDGET UTIL KNOWL...SOC CONCPT METH 20 OPEN/SPACE. PAGE 108 H2164
OP/RES COM/IND MUNIC CONTROL

S62
WALTER E.,"VERS UNE CLASSIFICATION SCIENTIFIQUE DE LA SOCIOLOGIA." UNIV CULTURE INTELL SOCIETY R+D ACT/RES LEGIT ROUTINE ATTIT KNOWL...JURID MGT TREND GEN/LAWS 20. PAGE 165 H3296
PLAN CONCPT

B63
DE VRIES E.,SOCIAL ASPECTS OF ECONOMIC DEVELOPMENT IN LATIN AMERICA. CULTURE SOCIETY STRATA FINAN INDUS INT/ORG DELIB/GP ACT/RES ECO/TAC EDU/PROP ADMIN ATTIT SUPEGO HEALTH KNOWL ORD/FREE...SOC STAT TREND ANTHOL TOT/POP VAL/FREE. PAGE 39 H0777
L/A+17C ECO/UNDEV

B63
HALPERIN M.H.,THE POLITICS OF SOCIAL CHANGE IN THE MIDDLE EAST AND NORTH AFRICA. ISLAM CULTURE ACT/RES REV ATTIT PERCEPT KNOWL...METH/CNCPT OBS TIME/SEQ GEN/METH TOT/POP VAL/FREE 20. PAGE 64 H1291
SOC TREND

B63
LERNER R.,MEDIEVAL POLITICAL PHILOSOPHY. ISLAM MORAL PWR CATHISM...CATH CONCPT OBS IDEA/COMP ANTHOL 9/15 JEWS CHRISTIAN BACON/R AQUINAS/T. PAGE 95 H1890
KNOWL PHIL/SCI

B63
MENZEL J.M.,THE CHINESE CIVIL SERVICE: CAREER OPEN TO TALENT? ASIA ROUTINE INGP/REL DISCRIM ATTIT ROLE KNOWL ANTHOL. PAGE 109 H2177
ADMIN NAT/G DECISION ELITES

B63
US ATOMIC ENERGY COMMISSION,ATOMIC ENERGY IN THE SOVIET UNION: TRIP REPORT OF THE US ATOMIC ENERGY DELEGATION, MAY 1933. USSR R+D NAT/G CONSULT CREATE DIPLOM ADMIN ROUTINE EFFICIENCY PRODUC KNOWL SKILL ...NAT/COMP 20 AEC TRAVEL TREATY. PAGE 159 H3176
METH/COMP OP/RES TEC/DEV NUC/PWR

L63
CORWIN A.F.,"CONTEMPORARY MEXICAN ATTITUDES TOWARD POPULATION, POVERTY, AND PUBLIC OPINION." L/A+17C CULTURE SOCIETY ACT/RES ECO/TAC EDU/PROP PERSON HEALTH KNOWL...GEOG PHIL/SCI STAT OBS INT SAMP MEXIC/AMER VAL/FREE 20. PAGE 34 H0672
ATTIT QU

L63
NASH M.,"PSYCHO-CULTURAL FACTORS IN ASIAN ECONOMIC GROWTH." ASIA ISLAM S/ASIA CULTURE ECO/UNDEV DELIB/GP EDU/PROP COERCE ATTIT PERSON HEALTH KNOWL ORD/FREE...PSY SOC STAT TREND ANTHOL VAL/FREE 20. PAGE 116 H2313
SOCIETY ECO/TAC

S63
DEUTSCHMANN P.J.,"THE MASS MEDIA IN AN UNDERDEVELOPED VILLAGE." L/A+17C EDU/PROP PERCEPT KNOWL ORD/FREE...SOC INT VAL/FREE 20. PAGE 40 H0809
COM/IND CULTURE

S63
HOSKINS H.L.,"ARAB SOCIALISM IN THE UAR." ISLAM USSR AGRI INDUS NAT/G TOP/EX CREATE DIPLOM EDU/PROP DRIVE KNOWL PWR SOCISM...POLICY CONCPT TREND SUEZ 20. PAGE 74 H1478
ECO/DEV PLAN UAR

S63
MAZRUI A.A.,"ON THE CONCEPT 'WE ARE ALL AFRICANS'." AFR CULTURE KIN LOC/G NAT/G DOMIN EDU/PROP LEGIT ATTIT PERCEPT PERSON KNOWL ORD/FREE...TIME/SEQ TOT/POP 20. PAGE 106 H2110
PROVS INT/ORG NAT/LISM

S63
MORISON D.,"AFRICAN STUDIES IN THE SOVIET UNION." AFR COM CULTURE INTELL REGION ATTIT KNOWL...HUM TREND 20. PAGE 113 H2258
EDU/PROP USSR

C63
BECKHAM R.S.,"A BASIC LIST OF BOOKS AND PERIODICALS FOR COLLEGE LIBRARIES." UNIV GP/REL...PSY SOC. PAGE 13 H0255
BIBLIOG SOCIETY CULTURE KNOWL

B64
BERRINGTON H.,HOW NATIONS ARE GOVERNED. FRANCE WOR+45 ECO/UNDEV INT/ORG POL/PAR CHOOSE TOTALISM KNOWL...MAJORIT T 20 UN COMMONWLTH THIRD/WRLD. PAGE 16 H0320
NAT/G GOV/COMP ECO/DEV CONSTN

B64
CAUTE D.,COMMUNISM AND THE FRENCH INTELLECTUALS, 1914-1960. COM EUR+WWI MOD/EUR NAT/G PERF/ART PROF/ORG CREATE EDU/PROP ATTIT PERSON KNOWL MARXISM ...SOC TIME/SEQ MARX/KARL 20 MALRAUX/A GIDE/A SARTRE/J. PAGE 28 H0563
POL/PAR INTELL

B64
CURTIN P.D.,THE IMAGE OF AFRICA: BRITISH IDEAS AND ACTION, 1780-1850. MOD/EUR SOCIETY FORCES ACT/RES DOMIN EDU/PROP COERCE ATTIT PERCEPT RIGID/FLEX SUPEGO HEALTH KNOWL MORAL ORD/FREE WEALTH...CONCPT WORK VAL/FREE. PAGE 36 H0726
AFR CULTURE UK DIPLOM

B64
LATORRE A.,UNIVERSIDAD Y SOCIEDAD. SPAIN EDU/PROP LEAD GP/REL PERS/REL ATTIT KNOWL. PAGE 92 H1837
ACADEM CULTURE ROLE INTELL

B64
VALEN H.,POLITICAL PARTIES IN NORWAY. NORWAY ACADEM PARTIC ROUTINE INGP/REL KNOWL...QU 20. PAGE 161 H3220
LOC/G POL/PAR PERSON

L64
SYMONDS R.,"REFLECTIONS IN LOCALISATION." AFR S/ASIA UK STRATA INT/ORG NAT/G SCHOOL EDU/PROP LEGIT KNOWL ORD/FREE PWR RESPECT CMN/WLTH 20. PAGE 151 H3023
ADMIN MGT COLONIAL

S64
GRUNER E.,"PRENSA, PARTIDOS POLITICOS, Y GRUPOS DE PRESION EN SUIZA." EUR+WWI MOD/EUR NAT/G EDU/PROP LEGIT PRESS ATTIT KNOWL ORD/FREE...CONCPT STAT CON/ANAL CHARTS 20. PAGE 62 H1241
POL/PAR SWITZERLND

S64
JOHNSON K.F.,"CAUSAL FACTORS IN LATIN AMERICAN POLITICAL INSTABILITY." CULTURE NAT/G VOL/ASSN EX/STRUC FORCES EDU/PROP LEGIT ADMIN COERCE REV ATTIT KNOWL PWR...STYLE RECORD CHARTS WORK 20. PAGE 81 H1624
L/A+17C PERCEPT ELITES

S64
TINKER H.,"POLITICS IN SOUTHEAST ASIA." INT/ORG NAT/G CREATE PLAN TEC/DEV GUERRILLA KNOWL ORD/FREE COLD/WAR. PAGE 155 H3103
S/ASIA ACT/RES REGION

B65
SLOTKIN J.S.,READINGS IN EARLY ANTHROPOLOGY. INTELL SECT CREATE ATTIT KNOWL...HUM PHIL/SCI PSY LING 1/18. PAGE 145 H2902
SOC CULTURE GP/COMP

B65
VON STACKELBERG K.,ALLE KRETER LUGEN VORURTEILE UBER MENSCHEN UND VOLKER. DIPLOM DOMIN RUMOR NAT/LISM PERSON KNOWL...SOC QU BIBLIOG 20. PAGE 164 H3277
NAT/COMP ATTIT EDU/PROP SAMP

L65
LASSWELL H.D.,"THE POLICY SCIENCES OF DEVELOPMENT." CULTURE SOCIETY EX/STRUC CREATE ADMIN ATTIT KNOWL ...SOC CONCPT SIMUL GEN/METH. PAGE 92 H1835
PWR METH/CNCPT DIPLOM

B66
DEXTER N.C.,GUIDE TO CONTEMPORARY POLITICS. EUR+WWI UK PARL/PROC GP/REL KNOWL...POLICY MAJORIT IDEA/COMP 20. PAGE 41 H0815
POL/PAR CONCPT NAT/G

B66
IOWA STATE U CTR AGRI AND ECO,RESEARCH AND EDUCATION FOR REGIONAL AND AREA DEVELOPMENT. FUT LAW CULTURE R+D LOC/G PLAN KNOWL...POLICY CHARTS ANTHOL 20. PAGE 78 H1565
REGION ACT/RES ECO/TAC INDUS

B66
LAVEN P.,RENAISSANCE ITALY: 1464-1534. ITALY AGRI EXTR/IND FINAN MUNIC INT/TRADE DRIVE...CATH GEOG CHARTS BIBLIOG/A 15. PAGE 92 H1841
CULTURE HUM TEC/DEV KNOWL

B67
COWLES M.,PERSPECTIVES IN THE EDUCATION OF DISADVANTAGED CHILDREN. CULTURE OP/RES PLAN PERS/REL ADJUST HABITAT PERCEPT KNOWL WEALTH ...SOC/WK IDEA/COMP ANTHOL 20. PAGE 34 H0686
EDU/PROP AGE/C TEC/DEV SCHOOL

B67
LAQUER W.,THE FATE OF THE REVOLUTION: INTERPRETATIONS OF SOVIET HISTORY. RUSSIA NAT/G MARXISM...BIBLIOG 20 STALIN/J. PAGE 91 H1816
REV KNOWL HIST/WRIT IDEA/COMP

B67
MICKIEWICZ E.P.,SOVIET POLITICAL SCHOOLS: THE COMMUNIST PARTY ADULT INSTRUCTION SYSTEM. COM USSR INTELL SCHOOL WORKER CREATE PRESS ADMIN CONTROL ATTIT KNOWL...PROG/TEAC SOC/INTEG 20 COM/PARTY. PAGE 110 H2200
NAT/G EDU/PROP AGE/A MARXISM

B67
SALISBURY H.E.,BEHIND THE LINES - HANOI. VIETNAM/N
WAR

NAT/G GUERRILLA CIVMIL/REL NAT/LISM KNOWL 20. PAGE 137 H2741 — PROB/SOLV DIPLOM OBS

S67 HUNTINGTON S.P.,"INTRODUCTION: SOCIAL SCIENCE AND VIETNAM." VIETNAM CULTURE 20. PAGE 75 H1506 — ACADEM KNOWL PROF/ORG SOCIETY

S67 KINGSBURY E.C.,"LAW AS COMPACT: ANCIENT ISRAEL'S CONTRIBUTION TO THE UNDERSTANDING OF LAW." ISRAEL MEDIT-7 CULTURE KIN KNOWL...JURID CONCPT TREND IDEA/COMP METH/COMP WORSHIP JEWS DEITY. PAGE 86 H1716 — LAW AGREE CONSTN INGP/REL

S67 SLOAN P.,"FIFTY YEARS OF SOVIET RULE." USSR INDUS EDU/PROP EFFICIENCY PRODUC HEALTH KNOWL MORAL WEALTH MARXISM...POLICY 20. PAGE 145 H2900 — CREATE NAT/G PLAN INSPECT

S67 SULLIVAN J.H.,"THE PRESS AND POLITICS IN INDONESIA." INDONESIA NAT/G WRITING REV...TREND GOV/COMP 20. PAGE 150 H3007 — CIVMIL/REL KNOWL TOTALISM

C67 GEHLEN M.P.,"THE POLITICS OF COEXISTENCE: SOVIET METHODS AND MOTIVES." COM USSR NAT/G INT/TRADE EDU/PROP ARMS/CONT DETER KNOWL...CHARTS IDEA/COMP 20 COLD/WAR. PAGE 55 H1108 — BIBLIOG PEACE DIPLOM MARXISM

KNOWLEDGE TEST....SEE KNO/TEST

KNOWLES A.F. H1735

KNOX/HENRY....HENRY KNOX (SECRETARY OF WAR 1789)

KOENTJARANINGRAT R. H1736

KOGAN N. H1737

KOH S.J. H1738

KOHLER/J....JOSEF KOHLER

KOHN H. H1739,H1740,H1741,H1742,H1743,H1744,H1745,H1746,H1747

KOHN W.S.G. H1748

KOLAJA J. H1280

KOLARZ W. H1749,H1750,H1751,H1752

KOLKOWICZ R. H1753

KOMIYA R. H1754

KONCZACKI Z.A. H1755

KORBONSKI A. H0117

KOREA....KOREA IN GENERAL; SEE ALSO ASIA

B39 KERNER R.J.,NORTHEAST ASIA: A SELECTED BIBLIOGRAPHY (2 VOLS.). KOREA RUSSIA NAT/G DIPLOM...GEOG 19/20 CHINJAP. PAGE 85 H1696 — BIBLIOG ASIA SOCIETY CULTURE

B50 JONES H.D.,KOREA, AN ANNOTATED BIBLIOGRAPHY OF PUBLICATIONS IN WESTERN LANGUAGES. KOREA CULTURE MUNIC SECT FORCES DIPLOM HEALTH WEALTH...ART/METH GEOG SOC LING 20. PAGE 82 H1632 — BIBLIOG/A ASIA NAT/G ECO/UNDEV

B54 EPSTEIN L.D.,BRITAIN - UNEASY ALLY. KOREA UK USA+45 NAT/G POL/PAR ECO/TAC FOR/AID INT/TRADE WAR LABOR/PAR CONSRV/PAR. PAGE 47 H0934 — DIPLOM ATTIT POLICY NAT/COMP

B54 HAZARD B.H. JR.,KOREAN STUDIES GUIDE. KOREA CONSTN CULTURE AGRI FAM SECT CREATE WAR NAT/LISM HABITAT PWR...CHARTS 14/20. PAGE 68 H1371 — BIBLIOG/A ELITES GP/REL

B54 WILLIAMSON H.F.,ECONOMIC DEVELOPMENT - PRINCIPLES AND PATTERNS. INDIA KOREA CULTURE ECO/DEV ECO/UNDEV TEC/DEV...CENSUS NAT/COMP 20 CHINJAP MEXIC/AMER RESOURCE/N. PAGE 168 H3369 — ECO/TAC GEOG LABOR

B59 NAHM A.C.,JAPANESE PENETRATION OF KOREA, 1894-1910. ASIA KOREA NAT/G...POLICY 20 CHINJAP. PAGE 115 H2303 — BIBLIOG/A DIPLOM WAR COLONIAL

B59 VINACKE H.M.,A HISTORY OF THE FAR EAST IN MODERN TIMES (6TH ED.). KOREA S/ASIA USSR CONSTN CULTURE STRATA ECO/UNDEV NAT/G CHIEF FOR/AID INT/TRADE GP/REL...SOC NAT/COMP 19/20 CHINJAP. PAGE 163 H3255 — STRUCT ASIA

B61 TACHAKKYO K.,BIBLIOGRAPHY OF KOREAN STUDIES: A BIBLIOGRAPHICAL GUIDE TO KOREAN PUBLICATIONS ON KOREAN STUDIES APPEARING 1945-1958. KOREA LAW...HUM JURID PHIL/SCI LING 19/20. PAGE 152 H3033 — BIBLIOG/A SOCIETY CULTURE WAR

B62 SILBERMAN B.S.,JAPAN AND KOREA; A CRITICAL BIBLIOGRAPHY. KOREA LAW STRATA STRUCT AGRI INDUS NAT/G POL/PAR SECT...HUM LING IDEA/COMP 5/20 CHINJAP. PAGE 144 H2872 — BIBLIOG/A CULTURE S/ASIA

B63 ATTIA G.E.D.,LES FORCES ARMEES DES NATIONS UNIES EN COREE ET AU MOYENORIENT. KOREA CONSTN NAT/G DELIB/GP LEGIS PWR...IDEA/COMP NAT/COMP BIBLIOG UN SUEZ. PAGE 9 H0177 — FORCES INT/LAW

B63 LEE C.,THE POLITICS OF KOREAN NATIONALISM. KOREA S/ASIA DIPLOM REV WAR 14/20 CHINJAP. PAGE 93 H1855 — NAT/LISM SOVEREIGN COLONIAL

C63 ATTIA G.E.O.,"LES FORCES ARMEES DES NATIONS UNIES EN COREE ET AU MOYENORIENT." KOREA CONSTN DELIB/GP LEGIS PWR...IDEA/COMP NAT/COMP BIBLIOG UN SUEZ. PAGE 9 H0178 — FORCES NAT/G INT/LAW

B64 INTL CONF ON POPULATION,POPULATION DYNAMICS: INTERNATIONAL ACTION AND TRAINING PROGRAMS. INDIA KOREA L/A+17C TAIWAN USA+45 WOR+45 FAM PLAN CONFER ...NEW/IDEA ANTHOL 20 CHINJAP BIRTH/CON. PAGE 78 H1561 — NAT/COMP CONTROL ATTIT EDU/PROP

S64 LANGER P.F.,"JAPAN'S RELATIONS WITH CHINA." ASIA CHINA/COM KOREA S/ASIA ECO/DEV NAT/G POL/PAR EDU/PROP ATTIT ALL/VALS...METH/CNCPT TIME/SEQ TREND 20 CHINJAP. PAGE 91 H1808 — RIGID/FLEX ECO/TAC

S64 LEWIS R.,"OPINION SURVEYING IN KOREA." ASIA FUT KOREA LEGIS EDU/PROP EXEC ALL/VALS...POLICY CONCPT MYTH TESTS CON/ANAL GEN/METH TOT/POP VAL/FREE 20. PAGE 96 H1915 — NAT/G QU

B65 CHUNG Y.S.,KOREA: A SELECTED BIBLIOGRAPHY 1959-1963. ASIA KOREA NAT/G DIPLOM 20. PAGE 30 H0601 — BIBLIOG/A SOC

B65 SAKAI R.K.,STUDIES ON ASIA, 1965. INDIA KOREA S/ASIA USA+45 CONSTN KIN SECT PARTIC SUFF NAT/LISM ...POLICY SOC 19/20 CHINJAP. PAGE 137 H2737 — PARL/PROC ASIA

B66 FITZGERALD C.P.,A CONCISE HISTORY OF EAST ASIA. ASIA KOREA S/ASIA INT/TRADE REGION MARXISM 20 CHINJAP. PAGE 51 H1017 — ECO/UNDEV COLONIAL CULTURE

B66 KOH S.J.,STAGES OF INDUSTRIAL DEVELOPMENT IN ASIA. ASIA INDIA KOREA STRATA STRUCT NAT/G INT/TRADE ...CHARTS 19/20 CHINJAP. PAGE 87 H1738 — INDUS ECO/UNDEV ECO/DEV LABOR

B67 MCNELLY T.,SOURCES IN MODERN EAST ASIAN HISTORY AND POLITICS. KOREA VIETNAM CULTURE DIPLOM COLONIAL REV WAR PWR ALL/IDEOS MARXISM...ANTHOL 20 CHINJAP. PAGE 107 H2147 — NAT/COMP ASIA S/ASIA SOCIETY

KOREA/N....NORTH KOREA

N KYRIAK T.E.,ASIAN DEVELOPMENTS: A BIBLIOGRAPHY. INDONESIA KOREA/N VIETNAM/N CULTURE SOCIETY ECO/UNDEV NAT/G DIPLOM...SOC TREND 20 MONGOLIA. PAGE 90 H1788 — BIBLIOG/A ALL/IDEOS S/ASIA ASIA

S63 HALPERN A.M.,"THE EMERGENCE OF AN ASIAN COMMUNIST BLOC." ASIA CHINA/COM COM FUT KOREA/N S/ASIA VIETNAM/N STRATA NAT/G DELIB/GP FORCES TOP/EX PLAN BAL/PWR COERCE DETER PWR COLD/WAR WORK 20. PAGE 65 H1295 — POL/PAR EDU/PROP DIPLOM

S63 TANG P.S.H.,"SINO-SOVIET TENSIONS." ASIA CHINA/COM COM CUBA KOREA/N VIETNAM/N NAT/G VOL/ASSN DELIB/GP PEACE PERCEPT PWR...METH/CNCPT MYTH RECORD TREND GEN/LAWS 20. PAGE 152 H3041 — ACT/RES EDU/PROP REV

KOREA/S....SOUTH KOREA

S67 SUNG C.H.,"POLITICAL DIAGNOSIS OF KOREAN SOCIETY* A SURVEY OF MILITARY AND CIVILIAN VALUES." KOREA/S ECO/UNDEV NAT/G CIVMIL/REL...QU SAMP GP/COMP. PAGE 151 H3009 — ELITES FORCES ATTIT ORD/FREE

KORNBERG A. H1756

KORNHAUSER W. H1757

KORNILOV/L....LAVR GEORGIEVICH KORNILOV

KOSAMBI D.D. H1758

KOSSACK G. H1269

KOUSOULAS D.G. H1759

KOVNER M. H1760

KRABBE H. H1761

KRACKE E.A. H1762

KRADER L. H1763

KRAEHE E. H1764

KRAWIETZ W. H3276

KRECH D. H1765

KRENZ F.E. H1766

KREY A.C. H1767

KRIS E. H1768

KRISTOF L.K.D. H1769

KROEBER A.L. H1770,H1771,H1772

KROGER K. H1773

KROLL M. H1774

KROPOTKIN P. H1775,H1776

KRUEGER H. H1777

KRUGLAK T.E. H1778

KRUSE H. H1779

KU KLUX KLAN....SEE KKK

KUNSTADTER P. H1780

KUOMINTANG....KUOMINTANG

KUPER H. H1781

KUPER L. H1782,H1783

KURL S. H1784

KURZMAN D. H1785

KUWAIT....SEE ALSO ISLAM

B58

MACRO E.,BIBLIOGRAPHY OF THE ARABIAN PENINSULA (PAMPHLET). KUWAIT SAUDI/ARAB YEMEN COLONIAL...GEOG 19/20. PAGE 101 H2012 — BIBLIOG ISLAM CULTURE NAT/G

S61

VALLET R.,"IRAN: KEY TO THE MIDDLE EAST." COM IRAQ ISLAM KUWAIT LEBANON SAUDI/ARAB TURKEY ELITES SOCIETY INDUS PROC/MFG POL/PAR TOP/EX PLAN BAL/PWR DIPLOM ECO/TAC ALL/VALS...TREND CENTO 20. PAGE 161 H3224 — NAT/G ECO/UNDEV IRAN

B65

INT. BANK RECONSTR. DEVELOP.,ECONOMIC DEVELOPMENT OF KUWAIT. ISLAM KUWAIT AGRI FINAN MARKET EX/STRUC TEC/DEV ECO/TAC ADMIN WEALTH...OBS CON/ANAL CHARTS 20. PAGE 77 H1541 — INDUS NAT/G

KUZNETS S. H1786

KUZNETS....KUZNETS SCALE

KY/NGUYEN....NGUYEN KY

B66

VIEN N.C.,SEEKING THE TRUTH. VIETNAM DELIB/GP DOMIN RISK MARXISM 20 KY/NGUYEN. PAGE 162 H3250 — NAT/G COLONIAL PWR SOVEREIGN

KYLE K. H1787

KYRIAK T.E. H1788,H1789

L

L/A+17C....LATIN AMERICA SINCE 1700; SEE ALSO APPROPRIATE NATIONS

N

BIBLIOTECH NACIONAL,CATALOGO BREVE DE LA BIBLIOTECA AMERICANA DE JT MEDINA (2 VOLS.). CHILE NAT/G PERSON HUM. PAGE 16 H0330 — BIBLIOG/A CHARTS L/A+17C

N

UNIVERSITY OF FLORIDA LIBRARY,DOORS TO LATIN AMERICA; RECENT BOOKS AND PAMPHLETS. CONSTN CULTURE SOCIETY ECO/UNDEV COLONIAL LEAD GOV/REL NAT/LISM ATTIT...HUM SOC 20. PAGE 159 H3170 — BIBLIOG/A L/A+17C DIPLOM NAT/G

N

HANDBOOK OF LATIN AMERICAN STUDIES. LAW CULTURE ECO/UNDEV POL/PAR ADMIN LEAD...SOC 20. PAGE 1 H0016 — BIBLIOG/A L/A+17C NAT/G DIPLOM

N

CARIBBEAN COMMISSION,CURRENT CARIBBEAN BIBLIOGRAPHY. FRANCE NETHERLAND UK CULTURE ECO/UNDEV PRESS LEAD ATTIT...GEOG SOC 20. PAGE 26 H0530 — BIBLIOG NAT/G L/A+17C DIPLOM

N

INSTITUTE OF HISPANIC STUDIES,HISPANIC AMERICAN REPORT. EUR+WWI SPAIN LAW CONSTN ECO/UNDEV POL/PAR EX/STRUC LEGIS LEAD...HUM SOC 20. PAGE 77 H1538 — BIBLIOG/A L/A+17C NAT/G DIPLOM

N

UNIVERSITY OF CALIFORNIA,STATISTICAL ABSTRACT OF LATIN AMERICA. L/A+17C DIPLOM 20. PAGE 158 H3169 — BIBLIOG NAT/G ECO/UNDEV STAT

B01

GRIFFIN A.P.C.,A LIST OF BOOKS ON THE DANISH WEST INDIES (PAMPHLET). L/A+17C WEST/IND CULTURE LOC/G ...GEOG MGT 18/20. PAGE 61 H1214 — BIBLIOG/A SOCIETY COLONIAL ADMIN

B17

DOS SANTOS M.,BIBLIOGRAPHIA GERAL, A DESCRIPCAO BIBLIOGRAFICA DE LIVROS TANTO DE AUTORES PORTUGUEZES COMO BRASILEIROS... BRAZIL PORTUGAL NAT/G LEAD GP/REL 15/20. PAGE 42 H0840 — BIBLIOG/A L/A+17C DIPLOM COLONIAL

N19

OPERATIONS AND POLICY RESEARCH,PERU ELECTION MEMORANDA (PAMPHLET). L/A+17C PERU POL/PAR LEGIS EXEC APPORT REPRESENT 20. PAGE 121 H2421 — CHOOSE CONSTN SUFF NAT/G

N19

ROWE J.W.,THE ARGENTINE ELECTIONS OF 1963 (PAMPHLET). L/A+17C LOC/G NAT/G LEGIS REPRESENT 20 ARGEN. PAGE 135 H2703 — CHOOSE CONSTN APPORT POL/PAR

B29

ROBERTS S.H.,HISTORY OF FRENCH COLONIAL POLICY. AFR ASIA L/A+17C S/ASIA CULTURE ECO/DEV ECO/UNDEV FINAN NAT/G PLAN ECO/TAC DOMIN ROUTINE SOVEREIGN...OBS HIST/WRIT TREND CHARTS VAL/FREE 19/20. PAGE 132 H2642 — INT/ORG ACT/RES FRANCE COLONIAL

B31

KIRKPATRICK F.A.,A HISTORY OF THE ARGENTINE REPUBLIC. SPAIN UK CONSTN SOCIETY ECO/UNDEV EX/STRUC DIPLOM FOR/AID LEAD WAR ATTIT...BIOG CHARTS 16/20 ARGEN SAN/MARTIN. PAGE 86 H1724 — NAT/G L/A+17C COLONIAL

B32

CATALOGUE OF BOOKS, MANSUCRIPTS, ETC. IN THE CARIBBEANA SECTION OF THE N.M. WILLIAMS MEMORIAL ETHNOLOGICAL COLLECTION. JAMAICA WEST/IND GP/REL ATTIT SOC. PAGE 2 H0031 — BIBLIOG L/A+17C CULTURE SOCIETY

B32

CHILDS J.B.,THE MEMORIAS OF THE REPUBLICS OF CENTRAL AMERICA AND OF THE ANTILLES. L/A+17C 19/20 CENTRAL/AM. PAGE 29 H0592 — BIBLIOG GOV/REL NAT/G EX/STRUC

B38

DEL TORO J.,A BIBLIOGRAPHY OF THE COLLECTIVE BIOGRAPHY OF SPANISH AMERICA. ELITES NAT/G WRITING LEAD PERSON 19/20. PAGE 39 H0786 — BIBLIOG/A L/A+17C BIOG

B41

CHILDS J.B.,COLOMBIAN GOVERNMENT PUBLICATIONS (PAMPHLET). L/A+17C SOCIETY 19/20 COLOMB. PAGE 30 H0593 — BIBLIOG GOV/REL NAT/G EX/STRUC

B42

PAGINSKY P.,GERMAN WORKS RELATING TO AMERICA, 1493-1800; A LIST COMPILED FROM THE COLLECTIONS OF THE NEW YORK PUBLIC LIBRARY. GERMANY PRE/AMER CULTURE COLONIAL ATTIT...POLICY SOC 15/19. PAGE 122 H2442 — BIBLIOG/A NAT/G L/A+17C DIPLOM

B42

SIMOES DOS REIS A.,BIBLIOGRAFIA DAS BIBLIOGRAFIAS BRASILEIRAS. BRAZIL ADMIN COLONIAL 20. PAGE 144 H2879 — BIBLIOG NAT/G DIPLOM L/A+17C

B43

BROWN A.D.,BRITISH POSSESSIONS IN THE CARIBBEAN AREA: A SELECTED LIST OF REFERENCES. UK NAT/G DIPLOM...GEOG 20 CARIBBEAN. PAGE 22 H0437 — BIBLIOG COLONIAL ECO/UNDEV L/A+17C

B43

DURON J.F.,REPERTORIO BIBLIOGRAFICO HONDURENO. HONDURAS WRITING. PAGE 44 H0871 — BIBLIOG NAT/G

L/A+17C
B43
JONES C.K.,A BIBLIOGRAPHY OF LATIN AMERICAN BIBLIOGRAPHIES (2ND ED.). CULTURE ALL/VALS...POLICY GEOG HUM SOC LING BIOG TREND 20. PAGE 82 H1629 BIBLIOG/A L/A+17C HIST/WRIT
B44
SHELBY C.,LATIN AMERICAN PERIODICALS CURRENTLY RECEIVED IN THE LIBRARY OF CONGRESS AND IN LIBRARY OF DEPARTMENT OF AGRICULTURE. SOCIETY AGRI INDUS LABOR POL/PAR INT/TRADE...GEOG SOC 20. PAGE 143 H2856 BIBLIOG ECO/UNDEV CULTURE L/A+17C
B45
PERAZA SARAUSA F.,BIBLIOGRAFIAS CUBANAS. CUBA CULTURE ECO/UNDEV AGRI EDU/PROP PRESS CIVMIL/REL ...POLICY GEOG PHIL/SCI BIOG 19/20. PAGE 125 H2489 BIBLIOG/A L/A+17C NAT/G DIPLOM
B47
BEHAR D.,BIBLIOGRAFIA HISPANOAMERICANA. LIBROS ANTIGUOS Y MODERNOS REFERENTES A AMERICA Y ESPANA. PORTUGAL SPAIN CONSTN NAT/G SECT CREATE REV WAR GOV/REL...ART/METH GEOG PHIL/SCI LING 20 ARGEN. PAGE 13 H0260 BIBLIOG L/A+17C CULTURE
B48
GUIDE TO THE RECORDS IN THE NATIONAL ARCHIVES. ECO/UNDEV ADMIN COLONIAL 16/20. PAGE 2 H0034 BIBLIOG NAT/G L/A+17C DIPLOM
B48
FLOREN LOZANO L.,BIBLIOGRAFIA DE LA BIBLIOGRAFIA DOMINICANA. DOMIN/REP NAT/G DIPLOM EDU/PROP CIVMIL/REL...POLICY ART/METH GEOG PHIL/SCI HIST/WRIT 20. PAGE 51 H1027 BIBLIOG/A BIOG L/A+17C CULTURE
B48
US LIBRARY OF CONGRESS,BRAZIL: A GUIDE TO THE OFFICIAL PUBLICATIONS OF BRAZIL. BRAZIL L/A+17C CONSULT DELIB/GP LEGIS CT/SYS 19/20. PAGE 160 H3206 BIBLIOG/A NAT/G ADMIN TOP/EX
B49
BORBA DE MORAES R.,MANUAL BIBLIOGRAFICO DE ESTUDOS BRASILEIROS. BRAZIL DIPLOM ADMIN LEAD...SOC 20. PAGE 19 H0374 BIBLIOG L/A+17C NAT/G ECO/UNDEV
S49
DEXTER L.A.,"A DIALOGUE ON THE SOCIAL PSYCHOLOGY OF COLONIALISM AND ON CERTAIN PUERTO RICAN PROFESSIONAL PERSONALITY PATTERNS." L/A+17C PUERT/RICO STRATA STRUCT DOMIN ISOLAT DRIVE ...NAT/COMP PERS/COMP HYPO/EXP 20 JEWS NEGRO. PAGE 41 H0813 COLONIAL SOC PSY PERSON
C50
STOKES W.S.,"HONDURAS: AN AREA STUDY IN GOVERNMENT." HONDURAS NAT/G POL/PAR COLONIAL CT/SYS ROUTINE CHOOSE REPRESENT...GEOG RECORD BIBLIOG 19/20. PAGE 149 H2988 CONSTN LAW L/A+17C ADMIN
B51
CATALOGO GENERAL DE LA LIBRERIA ESPANOLA E HISPANOAMERICANA 1901-1930; AUTORES (5 VOLS., 1932-1951). SPAIN COLONIAL GOV/REL...SOC 20. PAGE 2 H0036 BIBLIOG L/A+17C DIPLOM NAT/G
B51
BISSAINTHE M.,DICTIONNAIRE DE BIBLIOGRAPHIE HAITIENNE. HAITI ELITES AGRI LEGIS DIPLOM INT/TRADE WRITING ORD/FREE CATHISM...ART/METH GEOG 19/20 NEGRO TREATY. PAGE 17 H0347 BIBLIOG L/A+17C SOCIETY NAT/G
B51
CHRISTENSEN A.N.,THE EVOLUTION OF LATIN AMERICAN GOVERNMENT: A BOOK OF READINGS. ECO/UNDEV INDUS LOC/G POL/PAR EX/STRUC LEGIS FOR/AID CT/SYS ...SOC/WK 20 SOUTH/AMER. PAGE 30 H0599 NAT/G CONSTN DIPLOM L/A+17C
B52
DILLON D.R.,LATIN AMERICA, 1935-1949; A SELECTED BIBLIOGRAPHY. LAW EDU/PROP...SOC 20. PAGE 41 H0826 BIBLIOG L/A+17C NAT/G DIPLOM
B52
FORDE L.D.,HABITAT, ECONOMY AND SOCIETY. AFR L/A+17C S/ASIA STRUCT AGRI INGP/REL...GEOG OBS BIBLIOG 20. PAGE 52 H1037 SOC HABITAT CULTURE ECO/UNDEV
B52
TAX S.,HERITAGE OF CONQUEST. L/A+17C ECO/UNDEV LOC/G WEALTH...POLICY ANTHOL WORSHIP 20 MEXIC/AMER CENTRAL/AM. PAGE 153 H3052 PHIL/SCI CULTURE SOCIETY
B53
KANTOR H.,A BIBLIOGRAPHY OF UNPUBLISHED DOCTORAL DISSERTATIONS AND MASTERS' THESES DEALING WITH GOVTS, POL, INT REL OF LAT AM. L/A+17C INT/ORG POL/PAR ACT/RES OP/RES CONFER ATTIT...INT/LAW PHIL/SCI 20. PAGE 83 H1656 BIBLIOG ACADEM DIPLOM NAT/G
B53
ROSCIO J.G.,OBRAS. L/A+17C SPAIN DIPLOM REV WAR NAT/LISM TOTALISM PWR SOVEREIGN 19. PAGE 134 H2671 ORD/FREE COLONIAL NAT/G PHIL/SCI
B53
WAGLEY C.,AMAZON TOWN: A STUDY OF MAN IN THE TROPICS. BRAZIL L/A+17C STRATA STRUCT ECO/UNDEV AGRI EX/STRUC RACE/REL DISCRIM HABITAT WEALTH...OBS SOC/EXP 20. PAGE 164 H3285 SOC NEIGH CULTURE INGP/REL
B54
GIRALSO JARAMLLO G.,BIBLIOGRAFIA DE BIBLIOGRAFIAS COLOMBIANAS. L/A+17C ACADEM SECT CREATE EDU/PROP ...ART/METH GEOG LING TREND 20 COLOMB. PAGE 57 H1135 BIBLIOG/A CULTURE PHIL/SCI ECO/UNDEV
B55
JONES T.B.,A BIBLIOGRAPHY ON SOUTH AMERICAN ECONOMIC AFFAIRS: ARTICLES IN NINETEENTH CENTURY PERIODICALS (PAMPHLET). AGRI COM/IND DIST/IND EXTR/IND FINAN INDUS LABOR NAT/G 19. PAGE 82 H1634 BIBLIOG ECO/UNDEV L/A+17C TEC/DEV
B56
READ M.,EDUCATION AND SOCIAL CHANGE IN TROPICAL AREAS. AFR L/A+17C SOCIETY LITERACY PERCEPT PERSON WEALTH...HEAL PHIL/SCI SOC 20. PAGE 130 H2603 EDU/PROP HABITAT DRIVE CULTURE
B57
BUCK P.W.,CONTOL OF FOREIGN RELATIONS IN MODERN NATIONS. FRANCE L/A+17C NETHERLAND USSR WOR+45 INT/ORG TOP/EX BAL/PWR DOMIN EDU/PROP COERCE PEACE ATTIT...CONCPT TREND 20 CMN/WLTH. PAGE 23 H0465 NAT/G PWR DIPLOM
B57
CARIBBEAN COMMISSION,A CATALOGUE OF CARIBBEAN COMMISSION PUBLICATIONS (PAMPHLET). WEST/IND CULTURE ECO/UNDEV LOC/G DIPLOM SOC. PAGE 26 H0531 BIBLIOG L/A+17C INT/ORG NAT/G
B57
DEAN V.M.,THE NATURE OF THE NON-WESTERN WORLD. AFR ASIA L/A+17C S/ASIA CULTURE SOCIETY STRATA ECO/DEV DIPLOM ECO/TAC FOR/AID ATTIT DRIVE ALL/VALS ...RELATIV SOC CONCPT TIME/SEQ TREND TOT/POP 20. PAGE 39 H0778 ECO/UNDEV STERTYP NAT/LISM
B57
HALLGARTEN G.W.,DAMONEN ODER RETTER. ASIA L/A+17C CAP/ISM ATTIT MARXISM SOCISM...NAT/COMP. PAGE 64 H1289 TOTALISM FASCISM COERCE DOMIN
B57
HERNANDEZ-ARREGU J.,IMPERIALISMO Y CULTURA (LA POLITICA EN LA INTELIGENCIA ARGENTINA). L/A+17C CULTURE ELITES WRITING COLONIAL CROWD ATTIT FASCISM MARXISM SOCISM...BIOG IDEA/COMP 20 ARGEN PERON/JUAN COM/PARTY. PAGE 70 H1403 INTELL CREATE ART/METH HUM
B57
PALACIOS A.L.,PETROLEO, MONOPOLIOS, Y LATIFUNDIOS. L/A+17C EXTR/IND NAT/G TEC/DEV ECO/TAC CONTROL PRODUC 20 ARGEN MONOPOLY RESOURCE/N. PAGE 123 H2448 ECO/UNDEV NAT/LISM INDUS AGRI
B57
US SENATE SPEC COMM FOR AID,COMPILATION OF STUDIES AND SURVEYS. AFR ASIA L/A+17C USA+45 ECO/UNDEV AGRI INT/ORG CONSULT TEC/DEV CONFER TOTALISM...NAT/COMP 20 CONGRESS. PAGE 161 H3216 FOR/AID DIPLOM ORD/FREE DELIB/GP
B58
HUMPHREYS R.A.,LATIN AMERICAN HISTORY: A GUIDE TO THE LITERATURE IN ENGLISH. CULTURE NAT/G DIPLOM BIOG. PAGE 75 H1495 BIBLIOG/A L/A+17C
B58
JOHNSON J.J.,POLITICAL CHANGE IN LATIN AMERICA: THE EMERGENCE OF THE MIDDLE SECTORS. INTELL STRATA STRUCT ECO/UNDEV MUNIC TEC/DEV LEAD REV...DECISION TREND GOV/COMP BIBLIOG/A 20. PAGE 81 H1621 L/A+17C ELITES GP/REL DOMIN
B58
PAN AMERICAN UNION,REPERTORIO DE PUBLICACIONES PERIODICAS ACTUALES LATINO-AMERICANAS. CULTURE ECO/UNDEV ADMIN LEAD GOV/REL 20 OAS. PAGE 123 H2455 BIBLIOG L/A+17C NAT/G DIPLOM
B59
CORDONA G.D.,INDICE BIBLIOGRAFICO GUATEMALTECO 1958. GUATEMALA...SOC 20. PAGE 33 H0666 BIBLIOG NAT/G LOC/G L/A+17C
B59
INTERAMERICAN CULTURAL COUN,LISTA DE LIBROS REPRESENTAVOS DE AMERICA. CULTURE DIPLOM ADMIN 20. PAGE 77 H1542 BIBLIOG/A NAT/G L/A+17C SOC
B59
LOPEZ M.M.,CATALOGOS DE PUBLICACIONES PERIODICAS MEXICANAS. L/A+17C CULTURE NAT/G DIPLOM 20 MEXIC/AMER. PAGE 98 H1965 BIBLIOG PRESS CON/ANAL
B59
MARTZ J.D.,CENTRAL AMERICA: THE CRISIS AND THE CHALLENGE. L/A+17C POL/PAR CHIEF CHOOSE SOVEREIGN ...BIOG TREND BIBLIOG 20 CENTRAL/AM. PAGE 104 H2071 NAT/G GOV/REL DIPLOM GOV/COMP
B59
PANAMERICAN UNION,PUBLICATIONS: PAU AND OFFICIAL RECORDS OF THE OAS, IN ENGLISH, SPANISH, PORTUGUESE, AND FRENCH, 1958-59. NAT/G ATTIT...SOC 20 OAS. PAGE 123 H2456 BIBLIOG L/A+17C INT/LAW DIPLOM
B59
ROCHE J.,LA COLONISATION ALLEMANDE ET LE RIO GRANDE DO SUL. BRAZIL L/A+17C NAT/G PROVS INGP/REL ECO/UNDEV GP/REL

RACE/REL DISCRIM HABITAT...GEOG SOC/INTEG 19/20 MIGRATION. PAGE 133 H2652
ATTIT

B59
SZLUC T.,TWILIGHT OF THE TYRANTS. BRAZIL L/A+17C PERU VENEZUELA NAT/G FORCES CONTROL PERSON MORAL ORD/FREE PWR...CONCPT 20 ARGEN COLOMB. PAGE 151 H3028
TOTALISM CHIEF REV FASCISM

S59
MECHAM J.L.,"LATIN AMERICAN CONSTITUTIONS: NOMINAL AND REAL" (BMR)" L/A+17C REV...CON/ANAL NAT/COMP 20. PAGE 108 H2156
CONSTN CHOOSE CONCPT NAT/G

S59
PLAZA G.,"FOR A REGIONAL MARKET IN LATIN AMERICA." FUT L/A+17C CULTURE INDUS NAT/G ECO/TAC INT/TRADE ATTIT WEALTH...NEW/IDEA TREND OAS 20. PAGE 126 H2527
MARKET INT/ORG REGION

B60
ALMOND G.A.,THE POLITICS OF THE DEVELOPING AREAS. AFR ISLAM L/A+17C S/ASIA SOCIETY ECO/UNDEV NAT/G ADMIN PERCEPT KNOWL SOVEREIGN...CONCPT GEN/LAWS 20. PAGE 6 H0112
EX/STRUC ATTIT NAT/LISM

B60
DE HERRERA C.D.,LISTA BIBLIOGRAFICA DE LOS TRABAJOS DE GRADUACION Y TESIS PRESENTADOS EN LA UNIVERSIDAD, 1939-1960. PANAMA DIPLOM LEAD...SOC 20. PAGE 38 H0754
BIBLIOG L/A+17C NAT/G ACADEM

B60
FLORES R.H.,CATALOGO DE TESIS DOCTORALES DE LAS FACULTADES DE LA UNIVERSIDAD DE EL SALVADOR. EL/SALVADR LAW DIPLOM ADMIN LEAD GOV/REL...SOC 19/20. PAGE 52 H1030
BIBLIOG ACADEM L/A+17C NAT/G

B60
MOCTEZUMA A.P.,EL CONFLICTO RELIGIOSO DE 1926 (2ND ED.). L/A+17C LAW NAT/G LOBBY COERCE GP/REL ATTIT ...POLICY 20 MEXIC/AMER CHURCH/STA. PAGE 112 H2233
SECT ORD/FREE DISCRIM REV

B60
PINTO F.B.M.,ENRIQUECIMENTO ILICITO NO EXERCICIO DE CARGOS PUBLICOS. BRAZIL L/A+17C USA+45 ELITES TRIBUTE CONTROL INGP/REL ORD/FREE PWR...NAT/COMP 20. PAGE 126 H2513
ADMIN NAT/G CRIME LAW

B60
THORD-GRAY I.,GRINGO REBEL. L/A+17C NAT/G CONTROL LEAD ATTIT...OBS 20 MEXIC/AMER. PAGE 154 H3087
REV FORCES CIVMIL/REL ORD/FREE

B60
US LIBRARY OF CONGRESS,INDEX TO LATIN AMERICAN LEGISLATION: 1950-1960 (2 VOLS.). NAT/G DELIB/GP ADMIN PARL/PROC 20. PAGE 161 H3211
BIBLIOG/A LEGIS L/A+17C JURID

S60
"THE EMERGING COMMON MARKETS IN LATIN AMERICA." FUT L/A+17C STRATA DIST/IND INDUS LABOR NAT/G LEGIS ECO/TAC ADMIN RIGID/FLEX HEALTH...NEW/IDEA TIME/SEQ OAS 20. PAGE 2 H0038
FINAN ECO/UNDEV INT/TRADE

S60
FITZGIBBON R.H.,"DICTATORSHIP AND DEMOCRACY IN LATIN AMERICA." FUT ECO/DEV ECO/UNDEV INT/ORG LOC/G NAT/G TOP/EX PLAN TEC/DEV ECO/TAC CHOOSE ATTIT DRIVE PERSON ALL/VALS OAS TOT/POP 20. PAGE 51 H1019
L/A+17C ACT/RES INT/TRADE

S60
JAFFEE A.J.,"POPULATION TRENDS AND CONTROLS IN UNDERDEVELOPED COUNTRIES." AFR FUT ISLAM L/A+17C S/ASIA CULTURE R+D FAM ACT/RES PLAN EDU/PROP BIO/SOC RIGID/FLEX HEALTH...SOC STAT OBS CHARTS 20. PAGE 79 H1582
ECO/UNDEV GEOG

S60
WYCKOFF T.,"THE ROLE OF THE MILITARY IN LATIN AMERICAN POLITICS." L/A+17C CONSTN CULTURE ECO/UNDEV POL/PAR FORCES LEGIS TOP/EX LEGIT GUERRILLA REV CHOOSE ORD/FREE PWR...TIME/SEQ VAL/FREE 20. PAGE 171 H3430
NAT/G COERCE TOTALISM

B61
BAYITCH S.A.,LATIN AMERICA: A BIBLIOGRAPHICAL GUIDE. LAW CONSTN LEGIS JUDGE ADJUD CT/SYS 20. PAGE 12 H0243
BIBLIOG L/A+17C NAT/G JURID

B61
ESTEBAN J.C.,IMPERIALISMO Y DESARROLLO ECONOMICO. L/A+17C FINAN INDUS NAT/G ECO/TAC CONTROL ROLE. PAGE 47 H0941
ECO/UNDEV NAT/LISM DIPLOM BAL/PAY

B61
ESTEVEZ A.,ASPECTOS ECONOMICO-FINANCIEROS DE LA CAMPANA SANMARITANA. L/A+17C SPAIN FINAN COLONIAL LEAD ROLE ORD/FREE WEALTH 19 SOUTH/AMER SAN/MARTIN. PAGE 47 H0942
ECO/UNDEV REV BUDGET NAT/G

B61
FREYRE G.,THE PORTUGUESE AND THE TROPICS. L/A+17C PORTUGAL SOCIETY PERF/ART ADMIN TASK GP/REL ...ART/METH CONCPT SOC/INTEG 20. PAGE 53 H1060
COLONIAL METH PLAN CULTURE

B61
GRASES P.,ESTUDIOS BIBLIOGRAFICOS. VENEZUELA...SOC 20. PAGE 60 H1197
BIBLIOG NAT/G DIPLOM L/A+17C

B61
GUEVARA E.,GUERRILLA WARFARE. L/A+17C ECO/UNDEV NAT/G POL/PAR VOL/ASSN PLAN DOMIN REV DRIVE PWR WEALTH...NEW/IDEA RECORD BIOG COLD/WAR MARX/KARL OAS 20. PAGE 62 H1247
FORCES COERCE GUERRILLA CUBA

B61
HADDAD J.A.,REVOLUCAO CUBANA E REVOLUCAO BRASILEIRA. BRAZIL CUBA L/A+17C STRATA AGRI WORKER EDU/PROP REGION...POLICY NAT/COMP 20. PAGE 63 H1272
REV ORD/FREE DIPLOM ECO/UNDEV

B61
LUZ N.V.,A LUTA PELA INDUSTRIALIZACAO DO BRAZIL. BRAZIL L/A+17C AGRI NAT/G TEC/DEV COLONIAL 19/20. PAGE 99 H1981
ECO/UNDEV INDUS NAT/LISM POLICY

B61
ROIG E.,MARTI, ANTIIMPERIALISTA. CUBA L/A+17C DIPLOM DOMIN COLONIAL CONTROL LEAD PWR SOVEREIGN ...PHIL/SCI 19 MARTI/JOSE INTERVENT. PAGE 133 H2664
PERSON NAT/LISM ECO/UNDEV ORD/FREE

B61
STARK H.,SOCIAL AND ECONOMIC FRONTIERS IN LATIN AMERICA (2ND ED.). CUBA FUT CULTURE AGRI INDUS ECO/TAC PRODUC ATTIT MARXISM...NAT/COMP BIBLIOG T 20. PAGE 149 H2971
L/A+17C SOCIETY DIPLOM ECO/UNDEV

B61
ZIMMERMAN I.,A GUIDE TO CURRENT LATIN AMERICAN PERIODICALS: HUMANITIES AND SOCIAL SCIENCES. LABOR SECT EDU/PROP...GEOG HUM SOC LING STAT NAT/COMP 20. PAGE 173 H3456
BIBLIOG/A DIPLOM L/A+17C PHIL/SCI

S61
FITZGIBBON R.H.,"MEASUREMENT OF LATIN AMERICAN POLITICAL CHANGE." L/A+17C CONSTN CULTURE SOCIETY ECO/UNDEV NAT/G POL/PAR PUB/INST ACT/RES EDU/PROP PERCEPT KNOWL ORD/FREE SOVEREIGN...METH/CNCPT TREND OAS 20. PAGE 51 H1020
CHOOSE ATTIT

S61
NEEDLER M.C.,"THE POLITICAL DEVELOPMENT OF MEXICO." STRUCT NAT/G ADMIN RIGID/FLEX...TIME/SEQ TREND MEXIC/AMER TOT/POP VAL/FREE 19/20. PAGE 116 H2328
L/A+17C POL/PAR

S61
RANDALL F.B.,"COMMUNISM IN THE HIGH ANDES." L/A+17C PERU USSR SOCIETY PLAN EDU/PROP TOTALISM ATTIT RIGID/FLEX PWR WEALTH...HUM CONCPT GEN/LAWS 20 BOLIV EQUADOR. PAGE 129 H2589
CULTURE DRIVE

B62
THREE PRELIMINARY BIBLIOGRAPHIES OF WORKS RELATED TO THE SOCIAL SCIENCES IN LATIN AMERICA. BRAZIL CULTURE SOCIETY NAT/G PLAN PROB/SOLV...PSY 20 MEXIC/AMER. PAGE 2 H0040
BIBLIOG L/A+17C SOC AGRI

B62
BROWN L.C.,LATIN AMERICA, A BIBLIOGRAPHY. EX/STRUC ADMIN LEAD ATTIT...POLICY 20. PAGE 22 H0445
BIBLIOG L/A+17C DIPLOM NAT/G

B62
DE MADARIAGA S.,L'AMERIQUE LATINE ENTRE L'OURS ET L'AIGLE. L/A+17C SOCIETY NAT/G ECO/TAC EDU/PROP REGION COERCE ATTIT ALL/VALS...MAJORIT TIME/SEQ STERTYP COLD/WAR OAS 20. PAGE 38 H0760
POL/PAR ECO/UNDEV

B62
DEBUYST F.,LAS CLASES SOCIALES EN AMERICA LATINA. L/A+17C SOCIETY STRUCT WORKER EDU/PROP RACE/REL ATTIT HABITAT ROLE...GEOG SOC NAT/COMP SOC/INTEG 20. PAGE 39 H0780
STRATA GP/REL WEALTH

B62
DIAZ J.S.,MANUAL DE BIBLIOGRAFIA DE LA LITERATURA ESPANOLA. PRE/AMER SPAIN ECO/UNDEV DIPLOM LEAD ATTIT...SOC 15/20. PAGE 41 H0820
BIBLIOG L/A+17C NAT/G COLONIAL

B62
ESCUELA SUPERIOR DE ADMIN PUBL,INFORME DEL SEMINARIO SOBRE SERVICIO CIVIL O CARRERA ADMINISTRATIVA. L/A+17C ELITES STRATA CONFER CONTROL GOV/REL INGP/REL SUPEGO 20 CENTRAL/AM CIVIL/SERV. PAGE 47 H0939
ADMIN NAT/G PROB/SOLV ATTIT

B62
JOHNSON J.J.,THE ROLE OF THE MILITARY IN UNDERDEVELOPED COUNTRIES. AFR BURMA INDONESIA ISLAM ISRAEL L/A+17C S/ASIA THAILAND CULTURE ECO/UNDEV KIN PROVS CONSULT ACT/RES COERCE REV DRIVE RIGID/FLEX ORD/FREE...RECORD ANTHOL 20. PAGE 81 H1622
FORCES CONCPT

B62
KIDDER F.E.,THESES ON PAN AMERICAN TOPICS. LAW CULTURE NAT/G SECT DIPLOM HEALTH...ART/METH GEOG SOC 13/20. PAGE 86 H1709
BIBLIOG CHRIST-17C L/A+17C SOCIETY

B62
MARTINS A.F.,REVOLUCAO BRANCA NO CAMPO. L/A+17C SERV/IND DEMAND EFFICIENCY PRODUC...POLICY METH/COMP. PAGE 104 H2070
AGRI ECO/UNDEV TEC/DEV NAT/COMP

S62
BELL W.,"EQUALITY AND ATTITUDES OF ELITES IN JAMAICA" L/A+17C STRATA PWR WEALTH...SOC QU TREND. PAGE 13 H0266
ELITES FUT SOCIETY CULTURE

S62
HYDE D.,"COMMUNISM IN LATIN AMERICA." L/A+17C ECO/DEV NAT/G SECT EDU/PROP ATTIT ALL/VALS MARXISM ...SOC CONCPT TOT/POP COLD/WAR OAS 20. PAGE 76 H1515
COM POL/PAR REV

S62
SPRINGER H.W.,"FEDERATION IN THE CARIBBEAN: AN ATTEMPT THAT FAILED." L/A+17C ECO/UNDEV INT/ORG POL/PAR PROVS LEGIS CREATE PLAN LEGIT ADMIN FEDERAL ATTIT DRIVE PERSON ORD/FREE PWR...POLICY GEOG PSY CONCPT OBS CARIBBEAN CMN/WLTH 20. PAGE 148 H2955
VOL/ASSN NAT/G REGION

B63
BELFRAGE C.,THE MAN AT THE DOOR WITH THE GUN. CUBA L/A+17C NAT/G LEAD PARTIC GP/REL PWR...POLICY 20 CASTRO/F. PAGE 13 H0261
REGION ECO/UNDEV STRUCT ATTIT

B63
BRODOWSKI J.H.,LATIN AMERICA TODAY. CULTURE LEAD ...SOC 20. PAGE 21 H0426
BIBLIOG/A L/A+17C NAT/G DIPLOM

B63
CANELAS O.A.,RADIOGRAFIA DE LA ALIANZA PARA EL ATRASO. L/A+17C USA+45 ECO/TAC DOMIN COLONIAL NAT/LISM...SOCIALIST NAT/COMP 20. PAGE 26 H0519
REV DIPLOM ECO/UNDEV REGION

B63
COMISION DE HISTORIO,GUIA DE LOS DOCUMENTOS MICROFOTOGRAFIADOS POR LA UNIDAD MOVIL DE LA UNESCO. SOCIETY ECO/UNDEV INT/ORG ADMIN...SOC 20 UNESCO. PAGE 32 H0637
BIBLIOG NAT/G L/A+17C DIPLOM

B63
DE VRIES E.,SOCIAL ASPECTS OF ECONOMIC DEVELOPMENT IN LATIN AMERICA. CULTURE SOCIETY STRATA FINAN INDUS INT/ORG DELIB/GP ACT/RES ECO/TAC EDU/PROP ADMIN ATTIT SUPEGO HEALTH KNOWL ORD/FREE...SOC STAT TREND ANTHOL TOT/POP VAL/FREE. PAGE 39 H0777
L/A+17C ECO/UNDEV

B63
FURTADO C.,THE ECONOMIC GROWTH OF BRAZIL: A SURVEY FROM COLONIAL TO MODERN TIMES. L/A+17C AGRI DIST/IND EXTR/IND INDUS WORKER COLONIAL RACE/REL OWN GOV/COMP. PAGE 54 H1082
ECO/UNDEV TEC/DEV LABOR DOMIN

B63
GLADE W.P. JR.,THE POLITICAL ECONOMY OF MEXICO. FUT L/A+17C CULTURE SOCIETY AGRI INDUS DELIB/GP ACT/RES ECO/TAC ATTIT HEALTH ORD/FREE...STAT TIME/SEQ TREND MEXIC/AMER TOT/POP VAL/FREE 20. PAGE 57 H1138
FINAN ECO/UNDEV

B63
O'LEARY T.J.,ETHNOGRAPHIC BIBLIOGRAPHY OF SOUTH AMERICA. SOCIETY KIN...GEOG 19/20 SOUTH/AMER. PAGE 120 H2389
SOC CULTURE L/A+17C BIBLIOG

B63
PEREZ ORTIZ R.,ANUARIO BIBLIOGRAFICO COLOMBIANO, 1961. AGRI...INT/LAW JURID SOC LING 20 COLOMB. PAGE 125 H2491
BIBLIOG L/A+17C NAT/G

B63
RONNING C.N.,LAW AND POLITICS IN INTER-AMERICAN DIPLOMACY. L/A+17C ECO/UNDEV NAT/G CONSULT DELIB/GP CREATE CAP/ISM ECO/TAC LEGIT REGION RIGID/FLEX ...METH/CNCPT GEN/LAWS OAS 20. PAGE 133 H2668
VOL/ASSN ALL/VALS DIPLOM

B63
SCHECHTMAN J.B.,THE REFUGEE IN THE WORLD: DISPLACEMENT AND INTEGRATION. AFR ASIA EUR+WWI ISLAM L/A+17C S/ASIA CULTURE STRATA LOC/G EX/STRUC PLAN ECO/TAC ROUTINE...CONCPT TIME/SEQ VAL/FREE 20. PAGE 139 H2779
INT/ORG SOC

B63
WAGLEY C.,INTRODUCTION TO BRAZIL. BRAZIL L/A+17C FAM KIN SCHOOL SECT ATTIT WEALTH...GEOG SOC. PAGE 164 H3286
ECO/UNDEV ELITES HABITAT STRATA

L63
CORWIN A.F.,"CONTEMPORARY MEXICAN ATTITUDES TOWARD POPULATION, POVERTY, AND PUBLIC OPINION." L/A+17C CULTURE SOCIETY ACT/RES ECO/TAC EDU/PROP PERSON HEALTH KNOWL...GEOG PHIL/SCI STAT OBS INT SAMP MEXIC/AMER VAL/FREE 20. PAGE 34 H0672
ATTIT QU

S63
DEUTSCHMANN P.J.,"THE MASS MEDIA IN AN UNDERDEVELOPED VILLAGE." L/A+17C EDU/PROP PERCEPT KNOWL ORD/FREE...SOC INT VAL/FREE 20. PAGE 40 H0809
COM/IND CULTURE

S63
GILLIN J.P.,"POSSIBLE CULTURAL MALADJUSTMENT IN MODERN LATIN AMERICA." ATTIT ORD/FREE...SOC TREND GEN/LAWS 20. PAGE 56 H1128
L/A+17C CULTURE

S63
LAMBERT D.,"LA TRANSPOSITION DU REGIME PRESIDENTIEL HORS DES ETATSUNIS; LE CAS DE L'AMERIQUE LATINE." NAT/G EX/STRUC LEGIS PARL/PROC PWR 18/20 PRESIDENT CENTRAL/AM SOUTH/AMER. PAGE 90 H1800
DELIB/GP CHIEF L/A+17C GOV/REL

S63
POPPINO R.E.,"IMBALANCE IN BRAZIL." L/A+17C NAT/G TOP/EX PLAN DIPLOM LEGIT DRIVE WEALTH...CON/ANAL LAFTA 20. PAGE 127 H2544
POL/PAR ECO/TAC BRAZIL

S63
WELLS H.,"THE OAS AND THE DOMINICAN ELECTIONS." L/A+17C INT/ORG NAT/G POL/PAR TEC/DEV ECO/TAC EDU/PROP PERCEPT...TIME/SEQ OAS TOT/POP 20. PAGE 166 H3332
CONSULT CHOOSE DOMIN/REP

B64
ANDREWS D.H.,LATIN AMERICA: A BIBLIOGRAPHY OF PAPERBACK BOOKS. SECT INT/TRADE EDU/PROP WAR GOV/REL ADJUST NAT/LISM ATTIT...ART/METH LING BIOG 20. PAGE 7 H0138
BIBLIOG L/A+17C CULTURE NAT/G

B64
BERNSTEIN H.,A BOOKSHELF ON BRAZIL. BRAZIL ADMIN COLONIAL...HUM JURID SOC 20. PAGE 16 H0315
BIBLIOG/A NAT/G L/A+17C ECO/UNDEV

B64
BERNSTEIN H.,VENEZUELA AND COLOMBIA. L/A+17C VENEZUELA INTELL COLONIAL ATTIT 20 COLOMB. PAGE 16 H0316
CULTURE NAT/LISM LEAD

B64
CORFO,CHILE, A SELECTED BIBLIOGRAPHY IN ENGLISH (PAMPHLET). CHILE DIPLOM...SOC 20. PAGE 33 H0669
BIBLIOG NAT/G POLICY L/A+17C

B64
HARRIS M.,PATTERNS OF RACE IN THE AMERICAS. BRAZIL L/A+17C STRATA ECO/UNDEV AGRI KIN MUNIC SECT COLONIAL RACE/REL...SOC SOC/INTEG 17/20 NEGRO INDIAN/AM. PAGE 67 H1342
STRUCT PRE/AMER CULTURE SOCIETY

B64
HOROWITZ I.L.,REVOLUTION IN BRAZIL. BRAZIL L/A+17C ELITES STRATA NAT/G BAL/PWR PARTIC ATTIT 20. PAGE 74 H1473
ECO/UNDEV DIPLOM POLICY ORD/FREE

B64
IBERO-AMERICAN INSTITUTES,IBEROAMERICANA. STRUCT ADMIN SOC. PAGE 76 H1519
BIBLIOG L/A+17C NAT/G DIPLOM

B64
INTL CONF ON POPULATION,POPULATION DYNAMICS: INTERNATIONAL ACTION AND TRAINING PROGRAMS. INDIA KOREA L/A+17C TAIWAN USA+45 WOR+45 FAM PLAN CONFER ...NEW/IDEA ANTHOL 20 CHINJAP BIRTH/CON. PAGE 78 H1561
NAT/COMP CONTROL ATTIT EDU/PROP

B64
JOHNSON J.J.,CONTINUITY AND CHANGE IN LATIN AMERICA. L/A+17C INTELL FORCES WORKER CIVMIL/REL CHINJAP. PAGE 81 H1623
ANTHOL CULTURE STRATA GP/COMP

B64
LEWIN P.,THE FOREIGN TRADE OF COMMUNIST CHINA* ITS IMPACT ON THE FREE WORLD. AFR EUR+WWI L/A+17C S/ASIA ECO/UNDEV CREATE FOR/AID...STAT NET/THEORY TREND CHARTS. PAGE 96 H1910
ASIA INT/TRADE NAT/COMP USSR

B64
LIEVWEN E.,GENERALS VS PRESIDENTS: WEOMILITARISM IN LATIN AMERICA. L/A+17C FORCES DIPLOM FOR/AID LEAD ...NAT/COMP 20 PRESIDENT. PAGE 97 H1929
CIVMIL/REL REV CONSERVE ORD/FREE

B64
MAIER J.,POLITICS OF CHANGE IN LATIN AMERICA. BRAZIL L/A+17C STRATA INT/ORG NAT/G POL/PAR FOR/AID REV 20. PAGE 101 H2019
SOCIETY NAT/LISM DIPLOM REGION

B64
MARTINEZ J.R.,THREE CASES OF COMMUNISM: CUBA, BRAZIL, AND MEXICO. BRAZIL CUBA L/A+17C CONSTN NAT/G DIPLOM ECO/TAC GP/REL INGP/REL...GP/COMP BIBLIOG 20 MEXIC/AMER COM/PARTY. PAGE 103 H2068
MARXISM BIOG REV NAT/COMP

B64
MUSEUM FUR VOLKERKUNDE WIEN,ZENTRALAMERIKA MEXIKO VOLKER UND KULTUREN. COSTA/RICA GUATEMALA L/A+17C PANAMA SECT WAR GP/REL SOVEREIGN...ART/METH 20 CENTRAL/AM MEXIC/AMER. PAGE 115 H2300
SOCIETY STRUCT CULTURE AGRI

B64
MUSSO AMBROSI L.A.,BIBLIOGRAFIA DE BIBLIOGRAFIAS URUGUAYAS. URUGUAY DIPLOM ADMIN ATTIT...SOC 20. PAGE 115 H2301
BIBLIOG NAT/G L/A+17C PRESS

B64
PERAZA SARAUSA F.,DIRECTORIO DE REVISTAS Y PERIODICOS DE CUBA. CUBA L/A+17C NAT/G ATTIT 20. PAGE 125 H2490
BIBLIOG/A PRESS SERV/IND LEAD

B64
PIKE F.B.,THE CONFLICT BETWEEN CHURCH AND STATE IN LATIN AMERICA. L/A+17C CULTURE SOCIETY STRATA DOMIN EDU/PROP LEGIT COERCE ATTIT ORD/FREE PWR WEALTH ...CONCPT TIME/SEQ TREND VAL/FREE. PAGE 125 H2510
SECT NAT/G

B64
POWELSON J.P.,LATIN AMERICA: TODAY'S ECONOMIC AND
ECO/UNDEV

SOCIAL REVOLUTION. L/A+17C INTELL SOCIETY STRUCT AGRI INDUS NAT/G DIPLOM ECO/TAC REV...POLICY 20. PAGE 128 H2552
WEALTH ADJUST PLAN

B64
TEPASKE J.J.,EXPLOSIVE FORCES IN LATIN AMERICA. CULTURE INTELL ECO/UNDEV INT/ORG NAT/G SECT FORCES ECO/TAC EDU/PROP PWR WEALTH SOC. PAGE 153 H3063
L/A+17C RIGID/FLEX FOR/AID USSR

B64
THORNTON T.P.,THE THIRD WORLD IN SOVIET PERSPECTIVE: STUDIES BY SOVIET WRITERS ON THE DEVELOPING AREAS. AFR L/A+17C S/ASIA STRATA AGRI INDUS MARKET NAT/G POL/PAR ECO/TAC COLONIAL PERCEPT PWR WEALTH...MARXIST STAT CHARTS WORK MARX/KARL 20. PAGE 155 H3090
ECO/UNDEV ACT/RES USSR DIPLOM

B64
TURNER M.C.,LIBROS EN VENTA EN HISPANOAMERICA Y ESPANA. SPAIN LAW CONSTN CULTURE ADMIN LEAD...HUM SOC 20. PAGE 157 H3141
BIBLIOG L/A+17C NAT/G DIPLOM

B64
URQUIDI V.L.,THE CHALLENGE OF DEVELOPMENT IN LATIN AMERICA. L/A+17C FINAN INT/ORG TEC/DEV DIPLOM INT/TRADE PRICE REGION PRODUC...CHARTS 20. PAGE 159 H3175
ECO/UNDEV ECO/TAC NAT/G TREND

B64
WHITEFORD A.H.,TWO CITIES OF LATIN AMERICA: A COMPARATIVE DESCRIPTION OF SOCIAL CLASSES. L/A+17C CULTURE SOCIETY MUNIC DOMIN LEGIT ATTIT ALL/VALS ...STAT OBS VAL/FREE 20. PAGE 167 H3352
STRATA SOC

L64
BERELSON B.,"SAMPLE SURVEYS AND POPULATION CONTROL." ASIA FUT ISLAM L/A+17C CULTURE SOCIETY FAM NAT/G CONSULT PLAN EDU/PROP ATTIT DRIVE ALL/VALS...POLICY RELATIV HEAL PSY SOC CONCPT METH/CNCPT OBS OBS/ENVIR TOT/POP. PAGE 15 H0297
BIO/SOC SAMP

L64
HAAS E.B.,"ECONOMICS AND DIFFERENTIAL PATTERNS OF POLITICAL INTEGRATION: PROJECTIONS ABOUT UNITY IN LATIN AMERICA." SOCIETY NAT/G DELIB/GP ACT/RES CREATE PLAN ECO/TAC REGION ROUTINE ATTIT DRIVE PWR WEALTH...CONCPT TREND CHARTS LAFTA 20. PAGE 63 H1266
L/A+17C INT/ORG MARKET

S64
ADAMS R.,"POLITICS AND SOCIAL ANTHROPOLOGY IN SPANISH AMERICA." FUT CULTURE SOCIETY NAT/G PROF/ORG EDU/PROP ATTIT RIGID/FLEX ALL/VALS ...POLICY GEOG METH/CNCPT MYTH TREND VAL/FREE 20. PAGE 3 H0065
L/A+17C SOC

S64
CATTELL D.T.,"SOVIET POLICIES IN LATIN AMERICA." COM CUBA L/A+17C USSR SOCIETY NAT/G POL/PAR FORCES CREATE ECO/TAC EDU/PROP REGION REV RIGID/FLEX ...GEN/LAWS COLD/WAR 20. PAGE 28 H0560
DRIVE PWR

S64
JOHNSON K.F.,"CAUSAL FACTORS IN LATIN AMERICAN POLITICAL INSTABILITY." CULTURE NAT/G VOL/ASSN EX/STRUC FORCES EDU/PROP LEGIT ADMIN COERCE REV ATTIT KNOWL PWR...STYLE RECORD CHARTS WORK 20. PAGE 81 H1624
L/A+17C PERCEPT ELITES

S64
NASH M.,"SOCIAL PREREQUISITES TO ECONOMIC GROWTH IN LATIN AMERICA AND SOUTHEAST ASIA." L/A+17C S/ASIA CULTURE SOCIETY ECO/UNDEV AGRI INDUS NAT/G PLAN TEC/DEV EDU/PROP ROUTINE ALL/VALS...POLICY RELATIV SOC NAT/COMP WORK TOT/POP 20. PAGE 116 H2314
ECO/DEV PERCEPT

C64
SCOTT R.E.,"MEXICAN GOVERNMENT IN TRANSITION (REV ED)" CULTURE STRUCT POL/PAR CHIEF ADMIN LOBBY REV CHOOSE GP/REL DRIVE...BIBLIOG METH 20 MEXIC/AMER. PAGE 141 H2816
NAT/G L/A+17C ROUTINE CONSTN

B65
AIR UNIVERSITY LIBRARY,LATIN AMERICA, SELECTED REFERENCES. ECO/UNDEV FORCES EDU/PROP MARXISM 20 OAS. PAGE 4 H0084
BIBLIOG L/A+17C NAT/G DIPLOM

B65
ALEXANDER R.J.,ORGANIZED LABOR IN LATIN AMERICA. L/A+17C INT/ORG LEGIS WORKER TEC/DEV BARGAIN INT/TRADE REV...NAT/COMP BIBLIOG 20. PAGE 5 H0102
LABOR POL/PAR ECO/UNDEV POLICY

B65
APTER D.E.,THE POLITICS OF MODERNIZATION. AFR L/A+17C CULTURE NAT/G POL/PAR ADMIN COLONIAL NAT/LISM ATTIT RIGID/FLEX PWR...SOC CONCPT. PAGE 8 H0154
ECO/UNDEV GEN/LAWS STRATA CREATE

B65
CHANDLER M.J.,A GUIDE TO RECORDS IN BARBADOS. WEST/IND PUB/INST SCHOOL SECT...HIST/WRIT 20. PAGE 28 H0573
BIBLIOG LOC/G L/A+17C NAT/G

B65
FAGG J.E.,CUBA, HAITI, AND THE DOMINICAN REPUBLIC. CUBA DOMIN/REP HAITI L/A+17C NAT/G DIPLOM ECO/TAC DOMIN CHOOSE AUTHORIT ROLE SOVEREIGN POPULISM 17/20. PAGE 48 H0959
COLONIAL ECO/UNDEV REV GOV/COMP

B65
FORM W.H.,INDUSTRIAL RELATIONS AND SOCIAL CHANGE IN LATIN AMERICA. L/A+17C AGRI LABOR NAT/G PLAN PROB/SOLV DIPLOM...MGT SOC ANTHOL BIBLIOG/A METH 20. PAGE 52 H1038
INDUS GP/REL NAT/COMP ECO/UNDEV

B65
GREGG J.L.,POLITICAL PARTIES AND PARTY SYSTEMS IN GUATEMALA, 1944-1963. GUATEMALA L/A+17C EX/STRUC FORCES CREATE CONTROL REV CHOOSE PWR...TREND IDEA/COMP 20. PAGE 60 H1209
LEAD POL/PAR NAT/G CHIEF

B65
HAMIL H.M.,DICTATORSHIP IN SPANISH AMERICA. NAT/G COERCE MORAL ORD/FREE...POLICY PSY SOC ANTHOL 18/20. PAGE 65 H1300
TOTALISM CHIEF L/A+17C FASCISM

B65
HARBISON F.,MANPOWER AND EDUCATION. AFR CHINA/COM IRAN L/A+17C S/ASIA TEC/DEV ADJUST OPTIMAL SKILL ...ANTHOL 20. PAGE 66 H1325
ECO/UNDEV EDU/PROP WORKER NAT/COMP

B65
HISPANIC SOCIETY OF AMERICA,CATALOGUE (10 VOLS.). PORTUGAL PRE/AMER SPAIN NAT/G ADMIN...POLICY SOC 15/20. PAGE 71 H1426
BIBLIOG L/A+17C COLONIAL DIPLOM

B65
IANNI O.,ESTADO E CAPITALISMO. L/A+17C FINAN TEC/DEV ECO/TAC ORD/FREE WEALTH POLICY. PAGE 76 H1518
ECO/UNDEV STRUCT INDUS NAT/G

B65
RODRIGUEZ M.,CENTRAL AMERICA. COSTA/RICA GUATEMALA L/A+17C NICARAGUA DIPLOM COLONIAL REGION NAT/LISM ALL/IDEOS SOCISM...MAJORIT TIME/SEQ BIBLIOG 19/20. PAGE 133 H2656
CULTURE NAT/COMP NAT/G ECO/UNDEV

B65
SABLE M.H.,MASTER DIRECTORY FOR LATIN AMERICA. AGRI COM/IND FINAN R+D ACADEM LABOR NAT/G POL/PAR VOL/ASSN INT/TRADE EDU/PROP 20. PAGE 136 H2728
INDEX L/A+17C INT/ORG DIPLOM

B65
SLATER J.,A REVALUATION OF COLLECTIVE SECURITY* THE OAS IN ACTION. L/A+17C USA+45 NAT/G ADMIN COERCE ORD/FREE PWR...GOV/COMP IDEA/COMP GEN/LAWS OAS. PAGE 145 H2899
REGION INT/ORG FORCES

L65
WIONCZEK M.,"LATIN AMERICA FREE TRADE ASSOCIATION." AGRI DIST/IND FINAN INDUS INT/ORG LABOR NAT/G TEC/DEV ECO/TAC HEALTH SKILL WEALTH...POLICY RELATIV MGT LAFTA 20. PAGE 169 H3390
L/A+17C MARKET REGION

S65
BRANDENBURG F.,"THE RELEVANCE OF MEXICAN EXPERIENCE TO LATIN AMERICAN DEVELOPMENT." BRAZIL CHILE VENEZUELA STRUCT ECO/UNDEV AGRI CREATE ECO/TAC ...STAT RECORD MEXIC/AMER ARGEN COLOMB. PAGE 20 H0405
L/A+17C GOV/COMP

S65
MARK M.,"MUST WE FIGHT SOCIAL REVOLUTIONS OF THE LEFT?" L/A+17C USA+45 ECO/UNDEV DIPLOM ADJUST PERCEPT...IDEA/COMP NAT/COMP. PAGE 103 H2053
NAT/LISM REV MARXISM CREATE

S65
MCALISTER L.N.,"CHANGING CONCEPTS OF THE ROLE OF THE MILITARY IN LATIN AMERICA." CULTURE NAT/G CREATE REGION NAT/LISM ATTIT SOVEREIGN...NAT/COMP GEN/LAWS. PAGE 106 H2120
L/A+17C FORCES IDEA/COMP PWR

S65
POWELL J.D.,"MILITARY ASSISTANCE AND MILITARISM IN LATIN AMERICA." USA+45 INT/ORG NAT/G CONTROL REGION PRODUC WEALTH...CLASSIF STAT NAT/COMP CONGRESS. PAGE 128 H2550
L/A+17C FORCES FOR/AID PWR

S65
WOLF C. JR.,"THE POLITICAL EFFECTS OF SOME MILITARY PROGRAMS* SOME INDICATIONS FROM LATIN AMERICA." ELITES STRATA BUDGET FOR/AID WEAPON ATTIT PERCEPT PWR...REGRESS SYS/QU CHARTS NAT/COMP. PAGE 170 H3397
L/A+17C FORCES CIVMIL/REL PROBABIL

B66
BROWN R.T.,TRANSPORT AND THE ECONOMIC INTEGRATION OF SOUTH AMERICA. L/A+17C ECO/UNDEV NAT/G OP/RES DIPLOM INT/TRADE REGION WEALTH...ECOMETRIC GEOG STAT LAFTA TIME. PAGE 22 H0449
MARKET DIST/IND SIMUL

B66
CANNING HOUSE LIBRARY,AUTHOR AND SUBJECT CATALOGUES OF THE CANNING HOUSE LIBRARY (5 VOLS.). UK CULTURE LEAD...SOC 19/20. PAGE 26 H0520
BIBLIOG L/A+17C NAT/G DIPLOM

B66
HANKE L.,HANDBOOK OF LATIN AMERICAN STUDIES. ECO/UNDEV ADMIN LEAD...HUM SOC 20. PAGE 65 H1313
BIBLIOG/A L/A+17C INDEX NAT/G

B66
MASUR G.,NATIONALISM IN LATIN AMERICA* DIVERSITY AND UNITY. CHRIST-17C PRE/AMER ELITES ECO/UNDEV CREATE DIPLOM INT/TRADE COLONIAL REV SOVEREIGN SOC.
L/A+17C NAT/LISM CULTURE

PAGE 105 H2089

B66
US DEPARTMENT OF STATE,RESEARCH ON THE AMERICAN REPUBLICS (EXTERNAL RESEARCH LIST NO 6-25). CULTURE SOCIETY POL/PAR DIPLOM EDU/PROP MARXISM WORSHIP 20 OAS. PAGE 159 H3189 BIBLIOG/A L/A+17C REGION NAT/G

B66
WHITAKER A.P.,NATIONALISM IN CONTEMPORARY LATIN AMERICA. AGRI NAT/G WEALTH...POLICY SOC CONCPT OBS TREND 20. PAGE 167 H3344 NAT/LISM L/A+17C DIPLOM ECO/UNDEV

B66
ZABLOCKI C.J.,SINO-SOVIET RIVALRY. AFR ASIA CHINA/COM CUBA EUR+WWI L/A+17C USA+45 USSR WOR+45 POL/PAR FORCES COERCE NUC/PWR...GOV/COMP IDEA/COMP 20 MAO KHRUSH/N. PAGE 172 H3444 DIPLOM MARXISM COM

S66
LODGE G.C.,"REVOLUTION IN LATIN AMERICA." USA+45 ELITES INDUS LABOR PROF/ORG SECT TEC/DEV CAP/ISM SKILL MARXISM...POLICY NAT/COMP. PAGE 98 H1950 ATTIT REV L/A+17C IDEA/COMP

S66
MARTZ J.D.,"THE PLACE OF LATIN AMERICA IN THE STUDY OF COMPARATIVE POLITICS." AFR ASIA CULTURE STRUCT ECO/UNDEV ACADEM CREATE...CLASSIF NAT/COMP. PAGE 104 H2072 L/A+17C GOV/COMP STERTYP GEN/LAWS

S66
MERRITT R.L.,"SELECTED ARTICLES AND DOCUMENTS ON COMPARATIVE GOVERNMENT AND CROSS-NATIONAL RESEARCH." AFR ASIA EUR+WWI L/A+17C MOD/EUR ELITES R+D ACT/RES DIPLOM PWR...SOC CONCPT 18/20. PAGE 109 H2185 BIBLIOG GOV/COMP NAT/G GOV/REL

S66
SNOW P.G.,"A SCALOGRAM ANALYSIS OF POLITICAL DEVELOPMENT." STRATA ECO/UNDEV POL/PAR REGION ALL/VALS PWR...SOC CHARTS. PAGE 146 H2924 L/A+17C NAT/COMP TESTS CLASSIF

S66
TOUVAL S.,"AFRICA'S FRONTIERS* REACTIONS TO A COLONIAL LEGACY." L/A+17C CONFER ADJUD COLONIAL APPORT CONSEN NAT/LISM RESPECT...RECORD NAT/COMP. PAGE 156 H3120 AFR GEOG SOVEREIGN WAR

N66
HISPANIC LUSO-BRAZILIAN COUN,LATIN AMERICA; AN INTRODUCTION TO MODERN BOOKS IN ENGLISH CONCERNING THE COUNTRIES OF LATIN AMERICA (2ND ED., PAMPH). CULTURE GOV/REL GEOG. PAGE 71 H1425 BIBLIOG/A ECO/UNDEV NAT/G L/A+17C

B67
ANDERSON C.W.,POLITICS AND ECONOMIC CHANGE IN LATIN AMERICA. L/A+17C INDUS NAT/G OP/RES ADMIN DEMAND ...POLICY STAT CHARTS NAT/COMP 20. PAGE 6 H0125 ECO/UNDEV PROB/SOLV PLAN ECO/TAC

B67
BURR R.N.,OUR TROUBLED HEMISPHERE: PERSPECTIVES ON UNITED STATES-LATIN AMERICAN RELATIONS. L/A+17C USA+45 USA-45 INT/ORG FOR/AID COLONIAL PWR 19/20 OAS. PAGE 25 H0493 DIPLOM NAT/COMP NAT/G POLICY

B67
DIX R.H.,COLOMBIA: THE POLITICAL DIMENSIONS OF CHANGE. ELITES POL/PAR DOMIN REV...AUD/VIS 20 COLOMB. PAGE 41 H0828 L/A+17C NAT/G TEC/DEV LEAD

B67
LAMBERT J.,LATIN AMERICA: SOCIAL STRUCTURES AND POLITICAL INSTITUTIONS. STRUCT TEC/DEV DIPLOM ADMIN COLONIAL LEAD ATTIT...SOC CLASSIF NAT/COMP 17/20. PAGE 90 H1801 L/A+17C NAT/G ECO/UNDEV SOCIETY

B67
NASH M.,MACHINE AGE MAYA. GUATEMALA L/A+17C STRUCT AGRI WORKER CREATE INCOME ATTIT RIGID/FLEX ROLE ...IDEA/COMP SOC/EXP WORSHIP 20 INDIAN/AM. PAGE 116 H2315 INDUS CULTURE SOC MUNIC

B67
PIKE F.B.,FREEDOM AND REFORM IN LATIN AMERICA. BRAZIL URUGUAY CONSTN CULTURE SECT DIPLOM EDU/PROP PARTIC DRIVE ALL/VALS CATHISM...GEOG ANTHOL BIBLIOG REFORMERS BOLIV. PAGE 126 H2511 L/A+17C ORD/FREE ECO/UNDEV REV

B67
PLANK J.,CUBA AND THE UNITED STATES: LONG RANGE PERSPECTIVES. CUBA L/A+17C USSR ECO/UNDEV NAT/G FORCES ECO/TAC INT/TRADE AGREE REV...PREDICT TREND ANTHOL 20 CASTRO/F COLD/WAR OAS. PAGE 126 H2520 DIPLOM

L67
EINAUDI L.,"ANNOTATED BIBLIOGRAPHY OF LATIN AMERICAN MILITARY JOURNALS" LAW TEC/DEV DOMIN EDU/PROP COERCE WAR CIVMIL/REL 20. PAGE 45 H0899 BIBLIOG/A NAT/G FORCES L/A+17C

L67
LATIN AMERICAN STUDIES ASSN,"RESEARCH ON EDUCATION IN LATIN AMERICA." L/A+17C NAT/G HABITAT...GOV/COMP ANTHOL 20. PAGE 92 H1836 EDU/PROP SCHOOL ACADEM R+D

L67
ROTH A.R.,"CAPITAL-MARKET DEVELOPMENT IN ISRAEL AND BRAZIL: TWO EXAMPLES OF THE ROLE OF LAW IN DEVELOPMENT." BRAZIL ISRAEL L/A+17C INDUS MARKET ECO/TAC FOR/AID INT/TRADE CONTROL BAL/PAY 20. PAGE 135 H2694 LAW ECO/UNDEV NAT/COMP FINAN

L67
RUTH J.M.,"THE ADMINISTRATION OF WATER RESOURCES IN GUATEMALA." GUATEMALA L/A+17C DIST/IND LOC/G NAT/G EX/STRUC ADMIN GOV/REL DEMAND EQUILIB WEALTH...GEOG MGT 20. PAGE 136 H2723 EFFICIENCY ECO/UNDEV PLAN ACT/RES

L67
SEGAL A.,"THE INTEGRATION OF DEVELOPING COUNTRIES: SOME THOUGHTS ON EAST AFRICA AND CENTRAL AMERICA." AFR L/A+17C INT/ORG NAT/G VOL/ASSN FOR/AID INT/TRADE EQUILIB NAT/LISM PWR 20. PAGE 141 H2820 ECO/UNDEV DIPLOM REGION

L67
TABORSKY E.,"THE COMMUNIST PARTIES OF THE 'THIRD WORLD' IN SOVIET STRATEGY." AFR ASIA L/A+17C USSR INTELL NAT/G WORKER PLAN CONTROL LEAD PARTIC REV ...GOV/COMP 20 COM/PARTY THIRD/WRLD. PAGE 152 H3032 POL/PAR MARXISM ECO/UNDEV DIPLOM

L67
WRIGHT W.R.,"FOREIGN-OWNED RAILWAYS IN ARGENTINA: A CASE STUDY OF ECONOMIC NATIONALISM." L/A+17C UK ECO/UNDEV SERV/IND LG/CO NAT/G TEC/DEV BAL/PWR EQUILIB ARGEN. PAGE 171 H3423 NAT/LISM CAP/ISM ECO/TAC COLONIAL

S67
ADAMS R.N.,"ETHICS AND THE SOCIAL ANTHROPOLOGIST IN LATIN AMERICA." USA+45 INTELL PROB/SOLV ECO/TAC LEAD...DECISION SOC NAT/COMP PERS/COMP. PAGE 3 H0066 L/A+17C POLICY ECO/UNDEV CONSULT

S67
BAER W.,"THE INFLATION CONTROVERSY IN LATIN AMERICA: SURVEY." L/A+17C ECO/UNDEV AGRI FINAN INDUS PLAN PROB/SOLV TEC/DEV...BIBLIOG/A 20. PAGE 10 H0194 NAT/G BAL/PAY ECO/TAC BUDGET

S67
BRANCO R.,"LAND REFORM* THE ANSWER TO LATIN AMERICA'S AGRICULTURAL DEVELOPMENT?" L/A+17C NAT/G PLAN TEC/DEV BUDGET RENT EFFICIENCY 20. PAGE 20 H0404 ECO/UNDEV AGRI TAX OWN

S67
COHEN A.,"REVOLUTION IN ARGENTINA?" L/A+17C NAT/G POL/PAR CHIEF PROB/SOLV ECO/TAC 20 ARGEN. PAGE 31 H0615 REV ECO/UNDEV CONTROL BIOG

S67
COLLINS B.A.,"SOME NOTES ON PUBLIC SERVICE COMMISSIONS IN THE COMMONWEALTH CARIBBEAN." JAMAICA L/A+17C TRINIDAD UK NAT/G OP/RES DOMIN SENIOR COLONIAL CONTROL INGP/REL CENTRAL EFFICIENCY PWR ...DECISION 20. PAGE 31 H0631 ADMIN EX/STRUC ECO/UNDEV CHOOSE

S67
CUMMINS L.,"THE FORMULATION OF THE "PLATT" AMENDMENT." CUBA L/A+17C NAT/G DELIB/GP CONFER ...POLICY 20. PAGE 36 H0720 DIPLOM INT/LAW LEGIS

S67
DANA MONTANO S.M.,"APLICACIONES CONCRETAS DE LAS RESOLUCIONES Y RECOMENDACIONES DE LAS CONFERENCIAS INTERAMERICANAS DE ABOGADOS" L/A+17C NAT/G PROVS GOV/REL PERCEPT 20 ARGEN. PAGE 37 H0739 JURID CT/SYS ORD/FREE BAL/PWR

S67
GONZALEZ M.P.,"CUBA, UNA REVOLUCION EN MARCHA." CUBA L/A+17C USA+45 VIETNAM ECO/UNDEV FORCES DIPLOM DOMIN...POLICY MARXIST NAT/COMP CASTRO/F. PAGE 58 H1163 REV NAT/G COLONIAL SOVEREIGN

S67
GOODSELL J.N.,"BALAGUER'S DOMINICAN REPUBLIC." DOMIN/REP FUT L/A+17C POL/PAR PROB/SOLV ECO/TAC 20. PAGE 59 H1174 ECO/UNDEV CHIEF POLICY NAT/G

S67
GRAHAM R.,"BRAZIL'S DILEMMA." BRAZIL FUT L/A+17C NAT/G CHIEF PROB/SOLV ECO/TAC PWR 20. PAGE 60 H1193 ECO/UNDEV CONSTN POL/PAR POLICY

S67
GRANT C.H.,"RURAL LOCAL GOVERNMENT IN GUYANA AND BRITISH HONDURAS." GUYANA HONDURAS L/A+17C AGRI NAT/G EX/STRUC ACT/RES REGION GOV/REL EFFICIENCY ORD/FREE 20. PAGE 60 H1196 ECO/UNDEV LOC/G ADMIN MUNIC

S67
GRIEB K.J.,"THE UNITED STATES AND THE CENTRAL AMERICAN CONFEDERATION." COSTA/RICA EL/SALVADR GUATEMALA HONDURAS L/A+17C NICARAGUA NAT/G FORCES CONFER AGREE EXEC ARMS/CONT REV WAR PEACE ATTIT 20. PAGE 60 H1212 INT/ORG DIPLOM POLICY REGION

S67
HASSAN M.F.,"THE SECOND FOUR-YEAR PLAN OF VENEZUELA." L/A+17C VENEZUELA AGRI INDUS NAT/G PLAN RATION CONTROL HABITAT...MATH STAT 20. PAGE 67 H1352 ECO/UNDEV FINAN BUDGET PROB/SOLV

S67
HEATH D.B.,"BOLIVIA UNDER BARRIENTOS." L/A+17C NAT/G CHIEF DIPLOM ECO/TAC...POLICY 20 BOLIV. PAGE 69 H1379 ECO/UNDEV POL/PAR REV CONSTN

S67
KROLL M.,"POLITICAL LEADERSHIP AND ADMINISTRATIVE COMMUNICATIONS IN NEW NATION STATES* CASE STUDY OF NAT/G ADMIN

TRINIDAD AND TOBAGO." L/A+17C TRINIDAD INTELL OP/RES DOMIN COLONIAL LEAD GP/REL CENTRAL EFFICIENCY...DECISION OBS METH/COMP 20. PAGE 89 H1774 — EDU/PROP CONTROL

S67
PETRAS J.,"GUERRILLA MOVEMENTS IN LATIN AMERICA - I." GUATEMALA PERU VENEZUELA NAT/G COLONIAL LEAD ATTIT PWR...TIME/SEQ METH/COMP 20 COLOMB. PAGE 125 H2497 — GUERRILLA REV L/A+17C MARXISM

S67
RAMA C.M.,"PASADO Y PRESENTE DE LA RELIGION EN AMERICA LATINA." L/A+17C ELITES SOCIETY STRATA MARXISM...STAT WORSHIP PROTESTANT. PAGE 129 H2585 — SECT CATHISM STRUCT NAT/COMP

S67
SANCHEZ J.D.,"DESARROLLO ECONOMICO Y FUTURO DE COLOMBIA." L/A+17C AGRI EXTR/IND FINAN INDUS MARKET INT/TRADE CONTROL...STAT TREND COLOMB. PAGE 137 H2748 — ECO/UNDEV FUT NAT/G ECO/TAC

S67
TANTER R.,"A THEORY OF REVOLUTION." ASIA CUBA L/A+17C S/ASIA SOCIETY NAT/G ADJUST...CONCPT CHARTS. PAGE 152 H3046 — REV ECO/UNDEV EDU/PROP METH/COMP

S67
TAYLOR P.B. JR.,"PROGRESS IN VENEZUELA." L/A+17C VENEZUELA AGRI INDUS LG/CO NAT/G SML/CO CHOOSE ...POLICY 20. PAGE 153 H3057 — ECO/UNDEV ECO/TAC POL/PAR ORD/FREE

LA BOETIE E. H1790

LA DOCUMENTATION FRANCAISE H1791

LA PONCE J.A. H1793,H1794

LAB/EXP....LABORATORY EXPERIMENTS

B58
SCOTT J.P.,AGGRESSION. CULTURE FAM SCHOOL ATTIT DISPL HEALTH...SOC CONCPT NEW/IDEA CHARTS LAB/EXP. PAGE 141 H2814 — DRIVE PSY WAR

LABEDZ L. H1626,H1795,H1820,H1821

LABOR FORCE....SEE WORKER

LABOR RELATIONS....SEE LABOR, ALSO RELATIONS INDEX

LABOR UNIONS....SEE LABOR

LABOR....LABOR UNIONS (BUT NOT GUILDS)

N
CANADIAN GOVERNMENT PUBLICATIONS (1955-). CANADA AGRI FINAN LABOR FORCES INT/TRADE HEALTH...JURID 20 PARLIAMENT. PAGE 1 H0003 — BIBLIOG/A NAT/G DIPLOM INT/ORG

N
INDIA: A REFERENCE ANNUAL. INDIA CULTURE COM/IND R+D FORCES PLAN RECEIVE EDU/PROP HEALTH...STAT CHARTS BIBLIOG 20. PAGE 1 H0017 — CONSTN LABOR INT/ORG

N
AFRICAN BIBLIOGRAPHIC CENTER,A CURRENT BIBLIOGRAPHY ON AFRICAN AFFAIRS. LAW CULTURE ECO/UNDEV LABOR SECT DIPLOM FOR/AID COLONIAL NAT/LISM...LING 20. PAGE 4 H0075 — BIBLIOG/A AFR NAT/G REGION

N
INTERNATIONAL CENTRE AFRICAN,BULLETIN OF INFORMATION ON THESES AND STUDIES IN PROGRESS OR PROPOSED. LAW CULTURE FINAN INDUS LABOR TEC/DEV EDU/PROP...GEOG SOC NAT/COMP 20. PAGE 78 H1554 — BIBLIOG/A ACT/RES ACADEM INTELL

C06
MONTGOMERY H.,"A DICTIONARY OF POLITICAL PHRASES AND ILLUSIONS WITH A SHORT BIBLIOGRAPHY." EUR+WWI MOD/EUR UK AGRI LABOR LOC/G NAT/G COLONIAL CHOOSE RACE/REL. PAGE 112 H2245 — BIBLIOG DICTIONARY POLICY DIPLOM

B10
MENDELSSOHN S.,SOUTH AFRICAN BIBLIOGRAPHY (2 VOLS.). SOUTH/AFR EXTR/IND LABOR SECT DIPLOM INT/TRADE COLONIAL RACE/REL DISCRIM...GEOG 20. PAGE 109 H2172 — BIBLIOG/A AFR NAT/G NAT/LISM

B14
LEVINE L.,SYNDICALISM IN FRANCE (2ND ED.). FRANCE LAW SOCIETY ECO/DEV NAT/G ECO/TAC LEAD ATTIT ...POLICY CONCPT STAT BIBLIOG 18/20 REFORMERS. PAGE 95 H1902 — LABOR INDUS SOCISM REV

N19
BUSINESS ECONOMISTS' GROUP,INCOME POLICIES (PAMPHLET). UK INDUS LABOR TOP/EX PAY COST PRODUC ...ECOMETRIC GOV/COMP SIMUL ANTHOL 20. PAGE 25 H0497 — INCOME WORKER WEALTH POLICY

N19
INTERNATIONAL LABOUR OFFICE,EMPLOYMENT, UNEMPLOYMENT AND LABOUR FORCE STATISTICS (PAMPHLET). EUR+WWI STRATA AGRI INDUS NAT/G PROB/SOLV PAY AGE SEX...SAMP NAT/COMP METH 20 ILO. PAGE 78 H1557 — WORKER LABOR STAT ECO/DEV

B20
WEBB S.,INDUSTRIAL DEMOCRACY. UK PARTIC GP/REL ...SOC OBS RECORD CHARTS 18/20. PAGE 166 H3317 — LABOR NAT/G VOL/ASSN MAJORIT

B28
BUELL R.,THE NATIVE PROBLEM IN AFRICA. KIN LABOR LOC/G ECO/TAC ROUTINE ORD/FREE...REC/INT KNO/TEST CENSUS TREND CHARTS SOC/EXP STERTYP 20. PAGE 23 H0466 — AFR CULTURE

C28
SCHNEIDER H.W.,"MAKING THE FASCIST STATE." ITALY CULTURE LABOR DIPLOM REV WAR NAT/LISM TOTALISM ATTIT DRIVE SOCISM...BIBLIOG PARLIAMENT 20. PAGE 140 H2792 — FASCISM POLICY POL/PAR

B30
HULL W.I.,INDIA'S POLITICAL CRISIS. INDIA UK INT/ORG LABOR SECT DELIB/GP LEGIS DIPLOM NEUTRAL REGION CROWD GOV/REL MAJORITY ATTIT 20 NEHRU/J GANDHI/M COMMONWLTH. PAGE 75 H1492 — ORD/FREE NAT/G COLONIAL NAT/LISM

B31
CROOK W.H.,THE GENERAL STRIKE: A STUDY OF LABOR'S TRAGIC WEAPON IN THEORY AND PRACTICE. BELGIUM FRANCE SWEDEN UK WOR-45 PROB/SOLV ECO/TAC DOMIN PWR ...POLICY TIME/SEQ NAT/COMP GEN/LAWS 19/20 STRIKE. PAGE 35 H0707 — LABOR WORKER LG/CO BARGAIN

B33
MOSS W.,POLITICAL PARTIES IN THE IRISH FREE STATE. IRELAND UK LAW FINAN LABOR DELIB/GP TOP/EX TARIFFS EDU/PROP...CHARTS GP/COMP 20. PAGE 113 H2269 — POL/PAR NAT/G CHOOSE POLICY

B34
LIPPMANN W.,THE METHOD OF FREEDOM. SOCIETY INDUS LABOR LOBBY WAR REPRESENT...POLICY IDEA/COMP METH/COMP 19/20. PAGE 97 H1936 — CONCPT MAJORIT NAT/G

B35
NORDSKOG J.E.,SOCIAL REFORM IN NORWAY. NORWAY INDUS NAT/G POL/PAR LEGIS ADJUD...SOC BIBLIOG SOC/INTEG 20. PAGE 119 H2371 — LABOR ADJUST

B38
FIELD G.L.,THE SYNDICAL AND CORPORATIVE INSTITUTIONS OF ITALIAN FASCISM. ITALY CONSTN STRATA LABOR EX/STRUC TOP/EX ADJUD ADMIN LEAD TOTALISM AUTHORIT...MGT 20 MUSSOLIN/B. PAGE 50 H0991 — FASCISM INDUS NAT/G WORKER

B38
REICH N.,LABOR RELATIONS IN REPUBLICAN GERMANY. GERMANY CONSTN ECO/DEV INDUS NAT/G ADMIN CONTROL GP/REL FASCISM POPULISM 20 WEIMAR/REP. PAGE 130 H2609 — WORKER MGT LABOR BARGAIN

B39
HITLER A.,MEIN KAMPF. EUR+WWI FUT MOD/EUR STRUCT INT/ORG LABOR NAT/G POL/PAR FORCES CREATE PLAN BAL/PWR DIPLOM ECO/TAC DOMIN EDU/PROP ADMIN COERCE ATTIT...SOCIALIST BIOG TREND NAZI. PAGE 71 H1428 — PWR NEW/IDEA WAR

B39
MARQUAND H.A.,ORGANIZED LABOUR IN FOUR CONTINENTS. EUR+WWI USA-45 INDUS NAT/G PAY GP/REL TOTALISM ATTIT WEALTH ALL/IDEOS...TREND NAT/COMP 20 ILO AFL/CIO EUROPE CHINJAP MEXIC/AMER. PAGE 103 H2055 — LABOR WORKER CONCPT ANTHOL

S39
HECKSCHER G.,"GROUP ORGANIZATION IN SWEDEN." SWEDEN STRATA ECO/DEV AGRI INDUS LABOR NAT/G PROF/ORG ECO/TAC CENTRAL SOCISM...MGT 19/20. PAGE 69 H1382 — LAISSEZ SOC

B40
MCHENRY D.E.,HIS MAJESTY'S OPPOSITION: STRUCTURE AND PROBLEMS OF THE BRITISH LABOUR PARTY 1931-1938. UK FINAN LABOR LOC/G DELIB/GP LEGIS EDU/PROP LEAD PARTIC CHOOSE GP/REL SOCISM...TREND 20 LABOR/PAR. PAGE 107 H2130 — POL/PAR MGT NAT/G POLICY

B40
WUNDERLICH F.,LABOR UNDER GERMAN DEMOCRACY, ARBITRATION 1918-1933. GERMANY NAT/G PAY REPAR ADJUD CT/SYS GP/REL...MAJORIT 20. PAGE 171 H3426 — LABOR WORKER INDUS BARGAIN

B42
CONOVER H.F.,THE NETHERLANDS EAST INDIES: A SELECTED LIST OF REFERENCES. ECO/UNDEV AGRI EXTR/IND LABOR SCHOOL SECT INT/TRADE COLONIAL HEALTH...GEOG 19/20. PAGE 32 H0642 — BIBLIOG S/ASIA CULTURE

B42
CONOVER H.F.,NEW ZEALAND: A SELECTED LIST OF REFERENCES (PAMPHLET). NEW/ZEALND ECO/UNDEV AGRI INDUS LABOR NAT/G SCHOOL FORCES DIPLOM COLONIAL WAR ...HUM 20. PAGE 32 H0643 — BIBLIOG/A S/ASIA CULTURE

B42
ROBBINS J.J.,THE GOVERNMENT OF LABOR RELATIONS IN SWEDEN. SWEDEN LAW CONSTN ADJUD CT/SYS GP/REL ...JURID 20. PAGE 132 H2638 — NAT/G BARGAIN LABOR INDUS

B43
BROWN A.D.,GREECE: SELECTED LIST OF REFERENCES. GREECE ECO/UNDEV AGRI FINAN INDUS LABOR SECT TEC/DEV INT/TRADE LEAD...SOC 20. PAGE 22 H0438 — BIBLIOG/A WAR DIPLOM

NAT/G

B44
SHELBY C.,LATIN AMERICAN PERIODICALS CURRENTLY BIBLIOG
RECEIVED IN THE LIBRARY OF CONGRESS AND IN LIBRARY ECO/UNDEV
OF DEPARTMENT OF AGRICULTURE. SOCIETY AGRI INDUS CULTURE
LABOR POL/PAR INT/TRADE...GEOG SOC 20. PAGE 143 L/A+17C
H2856

N47
CANNON J.P.,AMERICAN STALINISM AND ANTI-STALINISM (LABOR
PAMPHLET). NAT/G WORKER DOMIN EDU/PROP REV GP/REL MARXISM
...MARXIST CONCPT 20 STALIN/J TROTSKY/L. PAGE 26 CAP/ISM
H0521 POL/PAR

B49
HEADLAM-MORLEY,BIBLIOGRAPHY IN POLITICS FOR THE BIBLIOG
HONOUR SCHOOL OF PHILOSOPHY, POLITICS AND ECONOMICS NAT/G
(PAMPHLET). UK CONSTN LABOR MUNIC DIPLOM ADMIN PHIL/SCI
19/20. PAGE 69 H1375 GOV/REL

B50
BERMAN H.J.,JUSTICE IN RUSSIA; AN INTERPRETATION OF JURID
SOVIET LAW. USSR LAW STRUCT LABOR FORCES AGREE ADJUD
GP/REL ORD/FREE SOCISM...TIME/SEQ 20. PAGE 15 H0309 MARXISM
COERCE

B51
HALEVY E.,IMPERIALISM AND THE RISE OF LABOR (2ND COLONIAL
ED.). UK NAT/G POL/PAR TOP/EX ATTIT ORD/FREE PWR LABOR
19/20 PARLIAMENT LABOR/PAR. PAGE 64 H1284 POLICY
WAR

B51
MARX K.,THE EIGHTEENTH BRUMAIRE OF LOUIS BONAPARTE REV
(1852). FRANCE STRATA FINAN INDUS LABOR CHIEF MARXISM
FORCES WORKER CAP/ISM ECO/TAC PARL/PROC ORD/FREE ELITES
...MARXIST 19. PAGE 104 H2080 NAT/G

C52
LEWIS B.W.,"BRITISH PLANNING AND NATIONALIZATION." NEW/LIB
UK INDUS SERV/IND LABOR NAT/G OP/RES TEC/DEV TAX ECO/DEV
WEALTH...CHARTS BIBLIOG 20. PAGE 96 H1912 POL/PAR
PLAN

B53
FLORENCE P.S.,THE LOGIC OF BRITISH AND AMERICAN INDUS
INDUSTRY; A REALISTIC ANALYSIS OF ECONOMIC ECO/DEV
STRUCTURE AND GOVERNMENT. UK USA+45 USA-45 FINAN NAT/G
LABOR CAP/ISM INGP/REL EFFICIENCY...MGT CONCPT STAT NAT/COMP
CHARTS METH 20. PAGE 51 H1028

S53
BAUER R.A.,"WORD-OF-MOUTH COMMUNICATION IN THE CULTURE
SOVIET UNION." COM INTELL SOCIETY LABOR ATTIT KNOWL USSR
...INT QU SAMP CHARTS 20. PAGE 12 H0239

S53
DRUCKER P.F.,"THE EMPLOYEE SOCIETY." STRUCT BAL/PWR LABOR
PARTIC REPRESENT PWR...DECISION CONCPT. PAGE 42 MGT
H0849 WORKER
CULTURE

B54
BERGER M.,FREEDOM AND CONTROL IN MODERN SOCIETY. ORD/FREE
LABOR NAT/G VOL/ASSN AUTHORIT DRIVE PLURISM CONTROL
...METH/CNCPT CLASSIF. PAGE 15 H0300 INGP/REL

B54
BINANI G.D.,INDIA AT A GLANCE (REV. ED.). INDIA INDEX
COM/IND FINAN INDUS LABOR PROVS SCHOOL PLAN DIPLOM CON/ANAL
INT/TRADE ADMIN...JURID 20. PAGE 17 H0335 NAT/G
ECO/UNDEV

B54
MOSK S.A.,INDUSTRIAL REVOLUTION IN MEXICO. MARKET INDUS
LABOR CREATE CAP/ISM ADMIN ATTIT SOCISM...POLICY 20 TEC/DEV
MEXIC/AMER. PAGE 113 H2268 ECO/UNDEV
NAT/G

B54
WILLIAMSON H.F.,ECONOMIC DEVELOPMENT - PRINCIPLES ECO/TAC
AND PATTERNS. INDIA KOREA CULTURE ECO/DEV ECO/UNDEV GEOG
TEC/DEV...CENSUS NAT/COMP 20 CHINJAP MEXIC/AMER LABOR
RESOURCE/N. PAGE 168 H3369

B55
INTERNATIONAL COMN JURISTS,JUSTICE ENSLAVED. COM SOCISM
CONSTN LABOR NAT/G CONTROL CHOOSE 20. PAGE 78 H1555 TOTALISM
ORD/FREE
COERCE

B55
JONES T.B.,A BIBLIOGRAPHY ON SOUTH AMERICAN BIBLIOG
ECONOMIC AFFAIRS: ARTICLES IN NINETEENTH CENTURY ECO/UNDEV
PERIODICALS (PAMPHLET). AGRI COM/IND DIST/IND L/A+17C
EXTR/IND FINAN INDUS LABOR NAT/G 19. PAGE 82 H1634 TEC/DEV

B55
RUSTOW D.A.,THE POLITICS OF COMPROMISE. SWEDEN POL/PAR
LABOR EX/STRUC LEGIS PLAN REPRESENT SOCISM...SOC NAT/G
19/20. PAGE 136 H2720 POLICY
ECO/TAC

B55
SERRANO MOSCOSO E.,A STATEMENT OF THE LAWS OF FINAN
ECUADOR IN MATTERS AFFECTING BUSINESS (2ND ED.). ECO/UNDEV
ECUADOR INDUS LABOR LG/CO NAT/G LEGIS TAX CONTROL LAW
MARRIAGE 20. PAGE 141 H2830 CONSTN

B56
INTERNATIONAL AFRICAN INST,SOCIAL IMPLICATIONS OF AFR
INDUSTRIALIZATION AND URBANIZATION IN AFRICA SOUTH ECO/UNDEV
OF THE SAHARA. SOUTH/AFR INDUS LABOR MUNIC WORKER ADJUST
TEC/DEV...SOC OBS TREND ANTHOL 20. PAGE 77 H1549 CULTURE

L56
EPSTEIN L.D.,"BRITISH MASS PARTIES IN COMPARISON POL/PAR
WITH AMERICAN PARTIES" UK USA+45 STRATA ECO/DEV NAT/COMP
LABOR...CON/ANAL 20. PAGE 47 H0936 PARTIC
CHOOSE

B57
IKE N.,JAPANESE POLITICS. INTELL STRUCT AGRI INDUS NAT/G
FAM KIN LABOR PRESS CHOOSE ATTIT...DECISION BIBLIOG ADMIN
19/20 CHINJAP. PAGE 76 H1523 POL/PAR
CULTURE

B57
SHEIKH N.A.,SOME ASPECTS OF THE CONSTITUTION AND ISLAM
THE ECONOMICS OF ISLAM. PAKISTAN CULTURE AGRI FINAN POLICY
LABOR NAT/G SECT INT/TRADE 20 MUSLIM. PAGE 143 ECO/TAC
H2855 CONSTN

L57
BENDIX R.,"POLITICAL SOCIOLOGY." CULTURE INTELL BIBLIOG/A
LABOR POL/PAR SECT LEGIS EDU/PROP ADMIN CHOOSE ACT/RES
CIVMIL/REL ATTIT...IDEA/COMP 20. PAGE 14 H0274 SOC

B58
CUNNINGHAM W.B.,COMPULSORY CONCILIATION AND POLICY
COLLECTIVE BARGAINING. CANADA NAT/G LEGIS ADJUD BARGAIN
CT/SYS GP/REL...MGT 20 NEW/BRUNS STRIKE CASEBOOK. LABOR
PAGE 36 H0722 INDUS

B58
WOODS H.D.,PATTERNS OF INDUSTRIAL DISPUTE BARGAIN
SETTLEMENT IN FIVE CANADIAN INDUSTRIES. CANADA INDUS
USA+45 CONSULT ADJUD GP/REL...JURID GOV/COMP LABOR
METH/COMP ANTHOL 20. PAGE 170 H3408 NAT/G

C58
BLANCHARD W.,"THAILAND." THAILAND CULTURE AGRI NAT/G
FINAN INDUS FAM LABOR INT/TRADE ATTIT...GEOG HEAL DIPLOM
SOC BIBLIOG 20. PAGE 18 H0354 ECO/UNDEV
S/ASIA

B59
BRIGGS A.,CHARTIST STUDIES. UK LAW NAT/G WORKER INDUS
EDU/PROP COERCE SUFF GP/REL ATTIT...ANTHOL 19. STRATA
PAGE 21 H0416 LABOR
POLICY

B59
DAHRENDORF R.,CLASS AND CLASS CONFLICT IN VOL/ASSN
INDUSTRIAL SOCIETY. LABOR NAT/G COERCE ROLE PLURISM STRUCT
...POLICY MGT CONCPT CLASSIF. PAGE 37 H0734 SOC
GP/REL

B59
EPSTEIN F.T.,EAST GERMANY: A SELECTED BIBLIOGRAPHY BIBLIOG/A
(PAMPHLET). COM GERMANY/E LAW AGRI FINAN INDUS INTELL
LABOR POL/PAR EDU/PROP ADMIN AGE/Y 20. PAGE 47 MARXISM
H0932 NAT/G

B59
GINSBURG M.,LAW AND OPINION IN ENGLAND. UK CULTURE JURID
KIN LABOR LEGIS EDU/PROP ADMIN CT/SYS CRIME OWN POLICY
HEALTH...ANTHOL 20 ENGLSH/LAW. PAGE 56 H1132 ECO/TAC

B59
LANDAUER C.,EUROPEAN SOCIALISM (2 VOLS.). COM SOCISM
EUR+WWI MOD/EUR INTELL INDUS REV WAR...MAJORIT NAT/COMP
IDEA/COMP BIBLIOG 19/20 HITLER/A. PAGE 90 H1805 LABOR
MARXISM

B59
MAC MILLAN W.M.,THE ROAD TO SELF-RULE. SOUTH/AFR UK AFR
CULTURE SOCIETY AGRI LABOR NAT/G INT/TRADE CONTROL COLONIAL
GP/REL...SOC 19/20. PAGE 100 H1988 SOVEREIGN
POLICY

B59
MILLER A.S.,PRIVATE GOVERNMENTS AND THE FEDERAL
CONSTITUTION (PAMPHLET). LAW LABOR NAT/G ROLE PWR CONSTN
PLURISM...POLICY DECISION. PAGE 111 H2211 VOL/ASSN
CONSEN

B60
JOHNSON H.M.,SOCIOLOGY: A SYSTEMATIC INTRODUCTION. SOC
MARKET FAM LABOR POL/PAR CHOOSE DISCRIM MARRIAGE SOCIETY
ALL/IDEOS...BIBLIOG T WORSHIP. PAGE 81 H1620 CULTURE
GEN/LAWS

B60
MOORE W.E.,LABOR COMMITMENT AND SOCIAL CHANGE IN LABOR
DEVELOPING AREAS. SOCIETY STRATA ECO/UNDEV MARKET ORD/FREE
VOL/ASSN WORKER AUTHORIT SKILL...MGT NAT/COMP ATTIT
SOC/INTEG 20. PAGE 113 H2250 INDUS

B60
ROBERTSON D.,THE CONTROL OF INDUSTRY. UK MARKET INDUS
LABOR WORKER PRICE CONTROL GP/REL COST DEMAND FINAN
ORD/FREE WEALTH NEW/LIB SOCISM 20. PAGE 132 H2646 NAT/G
ECO/DEV

B60
SCHAPIRO L.,THE COMMUNIST PARTY OF THE SOVIET INTELL
UNION. COM LAW SOCIETY STRATA STRUCT ECO/DEV LABOR PWR
NAT/G POL/PAR CREATE DOMIN EDU/PROP COERCE TOTALISM USSR
MARXISM...POLICY CONCPT MYTH TIME/SEQ WORK TOT/POP
20 LENIN/VI STALIN/J. PAGE 139 H2772

B60
SLOTKIN J.S.,FROM FIELD TO FACTORY; NEW INDUSTRIAL INDUS
EMPLOYEES. HABITAT...MGT NEW/IDEA NAT/COMP BIBLIOG LABOR
SOC/INTEG 20. PAGE 145 H2901 CULTURE
WORKER

B60
WEINER H.E.,BRITISH LABOR AND PUBLIC OWNERSHIP. UK LABOR

SERV/IND LG/CO WORKER CONTROL OWN 20. PAGE 166 H3327 — NAT/G INDUS ATTIT

L60
KAPLAN M.A.,"COMMUNIST COUP IN CZECHOSLOVAKIA." COM EUR+WWI INTELL LABOR LOC/G NAT/G POL/PAR FORCES EDU/PROP EXEC MARXISM...TIME/SEQ HYPO/EXP 20. PAGE 83 H1659 — STRUCT COERCE CZECHOSLVK

S60
"THE EMERGING COMMON MARKETS IN LATIN AMERICA." FUT L/A+17C STRATA DIST/IND INDUS LABOR NAT/G LEGIS ECO/TAC ADMIN RIGID/FLEX HEALTH...NEW/IDEA TIME/SEQ OAS 20. PAGE 2 H0038 — FINAN ECO/UNDEV INT/TRADE

B61
CARNELL F.,THE POLITICS OF THE NEW STATES: A SELECT ANNOTATED BIBLIOGRAPHY WITH SPECIAL REFERENCE TO THE COMMONWEALTH. CONSTN ELITES LABOR NAT/G POL/PAR EX/STRUC DIPLOM ADJUD ADMIN...GOV/COMP 20 COMMONWLTH. PAGE 27 H0534 — BIBLIOG/A AFR ASIA COLONIAL

B61
CARROTHERS A.W.R.,LABOR ARBITRATION IN CANADA. CANADA LAW NAT/G CONSULT LEGIS WORKER ADJUD ADMIN CT/SYS 20. PAGE 27 H0542 — LABOR MGT GP/REL BARGAIN

B61
GANGULI B.N.,ECONOMIC INTEGRATION. FINAN LABOR CAP/ISM DIPLOM WEALTH...NAT/COMP 20. PAGE 55 H1096 — ECO/TAC METH/CNCPT EQUILIB ECO/UNDEV

B61
HALPERIN S.,THE POLITICAL WORLD OF AMERICAN ZIONISM. ISRAEL FINAN LABOR VOL/ASSN GIVE LOBBY REPRESENT GP/REL ATTIT POLICY. PAGE 64 H1293 — CULTURE SECT EDU/PROP DELIB/GP

B61
LENIN V.I.,WHAT IS TO BE DONE? (1902). RUSSIA LABOR NAT/G POL/PAR WORKER CAP/ISM ECO/TAC ADMIN PARTIC ...MARXIST IDEA/COMP GEN/LAWS 19/20. PAGE 94 H1881 — EDU/PROP PRESS MARXISM METH/COMP

B61
LYFORD J.P.,THE AGREEABLE AUTOCRACIES. SOCIETY LABOR POL/PAR SECT DIPLOM CHOOSE...CONCPT 20 WHITE/T NIEBUHR/R. PAGE 99 H1982 — ATTIT POPULISM PRESS NAT/G

B61
MARX K.,THE COMMUNIST MANIFESTO. IN (MENDEL A. ESSENTIAL WORKS OF MARXISM, NEW YORK: BANTAM. FUT MOD/EUR CULTURE ECO/DEV ECO/UNDEV AGRI FINAN INDUS MARKET PROC/MFG LABOR MUNIC POL/PAR CONSULT FORCES CREATE PLAN ADMIN ATTIT DRIVE RIGID/FLEX ORD/FREE PWR RESPECT MARX/KARL WORK. PAGE 104 H2081 — COM NEW/IDEA CAP/ISM REV

B61
ZIMMERMAN I.,A GUIDE TO CURRENT LATIN AMERICAN PERIODICALS: HUMANITIES AND SOCIAL SCIENCES. LABOR SECT EDU/PROP...GEOG HUM SOC LING STAT NAT/COMP 20. PAGE 173 H3456 — BIBLIOG/A DIPLOM L/A+17C PHIL/SCI

B62
BELL D.,THE END OF IDEOLOGY (REV. ED.). USA+45 USA-45 ELITES STRATA LABOR CREATE CRIME PWR MARXISM ...PHIL/SCI METH/COMP 20 EUROPE. PAGE 13 H0265 — CROWD CAP/ISM SOCISM IDEA/COMP

B62
GALENSON W.,LABOR IN DEVELOPING COUNTRIES. BRAZIL INDONESIA ISRAEL PAKISTAN TURKEY AGRI INDUS WORKER PAY PRICE GP/REL WEALTH...MGT CHARTS METH/COMP NAT/COMP 20. PAGE 54 H1088 — LABOR ECO/UNDEV BARGAIN POL/PAR

B62
PASTOR R.S.,A STATEMENT OF THE LAWS OF PARAGUAY IN MATTERS AFFECTING BUSINESS (2ND ED.). PARAGUAY INDUS FAM LABOR LG/CO NAT/G LEGIS TAX CONTROL MARRIAGE 20. PAGE 124 H2474 — FINAN ECO/UNDEV LAW CONSTN

B62
WOODS H.D.,LABOUR POLICY AND LABOUR ECONOMICS IN CANADA. CANADA FUT NAT/G VOL/ASSN WORKER BARGAIN ECO/TAC PAY CONFER GP/REL 20. PAGE 170 H3409 — LABOR POLICY INDUS ECO/DEV

B63
BERGSON A.,ECONOMIC TRENDS IN THE SOVIET UNION. USSR ECO/UNDEV AGRI NAT/G FORCES PLAN TEC/DEV INT/TRADE BAL/PAY...POLICY ANTHOL 20. PAGE 15 H0302 — ECO/DEV NAT/COMP INDUS LABOR

B63
CROSS C.,THE FASCISTS IN BRITAIN. UK ELITES LABOR NAT/G DOMIN PARTIC DISCRIM TOTALISM ATTIT...STERTYP 20. PAGE 35 H0708 — POL/PAR FASCISM RACE/REL LEAD

B63
FISCHER-GALATI S.A.,RUMANIA; A BIBLIOGRAPHIC GUIDE (PAMPHLET). ROMANIA INTELL ECO/DEV LABOR SECT WEALTH...GEOG SOC/WK LING 20. PAGE 51 H1012 — BIBLIOG/A NAT/G COM LAW

B63
FURTADO C.,THE ECONOMIC GROWTH OF BRAZIL: A SURVEY FROM COLONIAL TO MODERN TIMES. L/A+17C AGRI DIST/IND EXTR/IND INDUS WORKER COLONIAL RACE/REL OWN GOV/COMP. PAGE 54 H1082 — ECO/UNDEV TEC/DEV LABOR DOMIN

B63
GOURNAY B.,PUBLIC ADMINISTRATION. FRANCE LAW CONSTN AGRI FINAN LABOR SCHOOL EX/STRUC CHOOSE...MGT METH/COMP 20. PAGE 59 H1189 — BIBLIOG/A ADMIN NAT/G LOC/G

B63
PAUW B.A.,THE SECOND GENERATION. SOUTH/AFR INDUS FAM LABOR SECT EDU/PROP MARRIAGE ATTIT...SOC 20. PAGE 124 H2478 — KIN CULTURE STRUCT SOCIETY

B63
PELLING H.M.,A HISTORY OF BRITISH TRADE UNIONISM. UK ELITES ECO/DEV POL/PAR GP/REL PWR NEW/LIB 19/20. PAGE 124 H2485 — LABOR VOL/ASSN NAT/G

B64
FAINSOD M.,HOW RUSSIA IS RULED (REV. ED.). RUSSIA USSR AGRI PROC/MFG LABOR POL/PAR EX/STRUC CONTROL PWR...POLICY BIBLIOG 19/20 KHRUSH/N COM/PARTY. PAGE 48 H0963 — NAT/G REV MARXISM

B64
FRIEDLAND W.H.,AFRICAN SOCIALISM. ECO/UNDEV MARKET LABOR NAT/G POL/PAR PLAN CAP/ISM ECO/TAC EDU/PROP CHOOSE ATTIT DRIVE PWR WEALTH...POLICY CONCPT RECORD STERTYP 20. PAGE 53 H1063 — AFR SOCISM

B64
FROMM E.,MARX'S CONCEPT OF MAN. LABOR OWN PERSON ...HUM IDEA/COMP GEN/LAWS 17 MARX/KARL EUROPE SPINOZA/B GOETHE/J HEGEL/GWF. PAGE 54 H1072 — INGP/REL CONCPT MARXISM SOCISM

B64
GESELLSCHAFT RECHTSVERGLEICH,BIBLIOGRAPHIE DES DEUTSCHEN RECHTS (BIBLIOGRAPHY OF GERMAN LAW, TRANS. BY COURTLAND PETERSON). GERMANY FINAN INDUS LABOR SECT FORCES CT/SYS PARL/PROC CRIME...INT/LAW SOC NAT/COMP 20. PAGE 56 H1117 — BIBLIOG/A JURID CONSTN ADMIN

B64
GILLY A.,INSIDE THE CUBAN REVOLUTION. CUBA AGRI INDUS LABOR CREATE DIPLOM...METH/COMP 20. PAGE 56 H1129 — REV PLAN MARXISM ECO/UNDEV

B64
HAMILTON W.B.,THE TRANSFER OF INSTITUTIONS. CANADA INDIA UK LAW AGRI LABOR SECT COLONIAL 18/20. PAGE 65 H1301 — NAT/COMP ECO/UNDEV EDU/PROP CULTURE

B64
HARBISON F.H.,EDUCATION, MANPOWER, AND ECONOMIC GROWTH. WOR+45 ECO/DEV ECO/UNDEV ACADEM LABOR SCHOOL WORKER UTIL...IDEA/COMP NAT/COMP. PAGE 66 H1326 — PLAN TEC/DEV EDU/PROP SKILL

B64
HAZLEWOOD A.,THE ECONOMICS OF DEVELOPMENT: AN ANNOTATED LIST OF BOOKS AND ARTICLES PUBLISHED 1958-1962. AGRI FINAN INDUS LABOR NAT/G DIPLOM INT/TRADE INCOME...MGT 20. PAGE 69 H1374 — BIBLIOG/A ECO/UNDEV TEC/DEV

B64
IMAZ J.L.,LOS QUE MANDAN. INDUS LABOR NAT/G POL/PAR PROVS SECT CHIEF TOP/EX CONTROL 20 ARGEN. PAGE 76 H1524 — LEAD FORCES ELITES ATTIT

B64
LI C.M.,INDUSTRIAL DEVELOPMENT IN COMMUNIST CHINA. CHINA/COM ECO/DEV ECO/UNDEV AGRI FINAN INDUS MARKET LABOR NAT/G ECO/TAC INT/TRADE EXEC ALL/VALS ...POLICY RELATIV TREND WORK TOT/POP VAL/FREE 20. PAGE 96 H1921 — ASIA TEC/DEV

B64
MILIBAND R.,THE SOCIALIST REGISTER: 1964. GERMANY/W ITALY UK LABOR POL/PAR ECO/TAC FOR/AID NUC/PWR ...POLICY SOCIALIST IDEA/COMP 20 MAO NASSER/G. PAGE 110 H2204 — MARXISM SOCISM CAP/ISM PROB/SOLV

B64
MORGAN H.W.,AMERICAN SOCIALISM 1900-1960. USA+45 USA-45 INTELL AGRI LABOR WORKER BARGAIN ECO/TAC GP/REL RACE/REL 20 NEGRO MIGRATION GOLD/STAND. PAGE 113 H2254 — SOCISM POL/PAR ECO/DEV STRATA

B64
SOLOW R.M.,THE NATURE AND SOURCES OF UNEMPLOYMENT IN THE UNITED STATES (PAMPHLET). USA+45 INDUS LABOR TEC/DEV ECO/TAC SKILL WEALTH...TREND NAT/COMP 20. PAGE 147 H2930 — ECO/DEV WORKER STAT PRODUC

B64
WERNETTE J.P.,GOVERNMENT AND BUSINESS. LABOR CAP/ISM ECO/TAC INT/TRADE TAX ADMIN AUTOMAT NUC/PWR CIVMIL/REL DEMAND...MGT 20 MONOPOLY. PAGE 167 H3333 — NAT/G FINAN ECO/DEV CONTROL

B65
AIYAR S.P.,STUDIES IN INDIAN DEMOCRACY. INDIA STRATA ECO/UNDEV LABOR POL/PAR LEGIS DIPLOM LOBBY REGION CHOOSE ATTIT SOCISM...ANTHOL 20. PAGE 4 H0086 — ORD/FREE REPRESENT ADMIN NAT/G

B65
ALEXANDER R.J.,ORGANIZED LABOR IN LATIN AMERICA. L/A+17C INT/ORG LEGIS WORKER TEC/DEV BARGAIN INT/TRADE REV...NAT/COMP BIBLIOG 20. PAGE 5 H0102 — LABOR POL/PAR ECO/UNDEV POLICY

B65
BARRY E.E.,NATIONALISATION IN BRITISH POLITICS: THE HISTORICAL BACKGROUND. UK AGRI DIST/IND EXTR/IND LABOR LG/CO ATTIT CONSERVE SOCISM 19/20 LABOR/PAR. PAGE 12 H0231
NAT/G OWN INDUS POL/PAR

B65
CHENG C.-.Y.,SCIENTIFIC AND ENGINEERING MANPOWER IN COMMUNIST CHINA, 1949-1963. CHINA/COM USSR ELITES ECO/DEV R+D ACADEM LABOR NAT/G EDU/PROP CONTROL UTIL...POLICY BIBLIOG 20. PAGE 29 H0588
WORKER CONSULT MARXISM BIOG

B65
COLLINS H.,KARL MARX AND THE BRITISH LABOR MOVEMENT, YEARS OF THE FIRST INTERNATIONAL. EUR+WWI MOD/EUR UK STRATA INDUS NAT/G POL/PAR SOCISM ...CONCPT 19/20 MARX/KARL. PAGE 32 H0633
MARXISM LABOR INT/ORG WORKER

B65
EDELMAN M.,THE POLITICS OF WAGE-PRICE DECISIONS. GERMANY ITALY NETHERLAND UK INDUS LABOR POL/PAR PROB/SOLV BARGAIN PRICE ROUTINE BAL/PAY COST DEMAND 20. PAGE 44 H0888
GOV/COMP CONTROL ECO/TAC PLAN

B65
FORM W.H.,INDUSTRIAL RELATIONS AND SOCIAL CHANGE IN LATIN AMERICA. L/A+17C AGRI LABOR NAT/G PLAN PROB/SOLV DIPLOM...MGT SOC ANTHOL BIBLIOG/A METH 20. PAGE 52 H1038
INDUS GP/REL NAT/COMP ECO/UNDEV

B65
HALEVY E.,THE ERA OF TYRANNIES (TRANS. BY R. K. WEBB). FRANCE MOD/EUR UK ECO/DEV LABOR NAT/G BAL/PWR FEDERAL ALL/VALS...OLD/LIB TREND 18/20 SAINTSIMON. PAGE 64 H1285
SOCISM CONCPT UTOPIA ORD/FREE

B65
HERRICK B.H.,URBAN MIGRATION AND ECONOMIC DEVELOPMENT IN CHILE. CHILE AGRI INDUS LABOR NAT/G CENTRAL PRODUC...STAT SAMP CHARTS BIBLIOG/A 20 MIGRATION. PAGE 70 H1404
HABITAT GEOG MUNIC ECO/UNDEV

B65
PELLING H.,A SHORT HISTORY OF THE LABOUR PARTY (2ND ED.). UK NAT/G CHIEF PARL/PROC GP/REL INGP/REL 20 LABOR/PAR PARLIAMENT WILSON/H. PAGE 124 H2484
POL/PAR NEW/LIB LEAD LABOR

B65
PROEHL P.O.,FOREIGN ENTERPRISE IN NIGERIA. NIGERIA FINAN LABOR NAT/G TAX 20. PAGE 128 H2562
ECO/UNDEV ECO/TAC JURID CAP/ISM

B65
RENNER K.,MENSCH UND GESELLSCHAFT - GRUNDRISS EINER SOZIOLOGIE (2ND ED.). STRATA FAM LABOR PROF/ORG WAR ...JURID CLASSIF 20. PAGE 131 H2616
SOC STRUCT NAT/G SOCIETY

B65
SABLE M.H.,MASTER DIRECTORY FOR LATIN AMERICA. AGRI COM/IND FINAN R+D ACADEM LABOR NAT/G POL/PAR VOL/ASSN INT/TRADE EDU/PROP 20. PAGE 136 H2728
INDEX L/A+17C INT/ORG DIPLOM

B65
UN,SPACE ACTIVITIES AND RESOURCES: REVIEW OF UNITED NATION'S NATIONAL AND INTERNATIONAL PROGRAMS. INT/ORG LABOR PLAN TEC/DEV DIPLOM EFFICIENCY HEALTH ...GOV/COMP 20 UN. PAGE 158 H3155
SPACE NUC/PWR FOR/AID PEACE

B65
WURFEL S.W.,FOREIGN ENTERPRISE IN COLOMBIA. FINAN LABOR NAT/G ECO/TAC TAX REGION 20 COLOMB. PAGE 171 H3429
ECO/UNDEV INT/TRADE JURID CAP/ISM

L65
MATTHEWS D.G.,"A CURRENT BIBLIOGRAPHY ON ETHIOPIAN AFFAIRS: A SELECT BIBLIOGRAPHY FROM 1950-1964." ETHIOPIA LAW CULTURE ECO/UNDEV INDUS LABOR SECT FORCES DIPLOM CIVMIL/REL RACE/REL...LING STAT 20. PAGE 105 H2093
BIBLIOG/A ADMIN POL/PAR NAT/G

L65
MATTHEWS D.G.,"A CURRENT BIBLIOGRAPHY ON SUDANESE AFFAIRS; A SELECT BIBLIOGRAPHY FROM 1960-1964." SUDAN LAW CULTURE AGRI FINAN INDUS LABOR POL/PAR TEC/DEV FOR/AID RACE/REL LITERACY...LING 20. PAGE 105 H2094
BIBLIOG ECO/UNDEV NAT/G DIPLOM

L65
WIONCZEK M.,"LATIN AMERICA FREE TRADE ASSOCIATION." AGRI DIST/IND FINAN INDUS INT/ORG LABOR NAT/G TEC/DEV ECO/TAC HEALTH SKILL WEALTH...POLICY RELATIV MGT LAFTA 20. PAGE 169 H3390
L/A+17C MARKET REGION

S65
KINDLEBERGER C.P.,"MASS MIGRATION, THEN AND NOW." LAW ECO/DEV ECO/UNDEV INDUS LABOR INT/TRADE FEEDBACK REGION RIGID/FLEX...SOC NAT/COMP EEC. PAGE 86 H1714
EUR+WWI USA-45 WORKER IDEA/COMP

S65
MULLER A.L.,"SOME NON-ECONOMIC DETERMINANTS OF THE ECONOMIC STATUS OF ASIANS IN AFRICA." AFR SOUTH/AFR CULTURE 20. PAGE 114 H2283
DISCRIM RACE/REL LABOR SECT

B66
BRODERSEN A.,THE SOVIET WORKER: LABOR AND GOVERNMENT IN SOVIET SOCIETY. USSR STRUCT INDUS LABOR PLAN PAY INGP/REL PRODUC...POLICY GEN/LAWS BIBLIOG 20 STALIN/J LENIN/VI BOLSHEVISM KHRUSH/N. PAGE 21 H0425
WORKER ROLE NAT/G MARXISM

B66
COLE A.B.,SOCIALIST PARTIES IN POSTWAR JAPAN. STRATA AGRI LABOR PLAN DIPLOM ECO/TAC AGREE LEAD CHOOSE ATTIT...CHARTS 20 CHINJAP SOC/DEMPAR. PAGE 31 H0620
POL/PAR POLICY SOCISM NAT/G

B66
DOBB M.,SOVIET ECONOMIC DEVELOPMENT SINCE 1917. USSR ECO/DEV ECO/UNDEV LABOR NAT/G TEC/DEV ECO/TAC ROUTINE PRODUC MARXISM 20. PAGE 41 H0829
PLAN INDUS WORKER

B66
FINER S.E.,ANONYMOUS EMPIRE: STUDY OF THE LOBBY IN GREAT BRITAIN. UK CONSTN LABOR POL/PAR SECT DOMIN EDU/PROP PRESS CHOOSE...CONCPT CHARTS 20 PARLIAMENT. PAGE 50 H1004
LOBBY NAT/G LEGIS PWR

B66
FORD P.,CARDINAL MORAN AND THE A. L. P. NAT/G POL/PAR SECT DELIB/GP LOBBY REV CHOOSE ORD/FREE MARXISM 19/20 AUSTRAL PROTESTANT LABOR/PAR. PAGE 52 H1035
CATHISM SOCISM LABOR SOCIETY

B66
HACKETT J.,L'ECONOMIE BRITANNIQUE: PROBLEMES ET PERSPECTIVES. FRANCE UK LABOR MUNIC NAT/G EX/STRUC PROB/SOLV BAL/PAY INCOME RIGID/FLEX...MGT PHIL/SCI CHARTS 20. PAGE 63 H1271
ECO/DEV FINAN ECO/TAC PLAN

B66
KOH S.J.,STAGES OF INDUSTRIAL DEVELOPMENT IN ASIA. ASIA INDIA KOREA STRATA STRUCT NAT/G INT/TRADE ...CHARTS 19/20 CHINJAP. PAGE 87 H1738
INDUS ECO/UNDEV ECO/DEV LABOR

B66
MADAN G.R.,ECONOMIC THINKING IN INDIA. INDIA ECO/UNDEV AGRI FINAN INDUS LABOR PLAN CAP/ISM INT/TRADE MARXISM SOCISM...POLICY 1/20. PAGE 101 H2013
ECO/TAC PHIL/SCI NAT/G POL/PAR

B66
MILONE P.D.,URBAN AREAS IN INDONESIA. INDONESIA LABOR NAT/G COLONIAL GP/REL...CENSUS CHARTS 17/20. PAGE 111 H2218
MUNIC GEOG STRUCT SOCIETY

B66
ROSS A.M.,INDUSTRIAL RELATIONS AND ECONOMIC DEVELOPMENT. POL/PAR LEGIS WORKER BARGAIN PRICE EXEC LOBBY INCOME PWR...DECISION ANTHOL BIBLIOG 20. PAGE 134 H2686
ECO/UNDEV LABOR NAT/G GP/REL

B66
SCHATTEN F.,COMMUNISM IN AFRICA. AFR GHANA GUINEA MALI CULTURE ECO/UNDEV LABOR SECT ECO/TAC EDU/PROP REV 20. PAGE 139 H2774
COLONIAL NAT/LISM MARXISM DIPLOM

B66
SMITH H.E.,READINGS IN ECONOMIC DEVELOPMENT AND ADMINISTRATION IN TANZANIA. TANZANIA FINAN INDUS LABOR NAT/G PLAN PROB/SOLV INT/TRADE COLONIAL REGION...ANTHOL BIBLIOG 20 AFRICA/E. PAGE 146 H2910
TEC/DEV ADMIN GOV/REL

S66
LODGE G.C.,"REVOLUTION IN LATIN AMERICA." USA+45 ELITES INDUS LABOR PROF/ORG SECT TEC/DEV CAP/ISM SKILL MARXISM...POLICY NAT/COMP. PAGE 98 H1950
ATTIT REV L/A+17C IDEA/COMP

S66
MATTHEWS D.G.,"ETHIOPIAN OUTLINE: A BIBLIOGRAPHIC RESEARCH GUIDE." ETHIOPIA LAW STRUCT ECO/UNDEV AGRI LABOR SECT CHIEF DELIB/GP EX/STRUC ADMIN...LING ORG/CHARTS 20. PAGE 105 H2095
BIBLIOG NAT/G DIPLOM POL/PAR

C66
WINT G.,"ASIA: A HANDBOOK." ASIA S/ASIA INDUS LABOR SECT PRESS RACE/REL MARXISM...STAT CHARTS BIBLIOG 20. PAGE 169 H3388
ECO/UNDEV DIPLOM NAT/G SOCIETY

B67
BADGLEY R.F.,DOCTORS' STRIKE; MEDICAL CARE AND CONFLICT IN SASKATCHEWAN. CANADA NAT/G PROF/ORG GP/REL ADJUST ATTIT...HEAL SOC 20. PAGE 10 H0192
HEALTH PLAN LABOR BARGAIN

B67
DILLARD D.,ECONOMIC DEVELOPMENT OF THE NORTH ATLANTIC COMMUNITY. EUR+WWI MOD/EUR USA+45 USA-45 ECO/UNDEV LABOR CAP/ISM WAR BAL/PAY...NAT/COMP 15/20. PAGE 41 H0824
ECO/DEV INT/TRADE INDUS DIPLOM

B67
GALBRAITH J.K.,THE NEW INDUSTRIAL STATE. INDUS LABOR LG/CO NAT/G POL/PAR SCHOOL OP/RES CAP/ISM EXEC TREND. PAGE 54 H1087
TEC/DEV ECO/DEV SOCIETY MARKET

B67
HAWTREY R.,INCOMES AND MONEY. EUR+WWI FUT UK LABOR WORKER INT/TRADE TAX PAY BAL/PAY COST WEALTH 20. PAGE 68 H1363
FINAN NAT/G POLICY ECO/DEV

B67
HOLLERMAN L.,JAPAN'S DEPENDENCE ON THE WORLD ECONOMY. INDUS MARKET LABOR NAT/G DIPLOM 20 CHINJAP. PAGE 73 H1457
PLAN ECO/DEV ECO/TAC INT/TRADE

B67
RUDMAN H.C.,THE SCHOOL AND STATE IN THE USSR. COM USSR ACADEM LABOR LOC/G PUB/INST EDU/PROP GP/REL ROLE...POLICY DECISION MGT CHARTS 20. PAGE 136 H2712
SCHOOL ADMIN NAT/G POL/PAR

S67
BAIKALOV A.,"EMERGENCY LEGISLATION IN WEST GERMANY." GERMANY/W LABOR NAT/G POL/PAR SANCTION ...MARXIST 20. PAGE 10 H0199
LAW TOTALISM LEGIS PARL/PROC

S67
DERRICK P.,"THE WHITE PAPER ON INCOMES." EUR+WWI UK LAW LABOR NAT/G PLAN PROB/SOLV GP/REL...GOV/COMP PARLIAMENT. PAGE 40 H0794
INCOME POL/PAR POLICY

S67
DEWHURST A.,"THE WAGE MOVEMENT IN CANADA." CANADA AGRI NAT/G PARTIC COST PRODUC PROFIT 20. PAGE 41 H0811
WORKER MARXIST INDUS LABOR

S67
JENCKS C.E.,"SOCIAL STATUS OF COAL MINERS IN BRITAIN SINCE NATIONALIZATION." UK STRATA STRUCT LABOR RECEIVE GP/REL INCOME OWN ATTIT HABITAT...MGT T 20. PAGE 80 H1600
EXTR/IND WORKER CONTROL NAT/G

S67
NEALE R.S.,"WORKING CLASS WOMEN AND WOMEN'S SUFFRAGE." UK LAW CONSTN LABOR NAT/G DELIB/GP LEGIS WORKER PAY PARTIC CHOOSE 19 FEMALE/SEX. PAGE 116 H2326
STRATA SEX SUFF DISCRIM

B68
PROUDHON J.P.,IDEE GENERALE DE LA REVOLUTION AU XIXE SIECLE (1851). FRANCE UNIV NAT/G CREATE AGREE UTOPIA ORD/FREE...ANARCH 19. PAGE 128 H2563
REV SOCIETY WORKER LABOR

LABOR/PAR....LABOR PARTY (ALL NATIONS)

B13
BARDOUX J.,L'ANGLETERRE RADICALE; ESSAI DE LA PSYCHOLOGIE SOCIALE (1906-1913). UK CONSTN NAT/G WORKER CREATE BUDGET ECO/TAC ATTIT...POLICY 20 PARLIAMENT LABOR/PAR STRIKE NAVY. PAGE 11 H0215
POL/PAR CHOOSE COLONIAL LEGIS

B38
DAVIES E.,"NATIONAL" CAPITALISM: THE GOVERNMENT'S RECORD AS PROTECTOR OF PRIVATE MONOPOLY. UK ELITES SOCIETY STRATA POL/PAR WORKER PROB/SOLV CONTROL SOCISM 20 MONOPOLY LABOR/PAR CHAMBRLN/N. PAGE 37 H0747
CAP/ISM NAT/G INDUS POLICY

B40
MCHENRY D.E.,HIS MAJESTY'S OPPOSITION: STRUCTURE AND PROBLEMS OF THE BRITISH LABOUR PARTY 1931-1938. UK FINAN LABOR LOC/G DELIB/GP LEGIS EDU/PROP LEAD PARTIC CHOOSE GP/REL SOCISM...TREND 20 LABOR/PAR. PAGE 107 H2130
POL/PAR MGT NAT/G POLICY

B50
MCHENRY D.E.,THE THIRD FORCE IN CANADA: THE COOPERATIVE COMMONWEALTH FEDERATION, 1932-1948. CANADA EX/STRUC LEGIS REPRESENT 20 LABOR/PAR. PAGE 107 H2131
POL/PAR ADMIN CHOOSE POLICY

B51
HALEVY E.,IMPERIALISM AND THE RISE OF LABOR (2ND ED.). UK NAT/G POL/PAR TOP/EX ATTIT ORD/FREE PWR 19/20 PARLIAMENT LABOR/PAR. PAGE 64 H1284
COLONIAL LABOR POLICY WAR

B54
EPSTEIN L.D.,BRITAIN - UNEASY ALLY. KOREA UK USA+45 NAT/G POL/PAR ECO/TAC FOR/AID INT/TRADE WAR LABOR/PAR CONSRV/PAR. PAGE 47 H0934
DIPLOM ATTIT POLICY NAT/COMP

B59
JENKINS C.,POWER AT THE TOP: A CRITICAL SURVEY OF THE NATIONALIZED INDUSTRIES. UK POL/PAR CONTROL ...WELF/ST CHARTS 20 LABOR/PAR. PAGE 80 H1601
NAT/G OWN INDUS NEW/LIB

B61
JENNINGS I.,PARTY POLITICS: THE GROWTH OF PARTIES (VOL. II). UK SOCIETY NAT/G LEGIS ATTIT 18/20 LABOR/PAR LIB/PARTY CONSRV/PAR. PAGE 80 H1606
CHOOSE POL/PAR PWR POLICY

B61
MILIBAND R.,PARLIAMENTARY SOCIALISM. EUR+WWI UK EXEC LEAD PARL/PROC GP/REL...POLICY 20 PARLIAMENT LABOR/PAR. PAGE 110 H2203
POL/PAR NAT/G PWR SOCISM

B65
BARRY E.E.,NATIONALISATION IN BRITISH POLITICS: THE HISTORICAL BACKGROUND. UK AGRI DIST/IND EXTR/IND LABOR LG/CO ATTIT CONSERVE SOCISM 19/20 LABOR/PAR. PAGE 12 H0231
NAT/G OWN INDUS POL/PAR

B65
BULMER-THOMAS I.,THE GROWTH OF THE BRITISH PARTY SYSTEM (VOL. II) 1924-1964. UK ECO/DEV BARGAIN WAR CHOOSE ATTIT ORD/FREE 20 LABOR/PAR CONSRV/PAR. PAGE 23 H0472
CHIEF POL/PAR PARL/PROC NAT/G

B65
PELLING H.,A SHORT HISTORY OF THE LABOUR PARTY (2ND ED.). UK NAT/G CHIEF PARL/PROC GP/REL INGP/REL 20 LABOR/PAR PARLIAMENT WILSON/H. PAGE 124 H2484
POL/PAR NEW/LIB LEAD LABOR

B66
FORD P.,CARDINAL MORAN AND THE A. L. P. NAT/G POL/PAR SECT DELIB/GP LOBBY REV CHOOSE ORD/FREE MARXISM 19/20 AUSTRAL PROTESTANT LABOR/PAR. PAGE 52 H1035
CATHISM SOCISM LABOR SOCIETY

B66
LONDON DAILY TELEGRAPH,ELECTION '66: GALLUP ANALYSIS OF THE VOTING RESULTS. UK LEGIS COMPUTER ATTIT...QU SAMP CHARTS 20 LABOR/PAR HOUSE/CMNS. PAGE 98 H1959
STAT CHOOSE REPRESENT POL/PAR

S67
MARWICK A.,"THE LABOUR PARTY AND THE WELFARE STATE IN BRITAIN, 19001948." UK SOCIETY STRUCT ECO/DEV WORKER CREATE PRICE CHOOSE WEALTH NEW/LIB SOCISM ...POLICY HEAL 20 PARLIAMENT LABOR/PAR. PAGE 104 H2074
POL/PAR RECEIVE LEGIS NAT/G

LABORATORY EXPERIMENTS....SEE LAB/EXP

LAFTA....LATIN AMERICAN FREE TRADE ASSOCIATION; SEE ALSO INT/ORG, VOL/ASSN, INT/TRADE

S63
POPPINO R.E.,"IMBALANCE IN BRAZIL." L/A+17C NAT/G TOP/EX PLAN DIPLOM LEGIT DRIVE WEALTH...CON/ANAL LAFTA 20. PAGE 127 H2544
POL/PAR ECO/TAC BRAZIL

L64
HAAS E.B.,"ECONOMICS AND DIFFERENTIAL PATTERNS OF POLITICAL INTEGRATION: PROJECTIONS ABOUT UNITY IN LATIN AMERICA." SOCIETY NAT/G DELIB/GP ACT/RES CREATE PLAN ECO/TAC REGION ROUTINE ATTIT DRIVE PWR WEALTH...CONCPT TREND CHARTS LAFTA 20. PAGE 63 H1266
L/A+17C INT/ORG MARKET

L65
WIONCZEK M.,"LATIN AMERICA FREE TRADE ASSOCIATION." AGRI DIST/IND FINAN INDUS INT/ORG LABOR NAT/G TEC/DEV ECO/TAC HEALTH SKILL WEALTH...POLICY RELATIV MGT LAFTA 20. PAGE 169 H3390
L/A+17C MARKET REGION

B66
BROWN R.T.,TRANSPORT AND THE ECONOMIC INTEGRATION OF SOUTH AMERICA. L/A+17C ECO/UNDEV NAT/G OP/RES DIPLOM INT/TRADE REGION WEALTH...ECOMETRIC GEOG STAT LAFTA TIME. PAGE 22 H0449
MARKET DIST/IND SIMUL

LAGUARD/F....FIORELLO LAGUARDIA

LAHAYE R. H1796

LAHBABI M. H1797

LAISSEZ....LAISSEZ-FAIRE-ISM; SEE ALSO OLD/LIB

B20
MALTHUS T.R.,PRINCIPLES OF POLITICAL ECONOMY. UK AGRI INDUS MARKET NAT/G DIPLOM PRICE CONTROL BAL/PAY COST OWN PWR LAISSEZ 18/19. PAGE 102 H2034
GEN/LAWS DEMAND WEALTH

B21
BERGSTRASSER L.,GESCHICHTE DER POLITISCHEN PARTEIEN. GERMANY MOD/EUR NAT/G PRESS PWR ...TIME/SEQ 17/20. PAGE 15 H0303
POL/PAR LAISSEZ CONSERVE

B26
TAWNEY R.H.,RELIGION AND THE RISE OF CAPITALISM. UK CULTURE NAT/G TEC/DEV OWN LAISSEZ...POLICY SOC TIME/SEQ 16/19. PAGE 153 H3050
SECT WEALTH INDUS CAP/ISM

C31
MOGI S.,"THE PROBLEM OF FEDERALISM: A STUDY IN THE HISTORY OF POLITICAL THEORY." CONSTN COLONIAL NAT/LISM SOVEREIGN LAISSEZ PLURISM 18/20. PAGE 112 H2235
FEDERAL CONCPT NAT/G

B36
SMITH T.V.,THE PROMISE OF AMERICAN POLITICS. USA-45 WOR-45 LAW CONSTN STRATA PARTIC FASCISM LAISSEZ MARXISM...MAJORIT METH/COMP 18/20 JEFFERSN/T LOCKE/JOHN BENTHAM/J. PAGE 146 H2920
CONCPT ORD/FREE IDEA/COMP NAT/COMP

S38
HALL R.C.,"REPRESENTATION OF BIG BUSINESS IN THE HOUSE OF COMMONS." UK ECO/DEV INDUS PROF/ORG LEGIS CAP/ISM ECO/TAC LAISSEZ...POLICY OLD/LIB PLURIST MGT 20 HOUSE/CMNS. PAGE 64 H1287
LOBBY NAT/G

S39
HECKSCHER G.,"GROUP ORGANIZATION IN SWEDEN." SWEDEN STRATA ECO/DEV AGRI INDUS LABOR NAT/G PROF/ORG ECO/TAC CENTRAL SOCISM...MGT 19/20. PAGE 69 H1382
LAISSEZ SOC

B40
MANNHEIM K.,MAN AND SOCIETY IN AN AGE OF RECONSTRUCTION. MOD/EUR CULTURE ECO/DEV PLAN TEC/DEV PERSON LAISSEZ NEW/LIB...NEW/IDEA IDEA/COMP BIBLIOG 19/20. PAGE 102 H2038
CONCPT ATTIT SOCIETY TOTALISM

B41
GREEN T.H.,PRINCIPLES OF PUBLIC ADMINISTRATION. UNIV CONSTN VOL/ASSN INGP/REL MORAL ORD/FREE ...GOV/COMP IDEA/COMP GEN/LAWS 20. PAGE 60 H1208
POLICY LAISSEZ MAJORIT

B44
HAYEK F.A.,THE ROAD TO SERFDOM. NAT/G POL/PAR CREATE EDU/PROP ATTIT WEALTH LAISSEZ...OLD/LIB CONCPT TREND 20. PAGE 68 H1368 — FUT PLAN ECO/TAC SOCISM

C49
SCHAPIRO J.S.,"LIBERALISM AND THE CHALLENGE OF FASCISM." FRANCE UK STRATA PERSON...CONCPT BIOG IDEA/COMP BIBLIOG 18/20. PAGE 139 H2771 — FASCISM LAISSEZ ATTIT

B51
EUCKEN W.,THIS UNSUCCESSFUL AGE. GERMANY NAT/G WORKER TEC/DEV ECO/TAC ORD/FREE 20. PAGE 47 H0947 — ECO/DEV PLAN LAISSEZ NEW/LIB

C52
HUME D.,"OF TAXES" IN D. HUME, POLITICAL DISCOURSES (1752)" UK NAT/G COST INCOME LAISSEZ...GEN/LAWS 18. PAGE 75 H1493 — TAX FINAN WEALTH POLICY

B53
BARZEL R.,DIE DEUTSCHEN PARTEIEN. GERMANY MARXISM SOCISM...CONCPT IDEA/COMP 19/20 SOC/DEMPAR CHRIS/DEM. PAGE 12 H0232 — POL/PAR NAT/G LAISSEZ

B56
KALLEN H.M.,CULTURAL PLURALISM AND THE AMERICAN IDEA. RACE/REL ADJUST PERSON ORD/FREE LAISSEZ ...PLURIST GEN/LAWS ANTHOL. PAGE 83 H1652 — PLURISM CULTURE GP/REL SECT

B57
BULLOCK A.,THE LIBERAL TRADITION FROM FOX TO KEYNES. UK CULTURE INTELL CREATE WRITING COLONIAL PERS/REL ATTIT ORD/FREE...POLICY OLD/LIB TRADIT CONCPT 18/20 CHURCHLL/W MILL/JS KEYNES/JM ASQUITH/HH. PAGE 23 H0469 — ANTHOL DEBATE LAISSEZ

B57
LONG H.A.,USURPERS - FOES OF FREE MAN. LAW NAT/G CHIEF LEGIS DOMIN ADJUD REPRESENT GOV/REL ORD/FREE LAISSEZ POPULISM...POLICY 18/20 SUPREME/CT ROOSEVLT/F CONGRESS CON/INTERP. PAGE 98 H1961 — CT/SYS CENTRAL FEDERAL CONSTN

B59
BROSE O.J.,CHURCH AND PARLIAMENT: THE RESHAPING OF THE CHURCH OF ENGLAND 1828-1860. UK SOCIETY TEC/DEV ATTIT LAISSEZ...BIBLIOG 19 CHURCH/STA. PAGE 22 H0434 — SECT LEGIS GP/REL NAT/G

B60
GRAMPP W.D.,THE MANCHESTER SCHOOL OF ECONOMICS. UK LAW ECO/DEV COERCE ATTIT ORD/FREE LAISSEZ ...PHIL/SCI IDEA/COMP 19/20 MANCHESTER CORN/LAWS. PAGE 60 H1194 — ECO/TAC VOL/ASSN LOBBY NAT/G

B60
STRACHEY J.,THE END OF EMPIRE. UK WOR+45 WOR-45 DIPLOM INT/TRADE DOMIN ADJUST ORD/FREE WEALTH ...SOCIALIST GOV/COMP TIME COMMONWLTH. PAGE 150 H2991 — COLONIAL ECO/DEV BAL/PWR LAISSEZ

B63
CARY J.,POWER IN MEN. NAT/G ORD/FREE...GEN/LAWS 20. PAGE 28 H0553 — PHIL/SCI OLD/LIB LAISSEZ PWR

L63
BOLGAR V.,"THE PUBLIC INTEREST: A JURISPRUDENTIAL AND COMPARATIVE OVERVIEW OF SYMPOSIUM ON FUNDAMENTAL CONCEPTS OF PUBLIC LAW" COM FRANCE GERMANY SWITZERLND LAW ADJUD ADMIN AGREE LAISSEZ ...JURID GEN/LAWS 20 EUROPE/E. PAGE 18 H0369 — CONCPT ORD/FREE CONTROL NAT/COMP

B64
RAISON T.,WHY CONSERVATIVE? UK FORCES DIPLOM ECO/TAC GIVE EDU/PROP ORD/FREE WEALTH LAISSEZ ...GOV/COMP 20 TORY/PARTY CONSRV/PAR. PAGE 129 H2583 — PLURISM CONSERVE POL/PAR NAT/G

B65
ONUOHA B.,THE ELEMENTS OF AFRICAN SOCIALISM. AFR FINAN SECT TEC/DEV FOR/AID GP/REL OWN LAISSEZ MARXISM...CONCPT BIBLIOG 20. PAGE 121 H2419 — SOCISM ECO/UNDEV NAT/G EX/STRUC

B65
SALVADORI M.,ITALY. AUSTRIA FRANCE GERMANY ITALY SPAIN CULTURE NAT/G POL/PAR DIPLOM WAR FASCISM LAISSEZ MARXISM...TIME/SEQ CHARTS BIBLIOG/A. PAGE 137 H2744 — NAT/LISM CATHISM SOCIETY

L66
HUNTINGTON S.P.,"POLITICAL MODERNIZATION* AMERICA VS EUROPE." EUR+WWI MOD/EUR UK USA+45 LAW ECO/UNDEV PWR SOVEREIGN CONSERVE LAISSEZ GOV/COMP. PAGE 75 H1505 — STRUCT CREATE OBS

B67
BODENHEIMER E.,TREATISE ON JUSTICE. INT/ORG NAT/G PUB/INST ACT/RES RISK CRIME INGP/REL DISCRIM DRIVE LAISSEZ 20. PAGE 18 H0363 — ALL/VALS STRUCT JURID CONCPT

S67
SCOVILLE W.J.,"GOVERNMENT REGULATION AND GROWTH IN THE FRENCH PAPER INDUSTRY DURING THE EIGHTEENTH CENTURY." FRANCE MOD/EUR FINAN CAP/ISM TAX ADMIN CONTROL PRIVIL LAISSEZ...POLICY 18. PAGE 141 H2818 — NAT/G PROC/MFG ECO/DEV INGP/REL

B76
SMITH A.,THE WEALTH OF NATIONS. UK STRUCT WORKER DIPLOM ECO/TAC OPTIMAL DRIVE PERSON ORD/FREE ...OLD/LIB GEN/LAWS 17/18. PAGE 145 H2905 — WEALTH PRODUC INDUS LAISSEZ

B79
BRODERICK G.C.,POLITICAL STUDIES. IRELAND UK ROMAN/EMP LAW ACADEM LOC/G NAT/G DIPLOM PARL/PROC SUFF GP/REL LAISSEZ...ANTHOL. PAGE 21 H0424 — CONSTN COLONIAL

LAKEWOOD....LAKEWOOD, CALIFORNIA

LAKOFF/SA....SANFORD A. LAKOFF

LALL B.G. H1798

LAMB B.P. H1799

LAMBERT D. H1800

LAMBERT J. H1801

LAMBERT W.E. H1802

LAMBIRI I. H1803

LAND REFORM....SEE AGRI + CREATE

LAND/LEAG....LAND LEAGUE (IRELAND)

LAND/VALUE....LAND VALUE TAX

LANDAU J.M. H1804

LANDAUER C. H1805

LANDE C.H. H1806

LANDRAT....COUNTY CHIEF EXECUTIVE (GERMANY)

S49
STEINMETZ H.,"THE PROBLEMS OF THE LANDRAT: A STUDY OF COUNTY GOVERNMENT IN THE US ZONE OF GERMANY." GERMANY/W USA+45 INDUS PLAN DIPLOM EDU/PROP CONTROL WAR GOV/REL FEDERAL WEALTH PLURISM...GOV/COMP 20 LANDRAT. PAGE 149 H2977 — LOC/G COLONIAL MGT TOP/EX

LANDRM/GRF....LANDRUM-GRIFFIN ACT

LANDRUM-GRIFFIN ACT....SEE LANDRM/GRF

LANE J.P. H1807

LANGER P.F. H1808

LANGER W.L. H1809,H1810

LANGERHANS H. H1811

LANGLEY....LANGLEY-PORTER NEUROPSYCHIATRIC INSTITUTE

LANGUAGE....SEE LING, ALSO LOGIC, MATHEMATICS, AND LANGUAGE INDEX, P. XIV

LANGUEDOC....LANGUEDOC, SOUTHERN FRANCE

LAO/TZU....LAO TZU

LAOS....SEE ALSO S/ASIA

B12
CORDIER H.,BIBLIOTHECA INDOSINICA: DICTIONAIRE BIBLIOGRAPHIQUE DES OUVRAGES RELATIFS A LA PENINSULE INDOCHINOISE. BURMA LAOS MALAYSIA S/ASIA THAILAND VIETNAM SECT...LING 20. PAGE 33 H0665 — BIBLIOG/A GEOG NAT/G

N19
BRIMMELL G.H.,COMMUNISM IN SOUTHEAST ASIA (PAMPHLET). BURMA CAMBODIA COM INDIA INDONESIA LAOS MOD/EUR NAT/G POL/PAR FORCES CAP/ISM CONTROL WEALTH ...MYTH 20. PAGE 21 H0420 — MARXISM S/ASIA REV ECO/UNDEV

B50
EMBREE J.F.,BIBLIOGRAPHY OF THE PEOPLES AND CULTURES OF MAINLAND SOUTHEAST ASIA. CAMBODIA LAOS THAILAND VIETNAM LAW...GEOG HUM SOC MYTH LING CHARTS WORSHIP 20. PAGE 46 H0915 — BIBLIOG/A CULTURE S/ASIA

B51
BERNATZIK H.A.,THE SPIRITS OF THE YELLOW LEAVES. BURMA LAOS S/ASIA THAILAND VIETNAM SOCIETY AGRI COLONIAL LEISURE GP/REL PERS/REL ISOLAT AGE HABITAT SEX WORSHIP 20. PAGE 16 H0310 — SOC KIN ECO/UNDEV CULTURE

B55
THOMPSON V.,MINORITY PROBLEMS IN SOUTHEAST ASIA. CAMBODIA CHINA/COM LAOS S/ASIA KIN NAT/G SECT PROB/SOLV EDU/PROP REGION GP/REL RACE/REL MARXISM ...SOC 20 BUDDHISM UN. PAGE 154 H3085 — INGP/REL GEOG DIPLOM STRUCT

B64
HALPERN J.M.,GOVERNMENT, POLITICS, AND SOCIAL STRUCTURE IN LAOS. LAOS CULTURE SOCIETY STRATA STRUCT FAM DIPLOM DOMIN MARXISM...INT GOV/COMP WORSHIP SOC/INTEG 20. PAGE 65 H1297 NAT/G SOC LOC/G

B64
HOBBS C.C.,SOUTHEAST ASIA: AN ANNOTATED BIBLIOGRAPHY OF SELECTED REFERENCES IN WESTERN LANGUAGES (REV. ED.). CAMBODIA INDONESIA LAOS THAILAND VIETNAM CONSTN NAT/G...SOC WORSHIP 20. PAGE 72 H1437 BIBLIOG/A S/ASIA CULTURE SOCIETY

B66
COEDES G.,THE MAKING OF SOUTH EAST ASIA. BURMA CAMBODIA LAOS S/ASIA THAILAND VIETNAM REV WAR CIVMIL/REL...GEOG 6/13. PAGE 31 H0614 CULTURE FORCES DOMIN

L67
MCALLISTER J.T. JR.,"THE POSSIBILITIES FOR DIPLOMACY IN SOUTHEAST ASIA." LAOS VIETNAM INT/ORG NAT/G PROVS BAL/PWR DOMIN AGREE COLONIAL WAR PWR 17/20 TREATY. PAGE 106 H2121 DIPLOM S/ASIA

LAPENNA I. H1812

LAPIERRE J.W. H1813

LAPONCE J.A. H1814

LAPRADE W.T. H1815

LAQUEUR W.Z. H1816,H1817,H1818,H1819,H1820,H1821,H1822

LARCENY....LARCENY

LARKIN E. H1823

LARSON A. H1824

LARTEH....LARTEH, GHANA

LARUS J. H1825

LASKER B. H1826

LASKI H.J. H1828,H1829,H1830

LASKI H.S. H1831

LASKI/H....HAROLD LASKI

LASKIN B. H1832

LASSALLE/F....FERDINAND LASSALLE

B50
CARR E.H.,STUDIES IN REVOLUTION. CREATE WAR PERSON ALL/IDEOS MARXISM SOCISM...PHIL/SCI METH/COMP ANTHOL 18/20 SAINTSIMON MARX/KARL PROUDHON/P LASSALLE/F PLEKHNV/GV. PAGE 27 H0537 REV IDEA/COMP COERCE BIOG

LASSWELL H.D. H1833,H1834,H1835

LASSWELL/H....HAROLD D. LASSWELL

S58
EULAU H.,"HD LASSWELL'S DEVELOPMENTAL ANALYSIS." FUT CULTURE TOP/EX PLAN CHOOSE SUPEGO PWR...TREND HYPO/EXP SIMUL GEN/METH VAL/FREE 20 LASSWELL/H. PAGE 47 H0948 CONCPT NEW/IDEA ELITES

LATIN AMERICA....SEE L/A+17C

LATIN AMERICAN FREE TRADE ASSOCIATION....SEE LAFTA

LATIN AMERICAN STUDIES ASSN H1836

LATORRE A. H1837

LATOURETTE K.S. H1838

LATVIA....SEE ALSO USSR

LAULICHT J. H1839

LAUNDY P. H3363

LAURIER/W....SIR WILFRED LAURIER

LAUTERBACH A. H1840

LAVEN P. H1841

LAVRIN J. H1842

LAVROFF D.-G. H1843

LAW....LAW, ETHICAL DIRECTIVES IN A COMMUNITY; SEE ALSO JURID

N
ACAD RUMANIAN SCI DOC CTR,RUMANIAN SCIENTIFIC ABSTRACTS: SOCIAL SCIENCES. ROMANIA FINAN HABITAT ...ART/METH GEOG HUM JURID PSY 20. PAGE 3 H0059 BIBLIOG/A CULTURE LING LAW

N
SCHADERA I.,SELECT BIBLIOGRAPHY OF SOUTH AFRICAN NATIVE LIFE AND PROBLEMS. SOUTH/AFR LAW CULTURE ECO/UNDEV COLONIAL PARTIC...POLICY LING 20. PAGE 138 H2768 BIBLIOG/A SOC AFR STRUCT

B
DEUTSCHE BIBLIOTH FRANKF A M,DEUTSCHE BIBLIOGRAPHIE. EUR+WWI GERMANY ECO/DEV FORCES DIPLOM LEAD...POLICY PHIL/SCI SOC 20. PAGE 40 H0802 BIBLIOG LAW ADMIN NAT/G

N
AUSTRALIAN PUBLIC AFFAIRS INFORMATION SERVICE. LAW ...HEAL HUM MGT SOC CON/ANAL 20 AUSTRAL. PAGE 1 H0011 BIBLIOG NAT/G CULTURE DIPLOM

N
BIBLIOGRAPHIE DE LA PHILOSOPHIE. LAW CULTURE SECT EDU/PROP MORAL...HUM METH/CNCPT 20. PAGE 1 H0012 BIBLIOG/A PHIL/SCI CONCPT LOG

N
HANDBOOK OF LATIN AMERICAN STUDIES. LAW CULTURE ECO/UNDEV POL/PAR ADMIN LEAD...SOC 20. PAGE 1 H0016 BIBLIOG/A L/A+17C NAT/G DIPLOM

N
LONDON TIMES OFFICIAL INDEX. UK LAW ECO/DEV NAT/G DIPLOM LEAD ATTIT 20. PAGE 1 H0018 BIBLIOG INDEX PRESS WRITING

N
PUBLISHERS' CIRCULAR, THE OFFICIAL ORGAN OF THE PUBLISHERS' ASSOCIATION OF GREAT BRITAIN AND IRELAND. EUR+WWI MOD/EUR UK LAW PROB/SOLV DIPLOM COLONIAL ATTIT...HUM 19/20 CMN/WLTH. PAGE 1 H0019 BIBLIOG NAT/G WRITING LEAD

N
PUBLISHERS' TRADE LIST ANNUAL. LAW POL/PAR ADMIN PERSON ALL/IDEOS...HUM SOC 19/20. PAGE 1 H0020 BIBLIOG NAT/G DIPLOM POLICY

N
SUBJECT GUIDE TO BOOKS IN PRINT: AN INDEX TO THE PUBLISHERS' TRADE LIST ANNUAL. UNIV LAW LOC/G DIPLOM WRITING ADMIN LEAD PERSON...MGT SOC. PAGE 2 H0024 BIBLIOG ECO/DEV POL/PAR NAT/G

N
SUMMARIES OF SELECTED JAPANESE MAGAZINES. LAW CULTURE ADMIN LEAD 20 CHINJAP. PAGE 2 H0025 BIBLIOG/A ATTIT NAT/G ASIA

N
NEUE POLITISCHE LITERATUR; BERICHTE UBER DAS INTERNATIONALE SCHRIFTTUM ZUR POLITIK. WOR+45 LAW CONSTN POL/PAR ADMIN LEAD GOV/REL...POLICY IDEA/COMP. PAGE 2 H0027 BIBLIOG/A DIPLOM NAT/G NAT/COMP

N
"PROLOG",DIGEST OF THE SOVIET UKRANIAN PRESS. USSR LAW AGRI INDUS PROVS SCHOOL DIPLOM GOV/REL ATTIT ...HUM LING 20. PAGE 3 H0053 BIBLIOG/A NAT/G PRESS COM

N
AFRICAN BIBLIOGRAPHIC CENTER,A CURRENT BIBLIOGRAPHY ON AFRICAN AFFAIRS. LAW CULTURE ECO/UNDEV LABOR SECT DIPLOM FOR/AID COLONIAL NAT/LISM...LING 20. PAGE 4 H0075 BIBLIOG/A AFR NAT/G REGION

N
ASIA FOUNDATION,LIBRARY NOTES. LAW CONSTN CULTURE SOCIETY ECO/UNDEV INT/ORG NAT/G COLONIAL LEAD REGION NAT/LISM ATTIT 20 UN. PAGE 9 H0176 BIBLIOG/A ASIA S/ASIA DIPLOM

N
CORNELL UNIVERSITY LIBRARY,SOUTHEAST ASIA ACCESSIONS LIST. LAW SOCIETY STRUCT ECO/UNDEV POL/PAR TEC/DEV DIPLOM LEAD REGION. PAGE 34 H0671 BIBLIOG S/ASIA NAT/G CULTURE

N
DEUTSCHE BUCHEREI,JAHRESVERZEICHNIS DES DEUTSCHEN SCHRIFTUMS. AUSTRIA EUR+WWI GERMANY SWITZERLND LAW LOC/G DIPLOM ADMIN...MGT SOC 19/20. PAGE 40 H0804 BIBLIOG WRITING NAT/G

N
DEUTSCHE BUCHEREI,DEUTSCHES BUCHERVERZEICHNIS. GERMANY LAW CULTURE POL/PAR ADMIN LEAD ATTIT PERSON ...SOC 20. PAGE 40 H0805 BIBLIOG NAT/G DIPLOM ECO/DEV

N
INADA S.,INTRODUCTION TO SCIENTIFIC WORKS IN BIBLIOG/A

HUMANITIES AND SOCIAL SCIENCES PUBLISHED IN JAPAN. LAW CULTURE ACADEM EDU/PROP...ART/METH HUM 20 CHINJAP. PAGE 76 H1525 NAT/G SOC S/ASIA

N
INSTITUTE OF HISPANIC STUDIES,HISPANIC AMERICAN REPORT. EUR+WWI SPAIN LAW CONSTN ECO/UNDEV POL/PAR EX/STRUC LEGIS LEAD...HUM SOC 20. PAGE 77 H1538 BIBLIOG/A L/A+17C NAT/G DIPLOM

N
INTERNATIONAL CENTRE AFRICAN,BULLETIN OF INFORMATION ON THESES AND STUDIES IN PROGRESS OR PROPOSED. LAW CULTURE FINAN INDUS LABOR TEC/DEV EDU/PROP...GEOG SOC NAT/COMP 20. PAGE 78 H1554 BIBLIOG/A ACT/RES ACADEM INTELL

N
MINISTERE DE L'EDUC NATIONALE,CATALOGUE DES THESES DE DOCTORAT SOUTENNES DEVANT LES UNIVERSITAIRES FRANCAISES. FRANCE LAW DIPLOM ADMIN...HUM SOC 20. PAGE 111 H2223 BIBLIOG ACADEM KNOWL NAT/G

N
MINISTRY OF OVERSEAS DEVELOPME,TECHNICAL CO-OPERATION -- A BIBLIOGRAPHY. UK LAW SOCIETY DIPLOM ECO/TAC FOR/AID...STAT 20 CMN/WLTH. PAGE 111 H2225 BIBLIOG TEC/DEV ECO/DEV NAT/G

N
SOUTH AFRICA STATE LIBRARY,SOUTH AFRICAN NATIONAL BIBLIOGRAPHY, SANB. SOUTH/AFR LAW NAT/G EDU/PROP ...MGT PSY SOC 20. PAGE 147 H2937 BIBLIOG PRESS WRITING

B00
MAINE H.S.,ANCIENT LAW. MEDIT-7 CULTURE SOCIETY KIN SECT LEGIS LEGIT ROUTINE...JURID HIST/WRIT CON/ANAL TOT/POP VAL/FREE. PAGE 101 H2020 FAM LAW

B01
BRYCE J.,STUDIES IN HISTORY AND JURISPRUDENCE (2 VOLS.). ICELAND SOUTH/AFR UK LAW PROB/SOLV SOVEREIGN...PHIL/SCI NAT/COMP ROME/ANC ROMAN/LAW. PAGE 23 H0455 IDEA/COMP CONSTN JURID

B03
FAGUET E.,LE LIBERALISME. FRANCE PRESS ADJUD ADMIN DISCRIM CONSERVE SOCISM...TRADIT SOC LING WORSHIP PARLIAMENT. PAGE 48 H0960 ORD/FREE EDU/PROP NAT/G LAW

B03
FORTESCUE G.K.,SUBJECT INDEX OF THE MODERN WORKS ADDED TO THE LIBRARY OF THE BRITISH MUSEUM IN THE YEARS 1881-1900 (3 VOLS.). UK LAW CONSTN FINAN NAT/G FORCES INT/TRADE COLONIAL 19. PAGE 52 H1041 BIBLIOG INDEX WRITING

C05
DUNNING W.A.,"HISTORY OF POLITICAL THEORIES FROM LUTHER TO MONTESQUIEU." LAW NAT/G SECT DIPLOM REV WAR ORD/FREE SOVEREIGN CONSERVE...TRADIT BIBLIOG 16/18. PAGE 43 H0867 PHIL/SCI CONCPT GEN/LAWS

B07
BENTHAM J.,AN INTRODUCTION TO THE PRINCIPLES OF MORALS AND LEGISLATION. UNIV CONSTN CULTURE SOCIETY NAT/G CONSULT LEGIS JUDGE ADJUD CT/SYS...JURID CONCPT NEW/IDEA. PAGE 14 H0287 LAW GEN/LAWS

B09
JUSTINIAN,THE DIGEST (DIGESTA CORPUS JURIS CIVILIS) (2 VOLS.) (TRANS. BY C. H. MONRO). ROMAN/EMP LAW FAM LOC/G LEGIS EDU/PROP CONTROL MARRIAGE OWN ROLE CIVIL/LAW. PAGE 82 H1645 JURID CT/SYS NAT/G STRATA

B09
LOBINGIER C.S.,THE PEOPLE'S LAW OR POPULAR PARTICIPATION IN LAW-MAKING. FRANCE SWITZERLND UK LOC/G NAT/G PROVS LEGIS SUFF MAJORITY PWR POPULISM ...GOV/COMP BIBLIOG 19. PAGE 97 H1945 CONSTN LAW PARTIC

C09
SCHAPIRO J.S.,"SOCIAL REFORM AND THE REFORMATION." CHRIST-17C GERMANY LAW CONSTN LG/CO NAT/G WORKER PROB/SOLV CT/SYS REV...BIBLIOG 16. PAGE 138 H2770 ORD/FREE SECT ECO/TAC BIOG

B10
MCILWAIN C.H.,THE HIGH COURT OF PARLIAMENT AND ITS SUPREMACY B1910 1878 408. UK EX/STRUC PARL/PROC GOV/REL INGP/REL PRIVIL 12/20 PARLIAMENT ENGLSH/LAW. PAGE 107 H2132 LAW LEGIS CONSTN NAT/G

B11
PHILLIPSON C.,THE INTERNATIONAL LAW AND CUSTOM OF ANCIENT GREECE AND ROME. MEDIT-7 UNIV INTELL SOCIETY STRUCT NAT/G LEGIS EXEC PERSON...CONCPT OBS CON/ANAL ROM/EMP. PAGE 125 H2504 INT/ORG LAW INT/LAW

B12
POLLOCK F.,THE GENIUS OF THE COMMON LAW. CHRIST-17C UK FINAN CHIEF ACT/RES ADMIN GP/REL ATTIT SOCISM ...ANARCH JURID. PAGE 127 H2537 LAW CULTURE CREATE

B14
FIGGIS J.N.,CHURCHES IN THE MODERN STATE (2ND ED.). LAW CHIEF BAL/PWR PWR...CONCPT CHURCH/STA POPE. PAGE 50 H0998 SECT NAT/G SOCIETY ORD/FREE

B14
LEVINE L.,SYNDICALISM IN FRANCE (2ND ED.). FRANCE LAW SOCIETY ECO/DEV NAT/G ECO/TAC LEAD ATTIT ...POLICY CONCPT STAT BIBLIOG 18/20 REFORMERS. PAGE 95 H1902 LABOR INDUS SOCISM REV

B16
PUFENDORF S.,LAW OF NATURE AND OF NATIONS (ABRIDGED). UNIV LAW NAT/G DIPLOM AGREE WAR PERSON ALL/VALS PWR...POLICY 18 DEITY NATURL/LAW. PAGE 128 H2565 CONCPT INT/LAW SECT MORAL

B17
DE MAISTRE J.,DU PAPE (1817). FRANCE LAW SOCIETY SECT DOMIN REV HAPPINESS PWR SOVEREIGN 18/19 PROTESTANT. PAGE 38 H0761 CATH CHIEF LEGIT NAT/G

B18
EYBERS G.W.,SELECT CONSTITUTIONAL DOCUMENTS ILLUSTRATING SOUTH AFRICAN HISTORY 1795-1910. SOUTH/AFR LOC/G LEGIS CT/SYS...JURID ANTHOL 18/20 NATAL CAPE/HOPE ORANGE/STA. PAGE 48 H0955 CONSTN LAW NAT/G COLONIAL

B19
DUGUIT L.,LAW IN THE MODERN STATE (TRANS. BY FRIDA AND HAROLD LASKI). CONSTN SOCIETY STRUCT MORAL ORD/FREE SOVEREIGN 20. PAGE 43 H0860 GEN/LAWS CONCPT NAT/G LAW

N19
COUTROT A.,THE FIGHT OVER THE 1959 PRIVATE EDUCATION LAW IN FRANCE (PAMPHLET). FRANCE NAT/G SECT GIVE EDU/PROP GP/REL ATTIT RIGID/FLEX ORD/FREE 20 CHURCH/STA. PAGE 34 H0681 SCHOOL PARL/PROC CATHISM LAW

N19
GRIFFITH W.,THE PUBLIC SERVICE (PAMPHLET). UK LAW LOC/G NAT/G PARTIC CHOOSE DRIVE ROLE SKILL...CHARTS 20 CIVIL/SERV. PAGE 61 H1222 ADMIN EFFICIENCY EDU/PROP GOV/REL

N19
OPERATIONS AND POLICY RESEARCH,URUGUAY: ELECTION FACTBOOK: NOVEMBER 27, 1966 (PAMPHLET). URUGUAY LAW NAT/G LEAD REPRESENT...STAT BIOG CHARTS 20. PAGE 121 H2422 POL/PAR CHOOSE PLAN ATTIT

B20
COX H.,ECONOMIC LIBERTY. UNIV LAW INT/TRADE RATION TARIFFS RACE/REL SOCISM POLICY. PAGE 34 H0687 NAT/G ORD/FREE ECO/TAC PERSON

B22
KRABBE H.,THE MODERN IDEA OF THE STATE. LAW CHIEF DIPLOM DOMIN ADMIN REPRESENT CENTRAL ORD/FREE ...NEW/IDEA GOV/COMP IDEA/COMP. PAGE 88 H1761 SOVEREIGN CONSTN PHIL/SCI

B23
LEES-SMITH H.B.,SECOND CHAMBERS IN THEORY AND PRACTICE. IRELAND NORWAY SOUTH/AFR UK LAW POL/PAR LEGIS CONTROL 20 CMN/WLTH. PAGE 93 H1858 PARL/PROC DELIB/GP REPRESENT GP/COMP

B23
POUND R.,INTERPRETATIONS OF LEGAL HISTORY. CULTURE ...PHIL/SCI NEW/IDEA CLASSIF SIMUL GEN/LAWS 19/20. PAGE 127 H2547 LAW IDEA/COMP JURID

B24
HOLDSWORTH W.S.,A HISTORY OF ENGLISH LAW; THE COMMON LAW AND ITS RIVALS (VOL. IV). UK SEA AGRI CHIEF ADJUD CONTROL CRIME GOV/REL...INT/LAW JURID NAT/COMP 16/17 PARLIAMENT COMMON/LAW CANON/LAW ENGLSH/LAW. PAGE 72 H1449 LAW LEGIS CT/SYS CONSTN

B25
WEBSTER C.,THE FOREIGN POLICY OF CASTLEREAGH: 1815-1822. LAW NAT/G DELIB/GP TOP/EX BAL/PWR ORD/FREE PWR RESPECT 19. PAGE 166 H3322 MOD/EUR DIPLOM UK

B26
FORTESCUE J.,THE GOVERNANCE OF ENGLAND (1471-76). UK LAW FINAN SECT LEGIS PROB/SOLV TAX DOMIN ADMIN GP/REL COST ORD/FREE PWR 14/15. PAGE 52 H1042 CONSERVE CONSTN CHIEF NAT/G

B26
MALINOWSKI B.,CRIME AND CUSTOM IN SAVAGE SOCIETY. SOCIETY FAM SECT LEGIT SANCTION MARRIAGE MYSTISM ...PSY SOC 19/20 MELANESIA CANON/LAW. PAGE 102 H2030 LAW CULTURE CRIME ADJUD

B26
MCIVER R.M.,THE MODERN STATE. UNIV LAW AUTHORIT SOVEREIGN IDEA/COMP. PAGE 107 H2136 GEN/LAWS CONSTN NAT/G PWR

B27
GOOCH G.P.,ENGLISH DEMOCRATIC IDEAS IN THE SEVENTEENTH CENTURY (2ND ED.). UK LAW SECT FORCES DIPLOM LEAD PARL/PROC REV ATTIT AUTHORIT...ANARCH CONCPT 17 PARLIAMENT CMN/WLTH REFORMERS. PAGE 58 H1167 IDEA/COMP MAJORIT EX/STRUC CONSERVE

B27
JOHN OF SALISBURY,THE STATESMAN'S BOOK (1159) (TRANS. BY J. DICKINSON). DOMIN GP/REL MORAL ORD/FREE PWR CONSERVE...CATH CONCPT 12. PAGE 81 H1617 NAT/G SECT CHIEF LAW

B28
CORBETT P.E.,CANADA AND WORLD POLITICS. LAW CULTURE SOCIETY STRUCT MARKET INT/ORG FORCES ACT/RES PLAN ECO/TAC LEGIT ORD/FREE PWR RESPECT...SOC CONCPT TIME/SEQ TREND CMN/WLTH 20 LEAGUE/NAT. PAGE 33 H0662 NAT/G CANADA

B28
HOBBES T.,THE ELEMENTS OF LAW, NATURAL AND POLITIC (1650). STRATA NAT/G SECT CHIEF AGREE ATTIT ALL/VALS MORAL ORD/FREE POPULISM...POLICY CONCPT. PAGE 71 H1432 PERSON LAW SOVEREIGN CONSERVE

B28
HOLDSWORTH W.S.,THE HISTORIANS OF ANGLO-AMERICAN LAW. UK USA-45 INTELL LEGIS RESPECT...BIOG NAT/COMP 17/20 COMMON/LAW. PAGE 72 H1450 HIST/WRIT LAW JURID

B28
YANG KUNG-SUN,THE BOOK OF LORD SHANG. LAW ECO/UNDEV LOC/G NAT/G NEIGH PLAN ECO/TAC LEGIT ATTIT SKILL ...CONCPT CON/ANAL WORK TOT/POP. PAGE 172 H3434 ASIA JURID

B29
CAM H.M.,BIBLIOGRAPHY OF ENGLISH CONSTITUTIONAL HISTORY (PAMPHLET). UK LAW LOC/G NAT/G POL/PAR SECT DELIB/GP ADJUD ORD/FREE 19/20 PARLIAMENT. PAGE 25 H0510 BIBLIOG/A CONSTN ADMIN PARL/PROC

B30
BENTHAM J.,THE RATIONALE OF PUNISHMENT. UK LAW LOC/G NAT/G LEGIS CONTROL...JURID GEN/LAWS COURT/SYS 19. PAGE 14 H0289 CRIME SANCTION COERCE ORD/FREE

B30
BURLAMAQUI J.J.,PRINCIPLES OF NATURAL AND POLITIC LAW (2 VOLS.) (1747-51). EX/STRUC LEGIS AGREE CT/SYS CHOOSE ROLE SOVEREIGN 18 NATURL/LAW. PAGE 24 H0490 LAW NAT/G ORD/FREE CONCPT

B30
BYNKERSHOEK C.,QUAESTIONUM JURIS PUBLICI LIBRI DUO. CHRIST-17C MOD/EUR CONSTN ELITES SOCIETY NAT/G PROVS EX/STRUC FORCES TOP/EX BAL/PWR DIPLOM ATTIT MORAL...TRADIT CONCPT. PAGE 25 H0502 INT/ORG LAW NAT/LISM INT/LAW

B32
GREAT BRIT COMM MINISTERS PWR,REPORT. UK LAW CONSTN CONSULT LEGIS PARL/PROC SANCTION SOVEREIGN ...DECISION JURID 20 PARLIAMENT. PAGE 60 H1201 EX/STRUC NAT/G PWR CONTROL

B32
LUNT D.C.,THE ROAD TO THE LAW. UK USA-45 LEGIS EDU/PROP OWN ORD/FREE...DECISION TIME/SEQ NAT/COMP 16/20 AUSTRAL ENGLSH/LAW COMMON/LAW. PAGE 99 H1980 ADJUD LAW JURID CT/SYS

B33
ENSOR R.C.K.,COURTS AND JUDGES IN FRANCE, GERMANY, AND ENGLAND. FRANCE GERMANY UK LAW PROB/SOLV ADMIN ROUTINE CRIME ROLE...METH/COMP 20 CIVIL/LAW. PAGE 46 H0930 CT/SYS EX/STRUC ADJUD NAT/COMP

B33
MOSS W.,POLITICAL PARTIES IN THE IRISH FREE STATE. IRELAND UK LAW FINAN LABOR DELIB/GP TOP/EX TARIFFS EDU/PROP...CHARTS GP/COMP 20. PAGE 113 H2269 POL/PAR NAT/G CHOOSE POLICY

B33
PUBLIC OPINION AND WORLD POLITICS. UNIV LAW CULTURE NAT/G PRESS REV GP/REL...MAJORIT METH/COMP ANTHOL 20. PAGE 171 H3420 DIPLOM EDU/PROP ATTIT MAJORITY

B35
MORE T.,UTOPIA (1516) (TRANS. BY R. ROBYNSON). LAW CULTURE SOCIETY STRUCT FAM SECT EDU/PROP WAR OWN UTIL KNOWL WEALTH 16. PAGE 113 H2253 UTOPIA NAT/G ECO/TAC GEN/LAWS

B35
RAM J.,THE SCIENCE OF LEGAL JUDGMENT: A TREATISE... UK CONSTN NAT/G LEGIS CREATE PROB/SOLV AGREE CT/SYS ...INT/LAW CONCPT 19 ENGLSH/LAW CANON/LAW CIVIL/LAW CTS/WESTM. PAGE 129 H2584 LAW JURID EX/STRUC ADJUD

B36
CULVER D.C.,METHODOLOGY OF SOCIAL SCIENCE RESEARCH: A BIBLIOGRAPHY. LAW CULTURE...CRIMLGY GEOG STAT OBS INT QU HIST/WRIT CHARTS 20. PAGE 36 H0719 BIBLIOG/A METH SOC

B36
SMITH T.V.,THE PROMISE OF AMERICAN POLITICS. USA-45 WOR-45 LAW CONSTN STRATA PARTIC FASCISM LAISSEZ MARXISM...MAJORIT METH/COMP 18/20 JEFFERSN/T LOCKE/JOHN BENTHAM/J. PAGE 146 H2920 CONCPT ORD/FREE IDEA/COMP NAT/COMP

B37
BORGESE G.A.,GOLIATH: THE MARCH OF FASCISM. GERMANY ITALY LAW POL/PAR SECT DIPLOM SOCISM...JURID MYTH 20 DANTE MACHIAVELL MUSSOLIN/B. PAGE 19 H0375 POLICY NAT/LISM FASCISM NAT/G

B38
DUNHAM W.H. JR.,COMPLAINT AND REFORM IN ENGLAND 1436-1714. UK LAW ACADEM NAT/G POL/PAR SCHOOL PRESS COLONIAL PARL/PROC MORAL...SOC/WK ANTHOL 15/18 HAKLUYT/R COWPER/W. PAGE 43 H0865 ATTIT SOCIETY SECT

B38
HARPER S.N.,THE GOVERNMENT OF THE SOVIET UNION. COM USSR LAW CONSTN ECO/DEV PLAN TEC/DEV DIPLOM INT/TRADE ADMIN REV NAT/LISM...POLICY 20. PAGE 67 H1337 MARXISM NAT/G LEAD POL/PAR

B38
HOLDSWORTH W.S.,A HISTORY OF ENGLISH LAW; THE CENTURIES OF SETTLEMENT AND REFORM (VOL. X). INDIA UK CONSTN NAT/G CHIEF LEGIS ADMIN COLONIAL CT/SYS CHOOSE ORD/FREE PWR...JURID 18 PARLIAMENT COMMONWLTH COMMON/LAW. PAGE 72 H1451 LAW LOC/G EX/STRUC ADJUD

B38
HOLDSWORTH W.S.,A HISTORY OF ENGLISH LAW; THE CENTURIES OF SETTLEMENT AND REFORM (VOL. XI). UK CONSTN NAT/G EX/STRUC DIPLOM ADJUD CT/SYS LEAD CRIME ATTIT...INT/LAW JURID 18 CMN/WLTH PARLIAMENT ENGLSH/LAW. PAGE 73 H1452 LAW COLONIAL LEGIS PARL/PROC

B38
MARX K.,THE GERMAN IDEOLOGY, PARTS 1 AND 3 (1846). MOD/EUR LAW STRATA WORKER DOMIN REV UTOPIA SOCISM 19 MARX/KARL. PAGE 104 H2079 MARXIST OWN PRODUC ECO/TAC

B38
MCNAIR A.D.,THE LAW OF TREATIES: BRITISH PRACTICE AND OPINIONS. UK CREATE DIPLOM LEGIT WRITING ADJUD WAR...INT/LAW JURID TREATY. PAGE 107 H2144 AGREE LAW CT/SYS NAT/G

B38
POUND R.,THE FORMATIVE ERA OF AMERICAN LAW. CULTURE NAT/G PROVS LEGIS ADJUD CT/SYS PERSON SOVEREIGN ...POLICY IDEA/COMP GEN/LAWS 18/19. PAGE 127 H2548 CONSTN LAW CREATE JURID

B38
RAWLINSON H.G.,INDIA: A SHORT CULTURAL HISTORY. INDIA LAW STRATA FORCES INT/TRADE ADMIN COLONIAL PERSON...GEOG HUM BIBLIOG WORSHIP 20. PAGE 130 H2598 CULTURE SECT MYTH ART/METH

B39
AKIGA,AKIGA'S STORY: THE TIV TRIBE AS SEEN BY ONE OF ITS MEMBERS. NIGERIA LAW STRUCT ECO/UNDEV FAM LEAD GP/REL MARRIAGE...LING WORSHIP 20. PAGE 4 H0089 KIN SECT SOC CULTURE

B39
HILL R.L.,A BIBLIOGRAPHY OF THE ANGLO-EGYPTIAN SUDAN FROM THE EARLIEST TIMES TO 1937. AFR ETHIOPIA SUDAN UAR LAW COM/IND SECT RACE/REL...GEOG HEAL SOC LING 19/20 NEGRO. PAGE 71 H1417 BIBLIOG CULTURE NAT/COMP GP/COMP

B39
SIEYES E.J.,LES DISCOURS DE SIEYES DANS LES DEBATS CONSTITUTIONNELS DE L'AN III (2 ET 18 THERMIDOR). FRANCE LAW NAT/G PROB/SOLV BAL/PWR GOV/REL 18 JURY. PAGE 144 H2871 CONSTN ADJUD LEGIS EX/STRUC

B40
MCILWAIN C.H.,CONSTITUTIONALISM, ANCIENT AND MODERN. CHRIST-17C MOD/EUR NAT/G CHIEF PROB/SOLV INSPECT AUTHORIT ORD/FREE PWR...TIME/SEQ ROMAN/REP. PAGE 107 H2134 CONSTN GEN/LAWS LAW

B40
TONNIES F.,FUNDAMENTAL CONCEPTS OF SOCIOLOGY (1887) (TRANS. BY C. LOOMIS). LAW STRATA STRUCT FAM MUNIC NAT/G DOMIN LEGIT SANCTION COERCE CRIME PERSON 19. PAGE 156 H3115 CULTURE SOCIETY GEN/LAWS SOC

S40
GURVITCH G.,"MAJOR PROBLEMS OF THE SOCIOLOGY OF LAW." CULTURE SANCTION KNOWL MORAL...POLICY EPIST JURID WORSHIP. PAGE 63 H1255 SOC LAW PHIL/SCI

B41
GILMORE M.P.,ARGUMENT FROM ROMAN LAW IN POLITICAL THOUGHT, 1200-1600. INTELL LICENSE CONTROL CT/SYS GOV/REL PRIVIL PWR...IDEA/COMP BIBLIOG 13/16. PAGE 56 H1130 JURID LAW CONCPT NAT/G

B41
GRISMER R.,A NEW BIBLIOGRAPHY OF THE LITERATURES OF SPAIN AND SPANISH AMERICA. CHRIST-17C MOD/EUR PRE/AMER SPAIN CULTURE DIPLOM EDU/PROP...ART/METH GEOG HUM PHIL/SCI 20. PAGE 61 H1229 BIBLIOG LAW NAT/G ECO/UNDEV

B42
CRAIG A.,ABOVE ALL LIBERTIES. FRANCE UK USA-45 LAW CONSTN CULTURE INTELL NAT/G SECT JUDGE...IDEA/COMP BIBLIOG 18/20. PAGE 35 H0692 ORD/FREE MORAL WRITING EDU/PROP

B42
FORTESCU J.,IN PRAISE OF ENGLISH LAW (1464) (TRANS. BY S.B. CHRIMES). UK ELITES CHIEF FORCES CT/SYS COERCE CRIME GOV/REL ILLEGIT...JURID GOV/COMP GEN/LAWS 15. PAGE 52 H1040 LAW CONSTN LEGIS ORD/FREE

B42
HEGEL G.W.F.,PHILOSOPHY OF RIGHT. UNIV FAM SECT CHIEF AGREE WAR MARRIAGE OWN ORD/FREE...POLICY CONCPT. PAGE 69 H1383 NAT/G LAW RATIONAL

B42
ROBBINS J.J.,THE GOVERNMENT OF LABOR RELATIONS IN SWEDEN. SWEDEN LAW CONSTN ADJUD CT/SYS GP/REL ...JURID 20. PAGE 132 H2638 NAT/G BARGAIN LABOR INDUS

C42
CRAIG A.,"ABOVE ALL LIBERTIES." FRANCE UK LAW CULTURE INTELL SECT ORD/FREE 18/20. PAGE 35 H0693 BIBLIOG/A EDU/PROP WRITING MORAL

B43
SERENI A.P.,THE ITALIAN CONCEPTION OF INTERNATIONAL LAW. EUR+WWI MOD/EUR INT/ORG NAT/G DOMIN COERCE ORD/FREE FASCISM...OBS/ENVIR TREND 20. PAGE 141 H2829 LAW TIME/SEQ INT/LAW ITALY

C43
BENTHAM J.,"ON THE LIBERTY OF THE PRESS, AND PUBLIC DISCUSSION" IN J. BOWRING, ED., THE WORKS OF JEREMY BENTHAM." SPAIN UK LAW ELITES NAT/G LEGIS INSPECT LEGIT WRITING CONTROL PRIVIL TOTALISM AUTHORIT ...TRADIT 19 FREE/SPEE. PAGE 15 H0290
ORD/FREE PRESS CONFER CONSERVE

B44
SUAREZ F.,A TREATISE ON LAWS AND GOD THE LAWGIVER (1612) IN SELECTIONS FROM THREE WORKS, VOL. II. FRANCE ITALY UK CULTURE NAT/G SECT CHIEF LEGIS DOMIN LEGIT CT/SYS ORD/FREE PWR WORSHIP 16/17. PAGE 150 H3004
LAW JURID GEN/LAWS CATH

B44
US LIBRARY OF CONGRESS,RUSSIA: A CHECK LIST PRELIMINARY TO A BASIC BIBLIOGRAPHY OF MATERIALS IN THE RUSSIAN LANGUAGE. COM USSR CULTURE EDU/PROP MARXISM...ART/METH HUM LING 19/20. PAGE 160 H3204
BIBLIOG LAW SECT

N45
INDIA QUARTERLY, A JOURNAL OF INTERNATIONAL AFFAIRS. INDIA LAW CONSTN ECO/UNDEV INT/ORG POL/PAR COLONIAL LEAD PARL/PROC WAR ATTIT...SOC 20 CMN/WLTH. PAGE 2 H0033
BIBLIOG/A S/ASIA DIPLOM NAT/G

B45
US LIBRARY OF CONGRESS,NETHERLANDS EAST INDIES. INDONESIA LAW CULTURE AGRI INDUS SCHOOL COLONIAL HEALTH...GEOG JURID SOC 19/20 NETH/IND. PAGE 160 H3205
BIBLIOG/A S/ASIA NAT/G

B46
BLUM L.,FOR ALL MANKIND (TRANS. BY W. PICKLES). FRANCE GERMANY USSR LAW SOCIETY STRUCT POL/PAR WORKER DIPLOM DOMIN CHOOSE ORD/FREE FASCISM 20. PAGE 18 H0361
POPULISM SOCIALIST NAT/G WAR

S46
SILBERNER E.,"THE PROBLEM OF WAR IN NINETEENTH CENTURY ECONOMIC THOUGHT." EUR+WWI MOD/EUR UNIV LAW ECO/DEV ECO/UNDEV FINAN INDUS MARKET INT/ORG NAT/G CONSULT FORCES...CONCPT GEN/LAWS GEN/METH 19. PAGE 144 H2875
ATTIT ECO/TAC WAR

B47
DE NOIA J.,GUIDE TO OFFICIAL PUBLICATIONS OF OTHER AMERICAN REPUBLICS: ECUADOR (VOL. IX). ECUADOR LAW FINAN LEGIS BUDGET CT/SYS 19/20. PAGE 38 H0763
BIBLIOG/A CONSTN NAT/G EDU/PROP

B47
DE NOIA J.,GUIDE TO OFFICIAL PUBLICATIONS OF THE OTHER AMERICAN REPUBLICS: EL SALVADOR. EL/SALVADR LAW LEGIS EDU/PROP CT/SYS 20. PAGE 38 H0764
BIBLIOG/A CONSTN NAT/G ADMIN

B47
DE NOIA J.,GUIDE TO OFFICIAL PUBLICATIONS OF THE OTHER AMERICAN REPUBLICS: NICARAGUA (VOL. XIV). NICARAGUA LAW LEGIS ADMIN CT/SYS...JURID 19/20. PAGE 38 H0765
BIBLIOG/A EDU/PROP NAT/G CONSTN

B47
DE NOIA J.,GUIDE TO OFFICIAL PUBLICATIONS OF THE OTHER AMERICAN REPUBLICS: PANAMA (VOL. XV). PANAMA LAW LEGIS EDU/PROP CT/SYS 20. PAGE 38 H0766
BIBLIOG/A CONSTN ADMIN NAT/G

B47
LOCKE J.,TWO TREATISES OF GOVERNMENT (1690). UK LAW SOCIETY LEGIS LEGIT AGREE REV OWN HEREDITY MORAL CONSERVE...POLICY MAJORIT 17 WILLIAM/3 NATURL/LAW. PAGE 97 H1946
CONCPT ORD/FREE NAT/G CONSEN

B47
MCILWAIN C.H.,CONSTITUTIONALISM: ANCIENT AND MODERN. USA+45 ROMAN/EMP LAW CHIEF LEGIS CT/SYS GP/REL ORD/FREE SOVEREIGN...POLICY TIME/SEQ ROMAN/REP EUROPE. PAGE 107 H2135
CONSTN NAT/G PARL/PROC GOV/COMP

B47
NEUBURGER O.,GUIDE TO OFFICIAL PUBLICATIONS OF OTHER AMERICAN REPUBLICS: HONDURAS (VOL. XIII). HONDURAS LAW LEGIS ADMIN CT/SYS...JURID 19/20. PAGE 117 H2333
BIBLIOG/A NAT/G EDU/PROP CONSTN

B47
NEUBURGER O.,GUIDE TO OFFICIAL PUBLICATIONS OF THE OTHER AMERICAN REPUBLICS: HAITI (VOL. XII). HAITI LAW FINAN LEGIS PRESS...JURID 20. PAGE 117 H2334
BIBLIOG/A CONSTN NAT/G EDU/PROP

B48
DE NOIA J.,GUIDE TO OFFICIAL PUBLICATIONS OF OTHER AMERICAN REPUBLICS: PERU (VOL. XVII). PERU LAW LEGIS ADMIN CT/SYS...JURID 19/20. PAGE 38 H0767
BIBLIOG/A CONSTN NAT/G EDU/PROP

B48
NEUBURGER O.,GUIDE TO OFFICIAL PUBLICATIONS OF THE OTHER AMERICAN REPUBLICS: VENEZUELA (VOL. XIX). VENEZUELA FINAN LEGIS PLAN BUDGET DIPLOM CT/SYS PARL/PROC 19/20. PAGE 117 H2335
BIBLIOG/A NAT/G CONSTN LAW

S48
ALEXANDER L.,"WAR CRIMES, THEIR SOCIAL-PSYCHOLOGICAL ASPECTS." EUR+WWI GERMANY LAW CULTURE ELITES KIN POL/PAR PUB/INST FORCES DOMIN EDU/PROP COERCE CRIME ATTIT SUPEGO HEALTH MORAL PWR FASCISM ...PSY OBS TREND GEN/LAWS NAZI 20. PAGE 5 H0100
DRIVE WAR

B49
DENNING A.,FREEDOM UNDER THE LAW. MOD/EUR UK LAW SOCIETY CHIEF EX/STRUC LEGIS ADJUD CT/SYS PERS/REL PERSON 17/20 ENGLSH/LAW. PAGE 40 H0793
ORD/FREE JURID NAT/G

B49
HOLLERAN M.P.,CHURCH AND STATE IN GUATEMALA. GUATEMALA LAW STRUCT CATHISM...SOC SOC/INTEG 17/20 CHURCH/STA. PAGE 73 H1456
SECT NAT/G GP/REL CULTURE

B49
SCHONS D.,BOOK CENSORSHIP IN NEW SPAIN (NEW WORLD STUDIES, BOOK II). SPAIN LAW CULTURE INSPECT ADJUD CT/SYS SANCTION GP/REL ORD/FREE 14/17. PAGE 140 H2797
CHRIST-17C EDU/PROP CONTROL PRESS

B49
SCHWARTZ B.,LAW AND THE EXECUTIVE IN BRITAIN: A COMPARATIVE STUDY. UK USA+45 LAW EX/STRUC PWR ...GOV/COMP 20. PAGE 140 H2807
ADMIN EXEC CONTROL REPRESENT

B49
US DEPARTMENT OF STATE,SOVIET BIBLIOGRAPHY (PAMPHLET). CHINA/COM COM USSR LAW AGRI INT/ORG ECO/TAC EDU/PROP...POLICY GEOG 20. PAGE 159 H3185
BIBLIOG/A MARXISM CULTURE DIPLOM

B49
WORMUTH F.D.,THE ORIGINS OF MODERN CONSTITUTIONALISM. GREECE UK LEGIS CREATE TEC/DEV BAL/PWR DOMIN ADJUD REV WAR PWR...JURID ROMAN/REP CROMWELL/O. PAGE 170 H3412
NAT/G CONSTN LAW

B50
BERMAN H.J.,JUSTICE IN RUSSIA; AN INTERPRETATION OF SOVIET LAW. USSR LAW STRUCT LABOR FORCES AGREE GP/REL ORD/FREE SOCISM...TIME/SEQ 20. PAGE 15 H0309
JURID ADJUD MARXISM COERCE

B50
DUCLOS P.,L'EVOLUTION DES RAPPORTS POLITIQUES DEPUIS 1750 (LIBERTE, INTEGRATION, UNITE). LAW INT/ORG FEDERAL TOTALISM ATTIT PWR...MAJORIT BIBLIOG 18/20 PARLIAMENT EUROPE. PAGE 43 H0852
ORD/FREE DIPLOM NAT/G GOV/COMP

B50
EMBREE J.F.,BIBLIOGRAPHY OF THE PEOPLES AND CULTURES OF MAINLAND SOUTHEAST ASIA. CAMBODIA LAOS THAILAND VIETNAM LAW...GEOG HUM SOC MYTH LING CHARTS WORSHIP 20. PAGE 46 H0915
BIBLIOG/A CULTURE S/ASIA

B50
HARLEY G.W.,MASKS AS AGENTS OF SOCIAL CONTROL IN NORTHEAST LIBERIA. AFR LIBERIA LAW CULTURE ADJUST CONSEN MORAL...GEOG SOC WORSHIP 20. PAGE 66 H1332
CONTROL ECO/UNDEV SECT CHIEF

B50
HOBBES T.,LEVIATHAN. UNIV CONSTN SOCIETY LOC/G NAT/G CONSULT TOP/EX DOMIN DRIVE PERSON PWR ...PHIL/SCI CONCPT SELF/OBS GEN/LAWS TOT/POP. PAGE 72 H1434
LAW ORD/FREE

B50
HOOKER R.,OF THE LAWS OF ECCLESIASTICAL POLITY (1594) (ABR. BY J. S. MARSHALL). UK UNIV CHIEF PARTIC MORAL...JURID GEN/LAWS WORSHIP 16. PAGE 73 H1463
SECT CONCPT LAW NAT/G

B50
MACIVER R.M.,GREAT EXPRESSIONS OF HUMAN RIGHTS. LAW CONSTN CULTURE INTELL SOCIETY R+D INT/ORG ATTIT DRIVE...JURID OBS HIST/WRIT GEN/LAWS. PAGE 100 H1999
UNIV CONCPT

B50
WADE E.C.S.,CONSTITUTIONAL LAW; AN OUTLINE OF THE LAW AND PRACTICE OF THE CONSTITUTION. UK LEGIS DOMIN ADMIN GP/REL 16/20 CMN/WLTH PARLIAMENT ENGLSH/LAW. PAGE 164 H3283
CONSTN NAT/G PARL/PROC LAW

B50
WARD R.E.,A GUIDE TO JAPANESE REFERENCE AND RESEARCH MATERIALS IN THE FIELD OF POLITICAL SCIENCE. LAW CONSTN LOC/G PRESS ADMIN...SOC CON/ANAL METH 19/20 CHINJAP. PAGE 165 H3305
BIBLIOG/A ASIA NAT/G

C50
NUMELIN R.,"THE BEGINNINGS OF DIPLOMACY." INT/TRADE WAR GP/REL PEACE STRANGE ATTIT...INT/LAW CONCPT BIBLIOG. PAGE 119 H2380
DIPLOM KIN CULTURE LAW

C50
STOKES W.S.,"HONDURAS: AN AREA STUDY IN GOVERNMENT." HONDURAS NAT/G POL/PAR COLONIAL CT/SYS ROUTINE CHOOSE REPRESENT...GEOG RECORD BIBLIOG 19/20. PAGE 149 H2988
CONSTN LAW L/A+17C ADMIN

B51
HUXLEY J.,FREEDOM AND CULTURE. UNIV LAW SOCIETY R+D ACADEM SCHOOL CREATE SANCTION ATTIT KNOWL...HUM ANTHOL 20. PAGE 76 H1512
CULTURE ORD/FREE PHIL/SCI IDEA/COMP

B51
WEBSTER C.,THE FOREIGN POLICY OF PALMERSTON - 1830 TO 1841. MOD/EUR UK LAW CONSTN INTELL SOCIETY STRUCT NAT/G FORCES TOP/EX CREATE BAL/PWR PWR 19. PAGE 166 H3323
ADMIN PERSON DIPLOM

B51
WHEARE K.C.,MODERN CONSTITUTIONS (HOME UNIVERSITY LIBRARY). UNIV LAW NAT/G LEGIS...CONCPT TREND BIBLIOG. PAGE 167 H3336
CONSTN CLASSIF PWR

CREATE
B52
BENTHAM A.,HANDBOOK OF POLITICAL FALLACIES. FUT MOD/EUR LAW INTELL LOC/G MUNIC NAT/G DELIB/GP LEGIS CREATE EDU/PROP CT/SYS ATTIT RIGID/FLEX KNOWL PWR ...RELATIV PSY SOC CONCPT SELF/OBS TREND STERTYP TOT/POP. PAGE 14 H0286 POL/PAR

B52
DILLON D.R.,LATIN AMERICA, 1935-1949; A SELECTED BIBLIOGRAPHY. LAW EDU/PROP...SOC 20. PAGE 41 H0826 BIBLIOG L/A+17C NAT/G DIPLOM

B52
ETTINGHAUSEN R.,SELECTED AND ANNOTATED BIBLIOGRAPHY OF BOOKS AND PERIODICALS IN WESTERN LANGUAGES DEALING WITH NEAR AND MIDDLE EAST. LAW CULTURE SECT ...ART/METH GEOG SOC. PAGE 47 H0944 BIBLIOG/A ISLAM MEDIT-7

B52
KOLARZ W.,RUSSIA AND HER COLONIES. COM RUSSIA LAW CULTURE ECO/DEV KIN LOC/G SECT TEC/DEV ECO/TAC EDU/PROP REGION COERCE ATTIT PWR SOVEREIGN...SOC TIME/SEQ CON/ANAL VAL/FREE 19/20. PAGE 88 H1749 NAT/G DOMIN USSR COLONIAL

B52
MONTAGU A.,MAN'S MOST DANGEROUS MYTH: THE FALLACY OF RACE. LAW PROB/SOLV WAR HABITAT POPULISM...PSY CONCPT CHARTS BIBLIOG NEGRO JEWS. PAGE 112 H2242 DISCRIM MYTH CULTURE RACE/REL

B52
SCHATTSCHNEIDER E.E.,A GUIDE TO THE STUDY OF PUBLIC AFFAIRS. LAW LOC/G NAT/G LEGIS BUDGET PRESS ADMIN LOBBY...JURID CHARTS 20. PAGE 139 H2775 ACT/RES INTELL ACADEM METH/COMP

B52
US DEPARTMENT OF STATE,RESEARCH ON EASTERN EUROPE (EXCLUDING USSR). EUR+WWI LAW ECO/DEV NAT/G PROB/SOLV DIPLOM ADMIN LEAD MARXISM...TREND 19/20. PAGE 159 H3187 BIBLIOG R+D ACT/RES COM

B53
BROWN D.M.,THE WHITE UMBRELLA: INDIAN POLITICAL THOUGHT FROM MANU TO GANDHI. INDIA LAW NAT/G SECT WRITING NAT/LISM...ANTHOL BIBLIOG 20 HINDU GANDHI/M MANU. PAGE 22 H0442 CONCPT DOMIN CONSERVE

B53
ORFIELD L.B.,THE GROWTH OF SCANDINAVIAN LAW. DENMARK ICELAND NORWAY SWEDEN LAW DIPLOM...BIBLIOG 9/20. PAGE 121 H2426 JURID CT/SYS NAT/G

B53
PIERCE R.A.,RUSSIAN CENTRAL ASIA, 1867-1917: A SELECTED BIBLIOGRAPHY (PAMPHLET). USSR LAW CULTURE NAT/G EDU/PROP WAR...GEOG SOC 19/20. PAGE 125 H2508 BIBLIOG COLONIAL ADMIN COM

B54
FRIEDMAN W.,THE PUBLIC CORPORATION: A COMPARATIVE SYMPOSIUM (UNIVERSITY OF TORONTO SCHOOL OF LAW COMPARATIVE LAW SERIES, VOL. I). SWEDEN USA+45 INDUS INT/ORG NAT/G REGION CENTRAL FEDERAL...POLICY JURID IDEA/COMP NAT/COMP ANTHOL 20 COMMONWLTH MONOPOLY EUROPE. PAGE 53 H1065 LAW SOCISM LG/CO OWN

B54
LEWIS E.,MEDIEVAL POLITICAL IDEAS. LAW CULTURE SOCIETY ECO/UNDEV NAT/G SECT GOV/REL ATTIT ...BIBLIOG/A T 11/15. PAGE 96 H1913 CHRIST-17C IDEA/COMP INTELL CONCPT

B54
SCHWARTZ B.,FRENCH ADMINISTRATIVE LAW AND THE COMMON-LAW WORLD. FRANCE CULTURE LOC/G NAT/G PROVS DELIB/GP EX/STRUC LEGIS PROB/SOLV CT/SYS EXEC GOV/REL...IDEA/COMP ENGLSH/LAW. PAGE 140 H2808 JURID LAW METH/COMP ADJUD

B54
TITIEV M.,THE SCIENCE OF MAN. LAW STRATA KIN GP/REL PERS/REL HABITAT HEREDITY KNOWL...LING CHARTS BIBLIOG WORSHIP. PAGE 155 H3107 SOC PSY CULTURE

B54
TOTOK W.,HANDBUCH DER BIBLIOGRAPHISCHEN NACHSCHLAGEWERKE. GERMANY LAW CULTURE ADMIN...SOC 20. PAGE 156 H3117 BIBLIOG/A NAT/G DIPLOM POLICY

C54
GUINS G.C.,"SOVIET LAW AND SOVIET SOCIETY." COM USSR STRATA FAM NAT/G WORKER DOMIN RACE/REL ...BIBLIOG 20. PAGE 62 H1249 LAW STRUCT PLAN

B55
CHARMATZ J.P.,COMPARATIVE STUDIES IN COMMUNITY PROPERTY LAW. FRANCE USA+45...JURID GOV/COMP ANTHOL 20. PAGE 29 H0583 MARRIAGE LAW OWN MUNIC

B55
KHADDURI M.,LAW IN THE MIDDLE EAST. LAW CONSTN ACADEM FAM EDU/PROP CT/SYS SANCTION CRIME...INT/LAW GOV/COMP ANTHOL 6/20 MID/EAST. PAGE 85 H1703 ADJUD JURID ISLAM

B55
MAZZINI J.,THE DUTIES OF MAN. MOD/EUR LAW SOCIETY FAM NAT/G POL/PAR SECT VOL/ASSN EX/STRUC ACT/RES CREATE REV PEACE ATTIT ALL/VALS...GEN/LAWS WORK 19. PAGE 106 H2113 SUPEGO CONCPT NAT/LISM

B55
MID-EUROPEAN LAW PROJECT,CHURCH AND STATE BEHIND THE IRON CURTAIN. COM CZECHOSLVK HUNGARY POLAND USSR CULTURE SECT EDU/PROP GOV/REL CATHISM...CHARTS ANTHOL BIBLIOG WORSHIP 20 CHURCH/STA. PAGE 110 H2202 LAW MARXISM POLICY

B55
MOHL R.V.,DIE GESCHICHTE UND LITERATUR DER STAATSWISSENSCHAFTEN (3 VOLS.). LAW NAT/G...JURID METH/COMP METH. PAGE 112 H2236 PHIL/SCI MOD/EUR

B55
SERRANO MOSCOSO E.,A STATEMENT OF THE LAWS OF ECUADOR IN MATTERS AFFECTING BUSINESS (2ND ED.). ECUADOR INDUS LABOR LG/CO NAT/G LEGIS TAX CONTROL MARRIAGE 20. PAGE 141 H2830 FINAN ECO/UNDEV LAW CONSTN

B55
SMITH G.,A CONSTITUTIONAL AND LEGAL HISTORY OF ENGLAND. UK ELITES NAT/G LEGIS ADJUD OWN HABITAT POPULISM...JURID 20 ENGLSH/LAW. PAGE 145 H2909 CONSTN PARTIC LAW CT/SYS

B56
BECKER H.,MAN IN RECIPROCITY: INTRODUCTORY LECTURES ON CULTURE, SOCIETY, AND PERSONALITY. LAW FAM SECT REGION GP/REL ADJUST ATTIT PERSON...BIBLIOG 20. PAGE 13 H0253 CULTURE STRUCT SOC PSY

B56
DOUGLAS W.O.,WE THE JUDGES. INDIA USA+45 USA-45 LAW NAT/G SECT LEGIS PRESS CRIME FEDERAL ORD/FREE ...POLICY GOV/COMP 19/20 WARRN/EARL MARSHALL/J SUPREME/CT. PAGE 42 H0841 ADJUD CT/SYS CONSTN GOV/REL

B56
EMDEN C.S.,THE PEOPLE AND THE CONSTITUTION (2ND ED.). UK LEGIS POPULISM 17/20 PARLIAMENT. PAGE 46 H0916 CONSTN PARL/PROC NAT/G LAW

B56
EVANS-PRITCHARD E.E.,THE INSTITUTIONS OF PRIMITIVE SOCIETY. LAW SOCIETY KIN ACT/RES CREATE ALL/VALS ...ART/METH SOC METH/CNCPT WORSHIP 20. PAGE 48 H0953 STRUCT PHIL/SCI CULTURE CONCPT

B56
KUPER L.,PASSIVE RESISTANCE IN SOUTH AFRICA. SOUTH/AFR LAW NAT/G POL/PAR VOL/ASSN DISCRIM ...POLICY SOC AUD/VIS 20. PAGE 89 H1782 ORD/FREE RACE/REL ATTIT

B56
SYKES G.M.,CRIME AND SOCIETY. LAW STRATA STRUCT ACT/RES ROUTINE ANOMIE WEALTH...POLICY SOC/INTEG 20. PAGE 151 H3021 CRIMLGY CRIME CULTURE INGP/REL

C56
FALL B.B.,"THE VIET-MINH REGIME." VIETNAM LAW ECO/UNDEV POL/PAR FORCES DOMIN WAR ATTIT MARXISM ...BIOG PREDICT BIBLIOG/A 20. PAGE 48 H0967 NAT/G ADMIN EX/STRUC LEAD

B57
DONALDSON A.G.,SOME COMPARATIVE ASPECTS OF IRISH LAW. IRELAND NAT/G DIPLOM ADMIN CT/SYS LEAD ATTIT SOVEREIGN...JURID BIBLIOG/A 12/20 CMN/WLTH. PAGE 42 H0835 CONSTN LAW NAT/COMP INT/LAW

B57
KANTOROWICZ E.,THE KING'S TWO BODIES; A STUDY IN MEDIEVAL POLITICAL THEOLOGY. UK LAW CONSTN NAT/G CT/SYS...ART/METH HUM CONCPT MYTH TIME/SEQ BIBLIOG 4/17 ELIZABTH/I POPE CHURCH/STA. PAGE 83 H1657 JURID SECT CHIEF SOVEREIGN

B57
LONG H.A.,USURPERS - FOES OF FREE MAN. LAW NAT/G CHIEF LEGIS DOMIN ADJUD REPRESENT GOV/REL ORD/FREE LAISSEZ POPULISM...POLICY 18/20 SUPREME/CT ROOSEVLT/F CONGRESS CON/INTERP. PAGE 98 H1961 CT/SYS CENTRAL FEDERAL CONSTN

B57
PLAYFAIR G.,THE OFFENDERS: THE CASE AGAINST LEGAL VENGEANCE. UNIV LAW SOCIETY NAT/G PROB/SOLV DEATH PERSON ORD/FREE...HEAL INT/LAW BIBLIOG 20 REFORMERS. PAGE 126 H2524 CRIME TEC/DEV SANCTION CT/SYS

B57
SCARROW H.A.,THE HIGHER PUBLIC SERVICE OF THE COMMONWEALTH OF AUSTRALIA. LAW SENIOR LOBBY ROLE 20 AUSTRAL CIVIL/SERV COMMONWLTH. PAGE 138 H2766 ADMIN NAT/G EX/STRUC GOV/COMP

B57
SCHLESINGER J.A.,HOW THEY BECAME GOVERNOR; A STUDY OF COMPARATIVE STATE POLITICS, 1870-1950. USA+45 USA-45 LAW POL/PAR LEGIS EDU/PROP REGION...STAT TREND CHARTS TIME 19/20 GOVERNOR. PAGE 139 H2788 PROVS CHIEF GOV/COMP CHOOSE

B57
WILSON P.,SOUTH ASIA; A SELECTED BIBLIOGRAPHY ON INDIA, PAKISTAN, CEYLON (PAMPHLET). CEYLON INDIA PAKISTAN LAW ECO/UNDEV PLAN DIPLOM 20. PAGE 169 H3381 BIBLIOG S/ASIA CULTURE NAT/G

S57
KILSON M.L.,"LAND AND POLITICS IN KENYA: AN ANALYSIS OF AFRICAN POLITICS IN A PLURAL SOCIETY." FUT LAW CULTURE KIN NAT/G ECO/TAC DOMIN REV NAT/LISM ORD/FREE PWR RESPECT SOVEREIGN WEALTH ...SOC OBS TREND WORK VAL/FREE CMN/WLTH 20. PAGE 86 H1710 AFR ECO/UNDEV

B58
BRADY A.,DEMOCRACY IN THE DOMINIONS (3RD ED.). CANADA NEW/ZEALND SOUTH/AFR WOR+45 LAW EX/STRUC DOMIN COLONIAL PARL/PROC REPRESENT RACE/REL NAT/LISM WEALTH 20 AUSTRAL CMN/WLTH. PAGE 20 H0399
GOV/COMP POL/PAR POPULISM NAT/G

B58
EUSDEN J.D.,PURITANS, LAWYERS, AND POLITICS IN EARLY SEVENTEENTH-CENTURY ENGLAND. UK CT/SYS PARL/PROC RATIONAL PWR SOVEREIGN...IDEA/COMP BIBLIOG 17 PURITAN COMMON/LAW. PAGE 48 H0951
GP/REL SECT NAT/G LAW

B58
KURL S.,ESTONIA: A SELECTED BIBLIOGRAPHY. USSR ESTONIA LAW INTELL SECT...ART/METH GEOG HUM SOC 20. PAGE 89 H1784
BIBLIOG CULTURE NAT/G

B58
LEPOINTE G.,ELEMENTS DE BIBLIOGRAPHIE SUR L'HISTOIRE DES INSTITUTIONS ET DES FAITS SOCIAUX, 987-1875. FRANCE SOCIETY NAT/G PROVS SECT ...PHIL/SCI 19/20. PAGE 94 H1887
BIBLIOG LAW

B58
PAYNO M.,LA REFORMA SOCIAL EN ESPANA Y MEXICO. SPAIN ECO/TAC TAX LOBBY COERCE REV OWN CATHISM 19/20 MEXIC/AMER. PAGE 124 H2479
SECT NAT/G LAW ELITES

B58
STRONG C.F.,MODERN POLITICAL CONSTITUTIONS. LAW CHIEF DELIB/GP EX/STRUC LEGIS ADJUD CHOOSE FEDERAL POPULISM...CONCPT BIBLIOG 20 UN. PAGE 150 H2998
CONSTN IDEA/COMP NAT/G

C58
MORRALL J.B.,"POLITICAL THOUGHT IN MEDIEVAL TIMES." LAW NAT/G SECT DOMIN ATTIT PWR...BIOG HIST/WRIT BIBLIOG. PAGE 113 H2260
CHRIST-17C CONCPT

C58
WILDING N.,"AN ENCYCLOPEDIA OF PARLIAMENT." UK LAW CONSTN CHIEF PROB/SOLV DIPLOM DEBATE WAR INGP/REL PRIVIL...BIBLIOG DICTIONARY 13/20 CMN/WLTH PARLIAMENT. PAGE 168 H3363
PARL/PROC POL/PAR NAT/G ADMIN

B59
BRIGGS A.,CHARTIST STUDIES. UK LAW NAT/G WORKER EDU/PROP COERCE SUFF GP/REL ATTIT...ANTHOL 19. PAGE 21 H0416
INDUS STRATA LABOR POLICY

B59
CUCCORESE H.J.,HISTORIA DE LA CONVERSION DEL PAPEL MONEDA EN BUENOS AIRES, 1861-1867. LAW LOC/G NAT/G ATTIT...POLICY BIBLIOG 19 ARGEN BUENOS/AIR GOLD/STAND. PAGE 36 H0717
FINAN PLAN LEGIS

B59
EPSTEIN F.T.,EAST GERMANY: A SELECTED BIBLIOGRAPHY (PAMPHLET). COM GERMANY/E LAW AGRI FINAN INDUS LABOR POL/PAR EDU/PROP ADMIN AGE/Y 20. PAGE 47 H0932
BIBLIOG/A INTELL MARXISM NAT/G

B59
HANSON A.H.,THE STRUCTURE AND CONTROL OF STATE ENTERPRISES IN TURKEY. TURKEY LAW ADMIN GOV/REL EFFICIENCY...CHARTS 20. PAGE 66 H1319
NAT/G LG/CO OWN CONTROL

B59
MILLER A.S.,PRIVATE GOVERNMENTS AND THE CONSTITUTION (PAMPHLET). LAW LABOR NAT/G ROLE PWR PLURISM...POLICY DECISION. PAGE 111 H2211
FEDERAL CONSTN VOL/ASSN CONSEN

B59
SANCHEZ A.L.,EL CONCEPTO DEL ESTADO EN EL PENSAMIENTO ESPANOL DEL SIGLO XVI. SPAIN LEGIS JUDGE BAL/PWR LEGIT EXEC WAR PWR...MAJORIT 16. PAGE 137 H2747
NAT/G PHIL/SCI LAW SOVEREIGN

B59
SISSON C.H.,THE SPIRIT OF BRITISH ADMINISTRATION AND SOME EUROPEAN COMPARISONS. FRANCE GERMANY/W SWEDEN UK LAW EX/STRUC INGP/REL EFFICIENCY ORD/FREE ...DECISION 20. PAGE 144 H2890
GOV/COMP ADMIN ELITES ATTIT

S59
CHAPMAN B.,"THE FRENCH CONSEIL D'ETAT." FRANCE NAT/G CONSULT OP/RES PROB/SOLV PWR...OBS 20. PAGE 29 H0580
ADMIN LAW CT/SYS LEGIS

S59
JENKS C.W.,"THE CHALLENGE OF UNIVERSALITY." FUT UNIV CONSTN CULTURE CONSULT CREATE PLAN LEGIT ATTIT MORAL ORD/FREE RESPECT...MAJORIT JURID 20. PAGE 80 H1602
INT/ORG LAW PEACE INT/LAW

C59
COLLINS I.,"THE GOVERNMENT AND THE NEWSPAPER PRESS IN FRANCE, 1814-1881. FRANCE LAW ADMIN CT/SYS ...CON/ANAL BIBLIOG 19. PAGE 32 H0634
PRESS ORD/FREE NAT/G EDU/PROP

C59
EASTON D.,"POLITICAL ANTHROPOLOGY" IN BIENNIAL REVIEW OF ANTHROPOLOGY" UNIV LAW CULTURE ELITES SOCIETY CREATE...PSY CONCPT GP/COMP GEN/METH 20. PAGE 44 H0880
SOC BIBLIOG/A NEW/IDEA

B60
ALBI F.,TRATADO DE LOS MODOS DE GESTION DE LAS CORPORACIONES LOCALES. SPAIN FINAN NAT/G BUDGET CONTROL EXEC ROUTINE GOV/REL ORD/FREE SOVEREIGN ...MGT 20. PAGE 5 H0092
LOC/G LAW ADMIN MUNIC

B60
CASTBERG F.,FREEDOM OF SPEECH IN THE WEST. FRANCE GERMANY USA+45 USA-45 LAW CONSTN CHIEF PRESS DISCRIM...CONCPT 18/20. PAGE 28 H0558
ORD/FREE SANCTION ADJUD NAT/COMP

B60
FLORES R.H.,CATALOGO DE TESIS DOCTORALES DE LAS FACULTADES DE LA UNIVERSIDAD DE EL SALVADOR. EL/SALVADR LAW DIPLOM ADMIN LEAD GOV/REL...SOC 19/20. PAGE 52 H1030
BIBLIOG ACADEM L/A+17C NAT/G

B60
GRAMPP W.D.,THE MANCHESTER SCHOOL OF ECONOMICS. UK LAW ECO/DEV COERCE ATTIT ORD/FREE LAISSEZ ...PHIL/SCI IDEA/COMP 19/20 MANCHESTER CORN/LAWS. PAGE 60 H1194
ECO/TAC VOL/ASSN LOBBY NAT/G

B60
HAYEK F.A.,THE CONSTITUTION OF LIBERTY. UNIV LAW CONSTN WORKER TAX EDU/PROP ADMIN CT/SYS COERCE DISCRIM...IDEA/COMP 20. PAGE 68 H1369
ORD/FREE CHOOSE NAT/G CONCPT

B60
LASKIN B.,CANADIAN CONSTITUTIONAL LAW: TEXT AND NOTES ON DISTRIBUTION OF LEGISLATIVE POWER (2ND ED.). CANADA LOC/G ECO/TAC TAX CONTROL CT/SYS CRIME FEDERAL PWR...JURID 20 PARLIAMENT. PAGE 92 H1832
CONSTN NAT/G LAW LEGIS

B60
MOCTEZUMA A.P.,EL CONFLICTO RELIGIOSO DE 1926 (2ND ED.). L/A+17C LAW NAT/G LOBBY COERCE GP/REL ATTIT ...POLICY 20 MEXIC/AMER CHURCH/STA. PAGE 112 H2233
SECT ORD/FREE DISCRIM REV

B60
PINTO F.B.M.,ENRIQUECIMENTO ILICITO NO EXERCICIO DE CARGOS PUBLICOS. BRAZIL L/A+17C USA+45 ELITES TRIBUTE CONTROL INGP/REL ORD/FREE PWR...NAT/COMP 20. PAGE 126 H2513
ADMIN NAT/G CRIME LAW

B60
SCHAPIRO L.,THE COMMUNIST PARTY OF THE SOVIET UNION. COM LAW SOCIETY STRATA STRUCT ECO/DEV LABOR NAT/G POL/PAR CREATE DOMIN EDU/PROP COERCE TOTALISM MARXISM...POLICY CONCPT MYTH TIME/SEQ WORK TOT/POP 20 LENIN/VI STALIN/J. PAGE 139 H2772
INTELL PWR USSR

B60
SCHEIBER H.N.,THE WILSON ADMINISTRATION AND CIVIL LIBERTIES 1917-1921. LAW GOV/REL ATTIT 20 WILSON/W CIVIL/LIB. PAGE 139 H2782
ORD/FREE WAR NAT/G CONTROL

B60
RUDD J.,TABOO, A STUDY OF MALAGASY CUSTOMS AND BELIEFS. MADAGASCAR LAW FAM CONTROL CRIME PERSON ...CONCPT 20. PAGE 173 H3466
CULTURE DOMIN SECT SANCTION

S60
EMERSON R.,"THE EROSION OF DEMOCRACY." AFR FUT LAW CULTURE INTELL SOCIETY ECO/UNDEV FAM LOC/G NAT/G FORCES PLAN TEC/DEV ECO/TAC ADMIN CT/SYS ATTIT ORD/FREE PWR...SOCIALIST SOC CONCPT STAND/INT TIME/SEQ WORK 20. PAGE 46 H0918
S/ASIA POL/PAR

C60
HAZARD J.N.,"SETTLING DISPUTES IN SOVIET SOCIETY: THE FORMATIVE YEARS OF LEGAL INSTITUTIONS." USSR NAT/G PROF/ORG PROB/SOLV CONTROL CT/SYS ROUTINE REV CENTRAL...JURID BIBLIOG 20. PAGE 68 H1372
ADJUD LAW COM POLICY

N60
RHODESIA-NYASA NATL ARCHIVES,A SELECT BIBLIOGRAPHY OF RECENT PUBLICATIONS CONCERNING THE FEDERATION OF RHODESIA AND NYASALAND (PAMPHLET). MALAWI RHODESIA LAW CULTURE STRUCT ECO/UNDEV LEGIS...GEOG 20. PAGE 131 H2620
BIBLIOG ADMIN ORD/FREE NAT/G

B61
BAYITCH S.A.,LATIN AMERICA: A BIBLIOGRAPHICAL GUIDE. LAW CONSTN LEGIS JUDGE ADJUD CT/SYS 20. PAGE 12 H0243
BIBLIOG L/A+17C NAT/G JURID

B61
BEDFORD S.,THE FACES OF JUSTICE: A TRAVELLER'S REPORT. AUSTRIA FRANCE GERMANY/W SWITZERLND UK UNIV WOR+45 WOR-45 CULTURE PARTIC GOV/REL MORAL...JURID OBS GOV/COMP 20. PAGE 13 H0257
CT/SYS ORD/FREE PERSON LAW

B61
BURDETTE F.L.,POLITICAL SCIENCE: A SELECTED BIBLIOGRAPHY OF BOOKS IN PRINT, WITH ANNOTATIONS (PAMPHLET). LAW LOC/G NAT/G POL/PAR PROVS DIPLOM EDU/PROP ADMIN CHOOSE ATTIT 20. PAGE 24 H0479
BIBLIOG/A GOV/COMP CONCPT ROUTINE

B61
CARROTHERS A.W.R.,LABOR ARBITRATION IN CANADA. CANADA LAW NAT/G CONSULT LEGIS WORKER ADJUD ADMIN CT/SYS 20. PAGE 27 H0542
LABOR MGT GP/REL BARGAIN

B61
CASSINELLI C.W.,THE POLITICS OF FREEDOM. FUT UNIV LAW POL/PAR CHOOSE ORD/FREE...POLICY CONCPT MYTH BIBLIOG. PAGE 28 H0555
MAJORIT NAT/G PARL/PROC PARTIC

B61
GUIZOT F.P.G.,HISTORY OF THE ORIGIN OF
LEGIS

REPRESENTATIVE GOVERNMENT IN EUROPE. CHRIST-17C FRANCE MOD/EUR SPAIN UK LAW CHIEF FORCES POPULISM ...MAJORIT TIME/SEQ GOV/COMP NAT/COMP 4/19 PARLIAMENT. PAGE 62 H1250
REPRESENT CONSTN NAT/G

B61
JUSTICE,THE CITIZEN AND THE ADMINISTRATION: THE REDRESS OF GRIEVANCES (PAMPHLET). EUR+WWI UK LAW CONSTN STRATA NAT/G CT/SYS PARTIC COERCE...NEW/IDEA IDEA/COMP 20 OMBUDSMAN. PAGE 82 H1644
INGP/REL CONSULT ADJUD REPRESENT

B61
LA PONCE J.A.,THE GOVERNMENT OF THE FIFTH REPUBLIC: FRENCH POLITICAL PARTIES AND THE CONSTITUTION. ALGERIA FRANCE LAW NAT/G DELIB/GP LEGIS ECO/TAC MARXISM SOCISM...CHARTS BIBLIOG/A 20 DEGAULLE/C. PAGE 90 H1794
PWR POL/PAR CONSTN CHIEF

B61
LAHAYE R.,LES ENTREPRISES PUBLIQUES AU MAROC. FRANCE MOROCCO LAW DIST/IND EXTR/IND FINAN CONSULT PLAN TEC/DEV ADMIN AGREE CONTROL OWN...POLICY 20. PAGE 90 H1796
NAT/G INDUS ECO/UNDEV ECO/TAC

B61
TACHAKKYO K.,BIBLIOGRAPHY OF KOREAN STUDIES: A BIBLIOGRAPHICAL GUIDE TO KOREAN PUBLICATIONS ON KOREAN STUDIES APPEARING 1945-1958. KOREA LAW...HUM JURID PHIL/SCI LING 19/20. PAGE 152 H3033
BIBLIOG/A SOCIETY CULTURE WAR

B61
ULLMAN W.,PRINCIPLES OF GOVERNMENT AND POLITICS IN THE MIDDLE AGES. LAW CONSTN DOMIN EDU/PROP LEGIT TOTALISM SOVEREIGN POPULISM...POLICY GOV/COMP IDEA/COMP 12/16 POPE KING CHURCH/STA. PAGE 158 H3152
SECT CHIEF NAT/G LEGIS

B61
WARD R.E.,JAPANESE POLITICAL SCIENCE: A GUIDE TO JAPANESE REFERENCE AND RESEARCH MATERIALS (2ND ED.). LAW CONSTN STRATA NAT/G POL/PAR DELIB/GP LEGIS ADMIN CHOOSE GP/REL...INT/LAW 19/20 CHINJAP. PAGE 165 H3306
BIBLIOG/A PHIL/SCI

L61
KAUPER P.G.,"CHURCH AND STATE: COOPERATIVE SEPARATISM." NAT/G LEGIS OP/RES TAX EDU/PROP GP/REL TREND. PAGE 84 H1671
SECT CONSTN LAW POLICY

C61
MOODIE G.C.,"THE GOVERNMENT OF GREAT BRITAIN." UK LAW STRUCT LOC/G POL/PAR DIPLOM RECEIVE ADMIN COLONIAL CHOOSE...BIBLIOG 20 PARLIAMENT. PAGE 112 H2247
NAT/G SOCIETY PARL/PROC GOV/COMP

B62
COSTA RICA UNIVERSIDAD BIBL,LISTA DE TESIS DE GRADO DE LA UNIVERSIDAD DE COSTA RICA. COSTA/RICA LAW LOC/G ADMIN LEAD...SOC 20. PAGE 34 H0675
BIBLIOG/A NAT/G DIPLOM ECO/UNDEV

B62
FEIT E.,SOUTH AFRICA, THE DYNAMICS OF THE AFRICAN NATIONAL CONGRESS. AFR SOUTH/AFR LAW INTELL STRATA KIN NAT/G POL/PAR ECO/TAC DOMIN RISK COERCE 20 NEGRO. PAGE 49 H0984
RACE/REL ELITES CONTROL STRUCT

B62
FINER S.E.,THE MAN ON HORSEBACK: ROLE OF THE MILITARY IN POLITICS. UNIV LAW CONSTN ELITES SOCIETY POL/PAR BAL/PWR DOMIN EDU/PROP LEGIT COERCE GUERRILLA REV WAR WEAPON DRIVE SUPEGO ORD/FREE PWR RESPECT...POLICY CONCPT GEN/METH. PAGE 50 H1003
NAT/G FORCES TOTALISM

B62
GROGAN V.,ADMINISTRATIVE TRIBUNALS IN THE PUBLIC SERVICE. IRELAND UK NAT/G CONTROL CT/SYS...JURID GOV/COMP 20. PAGE 61 H1231
ADMIN LAW ADJUD DELIB/GP

B62
GRZYBOWSKI K.,SOVIET LEGAL INSTITUTIONS. USA+45 USSR ECO/DEV NAT/G EDU/PROP CONTROL CT/SYS CRIME OWN ATTIT PWR SOCISM...NAT/COMP 20. PAGE 62 H1242
ADJUD LAW JURID

B62
KIDDER F.E.,THESES ON PAN AMERICAN TOPICS. LAW CULTURE NAT/G SECT DIPLOM HEALTH...ART/METH GEOG SOC 13/20. PAGE 86 H1709
BIBLIOG CHRIST-17C L/A+17C SOCIETY

B62
KINDERSLEY R.,THE FIRST RUSSIAN REVISIONISTS. COM USSR LAW ELITES INTELL NAT/G LEGIS ECO/TAC EDU/PROP CONTROL LEAD GP/REL SOCISM 19/20 MARX/KARL BOLSHEVISM. PAGE 86 H1712
CONSTN MARXISM POPULISM BIOG

B62
LAQUEUR W.,THE FUTURE OF COMMUNIST SOCIETY. CHINA/COM USSR LAW ECO/DEV NAT/G POL/PAR PLAN PROB/SOLV DIPLOM LEAD...POLICY CONCPT IDEA/COMP ANTHOL 20. PAGE 91 H1820
MARXISM COM FUT SOCIETY

B62
PAIKERT G.C.,THE GERMAN EXODUS. EUR+WWI GERMANY/W LAW CULTURE SOCIETY STRUCT INDUS NAT/LISM RESPECT SOVEREIGN...CHARTS BIBLIOG SOC/INTEG 20 MIGRATION. PAGE 122 H2444
INGP/REL STRANGE GEOG GP/REL

B62
PASTOR R.S.,A STATEMENT OF THE LAWS OF PARAGUAY IN MATTERS AFFECTING BUSINESS (2ND ED.). PARAGUAY INDUS FAM LABOR LG/CO NAT/G LEGIS TAX CONTROL MARRIAGE 20. PAGE 124 H2474
FINAN ECO/UNDEV LAW CONSTN

B62
ROUSSEAU J.J.,THE SOCIAL CONTRACT. LAW CONSTN CHIEF DOMIN REPRESENT GP/REL ORD/FREE POPULISM...MAJORIT GOV/COMP 18. PAGE 135 H2700
GEN/LAWS AGREE REV

B62
SILBERMAN B.S.,JAPAN AND KOREA; A CRITICAL BIBLIOGRAPHY. KOREA LAW STRATA STRUCT AGRI INDUS NAT/G POL/PAR SECT...HUM LING IDEA/COMP 5/20 CHINJAP. PAGE 144 H2872
BIBLIOG/A CULTURE S/ASIA

B62
UNECA LIBRARY,NEW ACQUISITIONS IN THE UNECA LIBRARY. LAW NAT/G PLAN PROB/SOLV TEC/DEV ADMIN REGION...GEOG SOC 20 UN. PAGE 158 H3161
BIBLIOG AFR ECO/UNDEV INT/ORG

L62
"AMERICAN BEHAVIORAL SCIENTIST." USSR LAW NAT/G ...SOC 20 UN. PAGE 2 H0039
BIBLIOG AFR R+D

L62
CORET A.,"L'INDEPENDANCE DU SAMOA OCCIDENTAL." S/ASIA LAW INT/ORG EXEC ALL/VALS SAMOA UN 20. PAGE 33 H0668
NAT/G STRUCT SOVEREIGN

L62
MURACCIOLE L.,"LA BANQUE CENTRALE DES ETATS DE L'AFRIQUE DE L'OUEST." AFR LAW ECO/UNDEV INT/ORG NAT/G CONSULT ECO/TAC ROUTINE...CHARTS 20. PAGE 115 H2292
ISLAM FINAN INT/TRADE

L62
ORDONNEAU P.,"LES PROBLEMES POSES PAR L'INDEPENDANCE DES NOUVEAUX ETATS AFRICAINS ET MALGACHE SUR LE PLAN DU CONTENTIEUX." FRANCE ISLAM MADAGASCAR LAW STRATA ECO/UNDEV NAT/G LEGIS LEGIT ...JURID TIME/SEQ 20. PAGE 121 H2425
AFR ADJUD COLONIAL SOVEREIGN

S62
BRAIBANTI R.,"REFLECTIONS ON BUREAUCRATIC CORRPUTION." LAW REPRESENT 20. PAGE 20 H0400
CONTROL MORAL ADMIN GOV/COMP

S62
VIGNES D.,"L'AUTORITE DES TRAITES INTERNATIONAUX EN DROIT INTERNE." EUR+WWI UNIV LAW CONSTN INTELL NAT/G POL/PAR DIPLOM ATTIT PERCEPT ALL/VALS ...POLICY INT/LAW JURID CONCPT TIME/SEQ 20 TREATY. PAGE 163 H3252
STRUCT LEGIT FRANCE

B63
DALAND R.T.,PERSPECTIVES OF BRAZILIAN PUBLIC ADMINISTRATION (VOL. I). BRAZIL LAW ECO/UNDEV SCHOOL CHIEF TEC/DEV CONFER CONTROL GP/REL ATTIT ROLE PWR...ANTHOL 20. PAGE 37 H0735
ADMIN NAT/G PLAN GOV/REL

B63
DECOTTIGNIES R.,LES NATIONALITES AFRICAINES. AFR NAT/G PROB/SOLV DIPLOM COLONIAL ORD/FREE...CHARTS GOV/COMP 20. PAGE 39 H0781
NAT/LISM JURID LEGIS LAW

B63
EDDY J.P.,JUSTICE OF THE PEACE. UK LAW CONSTN CULTURE 14/20 COMMON/LAW. PAGE 44 H0887
CRIME JURID CT/SYS ADJUD

B63
ELIAS T.O.,GOVERNMENT AND POLITICS IN AFRICA. CONSTN CULTURE SOCIETY NAT/G POL/PAR DIPLOM REPRESENT PERSON...SOC TREND BIBLIOG 4/20. PAGE 45 H0906
AFR NAT/LISM COLONIAL LAW

B63
FAWCETT J.E.S.,THE BRITISH COMMONWEALTH IN INTERNATIONAL LAW. LAW INT/ORG NAT/G VOL/ASSN OP/RES DIPLOM ADJUD CENTRAL CONSEN...NET/THEORY CMN/WLTH TREATY. PAGE 49 H0977
INT/LAW STRUCT COLONIAL

B63
FISCHER-GALATI S.A.,RUMANIA; A BIBLIOGRAPHIC GUIDE (PAMPHLET). ROMANIA INTELL ECO/DEV LABOR SECT WEALTH...GEOG SOC/WK LING 20. PAGE 51 H1012
BIBLIOG/A NAT/G COM LAW

B63
GEERTZ C.,OLD SOCIETIES AND NEW STATES: THE QUEST FOR MODERNITY IN ASIA AND AFRICA. AFR ASIA LAW CULTURE SECT EDU/PROP REV...GOV/COMP NAT/COMP 20. PAGE 55 H1107
ECO/UNDEV TEC/DEV NAT/LISM SOVEREIGN

B63
GLUCKMAN M.,ORDER AND REBELLION IN TRIBAL AFRICA. EUR+WWI LAW CULTURE STRATA KIN MUNIC DELIB/GP ACT/RES DOMIN EDU/PROP LEGIT ADMIN COERCE CHOOSE ATTIT PERSON ORD/FREE PWR...SOC CHARTS GEN/LAWS TOT/POP VAL/FREE. PAGE 57 H1147
AFR SOCIETY

B63
GOURNAY B.,PUBLIC ADMINISTRATION. FRANCE LAW CONSTN AGRI FINAN LABOR SCHOOL EX/STRUC CHOOSE...MGT METH/COMP 20. PAGE 59 H1189
BIBLIOG/A ADMIN NAT/G LOC/G

B63
HARDY M.J.L.,BLOOD FEUDS AND THE PAYMENT OF BLOOD MONEY IN THE MIDDLE EAST. ISLAM SOCIETY SECT REGION SANCTION COERCE DEATH MURDER 7/20 ARABS. PAGE 66 H1329
KIN TRIBUTE LAW CULTURE

B63
JACOB H.,GERMAN ADMINISTRATION SINCE BISMARCK: CENTRAL AUTHORITY VERSUS LOCAL AUTONOMY. GERMANY GERMANY/W LAW POL/PAR CONTROL CENTRAL TOTALISM FASCISM...MAJORIT DECISION STAT CHARTS GOV/COMP 19/20 BISMARCK/O HITLER/A WEIMAR/REP. PAGE 79 H1577
ADMIN NAT/G LOC/G POLICY

B63
JUDD P.,AFRICAN INDEPENDENCE: THE EXPLODING EMERGENCE OF THE NEW AFRICAN NATIONS. AFR UK LAW CONSTN CULTURE KIN DIPLOM ATTIT...CHARTS BIBLIOG 20 UN DEGAULLE/C NEGRO THIRD/WRLD. PAGE 82 H1640
ORD/FREE POLICY DOMIN LOC/G

B63
LAVROFF D.-G.,LES LIBERTES PUBLIQUES EN UNION SOVIETIQUE (REV. ED.). USSR NAT/G WORKER SANCTION CRIME MARXISM NEW/LIB...JURID BIBLIOG WORSHIP 20. PAGE 92 H1843
ORD/FREE LAW ATTIT COM

B63
LEWIN J.,POLITICS AND LAW IN SOUTH AFRICA. SOUTH/AFR UK POL/PAR BAL/PWR ECO/TAC COLONIAL CONTROL GP/REL DISCRIM PWR 20 NEGRO. PAGE 96 H1909
NAT/LISM POLICY LAW RACE/REL

B63
MAC MILLAN W.M.,BANTU, BOER, AND BRITON: THE MAKING OF THE SOUTH AFRICAN NATIVE PROBLEM. SOUTH/AFR UK LAW KIN NAT/G SECT LEGIS COLONIAL ISOLAT ATTIT ...BIOG 18/20 BANTU NEGRO PHILIP/J MISSION. PAGE 100 H1989
AFR RACE/REL ELITES

B63
MAJUMDAR O.N.,AN INTRODUCTION TO SOCIAL ANTHROPOLOGY. INDIA LAW STRATA ECO/UNDEV KIN DEMAND MARRIAGE...GP/COMP BIBLIOG T WORSHIP 20. PAGE 101 H2026
SOC CULTURE STRUCT GP/REL

B63
SCHUMAN S.I.,LEGAL POSITIVISM: ITS SCOPE AND LIMITATIONS. CONSTN NAT/G DIPLOM PARTIC UTOPIA ...POLICY DECISION PHIL/SCI CONCPT 20. PAGE 140 H2802
GEN/METH LAW METH/COMP

B63
STRAUSS L.,HISTORY OF POLITICAL PHILOSOPHY. LAW SOCIETY CAP/ISM MARXISM 19 AQUINAS/T BACON/F HEGEL/GWF MILL/JS NIETZSCH/F. PAGE 150 H2995
IDEA/COMP PHIL/SCI ANTHOL

B63
WALKER A.A.,OFFICIAL PUBLICATIONS OF SIERRA LEONE AND GAMBIA. GAMBIA SIER/LEONE UK LAW CONSTN LEGIS PLAN BUDGET DIPLOM...SOC SAMP CON/ANAL 20. PAGE 164 H3290
BIBLIOG NAT/G COLONIAL ADMIN

L63
BOLGAR V.,"THE PUBLIC INTEREST: A JURISPRUDENTIAL AND COMPARATIVE OVERVIEW OF SYMPOSIUM ON FUNDAMENTAL CONCEPTS OF PUBLIC LAW" COM FRANCE GERMANY SWITZERLND LAW ADJUD ADMIN AGREE LAISSEZ ...JURID GEN/LAWS 20 EUROPE/E. PAGE 18 H0369
CONCPT ORD/FREE CONTROL NAT/COMP

L63
ROSE R.,"COMPARATIVE STUDIES IN POLITICAL FINANCE: A SYMPOSIUM." ASIA EUR+WWI S/ASIA LAW CULTURE DELIB/GP LEGIS ACT/RES ECO/TAC EDU/PROP CHOOSE ATTIT RIGID/FLEX SUPEGO PWR SKILL WEALTH...STAT ANTHOL VAL/FREE. PAGE 134 H2674
FINAN POL/PAR

S63
GLUCKMAN M.,"CIVIL WAR AND THEORIES OF POWER IN BAROTSE-LAND: AFRICAN AND MEDIEVAL ANALOGIES." AFR CHRIST-17C LAW CONSTN CULTURE STRATA KIN DELIB/GP FORCES DOMIN LEGIT COERCE PERCEPT ORD/FREE...SOC INT TIME/SEQ GEN/LAWS VAL/FREE. PAGE 57 H1148
TOP/EX PWR WAR

S63
WEISSBERG G.,"MAPS AS EVIDENCE IN INTERNATIONAL BOUNDARY DISPUTES: A REAPPRAISAL." CHINA/COM EUR+WWI INDIA MOD/EUR S/ASIA INT/ORG NAT/G LEGIT PERCEPT...JURID CHARTS 20. PAGE 166 H3331
LAW GEOG SOVEREIGN

B64
BEATTIE J.,OTHER CULTURES. UNIV LAW FAM POL/PAR SECT ADJUD OWN ALL/VALS WEALTH...SOC NAT/COMP SOC/INTEG 20. PAGE 13 H0251
METH/CNCPT CULTURE STRUCT

B64
CULLINGWORTH J.B.,TOWN AND COUNTRY PLANNING IN ENGLAND AND WALES. UK LAW SOCIETY CONSULT ACT/RES ADMIN ROUTINE LEISURE INGP/REL ADJUST PWR...GEOG 20 OPEN/SPACE URBAN/RNWL. PAGE 36 H0718
MUNIC PLAN NAT/G PROB/SOLV

B64
FREISEN J.,STAAT UND KATHOLISCHE KIRCHE IN DEN DEUTSCHEN BUNDESSTAATEN (2 VOLS.). GERMANY LAW FAM NAT/G EDU/PROP GP/REL MARRIAGE WEALTH 19/20 CHURCH/STA. PAGE 53 H1056
SECT CATHISM JURID PROVS

B64
GOODNOW H.F.,THE CIVIL SERVICE OF PAKISTAN: BUREAUCRACY IN A NEW NATION. INDIA PAKISTAN S/ASIA ECO/UNDEV PROVS CHIEF PARTIC CHOOSE EFFICIENCY PWR ...BIBLIOG 20. PAGE 59 H1173
ADMIN GOV/REL LAW NAT/G

B64
GROVES H.E.,THE CONSTITUTION OF MALAYSIA. MALAYSIA POL/PAR CHIEF CONSULT DELIB/GP CT/SYS PARL/PROC CHOOSE FEDERAL ORD/FREE 20. PAGE 62 H1238
CONSTN NAT/G LAW

B64
HAAR C.M.,LAW AND LAND: ANGLO-AMERICAN PLANNING PRACTICE. UK USA+45 NAT/G TEC/DEV BUDGET CT/SYS INGP/REL EFFICIENCY OWN...JURID 20. PAGE 63 H1263
LAW PLAN MUNIC NAT/COMP

B64
HAMILTON W.B.,THE TRANSFER OF INSTITUTIONS. CANADA INDIA UK LAW AGRI LABOR SECT COLONIAL 18/20. PAGE 65 H1301
NAT/COMP ECO/UNDEV EDU/PROP CULTURE

B64
HANNA W.J.,POLITICS IN BLACK AFRICA: A SELECTIVE BIBLIOGRAPHY OF RELEVANT PERIODICAL LITERATURE. AFR LAW LOC/G MUNIC NAT/G POL/PAR LOBBY CHOOSE RACE/REL SOVEREIGN 20. PAGE 66 H1315
BIBLIOG NAT/LISM COLONIAL

B64
HEIMSATH C.H.,INDIAN NATIONALISM AND HINDU SOCIAL REFORM. S/ASIA LAW CULTURE SOCIETY STRATA PROVS VOL/ASSN DELIB/GP LEGIS TOP/EX DOMIN EDU/PROP LEGIT ATTIT ALL/VALS...POLICY SOC TIME/SEQ STERTYP VAL/FREE 19/20. PAGE 69 H1385
SECT NAT/G

B64
HOLDSWORTH W.S.,A HISTORY OF ENGLISH LAW; THE CENTURIES OF DEVELOPMENT AND REFORM (VOL. XIV). UK CONSTN LOC/G NAT/G POL/PAR CHIEF EX/STRUC ADJUD COLONIAL ATTIT...INT/LAW JURID 18/19 TORY/PARTY COMMONWLTH WHIG/PARTY COMMON/LAW. PAGE 73 H1453
LAW LEGIS LEAD CT/SYS

B64
JOHNSON A.F.,BIBLIOGRAPHY OF GHANA: 1930-1961. GHANA LAW AGRI INDUS NAT/G INT/TRADE EDU/PROP HEALTH...GEOG AUD/VIS CHARTS 20. PAGE 81 H1618
BIBLIOG/A CULTURE SOC

B64
LAPENNA I.,STATE AND LAW: SOVIET AND YUGOSLAV THEORY. USSR YUGOSLAVIA STRATA STRUCT NAT/G DOMIN COERCE MARXISM...GOV/COMP IDEA/COMP 20. PAGE 91 H1812
JURID COM LAW SOVEREIGN

B64
LEDERMAN W.R.,THE COURTS AND THE CANDIAN CONSTITUTION. CANADA PARL/PROC...POLICY JURID GOV/COMP ANTHOL 19/20 SUPREME/CT PARLIAMENT. PAGE 93 H1854
CONSTN CT/SYS LEGIS LAW

B64
LIGGETT E.,BRITISH POLITICAL ISSUES: VOLUME 1. UK LAW CONSTN LOC/G NAT/G ADJUD 20. PAGE 97 H1930
POL/PAR GOV/REL CT/SYS DIPLOM

B64
O'HEARN P.J.T.,PEACE, ORDER AND GOOD GOVERNMENT; A NEW CONSTITUTION FOR CANADA. CANADA EX/STRUC LEGIS CT/SYS PARL/PROC...BIBLIOG 20. PAGE 120 H2388
NAT/G CONSTN LAW CREATE

B64
PERKINS D.,THE AMERICAN DEMOCRACY: ITS RISE TO POWER. ASIA USSR LAW CULTURE FINAN EDU/PROP COLONIAL CHOOSE...POLICY CHARTS BIBLIOG WORSHIP PRESIDENT 15/20 NEGRO. PAGE 125 H2492
LOC/G ECO/TAC WAR DIPLOM

B64
RAGHAVAN M.D.,INDIA IN CEYLONESE HISTORY, SOCIETY AND CULTURE. CEYLON INDIA S/ASIA LAW SOCIETY INT/TRADE ATTIT...ART/METH JURID SOC LING 20. PAGE 129 H2581
DIPLOM CULTURE SECT STRUCT

B64
SIEKANOWICZ P.,LEGAL SOURCES AND BIBLIOGRAPHY OF POLAND. COM POLAND CONSTN NAT/G PARL/PROC SANCTION CRIME MARXISM 16/20. PAGE 143 H2870
BIBLIOG ADJUD LAW JURID

B64
SKINNER E.P.,THE MOSSI OF UPPER VOLTA: THE POLITICAL DEVELOPMENT OF A SUDANESE PEOPLE. AFR LAW AGRI FAM KIN POL/PAR PROVS SECT DELIB/GP EX/STRUC FORCES TOP/EX DOMIN EDU/PROP LEGIT CT/SYS COERCE CHOOSE ORD/FREE PWR WEALTH...SOC MYTH VAL/FREE. PAGE 145 H2897
CULTURE OBS UPPER/VOLT

B64
SZLADITS C.,BIBLIOGRAPHY ON FOREIGN AND COMPARATIVE LAW: BOOKS AND ARTICLES IN ENGLISH (SUPPLEMENT 1962). FINAN INDUS JUDGE LICENSE ADMIN CT/SYS PARL/PROC OWN...INT/LAW CLASSIF METH/COMP NAT/COMP 20. PAGE 151 H3027
BIBLIOG/A JURID ADJUD LAW

B64
TURNER M.C.,LIBROS EN VENTA EN HISPANOAMERICA Y ESPANA. SPAIN LAW CONSTN CULTURE ADMIN LEAD...HUM SOC 20. PAGE 157 H3141
BIBLIOG L/A+17C NAT/G DIPLOM

B64
WALDMAN E.,THE GOOSE STEP IS VERBOTEN: THE GERMAN ARMY TODAY. GERMANY/W LAW CONSTN LEGIS PROB/SOLV DOMIN CONTROL CIVMIL/REL GOV/REL INGP/REL ATTIT ...DEEP/QU 20. PAGE 164 H3289
SOC FORCES NAT/G

B64
WITHERELL J.W.,OFFICIAL PUBLICATIONS OF FRENCH EQUATORIAL AFRICA, FRENCH CAMEROONS, AND TOGO, 1946-1958 (PAMPHLET). CAMEROON CHAD FRANCE GABON TOGO LAW ECO/UNDEV EXTR/IND INT/TRADE...GEOG HEAL 20. PAGE 169 H3392
BIBLIOG/A AFR NAT/G ADMIN

B64
WRAITH R.,CORRUPTION IN DEVELOPING COUNTRIES. NIGERIA UK LAW ELITES STRATA INDUS LOC/G NAT/G SECT FORCES EDU/PROP ADMIN PWR WEALTH 18/20. PAGE 171 H3414
ECO/UNDEV CRIME SANCTION ATTIT

B64
WRIGHT G.,RURAL REVOLUTION IN FRANCE: THE PEASANTRY IN THE TWENTIETH CENTURY. EUR+WWI MOD/EUR LAW CULTURE AGRI POL/PAR DELIB/GP LEGIS ECO/TAC EDU/PROP COERCE CHOOSE ATTIT RIGID/FLEX HEALTH ...STAT CENSUS CHARTS VAL/FREE 20. PAGE 171 H3419
PWR STRATA FRANCE REV

B64
WRIGHT Q.,A STUDY OF WAR. LAW NAT/G PROB/SOLV BAL/PWR NAT/LISM PEACE ATTIT SOVEREIGN...CENSUS SOC/INTEG. PAGE 171 H3421
WAR CONCPT DIPLOM CONTROL

B65
BERNDT R.M.,ABORIGINAL MAN IN AUSTRALIA. LAW DOMIN ADMIN COLONIAL MARRIAGE HABITAT ORD/FREE...LING CHARTS ANTHOL BIBLIOG WORSHIP 20 AUSTRAL ABORIGINES MUSIC ELKIN/AP. PAGE 16 H0312
SOC CULTURE SOCIETY STRUCT

B65
CARTER G.M.,POLITICS IN EUROPE. EUR+WWI FRANCE GERMANY/W UK USSR LAW CONSTN POL/PAR VOL/ASSN PRESS LOBBY PWR...ANTHOL SOC/INTEG EEC. PAGE 27 H0548
GOV/COMP OP/RES ECO/DEV

B65
CHEN T.H.,THE CHINESE COMMUNIST REGIME: A DOCUMENTARY STUDY (2 VOLS.). CHINA/COM LAW CONSTN ELITES ECO/UNDEV LEGIS ECO/TAC ADMIN CONTROL PWR ...SOC 20. PAGE 29 H0587
MARXISM POL/PAR NAT/G

B65
GAJENDRAGADKAR P.B.,LAW, LIBERTY AND SOCIAL JUSTICE. INDIA CONSTN NAT/G SECT PLAN ECO/TAC PRESS POPULISM...SOC METH/COMP 20 HINDU. PAGE 54 H1086
ORD/FREE LAW ADJUD JURID

B65
HARMON R.B.,POLITICAL SCIENCE: A BIBLIOGRAPHICAL GUIDE TO THE LITERATURE. WOR+45 WOR-45 R+D INT/ORG LOC/G NAT/G DIPLOM ADMIN...CONCPT METH. PAGE 67 H1334
BIBLIOG POL/PAR LAW GOV/COMP

B65
HESS A.G.,CHASING THE DRAGON: A REPORT ON DRUG ADDICTION IN HONG KONG. ASIA CULTURE PROB/SOLV TRIBUTE...POLICY PSY SOC CLASSIF STAT 17/20 HONG/KONG. PAGE 70 H1411
BIO/SOC CRIME SOCIETY LAW

B65
KUPER L.,AN AFRICAN BOURGEOISIE. SOUTH/AFR LAW INTELL NAT/G POL/PAR VOL/ASSN DISCRIM...POLICY 20. PAGE 89 H1783
RACE/REL SOC STRUCT

B65
MAIR L.,AN INTRODUCTION TO SOCIAL ANTHROPOLOGY. LAW STRATA FINAN FAM KIN SECT INT/TRADE RACE/REL ADJUST PRODUC...T 20. PAGE 101 H2023
SOC STRUCT CULTURE SOCIETY

B65
PEASLEE A.J.,CONSTITUTIONS OF NATIONS* THIRD REVISED EDITION (VOLUME I* AFRICA). LAW EX/STRUC LEGIS TOP/EX LEGIT CT/SYS ROUTINE ORD/FREE PWR SOVEREIGN...CON/ANAL CHARTS. PAGE 124 H2481
AFR CHOOSE CONSTN NAT/G

B65
POBEDONOSTSEV K.P.,REFLECTIONS OF A RUSSIAN STATESMAN. RUSSIA LAW ELITES EDU/PROP PRESS ADJUD MARRIAGE ATTIT PWR...MAJORIT TRADIT 19 CHURCH/STA. PAGE 127 H2531
TOTALISM POLICY CONSTN NAT/G

B65
PUNDEEF M.V.,BULGARIA; A BIBLIOGRAPHIC GUIDE. BULGARIA LAW CULTURE INTELL ECO/DEV LEAD MARXISM 20. PAGE 128 H2566
BIBLIOG/A NAT/G COM SOCISM

B65
SAUVAGET J.,INTRODUCTION TO THE HISTORY OF THE MIDDLE EAST (A BIBLIOGRAPHICAL GUIDE). LAW CULTURE GEOG. PAGE 138 H2757
BIBLIOG/A ISLAM GOV/COMP

B65
ULLMANN W.,A HISTORY OF POLITICAL THOUGHT: THE MIDDLE AGES. CHRIST-17C LOC/G NAT/G CENTRAL PWR ...PHIL/SCI LOG BIBLIOG 6/15. PAGE 158 H3153
IDEA/COMP SOVEREIGN SECT LAW

L65
MATTHEWS D.G.,"A CURRENT BIBLIOGRAPHY ON ETHIOPIAN AFFAIRS: A SELECT BIBLIOGRAPHY FROM 1950-1964." ETHIOPIA LAW CULTURE ECO/UNDEV INDUS LABOR SECT FORCES DIPLOM CIVMIL/REL RACE/REL...LING STAT 20. PAGE 105 H2093
BIBLIOG/A ADMIN POL/PAR NAT/G

L65
MATTHEWS D.G.,"A CURRENT BIBLIOGRAPHY ON SUDANESE AFFAIRS; A SELECT BIBLIOGRAPHY FROM 1960-1964." SUDAN LAW CULTURE AGRI FINAN INDUS LABOR POL/PAR TEC/DEV FOR/AID RACE/REL LITERACY...LING 20. PAGE 105 H2094
BIBLIOG ECO/UNDEV NAT/G DIPLOM

L65
SHARMA S.P.,"THE INDIA-CHINA BORDER DISPUTE: AN INDIAN PERSPECTIVE." ASIA CHINA/COM S/ASIA NAT/G LEGIT CT/SYS NAT/LISM DRIVE MORAL ORD/FREE PWR 20. PAGE 142 H2850
LAW ATTIT SOVEREIGN INDIA

S65
KINDLEBERGER C.P.,"MASS MIGRATION, THEN AND NOW." LAW ECO/DEV ECO/UNDEV INDUS LABOR INT/TRADE FEEDBACK REGION RIGID/FLEX...SOC NAT/COMP EEC. PAGE 86 H1714
EUR+WWI USA-45 WORKER IDEA/COMP

S65
PRABHAKAR P.,"SURVEY OF RESEARCH AND SOURCE MATERIALS; THE SINO-INDIAN BORDER DISPUTE." CHINA/COM INDIA LAW NAT/G PLAN BAL/PWR WAR...POLICY 20 COLD/WAR. PAGE 128 H2553
BIBLIOG ASIA S/ASIA DIPLOM

B66
ARCHER P.,FREEDOM AT STAKE. UK LAW NAT/G LEGIS JUDGE CRIME MORAL...CONCPT 20 CIVIL/LIB. PAGE 8 H0159
ORD/FREE NAT/COMP POLICY

B66
BARRETT J.,THAT BETTER COUNTRY: RELIGIOUS ASPECT OF LIFE IN EASTERN AUSTRALIA, 1835-1850. LAW ECO/UNDEV SCHOOL TEC/DEV EDU/PROP CONTROL HABITAT MORAL WORSHIP 19 AUSTRAL CHURCH/STA. PAGE 11 H0229
SECT CULTURE GOV/REL

B66
BRAIBANTI R.,RESEARCH ON THE BUREAUCRACY OF PAKISTAN. PAKISTAN LAW CULTURE INTELL ACADEM LOC/G SECT PRESS CT/SYS...LING CHARTS 20 BUREAUCRCY. PAGE 20 H0402
HABITAT NAT/G ADMIN CONSTN

B66
COLEMAN-NORTON P.R.,ROMAN STATE AND CHRISTIAN CHURCH: A COLLECTION OF LEGAL DOCUMENTS TO A.D. 535 (3 VOLS.). CHRIST-17C ROMAN/EMP...ANTHOL DICTIONARY 6 CHRISTIAN CHURCH/STA. PAGE 31 H0630
GP/REL NAT/G SECT LAW

B66
DALLIN A.,POLITICS IN THE SOVIET UNION: 7 CASES. COM USSR LAW POL/PAR CHIEF FORCES WRITING CONTROL PARL/PROC CIVMIL/REL TOTALISM...ANTHOL 20 KHRUSH/N STALIN/J CASEBOOK COM/PARTY. PAGE 37 H0736
MARXISM DOMIN ORD/FREE GOV/REL

B66
FEINE H.E.,REICH UND KIRCHE. CHRIST-17C MOD/EUR ROMAN/EMP LAW CHOOSE ATTIT 10/19 CHURCH/STA ROMAN/LAW. PAGE 49 H0982
JURID SECT NAT/G GP/REL

B66
HAHN C.H.L.,THE NATIVE TRIBES OF SOUTH WEST AFRICA. LAW FAM SECT HABITAT SKILL...SOC AUD/VIS WORSHIP RITUAL 20 AFRICA/SW. PAGE 64 H1275
CULTURE SOCIETY STRUCT AFR

B66
HAMILTON W.B.,A DECADE OF THE COMMONWEALTH, 1955-1964. UK LAW ELITES FINAN FOR/AID CONFER COLONIAL PWR...GEOG CHARTS ANTHOL 20 CMN/WLTH UN. PAGE 65 H1302
INT/ORG INGP/REL DIPLOM NAT/G

B66
HAY P.,FEDERALISM AND SUPRANATIONAL ORGANIZATIONS: PATTERNS FOR NEW LEGAL STRUCTURES. EUR+WWI LAW NAT/G VOL/ASSN DIPLOM PWR...NAT/COMP TREATY EEC. PAGE 68 H1364
SOVEREIGN FEDERAL INT/ORG INT/LAW

B66
HOLDSWORTH W.S.,A HISTORY OF ENGLISH LAW; THE CENTURIES OF SETTLEMENT AND REFORM (VOL. XVI). UK LOC/G NAT/G EX/STRUC LEGIS CT/SYS LEAD ATTIT ...POLICY DECISION JURID IDEA/COMP 18 PARLIAMENT. PAGE 73 H1454
BIOG PERSON PROF/ORG LAW

B66
HOPKINS J.F.K.,ARABIC PERIODICAL LITERATURE, 1961. ISLAM LAW CULTURE SECT...GEOG HEAL PHIL/SCI PSY SOC 20. PAGE 73 H1466
BIBLIOG/A NAT/LISM TEC/DEV INDUS

B66
IBRAHIM-HILMY,THE LITERATURE OF EGYPT AND THE SOUDAN: FROM THE EARLIEST TIMES TO THE YEAR 1885 INCLUSIVE (2 VOLS.). MEDIT-7 SUDAN UAR LAW SOCIETY SECT ATTIT EGYPT/ANC. PAGE 76 H1520
BIBLIOG CULTURE ISLAM NAT/G

B66
INSTITUTE COMP STUDY POL SYS,DOMINICAN REPUBLIC ELECTION FACT BOOK. DOMIN/REP LAW LEGIS REPRESENT ...JURID CHARTS 20. PAGE 77 H1536
SUFF CHOOSE POL/PAR NAT/G

B66
IOWA STATE U CTR AGRI AND ECO,RESEARCH AND EDUCATION FOR REGIONAL AND AREA DEVELOPMENT. FUT LAW CULTURE R+D LOC/G PLAN KNOWL...POLICY CHARTS ANTHOL 20. PAGE 78 H1565
REGION ACT/RES ECO/TAC INDUS

B66
KASUNMU A.B.,NIGERIAN FAMILY LAW. NIGERIA KIN LEGIT ILLEGIT MARRIAGE AGE DRIVE HABITAT ALL/VALS...JURID IDEA/COMP T 20 ENGLSH/LAW. PAGE 83 H1667
FAM LAW CULTURE AFR

B66
KEAY E.A.,THE NATIVE AND CUSTOMARY COURTS OF NIGERIA. NIGERIA CONSTN ELITES NAT/G TOP/EX PARTIC REGION...DECISION JURID 19/20. PAGE 84 H1673
AFR ADJUD LAW

B66
KERR M.H.,ISLAMIC REFORM: THE POLITICAL AND LEGAL THEORIES OF MUHAMMAD 'ABDUH AND RASHID RIDA. NAT/G SECT LEAD SOVEREIGN CONSERVE...JURID BIBLIOG WORSHIP 20. PAGE 85 H1698
LAW CONCPT ISLAM

B66
LEIGH M.B.,CHECK LIST OF HOLDINGS ON BORNEO IN THE CORNELL UNIVERSITY LIBRARIES (PAMPHLET). BORNEO MALAYSIA LAW CONSTN GP/REL SOC. PAGE 93 H1866
BIBLIOG S/ASIA DIPLOM NAT/G

B66
MERILLAT H.C.L.,LEGAL ADVISERS AND INTERNATIONAL
INT/ORG

ORGANIZATIONS. LAW NAT/G CONSULT OP/RES ADJUD SANCTION TASK CONSEN ORG/CHARTS. PAGE 109 H2178 INT/LAW CREATE OBS

B66
MULLER C.F.J.,A SELECT BIBLIOGRAPHY OF SOUTH AFRICAN HISTORY; A GUIDE FOR HISTORICAL RESEARCH. SOUTH/AFR UK LAW CONSTN SOCIETY STRUCT AGRI SECT DIPLOM COLONIAL LEAD RACE/REL...POLICY 17/20 NEGRO. PAGE 114 H2284 BIBLIOG AFR NAT/G

B66
SWEET E.C.,CIVIL LIBERTIES IN AMERICA. LAW CONSTN NAT/G PRESS CT/SYS DISCRIM ATTIT WORSHIP 20 CIVIL/LIB. PAGE 151 H3018 ADJUD ORD/FREE SUFF COERCE

B66
US DEPARTMENT OF STATE,RESEARCH ON AFRICA (EXTERNAL RESEARCH LIST NO 5-25). LAW CULTURE ECO/UNDEV POL/PAR DIPLOM EDU/PROP LEAD REGION MARXISM...GEOG LING WORSHIP 20. PAGE 159 H3188 BIBLIOG/A ASIA S/ASIA NAT/G

B66
US DEPARTMENT OF STATE,RESEARCH ON THE USSR AND EASTERN EUROPE (EXTERNAL RESEARCH LIST NO 1-25). USSR LAW CULTURE SOCIETY NAT/G TEC/DEV DIPLOM EDU/PROP REGION...GEOG LING. PAGE 160 H3191 BIBLIOG/A EUR+WWI COM MARXISM

B66
US DEPARTMENT OF STATE,RESEARCH ON WESTERN EUROPE, GREAT BRITAIN, AND CANADA (EXTERNAL RESEARCH LIST NO 3-25). CANADA GERMANY/W UK LAW CULTURE NAT/G POL/PAR FORCES EDU/PROP REGION MARXISM...GEOG SOC WORSHIP 20 CMN/WLTH. PAGE 160 H3192 BIBLIOG/A EUR+WWI DIPLOM

B66
ZINKIN T.,CHALLENGES IN INDIA. INDIA PAKISTAN LAW AGRI FINAN INDUS TOP/EX TEC/DEV CONTROL ROUTINE ORD/FREE PWR 20 NEHRU/J SHASTRI/LB CIVIL/SERV. PAGE 173 H3458 NAT/G ECO/TAC POLICY ADMIN

L66
HUNTINGTON S.P.,"POLITICAL MODERNIZATION* AMERICA VS EUROPE." EUR+WWI MOD/EUR UK USA+45 LAW ECO/UNDEV PWR SOVEREIGN CONSERVE LAISSEZ GOV/COMP. PAGE 75 H1505 STRUCT CREATE OBS

L66
KRENZ F.E.,"THE REFUGEE AS A SUBJECT OF INTERNATIONAL LAW." FUT LAW NAT/G CREATE ADJUD ISOLAT STRANGE...RECORD UN. PAGE 88 H1766 INT/LAW DISCRIM NEW/IDEA

L66
SEYLER W.C.,"DOCTORAL DISSERTATIONS IN POLITICAL SCIENCE IN UNIVERSITIES OF THE UNITED STATES AND CANADA." INT/ORG LOC/G ADMIN...INT/LAW MGT GOV/COMP. PAGE 142 H2836 BIBLIOG LAW NAT/G

S66
MATTHEWS D.G.,"ETHIOPIAN OUTLINE: A BIBLIOGRAPHIC RESEARCH GUIDE." ETHIOPIA LAW STRUCT ECO/UNDEV AGRI LABOR SECT CHIEF DELIB/GP EX/STRUC ADMIN...LING ORG/CHARTS 20. PAGE 105 H2095 BIBLIOG NAT/G DIPLOM POL/PAR

S66
MATTHEWS D.G.,"PRELUDE-COUP D'ETAT-MILITARY GOVERNMENT: A BIBLIOGRAPHICAL AND RESEARCH GUIDE TO NIGERIAN POL AND GOVT, JAN, 1965-66." AFR NIGER LAW CONSTN POL/PAR LEGIS CIVMIL/REL GOV/REL...STAT 20. PAGE 105 H2096 BIBLIOG NAT/G ADMIN CHOOSE

B67
ANDERSON E.N.,POLITICAL INSTITUTIONS AND SOCIAL CHANGE IN CONTINENTAL EUROPE IN THE NINETEENTH CENTURY. MOD/EUR LAW CONSTN SOCIETY POL/PAR TEC/DEV LEAD REV ATTIT...BIBLIOG 19. PAGE 6 H0127 NAT/G NAT/COMP METH/COMP INDUS

B67
ANDERSON O.,A LIBERAL STATE AT WAR. MOD/EUR UK LAW CULTURE STRUCT ECO/DEV NAT/G DIPLOM PARL/PROC GP/REL ALL/VALS...CONCPT 19. PAGE 7 H0131 WAR FORCES

B67
BOHANNAN P.,LAW AND WARFARE. CULTURE CT/SYS COERCE REV PEACE...JURID SOC CONCPT ANTHOL 20. PAGE 18 H0367 METH/COMP ADJUD WAR LAW

B67
BROWN L.N.,FRENCH ADMINISTRATIVE LAW. FRANCE UK CONSTN NAT/G LEGIS DOMIN CONTROL EXEC PARL/PROC PWR ...JURID METH/COMP GEN/METH. PAGE 22 H0447 EX/STRUC LAW IDEA/COMP CT/SYS

B67
BUNN R.F.,POLITICS AND CIVIL LIBERTIES IN EUROPE: FOUR CASE STUDIES. FRANCE GERMANY/W UK USSR NAT/G PRESS CRIME CROWD PRIVIL ATTIT 20. PAGE 24 H0476 ORD/FREE CONSTN NAT/COMP LAW

B67
CANTOR N.F.,THE ENGLISH TRADITION* TWENTIETH-CENTURY VIEWS OF ENGLISH HISTORY (2VOLS.). UK STRATA NAT/G SECT WAR...POLICY GOV/COMP IDEA/COMP ANTHOL T PARLIAMENT CMN/WLTH. PAGE 26 H0522 CT/SYS LAW POL/PAR

B67
GELLHORN W.,OMBUDSMEN AND OTHERS: CITIZENS' PROTECTORS IN NINE COUNTRIES. WOR+45 LAW CONSTN LEGIS INSPECT ADJUD ADMIN CONTROL CT/SYS CHOOSE PERS/REL...STAT CHARTS 20. PAGE 55 H1109 NAT/COMP REPRESENT INGP/REL PROB/SOLV

B67
HODGKINSON R.G.,THE ORIGINS OF THE NATIONAL HEALTH SERVICE: THE MEDICAL SERVICES OF THE NEW POOR LAW, 1834-1871. UK INDUS MUNIC WORKER PROB/SOLV EFFICIENCY ATTIT HEALTH WEALTH SOCISM...JURID SOC/WK 19/20. PAGE 72 H1445 HEAL NAT/G POLICY LAW

B67
LENG S.C.,JUSTICE IN COMMUNIST CHINA: A SURVEY OF THE JUDICIAL SYSTEM OF THE CHINESE PEOPLE'S REPUBLIC. CHINA/COM LAW CONSTN LOC/G NAT/G PROF/ORG CONSULT FORCES ADMIN CRIME ORD/FREE...BIBLIOG 20 MAO. PAGE 94 H1877 CT/SYS ADJUD JURID MARXISM

B67
OPERATIONS AND POLICY RESEARCH,NICARAGUA: ELECTION FACTBOOK: FEBRUARY 5, 1967 (PAMPHLET). NICARAGUA LAW NAT/G LEAD REPRESENT...STAT BIOG CHARTS 20. PAGE 121 H2423 POL/PAR CHOOSE PLAN ATTIT

B67
POMEROY W.J.,HALF A CENTURY OF SOCIALISM. USSR LAW AGRI INDUS NAT/G CREATE DIPLOM EDU/PROP PERSON ORD/FREE WEALTH...POLICY TREND 20. PAGE 127 H2541 SOCISM MARXISM COM SOCIETY

B67
SCHWARTZ B.,THE ROOTS OF FREEDOM: A CONSTITUTIONAL HISTORY OF ENGLAND. UK LAW POL/PAR DELIB/GP LEGIS REV REPRESENT...JURID BIBLIOG/A 13/20. PAGE 140 H2809 CONSTN PARL/PROC NAT/G

B67
WIENER F.B.,CIVILIANS UNDER MILITARY JUSTICE; THE BRITISH PRACTICE SINCE 1689 ESPECIALLY IN NORTH AMERICA. UK USA-45 LAW CONSTN CRIME REV...DECISION CHARTS NAT/COMP BIBLIOG 17/20. PAGE 168 H3356 CT/SYS FORCES ADJUD

L67
CRIBBET J.E.,"SOME REFLECTIONS ON THE LAW OF LAND - A VIEW FROM SCANDINAVIA." DENMARK NETHERLAND NORWAY SWEDEN INDUS MUNIC NEIGH RACE/REL ATTIT HABITAT ...IDEA/COMP 20. PAGE 35 H0701 LAW PLAN CONTROL NAT/G

L67
EINAUDI L.,"ANNOTATED BIBLIOGRAPHY OF LATIN AMERICAN MILITARY JOURNALS" LAW TEC/DEV DOMIN EDU/PROP COERCE WAR CIVMIL/REL 20. PAGE 45 H0899 BIBLIOG/A NAT/G FORCES L/A+17C

L67
GOOD E.M.,"CAPITAL PUNISHMENT AND ITS ALTERNATIVES IN ANCIENT NEAR EASTERN LAW." SOCIETY SECT INGP/REL CONSEN ATTIT SEX MORAL...CRIMLGY GP/COMP. PAGE 58 H1168 MEDIT-7 LAW JURID CULTURE

L67
ROTH A.R.,"CAPITAL-MARKET DEVELOPMENT IN ISRAEL AND BRAZIL: TWO EXAMPLES OF THE ROLE OF LAW IN DEVELOPMENT." BRAZIL ISRAEL L/A+17C INDUS MARKET ECO/TAC FOR/AID INT/TRADE CONTROL BAL/PAY 20. PAGE 135 H2694 LAW ECO/UNDEV NAT/COMP FINAN

L67
WAELBROECK M.,"THE APPLICATION OF EEC LAW BY NATIONAL COURTS." EUR+WWI INT/ORG CT/SYS...JURID EEC TREATY. PAGE 164 H3284 INT/LAW NAT/G LAW PROB/SOLV

S67
ADOKO A.,"THE CONSTITUTION OF UGANDA." AFR UGANDA LOC/G CHIEF FORCES LEGIS ADJUD EXEC CHOOSE NAT/LISM ...IDEA/COMP 20. PAGE 4 H0072 NAT/G CONSTN ORD/FREE LAW

S67
BAIKALOV A.,"EMERGENCY LEGISLATION IN WEST GERMANY." GERMANY/W LABOR NAT/G POL/PAR SANCTION ...MARXIST 20. PAGE 10 H0199 LAW TOTALISM LEGIS PARL/PROC

S67
BRADLEY A.W.,"CONSTITUTION-MAKING IN UGANDA." UGANDA LAW CHIEF DELIB/GP LEGIS ADMIN EXEC PARL/PROC RACE/REL ORD/FREE...GOV/COMP 20. PAGE 20 H0397 NAT/G CREATE CONSTN FEDERAL

S67
DERRICK P.,"THE WHITE PAPER ON INCOMES." EUR+WWI UK LAW LABOR NAT/G PLAN PROB/SOLV GP/REL...GOV/COMP PARLIAMENT. PAGE 40 H0794 INCOME POL/PAR POLICY

S67
DRYDEN S.,"LOCAL GOVERNMENT IN TANZANIA PART II" TANZANIA LAW NAT/G POL/PAR CONTROL PARTIC REPRESENT ...DECISION 20. PAGE 42 H0850 LOC/G GOV/REL ADMIN STRUCT

S67
KASFIR N.,"THE UGANDA CONSTITUENT ASSEMBLY DEBATE." UGANDA REPRESENT FEDERAL ORD/FREE POPULISM...POLICY DECISION 20. PAGE 83 H1665 CONSTN CONFER LAW NAT/G

S67
KINGSBURY E.C.,"LAW AS COMPACT: ANCIENT ISRAEL'S CONTRIBUTION TO THE UNDERSTANDING OF LAW." ISRAEL MEDIT-7 CULTURE KIN KNOWL...JURID CONCPT TREND IDEA/COMP METH/COMP WORSHIP JEWS DEITY. PAGE 86 H1716 LAW AGREE CONSTN INGP/REL

S67
LEGRES A.,"LES FONCTIONS D'UN PARLEMENT MODERNE." FRANCE DEBATE PARL/PROC SANCTION ATTIT PWR 20 PARLIAMENT. PAGE 93 H1860 NAT/G LAW LEGIS CHOOSE

S67
MAIR L.,"BUSOGA LOCAL GOVERNMENT" AFR UGANDA UK CONSTN GP/REL...GOV/COMP METH/COMP 20. PAGE 101 H2024
LOC/G COLONIAL LAW ATTIT

S67
MAYANJA A.,"THE GOVERNMENT'S PROPOSALS ON THE NEW CONSTITUTION." AFR UGANDA LAW CHIEF LEGIS ADJUD REPRESENT FEDERAL PWR 20. PAGE 105 H2105
CONSTN CONFER ORD/FREE NAT/G

S67
NEALE R.S.,"WORKING CLASS WOMEN AND WOMEN'S SUFFRAGE." UK LAW CONSTN LABOR NAT/G DELIB/GP LEGIS WORKER PAY PARTIC CHOOSE 19 FEMALE/SEX. PAGE 116 H2326
STRATA SEX SUFF DISCRIM

S67
RUCKER B.W.,"WHAT SOLUTIONS DO PEOPLE ENDORSE IN FREE PRESS-FAIR TRIAL DILEMMA?" LAW NAT/G CT/SYS ATTIT...NET/THEORY SAMP CHARTS IDEA/COMP METH 20. PAGE 136 H2710
CONCPT PRESS ADJUD ORD/FREE

S67
SEIDLER G.L.,"MARXIST LEGAL THOUGHT IN POLAND." POLAND SOCIETY R+D LOC/G NAT/G ACT/RES ADJUD CT/SYS SUPEGO PWR...SOC TREND 20 MARX/KARL. PAGE 141 H2822
MARXISM LAW CONCPT EFFICIENCY

S67
ULC O.,"CLASS STRUGGLE AND SOCIALIST JUSTICE: THE CASE OF CZECHOSLOVAKIA." COM CZECHOSLVK LAW CONSTN ELITES STRUCT NAT/G CRIME GP/REL MARXISM 20. PAGE 158 H3151
TOTALISM CT/SYS ADJUD STRATA

S67
WILLIAMS F.R.A.,"FUNDAMENTAL RIGHTS AND THE PROSPECT FOR DEMOCRACY IN NIGERIA." FUT NIGERIA SOCIETY ECO/UNDEV LEGIS ADJUD CHOOSE 20. PAGE 168 H3366
CONSTN LAW ORD/FREE NAT/G

S68
BURGESS J.W.,"VON HOLST'S PUBLIC LAW OF THE UNITED STATES" USA-45 LAW GOV/REL...GOV/COMP IDEA/COMP 19. PAGE 24 H0480
CONSTN FEDERAL NAT/G JURID

B75
MAINE H.S.,LECTURES ON THE EARLY HISTORY OF INSTITUTIONS. IRELAND UK CONSTN ELITES STRUCT FAM KIN CHIEF LEGIS CT/SYS OWN SOVEREIGN...CONCPT 16 BENTHAM/J BREHON ROMAN/LAW. PAGE 101 H2021
CULTURE LAW INGP/REL

B79
BRODERICK G.C.,POLITICAL STUDIES. IRELAND UK ROMAN/EMP LAW ACADEM LOC/G NAT/G DIPLOM PARL/PROC SUFF GP/REL LAISSEZ...ANTHOL. PAGE 21 H0424
CONSTN COLONIAL

B89
FERNEUIL T.,LES PRINCIPES DE 1789 ET LA SCIENCE SOCIALE. FRANCE NAT/G REV ATTIT...CONCPT TREND IDEA/COMP 18/19. PAGE 49 H0986
CONSTN POLICY LAW

B91
BENTHAM J.,A FRAGMENT ON GOVERNMENT (1776). CONSTN MUNIC NAT/G SECT AGREE HAPPINESS UTIL MORAL ORD/FREE...JURID CONCPT. PAGE 15 H0292
SOVEREIGN LAW DOMIN

B91
SIDGWICK H.,THE ELEMENTS OF POLITICS. LOC/G NAT/G LEGIS DIPLOM ADJUD CONTROL EXEC PARL/PROC REPRESENT GOV/REL SOVEREIGN ALL/IDEOS 19 MILL/JS BENTHAM/J. PAGE 143 H2868
POLICY LAW CONCPT

B94
BENOIST C.,LA POLITIQUE. FRANCE LAW SOCIETY STRUCT POL/PAR PARL/PROC GP/REL ATTIT PWR 19/20. PAGE 14 H0283
NAT/G REPRESENT ORD/FREE

B96
DE VATTEL E.,THE LAW OF NATIONS. AGRI FINAN CHIEF DIPLOM INT/TRADE AGREE OWN ALL/VALS MORAL ORD/FREE SOVEREIGN...GEN/LAWS 18 NATURL/LAW WOLFF/C. PAGE 39 H0774
LAW CONCPT NAT/G INT/LAW

B96
ESMEIN A.,ELEMENTS DE DROIT CONSTITUTIONNEL. FRANCE UK CHIEF EX/STRUC LEGIS ADJUD CT/SYS PARL/PROC REV GOV/REL ORD/FREE...JURID METH/COMP 18/19. PAGE 47 H0940
LAW CONSTN NAT/G CONCPT

B97
JENKS E.J.,LAW AND POLITICS IN THE MIDDLE AGES. CHRIST-17C CULTURE STRUCT KIN NAT/G SECT CT/SYS GP/REL...CLASSIF CHARTS IDEA/COMP BIBLIOG 8/16. PAGE 80 H1603
LAW SOCIETY ADJUST

B98
POLLOCK F.,THE HISTORY OF ENGLISH LAW BEFORE THE TIME OF EDWARD I (2 VOLS, 2ND ED.). UK CULTURE LOC/G LEGIS LICENSE AGREE CONTROL CT/SYS SANCTION CRIME...TIME/SEQ 13 COMMON/LAW CANON/LAW. PAGE 127 H2538
LAW ADJUD JURID

B99
KINGSLEY M.H.,WEST AFRICAN STUDIES. GHANA NIGERIA SIER/LEONE LAW EXTR/IND SECT DIPLOM INT/TRADE DOMIN RACE/REL OWN HEALTH...SOC 19. PAGE 86 H1717
AFR HEREDITY COLONIAL CULTURE

B99
LECKY W.E.H.,DEMOCRACY AND LIBERTY (2 VOLS.). LAW CONSTN STRATA POL/PAR SECT WORKER DIPLOM ADJUD REPRESENT NAT/LISM CONSERVE. PAGE 93 H1851
LEGIS NAT/G POPULISM

ORD/FREE

LAW/ETHIC....ETHICS OF LAW AND COURT PROCESSES

LAWLEY F.E. H1844,H1845

LAWRENC/TE....THOMAS EDWARD LAWRENCE

LAWRENCE P. H1846,H1847

LAWRIE G. H1848

LAZARFELD P. H1579

LAZRSFLD/P....PAUL LAZARSFELD (AND LAZARSFELD SCALE)

LEAD....LEADING, CONTRIBUTING MORE THAN AVERAGE

N
UNIVERSITY OF FLORIDA LIBRARY,DOORS TO LATIN AMERICA; RECENT BOOKS AND PAMPHLETS. CONSTN CULTURE SOCIETY ECO/UNDEV COLONIAL LEAD GOV/REL NAT/LISM ATTIT...HUM SOC 20. PAGE 159 H3170
BIBLIOG/A L/A+17C DIPLOM NAT/G

B
DEUTSCHE BIBLIOTH FRANKF A M,DEUTSCHE BIBLIOGRAPHIE. EUR+WWI GERMANY ECO/DEV FORCES DIPLOM LEAD...POLICY PHIL/SCI SOC 20. PAGE 40 H0802
BIBLIOG LAW ADMIN NAT/G

N
BULLETIN ANALYTIQUE DE DOCUMENTATION POLITIQUE, ECONOMIQUE, ET SOCIAL CONTEMPORAIRE. FRANCE WOR+45 SOCIETY ECO/DEV ECO/UNDEV INT/ORG LOC/G PROB/SOLV FOR/AID LEAD REGION SOC. PAGE 1 H0002
BIBLIOG/A DIPLOM NAT/COMP NAT/G

N
INTERNATIONAL BIBLIOGRAPHIE DER DEUTSCHEN ZEITSCHRIFTENLITERATUR. EUR+WWI GERMANY MOD/EUR ECO/DEV POL/PAR LEAD WAR NAT/LISM ATTIT...EPIST PHIL/SCI 19/20. PAGE 1 H0004
BIBLIOG/A NAT/G PERSON CULTURE

N
JOURNAL OF MODERN HISTORY. WOR+45 WOR-45 LEAD WAR ...TIME/SEQ TREND NAT/COMP 20. PAGE 1 H0006
BIBLIOG/A DIPLOM NAT/G

N
MIDDLE EAST JOURNAL. CULTURE SECT DIPLOM LEAD GOV/REL ATTIT...POLICY PHIL/SCI SOC LING BIOG 20. PAGE 1 H0007
BIBLIOG ISLAM NAT/G ECO/UNDEV

N
NEUE POLITISCHE LITERATUR. AFR ASIA EUR+WWI GERMANY RUSSIA SOCIETY ECO/DEV ECO/UNDEV PLAN PROB/SOLV LEAD MARXISM...PHIL/SCI CONCPT 20. PAGE 1 H0008
BIBLIOG DIPLOM COM NAT/G

N
DAILY SUMMARY OF THE JAPANESE PRESS. NAT/G DIPLOM LEAD 20 CHINJAP. PAGE 1 H0013
BIBLIOG PRESS ASIA ATTIT

N
HANDBOOK OF LATIN AMERICAN STUDIES. LAW CULTURE ECO/UNDEV POL/PAR ADMIN LEAD...SOC 20. PAGE 1 H0016
BIBLIOG/A L/A+17C NAT/G DIPLOM

N
LONDON TIMES OFFICIAL INDEX. UK LAW ECO/DEV NAT/G DIPLOM LEAD ATTIT 20. PAGE 1 H0018
BIBLIOG INDEX PRESS WRITING

N
PUBLISHERS' CIRCULAR, THE OFFICIAL ORGAN OF THE PUBLISHERS' ASSOCIATION OF GREAT BRITAIN AND IRELAND. EUR+WWI MOD/EUR UK LAW PROB/SOLV DIPLOM COLONIAL ATTIT...HUM 19/20 CMN/WLTH. PAGE 1 H0019
BIBLIOG NAT/G WRITING LEAD

N
SUBJECT GUIDE TO BOOKS IN PRINT: AN INDEX TO THE PUBLISHERS' TRADE LIST ANNUAL. UNIV LAW LOC/G DIPLOM WRITING ADMIN LEAD PERSON...MGT SOC. PAGE 2 H0024
BIBLIOG ECO/DEV POL/PAR NAT/G

N
SUMMARIES OF SELECTED JAPANESE MAGAZINES. LAW CULTURE ADMIN LEAD 20 CHINJAP. PAGE 2 H0025
BIBLIOG/A ATTIT NAT/G ASIA

N
NEUE POLITISCHE LITERATUR; BERICHTE UBER DAS INTERNATIONALE SCHRIFTTUM ZUR POLITIK. WOR+45 LAW CONSTN POL/PAR ADMIN LEAD GOV/REL...POLICY IDEA/COMP. PAGE 2 H0027
BIBLIOG/A DIPLOM NAT/G NAT/COMP

N
ASIA FOUNDATION,LIBRARY NOTES. LAW CONSTN CULTURE SOCIETY ECO/UNDEV INT/ORG NAT/G COLONIAL LEAD REGION NAT/LISM ATTIT 20 UN. PAGE 9 H0176
BIBLIOG/A ASIA S/ASIA DIPLOM

N
CARIBBEAN COMMISSION,CURRENT CARIBBEAN BIBLIOGRAPHY. FRANCE NETHERLAND UK CULTURE ECO/UNDEV PRESS LEAD ATTIT...GEOG SOC 20. PAGE 26
BIBLIOG NAT/G L/A+17C

H0530 DIPLOM

N
CORNELL UNIVERSITY LIBRARY,SOUTHEAST ASIA ACCESSIONS LIST. LAW SOCIETY STRUCT ECO/UNDEV POL/PAR TEC/DEV DIPLOM LEAD REGION. PAGE 34 H0671 BIBLIOG S/ASIA NAT/G CULTURE

N
DEUTSCHE BUCHEREI,DEUTSCHE NATIONALBIBLIOGRAPHIE. GERMANY ECO/DEV DIPLOM AGE/Y ATTIT...PHIL/SCI SOC 20. PAGE 40 H0803 BIBLIOG NAT/G LEAD POLICY

N
DEUTSCHE BUCHEREI,DEUTSCHES BUCHERVERZEICHNIS. GERMANY LAW CULTURE POL/PAR ADMIN LEAD ATTIT PERSON ...SOC 20. PAGE 40 H0805 BIBLIOG NAT/G DIPLOM ECO/DEV

N
INSTITUTE OF HISPANIC STUDIES,HISPANIC AMERICAN REPORT. EUR+WWI SPAIN LAW CONSTN ECO/UNDEV POL/PAR EX/STRUC LEGIS LEAD...HUM SOC 20. PAGE 77 H1538 BIBLIOG/A L/A+17C NAT/G DIPLOM

N
US CONSOLATE GENERAL HONG KONG,REVIEW OF THE HONG KONG CHINESE PRESS. ECO/UNDEV LOC/G NAT/G PLAN DIPLOM EDU/PROP LEAD GP/REL MARXISM...POLICY INDEX 20. PAGE 159 H3178 BIBLIOG/A ASIA PRESS ATTIT

N
US CONSULATE GENERAL HONG KONG,CURRENT BACKGROUND. CHINA/COM ECO/UNDEV LOC/G NAT/G PLAN DIPLOM EDU/PROP LEAD REV ATTIT...POLICY INDEX 20. PAGE 159 H3179 BIBLIOG/A MARXIST ASIA PRESS

N
US CONSULATE GENERAL HONG KONG,EXTRACTS FROM CHINA MAINLAND MAGAZINES. ASIA CHINA/COM ECO/UNDEV NAT/G CHIEF LEAD ATTIT...MARXIST INDEX 20. PAGE 159 H3180 BIBLIOG MARXISM PRESS

N
US CONSULATE GENERAL HONG KONG,SURVEY OF CHINA MAINLAND PRESS. CHINA/COM ECO/UNDEV LOC/G NAT/G PLAN DIPLOM EDU/PROP LEAD REV ATTIT...POLICY INDEX 20. PAGE 159 H3181 BIBLIOG/A MARXIST ASIA PRESS

N
US CONSULATE GENERAL HONG KONG,US CONSULATE GENERAL, HONG KONG, PRESS SUMMARIES. CHINA/COM ECO/UNDEV LOC/G NAT/G PLAN DIPLOM EDU/PROP LEAD REV ATTIT...POLICY INDEX 20. PAGE 159 H3182 BIBLIOG/A MARXIST ASIA PRESS

N
US LIBRARY OF CONGRESS,ACCESSIONS LIST - INDIA. INDIA CULTURE AGRI LOC/G POL/PAR PLAN PROB/SOLV TEC/DEV DIPLOM EDU/PROP LEAD GP/REL ATTIT 20. PAGE 160 H3199 BIBLIOG S/ASIA ECO/UNDEV NAT/G

N
US LIBRARY OF CONGRESS,ACCESSIONS LIST -- ISRAEL. ISRAEL CULTURE ECO/UNDEV POL/PAR PLAN PROB/SOLV TEC/DEV DIPLOM EDU/PROP LEAD WAR ATTIT 20 JEWS. PAGE 160 H3200 BIBLIOG ISLAM NAT/G GP/REL

B00
MARKHAM V.R.,SOUTH AFRICA, PAST AND PRESENT. NETHERLAND SOUTH/AFR CULTURE LEGIS EDU/PROP COLONIAL CHOOSE REPRESENT DISCRIM ATTIT...OBS TIME/SEQ 17/19 NEGRO BOER/WAR. PAGE 103 H2054 WAR LEAD RACE/REL

B10
TEMPERLEY H.W.V.,SENATES AND UPPER CHAMBERS; THEIR USE AND FUNCTION IN THE MODERN STATE... UK WOR-45 CONSTN NAT/G POL/PAR PROVS SECT COLONIAL LEAD CHOOSE REPRESENT PWR...BIBLIOG 19/20 PARLIAMENT SENATE CMN/WLTH HOUSE/LORD. PAGE 153 H3059 PARL/PROC NAT/COMP LEGIS EX/STRUC

B14
LEVINE L.,SYNDICALISM IN FRANCE (2ND ED.). FRANCE LAW SOCIETY ECO/DEV NAT/G ECO/TAC LEAD ATTIT ...POLICY CONCPT STAT BIBLIOG 18/20 REFORMERS. PAGE 95 H1902 LABOR INDUS SOCISM REV

B15
MICHELS R.,POLITICAL PARTIES. NAT/G BAL/PWR CHOOSE REPRESENT ATTIT SOCISM...PSY SOC CONCPT OBS 20 MONOPOLY. PAGE 110 H2198 POL/PAR CENTRAL LEAD PWR

B17
BARRES M.,THE UNDYING SPIRIT OF FRANCE (TRANS. BY M. CORWIN). FRANCE DOMIN LEAD DEATH ATTIT RESPECT ...NAT/COMP 20 WWI. PAGE 11 H0226 NAT/LISM FORCES WAR CULTURE

B17
DOS SANTOS M.,BIBLIOGRAPHIA GERAL, A DESCRIPCAO BIBLIOGRAFICA DE LIVROS TANTO DE AUTORES PORTUGUEZES COMO BRASILEIROS... BRAZIL PORTUGAL NAT/G LEAD GP/REL 15/20. PAGE 42 H0840 BIBLIOG/A L/A+17C DIPLOM COLONIAL

B17
HARLOW R.V.,THE HISTORY OF LEGISLATIVE METHODS IN THE PERIOD BEFORE 1825. USA-45 EX/STRUC ADMIN COLONIAL LEAD PARL/PROC ROUTINE...GP/COMP GOV/COMP HOUSE/REP. PAGE 66 H1333 LEGIS DELIB/GP PROVS POL/PAR

N19
BARRES M.,"THE WAR AND THE SPIRIT OF YOUTH" (PAMPHLET). FRANCE FORCES DOMIN LEAD DEATH AGE/Y ATTIT RESPECT...FASCIST 20 WWI. PAGE 11 H0228 WAR NAT/LISM CULTURE MYSTIC

N19
GOODMAN G.K.,IMPERIAL JAPAN AND ASIA: A REASSESSMENT (PAMPHLET). ASIA S/ASIA ECO/DEV FORCES LEAD WAR NAT/LISM ATTIT...DECISION CONCPT BIBLIOG 19/20 CHINJAP. PAGE 59 H1172 DIPLOM NAT/G POLICY COLONIAL

N19
HAJDA J.,THE COLD WAR VIEWED AS A SOCIOLOGICAL PROBLEM (PAMPHLET). COM CZECHOSLVK EUR+WWI SOCIETY PLAN EDU/PROP CONTROL TASK ATTIT MARXISM...POLICY 20 COLD/WAR MIGRATION. PAGE 64 H1280 DIPLOM LEAD PWR NAT/G

N19
OPERATIONS AND POLICY RESEARCH,URUGUAY: ELECTION FACTBOOK: NOVEMBER 27, 1966 (PAMPHLET). URUGUAY LAW NAT/G LEAD REPRESENT...STAT BIOG CHARTS 20. PAGE 121 H2422 POL/PAR CHOOSE PLAN ATTIT

B21
KREY A.C.,THE FIRST CRUSADE. CHRIST-17C SOCIETY STRATA NAT/G SECT FORCES WORKER WRITING LEAD ATTIT ...CHARTS 11 CHRISTIAN CRUSADES. PAGE 88 H1767 WAR CATH DIPLOM PARTIC

B21
WALLAS G.,HUMAN NATURE IN POLITICS (3RD ED.). UNIV NAT/G LEAD CHOOSE REPRESENT GP/REL NAT/LISM RATIONAL BIO/SOC HEREDITY ALL/VALS MAJORIT. PAGE 165 H3293 PSY DRIVE PERSON

S21
MALINOWSKI B.,"THE PRIMITIVE ECONOMICS OF THE TROBRIAND ISLANDERS" (BMR)" CULTURE SOCIETY NAT/G CHIEF LEAD OWN...SOC MYTH WORSHIP 20 NEW/GUINEA TROBRIAND RESOURCE/N. PAGE 101 H2029 ECO/UNDEV AGRI PRODUC STRUCT

B26
SMITH T.V.,THE DEMOCRATIC WAY OF LIFE. UNIV SOCIETY NAT/G WORKER TASK CHOOSE ALL/VALS...IDEA/COMP WORSHIP. PAGE 146 H2919 MAJORIT CONCPT ORD/FREE LEAD

B27
BELLOC H.,THE SERVILE STATE (1912) (3RD ED.). PRUSSIA UK CULTURE STRATA INDUS NAT/G ECO/TAC CONTROL LEAD SUFF DISCRIM EQUILIB ORD/FREE WEALTH 20. PAGE 13 H0269 WORKER CAP/ISM DOMIN CATH

B27
ENGELS F.,THE PEASANT WAR IN GERMANY (1850). GERMANY MOD/EUR AGRI WORKER LEAD COERCE INGP/REL ...TREND 16/19. PAGE 46 H0924 WAR STRATA REV MARXIST

B27
GOOCH G.P.,ENGLISH DEMOCRATIC IDEAS IN THE SEVENTEENTH CENTURY (2ND ED.). UK LAW SECT FORCES DIPLOM LEAD PARL/PROC REV ATTIT AUTHORIT...ANARCH CONCPT 17 PARLIAMENT CMN/WLTH REFORMERS. PAGE 58 H1167 IDEA/COMP MAJORIT EX/STRUC CONSERVE

S27
MICHELS R.,"SOME REFLECTIONS ON THE SOCIOLOGICAL CHARACTER OF POLITICAL PARTIES" (BMR)" WOR-45 STRATA MAJORITY DRIVE...GOV/COMP 20. PAGE 110 H2199 POL/PAR PWR LEAD CONCPT

B28
FYFE H.,THE BRITISH LIBERAL PARTY. UK SECT ADMIN LEAD CHOOSE GP/REL PWR SOCISM...MAJORIT TIME/SEQ 19/20 LIB/PARTY CONSRV/PAR. PAGE 54 H1084 POL/PAR NAT/G REPRESENT POPULISM

B28
LODGE H.C.,THE HISTORY OF NATIONS (25 VOLS.). UNIV LEAD...ANTHOL BIBLIOG INDEX. PAGE 98 H1951 DIPLOM SOCIETY NAT/G

B31
KIRKPATRICK F.A.,A HISTORY OF THE ARGENTINE REPUBLIC. SPAIN UK CONSTN SOCIETY ECO/UNDEV EX/STRUC DIPLOM FOR/AID LEAD WAR ATTIT...BIOG CHARTS 16/20 ARGEN SAN/MARTIN. PAGE 86 H1724 NAT/G L/A+17C COLONIAL

C33
MURET C.T.,"FRENCH ROYALIST DOCTRINES SINCE THE REVOLUTION." FRANCE CONSTN NAT/G SECT ADMIN LEAD SOVEREIGN...POLICY BIOG IDEA/COMP BIBLIOG 18/20. PAGE 115 H2295 POL/PAR ATTIT INTELL CONSERVE

B34
DE CENIVAL P.,BIBLIOGRAPHIE MAROCAINE: 1923-1933. FRANCE MOROCCO SECT ADMIN LEAD GP/REL ATTIT...LING 20. PAGE 37 H0750 BIBLIOG/A ISLAM NAT/G COLONIAL

B36
BATTAGLIA F.,LINEAMENTI DI STORIA DELLE DOCTRINE POLITICHE CON APPENDICI BIBLIOGRAFICHE. ITALY PROB/SOLV LEAD 20. PAGE 12 H0237 BIBLIOG PHIL/SCI CONCPT NAT/G

B36
LAPRADE W.T.,PUBLIC OPINION AND POLITICS IN EIGHTEENTH CENTURY ENGLAND. UK CULTURE POL/PAR CHIEF TOP/EX LEAD REV NAT/LISM PWR 18 PROTESTANT PROTESTANT CHURCH/STA. PAGE 91 H1815 POLICY ELITES ATTIT TIME/SEQ

B36
PREVITE-ORTON C.W.,THE CAMBRIDGE MEDIEVAL HISTORY (8 VOLS.). CHRIST-17C NAT/G PROB/SOLV TEC/DEV LEAD ...POLICY CONCPT WORSHIP. PAGE 128 H2559 BIBLIOG IDEA/COMP TREND

B37
MUNZENBERG W.,PROPAGANDA ALS WAFFE. COM/IND PRESS EDU/PROP

COERCE WAR...PSY 20. PAGE 115 H2290 DOMIN NAT/G LEAD

B38
DEL TORO J.,A BIBLIOGRAPHY OF THE COLLECTIVE BIOGRAPHY OF SPANISH AMERICA. ELITES NAT/G WRITING LEAD PERSON 19/20. PAGE 39 H0786 BIBLIOG/A L/A+17C BIOG

B38
FIELD G.L.,THE SYNDICAL AND CORPORATIVE INSTITUTIONS OF ITALIAN FASCISM. ITALY CONSTN STRATA LABOR EX/STRUC TOP/EX ADJUD ADMIN LEAD TOTALISM AUTHORIT...MGT 20 MUSSOLIN/B. PAGE 50 H0991 FASCISM INDUS NAT/G WORKER

B38
HARPER S.N.,THE GOVERNMENT OF THE SOVIET UNION. COM USSR LAW CONSTN ECO/DEV PLAN TEC/DEV DIPLOM INT/TRADE ADMIN REV NAT/LISM...POLICY 20. PAGE 67 H1337 MARXISM NAT/G LEAD POL/PAR

B38
HOLDSWORTH W.S.,A HISTORY OF ENGLISH LAW; THE CENTURIES OF SETTLEMENT AND REFORM (VOL. XI). UK CONSTN NAT/G EX/STRUC DIPLOM ADJUD CT/SYS LEAD CRIME ATTIT...INT/LAW JURID 18 CMN/WLTH PARLIAMENT ENGLSH/LAW. PAGE 73 H1452 LAW COLONIAL LEGIS PARL/PROC

B39
AKIGA,AKIGA'S STORY: THE TIV TRIBE AS SEEN BY ONE OF ITS MEMBERS. NIGERIA LAW STRUCT ECO/UNDEV FAM LEAD GP/REL MARRIAGE...LING WORSHIP 20. PAGE 4 H0089 KIN SECT SOC CULTURE

B39
COBBAN A.,DICTATORSHIP: ITS HISTORY AND THEORY. EUR+WWI MOD/EUR SOCIETY STRUCT NAT/G TEC/DEV LEAD NAT/LISM SOVEREIGN...IDEA/COMP 14/20. PAGE 30 H0610 TOTALISM FASCISM CONCPT

B39
JENNINGS W.I.,PARLIAMENT. UK POL/PAR OP/RES BUDGET LEAD CHOOSE GP/REL...MGT 20 PARLIAMENT HOUSE/LORD HOUSE/CMNS. PAGE 80 H1609 PARL/PROC LEGIS CONSTN NAT/G

B40
HUNTER R.,REVOLUTION: WHY, HOW, WHEN? NAT/G ECO/TAC EDU/PROP COERCE ORD/FREE FASCISM POPULISM SOCISM 18/20 HITLER/A LENIN/VI. PAGE 75 H1502 REV METH/COMP LEAD CONSTN

B40
LEDERER E.,STATE OF THE MASSES. GERMANY ITALY SOCIETY NAT/G ECO/TAC EDU/PROP LEAD TOTALISM ...SOCIALIST PSY 20. PAGE 93 H1852 CROWD FASCISM AUTHORIT PERSON

B40
MCHENRY D.E.,HIS MAJESTY'S OPPOSITION: STRUCTURE AND PROBLEMS OF THE BRITISH LABOUR PARTY 1931-1938. UK FINAN LABOR LOC/G DELIB/GP LEGIS EDU/PROP LEAD PARTIC CHOOSE GP/REL SOCISM...TREND 20 LABOR/PAR. PAGE 107 H2130 POL/PAR MGT NAT/G POLICY

B41
KEESING F.M.,THE SOUTH SEAS IN THE MODERN WORLD. INDONESIA STRUCT FAM SECT EDU/PROP LEAD INCOME WEALTH...HEAL SOC 20. PAGE 84 H1678 CULTURE ECO/UNDEV GOV/COMP DIPLOM

S41
DENNERY E.,"DEMOCRACY AND THE FRENCH ARMY." FRANCE NAT/G EX/STRUC LEAD REV ROLE 18/20. PAGE 40 H0792 FORCES POPULISM STRATA CIVMIL/REL

B42
BARKER E.,REFLECTIONS ON GOVERNMENT. EUR+WWI SOCIETY LEGIS EDU/PROP ADMIN LEAD PARTIC CHOOSE TOTALISM AUTHORIT ORD/FREE SOCISM 20. PAGE 11 H0218 NAT/G POPULISM ACT/RES GEN/LAWS

B43
BROWN A.D.,GREECE: SELECTED LIST OF REFERENCES. GREECE ECO/UNDEV AGRI FINAN INDUS LABOR SECT TEC/DEV INT/TRADE LEAD...SOC 20. PAGE 22 H0438 BIBLIOG/A WAR DIPLOM NAT/G

B43
GRIERSON P.,BOOKS ON SOVIET RUSSIA 1917-42: A BIBLIOGRAPHY AND A GUIDE TO READING. USSR CULTURE ELITES NAT/G PLAN DIPLOM REV...GEOG 20. PAGE 61 H1213 BIBLIOG/A COM MARXISM LEAD

B43
LENIN V.I.,LEFT WING COMMUNISM: AN INFANTILE DISORDER (1920). GERMANY MOD/EUR USSR STRUCT CHIEF DOMIN EDU/PROP LEGIT LEAD REPRESENT POPULISM ...METH/COMP 19 LENIN/VI COM/PARTY MENSHEVIK. PAGE 94 H1879 COM MARXISM NAT/G REV

B43
LEWIN E.,ROYAL EMPIRE SOCIETY BIBLIOGRAPHIES NO. 9: SUB-SAHARA AFRICA. ECO/UNDEV TEC/DEV DIPLOM ADMIN COLONIAL LEAD 20. PAGE 96 H1908 BIBLIOG AFR NAT/G SOCIETY

N45
INDIA QUARTERLY, A JOURNAL OF INTERNATIONAL AFFAIRS. INDIA LAW CONSTN ECO/UNDEV INT/ORG POL/PAR COLONIAL LEAD PARL/PROC WAR ATTIT...SOC 20 CMN/WLTH. PAGE 2 H0033 BIBLIOG/A S/ASIA DIPLOM NAT/G

B45
MERRIAM C.E.,SYSTEMATIC POLITICS. FUT POL/PAR DELIB/GP DIPLOM ADJUD ADMIN LEAD CHOOSE ATTIT...MGT PHIL/SCI TREND. PAGE 109 H2183 NAT/G METH/CNCPT CREATE

B48
WOLFE B.D.,THREE WHO MADE A REVOLUTION. USSR CONSTN NAT/G CAP/ISM EDU/PROP CONTROL WAR GP/REL INGP/REL PERS/REL ROLE 20 STALIN/J LENIN/VI TROTSKY/L BOLSHEVISM. PAGE 170 H3398 BIOG REV LEAD MARXISM

B48
WRIGHT G.,THE RESHAPING OF FRENCH DEMOCRACY. FRANCE NAT/G POL/PAR SECT LEAD CHOOSE GP/REL INGP/REL MARXISM SOCISM...CHARTS BIBLIOG 20 DEGAULLE/C. PAGE 171 H3418 CONSTN POPULISM CREATE LEGIS

B49
BORBA DE MORAES R.,MANUAL BIBLIOGRAFICO DE ESTUDOS BRASILEIROS. BRAZIL DIPLOM ADMIN LEAD...SOC 20. PAGE 19 H0374 BIBLIOG L/A+17C NAT/G ECO/UNDEV

B49
GORER G.,THE PEOPLE OF GREAT RUSSIA: A PSYCHOLOGICAL STUDY. RUSSIA USSR NAT/G DIPLOM LEAD AGE/C ANOMIE ATTIT DRIVE...POLICY 20. PAGE 59 H1182 ISOLAT PERSON PSY SOCIETY

B50
COUNCIL BRITISH NATIONAL BIB,BRITISH NATIONAL BIBLIOGRAPHY. UK AGRI CONSTRUC PERF/ART POL/PAR SECT CREATE INT/TRADE LEAD...HUM JURID PHIL/SCI 20. PAGE 34 H0677 BIBLIOG/A NAT/G TEC/DEV DIPLOM

B50
MACHIAVELLI N.,THE DISCOURSES (1516). NAT/G SECT FORCES DOMIN LEGIT CONTROL LEAD COERCE TOTALISM ORD/FREE. PAGE 100 H1995 PWR GEN/LAWS CHIEF

B50
TENG S.,AN ANNOTATED BIBLIOGRAPHY OF SELECTED CHINESE REFERENCE WORKS (REV. ED.). CULTURE ECO/UNDEV LEAD MARXISM...LING INDEX 3/20. PAGE 153 H3062 BIBLIOG/A ASIA NAT/G

B51
JENNINGS S.I.,THE COMMONWEALTH IN ASIA. CEYLON INDIA PAKISTAN S/ASIA UK CONSTN CULTURE SOCIETY STRATA STRUCT NAT/G POL/PAR EDU/PROP LEAD WAR 20 CMN/WLTH. PAGE 80 H1608 NAT/LISM REGION COLONIAL DIPLOM

B51
US LIBRARY OF CONGRESS,EAST EUROPEAN ACCESSIONS LIST (VOL. I). POL/PAR DIPLOM ADMIN LEAD 20. PAGE 160 H3207 BIBLIOG/A COM SOCIETY NAT/G

S51
MACRAE D.G.,"THE BOLSHEVIK IDEOLOGY; THE INTELLECTUAL AND EMOTIONAL FACTORS IN COMMUNIST AFFILIATION" (BMR)" COM LEAD REV ATTIT ORD/FREE ...SOC CON/ANAL 20 BOLSHEVISM. PAGE 100 H2008 MARXISM INTELL PHIL/SCI SECT

N51
MEYER E.W.,POLITICAL PARTIES IN WESTERN GERMANY (PAMPHLET). EUR+WWI GERMANY/W PRESS LEAD CHOOSE REPRESENT ATTIT 20. PAGE 109 H2189 BIBLIOG POL/PAR NAT/G VOL/ASSN

B52
SPENCER F.A.,WAR AND POSTWAR GREECE: AN ANALYSIS BASED ON GREEK WRITINGS. GREECE SOCIETY NAT/G POL/PAR FORCES CREATE DIPLOM LEAD MARXISM...SOC 20. PAGE 147 H2943 BIBLIOG/A WAR REV

B52
SPICER E.H.,HUMAN PROBLEMS IN TECHNOLOGICAL CHANGE. ECO/UNDEV AGRI INDUS NAT/G ACT/RES LEAD GP/REL INGP/REL ROLE...INT METH 20 CASEBOOK. PAGE 147 H2947 TEC/DEV CULTURE STRUCT OP/RES

B52
US DEPARTMENT OF STATE,RESEARCH ON EASTERN EUROPE (EXCLUDING USSR). EUR+WWI LAW ECO/DEV NAT/G PROB/SOLV DIPLOM ADMIN LEAD MARXISM...TREND 19/20. PAGE 159 H3187 BIBLIOG R+D ACT/RES COM

B53
CURTISS J.S.,THE RUSSIAN CHURCH AND THE SOVIET STATE 1917-1950. COM USSR CONTROL LEAD REV MARXISM ...POLICY BIBLIOG 20 CHURCH/STA ORTHO/RUSS. PAGE 36 H0728 GP/REL NAT/G SECT PWR

B53
ELAHI K.N.,A GUIDE TO WORKS OF REFERENCE PUBLISHED IN PAKISTAN (PAMPHLET). PAKISTAN DIPLOM COLONIAL LEAD. PAGE 45 H0903 BIBLIOG S/ASIA NAT/G

B53
MIT CENTER INTERNATIONAL STU,BIBLIOGRAPHY OF THE ECONOMIC AND POLITICAL DEVELOPMENT OF INDONESIA. INDONESIA STRUCT NAT/G COLONIAL LEAD...STAT 20. PAGE 111 H2226 BIBLIOG ECO/UNDEV TEC/DEV S/ASIA

B54
KOLARZ W.,THE PEOPLES OF THE SOVIET FAR EAST. RUSSIA USSR STRUCT LEAD ISOLAT NAT/LISM...CHARTS 20. PAGE 88 H1750 COLONIAL RACE/REL ADJUST CULTURE

B54
MATTHEWS D.R.,THE SOCIAL BACKGROUND OF POLITICAL DECISION-MAKERS. CULTURE SOCIETY STRATA FAM EX/STRUC LEAD ATTIT BIO/SOC DRIVE PERSON ALL/VALS DECISION BIOG SOC

HIST/WRIT. PAGE 105 H2097

B54
SALVEMINI G.,PRELUDE TO WORLD WAR II. ITALY MOD/EUR INT/ORG BAL/PWR EDU/PROP CONTROL TOTALISM...TREND NAT/COMP BIBLIOG 19 HITLER/A LEAGUE/NAT MUSSOLIN/B. PAGE 137 H2745
WAR FASCISM LEAD PWR

C54
DE GRAZIA A.,"THE COMPARATIVE SURVEY OF EUROPEAN-AMERICAN POLITICAL BEHAV IOR; A RESEARCH PROSPECTUS (PAPER)" EUR+WWI FRANCE GERMANY SPAIN UK USA+45 WOR+45 STRATA POL/PAR DIPLOM EDU/PROP COLONIAL LEAD WAR NAT/LISM CONCPT. PAGE 37 H0752
BIBLIOG R+D METH NAT/COMP

B55
DUVERGER M.,THE POLITICAL ROLE OF WOMEN. FRANCE GERMANY/W NORWAY YUGOSLAVIA STRATA LOBBY AGE ATTIT ROLE...STAT SAMP CHARTS METH/COMP NAT/COMP HYPO/EXP FEMALE/SEX. PAGE 44 H0875
SEX LEAD PARTIC CHOOSE

B55
GALLOWAY G.B.,CONGRESS AND PARLIAMENT: THEIR ORGANIZATION AND OPERATION IN THE US AND THE UK: PLANNING PAMPHLET NO. 93. POL/PAR EX/STRUC DEBATE CONTROL LEAD ROUTINE EFFICIENCY PWR...POLICY CONGRESS PARLIAMENT. PAGE 54 H1089
DELIB/GP LEGIS PARL/PROC GOV/COMP

B55
INSTITUTE POLITISCHE WISSEN,POLITISCHE LITERATUR (3 VOLS.). INT/ORG LEAD WAR PEACE...CONCPT TREND NAT/COMP 20. PAGE 77 H1540
BIBLIOG/A NAT/G DIPLOM POLICY

B55
WHEARE K.C.,GOVERNMENT BY COMMITTEE; AN ESSAY ON THE BRITISH CONSTITUTION. UK NAT/G LEGIS INSPECT CONFER ADJUD ADMIN CONTROL TASK EFFICIENCY ROLE POPULISM 20. PAGE 167 H3337
DELIB/GP CONSTN LEAD GP/COMP

C55
OLIVER D.L.,"A LEADER IN ACTION," IN D. A. OLIVER, SOLOMON ISLAND SOCIETY." S/ASIA SOCIETY STRUCT CONTROL TASK PWR...OBS/ENVIR WORSHIP 20. PAGE 121 H2413
LEAD RESPECT CULTURE KIN

B56
HERNANDEZ URBINA A.,LOS PARTIDOS Y LA CRISIS DEL APRA. PERU NAT/G LEAD LOBBY CHOOSE SOCISM...POLICY DECISION 20 COM/PARTY APRA CONGRESS. PAGE 70 H1402
POL/PAR PARTIC PARL/PROC GP/REL

B56
PHILIPPINE STUDIES PROGRAM,SELECTED BIBLIOGRAPHY ON THE PHILIPPINES, TOPICALLY ARRANGED AND ANNOTATED. PHILIPPINE SECT DIPLOM COLONIAL LEAD...SOC 18/20. PAGE 125 H2501
BIBLIOG/A S/ASIA NAT/G ECO/UNDEV

B56
SPINKA M.,THE CHURCH IN SOVIET RUSSIA. USSR CONTROL LEAD TASK COERCE 20. PAGE 147 H2949
GP/REL NAT/G SECT PWR

B56
VON BECKERATH E.,HANDWORTERBUCH DER SOCIALWISSENSCHAFTEN (II VOLS.). EUR+WWI GERMANY POL/PAR WORKER DIPLOM LEAD CHOOSE SUFF WEALTH...SOC 20. PAGE 163 H3263
BIBLIOG INT/TRADE NAT/G ECO/DEV

B56
VUCINICH A.,THE SOVIET ACADEMY OF SCIENCES. USSR STRUCT ACADEM NAT/G EDU/PROP ADMIN LEAD ROLE ...BIBLIOG 20 ACADEM/SCI. PAGE 164 H3280
PHIL/SCI CREATE INTELL PROF/ORG

B56
WEBER M.,STAATSSOZIOLOGIE. STRUCT LEGIT ADMIN PARL/PROC SUPEGO CONSERVE JURID. PAGE 166 H3320
SOC NAT/G POL/PAR LEAD

B56
WEBER M.,WIRTSCHAFT UND GESELLSCHAFT (2ND VOL.). STRUCT NAT/G POL/PAR LEAD PWR OBJECTIVE IDEA/COMP. PAGE 166 H3321
LEGIT JURID SOC

S56
MACRAE D. JR.,"ROLL CALL VOTES AND LEADERSHIP." ACT/RES LEAD CHOOSE DRIVE CONSERVE NEW/LIB...STAT STYLE. PAGE 100 H2007
POL/PAR GOV/COMP LEGIS SUPEGO

C56
FALL B.B.,"THE VIET-MINH REGIME." VIETNAM LAW ECO/UNDEV POL/PAR FORCES DOMIN WAR ATTIT MARXISM ...BIOG PREDICT BIBLIOG/A 20. PAGE 48 H0967
NAT/G ADMIN EX/STRUC LEAD

C56
NEUMANN S.,"MODERN POLITICAL PARTIES: APPROACHES TO COMPARATIVE POLITIC. FRANCE UK EX/STRUC DOMIN ADMIN LEAD REPRESENT TOTALISM ATTIT...POLICY TREND METH/COMP ANTHOL BIBLIOG/A 20 CMN/WLTH. PAGE 117 H2338
POL/PAR GOV/COMP ELITES MAJORIT

B57
BISHOP O.B.,PUBLICATIONS OF THE GOVERNMENTS OF NOVA SCOTIA, PRINCE EDWARD ISLAND, NEW BRUNSWICK 1758-1952. CANADA UK ADMIN COLONIAL LEAD...POLICY 18/20. PAGE 17 H0345
BIBLIOG NAT/G DIPLOM

B57
DONALDSON A.G.,SOME COMPARATIVE ASPECTS OF IRISH LAW. IRELAND NAT/G DIPLOM ADMIN CT/SYS LEAD ATTIT SOVEREIGN...JURID BIBLIOG/A 12/20 CMN/WLTH. PAGE 42 H0835
CONSTN LAW NAT/COMP INT/LAW

B57
KENNEDY M.D.,A SHORT HISTORY OF COMMUNISM IN ASIA. ASIA BURMA INDIA S/ASIA THAILAND NAT/G POL/PAR LEAD REV WAR MARXISM SOCISM...POLICY 20 CHINJAP. PAGE 85 H1688
DIPLOM NAT/LISM TOTALISM COERCE

C57
WITTFOGEL K.A.,"ORIENTAL DESPOTISM: A COMPARATIVE STUDY OF TOTAL POWER." ASIA CULTURE STRATA NAT/G LEAD OWN ORD/FREE PWR...CONCPT TREND BIBLIOG 20. PAGE 170 H3393
TOTALISM HABITAT DOMIN ELITES

B58
CRAIG G.A.,FROM BISMARCK TO ADENAUER: ASPECTS OF GERMAN STATECRAFT. GERMANY INTELL FORCES ECO/TAC CONFER COERCE WAR GP/REL ORD/FREE PWR CONSERVE 19/20 BISMARCK/O ADENAUER/K. PAGE 35 H0695
DIPLOM LEAD NAT/G

B58
FLORES X.,LA TRADICION CATOLICA Y EL FUTURO POLITICO DE ESPANA (PAMPHLET). SPAIN NAT/G ACT/RES LEAD GP/REL CATHISM 20 CHRISTIAN CHURCH/STA. PAGE 52 H1031
SECT POL/PAR ATTIT ORD/FREE

B58
HSU U.T.,THE INVISIBLE CONFLICT. ASIA USSR ELITES NAT/G CONTROL LEAD COERCE REV WAR NAT/LISM ORD/FREE PWR 20 COM/PARTY ESPIONAGE. PAGE 74 H1485
MARXISM POL/PAR EDU/PROP FORCES

B58
JOHNSON J.J.,POLITICAL CHANGE IN LATIN AMERICA: THE EMERGENCE OF THE MIDDLE SECTORS. INTELL STRATA STRUCT ECO/UNDEV MUNIC TEC/DEV LEAD REV...DECISION TREND GOV/COMP BIBLIOG/A 20. PAGE 81 H1621
L/A+17C ELITES GP/REL DOMIN

B58
PAN AMERICAN UNION,REPERTORIO DE PUBLICACIONES PERIODICAS ACTUALES LATINO-AMERICANAS. CULTURE ECO/UNDEV ADMIN LEAD GOV/REL 20 OAS. PAGE 123 H2455
BIBLIOG L/A+17C NAT/G DIPLOM

B58
WILMERDING L. JR.,THE ELECTORAL COLLEGE. CONSTN NAT/G POL/PAR DELIB/GP LEGIS PROB/SOLV CONFER EXEC LEAD APPORT REPRESENT. PAGE 169 H3377
CHOOSE DECISION ACT/RES

S58
GARCEAU O.,"INTEREST GROUP THEORY IN POLITICAL RESEARCH." ELITES NAT/G PLAN LEAD REPRESENT INGP/REL POLICY. PAGE 55 H1098
GP/COMP GP/REL LOBBY PLURISM

S58
LOCKWOOD W.W.,"THE SOCIALISTIC SOCIETY: INDIA AND JAPAN." INDIA ECO/DEV ECO/UNDEV INDUS NAT/G CONTROL LEAD PRODUC WEALTH 20 CHINJAP. PAGE 98 H1948
ECO/TAC NAT/COMP FINAN SOCISM

S58
PYE L.W.,"THE NON-WESTERN POLITICAL PROCESS" (BMR)" AFR ASIA ISLAM S/ASIA DIPLOM ADMIN LEAD LOBBY ROUTINE CONSEN...DECISION 20. PAGE 128 H2567
CULTURE POL/PAR NAT/G LOC/G

B59
DEHIO L.,GERMANY AND WORLD POLITICS IN THE TWENTIETH CENTURY. EUR+WWI FRANCE GERMANY MOD/EUR UK USSR NAT/G CHIEF BAL/PWR DOMIN COLONIAL CONTROL LEAD...IDEA/COMP 20 VERSAILLES. PAGE 39 H0783
DIPLOM WAR NAT/LISM SOVEREIGN

B59
GOPAL R.,INDIAN MUSLIMS: A POLITICAL HISTORY (1858-1947). INDIA ISLAM PAKISTAN NAT/G SECT LEGIS LEAD COERCE WAR REPRESENT ISOLAT ORD/FREE 19/20 HINDU MUSLIM. PAGE 59 H1175
COLONIAL GP/REL POL/PAR REGION

B59
HENDEL S.,THE SOVIET CRUCIBLE. USSR LEAD COERCE NAT/LISM UTOPIA PWR...POLICY CONCPT ANTHOL 20 STALIN/J LENIN/VI MARX/KARL BOLSHEVIK. PAGE 70 H1393
COM MARXISM REV TOTALISM

B59
OVERSTREET G.D.,COMMUNISM IN INDIA. INDIA S/ASIA CONSTN INT/ORG LEAD GP/REL...CHARTS BIBLIOG 20. PAGE 122 H2435
MARXISM NAT/LISM POL/PAR WAR

B59
PARK R.L.,LEADERSHIP AND POLITICAL INSTITUTIONS IN INDIA. S/ASIA CULTURE ECO/UNDEV LOC/G MUNIC PROVS LEGIS PLAN ADMIN LEAD ORD/FREE WEALTH...GEOG SOC BIOG TOT/POP VAL/FREE 20. PAGE 123 H2468
NAT/G EXEC INDIA

B60
ABERNATHY G.L.,PAKISTAN: A SELECTED, ANNOTATED BIBLIOGRAPHY (2ND ED., PAMPHLET). PAKISTAN CULTURE LEAD 20. PAGE 3 H0056
BIBLIOG/A SOC

B60
DE HERRERA C.D.,LISTA BIBLIOGRAFICA DE LOS TRABAJOS DE GRADUACION Y TESIS PRESENTADOS EN LA UNIVERSIDAD, 1939-1960. PANAMA DIPLOM LEAD...SOC 20. PAGE 38 H0754
BIBLIOG L/A+17C NAT/G ACADEM

B60
FISCHER L.,THE SOVIETS IN WORLD AFFAIRS. CHINA/COM COM EUR+WWI USSR INT/ORG CONFER LEAD ARMS/CONT REV PWR...CHARTS 20 TREATY VERSAILLES. PAGE 51 H1010
DIPLOM NAT/G POLICY MARXISM

B60
FLORES R.H.,CATALOGO DE TESIS DOCTORALES DE LAS FACULTADES DE LA UNIVERSIDAD DE EL SALVADOR. EL/SALVADR LAW DIPLOM ADMIN LEAD GOV/REL...SOC 19/20. PAGE 52 H1030
BIBLIOG ACADEM L/A+17C NAT/G

B60
LOMBARDO TOLEDANO V,EL NEONAZISMO; SUS CHARACTERISTICAS Y PELIGROS. GERMANY/W POL/PAR COLONIAL LEAD LOBBY ATTIT 20 NAZI. PAGE 98 H1956
NAT/G FASCISM POLICY DIPLOM

B60
MANIS J.G.,MAN AND SOCIETY. STRATA LEAD INGP/REL PERS/REL ATTIT PWR...PSY ANTHOL T SOC/INTEG MARX/KARL MILL/JS FREUD/S CHURCHLL/W SPENCER/H RUSSELL/B. PAGE 102 H2036
SOC SOCIETY STRUCT CULTURE

B60
MINIFIE J.M.,PEACEMAKER OR POWDER-MONKEY. CANADA INT/ORG NAT/G FORCES LEAD WAR...PREDICT 20. PAGE 111 H2222
DIPLOM POLICY NEUTRAL PEACE

B60
THORD-GRAY I.,GRINGO REBEL. L/A+17C NAT/G CONTROL LEAD ATTIT...OBS 20 MEXIC/AMER. PAGE 154 H3087
REV FORCES CIVMIL/REL ORD/FREE

B61
ASHLEY M.P.,GREAT BRITAIN TO 1688: A MODERN HISTORY. UK NAT/G CHIEF LEAD REV WAR...POLICY BIBLIOG 1/17. PAGE 9 H0174
DOMIN CONSERVE

B61
BROWN D.M.,THE NATIONALIST MOVEMENT. INDIA CULTURE STRATA REV MORAL ORD/FREE...BIBLIOG 20 HINDU. PAGE 22 H0443
NAT/LISM LEAD CHIEF POL/PAR

B61
CATHERINE R.,LE FONCTIONNAIRE FRANCAIS. FRANCE NAT/G INGP/REL ATTIT MORAL ORD/FREE...T CIVIL/SERV. PAGE 28 H0559
ADMIN GP/REL LEAD SUPEGO

B61
CONOVER H.F.,SERIALS FOR AFRICAN STUDIES. ECO/UNDEV DIPLOM LEAD NAT/LISM ATTIT...SOC 20. PAGE 33 H0653
BIBLIOG AFR NAT/G

B61
DELEFORTRIE-SOU N.,LES DIRIGEANTS DE L'INDUSTRIE FRANCAISE. FRANCE CULTURE ELITES PROB/SOLV ...DECISION STAT CHARTS 20. PAGE 39 H0789
INDUS STRATA TOP/EX LEAD

B61
ESTEVEZ A.,ASPECTOS ECONOMICO-FINANCIEROS DE LA CAMPANA SANMARITANA. L/A+17C SPAIN FINAN COLONIAL LEAD ROLE ORD/FREE WEALTH 19 SOUTH/AMER SAN/MARTIN. PAGE 47 H0942
ECO/UNDEV REV BUDGET NAT/G

B61
HISTORICAL RESEARCH INSTITUTE,A SHORT BIBLIOGRAPHY OF INDO-MUSLIM HISTORY. INDIA S/ASIA DIPLOM EDU/PROP COLONIAL LEAD NAT/LISM ATTIT...BIOG 19/20. PAGE 71 H1427
BIBLIOG NAT/G SECT POL/PAR

B61
INDIAN NATIONAL CONGRESS,SOUVENIR, 66TH SESSION. INDIA S/ASIA CONSTN CULTURE LEGIS CREATE TEC/DEV LEAD TASK...GEOG CHARTS 20. PAGE 77 H1533
CONFER PLAN NAT/G POLICY

B61
LEVIN L.A.,BIBLIOGRAFIIA BIBLIOGRAFII PROIZVEDENII K. MARKSA, F. ENGELSA, V.I. LENINA. COM USSR NAT/G POL/PAR WORKER LEAD REV ATTIT...POLICY IDEA/COMP 20 MARX/KARL LENIN/VI ENGELS. PAGE 95 H1899
BIBLIOG/A MARXISM MARXIST CONCPT

B61
MILIBAND R.,PARLIAMENTARY SOCIALISM. EUR+WWI UK EXEC LEAD PARL/PROC GP/REL...POLICY 20 PARLIAMENT LABOR/PAR. PAGE 110 H2203
POL/PAR NAT/G PWR SOCISM

B61
PANIKKAR K.M.,REVOLUTION IN AFRICA. AFR GUINEA ECO/UNDEV POL/PAR DIPLOM COLONIAL EXEC LEAD SOVEREIGN...CHARTS 20. PAGE 123 H2461
NAT/LISM NAT/G CHIEF

B61
ROIG E.,MARTI, ANTIIMPERIALISTA. CUBA L/A+17C DIPLOM DOMIN COLONIAL CONTROL LEAD PWR SOVEREIGN ...PHIL/SCI 19 MARTI/JOSE INTERVENT. PAGE 133 H2664
PERSON NAT/LISM ECO/UNDEV ORD/FREE

B61
YUAN TUNG-LI,A GUIDE TO DOCTORAL DISSERTATIONS BY CHINESE STUDENTS IN AMERICA, 1905-1960. ASIA CULTURE SOCIETY ECO/UNDEV NAT/G PROB/SOLV DIPLOM LEAD ATTIT...HUM SOC STAT 20. PAGE 172 H3442
BIBLIOG ACADEM ACT/RES OP/RES

S61
LOEWENBERG G.,"PARLIAMENTARISM IN WESTERN GERMANY: THE FUNCTIONING OF THE BUNDESTAG" (BMR)" GERMANY/W NAT/G POL/PAR CHIEF LEAD 20 PARLIAMENT. PAGE 98 H1952
LEGIS CHOOSE CONSTN PARL/PROC

B62
ANDREWS W.G.,EUROPEAN POLITICAL INSTITUTIONS. FRANCE GERMANY UK USSR TOP/EX LEAD PARL/PROC CHOOSE 20. PAGE 7 H0139
NAT/COMP POL/PAR EX/STRUC

LEGIS

B62
BROWN L.C.,LATIN AMERICA, A BIBLIOGRAPHY. EX/STRUC ADMIN LEAD ATTIT...POLICY 20. PAGE 22 H0445
BIBLIOG L/A+17C DIPLOM NAT/G

B62
CARTER G.M.,THE GOVERNMENT OF THE SOVIET UNION. USSR CULTURE LOC/G DIPLOM ECO/TAC ADJUD CT/SYS LEAD WEALTH...CHARTS T 20 COM/PARTY. PAGE 27 H0546
NAT/G MARXISM POL/PAR EX/STRUC

B62
CHAPMAN R.M.,NEW ZEALAND POLITICS IN ACTION: THE 1960 GENERAL ELECTION. NEW/ZEALND LEGIS EDU/PROP PRESS TV LEAD ATTIT...STAND/INT 20. PAGE 29 H0582
NAT/G CHOOSE POL/PAR

B62
COSTA RICA UNIVERSIDAD BIBL,LISTA DE TESIS DE GRADO DE LA UNIVERSIDAD DE COSTA RICA. COSTA/RICA LAW LOC/G ADMIN LEAD...SOC 20. PAGE 34 H0675
BIBLIOG/A NAT/G DIPLOM ECO/UNDEV

B62
DIAZ J.S.,MANUAL DE BIBLIOGRAFIA DE LA LITERATURA ESPANOLA. PRE/AMER SPAIN ECO/UNDEV DIPLOM LEAD ATTIT...SOC 15/20. PAGE 41 H0820
BIBLIOG L/A+17C NAT/G COLONIAL

B62
HABERMAS J.,STRUKTURWANDEL DER OFFENTLICHKEIT. NAT/G EDU/PROP PRESS LEAD PARTIC PWR 20. PAGE 63 H1268
ATTIT CONCPT DOMIN

B62
KINDERSLEY R.,THE FIRST RUSSIAN REVISIONISTS. COM USSR LAW ELITES INTELL NAT/G LEGIS ECO/TAC EDU/PROP CONTROL LEAD GP/REL SOCISM 19/20 MARX/KARL BOLSHEVISM. PAGE 86 H1712
CONSTN MARXISM POPULISM BIOG

B62
KIRPICEVA I.K.,HANDBUCH DER RUSSISCHEN UND SOWJETISCHEN BIBLIOGRAPHIEN (5 VOLS.). USSR STRUCT ECO/DEV DIPLOM LEAD ATTIT 18/20. PAGE 86 H1726
BIBLIOG/A NAT/G MARXISM COM

B62
KRECH D.,INDIVIDUAL IN SOCIETY; A TEXTBOOK OF SOCIAL PSYCHOLOGY. UNIV CULTURE LEAD INGP/REL ATTIT DRIVE PERCEPT ROLE...PHIL/SCI BIBLIOG T. PAGE 88 H1765
PSY SOC SOCIETY PERS/REL

B62
LAQUEUR W.,THE FUTURE OF COMMUNIST SOCIETY. CHINA/COM USSR LAW ECO/DEV NAT/G POL/PAR PLAN PROB/SOLV DIPLOM LEAD...POLICY CONCPT IDEA/COMP ANTHOL 20. PAGE 91 H1820
MARXISM COM FUT SOCIETY

B62
LAQUEUR W.,POLYCENTRISM. CHINA/COM COM USSR WOR+45 INT/ORG NAT/G ECO/TAC DOMIN LEAD ATTIT PWR SOVEREIGN...ANTHOL 20. PAGE 91 H1821
MARXISM DIPLOM BAL/PWR POLICY

B62
MEYER A.G.,LENINISM. USSR STRUCT NAT/G CAP/ISM LEAD WAR PWR SOVEREIGN...BIBLIOG 20 LENIN/VI. PAGE 109 H2187
POL/PAR REV MARXISM PHIL/SCI

B62
MILLER J.D.B.,THE NATURE OF POLITICS. NAT/G DOMIN LEGIT LEAD...CONCPT METH. PAGE 111 H2213
METH/COMP IDEA/COMP PHIL/SCI

B62
OLLE-LAPRUNE J.,LA STABILITE DES MINISTRES SOUS LA TROISIEME REPUBLIQUE, 1879-1940. FRANCE CONSTN POL/PAR LEAD WAR INGP/REL RIGID/FLEX PWR...POLICY CHARTS 19/20. PAGE 121 H2415
LEGIS NAT/G ADMIN PERSON

B62
US DEPARTMENT OF THE ARMY,GUIDE TO JAPANESE MONOGRAPHS AND JAPANESE STUDIES ON MANCHURIA: 1945-1960. CHINA/COM NAT/G DIPLOM LEAD COERCE WAR ...CHARTS 19/20 CHINJAP. PAGE 160 H3193
BIBLIOG/A FORCES ASIA S/ASIA

B62
WHITING K.R.,THE SOVIET UNION TODAY: A CONCISE HANDBOOK. USSR ELITES AGRI INDUS POL/PAR FORCES DIPLOM EDU/PROP LEAD...GEOG TREND 19/20. PAGE 168 H3354
NAT/G ATTIT MARXISM POLICY

C62
BACON F.,"OF SEDITIONS AND TROUBLES" (1625) IN F. BACON, ESSAYS." INDUS MARKET CHIEF ECO/TAC EDU/PROP CONTROL LEAD PEACE WEALTH 17 MACHIAVELL. PAGE 9 H0191
REV ORD/FREE NAT/G GEN/LAWS

B63
BELFRAGE C.,THE MAN AT THE DOOR WITH THE GUN. CUBA L/A+17C NAT/G LEAD PARTIC GP/REL PWR...POLICY 20 CASTRO/F. PAGE 13 H0261
REGION ECO/UNDEV STRUCT ATTIT

B63
BISHOP O.B.,PUBLICATIONS OF THE GOVERNMENT OF THE PROVINCE OF CANADA 1841-1867. CANADA DIPLOM COLONIAL LEAD...POLICY 18. PAGE 17 H0346
BIBLIOG NAT/G ATTIT

B63
BRODOWSKI J.H.,LATIN AMERICA TODAY. CULTURE LEAD ...SOC 20. PAGE 21 H0426
BIBLIOG/A L/A+17C NAT/G

DIPLOM

B63
BROGAN D.W.,POLITICAL PATTERNS IN TODAY'S WORLD. FRANCE USA+45 USSR WOR+45 CONSTN STRUCT PLAN DIPLOM ADMIN LEAD ROLE SUPEGO...PHIL/SCI 20. PAGE 21 H0429 NAT/COMP NEW/LIB COM TOTALISM

B63
CROSS C.,THE FASCISTS IN BRITAIN. UK ELITES LABOR NAT/G DOMIN PARTIC DISCRIM TOTALISM ATTIT...STERTYP 20. PAGE 35 H0708 POL/PAR FASCISM RACE/REL LEAD

B63
DEUTSCH K.W.,THE NERVES OF GOVERNMENT. NAT/G CREATE EDU/PROP CONTROL LEAD PWR...CONCPT GEN/LAWS 20. PAGE 40 H0799 DECISION GAME SIMUL OP/RES

B63
GAMBLE S.D.,NORTH CHINA VILLAGES: SOCIAL, POLITICAL, AND ECONOMIC ACTIVITIES BEFORE 1933. ASIA CULTURE STRUCT FAM DOMIN EDU/PROP WORSHIP 20. PAGE 55 H1093 MUNIC AGRI LEAD FINAN

B63
KLEIMAN R.,ATLANTIC CRISIS; AMERICAN DIPLOMACY CONFRONTS A RESURGENT EUROPE. EUR+WWI USA+45 ECO/DEV AGRI NAT/G CHIEF FORCES PLAN LEAD ATTIT ...CONCPT 20 NATO KENNEDY/JF DEGAULLE/C EEC JOHNSON/LB. PAGE 87 H1731 DIPLOM REGION POLICY

B63
MERKL P.H.,THE ORIGIN OF THE WEST GERMAN REPUBLIC. GERMANY/W WOR+45 POL/PAR DIPLOM LEAD LOBBY REPRESENT GP/REL NAT/LISM 20. PAGE 109 H2179 CONSTN PARL/PROC CONTROL BAL/PWR

B63
SILVERT K.H.,EXPECTANT PEOPLES: NATIONALISM AND DEVELOPMENT. CULTURE STRATA SECT LEAD REGION RACE/REL ALL/IDEOS...GEN/LAWS SOC/INTEG 20. PAGE 144 H2877 NAT/LISM ECO/UNDEV ALL/VALS

B63
SWEARER H.R.,CONTEMPORARY COMMUNISM: THEORY AND PRACTICE. COM USSR SOCIETY ECO/DEV POL/PAR FORCES PLAN ADMIN LEAD NAT/LISM...POLICY ANTHOL 20 LENIN/VI COM/PARTY. PAGE 151 H3015 MARXISM CONCPT DIPLOM NAT/G

S63
OGOT B.,"FROM CHIEF TO PRESIDENT." AFR SECT REGION NAT/LISM...SOC GOV/COMP NAT/COMP 20 PRESIDENT. PAGE 121 H2410 CHIEF CULTURE LEAD ORD/FREE

S63
ZOLBERG A.R.,"MASS PARTIES AND NATIONAL INTEGRATION: THE CASE OF THE IVORY COAST" (BMR)" AFR IVORY/CST CONSTN VOL/ASSN DIPLOM LEAD GP/REL INGP/REL 20. PAGE 173 H3461 POL/PAR ECO/UNDEV NAT/G ADJUST

B64
ALDEFER H.F.,A BIBLIOGRAPHY OF AFRICAN GOVERNMENT: 1950-1964. ALGERIA GUINEA LIBERIA UAR ECO/UNDEV POL/PAR LEGIS COLONIAL LEAD PARL/PROC NAT/LISM 20. PAGE 5 H0098 BIBLIOG AFR LOC/G NAT/G

B64
BELL W.,JAMAICAN LEADERS: POLITICAL ATTITUDES IN A NEW NATION. JAMAICA STRUCT ACT/RES CREATE PROB/SOLV DIPLOM COLONIAL LEAD...QU 20. PAGE 13 H0267 NAT/LISM ATTIT DRIVE SOVEREIGN

B64
BERNSTEIN H.,VENEZUELA AND COLOMBIA. L/A+17C VENEZUELA INTELL COLONIAL ATTIT 20 COLOMB. PAGE 16 H0316 CULTURE NAT/LISM LEAD

B64
BRZEZINSKI Z.,POLITICAL POWER: USA/USSR. USA+45 USSR AGRI POL/PAR FORCES CREATE CHOOSE ATTIT ORD/FREE PWR MARXISM...MYTH 20 KENNEDY/JF. PAGE 23 H0457 NAT/G NAT/COMP POLICY LEAD

B64
BURKE F.G.,AFRICA'S QUEST FOR ORDER. AFR CULTURE KIN MUNIC NAT/G DIPLOM COLONIAL REV DISCRIM NAT/LISM AGE/Y 20. PAGE 24 H0488 ORD/FREE CONSEN RACE/REL LEAD

B64
BUTWELL R.,SOUTHEAST ASIA TODAY - AND TOMORROW. NAT/G COLONIAL LEAD REGION WAR CHOOSE WEALTH MARXISM 20. PAGE 25 H0500 S/ASIA DIPLOM ECO/UNDEV NAT/LISM

B64
DOOLIN D.J.,COMMUNIST CHINA: THE POLITICS OF STUDENT OPPOSITION. CHINA/COM ELITES STRATA ACADEM NAT/G WRITING CT/SYS LEAD PARTIC COERCE TOTALISM 20. PAGE 42 H0838 MARXISM DEBATE AGE/Y PWR

B64
ETZIONI A.,MODERN ORGANIZATIONS. CLIENT STRUCT DOMIN CONTROL LEAD PERS/REL AUTHORIT...CLASSIF BUREAUCRCY. PAGE 47 H0946 MGT ADMIN PLAN CULTURE

B64
FISCHER L.,THE LIFE OF LENIN. USSR LEAD REV WAR ...SOC 19/20 LENIN/VI COM/PARTY BOLSHEVISM. PAGE 51 H1011 BIOG MARXISM PERSON CHIEF

B64
HALPERIN S.W.,MUSSOLINI AND ITALIAN FASCISM. ITALY NAT/G POL/PAR SECT ECO/TAC LEAD PWR SOCISM...POLICY 20 MUSSOLIN/B. PAGE 64 H1294 FASCISM NAT/LISM EDU/PROP CHIEF

B64
HELMREICH E.,A FREE CHURCH IN A FREE STATE? FRANCE GERMANY ITALY SECT LEAD PWR CATHISM...POLICY ANTHOL WORSHIP 19/20 CHURCH/STA. PAGE 69 H1389 GP/REL NAT/G

B64
HOLDSWORTH W.S.,A HISTORY OF ENGLISH LAW; THE CENTURIES OF DEVELOPMENT AND REFORM (VOL. XIV). UK CONSTN LOC/G NAT/G POL/PAR CHIEF EX/STRUC ADJUD COLONIAL ATTIT...INT/LAW JURID 18/19 TORY/PARTY COMMONWLTH WHIG/PARTY COMMON/LAW. PAGE 73 H1453 LAW LEGIS LEAD CT/SYS

B64
IMAZ J.L.,LOS QUE MANDAN. INDUS LABOR NAT/G POL/PAR PROVS SECT CHIEF TOP/EX CONTROL 20 ARGEN. PAGE 76 H1524 LEAD FORCES ELITES ATTIT

B64
KOLARZ W.,BOOKS ON COMMUNISM. USSR WOR+45 CULTURE NAT/G POL/PAR DIPLOM LEAD...CONCPT GOV/COMP IDEA/COMP. PAGE 88 H1752 BIBLIOG/A SOCIETY COM MARXISM

B64
LATORRE A.,UNIVERSIDAD Y SOCIEDAD. SPAIN EDU/PROP LEAD GP/REL PERS/REL ATTIT KNOWL. PAGE 92 H1837 ACADEM CULTURE ROLE INTELL

B64
LIEVWEN E.,GENERALS VS PRESIDENTS: WEOMILITARISM IN LATIN AMERICA. L/A+17C FORCES DIPLOM FOR/AID LEAD ...NAT/COMP 20 PRESIDENT. PAGE 97 H1929 CIVMIL/REL REV CONSERVE ORD/FREE

B64
MAHAR J.M.,INDIA: A CRITICAL BIBLIOGRAPHY. INDIA PAKISTAN CULTURE ECO/UNDEV LOC/G POL/PAR SECT PROB/SOLV DIPLOM ADMIN COLONIAL PARL/PROC ATTIT 20. PAGE 101 H2016 BIBLIOG/A S/ASIA NAT/G LEAD

B64
NICOL D.,AFRICA - A SUBJECTIVE VIEW. AFR INT/ORG PLAN ADMIN COLONIAL PARL/PROC PARTIC REGION GOV/REL LITERACY ATTIT...BIBLIOG 20 CIVIL/SERV. PAGE 118 H2350 NAT/G LEAD CULTURE ACADEM

B64
PERAZA SARAUSA F.,DIRECTORIO DE REVISTAS Y PERIODICOS DE CUBA. CUBA L/A+17C NAT/G ATTIT 20. PAGE 125 H2490 BIBLIOG/A PRESS SERV/IND LEAD

B64
QUIGG P.W.,AFRICA: A FOREIGN AFFAIRS READER. AFR FRANCE PORTUGAL UK DIPLOM LEAD PARL/PROC MARXISM ...MAJORIT METH/CNCPT GOV/COMP IDEA/COMP ANTHOL 19/20. PAGE 129 H2575 COLONIAL SOVEREIGN NAT/LISM RACE/REL

B64
TINKER H.,BALLOT BOX AND BAYONET - PEOPLE AND GOVERNMENT IN EMERGENT ASIAN COUNTRIES. CEYLON INDIA INDONESIA PHILIPPINE POL/PAR ADMIN COLONIAL LEAD PARL/PROC CHOOSE CONSEN ORD/FREE SOVEREIGN PLURISM...GOV/COMP THIRD/WRLD. PAGE 155 H3104 MYTH S/ASIA NAT/COMP NAT/LISM

B64
TURNER M.C.,LIBROS EN VENTA EN HISPANOAMERICA Y ESPANA. SPAIN LAW CONSTN CULTURE ADMIN LEAD...HUM SOC 20. PAGE 157 H3141 BIBLIOG L/A+17C NAT/G DIPLOM

S64
SWEARER H.R.,"AFTER KHRUSHCHEV: WHAT NEXT." COM FUT USSR CONSTN ELITES NAT/G POL/PAR CHIEF DELIB/GP LEGIS DOMIN LEAD...RECORD TREND STERTYP GEN/METH 20. PAGE 151 H3016 EX/STRUC PWR

B65
ALLEN W.S.,THE NAZI SEIZURE OF POWER. GERMANY NAT/G CHIEF LEAD COERCE CHOOSE REPRESENT GOV/REL AUTHORIT ...DECISION 20 HITLER/A NAZI. PAGE 5 H0106 MUNIC FASCISM TOTALISM LOC/G

B65
ARENSBERG C.M.,CULTURE AND COMMUNITY. UNIV FACE/GP ACT/RES EDU/PROP LEAD REGION GP/REL PERS/REL HABITAT ALL/VALS...SOC CONCPT 20. PAGE 8 H0162 SOCIETY CULTURE NEIGH NEW/IDEA

B65
BAYNE E.A.,FOUR WAYS OF POLITICS: STATE AND NATION IN ITALY, SOMALIA, ISRAEL, AND IRAN. IRAN ISRAEL ITALY SOMALIA LEAD CHOOSE MAJORITY GOV/COMP. PAGE 12 H0244 ECO/UNDEV NAT/G DECISION TOP/EX

B65
CARTER G.M.,GOVERNMENT AND POLITICS IN THE TWENTIETH CENTURY (REV. ED.). WOR+45 NAT/G POL/PAR LEGIS DIPLOM LEAD PARL/PROC CHOOSE TOTALISM 20. PAGE 27 H0549 GOV/COMP ECO/UNDEV ALL/IDEOS ECO/DEV

B65
COWAN L.G.,EDUCATION AND NATION-BUILDING IN AFRICA. AFR CULTURE ECO/UNDEV POL/PAR ACT/RES LEAD SOVEREIGN...METH/COMP ANTHOL BIBLIOG 20. PAGE 34 H0684 EDU/PROP COLONIAL ACADEM NAT/LISM

B65
EDINGER L.J.,KURT SCHUMACHER: A STUDY IN PERSONALITY AND POLITICAL BEHAVIOR. EUR+WWI GERMANY NAT/G DRIVE ROLE PWR SOCISM...BIBLIOG 20 SOC/DEMPAR SCHUMCHR/K. PAGE 44 H0889
TOP/EX LEAD PERSON BIOG

B65
FAUST J.J.,A REVOLUCAO DEVORA SEUS PRESIDENTES. BRAZIL NAT/G POL/PAR LEAD CHOOSE CIVMIL/REL ORD/FREE 20 PRESIDENT. PAGE 49 H0976
PARTIC REV FORCES GP/REL

B65
GEORGE M.,THE WARPED VISION. EUR+WWI UK NAT/G POL/PAR LEGIS PARL/PROC SANCTION COERCE WAR GOV/REL PEACE RESPECT 20 CONSRV/PAR. PAGE 56 H1113
LEAD ATTIT DIPLOM POLICY

B65
GRAHAM G.S.,THE POLITICS OF NAVAL SUPREMACY; STUDIES IN BRITISH MARITIME ASCENDANCY. UK SEA NAT/G BAL/PWR LEAD WAR WEAPON PEACE...POLICY 18/19 COMMONWLTH. PAGE 60 H1191
FORCES PWR COLONIAL DIPLOM

B65
GREGG J.L.,POLITICAL PARTIES AND PARTY SYSTEMS IN GUATEMALA, 1944-1963. GUATEMALA L/A+17C EX/STRUC FORCES CREATE CONTROL REV CHOOSE PWR...TREND IDEA/COMP 20. PAGE 60 H1209
LEAD POL/PAR NAT/G CHIEF

B65
HADWIGER D.F.,PRESSURES AND PROTEST. NAT/G LEGIS PLAN LEAD PARTIC ROUTINE ATTIT POLICY. PAGE 63 H1273
AGRI GP/REL LOBBY CHOOSE

B65
HART B.H.L.,THE MEMOIRS OF CAPTAIN LIDDELL HART (VOL. I). UK NAT/G PLAN TEC/DEV DIPLOM ADMIN WEAPON GOV/REL PERS/REL ATTIT PWR FASCISM...POLICY 20. PAGE 67 H1348
FORCES BIOG LEAD WAR

B65
HUNT G.L.,CALVINISM AND THE POLITICAL ORDER. NAT/G LEAD...POLICY IDEA/COMP ANTHOL WORSHIP 20. PAGE 75 H1498
SECT CONCPT

B65
LANDE C.H.,LEADERS, FACTIONS, AND PARTIES. PHILIPPINE CONSTN LOC/G NAT/G PARTIC...CHARTS BIBLIOG 20. PAGE 90 H1806
LEAD POL/PAR POLICY

B65
MERKL P.H.,GERMANY: YESTERDAY AND TOMORROW. GERMANY POL/PAR PLAN DIPLOM LEAD FEDERAL 19/20. PAGE 109 H2181
NAT/G FUT

B65
NAMIER L.B.,THE STRUCTURE OF POLITICS AT THE ACCESSION OF GEORGE III. UK LOC/G TOP/EX COLONIAL LEAD PARTIC REV CHOOSE REPRESENT GOV/REL PERSON SOVEREIGN...GOV/COMP 18 PARLIAMENT. PAGE 115 H2309
PARL/PROC LEGIS NAT/G POL/PAR

B65
PARRIS H.W.,GOVERNMENT AND THE RAILWAYS IN NINETEENTH-CENTURY BRITAIN. UK DELIB/GP CONTROL LEAD CENTRAL 19 RAILROAD. PAGE 124 H2470
DIST/IND NAT/G PLAN GP/REL

B65
PELLING H.,A SHORT HISTORY OF THE LABOUR PARTY (2ND ED.). UK NAT/G CHIEF PARL/PROC GP/REL INGP/REL 20 LABOR/PAR PARLIAMENT WILSON/H. PAGE 124 H2484
POL/PAR NEW/LIB LEAD LABOR

B65
PUNDEEF M.V.,BULGARIA; A BIBLIOGRAPHIC GUIDE. BULGARIA LAW CULTURE INTELL ECO/DEV LEAD MARXISM 20. PAGE 128 H2566
BIBLIOG/A NAT/G COM SOCISM

B65
ULAM A.,THE BOLSHEVIKS. COM USSR NAT/G CHIEF ECO/TAC ADMIN LEAD WAR POPULISM...POLICY 19/20 LENIN/VI BOLSHEVISM. PAGE 157 H3148
SOCISM POL/PAR TOP/EX REV

B65
WOLFE B.D.,MARXISM; ONE HUNDRED YEARS IN THE LIFE OF A DOCTRINE. USSR WAR NAT/LISM PEACE TOTALISM ...MAJORIT 20 MARX/KARL. PAGE 170 H3399
MARXISM LEAD ATTIT

S65
LAULICHT J.,"PUBLIC OPINION AND FOREIGN POLICY DECISIONS." CANADA ELITES NAT/G FOR/AID LEAD NUC/PWR PERCEPT...INT QU CHARTS UN COLD/WAR. PAGE 92 H1839
DIPLOM ATTIT CON/ANAL SAMP

C65
NEUMANN S.,"PERMANENT REVOLUTION: TOTALITARIANISM IN THE AGE OF INTERNA TIONAL CIVIL WAR (2ND ED.)" EUR+WWI ELITES POL/PAR DOMIN EDU/PROP LEAD CROWD REPRESENT...MAJORIT GOV/COMP BIBLIOG 20. PAGE 117 H2340
TOTALISM REV FASCISM STRUCT

B66
ASHRAF A.,THE CITY GOVERNMENT OF CALCUTTA: A STUDY OF INERTIA. INDIA ELITES INDUS NAT/G EX/STRUC ACT/RES PLAN PROB/SOLV LEAD HABITAT...BIBLIOG 20 CALCUTTA. PAGE 9 H0175
LOC/G MUNIC ADMIN ECO/UNDEV

B66
BARNETT D.L.,MAU MAU FROM WITHIN. AFR UK POL/PAR LEAD GUERRILLA AUTHORIT ORD/FREE...SOC BIOG 20 NEGRO MAU/MAU. PAGE 11 H0225
REV CULTURE NAT/G

B66
BLACK C.E.,THE DYNAMICS OF MODERNIZATION: A STUDY IN COMPARATIVE HISTORY. STRUCT ECO/DEV ECO/UNDEV NAT/G DIPLOM LEAD REV...PREDICT TIME/SEQ TREND SOC/INTEG 17/20. PAGE 17 H0350
SOCIETY SOC NAT/COMP

B66
CANNING HOUSE LIBRARY,AUTHOR AND SUBJECT CATALOGUES OF THE CANNING HOUSE LIBRARY (5 VOLS.). UK CULTURE LEAD...SOC 19/20. PAGE 26 H0520
BIBLIOG L/A+17C NAT/G DIPLOM

B66
COLE A.B.,SOCIALIST PARTIES IN POSTWAR JAPAN. STRATA AGRI LABOR PLAN DIPLOM ECO/TAC AGREE LEAD CHOOSE ATTIT...CHARTS 20 CHINJAP SOC/DEMPAR. PAGE 31 H0620
POL/PAR POLICY SOCISM NAT/G

B66
DARLING M.,APPRENTICE TO POWER INDIA 1904-1908. INDIA LEAD GP/REL PERSON...GEOG 20. PAGE 37 H0742
OBS SOCIETY ADMIN NAT/G

B66
DE VORE B.B.,LAND AND LIBERTY; A HISTORY OF THE MEXICAN REVOLUTION. CONSTN INTELL NAT/G CONTROL LEAD CHOOSE TOTALISM AUTHORIT...BIBLIOG 19/20 MEXIC/AMER DIAZ/P LIB/PARTY MAGON/F MADERO/F. PAGE 39 H0776
REV CHIEF POL/PAR

B66
DEUTSCHER I.,STALIN: A POLITICAL BIOGRAPHY. EUR+WWI USSR POL/PAR FORCES DIPLOM ADMIN LEAD REV WAR TOTALISM PERSON 20 STALIN/J ROOSEVLT/F LENIN/VI HITLER/A. PAGE 40 H0807
BIOG MARXISM TOP/EX PWR

B66
DODGE D.,AFRICAN POLITICS IN PERSPECTIVE. ELITES POL/PAR PROB/SOLV LEAD...POLICY 20 THIRD/WRLD. PAGE 41 H0831
AFR NAT/G COLONIAL SOVEREIGN

B66
HANKE L.,HANDBOOK OF LATIN AMERICAN STUDIES. ECO/UNDEV ADMIN LEAD...HUM SOC 20. PAGE 65 H1313
BIBLIOG/A L/A+17C INDEX NAT/G

B66
HIDAYATULLAH M.,DEMOCRACY IN INDIA AND THE JUDICIAL PROCESS. INDIA EX/STRUC LEGIS LEAD GOV/REL ATTIT ORD/FREE...MAJORIT CONCPT 20 NEHRU/J. PAGE 71 H1415
NAT/G CT/SYS CONSTN JURID

B66
HINTON W.,FANSHEN: A DOCUMENTARY OF REVOLUTION IN A CHINESE VILLAGE. ASIA ELITES MUNIC NAT/G POL/PAR SECT WORKER LEAD WAR PRIVIL PWR 20 MAO. PAGE 71 H1422
MARXISM REV NEIGH OWN

B66
HOLDSWORTH W.S.,A HISTORY OF ENGLISH LAW; THE CENTURIES OF SETTLEMENT AND REFORM (VOL. XVI). UK LOC/G NAT/G EX/STRUC LEGIS CT/SYS LEAD ATTIT ...POLICY DECISION JURID IDEA/COMP 18 PARLIAMENT. PAGE 73 H1454
BIOG PERSON PROF/ORG LAW

B66
KAUNDA K.,ZAMBIA: INDEPENDENCE AND BEYOND: THE SPEECHES OF KENNETH KAUNDA. AFR FUT ZAMBIA SOCIETY ECO/UNDEV NAT/G PROB/SOLV ECO/TAC ADMIN RACE/REL SOVEREIGN 20. PAGE 84 H1670
ORD/FREE COLONIAL CONSTN LEAD

B66
KERR M.H.,ISLAMIC REFORM: THE POLITICAL AND LEGAL THEORIES OF MUHAMMAD 'ABDUH AND RASHID RIDA. NAT/G SECT LEAD SOVEREIGN CONSERVE...JURID BIBLIOG WORSHIP 20. PAGE 85 H1698
LAW CONCPT ISLAM

B66
KEYES J.G.,A BIBLIOGRAPHY OF WESTERN LANGUAGE PUBLICATIONS CONCERNING NORTH VIETNAM IN THE CORNELL LIBRARY. VIETNAM/N NAT/G FORCES TEC/DEV DIPLOM LEAD RACE/REL...GEOG SOC 20. PAGE 85 H1700
BIBLIOG/A CULTURE ECO/UNDEV S/ASIA

B66
LOVEDAY P.,PARLIAMENT FACTIONS AND PARTIES: THE FIRST THIRTY YEARS OF RESPONSIBLE GOVERNMENT IN NEW SOUTH WALES, 1856-1889. PROVS LEAD PARL/PROC PARTIC GP/REL INGP/REL MAJORITY PWR...GP/COMP 19 AUSTRAL. PAGE 99 H1970
POL/PAR ELITES NAT/G LEGIS

B66
MAICHEL K.,CATALOG OF SOVIET AND RUSSIAN NEWSPAPERS AT THE HOOVER INSTITUTION OF WAR, REVOLUTION AND PEACE. USSR NAT/G EDU/PROP LEAD REV WAR PEACE ATTIT 19/20. PAGE 101 H2017
BIBLIOG/A PRESS COM MARXISM

B66
MATTHEWS R.,AFRICAN POWDER KEG: REVOLT AND DISSENT IN SIX EMERGENT NATIONS. AFR ALGERIA DAHOMEY GABON GHANA MALAWI GAMBLE LEAD PARTIC REV DRIVE...BIOG TREND GOV/COMP 20. PAGE 105 H2098
ELITES ECO/UNDEV TOP/EX CONTROL

B66
MULLER C.F.J.,A SELECT BIBLIOGRAPHY OF SOUTH AFRICAN HISTORY; A GUIDE FOR HISTORICAL RESEARCH. SOUTH/AFR UK LAW CONSTN SOCIETY STRUCT AGRI SECT DIPLOM COLONIAL LEAD RACE/REL...POLICY 17/20 NEGRO. PAGE 114 H2284
BIBLIOG AFR NAT/G

B66
NIEDERGANG M.,LA REVOLUTION DE SAINT-DOMINGUE.
REV

DOMIN/REP INT/ORG NAT/G CONTROL LEAD GP/REL ORD/FREE MARXISM 20. PAGE 118 H2361 FORCES DIPLOM B66

NOEL G.E.,THE NEW BRITAIN AND HAROLD WILSON: INTERIM REPORT, 1966 GENERAL ELECTION. UK POL/PAR CONSULT PROB/SOLV BUDGET DIPLOM ECO/TAC LEAD CHOOSE ATTIT 20 WILSON/H PARLIAMENT. PAGE 118 H2366 BIOG PERSON NAT/G CHIEF B66

O'NEILL R.J.,THE GERMAN ARMY AND THE NAZI PARTY, 1933-1939. GERMANY ELITES NAT/G EDU/PROP CONTROL LEAD COERCE WAR...POLICY INT TIME/SEQ BIBLIOG 20 HITLER/A NAZI. PAGE 120 H2391 CIVMIL/REL FORCES FASCISM POL/PAR B66

ROOS H.,A HISTORY OF MODERN POLAND FROM THE FOUNDATION OF THE STATE IN THE FIRST WORLD WAR TO THE PRESENT DAY. EUR+WWI POLAND INTELL SOCIETY ECO/TAC LEAD REV ATTIT ORD/FREE MARXISM...BIBLIOG 20 WWI PARTITION. PAGE 133 H2669 NAT/G WAR DIPLOM B66

SILBERMAN B.S.,MODERN JAPANESE LEADERSHIP; TRANSITION AND CHANGE. NAT/G POL/PAR CHIEF ADMIN REPRESENT GP/REL ADJUST RIGID/FLEX...SOC METH/COMP ANTHOL 19/20 CHINJAP CHRISTIAN. PAGE 144 H2873 LEAD CULTURE ELITES MUNIC B66

SPEARS E.L.,TWO MEN WHO SAVED FRANCE: PETAIN AND DE GAULLE. FRANCE CONSTN FORCES DIPLOM WAR PERSON 20 WWI PETAIN/HP DEGAULLE/C. PAGE 147 H2942 BIOG LEAD CHIEF NAT/G B66

SWEARINGEN A.R.,SOVIET AND CHINESE COMMUNIST POWER IN THE WORLD TODAY. COM USA+45 ECO/UNDEV CREATE LEAD WAR ADJUST...TREND NAT/COMP ANTHOL COLD/WAR KHRUSH/N. PAGE 151 H3017 USSR ASIA DIPLOM ATTIT B66

US DEPARTMENT OF STATE,RESEARCH ON AFRICA (EXTERNAL RESEARCH LIST NO 5-25). LAW CULTURE ECO/UNDEV POL/PAR DIPLOM EDU/PROP LEAD REGION MARXISM...GEOG LING WORSHIP 20. PAGE 159 H3188 BIBLIOG/A ASIA S/ASIA NAT/G B66

US DEPARTMENT OF THE ARMY,SOUTH ASIA: A STRATEGIC SURVEY (PAMPHLET NO. 550-3). AFGHANISTN INDIA NEPAL PAKISTAN ECO/UNDEV INT/ORG POL/PAR FORCES FOR/AID INT/TRADE LEAD WAR...POLICY SOC TREND 20. PAGE 160 H3195 BIBLIOG/A S/ASIA DIPLOM NAT/G B66

WANG Y.C.,CHINESE INTELLECTUALS AND THE WEST 1872-1949. ASIA ELITES LEAD STRANGE ROLE MARXISM ...CHARTS 19/20. PAGE 165 H3301 INTELL EDU/PROP CULTURE SOCIETY B66

WEINSTEIN B.,GABON: NATION-BUILDING ON THE OGOOUE. AFR GABON WOR+45 CULTURE SOCIETY PLAN DIPLOM COLONIAL INGP/REL ANOMIE HABITAT SUPEGO 20. PAGE 166 H3329 ECO/UNDEV GP/REL LEAD NAT/G B66

ZEINE Z.N.,THE EMERGENCE OF ARAB NATIONALISM (REV. ED.). TURKEY UK NAT/G SECT TEC/DEV LEAD REV WAR AGE/Y ROLE ORD/FREE...TRADIT CHARTS BIBLIOG 20 ARABS OTTOMAN. PAGE 173 H3453 ISLAM NAT/LISM DIPLOM S66

"FURTHER READING." INDIA LEAD ATTIT...CONCPT 20. PAGE 2 H0048 BIBLIOG NAT/G DIPLOM POLICY S66

COWAN L.G.,"THE MILITARY AND AFRICAN POLITICS." AFR FUT NAT/G POL/PAR PARTIC REV 20. PAGE 34 H0685 CIVMIL/REL FORCES PWR LEAD S66

GAMER R.E.,"URGENT SINGAPORE, PATIENT MALAYSIA." MALAYSIA S/ASIA ECO/UNDEV POL/PAR CHIEF TARIFFS TAX CONTROL LEAD REGION PWR 20 SINGAPORE. PAGE 55 H1094 DIPLOM NAT/G POLICY ECO/TAC C66

ROSENBERG C.G. JR.,"THE MYTH OF "MAU-MAU:" NATIONALISM IN KENYA." AFR CULTURE NAT/G POL/PAR COERCE REV RACE/REL ATTIT ORD/FREE SOVEREIGN...MYTH BIBLIOG 20. PAGE 134 H2678 NAT/LISM COLONIAL MAJORIT LEAD B67

ANDERSON E.N.,POLITICAL INSTITUTIONS AND SOCIAL CHANGE IN CONTINENTAL EUROPE IN THE NINETEENTH CENTURY. MOD/EUR LAW CONSTN SOCIETY POL/PAR TEC/DEV LEAD REV ATTIT...BIBLIOG 19. PAGE 6 H0127 NAT/G NAT/COMP METH/COMP INDUS B67

BANKWITZ P.C.,MAXINE WEYGAND AND CIVIL-MILITARY RELATIONS IN MODERN FRANCE. FRANCE LEAD WAR PWR ...INT BIBLIOG 20. PAGE 11 H0212 CIVMIL/REL FORCES NAT/G TOP/EX B67

DAVIDSON E.,THE TRIAL OF THE GERMANS* NUREMBERG* 1946-48. EUR+WWI GERMANY CULTURE NAT/G LEAD PERSON HEALTH...CRIMLGY PSY SOC BIOG JEWS. PAGE 37 H0745 FASCISM ADJUD TOTALISM WAR B67

DIX R.H.,COLOMBIA: THE POLITICAL DIMENSIONS OF CHANGE. ELITES POL/PAR DOMIN REV...AUD/VIS 20 COLOMB. PAGE 41 H0828 L/A+17C NAT/G TEC/DEV LEAD B67

ERDMAN H.L.,THE SWATANTRA PARTY AND INDIAN CONSERVATISM. INDIA S/ASIA SOCIETY STRATA LOC/G NAT/G LEAD PARTIC GP/REL ATTIT...CONCPT GP/COMP BIBLIOG 20 SWATANTRA. PAGE 47 H0938 POL/PAR CONSERVE CHOOSE POLICY B67

FANON F.,TOWARD THE AFRICAN REVOLUTION. AFR FRANCE CULTURE ELITES LEAD REV GP/REL ORD/FREE SOVEREIGN 20. PAGE 49 H0969 COLONIAL DOMIN ECO/UNDEV RACE/REL B67

FAY S.B.,THE ORIGINS OF THE WORLD WAR (2ND REV. ED. 2 VOLS.). NAT/G FORCES DIPLOM CONFER LEAD PEACE ...REALPOL GOV/COMP 19/20. PAGE 49 H0978 MOD/EUR WAR REGION INT/ORG B67

GIFFORD P.,BRITAIN AND GERMANY IN AFRICA. AFR GERMANY UK ECO/UNDEV LEAD WAR NAT/LISM ATTIT ...POLICY HIST/WRIT METH/COMP ANTHOL BIBLIOG 19/20 WWI. PAGE 56 H1123 COLONIAL ADMIN DIPLOM NAT/COMP B67

KENNETT L.,THE FRENCH ARMIES IN THE SEVEN YEARS' WAR. FRANCE NAT/G CONTROL LEAD WAR CIVMIL/REL EFFICIENCY ATTIT PWR SKILL CONSERVE 18. PAGE 85 H1690 FORCES CHIEF METH/COMP B67

LAMBERT J.,LATIN AMERICA: SOCIAL STRUCTURES AND POLITICAL INSTITUTIONS. STRUCT TEC/DEV DIPLOM ADMIN COLONIAL LEAD ATTIT...SOC CLASSIF NAT/COMP 17/20. PAGE 90 H1801 L/A+17C NAT/G ECO/UNDEV SOCIETY B67

MENDEL A.P.,POLITICAL MEMOIRS 1905-1917 BY PAUL MILIUKOV (TRANS. BY CARL GOLDBERG). USSR AGRI DIPLOM ECO/TAC POPULISM...MAJORIT 20. PAGE 109 H2170 BIOG LEAD NAT/G CONSTN B67

ODINGA O.,NOT YET UHURU. NAT/G POL/PAR PROB/SOLV COERCE REV WAR PERS/REL PERSON ORD/FREE...POLICY 20 ODINGA/O KENYATTA. PAGE 120 H2395 ATTIT BIOG LEAD AFR B67

OPERATIONS AND POLICY RESEARCH,NICARAGUA: ELECTION FACTBOOK: FEBRUARY 5, 1967 (PAMPHLET). NICARAGUA LAW NAT/G LEAD REPRESENT...STAT BIOG CHARTS 20. PAGE 121 H2423 POL/PAR CHOOSE PLAN ATTIT B67

ROELOFS H.M.,THE LANGUAGE OF MODERN POLITICS: AN INTRODUCTION TO THE STUDY OF GOVERNMENT. DIPLOM ADMIN MARXISM NEW/LIB...JURID CONCPT METH/COMP T 20. PAGE 133 H2657 LEAD NAT/COMP PERS/REL NAT/G B67

RUSTOW D.A.,A WORLD OF NATIONS; PROBLEMS OF POLITICAL MODERNIZATION. CONSTN NAT/G POL/PAR FORCES DIPLOM LEAD AUTHORIT...CHARTS IDEA/COMP 20. PAGE 136 H2722 PROB/SOLV ECO/UNDEV CONCPT NAT/COMP B67

SCHECTER J.,THE NEW FACE OF BUDDHA: BUDDHISM AND POLITICAL POWER IN SOUTHEAST ASIA. S/ASIA NAT/G POL/PAR NAT/LISM ATTIT MARXISM...BIBLIOG 20. PAGE 139 H2780 SECT POLICY PWR LEAD B67

SCHWARTZ M.A.,PUBLIC OPINION AND CANADIAN IDENTITY. CANADA SOCIETY LOC/G DIPLOM ADMIN LEAD REGION GP/REL SAMP. PAGE 141 H2812 ATTIT NAT/G NAT/LISM POL/PAR B67

SETON-WATSON H.,THE RUSSIAN EMPIRE, 1801-1917. COM RUSSIA STRATA ECO/DEV AGRI INDUS POL/PAR DIPLOM NAT/LISM MARXISM...IDEA/COMP BIBLIOG 19/20 MARX/KARL. PAGE 142 H2834 SOCIETY NAT/G LEAD POLICY B67

SHAKABPA T.W.D.,TIBET: A POLITICAL HISTORY. CHINA/COM UK CHIEF LEAD...INT BIBLIOG 20 TIBET. PAGE 142 H2839 DIPLOM SECT NAT/G B67

VENKATESWARAN R.J.,CABINET GOVERNMENT IN INDIA. INDIA UK SOCIETY OP/RES COLONIAL LEAD EFFICIENCY ORD/FREE 20. PAGE 162 H3241 DELIB/GP ADMIN CONSTN NAT/G B67

WARREN S.,THE AMERICAN PRESIDENT. POL/PAR FORCES LEGIS DIPLOM ECO/TAC ADMIN EXEC PWR...ANTHOL 18/20 ROOSEVLT/F KENNEDY/JF JOHNSON/LB TRUMAN/HS WILSON/W. PAGE 165 H3312 CHIEF LEAD NAT/G CONSTN B67

WISEMAN H.V.,BRITAIN AND THE COMMONWEALTH. EUR+WWI FUT UK ECO/DEV POL/PAR TEC/DEV INT/TRADE LEAD ROLE SOVEREIGN...SOC TREND 20 CMN/WLTH. PAGE 169 H3391 INT/ORG DIPLOM NAT/G NAT/COMP B67

YAMAMURA K.,ECONOMIC POLICY IN POSTWAR JAPAN. ASIA FINAN POL/PAR DIPLOM LEAD NAT/LISM ATTIT NEW/LIB POPULISM 20 CHINJAP. PAGE 171 H3432 ECO/DEV POLICY NAT/G

TEC/DEV

L67
BRIDGHAM P.,"MAO'S "CULTURAL REVOLUTION"* ORIGIN AND DEVELOPMENT." NAT/G LEAD CIVMIL/REL NAT/LISM TOTALISM ATTIT DRIVE PWR MARXISM 20. PAGE 21 H0413
CHINA/COM CULTURE REV CROWD

L67
TABORSKY E.,"THE COMMUNIST PARTIES OF THE 'THIRD WORLD' IN SOVIET STRATEGY." AFR ASIA L/A+17C USSR INTELL NAT/G WORKER PLAN CONTROL LEAD PARTIC REV ...GOV/COMP 20 COM/PARTY THIRD/WRLD. PAGE 152 H3032
POL/PAR MARXISM ECO/UNDEV DIPLOM

S67
ABDEL-MALEK A.,"THE CRISIS IN NASSER'S EGYPT." ISLAM UAR STRUCT POL/PAR EX/STRUC CREATE PLAN WAR ATTIT ORD/FREE PWR...POLICY DECISION 20. PAGE 3 H0054
FORCES LEAD PROB/SOLV NAT/G

S67
ADAMS R.N.,"ETHICS AND THE SOCIAL ANTHROPOLOGIST IN LATIN AMERICA." USA+45 INTELL PROB/SOLV ECO/TAC LEAD...DECISION SOC NAT/COMP PERS/COMP. PAGE 3 H0066
L/A+17C POLICY ECO/UNDEV CONSULT

S67
AKE C.,"POLITICAL INTEGRATION AND POLITICAL STABILITY." ELITES POL/PAR LEAD ADJUST EFFICIENCY ATTIT AUTHORIT DRIVE...CONCPT 20. PAGE 4 H0088
CULTURE NAT/G CONTROL GP/REL

S67
BELGION M.,"THE CASE FOR REHABILITATING MARSHAL PETAIN." EUR+WWI FRANCE NAT/G DIPLOM ATTIT PERSON MORAL PETAIN/HP. PAGE 13 H0262
WAR FORCES LEAD

S67
CARR E.H.,"REVOLUTION FROM ABOVE." USSR STRATA FINAN INDUS NAT/G DOMIN LEAD GP/REL INGP/REL OWN PRODUC PWR 20 STALIN/J. PAGE 27 H0538
AGRI POLICY COM EFFICIENCY

S67
CATTELL D.T.,"THE FIFTIETH ANNIVERSARY: A SOVIET WATERSHED?" USSR CONSTN ECO/DEV NAT/G LEAD TOTALISM 20 KHRUSH/N. PAGE 28 H0562
MARXISM CHIEF POLICY ADJUST

S67
CHIU S.M.,"CHINA'S MILITARY POSTURE." CHINA/COM ELITES NAT/G POL/PAR TEC/DEV ECO/TAC DOMIN CONTROL LEAD REV MARXISM 20 MAO. PAGE 30 H0595
FORCES CIVMIL/REL NUC/PWR DIPLOM

S67
FRANCIS M.J.,"THE US PRESS AND CASTRO: A STUDY IN DECLINING RELATIONS." COM DIPLOM WAR TOTALISM ATTIT SOCISM...POLICY IDEA/COMP 20. PAGE 52 H1046
PRESS LEAD REV NAT/G

S67
KROLL M.,"POLITICAL LEADERSHIP AND ADMINISTRATIVE COMMUNICATIONS IN NEW NATION STATES* CASE STUDY OF TRINIDAD AND TOBAGO." L/A+17C TRINIDAD INTELL OP/RES DOMIN COLONIAL LEAD GP/REL CENTRAL EFFICIENCY...DECISION OBS METH/COMP 20. PAGE 89 H1774
NAT/G ADMIN EDU/PROP CONTROL

S67
LOFCHIE M.F.,"OKELLO'S REVOLUTION." TANZANIA NAT/G POL/PAR FORCES PLAN CONTROL 20. PAGE 98 H1954
AFR REV LEAD CHIEF

S67
MATTHEWS R.O.,"THE SUEZ CANAL DISPUTE* A CASE STUDY IN PEACEFUL SETTLEMENT." FRANCE ISRAEL UAR UK NAT/G CONTROL LEAD COERCE WAR NAT/LISM ROLE ORD/FREE PWR ...INT/LAW UN 20. PAGE 105 H2099
PEACE DIPLOM ADJUD

S67
MENDL W.,"FRENCH ATTITUDES ON DISARMAMENT." FRANCE CULTURE CHIEF FORCES DIPLOM LEAD WAR...TIME/SEQ 20 DEGAULLE/C. PAGE 109 H2175
NUC/PWR WEAPON ARMS/CONT POLICY

S67
PERKINS D.H.,"ECONOMIC GROWTH IN CHINA AND THE CULTURAL REVOLUTION(1960APRIL 1967)" CHINA/COM FUT AGRI INDUS PLAN LEAD MARXISM...CHARTS 20 MAO. PAGE 125 H2493
ECO/TAC CULTURE REV ECO/UNDEV

S67
PETRAS J.,"GUERRILLA MOVEMENTS IN LATIN AMERICA - I." GUATEMALA PERU VENEZUELA NAT/G COLONIAL LEAD ATTIT PWR...TIME/SEQ METH/COMP 20 COLOMB. PAGE 125 H2497
GUERRILLA REV L/A+17C MARXISM

S67
RAUM O.,"THE MODERN LEADERSHIP GROUP AMONG THE SOUTH AFRICAN XHOSA." SOUTH/AFR SOCIETY SECT EX/STRUC REPRESENT GP/REL INGP/REL PERSON ...METH/COMP 17/20 XHOSA NEGRO. PAGE 130 H2596
RACE/REL KIN LEAD CULTURE

S67
SHIGEO N.,"THE GREAT CULTURAL REVOLUTION." ASIA ECO/UNDEV AGRI NAT/G CHIEF ECO/TAC EDU/PROP CONTROL LEAD PWR 20 MAO. PAGE 143 H2860
CREATE REV CULTURE POL/PAR

S67
SZALAY L.B.,"SOVIET DOMESTIC PROPAGANDA AND LIBERALIZATION." COM USSR SOCIETY COM/IND NAT/G POL/PAR EX/STRUC TEC/DEV LEAD ATTIT ROLE MARXISM ...METH/COMP 20. PAGE 151 H3026
EDU/PROP TOTALISM PERSON PERCEPT

S67
TATU M.,"URSS: LES FLOTTEMENTS DE LA DIRECTION COLLEGIALE." UAR USSR CHIEF LEAD INGP/REL EFFICIENCY...DECISION TREND 20 MID/EAST. PAGE 152 H3047
POLICY NAT/G EX/STRUC DIPLOM

S67
VON LAUE T.H.,"WESTERNIZATION, REVOLUTION AND THE SEARCH FOR A BASIS OF AUTHORITY - RUSSIA IN 1917." USSR ELITES INTELL ECO/UNDEV NAT/G WORKER ECO/TAC TAX ADMIN LEAD AUTHORIT 20 LENIN/VI. PAGE 164 H3274
MARXISM REV COM DOMIN

S67
WHITE W.L.,"THE TREASURY BOARD AND PARLIAMENT." CANADA CONSTN CONSULT LEGIS LEAD PARL/PROC GP/REL ...DECISION 20. PAGE 167 H3351
FINAN DELIB/GP NAT/G ADMIN

S67
YEFROMEV A.,"THE TRUE FACE OF THE WEST GERMAN NATIONAL-DEMOCRATS." GERMANY/W NAT/G DOMIN LEAD SANCTION WAR ATTIT PERSON...MARXIST 20. PAGE 172 H3436
POL/PAR TOTALISM PARL/PROC DIPLOM

L68
CURRENT HISTORY,"DE GAULLE'S FRANCE." FRANCE MOD/EUR WOR+45 INDUS MARKET INT/ORG BUDGET DIPLOM AUTHORIT DRIVE...GOV/COMP IDEA/COMP 20 DEGAULLE/C EEC. PAGE 36 H0723
INT/TRADE PERSON LEAD NAT/LISM

S68
SHAPIRO J.P.,"SOVIET HISTORIOGRAPHY AND THE MOSCOW TRIALS: AFTER THIRTY YEARS." USSR NAT/G LEGIT PRESS CONTROL LEAD ATTIT MARXISM...NEW/IDEA METH 20 TROTSKY/L STALIN/J KHRUSH/N. PAGE 142 H2843
HIST/WRIT EDU/PROP SANCTION ADJUD

B75
NEWMAN J.H.,A LETTER ADDRESSED TO THE DUKE OF NORFOLK ON THE OCCASION OF MR. GLADSTONE'S RECENT EXPOSTULATION. NAT/G SECT CHIEF LEGIS CONTROL LEAD GP/REL SUPEGO SOC/INTEG WORSHIP 19 ENGLAND. PAGE 117 H2346
POLICY DOMIN SOVEREIGN CATHISM

B85
TAINE H.A.,THE FRENCH REVOLUTION (3 VOLS.) (TRANS. BY J. DURAND). FRANCE MOD/EUR SOCIETY STRATA POL/PAR ECO/TAC DOMIN EDU/PROP GP/REL PWR ...GOV/COMP IDEA/COMP 18. PAGE 152 H3036
REV NAT/G EX/STRUC LEAD

B93
ROYAL GEOGRAPHIC SOCIETY,BIBLIOGRAPHY OF BARBARY STATES (4 SUPPLEMENTARY PAPERS). ALGERIA LIBYA MOROCCO SOCIETY STRUCT DIPLOM LEAD 14/19 TUNIS. PAGE 135 H2706
BIBLIOG ISLAM NAT/G COLONIAL

B96
LOWELL A.L.,GOVERNMENTS AND PARTIES IN CONTINENTAL EUROPE, VOL. II. AUSTRIA GERMANY HUNGARY MOD/EUR SWITZERLND SOCIETY EX/STRUC LEGIS DIPLOM AGREE LEAD PARL/PROC PWR...POLICY 19. PAGE 99 H1974
POL/PAR NAT/G GOV/REL ELITES

B98
FORTES M.,AFRICAN POLITICAL SYSTEMS. ECO/UNDEV KIN LOC/G NEIGH POL/PAR SECT LEAD GP/REL ORD/FREE...SOC 20 NEGRO. PAGE 52 H1039
AFR CULTURE STRUCT

LEADING....SEE LEAD

LEAGUE OF WOMEN VOTERS....SEE LEAGUE/WV

LEAGUE/NAT....LEAGUE OF NATIONS; SEE ALSO INT/ORG

B27
CHILDS J.B.,AN ACCOUNT OF GOVERNMENT DOCUMENT BIBLIOGRAPHY IN THE UNITED STATES AND ELSEWHERE (A PAPER). LOC/G PRESS CENTRAL KNOWL...METH 19/20 LEAGUE/NAT. PAGE 29 H0590
BIBLIOG/A CON/ANAL NAT/G

B28
CORBETT P.E.,CANADA AND WORLD POLITICS. LAW CULTURE SOCIETY STRUCT MARKET INT/ORG FORCES ACT/RES PLAN ECO/TAC LEGIT ORD/FREE PWR RESPECT...SOC CONCPT TIME/SEQ TREND CMN/WLTH 20 LEAGUE/NAT. PAGE 33 H0662
NAT/G CANADA

B29
STURZO L.,THE INTERNATIONAL COMMUNITY AND THE RIGHT OF WAR (TRANS. BY BARBARA BARCLAY CARTER). CULTURE CREATE PROB/SOLV DIPLOM ADJUD CONTROL PEACE PERSON ORD/FREE...INT/LAW IDEA/COMP PACIFIST 20 LEAGUE/NAT. PAGE 150 H3003
INT/ORG PLAN WAR CONCPT

B30
SMUTS J.C.,AFRICA AND SOME WORLD PROBLEMS. RHODESIA SOUTH/AFR CULTURE ECO/UNDEV INDUS INT/ORG SECT PROB/SOLV REGION GOV/REL DISCRIM ATTIT 19/20 LEAGUE/NAT LIVNGSTN/D NEGRO. PAGE 146 H2921
LEGIS AFR COLONIAL RACE/REL

B36
RAPPARD W.E.,THE GOVERNMENT OF SWITZERLAND. SWITZERLND INT/ORG POL/PAR EX/STRUC DIPLOM NEUTRAL PARL/PROC REGION WAR HABITAT SOVEREIGN...NAT/COMP SOC/INTEG 20 LEAGUE/NAT WWI. PAGE 130 H2594
CONSTN NAT/G CULTURE FEDERAL

B37
UNION OF SOUTH AFRICA,REPORT CONCERNING ADMINISTRATION OF SOUTH WEST AFRICA (6 VOLS.). SOUTH/AFR INDUS PUB/INST FORCES LEGIS BUDGET DIPLOM
NAT/G ADMIN COLONIAL

EDU/PROP ADJUD CT/SYS...GEOG CHARTS 20 AFRICA/SW LEAGUE/NAT. PAGE 158 H3166 — CONSTN

B39
BENES E.,INTERNATIONAL SECURITY. GERMANY UK NAT/G DELIB/GP PLAN BAL/PWR ATTIT ORD/FREE PWR LEAGUE/NAT 20 TREATY. PAGE 14 H0280 — EUR+WWI INT/ORG WAR

B39
BENES E.,DEMOCRACY TODAY AND TOMORROW. EUR+WWI SOCIETY ECO/DEV DELIB/GP ECO/TAC REGION ATTIT PWR FASCISM...CONCPT LEAGUE/NAT 20. PAGE 14 H0281 — NAT/G LEGIT NAT/LISM

B52
WALTERS F.P.,A HISTORY OF THE LEAGUE OF NATIONS. EUR+WWI CONSTN NAT/G LEGIS TOP/EX ACT/RES PLAN EDU/PROP LEGIT ROUTINE ATTIT...TREND LEAGUE/NAT 20 CHINJAP. PAGE 165 H3297 — INT/ORG TIME/SEQ NAT/LISM

C52
FIFIELD R.H.,"WOODROW WILSON AND THE FAR EAST." ASIA CHIEF DELIB/GP BAL/PWR CONFER COLONIAL ARMS/CONT WAR...TIME/SEQ NAT/COMP 19/20 WILSON/W LEAGUE/NAT. PAGE 50 H0995 — BIBLIOG DIPLOM INT/ORG

B54
SALVEMINI G.,PRELUDE TO WORLD WAR II. ITALY MOD/EUR INT/ORG BAL/PWR EDU/PROP CONTROL TOTALISM...TREND NAT/COMP BIBLIOG 19 HITLER/A LEAGUE/NAT MUSSOLIN/B. PAGE 137 H2745 — WAR FASCISM LEAD PWR

S54
DODD S.C.,"THE SCIENTIFIC MEASUREMENT OF FITNESS FOR SELF-GOVERNMENT." FUT CONSTN ECO/UNDEV INT/ORG PLAN PWR...CONCPT QUANT CON/ANAL SOC/EXP UN LEAGUE/NAT 20. PAGE 41 H0830 — NAT/G STAT SOVEREIGN

B55
WOYTINSKY W.S.,WORLD COMMERCE AND GOVERNMENTS: TRENDS AND OUTLOOK. WOR+45 FINAN POL/PAR DIPLOM ECO/TAC FOR/AID DOMIN WAR CHOOSE...CHARTS BIBLIOG 20 LEAGUE/NAT UN ILO. PAGE 171 H3413 — INT/TRADE DIST/IND NAT/COMP NAT/G

B60
THE AFRICA 1960 COMMITTEE,MANDATE IN TRUST; THE PROBLEM OF SOUTH WEST AFRICA. GERMANY STRUCT REGION SANCTION CHOOSE DISCRIM...INT/LAW 20 AFRICA/SW UN LEAGUE/NAT TRUST/TERR. PAGE 153 H3066 — NAT/G DIPLOM COLONIAL RACE/REL

B62
DUTOIT B.,LA NEUTRALITE SUISSE A L'HEURE EUROPEENNE. EUR+WWI MOD/EUR INT/ORG NAT/G VOL/ASSN PLAN BAL/PWR LEGIT NEUTRAL REGION PEACE ORD/FREE SOVEREIGN...CONCPT OBS TIME/SEQ TREND STERTYP VAL/FREE LEAGUE/NAT UN 20. PAGE 44 H0873 — ATTIT DIPLOM SWITZERLND

B62
GANJI M.,INTERNATIONAL PROTECTION OF HUMAN RIGHTS. WOR+45 CONSTN INT/TRADE CT/SYS SANCTION CRIME WAR RACE/REL...CHARTS IDEA/COMP NAT/COMP BIBLIOG 20 TREATY NEGRO LEAGUE/NAT UN CIVIL/LIB. PAGE 55 H1097 — ORD/FREE DISCRIM LEGIS DELIB/GP

L62
NOLTE E.,"ZUR PHANOMENOLOGIE DES FASCHIMUS." EUR+WWI GERMANY ITALY TURKEY INTELL NAT/G CHIEF CONSULT FORCES CREATE DOMIN EDU/PROP COERCE WAR CHOOSE DRIVE FASCISM...PSY CONCPT MYTH GEN/METH LEAGUE/NAT NAZI 20. PAGE 118 H2367 — ATTIT PWR

B63
NICOLSON H.,DIPLOMACY (3RD ED.). INT/ORG NAT/G CONSULT DELIB/GP CONFER 19/20 LEAGUE/NAT UN. PAGE 118 H2354 — DIPLOM CONCPT NAT/COMP

B66
DOUMA J.,BIBLIOGRAPHY ON THE INTERNATIONAL COURT INCLUDING THE PERMANENT COURT, 1918-1964. WOR+45 WOR-45 DELIB/GP WAR PRIVIL...JURID NAT/COMP 20 UN LEAGUE/NAT. PAGE 42 H0844 — BIBLIOG/A INT/ORG CT/SYS DIPLOM

B66
US LIBRARY OF CONGRESS,NIGERIA: A GUIDE TO OFFICIAL PUBLICATIONS. CAMEROON NIGERIA UK DIPLOM...POLICY 19/20 UN LEAGUE/NAT. PAGE 161 H3215 — BIBLIOG ADMIN NAT/G COLONIAL

S68
DUGARD J.,"THE REVOCATION OF THE MANDATE FOR SOUTH WEST AFRICA." SOUTH/AFR WOR+45 STRATA NAT/G DELIB/GP DIPLOM ADJUD SANCTION CHOOSE RACE/REL ...POLICY NAT/COMP 20 AFRICA/SW UN TRUST/TERR LEAGUE/NAT. PAGE 43 H0858 — AFR INT/ORG DISCRIM COLONIAL

LEAGUE/WV....LEAGUE OF WOMEN VOTERS

LEARNING....SEE PERCEPT

LEASE....SEE RENT

LEBANON....SEE ALSO ISLAM

C55
GRASSMUCK G.L.,"A MANUAL OF LEBANESE ADMINISTRATION." LEBANON PLAN...CHARTS BIBLIOG/A 20. PAGE 60 H1198 — ADMIN NAT/G ISLAM EX/STRUC

B58
LERNER D.,THE PASSING OF TRADITIONAL SOCIETY: MODERNIZING THE MIDDLE EAST. IRAN ISLAM LEBANON SYRIA TURKEY UAR CULTURE INTELL STRATA KIN NAT/G NEIGH SECT EDU/PROP ATTIT PERSON...MYTH OBS 20. PAGE 95 H1888 — ECO/UNDEV RIGID/FLEX

S61
VALLET R.,"IRAN: KEY TO THE MIDDLE EAST." COM IRAQ ISLAM KUWAIT LEBANON SAUDI/ARAB TURKEY ELITES SOCIETY INDUS PROC/MFG POL/PAR TOP/EX PLAN BAL/PWR DIPLOM ECO/TAC ALL/VALS...TREND CENTO 20. PAGE 161 H3224 — NAT/G ECO/UNDEV IRAN

S63
HUREWITZ J.C.,"LEBANESE DEMOCRACY IN ITS INTERNATIONAL SETTING." FRANCE ISLAM UK LOC/G NAT/G SECT DOMIN EDU/PROP EXEC ATTIT PWR...TIME/SEQ 20. PAGE 75 H1507 — STRUCT LEBANON

S64
LEWIS B.,"THE QUEST FOR FREEDOM--A SAD STORY OF THE MIDDLE EAST." ISLAM ISRAEL LEBANON TURKEY CULTURE NAT/G SECT LEGIS TOP/EX DOMIN EDU/PROP LEGIT ORD/FREE PWR RESPECT...POLICY TIME/SEQ VAL/FREE 20. PAGE 96 H1911 — CONSTN ATTIT NAT/LISM

B66
RIZK C.,LE REGIME POLITIQUE LIBANAIS. ISLAM LEBANON STRUCT POL/PAR SECT LOBBY GP/REL 20 ARABS MUSLIM CHRISTIAN. PAGE 132 H2637 — ECO/UNDEV NAT/G CULTURE

LEBON J.H.C. H1849

LEBRUN J. H1850

LECKY W.E.H. H1851

LEDERER E. H1852

LEDERER W. H1853

LEDERMAN W.R. H1854

LEDYARD/J....JOHN LEDYARD

B64
BEDERMAN S.H.,THE ETHNOLOGICAL CONTRIBUTIONS OF JOHN LEDYARD (PAMPHLET). ASIA PRE/AMER S/ASIA...SOC 18 LEDYARD/J KAMCHATKA TAHITI TARTARS INDIAN/AM. PAGE 13 H0256 — CULTURE BIOG METH/CNCPT STRUCT

LEE C. H1855

LEE D. H1856

LEE J.M. H1857

LEE/IVY....IVY LEE

LEES-SMITH H.B. H1858

LEEVILLE....LEEVILLE, TEXAS

LEFEVRE P.C. H1850

LEFEVRE R. H1859

LEGAL SYSTEM....SEE LAW

LEGAL PERMIT....SEE LICENSE

LEGION OF DECENCY....SEE LEGION/DCY

LEGION/DCY....LEGION OF DECENCY

LEGIS....LEGISLATURES; SEE ALSO PARLIAMENT, CONGRESS

N
INSTITUTE OF HISPANIC STUDIES,HISPANIC AMERICAN REPORT. EUR+WWI SPAIN LAW CONSTN ECO/UNDEV POL/PAR EX/STRUC LEGIS LEAD...HUM SOC 20. PAGE 77 H1538 — BIBLIOG/A L/A+17C NAT/G DIPLOM

NSY
MACKENZIE K.R.,THE ENGLISH PARLIAMENT. UK POL/PAR CHIEF DIPLOM TAX TASK WAR AUTHORIT...POLICY TREND 12/20 PARLIAMENT. PAGE 100 H2000 — ORD/FREE LEGIS NAT/G

B00
MAINE H.S.,ANCIENT LAW. MEDIT-7 CULTURE SOCIETY KIN SECT LEGIS LEGIT ROUTINE...JURID HIST/WRIT CON/ANAL TOT/POP VAL/FREE. PAGE 101 H2020 — FAM LAW

B00
MARKHAM V.R.,SOUTH AFRICA, PAST AND PRESENT. NETHERLAND SOUTH/AFR CULTURE LEGIS EDU/PROP COLONIAL CHOOSE REPRESENT DISCRIM ATTIT...OBS TIME/SEQ 17/19 NEGRO BOER/WAR. PAGE 103 H2054 — WAR LEAD RACE/REL

B02
JELLINEK G.,LA DECLARATION DES DROITS DE L'HOMME ET DU CITOYEN (1895) (TRANSLATED FROM GERMAN BY G. FARDIS). FRANCE GERMANY USA-45 NAT/G SECT LEGIS 18. PAGE 80 H1598 — ORD/FREE CONCPT REV

B07
BENTHAM J.,AN INTRODUCTION TO THE PRINCIPLES OF MORALS AND LEGISLATION. UNIV CONSTN CULTURE SOCIETY NAT/G CONSULT LEGIS JUDGE ADJUD CT/SYS...JURID — LAW GEN/LAWS

CONCPT NEW/IDEA. PAGE 14 H0287

B08
THE GOVERNMENT OF SOUTH AFRICA (VOL. II). SOUTH/AFR CONSTN
STRATA EXTR/IND EX/STRUC TOP/EX BUDGET ADJUD ADMIN FINAN
CT/SYS PRODUC...CORREL CENSUS 19 RAILROAD LEGIS
CIVIL/SERV POSTAL/SYS. PAGE 2 H0030 NAT/G

B08
NIRRNHEIM O.,DAS ERSTE JAHR DES MINISTERIUMS CHIEF
BISMARCK UND DIE OEFFENTLICHE MEINUNG (HEIDELBERGER PRESS
ABHANDLUNGEN, 20. HEFT). GERMANY MOD/EUR LEGIS NAT/G
DIPLOM EDU/PROP INGP/REL...BIOG GOV/COMP IDEA/COMP ATTIT
BIBLIOG 19 BISMARCK/O. PAGE 118 H2363

B09
JUSTINIAN,THE DIGEST (DIGESTA CORPUS JURIS CIVILIS) JURID
(2 VOLS.) (TRANS. BY C. H. MONRO). ROMAN/EMP LAW CT/SYS
FAM LOC/G LEGIS EDU/PROP CONTROL MARRIAGE OWN ROLE NAT/G
CIVIL/LAW. PAGE 82 H1645 STRATA

B09
LOBINGIER C.S.,THE PEOPLE'S LAW OR POPULAR CONSTN
PARTICIPATION IN LAW-MAKING. FRANCE SWITZERLND UK LAW
LOC/G NAT/G PROVS LEGIS SUFF MAJORITY PWR POPULISM PARTIC
...GOV/COMP BIBLIOG 19. PAGE 97 H1945

B10
MCILWAIN C.H.,THE HIGH COURT OF PARLIAMENT AND ITS LAW
SUPREMACY B1910 1878 408. UK EX/STRUC PARL/PROC LEGIS
GOV/REL INGP/REL PRIVIL 12/20 PARLIAMENT CONSTN
ENGLSH/LAW. PAGE 107 H2132 NAT/G

B10
TEMPERLEY H.W.V.,SENATES AND UPPER CHAMBERS; THEIR PARL/PROC
USE AND FUNCTION IN THE MODERN STATE... UK WOR-45 NAT/COMP
CONSTN NAT/G POL/PAR PROVS SECT COLONIAL LEAD LEGIS
CHOOSE REPRESENT PWR...BIBLIOG 19/20 PARLIAMENT EX/STRUC
SENATE CMN/WLTH HOUSE/LORD. PAGE 153 H3059

B11
PHILLIPSON C.,THE INTERNATIONAL LAW AND CUSTOM OF INT/ORG
ANCIENT GREECE AND ROME. MEDIT-7 UNIV INTELL LAW
SOCIETY STRUCT NAT/G LEGIS EXEC PERSON...CONCPT OBS INT/LAW
CON/ANAL ROM/EMP. PAGE 125 H2504

B12
HARIOU M.,LA SOUVERAINTE NATIONALE. EX/STRUC FORCES SOVEREIGN
LEGIS CHOOSE PWR JURID. PAGE 66 H1331 CONCPT
NAT/G
REPRESENT

B13
BARDOUX J.,L'ANGLETERRE RADICALE; ESSAI DE LA POL/PAR
PSYCHOLOGIE SOCIALE (1906-1913). UK CONSTN NAT/G CHOOSE
WORKER CREATE BUDGET ECO/TAC ATTIT...POLICY 20 COLONIAL
PARLIAMENT LABOR/PAR STRIKE NAVY. PAGE 11 H0215 LEGIS

B16
TREITSCHKE H.,POLITICS. UNIV SOCIETY STRATA NAT/G EXEC
EX/STRUC LEGIS DOMIN EDU/PROP ATTIT PWR RESPECT ELITES
...CONCPT TIME/SEQ GEN/LAWS TOT/POP 20. PAGE 157 GERMANY
H3129

N16
MILTON J.,THE READIE AND EASY WAY TO ESTABLISH A ORD/FREE
FREE COMMONWEALTH. CONSTN LEGIS PARL/PROC CONSERVE NAT/G
...MAJORIT 17. PAGE 111 H2219 CHIEF
POPULISM

B17
HARLOW R.V.,THE HISTORY OF LEGISLATIVE METHODS IN LEGIS
THE PERIOD BEFORE 1825. USA-45 EX/STRUC ADMIN DELIB/GP
COLONIAL LEAD PARL/PROC ROUTINE...GP/COMP GOV/COMP PROVS
HOUSE/REP. PAGE 66 H1333 POL/PAR

N17
BURKE E.,THOUGHTS ON THE CAUSE OF THE PRESENT ORD/FREE
DISCONTENTS (PAMPHLET). MOD/EUR UK CONSTN CHIEF REV
LEGIS DOMIN CONTROL EXEC REPRESENT POPULISM PARL/PROC
...TRADIT NEW/IDEA METH/COMP 18 BURKE/EDM. PAGE 24 NAT/G
H0484

B18
EYBERS G.W.,SELECT CONSTITUTIONAL DOCUMENTS CONSTN
ILLUSTRATING SOUTH AFRICAN HISTORY 1795-1910. LAW
SOUTH/AFR LOC/G LEGIS CT/SYS...JURID ANTHOL 18/20 NAT/G
NATAL CAPE/HOPE ORANGE/STA. PAGE 48 H0955 COLONIAL

B18
WILSON W.,THE STATE: ELEMENTS OF HISTORICAL AND NAT/G
PRACTICAL POLITICS. FRANCE GERMANY ITALY UK USSR JURID
CONSTN EX/STRUC LEGIS CT/SYS WAR PWR...POLICY CONCPT
GOV/COMP 20. PAGE 169 H3385 NAT/COMP

B19
NATHAN M.,THE SOUTH AFRICAN COMMONWEALTH: CONSTN
CONSTITUTION, PROBLEMS, SOCIAL CONDITIONS. NAT/G
SOUTH/AFR UK CULTURE INDUS EX/STRUC LEGIS BUDGET POL/PAR
EDU/PROP ADMIN CT/SYS GP/REL RACE/REL...LING 19/20 SOCIETY
CMN/WLTH. PAGE 116 H2317

N19
CANADA CIVIL SERV COMM,THE ANALYSIS OF ORGANIZATION NAT/G
IN THE GOVERNMENT OF CANADA (PAMPHLET). CANADA MGT
CONSTN EX/STRUC LEGIS TOP/EX CREATE PLAN CONTROL ADMIN
GP/REL 20. PAGE 26 H0517 DELIB/GP

N19
GORWALA A.D.,THE ADMINISTRATIVE JUNGLE (PAMPHLET). ADMIN
INDIA NAT/G LEGIS ECO/TAC CONTROL GOV/REL POLICY
...METH/COMP 20. PAGE 59 H1183 PLAN
ECO/UNDEV

N19
OPERATIONS AND POLICY RESEARCH,PERU ELECTION CHOOSE
MEMORANDA (PAMPHLET). L/A+17C PERU POL/PAR LEGIS CONSTN
EXEC APPORT REPRESENT 20. PAGE 121 H2421 SUFF
NAT/G

N19
ROWE J.W.,THE ARGENTINE ELECTIONS OF 1963 CHOOSE
(PAMPHLET). L/A+17C LOC/G NAT/G LEGIS REPRESENT 20 CONSTN
ARGEN. PAGE 135 H2703 APPORT
POL/PAR

N19
TREVELYAN G.M.,THE TWO-PARTY SYSTEM IN ENGLISH PARL/PROC
POLITICAL HISTORY (PAMPHLET). UK CHIEF LEGIS POL/PAR
COLONIAL EXEC REV CHOOSE 17/19. PAGE 157 H3131 NAT/G
PWR

B20
BOSANQUET B.,THE PHILOSOPHICAL THEORY OF THE STATE GEN/LAWS
(3RD ED.). SECT LEGIS EDU/PROP ORD/FREE...POLICY CONSTN
SOC GOV/COMP IDEA/COMP NAT/COMP. PAGE 19 H0380 NAT/G

C20
BLACHLY F.F.,"THE GOVERNMENT AND ADMINISTRATION OF NAT/G
GERMANY." GERMANY CONSTN LOC/G PROVS DELIB/GP GOV/REL
EX/STRUC FORCES LEGIS TOP/EX CT/SYS...BIBLIOG/A ADMIN
19/20. PAGE 17 H0348 PHIL/SCI

B23
FRANK T.,A HISTORY OF ROME. MEDIT-7 INTELL SOCIETY EXEC
LOC/G NAT/G POL/PAR FORCES LEGIS DOMIN LEGIT STRUCT
ALL/VALS...POLICY CONCPT TIME/SEQ GEN/LAWS ROM/EMP ELITES
ROM/EMP. PAGE 53 H1050

B23
LEES-SMITH H.B.,SECOND CHAMBERS IN THEORY AND PARL/PROC
PRACTICE. IRELAND NORWAY SOUTH/AFR UK LAW POL/PAR DELIB/GP
LEGIS CONTROL 20 CMN/WLTH. PAGE 93 H1858 REPRESENT
GP/COMP

B23
ROBERT H.M.,PARLIAMENTARY LAW. POL/PAR LEGIS PARTIC PARL/PROC
CHOOSE REPRESENT GP/REL. PAGE 132 H2640 DELIB/GP
NAT/G
JURID

B24
HOLDSWORTH W.S.,A HISTORY OF ENGLISH LAW; THE LAW
COMMON LAW AND ITS RIVALS (VOL. IV). UK SEA AGRI LEGIS
CHIEF ADJUD CONTROL CRIME GOV/REL...INT/LAW JURID CT/SYS
NAT/COMP 16/17 PARLIAMENT COMMON/LAW CANON/LAW CONSTN
ENGLSH/LAW. PAGE 72 H1449

B26
FORTESCUE J.,THE GOVERNANCE OF ENGLAND (1471-76). CONSERVE
UK LAW FINAN SECT LEGIS PROB/SOLV TAX DOMIN ADMIN CONSTN
GP/REL COST ORD/FREE PWR 14/15. PAGE 52 H1042 CHIEF
NAT/G

B26
POLLARD A.F.,THE EVOLUTION OF PARLIAMENT. UK CONSTN LEGIS
POL/PAR EX/STRUC GOV/REL INGP/REL PRIVIL RIGID/FLEX PARL/PROC
...TIME/SEQ 11/20 CMN/WLTH PARLIAMENT. PAGE 127 NAT/G
H2536

B27
FLOURNOY F.,PARLIAMENT AND WAR. MOD/EUR UK NAT/G COERCE
FORCES LEGIS TOP/EX DIPLOM LEGIT DEBATE ATTIT WAR
RIGID/FLEX PWR...DECISION TIME/SEQ PARLIAMENT
19/20. PAGE 52 H1032

B27
MCCOWN A.C.,THE CONGRESSIONAL CONFERENCE COMMITTEE. DELIB/GP
FACE/GP CONTROL. PAGE 106 H2128 GOV/COMP
LEGIS
CONFER

B27
WILLOUGHBY W.F.,PRINCIPLES OF PUBLIC ADMINISTRATION NAT/G
WITH SPECIAL REFERENCE TO THE NATIONAL AND STATE EX/STRUC
GOVERNMENTS OF THE UNITED STATES. FINAN PROVS CHIEF OP/RES
CONSULT LEGIS CREATE BUDGET EXEC ROUTINE GOV/REL ADMIN
CENTRAL...MGT 20 BUR/BUDGET CONGRESS PRESIDENT.
PAGE 169 H3373

B28
CHILDS J.B.,FOREIGN GOVERNMENT PUBLICATIONS BIBLIOG
(PAMPHLET). LEGIS DIPLOM 19/20. PAGE 29 H0591 PRESS
NAT/G

B28
HOLDSWORTH W.S.,THE HISTORIANS OF ANGLO-AMERICAN HIST/WRIT
LAW. UK USA-45 INTELL LEGIS RESPECT...BIOG NAT/COMP LAW
17/20 COMMON/LAW. PAGE 72 H1450 JURID

B30
BENTHAM J.,THE RATIONALE OF PUNISHMENT. UK LAW CRIME
LOC/G NAT/G LEGIS CONTROL...JURID GEN/LAWS SANCTION
COURT/SYS 19. PAGE 14 H0289 COERCE
ORD/FREE

B30
BURLAMAQUI J.J.,PRINCIPLES OF NATURAL AND POLITIC LAW
LAW (2 VOLS.) (1747-51). EX/STRUC LEGIS AGREE NAT/G
CT/SYS CHOOSE ROLE SOVEREIGN 18 NATURL/LAW. PAGE 24 ORD/FREE
H0490 CONCPT

B30
HULL W.I.,INDIA'S POLITICAL CRISIS. INDIA UK ORD/FREE
INT/ORG LABOR SECT DELIB/GP LEGIS DIPLOM NEUTRAL NAT/G
REGION CROWD GOV/REL MAJORITY ATTIT 20 NEHRU/J COLONIAL
GANDHI/M COMMONWLTH. PAGE 75 H1492 NAT/LISM

B30
SMUTS J.C.,AFRICA AND SOME WORLD PROBLEMS. RHODESIA SOUTH/AFR CULTURE ECO/UNDEV INDUS INT/ORG SECT PROB/SOLV REGION GOV/REL DISCRIM ATTIT 19/20 LEAGUE/NAT LIVNGSTN/D NEGRO. PAGE 146 H2921 LEGIS AFR COLONIAL RACE/REL

B30
WILLOUGHBY W.W.,THE ETHICAL BASIS OF POLITICAL AUTHORITY. NAT/G LEGIS PARL/PROC INGP/REL UTOPIA ORD/FREE 16/20. PAGE 169 H3374 MORAL POLICY CONSTN

B31
DUFFIELD M.,KING LEGION. NAT/G PROVS SECT LEGIS EDU/PROP PRESS GP/REL AGE/Y MARXISM POLICY. PAGE 43 H0856 SUPEGO FORCES VOL/ASSN LOBBY

B32
GREAT BRIT COMM MINISTERS PWR,REPORT. UK LAW CONSTN CONSULT LEGIS PARL/PROC SANCTION SOVEREIGN ...DECISION JURID 20 PARLIAMENT. PAGE 60 H1201 EX/STRUC NAT/G PWR CONTROL

B32
LUNT D.C.,THE ROAD TO THE LAW. UK USA-45 LEGIS EDU/PROP OWN ORD/FREE...DECISION TIME/SEQ NAT/COMP 16/20 AUSTRAL ENGLSH/LAW COMMON/LAW. PAGE 99 H1980 ADJUD LAW JURID CT/SYS

B32
MCKISACK M.,THE PARLIAMENTARY REPRESENTATION OF THE ENGLISH BOROUGHS DURING THE MIDDLE AGES. UK CONSTN CULTURE ELITES EX/STRUC TAX PAY ADJUD PARL/PROC APPORT FEDERAL...POLICY 13/15 PARLIAMENT. PAGE 107 H2139 NAT/G MUNIC LEGIS CHOOSE

L34
GOSNELL H.F.,"BRITISH ROYAL COMMISSIONS OF INQUIRY" UK CONSTN LEGIS PRESS ADMIN PARL/PROC...DECISION 20 PARLIAMENT. PAGE 59 H1184 DELIB/GP INSPECT POLICY NAT/G

B35
NORDSKOG J.E.,SOCIAL REFORM IN NORWAY. NORWAY INDUS NAT/G POL/PAR LEGIS ADJUD...SOC BIBLIOG SOC/INTEG 20. PAGE 119 H2371 LABOR ADJUST

B35
RAM J.,THE SCIENCE OF LEGAL JUDGMENT: A TREATISE... UK CONSTN NAT/G LEGIS CREATE PROB/SOLV AGREE CT/SYS ...INT/LAW CONCPT 19 ENGLSH/LAW CANON/LAW CIVIL/LAW CTS/WESTM. PAGE 129 H2584 LAW JURID EX/STRUC ADJUD

B35
TAKEUCHI T.,WAR AND DIPLOMACY IN THE JAPANESE EMPIRE. ASIA ELITES STRATA NAT/G SECT LEGIS ACT/RES PLAN LEGIT PARL/PROC ROUTINE WAR...MGT BIOG CHINJAP TOT/POP 19/20 CHINJAP. PAGE 152 H3038 EXEC STRUCT

B36
CLARKE M.V.,MEDIEVAL REPRESENTATION AND CONSENT. IRELAND UK REPRESENT SUFF. PAGE 30 H0603 PARL/PROC LEGIS NAT/G

B36
CLOKIE H.M.,THE ORIGIN AND NATURE OF CONSTITUTIONAL GOVERNMENT. UK NAT/G POL/PAR CONSULT LEGIS ...GOV/COMP 14/20 CABINET PARLIAMENT. PAGE 30 H0606 CONCPT CONSTN PARL/PROC

B37
UNION OF SOUTH AFRICA,REPORT CONCERNING ADMINISTRATION OF SOUTH WEST AFRICA (6 VOLS.). SOUTH/AFR INDUS PUB/INST FORCES LEGIS BUDGET DIPLOM EDU/PROP ADJUD CT/SYS...GEOG CHARTS 20 AFRICA/SW LEAGUE/NAT. PAGE 158 H3166 NAT/G ADMIN COLONIAL CONSTN

B38
HOLDSWORTH W.S.,A HISTORY OF ENGLISH LAW; THE CENTURIES OF SETTLEMENT AND REFORM (VOL. X). INDIA UK CONSTN NAT/G CHIEF LEGIS ADMIN COLONIAL CT/SYS CHOOSE ORD/FREE PWR...JURID 18 PARLIAMENT COMMONWLTH COMMON/LAW. PAGE 72 H1451 LAW LOC/G EX/STRUC ADJUD

B38
HOLDSWORTH W.S.,A HISTORY OF ENGLISH LAW; THE CENTURIES OF SETTLEMENT AND REFORM (VOL. XI). UK CONSTN NAT/G EX/STRUC DIPLOM ADJUD CT/SYS LEAD CRIME ATTIT...INT/LAW JURID 18 CMN/WLTH PARLIAMENT ENGLSH/LAW. PAGE 73 H1452 LAW COLONIAL LEGIS PARL/PROC

B38
POUND R.,THE FORMATIVE ERA OF AMERICAN LAW. CULTURE NAT/G PROVS LEGIS ADJUD CT/SYS PERSON SOVEREIGN ...POLICY IDEA/COMP GEN/LAWS 18/19. PAGE 127 H2548 CONSTN LAW CREATE JURID

S38
HALL R.C.,"REPRESENTATION OF BIG BUSINESS IN THE HOUSE OF COMMONS." UK ECO/DEV INDUS PROF/ORG LEGIS CAP/ISM ECO/TAC LAISSEZ...POLICY OLD/LIB PLURIST MGT 20 HOUSE/CMNS. PAGE 64 H1287 LOBBY NAT/G

B39
JENNINGS W.I.,PARLIAMENT. UK POL/PAR OP/RES BUDGET LEAD CHOOSE GP/REL...MGT 20 PARLIAMENT HOUSE/LORD HOUSE/CMNS. PAGE 80 H1609 PARL/PROC LEGIS CONSTN NAT/G

B39
MCILWAIN C.H.,CONSTITUTIONALISM AND THE CHANGING WORLD. UK USA-45 LEGIS PRIVIL AUTHORIT SOVEREIGN ...GOV/COMP 15/20 MAGNA/CART HOUSE/CMNS. PAGE 107 H2133 CONSTN POLICY JURID

B39
SIEYES E.J.,LES DISCOURS DE SIEYES DANS LES DEBATS CONSTITUTIONNELS DE L'AN III (2 ET 18 THERMIDOR). FRANCE LAW NAT/G PROB/SOLV BAL/PWR GOV/REL 18 JURY. PAGE 144 H2871 CONSTN ADJUD LEGIS EX/STRUC

B39
TAGGART F.J.,ROME AND CHINA. MEDIT-7 INT/ORG NAT/G FORCES LEGIS TOP/EX PLAN PWR SOVEREIGN...CHARTS TOT/POP ROM/EMP. PAGE 152 H3034 ASIA WAR

S39
AIKEN C.,"THE BRITISH BUREAUCRACY AND THE ORIGINS OF PARLIAMENTARY DEMOCRACY" UK TOP/EX ADMIN. PAGE 4 H0082 MGT NAT/G LEGIS

C39
BURKE E.,"ON THE REFORM OF THE REPRESENTATION IN THE HOUSE OF COMMONS" (1782) IN COLLECTED WORKS (VOL. 5)" UK ELITES STRATA NAT/G REPRESENT ORD/FREE PWR POPULISM...POLICY NEW/IDEA GEN/LAWS 18 BURKE/EDM. PAGE 24 H0486 TRADIT CONSTN PARL/PROC LEGIS

C39
REISCHAUER R.,"JAPAN'S GOVERNMENT--POLITICS." CONSTN STRATA POL/PAR FORCES LEGIS DIPLOM ADMIN EXEC CENTRAL...POLICY BIBLIOG 20 CHINJAP. PAGE 131 H2610 NAT/G S/ASIA CONCPT ROUTINE

B40
BROGAN D.W.,THE DEVELOPMENT OF MODERN FRANCE (1870-1939). FRANCE GERMANY UK USSR CONSTN CHIEF LEGIS DIPLOM AGREE COLONIAL WAR NAT/LISM PEACE SOCISM 19/20 TREATY. PAGE 21 H0428 MOD/EUR NAT/G

B40
KER A.M.,MEXICAN GOVERNMENT PUBLICATIONS: A GUIDE TO THE MORE IMPORTANT PUBLICATIONS OF THE GOVERNMENT OF MEXICO, 1821-1936. CHIEF ADJUD 19/20 MEXIC/AMER. PAGE 85 H1693 BIBLIOG NAT/G EXEC LEGIS

B40
MCHENRY D.E.,HIS MAJESTY'S OPPOSITION: STRUCTURE AND PROBLEMS OF THE BRITISH LABOUR PARTY 1931-1938. UK FINAN LABOR LOC/G DELIB/GP LEGIS EDU/PROP LEAD PARTIC CHOOSE GP/REL SOCISM...TREND 20 LABOR/PAR. PAGE 107 H2130 POL/PAR MGT NAT/G POLICY

S40
BROMAGE A.W.,"THE VOCATIONAL SENATE IN IRELAND" EUR+WWI IRELAND. PAGE 21 H0430 PWR NAT/G REPRESENT LEGIS

S40
FAHS C.B.,"POLITICAL GROUPS IN THE JAPANESE HOUSE OF PEERS." ELITES NAT/G ADMIN GP/REL...TREND CHINJAP. PAGE 48 H0961 ROUTINE POL/PAR LEGIS

C40
FAHS C.B.,"GOVERNMENT IN JAPAN." FINAN FORCES LEGIS TOP/EX BUDGET INT/TRADE EDU/PROP SOVEREIGN ...CON/ANAL BIBLIOG/A 20 CHINJAP. PAGE 48 H0962 ASIA DIPLOM NAT/G ADMIN

B41
CHILDS J.B.,A GUIDE TO THE OFFICIAL PUBLICATIONS OF THE OTHER AMERICAN REPUBLICS: ARGENTINA. CHIEF DIPLOM GOV/REL...BIBLIOG 18/19 ARGEN. PAGE 30 H0594 NAT/G EX/STRUC METH/CNCPT LEGIS

B42
BARKER E.,REFLECTIONS ON GOVERNMENT. EUR+WWI SOCIETY LEGIS EDU/PROP ADMIN LEAD PARTIC CHOOSE TOTALISM AUTHORIT ORD/FREE SOCISM 20. PAGE 11 H0218 NAT/G POPULISM ACT/RES GEN/LAWS

B42
FORTESCU J.,IN PRAISE OF ENGLISH LAW (1464) (TRANS. BY S.B. CHRIMES). UK ELITES CHIEF FORCES CT/SYS COERCE CRIME GOV/REL ILLEGIT...JURID GOV/COMP GEN/LAWS 15. PAGE 52 H1040 LAW CONSTN LEGIS ORD/FREE

S43
PRICE D.K.,"THE PARLIAMENTARY AND PRESIDENTIAL SYSTEMS" (BMR)" USA-45 NAT/G EX/STRUC PARL/PROC GOV/REL PWR 20 PRESIDENT CONGRESS PARLIAMENT. PAGE 128 H2561 LEGIS REPRESENT ADMIN GOV/COMP

C43
BENTHAM J.,"ON THE LIBERTY OF THE PRESS, AND PUBLIC DISCUSSION" IN J. BOWRING, ED., THE WORKS OF JEREMY BENTHAM." SPAIN UK LAW ELITES NAT/G LEGIS INSPECT LEGIT WRITING CONTROL PRIVIL TOTALISM AUTHORIT ...TRADIT 19 FREE/SPEE. PAGE 15 H0290 ORD/FREE PRESS CONFER CONSERVE

B44
SUAREZ F.,A TREATISE ON LAWS AND GOD THE LAWGIVER (1612) IN SELECTIONS FROM THREE WORKS, VOL. II. FRANCE ITALY UK CULTURE NAT/G SECT CHIEF LEGIS DOMIN LEGIT CT/SYS ORD/FREE PWR WORSHIP 16/17. PAGE 150 H3004 LAW JURID GEN/LAWS CATH

B45
HORN O.B.,BRITISH PUBLIC OPINION AND THE FIRST PARTITION OF POLAND. POLAND UK LEGIS PRESS RUMOR CONTROL PARTIC NAT/LISM SOVEREIGN 18/19. PAGE 73 H1469 DIPLOM POLICY ATTIT NAT/G

B47
DE NOIA J.,GUIDE TO OFFICIAL PUBLICATIONS OF OTHER AMERICAN REPUBLICS: ECUADOR (VOL. IX). ECUADOR LAW FINAN LEGIS BUDGET CT/SYS 19/20. PAGE 38 H0763 BIBLIOG/A CONSTN NAT/G EDU/PROP

B47
DE NOIA J.,GUIDE TO OFFICIAL PUBLICATIONS OF THE OTHER AMERICAN REPUBLICS: EL SALVADOR. EL/SALVADR LAW LEGIS EDU/PROP CT/SYS 20. PAGE 38 H0764
BIBLIOG/A CONSTN NAT/G ADMIN

B47
DE NOIA J.,GUIDE TO OFFICIAL PUBLICATIONS OF THE OTHER AMERICAN REPUBLICS: NICARAGUA (VOL. XIV). NICARAGUA LAW LEGIS ADMIN CT/SYS...JURID 19/20. PAGE 38 H0765
BIBLIOG/A EDU/PROP NAT/G CONSTN

B47
DE NOIA J.,GUIDE TO OFFICIAL PUBLICATIONS OF THE OTHER AMERICAN REPUBLICS: PANAMA (VOL. XV). PANAMA LAW LEGIS EDU/PROP CT/SYS 20. PAGE 38 H0766
BIBLIOG/A CONSTN ADMIN NAT/G

B47
LOCKE J.,TWO TREATISES OF GOVERNMENT (1690). UK LAW SOCIETY LEGIS LEGIT AGREE REV OWN HEREDITY MORAL CONSERVE...POLICY MAJORIT 17 WILLIAM/3 NATURL/LAW. PAGE 97 H1946
CONCPT ORD/FREE NAT/G CONSEN

B47
MCILWAIN C.H.,CONSTITUTIONALISM: ANCIENT AND MODERN. USA+45 ROMAN/EMP LAW CHIEF LEGIS CT/SYS GP/REL ORD/FREE SOVEREIGN...POLICY TIME/SEQ ROMAN/REP EUROPE. PAGE 107 H2135
CONSTN NAT/G PARL/PROC GOV/COMP

B47
NEUBURGER O.,GUIDE TO OFFICIAL PUBLICATIONS OF OTHER AMERICAN REPUBLICS: HONDURAS (VOL. XIII). HONDURAS LAW LEGIS ADMIN CT/SYS...JURID 19/20. PAGE 117 H2333
BIBLIOG/A NAT/G EDU/PROP CONSTN

B47
NEUBURGER O.,GUIDE TO OFFICIAL PUBLICATIONS OF THE OTHER AMERICAN REPUBLICS: HAITI (VOL. XII). HAITI LAW FINAN LEGIS PRESS...JURID 20. PAGE 117 H2334
BIBLIOG/A CONSTN NAT/G EDU/PROP

B48
DE NOIA J.,GUIDE TO OFFICIAL PUBLICATIONS OF OTHER AMERICAN REPUBLICS: PERU (VOL. XVII). PERU LAW LEGIS ADMIN CT/SYS...JURID 19/20. PAGE 38 H0767
BIBLIOG/A CONSTN NAT/G EDU/PROP

B48
NEUBURGER O.,GUIDE TO OFFICIAL PUBLICATIONS OF THE OTHER AMERICAN REPUBLICS: VENEZUELA (VOL. XIX). VENEZUELA FINAN LEGIS PLAN BUDGET DIPLOM CT/SYS PARL/PROC 19/20. PAGE 117 H2335
BIBLIOG/A NAT/G CONSTN LAW

B48
US LIBRARY OF CONGRESS,BRAZIL: A GUIDE TO THE OFFICIAL PUBLICATIONS OF BRAZIL. BRAZIL L/A+17C CONSULT DELIB/GP LEGIS CT/SYS 19/20. PAGE 160 H3206
BIBLIOG/A NAT/G ADMIN TOP/EX

B48
WRIGHT G.,THE RESHAPING OF FRENCH DEMOCRACY. FRANCE NAT/G POL/PAR SECT LEAD CHOOSE GP/REL INGP/REL MARXISM SOCISM...CHARTS BIBLIOG 20 DEGAULLE/C. PAGE 171 H3418
CONSTN POPULISM CREATE LEGIS

B49
DENNING A.,FREEDOM UNDER THE LAW. MOD/EUR UK LAW SOCIETY CHIEF EX/STRUC LEGIS ADJUD CT/SYS PERS/REL PERSON 17/20 ENGLSH/LAW. PAGE 40 H0793
ORD/FREE JURID NAT/G

B49
WORMUTH F.D.,THE ORIGINS OF MODERN CONSTITUTIONALISM. GREECE UK LEGIS CREATE TEC/DEV BAL/PWR DOMIN ADJUD REV WAR PWR...JURID ROMAN/REP CROMWELL/O. PAGE 170 H3412
NAT/G CONSTN LAW

L49
BRECHT A.,"THE NEW GERMAN CONSTITUTION." GERMANY/W NAT/G CHIEF EX/STRUC LEGIS PROB/SOLV ADMIN REPRESENT TOTALISM ORD/FREE PLURISM...MAJORIT CHARTS 20. PAGE 20 H0409
CONSTN DIPLOM SOVEREIGN FEDERAL

L49
LOEWENSTEIN K.,"THE PRESIDENCY OUTSIDE THE UNITED STATES: A STUDY IN COMPARATIVE POLITICAL INSTITUTIONS." WOR-45 LEGIS GP/REL...POLICY 18/20. PAGE 98 H1953
CHIEF CONSTN GOV/COMP NAT/G

S49
BOUSCAREN A.T.,"THE EUROPEAN CHRISTIAN DEMOCRATS" EUR+WWI NAT/G LEGIS 19/20 CHRIS/DEM EUROPE. PAGE 19 H0387
REPRESENT POL/PAR

B50
ALBRECHT-CARRIE R.,ITALY FROM NAPOLEON TO MUSSOLINI. GERMANY ITALY SPAIN SOCIETY ECO/DEV POL/PAR LEGIS AGREE CONTROL WAR NAT/LISM TOTALISM PWR SOCISM...SOC 19/20 TREATY. PAGE 5 H0095
FASCISM NAT/G

B50
HALLOWELL J.H.,MAIN CURRENTS IN MODERN POLITICAL THOUGHT. CONSTN SECT LEGIS...MAJORIT CONCPT 17/20 MARX/KARL MILL/JS HOBBES/T LENIN/VI. PAGE 64 H1290
IDEA/COMP POPULISM SOCISM

B50
LYONS F.S.L.,THE IRISH PARLIAMENTARY PARTY, 1890-1910: STUDIES IN IRISH HISTORY (VOL. 4). IRELAND DELIB/GP LEGIS PAY EDU/PROP ADMIN GP/REL ATTIT...BIBLIOG 19/20 PARLIAMENT PARNELL/CS DIRECT/NAT. PAGE 99 H1986
POL/PAR CHOOSE NAT/G POLICY

B50
MCHENRY D.E.,THE THIRD FORCE IN CANADA: THE COOPERATIVE COMMONWEALTH FEDERATION, 1932-1948. CANADA EX/STRUC LEGIS REPRESENT 20 LABOR/PAR. PAGE 107 H2131
POL/PAR ADMIN CHOOSE POLICY

B50
WADE E.C.S.,CONSTITUTIONAL LAW; AN OUTLINE OF THE LAW AND PRACTICE OF THE CONSTITUTION. UK LEGIS DOMIN ADMIN GP/REL 16/20 CMN/WLTH PARLIAMENT ENGLSH/LAW. PAGE 164 H3283
CONSTN NAT/G PARL/PROC LAW

B51
BISSAINTHE M.,DICTIONNAIRE DE BIBLIOGRAPHIE HAITIENNE. HAITI ELITES AGRI LEGIS DIPLOM INT/TRADE WRITING ORD/FREE CATHISM...ART/METH GEOG 19/20 NEGRO TREATY. PAGE 17 H0347
BIBLIOG L/A+17C SOCIETY NAT/G

B51
CHRISTENSEN A.N.,THE EVOLUTION OF LATIN AMERICAN GOVERNMENT: A BOOK OF READINGS. ECO/UNDEV INDUS LOC/G POL/PAR EX/STRUC LEGIS FOR/AID CT/SYS ...SOC/WK 20 SOUTH/AMER. PAGE 30 H0599
NAT/G CONSTN DIPLOM L/A+17C

B51
JENNINGS I.,THE COMMONWEALTH IN ASIA. CEYLON INDIA PAKISTAN CULTURE STRATA NAT/G LEGIS DIPLOM COLONIAL ATTIT...DECISION 20 CMN/WLTH. PAGE 80 H1604
CONSTN INT/ORG POLICY PLAN

B51
LEONARD L.L.,INTERNATIONAL ORGANIZATION. WOR+45 WOR-45 EX/STRUC FORCES LEGIS ECO/TAC INT/TRADE COLONIAL ARMS/CONT...SOC/WK GOV/COMP BIBLIOG. PAGE 94 H1884
NAT/G DIPLOM INT/ORG DELIB/GP

B51
WHEARE K.C.,MODERN CONSTITUTIONS (HOME UNIVERSITY LIBRARY). UNIV LAW NAT/G LEGIS...CONCPT TREND BIBLIOG. PAGE 167 H3336
CONSTN CLASSIF PWR CREATE

B52
APPADORAI A.,THE SUBSTANCE OF POLITICS (6TH ED.). EX/STRUC LEGIS DIPLOM CT/SYS CHOOSE FASCISM MARXISM SOCISM...BIBLIOG T. PAGE 7 H0145
PHIL/SCI NAT/G

B52
BAILEY S.D.,THE BRITISH PARTY SYSTEM. UK LEGIS ...POLICY GP/COMP ANTHOL 11/20. PAGE 10 H0200
POL/PAR LOC/G NAT/G DELIB/GP

B52
BENTHAM A.,HANDBOOK OF POLITICAL FALLACIES. FUT MOD/EUR LAW INTELL LOC/G MUNIC NAT/G DELIB/GP LEGIS CREATE EDU/PROP CT/SYS ATTIT RIGID/FLEX KNOWL PWR ...RELATIV PSY SOC CONCPT SELF/OBS TREND STERTYP TOT/POP. PAGE 14 H0286
POL/PAR

B52
HIMMELFARB G.,LORD ACTON: A STUDY IN CONSCIENCE AND POLITICS. MOD/EUR NAT/G POL/PAR SECT LEGIS TOP/EX EDU/PROP ADMIN NAT/LISM ATTIT PERSON SUPEGO MORAL ORD/FREE...CONCPT PARLIAMENT 19 ACTON/LORD. PAGE 71 H1419
PWR BIOG

B52
SCHATTSCHNEIDER E.E.,A GUIDE TO THE STUDY OF PUBLIC AFFAIRS. LAW LOC/G NAT/G LEGIS BUDGET PRESS ADMIN LOBBY...JURID CHARTS 20. PAGE 139 H2775
ACT/RES INTELL ACADEM METH/COMP

B52
THOM J.M.,GUIDE TO RESEARCH MATERIAL IN POLITICAL SCIENCE (PAMPHLET). ELITES LOC/G MUNIC NAT/G LEGIS DIPLOM ADJUD CIVMIL/REL GOV/REL PWR MGT. PAGE 154 H3074
BIBLIOG/A KNOWL

B52
WALTERS F.P.,A HISTORY OF THE LEAGUE OF NATIONS. EUR+WWI CONSTN NAT/G LEGIS TOP/EX ACT/RES PLAN EDU/PROP LEGIT ROUTINE ATTIT...TREND LEAGUE/NAT 20 CHINJAP. PAGE 165 H3297
INT/ORG TIME/SEQ NAT/LISM

B54
JENNINGS I.,THE QUEEN'S GOVERNMENT. UK POL/PAR DELIB/GP ADJUD ADMIN CT/SYS PARL/PROC REPRESENT CONSERVE 13/20 PARLIAMENT. PAGE 80 H1605
NAT/G CONSTN LEGIS CHIEF

B54
MORRISON H.,GOVERNMENT AND PARLIAMENT. UK NAT/G PARLIAMENT. PAGE 113 H2266
GOV/REL EX/STRUC LEGIS PARL/PROC

B54
SCHWARTZ B.,FRENCH ADMINISTRATIVE LAW AND THE COMMON-LAW WORLD. FRANCE CULTURE LOC/G NAT/G PROVS DELIB/GP EX/STRUC LEGIS PROB/SOLV CT/SYS EXEC GOV/REL...IDEA/COMP ENGLSH/LAW. PAGE 140 H2808
JURID LAW METH/COMP ADJUD

L54
FURNISS E.S.,"WEAKNESSES IN FRENCH FOREIGN POLICY-MAKING." EUR+WWI LEGIS LEGIT EXEC ATTIT RIGID/FLEX ORD/FREE...SOC CONCPT METH/CNCPT OBS 20. PAGE 54 H1078
NAT/G STRUCT DIPLOM FRANCE

C54
LANDAU J.M.,"PARLIAMENTS AND PARTIES IN EGYPT." UAR NAT/G SECT CONSULT LEGIS TOP/EX PROB/SOLV ADMIN COLONIAL...GEN/LAWS BIBLIOG 19/20. PAGE 90 H1804
ISLAM NAT/LISM PARL/PROC POL/PAR

B55
APTER D.E.,THE GOLD COAST IN TRANSITION. FUT CONSTN CULTURE SOCIETY ECO/UNDEV FAM KIN LOC/G NAT/G
AFR SOVEREIGN

POL/PAR LEGIS TOP/EX EDU/PROP LEGIT ADMIN ATTIT PERSON PWR...CONCPT STAT INT CENSUS TOT/POP VAL/FREE. PAGE 7 H0149

B55
BAILEY S.K.,RESEARCH FRONTIERS IN POLITICS AND GOVERNMENT. CONSTN LEGIS ADMIN REV CHOOSE...CONCPT IDEA/COMP GAME ANTHOL 20. PAGE 10 H0201
R+D METH NAT/G

B55
GALLOWAY G.B.,CONGRESS AND PARLIAMENT: THEIR ORGANIZATION AND OPERATION IN THE US AND THE UK: PLANNING PAMPHLET NO. 93. POL/PAR EX/STRUC DEBATE CONTROL LEAD ROUTINE EFFICIENCY PWR...POLICY CONGRESS PARLIAMENT. PAGE 54 H1089
DELIB/GP LEGIS PARL/PROC GOV/COMP

B55
RUSTOW D.A.,THE POLITICS OF COMPROMISE. SWEDEN LABOR EX/STRUC LEGIS PLAN REPRESENT SOCISM...SOC 19/20. PAGE 136 H2720
POL/PAR NAT/G POLICY ECO/TAC

B55
SERRANO MOSCOSO E.,A STATEMENT OF THE LAWS OF ECUADOR IN MATTERS AFFECTING BUSINESS (2ND ED.). ECUADOR INDUS LABOR LG/CO NAT/G LEGIS TAX CONTROL MARRIAGE 20. PAGE 141 H2830
FINAN ECO/UNDEV LAW CONSTN

B55
SMITH G.,A CONSTITUTIONAL AND LEGAL HISTORY OF ENGLAND. UK ELITES NAT/G LEGIS ADJUD OWN HABITAT POPULISM...JURID 20 ENGLSH/LAW. PAGE 145 H2909
CONSTN PARTIC LAW CT/SYS

B55
WHEARE K.C.,GOVERNMENT BY COMMITTEE; AN ESSAY ON THE BRITISH CONSTITUTION. UK NAT/G LEGIS INSPECT CONFER ADJUD ADMIN CONTROL TASK EFFICIENCY ROLE POPULISM 20. PAGE 167 H3337
DELIB/GP CONSTN LEAD GP/COMP

S55
BENN S.I.,"THE USES OF 'SOVEREIGNTY'." UNIV NAT/G LEGIS DIPLOM COERCE...METH/CNCPT GEN/LAWS. PAGE 14 H0282
SOVEREIGN IDEA/COMP CONCPT PWR

C55
APTER D.E.,"THE GOLD COAST IN TRANSITION." AFR CONSTN LOC/G LEGIS DIPLOM COLONIAL CONTROL GOV/REL ...CHARTS BIBLIOG 20 CMN/WLTH. PAGE 7 H0150
ORD/FREE REPRESENT PARL/PROC NAT/G

356
DOUGLAS W.O.,WE THE JUDGES. INDIA USA+45 USA-45 LAW NAT/G SECT LEGIS PRESS CRIME FEDERAL ORD/FREE ...POLICY GOV/COMP 19/20 WARRN/EARL MARSHALL/J SUPREME/CT. PAGE 42 H0841
ADJUD CT/SYS CONSTN GOV/REL

B56
EMDEN C.S.,THE PEOPLE AND THE CONSTITUTION (2ND ED.). UK LEGIS POPULISM 17/20 PARLIAMENT. PAGE 46 H0916
CONSTN PARL/PROC NAT/G LAW

B56
JENNINGS W.I.,THE APPROACH TO SELF-GOVERNMENT. CEYLON INDIA PAKISTAN S/ASIA UK SOCIETY POL/PAR DELIB/GP LEGIS ECO/TAC EDU/PROP ADMIN EXEC CHOOSE ATTIT ALL/VALS...JURID CONCPT GEN/METH TOT/POP 20. PAGE 81 H1610
NAT/G CONSTN COLONIAL

B56
RIESENBERG P.N.,INALIENABILITY OF SOVEREIGNTY IN MEDIEVAL POLITICAL THOUGHT. CHRIST-17C INTELL NAT/G SECT CHIEF LEGIS SANCTION AUTHORIT ORD/FREE CONSERVE...IDEA/COMP BIBLIOG 12/16. PAGE 131 H2627
SOVEREIGN ATTIT

S56
KHAMA T.,"POLITICAL CHANGE IN AFRICAN SOCIETY." CONSTN SOCIETY LOC/G NAT/G POL/PAR EX/STRUC LEGIS LEGIT ADMIN CHOOSE REPRESENT NAT/LISM MORAL ORD/FREE PWR...CONCPT OBS TREND GEN/METH CMN/WLTH 17/20. PAGE 85 H1706
AFR ELITES

S56
MACRAE D. JR.,"ROLL CALL VOTES AND LEADERSHIP." ACT/RES LEAD CHOOSE DRIVE CONSERVE NEW/LIB...STAT STYLE. PAGE 100 H2007
POL/PAR GOV/COMP LEGIS SUPEGO

B57
HODGKIN T.,NATIONALISM IN COLONIAL AFRICA. STRATA STRUCT MUNIC NAT/G POL/PAR LEGIS ATTIT SOVEREIGN ...POLICY TREND BIBLIOG 20. PAGE 72 H1444
AFR COLONIAL NAT/LISM DIPLOM

B57
HOUN F.W.,CENTRAL GOVERNMENT OF CHINA, 1912-1928. ASIA CONSTN CHIEF LEGIS CONTROL PWR...BIBLIOG 20. PAGE 74 H1480
POL/PAR ATTIT NAT/G PLAN

B57
LONG H.A.,USURPERS - FOES OF FREE MAN. LAW NAT/G CHIEF LEGIS DOMIN ADJUD REPRESENT GOV/REL ORD/FREE LAISSEZ POPULISM...POLICY 18/20 SUPREME/CT ROOSEVLT/F CONGRESS CON/INTERP. PAGE 98 H1961
CT/SYS CENTRAL FEDERAL CONSTN

B57
MUELLER-DEHAM A.,HUMAN RELATIONS AND POWER; SOCIO-POLITICAL ANALYSIS AND SYNTHESIS. CONSTN SOCIETY NAT/G POL/PAR PROVS LEGIS POPULISM...SOC NEW/IDEA. PAGE 114 H2280
GEN/LAWS PERS/REL PWR CONCPT

B57
ROBERTSON H.M.,SOUTH AFRICA, ECONOMIC AND POLITICAL ASPECTS. SOUTH/AFR CONSTN CULTURE POL/PAR LEGIS DIPLOM DOMIN COLONIAL...SOC BIBLIOG 19/20. PAGE 132 H2647
RACE/REL ECO/UNDEV ECO/TAC DISCRIM

B57
SCHLESINGER J.A.,HOW THEY BECAME GOVERNOR; A STUDY OF COMPARATIVE STATE POLITICS, 1870-1950. USA+45 USA-45 LAW POL/PAR LEGIS EDU/PROP REGION...STAT TREND CHARTS TIME 19/20 GOVERNOR. PAGE 139 H2788
PROVS CHIEF GOV/COMP CHOOSE

L57
BENDIX R.,"POLITICAL SOCIOLOGY." CULTURE INTELL LABOR POL/PAR SECT LEGIS EDU/PROP ADMIN CHOOSE CIVMIL/REL ATTIT...IDEA/COMP 20. PAGE 14 H0274
BIBLIOG/A ACT/RES SOC

S57
LEWIS E.G.,"PARLIAMENTARY CONTROL OF NATIONALIZED INDUSTRY IN FRANCE." FRANCE NAT/G DELIB/GP ACT/RES PLAN PROB/SOLV ECO/TAC DOMIN CENTRAL. PAGE 96 H1914
PWR LEGIS INDUS CONTROL

S57
MARCH J.C.,"PARTY LEGISLATIVE REPRESENTATION AS A FUNCTION OF ELECTION RESULTS." DRIVE...PROBABIL REGRESS STYLE CHARTS HYPO/EXP SIMUL. PAGE 102 H2046
REPRESENT GOV/COMP LEGIS CHOOSE

C57
MORRIS-JONES W.H.,"PARLIAMENT IN INDIA." INDIA CONSTN LEGIS CONFER COLONIAL CHOOSE PRIVIL ATTIT ...GOV/COMP BIBLIOG 20. PAGE 113 H2264
PARL/PROC EX/STRUC NAT/G POL/PAR

B58
BRIERLY J.L.,THE BASIS OF OBLIGATION IN INTERNATIONAL LAW, AND OTHER PAPERS. WOR+45 WOR-45 LEGIS...JURID CONCPT NAT/COMP ANTHOL 20. PAGE 21 H0415
INT/LAW DIPLOM ADJUD SOVEREIGN

B58
COWAN L.G.,LOCAL GOVERNMENT IN WEST AFRICA. AFR FRANCE UK CULTURE KIN POL/PAR CHIEF LEGIS CREATE ADMIN PARTIC GOV/REL GP/REL...METH/COMP 20. PAGE 34 H0682
LOC/G COLONIAL SOVEREIGN REPRESENT

B58
CUNNINGHAM W.B.,COMPULSORY CONCILIATION AND COLLECTIVE BARGAINING. CANADA NAT/G LEGIS ADJUD CT/SYS GP/REL...MGT 20 NEW/BRUNS STRIKE CASEBOOK. PAGE 36 H0722
POLICY BARGAIN LABOR INDUS

B58
DWARKADAS R.,ROLE OF HIGHER CIVIL SERVICE IN INDIA. INDIA ECO/UNDEV LEGIS PROB/SOLV GP/REL PERS/REL ...POLICY WELF/ST DECISION ORG/CHARTS BIBLIOG 20 CIVIL/SERV INTRVN/ECO. PAGE 44 H0876
ADMIN NAT/G ROLE PLAN

B58
INDIA (REPUBLIC) PARLIAMENT,CLASSIFIED LIST OF PUBLIC UNDERTAKINGS AND OTHER BODIES IN INDIA. INDIA ACADEM LG/CO CONSULT LEGIT CONFER GOV/REL 20. PAGE 76 H1528
NAT/G LEGIS LICENSE PROF/ORG

B58
KINTNER W.R.,ORGANIZING FOR CONFLICT: A PROPOSAL. USSR STRUCT NAT/G LEGIS ADMIN EXEC PEACE ORD/FREE PWR...CONCPT OBS TREND NAT/COMP VAL/FREE COLD/WAR 20. PAGE 86 H1719
USA+45 PLAN DIPLOM

B58
LAHBABI M.,LE GOUVERNEMENT MAROCAIN A L'AUBE DU XXE SIECLE. FRANCE MOROCCO CHIEF EX/STRUC LEGIS ORD/FREE PWR...JURID BIBLIOG 19/20. PAGE 90 H1797
NAT/G COLONIAL SOVEREIGN

B58
OGILVIE C.,THE KING'S GOVERNMENT AND THE COMMON LAW, 1471-1641. UK STRUCT NAT/G CHIEF LEGIS WORKER BAL/PWR GP/REL AUTHORIT 15/17 COMMON/LAW. PAGE 120 H2408
CONSTN ELITES DOMIN

B58
PALMER E.E.,"POLITICAL MAN" IN E. PALMER, PROBLEMS IN DEMOCRATIC CITIZENSHIP. LOC/G NAT/G LEGIS PRESS CHOOSE REPRESENT GP/REL...DECISION SOC IDEA/COMP ANTHOL 20. PAGE 123 H2449
PARTIC POL/PAR EDU/PROP MAJORIT

B58
STRONG C.F.,MODERN POLITICAL CONSTITUTIONS. LAW CHIEF DELIB/GP EX/STRUC LEGIS ADJUD CHOOSE FEDERAL POPULISM...CONCPT BIBLIOG 20 UN. PAGE 150 H2998
CONSTN IDEA/COMP NAT/G

B58
WILMERDING L. JR.,THE ELECTORAL COLLEGE. CONSTN NAT/G POL/PAR DELIB/GP LEGIS PROB/SOLV CONFER EXEC LEAD APPORT REPRESENT. PAGE 169 H3377
CHOOSE DECISION ACT/RES

S58
STAAR R.F.,"ELECTIONS IN COMMUNIST POLAND." EUR+WWI SOCIETY INT/ORG NAT/G POL/PAR LEGIS ACT/RES ECO/TAC EDU/PROP ADJUD ADMIN ROUTINE COERCE TOTALISM ATTIT ORD/FREE PWR 20. PAGE 148 H2963
COM CHOOSE POLAND

B59
BARRON R.,PARTIES AND POLITICS IN MODERN FRANCE. FRANCE LOC/G DELIB/GP LEGIS TOP/EX EDU/PROP LEGIT TV FEEDBACK 20. PAGE 12 H0230
POL/PAR ALL/IDEOS CHOOSE PARTIC

B59
BROSE O.J.,CHURCH AND PARLIAMENT: THE RESHAPING OF THE CHURCH OF ENGLAND 1828-1860. UK SOCIETY TEC/DEV ATTIT LAISSEZ...BIBLIOG 19 CHURCH/STA. PAGE 22 H0434
SECT LEGIS GP/REL NAT/G

B59
BROWN D.F.,THE GROWTH OF DEMOCRATIC GOVERNMENT. WOR+45 BARGAIN EDU/PROP LOBBY APPORT CHOOSE 20. PAGE 22 H0441
GOV/COMP LEGIS POL/PAR CHIEF

B59
CUCCORESE H.J.,HISTORIA DE LA CONVERSION DEL PAPEL MONEDA EN BUENOS AIRES, 1861-1867. LAW LOC/G NAT/G ATTIT...POLICY BIBLIOG 19 ARGEN BUENOS/AIR GOLD/STAND. PAGE 36 H0717
FINAN PLAN LEGIS

B59
GINSBURG M.,LAW AND OPINION IN ENGLAND. UK CULTURE KIN LABOR LEGIS EDU/PROP ADMIN CT/SYS CRIME OWN HEALTH...ANTHOL 20 ENGLSH/LAW. PAGE 56 H1132
JURID POLICY ECO/TAC

B59
GOPAL R.,INDIAN MUSLIMS: A POLITICAL HISTORY (1858-1947). INDIA ISLAM PAKISTAN NAT/G SECT LEGIS LEAD COERCE WAR REPRESENT ISOLAT ORD/FREE 19/20 HINDU MUSLIM. PAGE 59 H1175
COLONIAL GP/REL POL/PAR REGION

B59
LEITES N.,ON THE GAME OF POLITICS IN FRANCE. ALGERIA FRANCE CONSTN SECT VOL/ASSN ECO/TAC INT/TRADE PARL/PROC WAR SOCISM 20 DEGAULLE/C EEC. PAGE 94 H1871
POL/PAR NAT/G LEGIS IDEA/COMP

B59
MADHOK B.,POLITICAL TRENDS IN INDIA. INDIA PAKISTAN UK STRATA ECO/UNDEV POL/PAR LEGIS CAP/ISM DIPLOM COLONIAL CHOOSE MARXISM...SOC TREND 20 GANDHI/M NEHRU/J. PAGE 101 H2014
GEOG NAT/G

B59
PARK R.L.,LEADERSHIP AND POLITICAL INSTITUTIONS IN INDIA. S/ASIA CULTURE ECO/UNDEV LOC/G MUNIC PROVS LEGIS PLAN ADMIN LEAD ORD/FREE WEALTH...GEOG SOC BIOG TOT/POP VAL/FREE 20. PAGE 123 H2468
NAT/G EXEC INDIA

B59
PAULSEN M.G.,LEGAL INSTITUTIONS TODAY AND TOMORROW. UK USA+45 NAT/G PROF/ORG PROVS ADMIN PARL/PROC ORD/FREE NAT/COMP. PAGE 124 H2477
JURID ADJUD JUDGE LEGIS

B59
SANCHEZ A.L.,EL CONCEPTO DEL ESTADO EN EL PENSAMIENTO ESPANOL DEL SIGLO XVI. SPAIN LEGIS JUDGE BAL/PWR LEGIT EXEC WAR PWR...MAJORIT 16. PAGE 137 H2747
NAT/G PHIL/SCI LAW SOVEREIGN

B59
SISSONS C.B.,CHURCH AND STATE IN CANADIAN EDUCATION: AN HISTORICAL STUDY. CANADA ACADEM NAT/G SCHOOL LEGIS REGION MAJORITY...MAJORIT WORSHIP 18/20 CHURCH/STA. PAGE 145 H2891
SECT EDU/PROP PROVS GP/REL

B59
VERNEY D.V.,PUBLIC ENTERPRISE IN SWEDEN. FUT SWEDEN UK INDUS POL/PAR LEGIS PROB/SOLV CAP/ISM INT/TRADE CONTROL SOCISM...MGT CONCPT NAT/COMP 20 SOCDEM/PAR CIVIL/SERV. PAGE 162 H3246
ECO/DEV POLICY LG/CO NAT/G

L59
JANIS I.L.,"DECISIONAL CONFLICT: A THEORETICAL ANALYSIS." INTELL NAT/G POL/PAR DELIB/GP LEGIS TOP/EX PLAN...DECISION CONGRESS NAZI 20 WWI. PAGE 80 H1590
ACT/RES PSY DIPLOM

S59
CHAPMAN B.,"THE FRENCH CONSEIL D'ETAT." FRANCE NAT/G CONSULT OP/RES PROB/SOLV PWR...OBS 20. PAGE 29 H0580
ADMIN LAW CT/SYS LEGIS

S59
MENDELSON W.,"JUDICIAL REVIEW AND PARTY POLITICS" (BMR)" UK USA+45 USA-45 NAT/G LEGIS PROB/SOLV EDU/PROP ADJUD EFFICIENCY...POLICY NAT/COMP 19/20 AUSTRAL SUPREME/CT. PAGE 109 H2171
CT/SYS POL/PAR BAL/PWR JURID

B60
JUNZ A.J.,PRESENT TRENDS IN AMERICAN NATIONAL GOVERNMENT. LEGIS DIPLOM ADMIN CT/SYS ORD/FREE ...CONCPT ANTHOL 20 CONGRESS PRESIDENT SUPREME/CT. PAGE 3 H0052
POL/PAR CHOOSE CONSTN NAT/G

B60
AYEARST M.,THE BRITISH WEST INDIES: THE SEARCH FOR SELF-GOVERNMENT. FUT WEST/IND LOC/G POL/PAR EX/STRUC LEGIS CHOOSE FEDERAL...NAT/COMP BIBLIOG 17/20. PAGE 9 H0186
CONSTN COLONIAL REPRESENT NAT/G

B60
BANERJEE D.N.,OUR FUNDAMENTAL RIGHTS: THEIR NATURE AND EXTENT (AS JUDICIALLY DETERMINED). INDIA UK CULTURE STRATA NAT/G WORKER EDU/PROP CONTROL DISCRIM OWN...IDEA/COMP WORSHIP 20 REFORMERS COMMONWLTH. PAGE 10 H0207
CONSTN ORD/FREE LEGIS POLICY

B60
JEFFRIES C.,TRANSFER OF POWER: PROBLEMS OF THE PASSAGE TO SELFGOVERNMENT. CEYLON GHANA MALAYSIA NIGERIA UK INT/ORG CONSULT DELIB/GP LEGIS DIPLOM CONFER PARL/PROC 20. PAGE 80 H1595
SOVEREIGN COLONIAL ORD/FREE NAT/G

B60
JHA C.,INDIAN GOVERNMENT AND POLITICS. INDIA SERV/IND POL/PAR PROVS LEGIS CT/SYS CHOOSE GOV/REL FEDERAL 20. PAGE 81 H1616
NAT/G PARL/PROC CONSTN ADJUST

B60
KERSELL J.E.,PARLIAMENTARY SUPERVISION OF DELEGATED LEGISLATION. UK EFFICIENCY PWR...POLICY CHARTS BIBLIOG METH 20 PARLIAMENT. PAGE 85 H1699
LEGIS CONTROL NAT/G EX/STRUC

B60
LASKIN B.,CANADIAN CONSTITUTIONAL LAW: TEXT AND NOTES ON DISTRIBUTION OF LEGISLATIVE POWER (2ND ED.). CANADA LOC/G ECO/TAC TAX CONTROL CT/SYS CRIME FEDERAL PWR...JURID 20 PARLIAMENT. PAGE 92 H1832
CONSTN NAT/G LAW LEGIS

B60
LINDSAY K.,EUROPEAN ASSEMBLIES: THE EXPERIMENTAL PERIOD 1949-1959. EUR+WWI ECO/DEV NAT/G POL/PAR LEGIS TOP/EX ACT/RES PLAN ECO/TAC DOMIN LEGIT ROUTINE ATTIT DRIVE ORD/FREE PWR SKILL...SOC CONCPT TREND CHARTS GEN/LAWS VAL/FREE. PAGE 97 H1932
VOL/ASSN INT/ORG REGION

B60
MACRIDIS R.C.,THE DE GAULLE REPUBLIC: QUEST FOR UNITY. EUR+WWI NAT/G POL/PAR LEGIS LEGIT NAT/LISM ATTIT RIGID/FLEX ORD/FREE PWR...JURID CONCPT TIME/SEQ 20 DEGAULLE/C. PAGE 100 H2009
TOP/EX STRUCT FRANCE

B60
PRASAD B.,THE ORIGINS OF PROVINCIAL AUTONOMY. INDIA UK FINAN LOC/G FORCES LEGIS CONTROL CT/SYS PWR ...JURID 19/20. PAGE 128 H2554
CENTRAL PROVS COLONIAL NAT/G

B60
SOUTH AFRICAN CONGRESS OF DEM,FACE THE FUTURE. SOUTH/AFR ELITES LEGIS ADMIN REGION COERCE PEACE ATTIT 20. PAGE 147 H2938
RACE/REL DISCRIM CONSTN NAT/G

B60
US LIBRARY OF CONGRESS,INDEX TO LATIN AMERICAN LEGISLATION: 1950-1960 (2 VOLS.). NAT/G DELIB/GP ADMIN PARL/PROC 20. PAGE 161 H3211
BIBLIOG/A LEGIS L/A+17C JURID

S60
"THE EMERGING COMMON MARKETS IN LATIN AMERICA." FUT L/A+17C STRATA DIST/IND INDUS LABOR NAT/G LEGIS ECO/TAC ADMIN RIGID/FLEX HEALTH...NEW/IDEA TIME/SEQ OAS 20. PAGE 2 H0038
FINAN ECO/UNDEV INT/TRADE

S60
FRANKEL S.H.,"ECONOMIC ASPECTS OF POLITICAL INDEPENDENCE IN AFRICA." AFR FUT SOCIETY ECO/UNDEV COM/IND FINAN LEGIS PLAN TEC/DEV CAP/ISM ECO/TAC INT/TRADE ADMIN ATTIT DRIVE RIGID/FLEX PWR WEALTH ...MGT NEW/IDEA MATH TIME/SEQ VAL/FREE 20. PAGE 53 H1052
NAT/G FOR/AID

S60
HOWARD M.,"BRITAIN'S DEFENSE: COMMITMENTS AND CAPABILITIES." EUR+WWI ECO/DEV NAT/G FORCES LEGIS PLAN DETER ORD/FREE WEALTH...POLICY CONCPT TIME/SEQ GEN/METH 20. PAGE 74 H1481
FUT PWR DIPLOM UK

S60
WYCKOFF T.,"THE ROLE OF THE MILITARY IN LATIN AMERICAN POLITICS." L/A+17C CONSTN CULTURE ECO/UNDEV POL/PAR FORCES LEGIS TOP/EX LEGIT GUERRILLA REV CHOOSE ORD/FREE PWR...TIME/SEQ VAL/FREE 20. PAGE 171 H3430
NAT/G COERCE TOTALISM

N60
RHODESIA-NYASA NATL ARCHIVES,A SELECT BIBLIOGRAPHY OF RECENT PUBLICATIONS CONCERNING THE FEDERATION OF RHODESIA AND NYASALAND (PAMPHLET). MALAWI RHODESIA LAW CULTURE STRUCT ECO/UNDEV LEGIS...GEOG 20. PAGE 131 H2620
BIBLIOG ADMIN ORD/FREE NAT/G

B61
BAYITCH S.A.,LATIN AMERICA: A BIBLIOGRAPHICAL GUIDE. LAW CONSTN LEGIS JUDGE ADJUD CT/SYS 20. PAGE 12 H0243
BIBLIOG L/A+17C NAT/G JURID

B61
BINDER L.,RELIGION AND POLITICS IN PAKISTAN. ISLAM PAKISTAN NAT/G SECT LEGIS CREATE CHOOSE GP/REL ...MAJORIT TRADIT 20. PAGE 17 H0336
CONSTN CONFER NAT/LISM POL/PAR

B61
BISHOP D.G.,THE ADMINISTRATION OF BRITISH FOREIGN RELATIONS. EUR+WWI MOD/EUR INT/ORG NAT/G POL/PAR DELIB/GP LEGIS TOP/EX ECO/TAC DOMIN EDU/PROP ADMIN COERCE 20. PAGE 17 H0344
ROUTINE PWR DIPLOM UK

B61
BURDEAU G.,O PODER EXECUTIVO NA FRANCA. EUR+WWI FRANCE CONSTN DELIB/GP LEGIT ADMIN ATTIT ALL/VALS CONCPT. PAGE 24 H0478
TOP/EX POL/PAR NAT/G LEGIS

B61
CARROTHERS A.W.R.,LABOR ARBITRATION IN CANADA. CANADA LAW NAT/G CONSULT LEGIS WORKER ADJUD ADMIN CT/SYS 20. PAGE 27 H0542
LABOR MGT GP/REL BARGAIN

B61
DRAGNICH A.N.,MAJOR EUROPEAN GOVERNMENTS. FRANCE GERMANY/W UK USSR LOC/G EX/STRUC CT/SYS PARL/PROC ATTIT MARXISM...JURID MGT NAT/COMP 19/20. PAGE 42 H0846
NAT/G LEGIS CONSTN POL/PAR

B61
GUIZOT F.P.G.,HISTORY OF THE ORIGIN OF REPRESENTATIVE GOVERNMENT IN EUROPE. CHRIST-17C FRANCE MOD/EUR SPAIN UK LAW CHIEF FORCES POPULISM ...MAJORIT TIME/SEQ GOV/COMP NAT/COMP 4/19 PARLIAMENT. PAGE 62 H1250 — LEGIS REPRESENT CONSTN NAT/G

B61
HARE T.,A TREATISE ON THE ELECTION OF REPRESENTATIVES, PARLIAMENTARY AND MUNICIPAL. UK CONSTN NAT/G PARL/PROC CHOOSE ATTIT...MAJORIT 18/19 PARLIAMENT. PAGE 66 H1330 — LEGIS GOV/REL CONSEN REPRESENT

B61
INDIAN NATIONAL CONGRESS,SOUVENIR, 66TH SESSION. INDIA S/ASIA CONSTN CULTURE LEGIS CREATE TEC/DEV LEAD TASK...GEOG CHARTS 20. PAGE 77 H1533 — CONFER PLAN NAT/G POLICY

B61
JENNINGS I.,PARTY POLITICS: THE GROWTH OF PARTIES (VOL. II). UK SOCIETY NAT/G LEGIS ATTIT 18/20 LABOR/PAR LIB/PARTY CONSRV/PAR. PAGE 80 H1606 — CHOOSE POL/PAR PWR POLICY

B61
KHALIQUZZAMAN C.,PATHWAY TO PAKISTAN. INDIA PAKISTAN UK SECT LEGIS CHOOSE RACE/REL ATTIT ORD/FREE 20 MUSLIM. PAGE 85 H1705 — GP/REL NAT/G COLONIAL SOVEREIGN

B61
KHAN A.W.,INDIA WINS FREEDOM: THE OTHER SIDE. INDIA PAKISTAN CULTURE LEGIS DIPLOM PARL/PROC REV WAR NAT/LISM 20. PAGE 85 H1707 — SOVEREIGN GP/REL RACE/REL ORD/FREE

B61
LA PONCE J.A.,THE GOVERNMENT OF THE FIFTH REPUBLIC: FRENCH POLITICAL PARTIES AND THE CONSTITUTION. ALGERIA FRANCE LAW NAT/G DELIB/GP LEGIS ECO/TAC MARXISM SOCISM...CHARTS BIBLIOG/A 20 DEGAULLE/C. PAGE 90 H1794 — PWR POL/PAR CONSTN CHIEF

B61
MACLURE M.,AFRICA: THE POLITICAL PATTERN. SOUTH/AFR CULTURE LEGIS DIPLOM COLONIAL RACE/REL 20. PAGE 100 H2005 — AFR POLICY NAT/G

B61
MARVICK D.,POLITICAL DECISION-MAKERS. INTELL STRATA NAT/G POL/PAR EX/STRUC LEGIS DOMIN EDU/PROP ATTIT PERSON PWR...PSY STAT OBS CONT/OBS STAND/INT UNPLAN/INT TIME/SEQ CHARTS STERTYP VAL/FREE. PAGE 104 H2073 — TOP/EX BIOG ELITES

B61
PANIKKAR K.M.,THE VOICE OF FREEDOM: SELECTED SPEECHES OF PANDIT MOTILAL NEHRU. INDIA UK CONSTN FINAN FORCES LEGIS DIPLOM TAX COLONIAL...POLICY MAJORIT ANTHOL 20 NEHRU/PM. PAGE 123 H2460 — NAT/LISM ORD/FREE CHIEF NAT/G

B61
SANTHANAM K.,DEMOCRATIC PLANNING. INDIA AGRI FINAN LEGIS DIPLOM PARL/PROC ORD/FREE 20. PAGE 138 H2753 — PLAN NAT/G CONSTN POLICY

B61
SCHNAPPER B.,LA POLITIQUE ET LE COMMERCE FRANCAIS DANS LE GOLFE DE GUINEE DE 1838 A 1871. FRANCE GUINEA UK SEA EXTR/IND NAT/G DELIB/GP LEGIS ADMIN ORD/FREE...POLICY GEOG CENSUS CHARTS BIBLIOG 19. PAGE 139 H2791 — COLONIAL INT/TRADE DOMIN AFR

B61
SHARMA T.R.,THE WORKING OF STATE ENTERPRISES IN INDIA. INDIA DELIB/GP LEGIS WORKER BUDGET PRICE CONTROL GP/REL OWN ATTIT...MGT CHARTS 20. PAGE 142 H2851 — NAT/G INDUS ADMIN SOCISM

B61
TREVE W.,DEUTSCHE PARTEIPROGRAMME 1861-1961. GERMANY GERMANY/W DELIB/GP CONFER CHOOSE REPRESENT 19/20. PAGE 157 H3130 — POL/PAR NAT/G LEGIS PARL/PROC

B61
ULLMAN W.,PRINCIPLES OF GOVERNMENT AND POLITICS IN THE MIDDLE AGES. LAW CONSTN DOMIN EDU/PROP LEGIT TOTALISM SOVEREIGN POPULISM...POLICY GOV/COMP IDEA/COMP 12/16 POPE KING CHURCH/STA. PAGE 158 H3152 — SECT CHIEF NAT/G LEGIS

B61
WARD R.E.,JAPANESE POLITICAL SCIENCE: A GUIDE TO JAPANESE REFERENCE AND RESEARCH MATERIALS (2ND ED.). LAW CONSTN STRATA NAT/G POL/PAR DELIB/GP LEGIS ADMIN CHOOSE GP/REL...INT/LAW 19/20 CHINJAP. PAGE 165 H3306 — BIBLIOG/A PHIL/SCI

B61
WEST F.J.,POLITICAL ADVANCEMENT IN THE SOUTH PACIFIC. CONSTN CULTURE POL/PAR LEGIS DOMIN ADMIN CHOOSE SOVEREIGN VAL/FREE 20 FIJI TAHITI SAMOA. PAGE 167 H3335 — S/ASIA LOC/G COLONIAL

L61
KAUPER P.G.,"CHURCH AND STATE: COOPERATIVE SEPARATISM." NAT/G LEGIS OP/RES TAX EDU/PROP GP/REL TREND. PAGE 84 H1671 — SECT CONSTN LAW POLICY

S61
LOEWENBERG G.,"PARLIAMENTARISM IN WESTERN GERMANY: THE FUNCTIONING OF THE BUNDESTAG" (BMR)" GERMANY/W NAT/G POL/PAR CHIEF LEAD 20 PARLIAMENT. PAGE 98 H1952 — LEGIS CHOOSE CONSTN PARL/PROC

C61
LAPONCE J.A.,"THE GOVERNMENT OF THE FIFTH REPUBLIC." FRANCE CHIEF LEGIS PARL/PROC CHOOSE ...CHARTS GP/COMP IDEA/COMP BIBLIOG/A 20. PAGE 91 H1814 — POL/PAR NAT/G CONSTN DOMIN

B62
ANDREWS W.G.,EUROPEAN POLITICAL INSTITUTIONS. FRANCE GERMANY UK USSR TOP/EX LEAD PARL/PROC CHOOSE 20. PAGE 7 H0139 — NAT/COMP POL/PAR EX/STRUC LEGIS

B62
ANDREWS W.G.,FRENCH POLITICS AND ALGERIA: THE PROCESS OF POLICY FORMATION 1954-1962. ALGERIA FRANCE CONSTN ELITES POL/PAR CHIEF DELIB/GP LEGIS DIPLOM PRESS CHOOSE 20. PAGE 7 H0140 — GOV/COMP EXEC COLONIAL

B62
ARNE S.,LE PRESIDENT DU CONSEIL DES MINISTRES SOUS LA IV REPUBLIQUE. EUR+WWI FRANCE LEGIT PWR...BIOG CHARTS. PAGE 8 H0165 — DELIB/GP POL/PAR NAT/G LEGIS

B62
BRETTON H.L.,POWER AND STABILITY IN NIGERIA: THE POLITICS OF DECOLONIZATION. AFR CONSTN INTELL ECO/UNDEV COM/IND KIN NAT/G POL/PAR PROVS VOL/ASSN LEGIS DOMIN EDU/PROP LEGIT EXEC ROUTINE CHOOSE NAT/LISM ATTIT PERCEPT ALL/VALS. PAGE 20 H0411 — CULTURE OBS NIGERIA

B62
BROWN B.E.,NEW DIRECTIONS IN COMPARATIVE POLITICS. AUSTRIA FRANCE GERMANY UK WOR+45 EX/STRUC LEGIS ORD/FREE 20. PAGE 22 H0439 — NAT/COMP METH POL/PAR FORCES

B62
CHAPMAN R.M.,NEW ZEALAND POLITICS IN ACTION: THE 1960 GENERAL ELECTION. NEW/ZEALND LEGIS EDU/PROP PRESS TV LEAD ATTIT...STAND/INT 20. PAGE 29 H0582 — NAT/G CHOOSE POL/PAR

B62
GANJI M.,INTERNATIONAL PROTECTION OF HUMAN RIGHTS. WOR+45 CONSTN INT/TRADE CT/SYS SANCTION CRIME WAR RACE/REL...CHARTS IDEA/COMP NAT/COMP BIBLIOG 20 TREATY NEGRO LEAGUE/NAT UN CIVIL/LIB. PAGE 55 H1097 — ORD/FREE DISCRIM LEGIS DELIB/GP

B62
HOOK S.,THE PARADOXES OF FREEDOM. UNIV CONSTN INTELL LEGIS CONTROL REV CHOOSE SUPEGO...POLICY JURID IDEA/COMP 19/20 CIV/RIGHTS. PAGE 73 H1461 — CONCPT MAJORIT ORD/FREE ALL/VALS

B62
HUNKIN P.,ENSEIGNEMENT ET POLITIQUE EN FRANCE ET EN ANGLETERRE. FRANCE UK CONSTN ACADEM SECT CHIEF DELIB/GP PROB/SOLV CONTROL REV ORD/FREE CONSERVE ...BIBLIOG 18/20. PAGE 75 H1496 — EDU/PROP LEGIS IDEA/COMP NAT/G

B62
JAIN R.S.,THE GROWTH AND DEVELOPMENT OF GOVERNOR-GENERAL'S EXECUTIVE COUNCIL 1858-1919. INDIA UK CONSTN EX/STRUC LEGIS ADJUD ADMIN INGP/REL ATTIT 19/20. PAGE 79 H1585 — NAT/G DELIB/GP CHIEF CONSULT

B62
KARNJAHAPRAKORN C.,MUNICIPAL GOVERNMENT IN THAILAND AS AN INSTITUTION AND PROCESS OF SELF-GOVERNMENT. THAILAND CULTURE FINAN EX/STRUC LEGIS PLAN CONTROL GOV/REL EFFICIENCY ATTIT...POLICY 20. PAGE 83 H1662 — LOC/G MUNIC ORD/FREE ADMIN

B62
KASTARI P.,LA PRESIDENCE DE LA REPUBLIQUE EN FINLANDE. FINLAND CONSTN NAT/G POL/PAR LEGIS LEGIT ATTIT...JURID CONCPT 20 PRESIDENT. PAGE 83 H1666 — PARL/PROC CHIEF PWR DECISION

B62
KINDERSLEY R.,THE FIRST RUSSIAN REVISIONISTS. COM USSR LAW ELITES INTELL NAT/G LEGIS ECO/TAC EDU/PROP CONTROL LEAD GP/REL SOCISM 19/20 MARX/KARL BOLSHEVISM. PAGE 86 H1712 — CONSTN MARXISM POPULISM BIOG

B62
MANSERGH N.,SOUTH AFRICA 1906-1961: THE PRICE OF MAGNANIMITY. SOUTH/AFR LEGIS LEGIT SUFF NAT/LISM ATTIT ORD/FREE 20 NEGRO 20. PAGE 102 H2041 — COLONIAL DISCRIM NAT/G

B62
OLLE-LAPRUNE J.,LA STABILITE DES MINISTRES SOUS LA TROISIEME REPUBLIQUE, 1879-1940. FRANCE CONSTN POL/PAR LEAD WAR INGP/REL RIGID/FLEX PWR...POLICY CHARTS 19/20. PAGE 121 H2415 — LEGIS NAT/G ADMIN PERSON

B62
PASTOR R.S.,A STATEMENT OF THE LAWS OF PARAGUAY IN MATTERS AFFECTING BUSINESS (2ND ED.). PARAGUAY INDUS FAM LABOR LG/CO NAT/G LEGIS TAX CONTROL MARRIAGE 20. PAGE 124 H2474 — FINAN ECO/UNDEV LAW CONSTN

B62
PHILLIPS O.H.,CONSTITUTIONAL AND ADMINISTRATIVE LAW (3RD ED.). UK INT/ORG LOC/G CHIEF EX/STRUC LEGIS BAL/PWR ADJUD COLONIAL CT/SYS PWR...CHARTS 20. PAGE 125 H2503 — JURID ADMIN CONSTN NAT/G

B62
STARR R.E.,POLAND 1944-1962: THE SOVIETIZATION OF A — MARXISM

CAPTIVE PEOPLE. COM POLAND USSR POL/PAR SECT LEGIS DIPLOM DOMIN EDU/PROP CHOOSE ORD/FREE...POLICY CHARTS BIBLIOG 20. PAGE 149 H2973
NAT/G TOTALISM NAT/COMP

B62
TATZ C.M.,SHADOW AND SUBSTANCE IN SOUTH AFRICA. SOUTH/AFR AGRI NAT/G POL/PAR DOMIN GP/REL ATTIT PWR 20. PAGE 152 H3048
RACE/REL REPRESENT DISCRIM LEGIS

L62
ORDONNEAU P.,"LES PROBLEMES POSES PAR L'INDEPENDANCE DES NOUVEAUX ETATS AFRICAINS ET MALGACHE SUR LE PLAN DU CONTENTIEUX." FRANCE ISLAM MADAGASCAR LAW STRATA ECO/UNDEV NAT/G LEGIS LEGIT ...JURID TIME/SEQ 20. PAGE 121 H2425
AFR ADJUD COLONIAL SOVEREIGN

S62
MURACCIOLE L.,"LES CONSTITUTIONS DES ETATS AFRICAINS D'EXPRESSION FRANCAISE: LA CONSTITUTION DU 16 AVRIL 1962 DE LA REPUBLIQUE DU" AFR CHAD CHIEF LEGIS LEGIT COLONIAL EXEC ROUTINE ORD/FREE SOVEREIGN...SOC CONCPT 20. PAGE 115 H2291
NAT/G CONSTN

S62
SPRINGER H.W.,"FEDERATION IN THE CARIBBEAN: AN ATTEMPT THAT FAILED." L/A+17C ECO/UNDEV INT/ORG POL/PAR PROVS LEGIS CREATE PLAN LEGIT ADMIN FEDERAL ATTIT DRIVE PERSON ORD/FREE PWR...POLICY GEOG PSY CONCPT OBS CARIBBEAN CMN/WLTH 20. PAGE 148 H2955
VOL/ASSN NAT/G REGION

S62
THOMPSON D.,"THE UNITED KINGDOM AND THE TREATY OF ROME." EUR+WWI INT/ORG NAT/G DELIB/GP LEGIS INT/TRADE RIGID/FLEX...CONCPT EEC PARLIAMENT CMN/WLTH 20. PAGE 154 H3079
ADJUD JURID

B63
ADRIAN C.R.,GOVERNING OVER FIFTY STATES AND THEIR COMMUNITIES. USA+45 CONSTN FINAN MUNIC NAT/G POL/PAR EX/STRUC LEGIS ADMIN CONTROL CT/SYS ...CHARTS 20. PAGE 4 H0073
PROVS LOC/G GOV/REL GOV/COMP

B63
ARAZI A.,LE SYSTEME ELECTORAL ISRAELIEN. ISRAEL NAT/G ADMIN ALL/VALS PARLIAMENT. PAGE 8 H0158
LEGIS CHOOSE POL/PAR

B63
ATTIA G.E.D.,LES FORCES ARMEES DES NATIONS UNIES EN COREE ET AU MOYENORIENT. KOREA CONSTN NAT/G DELIB/GP LEGIS PWR...IDEA/COMP NAT/COMP BIBLIOG UN SUEZ. PAGE 9 H0177
FORCES INT/LAW

B63
BADI J.,THE GOVERNMENT OF THE STATE OF ISRAEL: A CRITICAL ACCOUNT OF ITS PARLIAMENT, EXECUTIVE, AND JUDICIARY. ISRAEL ECO/DEV CHIEF DELIB/GP LEGIS DIPLOM CT/SYS INGP/REL PEACE ORD/FREE...BIBLIOG 20 PARLIAMENT ARABS MIGRATION. PAGE 10 H0193
NAT/G CONSTN EX/STRUC POL/PAR

B63
BLONDEL J.,VOTERS, PARTIES, AND LEADERS. UK ELITES LOC/G NAT/G PROVS ACT/RES DOMIN REPRESENT GP/REL INGP/REL...SOC BIBLIOG 20. PAGE 18 H0358
POL/PAR STRATA LEGIS ADMIN

B63
CARTER G.M.,FIVE AFRICAN STATES: RESPONSES TO DIVERSITY. CONSTN CULTURE STRATA LEGIS PLAN ECO/TAC DOMIN EDU/PROP CT/SYS EXEC CHOOSE ATTIT HEALTH ORD/FREE PWR...TIME/SEQ TOT/POP VAL/FREE. PAGE 27 H0547
AFR SOCIETY

B63
CRUICKSHANK M.,CHURCH AND STATE IN ENGLISH EDUCATION 1870 TO PRESENT. UK LEGIS TAX GIVE DOMIN LEGIT ORD/FREE 19/20 CHURCH/STA. PAGE 36 H0715
NAT/G SECT EDU/PROP GP/REL

B63
DECOTTIGNIES R.,LES NATIONALITES AFRICAINES. AFR NAT/G PROB/SOLV DIPLOM COLONIAL ORD/FREE...CHARTS GOV/COMP 20. PAGE 39 H0781
NAT/LISM JURID LEGIS LAW

B63
ECKSTEIN H.,COMPARATIVE POLITICS. POL/PAR LEGIS CT/SYS CHOOSE TOTALISM PWR POPULISM...METH/COMP GEN/METH ANTHOL BIBLIOG 20. PAGE 44 H0886
NAT/COMP CONSTN REPRESENT NAT/G

B63
FRANKEL J.,THE MAKING OF FOREIGN POLICY: AN ANALYSIS OF DECISION-MAKING. CHINA/COM EUR+WWI USA+45 ELITES INTELL FORCES LEGIS PLAN ATTIT ALL/VALS MORAL CONSERVE...GOV/COMP 20 PRESIDENT UN TREATY. PAGE 53 H1051
POLICY DECISION PROB/SOLV DIPLOM

B63
GARDINIER D.E.,CAMEROON: UNITED NATIONS CHALLENGE TO FRENCH POLICY. AFR CAMEROON FRANCE NAT/G LEGIS CONTROL SOVEREIGN 20 UN. PAGE 55 H1101
DIPLOM POLICY INT/ORG COLONIAL

B63
GORDON M.S.,THE ECONOMICS OF WELFARE POLICIES. INDUS LOC/G NAT/G LEGIS WORKER INCOME AGE/O SKILL WEALTH...METH/COMP NAT/COMP 20. PAGE 59 H1180
METH/CNCPT ECO/TAC POLICY

B63
GRIMOND J.,THE LIBERAL CHALLENGE. UK SOCIETY INDUS POL/PAR LEGIS PLAN CAP/ISM DIPLOM EDU/PROP GOV/REL CONSERVE 20 PARLIAMENT REFORMERS. PAGE 61 H1227
NAT/G NEW/LIB ECO/DEV

POLICY

B63
HUGHES A.J.,EAST AFRICA: THE SEARCH FOR UNITY- KENYA, TANGANYIKA, UGANDA, AND ZANZIBAR. TANZANIA UGANDA CONSTN POL/PAR SECT CHIEF DELIB/GP LEGIS WAR CHOOSE NAT/LISM MARXISM...POLICY CHARTS 20 NEGRO UN. PAGE 74 H1488
NAT/G DOMIN LOC/G AFR

B63
KOGAN N.,THE POLITICS OF ITALIAN FOREIGN POLICY. EUR+WWI LEGIS DOMIN LEGIT EXEC PWR RESPECT SKILL ...POLICY DECISION HUM SOC METH/CNCPT OBS INT CHARTS 20. PAGE 87 H1737
NAT/G ROUTINE DIPLOM ITALY

B63
LEVIN M.G.,ETHNIC ORIGINS OF THE PEOPLES OF NORTHEASTERN ASIA. CONSTN LEGIS...STAT CENSUS CHARTS 20 TEXAS MAPS. PAGE 95 H1901
HEREDITY HABITAT CULTURE GEOG

B63
MAC MILLAN W.M.,BANTU, BOER, AND BRITON: THE MAKING OF THE SOUTH AFRICAN NATIVE PROBLEM. SOUTH/AFR UK LAW KIN NAT/G SECT LEGIS COLONIAL ISOLAT ATTIT ...BIOG 18/20 BANTU NEGRO PHILIP/J MISSION. PAGE 100 H1989
AFR RACE/REL ELITES

B63
MONGER G.W.,THE END OF ISOLATION. FRANCE MOD/EUR RUSSIA UK NAT/G LEGIS TOP/EX GOV/REL PWR 20 TREATY CHINJAP. PAGE 112 H2239
DIPLOM POLICY WAR

B63
RICHARDSON H.G.,THE ADMINISTRATION OF IRELAND 1172-1377. IRELAND CONSTN EX/STRUC LEGIS JUDGE CT/SYS PARL/PROC...CHARTS BIBLIOG 12/14. PAGE 131 H2621
ADMIN NAT/G PWR

B63
SHANKS M.,THE LESSONS OF PUBLIC ENTERPRISE. UK LEGIS WORKER ECO/TAC ADMIN PARL/PROC GOV/REL ATTIT ...POLICY MGT METH/COMP NAT/COMP ANTHOL 20 PARLIAMENT. PAGE 142 H2840
SOCISM OWN NAT/G INDUS

B63
SINGH H.L.,PROBLEMS AND POLICIES OF THE BRITISH IN INDIA, 1885-1898. INDIA UK NAT/G FORCES LEGIS PROB/SOLV CONTROL RACE/REL ADJUST DISCRIM NAT/LISM RIGID/FLEX...MGT 19 CIVIL/SERV. PAGE 144 H2885
COLONIAL PWR POLICY ADMIN

B63
SKLAR R.L.,NIGERIAN POLITICAL PARTIES: POWER IN AN EMERGENT AFRICAN NATION. AFR EUR+WWI CULTURE STRATA NAT/G DELIB/GP EX/STRUC LEGIS DOMIN EDU/PROP ROUTINE CHOOSE ATTIT PERCEPT ORD/FREE PWR...SOC CONCPT OBS TOT/POP VAL/FREE. PAGE 145 H2898
POL/PAR SOCIETY NAT/LISM NIGERIA

B63
TOUVAL S.,SOMALI NATIONALISM: INTERNATIONAL POLITICS AND THE DRIVE FOR UNITY IN THE HORN OF AFRICA. AFR CULTURE PROVS LEGIS EDU/PROP REGION COERCE ATTIT...MYTH UNPLAN/INT TIME/SEQ SOMALI VAL/FREE 20. PAGE 156 H3118
SOCIETY EXEC NAT/LISM

B63
WALKER A.A.,OFFICIAL PUBLICATIONS OF SIERRA LEONE AND GAMBIA. GAMBIA SIER/LEONE UK LAW CONSTN LEGIS PLAN BUDGET DIPLOM...SOC SAMP CON/ANAL 20. PAGE 164 H3290
BIBLIOG NAT/G COLONIAL ADMIN

B63
WHEARE K.C.,LEGISLATURES. POL/PAR DELIB/GP WAR PEACE CONCPT. PAGE 167 H3338
LEGIS PARL/PROC JURID GOV/COMP

L63
ROSE R.,"COMPARATIVE STUDIES IN POLITICAL FINANCE: A SYMPOSIUM." ASIA EUR+WWI S/ASIA LAW CULTURE DELIB/GP LEGIS ACT/RES ECO/TAC EDU/PROP CHOOSE ATTIT RIGID/FLEX SUPEGO PWR SKILL WEALTH...STAT ANTHOL VAL/FREE. PAGE 134 H2674
FINAN POL/PAR

S63
BANFIELD J.,"FEDERATION IN EAST-AFRICA." AFR UGANDA ELITES INT/ORG NAT/G VOL/ASSN LEGIS ECO/TAC FEDERAL ATTIT SOVEREIGN TOT/POP 20 TANGANYIKA. PAGE 10 H0210
EX/STRUC PWR REGION

S63
DUDLEY B.J.,"THE NOMINATION OF PARLIAMENTARY CANDIDATES IN NORTHERN NIGERIA." AFR CONSTN CULTURE ELITES STRATA DELIB/GP LEGIS DOMIN EDU/PROP COERCE ATTIT SUPEGO PWR...STAT VAL/FREE 20. PAGE 43 H0854
POL/PAR CHOOSE NIGERIA

S63
EMERI C.,"LES FORCES POLITIQUES AU PARLEMENT" EUR+WWI FRANCE ELITES DELIB/GP TOP/EX LEGIT ATTIT ...SOC 20 PARLIAMENT. PAGE 46 H0917
POL/PAR LEGIS PWR NAT/G

S63
LAMBERT D.,"LA TRANSPOSITION DU REGIME PRESIDENTIEL HORS DES ETATSUNIS; LE CAS DE L'AMERIQUE LATINE." NAT/G EX/STRUC LEGIS PARL/PROC PWR 18/20 PRESIDENT CENTRAL/AM SOUTH/AMER. PAGE 90 H1800
DELIB/GP CHIEF L/A+17C GOV/REL

S63
LEE J.M.,"PARLIAMENT IN REPUBLICAN GHANA." AFR CONSTN CULTURE SOCIETY STRATA POL/PAR DELIB/GP TOP/EX DOMIN EDU/PROP LEGIT COERCE CHOOSE ATTIT ALL/VALS...CONCPT STAT TIME/SEQ VAL/FREE 20. PAGE 93 H1857
LEGIS GHANA

S63
NICHOLAS W.,"VILLAGE FACTIONS AND POLITICAL PARTIES IN RURAL WEST BENGAL." S/ASIA CULTURE STRATA FACE/GP KIN MUNIC DELIB/GP LEGIS DOMIN EDU/PROP COERCE CHOOSE ATTIT ALL/VALS...STAT TOT/POP VAL/FREE 20. PAGE 117 H2348
NEIGH POL/PAR

C63
ATTIA G.E.O.,"LES FORCES ARMEES DES NATIONS UNIES EN COREE ET AU MOYENORIENT." KOREA CONSTN DELIB/GP LEGIS PWR...IDEA/COMP NAT/COMP BIBLIOG UN SUEZ. PAGE 9 H0178
FORCES NAT/G INT/LAW

B64
AGGARWALA R.C.,CONSTITUTIONAL HISTORY OF INDIA AND NATIONAL MOVEMENT INCLUDING COMPARATIVE STUDY OF MODERN INDIA CONSTITUTION. INDIA S/ASIA SECT VOL/ASSN EX/STRUC LEGIS COERCE REV INGP/REL ORD/FREE...SOC BIBLIOG 18/20 CMN/WLTH. PAGE 4 H0077
CONSTN COLONIAL DOMIN NAT/G

B64
ALDEFER H.F.,A BIBLIOGRAPHY OF AFRICAN GOVERNMENT: 1950-1964. ALGERIA GUINEA LIBERIA UAR ECO/UNDEV POL/PAR LEGIS COLONIAL LEAD PARL/PROC NAT/LISM 20. PAGE 5 H0098
BIBLIOG AFR LOC/G NAT/G

B64
ANDREN N.,GOVERNMENT AND POLITICS IN THE NORDIC COUNTRIES: DENMARK, FINLAND, ICELAND, NORWAY, SWEDEN. DENMARK FINLAND ICELAND NORWAY SWEDEN POL/PAR CHIEF LEGIS ADMIN REGION REPRESENT ATTIT CONSERVE...CHARTS BIBLIOG/A 20. PAGE 7 H0137
CONSTN NAT/G CULTURE GOV/COMP

B64
AVASTHI A.,ASPECTS OF ADMINISTRATION. INDIA UK USA+45 FINAN ACADEM DELIB/GP LEGIS RECEIVE PARL/PROC PRIVIL...NAT/COMP 20. PAGE 9 H0183
MGT ADMIN SOC/WK ORD/FREE

B64
BAGEHOT W.,THE ENGLISH CONSTITUTION. UK CHIEF CONSULT LEGIS BAL/PWR PWR...BIBLIOG 18/19 PARLIAMENT. PAGE 10 H0198
CONSTN PARL/PROC NAT/G CONCPT

B64
COONDOO R.,THE DIVISION OF POWERS IN THE INDIAN CONSTITUTION. INDIA ECO/UNDEV FINAN TEC/DEV WAR CENTRAL EFFICIENCY NAT/LISM PWR WEALTH NEW/LIB ...BIBLIOG 18/20. PAGE 33 H0659
CONSTN LEGIS WELF/ST GOV/COMP

B64
DE SMITH S.A.,THE NEW COMMONWEALTH AND ITS CONSTITUTIONS. AFR CYPRUS PAKISTAN S/ASIA INT/ORG NAT/G LEGIS LEGIT RIGID/FLEX PWR...CONCPT TIME/SEQ CMN/WLTH 20. PAGE 38 H0770
EX/STRUC CONSTN SOVEREIGN

B64
HALLER W.,DER SCHWEDISCHE JUSTITIEOMBUDSMAN. DENMARK FINLAND NORWAY SWEDEN LEGIS ADJUD CONTROL PERSON ORD/FREE...NAT/COMP 20 OMBUDSMAN. PAGE 64 H1288
JURID PARL/PROC ADMIN CHIEF

B64
HEIMSATH C.H.,INDIAN NATIONALISM AND HINDU SOCIAL REFORM. S/ASIA LAW CULTURE SOCIETY STRATA PROVS VOL/ASSN DELIB/GP LEGIS TOP/EX DOMIN EDU/PROP LEGIT ATTIT ALL/VALS...POLICY SOC TIME/SEQ STERTYP VAL/FREE 19/20. PAGE 69 H1385
SECT NAT/G

B64
HOLDSWORTH W.S.,A HISTORY OF ENGLISH LAW; THE CENTURIES OF DEVELOPMENT AND REFORM (VOL. XIV). UK CONSTN LOC/G NAT/G POL/PAR CHIEF EX/STRUC ADJUD COLONIAL ATTIT...INT/LAW JURID 18/19 TORY/PARTY COMMONWLTH WHIG/PARTY COMMON/LAW. PAGE 73 H1453
LAW LEGIS LEAD CT/SYS

B64
HOPKINSON T.,SOUTH AFRICA. SOUTH/AFR UK NAT/G POL/PAR LEGIS ECO/TAC PARL/PROC WAR...JURID AUD/VIS 19/20. PAGE 73 H1467
SOCIETY RACE/REL DISCRIM

B64
INDIAN COMM PREVENTION CORRUPT,REPORT, 1964. INDIA NAT/G GOV/REL ATTIT ORD/FREE...CRIMLGY METH 20. PAGE 76 H1530
CRIME ADMIN LEGIS LOC/G

B64
LEDERMAN W.R.,THE COURTS AND THE CANDIAN CONSTITUTION. CANADA PARL/PROC...POLICY JURID GOV/COMP ANTHOL 19/20 SUPREME/CT PARLIAMENT. PAGE 93 H1854
CONSTN CT/SYS LEGIS LAW

B64
MINAR D.W.,IDEAS AND POLITICS: THE AMERICAN EXPERIENCE. SECT CHIEF LEGIS CREATE ADJUD EXEC REV PWR...PHIL/SCI CONCPT IDEA/COMP 18/20 HAMILTON/A JEFFERSN/T DECLAR/IND JACKSON/A PRESIDENT. PAGE 111 H2220
CONSTN NAT/G FEDERAL

B64
MORGENTHAU R.S.,POLITICAL PARTIES IN FRENCH-SPEAKING WEST AFRICA. AFR FRANCE GUINEA IVORY/CST MALI SENEGAL CONSTN LEGIS CREATE PLAN LOBBY PARTIC GP/REL...POLICY BIBLIOG 20. PAGE 113 H2257
POL/PAR NAT/G SOVEREIGN COLONIAL

B64
O'HEARN P.J.T.,PEACE, ORDER AND GOOD GOVERNMENT; A NEW CONSTITUTION FOR CANADA. CANADA EX/STRUC LEGIS CT/SYS PARL/PROC...BIBLIOG 20. PAGE 120 H2388
NAT/G CONSTN LAW CREATE

B64
PHILLIPS C.S.,THE DEVELOPMENT OF NIGERIAN FOREIGN POLICY. AFR CONSTN CULTURE STRATA NAT/G LEGIS DOMIN LEGIT EXEC...RELATIV SOC TIME/SEQ TREND TOT/POP 20. PAGE 125 H2502
CHOOSE POLICY DIPLOM NIGERIA

B64
PIPES R.,THE FORMATION OF THE SOVIET UNION. EUR+WWI MOD/EUR STRUCT ECO/UNDEV NAT/G LEGIS DOMIN LEGIT CT/SYS EXEC COERCE ALL/VALS...POLICY RELATIV HIST/WRIT TIME/SEQ TOT/POP 19/20. PAGE 126 H2514
COM USSR RUSSIA

B64
RIES J.C.,THE MANAGEMENT OF DEFENSE: ORGANIZATION AND CONTROL OF THE US ARMED SERVICES. PROF/ORG DELIB/GP EX/STRUC LEGIS GOV/REL PERS/REL CENTRAL RATIONAL PWR...POLICY TREND GOV/COMP BIBLIOG. PAGE 131 H2626
FORCES ACT/RES DECISION CONTROL

B64
STRONG C.F.,HISTORY OF MODERN POLITICAL CONSTITUTIONS. STRUCT INT/ORG NAT/G LEGIS TEC/DEV DIPLOM INT/TRADE CT/SYS EXEC...METH/COMP T 12/20 UN. PAGE 150 H2999
CONSTN CONCPT

B64
THORNBURG M.W.,PEOPLE AND POLICY IN THE MIDDLE EAST. ISLAM ECO/UNDEV FAM KIN MUNIC NAT/G NEIGH POL/PAR SECT DELIB/GP LEGIS PLAN ECO/TAC DOMIN ADMIN ATTIT HEALTH RESPECT...SOC CONCPT METH/CNCPT OBS TIME/SEQ TOT/POP VAL/FREE. PAGE 154 H3088
TEC/DEV CULTURE

B64
US HOUSE COMM BANKING-CURR,INTERNATIONAL DEVELOPMENT ASSOCIATION ACT AMENDMENT. CHINA/COM USA+45 USSR FINAN FORCES LEGIS DIPLOM CONFER EFFICIENCY...CHARTS GOV/COMP 20 PRESIDENT CONGRESS INTL/DEV. PAGE 160 H3196
BAL/PAY FOR/AID RECORD ECO/TAC

B64
UTECHIN S.V.,RUSSIAN POLITICAL THOUGHT: A CONCISE HISTORY. RUSSIA USSR INTELL STRATA POL/PAR SECT LEGIS EDU/PROP REV WAR MARXISM...ANARCH BIBLIOG 9/20 REFORMERS SLAVS. PAGE 161 H3218
IDEA/COMP ATTIT ALL/IDEOS NAT/G

B64
VECCHIO G.D.,L'ETAT ET LE DROIT. ITALY CONSTN EX/STRUC LEGIS DIPLOM CT/SYS...JURID 20 UN. PAGE 162 H3238
NAT/G SOVEREIGN CONCPT INT/LAW

B64
WALDMAN E.,THE GOOSE STEP IS VERBOTEN: THE GERMAN ARMY TODAY. GERMANY/W LAW CONSTN LEGIS PROB/SOLV DOMIN CONTROL CIVMIL/REL GOV/REL INGP/REL ATTIT ...DEEP/QU 20. PAGE 164 H3289
SOC FORCES NAT/G

B64
WHEARE K.C.,FEDERAL GOVERNMENT (4TH ED.). WOR+45 WOR-45 POL/PAR LEGIS BAL/PWR CT/SYS...POLICY JURID CONCPT GOV/COMP 17/20. PAGE 167 H3339
FEDERAL CONSTN EX/STRUC NAT/COMP

B64
WRIGHT G.,RURAL REVOLUTION IN FRANCE: THE PEASANTRY IN THE TWENTIETH CENTURY. EUR+WWI MOD/EUR LAW CULTURE AGRI POL/PAR DELIB/GP LEGIS ECO/TAC EDU/PROP COERCE CHOOSE ATTIT RIGID/FLEX HEALTH ...STAT CENSUS CHARTS VAL/FREE 20. PAGE 171 H3419
PWR STRATA FRANCE REV

S64
GIROD R.,"LE SYSTEME DES PARTIS EN SUISSE." CONSTN LOC/G DELIB/GP FEDERAL ALL/VALS. PAGE 57 H1136
POL/PAR LEGIS NAT/G PARL/PROC

S64
GROSS J.A.,"WHITEHALL AND THE COMMONWEALTH." EUR+WWI MOD/EUR INT/ORG NAT/G CONSULT DELIB/GP LEGIS DOMIN ADMIN COLONIAL ROUTINE PWR CMN/WLTH 19/20. PAGE 62 H1233
EX/STRUC ATTIT TREND

S64
LEWIS B.,"THE QUEST FOR FREEDOM--A SAD STORY OF THE MIDDLE EAST." ISLAM ISRAEL LEBANON TURKEY CULTURE NAT/G SECT LEGIS TOP/EX DOMIN EDU/PROP LEGIT ORD/FREE PWR RESPECT...POLICY TIME/SEQ VAL/FREE 20. PAGE 96 H1911
CONSTN ATTIT NAT/LISM

S64
LEWIS R.,"OPINION SURVEYING IN KOREA." ASIA FUT KOREA LEGIS EDU/PROP EXEC ALL/VALS...POLICY CONCPT MYTH TESTS CON/ANAL GEN/METH TOT/POP VAL/FREE 20. PAGE 96 H1915
NAT/G QU

S64
RUDOLPH L.I.,"GENERALS AND POLITICIANS IN INDIA." INDIA S/ASIA CULTURE STRATA NAT/G LEGIS TOP/EX EDU/PROP ATTIT ORD/FREE PWR RESPECT SKILL...POLICY BIOG TIME/SEQ STERTYP VAL/FREE 20. PAGE 136 H2713
FORCES COERCE

S64
SCHEFFLER H.W.,"THE GENESIS AND REPRESSION OF CONFLICT: CHOISEUL ISLAND." S/ASIA LOC/G NAT/G FORCES LEGIS DIPLOM DOMIN LEGIT EXEC CHOOSE ATTIT RESPECT SKILL...POLICY JURID OBS TREND GEN/METH 20. PAGE 139 H2781
PWR COERCE WAR

S64
SWEARER H.R.,"AFTER KHRUSHCHEV: WHAT NEXT." COM FUT USSR CONSTN ELITES NAT/G POL/PAR CHIEF DELIB/GP LEGIS DOMIN LEAD...RECORD TREND STERTYP GEN/METH 20. PAGE 151 H3016
EX/STRUC PWR

S64
UNRUH J.M.,"SCIENTIFIC INPUTS TO LEGISLATIVE DECISION-MAKING (SUPPLEMENT)" USA+45 ACADEM NAT/G PROVS GOV/REL GOV/COMP. PAGE 159 H3171
CREATE DECISION LEGIS PARTIC

B65
AIYAR S.P.,STUDIES IN INDIAN DEMOCRACY. INDIA STRATA ECO/UNDEV LABOR POL/PAR LEGIS DIPLOM LOBBY REGION CHOOSE ATTIT SOCISM...ANTHOL 20. PAGE 4 H0086
ORD/FREE REPRESENT ADMIN NAT/G

B65
ALEXANDER R.J.,ORGANIZED LABOR IN LATIN AMERICA. L/A+17C INT/ORG LEGIS WORKER TEC/DEV BARGAIN INT/TRADE REV...NAT/COMP BIBLIOG 20. PAGE 5 H0102
LABOR POL/PAR ECO/UNDEV POLICY

B65
BETTISON D.G.,THE PAPUA-GUINEA ELECTIONS 1964. S/ASIA CONSTN POL/PAR EDU/PROP PARTIC SUFF CENTRAL CONSEN...OBS CHARTS BIBLIOG 20. PAGE 16 H0324
NAT/G LEGIS CHOOSE REPRESENT

B65
BLITZ L.F.,THE POLITICS AND ADMINISTRATION OF NIGERIAN GOVERNMENT. NIGER CULTURE LOC/G LEGIS DIPLOM COLONIAL CT/SYS SOVEREIGN...GEOG SOC ANTHOL 20. PAGE 18 H0357
NAT/G GOV/REL POL/PAR

B65
BORTOLI G.,SOCIOLOGIE DU REFERENDUM DANS LA FRANCE MODERNE. FRANCE CONSTN EDU/PROP SUFF ATTIT ORD/FREE ...POLICY DECISION CHARTS BIBLIOG 20 DEGAULLE/C. PAGE 19 H0379
LEGIS SOCIETY PWR NAT/G

B65
BRASS P.R.,FACTIONAL POLITICS IN AN INDIAN STATE: THE CONGRESS PARTY IN UTTAR PRADESH. INDIA UK CONSTN CULTURE ECO/UNDEV LOC/G DOMIN COLONIAL CROWD GP/REL ADJUST CENTRAL RIGID/FLEX SOVEREIGN 20 UTTAR/PRAD CONGRESS/P. PAGE 20 H0406
POL/PAR PROVS LEGIS CHOOSE

B65
CAMPBELL G.A.,THE CIVIL SERVICE IN BRITAIN (2ND ED.). UK DELIB/GP FORCES WORKER CREATE PLAN ...POLICY AUD/VIS 19/20 CIVIL/SERV. PAGE 26 H0515
ADMIN LEGIS NAT/G FINAN

B65
CARTER G.M.,GOVERNMENT AND POLITICS IN THE TWENTIETH CENTURY (REV. ED.). WOR+45 NAT/G POL/PAR LEGIS DIPLOM LEAD PARL/PROC CHOOSE TOTALISM 20. PAGE 27 H0549
GOV/COMP ECO/UNDEV ALL/IDEOS ECO/DEV

B65
CHANDA A.,FEDERALISM IN INDIA. INDIA UK ELITES FINAN NAT/G POL/PAR EX/STRUC LEGIS DIPLOM TAX GOV/REL POPULISM...POLICY 20. PAGE 28 H0572
CONSTN CENTRAL FEDERAL

B65
CHARNAY J.P.,LE SUFFRAGE POLITIQUE EN FRANCE; ELECTIONS PARLEMENTAIRES, ELECTION PRESIDENTIELLE, REFERENDUMS. FRANCE CONSTN CHIEF DELIB/GP ECO/TAC EDU/PROP CRIME INGP/REL MORAL ORD/FREE PWR CATHISM 20 PARLIAMENT PRESIDENT. PAGE 29 H0584
CHOOSE SUFF NAT/G LEGIS

B65
CHEN T.H.,THE CHINESE COMMUNIST REGIME: A DOCUMENTARY STUDY (2 VOLS.). CHINA/COM LAW CONSTN ELITES ECO/UNDEV LEGIS ECO/TAC ADMIN CONTROL PWR ...SOC 20. PAGE 29 H0587
MARXISM POL/PAR NAT/G

B65
CHRIMES S.B.,ENGLISH CONSTITUTIONAL HISTORY (3RD ED.). UK CHIEF CONSULT DELIB/GP LEGIS CT/SYS 15/20 COMMON/LAW PARLIAMENT. PAGE 30 H0598
CONSTN BAL/PWR NAT/G

B65
GEORGE M.,THE WARPED VISION. EUR+WWI UK NAT/G POL/PAR LEGIS PARL/PROC SANCTION COERCE WAR GOV/REL PEACE RESPECT 20 CONSRV/PAR. PAGE 56 H1113
LEAD ATTIT DIPLOM POLICY

B65
GWYN R.J.,THE SHAPE OF SCANDAL: A STUDY OF A GOVERNMENT IN CRISIS. CANADA LEGIS ADJUD CT/SYS SANCTION CMN/WLTH 20 PEARSON/L. PAGE 63 H1260
ELITES NAT/G CRIME

B65
HADWIGER D.F.,PRESSURES AND PROTEST. NAT/G LEGIS PLAN LEAD PARTIC ROUTINE ATTIT POLICY. PAGE 63 H1273
AGRI GP/REL LOBBY CHOOSE

B65
JACKSON G.,THE SPANISH REPUBLIC AND THE CIVIL WAR, 1931-1939. EUR+WWI INTELL STRUCT COM/IND NAT/G POL/PAR LEGIS EDU/PROP EXEC COERCE NAT/LISM DRIVE PWR...INT TIME/SEQ TOT/POP 20. PAGE 79 H1574
ATTIT GUERRILLA SPAIN

B65
JACOB H.,POLITICS IN THE AMERICAN STATES; A COMPARATIVE ANALYSIS. USA+45 POL/PAR CHIEF LEGIS TAX EDU/PROP CONTROL CT/SYS LOBBY PARTIC...DECISION CHARTS 20. PAGE 79 H1578
PROVS GOV/COMP PWR

B65
MCWHINNEY E.,JUDICIAL REVIEW IN THE ENGLISH-SPEAKING WORLD (3RD ED.). CANADA UK WOR+45 LEGIS CONTROL EXEC PARTIC...JURID 20 AUSTRAL. PAGE 108 H2151
GOV/COMP CT/SYS ADJUD CONSTN

B65
MONTESQUIEU C DE S.,CONSIDERATIONS ON THE CAUSES OF THE GREATNESS OF THE ROMANS AND THEIR DECLINE (1748 TRANS. BY D. LOWENTHAL). ROMAN/EMP SECT CHIEF EX/STRUC FORCES LEGIS DOMIN WAR POPULISM...POLICY REALPOL ROME/ANC. PAGE 112 H2244
NAT/G PWR COLONIAL MORAL

B65
NAMIER L.B.,THE STRUCTURE OF POLITICS AT THE ACCESSION OF GEORGE III. UK LOC/G TOP/EX COLONIAL LEAD PARTIC REV CHOOSE REPRESENT GOV/REL PERSON SOVEREIGN...GOV/COMP 18 PARLIAMENT. PAGE 115 H2309
PARL/PROC LEGIS NAT/G POL/PAR

B65
O'CONNELL M.R.,IRISH POLITICS AND SOCIAL CONFLICT IN THE AGE OF THE AMERICAN REVOLUTION. FRANCE IRELAND MOD/EUR STRATA SECT LEGIS DIPLOM INT/TRADE DOMIN REV WAR...BIBLIOG 18 PARLIAMENT. PAGE 119 H2387
CATHISM ATTIT NAT/G DELIB/GP

B65
OGILVY-WEBB M.,THE GOVERNMENT EXPLAINS: A STUDY OF THE INFORMATION SERVICES. UK DELIB/GP LEGIS WORKER BUDGET DIPLOM 20. PAGE 121 H2409
EDU/PROP ATTIT NAT/G ADMIN

B65
PEASLEE A.J.,CONSTITUTIONS OF NATIONS* THIRD REVISED EDITION (VOLUME I* AFRICA). LAW EX/STRUC LEGIS TOP/EX LEGIT CT/SYS ROUTINE ORD/FREE PWR SOVEREIGN...CON/ANAL CHARTS. PAGE 124 H2481
AFR CHOOSE CONSTN NAT/G

B65
QURESHI I.H.,THE STRUGGLE FOR PAKISTAN. INDIA PAKISTAN UK CULTURE LEGIS DIPLOM EDU/PROP COLONIAL ATTIT SOVEREIGN 19/20 MUSLIM. PAGE 129 H2576
GP/REL RACE/REL WAR SECT

B65
SHARMA S.A.,PARLIAMENTARY GOVERNMENT IN INDIA. INDIA FINAN LOC/G PROVS DELIB/GP PLAN ADMIN CT/SYS FEDERAL...JURID 20. PAGE 142 H2849
NAT/G CONSTN PARL/PROC LEGIS

S65
PLISCHKE E.,"INTEGRATING BERLIN AND THE FEDERAL REPUBLIC OF GERMANY." EUR+WWI GERMANY/W LEGIS TEC/DEV DOMIN ORD/FREE PWR...JURID 20 BERLIN. PAGE 126 H2528
DIPLOM NAT/G MUNIC

S65
RUBINSTEIN A.Z.,"YUGOSLAVIA'S OPENING SOCIETY." COM USSR INTELL NAT/G LEGIS TOP/EX LEGIT CT/SYS RIGID/FLEX ALL/VALS SOCISM...HUM TIME/SEQ TREND 20. PAGE 135 H2708
CONSTN EX/STRUC YUGOSLAVIA

C65
BORTOLI G.,"SOCIOLOGIE DU REFERENDUM DANS LA FRANCE MODERNE." FRANCE CONSTN NAT/G EDU/PROP SUFF ATTIT ORD/FREE...POLICY DECISION SOC CHARTS 20. PAGE 19 H0378
BIBLIOG LEGIS SOCIETY PWR

B66
ADAMS J.C.,THE GOVERNMENT OF REPUBLICAN ITALY (2ND ED.). ITALY LOC/G POL/PAR DELIB/GP LEGIS WORKER ADMIN CT/SYS FASCISM...CHARTS BIBLIOG 20 PARLIAMENT. PAGE 3 H0064
NAT/G CHOOSE EX/STRUC CONSTN

B66
ANDERSON S.V.,CANADIAN OMBUDSMAN PROPOSALS. CANADA LEGIS DEBATE PARL/PROC...MAJORIT JURID TIME/SEQ IDEA/COMP 20 OMBUDSMAN PARLIAMENT. PAGE 7 H0133
NAT/G CREATE ADMIN POL/PAR

B66
ARCHER P.,FREEDOM AT STAKE. UK LAW NAT/G LEGIS JUDGE CRIME MORAL...CONCPT 20 CIVIL/LIB. PAGE 8 H0159
ORD/FREE NAT/COMP POLICY

B66
CHAPMAN B.,THE PROFESSION OF GOVERNMENT: THE PUBLIC SERVICE IN EUROPE. CONSTN NAT/G POL/PAR EX/STRUC LEGIS TOP/EX PROB/SOLV DEBATE EXEC PARL/PROC PARTIC 20. PAGE 29 H0581
BIBLIOG ADMIN EUR+WWI GOV/COMP

B66
DAHL R.A.,POLITICAL OPPOSITIONS IN WESTERN DEMOCRACIES. EUR+WWI USA+45 USA-45 SOCIETY STRATA ECO/DEV NAT/G LEGIS REPRESENT...TREND NAT/COMP ANTHOL 20. PAGE 37 H0732
POL/PAR CHOOSE PARTIC PLURISM

B66
FINER S.E.,ANONYMOUS EMPIRE: STUDY OF THE LOBBY IN GREAT BRITAIN. UK CONSTN LABOR POL/PAR SECT DOMIN EDU/PROP PRESS CHOOSE...CONCPT CHARTS 20 PARLIAMENT. PAGE 50 H1004
LOBBY NAT/G LEGIS PWR

B66
FRANK E.,LAWMAKERS IN A CHANGING WORLD. FRANCE UK USSR WOR+45 PARTIC EFFICIENCY ROLE ALL/IDEOS ...CHARTS ANTHOL PARLIAMENT 20 UN COLD/WAR. PAGE 52 H1049
GOV/COMP LEGIS NAT/G DIPLOM

B66
FRIED R.C.,COMPARATIVE POLITICAL INSTITUTIONS. USSR EX/STRUC FORCES LEGIS JUDGE CONTROL REPRESENT ALL/IDEOS 20 CONGRESS BUREAUCRCY. PAGE 53 H1062
NAT/G PWR EFFICIENCY GOV/COMP

B66
GHOSH P.K.,THE CONSTITUTION OF INDIA: HOW IT HAS BEEN FRAMED. INDIA LOC/G DELIB/GP EX/STRUC PROB/SOLV BUDGET INT/TRADE CT/SYS CHOOSE...LING 20. PAGE 56 H1121
CONSTN NAT/G LEGIS FEDERAL

B66
GUNN G.E.,THE POLITICAL HISTORY OF NEWFOUNDLAND
POL/PAR

1832-1864. CANADA FINAN LEGIS CHOOSE REPRESENT ...CHARTS 19. PAGE 62 H1252 NAT/G CONSTN

B66
HIDAYATULLAH M.,DEMOCRACY IN INDIA AND THE JUDICIAL PROCESS. INDIA EX/STRUC LEGIS LEAD GOV/REL ATTIT ORD/FREE...MAJORIT CONCPT 20 NEHRU/J. PAGE 71 H1415 NAT/G CT/SYS CONSTN JURID

B66
HOLDSWORTH W.S.,A HISTORY OF ENGLISH LAW; THE CENTURIES OF SETTLEMENT AND REFORM (VOL. XVI). UK LOC/G NAT/G EX/STRUC LEGIS CT/SYS LEAD ATTIT ...POLICY DECISION JURID IDEA/COMP 18 PARLIAMENT. PAGE 73 H1454 BIOG PERSON PROF/ORG LAW

B66
INSTITUTE COMP STUDY POL SYS,DOMINICAN REPUBLIC ELECTION FACT BOOK. DOMIN/REP LAW LEGIS REPRESENT ...JURID CHARTS 20. PAGE 77 H1536 SUFF CHOOSE POL/PAR NAT/G

B66
INTERPARLIAMENTARY UNION,PARLIAMENTS: COMPARATIVE STUDY ON STRUCTURE AND FUNCTIONING OF REPRESENTATIVE INSTITUTIONS IN FIFTY-FIVE COUNTRIES. WOR+45 POL/PAR DELIB/GP BUDGET ADMIN CONTROL CHOOSE. PAGE 78 H1560 PARL/PROC LEGIS GOV/COMP EX/STRUC

B66
JOHNSON N.,PARLIAMENT AND ADMINISTRATION: THE ESTIMATES COMMITTEE 1945-65. FUT UK NAT/G EX/STRUC PLAN BUDGET ORD/FREE...T 20 PARLIAMENT HOUSE/CMNS. PAGE 81 H1625 LEGIS ADMIN FINAN DELIB/GP

B66
LEROY P.,L'ORGANIZATION CONSTITUTIONNELLE ET LES CRISES. FRANCE NAT/G ADJUD CONTROL PARL/PROC WAR ...POLICY BIBLIOG 20. PAGE 95 H1892 CONSTN PWR EXEC LEGIS

B66
LONDON DAILY TELEGRAPH,ELECTION '66: GALLUP ANALYSIS OF THE VOTING RESULTS. UK LEGIS COMPUTER ATTIT...QU SAMP CHARTS 20 LABOR/PAR HOUSE/CMNS. PAGE 98 H1959 STAT CHOOSE REPRESENT POL/PAR

B66
LOVEDAY P.,PARLIAMENT FACTIONS AND PARTIES: THE FIRST THIRTY YEARS OF RESPONSIBLE GOVERNMENT IN NEW SOUTH WALES, 1856-1889. PROVS LEAD PARL/PROC PARTIC GP/REL INGP/REL MAJORITY PWR...GP/COMP 19 AUSTRAL. PAGE 99 H1970 POL/PAR ELITES NAT/G LEGIS

B66
NEUMANN R.G.,THE GOVERNMENT OF THE GERMAN FEDERAL REPUBLIC. EUR+WWI GERMANY/W LOC/G EX/STRUC LEGIS CT/SYS INGP/REL PWR...BIBLIOG 20 ADENAUER/K. PAGE 117 H2336 NAT/G POL/PAR DIPLOM CONSTN

B66
POLE J.R.,POLITICAL REPRESENTATION IN ENGLAND AND THE ORIGINS OF THE AMERICAN REPUBLIC. UK USA-45 CONSTN ELITES NAT/G POL/PAR LEGIS PARL/PROC ...MAJORIT 17/19. PAGE 127 H2534 REPRESENT GOV/COMP

B66
ROSS A.M.,INDUSTRIAL RELATIONS AND ECONOMIC DEVELOPMENT. POL/PAR LEGIS WORKER BARGAIN PRICE EXEC LOBBY INCOME PWR...DECISION ANTHOL BIBLIOG 20. PAGE 134 H2686 ECO/UNDEV LABOR NAT/G GP/REL

B66
SAINDERICHIN P.,HISTORIE SECRETE D'UNE ELECTION, DECEMBER 5-19, 1965. FRANCE NAT/G DELIB/GP LEGIS PLAN EDU/PROP TV SOCISM...MARXIST 20 DEGAULLE/C. PAGE 137 H2731 CHOOSE CHIEF PROB/SOLV POL/PAR

B66
SHARMA B.M.,THE REPUBLIC OF INDIA; CONSTITUTION AND GOVERNMENT. INDIA POL/PAR LEGIS EFFICIENCY ...TIME/SEQ GOV/COMP 20. PAGE 142 H2846 PROVS NAT/G CONSTN

B66
TIVEY L.J.,NATIONALISATION IN BRITISH INDUSTRY. UK LEGIS PARL/PROC GP/REL OWN ATTIT SOCISM 20. PAGE 156 H3109 NAT/G INDUS CONTROL LG/CO

B66
WUEST J.J.,NEW SOURCE BOOK IN MAJOR EUROPEAN GOVERNMENTS. CHRIST-17C EUR+WWI FRANCE GERMANY ITALY MOD/EUR UK USSR LOC/G POL/PAR CHIEF EX/STRUC CHOOSE CONSERVE MARXISM...JURID T 13/20. PAGE 171 H3425 NAT/G CONSTN LEGIS

S66
DETTER I.,"THE PROBLEM OF UNEQUAL TREATIES." CONSTN NAT/G LEGIS COLONIAL COERCE PWR...GEOG UN TIME TREATY. PAGE 40 H0796 SOVEREIGN DOMIN INT/LAW ECO/UNDEV

S66
MATTHEWS D.G.,"PRELUDE-COUP D'ETAT-MILITARY GOVERNMENT: A BIBLIOGRAPHICAL AND RESEARCH GUIDE TO NIGERIAN POL AND GOVT, JAN, 1965-66." AFR NIGER LAW CONSTN POL/PAR LEGIS CIVMIL/REL GOV/REL...STAT 20. PAGE 105 H2096 BIBLIOG NAT/G ADMIN CHOOSE

B67
ANDERSON S.V.,THE NORDIC COUNCIL: A STUDY OF SCANDINAVIAN REGIONALISM. DENMARK FINLAND ICELAND NORWAY SWEDEN MARKET NAT/G VOL/ASSN CONSULT PARL/PROC ATTIT...TIME/SEQ BIBLIOG 20. PAGE 7 H0134 INT/ORG REGION DIPLOM LEGIS

B67
BROWN L.N.,FRENCH ADMINISTRATIVE LAW. FRANCE UK CONSTN NAT/G LEGIS DOMIN CONTROL EXEC PARL/PROC PWR ...JURID METH/COMP GEN/METH. PAGE 22 H0447 EX/STRUC LAW IDEA/COMP CT/SYS

B67
GELLHORN W.,OMBUDSMEN AND OTHERS: CITIZENS' PROTECTORS IN NINE COUNTRIES. WOR+45 LAW CONSTN LEGIS INSPECT ADJUD ADMIN CONTROL CT/SYS CHOOSE PERS/REL...STAT CHARTS 20. PAGE 55 H1109 NAT/COMP REPRESENT INGP/REL PROB/SOLV

B67
KORNBERG A.,CANADIAN LEGISLATIVE BEHAVIOR: A STUDY OF THE 25TH PARLIAMENT. CANADA NAT/G POL/PAR PARL/PROC CHOOSE INGP/REL ADJUST ANOMIE RIGID/FLEX ...SOC STAND/INT CHARTS SOC/EXP 20 PARLIAMENT. PAGE 88 H1756 ATTIT LEGIS ROLE

B67
MILNE R.S.,GOVERNMENT AND POLITICS IN MALAYSIA. INDONESIA MALAYSIA LOC/G EX/STRUC FORCES DIPLOM GP/REL 20 SINGAPORE. PAGE 111 H2217 NAT/G LEGIS ADMIN

B67
MORRIS A.J.A.,PARLIAMENTARY DEMOCRACY IN THE NINETEENTH CENTURY. UK INDUS LOC/G NAT/G POL/PAR CONSULT LEGIS INT/TRADE ADMIN CHOOSE SUFF SOVEREIGN 19 PARLIAMENT. PAGE 113 H2261 TIME/SEQ CONSTN PARL/PROC POPULISM

B67
SCHWARTZ B.,THE ROOTS OF FREEDOM: A CONSTITUTIONAL HISTORY OF ENGLAND. UK LAW POL/PAR DELIB/GP LEGIS REV REPRESENT...JURID BIBLIOG/A 13/20. PAGE 140 H2809 CONSTN PARL/PROC NAT/G

B67
WARREN S.,THE AMERICAN PRESIDENT. POL/PAR FORCES LEGIS DIPLOM ECO/TAC ADMIN EXEC PWR...ANTHOL 18/20 ROOSEVLT/F KENNEDY/JF JOHNSON/LB TRUMAN/HS WILSON/W. PAGE 165 H3312 CHIEF LEAD NAT/G CONSTN

L67
"A PROPOS DES INCITATIONS FINANCIERES AUX GROUPEMENTS DES COMMUNES: ESSAI D'INTERPRETATION." FRANCE NAT/G LEGIS ADMIN GOV/REL CENTRAL 20. PAGE 3 H0051 LOC/G ECO/TAC APPORT ADJUD

L67
WILBER L.A.,"THE GOVERNMENTAL STRUCTURE OF MISSISSIPPI: ITS STRENGTHS AND WEAKNESSES." AGRI LOC/G SCHOOL EX/STRUC LEGIS TOP/EX BUDGET CT/SYS APPORT RACE/REL...GOV/COMP 20 MISSISSIPP. PAGE 168 H3359 CONSTN PROVS STAT CON/ANAL

S67
ADNITT F.W.,"THE RISE OF ENGLISH RADICALISM -- PART 2." UK NAT/G WORKER INCOME WEALTH...BIOG 19 PARLIAMENT. PAGE 4 H0071 LEGIS LOBBY

S67
ADOKO A.,"THE CONSTITUTION OF UGANDA." AFR UGANDA LOC/G CHIEF FORCES LEGIS ADJUD EXEC CHOOSE NAT/LISM ...IDEA/COMP 20. PAGE 4 H0072 NAT/G CONSTN ORD/FREE LAW

S67
BAIKALOV A.,"EMERGENCY LEGISLATION IN WEST GERMANY." GERMANY/W LABOR NAT/G POL/PAR SANCTION ...MARXIST 20. PAGE 10 H0199 LAW TOTALISM LEGIS PARL/PROC

S67
BRADLEY A.W.,"CONSTITUTION-MAKING IN UGANDA." UGANDA LAW CHIEF DELIB/GP LEGIS ADMIN EXEC PARL/PROC RACE/REL ORD/FREE...GOV/COMP 20. PAGE 20 H0397 NAT/G CREATE CONSTN FEDERAL

S67
CUMMINS L.,"THE FORMULATION OF THE "PLATT" AMENDMENT." CUBA L/A+17C NAT/G DELIB/GP CONFER ...POLICY 20. PAGE 36 H0720 DIPLOM INT/LAW LEGIS

S67
DOERN G.B.,"THE ROYAL COMMISSIONS IN THE GENERAL POLICY PROCESS AND IN FEDERAL-PROVINCIAL RELATIONS." CANADA CONSTN ACADEM PROVS CONSULT DELIB/GP LEGIS ACT/RES PROB/SOLV CONFER CONTROL EFFICIENCY...METH/COMP 20 SENATE ROYAL/COMM. PAGE 42 H0832 R+D EX/STRUC GOV/REL NAT/G

S67
FUSARO A.,"THE EFFECT OF PROPORTIONAL REPRESENTATION ON VOTING IN THE AUSTRALIAN SENATE." S/ASIA CONSTN POL/PAR CONTROL GP/REL PWR...CHARTS 20 AUSTRAL HOUSE/REP SENATE. PAGE 54 H1083 LEGIS CHOOSE REPRESENT NAT/G

S67
GREGORY R.,"THE MINISTER'S LINE: OR, THE M4 COMES TO BERKSHIRE. PART I." UK CONSTN DIST/IND LEGIS TOP/EX PLAN ADJUD...GEOG 20. PAGE 60 H1210 DECISION CONSTRUC NAT/G DELIB/GP

S67
HANSON A.H.,"INDIA AFTER THE ELECTIONS." INDIA ECO/UNDEV LEGIS TEC/DEV FOR/AID GP/REL FEDERAL ATTIT 20. PAGE 66 H1321 NAT/G POL/PAR REGION CENTRAL

S67
HARNON E.,"CRIMINAL PROCEDURE IN ISRAEL - SOME COMPARATIVE ASPECTS." ISRAEL USA+45 CLIENT EX/STRUC LEGIS...JURID NAT/COMP 20. PAGE 67 H1336 ADJUD CONSTN CT/SYS CRIME

S67
INDER S.,"AFTER THE CORONATION." CONSTN ECO/UNDEV EX/STRUC LEGIS INT/TRADE CONTROL SOVEREIGN ...TIME/SEQ 20 TONGA COMMONWLTH INAUGURATE. PAGE 76 H1527 — CHIEF NAT/G POLICY

S67
LEGRES A.,"LES FONCTIONS D'UN PARLEMENT MODERNE." FRANCE DEBATE PARL/PROC SANCTION ATTIT PWR 20 PARLIAMENT. PAGE 93 H1860 — NAT/G LAW LEGIS CHOOSE

S67
LEHMBRUCH G.,"WAHLREFORM UND POLITISCHES SYSTEM." NETHERLAND NAT/G LEGIS PARL/PROC...SOC 20. PAGE 93 H1864 — CHOOSE POL/PAR METH/CNCPT GP/COMP

S67
MARWICK A.,"THE LABOUR PARTY AND THE WELFARE STATE IN BRITAIN, 19001948." UK SOCIETY STRUCT ECO/DEV WORKER CREATE PRICE CHOOSE WEALTH NEW/LIB SOCISM ...POLICY HEAL 20 PARLIAMENT LABOR/PAR. PAGE 104 H2074 — POL/PAR RECEIVE LEGIS NAT/G

S67
MAYANJA A.,"THE GOVERNMENT'S PROPOSALS ON THE NEW CONSTITUTION." AFR UGANDA LAW CHIEF LEGIS ADJUD REPRESENT FEDERAL PWR 20. PAGE 105 H2105 — CONSTN CONFER ORD/FREE NAT/G

S67
NEALE R.S.,"WORKING CLASS WOMEN AND WOMEN'S SUFFRAGE." UK LAW CONSTN LABOR NAT/G DELIB/GP LEGIS WORKER PAY PARTIC CHOOSE 19 FEMALE/SEX. PAGE 116 H2326 — STRATA SEX SUFF DISCRIM

S67
PAI G.A.,"TAXATION AND PLANNING IN INDIA: A BIRDS-EYE VIEW." INDIA ELITES NAT/G LEGIS BUDGET CONTROL LOBBY INCOME...STAT CHARTS 20. PAGE 122 H2443 — TAX PLAN WEALTH STRATA

S67
SIPPEL D.,"INDIENS UNSICHERE ZUKUNFT." INDIA CULTURE ACADEM POL/PAR LEGIS COLONIAL CHOOSE SOVEREIGN...JURID 20. PAGE 144 H2888 — SOCIETY STRUCT ECO/UNDEV NAT/G

S67
STRAFFORD P.,"FRENCH ELECTIONS." FRANCE NAT/G CHIEF LEGIS BAL/PWR ECO/TAC PARL/PROC PARTIC ATTIT 20. PAGE 150 H2993 — POL/PAR SOCISM CENTRAL MARXISM

S67
WHITE W.L.,"THE TREASURY BOARD AND PARLIAMENT." CANADA CONSTN CONSULT LEGIS LEAD PARL/PROC GP/REL ...DECISION 20. PAGE 167 H3351 — FINAN DELIB/GP NAT/G ADMIN

S67
WILLIAMS F.R.A.,"FUNDAMENTAL RIGHTS AND THE PROSPECT FOR DEMOCRACY IN NIGERIA." FUT NIGERIA SOCIETY ECO/UNDEV LEGIS ADJUD CHOOSE 20. PAGE 168 H3366 — CONSTN LAW ORD/FREE NAT/G

B73
STEPHEN J.F.,LIBERTY, EQUALITY, FRATERNITY. UNIV SOCIETY NAT/G LEGIS DOMIN AGREE PERS/REL ATTIT MORAL...IDEA/COMP 19 MILL/JS. PAGE 149 H2978 — ORD/FREE CONCPT COERCE SECT

B75
MAINE H.S.,LECTURES ON THE EARLY HISTORY OF INSTITUTIONS. IRELAND UK CONSTN ELITES STRUCT FAM KIN CHIEF LEGIS CT/SYS OWN SOVEREIGN...CONCPT 16 BENTHAM/J BREHON ROMAN/LAW. PAGE 101 H2021 — CULTURE LAW INGP/REL

B75
NEWMAN J.H.,A LETTER ADDRESSED TO THE DUKE OF NORFOLK ON THE OCCASION OF MR. GLADSTONE'S RECENT EXPOSTULATION. NAT/G SECT CHIEF LEGIS CONTROL LEAD GP/REL SUPEGO SOC/INTEG WORSHIP 19 ENGLAND. PAGE 117 H2346 — POLICY DOMIN SOVEREIGN CATHISM

B83
AMOS S.,THE SCIENCE OF POLITICS. MOD/EUR CONSTN LOC/G NAT/G EX/STRUC LEGIS DIPLOM...METH/COMP 19/20. PAGE 6 H0124 — NEW/IDEA PHIL/SCI CONCPT

B85
BLUNTSCHLI J.K.,THE THEORY OF THE STATE. GERMANY CONSTN INGP/REL NAT/LISM PERSON SOVEREIGN CONSERVE ...SOC. PAGE 18 H0362 — CONCPT LEGIS NAT/G

B87
ADAMS J.,A DEFENSE OF THE CONSTITUTIONS OF GOVERNMENT OF THE UNITED STATES OF AMERICA. USA-45 STRATA CHIEF EX/STRUC LEGIS CT/SYS CONSERVE POPULISM...CONCPT CON/ANAL GOV/COMP. PAGE 3 H0063 — CONSTN BAL/PWR PWR NAT/G

B91
SIDGWICK H.,THE ELEMENTS OF POLITICS. LOC/G NAT/G LEGIS DIPLOM ADJUD CONTROL EXEC PARL/PROC REPRESENT GOV/REL SOVEREIGN ALL/IDEOS 19 MILL/JS BENTHAM/J. PAGE 143 H2868 — POLICY LAW CONCPT

B96
ESMEIN A.,ELEMENTS DE DROIT CONSTITUTIONNEL. FRANCE UK CHIEF EX/STRUC LEGIS ADJUD CT/SYS PARL/PROC REV GOV/REL ORD/FREE...JURID METH/COMP 18/19. PAGE 47 H0940 — LAW CONSTN NAT/G CONCPT

B96
LOWELL A.L.,GOVERNMENTS AND PARTIES IN CONTINENTAL EUROPE (VOL. I). MOD/EUR LOC/G NAT/G SECT CHIEF LEGIS PARL/PROC GOV/REL...POLICY 19. PAGE 99 H1973 — POL/PAR GOV/COMP CONSTN EX/STRUC

B96
LOWELL A.L.,GOVERNMENTS AND PARTIES IN CONTINENTAL EUROPE, VOL. II. AUSTRIA GERMANY HUNGARY MOD/EUR SWITZERLND SOCIETY EX/STRUC LEGIS DIPLOM AGREE LEAD PARL/PROC PWR...POLICY 19. PAGE 99 H1974 — POL/PAR NAT/G GOV/REL ELITES

B98
POLLOCK F.,THE HISTORY OF ENGLISH LAW BEFORE THE TIME OF EDWARD I (2 VOLS, 2ND ED.). UK CULTURE LOC/G LEGIS LICENSE AGREE CONTROL CT/SYS SANCTION CRIME...TIME/SEQ 13 COMMON/LAW CANON/LAW. PAGE 127 H2538 — LAW ADJUD JURID

B99
LECKY W.E.H.,DEMOCRACY AND LIBERTY (2 VOLS.). LAW CONSTN STRATA POL/PAR SECT WORKER DIPLOM ADJUD REPRESENT NAT/LISM CONSERVE. PAGE 93 H1851 — LEGIS NAT/G POPULISM ORD/FREE

LEGISLATION....SEE CONGRESS, LEGIS, SENATE, HOUSE/REP

LEGISLATIVE APPORTIONMENT....SEE APPORT

LEGISLATURES....SEE LEGIS

LEGIT....LEGITIMACY

B00
MAINE H.S.,ANCIENT LAW. MEDIT-7 CULTURE SOCIETY KIN SECT LEGIS LEGIT ROUTINE...JURID HIST/WRIT CON/ANAL TOT/POP VAL/FREE. PAGE 101 H2020 — FAM LAW

B04
DANTE ALIGHIERI,DE MONARCHIA (CA .1310). CHRIST-17C ITALY DOMIN LEGIT ATTIT PWR...CATH CONCPT TIME/SEQ. PAGE 37 H0741 — SECT NAT/G SOVEREIGN

B17
DE MAISTRE J.,DU PAPE (1817). FRANCE LAW SOCIETY SECT DOMIN REV HAPPINESS PWR SOVEREIGN 18/19 PROTESTANT. PAGE 38 H0761 — CATH CHIEF LEGIT NAT/G

N19
MAO TSE-TUNG,ON SOME IMPORTANT PROBLEMS OF THE PARTY'S PRESENT POLICY. CHINA/COM CONSTN ELITES INTELL AGRI DOMIN EDU/PROP REV REPRESENT GP/REL OWN PEACE ORD/FREE 20 COM/PARTY. PAGE 102 H2044 — POLICY NAT/G CHIEF LEGIT

N19
TEMPLE W.,AN ESSAY UPON THE ORIGINAL AND NATURE OF GOVERNMENT (PAMPHLET). CHRIST-17C UK FAM LOC/G LEGIT ORD/FREE CONSERVE 17. PAGE 153 H3060 — NAT/G CONCPT PWR SOCIETY

B20
HALDANE R.B.,BEFORE THE WAR. MOD/EUR SOCIETY INT/ORG NAT/G DELIB/GP PLAN DOMIN EDU/PROP LEGIT ADMIN COERCE ATTIT DRIVE MORAL ORD/FREE PWR...SOC CONCPT SELF/OBS RECORD BIOG TIME/SEQ. PAGE 64 H1282 — POLICY DIPLOM UK

B23
FRANK T.,A HISTORY OF ROME. MEDIT-7 INTELL SOCIETY LOC/G NAT/G POL/PAR FORCES LEGIS DOMIN LEGIT ALL/VALS...POLICY CONCPT TIME/SEQ GEN/LAWS ROM/EMP ROM/EMP. PAGE 53 H1050 — EXEC STRUCT ELITES

B26
HOCKING W.E.,PRESENT STATUS OF THE PHILOSOPHY OF LAW AND OF RIGHTS. UNIV CULTURE INTELL SOCIETY NAT/G CREATE LEGIT SANCTION ALL/VALS SOC/INTEG 18/20. PAGE 72 H1442 — JURID PHIL/SCI ORD/FREE

B26
MALINOWSKI B.,CRIME AND CUSTOM IN SAVAGE SOCIETY. SOCIETY FAM SECT LEGIT SANCTION MARRIAGE MYSTISM ...PSY SOC 19/20 MELANESIA CANON/LAW. PAGE 102 H2030 — LAW CULTURE CRIME ADJUD

B27
FLOURNOY F.,PARLIAMENT AND WAR. MOD/EUR UK NAT/G FORCES LEGIS TOP/EX DIPLOM LEGIT DEBATE ATTIT RIGID/FLEX PWR...DECISION TIME/SEQ PARLIAMENT 19/20. PAGE 52 H1032 — COERCE WAR

B28
CORBETT P.E.,CANADA AND WORLD POLITICS. LAW CULTURE SOCIETY STRUCT MARKET INT/ORG FORCES ACT/RES PLAN ECO/TAC LEGIT ORD/FREE PWR RESPECT...SOC CONCPT TIME/SEQ TREND CMN/WLTH 20 LEAGUE/NAT. PAGE 33 H0662 — NAT/G CANADA

B28
MARSILIUS/PADUA,DEFENSOR PACIS (1324). CHRIST-17C CONSTN NAT/G DIPLOM DOMIN LEGIT CONTROL WAR PEACE ORD/FREE SOVEREIGN POPULISM 14 POPE. PAGE 103 H2059 — CATH SECT GEN/LAWS

B28
YANG KUNG-SUN,THE BOOK OF LORD SHANG. LAW ECO/UNDEV LOC/G NAT/G NEIGH PLAN ECO/TAC LEGIT ATTIT SKILL ...CONCPT CON/ANAL WORK TOT/POP. PAGE 172 H3434 — ASIA JURID

B34
GONZALEZ PALENCIA A,ESTUDIO HISTORICO SOBRE LA CENSURA GUBERNATIVA EN ESPANA 1800-1833. NAT/G COERCE INGP/REL ATTIT AUTHORIT KNOWL...POLICY JURID — LEGIT EDU/PROP PRESS

19. PAGE 58 H1165 CONTROL

B35
MARRIOTT J.A.,DICTATORSHIP AND DEMOCRACY. GERMANY GREECE UK CHIEF DIPLOM DOMIN LEGIT PEACE ORD/FREE CONSERVE...TREND ROME HITLER/A. PAGE 103 H2057
TOTALISM POPULISM PLURIST NAT/G

B35
TAKEUCHI T.,WAR AND DIPLOMACY IN THE JAPANESE EMPIRE. ASIA ELITES STRATA NAT/G SECT LEGIS ACT/RES PLAN LEGIT PARL/PROC ROUTINE WAR...MGT BIOG CHINJAP TOT/POP 19/20 CHINJAP. PAGE 152 H3038
EXEC STRUCT

L37
NICOLSON H.,"THE MEANING OF PRESTIGE." EUR+WWI MOD/EUR UK CULTURE SOCIETY NAT/G DIPLOM DOMIN LEGIT ATTIT DRIVE PWR...METH/CNCPT RECORD TIME/SEQ GEN/METH CMN/WLTH TOT/POP 20. PAGE 118 H2351
CONCPT STERTYP

B38
MCNAIR A.D.,THE LAW OF TREATIES: BRITISH PRACTICE AND OPINIONS. UK CREATE DIPLOM LEGIT WRITING ADJUD WAR...INT/LAW JURID TREATY. PAGE 107 H2144
AGREE LAW CT/SYS NAT/G

B39
BENES E.,DEMOCRACY TODAY AND TOMORROW. EUR+WWI SOCIETY ECO/DEV DELIB/GP ECO/TAC REGION ATTIT PWR FASCISM...CONCPT LEAGUE/NAT 20. PAGE 14 H0281
NAT/G LEGIT NAT/LISM

B40
HOBBES T.,BEHEMOTH (1668). UK CONSTN SECT DOMIN LEGIT UTIL ORD/FREE CATHISM...POLICY CONCPT GEN/LAWS 17 CHARLES/I CROMWELL/O PROTESTANT. PAGE 71 H1433
REV NAT/G CHIEF

B40
JORDAN W.K.,THE DEVELOPMENT OF RELIGIOUS TOLERATION IN ENGLAND. CHRIST-17C CULTURE SOCIETY LEGIT ATTIT RESPECT...POLICY CONCPT RECORD TIME/SEQ STERTYP GEN/LAWS TOT/POP 16/17. PAGE 82 H1635
SECT UK

B40
TONNIES F.,FUNDAMENTAL CONCEPTS OF SOCIOLOGY (1887) (TRANS. BY C. LOOMIS). LAW STRATA STRUCT FAM MUNIC NAT/G DOMIN LEGIT SANCTION COERCE CRIME PERSON 19. PAGE 156 H3115
CULTURE SOCIETY GEN/LAWS SOC

B42
FEFFERO G.,THE PRINCIPLES OF POWER (TRANS. BY T. JAECKEL). MOD/EUR CONSTN NAT/G CHIEF CONTROL REV WAR ORD/FREE CONSERVE FASCISM POPULISM...GEN/LAWS 18/20 EUROPE. PAGE 49 H0980
PWR LEGIT TRADIT ELITES

B42
LA BOETIE E.,ANTI-DICTATOR (1548) (TRANS. BY H. KUNZ). CONSTN NAT/G CHIEF DOMIN LEGIT CONTROL POPULISM. PAGE 90 H1790
PWR ORD/FREE TOTALISM GEN/LAWS

B43
LENIN V.I.,LEFT WING COMMUNISM: AN INFANTILE DISORDER (1920). GERMANY MOD/EUR USSR STRUCT CHIEF DOMIN EDU/PROP LEGIT LEAD REPRESENT POPULISM ...METH/COMP 19 LENIN/VI COM/PARTY MENSHEVIK. PAGE 94 H1879
COM MARXISM NAT/G REV

B43
MARITAIN J.,THE RIGHTS OF MAN AND NATURAL LAW. CONSTN NAT/G DOMIN LEGIT INGP/REL TOTALISM MORAL POPULISM WORSHIP 19/20 CIVIL/LIB CHURCH/STA NATURL/LAW. PAGE 103 H2051
PLURIST ORD/FREE GEN/LAWS

C43
BENTHAM J.,"ON THE LIBERTY OF THE PRESS, AND PUBLIC DISCUSSION" IN J. BOWRING, ED., THE WORKS OF JEREMY BENTHAM." SPAIN UK LAW ELITES NAT/G LEGIS INSPECT LEGIT WRITING CONTROL PRIVIL TOTALISM AUTHORIT ...TRADIT 19 FREE/SPEE. PAGE 15 H0290
ORD/FREE PRESS CONFER CONSERVE

B44
GYORGY A.,GEOPOLITICS: THE NEW GERMAN SCIENCE. EUR+WWI GERMANY STRATA NAT/G PROVS DOMIN EDU/PROP ATTIT DRIVE FASCISM...GEOG NAZI 20. PAGE 63 H1261
PWR LEGIT WAR

B44
SUAREZ F.,A TREATISE ON LAWS AND GOD THE LAWGIVER (1612) IN SELECTIONS FROM THREE WORKS, VOL. II. FRANCE ITALY UK CULTURE NAT/G SECT CHIEF LEGIS DOMIN LEGIT CT/SYS ORD/FREE PWR WORSHIP 16/17. PAGE 150 H3004
LAW JURID GEN/LAWS CATH

C44
SUAREZ F.,"ON WAR" (1621) IN SELECTIONS FROM THREE WORKS, VOL. I." NAT/G SECT CHIEF DIPLOM LEGIT MORAL PWR...POLICY INT/LAW 17. PAGE 150 H3005
WAR REV ORD/FREE CATH

B46
MILL J.S.,ON LIBERTY. NAT/G LEGIT CONTROL PERS/REL PERCEPT...CONCPT 19. PAGE 110 H2206
ORD/FREE SOCIETY PERSON GEN/LAWS

B46
NICOLSON H.,THE CONGRESS OF VIENNA. MOD/EUR NAT/G FORCES BAL/PWR DOMIN LEGIT COERCE PERSON PWR ...RECORD TIME/SEQ STERTYP 19 CONG/VIENN. PAGE 118 H2353
CONCPT POLICY DIPLOM

B47
LOCKE J.,TWO TREATISES OF GOVERNMENT (1690). UK LAW SOCIETY LEGIS LEGIT AGREE REV OWN HEREDITY MORAL CONSERVE...POLICY MAJORIT 17 WILLIAM/3 NATURL/LAW.
CONCPT ORD/FREE NAT/G

PAGE 97 H1946 CONSEN

S48
ALMOND G.A.,"THE CHRISTIAN PARTIES OF WESTEN EUROPE." EUR+WWI NAT/G EDU/PROP LEGIT TOTALISM ORD/FREE PWR MARXISM...TREND CHARTS STERTYP GEN/LAWS COLD/WAR 20. PAGE 5 H0110
POL/PAR CATH SOCISM

B49
HAUSER R.,AUTORITAT UND MACHT. SOCIETY SECT PWR CATHISM...JURID CONCPT 16/20 PROTESTANT LUTHER/M CALVIN/J CHURCH/STA. PAGE 68 H1360
SOVEREIGN NAT/G LEGIT

B50
MACHIAVELLI N.,THE DISCOURSES (1516). NAT/G SECT FORCES DOMIN LEGIT CONTROL LEAD COERCE TOTALISM ORD/FREE. PAGE 100 H1995
PWR GEN/LAWS CHIEF

S51
NORTHROP F.S.C.,"ASIAN MENTALITY AND UNITED STATES FOREIGN POLICY." ASIA ISLAM USA+45 CULTURE SOCIETY SECT EDU/PROP LEGIT COERCE DRIVE MORAL ORD/FREE ...POLICY RELATIV TOT/POP 20. PAGE 119 H2376
S/ASIA ATTIT DIPLOM

C51
HAMMOND M.,"CITY-STATE AND WORLD STATE." CONSTN INTELL LOC/G LEGIT CENTRAL RATIONAL BIBLIOG. PAGE 65 H1308
NAT/G ATTIT REGION MEDIT-7

B52
LEYS W.,ETHICS FOR POLICY DECISIONS. INTELL NAT/G CONSULT PLAN DOMIN EDU/PROP LEGIT COERCE KNOWL MORAL PWR...HUM GEN/LAWS. PAGE 96 H1920
ACT/RES POLICY

B52
LOPEZ-AMO A.,LA MONARQUIA DE LA REFORMA SOCIAL. MOD/EUR SPAIN CONSTN NAT/G TASK EFFICIENCY CONSERVE ...ANARCH TRADIT SOC CONCPT IDEA/COMP 19/20. PAGE 98 H1967
MARXISM REV LEGIT ORD/FREE

B52
WALTERS F.P.,A HISTORY OF THE LEAGUE OF NATIONS. EUR+WWI CONSTN NAT/G LEGIS TOP/EX ACT/RES PLAN EDU/PROP LEGIT ROUTINE ATTIT...TREND LEAGUE/NAT 20 CHINJAP. PAGE 165 H3297
INT/ORG TIME/SEQ NAT/LISM

B53
MEYER P.,THE JEWS IN THE SOVIET SATELLITES. CZECHOSLVK POLAND SOCIETY STRATA NAT/G BAL/PWR ECO/TAC EDU/PROP LEGIT ADMIN COERCE ATTIT DISPL PERCEPT HEALTH PWR RESPECT WEALTH...METH/CNCPT JEWS VAL/FREE NAZI 20. PAGE 110 H2192
COM SECT TOTALISM USSR

B53
NELSON G.R.,FREEDOM AND WELFARE: SOCIAL PATTERNS IN THE NORTHERN COUNTRIES OF EUROPE. EUR+WWI ECO/DEV NAT/G EDU/PROP LEGIT HEALTH ORD/FREE SKILL WEALTH ...STAT AUD/VIS SCANDINAV WORK TOT/POP 20. PAGE 116 H2329
PLAN ECO/TAC

B54
FRIEDRICH C.J.,TOTALITARIAN DICTATORSHIP AND AUTOCRACY. COM EUR+WWI GERMANY ITALY USSR INTELL ECO/DEV NAT/G POL/PAR FORCES TOP/EX ECO/TAC EDU/PROP LEGIT COERCE ATTIT ORD/FREE PWR FASCISM ...CONCPT TIME/SEQ GEN/LAWS NAZI 20. PAGE 53 H1068
SOCIETY DOMIN TOTALISM

L54
FURNISS E.S.,"WEAKNESSES IN FRENCH FOREIGN POLICY-MAKING." EUR+WWI LEGIS LEGIT EXEC ATTIT RIGID/FLEX ORD/FREE...SOC CONCPT METH/CNCPT OBS 20. PAGE 54 H1078
NAT/G STRUCT DIPLOM FRANCE

B55
APTER D.E.,THE GOLD COAST IN TRANSITION. FUT CONSTN CULTURE SOCIETY ECO/UNDEV FAM KIN LOC/G NAT/G POL/PAR LEGIS TOP/EX EDU/PROP LEGIT ADMIN ATTIT PERSON PWR...CONCPT STAT INT CENSUS TOT/POP VAL/FREE. PAGE 7 H0149
AFR SOVEREIGN

B56
CARRIL B.,PROBLEMAS DE LA REVOLUCION Y LA DEMOCRACIA. CONSTN FORCES DOMIN CONTROL TOTALISM PWR 20. PAGE 27 H0539
REV ORD/FREE LEGIT NAT/G

B56
CEPEDA U.A.,EN TORNO AL CONCEPTO DEL ESTADO EN LOS REYES CATHOLICOS. SPAIN SOCIETY STRUCT SECT LEGIT WAR ATTIT WORSHIP 15/17. PAGE 28 H0569
NAT/G PHIL/SCI CHIEF PWR

B56
WEBER M.,STAATSSOZIOLOGIE. STRUCT LEGIT ADMIN PARL/PROC SUPEGO CONSERVE JURID. PAGE 166 H3320
SOC NAT/G POL/PAR LEAD

B56
WEBER M.,WIRTSCHAFT UND GESELLSCHAFT (2ND VOL.). STRUCT NAT/G POL/PAR LEAD PWR OBJECTIVE IDEA/COMP. PAGE 166 H3321
LEGIT JURID SOC

S56
GORDON L.,"THE ORGANIZATION FOR EUROPEAN ECONOMIC COOPERATION." EUR+WWI INDUS INT/ORG NAT/G CONSULT DELIB/GP ACT/RES CREATE PLAN TEC/DEV EDU/PROP LEGIT WEALTH OEEC 20. PAGE 59 H1178
VOL/ASSN ECO/DEV

S56
KHAMA T.,"POLITICAL CHANGE IN AFRICAN SOCIETY." CONSTN SOCIETY LOC/G NAT/G POL/PAR EX/STRUC LEGIS LEGIT ADMIN CHOOSE REPRESENT NAT/LISM MORAL ORD/FREE PWR...CONCPT OBS TREND GEN/METH CMN/WLTH
AFR ELITES

17/20. PAGE 85 H1706

B57
COLE G.D.H.,THE POST WAR CONDITIONS OF BRITAIN. EUR+WWI STRUCT NAT/G PLAN EDU/PROP LEGIT RIGID/FLEX ORD/FREE WEALTH...SOCIALIST WELF/ST STAT TREND CON/ANAL CHARTS PARLIAMENT WORK 20. PAGE 31 H0624 ECO/DEV UK

B57
LAQUER W.Z.,COMMUNISM AND NATIONALISM IN THE MIDDLE EAST. ELITES INTELL STRATA NAT/G POL/PAR SECT VOL/ASSN TOP/EX DOMIN LEGIT REGION COERCE ATTIT PERSON PWR...CONCPT HIST/WRIT TIME/SEQ TREND GEN/LAWS VAL/FREE. PAGE 91 H1817 ISLAM NAT/LISM

B58
HAAS E.B.,THE UNITING OF EUROPE. EUR+WWI INT/ORG NAT/G POL/PAR TOP/EX ECO/TAC EDU/PROP LEGIT FEDERAL NAT/LISM DRIVE RIGID/FLEX ORD/FREE PWR PLURISM ...POLICY CONCPT INT GEN/LAWS ECSC EEC 20. PAGE 63 H1264 VOL/ASSN ECO/DEV

B58
INDIA (REPUBLIC) PARLIAMENT,CLASSIFIED LIST OF PUBLIC UNDERTAKINGS AND OTHER BODIES IN INDIA. INDIA ACADEM LG/CO CONSULT LEGIT CONFER GOV/REL 20. PAGE 76 H1528 NAT/G LEGIS LICENSE PROF/ORG

B59
BARRON R.,PARTIES AND POLITICS IN MODERN FRANCE. FRANCE LOC/G DELIB/GP LEGIS TOP/EX EDU/PROP LEGIT TV FEEDBACK 20. PAGE 12 H0230 POL/PAR ALL/IDEOS CHOOSE PARTIC

B59
EAENZA L.,COMMUNISMO E CATTOLICESIMO IN UNA PARROCHIA DI CAMPAGNA. ITALY CULTURE ELITES ECO/DEV AGRI KIN POL/PAR DOMIN LEGIT RIGID/FLEX...DECISION OBS IDEA/COMP 20 COM/PARTY CHURCH/STA. PAGE 44 H0878 ATTIT CATHISM NEIGH MARXISM

B59
INTERNATIONAL PRESS INSTITUTE,THE PRESS IN AUTHORITARIAN COUNTRIES. COM PORTUGAL SPAIN UAR USSR NAT/G DOMIN LEGIT ORD/FREE FASCISM SOCISM 20. PAGE 78 H1559 PRESS CONTROL TOTALISM EDU/PROP

B59
SANCHEZ A.L.,EL CONCEPTO DEL ESTADO EN EL PENSAMIENTO ESPANOL DEL SIGLO XVI. SPAIN LEGIS JUDGE BAL/PWR LEGIT EXEC WAR PWR...MAJORIT 16. PAGE 137 H2747 NAT/G PHIL/SCI LAW SOVEREIGN

B59
SCHORN H.,DER RICHTER IM DRITTEN REICH; GESCHICHTE UND DOKUMENTE. GERMANY NAT/G LEGIT CT/SYS INGP/REL MORAL ORD/FREE RESPECT...JURID GP/COMP 20. PAGE 140 H2798 ADJUD JUDGE FASCISM

S59
JENKS C.W.,"THE CHALLENGE OF UNIVERSALITY." FUT UNIV CONSTN CULTURE CONSULT CREATE PLAN LEGIT ATTIT MORAL ORD/FREE RESPECT...MAJORIT JURID 20. PAGE 80 H1602 INT/ORG LAW PEACE INT/LAW

S59
LABEDZ L.,"IDEOLOGY: THE FOURTH STAGE." COM USSR NAT/G TOP/EX LEGIT ATTIT PWR MARXISM...METH/CNCPT HIST/WRIT STERTYP TOT/POP 20. PAGE 90 H1795 CONCPT GEN/LAWS

S59
WARBURG J.P.,"THE CENTRAL EUROPEAN CRISIS: A PROPOSAL FOR WESTERN INITIATIVE." EUR+WWI INT/ORG NAT/G LEGIT DETER WAR...CONCPT BER/BLOC UN 20. PAGE 165 H3302 PLAN GERMANY

B60
LINDSAY K.,EUROPEAN ASSEMBLIES: THE EXPERIMENTAL PERIOD 1949-1959. EUR+WWI ECO/DEV NAT/G POL/PAR LEGIS TOP/EX ACT/RES PLAN ECO/TAC DOMIN LEGIT ROUTINE ATTIT DRIVE ORD/FREE PWR SKILL...SOC CONCPT TREND CHARTS GEN/LAWS VAL/FREE. PAGE 97 H1932 VOL/ASSN INT/ORG REGION

B60
MACRIDIS R.C.,THE DE GAULLE REPUBLIC: QUEST FOR UNITY. EUR+WWI NAT/G POL/PAR LEGIS LEGIT NAT/LISM ATTIT RIGID/FLEX ORD/FREE PWR...JURID CONCPT TIME/SEQ 20 DEGAULLE/C. PAGE 100 H2009 TOP/EX STRUCT FRANCE

S60
BERG E.J.,"ECONOMIC BASIS OF POLITICAL CHOICE IN FRENCH WEST AFRICA." FRANCE ECO/UNDEV AGRI INDUS NAT/G PLAN LEGIT COLONIAL REGION ATTIT PWR WEALTH ...CONCPT 20. PAGE 15 H0299 AFR ECO/TAC

S60
GINSBURGS G.,"PEKING-LHASA-NEW DELHI." CHINA/COM FUT INDIA S/ASIA KIN NAT/G PROVS SECT FORCES BAL/PWR ECO/TAC DOMIN EDU/PROP LEGIT ADMIN REGION GUERRILLA PWR...TREND TIBET 20. PAGE 57 H1134 ASIA COERCE DIPLOM

S60
PERLMANN H.,"UPHEAVAL IN TURKEY." EUR+WWI ISLAM NAT/G FORCES TOP/EX LEGIT COERCE CHOOSE DRIVE ORD/FREE PWR...TIME/SEQ TOT/POP 20. PAGE 125 H2494 CONSTN TURKEY

S60
SHILS E.,"THE INTELLECTUALS IN THE POLITICAL DEVELOPMENT OF THE NEW STATES." AFR ASIA S/ASIA ELITES LOC/G NAT/G CONSULT EX/STRUC CREATE PLAN ECO/TAC DOMIN LEGIT DRIVE PWR...TRADIT CONCPT STERTYP GEN/LAWS 20. PAGE 143 H2861 POL/PAR INTELL NAT/LISM

S60
WYCKOFF T.,"THE ROLE OF THE MILITARY IN LATIN AMERICAN POLITICS." L/A+17C CONSTN CULTURE ECO/UNDEV POL/PAR FORCES LEGIS TOP/EX LEGIT GUERRILLA REV CHOOSE ORD/FREE PWR...TIME/SEQ VAL/FREE 20. PAGE 171 H3430 NAT/G COERCE TOTALISM

B61
BURDEAU G.,O PODER EXECUTIVO NA FRANCA. EUR+WWI FRANCE CONSTN DELIB/GP LEGIT ADMIN ATTIT ALL/VALS CONCPT. PAGE 24 H0478 TOP/EX POL/PAR NAT/G LEGIS

B61
ULLMAN W.,PRINCIPLES OF GOVERNMENT AND POLITICS IN THE MIDDLE AGES. LAW CONSTN DOMIN EDU/PROP LEGIT TOTALISM SOVEREIGN POPULISM...POLICY GOV/COMP IDEA/COMP 12/16 POPE KING CHURCH/STA. PAGE 158 H3152 SECT CHIEF NAT/G LEGIS

B61
VON MERING O.,A GRAMMAR OF HUMAN VALUES. WOR+45 CULTURE FACE/GP NEIGH CREATE EDU/PROP LEGIT ATTIT DRIVE PERSON ORD/FREE...PSY SOC METH/CNCPT OBS RECORD INT REC/INT STAND/INT QU CHARTS VAL/FREE. PAGE 164 H3275 SOCIETY MORAL

S61
DOGAN M.,"LES OFFICIERS DANS LA CARRIERE POLITIQUE DE MARECHAL MACMAHON AU GENERAL DE GAULLE." EUR+WWI FRANCE MOD/EUR ELITES STRATA POL/PAR LEGIT ATTIT ALL/VALS...SOC CONCPT 19/20. PAGE 42 H0833 PROF/ORG FORCES NAT/G DELIB/GP

S61
MILLER E.,"LEGAL ASPECTS OF UN ACTION IN THE CONGO." AFR CULTURE ADMIN PEACE DRIVE RIGID/FLEX ORD/FREE...WELF/ST JURID OBS UN CONGO 20. PAGE 111 H2212 INT/ORG LEGIT

S61
TANHAM B.K.,"COMMUNIST REVOLUTIONARY WARFARE: THE VIETMINH IN INDOCHINA." EUR+WWI S/ASIA VIETNAM NAT/G EDU/PROP LEGIT GUERRILLA ATTIT PWR...CONCPT GEN/LAWS 20. PAGE 152 H3042 FORCES ECO/TAC WAR FRANCE

B62
ABRAHAM W.E.,THE MIND OF AFRICA. AFR SOCIETY STRATA KIN ECO/TAC DOMIN EDU/PROP LEGIT COERCE ATTIT ALL/VALS...MAJORIT SOC OBS HIST/WRIT TIME/SEQ TREND TOT/POP 20. PAGE 3 H0058 CULTURE SIMUL GHANA

B62
ARNE S.,LE PRESIDENT DU CONSEIL DES MINISTRES SOUS LA IV REPUBLIQUE. EUR+WWI FRANCE LEGIT PWR...BIOG CHARTS. PAGE 8 H0165 DELIB/GP POL/PAR NAT/G LEGIS

B62
BINDER L.,IRAN: POLITICAL DEVELOPMENT IN A CHANGING SOCIETY. IRAN OP/RES REV GP/REL CENTRAL RATIONAL PWR...PHIL/SCI NAT/COMP GEN/LAWS 20. PAGE 17 H0337 LEGIT NAT/G ADMIN STRUCT

B62
BRETTON H.L.,POWER AND STABILITY IN NIGERIA: THE POLITICS OF DECOLONIZATION. AFR CONSTN INTELL ECO/UNDEV COM/IND KIN NAT/G POL/PAR PROVS VOL/ASSN LEGIS DOMIN EDU/PROP LEGIT EXEC ROUTINE CHOOSE NAT/LISM ATTIT PERCEPT ALL/VALS. PAGE 20 H0411 CULTURE OBS NIGERIA

B62
DUTOIT B.,LA NEUTRALITE SUISSE A L'HEURE EUROPEENNE. EUR+WWI MOD/EUR INT/ORG NAT/G VOL/ASSN PLAN BAL/PWR LEGIT NEUTRAL REGION PEACE ORD/FREE SOVEREIGN...CONCPT OBS TIME/SEQ TREND STERTYP VAL/FREE LEAGUE/NAT UN 20. PAGE 44 H0873 ATTIT DIPLOM SWITZERLND

B62
FINER S.E.,THE MAN ON HORSEBACK: ROLE OF THE MILITARY IN POLITICS. UNIV LAW CONSTN ELITES SOCIETY POL/PAR BAL/PWR DOMIN EDU/PROP LEGIT COERCE GUERRILLA REV WAR WEAPON DRIVE SUPEGO ORD/FREE PWR RESPECT...POLICY CONCPT GEN/METH. PAGE 50 H1003 NAT/G FORCES TOTALISM

B62
HATCH J.,AFRICA TODAY-AND TOMORROW: AN OUTLINE OF BASIC FACTS AND MAJOR PROBLEMS. AFR FUT ISLAM STRATA ECO/UNDEV INT/ORG NAT/G POL/PAR DELIB/GP TOP/EX EDU/PROP LEGIT CHOOSE ATTIT...TIME/SEQ TOT/POP COLD/WAR 20. PAGE 67 H1353 PLAN CONSTN NAT/LISM

B62
KASTARI P.,LA PRESIDENCE DE LA REPUBLIQUE EN FINLANDE. FINLAND CONSTN NAT/G POL/PAR LEGIS LEGIT ATTIT...JURID CONCPT 20 PRESIDENT. PAGE 83 H1666 PARL/PROC CHIEF PWR DECISION

B62
MANSERGH N.,SOUTH AFRICA 1906-1961: THE PRICE OF MAGNANIMITY. SOUTH/AFR LEGIS LEGIT SUFF NAT/LISM ATTIT ORD/FREE 20 NEGRO 20. PAGE 102 H2041 COLONIAL DISCRIM NAT/G

B62
MELADY T.,THE WHITE MAN'S FUTURE IN BLACK AFRICA. FUT CULTURE SOCIETY NAT/G POL/PAR PLAN ECO/TAC DOMIN EDU/PROP LEGIT COLONIAL RACE/REL ATTIT DRIVE ALL/VALS...PSY SOC CONCPT TIME/SEQ TOT/POP VAL/FREE 20. PAGE 108 H2167 AFR STRATA ELITES

B62
MILLER J.D.B.,THE NATURE OF POLITICS. NAT/G DOMIN LEGIT LEAD...CONCPT METH. PAGE 111 H2213 METH/COMP IDEA/COMP PHIL/SCI

B62
THIERRY S.S.,LE VATICAN SECRET. CHRIST-17C EUR+WWI ADMIN

MOD/EUR VATICAN NAT/G SECT DELIB/GP DOMIN LEGIT SOVEREIGN. PAGE 154 H3072 EX/STRUC CATHISM DECISION

L62
ORDONNEAU P.,"LES PROBLEMES POSES PAR L'INDEPENDANCE DES NOUVEAUX ETATS AFRICAINS ET MALGACHE SUR LE PLAN DU CONTENTIEUX." FRANCE ISLAM MADAGASCAR LAW STRATA ECO/UNDEV NAT/G LEGIS LEGIT ...JURID TIME/SEQ 20. PAGE 121 H2425 AFR ADJUD COLONIAL SOVEREIGN

S62
FESLER J.W.,"FRENCH FIELD ADMINISTRATION: THE BEGINNINGS." CHRIST-17C CULTURE SOCIETY STRATA NAT/G ECO/TAC DOMIN EDU/PROP LEGIT ADJUD COERCE ATTIT ALL/VALS...TIME/SEQ CON/ANAL GEN/METH VAL/FREE 13/15. PAGE 49 H0988 EX/STRUC FRANCE

S62
MOUSKHELY M.,"LA NAISSANCE DES ETATS EN DROIT INTERNATIONAL PUBLIC." UNIV SOCIETY INT/ORG VOL/ASSN LEGIT ATTIT RIGID/FLEX...JURID TIME/SEQ 20. PAGE 114 H2272 NAT/G STRUCT INT/LAW

S62
MURACCIOLE L.,"LES CONSTITUTIONS DES ETATS AFRICAINS D'EXPRESSION FRANCAISE: LA CONSTITUTION DU 16 AVRIL 1962 DE LA REPUBLIQUE DU" AFR CHAD CHIEF LEGIS LEGIT COLONIAL EXEC ROUTINE ORD/FREE SOVEREIGN...SOC CONCPT 20. PAGE 115 H2291 NAT/G CONSTN

S62
PIQUEMAL M.,"LES PROBLEMES DES UNIONS D'ETATS EN AFRIQUE NOIRE." FRANCE SOCIETY INT/ORG NAT/G DELIB/GP PLAN LEGIT ADMIN COLONIAL ROUTINE ATTIT ORD/FREE PWR...GEOG METH/CNCPT 20. PAGE 126 H2515 AFR ECO/UNDEV REGION

S62
SPRINGER H.W.,"FEDERATION IN THE CARIBBEAN: AN ATTEMPT THAT FAILED." L/A+17C ECO/UNDEV INT/ORG POL/PAR PROVS LEGIS CREATE PLAN LEGIT ADMIN FEDERAL ATTIT DRIVE PERSON ORD/FREE PWR...POLICY GEOG PSY CONCPT OBS CARIBBEAN CMN/WLTH 20. PAGE 148 H2955 VOL/ASSN NAT/G REGION

S62
VIGNES D.,"L'AUTORITE DES TRAITES INTERNATIONAUX EN DROIT INTERNE." EUR+WWI UNIV LAW CONSTN INTELL NAT/G POL/PAR DIPLOM ATTIT PERCEPT ALL/VALS ...POLICY INT/LAW JURID CONCPT TIME/SEQ 20 TREATY. PAGE 163 H3252 STRUCT LEGIT FRANCE

S62
WALTER E.,"VERS UNE CLASSIFICATION SCIENTIFIQUE DE LA SOCIOLOGIA." UNIV CULTURE INTELL SOCIETY R+D ACT/RES LEGIT ROUTINE ATTIT KNOWL...JURID MGT TREND GEN/LAWS 20. PAGE 165 H3296 PLAN CONCPT

B63
CREMEANS C.,THE ARABS AND THE WORLD: NASSER'S ARAB NATIONALIST POLICY. FUT ISLAM UAR USA+45 SOCIETY STRATA NAT/G POL/PAR PLAN DIPLOM EDU/PROP LEGIT DRIVE ALL/VALS...INT TIME/SEQ CHARTS 20 NASSER/G. PAGE 35 H0700 TOP/EX ATTIT REGION NAT/LISM

B63
CRUICKSHANK M.,CHURCH AND STATE IN ENGLISH EDUCATION 1870 TO PRESENT. UK LEGIS TAX GIVE DOMIN LEGIT ORD/FREE 19/20 CHURCH/STA. PAGE 36 H0715 NAT/G SECT EDU/PROP GP/REL

B63
DEBRAY P.,LE PORTUGAL ENTRE DEUX REVOLUTIONS. EUR+WWI PORTUGAL CONSTN LEGIT ADMIN ATTIT ALL/VALS ...DECISION CONCPT 20 SALAZAR/A. PAGE 39 H0779 NAT/G DELIB/GP TOP/EX

B63
GLUCKMAN M.,ORDER AND REBELLION IN TRIBAL AFRICA. EUR+WWI LAW CULTURE STRATA KIN MUNIC DELIB/GP ACT/RES DOMIN EDU/PROP LEGIT ADMIN COERCE CHOOSE ATTIT PERSON ORD/FREE PWR...SOC CHARTS GEN/LAWS TOT/POP VAL/FREE. PAGE 57 H1147 AFR SOCIETY

B63
KHADDURI M.,MODERN LIBYA: A STUDY IN POLITICAL DEVELOPMENT. EUR+WWI ISLAM LIBYA ELITES INT/ORG POL/PAR FORCES DIPLOM FOR/AID DOMIN EDU/PROP LEGIT NAT/LISM DRIVE RIGID/FLEX SKILL...CONCPT TIME/SEQ TREND 20. PAGE 85 H1704 NAT/G STRUCT

B63
KOGAN N.,THE POLITICS OF ITALIAN FOREIGN POLICY. EUR+WWI LEGIS DOMIN LEGIT EXEC PWR RESPECT SKILL ...POLICY DECISION HUM SOC METH/CNCPT OBS INT CHARTS 20. PAGE 87 H1737 NAT/G ROUTINE DIPLOM ITALY

B63
MAYNE R.,THE COMMUNITY OF EUROPE. UK CONSTN NAT/G CONSULT DELIB/GP CREATE PLAN ECO/TAC LEGIT ADMIN ROUTINE ORD/FREE PWR WEALTH...CONCPT TIME/SEQ EEC EURATOM 20. PAGE 105 H2107 EUR+WWI INT/ORG REGION

B63
QUAISON-SACKEY A.,AFRICA UNBOUND: REFLECTIONS OF AN AFRICAN STATESMAN. ISLAM CULTURE INTELL INT/ORG POL/PAR TOP/EX DOMIN EDU/PROP LEGIT ATTIT PERSON ...CONCPT OBS TIME/SEQ CHARTS STERTYP 20 UN. PAGE 129 H2571 AFR BIOG

B63
REYNOLDS B.,MAGIC, DIVINATION AND WITCHCRAFT AMONG THE BAROTSE OF NORTHERN RHODESIA. RHODESIA CULTURE KIN CREATE LEGIT PARTIC DEATH DREAM STRANGE HABITAT PERSON...AUD/VIS WORSHIP 20. PAGE 131 H2619 AFR SOC MYTH SECT

B63
RONNING C.N.,LAW AND POLITICS IN INTER-AMERICAN DIPLOMACY. L/A+17C ECO/UNDEV NAT/G CONSULT DELIB/GP CREATE CAP/ISM ECO/TAC LEGIT REGION RIGID/FLEX ...METH/CNCPT GEN/LAWS OAS 20. PAGE 133 H2668 VOL/ASSN ALL/VALS DIPLOM

B63
SETON-WATSON H.,THE NEW IMPERIALISM. COM EUR+WWI MOD/EUR ECO/UNDEV NAT/G FORCES DIPLOM DOMIN EDU/PROP LEGIT COLONIAL EXEC COERCE GP/REL RACE/REL DISCRIM ATTIT...TIME/SEQ 20. PAGE 142 H2833 ECO/TAC RUSSIA USSR

B63
ULAM A.B.,THE NEW FACE OF SOVIET TOTALITARIANISM. FUT INTELL NAT/G POL/PAR EX/STRUC TOP/EX DIPLOM ECO/TAC DOMIN EDU/PROP LEGIT COERCE ATTIT RIGID/FLEX...OBS HIST/WRIT TREND TOT/POP VAL/FREE COLD/WAR. PAGE 158 H3150 COM PWR TOTALISM USSR

B63
VON DER MEHDEN F.R.,RELIGION AND NATIONALISM IN SOUTHEAST ASIA. BURMA PHILIPPINE S/ASIA INTELL SOCIETY DOMIN EDU/PROP LEGIT ATTIT MORAL ORD/FREE ...SOC CENSUS HIST/WRIT TOT/POP VAL/FREE 20 WORSHIP LONDON. PAGE 163 H3265 SECT CULTURE NAT/LISM

B63
ZARTMAN I.W.,GOVERNMENT AND POLITICS IN NORTHERN AFRICA. AFR ALGERIA ISLAM LIBYA MOROCCO UAR ELITES SOCIETY PLAN ECO/TAC DOMIN EDU/PROP LEGIT ATTIT ...GEOG CONCPT TIME/SEQ 20 TUNIS. PAGE 172 H3448 CULTURE DRIVE NAT/LISM

L63
FREUND G.,"ADENAUER AND THE FUTURE OF GERMANY." EUR+WWI FUT GERMANY/W FORCES LEGIT ADMIN ROUTINE ATTIT DRIVE PERSON PWR...POLICY TIME/SEQ TREND VAL/FREE 20 ADENAUER/K. PAGE 53 H1058 NAT/G BIOG DIPLOM GERMANY

L63
ZARTMAN I.W.,"THE SAHARA--BRIDGE OR BARRIER." ISLAM CULTURE SOCIETY NAT/G DELIB/GP DOMIN EDU/PROP LEGIT ATTIT...HIST/WRIT TIME/SEQ CHARTS TOT/POP VAL/FREE 20. PAGE 172 H3447 INT/ORG PWR NAT/LISM

S63
ANTHON C.G.,"THE END OF THE ADENAUER ERA." EUR+WWI GERMANY/W CONSTN EX/STRUC CREATE DIPLOM LEGIT ATTIT PERSON ALL/VALS...RECORD 20 ADENAUER/K. PAGE 7 H0144 NAT/G TOP/EX BAL/PWR GERMANY

S63
EMERI C.,"LES FORCES POLITIQUES AU PARLEMENT" EUR+WWI FRANCE ELITES DELIB/GP TOP/EX LEGIT ATTIT ...SOC 20 PARLIAMENT. PAGE 46 H0917 POL/PAR LEGIS PWR NAT/G

S63
GLUCKMAN M.,"CIVIL WAR AND THEORIES OF POWER IN BAROTSE-LAND: AFRICAN AND MEDIEVAL ANALOGIES." AFR CHRIST-17C LAW CONSTN CULTURE STRATA KIN DELIB/GP FORCES DOMIN LEGIT COERCE PERCEPT ORD/FREE...SOC INT TIME/SEQ GEN/LAWS VAL/FREE. PAGE 57 H1148 TOP/EX PWR WAR

S63
HARRIS R.L.,"A COMPARATIVE ANALYSIS OF THE ADMINISTRATIVE SYSTEMS OF CANADA AND CEYLON." S/ASIA CULTURE SOCIETY STRATA TOP/EX ACT/RES DOMIN EDU/PROP LEGIT COERCE ATTIT SUPEGO ALL/VALS...MGT CHARTS GEN/LAWS VAL/FREE 20. PAGE 67 H1343 DELIB/GP EX/STRUC CANADA CEYLON

S63
LEE J.M.,"PARLIAMENT IN REPUBLICAN GHANA." AFR CONSTN CULTURE SOCIETY STRATA POL/PAR DELIB/GP TOP/EX DOMIN EDU/PROP LEGIT COERCE CHOOSE ATTIT ALL/VALS...CONCPT STAT TIME/SEQ VAL/FREE 20. PAGE 93 H1857 LEGIS GHANA

S63
MAZRUI A.A.,"ON THE CONCEPT 'WE ARE ALL AFRICANS'." AFR CULTURE KIN LOC/G NAT/G DOMIN EDU/PROP LEGIT ATTIT PERCEPT PERSON KNOWL ORD/FREE...TIME/SEQ TOT/POP 20. PAGE 106 H2110 PROVS INT/ORG NAT/LISM

S63
POPPINO R.E.,"IMBALANCE IN BRAZIL." L/A+17C NAT/G TOP/EX PLAN DIPLOM LEGIT DRIVE WEALTH...CON/ANAL LAFTA 20. PAGE 127 H2544 POL/PAR ECO/TAC BRAZIL

S63
TILMAN R.O.,"MALAYSIA: THE PROBLEMS OF FEDERATION." ISLAM S/ASIA CONSTN PROVS SECT DELIB/GP DOMIN EDU/PROP LEGIT EXEC COERCE CHOOSE ATTIT HEALTH ORD/FREE PWR...STAT TOT/POP VAL/FREE 20. PAGE 155 H3097 NAT/G CULTURE MALAYSIA

S63
WEISSBERG G.,"MAPS AS EVIDENCE IN INTERNATIONAL BOUNDARY DISPUTES: A REAPPRAISAL." CHINA/COM EUR+WWI INDIA MOD/EUR S/ASIA INT/ORG NAT/G LEGIT PERCEPT...JURID CHARTS 20. PAGE 166 H3331 LAW GEOG SOVEREIGN

B64
DE SMITH S.A.,THE NEW COMMONWEALTH AND ITS CONSTITUTIONS. AFR CYPRUS PAKISTAN S/ASIA INT/ORG NAT/G LEGIS LEGIT RIGID/FLEX PWR...CONCPT TIME/SEQ CMN/WLTH 20. PAGE 38 H0770 EX/STRUC CONSTN SOVEREIGN

B64
HEIMSATH C.H.,INDIAN NATIONALISM AND HINDU SOCIAL REFORM. S/ASIA LAW CULTURE SOCIETY STRATA PROVS VOL/ASSN DELIB/GP LEGIS TOP/EX DOMIN EDU/PROP LEGIT ATTIT ALL/VALS...POLICY SOC TIME/SEQ STERTYP VAL/FREE 19/20. PAGE 69 H1385 SECT NAT/G

B64
PHILLIPS C.S.,THE DEVELOPMENT OF NIGERIAN FOREIGN POLICY. AFR CONSTN CULTURE STRATA NAT/G LEGIS DOMIN LEGIT EXEC...RELATIV SOC TIME/SEQ TREND TOT/POP 20. PAGE 125 H2502 CHOOSE POLICY DIPLOM NIGERIA

B64
PIKE F.B.,THE CONFLICT BETWEEN CHURCH AND STATE IN LATIN AMERICA. L/A+17C CULTURE SOCIETY STRATA DOMIN EDU/PROP LEGIT COERCE ATTIT ORD/FREE PWR WEALTH ...CONCPT TIME/SEQ TREND VAL/FREE. PAGE 125 H2510 SECT NAT/G

B64
PIPES R.,THE FORMATION OF THE SOVIET UNION. EUR+WWI MOD/EUR STRUCT ECO/UNDEV NAT/G LEGIS DOMIN LEGIT CT/SYS EXEC COERCE ALL/VALS...POLICY RELATIV HIST/WRIT TIME/SEQ TOT/POP 19/20. PAGE 126 H2514 COM USSR RUSSIA

B64
SINGER M.R.,THE EMERGING ELITE: A STUDY OF POLITICAL LEADERSHIP IN CEYLON. S/ASIA ECO/UNDEV AGRI KIN NAT/G SECT EX/STRUC LEGIT ATTIT PWR RESPECT...SOC STAT CHARTS 20. PAGE 144 H2883 TOP/EX STRATA NAT/LISM CEYLON

B64
SKINNER E.P.,THE MOSSI OF UPPER VOLTA: THE POLITICAL DEVELOPMENT OF A SUDANESE PEOPLE. AFR LAW AGRI FAM KIN POL/PAR PROVS SECT DELIB/GP EX/STRUC FORCES TOP/EX DOMIN EDU/PROP LEGIT CT/SYS COERCE CHOOSE ORD/FREE PWR WEALTH...SOC MYTH VAL/FREE. PAGE 145 H2897 CULTURE OBS UPPER/VOLT

B64
WAINHOUSE D.W.,REMNANTS OF EMPIRE: THE UNITED NATIONS AND THE END OF COLONIALISM. FUT PORTUGAL WOR+45 NAT/G CONSULT DOMIN LEGIT ADMIN ROUTINE ATTIT ORD/FREE...POLICY JURID RECORD INT TIME/SEQ UN CMN/WLTH 20. PAGE 164 H3287 INT/ORG TREND COLONIAL

B64
WARD R.E.,POLITICAL MODERNIZATION IN JAPAN AND TURKEY. ASIA ISLAM S/ASIA CONSTN CULTURE STRATA COM/IND POL/PAR FORCES ACT/RES ECO/TAC DOMIN EDU/PROP LEGIT ADMIN CHOOSE ATTIT ALL/VALS...STAT TIME/SEQ VAL/FREE CHINJAP. PAGE 165 H3307 SOCIETY TURKEY

B64
WHITEFORD A.H.,TWO CITIES OF LATIN AMERICA: A COMPARATIVE DESCRIPTION OF SOCIAL CLASSES. L/A+17C CULTURE SOCIETY MUNIC DOMIN LEGIT ATTIT ALL/VALS ...STAT OBS VAL/FREE 20. PAGE 167 H3352 STRATA SOC

L64
MACKINTOSH J.P.,"NIGERIA'S EXTERNAL AFFAIRS." UK CULTURE ECO/UNDEV NAT/G VOL/ASSN EDU/PROP LEGIT ADMIN ATTIT ORD/FREE PWR 20. PAGE 100 H2002 AFR DIPLOM NIGERIA

L64
ROTBERG R.,"THE FEDERATION MOVEMENT IN BRITISH EAST AND CENTRAL AFRICA." AFR RHODESIA UGANDA ECO/UNDEV NAT/G POL/PAR FORCES DOMIN LEGIT ADMIN COERCE ATTIT ...CONCPT TREND 20 TANGANYIKA. PAGE 135 H2691 VOL/ASSN PWR REGION

L64
SYMONDS R.,"REFLECTIONS IN LOCALISATION." AFR S/ASIA UK STRATA INT/ORG NAT/G SCHOOL EDU/PROP LEGIT KNOWL ORD/FREE PWR RESPECT CMN/WLTH 20. PAGE 151 H3023 ADMIN MGT COLONIAL

S64
BRADLEY C.P.,"THE FORMATION OF MALAYSIA." INDIA S/ASIA POL/PAR VOL/ASSN TOP/EX LEGIT RACE/REL ORD/FREE 20. PAGE 20 H0398 NAT/G CREATE COLONIAL MALAYSIA

S64
CLIFFE L.,"TANGANYIKA'S TWO YEARS OF INDEPENDENCE." AFR INDUS MARKET NAT/G POL/PAR DELIB/GP CREATE ECO/TAC LEGIT DRIVE ALL/VALS...METH/CNCPT RECORD 20 TANGANYIKA. PAGE 30 H0604 ECO/UNDEV PLAN

S64
CLIGNET R.,"POTENTIAL ELITES IN GHANA AND THE IVORY COAST: A PRELIMINARY SURVEY." AFR CULTURE ELITES STRATA KIN NAT/G SECT DOMIN EXEC ORD/FREE RESPECT SKILL...POLICY RELATIV GP/COMP NAT/COMP 20. PAGE 30 H0605 PWR LEGIT IVORY/CST GHANA

S64
ENNIS T.E.,"VIETNAM: LAND WITHOUT LAUGHTER." S/ASIA VIETNAM VIETNAM/S INTELL SOCIETY SECT FORCES DIPLOM LEGIT COERCE WAR ATTIT RIGID/FLEX ORD/FREE COLD/WAR 20. PAGE 46 H0929 NAT/G TOP/EX GUERRILLA

S64
GRUNER E.,"PRENSA, PARTIDOS POLITICOS, Y GRUPOS DE PRESION EN SUIZA." EUR+WWI MOD/EUR NAT/G EDU/PROP LEGIT PRESS ATTIT KNOWL ORD/FREE...CONCPT STAT CON/ANAL CHARTS 20. PAGE 62 H1241 POL/PAR SWITZERLND

S64
JOHNSON K.F.,"CAUSAL FACTORS IN LATIN AMERICAN POLITICAL INSTABILITY." CULTURE NAT/G VOL/ASSN EX/STRUC FORCES EDU/PROP LEGIT ADMIN COERCE REV ATTIT KNOWL PWR...STYLE RECORD CHARTS WORK 20. PAGE 81 H1624 L/A+17C PERCEPT ELITES

S64
LEVI W.,"INDIAN NEUTRALISM RECONSIDERED." ASIA CHINA/COM S/ASIA SOCIETY NAT/G ACT/RES LEGIT NEUTRAL COERCE ATTIT DRIVE PERCEPT RIGID/FLEX HEALTH LOVE PWR...DECISION RECORD TREND STERTYP 20. PAGE 95 H1896 ORD/FREE CONCPT INDIA

S64
LEWIS B.,"THE QUEST FOR FREEDOM--A SAD STORY OF THE MIDDLE EAST." ISLAM ISRAEL LEBANON TURKEY CULTURE NAT/G SECT LEGIS TOP/EX DOMIN EDU/PROP LEGIT ORD/FREE PWR RESPECT...POLICY TIME/SEQ VAL/FREE 20. PAGE 96 H1911 CONSTN ATTIT NAT/LISM

S64
LOW D.A.,"LION RAMPANT." EUR+WWI MOD/EUR S/ASIA ECO/UNDEV NAT/G FORCES TEC/DEV ECO/TAC LEGIT ADMIN COLONIAL COERCE ORD/FREE RESPECT 19/20. PAGE 99 H1972 AFR DOMIN DIPLOM UK

S64
MERKL P.H.,"EUROPEAN ASSEMBLY PARTIES AND NATIONAL DELEGATIONS." INT/ORG DELIB/GP DOMIN EDU/PROP LEGIT CHOOSE PWR...STAT VAL/FREE 20. PAGE 109 H2180 EUR+WWI POL/PAR REGION

S64
SAAB H.,"THE ARAB SEARCH FOR A FEDERAL UNION." SOCIETY INT/ORG NAT/G DELIB/GP FORCES ACT/RES TEC/DEV ECO/TAC DOMIN LEGIT REGION ROUTINE ATTIT DRIVE RIGID/FLEX ALL/VALS...SOC CONCPT NEW/IDEA TIME/SEQ TREND. PAGE 136 H2726 ISLAM PLAN

S64
SAYEED K.,"PATHAN REGIONALISM." ISLAM PAKISTAN S/ASIA CULTURE SOCIETY NAT/G NEIGH DIPLOM LEGIT COERCE CHOOSE ATTIT DISPL PERCEPT ALL/VALS SOVEREIGN...POLICY RELATIV SOC TIME/SEQ TOT/POP 20. PAGE 138 H2761 SECT NAT/LISM REGION

S64
SCHEFFLER H.W.,"THE GENESIS AND REPRESSION OF CONFLICT: CHOISEUL ISLAND." S/ASIA LOC/G NAT/G FORCES LEGIS DIPLOM DOMIN LEGIT EXEC CHOOSE ATTIT RESPECT SKILL...POLICY JURID OBS TREND GEN/METH 20. PAGE 139 H2781 PWR COERCE WAR

S64
TOUVAL S.,"THE SOMALI REPUBLIC." AFR ISLAM SOMALIA FAM KIN NAT/G CREATE FOR/AID LEGIT ATTIT ALL/VALS ...RECORD TREND 20. PAGE 156 H3119 ECO/UNDEV RIGID/FLEX

B65
ADAM T.R.,GOVERNMENT AND POLITICS IN AFRICA SOUTH OF THE SAHARA. AFR EUR+WWI CONSTN CULTURE INTELL POL/PAR TOP/EX LEGIT REGION DRIVE...OBS TREND CMN/WLTH 20. PAGE 3 H0062 NAT/G TIME/SEQ RACE/REL COLONIAL

B65
PEASLEE A.J.,CONSTITUTIONS OF NATIONS* THIRD REVISED EDITION (VOLUME I* AFRICA). LAW EX/STRUC LEGIS TOP/EX LEGIT CT/SYS ROUTINE ORD/FREE PWR SOVEREIGN...CON/ANAL CHARTS. PAGE 124 H2481 AFR CHOOSE CONSTN NAT/G

B65
SCALAPINO R.A.,THE COMMUNIST REVOLUTION IN ASIA* TACTICS, GOALS, AND ACHIEVEMENTS. INDIA INTELL POL/PAR FORCES DOMIN EDU/PROP LEGIT COERCE REV ATTIT CHINJAP. PAGE 138 H2763 ASIA S/ASIA MARXISM NAT/COMP

L65
SHARMA S.P.,"THE INDIA-CHINA BORDER DISPUTE: AN INDIAN PERSPECTIVE." ASIA CHINA/COM S/ASIA NAT/G LEGIT CT/SYS NAT/LISM DRIVE MORAL ORD/FREE PWR 20. PAGE 142 H2850 LAW ATTIT SOVEREIGN INDIA

S65
RUBINSTEIN A.Z.,"YUGOSLAVIA'S OPENING SOCIETY." COM USSR INTELL NAT/G LEGIS TOP/EX LEGIT CT/SYS RIGID/FLEX ALL/VALS SOCISM...HUM TIME/SEQ TREND 20. PAGE 135 H2708 CONSTN EX/STRUC YUGOSLAVIA

S65
VUCINICH W.S.,"WHITHER RUMANIA." COM USSR YUGOSLAVIA NAT/G VOL/ASSN DELIB/GP TOP/EX LEGIT NAT/LISM TOTALISM ATTIT DRIVE RIGID/FLEX ORD/FREE WEALTH SOCISM...TIME/SEQ TREND 20. PAGE 164 H3281 ECO/DEV CREATE ROMANIA

B66
KASUNMU A.B.,NIGERIAN FAMILY LAW. NIGERIA KIN LEGIT ILLEGIT MARRIAGE AGE DRIVE HABITAT ALL/VALS...JURID IDEA/COMP T 20 ENGLSH/LAW. PAGE 83 H1667 FAM LAW CULTURE AFR

B66
NOLTE E.,THREE FACES OF FASCISM. FRANCE GERMANY DOMIN LEGIT COERCE CROWD REV WAR GP/REL RACE/REL SOVEREIGN...GOV/COMP IDEA/COMP 19/20 HITLER/A MUSSOLIN/B MARX/KARL. PAGE 118 H2368 FASCISM TOTALISM NAT/G POL/PAR

B66
WEINSTEIN F.B.,VIETNAM'S UNHELD ELECTIONS: THE FAILURE TO CARRY OUT THE 1956 REUNIFICATION ELECTIONS... (MONOGRAPH). VIETNAM/S VIETNAM/N LEGIT CONFER ADJUD WAR PEACE 20 TREATY GENEVA/CON UNIFICA. PAGE 166 H3330 AGREE NAT/G CHOOSE DIPLOM

B66
WILLNER A.R.,THE NEOTRADITIONAL ACCOMMODATION TO POLITICAL INDEPENDENCE* THE CASE OF INDONESIA * RESEARCH MONOGRAPH NO. 26. CULTURE ECO/UNDEV CREATE PROB/SOLV FOR/AID LEGIT COLONIAL EFFICIENCY NAT/LISM ALL/VALS SOC. PAGE 168 H3371 INDONESIA CONSERVE ELITES ADMIN

S66
KAPIL R.L.,"ON THE CONFLICT POTENTIAL OF INHERITED BOUNDARIES IN AFRICA." MOD/EUR MOROCCO UAR EX/STRUC DIPLOM LEGIT REGION ADJUST...RECORD NAT/COMP GEN/LAWS. PAGE 83 H1658 AFR COLONIAL PREDICT GEOG

S67
BHATNAGAR J.K.,"THE VALUES AND ATTITUDES OF SOME NAT/COMP

INDIAN AND BRITISH STUDENTS." INDIA UK ECO/UNDEV LEGIT COLONIAL GP/REL SOVEREIGN...QU 20. PAGE 16 H0328 ATTIT EDU/PROP ACADEM

S67
KYLE K.,"BACKGROUND TO THE CRISIS" ISLAM ISRAEL UAR UK USSR NAT/G PROB/SOLV LEGIT CONTROL REGION STRANGE MORAL 20 JEWS. PAGE 89 H1787 DIPLOM POLICY SOVEREIGN COERCE

S67
MITCHELL W.C.,"THE SHAPE OF POLITICAL THEORY TO COME: FROM POLITICAL SOCIOLOGY TO POLITICAL ECONOMY." ACADEM NAT/G BUDGET TAX LEGIT LOBBY GOV/REL INGP/REL...SOC NEW/IDEA TREND CHARTS 20 MONEY. PAGE 112 H2231 ECO/TAC GEN/LAWS

S67
POWELL D.,"THE EFFECTIVENESS OF SOVIET ANTI-RELIGIOUS PROPAGANDA." USSR NAT/G DOMIN LEGIT NAT/LISM 20. PAGE 127 H2549 EDU/PROP ATTIT SECT CONTROL

S68
SHAPIRO J.P.,"SOVIET HISTORIOGRAPHY AND THE MOSCOW TRIALS: AFTER THIRTY YEARS." USSR NAT/G LEGIT PRESS CONTROL LEAD ATTIT MARXISM...NEW/IDEA METH 20 TROTSKY/L STALIN/J KHRUSH/N. PAGE 142 H2843 HIST/WRIT EDU/PROP SANCTION ADJUD

B90
BURKE E.,REFLECTIONS ON THE REVOLUTION IN FRANCE. FRANCE UK NAT/G DOMIN LEGIT PEACE PWR SOVEREIGN CONSERVE...POLICY GEN/LAWS 18. PAGE 24 H0487 REV ORD/FREE CHIEF TRADIT

B91
PAINE T.,RIGHTS OF MAN. FRANCE MOD/EUR CONSTN NAT/G CHIEF DOMIN LEGIT SOVEREIGN...MAJORIT IDEA/COMP 18 BURKE/EDM CIVIL/LIB. PAGE 122 H2446 GEN/LAWS ORD/FREE REV AGREE

B99
BROOKS S.,BRITAIN AND THE BOERS. AFR SOUTH/AFR UK CULTURE INSPECT LEGIT...INT/LAW 19/20 BOER/WAR. PAGE 22 H0433 WAR DIPLOM NAT/G

LEGRES A. H1860

LEGUM C. H1861,H1862

LEHMAN R.L. H1863

LEHMBRUCH G. H1864

LEIB B.S. H1192

LEIBLER I. H1865

LEIBNITZ/G....GOTTFRIED WILHELM VON LEIBNITZ

B58
HERRMANN K.,DAS STAATSDENKEN BEI LEIBNIZ. GP/REL ATTIT ORD/FREE...CONCPT IDEA/COMP 17 LEIBNITZ/G CHURCH/STA. PAGE 70 H1406 NAT/G JURID SECT EDU/PROP

LEIGH M.B. H1866

LEIGHTON A.H. H1867

LEIGHTON D.C. H1868

LEISURE....UNOBLIGATED TIME EXPENDITURES

B04
REED W.A.,ETHNOLOGICAL SURVEY PUBLICATIONS (VOL. II). PHILIPPINE STRUCT INDUS SECT DEATH LEISURE HABITAT...AUD/VIS CHARTS WORSHIP 20 NABOLOI NEGRITO BATAK. PAGE 130 H2607 CULTURE SOCIETY SOC OBS

B40
ZWEIG F.,THE WORKER IN AN AFFLUENT SOCIETY: FAMILY LIFE AND INDUSTRY. UK STRATA LG/CO ECO/TAC LEISURE INGP/REL HAPPINESS HEALTH...PSY SOC/WK INT CHARTS WORSHIP 20 FEMALE/SEX. PAGE 173 H3465 MARRIAGE ATTIT FINAN CULTURE

B51
BERNATZIK H.A.,THE SPIRITS OF THE YELLOW LEAVES. BURMA LAOS S/ASIA THAILAND VIETNAM SOCIETY AGRI COLONIAL LEISURE GP/REL PERS/REL ISOLAT AGE HABITAT SEX WORSHIP 20. PAGE 16 H0310 SOC KIN ECO/UNDEV CULTURE

B58
CROWE S.,THE LANDSCAPE OF POWER. UK CULTURE SERV/IND NAT/G CONSULT PARTIC NUC/PWR LEISURE...SOC EXHIBIT 20. PAGE 36 H0712 HABITAT TEC/DEV PLAN CONTROL

B61
VAN GULIK R.H.,SEXUAL LIFE IN ANCIENT CHINA. ASIA LEISURE...CHARTS. PAGE 161 H3230 SEX CULTURE MARRIAGE LOVE

B64
CULLINGWORTH J.B.,TOWN AND COUNTRY PLANNING IN ENGLAND AND WALES. UK LAW SOCIETY CONSULT ACT/RES ADMIN ROUTINE LEISURE INGP/REL ADJUST PWR...GEOG 20 OPEN/SPACE URBAN/RNWL. PAGE 36 H0718 MUNIC PLAN NAT/G PROB/SOLV

B64
JOSEPHSON E.,MAN ALONE: ALIENATION IN MODERN SOCIETY. WOR+45 ECO/DEV WORKER WAR LEISURE RACE/REL ANOMIE ATTIT PERCEPT PERSON ALL/VALS...ANTHOL 20. PAGE 82 H1636 STRANGE CULTURE SOCIETY ADJUST

B64
PINNICK A.W.,COUNTRY PLANNERS IN ACTION. UK FINAN SERV/IND NAT/G CONSULT DELIB/GP PRICE CONTROL ROUTINE LEISURE AGE/C...GEOG 20 URBAN/RNWL. PAGE 126 H2512 MUNIC PLAN INDUS ATTIT

B64
SCHNITGER F.M.,FORGOTTEN KINGDOMS IN SUMATRA. FAM SECT LEISURE HABITAT...OBS AUD/VIS WORSHIP 20 SUMATRA. PAGE 140 H2793 CULTURE AFR SOCIETY STRUCT

B65
LAMBIRI I.,SOCIAL CHANGE IN A GREEK COUNTRY TOWN. GREECE FAM PROB/SOLV ROUTINE TASK LEISURE INGP/REL CONSEN ORD/FREE...SOC INT QU CHARTS 20. PAGE 90 H1803 INDUS WORKER CULTURE NEIGH

LEITES N. H1834,H1869,H1870,H1871

LEITZ F. H1872

LEMARCHAND R. H1873,H1874

LEMBERG E. H1875

LEMERT E.M. H1876

LEND/LEASE....LEND-LEASE PROGRAM(S)

LENG S.C. H1877

LENIN V.I. H1878,H1879,H1880,H1881

LENIN/VI....VLADIMIR ILYICH LENIN

B34
STALIN J.,PROBLEMS OF LENINISM. USSR STRATA INDUS LOC/G POL/PAR ECO/TAC CONTROL TOTALISM PWR SOCISM LENIN/VI STALIN/J. PAGE 148 H2968 MARXISM REV ELITES NAT/G

B40
HUNTER R.,REVOLUTION: WHY, HOW, WHEN? NAT/G ECO/TAC EDU/PROP COERCE ORD/FREE FASCISM POPULISM SOCISM 18/20 HITLER/A LENIN/VI. PAGE 75 H1502 REV METH/COMP LEAD CONSTN

B43
LENIN V.I.,LEFT WING COMMUNISM: AN INFANTILE DISORDER (1920). GERMANY MOD/EUR USSR STRUCT CHIEF DOMIN EDU/PROP LEGIT LEAD REPRESENT POPULISM ...METH/COMP 19 LENIN/VI COM/PARTY MENSHEVIK. PAGE 94 H1879 COM MARXISM NAT/G REV

B48
TOWSTER J.,POLITICAL POWER IN THE USSR: 1917-1947. USSR CONSTN CULTURE ELITES CREATE PLAN COERCE CENTRAL ATTIT RIGID/FLEX ORD/FREE...BIBLIOG SOC/INTEG 20 LENIN/VI STALIN/J. PAGE 156 H3122 EX/STRUC NAT/G MARXISM PWR

B48
WOLFE B.D.,THREE WHO MADE A REVOLUTION. USSR CONSTN NAT/G CAP/ISM EDU/PROP CONTROL WAR GP/REL INGP/REL PERS/REL ROLE 20 STALIN/J LENIN/VI TROTSKY/L BOLSHEVISM. PAGE 170 H3398 BIOG REV LEAD MARXISM

B50
HALLOWELL J.H.,MAIN CURRENTS IN MODERN POLITICAL THOUGHT. CONSTN SECT LEGIS...MAJORIT CONCPT 17/20 MARX/KARL MILL/JS HOBBES/T LENIN/VI. PAGE 64 H1290 IDEA/COMP POPULISM SOCISM

B54
LENIN V.I.,SELECTED WORKS (12 VOLS.). USSR INTELL SOCIETY STRATA STRUCT NAT/G POL/PAR WORKER CAP/ISM REV WAR...MARXIST PHIL/SCI 20 MARX/KARL LENIN/VI. PAGE 94 H1880 COM MARXISM

B55
MAYO H.B.,DEMOCRACY AND MARXISM. COM USSR STRATA NAT/G WORKER ECO/TAC REV MORAL...PHIL/SCI HIST/WRIT IDEA/COMP WORSHIP 20 MARX/KARL LENIN/VI STALIN/J TROTSKY/L. PAGE 105 H2108 MARXISM CAP/ISM

B58
DUNAYEVSKAYA R.,MARXISM AND FREEDOM: FROM 1776 UNTIL TODAY. COM USSR WORKER CAP/ISM DOMIN REV GP/REL TOTALISM ALL/VALS...MYTH BIOG IDEA/COMP 18/20 MARX/KARL LENIN/VI STALIN/J. PAGE 43 H0861 MARXISM CONCPT ORD/FREE

B58
PALMER E.E.,THE COMMUNIST CHALLENGE. COM USA+45 USA-45 ECO/DEV ECO/UNDEV NEUTRAL ORD/FREE POPULISM ...CONCPT NAT/COMP ANTHOL 19/20 LENIN/VI STALIN/J MAO MARX/KARL COM/PARTY. PAGE 123 H2450 MARXISM DIPLOM IDEA/COMP POLICY

B59
HENDEL S.,THE SOVIET CRUCIBLE. USSR LEAD COERCE NAT/LISM UTOPIA PWR...POLICY CONCPT ANTHOL 20 STALIN/J LENIN/VI MARX/KARL BOLSHEVIK. PAGE 70 H1393 COM MARXISM REV TOTALISM

B59
PAGE S.W.,LENIN AND WORLD REVOLUTION. COM USSR NAT/G DOMIN COERCE CROWD UTOPIA ATTIT AUTHORIT DRIVE PWR...CONCPT MYTH 19/20 LENIN/VI MARX/KARL. PAGE 122 H2441 REV PERSON MARXISM BIOG

B60
SCHAPIRO L.,THE COMMUNIST PARTY OF THE SOVIET UNION. COM LAW SOCIETY STRATA STRUCT ECO/DEV LABOR NAT/G POL/PAR CREATE DOMIN EDU/PROP COERCE TOTALISM MARXISM...POLICY CONCPT MYTH TIME/SEQ WORK TOT/POP 20 LENIN/VI STALIN/J. PAGE 139 H2772 INTELL PWR USSR

B61
LEVIN L.A.,BIBLIOGRAFIIA BIBLIOGRAFII PROIZVEDENII K. MARKSA, F. ENGELSA, V.I. LENINA. COM USSR NAT/G POL/PAR WORKER LEAD REV ATTIT...POLICY IDEA/COMP 20 MARX/KARL LENIN/VI ENGELS. PAGE 95 H1899 BIBLIOG/A MARXISM MARXIST CONCPT

B62
EBENSTEIN W.,TWO WAYS OF LIFE. USA+45 CULTURE ECO/DEV PLAN EDU/PROP CONTROL ORD/FREE...GOV/COMP IDEA/COMP T 20 MARX/KARL ENGELS/F LENIN/VI LOCKE/JOHN MILL/JS. PAGE 44 H0885 MARXISM POPULISM ECO/TAC DIPLOM

B62
MEHNERT K.,SOVIET MAN AND HIS WORLD. COM USSR INTELL FAM WORKER PLAN EDU/PROP REV PRODUC MARXISM ...SOC TREND SOC/INTEG 20 LENIN/VI STALIN/J KHRUSH/N. PAGE 108 H2162 SOCIETY CULTURE ECO/DEV

B62
MEYER A.G.,LENINISM. USSR STRUCT NAT/G CAP/ISM LEAD WAR PWR SOVEREIGN...BIBLIOG 20 LENIN/VI. PAGE 109 H2187 POL/PAR REV MARXISM PHIL/SCI

B63
MCNEAL R.H.,THE BOLSHEVIK TRADITION: LENIN, STALIN, KHRUSHCHEV. USSR NAT/G SUPEGO CONSERVE...IDEA/COMP GEN/LAWS 20 LENIN/VI STALIN/J KHRUSH/N. PAGE 107 H2145 INTELL BIOG PERS/COMP

B63
MILLER W.J.,THE MEANING OF COMMUNISM. USSR SOCIETY ECO/DEV EX/STRUC WORKER TEC/DEV ADMIN TOTALISM ...POLICY CONCPT CHARTS BIBLIOG T 20 COLD/WAR LENIN/VI STALIN/J. PAGE 111 H2215 MARXISM TRADIT DIPLOM NAT/G

B63
SWEARER H.R.,CONTEMPORARY COMMUNISM: THEORY AND PRACTICE. COM USSR SOCIETY ECO/DEV POL/PAR FORCES PLAN ADMIN LEAD NAT/LISM...POLICY ANTHOL 20 LENIN/VI COM/PARTY. PAGE 151 H3015 MARXISM CONCPT DIPLOM NAT/G

B64
FISCHER L.,THE LIFE OF LENIN. USSR LEAD REV WAR ...SOC 19/20 LENIN/VI COM/PARTY BOLSHEVISM. PAGE 51 H1011 BIOG MARXISM PERSON CHIEF

B64
RESHETAR J.S. JR.,A CONCISE HISTORY OF THE COMMUNIST PARTY OF THE SOVIET UNION (REV. ED.). COM USSR NAT/G EXEC 19/20 LENIN/VI STALIN/J KHRUSH/N. PAGE 131 H2618 CHIEF POL/PAR MARXISM PWR

B65
ULAM A.,THE BOLSHEVIKS. COM USSR NAT/G CHIEF ECO/TAC ADMIN LEAD WAR POPULISM...POLICY 19/20 LENIN/VI BOLSHEVISM. PAGE 157 H3148 SOCISM POL/PAR TOP/EX REV

B66
BRODERSEN A.,THE SOVIET WORKER: LABOR AND GOVERNMENT IN SOVIET SOCIETY. USSR STRUCT INDUS LABOR PLAN PAY INGP/REL PRODUC...POLICY GEN/LAWS BIBLIOG 20 STALIN/J LENIN/VI BOLSHEVISM KHRUSH/N. PAGE 21 H0425 WORKER ROLE NAT/G MARXISM

B66
DEUTSCHER I.,STALIN: A POLITICAL BIOGRAPHY. EUR+WWI USSR POL/PAR FORCES DIPLOM ADMIN LEAD REV WAR TOTALISM PERSON 20 STALIN/J ROOSEVLT/F LENIN/VI HITLER/A. PAGE 40 H0807 BIOG MARXISM TOP/EX PWR

B66
HERMANN F.G.,DER KAMPF GEGEN RELIGION UND KIRCHE IN DER SOWJETISCHEN BESATZUNGSZONE DEUTSCHLANDS. GERMANY/E EDU/PROP ATTIT PERSON MORAL MARXISM 20 LENIN/VI STALIN/J KHRUSH/N. PAGE 70 H1400 SECT ORD/FREE GP/REL NAT/G

B67
BRZEZINSKI Z.K.,THE SOVIET BLOC: UNITY AND CONFLICT (2ND ED., REV., ENLARGED). COM POLAND USSR INTELL CHIEF EX/STRUC CONTROL EXEC GOV/REL PWR MARXISM ...TREND IDEA/COMP 20 LENIN/VI MARX/KARL STALIN/J. PAGE 23 H0463 NAT/G DIPLOM

B67
TOMPKINS S.R.,THE TRIUMPH OF BOLSHEVISM: REVOLUTION OR REACTION? USSR WORKER PRESS WEALTH MARXISM POPULISM...BIOG TREND IDEA/COMP BIBLIOG 19/20 LENIN/VI. PAGE 156 H3113 REV NAT/G POL/PAR NAT/LISM

S67
VON LAUE T.H.,"WESTERNIZATION, REVOLUTION AND THE SEARCH FOR A BASIS OF AUTHORITY - RUSSIA IN 1917." USSR ELITES INTELL ECO/UNDEV NAT/G WORKER ECO/TAC TAX ADMIN LEAD AUTHORIT 20 LENIN/VI. PAGE 164 H3274 MARXISM REV COM DOMIN

LENSKI G.E. H1882

LENZ F. H1883

LEONARD L.L. H1884

LEONARD T.J. H1885

LEONTIEF W. H1886

LEPOINTE G. H1887

LERNER D. H1179,H1888,H1889

LERNER R. H1890

LERNER W. H1891

LEROY P. H1892

LESAGE/J....J. LESAGE

LETHBRIDGE H.J. H1893,H1894

LEVCIK B. H1895

LEVELLERS....LEVELLERS PARTY

B44
WOLFE D.M.,LEVELLER MANIFESTOES OF THE PURITAN REVOLUTION. UK CONSTN NAT/G SECT...CONCPT ANTHOL 17 LEVELLERS DECLAR/IND PURITAN LOCKE/JOHN. PAGE 170 H3400 POL/PAR REV ORD/FREE ATTIT

LEVI W. H1896,H1897,H1898

LEVIN L.A. H1899

LEVIN M.G. H1900,H1901

LEVINE L. H1902

LEVINE R.A. H1903,H1904,H1905

LEVY J-P. H1906

LEVY M. H1907

LEWIN E. H1908

LEWIN J. H1909

LEWIN P. H1910

LEWIS B. H1911

LEWIS B.W. H1912

LEWIS E. H1913

LEWIS E.G. H1914

LEWIS J.D. H0248

LEWIS R. H1915

LEWIS W.A. H1916

LEWIS/A....ARTHUR LEWIS

LEWIS/JL....JOHN L. LEWIS

LEYBURN J.G. H1917

LEYDER J. H1918

LEYS C. H1919

LEYS W. H1920

LFNA....LEAGUE OF FREE NATIONS ASSOCIATION

LG/CO....LARGE COMPANY

C09
SCHAPIRO J.S.,"SOCIAL REFORM AND THE REFORMATION." CHRIST-17C GERMANY LAW CONSTN LG/CO NAT/G WORKER PROB/SOLV CT/SYS REV...BIBLIOG 16. PAGE 138 H2770 ORD/FREE SECT ECO/TAC BIOG

B29
LEITZ F.,DIE PUBLIZITAT DER AKTIENGESELLSCHAFT. BELGIUM FRANCE GERMANY UK FINAN PRESS GP/REL PROFIT KNOWL 20. PAGE 94 H1872 LG/CO JURID ECO/TAC NAT/COMP

B31
CROOK W.H.,THE GENERAL STRIKE: A STUDY OF LABOR'S TRAGIC WEAPON IN THEORY AND PRACTICE. BELGIUM FRANCE SWEDEN UK WOR-45 PROB/SOLV ECO/TAC DOMIN PWR LABOR WORKER LG/CO

...POLICY TIME/SEQ NAT/COMP GEN/LAWS 19/20 STRIKE. BARGAIN
PAGE 35 H0707

B40
ZWEIG F.,THE WORKER IN AN AFFLUENT SOCIETY: FAMILY MARRIAGE
LIFE AND INDUSTRY. UK STRATA LG/CO ECO/TAC LEISURE ATTIT
INGP/REL HAPPINESS HEALTH...PSY SOC/WK INT CHARTS FINAN
WORSHIP 20 FEMALE/SEX. PAGE 173 H3465 CULTURE

B46
ALLEN J.S.,WORLD MONOPOLY AND PEACE. GERMANY UK CAP/ISM
USSR FINAN INDUS LG/CO DOMIN CONTROL PEACE PWR DIPLOM
WEALTH SOCISM...NAT/COMP 20 MONOPOLY. PAGE 5 H0105 WAR
COLONIAL

B46
DAVIES E.,NATIONAL ENTERPRISE: THE DEVELOPMENT OF ADMIN
THE PUBLIC CORPORATION. UK LG/CO EX/STRUC WORKER NAT/G
PROB/SOLV COST ATTIT SOCISM 20. PAGE 37 H0748 CONTROL
INDUS

B47
BOWEN R.H.,GERMAN THEORIES OF THE CORPORATIVE IDEA/COMP
STATE, WITH SPECIAL REFERENCES TO THE PERIOD CENTRAL
1870-1919. GERMANY INDUS LG/CO CATHISM SOCISM...SOC NAT/G
18/20. PAGE 19 H0389 POLICY

B54
FRIEDMAN W.,THE PUBLIC CORPORATION: A COMPARATIVE LAW
SYMPOSIUM (UNIVERSITY OF TORONTO SCHOOL OF LAW SOCISM
COMPARATIVE LAW SERIES, VOL. I). SWEDEN USA+45 LG/CO
INDUS INT/ORG NAT/G REGION CENTRAL FEDERAL...POLICY OWN
JURID IDEA/COMP NAT/COMP ANTHOL 20 COMMONWLTH
MONOPOLY EUROPE. PAGE 53 H1065

C54
BERLE A.A. JR.,"THE 20TH CENTURY CAPITALIST LG/CO
REVOLUTION." ECO/DEV NAT/G DIPLOM PRICE CONTROL CAP/ISM
ATTIT...BIBLIOG/A 20. PAGE 15 H0306 MGT
PWR

B55
SERRANO MOSCOSO E.,A STATEMENT OF THE LAWS OF FINAN
ECUADOR IN MATTERS AFFECTING BUSINESS (2ND ED.). ECO/UNDEV
ECUADOR INDUS LABOR LG/CO NAT/G LEGIS TAX CONTROL LAW
MARRIAGE 20. PAGE 141 H2830 CONSTN

B58
INDIA (REPUBLIC) PARLIAMENT,CLASSIFIED LIST OF NAT/G
PUBLIC UNDERTAKINGS AND OTHER BODIES IN INDIA. LEGIS
INDIA ACADEM LG/CO CONSULT LEGIT CONFER GOV/REL 20. LICENSE
PAGE 76 H1528 PROF/ORG

B58
MCIVOR R.C.,CANADIAN MONETARY, BANKING, AND FISCAL ECO/TAC
DEVELOPMENT. CANADA INDUS LG/CO NAT/G SML/CO FINAN
CONTROL WAR...GEN/LAWS BIBLIOG 17/20. PAGE 107 ECO/DEV
H2137 WEALTH

B59
FAYERWEATHER J.,THE EXECUTIVE OVERSEAS: INT/TRADE
ADMINISTRATIVE ATTITUDES AND RELATIONSHIPS IN A TOP/EX
FOREIGN CULTURE. USA+45 WOR+45 CULTURE LG/CO SML/CO NAT/COMP
ATTIT...MGT PERS/COMP 20 MEXIC/AMER. PAGE 49 H0979 PERS/REL

B59
HANSON A.H.,THE STRUCTURE AND CONTROL OF STATE NAT/G
ENTERPRISES IN TURKEY. TURKEY LAW ADMIN GOV/REL LG/CO
EFFICIENCY...CHARTS 20. PAGE 66 H1319 OWN
CONTROL

B59
VERNEY D.V.,PUBLIC ENTERPRISE IN SWEDEN. FUT SWEDEN ECO/DEV
UK INDUS POL/PAR LEGIS PROB/SOLV CAP/ISM INT/TRADE POLICY
CONTROL SOCISM...MGT CONCPT NAT/COMP 20 SOCDEM/PAR LG/CO
CIVIL/SERV. PAGE 162 H3246 NAT/G

B60
WEINER H.E.,BRITISH LABOR AND PUBLIC OWNERSHIP. UK LABOR
SERV/IND LG/CO WORKER CONTROL OWN 20. PAGE 166 NAT/G
H3327 INDUS
ATTIT

B61
MIT CENTER INTERNATIONAL STU,OFFICIAL SERIAL BIBLIOG
PUBLICATIONS RELATING TO ECONOMIC DEVELOPMENT IN ECO/UNDEV
AFRICA SOUTH OF THE SAHARA. AFR SOCIETY AGRI FINAN ECO/TAC
INDUS LG/CO ADMIN 20. PAGE 111 H2228 NAT/G

L61
LEVINE R.A.,"THE ANTHROPOLOGY OF CONFLICT." FUT SOCIETY
CULTURE INTELL FAM INT/ORG LG/CO SML/CO ATTIT KNOWL ACT/RES
...METH/CNCPT VAL/FREE 20. PAGE 95 H1905

B62
KAGZI M.C.,THE INDIAN ADMINISTRATIVE LAW. INDIA JURID
LG/CO CONTROL CT/SYS...CONCPT 20. PAGE 83 H1649 ADJUD
DELIB/GP
NAT/G

B62
PASTOR R.S.,A STATEMENT OF THE LAWS OF PARAGUAY IN FINAN
MATTERS AFFECTING BUSINESS (2ND ED.). PARAGUAY ECO/UNDEV
INDUS FAM LABOR LG/CO NAT/G LEGIS TAX CONTROL LAW
MARRIAGE 20. PAGE 124 H2474 CONSTN

B64
BAUCHET P.,ECONOMIC PLANNING. FRANCE STRATA LG/CO ECO/DEV
CAP/ISM ADMIN PARL/PROC DEMAND OPTIMAL ATTIT PWR NAT/G
SOCISM...POLICY CHARTS 20. PAGE 12 H0238 PLAN
ECO/TAC

B64
FLORENCE P.S.,ECONOMICS AND SOCIOLOGY OF INDUSTRY; INDUS
A REALISTIC ANALYSIS OF DEVELOPMENT. ECO/UNDEV SOC
LG/CO NAT/G PLAN...GEOG MGT BIBLIOG 20. PAGE 51 ADMIN
H1029

B64
HALE O.J.,THE CAPTIVE PRESS IN THE THIRD REICH. COM/IND
GERMANY CULTURE LG/CO NAT/G POL/PAR PLAN DOMIN TASK PRESS
CENTRAL OWN TOTALISM PWR...BIBLIOG 20 HITLER/A NAZI CONTROL
AMMAN/MAX. PAGE 64 H1283 FASCISM

B65
BARRY E.E.,NATIONALISATION IN BRITISH POLITICS: THE NAT/G
HISTORICAL BACKGROUND. UK AGRI DIST/IND EXTR/IND OWN
LABOR LG/CO ATTIT CONSERVE SOCISM 19/20 LABOR/PAR. INDUS
PAGE 12 H0231 POL/PAR

B65
GOLEMBIEWSKI R.T.,MEN, MANAGEMENT, AND MORALITY; LG/CO
TOWARD A NEW ORGANIZATIONAL ETHIC. CONSTN EX/STRUC MGT
CREATE ADMIN CONTROL INGP/REL PERSON SUPEGO MORAL PROB/SOLV
PWR...GOV/COMP METH/COMP 20 BUREAUCRCY. PAGE 58
H1161

B66
BIRKHEAD G.S.,ADMINISTRATIVE PROBLEMS IN PAKISTAN. ADMIN
PAKISTAN AGRI FINAN INDUS LG/CO ECO/TAC CONTROL PWR NAT/G
...CHARTS ANTHOL 20. PAGE 17 H0340 ORD/FREE
ECO/UNDEV

B66
TIVEY L.J.,NATIONALISATION IN BRITISH INDUSTRY. UK NAT/G
LEGIS PARL/PROC GP/REL OWN ATTIT SOCISM 20. INDUS
PAGE 156 H3109 CONTROL
LG/CO

B67
GALBRAITH J.K.,THE NEW INDUSTRIAL STATE. INDUS TEC/DEV
LABOR LG/CO NAT/G POL/PAR SCHOOL OP/RES CAP/ISM ECO/DEV
EXEC TREND. PAGE 54 H1087 SOCIETY
MARKET

B67
THOMAN R.S.,GEOGRAPHY OF INTERNATIONAL TRADE. INT/TRADE
WOR+45 ECO/DEV ECO/UNDEV INT/ORG LG/CO PLAN BAL/PAY GEOG
...STAT CHARTS NAT/COMP 20. PAGE 154 H3075 ECO/TAC
DIPLOM

L67
WRIGHT W.R.,"FOREIGN-OWNED RAILWAYS IN ARGENTINA: A NAT/LISM
CASE STUDY OF ECONOMIC NATIONALISM." L/A+17C UK CAP/ISM
ECO/UNDEV SERV/IND LG/CO NAT/G TEC/DEV BAL/PWR ECO/TAC
EQUILIB ARGEN. PAGE 171 H3423 COLONIAL

S67
ALPANDER G.G.,"ENTREPRENEURS AND PRIVATE ENTERPRISE ECO/UNDEV
IN TURKEY." TURKEY INDUS PROC/MFG EDU/PROP ATTIT LG/CO
DRIVE WEALTH...GEOG MGT SOC STAT TREND CHARTS 20. NAT/G
PAGE 6 H0114 POLICY

S67
BOSHER J.F.,"GOVERNMENT AND PRIVATE INTERESTS IN NAT/G
NEW FRANCE." CANADA FRANCE INDUS LG/CO SML/CO FINAN
CAP/ISM INT/TRADE COLONIAL GP/REL...HIST/WRIT ADMIN
17/18. PAGE 19 H0381 CONTROL

S67
TAYLOR P.B. JR.,"PROGRESS IN VENEZUELA." L/A+17C ECO/UNDEV
VENEZUELA AGRI INDUS LG/CO NAT/G SML/CO CHOOSE ECO/TAC
...POLICY 20. PAGE 153 H3057 POL/PAR
ORD/FREE

S67
WRAITH R.E.,"ADMINISTRATIVE CHANGE IN THE NEW ADMIN
AFRICA." AFR LG/CO ADJUD INGP/REL PWR...RECORD NAT/G
GP/COMP 20. PAGE 171 H3416 LOC/G
ECO/UNDEV

LI C.M. H1921

LIB/INTRNT....LIBERAL INTERNATIONAL

LIB/PARTY....LIBERAL PARTY (ALL NATIONS)

B28
FYFE H.,THE BRITISH LIBERAL PARTY. UK SECT ADMIN POL/PAR
LEAD CHOOSE GP/REL PWR SOCISM...MAJORIT TIME/SEQ NAT/G
19/20 LIB/PARTY CONSRV/PAR. PAGE 54 H1084 REPRESENT
POPULISM

B61
JENNINGS I.,PARTY POLITICS: THE GROWTH OF PARTIES CHOOSE
(VOL. II). UK SOCIETY NAT/G LEGIS ATTIT 18/20 POL/PAR
LABOR/PAR LIB/PARTY CONSRV/PAR. PAGE 80 H1606 PWR
POLICY

B66
DE VORE B.B.,LAND AND LIBERTY; A HISTORY OF THE REV
MEXICAN REVOLUTION. CONSTN INTELL NAT/G CONTROL CHIEF
LEAD CHOOSE TOTALISM AUTHORIT...BIBLIOG 19/20 POL/PAR
MEXIC/AMER DIAZ/P LIB/PARTY MAGON/F MADERO/F.
PAGE 39 H0776

LIBERALISM....SEE NEW/LIB, WELF/ST, OLD/LIB, LAISSEZ

LIBERIA....SEE ALSO AFR

B50
HARLEY G.W.,MASKS AS AGENTS OF SOCIAL CONTROL IN CONTROL
NORTHEAST LIBERIA. AFR LIBERIA LAW CULTURE ADJUST ECO/UNDEV
CONSEN MORAL...GEOG SOC WORSHIP 20. PAGE 66 H1332 SECT
CHIEF

B62
CARTER G.M.,AFRICAN ONE-PARTY STATES. ISLAM IVORY/CST LIBERIA CONSTN CULTURE SOCIETY POL/PAR PLAN DOMIN EDU/PROP EXEC REGION CHOOSE ATTIT ALL/VALS...CONCPT TIME/SEQ CHARTS VAL/FREE 20 TANGANYIKA. PAGE 27 H0545 — AFR NAT/LISM

B64
ALDEFER H.F.,A BIBLIOGRAPHY OF AFRICAN GOVERNMENT: 1950-1964. ALGERIA GUINEA LIBERIA UAR ECO/UNDEV POL/PAR LEGIS COLONIAL LEAD PARL/PROC NAT/LISM 20. PAGE 5 H0098 — BIBLIOG AFR LOC/G NAT/G

LIBERTY....SEE ORD/FREE

LIBRARY HUNGARIAN ACADEMY SCI H1922

LIBYA....SEE ALSO ISLAM

B48
MAUGHAM R.,NORTH AFRICAN NOTEBOOK. ALGERIA ISLAM LIBYA MOROCCO STRUCT ECO/UNDEV COLONIAL...SOC OBS AUD/VIS NAT/COMP WORSHIP 20 TUNIS. PAGE 105 H2102 — SOCIETY RECORD NAT/LISM

B55
KRUSE H.,DAS STAATSANGEHORIGKEITSRECHT DER ARABISCHEN STAATEN. ISLAM JORDAN LIBYA SYRIA UAR NAT/G SECT RACE/REL...INT/LAW 6/20 TREATY. PAGE 89 H1779 — JURID NAT/LISM DIPLOM GP/REL

B61
NATIONAL BANK OF LIBYA,INFLATION IN LIBYA (PAMPHLET). LIBYA SOCIETY NAT/G PLAN INT/TRADE ...STAT CHARTS 20 GOLD/STAND. PAGE 116 H2318 — ECO/TAC ECO/UNDEV FINAN BUDGET

B63
KHADDURI M.,MODERN LIBYA: A STUDY IN POLITICAL DEVELOPMENT. EUR+WWI ISLAM LIBYA ELITES INT/ORG POL/PAR FORCES DIPLOM FOR/AID DOMIN EDU/PROP LEGIT NAT/LISM DRIVE RIGID/FLEX SKILL...CONCPT TIME/SEQ TREND 20. PAGE 85 H1704 — NAT/G STRUCT

B63
ZARTMAN I.W.,GOVERNMENT AND POLITICS IN NORTHERN AFRICA. AFR ALGERIA ISLAM LIBYA MOROCCO UAR ELITES SOCIETY PLAN ECO/TAC DOMIN EDU/PROP LEGIT ATTIT ...GEOG CONCPT TIME/SEQ 20 TUNIS. PAGE 172 H3448 — CULTURE DRIVE NAT/LISM

B66
BROWN L.C.,STATE AND SOCIETY IN INDEPENDENT NORTH AFRICA. ALGERIA LIBYA MOROCCO AGRI INDUS INT/ORG POL/PAR SECT PLAN DIPLOM COLONIAL...LING NAT/COMP ANTHOL BIBLIOG 20 TUNIS MUSLIM. PAGE 22 H0446 — NAT/G SOCIETY CULTURE ECO/UNDEV

B93
ROYAL GEOGRAPHIC SOCIETY,BIBLIOGRAPHY OF BARBARY STATES (4 SUPPLEMENTARY PAPERS). ALGERIA LIBYA MOROCCO SOCIETY STRUCT DIPLOM LEAD 14/19 TUNIS. PAGE 135 H2706 — BIBLIOG ISLAM NAT/G COLONIAL

LICENSE....LEGAL PERMIT

B41
GILMORE M.P.,ARGUMENT FROM ROMAN LAW IN POLITICAL THOUGHT, 1200-1600. INTELL LICENSE CONTROL CT/SYS GOV/REL PRIVIL PWR...IDEA/COMP BIBLIOG 13/16. PAGE 56 H1130 — JURID LAW CONCPT NAT/G

B58
INDIA (REPUBLIC) PARLIAMENT,CLASSIFIED LIST OF PUBLIC UNDERTAKINGS AND OTHER BODIES IN INDIA. INDIA ACADEM LG/CO CONSULT LEGIT CONFER GOV/REL 20. PAGE 76 H1528 — NAT/G LEGIS LICENSE PROF/ORG

B62
SWAYZE H.,POLITICAL CONTROL OF LITERATURE IN THE USSR, 1946-1959. USSR NAT/G CREATE LICENSE...JURID 20. PAGE 151 H3014 — MARXISM WRITING CONTROL DOMIN

B64
SZLADITS C.,BIBLIOGRAPHY ON FOREIGN AND COMPARATIVE LAW: BOOKS AND ARTICLES IN ENGLISH (SUPPLEMENT 1962). FINAN INDUS JUDGE LICENSE ADMIN CT/SYS PARL/PROC OWN...INT/LAW CLASSIF METH/COMP NAT/COMP 20. PAGE 151 H3027 — BIBLIOG/A JURID ADJUD LAW

B98
POLLOCK F.,THE HISTORY OF ENGLISH LAW BEFORE THE TIME OF EDWARD I (2 VOLS, 2ND ED.). UK CULTURE LOC/G LEGIS LICENSE AGREE CONTROL CT/SYS SANCTION CRIME...TIME/SEQ 13 COMMON/LAW CANON/LAW. PAGE 127 H2538 — LAW ADJUD JURID

LICHFIELD N. H1923

LICHTHEIM G. H1924

LIEBER F. H1925

LIEBERSON S. H1926

LIEBESNY H.J. H1703

LIEBKNECHT W.P.C. H1927

LIECHTENST....LIECHTENSTEIN; SEE ALSO APPROPRIATE TIME/SPACE/CULTURE INDEX

S59
LEYS C.,"MODELS, THEORIES, AND THE THEORY OF POLITICAL PARTIES" CANADA LIECHTENST UK LOC/G NAT/G PARTIC REPRESENT GP/REL CONSEN EQUILIB MAJORITY ...NEW/IDEA MATH CHARTS 20. PAGE 96 H1919 — POL/PAR CHOOSE METH/CNCPT SIMUL

S67
KOHN W.S.G.,"THE SOVEREIGNTY OF LIECHTENSTEIN." LIECHTENST SWITZERLND USSR CONSTN DEBATE WAR CONSERVE 18/20 UN. PAGE 88 H1748 — SOVEREIGN NAT/G PWR DIPLOM

LIENHARDT G. H1928

LIESNER H.H. H2154

LIEUWEN E. H1929

LIGGETT E. H1930

LIGHTFT/PM....PHIL M. LIGHTFOOT

LIGOT M. H1931

LIKERT/R....RENSIS LIKERT

LIN/PIAO....LIN PIAO

LINCOLN/A....PRESIDENT ABRAHAM LINCOLN

LINDAHL/E....ERIK LINDAHL

LINDSAY H.A. H3099

LINDSAY K. H1932

LINEBARGER P. H1933

LING D.L. H1934

LING....LINGUISTICS, LANGUAGE

N
ACAD RUMANIAN SCI DOC CTR,RUMANIAN SCIENTIFIC ABSTRACTS: SOCIAL SCIENCES. ROMANIA FINAN HABITAT ...ART/METH GEOG HUM JURID PSY 20. PAGE 3 H0059 — BIBLIOG/A CULTURE LING LAW

N
SCHADERA I.,SELECT BIBLIOGRAPHY OF SOUTH AFRICAN NATIVE LIFE AND PROBLEMS. SOUTH/AFR LAW CULTURE ECO/UNDEV COLONIAL PARTIC...POLICY LING 20. PAGE 138 H2768 — BIBLIOG/A SOC AFR STRUCT

N
MIDDLE EAST JOURNAL. CULTURE SECT DIPLOM LEAD GOV/REL ATTIT...POLICY PHIL/SCI SOC LING BIOG 20. PAGE 1 H0007 — BIBLIOG ISLAM NAT/G ECO/UNDEV

N
"PROLOG",DIGEST OF THE SOVIET UKRANIAN PRESS. USSR LAW AGRI INDUS PROVS SCHOOL DIPLOM GOV/REL ATTIT ...HUM LING 20. PAGE 3 H0053 — BIBLIOG/A NAT/G PRESS COM

N
AFRICAN BIBLIOGRAPHIC CENTER,A CURRENT BIBLIOGRAPHY ON AFRICAN AFFAIRS. LAW CULTURE ECO/UNDEV LABOR SECT DIPLOM FOR/AID COLONIAL NAT/LISM...LING 20. PAGE 4 H0075 — BIBLIOG/A AFR NAT/G REGION

N
MIDDLE EAST INSTITUTE,CURRENT RESEARCH ON THE MIDDLE EAST....PHIL/SCI PSY SOC LING 20. PAGE 110 H2201 — BIBLIOG R+D ISLAM NAT/G

N
US LIBRARY OF CONGRESS,SOUTHERN ASIA ACCESSIONS LIST. BURMA CEYLON INDIA NEPAL PAKISTAN S/ASIA THAILAND AGRI INDUS SCHOOL WORKER...ART/METH GEOG HEAL PHIL/SCI LING 20. PAGE 160 H3201 — BIBLIOG/A SOCIETY CULTURE ECO/UNDEV

B03
FAGUET E.,LE LIBERALISME. FRANCE PRESS ADJUD ADMIN DISCRIM CONSERVE SOCISM...TRADIT SOC LING WORSHIP PARLIAMENT. PAGE 48 H0960 — ORD/FREE EDU/PROP NAT/G LAW

B05
PHILIPPINE ISLANDS BUREAU SCI,ETHNOLOGICAL SURVEY: THE BONTOC IGOROT. ECO/UNDEV AGRI FAM MARRIAGE HEALTH WEALTH...LING OBS AUD/VIS CHARTS WORSHIP 20 LUZON BONTOC. PAGE 125 H2500 — CULTURE INGP/REL KIN STRUCT

B12
CORDIER H.,BIBLIOTHECA INDOSINICA: DICTIONAIRE BIBLIOGRAPHIQUE DES OUVRAGES RELATIFS A LA PENINSULE INDOCHINOISE. BURMA LAOS MALAYSIA S/ASIA THAILAND VIETNAM SECT...LING 20. PAGE 33 H0665 — BIBLIOG/A GEOG NAT/G

N13
H T.,GRUNDZUGE DES CHINESISCHEN VOLKSCHARACTERS. ASIA CULTURE SOCIETY...HUM 19/20. PAGE 63 H1262
ATTIT PERSON ART/METH LING

B18
KERNER R.J.,SLAVIC EUROPE: A SELECTED BIBLIOGRAPHY IN THE WESTERN EUROPEAN LANGUAGES. BULGARIA CZECHOSLVK GERMANY/E POLAND RUSSIA YUGOSLAVIA NAT/G DIPLOM MARXISM...LING 19/20. PAGE 85 H1695
BIBLIOG SOCIETY CULTURE COM

B19
NATHAN M.,THE SOUTH AFRICAN COMMONWEALTH: CONSTITUTION, PROBLEMS, SOCIAL CONDITIONS. SOUTH/AFR UK CULTURE INDUS EX/STRUC LEGIS BUDGET EDU/PROP ADMIN CT/SYS GP/REL RACE/REL...LING 19/20 CMN/WLTH. PAGE 116 H2317
CONSTN NAT/G POL/PAR SOCIETY

B22
FICHTE J.G.,ADDRESSES TO THE GERMAN NATION. GERMANY PRUSSIA ELITES NAT/G SECT CREATE INT/TRADE HEREDITY ...ART/METH LING 19 FRANK/PARL. PAGE 50 H0989
NAT/LISM CULTURE EDU/PROP REGION

B27
SMITH E.W.,THE GOLDEN STOOL: SOME ASPECTS OF THE CONFLICT OF CULTURES IN AFRICA. AFR FINAN INDUS SECT INT/TRADE COERCE CHOOSE RACE/REL ATTIT...GEOG LING 20 NEGRO. PAGE 145 H2907
COLONIAL CULTURE GP/REL EDU/PROP

B29
PRATT I.A.,MODERN EGYPT: A LIST OF REFERENCES TO MATERIAL IN THE NEW YORK PUBLIC LIBRARY. UAR ECO/UNDEV...GEOG JURID SOC LING 20. PAGE 128 H2555
BIBLIOG ISLAM DIPLOM NAT/G

B31
KROEBER A.L.,SOURCE BOOK IN ANTHROPOLOGY. PREHIST SECT RACE/REL...LING GP/COMP ANTHOL. PAGE 89 H1770
SOC HEREDITY CULTURE ALL/VALS

B34
DE CENIVAL P.,BIBLIOGRAPHIE MAROCAINE: 1923-1933. FRANCE MOROCCO SECT ADMIN LEAD GP/REL ATTIT...LING 20. PAGE 37 H0750
BIBLIOG/A ISLAM NAT/G COLONIAL

B37
HAMILTON W.H.,THE POWER TO GOVERN. ECO/DEV FINAN INDUS ECO/TAC INT/TRADE TARIFFS TAX CONTROL CT/SYS WAR COST PWR 18/20 SUPREME/CT. PAGE 65 H1303
LING CONSTN NAT/G POLICY

B38
CARVALHO C.M.,GEOGRAPHIA HUMANA; POLITICA E ECONOMICA (3RD ED.). BRAZIL CULTURE AGRI INDUS DIPLOM COLONIAL GP/REL RACE/REL...LING 20 RESOURCE/N. PAGE 27 H0551
GEOG HABITAT

B39
AKIGA,AKIGA'S STORY: THE TIV TRIBE AS SEEN BY ONE OF ITS MEMBERS. NIGERIA LAW STRUCT ECO/UNDEV FAM LEAD GP/REL MARRIAGE...LING WORSHIP 20. PAGE 4 H0089
KIN SECT SOC CULTURE

B39
HILL R.L.,A BIBLIOGRAPHY OF THE ANGLO-EGYPTIAN SUDAN FROM THE EARLIEST TIMES TO 1937. AFR ETHIOPIA SUDAN UAR LAW COM/IND SECT RACE/REL...GEOG HEAL SOC LING 19/20 NEGRO. PAGE 71 H1417
BIBLIOG CULTURE NAT/COMP GP/COMP

B39
MILLER P.,THE NEW ENGLAND MIND: THE SEVENTEENTH CENTURY. CULTURE DOMIN WRITING INGP/REL CONSEN MAJORITY PERCEPT KNOWL MORAL...CONCPT LING WORSHIP 17 NEW/ENGLND PROTESTANT. PAGE 111 H2214
SECT REGION SOC ATTIT

S39
LASSWELL H.D.,"PERSON, PERSONALITY, GROUP, CULTURE" (BMR)" UNIV CREATE EDU/PROP...EPIST CONCPT LING METH. PAGE 92 H1833
PERSON GP/REL CULTURE PERS/REL

B41
HAYAKAWA S.I.,LANGUAGE IN ACTION. CULTURE INTELL SOCIETY KNOWL...METH/CNCPT LING LOG RECORD STERTYP GEN/METH TOT/POP 20. PAGE 68 H1366
EDU/PROP SOC

C41
KLUCKHOHN C.,"PATTERNING AS EXEMPLIFIED IN NAVAHO CULTURE" IN EDWARD SAPIR, LANGUAGE, CULTURE, AND PERSONALITY (BMR)" KIN PERS/REL ATTIT PERSON...SOC CONCPT METH/CNCPT LING OBS/ENVIR CON/ANAL BIBLIOG SOC/INTEG 20 NAVAHO INDIAN/AM SAPIR/EDW. PAGE 87 H1733
CULTURE INGP/REL STRUCT

B43
JONES C.K.,A BIBLIOGRAPHY OF LATIN AMERICAN BIBLIOGRAPHIES (2ND ED.). CULTURE ALL/VALS...POLICY GEOG HUM SOC LING BIOG TREND 20. PAGE 82 H1629
BIBLIOG/A L/A+17C HIST/WRIT

B44
US LIBRARY OF CONGRESS,RUSSIA: A CHECK LIST PRELIMINARY TO A BASIC BIBLIOGRAPHY OF MATERIALS IN THE RUSSIAN LANGUAGE. COM USSR CULTURE EDU/PROP MARXISM...ART/METH HUM LING 19/20. PAGE 160 H3204
BIBLIOG LAW SECT

C44
VAN VALKENBURG S.,"ELEMENTS OF POLITICAL GEOGRAPHY." FRANCE COM/IND INDUS NAT/G SECT RACE/REL...LING TREND GEN/LAWS BIBLIOG 20. PAGE 162 H3232
GEOG DIPLOM COLONIAL

B46
CASSIRER E.,THE MYTH OF THE STATE. WOR-45 SOCIETY RACE/REL RATIONAL PWR FASCISM...PHIL/SCI PSY LING TREND HEGEL/GWF MACHIAVELL. PAGE 28 H0557
MYTH CONCPT NAT/G IDEA/COMP

N46
HOBBS C.C.,SOUTHEAST ASIA, 1935-45: A SELECTED LIST OF REFERENCE BOOKS (PAMPHLET). S/ASIA AGRI INDUS NAT/G SECT DIPLOM WAR...ART/METH GEOG SOC LING 20. PAGE 72 H1435
BIBLIOG/A CULTURE HABITAT

B47
BEHAR D.,BIBLIOGRAFIA HISPANOAMERICANA. LIBROS ANTIGUOS Y MODERNOS REFERENTES A AMERICA Y ESPANA. PORTUGAL SPAIN CONSTN NAT/G SECT CREATE REV WAR GOV/REL...ART/METH GEOG PHIL/SCI LING 20 ARGEN. PAGE 13 H0260
BIBLIOG L/A+17C CULTURE

B47
HERSKOVITS M.U.,MAN AND HIS WORK. UNIV SECT TEC/DEV PARTIC...PHIL/SCI LING AUD/VIS BIBLIOG. PAGE 70 H1409
SOC CULTURE INGP/REL HABITAT

B50
EMBREE J.F.,BIBLIOGRAPHY OF THE PEOPLES AND CULTURES OF MAINLAND SOUTHEAST ASIA. CAMBODIA LAOS THAILAND VIETNAM LAW...GEOG HUM SOC MYTH LING CHARTS WORSHIP 20. PAGE 46 H0915
BIBLIOG/A CULTURE S/ASIA

B50
HOBBS C.C.,INDOCHINA, A BIBLIOGRAPHY OF THE LAND AND PEOPLE. VIETNAM CULTURE AGRI INDUS NAT/G SECT ...ART/METH GEOG SOC LING 20. PAGE 72 H1436
BIBLIOG/A S/ASIA COLONIAL ECO/UNDEV

B50
JONES H.D.,KOREA, AN ANNOTATED BIBLIOGRAPHY OF PUBLICATIONS IN WESTERN LANGUAGES. KOREA CULTURE MUNIC SECT FORCES DIPLOM HEALTH WEALTH...ART/METH GEOG SOC LING 20. PAGE 82 H1632
BIBLIOG/A ASIA NAT/G ECO/UNDEV

B50
TENG S.,AN ANNOTATED BIBLIOGRAPHY OF SELECTED CHINESE REFERENCE WORKS (REV. ED.). CULTURE ECO/UNDEV LEAD MARXISM...LING INDEX 3/20. PAGE 153 H3062
BIBLIOG/A ASIA NAT/G

B54
GIRALSO JARAMLLO G.,BIBLIOGRAFIA DE BIBLIOGRAFIAS COLOMBIANAS. L/A+17C ACADEM SECT CREATE EDU/PROP ...ART/METH GEOG LING TREND 20 COLOMB. PAGE 57 H1135
BIBLIOG/A CULTURE PHIL/SCI ECO/UNDEV

B54
TITIEV M.,THE SCIENCE OF MAN. LAW STRATA KIN GP/REL PERS/REL HABITAT HEREDITY KNOWL...LING CHARTS BIBLIOG WORSHIP. PAGE 155 H3107
SOC PSY CULTURE

B56
DEUTSCH K.W.,AN INTERDISCIPLINARY BIBLIOGRAPHY ON NATIONALISM, 1935-1953. CULTURE SOCIETY SECT ATTIT HABITAT HEREDITY PERCEPT ROLE WEALTH...METH/CNCPT LING 20. PAGE 40 H0798
BIBLIOG/A NAT/LISM COLONIAL ADJUST

B56
INTERNATIONAL AFRICAN INST,ETHNOGRAPHIC SURVEY OF AFRICA; WESTERN AFRICA: PAGAN PEOPLES OF CENTRAL AREA OF NORTHERN NIGERIA (VOL. XII). NIGERIA FAM KIN SECT ECO/TAC GOV/REL GP/REL ATTIT...LING CHARTS 20. PAGE 77 H1548
STRUCT INGP/REL HABITAT CULTURE

B56
SHAPIRO H.L.,MAN, CULTURE, AND SOCIETY. STRUCT FAM SECT GP/REL INGP/REL...ART/METH GEOG PSY LING ANTHOL BIBLIOG. PAGE 142 H2842
CULTURE PERSON SOC

B57
BYRNES R.F.,BIBLIOGRAPHY OF AMERICAN PUBLICATIONS ON EAST CENTRAL EUROPE, 1945-1957 (VOL. XXII). SECT DIPLOM EDU/PROP RACE/REL...ART/METH GEOG JURID SOC LING 20 JEWS. PAGE 25 H0503
BIBLIOG/A COM MARXISM NAT/G

B57
CENTRAL ASIAN RESEARCH CENTRE,BIBLIOGRAPHY OF RECENT SOVIET SOURCE MATERIAL ON SOVIET CENTRAL ASIA AND THE BORDERLANDS. AFGHANISTN INDIA PAKISTAN UAR USSR ECO/UNDEV AGRI EXTR/IND INDUS ACADEM ADMIN ...HEAL HUM LING CON/ANAL 20. PAGE 28 H0567
BIBLIOG/A COM CULTURE NAT/G

B58
BAGBY P.,CULTURE AND HISTORY....PHIL/SCI CONCPT LING LOG IDEA/COMP GEN/LAWS BIBLIOG 20. PAGE 10 H0196
HIST/WRIT CULTURE GP/COMP NAT/COMP

B58
HENLE P.,LANGUAGE, THOUGHT AND CULTURE. CULTURE GP/REL PERCEPT...PSY TREND ANTHOL 20. PAGE 70 H1397
LING RATIONAL CONCPT SOC

B58
MASON J.B.,THAILAND BIBLIOGRAPHY. S/ASIA THAILAND CULTURE EDU/PROP ADMIN...GEOG SOC LING 20. PAGE 104 H2087
BIBLIOG/A ECO/UNDEV DIPLOM NAT/G

B59
MURDOCK G.P.,AFRICA: ITS PEOPLES AND THEIR CULTURE HISTORY. AFR CULTURE AGRI LOC/G INGP/REL HABITAT ...GEOG SOC LING CHARTS BIBLIOG 20 NEGRO EGYPT/ANC. PAGE 115 H2293
SOCIETY ECO/TAC GP/COMP KIN

B59
WARNER W.L.,THE LIVING AND THE DEAD: A STUDY OF SYMBOLIC LIFE OF AMERICANS. INTELL KIN DEATH ALL/VALS ALL/IDEOS...CONCPT MYTH LING OBS/ENVIR CHARTS BIBLIOG WORSHIP 18/20. PAGE 165 H3311 — CULTURE SOC TIME/SEQ IDEA/COMP

B60
BRIGGS L.C.,TRIBES OF THE SAHARA. AFR MOROCCO STRATA AGRI GP/REL HEALTH...GEOG SOC MYTH LING BIBLIOG 13/20 ARABS. PAGE 21 H0418 — CULTURE HABITAT KIN SELF/OBS

B60
CHATTERJI S.K.,AFRICANISM: THE AFRICAN PERSONALITY. KIN NAT/G SECT CREATE DIPLOM COLONIAL GP/REL ATTIT ORD/FREE...LING WORSHIP 20. PAGE 29 H0585 — PERSON NAT/LISM AFR CULTURE

B60
HARRISON S.S.,INDIA: THE MOST DANGEROUS DECADES. INDIA CONSTN STRATA POL/PAR SECT PLAN ADMIN CHOOSE GP/REL TOTALISM MARXISM...LING 20 NEHRU/J. PAGE 67 H1347 — CULTURE ECO/UNDEV PROB/SOLV REGION

B60
KEPHART C.,RACES OF MAN. GP/REL HABITAT...LING SOC/INTEG 20 MIGRATION MISCEGEN. PAGE 85 H1692 — CULTURE RACE/REL HEREDITY GEOG

B60
NAKAMURA H.,THE WAYS OF THINKING OF EASTERN PEOPLES. ASIA INDIA PERSON...HUM SOC LING LOG WORSHIP CHINJAP. PAGE 115 H2305 — CULTURE SECT ATTIT

B60
SZTARAY Z.,BIBLIOGRAPHY ON HUNGARY. HUNGARY MOD/EUR CULTURE INDUS SECT DIPLOM REV...ART/METH SOC LING 18/20. PAGE 151 H3029 — BIBLIOG NAT/G COM MARXISM

B60
WILLIAMS L.E.,OVERSEAS CHINESE NATIONALISM: THE GENESIS OF THE PAN-CHINESE MOVEMENT IN INDONESIA, 1900-1916. ASIA COM INDONESIA AGRI INT/ORG LOC/G DIPLOM EDU/PROP HABITAT PWR POPULISM...GEOG LING CENSUS 20. PAGE 168 H3367 — NAT/LISM GP/REL DECISION NAT/G

B60
ZENKOVSKY S.A.,PAN-TURKISM AND ISLAM IN RUSSIA. ASIA RUSSIA USSR CULTURE POL/PAR DOMIN REV GP/REL MARXISM...LING GP/COMP BIBLIOG 19/20 TURKIC. PAGE 173 H3454 — SECT NAT/LISM COM ISLAM

B61
DOOB L.W.,COMMUNICATION IN AFRICA: A SEARCH FOR BOUNDARIES. CULTURE SOCIETY EDU/PROP WRITING INGP/REL DRIVE ORD/FREE...ART/METH SOC LING BIBLIOG 20. PAGE 42 H0837 — AFR FEEDBACK PERCEPT PERS/REL

B61
JONES R.,AFRICA BIBLIOGRAPHY SERIES: SOUTH EAST CENTRAL AFRICA AND MADAGASCAR. AFR MADAGASCAR RHODESIA SECT BIO/SOC...JURID NAT/COMP 20. PAGE 82 H1633 — BIBLIOG/A SOC CULTURE LING

B61
MARTINEZ RIOS J.,BIBLIOGRAFIA ANTROPOLOGICA Y SOCIOLOGICA DEL ESTADO DE OAXACA. WRITING...LING 12/20 INDIAN/AM MEXIC/AMER. PAGE 103 H2069 — BIBLIOG SOC PROVS CULTURE

B61
TACHAKKYO K.,BIBLIOGRAPHY OF KOREAN STUDIES: A BIBLIOGRAPHICAL GUIDE TO KOREAN PUBLICATIONS ON KOREAN STUDIES APPEARING 1945-1958. KOREA LAW...HUM JURID PHIL/SCI LING 19/20. PAGE 152 H3033 — BIBLIOG/A SOCIETY CULTURE WAR

B61
TURNBULL C.M.,THE FOREST PEOPLE. EATING GP/REL INGP/REL RACE/REL ISOLAT HABITAT HEREDITY...GEOG SOC LING DICTIONARY WORSHIP 20 CONGO NEGRO BA/MBUTI. PAGE 157 H3138 — AFR CULTURE KIN RECORD

B61
ZIMMERMAN I.,A GUIDE TO CURRENT LATIN AMERICAN PERIODICALS: HUMANITIES AND SOCIAL SCIENCES. LABOR SECT EDU/PROP...GEOG HUM SOC LING STAT NAT/COMP 20. PAGE 173 H3456 — BIBLIOG/A DIPLOM L/A+17C PHIL/SCI

B62
DAVAR F.C.,IRAN AND INDIA THROUGH THE AGES. INDIA IRAN ELITES SECT CREATE ORD/FREE...LING BIBLIOG. PAGE 37 H0743 — NAT/COMP DIPLOM CULTURE

B62
HACHMANN R.,VOLKER ZWISCHEN GERMANEN UND KELTEN. GERMANY CULTURE STRUCT MUNIC...ART/METH CHARTS MAPS. PAGE 63 H1269 — LING SOC KIN GP/REL

B62
KEESING F.M.,THE ETHNOHISTORY OF NORTHERN LUZON. PHILIPPINE ECO/UNDEV FAM SECT CHIEF REGION GP/REL HABITAT...GEOG LING BIBLIOG WORSHIP 20. PAGE 84 H1680 — CULTURE SOC KIN

B62
KENNEDY R.,BIBLIOGRAPHY OF INDONESIAN PEOPLES AND CULTURES (2ND REV. ED.). INDONESIA STRUCT ECO/UNDEV SCHOOL EDU/PROP COLONIAL...GEOG SOC LING NAT/COMP 20. PAGE 85 H1689 — BIBLIOG S/ASIA CULTURE KIN

B62
MICHAEL H.N.,STUDIES IN SIBERIAN ETHNOGENESIS. USSR KIN...ART/METH SOC 20 SIBERIA. PAGE 110 H2196 — HABITAT HEREDITY CULTURE LING

B62
SILBERMAN B.S.,JAPAN AND KOREA; A CRITICAL BIBLIOGRAPHY. KOREA LAW STRATA STRUCT AGRI INDUS NAT/G POL/PAR SECT...HUM LING IDEA/COMP 5/20 CHINJAP. PAGE 144 H2872 — BIBLIOG/A CULTURE S/ASIA

B62
YOUNG G.,THE HILL TRIBES OF NORTHERN THAILAND. S/ASIA THAILAND FAM KIN LOC/G GP/REL HABITAT...GEOG LING OBS 20. PAGE 172 H3438 — CULTURE STRUCT ECO/UNDEV SECT

B63
CONFERENCE ABORIGINAL STUDIES,AUSTRALIAN ABORIGINAL STUDIES. ECO/UNDEV INT/TRADE COLONIAL ADJUST HABITAT HEREDITY...GEOG PSY LING SOC/EXP ANTHOL WORSHIP 20 AUSTRAL ABORIGINES. PAGE 32 H0638 — SOC SOCIETY CULTURE STRUCT

B63
FISCHER-GALATI S.A.,RUMANIA; A BIBLIOGRAPHIC GUIDE (PAMPHLET). ROMANIA INTELL ECO/DEV LABOR SECT WEALTH...GEOG SOC/WK LING 20. PAGE 51 H1012 — BIBLIOG/A NAT/G COM LAW

B63
JAIRAZBHOY R.A.,FOREIGN INFLUENCE IN ANCIENT INDIA. INDIA ELITES SECT DIPLOM EDU/PROP COLONIAL REGION GP/REL...ART/METH LING WORSHIP +/14 GRECO/ROMN MESOPOTAM PERSIA PARTH/SASS. PAGE 79 H1587 — CULTURE SOCIETY COERCE DOMIN

B63
PEREZ ORTIZ R.,ANUARIO BIBLIOGRAFICO COLOMBIANO, 1961. AGRI...INT/LAW JURID SOC LING 20 COLOMB. PAGE 125 H2491 — BIBLIOG L/A+17C NAT/G

B63
SAKAI R.K.,STUDIES ON ASIA, 1963. ASIA INDIA ISRAEL S/ASIA USA+45 PERF/ART POL/PAR SECT REGION NAT/LISM ...SOC LING TREND ANTHOL 19/20 CHINJAP. PAGE 137 H2735 — PWR CULTURE

B63
SINOR D.,INTRODUCTION A L'ETUDE DE L'EURASIE CENTRALE. ASIA CULTURE KIN. PAGE 144 H2887 — BIBLIOG SOC LING

B63
STUCKI C.W.,AMERICAN DOCTORAL DISSERTATIONS ON ASIA 1933-62 (A PAPER). PREHIST INDUS NAT/G GOV/REL ALL/IDEOS...ART/METH GEOG SOC LING 20. PAGE 150 H3002 — BIBLIOG ASIA SOCIETY S/ASIA

B64
ANDREWS D.H.,LATIN AMERICA: A BIBLIOGRAPHY OF PAPERBACK BOOKS. SECT INT/TRADE EDU/PROP WAR GOV/REL ADJUST NAT/LISM ATTIT...ART/METH LING BIOG 20. PAGE 7 H0138 — BIBLIOG L/A+17C CULTURE NAT/G

B64
GRIFFITH W.,THE WELSH (2ND ED.). UK SOCIETY STRUCT SECT WRITING NAT/LISM...ART/METH MODAL OBS/ENVIR TREND SOC/INTEG WALES PURITAN MUSIC. PAGE 61 H1223 — CULTURE SOC LING

B64
KIDD K.E.,BRIEF BIBLIOGRAPHY OF ONTARIO ANTHROPOLOGY (PAMPHLET). CANADA PREHIST HABITAT ...MYTH WORSHIP. PAGE 86 H1708 — BIBLIOG SOC LING CULTURE

B64
MCCALL D.F.,AFRICA IN TIME PERSPECTIVE. AFR EXTR/IND KIN SECT CREATE PERS/REL HABITAT...GEOG METH/CNCPT LING BIBLIOG/A TIME 20. PAGE 106 H2124 — HIST/WRIT OBS/ENVIR CULTURE

B64
MOUMOUNI A.,L'EDUCATION EN AFRIQUE. UNIV CULTURE ELITES INTELL EDU/PROP ADMIN COLONIAL...LING TREND BIBLIOG 20. PAGE 114 H2271 — SCHOOL AFR PROB/SOLV

B64
RAGHAVAN M.D.,INDIA IN CEYLONESE HISTORY, SOCIETY AND CULTURE. CEYLON INDIA S/ASIA LAW SOCIETY INT/TRADE ATTIT...ART/METH JURID SOC LING 20. PAGE 129 H2581 — DIPLOM CULTURE SECT STRUCT

B64
WICKENS G.M.,PERSIA IN ISLAMIC TIMES: A PRACTICAL BIBLIOGRAPHY OF ITS HISTORY, CULTURE AND LANGUAGE (PAMPHLET). IRAN ISLAM SECT. PAGE 168 H3355 — BIBLIOG CULTURE LING

B65
BERNDT R.M.,ABORIGINAL MAN IN AUSTRALIA. LAW DOMIN ADMIN COLONIAL MARRIAGE HABITAT ORD/FREE...LING CHARTS ANTHOL BIBLIOG WORSHIP 20 AUSTRAL ABORIGINES MUSIC ELKIN/AP. PAGE 16 H0312 — SOC CULTURE SOCIETY STRUCT

B65
CENTRAL GAZETTEERS UNIT,THE GAZETTEER OF INDIA (VOL. I). INDIA SOCIETY STRATA PLAN EDU/PROP NAT/LISM ORD/FREE WEALTH...GEOG LING CHARTS SOC/INTEG 20. PAGE 28 H0568 — PRESS CULTURE SECT STRUCT

B65
HYMES D.,THE USE OF COMPUTERS IN ANTHROPOLOGY. CULTURE PROF/ORG CONSULT CREATE EFFICIENCY PERCEPT ...CLASSIF LING CON/ANAL COMPUT/IR METH/COMP ANTHOL 20. PAGE 76 H1517 — METH COMPUTER TEC/DEV SOC

B65
KUPER H.,URBANIZATION AND MIGRATION IN WEST AFRICA. UPPER/VOLT CULTURE ECO/UNDEV WORKER REGION GOV/REL ...LING ANTHOL SOC/INTEG 20 AFRICA/W OSHOGBO MOSSI — AFR HABITAT MUNIC

MIGRATION. PAGE 89 H1781 GEOG

B65
SLOTKIN J.S.,READINGS IN EARLY ANTHROPOLOGY. INTELL SECT CREATE ATTIT KNOWL...HUM PHIL/SCI PSY LING 1/18. PAGE 145 H2902 SOC CULTURE GP/COMP

L65
MATTHEWS D.G.,"A CURRENT BIBLIOGRAPHY ON ETHIOPIAN AFFAIRS: A SELECT BIBLIOGRAPHY FROM 1950-1964." ETHIOPIA LAW CULTURE ECO/UNDEV INDUS LABOR SECT FORCES DIPLOM CIVMIL/REL RACE/REL...LING STAT 20. PAGE 105 H2093 BIBLIOG/A ADMIN POL/PAR NAT/G

L65
MATTHEWS D.G.,"A CURRENT BIBLIOGRAPHY ON SUDANESE AFFAIRS; A SELECT BIBLIOGRAPHY FROM 1960-1964." SUDAN LAW CULTURE AGRI FINAN INDUS LABOR POL/PAR TEC/DEV FOR/AID RACE/REL LITERACY...LING 20. PAGE 105 H2094 BIBLIOG ECO/UNDEV NAT/G DIPLOM

B66
BRAIBANTI R.,RESEARCH ON THE BUREAUCRACY OF PAKISTAN. PAKISTAN LAW CULTURE INTELL ACADEM LOC/G SECT PRESS CT/SYS...LING CHARTS 20 BUREAUCRCY. PAGE 20 H0402 HABITAT NAT/G ADMIN CONSTN

B66
BRECHER M.,SUCCESSION IN INDIA. INDIA USA+45 CONSTN AGRI POL/PAR PROVS SECT DELIB/GP FORCES PROB/SOLV ECO/TAC PWR...LING 20 CONGRESS NEHRU/J. PAGE 20 H0408 CHIEF DECISION CHOOSE

B66
BROWN L.C.,STATE AND SOCIETY IN INDEPENDENT NORTH AFRICA. ALGERIA LIBYA MOROCCO AGRI INDUS INT/ORG POL/PAR SECT PLAN DIPLOM COLONIAL...LING NAT/COMP ANTHOL BIBLIOG 20 TUNIS MUSLIM. PAGE 22 H0446 NAT/G SOCIETY CULTURE ECO/UNDEV

B66
CAPELL A.,STUDIES IN SOCIO-LINGUISTICS. CULTURE ADJUST...CLASSIF IDEA/COMP SOC/EXP BIBLIOG 20. PAGE 26 H0525 LING SOC PHIL/SCI CORREL

B66
ELLIS A.B.,THE EWE-SPEAKING PEOPLES OF THE SLAVE COAST OF WEST AFRICA. AFR FORCES ADJUST...LING RECORD GP/COMP WORSHIP 20 AFRICA/W DEITY. PAGE 45 H0910 MYTH CULTURE HABITAT

B66
GHOSH P.K.,THE CONSTITUTION OF INDIA: HOW IT HAS BEEN FRAMED. INDIA LOC/G DELIB/GP EX/STRUC PROB/SOLV BUDGET INT/TRADE CT/SYS CHOOSE...LING 20. PAGE 56 H1121 CONSTN NAT/G LEGIS FEDERAL

B66
JONES D.H.,AFRICA BIBLIOGRAPHY SERIES: EAST AFRICA. AFR UGANDA SECT BIO/SOC...JURID NAT/COMP 20. PAGE 82 H1630 BIBLIOG/A SOC CULTURE LING

B66
US DEPARTMENT OF STATE,RESEARCH ON AFRICA (EXTERNAL RESEARCH LIST NO 5-25). LAW CULTURE ECO/UNDEV POL/PAR DIPLOM EDU/PROP LEAD REGION MARXISM...GEOG LING WORSHIP 20. PAGE 159 H3188 BIBLIOG/A ASIA S/ASIA NAT/G

B66
US DEPARTMENT OF STATE,RESEARCH ON THE USSR AND EASTERN EUROPE (EXTERNAL RESEARCH LIST NO 1-25). USSR LAW CULTURE SOCIETY NAT/G TEC/DEV DIPLOM EDU/PROP REGION...GEOG LING. PAGE 160 H3191 BIBLIOG/A EUR+WWI COM MARXISM

S66
MATTHEWS D.G.,"ETHIOPIAN OUTLINE: A BIBLIOGRAPHIC RESEARCH GUIDE." ETHIOPIA LAW STRUCT ECO/UNDEV AGRI LABOR SECT CHIEF DELIB/GP EX/STRUC ADMIN...LING ORG/CHARTS 20. PAGE 105 H2095 BIBLIOG NAT/G DIPLOM POL/PAR

C66
DEUTSCH K.W.,"NATIONALISM AND SOCIAL COMMUNICATION." CULTURE INGP/REL ATTIT PWR...PSY SOC CONCPT LING IDEA/COMP 20. PAGE 40 H0800 BIBLIOG NAT/LISM GEN/LAWS

B67
ALLWORTH E.,CENTRAL ASIA: A CENTURY OF RUSSIAN RULE. USSR INTELL SOCIETY AGRI INDUS COLONIAL REV WAR NAT/LISM...ART/METH GEOG LING 19/20. PAGE 5 H0108 ASIA CULTURE NAT/G

B67
COLLINS R.O.,EGYPT AND THE SUDAN. COM FRANCE ISLAM SUDAN UAR UK SOCIETY NAT/G COLONIAL NAT/LISM...GEOG SOC LING TREND SOC/INTEG 7/20 SUEZ. PAGE 32 H0635 AGRI CULTURE ECO/UNDEV

B67
THOMPSON E.T.,PERSPECTIVES ON THE SOUTH: AGENDA FOR RESEARCH. CULTURE ECO/UNDEV SECT GP/REL EFFICIENCY ALL/VALS...HUM SOC CONCPT LING 20 NEGRO. PAGE 154 H3080 PROB/SOLV IDEA/COMP REGION ACT/RES

L67
TAMBIAH S.J.,"THE POLITICS OF LANGUAGE IN INDIA AND CEYLON." CEYLON INDIA NAT/G DOMIN ADMIN...SOC 20. PAGE 152 H3039 POL/PAR LING NAT/LISM REGION

S67
EPSTEIN E.H.,"NATIONAL IDENTITY AND THE LANGUAGE ISSUE IN PUERTO RICO." PUERT/RICO CULTURE STRUCT NAT/G PROB/SOLV SKILL...JURID STAT METH/COMP 20. PAGE 47 H0931 EDU/PROP SCHOOL LING NAT/LISM

LINGUISTICS....SEE LING

LINK/AS....ARTHUR S. LINK

LINTON R. H1935

LIPMAN E.J. H3279

LIPPMANN W. H1936

LIPPMANN/W....WALTER LIPPMANN

LIPSCOMB J.F. H1937

LIPSET S.M. H0273,H0274,H1938,H1939,H1940,H2904

LISTER L. H1941

LITERACY....ABILITY TO READ AND WRITE

B56
READ M.,EDUCATION AND SOCIAL CHANGE IN TROPICAL AREAS. AFR L/A+17C SOCIETY LITERACY PERCEPT PERSON WEALTH...HEAL PHIL/SCI SOC 20. PAGE 130 H2603 EDU/PROP HABITAT DRIVE CULTURE

B61
KEE R.,REFUGEE WORLD. AUSTRIA EUR+WWI GERMANY NEIGH EX/STRUC WORKER PROB/SOLV ECO/TAC RENT EDU/PROP INGP/REL COST LITERACY HABITAT 20 MIGRATION. PAGE 84 H1676 NAT/G GIVE WEALTH STRANGE

B63
HUNTER G.,EDUCATION FOR A DEVELOPING REGION; A STUDY IN EAST AFRICA. AFR TANZANIA UGANDA NAT/G TEC/DEV INGP/REL ADJUST LITERACY ATTIT 20 AFRICA/E. PAGE 75 H1501 EDU/PROP POLICY ECO/UNDEV EFFICIENCY

B64
NICOL D.,AFRICA - A SUBJECTIVE VIEW. AFR INT/ORG PLAN ADMIN COLONIAL PARL/PROC PARTIC REGION GOV/REL LITERACY ATTIT...BIBLIOG 20 CIVIL/SERV. PAGE 118 H2350 NAT/G LEAD CULTURE ACADEM

B65
FOSTER P.,EDUCATION AND SOCIAL CHANGE IN GHANA. GHANA CULTURE STRUCT ECO/UNDEV TEC/DEV REGION EFFICIENCY LITERACY ALL/VALS SOVEREIGN...STAT METH/COMP 19/20 GOLD/COAST. PAGE 52 H1043 SCHOOL CREATE SOCIETY

B65
HAVIGHURST R.J.,SOCIETY AND EDUCATION IN BRAZIL. BRAZIL PORTUGAL ECO/UNDEV INDUS NAT/G CREATE INSPECT COLONIAL ADJUST DEMAND LITERACY...CENSUS TREND CHARTS 16/20. PAGE 68 H1362 SCHOOL ACADEM ACT/RES CULTURE

L65
MATTHEWS D.G.,"A CURRENT BIBLIOGRAPHY ON SUDANESE AFFAIRS; A SELECT BIBLIOGRAPHY FROM 1960-1964." SUDAN LAW CULTURE AGRI FINAN INDUS LABOR POL/PAR TEC/DEV FOR/AID RACE/REL LITERACY...LING 20. PAGE 105 H2094 BIBLIOG ECO/UNDEV NAT/G DIPLOM

B66
FISK E.K.,NEW GUINEA ON THE THRESHOLD; ASPECTS OF SOCIAL, POLITICAL, AND ECONOMIC DEVELOPMENT. AGRI NAT/G INT/TRADE ADMIN ADJUST LITERACY ROLE...CHARTS ANTHOL 20 NEW/GUINEA. PAGE 51 H1015 ECO/UNDEV SOCIETY

S67
CRITTENDEN J.,"DIMENSIONS OF MODERNIZATION IN THE AMERICAN STATES." USA+45 STRUCT MUNIC PROB/SOLV CONTROL LITERACY HABITAT...CONCPT METH/CNCPT CORREL CONT/OBS CENSUS 20. PAGE 35 H0702 PROVS GOV/COMP STAT ECO/DEV

S67
SCOTT J.W.,"SOURCES OF SOCIAL CHANGE IN COMMUNITY, FAMILY, AND FERTILITY IN A PUERTO RICAN TOWN." PUERT/RICO CULTURE STRUCT ECO/UNDEV INDUS PERS/REL ROLE...SOC STAND/INT. PAGE 141 H2815 FAM MARRIAGE LITERACY ATTIT

B82
MACDONALD D.,AFRICANA; OR, THE HEART OF HEATHEN AFRICA, VOL. II: MISSION LIFE. SOCIETY STRATA KIN CREATE EDU/PROP ADMIN COERCE LITERACY HEALTH...MYTH WORSHIP 19 LIVNGSTN/D MISSION NEGRO. PAGE 100 H1990 SECT AFR CULTURE ORD/FREE

LITERARY ANALYSIS....SEE HUM

LITHUANIA....SEE ALSO USSR

B61
BALYS J.,LITHUANIA AND LITHUANIANS: A SELECTED BIBLIOGRAPHY. LITHUANIA SOC. PAGE 10 H0206 BIBLIOG POLICY NAT/G COM

S67
"PROTEST AGAINST SOVIET INDUSTRIALIZATION ILLS IN LITHUANIA* A MEMORANDUM." USSR LITHUANIA NAT/G PROVS COST GEOG. PAGE 2 H0050 INDUS COLONIAL NAT/LISM PLAN

LITT T. H1942

LIU/SHAO....LIU SHAO-CHI

LIVINGSTON H.H. H2375

LIVINGSTON W.S. H1943

LIVNGSTN/D....DAVID LIVINGSTON

B30
SMUTS J.C.,AFRICA AND SOME WORLD PROBLEMS. RHODESIA SOUTH/AFR CULTURE ECO/UNDEV INDUS INT/ORG SECT PROB/SOLV REGION GOV/REL DISCRIM ATTIT 19/20 LEAGUE/NAT LIVNGSTN/D NEGRO. PAGE 146 H2921
LEGIS AFR COLONIAL RACE/REL

B82
MACDONALD D.,AFRICANA; OR, THE HEART OF HEATHEN AFRICA, VOL. II: MISSION LIFE. SOCIETY STRATA KIN CREATE EDU/PROP ADMIN COERCE LITERACY HEALTH...MYTH WORSHIP 19 LIVNGSTN/D MISSION NEGRO. PAGE 100 H1990
SECT AFR CULTURE ORD/FREE

LIVY....LIVY

LLOYD H.D. H1944

LLOYD/HD....HENRY D. LLOYD

LLOYD-GEO/D....DAVID LLOYD GEORGE

LOANS....SEE RENT+GIVE+FOR/AID+FINAN

LOBBY....PRESSURE GROUP

B31
DUFFIELD M.,KING LEGION. NAT/G PROVS SECT LEGIS EDU/PROP PRESS GP/REL AGE/Y MARXISM POLICY. PAGE 43 H0856
SUPEGO FORCES VOL/ASSN LOBBY

B34
LIPPMANN W.,THE METHOD OF FREEDOM. SOCIETY INDUS LABOR LOBBY WAR REPRESENT...POLICY IDEA/COMP METH/COMP 19/20. PAGE 97 H1936
CONCPT MAJORIT NAT/G

S38
HALL R.C.,"REPRESENTATION OF BIG BUSINESS IN THE HOUSE OF COMMONS." UK ECO/DEV INDUS PROF/ORG LEGIS CAP/ISM ECO/TAC LAISSEZ...POLICY OLD/LIB PLURIST MGT 20 HOUSE/CMNS. PAGE 64 H1287
LOBBY NAT/G

B51
MEYER E.W.,POLITICAL PARTIES IN WESTERN GERMANY (PAMPHLET). GERMANY/W MUNIC NAT/G GOV/REL ALL/IDEOS 20 UNIFICA BERLIN. PAGE 109 H2190
POL/PAR LOBBY CHOOSE CONSTN

B52
SCHATTSCHNEIDER E.E.,A GUIDE TO THE STUDY OF PUBLIC AFFAIRS. LAW LOC/G NAT/G LEGIS BUDGET PRESS ADMIN LOBBY...JURID CHARTS 20. PAGE 139 H2775
ACT/RES INTELL ACADEM METH/COMP

B55
DUVERGER M.,THE POLITICAL ROLE OF WOMEN. FRANCE GERMANY/W NORWAY YUGOSLAVIA STRATA LOBBY AGE ATTIT ROLE...STAT SAMP CHARTS METH/COMP NAT/COMP HYPO/EXP FEMALE/SEX. PAGE 44 H0875
SEX LEAD PARTIC CHOOSE

B56
HERNANDEZ URBINA A.,LOS PARTIDOS Y LA CRISIS DEL APRA. PERU NAT/G LEAD LOBBY CHOOSE SOCISM...POLICY DECISION 20 COM/PARTY APRA CONGRESS. PAGE 70 H1402
POL/PAR PARTIC PARL/PROC GP/REL

B57
SCARROW H.A.,THE HIGHER PUBLIC SERVICE OF THE COMMONWEALTH OF AUSTRALIA. LAW SENIOR LOBBY ROLE 20 AUSTRAL CIVIL/SERV COMMONWLTH. PAGE 138 H2766
ADMIN NAT/G EX/STRUC GOV/COMP

B58
PAYNO M.,LA REFORMA SOCIAL EN ESPANA Y MEXICO. SPAIN ECO/TAC TAX LOBBY COERCE REV OWN CATHISM 19/20 MEXIC/AMER. PAGE 124 H2479
SECT NAT/G LAW ELITES

S58
GARCEAU O.,"INTEREST GROUP THEORY IN POLITICAL RESEARCH." ELITES NAT/G PLAN LEAD REPRESENT INGP/REL POLICY. PAGE 55 H1098
GP/COMP GP/REL LOBBY PLURISM

S58
PYE L.W.,"THE NON-WESTERN POLITICAL PROCESS" (BMR)" AFR ASIA ISLAM S/ASIA DIPLOM ADMIN LEAD LOBBY ROUTINE CONSEN...DECISION 20. PAGE 128 H2567
CULTURE POL/PAR NAT/G LOC/G

S58
SCHUMM S.,"INTEREST REPRESENTATION IN FRANCE AND GERMANY." EUR+WWI FRANCE GERMANY INSPECT PARL/PROC REPRESENT 20 WEIMAR/REP. PAGE 140 H2803
LOBBY DELIB/GP NAT/G

B59
BROWN D.F.,THE GROWTH OF DEMOCRATIC GOVERNMENT. WOR+45 BARGAIN EDU/PROP LOBBY APPORT CHOOSE 20. PAGE 22 H0441
GOV/COMP LEGIS POL/PAR CHIEF

B60
GRAMPP W.D.,THE MANCHESTER SCHOOL OF ECONOMICS. UK LAW ECO/DEV COERCE ATTIT ORD/FREE LAISSEZ ...PHIL/SCI IDEA/COMP 19/20 MANCHESTER CORN/LAWS. PAGE 60 H1194
ECO/TAC VOL/ASSN LOBBY NAT/G

B60
LOMBARDO TOLEDANO V,EL NEONAZISMO; SUS CHARACTERISTICAS Y PELIGROS. GERMANY/W POL/PAR COLONIAL LEAD LOBBY ATTIT 20 NAZI. PAGE 98 H1956
NAT/G FASCISM POLICY DIPLOM

B60
MOCTEZUMA A.P.,EL CONFLICTO RELIGIOSO DE 1926 (2ND ED.). L/A+17C LAW NAT/G LOBBY COERCE GP/REL ATTIT ...POLICY 20 MEXIC/AMER CHURCH/STA. PAGE 112 H2233
SECT ORD/FREE DISCRIM REV

S60
TAYLOR M.G.,"THE ROLE OF THE MEDICAL PROFESSION IN THE FORMULATION AND EXECUTION OF PUBLIC POLICY" (BMR)" CANADA NAT/G CONSULT ADMIN REPRESENT GP/REL ROLE SOVEREIGN...DECISION 20 CMA. PAGE 153 H3056
PROF/ORG HEALTH LOBBY POLICY

B61
HALPERIN S.,THE POLITICAL WORLD OF AMERICAN ZIONISM. ISRAEL FINAN LABOR VOL/ASSN GIVE LOBBY REPRESENT GP/REL ATTIT POLICY. PAGE 64 H1293
CULTURE SECT EDU/PROP DELIB/GP

S61
EHRMANN H.W.,"FRENCH BUREAUCRACY AND ORGANIZED INTERESTS" (BMR)" FRANCE NAT/G DELIB/GP ROUTINE ...INT 20 BUREAUCRCY CIVIL/SERV. PAGE 45 H0897
ADMIN DECISION PLURISM LOBBY

S61
MACRIDIS R.C.,"INTEREST GROUPS IN COMPARATIVE ANALYSIS." CULTURE OP/RES LOBBY REPRESENT GP/REL AUTHORIT ORD/FREE PWR...POLICY DECISION METH/CNCPT CLASSIF. PAGE 101 H2010
GP/COMP CONCPT PLURISM

S62
ROSE R.,"THE POLITICAL IDEALS OF ENGLISH PARTY ACTIVISTS" (BMR)" UK PARL/PROC PARTIC ATTIT ROLE ...SAMP/SIZ CHARTS 20. PAGE 134 H2673
POL/PAR LOBBY REPRESENT NAT/G

B63
MERKL P.H.,THE ORIGIN OF THE WEST GERMAN REPUBLIC. GERMANY/W WOR+45 POL/PAR DIPLOM LEAD LOBBY REPRESENT GP/REL NAT/LISM 20. PAGE 109 H2179
CONSTN PARL/PROC CONTROL BAL/PWR

B64
HANNA W.J.,POLITICS IN BLACK AFRICA: A SELECTIVE BIBLIOGRAPHY OF RELEVANT PERIODICAL LITERATURE. AFR LAW LOC/G MUNIC NAT/G POL/PAR LOBBY CHOOSE RACE/REL SOVEREIGN 20. PAGE 66 H1315
BIBLIOG NAT/LISM COLONIAL

B64
MORGENTHAU R.S.,POLITICAL PARTIES IN FRENCH-SPEAKING WEST AFRICA. AFR FRANCE GUINEA IVORY/CST MALI SENEGAL CONSTN LEGIS CREATE PLAN LOBBY PARTIC GP/REL...POLICY BIBLIOG 20. PAGE 113 H2257
POL/PAR NAT/G SOVEREIGN COLONIAL

C64
SCOTT R.E.,"MEXICAN GOVERNMENT IN TRANSITION (REV ED)" CULTURE STRUCT POL/PAR CHIEF ADMIN LOBBY REV CHOOSE GP/REL DRIVE...BIBLIOG METH 20 MEXIC/AMER. PAGE 141 H2816
NAT/G L/A+17C ROUTINE CONSTN

B65
AIYAR S.P.,STUDIES IN INDIAN DEMOCRACY. INDIA STRATA ECO/UNDEV LABOR POL/PAR LEGIS DIPLOM LOBBY REGION CHOOSE ATTIT SOCISM...ANTHOL 20. PAGE 4 H0086
ORD/FREE REPRESENT ADMIN NAT/G

B65
CARTER G.M.,POLITICS IN EUROPE. EUR+WWI FRANCE GERMANY/W UK USSR LAW CONSTN POL/PAR VOL/ASSN PRESS LOBBY PWR...ANTHOL SOC/INTEG EEC. PAGE 27 H0548
GOV/COMP OP/RES ECO/DEV

B65
HADWIGER D.F.,PRESSURES AND PROTEST. NAT/G LEGIS PLAN LEAD PARTIC ROUTINE ATTIT POLICY. PAGE 63 H1273
AGRI GP/REL LOBBY CHOOSE

B65
JACOB H.,POLITICS IN THE AMERICAN STATES; A COMPARATIVE ANALYSIS. USA+45 POL/PAR CHIEF LEGIS TAX EDU/PROP CONTROL CT/SYS LOBBY PARTIC...DECISION CHARTS 20. PAGE 79 H1578
PROVS GOV/COMP PWR

B66
FINER S.E.,ANONYMOUS EMPIRE: STUDY OF THE LOBBY IN GREAT BRITAIN. UK CONSTN LABOR POL/PAR SECT DOMIN EDU/PROP PRESS CHOOSE...CONCPT CHARTS 20 PARLIAMENT. PAGE 50 H1004
LOBBY NAT/G LEGIS PWR

B66
FORD P.,CARDINAL MORAN AND THE A. L. P. NAT/G POL/PAR SECT DELIB/GP LOBBY REV CHOOSE ORD/FREE MARXISM 19/20 AUSTRAL PROTESTANT LABOR/PAR. PAGE 52 H1035
CATHISM SOCISM LABOR SOCIETY

B66
RIZK C.,LE REGIME POLITIQUE LIBANAIS. ISLAM LEBANON STRUCT POL/PAR SECT LOBBY GP/REL 20 ARABS MUSLIM CHRISTIAN. PAGE 132 H2637
ECO/UNDEV NAT/G CULTURE

B66
ROSS A.M.,INDUSTRIAL RELATIONS AND ECONOMIC DEVELOPMENT. POL/PAR LEGIS WORKER BARGAIN PRICE EXEC LOBBY INCOME PWR...DECISION ANTHOL BIBLIOG 20. PAGE 134 H2686
ECO/UNDEV LABOR NAT/G GP/REL

S66
FELD W.,"NATIONAL ECONOMIC INTEREST GROUPS AND
LOBBY

POLICY FORMATION IN THE EEC." NAT/G POL/PAR REGION CENTRAL SOVEREIGN...INT NET/THEORY EEC. PAGE 49 H0985
ELITES DECISION

B67
HANRIEDER W.F.,WEST GERMAN FOREIGN POLICY 1949-1963: INTERNATIONAL PRESSURE AND DOMESTIC RESPONSE. EUR+WWI GERMANY/W POL/PAR LOBBY CONSEN 20. PAGE 66 H1316
DIPLOM POLICY NAT/G ATTIT

B67
MENARD O.D.,THE ARMY AND THE FIFTH REPUBLIC. ALGERIA FRANCE VIETNAM ELITES STRATA COLONIAL CONTROL LOBBY WAR CIVMIL/REL ROLE PWR...POLICY 20 DEGAULLE/C. PAGE 108 H2169
FORCES ATTIT NAT/G

L67
GLAZER M.,"LAS ACTITUDES Y ACTIVIDADES POLITICAS DE LOS ESTUDIANTES DE LA UNIVERSIDAD DE CHILE." CHILE NAT/G POL/PAR EDU/PROP LOBBY ATTIT 20. PAGE 57 H1141
ACADEM AGE/Y PARTIC ELITES

L67
ISRAEL J.,"THE RED GUARDS IN HISTORICAL PERSPECTIVE: CONTINUITY AND CHANGE IN THE CHINESE YOUTH MOVEMENT." CHINA/COM FUT POL/PAR CONTROL REV GP/REL 20. PAGE 79 H1572
AGE/Y LOBBY MARXISM NAT/G

S67
ADNITT F.W.,"THE RISE OF ENGLISH RADICALISM -- PART 2." UK NAT/G WORKER INCOME WEALTH...BIOG 19 PARLIAMENT. PAGE 4 H0071
LEGIS LOBBY

S67
HOFMANN W.,"THE PUBLIC INTEREST PRESSURE GROUP: THE CASE OF THE DEUTSCHE STADTETAG." GERMANY GERMANY/W CONSTN STRUCT NAT/G CENTRAL FEDERAL PWR...TIME/SEQ 20. PAGE 72 H1447
LOC/G VOL/ASSN LOBBY ADMIN

S67
MITCHELL W.C.,"THE SHAPE OF POLITICAL THEORY TO COME: FROM POLITICAL SOCIOLOGY TO POLITICAL ECONOMY." ACADEM NAT/G BUDGET TAX LEGIT LOBBY GOV/REL INGP/REL...SOC NEW/IDEA TREND CHARTS 20 MONEY. PAGE 112 H2231
ECO/TAC GEN/LAWS

S67
PAI G.A.,"TAXATION AND PLANNING IN INDIA: A BIRDS-EYE VIEW." INDIA ELITES NAT/G LEGIS BUDGET CONTROL LOBBY INCOME...STAT CHARTS 20. PAGE 122 H2443
TAX PLAN WEALTH STRATA

S67
TIVEY L.,"THE POLITICAL CONSEQUENCES OF ECONOMIC PLANNING." UK CONSTN INDUS ACT/RES ADMIN CONTROL LOBBY REPRESENT EFFICIENCY SUPEGO SOVEREIGN ...DECISION 20. PAGE 155 H3108
PLAN POLICY NAT/G

LOBBYING....SEE LOBBY

LOBINGIER C.S. H1945

LOC/G....LOCAL GOVERNMENT

N
AUSTRALIAN NATIONAL RES COUN,AUSTRALIAN SOCIAL SCIENCE ABSTRACTS. NEW/ZEALND CULTURE SOCIETY LOC/G CT/SYS PARL/PROC...HEAL JURID PSY SOC 20 AUSTRAL. PAGE 9 H0181
BIBLIOG/A POLICY NAT/G ADMIN

N
BULLETIN ANALYTIQUE DE DOCUMENTATION POLITIQUE, ECONOMIQUE, ET SOCIAL CONTEMPORAIRE. FRANCE WOR+45 SOCIETY ECO/DEV ECO/UNDEV INT/ORG LOC/G PROB/SOLV FOR/AID LEAD REGION SOC. PAGE 1 H0002
BIBLIOG/A DIPLOM NAT/COMP NAT/G

N
SUBJECT GUIDE TO BOOKS IN PRINT: AN INDEX TO THE PUBLISHERS' TRADE LIST ANNUAL. UNIV LAW LOC/G DIPLOM WRITING ADMIN LEAD PERSON...MGT SOC. PAGE 2 H0024
BIBLIOG ECO/DEV POL/PAR NAT/G

N
DEUTSCHE BUCHEREI,JAHRESVERZEICHNIS DES DEUTSCHEN SCHRIFTUMS. AUSTRIA EUR+WWI GERMANY SWITZERLND LAW LOC/G DIPLOM ADMIN...MGT SOC 19/20. PAGE 40 H0804
BIBLIOG WRITING NAT/G

N
US CONSULATE GENERAL HONG KONG,REVIEW OF THE HONG KONG CHINESE PRESS. ECO/UNDEV LOC/G NAT/G PLAN DIPLOM EDU/PROP LEAD GP/REL MARXISM...POLICY INDEX 20. PAGE 159 H3178
BIBLIOG/A ASIA PRESS ATTIT

N
US CONSULATE GENERAL HONG KONG,CURRENT BACKGROUND. CHINA/COM ECO/UNDEV LOC/G NAT/G PLAN DIPLOM EDU/PROP LEAD REV ATTIT...POLICY INDEX 20. PAGE 159 H3179
BIBLIOG/A MARXIST ASIA PRESS

N
US CONSULATE GENERAL HONG KONG,SURVEY OF CHINA MAINLAND PRESS. CHINA/COM ECO/UNDEV LOC/G NAT/G PLAN DIPLOM EDU/PROP LEAD REV ATTIT...POLICY INDEX 20. PAGE 159 H3181
BIBLIOG/A MARXIST ASIA PRESS

N
US CONSULATE GENERAL HONG KONG,US CONSULATE GENERAL, HONG KONG, PRESS SUMMARIES. CHINA/COM ECO/UNDEV LOC/G NAT/G PLAN DIPLOM EDU/PROP LEAD REV ATTIT...POLICY INDEX 20. PAGE 159 H3182
BIBLIOG/A MARXIST ASIA PRESS

N
US LIBRARY OF CONGRESS,ACCESSIONS LIST - INDIA. INDIA CULTURE AGRI LOC/G POL/PAR PLAN PROB/SOLV TEC/DEV DIPLOM EDU/PROP LEAD GP/REL ATTIT 20. PAGE 160 H3199
BIBLIOG S/ASIA ECO/UNDEV NAT/G

B01
GRIFFIN A.P.C.,A LIST OF BOOKS ON THE DANISH WEST INDIES (PAMPHLET). L/A+17C WEST/IND CULTURE LOC/G ...GEOG MGT 18/20. PAGE 61 H1214
BIBLIOG/A SOCIETY COLONIAL ADMIN

B01
GRIFFIN A.P.C.,A LIST OF BOOKS ON PORTO RICO. PUERT/RICO CULTURE LOC/G...GEOG MGT 19/20. PAGE 61 H1215
BIBLIOG/A SOCIETY COLONIAL ADMIN

C06
MONTGOMERY H.,"A DICTIONARY OF POLITICAL PHRASES AND ILLUSIONS WITH A SHORT BIBLIOGRAPHY." EUR+WWI MOD/EUR UK AGRI LABOR LOC/G NAT/G COLONIAL CHOOSE RACE/REL. PAGE 112 H2245
BIBLIOG DICTIONARY POLICY DIPLOM

B09
JUSTINIAN,THE DIGEST (DIGESTA CORPUS JURIS CIVILIS) (2 VOLS.) (TRANS. BY C. H. MONRO). ROMAN/EMP LAW FAM LOC/G LEGIS EDU/PROP CONTROL MARRIAGE OWN ROLE CIVIL/LAW. PAGE 82 H1645
JURID CT/SYS NAT/G STRATA

B09
LOBINGIER C.S.,THE PEOPLE'S LAW OR POPULAR PARTICIPATION IN LAW-MAKING. FRANCE SWITZERLND UK LOC/G NAT/G PROVS LEGIS SUFF MAJORITY PWR POPULISM ...GOV/COMP BIBLIOG 19. PAGE 97 H1945
CONSTN LAW PARTIC

B18
EYBERS G.W.,SELECT CONSTITUTIONAL DOCUMENTS ILLUSTRATING SOUTH AFRICAN HISTORY 1795-1910. SOUTH/AFR LOC/G LEGIS CT/SYS...JURID ANTHOL 18/20 NATAL CAPE/HOPE ORANGE/STA. PAGE 48 H0955
CONSTN LAW NAT/G COLONIAL

N19
GRIFFITH W.,THE PUBLIC SERVICE (PAMPHLET). UK LAW LOC/G NAT/G PARTIC CHOOSE DRIVE ROLE SKILL...CHARTS 20 CIVIL/SERV. PAGE 61 H1222
ADMIN EFFICIENCY EDU/PROP GOV/REL

N19
ROWE J.W.,THE ARGENTINE ELECTIONS OF 1963 (PAMPHLET). L/A+17C LOC/G NAT/G LEGIS REPRESENT 20 ARGEN. PAGE 135 H2703
CHOOSE CONSTN APPORT POL/PAR

N19
TEMPLE W.,AN ESSAY UPON THE ORIGINAL AND NATURE OF GOVERNMENT (PAMPHLET). CHRIST-17C UK FAM LOC/G LEGIT ORD/FREE CONSERVE 17. PAGE 153 H3060
NAT/G CONCPT PWR SOCIETY

B20
COLE G.D.H.,SOCIAL THEORY. CULTURE LOC/G SECT REGION REPRESENT ATTIT DRIVE...PSY SOC BIBLIOG. PAGE 31 H0621
CONCPT NAT/G PHIL/SCI

C20
BLACHLY F.F.,"THE GOVERNMENT AND ADMINISTRATION OF GERMANY." GERMANY CONSTN LOC/G PROVS DELIB/GP EX/STRUC FORCES LEGIS TOP/EX CT/SYS...BIBLIOG/A 19/20. PAGE 17 H0348
NAT/G GOV/REL ADMIN PHIL/SCI

B23
FRANK T.,A HISTORY OF ROME. MEDIT-7 INTELL SOCIETY LOC/G NAT/G POL/PAR FORCES LEGIS DOMIN LEGIT ALL/VALS...POLICY CONCPT TIME/SEQ GEN/LAWS ROM/EMP ROM/EMP. PAGE 53 H1050
EXEC STRUCT ELITES

B27
CHILDS J.B.,AN ACCOUNT OF GOVERNMENT DOCUMENT BIBLIOGRAPHY IN THE UNITED STATES AND ELSEWHERE (A PAPER). LOC/G PRESS CENTRAL KNOWL...METH 19/20 LEAGUE/NAT. PAGE 29 H0590
BIBLIOG/A CON/ANAL NAT/G

B28
BUELL R.,THE NATIVE PROBLEM IN AFRICA. KIN LABOR LOC/G ECO/TAC ROUTINE ORD/FREE...REC/INT KNO/TEST CENSUS TREND CHARTS SOC/EXP STERTYP 20. PAGE 23 H0466
AFR CULTURE

B28
YANG KUNG-SUN,THE BOOK OF LORD SHANG. LAW ECO/UNDEV LOC/G NAT/G NEIGH PLAN ECO/TAC LEGIT ATTIT SKILL ...CONCPT CON/ANAL WORK TOT/POP. PAGE 172 H3434
ASIA JURID

B29
CAM H.M.,BIBLIOGRAPHY OF ENGLISH CONSTITUTIONAL HISTORY (PAMPHLET). UK LAW LOC/G NAT/G POL/PAR SECT DELIB/GP ADJUD ORD/FREE 19/20 PARLIAMENT. PAGE 25 H0510
BIBLIOG/A CONSTN ADMIN PARL/PROC

B30
BENTHAM J.,THE RATIONALE OF PUNISHMENT. UK LAW LOC/G NAT/G LEGIS CONTROL...JURID GEN/LAWS COURT/SYS 19. PAGE 14 H0289
CRIME SANCTION COERCE ORD/FREE

B34
RIDLEY C.E.,THE CITY-MANAGER PROFESSION. CHIEF PLAN ADMIN CONTROL ROUTINE CHOOSE...TECHNIC CHARTS GOV/COMP BIBLIOG 20. PAGE 131 H2624
MUNIC EX/STRUC LOC/G EXEC

B34
STALIN J.,PROBLEMS OF LENINISM. USSR STRATA INDUS LOC/G POL/PAR ECO/TAC CONTROL TOTALISM PWR SOCISM LENIN/VI STALIN/J. PAGE 148 H2968
MARXISM REV ELITES NAT/G

B35
DE TOCQUEVILLE A.,DEMOCRACY IN AMERICA (4 VOLS.) (TRANS. BY HENRY REEVE). CONSTN STRUCT LOC/G NAT/G POL/PAR PROVS ETIQUET CT/SYS MAJORITY ATTIT 18/19. PAGE 39 H0772
POPULISM MAJORIT ORD/FREE SOCIETY

B35
GORER G.,AFRICA DANCES: A BOOK ABOUT WEST AFRICAN NEGROES. STRUCT LOC/G SECT FORCES TAX ADMIN COLONIAL...ART/METH MYTH WORSHIP 20 NEGRO AFRICA/W CHRISTIAN RITUAL. PAGE 59 H1181
AFR ATTIT CULTURE SOCIETY

B38
HOLDSWORTH W.S.,A HISTORY OF ENGLISH LAW; THE CENTURIES OF SETTLEMENT AND REFORM (VOL. X). INDIA UK CONSTN NAT/G CHIEF LEGIS ADMIN COLONIAL CT/SYS CHOOSE ORD/FREE PWR...JURID 18 PARLIAMENT COMMONWLTH COMMON/LAW. PAGE 72 H1451
LAW LOC/G EX/STRUC ADJUD

B39
ANDERSON W.,LOCAL GOVERNMENT IN EUROPE. FRANCE GERMANY ITALY UK USSR MUNIC PROVS ADMIN GOV/REL CENTRAL SOVEREIGN 20. PAGE 7 H0136
GOV/COMP NAT/COMP LOC/G CONSTN

B40
MCHENRY D.E.,HIS MAJESTY'S OPPOSITION: STRUCTURE AND PROBLEMS OF THE BRITISH LABOUR PARTY 1931-1938. UK FINAN LABOR LOC/G DELIB/GP LEGIS EDU/PROP LEAD PARTIC CHOOSE GP/REL SOCISM...TREND 20 LABOR/PAR. PAGE 107 H2130
POL/PAR MGT NAT/G POLICY

B42
BLANCHARD L.R.,MARTINIQUE: A SELECTED LIST OF REFERENCES (PAMPHLET). WEST/IND AGRI LOC/G SCHOOL ...ART/METH GEOG JURID CHARTS 20. PAGE 18 H0353
BIBLIOG/A SOCIETY CULTURE COLONIAL

B42
CONOVER H.F.,FRENCH COLONIES IN AFRICA: A LIST OF REFERENCES. ALGERIA FRANCE MOROCCO SOMALIA SUDAN CULTURE AGRI LOC/G SECT FORCES DIPLOM INT/TRADE NAT/LISM HEALTH...CON/ANAL 20. PAGE 32 H0641
BIBLIOG AFR ECO/UNDEV COLONIAL

B45
CONOVER H.F.,THE GOVERNMENTS OF THE MAJOR FOREIGN POWERS: A BIBLIOGRAPHY. FRANCE GERMANY ITALY UK USSR CONSTN LOC/G POL/PAR EX/STRUC FORCES ADMIN CT/SYS CIVMIL/REL TOTALISM...POLICY 19/20. PAGE 32 H0645
BIBLIOG NAT/G DIPLOM

B45
DITTMANN,DAS POLITISCHE DEUTSCHLAND VOR HITLER. GERMANY LOC/G PROVS...CHARTS GP/COMP 20. PAGE 41 H0827
POL/PAR NAT/G PARTIC

B46
HUTTON J.,THE CONSTITUTION OF THE UNION OF SOUTH AFRICA: BIBLIOGRAPHY (PAMPHLET). SOUTH/AFR MUNIC DIPLOM RACE/REL 20. PAGE 75 H1510
BIBLIOG CONSTN NAT/G LOC/G

B48
HARRIS G.M.,COMPARATIVE LOCAL GOVERNMENT. FINAN CHOOSE ALL/VALS. PAGE 67 H1339
PARTIC GOV/REL LOC/G GOV/COMP

B48
LASKI H.S.,THE AMERICAN DEMOCRACY. CULTURE INDUS SECT WORKER DIPLOM EDU/PROP REPRESENT RACE/REL ORD/FREE PWR...NAT/COMP 18/20. PAGE 92 H1831
NAT/G LOC/G USA-45 POPULISM

S49
STEINMETZ H.,"THE PROBLEMS OF THE LANDRAT: A STUDY OF COUNTY GOVERNMENT IN THE US ZONE OF GERMANY." GERMANY/W USA+45 INDUS PLAN DIPLOM EDU/PROP CONTROL WAR GOV/REL FEDERAL WEALTH PLURISM...GOV/COMP 20 LANDRAT. PAGE 149 H2977
LOC/G COLONIAL MGT TOP/EX

B50
HOBBES T.,LEVIATHAN. UNIV CONSTN SOCIETY LOC/G NAT/G CONSULT TOP/EX DOMIN DRIVE PERSON PWR ...PHIL/SCI CONCPT SELF/OBS GEN/LAWS TOT/POP. PAGE 72 H1434
LAW ORD/FREE

B50
WARD R.E.,A GUIDE TO JAPANESE REFERENCE AND RESEARCH MATERIALS IN THE FIELD OF POLITICAL SCIENCE. LAW CONSTN LOC/G PRESS ADMIN...SOC CON/ANAL METH 19/20 CHINJAP. PAGE 165 H3305
BIBLIOG/A ASIA NAT/G

B51
CHRISTENSEN A.N.,THE EVOLUTION OF LATIN AMERICAN GOVERNMENT: A BOOK OF READINGS. ECO/UNDEV INDUS LOC/G POL/PAR EX/STRUC LEGIS FOR/AID CT/SYS ...SOC/WK 20 SOUTH/AMER. PAGE 30 H0599
NAT/G CONSTN DIPLOM L/A+17C

C51
HAMMOND M.,"CITY-STATE AND WORLD STATE." CONSTN INTELL LOC/G LEGIT CENTRAL RATIONAL BIBLIOG. PAGE 65 H1308
NAT/G ATTIT REGION MEDIT-7

B52
BAILEY S.D.,THE BRITISH PARTY SYSTEM. UK LEGIS ...POLICY GP/COMP ANTHOL 11/20. PAGE 10 H0200
POL/PAR LOC/G NAT/G DELIB/GP

B52
BENTHAM A.,HANDBOOK OF POLITICAL FALLACIES. FUT MOD/EUR LAW INTELL LOC/G MUNIC NAT/G DELIB/GP LEGIS CREATE EDU/PROP CT/SYS ATTIT RIGID/FLEX KNOWL PWR ...RELATIV PSY SOC CONCPT SELF/OBS TREND STERTYP TOT/POP. PAGE 14 H0286
POL/PAR

B52
KOLARZ W.,RUSSIA AND HER COLONIES. COM RUSSIA LAW CULTURE ECO/DEV KIN LOC/G SECT TEC/DEV ECO/TAC EDU/PROP REGION COERCE ATTIT PWR SOVEREIGN...SOC TIME/SEQ CON/ANAL VAL/FREE 19/20. PAGE 88 H1749
NAT/G DOMIN USSR COLONIAL

B52
SCHATTSCHNEIDER E.E.,A GUIDE TO THE STUDY OF PUBLIC AFFAIRS. LAW LOC/G NAT/G LEGIS BUDGET PRESS ADMIN LOBBY...JURID CHARTS 20. PAGE 139 H2775
ACT/RES INTELL ACADEM METH/COMP

B52
TAX S.,HERITAGE OF CONQUEST. L/A+17C ECO/UNDEV LOC/G WEALTH...POLICY ANTHOL WORSHIP 20 MEXIC/AMER CENTRAL/AM. PAGE 153 H3052
PHIL/SCI CULTURE SOCIETY

B52
THOM J.M.,GUIDE TO RESEARCH MATERIAL IN POLITICAL SCIENCE (PAMPHLET). ELITES LOC/G MUNIC NAT/G LEGIS DIPLOM ADJUD CIVMIL/REL GOV/REL PWR MGT. PAGE 154 H3074
BIBLIOG/A KNOWL

B53
APPLEBY P.H.,PUBLIC ADMINISTRATION IN INDIA: REPORT OF A SURVEY. INDIA LOC/G OP/RES ATTIT ORD/FREE 20. PAGE 7 H0147
ADMIN NAT/G EX/STRUC GOV/REL

B53
LEITES N.,A STUDY OF BOLSHEVISM. ELITES STRATA INT/ORG LOC/G POL/PAR WORKER EDU/PROP REV TOTALISM UTOPIA PWR...CONCPT 20 BOLSHEVISM. PAGE 94 H1870
MARXISM PLAN COM

B53
STOUT H.M.,BRITISH GOVERNMENT. UK FINAN LOC/G POL/PAR DELIB/GP DIPLOM ADMIN COLONIAL CHOOSE ORD/FREE...JURID BIBLIOG 20 COMMONWLTH. PAGE 150 H2990
NAT/G PARL/PROC CONSTN NEW/LIB

B54
SCHWARTZ B.,FRENCH ADMINISTRATIVE LAW AND THE COMMON-LAW WORLD. FRANCE CULTURE LOC/G NAT/G PROVS DELIB/GP EX/STRUC LEGIS PROB/SOLV CT/SYS EXEC GOV/REL...IDEA/COMP ENGLSH/LAW. PAGE 140 H2808
JURID LAW METH/COMP ADJUD

B55
APTER D.E.,THE GOLD COAST IN TRANSITION. FUT CONSTN CULTURE SOCIETY ECO/UNDEV FAM KIN LOC/G NAT/G POL/PAR LEGIS TOP/EX EDU/PROP LEGIT ADMIN ATTIT PERSON PWR...CONCPT STAT INT CENSUS TOT/POP VAL/FREE. PAGE 7 H0149
AFR SOVEREIGN

B55
POLLOCK J.K.,GERMAN DEMOCRACY AT WORK. GERMANY/W LOC/G NAT/G DIPLOM PARL/PROC...OBS IDEA/COMP 20. PAGE 127 H2539
PARTIC POL/PAR CHOOSE EDU/PROP

C55
APTER D.E.,"THE GOLD COAST IN TRANSITION." AFR CONSTN LOC/G LEGIS DIPLOM COLONIAL CONTROL GOV/REL ...CHARTS BIBLIOG 20 CMN/WLTH. PAGE 7 H0150
ORD/FREE REPRESENT PARL/PROC NAT/G

B56
WILSON P.,GOVERNMENT AND POLITICS OF INDIA AND PAKISTAN: 1885-1955; A BIBLIOGRAPHY OF WORKS IN WESTERN LANGUAGES. INDIA PAKISTAN CONSTN LOC/G POL/PAR FORCES DIPLOM ADMIN WAR CHOOSE...BIOG CON/ANAL 19/20. PAGE 169 H3380
BIBLIOG COLONIAL NAT/G S/ASIA

S56
KHAMA T.,"POLITICAL CHANGE IN AFRICAN SOCIETY." CONSTN SOCIETY LOC/G NAT/G POL/PAR EX/STRUC LEGIS LEGIT ADMIN CHOOSE REPRESENT NAT/LISM MORAL ORD/FREE PWR...CONCPT OBS TREND GEN/METH CMN/WLTH 17/20. PAGE 85 H1706
AFR ELITES

B57
CARIBBEAN COMMISSION,A CATALOGUE OF CARIBBEAN COMMISSION PUBLICATIONS (PAMPHLET). WEST/IND CULTURE ECO/UNDEV LOC/G DIPLOM SOC. PAGE 26 H0531
BIBLIOG L/A+17C INT/ORG NAT/G

S57
HAILEY,"TOMORROW IN AFRICA." CONSTN SOCIETY LOC/G NAT/G DOMIN ADJUD ADMIN GP/REL DISCRIM NAT/LISM ATTIT MORAL ORD/FREE...PSY SOC CONCPT OBS RECORD TREND GEN/LAWS CMN/WLTH 20. PAGE 64 H1277
AFR PERSON ELITES RACE/REL

B58
CARTER G.M.,TRANSITION IN AFRICA; STUDIES IN POLITICAL ADAPTATION. AFR CENTRL/AFR GHANA NIGERIA CONSTN LOC/G POL/PAR ADMIN GP/REL FEDERAL...MAJORIT BIBLIOG 20. PAGE 27 H0543
NAT/COMP PWR CONTROL NAT/G

B58
COLEMAN J.S.,NIGERIA: BACKGROUND TO NATIONALISM. AFR SOCIETY ECO/DEV KIN LOC/G POL/PAR TEC/DEV DOMIN ADMIN DRIVE PWR RESPECT...TRADIT SOC INT SAMP TIME/SEQ 20. PAGE 31 H0627
NAT/G NAT/LISM NIGERIA

B58
COWAN L.G.,LOCAL GOVERNMENT IN WEST AFRICA. AFR FRANCE UK CULTURE KIN POL/PAR CHIEF LEGIS CREATE ADMIN PARTIC GOV/REL GP/REL...METH/COMP 20. PAGE 34 H0682
LOC/G COLONIAL SOVEREIGN REPRESENT

B58
NICULESCU B.,COLONIAL PLANNING: A COMPARATIVE
PLAN

STUDY. AFR AGRI LOC/G MUNIC NAT/G DELIB/GP COLONIAL 20. PAGE 118 H2356
ECO/UNDEV TEC/DEV NAT/COMP

B58
PALMER E.E.,"POLITICAL MAN" IN E. PALMER, PROBLEMS IN DEMOCRATIC CITIZENSHIP. LOC/G NAT/G LEGIS PRESS CHOOSE REPRESENT GP/REL...DECISION SOC IDEA/COMP ANTHOL 20. PAGE 123 H2449
PARTIC POL/PAR EDU/PROP MAJORIT

B58
SHAW S.J.,THE FINANCIAL AND ADMINISTRATIVE ORGANIZATION AND DEVELOPMENT OF OTTOMAN EGYPT 1517-1798. UAR LOC/G FORCES BUDGET INT/TRADE TAX EATING INCOME WEALTH...CHARTS BIBLIOG 16/18 OTTOMAN NAPOLEON/B. PAGE 143 H2853
FINAN ADMIN GOV/REL CULTURE

S58
MAIR L.P.,"REPRESENTATIVE LOCAL GOVERNMENT AS A PROBLEM IN SOCIAL CHANGE." ECO/UNDEV KIN LOC/G NAT/G SCHOOL JUDGE ADMIN ROUTINE REPRESENT RIGID/FLEX RESPECT...CONCPT STERTYP CMN/WLTH 20. PAGE 101 H2025
AFR PWR ELITES

S58
PYE L.W.,"THE NON-WESTERN POLITICAL PROCESS" (BMR)" AFR ASIA ISLAM S/ASIA DIPLOM ADMIN LEAD LOBBY ROUTINE CONSEN...DECISION 20. PAGE 128 H2567
CULTURE POL/PAR NAT/G LOC/G

B59
BARRON R.,PARTIES AND POLITICS IN MODERN FRANCE. FRANCE LOC/G DELIB/GP LEGIS TOP/EX EDU/PROP LEGIT TV FEEDBACK 20. PAGE 12 H0230
POL/PAR ALL/IDEOS CHOOSE PARTIC

B59
CORDONA G.D.,INDICE BIBLIOGRAFICO GUATEMALTECO 1958. GUATEMALA...SOC 20. PAGE 33 H0666
BIBLIOG NAT/G LOC/G L/A+17C

B59
CUCCORESE H.J.,HISTORIA DE LA CONVERSION DEL PAPEL MONEDA EN BUENOS AIRES, 1861-1867. LAW LOC/G NAT/G ATTIT...POLICY BIBLIOG 19 ARGEN BUENOS/AIR GOLD/STAND. PAGE 36 H0717
FINAN PLAN LEGIS

B59
MURDOCK G.P.,AFRICA: ITS PEOPLES AND THEIR CULTURE HISTORY. AFR CULTURE AGRI LOC/G INGP/REL HABITAT ...GEOG SOC LING CHARTS BIBLIOG 20 NEGRO EGYPT/ANC. PAGE 115 H2293
SOCIETY ECO/TAC GP/COMP KIN

B59
PARK R.L.,LEADERSHIP AND POLITICAL INSTITUTIONS IN INDIA. S/ASIA CULTURE ECO/UNDEV LOC/G MUNIC PROVS LEGIS PLAN ADMIN LEAD ORD/FREE WEALTH...GEOG SOC BIOG TOT/POP VAL/FREE 20. PAGE 123 H2468
NAT/G EXEC INDIA

B59
WRAITH R.E.,EAST AFRICAN CITIZEN. AFR GHANA UK AGRI INDUS LOC/G POL/PAR PROB/SOLV CONTROL REGION REPRESENT NAT/LISM PWR...OBS 20 AFRICA/E AFRICA/W. PAGE 171 H3415
ECO/UNDEV RACE/REL NAT/G NAT/COMP

S59
LEYS C.,"MODELS, THEORIES, AND THE THEORY OF POLITICAL PARTIES" CANADA LIECHTENST UK LOC/G NAT/G PARTIC REPRESENT GP/REL CONSEN EQUILIB MAJORITY ...NEW/IDEA MATH CHARTS 20. PAGE 96 H1919
POL/PAR CHOOSE METH/CNCPT SIMUL

B60
ALBI F.,TRATADO DE LOS MODOS DE GESTION DE LAS CORPORACIONES LOCALES. SPAIN FINAN NAT/G BUDGET CONTROL EXEC ROUTINE GOV/REL ORD/FREE SOVEREIGN ...MGT 20. PAGE 5 H0092
LOC/G LAW ADMIN MUNIC

B60
AYEARST M.,THE BRITISH WEST INDIES: THE SEARCH FOR SELF-GOVERNMENT. FUT WEST/IND LOC/G POL/PAR EX/STRUC LEGIS CHOOSE FEDERAL...NAT/COMP BIBLIOG 17/20. PAGE 9 H0186
CONSTN COLONIAL REPRESENT NAT/G

B60
LASKIN B.,CANADIAN CONSTITUTIONAL LAW: TEXT AND NOTES ON DISTRIBUTION OF LEGISLATIVE POWER (2ND ED.). CANADA LOC/G ECO/TAC TAX CONTROL CT/SYS CRIME FEDERAL PWR...JURID 20 PARLIAMENT. PAGE 92 H1832
CONSTN NAT/G LAW LEGIS

B60
PRASAD B.,THE ORIGINS OF PROVINCIAL AUTONOMY. INDIA UK FINAN LOC/G FORCES LEGIS CONTROL CT/SYS PWR ...JURID 19/20. PAGE 128 H2554
CENTRAL PROVS COLONIAL NAT/G

B60
SMITH M.G.,GOVERNMENT IN ZAZZAU 1800-1950. NIGERIA UK CULTURE SOCIETY LOC/G ADMIN COLONIAL ...METH/CNCPT NEW/IDEA METH 19/20. PAGE 146 H2914
REGION CONSTN KIN ECO/UNDEV

B60
WILLIAMS L.E.,OVERSEAS CHINESE NATIONALISM: THE GENESIS OF THE PAN-CHINESE MOVEMENT IN INDONESIA, 1900-1916. ASIA COM INDONESIA AGRI INT/ORG LOC/G DIPLOM EDU/PROP HABITAT PWR POPULISM...GEOG LING CENSUS 20. PAGE 168 H3367
NAT/LISM GP/REL DECISION NAT/G

L60
KAPLAN M.A.,"COMMUNIST COUP IN CZECHOSLOVAKIA." COM EUR+WWI INTELL LABOR LOC/G NAT/G POL/PAR FORCES EDU/PROP EXEC MARXISM...TIME/SEQ HYPO/EXP 20. PAGE 83 H1659
STRUCT COERCE CZECHOSLVK

S60
BANFIELD E.C.,"THE POLITICAL IMPLICATIONS OF METROPOLITAN GROWTH" (BMR)" UK USA+45 LOC/G PROB/SOLV ADMIN GP/REL...METH/COMP NAT/COMP 20. PAGE 10 H0209
TASK MUNIC GOV/COMP CENSUS

S60
EMERSON R.,"THE EROSION OF DEMOCRACY." AFR FUT LAW CULTURE INTELL SOCIETY ECO/UNDEV FAM LOC/G NAT/G FORCES PLAN TEC/DEV ECO/TAC ADMIN CT/SYS ATTIT ORD/FREE PWR...SOCIALIST SOC CONCPT STAND/INT TIME/SEQ WORK 20. PAGE 46 H0918
S/ASIA POL/PAR

S60
FITZGIBBON R.H.,"DICTATORSHIP AND DEMOCRACY IN LATIN AMERICA." FUT ECO/DEV ECO/UNDEV INT/ORG LOC/G NAT/G TOP/EX PLAN TEC/DEV ECO/TAC CHOOSE ATTIT DRIVE PERSON ALL/VALS OAS TOT/POP 20. PAGE 51 H1019
L/A+17C ACT/RES INT/TRADE

S60
LEVINE R.A.,"THE INTERNALIZATION OF POLITICAL VALUES IN STATELESS SOCIETIES." AFR FAM KIN LOC/G PROVS JUDGE PERSON RIGID/FLEX...DECISION SOC TIME/SEQ 20. PAGE 95 H1904
CULTURE ATTIT

S60
SHILS E.,"THE INTELLECTUALS IN THE POLITICAL DEVELOPMENT OF THE NEW STATES." AFR ASIA S/ASIA ELITES LOC/G NAT/G CONSULT EX/STRUC CREATE PLAN ECO/TAC DOMIN LEGIT DRIVE PWR...TRADIT CONCPT STERTYP GEN/LAWS 20. PAGE 143 H2861
POL/PAR INTELL NAT/LISM

C60
HOSELITZ B.,"THE ROLE OF CITIES IN THE ECONOMIC GROWTH OF UNDERDEVELOPED COUNTRIES" IN "SOCIOLOGICAL ASPECTS OF ECONOMIC GROWTH"(BMR). CULTURE LOC/G ACT/RES...SOC IDEA/COMP METH/COMP METH 14/20 REDFIELD/R. PAGE 74 H1474
METH/CNCPT MUNIC TEC/DEV ECO/UNDEV

B61
BURDETTE F.L.,POLITICAL SCIENCE: A SELECTED BIBLIOGRAPHY OF BOOKS IN PRINT, WITH ANNOTATIONS (PAMPHLET). LAW LOC/G NAT/G POL/PAR PROVS DIPLOM EDU/PROP ADMIN CHOOSE ATTIT 20. PAGE 24 H0479
BIBLIOG/A GOV/COMP CONCPT ROUTINE

B61
DONNISON F.S.V.,CIVIL AFFAIRS AND MILITARY GOVERNMENT NORTH-WEST EUROPE 1944-1946. EUR+WWI FRANCE GERMANY UK USSR LOC/G PROVS PLAN PROB/SOLV BAL/PWR ECO/TAC CONTROL PWR...CHARTS 20. PAGE 42 H0836
NAT/G WAR FORCES CIVMIL/REL

B61
DRAGNICH A.N.,MAJOR EUROPEAN GOVERNMENTS. FRANCE GERMANY/W UK USSR LOC/G EX/STRUC CT/SYS PARL/PROC ATTIT MARXISM...JURID MGT NAT/COMP 19/20. PAGE 42 H0846
NAT/G LEGIS CONSTN POL/PAR

B61
GARCIA E.,LA ADMINISTRACION ESPANOLA. SPAIN GOV/REL ...CONCPT METH/COMP 20. PAGE 55 H1099
ADMIN NAT/G LOC/G DECISION

B61
HICKS U.K.,DEVELOPMENT FROM BELOW. UK INDUS ADMIN COLONIAL ROUTINE GOV/REL...POLICY METH/CNCPT CHARTS 19/20 CMN/WLTH. PAGE 71 H1414
ECO/UNDEV LOC/G GOV/COMP METH/COMP

B61
INTL UNION LOCAL AUTHORITIES,METROPOLIS. WOR+45 DIST/IND FINAN GIVE EDU/PROP CRIME COST HEALTH WEALTH 20. PAGE 78 H1563
MUNIC GOV/COMP LOC/G BIBLIOG

B61
NARAIN J.P.,SWARAJ FOR THE PEOPLE. INDIA CONSTN LOC/G MUNIC POL/PAR CHOOSE REPRESENT EFFICIENCY ATTIT PWR SOVEREIGN 20. PAGE 116 H2311
NAT/G ORD/FREE EDU/PROP EX/STRUC

B61
WEST F.J.,POLITICAL ADVANCEMENT IN THE SOUTH PACIFIC. CONSTN CULTURE POL/PAR LEGIS DOMIN ADMIN CHOOSE SOVEREIGN VAL/FREE 20 FIJI TAHITI SAMOA. PAGE 167 H3335
S/ASIA LOC/G COLONIAL

S61
ELAZAR D.J.,"CHURCHES AS MOLDERS OF AMERICAN POLITICS." STRATA MUNIC EDU/PROP RACE/REL ORD/FREE SOC. PAGE 45 H0904
SECT CULTURE REPRESENT LOC/G

C61
MOODIE G.C.,"THE GOVERNMENT OF GREAT BRITAIN." UK LAW STRUCT LOC/G POL/PAR DIPLOM RECEIVE ADMIN COLONIAL CHOOSE...BIBLIOG 20 PARLIAMENT. PAGE 112 H2247
NAT/G SOCIETY PARL/PROC GOV/COMP

B62
CARTER G.M.,THE GOVERNMENT OF THE SOVIET UNION. USSR CULTURE LOC/G DIPLOM ECO/TAC ADJUD CT/SYS LEAD WEALTH...CHARTS T 20 COM/PARTY. PAGE 27 H0546
NAT/G MARXISM POL/PAR EX/STRUC

B62
CARY J.,THE CASE FOR AFRICAN FREEDOM AND OTHER WRITINGS ON AFRICA. AFR UK INDUS LOC/G NAT/G SECT INT/TRADE EDU/PROP GOV/REL RACE/REL ORD/FREE ...CONCPT ANTHOL 19/20. PAGE 27 H0552
NAT/LISM COLONIAL TREND ECO/UNDEV

B62
COSTA RICA UNIVERSIDAD BIBL,LISTA DE TESIS DE GRADO
BIBLIOG/A

DE LA UNIVERSIDAD DE COSTA RICA. COSTA/RICA LAW LOC/G ADMIN LEAD...SOC 20. PAGE 34 H0675
NAT/G DIPLOM ECO/UNDEV

B62
GROVE J.W.,GOVERNMENT AND INDUSTRY IN BRITAIN. UK FINAN LOC/G CONSULT DELIB/GP INT/TRADE ADMIN CONTROL...BIBLIOG 20. PAGE 62 H1237
ECO/TAC INDUS NAT/G GP/REL

B62
INAYATULLAH,BUREAUCRACY AND DEVELOPMENT IN PAKISTAN. PAKISTAN ECO/UNDEV EDU/PROP CONFER ...ANTHOL DICTIONARY 20 BUREAUCRCY. PAGE 76 H1526
EX/STRUC ADMIN NAT/G LOC/G

B62
KARNJAHAPRAKORN C.,MUNICIPAL GOVERNMENT IN THAILAND AS AN INSTITUTION AND PROCESS OF SELF-GOVERNMENT. THAILAND CULTURE FINAN EX/STRUC LEGIS PLAN CONTROL GOV/REL EFFICIENCY ATTIT...POLICY 20. PAGE 83 H1662
LOC/G MUNIC ORD/FREE ADMIN

B62
STATE AND LOCAL GOVERNMENT. MUNIC NAT/G NEIGH PRESS CONTROL CHOOSE REPRESENT...BIBLIOG 20. PAGE 104 H2076
PROVS LOC/G GOV/REL PWR

B62
MUKERJI S.N.,ADMINISTRATION OF EDUCATION IN INDIA. ACADEM LOC/G PROVS ROUTINE...POLICY STAT CHARTS 20. PAGE 114 H2282
SCHOOL ADMIN NAT/G EDU/PROP

B62
PHILLIPS O.H.,CONSTITUTIONAL AND ADMINISTRATIVE LAW (3RD ED.). UK INT/ORG LOC/G CHIEF EX/STRUC LEGIS BAL/PWR ADJUD COLONIAL CT/SYS PWR...CHARTS 20. PAGE 125 H2503
JURID ADMIN CONSTN NAT/G

B62
YOUNG G.,THE HILL TRIBES OF NORTHERN THAILAND. S/ASIA THAILAND FAM KIN LOC/G GP/REL HABITAT...GEOG LING OBS 20. PAGE 172 H3438
CULTURE STRUCT ECO/UNDEV SECT

S62
GUETZKOW H.,"THE POTENTIAL OF CASE STUDY IN ANALYZING INTERNATIONAL CONFLICT." EUR+WWI FUT GERMANY INTELL SOCIETY STRUCT INT/ORG LOC/G NAT/G CONSULT CREATE PLAN CHOOSE ATTIT RIGID/FLEX ...POLICY SAAR 20. PAGE 62 H1246
EDU/PROP METH/CNCPT COERCE FRANCE

B63
ADRIAN C.R.,GOVERNING OVER FIFTY STATES AND THEIR COMMUNITIES. USA+45 CONSTN FINAN MUNIC NAT/G POL/PAR EX/STRUC LEGIS ADMIN CONTROL CT/SYS ...CHARTS 20. PAGE 4 H0073
PROVS LOC/G GOV/REL GOV/COMP

B63
BLONDEL J.,VOTERS, PARTIES, AND LEADERS. UK ELITES LOC/G NAT/G PROVS ACT/RES DOMIN REPRESENT GP/REL INGP/REL...SOC BIBLIOG 20. PAGE 18 H0358
POL/PAR STRATA LEGIS ADMIN

B63
ELLIOT J.H.,THE REVOLT OF THE CATALANS. SPAIN LOC/G PROVS FORCES DIPLOM TASK WAR GOV/REL INGP/REL ...POLICY 17 OLIVARES. PAGE 45 H0909
REV NAT/G TOP/EX DOMIN

B63
FRIEDRICH C.J.,MAN AND HIS GOVERNMENT: AN EMPIRICAL THEORY OF POLITICS. UNIV LOC/G NAT/G ADJUD REV INGP/REL DISCRIM PWR BIBLIOG. PAGE 53 H1069
PERSON ORD/FREE PARTIC CONTROL

B63
GORDON M.S.,THE ECONOMICS OF WELFARE POLICIES. INDUS LOC/G NAT/G LEGIS WORKER INCOME AGE/O SKILL WEALTH...METH/COMP NAT/COMP 20. PAGE 59 H1180
METH/CNCPT ECO/TAC POLICY

B63
GOURNAY B.,PUBLIC ADMINISTRATION. FRANCE LAW CONSTN AGRI FINAN LABOR SCHOOL EX/STRUC CHOOSE...MGT METH/COMP 20. PAGE 59 H1189
BIBLIOG/A ADMIN NAT/G LOC/G

B63
HUGHES A.J.,EAST AFRICA: THE SEARCH FOR UNITY- KENYA, TANGANYIKA, UGANDA, AND ZANZIBAR. TANZANIA UGANDA CONSTN POL/PAR SECT CHIEF DELIB/GP LEGIS WAR CHOOSE NAT/LISM MARXISM...POLICY CHARTS 20 NEGRO UN. PAGE 74 H1488
NAT/G DOMIN LOC/G AFR

B63
JACOB H.,GERMAN ADMINISTRATION SINCE BISMARCK: CENTRAL AUTHORITY VERSUS LOCAL AUTONOMY. GERMANY GERMANY/W LAW POL/PAR CONTROL CENTRAL TOTALISM FASCISM...MAJORIT DECISION STAT CHARTS GOV/COMP 19/20 BISMARCK/O HITLER/A WEIMAR/REP. PAGE 79 H1577
ADMIN NAT/G LOC/G POLICY

B63
JUDD P.,AFRICAN INDEPENDENCE: THE EXPLODING EMERGENCE OF THE NEW AFRICAN NATIONS. AFR UK LAW CONSTN CULTURE KIN DIPLOM ATTIT...CHARTS BIBLIOG 20 UN DEGAULLE/C NEGRO THIRD/WRLD. PAGE 82 H1640
ORD/FREE POLICY DOMIN LOC/G

B63
LIVINGSTON W.S.,FEDERALISM IN THE COMMONWEALTH - A BIBLIOGRAPHICAL COMMENTARY. CANADA INDIA PAKISTAN UK STRUCT LOC/G NAT/G POL/PAR...NAT/COMP 20 AUSTRAL. PAGE 97 H1943
BIBLIOG JURID FEDERAL CONSTN

B63
RIVKIN A.,THE AFRICAN PRESENCE IN WORLD AFFAIRS. ECO/UNDEV AGRI INT/ORG LOC/G NAT/LISM...OBS PREDICT GOV/COMP 20. PAGE 132 H2635
AFR NAT/G DIPLOM BAL/PWR

B63
SCHECHTMAN J.B.,THE REFUGEE IN THE WORLD: DISPLACEMENT AND INTEGRATION. AFR ASIA EUR+WWI ISLAM L/A+17C S/ASIA CULTURE STRATA LOC/G EX/STRUC PLAN ECO/TAC ROUTINE...CONCPT TIME/SEQ VAL/FREE 20. PAGE 139 H2779
INT/ORG SOC

S63
HUREWITZ J.C.,"LEBANESE DEMOCRACY IN ITS INTERNATIONAL SETTING." FRANCE ISLAM UK LOC/G NAT/G SECT DOMIN EDU/PROP EXEC ATTIT PWR...TIME/SEQ 20. PAGE 75 H1507
STRUCT LEBANON

S63
MAZRUI A.A.,"ON THE CONCEPT 'WE ARE ALL AFRICANS'." AFR CULTURE KIN LOC/G NAT/G DOMIN EDU/PROP LEGIT ATTIT PERCEPT PERSON KNOWL ORD/FREE...TIME/SEQ TOT/POP 20. PAGE 106 H2110
PROVS INT/ORG NAT/LISM

B64
AGGER R.E.,THE RULERS AND THE RULED: POLITICAL POWER AND IMPOTENCE IN AMERICAN COMMUNITIES. CULTURE DOMIN CHOOSE ATTIT ALL/VALS...DECISION SOC CONCPT OBS QU CHARTS. PAGE 4 H0079
PWR STRUCT LOC/G MUNIC

B64
ALDEFER H.F.,A BIBLIOGRAPHY OF AFRICAN GOVERNMENT: 1950-1964. ALGERIA GUINEA LIBERIA UAR ECO/UNDEV POL/PAR LEGIS COLONIAL LEAD PARL/PROC NAT/LISM 20. PAGE 5 H0098
BIBLIOG AFR LOC/G NAT/G

B64
BENDIX R.,NATION-BUILDING AND CITIZENSHIP: STUDIES OF OUR CHANGING SOCIAL ORDER. WOR+45 CULTURE LOC/G GOV/REL INGP/REL ORD/FREE PWR 20. PAGE 14 H0275
PARTIC NAT/COMP ADMIN AUTHORIT

B64
GREBLER L.,URBAN RENEWAL IN EUROPEAN COUNTRIES: ITS EMERGENCE AND POTENTIALS. EUR+WWI UK ECO/DEV LOC/G NEIGH CREATE ADMIN ATTIT...TREND NAT/COMP 20 URBAN/RNWL. PAGE 60 H1205
MUNIC PLAN CONSTRUC NAT/G

B64
HALPERN J.M.,GOVERNMENT, POLITICS, AND SOCIAL STRUCTURE IN LAOS. LAOS CULTURE SOCIETY STRATA STRUCT FAM DIPLOM DOMIN MARXISM...INT GOV/COMP WORSHIP SOC/INTEG 20. PAGE 65 H1297
NAT/G SOC LOC/G

B64
HANNA W.J.,POLITICS IN BLACK AFRICA: A SELECTIVE BIBLIOGRAPHY OF RELEVANT PERIODICAL LITERATURE. AFR LAW LOC/G MUNIC NAT/G POL/PAR LOBBY CHOOSE RACE/REL SOVEREIGN 20. PAGE 66 H1315
BIBLIOG NAT/LISM COLONIAL

B64
HILL C.R.,BANTUSTANS: THE FRAGMENTATION OF SOUTH AFRICA. AFR SOUTH/AFR ELITES SOCIETY KIN CONTROL DISCRIM ANOMIE ATTIT...POLICY CHARTS GOV/COMP 20 NEGRO BANTUSTANS TRANSKEI NATAL. PAGE 71 H1416
RACE/REL CULTURE LOC/G ORD/FREE

B64
HOLDSWORTH W.S.,A HISTORY OF ENGLISH LAW; THE CENTURIES OF DEVELOPMENT AND REFORM (VOL. XIV). UK CONSTN LOC/G NAT/G POL/PAR CHIEF EX/STRUC ADJUD COLONIAL ATTIT...INT/LAW JURID 18/19 TORY/PARTY COMMONWLTH WHIG/PARTY COMMON/LAW. PAGE 73 H1453
LAW LEGIS LEAD CT/SYS

B64
INDIAN COMM PREVENTION CORRUPT,REPORT, 1964. INDIA NAT/G GOV/REL ATTIT ORD/FREE...CRIMLGY METH 20. PAGE 76 H1530
CRIME ADMIN LEGIS LOC/G

B64
LIGGETT E.,BRITISH POLITICAL ISSUES: VOLUME 1. UK LAW CONSTN LOC/G NAT/G ADJUD 20. PAGE 97 H1930
POL/PAR GOV/REL CT/SYS DIPLOM

B64
MAHAR J.M.,INDIA: A CRITICAL BIBLIOGRAPHY. INDIA PAKISTAN CULTURE ECO/UNDEV LOC/G POL/PAR SECT PROB/SOLV DIPLOM ADMIN COLONIAL PARL/PROC ATTIT 20. PAGE 101 H2016
BIBLIOG/A S/ASIA NAT/G LEAD

B64
NATIONAL BOOK LEAGUE,THE COMMONWEALTH IN BOOKS: AN ANNOTATED LIST. CANADA UK LOC/G SECT ADMIN...SOC BIOG 20 CMN/WLTH. PAGE 116 H2320
BIBLIOG/A JURID NAT/G

B64
PERKINS D.,THE AMERICAN DEMOCRACY: ITS RISE TO POWER. ASIA USSR LAW CULTURE FINAN EDU/PROP COLONIAL CHOOSE...POLICY CHARTS BIBLIOG WORSHIP PRESIDENT 15/20 NEGRO. PAGE 125 H2492
LOC/G ECO/TAC WAR DIPLOM

B64
VALEN H.,POLITICAL PARTIES IN NORWAY. NORWAY ACADEM PARTIC ROUTINE INGP/REL KNOWL...QU 20. PAGE 161 H3220
LOC/G POL/PAR PERSON

B64
WRAITH R.,CORRUPTION IN DEVELOPING COUNTRIES. NIGERIA UK LAW ELITES STRATA INDUS LOC/G NAT/G SECT FORCES EDU/PROP ADMIN PWR WEALTH 18/20. PAGE 171 H3414
ECO/UNDEV CRIME SANCTION ATTIT

S64
GIROD R.,"LE SYSTEME DES PARTIS EN SUISSE." CONSTN LOC/G DELIB/GP FEDERAL ALL/VALS. PAGE 57 H1136
POL/PAR LEGIS NAT/G PARL/PROC

S64
NEEDHAM T.,"SCIENCE AND SOCIETY IN EAST AND WEST." INTELL STRATA R+D LOC/G NAT/G PROVS CONSULT ACT/RES CREATE PLAN TEC/DEV EDU/PROP ADMIN ATTIT ALL/VALS ...POLICY RELATIV MGT CONCPT NEW/IDEA TIME/SEQ WORK WORK. PAGE 116 H2327
ASIA STRUCT

S64
SCHEFFLER H.W.,"THE GENESIS AND REPRESSION OF CONFLICT: CHOISEUL ISLAND." S/ASIA LOC/G NAT/G FORCES LEGIS DIPLOM DOMIN LEGIT EXEC CHOOSE ATTIT RESPECT SKILL...POLICY JURID OBS TREND GEN/METH 20. PAGE 139 H2781
PWR COERCE WAR

B65
ALLEN W.S.,THE NAZI SEIZURE OF POWER. GERMANY NAT/G CHIEF LEAD COERCE CHOOSE REPRESENT GOV/REL AUTHORIT ...DECISION 20 HITLER/A NAZI. PAGE 5 H0106
MUNIC FASCISM TOTALISM LOC/G

B65
BLITZ L.F.,THE POLITICS AND ADMINISTRATION OF NIGERIAN GOVERNMENT. NIGER CULTURE LOC/G LEGIS DIPLOM COLONIAL CT/SYS SOVEREIGN...GEOG SOC ANTHOL 20. PAGE 18 H0357
NAT/G GOV/REL POL/PAR

B65
BRASS P.R.,FACTIONAL POLITICS IN AN INDIAN STATE: THE CONGRESS PARTY IN UTTAR PRADESH. INDIA UK CONSTN CULTURE ECO/UNDEV LOC/G DOMIN COLONIAL CROWD GP/REL ADJUST CENTRAL RIGID/FLEX SOVEREIGN 20 UTTAR/PRAD CONGRESS/P. PAGE 20 H0406
POL/PAR PROVS LEGIS CHOOSE

B65
CHANDLER M.J.,A GUIDE TO RECORDS IN BARBADOS. WEST/IND PUB/INST SCHOOL SECT...HIST/WRIT 20. PAGE 28 H0573
BIBLIOG LOC/G L/A+17C NAT/G

B65
HARMON R.B.,POLITICAL SCIENCE: A BIBLIOGRAPHICAL GUIDE TO THE LITERATURE. WOR+45 WOR-45 R+D INT/ORG LOC/G NAT/G DIPLOM ADMIN...CONCPT METH. PAGE 67 H1334
BIBLIOG POL/PAR LAW GOV/COMP

B65
LANDE C.H.,LEADERS, FACTIONS, AND PARTIES. PHILIPPINE CONSTN LOC/G NAT/G PARTIC...CHARTS BIBLIOG 20. PAGE 90 H1806
LEAD POL/PAR POLICY

B65
MOORE C.H.,TUNISIA SINCE INDEPENDENCE. ELITES LOC/G POL/PAR ADMIN COLONIAL CONTROL EXEC GOV/REL TOTALISM MARXISM...INT 20 TUNIS. PAGE 112 H2248
NAT/G EX/STRUC SOCISM

B65
NAMIER L.B.,THE STRUCTURE OF POLITICS AT THE ACCESSION OF GEORGE III. UK LOC/G TOP/EX COLONIAL LEAD PARTIC REV CHOOSE REPRESENT GOV/REL PERSON SOVEREIGN...GOV/COMP 18 PARLIAMENT. PAGE 115 H2309
PARL/PROC LEGIS NAT/G POL/PAR

B65
SHARMA S.A.,PARLIAMENTARY GOVERNMENT IN INDIA. INDIA FINAN LOC/G PROVS DELIB/GP PLAN ADMIN CT/SYS FEDERAL...JURID 20. PAGE 142 H2849
NAT/G CONSTN PARL/PROC LEGIS

B65
STEINER K.,LOCAL GOVERNMENT IN JAPAN. CONSTN CULTURE NAT/G ADMIN CHOOSE...SOC STAT 20 CHINJAP. PAGE 149 H2976
LOC/G SOCIETY JURID ORD/FREE

B65
ULLMANN W.,A HISTORY OF POLITICAL THOUGHT: THE MIDDLE AGES. CHRIST-17C LOC/G NAT/G CENTRAL PWR ...PHIL/SCI LOG BIBLIOG 6/15. PAGE 158 H3153
IDEA/COMP SOVEREIGN SECT LAW

B65
US LIBRARY OF CONGRESS,RARE BOOKS DIVISION: GUIDE TO ITS COLLECTION AND SERVICES. LOC/G SECT WAR. PAGE 161 H3214
BIBLIOG/A NAT/G DIPLOM

S65
KEE W.S.,"CENTRAL CITY EXPENDITURES AND METROPOLITAN AREAS." PLAN BUDGET ECO/TAC TAX GP/REL WEALTH...CHARTS 20. PAGE 84 H1677
LOC/G MUNIC GOV/COMP NEIGH

N65
MOTE M.E.,SOVIET LOCAL AND REPUBLIC ELECTIONS. COM USSR NAT/G PLAN PARTIC GOV/REL TOTALISM PWR ...CHARTS 20. PAGE 114 H2270
CHOOSE ADMIN CONTROL LOC/G

B66
ADAMS J.C.,THE GOVERNMENT OF REPUBLICAN ITALY (2ND ED.). ITALY LOC/G POL/PAR DELIB/GP LEGIS WORKER ADMIN CT/SYS FASCISM...CHARTS BIBLIOG 20 PARLIAMENT. PAGE 3 H0064
NAT/G CHOOSE EX/STRUC CONSTN

B66
ASHRAF A.,THE CITY GOVERNMENT OF CALCUTTA: A STUDY OF INERTIA. INDIA ELITES INDUS NAT/G EX/STRUC ACT/RES PLAN PROB/SOLV LEAD HABITAT...BIBLIOG 20 CALCUTTA. PAGE 9 H0175
LOC/G MUNIC ADMIN ECO/UNDEV

B66
BHALERAO C.N.,PUBLIC SERVICE COMMISSIONS OF INDIA: A STUDY. INDIA SERV/IND EX/STRUC ROUTINE CHOOSE GOV/REL INGP/REL...KNO/TEST EXHIBIT 20. PAGE 16 H0326
NAT/G OP/RES LOC/G ADMIN

B66
BRAIBANTI R.,RESEARCH ON THE BUREAUCRACY OF PAKISTAN. PAKISTAN LAW CULTURE INTELL ACADEM LOC/G SECT PRESS CT/SYS...LING CHARTS 20 BUREAUCRCY. PAGE 20 H0402
HABITAT NAT/G ADMIN CONSTN

B66
BUTLER D.E.,THE BRITISH GENERAL ELECTION OF 1966. UK LOC/G NAT/G OP/RES CONFER CHOOSE MAJORITY ATTIT ...CHARTS TIME 20. PAGE 25 H0498
POL/PAR REPRESENT GP/REL PERS/REL

B66
DUNCOMBE H.S.,COUNTY GOVERNMENT IN AMERICA. USA+45 FINAN MUNIC ADMIN ROUTINE GOV/REL...GOV/COMP 20. PAGE 43 H0863
LOC/G PROVS CT/SYS TOP/EX

B66
EPSTEIN F.T.,THE AMERICAN BIBLIOGRAPHY OF RUSSIAN AND EAST EUROPEAN STUDIES FOR 1964. USSR LOC/G NAT/G POL/PAR FORCES ADMIN ARMS/CONT...JURID CONCPT 20 UN. PAGE 47 H0933
BIBLIOG COM MARXISM DIPLOM

B66
GHOSH P.K.,THE CONSTITUTION OF INDIA: HOW IT HAS BEEN FRAMED. INDIA LOC/G DELIB/GP EX/STRUC PROB/SOLV BUDGET INT/TRADE CT/SYS CHOOSE...LING 20. PAGE 56 H1121
CONSTN NAT/G LEGIS FEDERAL

B66
HARMON R.B.,SOURCES AND PROBLEMS OF BIBLIOGRAPHY IN POLITICAL SCIENCE (PAMPHLET). INT/ORG LOC/G MUNIC POL/PAR ADMIN GOV/REL ALL/IDEOS...JURID MGT CONCPT 19/20. PAGE 67 H1335
BIBLIOG DIPLOM INT/LAW NAT/G

B66
HOLDSWORTH W.S.,A HISTORY OF ENGLISH LAW; THE CENTURIES OF SETTLEMENT AND REFORM (VOL. XVI). UK LOC/G NAT/G EX/STRUC LEGIS CT/SYS LEAD ATTIT ...POLICY DECISION JURID IDEA/COMP 18 PARLIAMENT. PAGE 73 H1454
BIOG PERSON PROF/ORG LAW

B66
IOWA STATE U CTR AGRI AND ECO,RESEARCH AND EDUCATION FOR REGIONAL AND AREA DEVELOPMENT. FUT LAW CULTURE R+D LOC/G PLAN KNOWL...POLICY CHARTS ANTHOL 20. PAGE 78 H1565
REGION ACT/RES ECO/TAC INDUS

B66
NEUMANN R.G.,THE GOVERNMENT OF THE GERMAN FEDERAL REPUBLIC. EUR+WWI GERMANY/W LOC/G EX/STRUC LEGIS CT/SYS INGP/REL PWR...BIBLIOG 20 ADENAUER/K. PAGE 117 H2336
NAT/G POL/PAR DIPLOM CONSTN

B66
SCHURMANN F.,IDEOLOGY AND ORGANIZATION IN COMMUNIST CHINA. CHINA/COM LOC/G MUNIC POL/PAR ECO/TAC CONTROL ATTIT...MGT STERTYP 20 COM/PARTY. PAGE 140 H2805
MARXISM STRUCT ADMIN NAT/G

B66
SWARTZ M.J.,POLITICAL ANTHROPOLOGY. WOR+45 POL/PAR ACT/RES REV GP/REL DRIVE...SOC CONCPT TIME/SEQ GP/COMP ANTHOL WORSHIP 20. PAGE 151 H3013
PARTIC RIGID/FLEX LOC/G CREATE

B66
WUEST J.J.,NEW SOURCE BOOK IN MAJOR EUROPEAN GOVERNMENTS. CHRIST-17C EUR+WWI FRANCE GERMANY ITALY MOD/EUR UK USSR LOC/G POL/PAR CHIEF EX/STRUC CHOOSE CONSERVE MARXISM...JURID T 13/20. PAGE 171 H3425
NAT/G CONSTN LEGIS

L66
SEYLER W.C.,"DOCTORAL DISSERTATIONS IN POLITICAL SCIENCE IN UNIVERSITIES OF THE UNITED STATES AND CANADA." INT/ORG LOC/G ADMIN...INT/LAW MGT GOV/COMP. PAGE 142 H2836
BIBLIOG LAW NAT/G

L66
"FEDERAL, STATE AND LOCAL GOVERNMENT PUBLICATIONS." ACADEM LOC/G NAT/G PROVS SCHOOL EFFICIENCY ...PHIL/SCI ANTHOL. PAGE 143 H2854
BIBLIOG OP/RES METH

S66
"RESEARCH WORK 1965-1966." NEW/ZEALND ELITES ACADEM LOC/G MUNIC POL/PAR PROVS DIPLOM COLONIAL...SOC 20 AUSTRAL. PAGE 2 H0047
BIBLIOG NAT/G CULTURE S/ASIA

S66
"FURTHER READING." INDIA LOC/G NAT/G PLAN ADMIN WEALTH...GEOG SOC CONCPT CENSUS 20. PAGE 2 H0049
BIBLIOG ECO/UNDEV TEC/DEV PROVS

B67
BARNETT A.D.,CADRES, BUREAUCRACY, AND POLITICAL POWER IN COMMUNIST CHINA. CHINA/COM ELITES LOC/G NAT/G INGP/REL...SOC INT DICTIONARY 20. PAGE 11 H0224
GOV/REL STRUCT MARXISM EDU/PROP

B67
CORDIER A.W.,COLUMBIA ESSAYS IN INTERNATIONAL AFFAIRS. ASIA CHINA/COM FRANCE S/ASIA SPAIN UAR ECO/UNDEV LOC/G ECO/TAC GUERRILLA PWR...BIOG ANTHOL 18/20 MAU/MAU. PAGE 33 H0663
NAT/G DIPLOM MARXISM POLICY

B67
ERDMAN H.L.,THE SWATANTRA PARTY AND INDIAN CONSERVATISM. INDIA S/ASIA SOCIETY STRATA LOC/G NAT/G LEAD PARTIC GP/REL ATTIT...CONCPT GP/COMP BIBLIOG 20 SWATANTRA. PAGE 47 H0938 POL/PAR CONSERVE CHOOSE POLICY

B67
LENG S.C.,JUSTICE IN COMMUNIST CHINA: A SURVEY OF THE JUDICIAL SYSTEM OF THE CHINESE PEOPLE'S REPUBLIC. CHINA/COM LAW CONSTN LOC/G NAT/G PROF/ORG CONSULT FORCES ADMIN CRIME ORD/FREE...BIBLIOG 20 MAO. PAGE 94 H1877 CT/SYS ADJUD JURID MARXISM

B67
MILNE R.S.,GOVERNMENT AND POLITICS IN MALAYSIA. INDONESIA MALAYSIA LOC/G EX/STRUC FORCES DIPLOM GP/REL 20 SINGAPORE. PAGE 111 H2217 NAT/G LEGIS ADMIN

B67
MORRIS A.J.A.,PARLIAMENTARY DEMOCRACY IN THE NINETEENTH CENTURY. UK INDUS LOC/G NAT/G POL/PAR CONSULT LEGIS INT/TRADE ADMIN CHOOSE SUFF SOVEREIGN 19 PARLIAMENT. PAGE 113 H2261 TIME/SEQ CONSTN PARL/PROC POPULISM

B67
POGANY A.H.,POLITICAL SCIENCE AND INTERNATIONAL RELATIONS, BOOKS RECOMMENDED FOR AMERICAN CATHOLIC COLLEGE LIBRARIES. INT/ORG LOC/G NAT/G FORCES BAL/PWR ECO/TAC NUC/PWR...CATH INT/LAW TREATY 20. PAGE 127 H2532 BIBLIOG DIPLOM

B67
RUDMAN H.C.,THE SCHOOL AND STATE IN THE USSR. COM USSR ACADEM LABOR LOC/G PUB/INST EDU/PROP GP/REL ROLE...POLICY DECISION MGT CHARTS 20. PAGE 136 H2712 SCHOOL ADMIN NAT/G POL/PAR

B67
SCHWARTZ M.A.,PUBLIC OPINION AND CANADIAN IDENTITY. CANADA SOCIETY LOC/G DIPLOM ADMIN LEAD REGION GP/REL SAMP. PAGE 141 H2812 ATTIT NAT/G NAT/LISM POL/PAR

B67
WINTER E.H.,CONTEMPORARY CHANGE IN TRADITIONAL SOCIETIES: VOLUME I INTRODUCTION AND AFRICAN TRIBES. NIGERIA AGRI LOC/G NAT/G CREATE DOMIN COLONIAL CONTROL GP/REL PWR SOVEREIGN...SOC OBS 20 TANGANYIKA. PAGE 169 H3389 SOCIETY AFR CONSERVE KIN

L67
"A PROPOS DES INCITATIONS FINANCIERES AUX GROUPEMENTS DES COMMUNES: ESSAI D'INTERPRETATION." FRANCE NAT/G LEGIS ADMIN GOV/REL CENTRAL 20. PAGE 3 H0051 LOC/G ECO/TAC APPORT ADJUD

L67
RUTH J.M.,"THE ADMINISTRATION OF WATER RESOURCES IN GUATEMALA." GUATEMALA L/A+17C DIST/IND LOC/G NAT/G EX/STRUC ADMIN GOV/REL DEMAND EQUILIB WEALTH...GEOG MGT 20. PAGE 136 H2723 EFFICIENCY ECO/UNDEV PLAN ACT/RES

L67
WILBER L.A.,"THE GOVERNMENTAL STRUCTURE OF MISSISSIPPI: ITS STRENGTHS AND WEAKNESSES." AGRI LOC/G SCHOOL EX/STRUC LEGIS TOP/EX BUDGET CT/SYS APPORT RACE/REL...GOV/COMP 20 MISSISSIPP. PAGE 168 H3359 CONSTN PROVS STAT CON/ANAL

S67
ADOKO A.,"THE CONSTITUTION OF UGANDA." AFR UGANDA LOC/G CHIEF FORCES LEGIS ADJUD EXEC CHOOSE NAT/LISM ...IDEA/COMP 20. PAGE 4 H0072 NAT/G CONSTN ORD/FREE LAW

S67
DRYDEN S.,"LOCAL GOVERNMENT IN TANZANIA PART II" TANZANIA LAW NAT/G POL/PAR CONTROL PARTIC REPRESENT ...DECISION 20. PAGE 42 H0850 LOC/G GOV/REL ADMIN STRUCT

S67
GRANT C.H.,"RURAL LOCAL GOVERNMENT IN GUYANA AND BRITISH HONDURAS." GUYANA HONDURAS L/A+17C AGRI NAT/G EX/STRUC ACT/RES REGION GOV/REL EFFICIENCY ORD/FREE 20. PAGE 60 H1196 ECO/UNDEV LOC/G ADMIN MUNIC

S67
HEBAL J.J.,"APPROACHES TO REGIONAL AND METROPOLITAN GOVERNMENTS IN THE UNITED STATES AND CANADA." CANADA FUT USA+45 MUNIC...TREND 20. PAGE 69 H1380 ADMIN REGION LOC/G NAT/COMP

S67
HOFMANN W.,"THE PUBLIC INTEREST PRESSURE GROUP: THE CASE OF THE DEUTSCHE STADTETAG." GERMANY GERMANY/W CONSTN STRUCT NAT/G CENTRAL FEDERAL PWR...TIME/SEQ 20. PAGE 72 H1447 LOC/G VOL/ASSN LOBBY ADMIN

S67
LAQUEUR W.,"BONN IS NOT WEIMAR* REFLECTIONS ON THE RADICAL RIGHT IN GER MANY." CULTURE LOC/G NAT/G PARTIC CHOOSE. PAGE 91 H1822 GERMANY/W FASCISM NAT/LISM

S67
MAIR L.,"BUSOGA LOCAL GOVERNMENT" AFR UGANDA UK CONSTN GP/REL...GOV/COMP METH/COMP 20. PAGE 101 H2024 LOC/G COLONIAL LAW ATTIT

S67
SALYZYN V.,"FEDERAL-PROVINCIAL TAX SHARING SCHEMES." CANADA LOC/G PROB/SOLV TEC/DEV BUDGET GOV/REL EFFICIENCY 20. PAGE 137 H2746 PROVS TAX MUNIC

NAT/G

S67
SEIDLER G.L.,"MARXIST LEGAL THOUGHT IN POLAND." POLAND SOCIETY R+D LOC/G NAT/G ACT/RES ADJUD CT/SYS SUPEGO PWR...SOC TREND 20 MARX/KARL. PAGE 141 H2822 MARXISM LAW CONCPT EFFICIENCY

S67
SHARKANSKY I.,"ECONOMIC AND POLITICAL CORRELATES OF STATE GOVERNMENT EXPENDITURE: GENERAL TENDENCIES AND DEVIANT CASES." USA+45 LOC/G NAT/G TAX GIVE INCOME...CENSUS CHARTS. PAGE 142 H2845 PROVS BUDGET GOV/COMP

S67
SUBRAMANIAM V.,"REPRESENTATIVE BUREAUCRACY: A REASSESSMENT." USA+45 ELITES LOC/G NAT/G ADMIN GOV/REL PRIVIL DRIVE ROLE...POLICY CENSUS 20 CIVIL/SERV BUREAUCRCY. PAGE 150 H3006 STRATA GP/REL MGT GOV/COMP

S67
WRAITH R.E.,"ADMINISTRATIVE CHANGE IN THE NEW AFRICA." AFR LG/CO ADJUD INGP/REL PWR...RECORD GP/COMP 20. PAGE 171 H3416 ADMIN NAT/G LOC/G ECO/UNDEV

B79
BRODERICK G.C.,POLITICAL STUDIES. IRELAND UK ROMAN/EMP LAW ACADEM LOC/G NAT/G DIPLOM PARL/PROC SUFF GP/REL LAISSEZ...ANTHOL. PAGE 21 H0424 CONSTN COLONIAL

B83
AMOS S.,THE SCIENCE OF POLITICS. MOD/EUR CONSTN LOC/G NAT/G EX/STRUC LEGIS DIPLOM...METH/COMP 19/20. PAGE 6 H0124 NEW/IDEA PHIL/SCI CONCPT

L86
BURGESS J.W.,"THE RECENT CONSTITUTIONAL CRISIS IN NORWAY" MOD/EUR NORWAY SWEDEN LOC/G NAT/G CHIEF BAL/PWR NAT/LISM ORD/FREE 19. PAGE 24 H0481 CONSTN SOVEREIGN GOV/REL

B87
KINNEAR J.B.,PRINCIPLES OF CIVIL GOVERNMENT. MOD/EUR USA-45 CONSTN LOC/G EX/STRUC ADMIN PARL/PROC RACE/REL...CONCPT 18/19. PAGE 86 H1718 POL/PAR NAT/G GOV/COMP REPRESENT

B91
SIDGWICK H.,THE ELEMENTS OF POLITICS. LOC/G NAT/G LEGIS DIPLOM ADJUD CONTROL EXEC PARL/PROC REPRESENT GOV/REL SOVEREIGN ALL/IDEOS 19 MILL/JS BENTHAM/J. PAGE 143 H2868 POLICY LAW CONCPT

B95
SELIGMAN E.R.A.,ESSAYS IN TAXATION. NEW/ZEALND PRUSSIA UK USA-45 MARKET LOC/G CREATE PRICE CONTROL INCOME OWN WEALTH...GOV/COMP METH/COMP 19. PAGE 141 H2824 TAX TARIFFS INDUS NAT/G

B96
LOWELL A.L.,GOVERNMENTS AND PARTIES IN CONTINENTAL EUROPE (VOL. I). MOD/EUR LOC/G NAT/G SECT CHIEF LEGIS PARL/PROC GOV/REL...POLICY 19. PAGE 99 H1973 POL/PAR GOV/COMP CONSTN EX/STRUC

B98
FORTES M.,AFRICAN POLITICAL SYSTEMS. ECO/UNDEV KIN LOC/G NEIGH POL/PAR SECT LEAD GP/REL ORD/FREE...SOC 20 NEGRO. PAGE 52 H1039 AFR CULTURE STRUCT

B98
POLLOCK F.,THE HISTORY OF ENGLISH LAW BEFORE THE TIME OF EDWARD I (2 VOLS, 2ND ED.). UK CULTURE LOC/G LEGIS LICENSE AGREE CONTROL CT/SYS SANCTION CRIME...TIME/SEQ 13 COMMON/LAW CANON/LAW. PAGE 127 H2538 LAW ADJUD JURID

LOCAL GOVERNMENT....SEE LOC/G

LOCKE J. H1946,H1947

LOCKE/JOHN....JOHN LOCKE

B36
SMITH T.V.,THE PROMISE OF AMERICAN POLITICS. USA-45 WOR-45 LAW CONSTN STRATA PARTIC FASCISM LAISSEZ MARXISM...MAJORIT METH/COMP 18/20 JEFFERSN/T LOCKE/JOHN BENTHAM/J. PAGE 146 H2920 CONCPT ORD/FREE IDEA/COMP NAT/COMP

B44
WOLFE D.M.,LEVELLER MANIFESTOES OF THE PURITAN REVOLUTION. UK CONSTN NAT/G SECT...CONCPT ANTHOL 17 LEVELLERS DECLAR/IND PURITAN LOCKE/JOHN. PAGE 170 H3400 POL/PAR REV ORD/FREE ATTIT

B62
EBENSTEIN W.,TWO WAYS OF LIFE. USA+45 CULTURE ECO/DEV PLAN EDU/PROP CONTROL ORD/FREE...GOV/COMP IDEA/COMP T 20 MARX/KARL ENGELS/F LENIN/VI LOCKE/JOHN MILL/JS. PAGE 44 H0885 MARXISM POPULISM ECO/TAC DIPLOM

B62
MACPHERSON C.B.,THE POLITICAL THEORY OF POSSESSIVE INDIVIDUALISM. UK MARKET NAT/G PERS/REL RATIONAL ...IDEA/COMP 17/19 LOCKE/JOHN. PAGE 100 H2006 PHIL/SCI OWN

B65
GEWIRTH A.,POLITICAL PHILOSOPHY. UNIV SOCIETY NAT/G GP/REL INGP/REL CONSEN PWR...IDEA/COMP GEN/LAWS 17/19 HOBBES/T LOCKE/JOHN MARX/KARL MILL/JS ROUSSEAU/J. PAGE 56 H1118 ORD/FREE SOVEREIGN PHIL/SCI

LOCKWOOD W.W. H1948

LODGE G.C. H1950

LODGE H.C. H1951

LODGE/HC....HENRY CABOT LODGE

LOEWENBERG G. H1952

LOEWENSTEIN K. H1953

LOFCHIE M.F. H1954

LOG....LOGIC

N
BIBLIOGRAPHIE DE LA PHILOSOPHIE. LAW CULTURE SECT EDU/PROP MORAL...HUM METH/CNCPT 20. PAGE 1 H0012 — BIBLIOG/A PHIL/SCI CONCPT LOG

B41
HAYAKAWA S.I.,LANGUAGE IN ACTION. CULTURE INTELL SOCIETY KNOWL...METH/CNCPT LING LOG RECORD STERTYP GEN/METH TOT/POP 20. PAGE 68 H1366 — EDU/PROP SOC

B58
BAGBY P.,CULTURE AND HISTORY....PHIL/SCI CONCPT LING LOG IDEA/COMP GEN/LAWS BIBLIOG 20. PAGE 10 H0196 — HIST/WRIT CULTURE GP/COMP NAT/COMP

B60
NAKAMURA H.,THE WAYS OF THINKING OF EASTERN PEOPLES. ASIA INDIA PERSON...HUM SOC LING LOG WORSHIP CHINJAP. PAGE 115 H2305 — CULTURE SECT ATTIT

B61
NEWMAN R.P.,RECOGNITION OF COMMUNIST CHINA? A STUDY IN ARGUMENT. CHINA/COM NAT/G PROB/SOLV RATIONAL ...INT/LAW LOG IDEA/COMP BIBLIOG 20. PAGE 117 H2347 — MARXISM ATTIT DIPLOM POLICY

B65
ULLMANN W.,A HISTORY OF POLITICAL THOUGHT: THE MIDDLE AGES. CHRIST-17C LOC/G NAT/G CENTRAL PWR ...PHIL/SCI LOG BIBLIOG 6/15. PAGE 158 H3153 — IDEA/COMP SOVEREIGN SECT LAW

LOGERECI A. H1955

LOGIC....SEE LOG

LOGIST/MGT....LOGISTICS MANAGEMENT INSTITUTE

LOGISTICS MANAGEMENT INSTITUTE....SEE LOGIST/MGT

LOMBARDO TOLEDANO V H1956

LONDON K. H1957,H1958

LONDON....LONDON, ENGLAND

B63
VON DER MEHDEN F.R.,RELIGION AND NATIONALISM IN SOUTHEAST ASIA. BURMA PHILIPPINE S/ASIA INTELL SOCIETY DOMIN EDU/PROP LEGIT ATTIT MORAL ORD/FREE ...SOC CENSUS HIST/WRIT TOT/POP VAL/FREE 20 WORSHIP LONDON. PAGE 163 H3265 — SECT CULTURE NAT/LISM

LONDON DAILY TELEGRAPH H1959

LONDON LIBRARY ASSOCIATION H1960

LONG H.A. H1961

LONG/FAMLY....THE LONG FAMILY OF LOUISIANA

LONGAKER R.P. H3015

LONGE/FD....F.D. LONGE

LOOMIE A.J. H1962

LOOMIS C.P. H1963

LOOS W.A. H1964

LOPEZ M.M. H1965

LOPEZIBOR J. H1966

LOPEZ-AMO A. H1967

LORWIN L.L. H1968

LOS/ANG....LOS ANGELES

LOUCKS W.N. H1969

LOUIS W.R. H1123

LOUISIANA....LOUISIANA

B66
O'NEILL C.E.,CHURCH AND STATE IN FRENCH COLONIAL LOUISIANA: POLICY AND POLITICS TO 1732. PROVS VOL/ASSN DELIB/GP ADJUD ADMIN GP/REL ATTIT DRIVE ...POLICY BIBLIOG 17/18 LOUISIANA CHURCH/STA. PAGE 120 H2390 — COLONIAL NAT/G SECT PWR

LOUISVILLE....LOUISVILLE, KENTUCKY

LOUVERT/T....LOOUVERTURE TOUSSANT

LOVE....AFFECTION, FRIENDSHIP, SEX RELATIONS

B21
BALFOUR A.J.,ESSAYS SPECULATIVE AND POLITICAL. SEA CULTURE CREATE WAR NAT/LISM PEACE LOVE...ART/METH INT/LAW CONCPT ANTHOL 20 JEWS. PAGE 10 H0204 — PHIL/SCI SOCIETY DIPLOM

B37
HORNEY K.,THE NEUROTIC PERSONALITY OF OUR TIME. SOCIETY PERS/REL ADJUST HAPPINESS ANOMIE ATTIT DRIVE SEX LOVE PWR CONCPT. PAGE 74 H1472 — PSY PERSON STRANGE CULTURE

B49
SARGENT S.S.,CULTURE AND PERSONALITY. FUT UNIV SOCIETY FAM KIN NEIGH BIO/SOC DRIVE PERCEPT RIGID/FLEX LOVE RESPECT...PSY SOC CONCPT OBS TIME/SEQ TREND CON/ANAL CHARTS HYPO/EXP SIMUL TOT/POP. PAGE 138 H2754 — CULTURE PERSON

B50
GLEASON J.H.,THE GENESIS OF RUSSOPHOBIA IN GREAT BRITAIN: A STUDY OF THE INTERACTION OF POLICY AND OPINION. ASIA RUSSIA UK NAT/G AGREE CONTROL REV WAR LOVE PWR TREATY 19. PAGE 57 H1142 — DIPLOM POLICY DOMIN COLONIAL

B54
CAMPANELLA T.,A DISCOURSE TOUCHING THE SPANISH MONARCHY... (1640). SPAIN UNIV SEA STRATA FINAN SECT FORCES SUPEGO LOVE ORD/FREE...CONCPT 17. PAGE 26 H0514 — CONSERVE CHIEF NAT/G DIPLOM

C55
SANTAYANA G.,"REASON IN SOCIETY" IN G. SANTAYANA, THE LIFE OF REASON." INDUS FAM NAT/G WAR GP/REL HAPPINESS PRODUC LOVE WEALTH CONSERVE POPULISM CONCPT. PAGE 138 H2752 — RATIONAL SOCIETY CULTURE ATTIT

B56
MANNONI D.O.,PROSPERO AND CALIBAN: THE PSYCHOLOGY OF COLONIZATION. AFR EUR+WWI FAM KIN MUNIC SECT DOMIN ADMIN ATTIT DRIVE LOVE PWR RESPECT...PSY SOC CONCPT MYTH OBS DEEP/INT BIOG GEN/METH MALAGASY 20. PAGE 102 H2040 — CULTURE COLONIAL

B59
LEE D.,FREEDOM AND CULTURE. WOR+45 WOR-45 FAM HABITAT PERSON LOVE MORAL...PSY SOC OBS NAT/COMP WORSHIP 20. PAGE 93 H1856 — CULTURE SOCIETY CONCPT INGP/REL

S59
LYNN D.B.,"THE EFFECTS OF FATHER-ABSENCE ON NORWEGIAN BOYS AND GIRLS." NORWAY CULTURE PERS/REL ADJUST DISPL LOVE...PSY CORREL STAT INT CON/ANAL CHARTS SOC/INTEG 20. PAGE 99 H1983 — SOC FAM AGE/C ANOMIE

B61
BERKOWITZ L.,AGGRESSION: AS A SOCIAL PSYCHOLOGICAL ANALYSIS. UNIV CULTURE FACE/GP FAM KIN NEIGH EDU/PROP DISPL DRIVE HEALTH LOVE ORD/FREE...PSY SOC CONCPT OBS TREND. PAGE 15 H0305 — SOCIETY COERCE WAR

B61
VAN GULIK R.H.,SEXUAL LIFE IN ANCIENT CHINA. ASIA LEISURE...CHARTS. PAGE 161 H3230 — SEX CULTURE MARRIAGE LOVE

B63
BROOKES E.H.,POWER, LAW, RIGHT, AND LOVE: A STUDY IN POLITICAL VALUES. SOUTH/AFR NAT/G PERSON ...CONCPT IDEA/COMP 20. PAGE 21 H0432 — PWR ORD/FREE JURID LOVE

B63
ROBERTSON A.H.,HUMAN RIGHTS IN EUROPE. CONSTN SOCIETY INT/ORG NAT/G VOL/ASSN DELIB/GP ACT/RES PLAN ADJUD REGION ROUTINE ATTIT LOVE ORD/FREE RESPECT...JURID SOC CONCPT SOC/EXP UN 20. PAGE 132 H2645 — EUR+WWI PERSON

S64
HIRAI N.,"SHINTO AND INTERNATIONAL PROBLEMS." SOCIETY NAT/G PLAN EDU/PROP RACE/REL PEACE ATTIT PERCEPT LOVE MORAL...HUM MYTH RECORD SAMP TREND STERTYP TOT/POP 20 UN CHINJAP SHINTO. PAGE 71 H1423 — ASIA SECT

S64
LEVI W.,"INDIAN NEUTRALISM RECONSIDERED." ASIA CHINA/COM S/ASIA SOCIETY NAT/G ACT/RES LEGIT NEUTRAL COERCE ATTIT DRIVE PERCEPT RIGID/FLEX HEALTH LOVE PWR...DECISION RECORD TREND STERTYP 20. PAGE 95 H1896 — ORD/FREE CONCPT INDIA

S65
HAYTER T.,"FRENCH AID TO AFRICA* ITS SCOPE AND ACHIEVEMENTS." CULTURE ECO/TAC INT/TRADE ADMIN — AFR FRANCE

REGION CENTRAL FEDERAL LOVE PWR SOVEREIGN EEC. PAGE 68 H1370 — FOR/AID COLONIAL

S65
LEVI W.,"THE CONCEPT OF INTEGRATION IN RESEARCH ON PEACE." NAT/G VOL/ASSN DIPLOM TASK ADJUST NAT/LISM PEACE DRIVE LOVE...PSY NET/THEORY GEN/LAWS. PAGE 95 H1897 — CONCPT IDEA/COMP INT/ORG CENTRAL

S67
THEROUX P.,"HATING THE ASIANS." TANZANIA UGANDA CONSTN INDUS NAT/G POL/PAR WORKER ECO/TAC HABITAT LOVE...POLICY GEOG 20 MIGRATION. PAGE 154 H3069 — AFR RACE/REL SOVEREIGN ATTIT

LOVEDAY P. H1970

LOVELL R.I. H1971

LOVESTN/J....JAY LOVESTONE

LOW D.A. H1972

LOWELL A.L. H1973,H1974

LOWENSTEIN A.K. H1975

LOWER A.R.M. H1976

LOYALTY....SEE SUPEGO

LUA....LUA, OR LAWA: VILLAGE PEOPLES OF NORTHERN THAILAND

B65
KUNSTADTER P.,THE LUA (LAWA) OF NORTHERN THAILAND: ASPECTS OF SOCIAL STRUCTURE, AGRICULTURE, AND RELIGION. THAILAND AGRI FAM KIN INGP/REL ISOLAT MARRIAGE HEALTH WORSHIP 20 BUDDHISM LUA. PAGE 89 H1780 — STRUCT ECO/UNDEV CULTURE

LUANDA....LUANDA, ANGOLA

LUBBOCK/TX....LUBBOCK, TEXAS

LUDWIG/BAV....LUDWIG THE BAVARIAN

LUKASZEWSKI J. H1977

LUMBERING....SEE EXTR/IND

LUNDBERG G.A. H1978,H1979

LUNT D.C. H1980

LUTHER/M....MARTIN LUTHER

B49
HAUSER R.,AUTORITAT UND MACHT. SOCIETY SECT PWR CATHISM...JURID CONCPT 16/20 PROTESTANT LUTHER/M CALVIN/J CHURCH/STA. PAGE 68 H1360 — SOVEREIGN NAT/G LEGIT

LUVALE....LUVALE TRIBE, CENTRAL AFRICA

LUXEMBOURG....SEE ALSO APPROPRIATE TIME/SPACE/CULTURE INDEX

B62
MEADE J.E.,CASE STUDIES IN EUROPEAN ECONOMIC UNION. BELGIUM EUR+WWI LUXEMBOURG NAT/G INT/TRADE REGION ROUTINE WEALTH...METH/CNCPT STAT CHARTS ECSC TOT/POP OEEC EEC 20. PAGE 108 H2154 — INT/ORG ECO/TAC

LUZ N.V. H1981

LUZON....LUZON, PHILIPPINES

B05
PHILIPPINE ISLANDS BUREAU SCI,ETHNOLOGICAL SURVEY: THE BONTOC IGOROT. ECO/UNDEV AGRI FAM MARRIAGE HEALTH WEALTH...LING OBS AUD/VIS CHARTS WORSHIP 20 LUZON BONTOC. PAGE 125 H2500 — CULTURE INGP/REL KIN STRUCT

LYFORD J.P. H1982

LYNN D.B. H1983

LYON B. H1984

LYON P. H1985

LYONS D. H2454

LYONS F.S.L. H1986

M

MAC DONALD H.M. H1987

MAC MILLAN W.M. H1988,H1989

MACAO....MACAO

MACAPAGL/D....DIOSDADO MACAPAGAL

MACARTHR/D....DOUGLAS MACARTHUR

MACDONALD D. H1990

MACFARQUHAR R. H1991,H1992

MACHIAVELLI N. H1993,H1995

MACHIAVELL....NICCOLO MACHIAVELLI

MACHIAVELLISM....SEE REALPOL, MACHIAVELL

B37
BORGESE G.A.,GOLIATH: THE MARCH OF FASCISM. GERMANY ITALY LAW POL/PAR SECT DIPLOM SOCISM...JURID MYTH 20 DANTE MACHIAVELL MUSSOLIN/B. PAGE 19 H0375 — POLICY NAT/LISM FASCISM NAT/G

B46
CASSIRER E.,THE MYTH OF THE STATE. WOR-45 SOCIETY RACE/REL RATIONAL PWR FASCISM...PHIL/SCI PSY LING TREND HEGEL/GWF MACHIAVELL. PAGE 28 H0557 — MYTH CONCPT NAT/G IDEA/COMP

B55
KOHN H.,NATIONALISM: ITS MEANING AND HISTORY. GP/REL INGP/REL ATTIT...CONCPT NAT/COMP 16/20 MACHIAVELL. PAGE 87 H1743 — NAT/LISM DIPLOM FASCISM REV

B57
MEINECKE F.,MACHIAVELLISM. CHRIST-17C FRANCE GERMANY ITALY MOD/EUR BAL/PWR PARL/PROC TOTALISM ...PHIL/SCI 15/20 MACHIAVELL. PAGE 108 H2166 — NAT/LISM NAT/G PWR

C62
BACON F.,"OF SEDITIONS AND TROUBLES" (1625) IN F. BACON, ESSAYS." INDUS MARKET CHIEF ECO/TAC EDU/PROP CONTROL LEAD PEACE WEALTH 17 MACHIAVELL. PAGE 9 H0191 — REV ORD/FREE NAT/G GEN/LAWS

MACIVER R.M. H1996,H1997,H1998,H1999

MACKENZIE K.R. H2000

MACKENZIE R.D. H2001

MACKINTOSH J.P. H2002

MACLEISH/A....ARCHIBALD MACLEISH

MACLEOD I. H2003

MACLEOD W.C. H2004

MACLURE M. H2005

MACMILLAN W.M. H2158

MACMILLN/H....HAROLD MACMILLAN, PRIME MINISTER

MACPHERSON C.B. H2006

MACRAE D. H2007

MACRAE D.G. H2008

MACRIDIS R.C. H2009,H2010,H2011

MACRO E. H2012

MADAGASCAR....SEE ALSO AFR

N
CONOVER H.F.,MADAGASCAR: A SELECTED LIST OF REFERENCES. MADAGASCAR STRUCT ECO/UNDEV NAT/G ADMIN ...SOC 19/20. PAGE 32 H0639 — BIBLIOG/A SOCIETY CULTURE COLONIAL

B60
RUUD J.,TABOO, A STUDY OF MALAGASY CUSTOMS AND BELIEFS. MADAGASCAR LAW FAM CONTROL CRIME PERSON ...CONCPT 20. PAGE 173 H3466 — CULTURE DOMIN SECT SANCTION

B61
JONES R.,AFRICA BIBLIOGRAPHY SERIES: SOUTH EAST CENTRAL AFRICA AND MADAGASCAR. AFR MADAGASCAR RHODESIA SECT BIO/SOC...JURID NAT/COMP 20. PAGE 82 H1633 — BIBLIOG/A SOC CULTURE LING

L62
ORDONNEAU P.,"LES PROBLEMES POSES PAR L'INDEPENDANCE DES NOUVEAUX ETATS AFRICAINS ET MALGACHE SUR LE PLAN DU CONTENTIEUX." FRANCE ISLAM MADAGASCAR LAW STRATA ECO/UNDEV NAT/G LEGIS LEGIT ...JURID TIME/SEQ 20. PAGE 121 H2425 — AFR ADJUD COLONIAL SOVEREIGN

S62
RAZAFIMBAHINY J.,"L'ORGANISATION AFRICAINE ET — INT/ORG

MALGACHE DE COOPERATION ECONOMIQUE." AFR ISLAM MADAGASCAR NAT/G ACT/RES ECO/TAC ALL/VALS ...TIME/SEQ 20. PAGE 130 H2601 ECO/UNDEV

S68
LAPIERRE J.W.,"TRADITION ET MODERNITE A MADAGASCAR." ISLAM MADAGASCAR AGRI FINAN KIN NAT/G CREATE OP/RES GP/REL INGP/REL ATTIT CONSERVE...PSY 20. PAGE 91 H1813 ECO/UNDEV FOR/AID CULTURE TEC/DEV

MADAN G.R. H2013

MADAN T.N. H2026

MADERO/F....FRANCISCO MADERO

B66
DE VORE B.B.,LAND AND LIBERTY; A HISTORY OF THE MEXICAN REVOLUTION. CONSTN INTELL NAT/G CONTROL LEAD CHOOSE TOTALISM AUTHORIT...BIBLIOG 19/20 MEXIC/AMER DIAZ/P LIB/PARTY MAGON/F MADERO/F. PAGE 39 H0776 REV CHIEF POL/PAR

MADHOK B. H2014

MADISON/J....PRESIDENT JAMES MADISON

MAFIA....MAFIA

B66
HOEVELER H.J.,INTERNATIONALE BEKAMPFUNG DES VERBRECHENS. AUSTRIA SWITZERLND WOR+45 INT/ORG CONTROL BIO/SOC...METH/COMP NAT/COMP 20 MAFIA SCOT/YARD FBI. PAGE 72 H1446 CRIMLGY CRIME DIPLOM INT/LAW

MAGATHAN W. H2015

MAGHREB....SEE ALSO ISLAM

S67
ZARTMAN I.W.," NAT/G POL/PAR VOL/ASSN NAT/LISM ORD/FREE PWR...CONCPT NAT/COMP ORG/CHARTS OAU MAGHREB. PAGE 172 H3451 AFR ISLAM DIPLOM REGION

MAGNA/CART....MAGNA CARTA

B39
MCILWAIN C.H.,CONSTITUTIONALISM AND THE CHANGING WORLD. UK USA-45 LEGIS PRIVIL AUTHORIT SOVEREIGN ...GOV/COMP 15/20 MAGNA/CART HOUSE/CMNS. PAGE 107 H2133 CONSTN POLICY JURID

MAGON/F....FLORES MAGON

B66
DE VORE B.B.,LAND AND LIBERTY; A HISTORY OF THE MEXICAN REVOLUTION. CONSTN INTELL NAT/G CONTROL LEAD CHOOSE TOTALISM AUTHORIT...BIBLIOG 19/20 MEXIC/AMER DIAZ/P LIB/PARTY MAGON/F MADERO/F. PAGE 39 H0776 REV CHIEF POL/PAR

MAHAR J.M. H2016

MAHDI M. H1890

MAICHEL K. H2017

MAIER H. H2018

MAIER J. H2019

MAIMONIDES....MAIMONIDES

MAINE H.S. H2020,H2021

MAINE....MAINE

MAIR L.P. H2022,H2023,H2024

MAITLAND F.W. H2538

MAITLAND/F....FREDERIC WILLIAM MAITLAND

B28
BARKER E.,POLITICAL THOUGHT IN ENGLAND: FROM HERBERT SPENCER TO THE PRESENT DAY. UK ALL/IDEOS ...PHIL/SCI 19/20 SPENCER/H GREEN/TH BENTHAM/J MAITLAND/F. PAGE 11 H0217 INTELL GEN/LAWS IDEA/COMP

MAJORIT....MAJORITARIAN

NCO
CARRINGTON C.E.,THE COMMONWEALTH IN AFRICA (PAMPHLET). UK STRUCT NAT/G COLONIAL REPRESENT GOV/REL RACE/REL NAT/LISM...MAJORIT 20 EEC NEGRO COLD/WAR. PAGE 27 H0540 ECO/UNDEV AFR DIPLOM PLAN

B15
VEBLEN T.,IMPERIAL GERMANY AND THE INDUSTRIAL REVOLUTION. GERMANY MOD/EUR UK USA-45 NAT/G TEC/DEV CAP/ISM...MAJORIT NAT/COMP 19/20 CHINJAP. PAGE 162 H3236 ECO/DEV INDUS TECHNIC BAL/PWR

N16
MILTON J.,THE READIE AND EASY WAY TO ESTABLISH A FREE COMMONWEALTH. CONSTN LEGIS PARL/PROC CONSERVE ...MAJORIT 17. PAGE 111 H2219 ORD/FREE NAT/G CHIEF POPULISM

B18
YUKIO O.,THE VOICE OF JAPANESE DEMOCRACY, AN ESSAY ON CONSTITUTIONAL LOYALTY (TRANS BY J. E. BECKER). ASIA POL/PAR DELIB/GP EX/STRUC RIGID/FLEX ORD/FREE PWR...POLICY JURID METH/COMP 19/20 CHINJAP. PAGE 172 H3443 CONSTN MAJORIT CHOOSE NAT/G

B20
WEBB S.,INDUSTRIAL DEMOCRACY. UK PARTIC GP/REL ...SOC OBS RECORD CHARTS 18/20. PAGE 166 H3317 LABOR NAT/G VOL/ASSN MAJORIT

B21
WALLAS G.,HUMAN NATURE IN POLITICS (3RD ED.). UNIV NAT/G LEAD CHOOSE REPRESENT GP/REL NAT/LISM RATIONAL BIO/SOC HEREDITY ALL/VALS MAJORIT. PAGE 165 H3293 PSY DRIVE PERSON

B26
SMITH T.V.,THE DEMOCRATIC WAY OF LIFE. UNIV SOCIETY NAT/G WORKER TASK CHOOSE ALL/VALS...IDEA/COMP WORSHIP. PAGE 146 H2919 MAJORIT CONCPT ORD/FREE LEAD

B27
GOOCH G.P.,ENGLISH DEMOCRATIC IDEAS IN THE SEVENTEENTH CENTURY (2ND ED.). UK LAW SECT FORCES DIPLOM LEAD PARL/PROC REV ATTIT AUTHORIT...ANARCH CONCPT 17 PARLIAMENT CMN/WLTH REFORMERS. PAGE 58 H1167 IDEA/COMP MAJORIT EX/STRUC CONSERVE

B28
FYFE H.,THE BRITISH LIBERAL PARTY. UK SECT ADMIN LEAD CHOOSE GP/REL PWR SOCISM...MAJORIT TIME/SEQ 19/20 LIB/PARTY CONSRV/PAR. PAGE 54 H1084 POL/PAR NAT/G REPRESENT POPULISM

B30
HATTERSLEY A.F.,A SHORT HISTORY OF DEMOCRACY. WOR-45 CONSTN NAT/G SECT DOMIN WAR CHOOSE ORD/FREE PWR...CONCPT GOV/COMP BIBLIOG ATHENS ROME. PAGE 68 H1355 REPRESENT MAJORIT POPULISM

B33
PUBLIC OPINION AND WORLD POLITICS. UNIV LAW CULTURE NAT/G PRESS REV GP/REL...MAJORIT METH/COMP ANTHOL 20. PAGE 171 H3420 DIPLOM EDU/PROP ATTIT MAJORITY

B34
LIPPMANN W.,THE METHOD OF FREEDOM. SOCIETY INDUS LABOR LOBBY WAR REPRESENT...POLICY IDEA/COMP METH/COMP 19/20. PAGE 97 H1936 CONCPT MAJORIT NAT/G

B35
DE TOCQUEVILLE A.,DEMOCRACY IN AMERICA (4 VOLS.) (TRANS. BY HENRY REEVE). CONSTN STRUCT LOC/G NAT/G POL/PAR PROVS ETIQUET CT/SYS MAJORITY ATTIT 18/19. PAGE 39 H0772 POPULISM MAJORIT ORD/FREE SOCIETY

B36
BELLOC H.,THE RESTORATION OF PROPERTY. UK STRATA NAT/G PROF/ORG DELIB/GP WORKER CREATE PROB/SOLV ECO/TAC PARTIC UTOPIA ORD/FREE SOCISM 20. PAGE 13 H0270 CONTROL MAJORIT CAP/ISM OWN

B36
SMITH T.V.,THE PROMISE OF AMERICAN POLITICS. USA-45 WOR-45 LAW CONSTN STRATA PARTIC FASCISM LAISSEZ MARXISM...MAJORIT METH/COMP 18/20 JEFFERSN/T LOCKE/JOHN BENTHAM/J. PAGE 146 H2920 CONCPT ORD/FREE IDEA/COMP NAT/COMP

B38
HEIMANN E.,COMMUNISM, FASCISM, OR DEMOCRACY? WOR-45 CONSTN SOCIETY STRATA AGRI CAP/ISM MORAL ORD/FREE ...MAJORIT METH/COMP NAT/COMP 19/20. PAGE 69 H1384 SOCISM MARXISM FASCISM PLURISM

B40
WUNDERLICH F.,LABOR UNDER GERMAN DEMOCRACY, ARBITRATION 1918-1933. GERMANY NAT/G PAY REPAR ADJUD CT/SYS GP/REL...MAJORIT 20. PAGE 171 H3426 LABOR WORKER INDUS BARGAIN

B41
GREEN T.H.,PRINCIPLES OF POLITICAL ADMINISTRATION. UNIV CONSTN VOL/ASSN INGP/REL MORAL ORD/FREE ...GOV/COMP IDEA/COMP GEN/LAWS 20. PAGE 60 H1208 POLICY LAISSEZ MAJORIT

C41
WASSERMAN L.,"HANDBOOK OF POLITICAL "ISMS" CAP/ISM REPRESENT TOTALISM MARXISM NEW/LIB SOCISM...MAJORIT BIBLIOG 20. PAGE 166 H3313 IDEA/COMP PHIL/SCI OWN NAT/G

B47
LOCKE J.,TWO TREATISES OF GOVERNMENT (1690). UK LAW SOCIETY LEGIS LEGIT AGREE REV OWN HEREDITY MORAL CONSERVE...POLICY MAJORIT 17 WILLIAM/3 NATURL/LAW. CONCPT ORD/FREE NAT/G

PAGE 97 H1946 — CONSEN

B48
COX O.C.,CASTE, CLASS, AND RACE. INDIA WOR+45 WOR-45 SECT TEC/DEV MARRIAGE ROLE MARXISM...MAJORIT NAT/COMP SOC/INTEG 20 NEGRO HINDU. PAGE 34 H0688
RACE/REL STRUCT STRATA DISCRIM

B49
VIERECK P.,CONSERVATISM REVISITED: THE REVOLT AGAINST REVOLT 1815-1949. EUR+WWI ELITES NAT/G FORCES PARTIC GOV/REL NAT/LISM...MAJORIT CONCPT GOV/COMP METTRNCH/K. PAGE 163 H3251
CONSERVE MARXISM REALPOL

L49
BRECHT A.,"THE NEW GERMAN CONSTITUTION." GERMANY/W NAT/G CHIEF EX/STRUC LEGIS PROB/SOLV ADMIN REPRESENT TOTALISM ORD/FREE PLURISM...MAJORIT CHARTS 20. PAGE 20 H0409
CONSTN DIPLOM SOVEREIGN FEDERAL

B50
DUCLOS P.,L'EVOLUTION DES RAPPORTS POLITIQUES DEPUIS 1750 (LIBERTE, INTEGRATION, UNITE). LAW INT/ORG FEDERAL TOTALISM ATTIT PWR...MAJORIT BIBLIOG 18/20 PARLIAMENT EUROPE. PAGE 43 H0852
ORD/FREE DIPLOM NAT/G GOV/COMP

B50
HALLOWELL J.H.,MAIN CURRENTS IN MODERN POLITICAL THOUGHT. CONSTN SECT LEGIS...MAJORIT CONCPT 17/20 MARX/KARL MILL/JS HOBBES/T LENIN/VI. PAGE 64 H1290
IDEA/COMP POPULISM SOCISM

B56
ROBERTS H.L.,RUSSIA AND AMERICA. CHINA/COM S/ASIA USSR FORCES TEC/DEV FOR/AID NUC/PWR ALL/IDEOS ...MAJORIT TREND NAT/COMP 20 COLD/WAR UN NATO. PAGE 132 H2641
DIPLOM INT/ORG BAL/PWR TOTALISM

C56
NEUMANN S.,"MODERN POLITICAL PARTIES: APPROACHES TO COMPARATIVE POLITIC. FRANCE UK EX/STRUC DOMIN ADMIN LEAD REPRESENT TOTALISM ATTIT...POLICY TREND METH/COMP ANTHOL BIBLIOG/A 20 CMN/WLTH. PAGE 117 H2338
POL/PAR GOV/COMP ELITES MAJORIT

B58
CARTER G.M.,TRANSITION IN AFRICA; STUDIES IN POLITICAL ADAPTATION. AFR CENTRL/AFR GHANA NIGERIA CONSTN LOC/G POL/PAR ADMIN GP/REL FEDERAL...MAJORIT BIBLIOG 20. PAGE 27 H0543
NAT/COMP PWR CONTROL NAT/G

B58
PALMER E.E.,"POLITICAL MAN" IN E. PALMER, PROBLEMS IN DEMOCRATIC CITIZENSHIP. LOC/G NAT/G LEGIS PRESS CHOOSE REPRESENT GP/REL...DECISION SOC IDEA/COMP ANTHOL 20. PAGE 123 H2449
PARTIC POL/PAR EDU/PROP MAJORIT

B59
LANDAUER C.,EUROPEAN SOCIALISM (2 VOLS.). COM EUR+WWI MOD/EUR INTELL INDUS REV WAR...MAJORIT IDEA/COMP BIBLIOG 19/20 HITLER/A. PAGE 90 H1805
SOCISM NAT/COMP LABOR MARXISM

B59
SANCHEZ A.L.,EL CONCEPTO DEL ESTADO EN EL PENSAMIENTO ESPANOL DEL SIGLO XVI. SPAIN LEGIS JUDGE BAL/PWR LEGIT EXEC WAR PWR...MAJORIT 16. PAGE 137 H2747
NAT/G PHIL/SCI LAW SOVEREIGN

B59
SISSONS C.B.,CHURCH AND STATE IN CANADIAN EDUCATION: AN HISTORICAL STUDY. CANADA ACADEM NAT/G SCHOOL LEGIS REGION MAJORITY...MAJORIT WORSHIP 18/20 CHURCH/STA. PAGE 145 H2891
SECT EDU/PROP PROVS GP/REL

S59
JENKS C.W.,"THE CHALLENGE OF UNIVERSALITY." FUT UNIV CONSTN CULTURE CONSULT CREATE PLAN LEGIT ATTIT MORAL ORD/FREE RESPECT...MAJORIT JURID 20. PAGE 80 H1602
INT/ORG LAW PEACE INT/LAW

B61
BINDER L.,RELIGION AND POLITICS IN PAKISTAN. ISLAM PAKISTAN NAT/G SECT LEGIS CREATE CHOOSE GP/REL ...MAJORIT TRADIT 20. PAGE 17 H0336
CONSTN CONFER NAT/LISM POL/PAR

B61
CASSINELLI C.W.,THE POLITICS OF FREEDOM. FUT UNIV LAW POL/PAR CHOOSE ORD/FREE...POLICY CONCPT MYTH BIBLIOG. PAGE 28 H0555
MAJORIT NAT/G PARL/PROC PARTIC

B61
GUIZOT F.P.G.,HISTORY OF THE ORIGIN OF REPRESENTATIVE GOVERNMENT IN EUROPE. CHRIST-17C FRANCE MOD/EUR SPAIN UK LAW CHIEF FORCES POPULISM ...MAJORIT TIME/SEQ GOV/COMP NAT/COMP 4/19 PARLIAMENT. PAGE 62 H1250
LEGIS REPRESENT CONSTN NAT/G

B61
HARE T.,A TREATISE ON THE ELECTION OF REPRESENTATIVES, PARLIAMENTARY AND MUNICIPAL. UK CONSTN NAT/G PARL/PROC CHOOSE ATTIT...MAJORIT 18/19 PARLIAMENT. PAGE 66 H1330
LEGIS GOV/REL CONSEN REPRESENT

B61
PANIKKAR K.M.,THE VOICE OF FREEDOM: SELECTED SPEECHES OF PANDIT MOTILAL NEHRU. INDIA UK CONSTN FINAN FORCES LEGIS DIPLOM TAX COLONIAL...POLICY MAJORIT ANTHOL 20 NEHRU/PM. PAGE 123 H2460
NAT/LISM ORD/FREE CHIEF NAT/G

B61
STAHL W.,EDUCATION FOR DEMOCRACY IN WEST GERMANY: ACHIEVEMENT SHORTCOMINGS - PROSPECTS. GERMANY/W SOCIETY NAT/G FORCES PLAN PROB/SOLV PRESS ALL/VALS
EDU/PROP POPULISM AGE/Y

...POLICY MAJORIT CONCPT ANTHOL 20. PAGE 148 H2967 — ADJUST

B62
ABRAHAM W.E.,THE MIND OF AFRICA. AFR SOCIETY STRATA KIN ECO/TAC DOMIN EDU/PROP LEGIT COERCE ATTIT ALL/VALS...MAJORIT SOC OBS HIST/WRIT TIME/SEQ TREND TOT/POP 20. PAGE 3 H0058
CULTURE SIMUL GHANA

B62
DE MADARIAGA S.,L'AMERIQUE LATINE ENTRE L'OURS ET L'AIGLE. L/A+17C SOCIETY NAT/G ECO/TAC EDU/PROP REGION COERCE ATTIT ALL/VALS...MAJORIT TIME/SEQ STERTYP COLD/WAR OAS 20. PAGE 38 H0760
POL/PAR ECO/UNDEV

B62
HOOK S.,THE PARADOXES OF FREEDOM. UNIV CONSTN INTELL LEGIS CONTROL REV CHOOSE SUPEGO...POLICY JURID IDEA/COMP 19/20 CIV/RIGHTS. PAGE 73 H1461
CONCPT MAJORIT ORD/FREE ALL/VALS

B62
RANNEY A.,THE DOCTRINE OF RESPONSIBLE PARTY GOVERNMENT. USA+45 USA-45 CONSTN PLAN CHOOSE ...MAJORIT GOV/COMP IDEA/COMP 20. PAGE 130 H2591
POL/PAR POLICY REPRESENT NAT/G

B62
ROUSSEAU J.J.,THE SOCIAL CONTRACT. LAW CONSTN CHIEF DOMIN REPRESENT GP/REL ORD/FREE POPULISM...MAJORIT GOV/COMP 18. PAGE 135 H2700
GEN/LAWS AGREE REV

B63
JACOB H.,GERMAN ADMINISTRATION SINCE BISMARCK: CENTRAL AUTHORITY VERSUS LOCAL AUTONOMY. GERMANY GERMANY/W LAW POL/PAR CONTROL CENTRAL TOTALISM FASCISM...MAJORIT DECISION STAT CHARTS GOV/COMP 19/20 BISMARCK/O HITLER/A WEIMAR/REP. PAGE 79 H1577
ADMIN NAT/G LOC/G POLICY

B63
MULLER H.J.,FREEDOM IN THE WESTERN WORLD. PREHIST CULTURE SECT CREATE TEC/DEV DOMIN PWR WEALTH ...MAJORIT SOC CONCPT. PAGE 114 H2285
ORD/FREE TIME/SEQ SOCIETY

B64
BERRINGTON H.,HOW NATIONS ARE GOVERNED. FRANCE WOR+45 ECO/UNDEV INT/ORG POL/PAR CHOOSE TOTALISM KNOWL...MAJORIT T 20 UN COMMONWLTH THIRD/WRLD. PAGE 16 H0320
NAT/G GOV/COMP ECO/DEV CONSTN

B64
DOWNIE R.S.,GOVERNMENT ACTION AND MORALITY: SOME PRINCIPLES AND CONCEPTS OF LIBERAL-DEMOCRACY. UK PARL/PROC ATTIT ROLE...MAJORIT DECISION CONCPT 20. PAGE 42 H0845
NAT/G MORAL POLICY GEN/LAWS

B64
QUIGG P.W.,AFRICA: A FOREIGN AFFAIRS READER. AFR FRANCE PORTUGAL UK DIPLOM LEAD PARL/PROC MARXISM ...MAJORIT METH/CNCPT GOV/COMP IDEA/COMP ANTHOL 19/20. PAGE 129 H2575
COLONIAL SOVEREIGN NAT/LISM RACE/REL

B64
TAWNEY R.H.,EQUALITY. UK CULTURE STRATA ECO/TAC EDU/PROP REPRESENT OWN NEW/LIB...MAJORIT WELF/ST SOC 20. PAGE 153 H3051
WEALTH STRUCT ELITES POPULISM

B65
DAHL R.A.,MODERN POLITICAL ANALYSIS. UNIV COERCE ...MAJORIT DECISION METH. PAGE 36 H0731
CONCPT GOV/COMP PWR

B65
NATIONAL BOOK CENTRE PAKISTAN,BOOKS ON PAKISTAN: A BIBLIOGRAPHY. PAKISTAN CULTURE DIPLOM ADMIN ATTIT ...MAJORIT SOC CONCPT 20. PAGE 116 H2319
BIBLIOG CONSTN S/ASIA NAT/G

B65
NORDEN A.,WAR AND NAZI CRIMINALS IN WEST GERMANY: STATE, ECONOMY, ADMINISTRATION, ARMY, JUSTICE, SCIENCE. GERMANY GERMANY/W MOD/EUR ECO/DEV ACADEM EX/STRUC FORCES DOMIN ADMIN CT/SYS...POLICY MAJORIT PACIFIST 20. PAGE 119 H2370
FASCIST WAR NAT/G TOP/EX

B65
POBEDONOSTSEV K.P.,REFLECTIONS OF A RUSSIAN STATESMAN. RUSSIA LAW ELITES EDU/PROP PRESS ADJUD MARRIAGE ATTIT PWR...MAJORIT TRADIT 19 CHURCH/STA. PAGE 127 H2531
TOTALISM POLICY CONSTN NAT/G

B65
RODRIGUEZ M.,CENTRAL AMERICA. COSTA/RICA GUATEMALA L/A+17C NICARAGUA DIPLOM COLONIAL REGION NAT/LISM ALL/IDEOS SOCISM...MAJORIT TIME/SEQ BIBLIOG 19/20. PAGE 133 H2656
CULTURE NAT/COMP NAT/G ECO/UNDEV

B65
WOLFE B.D.,MARXISM; ONE HUNDRED YEARS IN THE LIFE OF A DOCTRINE. USSR WAR NAT/LISM PEACE TOTALISM ...MAJORIT 20 MARX/KARL. PAGE 170 H3399
MARXISM LEAD ATTIT

C65
NEUMANN S.,"PERMANENT REVOLUTION: TOTALITARIANISM IN THE AGE OF INTERNA TIONAL CIVIL WAR (2ND ED.)" EUR+WWI ELITES POL/PAR DOMIN EDU/PROP LEAD CROWD REPRESENT...MAJORIT GOV/COMP BIBLIOG 20. PAGE 117 H2340
TOTALISM REV FASCISM STRUCT

B66
ANDERSON S.V.,CANADIAN OMBUDSMAN PROPOSALS. CANADA LEGIS DEBATE PARL/PROC...MAJORIT JURID TIME/SEQ IDEA/COMP 20 OMBUDSMAN PARLIAMENT. PAGE 7 H0133
NAT/G CREATE ADMIN POL/PAR

B66
BEER S.H.,BRITISH POLITICS IN THE COLLECTIVIST AGE. UK NAT/G CONTROL CHOOSE GP/REL ATTIT PWR PLURISM ...MAJORIT WELF/ST 16/20. PAGE 13 H0258
POL/PAR SOCISM TRADIT GP/COMP

B66
BERELSON B.,READER IN PUBLIC OPINION AND COMMUNICATION (2ND ED.). UNIV NAT/G PRESS GP/REL PERS/REL PERCEPT RIGID/FLEX...MAJORIT QUANT METH/COMP ANTHOL BIBLIOG 20. PAGE 15 H0298
EDU/PROP ATTIT CONCPT COM/IND

B66
BRACKMAN A.C.,SOUTHEAST ASIA'S SECOND FRONT: THE POWER STRUGGLE IN THE MALAY ARCHIPELAGO. CHINA/COM INDONESIA MALAYSIA ECO/UNDEV INT/ORG NAT/G FORCES DIPLOM EDU/PROP REGION COERCE GUERRILLA AUTHORIT POPULISM...MAJORIT 20 KENNEDY/JF SEATO. PAGE 20 H0396
S/ASIA MARXISM REV

B66
DE TOCQUEVILLE A,DEMOCRACY IN AMERICA (1834-1840) (2 VOLS. IN I; TRANS. BY G. LAWRENCE). FRANCE CULTURE STRATA POL/PAR CT/SYS REPRESENT FEDERAL ORD/FREE SOVEREIGN...MAJORIT TREND GEN/LAWS 18/19. PAGE 39 H0773
POPULISM USA-45 CONSTN NAT/COMP

B66
DEXTER N.C.,GUIDE TO CONTEMPORARY POLITICS. EUR+WWI UK PARL/PROC GP/REL KNOWL...POLICY MAJORIT IDEA/COMP 20. PAGE 41 H0815
POL/PAR CONCPT NAT/G

B66
HIDAYATULLAH M.,DEMOCRACY IN INDIA AND THE JUDICIAL PROCESS. INDIA EX/STRUC LEGIS LEAD GOV/REL ATTIT ORD/FREE...MAJORIT CONCPT 20 NEHRU/J. PAGE 71 H1415
NAT/G CT/SYS CONSTN JURID

B66
POLE J.R.,POLITICAL REPRESENTATION IN ENGLAND AND THE ORIGINS OF THE AMERICAN REPUBLIC. UK USA-45 CONSTN ELITES NAT/G POL/PAR LEGIS PARL/PROC ...MAJORIT 17/19. PAGE 127 H2534
REPRESENT GOV/COMP

C66
ROSENBERG C.G. JR.,"THE MYTH OF "MAU-MAU:" NATIONALISM IN KENYA." AFR CULTURE NAT/G POL/PAR COERCE REV RACE/REL ATTIT ORD/FREE SOVEREIGN...MYTH BIBLIOG 20. PAGE 134 H2678
NAT/LISM COLONIAL MAJORIT LEAD

B67
MENDEL A.P.,POLITICAL MEMOIRS 1905-1917 BY PAUL MILIUKOV (TRANS. BY CARL GOLDBERG). USSR AGRI DIPLOM ECO/TAC POPULISM...MAJORIT 20. PAGE 109 H2170
BIOG LEAD NAT/G CONSTN

S67
IDENBURG P.J.,"POLITICAL STRUCTURAL DEVELOPMENT IN TROPICAL AFRICA." UK ECO/UNDEV KIN POL/PAR CHIEF EX/STRUC CREATE COLONIAL CONTROL REPRESENT RACE/REL ...MAJORIT TREND 20. PAGE 76 H1521
AFR CONSTN NAT/G GOV/COMP

S67
NEUBAUER D.E.,"SOME CONDITIONS OF DEMOCRACY." ECO/DEV COM/IND DIST/IND POL/PAR EDU/PROP REPRESENT ...SOC STAT NAT/COMP 20. PAGE 117 H2331
NAT/G CHOOSE MAJORIT ECO/UNDEV

C80
ARNOLD M.,"DEMOCRACY" IN MIXED ESSAYS (2ND ED.)" UK SOCIETY STRUCT...CONCPT METH/COMP 19. PAGE 8 H0166
NAT/G MAJORIT EX/STRUC ELITES

B91
PAINE T.,RIGHTS OF MAN. FRANCE MOD/EUR CONSTN NAT/G CHIEF DOMIN LEGIT SOVEREIGN...MAJORIT IDEA/COMP 18 BURKE/EDM CIVIL/LIB. PAGE 122 H2446
GEN/LAWS ORD/FREE REV AGREE

MAJORITY....BEHAVIOR OF MAJOR PARTS OF A GROUP; SEE ALSO CONSEN, MAJORIT

B09
LOBINGIER C.S.,THE PEOPLE'S LAW OR POPULAR PARTICIPATION IN LAW-MAKING. FRANCE SWITZERLND UK LOC/G NAT/G PROVS LEGIS SUFF MAJORITY PWR POPULISM ...GOV/COMP BIBLIOG 19. PAGE 97 H1945
CONSTN LAW PARTIC

B23
DELBRUCK H.,GOVERNMENT AND THE WILL OF THE PEOPLE (TRANS. BY ROY S. MACELWEE). MOD/EUR NAT/G CHOOSE REPRESENT...CONCPT 19/20. PAGE 39 H0788
SOVEREIGN ORD/FREE MAJORITY POL/PAR

S27
MICHELS R.,"SOME REFLECTIONS ON THE SOCIOLOGICAL CHARACTER OF POLITICAL PARTIES" (BMR)" WOR-45 STRATA MAJORITY DRIVE...GOV/COMP 20. PAGE 110 H2199
POL/PAR PWR LEAD CONCPT

B30
HULL W.I.,INDIA'S POLITICAL CRISIS. INDIA UK INT/ORG LABOR SECT DELIB/GP LEGIS DIPLOM NEUTRAL REGION CROWD GOV/REL MAJORITY ATTIT 20 NEHRU/J GANDHI/M COMMONWLTH. PAGE 75 H1492
ORD/FREE NAT/G COLONIAL NAT/LISM

S31
HEINBERG J.G.,"THE PERSONNEL OF FRENCH CABINETS, 1871-1930." FRANCE STRATA CHIEF CHOOSE REPRESENT MAJORITY...STAT QU CENSUS TREND CHARTS PERS/COMP 19/20 CHAMBR/DEP. PAGE 69 H1386
ELITES NAT/G DELIB/GP TOP/EX

B33
PUBLIC OPINION AND WORLD POLITICS. UNIV LAW CULTURE NAT/G PRESS REV GP/REL...MAJORIT METH/COMP ANTHOL 20. PAGE 171 H3420
DIPLOM EDU/PROP ATTIT MAJORITY

B35
DE TOCQUEVILLE A.,DEMOCRACY IN AMERICA (4 VOLS.) (TRANS. BY HENRY REEVE). CONSTN STRUCT LOC/G NAT/G POL/PAR PROVS ETIQUET CT/SYS MAJORITY ATTIT 18/19. PAGE 39 H0772
POPULISM MAJORIT ORD/FREE SOCIETY

B39
MILLER P.,THE NEW ENGLAND MIND: THE SEVENTEENTH CENTURY. CULTURE DOMIN WRITING INGP/REL CONSEN MAJORITY PERCEPT KNOWL MORAL...CONCPT LING WORSHIP 17 NEW/ENGLND PROTESTANT. PAGE 111 H2214
SECT REGION SOC ATTIT

S45
SPENCER R.C.,"PARTY GOVERNMENT AND THE SWEDISH RISKDAG." SWEDEN CHOOSE MAJORITY. PAGE 147 H2946
GOV/COMP NAT/G POL/PAR PARL/PROC

B59
SISSONS C.B.,CHURCH AND STATE IN CANADIAN EDUCATION: AN HISTORICAL STUDY. CANADA ACADEM NAT/G SCHOOL LEGIS REGION MAJORITY...MAJORIT WORSHIP 18/20 CHURCH/STA. PAGE 145 H2891
SECT EDU/PROP PROVS GP/REL

S59
LEYS C.,"MODELS, THEORIES, AND THE THEORY OF POLITICAL PARTIES" CANADA LIECHTENST UK LOC/G NAT/G PARTIC REPRESENT GP/REL CONSEN EQUILIB MAJORITY ...NEW/IDEA MATH CHARTS 20. PAGE 96 H1919
POL/PAR CHOOSE METH/CNCPT SIMUL

B65
BAYNE E.A.,FOUR WAYS OF POLITICS: STATE AND NATION IN ITALY, SOMALIA, ISRAEL, AND IRAN. IRAN ISRAEL ITALY SOMALIA LEAD CHOOSE MAJORITY GOV/COMP. PAGE 12 H0244
ECO/UNDEV NAT/G DECISION TOP/EX

B66
BUTLER D.E.,THE BRITISH GENERAL ELECTION OF 1966. UK LOC/G NAT/G OP/RES CONFER CHOOSE MAJORITY ATTIT ...CHARTS TIME 20. PAGE 25 H0498
POL/PAR REPRESENT GP/REL PERS/REL

B66
LOVEDAY P.,PARLIAMENT FACTIONS AND PARTIES: THE FIRST THIRTY YEARS OF RESPONSIBLE GOVERNMENT IN NEW SOUTH WALES, 1856-1889. PROVS LEAD PARL/PROC PARTIC GP/REL INGP/REL MAJORITY PWR...GP/COMP 19 AUSTRAL. PAGE 99 H1970
POL/PAR ELITES NAT/G LEGIS

B67
RAE D.,THE POLITICAL CONSEQUENCES OF ELECTORAL LAWS. EUR+WWI ICELAND ISRAEL NEW/ZEALND UK USA+45 ADJUD APPORT GP/REL MAJORITY...MATH STAT CENSUS CHARTS BIBLIOG 20 AUSTRAL. PAGE 129 H2579
POL/PAR CHOOSE NAT/COMP REPRESENT

S67
ANTHEM T.,"CYPRUS* WHAT NOW?" CYPRUS GREECE TURKEY NAT/G BUDGET MAJORITY 20 NATO. PAGE 7 H0143
DIPLOM COERCE INT/TRADE ADJUD

S67
BASKIN D.B.,"NATIONALITY DOCTRINE AND ANTI-SEMITISM IN THE USSR." USSR CULTURE STRATA ISOLAT MAJORITY ATTIT RIGID/FLEX RESPECT...GP/COMP JEWS. PAGE 12 H0234
NAT/LISM MARXISM GP/REL DISCRIM

MAJUMDAR D.N. H2026

MALAGASY....MALAGASY REPUBLIC

B56
MANNONI D.O.,PROSPERO AND CALIBAN: THE PSYCHOLOGY OF COLONIZATION. AFR EUR+WWI FAM KIN MUNIC SECT DOMIN ADMIN ATTIT DRIVE LOVE PWR RESPECT...PSY SOC CONCPT MYTH OBS DEEP/INT BIOG GEN/METH MALAGASY 20. PAGE 102 H2040
CULTURE COLONIAL

MALAN V.D. H2027

MALAWI....SEE ALSO AFR

N60
RHODESIA-NYASA NATL ARCHIVES,A SELECT BIBLIOGRAPHY OF RECENT PUBLICATIONS CONCERNING THE FEDERATION OF RHODESIA AND NYASALAND (PAMPHLET). MALAWI RHODESIA LAW CULTURE STRUCT ECO/UNDEV LEGIS...GEOG 20. PAGE 131 H2620
BIBLIOG ADMIN ORD/FREE NAT/G

B63
STIRNIMANN H.,NGUNI UND GNONI; EINE KULTURGESCHICHTLICHE STUDIE (ACTA ETHNOLOGICA ET LINGUISTICA, NUMBER 6). AFR MALAWI SOUTH/AFR FORCES HABITAT...RECORD CHARTS BIBLIOG WORSHIP 19/20 NATAL. PAGE 149 H2987
CULTURE GP/COMP SOCIETY

B64
FRANCK T.M.,EAST AFRICAN UNITY THROUGH LAW. MALAWI TANZANIA UGANDA UK ZAMBIA CONSTN INT/ORG NAT/G ADMIN ROUTINE TASK NAT/LISM ATTIT SOVEREIGN ...RECORD IDEA/COMP NAT/COMP. PAGE 52 H1048
AFR FEDERAL REGION INT/LAW

B66
MATTHEWS R.,AFRICAN POWER KEG: REVOLT AND DISSENT
ELITES

IN SIX EMERGENT NATIONS. AFR ALGERIA DAHOMEY GABON GHANA MALAWI GAMBLE LEAD PARTIC REV DRIVE...BIOG TREND GOV/COMP 20. PAGE 105 H2098 ECO/UNDEV TOP/EX CONTROL

MALAYA....MALAYA

B49
PELZER K.J.,SELECTED BIBLIOGRAPHY ON THE GEOGRAPHY OF SOUTHEAST ASIA (3 VOLS., 1949-1956). PHILIPPINE CULTURE...SOC 20 MALAYA. PAGE 124 H2486 BIBLIOG S/ASIA GEOG

B60
SAKAI R.K.,STUDIES ON ASIA, 1960. ASIA CHINA/COM S/ASIA COM/IND ECO/TAC...ANTHOL 17/20 MALAYA. PAGE 137 H2733 ECO/UNDEV SOC

MALAYSIA....SEE ALSO S/ASIA

B12
CORDIER H.,BIBLIOTHECA INDOSINICA: DICTIONAIRE BIBLIOGRAPHIQUE DES OUVRAGES RELATIFS A LA PENINSULE INDOCHINOISE. BURMA LAOS MALAYSIA S/ASIA THAILAND VIETNAM SECT...LING 20. PAGE 33 H0665 BIBLIOG/A GEOG NAT/G

B43
US LIBRARY OF CONGRESS,BRITISH MALAYA AND BRITISH NORTH BORNEO. BORNEO MALAYSIA CONSTN AGRI COM/IND INDUS EDU/PROP 19/20. PAGE 160 H3203 BIBLIOG CULTURE

B50
CORNELL U DEPT ASIAN STUDIES,SOUTHEAST ASIA PROGRAM DATA PAPER. BURMA CAMBODIA INDONESIA MALAYSIA VIETNAM SOCIETY STRUCT NAT/G SECT DIPLOM FOR/AID PWR WEALTH...SOC 20. PAGE 33 H0670 BIBLIOG/A CULTURE S/ASIA ECO/UNDEV

S55
GOODENOUGH W.H.,"A PROBLEM IN MALAYO-POLYNESIAN SOCIAL ORGANIZATION" (BMR)" MALAYSIA S/ASIA CULTURE AGRI PROB/SOLV OWN HABITAT...SOC 20 20 POLYNESIA. PAGE 58 H1170 KIN STRUCT FAM ECO/UNDEV

C58
GINSBURG N.,"MALAYA." MALAYSIA PROB/SOLV REGION NAT/LISM KNOWL WEALTH...GEOG SOC CHARTS BIBLIOG 20. PAGE 57 H1133 COM/IND ECO/UNDEV CULTURE NAT/G

B60
JEFFRIES C.,TRANSFER OF POWER: PROBLEMS OF THE PASSAGE TO SELFGOVERNMENT. CEYLON GHANA MALAYSIA NIGERIA UK INT/ORG CONSULT DELIB/GP LEGIS DIPLOM CONFER PARL/PROC 20. PAGE 80 H1595 SOVEREIGN COLONIAL ORD/FREE NAT/G

S63
TILMAN R.O.,"MALAYSIA: THE PROBLEMS OF FEDERATION." ISLAM S/ASIA CONSTN PROVS SECT DELIB/GP DOMIN EDU/PROP LEGIT EXEC COERCE CHOOSE ATTIT HEALTH ORD/FREE PWR...STAT TOT/POP VAL/FREE 20. PAGE 155 H3097 NAT/G CULTURE MALAYSIA

B64
GROVES H.E.,THE CONSTITUTION OF MALAYSIA. MALAYSIA POL/PAR CHIEF CONSULT DELIB/GP CT/SYS PARL/PROC CHOOSE FEDERAL ORD/FREE 20. PAGE 62 H1238 CONSTN NAT/G LAW

B64
SAKAI R.K.,STUDIES ON ASIA, 1964. ASIA CHINA/COM ISRAEL MALAYSIA S/ASIA USA+45 USSR ECO/UNDEV FAM POL/PAR SECT CONSULT NAT/LISM...POLICY SOC 20 CHINJAP. PAGE 137 H2736 PWR DIPLOM

B64
TILMAN R.O.,BUREAUCRATIC TRANSITION IN MALAYA. MALAYSIA S/ASIA UK NAT/G EX/STRUC DIPLOM...CHARTS BIBLIOG 20. PAGE 155 H3098 ADMIN COLONIAL SOVEREIGN EFFICIENCY

S64
BRADLEY C.P.,"THE FORMATION OF MALAYSIA." INDIA S/ASIA POL/PAR VOL/ASSN TOP/EX LEGIT RACE/REL ORD/FREE 20. PAGE 20 H0398 NAT/G CREATE COLONIAL MALAYSIA

B65
ONSLOW C.,ASIAN ECONOMIC DEVELOPMENT. BURMA CEYLON INDIA MALAYSIA PAKISTAN S/ASIA AGRI INDUS MARKET PROB/SOLV CAP/ISM FOR/AID INT/TRADE DEMAND WEALTH ...POLICY ANTHOL 20. PAGE 121 H2418 ECO/UNDEV ECO/TAC PLAN NAT/G

B65
SWIFT M.G.,MALAY PEASANT SOCIETY IN JELEBU. MALAYSIA FAM INT/TRADE ADJUD OWN WEALTH...SOC WORSHIP 20. PAGE 151 H3020 STRUCT ECO/UNDEV CULTURE SOCIETY

S65
SANDERS R.,"MASS SUPPORT AND COMMUNIST INSURRECTION." GREECE MALAYSIA PHILIPPINE VIETNAM STRUCT ECO/UNDEV POL/PAR FORCES CREATE REV ...GP/COMP IDEA/COMP. PAGE 138 H2751 GUERRILLA MARXISM GOV/COMP

B66
BRACKMAN A.C.,SOUTHEAST ASIA'S SECOND FRONT: THE POWER STRUGGLE IN THE MALAY ARCHIPELAGO. CHINA/COM INDONESIA MALAYSIA ECO/UNDEV INT/ORG NAT/G FORCES DIPLOM EDU/PROP REGION COERCE GUERRILLA AUTHORIT POPULISM...MAJORIT 20 KENNEDY/JF SEATO. PAGE 20 H0396 S/ASIA MARXISM REV

B66
LEIGH M.B.,CHECK LIST OF HOLDINGS ON BORNEO IN THE CORNELL UNIVERSITY LIBRARIES (PAMPHLET). BORNEO MALAYSIA LAW CONSTN GP/REL SOC. PAGE 93 H1866 BIBLIOG S/ASIA DIPLOM NAT/G

S66
GAMER R.E.,"URGENT SINGAPORE, PATIENT MALAYSIA." MALAYSIA S/ASIA ECO/UNDEV POL/PAR CHIEF TARIFFS TAX CONTROL LEAD REGION PWR 20 SINGAPORE. PAGE 55 H1094 DIPLOM NAT/G POLICY ECO/TAC

B67
MILNE R.S.,GOVERNMENT AND POLITICS IN MALAYSIA. INDONESIA MALAYSIA LOC/G EX/STRUC FORCES DIPLOM GP/REL 20 SINGAPORE. PAGE 111 H2217 NAT/G LEGIS ADMIN

B67
NESS G.D.,BUREAUCRACY AND RURAL DEVELOPMENT IN MALAYSIA. MALAYSIA UK SOCIETY FINAN INDUS WORKER TEC/DEV ECO/TAC COLONIAL EQUILIB ORD/FREE...STAT CHARTS 20. PAGE 117 H2330 ECO/UNDEV PLAN NAT/G ADMIN

MALCOLM/X....MALCOLM X

MALDIVE....MALDIVE ISLAND; SEE ALSO S/ASIA, COMMONWLTH

MALE/SEX....MALE SEX

MALENBAUM W. H2028

MALI....SEE ALSO AFR

N19
SENGHOR L.S.,AFRICAN SOCIALISM (PAMPHLET). AFR FRANCE MALI USSR ELITES ECO/UNDEV NAT/G DIPLOM DOMIN EDU/PROP ATTIT 20 NEGRO. PAGE 141 H2827 SOCISM MARXISM ORD/FREE NAT/LISM

B59
SENGHOR L.S.,RAPPORT SUR LA DOCTRINE ET LA PROGRAMME DU PART I. FRANCE MALI CONSTN POL/PAR PLAN CHOOSE OWN ORD/FREE MARXISM...SOCIALIST 20 NEGRO. PAGE 141 H2828 ATTIT NAT/G AFR SOCISM

B64
MORGENTHAU R.S.,POLITICAL PARTIES IN FRENCH-SPEAKING WEST AFRICA. AFR FRANCE GUINEA IVORY/CST MALI SENEGAL CONSTN LEGIS CREATE PLAN LOBBY PARTIC GP/REL...POLICY BIBLIOG 20. PAGE 113 H2257 POL/PAR NAT/G SOVEREIGN COLONIAL

B66
SCHATTEN F.,COMMUNISM IN AFRICA. AFR GHANA GUINEA MALI CULTURE ECO/UNDEV LABOR SECT ECO/TAC EDU/PROP REV 20. PAGE 139 H2774 COLONIAL NAT/LISM MARXISM DIPLOM

B67
JOHNSON H.G.,ECONOMIC NATIONALISM IN OLD AND NEW STATES. CANADA CHINA/COM MALI UK DIPLOM...SIMUL GEN/LAWS 19/20 MEXIC/AMER. PAGE 81 H1619 NAT/LISM ECO/UNDEV ECO/DEV NAT/COMP

MALINOWSKI B. H2029,H2030,H2031,H2032

MALLORY J.R. H2033

MALOF P. H1021

MALRAUX/A....ANDRE MALRAUX

B64
CAUTE D.,COMMUNISM AND THE FRENCH INTELLECTUALS, 1914-1960. COM EUR+WWI MOD/EUR NAT/G PERF/ART PROF/ORG CREATE EDU/PROP ATTIT PERSON KNOWL MARXISM ...SOC TIME/SEQ MARX/KARL 20 MALRAUX/A GIDE/A SARTRE/J. PAGE 28 H0563 POL/PAR INTELL

MALTA....SEE ALSO APPROPRIATE TIME/SPACE/CULTURE INDEX

B65
BOISSEVAIN J.,SAINTS AND FIREWORKS: RELIGION AND POLITICS IN RURAL MALTA. MALTA STRUCT FAM NEIGH POL/PAR REPRESENT INGP/REL CENTRAL...CHARTS BIBLIOG 20. PAGE 18 H0368 GP/REL NAT/G SECT MUNIC

MALTHUS T.R. H2034

MALTHUS....THOMAS ROBERT MALTHUS

MANAGEMENT....SEE MGT, EX/STRUC, ADMIN

MANAGEMENT BY OBJECTIVES....SEE MGT/OBJECT

MANCHESTER....MANCHESTER, ENGLAND

B60
GRAMPP W.D.,THE MANCHESTER SCHOOL OF ECONOMICS. UK LAW ECO/DEV COERCE ATTIT ORD/FREE LAISSEZ ...PHIL/SCI IDEA/COMP 19/20 MANCHESTER CORN/LAWS. PAGE 60 H1194 ECO/TAC VOL/ASSN LOBBY NAT/G

MANCHU/DYN....MANCHU DYNASTY

B50
FITZGERALD C.P.,CHINA, A SHORT CULTURAL HISTORY. NAT/G

ASIA DIPLOM INT/TRADE...ART/METH SOC MANCHU/DYN. PAGE 51 H1016 — SOCIETY

MANGLAPUS R.S. H2035

MANIS J.G. H2036

MANITOBA....MANITOBA, CANADA

MANNERS R.A. H0857

MANNERS....SEE ETIQUET

MANNHEIM E. H2037

MANNHEIM K. H2038

MANNHEIM/K....KARL MANNHEIM

MANNING H.T. H2039

MANNONI D.O. H2040

MANPOWER....SEE LABOR

MANSERGH N. H2041,H2042

MANSSELL G. H0713

MANSUR F. H2043

MANTON/M....MART MANTON

MANU

B53
BROWN D.M.,THE WHITE UMBRELLA: INDIAN POLITICAL THOUGHT FROM MANU TO GANDHI. INDIA LAW NAT/G SECT WRITING NAT/LISM...ANTHOL BIBLIOG 20 HINDU GANDHI/M MANU. PAGE 22 H0442 — CONCPT DOMIN CONSERVE

MANUFACTURING INDUSTRY....SEE PROC/MFG

MAO....MAO TSE-TUNG

B56
SMEDLEY A.,THE GREAT ROAD: THE LIFE AND TIMES OF CHU TEH. ASIA USSR NAT/G POL/PAR DIPLOM COERCE GUERRILLA CIVMIL/REL NAT/LISM PERSON SKILL MARXISM ...BIOG 20 CHINJAP MAO. PAGE 145 H2903 — REV WAR FORCES

B58
PALMER E.E.,THE COMMUNIST CHALLENGE. COM USA+45 USA-45 ECO/DEV ECO/UNDEV NEUTRAL ORD/FREE POPULISM ...CONCPT NAT/COMP ANTHOL 19/20 LENIN/VI STALIN/J MAO MARX/KARL COM/PARTY. PAGE 123 H2450 — MARXISM DIPLOM IDEA/COMP POLICY

B60
MACFARQUHAR R.,THE HUNDRED FLOWERS. ASIA NAT/G WORKER GP/REL ORD/FREE MARXISM 20 MAO. PAGE 100 H1991 — DEBATE PRESS POL/PAR ATTIT

S60
NORTH R.C.,"THE NEW EXPANSIONISM." ASIA CHINA/COM FUT INDIA CULTURE SOCIETY NAT/G TOP/EX DOMIN COERCE PWR MARXISM...CONCPT TIME/SEQ TREND GEN/LAWS COLD/WAR 20 MAO. PAGE 119 H2372 — ATTIT DRIVE NAT/LISM

S61
ZAGORIA D.S.,"THE FUTURE OF SINO-SOVIET RELATIONS." CHINA/COM INT/ORG NAT/G POL/PAR VOL/ASSN ACT/RES PLAN PERSON...METH/CNCPT TIME/SEQ TOT/POP VAL/FREE 20 MAO KHRUSH/N. PAGE 172 H3445 — ASIA COM TOTALISM USSR

B63
HAMM H.,ALBANIA - CHINA'S BEACHHEAD IN EUROPE. ALBANIA CHINA/COM USSR YUGOSLAVIA ELITES SOCIETY POL/PAR DELIB/GP FORCES ECO/TAC COERCE ISOLAT PEACE MARXISM...IDEA/COMP 20 MAO. PAGE 65 H1304 — DIPLOM REV NAT/G POLICY

B64
MILIBAND R.,THE SOCIALIST REGISTER: 1964. GERMANY/W ITALY UK LABOR POL/PAR ECO/TAC FOR/AID NUC/PWR ...POLICY SOCIALIST IDEA/COMP 20 MAO NASSER/G. PAGE 110 H2204 — MARXISM SOCISM CAP/ISM PROB/SOLV

B66
HINTON W.,FANSHEN: A DOCUMENTARY OF REVOLUTION IN A CHINESE VILLAGE. ASIA ELITES MUNIC NAT/G POL/PAR SECT WORKER LEAD WAR PRIVIL PWR 20 MAO. PAGE 71 H1422 — MARXISM REV NEIGH OWN

B66
MACFARQUHAR R.,CHINA UNDER MAO: POLITICS TAKES COMMAND. CHINA/COM COM AGRI INDUS CHIEF FORCES DIPLOM INT/TRADE EDU/PROP TASK REV ADJUST...ANTHOL 20 MAO. PAGE 100 H1992 — ECO/UNDEV TEC/DEV ECO/TAC ADMIN

B66
SCHRAM S.,MAO TSE-TUNG. ASIA CHINA/COM CONTROL REGION ATTIT...POLICY IDEA/COMP 20 MAO. PAGE 140 H2799 — BIOG MARXISM TOP/EX GUERRILLA

B66
ZABLOCKI C.J.,SINO-SOVIET RIVALRY. AFR ASIA CHINA/COM CUBA EUR+WWI L/A+17C USA+45 USSR WOR+45 POL/PAR FORCES COERCE NUC/PWR...GOV/COMP IDEA/COMP 20 MAO KHRUSH/N. PAGE 172 H3444 — DIPLOM MARXISM COM

B67
LENG S.C.,JUSTICE IN COMMUNIST CHINA: A SURVEY OF THE JUDICIAL SYSTEM OF THE CHINESE PEOPLE'S REPUBLIC. CHINA/COM LAW CONSTN LOC/G NAT/G PROF/ORG CONSULT FORCES ADMIN CRIME ORD/FREE...BIBLIOG 20 MAO. PAGE 94 H1877 — CT/SYS ADJUD JURID MARXISM

S67
CHIU S.M.,"CHINA'S MILITARY POSTURE." CHINA/COM ELITES NAT/G POL/PAR TEC/DEV ECO/TAC DOMIN CONTROL LEAD REV MARXISM 20 MAO. PAGE 30 H0595 — FORCES CIVMIL/REL NUC/PWR DIPLOM

S67
CHU-YUAN CHENG,"THE CULTURAL REVOLUTION AND CHINA'S ECONOMY." CHINA/COM AGRI DIST/IND INDUS MARKET NAT/G WORKER PLAN INT/TRADE DOMIN DEMAND PRODUC ...CHARTS 20 MAO. PAGE 30 H0600 — ECO/DEV ECO/TAC REV SOCISM

S67
PAK H.,"CHINA'S MILITIA AND MAO TSE-TUNG'S 'PEOPLE'S WAR'." CHINA/COM SOCIETY POL/PAR EX/STRUC PROB/SOLV PARTIC COERCE WAR CIVMIL/REL ATTIT DRIVE MARXISM...METH/COMP 20 MAO. PAGE 122 H2447 — FORCES NAT/G WORKER CHIEF

S67
PERKINS D.H.,"ECONOMIC GROWTH IN CHINA AND THE CULTURAL REVOLUTION(1960APRIL 1967)" CHINA/COM FUT AGRI INDUS PLAN LEAD MARXISM...CHARTS 20 MAO. PAGE 125 H2493 — ECO/TAC CULTURE REV ECO/UNDEV

S67
SHIGEO N.,"THE GREAT CULTURAL REVOLUTION." ASIA ECO/UNDEV AGRI NAT/G CHIEF ECO/TAC EDU/PROP CONTROL LEAD PWR 20 MAO. PAGE 143 H2860 — CREATE REV CULTURE POL/PAR

MAO TSE-TUNG H2044,H2045

MAPS....MAPS AND ATLASES; SEE ALSO CHARTS

B18
CVIJIC J.,THE BALKAN PENINSULA. MOD/EUR COERCE ...SOC CHARTS GP/COMP NAT/COMP 20 BALKANS MAPS. PAGE 36 H0729 — GEOG HABITAT GOV/COMP CULTURE

B44
FULLER G.H.,TURKEY: A SELECTED LIST OF REFERENCES. ISLAM TURKEY CULTURE ECO/UNDEV AGRI DIPLOM NAT/LISM CONSERVE...GEOG HUM INT/LAW SOC 7/20 MAPS. PAGE 54 H1075 — BIBLIOG/A ALL/VALS

B49
UNSTEAD J.F.,A WORLD SURVEY FROM THE HUMAN ASPECT. AGRI INDUS...SOC CENSUS CHARTS 20 MAPS MIGRATION. PAGE 159 H3172 — CULTURE HABITAT GEOG ATTIT

B58
WARNER W.L.,A BLACK CIVILIZATION - A SOCIAL STUDY OF AN AUSTRALIAN TRIBE. SOCIETY FAM MARRIAGE...PSY SOC MYTH CHARTS 20 AUSTRAL MAPS MURNGIN RITUAL. PAGE 165 H3310 — CULTURE KIN STRUCT DEATH

B59
GOLDWIN R.A.,READINGS IN RUSSIAN FOREIGN POLICY. HUNGARY USSR YUGOSLAVIA ELITES INT/ORG NAT/G REV WAR NAT/LISM PERSON SOCISM...CHARTS 20 MAPS BOLSHEVISM. PAGE 58 H1160 — COM MARXISM DIPLOM POLICY

B62
HACHMANN R.,VOLKER ZWISCHEN GERMANEN UND KELTEN. GERMANY CULTURE STRUCT MUNIC...ART/METH CHARTS MAPS. PAGE 63 H1269 — LING SOC KIN GP/REL

B63
LEVIN M.G.,ETHNIC ORIGINS OF THE PEOPLES OF NORTHEASTERN ASIA. CONSTN LEGIS...STAT CENSUS CHARTS 20 TEXAS MAPS. PAGE 95 H1901 — HEREDITY HABITAT CULTURE GEOG

B64
COWAN L.G.,THE DILEMMAS OF AFRICAN INDEPENDENCE. AFR INDUS NAT/G SECT DIPLOM ECO/TAC REGION MARXISM ...CHARTS BIBLIOG 20 MAPS. PAGE 34 H0683 — ORD/FREE COLONIAL REV ECO/UNDEV

B66
FLINT J.E.,NIGERIA AND GHANA. AFR GHANA NIGERIA UK NAT/G DOMIN DISCRIM...CHARTS BIBLIOG/A 15/20 NEGRO MAPS. PAGE 51 H1026 — CULTURE COLONIAL NAT/LISM

MARAJO....MARAJO, A BRAZILIAN ISLAND

MARANHAO....MARANHAO, BRAZIL

B48
EDUARDO O.D.C.,THE NEGRO IN NORTHERN BRAZIL: A STUDY IN ACCULTURATION. BRAZIL ECO/UNDEV FAM SECT PAY REGION HABITAT CATHISM MYSTISM...GEOG OBS SOC/INTEG WORSHIP 20 NEGRO MARANHAO. PAGE 44 H0890 — CULTURE ADJUST GP/REL

MARCANT/V....VITO MARCANTONIO

MARCH J.G. H2046

MARCUSE/H....HERBERT MARCUSE

MARES V.E. H2047

MARIAS J. H2048

MARITAIN J. H2049,H2050,H2051,H2052

MARITAIN/J....JACQUES MARITAIN

N19
WEBB L.C.,CHURCH AND STATE IN ITALY: 1947-1957 (PAMPHLET). GERMANY ITALY CONSTN POL/PAR AGREE CONTROL PARTIC CHOOSE ATTIT ORD/FREE FASCISM MARXISM 20 CHURCH/STA MARITAIN/J SALO. PAGE 166 H3316
SECT CATHISM NAT/G GP/REL

B64
KARIEL H.S.,IN SEARCH OF AUTHORITY: TWENTIETH-CENTURY POLITICAL THOUGHT. WOR+45 WOR-45 NAT/G EX/STRUC TOTALISM DRIVE PWR...MGT PHIL/SCI GEN/LAWS 19/20 NIETZSCH/F FREUD/S WEBER/MAX NIEBUHR/R MARITAIN/J. PAGE 83 H1661
CONSTN CONCPT ORD/FREE IDEA/COMP

MARITIME....MARITIME PROVINCES

MARK M. H2053

MARKET RESEARCH....SEE MARKET

MARKET....MARKETING SYSTEM

B04
GRIFFIN A.P.C.,LIST OF REFERENCES ON BUDGETS OF FOREIGN COUNTRIES (PAMPHLET). MOD/EUR FINAN MARKET TAX...MGT STAT 19/20. PAGE 61 H1218
BIBLIOG/A BUDGET NAT/G

B13
DIE REKLAME IHRE KUNST UND WISSENSCHAFT. GERMANY POLAND SWITZERLND USA+45 TEC/DEV CAP/ISM DEMAND ...ART/METH EXHIBIT METH/COMP ANTHOL 20. PAGE 135 H2707
EDU/PROP MARKET NAT/COMP ATTIT

B20
MALTHUS T.R.,PRINCIPLES OF POLITICAL ECONOMY. UK AGRI INDUS MARKET NAT/G DIPLOM PRICE CONTROL BAL/PAY COST OWN PWR LAISSEZ 18/19. PAGE 102 H2034
GEN/LAWS DEMAND WEALTH

B22
URE P.N.,THE ORIGIN OF TYRANNY. MEDIT-7 FINAN INDUS CHIEF FORCES ECO/TAC WEALTH. PAGE 159 H3174
AUTHORIT PWR NAT/G MARKET

B27
WEBER M.,GENERAL ECONOMIC HISTORY. CHRIST-17C MOD/EUR STRUCT AGRI EXTR/IND FINAN INDUS MARKET FAM MUNIC NAT/G PROF/ORG SECT ECO/TAC 8/20. PAGE 166 H3319
ECO/DEV CAP/ISM

B28
CORBETT P.E.,CANADA AND WORLD POLITICS. LAW CULTURE SOCIETY STRUCT MARKET INT/ORG FORCES ACT/RES PLAN ECO/TAC LEGIT ORD/FREE PWR RESPECT...SOC CONCPT TIME/SEQ TREND CMN/WLTH 20 LEAGUE/NAT. PAGE 33 H0662
NAT/G CANADA

B37
PARSONS T.,THE STRUCTURE OF SOCIAL ACTION. UNIV INTELL SOCIETY INDUS MARKET ECO/TAC ROUTINE CHOOSE ALL/VALS...CONCPT OBS BIOG TREND GEN/LAWS 20. PAGE 124 H2471
CULTURE ATTIT CAP/ISM

B38
COUPLAND R.,EAST AFRICA AND ITS INVADERS. AFR ISLAM STRATA SECT FORCES DIPLOM TRIBUTE CONTROL DISCRIM NAT/LISM 19 AFRICA/E EUROPE MISSION. PAGE 34 H0680
CULTURE ELITES COLONIAL MARKET

S46
SILBERNER E.,"THE PROBLEM OF WAR IN NINETEENTH CENTURY ECONOMIC THOUGHT." EUR+WWI MOD/EUR UNIV LAW ECO/DEV ECO/UNDEV FINAN INDUS MARKET INT/ORG NAT/G CONSULT FORCES...CONCPT GEN/LAWS GEN/METH 19. PAGE 144 H2875
ATTIT ECO/TAC WAR

B54
MOSK S.A.,INDUSTRIAL REVOLUTION IN MEXICO. MARKET LABOR CREATE CAP/ISM ADMIN ATTIT SOCISM...POLICY 20 MEXIC/AMER. PAGE 113 H2268
INDUS TEC/DEV ECO/UNDEV NAT/G

B57
NEUMARK S.D.,ECONOMIC INFLUENCES ON THE SOUTH AFRICAN FRONTIER, 1652-1836. SOUTH/AFR SEA AGRI NAT/G FORCES WORKER DIPLOM INT/TRADE PRICE DEMAND PRODUC...STAT CHARTS 17/19 FRONTIER. PAGE 117 H2341
COLONIAL ECO/UNDEV ECO/TAC MARKET

B59
ETSCHMANN R.,DIE WAHRUNGS- UND DEVISENPOLITIK DES OSTBLOCKS UND IHRE AUSWIRKUNGEN AUF DIE WIRTSCHAFTSBEZIEHUNGEN ZWISCHEN OST U WEST. BULGARIA CZECHOSLVK HUNGARY POLAND USSR MARKET NAT/G PLAN DIPLOM...NAT/COMP 20. PAGE 47 H0943
ECO/TAC FINAN POLICY INT/TRADE

B59
MEYER A.J.,MIDDLE EASTERN CAPITALISM: NINE ESSAYS. ISLAM CULTURE ECO/UNDEV INDUS MARKET NAT/G PLAN ATTIT RIGID/FLEX...STAT OBS TREND GEN/LAWS. PAGE 109 H2188
TEC/DEV ECO/TAC ANTHOL

L59
MURPHY J.C.,"SOME IMPLICATIONS OF EUROPE'S COMMON MARKET. IN (COOK P, ECONOMIC DEVELOPMENT AND INTERNATIONAL TRADE,." EUR+WWI ECO/DEV DIST/IND INDUS NAT/G PLAN ECO/TAC INT/TRADE WEALTH...STAT TREND OEEC TOT/POP 20 EEC. PAGE 115 H2298
MARKET INT/ORG REGION

S59
PLAZA G.,"FOR A REGIONAL MARKET IN LATIN AMERICA." FUT L/A+17C CULTURE INDUS NAT/G ECO/TAC INT/TRADE ATTIT WEALTH...NEW/IDEA TREND OAS 20. PAGE 126 H2527
MARKET INT/ORG REGION

S59
ZAUBERMAN A.,"SOVIET BLOC ECONOMIC INTEGRATION." COM CULTURE INTELL ECO/DEV INDUS TOP/EX ACT/RES PLAN ECO/TAC INT/TRADE ROUTINE CHOOSE ATTIT ...TIME/SEQ 20. PAGE 172 H3452
MARKET INT/ORG USSR TOTALISM

B60
BAYER H.,WIRTSCHAFTSPROGNOSE UND WIRTSCHAFTSGESTALTUNG. GERMANY NETHERLAND MARKET PLAN CAP/ISM DEBATE...NAT/COMP 20. PAGE 12 H0242
ECO/DEV ECO/UNDEV FINAN POLICY

B60
JOHNSON H.M.,SOCIOLOGY: A SYSTEMATIC INTRODUCTION. MARKET FAM LABOR POL/PAR CHOOSE DISCRIM MARRIAGE ALL/IDEOS...BIBLIOG T WORSHIP. PAGE 81 H1620
SOC SOCIETY CULTURE GEN/LAWS

B60
LISTER L.,EUROPE'S COAL AND STEEL COMMUNITY. FRANCE GERMANY STRUCT ECO/DEV EXTR/IND INDUS MARKET NAT/G DELIB/GP ECO/TAC INT/TRADE EDU/PROP ATTIT RIGID/FLEX ORD/FREE PWR WEALTH...CONCPT STAT TIME/SEQ CHARTS ECSC 20. PAGE 97 H1941
EUR+WWI INT/ORG REGION

B60
MOORE W.E.,LABOR COMMITMENT AND SOCIAL CHANGE IN DEVELOPING AREAS. SOCIETY STRATA ECO/UNDEV MARKET VOL/ASSN WORKER AUTHORIT SKILL...MGT NAT/COMP SOC/INTEG 20. PAGE 113 H2250
LABOR ORD/FREE ATTIT INDUS

B60
ROBERTSON D.,THE CONTROL OF INDUSTRY. UK MARKET LABOR WORKER PRICE CONTROL GP/REL COST DEMAND ORD/FREE WEALTH NEW/LIB SOCISM 20. PAGE 132 H2646
INDUS FINAN NAT/G ECO/DEV

B61
MARX K.,THE COMMUNIST MANIFESTO. IN (MENDEL A. ESSENTIAL WORKS OF MARXISM, NEW YORK: BANTAM. FUT MOD/EUR CULTURE ECO/DEV ECO/UNDEV AGRI FINAN INDUS MARKET PROC/MFG LABOR MUNIC POL/PAR CONSULT FORCES CREATE PLAN ADMIN ATTIT DRIVE RIGID/FLEX ORD/FREE PWR RESPECT MARX/KARL WORK. PAGE 104 H2081
COM NEW/IDEA CAP/ISM REV

B61
WILLSON F.M.G.,ADMINISTRATORS IN ACTION. UK MARKET TEC/DEV PARL/PROC 20. PAGE 169 H3376
ADMIN NAT/G CONSTN

B62
MACPHERSON C.B.,THE POLITICAL THEORY OF POSSESSIVE INDIVIDUALISM. UK MARKET NAT/G PERS/REL RATIONAL ...IDEA/COMP 17/19 LOCKE/JOHN. PAGE 100 H2006
PHIL/SCI OWN

B62
MICHAELY M.,CONCENTRATION IN INTERNATIONAL TRADE. ECO/DEV ECO/UNDEV PRICE INCOME...CHARTS NAT/COMP 20. PAGE 110 H2197
INT/TRADE MARKET FINAN GEOG

B62
MODELSKI G.,SEATO-SIX STUDIES. ASIA CHINA/COM INDIA S/ASIA INT/ORG NAT/G ECO/TAC DETER ATTIT ORD/FREE PWR...TIME/SEQ COLD/WAR TOT/POP 20 SEATO. PAGE 112 H2234
MARKET ECO/UNDEV INT/TRADE

C62
BACON F.,"OF SEDITIONS AND TROUBLES" (1625) IN F. BACON, ESSAYS." INDUS MARKET CHIEF ECO/TAC EDU/PROP CONTROL LEAD PEACE WEALTH 17 MACHIAVELL. PAGE 9 H0191
REV ORD/FREE NAT/G GEN/LAWS

B63
SELF P.,THE STATE AND THE FARMER. UK ECO/DEV MARKET WORKER PRICE CONTROL GP/REL...WELF/ST 20 DEPT/AGRI. PAGE 141 H2823
AGRI NAT/G ADMIN VOL/ASSN

S63
APPERT K.,"BERECHTIGE VORBEHALTE DER SCHWEIZERISCHEN ZUR INTEGRATION." EUR+WWI UK MARKET SERV/IND NAT/G PLAN RIGID/FLEX OEEC 20 EEC. PAGE 7 H0146
FINAN ATTIT SWITZERLND

B64
FRIEDLAND W.H.,AFRICAN SOCIALISM. ECO/UNDEV MARKET LABOR NAT/G POL/PAR PLAN CAP/ISM ECO/TAC EDU/PROP CHOOSE ATTIT DRIVE PWR WEALTH...POLICY CONCPT RECORD STERTYP 20. PAGE 53 H1063
AFR SOCISM

B64
LI C.M.,INDUSTRIAL DEVELOPMENT IN COMMUNIST CHINA. CHINA/COM ECO/DEV ECO/UNDEV AGRI FINAN INDUS MARKET LABOR NAT/G ECO/TAC INT/TRADE EXEC ALL/VALS
ASIA TEC/DEV

...POLICY RELATIV TREND WORK TOT/POP VAL/FREE 20. PAGE 96 H1921

B64
RAMAZANI R.K.,THE MIDDLE EAST AND THE EUROPEAN COMMON MARKET. EUR+WWI ISLAM ECO/DEV EXTR/IND MARKET PROC/MFG INT/ORG NAT/G TEC/DEV ECO/TAC REGION DRIVE WEALTH...STAT CHARTS EEC TOT/POP 20. PAGE 129 H2587
ECO/UNDEV ATTIT INT/TRADE

B64
SANDEE J.,EUROPE'S FUTURE CONSUMPTION. EUR+WWI FUT EDU/PROP...IDEA/COMP NAT/COMP ANTHOL 20 EUROPE. PAGE 137 H2750
MARKET ECO/DEV PREDICT PRICE

B64
THORNTON T.P.,THE THIRD WORLD IN SOVIET PERSPECTIVE: STUDIES BY SOVIET WRITERS ON THE DEVELOPING AREAS. AFR L/A+17C S/ASIA STRATA AGRI INDUS MARKET NAT/G POL/PAR ECO/TAC COLONIAL PERCEPT PWR WEALTH...MARXIST STAT CHARTS WORK MARX/KARL 20. PAGE 155 H3090
ECO/UNDEV ACT/RES USSR DIPLOM

L64
HAAS E.B.,"ECONOMICS AND DIFFERENTIAL PATTERNS OF POLITICAL INTEGRATION: PROJECTIONS ABOUT UNITY IN LATIN AMERICA." SOCIETY NAT/G DELIB/GP ACT/RES CREATE PLAN ECO/TAC REGION ROUTINE ATTIT DRIVE PWR WEALTH...CONCPT TREND CHARTS LAFTA 20. PAGE 63 H1266
L/A+17C INT/ORG MARKET

S64
CLIFFE L.,"TANGANYIKA'S TWO YEARS OF INDEPENDENCE." AFR INDUS MARKET NAT/G POL/PAR DELIB/GP CREATE ECO/TAC LEGIT DRIVE ALL/VALS...METH/CNCPT RECORD 20 TANGANYIKA. PAGE 30 H0604
ECO/UNDEV PLAN

S64
CROUZET F.,"WARS, BLOCKADE, AND ECONOMIC CHANGE IN EUROPE, 1792-1815." UK INDUS NAT/G TEC/DEV ECO/TAC WEALTH...POLICY RELATIV HIST/WRIT TIME/SEQ 18/19. PAGE 35 H0710
MOD/EUR MARKET

B65
INT. BANK RECONSTR. DEVELOP.,ECONOMIC DEVELOPMENT OF KUWAIT. ISLAM KUWAIT AGRI FINAN MARKET EX/STRUC TEC/DEV ECO/TAC ADMIN WEALTH...OBS CON/ANAL CHARTS 20. PAGE 77 H1541
INDUS NAT/G

B65
ONSLOW C.,ASIAN ECONOMIC DEVELOPMENT. BURMA CEYLON INDIA MALAYSIA PAKISTAN S/ASIA AGRI INDUS MARKET PROB/SOLV CAP/ISM FOR/AID INT/TRADE DEMAND WEALTH ...POLICY ANTHOL 20. PAGE 121 H2418
ECO/UNDEV ECO/TAC PLAN NAT/G

L65
WIONCZEK M.,"LATIN AMERICA FREE TRADE ASSOCIATION." AGRI DIST/IND FINAN INDUS INT/ORG LABOR NAT/G TEC/DEV ECO/TAC HEALTH SKILL WEALTH...POLICY RELATIV MGT LAFTA 20. PAGE 169 H3390
L/A+17C MARKET REGION

B66
BROWN R.T.,TRANSPORT AND THE ECONOMIC INTEGRATION OF SOUTH AMERICA. L/A+17C ECO/UNDEV NAT/G OP/RES DIPLOM INT/TRADE REGION WEALTH...ECOMETRIC GEOG STAT LAFTA TIME. PAGE 22 H0449
MARKET DIST/IND SIMUL

B67
ANDERSON S.V.,THE NORDIC COUNCIL: A STUDY OF SCANDINAVIAN REGIONALISM. DENMARK FINLAND ICELAND NORWAY SWEDEN MARKET NAT/G VOL/ASSN CONSULT PARL/PROC ATTIT...TIME/SEQ BIBLIOG 20. PAGE 7 H0134
INT/ORG REGION DIPLOM LEGIS

B67
GALBRAITH J.K.,THE NEW INDUSTRIAL STATE. INDUS LABOR LG/CO NAT/G POL/PAR SCHOOL OP/RES CAP/ISM EXEC TREND. PAGE 54 H1087
TEC/DEV ECO/DEV SOCIETY MARKET

B67
HOLLERMAN L.,JAPAN'S DEPENDENCE ON THE WORLD ECONOMY. INDUS MARKET LABOR NAT/G DIPLOM 20 CHINJAP. PAGE 73 H1457
PLAN ECO/DEV ECO/TAC INT/TRADE

L67
KELLEHER G.W.,"THE COMMON MARKET ANTITRUST LAWS: THE FIRST TEN YEARS." EUR+WWI INDUS PRICE ADJUD AGREE CONTROL PROFIT...POLICY 20 EEC. PAGE 84 H1684
INT/ORG INT/TRADE MARKET NAT/G

L67
ROTH A.R.,"CAPITAL-MARKET DEVELOPMENT IN ISRAEL AND BRAZIL: TWO EXAMPLES OF THE ROLE OF LAW IN DEVELOPMENT." BRAZIL ISRAEL L/A+17C INDUS MARKET ECO/TAC FOR/AID INT/TRADE CONTROL BAL/PAY 20. PAGE 135 H2694
LAW ECO/UNDEV NAT/COMP FINAN

S67
CHU-YUAN CHENG,"THE CULTURAL REVOLUTION AND CHINA'S ECONOMY." CHINA/COM AGRI DIST/IND INDUS MARKET NAT/G WORKER PLAN INT/TRADE DOMIN DEMAND PRODUC ...CHARTS 20 MAO. PAGE 30 H0600
ECO/DEV ECO/TAC REV SOCISM

S67
SANCHEZ J.D.,"DESARROLLO ECONOMICO Y FUTURO DE COLOMBIA." L/A+17C AGRI EXTR/IND FINAN INDUS MARKET INT/TRADE CONTROL...STAT TREND COLOMB. PAGE 137 H2748
ECO/UNDEV FUT NAT/G ECO/TAC

S67
SCHACHTER G.,"REGIONAL DEVELOPMENT IN THE ITALIAN DUAL ECONOMY" ITALY AGRI INDUS MARKET WORKER ECO/TAC CONTROL INCOME PRODUC 20. PAGE 138 H2767
REGION ECO/UNDEV NAT/G PROB/SOLV

L68
CURRENT HISTORY,"DE GAULLE'S FRANCE." FRANCE MOD/EUR WOR+45 INDUS MARKET INT/ORG BUDGET DIPLOM AUTHORIT DRIVE...GOV/COMP IDEA/COMP 20 DEGAULLE/C EEC. PAGE 36 H0723
INT/TRADE PERSON LEAD NAT/LISM

B95
SELIGMAN E.R.A.,ESSAYS IN TAXATION. NEW/ZEALND PRUSSIA UK USA-45 MARKET LOC/G CREATE PRICE CONTROL INCOME OWN WEALTH...GOV/COMP METH/COMP 19. PAGE 141 H2824
TAX TARIFFS INDUS NAT/G

MARKETING SYSTEM....SEE MARKET

MARKHAM V.R. H2054

MARQUAND H.A. H2055

MARRARO H.R. H2056

MARRIAGE....WEDLOCK; SEE ALSO LOVE

N
KRADER L.,SOCIAL ORGANIZATION OF THE MONGOL-TURKIC PASTORAL NOMADS. SOCIETY FAM KIN NEIGH GP/REL MARRIAGE 16/20 MONGOLIA TURKIC MIGRATION. PAGE 88 H1763
BIO/SOC HABITAT CULTURE STRUCT

B05
PHILIPPINE ISLANDS BUREAU SCI,ETHNOLOGICAL SURVEY: THE BONTOC IGOROT. ECO/UNDEV AGRI FAM MARRIAGE HEALTH WEALTH...LING OBS AUD/VIS CHARTS WORSHIP 20 LUZON BONTOC. PAGE 125 H2500
CULTURE INGP/REL KIN STRUCT

B06
SUMNER W.G.,FOLKWAYS: STUDY OF THE SOCIOLOGICAL IMPORTANCE OF USAGES, MANNERS, CUSTOMS, MORES, AND MORALS. STRUCT KIN ETIQUET ROUTINE MURDER MARRIAGE PEACE SEX ALL/VALS WEALTH BIBLIOG. PAGE 150 H3008
CULTURE SOC SANCTION MORAL

B09
JUSTINIAN,THE DIGEST (DIGESTA CORPUS JURIS CIVILIS) (2 VOLS.) (TRANS. BY C. H. MONRO). ROMAN/EMP LAW FAM LOC/G LEGIS EDU/PROP CONTROL MARRIAGE OWN ROLE CIVIL/LAW. PAGE 82 H1645
JURID CT/SYS NAT/G STRATA

B26
MALINOWSKI B.,CRIME AND CUSTOM IN SAVAGE SOCIETY. SOCIETY FAM SECT LEGIT SANCTION MARRIAGE MYSTISM ...PSY SOC 19/20 MELANESIA CANON/LAW. PAGE 102 H2030
LAW CULTURE CRIME ADJUD

B39
AKIGA,AKIGA'S STORY: THE TIV TRIBE AS SEEN BY ONE OF ITS MEMBERS. NIGERIA LAW STRUCT ECO/UNDEV FAM LEAD GP/REL MARRIAGE...LING WORSHIP 20. PAGE 4 H0089
KIN SECT SOC CULTURE

B40
ZWEIG F.,THE WORKER IN AN AFFLUENT SOCIETY: FAMILY LIFE AND INDUSTRY. UK STRATA LG/CO ECO/TAC LEISURE INGP/REL HAPPINESS HEALTH...PSY SOC/WK INT CHARTS WORSHIP 20 FEMALE/SEX. PAGE 173 H3465
MARRIAGE ATTIT FINAN CULTURE

B42
HEGEL G.W.F.,PHILOSOPHY OF RIGHT. UNIV FAM SECT CHIEF AGREE WAR MARRIAGE OWN ORD/FREE...POLICY CONCPT. PAGE 69 H1383
NAT/G LAW RATIONAL

B48
COX O.C.,CASTE, CLASS, AND RACE. INDIA WOR+45 WOR-45 SECT TEC/DEV MARRIAGE ROLE MARXISM...MAJORIT NAT/COMP SOC/INTEG 20 NEGRO HINDU. PAGE 34 H0688
RACE/REL STRUCT STRATA DISCRIM

B55
CHARMATZ J.P.,COMPARATIVE STUDIES IN COMMUNITY PROPERTY LAW. FRANCE USA+45...JURID GOV/COMP ANTHOL 20. PAGE 29 H0583
MARRIAGE LAW OWN MUNIC

B55
SERRANO MOSCOSO E.,A STATEMENT OF THE LAWS OF ECUADOR IN MATTERS AFFECTING BUSINESS (2ND ED.). ECUADOR INDUS LABOR LG/CO NAT/G LEGIS TAX CONTROL MARRIAGE 20. PAGE 141 H2830
FINAN ECO/UNDEV LAW CONSTN

B55
WRONG D.H.,AMERICAN AND CANADIAN VIEWPOINTS. CANADA USA+45 CONSTN STRATA FAM SECT WORKER ECO/TAC EDU/PROP ADJUD MARRIAGE...IDEA/COMP 20. PAGE 171 H3424
DIPLOM ATTIT NAT/COMP CULTURE

B57
KOENTJARANINGRAT R.,A PRELIMINARY DESCRIPTION OF THE JAVANESE KINSHIP SYSTEM. INDONESIA STRATA FAM INGP/REL ADJUST MARRIAGE AGE/C AGE/Y AGE/A PERSON ...OBS CHARTS DICTIONARY 20 JAVA. PAGE 87 H1736
KIN STRUCT ELITES CULTURE

B58
WARNER W.L.,A BLACK CIVILIZATION - A SOCIAL STUDY OF AN AUSTRALIAN TRIBE. SOCIETY FAM MARRIAGE...PSY SOC MYTH CHARTS 20 AUSTRAL MAPS MURNGIN RITUAL. PAGE 165 H3310
CULTURE KIN STRUCT DEATH

B59
VORSPAN A.,JUSTICE AND JUDAISM. FAM DIPLOM ECO/TAC EDU/PROP CRIME RACE/REL MARRIAGE ANOMIE ATTIT ORD/FREE...POLICY 20 UN. PAGE 164 H3279
SECT CULTURE ACT/RES

GP/REL

B60
JOHNSON H.M.,SOCIOLOGY: A SYSTEMATIC INTRODUCTION. MARKET FAM LABOR POL/PAR CHOOSE DISCRIM MARRIAGE ALL/IDEOS...BIBLIOG T WORSHIP. PAGE 81 H1620
SOC SOCIETY CULTURE GEN/LAWS

B60
OTTENBERG S.,CULTURES AND SOCIETIES OF AFRICA. AFR KIN TEC/DEV GP/REL MARRIAGE ATTIT HABITAT HEREDITY ...ANTHOL BIBLIOG T WORSHIP 20. PAGE 122 H2433
SOCIETY INGP/REL STRUCT CULTURE

B61
BLAKE J.,FAMILY STRUCTURE IN JAMAICA. JAMAICA CULTURE SOCIETY ACT/RES CONTROL MARRIAGE AGE ...POLICY SOC BIBLIOG 20. PAGE 18 H0351
FAM SEX STRUCT ATTIT

B61
SOUTHALL A.,SOCIAL CHANGE IN MODERN AFRICA. CULTURE STRATA ECO/UNDEV AGRI FAM KIN MUNIC GP/REL INGP/REL MARRIAGE...GEOG ANTHOL 20. PAGE 147 H2940
AFR TREND SOCIETY SOC

B61
VAN GULIK R.H.,SEXUAL LIFE IN ANCIENT CHINA. ASIA LEISURE...CHARTS. PAGE 161 H3230
SEX CULTURE MARRIAGE LOVE

B62
BERNOT R.M.,EXCESS AND RESTRAINT: SOCIAL CONTROL AMONG GUINEA MOUNTAIN PEOPLE. CULTURE FAM KIN CT/SYS COERCE WAR PERS/REL MARRIAGE HABITAT SEX ...MYTH 20 NEW/GUINEA. PAGE 16 H0314
SOCIETY CONTROL STRUCT ADJUST

B62
EDWARDS A.C.,THE OVIMBUNDU UNDER TWO SOVEREIGNTIES. CULTURE STRUCT FAM MARRIAGE HABITAT...SOC 19/20 OVIMBUNDU. PAGE 45 H0891
KIN NEIGH SOCIETY CONTROL

B62
FALKENBERG J.,KIN AND TOTEM; GROUP RELATIONS OF AUSTRALIAN ABORIGINES IN THE PORT KEATS DISTRICT. SOCIETY STRATA STRUCT GP/REL PERS/REL MARRIAGE AGE ATTIT SEX...SOC STAT CHARTS AUSTRAL ABORIGINES. PAGE 48 H0964
KIN INGP/REL CULTURE FAM

B62
MALINOWSKI B.,SEX, CULTURE, AND MYTH. UNIV SOCIETY FAM PERS/REL MARRIAGE RATIONAL HABITAT PERSON SUPEGO MORAL WORSHIP 20. PAGE 102 H2032
MYTH SECT SEX CULTURE

B62
PASTOR R.S.,A STATEMENT OF THE LAWS OF PARAGUAY IN MATTERS AFFECTING BUSINESS (2ND ED.). PARAGUAY INDUS FAM LABOR LG/CO NAT/G LEGIS TAX CONTROL MARRIAGE 20. PAGE 124 H2474
FINAN ECO/UNDEV LAW CONSTN

B62
SMITH M.G.,KINSHIP AND COMMUNITY IN CARRIACOU. WEST/IND STRATA AGRI FAM SECT WORKER MARRIAGE OWN HEREDITY WEALTH...SOC 18/20. PAGE 146 H2915
CULTURE HABITAT KIN STRUCT

B62
VILAKAZI A.,ZULU TRANSFORMATIONS: A STUDY OF THE DYNAMICS OF SOCIAL CHANGE. AFR CULTURE ECO/UNDEV KIN NEIGH SEX...GEOG QU TREND CHARTS BIBLIOG 19/20. PAGE 163 H3254
MARRIAGE SECT SOC EDU/PROP

B63
BOHANNAN P.,SOCIAL ANTHROPOLOGY. ECO/DEV GP/REL DEMAND MARRIAGE HABITAT...CHARTS GP/COMP BIBLIOG T WORSHIP 20. PAGE 18 H0366
SOC STRUCT FAM CULTURE

B63
DRIVER H.E.,ETHNOGRAPHY AND ACCULTURATION OF THE CHICHIMECA-JONAZ OF NORTHEAST MEXICO. ECO/UNDEV AGRI FAM KIN EDU/PROP MARRIAGE HEALTH...GEOG INT CHARTS WORSHIP 18/20 MEXIC/AMER. PAGE 42 H0848
CULTURE HABITAT STRUCT GP/REL

B63
GOODE W.J.,WORLD REVOLUTION AND FAMILY PATTERNS. AFR CHINA/COM INDIA UAR CREATE ADJUST ATTIT SEX ...SOC 20 CHINJAP. PAGE 58 H1169
FAM NAT/COMP CULTURE MARRIAGE

B63
MAJUMDAR O.N.,AN INTRODUCTION TO SOCIAL ANTHROPOLOGY. INDIA LAW STRATA ECO/UNDEV KIN DEMAND MARRIAGE...GP/COMP BIBLIOG T WORSHIP 20. PAGE 101 H2026
SOC CULTURE STRUCT GP/REL

B63
PAUW B.A.,THE SECOND GENERATION. SOUTH/AFR INDUS FAM LABOR SECT EDU/PROP MARRIAGE ATTIT...SOC 20. PAGE 124 H2478
KIN CULTURE STRUCT SOCIETY

S63
ROBINSON W.C.,"URBANIZATION AND FERTILITY: THE NON-WESTERN EXPERIENCE (BMR)" DEATH MARRIAGE AGE/C BIO/SOC...STAT CENSUS CON/ANAL CHARTS NAT/COMP 20 THIRD/WRLD. PAGE 133 H2651
GEOG MUNIC FAM ECO/UNDEV

B64
ELKIN A.P.,THE AUSTRALIAN ABORIGINES - HOW TO UNDERSTAND THEM (4TH ED.). FAM NEIGH DEATH MARRIAGE ATTIT BIO/SOC HABITAT...PSY SOC MYTH WORSHIP AUSTRAL ABORIGINES. PAGE 45 H0908
CULTURE STRUCT SOCIETY KIN

B64
FREISEN J.,STAAT UND KATHOLISCHE KIRCHE IN DEN DEUTSCHEN BUNDESSTAATEN (2 VOLS.). GERMANY LAW FAM NAT/G EDU/PROP GP/REL MARRIAGE WEALTH 19/20 CHURCH/STA. PAGE 53 H1056
SECT CATHISM JURID PROVS

B64
MORGAN L.H.,ANCIENT SOCIETY (1877). SOCIETY FAM OWN ...INT QU GEN/LAWS SOC/INTEG. PAGE 113 H2255
KIN MARRIAGE CULTURE

B65
BERNDT R.M.,ABORIGINAL MAN IN AUSTRALIA. LAW DOMIN ADMIN COLONIAL MARRIAGE HABITAT ORD/FREE...LING CHARTS ANTHOL BIBLIOG WORSHIP 20 AUSTRAL ABORIGINES MUSIC ELKIN/AP. PAGE 16 H0312
SOC CULTURE SOCIETY STRUCT

B65
KUNSTADTER P.,THE LUA (LAWA) OF NORTHERN THAILAND: ASPECTS OF SOCIAL STRUCTURE, AGRICULTURE, AND RELIGION. THAILAND AGRI FAM KIN INGP/REL ISOLAT MARRIAGE HEALTH WORSHIP 20 BUDDHISM LUA. PAGE 89 H1780
STRUCT ECO/UNDEV CULTURE

B65
POBEDONOSTSEV K.P.,REFLECTIONS OF A RUSSIAN STATESMAN. RUSSIA LAW ELITES EDU/PROP PRESS ADJUD MARRIAGE ATTIT PWR...MAJORIT TRADIT 19 CHURCH/STA. PAGE 127 H2531
TOTALISM POLICY CONSTN NAT/G

B65
SPENCER P.,THE SAMBURU: A STUDY OF GERONTOCRACY IN A NOMADIC TRIBE. AFR SOCIETY ECO/UNDEV AGRI FAM NEIGH SECT GP/REL MARRIAGE WORSHIP 20 SAMBURU. PAGE 147 H2945
KIN STRUCT AGE/O CULTURE

B65
SVALASTOGA K.,SOCIAL DIFFERENTIATION. CULTURE ELITES SOCIETY MARRIAGE...CONCPT SIMUL. PAGE 151 H3011
SOC STRATA STRUCT GP/REL

B66
KASUNMU A.B.,NIGERIAN FAMILY LAW. NIGERIA KIN LEGIT ILLEGIT MARRIAGE AGE DRIVE HABITAT ALL/VALS...JURID IDEA/COMP T 20 ENGLSH/LAW. PAGE 83 H1667
FAM LAW CULTURE AFR

B66
KEIL S.,SEXUALITAT - ERKENNTNISSE UND MASS-STABE. CULTURE DOMIN MARRIAGE AGE/Y AGE/A PERSON SUPEGO PLURISM 17/20. PAGE 84 H1681
SEX ATTIT STRUCT SOCIETY

B66
LEYBURN J.G.,THE HAITIAN PEOPLE (REV. ED.). HAITI SOCIETY FAM SECT DOMIN COLONIAL MARRIAGE...SOC CHARTS BIBLIOG/A 18/10. PAGE 96 H1917
STRUCT STRATA INGP/REL CULTURE

B67
PATAI R.,GOLDEN RIVER TO GOLDEN ROAD: SOCIETY, CULTURE, AND CHANGE IN THE MIDDLE EAST (2ND ED.). ELITES FAM KIN TEC/DEV MARRIAGE NAT/LISM SEX ORD/FREE...TREND GP/COMP WORSHIP 20. PAGE 124 H2476
CULTURE SOCIETY ISLAM STRUCT

S67
SCOTT J.W.,"SOURCES OF SOCIAL CHANGE IN COMMUNITY, FAMILY, AND FERTILITY IN A PUERTO RICAN TOWN." PUERT/RICO CULTURE STRUCT ECO/UNDEV INDUS PERS/REL ROLE...SOC STAND/INT. PAGE 141 H2815
FAM MARRIAGE LITERACY ATTIT

B84
ENGELS F.,THE ORIGIN OF THE FAMILY, PRIVATE PROPERTY, AND THE STATE (TRANS. BY E. UNTERMANN). UNIV ELITES SOCIETY CAP/ISM ECO/TAC MARRIAGE ORD/FREE POPULISM...MARXIST SOC ENGELS. PAGE 46 H0926
FAM OWN WEALTH SOCISM

B90
TAINE H.A.,MODERN REGIME (2 VOLS.). FRANCE FAM REV CENTRAL MARRIAGE PWR...TREND 19 NAPOLEON/B. PAGE 152 H3037
STRUCT NAT/G OLD/LIB MORAL

MARRIOTT J.A. H2057

MARSH D.C. H2058

MARSH N.S. H3079

MARSHALL/A....ALFRED MARSHALL

N19
HABERLER G.,A SURVEY OF INTERNATIONAL TRADE THEORY (PAMPHLET). FINAN NAT/G COST INCOME 18/20 MONEY HUME/D MARSHALL/A. PAGE 63 H1267
INT/TRADE BAL/PAY GEN/LAWS POLICY

MARSHALL/J....JOHN MARSHALL

B56
DOUGLAS W.O.,WE THE JUDGES. INDIA USA+45 USA-45 LAW NAT/G SECT LEGIS PRESS CRIME FEDERAL ORD/FREE ...POLICY GOV/COMP 19/20 WARRN/EARL MARSHALL/J SUPREME/CT. PAGE 42 H0841
ADJUD CT/SYS CONSTN GOV/REL

MARSHL/PLN....MARSHALL PLAN

B57
REISS J.,GEORGE KENNANS POLITIK DER EINDAMMUNG. USSR NAT/G FORCES TOTALISM ATTIT ORD/FREE...POLICY 20 NATO TRUMAN/HS MARSHL/PLN KENNAN/G. PAGE 131 H2613 DIPLOM DETER PEACE

MARSILIUS/PADUA H2059

MARTELLI G. H2060

MARTI/JOSE....JOSE MARTI

B61
ROIG E.,MARTI, ANTIIMPERIALISTA. CUBA L/A+17C DIPLOM DOMIN COLONIAL CONTROL LEAD PWR SOVEREIGN ...PHIL/SCI 19 MARTI/JOSE INTERVENT. PAGE 133 H2664 PERSON NAT/LISM ECO/UNDEV ORD/FREE

MARTIN A.W. H1970

MARTIN B.K. H2061

MARTIN L.W. H2063,H2064

MARTINDALE D. H2065,H2066

MARTINET G. H2067

MARTINEZ J.R. H2068

MARTINEZ RIOS J. H2069

MARTINS A.F. H2070

MARTZ J.D. H2071,H2072

MARVICK D. H2073

MARWICK A. H2074

MARX F.M. H2075

MARX K. H2077,H2078,H2079,H2080,H2081,H2082,H2083

MARX/KARL....KARL MARX

B30
MASON E.S.,THE PARIS COMMUNE: AN EPISODE IN THE HISTORY OF THE SOCIALIST MOVEMENT. FRANCE MOD/EUR ELITES SOCIETY STRATA ECO/DEV WORKER EDU/PROP CHOOSE INGP/REL SOCISM 19 MARX/KARL PARIS. PAGE 104 H2085 NAT/G REV MARXISM

B38
MARX K.,THE GERMAN IDEOLOGY, PARTS 1 AND 3 (1846). MOD/EUR LAW STRATA WORKER DOMIN REV UTOPIA SOCISM 19 MARX/KARL. PAGE 104 H2079 MARXIST OWN PRODUC ECO/TAC

B45
VENABLE V.,HUMAN NATURE: THE MARXIAN VIEW. UNIV STRATA CAP/ISM REV GP/REL PERS/REL PRODUC KNOWL ...PHIL/SCI CONCPT IDEA/COMP 19 MARX/KARL ENGELS/F. PAGE 162 H3240 PERSON MARXISM WORKER UTOPIA

B50
CARR E.H.,STUDIES IN REVOLUTION. CREATE WAR PERSON ALL/IDEOS MARXISM SOCISM...PHIL/SCI METH/COMP ANTHOL 18/20 SAINTSIMON MARX/KARL PROUDHON/P LASSALLE/F PLEKHNV/GV. PAGE 27 H0537 REV IDEA/COMP COERCE BIOG

B50
HALLOWELL J.H.,MAIN CURRENTS IN MODERN POLITICAL THOUGHT. CONSTN SECT LEGIS...MAJORIT CONCPT 17/20 MARX/KARL MILL/JS HOBBES/T LENIN/VI. PAGE 64 H1290 IDEA/COMP POPULISM SOCISM

B50
SCHUMPETER J.A.,CAPITALISM, SOCIALISM, AND DEMOCRACY (3RD ED.). USA-45 USSR WOR+45 WOR-45 INTELL ECO/DEV ECO/UNDEV ECO/TAC WAR PRODUC ORD/FREE...MGT SOC 20 MARX/KARL. PAGE 140 H2804 SOCIALIST CAP/ISM MARXISM IDEA/COMP

B50
TRAGER F.N.,MARXISM IN SOUTHEAST ASIA. BURMA INDONESIA THAILAND VIETNAM CULTURE SOCIETY NAT/G VOL/ASSN EXEC ROUTINE COERCE ATTIT RIGID/FLEX PWR ...METH/CNCPT TIME/SEQ STERTYP GEN/LAWS MARX/KARL VAL/FREE COLD/WAR NAM 20. PAGE 156 H3126 S/ASIA POL/PAR REV

B54
LENIN V.I.,SELECTED WORKS (12 VOLS.). USSR INTELL SOCIETY STRATA STRUCT NAT/G POL/PAR WORKER CAP/ISM REV WAR...MARXIST PHIL/SCI 20 MARX/KARL LENIN/VI. PAGE 94 H1880 COM MARXISM

B55
MAYO H.B.,DEMOCRACY AND MARXISM. COM USSR STRATA NAT/G WORKER ECO/TAC REV MORAL...PHIL/SCI HIST/WRIT IDEA/COMP WORSHIP 20 MARX/KARL LENIN/VI STALIN/J TROTSKY/L. PAGE 105 H2108 MARXISM CAP/ISM

B58
ARON R.,SOCIOLOGIE DES SOCIETES INDUSTRIELLES: ESQUISSE D'UNE THEORIE DES REGIMES POLITIQUES. FRANCE SOCIETY NAT/G PROB/SOLV ATTIT RIGID/FLEX MARXISM POPULISM...POLICY SOC T 20 MARX/KARL TOCQUEVILL. PAGE 8 H0170 TOTALISM INDUS CONSTN GOV/COMP

B58
DUNAYEVSKAYA R.,MARXISM AND FREEDOM: FROM 1776 UNTIL TODAY. COM USSR WORKER CAP/ISM DOMIN REV GP/REL TOTALISM ALL/VALS...MYTH BIOG IDEA/COMP 18/20 MARX/KARL LENIN/VI STALIN/J. PAGE 43 H0861 MARXISM CONCPT ORD/FREE

B58
PALMER E.E.,THE COMMUNIST CHALLENGE. COM USA+45 USA-45 ECO/DEV ECO/UNDEV NEUTRAL ORD/FREE POPULISM ...CONCPT NAT/COMP ANTHOL 19/20 LENIN/VI STALIN/J MAO MARX/KARL COM/PARTY. PAGE 123 H2450 MARXISM DIPLOM IDEA/COMP POLICY

B59
HENDEL S.,THE SOVIET CRUCIBLE. USSR LEAD COERCE NAT/LISM UTOPIA PWR...POLICY CONCPT ANTHOL 20 STALIN/J LENIN/VI MARX/KARL BOLSHEVIK. PAGE 70 H1393 COM MARXISM REV TOTALISM

B59
LIPSET S.M.,SOCIAL MOBILITY IN INDUSTRIAL SOCIETY. EUR+WWI USA+45 USSR STRUCT INDUS WRITING GP/REL INGP/REL DRIVE...SOC CHARTS NAT/COMP SOC/INTEG 20 MARX/KARL ENGELS/F. PAGE 97 H1940 STRATA ECO/DEV SOCIETY

B59
PAGE S.W.,LENIN AND WORLD REVOLUTION. COM USSR NAT/G DOMIN COERCE CROWD UTOPIA ATTIT AUTHORIT DRIVE PWR...CONCPT MYTH 19/20 LENIN/VI MARX/KARL. PAGE 122 H2441 REV PERSON MARXISM BIOG

B60
MANIS J.G.,MAN AND SOCIETY. STRATA LEAD INGP/REL PERS/REL ATTIT PWR...PSY ANTHOL T SOC/INTEG MARX/KARL MILL/JS FREUD/S CHURCHLL/W SPENCER/H RUSSELL/B. PAGE 102 H2036 SOC SOCIETY STRUCT CULTURE

B61
GUEVARA E.,GUERRILLA WARFARE. L/A+17C ECO/UNDEV NAT/G POL/PAR VOL/ASSN PLAN DOMIN REV DRIVE PWR WEALTH...NEW/IDEA RECORD BIOG COLD/WAR MARX/KARL OAS 20. PAGE 62 H1247 FORCES COERCE GUERRILLA CUBA

B61
LEVIN L.A.,BIBLIOGRAFIIA BIBLIOGRAFII PROIZVEDENII K. MARKSA, F. ENGELSA, V.I. LENINA. COM USSR NAT/G POL/PAR WORKER LEAD REV ATTIT...POLICY IDEA/COMP 20 MARX/KARL LENIN/VI ENGELS. PAGE 95 H1899 BIBLIOG/A MARXISM MARXIST CONCPT

B61
MARX K.,THE COMMUNIST MANIFESTO. IN (MENDEL A. ESSENTIAL WORKS OF MARXISM, NEW YORK: BANTAM. FUT MOD/EUR CULTURE ECO/DEV ECO/UNDEV AGRI FINAN INDUS MARKET PROC/MFG LABOR MUNIC POL/PAR CONSULT FORCES CREATE PLAN ADMIN ATTIT DRIVE RIGID/FLEX ORD/FREE PWR RESPECT MARX/KARL WORK. PAGE 104 H2081 COM NEW/IDEA CAP/ISM REV

B62
EBENSTEIN W.,TWO WAYS OF LIFE. USA+45 CULTURE ECO/DEV PLAN EDU/PROP CONTROL ORD/FREE...GOV/COMP IDEA/COMP T 20 MARX/KARL ENGELS/F LENIN/VI LOCKE/JOHN MILL/JS. PAGE 44 H0885 MARXISM POPULISM ECO/TAC DIPLOM

B62
KINDERSLEY R.,THE FIRST RUSSIAN REVISIONISTS. COM USSR LAW ELITES INTELL NAT/G LEGIS ECO/TAC EDU/PROP CONTROL LEAD GP/REL SOCISM 19/20 MARX/KARL BOLSHEVISM. PAGE 86 H1712 CONSTN MARXISM POPULISM BIOG

S62
CROAN M.,"POLYCENTRISM: COMMUNIST INTERNATIONAL RELATIONS." ASIA STRUCT INT/ORG NAT/G POL/PAR CONSULT PLAN DOMIN EDU/PROP COERCE ATTIT RIGID/FLEX SOCISM...POLICY CONCPT TREND CON/ANAL GEN/LAWS MARX/KARL. PAGE 35 H0703 COM CREATE DIPLOM NAT/LISM

S62
KOLARZ W.,"THE IMPACT OF COMMUNISM ON WEST AFRICA." AFR FUT SOCIETY INT/ORG NAT/G CREATE PLAN DOMIN EDU/PROP COERCE NAT/LISM ATTIT RIGID/FLEX SOCISM ...POLICY CONCPT TREND MARX/KARL 20. PAGE 88 H1751 COM POL/PAR COLONIAL

S62
SARKISYANZ E.,"NATIONALISM, CAPITALISM, AND THE UNCOMMITED NATIONS: MARXISM AND ASIAN CULTURAL TRADITIONS." ASIA BURMA CHINA/COM COM CULTURE SOCIETY NAT/G POL/PAR PLAN DOMIN EDU/PROP COLONIAL COERCE ATTIT RIGID/FLEX...CONCPT TREND MARX/KARL 20 TIBET BUDDHISM. PAGE 138 H2755 S/ASIA SECT NAT/LISM CAP/ISM

B63
BERLIN I.,KARL MARX, HIS LIFE AND ENVIRONMENT (3RD ED.). MOD/EUR USSR INTELL EDU/PROP PARTIC REV ATTIT 19 MARX/KARL. PAGE 15 H0307 BIOG PERSON MARXISM CONCPT

B63
MARX K.,THE POVERTY OF PHILOSOPHY (1847). SOCIETY STRATA INDUS WORKER OWN UTOPIA SOCISM...GEN/LAWS MARX/KARL. PAGE 104 H2082 MARXIST PRODUC

L63
MICHAEL F.,"KHRUSHCHEV'S DISLOYAL OPPOSITION: STRUCTURAL CHANGE AND POWER STRUGGLE IN COMMUNIST BLOC." ASIA CHINA/COM FUT NAT/G POL/PAR CONSULT PLAN DOMIN ATTIT...POLICY CONCPT TREND MARX/KARL 20 KHRUSH/N. PAGE 110 H2195 COM STRUCT NAT/LISM USSR

B64
CAUTE D.,COMMUNISM AND THE FRENCH INTELLECTUALS, 1914-1960. COM EUR+WWI MOD/EUR NAT/G PERF/ART PROF/ORG CREATE EDU/PROP ATTIT PERSON KNOWL MARXISM POL/PAR INTELL

...SOC TIME/SEQ MARX/KARL 20 MALRAUX/A GIDE/A SARTRE/J. PAGE 28 H0563

B64
FROMM E.,MARX'S CONCEPT OF MAN. LABOR OWN PERSON ...HUM IDEA/COMP GEN/LAWS 17 MARX/KARL EUROPE SPINOZA/B GOETHE/J HEGEL/GWF. PAGE 54 H1072
INGP/REL CONCPT MARXISM SOCISM

B64
THORNTON T.P.,THE THIRD WORLD IN SOVIET PERSPECTIVE: STUDIES BY SOVIET WRITERS ON THE DEVELOPING AREAS. AFR L/A+17C S/ASIA STRATA AGRI INDUS MARKET NAT/G POL/PAR ECO/TAC COLONIAL PERCEPT PWR WEALTH...MARXIST STAT CHARTS WORK MARX/KARL 20. PAGE 155 H3090
ECO/UNDEV ACT/RES USSR DIPLOM

B65
COLLINS H.,KARL MARX AND THE BRITISH LABOR MOVEMENT, YEARS OF THE FIRST INTERNATIONAL. EUR+WWI MOD/EUR UK STRATA INDUS NAT/G POL/PAR SOCISM ...CONCPT 19/20 MARX/KARL. PAGE 32 H0633
MARXISM LABOR INT/ORG WORKER

B65
GEWIRTH A.,POLITICAL PHILOSOPHY. UNIV SOCIETY NAT/G GP/REL INGP/REL CONSEN PWR...IDEA/COMP GEN/LAWS 17/19 HOBBES/T LOCKE/JOHN MARX/KARL MILL/JS ROUSSEAU/J. PAGE 56 H1118
ORD/FREE SOVEREIGN PHIL/SCI

B65
ROSENBERG A.,DEMOCRACY AND SOCIALISM. COM EUR+WWI FRANCE MOD/EUR STRUCT INT/ORG NAT/G POL/PAR TOP/EX EDU/PROP COERCE PERSON PWR FASCISM MARXISM...CONCPT TIME/SEQ MARX/KARL 19/20. PAGE 134 H2677
ATTIT

B65
WOLFE B.D.,MARXISM; ONE HUNDRED YEARS IN THE LIFE OF A DOCTRINE. USSR WAR NAT/LISM PEACE TOTALISM ...MAJORIT 20 MARX/KARL. PAGE 170 H3399
MARXISM LEAD ATTIT

B66
LENSKI G.E.,POWER AND PRIVILEGE: A THEORY OF SOCIAL STRATIFICATION. SWEDEN UK UNIV USSR CULTURE ECO/UNDEV PRIVIL PWR...PHIL/SCI CONCPT CHARTS IDEA/COMP HYPO/EXP METH MARX/KARL. PAGE 94 H1882
SOC STRATA STRUCT SOCIETY

B66
NOLTE E.,THREE FACES OF FASCISM. FRANCE GERMANY DOMIN LEGIT COERCE CROWD REV WAR GP/REL RACE/REL SOVEREIGN...GOV/COMP IDEA/COMP 19/20 HITLER/A MUSSOLIN/B MARX/KARL. PAGE 118 H2368
FASCISM TOTALISM NAT/G POL/PAR

B67
BRZEZINSKI Z.K.,THE SOVIET BLOC: UNITY AND CONFLICT (2ND ED., REV., ENLARGED). COM POLAND USSR INTELL CHIEF EX/STRUC CONTROL EXEC GOV/REL PWR MARXISM ...TREND IDEA/COMP 20 LENIN/VI MARX/KARL STALIN/J. PAGE 23 H0463
NAT/G DIPLOM

B67
SETON-WATSON H.,THE RUSSIAN EMPIRE, 1801-1917. COM RUSSIA STRATA ECO/DEV AGRI INDUS POL/PAR DIPLOM NAT/LISM MARXISM...IDEA/COMP BIBLIOG 19/20 MARX/KARL. PAGE 142 H2834
SOCIETY NAT/G LEAD POLICY

S67
SEIDLER G.L.,"MARXIST LEGAL THOUGHT IN POLAND." POLAND SOCIETY R+D LOC/G NAT/G ACT/RES ADJUD CT/SYS SUPEGO PWR...SOC TREND 20 MARX/KARL. PAGE 141 H2822
MARXISM LAW CONCPT EFFICIENCY

S68
HOOK S.,"THE ENLIGHTENMENT AND MARXISM." CULTURE SOCIETY RATIONAL ORD/FREE PLURISM SOCISM...CONCPT HIST/WRIT 18/19 MARX/KARL HEGEL/GWF ENLIGHTNMT. PAGE 73 H1462
IDEA/COMP MARXISM OBJECTIVE

MARXISM....MARXISM, COMMUNISM; SEE ALSO MARXIST

N
BROCKWAY A.F.,AFRICAN SOCIALISM. EUR+WWI GHANA ISLAM UAR ECO/UNDEV CAP/ISM INT/TRADE COLONIAL COERCE GOV/REL DISCRIM 20 NEGRO NKRUMAH/K NASSER/G. PAGE 21 H0423
AFR SOCISM MARXISM

N
NEUE POLITISCHE LITERATUR. AFR ASIA EUR+WWI GERMANY RUSSIA SOCIETY ECO/DEV ECO/UNDEV PLAN PROB/SOLV LEAD MARXISM...PHIL/SCI CONCPT 20. PAGE 1 H0008
BIBLIOG DIPLOM COM NAT/G

N
PEKING REVIEW. CHINA/COM CULTURE AGRI INDUS DIPLOM EDU/PROP GUERRILLA ATTIT MARXISM...BIBLIOG 20. PAGE 1 H0009
MARXIST NAT/G POL/PAR PRESS

N
AVTOREFERATY DISSERTATSII. USSR INTELL ACADEM NAT/G DIPLOM GOV/REL KNOWL CONCPT. PAGE 2 H0029
BIBLIOG MARXISM MARXIST COM

N
KYRIAK T.E.,CHINA: A BIBLIOGRAPHY. ASIA CHINA/COM AGRI FINAN INDUS NAT/G INT/TRADE PRESS...SOC 20. PAGE 90 H1789
BIBLIOG/A MARXISM TOP/EX POL/PAR

N
US CONSOLATE GENERAL HONG KONG,REVIEW OF THE HONG KONG CHINESE PRESS. ECO/UNDEV LOC/G NAT/G PLAN DIPLOM EDU/PROP LEAD GP/REL MARXISM...POLICY INDEX 20. PAGE 159 H3178
BIBLIOG/A ASIA PRESS ATTIT

N
US CONSULATE GENERAL HONG KONG,EXTRACTS FROM CHINA MAINLAND MAGAZINES. ASIA CHINA/COM ECO/UNDEV NAT/G CHIEF LEAD ATTIT...MARXIST INDEX 20. PAGE 159 H3180
BIBLIOG MARXISM PRESS

N
US DEPARTMENT OF STATE,BIBLIOGRAPHY (PAMPHLETS). AGRI INDUS INT/ORG FOR/AID EDU/PROP WAR MARXISM ...SOC GOV/COMP METH/COMP 20. PAGE 159 H3184
BIBLIOG DIPLOM ECO/DEV NAT/G

B18
KERNER R.J.,SLAVIC EUROPE: A SELECTED BIBLIOGRAPHY IN THE WESTERN EUROPEAN LANGUAGES. BULGARIA CZECHOSLVK GERMANY/E POLAND RUSSIA YUGOSLAVIA NAT/G DIPLOM MARXISM...LING 19/20. PAGE 85 H1695
BIBLIOG SOCIETY CULTURE COM

N19
BRIMMELL G.H.,COMMUNISM IN SOUTHEAST ASIA (PAMPHLET). BURMA CAMBODIA COM INDIA INDONESIA LAOS MOD/EUR NAT/G POL/PAR FORCES CAP/ISM CONTROL WEALTH ...MYTH 20. PAGE 21 H0420
MARXISM S/ASIA REV ECO/UNDEV

N19
HAJDA J.,THE COLD WAR VIEWED AS A SOCIOLOGICAL PROBLEM (PAMPHLET). COM CZECHOSLVK EUR+WWI SOCIETY PLAN EDU/PROP CONTROL TASK ATTIT MARXISM...POLICY 20 COLD/WAR MIGRATION. PAGE 64 H1280
DIPLOM LEAD PWR NAT/G

N19
SENGHOR L.S.,AFRICAN SOCIALISM (PAMPHLET). AFR FRANCE MALI USSR ELITES ECO/UNDEV NAT/G DIPLOM DOMIN EDU/PROP ATTIT 20 NEGRO. PAGE 141 H2827
SOCISM MARXISM ORD/FREE NAT/LISM

N19
WEBB L.C.,CHURCH AND STATE IN ITALY: 1947-1957 (PAMPHLET). GERMANY ITALY CONSTN POL/PAR AGREE CONTROL PARTIC CHOOSE ATTIT ORD/FREE FASCISM MARXISM 20 CHURCH/STA MARITAIN/J SALO. PAGE 166 H3316
SECT CATHISM NAT/G GP/REL

C20
DUNNING W.A.,"A HISTORY OF POLITICAL THINKERS FROM ROUSSEAU TO SPENCER." NAT/G REV NAT/LISM UTIL CONSERVE MARXISM POPULISM...JURID BIBLIOG 18/19. PAGE 43 H0868
IDEA/COMP PHIL/SCI CONCPT GEN/LAWS

B29
DE REPARAZ G.,GEOGRAFIA Y POLITICA. CHILE SPAIN USSR NAT/G DIPLOM REV MARXISM...POLICY 19/20. PAGE 38 H0768
GEOG MOD/EUR

B30
MASON E.S.,THE PARIS COMMUNE: AN EPISODE IN THE HISTORY OF THE SOCIALIST MOVEMENT. FRANCE MOD/EUR ELITES SOCIETY STRATA ECO/DEV WORKER EDU/PROP CHOOSE INGP/REL SOCISM 19 MARX/KARL PARIS. PAGE 104 H2085
NAT/G REV MARXISM

B31
DUFFIELD M.,KING LEGION. NAT/G PROVS SECT LEGIS EDU/PROP PRESS GP/REL AGE/Y MARXISM POLICY. PAGE 43 H0856
SUPEGO FORCES VOL/ASSN LOBBY

B33
BERDYAEV N.,CHRISTIANITY AND CLASS WAR. UNIV SOCIETY WORKER CREATE PROB/SOLV ATTIT PERSON ORD/FREE...CONCPT CHRISTIAN. PAGE 15 H0296
SECT MARXISM STRATA GP/REL

B34
STALIN J.,PROBLEMS OF LENINISM. USSR STRATA INDUS LOC/G POL/PAR ECO/TAC CONTROL TOTALISM PWR SOCISM LENIN/VI STALIN/J. PAGE 148 H2968
MARXISM REV ELITES NAT/G

B36
HUBERMAN L.,MAN'S WORLDLY GOODS: THE STORY OF THE WEALTH OF NATIONS. CHRIST-17C EUR+WWI MOD/EUR SOCIETY DOMIN REV ORD/FREE...TIME/SEQ METH/COMP. PAGE 74 H1486
WEALTH CAP/ISM MARXISM CREATE

B36
MARITAIN J.,FREEDOM IN THE MODERN WORLD. CONSTN NAT/G SECT CAP/ISM MARXISM SOCISM...GOV/COMP IDEA/COMP 19/20 HUMANISM CHRISTIAN. PAGE 102 H2049
GEN/LAWS POLICY ORD/FREE

B36
SMITH T.V.,THE PROMISE OF AMERICAN POLITICS. USA-45 WOR-45 LAW CONSTN STRATA PARTIC FASCISM LAISSEZ MARXISM...MAJORIT METH/COMP 18/20 JEFFERSN/T LOCKE/JOHN BENTHAM/J. PAGE 146 H2920
CONCPT ORD/FREE IDEA/COMP NAT/COMP

B37
BERDYAEV N.,THE ORIGIN OF RUSSIAN COMMUNISM. MOD/EUR RUSSIA USSR INTELL SECT REV...ANARCH HUM 19/20 ORTHO/RUSS COM/PARTY CHRISTIAN. PAGE 15 H0294
MARXISM NAT/LISM CULTURE ATTIT

B38
HARPER S.N.,THE GOVERNMENT OF THE SOVIET UNION. COM USSR LAW CONSTN ECO/DEV PLAN TEC/DEV DIPLOM INT/TRADE ADMIN REV NAT/LISM...POLICY 20. PAGE 67 H1337
MARXISM NAT/G LEAD POL/PAR

B38
HEIMANN E.,COMMUNISM, FASCISM, OR DEMOCRACY? WOR-45 CONSTN SOCIETY STRATA AGRI CAP/ISM MORAL ORD/FREE ...MAJORIT METH/COMP NAT/COMP 19/20. PAGE 69 H1384
SOCISM MARXISM FASCISM PLURISM

B39
KOHN H.,REVOLUTIONS AND DICTATORSHIPS. COM EUR+WWI ISLAM MOD/EUR NAT/G CHIEF FORCES WAR CIVMIL/REL PWR MARXISM 18/20. PAGE 87 H1739
NAT/LISM TOTALISM REV FASCISM

B39
OAKESHOTT M.,THE SOCIAL AND POLITICAL DOCTRINES OF CONTEMPORARY EUROPE. EUR+WWI RATIONAL CATHISM FASCISM MARXISM POPULISM...POLICY ANTHOL 20 NAZI. PAGE 120 H2392
IDEA/COMP GOV/COMP ALL/IDEOS NAT/G

C41
WASSERMAN L.,"HANDBOOK OF POLITICAL "ISMS" CAP/ISM REPRESENT TOTALISM MARXISM NEW/LIB SOCISM...MAJORIT BIBLIOG 20. PAGE 166 H3313
IDEA/COMP PHIL/SCI OWN NAT/G

B42
NEUMANN S.,PERMANENT REVOLUTION: THE TOTAL STATE IN A WORLD AT WAR. COM EUR+WWI GERMANY USSR EX/STRUC DIPLOM CONTROL COERCE REPRESENT MARXISM...SOC GOV/COMP BIBLIOG 20 HITLER/A STALIN/J. PAGE 117 H2337
FASCISM TOTALISM DOMIN EDU/PROP

B43
CONOVER H.F.,SOVIET RUSSIA: SELECTED LIST OF REFERENCES. USSR CULTURE INDUS NAT/G TOP/EX TEC/DEV BUDGET WAR CIVMIL/REL EFFICIENCY MARXISM 20. PAGE 32 H0644
BIBLIOG ECO/DEV COM DIPLOM

B43
GRIERSON P.,BOOKS ON SOVIET RUSSIA 1917-42: A BIBLIOGRAPHY AND A GUIDE TO READING. USSR CULTURE ELITES NAT/G PLAN DIPLOM REV...GEOG 20. PAGE 61 H1213
BIBLIOG/A COM MARXISM LEAD

B43
LASKI H.J.,REFLECTIONS ON THE REVOLUTIONS OF OUR TIME. COM USSR NAT/G WORKER UTOPIA ORD/FREE WEALTH MARXISM SOCISM 19/20. PAGE 92 H1830
CAP/ISM WELF/ST ECO/TAC POLICY

B43
LENIN V.I.,STATE AND REVOLUTION. USSR CAP/ISM ...ANARCH MARXIST PHIL/SCI IDEA/COMP 20. PAGE 94 H1878
SOCIETY NAT/G REV MARXISM

B43
LENIN V.I.,LEFT WING COMMUNISM: AN INFANTILE DISORDER (1920). GERMANY MOD/EUR USSR STRUCT CHIEF DOMIN EDU/PROP LEGIT LEAD REPRESENT POPULISM ...METH/COMP 19 LENIN/VI COM/PARTY MENSHEVIK. PAGE 94 H1879
COM MARXISM NAT/G REV

B44
US LIBRARY OF CONGRESS,RUSSIA: A CHECK LIST PRELIMINARY TO A BASIC BIBLIOGRAPHY OF MATERIALS IN THE RUSSIAN LANGUAGE. COM USSR CULTURE EDU/PROP MARXISM...ART/METH HUM LING 19/20. PAGE 160 H3204
BIBLIOG LAW SECT

B45
CLAGETT H.L.,COMMUNIST CHINA: RUTHLESS ENEMY OR PAPER TIGER (PAMPHLET). CHINA/COM ECO/UNDEV AGRI INDUS NAT/G POL/PAR ECO/TAC INT/TRADE GUERRILLA ATTIT...CHARTS NAT/COMP ORG/CHARTS 20. PAGE 30 H0602
BIBLIOG/A MARXISM DIPLOM COERCE

B45
CROCE B.,POLITICS AND MORALS. UNIV NAT/G ECO/TAC ORD/FREE MARXISM POPULISM SOCISM...REALPOL 15/20 HEGEL/GWF ROUSSEAU/J. PAGE 35 H0704
MORAL GEN/LAWS IDEA/COMP

B45
VENABLE V.,HUMAN NATURE: THE MARXIAN VIEW. UNIV STRATA CAP/ISM REV GP/REL PERS/REL PRODUC KNOWL ...PHIL/SCI CONCPT IDEA/COMP 19 MARX/KARL ENGELS/F. PAGE 162 H3240
PERSON MARXISM WORKER UTOPIA

B47
NIEBUHR R.,THE CHILDREN OF LIGHT AND THE CHILDREN OF DARKNESS: A VINDICATION OF DEMOCRACY AND CRITIQUE OF TRADITIONAL DEFENSE. UNIV STRUCT NAT/G SECT INGP/REL OWN PEACE ORD/FREE MARXISM ...IDEA/COMP GEN/LAWS 20 CHRISTIAN. PAGE 118 H2358
POPULISM DIPLOM NEIGH GP/REL

N47
CANNON J.P.,AMERICAN STALINISM AND ANTI-STALINISM (PAMPHLET). NAT/G WORKER DOMIN EDU/PROP REV GP/REL ...MARXIST CONCPT 20 STALIN/J TROTSKY/L. PAGE 26 H0521
LABOR MARXISM CAP/ISM POL/PAR

B48
COX O.C.,CASTE, CLASS, AND RACE. INDIA WOR+45 WOR-45 SECT TEC/DEV MARRIAGE ROLE MARXISM...MAJORIT NAT/COMP SOC/INTEG 20 NEGRO HINDU. PAGE 34 H0688
RACE/REL STRUCT STRATA DISCRIM

B48
TOWSTER J.,POLITICAL POWER IN THE USSR: 1917-1947. USSR CONSTN CULTURE ELITES CREATE PLAN COERCE CENTRAL ATTIT RIGID/FLEX ORD/FREE...BIBLIOG SOC/INTEG 20 LENIN/VI STALIN/J. PAGE 156 H3122
EX/STRUC NAT/G MARXISM PWR

B48
TOYNBEE A.J.,CIVILIZATION ON TRIAL. FUT WOR-45 NAT/G CREATE CAP/ISM DIPLOM NUC/PWR CHOOSE MARXISM ...GEOG CONCPT WORSHIP. PAGE 156 H3125
SOCIETY TIME/SEQ NAT/COMP

B48
WOLFE B.D.,THREE WHO MADE A REVOLUTION. USSR CONSTN NAT/G CAP/ISM EDU/PROP CONTROL WAR GP/REL INGP/REL PERS/REL ROLE 20 STALIN/J LENIN/VI TROTSKY/L BOLSHEVISM. PAGE 170 H3398
BIOG REV LEAD MARXISM

B48
WRIGHT G.,THE RESHAPING OF FRENCH DEMOCRACY. FRANCE NAT/G POL/PAR SECT LEAD CHOOSE GP/REL INGP/REL MARXISM SOCISM...CHARTS BIBLIOG 20 DEGAULLE/C. PAGE 171 H3418
CONSTN POPULISM CREATE LEGIS

B48
YAKOBSON S.,FIVE HUNDRED RUSSIAN WORKS FOR COLLEGE LIBRARIES (PAMPHLET). MOD/EUR USSR MARXISM SOCISM ...ART/METH GEOG HUM JURID SOC 13/20. PAGE 171 H3431
BIBLIOG NAT/G CULTURE COM

S48
ALMOND G.A.,"THE CHRISTIAN PARTIES OF WESTEN EUROPE." EUR+WWI NAT/G EDU/PROP LEGIT TOTALISM ORD/FREE PWR MARXISM...TREND CHARTS STERTYP GEN/LAWS COLD/WAR 20. PAGE 5 H0110
POL/PAR CATH SOCISM

B49
MAO TSE-TUNG,NEW DEMOCRACY. CHINA/COM NAT/G DIPLOM ECO/TAC EDU/PROP REV...CONCPT METH SOC/INTEG 20. PAGE 102 H2045
SOCISM MARXISM POPULISM CULTURE

B49
US DEPARTMENT OF STATE,SOVIET BIBLIOGRAPHY (PAMPHLET). CHINA/COM COM USSR LAW AGRI INT/ORG ECO/TAC EDU/PROP...POLICY GEOG 20. PAGE 159 H3185
BIBLIOG/A MARXISM CULTURE DIPLOM

B49
VIERECK P.,CONSERVATISM REVISITED: THE REVOLT AGAINST REVOLT 1815-1949. EUR+WWI ELITES NAT/G FORCES PARTIC GOV/REL NAT/LISM...MAJORIT CONCPT GOV/COMP METTRNCH/K. PAGE 163 H3251
CONSERVE MARXISM REALPOL

B50
BERMAN H.J.,JUSTICE IN RUSSIA; AN INTERPRETATION OF SOVIET LAW. USSR LAW STRUCT LABOR FORCES AGREE GP/REL ORD/FREE SOCISM...TIME/SEQ 20. PAGE 15 H0309
JURID ADJUD MARXISM COERCE

B50
CARR E.H.,STUDIES IN REVOLUTION. CREATE WAR PERSON ALL/IDEOS MARXISM SOCISM...PHIL/SCI METH/COMP ANTHOL 18/20 SAINTSIMON MARX/KARL PROUDHON/P LASSALLE/F PLEKHNV/GV. PAGE 27 H0537
REV IDEA/COMP COERCE BIOG

B50
SCHUMPETER J.A.,CAPITALISM, SOCIALISM, AND DEMOCRACY (3RD ED.). USA-45 USSR WOR+45 WOR-45 INTELL ECO/DEV ECO/UNDEV ECO/TAC WAR PRODUC ORD/FREE...MGT SOC 20 MARX/KARL. PAGE 140 H2804
SOCIALIST CAP/ISM MARXISM IDEA/COMP

B50
TENG S.,AN ANNOTATED BIBLIOGRAPHY OF SELECTED CHINESE REFERENCE WORKS (REV. ED.). CULTURE ECO/UNDEV LEAD MARXISM...LING INDEX 3/20. PAGE 153 H3062
BIBLIOG/A ASIA NAT/G

B50
WILBUR C.M.,CHINESE SOURCES ON THE HISTORY OF THE CHINESE COMMUNIST MOVEMENT (PAMPHLET). CHINA/COM ECO/UNDEV PROVS FORCES WAR...PHIL/SCI 20. PAGE 168 H3360
BIBLIOG/A MARXISM REV NAT/G

B51
BORKENAU F.,EUROPEAN COMMUNISM. COM EUR+WWI GERMANY SPAIN USSR INT/ORG PLAN REV WAR ATTIT 20 STALIN/J HITLER/A. PAGE 19 H0376
MARXISM POLICY DIPLOM NAT/G

B51
MARX K.,THE EIGHTEENTH BRUMAIRE OF LOUIS BONAPARTE (1852). FRANCE STRATA FINAN INDUS LABOR CHIEF FORCES WORKER CAP/ISM ECO/TAC PARL/PROC ORD/FREE ...MARXIST 19. PAGE 104 H2080
REV MARXISM ELITES NAT/G

B51
MORLEY C.,GUIDE TO RESEARCH IN RUSSIAN HISTORY. USSR MARXISM...BIOG HIST/WRIT ANTHOL DICTIONARY. PAGE 113 H2259
BIBLIOG/A R+D NAT/G COM

S51
MACRAE D.G.,"THE BOLSHEVIK IDEOLOGY; THE INTELLECTUAL AND EMOTIONAL FACTORS IN COMMUNIST AFFILIATION" (BMR)" COM LEAD REV ATTIT ORD/FREE ...SOC CON/ANAL 20 BOLSHEVISM. PAGE 100 H2008
MARXISM INTELL PHIL/SCI SECT

C51
BEST H.,"THE SOVIET STATE AND ITS INCEPTION." USSR CULTURE INDUS DIPLOM WEALTH...GEOG SOC BIBLIOG 20. PAGE 16 H0322
COM GEN/METH REV MARXISM

B52
APPADORAI A.,THE SUBSTANCE OF POLITICS (6TH ED.). EX/STRUC LEGIS DIPLOM CT/SYS CHOOSE FASCISM MARXISM SOCISM...BIBLIOG T. PAGE 7 H0145
PHIL/SCI NAT/G

B52
LOPEZ-AMO A.,LA MONARQUIA DE LA REFORMA SOCIAL. MOD/EUR SPAIN CONSTN NAT/G TASK EFFICIENCY CONSERVE ...ANARCH TRADIT SOC CONCPT IDEA/COMP 19/20. PAGE 98 H1967
MARXISM REV LEGIT ORD/FREE

B52
SPENCER F.A.,WAR AND POSTWAR GREECE: AN ANALYSIS BASED ON GREEK WRITINGS. GREECE SOCIETY NAT/G POL/PAR FORCES CREATE DIPLOM LEAD MARXISM...SOC 20. PAGE 147 H2943
BIBLIOG/A WAR REV

B52
US DEPARTMENT OF STATE,RESEARCH ON EASTERN EUROPE (EXCLUDING USSR). EUR+WWI LAW ECO/DEV NAT/G PROB/SOLV DIPLOM ADMIN LEAD MARXISM...TREND 19/20. PAGE 159 H3187
BIBLIOG R+D ACT/RES COM

B53
BARZEL R.,DIE DEUTSCHEN PARTEIEN. GERMANY MARXISM SOCISM...CONCPT IDEA/COMP 19/20 SOC/DEMPAR CHRIS/DEM. PAGE 12 H0232
POL/PAR NAT/G LAISSEZ

B53
CURTISS J.S.,THE RUSSIAN CHURCH AND THE SOVIET STATE 1917-1950. COM USSR CONTROL LEAD REV MARXISM ...POLICY BIBLIOG 20 CHURCH/STA ORTHO/RUSS. PAGE 36 H0728
GP/REL NAT/G SECT PWR

B53
LEITES N.,A STUDY OF BOLSHEVISM. WOR+45 WOR-45 ELITES SOCIETY INT/ORG NAT/G EX/STRUC EDU/PROP EXEC ROUTINE ATTIT MORAL MARXISM...CONCPT OBS VAL/FREE 20. PAGE 94 H1869
COM POL/PAR USSR TOTALISM

B53
LEITES N.,A STUDY OF BOLSHEVISM. ELITES STRATA INT/ORG LOC/G POL/PAR WORKER EDU/PROP REV TOTALISM UTOPIA PWR...CONCPT 20 BOLSHEVISM. PAGE 94 H1870
MARXISM PLAN COM

B53
LENZ F.,DIE BEWEGUNGEN DER GROSSEN MACHTE. USA+45 USA-45 USSR SOCIETY STRATA STRUCT NAT/G PERSON MARXISM...CONCPT IDEA/COMP NAT/COMP 18/20. PAGE 94 H1883
BAL/PWR TREND DIPLOM HIST/WRIT

B53
MAXIMOFF G.P.,THE POLITICAL PHILOSOPHY OF BAKUNIN: SCIENTIFIC ANARCHISM. STRUCT INGP/REL FEDERAL MARXISM...ANARCH BIOG 19 BAKUNIN. PAGE 105 H2104
SOCIETY PHIL/SCI NAT/G IDEA/COMP

B53
SHIRATO I.,JAPANESE SOURCES ON THE HISTORY OF THE CHINESE COMMUNIST MOVEMENT (PAMPHLET). CHINA/COM USSR CONSTRUC NAT/G POL/PAR FORCES DIPLOM DOMIN EDU/PROP CONTROL WAR TOTALISM SOCISM 20. PAGE 143 H2863
BIBLIOG/A MARXISM ECO/UNDEV

S53
ARENDT H.,"IDEOLOGY AND TERROR: A NOVEL FORM OF GOVERNMENT." WOR-45 DOMIN STRANGE ATTIT SUPEGO MARXISM...GOV/COMP IDEA/COMP 20 NAZI. PAGE 8 H0160
TOTALISM ANOMIE ALL/IDEOS SOCIETY

B54
LENIN V.I.,SELECTED WORKS (12 VOLS.). USSR INTELL SOCIETY STRATA STRUCT NAT/G POL/PAR WORKER CAP/ISM REV WAR...MARXIST PHIL/SCI 20 MARX/KARL LENIN/VI. PAGE 94 H1880
COM MARXISM

B55
MAYO H.B.,DEMOCRACY AND MARXISM. COM USSR STRATA NAT/G WORKER ECO/TAC REV MORAL...PHIL/SCI HIST/WRIT IDEA/COMP WORSHIP 20 MARX/KARL LENIN/VI STALIN/J TROTSKY/L. PAGE 105 H2108
MARXISM CAP/ISM

B55
MID-EUROPEAN LAW PROJECT,CHURCH AND STATE BEHIND THE IRON CURTAIN. COM CZECHOSLVK HUNGARY POLAND USSR CULTURE SECT EDU/PROP GOV/REL CATHISM...CHARTS ANTHOL BIBLIOG WORSHIP 20 CHURCH/STA. PAGE 110 H2202
LAW MARXISM POLICY

B55
THOMPSON V.,MINORITY PROBLEMS IN SOUTHEAST ASIA. CAMBODIA CHINA/COM LAOS S/ASIA KIN NAT/G SECT PROB/SOLV EDU/PROP REGION GP/REL RACE/REL MARXISM ...SOC 20 BUDDHISM UN. PAGE 154 H3085
INGP/REL GEOG DIPLOM STRUCT

B55
VERGNAUD P.,L'IDEE DE LA NATIONALITE ET DE LA LIBRE DISPOSITION DES PEUPLES DANS SES RAPPORTS AVEC L'IDEE DE L'ETAT. STRATA NAT/G EDU/PROP RACE/REL AUTHORIT FASCISM MARXISM MYTH. PAGE 162 H3243
NAT/LISM DISCRIM ORD/FREE

L55
ROSTOW W.W.,"RUSSIA AND CHINA UNDER COMMUNISM." CHINA/COM USSR INTELL STRUCT INT/ORG NAT/G POL/PAR TOP/EX ACT/RES PLAN ADMIN ATTIT ALL/VALS MARXISM ...CONCPT OBS TIME/SEQ TREND GOV/COMP VAL/FREE 20. PAGE 134 H2689
COM ASIA

B56
PADMORE G.,PAN-AFRICANISM OR COMMUNISM. AFR FUT NIGERIA INTELL NAT/G COLONIAL FEDERAL ATTIT DRIVE PWR RESPECT WEALTH MARXISM...CONCPT AUD/VIS STERTYP 20. PAGE 122 H2440
POL/PAR NAT/LISM

B56
SMEDLEY A.,THE GREAT ROAD: THE LIFE AND TIMES OF CHU TEH. ASIA USSR NAT/G POL/PAR DIPLOM COERCE GUERRILLA CIVMIL/REL NAT/LISM PERSON SKILL MARXISM ...BIOG 20 CHINJAP MAO. PAGE 145 H2903
REV WAR FORCES

B56
VON HARPE W.,DIE SOWJETUNION FINNLAND UND SKANDANAVIEN, 1945-1955. EUR+WWI FINLAND GERMANY USSR WAR INGP/REL ORD/FREE SOVEREIGN MARXISM ...POLICY GOV/COMP BIBLIOG 20 STALIN/J. PAGE 163 H3270
DIPLOM COM NEUTRAL BAL/PWR

C56
FALL B.B.,"THE VIET-MINH REGIME." VIETNAM LAW ECO/UNDEV POL/PAR FORCES DOMIN WAR ATTIT MARXISM ...BIOG PREDICT BIBLIOG/A 20. PAGE 48 H0967
NAT/G ADMIN EX/STRUC

LEAD

B57
ARON R.,THE OPIUM OF THE INTELLECTUALS (TRANS. BY TERENCE KILMARTIN). FRANCE USSR WOR+45 CULTURE POL/PAR PLAN DOMIN EDU/PROP REV ATTIT ORD/FREE ...IDEA/COMP METH/COMP NAT/COMP 20 COM/PARTY. PAGE 8 H0169
INTELL UTOPIA MYTH MARXISM

B57
BYRNES R.F.,BIBLIOGRAPHY OF AMERICAN PUBLICATIONS ON EAST CENTRAL EUROPE, 1945-1957 (VOL. XXII). SECT DIPLOM EDU/PROP RACE/REL...ART/METH GEOG JURID SOC LING 20 JEWS. PAGE 25 H0503
BIBLIOG/A COM MARXISM NAT/G

B57
HALLGARTEN G.W.,DAMONEN ODER RETTER. ASIA L/A+17C CAP/ISM ATTIT MARXISM SOCISM...NAT/COMP. PAGE 64 H1289
TOTALISM FASCISM COERCE DOMIN

B57
HERNANDEZ-ARREGU J.,IMPERIALISMO Y CULTURA (LA POLITICA EN LA INTELIGENCIA ARGENTINA). L/A+17C CULTURE ELITES WRITING COLONIAL CROWD ATTIT FASCISM MARXISM SOCISM...BIOG IDEA/COMP 20 ARGEN PERON/JUAN COM/PARTY. PAGE 70 H1403
INTELL CREATE ART/METH HUM

B57
KENNEDY M.D.,A SHORT HISTORY OF COMMUNISM IN ASIA. ASIA BURMA INDIA S/ASIA THAILAND NAT/G POL/PAR LEAD REV WAR MARXISM SOCISM...POLICY 20 CHINJAP. PAGE 85 H1688
DIPLOM NAT/LISM TOTALISM COERCE

B57
LOUCKS W.N.,COMPARATIVE ECONOMIC SYSTEMS (5TH ED.). COM UK USSR INDUS POL/PAR PLAN CAP/ISM TOTALISM MARXISM...PHIL/SCI BIBLIOG 19/20. PAGE 99 H1969
NAT/COMP IDEA/COMP SOCISM

B57
PARK A.G.,BOLSHEVISM IN TURKESTAN 1917-1927. COM RUSSIA USSR CULTURE AGRI SECT DOMIN GP/REL INGP/REL NAT/LISM...BIBLIOG 20 TURKESTAN. PAGE 123 H2467
REV POLICY MARXISM ISLAM

B57
TOMASIC D.A.,NATIONAL COMMUNISM AND SOVIET STRATEGY. UK USSR YUGOSLAVIA NAT/G POL/PAR CHIEF CREATE DOMIN REV WAR PWR...BIOG TREND 20 TITO/MARSH STALIN/J. PAGE 156 H3112
COM NAT/LISM MARXISM DIPLOM

B57
VON HIPPEL E.,GESCHICHTE DER STAATSPHILOSOPHIE (2 VOLS.). ASIA GREECE INDIA PRE/AMER UAR NAT/LISM ORD/FREE MARXISM. PAGE 164 H3272
CULTURE CONCPT NAT/G

B58
ARON R.,SOCIOLOGIE DES SOCIETES INDUSTRIELLES: ESQUISSE D'UNE THEORIE DES REGIMES POLITIQUES. FRANCE SOCIETY NAT/G PROB/SOLV ATTIT RIGID/FLEX MARXISM POPULISM...POLICY SOC T 20 MARX/KARL TOCQUEVILL. PAGE 8 H0170
TOTALISM INDUS CONSTN GOV/COMP

B58
CHANG H.,WITHIN THE FOUR SEAS. ASIA WAR MORAL MARXISM...IDEA/COMP NAT/COMP 20 CONFUCIUS. PAGE 29 H0577
PEACE DIPLOM KNOWL CULTURE

B58
DUNAYEVSKAYA R.,MARXISM AND FREEDOM: FROM 1776 UNTIL TODAY. COM USSR WORKER CAP/ISM DOMIN REV GP/REL TOTALISM ALL/VALS...MYTH BIOG IDEA/COMP 18/20 MARX/KARL LENIN/VI STALIN/J. PAGE 43 H0861
MARXISM CONCPT ORD/FREE

B58
HSU U.T.,THE INVISIBLE CONFLICT. ASIA USSR ELITES NAT/G CONTROL LEAD COERCE REV WAR NAT/LISM ORD/FREE PWR 20 COM/PARTY ESPIONAGE. PAGE 74 H1485
MARXISM POL/PAR EDU/PROP FORCES

B58
LAQUER W.Z.,THE MIDDLE EAST IN TRANSITION. COM USSR ECO/UNDEV NAT/G VOL/ASSN EDU/PROP EXEC ATTIT DRIVE PWR MARXISM COLD/WAR TOT/POP 20. PAGE 91 H1818
ISLAM TREND NAT/LISM

B58
PALMER E.E.,THE COMMUNIST CHALLENGE. COM USA+45 USA-45 ECO/DEV ECO/UNDEV NEUTRAL ORD/FREE POPULISM ...CONCPT NAT/COMP ANTHOL 19/20 LENIN/VI STALIN/J MAO MARX/KARL COM/PARTY. PAGE 123 H2450
MARXISM DIPLOM IDEA/COMP POLICY

B58
SCOTT D.J.R.,RUSSIAN POLITICAL INSTITUTIONS. RUSSIA USSR CONSTN AGRI DELIB/GP PLAN EDU/PROP CONTROL CHOOSE EFFICIENCY ATTIT MARXISM...BIBLIOG/A 13/20. PAGE 141 H2813
NAT/G POL/PAR ADMIN DECISION

B58
TILLION G.,ALGERIA: THE REALITIES. ALGERIA FRANCE ISLAM CULTURE STRATA PROB/SOLV DOMIN REV NAT/LISM WEALTH MARXISM...GEOG 20. PAGE 155 H3094
ECO/UNDEV SOC COLONIAL DIPLOM

B58
VARG P.A.,MISSIONARIES, CHINESE, AND DIPLOMATS: THE AMERICAN PROTESTANT MISSIONARY MOVEMENT IN CHINA, 1890-1952. ASIA ECO/UNDEV NAT/G PROB/SOLV CAP/ISM EDU/PROP COLONIAL NAT/LISM ATTIT MARXISM...NAT/COMP STERTYP 20 CHINJAP PROTESTANT MISSION. PAGE 162 H3234
CULTURE DIPLOM SECT

L58
BELL D.,"TEN THEORIES IN SEARCH OF REALITY: THE PREDICTION OF SOVIET BEHAVIOR IN THE SOCIAL
MARXISM PREDICT

SCIENCES" (BMR)" COM USSR...POLICY SOC METH/COMP 20. PAGE 13 H0264 — IDEA/COMP

B59
CAREW-HUNT R.C.,BOOKS ON COMMUNISM. NAT/G POL/PAR DIPLOM REV...BIOG 19/20. PAGE 26 H0528 — BIBLIOG/A MARXISM COM ASIA

B59
EAENZA L.,COMMUNISMO E CATTOLICESIMO IN UNA PARROCHIA DI CAMPAGNA. ITALY CULTURE ELITES ECO/DEV AGRI KIN POL/PAR DOMIN LEGIT RIGID/FLEX...DECISION OBS IDEA/COMP 20 COM/PARTY CHURCH/STA. PAGE 44 H0878 — ATTIT CATHISM NEIGH MARXISM

B59
EPSTEIN F.T.,EAST GERMANY: A SELECTED BIBLIOGRAPHY (PAMPHLET). COM GERMANY/E LAW AGRI FINAN INDUS LABOR POL/PAR EDU/PROP ADMIN AGE/Y 20. PAGE 47 H0932 — BIBLIOG/A INTELL MARXISM NAT/G

B59
GOLDWIN R.A.,READINGS IN RUSSIAN FOREIGN POLICY. HUNGARY USSR YUGOSLAVIA ELITES INT/ORG NAT/G REV WAR NAT/LISM PERSON SOCISM...CHARTS 20 MAPS BOLSHEVISM. PAGE 58 H1160 — COM MARXISM DIPLOM POLICY

B59
HENDEL S.,THE SOVIET CRUCIBLE. USSR LEAD COERCE NAT/LISM UTOPIA PWR...POLICY CONCPT ANTHOL 20 STALIN/J LENIN/VI MARX/KARL BOLSHEVIK. PAGE 70 H1393 — COM MARXISM REV TOTALISM

B59
LANDAUER C.,EUROPEAN SOCIALISM (2 VOLS.). COM EUR+WWI MOD/EUR INTELL INDUS REV WAR...MAJORIT IDEA/COMP BIBLIOG 19/20 HITLER/A. PAGE 90 H1805 — SOCISM NAT/COMP LABOR MARXISM

B59
LEFEVRE R.,THE NATURE OF MAN AND HIS GOVERNMENT. EUR+WWI MOD/EUR CONSTN CULTURE MORAL MARXISM ...POLICY 18/20. PAGE 93 H1859 — NAT/G TASK ORD/FREE ATTIT

B59
MADHOK B.,POLITICAL TRENDS IN INDIA. INDIA PAKISTAN UK STRATA ECO/UNDEV POL/PAR LEGIS CAP/ISM DIPLOM COLONIAL CHOOSE MARXISM...SOC TREND 20 GANDHI/M NEHRU/J. PAGE 101 H2014 — GEOG NAT/G

B59
OVERSTREET G.D.,COMMUNISM IN INDIA. INDIA S/ASIA CONSTN INT/ORG LEAD GP/REL...CHARTS BIBLIOG 20. PAGE 122 H2435 — MARXISM NAT/LISM POL/PAR WAR

B59
PAGE S.W.,LENIN AND WORLD REVOLUTION. COM USSR NAT/G DOMIN COERCE CROWD UTOPIA ATTIT AUTHORIT DRIVE PWR...CONCPT MYTH 19/20 LENIN/VI MARX/KARL. PAGE 122 H2441 — REV PERSON MARXISM BIOG

B59
SENGHOR L.S.,RAPPORT SUR LA DOCTRINE ET LA PROGRAMME DU PART I. FRANCE MALI CONSTN POL/PAR PLAN CHOOSE OWN ORD/FREE MARXISM...SOCIALIST 20 NEGRO. PAGE 141 H2828 — ATTIT NAT/G AFR SOCISM

S59
LABEDZ L.,"IDEOLOGY: THE FOURTH STAGE." COM USSR NAT/G TOP/EX LEGIT ATTIT PWR MARXISM...METH/CNCPT HIST/WRIT STERTYP TOT/POP 20. PAGE 90 H1795 — CONCPT GEN/LAWS

S59
SKILLING H.G.,"COMMUNISM: NATIONAL OR INTERNATIONAL." CHINA/COM USSR YUGOSLAVIA NAT/G POL/PAR VOL/ASSN DOMIN REGION COERCE ATTIT PWR MARXISM SOCISM...CONCPT TOT/POP 20 TITO/MARSH. PAGE 145 H2894 — COM TREND

B60
EMERSON R.,FROM EMPIRE TO NATION: THE RISE TO SELF-ASSERTION OF ASIAN AND AFRICAN PEOPLES. S/ASIA CULTURE NAT/G SECT DIPLOM ATTIT SOVEREIGN MARXISM ...POLICY BIBLIOG 19/20. PAGE 46 H0919 — NAT/LISM COLONIAL AFR ASIA

B60
FISCHER L.,THE SOVIETS IN WORLD AFFAIRS. CHINA/COM COM EUR+WWI USSR INT/ORG CONFER LEAD ARMS/CONT REV PWR...CHARTS 20 TREATY VERSAILLES. PAGE 51 H1010 — DIPLOM NAT/G POLICY MARXISM

B60
FRANCIS R.G.,THE PREDICTIVE PROCESS. PLAN MARXISM ...DECISION SOC CONCPT NAT/COMP 19/20. PAGE 52 H1047 — PREDICT PHIL/SCI TREND

B60
HARRISON S.S.,INDIA: THE MOST DANGEROUS DECADES. INDIA CONSTN STRATA POL/PAR SECT PLAN ADMIN CHOOSE GP/REL TOTALISM MARXISM...LING 20 NEHRU/J. PAGE 67 H1347 — CULTURE ECO/UNDEV PROB/SOLV REGION

B60
MACFARQUHAR R.,THE HUNDRED FLOWERS. ASIA NAT/G WORKER GP/REL ORD/FREE MARXISM 20 MAO. PAGE 100 H1991 — DEBATE PRESS POL/PAR ATTIT

B60
MC CLELLAN G.S.,INDIA. CHINA/COM INDIA CONSTN ELITES STRATA AGRI POL/PAR FOR/AID ARMS/CONT REV MARXISM...CENSUS BIBLIOG 20 COLD/WAR GANDHI/M NEHRU/J. PAGE 106 H2117 — DIPLOM NAT/G SOCIETY ECO/UNDEV

B60
MCCLOSKY H.,THE SOVIET DICTATORSHIP. FUT CONSTN CULTURE INTELL SOCIETY POL/PAR SECT VOL/ASSN FORCES PLAN TEC/DEV DOMIN EDU/PROP COERCE PWR MARXISM ...POLICY CONCPT MYTH STERTYP 20. PAGE 106 H2127 — COM NAT/G TOTALISM USSR

B60
SCHAPIRO L.,THE COMMUNIST PARTY OF THE SOVIET UNION. COM LAW SOCIETY STRATA STRUCT ECO/DEV LABOR NAT/G POL/PAR CREATE DOMIN EDU/PROP COERCE TOTALISM MARXISM...POLICY CONCPT MYTH TIME/SEQ WORK TOT/POP 20 LENIN/VI STALIN/J. PAGE 139 H2772 — INTELL PWR USSR

B60
SZTARAY Z.,BIBLIOGRAPHY ON HUNGARY. HUNGARY MOD/EUR CULTURE INDUS SECT DIPLOM REV...ART/METH SOC LING 18/20. PAGE 151 H3029 — BIBLIOG NAT/G COM MARXISM

B60
WORLEY P.,ASIA TODAY (REV. ED.) (PAMPHLET). COM ECO/UNDEV AGRI FINAN INDUS POL/PAR FOR/AID ADMIN MARXISM 20. PAGE 170 H3411 — BIBLIOG/A ASIA DIPLOM NAT/G

B60
ZENKOVSKY S.A.,PAN-TURKISM AND ISLAM IN RUSSIA. ASIA RUSSIA USSR CULTURE POL/PAR DOMIN REV GP/REL MARXISM...LING GP/COMP BIBLIOG 19/20 TURKIC. PAGE 173 H3454 — SECT NAT/LISM COM ISLAM

L60
KAPLAN M.A.,"COMMUNIST COUP IN CZECHOSLOVAKIA." COM EUR+WWI INTELL LABOR LOC/G NAT/G POL/PAR FORCES EDU/PROP EXEC MARXISM...TIME/SEQ HYPO/EXP 20. PAGE 83 H1659 — STRUCT COERCE CZECHOSLVK

S60
CASSINELLI C.,"TOTALITARIANISM, IDEOLOGY AND PROPAGANDA." EUR+WWI CULTURE SOCIETY NAT/G DOMIN COERCE ORD/FREE FASCISM MARXISM...MARXIST CONCPT STERTYP GEN/LAWS TOT/POP 20. PAGE 28 H0554 — ATTIT EDU/PROP TOTALISM

S60
NORTH R.C.,"THE NEW EXPANSIONISM." ASIA CHINA/COM FUT INDIA CULTURE SOCIETY NAT/G TOP/EX DOMIN COERCE PWR MARXISM...CONCPT TIME/SEQ TREND GEN/LAWS COLD/WAR 20 MAO. PAGE 119 H2372 — ATTIT DRIVE NAT/LISM

B61
BURKS R.V.,THE DYNAMICS OF COMMUNISM IN EASTERN EUROPE. COM YUGOSLAVIA POL/PAR RACE/REL ISOLAT ...CORREL CON/ANAL CHARTS GP/COMP DICTIONARY 20 EUROPE/E SLAV/MACED. PAGE 24 H0489 — MARXISM STRUCT WORKER REPRESENT

B61
CONQUEST R.,POWER AND POLICY IN THE USSR. USSR NAT/G POL/PAR DIPLOM MARXISM 20. PAGE 33 H0655 — COM HIST/WRIT GOV/REL PWR

B61
DRAGNICH A.N.,MAJOR EUROPEAN GOVERNMENTS. FRANCE GERMANY/W UK USSR LOC/G EX/STRUC CT/SYS PARL/PROC ATTIT MARXISM...JURID MGT NAT/COMP 19/20. PAGE 42 H0846 — NAT/G LEGIS CONSTN POL/PAR

B61
HEMPSTONE S.,THE NEW AFRICA. AGRI INDUS KIN NAT/G COLONIAL MARXISM...SOC INT TREND NAT/COMP BIBLIOG/A 20. PAGE 69 H1392 — AFR ORD/FREE PERSON CULTURE

B61
LA PONCE J.A.,THE GOVERNMENT OF THE FIFTH REPUBLIC: FRENCH POLITICAL PARTIES AND THE CONSTITUTION. ALGERIA FRANCE LAW NAT/G DELIB/GP LEGIS ECO/TAC MARXISM SOCISM...CHARTS BIBLIOG/A 20 DEGAULLE/C. PAGE 90 H1794 — PWR POL/PAR CONSTN CHIEF

B61
LENIN V.I.,WHAT IS TO BE DONE? (1902). RUSSIA LABOR NAT/G POL/PAR WORKER CAP/ISM ECO/TAC ADMIN PARTIC ...MARXIST IDEA/COMP GEN/LAWS 19/20. PAGE 94 H1881 — EDU/PROP PRESS MARXISM METH/COMP

B61
LETHBRIDGE H.J.,CHINA'S URBAN COMMUNES. CHINA/COM FUT ECO/UNDEV DIPLOM EDU/PROP DEMAND INCOME MARXISM ...POLICY 20. PAGE 95 H1893 — MUNIC CONTROL ECO/TAC NAT/G

B61
LEVIN L.A.,BIBLIOGRAFIIA BIBLIOGRAFII PROIZVEDENII K. MARKSA, F. ENGELSA, V.I. LENINA. COM USSR NAT/G POL/PAR WORKER LEAD REV ATTIT...POLICY IDEA/COMP 20 MARX/KARL LENIN/VI ENGELS. PAGE 95 H1899 — BIBLIOG/A MARXISM MARXIST CONCPT

B61
LICHTHEIM G.,MARXISM. GERMANY SOCIETY WORKER CAP/ISM ECO/TAC NAT/LISM POPULISM...TIME/SEQ GOV/COMP NAT/COMP 18/20 COM/PARTY. PAGE 96 H1924 — MARXISM SOCISM IDEA/COMP CULTURE

B61
MOLLAU G.,INTERNATIONAL COMMUNISM AND WORLD REVOLUTION: HISTORY AND METHODS. RUSSIA USSR INT/ORG NAT/G POL/PAR VOL/ASSN FORCES BAL/PWR DIPLOM EXEC REGION WAR ATTIT PWR MARXISM...CONCPT TIME/SEQ COLD/WAR 19/20. PAGE 112 H2237 — COM REV

B61
NEWMAN R.P.,RECOGNITION OF COMMUNIST CHINA? A STUDY — MARXISM

IN ARGUMENT. CHINA/COM NAT/G PROB/SOLV RATIONAL ...INT/LAW LOG IDEA/COMP BIBLIOG 20. PAGE 117 H2347 — ATTIT DIPLOM POLICY

B61
NOVE A.,THE SOVIET ECONOMY. USSR ECO/DEV FINAN NAT/G ECO/TAC PRICE ADMIN EFFICIENCY MARXISM ...TREND BIBLIOG 20. PAGE 119 H2378 — PLAN PRODUC POLICY

B61
SCHWARTZ H.,THE RED PHOENIX: RUSSIA SINCE WORLD WAR II. USA+45 WOR+45 ELITES POL/PAR TEC/DEV ECO/TAC MARXISM. PAGE 140 H2810 — DIPLOM NAT/G ECO/DEV

B61
STARK H.,SOCIAL AND ECONOMIC FRONTIERS IN LATIN AMERICA (2ND ED.). CUBA FUT CULTURE AGRI INDUS ECO/TAC PRODUC ATTIT MARXISM...NAT/COMP BIBLIOG T 20. PAGE 149 H2971 — L/A+17C SOCIETY DIPLOM ECO/UNDEV

S61
TOMASIC D.,"POLITICAL LEADERSHIP IN CONTEMPORARY POLAND." COM EUR+WWI GERMANY NAT/G POL/PAR SECT DELIB/GP PLAN ECO/TAC DOMIN EDU/PROP PWR MARXISM ...MARXIST GEOG MGT CONCPT TIME/SEQ STERTYP 20. PAGE 156 H3111 — SOCIETY ROUTINE USSR POLAND

S61
TUCKER R.C.,"TOWARDS A COMPARATIVE POLITICS OF MOVEMENT-REGIMES" (BMR)" USSR CONSTN NAT/G CREATE PROB/SOLV DIPLOM DOMIN REV...GP/COMP IDEA/COMP METH 20 STALIN/J BOLSHEVISM. PAGE 157 H3135 — MARXISM POLICY GEN/LAWS PWR

B62
BAFFREY S.A.,THE RED MYTH: A HISTORY OF COMMUNISM FROM MARX TO KHRUSHCHEV. USSR NAT/G CHIEF CAP/ISM DIPLOM EDU/PROP REV WAR PEACE TOTALISM...POLICY 20 STALIN/J KHRUSH/N. PAGE 10 H0195 — CONCPT MARXISM TV

B62
BARNETT A.D.,COMMUNIST CHINA IN PERSPECTIVE. CHINA/COM FUT CULTURE ECO/UNDEV TEC/DEV CONTROL 20. PAGE 11 H0222 — REV MARXISM TREND PLAN

B62
BELL D.,THE END OF IDEOLOGY (REV. ED.). USA+45 USA-45 ELITES STRATA LABOR CREATE CRIME PWR MARXISM ...PHIL/SCI METH/COMP 20 EUROPE. PAGE 13 H0265 — CROWD CAP/ISM SOCISM IDEA/COMP

B62
BRUMBERG A.,RUSSIA UNDER KHRUSHCHEV. FUT USSR SOCIETY ECO/DEV AGRI PERF/ART WORKER PWR...SOC ANTHOL 20 KHRUSH/N. PAGE 22 H0453 — COM MARXISM NAT/G CHIEF

B62
CARTER G.M.,THE GOVERNMENT OF THE SOVIET UNION. USSR CULTURE LOC/G DIPLOM ECO/TAC ADJUD CT/SYS LEAD WEALTH...CHARTS T 20 COM/PARTY. PAGE 27 H0546 — NAT/G MARXISM POL/PAR EX/STRUC

B62
EBENSTEIN W.,TWO WAYS OF LIFE. USA+45 CULTURE ECO/DEV PLAN EDU/PROP CONTROL ORD/FREE...GOV/COMP IDEA/COMP T 20 MARX/KARL ENGELS/F LENIN/VI LOCKE/JOHN MILL/JS. PAGE 44 H0885 — MARXISM POPULISM ECO/TAC DIPLOM

B62
GOURE L.,CIVIL DEFENSE IN THE SOVIET UNION. COM USA+45 USSR MUNIC NAT/G DETER ATTIT MARXISM ...NAT/COMP 20 CIV/DEFENS. PAGE 59 H1188 — PLAN FORCES WAR COERCE

B62
HUCKER C.O.,CHINA: A CRITICAL BIBLIOGRAPHY (PAMPHLET). ASIA STRUCT AGRI FINAN INDUS HABITAT MARXISM...EPIST HUM. PAGE 74 H1487 — BIBLIOG/A CULTURE INTELL SOCIETY

B62
KINDERSLEY R.,THE FIRST RUSSIAN REVISIONISTS. COM USSR LAW ELITES INTELL NAT/G LEGIS ECO/TAC EDU/PROP CONTROL LEAD GP/REL SOCISM 19/20 MARX/KARL BOLSHEVISM. PAGE 86 H1712 — CONSTN MARXISM POPULISM BIOG

B62
KIRPICEVA I.K.,HANDBUCH DER RUSSISCHEN UND SOWJETISCHEN BIBLIOGRAPHIEN (5 VOLS.). USSR STRUCT ECO/DEV DIPLOM LEAD ATTIT 18/20. PAGE 86 H1726 — BIBLIOG/A NAT/G MARXISM COM

B62
LAQUEUR W.,THE FUTURE OF COMMUNIST SOCIETY. CHINA/COM USSR LAW ECO/DEV NAT/G POL/PAR PLAN PROB/SOLV DIPLOM LEAD...POLICY CONCPT IDEA/COMP ANTHOL 20. PAGE 91 H1820 — MARXISM COM FUT SOCIETY

B62
LAQUEUR W.,POLYCENTRISM. CHINA/COM COM USSR WOR+45 INT/ORG NAT/G ECO/TAC DOMIN LEAD ATTIT PWR SOVEREIGN...ANTHOL 20. PAGE 91 H1821 — MARXISM DIPLOM BAL/PWR POLICY

B62
LITT T.,FREIHEIT UND LEBENS ORDNUNG. COM NAT/G ATTIT KNOWL...POLICY 20. PAGE 97 H1942 — ORD/FREE MARXISM CONCPT IDEA/COMP

B62
MEHNERT K.,SOVIET MAN AND HIS WORLD. COM USSR INTELL FAM WORKER PLAN EDU/PROP REV PRODUC MARXISM ...SOC TREND SOC/INTEG 20 LENIN/VI STALIN/J KHRUSH/N. PAGE 108 H2162 — SOCIETY CULTURE ECO/DEV

B62
MEYER A.G.,LENINISM. USSR STRUCT NAT/G CAP/ISM LEAD WAR PWR SOVEREIGN...BIBLIOG 20 LENIN/VI. PAGE 109 H2187 — POL/PAR REV MARXISM PHIL/SCI

B62
STARR R.E.,POLAND 1944-1962: THE SOVIETIZATION OF A CAPTIVE PEOPLE. COM POLAND USSR POL/PAR SECT LEGIS DIPLOM DOMIN EDU/PROP CHOOSE ORD/FREE...POLICY CHARTS BIBLIOG 20. PAGE 149 H2973 — MARXISM NAT/G TOTALISM NAT/COMP

B62
SWAYZE H.,POLITICAL CONTROL OF LITERATURE IN THE USSR, 1946-1959. USSR NAT/G CREATE LICENSE...JURID 20. PAGE 151 H3014 — MARXISM WRITING CONTROL DOMIN

B62
WALSTON H.,AGRICULTURE UNDER COMMUNISM. CHINA/COM COM PROB/SOLV HAPPINESS RIGID/FLEX...POLICY METH/COMP 20. PAGE 165 H3295 — AGRI MARXISM PLAN CREATE

B62
WHITING K.R.,THE SOVIET UNION TODAY: A CONCISE HANDBOOK. USSR ELITES AGRI INDUS POL/PAR FORCES DIPLOM EDU/PROP LEAD...GEOG TREND 19/20. PAGE 168 H3354 — NAT/G ATTIT MARXISM POLICY

B62
YU LIEN YEN CHIU,INDEX TO THE CLASSIFIED FILES ON COMMUNIST CHINA. CHINA/COM CULTURE ECO/UNDEV CIVMIL/REL PWR WEALTH MARXISM...PSY SOC METH 20. PAGE 172 H3440 — BIBLIOG INDEX COM

B62
ZINKIN T.,REPORTING INDIA. INDIA PAKISTAN WOR+45 SOCIETY SECT FORCES EDU/PROP CROWD DISCRIM NAT/LISM MARXISM...POLICY 20. PAGE 173 H3457 — STRATA COLONIAL BAL/PWR CONTROL

S62
ANSPRENGER F.,"NATIONALISM, COMMUNISM, AND THE UNCOMMITTED NATIONS: AMERICAN PROFILES." FUT ISLAM CULTURE SOCIETY ECO/UNDEV NAT/G POL/PAR PLAN ECO/TAC EDU/PROP COERCE CHOOSE ALL/VALS MARXISM SOCISM...SOC CONCPT BIOG TREND 20. PAGE 7 H0142 — AFR COM NAT/LISM

S62
HYDE D.,"COMMUNISM IN LATIN AMERICA." L/A+17C ECO/DEV NAT/G SECT EDU/PROP ATTIT ALL/VALS MARXISM ...SOC CONCPT TOT/POP COLD/WAR OAS 20. PAGE 76 H1515 — COM POL/PAR REV

S62
IOVTCHOUK M.T.,"ON SOME THEORETICAL PRINCIPLES AND METHODS OF SOCIOLOGICAL INVESTIGATIONS (IN RUSSIAN)." FUT USA+45 STRATA R+D NAT/G POL/PAR TOP/EX ACT/RES PLAN ECO/TAC EDU/PROP ROUTINE ATTIT RIGID/FLEX MARXISM SOCISM...MARXIST METH/CNCPT OBS TREND NAT/COMP GEN/LAWS 20. PAGE 78 H1564 — COM ECO/DEV CAP/ISM USSR

S62
LONDON K.,"SINO-SOVIET RELATIONS IN THE CONTEXT OF THE 'WORLD SOCIALIST SYSTEM'." ASIA CHINA/COM COM USSR INT/ORG NAT/G TOP/EX BAL/PWR DIPLOM DOMIN ATTIT PERCEPT RIGID/FLEX PWR MARXISM...METH/CNCPT TREND 20. PAGE 98 H1957 — DELIB/GP CONCPT SOCISM

S62
PISTRAK L.,"SOVIET VIEWS ON AFRICA." AFR COM FUT ISLAM USSR INTELL STRUCT KIN POL/PAR PLAN EDU/PROP RIGID/FLEX PWR MARXISM...TIME/SEQ WORK TOT/POP 20. PAGE 126 H2516 — NAT/G ATTIT SOCISM

S62
SHATTEN F.,"POLYCENTRISM: AFRICA: NATIONALISM AND COMMUNISM." ASIA COM FUT ISLAM CULTURE SOCIETY ECO/UNDEV NAT/G PLAN DOMIN COLONIAL COERCE CHOOSE RIGID/FLEX ALL/VALS MARXISM...CONCPT TREND 20. PAGE 143 H2852 — AFR ATTIT NAT/LISM SOCISM

S62
STRACHEY J.,"COMMUNIST INTENTIONS." ASIA USSR YUGOSLAVIA INT/ORG NAT/G FORCES DOMIN EDU/PROP COERCE NUC/PWR NAT/LISM PEACE RIGID/FLEX PWR MARXISM...CONCPT MYTH OBS TIME/SEQ TREND COLD/WAR TOT/POP 20. PAGE 150 H2992 — COM ATTIT WAR

B63
BERLIN I.,KARL MARX, HIS LIFE AND ENVIRONMENT (3RD ED.). MOD/EUR USSR INTELL EDU/PROP PARTIC REV ATTIT 19 MARX/KARL. PAGE 15 H0307 — BIOG PERSON MARXISM CONCPT

B63
CHEN N.-R.,THE ECONOMY OF MAINLAND CHINA, 1949-1963: A BIBLIOGRAPHY OF MATERIALS IN ENGLISH. CHINA/COM ECO/UNDEV PRESS 20. PAGE 29 H0586 — BIBLIOG MARXISM NAT/G ASIA

B63
CHOU S.H.,THE CHINESE INFLATION 1937-1949. ASIA SOCIETY POL/PAR FOR/AID INT/TRADE BAL/PAY WEALTH MARXISM...STAT CHARTS 20 COM/PARTY GOLD/STAND. PAGE 30 H0597 — FINAN ECO/TAC BUDGET NAT/G

B63
CRANKSHAW E.,THE NEW COLD WAR: MOSCOW V. PEKIN. CHINA/COM USSR INTELL POL/PAR DELIB/GP CAP/ISM COERCE REV NAT/LISM TOTALISM DRIVE...POLICY — ATTIT DIPLOM NAT/COMP

IDEA/COMP 20 KHRUSH/N. PAGE 35 H0698
MARXISM

B63
HAMM H.,ALBANIA - CHINA'S BEACHHEAD IN EUROPE. ALBANIA CHINA/COM USSR YUGOSLAVIA ELITES SOCIETY POL/PAR DELIB/GP FORCES ECO/TAC COERCE ISOLAT PEACE MARXISM...IDEA/COMP 20 MAO. PAGE 65 H1304
DIPLOM REV NAT/G POLICY

B63
HOLLANDER P.,THE NEW MAN AND HIS ENEMIES: A STUDY OF THE STALINIST CONCEPTIONS OF GOOD AND EVIL PERSONIFIED (DOCTORAL THESIS). USSR SOCIETY ECO/DEV NAT/G EDU/PROP WRITING...SOC STERTYP BIBLIOG 20 STALIN/J. PAGE 73 H1455
CONTROL ATTIT TOTALISM MARXISM

B63
HUGHES A.J.,EAST AFRICA: THE SEARCH FOR UNITY- KENYA, TANGANYIKA, UGANDA, AND ZANZIBAR. TANZANIA UGANDA CONSTN POL/PAR SECT CHIEF DELIB/GP LEGIS WAR CHOOSE NAT/LISM MARXISM...POLICY CHARTS 20 NEGRO UN. PAGE 74 H1488
NAT/G DOMIN LOC/G AFR

B63
HYDE D.,THE PEACEFUL ASSAULT. COM UAR USSR ECO/DEV ECO/UNDEV NAT/G POL/PAR CAP/ISM PWR 20. PAGE 76 H1516
MARXISM CONTROL ECO/TAC DIPLOM

B63
LAVROFF D.-G.,LES LIBERTES PUBLIQUES EN UNION SOVIETIQUE (REV. ED.). USSR NAT/G WORKER SANCTION CRIME MARXISM NEW/LIB...JURID BIBLIOG WORSHIP 20. PAGE 92 H1843
ORD/FREE LAW ATTIT COM

B63
LETHBRIDGE H.J.,THE PEASANT AND THE COMMUNES. CHINA/COM COM USSR NEIGH PROB/SOLV ADJUST EFFICIENCY...POLICY METH/COMP NAT/COMP 20. PAGE 95 H1894
MARXISM ECO/TAC AGRI WORKER

B63
MILLER W.J.,THE MEANING OF COMMUNISM. USSR SOCIETY ECO/DEV EX/STRUC WORKER TEC/DEV ADMIN TOTALISM ...POLICY CONCPT CHARTS BIBLIOG T 20 COLD/WAR LENIN/VI STALIN/J. PAGE 111 H2215
MARXISM TRADIT DIPLOM NAT/G

B63
MOSELY P.E.,THE SOVIET UNION, 1922-1962: A FOREIGN AFFAIRS READER. ASIA POLAND USSR CULTURE INTELL AGRI POL/PAR WORKER INT/TRADE DOMIN WAR NAT/LISM MARXISM SOCISM 20 KHRUSH/N. PAGE 113 H2267
PWR POLICY DIPLOM

B63
STRAUSS L.,HISTORY OF POLITICAL PHILOSOPHY. LAW SOCIETY CAP/ISM MARXISM 19 AQUINAS/T BACON/F HEGEL/GWF MILL/JS NIETZSCH/F. PAGE 150 H2995
IDEA/COMP PHIL/SCI ANTHOL

B63
SWEARER H.R.,CONTEMPORARY COMMUNISM: THEORY AND PRACTICE. COM USSR SOCIETY ECO/DEV POL/PAR FORCES PLAN ADMIN LEAD NAT/LISM...POLICY ANTHOL 20 LENIN/VI COM/PARTY. PAGE 151 H3015
MARXISM CONCPT DIPLOM NAT/G

B63
TUCKER R.C.,THE SOVIET POLITICAL MIND. COM INTELL NAT/G TOP/EX EDU/PROP ADMIN COERCE TOTALISM ATTIT PWR MARXISM...PSY MYTH HYPO/EXP 20. PAGE 157 H3136
STRUCT RIGID/FLEX ELITES USSR

S63
HARRIS R.L.,"COMMUNISM AND ASIA: ILLUSIONS AND MISCONCEPTIONS." ASIA COM FUT S/ASIA ECO/UNDEV AGRI NAT/G POL/PAR EX/STRUC EDU/PROP COERCE ATTIT MARXISM COLD/WAR TOT/POP 20. PAGE 67 H1344
PWR GUERRILLA

S63
ROGIN M.,"ROUSSEAU IN AFRICA." AFR MARXISM POPULISM SOCISM 20 ROUSSEAU/J. PAGE 133 H2661
IDEA/COMP CULTURE CONSTN ORD/FREE

B64
AFRO ASIAN SOLIDARITY AGAINST IMPERIALISM. AFR ISLAM S/ASIA ECO/UNDEV NAT/G POL/PAR TOP/EX PRESS ...INT ANTHOL 20 CHOU/ENLAI. PAGE 2 H0043
MARXISM DIPLOM EDU/PROP CHIEF

B64
BRZEZINSKI Z.,POLITICAL POWER: USA/USSR. USA+45 USSR AGRI POL/PAR FORCES CREATE CHOOSE ATTIT ORD/FREE PWR MARXISM...MYTH 20 KENNEDY/JF. PAGE 23 H0457
NAT/G NAT/COMP POLICY LEAD

B64
BUTWELL R.,SOUTHEAST ASIA TODAY - AND TOMORROW. NAT/G COLONIAL LEAD REGION WAR CHOOSE WEALTH MARXISM 20. PAGE 25 H0500
S/ASIA DIPLOM ECO/UNDEV NAT/LISM

B64
CAUTE D.,COMMUNISM AND THE FRENCH INTELLECTUALS, 1914-1960. COM EUR+WWI MOD/EUR NAT/G PERF/ART PROF/ORG CREATE EDU/PROP ATTIT PERSON KNOWL MARXISM ...SOC TIME/SEQ MARX/KARL 20 MALRAUX/A GIDE/A SARTRE/J. PAGE 28 H0563
POL/PAR INTELL

B64
COWAN L.G.,THE DILEMMAS OF AFRICAN INDEPENDENCE. AFR INDUS NAT/G SECT DIPLOM ECO/TAC REGION MARXISM ...CHARTS BIBLIOG 20 MAPS. PAGE 34 H0683
ORD/FREE COLONIAL REV ECO/UNDEV

B64
DANIELS R.V.,RUSSIA. RUSSIA USSR STRUCT NAT/LISM TOTALISM ORD/FREE WEALTH...POLICY DECISION TREND. PAGE 37 H0740
MARXISM REV ECO/DEV DIPLOM

B64
DEL VAYO J.A.,CHINA TRIUMPHS. CHINA/COM CULTURE DIPLOM HEALTH 20. PAGE 39 H0787
MARXISM CREATE ORD/FREE POLICY

B64
DOOLIN D.J.,COMMUNIST CHINA: THE POLITICS OF STUDENT OPPOSITION. CHINA/COM ELITES STRATA ACADEM NAT/G WRITING CT/SYS LEAD PARTIC COERCE TOTALISM 20. PAGE 42 H0838
MARXISM DEBATE AGE/Y PWR

B64
EMBREE A.T.,A GUIDE TO PAPERBACKS ON ASIA; SELECTED AND ANNOTATED (PAMPHLET). CULTURE SOCIETY ECO/UNDEV SECT DIPLOM COLONIAL MARXISM...SOC 20. PAGE 46 H0913
BIBLIOG/A ASIA S/ASIA NAT/G

B64
FAINSOD M.,HOW RUSSIA IS RULED (REV. ED.). RUSSIA USSR AGRI PROC/MFG LABOR POL/PAR EX/STRUC CONTROL PWR...POLICY BIBLIOG 19/20 KHRUSH/N COM/PARTY. PAGE 48 H0963
NAT/G REV MARXISM

B64
FISCHER L.,THE LIFE OF LENIN. USSR LEAD REV WAR ...SOC 19/20 LENIN/VI COM/PARTY BOLSHEVISM. PAGE 51 H1011
BIOG MARXISM PERSON CHIEF

B64
FROMM E.,MARX'S CONCEPT OF MAN. LABOR OWN PERSON ...HUM IDEA/COMP GEN/LAWS 17 MARX/KARL EUROPE SPINOZA/B GOETHE/J HEGEL/GWF. PAGE 54 H1072
INGP/REL CONCPT MARXISM SOCISM

B64
GILLY A.,INSIDE THE CUBAN REVOLUTION. CUBA AGRI INDUS LABOR CREATE DIPLOM...METH/COMP 20. PAGE 56 H1129
REV PLAN MARXISM ECO/UNDEV

B64
GRIFFITH W.E.,COMMUNISM IN EUROPE (2 VOLS.). CZECHOSLVK USSR WOR+45 WOR-45 YUGOSLAVIA INGP/REL MARXISM SOCISM...ANTHOL 20 EUROPE/E. PAGE 61 H1225
COM POL/PAR DIPLOM GOV/COMP

B64
GUMPLOWICZ L.,RECHTSSTAAT UND SOZIALISMUS. STRATA ORD/FREE SOVEREIGN MARXISM...IDEA/COMP 16/20 KANT/I HOBBES/T. PAGE 62 H1251
JURID NAT/G SOCISM CONCPT

B64
HALPERN J.M.,GOVERNMENT, POLITICS, AND SOCIAL STRUCTURE IN LAOS. LAOS CULTURE SOCIETY STRATA STRUCT FAM DIPLOM DOMIN MARXISM...INT GOV/COMP WORSHIP SOC/INTEG 20. PAGE 65 H1297
NAT/G SOC LOC/G

B64
KIS T.I.,LES PAYS DE L'EUROPE DE L'EST: LEURS RAPPORTS MUTUELS ET LE PROBLEME DE LEUR INTEGRATION DANS L'ORBITE DE L'USSR. EUR+WWI RUSSIA USSR INT/ORG NAT/G REV ATTIT...JURID SOC BIBLIOG WARSAW/P COMECON EUROPE/E. PAGE 86 H1727
DIPLOM COM MARXISM REGION

B64
KOLARZ W.,BOOKS ON COMMUNISM. USSR WOR+45 CULTURE NAT/G POL/PAR DIPLOM LEAD...CONCPT GOV/COMP IDEA/COMP. PAGE 88 H1752
BIBLIOG/A SOCIETY COM MARXISM

B64
LAPENNA I.,STATE AND LAW: SOVIET AND YUGOSLAV THEORY. USSR YUGOSLAVIA STRATA STRUCT NAT/G DOMIN COERCE MARXISM...GOV/COMP IDEA/COMP 20. PAGE 91 H1812
JURID COM LAW SOVEREIGN

B64
LATOURETTE K.S.,CHINA. ASIA CHINA/COM FUT USSR ECO/UNDEV ECO/TAC WAR 19/20. PAGE 92 H1838
MARXISM NAT/G POLICY DIPLOM

B64
MARTINET G.,MARXISM OF OUR TIME: OR THE CONTRADICTIONS OF SOCIALISM. FRANCE NAT/G OPTIMAL RIGID/FLEX SOCISM...IDEA/COMP 20. PAGE 103 H2067
MARXISM MARXIST PROB/SOLV CREATE

B64
MARTINEZ J.R.,THREE CASES OF COMMUNISM: CUBA, BRAZIL, AND MEXICO. BRAZIL CUBA L/A+17C CONSTN NAT/G DIPLOM ECO/TAC GP/REL INGP/REL...GP/COMP BIBLIOG 20 MEXIC/AMER COM/PARTY. PAGE 103 H2068
MARXISM BIOG REV NAT/COMP

B64
MILIBAND R.,THE SOCIALIST REGISTER: 1964. GERMANY/W ITALY UK LABOR POL/PAR ECO/TAC FOR/AID NUC/PWR ...POLICY SOCIALIST IDEA/COMP 20 MAO NASSER/G. PAGE 110 H2204
MARXISM SOCISM CAP/ISM PROB/SOLV

B64
QUIGG P.W.,AFRICA: A FOREIGN AFFAIRS READER. AFR FRANCE PORTUGAL UK DIPLOM LEAD PARL/PROC MARXISM ...MAJORIT METH/CNCPT GOV/COMP IDEA/COMP ANTHOL 19/20. PAGE 129 H2575
COLONIAL SOVEREIGN NAT/LISM RACE/REL

B64
RESHETAR J.S. JR.,A CONCISE HISTORY OF THE COMMUNIST PARTY OF THE SOVIET UNION (REV. ED.). COM
CHIEF POL/PAR

USSR NAT/G EXEC 19/20 LENIN/VI STALIN/J KHRUSH/N. PAGE 131 H2618 — MARXISM PWR

B64

SIEKANOWICZ P.,LEGAL SOURCES AND BIBLIOGRAPHY OF POLAND. COM POLAND CONSTN NAT/G PARL/PROC SANCTION CRIME MARXISM 16/20. PAGE 143 H2870 — BIBLIOG ADJUD LAW JURID

B64

UTECHIN S.V.,RUSSIAN POLITICAL THOUGHT: A CONCISE HISTORY. RUSSIA USSR INTELL STRATA POL/PAR SECT LEGIS EDU/PROP REV WAR MARXISM...ANARCH BIBLIOG 9/20 REFORMERS SLAVS. PAGE 161 H3218 — IDEA/COMP ATTIT ALL/IDEOS NAT/G

B64

VON STEIN L.J.,THE HISTORY OF THE SOCIAL MOVEMENT IN FRANCE, 1789-1850 (TRANS. BY K. MENGELBERG). COM FRANCE MOD/EUR NAT/G EX/STRUC INGP/REL ALL/IDEOS CONSERVE MARXISM...SOC BIBLIOG 18/19. PAGE 164 H3278 — REV STRATA

S64

HORECKY P.L.,"LIBRARY OF CONGRESS PUBLICATIONS IN AID OF USSR AND EAST EUROPEAN RESEARCH." BULGARIA CZECHOSLVK POLAND USSR YUGOSLAVIA NAT/G POL/PAR DIPLOM ADMIN GOV/REL...CLASSIF 20. PAGE 73 H1468 — BIBLIOG/A COM MARXISM

S64

LERNER W.,"THE HISTORICAL ORIGINS OF THE SOVIET DOCTRINE OF PEACEFUL COEXISTENCE." COM USSR INT/ORG NAT/G VOL/ASSN PLAN PEACE ATTIT RIGID/FLEX PWR MARXISM...TIME/SEQ COLD/WAR 20. PAGE 95 H1891 — EDU/PROP DIPLOM

S64

SOLOVEYTCHIK G.,"BOOKS ON RUSSIA." USSR ELITES NAT/G PERF/ART REV GOV/REL MARXISM...AUD/VIS 20. PAGE 147 H2929 — BIBLIOG/A COM CULTURE

C64

GOLDMAN M.I.,"COMPARATIVE ECONOMIC SYSTEMS: A READER." COM ECO/UNDEV NAT/G BUDGET CAP/ISM ADMIN TOTALISM MARXISM SOCISM...MGT ANTHOL BIBLIOG 19/20. PAGE 58 H1157 — NAT/COMP CONTROL IDEA/COMP

B65

AIR UNIVERSITY LIBRARY,LATIN AMERICA, SELECTED REFERENCES. ECO/UNDEV FORCES EDU/PROP MARXISM 20 OAS. PAGE 4 H0084 — BIBLIOG L/A+17C NAT/G DIPLOM

B65

BROCK C.,A GUIDE TO LIBRARY RESOURCES FOR POLITICAL SCIENCE STUDENTS AT THE UNIVERSITY OF NORTH CAROLINA (PAMPHLET). USA+45 WOR+45 PROVS ATTIT MARXISM...POLICY NAT/COMP UN. PAGE 21 H0422 — BIBLIOG/A DIPLOM NAT/G INT/ORG

B65

CHEN T.H.,THE CHINESE COMMUNIST REGIME: A DOCUMENTARY STUDY (2 VOLS.). CHINA/COM LAW CONSTN ELITES ECO/UNDEV LEGIS ECO/TAC ADMIN CONTROL PWR ...SOC 20. PAGE 29 H0587 — MARXISM POL/PAR NAT/G

B65

CHENG C.-Y.,SCIENTIFIC AND ENGINEERING MANPOWER IN COMMUNIST CHINA, 1949-1963. CHINA/COM USSR ELITES ECO/DEV R+D ACADEM LABOR NAT/G EDU/PROP CONTROL UTIL...POLICY BIBLIOG 20. PAGE 29 H0588 — WORKER CONSULT MARXISM BIOG

B65

COLLINS H.,KARL MARX AND THE BRITISH LABOR MOVEMENT, YEARS OF THE FIRST INTERNATIONAL. EUR+WWI MOD/EUR UK STRATA INDUS NAT/G POL/PAR SOCISM ...CONCPT 19/20 MARX/KARL. PAGE 32 H0633 — MARXISM LABOR INT/ORG WORKER

B65

COX R.H.,THE STATE IN INTERNATIONAL RELATIONS. INT/ORG DIPLOM REV WAR PEACE MARXISM...CONCPT GOV/COMP. PAGE 34 H0690 — SOVEREIGN NAT/G FASCISM ORD/FREE

B65

HALPERIN M.H.,COMMUNIST CHINA AND ARMS CONTROL. CHINA/COM FUT USA+45 CULTURE FORCES TEC/DEV ECO/TAC WAR PEACE ORD/FREE MARXISM 20 COLD/WAR. PAGE 64 H1292 — ATTIT POLICY ARMS/CONT NUC/PWR

B65

HAPGOOD D.,AFRICA: FROM INDEPENDENCE TO TOMARROW. AFR GUINEA SENEGAL CULTURE ELITES ECO/UNDEV AGRI SCHOOL FOR/AID COLONIAL MARXISM...TREND 20. PAGE 66 H1323 — ECO/TAC SOCIETY NAT/G

B65

JAIN S.C.,THE STATE AND AGRICULTURE. INDIA S/ASIA ECO/UNDEV PROB/SOLV CAP/ISM MARXISM SOCISM 20. PAGE 79 H1586 — NAT/G POLICY AGRI ECO/TAC

B65

JASNY H.,KHRUSHCHEV'S CROP POLICY. USSR ECO/DEV PLAN MARXISM...STAT 20 KHRUSH/N RESOURCE/N. PAGE 80 H1593 — AGRI NAT/G POLICY ECO/TAC

B65

JELAVICH C.,THE BALKANS. ALBANIA BULGARIA GREECE ROMANIA YUGOSLAVIA ECO/UNDEV WAR SOVEREIGN MARXISM 6/20. PAGE 80 H1597 — NAT/LISM NAT/G

B65

JOHNSON P.,KHRUSHCHEV AND THE ARTS: POLITICS OF SOVIET CULTURE, 1962-1964. COM USSR NAT/G PERF/ART CONFER DEBATE GP/REL PERS/REL UTIL ATTIT DRIVE 20 KHRUSH/N. PAGE 81 H1626 — CULTURE MARXISM POLICY CHIEF

B65

KOUSOULAS D.G.,REVOLUTION AND DEFEAT; THE STORY OF THE GREEK COMMUNIST PARTY. GREECE INT/ORG EX/STRUC DIPLOM FOR/AID EDU/PROP PARL/PROC ADJUST ATTIT 20 COM/PARTY. PAGE 88 H1759 — REV MARXISM POL/PAR ORD/FREE

B65

MENON K.P.S.,MANY WORLDS. INDIA BAL/PWR CAP/ISM COLONIAL REV ORD/FREE PWR MARXISM...POLICY 20 COLD/WAR. PAGE 109 H2176 — BIOG DIPLOM NAT/G

B65

MOORE C.H.,TUNISIA SINCE INDEPENDENCE. ELITES LOC/G POL/PAR ADMIN COLONIAL CONTROL EXEC GOV/REL TOTALISM MARXISM...INT 20 TUNIS. PAGE 112 H2248 — NAT/G EX/STRUC SOCISM

B65

O'BRIEN F.,CRISIS IN WORLD COMMUNISM* MARXISM IN SEARCH OF EFFICIENCY. COM ECO/DEV PLAN INT/TRADE WAR ADJUST PEACE...STAT TIME/SEQ GOV/COMP NAT/COMP COLD/WAR. PAGE 119 H2384 — MARXISM USSR DRIVE EFFICIENCY

B65

OBUKAR C.,THE MODERN AFRICAN. AGRI INDUS WORKER CAP/ISM EDU/PROP PARTIC RACE/REL NAT/LISM ALL/VALS MARXISM...SOC IDEA/COMP 20. PAGE 120 H2393 — AFR ECO/UNDEV CULTURE SOVEREIGN

B65

ONUOHA B.,THE ELEMENTS OF AFRICAN SOCIALISM. AFR FINAN SECT TEC/DEV FOR/AID GP/REL OWN LAISSEZ MARXISM...CONCPT BIBLIOG 20. PAGE 121 H2419 — SOCISM ECO/UNDEV NAT/G EX/STRUC

B65

PUNDEEF M.V.,BULGARIA; A BIBLIOGRAPHIC GUIDE. BULGARIA LAW CULTURE INTELL ECO/DEV LEAD MARXISM 20. PAGE 128 H2566 — BIBLIOG/A NAT/G COM SOCISM

B65

RANDALL F.B.,STALIN'S RUSSIA. USSR STRUCT AGRI NAT/G PLAN DIPLOM WAR TOTALISM MARXISM...BIBLIOG/A 19/20 STALIN/J. PAGE 129 H2590 — BIOG INDUS ECO/DEV

B65

ROMEIN J.,THE ASIAN CENTURY. ASIA COM S/ASIA DIPLOM COLONIAL TIME 20. PAGE 133 H2666 — REV NAT/LISM CULTURE MARXISM

B65

ROSENBERG A.,DEMOCRACY AND SOCIALISM. COM EUR+WWI FRANCE MOD/EUR STRUCT INT/ORG NAT/G POL/PAR TOP/EX EDU/PROP COERCE PERSON PWR FASCISM MARXISM...CONCPT TIME/SEQ MARX/KARL 19/20. PAGE 134 H2677 — ATTIT

B65

SALVADORI M.,ITALY. AUSTRIA FRANCE GERMANY ITALY SPAIN CULTURE NAT/G POL/PAR DIPLOM WAR FASCISM LAISSEZ MARXISM...TIME/SEQ CHARTS BIBLIOG/A. PAGE 137 H2744 — NAT/LISM CATHISM SOCIETY

B65

SCALAPINO R.A.,THE COMMUNIST REVOLUTION IN ASIA* TACTICS, GOALS, AND ACHIEVEMENTS. INDIA INTELL POL/PAR FORCES DOMIN EDU/PROP LEGIT COERCE REV ATTIT CHINJAP. PAGE 138 H2763 — ASIA S/ASIA MARXISM NAT/COMP

B65

TUTSCH H.E.,FACETS OF ARAB NATIONALISM. ISLAM ISRAEL CULTURE STRUCT SECT RIGID/FLEX ORD/FREE MARXISM SOCISM 20. PAGE 157 H3143 — ECO/UNDEV NAT/LISM TEC/DEV SOCIETY

B65

WOLFE B.D.,MARXISM; ONE HUNDRED YEARS IN THE LIFE OF A DOCTRINE. USSR WAR NAT/LISM PEACE TOTALISM ...MAJORIT 20 MARX/KARL. PAGE 170 H3399 — MARXISM LEAD ATTIT

L65

HOUN F.S.,"THE COMMUNIST MONOLITH VERSUS THE CHINESE TRADITION." CULTURE INTELL SOCIETY STRUCT DOMIN GP/REL ORD/FREE CONSERVE PLURISM...GOV/COMP WORSHIP. PAGE 74 H1479 — ASIA MARXISM TOTALISM

S65

MARK M.,"MUST WE FIGHT SOCIAL REVOLUTIONS OF THE LEFT?" L/A+17C USA+45 ECO/UNDEV DIPLOM ADJUST PERCEPT...IDEA/COMP NAT/COMP. PAGE 103 H2053 — NAT/LISM REV MARXISM CREATE

S65

PLANK J.N.,"THE CARIBBEAN* INTERVENTION, WHEN AND HOW." CUBA GUATEMALA HAITI PANAMA USA+45 VENEZUELA FORCES PROB/SOLV RISK COERCE...NAT/COMP OAS TIME. PAGE 126 H2521 — SOVEREIGN MARXISM REV

S65

SANDERS R.,"MASS SUPPORT AND COMMUNIST INSURRECTION." GREECE MALAYSIA PHILIPPINE VIETNAM STRUCT ECO/UNDEV POL/PAR FORCES CREATE REV ...GP/COMP IDEA/COMP. PAGE 138 H2751 — GUERRILLA MARXISM GOV/COMP

S65

STAROBIN J.R.,"COMMUNISM IN WESTERN EUROPE." FRANCE GERMANY ITALY USA+45 USSR ECO/DEV FEDERAL PEACE ATTIT DRIVE PWR TREND. PAGE 149 H2972 — MARXISM EUR+WWI POL/PAR NAT/COMP

B66

BRACKMAN A.C.,SOUTHEAST ASIA'S SECOND FRONT: THE POWER STRUGGLE IN THE MALAY ARCHIPELAGO. CHINA/COM INDONESIA MALAYSIA ECO/UNDEV INT/ORG NAT/G FORCES DIPLOM EDU/PROP REGION COERCE GUERRILLA AUTHORIT — S/ASIA MARXISM REV

POPULISM...MAJORIT 20 KENNEDY/JF SEATO. PAGE 20 H0396

B66
BRODERSEN A.,THE SOVIET WORKER: LABOR AND GOVERNMENT IN SOVIET SOCIETY. USSR STRUCT INDUS LABOR PLAN PAY INGP/REL PRODUC...POLICY GEN/LAWS BIBLIOG 20 STALIN/J LENIN/VI BOLSHEVISM KHRUSH/N. PAGE 21 H0425
WORKER ROLE NAT/G MARXISM

B66
BROWN J.F.,THE NEW EASTERN EUROPE. ALBANIA BULGARIA HUNGARY POLAND ROMANIA CULTURE AGRI POL/PAR WAR NAT/LISM MARXISM...CHARTS BIBLIOG 20. PAGE 22 H0444
DIPLOM COM NAT/G ECO/UNDEV

B66
BUKHARIN N.,THE ABC OF COMMUNISM: A POPULAR EXPLANATION OF THE PROGRAM OF THE COMMUNIST PARTY OF RUSSIA. USSR STRATA SECT FORCES WORKER CAP/ISM RECEIVE EDU/PROP NAT/LISM TOTALISM 20. PAGE 23 H0468
MARXISM CONCPT POLICY REV

B66
CHANG,THE PARTY AND THE NATIONAL QUESTION IN CHINA (TRANS. BY GEORGE MOSELEY). CHINA/COM CULTURE CONTROL NAT/LISM...CHARTS BIBLIOG/A 20. PAGE 29 H0576
GP/REL REGION ISOLAT MARXISM

B66
COLE G.D.H.,THE MEANING OF MARXISM. USSR WOR+45 STRATA STRUCT NAT/G WORKER COST FASCISM...IDEA/COMP 20. PAGE 31 H0625
MARXISM CONCPT HIST/WRIT CAP/ISM

B66
DALLIN A.,POLITICS IN THE SOVIET UNION: 7 CASES. COM USSR LAW POL/PAR CHIEF FORCES WRITING CONTROL PARL/PROC CIVMIL/REL TOTALISM...ANTHOL 20 KHRUSH/N STALIN/J CASEBOOK COM/PARTY. PAGE 37 H0736
MARXISM DOMIN ORD/FREE GOV/REL

B66
DEUTSCHER I.,STALIN: A POLITICAL BIOGRAPHY. EUR+WWI USSR POL/PAR FORCES DIPLOM ADMIN LEAD REV WAR TOTALISM PERSON 20 STALIN/J ROOSEVLT/F LENIN/VI HITLER/A. PAGE 40 H0807
BIOG MARXISM TOP/EX PWR

B66
DOBB M.,SOVIET ECONOMIC DEVELOPMENT SINCE 1917. USSR ECO/DEV ECO/UNDEV LABOR NAT/G TEC/DEV ECO/TAC ROUTINE PRODUC MARXISM 20. PAGE 41 H0829
PLAN INDUS WORKER

B66
EPSTEIN F.T.,THE AMERICAN BIBLIOGRAPHY OF RUSSIAN AND EAST EUROPEAN STUDIES FOR 1964. USSR LOC/G NAT/G POL/PAR FORCES ADMIN ARMS/CONT...JURID CONCPT 20 UN. PAGE 47 H0933
BIBLIOG COM MARXISM DIPLOM

B66
FITZGERALD C.P.,A CONCISE HISTORY OF EAST ASIA. ASIA KOREA S/ASIA INT/TRADE REGION MARXISM 20 CHINJAP. PAGE 51 H1017
ECO/UNDEV COLONIAL CULTURE

B66
FITZGERALD C.P.,THE BIRTH OF COMMUNIST CHINA (2ND ED.). ASIA CHINA/COM STRUCT BAL/PWR DIPLOM ECO/TAC INT/TRADE WEALTH 20. PAGE 51 H1018
REV MARXISM ECO/UNDEV

B66
FORD P.,CARDINAL MORAN AND THE A. L. P. NAT/G POL/PAR SECT DELIB/GP LOBBY REV CHOOSE ORD/FREE MARXISM 19/20 AUSTRAL PROTESTANT LABOR/PAR. PAGE 52 H1035
CATHISM SOCISM LABOR SOCIETY

B66
FRIEDRICH C.J.,REVOLUTION: NOMOS VIII. NAT/G SOCISM ...OBS TREND IDEA/COMP ANTHOL 18/20. PAGE 54 H1070
REV MARXISM CONCPT DIPLOM

B66
HERMANN F.G.,DER KAMPF GEGEN RELIGION UND KIRCHE IN DER SOWJETISCHEN BESATZUNGSZONE DEUTSCHLANDS. GERMANY/E EDU/PROP ATTIT PERSON MORAL MARXISM 20 LENIN/VI STALIN/J KHRUSH/N. PAGE 70 H1400
SECT ORD/FREE GP/REL NAT/G

B66
HINTON W.,FANSHEN: A DOCUMENTARY OF REVOLUTION IN A CHINESE VILLAGE. ASIA ELITES MUNIC NAT/G POL/PAR SECT WORKER LEAD WAR PRIVIL PWR 20 MAO. PAGE 71 H1422
MARXISM REV NEIGH OWN

B66
INTL CONF ON WORLD POLITICS-5,EASTERN EUROPE IN TRANSITION. EUR+WWI USSR ECO/TAC NAT/LISM ATTIT SOVEREIGN...CHARTS ANTHOL 20 TREATY WARSAW/P. PAGE 78 H1562
COM NAT/COMP MARXISM DIPLOM

B66
JACKSON G.D.,COMINTERN AND PEASANT IN EAST EUROPE 1919-1930. BULGARIA COM CZECHOSLVK EUR+WWI POLAND ROMANIA YUGOSLAVIA STRATA AGRI VOL/ASSN DIPLOM CONTROL CROWD WEALTH...POLICY NAT/COMP 20. PAGE 79 H1575
MARXISM ECO/UNDEV WORKER INT/ORG

B66
LEIBLER I.,SOVIET JEWRY AND HUMAN RIGHTS. USSR INTELL NAT/G DOMIN ATTIT 20 AUSTRAL JEWS. PAGE 93 H1865
DISCRIM RACE/REL MARXISM POL/PAR

B66
LEONTIEF W.,ESSAYS IN ECONOMICS. ECO/UNDEV INDUS NAT/G CAP/ISM FOR/AID AUTOMAT MARXISM...ECOMETRIC CHARTS ANTHOL METH 20 KEYNES/JM. PAGE 94 H1886
CONCPT METH/CNCPT METH/COMP

B66
MADAN G.R.,ECONOMIC THINKING IN INDIA. INDIA ECO/UNDEV AGRI FINAN INDUS LABOR PLAN CAP/ISM INT/TRADE MARXISM SOCISM...POLICY 1/20. PAGE 101 H2013
ECO/TAC PHIL/SCI NAT/G POL/PAR

B66
MAICHEL K.,CATALOG OF SOVIET AND RUSSIAN NEWSPAPERS AT THE HOOVER INSTITUTION OF WAR, REVOLUTION AND PEACE. USSR NAT/G EDU/PROP LEAD REV WAR PEACE ATTIT 19/20. PAGE 101 H2017
BIBLIOG/A PRESS COM MARXISM

B66
NIEDERGANG M.,LA REVOLUTION DE SAINT-DOMINGUE. DOMIN/REP INT/ORG NAT/G CONTROL LEAD GP/REL ORD/FREE MARXISM 20. PAGE 118 H2361
REV FORCES DIPLOM

B66
PAN S.,VIETNAM CRISIS. ASIA FRANCE USA+45 USA-45 VIETNAM CULTURE SOCIETY INT/ORG ECO/TAC AGREE CONTROL WAR MARXISM 20. PAGE 123 H2454
ECO/UNDEV POLICY DIPLOM NAT/COMP

B66
ROOS H.,A HISTORY OF MODERN POLAND FROM THE FOUNDATION OF THE STATE IN THE FIRST WORLD WAR TO THE PRESENT DAY. EUR+WWI POLAND INTELL SOCIETY ECO/TAC LEAD REV ATTIT ORD/FREE MARXISM...BIBLIOG 20 WWI PARTITION. PAGE 133 H2669
NAT/G WAR DIPLOM

B66
SAKAI R.K.,STUDIES ON ASIA, 1966. CEYLON INDIA USA-45 INDUS POL/PAR DIPLOM ECO/TAC MARXISM ...POLICY 19/20 CHINJAP. PAGE 137 H2738
SECT ECO/UNDEV

B66
SCHATTEN F.,COMMUNISM IN AFRICA. AFR GHANA GUINEA MALI CULTURE ECO/UNDEV LABOR SECT ECO/TAC EDU/PROP REV 20. PAGE 139 H2774
COLONIAL NAT/LISM MARXISM DIPLOM

B66
SCHRAM S.,MAO TSE-TUNG. ASIA CHINA/COM CONTROL REGION ATTIT...POLICY IDEA/COMP 20 MAO. PAGE 140 H2799
BIOG MARXISM TOP/EX GUERRILLA

B66
SCHURMANN F.,IDEOLOGY AND ORGANIZATION IN COMMUNIST CHINA. CHINA/COM LOC/G MUNIC POL/PAR ECO/TAC CONTROL ATTIT...MGT STERTYP 20 COM/PARTY. PAGE 140 H2805
MARXISM STRUCT ADMIN NAT/G

B66
SKILLING H.G.,THE GOVERNMENTS OF COMMUNIST EAST EUROPE. COM EUR+WWI ELITES FORCES DIPLOM ECO/TAC CONTROL HABITAT SOCISM...DECISION BIBLIOG 20 EUROPE/E COM/PARTY. PAGE 145 H2895
MARXISM NAT/COMP GP/COMP DOMIN

B66
THOMPSON J.M.,RUSSIA, BOLSHEVISM, AND THE VERSAILLES PEACE. RUSSIA USSR INT/ORG NAT/G DELIB/GP AGREE REV WAR PWR 20 TREATY VERSAILLES BOLSHEVISM. PAGE 154 H3083
DIPLOM PEACE MARXISM

B66
TYSON G.,NEHRU: THE YEARS OF POWER. INDIA UK STRATA ECO/UNDEV FINAN SECT TASK WAR ORD/FREE MARXISM ...POLICY BIBLIOG 20 NEHRU/J. PAGE 157 H3145
CHIEF PWR DIPLOM NAT/G

B66
US DEPARTMENT OF STATE,RESEARCH ON AFRICA (EXTERNAL RESEARCH LIST NO 5-25). LAW CULTURE ECO/UNDEV POL/PAR DIPLOM EDU/PROP LEAD REGION MARXISM...GEOG LING WORSHIP 20. PAGE 159 H3188
BIBLIOG/A ASIA S/ASIA NAT/G

B66
US DEPARTMENT OF STATE,RESEARCH ON THE AMERICAN REPUBLICS (EXTERNAL RESEARCH LIST NO 6-25). CULTURE SOCIETY POL/PAR DIPLOM EDU/PROP MARXISM WORSHIP 20 OAS. PAGE 159 H3189
BIBLIOG/A L/A+17C REGION NAT/G

B66
US DEPARTMENT OF STATE,RESEARCH ON THE USSR AND EASTERN EUROPE (EXTERNAL RESEARCH LIST NO 1-25). USSR LAW CULTURE SOCIETY NAT/G TEC/DEV DIPLOM EDU/PROP REGION...GEOG LING. PAGE 160 H3191
BIBLIOG/A EUR+WWI COM MARXISM

B66
US DEPARTMENT OF STATE,RESEARCH ON WESTERN EUROPE, GREAT BRITAIN, AND CANADA (EXTERNAL RESEARCH LIST NO 3-25). CANADA GERMANY/W UK LAW CULTURE NAT/G POL/PAR FORCES EDU/PROP REGION MARXISM...GEOG SOC WORSHIP 20 CMN/WLTH. PAGE 160 H3192
BIBLIOG/A EUR+WWI DIPLOM

B66
US DEPARTMENT OF THE ARMY,COMMUNIST CHINA: A STRATEGIC SURVEY: A BIBLIOGRAPHY (PAMPHLET NO. 20-67). CHINA/COM COM INDIA USSR NAT/G POL/PAR EX/STRUC FORCES NUC/PWR REV ATTIT...POLICY GEOG CHARTS. PAGE 160 H3194
BIBLIOG/A MARXISM S/ASIA DIPLOM

B66
VIEN N.C.,SEEKING THE TRUTH. VIETNAM DELIB/GP DOMIN RISK MARXISM 20 KY/NGUYEN. PAGE 162 H3250
NAT/G COLONIAL PWR SOVEREIGN

B66
WANG Y.C.,CHINESE INTELLECTUALS AND THE WEST 1872-1949. ASIA ELITES LEAD STRANGE ROLE MARXISM ...CHARTS 19/20. PAGE 165 H3301
INTELL EDU/PROP CULTURE SOCIETY

B66
WUEST J.J.,NEW SOURCE BOOK IN MAJOR EUROPEAN GOVERNMENTS. CHRIST-17C EUR+WWI FRANCE GERMANY ITALY MOD/EUR UK USSR LOC/G POL/PAR CHIEF EX/STRUC CHOOSE CONSERVE MARXISM...JURID T 13/20. PAGE 171 H3425
NAT/G CONSTN LEGIS

B66
ZABLOCKI C.J.,SINO-SOVIET RIVALRY. AFR ASIA CHINA/COM CUBA EUR+WWI L/A+17C USA+45 USSR WOR+45 POL/PAR FORCES COERCE NUC/PWR...GOV/COMP IDEA/COMP 20 MAO KHRUSH/N. PAGE 172 H3444
DIPLOM MARXISM COM

S66
BLANC N.,"SPAIN: LEARNING THROUGH STRUGGLE" SPAIN STRATA STRUCT SECT FORCES PROB/SOLV AGE/Y ATTIT ORD/FREE PWR WEALTH MARXISM SOCISM 19/20 FRANCO/F SUCCESSION. PAGE 18 H0352
NAT/G FUT SOCIALIST TOTALISM

S66
CRANMER-BYNG J.L.,"THE CHINESE ATTITUDE TOWARDS EXTERNAL RELATIONS." ASIA CHINA/COM EXEC NAT/LISM MARXISM...POLICY 20. PAGE 35 H0699
ATTIT DIPLOM NAT/G

S66
GILBERT S.P.,"WARS OF LIBERATION AND SOVIET MILITARY AID POLICY." ASIA INDIA INDONESIA UAR USA+45 STRATA WAR PERCEPT MARXISM...STAT NAT/COMP. PAGE 56 H1124
USSR FOR/AID WEAPON DRIVE

S66
LODGE G.C.,"REVOLUTION IN LATIN AMERICA." USA+45 ELITES INDUS LABOR PROF/ORG SECT TEC/DEV CAP/ISM SKILL MARXISM...POLICY NAT/COMP. PAGE 98 H1950
ATTIT REV L/A+17C IDEA/COMP

S66
MCLANE C.B.,"SOVIET DOCTRINE AND THE MILITARY COUPS IN AFRICA." ALGERIA GHANA COLONIAL NAT/LISM RIGID/FLEX SOVEREIGN MARXISM...DECISION NAT/COMP. PAGE 107 H2140
USSR ATTIT AFR FORCES

S66
SCHWARTZ M.,"THE 1964 PRESIDENTIAL ELECTIONS THROUGH SOVIET EYES." ASIA POL/PAR DIPLOM ATTIT MARXISM...NAT/COMP COLD/WAR. PAGE 140 H2811
USSR USA+45 PERCEPT

S66
SKILLING H.G.,"THE RUMANIAN NATIONAL COURSE." COM EUR+WWI ROMANIA NAT/G ECO/TAC PWR 20. PAGE 145 H2896
NAT/LISM POLICY DIPLOM MARXISM

S66
STRAYER J.R.,"PROBLEMS OF DICTATORSHIP* THE RUSSIAN EXPERIENCE." ASIA MOD/EUR ELITES STRATA POL/PAR CREATE NAT/LISM MARXISM...GOV/COMP NAT/COMP. PAGE 150 H2997
NAT/G GEN/LAWS USSR TOTALISM

C66
WINT G.,"ASIA: A HANDBOOK." ASIA S/ASIA INDUS LABOR SECT PRESS RACE/REL MARXISM...STAT CHARTS BIBLIOG 20. PAGE 169 H3388
ECO/UNDEV DIPLOM NAT/G SOCIETY

B67
ANDERSON C.W.,ISSUES OF POLITICAL DEVELOPMENT. BURMA WOR+45 CULTURE TOP/EX ECO/TAC MARXISM ...CHARTS NAT/COMP 20 COLOMB CONGO/LEOP. PAGE 6 H0126
NAT/LISM COERCE ECO/UNDEV SOCISM

B67
ANDERSON T.,RUSSIAN POLITICAL THOUGHT; AN INTRODUCTION. USSR NAT/G POL/PAR CHIEF MARXISM ...TIME/SEQ BIBLIOG 9/20. PAGE 7 H0135
TREND CONSTN ATTIT

B67
BAIN C.A.,VIETNAM: THE ROOTS OF CONFLICT. FRANCE S/ASIA USSR VIETNAM POL/PAR SECT FORCES COLONIAL NAT/LISM PEACE ORD/FREE MARXISM...GEOG CHARTS 4/20. PAGE 10 H0202
NAT/G WAR CULTURE

B67
BARNETT A.D.,CADRES, BUREAUCRACY, AND POLITICAL POWER IN COMMUNIST CHINA. CHINA/COM ELITES LOC/G NAT/G INGP/REL...SOC INT DICTIONARY 20. PAGE 11 H0224
GOV/REL STRUCT MARXISM EDU/PROP

B67
BROMKE A.,POLAND'S POLITICS: IDEALISM VS. REALISM. COM GERMANY POLAND RUSSIA USSR POL/PAR CATHISM ...BIBLIOG 19/20. PAGE 21 H0431
NAT/G DIPLOM MARXISM

B67
BRZEZINSKI Z.K.,IDEOLOGY AND POWER IN SOVIET POLITICS. USSR NAT/G POL/PAR PWR...GEN/LAWS 19/20. PAGE 23 H0462
DIPLOM EX/STRUC MARXISM

B67
BRZEZINSKI Z.K.,THE SOVIET BLOC: UNITY AND CONFLICT (2ND ED., REV., ENLARGED). COM POLAND USSR INTELL CHIEF EX/STRUC CONTROL EXEC GOV/REL PWR MARXISM ...TREND IDEA/COMP 20 LENIN/VI MARX/KARL STALIN/J. PAGE 23 H0463
NAT/G DIPLOM

B67
CEFKIN J.L.,THE BACKGROUND OF CURRENT WORLD PROBLEMS. NAT/G MARXISM...T 20 UN COLD/WAR. PAGE 28 H0565
DIPLOM NAT/LISM ECO/UNDEV

B67
CORDIER A.W.,COLUMBIA ESSAYS IN INTERNATIONAL AFFAIRS. ASIA CHINA/COM FRANCE S/ASIA SPAIN UAR ECO/UNDEV LOC/G ECO/TAC GUERRILLA PWR...BIOG ANTHOL 18/20 MAU/MAU. PAGE 33 H0663
NAT/G DIPLOM MARXISM POLICY

B67
EVANS R.H.,COEXISTENCE: COMMUNISM AND ITS PRACTICE IN BOLOGNA, 1945-1965. ITALY CAP/ISM ADMIN CHOOSE PEACE ORD/FREE...SOC STAT DEEP/INT SAMP CHARTS BIBLIOG 20. PAGE 48 H0952
MARXISM CULTURE MUNIC POL/PAR

B67
FALL B.B.,HO CHI MINH ON REVOLUTION: SELECTED WRITINGS, 1920-66. COM VIETNAM ELITES NAT/G COERCE GUERRILLA RACE/REL MARXISM...MARXIST ANTHOL 20. PAGE 48 H0968
REV COLONIAL ECO/UNDEV S/ASIA

B67
FIELD M.G.,SOVIET SOCIALIZED MEDICINE. USSR FINAN R+D PROB/SOLV ADMIN SOCISM...MGT SOC CONCPT 20. PAGE 50 H0993
PUB/INST HEALTH NAT/G MARXISM

B67
KAROL K.S.,CHINA, THE OTHER COMMUNISM (TRANS. BY TOM BAISTOW). CHINA/COM CULTURE INDUS FORCES DIPLOM EDU/PROP CONTROL EXEC NUC/PWR ATTIT...SOC CHARTS 20. PAGE 83 H1663
NAT/G POL/PAR MARXISM INGP/REL

B67
KOLKOWICZ R.,THE SOVIET MILITARY AND THE COMMUNIST PARTY. COM USSR ELITES NAT/G CREATE CIVMIL/REL GP/REL...TREND BIBLIOG/A 20 COM/PARTY. PAGE 88 H1753
MARXISM CONSTN FORCES POL/PAR

B67
LAQUER W.,THE FATE OF THE REVOLUTION: INTERPRETATIONS OF SOVIET HISTORY. RUSSIA NAT/G MARXISM...BIBLIOG 20 STALIN/J. PAGE 91 H1816
REV KNOWL HIST/WRIT IDEA/COMP

B67
LENG S.C.,JUSTICE IN COMMUNIST CHINA: A SURVEY OF THE JUDICIAL SYSTEM OF THE CHINESE PEOPLE'S REPUBLIC. CHINA/COM LAW CONSTN LOC/G NAT/G PROF/ORG CONSULT FORCES ADMIN CRIME ORD/FREE...BIBLIOG 20 MAO. PAGE 94 H1877
CT/SYS ADJUD JURID MARXISM

B67
MCNELLY T.,SOURCES IN MODERN EAST ASIAN HISTORY AND POLITICS. KOREA VIETNAM CULTURE DIPLOM COLONIAL REV WAR PWR ALL/IDEOS MARXISM...ANTHOL 20 CHINJAP. PAGE 107 H2147
NAT/COMP ASIA S/ASIA SOCIETY

B67
MICKIEWICZ E.P.,SOVIET POLITICAL SCHOOLS: THE COMMUNIST PARTY ADULT INSTRUCTION SYSTEM. COM USSR INTELL SCHOOL WORKER CREATE PRESS ADMIN CONTROL ATTIT KNOWL...PROG/TEAC SOC/INTEG 20 COM/PARTY. PAGE 110 H2200
NAT/G EDU/PROP AGE/A MARXISM

B67
POMEROY W.J.,HALF A CENTURY OF SOCIALISM. USSR LAW AGRI INDUS NAT/G CREATE DIPLOM EDU/PROP PERSON ORD/FREE WEALTH...POLICY TREND 20. PAGE 127 H2541
SOCISM MARXISM COM SOCIETY

B67
RAMUNDO B.A.,PEACEFUL COEXISTENCE: INTERNATIONAL LAW IN THE BUILDING OF COMMUNISM. USSR INT/ORG DIPLOM COLONIAL ARMS/CONT ROLE SOVEREIGN...POLICY METH/COMP NAT/COMP BIBLIOG. PAGE 129 H2588
INT/LAW PEACE MARXISM METH/CNCPT

B67
REES D.,THE AGE OF CONTAINMENT. WOR+45 FORCES ARMS/CONT ATTIT PWR...CONCPT TREND METH/COMP BIBLIOG/A 20. PAGE 130 H2608
DIPLOM NUC/PWR MARXISM GOV/COMP

B67
ROELOFS H.M.,THE LANGUAGE OF MODERN POLITICS: AN INTRODUCTION TO THE STUDY OF GOVERNMENT. DIPLOM ADMIN MARXISM NEW/LIB...JURID CONCPT METH/COMP T 20. PAGE 133 H2657
LEAD NAT/COMP PERS/REL NAT/G

B67
SCHECTER J.,THE NEW FACE OF BUDDHA: BUDDHISM AND POLITICAL POWER IN SOUTHEAST ASIA. S/ASIA NAT/G POL/PAR NAT/LISM ATTIT MARXISM...BIBLIOG 20. PAGE 139 H2780
SECT POLICY PWR LEAD

B67
SETON-WATSON H.,THE RUSSIAN EMPIRE, 1801-1917. COM RUSSIA STRATA ECO/DEV AGRI INDUS POL/PAR DIPLOM NAT/LISM MARXISM...IDEA/COMP BIBLIOG 19/20 MARX/KARL. PAGE 142 H2834
SOCIETY NAT/G LEAD POLICY

B67
SHAFFER H.G.,THE COMMUNIST WORLD: MARXIST AND NON-MARXIST VIEWS. WOR+45 SOCIETY DIPLOM ECO/TAC CONTROL SOCISM...MARXIST ANTHOL BIBLIOG/A 20. PAGE 142 H2838
MARXISM NAT/COMP IDEA/COMP COM

B67
SHAPIRO P.S.,COMMUNICATIONS OR TRANSPORT: DECISION-MAKING IN DEVELOPING COUNTRIES. WOR+45 NAT/G PLAN ALL/IDEOS MARXISM...NAT/COMP GEN/LAWS. PAGE 142 H2844
BUDGET COM/IND DECISION ECO/DEV

B67
TOMPKINS S.R.,THE TRIUMPH OF BOLSHEVISM: REVOLUTION OR REACTION? USSR WORKER PRESS WEALTH MARXISM POPULISM...BIOG TREND IDEA/COMP BIBLIOG 19/20 LENIN/VI. PAGE 156 H3113
REV NAT/G POL/PAR NAT/LISM

B67
TREADGOLD D.W.,SOVIET AND CHINESE COMMUNISM* SIMILARITIES AND DIFFERENCES. CHINA/COM COM NAT/G PLAN DIPLOM CENTRAL PWR MARXISM...POLICY 20.
CULTURE NAT/LISM

PAGE 156 H3128

B67
ZALESKI E.,PLANNING REFORMS IN THE SOVIET UNION 1962-1966. COM USSR NAT/G CONFER CONTROL EFFICIENCY MARXISM...POLICY DECISION 20. PAGE 172 H3446 ECO/DEV PLAN ADMIN CENTRAL

L67
AUSTIN D.A.,"POLITICAL CONFLICT IN AFRICA." CONSTN NAT/G CREATE ADMIN COLONIAL ORD/FREE MARXISM POPULISM SOCISM...NAT/COMP ANTHOL 20. PAGE 9 H0180 ANOMIE AFR POL/PAR

L67
BRIDGHAM P.,"MAO'S "CULTURAL REVOLUTION"* ORIGIN AND DEVELOPMENT." NAT/G LEAD CIVMIL/REL NAT/LISM TOTALISM ATTIT DRIVE PWR MARXISM 20. PAGE 21 H0413 CHINA/COM CULTURE REV CROWD

L67
ISRAEL J.,"THE RED GUARDS IN HISTORICAL PERSPECTIVE: CONTINUITY AND CHANGE IN THE CHINESE YOUTH MOVEMENT." CHINA/COM FUT POL/PAR CONTROL REV GP/REL 20. PAGE 79 H1572 AGE/Y LOBBY MARXISM NAT/G

L67
ROBINSON T.W.,"A NATIONAL INTEREST ANALYSIS OF SINO-SOVIET RELATIONS." CHINA/COM USSR NAT/G NUC/PWR ATTIT PWR...CONCPT CHARTS 20. PAGE 132 H2650 MARXISM DIPLOM SOVEREIGN GEN/LAWS

L67
TABORSKY E.,"THE COMMUNIST PARTIES OF THE 'THIRD WORLD' IN SOVIET STRATEGY." AFR ASIA L/A+17C USSR INTELL NAT/G WORKER PLAN CONTROL LEAD PARTIC REV ...GOV/COMP 20 COM/PARTY THIRD/WRLD. PAGE 152 H3032 POL/PAR MARXISM ECO/UNDEV DIPLOM

L67
VAN DER KROEF J.M.,"INDONESIA: THE BATTLE OF THE 'OLD' AND THE 'NEW ORDER'." INDONESIA ISLAM ELITES POL/PAR DOMIN INGP/REL NAT/LISM PWR...IDEA/COMP 20. PAGE 161 H3229 FORCES MARXISM NAT/G BAL/PWR

S67
BASKIN D.B.,"NATIONALITY DOCTRINE AND ANTI-SEMITISM IN THE USSR." USSR CULTURE STRATA ISOLAT MAJORITY ATTIT RIGID/FLEX RESPECT...GP/COMP JEWS. PAGE 12 H0234 NAT/LISM MARXISM GP/REL DISCRIM

S67
BURGHART A.,"CATHOLIC SOCIAL THOUGHT IN AUSTRIA." AUSTRIA EUR+WWI NAT/G PAY PERS/REL OWN MARXISM SOCISM...SOC 20. PAGE 24 H0482 CATHISM ATTIT TREND SOCIETY

S67
CATTELL D.T.,"A NEO-MARXIST THEORY OF COMPARATIVE ANALYSIS." USSR STRATA INSPECT DOMIN CONTROL COERCE OWN TOTALISM PWR...FASCIST HYPO/EXP METH 20. PAGE 28 H0561 GOV/COMP MARXISM SIMUL CLASSIF

S67
CATTELL D.T.,"THE FIFTIETH ANNIVERSARY: A SOVIET WATERSHED?" USSR CONSTN ECO/DEV NAT/G LEAD TOTALISM 20 KHRUSH/N. PAGE 28 H0562 MARXISM CHIEF POLICY ADJUST

S67
CHIU S.M.,"CHINA'S MILITARY POSTURE." CHINA/COM ELITES NAT/G POL/PAR TEC/DEV ECO/TAC DOMIN CONTROL LEAD REV MARXISM 20 MAO. PAGE 30 H0595 FORCES CIVMIL/REL NUC/PWR DIPLOM

S67
EGBERT D.D.,"POLITICS AND ART IN COMMUNIST BULGARIA" BULGARIA COM USSR CULTURE DIPLOM INGP/REL TOTALISM...TREND 20. PAGE 45 H0894 CREATE ART/METH CONTROL MARXISM

S67
ELLISON H.J.,"THE SOCIALIST REVOLUTIONARIES." USSR ECO/UNDEV NAT/G INGP/REL EFFICIENCY ATTIT PWR MARXISM...CONCPT IDEA/COMP 20 SOC/REVPAR. PAGE 46 H0911 POL/PAR REV AGRI

S67
GAMARNIKOW M.,"THE NEW ROLE OF PRIVATE ENTERPRISE." ECO/DEV INDUS NAT/G SML/CO CREATE PROB/SOLV MARXISM ...POLICY TREND IDEA/COMP 20. PAGE 55 H1092 ECO/TAC ATTIT CAP/ISM COM

S67
LEVCIK B.,"WAGES AND EMPLOYMENT PROBLEMS IN THE NEW SYSTEM OF PLANNED MANAGEMENT IN CZECHOSLOVAKIA." CZECHOSLVK EUR+WWI NAT/G OP/RES PLAN ADMIN ROUTINE INGP/REL CENTRAL EFFICIENCY PRODUC DECISION. PAGE 95 H1895 MARXISM WORKER MGT PAY

S67
LOGERECI A.,"ALBANIA AND CHINA* THE INCONGRUOUS ALLIANCE." NAT/LISM PWR...GOV/COMP 20. PAGE 98 H1955 ALBANIA CHINA/COM DIPLOM MARXISM

S67
MCCLEERY W.,"AN INTERVIEW WITH J. DOUGLAS BROWN ON THE 'WAY' OF VIETNAM" COM VIETNAM INTELL ECO/DEV ACADEM NAT/G COERCE PERSON SUPEGO ORD/FREE 20. PAGE 106 H2125 ATTIT WAR COLONIAL MARXISM

S67
MOZINGO D.,"CHINA AND INDONESIA." CHINA/COM INDONESIA POL/PAR 20. PAGE 114 H2276 MARXISM CONTROL DIPLOM NAT/G

S67
NATSAGDORJ A.S.,"THE ECONOMIC BASIS OF FEUDALISM IN MONGOLIA." ASIA COM USSR OWN WEALTH CONSERVE...SOC 20 MONGOLIA. PAGE 116 H2324 ECO/TAC AGRI NAT/COMP MARXISM

S67
PAK H.,"CHINA'S MILITIA AND MAO TSE-TUNG'S 'PEOPLE'S WAR'." CHINA/COM SOCIETY POL/PAR EX/STRUC PROB/SOLV PARTIC COERCE WAR CIVMIL/REL ATTIT DRIVE MARXISM...METH/COMP 20 MAO. PAGE 122 H2447 FORCES NAT/G WORKER CHIEF

S67
PERKINS D.H.,"ECONOMIC GROWTH IN CHINA AND THE CULTURAL REVOLUTION(1960APRIL 1967)" CHINA/COM FUT AGRI INDUS PLAN LEAD MARXISM...CHARTS 20 MAO. PAGE 125 H2493 ECO/TAC CULTURE REV ECO/UNDEV

S67
PETRAS J.,"GUERRILLA MOVEMENTS IN LATIN AMERICA - I." GUATEMALA PERU VENEZUELA NAT/G COLONIAL LEAD ATTIT PWR...TIME/SEQ METH/COMP 20 COLOMB. PAGE 125 H2497 GUERRILLA REV L/A+17C MARXISM

S67
RAMA C.M.,"PASADO Y PRESENTE DE LA RELIGION EN AMERICA LATINA." L/A+17C ELITES SOCIETY STRATA MARXISM...STAT WORSHIP PROTESTANT. PAGE 129 H2585 SECT CATHISM STRUCT NAT/COMP

S67
RICHMAN B.M.,"CAPITALISTS & MANAGERS IN COMMUNIST CHINA." ASIA CHINA/COM ECO/UNDEV NAT/G CONSULT EX/STRUC PLAN EFFICIENCY PRODUC WEALTH MARXISM ...MGT CHARTS 20. PAGE 131 H2623 CAP/ISM INDUS

S67
SAVER W.,"NATIONAL SOCIALISM: TOTALITARIANISM OR FASCISM?" GERMANY STRUCT POL/PAR PROB/SOLV MARXISM ...SOC CONCPT HIST/WRIT IDEA/COMP 20 HITLER/A COLD/WAR. PAGE 138 H2760 SOCISM NAT/G TOTALISM FASCISM

S67
SEIDLER G.L.,"MARXIST LEGAL THOUGHT IN POLAND." POLAND SOCIETY R+D LOC/G NAT/G ACT/RES ADJUD CT/SYS SUPEGO PWR...SOC TREND 20 MARX/KARL. PAGE 141 H2822 MARXISM LAW CONCPT EFFICIENCY

S67
SHELDON C.H.,"PUBLIC OPINION AND HIGH COURTS: COMMUNIST PARTY CASES IN FOUR CONSTITUTIONAL SYSTEMS." CANADA GERMANY/W WOR+45 POL/PAR MARXISM ...METH/COMP NAT/COMP 20 AUSTRAL. PAGE 143 H2857 ATTIT CT/SYS CONSTN DECISION

S67
SLOAN P.,"FIFTY YEARS OF SOVIET RULE." USSR INDUS EDU/PROP EFFICIENCY PRODUC HEALTH KNOWL MORAL WEALTH MARXISM...POLICY 20. PAGE 145 H2900 CREATE NAT/G PLAN INSPECT

S67
SMITH J.E.,"THE GERMAN DEMOCRATIC REPUBLIC AND THE WEST." GERMANY/E ECO/DEV NAT/G PROB/SOLV CONTROL REV TOTALISM...GOV/COMP 20. PAGE 146 H2911 DIPLOM PWR MARXISM

S67
SMITH J.E.,"RED PRUSSIANISM OF THE GERMAN DEMOCRATIC REPUBLIC." GERMANY/E INTELL TOP/EX WORKER PLAN DIPLOM PRODUC ATTIT WEALTH MARXISM. PAGE 146 H2912 NAT/G TOTALISM INDUS NAT/LISM

S67
SMITH J.E.,"THE RED PRUSSIANISM OF THE GERMAN DEMOCRATIC REPUBLIC." GERMANY/E INTELL NAT/G SECT CHIEF...PREDICT TIME/SEQ 20. PAGE 146 H2913 MARXISM NAT/LISM GOV/COMP EDU/PROP

S67
SPITTMANN I.,"EAST GERMANY: THE SWINGING PENDULUM." COM GERMANY/E NAT/G EFFICIENCY MARXISM 20. PAGE 148 H2952 PRODUC POL/PAR WEALTH ATTIT

S67
STRAFFORD P.,"FRENCH ELECTIONS." FRANCE NAT/G CHIEF LEGIS BAL/PWR ECO/TAC PARL/PROC PARTIC ATTIT 20. PAGE 150 H2993 POL/PAR SOCISM CENTRAL MARXISM

S67
SZALAY L.B.,"SOVIET DOMESTIC PROPAGANDA AND LIBERALIZATION." COM USSR SOCIETY COM/IND NAT/G POL/PAR EX/STRUC TEC/DEV LEAD ATTIT ROLE MARXISM ...METH/COMP 20. PAGE 151 H3026 EDU/PROP TOTALISM PERSON PERCEPT

S67
TIKHOMIROV I.A.,"DIVISION OF POWERS OR DIVISION OF LABOR?" USSR NAT/G DELIB/GP ADJUD GP/REL MARXISM SOCISM 20. PAGE 155 H3093 BAL/PWR WORKER STRATA ADMIN

S67
ULC O.,"CLASS STRUGGLE AND SOCIALIST JUSTICE: THE CASE OF CZECHOSLOVAKIA." COM CZECHOSLVK LAW CONSTN ELITES STRUCT NAT/G CRIME GP/REL MARXISM 20. PAGE 158 H3151 TOTALISM CT/SYS ADJUD STRATA

S67
VON LAUE T.H.,"WESTERNIZATION, REVOLUTION AND THE SEARCH FOR A BASIS OF AUTHORITY - RUSSIA IN 1917." USSR ELITES INTELL ECO/UNDEV NAT/G WORKER ECO/TAC TAX ADMIN LEAD AUTHORIT 20 LENIN/VI. PAGE 164 H3274 MARXISM REV COM DOMIN

C67
GEHLEN M.P.,"THE POLITICS OF COEXISTENCE: SOVIET BIBLIOG

METHODS AND MOTIVES." COM USSR NAT/G INT/TRADE EDU/PROP ARMS/CONT DETER KNOWL...CHARTS IDEA/COMP 20 COLD/WAR. PAGE 55 H1108 — PEACE DIPLOM MARXISM

S68
BOSSCHERE G D.E.,"A L'EST DU NOUVEAU." CZECHOSLVK HUNGARY POLAND ROMANIA YUGOSLAVIA AGRI CREATE ECO/TAC COERCE GP/REL ATTIT MARXISM SOCISM 20. PAGE 19 H0382 — ORD/FREE COM NAT/G DIPLOM

S68
HOOK S.,"THE ENLIGHTENMENT AND MARXISM." CULTURE SOCIETY RATIONAL ORD/FREE PLURISM SOCISM...CONCPT HIST/WRIT 18/19 MARX/KARL HEGEL/GWF ENLIGHTNMT. PAGE 73 H1462 — IDEA/COMP MARXISM OBJECTIVE

S68
KANET R.E.,"RECENT SOVIET REASSESSMENT OF DEVELOPMENTS IN THE THIRD WORLD." ALGERIA GHANA INDONESIA USSR WOR+45 CONSTN ELITES INTELL STRUCT DOMIN CONTROL REV PWR MARXISM...IDEA/COMP METH 20 THIRD/WRLD. PAGE 83 H1653 — DIPLOM NEUTRAL NAT/G NAT/COMP

S68
LAVRIN J.,"THE TWO WORLDS." RUSSIA USSR SOCIETY STRUCT NAT/G DIPLOM ATTIT PERSON MARXISM...GEOG SOC IDEA/COMP PERS/COMP 18/20. PAGE 92 H1842 — NAT/COMP NAT/LISM CULTURE

S68
SHAPIRO J.P.,"SOVIET HISTORIOGRAPHY AND THE MOSCOW TRIALS: AFTER THIRTY YEARS." USSR NAT/G LEGIT PRESS CONTROL LEAD ATTIT MARXISM...NEW/IDEA METH 20 TROTSKY/L STALIN/J KHRUSH/N. PAGE 142 H2843 — HIST/WRIT EDU/PROP SANCTION ADJUD

MARXIST....MARXIST

N
PEKING REVIEW. CHINA/COM CULTURE AGRI INDUS DIPLOM EDU/PROP GUERRILLA ATTIT MARXISM...BIBLIOG 20. PAGE 1 H0009 — MARXIST NAT/G POL/PAR PRESS

N
AVTOREFERATY DISSERTATSII. USSR INTELL ACADEM NAT/G DIPLOM GOV/REL KNOWL CONCPT. PAGE 2 H0029 — BIBLIOG MARXISM MARXIST COM

N
US CONSULATE GENERAL HONG KONG,CURRENT BACKGROUND. CHINA/COM ECO/UNDEV LOC/G NAT/G PLAN DIPLOM EDU/PROP LEAD REV ATTIT...POLICY INDEX 20. PAGE 159 H3179 — BIBLIOG/A MARXIST ASIA PRESS

N
US CONSULATE GENERAL HONG KONG,EXTRACTS FROM CHINA MAINLAND MAGAZINES. ASIA CHINA/COM ECO/UNDEV NAT/G CHIEF LEAD ATTIT...MARXIST INDEX 20. PAGE 159 H3180 — BIBLIOG MARXISM PRESS

N
US CONSULATE GENERAL HONG KONG,SURVEY OF CHINA MAINLAND PRESS. CHINA/COM ECO/UNDEV LOC/G NAT/G PLAN DIPLOM EDU/PROP LEAD REV ATTIT...POLICY INDEX 20. PAGE 159 H3181 — BIBLIOG/A MARXIST ASIA PRESS

N
US CONSULATE GENERAL HONG KONG,US CONSULATE GENERAL, HONG KONG, PRESS SUMMARIES. CHINA/COM ECO/UNDEV LOC/G NAT/G PLAN DIPLOM EDU/PROP LEAD REV ATTIT...POLICY INDEX 20. PAGE 159 H3182 — BIBLIOG/A MARXIST ASIA PRESS

N
US LIBRARY OF CONGRESS,EAST EUROPEAN ACCESSIONS INDEX. NAT/G ISOLAT ATTIT KNOWL...POLICY 20. PAGE 160 H3202 — BIBLIOG COM MARXIST DIPLOM

B27
ENGELS F.,THE PEASANT WAR IN GERMANY (1850). GERMANY MOD/EUR AGRI WORKER LEAD COERCE INGP/REL ...TREND 16/19. PAGE 46 H0924 — WAR STRATA REV MARXIST

B34
MARX K.,THE CLASS STRUGGLES IN FRANCE. FRANCE INDUS WORKER CONSERVE...TREND GEN/LAWS 19. PAGE 104 H2077 — MARXIST STRATA REV INT/TRADE

B37
MARX K.,THE CIVIL WAR IN THE UNITED STATES. USA-45 WORKER DIPLOM INT/TRADE DOMIN RACE/REL ATTIT ...TREND 19. PAGE 104 H2078 — WAR REV MARXIST ORD/FREE

B38
MARX K.,THE GERMAN IDEOLOGY, PARTS 1 AND 3 (1846). MOD/EUR LAW STRATA WORKER DOMIN REV UTOPIA SOCISM 19 MARX/KARL. PAGE 104 H2079 — MARXIST OWN PRODUC ECO/TAC

B39
ENGELS F.,HERRN EUGEN DUHRING'S REVOLUTION IN SCIENCE (1878). CULTURE STRATA STRUCT FAM SECT ECO/TAC REV WAR SOCISM...MARXIST 19. PAGE 46 H0925 — PWR SOCIETY WEALTH GEN/LAWS

B43
LENIN V.I.,STATE AND REVOLUTION. USSR CAP/ISM ...ANARCH MARXIST PHIL/SCI IDEA/COMP 20. PAGE 94 H1878 — SOCIETY NAT/G REV MARXISM

N47
CANNON J.P.,AMERICAN STALINISM AND ANTI-STALINISM (PAMPHLET). NAT/G WORKER DOMIN EDU/PROP REV GP/REL ...MARXIST CONCPT 20 STALIN/J TROTSKY/L. PAGE 26 H0521 — LABOR MARXISM CAP/ISM POL/PAR

B51
MARX K.,THE EIGHTEENTH BRUMAIRE OF LOUIS BONAPARTE (1852). FRANCE STRATA FINAN INDUS LABOR CHIEF FORCES WORKER CAP/ISM ECO/TAC PARL/PROC ORD/FREE ...MARXIST 19. PAGE 104 H2080 — REV MARXISM ELITES NAT/G

B54
LENIN V.I.,SELECTED WORKS (12 VOLS.). USSR INTELL SOCIETY STRATA STRUCT NAT/G POL/PAR WORKER CAP/ISM REV WAR...MARXIST PHIL/SCI 20 MARX/KARL LENIN/VI. PAGE 94 H1880 — COM MARXISM

S60
CASSINELLI C.,"TOTALITARIANISM, IDEOLOGY AND PROPAGANDA." EUR+WWI CULTURE SOCIETY NAT/G DOMIN COERCE ORD/FREE FASCISM MARXISM...MARXIST CONCPT STERTYP GEN/LAWS TOT/POP 20. PAGE 28 H0554 — ATTIT EDU/PROP TOTALISM

B61
LENIN V.I.,WHAT IS TO BE DONE? (1902). RUSSIA LABOR NAT/G POL/PAR WORKER CAP/ISM ECO/TAC ADMIN PARTIC ...MARXIST IDEA/COMP GEN/LAWS 19/20. PAGE 94 H1881 — EDU/PROP PRESS MARXISM METH/COMP

B61
LEVIN L.A.,BIBLIOGRAFIIA BIBLIOGRAFII PROIZVEDENII K. MARKSA, F. ENGELSA, V.I. LENINA. COM USSR NAT/G POL/PAR WORKER LEAD REV ATTIT...POLICY IDEA/COMP 20 MARX/KARL LENIN/VI ENGELS. PAGE 95 H1899 — BIBLIOG/A MARXISM MARXIST CONCPT

S61
TOMASIC D.,"POLITICAL LEADERSHIP IN CONTEMPORARY POLAND." COM EUR+WWI GERMANY NAT/G POL/PAR SECT DELIB/GP PLAN ECO/TAC DOMIN EDU/PROP PWR MARXISM ...MARXIST GEOG MGT CONCPT TIME/SEQ STERTYP 20. PAGE 156 H3111 — SOCIETY ROUTINE USSR POLAND

S62
IOVTCHOUK M.T.,"ON SOME THEORETICAL PRINCIPLES AND METHODS OF SOCIOLOGICAL INVESTIGATIONS (IN RUSSIAN)." FUT USA+45 STRATA R+D NAT/G POL/PAR TOP/EX ACT/RES PLAN ECO/TAC EDU/PROP ROUTINE ATTIT RIGID/FLEX MARXISM SOCISM...MARXIST METH/CNCPT OBS TREND NAT/COMP GEN/LAWS 20. PAGE 78 H1564 — COM ECO/DEV CAP/ISM USSR

B63
MARX K.,THE POVERTY OF PHILOSOPHY (1847). SOCIETY STRATA INDUS WORKER OWN UTOPIA SOCISM...GEN/LAWS MARX/KARL. PAGE 104 H2082 — MARXIST PRODUC

B64
MARTINET G.,MARXISM OF OUR TIME: OR THE CONTRADICTIONS OF SOCIALISM. FRANCE NAT/G OPTIMAL RIGID/FLEX SOCISM...IDEA/COMP 20. PAGE 103 H2067 — MARXISM MARXIST PROB/SOLV CREATE

B64
THORNTON T.P.,THE THIRD WORLD IN SOVIET PERSPECTIVE: STUDIES BY SOVIET WRITERS ON THE DEVELOPING AREAS. AFR L/A+17C S/ASIA STRATA AGRI INDUS MARKET NAT/G POL/PAR ECO/TAC COLONIAL PERCEPT PWR WEALTH...MARXIST STAT CHARTS WORK MARX/KARL 20. PAGE 155 H3090 — ECO/UNDEV ACT/RES USSR DIPLOM

B66
SAINDERICHIN P.,HISTORIE SECRETE D'UNE ELECTION, DECEMBER 5-19, 1965. FRANCE NAT/G DELIB/GP LEGIS PLAN EDU/PROP TV SOCISM...MARXIST 20 DEGAULLE/C. PAGE 137 H2731 — CHOOSE CHIEF PROB/SOLV POL/PAR

B67
FALL B.B.,HO CHI MINH ON REVOLUTION: SELECTED WRITINGS, 1920-66. COM VIETNAM ELITES NAT/G COERCE GUERRILLA RACE/REL MARXISM...MARXIST ANTHOL 20. PAGE 48 H0968 — REV COLONIAL ECO/UNDEV S/ASIA

B67
SHAFFER H.G.,THE COMMUNIST WORLD: MARXIST AND NON-MARXIST VIEWS. WOR+45 SOCIETY DIPLOM ECO/TAC CONTROL SOCISM...MARXIST ANTHOL BIBLIOG/A 20. PAGE 142 H2838 — MARXISM NAT/COMP IDEA/COMP COM

S67
BAIKALOV A.,"EMERGENCY LEGISLATION IN WEST GERMANY." GERMANY/W LABOR NAT/G POL/PAR SANCTION ...MARXIST 20. PAGE 10 H0199 — LAW TOTALISM LEGIS PARL/PROC

S67
DEWHURST A.,"THE WAGE MOVEMENT IN CANADA." CANADA AGRI NAT/G PARTIC COST PRODUC PROFIT 20. PAGE 41 H0811 — WORKER MARXIST INDUS LABOR

S67
GONZALEZ M.P.,"CUBA, UNA REVOLUCION EN MARCHA." CUBA L/A+17C USA+45 VIETNAM ECO/UNDEV FORCES DIPLOM DOMIN...POLICY MARXIST NAT/COMP CASTRO/F. PAGE 58 H1163 — REV NAT/G COLONIAL SOVEREIGN

S67
PONOMARYOV B.,"THE OCTOBER REVOLUTION - BEGINNING OF THE EPOCH OF SOCIALISM AND COMMUNISM." COM FUT USSR WOR+45 SOCIETY STRATA CHIEF CREATE DIPLOM ECO/TAC EDU/PROP SOCISM...NAT/COMP 20. PAGE 127 H2542 — MARXIST WORKER INT/ORG POLICY

S67
ROCHET W.,"THE OCTOBER REVOLUTION AND THE STRUGGLE OF THE FRENCH COMMUNISTS." COM FRANCE ELITES SOCIETY STRATA ECO/TAC EDU/PROP GP/REL WEALTH ...MARXIST IDEA/COMP NAT/COMP 20. PAGE 133 H2654 — SOCISM CHOOSE METH/COMP NAT/G

S67
SAVELYEV N.,"MONOPOLY DRIVE IN INDIA." INDIA INDUS NAT/G INT/TRADE NEUTRAL SANCTION GOV/REL CONSERVE ...MARXIST 20. PAGE 138 H2759 — ECO/UNDEV POL/PAR ECO/TAC CONTROL

S67
YEFROMEV A.,"THE TRUE FACE OF THE WEST GERMAN NATIONAL-DEMOCRATS." GERMANY/W NAT/G DOMIN LEAD SANCTION WAR ATTIT PERSON...MARXIST 20. PAGE 172 H3436 — POL/PAR TOTALISM PARL/PROC DIPLOM

S68
DEUTSCHER I.,"GERMANY AND MARXISM." FUT GERMANY/W NAT/G...MARXIST TREND 20. PAGE 40 H0808 — SOCISM ORD/FREE POPULISM POL/PAR

B84
ENGELS F.,THE ORIGIN OF THE FAMILY, PRIVATE PROPERTY, AND THE STATE (TRANS. BY E. UNTERMANN). UNIV ELITES SOCIETY CAP/ISM ECO/TAC MARRIAGE ORD/FREE POPULISM...MARXIST SOC ENGELS. PAGE 46 H0926 — FAM OWN WEALTH SOCISM

B96
MARX K.,REVOLUTION AND COUNTER-REVOLUTION. GERMANY CONSTN ELITES INDUS NAT/G DIPLOM ECO/TAC WEALTH. PAGE 104 H2083 — MARXIST REV PWR STRATA

MARYLAND....MARYLAND

MAS LATRIE L. H2084

MASON E.S. H2085,H2086

MASON J.B. H2087

MASS MEDIA....SEE EDU/PROP, COM/IND

MASSACHU....MASSACHUSETTS

MASSEY V. H2088

MASUMI J. H2762

MASUR G. H2089

MATH....MATHEMATICS

B24
SHIROKOGOROFF S.M.,ETHNICAL UNIT AND MILIEU. GP/REL ...PHIL/SCI SOC MATH METH. PAGE 143 H2865 — IDEA/COMP HABITAT CULTURE SOCIETY

S59
LEYS C.,"MODELS, THEORIES, AND THE THEORY OF POLITICAL PARTIES" CANADA LIECHTENST UK LOC/G NAT/G PARTIC REPRESENT GP/REL CONSEN EQUILIB MAJORITY ...NEW/IDEA MATH CHARTS 20. PAGE 96 H1919 — POL/PAR CHOOSE METH/CNCPT SIMUL

B60
WOLF C.,FOREIGN AID: THEORY AND PRACTICE IN SOUTHERN ASIA. CEYLON INDONESIA PHILIPPINE S/ASIA CULTURE STRATA ECO/UNDEV PLAN EDU/PROP ATTIT ...METH/CNCPT MATH QUANT STAT CONT/OBS TIME/SEQ SIMUL TOT/POP 20. PAGE 170 H3396 — ACT/RES ECO/TAC FOR/AID

S60
FRANKEL S.H.,"ECONOMIC ASPECTS OF POLITICAL INDEPENDENCE IN AFRICA." AFR FUT SOCIETY ECO/UNDEV COM/IND FINAN LEGIS PLAN TEC/DEV CAP/ISM ECO/TAC INT/TRADE ADMIN ATTIT DRIVE RIGID/FLEX PWR WEALTH ...MGT NEW/IDEA MATH TIME/SEQ VAL/FREE 20. PAGE 53 H1052 — NAT/G FOR/AID

B61
FIELD H.,ANCIENT AND MODERN MAN IN SOUTHWESTERN ASIA: II. CULTURE SOCIETY...CLASSIF MATH GP/COMP NAT/COMP 20. PAGE 50 H0992 — STAT CHARTS PHIL/SCI RECORD

B63
MCPHEE W.N.,FORMAL THEORIES OF MASS BEHAVIOR. CULTURE STRUCT DOMIN EDU/PROP CHOOSE...MATH 20. PAGE 108 H2149 — SOC METH CONCPT ATTIT

S65
BANK A.S.,"GROUPING POLITICAL SYSTEMS* Q-FACTOR ANALYSIS OF A CROSSPOLITY SURVEY." CULTURE...CHARTS NAT/COMP. PAGE 11 H0211 — CLASSIF NAT/G WOR+45 MATH

S65
WRIGHT Q.,"THE ESCALATION OF INTERNATIONAL CONFLICTS." WOR+45 WOR-45 FORCES DIPLOM RISK COST ATTIT ALL/VALS...INT/LAW QUANT STAT NAT/COMP. PAGE 171 H3422 — WAR PERCEPT PREDICT MATH

B66
MERRITT R.L.,COMPARING NATIONS* THE USE OF QUANTITATIVE DATA IN CROSSNATIONAL RESEARCH. ACADEM DIPLOM GP/REL...PHIL/SCI STAT TREND GP/COMP PERS/COMP GEN/METH ANTHOL BIBLIOG INDEX. PAGE 109 H2184 — NAT/COMP MATH COMPUT/IR QUANT

B66
SASTRI K.V.S.,FEDERAL-STATE FISCAL RELATIONS IN INDIA: A STUDY OF THE FINANCE COMMISSION AND TECHNIQUES OF FINANCIAL ADJUSTMENT. INDIA PROVS DELIB/GP GOV/REL FEDERAL...MATH CHARTS 20. PAGE 138 H2756 — TAX BUDGET FINAN NAT/G

B67
RAE D.,THE POLITICAL CONSEQUENCES OF ELECTORAL LAWS. EUR+WWI ICELAND ISRAEL NEW/ZEALND UK USA+45 ADJUD APPORT GP/REL MAJORITY...MATH STAT CENSUS CHARTS BIBLIOG 20 AUSTRAL. PAGE 129 H2579 — POL/PAR CHOOSE NAT/COMP REPRESENT

S67
HASSAN M.F.,"THE SECOND FOUR-YEAR PLAN OF VENEZUELA." L/A+17C VENEZUELA AGRI INDUS NAT/G PLAN RATION CONTROL HABITAT...MATH STAT 20. PAGE 67 H1352 — ECO/UNDEV FINAN BUDGET PROB/SOLV

MATHEMATICS....SEE MATH, ALSO LOGIC, MATHEMATICS, AND LANGUAGE INDEX, P. XIV

MATHER F.C. H2090

MATOS J. H2091

MATTEI/E....ENRICO MATTEI

MATTHEWS D.G. H2092,H2093,H2094,H2095,H2096

MATTHEWS D.R. H2097

MATTHEWS N. H3288

MATTHEWS R. H2098

MATTHEWS R.O. H2099

MATTHIAS E. H2100

MAU/MAU....MAU MAU

B54
MITCHELL P.,AFRICAN AFTERTHOUGHTS. UGANDA CONSTN NAT/G ADJUD COERCE WAR 20 WWI MAU/MAU. PAGE 112 H2230 — BIOG CHIEF COLONIAL DOMIN

B66
BARNETT D.L.,MAU MAU FROM WITHIN. AFR UK POL/PAR LEAD GUERRILLA AUTHORIT ORD/FREE...SOC BIOG 20 NEGRO MAU/MAU. PAGE 11 H0225 — REV CULTURE NAT/G

B67
CORDIER A.W.,COLUMBIA ESSAYS IN INTERNATIONAL AFFAIRS. ASIA CHINA/COM FRANCE S/ASIA SPAIN UAR ECO/UNDEV LOC/G ECO/TAC GUERRILLA PWR...BIOG ANTHOL 18/20 MAU/MAU. PAGE 33 H0663 — NAT/G DIPLOM MARXISM POLICY

MAUD J. H2101

MAUD....MILITARY APPLICATIONS OF URANIUM DETONATION (MAUD) (U.K. - WWII)

MAUGHAM R. H2102

MAURITANIA....SEE ALSO AFR

MAURRAS C. H2103

MAURRAS/C....CHARLES MAURRAS

MAXIMOFF G.P. H2104

MAYANJA A. H2105

MAYNE A. H2106

MAYNE R. H2107

MAYO H.B. H2108,H2109

MAYO/ELTON....ELTON MAYO

MAYOR....MAYOR; SEE ALSO MUNIC, CHIEF

MAZRUI A.A. H2110,H2111

MAZZINI J. H2112,H2113

MBEKI G. H2114

MBEMBE....MBEMBE TRIBE

B65
HARRIS R.L.,POLITICAL ORGANIZATION OF THE MBEMBE NIGERIA. AFR NIGERIA SOCIETY AGRI SECT WORKER PAY ...SOC WORSHIP 20 MBEMBE. PAGE 67 H1345 STRUCT CHIEF CULTURE

MBOYA T. H2115,H2116

MC CLELLAN G.S. H2117

MC DOWELL R.B. H2118

MC WILLIAM M. H2119

MCALISTER L.N. H2120

MCALLISTER J.T. H2121

MCAUSLAN J.P.W. H2122

MCBRYDE F.W. H2123

MCCALL D.F. H2124

MCCARTHY/E....EUGENE MCCARTHY

MCCARTHY/J....JOSEPH MCCARTHY

MCCLEERY W. H2125

MCCLELLN/J....JOHN MCCLELLAN

MCCLINTOCK R. H2126

MCCLOSKY H. H2127

MCCOWN A.C. H2128

MCDOUGAL M.S. H2129

MCGEORGE H. H0764

MCHENRY D.E. H2130,H2131

MCILWAIN C.H. H2132,H2133,H2134,H2135

MCIVER R.M. H2136

MCIVOR R.C. H2137

MCKAY V. H2138

MCKINLEY/W....PRESIDENT WILLIAM MCKINLEY

MCKISACK M. H2139

MCLANE C.B. H2140

MCLAUGHLIN M.R. H2141

MCLEAN J.M. H2142

MCLENNAN B.N. H2143

MCLUHAN/M....MARSHALL MCLUHAN

MCMAHON....MCMAHON LINE

MCNAIR A.D. H2144

MCNAMARA/R....ROBERT MCNAMARA

MCNEAL R.H. H2145

MCNEIL E.B. H2146

MCNELLY T. H2147

MCPHEE A. H2148

MCPHEE W.N. H2149

MCRAE K.D. H0364

MCSHERRY J.E. H2150

MCWHINNEY E. H2151

MDTA....MANPOWER DEVELOPMENT AND TRAINING ACT (1962)

MEAD M. H2152,H2153

MEAD/GH....GEORGE HERBERT MEAD

MEAD/MARG....MARGARET MEAD

B63
RUITENBEER H.M.,THE DILEMMA OF ORGANIZATIONAL SOCIETY. CULTURE ECO/DEV MUNIC SECT TEC/DEV EDU/PROP NAT/LISM ORD/FREE...NAT/COMP 20 RIESMAN/D WHYTE/WF MERTON/R MEAD/MARG JASPERS/K. PAGE 136 H2716 PERSON ROLE ADMIN WORKER

MEADE J.E. H2154

MEADVIL/PA....MEADVILLE, PA.

MEADVILLE, PA.....SEE MEADVIL/PA

MEAGHER R.F. H2155

MECHAM J.L. H2156

MECRENSKY E. H2157

MEDIATION....SEE CONFER, CONSULT

MEDICAL CARE....SEE HEALTH

MEDITERRANEAN AND NEAR EAST, TO ISLAMIC PERIOD....SEE MEDIT-7

MEDIT-7....MEDITERRANEAN AND NEAR EAST TO THE ISLAMIC PERIOD (7TH CENTURY); SEE ALSO APPROPRIATE NATIONS

N
BURY J.B.,THE CAMBRIDGE ANCIENT HISTORY (12 VOLS.). MEDIT-7 DIPLOM COLONIAL WAR...HUM EGYPT/ANC ROME/EMP BABYLONIA GREECE/ANC. PAGE 25 H0495 BIBLIOG/A SOCIETY CULTURE NAT/G

B00
MAINE H.S.,ANCIENT LAW. MEDIT-7 CULTURE SOCIETY KIN SECT LEGIS LEGIT ROUTINE...JURID HIST/WRIT CON/ANAL TOT/POP VAL/FREE. PAGE 101 H2020 FAM LAW

B00
OMAN C.,A HISTORY OF THE ART OF WAR: THE MIDDLE AGES FROM THE FOURTH TO THE FOURTEENTH CENTURY. CHRIST-17C MEDIT-7 CULTURE SOCIETY INT/ORG ROUTINE PERSON...CONT/OBS HIST/WRIT CHARTS VAL/FREE. PAGE 121 H2417 FORCES SKILL WAR

B11
PHILLIPSON C.,THE INTERNATIONAL LAW AND CUSTOM OF ANCIENT GREECE AND ROME. MEDIT-7 UNIV INTELL SOCIETY STRUCT NAT/G LEGIS EXEC PERSON...CONCPT OBS CON/ANAL ROM/EMP. PAGE 125 H2504 INT/ORG LAW INT/LAW

B22
URE P.N.,THE ORIGIN OF TYRANNY. MEDIT-7 FINAN INDUS CHIEF FORCES ECO/TAC WEALTH. PAGE 159 H3174 AUTHORIT PWR NAT/G MARKET

B23
FRANK T.,A HISTORY OF ROME. MEDIT-7 INTELL SOCIETY LOC/G NAT/G POL/PAR FORCES LEGIS DOMIN LEGIT ALL/VALS...POLICY CONCPT TIME/SEQ GEN/LAWS ROM/EMP ROM/EMP. PAGE 53 H1050 EXEC STRUCT ELITES

B39
TAGGART F.J.,ROME AND CHINA. MEDIT-7 INT/ORG NAT/G FORCES LEGIS TOP/EX PLAN PWR SOVEREIGN...CHARTS TOT/POP ROM/EMP. PAGE 152 H3034 ASIA WAR

C51
HAMMOND M.,"CITY-STATE AND WORLD STATE." CONSTN INTELL LOC/G LEGIT CENTRAL RATIONAL BIBLIOG. PAGE 65 H1308 NAT/G ATTIT REGION MEDIT-7

B52
ETTINGHAUSEN R.,SELECTED AND ANNOTATED BIBLIOGRAPHY OF BOOKS AND PERIODICALS IN WESTERN LANGUAGES DEALING WITH NEAR AND MIDDLE EAST. LAW CULTURE SECT ...ART/METH GEOG SOC. PAGE 47 H0944 BIBLIOG/A ISLAM MEDIT-7

B59
HONINGMAN J.J.,THE WORLD OF MAN. CHRIST-17C MEDIT-7 PRE/AMER PREHIST CREATE INGP/REL BIO/SOC HABITAT ...PSY SOC BIBLIOG. PAGE 73 H1460 CULTURE METH PERSON STRUCT

B60
BARBU Z.,PROBLEMS OF HISTORICAL PSYCHOLOGY. GREECE MEDIT-7 UK CULTURE TEC/DEV ADJUST RATIONAL ATTIT PERCEPT...METH/CNCPT NEW/IDEA TIME/SEQ GEN/METH. PAGE 11 H0214 PERSON PSY HIST/WRIT IDEA/COMP

B63
THUCYDIDES,THE PELOPONESIAN WARS. MEDIT-7 CULTURE INT/ORG NAT/G FORCES TOP/EX PLAN ROUTINE PWR ...CONCPT. PAGE 155 H3091 ATTIT COERCE WAR

B66
IBRAHIM-HILMY,THE LITERATURE OF EGYPT AND THE SOUDAN: FROM THE EARLIEST TIMES TO THE YEAR 1885 INCLUSIVE (2 VOLS.). MEDIT-7 SUDAN UAR LAW SOCIETY SECT ATTIT EGYPT/ANC. PAGE 76 H1520 BIBLIOG CULTURE ISLAM NAT/G

B67
LEVY J.-P.,THE ECONOMIC LIFE OF THE ANCIENT WORLD. CULTURE SOCIETY INT/TRADE COLONIAL WEALTH ...BIBLIOG. PAGE 95 H1906 ECO/TAC ECO/UNDEV FINAN

MEDIT-7

L67
GOOD E.M.,"CAPITAL PUNISHMENT AND ITS ALTERNATIVES IN ANCIENT NEAR EASTERN LAW." SOCIETY SECT INGP/REL CONSEN ATTIT SEX MORAL...CRIMLGY GP/COMP. PAGE 58 H1168 — MEDIT-7 LAW JURID CULTURE

S67
KINGSBURY E.C.,"LAW AS COMPACT: ANCIENT ISRAEL'S CONTRIBUTION TO THE UNDERSTANDING OF LAW." ISRAEL MEDIT-7 CULTURE KIN KNOWL...JURID CONCPT TREND IDEA/COMP METH/COMP WORSHIP JEWS DEITY. PAGE 86 H1716 — LAW AGREE CONSTN INGP/REL

C93
PLAYFAIR R.L.,"A BIBLIOGRAPHY OF MOROCCO." MOROCCO CULTURE AGRI FORCES DIPLOM WAR HEALTH...GEOG JURID SOC CHARTS. PAGE 126 H2526 — BIBLIOG ISLAM MEDIT-7

MEEK C.K. H2158

MEGGITT M.J. H1847,H2159

MEHDI M.T. H2160

MEHNERT K. H2161,H2162

MEHROTRA S.R. H2163

MEIER R.L. H2164,H2165

MEIJI....MEIJI: THE REIGN OF EMPEROR MUTSUHITO OF JAPAN (1868-1912)

MEINECKE F. H2166

MELADY T. H2167,H2168

MELANESIA....MELANESIA

B26
MALINOWSKI B.,CRIME AND CUSTOM IN SAVAGE SOCIETY. SOCIETY FAM SECT LEGIT SANCTION MARRIAGE MYSTISM ...PSY SOC 19/20 MELANESIA CANON/LAW. PAGE 102 H2030 — LAW CULTURE CRIME ADJUD

L95
BELSHAW C.S.,"IN SEARCH OF WEALTH; STUDY OF EMERGENCE OF COMMERCIAL OPERA TIONS IN MELANESIAN SOCIETY OF SOUTHEASTERN PAPUA." S/ASIA CULTURE KIN ECO/TAC DEMAND INCOME 20 MELANESIA PAPUA. PAGE 14 H0272 — INT/TRADE ECO/UNDEV METH/COMP SOCIETY

MENARD O.D. H2169

MENDEL A.P. H2170

MENDELSON W. H2171

MENDELSSOHN S. H2172,H2173

MENDIETTA Y NUNE L. H2174

MENDL W. H2175

MENON K.P.S. H2176

MENON/KRSH....KRISHNA MENON

MENSHEVIK....MENSHEVIKS

B43
LENIN V.I.,LEFT WING COMMUNISM: AN INFANTILE DISORDER (1920). GERMANY MOD/EUR USSR STRUCT CHIEF DOMIN EDU/PROP LEGIT LEAD REPRESENT POPULISM ...METH/COMP 19 LENIN/VI COM/PARTY MENSHEVIK. PAGE 94 H1879 — COM MARXISM NAT/G REV

MENTAL DISORDERS....SEE HEALTH

MENTAL HEALTH....SEE HEALTH, PSY

MENTAL INSTITUTION....SEE PUB/INST

MENZEL J.M. H2177

MENZIES/RG....ROBERT G. MENZIES

MERCANTILISM....SEE ECO

MERCANTLST....MERCANTILIST ECONOMIC THEORY

B82
CUNNINGHAM W.,THE GROWTH OF ENGLISH INDUSTRY AND COMMERCE. FUT UK FINAN NAT/G CAP/ISM...POLICY 20 MERCANTLST CHRISTIAN POPE. PAGE 36 H0721 — INDUS INT/TRADE SML/CO CONSERVE

B96
SCHMOLLER G.,THE MERCANTILE SYSTEM AND ITS HISTORICAL SIGNIFICANCE: ILLUSTRATED CHIEFLY FROM PRUSSIAN HISTORY (TRANS.). PRUSSIA CULTURE INDUS KIN MUNIC NAT/G PROVS OP/RES ECO/TAC INT/TRADE SUPEGO PWR WEALTH 19 MERCANTLST. PAGE 139 H2790 — GEN/METH INGP/REL CONCPT

MERCIER/E....ERNEST MERCIER

MEREDITH/J....JAMES MEREDITH

MERGERS....SEE INDUS, EX/STRUC, FINAN

MERILLAT H.C.L. H2178

MERKL P.H. H2179,H2180,H2181

MERRIAM A. H2182

MERRIAM C.E. H2183

MERRITT R.L. H2184,H2185

MERTHYR....MERTHYR, WALES

MERTON R.K. H2186

MERTON/R....ROBERT MERTON

B63
RUITENBEER H.M.,THE DILEMMA OF ORGANIZATIONAL SOCIETY. CULTURE ECO/DEV MUNIC SECT TEC/DEV EDU/PROP NAT/LISM ORD/FREE...NAT/COMP 20 RIESMAN/D WHYTE/WF MERTON/R MEAD/MARG JASPERS/K. PAGE 136 H2716 — PERSON ROLE ADMIN WORKER

MESKILL J. H0914

MESOPOTAM....MESOPOTAMIA

B63
JAIRAZBHOY R.A.,FOREIGN INFLUENCE IN ANCIENT INDIA. INDIA ELITES SECT DIPLOM EDU/PROP COLONIAL REGION GP/REL...ART/METH LING WORSHIP +/14 GRECO/ROMN MESOPOTAM PERSIA PARTH/SASS. PAGE 79 H1587 — CULTURE SOCIETY COERCE DOMIN

METH....HEAVILY EMPHASIZED METHODOLOGY OR TECHNIQUE OF STUDY

N
AMERICAN POLITICAL SCIENCE REVIEW. USA+45 USA-45 WOR+45 WOR-45 INT/ORG ADMIN...INT/LAW PHIL/SCI CONCPT METH 20 UN. PAGE 1 H0001 — BIBLIOG/A DIPLOM NAT/G GOV/COMP

N19
INTERNATIONAL LABOUR OFFICE,EMPLOYMENT, UNEMPLOYMENT AND LABOUR FORCE STATISTICS (PAMPHLET). EUR+WWI STRATA AGRI INDUS NAT/G PROB/SOLV PAY AGE SEX...SAMP NAT/COMP METH 20 ILO. PAGE 78 H1557 — WORKER LABOR STAT ECO/DEV

B22
OGBURN W.F.,SOCIAL CHANGE WITH RESPECT TO CULTURE AND ORIGINAL NATURE. ACT/RES OP/RES CRIME GP/REL ANOMIE BIO/SOC PWR...PSY SOC TIME/SEQ METH SOC/INTEG. PAGE 120 H2405 — CULTURE CREATE TEC/DEV

B24
BAGEHOT W.,THE ENGLISH CONSTITUTION AND OTHER POLITICAL ESSAYS. UK DELIB/GP BAL/PWR ADMIN CONTROL EXEC ROUTINE CONSERVE...METH PARLIAMENT 19/20. PAGE 10 H0197 — NAT/G STRUCT CONCPT

B24
SHIROKOGOROFF S.M.,ETHNICAL UNIT AND MILIEU. GP/REL ...PHIL/SCI SOC MATH METH. PAGE 143 H2865 — IDEA/COMP HABITAT CULTURE SOCIETY

B27
CHILDS J.B.,AN ACCOUNT OF GOVERNMENT DOCUMENT BIBLIOGRAPHY IN THE UNITED STATES AND ELSEWHERE (A PAPER). LOC/G PRESS CENTRAL KNOWL...METH 19/20 LEAGUE/NAT. PAGE 29 H0590 — BIBLIOG/A CON/ANAL NAT/G

C31
MACLEOD W.C.,"THE ORIGIN AND HISTORY OF POLITICS." UNIV CULTURE NAT/G REPRESENT...SOC CONCPT TREND BIBLIOG. PAGE 100 H2004 — METH STRUCT SOCIETY

B36
CULVER D.C.,METHODOLOGY OF SOCIAL SCIENCE RESEARCH: A BIBLIOGRAPHY. LAW CULTURE...CRIMLGY GEOG STAT OBS INT QU HIST/WRIT CHARTS 20. PAGE 36 H0719 — BIBLIOG/A METH SOC

B39
FIRTH R.,PRIMITIVE POLYNESIAN ECONOMY. SOCIETY DIST/IND SECT CHIEF CAP/ISM PRODUC WEALTH...SOC OBS METH WORSHIP 20 POLYNESIA. PAGE 50 H1007 — ECO/UNDEV CULTURE AGRI ECO/TAC

S39
LASSWELL H.D.,"PERSON, PERSONALITY, GROUP, CULTURE" (BMR)" UNIV CREATE EDU/PROP...EPIST CONCPT LING METH. PAGE 92 H1833 — PERSON GP/REL CULTURE PERS/REL

B40
HERSKOVITS M.J.,THE ECONOMIC LIFE OF PRIMITIVE PEOPLES. INDUS OP/RES PLAN PROB/SOLV...BIBLIOG METH 20. PAGE 70 H1407
CULTURE ECO/TAC ECO/UNDEV PRODUC

B49
MAO TSE-TUNG,NEW DEMOCRACY. CHINA/COM NAT/G DIPLOM ECO/TAC EDU/PROP REV...CONCPT METH SOC/INTEG 20. PAGE 102 H2045
SOCISM MARXISM POPULISM CULTURE

B50
WARD R.E.,A GUIDE TO JAPANESE REFERENCE AND RESEARCH MATERIALS IN THE FIELD OF POLITICAL SCIENCE. LAW CONSTN LOC/G PRESS ADMIN...SOC CON/ANAL METH 19/20 CHINJAP. PAGE 165 H3305
BIBLIOG/A ASIA NAT/G

B52
SPICER E.H.,HUMAN PROBLEMS IN TECHNOLOGICAL CHANGE. ECO/UNDEV AGRI INDUS NAT/G ACT/RES LEAD GP/REL INGP/REL ROLE...INT METH 20 CASEBOOK. PAGE 147 H2947
TEC/DEV CULTURE STRUCT OP/RES

B52
UNESCO,DOCUMENTATION IN THE SOCIAL SCIENCES. CULTURE...GP/COMP METH 20 UNESCO. PAGE 158 H3162
BIBLIOG SOC

N52
COORDINATING COMM DOC SOC SCI,INTERNATIONAL REPERTORY OF SOCIAL SCIENCE DOCUMENTATION CENTERS (PAMPHLET). ACT/RES OP/RES WRITING KNOWL...CON/ANAL METH. PAGE 33 H0661
BIBLIOG/A R+D NAT/G INT/ORG

B53
BIDNEY D.,THEORETICAL ANTHROPOLOGY. DRIVE ROLE ORD/FREE...CONCPT METH/CNCPT MYTH CLASSIF OBS IDEA/COMP METH/COMP BIBLIOG METH 20. PAGE 17 H0331
CULTURE SOC PSY PHIL/SCI

B53
FLORENCE P.S.,THE LOGIC OF BRITISH AND AMERICAN INDUSTRY; A REALISTIC ANALYSIS OF ECONOMIC STRUCTURE AND GOVERNMENT. UK USA+45 USA-45 FINAN LABOR CAP/ISM INGP/REL EFFICIENCY...MGT CONCPT STAT CHARTS METH 20. PAGE 51 H1028
INDUS ECO/DEV NAT/G NAT/COMP

B54
GATZKE H.W.,STRESEMANN AND THE REARMAMENT OF GERMANY. EUR+WWI GERMANY USSR FINAN NAT/G ECO/TAC ATTIT...BIOG METH 20 STRESEMN/G. PAGE 55 H1105
FORCES INDUS PWR

B54
CHECKLIST OF ARCHIVES IN THE JAPANESE MINISTRY OF FOREIGN AFFAIRS....GEOG SOC METH 19/20 CHINJAP. PAGE 161 H3219
BIBLIOG/A NAT/G ASIA

C54
DE GRAZIA A.,"THE COMPARATIVE SURVEY OF EUROPEAN-AMERICAN POLITICAL BEHAV IOR; A RESEARCH PROSPECTUS (PAPER)" EUR+WWI FRANCE GERMANY SPAIN UK USA+45 WOR+45 STRATA POL/PAR DIPLOM EDU/PROP COLONIAL LEAD WAR NAT/LISM CONCPT. PAGE 37 H0752
BIBLIOG R+D METH NAT/COMP

B55
BAILEY S.K.,RESEARCH FRONTIERS IN POLITICS AND GOVERNMENT. CONSTN LEGIS ADMIN REV CHOOSE...CONCPT IDEA/COMP GAME ANTHOL 20. PAGE 10 H0201
R+D METH NAT/G

B55
MOHL R.V.,DIE GESCHICHTE UND LITERATUR DER STAATSWISSENSCHAFTEN (3 VOLS.). LAW NAT/G...JURID METH/COMP METH. PAGE 112 H2236
PHIL/SCI MOD/EUR

B55
RESHETAR J.S.,PROBLEMS OF ANALYZING AND PREDICTING SOVIET BEHAVIOR. USSR CULTURE ECO/DEV AGRI DIST/IND EXTR/IND PROC/MFG NAT/G SECT TOP/EX ACT/RES ADMIN PWR WEALTH...SOC METH TOT/POP VAL/FREE 20. PAGE 131 H2617
COM ATTIT

B56
DRIVER H.E.,AN INTEGRATION OF FUNCTIONAL, EVOLUTIONARY AND HISTORICAL THEORY BY MEANS OF CORRELATIONS. INGP/REL BIO/SOC HABITAT...PHIL/SCI GEN/LAWS. PAGE 42 H0847
CULTURE METH SOC CORREL

S56
ALMOND G.A.,"COMPARATIVE POLITICAL SYSTEMS" (BMR)" WOR+45 WOR-45 PROB/SOLV DIPLOM EFFICIENCY ...PHIL/SCI SOC METH 17/20. PAGE 5 H0111
GOV/COMP CONCPT ALL/IDEOS NAT/COMP

B57
ALEXANDER L.M.,WORLD POLITICAL PATTERNS. NAT/G PROVS CAP/ISM DIPLOM COLONIAL NAT/LISM...POLICY GEOG CHARTS METH/COMP NAT/COMP 20. PAGE 5 H0101
CONTROL METH GOV/COMP

B57
LOOMIS C.P.,RURAL SOCIOLOGY. CULTURE KIN NAT/G SECT VOL/ASSN ACT/RES EDU/PROP HEALTH. PAGE 98 H1963
SOC AGRI METH T

B57
ROSS R.,THE FABRIC OF SOCIETY. STRATA GP/REL PERSON ...CONCPT METH T 20. PAGE 134 H2687
SOC PHIL/SCI CULTURE STRUCT

S57
NEUMANN S.,"COMPARATIVE POLITICS: A HALF CENTURY APPRAISAL" USA+45 USA-45...SOC TIME/SEQ TREND NAT/COMP METH 20. PAGE 117 H2339
PHIL/SCI GOV/COMP GEN/METH

B58
INTERNATIONAL ECONOMIC ASSN,ECONOMICS OF INTERNATIONAL MIGRATION. WOR+45 WOR-45 ECO/UNDEV FINAN NAT/G REGION...NAT/COMP METH 20. PAGE 78 H1556
CENSUS GEOG DIPLOM ECO/TAC

S58
APTER D.E.,"A COMPARATIVE METHOD FOR THE STUDY OF POLITICS" (BMR)" UNIV SOCIETY STRATA NAT/G POL/PAR ...CHARTS SIMUL 20. PAGE 8 H0151
SOC METH METH/COMP

B59
HONINGMAN J.J.,THE WORLD OF MAN. CHRIST-17C MEDIT-7 PRE/AMER PREHIST CREATE INGP/REL BIO/SOC HABITAT ...PSY SOC BIBLIOG. PAGE 73 H1460
CULTURE METH PERSON STRUCT

B59
LEIGHTON A.H.,MY NAME IS LEGION; FOUNDATIONS FOR A THEORY OF MAN IN RELATION TO CULTURE (VOL. I). CULTURE STRANGE ANOMIE...SOC CONCPT METH/CNCPT CHARTS BIBLIOG METH 20 NOVA/SCOT. PAGE 93 H1867
HEALTH PSY SOCIETY HABITAT

B60
KERSELL J.E.,PARLIAMENTARY SUPERVISION OF DELEGATED LEGISLATION. UK EFFICIENCY PWR...POLICY CHARTS BIBLIOG METH 20 PARLIAMENT. PAGE 85 H1699
LEGIS CONTROL NAT/G EX/STRUC

B60
SCANLON D.G.,INTERNATIONAL EDUCATION: A DOCUMENTARY HISTORY. ADMIN CONTROL ATTIT PERCEPT...BIOG ANTHOL METH 20. PAGE 138 H2765
EDU/PROP INT/ORG NAT/COMP DIPLOM

B60
SMITH M.G.,GOVERNMENT IN ZAZZAU 1800-1950. NIGERIA UK CULTURE SOCIETY LOC/G ADMIN COLONIAL ...METH/CNCPT NEW/IDEA METH 19/20. PAGE 146 H2914
REGION CONSTN KIN ECO/UNDEV

C60
HOSELITZ B.,"THE ROLE OF CITIES IN THE ECONOMIC GROWTH OF UNDERDEVELOPED COUNTRIES" IN "SOCIOLOGICAL ASPECTS OF ECONOMIC GROWTH"(BMR). CULTURE LOC/G ACT/RES...SOC IDEA/COMP METH/COMP METH 14/20 REDFIELD/R. PAGE 74 H1474
METH/CNCPT MUNIC TEC/DEV ECO/UNDEV

B61
FREYRE G.,THE PORTUGUESE AND THE TROPICS. L/A+17C PORTUGAL SOCIETY PERF/ART ADMIN TASK GP/REL ...ART/METH CONCPT SOC/INTEG 20. PAGE 53 H1060
COLONIAL METH PLAN CULTURE

B61
NICOLSON H.G.,THE OLD DIPLOMACY AND THE NEW. NAT/G PLAN PROB/SOLV...METH 20. PAGE 118 H2355
DIPLOM POLICY INT/ORG

S61
TUCKER R.C.,"TOWARDS A COMPARATIVE POLITICS OF MOVEMENT-REGIMES" (BMR)" USSR CONSTN NAT/G CREATE PROB/SOLV DIPLOM DOMIN REV...GP/COMP IDEA/COMP METH 20 STALIN/J BOLSHEVISM. PAGE 157 H3135
MARXISM POLICY GEN/LAWS PWR

B62
BROWN B.E.,NEW DIRECTIONS IN COMPARATIVE POLITICS. AUSTRIA FRANCE GERMANY UK WOR+45 EX/STRUC LEGIS ORD/FREE 20. PAGE 22 H0439
NAT/COMP METH POL/PAR FORCES

B62
EVANS-PRITCHARD E.E.,ESSAYS IN SOCIAL ANTHROPOLOGY. AFR KIN REGION INGP/REL DRIVE HABITAT...OBS METH 20 ZANDE. PAGE 48 H0954
SOCIETY CULTURE SOC STRUCT

B62
MEIER R.L.,A COMMUNICATIONS THEORY OF URBAN GROWTH. CULTURE ECO/DEV COMPUTER BUDGET UTIL KNOWL...SOC CONCPT METH 20 OPEN/SPACE. PAGE 108 H2164
OP/RES COM/IND MUNIC CONTROL

B62
MILLER J.D.B.,THE NATURE OF POLITICS. NAT/G DOMIN LEGIT LEAD...CONCPT METH. PAGE 111 H2213
METH/COMP IDEA/COMP PHIL/SCI

B62
YU LIEN YEN CHIU,INDEX TO THE CLASSIFIED FILES ON COMMUNIST CHINA. CHINA/COM CULTURE ECO/UNDEV CIVMIL/REL PWR WEALTH MARXISM...PSY SOC METH 20. PAGE 172 H3440
BIBLIOG INDEX COM

B63
GERSCHENKRON A.,THE STABILITY OF DICTATORSHIPS. NAT/G EDU/PROP TASK ATTIT PERSON...POLICY PSY SOC METH 19/20. PAGE 56 H1116
TOTALISM CONCPT CONTROL ORD/FREE

B63
INDIAN INSTITUTE PUBLIC ADMIN,CASES IN INDIAN ADMINISTRATION. INDIA AGRI NAT/G PROB/SOLV TEC/DEV ECO/TAC ADMIN...ANTHOL METH 20. PAGE 77 H1532
DECISION PLAN MGT ECO/UNDEV

B63
MCPHEE W.N.,FORMAL THEORIES OF MASS BEHAVIOR. CULTURE STRUCT DOMIN EDU/PROP CHOOSE...MATH 20. PAGE 108 H2149
SOC METH CONCPT ATTIT

B63
OECD,FOOD AID: ITS ROLE IN ECONOMIC DEVELOPMENT. FINAN NAT/G PLAN DIPLOM GIVE TASK WEALTH
ECO/UNDEV FOR/AID

...METH/COMP METH 20. PAGE 120 H2397 INT/ORG POLICY N63

LEDERER W.,THE BALANCE ON FOREIGN TRANSACTIONS: PROBLEMS OF DEFINITION AND MEASUREMENT (PAMPHLET). USA+45 BUDGET DIPLOM ECO/TAC PRICE GOV/REL...POLICY STAT NAT/COMP METH 20. PAGE 93 H1853 FINAN BAL/PAY INT/TRADE ECO/DEV B64

HERRICK M.D.,CATALOG OF AFRICAN GOVERNMENT DOCUMENTS AND AFRICAN AREA INDEX (2ND REV. ED.) ....SOC INDEX METH 20. PAGE 70 H1405 BIBLIOG ECO/UNDEV AFR NAT/G B64

INDIAN COMM PREVENTION CORRUPT,REPORT, 1964. INDIA NAT/G GOV/REL ATTIT ORD/FREE...CRIMLGY METH 20. PAGE 76 H1530 CRIME ADMIN LEGIS LOC/G B64

JARVIE I.C.,THE REVOLUTION IN ANTHROPOLOGY. UNIV CULTURE SOCIETY SECT...MYTH 20 POPPER/K. PAGE 80 H1592 SOC TREND PHIL/SCI METH B64

LIENHARDT G.,SOCIAL ANTHROPOLOGY. SOCIETY FAM KIN ...CONCPT METH. PAGE 97 H1928 SOC HABITAT HEREDITY CULTURE CULTURE B64

MEAD M.,CONTINUITIES IN CULTURAL EVOLUTION. FACE/GP KIN ACT/RES EDU/PROP GP/REL INGP/REL DRIVE HEREDITY ROLE...TIME/SEQ TREND METH SOC/INTEG 20. PAGE 108 H2153 CULTURE SOC PERS/REL B64

NORTHROP F.S.,CROSS-CULTURAL UNDERSTANDING: EPISTEMOLOGY IN ANTHROPOLOGY. BURMA GREECE THAILAND HABITAT PERCEPT PERSON...PHIL/SCI SOC METH 20 MEXIC/AMER CHINJAP. PAGE 119 H2375 EPIST PSY CULTURE CONCPT B64

WERTHEIM W.F.,EAST-WEST PARALLELS. INDONESIA S/ASIA NAT/G SECT...TIME/SEQ METH REFORMERS S/EASTASIA. PAGE 167 H3334 SOC ECO/UNDEV CULTURE NAT/LISM C64

SCOTT R.E.,"MEXICAN GOVERNMENT IN TRANSITION (REV ED)" CULTURE STRUCT POL/PAR CHIEF ADMIN LOBBY REV CHOOSE GP/REL DRIVE...BIBLIOG METH 20 MEXIC/AMER. PAGE 141 H2816 NAT/G L/A+17C ROUTINE CONSTN B65

CANTRIL H.,THE PATTERN OF HUMAN CONCERNS. ELITES ECO/DEV ECO/UNDEV...STAT CHARTS METH 20. PAGE 26 H0524 ATTIT ALL/VALS NAT/COMP CULTURE B65

DAHL R.A.,MODERN POLITICAL ANALYSIS. UNIV COERCE ...MAJORIT DECISION METH. PAGE 36 H0731 CONCPT GOV/COMP PWR B65

DURKHEIM E.,THE ELEMENTARY FORMS OF THE RELIGIOUS LIFE. KIN PARTIC MORAL...PSY MYTH OBS IDEA/COMP METH WORSHIP 19/20. PAGE 43 H0870 SOC CULTURE CONCPT B65

FORM W.H.,INDUSTRIAL RELATIONS AND SOCIAL CHANGE IN LATIN AMERICA. L/A+17C AGRI LABOR NAT/G PLAN PROB/SOLV DIPLOM...MGT SOC ANTHOL BIBLIOG/A METH 20. PAGE 52 H1038 INDUS GP/REL NAT/COMP ECO/UNDEV B65

HARMON R.B.,POLITICAL SCIENCE: A BIBLIOGRAPHICAL GUIDE TO THE LITERATURE. WOR+45 WOR-45 R+D INT/ORG LOC/G NAT/G DIPLOM ADMIN...CONCPT METH. PAGE 67 H1334 BIBLIOG POL/PAR LAW GOV/COMP B65

HYMES D.,THE USE OF COMPUTERS IN ANTHROPOLOGY. CULTURE PROF/ORG CONSULT CREATE EFFICIENCY PERCEPT ...CLASSIF LING CON/ANAL COMPUT/IR METH/COMP ANTHOL 20. PAGE 76 H1517 METH COMPUTER TEC/DEV SOC B65

MURDOCK G.P.,CULTURE AND SOCIETY. SOCIETY STRATA STRUCT SECT CREATE CONTROL ORD/FREE...GP/COMP ANTHOL 20. PAGE 115 H2294 CULTURE PHIL/SCI METH IDEA/COMP B65

OECD,THE MEDITERRANEAN REGIONAL PROJECT: ITALY; EDUCATION AND DEVELOPMENT. ITALY SOCIETY STRATA FINAN NAT/G PROF/ORG WORKER PLAN PROB/SOLV ADMIN ...STAT CHARTS METH 20 OECD. PAGE 120 H2400 SCHOOL EDU/PROP ECO/UNDEV ACADEM B65

VON RENESSE E.A.,UNVOLLENDETE DEMOKRATIEN. AFR ISLAM S/ASIA SOCIETY ACT/RES COLONIAL...JURID CHARTS BIBLIOG METH 13/20. PAGE 164 H3276 ECO/UNDEV NAT/COMP SOVEREIGN S65

VAN DEN BERG M.,"SOME METHODOLOGICAL ASPECTS OF SOUTH AFRICA'S FIRST E.D.P." SOUTH/AFR NAT/G CREATE TEC/DEV CAP/ISM INCOME PRODUC...CON/ANAL CHARTS 20. PAGE 161 H3226 ECO/DEV PLAN METH STAT C65

COLEMAN J.S.,"EDUCATION AND POLITICAL DEVELOPMENT." ECO/UNDEV COM CULTURE INTELL STRUCT SCHOOL PERSON SOVEREIGN ...POLICY ANTHOL BIBLIOG/A METH 20. PAGE 31 H0629 NAT/LISM EDU/PROP TEC/DEV B66

AGGARWALA R.N.,FINANCIAL COMMITTEES OF THE INDIAN PARLIAMENT: A STUDY IN PARLIAMENTARY CONTROL OVER PUBLIC EXPENDITURE. INDIA FINAN NAT/G ROLE...CHARTS METH/COMP METH 20 PARLIAMENT. PAGE 4 H0078 PARL/PROC BUDGET CONTROL DELIB/GP B66

LENSKI G.E.,POWER AND PRIVILEGE: A THEORY OF SOCIAL STRATIFICATION. SWEDEN UK UNIV USSR CULTURE ECO/UNDEV PRIVIL PWR...PHIL/SCI CONCPT CHARTS IDEA/COMP HYPO/EXP METH MARX/KARL. PAGE 94 H1882 SOC STRATA STRUCT SOCIETY B66

LEONTIEF W.,ESSAYS IN ECONOMICS. ECO/UNDEV INDUS NAT/G CAP/ISM FOR/AID AUTOMAT MARXISM...ECOMETRIC CHARTS ANTHOL METH 20 KEYNES/JM. PAGE 94 H1886 CONCPT METH/CNCPT METH/COMP B66

PARETO V.,SOCIOLOGICAL WRITINGS (TRANS. BY DERICK MURFIN). UNIV NAT/G SOCISM. PAGE 123 H2466 SOC CONCPT METH SOCIETY B66

RADIN P.,THE METHOD AND THEORY OF ETHNOLOGY. CULTURE STRUCT BIO/SOC HABITAT...HUM OBS/ENVIR METH/COMP GEN/LAWS 20 HUMANISM. PAGE 129 H2578 PHIL/SCI SOC METH SOCIETY SOCIETY B66

SMELSER N.J.,SOCIAL STRUCTURE AND MOBILITY IN ECONOMIC DEVELOPMENT. CULTURE SOCIETY CONFER...PSY SOC CHARTS METH/COMP NAT/COMP ANTHOL METH 20. PAGE 145 H2904 STRUCT STRATA ECO/UNDEV ECO/DEV L66

"FEDERAL, STATE AND LOCAL GOVERNMENT PUBLICATIONS." ACADEM LOC/G NAT/G PROVS SCHOOL EFFICIENCY ...PHIL/SCI ANTHOL. PAGE 143 H2854 BIBLIOG OP/RES METH S66

MCLENNAN B.N.,"EVOLUTION OF CONCEPTS OF REPRESENTATION IN INDONESIA" INDONESIA...CONCPT IDEA/COMP METH 20. PAGE 107 H2143 REPRESENT NAT/G POPULISM PWR B67

DENISON E.F.,WHY GROWTH RATES DIFFER; POSTWAR EXPERIENCE IN NINE WESTERN COUNTRIES. WOR+45 FINAN WORKER TEC/DEV EDU/PROP PRICE PRODUC WEALTH ...ECOMETRIC STAT CHARTS BIBLIOG. PAGE 40 H0791 METH NAT/COMP ECO/DEV ECO/TAC S67

CATTELL D.T.,"A NEO-MARXIST THEORY OF COMPARATIVE ANALYSIS." USSR STRATA INSPECT DOMIN CONTROL COERCE OWN TOTALISM PWR...FASCIST HYPO/EXP METH 20. PAGE 28 H0561 GOV/COMP MARXISM SIMUL CLASSIF S67

RUCKER B.W.,"WHAT SOLUTIONS DO PEOPLE ENDORSE IN FREE PRESS-FAIR TRIAL DILEMMA?" LAW NAT/G CT/SYS ATTIT...NET/THEORY SAMP CHARTS IDEA/COMP METH 20. PAGE 136 H2710 CONCPT PRESS ADJUD ORD/FREE S68

KANET R.E.,"RECENT SOVIET REASSESSMENT OF DEVELOPMENTS IN THE THIRD WORLD." ALGERIA GHANA INDONESIA USSR WOR+45 CONSTN ELITES INTELL STRUCT DOMIN CONTROL REV PWR MARXISM...IDEA/COMP METH 20 THIRD/WRLD. PAGE 83 H1653 DIPLOM NEUTRAL NAT/G NAT/COMP S68

SHAPIRO J.P.,"SOVIET HISTORIOGRAPHY AND THE MOSCOW TRIALS: AFTER THIRTY YEARS." USSR NAT/G LEGIT PRESS CONTROL LEAD ATTIT MARXISM...NEW/IDEA METH 20 TROTSKY/L STALIN/J KHRUSH/N. PAGE 142 H2843 HIST/WRIT EDU/PROP SANCTION ADJUD

METH/CNCPT....METHODOLOGICAL CONCEPTS

METH/COMP....COMPARISON OF METHODS

N

US DEPARTMENT OF STATE,BIBLIOGRAPHY (PAMPHLETS). AGRI INDUS INT/ORG FOR/AID EDU/PROP WAR MARXISM ...SOC GOV/COMP METH/COMP 20. PAGE 159 H3184 BIBLIOG DIPLOM ECO/DEV NAT/G B13

DIE REKLAME IHRE KUNST UND WISSENSCHAFT. GERMANY POLAND SWITZERLND USA+45 TEC/DEV CAP/ISM DEMAND ...ART/METH EXHIBIT METH/COMP ANTHOL 20. PAGE 135 H2707 EDU/PROP MARKET NAT/COMP ATTIT N17

BURKE E.,THOUGHTS ON THE CAUSE OF THE PRESENT DISCONTENTS (PAMPHLET). MOD/EUR UK CONSTN CHIEF LEGIS DOMIN CONTROL EXEC REPRESENT POPULISM ...TRADIT NEW/IDEA METH/COMP 18 BURKE/EDM. PAGE 24 H0484 ORD/FREE REV PARL/PROC NAT/G B18

YUKIO O.,THE VOICE OF JAPANESE DEMOCRACY, AN ESSAY ON CONSTITUTIONAL LOYALTY (TRANS BY J. E. BECKER). ASIA POL/PAR DELIB/GP EX/STRUC RIGID/FLEX ORD/FREE PWR...POLICY JURID METH/COMP 19/20 CHINJAP. PAGE 172 H3443 CONSTN MAJORIT CHOOSE NAT/G N19

FREEMAN H.A.,COERCION OF STATES IN FEDERAL UNIONS FEDERAL

(PAMPHLET). WOR-45 DIPLOM CONTROL COERCE PEACE ORD/FREE...GOV/COMP METH/COMP NAT/COMP PACIFIST 20. PAGE 53 H1055
WAR INT/ORG PACIFISM
N19

GORWALA A.D.,THE ADMINISTRATIVE JUNGLE (PAMPHLET). INDIA NAT/G LEGIS ECO/TAC CONTROL GOV/REL ...METH/COMP 20. PAGE 59 H1183
ADMIN POLICY PLAN ECO/UNDEV
B23

KADEN E.H.,DER POLITISCHE CHARAKTER DER FRANZOSISCHEN KULTURPROPAGANDA AM RHEIN. FRANCE MOD/EUR DOMIN PRESS...GEOG METH/COMP 20. PAGE 82 H1648
EDU/PROP ATTIT DIPLOM NAT/G
B33

ENSOR R.C.K.,COURTS AND JUDGES IN FRANCE, GERMANY, AND ENGLAND. FRANCE GERMANY UK LAW PROB/SOLV ADMIN ROUTINE CRIME ROLE...METH/COMP 20 CIVIL/LAW. PAGE 46 H0930
CT/SYS EX/STRUC ADJUD NAT/COMP
B33

PUBLIC OPINION AND WORLD POLITICS. UNIV LAW CULTURE NAT/G PRESS REV GP/REL...MAJORIT METH/COMP ANTHOL 20. PAGE 171 H3420
DIPLOM EDU/PROP ATTIT MAJORITY
B34

LIPPMANN W.,THE METHOD OF FREEDOM. SOCIETY INDUS LABOR LOBBY WAR REPRESENT...POLICY IDEA/COMP METH/COMP 19/20. PAGE 97 H1936
CONCPT MAJORIT NAT/G
B36

HUBERMAN L.,MAN'S WORLDLY GOODS: THE STORY OF THE WEALTH OF NATIONS. CHRIST-17C EUR+WWI MOD/EUR SOCIETY DOMIN REV ORD/FREE...TIME/SEQ METH/COMP. PAGE 74 H1486
WEALTH CAP/ISM MARXISM CREATE
B36

SMITH T.V.,THE PROMISE OF AMERICAN POLITICS. USA-45 WOR-45 LAW CONSTN STRATA PARTIC FASCISM LAISSEZ MARXISM...MAJORIT METH/COMP 18/20 JEFFERSN/T LOCKE/JOHN BENTHAM/J. PAGE 146 H2920
CONCPT ORD/FREE IDEA/COMP NAT/COMP
B37

VON HAYEK F.A.,MONETARY NATIONALISM AND INTERNATIONAL STABILITY. WOR-45 ECO/DEV NAT/G PROB/SOLV INT/TRADE...POLICY CONCPT METH/COMP NAT/COMP 20. PAGE 163 H3271
ECO/TAC FINAN DIPLOM NAT/LISM
B38

HEIMANN E.,COMMUNISM, FASCISM, OR DEMOCRACY? WOR-45 CONSTN SOCIETY STRATA AGRI CAP/ISM MORAL ORD/FREE ...MAJORIT METH/COMP NAT/COMP 19/20. PAGE 69 H1384
SOCISM MARXISM FASCISM PLURISM
B38

LAWLEY F.E.,THE GROWTH OF COLLECTIVE ECONOMY VOL. 1: NATIONAL. EUR+WWI AGRI INDUS NAT/G BARGAIN CAP/ISM ECO/TAC WAR OPTIMAL WEALTH...GOV/COMP METH/COMP 19/20 MONOPOLY. PAGE 92 H1844
SOCISM PRICE CONTROL OWN
B40

HUNTER R.,REVOLUTION: WHY, HOW, WHEN? NAT/G ECO/TAC EDU/PROP COERCE ORD/FREE FASCISM POPULISM SOCISM 18/20 HITLER/A LENIN/VI. PAGE 75 H1502
REV METH/COMP LEAD CONSTN
B41

BAUMANN G.,GRUNDLAGEN UND PRAXIS DER INTERNATIONALEN PROPAGANDA. FRANCE GERMANY UK CULTURE COM/IND PRESS PWR...PSY METH/COMP 20. PAGE 12 H0241
EDU/PROP DOMIN ATTIT DIPLOM
B41

COHEN E.W.,THE GROWTH OF THE BRITISH CIVIL SERVICE 1780-1939. UK NAT/G SENIOR ROUTINE GOV/REL...MGT METH/COMP BIBLIOG 18/20. PAGE 31 H0616
OP/RES TIME/SEQ CENTRAL ADMIN
B43

LENIN V.I.,LEFT WING COMMUNISM: AN INFANTILE DISORDER (1920). GERMANY MOD/EUR USSR STRUCT CHIEF DOMIN EDU/PROP LEGIT LEAD REPRESENT POPULISM ...METH/COMP 19 LENIN/VI COM/PARTY MENSHEVIK. PAGE 94 H1879
COM MARXISM NAT/G REV
B44

KRIS E.,GERMAN RADIO PROPAGANDA: REPORT ON HOME BROADCASTS DURING THE WAR. EUR+WWI GERMANY CULTURE CONSULT PROB/SOLV FEEDBACK TASK INGP/REL DRIVE PWR FASCISM...CON/ANAL METH/COMP 20. PAGE 89 H1768
EDU/PROP DOMIN ACT/RES ATTIT
B48

FURNIVAL J.,COLONIAL POLICY AND PRACTICE A COMPARATIVE STUDY OF BURMA, AND NETHERLANDS INDIA. BURMA INDONESIA S/ASIA...GEOG OBS GOV/COMP METH/COMP 20. PAGE 54 H1080
COLONIAL NAT/LISM WEALTH SOVEREIGN
B48

TURNER A.C.,FREE SPEECH AND BROADCASTING. UK USA+45 ORD/FREE NAT/COMP. PAGE 157 H3140
COM/IND NAT/G CONTROL METH/COMP
B49

MCLEAN J.M.,THE PUBLIC SERVICE AND UNIVERSITY EDUCATION. UK USA-45 DELIB/GP EX/STRUC TOP/EX ADMIN ...GOV/COMP METH/COMP NAT/COMP ANTHOL 20. PAGE 107 H2142
ACADEM NAT/G EXEC EDU/PROP
B50

CARR E.H.,STUDIES IN REVOLUTION. CREATE WAR PERSON ALL/IDEOS MARXISM SOCISM...PHIL/SCI METH/COMP ANTHOL 18/20 SAINTSIMON MARX/KARL PROUDHON/P LASSALLE/F PLEKHNV/GV. PAGE 27 H0537
REV IDEA/COMP COERCE BIOG
B50

LIPSET S.M.,AGRARIAN SOCIALISM. CANADA POL/PAR OP/RES ECO/TAC ADMIN ATTIT...TIME/SEQ NAT/COMP SOC/EXP 20 SASKATCH. PAGE 97 H1938
SOCISM AGRI METH/COMP STRUCT
B52

SCHATTSCHNEIDER E.E.,A GUIDE TO THE STUDY OF PUBLIC AFFAIRS. LAW LOC/G NAT/G LEGIS BUDGET PRESS ADMIN LOBBY...JURID CHARTS 20. PAGE 139 H2775
ACT/RES INTELL ACADEM METH/COMP
B53

BENDIX R.,CLASS, STATUS AND POWER: A READER IN SOCIAL STRATIFICATION. USA+45 SOCIETY ACT/RES DOMIN ATTIT RIGID/FLEX...PSY SOC CONCPT METH/COMP NAT/COMP 20. PAGE 14 H0273
STRATA PWR STRUCT ROLE
B53

BIDNEY D.,THEORETICAL ANTHROPOLOGY. DRIVE ROLE ORD/FREE...CONCPT METH/CNCPT MYTH CLASSIF OBS IDEA/COMP METH/COMP BIBLIOG METH 20. PAGE 17 H0331
CULTURE SOC PSY PHIL/SCI
B53

MEAD M.,CULTURAL PATTERNS AND TECHNICAL CHANGE. BURMA GREECE NIGERIA ECO/UNDEV AGRI INDUS SCHOOL SECT CREATE FEEDBACK HABITAT...PSY METH/COMP BIBLIOG 20 UN. PAGE 108 H2152
HEALTH TEC/DEV CULTURE ADJUST
B54

SCHWARTZ B.,FRENCH ADMINISTRATIVE LAW AND THE COMMON-LAW WORLD. FRANCE CULTURE LOC/G NAT/G PROVS DELIB/GP EX/STRUC LEGIS PROB/SOLV CT/SYS EXEC GOV/REL...IDEA/COMP ENGLSH/LAW. PAGE 140 H2808
JURID LAW METH/COMP ADJUD
B55

DUVERGER M.,THE POLITICAL ROLE OF WOMEN. FRANCE GERMANY/W NORWAY YUGOSLAVIA STRATA LOBBY AGE ATTIT ROLE...STAT SAMP CHARTS METH/COMP NAT/COMP HYPO/EXP FEMALE/SEX. PAGE 44 H0875
SEX LEAD PARTIC CHOOSE
B55

MOHL R.V.,DIE GESCHICHTE UND LITERATUR DER STAATSWISSENSCHAFTEN (3 VOLS.). LAW NAT/G...JURID METH/COMP METH. PAGE 112 H2236
PHIL/SCI MOD/EUR
B55

STEWARD J.H.,THEORY OF CULTURE CHANGE; THE METHODOLOGY OF MULTILINEAR EVOLUTION. SOCIETY KIN SECT GP/REL INGP/REL...BIBLIOG SOC/INTEG 20. PAGE 149 H2984
CULTURE CONCPT METH/COMP HABITAT
C55

STEWARD J.H.,"THE CONCEPT AND METHOD OF CULTURAL ECOLOGY" IN T.H. STEWARD'S THEORY OF CULTURAL CHANGE." SOCIETY INGP/REL...CONCPT CON/ANAL METH/COMP 20. PAGE 149 H2985
HABITAT CULTURE CREATE ADJUST
C56

NEUMANN S.,"MODERN POLITICAL PARTIES: APPROACHES TO COMPARATIVE POLITIC. FRANCE UK EX/STRUC DOMIN ADMIN LEAD REPRESENT TOTALISM ATTIT...POLICY TREND METH/COMP ANTHOL BIBLIOG/A 20 CMN/WLTH. PAGE 117 H2338
POL/PAR GOV/COMP ELITES MAJORIT
B57

ALEXANDER L.M.,WORLD POLITICAL PATTERNS. NAT/G PROVS CAP/ISM DIPLOM COLONIAL NAT/LISM...POLICY GEOG CHARTS METH/COMP NAT/COMP 20. PAGE 5 H0101
CONTROL METH GOV/COMP
B57

ARON R.,THE OPIUM OF THE INTELLECTUALS (TRANS. BY TERENCE KILMARTIN). FRANCE USSR WOR+45 CULTURE POL/PAR PLAN DOMIN EDU/PROP REV ATTIT ORD/FREE ...IDEA/COMP METH/COMP NAT/COMP 20 COM/PARTY. PAGE 8 H0169
INTELL UTOPIA MYTH MARXISM
B58

COWAN L.G.,LOCAL GOVERNMENT IN WEST AFRICA. AFR FRANCE UK CULTURE KIN POL/PAR CHIEF LEGIS CREATE ADMIN PARTIC GOV/REL GP/REL...METH/COMP 20. PAGE 34 H0682
LOC/G COLONIAL SOVEREIGN REPRESENT
B58

GURVITCH G.,TRAITE DE SOCIOLOGIE (2 VOLS.). FRANCE CULTURE INDUS GP/REL INGP/REL...PSY BIBLIOG 20. PAGE 63 H1256
ANTHOL SOC METH/COMP METH/CNCPT
B58

MECRENSKY E.,SCIENTIFIC MANPOWER IN EUROPE. WOR+45 EDU/PROP GOV/REL SKILL...TECHNIC PHIL/SCI INT CHARTS BIBLIOG 20. PAGE 108 H2157
ECO/TAC TEC/DEV METH/COMP NAT/COMP
B58

OGDEN F.D.,THE POLL TAX IN THE SOUTH. USA+45 USA-45 CONSTN ADJUD ADMIN PARTIC CRIME...TIME/SEQ GOV/COMP METH/COMP 18/20 SOUTH/US. PAGE 120 H2407
TAX CHOOSE RACE/REL DISCRIM
B58

WOODS H.D.,PATTERNS OF INDUSTRIAL DISPUTE SETTLEMENT IN FIVE CANADIAN INDUSTRIES. CANADA USA+45 CONSULT ADJUD GP/REL...JURID GOV/COMP METH/COMP ANTHOL 20. PAGE 170 H3408
BARGAIN INDUS LABOR NAT/G
L58

BELL D.,"TEN THEORIES IN SEARCH OF REALITY: THE PREDICTION OF SOVIET BEHAVIOR IN THE SOCIAL SCIENCES" (BMR)" COM USSR...POLICY SOC METH/COMP
MARXISM PREDICT IDEA/COMP

20. PAGE 13 H0264

S58
APTER D.E.,"A COMPARATIVE METHOD FOR THE STUDY OF POLITICS" (BMR)" UNIV SOCIETY STRATA NAT/G POL/PAR ...CHARTS SIMUL 20. PAGE 8 H0151
SOC METH METH/COMP

B59
ELDRIDGE H.T.,THE MATERIALS OF DEMOGRAPHY: A SELECTED AND ANNOTATED BIBLIOGRAPHY. R+D DEATH ...SAMP METH/COMP NAT/COMP 20. PAGE 45 H0905
BIBLIOG/A GEOG STAT TREND

S59
DUNCAN O.D.,"CULTURAL, BEHAVIORAL, AND ECOLOGICAL PERSPECTIVES IN THE STUDY OF SOCIAL ORGANIZATION" (BMR)" UNIV STRATA EX/STRUC PROB/SOLV ADMIN ATTIT SOC/INTEG 20 BUREAUCRCY. PAGE 43 H0862
CULTURE METH/COMP SOCIETY HABITAT

B60
MEYRIAT J.,LA SCIENCE POLITIQUE EN FRANCE, 1945-1958; BIBLIOGRAPHIES FRANCAISES DE SCIENCES SOCIALES (VOL. I). EUR+WWI FRANCE POL/PAR DIPLOM ADMIN CHOOSE ATTIT...IDEA/COMP METH/COMP NAT/COMP 20. PAGE 110 H2193
BIBLIOG/A NAT/G CONCPT PHIL/SCI

B60
ROBINSON E.A.G.,ECONOMIC CONSEQUENCES OF THE SIZE OF NATIONS. AGRI INDUS DELIB/GP FOR/AID ADMIN EFFICIENCY...METH/COMP 20. PAGE 132 H2649
CONCPT INT/ORG NAT/COMP

B60
SAHLINS M.D.,EVOLUTION AND CULTURE. CREATE...MYTH METH/COMP BIBLIOG 20. PAGE 137 H2730
CULTURE NEW/IDEA CONCPT HABITAT

B60
STOLPER W.F.,GERMANY BETWEEN EAST AND WEST: THE ECONOMICS OF COMPETITIVE COEXISTENCE. FUT GERMANY/E GERMANY/W WOR+45 FINAN POL/PAR BUDGET ECO/TAC FOR/AID INT/TRADE...STAT CHARTS METH/COMP 20 COLD/WAR. PAGE 150 H2989
ECO/DEV DIPLOM GOV/COMP BAL/PWR

L60
ROKKAN S.,"NORWAY AND THE UNITED STATES OF AMERICA." NORWAY CHOOSE...SOC STAND/INT SAMP CHARTS GP/COMP METH/COMP 20. PAGE 133 H2665
STRUCT NAT/G PARTIC REPRESENT

S60
BANFIELD E.C.,"THE POLITICAL IMPLICATIONS OF METROPOLITAN GROWTH" (BMR)" UK USA+45 LOC/G PROB/SOLV ADMIN GP/REL...METH/COMP NAT/COMP 20. PAGE 10 H0209
TASK MUNIC GOV/COMP CENSUS

S60
TURNER R.H.,"SPONSORED AND CONTEST MOBILITY IN THE SCHOOL SYSTEM." UK USA+45 ELITES STRATA ACADEM FACE/GP EDU/PROP CONTROL INGP/REL ADJUST ATTIT PERSON...METH/COMP 20. PAGE 157 H3142
AGE/Y NAT/COMP SCHOOL STRUCT

C60
HOSELITZ B.,"THE ROLE OF CITIES IN THE ECONOMIC GROWTH OF UNDERDEVELOPED COUNTRIES" IN "SOCIOLOGICAL ASPECTS OF ECONOMIC GROWTH"(BMR). CULTURE LOC/G ACT/RES...SOC IDEA/COMP METH/COMP METH 14/20 REDFIELD/R. PAGE 74 H1474
METH/CNCPT MUNIC TEC/DEV ECO/UNDEV

B61
GARCIA E.,LA ADMINISTRACION ESPANOLA. SPAIN GOV/REL ...CONCPT METH/COMP 20. PAGE 55 H1099
ADMIN NAT/G LOC/G DECISION

B61
HICKS U.K.,DEVELOPMENT FROM BELOW. UK INDUS ADMIN COLONIAL ROUTINE GOV/REL...POLICY METH/CNCPT CHARTS 19/20 CMN/WLTH. PAGE 71 H1414
ECO/UNDEV LOC/G GOV/COMP METH/COMP

B61
LENIN V.I.,WHAT IS TO BE DONE? (1902). RUSSIA LABOR NAT/G POL/PAR WORKER CAP/ISM ECO/TAC ADMIN PARTIC ...MARXIST IDEA/COMP GEN/LAWS 19/20. PAGE 94 H1881
EDU/PROP PRESS MARXISM METH/COMP

B61
ROCHE J.P.,COURTS AND RIGHTS: THE AMERICAN JUDICIARY IN ACTION (2ND ED.). UK USA+45 USA-45 STRUCT TEC/DEV SANCTION PERS/REL RACE/REL ORD/FREE ...METH/CNCPT GOV/COMP METH/COMP T 13/20. PAGE 133 H2653
JURID CT/SYS NAT/G PROVS

B62
BELL D.,THE END OF IDEOLOGY (REV. ED.). USA+45 USA-45 ELITES STRATA LABOR CREATE CRIME PWR MARXISM ...PHIL/SCI METH/COMP 20 EUROPE. PAGE 13 H0265
CROWD CAP/ISM SOCISM IDEA/COMP

B62
GALENSON W.,LABOR IN DEVELOPING COUNTRIES. BRAZIL INDONESIA ISRAEL PAKISTAN TURKEY AGRI INDUS WORKER PAY PRICE GP/REL WEALTH...MGT CHARTS METH/COMP NAT/COMP 20. PAGE 54 H1088
LABOR ECO/UNDEV BARGAIN POL/PAR

B62
MARTINS A.F.,REVOLUCAO BRANCA NO CAMPO. L/A+17C SERV/IND DEMAND EFFICIENCY PRODUC...POLICY METH/COMP. PAGE 104 H2070
AGRI ECO/UNDEV TEC/DEV NAT/COMP

B62
MILLER J.D.B.,THE NATURE OF POLITICS. NAT/G DOMIN LEGIT LEAD...CONCPT METH. PAGE 111 H2213
METH/COMP IDEA/COMP PHIL/SCI

B62
NOBECOURT R.G.,LES SECRETS DE LA PROPAGANDE EN FRANCE OCCUPEE. FRANCE ELITES NAT/G DIPLOM GP/REL NAT/LISM TOTALISM ORD/FREE 20 VICHY VICHY. PAGE 118 H2365
METH/COMP EDU/PROP WAR CONTROL

B62
SCHECHTMAN J.B.,POSTWAR POPULATION TRANSFERS IN EUROPE: 1945-1955. COM CZECHOSLVK GERMANY POLAND USSR CULTURE SOCIETY PROB/SOLV AGREE NAT/LISM...SOC STAT TREND CHARTS METH/COMP 20 MIGRATION. PAGE 139 H2778
GEOG CENSUS EUR+WWI HABITAT

B62
WALSTON H.,AGRICULTURE UNDER COMMUNISM. CHINA/COM COM PROB/SOLV HAPPINESS RIGID/FLEX...POLICY METH/COMP 20. PAGE 165 H3295
AGRI MARXISM PLAN CREATE

N62
US CONGRESS JT ATOM ENRGY COMM,PEACEFUL USES OF ATOMIC ENERGY, HEARING. USA+45 USSR TEC/DEV ATTIT RIGID/FLEX...TESTS CHARTS EXHIBIT METH/COMP 20 CONGRESS. PAGE 159 H3177
NUC/PWR ACADEM SCHOOL NAT/COMP

B63
BIDNEY D.,THE CONCEPT OF FREEDOM IN ANTHROPOLOGY. UNIV CULTURE STRATA SECT CREATE NAT/LISM ...METH/COMP 20. PAGE 17 H0332
SOC PERSON ORD/FREE CONCPT

B63
DUE J.F.,STATE SALES TAX ADMINISTRATION. OP/RES BUDGET PAY ADMIN EXEC ROUTINE COST EFFICIENCY PROFIT...CHARTS METH/COMP 20. PAGE 43 H0855
PROVS TAX STAT GOV/COMP

B63
ECKSTEIN H.,COMPARATIVE POLITICS. POL/PAR LEGIS CT/SYS CHOOSE TOTALISM PWR POPULISM...METH/COMP GEN/METH ANTHOL BIBLIOG 20. PAGE 44 H0886
NAT/COMP CONSTN REPRESENT NAT/G

B63
FRIED R.C.,THE ITALIAN PREFECTS. ITALY STRATA ECO/DEV NAT/LISM ALL/IDEOS...TREND CHARTS METH/COMP BIBLIOG 17/20 PREFECT. PAGE 53 H1061
ADMIN NAT/G EFFICIENCY

B63
GORDON M.S.,THE ECONOMICS OF WELFARE POLICIES. INDUS LOC/G NAT/G LEGIS WORKER INCOME AGE/O SKILL WEALTH...METH/COMP NAT/COMP 20. PAGE 59 H1180
METH/CNCPT ECO/TAC POLICY

B63
GOURNAY B.,PUBLIC ADMINISTRATION. FRANCE LAW CONSTN AGRI FINAN LABOR SCHOOL EX/STRUC CHOOSE...MGT METH/COMP 20. PAGE 59 H1189
BIBLIOG/A ADMIN NAT/G LOC/G

B63
GUIMARAES A.P.,INFLACAO E MONOPOLIO NO BRASIL. BRAZIL FINAN NAT/G PLAN PAY...METH/COMP 20. PAGE 62 H1248
ECO/UNDEV PRICE INT/TRADE BAL/PAY

B63
INTERNATIONAL ASSOCIATION RES,AFRICAN STUDIES IN INCOME AND WEALTH. AFR NAT/G PROB/SOLV DEMAND INCOME...ECOMETRIC METH/COMP 20. PAGE 78 H1553
WEALTH PLAN ECO/UNDEV BUDGET

B63
LEONARD T.J.,THE FEDERAL SYSTEM OF INDIA. INDIA MUNIC NAT/G PROVS ADMIN SOVEREIGN...IDEA/COMP 20. PAGE 94 H1885
FEDERAL MGT NAT/COMP METH/COMP

B63
LETHBRIDGE H.J.,THE PEASANT AND THE COMMUNES. CHINA/COM COM USSR NEIGH PROB/SOLV ADJUST EFFICIENCY...POLICY METH/COMP NAT/COMP 20. PAGE 95 H1894
MARXISM ECO/TAC AGRI WORKER

B63
MARTINDALE D.,COMMUNITY, CHARACTER AND CIVILIZATION: STUDIES IN SOCIAL BEHAVIORISM. INTELL FAM NEIGH VOL/ASSN GP/REL NAT/LISM ATTIT PERSON ...CONCPT GP/COMP 20 BEHAVIORSM. PAGE 103 H2066
SOC METH/COMP CULTURE STRUCT

B63
OECD,FOOD AID: ITS ROLE IN ECONOMIC DEVELOPMENT. FINAN NAT/G PLAN DIPLOM GIVE TASK WEALTH ...METH/COMP METH 20. PAGE 120 H2397
ECO/UNDEV FOR/AID INT/ORG POLICY

B63
SCHUMAN S.I.,LEGAL POSITIVISM: ITS SCOPE AND LIMITATIONS. CONSTN NAT/G DIPLOM PARTIC UTOPIA ...POLICY DECISION PHIL/SCI CONCPT 20. PAGE 140 H2802
GEN/METH LAW METH/COMP

B63
SHANKS M.,THE LESSONS OF PUBLIC ENTERPRISE. UK LEGIS WORKER ECO/TAC ADMIN PARL/PROC GOV/REL ATTIT ...POLICY MGT METH/COMP NAT/COMP ANTHOL 20 PARLIAMENT. PAGE 142 H2840
SOCISM OWN NAT/G INDUS

B63
US ATOMIC ENERGY COMMISSION,ATOMIC ENERGY IN THE SOVIET UNION: TRIP REPORT OF THE US ATOMIC ENERGY DELEGATION, MAY 1933. USSR R+D NAT/G CONSULT CREATE DIPLOM ADMIN ROUTINE EFFICIENCY PRODUC KNOWL SKILL ...NAT/COMP 20 AEC TRAVEL TREATY. PAGE 159 H3176
METH/COMP OP/RES TEC/DEV NUC/PWR

B64
GILLY A.,INSIDE THE CUBAN REVOLUTION. CUBA AGRI INDUS LABOR CREATE DIPLOM...METH/COMP 20. PAGE 56 H1129
REV PLAN MARXISM ECO/UNDEV

B64
GLUCKMANN M.,CLOSED SYSTEMS AND OPEN MINDS: THE LIMITS OF NAIVETY IN SOCIAL ANTHROPOLOGY. AFR INDIA MUNIC...IDEA/COMP METH/COMP ANTHOL. PAGE 57 H1149
CULTURE OBS SOC

B64
INTERNATIONAL LABOUR OFFICE,EMPLOYMENT AND ECONOMIC GROWTH. ECO/DEV ECO/UNDEV NAT/G PLAN DIPLOM INT/TRADE CONTROL INCOME PRODUC WEALTH...STAT NAT/COMP 20 ILO. PAGE 78 H1558
WORKER METH/COMP ECO/TAC OPTIMAL

B64
KALDOR N.,ESSAYS ON ECONOMIC POLICY (VOL. II). CHILE GERMANY INDIA FINAN...GOV/COMP METH/COMP 20 KEYNES/JM. PAGE 83 H1651
BAL/PAY INT/TRADE METH/CNCPT ECO/UNDEV

B64
OECD SEMINAR REGIONAL DEV,REGIONAL DEVELOPMENT IN ISRAEL. ISRAEL STRUCT ECO/UNDEV NAT/G REGION...GEOG 20. PAGE 120 H2404
ADMIN PROVS PLAN METH/COMP

B64
ON CULTURE AND SOCIAL CHANGE. FAM NAT/G ACT/RES ECO/TAC RACE/REL...PSY TIME/SEQ TREND IDEA/COMP METH/COMP ANTHOL BIBLIOG 20. PAGE 120 H2406
CULTURE TEC/DEV STRUCT CREATE

B64
STRONG C.F.,HISTORY OF MODERN POLITICAL CONSTITUTIONS. STRUCT INT/ORG NAT/G LEGIS TEC/DEV DIPLOM INT/TRADE CT/SYS EXEC...METH/COMP T 12/20 UN. PAGE 150 H2999
CONSTN CONCPT

B64
SZLADITS C.,BIBLIOGRAPHY ON FOREIGN AND COMPARATIVE LAW: BOOKS AND ARTICLES IN ENGLISH (SUPPLEMENT 1962). FINAN INDUS JUDGE LICENSE ADMIN CT/SYS PARL/PROC OWN...INT/LAW CLASSIF METH/COMP NAT/COMP 20. PAGE 151 H3027
BIBLIOG/A JURID ADJUD LAW

S64
COLEMAN J.S.,"COLLECTIVE DECISIONS." CULTURE ATTIT PERCEPT PWR SOC. PAGE 31 H0628
DECISION INGP/REL PERSON METH/COMP

S64
KANOUTE P.,"AFRICAN SOCIALISM." AFR CONSTN NAT/G COLONIAL ORD/FREE...GOV/COMP METH/COMP 20 EUROPE. PAGE 83 H1655
SOCISM CULTURE STRUCT IDEA/COMP

B65
COWAN L.G.,EDUCATION AND NATION-BUILDING IN AFRICA. AFR CULTURE ECO/UNDEV POL/PAR ACT/RES LEAD SOVEREIGN...METH/COMP ANTHOL BIBLIOG 20. PAGE 34 H0684
EDU/PROP COLONIAL ACADEM NAT/LISM

B65
CRAMER J.F.,CONTEMPORARY EDUCATION: A COMPARATIVE STUDY OF NATIONAL SYSTEMS (2ND ED.). CHINA/COM EUR+WWI INDIA USA+45 FINAN PROB/SOLV ADMIN CONTROL ATTIT...IDEA/COMP METH/COMP 20 CHINJAP. PAGE 35 H0697
EDU/PROP NAT/COMP SCHOOL ACADEM

B65
EASTON D.,A SYSTEM ANALYSIS OF POLITICAL LIFE. UNIV STRUCT NAT/G FEEDBACK PARTIC PERS/REL EFFICIENCY ...TREND CHARTS METH/COMP 20. PAGE 44 H0881
SIMUL POLICY GEN/METH

B65
FOSTER P.,EDUCATION AND SOCIAL CHANGE IN GHANA. GHANA CULTURE STRUCT ECO/UNDEV TEC/DEV REGION EFFICIENCY LITERACY ALL/VALS SOVEREIGN...STAT METH/COMP 19/20 GOLD/COAST. PAGE 52 H1043
SCHOOL CREATE SOCIETY

B65
GAJENDRAGADKAR P.B.,LAW, LIBERTY AND SOCIAL JUSTICE. INDIA CONSTN NAT/G SECT PLAN ECO/TAC PRESS POPULISM...SOC METH/COMP 20 HINDU. PAGE 54 H1086
ORD/FREE LAW ADJUD JURID

B65
GOLEMBIEWSKI R.T.,MEN, MANAGEMENT, AND MORALITY; TOWARD A NEW ORGANIZATIONAL ETHIC. CONSTN EX/STRUC CREATE ADMIN CONTROL INGP/REL PERSON SUPEGO MORAL PWR...GOV/COMP METH/COMP 20 BUREAUCRCY. PAGE 58 H1161
LG/CO MGT PROB/SOLV

B65
HYMES D.,THE USE OF COMPUTERS IN ANTHROPOLOGY. CULTURE PROF/ORG CONSULT CREATE EFFICIENCY PERCEPT ...CLASSIF LING CON/ANAL COMPUT/IR METH/COMP ANTHOL 20. PAGE 76 H1517
METH COMPUTER TEC/DEV SOC

B65
ROWAT D.C.,THE OMBUDSMAN: CITIZEN'S DEFENDER. DENMARK FINLAND NEW/ZEALND NORWAY SWEDEN CONSULT PROB/SOLV FEEDBACK PARTIC GP/REL...SOC CONCPT NEW/IDEA METH/COMP ANTHOL BIBLIOG 20. PAGE 135 H2701
INSPECT CONSTN NAT/G ADMIN

B66
AGGARWALA R.N.,FINANCIAL COMMITTEES OF THE INDIAN PARLIAMENT: A STUDY IN PARLIAMENTARY CONTROL OVER PUBLIC EXPENDITURE. INDIA FINAN NAT/G ROLE...CHARTS METH/COMP METH 20 PARLIAMENT. PAGE 4 H0078
PARL/PROC BUDGET CONTROL DELIB/GP

B66
BERELSON B.,READER IN PUBLIC OPINION AND COMMUNICATION (2ND ED.). UNIV NAT/G PRESS GP/REL PERS/REL PERCEPT RIGID/FLEX...MAJORIT QUANT METH/COMP ANTHOL BIBLIOG 20. PAGE 15 H0298
EDU/PROP ATTIT CONCPT COM/IND

B66
HOEVELER H.J.,INTERNATIONALE BEKAMPFUNG DES VERBRECHENS. AUSTRIA SWITZERLND WOR+45 INT/ORG CONTROL BIO/SOC...METH/COMP NAT/COMP 20 MAFIA SCOT/YARD FBI. PAGE 72 H1446
CRIMLGY CRIME DIPLOM INT/LAW

B66
LEONTIEF W.,ESSAYS IN ECONOMICS. ECO/UNDEV INDUS NAT/G CAP/ISM FOR/AID AUTOMAT MARXISM...ECOMETRIC CHARTS ANTHOL METH 20 KEYNES/JM. PAGE 94 H1886
CONCPT METH/CNCPT METH/COMP

B66
OWEN G.,INDUSTRY IN THE UNITED STATES. UK USA+45 NAT/G WEALTH...DECISION NAT/COMP 20. PAGE 122 H2436
METH/COMP INDUS MGT PROB/SOLV

B66
RADIN P.,THE METHOD AND THEORY OF ETHNOLOGY. CULTURE STRUCT BIO/SOC HABITAT...HUM OBS/ENVIR METH/COMP GEN/LAWS 20 HUMANISM. PAGE 129 H2578
PHIL/SCI SOC METH SOCIETY

B66
SILBERMAN B.S.,MODERN JAPANESE LEADERSHIP; TRANSITION AND CHANGE. NAT/G POL/PAR CHIEF ADMIN REPRESENT GP/REL ADJUST RIGID/FLEX...SOC METH/COMP ANTHOL 19/20 CHINJAP CHRISTIAN. PAGE 144 H2873
LEAD CULTURE ELITES MUNIC

B66
SMELSER N.J.,SOCIAL STRUCTURE AND MOBILITY IN ECONOMIC DEVELOPMENT. CULTURE SOCIETY CONFER...PSY SOC CHARTS METH/COMP NAT/COMP ANTHOL METH 20. PAGE 145 H2904
STRUCT STRATA ECO/UNDEV ECO/DEV

B66
SOROKIN P.A.,SOCIOLOGICAL THEORIES OF TODAY. SOCIETY STRUCT FAM SECT GP/REL ADJUST...PHIL/SCI PSY TREND METH/COMP 20. PAGE 147 H2935
SOC CULTURE METH/CNCPT EPIST

B66
SPULBER N.,THE STATE AND ECONOMIC DEVELOPMENT IN EASTERN EUROPE. BULGARIA COM CZECHOSLVK HUNGARY POLAND YUGOSLAVIA CULTURE PLAN CAP/ISM INT/TRADE CONTROL...POLICY CHARTS METH/COMP BIBLIOG/A 19/20. PAGE 148 H2958
ECO/DEV ECO/UNDEV NAT/G TOTALISM

B66
WINKS R.W.,THE HISTORIOGRAPHY OF THE BRITISH EMPIRE-COMMONWEALTH. CANADA INDIA PAKISTAN UK CULTURE SOCIETY STRUCT POL/PAR...CONCPT NAT/COMP 20 AUSTRAL. PAGE 169 H3386
HIST/WRIT TREND IDEA/COMP METH/COMP

B67
ANDERSON E.N.,POLITICAL INSTITUTIONS AND SOCIAL CHANGE IN CONTINENTAL EUROPE IN THE NINETEENTH CENTURY. MOD/EUR LAW CONSTN SOCIETY POL/PAR TEC/DEV LEAD REV ATTIT...BIBLIOG 19. PAGE 6 H0127
NAT/G NAT/COMP METH/COMP INDUS

B67
ASHFORD D.E.,NATIONAL DEVELOPMENT AND LOCAL REFORM: POLITICAL PARTICIPATION IN MOROCCO, TUNISIA, AND PAKISTAN. MOROCCO PAKISTAN CULTURE PROB/SOLV ATTIT ...POLICY SOC METH/COMP NAT/COMP BIBLIOG 20 TUNIS. PAGE 9 H0173
PARTIC ECO/UNDEV ADJUST NAT/G

B67
BOHANNAN P.,LAW AND WARFARE. CULTURE CT/SYS COERCE REV PEACE...JURID SOC CONCPT ANTHOL 20. PAGE 18 H0367
METH/COMP ADJUD WAR LAW

B67
BROWN L.N.,FRENCH ADMINISTRATIVE LAW. FRANCE UK CONSTN NAT/G LEGIS DOMIN CONTROL EXEC PARL/PROC PWR ...JURID METH/COMP GEN/METH. PAGE 22 H0447
EX/STRUC LAW IDEA/COMP CT/SYS

B67
GIFFORD P.,BRITAIN AND GERMANY IN AFRICA. AFR GERMANY UK ECO/UNDEV LEAD WAR NAT/LISM ATTIT ...POLICY HIST/WRIT METH/COMP ANTHOL BIBLIOG 19/20 WWI. PAGE 56 H1123
COLONIAL ADMIN DIPLOM NAT/COMP

B67
GILL R.T.,ECONOMIC DEVELOPMENT: PAST AND PRESENT (2ND ED.). ASIA INDIA USA+45 USA-45 WOR+45 WOR-45 DEMAND EFFICIENCY NAT/LISM WEALTH...GOV/COMP METH/COMP 18/20. PAGE 56 H1127
ECO/DEV ECO/UNDEV PLAN PROB/SOLV

B67
KENNETT L.,THE FRENCH ARMIES IN THE SEVEN YEARS' WAR. FRANCE NAT/G CONTROL LEAD WAR CIVMIL/REL EFFICIENCY ATTIT PWR SKILL CONSERVE 18. PAGE 85 H1690
FORCES CHIEF METH/COMP

B67
LYON B.,MEDIEVAL FINANCE. CHRIST-17C...SOC 11/12. PAGE 99 H1984
FINAN METH/COMP ECO/TAC NAT/COMP

B67
RAMUNDO B.A.,PEACEFUL COEXISTENCE: INTERNATIONAL LAW IN THE BUILDING OF COMMUNISM. USSR INT/ORG DIPLOM COLONIAL ARMS/CONT ROLE SOVEREIGN...POLICY
INT/LAW PEACE MARXISM

METH/COMP NAT/COMP BIBLIOG. PAGE 129 H2588 METH/CNCPT

B67
REES D.,THE AGE OF CONTAINMENT. WOR+45 FORCES ARMS/CONT ATTIT PWR...CONCPT TREND METH/COMP BIBLIOG/A 20. PAGE 130 H2608
DIPLOM NUC/PWR MARXISM GOV/COMP

B67
ROELOFS H.M.,THE LANGUAGE OF MODERN POLITICS: AN INTRODUCTION TO THE STUDY OF GOVERNMENT. DIPLOM ADMIN MARXISM NEW/LIB...JURID CONCPT METH/COMP T 20. PAGE 133 H2657
LEAD NAT/COMP PERS/REL NAT/G

B67
ROSENTHAL A.H.,THE SOCIAL PROGRAMS OF SWEDEN. SWEDEN USA+45 FINAN NAT/G PLAN PROB/SOLV INSPECT ORD/FREE...POLICY HEAL SOC CHARTS NAT/COMP 20. PAGE 134 H2681
GIVE SOC/WK WEALTH METH/COMP

S67
CAMERON R.,"SOME LESSONS OF HISTORY FOR DEVELOPING NATIONS." WOR+45 WOR-45 FINAN NAT/G WORKER EDU/PROP PARTIC ROLE...DECISION METH/COMP 18/20. PAGE 25 H0511
ECO/UNDEV NAT/COMP POLICY CONCPT

S67
COHEN R.,"ANTHROPOLOGY AND POLITICAL SCIENCE: COURTSHIP OR MARRIAGE?" CULTURE STRATA STRUCT MUNIC REGION UTOPIA...NEW/IDEA TREND IDEA/COMP METH/COMP 20. PAGE 31 H0618
SOC INGP/REL AFR

S67
DOERN G.B.,"THE ROYAL COMMISSIONS IN THE GENERAL POLICY PROCESS AND IN FEDERAL-PROVINCIAL RELATIONS." CANADA CONSTN ACADEM PROVS CONSULT DELIB/GP LEGIS ACT/RES PROB/SOLV CONFER CONTROL EFFICIENCY...METH/COMP 20 SENATE ROYAL/COMM. PAGE 42 H0832
R+D EX/STRUC GOV/REL NAT/G

S67
EPSTEIN E.H.,"NATIONAL IDENTITY AND THE LANGUAGE ISSUE IN PUERTO RICO." PUERT/RICO CULTURE STRUCT NAT/G PROB/SOLV SKILL...JURID STAT METH/COMP 20. PAGE 47 H0931
EDU/PROP SCHOOL LING NAT/LISM

S67
KINGSBURY E.C.,"LAW AS COMPACT: ANCIENT ISRAEL'S CONTRIBUTION TO THE UNDERSTANDING OF LAW." ISRAEL MEDIT-7 CULTURE KIN KNOWL...JURID CONCPT TREND IDEA/COMP METH/COMP WORSHIP JEWS DEITY. PAGE 86 H1716
LAW AGREE CONSTN INGP/REL

S67
KNOWLES A.F.,"NOTES ON A CANADIAN MASS MEDIA POLICY." CANADA TV CONTROL ROLE...METH/COMP 20. PAGE 87 H1735
EDU/PROP COM/IND NAT/G POLICY

S67
KROLL M.,"POLITICAL LEADERSHIP AND ADMINISTRATIVE COMMUNICATIONS IN NEW NATION STATES* CASE STUDY OF TRINIDAD AND TOBAGO." L/A+17C TRINIDAD INTELL OP/RES DOMIN COLONIAL LEAD GP/REL CENTRAL EFFICIENCY...DECISION OBS METH/COMP 20. PAGE 89 H1774
NAT/G ADMIN EDU/PROP CONTROL

S67
MAIR L.,"BUSOGA LOCAL GOVERNMENT" AFR UGANDA UK CONSTN GP/REL...GOV/COMP METH/COMP 20. PAGE 101 H2024
LOC/G COLONIAL LAW ATTIT

S67
PAK H.,"CHINA'S MILITIA AND MAO TSE-TUNG'S 'PEOPLE'S WAR'." CHINA/COM SOCIETY POL/PAR EX/STRUC PROB/SOLV PARTIC COERCE WAR CIVMIL/REL ATTIT DRIVE MARXISM...METH/COMP 20 MAO. PAGE 122 H2447
FORCES NAT/G WORKER CHIEF

S67
PETRAS J.,"GUERRILLA MOVEMENTS IN LATIN AMERICA - I." GUATEMALA PERU VENEZUELA NAT/G COLONIAL LEAD ATTIT PWR...TIME/SEQ METH/COMP 20 COLOMB. PAGE 125 H2497
GUERRILLA REV L/A+17C MARXISM

S67
RAUM O.,"THE MODERN LEADERSHIP GROUP AMONG THE SOUTH AFRICAN XHOSA." SOUTH/AFR SOCIETY SECT EX/STRUC REPRESENT GP/REL INGP/REL PERSON ...METH/COMP 17/20 XHOSA NEGRO. PAGE 130 H2596
RACE/REL KIN LEAD CULTURE

S67
ROCHET W.,"THE OCTOBER REVOLUTION AND THE STRUGGLE OF THE FRENCH COMMUNISTS." COM FRANCE ELITES SOCIETY STRATA ECO/TAC EDU/PROP GP/REL WEALTH ...MARXIST IDEA/COMP NAT/COMP 20. PAGE 133 H2654
SOCISM CHOOSE METH/COMP NAT/G

S67
ROSE S.,"ASIAN NATIONALISM* THE SECOND STAGE." ASIA COM ECO/UNDEV NAT/G PROB/SOLV DIPLOM FOR/AID DOMIN NEUTRAL REGION TASK...METH/COMP 20. PAGE 134 H2675
NAT/LISM S/ASIA BAL/PWR COLONIAL

S67
SHELDON C.H.,"PUBLIC OPINION AND HIGH COURTS: COMMUNIST PARTY CASES IN FOUR CONSTITUTIONAL SYSTEMS." CANADA GERMANY/W WOR+45 POL/PAR MARXISM ...METH/COMP NAT/COMP 20 AUSTRAL. PAGE 143 H2857
ATTIT CT/SYS CONSTN DECISION

S67
SZALAY L.B.,"SOVIET DOMESTIC PROPAGANDA AND LIBERALIZATION." COM USSR SOCIETY COM/IND NAT/G POL/PAR EX/STRUC TEC/DEV LEAD ATTIT ROLE MARXISM ...METH/COMP 20. PAGE 151 H3026
EDU/PROP TOTALISM PERSON PERCEPT

S67
TANTER R.,"A THEORY OF REVOLUTION." ASIA CUBA L/A+17C S/ASIA SOCIETY NAT/G ADJUST...CONCPT CHARTS. PAGE 152 H3046
REV ECO/UNDEV EDU/PROP METH/COMP

C80
ARNOLD M.,"DEMOCRACY" IN MIXED ESSAYS (2ND ED.)" UK SOCIETY STRUCT...CONCPT METH/COMP 19. PAGE 8 H0166
NAT/G MAJORIT EX/STRUC ELITES

B83
AMOS S.,THE SCIENCE OF POLITICS. MOD/EUR CONSTN LOC/G NAT/G EX/STRUC LEGIS DIPLOM...METH/COMP 19/20. PAGE 6 H0124
NEW/IDEA PHIL/SCI CONCPT

B91
MILL J.S.,SOCIALISM (1859). MOD/EUR AGRI INDUS NAT/G REV INCOME PRODUC ORD/FREE POPULISM SOCISM ...GOV/COMP METH/COMP 19. PAGE 110 H2209
WEALTH SOCIALIST ECO/TAC OWN

B95
SELIGMAN E.R.A.,ESSAYS IN TAXATION. NEW/ZEALND PRUSSIA UK USA-45 MARKET LOC/G CREATE PRICE CONTROL INCOME OWN WEALTH...GOV/COMP METH/COMP 19. PAGE 141 H2824
TAX TARIFFS INDUS NAT/G

L95
BELSHAW C.S.,"IN SEARCH OF WEALTH; STUDY OF EMERGENCE OF COMMERCIAL OPERA TIONS IN MELANESIAN SOCIETY OF SOUTHEASTERN PAPUA." S/ASIA CULTURE KIN ECO/TAC DEMAND INCOME 20 MELANESIA PAPUA. PAGE 14 H0272
INT/TRADE ECO/UNDEV METH/COMP SOCIETY

B96
ESMEIN A.,ELEMENTS DE DROIT CONSTITUTIONNEL. FRANCE UK CHIEF EX/STRUC LEGIS ADJUD CT/SYS PARL/PROC REV GOV/REL ORD/FREE...JURID METH/COMP 18/19. PAGE 47 H0940
LAW CONSTN NAT/G CONCPT

METHOD, COMPARATIVE....SEE IDEA/COMP, METH/COMP

METHODOLOGY....SEE METH, PHIL/SCI, METHODOLOGICAL INDEXES, PP. XIII-XIV

METRO/COUN....METROPOLITAN COUNCIL

METROPOLITAN....SEE MUNIC

METROPOLITAN COUNCIL....SEE METRO/COUN

METTRNCH/K....PRINCE K. VON METTERNICH

B49
VIERECK P.,CONSERVATISM REVISITED: THE REVOLT AGAINST REVOLT 1815-1949. EUR+WWI ELITES NAT/G FORCES PARTIC GOV/REL NAT/LISM...MAJORIT CONCPT GOV/COMP METTRNCH/K. PAGE 163 H3251
CONSERVE MARXISM REALPOL

MEXIC/AMER....MEXICAN-AMERICANS; SEE ALSO SPAN/AMER

B33
TANNENBAUM F.,PEACE BY REVOLUTION. ECO/UNDEV AGRI SECT WORKER DIPLOM EDU/PROP DISCRIM OWN WEALTH POPULISM 17/20 MEXIC/AMER INDIAN/AM. PAGE 152 H3043
CULTURE COLONIAL RACE/REL REV

B39
MARQUAND H.A.,ORGANIZED LABOUR IN FOUR CONTINENTS. EUR+WWI USA-45 INDUS NAT/G PAY GP/REL TOTALISM ATTIT WEALTH ALL/IDEOS...TREND NAT/COMP 20 ILO AFL/CIO EUROPE CHINJAP MEXIC/AMER. PAGE 103 H2055
LABOR WORKER CONCPT ANTHOL

B40
KER A.M.,MEXICAN GOVERNMENT PUBLICATIONS: A GUIDE TO THE MORE IMPORTANT PUBLICATIONS OF THE GOVERNMENT OF MEXICO, 1821-1936. CHIEF ADJUD 19/20 MEXIC/AMER. PAGE 85 H1693
BIBLIOG NAT/G EXEC LEGIS

B42
REDFIELD R.,THE FOLK CULTURE OF YUCATAN. STRATA FAM KIN MUNIC SECT DISCRIM ISOLAT ANOMIE HEALTH ...BIBLIOG 20 MEXIC/AMER. PAGE 130 H2605
CULTURE NEIGH GP/COMP SOCIETY

B52
TAX S.,HERITAGE OF CONQUEST. L/A+17C ECO/UNDEV LOC/G WEALTH...POLICY ANTHOL WORSHIP 20 MEXIC/AMER CENTRAL/AM. PAGE 153 H3052
PHIL/SCI CULTURE SOCIETY

B54
MOSK S.A.,INDUSTRIAL REVOLUTION IN MEXICO. MARKET LABOR CREATE CAP/ISM ADMIN ATTIT SOCISM...POLICY 20 MEXIC/AMER. PAGE 113 H2268
INDUS TEC/DEV ECO/UNDEV NAT/G

B54
WILLIAMSON H.F.,ECONOMIC DEVELOPMENT - PRINCIPLES AND PATTERNS. INDIA KOREA CULTURE ECO/DEV ECO/UNDEV TEC/DEV...CENSUS NAT/COMP 20 CHINJAP MEXIC/AMER RESOURCE/N. PAGE 168 H3369
ECO/TAC GEOG LABOR

B58
PAYNO M.,LA REFORMA SOCIAL EN ESPANA Y MEXICO. SPAIN ECO/TAC TAX LOBBY COERCE REV OWN CATHISM 19/20 MEXIC/AMER. PAGE 124 H2479
SECT NAT/G LAW ELITES

B59
FAYERWEATHER J.,THE EXECUTIVE OVERSEAS: ADMINISTRATIVE ATTITUDES AND RELATIONSHIPS IN A FOREIGN CULTURE. USA+45 WOR+45 CULTURE LG/CO SML/CO ATTIT...MGT PERS/COMP 20 MEXIC/AMER. PAGE 49 H0979 INT/TRADE TOP/EX NAT/COMP PERS/REL

B59
LOPEZ M.M.,CATALOGOS DE PUBLICACIONES PERIODICAS MEXICANAS. L/A+17C CULTURE NAT/G DIPLOM 20 MEXIC/AMER. PAGE 98 H1965 BIBLIOG PRESS CON/ANAL

B60
GONZALEZ NAVARRO M.,LA COLONIZACION EN MEXICO, 1877-1910. AGRI NAT/G PLAN PROB/SOLV INCOME ...POLICY JURID CENSUS 19/20 MEXIC/AMER MIGRATION. PAGE 58 H1164 ECO/UNDEV GEOG HABITAT COLONIAL

B60
MOCTEZUMA A.P.,EL CONFLICTO RELIGIOSO DE 1926 (2ND ED.). L/A+17C LAW NAT/G LOBBY COERCE GP/REL ATTIT ...POLICY 20 MEXIC/AMER CHURCH/STA. PAGE 112 H2233 SECT ORD/FREE DISCRIM REV

B60
THORD-GRAY I.,GRINGO REBEL. L/A+17C NAT/G CONTROL LEAD ATTIT...OBS 20 MEXIC/AMER. PAGE 154 H3087 REV FORCES CIVMIL/REL ORD/FREE

B61
ERASMUS C.J.,MAN TAKES CONTROL: CULTURAL DEVELOPMENT AND AMERICAN AID. STRUCT OWN DRIVE PERCEPT...SOC 20 MEXIC/AMER. PAGE 47 H0937 ORD/FREE CULTURE ECO/UNDEV TEC/DEV

B61
MARTINEZ RIOS J.,BIBLIOGRAFIA ANTROPOLOGICA Y SOCIOLOGICA DEL ESTADO DE OAXACA. WRITING...LING 12/20 INDIAN/AM MEXIC/AMER. PAGE 103 H2069 BIBLIOG SOC PROVS CULTURE

B61
PAZ O.,THE LABYRINTH OF SOLITUDE; LIFE AND THOUGHT IN MEXICO (TRANS. BY LYSANDER KEMP). INTELL COLONIAL REV...PSY SOC TIME/SEQ 16/20 MEXIC/AMER. PAGE 124 H2480 CULTURE PERSON PERS/REL SOCIETY

S61
NEEDLER M.C.,"THE POLITICAL DEVELOPMENT OF MEXICO." STRUCT NAT/G ADMIN RIGID/FLEX...TIME/SEQ TREND MEXIC/AMER TOT/POP VAL/FREE 19/20. PAGE 116 H2328 L/A+17C POL/PAR

B62
THREE PRELIMINARY BIBLIOGRAPHIES OF WORKS RELATED TO THE SOCIAL SCIENCES IN LATIN AMERICA. BRAZIL CULTURE SOCIETY NAT/G PLAN PROB/SOLV...PSY 20 MEXIC/AMER. PAGE 2 H0040 BIBLIOG L/A+17C SOC AGRI

B63
ALMOND G.A.,THE CIVIC CULTURE: POLITICAL ATTITUDES AND DEMOCRACY IN FIVE NATIONS. GERMANY/W ITALY UK USA+45 SOCIETY STRUCT PARTIC...SOC DEEP/INT SAMP 20 MEXIC/AMER. PAGE 6 H0113 POPULISM CULTURE NAT/COMP ATTIT

B63
DRIVER H.E.,ETHNOGRAPHY AND ACCULTURATION OF THE CHICHIMECA-JONAZ OF NORTHEAST MEXICO. ECO/UNDEV AGRI FAM KIN EDU/PROP MARRIAGE HEALTH...GEOG INT CHARTS WORSHIP 18/20 MEXIC/AMER. PAGE 42 H0848 CULTURE HABITAT STRUCT GP/REL

B63
GLADE W.P. JR.,THE POLITICAL ECONOMY OF MEXICO. FUT L/A+17C CULTURE SOCIETY AGRI INDUS DELIB/GP ACT/RES ECO/TAC ATTIT HEALTH ORD/FREE...STAT TIME/SEQ TREND MEXIC/AMER TOT/POP VAL/FREE 20. PAGE 57 H1138 FINAN ECO/UNDEV

L63
CORWIN A.F.,"CONTEMPORARY MEXICAN ATTITUDES TOWARD POPULATION, POVERTY, AND PUBLIC OPINION." L/A+17C CULTURE SOCIETY ACT/RES ECO/TAC EDU/PROP PERSON HEALTH KNOWL...GEOG PHIL/SCI STAT OBS INT SAMP MEXIC/AMER VAL/FREE 20. PAGE 34 H0672 ATTIT QU

B64
MARTINEZ J.R.,THREE CASES OF COMMUNISM: CUBA, BRAZIL, AND MEXICO. BRAZIL CUBA L/A+17C CONSTN NAT/G DIPLOM ECO/TAC GP/REL INGP/REL...GP/COMP BIBLIOG 20 MEXIC/AMER COM/PARTY. PAGE 103 H2068 MARXISM BIOG REV NAT/COMP

B64
MUSEUM FUR VOLKERKUNDE WIEN,ZENTRALAMERIKA MEXIKO VOLKER UND KULTUREN. COSTA/RICA GUATEMALA L/A+17C PANAMA SECT WAR GP/REL SOVEREIGN...ART/METH 20 CENTRAL/AM MEXIC/AMER. PAGE 115 H2300 SOCIETY STRUCT CULTURE AGRI

B64
NORTHROP F.S.,CROSS-CULTURAL UNDERSTANDING: EPISTEMOLOGY IN ANTHROPOLOGY. BURMA GREECE THAILAND HABITAT PERCEPT PERSON...PHIL/SCI SOC METH 20 MEXIC/AMER CHINJAP. PAGE 119 H2375 EPIST PSY CULTURE CONCPT

C64
SCOTT R.E.,"MEXICAN GOVERNMENT IN TRANSITION (REV ED)" CULTURE STRUCT POL/PAR CHIEF ADMIN LOBBY REV CHOOSE GP/REL DRIVE...BIBLIOG METH 20 MEXIC/AMER. PAGE 141 H2816 NAT/G L/A+17C ROUTINE CONSTN

S65
BRANDENBURG F.,"THE RELEVANCE OF MEXICAN EXPERIENCE TO LATIN AMERICAN DEVELOPMENT." BRAZIL CHILE VENEZUELA STRUCT ECO/UNDEV AGRI CREATE ECO/TAC ...STAT RECORD MEXIC/AMER ARGEN COLOMB. PAGE 20 H0405 L/A+17C GOV/COMP

B66
DE VORE B.B.,LAND AND LIBERTY; A HISTORY OF THE MEXICAN REVOLUTION. CONSTN INTELL NAT/G CONTROL LEAD CHOOSE TOTALISM AUTHORIT...BIBLIOG 19/20 MEXIC/AMER DIAZ/P LIB/PARTY MAGON/F MADERO/F. PAGE 39 H0776 REV CHIEF POL/PAR

B67
ALBA V.,THE MEXICANS; THE MAKING OF A NATION. SOCIETY ECO/UNDEV AGRI INDUS SECT STRANGE ATTIT ...GEOG 20 MEXIC/AMER. PAGE 4 H0091 CONSTN NAT/G CULTURE ANOMIE

B67
JOHNSON H.G.,ECONOMIC NATIONALISM IN OLD AND NEW STATES. CANADA CHINA/COM MALI UK DIPLOM...SIMUL GEN/LAWS 19/20 MEXIC/AMER. PAGE 81 H1619 NAT/LISM ECO/UNDEV ECO/DEV NAT/COMP

MEXICO....SEE ALSO L/A+17C

MEYER A.G. H2187

MEYER A.J. H2188

MEYER E.W. H2189,H2190

MEYER F.S. H2191

MEYER P. H2192

MEYRIAT J. H2193

MEZERIK A.G. H2194

MGT....MANAGEMENT

N
AUSTRALIAN PUBLIC AFFAIRS INFORMATION SERVICE. LAW ...HEAL HUM MGT SOC CON/ANAL 20 AUSTRAL. PAGE 1 H0011 BIBLIOG NAT/G CULTURE DIPLOM

N
CIVIL SERVICE JOURNAL. PARTIC INGP/REL PERS/REL ...MGT BIBLIOG/A 20. PAGE 1 H0015 ADMIN NAT/G SERV/IND WORKER

N
SUBJECT GUIDE TO BOOKS IN PRINT: AN INDEX TO THE PUBLISHERS' TRADE LIST ANNUAL. UNIV LAW LOC/G DIPLOM WRITING ADMIN LEAD PERSON...MGT SOC. PAGE 2 H0024 BIBLIOG ECO/DEV POL/PAR NAT/G

N
DEUTSCHE BUCHEREI,JAHRESVERZEICHNIS DES DEUTSCHEN SCHRIFTUMS. AUSTRIA EUR+WWI GERMANY SWITZERLND LAW LOC/G DIPLOM ADMIN...MGT SOC 19/20. PAGE 40 H0804 BIBLIOG WRITING NAT/G

N
SOUTH AFRICA STATE LIBRARY,SOUTH AFRICAN NATIONAL BIBLIOGRAPHY, SANB. SOUTH/AFR LAW NAT/G EDU/PROP ...MGT PSY SOC 20. PAGE 147 H2937 BIBLIOG PRESS WRITING

B01
GRIFFIN A.P.C.,A LIST OF BOOKS ON THE DANISH WEST INDIES (PAMPHLET). L/A+17C WEST/IND CULTURE LOC/G ...GEOG MGT 18/20. PAGE 61 H1214 BIBLIOG/A SOCIETY COLONIAL ADMIN

B01
GRIFFIN A.P.C.,A LIST OF BOOKS ON PORTO RICO. PUERT/RICO CULTURE LOC/G...GEOG MGT 19/20. PAGE 61 H1215 BIBLIOG/A SOCIETY COLONIAL ADMIN

B03
GRIFFIN A.P.C.,SELECT LIST OF REFERENCES ON GOVERNMENT OWNERSHIP OF RAILROADS (PAMPHLET). MOD/EUR NAT/G ADMIN...MGT GOV/COMP 19/20. PAGE 61 H1217 BIBLIOG/A SOCISM OWN DIST/IND

B04
GRIFFIN A.P.C.,LIST OF REFERENCES ON BUDGETS OF FOREIGN COUNTRIES (PAMPHLET). MOD/EUR FINAN MARKET TAX...MGT STAT 19/20. PAGE 61 H1218 BIBLIOG/A BUDGET NAT/G

B05
MACHIAVELLI N.,THE ART OF WAR. CHRIST-17C TOP/EX DRIVE ORD/FREE PWR SKILL...MGT CHARTS. PAGE 100 H1993 NAT/G FORCES WAR ITALY

N19
CANADA CIVIL SERV COMM,THE ANALYSIS OF ORGANIZATION IN THE GOVERNMENT OF CANADA (PAMPHLET). CANADA CONSTN EX/STRUC LEGIS TOP/EX CREATE PLAN CONTROL GP/REL 20. PAGE 26 H0517 NAT/G MGT ADMIN DELIB/GP

B27
WILLOUGHBY W.F.,PRINCIPLES OF PUBLIC ADMINISTRATION WITH SPECIAL REFERENCE TO THE NATIONAL AND STATE GOVERNMENTS OF THE UNITED STATES. FINAN PROVS CHIEF CONSULT LEGIS CREATE BUDGET EXEC ROUTINE GOV/REL CENTRAL...MGT 20 BUR/BUDGET CONGRESS PRESIDENT. PAGE 169 H3373 NAT/G EX/STRUC OP/RES ADMIN

B31
DEKAT A.D.A.,COLONIAL POLICY. S/ASIA CULTURE DRIVE

EX/STRUC ECO/TAC DOMIN ADMIN COLONIAL ROUTINE SOVEREIGN WEALTH...POLICY MGT RECORD KNO/TEST SAMP. PAGE 39 H0785 PWR INDONESIA NETHERLAND

B35
TAKEUCHI T.,WAR AND DIPLOMACY IN THE JAPANESE EMPIRE. ASIA ELITES STRATA NAT/G SECT LEGIS ACT/RES PLAN LEGIT PARL/PROC ROUTINE WAR...MGT BIOG CHINJAP TOT/POP 19/20 CHINJAP. PAGE 152 H3038 EXEC STRUCT

B38
FIELD G.L.,THE SYNDICAL AND CORPORATIVE INSTITUTIONS OF ITALIAN FASCISM. ITALY CONSTN STRATA LABOR EX/STRUC TOP/EX ADJUD ADMIN LEAD TOTALISM AUTHORIT...MGT 20 MUSSOLIN/B. PAGE 50 H0991 FASCISM INDUS NAT/G WORKER

B38
REICH N.,LABOR RELATIONS IN REPUBLICAN GERMANY. GERMANY CONSTN ECO/DEV INDUS NAT/G ADMIN CONTROL GP/REL FASCISM POPULISM 20 WEIMAR/REP. PAGE 130 H2609 WORKER MGT LABOR BARGAIN

S38
HALL R.C.,"REPRESENTATION OF BIG BUSINESS IN THE HOUSE OF COMMONS." UK ECO/DEV INDUS PROF/ORG LEGIS CAP/ISM ECO/TAC LAISSEZ...POLICY OLD/LIB PLURIST MGT 20 HOUSE/CMNS. PAGE 64 H1287 LOBBY NAT/G

B39
JENNINGS W.I.,PARLIAMENT. UK POL/PAR OP/RES BUDGET LEAD CHOOSE GP/REL...MGT 20 PARLIAMENT HOUSE/LORD HOUSE/CMNS. PAGE 80 H1609 PARL/PROC LEGIS CONSTN NAT/G

S39
AIKEN C.,"THE BRITISH BUREAUCRACY AND THE ORIGINS OF PARLIAMENTARY DEMOCRACY" UK TOP/EX ADMIN. PAGE 4 H0082 MGT NAT/G LEGIS

S39
HECKSCHER G.,"GROUP ORGANIZATION IN SWEDEN." SWEDEN STRATA ECO/DEV AGRI INDUS LABOR NAT/G PROF/ORG ECO/TAC CENTRAL SOCISM...MGT 19/20. PAGE 69 H1382 LAISSEZ SOC

B40
MCHENRY D.E.,HIS MAJESTY'S OPPOSITION: STRUCTURE AND PROBLEMS OF THE BRITISH LABOUR PARTY 1931-1938. UK FINAN LABOR LOC/G DELIB/GP LEGIS EDU/PROP LEAD PARTIC CHOOSE GP/REL SOCISM...TREND 20 LABOR/PAR. PAGE 107 H2130 POL/PAR MGT NAT/G POLICY

B41
COHEN E.W.,THE GROWTH OF THE BRITISH CIVIL SERVICE 1780-1939. UK NAT/G SENIOR ROUTINE GOV/REL...MGT METH/COMP BIBLIOG 18/20. PAGE 31 H0616 OP/RES TIME/SEQ CENTRAL ADMIN

B45
MERRIAM C.E.,SYSTEMATIC POLITICS. FUT POL/PAR DELIB/GP DIPLOM ADJUD ADMIN LEAD CHOOSE ATTIT...MGT PHIL/SCI TREND. PAGE 109 H2183 NAT/G METH/CNCPT CREATE

B48
ROSENFARB J.,FREEDOM AND THE ADMINISTRATIVE STATE. NAT/G ROUTINE EFFICIENCY PRODUC RATIONAL UTIL ...TECHNIC WELF/ST MGT 20 BUREAUCRCY. PAGE 134 H2680 ECO/DEV INDUS PLAN WEALTH

S49
STEINMETZ H.,"THE PROBLEMS OF THE LANDRAT: A STUDY OF COUNTY GOVERNMENT IN THE US ZONE OF GERMANY." GERMANY/W USA+45 INDUS PLAN DIPLOM EDU/PROP CONTROL WAR GOV/REL FEDERAL WEALTH PLURISM...GOV/COMP 20 LANDRAT. PAGE 149 H2977 LOC/G COLONIAL MGT TOP/EX

B50
SCHUMPETER J.A.,CAPITALISM, SOCIALISM, AND DEMOCRACY (3RD ED.). USA-45 USSR WOR+45 WOR-45 INTELL ECO/DEV ECO/UNDEV ECO/TAC WAR PRODUC ORD/FREE...MGT SOC 20 MARX/KARL. PAGE 140 H2804 SOCIALIST CAP/ISM MARXISM IDEA/COMP

B52
THOM J.M.,GUIDE TO RESEARCH MATERIAL IN POLITICAL SCIENCE (PAMPHLET). ELITES LOC/G MUNIC NAT/G LEGIS DIPLOM ADJUD CIVMIL/REL GOV/REL PWR MGT. PAGE 154 H3074 BIBLIOG/A KNOWL

B53
FLORENCE P.S.,THE LOGIC OF BRITISH AND AMERICAN INDUSTRY; A REALISTIC ANALYSIS OF ECONOMIC STRUCTURE AND GOVERNMENT. UK USA+45 USA-45 FINAN LABOR CAP/ISM INGP/REL EFFICIENCY...MGT CONCPT STAT CHARTS METH 20. PAGE 51 H1028 INDUS ECO/DEV NAT/G NAT/COMP

S53
DRUCKER P.F.,"THE EMPLOYEE SOCIETY." STRUCT BAL/PWR PARTIC REPRESENT PWR...DECISION CONCPT. PAGE 42 H0849 LABOR MGT WORKER CULTURE

C54
BERLE A.A. JR.,"THE 20TH CENTURY CAPITALIST REVOLUTION." ECO/DEV NAT/G DIPLOM PRICE CONTROL ATTIT...BIBLIOG/A 20. PAGE 15 H0306 LG/CO CAP/ISM MGT PWR

B56
TRAGER F.N.,ANNOTATED BIBLIOGRAPHY OF BURMA. BURMA STRUCT NAT/G...GEOG JURID MGT SOC 20. PAGE 156 H3127 BIBLIOG/A S/ASIA CULTURE SOCIETY

B57
BARAN P.A.,THE POLITICAL ECONOMY OF GROWTH. MOD/EUR USA+45 USA-45 TEC/DEV TAX SOCISM...MGT CONCPT GOV/COMP. PAGE 11 H0213 CAP/ISM CONTROL ECO/UNDEV FINAN

B58
LIST OF PUBLICATIONS (PERIODICAL OR AD HOC) ISSUED BY VARIOUS MINISTRIES OF THE GOVERNMENT OF INDIA (3RD ED.). INDIA ECO/UNDEV PLAN...POLICY MGT 20. PAGE 2 H0037 BIBLIOG NAT/G ADMIN

B58
CUNNINGHAM W.B.,COMPULSORY CONCILIATION AND COLLECTIVE BARGAINING. CANADA NAT/G LEGIS ADJUD CT/SYS GP/REL...MGT 20 NEW/BRUNS STRIKE CASEBOOK. PAGE 36 H0722 POLICY BARGAIN LABOR INDUS

B58
SHARMA M.P.,PUBLIC ADMINISTRATION IN THEORY AND PRACTICE. INDIA UK USA+45 USA-45 EX/STRUC ADJUD ...POLICY CONCPT NAT/COMP 20. PAGE 142 H2847 MGT ADMIN DELIB/GP JURID

B59
DAHRENDORF R.,CLASS AND CLASS CONFLICT IN INDUSTRIAL SOCIETY. LABOR NAT/G COERCE ROLE PLURISM ...POLICY MGT CONCPT CLASSIF. PAGE 37 H0734 VOL/ASSN STRUCT SOC GP/REL

B59
FAYERWEATHER J.,THE EXECUTIVE OVERSEAS: ADMINISTRATIVE ATTITUDES AND RELATIONSHIPS IN A FOREIGN CULTURE. USA+45 WOR+45 CULTURE LG/CO SML/CO ATTIT...MGT PERS/COMP 20 MEXIC/AMER. PAGE 49 H0979 INT/TRADE TOP/EX NAT/COMP PERS/REL

B59
VERNEY D.V.,PUBLIC ENTERPRISE IN SWEDEN. FUT SWEDEN UK INDUS POL/PAR LEGIS PROB/SOLV CAP/ISM INT/TRADE CONTROL SOCISM...MGT CONCPT NAT/COMP 20 SOCDEM/PAR CIVIL/SERV. PAGE 162 H3246 ECO/DEV POLICY LG/CO NAT/G

B60
ALBI F.,TRATADO DE LOS MODOS DE GESTION DE LAS CORPORACIONES LOCALES. SPAIN FINAN NAT/G BUDGET CONTROL EXEC ROUTINE GOV/REL ORD/FREE SOVEREIGN ...MGT 20. PAGE 5 H0092 LOC/G LAW ADMIN MUNIC

B60
KERR C.,INDUSTRIALISM AND INDUSTRIAL MAN. CULTURE SOCIETY ECO/UNDEV NAT/G ADMIN PRODUC WEALTH ...PREDICT TREND NAT/COMP 19/20. PAGE 85 H1697 WORKER MGT ECO/DEV INDUS

B60
MOORE W.E.,LABOR COMMITMENT AND SOCIAL CHANGE IN DEVELOPING AREAS. SOCIETY STRATA ECO/UNDEV MARKET VOL/ASSN WORKER AUTHORIT SKILL...MGT NAT/COMP SOC/INTEG 20. PAGE 113 H2250 LABOR ORD/FREE ATTIT INDUS

B60
ROY N.C.,THE CIVIL SERVICE IN INDIA. INDIA POL/PAR ECO/TAC INCOME...JURID MGT 20 CIVIL/SERV. PAGE 135 H2705 ADMIN NAT/G DELIB/GP CONFER

B60
SLOTKIN J.S.,FROM FIELD TO FACTORY; NEW INDUSTRIAL EMPLOYEES. HABITAT...MGT NEW/IDEA NAT/COMP BIBLIOG SOC/INTEG 20. PAGE 145 H2901 INDUS LABOR CULTURE WORKER

S60
FRANKEL S.H.,"ECONOMIC ASPECTS OF POLITICAL INDEPENDENCE IN AFRICA." AFR FUT SOCIETY ECO/UNDEV COM/IND FINAN LEGIS PLAN TEC/DEV CAP/ISM ECO/TAC INT/TRADE ADMIN ATTIT DRIVE RIGID/FLEX PWR WEALTH ...MGT NEW/IDEA MATH TIME/SEQ VAL/FREE 20. PAGE 53 H1052 NAT/G FOR/AID

S60
RIVKIN A.,"AFRICAN ECONOMIC DEVELOPMENT: ADVANCED TECHNOLOGY AND THE STAGES OF GROWTH." CULTURE ECO/UNDEV AGRI COM/IND EXTR/IND PLAN ECO/TAC ATTIT DRIVE RIGID/FLEX SKILL WEALTH...MGT SOC GEN/LAWS WORK TOT/POP 20. PAGE 132 H2634 AFR TEC/DEV FOR/AID

B61
CARROTHERS A.W.R.,LABOR ARBITRATION IN CANADA. CANADA LAW NAT/G CONSULT LEGIS WORKER ADJUD ADMIN CT/SYS 20. PAGE 27 H0542 LABOR MGT GP/REL BARGAIN

B61
COHN B.S.,DEVELOPMENT AND IMPACT OF BRITISH ADMINISTRATION IN INDIA: A BIBLIOGRAPHIC ESSAY. INDIA UK ECO/UNDEV NAT/G DOMIN...POLICY MGT SOC 19/20. PAGE 31 H0619 BIBLIOG/A COLONIAL S/ASIA ADMIN

B61
DRAGNICH A.N.,MAJOR EUROPEAN GOVERNMENTS. FRANCE GERMANY/W UK USSR LOC/G EX/STRUC CT/SYS PARL/PROC ATTIT MARXISM...JURID MGT NAT/COMP 19/20. PAGE 42 H0846 NAT/G LEGIS CONSTN POL/PAR

B61
SHARMA T.R.,THE WORKING OF STATE ENTERPRISES IN INDIA. INDIA DELIB/GP LEGIS WORKER BUDGET PRICE CONTROL GP/REL OWN ATTIT...MGT CHARTS 20. PAGE 142 H2851 NAT/G INDUS ADMIN SOCISM

S61
BRZEZINSKI Z.K.,"THE ORGANIZATION OF THE COMMUNIST CAMP." COM CZECHOSLVK COM/IND NAT/G DELIB/GP INT/TRADE DOMIN EDU/PROP EXEC ROUTINE COERCE ATTIT PWR...MGT CONCPT TIME/SEQ CHARTS VAL/FREE 20 VOL/ASSN DIPLOM USSR

TREATY. PAGE 23 H0460

S61
TOMASIC D.,"POLITICAL LEADERSHIP IN CONTEMPORARY POLAND." COM EUR+WWI GERMANY NAT/G POL/PAR SECT DELIB/GP PLAN ECO/TAC DOMIN EDU/PROP PWR MARXISM ...MARXIST GEOG MGT CONCPT TIME/SEQ STERTYP 20. PAGE 156 H3111
SOCIETY ROUTINE USSR POLAND

B62
GALENSON W.,LABOR IN DEVELOPING COUNTRIES. BRAZIL INDONESIA ISRAEL PAKISTAN TURKEY AGRI INDUS WORKER PAY PRICE GP/REL WEALTH...MGT CHARTS METH/COMP NAT/COMP 20. PAGE 54 H1088
LABOR ECO/UNDEV BARGAIN POL/PAR

B62
HANSON A.H.,MANAGERIAL PROBLEMS IN PUBLIC ENTERPRISE. INDIA DELIB/GP GP/REL INGP/REL EFFICIENCY 20 PARLIAMENT. PAGE 66 H1320
MGT NAT/G INDUS PROB/SOLV

S62
WALTER E.,"VERS UNE CLASSIFICATION SCIENTIFIQUE DE LA SOCIOLOGIA." UNIV CULTURE INTELL SOCIETY R+D ACT/RES LEGIT ROUTINE ATTIT KNOWL...JURID MGT TREND GEN/LAWS 20. PAGE 165 H3296
PLAN CONCPT

B63
GOURNAY B.,PUBLIC ADMINISTRATION. FRANCE LAW CONSTN AGRI FINAN LABOR SCHOOL EX/STRUC CHOOSE...MGT METH/COMP 20. PAGE 59 H1189
BIBLIOG/A ADMIN NAT/G LOC/G

B63
INDIAN INSTITUTE PUBLIC ADMIN,CASES IN INDIAN ADMINISTRATION. INDIA AGRI NAT/G PROB/SOLV TEC/DEV ECO/TAC ADMIN...ANTHOL METH 20. PAGE 77 H1532
DECISION PLAN MGT ECO/UNDEV

B63
KAPP W.K.,HINDU CULTURE: ECONOMIC DEVELOPMENT AND ECONOMIC PLANNING IN INDIA. INDIA S/ASIA CULTURE ECO/TAC EDU/PROP ADMIN ALL/VALS...POLICY MGT TIME/SEQ VAL/FREE 20. PAGE 83 H1660
SECT ECO/UNDEV

B63
LEONARD T.J.,THE FEDERAL SYSTEM OF INDIA. INDIA MUNIC NAT/G PROVS ADMIN SOVEREIGN...IDEA/COMP 20. PAGE 94 H1885
FEDERAL MGT NAT/COMP METH/COMP

B63
SHANKS M.,THE LESSONS OF PUBLIC ENTERPRISE. UK LEGIS WORKER ECO/TAC ADMIN PARL/PROC GOV/REL ATTIT ...POLICY MGT METH/COMP NAT/COMP ANTHOL 20 PARLIAMENT. PAGE 142 H2840
SOCISM OWN NAT/G INDUS

B63
SINGH H.L.,PROBLEMS AND POLICIES OF THE BRITISH IN INDIA, 1885-1898. INDIA UK NAT/G FORCES LEGIS PROB/SOLV CONTROL RACE/REL ADJUST DISCRIM NAT/LISM RIGID/FLEX...MGT 19 CIVIL/SERV. PAGE 144 H2885
COLONIAL PWR POLICY ADMIN

B63
SPRING D.,THE ENGLISH LANDED ESTATE IN THE NINETEENTH CENTURY: ITS ADMINISTRATION. UK ELITES STRUCT AGRI NAT/G GP/REL OWN PWR WEALTH...BIBLIOG 19 HOUSE/LORD. PAGE 148 H2954
STRATA PERS/REL MGT

B63
UN SECRETARY GENERAL,PLANNING FOR ECONOMIC DEVELOPMENT. ECO/UNDEV FINAN BUDGET INT/TRADE TARIFFS TAX ADMIN 20 UN. PAGE 158 H3159
PLAN ECO/TAC MGT NAT/COMP

S63
ARASTEH R.,"THE ROLE OF INTELLECTUALS IN ADMINISTRATIVE DEVELOPMENT AND SOCIAL CHANGE IN MODERN IRAN." ISLAM CULTURE NAT/G CONSULT ACT/RES EDU/PROP EXEC ATTIT BIO/SOC PERCEPT SUPEGO ALL/VALS ...POLICY MGT PSY SOC CONCPT 20. PAGE 8 H0157
INTELL ADMIN IRAN

S63
HARRIS R.L.,"A COMPARATIVE ANALYSIS OF THE ADMINISTRATIVE SYSTEMS OF CANADA AND CEYLON." S/ASIA CULTURE SOCIETY STRATA TOP/EX ACT/RES DOMIN EDU/PROP LEGIT COERCE ATTIT SUPEGO ALL/VALS...MGT CHARTS GEN/LAWS VAL/FREE 20. PAGE 67 H1343
DELIB/GP EX/STRUC CANADA CEYLON

B64
AVASTHI A.,ASPECTS OF ADMINISTRATION. INDIA UK USA+45 FINAN ACADEM DELIB/GP LEGIS RECEIVE PARL/PROC PRIVIL...NAT/COMP 20. PAGE 9 H0183
MGT ADMIN SOC/WK ORD/FREE

B64
BRIGHT J.R.,RESEARCH, DEVELOPMENT AND TECHNOLOGICAL INNOVATION. CULTURE R+D CREATE PLAN PROB/SOLV AUTOMAT RISK PERSON...DECISION CONCPT PREDICT BIBLIOG. PAGE 21 H0419
TEC/DEV NEW/IDEA INDUS MGT

B64
ETZIONI A.,MODERN ORGANIZATIONS. CLIENT STRUCT DOMIN CONTROL LEAD PERS/REL AUTHORIT...CLASSIF BUREAUCRCY. PAGE 47 H0946
MGT ADMIN PLAN CULTURE

B64
FLORENCE P.S.,ECONOMICS AND SOCIOLOGY OF INDUSTRY; A REALISTIC ANALYSIS OF DEVELOPMENT. ECO/UNDEV LG/CO NAT/G PLAN...GEOG MGT BIBLIOG 20. PAGE 51 H1029
INDUS SOC ADMIN

B64
HAZLEWOOD A.,THE ECONOMICS OF DEVELOPMENT: AN ANNOTATED LIST OF BOOKS AND ARTICLES PUBLISHED 1958-1962. AGRI FINAN INDUS LABOR NAT/G DIPLOM INT/TRADE INCOME...MGT 20. PAGE 69 H1374
BIBLIOG/A ECO/UNDEV TEC/DEV

B64
JUCKER-FLEETWOOD E.,MONEY AND FINANCE IN AFRICA. ISLAM ECO/UNDEV SERV/IND NAT/G EX/STRUC PLAN ECO/TAC ROUTINE WEALTH...MGT TOT/POP 20. PAGE 82 H1639
AFR FINAN

B64
KARIEL H.S.,IN SEARCH OF AUTHORITY: TWENTIETH-CENTURY POLITICAL THOUGHT. WOR+45 WOR-45 NAT/G EX/STRUC TOTALISM DRIVE PWR...MGT PHIL/SCI GEN/LAWS 19/20 NIETZSCH/F FREUD/S WEBER/MAX NIEBUHR/R MARITAIN/J. PAGE 83 H1661
CONSTN CONCPT ORD/FREE IDEA/COMP

B64
PARANJAPE H.K.,THE FLIGHT OF TECHNICAL PERSONNEL IN PUBLIC UNDERTAKINGS. INDIA PAY DEMAND HAPPINESS ORD/FREE...MGT QU 20 MIGRATION. PAGE 123 H2464
ADMIN NAT/G WORKER PLAN

B64
WERNETTE J.P.,GOVERNMENT AND BUSINESS. LABOR CAP/ISM ECO/TAC INT/TRADE TAX ADMIN AUTOMAT NUC/PWR CIVMIL/REL DEMAND...MGT 20 MONOPOLY. PAGE 167 H3333
NAT/G FINAN ECO/DEV CONTROL

L64
SYMONDS R.,"REFLECTIONS IN LOCALISATION." AFR S/ASIA UK STRATA INT/ORG NAT/G SCHOOL EDU/PROP LEGIT KNOWL ORD/FREE PWR RESPECT CMN/WLTH 20. PAGE 151 H3023
ADMIN MGT COLONIAL

S64
NEEDHAM T.,"SCIENCE AND SOCIETY IN EAST AND WEST." INTELL STRATA R+D LOC/G NAT/G PROVS CONSULT ACT/RES CREATE PLAN TEC/DEV EDU/PROP ADMIN ATTIT ALL/VALS ...POLICY RELATIV MGT CONCPT NEW/IDEA TIME/SEQ WORK WORK. PAGE 116 H2327
ASIA STRUCT

C64
GOLDMAN M.I.,"COMPARATIVE ECONOMIC SYSTEMS: A READER." COM ECO/UNDEV NAT/G BUDGET CAP/ISM ADMIN TOTALISM MARXISM SOCISM...MGT ANTHOL BIBLIOG 19/20. PAGE 58 H1157
NAT/COMP CONTROL IDEA/COMP

B65
ACHTERBERG E.,BERLINER HOCHFINANZ - KAISER, FURSTEN, MILLIONARE UM 1900. GERMANY NAT/G EDU/PROP PERSON...MGT 19/20. PAGE 3 H0060
FINAN MUNIC BIOG ECO/TAC

B65
FORM W.H.,INDUSTRIAL RELATIONS AND SOCIAL CHANGE IN LATIN AMERICA. L/A+17C AGRI LABOR NAT/G PLAN PROB/SOLV DIPLOM...MGT SOC ANTHOL BIBLIOG/A METH 20. PAGE 52 H1038
INDUS GP/REL NAT/COMP ECO/UNDEV

B65
GOLEMBIEWSKI R.T.,MEN, MANAGEMENT, AND MORALITY; TOWARD A NEW ORGANIZATIONAL ETHIC. CONSTN EX/STRUC CREATE ADMIN CONTROL INGP/REL PERSON SUPEGO MORAL PWR...GOV/COMP METH/COMP 20 BUREAUCRCY. PAGE 58 H1161
LG/CO MGT PROB/SOLV

B65
MOORE W.E.,THE IMPACT OF INDUSTRY. CULTURE STRUCT ORD/FREE...TREND 20. PAGE 113 H2251
INDUS MGT TEC/DEV ECO/UNDEV

L65
WIONCZEK M.,"LATIN AMERICA FREE TRADE ASSOCIATION." AGRI DIST/IND FINAN INDUS INT/ORG LABOR NAT/G TEC/DEV ECO/TAC HEALTH SKILL WEALTH...POLICY RELATIV MGT LAFTA 20. PAGE 169 H3390
L/A+17C MARKET REGION

S65
HUGHES T.L.,"SCHOLARS AND FOREIGN POLICY* VARIETIES OF RESEARCH EXPERIENCE." COM/IND DIPLOM ADMIN EXEC ROUTINE...MGT OBS CONGRESS PRESIDENT CAMELOT. PAGE 75 H1491
ACT/RES ACADEM CONTROL NAT/G

S65
TABORSKY E.,"CHANGE IN CZECHOSLOVAKIA." COM USSR ELITES INTELL AGRI INDUS NAT/G DELIB/GP EX/STRUC ECO/TAC TOTALISM ATTIT RIGID/FLEX SOCISM...MGT CONCPT TREND 20. PAGE 152 H3031
ECO/DEV PLAN CZECHOSLVK

S65
TENDLER J.D.,"TECHNOLOGY AND ECONOMIC DEVELOPMENT* THE CASE OF HYDRO VS THERMAL POWER." CONSTRUC DIST/IND CREATE TEC/DEV INT/TRADE CENTRAL PWR SKILL WEALTH...MGT NAT/COMP ARGEN. PAGE 153 H3061
BRAZIL INDUS ECO/UNDEV

B66
BRAIBANTI R.,ASIAN BUREAUCRATIC SYSTEMS EMERGENT FROM THE BRITISH IMPERIAL TRADITION. BURMA CEYLON INDIA PAKISTAN UK ELITES ECO/UNDEV NAT/G...MGT SOC CHARTS ANTHOL 19/20. PAGE 20 H0401
GOV/COMP COLONIAL ADMIN S/ASIA

B66
HACKETT J.,L'ECONOMIE BRITANNIQUE: PROBLEMES ET PERSPECTIVES. FRANCE UK LABOR MUNIC NAT/G EX/STRUC PROB/SOLV BAL/PAY INCOME RIGID/FLEX...MGT PHIL/SCI CHARTS 20. PAGE 63 H1271
ECO/DEV FINAN ECO/TAC PLAN

B66
HARMON R.B.,SOURCES AND PROBLEMS OF BIBLIOGRAPHY IN POLITICAL SCIENCE (PAMPHLET). INT/ORG LOC/G MUNIC POL/PAR ADMIN GOV/REL ALL/IDEOS...JURID MGT CONCPT 19/20. PAGE 67 H1335
BIBLIOG DIPLOM INT/LAW NAT/G

B66
OWEN G.,INDUSTRY IN THE UNITED STATES. UK USA+45 NAT/G WEALTH...DECISION NAT/COMP 20. PAGE 122 H2436
METH/COMP INDUS MGT PROB/SOLV

B66
SCHURMANN F.,IDEOLOGY AND ORGANIZATION IN COMMUNIST CHINA. CHINA/COM LOC/G MUNIC POL/PAR ECO/TAC CONTROL ATTIT...MGT STERTYP 20 COM/PARTY. PAGE 140 H2805
MARXISM STRUCT ADMIN NAT/G

L66
SEYLER W.C.,"DOCTORAL DISSERTATIONS IN POLITICAL SCIENCE IN UNIVERSITIES OF THE UNITED STATES AND CANADA." INT/ORG LOC/G ADMIN...INT/LAW MGT GOV/COMP. PAGE 142 H2836
BIBLIOG LAW NAT/G

S66
FLEMING W.G.,"AUTHORITY, EFFICIENCY, AND ROLE STRESS: PROBLEMS IN THE DEVELOPMENT OF EAST AFRICAN BUREAUCRACIES." AFR UGANDA STRUCT PROB/SOLV ROUTINE INGP/REL ROLE...MGT SOC GP/COMP GOV/COMP 20 TANGANYIKA AFRICA/E. PAGE 51 H1024
DOMIN EFFICIENCY COLONIAL ADMIN

B67
DICKSON P.G.M.,THE FINANCIAL REVOLUTION IN ENGLAND. UK NAT/G TEC/DEV ADMIN GOV/REL...SOC METH/CNCPT CHARTS GP/COMP BIBLIOG 17/18. PAGE 41 H0823
ECO/DEV FINAN CAP/ISM MGT

B67
FIELD M.G.,SOVIET SOCIALIZED MEDICINE. USSR FINAN R+D PROB/SOLV ADMIN SOCISM...MGT SOC CONCPT 20. PAGE 50 H0993
PUB/INST HEALTH NAT/G MARXISM

B67
GROSS B.M.,ACTION UNDER PLANNING: THE GUIDANCE OF ECONOMIC DEVELOPMENT. STRUCT R+D NAT/G ACT/RES HABITAT...DECISION 20. PAGE 62 H1232
ECO/UNDEV PLAN ADMIN MGT

B67
JAIN R.K.,MANAGEMENT OF STATE ENTERPRISES. INDIA SOCIETY FINAN WORKER BUDGET ADMIN CONTROL OWN 20. PAGE 79 H1584
NAT/G SOCISM INDUS MGT

B67
RUDMAN H.C.,THE SCHOOL AND STATE IN THE USSR. COM USSR ACADEM LABOR LOC/G PUB/INST EDU/PROP GP/REL ROLE...POLICY DECISION MGT CHARTS 20. PAGE 136 H2712
SCHOOL ADMIN NAT/G POL/PAR

L67
RUTH J.M.,"THE ADMINISTRATION OF WATER RESOURCES IN GUATEMALA." GUATEMALA L/A+17C DIST/IND LOC/G NAT/G EX/STRUC ADMIN GOV/REL DEMAND EQUILIB WEALTH...GEOG MGT 20. PAGE 136 H2723
EFFICIENCY ECO/UNDEV PLAN ACT/RES

S67
ALPANDER G.G.,"ENTREPRENEURS AND PRIVATE ENTERPRISE IN TURKEY." TURKEY INDUS PROC/MFG EDU/PROP ATTIT DRIVE WEALTH...GEOG MGT SOC STAT TREND CHARTS 20. PAGE 6 H0114
ECO/UNDEV LG/CO NAT/G POLICY

S67
BEFU H.,"THE POLITICAL RELATION OF THE VILLAGE TO THE STATE." NAT/G DOMIN GOV/REL GP/REL MGT. PAGE 13 H0259
GOV/COMP NAT/LISM KIN MUNIC

S67
CARIAS B.,"EL CONTROL DE LAS EMPRESAS PUBLICAS POR GRUPOS DE INTERESES DE LA COMUNIDAD." FRANCE UK VENEZUELA INDUS NAT/G CONTROL OWN PWR...DECISION NAT/COMP 20. PAGE 26 H0529
WORKER REPRESENT MGT SOCISM

S67
JENCKS C.E.,"SOCIAL STATUS OF COAL MINERS IN BRITAIN SINCE NATIONALIZATION." UK STRATA STRUCT LABOR RECEIVE GP/REL INCOME OWN ATTIT HABITAT...MGT T 20. PAGE 80 H1600
EXTR/IND WORKER CONTROL NAT/G

S67
LEVCIK B.,"WAGES AND EMPLOYMENT PROBLEMS IN THE NEW SYSTEM OF PLANNED MANAGEMENT IN CZECHOSLOVAKIA." CZECHOSLVK EUR+WWI NAT/G OP/RES PLAN ADMIN ROUTINE INGP/REL CENTRAL EFFICIENCY PRODUC DECISION. PAGE 95 H1895
MARXISM WORKER MGT PAY

S67
RICHMAN B.M.,"CAPITALISTS & MANAGERS IN COMMUNIST CHINA." ASIA CHINA/COM ECO/UNDEV NAT/G CONSULT EX/STRUC PLAN EFFICIENCY PRODUC WEALTH MARXISM ...MGT CHARTS 20. PAGE 131 H2623
CAP/ISM INDUS

S67
SUBRAMANIAM V.,"REPRESENTATIVE BUREAUCRACY: A REASSESSMENT." USA+45 ELITES LOC/G NAT/G ADMIN GOV/REL PRIVIL DRIVE ROLE...POLICY CENSUS 20 CIVIL/SERV BUREAUCRCY. PAGE 150 H3006
STRATA GP/REL MGT GOV/COMP

MGT/OBJECT....MANAGEMENT BY OBJECTIVES

MICH/STA/U....MICHIGAN STATE UNIVERSITY

MICH/U....UNIVERSITY OF MICHIGAN

MICHAEL F. H2195

MICHAEL H.N. H2196

MICHAELY M. H2197

MICHELS R. H2198,H2199

MICHIGAN STATE UNIVERSITY....SEE MICH/STA/U

MICHIGAN....MICHIGAN

MICKIEWICZ E.P. H2200

MICRONESIA....MICRONESIA

MID/EAST....MIDDLE EAST

B55
KHADDURI M.,LAW IN THE MIDDLE EAST. LAW CONSTN ACADEM FAM EDU/PROP CT/SYS SANCTION CRIME...INT/LAW GOV/COMP ANTHOL 6/20 MID/EAST. PAGE 85 H1703
ADJUD JURID ISLAM

B62
HAIM S.G.,ARAB NATIONALISM. ISLAM CONSTN GP/REL ...ANTHOL BIBLIOG JEWS 20 MID/EAST ARABS. PAGE 64 H1279
NAT/LISM REV SECT DIPLOM

B64
VON GRUNEBAUM G.E.,MODERN ISLAM: THE SEARCH FOR CULTURAL IDENTITY. ACADEM NEIGH WRITING NAT/LISM ...HUM CONCPT 19/20 MUSLIM MID/EAST ARABS. PAGE 163 H3269
ISLAM CULTURE CREATE SECT

B65
BURLING R.,HILL FARMS AND PADI FIELDS. BURMA S/ASIA THAILAND VIETNAM AGRI NEIGH SECT GP/REL NAT/LISM ORD/FREE 20 MID/EAST MIGRATION. PAGE 24 H0491
SOCIETY STRUCT CULTURE SOVEREIGN

S67
TATU M.,"URSS: LES FLOTTEMENTS DE LA DIRECTION COLLEGIALE." UAR USSR CHIEF LEAD INGP/REL EFFICIENCY...DECISION TREND 20 MID/EAST. PAGE 152 H3047
POLICY NAT/G EX/STRUC DIPLOM

MIDDLE EAST INSTITUTE H2201

MIDDLETOWN....MIDDLETOWN: LOCATION OF LYND STUDY

MID-EUROPEAN LAW PROJECT H2202

MIDLARSKY M. H3046

MIDWEST/US....MIDWESTERN UNITED STATES

MIGRATION....MIGRATION; IMMIGRATION AND EMIGRATION; SEE ALSO HABITAT, GEOG

N
KRADER L.,SOCIAL ORGANIZATION OF THE MONGOL-TURKIC PASTORAL NOMADS. SOCIETY FAM KIN NEIGH GP/REL MARRIAGE 16/20 MONGOLIA TURKIC MIGRATION. PAGE 88 H1763
BIO/SOC HABITAT CULTURE STRUCT

N19
HAJDA J.,THE COLD WAR VIEWED AS A SOCIOLOGICAL PROBLEM (PAMPHLET). COM CZECHOSLVK EUR+WWI SOCIETY PLAN EDU/PROP CONTROL TASK ATTIT MARXISM...POLICY 20 COLD/WAR MIGRATION. PAGE 64 H1280
DIPLOM LEAD PWR NAT/G

B47
ISAAC J.,ECONOMICS OF MIGRATION. MOD/EUR CULTURE STRATA STRUCT NAT/G COLONIAL WEALTH...OLD/LIB TREND TIME 19/20 EUROPE/W MIGRATION. PAGE 78 H1569
HABITAT SOC GEOG

B49
UNSTEAD J.F.,A WORLD SURVEY FROM THE HUMAN ASPECT. AGRI INDUS...SOC CENSUS CHARTS 20 MAPS MIGRATION. PAGE 159 H3172
CULTURE HABITAT GEOG ATTIT

B52
LEBON J.H.C.,AN INTRODUCTION TO HUMAN GEOGRAPHY. CULTURE...GEOG SOC CONCPT CENSUS CHARTS 20 MIGRATION. PAGE 93 H1849
HABITAT GP/REL SOCIETY

B57
BUNDESMIN FUR VERTRIEBENE,DIE VERTREIBUNG DER DEUTSCHEN BEVOLKERUNG AUS DER TSCHECHOSLOWAKEI. CZECHOSLVK GERMANY NAT/G FORCES MURDER WAR INGP/REL ATTIT 20 MIGRATION. PAGE 24 H0474
GP/REL DOMIN COERCE DISCRIM

B58
BRIGGS L.C.,THE LIVING RACES OF THE SAHARA. STRATA AGRI KIN INT/TRADE HABITAT...GEOG AUD/VIS CHARTS BIBLIOG 20 SAHARA MIGRATION. PAGE 21 H0417
STRUCT SOCIETY SOC CULTURE

B59
BUNDESMIN FUR VERTRIEBENE,ZEITTAFEL DER VORGESCHICHTE UND DES ABLAUFS DER VERTREIBUNG SOWIE DER UNTERBRINGUNG UND EINGLIEDERUNG DER (2 VOLS.). GERMANY/E GERMANY/W NAT/G PROVS PROB/SOLV DIPLOM PARL/PROC ATTIT...BIBLIOG SOC/INTEG 20 MIGRATION PARLIAMENT. PAGE 24 H0475
JURID GP/REL INT/LAW

B59
LEMBERG E.,DIE VERTRIEBENEN IN WESTDEUTSCHLAND (3
GP/REL

B60
KEPHART C.,RACES OF MAN. GP/REL HABITAT...LING SOC/INTEG 20 MIGRATION MISCEGEN. PAGE 85 H1692 — CULTURE RACE/REL HEREDITY GEOG

B23
WILLOUGHBY W.C.,RACE PROBLEMS IN THE NEW AFRICA: A STUDY OF THE RELATION OF BANTU AND BRITONS IN THOSE PARTS OF BANTU AFRICA... AFR STRUCT SECT DOMIN EDU/PROP GP/REL ATTIT WORSHIP 20 BANTU EUROPE MISSION CHRISTIAN. PAGE 168 H3372 — KIN COLONIAL RACE/REL CULTURE

B38
COUPLAND R.,EAST AFRICA AND ITS INVADERS. AFR ISLAM STRATA SECT FORCES DIPLOM TRIBUTE CONTROL DISCRIM NAT/LISM 19 AFRICA/E EUROPE MISSION. PAGE 34 H0680 — CULTURE ELITES COLONIAL MARKET

B58
VARG P.A.,MISSIONARIES, CHINESE, AND DIPLOMATS: THE AMERICAN PROTESTANT MISSIONARY MOVEMENT IN CHINA, 1890-1952. ASIA ECO/UNDEV NAT/G PROB/SOLV CAP/ISM EDU/PROP COLONIAL NAT/LISM ATTIT MARXISM...NAT/COMP STERTYP 20 CHINJAP PROTESTANT MISSION. PAGE 162 H3234 — CULTURE DIPLOM SECT

B61
SHIELS W.E.,KING AND CHURCH: THE RISE AND FALL OF THE PATRONATO REAL. SPAIN INGP/REL...CONCPT WORSHIP 16/19 CHURCH/STA MISSION. PAGE 143 H2859 — SECT NAT/G CHIEF POLICY

B63
MAC MILLAN W.M.,BANTU, BOER, AND BRITON: THE MAKING OF THE SOUTH AFRICAN NATIVE PROBLEM. SOUTH/AFR UK LAW KIN NAT/G SECT LEGIS COLONIAL ISOLAT ATTIT ...BIOG 18/20 BANTU NEGRO PHILIP/J MISSION. PAGE 100 H1989 — AFR RACE/REL ELITES

B82
MACDONALD D.,AFRICANA; OR, THE HEART OF HEATHEN AFRICA, VOL. II: MISSION LIFE. SOCIETY STRATA KIN CREATE EDU/PROP ADMIN COERCE LITERACY HEALTH...MYTH WORSHIP 19 LIVNGSTN/D MISSION NEGRO. PAGE 100 H1990 — SECT AFR CULTURE ORD/FREE

L67
WILBER L.A.,"THE GOVERNMENTAL STRUCTURE OF MISSISSIPPI: ITS STRENGTHS AND WEAKNESSES." AGRI LOC/G SCHOOL EX/STRUC LEGIS TOP/EX BUDGET CT/SYS APPORT RACE/REL...GOV/COMP 20 MISSISSIPP. PAGE 168 H3359 — CONSTN PROVS STAT CON/ANAL

N
INTERNATIONAL BIBLIOGRAPHIE DER DEUTSCHEN ZEITSCHRIFTENLITERATUR. EUR+WWI GERMANY MOD/EUR ECO/DEV POL/PAR LEAD WAR NAT/LISM ATTIT...EPIST PHIL/SCI 19/20. PAGE 1 H0004 — BIBLIOG/A NAT/G PERSON CULTURE

N
PUBLISHERS' CIRCULAR, THE OFFICIAL ORGAN OF THE PUBLISHERS' ASSOCIATION OF GREAT BRITAIN AND IRELAND. EUR+WWI MOD/EUR UK LAW PROB/SOLV DIPLOM COLONIAL ATTIT...HUM 19/20 CMN/WLTH. PAGE 1 H0019 — BIBLIOG NAT/G WRITING LEAD

N
PRESSE UNIVERSITAIRES,ANNEE SOCIOLOGIQUE. EUR+WWI FRANCE MOD/EUR FAM ACT/RES WAR INGP/REL PERS/REL CONSEN DRIVE MORAL...CON/ANAL 19/20. PAGE 128 H2557 — BIBLIOG SOC CULTURE SOCIETY

B00
BENEDETTI V.,STUDIES IN DIPLOMACY. BELGIUM FRANCE GERMANY MOD/EUR CONSTN NAT/G CONSULT TOP/EX DOMIN EDU/PROP COERCE ATTIT...CONCPT INT BIOG TREND 19. PAGE 14 H0276 — PWR GEN/LAWS DIPLOM

B00
DE JOMINI A.H.,THE ART OF WAR. MOD/EUR NAT/G BAL/PWR DIPLOM DOMIN EXEC ROUTINE COERCE DRIVE PWR SKILL...POLICY CONCPT CHARTS STERTYP 19. PAGE 38 H0755 — PLAN FORCES WAR WEAPON

B00
VOLPICELLI Z.,RUSSIA ON THE PACIFIC AND THE SIBERIAN RAILWAY. MOD/EUR ECO/UNDEV INT/ORG FORCES PLAN DOMIN COLONIAL ROUTINE ATTIT ALL/VALS...OBS HIST/WRIT TIME/SEQ TREND CON/ANAL AUD/VIS CHARTS 18/19. PAGE 163 H3261 — NAT/G ACT/RES RUSSIA

B02
SEELEY J.R.,THE EXPANSION OF ENGLAND. MOD/EUR S/ASIA UK CULTURE NAT/G FORCES PLAN DOMIN EDU/PROP COLONIAL ROUTINE ATTIT ALL/VALS SOVEREIGN...CONCPT HIST/WRIT PARLIAMENT 18 CMN/WLTH. PAGE 141 H2819 — INT/ORG ACT/RES CAP/ISM INDIA

B03
GRIFFIN A.P.C.,LIST OF BOOKS ON THE CABINETS OF ENGLAND AND AMERICA (PAMPHLET). MOD/EUR UK USA-45 CONSTN NAT/G CONSULT EX/STRUC 19/20. PAGE 61 H1216 — BIBLIOG/A GOV/COMP ADMIN DELIB/GP

B03
GRIFFIN A.P.C.,SELECT LIST OF REFERENCES ON GOVERNMENT OWNERSHIP OF RAILROADS (PAMPHLET). MOD/EUR NAT/G ADMIN...MGT GOV/COMP 19/20. PAGE 61 H1217 — BIBLIOG/A SOCISM OWN DIST/IND

B04
GRIFFIN A.P.C.,LIST OF REFERENCES ON BUDGETS OF FOREIGN COUNTRIES (PAMPHLET). MOD/EUR FINAN MARKET TAX...MGT STAT 19/20. PAGE 61 H1218 — BIBLIOG/A BUDGET NAT/G

B05
GRIFFIN A.P.C.,LIST OF BOOKS ON RAILROADS IN FOREIGN COUNTRIES. MOD/EUR ECO/DEV NAT/G CONTROL SOCISM...JURID 19/20 RAILROAD. PAGE 61 H1219 — BIBLIOG/A SERV/IND ADMIN DIST/IND

C06
MONTGOMERY H.,"A DICTIONARY OF POLITICAL PHRASES AND ILLUSIONS WITH A SHORT BIBLIOGRAPHY." EUR+WWI MOD/EUR UK AGRI LABOR LOC/G NAT/G COLONIAL CHOOSE RACE/REL. PAGE 112 H2245 — BIBLIOG DICTIONARY POLICY DIPLOM

B08
NIRRNHEIM O.,DAS ERSTE JAHR DES MINISTERIUMS BISMARCK UND DIE OEFFENTLICHE MEINUNG (HEIDELBERGER ABHANDLUNGEN, 20. HEFT). GERMANY MOD/EUR LEGIS DIPLOM EDU/PROP INGP/REL...BIOG GOV/COMP IDEA/COMP BIBLIOG 19 BISMARCK/O. PAGE 118 H2363 — CHIEF PRESS NAT/G ATTIT

B12
HOBSON J.A.,THE EVOLUTION OF MODERN CAPITALISM. MOD/EUR UK STRATA ECO/DEV INDUS INCOME UTIL WEALTH ...SOC GEN/LAWS 7/20. PAGE 72 H1440 — CAP/ISM WORKER TEC/DEV TIME/SEQ

B14
BERHARDI F.,GERMANY AND THE NEXT WAR. MOD/EUR NAT/G SCHOOL FORCES ACT/RES DOMIN EDU/PROP SUPEGO PWR ...TIME/SEQ STERTYP TOT/POP 20 WWI. PAGE 15 H0304 — DRIVE COERCE WAR GERMANY

B14
BERNHARDI F.,ON THE WAR OF TODAY. MOD/EUR INT/ORG NAT/G TOP/EX PWR CHARTS. PAGE 16 H0313 — FORCES SKILL WAR

B15
FARIES J.C.,THE RISE OF INTERNATIONALISM. ASIA MOD/EUR NAT/G VOL/ASSN DELIB/GP BAL/PWR EDU/PROP ARMS/CONT RIGID/FLEX TREND. PAGE 49 H0971 — INT/ORG DIPLOM PEACE

B15
VEBLEN T.,IMPERIAL GERMANY AND THE INDUSTRIAL REVOLUTION. GERMANY MOD/EUR UK USA-45 NAT/G TEC/DEV CAP/ISM...MAJORIT NAT/COMP 19/20 CHINJAP. PAGE 162 H3236 — ECO/DEV INDUS TECHNIC BAL/PWR

N17
BURKE E.,THOUGHTS ON THE CAUSE OF THE PRESENT DISCONTENTS (PAMPHLET). MOD/EUR UK CONSTN CHIEF LEGIS DOMIN CONTROL EXEC REPRESENT POPULISM ...TRADIT NEW/IDEA METH/COMP 18 BURKE/EDM. PAGE 24 H0484 — ORD/FREE REV PARL/PROC NAT/G

B18
CVIJIC J.,THE BALKAN PENINSULA. MOD/EUR COERCE ...SOC CHARTS GP/COMP NAT/COMP 20 BALKANS MAPS. PAGE 36 H0729
GEOG HABITAT GOV/COMP CULTURE

N19
BRIMMELL G.H.,COMMUNISM IN SOUTHEAST ASIA (PAMPHLET). BURMA CAMBODIA COM INDIA INDONESIA LAOS MOD/EUR NAT/G POL/PAR FORCES CAP/ISM CONTROL WEALTH ...MYTH 20. PAGE 21 H0420
MARXISM S/ASIA REV ECO/UNDEV

N19
HANNA A.J.,EUROPEAN RULE IN AFRICA (PAMPHLET). BELGIUM FRANCE MOD/EUR UK WOR+45 WOR-45 ECO/UNDEV NAT/G PARTIC SOVEREIGN...NAT/COMP 19/20. PAGE 66 H1314
DIPLOM COLONIAL AFR NAT/LISM

N19
POUND R.,ORGANIZATION OF THE COURTS (PAMPHLET). MOD/EUR UK USA-45 ADJUD PWR...GOV/COMP 10/20 EUROPE. PAGE 127 H2546
CT/SYS JURID STRUCT ADMIN

B20
HALDANE R.B.,BEFORE THE WAR. MOD/EUR SOCIETY INT/ORG NAT/G DELIB/GP PLAN DOMIN EDU/PROP LEGIT ADMIN COERCE ATTIT DRIVE MORAL ORD/FREE PWR...SOC CONCPT SELF/OBS RECORD BIOG TIME/SEQ. PAGE 64 H1282
POLICY DIPLOM UK

B21
BERGSTRASSER L.,GESCHICHTE DER POLITISCHEN PARTEIEN. GERMANY MOD/EUR NAT/G PRESS PWR ...TIME/SEQ 17/20. PAGE 15 H0303
POL/PAR LAISSEZ CONSERVE

B21
STUART G.H.,FRENCH FOREIGN POLICY. CONSTN INT/ORG NAT/G POL/PAR EX/STRUC FORCES PLAN ECO/TAC DOMIN EDU/PROP ADJUD COERCE ATTIT DRIVE RIGID/FLEX ALL/VALS...POLICY OBS RECORD BIOG TIME/SEQ TREND. PAGE 150 H3000
MOD/EUR DIPLOM FRANCE

B23
DELBRUCK H.,GOVERNMENT AND THE WILL OF THE PEOPLE (TRANS. BY ROY S. MACELWEE). MOD/EUR NAT/G CHOOSE REPRESENT...CONCPT 19/20. PAGE 39 H0788
SOVEREIGN ORD/FREE MAJORITY POL/PAR

B23
KADEN E.H.,DER POLITISCHE CHARAKTER DER FRANZOSISCHEN KULTURPROPAGANDA AM RHEIN. FRANCE MOD/EUR DOMIN PRESS...GEOG METH/COMP 20. PAGE 82 H1648
EDU/PROP ATTIT DIPLOM NAT/G

B24
MARTIN B.K.,THE TRIUMPH OF LORD PALMERSTON. MOD/EUR RUSSIA TURKEY UK NAT/G DELIB/GP 19. PAGE 103 H2061
ATTIT WAR POL/PAR POLICY

B25
TEMPERLEY H.,THE FOREIGN POLICY OF CANNING: 1822-1827. MOD/EUR NAT/G TOP/EX EDU/PROP ROUTINE ATTIT RIGID/FLEX SUPEGO PWR SKILL...TIME/SEQ PARLIAMENT 20. PAGE 153 H3058
PERSON DIPLOM UK BIOG

B25
WEBSTER C.,THE FOREIGN POLICY OF CASTLEREAGH: 1815-1822. LAW NAT/G DELIB/GP TOP/EX BAL/PWR ORD/FREE PWR RESPECT 19. PAGE 166 H3322
MOD/EUR DIPLOM UK

B27
ENGELS F.,THE PEASANT WAR IN GERMANY (1850). GERMANY MOD/EUR AGRI WORKER LEAD COERCE INGP/REL ...TREND 16/19. PAGE 46 H0924
WAR STRATA REV MARXIST

B27
FLOURNOY F.,PARLIAMENT AND WAR. MOD/EUR UK NAT/G FORCES LEGIS TOP/EX DIPLOM LEGIT DEBATE ATTIT RIGID/FLEX PWR...DECISION TIME/SEQ PARLIAMENT 19/20. PAGE 52 H1032
COERCE WAR

B27
WEBER M.,GENERAL ECONOMIC HISTORY. CHRIST-17C MOD/EUR STRUCT AGRI EXTR/IND FINAN INDUS MARKET FAM MUNIC NAT/G PROF/ORG SECT ECO/TAC 8/20. PAGE 166 H3319
ECO/DEV CAP/ISM

B28
SOROKIN P.,CONTEMPORARY SOCIOLOGICAL THEORIES. MOD/EUR UNIV SOCIETY R+D SCHOOL ECO/TAC EDU/PROP ROUTINE ATTIT DRIVE...PSY CONCPT TIME/SEQ TREND GEN/LAWS 20. PAGE 147 H2934
CULTURE SOC WAR

B29
DE REPARAZ G.,GEOGRAFIA Y POLITICA. CHILE SPAIN USSR NAT/G DIPLOM REV MARXISM...POLICY 19/20. PAGE 38 H0768
GEOG MOD/EUR

B29
LANGER W.L.,THE FRANCO-RUSSIAN ALLIANCE: 1890-1894. FRANCE MOD/EUR UK USSR NAT/G CHIEF FORCES BAL/PWR AGREE WAR PEACE PWR...TIME/SEQ TREATY 19 BISMARCK/O. PAGE 91 H1809
DIPLOM

B30
BYNKERSHOEK C.,QUAESTIONUM JURIS PUBLICI LIBRI DUO. CHRIST-17C MOD/EUR CONSTN ELITES SOCIETY NAT/G PROVS EX/STRUC FORCES TOP/EX BAL/PWR DIPLOM ATTIT MORAL...TRADIT CONCPT. PAGE 25 H0502
INT/ORG LAW NAT/LISM INT/LAW

B30
MASON E.S.,THE PARIS COMMUNE: AN EPISODE IN THE HISTORY OF THE SOCIALIST MOVEMENT. FRANCE MOD/EUR ELITES SOCIETY STRATA ECO/DEV WORKER EDU/PROP CHOOSE INGP/REL SOCISM 19 MARX/KARL PARIS. PAGE 104 H2085
NAT/G REV MARXISM

B31
BONAR J.,THEORIES OF POPULATION FROM RALEIGH TO ARTHUR YOUNG. CHRIST-17C MOD/EUR CULTURE SOCIETY R+D CREATE ATTIT PERCEPT RIGID/FLEX...OLD/LIB CONCPT NEW/IDEA TIME/SEQ IDEA/COMP STERTYP GEN/LAWS. PAGE 19 H0372
GEOG BIOG

B32
BRYCE J.,THE HOLY ROMAN EMPIRE. GERMANY ITALY MOD/EUR CULTURE SOCIETY STRUCT INT/ORG NAT/G SECT DIPLOM DOMIN WAR SUPEGO ALL/VALS SOVEREIGN...GEOG SOC TIME/SEQ CHARTS STERTYP. PAGE 23 H0456
CHRIST-17C NAT/LISM

B36
HUBERMAN L.,MAN'S WORLDLY GOODS: THE STORY OF THE WEALTH OF NATIONS. CHRIST-17C EUR+WWI MOD/EUR SOCIETY DOMIN REV ORD/FREE...TIME/SEQ METH/COMP. PAGE 74 H1486
WEALTH CAP/ISM MARXISM CREATE

B36
WANDERSCHECK H.,WELTKRIEG UND PROPAGANDA. GERMANY MOD/EUR UK COM/IND NAT/G DOMIN PRESS ATTIT...POLICY 20 HITLER/A. PAGE 165 H3299
EDU/PROP PSY WAR KNOWL

B37
BERDYAEV N.,THE ORIGIN OF RUSSIAN COMMUNISM. MOD/EUR RUSSIA USSR INTELL SECT REV...ANARCH HUM 19/20 ORTHO/RUSS COM/PARTY CHRISTIAN. PAGE 15 H0294
MARXISM NAT/LISM CULTURE ATTIT

B37
THOMPSON J.W.,SECRET DIPLOMACY: A RECORD OF ESPIONAGE AND DOUBLE-DEALING: 1500-1815. CHRIST-17C MOD/EUR NAT/G WRITING RISK MORAL...ANTHOL BIBLIOG 16/19 ESPIONAGE. PAGE 154 H3084
DIPLOM CRIME

L37
NICOLSON H.,"THE MEANING OF PRESTIGE." EUR+WWI MOD/EUR UK CULTURE SOCIETY NAT/G DIPLOM DOMIN LEGIT ATTIT DRIVE PWR...METH/CNCPT RECORD TIME/SEQ GEN/METH CMN/WLTH TOT/POP 20. PAGE 118 H2351
CONCPT STERTYP

B38
MARX K.,THE GERMAN IDEOLOGY, PARTS 1 AND 3 (1846). MOD/EUR LAW STRATA WORKER DOMIN REV UTOPIA SOCISM 19 MARX/KARL. PAGE 104 H2079
MARXIST OWN PRODUC ECO/TAC

B39
ANDERSON P.R.,THE BACKGROUND OF ANTI-ENGLISH FEELING IN GERMANY, 1890-1902. GERMANY MOD/EUR UK NAT/G POL/PAR TOP/EX WAR...IDEA/COMP 19/20. PAGE 7 H0132
DIPLOM EDU/PROP ATTIT COLONIAL

B39
CARR E.H.,PROPAGANDA IN INTERNATIONAL POLITICS (PAMPHLET). EUR+WWI GERMANY MOD/EUR NAT/G AGREE WAR MORAL...POLICY 20 TREATY. PAGE 27 H0536
DIPLOM EDU/PROP CONTROL ATTIT

B39
COBBAN A.,DICTATORSHIP: ITS HISTORY AND THEORY. EUR+WWI MOD/EUR SOCIETY STRUCT NAT/G TEC/DEV LEAD NAT/LISM SOVEREIGN...IDEA/COMP 14/20. PAGE 30 H0610
TOTALISM FASCISM CONCPT

B39
HITLER A.,MEIN KAMPF. EUR+WWI FUT MOD/EUR STRUCT INT/ORG LABOR NAT/G POL/PAR FORCES CREATE PLAN BAL/PWR DIPLOM ECO/TAC DOMIN EDU/PROP ADMIN COERCE ATTIT...SOCIALIST BIOG TREND NAZI. PAGE 71 H1428
PWR NEW/IDEA WAR

B39
KOHN H.,REVOLUTIONS AND DICTATORSHIPS. COM EUR+WWI ISLAM MOD/EUR NAT/G CHIEF FORCES WAR CIVMIL/REL PWR MARXISM 18/20. PAGE 87 H1739
NAT/LISM TOTALISM REV FASCISM

B40
BROGAN D.W.,THE DEVELOPMENT OF MODERN FRANCE (1870-1939). FRANCE GERMANY UK USSR CONSTN CHIEF LEGIS DIPLOM AGREE COLONIAL WAR NAT/LISM PEACE SOCISM 19/20 TREATY. PAGE 21 H0428
MOD/EUR NAT/G

B40
MANNHEIM K.,MAN AND SOCIETY IN AN AGE OF RECONSTRUCTION. MOD/EUR CULTURE ECO/DEV PLAN TEC/DEV PERSON LAISSEZ NEW/LIB...NEW/IDEA IDEA/COMP BIBLIOG 19/20. PAGE 102 H2038
CONCPT ATTIT SOCIETY TOTALISM

B40
MCILWAIN C.H.,CONSTITUTIONALISM, ANCIENT AND MODERN. CHRIST-17C MOD/EUR NAT/G CHIEF PROB/SOLV INSPECT AUTHORIT ORD/FREE PWR...TIME/SEQ ROMAN/REP. PAGE 107 H2134
CONSTN GEN/LAWS LAW

B40
WANDERSCHECK H.,FRANKREICHS PROPAGANDA GEGEN DEUTSCHLAND. FRANCE GERMANY MOD/EUR UK NAT/G DIPLOM WAR 20 JEWS. PAGE 165 H3300
EDU/PROP ATTIT DOMIN PRESS

B41
GRISMER R.,A NEW BIBLIOGRAPHY OF THE LITERATURES OF SPAIN AND SPANISH AMERICA. CHRIST-17C MOD/EUR PRE/AMER SPAIN CULTURE DIPLOM EDU/PROP...ART/METH GEOG HUM PHIL/SCI 20. PAGE 61 H1229
BIBLIOG LAW NAT/G ECO/UNDEV

B41
HAUSHOFER K.,WEHR-GEOPOLITIK. EUR+WWI GERMANY MOD/EUR NAT/G ACT/RES BAL/PWR PWR...STAT TIME/SEQ
FORCES GEOG

CHARTS NAZI 20. PAGE 68 H1361 — WAR

B41
PALMER R.R.,TWELVE WHO RULED. MOD/EUR ELITES STRUCT NAT/G POL/PAR DELIB/GP DOMIN ATTIT SUPEGO PWR ...POLICY CONCPT 18. PAGE 123 H2453 — TOP/EX BIOG REV FRANCE

B42
FEFFERO G.,THE PRINCIPLES OF POWER (TRANS. BY T. JAECKEL). MOD/EUR CONSTN NAT/G CHIEF CONTROL REV WAR ORD/FREE CONSERVE FASCISM POPULISM...GEN/LAWS 18/20 EUROPE. PAGE 49 H0980 — PWR LEGIT TRADIT ELITES

B42
SINGTON D.,THE GOEBBELS EXPERIMENT. GERMANY MOD/EUR NAT/G EX/STRUC FORCES CONTROL ROUTINE WAR TOTALISM PWR...ART/METH HUM 20 NAZI GOEBBELS/J. PAGE 144 H2886 — FASCISM EDU/PROP ATTIT COM/IND

B43
EARLE E.M.,MAKERS OF MODERN STRATEGY: MILITARY THOUGHT FROM MACHIAVELLI TO HITLER. EUR+WWI MOD/EUR NAT/G ACT/RES BAL/PWR DOMIN COERCE ATTIT DRIVE RIGID/FLEX ALL/VALS...METH/CNCPT BIOG 16/20. PAGE 44 H0879 — PLAN FORCES WAR

B43
LENIN V.I.,LEFT WING COMMUNISM: AN INFANTILE DISORDER (1920). GERMANY MOD/EUR USSR STRUCT CHIEF DOMIN EDU/PROP LEGIT LEAD REPRESENT POPULISM ...METH/COMP 19 LENIN/VI COM/PARTY MENSHEVIK. PAGE 94 H1879 — COM MARXISM NAT/G REV

B43
SERENI A.P.,THE ITALIAN CONCEPTION OF INTERNATIONAL LAW. EUR+WWI MOD/EUR INT/ORG NAT/G DOMIN COERCE ORD/FREE FASCISM...OBS/ENVIR TREND 20. PAGE 141 H2829 — LAW TIME/SEQ INT/LAW ITALY

B46
NICOLSON H.,THE CONGRESS OF VIENNA. MOD/EUR NAT/G FORCES BAL/PWR DOMIN LEGIT COERCE PERSON PWR ...RECORD TIME/SEQ STERTYP 19 CONG/VIENN. PAGE 118 H2353 — CONCPT POLICY DIPLOM

S46
SILBERNER E.,"THE PROBLEM OF WAR IN NINETEENTH CENTURY ECONOMIC THOUGHT." EUR+WWI MOD/EUR UNIV LAW ECO/DEV ECO/UNDEV FINAN INDUS MARKET INT/ORG NAT/G CONSULT FORCES...CONCPT GEN/LAWS GEN/METH 19. PAGE 144 H2875 — ATTIT ECO/TAC WAR

B47
ISAAC J.,ECONOMICS OF MIGRATION. MOD/EUR CULTURE STRATA STRUCT NAT/G COLONIAL WEALTH...OLD/LIB TREND TIME 19/20 EUROPE/W MIGRATION. PAGE 78 H1569 — HABITAT SOC GEOG

B48
LAUTERBACH A.,ECONOMIC SECURITY AND INDIVIDUAL FREEDOM: CAN WE HAVE BOTH? COM EUR+WWI MOD/EUR UNIV WOR+45 CAP/ISM TOTALISM ALL/VALS...GOV/COMP BIBLIOG 20. PAGE 92 H1840 — ORD/FREE ECO/DEV DECISION INGP/REL

B48
YAKOBSON S.,FIVE HUNDRED RUSSIAN WORKS FOR COLLEGE LIBRARIES (PAMPHLET). MOD/EUR USSR MARXISM SOCISM ...ART/METH GEOG HUM JURID SOC 13/20. PAGE 171 H3431 — BIBLIOG NAT/G CULTURE COM

B49
DENNING A.,FREEDOM UNDER THE LAW. MOD/EUR UK LAW SOCIETY CHIEF EX/STRUC LEGIS ADJUD CT/SYS PERS/REL PERSON 17/20 ENGLSH/LAW. PAGE 40 H0793 — ORD/FREE JURID NAT/G

B50
CONOVER H.F.,INTRODUCTION TO EUROPE: A SELECTIVE GUIDE TO BACKGROUND READING. COM EUR+WWI NAT/G KNOWL...ART/METH GEOG SOC. PAGE 32 H0648 — BIBLIOG/A MOD/EUR HIST/WRIT

B50
GATZKE H.W.,GERMANY'S DRIVE TO THE WEST. BELGIUM GERMANY MOD/EUR AGRI INDUS POL/PAR FORCES DOMIN AGREE CONTROL REGION COERCE 20 TREATY WWI. PAGE 55 H1104 — WAR POLICY NAT/G DIPLOM

B50
KANN R.A.,THE MULTINATIONAL EMPIRE (2 VOLS.). AUSTRIA CZECHOSLVK GERMANY HUNGARY CULTURE NAT/G POL/PAR PROVS REGION REV FEDERAL...GEOG TREND CHARTS IDEA/COMP NAT/COMP 19/20. PAGE 83 H1654 — NAT/LISM MOD/EUR

B51
WEBSTER C.,THE FOREIGN POLICY OF PALMERSTON - 1830 TO 1841. MOD/EUR UK LAW CONSTN INTELL SOCIETY STRUCT NAT/G FORCES TOP/EX CREATE BAL/PWR PWR 19. PAGE 166 H3323 — ADMIN PERSON DIPLOM

B52
BENTHAM A.,HANDBOOK OF POLITICAL FALLACIES. FUT MOD/EUR LAW INTELL LOC/G MUNIC NAT/G DELIB/GP LEGIS CREATE EDU/PROP CT/SYS ATTIT RIGID/FLEX KNOWL PWR ...RELATIV PSY SOC CONCPT SELF/OBS TREND STERTYP TOT/POP. PAGE 14 H0286 — POL/PAR

B52
HIMMELFARB G.,LORD ACTON: A STUDY IN CONSCIENCE AND POLITICS. MOD/EUR NAT/G POL/PAR SECT LEGIS TOP/EX EDU/PROP ADMIN NAT/LISM ATTIT PERSON SUPEGO MORAL ORD/FREE...CONCPT PARLIAMENT 19 ACTON/LORD. PAGE 71 H1419 — PWR BIOG

B52
KOHN H.,PROPHETS AND PEOPLES: STUDIES IN NINETEENTH CENTURY NATIONALISM. MOD/EUR...IDEA/COMP 19. PAGE 87 H1741 — CONCPT NAT/LISM SOVEREIGN

B52
LOPEZ-AMO A.,LA MONARQUIA DE LA REFORMA SOCIAL. MOD/EUR SPAIN CONSTN NAT/G TASK EFFICIENCY CONSERVE ...ANARCH TRADIT SOC CONCPT IDEA/COMP 19/20. PAGE 98 H1967 — MARXISM REV LEGIT ORD/FREE

S52
MUEHLMANN W.E.,"L'IDEE NATIONALE ALLEMANDE ET L'IDEE NATIONALE FRANCAISE." EUR+WWI MOD/EUR SOCIETY KIN NAT/G PWR RESPECT...SOC CONCPT TIME/SEQ GEN/LAWS 19/20. PAGE 114 H2279 — CULTURE ATTIT FRANCE GERMANY

C53
DORWART R.A.,"THE ADMINISTRATIVE REFORMS OF FREDRICK WILLIAM I OF PRUSSIA. GERMANY MOD/EUR CHIEF CONTROL PWR...BIBLIOG 16/18. PAGE 42 H0839 — ADMIN NAT/G CENTRAL GOV/REL

B54
GERMANY FOREIGN MINISTRY,DOCUMENTS ON GERMAN FOREIGN POLICY 1918-1945, SERIES C (1933-1937) VOLS. I-V. GERMANY MOD/EUR FORCES PLAN ECO/TAC ...FASCIST CHARTS ANTHOL 20. PAGE 56 H1115 — NAT/G DIPLOM POLICY

B54
HAMSON C.J.,EXECUTIVE DISCRETION AND JUDICIAL CONTROL; AN ASPECT OF THE FRENCH CONSEIL D'ETAT. EUR+WWI FRANCE MOD/EUR UK NAT/G EX/STRUC PARTIC CONSERVE...JURID BIBLIOG/A 18/20 SUPREME/CT. PAGE 65 H1310 — ELITES ADJUD NAT/COMP

B54
SALVEMINI G.,PRELUDE TO WORLD WAR II. ITALY MOD/EUR INT/ORG BAL/PWR EDU/PROP CONTROL TOTALISM...TREND NAT/COMP BIBLIOG 19 HITLER/A LEAGUE/NAT MUSSOLIN/B. PAGE 137 H2745 — WAR FASCISM LEAD PWR

B54
SPENCER H.,SOCIAL STATICS. MOD/EUR UNIV SOCIETY ECO/DEV NAT/G ACT/RES PLAN EDU/PROP PERSON...POLICY CONCPT. PAGE 147 H2944 — MORAL ECO/TAC

B55
CRAIG G.A.,THE POLITICS OF THE PRUSSIAN ARMY 1640-1945. CHRIST-17C EUR+WWI MOD/EUR PRUSSIA STRUCT DIPLOM ADMIN REV WAR...SOC BIBLIOG 17/20. PAGE 35 H0694 — FORCES NAT/G ROLE CHIEF

B55
KOHN H.,THE MIND OF MODERN RUSSIA. COM MOD/EUR USSR SOCIETY NAT/G SECT FORCES TOP/EX COERCE TOTALISM DRIVE RIGID/FLEX PWR SOVEREIGN...CONCPT TIME/SEQ WORK. PAGE 87 H1742 — INTELL GEN/LAWS SOCISM RUSSIA

B55
MAZZINI J.,THE DUTIES OF MAN. MOD/EUR LAW SOCIETY FAM NAT/G POL/PAR SECT VOL/ASSN EX/STRUC ACT/RES CREATE REV PEACE ATTIT ALL/VALS...GEN/LAWS WORK 19. PAGE 106 H2113 — SUPEGO CONCPT NAT/LISM

B55
MOHL R.V.,DIE GESCHICHTE UND LITERATUR DER STAATSWISSENSCHAFTEN (3 VOLS.). LAW NAT/G...JURID METH/COMP METH. PAGE 112 H2236 — PHIL/SCI MOD/EUR

B55
NAMIER L.,PERSONALITIES AND POWERS. EUR+WWI MOD/EUR NAT/G POL/PAR TOP/EX EDU/PROP KNOWL...GEOG 17/20. PAGE 115 H2308 — TIME/SEQ DIPLOM UK

B55
ROWE C.,VOLTAIRE AND THE STATE. FRANCE MOD/EUR BAL/PWR CONTROL TASK SUPEGO ORD/FREE PWR...CONCPT 18 VOLTAIRE. PAGE 135 H2702 — NAT/G DIPLOM NAT/LISM ATTIT

B56
WOLFF R.L.,THE BALKANS IN OUR TIME. ALBANIA FUT MOD/EUR USSR YUGOSLAVIA CULTURE INT/ORG SECT DIPLOM EDU/PROP COERCE WAR ORD/FREE...CHARTS 4/20 BALKANS COMINFORM. PAGE 170 H3403 — GEOG COM

B57
BARAN P.A.,THE POLITICAL ECONOMY OF GROWTH. MOD/EUR USA+45 USA-45 TEC/DEV TAX SOCISM...MGT CONCPT GOV/COMP. PAGE 11 H0213 — CAP/ISM CONTROL ECO/UNDEV FINAN

B57
HIRSCH F.E.,EUROPE TODAY; A BIBLIOGRAPHY (2ND ED.). EUR+WWI MOD/EUR NAT/G WAR 20. PAGE 71 H1424 — BIBLIOG/A GEOG DIPLOM

B57
MEINECKE F.,MACHIAVELLISM. CHRIST-17C FRANCE GERMANY ITALY MOD/EUR BAL/PWR PARL/PROC TOTALISM ...PHIL/SCI 15/20 MACHIAVELL. PAGE 108 H2166 — NAT/LISM NAT/G PWR

B58
SYME R.,COLONIAL ELITES: ROME, SPAIN, AND THE AMERICAS. CHRIST-17C MOD/EUR SPAIN UK USA-45 CULTURE NAT/G CHIEF TOP/EX...GOV/COMP IDEA/COMP NAT/COMP ROM/EMP GIBBON/EDW TOYNBEE/A. PAGE 151 H3022 — COLONIAL ELITES DOMIN

B59
DEHIO L.,GERMANY AND WORLD POLITICS IN THE TWENTIETH CENTURY. EUR+WWI FRANCE GERMANY MOD/EUR UK USSR NAT/G CHIEF BAL/PWR DOMIN COLONIAL CONTROL LEAD...IDEA/COMP 20 VERSAILLES. PAGE 39 H0783 — DIPLOM WAR NAT/LISM SOVEREIGN

B59
LANDAUER C.,EUROPEAN SOCIALISM (2 VOLS.). COM EUR+WWI MOD/EUR INTELL INDUS REV WAR...MAJORIT — SOCISM NAT/COMP

IDEA/COMP BIBLIOG 19/20 HITLER/A. PAGE 90 H1805 LABOR MARXISM

B59
LEFEVRE R.,THE NATURE OF MAN AND HIS GOVERNMENT. EUR+WWI MOD/EUR CONSTN CULTURE MORAL MARXISM ...POLICY 18/20. PAGE 93 H1859 NAT/G TASK ORD/FREE ATTIT

B59
MAIER H.,REVOLUTION UND KIRCHE. FRANCE MOD/EUR SECT REV ORD/FREE...IDEA/COMP 18/19. PAGE 101 H2018 NAT/G CATHISM ATTIT POL/PAR

B60
ALBRECHT-CARRIE R.,FRANCE, EUROPE AND THE TWO WORLD WARS. EUR+WWI FRANCE GERMANY MOD/EUR UK ECO/DEV NAT/G FORCES BAL/PWR DOMIN ARMS/CONT PEACE PWR 20 TREATY EUROPE. PAGE 5 H0096 DIPLOM WAR

B60
BLACK C.E.,THE TRANSFORMATION OF RUSSIAN SOCIETY. COM MOD/EUR RUSSIA SOCIETY EDU/PROP COERCE ALL/VALS 19/20. PAGE 17 H0349 CULTURE RIGID/FLEX USSR

B60
KOHN H.,PAN-SLAVISM: ITS HISTORY AND IDEOLOGY. COM CZECHOSLVK EUR+WWI MOD/EUR USSR YUGOSLAVIA CULTURE ELITES INTELL KIN NAT/G EDU/PROP DRIVE SOVEREIGN ...HUM PHIL/SCI MYTH HIST/WRIT 19/20. PAGE 87 H1745 ATTIT CONCPT NAT/LISM

B60
SZTARAY Z.,BIBLIOGRAPHY ON HUNGARY. HUNGARY MOD/EUR CULTURE INDUS SECT DIPLOM REV...ART/METH SOC LING 18/20. PAGE 151 H3029 BIBLIOG NAT/G COM MARXISM

B61
BISHOP D.G.,THE ADMINISTRATION OF BRITISH FOREIGN RELATIONS. EUR+WWI MOD/EUR INT/ORG NAT/G POL/PAR DELIB/GP LEGIS TOP/EX ECO/TAC DOMIN EDU/PROP ADMIN COERCE 20. PAGE 17 H0344 ROUTINE PWR DIPLOM UK

B61
GUIZOT F.P.G.,HISTORY OF THE ORIGIN OF REPRESENTATIVE GOVERNMENT IN EUROPE. CHRIST-17C FRANCE MOD/EUR SPAIN UK LAW CHIEF FORCES POPULISM ...MAJORIT TIME/SEQ GOV/COMP NAT/COMP 4/19 PARLIAMENT. PAGE 62 H1250 LEGIS REPRESENT CONSTN NAT/G

B61
KEDOURIE E.,NATIONALISM (REV. ED.). MOD/EUR SOVEREIGN...CONCPT 19/20. PAGE 84 H1675 NAT/LISM NAT/G CREATE REV

B61
MARX K.,THE COMMUNIST MANIFESTO. IN (MENDEL A. ESSENTIAL WORKS OF MARXISM, NEW YORK: BANTAM. FUT MOD/EUR CULTURE ECO/DEV ECO/UNDEV AGRI FINAN INDUS MARKET PROC/MFG LABOR MUNIC POL/PAR CONSULT FORCES CREATE PLAN ADMIN ATTIT DRIVE RIGID/FLEX ORD/FREE PWR RESPECT MARX/KARL WORK. PAGE 104 H2081 COM NEW/IDEA CAP/ISM REV

B61
MONAS S.,THE THIRD SECTION: POLICE AND SOCIETY IN RUSSIA UNDER NICHOLAS I. MOD/EUR RUSSIA ELITES STRUCT NAT/G EX/STRUC ADMIN CONTROL PWR CONSERVE ...DECISION 19 NICHOLAS/I. PAGE 112 H2238 ORD/FREE COM FORCES COERCE

B61
ROBERTSON A.H.,THE LAW OF INTERNATIONAL INSTITUTIONS IN EUROPE. EUR+WWI MOD/EUR INT/ORG NAT/G VOL/ASSN DELIB/GP...JURID TIME/SEQ TOT/POP 20 TREATY. PAGE 132 H2644 RIGID/FLEX ORD/FREE

S61
ANDERSON O.,"ECONOMIC WARFARE IN THE CRIMEAN WAR." EUR+WWI MOD/EUR NAT/G ACT/RES WAR DRIVE PWR 19/20. PAGE 6 H0130 ECO/TAC UK RUSSIA

S61
DOGAN M.,"LES OFFICIERS DANS LA CARRIERE POLITIQUE DE MARECHAL MACMAHON AU GENERAL DE GAULLE." EUR+WWI FRANCE MOD/EUR ELITES STRATA POL/PAR LEGIT ATTIT ALL/VALS...SOC CONCPT 19/20. PAGE 42 H0833 PROF/ORG FORCES NAT/G DELIB/GP

B62
DUTOIT B.,LA NEUTRALITE SUISSE A L'HEURE EUROPEENNE. EUR+WWI MOD/EUR INT/ORG NAT/G VOL/ASSN PLAN BAL/PWR LEGIT NEUTRAL REGION PEACE ORD/FREE SOVEREIGN...CONCPT OBS TIME/SEQ TREND STERTYP VAL/FREE LEAGUE/NAT UN 20. PAGE 44 H0873 ATTIT DIPLOM SWITZERLND

B62
HENDERSON W.O.,THE GENESIS OF THE COMMON MARKET. EUR+WWI FRANCE MOD/EUR UK SEA COM/IND EXTR/IND COLONIAL DISCRIM...TIME/SEQ CHARTS BIBLIOG 18/20 EEC TREATY. PAGE 70 H1395 ECO/DEV INT/TRADE DIPLOM

B62
THIERRY S.S.,LE VATICAN SECRET. CHRIST-17C EUR+WWI MOD/EUR VATICAN NAT/G SECT DELIB/GP DOMIN LEGIT SOVEREIGN. PAGE 154 H3072 ADMIN EX/STRUC CATHISM DECISION

S62
LANGER W.L.,"FAREWELL TO EMPIRE." EUR+WWI MOD/EUR NAT/G DIPLOM EDU/PROP COLONIAL ATTIT ORD/FREE PWR SOVEREIGN WEALTH...CONCPT TIME/SEQ GEN/LAWS TOT/POP VAL/FREE CMN/WLTH 20. PAGE 91 H1810 DOMIN ECO/TAC NAT/LISM

B63
BERLIN I.,KARL MARX, HIS LIFE AND ENVIRONMENT (3RD ED.). MOD/EUR USSR INTELL EDU/PROP PARTIC REV ATTIT 19 MARX/KARL. PAGE 15 H0307 BIOG PERSON MARXISM CONCPT

B63
KRAEHE E.,METTERNICH'S GERMAN POLICY: THE CONTEST WITH NAPOLEON, 1799-1814, VOL. 1. FRANCE MOD/EUR NAT/G CONSULT TOP/EX PLAN BAL/PWR DOMIN COERCE ATTIT DRIVE PERCEPT PERSON SKILL...CONCPT RECORD TIME/SEQ TREND 18/19. PAGE 88 H1764 BIOG GERMANY DIPLOM

B63
MONGER G.W.,THE END OF ISOLATION. FRANCE MOD/EUR RUSSIA UK NAT/G LEGIS TOP/EX GOV/REL PWR 20 TREATY CHINJAP. PAGE 112 H2239 DIPLOM POLICY WAR

B63
NALBANDIAN L.,THE ARMENIAN REVOLUTIONARY MOVEMENT. MOD/EUR RUSSIA...IDEA/COMP NAT/COMP BIBLIOG 19 ARMENIA OTTOMAN. PAGE 115 H2306 NAT/LISM REV POL/PAR ORD/FREE

B63
OLSON M. JR.,THE ECONOMICS OF WARTIME SHORTAGE. FRANCE GERMANY MOD/EUR UK AGRI PROB/SOLV ADMIN DEMAND WEALTH...POLICY OLD/LIB 17/20. PAGE 121 H2416 WAR ADJUST ECO/TAC NAT/COMP

B63
SETON-WATSON H.,THE NEW IMPERIALISM. COM EUR+WWI MOD/EUR ECO/UNDEV NAT/G FORCES DIPLOM DOMIN EDU/PROP LEGIT COLONIAL EXEC COERCE GP/REL RACE/REL DISCRIM ATTIT...TIME/SEQ 20. PAGE 142 H2833 ECO/TAC RUSSIA USSR

B63
WILSON U.,EDUCATION AND CHANGING WEST AFRICAN CULTURE. AFR MOD/EUR UK CULTURE ECO/UNDEV MUNIC CONSULT 19/20 CMN/WLTH AFRICA/W. PAGE 169 H3384 COLONIAL POLICY SCHOOL

S63
LOPEZIBOR J.,"L'EUROPE, FORME DE VIE." CHRIST-17C EUR+WWI FUT MOD/EUR SOCIETY INT/ORG SECT EDU/PROP ATTIT RIGID/FLEX ALL/VALS...POLICY HUM SOC TIME/SEQ TREND GEN/LAWS. PAGE 98 H1966 NAT/G CULTURE

S63
SOEMARDJORN S.,"SOME SOCIAL AND CULTURAL IMPLICATIONS OF INDONESIA'S PLANNED AND UNPLANNED DEVELOPMENT." EUR+WWI FUT MOD/EUR S/ASIA CONSTN SOCIETY DELIB/GP ACT/RES PLAN ECO/TAC EDU/PROP COERCE ATTIT ALL/VALS...TIME/SEQ 20. PAGE 146 H2927 ECO/UNDEV CULTURE INDONESIA

S63
WEISSBERG G.,"MAPS AS EVIDENCE IN INTERNATIONAL BOUNDARY DISPUTES: A REAPPRAISAL." CHINA/COM EUR+WWI INDIA MOD/EUR S/ASIA INT/ORG NAT/G LEGIT PERCEPT...JURID CHARTS 20. PAGE 166 H3331 LAW GEOG SOVEREIGN

B64
CAUTE D.,COMMUNISM AND THE FRENCH INTELLECTUALS, 1914-1960. COM EUR+WWI MOD/EUR NAT/G PERF/ART PROF/ORG CREATE EDU/PROP ATTIT PERSON KNOWL MARXISM ...SOC TIME/SEQ MARX/KARL 20 MALRAUX/A GIDE/A SARTRE/J. PAGE 28 H0563 POL/PAR INTELL

B64
CURTIN P.D.,THE IMAGE OF AFRICA: BRITISH IDEAS AND ACTION, 1780-1850. MOD/EUR SOCIETY FORCES ACT/RES DOMIN EDU/PROP COERCE ATTIT PERCEPT RIGID/FLEX SUPEGO HEALTH KNOWL MORAL ORD/FREE WEALTH...CONCPT WORK VAL/FREE. PAGE 36 H0726 AFR CULTURE UK DIPLOM

B64
PIPES R.,THE FORMATION OF THE SOVIET UNION. EUR+WWI MOD/EUR STRUCT ECO/UNDEV NAT/G LEGIS DOMIN LEGIT CT/SYS EXEC COERCE ALL/VALS...POLICY RELATIV HIST/WRIT TIME/SEQ TOT/POP 19/20. PAGE 126 H2514 COM USSR RUSSIA

B64
TODD W.B.,A BIBLIOGRAPHY OF EDMUND BURKE. MOD/EUR UK NAT/G EDU/PROP ATTIT...HUM 18 BURKE/EDM. PAGE 156 H3110 BIBLIOG/A PHIL/SCI WRITING CONCPT

B64
VON STEIN L.J.,THE HISTORY OF THE SOCIAL MOVEMENT IN FRANCE, 1789-1850 (TRANS. BY K. MENGELBERG). COM FRANCE MOD/EUR NAT/G EX/STRUC INGP/REL ALL/IDEOS CONSERVE MARXISM...SOC BIBLIOG 18/19. PAGE 164 H3278 REV STRATA

B64
WRIGHT G.,RURAL REVOLUTION IN FRANCE: THE PEASANTRY IN THE TWENTIETH CENTURY. EUR+WWI MOD/EUR LAW CULTURE AGRI POL/PAR DELIB/GP LEGIS ECO/TAC EDU/PROP COERCE CHOOSE ATTIT RIGID/FLEX HEALTH ...STAT CENSUS CHARTS VAL/FREE 20. PAGE 171 H3419 PWR STRATA FRANCE REV

S64
CROUZET F.,"WARS, BLOCKADE, AND ECONOMIC CHANGE IN EUROPE, 1792-1815." UK INDUS NAT/G TEC/DEV ECO/TAC WEALTH...POLICY RELATIV HIST/WRIT TIME/SEQ 18/19. PAGE 35 H0710 MOD/EUR MARKET

S64
GROSS J.A.,"WHITEHALL AND THE COMMONWEALTH." EUR+WWI MOD/EUR INT/ORG NAT/G CONSULT DELIB/GP LEGIS DOMIN ADMIN COLONIAL ROUTINE PWR CMN/WLTH 19/20. PAGE 62 H1233 EX/STRUC ATTIT TREND

S64
GRUNER E.,"PRENSA, PARTIDOS POLITICOS, Y GRUPOS DE PRESION EN SUIZA." EUR+WWI MOD/EUR NAT/G EDU/PROP LEGIT PRESS ATTIT KNOWL ORD/FREE...CONCPT STAT POL/PAR SWITZERLND

CON/ANAL CHARTS 20. PAGE 62 H1241

S64
LOW D.A.,"LION RAMPANT." EUR+WWI MOD/EUR S/ASIA ECO/UNDEV NAT/G FORCES TEC/DEV ECO/TAC LEGIT ADMIN COLONIAL COERCE ORD/FREE RESPECT 19/20. PAGE 99 H1972 — AFR DOMIN DIPLOM UK

S64
REISS I.,"LE DECLENCHEMENT DE LA PREMIERE GUERRE MONDIALE." GERMANY RUSSIA NAT/G FORCES DOMIN EDU/PROP COERCE RIGID/FLEX PWR SOVEREIGN...RELATIV HIST/WRIT TOT/POP AUST/HUNG SERBIA 20. PAGE 131 H2612 — MOD/EUR BAL/PWR DIPLOM WAR

B65
COLLINS H.,KARL MARX AND THE BRITISH LABOR MOVEMENT, YEARS OF THE FIRST INTERNATIONAL. EUR+WWI MOD/EUR UK STRATA INDUS NAT/G POL/PAR SOCISM ...CONCPT 19/20 MARX/KARL. PAGE 32 H0633 — MARXISM LABOR INT/ORG WORKER

B65
GODECHOT J.,FRANCE AND THE ATLANTIC REVOLUTION OF THE EIGHTEENTH CENTURY 1770-1799. FRANCE CULTURE SOCIETY...GEOG 18. PAGE 57 H1150 — MOD/EUR NAT/G REV ECO/UNDEV

B65
HALEVY E.,THE ERA OF TYRANNIES (TRANS. BY R. K. WEBB). FRANCE MOD/EUR UK ECO/DEV LABOR NAT/G BAL/PWR FEDERAL ALL/VALS...OLD/LIB TREND 18/20 SAINTSIMON. PAGE 64 H1285 — SOCISM CONCPT UTOPIA ORD/FREE

B65
NORDEN A.,WAR AND NAZI CRIMINALS IN WEST GERMANY: STATE, ECONOMY, ADMINISTRATION, ARMY, JUSTICE, SCIENCE. GERMANY GERMANY/W MOD/EUR ECO/DEV ACADEM EX/STRUC FORCES DOMIN ADMIN CT/SYS...POLICY MAJORIT PACIFIST 20. PAGE 119 H2370 — FASCIST WAR NAT/G TOP/EX

B65
O'CONNELL M.R.,IRISH POLITICS AND SOCIAL CONFLICT IN THE AGE OF THE AMERICAN REVOLUTION. FRANCE IRELAND MOD/EUR STRATA SECT LEGIS DIPLOM INT/TRADE DOMIN REV WAR...BIBLIOG 18 PARLIAMENT. PAGE 119 H2387 — CATHISM ATTIT NAT/G DELIB/GP

B65
ROSENBERG A.,DEMOCRACY AND SOCIALISM. COM EUR+WWI FRANCE MOD/EUR STRUCT INT/ORG NAT/G POL/PAR TOP/EX EDU/PROP COERCE PERSON PWR FASCISM MARXISM...CONCPT TIME/SEQ MARX/KARL 19/20. PAGE 134 H2677 — ATTIT

B66
CAUTE D.,THE LEFT IN EUROPE SINCE 1789. EUR+WWI MOD/EUR NAT/G POL/PAR REV...TIME/SEQ GEN/LAWS BIBLIOG 18/20. PAGE 28 H0564 — ALL/IDEOS ORD/FREE CONCPT STRATA

B66
FEINE H.E.,REICH UND KIRCHE. CHRIST-17C MOD/EUR ROMAN/EMP LAW CHOOSE ATTIT 10/19 CHURCH/STA ROMAN/LAW. PAGE 49 H0982 — JURID SECT NAT/G GP/REL

B66
FUCHS W.P.,STAAT UND KIRCHE IM WANDEL DER JAHRHUNDERTE. EUR+WWI MOD/EUR UK REV...JURID CONCPT 4/20 EUROPE CHRISTIAN CHURCH/STA. PAGE 54 H1074 — SECT NAT/G ORD/FREE GP/REL

B66
MARTIN L.W.,DIPLOMACY IN MODERN EUROPEAN HISTORY. EUR+WWI MOD/EUR INT/ORG NAT/G EX/STRUC ROUTINE WAR PEACE TOTALISM PWR 15/20 COLD/WAR EUROPE/W. PAGE 103 H2064 — DIPLOM POLICY

B66
SETTON K.M.,GREAT PROBLEMS IN EUROPEAN CIVILIZATION. CHRIST-17C EUR+WWI MOD/EUR SECT GP/REL ALL/VALS ORD/FREE ALL/IDEOS...TREND ANTHOL T CHRISTIAN RENAISSAN PROTESTANT. PAGE 142 H2835 — CULTURE CONCPT IDEA/COMP

B66
WUEST J.J.,NEW SOURCE BOOK IN MAJOR EUROPEAN GOVERNMENTS. CHRIST-17C EUR+WWI FRANCE GERMANY ITALY MOD/EUR UK USSR LOC/G POL/PAR CHIEF EX/STRUC CHOOSE CONSERVE MARXISM...JURID T 13/20. PAGE 171 H3425 — NAT/G CONSTN LEGIS

L66
HUNTINGTON S.P.,"POLITICAL MODERNIZATION* AMERICA VS EUROPE." EUR+WWI MOD/EUR UK USA+45 LAW ECO/UNDEV PWR SOVEREIGN CONSERVE LAISSEZ GOV/COMP. PAGE 75 H1505 — STRUCT CREATE OBS

S66
KAPIL R.L.,"ON THE CONFLICT POTENTIAL OF INHERITED BOUNDARIES IN AFRICA." MOD/EUR MOROCCO UAR EX/STRUC DIPLOM LEGIT REGION ADJUST...RECORD NAT/COMP GEN/LAWS. PAGE 83 H1658 — AFR COLONIAL PREDICT GEOG

S66
MERRITT R.L.,"SELECTED ARTICLES AND DOCUMENTS ON COMPARATIVE GOVERNMENT AND CROSS-NATIONAL RESEARCH." AFR ASIA EUR+WWI L/A+17C MOD/EUR ELITES R+D ACT/RES DIPLOM PWR...SOC CONCPT 18/20. PAGE 109 H2185 — BIBLIOG GOV/COMP NAT/G GOV/REL

S66
STRAYER J.R.,"PROBLEMS OF DICTATORSHIP* THE RUSSIAN EXPERIENCE." ASIA MOD/EUR ELITES STRATA POL/PAR CREATE NAT/LISM MARXISM...GOV/COMP NAT/COMP. PAGE 150 H2997 — NAT/G GEN/LAWS USSR TOTALISM

B67
ALBINSKI H.S.,EUROPEAN POLITICAL PROCESSES: ESSAYS AND READINGS. EUR+WWI FRANCE GERMANY MOD/EUR UK ELITES POL/PAR PWR...CHARTS ANTHOL 18/20. PAGE 5 H0094 — NAT/COMP POLICY IDEA/COMP

B67
ANDERSON E.N.,POLITICAL INSTITUTIONS AND SOCIAL CHANGE IN CONTINENTAL EUROPE IN THE NINETEENTH CENTURY. MOD/EUR LAW CONSTN SOCIETY POL/PAR TEC/DEV LEAD REV ATTIT...BIBLIOG 19. PAGE 6 H0127 — NAT/G NAT/COMP METH/COMP INDUS

B67
ANDERSON O.,A LIBERAL STATE AT WAR. MOD/EUR UK LAW CULTURE STRUCT ECO/DEV NAT/G DIPLOM PARL/PROC GP/REL ALL/VALS...CONCPT 19. PAGE 7 H0131 — WAR FORCES

B67
DILLARD D.,ECONOMIC DEVELOPMENT OF THE NORTH ATLANTIC COMMUNITY. EUR+WWI MOD/EUR USA+45 USA-45 ECO/UNDEV LABOR CAP/ISM WAR BAL/PAY...NAT/COMP 15/20. PAGE 41 H0824 — ECO/DEV INT/TRADE INDUS DIPLOM

B67
FAY S.B.,THE ORIGINS OF THE WORLD WAR (2ND REV. ED. 2 VOLS.). NAT/G FORCES DIPLOM CONFER LEAD PEACE ...REALPOL GOV/COMP 19/20. PAGE 49 H0978 — MOD/EUR WAR REGION INT/ORG

B67
WOODRUFF W.,IMPACT OF WESTERN MAN. ECO/DEV INDUS CREATE PLAN PROB/SOLV COLONIAL GOV/REL...CHARTS GOV/COMP BIBLIOG 18/20. PAGE 170 H3407 — EUR+WWI MOD/EUR CAP/ISM

S67
SCOVILLE W.J.,"GOVERNMENT REGULATION AND GROWTH IN THE FRENCH PAPER INDUSTRY DURING THE EIGHTEENTH CENTURY." FRANCE MOD/EUR FINAN CAP/ISM TAX ADMIN CONTROL PRIVIL LAISSEZ...POLICY 18. PAGE 141 H2818 — NAT/G PROC/MFG ECO/DEV INGP/REL

L68
CURRENT HISTORY,"DE GAULLE'S FRANCE." FRANCE MOD/EUR WOR+45 INDUS MARKET INT/ORG BUDGET DIPLOM AUTHORIT DRIVE...GOV/COMP IDEA/COMP 20 DEGAULLE/C EEC. PAGE 36 H0723 — INT/TRADE PERSON LEAD NAT/LISM

C80
ARNOLD M.,"EQUALITY" IN MIXED ESSAYS." MOD/EUR UK ELITES STRATA NAT/G...CONCPT IDEA/COMP NAT/COMP SOC/INTEG 19. PAGE 8 H0167 — ORD/FREE UTOPIA SOCIETY STRUCT

C82
MILL J.S.,"CIVILIZATION" IN DISSERTATIONS AND DISCUSSIONS." MOD/EUR UK ECO/DEV CONTROL MORAL ORD/FREE PWR...SOC IDEA/COMP 19. PAGE 110 H2208 — SOCIETY NAT/G STRUCT CONCPT

B83
AMOS S.,THE SCIENCE OF POLITICS. MOD/EUR CONSTN LOC/G NAT/G EX/STRUC LEGIS DIPLOM...METH/COMP 19/20. PAGE 6 H0124 — NEW/IDEA PHIL/SCI CONCPT

B85
TAINE H.A.,THE FRENCH REVOLUTION (3 VOLS.) (TRANS. BY J. DURAND). FRANCE MOD/EUR SOCIETY STRATA POL/PAR ECO/TAC DOMIN EDU/PROP GP/REL PWR ...GOV/COMP IDEA/COMP 18. PAGE 152 H3036 — REV NAT/G EX/STRUC LEAD

L86
BURGESS J.W.,"THE RECENT CONSTITUTIONAL CRISIS IN NORWAY" MOD/EUR NORWAY SWEDEN LOC/G NAT/G CHIEF BAL/PWR NAT/LISM ORD/FREE 19. PAGE 24 H0481 — CONSTN SOVEREIGN GOV/REL

B87
KINNEAR J.B.,PRINCIPLES OF CIVIL GOVERNMENT. MOD/EUR USA-45 CONSTN LOC/G EX/STRUC ADMIN PARL/PROC RACE/REL...CONCPT 18/19. PAGE 86 H1718 — POL/PAR NAT/G GOV/COMP REPRESENT

B91
MILL J.S.,SOCIALISM (1859). MOD/EUR AGRI INDUS NAT/G REV INCOME PRODUC ORD/FREE POPULISM SOCISM ...GOV/COMP METH/COMP 19. PAGE 110 H2209 — WEALTH SOCIALIST ECO/TAC OWN

B91
PAINE T.,RIGHTS OF MAN. FRANCE MOD/EUR CONSTN NAT/G CHIEF DOMIN LEGIT SOVEREIGN...MAJORIT IDEA/COMP 18 BURKE/EDM CIVIL/LIB. PAGE 122 H2446 — GEN/LAWS ORD/FREE REV AGREE

B96
LOWELL A.L.,GOVERNMENTS AND PARTIES IN CONTINENTAL EUROPE (VOL. I). MOD/EUR LOC/G NAT/G SECT CHIEF LEGIS PARL/PROC GOV/REL...POLICY 19. PAGE 99 H1973 — POL/PAR GOV/COMP CONSTN EX/STRUC

B96
LOWELL A.L.,GOVERNMENTS AND PARTIES IN CONTINENTAL EUROPE, VOL. II. AUSTRIA GERMANY HUNGARY MOD/EUR SWITZERLND SOCIETY EX/STRUC LEGIS DIPLOM AGREE LEAD PARL/PROC PWR...POLICY 19. PAGE 99 H1974 — POL/PAR NAT/G GOV/REL ELITES

B99
RIPLEY W.Z.,A SELECTED BIBLIOGRAPHY OF THE ANTHROPOLOGY AND ETHNOLOGY OF EUROPE. SOCIETY STRATA STRUCT KIN SECT VOL/ASSN GP/REL INGP/REL HABITAT...GEOG 19. PAGE 132 H2632 — BIBLIOG/A MOD/EUR SOC CULTURE

MODAL....MODAL TYPES, FASHIONS

B64
GRIFFITH W.,THE WELSH (2ND ED.). UK SOCIETY STRUCT — CULTURE

SECT WRITING NAT/LISM...ART/METH MODAL OBS/ENVIR TREND SOC/INTEG WALES PURITAN MUSIC. PAGE 61 H1223 — SOC LING

S66
SMITH D.D.,"MODAL ATTITUDE CLUSTERS* A SUPPLEMENT FOR THE STUDY OF NATIONAL CHARACTER." CULTURE NAT/G PERCEPT...SOC NEW/IDEA MODAL RECORD GEN/METH. PAGE 145 H2906 — ATTIT PERSON PSY CONCPT

B67
RIESMAN D.,CONVERSATIONS IN JAPAN: MODERNIZATION, POLITICS, AND CULTURE. CHINA/COM STRATA STRUCT ECO/DEV INDUS ACADEM EDU/PROP...ART/METH SOC MODAL INT IDEA/COMP SOC/INTEG 20 CHINJAP HIROSHIMA. PAGE 131 H2629 — CULTURE SOCIETY ASIA

MODELS....SEE SIMUL, MATH, ALSO MODELS INDEX, P. XIV

MODELSKI G. H2234

MODERNIZATION....SEE MODERNIZE

MODERNIZE....MODERNIZATION

MOGI S. H2235

MOHL R.V. H2236

MOID A. H0903

MOLLAU G. H2237

MONACO....SEE ALSO APPROPRIATE TIME/SPACE/CULTURE INDEX

MONARCH....SEE CHIEF, KING

MONARCHY....SEE CONSERVE, CHIEF, KING

MONAS S. H2238

MONETARY POLICY....SEE FINAN, PLAN

MONEY....SEE FINAN, ECO

N19
HABERLER G.,A SURVEY OF INTERNATIONAL TRADE THEORY (PAMPHLET). FINAN NAT/G COST INCOME 18/20 MONEY HUME/D MARSHALL/A. PAGE 63 H1267 — INT/TRADE BAL/PAY GEN/LAWS POLICY

B61
HAUSER M.,DIE URSACHEN DER FRANZOSISCHEN INFLATION IN DEN JAHREN 1946-1952. FRANCE INDUS NAT/G BUDGET DIPLOM ECO/TAC FOR/AID COST MONEY 20 GOLD/STAND. PAGE 68 H1357 — ECO/DEV FINAN PRICE

B66
YEAGER L.B.,INTERNATIONAL MONETARY RELATIONS: THEORY, HISTORY, AND POLICY. WOR+45 WOR-45 INT/TRADE BAL/PAY...NAT/COMP 18/20 MONEY. PAGE 172 H3435 — FINAN DIPLOM ECO/TAC IDEA/COMP

S67
MITCHELL W.C.,"THE SHAPE OF POLITICAL THEORY TO COME: FROM POLITICAL SOCIOLOGY TO POLITICAL ECONOMY." ACADEM NAT/G BUDGET TAX LEGIT LOBBY GOV/REL INGP/REL...SOC NEW/IDEA TREND CHARTS 20 MONEY. PAGE 112 H2231 — ECO/TAC GEN/LAWS

MONGER G.W. H2239

MONGOLIA....SEE ALSO USSR

N
KRADER L.,SOCIAL ORGANIZATION OF THE MONGOL-TURKIC PASTORAL NOMADS. SOCIETY FAM KIN NEIGH GP/REL MARRIAGE 16/20 MONGOLIA TURKIC MIGRATION. PAGE 88 H1763 — BIO/SOC HABITAT CULTURE STRUCT

N
KYRIAK T.E.,ASIAN DEVELOPMENTS: A BIBLIOGRAPHY. INDONESIA KOREA/N VIETNAM/N CULTURE SOCIETY ECO/UNDEV NAT/G DIPLOM...SOC TREND 20 MONGOLIA. PAGE 90 H1788 — BIBLIOG/A ALL/IDEOS S/ASIA ASIA

S67
NATSAGDORJ A.S.,"THE ECONOMIC BASIS OF FEUDALISM IN MONGOLIA." ASIA COM USSR OWN WEALTH CONSERVE...SOC 20 MONGOLIA. PAGE 116 H2324 — ECO/TAC AGRI NAT/COMP MARXISM

MONNIER J.P. H2240

MONOPOLY....MONOPOLIES, OLIGOPOLIES, AND ANTI-TRUST ACTIONS

B08
LLOYD H.D.,THE SWISS DEMOCRACY. SWITZERLND INDUS NAT/G WORKER CHOOSE OWN ORD/FREE SOCISM...PLURIST 19/20 MONOPOLY. PAGE 97 H1944 — NAT/COMP GOV/COMP REPRESENT POPULISM

B15
MICHELS R.,POLITICAL PARTIES. NAT/G BAL/PWR CHOOSE REPRESENT ATTIT SOCISM...PSY SOC CONCPT OBS 20 MONOPOLY. PAGE 110 H2198 — POL/PAR CENTRAL LEAD PWR

B38
DAVIES E.,"NATIONAL" CAPITALISM: THE GOVERNMENT'S RECORD AS PROTECTOR OF PRIVATE MONOPOLY. UK ELITES SOCIETY STRATA POL/PAR WORKER PROB/SOLV CONTROL SOCISM 20 MONOPOLY LABOR/PAR CHAMBRLN/N. PAGE 37 H0747 — CAP/ISM NAT/G INDUS POLICY

B38
LAWLEY F.E.,THE GROWTH OF COLLECTIVE ECONOMY VOL. 1: NATIONAL. EUR+WWI AGRI INDUS NAT/G BARGAIN CAP/ISM ECO/TAC WAR OPTIMAL WEALTH...GOV/COMP METH/COMP 19/20 MONOPOLY. PAGE 92 H1844 — SOCISM PRICE CONTROL OWN

B38
LAWLEY F.E.,THE GROWTH OF COLLECTIVE ECONOMY VOL. 2: INTERNATIONAL. WOR-45 AGRI INDUS EQUILIB OPTIMAL OWN WEALTH...NAT/COMP 19/20 NAZI NEW/DEAL MONOPOLY. PAGE 92 H1845 — ECO/TAC SOCISM NAT/LISM CONTROL

B46
ALLEN J.S.,WORLD MONOPOLY AND PEACE. GERMANY UK USSR FINAN INDUS LG/CO DOMIN CONTROL PEACE PWR WEALTH SOCISM...NAT/COMP 20 MONOPOLY. PAGE 5 H0105 — CAP/ISM DIPLOM WAR COLONIAL

B54
FRIEDMAN W.,THE PUBLIC CORPORATION: A COMPARATIVE SYMPOSIUM (UNIVERSITY OF TORONTO SCHOOL OF LAW COMPARATIVE LAW SERIES, VOL. I). SWEDEN USA+45 INDUS INT/ORG NAT/G REGION CENTRAL FEDERAL...POLICY JURID IDEA/COMP NAT/COMP ANTHOL 20 COMMONWLTH MONOPOLY EUROPE. PAGE 53 H1065 — LAW SOCISM LG/CO OWN

B57
PALACIOS A.L.,PETROLEO, MONOPOLIOS, Y LATIFUNDIOS. L/A+17C EXTR/IND NAT/G TEC/DEV ECO/TAC CONTROL PRODUC 20 ARGEN MONOPOLY RESOURCE/N. PAGE 123 H2448 — ECO/UNDEV NAT/LISM INDUS AGRI

B64
WERNETTE J.P.,GOVERNMENT AND BUSINESS. LABOR CAP/ISM ECO/TAC INT/TRADE TAX ADMIN AUTOMAT NUC/PWR CIVMIL/REL DEMAND...MGT 20 MONOPOLY. PAGE 167 H3333 — NAT/G FINAN ECO/DEV CONTROL

MONROE A.D. H2241

MONROE/DOC....MONROE DOCTRINE

MONROE/J....PRESIDENT JAMES MONROE

MONTAGU A. H2242

MONTAGUE F.C. H0292

MONTAGUE J.B. H2243

MONTANA....MONTANA

MONTECARLO....MONTE CARLO - OPERATIONAL RESEARCH DECISION-MAKING MODEL

MONTESQ....MONTESQUIEU, CHARLES LOUIS DE SECONDAT

MONTESQUIEU C DE S. H2244

MONTGOMERY H. H2245

MONTGOMERY....MONTGOMERY, ALABAMA

MOODIE G.C. H2247

MOORE C.H. H2248

MOORE J.R. H2249

MOORE W.E. H2250,H2251

MOORTHY S.D. H2498

MORAES F. H2252

MORAL....RECTITUDE, MORALITY, GOODNESS (ALSO IMMORALITY)

N
BIBLIOGRAPHIE DE LA PHILOSOPHIE. LAW CULTURE SECT EDU/PROP MORAL...HUM METH/CNCPT 20. PAGE 1 H0012 — BIBLIOG/A PHIL/SCI CONCPT LOG

N
PRESSE UNIVERSITAIRES,ANNEE SOCIOLOGIQUE. EUR+WWI FRANCE MOD/EUR FAM ACT/RES WAR INGP/REL PERS/REL CONSEN DRIVE MORAL...CON/ANAL 19/20. PAGE 128 H2557 — BIBLIOG SOC CULTURE SOCIETY

B06
SUMNER W.G.,FOLKWAYS: STUDY OF THE SOCIOLOGICAL IMPORTANCE OF USAGES, MANNERS, CUSTOMS, MORES, AND MORALS. STRUCT KIN ETIQUET ROUTINE MURDER MARRIAGE PEACE SEX ALL/VALS WEALTH BIBLIOG. PAGE 150 H3008 — CULTURE SOC SANCTION MORAL

B10
MILL J.S.,UTILITARIANISM, LIBERTY, AND REPRESENTATIVE GOVERNMENT. CONTROL PERCEPT PERSON MORAL...CONCPT GEN/LAWS. PAGE 110 H2205
HAPPINESS ORD/FREE REPRESENT NAT/G

B13
KROPOTKIN P.,THE CONQUEST OF BREAD. SOCIETY STRATA AGRI INDUS WORKER REV HAPPINESS INCOME PRODUC HEALTH MORAL ORD/FREE. PAGE 89 H1775
ANARCH SOCIALIST OWN AGREE

B14
CRAIG J.,ELEMENTS OF POLITICAL SCIENCE (3 VOLS.). CONSTN AGRI INDUS SCHOOL FORCES TAX CT/SYS SUFF MORAL WEALTH...CONCPT 19 CIVIL/LIB. PAGE 35 H0696
PHIL/SCI NAT/G ORD/FREE

B16
PUFENDORF S.,LAW OF NATURE AND OF NATIONS (ABRIDGED). UNIV LAW NAT/G DIPLOM AGREE WAR PERSON ALL/VALS PWR...POLICY 18 DEITY NATURL/LAW. PAGE 128 H2565
CONCPT INT/LAW SECT MORAL

B17
DE VICTORIA F.,DE INDIS ET DE JURE BELLI (1557) IN F. DE VICTORIA, DE INDIS ET DE JURE BELLI REFLECTIONES. UNIV NAT/G SECT CHIEF PARTIC COERCE PEACE MORAL...POLICY 16 INDIAN/AM CHRISTIAN CONSCN/OBJ. PAGE 39 H0775
WAR INT/LAW OWN

B17
VEBLEN T.B.,AN INQUIRY INTO THE NATURE OF PEACE AND THE TERMS OF ITS PERPETUATION. UNIV STRATA FINAN EDU/PROP PRICE COST DISCRIM NAT/LISM MORAL ORD/FREE PACIFIST 20 WORLDUNITY. PAGE 162 H3237
PEACE DIPLOM WAR NAT/G

B19
DUGUIT L.,LAW IN THE MODERN STATE (TRANS. BY FRIDA AND HAROLD LASKI). CONSTN SOCIETY STRUCT MORAL ORD/FREE SOVEREIGN 20. PAGE 43 H0860
GEN/LAWS CONCPT NAT/G LAW

B20
HALDANE R.B.,BEFORE THE WAR. MOD/EUR SOCIETY INT/ORG NAT/G DELIB/GP PLAN DOMIN EDU/PROP LEGIT ADMIN COERCE ATTIT DRIVE MORAL ORD/FREE PWR...SOC CONCPT SELF/OBS RECORD BIOG TIME/SEQ. PAGE 64 H1282
POLICY DIPLOM UK

B27
JOHN OF SALISBURY,THE STATESMAN'S BOOK (1159) (TRANS. BY J. DICKINSON). DOMIN GP/REL MORAL ORD/FREE PWR CONSERVE...CATH CONCPT 12. PAGE 81 H1617
NAT/G SECT CHIEF LAW

B28
HOBBES T.,THE ELEMENTS OF LAW, NATURAL AND POLITIC (1650). STRATA NAT/G SECT CHIEF AGREE ATTIT ALL/VALS MORAL ORD/FREE POPULISM...POLICY CONCPT. PAGE 71 H1432
PERSON LAW SOVEREIGN CONSERVE

B30
BYNKERSHOEK C.,QUAESTIONUM JURIS PUBLICI LIBRI DUO. CHRIST-17C MOD/EUR CONSTN ELITES SOCIETY NAT/G PROVS EX/STRUC FORCES TOP/EX BAL/PWR DIPLOM ATTIT MORAL...TRADIT CONCPT. PAGE 25 H0502
INT/ORG LAW NAT/LISM INT/LAW

B30
WILLOUGHBY W.W.,THE ETHICAL BASIS OF POLITICAL AUTHORITY. NAT/G LEGIS PARL/PROC INGP/REL UTOPIA ORD/FREE 16/20. PAGE 169 H3374
MORAL POLICY CONSTN

B32
NIEBUHR R.,MORAL MAN AND IMMORAL SOCIETY* A STUDY IN ETHICS AND POLITICS. UNIV CULTURE SOCIETY STRUCT DIPLOM GOV/REL GP/REL PERS/REL...TREND IDEA/COMP. PAGE 118 H2357
MORAL PWR

B33
FERRERO G.,PEACE AND WAR (TRANS. BY BERTHA PRITCHARD). CULTURE FINAN SECT ATTIT SUPEGO MORAL ORD/FREE CONSERVE POPULISM SOCISM POLICY. PAGE 49 H0987
WAR PEACE DIPLOM PROB/SOLV

B37
CARLYLE T.,THE FRENCH REVOLUTION (2 VOLS.). FRANCE CONSTN NAT/G FORCES COERCE MURDER PEACE MORAL POPULISM...TIME/SEQ IDEA/COMP GEN/LAWS 18. PAGE 26 H0532
REV CHIEF TRADIT

B37
THOMPSON J.W.,SECRET DIPLOMACY: A RECORD OF ESPIONAGE AND DOUBLE-DEALING: 1500-1815. CHRIST-17C MOD/EUR NAT/G WRITING RISK MORAL...ANTHOL BIBLIOG 16/19 ESPIONAGE. PAGE 154 H3084
DIPLOM CRIME

B38
DUNHAM W.H. JR.,COMPLAINT AND REFORM IN ENGLAND 1436-1714. UK LAW ACADEM NAT/G POL/PAR SCHOOL PRESS COLONIAL PARL/PROC MORAL...SOC/WK ANTHOL 15/18 HAKLUYT/R COWPER/W. PAGE 43 H0865
ATTIT SOCIETY SECT

B38
HEIMANN E.,COMMUNISM, FASCISM, OR DEMOCRACY? WOR-45 CONSTN SOCIETY STRATA AGRI CAP/ISM MORAL ORD/FREE ...MAJORIT METH/COMP NAT/COMP 19/20. PAGE 69 H1384
SOCISM MARXISM FASCISM PLURISM

B39
CARR E.H.,PROPAGANDA IN INTERNATIONAL POLITICS (PAMPHLET). EUR+WWI GERMANY MOD/EUR NAT/G AGREE WAR MORAL...POLICY 20 TREATY. PAGE 27 H0536
DIPLOM EDU/PROP CONTROL ATTIT

B39
MILLER P.,THE NEW ENGLAND MIND: THE SEVENTEENTH CENTURY. CULTURE DOMIN WRITING INGP/REL CONSEN MAJORITY PERCEPT KNOWL MORAL...CONCPT LING WORSHIP 17 NEW/ENGLND PROTESTANT. PAGE 111 H2214
SECT REGION SOC ATTIT

S40
GURVITCH G.,"MAJOR PROBLEMS OF THE SOCIOLOGY OF LAW." CULTURE SANCTION KNOWL MORAL...POLICY EPIST JURID WORSHIP. PAGE 63 H1255
SOC LAW PHIL/SCI

B41
GREEN T.H.,PRINCIPLES OF PUBLIC ADMINISTRATION. UNIV CONSTN VOL/ASSN INGP/REL MORAL ORD/FREE ...GOV/COMP IDEA/COMP GEN/LAWS 20. PAGE 60 H1208
POLICY LAISSEZ MAJORIT

B42
BARNES H.E.,SOCIAL INSTITUTIONS IN AN ERA OF WORLD UPHEAVAL. INDUS FAM NAT/G PERF/ART SECT AUTOMAT PERSON MORAL...PREDICT 20. PAGE 11 H0221
SOCIETY CULTURE TECHRACY TREND

B42
CRAIG A.,ABOVE ALL LIBERTIES. FRANCE UK USA-45 LAW CONSTN CULTURE INTELL NAT/G SECT JUDGE...IDEA/COMP BIBLIOG 18/20. PAGE 35 H0692
ORD/FREE MORAL WRITING EDU/PROP

C42
CRAIG A.,"ABOVE ALL LIBERTIES." FRANCE UK LAW CULTURE INTELL SECT ORD/FREE 18/20. PAGE 35 H0693
BIBLIOG/A EDU/PROP WRITING MORAL

B43
MARITAIN J.,THE RIGHTS OF MAN AND NATURAL LAW. CONSTN NAT/G DOMIN LEGIT INGP/REL TOTALISM MORAL POPULISM WORSHIP 19/20 CIVIL/LIB CHURCH/STA NATURL/LAW. PAGE 103 H2051
PLURIST ORD/FREE GEN/LAWS

C43
BENTHAM J.,"PRINCIPLES OF INTERNATIONAL LAW" IN J. BOWRING, ED., THE WORKS OF JEREMY BENTHAM." UNIV NAT/G PLAN PROB/SOLV DIPLOM CONTROL SANCTION MORAL ORD/FREE PWR SOVEREIGN 19. PAGE 15 H0291
INT/LAW JURID WAR PEACE

C44
SUAREZ F.,"ON WAR" (1621) IN SELECTIONS FROM THREE WORKS, VOL. I." NAT/G SECT CHIEF DIPLOM LEGIT MORAL PWR...POLICY INT/LAW 17. PAGE 150 H3005
WAR REV ORD/FREE CATH

B45
CROCE B.,POLITICS AND MORALS. UNIV NAT/G ECO/TAC ORD/FREE MARXISM POPULISM SOCISM...REALPOL 15/20 HEGEL/GWF ROUSSEAU/J. PAGE 35 H0704
MORAL GEN/LAWS IDEA/COMP

B46
GODWIN W.,ENQUIRY CONCERNING POLITICAL JUSTICE AND ITS INFLUENCE ON MORALS AND HAPPINESS (1793). UNIV SOCIETY NAT/G GP/REL INGP/REL HAPPINESS ALL/VALS CONCPT. PAGE 58 H1151
MORAL PERSON ORD/FREE

B47
LOCKE J.,TWO TREATISES OF GOVERNMENT (1690). UK LAW SOCIETY LEGIS LEGIT AGREE REV OWN HEREDITY MORAL CONSERVE...POLICY MAJORIT 17 WILLIAM/3 NATURL/LAW. PAGE 97 H1946
CONCPT ORD/FREE NAT/G CONSEN

S48
ALEXANDER L.,"WAR CRIMES, THEIR SOCIAL-PSYCHOLOGICAL ASPECTS." EUR+WWI GERMANY LAW CULTURE ELITES KIN POL/PAR PUB/INST FORCES DOMIN EDU/PROP COERCE CRIME ATTIT SUPEGO HEALTH MORAL PWR FASCISM ...PSY OBS TREND GEN/LAWS NAZI 20. PAGE 5 H0100
DRIVE WAR

B50
HARLEY G.W.,MASKS AS AGENTS OF SOCIAL CONTROL IN NORTHEAST LIBERIA. AFR LIBERIA LAW CULTURE ADJUST CONSEN MORAL...GEOG SOC WORSHIP 20. PAGE 66 H1332
CONTROL ECO/UNDEV SECT CHIEF

B50
HOOKER R.,OF THE LAWS OF ECCLESIASTICAL POLITY (1594) (ABR. BY J. S. MARSHALL). UK UNIV CHIEF PARTIC MORAL...JURID GEN/LAWS WORSHIP 16. PAGE 73 H1463
SECT CONCPT LAW NAT/G

C50
ROUSSEAU J.J.,"DISCOURSE ON THE ORIGIN OF INEQUALITY" (1755) IN THE SOCIAL CONTRACT AND DISCOURSES." UNIV NAT/G PLAN BAL/PWR HAPPINESS UTOPIA BIO/SOC HEREDITY MORAL...WELF/ST CONCPT. PAGE 135 H2698
SOCIETY STRUCT PERSON GEN/LAWS

B51
LOOS W.A.,RELIGIOUS FAITH AND WORLD CULTURE. INTELL SOCIETY SECT EDU/PROP ROUTINE ATTIT PERSON ALL/VALS MORAL...CONCPT GEN/LAWS VAL/FREE. PAGE 98 H1964
UNIV CULTURE PEACE

S51
NORTHROP F.S.C.,"ASIAN MENTALITY AND UNITED STATES FOREIGN POLICY." ASIA ISLAM USA+45 CULTURE SOCIETY SECT EDU/PROP LEGIT COERCE DRIVE MORAL ORD/FREE ...POLICY RELATIV TOT/POP 20. PAGE 119 H2376
S/ASIA ATTIT DIPLOM

B52
HIMMELFARB G.,LORD ACTON: A STUDY IN CONSCIENCE AND POLITICS. MOD/EUR NAT/G POL/PAR SECT LEGIS TOP/EX EDU/PROP ADMIN NAT/LISM ATTIT PERSON SUPEGO MORAL ORD/FREE...CONCPT PARLIAMENT 19 ACTON/LORD. PAGE 71 H1419
PWR BIOG

B52
LEYS W.,ETHICS FOR POLICY DECISIONS. INTELL NAT/G CONSULT PLAN DOMIN EDU/PROP LEGIT COERCE KNOWL MORAL PWR...HUM GEN/LAWS. PAGE 96 H1920
ACT/RES POLICY

B53
COBLENTZ S.A.,FROM ARROW TO ATOM BOMB: THE PSYCHOLOGICAL HISTORY OF WAR. PREHIST CULTURE CROWD PEACE DRIVE MORAL PWR...GP/COMP IDEA/COMP. PAGE 31 H0613
WAR PSY SOCIETY

B53
LEITES N.,A STUDY OF BOLSHEVISM. WOR+45 WOR-45 ELITES SOCIETY INT/ORG NAT/G EX/STRUC EDU/PROP EXEC ROUTINE ATTIT MORAL MARXISM...CONCPT OBS VAL/FREE 20. PAGE 94 H1869
COM POL/PAR USSR TOTALISM

B53
REDFIELD R.,THE PRIMITIVE WORLD AND ITS TRANSFORMATIONS. UNIV CULTURE ATTIT MORAL...CONCPT TREND. PAGE 130 H2606
SOC CREATE PERSON SOCIETY

B54
SPENCER H.,SOCIAL STATICS. MOD/EUR UNIV SOCIETY ECO/DEV NAT/G ACT/RES PLAN EDU/PROP PERSON...POLICY CONCPT. PAGE 147 H2944
MORAL ECO/TAC

B55
MAYO H.B.,DEMOCRACY AND MARXISM. COM USSR STRATA NAT/G WORKER ECO/TAC REV MORAL...PHIL/SCI HIST/WRIT IDEA/COMP WORSHIP 20 MARX/KARL LENIN/VI STALIN/J TROTSKY/L. PAGE 105 H2108
MARXISM CAP/ISM

B55
VIGON J.,TEORIA DEL MILITARISMO. NAT/G DIPLOM COLONIAL COERCE GUERRILLA CIVMIL/REL NAT/LISM MORAL ALL/IDEOS PACIFISM 18/20. PAGE 163 H3253
FORCES PHIL/SCI WAR POLICY

B56
FIELD G.C.,POLITICAL THEORY. POL/PAR REPRESENT MORAL SOVEREIGN...JURID IDEA/COMP. PAGE 50 H0990
CONCPT NAT/G ORD/FREE DIPLOM

B56
GLUCKMAN M.,CUSTOM AND CONFLICT IN AFRICA. AFR FAM KIN NAT/G DOMIN DISCRIM DRIVE MORAL PWR...SOC BIBLIOG WORSHIP 20. PAGE 57 H1145
CULTURE CREATE PERS/REL GP/COMP

B56
MYERS F.M.,THE WARFARE OF DEMOCRATIC IDEALS. SECT KNOWL MORAL CATHISM...TRADIT CONCPT 20. PAGE 115 H2302
POPULISM CHOOSE REPRESENT PERCEPT

B56
WEIL E.,PHILOSOPHIE POLITIQUE. UNIV CULTURE RATIONAL PERSON ROLE. PAGE 166 H3326
SOCIETY NAT/G MORAL

S56
KHAMA T.,"POLITICAL CHANGE IN AFRICAN SOCIETY." CONSTN SOCIETY LOC/G NAT/G POL/PAR EX/STRUC LEGIS LEGIT ADMIN CHOOSE REPRESENT NAT/LISM MORAL ORD/FREE PWR...CONCPT OBS TREND GEN/METH CMN/WLTH 17/20. PAGE 85 H1706
AFR ELITES

S57
HAILEY,"TOMORROW IN AFRICA." CONSTN SOCIETY LOC/G NAT/G DOMIN ADJUD ADMIN GP/REL DISCRIM NAT/LISM ATTIT MORAL ORD/FREE...PSY SOC CONCPT OBS RECORD TREND GEN/LAWS CMN/WLTH 20. PAGE 64 H1277
AFR PERSON ELITES RACE/REL

B58
CHANG H.,WITHIN THE FOUR SEAS. ASIA WAR MORAL MARXISM...IDEA/COMP NAT/COMP 20 CONFUCIUS. PAGE 29 H0577
PEACE DIPLOM KNOWL CULTURE

B58
EMMET D.M.,FUNCTION, PURPOSE AND POWERS. SECT ATTIT MORAL PWR...CONCPT MYTH. PAGE 46 H0923
SOC CULTURE ALL/VALS GEN/LAWS

B58
GREAVES H.R.,THE FOUNDATIONS OF POLITICAL THEORY. WAR ATTIT SUPEGO ORD/FREE...IDEA/COMP SOC/INTEG. PAGE 60 H1203
CONCPT MORAL PERSON

B59
LEE D.,FREEDOM AND CULTURE. WOR+45 WOR-45 FAM HABITAT PERSON LOVE MORAL...PSY SOC OBS NAT/COMP WORSHIP 20. PAGE 93 H1856
CULTURE SOCIETY CONCPT INGP/REL

B59
LEFEVRE R.,THE NATURE OF MAN AND HIS GOVERNMENT. EUR+WWI MOD/EUR CONSTN CULTURE MORAL MARXISM ...POLICY 18/20. PAGE 93 H1859
NAT/G TASK ORD/FREE ATTIT

B59
SCHORN H.,DER RICHTER IM DRITTEN REICH; GESCHICHTE UND DOKUMENTE. GERMANY NAT/G LEGIT CT/SYS INGP/REL MORAL ORD/FREE RESPECT...JURID GP/COMP 20. PAGE 140 H2798
ADJUD JUDGE FASCISM

B59
SZLUC T.,TWILIGHT OF THE TYRANTS. BRAZIL L/A+17C PERU VENEZUELA NAT/G FORCES CONTROL PERSON MORAL ORD/FREE PWR...CONCPT 20 ARGEN COLOMB. PAGE 151 H3028
TOTALISM CHIEF REV FASCISM

S59
JENKS C.W.,"THE CHALLENGE OF UNIVERSALITY." FUT UNIV CONSTN CULTURE CONSULT CREATE PLAN LEGIT ATTIT MORAL ORD/FREE RESPECT...MAJORIT JURID 20. PAGE 80 H1602
INT/ORG LAW PEACE INT/LAW

S59
SCOTT W.A.,"EMPIRICAL ASSESSMENT OF VALUES AND IDEOLOGIES." CULTURE SOCIETY SECT CREATE DRIVE PERSON MORAL PWR...SOC METH/CNCPT STAT CONT/OBS DEEP/INT DEEP/QU CHARTS VAL/FREE. PAGE 141 H2817
ATTIT PSY

B61
BEDFORD S.,THE FACES OF JUSTICE: A TRAVELLER'S REPORT. AUSTRIA FRANCE GERMANY/W SWITZERLND UK UNIV WOR+45 WOR-45 CULTURE PARTIC GOV/REL MORAL...JURID OBS GOV/COMP 20. PAGE 13 H0257
CT/SYS ORD/FREE PERSON LAW

B61
BROWN D.M.,THE NATIONALIST MOVEMENT. INDIA CULTURE STRATA REV MORAL ORD/FREE...BIBLIOG 20 HINDU. PAGE 22 H0443
NAT/LISM LEAD CHIEF POL/PAR

B61
CATHERINE R.,LE FONCTIONNAIRE FRANCAIS. FRANCE NAT/G INGP/REL ATTIT MORAL ORD/FREE...T CIVIL/SERV. PAGE 28 H0559
ADMIN GP/REL LEAD SUPEGO

B61
FIRTH R.,ELEMENTS OF SOCIAL ORGANIZATION (3RD ED.). STRATA STRUCT ECO/UNDEV NEIGH CHIEF INGP/REL ATTIT MORAL...PHIL/SCI GP/COMP WORSHIP SOC/INTEG 20. PAGE 50 H1009
SOC CULTURE SOCIETY KIN

B61
VON MERING O.,A GRAMMAR OF HUMAN VALUES. WOR+45 CULTURE FACE/GP NEIGH CREATE EDU/PROP LEGIT ATTIT DRIVE PERSON ORD/FREE...PSY SOC METH/CNCPT OBS RECORD INT REC/INT STAND/INT QU CHARTS VAL/FREE. PAGE 164 H3275
SOCIETY MORAL

N61
PLATO,APOLOGY" IN PLATO, THE COLLECTED DIALOGUES, ED. BY E. HAMILTON AND H. CAIRNS (TRANS. BY H. TREDENNICK). GREECE SOCIETY NAT/G...CONCPT GEN/LAWS SOCRATES. PAGE 126 H2523
DEATH CT/SYS ATTIT MORAL

B62
INSTITUTE FOR STUDY OF USSR,YOUTH IN FERMENT. INTELL NAT/G PERF/ART POL/PAR SCHOOL VOL/ASSN FORCES EDU/PROP ATTIT DRIVE PERCEPT HEALTH KNOWL MORAL ORD/FREE RESPECT...SOC OBS HIST/WRIT VAL/FREE. PAGE 77 H1537
COM CULTURE USSR

B62
MALINOWSKI B.,SEX, CULTURE, AND MYTH. UNIV SOCIETY FAM PERS/REL MARRIAGE RATIONAL HABITAT PERSON SUPEGO MORAL WORSHIP 20. PAGE 102 H2032
MYTH SECT SEX CULTURE

B62
ZIESEL K.,DAS VERLORENE GEWISSEN. GERMANY/W NAT/G VOL/ASSN EDU/PROP PRESS SUPEGO...POLICY 20. PAGE 173 H3455
MORAL PWR ORD/FREE RESPECT

S62
BRAIBANTI R.,"REFLECTIONS ON BUREAUCRATIC CORRPUTION." LAW REPRESENT 20. PAGE 20 H0400
CONTROL MORAL ADMIN GOV/COMP

B63
FRANKEL J.,THE MAKING OF FOREIGN POLICY: AN ANALYSIS OF DECISION-MAKING. CHINA/COM EUR+WWI USA+45 ELITES INTELL FORCES LEGIS PLAN ATTIT ALL/VALS MORAL CONSERVE...GOV/COMP 20 PRESIDENT UN TREATY. PAGE 53 H1051
POLICY DECISION PROB/SOLV DIPLOM

B63
KATEB G.,UTOPIA AND ITS ENEMIES. CULTURE STRATA ECO/DEV INDUS REV MORAL...PSY IDEA/COMP 19/20. PAGE 84 H1668
UTOPIA SOCIETY PHIL/SCI PEACE

B63
LERNER R.,MEDIEVAL POLITICAL PHILOSOPHY. ISLAM MORAL PWR CATHISM...CATH CONCPT OBS IDEA/COMP ANTHOL 9/15 JEWS CHRISTIAN BACON/R AQUINAS/T. PAGE 95 H1890
KNOWL PHIL/SCI

B63
SILONE I.,THE SCHOOL FOR DICTATORS. EUR+WWI GERMANY ITALY SOCIETY NAT/G CHIEF EX/STRUC ATTIT MORAL PWR ...HIST/WRIT 20. PAGE 144 H2876
TOTALISM EDU/PROP ORD/FREE FASCISM

B63
VON DER MEHDEN F.R.,RELIGION AND NATIONALISM IN SOUTHEAST ASIA. BURMA PHILIPPINE S/ASIA INTELL SOCIETY DOMIN EDU/PROP LEGIT ATTIT MORAL ORD/FREE ...SOC CENSUS HIST/WRIT TOT/POP VAL/FREE 20 WORSHIP LONDON. PAGE 163 H3265
SECT CULTURE NAT/LISM

L63
JAY R.,"RELIGION AND POLITICS IN RURAL CENTRAL JAVA." S/ASIA SOCIETY NEIGH SECT PERSON HEALTH MORAL...SOC UNPLAN/INT TIME/SEQ JAVA VAL/FREE 20 WORSHIP. PAGE 80 H1594
CULTURE OBS

B64
COBBAN A.,ROUSSEAU AND THE MODERN STATE (2ND ED.). FRANCE PROB/SOLV NAT/LISM UTOPIA PERSON MORAL ...EPIST PHIL/SCI SOC IDEA/COMP 18 ROUSSEAU/J BURKE/EDM HOBBES/T HUME/D. PAGE 30 H0612
GEN/LAWS INGP/REL NAT/G ORD/FREE

B64
CURTIN P.D.,THE IMAGE OF AFRICA: BRITISH IDEAS AND ACTION, 1780-1850. MOD/EUR SOCIETY FORCES ACT/RES DOMIN EDU/PROP COERCE ATTIT PERCEPT RIGID/FLEX SUPEGO HEALTH KNOWL MORAL ORD/FREE WEALTH...CONCPT WORK VAL/FREE. PAGE 36 H0726
AFR CULTURE UK DIPLOM

B64
DOWNIE R.S.,GOVERNMENT ACTION AND MORALITY: SOME PRINCIPLES AND CONCEPTS OF LIBERAL-DEMOCRACY. UK PARL/PROC ATTIT ROLE...MAJORIT DECISION CONCPT 20. PAGE 42 H0845
NAT/G MORAL POLICY GEN/LAWS

B64
GROSSER A.,THE FEDERAL REPUBLIC OF GERMANY: A CONCISE HISTORY. GERMANY/W STRUCT MORAL ORD/FREE POPULISM SOCISM...SOC CONCPT 20. PAGE 62 H1235
NAT/G POL/PAR CHOOSE DIPLOM

B64
ROSENAU J.N.,INTERNATIONAL ASPECTS OF CIVIL STRIFE. CHINA/COM CUBA EUR+WWI USA+45 USSR BAL/PWR EDU/PROP NEUTRAL COERCE MORAL...NAT/COMP 20 COLD/WAR UN. PAGE 134 H2676
POLICY DIPLOM REV WAR

S64
HIRAI N.,"SHINTO AND INTERNATIONAL PROBLEMS." SOCIETY NAT/G PLAN EDU/PROP RACE/REL PEACE ATTIT PERCEPT LOVE MORAL...HUM MYTH RECORD SAMP TREND STERTYP TOT/POP 20 UN CHINJAP SHINTO. PAGE 71 H1423
ASIA SECT

S64
MARTELLI G.,"PORTUGAL AND THE UNITED NATIONS." AFR EUR+WWI ELITES INT/ORG NAT/G PROVS PLAN DIPLOM ECO/TAC DOMIN COLONIAL RIGID/FLEX MORAL ORD/FREE PWR WEALTH...MYTH UN 20. PAGE 103 H2060
ATTIT PORTUGAL

S64
SMYTHE H.H.,"NEHRU AND INDIAN FOREIGN POLICY." S/ASIA ECO/UNDEV NAT/G POL/PAR CONSULT PLAN DIPLOM NEUTRAL COERCE ATTIT DRIVE PERSON MORAL ORD/FREE RESPECT...GEOG CONCPT TIME/SEQ TREND GEN/LAWS 20 NEHRU/J. PAGE 146 H2922
TOP/EX BIOG INDIA

S64
TOYNBEE A.,"BRITAIN AND THE ARABS: THE NEED FOR A NEW START." NAT/G CREATE COLONIAL ATTIT RIGID/FLEX MORAL PWR...POLICY HIST/WRIT 20. PAGE 156 H3124
ISLAM ECO/TAC DIPLOM UK

B65
CHARNAY J.P.,LE SUFFRAGE POLITIQUE EN FRANCE; ELECTIONS PARLEMENTAIRES, ELECTION PRESIDENTIELLE, REFERENDUMS. FRANCE CONSTN CHIEF DELIB/GP ECO/TAC EDU/PROP CRIME INGP/REL MORAL ORD/FREE PWR CATHISM 20 PARLIAMENT PRESIDENT. PAGE 29 H0584
CHOOSE SUFF NAT/G LEGIS

B65
DOLCI D.,A NEW WORLD IN THE MAKING. GHANA SENEGAL USSR YUGOSLAVIA CULTURE INT/ORG PLAN EDU/PROP GP/REL PEACE MORAL...GEOG SOC 20 COLD/WAR. PAGE 42 H0834
SOCIETY ALL/VALS DRIVE PERSON

B65
DURKHEIM E.,THE ELEMENTARY FORMS OF THE RELIGIOUS LIFE. KIN PARTIC MORAL...PSY MYTH OBS IDEA/COMP METH WORSHIP 19/20. PAGE 43 H0870
SOC CULTURE CONCPT

B65
GOLEMBIEWSKI R.T.,MEN, MANAGEMENT, AND MORALITY; TOWARD A NEW ORGANIZATIONAL ETHIC. CONSTN EX/STRUC CREATE ADMIN CONTROL INGP/REL PERSON SUPEGO MORAL PWR...GOV/COMP METH/COMP 20 BUREAUCRCY. PAGE 58 H1161
LG/CO MGT PROB/SOLV

B65
HAMIL H.M.,DICTATORSHIP IN SPANISH AMERICA. NAT/G COERCE MORAL ORD/FREE...POLICY PSY SOC ANTHOL 18/20. PAGE 65 H1300
TOTALISM CHIEF L/A+17C FASCISM

B65
LARUS J.,COMPARATIVE WORLD POLITICS. ASIA INDIA WOR+45 WOR-45 BAL/PWR WAR PEACE RATIONAL MORAL PWR ...REALPOL INT/LAW MUSLIM. PAGE 91 H1825
GOV/COMP IDEA/COMP DIPLOM NAT/COMP

B65
MONTESQUIEU C DE S.,CONSIDERATIONS ON THE CAUSES OF THE GREATNESS OF THE ROMANS AND THEIR DECLINE (1748 TRANS. BY D. LOWENTHAL). ROMAN/EMP SECT CHIEF EX/STRUC FORCES LEGIS DOMIN WAR POPULISM...POLICY REALPOL ROME/ANC. PAGE 112 H2244
NAT/G PWR COLONIAL MORAL

L65
SHARMA S.P.,"THE INDIA-CHINA BORDER DISPUTE: AN INDIAN PERSPECTIVE." ASIA CHINA/COM S/ASIA NAT/G LEGIT CT/SYS NAT/LISM DRIVE MORAL ORD/FREE PWR 20. PAGE 142 H2850
LAW ATTIT SOVEREIGN INDIA

B66
ARCHER P.,FREEDOM AT STAKE. UK LAW NAT/G LEGIS JUDGE CRIME MORAL...CONCPT 20 CIVIL/LIB. PAGE 8 H0159
ORD/FREE NAT/COMP POLICY

B66
BARRETT J.,THAT BETTER COUNTRY: RELIGIOUS ASPECT OF LIFE IN EASTERN AUSTRALIA, 1835-1850. LAW ECO/UNDEV SCHOOL TEC/DEV EDU/PROP CONTROL HABITAT MORAL WORSHIP 19 AUSTRAL CHURCH/STA. PAGE 11 H0229
SECT CULTURE GOV/REL

B66
GARCON M.,LETTRE OUVERTE A LA JUSTICE. FRANCE NAT/G PROB/SOLV PAY EFFICIENCY MORAL 20. PAGE 55 H1100
ORD/FREE ADJUD

CT/SYS

B66
HERMANN F.G.,DER KAMPF GEGEN RELIGION UND KIRCHE IN DER SOWJETISCHEN BESATZUNGSZONE DEUTSCHLANDS. GERMANY/E EDU/PROP ATTIT PERSON MORAL MARXISM 20 LENIN/VI STALIN/J KHRUSH/N. PAGE 70 H1400
SECT ORD/FREE GP/REL NAT/G

B67
HUTCHINS F.G.,THE ILLUSION OF PERMANENCE: BRITISH IMPERIALISM IN INDIA. INDIA UK CULTURE STRUCT NAT/G REV GP/REL RACE/REL ADJUST DISCRIM ATTIT MORAL PWR SOC/INTEG 18/20. PAGE 75 H1509
COLONIAL CONTROL SOVEREIGN CONSERVE

B67
ZINN H.,VIETNAM THE LOGIC OF WITHDRAWAL. VIETNAM/S NAT/G DIPLOM DEATH MORAL 20. PAGE 173 H3459
WAR COST PACIFISM ATTIT

L67
GALTUNG J.,"ON THE EFFECTS OF INTERNATIONAL ECONOMIC SANCTIONS, WITH EXAMPLES FROM THE CASE OF RHODESIA." NAT/G DIPLOM EDU/PROP ADJUST EFFICIENCY ATTIT MORAL...OBS CHARTS 20. PAGE 55 H1091
SANCTION ECO/TAC INT/TRADE ECO/UNDEV

L67
GOOD E.M.,"CAPITAL PUNISHMENT AND ITS ALTERNATIVES IN ANCIENT NEAR EASTERN LAW." SOCIETY SECT INGP/REL CONSEN ATTIT SEX MORAL...CRIMLGY GP/COMP. PAGE 58 H1168
MEDIT-7 LAW JURID CULTURE

S67
BELGION M.,"THE CASE FOR REHABILITATING MARSHAL PETAIN." EUR+WWI FRANCE NAT/G DIPLOM ATTIT PERSON MORAL PETAIN/HP. PAGE 13 H0262
WAR FORCES LEAD

S67
BEVEL D.N.,"JOURNEY TO NORTH VIETNAM." VIETNAM/N CONSTN NAT/G FORCES PROB/SOLV DEATH CIVMIL/REL PEACE MORAL...ANTHOL 20 NEGRO. PAGE 16 H0325
ATTIT DIPLOM ORD/FREE WAR

S67
HAMMOND R.J.,"RACE ATTITUDES AND POLICIES IN PORTUGUESE AFRICA IN THE NINETEENTH AND TWENTIETH CENTURIES." AFR PORTUGAL NAT/G SECT EDU/PROP COLONIAL ATTIT RIGID/FLEX SEX MORAL RESPECT 19/20 NEGRO. PAGE 65 H1309
POLICY RACE/REL DISCRIM SOCIETY

S67
KYLE K.,"BACKGROUND TO THE CRISIS" ISLAM ISRAEL UAR UK USSR NAT/G PROB/SOLV LEGIT CONTROL REGION STRANGE MORAL 20 JEWS. PAGE 89 H1787
DIPLOM POLICY SOVEREIGN COERCE

S67
NIEBUHR R.,"THE ETHICS OF WAR AND PEACE IN THE NUCLEAR AGE." VIETNAM INTELL CONFER CONTROL WAR GOV/REL PERS/REL ORD/FREE...POLICY INT GOV/COMP NAT/COMP 20 UN. PAGE 118 H2360
MORAL PEACE NUC/PWR DIPLOM

S67
SLOAN P.,"FIFTY YEARS OF SOVIET RULE." USSR INDUS EDU/PROP EFFICIENCY PRODUC HEALTH KNOWL MORAL WEALTH MARXISM...POLICY 20. PAGE 145 H2900
CREATE NAT/G PLAN INSPECT

S67
WILSON J.Q.,"A GUIDE TO REAGAN COUNTRY* THE POLITICAL CULTURE OF SOUTHERN CALIFORNIA." NEIGH PROVS PARTIC CHOOSE ADJUST CONSEN PERSON CONSERVE CALIFORNIA REAGAN/RON. PAGE 169 H3379
CULTURE ATTIT MORAL

B73
STEPHEN J.F.,LIBERTY, EQUALITY, FRATERNITY. UNIV SOCIETY NAT/G LEGIS DOMIN AGREE PERS/REL ATTIT MORAL...IDEA/COMP 19 MILL/JS. PAGE 149 H2978
ORD/FREE CONCPT COERCE SECT

C82
MILL J.S.,"CIVILIZATION" IN DISSERTATIONS AND DISCUSSIONS." MOD/EUR UK ECO/DEV CONTROL MORAL ORD/FREE PWR...SOC IDEA/COMP 19. PAGE 110 H2208
SOCIETY NAT/G STRUCT CONCPT

B90
TAINE H.A.,MODERN REGIME (2 VOLS.). FRANCE FAM REV CENTRAL MARRIAGE PWR...TREND 19 NAPOLEON/B. PAGE 152 H3037
STRUCT NAT/G OLD/LIB MORAL

B91
BENTHAM J.,A FRAGMENT ON GOVERNMENT (1776). CONSTN MUNIC NAT/G SECT AGREE HAPPINESS UTIL MORAL ORD/FREE...JURID CONCPT. PAGE 15 H0292
SOVEREIGN LAW DOMIN

B96
DE VATTEL E.,THE LAW OF NATIONS. AGRI FINAN CHIEF DIPLOM INT/TRADE AGREE OWN ALL/VALS MORAL ORD/FREE SOVEREIGN...GEN/LAWS 18 NATURL/LAW WOLFF/C. PAGE 39 H0774
LAW CONCPT NAT/G INT/LAW

B96
KROPOTKIN P.,L'ANARCHIE. NAT/G VOL/ASSN REV MORAL WEALTH...POLICY 19. PAGE 89 H1776
SOCIETY ANARCH PERSON CONCPT

MORALITY....SEE MORAL, ALL/VALS

MORE T. H2253

MORE/THOM....SIR THOMAS MORE

C52
HUME D.,"IDEA OF A PERFECT COMMONWEALTH" IN D. HUME, POLITICAL DISCOURSES (1752)" UK NAT/G DOMIN GP/REL CONSERVE...POLICY CONCPT GEN/LAWS 18 MORE/THOM PLATO. PAGE 75 H1494 — CONSTN CHIEF SOCIETY GOV/COMP

MOREIRA J.R. H1362

MORGAN H.W. H2254

MORGAN L.H. H2255

MORGANTHAU H. H2360

MORGENSTERN O. H2256

MORGENTH/H.... HANS MORGENTHAU

MORGENTHAU R.S. H2257

MORISON D. H2258

MORL/MINTO....MORLEY-MINTO - ERA OF BRITISH RULE IN INDIA (1905-1910)

MORLEY C. H2259

MORLEY/J....JOHN MORLEY

MORMON....MORMON PEOPLE AND MORMON FAITH

B66
VOGT E.Z.,PEOPLE OF RIMROCK. STRATA STRUCT KIN SECT GP/REL HABITAT ALL/VALS...GEOG INT QU 20 TEXAS NAVAHO MORMON SPAN/AMER ZUNI. PAGE 163 H3260 — CULTURE GP/COMP SOC SOCIETY

MOROCCO....SEE ALSO ISLAM

B23
GRANT C.F.,STUDIES IN NORTH AFRICA. ALGERIA MOROCCO ROMAN/EMP CULTURE STRUCT NAT/G DIPLOM WAR ...NAT/COMP TUNIS EUROPE. PAGE 60 H1195 — ISLAM SECT DOMIN COLONIAL

B34
DE CENIVAL P.,BIBLIOGRAPHIE MAROCAINE: 1923-1933. FRANCE MOROCCO SECT ADMIN LEAD GP/REL ATTIT...LING 20. PAGE 37 H0750 — BIBLIOG/A ISLAM NAT/G COLONIAL

B42
CONOVER H.F.,FRENCH COLONIES IN AFRICA: A LIST OF REFERENCES. ALGERIA FRANCE MOROCCO SOMALIA SUDAN CULTURE AGRI LOC/G SECT FORCES DIPLOM INT/TRADE NAT/LISM HEALTH...CON/ANAL 20. PAGE 32 H0641 — BIBLIOG AFR ECO/UNDEV COLONIAL

B48
MAUGHAM R.,NORTH AFRICAN NOTEBOOK. ALGERIA ISLAM LIBYA MOROCCO STRUCT ECO/UNDEV COLONIAL...SOC OBS AUD/VIS NAT/COMP WORSHIP 20 TUNIS. PAGE 105 H2102 — SOCIETY RECORD NAT/LISM

B52
JULIEN C.A.,L'AFRIQUE DU NORD EN MARCHE: NATIONALISMES MUSULMANS ET SOUVERAINETE FRANCAISE (2ND ED). AFR ALGERIA FRANCE ISLAM MOROCCO NAT/G CONTROL ORD/FREE...POLICY 19/20 TUNIS MUSLIM. PAGE 82 H1641 — NAT/LISM COERCE DOMIN COLONIAL

B57
CONOVER H.F.,NORTH AND NORTHEAST AFRICA; A SELECTED ANNOTATED LIST OF WRITINGS. ALGERIA MOROCCO SUDAN UAR CULTURE INT/ORG PROB/SOLV ADJUD NAT/LISM PWR WEALTH...SOC 20 UN. PAGE 32 H0649 — BIBLIOG/A DIPLOM AFR ECO/UNDEV

B58
LAHBABI M.,LE GOUVERNEMENT MAROCAIN A L'AUBE DU XXE SIECLE. FRANCE MOROCCO CHIEF EX/STRUC LEGIS ORD/FREE PWR...JURID BIBLIOG 19/20. PAGE 90 H1797 — NAT/G COLONIAL SOVEREIGN

B60
BRIGGS L.C.,TRIBES OF THE SAHARA. AFR MOROCCO STRATA AGRI GP/REL HEALTH...GEOG SOC MYTH LING BIBLIOG 13/20 ARABS. PAGE 21 H0418 — CULTURE HABITAT KIN SELF/OBS

B61
LAHAYE R.,LES ENTREPRISES PUBLIQUES AU MAROC. FRANCE MOROCCO LAW DIST/IND EXTR/IND FINAN CONSULT PLAN TEC/DEV ADMIN AGREE CONTROL OWN...POLICY 20. PAGE 90 H1796 — NAT/G INDUS ECO/UNDEV ECO/TAC

B62
BAULIN J.,THE ARAB ROLE IN AFRICA. AFR ALGERIA FUT ISLAM MOROCCO UAR COLONIAL NEUTRAL REV...SOC 20 TUNIS BOURGUIBA. PAGE 12 H0240 — NAT/LISM DIPLOM NAT/G SECT

B62
DUROSELLE J.B.,LES NOUVEAUX ETATS DANS LES RELATIONS INTERNATIONALES. AFR CHINA/COM FRANCE MOROCCO S/ASIA USSR ECO/UNDEV INT/ORG PLAN ECO/TAC EDU/PROP ATTIT DRIVE...TREND TOT/POP TUNIS 20. PAGE 44 H0872 — NAT/G CONSTN DIPLOM

B63
ZARTMAN I.W.,GOVERNMENT AND POLITICS IN NORTHERN AFRICA. AFR ALGERIA ISLAM LIBYA MOROCCO UAR ELITES SOCIETY PLAN ECO/TAC DOMIN EDU/PROP LEGIT ATTIT ...GEOG CONCPT TIME/SEQ 20 TUNIS. PAGE 172 H3448 — CULTURE DRIVE NAT/LISM

B64
ZARTMAN I.W.,MOROCCO: PROBLEMS OF NEW POWER. ISLAM CULTURE ECO/UNDEV AGRI POL/PAR SCHOOL FORCES ADMIN ...CONCPT STAT INT CENSUS TIME/SEQ CHARTS WORK VAL/FREE 20. PAGE 172 H3449 — CHOOSE MOROCCO DELIB/GP DECISION

S65
ASHFORD D.E.,"BUREAUCRATS AND CITIZENS." MOROCCO PAKISTAN PARTIC 20 TUNIS. PAGE 9 H0172 — GOV/COMP ADMIN EX/STRUC ROLE

S65
THOMAS F.C. JR.,"THE PEACE CORPS IN MOROCCO." CULTURE MUNIC PROVS CREATE ROUTINE TASK ADJUST STRANGE...OBS PEACE/CORP. PAGE 154 H3077 — MOROCCO FRANCE FOR/AID EDU/PROP

B66
BROWN L.C.,STATE AND SOCIETY IN INDEPENDENT NORTH AFRICA. ALGERIA LIBYA MOROCCO AGRI INDUS INT/ORG POL/PAR SECT PLAN DIPLOM COLONIAL...LING NAT/COMP ANTHOL BIBLIOG 20 TUNIS MUSLIM. PAGE 22 H0446 — NAT/G SOCIETY CULTURE ECO/UNDEV

S66
KAPIL R.L.,"ON THE CONFLICT POTENTIAL OF INHERITED BOUNDARIES IN AFRICA." MOD/EUR MOROCCO UAR EX/STRUC DIPLOM LEGIT REGION ADJUST...RECORD NAT/COMP GEN/LAWS. PAGE 83 H1658 — AFR COLONIAL PREDICT GEOG

B67
ASHFORD D.E.,NATIONAL DEVELOPMENT AND LOCAL REFORM: POLITICAL PARTICIPATION IN MOROCCO, TUNISIA, AND PAKISTAN. MOROCCO PAKISTAN CULTURE PROB/SOLV ATTIT ...POLICY SOC METH/COMP NAT/COMP BIBLIOG 20 TUNIS. PAGE 9 H0173 — PARTIC ECO/UNDEV ADJUST NAT/G

B93
ROYAL GEOGRAPHIC SOCIETY,BIBLIOGRAPHY OF BARBARY STATES (4 SUPPLEMENTARY PAPERS). ALGERIA LIBYA MOROCCO SOCIETY STRUCT DIPLOM LEAD 14/19 TUNIS. PAGE 135 H2706 — BIBLIOG ISLAM NAT/G COLONIAL

C93
PLAYFAIR R.L.,"A BIBLIOGRAPHY OF MOROCCO." MOROCCO CULTURE AGRI FORCES DIPLOM WAR HEALTH...GEOG JURID SOC CHARTS. PAGE 126 H2526 — BIBLIOG ISLAM MEDIT-7

MORRALL J.B. H2260

MORRIS A.J.A. H2261

MORRIS I. H2262

MORRIS J. H2263

MORRIS/CW....C.W. MORRIS

MORRIS/G....G. MORRIS

MORRIS-JONES W.H. H2264

MORRISON C. H2265

MORRISON H. H2266

MORROW/DW....DWIGHT W. MORROW

MORSEY R. H2100

MOSCA/G....GAETANO MOSCA

MOSCOW....MOSCOW, U.S.S.R.

MOSELY P.E. H2267

MOSK S.A. H2268

MOSS W. H2269

MOSSI....MOSSI TRIBE

B65
KUPER H.,URBANIZATION AND MIGRATION IN WEST AFRICA. UPPER/VOLT CULTURE ECO/UNDEV WORKER REGION GOV/REL ...LING ANTHOL SOC/INTEG 20 AFRICA/W OSHOGBO MOSSI MIGRATION. PAGE 89 H1781 — AFR HABITAT MUNIC GEOG

MOTE M.E. H2270

MOTIVATION....SEE DRIVE

MOUMOUNI A. H2271

MOUSKHELY M. H2272

MOUSSA P. H2273

MOVIES....SEE FILM

MOYER K.E. H2274

MOYNI/RPRT....MOYNIHAN REPORT

MOYNIHAN REPORT....SEE MOYNI/RPRT

MOZAMBIQUE LIBERATION FRONT....SEE FRELIMO

MOZAMBIQUE....MOZAMBIQUE

MOZINGO D. H2275,H2276

MOZINGO D.P. H2277

MU FU-SHENG H2278

MUCKRAKER....MUCKRAKERS

MUEHLMANN W.E. H2279

MUELLER-DEHAM A. H2280

MUGWUMP....MUGWUMP

MUHAMMAD A.C. H2281

MUHLEN N. H0922

MUKERJI S.N. H2282

MULATTO....MULATTO

MULLER A.L. H2283

MULLER C.F.J. H2284

MULLER H.J. H2285

MULTIVAR....MULTIVARIATE ANALYSIS

MULTIVARIATE ANALYSIS....SEE MULTIVAR

MUMFORD L. H2286,H2287

MUNGER E.S. H2288,H2289

MUNIC....CITIES, TOWNS, VILLAGES

B18
BARRES M.,THE FAITH OF FRANCE (TRANS. BY ELISABETH MARBURY). FRANCE FAM MUNIC NEIGH POL/PAR SECT ALL/VALS 20. PAGE 11 H0227
TRADIT CULTURE WAR GP/REL

B27
WEBER M.,GENERAL ECONOMIC HISTORY. CHRIST-17C MOD/EUR STRUCT AGRI EXTR/IND FINAN INDUS MARKET FAM MUNIC NAT/G PROF/ORG SECT ECO/TAC 8/20. PAGE 166 H3319
ECO/DEV CAP/ISM

B31
HENNIG P.,GEOPOLITIK (2ND ED.). CULTURE MUNIC COLONIAL...CENSUS CHARTS 20. PAGE 70 H1398
GEOG HABITAT CREATE NEIGH

B32
MCKISACK M.,THE PARLIAMENTARY REPRESENTATION OF THE ENGLISH BOROUGHS DURING THE MIDDLE AGES. UK CONSTN CULTURE ELITES EX/STRUC TAX PAY ADJUD PARL/PROC APPORT FEDERAL...POLICY 13/15 PARLIAMENT. PAGE 107 H2139
NAT/G MUNIC LEGIS CHOOSE

B34
RIDLEY C.E.,THE CITY-MANAGER PROFESSION. CHIEF PLAN ADMIN CONTROL ROUTINE CHOOSE...TECHNIC CHARTS GOV/COMP BIBLIOG 20. PAGE 131 H2624
MUNIC EX/STRUC LOC/G EXEC

B39
ANDERSON W.,LOCAL GOVERNMENT IN EUROPE. FRANCE GERMANY ITALY UK USSR MUNIC PROVS ADMIN GOV/REL CENTRAL SOVEREIGN 20. PAGE 7 H0136
GOV/COMP NAT/COMP LOC/G CONSTN

B39
BARNES H.E.,SOCIETY IN TRANSITION: PROBLEMS OF A CHANGING ERA. USA-45 INDUS MUNIC PUB/INST EDU/PROP CRIME RACE/REL...SOC MYTH NAT/COMP. PAGE 11 H0220
SOCIETY CULTURE TECHRACY TEC/DEV

B40
TONNIES F.,FUNDAMENTAL CONCEPTS OF SOCIOLOGY (1887) (TRANS. BY C. LOOMIS). LAW STRATA STRUCT FAM MUNIC NAT/G DOMIN LEGIT SANCTION COERCE CRIME PERSON 19. PAGE 156 H3115
CULTURE SOCIETY GEN/LAWS SOC

B42
REDFIELD R.,THE FOLK CULTURE OF YUCATAN. STRATA FAM KIN MUNIC SECT DISCRIM ISOLAT ANOMIE HEALTH ...BIBLIOG 20 MEXIC/AMER. PAGE 130 H2605
CULTURE NEIGH GP/COMP

SOCIETY
S42
TISDALE H.,"THE PROCESS OF URBANIZATION" (BMR)" UNIV CULTURE...CENSUS GEN/LAWS. PAGE 155 H3106
MUNIC GEOG CONCPT TEC/DEV

B46
HUTTON J.,THE CONSTITUTION OF THE UNION OF SOUTH AFRICA: BIBLIOGRAPHY (PAMPHLET). SOUTH/AFR MUNIC DIPLOM RACE/REL 20. PAGE 75 H1510
BIBLIOG CONSTN NAT/G LOC/G

B49
HEADLAM-MORLEY,BIBLIOGRAPHY IN POLITICS FOR THE HONOUR SCHOOL OF PHILOSOPHY, POLITICS AND ECONOMICS (PAMPHLET). UK CONSTN LABOR MUNIC DIPLOM ADMIN 19/20. PAGE 69 H1375
BIBLIOG NAT/G PHIL/SCI GOV/REL

B50
JONES H.D.,KOREA, AN ANNOTATED BIBLIOGRAPHY OF PUBLICATIONS IN WESTERN LANGUAGES. KOREA CULTURE MUNIC SECT FORCES DIPLOM HEALTH WEALTH...ART/METH GEOG SOC LING 20. PAGE 82 H1632
BIBLIOG/A ASIA NAT/G ECO/UNDEV

B51
MEYER E.W.,POLITICAL PARTIES IN WESTERN GERMANY (PAMPHLET). GERMANY/W MUNIC NAT/G GOV/REL ALL/IDEOS 20 UNIFICA BERLIN. PAGE 109 H2190
POL/PAR LOBBY CHOOSE CONSTN

B52
BENTHAM A.,HANDBOOK OF POLITICAL FALLACIES. FUT MOD/EUR LAW INTELL LOC/G MUNIC NAT/G DELIB/GP LEGIS CREATE EDU/PROP CT/SYS ATTIT RIGID/FLEX KNOWL PWR ...RELATIV PSY SOC CONCPT SELF/OBS TREND STERTYP TOT/POP. PAGE 14 H0286
POL/PAR

B52
THOM J.M.,GUIDE TO RESEARCH MATERIAL IN POLITICAL SCIENCE (PAMPHLET). ELITES LOC/G MUNIC NAT/G LEGIS DIPLOM ADJUD CIVMIL/REL GOV/REL PWR MGT. PAGE 154 H3074
BIBLIOG/A KNOWL

B55
CHARMATZ J.P.,COMPARATIVE STUDIES IN COMMUNITY PROPERTY LAW. FRANCE USA+45...JURID GOV/COMP ANTHOL 20. PAGE 29 H0583
MARRIAGE LAW OWN MUNIC

B56
INTERNATIONAL AFRICAN INST,SOCIAL IMPLICATIONS OF INDUSTRIALIZATION AND URBANIZATION IN AFRICA SOUTH OF THE SAHARA. SOUTH/AFR INDUS LABOR MUNIC WORKER TEC/DEV...SOC OBS TREND ANTHOL 20. PAGE 77 H1549
AFR ECO/UNDEV ADJUST CULTURE

B56
MANNONI D.O.,PROSPERO AND CALIBAN: THE PSYCHOLOGY OF COLONIZATION. AFR EUR+WWI FAM KIN MUNIC SECT DOMIN ADMIN ATTIT DRIVE LOVE PWR RESPECT...PSY SOC CONCPT MYTH OBS DEEP/INT BIOG GEN/METH MALAGASY 20. PAGE 102 H2040
CULTURE COLONIAL

B57
BOUSTEDT O.,REGIONALE STRUKTUR- UND WIRTSCHAFTSFORSCHUNG. WOR+45 WOR-45 MUNIC PROVS STAT. PAGE 19 H0388
GEOG CONCPT NAT/COMP

B57
HODGKIN T.,NATIONALISM IN COLONIAL AFRICA. STRATA STRUCT MUNIC NAT/G POL/PAR LEGIS ATTIT SOVEREIGN ...POLICY TREND BIBLIOG 20. PAGE 72 H1444
AFR COLONIAL NAT/LISM DIPLOM

B58
JOHNSON J.J.,POLITICAL CHANGE IN LATIN AMERICA: THE EMERGENCE OF THE MIDDLE SECTORS. INTELL STRATA STRUCT ECO/UNDEV MUNIC TEC/DEV LEAD REV...DECISION TREND GOV/COMP BIBLIOG/A 20. PAGE 81 H1621
L/A+17C ELITES GP/REL DOMIN

B58
NICULESCU B.,COLONIAL PLANNING: A COMPARATIVE STUDY. AFR AGRI LOC/G MUNIC NAT/G DELIB/GP COLONIAL 20. PAGE 118 H2356
PLAN ECO/UNDEV TEC/DEV NAT/COMP

B59
CARPENTER G.W.,THE WAY IN AFRICA. AFR INDUS MUNIC DIPLOM DOMIN EDU/PROP COERCE DISCRIM NAT/LISM ORD/FREE 20 NEGRO CHRISTIAN. PAGE 27 H0535
CULTURE SECT ECO/UNDEV COLONIAL

B59
HENDERSON G.P.,REFERENCE MANUAL OF DIRECTORIES (16 VOLS.). MUNIC PROVS GOV/REL 20. PAGE 70 H1394
BIBLIOG/A NAT/COMP NAT/G INDUS

B59
PARK R.L.,LEADERSHIP AND POLITICAL INSTITUTIONS IN INDIA. S/ASIA CULTURE ECO/UNDEV LOC/G MUNIC PROVS LEGIS PLAN ADMIN LEAD ORD/FREE WEALTH...GEOG SOC BIOG TOT/POP VAL/FREE 20. PAGE 123 H2468
NAT/G EXEC INDIA

B60
ALBI F.,TRATADO DE LOS MODOS DE GESTION DE LAS CORPORACIONES LOCALES. SPAIN FINAN NAT/G BUDGET CONTROL EXEC ROUTINE GOV/REL ORD/FREE SOVEREIGN ...MGT 20. PAGE 5 H0092
LOC/G LAW ADMIN MUNIC

B60
COUGHLIN R.,DOUBLE IDENTITY: THE CHINESE AND MODERN THAILAND. CHINA/COM S/ASIA THAILAND ECO/UNDEV EXTR/IND FINAN INDUS KIN MUNIC NAT/G PROF/ORG
ASIA FAM CULTURE

SCHOOL SECT ATTIT DRIVE...CONCPT OBS 20. PAGE 34 H0676

B60
MINER H.M.,OASIS AND CASBAH: ALGERIAN CULTURE AND PERSONALITY IN CHANGE. ALGERIA FRANCE SOCIETY MUNIC COLONIAL ATTIT...INT PROJ/TEST CHARTS 20. PAGE 111 H2221
GP/COMP PERSON CULTURE ADJUST

S60
BANFIELD E.C.,"THE POLITICAL IMPLICATIONS OF METROPOLITAN GROWTH" (BMR)" UK USA+45 LOC/G PROB/SOLV ADMIN GP/REL...METH/COMP NAT/COMP 20. PAGE 10 H0209
TASK MUNIC GOV/COMP CENSUS

S60
COOK R.C.,"THE WORLD'S GREAT CITIES: EVOLUTION OR DEVOLUTION?" WOR+45 WOR-45 ECO/DEV ECO/UNDEV ACT/RES PROB/SOLV...GEOG TREND CHARTS NAT/COMP BIBLIOG 20. PAGE 33 H0658
MUNIC HABITAT PLAN CENSUS

S60
GRIMSHAW A.D.,"URBAN RACIAL VIOLENCE IN THE UNITED STATES: CHANGING ECOLOGICAL CONSIDERATIONS." STRUCT MUNIC FORCES PARTIC DISCRIM ATTIT HABITAT ...IDEA/COMP 20 NEGRO. PAGE 61 H1228
CROWD RACE/REL GOV/COMP NEIGH

S60
WOLFINGER R.E.,"REPUTATION AND REALITY IN THE STUDY OF COMMUNITY POWER." STRUCT PROB/SOLV INGP/REL ATTIT OBJECTIVE...SOC METH/CNCPT PERS/COMP. PAGE 170 H3404
CULTURE MUNIC DOMIN PWR

C60
HOSELITZ B.,"THE ROLE OF CITIES IN THE ECONOMIC GROWTH OF UNDERDEVELOPED COUNTRIES" IN "SOCIOLOGICAL ASPECTS OF ECONOMIC GROWTH"(BMR). CULTURE LOC/G ACT/RES...SOC IDEA/COMP METH/COMP METH 14/20 REDFIELD/R. PAGE 74 H1474
METH/CNCPT MUNIC TEC/DEV ECO/UNDEV

B61
BOURDIEU P.,THE ALGERIANS (TRANS. BY A.C. ROSS; REV. ED.). ALGERIA ISLAM CULTURE MUNIC CAP/ISM COLONIAL GP/REL ORD/FREE SOVEREIGN 20. PAGE 19 H0385
SOCIETY STRUCT ATTIT WAR

B61
INTL UNION LOCAL AUTHORITIES,METROPOLIS. WOR+45 DIST/IND FINAN GIVE EDU/PROP CRIME COST HEALTH WEALTH 20. PAGE 78 H1563
MUNIC GOV/COMP LOC/G BIBLIOG

B61
LETHBRIDGE H.J.,CHINA'S URBAN COMMUNES. CHINA/COM FUT ECO/UNDEV DIPLOM EDU/PROP DEMAND INCOME MARXISM ...POLICY 20. PAGE 95 H1893
MUNIC CONTROL ECO/TAC NAT/G

B61
MARX K.,THE COMMUNIST MANIFESTO. IN (MENDEL A. ESSENTIAL WORKS OF MARXISM, NEW YORK: BANTAM. FUT MOD/EUR CULTURE ECO/DEV ECO/UNDEV AGRI FINAN INDUS MARKET PROC/MFG LABOR MUNIC POL/PAR CONSULT FORCES CREATE PLAN ADMIN ATTIT DRIVE RIGID/FLEX ORD/FREE PWR RESPECT MARX/KARL WORK. PAGE 104 H2081
COM NEW/IDEA CAP/ISM REV

B61
MERRIAM A.,CONGO: BACKGROUND OF CONFLICT. AFR FUT KIN MUNIC NAT/G POL/PAR PROVS DELIB/GP PLAN DOMIN COERCE ATTIT...TIME/SEQ CHARTS CONGO 20. PAGE 109 H2182
CHOOSE GUERRILLA

B61
NARAIN J.P.,SWARAJ FOR THE PEOPLE. INDIA CONSTN LOC/G MUNIC POL/PAR CHOOSE REPRESENT EFFICIENCY ATTIT PWR SOVEREIGN 20. PAGE 116 H2311
NAT/G ORD/FREE EDU/PROP EX/STRUC

B61
SOUTHALL A.,SOCIAL CHANGE IN MODERN AFRICA. CULTURE STRATA ECO/UNDEV AGRI FAM KIN MUNIC GP/REL INGP/REL MARRIAGE...GEOG ANTHOL 20. PAGE 147 H2940
AFR TREND SOCIETY SOC

S61
ELAZAR D.J.,"CHURCHES AS MOLDERS OF AMERICAN POLITICS." STRATA MUNIC EDU/PROP RACE/REL ORD/FREE SOC. PAGE 45 H0904
SECT CULTURE REPRESENT LOC/G

S61
LIEBERSON S.,"THE IMPACT OF RESIDENTIAL SEGREGATION ON ETHNIC ASSIMILATION" (BMR)" CULTURE MUNIC GP/REL RACE/REL DISCRIM...GEOG STAT CON/ANAL CHARTS SOC/INTEG 20 MIGRATION. PAGE 96 H1926
HABITAT ISOLAT NEIGH

B62
BUSIA K.A.,THE CHALLENGE OF AFRICA. CULTURE KIN MUNIC NAT/G POL/PAR SCHOOL DELIB/GP PLAN ECO/TAC DOMIN EDU/PROP TOTALISM ATTIT PERSON ALL/VALS SOVEREIGN...SOC CONCPT STERTYP TOT/POP VAL/FREE 20. PAGE 25 H0496
AFR ECO/UNDEV NAT/LISM

B62
GOURE L.,CIVIL DEFENSE IN THE SOVIET UNION. COM USA+45 USSR MUNIC NAT/G DETER ATTIT MARXISM ...NAT/COMP 20 CIV/DEFENS. PAGE 59 H1188
PLAN FORCES WAR COERCE

B62
HACHMANN R.,VOLKER ZWISCHEN GERMANEN UND KELTEN. GERMANY CULTURE STRUCT MUNIC...ART/METH CHARTS MAPS. PAGE 63 H1269
LING SOC KIN GP/REL

B62
HO PING-TI,THE LADDER OF SUCCESS IN IMPERIAL CHINA: ASPECTS OF SOCIAL MOBILITY, 1368-1911. INTELL STRATA FAM KIN MUNIC NAT/G PROVS SCHOOL DELIB/GP DOMIN EDU/PROP ADMIN ROUTINE PERSON ALL/VALS...SOC STAT BIOG HIST/WRIT TIME/SEQ VAL/FREE. PAGE 71 H1431
ASIA CULTURE

B62
HUNTER G.,THE NEW SOCIETIES OF TROPICAL AFRICA. CULTURE INDUS KIN MUNIC WORKER INT/TRADE EDU/PROP ORD/FREE...INT TREND 20. PAGE 75 H1500
AFR GOV/COMP ECO/UNDEV SOCIETY

B62
KARNJAHAPRAKORN C.,MUNICIPAL GOVERNMENT IN THAILAND AS AN INSTITUTION AND PROCESS OF SELF-GOVERNMENT. THAILAND CULTURE FINAN EX/STRUC LEGIS PLAN CONTROL GOV/REL EFFICIENCY ATTIT...POLICY 20. PAGE 83 H1662
LOC/G MUNIC ORD/FREE ADMIN

B62
STATE AND LOCAL GOVERNMENT. MUNIC NAT/G NEIGH PRESS CONTROL CHOOSE REPRESENT...BIBLIOG 20. PAGE 104 H2076
PROVS LOC/G GOV/REL PWR

B62
MEIER R.L.,A COMMUNICATIONS THEORY OF URBAN GROWTH. CULTURE ECO/DEV COMPUTER BUDGET UTIL KNOWL...SOC CONCPT METH 20 OPEN/SPACE. PAGE 108 H2164
OP/RES COM/IND MUNIC CONTROL

B62
TURNBULL C.M.,THE LONELY AFRICAN. AFR MUNIC SECT ANOMIE ALL/VALS...DECISION 20. PAGE 157 H3139
CULTURE ISOLAT KIN TRADIT

B62
UMENDRAS H.,LES SOCIETESRFRANCAISES; BIBLIOGRAPHIES FRANCAISES DE SCIENCE SOCIALES (VOL. III). FRANCE SECT WORKER 20. PAGE 158 H3154
BIBLIOG/A AGRI MUNIC CULTURE

B62
VERHAEGEN P.,BIBLIOGRAPHIE DE L'URBANISATION DE L'AFRIQUE NOIRE: SON CADRE, SES CAUSES, ET SES CONSEQUENCES ECONOMIQUES, SOCIALES... AFR...SOC 20. PAGE 162 H3244
BIBLIOG ECO/UNDEV MUNIC CULTURE

L62
COHEN R.,"POWER IN COMPLEX SOCIETIES IN AFRICA." AFR KIN MUNIC POL/PAR DELIB/GP DOMIN ROUTINE ATTIT ALL/VALS...SOC STAT OBS INT QU CHARTS ANTHOL 20. PAGE 31 H0617
CULTURE STRATA ELITES

B63
ADRIAN C.R.,GOVERNING OVER FIFTY STATES AND THEIR COMMUNITIES. USA+45 CONSTN FINAN MUNIC NAT/G POL/PAR EX/STRUC LEGIS ADMIN CONTROL CT/SYS ...CHARTS 20. PAGE 4 H0073
PROVS LOC/G GOV/REL GOV/COMP

B63
BERREMAN G.D.,HINDUS OF THE HIMALAYAS. INDIA STRATA STRUCT KIN MUNIC 20 HINDU. PAGE 16 H0319
CULTURE SECT GP/REL ECO/UNDEV

B63
GAMBLE S.D.,NORTH CHINA VILLAGES: SOCIAL, POLITICAL, AND ECONOMIC ACTIVITIES BEFORE 1933. ASIA CULTURE STRUCT FAM DOMIN EDU/PROP WORSHIP 20. PAGE 55 H1093
MUNIC AGRI LEAD FINAN

B63
GEERTZ C.,PEDDLERS AND PRINCES: SOCIAL DEVELOPMENT AND ECONOMIC CHANGE IN TWO INDONESIAN TOWNS. S/ASIA CULTURE SOCIETY STRATA FACE/GP MUNIC CREATE TEC/DEV ECO/TAC ORD/FREE WEALTH...OBS INT CENSUS CHARTS WORK TOT/POP VAL/FREE 20. PAGE 55 H1106
ECO/UNDEV SOC ELITES INDONESIA

B63
GLUCKMAN M.,ORDER AND REBELLION IN TRIBAL AFRICA. EUR+WWI LAW CULTURE STRATA KIN MUNIC DELIB/GP ACT/RES DOMIN EDU/PROP LEGIT ADMIN COERCE CHOOSE ATTIT PERSON ORD/FREE PWR...SOC CHARTS GEN/LAWS TOT/POP VAL/FREE. PAGE 57 H1147
AFR SOCIETY

B63
LEONARD T.J.,THE FEDERAL SYSTEM OF INDIA. INDIA MUNIC NAT/G PROVS ADMIN SOVEREIGN...IDEA/COMP 20. PAGE 94 H1885
FEDERAL MGT NAT/COMP METH/COMP

B63
MAIR L.,NEW NATIONS. AFR FAM MUNIC SECT DOMIN CHOOSE NAT/LISM ORD/FREE...SOC 19/20. PAGE 101 H2022
COLONIAL CULTURE TEC/DEV ECO/UNDEV

B63
RUITENBEER H.M.,THE DILEMMA OF ORGANIZATIONAL SOCIETY. CULTURE ECO/DEV MUNIC SECT TEC/DEV EDU/PROP NAT/LISM ORD/FREE...NAT/COMP 20 RIESMAN/D WHYTE/WF MERTON/R MEAD/MARG JASPERS/K. PAGE 136 H2716
PERSON ROLE ADMIN WORKER

B63
THOMPSON F.M.L.,ENGLISH LANDED SOCIETY IN THE NINETEENTH CENTURY. UK STRUCT MUNIC NAT/G CONTROL WAR GP/REL OWN WEALTH...BIBLIOG 18/20. PAGE 154 H3081
STRATA PWR ELITES GOV/REL

B63
WILSON U.,EDUCATION AND CHANGING WEST AFRICAN CULTURE. AFR MOD/EUR UK CULTURE ECO/UNDEV MUNIC CONSULT 19/20 CMN/WLTH AFRICA/W. PAGE 169 H3384
COLONIAL POLICY SCHOOL

S63
NICHOLAS W.,"VILLAGE FACTIONS AND POLITICAL PARTIES IN RURAL WEST BENGAL." S/ASIA CULTURE STRATA FACE/GP KIN MUNIC DELIB/GP LEGIS DOMIN EDU/PROP COERCE CHOOSE ATTIT ALL/VALS...STAT TOT/POP VAL/FREE 20. PAGE 117 H2348
NEIGH POL/PAR

S63
ROBINSON W.C.,"URBANIZATION AND FERTILITY: THE NON-WESTERN EXPERIENCE (BMR)" DEATH MARRIAGE AGE/C BIO/SOC...STAT CENSUS CON/ANAL CHARTS NAT/COMP 20 THIRD/WRLD. PAGE 133 H2651
GEOG MUNIC FAM ECO/UNDEV

B64
AGGER R.E.,THE RULERS AND THE RULED: POLITICAL POWER AND IMPOTENCE IN AMERICAN COMMUNITIES. CULTURE DOMIN CHOOSE ATTIT ALL/VALS...DECISION SOC CONCPT OBS QU CHARTS. PAGE 4 H0079
PWR STRUCT LOC/G MUNIC

B64
BURKE F.G.,AFRICA'S QUEST FOR ORDER. AFR CULTURE KIN MUNIC NAT/G DIPLOM COLONIAL REV DISCRIM NAT/LISM AGE/Y 20. PAGE 24 H0488
ORD/FREE CONSEN RACE/REL LEAD

B64
CULLINGWORTH J.B.,TOWN AND COUNTRY PLANNING IN ENGLAND AND WALES. UK LAW SOCIETY CONSULT ACT/RES ADMIN ROUTINE LEISURE INGP/REL ADJUST PWR...GEOG 20 OPEN/SPACE URBAN/RNWL. PAGE 36 H0718
MUNIC PLAN NAT/G PROB/SOLV

B64
GLUCKMANN M.,CLOSED SYSTEMS AND OPEN MINDS: THE LIMITS OF NAIVETY IN SOCIAL ANTHROPOLOGY. AFR INDIA MUNIC...IDEA/COMP METH/COMP ANTHOL. PAGE 57 H1149
CULTURE OBS SOC

B64
GREBLER L.,URBAN RENEWAL IN EUROPEAN COUNTRIES: ITS EMERGENCE AND POTENTIALS. EUR+WWI UK ECO/DEV LOC/G NEIGH CREATE ADMIN ATTIT...TREND NAT/COMP 20 URBAN/RNWL. PAGE 60 H1205
MUNIC PLAN CONSTRUC NAT/G

B64
GREEN M.M.,IBO VILLAGE AFFAIRS. AFR FORCES PERS/REL ADJUST ISOLAT ATTIT HABITAT PERSON ALL/VALS...JURID RECORD SOC/INTEG 20 IBO. PAGE 60 H1207
MUNIC CULTURE ECO/UNDEV SOC

B64
HAAR C.M.,LAW AND LAND: ANGLO-AMERICAN PLANNING PRACTICE. UK USA+45 NAT/G TEC/DEV BUDGET CT/SYS INGP/REL EFFICIENCY OWN...JURID 20. PAGE 63 H1263
LAW PLAN MUNIC NAT/COMP

B64
HANNA W.J.,POLITICS IN BLACK AFRICA: A SELECTIVE BIBLIOGRAPHY OF RELEVANT PERIODICAL LITERATURE. AFR LAW LOC/G MUNIC NAT/G POL/PAR LOBBY CHOOSE RACE/REL SOVEREIGN 20. PAGE 66 H1315
BIBLIOG NAT/LISM COLONIAL

B64
HARRIS M.,PATTERNS OF RACE IN THE AMERICAS. BRAZIL L/A+17C STRATA ECO/UNDEV AGRI KIN MUNIC SECT COLONIAL RACE/REL...SOC SOC/INTEG 17/20 NEGRO INDIAN/AM. PAGE 67 H1342
STRUCT PRE/AMER CULTURE SOCIETY

B64
MORRIS J.,THE PRESENCE OF SPAIN. SPAIN MUNIC NAT/G FORCES ATTIT CATHISM...AUD/VIS 16/20. PAGE 113 H2263
CULTURE HABITAT SOCIETY GEOG

B64
PINNICK A.W.,COUNTRY PLANNERS IN ACTION. UK FINAN SERV/IND NAT/G CONSULT DELIB/GP PRICE CONTROL ROUTINE LEISURE AGE/C...GEOG 20 URBAN/RNWL. PAGE 126 H2512
MUNIC PLAN INDUS ATTIT

B64
THORNBURG M.W.,PEOPLE AND POLICY IN THE MIDDLE EAST. ISLAM ECO/UNDEV FAM KIN MUNIC NAT/G NEIGH POL/PAR SECT DELIB/GP LEGIS PLAN ECO/TAC DOMIN ADMIN ATTIT HEALTH RESPECT...SOC CONCPT METH/CNCPT OBS TIME/SEQ TOT/POP VAL/FREE. PAGE 154 H3088
TEC/DEV CULTURE

B64
WHITEFORD A.H.,TWO CITIES OF LATIN AMERICA: A COMPARATIVE DESCRIPTION OF SOCIAL CLASSES. L/A+17C CULTURE SOCIETY MUNIC DOMIN LEGIT ATTIT ALL/VALS ...STAT OBS VAL/FREE 20. PAGE 167 H3352
STRATA SOC

S64
EISTER A.W.,"PERSPECTIVE ON FUNCTIONS OF RELIGION IN A DEVELOPING COUNTRY: ISLAM IN PAKISTAN." ISLAM CULTURE MUNIC ACT/RES CREATE PROB/SOLV TEC/DEV WORSHIP. PAGE 45 H0902
ATTIT SECT ECO/DEV

B65
ACHTERBERG E.,BERLINER HOCHFINANZ - KAISER, FURSTEN, MILLIONARE UM 1900. GERMANY NAT/G EDU/PROP PERSON...MGT 19/20. PAGE 3 H0060
FINAN MUNIC BIOG ECO/TAC

B65
ALLEN W.S.,THE NAZI SEIZURE OF POWER. GERMANY NAT/G CHIEF LEAD COERCE CHOOSE REPRESENT GOV/REL AUTHORIT ...DECISION 20 HITLER/A NAZI. PAGE 5 H0106
MUNIC FASCISM TOTALISM LOC/G

B65
BETEILLE A.,CASTE, CLASS, AND POWER. INDIA MUNIC SECT REGION GP/REL PERS/REL ATTIT HABITAT RIGID/FLEX...SOC 20. PAGE 16 H0323
STRATA CULTURE PWR STRUCT

B65
BOISSEVAIN J.,SAINTS AND FIREWORKS: RELIGION AND POLITICS IN RURAL MALTA. MALTA STRUCT FAM NEIGH POL/PAR REPRESENT INGP/REL CENTRAL...CHARTS BIBLIOG 20. PAGE 18 H0368
GP/REL NAT/G SECT MUNIC

B65
DUGGAR G.S.,RENEWAL OF TOWN AND VILLAGE I: A WORLD-WIDE SURVEY OF LOCAL GOVERNMENT EXPERIENCE. WOR+45 CONSTRUC INDUS CREATE BUDGET REGION GOV/REL...QU NAT/COMP 20 URBAN/RNWL. PAGE 43 H0859
MUNIC NEIGH PLAN ADMIN

B65
GOULD J.,PENGUIN SURVEY OF THE SOCIAL SCIENCES* 1965. CULTURE SOCIETY R+D FAM KIN MUNIC ACT/RES DIPLOM SKILL. PAGE 59 H1186
SOC PHIL/SCI USSR UK

B65
HAUSER P.M.,THE STUDY OF URBANIZATION. S/ASIA ECO/DEV ECO/UNDEV NEIGH ACT/RES GEOG. PAGE 68 H1359
CULTURE MUNIC SOC

B65
HERRICK B.H.,URBAN MIGRATION AND ECONOMIC DEVELOPMENT IN CHILE. CHILE AGRI INDUS LABOR NAT/G CENTRAL PRODUC...STAT SAMP CHARTS BIBLIOG/A 20 MIGRATION. PAGE 70 H1404
HABITAT GEOG MUNIC ECO/UNDEV

B65
KUPER H.,URBANIZATION AND MIGRATION IN WEST AFRICA. UPPER/VOLT CULTURE ECO/UNDEV WORKER REGION GOV/REL ...LING ANTHOL SOC/INTEG 20 AFRICA/W OSHOGBO MOSSI MIGRATION. PAGE 89 H1781
AFR HABITAT MUNIC GEOG

B65
SIMMS R.P.,URBANIZATION IN WEST AFRICA; A REVIEW OF CURRENT LITERATURE. AFR PLAN TEC/DEV...SOC OBS NAT/COMP 20. PAGE 144 H2878
BIBLIOG/A MUNIC ECO/DEV ECO/UNDEV

B65
SIRISKAR V.M.,POLITICAL BEHAVIOR IN INDIA. INDIA SOCIETY MUNIC NAT/G PROVS ACT/RES SUFF...OBS CHARTS 20 POONA. PAGE 144 H2889
CHOOSE POL/PAR PWR ATTIT

B65
VAN DEN BERGHE P.L.,AFRICA: SOCIAL PROBLEMS OF CHANGE AND CONFLICT. ELITES STRATA ECO/UNDEV KIN MUNIC DIPLOM GP/REL RACE/REL NAT/LISM...ANTHOL BIBLIOG 20. PAGE 161 H3228
SOC CULTURE AFR STRUCT

S65
KEE W.S.,"CENTRAL CITY EXPENDITURES AND METROPOLITAN AREAS." PLAN BUDGET ECO/TAC TAX GP/REL WEALTH...CHARTS 20. PAGE 84 H1677
LOC/G MUNIC GOV/COMP NEIGH

S65
PLISCHKE E.,"INTEGRATING BERLIN AND THE FEDERAL REPUBLIC OF GERMANY." EUR+WWI GERMANY/W LEGIS TEC/DEV DOMIN ORD/FREE PWR...JURID 20 BERLIN. PAGE 126 H2528
DIPLOM NAT/G MUNIC

S65
THOMAS F.C. JR.,"THE PEACE CORPS IN MOROCCO." CULTURE MUNIC PROVS CREATE ROUTINE TASK ADJUST STRANGE...OBS PEACE/CORP. PAGE 154 H3077
MOROCCO FRANCE FOR/AID EDU/PROP

B66
ASHRAF A.,THE CITY GOVERNMENT OF CALCUTTA: A STUDY OF INERTIA. INDIA ELITES INDUS NAT/G EX/STRUC ACT/RES PLAN PROB/SOLV LEAD HABITAT...BIBLIOG 20 CALCUTTA. PAGE 9 H0175
LOC/G MUNIC ADMIN ECO/UNDEV

B66
DUNCOMBE H.S.,COUNTY GOVERNMENT IN AMERICA. USA+45 FINAN MUNIC ADMIN ROUTINE GOV/REL...GOV/COMP 20. PAGE 43 H0863
LOC/G PROVS CT/SYS TOP/EX

B66
HACKETT J.,L'ECONOMIE BRITANNIQUE: PROBLEMES ET PERSPECTIVES. FRANCE UK LABOR MUNIC NAT/G EX/STRUC PROB/SOLV BAL/PAY INCOME RIGID/FLEX...MGT PHIL/SCI CHARTS 20. PAGE 63 H1271
ECO/DEV FINAN ECO/TAC PLAN

B66
HARMON R.B.,SOURCES AND PROBLEMS OF BIBLIOGRAPHY IN POLITICAL SCIENCE (PAMPHLET). INT/ORG LOC/G MUNIC POL/PAR ADMIN GOV/REL ALL/IDEOS...JURID MGT CONCPT 19/20. PAGE 67 H1335
BIBLIOG DIPLOM INT/LAW NAT/G

B66
HINTON W.,FANSHEN: A DOCUMENTARY OF REVOLUTION IN A CHINESE VILLAGE. ASIA ELITES MUNIC NAT/G POL/PAR SECT WORKER LEAD WAR PRIVIL PWR 20 MAO. PAGE 71 H1422
MARXISM REV NEIGH OWN

B66
LAVEN P.,RENAISSANCE ITALY: 1464-1534. ITALY AGRI EXTR/IND FINAN MUNIC INT/TRADE DRIVE...CATH GEOG CHARTS BIBLIOG/A 15. PAGE 92 H1841
CULTURE HUM TEC/DEV KNOWL

B66
MILONE P.D.,URBAN AREAS IN INDONESIA. INDONESIA
MUNIC

LABOR NAT/G COLONIAL GP/REL...CENSUS CHARTS 17/20. PAGE 111 H2218 GEOG STRUCT SOCIETY

B66
SCHURMANN F.,IDEOLOGY AND ORGANIZATION IN COMMUNIST CHINA. CHINA/COM LOC/G MUNIC POL/PAR ECO/TAC CONTROL ATTIT...MGT STERTYP 20 COM/PARTY. PAGE 140 H2805 MARXISM STRUCT ADMIN NAT/G

B66
SILBERMAN B.S.,MODERN JAPANESE LEADERSHIP; TRANSITION AND CHANGE. NAT/G POL/PAR CHIEF ADMIN REPRESENT GP/REL ADJUST RIGID/FLEX...SOC METH/COMP ANTHOL 19/20 CHINJAP CHRISTIAN. PAGE 144 H2873 LEAD CULTURE ELITES MUNIC

S66
"RESEARCH WORK 1965-1966." NEW/ZEALND ELITES ACADEM LOC/G MUNIC POL/PAR PROVS DIPLOM COLONIAL...SOC 20 AUSTRAL. PAGE 2 H0047 BIBLIOG NAT/G CULTURE S/ASIA

B67
DEGLER C.N.,THE AGE OF THE ECONOMIC REVOLUTION 1876-1900. USA-45 AGRI MUNIC POL/PAR SECT ECO/TAC CHOOSE...PHIL/SCI CHARTS NAT/COMP 19 NEGRO. PAGE 39 H0782 INDUS SOCIETY ECO/DEV TEC/DEV

B67
EVANS R.H.,COEXISTENCE: COMMUNISM AND ITS PRACTICE IN BOLOGNA, 1945-1965. ITALY CAP/ISM ADMIN CHOOSE PEACE ORD/FREE...SOC STAT DEEP/INT SAMP CHARTS BIBLIOG 20. PAGE 48 H0952 MARXISM CULTURE MUNIC POL/PAR

B67
HODGKINSON R.G.,THE ORIGINS OF THE NATIONAL HEALTH SERVICE: THE MEDICAL SERVICES OF THE NEW POOR LAW, 1834-1871. UK INDUS MUNIC WORKER PROB/SOLV EFFICIENCY ATTIT HEALTH WEALTH SOCISM...JURID SOC/WK 19/20. PAGE 72 H1445 HEAL NAT/G POLICY LAW

B67
KING M.L. JR.,WHERE DO WE GO FROM HERE: CHAOS OR COMMUNITY? MUNIC NAT/G PARTIC INGP/REL ALL/VALS ...POLICY CONCPT BIOG 20. PAGE 86 H1715 RACE/REL DISCRIM STRUCT PWR

B67
NASH M.,MACHINE AGE MAYA. GUATEMALA L/A+17C STRUCT AGRI WORKER CREATE INCOME ATTIT RIGID/FLEX ROLE ...IDEA/COMP SOC/EXP WORSHIP 20 INDIAN/AM. PAGE 116 H2315 INDUS CULTURE SOC MUNIC

L67
CRIBBET J.E.,"SOME REFLECTIONS ON THE LAW OF LAND - A VIEW FROM SCANDINAVIA." DENMARK NETHERLAND NORWAY SWEDEN INDUS MUNIC NEIGH RACE/REL ATTIT HABITAT ...IDEA/COMP 20. PAGE 35 H0701 LAW PLAN CONTROL NAT/G

S67
BEFU H.,"THE POLITICAL RELATION OF THE VILLAGE TO THE STATE." NAT/G DOMIN GOV/REL GP/REL MGT. PAGE 13 H0259 GOV/COMP NAT/LISM KIN MUNIC

S67
COHEN R.,"ANTHROPOLOGY AND POLITICAL SCIENCE: COURTSHIP OR MARRIAGE?" CULTURE STRATA STRUCT MUNIC REGION UTOPIA...NEW/IDEA TREND IDEA/COMP METH/COMP 20. PAGE 31 H0618 SOC INGP/REL AFR

S67
CRITTENDEN J.,"DIMENSIONS OF MODERNIZATION IN THE AMERICAN STATES." USA+45 STRUCT MUNIC PROB/SOLV CONTROL LITERACY HABITAT...CONCPT METH/CNCPT CORREL CONT/OBS CENSUS 20. PAGE 35 H0702 PROVS GOV/COMP STAT ECO/DEV

S67
GRANT C.H.,"RURAL LOCAL GOVERNMENT IN GUYANA AND BRITISH HONDURAS." GUYANA HONDURAS L/A+17C AGRI NAT/G EX/STRUC ACT/RES REGION GOV/REL EFFICIENCY ORD/FREE 20. PAGE 60 H1196 ECO/UNDEV LOC/G ADMIN MUNIC

S67
HEBAL J.J.,"APPROACHES TO REGIONAL AND METROPOLITAN GOVERNMENTS IN THE UNITED STATES AND CANADA." CANADA FUT USA+45 MUNIC...TREND 20. PAGE 69 H1380 ADMIN REGION LOC/G NAT/COMP

S67
LICHFIELD N.,"THE EVALUATION OF CAPITAL INVESTMENT PROJECTS IN TOWN CENTRE REDEVELOPMENT." UK CONSTRUC MUNIC CONSULT COST...METH/CNCPT IDEA/COMP 20. PAGE 96 H1923 PLAN ECO/TAC NAT/G DECISION

S67
MALAN V.D.,"THE SILENT VILLAGE." KIN MUNIC NEIGH CHOOSE ISOLAT ROLE...SOC INDIAN/AM. PAGE 101 H2027 CULTURE STRUCT PREDICT

S67
SALYZYN V.,"FEDERAL-PROVINCIAL TAX SHARING SCHEMES." CANADA LOC/G PROB/SOLV TEC/DEV BUDGET GOV/REL EFFICIENCY 20. PAGE 137 H2746 PROVS TAX MUNIC NAT/G

B91
BENTHAM J.,A FRAGMENT ON GOVERNMENT (1776). CONSTN MUNIC NAT/G SECT AGREE HAPPINESS UTIL MORAL ORD/FREE...JURID CONCPT. PAGE 15 H0292 SOVEREIGN LAW DOMIN

B95
HAMMOND B.E.,THE POLITICAL INSTITUTIONS OF THE ANCIENT GREEKS. GREECE MUNIC PROVS COERCE WAR ORD/FREE ARISTOTLE. PAGE 65 H1307 GOV/COMP NAT/G IDEA/COMP

CONCPT

B96
SCHMOLLER G.,THE MERCANTILE SYSTEM AND ITS HISTORICAL SIGNIFICANCE: ILLUSTRATED CHIEFLY FROM PRUSSIAN HISTORY (TRANS.). PRUSSIA CULTURE INDUS KIN MUNIC NAT/G PROVS OP/RES ECO/TAC INT/TRADE SUPEGO PWR WEALTH 19 MERCANTLST. PAGE 139 H2790 GEN/METH INGP/REL CONCPT

MUNICH....MUNICH, GERMANY

MUNICIPALITIES....SEE MUNIC

MUNZENBERG W. H2290

MURACCIOLE L. H2291,H2292

MURDER....MURDER, ASSASSINATION; SEE ALSO CRIME

B06
SUMNER W.G.,FOLKWAYS: STUDY OF THE SOCIOLOGICAL IMPORTANCE OF USAGES, MANNERS, CUSTOMS, MORES, AND MORALS. STRUCT KIN ETIQUET ROUTINE MURDER MARRIAGE PEACE SEX ALL/VALS WEALTH BIBLIOG. PAGE 150 H3008 CULTURE SOC SANCTION MORAL

N17
BURKE E.,THOUGHTS ON THE PROSPECT OF A REGICIDE PEACE (PAMPHLET). FRANCE UK SECT DOMIN MURDER PEACE ORD/FREE SOVEREIGN POPULISM...POLICY GOV/COMP IDEA/COMP 18 JACOBINISM COEXIST. PAGE 24 H0483 REV CHIEF NAT/G DIPLOM

B37
CARLYLE T.,THE FRENCH REVOLUTION (2 VOLS.). FRANCE CONSTN NAT/G FORCES COERCE MURDER PEACE MORAL POPULISM...TIME/SEQ IDEA/COMP GEN/LAWS 18. PAGE 26 H0532 REV CHIEF TRADIT

B57
BUNDESMIN FUR VERTRIEBENE,DIE VERTREIBUNG DER DEUTSCHEN BEVOLKERUNG AUS DER TSCHECHOSLOWAKEI. CZECHOSLVK GERMANY NAT/G FORCES MURDER WAR INGP/REL ATTIT 20 MIGRATION. PAGE 24 H0474 GP/REL DOMIN COERCE DISCRIM

B63
HARDY M.J.L.,BLOOD FEUDS AND THE PAYMENT OF BLOOD MONEY IN THE MIDDLE EAST. ISLAM SOCIETY SECT REGION SANCTION COERCE DEATH MURDER 7/20 ARABS. PAGE 66 H1329 KIN TRIBUTE LAW CULTURE

MURDOCK G.P. H2293,H2294

MURET C.T. H2295

MURNGIN....MURNGIN, AN AUSTRALIAN TRIBE

B58
WARNER W.L.,A BLACK CIVILIZATION - A SOCIAL STUDY OF AN AUSTRALIAN TRIBE. SOCIETY FAM MARRIAGE...PSY SOC MYTH CHARTS 20 AUSTRAL MAPS MURNGIN RITUAL. PAGE 165 H3310 CULTURE KIN STRUCT DEATH

MUROMCEW C. H3324

MURPHEY R. H2296

MURPHY G. H2297

MURPHY J.C. H2298

MURRAY/JC....JOHN COURTNEY MURRAY

MURVAR V. H2299

MUSCAT....MUSCAT AND OMAN; SEE ALSO ISLAM

MUSEUM FUR VOLKERKUNDE WIEN H2300

MUSIC....MUSIC AND SONGS

B49
ROGERS C.B.,THE SPIRIT OF REVOLUTION IN 1789: A STUDY OF PUBLIC OPINION ...AT THE BEGINNING OF THE FRENCH REVOLUTION. FRANCE CULTURE ELITES EDU/PROP COERCE CROWD...BIBLIOG 18 MUSIC. PAGE 133 H2658 ATTIT POPULISM REV CREATE

B64
GRIFFITH W.,THE WELSH (2ND ED.). UK SOCIETY STRUCT SECT WRITING NAT/LISM...ART/METH MODAL OBS/ENVIR TREND SOC/INTEG WALES PURITAN MUSIC. PAGE 61 H1223 CULTURE SOC LING

B65
BERNDT R.M.,ABORIGINAL MAN IN AUSTRALIA. LAW DOMIN ADMIN COLONIAL MARRIAGE HABITAT ORD/FREE...LING CHARTS ANTHOL BIBLIOG WORSHIP 20 AUSTRAL ABORIGINES MUSIC ELKIN/AP. PAGE 16 H0312 SOC CULTURE SOCIETY STRUCT

MUSLIM....MUSLIM PEOPLE AND RELIGION

B52
JULIEN C.A.,L'AFRIQUE DU NORD EN MARCHE: NATIONALISMES MUSULMANS ET SOUVERAINETE FRANCAISE (2ND ED). AFR ALGERIA FRANCE ISLAM MOROCCO NAT/G CONTROL ORD/FREE...POLICY 19/20 TUNIS MUSLIM. NAT/LISM COERCE DOMIN COLONIAL

PAGE 82 H1641

B57
SHEIKH N.A.,SOME ASPECTS OF THE CONSTITUTION AND THE ECONOMICS OF ISLAM. PAKISTAN CULTURE AGRI FINAN LABOR NAT/G SECT INT/TRADE 20 MUSLIM. PAGE 143 H2855
ISLAM POLICY ECO/TAC CONSTN

B59
GOPAL R.,INDIAN MUSLIMS: A POLITICAL HISTORY (1858-1947). INDIA ISLAM PAKISTAN NAT/G SECT LEGIS LEAD COERCE WAR REPRESENT ISOLAT ORD/FREE 19/20 HINDU MUSLIM. PAGE 59 H1175
COLONIAL GP/REL POL/PAR REGION

B60
AUSTRUY J.,STRUCTURE ECONOMIQUE ET CIVILISATION: L'EGYPTE ET LE DESTIN ECONOMIQUE DE L'ISLAM. ISLAM UAR CREATE OP/RES ECO/TAC...SOC BIBLIOG 20 MUSLIM. PAGE 9 H0182
ECO/UNDEV CULTURE STRUCT

L60
WHEELER G.,"RACIAL PROBLEMS IN SOVIET MUSLIM ASIA." COM CULTURE SOCIETY NEIGH SECT DOMIN EDU/PROP DISCRIM DISPL DRIVE PWR SOVEREIGN...CENSUS SAMP TREND 20 MUSLIM. PAGE 167 H3340
PERSON ATTIT USSR RACE/REL

B61
KHALIQUZZAMAN C.,PATHWAY TO PAKISTAN. INDIA PAKISTAN UK SECT LEGIS CHOOSE RACE/REL ATTIT ORD/FREE 20 MUSLIM. PAGE 85 H1705
GP/REL NAT/G COLONIAL SOVEREIGN

B64
VON GRUNEBAUM G.E.,MODERN ISLAM: THE SEARCH FOR CULTURAL IDENTITY. ACADEM NEIGH WRITING NAT/LISM ...HUM CONCPT 19/20 MUSLIM MID/EAST ARABS. PAGE 163 H3269
ISLAM CULTURE CREATE SECT

B65
LARUS J.,COMPARATIVE WORLD POLITICS. ASIA INDIA WOR+45 WOR-45 BAL/PWR WAR PEACE RATIONAL MORAL PWR ...REALPOL INT/LAW MUSLIM. PAGE 91 H1825
GOV/COMP IDEA/COMP DIPLOM NAT/COMP

B65
QURESHI I.H.,THE STRUGGLE FOR PAKISTAN. INDIA PAKISTAN UK CULTURE LEGIS DIPLOM EDU/PROP COLONIAL ATTIT SOVEREIGN 19/20 MUSLIM. PAGE 129 H2576
GP/REL RACE/REL WAR SECT

B66
BROWN L.C.,STATE AND SOCIETY IN INDEPENDENT NORTH AFRICA. ALGERIA LIBYA MOROCCO AGRI INDUS INT/ORG POL/PAR SECT PLAN DIPLOM COLONIAL...LING NAT/COMP ANTHOL BIBLIOG 20 TUNIS MUSLIM. PAGE 22 H0446
NAT/G SOCIETY CULTURE ECO/UNDEV

B66
RIZK C.,LE REGIME POLITIQUE LIBANAIS. ISLAM LEBANON STRUCT POL/PAR SECT LOBBY GP/REL 20 ARABS MUSLIM CHRISTIAN. PAGE 132 H2637
ECO/UNDEV NAT/G CULTURE

MUSLIM/LG....MUSLIM LEAGUE

MUSSO AMBROSI L.A. H2301

MUSSOLIN/B....BENITO MUSSOLINI

B37
BORGESE G.A.,GOLIATH: THE MARCH OF FASCISM. GERMANY ITALY LAW POL/PAR SECT DIPLOM SOCISM...JURID MYTH 20 DANTE MACHIAVELL MUSSOLIN/B. PAGE 19 H0375
POLICY NAT/LISM FASCISM NAT/G

B38
FIELD G.L.,THE SYNDICAL AND CORPORATIVE INSTITUTIONS OF ITALIAN FASCISM. ITALY CONSTN STRATA LABOR EX/STRUC TOP/EX ADJUD ADMIN LEAD TOTALISM AUTHORIT...MGT 20 MUSSOLIN/B. PAGE 50 H0991
FASCISM INDUS NAT/G WORKER

B54
SALVEMINI G.,PRELUDE TO WORLD WAR II. ITALY MOD/EUR INT/ORG BAL/PWR EDU/PROP CONTROL TOTALISM...TREND NAT/COMP BIBLIOG 19 HITLER/A LEAGUE/NAT MUSSOLIN/B. PAGE 137 H2745
WAR FASCISM LEAD PWR

B55
ALFIERI D.,DICTATORS FACE TO FACE. NAT/G TOP/EX DIPLOM EXEC COERCE ORD/FREE FASCISM...POLICY OBS 20 HITLER/A MUSSOLIN/B. PAGE 5 H0103
WAR CHIEF TOTALISM PERS/REL

B64
HALPERIN S.W.,MUSSOLINI AND ITALIAN FASCISM. ITALY NAT/G POL/PAR SECT ECO/TAC LEAD PWR SOCISM...POLICY 20 MUSSOLIN/B. PAGE 64 H1294
FASCISM NAT/LISM EDU/PROP CHIEF

B66
NOLTE E.,THREE FACES OF FASCISM. FRANCE GERMANY DOMIN LEGIT COERCE CROWD REV WAR GP/REL RACE/REL SOVEREIGN...GOV/COMP IDEA/COMP 19/20 HITLER/A MUSSOLIN/B MARX/KARL. PAGE 118 H2368
FASCISM TOTALISM NAT/G POL/PAR

MYERS C.A. H1325,H1326

MYERS F.M. H2302

MYRDAL/G....GUNNAR MYRDAL

MYSTIC....MYSTICAL

N19
BARRES M.,"THE WAR AND THE SPIRIT OF YOUTH" (PAMPHLET). FRANCE FORCES DOMIN LEAD DEATH AGE/Y ATTIT RESPECT...FASCIST 20 WWI. PAGE 11 H0228
WAR NAT/LISM CULTURE MYSTIC

B40
THE GUIDE TO CATHOLIC LITERATURE, 1888-1940. ALL/VALS...POLICY MYSTIC HUM PHIL/SCI 19/20. PAGE 2 H0032
BIBLIOG/A CATHISM DIPLOM CULTURE

B60
SHIRER W.L.,THE RISE AND FALL OF THE THIRD REICH: A HISTORY OF NAZI GERMANY. EUR+WWI CULTURE ECO/DEV INDUS NAT/G POL/PAR FORCES PLAN TEC/DEV ECO/TAC COERCE ATTIT DRIVE PERSON PWR...MYSTIC PSY SOC MYTH STAT CHARTS EXHIBIT WORK VAL/FREE. PAGE 143 H2864
STRUCT GERMANY TOTALISM

MYSTICISM....SEE MYSTISM

MYSTISM....MYSTICISM

B26
MALINOWSKI B.,CRIME AND CUSTOM IN SAVAGE SOCIETY. SOCIETY FAM SECT LEGIT SANCTION MARRIAGE MYSTISM ...PSY SOC 19/20 MELANESIA CANON/LAW. PAGE 102 H2030
LAW CULTURE CRIME ADJUD

B48
EDUARDO O.D.C.,THE NEGRO IN NORTHERN BRAZIL: A STUDY IN ACCULTURATION. BRAZIL ECO/UNDEV FAM SECT PAY REGION HABITAT CATHISM MYSTISM...GEOG OBS SOC/INTEG WORSHIP 20 NEGRO MARANHAO. PAGE 44 H0890
CULTURE ADJUST GP/REL

B66
KIRKLAND E.C.,A BIBLIOGRAPHY OF SOUTH ASIAN FOLKLORE. WRITING HABITAT ALL/VALS MYSTISM ...ART/METH GEOG PSY SOC MYTH WORSHIP 13/20. PAGE 86 H1723
BIBLIOG S/ASIA CULTURE CREATE

MYTH....FICTION

N19
BRIMMELL G.H.,COMMUNISM IN SOUTHEAST ASIA (PAMPHLET). BURMA CAMBODIA COM INDIA INDONESIA LAOS MOD/EUR NAT/G POL/PAR FORCES CAP/ISM CONTROL WEALTH ...MYTH 20. PAGE 21 H0420
MARXISM S/ASIA REV ECO/UNDEV

S21
MALINOWSKI B.,"THE PRIMITIVE ECONOMICS OF THE TROBRIAND ISLANDERS" (BMR)" CULTURE SOCIETY NAT/G CHIEF LEAD OWN...SOC MYTH WORSHIP 20 NEW/GUINEA TROBRIAND RESOURCE/N. PAGE 101 H2029
ECO/UNDEV AGRI PRODUC STRUCT

B27
HOCART A.M.,KINGSHIP. UNIV CULTURE EX/STRUC TRIBUTE ROUTINE CHOOSE ROLE SOVEREIGN RITUAL 20 KING. PAGE 72 H1441
CHIEF MYTH IDEA/COMP

B35
GORER G.,AFRICA DANCES: A BOOK ABOUT WEST AFRICAN NEGROES. STRUCT LOC/G SECT FORCES TAX ADMIN COLONIAL...ART/METH MYTH WORSHIP 20 NEGRO AFRICA/W CHRISTIAN RITUAL. PAGE 59 H1181
AFR ATTIT CULTURE SOCIETY

B37
BORGESE G.A.,GOLIATH: THE MARCH OF FASCISM. GERMANY ITALY LAW POL/PAR SECT DIPLOM SOCISM...JURID MYTH 20 DANTE MACHIAVELL MUSSOLIN/B. PAGE 19 H0375
POLICY NAT/LISM FASCISM NAT/G

B38
RAWLINSON H.G.,INDIA: A SHORT CULTURAL HISTORY. INDIA LAW STRATA FORCES INT/TRADE ADMIN COLONIAL PERSON...GEOG HUM BIBLIOG WORSHIP 20. PAGE 130 H2598
CULTURE SECT MYTH ART/METH

B39
BARNES H.E.,SOCIETY IN TRANSITION: PROBLEMS OF A CHANGING ERA. USA-45 INDUS MUNIC PUB/INST EDU/PROP CRIME RACE/REL...SOC MYTH NAT/COMP. PAGE 11 H0220
SOCIETY CULTURE TECHRACY TEC/DEV

B44
CASSIRER E.,AN ESSAY ON MAN: AN INTRODUCTION TO A PHILOSOPHY OF HUMAN CULTURE. UNIV SECT CREATE EDU/PROP ATTIT KNOWL...HUM CONCPT MYTH TOT/POP. PAGE 28 H0556
CULTURE SOC

B46
CASSIRER E.,THE MYTH OF THE STATE. WOR-45 SOCIETY RACE/REL RATIONAL PWR FASCISM...PHIL/SCI PSY LING TREND HEGEL/GWF MACHIAVELL. PAGE 28 H0557
MYTH CONCPT NAT/G IDEA/COMP

B47
GITLOW A.L.,ECONOMICS OF THE MOUNT HAGEN TRIBES, NEW GUINEA. S/ASIA STRUCT AGRI FAM...GEOG MYTH 20 NEW/GUINEA. PAGE 57 H1137
HABITAT ECO/UNDEV CULTURE KIN

B49
SAUVY A.,LE POUVOIR ET L'OPINION. FRANCE STRATA NAT/G PERCEPT...POLICY PSY 20. PAGE 138 H2758
EDU/PROP MYTH PARTIC ATTIT

B50
EMBREE J.F.,BIBLIOGRAPHY OF THE PEOPLES AND CULTURES OF MAINLAND SOUTHEAST ASIA. CAMBODIA LAOS
BIBLIOG/A CULTURE

THAILAND VIETNAM LAW...GEOG HUM SOC MYTH LING S/ASIA
CHARTS WORSHIP 20. PAGE 46 H0915

B50
SMITH E.W.,AFRICAN IDEAS OF GOD. ATTIT...CONCPT SOC
MYTH IDEA/COMP ANTHOL BIBLIOG. PAGE 145 H2908 AFR
CULTURE
SECT

B52
MONTAGU A.,MAN'S MOST DANGEROUS MYTH: THE FALLACY DISCRIM
OF RACE. LAW PROB/SOLV WAR HABITAT POPULISM...PSY MYTH
CONCPT CHARTS BIBLIOG NEGRO JEWS. PAGE 112 H2242 CULTURE
RACE/REL

B53
BIDNEY D.,THEORETICAL ANTHROPOLOGY. DRIVE ROLE CULTURE
ORD/FREE...CONCPT METH/CNCPT MYTH CLASSIF OBS SOC
IDEA/COMP METH/COMP BIBLIOG METH 20. PAGE 17 H0331 PSY
PHIL/SCI

B54
MALINOWSKI B.,MAGIC, SCIENCE AND RELIGION. AGRI KIN CULTURE
GP/REL ALL/VALS...MYTH OBS RECORD IDEA/COMP WORSHIP ATTIT
20 NEW/GUINEA. PAGE 102 H2031 SOC

B54
PARRINDER G.,AFRICAN TRADITIONAL RELIGION. AFR SECT
SOCIETY EDU/PROP GP/REL PWR...SOC CONCPT IDEA/COMP MYTH
WORSHIP 20 DEITY. PAGE 124 H2469 ATTIT
CULTURE

B55
SHAFER B.C.,NATIONALISM: MYTH AND REALITY. FRANCE NAT/LISM
UK USA+45 USA-45 CULTURE SOCIETY STRUCT ECO/DEV WAR MYTH
PWR...NAT/COMP BIBLIOG 18/20. PAGE 142 H2837 NAT/G
CONCPT

B55
VERGNAUD P.,L'IDEE DE LA NATIONALITE ET DE LA LIBRE NAT/LISM
DISPOSITION DES PEUPLES DANS SES RAPPORTS AVEC DISCRIM
L'IDEE DE L'ETAT. STRATA NAT/G EDU/PROP RACE/REL ORD/FREE
AUTHORIT FASCISM MARXISM MYTH. PAGE 162 H3243

B56
DE JONG L.,THE GERMAN FIFTH COLUMN IN THE SECOND EDU/PROP
WORLD WAR. EUR+WWI GERMANY NAT/G DIPLOM ATTIT WAR
FASCISM...MYTH 20 NAZI. PAGE 38 H0756 RUMOR

B56
MANNONI D.O.,PROSPERO AND CALIBAN: THE PSYCHOLOGY CULTURE
OF COLONIZATION. AFR EUR+WWI FAM KIN MUNIC SECT COLONIAL
DOMIN ADMIN ATTIT DRIVE LOVE PWR RESPECT...PSY SOC
CONCPT MYTH OBS DEEP/INT BIOG GEN/METH MALAGASY 20.
PAGE 102 H2040

B56
MUMFORD L.,THE TRANSFORMATIONS OF MAN. UNIV CULTURE IDEA/COMP
INGP/REL HABITAT HEREDITY ALL/VALS ORD/FREE...MYTH PERSON
TIME/SEQ TREND WORSHIP. PAGE 114 H2287 CONCPT

B57
ARON R.,THE OPIUM OF THE INTELLECTUALS (TRANS. BY INTELL
TERENCE KILMARTIN). FRANCE USSR WOR+45 CULTURE UTOPIA
POL/PAR PLAN DOMIN EDU/PROP REV ATTIT ORD/FREE MYTH
...IDEA/COMP METH/COMP NAT/COMP 20 COM/PARTY. MARXISM
PAGE 8 H0169

B57
KANTOROWICZ E.,THE KING'S TWO BODIES; A STUDY IN JURID
MEDIEVAL POLITICAL THEOLOGY. UK LAW CONSTN NAT/G SECT
CT/SYS...ART/METH HUM CONCPT MYTH TIME/SEQ BIBLIOG CHIEF
4/17 ELIZABTH/I POPE CHURCH/STA. PAGE 83 H1657 SOVEREIGN

S57
SPROUT H.,"ENVIRONMENTAL FACTORS IN THE STUDY OF DECISION
INTERNATIONAL POLITICS." UNIV SOCIETY ECO/DEV NAT/G GEN/LAWS
DELIB/GP TOP/EX ROUTINE ATTIT PERCEPT...POLICY GEOG DIPLOM
CONCPT MYTH TIME/SEQ. PAGE 148 H2957

B58
DUNAYEVSKAYA R.,MARXISM AND FREEDOM: FROM 1776 MARXISM
UNTIL TODAY. COM USSR WORKER CAP/ISM DOMIN REV CONCPT
GP/REL TOTALISM ALL/VALS...MYTH BIOG IDEA/COMP ORD/FREE
18/20 MARX/KARL LENIN/VI STALIN/J. PAGE 43 H0861

B58
EMMET D.M.,FUNCTION, PURPOSE AND POWERS. SECT ATTIT SOC
MORAL PWR...CONCPT MYTH. PAGE 46 H0923 CULTURE
ALL/VALS
GEN/LAWS

B58
LERNER D.,THE PASSING OF TRADITIONAL SOCIETY: ECO/UNDEV
MODERNIZING THE MIDDLE EAST. IRAN ISLAM LEBANON RIGID/FLEX
SYRIA TURKEY UAR CULTURE INTELL STRATA KIN NAT/G
NEIGH SECT EDU/PROP ATTIT PERSON...MYTH OBS 20.
PAGE 95 H1888

B58
WARNER W.L.,A BLACK CIVILIZATION - A SOCIAL STUDY CULTURE
OF AN AUSTRALIAN TRIBE. SOCIETY FAM MARRIAGE...PSY KIN
SOC MYTH CHARTS 20 AUSTRAL MAPS MURNGIN RITUAL. STRUCT
PAGE 165 H3310 DEATH

B59
PAGE S.W.,LENIN AND WORLD REVOLUTION. COM USSR REV
NAT/G DOMIN COERCE CROWD UTOPIA ATTIT AUTHORIT PERSON
DRIVE PWR...CONCPT MYTH 19/20 LENIN/VI MARX/KARL. MARXISM
PAGE 122 H2441 BIOG

B59
WARNER W.L.,THE LIVING AND THE DEAD: A STUDY OF CULTURE
SYMBOLIC LIFE OF AMERICANS. INTELL KIN DEATH SOC
ALL/VALS ALL/IDEOS...CONCPT MYTH LING OBS/ENVIR TIME/SEQ
CHARTS BIBLIOG WORSHIP 18/20. PAGE 165 H3311 IDEA/COMP

B60
BRIGGS L.C.,TRIBES OF THE SAHARA. AFR MOROCCO CULTURE
STRATA AGRI GP/REL HEALTH...GEOG SOC MYTH LING HABITAT
BIBLIOG 13/20 ARABS. PAGE 21 H0418 KIN
SELF/OBS

B60
BRZEZINSKI Z.K.,THE SOVIET BLOC-UNITY AND CONFLICT. ATTIT
COM USSR CONSTN DOMIN ADMIN TOTALISM PWR...SOC MYTH EDU/PROP
RECORD TREND STERTYP GEN/LAWS GEN/METH TOT/POP 20.
PAGE 23 H0458

B60
BURRIDGE K.,MAMBU: A MELANESIAN MILLENNIUM. S/ASIA
ECO/UNDEV PROC/MFG FAM KIN CHIEF COLONIAL COERCE SECT
GP/REL DRIVE WEALTH WORSHIP 20 NEW/GUINEA. PAGE 25 CULTURE
H0494 MYTH

B60
KOHN H.,PAN-SLAVISM: ITS HISTORY AND IDEOLOGY. COM ATTIT
CZECHOSLVK EUR+WWI MOD/EUR USSR YUGOSLAVIA CULTURE CONCPT
ELITES INTELL KIN NAT/G EDU/PROP DRIVE SOVEREIGN NAT/LISM
...HUM PHIL/SCI MYTH HIST/WRIT 19/20. PAGE 87 H1745

B60
MCCLOSKY H.,THE SOVIET DICTATORSHIP. FUT CONSTN COM
CULTURE INTELL SOCIETY POL/PAR SECT VOL/ASSN FORCES NAT/G
PLAN TEC/DEV DOMIN EDU/PROP COERCE PWR MARXISM TOTALISM
...POLICY CONCPT MYTH STERTYP 20. PAGE 106 H2127 USSR

B60
SAHLINS M.D.,EVOLUTION AND CULTURE. CREATE...MYTH CULTURE
METH/COMP BIBLIOG 20. PAGE 137 H2730 NEW/IDEA
CONCPT
HABITAT

B60
SCHAPIRO L.,THE COMMUNIST PARTY OF THE SOVIET INTELL
UNION. COM LAW SOCIETY STRATA STRUCT ECO/DEV LABOR PWR
NAT/G POL/PAR CREATE DOMIN EDU/PROP COERCE TOTALISM USSR
MARXISM...POLICY CONCPT MYTH TIME/SEQ WORK TOT/POP
20 LENIN/VI STALIN/J. PAGE 139 H2772

B60
SHIRER W.L.,THE RISE AND FALL OF THE THIRD REICH: A STRUCT
HISTORY OF NAZI GERMANY. EUR+WWI CULTURE ECO/DEV GERMANY
INDUS NAT/G POL/PAR FORCES PLAN TEC/DEV ECO/TAC TOTALISM
COERCE ATTIT DRIVE PERSON PWR...MYSTIC PSY SOC MYTH
STAT CHARTS EXHIBIT WORK VAL/FREE. PAGE 143 H2864

S60
NORTH R.C.,"DIE DISKREPANZ ZWISCHEN REALITAT UND SOCIETY
WUNSCHBILD ALS INNENPOLITISCHER FAKTOR." ASIA ECO/TAC
CHINA/COM COM FUT ECO/UNDEV NAT/G PLAN DOMIN ADMIN
COERCE PERCEPT...SOC MYTH GEN/METH WORK TOT/POP 20.
PAGE 119 H2373

S60
NORTHEDGE F.S.,"BRITISH FOREIGN POLICY AND THE POL/PAR
PARTY SYSTEM." EUR+WWI FUT INT/ORG NAT/G EDU/PROP CHOOSE
ATTIT PWR...POLICY CONCPT MYTH TIME/SEQ TREND 20 DIPLOM
UN. PAGE 119 H2374 UK

B61
CASSINELLI C.W.,THE POLITICS OF FREEDOM. FUT UNIV MAJORIT
LAW POL/PAR CHOOSE ORD/FREE...POLICY CONCPT MYTH NAT/G
BIBLIOG. PAGE 28 H0555 PARL/PROC
PARTIC

B61
FIRTH R.,HISTORY AND TRADITIONS OF TIKOPIA. S/ASIA CULTURE
KIN SECT RUMOR WAR...MYTH WORSHIP 20 POLYNESIA. STRUCT
PAGE 50 H1008 HUM

L61
EZELLPH,"THE HISPANIC AGRICULTURATION OF THE GILA CULTURE
RIVER PIMAS." FAM TEC/DEV PERS/REL ADJUST...GEOG SOC
MYTH CHARTS BIBLIOG WORSHIP 17/20. PAGE 48 H0956 AGRI
DRIVE

B62
BERNOT R.M.,EXCESS AND RESTRAINT: SOCIAL CONTROL SOCIETY
AMONG GUINEA MOUNTAIN PEOPLE. CULTURE FAM KIN CONTROL
CT/SYS COERCE WAR PERS/REL MARRIAGE HABITAT SEX STRUCT
...MYTH 20 NEW/GUINEA. PAGE 16 H0314 ADJUST

B62
CHAKRAVARTI P.C.,INDIA'S CHINA POLICY. ASIA RIGID/FLEX
CHINA/COM S/ASIA CULTURE NAT/G TOP/EX ACT/RES TREND
EDU/PROP DRIVE ALL/VALS...MYTH 20. PAGE 28 H0571 INDIA

B62
KOSAMBI D.D.,MYTH AND REALITY. INDIA AGRI KIN SECT CULTURE
HABITAT...SOC 20. PAGE 88 H1758 SOCIETY
MYTH
ATTIT

B62
MALINOWSKI B.,SEX, CULTURE, AND MYTH. UNIV SOCIETY MYTH
FAM PERS/REL MARRIAGE RATIONAL HABITAT PERSON SECT
SUPEGO MORAL WORSHIP 20. PAGE 102 H2032 SEX
CULTURE

B62
MEGGITT M.J.,DESERT PEOPLE. ECO/UNDEV KIN CREATE ADJUST
PROB/SOLV CONTROL DRIVE ROLE...GEOG SOC MYTH CHARTS CULTURE
BIBLIOG 20 AUSTRAL. PAGE 108 H2159 INGP/REL
HABITAT

B62
RUDY Z.,ETHNOSOZIOLOGIE SOWJETISCHER VOLKER. USSR MYTH
SOCIETY STRUCT FAM SECT GP/REL ATTIT...SOC CULTURE
SOC/INTEG 20. PAGE 136 H2714 KIN

L62
NOLTE E.,"ZUR PHANOMENOLOGIE DES FASCHIMUS." ATTIT
EUR+WWI GERMANY ITALY TURKEY INTELL NAT/G CHIEF PWR
CONSULT FORCES CREATE DOMIN EDU/PROP COERCE WAR
CHOOSE DRIVE FASCISM...PSY CONCPT MYTH GEN/METH
LEAGUE/NAT NAZI 20. PAGE 118 H2367

S62
STRACHEY J.,"COMMUNIST INTENTIONS." ASIA USSR COM
YUGOSLAVIA INT/ORG NAT/G FORCES DOMIN EDU/PROP ATTIT
COERCE NUC/PWR NAT/LISM PEACE RIGID/FLEX PWR WAR
MARXISM...CONCPT MYTH OBS TIME/SEQ TREND COLD/WAR
TOT/POP 20. PAGE 150 H2992

B63
FARMER B.H.,CEYLON: A DIVIDED NATION. CEYLON INDIA DOMIN
NETHERLAND PORTUGAL UK ELITES POL/PAR COLONIAL ORD/FREE
...SOC MYTH CHARTS GOV/COMP WORSHIP 20. PAGE 49 ECO/UNDEV
H0972 POLICY

B63
REYNOLDS B.,MAGIC, DIVINATION AND WITCHCRAFT AMONG AFR
THE BAROTSE OF NORTHERN RHODESIA. RHODESIA CULTURE SOC
KIN CREATE LEGIT PARTIC DEATH DREAM STRANGE HABITAT MYTH
PERSON...AUD/VIS WORSHIP 20. PAGE 131 H2619 SECT

B63
TINDALE N.B.,ABORIGINAL AUSTRALIANS. KIN CREATE CULTURE
ROLE...SOC MYTH TREND 20 AUSTRAL ABORIGINES DRIVE
MIGRATION. PAGE 155 H3099 ECO/UNDEV
HABITAT

B63
TOUVAL S.,SOMALI NATIONALISM: INTERNATIONAL SOCIETY
POLITICS AND THE DRIVE FOR UNITY IN THE HORN OF EXEC
AFRICA. AFR CULTURE PROVS LEGIS EDU/PROP REGION NAT/LISM
COERCE ATTIT...MYTH UNPLAN/INT TIME/SEQ SOMALI
VAL/FREE 20. PAGE 156 H3118

B63
TUCKER R.C.,THE SOVIET POLITICAL MIND. COM INTELL STRUCT
NAT/G TOP/EX EDU/PROP ADMIN COERCE TOTALISM ATTIT RIGID/FLEX
PWR MARXISM...PSY MYTH HYPO/EXP 20. PAGE 157 H3136 ELITES
USSR

S63
STAAR R.F.,"HOW STRONG IS THE SOVIET BLOC." COM FORCES
USSR ECO/DEV NAT/G DELIB/GP ECO/TAC RIGID/FLEX MYTH
...CONCPT RECORD CHARTS 20. PAGE 148 H2964 TOTALISM

S63
TANG P.S.H.,"SINO-SOVIET TENSIONS." ASIA CHINA/COM ACT/RES
COM CUBA KOREA/N VIETNAM/N NAT/G VOL/ASSN DELIB/GP EDU/PROP
PEACE PERCEPT PWR...METH/CNCPT MYTH RECORD TREND REV
GEN/LAWS 20. PAGE 152 H3041

B64
BERNDT R.M.,THE WORLD OF THE FIRST AUSTRALIANS. CULTURE
S/ASIA ECO/UNDEV WORKER PROB/SOLV EFFICIENCY ROLE KIN
...SOC MYTH WORSHIP AUSTRAL ABORIGINES. PAGE 16 STRUCT
H0311 DRIVE

B64
BINDER L.,THE IDEOLOGICAL REVOLUTION IN THE MIDDLE POL/PAR
EAST. ISLAM STRUCT INT/ORG KIN SECT EX/STRUC TOP/EX NAT/G
PLAN ATTIT DRIVE RIGID/FLEX PWR...MYTH TOT/POP 20. NAT/LISM
PAGE 17 H0338

B64
BRZEZINSKI Z.,POLITICAL POWER: USA/USSR. USA+45 NAT/G
USSR AGRI POL/PAR FORCES CREATE CHOOSE ATTIT NAT/COMP
ORD/FREE PWR MARXISM...MYTH 20 KENNEDY/JF. PAGE 23 POLICY
H0457 LEAD

B64
ELKIN A.P.,THE AUSTRALIAN ABORIGINES - HOW TO CULTURE
UNDERSTAND THEM (4TH ED.). FAM NEIGH DEATH MARRIAGE STRUCT
ATTIT BIO/SOC HABITAT...PSY SOC MYTH WORSHIP SOCIETY
AUSTRAL ABORIGINES. PAGE 45 H0908 KIN

B64
JARVIE I.C.,THE REVOLUTION IN ANTHROPOLOGY. UNIV SOC
CULTURE SOCIETY SECT...MYTH 20 POPPER/K. PAGE 80 TREND
H1592 PHIL/SCI
METH

B64
KAUFMANN R.,MILLENARISME ET ACCULTURATION. SOCIETY AFR
DOMIN COLONIAL NAT/LISM ATTIT...SOC BIBLIOG 20 SECT
JEHOVA/WIT SEVENTHDAY. PAGE 84 H1669 MYTH
CULTURE

B64
KIDD K.E.,BRIEF BIBLIOGRAPHY OF ONTARIO BIBLIOG
ANTHROPOLOGY (PAMPHLET). CANADA PREHIST HABITAT SOC
...MYTH WORSHIP. PAGE 86 H1708 LING
CULTURE

B64
LAWRENCE P.,ROAD BELONG CARGO: A STUDY OF CARGO SOC
MOVEMENT IN SOUTHERN MADANG DISTRICT, NEW GUINEA. SECT
S/ASIA CULTURE ECO/UNDEV PROC/MFG KIN CHIEF ALL/VALS
COLONIAL COERCE GP/REL DRIVE WEALTH WORSHIP 20 MYTH
NEW/GUINEA. PAGE 92 H1846

B64
SKINNER E.P.,THE MOSSI OF UPPER VOLTA: THE CULTURE
POLITICAL DEVELOPMENT OF A SUDANESE PEOPLE. AFR LAW OBS
AGRI FAM KIN POL/PAR PROVS SECT DELIB/GP EX/STRUC UPPER/VOLT
FORCES TOP/EX DOMIN EDU/PROP LEGIT CT/SYS COERCE
CHOOSE ORD/FREE PWR WEALTH...SOC MYTH VAL/FREE.
PAGE 145 H2897

B64
TAYLOR E.,RICHER BY ASIA. S/ASIA CULTURE VOL/ASSN SOCIETY
ACT/RES ATTIT DISPL PERSON ALL/VALS...INT/LAW MYTH RIGID/FLEX
SELF/OBS 20. PAGE 153 H3054 INDIA

B64
TINKER H.,BALLOT BOX AND BAYONET - PEOPLE AND MYTH
GOVERNMENT IN EMERGENT ASIAN COUNTRIES. CEYLON S/ASIA
INDIA INDONESIA PHILIPPINE POL/PAR ADMIN COLONIAL NAT/COMP
LEAD PARL/PROC CHOOSE CONSEN ORD/FREE SOVEREIGN NAT/LISM
PLURISM...GOV/COMP THIRD/WRLD. PAGE 155 H3104

S64
ADAMS R.,"POLITICS AND SOCIAL ANTHROPOLOGY IN L/A+17C
SPANISH AMERICA." FUT CULTURE SOCIETY NAT/G SOC
PROF/ORG EDU/PROP ATTIT RIGID/FLEX ALL/VALS
...POLICY GEOG METH/CNCPT MYTH TREND VAL/FREE 20.
PAGE 3 H0065

S64
HIRAI N.,"SHINTO AND INTERNATIONAL PROBLEMS." ASIA
SOCIETY NAT/G PLAN EDU/PROP RACE/REL PEACE ATTIT SECT
PERCEPT LOVE MORAL...HUM MYTH RECORD SAMP TREND
STERTYP TOT/POP 20 UN CHINJAP SHINTO. PAGE 71 H1423

S64
LEWIS R.,"OPINION SURVEYING IN KOREA." ASIA FUT NAT/G
KOREA LEGIS EDU/PROP EXEC ALL/VALS...POLICY CONCPT QU
MYTH TESTS CON/ANAL GEN/METH TOT/POP VAL/FREE 20.
PAGE 96 H1915

S64
MARTELLI G.,"PORTUGAL AND THE UNITED NATIONS." AFR ATTIT
EUR+WWI ELITES INT/ORG NAT/G PROVS PLAN DIPLOM PORTUGAL
ECO/TAC DOMIN COLONIAL RIGID/FLEX MORAL ORD/FREE
PWR WEALTH...MYTH UN 20. PAGE 103 H2060

B65
DURKHEIM E.,THE ELEMENTARY FORMS OF THE RELIGIOUS SOC
LIFE. KIN PARTIC MORAL...PSY MYTH OBS IDEA/COMP CULTURE
METH WORSHIP 19/20. PAGE 43 H0870 CONCPT

B65
LAWRENCE P.,GODS, GHOSTS, AND MEN IN MELANESIA: MYTH
SOME RELIGIONS OF AUSTRALIAN NEW GUINEA AND THE NEW S/ASIA
HEBRIDES. SOCIETY ECO/UNDEV FAM GP/REL INGP/REL SECT
HABITAT PERSON...GEOG SOC ANTHOL BIBLIOG WORSHIP 20 CULTURE
NEW/GUINEA. PAGE 92 H1847

B65
STERN F.,THE POLITICS OF CULTURAL DESPAIR. EUR+WWI CULTURE
GERMANY POL/PAR SECT RACE/REL STRANGE TOTALISM ATTIT
...ART/METH MYTH BIBLIOG 20 JEWS. PAGE 149 H2980 NAT/LISM
FASCISM

S65
GRIFFITH S.B.,"COMMUNIST CHINA'S CAPACITY TO MAKE FORCES
WAR." CHINA/COM COM NAT/G TOP/EX PLAN DOMIN COERCE PWR
NUC/PWR ATTIT RESPECT SKILL...CONCPT MYTH TIME/SEQ WEAPON
TREND COLD/WAR 20. PAGE 61 H1221 ASIA

B66
BASDEN G.T.,NIGER IBOS. NIGERIA STRUCT SECT CHIEF CULTURE
COLONIAL HABITAT...POLICY SOC MYTH OBS WORSHIP 20 AFR
IBO. PAGE 12 H0233 SOCIETY

B66
ELLIS A.B.,THE EWE-SPEAKING PEOPLES OF THE SLAVE MYTH
COAST OF WEST AFRICA. AFR FORCES ADJUST...LING CULTURE
RECORD GP/COMP WORSHIP 20 AFRICA/W DEITY. PAGE 45 HABITAT
H0910

B66
KIRKLAND E.C.,A BIBLIOGRAPHY OF SOUTH ASIAN BIBLIOG
FOLKLORE. WRITING HABITAT ALL/VALS MYSTISM S/ASIA
...ART/METH GEOG PSY SOC MYTH WORSHIP 13/20. CULTURE
PAGE 86 H1723 CREATE

C66
ROSENBERG C.G. JR.,"THE MYTH OF "MAU-MAU:" NAT/LISM
NATIONALISM IN KENYA." AFR CULTURE NAT/G POL/PAR COLONIAL
COERCE REV RACE/REL ATTIT ORD/FREE SOVEREIGN...MYTH MAJORIT
BIBLIOG 20. PAGE 134 H2678 LEAD

S67
KRISTOF L.K.D.,"THE STATE-IDEA, THE NATIONAL IDEA GEOG
AND THE IMAGE OF THE FATHERLAND." CONSTN CULTURE CONCPT
INTELL SOCIETY WORKER TASK DRIVE HABITAT...MYTH NAT/G
GOV/COMP IDEA/COMP. PAGE 89 H1769 PERCEPT

S67
NIEBUHR R.,"THE SOCIAL MYTHS IN THE COLD WAR." MYTH
USA+45 USSR VIETNAM PROB/SOLV BAL/PWR ARMS/CONT DIPLOM
NAT/LISM PWR ALL/IDEOS CONCPT. PAGE 118 H2359 GOV/COMP

B82
MACDONALD D.,AFRICANA; OR, THE HEART OF HEATHEN SECT
AFRICA, VOL. II: MISSION LIFE. SOCIETY STRATA KIN AFR
CREATE EDU/PROP ADMIN COERCE LITERACY HEALTH...MYTH CULTURE
WORSHIP 19 LIVNGSTN/D MISSION NEGRO. PAGE 100 H1990 ORD/FREE

N

NAACP....NATIONAL ASSOCIATION FOR THE ADVANCEMENT OF
COLORED PEOPLE

NABALOI....NABALOI TRIBE, PHILIPPINES

B04
REED W.A.,ETHNOLOGICAL SURVEY PUBLICATIONS (VOL. CULTURE
II). PHILIPPINE STRUCT INDUS SECT DEATH LEISURE SOCIETY
HABITAT...AUD/VIS CHARTS WORSHIP 20 NABOLOI NEGRITO SOC

BATAK. PAGE 130 H2607 OBS

NAFTA....NORTH ATLANTIC FREE TRADE AREA

NAHM A.C. H2303

NAHUMI M. H2304

NAKAMURA H. H2305

NALBANDIAN L. H2306

NAM....NATIONAL ASSOCIATION OF MANUFACTURERS

B50
TRAGER F.N.,MARXISM IN SOUTHEAST ASIA. BURMA INDONESIA THAILAND VIETNAM CULTURE SOCIETY NAT/G VOL/ASSN EXEC ROUTINE COERCE ATTIT RIGID/FLEX PWR ...METH/CNCPT TIME/SEQ STERTYP GEN/LAWS MARX/KARL VAL/FREE COLD/WAR NAM 20. PAGE 156 H3126 S/ASIA POL/PAR REV

NAM/TIEN....NAM TIEN

NAMBOODIRIPAD E.M. H2307

NAMIER L. H2308

NAMIER L.B. H2309

NAPOLEON/B....NAPOLEON BONAPARTE

B58
SHAW S.J.,THE FINANCIAL AND ADMINISTRATIVE ORGANIZATION AND DEVELOPMENT OF OTTOMAN EGYPT 1517-1798. UAR LOC/G FORCES BUDGET INT/TRADE TAX EATING INCOME WEALTH...CHARTS BIBLIOG 16/18 OTTOMAN NAPOLEON/B. PAGE 143 H2853 FINAN ADMIN GOV/REL CULTURE

B90
TAINE H.A.,MODERN REGIME (2 VOLS.). FRANCE FAM REV CENTRAL MARRIAGE PWR...TREND 19 NAPOLEON/B. PAGE 152 H3037 STRUCT NAT/G OLD/LIB MORAL

NARAIN D. H2310

NARAIN J.P. H2311

NARASIMHAN V.K. H2312

NARAYAN/J....JAYPRAKASH NARAYAN

NARCO/ACT....UNIFORM NARCOTIC DRUG ACT

NASA....NATIONAL AERONAUTIC AND SPACE ADMINISTRATION

NASH M. H2313,H2314,H2315

NASHVILLE....NASHVILLE, TENNESSEE

NASRI A.R. H2316

NASSER/G....GAMAL ABDUL NASSER

N
BROCKWAY A.F.,AFRICAN SOCIALISM. EUR+WWI GHANA ISLAM UAR ECO/UNDEV CAP/ISM INT/TRADE COLONIAL COERCE GOV/REL DISCRIM 20 NEGRO NKRUMAH/K NASSER/G. PAGE 21 H0423 AFR SOCISM MARXISM

B63
CREMEANS C.,THE ARABS AND THE WORLD: NASSER'S ARAB NATIONALIST POLICY. FUT ISLAM UAR USA+45 SOCIETY STRATA NAT/G POL/PAR PLAN DIPLOM EDU/PROP LEGIT DRIVE ALL/VALS...INT TIME/SEQ CHARTS 20 NASSER/G. PAGE 35 H0700 TOP/EX ATTIT REGION NAT/LISM

B64
MILIBAND R.,THE SOCIALIST REGISTER: 1964. GERMANY/W ITALY UK LABOR POL/PAR ECO/TAC FOR/AID NUC/PWR ...POLICY SOCIALIST IDEA/COMP 20 MAO NASSER/G. PAGE 110 H2204 MARXISM SOCISM CAP/ISM PROB/SOLV

NAT/COMP....COMPARISON OF NATIONS

NAT/FARMER....NATIONAL FARMERS' ASSOCIATION

NAT/G....NATIONAL GOVERNMENT

NAT/LISM....NATIONALISM

N
UNIVERSITY OF FLORIDA LIBRARY,DOORS TO LATIN AMERICA; RECENT BOOKS AND PAMPHLETS. CONSTN CULTURE SOCIETY ECO/UNDEV COLONIAL LEAD GOV/REL NAT/LISM ATTIT...HUM SOC 20. PAGE 159 H3170 BIBLIOG/A L/A+17C DIPLOM NAT/G

N
INTERNATIONAL BIBLIOGRAPHIE DER DEUTSCHEN ZEITSCHRIFTENLITERATUR. EUR+WWI GERMANY MOD/EUR ECO/DEV POL/PAR LEAD WAR NAT/LISM ATTIT...EPIST PHIL/SCI 19/20. PAGE 1 H0004 BIBLIOG/A NAT/G PERSON CULTURE

N
JOURNAL OF ASIAN STUDIES. CULTURE ECO/DEV SECT DIPLOM EDU/PROP WAR NAT/LISM...PHIL/SCI SOC 20. PAGE 1 H0005 BIBLIOG ASIA S/ASIA NAT/G

N
AFRICAN BIBLIOGRAPHIC CENTER,A CURRENT BIBLIOGRAPHY ON AFRICAN AFFAIRS. LAW CULTURE ECO/UNDEV LABOR SECT DIPLOM FOR/AID COLONIAL NAT/LISM...LING 20. PAGE 4 H0075 BIBLIOG/A AFR NAT/G REGION

N
ASIA FOUNDATION,LIBRARY NOTES. LAW CONSTN CULTURE SOCIETY ECO/UNDEV INT/ORG NAT/G COLONIAL LEAD REGION NAT/LISM ATTIT 20 UN. PAGE 9 H0176 BIBLIOG/A ASIA S/ASIA DIPLOM

N
HOOVER INSTITUTION,UNITED STATES AND CANADIAN PUBLICATIONS ON AFRICA. CULTURE ECO/UNDEV AGRI TEC/DEV EDU/PROP COLONIAL RACE/REL NAT/LISM ATTIT HEALTH...SOC SOC/WK 20. PAGE 73 H1464 BIBLIOG DIPLOM NAT/G AFR

N
LONDON LIBRARY ASSOCIATION,ATHENAEUM SUBJECT INDEX. 1915-1918. NAT/G DIPLOM NAT/LISM 20. PAGE 98 H1960 BIBLIOG CON/ANAL SOC

N
NORTHWESTERN UNIVERSITY LIB,JOINT ACQUISITIONS LIST OF AFRICANA. AFR SOCIETY STRUCT EDU/PROP COLONIAL GP/REL RACE/REL NAT/LISM SOVEREIGN...SOC 20. PAGE 119 H2377 BIBLIOG CULTURE ECO/UNDEV INDUS

NCO
CARRINGTON C.E.,THE COMMONWEALTH IN AFRICA (PAMPHLET). UK STRUCT NAT/G COLONIAL REPRESENT GOV/REL RACE/REL NAT/LISM...MAJORIT 20 EEC NEGRO COLD/WAR. PAGE 27 H0540 ECO/UNDEV AFR DIPLOM PLAN

B10
MENDELSSOHN S.,SOUTH AFRICAN BIBLIOGRAPHY (2 VOLS.). SOUTH/AFR EXTR/IND LABOR SECT DIPLOM INT/TRADE COLONIAL RACE/REL DISCRIM...GEOG 20. PAGE 109 H2172 BIBLIOG/A AFR NAT/G NAT/LISM

B17
BARRES M.,THE UNDYING SPIRIT OF FRANCE (TRANS. BY M. CORWIN). FRANCE DOMIN LEAD DEATH ATTIT RESPECT ...NAT/COMP 20 WWI. PAGE 11 H0226 NAT/LISM FORCES WAR CULTURE

B17
VEBLEN T.B.,AN INQUIRY INTO THE NATURE OF PEACE AND THE TERMS OF ITS PERPETUATION. UNIV STRATA FINAN EDU/PROP PRICE COST DISCRIM NAT/LISM MORAL ORD/FREE PACIFIST 20 WORLDUNITY. PAGE 162 H3237 PEACE DIPLOM WAR NAT/G

N19
BARRES M.,"THE WAR AND THE SPIRIT OF YOUTH" (PAMPHLET). FRANCE FORCES DOMIN LEAD DEATH AGE/Y ATTIT RESPECT...FASCIST 20 WWI. PAGE 11 H0228 WAR NAT/LISM CULTURE MYSTIC

N19
GOODMAN G.K.,IMPERIAL JAPAN AND ASIA: A REASSESSMENT (PAMPHLET). ASIA S/ASIA ECO/DEV FORCES LEAD WAR NAT/LISM ATTIT...DECISION CONCPT BIBLIOG 19/20 CHINJAP. PAGE 59 H1172 DIPLOM NAT/G POLICY COLONIAL

N19
HANNA A.J.,EUROPEAN RULE IN AFRICA (PAMPHLET). BELGIUM FRANCE MOD/EUR UK WOR+45 WOR-45 ECO/UNDEV NAT/G PARTIC SOVEREIGN...NAT/COMP 19/20. PAGE 66 H1314 DIPLOM COLONIAL AFR NAT/LISM

N19
MASSEY V.,CANADIANS AND THEIR COMMONWEALTH: THE ROMANES LECTURE DELIVERED IN THE SHELDONIAN THEATRE JUNE 1, 1961 (PAMPHLET). CANADA UK CULTURE ECO/DEV REPRESENT NAT/LISM PEACE PWR CONSERVE 20 CMN/WLTH. PAGE 104 H2088 ATTIT DIPLOM NAT/G SOVEREIGN

N19
PROVISIONS SECTION OAU,ORGANIZATION OF AFRICAN UNITY: BASIC DOCUMENTS AND RESOLUTIONS (PAMPHLET). AFR CULTURE ECO/UNDEV DIPLOM ECO/TAC EDU/PROP COLONIAL ARMS/CONT NUC/PWR RACE/REL DISCRIM NAT/LISM 20 UN OAU. PAGE 128 H2564 CONSTN EX/STRUC SOVEREIGN INT/ORG

N19
SENGHOR L.S.,AFRICAN SOCIALISM (PAMPHLET). AFR FRANCE MALI USSR ELITES ECO/UNDEV NAT/G DIPLOM DOMIN EDU/PROP ATTIT 20 NEGRO. PAGE 141 H2827 SOCISM MARXISM ORD/FREE NAT/LISM

C20
DUNNING W.A.,"A HISTORY OF POLITICAL THINKERS FROM ROUSSEAU TO SPENCER." NAT/G REV NAT/LISM UTIL CONSERVE MARXISM POPULISM...JURID BIBLIOG 18/19. PAGE 43 H0868 IDEA/COMP PHIL/SCI CONCPT GEN/LAWS

B21
BALFOUR A.J.,ESSAYS SPECULATIVE AND POLITICAL. SEA CULTURE CREATE WAR NAT/LISM PEACE LOVE...ART/METH INT/LAW CONCPT ANTHOL 20 JEWS. PAGE 10 H0204 PHIL/SCI SOCIETY DIPLOM

B21
WALLAS G.,HUMAN NATURE IN POLITICS (3RD ED.). UNIV NAT/G LEAD CHOOSE REPRESENT GP/REL NAT/LISM RATIONAL BIO/SOC HEREDITY ALL/VALS MAJORIT. PSY DRIVE PERSON

PAGE 165 H3293

B22
FICHTE J.G.,ADDRESSES TO THE GERMAN NATION. GERMANY PRUSSIA ELITES NAT/G SECT CREATE INT/TRADE HEREDITY ...ART/METH LING 19 FRANK/PARL. PAGE 50 H0989
NAT/LISM CULTURE EDU/PROP REGION

C28
SCHNEIDER H.W.,"MAKING THE FASCIST STATE." ITALY CULTURE LABOR DIPLOM REV WAR NAT/LISM TOTALISM ATTIT DRIVE SOCISM...BIBLIOG PARLIAMENT 20. PAGE 140 H2792
FASCISM POLICY POL/PAR

C28
WARD P.W.,"SOVEREIGNTY: A STUDY OF A CONTEMPORARY POLITICAL NOTION." CONSTN NAT/G DIPLOM REPRESENT PLURISM...IDEA/COMP BIBLIOG. PAGE 165 H3304
SOVEREIGN CONCPT NAT/LISM

B30
BYNKERSHOEK C.,QUAESTIONUM JURIS PUBLICI LIBRI DUO. CHRIST-17C MOD/EUR CONSTN ELITES SOCIETY NAT/G PROVS EX/STRUC FORCES TOP/EX BAL/PWR DIPLOM ATTIT MORAL...TRADIT CONCPT. PAGE 25 H0502
INT/ORG LAW NAT/LISM INT/LAW

B30
HULL W.I.,INDIA'S POLITICAL CRISIS. INDIA UK INT/ORG LABOR SECT DELIB/GP LEGIS DIPLOM NEUTRAL REGION CROWD GOV/REL MAJORITY ATTIT 20 NEHRU/J GANDHI/M COMMONWLTH. PAGE 75 H1492
ORD/FREE NAT/G COLONIAL NAT/LISM

C31
MOGI S.,"THE PROBLEM OF FEDERALISM: A STUDY IN THE HISTORY OF POLITICAL THEORY." CONSTN COLONIAL NAT/LISM SOVEREIGN LAISSEZ PLURISM 18/20. PAGE 112 H2235
FEDERAL CONCPT NAT/G

B32
BRYCE J.,THE HOLY ROMAN EMPIRE. GERMANY ITALY MOD/EUR CULTURE SOCIETY STRUCT INT/ORG NAT/G SECT DIPLOM DOMIN WAR SUPEGO ALL/VALS SOVEREIGN...GEOG SOC TIME/SEQ CHARTS STERTYP. PAGE 23 H0456
CHRIST-17C NAT/LISM

B32
MARRARO H.R.,AMERICAN OPINION ON THE UNIFICATION OF ITALY. ITALY FORCES DIPLOM SOVEREIGN CATHISM CONSERVE...CONCPT NAT/COMP BIBLIOG 19. PAGE 103 H2056
ORD/FREE NAT/LISM REV CONSTN

B32
THIBAUDET A.,LES IDEES POLITIQUES DE LA FRANCE. FRANCE NAT/G SECT PRESS REV NAT/LISM PEACE ATTIT ...PSY 19/20 JACOBINISM JAURES/JL. PAGE 154 H3070
IDEA/COMP ALL/IDEOS CATHISM

B36
BOYCE A.N.,EUROPE AND SOUTH AFRICA. FRANCE GERMANY ITALY SOUTH/AFR UK INDUS NAT/G CONTROL REV WAR NAT/LISM...CONCPT HIST/WRIT 20. PAGE 20 H0392
COLONIAL GOV/COMP NAT/COMP DIPLOM

B36
LAPRADE W.T.,PUBLIC OPINION AND POLITICS IN EIGHTEENTH CENTURY ENGLAND. UK CULTURE POL/PAR CHIEF TOP/EX LEAD REV NAT/LISM PWR 18 PROTESTANT PROTESTANT CHURCH/STA. PAGE 91 H1815
POLICY ELITES ATTIT TIME/SEQ

C36
MAZZINI J.,"FROM THE COUNCIL TO GOD" (1870) IN J. MAZZINI, ESSAYS." ITALY NAT/G EDU/PROP PARTIC ORD/FREE PWR SOVEREIGN 19 POPE CHRISTIAN DEITY. PAGE 106 H2112
CATHISM DOMIN NAT/LISM SUPEGO

B37
BERDYAEV N.,THE ORIGIN OF RUSSIAN COMMUNISM. MOD/EUR RUSSIA USSR INTELL SECT REV...ANARCH HUM 19/20 ORTHO/RUSS COM/PARTY CHRISTIAN. PAGE 15 H0294
MARXISM NAT/LISM CULTURE ATTIT

B37
BORGESE G.A.,GOLIATH: THE MARCH OF FASCISM. GERMANY ITALY LAW POL/PAR SECT DIPLOM SOCISM...JURID MYTH 20 DANTE MACHIAVELL MUSSOLIN/B. PAGE 19 H0375
POLICY NAT/LISM FASCISM NAT/G

B37
VON HAYEK F.A.,MONETARY NATIONALISM AND INTERNATIONAL STABILITY. WOR-45 ECO/DEV NAT/G PROB/SOLV INT/TRADE...POLICY CONCPT METH/COMP NAT/COMP 20. PAGE 163 H3271
ECO/TAC FINAN DIPLOM NAT/LISM

B38
COUPLAND R.,EAST AFRICA AND ITS INVADERS. AFR ISLAM STRATA SECT FORCES DIPLOM TRIBUTE CONTROL DISCRIM NAT/LISM 19 AFRICA/E EUROPE MISSION. PAGE 34 H0680
CULTURE ELITES COLONIAL MARKET

B38
HARPER S.N.,THE GOVERNMENT OF THE SOVIET UNION. COM USSR LAW CONSTN ECO/DEV PLAN TEC/DEV DIPLOM INT/TRADE ADMIN REV NAT/LISM...POLICY 20. PAGE 67 H1337
MARXISM NAT/G LEAD POL/PAR

B38
LAWLEY F.E.,THE GROWTH OF COLLECTIVE ECONOMY VOL. 2: INTERNATIONAL. WOR-45 AGRI INDUS EQUILIB OPTIMAL OWN WEALTH...NAT/COMP 19/20 NAZI NEW/DEAL MONOPOLY. PAGE 92 H1845
ECO/TAC SOCISM NAT/LISM CONTROL

B39
BENES E.,DEMOCRACY TODAY AND TOMORROW. EUR+WWI SOCIETY ECO/DEV DELIB/GP ECO/TAC REGION ATTIT PWR FASCISM...CONCPT LEAGUE/NAT 20. PAGE 14 H0281
NAT/G LEGIT NAT/LISM

B39
COBBAN A.,DICTATORSHIP: ITS HISTORY AND THEORY. EUR+WWI MOD/EUR SOCIETY STRUCT NAT/G TEC/DEV LEAD NAT/LISM SOVEREIGN...IDEA/COMP 14/20. PAGE 30 H0610
TOTALISM FASCISM CONCPT

B39
KOHN H.,REVOLUTIONS AND DICTATORSHIPS. COM EUR+WWI ISLAM MOD/EUR NAT/G CHIEF FORCES WAR CIVMIL/REL PWR MARXISM 18/20. PAGE 87 H1739
NAT/LISM TOTALISM REV FASCISM

B40
BROGAN D.W.,THE DEVELOPMENT OF MODERN FRANCE (1870-1939). FRANCE GERMANY UK USSR CONSTN CHIEF LEGIS DIPLOM AGREE COLONIAL WAR NAT/LISM PEACE SOCISM 19/20 TREATY. PAGE 21 H0428
MOD/EUR NAT/G

B41
CROTHERS G.D.,THE GERMAN ELECTIONS OF 1907. GERMANY NAT/G EDU/PROP COLONIAL ATTIT. PAGE 35 H0709
CHOOSE PARL/PROC NAT/LISM POL/PAR

B41
HITLER A.,MEIN KAMPF (UNABR. ENG. VERSION) (1925). GERMANY CONSTN TEC/DEV RACE/REL NAT/LISM TOTALISM SOVEREIGN...BIOG 20 HITLER/A TREATY. PAGE 71 H1429
EDU/PROP WAR PLAN FASCISM

B42
BAYNES N.H.,INTELLECTUAL LIBERTY AND TOTALITARIAN CLAIMS. EUR+WWI GERMANY ITALY INTELL POL/PAR CIVMIL/REL NAT/LISM SOCISM CONCPT. PAGE 12 H0245
KNOWL FASCISM EDU/PROP ACADEM

B42
CONOVER H.F.,FRENCH COLONIES IN AFRICA: A LIST OF REFERENCES. ALGERIA FRANCE MOROCCO SOMALIA SUDAN CULTURE AGRI LOC/G SECT FORCES DIPLOM INT/TRADE NAT/LISM HEALTH...CON/ANAL 20. PAGE 32 H0641
BIBLIOG AFR ECO/UNDEV COLONIAL

B44
BERDYAEV N.,SLAVERY AND FREEDOM. NAT/G REV WAR NAT/LISM OWN AUTHORIT SEX CONSERVE SOCISM...TRADIT PHIL/SCI CIVIL/LIB. PAGE 15 H0295
ORD/FREE PERSON ELITES SOCIETY

B44
FULLER G.H.,TURKEY: A SELECTED LIST OF REFERENCES. ISLAM TURKEY CULTURE ECO/UNDEV AGRI DIPLOM NAT/LISM CONSERVE...GEOG HUM INT/LAW SOC 7/20 MAPS. PAGE 54 H1075
BIBLIOG/A ALL/VALS

B44
KOHN H.,THE IDEA OF NATIONALISM. UNIV SOCIETY KIN CREATE REGION CENTRAL SOVEREIGN. PAGE 87 H1740
NAT/LISM CONCPT NAT/G GP/REL

B45
HORN O.B.,BRITISH PUBLIC OPINION AND THE FIRST PARTITION OF POLAND. POLAND UK LEGIS PRESS RUMOR CONTROL PARTIC NAT/LISM SOVEREIGN 18/19. PAGE 73 H1469
DIPLOM POLICY ATTIT NAT/G

B45
LASKER B.,ASIA ON THE MOVE. ASIA BURMA S/ASIA THAILAND USSR ECO/UNDEV FAM KIN WAR NAT/LISM ATTIT ...GEOG CENSUS TREND AUSTRAL 20. PAGE 91 H1826
CULTURE RIGID/FLEX

B45
WOOLBERT R.G.,FOREIGN AFFAIRS BIBLIOGRAPHY, 1932-1942. INT/ORG SECT INT/TRADE COLONIAL RACE/REL NAT/LISM...GEOG INT/LAW GOV/COMP IDEA/COMP 20. PAGE 170 H3410
BIBLIOG/A DIPLOM WAR

B48
FURNIVAL J.,COLONIAL POLICY AND PRACTICE A COMPARATIVE STUDY OF BURMA, AND NETHERLANDS INDIA. BURMA INDONESIA S/ASIA...GEOG OBS GOV/COMP METH/COMP 20. PAGE 54 H1080
COLONIAL NAT/LISM WEALTH SOVEREIGN

B48
MAUGHAM R.,NORTH AFRICAN NOTEBOOK. ALGERIA ISLAM LIBYA MOROCCO STRUCT ECO/UNDEV COLONIAL...SOC OBS AUD/VIS NAT/COMP WORSHIP 20 TUNIS. PAGE 105 H2102
SOCIETY RECORD NAT/LISM

L48
SHILS E.A.,"COHESION AND DISINTEGRATION IN THE WEHRMACHT IN WORLD WAR II." GERMANY STRUCT DOMIN WAR INGP/REL ISOLAT NAT/LISM ATTIT AUTHORIT SUPEGO RESPECT...PSY CON/ANAL 20 NAZI. PAGE 143 H2862
EDU/PROP DRIVE PERS/REL FORCES

B49
HINDEN R.,EMPIRE AND AFTER. UK POL/PAR BAL/PWR DIPLOM INT/TRADE WAR NAT/LISM PWR 17/20. PAGE 71 H1420
NAT/G COLONIAL ATTIT POLICY

B49
VIERECK P.,CONSERVATISM REVISITED: THE REVOLT AGAINST REVOLT 1815-1949. EUR+WWI ELITES NAT/G FORCES PARTIC GOV/REL NAT/LISM...MAJORIT CONCPT GOV/COMP METTRNCH/K. PAGE 163 H3251
CONSERVE MARXISM REALPOL

C49
YANAGA C.,"JAPAN SINCE PERRY." S/ASIA CULTURE ECO/DEV FORCES WAR 19/20 CHINJAP. PAGE 172 H3433
DIPLOM POL/PAR CIVMIL/REL NAT/LISM

B50
ALBRECHT-CARRIE R.,ITALY FROM NAPOLEON TO MUSSOLINI. GERMANY ITALY SPAIN SOCIETY ECO/DEV POL/PAR LEGIS AGREE CONTROL WAR NAT/LISM TOTALISM PWR SOCISM...SOC 19/20 TREATY. PAGE 5 H0095
FASCISM NAT/G

B50
KANN R.A.,THE MULTINATIONAL EMPIRE (2 VOLS.).
NAT/LISM

AUSTRIA CZECHOSLVK GERMANY HUNGARY CULTURE NAT/G POL/PAR PROVS REGION REV FEDERAL...GEOG TREND CHARTS IDEA/COMP NAT/COMP 19/20. PAGE 83 H1654
MOD/EUR

B50
US DEPARTMENT OF STATE,DOCUMENTS ON GERMAN FOREIGN POLICY, 1918-1945 (13 VOLS.). EUR+WWI GERMANY NAT/G PLAN DIPLOM DOMIN EDU/PROP CONTROL NAT/LISM ...ANTHOL 20. PAGE 159 H3186
BIBLIOG/A WAR POLICY FASCIST

B51
CARRINGTON C.E.,THE LIQUIDATION OF THE BRITISH EMPIRE. AFR NAT/G INT/TRADE COLONIAL RACE/REL ATTIT ORD/FREE...POLICY NAT/COMP 20 CMN/WLTH. PAGE 27 H0541
SOVEREIGN NAT/LISM DIPLOM GP/REL

B51
JENNINGS S.I.,THE COMMONWEALTH IN ASIA. CEYLON INDIA PAKISTAN S/ASIA UK CONSTN CULTURE SOCIETY STRATA STRUCT NAT/G POL/PAR EDU/PROP LEAD WAR 20 CMN/WLTH. PAGE 80 H1608
NAT/LISM REGION COLONIAL DIPLOM

B51
WABEKE B.H.,A GUIDE TO DUTCH BIBLIOGRAPHIES. BELGIUM INDONESIA NETHERLAND DIPLOM INT/TRADE WAR NAT/LISM KNOWL...ART/METH HUM JURID CON/ANAL 14/20. PAGE 164 H3282
BIBLIOG/A NAT/G CULTURE COLONIAL

B52
GURLAND A.R.L.,POLITICAL SCIENCE IN WESTERN GERMANY: THOUGHTS AND WRITINGS, 1950-1952 (PAMPHLET). EUR+WWI GERMANY/W ELITES SOCIETY NAT/G NAT/LISM TOTALISM 20. PAGE 63 H1253
BIBLIOG/A DIPLOM CIVMIL/REL FASCISM

B52
HIMMELFARB G.,LORD ACTON: A STUDY IN CONSCIENCE AND POLITICS. MOD/EUR NAT/G POL/PAR SECT LEGIS TOP/EX EDU/PROP ADMIN NAT/LISM ATTIT PERSON SUPEGO MORAL ORD/FREE...CONCPT PARLIAMENT 19 ACTON/LORD. PAGE 71 H1419
PWR BIOG

B52
ISAACS H.R.,AFRICA: NEW CRISES IN THE MAKING (PAMPHLET). EUR+WWI USA+45 ELITES ECO/UNDEV WAR DISCRIM NAT/LISM ATTIT...POLICY NEW/IDEA CHARTS GOV/COMP 20 NEGRO COLD/WAR. PAGE 78 H1570
COLONIAL AFR RACE/REL ORD/FREE

B52
JULIEN C.A.,L'AFRIQUE DU NORD EN MARCHE: NATIONALISMES MUSULMANS ET SOUVERAINETE FRANCAISE (2ND ED). AFR ALGERIA FRANCE ISLAM MOROCCO NAT/G CONTROL ORD/FREE...POLICY 19/20 TUNIS MUSLIM. PAGE 82 H1641
NAT/LISM COERCE DOMIN COLONIAL

B52
KOHN H.,PROPHETS AND PEOPLES: STUDIES IN NINETEENTH CENTURY NATIONALISM. MOD/EUR...IDEA/COMP 19. PAGE 87 H1741
CONCPT NAT/LISM SOVEREIGN

B52
WALTERS F.P.,A HISTORY OF THE LEAGUE OF NATIONS. EUR+WWI CONSTN NAT/G LEGIS TOP/EX ACT/RES PLAN EDU/PROP LEGIT ROUTINE ATTIT...TREND LEAGUE/NAT 20 CHINJAP. PAGE 165 H3297
INT/ORG TIME/SEQ NAT/LISM

S52
MCDOUGAL M.S.,"THE COMPARATIVE STUDY OF LAW FOR POLICY PURPOSES." FUT NAT/G POL/PAR CONSULT ADJUD PWR SOVEREIGN...METH/CNCPT IDEA/COMP SIMUL 20. PAGE 106 H2129
PLAN JURID NAT/LISM

B53
BROWN D.M.,THE WHITE UMBRELLA: INDIAN POLITICAL THOUGHT FROM MANU TO GANDHI. INDIA LAW NAT/G SECT WRITING NAT/LISM...ANTHOL BIBLIOG 20 HINDU GANDHI/M MANU. PAGE 22 H0442
CONCPT DOMIN CONSERVE

B53
ROSCIO J.G.,OBRAS. L/A+17C SPAIN DIPLOM REV WAR NAT/LISM TOTALISM PWR SOVEREIGN 19. PAGE 134 H2671
ORD/FREE COLONIAL NAT/G PHIL/SCI

L53
DEUTSCH K.W.,"THE GROWTH OF NATIONS: SOME RECURRENT PATTERNS OF POLITICAL AND SOCIAL INTEGRATION" (BMR)" UNIV CULTURE SOCIETY ECO/DEV ECO/UNDEV NAT/G CREATE GP/REL...CONCPT GEN/LAWS SOC/INTEG 11/20. PAGE 40 H0797
TREND NAT/LISM ORD/FREE

B54
HAZARD B.H. JR.,KOREAN STUDIES GUIDE. KOREA CONSTN CULTURE AGRI FAM SECT CREATE WAR NAT/LISM HABITAT PWR...CHARTS 14/20. PAGE 68 H1371
BIBLIOG/A ELITES GP/REL

B54
KOLARZ W.,THE PEOPLES OF THE SOVIET FAR EAST. RUSSIA USSR STRUCT LEAD ISOLAT NAT/LISM...CHARTS 20. PAGE 88 H1750
COLONIAL RACE/REL ADJUST CULTURE

C54
DE GRAZIA A.,"THE COMPARATIVE SURVEY OF EUROPEAN-AMERICAN POLITICAL BEHAV IOR; A RESEARCH PROSPECTUS (PAPER)" EUR+WWI FRANCE GERMANY SPAIN UK USA+45 WOR+45 STRATA POL/PAR DIPLOM EDU/PROP COLONIAL LEAD WAR NAT/LISM CONCPT. PAGE 37 H0752
BIBLIOG R+D METH NAT/COMP

C54
HAMMER E.J.,"THE STRUGGLE FOR INDOCHINA." COM VIETNAM POL/PAR REV CENTRAL NAT/LISM ATTIT...POLICY CHARTS BIBLIOG 20. PAGE 65 H1305
WAR COLONIAL S/ASIA NAT/G

C54
LANDAU J.M.,"PARLIAMENTS AND PARTIES IN EGYPT." UAR NAT/G SECT CONSULT LEGIS TOP/EX PROB/SOLV ADMIN COLONIAL...GEN/LAWS BIBLIOG 19/20. PAGE 90 H1804
ISLAM NAT/LISM PARL/PROC POL/PAR

B55
FRANZ G.,KULTURKAMPF. AUSTRIA GERMANY PRUSSIA SWITZERLND POL/PAR DIPLOM GP/REL ATTIT ORD/FREE 18/19 CHURCH/STA. PAGE 53 H1053
NAT/LISM CATHISM NAT/G REV

B55
KOHN H.,NATIONALISM: ITS MEANING AND HISTORY. GP/REL INGP/REL ATTIT...CONCPT NAT/COMP 16/20 MACHIAVELL. PAGE 87 H1743
NAT/LISM DIPLOM FASCISM REV

B55
KRUSE H.,DAS STAATSANGEHORIGKEITSRECHT DER ARABISCHEN STAATEN. ISLAM JORDAN LIBYA SYRIA UAR NAT/G SECT RACE/REL...INT/LAW 6/20 TREATY. PAGE 89 H1779
JURID NAT/LISM DIPLOM GP/REL

B55
MAZZINI J.,THE DUTIES OF MAN. MOD/EUR LAW SOCIETY FAM NAT/G POL/PAR SECT VOL/ASSN EX/STRUC ACT/RES CREATE REV PEACE ATTIT ALL/VALS...GEN/LAWS WORK 19. PAGE 106 H2113
SUPEGO CONCPT NAT/LISM

B55
ROWE C.,VOLTAIRE AND THE STATE. FRANCE MOD/EUR BAL/PWR CONTROL TASK SUPEGO ORD/FREE PWR...CONCPT 18 VOLTAIRE. PAGE 135 H2702
NAT/G DIPLOM NAT/LISM ATTIT

B55
SHAFER B.C.,NATIONALISM: MYTH AND REALITY. FRANCE UK USA+45 USA-45 CULTURE SOCIETY STRUCT ECO/DEV WAR PWR...NAT/COMP BIBLIOG 18/20. PAGE 142 H2837
NAT/LISM MYTH NAT/G CONCPT

B55
TAN C.C.,THE BOXER CATASTROPHE. ASIA UK USSR ELITES POL/PAR VOL/ASSN FORCES PROB/SOLV DIPLOM ADMIN COLONIAL NAT/LISM PEACE TREATY 19/20 BOXER/REBL. PAGE 152 H3040
REV NAT/G WAR

B55
VERGNAUD P.,L'IDEE DE LA NATIONALITE ET DE LA LIBRE DISPOSITION DES PEUPLES DANS SES RAPPORTS AVEC L'IDEE DE L'ETAT. STRATA NAT/G EDU/PROP RACE/REL AUTHORIT FASCISM MARXISM MYTH. PAGE 162 H3243
NAT/LISM DISCRIM ORD/FREE

B55
VIGON J.,TEORIA DEL MILITARISMO. NAT/G DIPLOM COLONIAL COERCE GUERRILLA CIVMIL/REL NAT/LISM MORAL ALL/IDEOS PACIFISM 18/20. PAGE 163 H3253
FORCES PHIL/SCI WAR POLICY

S55
DE SMITH S.A.,"CONSTITUTIONAL MONARCHY IN BURGANDA." AFR UGANDA UK STRUCT CHIEF REGION INGP/REL ADJUST NAT/LISM SOVEREIGN CONSERVE ...POLICY 19/20 BURGANDA. PAGE 38 H0769
NAT/G DIPLOM CONSTN COLONIAL

B56
DEUTSCH K.W.,AN INTERDISCIPLINARY BIBLIOGRAPHY ON NATIONALISM, 1935-1953. CULTURE SOCIETY SECT ATTIT HABITAT HEREDITY PERCEPT ROLE WEALTH...METH/CNCPT LING 20. PAGE 40 H0798
BIBLIOG/A NAT/LISM COLONIAL ADJUST

B56
HATCH J.C.,NEW FROM AFRICA. AFR FUT UK NAT/G GUERRILLA ATTIT ORD/FREE PWR...AUD/VIS CHARTS 20. PAGE 68 H1354
NAT/LISM COLONIAL RACE/REL

B56
PADMORE G.,PAN-AFRICANISM OR COMMUNISM. AFR FUT NIGERIA INTELL NAT/G COLONIAL FEDERAL ATTIT DRIVE PWR RESPECT WEALTH MARXISM...CONCPT AUD/VIS STERTYP 20. PAGE 122 H2440
POL/PAR NAT/LISM

B56
SMEDLEY A.,THE GREAT ROAD: THE LIFE AND TIMES OF CHU TEH. ASIA USSR NAT/G POL/PAR DIPLOM COERCE GUERRILLA CIVMIL/REL NAT/LISM PERSON SKILL MARXISM ...BIOG 20 CHINJAP MAO. PAGE 145 H2903
REV WAR FORCES

S56
KHAMA T.,"POLITICAL CHANGE IN AFRICAN SOCIETY." CONSTN SOCIETY LOC/G NAT/G POL/PAR EX/STRUC LEGIS LEGIT ADMIN CHOOSE REPRESENT NAT/LISM MORAL ORD/FREE PWR...CONCPT OBS TREND GEN/METH CMN/WLTH 17/20. PAGE 85 H1706
AFR ELITES

N56
US HOUSE COMM FOREIGN AFFAIRS,REPORT OF THE SPECIAL STUDY MISSION TO AFRICA, SOUTH AND EAST OF THE SAHARA (PAMPHLET). AFR SOUTH/AFR USA+45 STRUCT INT/TRADE PARL/PROC NAT/LISM ATTIT ALL/VALS HEALTH ...POLICY 20 CONGRESS. PAGE 160 H3197
FOR/AID COLONIAL ECO/UNDEV DIPLOM

B57
ALEXANDER L.M.,WORLD POLITICAL PATTERNS. NAT/G PROVS CAP/ISM DIPLOM COLONIAL NAT/LISM...POLICY GEOG CHARTS METH/COMP NAT/COMP 20. PAGE 5 H0101
CONTROL METH GOV/COMP

B57
ARON R.,L'UNIFICATION ECONOMIQUE DE L'EUROPE. EUR+WWI SWITZERLND UK INT/ORG NAT/G REGION NAT/LISM ORD/FREE PWR...CONCPT METH/CNCPT OBS TREND STERTYP GEN/LAWS EEC 20. PAGE 8 H0168
VOL/ASSN ECO/TAC

B57
CONOVER H.F.,NORTH AND NORTHEAST AFRICA; A SELECTED ANNOTATED LIST OF WRITINGS. ALGERIA MOROCCO SUDAN UAR CULTURE INT/ORG PROB/SOLV ADJUD NAT/LISM PWR WEALTH...SOC 20 UN. PAGE 32 H0649 BIBLIOG/A DIPLOM AFR ECO/UNDEV

B57
DEAN V.M.,THE NATURE OF THE NON-WESTERN WORLD. AFR ASIA L/A+17C S/ASIA CULTURE SOCIETY STRATA ECO/DEV DIPLOM ECO/TAC FOR/AID ATTIT DRIVE ALL/VALS ...RELATIV SOC CONCPT TIME/SEQ TREND TOT/POP 20. PAGE 39 H0778 ECO/UNDEV STERTYP NAT/LISM

B57
HODGKIN T.,NATIONALISM IN COLONIAL AFRICA. STRATA STRUCT MUNIC NAT/G POL/PAR LEGIS ATTIT SOVEREIGN ...POLICY TREND BIBLIOG 20. PAGE 72 H1444 AFR COLONIAL NAT/LISM DIPLOM

B57
KENNEDY M.D.,A SHORT HISTORY OF COMMUNISM IN ASIA. ASIA BURMA INDIA S/ASIA THAILAND NAT/G POL/PAR LEAD REV WAR MARXISM SOCISM...POLICY 20 CHINJAP. PAGE 85 H1688 DIPLOM NAT/LISM TOTALISM COERCE

B57
KOHN H.,AMERICAN NATIONALISM. EUR+WWI USA+45 USA-45 COLONIAL REGION 18/20. PAGE 87 H1744 NAT/LISM NAT/COMP FEDERAL DIPLOM

B57
LAQUER W.Z.,COMMUNISM AND NATIONALISM IN THE MIDDLE EAST. ELITES INTELL STRATA NAT/G POL/PAR SECT VOL/ASSN TOP/EX DOMIN LEGIT REGION COERCE ATTIT PERSON PWR...CONCPT HIST/WRIT TIME/SEQ TREND GEN/LAWS VAL/FREE. PAGE 91 H1817 ISLAM NAT/LISM

B57
MEINECKE F.,MACHIAVELLISM. CHRIST-17C FRANCE GERMANY ITALY MOD/EUR BAL/PWR PARL/PROC TOTALISM ...PHIL/SCI 15/20 MACHIAVELL. PAGE 108 H2166 NAT/LISM NAT/G PWR

B57
PALACIOS A.L.,PETROLEO, MONOPOLIOS, Y LATIFUNDIOS. L/A+17C EXTR/IND NAT/G TEC/DEV ECO/TAC CONTROL PRODUC 20 ARGEN MONOPOLY RESOURCE/N. PAGE 123 H2448 ECO/UNDEV NAT/LISM INDUS AGRI

B57
PARK A.G.,BOLSHEVISM IN TURKESTAN 1917-1927. COM RUSSIA USSR CULTURE AGRI SECT DOMIN GP/REL INGP/REL NAT/LISM...BIBLIOG 20 TURKESTAN. PAGE 123 H2467 REV POLICY MARXISM ISLAM

B57
POPLAI S.L.,NATIONAL POLITICS AND 1957 ELECTIONS IN INDIA. INDIA BARGAIN PARL/PROC CONSEN NAT/LISM PWR WEALTH 20. PAGE 127 H2543 POL/PAR CHOOSE POLICY NAT/G

B57
TAYLOR J.V.,CHRISTIANITY AND POLITICS IN AFRICA. AFR CONTROL PARTIC GP/REL RACE/REL ATTIT...POLICY BIBLIOG/A WORSHIP 20. PAGE 153 H3055 SECT NAT/G NAT/LISM

B57
TOMASIC D.A.,NATIONAL COMMUNISM AND SOVIET STRATEGY. UK USSR YUGOSLAVIA NAT/G POL/PAR CHIEF CREATE DOMIN REV WAR PWR...BIOG TREND 20 TITO/MARSH STALIN/J. PAGE 156 H3112 COM NAT/LISM MARXISM DIPLOM

B57
VON HIPPEL E.,GESCHICHTE DER STAATSPHILOSOPHIE (2 VOLS.). ASIA GREECE INDIA PRE/AMER UAR NAT/LISM ORD/FREE MARXISM. PAGE 164 H3272 CULTURE CONCPT NAT/G

S57
HAILEY,"TOMORROW IN AFRICA." CONSTN SOCIETY LOC/G NAT/G DOMIN ADJUD ADMIN GP/REL DISCRIM NAT/LISM ATTIT MORAL ORD/FREE...PSY SOC CONCPT OBS RECORD TREND GEN/LAWS CMN/WLTH 20. PAGE 64 H1277 AFR PERSON ELITES RACE/REL

S57
KILSON M.L.,"LAND AND POLITICS IN KENYA: AN ANALYSIS OF AFRICAN POLITICS IN A PLURAL SOCIETY." FUT LAW CULTURE KIN NAT/G ECO/TAC DOMIN REV NAT/LISM ORD/FREE PWR RESPECT SOVEREIGN WEALTH ...SOC OBS TREND WORK VAL/FREE CMN/WLTH 20. PAGE 86 H1710 AFR ECO/UNDEV

N57
JENNINGS W.I.,NATIONALISM, COLONIALISM, AND NEUTRALISM (PAMPHLET). ASIA INDIA S/ASIA UK INTELL ACADEM POL/PAR 20. PAGE 81 H1611 NAT/LISM COLONIAL NEUTRAL ATTIT

B58
BRADY A.,DEMOCRACY IN THE DOMINIONS (3RD ED.). CANADA NEW/ZEALND SOUTH/AFR WOR+45 LAW EX/STRUC DOMIN COLONIAL PARL/PROC REPRESENT RACE/REL NAT/LISM WEALTH 20 AUSTRAL CMN/WLTH. PAGE 20 H0399 GOV/COMP POL/PAR POPULISM NAT/G

B58
COLEMAN J.S.,NIGERIA: BACKGROUND TO NATIONALISM. AFR SOCIETY ECO/DEV KIN LOC/G POL/PAR TEC/DEV DOMIN ADMIN DRIVE PWR RESPECT...TRADIT SOC INT SAMP TIME/SEQ 20. PAGE 31 H0627 NAT/G NAT/LISM NIGERIA

B58
DUCLOUX L.,FROM BLACKMAIL TO TREASON. FRANCE PLAN DIPLOM EDU/PROP PRESS RUMOR NAT/LISM...CRIMLGY 20. PAGE 43 H0853 COERCE CRIME NAT/G PWR

B58
GLUCKMAN M.,ANALYSIS OF A SOCIAL SITUATION IN MODERN ZULULAND. AFR PERS/REL ADJUST DISCRIM EQUILIB NAT/LISM...SOC RECORD AUD/VIS 20 ZULULAND. PAGE 57 H1146 CULTURE RACE/REL STRUCT GP/REL

B58
HAAS E.B.,THE UNITING OF EUROPE. EUR+WWI INT/ORG NAT/G POL/PAR TOP/EX ECO/TAC EDU/PROP LEGIT FEDERAL NAT/LISM DRIVE RIGID/FLEX ORD/FREE PWR PLURISM ...POLICY CONCPT INT GEN/LAWS ECSC EEC 20. PAGE 63 H1264 VOL/ASSN ECO/DEV

B58
HSU U.T.,THE INVISIBLE CONFLICT. ASIA USSR ELITES NAT/G CONTROL LEAD COERCE REV WAR NAT/LISM ORD/FREE PWR 20 COM/PARTY ESPIONAGE. PAGE 74 H1485 MARXISM POL/PAR EDU/PROP FORCES

B58
LAQUER W.Z.,THE MIDDLE EAST IN TRANSITION. COM USSR ECO/UNDEV NAT/G VOL/ASSN EDU/PROP EXEC ATTIT DRIVE PWR MARXISM COLD/WAR TOT/POP 20. PAGE 91 H1818 ISLAM TREND NAT/LISM

B58
LOWER A.R.M.,EVOLVING CANADIAN FEDERALISM. CANADA WEST/IND CONSTN PROB/SOLV COLONIAL REGION NAT/LISM ...ANTHOL 20. PAGE 99 H1976 FEDERAL NAT/G DIPLOM RACE/REL

B58
TILLION G.,ALGERIA: THE REALITIES. ALGERIA FRANCE ISLAM CULTURE STRATA PROB/SOLV DOMIN REV NAT/LISM WEALTH MARXISM...GEOG 20. PAGE 155 H3094 ECO/UNDEV SOC COLONIAL DIPLOM

B58
VARG P.A.,MISSIONARIES, CHINESE, AND DIPLOMATS: THE AMERICAN PROTESTANT MISSIONARY MOVEMENT IN CHINA, 1890-1952. ASIA ECO/UNDEV NAT/G PROB/SOLV CAP/ISM EDU/PROP COLONIAL NAT/LISM ATTIT MARXISM...NAT/COMP STERTYP 20 CHINJAP PROTESTANT MISSION. PAGE 162 H3234 CULTURE DIPLOM SECT

C58
FIFIELD R.H.,"THE DIPLOMACY OF SOUTHEAST ASIA: 1945-1958." INT/ORG NAT/G COLONIAL REGION...CHARTS BIBLIOG 20 UN. PAGE 50 H0996 S/ASIA DIPLOM NAT/LISM

C58
GINSBURG N.,"MALAYA." MALAYSIA PROB/SOLV REGION NAT/LISM KNOWL WEALTH...GEOG SOC CHARTS BIBLIOG 20. PAGE 57 H1133 COM/IND ECO/UNDEV CULTURE NAT/G

B59
CARPENTER G.W.,THE WAY IN AFRICA. AFR INDUS MUNIC DIPLOM DOMIN EDU/PROP COERCE DISCRIM NAT/LISM ORD/FREE 20 NEGRO CHRISTIAN. PAGE 27 H0535 CULTURE SECT ECO/UNDEV COLONIAL

B59
DEHIO L.,GERMANY AND WORLD POLITICS IN THE TWENTIETH CENTURY. EUR+WWI FRANCE GERMANY MOD/EUR UK USSR NAT/G CHIEF BAL/PWR DOMIN COLONIAL CONTROL LEAD...IDEA/COMP 20 VERSAILLES. PAGE 39 H0783 DIPLOM WAR NAT/LISM SOVEREIGN

B59
GOLDWIN R.A.,READINGS IN RUSSIAN FOREIGN POLICY. HUNGARY USSR YUGOSLAVIA ELITES INT/ORG NAT/G REV WAR NAT/LISM PERSON SOCISM...CHARTS 20 MAPS BOLSHEVISM. PAGE 58 H1160 COM MARXISM DIPLOM POLICY

B59
HENDEL S.,THE SOVIET CRUCIBLE. USSR LEAD COERCE NAT/LISM UTOPIA PWR...POLICY CONCPT ANTHOL 20 STALIN/J LENIN/VI MARX/KARL BOLSHEVIK. PAGE 70 H1393 COM MARXISM REV TOTALISM

B59
LAQUER W.Z.,THE SOVIET UNION AND THE MIDDLE EAST. COM UAR USSR ECO/UNDEV NAT/G VOL/ASSN ECO/TAC EDU/PROP COLONIAL EXEC PWR...TIME/SEQ TREND COLD/WAR 20. PAGE 91 H1819 ISLAM DRIVE FOR/AID NAT/LISM

B59
OVERSTREET G.D.,COMMUNISM IN INDIA. INDIA S/ASIA CONSTN INT/ORG LEAD GP/REL...CHARTS BIBLIOG 20. PAGE 122 H2435 MARXISM NAT/LISM POL/PAR WAR

B59
SITHOLE N.,AFRICAN NATIONALISM. UNIV CULTURE SECT ADMIN COLONIAL CHOOSE. PAGE 145 H2892 RACE/REL AFR NAT/LISM PERSON

B59
VITTACHIT,EMERGENCY '58. CEYLON UK STRUCT NAT/G FORCES ADJUD CRIME REV NAT/LISM 20. PAGE 163 H3258 RACE/REL DISCRIM DIPLOM SOVEREIGN

B59
WRAITH R.E.,EAST AFRICAN CITIZEN. AFR GHANA UK AGRI INDUS LOC/G POL/PAR PROB/SOLV CONTROL REGION REPRESENT NAT/LISM PWR...OBS 20 AFRICA/E AFRICA/W. PAGE 171 H3415 ECO/UNDEV RACE/REL NAT/G NAT/COMP

C59
KARPAT K.H.,"TURKEY'S POLITICS: THE TRANSITION TO A MULTI-PARTY SYSTEM." COM TURKEY CULTURE ECO/UNDEV SECT TEC/DEV NAT/LISM ATTIT...SOC CON/ANAL BIBLIOG 20. PAGE 83 H1664 POL/PAR NAT/G

B60
ALMOND G.A.,THE POLITICS OF THE DEVELOPING AREAS. AFR ISLAM L/A+17C S/ASIA SOCIETY ECO/UNDEV NAT/G ADMIN PERCEPT KNOWL SOVEREIGN...CONCPT GEN/LAWS 20. PAGE 6 H0112
EX/STRUC ATTIT NAT/LISM

B60
CARTER G.M.,INDEPENDENCE FOR AFRICA. AFR FUT SOCIETY STRATA ECO/DEV POL/PAR DELIB/GP PLAN DOMIN EDU/PROP COLONIAL REGION ATTIT DRIVE SOVEREIGN ...RECORD INT TIME/SEQ CHARTS 20. PAGE 27 H0544
NAT/G PWR NAT/LISM

B60
CHATTERJI S.K.,AFRICANISM: THE AFRICAN PERSONALITY. KIN NAT/G SECT CREATE DIPLOM COLONIAL GP/REL ATTIT ORD/FREE...LING WORSHIP 20. PAGE 29 H0585
PERSON NAT/LISM AFR CULTURE

B60
EMERSON R.,FROM EMPIRE TO NATION: THE RISE TO SELF-ASSERTION OF ASIAN AND AFRICAN PEOPLES. S/ASIA CULTURE NAT/G SECT DIPLOM ATTIT SOVEREIGN MARXISM ...POLICY BIBLIOG 19/20. PAGE 46 H0919
NAT/LISM COLONIAL AFR ASIA

B60
HAMADY S.,TEMPERAMENT AND CHARACTER OF THE ARABS. FAM NAT/G SECT DIPLOM NAT/LISM...POLICY 20 ARABS. PAGE 65 H1299
NAT/COMP PERSON CULTURE ISLAM

B60
HAUSER O.,PREUSSISCHE STAATSRASON UND NATIONALER GEDANKE. PRUSSIA SOCIETY PRESS ADMIN...CONCPT 19/20. PAGE 68 H1358
NAT/LISM NAT/G ATTIT PROVS

B60
KOHN H.,PAN-SLAVISM: ITS HISTORY AND IDEOLOGY. COM CZECHOSLVK EUR+WWI MOD/EUR USSR YUGOSLAVIA CULTURE ELITES INTELL KIN NAT/G EDU/PROP DRIVE SOVEREIGN ...HUM PHIL/SCI MYTH HIST/WRIT 19/20. PAGE 87 H1745
ATTIT CONCPT NAT/LISM

B60
MACRIDIS R.C.,THE DE GAULLE REPUBLIC: QUEST FOR UNITY. EUR+WWI NAT/G POL/PAR LEGIS LEGIT NAT/LISM ATTIT RIGID/FLEX ORD/FREE PWR...JURID CONCPT TIME/SEQ 20 DEGAULLE/C. PAGE 100 H2009
TOP/EX STRUCT FRANCE

B60
MORRIS I.,NATIONALISM AND THE RIGHT WING IN JAPAN: A STUDY OF POST WAR TRENDS. ASIA ELITES NAT/G DELIB/GP FORCES TOP/EX CHOOSE ATTIT...INT GEN/LAWS CONGRESS 20 CHINJAP. PAGE 113 H2262
POL/PAR TREND NAT/LISM

B60
PIERCE R.A.,RUSSIAN CENTRAL ASIA, 1867-1917. ASIA RUSSIA CULTURE AGRI INDUS EDU/PROP REV NAT/LISM ...CHARTS BIBLIOG 19/20 BOLSHEVISM INTERVENT. PAGE 125 H2509
COLONIAL DOMIN ADMIN ECO/UNDEV

B60
WILLIAMS L.E.,OVERSEAS CHINESE NATIONALISM: THE GENESIS OF THE PAN-CHINESE MOVEMENT IN INDONESIA, 1900-1916. ASIA COM INDONESIA AGRI INT/ORG LOC/G DIPLOM EDU/PROP HABITAT PWR POPULISM...GEOG LING CENSUS 20. PAGE 168 H3367
NAT/LISM GP/REL DECISION NAT/G

B60
ZENKOVSKY S.A.,PAN-TURKISM AND ISLAM IN RUSSIA. ASIA RUSSIA USSR CULTURE POL/PAR DOMIN REV GP/REL MARXISM...LING GP/COMP BIBLIOG 19/20 TURKIC. PAGE 173 H3454
SECT NAT/LISM COM ISLAM

S60
APTER D.E.,"THE ROLE OF TRADITIONALISM IN THE POLITICAL MODERNIZATION OF GHANA AND UGANDA" (BMR)" AFR GHANA UGANDA CULTURE NAT/G POL/PAR NAT/LISM ...CON/ANAL 20. PAGE 8 H0152
CONSERVE ADMIN GOV/COMP PROB/SOLV

S60
CROZIER B.,"FRANCE AND ALGERIA." ALGERIA EUR+WWI FRANCE FUT ISLAM ECO/UNDEV NEIGH CONSULT DELIB/GP ECO/TAC COLONIAL COERCE ATTIT...SOC INT CON/ANAL 20. PAGE 36 H0713
NAT/G FORCES GUERRILLA NAT/LISM

S60
KELLEY G.A.,"THE POLITICAL BACKGROUND OF THE FRENCH A-BOMB." EUR+WWI USSR FORCES TOP/EX TEC/DEV NUC/PWR ATTIT PWR...CONCPT OBS/ENVIR TREND 20. PAGE 84 H1686
NAT/G RESPECT NAT/LISM FRANCE

S60
NORTH R.C.,"THE NEW EXPANSIONISM." ASIA CHINA/COM FUT INDIA CULTURE SOCIETY NAT/G TOP/EX DOMIN COERCE PWR MARXISM...CONCPT TIME/SEQ TREND GEN/LAWS COLD/WAR 20 MAO. PAGE 119 H2372
ATTIT DRIVE NAT/LISM

S60
SHILS E.,"THE INTELLECTUALS IN THE POLITICAL DEVELOPMENT OF THE NEW STATES." AFR ASIA S/ASIA ELITES LOC/G NAT/G CONSULT EX/STRUC CREATE PLAN ECO/TAC DOMIN LEGIT DRIVE PWR...TRADIT CONCPT STERTYP GEN/LAWS 20. PAGE 143 H2861
POL/PAR INTELL NAT/LISM

S60
SPIRO H.J.,"NEW CONSTITUTIONAL FORMS IN AFRICA." FUT CULTURE SOCIETY ECO/UNDEV NAT/G POL/PAR VOL/ASSN EDU/PROP ATTIT DRIVE ORD/FREE PWR RESPECT ...POLICY CONCPT OBS TREND CON/ANAL STERTYP GEN/LAWS VAL/FREE. PAGE 148 H2950
AFR CONSTN FOR/AID NAT/LISM

C60
EBENSTEIN W.,"MODERN POLITICAL THOUGHT (2ND ED.)" NAT/G CAP/ISM NAT/LISM PERSON ORD/FREE PWR ALL/IDEOS NEW/LIB SOCISM...TRADIT PSY BIBLIOG/A 18/20. PAGE 44 H0884
IDEA/COMP PHIL/SCI CONCPT GEN/LAWS

C60
WRIGGINS W.H.,"CEYLON: DILEMMAS OF A NEW NATION." ASIA CEYLON CONSTN STRUCT POL/PAR SECT FORCES DIPLOM GOV/REL NAT/LISM...CHARTS BIBLIOG 20. PAGE 171 H3417
PROB/SOLV NAT/G ECO/UNDEV

B61
ANSPRENGER F.,POLITIK IM SCHWARZEN AFRIKA. FRANCE NAT/G DIPLOM REGION REV NAT/LISM...CHARTS BIBLIOG 19/20. PAGE 7 H0141
AFR COLONIAL SOVEREIGN

B61
APTER D.E.,THE POLITICAL KINGDOM IN UGANDA. UGANDA CULTURE ECO/UNDEV AGRI KIN SECT TOP/EX REGION ATTIT HABITAT CONSERVE...GEOG AUD/VIS 20. PAGE 8 H0153
NAT/LISM POL/PAR COLONIAL ECO/TAC

B61
ATTLEE C.R.,EMPIRE INTO COMMONWEALTH. AFR ASIA CANADA UK NAT/G WAR NAT/LISM ATTIT...POLICY 20 AUSTRAL. PAGE 9 H0179
DIPLOM GP/REL COLONIAL SOVEREIGN

B61
BINDER L.,RELIGION AND POLITICS IN PAKISTAN. ISLAM PAKISTAN NAT/G SECT LEGIS CREATE CHOOSE GP/REL ...MAJORIT TRADIT 20. PAGE 17 H0336
CONSTN CONFER NAT/LISM POL/PAR

B61
BROUGHTON M.,PRESS AND POLITICS OF SOUTH AFRICA. SOUTH/AFR NAT/G COLONIAL GP/REL ADJUST 20. PAGE 22 H0435
NAT/LISM PRESS PWR CULTURE

B61
BROWN D.M.,THE NATIONALIST MOVEMENT. INDIA CULTURE STRATA REV MORAL ORD/FREE...BIBLIOG 20 HINDU. PAGE 22 H0443
NAT/LISM LEAD CHIEF POL/PAR

B61
BULLOCK A.,HITLER: A STUDY IN TYRANNY. EUR+WWI GERMANY SOCIETY STRUCT NAT/G POL/PAR FORCES CREATE DOMIN EDU/PROP EXEC COERCE WAR NAT/LISM DISPL DRIVE PERSON PWR...PSY NAZI 20 HITLER/A. PAGE 23 H0470
ATTIT BIOG TOTALISM

B61
CONOVER H.F.,SERIALS FOR AFRICAN STUDIES. ECO/UNDEV DIPLOM LEAD NAT/LISM ATTIT...SOC 20. PAGE 33 H0653
BIBLIOG AFR NAT/G

B61
DIA M.,THE AFRICAN NATIONS AND WORLD SOLIDARITY. ISLAM CULTURE ELITES ECO/DEV ECO/UNDEV INT/ORG NAT/G PLAN ECO/TAC INT/TRADE EDU/PROP NAT/LISM ATTIT DRIVE ORD/FREE WEALTH...SOCIALIST CONCPT CON/ANAL GEN/LAWS TOT/POP 20. PAGE 41 H0817
AFR REGION SOCISM

B61
DUFFY J.,AFRICA SPEAKS. GHANA TOGO CULTURE ECO/UNDEV PROB/SOLV COLONIAL NEUTRAL DISCRIM NAT/LISM SOVEREIGN ALL/IDEOS...CONCPT ANTHOL SOC/INTEG 20 NEGRO THIRD/WRLD. PAGE 43 H0857
AFR NAT/G FUT STRUCT

B61
ESTEBAN J.C.,IMPERIALISMO Y DESARROLLO ECONOMICO. L/A+17C FINAN INDUS NAT/G ECO/TAC CONTROL ROLE. PAGE 47 H0941
ECO/UNDEV NAT/LISM DIPLOM BAL/PAY

B61
HISTORICAL RESEARCH INSTITUTE,A SHORT BIBLIOGRAPHY OF INDO-MUSLIM HISTORY. INDIA S/ASIA DIPLOM EDU/PROP COLONIAL LEAD NAT/LISM ATTIT...BIOG 19/20. PAGE 71 H1427
BIBLIOG NAT/G SECT POL/PAR

B61
KEDOURIE E.,NATIONALISM (REV. ED.). MOD/EUR SOVEREIGN...CONCPT 19/20. PAGE 84 H1675
NAT/LISM NAT/G CREATE REV

B61
KEREKES T.,THE ARAB MIDDLE EAST AND MUSLIM AFRICA. ISLAM SOCIETY ECO/UNDEV SECT VOL/ASSN TOP/EX REGION ATTIT PWR...GEOG CONCPT TIME/SEQ GEN/LAWS 20. PAGE 85 H1694
NAT/G TREND NAT/LISM

B61
KHAN A.W.,INDIA WINS FREEDOM: THE OTHER SIDE. INDIA PAKISTAN CULTURE LEGIS DIPLOM PARL/PROC REV WAR NAT/LISM 20. PAGE 85 H1707
SOVEREIGN GP/REL RACE/REL ORD/FREE

B61
LEHMAN R.L.,AFRICA SOUTH OF THE SAHARA (PAMPHLET). DIPLOM COLONIAL NAT/LISM. PAGE 93 H1863
BIBLIOG/A AFR CULTURE NAT/G

B61
LICHTHEIM G.,MARXISM. GERMANY SOCIETY WORKER CAP/ISM ECO/TAC NAT/LISM POPULISM...TIME/SEQ GOV/COMP NAT/COMP 18/20 COM/PARTY. PAGE 96 H1924
MARXISM SOCISM IDEA/COMP CULTURE

B61
LUZ N.V.,A LUTA PELA INDUSTRIALIZACAO DO BRAZIL. BRAZIL L/A+17C AGRI NAT/G TEC/DEV COLONIAL 19/20. PAGE 99 H1981
ECO/UNDEV INDUS NAT/LISM POLICY

B61
PALMER N.D.,THE INDIAN POLITICAL SYSTEM. INDIA ECO/UNDEV SECT CHIEF COLONIAL CHOOSE ALL/IDEOS SOCISM...CHARTS BIBLIOG/A 20. PAGE 123 H2452
NAT/LISM POL/PAR NAT/G DIPLOM

B61
PANIKKAR K.M.,THE VOICE OF FREEDOM: SELECTED SPEECHES OF PANDIT MOTILAL NEHRU. INDIA UK CONSTN FINAN FORCES LEGIS DIPLOM TAX COLONIAL...POLICY MAJORIT ANTHOL 20 NEHRU/PM. PAGE 123 H2460
NAT/LISM ORD/FREE CHIEF NAT/G

B61
PANIKKAR K.M.,REVOLUTION IN AFRICA. AFR GUINEA ECO/UNDEV POL/PAR DIPLOM COLONIAL EXEC LEAD SOVEREIGN...CHARTS 20. PAGE 123 H2461
NAT/LISM NAT/G CHIEF

B61
ROIG E.,MARTI, ANTIIMPERIALISTA. CUBA L/A+17C DIPLOM DOMIN COLONIAL CONTROL LEAD PWR SOVEREIGN ...PHIL/SCI 19 MARTI/JOSE INTERVENT. PAGE 133 H2664
PERSON NAT/LISM ECO/UNDEV ORD/FREE

B61
SAFRAN M.,EGYPT IN SEARCH OF POLITICAL COMMUNITY: AN ANALYSIS OF THE INTELLECTUAL AND POLITICAL EVOLUTION OF EGYPT, 1804-1952. ISLAM NAT/G SECT EDU/PROP COERCE ATTIT DRIVE KNOWL PWR...TIME/SEQ 20. PAGE 137 H2729
INTELL NAT/LISM UAR

B61
SAKAI R.K.,STUDIES ON ASIA, 1961. ASIA BURMA INDIA S/ASIA FINAN ECO/TAC NAT/LISM SOCISM...POLICY ANTHOL 19/20 CHINJAP. PAGE 137 H2734
ECO/UNDEV SECT

B62
AMERICAN SOCIETY AFR CULTURE,PAN-AFRICANISM RECONSIDERED. AFR SOCIETY STRUCT SCHOOL CAP/ISM EDU/PROP...ART/METH NEW/IDEA PREDICT ANTHOL 20 PANAF/FREE NEGRO. PAGE 6 H0123
DIPLOM FEDERAL NAT/LISM CULTURE

B62
BAULIN J.,THE ARAB ROLE IN AFRICA. AFR ALGERIA FUT ISLAM MOROCCO UAR COLONIAL NEUTRAL REV...SOC 20 TUNIS BOURGUIBA. PAGE 12 H0240
NAT/LISM DIPLOM NAT/G SECT

B62
BERGER M.,THE ARAB WORLD TODAY. CULTURE FAM INT/ORG NAT/G SECT FORCES ECO/TAC NAT/LISM HABITAT...CHARTS BIBLIOG 20 ARABS. PAGE 15 H0301
ISLAM PERSON STRUCT SOCIETY

B62
BRETTON H.L.,POWER AND STABILITY IN NIGERIA: THE POLITICS OF DECOLONIZATION. AFR CONSTN INTELL ECO/UNDEV COM/IND KIN NAT/G POL/PAR PROVS VOL/ASSN LEGIS DOMIN EDU/PROP LEGIT EXEC ROUTINE CHOOSE NAT/LISM ATTIT PERCEPT ALL/VALS. PAGE 20 H0411
CULTURE OBS NIGERIA

B62
BUSIA K.A.,THE CHALLENGE OF AFRICA. CULTURE KIN MUNIC NAT/G POL/PAR SCHOOL DELIB/GP PLAN ECO/TAC DOMIN EDU/PROP TOTALISM ATTIT PERSON ALL/VALS SOVEREIGN...SOC CONCPT STERTYP TOT/POP VAL/FREE 20. PAGE 25 H0496
AFR ECO/UNDEV NAT/LISM

B62
CARTER G.M.,AFRICAN ONE-PARTY STATES. ISLAM IVORY/CST LIBERIA CONSTN CULTURE SOCIETY POL/PAR PLAN DOMIN EDU/PROP EXEC REGION CHOOSE ATTIT ALL/VALS...CONCPT TIME/SEQ CHARTS VAL/FREE 20 TANGANYIKA. PAGE 27 H0545
AFR NAT/LISM

B62
CARY J.,THE CASE FOR AFRICAN FREEDOM AND OTHER WRITINGS ON AFRICA. AFR UK INDUS LOC/G NAT/G SECT INT/TRADE EDU/PROP GOV/REL RACE/REL ORD/FREE ...CONCPT ANTHOL 19/20. PAGE 27 H0552
NAT/LISM COLONIAL TREND ECO/UNDEV

B62
GREEN L.P.,DEVELOPMENT IN AFRICA. AFR CENTRL/AFR GHANA RHODESIA SOUTH/AFR AGRI PROC/MFG INT/TRADE DEMAND NAT/LISM PRODUC WEALTH...GEOG METH/CNCPT CHARTS BIBLIOG 20. PAGE 60 H1206
CULTURE ECO/UNDEV GOV/REL TREND

B62
GUENA Y.,HISTORIQUE DE LA COMMUNAUTE. FUT ECO/UNDEV NAT/G PLAN EDU/PROP COLONIAL REGION NAT/LISM ALL/VALS SOVEREIGN...CONCPT OBS CHARTS 20. PAGE 62 H1244
AFR VOL/ASSN FOR/AID FRANCE

B62
HAIM S.G.,ARAB NATIONALISM. ISLAM CONSTN GP/REL ...ANTHOL BIBLIOG JEWS 20 MID/EAST ARABS. PAGE 64 H1279
NAT/LISM REV SECT DIPLOM

B62
HATCH J.,AFRICA TODAY-AND TOMORROW: AN OUTLINE OF BASIC FACTS AND MAJOR PROBLEMS. AFR FUT ISLAM STRATA ECO/UNDEV INT/ORG NAT/G POL/PAR DELIB/GP TOP/EX EDU/PROP LEGIT CHOOSE ATTIT...TIME/SEQ TOT/POP COLD/WAR 20. PAGE 67 H1353
PLAN CONSTN NAT/LISM

B62
INGHAM K.,A HISTORY OF EAST AFRICA. NAT/G DIPLOM ADMIN WAR NAT/LISM...SOC BIOG BIBLIOG. PAGE 77 H1534
AFR CONSTN COLONIAL

B62
JENNINGS I.,PARTY POLITICS: THE STUFF OF POLITICS (VOL.III). UK NAT/G SECT CHIEF INT/TRADE RECEIVE COLONIAL GP/REL NAT/LISM ORD/FREE SOCISM 19/20 CHURCH/STA WHIG/PARTY. PAGE 80 H1607
POL/PAR CONSTN PWR ALL/IDEOS

B62
LEGUM C.,PAN-AFRICANISM: A SHORT POLITICAL GUIDE. ISLAM CULTURE INTELL ECO/DEV NAT/G POL/PAR DELIB/GP PLAN EDU/PROP FEDERAL NAT/LISM ATTIT DRIVE PERSON ...RECORD TIME/SEQ CHARTS STERTYP 20. PAGE 93 H1861
AFR CONCPT

B62
MANNING H.T.,THE REVOLT OF FRENCH CANADA 1800-1835. CANADA UK CULTURE GOV/REL RACE/REL...BIBLIOG 19. PAGE 102 H2039
NAT/LISM COLONIAL GEOG

B62
MANSERGH N.,SOUTH AFRICA 1906-1961: THE PRICE OF MAGNANIMITY. SOUTH/AFR LEGIS LEGIT SUFF NAT/LISM ATTIT ORD/FREE 20 NEGRO 20. PAGE 102 H2041
COLONIAL DISCRIM NAT/G

B62
NOBECOURT R.G.,LES SECRETS DE LA PROPAGANDE EN FRANCE OCCUPEE. FRANCE ELITES NAT/G DIPLOM GP/REL NAT/LISM TOTALISM ORD/FREE 20 VICHY VICHY. PAGE 118 H2365
METH/COMP EDU/PROP WAR CONTROL

B62
PAIKERT G.C.,THE GERMAN EXODUS. EUR+WWI GERMANY/W LAW CULTURE SOCIETY STRUCT INDUS NAT/LISM RESPECT SOVEREIGN...CHARTS BIBLIOG SOC/INTEG 20 MIGRATION. PAGE 122 H2444
INGP/REL STRANGE GEOG GP/REL

B62
ROSENZWEIG F.,HEGEL UND DER STAAT. GERMANY SOCIETY FAM POL/PAR NAT/LISM...BIOG 19. PAGE 134 H2682
JURID NAT/G CONCPT PHIL/SCI

B62
SCALAPINO R.A.,PARTIES AND POLITICS IN CONTEMPORARY JAPAN. EX/STRUC DIPLOM CHOOSE NAT/LISM ATTIT ...POLICY 20 CHINJAP. PAGE 138 H2762
POL/PAR PARL/PROC ELITES DECISION

B62
SCHECHTMAN J.B.,POSTWAR POPULATION TRANSFERS IN EUROPE: 1945-1955. COM CZECHOSLVK GERMANY POLAND USSR CULTURE SOCIETY PROB/SOLV AGREE NAT/LISM...SOC STAT TREND CHARTS METH/COMP 20 MIGRATION. PAGE 139 H2778
GEOG CENSUS EUR+WWI HABITAT

B62
SCHMIDT-VOLKMAR E.,DER KULTURKAMPF IN DEUTSCHLAND 1871-1890. GERMANY PRUSSIA SOCIETY STRUCT SECT DIPLOM GP/REL NAT/LISM 19 CHURCH/STA BISMARCK/O. PAGE 139 H2789
POL/PAR CATHISM ATTIT NAT/G

B62
VAN RENSBURG P.,GUILTY LAND: THE HISTORY OF APARTHEID. SOUTH/AFR NAT/G POL/PAR DOMIN CHOOSE ...SOC 19/20 NEGRO. PAGE 162 H3231
RACE/REL DISCRIM NAT/LISM POLICY

B62
WEHLER H.V.,SOZIALDEMOKRATIE UND NATIONALSTAAT. GERMANY POLAND USSR CULTURE SOCIETY STRUCT NAT/G POL/PAR DIPLOM ORD/FREE 19/20. PAGE 166 H3325
NAT/LISM SOVEREIGN GP/REL ATTIT

B62
ZINKIN T.,REPORTING INDIA. INDIA PAKISTAN WOR+45 SOCIETY SECT FORCES EDU/PROP CROWD DISCRIM NAT/LISM MARXISM...POLICY 20. PAGE 173 H3457
STRATA COLONIAL BAL/PWR CONTROL

S62
ANSPRENGER F.,"NATIONALISM, COMMUNISM, AND THE UNCOMMITTED NATIONS: AMERICAN PROFILES." FUT ISLAM CULTURE SOCIETY ECO/UNDEV NAT/G POL/PAR PLAN ECO/TAC EDU/PROP COERCE CHOOSE ALL/VALS MARXISM SOCISM...SOC CONCPT BIOG TREND 20. PAGE 7 H0142
AFR COM NAT/LISM

S62
CROAN M.,"POLYCENTRISM: COMMUNIST INTERNATIONAL RELATIONS." ASIA STRUCT INT/ORG NAT/G POL/PAR CONSULT PLAN DOMIN EDU/PROP COERCE ATTIT RIGID/FLEX SOCISM...POLICY CONCPT TREND CON/ANAL GEN/LAWS MARX/KARL. PAGE 35 H0703
COM CREATE DIPLOM NAT/LISM

S62
KOLARZ W.,"THE IMPACT OF COMMUNISM ON WEST AFRICA." AFR FUT SOCIETY INT/ORG NAT/G CREATE PLAN DOMIN EDU/PROP COERCE NAT/LISM ATTIT RIGID/FLEX SOCISM ...POLICY CONCPT TREND MARX/KARL 20. PAGE 88 H1751
COM POL/PAR COLONIAL

S62
LANGER W.L.,"FAREWELL TO EMPIRE." EUR+WWI MOD/EUR NAT/G DIPLOM EDU/PROP COLONIAL ATTIT ORD/FREE PWR SOVEREIGN WEALTH...CONCPT TIME/SEQ GEN/LAWS TOT/POP VAL/FREE CMN/WLTH 20. PAGE 91 H1810
DOMIN ECO/TAC NAT/LISM

S62
LEGUM C.,"THE DANGERS OF INDEPENDENCE" AFR UGANDA NAT/G DIPLOM DOMIN REGION CENTRAL ATTIT POPULISM 20. PAGE 93 H1862
ORD/FREE SOVEREIGN NAT/LISM GOV/COMP

S62
MBOYA T.,"RELATIONS BETWEEN THE PRESS AND GOVERNMENT IN AFRICA." AFR DIPLOM EDU/PROP NAT/LISM ORD/FREE SOVEREIGN 20. PAGE 106 H2115
PRESS GP/REL ATTIT NAT/G

S62
PASSIN H.,"THE SOURCES OF PROTEST IN JAPAN." CULTURE SOCIETY EDU/PROP COERCE NAT/LISM DISPL DRIVE PWR RESPECT...POLICY SOC TREND 20 CHINJAP.
ASIA ATTIT REV

PAGE 124 H2473

S62
ROTBERG R.,"THE RISE OF AFRICAN NATIONALISM: THE CASE OF EAST AND CENTRAL AFRICA." AFR CULTURE SOCIETY NEIGH DIPLOM DOMIN COLONIAL COERCE DISPL PERCEPT PWR SOVEREIGN...POLICY OBS/ENVIR TREND WORK 20. PAGE 135 H2690 — ATTIT DRIVE NAT/LISM REV

S62
SARKISYANZ E.,"NATIONALISM, CAPITALISM, AND THE UNCOMMITED NATIONS: MARXISM AND ASIAN CULTURAL TRADITIONS." ASIA BURMA CHINA/COM COM CULTURE SOCIETY NAT/G POL/PAR PLAN DOMIN EDU/PROP COLONIAL COERCE ATTIT RIGID/FLEX...CONCPT TREND MARX/KARL 20 TIBET BUDDHISM. PAGE 138 H2755 — S/ASIA SECT NAT/LISM CAP/ISM

S62
SHATTEN F.,"POLYCENTRISM: AFRICA: NATIONALISM AND COMMUNISM." ASIA COM FUT ISLAM CULTURE SOCIETY ECO/UNDEV NAT/G PLAN DOMIN COLONIAL COERCE CHOOSE RIGID/FLEX ALL/VALS MARXISM...CONCPT TREND 20. PAGE 143 H2852 — AFR ATTIT NAT/LISM SOCISM

S62
STRACHEY J.,"COMMUNIST INTENTIONS." ASIA USSR YUGOSLAVIA INT/ORG NAT/G FORCES DOMIN EDU/PROP COERCE NUC/PWR NAT/LISM PEACE RIGID/FLEX PWR MARXISM...CONCPT MYTH OBS TIME/SEQ TREND COLD/WAR TOT/POP 20. PAGE 150 H2992 — COM ATTIT WAR

B63
BIDNEY D.,THE CONCEPT OF FREEDOM IN ANTHROPOLOGY. UNIV CULTURE STRATA SECT CREATE NAT/LISM ...METH/COMP 20. PAGE 17 H0332 — SOC PERSON ORD/FREE CONCPT

B63
CANELAS O.A.,RADIOGRAFIA DE LA ALIANZA PARA EL ATRASO. L/A+17C USA+45 ECO/TAC DOMIN COLONIAL NAT/LISM...SOCIALIST NAT/COMP 20. PAGE 26 H0519 — REV DIPLOM ECO/UNDEV REGION

B63
CONZE W.,DIE DEUTSCHE NATION. GERMANY NAT/G POL/PAR WAR ORD/FREE...TREND 8/20 NAZI. PAGE 33 H0657 — NAT/LISM FASCISM ATTIT SOCIETY

B63
CRANKSHAW E.,THE NEW COLD WAR: MOSCOW V. PEKIN. CHINA/COM USSR INTELL POL/PAR DELIB/GP CAP/ISM COERCE REV NAT/LISM TOTALISM DRIVE...POLICY IDEA/COMP 20 KHRUSH/N. PAGE 35 H0698 — ATTIT DIPLOM NAT/COMP MARXISM

B63
CREMEANS C.,THE ARABS AND THE WORLD: NASSER'S ARAB NATIONALIST POLICY. FUT ISLAM UAR USA+45 SOCIETY STRATA NAT/G POL/PAR PLAN DIPLOM EDU/PROP LEGIT DRIVE ALL/VALS...INT TIME/SEQ CHARTS 20 NASSER/G. PAGE 35 H0700 — TOP/EX ATTIT REGION NAT/LISM

B63
DECOTTIGNIES R.,LES NATIONALITES AFRICAINES. AFR NAT/G PROB/SOLV DIPLOM COLONIAL ORD/FREE...CHARTS GOV/COMP 20. PAGE 39 H0781 — NAT/LISM JURID LEGIS LAW

B63
ELIAS T.O.,GOVERNMENT AND POLITICS IN AFRICA. CONSTN CULTURE SOCIETY NAT/G POL/PAR DIPLOM REPRESENT PERSON...SOC TREND BIBLIOG 4/20. PAGE 45 H0906 — AFR NAT/LISM COLONIAL LAW

B63
FABER K.,DIE NATIONALISTISCHE PUBLIZISTIK DEUTSCHLANDS VON 1866 BIS 1871 (2 VOLS.). EUR+WWI GERMANY DIPLOM EDU/PROP 19. PAGE 48 H0957 — BIBLIOG/A NAT/G NAT/LISM POL/PAR

B63
FRANZ G.,TEILUNG UND WIEDERVEREINIGUNG. GERMANY IRELAND ITALY NETHERLAND POLAND CULTURE BAL/PWR CHOOSE NAT/LISM ORD/FREE SOVEREIGN 19/20. PAGE 53 H1054 — DIPLOM WAR NAT/COMP ATTIT

B63
FRIED R.C.,THE ITALIAN PREFECTS. ITALY STRATA ECO/DEV NAT/LISM ALL/IDEOS...TREND CHARTS METH/COMP BIBLIOG 17/20 PREFECT. PAGE 53 H1061 — ADMIN NAT/G EFFICIENCY

B63
GEERTZ C.,OLD SOCIETIES AND NEW STATES: THE QUEST FOR MODERNITY IN ASIA AND AFRICA. AFR ASIA LAW CULTURE SECT EDU/PROP REV...GOV/COMP NAT/COMP 20. PAGE 55 H1107 — ECO/UNDEV TEC/DEV NAT/LISM SOVEREIGN

B63
HUGHES A.J.,EAST AFRICA: THE SEARCH FOR UNITY- KENYA, TANGANYIKA, UGANDA, AND ZANZIBAR. TANZANIA UGANDA CONSTN POL/PAR SECT CHIEF DELIB/GP LEGIS WAR CHOOSE NAT/LISM MARXISM...POLICY CHARTS 20 NEGRO UN. PAGE 74 H1488 — NAT/G DOMIN LOC/G AFR

B63
ISSAWI C.,EGYPT IN REVOLUTION: AN ECONOMIC ANALYSIS. ISLAM STRUCT ECO/UNDEV AGRI FINAN INDUS PLAN EXEC REV NAT/LISM ATTIT RIGID/FLEX WEALTH SOCISM...STAT WORK 20. PAGE 79 H1573 — NAT/G UAR

B63
JENNINGS W.I.,DEMOCRACY IN AFRICA. UK CULTURE STRUCT ECO/UNDEV DIPLOM COLONIAL GP/REL ADJUST NAT/LISM ORD/FREE...GOV/COMP 20 THIRD/WRLD. PAGE 81 H1613 — PROB/SOLV AFR CONSTN POPULISM

B63
KHADDURI M.,MODERN LIBYA: A STUDY IN POLITICAL DEVELOPMENT. EUR+WWI ISLAM LIBYA ELITES INT/ORG POL/PAR FORCES DIPLOM FOR/AID DOMIN EDU/PROP LEGIT NAT/LISM DRIVE RIGID/FLEX SKILL...CONCPT TIME/SEQ TREND 20. PAGE 85 H1704 — NAT/G STRUCT

B63
LEE C.,THE POLITICS OF KOREAN NATIONALISM. KOREA S/ASIA DIPLOM REV WAR 14/20 CHINJAP. PAGE 93 H1855 — NAT/LISM SOVEREIGN COLONIAL

B63
LEWIN J.,POLITICS AND LAW IN SOUTH AFRICA. SOUTH/AFR UK POL/PAR BAL/PWR ECO/TAC COLONIAL CONTROL GP/REL DISCRIM PWR 20 NEGRO. PAGE 96 H1909 — NAT/LISM POLICY LAW RACE/REL

B63
LYON P.,NEUTRALISM. ECO/UNDEV EDU/PROP COLONIAL ALL/IDEOS...IDEA/COMP 20 COLD/WAR UN. PAGE 99 H1985 — NAT/COMP NAT/LISM DIPLOM NEUTRAL

B63
MAIR L.,NEW NATIONS. AFR FAM MUNIC SECT DOMIN CHOOSE NAT/LISM ORD/FREE...SOC 19/20. PAGE 101 H2022 — COLONIAL CULTURE TEC/DEV ECO/UNDEV

B63
MARTINDALE D.,COMMUNITY, CHARACTER AND CIVILIZATION: STUDIES IN SOCIAL BEHAVIORISM. INTELL FAM NEIGH VOL/ASSN GP/REL NAT/LISM ATTIT PERSON ...CONCPT GP/COMP 20 BEHAVIORSM. PAGE 103 H2066 — SOC METH/COMP CULTURE STRUCT

B63
MERKL P.H.,THE ORIGIN OF THE WEST GERMAN REPUBLIC. GERMANY/W WOR+45 POL/PAR DIPLOM LEAD LOBBY REPRESENT GP/REL NAT/LISM 20. PAGE 109 H2179 — CONSTN PARL/PROC CONTROL BAL/PWR

B63
MONTAGUE J.B. JR.,CLASS AND NATIONALITY; ENGLISH AND AMERICAN STUDIES. UK USA+45 ELITES STRUCT WORKER ATTIT PWR...SOC CHARTS SOC/EXP 20. PAGE 112 H2243 — STRATA NAT/LISM PERSON NAT/COMP

B63
MOSELY P.E.,THE SOVIET UNION, 1922-1962: A FOREIGN AFFAIRS READER. ASIA POLAND USSR CULTURE INTELL AGRI POL/PAR WORKER INT/TRADE DOMIN WAR NAT/LISM MARXISM SOCISM 20 KHRUSH/N. PAGE 113 H2267 — PWR POLICY DIPLOM

B63
NALBANDIAN L.,THE ARMENIAN REVOLUTIONARY MOVEMENT. MOD/EUR RUSSIA...IDEA/COMP NAT/COMP BIBLIOG 19 ARMENIA OTTOMAN. PAGE 115 H2306 — NAT/LISM REV POL/PAR ORD/FREE

B63
OTERO L.M.,HONDURAS. HONDURAS SPAIN STRUCT SECT COLONIAL REV WAR ATTIT PWR...GEOG WORSHIP 16/20. PAGE 122 H2432 — NAT/G SOCIETY NAT/LISM ECO/UNDEV

B63
RIVKIN A.,THE AFRICAN PRESENCE IN WORLD AFFAIRS. ECO/UNDEV AGRI INT/ORG LOC/G NAT/LISM...OBS PREDICT GOV/COMP 20. PAGE 132 H2635 — AFR NAT/G DIPLOM BAL/PWR

B63
RUITENBEER H.M.,THE DILEMMA OF ORGANIZATIONAL SOCIETY. CULTURE ECO/DEV MUNIC SECT TEC/DEV EDU/PROP NAT/LISM ORD/FREE...NAT/COMP 20 RIESMAN/D WHYTE/WF MERTON/R MEAD/MARG JASPERS/K. PAGE 136 H2716 — PERSON ROLE ADMIN WORKER

B63
SAKAI R.K.,STUDIES ON ASIA, 1963. ASIA INDIA ISRAEL S/ASIA USA+45 PERF/ART POL/PAR SECT REGION NAT/LISM ...SOC LING TREND ANTHOL 19/20 CHINJAP. PAGE 137 H2735 — PWR CULTURE

B63
SILVERT K.H.,EXPECTANT PEOPLES: NATIONALISM AND DEVELOPMENT. CULTURE STRATA SECT LEAD REGION RACE/REL ALL/IDEOS...GEN/LAWS SOC/INTEG 20. PAGE 144 H2877 — NAT/LISM ECO/UNDEV ALL/VALS

B63
SINGH H.L.,PROBLEMS AND POLICIES OF THE BRITISH IN INDIA, 1885-1898. INDIA UK NAT/G FORCES LEGIS PROB/SOLV CONTROL RACE/REL ADJUST DISCRIM NAT/LISM RIGID/FLEX...MGT 19 CIVIL/SERV. PAGE 144 H2885 — COLONIAL PWR POLICY ADMIN

B63
SKLAR R.L.,NIGERIAN POLITICAL PARTIES: POWER IN AN EMERGENT AFRICAN NATION. AFR EUR+WWI CULTURE STRATA NAT/G DELIB/GP EX/STRUC LEGIS DOMIN EDU/PROP ROUTINE CHOOSE ATTIT PERCEPT ORD/FREE PWR...SOC CONCPT OBS TOT/POP VAL/FREE. PAGE 145 H2898 — POL/PAR SOCIETY NAT/LISM NIGERIA

B63
STEVENS G.G.,EGYPT YESTERDAY AND TODAY. CONSTN ECO/UNDEV AGRI INDUS NAT/G POL/PAR FORCES ECO/TAC EDU/PROP COERCE WAR NAT/LISM DRIVE ALL/VALS ...TIME/SEQ WORK SUEZ 20. PAGE 149 H2983 — ISLAM TOP/EX REV UAR

B63
SWEARER H.R.,CONTEMPORARY COMMUNISM: THEORY AND PRACTICE. COM USSR SOCIETY ECO/DEV POL/PAR FORCES — MARXISM CONCPT

PLAN ADMIN LEAD NAT/LISM...POLICY ANTHOL 20 LENIN/VI COM/PARTY. PAGE 151 H3015 DIPLOM NAT/G

B63
TOUVAL S.,SOMALI NATIONALISM: INTERNATIONAL POLITICS AND THE DRIVE FOR UNITY IN THE HORN OF AFRICA. AFR CULTURE PROVS LEGIS EDU/PROP REGION COERCE ATTIT...MYTH UNPLAN/INT TIME/SEQ SOMALI VAL/FREE 20. PAGE 156 H3118 SOCIETY EXEC NAT/LISM

B63
VALJAVEC F.,AUSGEWAHLTE AUFSATZE. GERMANY HUNGARY STRUCT ATTIT...CONCPT IDEA/COMP 18/20 BALKANS. PAGE 161 H3223 SOCIETY CULTURE GP/REL NAT/LISM

B63
VIARD R.,LA FIN DE L'EMPIRE COLONIAL FRANCAIS. AFR FUT S/ASIA ECO/UNDEV NAT/G CONSULT PLAN ECO/TAC EDU/PROP REGION NAT/LISM ALL/VALS...CONCPT TIME/SEQ TREND VAL/FREE 20. PAGE 162 H3248 VOL/ASSN COLONIAL FRANCE

B63
VON DER MEHDEN F.R.,RELIGION AND NATIONALISM IN SOUTHEAST ASIA. BURMA PHILIPPINE S/ASIA INTELL SOCIETY DOMIN EDU/PROP LEGIT ATTIT MORAL ORD/FREE ...SOC CENSUS HIST/WRIT TOT/POP VAL/FREE 20 WORSHIP LONDON. PAGE 163 H3265 SECT CULTURE NAT/LISM

B63
WILCOX W.A.,PAKISTAN; THE CONSOLIDATION OF A NATION. INDIA PAKISTAN CONSTN SECT PROB/SOLV COLONIAL PARTIC GP/REL FEDERAL...POLICY 19/20. PAGE 168 H3361 NAT/LISM ECO/UNDEV DIPLOM STRUCT

B63
ZARTMAN I.W.,GOVERNMENT AND POLITICS IN NORTHERN AFRICA. AFR ALGERIA ISLAM LIBYA MOROCCO UAR ELITES SOCIETY PLAN ECO/TAC DOMIN EDU/PROP LEGIT ATTIT ...GEOG CONCPT TIME/SEQ 20 TUNIS. PAGE 172 H3448 CULTURE DRIVE NAT/LISM

L63
MICHAEL F.,"KHRUSHCHEV'S DISLOYAL OPPOSITION: STRUCTURAL CHANGE AND POWER STRUGGLE IN COMMUNIST BLOC." ASIA CHINA/COM FUT NAT/G POL/PAR CONSULT PLAN DOMIN ATTIT...POLICY CONCPT TREND MARX/KARL 20 KHRUSH/N. PAGE 110 H2195 COM STRUCT NAT/LISM USSR

L63
ZARTMAN I.W.,"THE SAHARA--BRIDGE OR BARRIER." ISLAM CULTURE SOCIETY NAT/G DELIB/GP DOMIN EDU/PROP LEGIT ATTIT...HIST/WRIT TIME/SEQ CHARTS TOT/POP VAL/FREE 20. PAGE 172 H3447 INT/ORG PWR NAT/LISM

S63
AYAL E.B.,"VALUE SYSTEM AND ECONOMIC DEVELOPMENT IN JAPAN AND THAILAND." ASIA S/ASIA THAILAND CULTURE ECO/DEV CAP/ISM DOMIN NAT/LISM DRIVE RIGID/FLEX SOCISM...WELF/ST OBS TREND CON/ANAL GEN/LAWS 20 CHINJAP. PAGE 9 H0185 ECO/UNDEV ALL/VALS

S63
LERNER D.,"WILL EUROPEAN UNION BRING ABOUT MERGED NATIONAL GOALS." EUR+WWI FRANCE GERMANY UK ECO/DEV NAT/G VOL/ASSN DELIB/GP BAL/PWR ECO/TAC NAT/LISM EEC 20 DEGAULLE/C. PAGE 95 H1889 ATTIT STERTYP ELITES REGION

S63
MAZRUI A.A.,"ON THE CONCEPT 'WE ARE ALL AFRICANS'." AFR CULTURE KIN LOC/G NAT/G DOMIN EDU/PROP LEGIT ATTIT PERCEPT PERSON KNOWL ORD/FREE...TIME/SEQ TOT/POP 20. PAGE 106 H2110 PROVS INT/ORG NAT/LISM

S63
MBOYA T.,"AFRICAN SOCIALISM." ECO/UNDEV INT/ORG DIPLOM FOR/AID INT/TRADE REGION GP/REL ATTIT ORD/FREE EACM. PAGE 106 H2116 AFR SOCISM CULTURE NAT/LISM

S63
NYE J.,"TANGANYIKA'S SELF-HELP." TANZANIA NAT/G GIVE COST EFFICIENCY NAT/LISM 20. PAGE 119 H2381 ECO/TAC POL/PAR ECO/UNDEV WORKER

S63
OGOT B.,"FROM CHIEF TO PRESIDENT." AFR SECT REGION NAT/LISM...SOC GOV/COMP NAT/COMP 20 PRESIDENT. PAGE 121 H2410 CHIEF CULTURE LEAD ORD/FREE

S63
RUSTOW D.A.,"THE MILITARY IN MIDDLE EASTERN SOCIETY AND POLITICS." FUT ISLAM CONSTN SOCIETY FACE/GP NAT/G POL/PAR PROF/ORG CONSULT DOMIN ADMIN EXEC REGION COERCE NAT/LISM ATTIT DRIVE PERSON ORD/FREE PWR...POLICY CONCPT OBS STERTYP 20. PAGE 136 H2721 FORCES ELITES

S63
TANNER R.,"WHO GOES HOME?" CULTURE GP/REL SOC/INTEG 20 TANGANYIKA MIGRATION. PAGE 152 H3045 ADMIN COLONIAL NAT/G NAT/LISM

B64
AKZIN B.,STATE AND NATION. UNIV ECO/UNDEV DIPLOM RACE/REL NAT/LISM ATTIT PLURISM...CONCPT IDEA/COMP 20. PAGE 4 H0090 GP/REL NAT/G KIN

B64
ALDEFER H.F.,A BIBLIOGRAPHY OF AFRICAN GOVERNMENT: 1950-1964. ALGERIA GUINEA LIBERIA UAR ECO/UNDEV POL/PAR LEGIS COLONIAL LEAD PARL/PROC NAT/LISM 20. PAGE 5 H0098 BIBLIOG AFR LOC/G NAT/G

B64
ANDREWS D.H.,LATIN AMERICA: A BIBLIOGRAPHY OF PAPERBACK BOOKS. SECT INT/TRADE EDU/PROP WAR GOV/REL ADJUST NAT/LISM ATTIT...ART/METH LING BIOG 20. PAGE 7 H0138 BIBLIOG L/A+17C CULTURE NAT/G

B64
ARASARATNAM S.,CEYLON. CEYLON NETHERLAND PORTUGAL S/ASIA UK STRUCT ECO/UNDEV SECT DIPLOM DOMIN RACE/REL NAT/LISM 17/20 CMN/WLTH. PAGE 8 H0156 COLONIAL NAT/G PROB/SOLV CULTURE

B64
BELL W.,JAMAICAN LEADERS: POLITICAL ATTITUDES IN A NEW NATION. JAMAICA STRUCT ACT/RES CREATE PROB/SOLV DIPLOM COLONIAL LEAD...QU 20. PAGE 13 H0267 NAT/LISM ATTIT DRIVE SOVEREIGN

B64
BERNSTEIN H.,VENEZUELA AND COLOMBIA. L/A+17C VENEZUELA INTELL COLONIAL ATTIT 20 COLOMB. PAGE 16 H0316 CULTURE NAT/LISM LEAD

B64
BINDER L.,THE IDEOLOGICAL REVOLUTION IN THE MIDDLE EAST. ISLAM STRUCT INT/ORG KIN SECT EX/STRUC TOP/EX PLAN ATTIT DRIVE RIGID/FLEX PWR...MYTH TOT/POP 20. PAGE 17 H0338 POL/PAR NAT/G NAT/LISM

B64
BUNTING B.P.,THE RISE OF THE SOUTH AFRICAN REICH. SOUTH/AFR INT/ORG NAT/G FORCES DIPLOM CONTROL WAR TOTALISM ATTIT...GOV/COMP 19/20. PAGE 24 H0477 RACE/REL DISCRIM NAT/LISM TREND

B64
BURKE F.G.,AFRICA'S QUEST FOR ORDER. AFR CULTURE KIN MUNIC NAT/G DIPLOM COLONIAL REV DISCRIM NAT/LISM AGE/Y 20. PAGE 24 H0488 ORD/FREE CONSEN RACE/REL LEAD

B64
BUTWELL R.,SOUTHEAST ASIA TODAY - AND TOMORROW. NAT/G COLONIAL LEAD REGION WAR CHOOSE WEALTH MARXISM 20. PAGE 25 H0500 S/ASIA DIPLOM ECO/UNDEV NAT/LISM

B64
COBBAN A.,ROUSSEAU AND THE MODERN STATE (2ND ED.). FRANCE PROB/SOLV NAT/LISM UTOPIA PERSON MORAL ...EPIST PHIL/SCI SOC IDEA/COMP 18 ROUSSEAU/J BURKE/EDM HOBBES/T HUME/D. PAGE 30 H0612 GEN/LAWS INGP/REL NAT/G ORD/FREE

B64
COONDOO R.,THE DIVISION OF POWERS IN THE INDIAN CONSTITUTION. INDIA ECO/UNDEV FINAN TEC/DEV WAR CENTRAL EFFICIENCY NAT/LISM PWR WEALTH NEW/LIB ...BIBLIOG 18/20. PAGE 33 H0659 CONSTN LEGIS WELF/ST GOV/COMP

B64
DANIELS R.V.,RUSSIA. RUSSIA USSR STRUCT NAT/LISM TOTALISM ORD/FREE WEALTH...POLICY DECISION TREND. PAGE 37 H0740 MARXISM REV ECO/DEV DIPLOM

B64
FRANCK T.M.,EAST AFRICAN UNITY THROUGH LAW. MALAWI TANZANIA UGANDA UK ZAMBIA CONSTN INT/ORG NAT/G ADMIN ROUTINE TASK NAT/LISM ATTIT SOVEREIGN ...RECORD IDEA/COMP NAT/COMP. PAGE 52 H1048 AFR FEDERAL REGION INT/LAW

B64
GREAT BRITAIN CENTRAL OFF INF,CONSTITUTIONAL DEVELOPMENT IN THE COMMONWEALTH. VOL/ASSN PLAN DIPLOM COLONIAL INGP/REL NAT/LISM ORD/FREE PWR 17/20 CMN/WLTH. PAGE 60 H1202 REGION CONSTN NAT/G SOVEREIGN

B64
GRIFFITH W.,THE WELSH (2ND ED.). UK SOCIETY STRUCT SECT WRITING NAT/LISM...ART/METH MODAL OBS/ENVIR TREND SOC/INTEG WALES PURITAN MUSIC. PAGE 61 H1223 CULTURE SOC LING

B64
HALPERIN S.W.,MUSSOLINI AND ITALIAN FASCISM. ITALY NAT/G POL/PAR SECT ECO/TAC LEAD PWR SOCISM...POLICY 20 MUSSOLIN/B. PAGE 64 H1294 FASCISM NAT/LISM EDU/PROP CHIEF

B64
HANNA W.J.,POLITICS IN BLACK AFRICA: A SELECTIVE BIBLIOGRAPHY OF RELEVANT PERIODICAL LITERATURE. AFR LAW LOC/G MUNIC NAT/G POL/PAR LOBBY CHOOSE RACE/REL SOVEREIGN 20. PAGE 66 H1315 BIBLIOG NAT/LISM COLONIAL

B64
KAUFMANN R.,MILLENARISME ET ACCULTURATION. SOCIETY DOMIN COLONIAL NAT/LISM ATTIT...SOC BIBLIOG 20 JEHOVA/WIT SEVENTHDAY. PAGE 84 H1669 AFR SECT MYTH CULTURE

B64
LEMARCHAND R.,POLITICAL AWAKENING IN THE BELGIAN CONGO. ECO/UNDEV VOL/ASSN DOMIN CHOOSE GP/REL INGP/REL DISCRIM ORD/FREE PWR...CHARTS 20 CONGO ARABS. PAGE 94 H1873 NAT/LISM COLONIAL POL/PAR RACE/REL

B64
MAIER J.,POLITICS OF CHANGE IN LATIN AMERICA. BRAZIL L/A+17C STRATA INT/ORG NAT/G POL/PAR FOR/AID REV 20. PAGE 101 H2019 SOCIETY NAT/LISM DIPLOM REGION

B64
MATTHEWS D.G.,A CURRENT VIEW OF AFRICANA (PAMPHLET). CULTURE ECO/UNDEV DIPLOM RACE/REL ATTIT BIBLIOG/A AFR

20. PAGE 105 H2092 — NAT/G NAT/LISM

B64
MBEKI G.,SOUTH AFRICA: THE PEASANT'S REVOLT. SOUTH/AFR POL/PAR COERCE REV NAT/LISM ORD/FREE SOVEREIGN 20 NEGRO. PAGE 106 H2114 — COLONIAL RACE/REL DISCRIM DOMIN

B64
MELADY T.,FACES OF AFRICA. AFR FUT ISLAM NAT/G POL/PAR SCHOOL DELIB/GP PLAN ECO/TAC EDU/PROP ATTIT ALL/VALS...CHARTS TOT/POP VAL/FREE 20. PAGE 108 H2168 — ECO/UNDEV TREND NAT/LISM

B64
QUIGG P.W.,AFRICA: A FOREIGN AFFAIRS READER. AFR FRANCE PORTUGAL UK DIPLOM LEAD PARL/PROC MARXISM ...MAJORIT METH/CNCPT GOV/COMP IDEA/COMP ANTHOL 19/20. PAGE 129 H2575 — COLONIAL SOVEREIGN NAT/LISM RACE/REL

B64
ROBERTS HL,FOREIGN AFFAIRS BIBLIOGRAPHY, 1952-1962. ECO/DEV SECT PLAN FOR/AID INT/TRADE ARMS/CONT NAT/LISM ATTIT...INT/LAW GOV/COMP IDEA/COMP 20. PAGE 132 H2643 — BIBLIOG/A DIPLOM INT/ORG WAR

B64
SAKAI R.K.,STUDIES ON ASIA, 1964. ASIA CHINA/COM ISRAEL MALAYSIA S/ASIA USA+45 USSR ECO/UNDEV FAM POL/PAR SECT CONSULT NAT/LISM...POLICY SOC 20 CHINJAP. PAGE 137 H2736 — PWR DIPLOM

B64
SANCHEZ J.M.,REFORM AND REACTION. SPAIN STRATA NAT/LISM TOTALISM 20. PAGE 137 H2749 — NAT/G SECT GP/REL REV

B64
SINGER M.R.,THE EMERGING ELITE: A STUDY OF POLITICAL LEADERSHIP IN CEYLON. S/ASIA ECO/UNDEV AGRI KIN NAT/G SECT EX/STRUC LEGIT ATTIT PWR RESPECT...SOC STAT CHARTS 20. PAGE 144 H2883 — TOP/EX STRATA NAT/LISM CEYLON

B64
TINKER H.,BALLOT BOX AND BAYONET - PEOPLE AND GOVERNMENT IN EMERGENT ASIAN COUNTRIES. CEYLON INDIA INDONESIA PHILIPPINE POL/PAR ADMIN COLONIAL LEAD PARL/PROC CHOOSE CONSEN ORD/FREE SOVEREIGN PLURISM...GOV/COMP THIRD/WRLD. PAGE 155 H3104 — MYTH S/ASIA NAT/COMP NAT/LISM

B64
VON GRUNEBAUM G.E.,MODERN ISLAM: THE SEARCH FOR CULTURAL IDENTITY. ACADEM NEIGH WRITING NAT/LISM ...HUM CONCPT 19/20 MUSLIM MID/EAST ARABS. PAGE 163 H3269 — ISLAM CULTURE CREATE SECT

B64
WALLBANK T.W.,DOCUMENTS ON MODERN AFRICA. NAT/G COLONIAL GP/REL ATTIT PWR...BIBLIOG 19/20. PAGE 165 H3294 — AFR NAT/LISM ECO/UNDEV DIPLOM

B64
WERTHEIM W.F.,EAST-WEST PARALLELS. INDONESIA S/ASIA NAT/G SECT...TIME/SEQ METH REFORMERS S/EASTASIA. PAGE 167 H3334 — SOC ECO/UNDEV CULTURE NAT/LISM

B64
WHITE D.S.,SEEDS OF DISCORD. EUR+WWI FRANCE NAT/G VOL/ASSN FORCES DIPLOM DOMIN NAT/LISM DISPL RIGID/FLEX PWR...RECORD INT BIOG 20 DEGAULLE/C ROOSEVLT/F CHURCHLL/W HULL. PAGE 167 H3347 — TOP/EX ATTIT

B64
WRIGHT Q.,A STUDY OF WAR. LAW NAT/G PROB/SOLV BAL/PWR NAT/LISM PEACE ATTIT SOVEREIGN...CENSUS SOC/INTEG. PAGE 171 H3421 — WAR CONCPT DIPLOM CONTROL

S64
GARMARNIKOW M.,"INFLUENCE-BUYING IN WEST AFRICA." COM FUT USSR INTELL NAT/G PLAN TEC/DEV ECO/TAC DOMIN EDU/PROP REGION NAT/LISM ATTIT DRIVE ALL/VALS SOVEREIGN...POLICY PSY SOC CONCPT TREND STERTYP WORK COLD/WAR 20. PAGE 55 H1102 — AFR ECO/UNDEV FOR/AID SOCISM

S64
IRELE A.,"A DEFENSE OF NEGRITUDE." AFR NAT/LISM ...HUM 20 NEGRO. PAGE 78 H1566 — CONCPT CULTURE NAT/COMP KIN

S64
LEWIS B.,"THE QUEST FOR FREEDOM--A SAD STORY OF THE MIDDLE EAST." ISLAM ISRAEL LEBANON TURKEY CULTURE NAT/G SECT LEGIS TOP/EX DOMIN EDU/PROP LEGIT ORD/FREE PWR RESPECT...POLICY TIME/SEQ VAL/FREE 20. PAGE 96 H1911 — CONSTN ATTIT NAT/LISM

S64
MARES V.E.,"EAST EUROPE'S SECOND CHANCE." COM EUR+WWI HUNGARY ROMANIA USSR YUGOSLAVIA ECO/UNDEV NAT/G TOP/EX CREATE PLAN TEC/DEV REGION NAT/LISM RIGID/FLEX PWR...CONCPT STAT COMECON 20. PAGE 102 H2047 — VOL/ASSN ECO/TAC

S64
SAYEED K.,"PATHAN REGIONALISM." ISLAM PAKISTAN S/ASIA CULTURE SOCIETY NAT/G NEIGH DIPLOM LEGIT COERCE CHOOSE ATTIT DISPL PERCEPT ALL/VALS SOVEREIGN...POLICY RELATIV SOC TIME/SEQ TOT/POP 20. PAGE 138 H2761 — SECT NAT/LISM REGION

B65
APTER D.E.,THE POLITICS OF MODERNIZATION. AFR L/A+17C CULTURE NAT/G POL/PAR ADMIN COLONIAL NAT/LISM ATTIT RIGID/FLEX PWR...SOC CONCPT. PAGE 8 H0154 — ECO/UNDEV GEN/LAWS STRATA CREATE

B65
BURLING R.,HILL FARMS AND PADI FIELDS. BURMA S/ASIA THAILAND VIETNAM AGRI NEIGH SECT GP/REL NAT/LISM ORD/FREE 20 MID/EAST MIGRATION. PAGE 24 H0491 — SOCIETY STRUCT CULTURE SOVEREIGN

B65
CALLEO D.P.,EUROPE'S FUTURE: THE GRAND ALTERNATIVES. UK INT/ORG DIPLOM PWR SOVEREIGN ...CONCPT IDEA/COMP NAT/COMP BIBLIOG 20 EEC EUROPE DEGAULLE/C NATO. PAGE 25 H0506 — FUT EUR+WWI FEDERAL NAT/LISM

B65
CENTRAL GAZETTEERS UNIT,THE GAZETTEER OF INDIA (VOL. I). INDIA SOCIETY STRATA PLAN EDU/PROP NAT/LISM ORD/FREE WEALTH...GEOG LING CHARTS SOC/INTEG 20. PAGE 28 H0568 — PRESS CULTURE SECT STRUCT

B65
COSTA H DE L.A.,THE BACKGROUND OF NATIONALISM AND OTHER ESSAYS. ASIA PHILIPPINE ATTIT PERCEPT CATHISM ...ANTHOL 20. PAGE 34 H0674 — NAT/LISM CULTURE ANOMIE NAT/G

B65
COWAN L.G.,EDUCATION AND NATION-BUILDING IN AFRICA. AFR CULTURE ECO/UNDEV POL/PAR ACT/RES LEAD SOVEREIGN...METH/COMP ANTHOL BIBLIOG 20. PAGE 34 H0684 — EDU/PROP COLONIAL ACADEM NAT/LISM

B65
INST INTL DES CIVILISATION DIF,THE CONSTITUTIONS AND ADMINISTRATIVE INSTITUTIONS OF THE NEW STATES. AFR ISLAM S/ASIA NAT/G POL/PAR DELIB/GP EX/STRUC CONFER EFFICIENCY NAT/LISM...JURID SOC 20. PAGE 77 H1535 — CONSTN ADMIN ADJUD ECO/UNDEV

B65
JACKSON G.,THE SPANISH REPUBLIC AND THE CIVIL WAR, 1931-1939. EUR+WWI INTELL STRUCT COM/IND NAT/G POL/PAR LEGIS EDU/PROP EXEC COERCE NAT/LISM DRIVE PWR...INT TIME/SEQ TOT/POP 20. PAGE 79 H1574 — ATTIT GUERRILLA SPAIN

B65
JELAVICH C.,THE BALKANS. ALBANIA BULGARIA GREECE ROMANIA YUGOSLAVIA ECO/UNDEV WAR SOVEREIGN MARXISM 6/20. PAGE 80 H1597 — NAT/LISM NAT/G

B65
KIRKWOOD K.,BRITAIN AND AFRICA. AFR UK ECO/UNDEV ECO/TAC WAR NAT/LISM SOVEREIGN 19/20. PAGE 86 H1725 — NAT/G DIPLOM POLICY COLONIAL

B65
KOHN H.,AFRICAN NATIONALISM IN THE TWENTIETH CENTURY. AFR NAT/G POL/PAR COLONIAL REGION DISCRIM SOVEREIGN 20. PAGE 87 H1747 — NAT/LISM CULTURE ATTIT

B65
MEHROTRA S.R.,INDIA AND THE COMMONWEALTH 1885-1929. INDIA UK INT/ORG VOL/ASSN GP/REL ATTIT...POLICY BIBLIOG 19/20 CMN/WLTH. PAGE 108 H2163 — DIPLOM NAT/G POL/PAR NAT/LISM

B65
MEYER F.S.,THE AFRICAN NETTLE. SOUTH/AFR NAT/LISM SOVEREIGN...ANTHOL 20 EUROPE. PAGE 110 H2191 — AFR COLONIAL RACE/REL ECO/UNDEV

B65
NYE J.S. JR.,PAN-AFRICANISM AND EAST AFRICAN INTEGRATION. TANZANIA UGANDA STRUCT ECO/UNDEV NAT/G DIPLOM FEDERAL NAT/LISM...STAT SOC/EXP BIBLIOG EEC OAU. PAGE 119 H2382 — REGION ATTIT GEN/LAWS AFR

B65
O'BRIEN W.V.,THE NEW NATIONS IN INTERNATIONAL LAW AND DIPLOMACY* THE YEAR BOOK OF WORLD POLITY* VOLUME III. USA+45 ECO/UNDEV INT/ORG FORCES DIPLOM COLONIAL NEUTRAL REV NAT/LISM ATTIT RESPECT. PAGE 119 H2385 — INT/LAW CULTURE SOVEREIGN ANTHOL

B65
OBUKAR C.,THE MODERN AFRICAN. AGRI INDUS WORKER CAP/ISM EDU/PROP PARTIC RACE/REL NAT/LISM ALL/VALS MARXISM...SOC IDEA/COMP 20. PAGE 120 H2393 — AFR ECO/UNDEV CULTURE SOVEREIGN

B65
POLK W.R.,THE UNITED STATES AND THE ARAB WORLD. USA+45 ECO/UNDEV EXTR/IND SECT WAR NAT/LISM ATTIT ...NAT/COMP COLD/WAR. PAGE 127 H2535 — ISLAM REGION CULTURE DIPLOM

B65
RIVLIN B.,THE CONTEMPORARY MIDDLE EAST* TRADITION AND INNOVATION. CULTURE SOCIETY ECO/UNDEV NAT/G TREND. PAGE 132 H2636 — ANTHOL ISLAM NAT/LISM DIPLOM

B65
RODRIGUEZ M.,CENTRAL AMERICA. COSTA/RICA GUATEMALA L/A+17C NICARAGUA DIPLOM COLONIAL REGION NAT/LISM ALL/IDEOS SOCISM...MAJORIT TIME/SEQ BIBLIOG 19/20. PAGE 133 H2656 — CULTURE NAT/COMP NAT/G ECO/UNDEV

B65
ROMEIN J.,THE ASIAN CENTURY. ASIA COM S/ASIA DIPLOM COLONIAL TIME 20. PAGE 133 H2666 REV NAT/LISM CULTURE MARXISM

B65
ROTBERG R.I.,A POLITICAL HISTORY OF TROPICAL AFRICA. EX/STRUC DIPLOM INT/TRADE DOMIN ADMIN RACE/REL NAT/LISM PWR SOVEREIGN...GEOG TIME/SEQ BIBLIOG 1/20. PAGE 135 H2692 AFR CULTURE COLONIAL

B65
SAKAI R.K.,STUDIES ON ASIA, 1965. INDIA KOREA S/ASIA USA+45 CONSTN KIN SECT PARTIC SUFF NAT/LISM ...POLICY SOC 19/20 CHINJAP. PAGE 137 H2737 PARL/PROC ASIA

B65
SALVADORI M.,ITALY. AUSTRIA FRANCE GERMANY ITALY SPAIN CULTURE NAT/G POL/PAR DIPLOM WAR FASCISM LAISSEZ MARXISM...TIME/SEQ CHARTS BIBLIOG/A. PAGE 137 H2744 NAT/LISM CATHISM SOCIETY

B65
STERN F.,THE POLITICS OF CULTURAL DESPAIR. EUR+WWI GERMANY POL/PAR SECT RACE/REL STRANGE TOTALISM ...ART/METH MYTH BIBLIOG 20 JEWS. PAGE 149 H2980 CULTURE ATTIT NAT/LISM FASCISM

B65
TUTSCH H.E.,FACETS OF ARAB NATIONALISM. ISLAM ISRAEL CULTURE STRUCT SECT RIGID/FLEX ORD/FREE MARXISM SOCISM 20. PAGE 157 H3143 ECO/UNDEV NAT/LISM TEC/DEV SOCIETY

B65
VAN DEN BERGHE P.L.,AFRICA: SOCIAL PROBLEMS OF CHANGE AND CONFLICT. ELITES STRATA ECO/UNDEV KIN MUNIC DIPLOM GP/REL RACE/REL NAT/LISM...ANTHOL BIBLIOG 20. PAGE 161 H3228 SOC CULTURE AFR STRUCT

B65
VATCHER W.H. JR.,WHITE LAAGER: THE RISE OF AFRIKANER NATIONALISM. AFR SOUTH/AFR CULTURE TOTALISM 20. PAGE 162 H3235 NAT/LISM POL/PAR RACE/REL DISCRIM

B65
VON STACKELBERG K.,ALLE KRETER LUGEN VORURTEILE UBER MENSCHEN UND VOLKER. DIPLOM DOMIN RUMOR NAT/LISM PERSON KNOWL...SOC QU BIBLIOG 20. PAGE 164 H3277 NAT/COMP ATTIT EDU/PROP SAMP

B65
WOLFE B.D.,MARXISM; ONE HUNDRED YEARS IN THE LIFE OF A DOCTRINE. USSR WAR NAT/LISM PEACE TOTALISM ...MAJORIT 20 MARX/KARL. PAGE 170 H3399 MARXISM LEAD ATTIT

B65
WOLPERT S.,INDIA. INDIA UK ECO/UNDEV DIPLOM GP/REL WEALTH 20 NEHRU/J. PAGE 170 H3405 CULTURE COLONIAL NAT/LISM SECT

L65
SHARMA S.P.,"THE INDIA-CHINA BORDER DISPUTE: AN INDIAN PERSPECTIVE." ASIA CHINA/COM S/ASIA NAT/G LEGIT CT/SYS NAT/LISM DRIVE MORAL ORD/FREE PWR 20. PAGE 142 H2850 LAW ATTIT SOVEREIGN INDIA

S65
LEVI W.,"THE CONCEPT OF INTEGRATION IN RESEARCH ON PEACE." NAT/G VOL/ASSN DIPLOM TASK ADJUST NAT/LISM PEACE DRIVE LOVE...PSY NET/THEORY GEN/LAWS. PAGE 95 H1897 CONCPT IDEA/COMP INT/ORG CENTRAL

S65
MARK M.,"MUST WE FIGHT SOCIAL REVOLUTIONS OF THE LEFT?" L/A+17C USA+45 ECO/UNDEV DIPLOM ADJUST PERCEPT...IDEA/COMP NAT/COMP. PAGE 103 H2053 NAT/LISM REV MARXISM CREATE

S65
MCALISTER L.N.,"CHANGING CONCEPTS OF THE ROLE OF THE MILITARY IN LATIN AMERICA." CULTURE NAT/G CREATE REGION NAT/LISM ATTIT SOVEREIGN...NAT/COMP GEN/LAWS. PAGE 106 H2120 L/A+17C FORCES IDEA/COMP PWR

S65
VUCINICH W.S.,"WHITHER RUMANIA." COM USSR YUGOSLAVIA NAT/G VOL/ASSN DELIB/GP TOP/EX LEGIT NAT/LISM TOTALISM ATTIT DRIVE RIGID/FLEX ORD/FREE WEALTH SOCISM...TIME/SEQ TREND 20. PAGE 164 H3281 ECO/DEV CREATE ROMANIA

C65
COLEMAN J.S.,"EDUCATION AND POLITICAL DEVELOPMENT." COM CULTURE INTELL STRUCT SCHOOL PERSON SOVEREIGN ...POLICY ANTHOL BIBLIOG/A METH 20. PAGE 31 H0629 ECO/UNDEV NAT/LISM EDU/PROP TEC/DEV

C65
STERN F.,"THE POLITICS OF CULTURAL DESPAIR." NAT/LISM...IDEA/COMP BIBLIOG 19/20. PAGE 149 H2979 CULTURE PHIL/SCI CONSERVE TOTALISM

B66
AIYAR S.P.,PERSPECTIVES ON THE WELFARE STATE. INDIA S/ASIA UK CONSTN ECO/UNDEV NAT/G INGP/REL CENTRAL NAT/LISM ATTIT...CONCPT ANTHOL BIBLIOG 20. PAGE 4 H0087 NEW/LIB WELF/ST IDEA/COMP ADJUST

B66
BROWN J.F.,THE NEW EASTERN EUROPE. ALBANIA BULGARIA HUNGARY POLAND ROMANIA CULTURE AGRI POL/PAR WAR NAT/LISM MARXISM...CHARTS BIBLIOG 20. PAGE 22 H0444 DIPLOM COM NAT/G ECO/UNDEV

B66
BUKHARIN N.,THE ABC OF COMMUNISM: A POPULAR EXPLANATION OF THE PROGRAM OF THE COMMUNIST PARTY OF RUSSIA. USSR STRATA SECT FORCES WORKER CAP/ISM RECEIVE EDU/PROP NAT/LISM TOTALISM 20. PAGE 23 H0468 MARXISM CONCPT POLICY REV

B66
CHANG,THE PARTY AND THE NATIONAL QUESTION IN CHINA (TRANS. BY GEORGE MOSELEY). CHINA/COM CULTURE CONTROL NAT/LISM...CHARTS BIBLIOG/A 20. PAGE 29 H0576 GP/REL REGION ISOLAT MARXISM

B66
CROWDER M.,A SHORT HISTORY OF NIGERIA. AFR NIGERIA UK ECO/UNDEV CHIEF INT/TRADE RACE/REL NAT/LISM ORD/FREE...GEOG SOC CHARTS BIBLIOG 14/20. PAGE 36 H0711 COLONIAL NAT/G CULTURE

B66
FLINT J.E.,NIGERIA AND GHANA. AFR GHANA NIGERIA UK NAT/G DOMIN DISCRIM...CHARTS BIBLIOG/A 15/20 NEGRO MAPS. PAGE 51 H1026 CULTURE COLONIAL NAT/LISM

B66
GRAHAM I.C.C.,PUBLICATIONS OF THE SOCIAL SCIENCE DEPARTMENT, THE RAND CORPORATION, 1948-1966. USSR WOR+45 NAT/G ARMS/CONT DETER WAR NAT/LISM...SOC GOV/COMP. PAGE 60 H1192 BIBLIOG DIPLOM NUC/PWR FORCES

B66
HARRISON B.,SOUTH-EAST ASIA: A SHORT HISTORY (3RD ED.). ECO/UNDEV INDUS NAT/G SECT BAL/PWR NAT/LISM ...SOC 15/20 S/EASTASIA. PAGE 67 H1346 COLONIAL S/ASIA CULTURE

B66
HATTICH M.,NATIONALBEWUSSTSEIN UND STAATSBEWUSSTSEIN IN DER PLURALISTISCHEN GESELLSCHAFT. GERMANY GP/REL ATTIT SOVEREIGN SOC/INTEG 20. PAGE 68 H1356 NAT/G NAT/LISM SOCIETY OBJECTIVE

B66
HEYMANN F.G.,POLAND AND CZECHOSLOVAKIA. COM CZECHOSLVK POLAND...CHARTS BIBLIOG/A 9/20. PAGE 70 H1413 CULTURE NAT/LISM ORD/FREE WAR

B66
HOPKINS J.F.K.,ARABIC PERIODICAL LITERATURE, 1961. ISLAM LAW CULTURE SECT...GEOG HEAL PHIL/SCI PSY SOC 20. PAGE 73 H1466 BIBLIOG/A NAT/LISM TEC/DEV INDUS

B66
INTL CONF ON WORLD POLITICS-5,EASTERN EUROPE IN TRANSITION. EUR+WWI USSR ECO/TAC NAT/LISM ATTIT SOVEREIGN...CHARTS ANTHOL 20 TREATY WARSAW/P. PAGE 78 H1562 COM NAT/COMP MARXISM DIPLOM

B66
KAZAMIAS A.M.,EDUCATION AND QUEST FOR MODERNITY IN TURKEY. ISLAM SOCIETY SECT NAT/LISM ATTIT ORD/FREE SOVEREIGN TURKS. PAGE 84 H1672 NAT/G EDU/PROP STRATA CULTURE

B66
LONDON K.,EASTERN EUROPE IN TRANSITION. CHINA/COM USSR DOMIN COLONIAL CENTRAL RIGID/FLEX PWR...SOC ANTHOL 20. PAGE 98 H1958 SOVEREIGN COM NAT/LISM DIPLOM

B66
MASUR G.,NATIONALISM IN LATIN AMERICA* DIVERSITY AND UNITY. CHRIST-17C PRE/AMER ELITES ECO/UNDEV CREATE DIPLOM INT/TRADE COLONIAL REV SOVEREIGN SOC. PAGE 105 H2089 L/A+17C NAT/LISM CULTURE

B66
RICHERT F.,DIE NATIONALE WELLE. GERMANY GERMANY/W PARL/PROC ORD/FREE FASCISM...TREND 19/20. PAGE 131 H2622 POL/PAR ATTIT NAT/LISM NAT/G

B66
RINGHOFER K.,STRUKTURPROBLEME DES RECHTES. AUSTRIA ATTIT ORD/FREE...IDEA/COMP 20. PAGE 132 H2630 JURID PROVS NAT/G NAT/LISM

B66
ROSNER J.,DER FASCHISMUS. AUSTRIA GERMANY ITALY STRATA NAT/G POL/PAR COERCE RACE/REL TOTALISM ATTIT AUTHORIT...IDEA/COMP 20 NAZI ANTI/SEMIT. PAGE 134 H2684 NAT/LISM FASCISM ORD/FREE WAR

B66
SCHATTEN F.,COMMUNISM IN AFRICA. AFR GHANA GUINEA MALI CULTURE ECO/UNDEV LABOR SECT ECO/TAC EDU/PROP REV 20. PAGE 139 H2774 COLONIAL NAT/LISM MARXISM DIPLOM

B66
US DEPARTMENT OF STATE,RESEARCH ON THE MIDDLE EAST (EXTERNAL RESEARCH LIST NO 4-25). GREECE ISRAEL SYRIA UAR YEMEN CULTURE SOCIETY POL/PAR SECT DIPLOM EDU/PROP WAR NAT/LISM...GEOG GOV/COMP 20. PAGE 160 H3190 BIBLIOG/A ISLAM NAT/G REGION

B66
WEBER J.,EOTVOS UND DIE UNGARISCHE NATIONALITATENFRAGE. HUNGARY CULTURE SOCIETY REV ORD/FREE SOVEREIGN...BIOG 19. PAGE 166 H3318 NAT/LISM GP/REL ATTIT

CONCPT

B66

WHITAKER A.P.,NATIONALISM IN CONTEMPORARY LATIN AMERICA. AGRI NAT/G WEALTH...POLICY SOC CONCPT OBS TREND 20. PAGE 167 H3344
NAT/LISM L/A+17C DIPLOM ECO/UNDEV

B66

WILLNER A.R.,THE NEOTRADITIONAL ACCOMMODATION TO POLITICAL INDEPENDENCE* THE CASE OF INDONESIA * RESEARCH MONOGRAPH NO. 26. CULTURE ECO/UNDEV CREATE PROB/SOLV FOR/AID LEGIT COLONIAL EFFICIENCY NAT/LISM ALL/VALS SOC. PAGE 168 H3371
INDONESIA CONSERVE ELITES ADMIN

B66

ZEINE Z.N.,THE EMERGENCE OF ARAB NATIONALISM (REV. ED.). TURKEY UK NAT/G SECT TEC/DEV LEAD REV WAR AGE/Y ROLE ORD/FREE...TRADIT CHARTS BIBLIOG 20 ARABS OTTOMAN. PAGE 173 H3453
ISLAM NAT/LISM DIPLOM

B66

ZOLBERG A.R.,CREATING POLITICAL ORDER. AFR CONGO/BRAZ GHANA NIGER KIN NAT/G DOMIN COLONIAL REGION CENTRAL NAT/LISM ATTIT PWR 20 CONGO/LEOP. PAGE 173 H3462
SOVEREIGN ORD/FREE CONSTN POL/PAR

S66

ADAMS T.W.,"THE FIRST REPUBLIC OF CYPRUS: A REVIEW OF AN UNWORKABLE CONSTITUTION." CYPRUS FUT PLAN NAT/LISM POPULISM 20. PAGE 3 H0067
CONSTN NAT/G PROB/SOLV

S66

CRANMER-BYNG J.L.,"THE CHINESE ATTITUDE TOWARDS EXTERNAL RELATIONS." ASIA CHINA/COM EXEC NAT/LISM MARXISM...POLICY 20. PAGE 35 H0699
ATTIT DIPLOM NAT/G

S66

GRUNDY K.W.,"RECENT CONTRIBUTIONS TO THE STUDY OF AFRICAN POLITICAL THOUGHT." DIPLOM NAT/LISM ALL/IDEOS...NEW/IDEA GOV/COMP 20. PAGE 62 H1239
BIBLIOG/A AFR ATTIT IDEA/COMP

S66

HEAPHEY J.,"THE ORGANIZATION OF EGYPT* INADEQUACIES OF A NONPOLITICAL MODEL FOR NATION-BUILDING." STRATA NAT/G CREATE PROB/SOLV ECO/TAC NAT/LISM SOCISM RECORD. PAGE 69 H1377
UAR ECO/UNDEV OBS

S66

MCLANE C.B.,"SOVIET DOCTRINE AND THE MILITARY COUPS IN AFRICA." ALGERIA GHANA COLONIAL NAT/LISM RIGID/FLEX SOVEREIGN MARXISM...DECISION NAT/COMP. PAGE 107 H2140
USSR ATTIT AFR FORCES

S66

O'BRIEN W.V.,"EVENTS AND TRENDS: PATTERNS OF AFRICAN INTERNATIONAL POLITICAL BEHAVIOR." CULTURE SOCIETY NAT/G NAT/LISM SOCISM. PAGE 119 H2386
BIBLIOG/A AFR TREND DIPLOM

S66

ROTHCHILD D.,"THE LIMITS OF FEDERALISM: AN EXAMINATION OF POLITICAL INSTITUTIONAL TRANSFER IN AFRICA." AFR CONSTN CULTURE ELITES ECO/UNDEV KIN PROB/SOLV ADMIN ORD/FREE PWR...POLICY 20. PAGE 135 H2695
FEDERAL NAT/G NAT/LISM COLONIAL

S66

SKILLING H.G.,"THE RUMANIAN NATIONAL COURSE." COM EUR+WWI ROMANIA NAT/G ECO/TAC PWR 20. PAGE 145 H2896
NAT/LISM POLICY DIPLOM MARXISM

S66

STRAYER J.R.,"PROBLEMS OF DICTATORSHIP* THE RUSSIAN EXPERIENCE." ASIA MOD/EUR ELITES STRATA POL/PAR CREATE NAT/LISM MARXISM...GOV/COMP NAT/COMP. PAGE 150 H2997
NAT/G GEN/LAWS USSR TOTALISM

S66

TOUVAL S.,"AFRICA'S FRONTIERS* REACTIONS TO A COLONIAL LEGACY." L/A+17C CONFER ADJUD COLONIAL APPORT CONSEN NAT/LISM RESPECT...RECORD NAT/COMP. PAGE 156 H3120
AFR GEOG SOVEREIGN WAR

C66

DEUTSCH K.W.,"NATIONALISM AND SOCIAL COMMUNICATION." CULTURE INGP/REL ATTIT PWR...PSY SOC CONCPT LING IDEA/COMP 20. PAGE 40 H0800
BIBLIOG NAT/LISM GEN/LAWS

C66

ROSENBERG C.G. JR.,"THE MYTH OF "MAU-MAU:" NATIONALISM IN KENYA." AFR CULTURE NAT/G POL/PAR COERCE REV RACE/REL ATTIT ORD/FREE SOVEREIGN...MYTH BIBLIOG 20. PAGE 134 H2678
NAT/LISM COLONIAL MAJORIT LEAD

B67

ALLWORTH E.,CENTRAL ASIA: A CENTURY OF RUSSIAN RULE. USSR INTELL SOCIETY AGRI INDUS COLONIAL REV WAR NAT/LISM...ART/METH GEOG LING 19/20. PAGE 5 H0108
ASIA CULTURE NAT/G

B67

ANDERSON C.W.,ISSUES OF POLITICAL DEVELOPMENT. BURMA WOR+45 CULTURE TOP/EX ECO/TAC MARXISM ...CHARTS NAT/COMP 20 COLOMB CONGO/LEOP. PAGE 6 H0126
NAT/LISM COERCE ECO/UNDEV SOCISM

B67

ARIKPO O.,THE DEVELOPMENT OF MODERN NIGERIA. AFR NIGERIA SOCIETY ECO/UNDEV KIN ADMIN FEDERAL NAT/LISM ORD/FREE WEALTH...POLICY GEOG BIBLIOG 19/20. PAGE 8 H0163
NAT/G CULTURE CONSTN COLONIAL

B67

BAIN C.A.,VIETNAM: THE ROOTS OF CONFLICT. FRANCE S/ASIA USSR VIETNAM POL/PAR SECT FORCES COLONIAL NAT/LISM PEACE ORD/FREE MARXISM...GEOG CHARTS 4/20. PAGE 10 H0202
NAT/G WAR CULTURE

B67

CEFKIN J.L.,THE BACKGROUND OF CURRENT WORLD PROBLEMS. NAT/G MARXISM...T 20 UN COLD/WAR. PAGE 28 H0565
DIPLOM NAT/LISM ECO/UNDEV

B67

CHILCOTE R.H.,PORTUGUESE AFRICA. PORTUGAL CULTURE SOCIETY ECO/UNDEV DOMIN NAT/LISM...TREND IDEA/COMP NAT/COMP BIBLIOG 15/20. PAGE 29 H0589
AFR COLONIAL ORD/FREE PROB/SOLV

B67

COLLINS R.O.,EGYPT AND THE SUDAN. COM FRANCE ISLAM SUDAN UAR UK SOCIETY NAT/G COLONIAL NAT/LISM...GEOG SOC LING TREND SOC/INTEG 7/20 SUEZ. PAGE 32 H0635
AGRI CULTURE ECO/UNDEV

B67

DEUTSCH K.W.,FRANCE, GERMANY AND THE WESTERN ALLIANCE. FRANCE GERMANY/W INT/ORG ARMS/CONT NAT/LISM SOVEREIGN...INT NAT/COMP 20. PAGE 40 H0801
ELITES ATTIT DIPLOM POLICY

B67

GIFFORD P.,BRITAIN AND GERMANY IN AFRICA. AFR GERMANY UK ECO/UNDEV LEAD WAR NAT/LISM ATTIT ...POLICY HIST/WRIT METH/COMP ANTHOL BIBLIOG 19/20 WWI. PAGE 56 H1123
COLONIAL ADMIN DIPLOM NAT/COMP

B67

GILL R.T.,ECONOMIC DEVELOPMENT: PAST AND PRESENT (2ND ED.). ASIA INDIA USA+45 USA-45 WOR+45 WOR-45 DEMAND EFFICIENCY NAT/LISM WEALTH...GOV/COMP METH/COMP 18/20. PAGE 56 H1127
ECO/DEV ECO/UNDEV PLAN PROB/SOLV

B67

JOHNSON H.G.,ECONOMIC NATIONALISM IN OLD AND NEW STATES. CANADA CHINA/COM MALI UK DIPLOM...SIMUL GEN/LAWS 19/20 MEXIC/AMER. PAGE 81 H1619
NAT/LISM ECO/UNDEV ECO/DEV NAT/COMP

B67

MACRIDIS R.C.,FOREIGN POLICY IN WORLD POLITICS (3RD ED.). EX/STRUC BAL/PWR COLONIAL NAT/LISM SKILL SOVEREIGN WEALTH...CONCPT TIME/SEQ ANTHOL 20 COLD/WAR. PAGE 101 H2011
DIPLOM POLICY NAT/G IDEA/COMP

B67

MAZRUI A.A.,THE ANGLO-AFRICAN COMMONWEALTH; POLITICAL FRICTION AND CULTURAL FUSION. AFR INT/ORG VOL/ASSN CHIEF GP/REL INGP/REL RACE/REL NAT/LISM 20 CMN/WLTH EEC. PAGE 106 H2111
COLONIAL SOVEREIGN DIPLOM CULTURE

B67

MEHDI M.T.,PEACE IN THE MIDDLE EAST. ISRAEL SOCIETY NAT/G PLAN EDU/PROP NAT/LISM DRIVE...IDEA/COMP 20 JEWS. PAGE 108 H2160
ISLAM DIPLOM GP/REL COERCE

B67

MUHAMMAD A.C.,THE EMERGENCE OF PAKISTAN. PAKISTAN S/ASIA CONSTN ECO/UNDEV NAT/G CONTROL NAT/LISM 20. PAGE 114 H2281
DIPLOM COLONIAL SECT PROB/SOLV

B67

MUNGER E.S.,AFRIKANER AND AFRICAN NATIONALISM: SOUTH AFRICAN PARALLELS AND PARAMETERS. SOUTH/AFR WOR+45 CULTURE ELITES STRUCT NAT/G PROB/SOLV DOMIN CONTROL PERS/REL NAT/LISM...SOC 20. PAGE 115 H2289
AFR RACE/REL

B67

PATAI R.,GOLDEN RIVER TO GOLDEN ROAD: SOCIETY, CULTURE, AND CHANGE IN THE MIDDLE EAST (2ND ED.). ELITES FAM KIN TEC/DEV MARRIAGE NAT/LISM SEX ORD/FREE...TREND GP/COMP WORSHIP 20. PAGE 124 H2476
CULTURE SOCIETY ISLAM STRUCT

B67

RAVKIN A.,THE NEW STATES OF AFRICA (HEADLINE SERIES, NO. 183((PAMPHLET). CULTURE STRUCT INDUS COLONIAL NAT/LISM...SOC 20. PAGE 130 H2597
AFR ECO/UNDEV SOCIETY ADMIN

B67

SALISBURY H.E.,BEHIND THE LINES - HANOI. VIETNAM/N NAT/G GUERRILLA CIVMIL/REL NAT/LISM KNOWL 20. PAGE 137 H2741
WAR PROB/SOLV DIPLOM OBS

B67

SCHECTER J.,THE NEW FACE OF BUDDHA: BUDDHISM AND POLITICAL POWER IN SOUTHEAST ASIA. S/ASIA NAT/G POL/PAR NAT/LISM ATTIT MARXISM...BIBLIOG 20. PAGE 139 H2780
SECT POLICY PWR LEAD

B67

SCHWARTZ M.A.,PUBLIC OPINION AND CANADIAN IDENTITY. CANADA SOCIETY LOC/G DIPLOM ADMIN LEAD REGION GP/REL SAMP. PAGE 141 H2812
ATTIT NAT/G NAT/LISM POL/PAR

B67

SETON-WATSON H.,THE RUSSIAN EMPIRE, 1801-1917. COM RUSSIA STRATA ECO/DEV AGRI INDUS POL/PAR DIPLOM NAT/LISM MARXISM...IDEA/COMP BIBLIOG 19/20 MARX/KARL. PAGE 142 H2834
SOCIETY NAT/G LEAD POLICY

B67

SPIRO H.S.,PATTERNS OF AFRICAN DEVLOPMENT: FIVE COMPARISONS. STRUCT ECO/UNDEV NAT/G CONSERVE SOCISM
AFR CONSTN

...PREDICT NAT/COMP 20 CHINJAP. PAGE 148 H2951 NAT/LISM TREND

B67
TOMPKINS S.R.,THE TRIUMPH OF BOLSHEVISM: REVOLUTION OR REACTION? USSR WORKER PRESS WEALTH MARXISM POPULISM...BIOG TREND IDEA/COMP BIBLIOG 19/20 LENIN/VI. PAGE 156 H3113 REV NAT/G POL/PAR NAT/LISM

B67
TREADGOLD D.W.,SOVIET AND CHINESE COMMUNISM* SIMILARITIES AND DIFFERENCES. CHINA/COM COM NAT/G PLAN DIPLOM CENTRAL PWR MARXISM...POLICY 20. PAGE 156 H3128 CULTURE NAT/LISM

B67
YAMAMURA K.,ECONOMIC POLICY IN POSTWAR JAPAN. ASIA FINAN POL/PAR DIPLOM LEAD NAT/LISM ATTIT NEW/LIB POPULISM 20 CHINJAP. PAGE 171 H3432 ECO/DEV POLICY NAT/G TEC/DEV

L67
BRIDGHAM P.,"MAO'S "CULTURAL REVOLUTION"* ORIGIN AND DEVELOPMENT." NAT/G LEAD CIVMIL/REL NAT/LISM TOTALISM ATTIT DRIVE PWR MARXISM 20. PAGE 21 H0413 CHINA/COM CULTURE REV CROWD

L67
SEGAL A.,"THE INTEGRATION OF DEVELOPING COUNTRIES: SOME THOUGHTS ON EAST AFRICA AND CENTRAL AMERICA." AFR L/A+17C INT/ORG NAT/G VOL/ASSN FOR/AID INT/TRADE EQUILIB NAT/LISM PWR 20. PAGE 141 H2820 ECO/UNDEV DIPLOM REGION

L67
TAMBIAH S.J.,"THE POLITICS OF LANGUAGE IN INDIA AND CEYLON." CEYLON INDIA NAT/G DOMIN ADMIN...SOC 20. PAGE 152 H3039 POL/PAR LING NAT/LISM REGION

L67
TOUVAL S.,"THE ORGANIZATION OF AFRICAN UNITY AND AFRICAN BORDERS." DEBATE REGION TASK REV ATTIT ORD/FREE...DECISION UN 20 OAU. PAGE 156 H3121 AFR NAT/G COLONIAL NAT/LISM

L67
VAN DER KROEF J.M.,"INDONESIA: THE BATTLE OF THE 'OLD' AND THE 'NEW ORDER'." INDONESIA ISLAM ELITES POL/PAR DOMIN INGP/REL NAT/LISM PWR...IDEA/COMP 20. PAGE 161 H3229 FORCES MARXISM NAT/G BAL/PWR

L67
WRIGHT W.R.,"FOREIGN-OWNED RAILWAYS IN ARGENTINA: A CASE STUDY OF ECONOMIC NATIONALISM." L/A+17C UK ECO/UNDEV SERV/IND LG/CO NAT/G TEC/DEV BAL/PWR EQUILIB ARGEN. PAGE 171 H3423 NAT/LISM CAP/ISM ECO/TAC COLONIAL

S67
"PROTEST AGAINST SOVIET INDUSTRIALIZATION ILLS IN LITHUANIA* A MEMORANDUM." USSR LITHUANIA NAT/G PROVS COST GEOG. PAGE 2 H0050 INDUS COLONIAL NAT/LISM PLAN

S67
ADOKO A.,"THE CONSTITUTION OF UGANDA." AFR UGANDA LOC/G CHIEF FORCES LEGIS ADJUD EXEC CHOOSE NAT/LISM ...IDEA/COMP 20. PAGE 4 H0072 NAT/G CONSTN ORD/FREE LAW

S67
ALBINSKI H.S.,"POLITICS AND BICULTURISM IN CANADA: THE FLAG DEBATE." CANADA SOCIETY NAT/G PROVS DELIB/GP DEBATE REGION SOVEREIGN PLURISM...POLICY SOC/INTEG 20. PAGE 5 H0093 NAT/LISM GP/REL POL/PAR CULTURE

S67
BASKIN D.B.,"NATIONALITY DOCTRINE AND ANTI-SEMITISM IN THE USSR." USSR CULTURE STRATA ISOLAT MAJORITY ATTIT RIGID/FLEX RESPECT...GP/COMP JEWS. PAGE 12 H0234 NAT/LISM MARXISM GP/REL DISCRIM

S67
BEFU H.,"THE POLITICAL RELATION OF THE VILLAGE TO THE STATE." NAT/G DOMIN GOV/REL GP/REL MGT. PAGE 13 H0259 GOV/COMP NAT/LISM KIN MUNIC

S67
EPSTEIN E.H.,"NATIONAL IDENTITY AND THE LANGUAGE ISSUE IN PUERTO RICO." PUERT/RICO CULTURE STRUCT NAT/G PROB/SOLV SKILL...JURID STAT METH/COMP 20. PAGE 47 H0931 EDU/PROP SCHOOL LING NAT/LISM

S67
FINLAY D.J.,"THE GHANA COUP...ONE YEAR LATER." GHANA FORCES FOR/AID PRESS CONTROL CIVMIL/REL NAT/LISM AUTHORIT PWR...PREDICT 20. PAGE 50 H1005 REV NAT/G ATTIT ECO/UNDEV

S67
FLETCHER-COOKE J.,"THE EMERGING AFRICAN STATE." AFR GP/REL NAT/LISM. PAGE 51 H1025 ECO/UNDEV NAT/COMP DIPLOM ATTIT

S67
GRUNDY K.W.,"AFRICA IN THE WORLD ARENA." ECO/UNDEV BAL/PWR FOR/AID NEUTRAL REV NAT/LISM GOV/COMP. PAGE 62 H1240 AFR DIPLOM INT/ORG COLONIAL

S67
HEASMAN D.J.,"THE GIBRALTAR AFFAIR." SPAIN UK NAT/G BAL/PWR CONSEN NAT/LISM ATTIT...REALPOL 20. PAGE 69 H1378 DIPLOM COLONIAL REGION

S67
LAQUEUR W.,"BONN IS NOT WEIMAR* REFLECTIONS ON THE RADICAL RIGHT IN GER MANY." CULTURE LOC/G NAT/G PARTIC CHOOSE. PAGE 91 H1822 GERMANY/W FASCISM NAT/LISM

S67
LEVI W.,"THE ELITIST NATURE OF NEW ASIA'S FOREIGN POLICY." CULTURE ECO/UNDEV NAT/G PROB/SOLV EDU/PROP COLONIAL CONTROL REGION NAT/LISM...NAT/COMP 20. PAGE 95 H1898 POLICY ELITES DIPLOM CREATE

S67
LOGERECI A.,"ALBANIA AND CHINA* THE INCONGRUOUS ALLIANCE." NAT/LISM PWR...GOV/COMP 20. PAGE 98 H1955 ALBANIA CHINA/COM DIPLOM MARXISM

S67
MATTHEWS R.O.,"THE SUEZ CANAL DISPUTE* A CASE STUDY IN PEACEFUL SETTLEMENT." FRANCE ISRAEL UAR UK NAT/G CONTROL LEAD COERCE WAR NAT/LISM ROLE ORD/FREE PWR ...INT/LAW UN 20. PAGE 105 H2099 PEACE DIPLOM ADJUD

S67
MOZINGO D.,"CONTAINMENT IN ASIA RECONSIDERED." NAT/G DIPLOM REV PEACE ORD/FREE 20. PAGE 114 H2275 ATTIT CONTROL NAT/LISM EFFICIENCY

S67
NAHUMI M.,"THE POWERS IN THE MIDDLE EAST CONFLICT." ISLAM ISRAEL JORDAN UAR NAT/G PEACE ATTIT 20 JEWS. PAGE 115 H2304 DIPLOM WAR NAT/LISM

S67
NIEBUHR R.,"THE SOCIAL MYTHS IN THE COLD WAR." USA+45 USSR VIETNAM PROB/SOLV BAL/PWR ARMS/CONT NAT/LISM PWR ALL/IDEOS CONCPT. PAGE 118 H2359 MYTH DIPLOM GOV/COMP

S67
POWELL D.,"THE EFFECTIVENESS OF SOVIET ANTI-RELIGIOUS PROPAGANDA." USSR NAT/G DOMIN LEGIT NAT/LISM 20. PAGE 127 H2549 EDU/PROP ATTIT SECT CONTROL

S67
ROSE S.,"ASIAN NATIONALISM* THE SECOND STAGE." ASIA COM ECO/UNDEV NAT/G PROB/SOLV DIPLOM FOR/AID DOMIN NEUTRAL REGION TASK...METH/COMP 20. PAGE 134 H2675 NAT/LISM S/ASIA BAL/PWR COLONIAL

S67
SMITH J.E.,"RED PRUSSIANISM OF THE GERMAN DEMOCRATIC REPUBLIC." GERMANY/E INTELL TOP/EX WORKER PLAN DIPLOM PRODUC ATTIT WEALTH MARXISM. PAGE 146 H2912 NAT/G TOTALISM INDUS NAT/LISM

S67
SMITH J.E.,"THE RED PRUSSIANISM OF THE GERMAN DEMOCRATIC REPUBLIC." GERMANY/E INTELL NAT/G SECT CHIEF...PREDICT TIME/SEQ 20. PAGE 146 H2913 MARXISM NAT/LISM GOV/COMP EDU/PROP

S67
SNELLEN I.T.,"APARTHEID* CHECKS AND CHANGES." SOUTH/AFR NAT/G PROB/SOLV COLONIAL REGION TASK GP/REL RACE/REL EFFICIENCY PRIVIL ORD/FREE 20. PAGE 146 H2923 DISCRIM NAT/LISM EQUILIB CONTROL

S67
SOMMER T.,"BONN CHANGES COURSE." GERMANY/W NAT/G POL/PAR PROB/SOLV NAT/LISM 20 NATO BERLIN/BLO. PAGE 147 H2932 DIPLOM BAL/PWR INT/ORG

S67
SPINELLI A.,"EUROPEAN UNION IN THE RESISTANCE." NAT/G BAL/PWR DIPLOM CONFER REGION TOTALISM ORD/FREE POLICY. PAGE 147 H2948 NAT/LISM FEDERAL EUR+WWI INT/ORG

S67
SYRKIN M.,"THE RIGHT TO BE ORDINARY." ISLAM ISRAEL NAT/G COERCE NAT/LISM RIGID/FLEX 20. PAGE 151 H3025 SOVEREIGN WAR FORCES DIPLOM

S67
WILLIAMS P.M.,"THE FRENCH GENERAL ELECTION OF MARCH 1967." FRANCE INDUS WORKER NAT/LISM PWR SOCISM 20. PAGE 168 H3368 POL/PAR NAT/G ATTIT CHOOSE

S67
ZARTMAN I.W.," NAT/G POL/PAR VOL/ASSN NAT/LISM ORD/FREE PWR...CONCPT NAT/COMP ORG/CHARTS OAU MAGHREB. PAGE 172 H3451 AFR ISLAM DIPLOM REGION

C67
LING D.L.,"TUNISIA: FROM PROTECTORATE TO REPUBLIC." CULTURE NAT/G POL/PAR CHIEF DIPLOM COERCE WAR PWR ...BIBLIOG 19/20 TUNIS. PAGE 97 H1934 AFR NAT/LISM COLONIAL PROB/SOLV

L68
CURRENT HISTORY,"DE GAULLE'S FRANCE." FRANCE MOD/EUR WOR+45 INDUS MARKET INT/ORG BUDGET DIPLOM AUTHORIT DRIVE...GOV/COMP IDEA/COMP 20 DEGAULLE/C EEC. PAGE 36 H0723 INT/TRADE PERSON LEAD NAT/LISM

L68
CURRENT HISTORY,"AFRICA, 1968." ETHIOPIA GHANA NIGERIA SOUTH/AFR CULTURE ECO/UNDEV KIN SECT CHIEF EX/STRUC WAR WEAPON CHOOSE CIVMIL/REL...GOV/COMP 20 AFRICA/E. PAGE 36 H0724 RACE/REL NAT/LISM FORCES AFR

S68
LAVRIN J.,"THE TWO WORLDS." RUSSIA USSR SOCIETY STRUCT NAT/G DIPLOM ATTIT PERSON MARXISM...GEOG SOC IDEA/COMP PERS/COMP 18/20. PAGE 92 H1842 NAT/COMP NAT/LISM CULTURE

B85
BLUNTSCHLI J.K.,THE THEORY OF THE STATE. GERMANY CONSTN INGP/REL NAT/LISM PERSON SOVEREIGN CONSERVE ...SOC. PAGE 18 H0362 CONCPT LEGIS NAT/G

L86
BURGESS J.W.,"THE RECENT CONSTITUTIONAL CRISIS IN NORWAY" MOD/EUR NORWAY SWEDEN LOC/G NAT/G CHIEF BAL/PWR NAT/LISM ORD/FREE 19. PAGE 24 H0481 CONSTN SOVEREIGN GOV/REL

B99
LECKY W.E.H.,DEMOCRACY AND LIBERTY (2 VOLS.). LAW CONSTN STRATA POL/PAR SECT WORKER DIPLOM ADJUD REPRESENT NAT/LISM CONSERVE. PAGE 93 H1851 LEGIS NAT/G POPULISM ORD/FREE

NAT/SAFETY....NATIONAL SAFETY COUNCIL

NAT/SERV....COMPULSORY NATIONAL SERVICE

NAT/UNITY....NATIONAL UNITY COMMITTEE (TURKEY)

NATAL ....SEE ALSO AFR

B18
EYBERS G.W.,SELECT CONSTITUTIONAL DOCUMENTS ILLUSTRATING SOUTH AFRICAN HISTORY 1795-1910. SOUTH/AFR LOC/G LEGIS CT/SYS...JURID ANTHOL 18/20 NATAL CAPE/HOPE ORANGE/STA. PAGE 48 H0955 CONSTN LAW NAT/G COLONIAL

B63
STIRNIMANN H.,NGUNI UND GNONI; EINE KULTURGESCHICHTLICHE STUDIE (ACTA ETHNOLOGICA ET LINGUISTICA, NUMBER 6). AFR MALAWI SOUTH/AFR FORCES HABITAT...RECORD CHARTS BIBLIOG WORSHIP 19/20 NATAL. PAGE 149 H2987 CULTURE GP/COMP SOCIETY

B64
HILL C.R.,BANTUSTANS: THE FRAGMENTATION OF SOUTH AFRICA. AFR SOUTH/AFR ELITES SOCIETY KIN CONTROL DISCRIM ANOMIE ATTIT...POLICY CHARTS GOV/COMP 20 NEGRO BANTUSTANS TRANSKEI NATAL. PAGE 71 H1416 RACE/REL CULTURE LOC/G ORD/FREE

B67
KONCZACKI Z.A.,PUBLIC FINANCE AND ECONOMIC DEVELOPMENT OF NATAL 1893-1910. TAX ADMIN COLONIAL ...STAT CHARTS BIBLIOG 19/20 NATAL. PAGE 88 H1755 ECO/TAC FINAN NAT/G ECO/UNDEV

NATHAN M. H2317

NATIONAL ASSOCIATION FOR THE ADVANCEMENT OF COLORED PEOPLE....SEE NAACP

NATIONAL ASSOCIATION OF MANUFACTURERS....SEE NAM

NATIONAL BELLAS HESS....SEE BELLAS/HES

NATIONAL COUNCIL OF CHURCHES....SEE NCC

NATIONAL DEBT....SEE DEBT

NATIONAL DIRECTORY (IRELAND)....SEE DIRECT/NAT

NATIONAL EDUCATION ASSOCIATION....SEE NEA

NATIONAL FARMERS' ASSOCIATION....SEE NAT/FARMER

NATIONAL GUARD....SEE NATL/GUARD

NATIONAL INSTITUTE OF HEALTH....SEE NIH

NATIONAL INSTITUTE OF PUBLIC ADMINISTRATION....SEE NIPA

NATIONAL LABOR RELATIONS BOARD....SEE NLRB

NATIONAL LIBERATION COUNCIL IN GHANA....SEE NLC

NATIONAL LIBERATION FRONT (OF SOUTH VIETNAM)....SEE NLF

NATIONAL RECOVERY ADMINISTRATION....SEE NRA

NATIONAL SAFETY COUNCIL....SEE NAT/SAFETY

NATIONAL SCIENCE FOUNDATION....SEE NSF

NATIONAL SECURITY COUNCIL....SEE NSC

NATIONAL SECURITY....SEE ORD/FREE

NATIONAL SOCIAL SCIENCE FOUNDATION....SEE NSSF

NATIONAL UNITY COMMITTEE....SEE NUC

NATIONAL WEALTH....SEE NAT/G+WEALTH

NATIONAL BANK OF LIBYA H2318

NATIONAL BOOK CENTRE PAKISTAN H2319

NATIONAL BOOK LEAGUE H2320

NATIONAL OFF STATE GOVT THAI H2321

NATIONAL REFERRAL CENTER SCI H2322

NATIONAL SCIENCE FOUNDATION H2323

NATIONALISM....SEE NAT/LISM

NATIONALIST CHINA....SEE TAIWAN

NATIONALIZATION....SEE SOCISM

NATL/GUARD....NATIONAL GUARD

NATO....NORTH ATLANTIC TREATY ORGANIZATION; SEE ALSO VOL/ASSN, INT/ORG, FORCES, DETER

B56
ROBERTS H.L.,RUSSIA AND AMERICA. CHINA/COM S/ASIA USSR FORCES TEC/DEV FOR/AID NUC/PWR ALL/IDEOS ...MAJORIT TREND NAT/COMP 20 COLD/WAR UN NATO. PAGE 132 H2641 DIPLOM INT/ORG BAL/PWR TOTALISM

B57
REISS J.,GEORGE KENNANS POLITIK DER EINDAMMUNG. USSR NAT/G FORCES TOTALISM ATTIT ORD/FREE...POLICY 20 NATO TRUMAN/HS MARSHL/PLN KENNAN/G. PAGE 131 H2613 DIPLOM DETER PEACE

B62
MORGENSTERN O.,STRATEGIE - HEUTE (2ND ED.). USA+45 USSR ECO/DEV DELIB/GP WAR PEACE ORD/FREE...GOV/COMP NAT/COMP 20 COLD/WAR NATO. PAGE 113 H2256 NUC/PWR DIPLOM FORCES TEC/DEV

B63
BROEKMEIJER M.W.,DEVELOPING COUNTRIES AND NATO. USSR FORCES DIPLOM NUC/PWR WAR PEACE TOTALISM 20 NATO. PAGE 21 H0427 ECO/UNDEV FOR/AID ORD/FREE NAT/G

B63
KLEIMAN R.,ATLANTIC CRISIS; AMERICAN DIPLOMACY CONFRONTS A RESURGENT EUROPE. EUR+WWI USA+45 ECO/DEV AGRI NAT/G CHIEF FORCES PLAN LEAD ATTIT ...CONCPT 20 NATO KENNEDY/JF DEGAULLE/C EEC JOHNSON/LB. PAGE 87 H1731 DIPLOM REGION POLICY

S63
KOHN H.,"GERMANY IN WORLD POLITICS." EUR+WWI GERMANY GERMANY/W USSR NAT/G POL/PAR TOP/EX ATTIT ...CONCPT TREND GEN/LAWS 20 NATO ADENAUER/K. PAGE 87 H1746 ACT/RES ORD/FREE BAL/PWR

B64
BROWN N.,NUCLEAR WAR* THE IMPENDING STRATEGIC DEADLOCK. USA+45 USSR TEC/DEV BUDGET RISK ARMS/CONT NUC/PWR WEAPON COST BIO/SOC...GEOG IDEA/COMP NAT/COMP GAME NATO WARSAW/P. PAGE 22 H0448 FORCES OP/RES WAR GEN/LAWS

B65
ADENAUER K.,MEMOIRS 1945-53. EUR+WWI GERMANY/W ECO/DEV CHIEF FORCES ECO/TAC WAR GOV/REL PWR SOVEREIGN 20 NATO ADENAUER/K. PAGE 3 H0068 BIOG DIPLOM NAT/G PERS/REL

B65
CALLEO D.P.,EUROPE'S FUTURE: THE GRAND ALTERNATIVES. UK INT/ORG DIPLOM PWR SOVEREIGN ...CONCPT IDEA/COMP NAT/COMP BIBLIOG 20 EEC EUROPE DEGAULLE/C NATO. PAGE 25 H0506 FUT EUR+WWI FEDERAL NAT/LISM

B65
US DEPARTMENT OF DEFENSE,US SECURITY ARMS CONTROL, AND DISARMAMENT 1961-1965 (PAMPHLET). CHINA/COM COM GERMANY/W ISRAEL SPACE USA+45 USSR WOR+45 FORCES EDU/PROP DETER EQUILIB PEACE ALL/VALS...GOV/COMP 20 NATO. PAGE 159 H3183 BIBLIOG/A ARMS/CONT NUC/PWR DIPLOM

S65
GORDON M.,"THE SETTING FOR EUROPEAN ARMS CONTROLS* POLITICAL AND STRATEGIC CHOICES OF EUROPEAN ELITES." FRANCE GERMANY UK USA+45 USSR ARMS/CONT DETER ATTIT ORD/FREE...SAMP NAT/COMP NATO. PAGE 59 H1179 REC/INT ELITES RISK WAR

S65
SPAAK P.H.,"THE SEARCH FOR CONSENSUS: A NEW EFFORT TO BUILD EUROPE." FRANCE GERMANY ECO/DEV NAT/G CONSULT FORCES PLAN EDU/PROP REGION CONSEN ATTIT ...SOC METH/CNCPT OBS TREND EEC NATO WORK 20. PAGE 147 H2941 EUR+WWI INT/ORG

S66
GALTUNG J.,"EAST-WEST INTERACTION PATTERNS." DIPLOM INT/TRADE...NET/THEORY CON/ANAL CHARTS NAT/COMP INDEX NATO COLD/WAR UN WARSAW/P. PAGE 55 H1090 STAT HYPO/EXP

S67
ANTHEM T.,"CYPRUS* WHAT NOW?" CYPRUS GREECE TURKEY NAT/G BUDGET MAJORITY 20 NATO. PAGE 7 H0143 DIPLOM COERCE INT/TRADE ADJUD

S67
ROOT W.,"REPORT FROM PARIS - DE GAULLE: WHICH WAY TO THE FUTURE?" CANADA FRANCE ISLAM UK INT/ORG CHIEF CREATE AGREE CONTROL ARMS/CONT NUC/PWR EQUILIB PEACE PWR 20 DEGAULLE/C NATO. PAGE 134 H2670
POLICY DIPLOM NAT/G BAL/PWR

S67
SOMMER T.,"BONN CHANGES COURSE." GERMANY/W NAT/G POL/PAR PROB/SOLV NAT/LISM 20 NATO BERLIN/BLO. PAGE 147 H2932
DIPLOM BAL/PWR INT/ORG

NATSAGDORJ A.S. H2324

NATURL/LAW....NATURAL LAW

B16
PUFENDORF S.,LAW OF NATURE AND OF NATIONS (ABRIDGED). UNIV LAW NAT/G DIPLOM AGREE WAR PERSON ALL/VALS PWR...POLICY 18 DEITY NATURL/LAW. PAGE 128 H2565
CONCPT INT/LAW SECT MORAL

B30
BURLAMAQUI J.J.,PRINCIPLES OF NATURAL AND POLITIC LAW (2 VOLS.) (1747-51). EX/STRUC LEGIS AGREE CT/SYS CHOOSE ROLE SOVEREIGN 18 NATURL/LAW. PAGE 24 H0490
LAW NAT/G ORD/FREE CONCPT

B43
MARITAIN J.,THE RIGHTS OF MAN AND NATURAL LAW. CONSTN NAT/G DOMIN LEGIT INGP/REL TOTALISM MORAL POPULISM WORSHIP 19/20 CIVIL/LIB CHURCH/STA NATURL/LAW. PAGE 103 H2051
PLURIST ORD/FREE GEN/LAWS

B47
LOCKE J.,TWO TREATISES OF GOVERNMENT (1690). UK LAW SOCIETY LEGIS LEGIT AGREE REV OWN HEREDITY MORAL CONSERVE...POLICY MAJORIT 17 WILLIAM/3 NATURL/LAW. PAGE 97 H1946
CONCPT ORD/FREE NAT/G CONSEN

B53
MARITAIN J.,L'HOMME ET L'ETAT. SECT DIPLOM GP/REL PEACE ORD/FREE...IDEA/COMP 17/20 CHURCH/STA NATURL/LAW. PAGE 103 H2052
CONCPT NAT/G SOVEREIGN COERCE

B66
LOCKE J.,THE SECOND TREATISE OF GOVERNMENT: AN ESSAY CONCERNING THE TRUE ORIGINAL EXTENT AND END OF CIVIL GOVERNMENT (3RD ED.). CONSTN SOCIETY CONTROL OWN...PHIL/SCI 17 NATURL/LAW. PAGE 97 H1947
NAT/G PWR GEN/LAWS ORD/FREE

B96
DE VATTEL E.,THE LAW OF NATIONS. AGRI FINAN CHIEF DIPLOM INT/TRADE AGREE OWN ALL/VALS MORAL ORD/FREE SOVEREIGN...GEN/LAWS 18 NATURL/LAW WOLFF/C. PAGE 39 H0774
LAW CONCPT NAT/G INT/LAW

NAVAHO....NAVAHO INDIANS

C41
KLUCKHOHN C.,"PATTERNING AS EXEMPLIFIED IN NAVAHO CULTURE" IN EDWARD SAPIR, LANGUAGE, CULTURE, AND PERSONALITY (BMR)" KIN PERS/REL ATTIT PERSON...SOC CONCPT METH/CNCPT LING OBS/ENVIR CON/ANAL BIBLIOG SOC/INTEG 20 NAVAHO INDIAN/AM SAPIR/EDW. PAGE 87 H1733
CULTURE INGP/REL STRUCT

B66
VOGT E.Z.,PEOPLE OF RIMROCK. STRATA STRUCT KIN SECT GP/REL HABITAT ALL/VALS...GEOG INT QU 20 TEXAS NAVAHO MORMON SPAN/AMER ZUNI. PAGE 163 H3260
CULTURE GP/COMP SOC SOCIETY

NAVAL/RES....OFFICE OF NAVAL RESEARCH

NAVY....NAVY (ALL NATIONS)

B13
BARDOUX J.,L'ANGLETERRE RADICALE; ESSAI DE LA PSYCHOLOGIE SOCIALE (1906-1913). UK CONSTN NAT/G WORKER CREATE BUDGET ECO/TAC ATTIT...POLICY 20 PARLIAMENT LABOR/PAR STRIKE NAVY. PAGE 11 H0215
POL/PAR CHOOSE COLONIAL LEGIS

S67
HARBRON J.D.,"UNIFICATION IN CANADA: FAIT ACCOMPLI" CANADA STRATA NAT/G DELIB/GP BUDGET GP/REL 20 NAVY. PAGE 66 H1327
INGP/REL FORCES PLAN ATTIT

NAZI....NAZI MOVEMENT (ALL NATIONS); SEE ALSO GERMANY, NAT/LISM, FASCIST

B38
LAWLEY F.E.,THE GROWTH OF COLLECTIVE ECONOMY VOL. 2: INTERNATIONAL. WOR-45 AGRI INDUS EQUILIB OPTIMAL OWN WEALTH...NAT/COMP 19/20 NAZI NEW/DEAL MONOPOLY. PAGE 92 H1845
ECO/TAC SOCISM NAT/LISM CONTROL

B39
HITLER A.,MEIN KAMPF. EUR+WWI FUT MOD/EUR STRUCT INT/ORG LABOR NAT/G POL/PAR FORCES CREATE PLAN BAL/PWR DIPLOM ECO/TAC DOMIN EDU/PROP ADMIN COERCE ATTIT...SOCIALIST BIOG TREND NAZI. PAGE 71 H1428
PWR NEW/IDEA WAR

B39
OAKESHOTT M.,THE SOCIAL AND POLITICAL DOCTRINES OF CONTEMPORARY EUROPE. EUR+WWI RATIONAL CATHISM FASCISM MARXISM POPULISM...POLICY ANTHOL 20 NAZI. PAGE 120 H2392
IDEA/COMP GOV/COMP ALL/IDEOS NAT/G

S39
COLE G.D.H.,"NAZI ECONOMICS: HOW DO THEY MANAGE IT?" GERMANY FORCES WORKER BUDGET INT/TRADE ROUTINE COERCE WAR 20 HITLER/A NAZI. PAGE 31 H0622
FASCISM ECO/TAC ATTIT PLAN

B41
HAUSHOFER K.,WEHR-GEOPOLITIK. EUR+WWI GERMANY MOD/EUR NAT/G ACT/RES BAL/PWR PWR...STAT TIME/SEQ CHARTS NAZI 20. PAGE 68 H1361
FORCES GEOG WAR

B42
NEUBURGER O.,OFFICIAL PUBLICATIONS OF PRESENT-DAY GERMANY: GOVERNMENT, CORPORATE ORGANIZATIONS, AND NATIONAL SOCIALIST PARTY. GERMANY CONSTN COM/IND POL/PAR EDU/PROP PRESS 20 NAZI. PAGE 117 H2332
BIBLIOG/A FASCISM NAT/G ADMIN

B42
SINGTON D.,THE GOEBBELS EXPERIMENT. GERMANY MOD/EUR NAT/G EX/STRUC FORCES CONTROL ROUTINE WAR TOTALISM PWR...ART/METH HUM 20 NAZI GOEBBELS/J. PAGE 144 H2886
FASCISM EDU/PROP ATTIT COM/IND

B44
GYORGY A.,GEOPOLITICS: THE NEW GERMAN SCIENCE. EUR+WWI GERMANY STRATA NAT/G PROVS DOMIN EDU/PROP ATTIT DRIVE FASCISM...GEOG NAZI 20. PAGE 63 H1261
PWR LEGIT WAR

L48
SHILS E.A.,"COHESION AND DISINTEGRATION IN THE WEHRMACHT IN WORLD WAR II." GERMANY STRUCT DOMIN WAR INGP/REL ISOLAT NAT/LISM ATTIT AUTHORIT SUPEGO RESPECT...PSY CON/ANAL 20 NAZI. PAGE 143 H2862
EDU/PROP DRIVE PERS/REL FORCES

S48
ALEXANDER L.,"WAR CRIMES, THEIR SOCIAL-PSYCHOLOGICAL ASPECTS." EUR+WWI GERMANY LAW CULTURE ELITES KIN POL/PAR PUB/INST FORCES DOMIN EDU/PROP COERCE CRIME ATTIT SUPEGO HEALTH MORAL PWR FASCISM ...PSY OBS TREND GEN/LAWS NAZI 20. PAGE 5 H0100
DRIVE WAR

S51
GOULD J.,"THE KOMSOMOL AND THE HITLER JUGEND." COM EUR+WWI GERMANY SOCIETY NAT/G POL/PAR SCHOOL TOTALISM DRIVE PERCEPT KNOWL FASCISM...SOC NAZI TOT/POP 20. PAGE 59 H1185
EDU/PROP CON/ANAL SOCISM

B53
MEYER P.,THE JEWS IN THE SOVIET SATELLITES. CZECHOSLVK POLAND SOCIETY STRATA NAT/G BAL/PWR ECO/TAC EDU/PROP LEGIT ADMIN COERCE ATTIT DISPL PERCEPT HEALTH PWR RESPECT WEALTH...METH/CNCPT JEWS VAL/FREE NAZI 20. PAGE 110 H2192
COM SECT TOTALISM USSR

S53
ARENDT H.,"IDEOLOGY AND TERROR: A NOVEL FORM OF GOVERNMENT." WOR-45 DOMIN STRANGE ATTIT SUPEGO MARXISM...GOV/COMP IDEA/COMP 20 NAZI. PAGE 8 H0160
TOTALISM ANOMIE ALL/IDEOS SOCIETY

B54
FRIEDRICH C.J.,TOTALITARIAN DICTATORSHIP AND AUTOCRACY. COM EUR+WWI GERMANY ITALY USSR INTELL ECO/DEV NAT/G POL/PAR FORCES TOP/EX ECO/TAC EDU/PROP LEGIT COERCE ATTIT ORD/FREE PWR FASCISM ...CONCPT TIME/SEQ GEN/LAWS NAZI 20. PAGE 53 H1068
SOCIETY DOMIN TOTALISM

L54
FRIEDRICH C.J.,"TOTALITARIANISM." COM EUR+WWI NAT/G POL/PAR SECT FORCES PLAN ECO/TAC DOMIN EDU/PROP EXEC COERCE REV ORD/FREE PWR...SOC CONCPT NAZI 20. PAGE 53 H1067
ATTIT TOTALISM

B56
DE JONG L.,THE GERMAN FIFTH COLUMN IN THE SECOND WORLD WAR. EUR+WWI GERMANY NAT/G DIPLOM ATTIT FASCISM...MYTH 20 NAZI. PAGE 38 H0756
EDU/PROP WAR RUMOR

L59
JANIS I.L.,"DECISIONAL CONFLICT: A THEORETICAL ANALYSIS." INTELL NAT/G POL/PAR DELIB/GP LEGIS TOP/EX PLAN...DECISION CONGRESS NAZI 20 WWI. PAGE 80 H1590
ACT/RES PSY DIPLOM

B60
LOMBARDO TOLEDANO V,EL NEONAZISMO; SUS CHARACTERISTICAS Y PELIGROS. GERMANY/W POL/PAR COLONIAL LEAD LOBBY ATTIT 20 NAZI. PAGE 98 H1956
NAT/G FASCISM POLICY DIPLOM

B61
BULLOCK A.,HITLER: A STUDY IN TYRANNY. EUR+WWI GERMANY SOCIETY STRUCT NAT/G POL/PAR FORCES CREATE DOMIN EDU/PROP EXEC COERCE WAR NAT/LISM DISPL DRIVE PERSON PWR...PSY NAZI 20 HITLER/A. PAGE 23 H0470
ATTIT BIOG TOTALISM

B61
SETON-WATSON H.,FROM LENIN TO KHRUSHCHEV: THE HISTORY OF WORLD COMMUNISM. ASIA COM EUR+WWI ISLAM S/ASIA ECO/DEV ECO/UNDEV NAT/G POL/PAR DIPLOM ECO/TAC EDU/PROP COERCE GUERRILLA ATTIT DRIVE WORK TOT/POP NAZI 20. PAGE 141 H2832
PWR REV USSR

L62
NOLTE E.,"ZUR PHANOMENOLOGIE DES FASCHIMUS." EUR+WWI GERMANY ITALY TURKEY INTELL NAT/G CHIEF CONSULT FORCES CREATE DOMIN EDU/PROP COERCE WAR CHOOSE DRIVE FASCISM...PSY CONCPT MYTH GEN/METH LEAGUE/NAT NAZI 20. PAGE 118 H2367
ATTIT PWR

B63
CONZE W.,DIE DEUTSCHE NATION. GERMANY NAT/G POL/PAR WAR ORD/FREE...TREND 8/20 NAZI. PAGE 33 H0657 NAT/LISM FASCISM ATTIT SOCIETY

B64
HALE O.J.,THE CAPTIVE PRESS IN THE THIRD REICH. GERMANY CULTURE LG/CO NAT/G POL/PAR PLAN DOMIN TASK CENTRAL OWN TOTALISM PWR...BIBLIOG 20 HITLER/A NAZI AMMAN/MAX. PAGE 64 H1283 COM/IND PRESS CONTROL FASCISM

S64
BARIETY J.,"LA POLITIQUE EXTERIEURE ALLEMANDE DANS L'HIVER 1939-1940." COM FINLAND GERMANY ISLAM ITALY USSR NAT/G FORCES ECO/TAC DOMIN EDU/PROP COERCE WAR PWR WEALTH...HIST/WRIT NAZI TOT/POP VAL/FREE 20. PAGE 11 H0216 EUR+WWI DIPLOM

B65
ALLEN W.S.,THE NAZI SEIZURE OF POWER. GERMANY NAT/G CHIEF LEAD COERCE CHOOSE REPRESENT GOV/REL AUTHORIT ...DECISION 20 HITLER/A NAZI. PAGE 5 H0106 MUNIC FASCISM TOTALISM LOC/G

B65
BRAMSTED E.K.,GOEBBELS AND NATIONAL SOCIALIST PROPAGANDA, 1925-1945. EUR+WWI GERMANY UK USSR NAT/G FORCES WAR FASCISM...TIME/SEQ 20 GOEBBELS/J NAZI. PAGE 20 H0403 EDU/PROP PSY COM/IND

B66
O'NEILL R.J.,THE GERMAN ARMY AND THE NAZI PARTY, 1933-1939. GERMANY ELITES NAT/G EDU/PROP CONTROL LEAD COERCE WAR...POLICY INT TIME/SEQ BIBLIOG 20 HITLER/A NAZI. PAGE 120 H2391 CIVMIL/REL FORCES FASCISM POL/PAR

B66
ROSNER J.,DER FASCHISMUS. AUSTRIA GERMANY ITALY STRATA NAT/G POL/PAR COERCE RACE/REL TOTALISM ATTIT AUTHORIT...IDEA/COMP 20 NAZI ANTI/SEMIT. PAGE 134 H2684 NAT/LISM FASCISM ORD/FREE WAR

B66
THORNTON M.J.,NAZISM, 1918-1945. GERMANY INT/ORG DIPLOM REV PEACE FASCISM...CONCPT 20 HITLER/A WEIMAR/REP NAZI. PAGE 155 H3089 TOTALISM POL/PAR NAT/G WAR

NCC....NATIONAL COUNCIL OF CHURCHES

NE/WIN....NE WIN

NEA....NATIONAL EDUCATION ASSOCIATION

NEALE A.D. H2325

NEALE R.S. H2326

NEAR EAST....SEE MEDIT-7, ISLAM

NEBRASKA....NEBRASKA

NEEDHAM T. H2327

NEEDLER M.C. H2328

NEG/INCOME....NEGATIVE INCOME TAX

NEGATIVE INCOME TAX....SEE NEG/INCOME

NEGRITO....NEGRITO TRIBE, PHILIPPINES

B04
REED W.A.,ETHNOLOGICAL SURVEY PUBLICATIONS (VOL. II). PHILIPPINE STRUCT INDUS SECT DEATH LEISURE HABITAT...AUD/VIS CHARTS WORSHIP 20 NABOLOI NEGRITO BATAK. PAGE 130 H2607 CULTURE SOCIETY SOC OBS

NEGRO....NEGRO

N
BROCKWAY A.F.,AFRICAN SOCIALISM. EUR+WWI GHANA ISLAM UAR ECO/UNDEV CAP/ISM INT/TRADE COLONIAL COERCE GOV/REL DISCRIM 20 NEGRO NKRUMAH/K NASSER/G. PAGE 21 H0423 AFR SOCISM MARXISM

NCO
CARRINGTON C.E.,THE COMMONWEALTH IN AFRICA (PAMPHLET). UK STRUCT NAT/G COLONIAL REPRESENT GOV/REL RACE/REL NAT/LISM...MAJORIT 20 EEC NEGRO COLD/WAR. PAGE 27 H0540 ECO/UNDEV AFR DIPLOM PLAN

B00
HOBSON J.A.,THE WAR IN SOUTH AFRICA: ITS CAUSES AND EFFECTS. NETHERLAND SOUTH/AFR UK ELITES AGRI EXTR/IND POL/PAR DIPLOM PRESS RACE/REL ATTIT ORD/FREE SOVEREIGN...INT 19 NEGRO. PAGE 72 H1439 WAR DOMIN POLICY NAT/G

B00
MARKHAM V.R.,SOUTH AFRICA, PAST AND PRESENT. NETHERLAND SOUTH/AFR CULTURE LEGIS EDU/PROP COLONIAL CHOOSE REPRESENT DISCRIM ATTIT...OBS TIME/SEQ 17/19 NEGRO BOER/WAR. PAGE 103 H2054 WAR LEAD RACE/REL

B12
SONOLET L.,L'AFRIQUE OCCIDENTALE FRANCAISE. FRANCE AGRI INDUS NAT/G SECT FORCES INT/TRADE EDU/PROP RACE/REL HEALTH ORD/FREE...CHARTS 19/20 NEGRO AFRICA/W. PAGE 147 H2933 DOMIN ADMIN COLONIAL AFR

N19
SENGHOR L.S.,AFRICAN SOCIALISM (PAMPHLET). AFR FRANCE MALI USSR ELITES ECO/UNDEV NAT/G DIPLOM DOMIN EDU/PROP ATTIT 20 NEGRO. PAGE 141 H2827 SOCISM MARXISM ORD/FREE NAT/LISM

B24
WALKER F.D.,AFRICA AND HER PEOPLES. ISLAM STRUCT FAM SECT EDU/PROP INGP/REL RACE/REL HABITAT...GEOG SOC IDEA/COMP WORSHIP 20 NEGRO. PAGE 164 H3292 CULTURE AFR GP/COMP KIN

B27
SMITH E.W.,THE GOLDEN STOOL: SOME ASPECTS OF THE CONFLICT OF CULTURES IN AFRICA. AFR FINAN INDUS SECT INT/TRADE COERCE CHOOSE RACE/REL ATTIT...GEOG LING 20 NEGRO. PAGE 145 H2907 COLONIAL CULTURE GP/REL EDU/PROP

B30
OLDMAN J.H.,WHITE AND BLACK IN AFRICA. AFR STRUCT COLONIAL PARTIC DISCRIM ISOLAT PRIVIL 20 SMUTS/JAN NEGRO WHITE/SUP. PAGE 121 H2412 SOVEREIGN ORD/FREE RACE/REL NAT/G

B30
SMUTS J.C.,AFRICA AND SOME WORLD PROBLEMS. RHODESIA SOUTH/AFR CULTURE ECO/UNDEV INDUS INT/ORG SECT PROB/SOLV REGION GOV/REL DISCRIM ATTIT 19/20 LEAGUE/NAT LIVNGSTN/D NEGRO. PAGE 146 H2921 LEGIS AFR COLONIAL RACE/REL

B35
GORER G.,AFRICA DANCES: A BOOK ABOUT WEST AFRICAN NEGROES. STRUCT LOC/G SECT FORCES TAX ADMIN COLONIAL...ART/METH MYTH WORSHIP 20 NEGRO AFRICA/W CHRISTIAN RITUAL. PAGE 59 H1181 AFR ATTIT CULTURE SOCIETY

B39
HILL R.L.,A BIBLIOGRAPHY OF THE ANGLO-EGYPTIAN SUDAN FROM THE EARLIEST TIMES TO 1937. AFR ETHIOPIA SUDAN UAR LAW COM/IND SECT RACE/REL...GEOG HEAL SOC LING 19/20 NEGRO. PAGE 71 H1417 BIBLIOG CULTURE NAT/COMP GP/COMP

B48
COX O.C.,CASTE, CLASS, AND RACE. INDIA WOR+45 WOR-45 SECT TEC/DEV MARRIAGE ROLE MARXISM...MAJORIT NAT/COMP SOC/INTEG 20 NEGRO HINDU. PAGE 34 H0688 RACE/REL STRUCT STRATA DISCRIM

B48
EDUARDO O.D.C.,THE NEGRO IN NORTHERN BRAZIL: A STUDY IN ACCULTURATION. BRAZIL ECO/UNDEV FAM SECT PAY REGION HABITAT CATHISM MYSTISM...GEOG OBS SOC/INTEG WORSHIP 20 NEGRO MARANHAO. PAGE 44 H0890 CULTURE ADJUST GP/REL

S49
DEXTER L.A.,"A DIALOGUE ON THE SOCIAL PSYCHOLOGY OF COLONIALISM AND ON CERTAIN PUERTO RICAN PROFESSIONAL PERSONALITY PATTERNS." L/A+17C PUERT/RICO STRATA STRUCT DOMIN ISOLAT DRIVE ...NAT/COMP PERS/COMP HYPO/EXP 20 JEWS NEGRO. PAGE 41 H0813 COLONIAL SOC PSY PERSON

S49
HUGHES E.C.,"SOCIAL CHANGE AND STATUS PROTEST: AN ESSAY ON THE MARGINAL MAN" (BMR)" EUR+WWI UK USA+45 CULTURE SOCIETY STRUCT RACE/REL...SOC NAT/COMP SOC/INTEG 19/20 NEGRO PARK/R. PAGE 74 H1490 STRATA ATTIT DISCRIM

B51
BISSAINTHE M.,DICTIONNAIRE DE BIBLIOGRAPHIE HAITIENNE. HAITI ELITES AGRI LEGIS DIPLOM INT/TRADE WRITING ORD/FREE CATHISM...ART/METH GEOG 19/20 NEGRO TREATY. PAGE 17 H0347 BIBLIOG L/A+17C SOCIETY NAT/G

B52
ISAACS H.R.,AFRICA: NEW CRISES IN THE MAKING (PAMPHLET). EUR+WWI USA+45 ELITES ECO/UNDEV WAR DISCRIM NAT/LISM ATTIT...POLICY NEW/IDEA CHARTS GOV/COMP 20 NEGRO COLD/WAR. PAGE 78 H1570 COLONIAL AFR RACE/REL ORD/FREE

B52
MONTAGU A.,MAN'S MOST DANGEROUS MYTH: THE FALLACY OF RACE. LAW PROB/SOLV WAR HABITAT POPULISM...PSY CONCPT CHARTS BIBLIOG NEGRO JEWS. PAGE 112 H2242 DISCRIM MYTH CULTURE RACE/REL

B59
CARPENTER G.W.,THE WAY IN AFRICA. AFR INDUS MUNIC DIPLOM DOMIN EDU/PROP COERCE DISCRIM NAT/LISM ORD/FREE 20 NEGRO CHRISTIAN. PAGE 27 H0535 CULTURE SECT ECO/UNDEV COLONIAL

B59
MURDOCK G.P.,AFRICA: ITS PEOPLES AND THEIR CULTURE HISTORY. AFR CULTURE AGRI LOC/G INGP/REL HABITAT ...GEOG SOC LING CHARTS BIBLIOG 20 NEGRO EGYPT/ANC. PAGE 115 H2293 SOCIETY ECO/TAC GP/COMP KIN

B59
SENGHOR L.S.,RAPPORT SUR LA DOCTRINE ET LA PROGRAMME DU PART I. FRANCE MALI CONSTN POL/PAR PLAN CHOOSE OWN ORD/FREE MARXISM...SOCIALIST 20 NEGRO. PAGE 141 H2828 ATTIT NAT/G AFR SOCISM

B60
LEYDER J.,BIBLIOGRAPHIE DE L'ENSEIGNEMENT SUPERIEUR ET DE LA RECHERCHE SCIENTIFIQUE EN AFRIQUE INTERTROPICALE (2 VOLS.). AFR CULTURE ECO/UNDEV AGRI PLAN EDU/PROP ADMIN COLONIAL...GEOG SOC/INTEG 20 NEGRO. PAGE 96 H1918 BIBLIOG/A ACT/RES ACADEM R+D

S60
BERREMAN G.D.,"CASTE IN INDIA AND THE UNITED STATES" (BMR)" INDIA USA+45 CULTURE SOCIETY STRUCT SECT GP/REL DISCRIM HEREDITY...SOC STERTYP 20 NEGRO HINDU. PAGE 16 H0318
STRATA RACE/REL NAT/COMP ATTIT

S60
GRIMSHAW A.D.,"URBAN RACIAL VIOLENCE IN THE UNITED STATES: CHANGING ECOLOGICAL CONSIDERATIONS." STRUCT MUNIC FORCES PARTIC DISCRIM ATTIT HABITAT ...IDEA/COMP 20 NEGRO. PAGE 61 H1228
CROWD RACE/REL GOV/COMP NEIGH

B61
ALLIGHAN G.,VERWOERD - THE END. SOUTH/AFR TOP/EX DIPLOM COLONIAL DISCRIM TOTALISM ATTIT AUTHORIT ...BIOG 20 NEGRO VERWOERD/H. PAGE 5 H0107
CONTROL CHIEF RACE/REL NAT/G

B61
DUFFY J.,AFRICA SPEAKS. GHANA TOGO CULTURE ECO/UNDEV PROB/SOLV COLONIAL NEUTRAL DISCRIM NAT/LISM SOVEREIGN ALL/IDEOS...CONCPT ANTHOL SOC/INTEG 20 NEGRO THIRD/WRLD. PAGE 43 H0857
AFR NAT/G FUT STRUCT

B61
SPOONER F.P.,SOUTH AFRICAN PREDICAMENT. FUT SOUTH/AFR INDUS POL/PAR RACE/REL INCOME...CHARTS 20 NEGRO. PAGE 148 H2953
ECO/DEV DISCRIM ECO/TAC POLICY

B61
TURNBULL C.M.,THE FOREST PEOPLE. EATING GP/REL INGP/REL RACE/REL ISOLAT HABITAT HEREDITY...GEOG SOC LING DICTIONARY WORSHIP 20 CONGO NEGRO BA/MBUTI. PAGE 157 H3138
AFR CULTURE KIN RECORD

B62
AMERICAN SOCIETY AFR CULTURE,PAN-AFRICANISM RECONSIDERED. AFR SOCIETY STRUCT SCHOOL CAP/ISM EDU/PROP...ART/METH NEW/IDEA PREDICT ANTHOL 20 PANAF/FREE NEGRO. PAGE 6 H0123
DIPLOM FEDERAL NAT/LISM CULTURE

B62
FEIT E.,SOUTH AFRICA, THE DYNAMICS OF THE AFRICAN NATIONAL CONGRESS. AFR SOUTH/AFR LAW INTELL STRATA KIN NAT/G POL/PAR ECO/TAC DOMIN RISK COERCE 20 NEGRO. PAGE 49 H0984
RACE/REL ELITES CONTROL STRUCT

B62
GANJI M.,INTERNATIONAL PROTECTION OF HUMAN RIGHTS. WOR+45 CONSTN INT/TRADE CT/SYS SANCTION CRIME WAR RACE/REL...CHARTS IDEA/COMP NAT/COMP BIBLIOG 20 TREATY NEGRO LEAGUE/NAT UN CIVIL/LIB. PAGE 55 H1097
ORD/FREE DISCRIM LEGIS DELIB/GP

B62
MANSERGH N.,SOUTH AFRICA 1906-1961: THE PRICE OF MAGNANIMITY. SOUTH/AFR LEGIS LEGIT SUFF NAT/LISM ATTIT ORD/FREE 20 NEGRO 20. PAGE 102 H2041
COLONIAL DISCRIM NAT/G

B62
VAN RENSBURG P.,GUILTY LAND: THE HISTORY OF APARTHEID. SOUTH/AFR NAT/G POL/PAR DOMIN CHOOSE ...SOC 19/20 NEGRO. PAGE 162 H3231
RACE/REL DISCRIM NAT/LISM POLICY

B63
HUGHES A.J.,EAST AFRICA: THE SEARCH FOR UNITY- KENYA, TANGANYIKA, UGANDA, AND ZANZIBAR. TANZANIA UGANDA CONSTN POL/PAR SECT CHIEF DELIB/GP LEGIS WAR CHOOSE NAT/LISM MARXISM...POLICY CHARTS 20 NEGRO UN. PAGE 74 H1488
NAT/G DOMIN LOC/G AFR

B63
JUDD P.,AFRICAN INDEPENDENCE: THE EXPLODING EMERGENCE OF THE NEW AFRICAN NATIONS. AFR UK LAW CONSTN CULTURE KIN DIPLOM ATTIT...CHARTS BIBLIOG 20 UN DEGAULLE/C NEGRO THIRD/WRLD. PAGE 82 H1640
ORD/FREE POLICY DOMIN LOC/G

B63
LEWIN J.,POLITICS AND LAW IN SOUTH AFRICA. SOUTH/AFR UK POL/PAR BAL/PWR ECO/TAC COLONIAL CONTROL GP/REL DISCRIM PWR 20 NEGRO. PAGE 96 H1909
NAT/LISM POLICY LAW RACE/REL

B63
MAC MILLAN W.M.,BANTU, BOER, AND BRITON: THE MAKING OF THE SOUTH AFRICAN NATIVE PROBLEM. SOUTH/AFR UK LAW KIN NAT/G SECT LEGIS COLONIAL ISOLAT ATTIT ...BIOG 18/20 BANTU NEGRO PHILIP/J MISSION. PAGE 100 H1989
AFR RACE/REL ELITES

B64
HARRIS M.,PATTERNS OF RACE IN THE AMERICAS. BRAZIL L/A+17C STRATA ECO/UNDEV AGRI KIN MUNIC SECT COLONIAL RACE/REL...SOC SOC/INTEG 17/20 NEGRO INDIAN/AM. PAGE 67 H1342
STRUCT PRE/AMER CULTURE SOCIETY

B64
HILL C.R.,BANTUSTANS: THE FRAGMENTATION OF SOUTH AFRICA. AFR SOUTH/AFR ELITES SOCIETY KIN CONTROL DISCRIM ANOMIE ATTIT...POLICY CHARTS GOV/COMP 20 NEGRO BANTUSTANS TRANSKEI NATAL. PAGE 71 H1416
RACE/REL CULTURE LOC/G ORD/FREE

B64
MBEKI G.,SOUTH AFRICA: THE PEASANT'S REVOLT. SOUTH/AFR POL/PAR COERCE REV NAT/LISM ORD/FREE SOVEREIGN 20 NEGRO. PAGE 106 H2114
COLONIAL RACE/REL DISCRIM DOMIN

B64
MORGAN H.W.,AMERICAN SOCIALISM 1900-1960. USA+45 USA-45 INTELL AGRI LABOR WORKER BARGAIN ECO/TAC GP/REL RACE/REL 20 NEGRO MIGRATION GOLD/STAND. PAGE 113 H2254
SOCISM POL/PAR ECO/DEV STRATA

B64
PERKINS D.,THE AMERICAN DEMOCRACY: ITS RISE TO POWER. ASIA USSR LAW CULTURE FINAN EDU/PROP COLONIAL CHOOSE...POLICY CHARTS BIBLIOG WORSHIP PRESIDENT 15/20 NEGRO. PAGE 125 H2492
LOC/G ECO/TAC WAR DIPLOM

S64
IRELE A.,"A DEFENSE OF NEGRITUDE." AFR NAT/LISM ...HUM 20 NEGRO. PAGE 78 H1566
CONCPT CULTURE NAT/COMP KIN

B65
GINIEWSKI P.,THE TWO FACES OF APARTHEID. AFR SOUTH/AFR STRATA AGRI INDUS COLONIAL PARTIC SOVEREIGN...CONCPT GOV/COMP NAT/COMP 19/20 NEGRO. PAGE 56 H1131
DISCRIM NAT/G RACE/REL STRUCT

B66
BARNETT D.L.,MAU MAU FROM WITHIN. AFR UK POL/PAR LEAD GUERRILLA AUTHORIT ORD/FREE...SOC BIOG 20 NEGRO MAU/MAU. PAGE 11 H0225
REV CULTURE NAT/G

B66
FLINT J.E.,NIGERIA AND GHANA. AFR GHANA NIGERIA UK NAT/G DOMIN DISCRIM...CHARTS BIBLIOG/A 15/20 NEGRO MAPS. PAGE 51 H1026
CULTURE COLONIAL NAT/LISM

B66
KEITH G.,THE FADING COLOUR BAR. AFR CENTRL/AFR UK ZAMBIA CULTURE SCHOOL EDU/PROP PERS/REL DISCRIM AGE ...AUD/VIS NAT/COMP SOC/INTEG 20 NEGRO. PAGE 84 H1682
RACE/REL STRUCT ATTIT NAT/G

B66
MULLER C.F.J.,A SELECT BIBLIOGRAPHY OF SOUTH AFRICAN HISTORY; A GUIDE FOR HISTORICAL RESEARCH. SOUTH/AFR UK LAW CONSTN SOCIETY STRUCT AGRI SECT DIPLOM COLONIAL LEAD RACE/REL...POLICY 17/20 NEGRO. PAGE 114 H2284
BIBLIOG AFR NAT/G

B67
CURTIN P.D.,AFRICA REMEMBERED. NIGERIA SENEGAL CULTURE DIPLOM INT/TRADE GP/REL RACE/REL...RECORD ANTHOL 18/19 NEGRO. PAGE 36 H0727
DOMIN ORD/FREE AFR DISCRIM

B67
DEGLER C.N.,THE AGE OF THE ECONOMIC REVOLUTION 1876-1900. USA-45 AGRI MUNIC POL/PAR SECT ECO/TAC CHOOSE...PHIL/SCI CHARTS NAT/COMP 19 NEGRO. PAGE 39 H0782
INDUS SOCIETY ECO/DEV TEC/DEV

B67
FANON F.,BLACK SKIN, WHITE MASKS: THE EXPERIENCES OF A BLACK MAN IN A WHITE WORLD. CULTURE COLONIAL HAPPINESS ISOLAT STRANGE ATTIT HABITAT RIGID/FLEX SEX...BIOG STERTYP SOC/INTEG 20 NEGRO. PAGE 49 H0970
DISCRIM PERS/REL RACE/REL PSY

B67
FISHEL L.H. JR.,THE NEGRO AMERICAN: A DOCUMENTARY HISTORY. SOCIETY NAT/G ROLE...POLICY ANTHOL 15/20 NEGRO. PAGE 51 H1013
ORD/FREE DISCRIM RACE/REL STRATA

B67
THOMPSON E.T.,PERSPECTIVES ON THE SOUTH: AGENDA FOR RESEARCH. CULTURE ECO/UNDEV SECT GP/REL EFFICIENCY ALL/VALS...HUM SOC CONCPT LING 20 NEGRO. PAGE 154 H3080
PROB/SOLV IDEA/COMP REGION ACT/RES

S67
BEVEL D.N.,"JOURNEY TO NORTH VIETNAM." VIETNAM/N CONSTN NAT/G FORCES PROB/SOLV DEATH CIVMIL/REL PEACE MORAL...ANTHOL 20 NEGRO. PAGE 16 H0325
ATTIT DIPLOM ORD/FREE WAR

S67
HAMMOND R.J.,"RACE ATTITUDES AND POLICIES IN PORTUGUESE AFRICA IN THE NINETEENTH AND TWENTIETH CENTURIES." AFR PORTUGAL NAT/G SECT EDU/PROP COLONIAL ATTIT RIGID/FLEX SEX MORAL RESPECT 19/20 NEGRO. PAGE 65 H1309
POLICY RACE/REL DISCRIM SOCIETY

S67
RAUM O.,"THE MODERN LEADERSHIP GROUP AMONG THE SOUTH AFRICAN XHOSA." SOUTH/AFR SOCIETY SECT EX/STRUC REPRESENT GP/REL INGP/REL PERSON ...METH/COMP 17/20 XHOSA NEGRO. PAGE 130 H2596
RACE/REL KIN LEAD CULTURE

B82
MACDONALD D.,AFRICANA; OR, THE HEART OF HEATHEN AFRICA, VOL. II: MISSION LIFE. SOCIETY STRATA KIN CREATE EDU/PROP ADMIN COERCE LITERACY HEALTH...MYTH WORSHIP 19 LIVNGSTN/D MISSION NEGRO. PAGE 100 H1990
SECT AFR CULTURE ORD/FREE

B98
FORTES M.,AFRICAN POLITICAL SYSTEMS. ECO/UNDEV KIN LOC/G NEIGH POL/PAR SECT LEAD GP/REL ORD/FREE...SOC 20 NEGRO. PAGE 52 H1039
AFR CULTURE STRUCT

B99
DU BOIS W.E.B.,THE PHILADELPHIA NEGRO: A SOCIAL STUDY. CULTURE STRATA KIN CRIME SUFF ADJUST DISCRIM ISOLAT HABITAT HEREDITY ALL/VALS SOC/INTEG 17/19 NEGRO PHILADELPH. PAGE 42 H0851
INGP/REL RACE/REL SOC CENSUS

NEHRU/J....JAWAHARLAL NEHRU

B30
HULL W.I.,INDIA'S POLITICAL CRISIS. INDIA UK INT/ORG LABOR SECT DELIB/GP LEGIS DIPLOM NEUTRAL
ORD/FREE NAT/G

REGION CROWD GOV/REL MAJORITY ATTIT 20 NEHRU/J GANDHI/M COMMONWLTH. PAGE 75 H1492
COLONIAL NAT/LISM

B59
MADHOK B.,POLITICAL TRENDS IN INDIA. INDIA PAKISTAN UK STRATA ECO/UNDEV POL/PAR LEGIS CAP/ISM DIPLOM COLONIAL CHOOSE MARXISM...SOC TREND 20 GANDHI/M NEHRU/J. PAGE 101 H2014
GEOG NAT/G

B60
HARRISON S.S.,INDIA: THE MOST DANGEROUS DECADES. INDIA CONSTN STRATA POL/PAR SECT PLAN ADMIN CHOOSE GP/REL TOTALISM MARXISM...LING 20 NEHRU/J. PAGE 67 H1347
CULTURE ECO/UNDEV PROB/SOLV REGION

B60
MC CLELLAN G.S.,INDIA. CHINA/COM INDIA CONSTN ELITES STRATA AGRI POL/PAR FOR/AID ARMS/CONT REV MARXISM...CENSUS BIBLIOG 20 COLD/WAR GANDHI/M NEHRU/J. PAGE 106 H2117
DIPLOM NAT/G SOCIETY ECO/UNDEV

B61
CHAKRABARTI A.,NEHRU: HIS DEMOCRACY AND INDIA. ASIA INDIA UK CONSTN ECO/UNDEV SECT DIPLOM COLONIAL PEACE WEALTH...BIBLIOG 20 CONGRESS NEHRU/J GANDHI/M. PAGE 28 H0570
ORD/FREE STRATA NAT/G CHIEF

S64
"FURTHER READING." INDIA ATTIT...POLICY 20 NEHRU/J. PAGE 2 H0042
BIBLIOG S/ASIA CHIEF NAT/G

S64
LANGERHANS H.,"NEHRU'S BITTERNESS." FUT INDIA S/ASIA CONSTN CULTURE ECO/UNDEV ECO/TAC DOMIN EDU/PROP ATTIT PERCEPT PERSON...POLICY 20 NEHRU/J. PAGE 91 H1811
ECO/DEV BIOG

S64
SMYTHE H.H.,"NEHRU AND INDIAN FOREIGN POLICY." S/ASIA ECO/UNDEV NAT/G POL/PAR CONSULT PLAN DIPLOM NEUTRAL COERCE ATTIT DRIVE PERSON MORAL ORD/FREE RESPECT...GEOG CONCPT TIME/SEQ TREND GEN/LAWS 20 NEHRU/J. PAGE 146 H2922
TOP/EX BIOG INDIA

B65
WOLPERT S.,INDIA. INDIA UK ECO/UNDEV DIPLOM GP/REL WEALTH 20 NEHRU/J. PAGE 170 H3405
CULTURE COLONIAL NAT/LISM SECT

B66
BRECHER M.,SUCCESSION IN INDIA. INDIA USA+45 CONSTN AGRI POL/PAR PROVS SECT DELIB/GP FORCES PROB/SOLV ECO/TAC PWR...LING 20 CONGRESS NEHRU/J. PAGE 20 H0408
CHIEF DECISION CHOOSE

B66
HIDAYATULLAH M.,DEMOCRACY IN INDIA AND THE JUDICIAL PROCESS. INDIA EX/STRUC LEGIS LEAD GOV/REL ATTIT ORD/FREE...MAJORIT CONCPT 20 NEHRU/J. PAGE 71 H1415
NAT/G CT/SYS CONSTN JURID

B66
TYSON G.,NEHRU: THE YEARS OF POWER. INDIA UK STRATA ECO/UNDEV FINAN SECT TASK WAR ORD/FREE MARXISM ...POLICY BIBLIOG 20 NEHRU/J. PAGE 157 H3145
CHIEF PWR DIPLOM NAT/G

B66
ZINKIN T.,CHALLENGES IN INDIA. INDIA PAKISTAN LAW AGRI FINAN INDUS TOP/EX TEC/DEV CONTROL ROUTINE ORD/FREE PWR 20 NEHRU/J SHASTRI/LB CIVIL/SERV. PAGE 173 H3458
NAT/G ECO/TAC POLICY ADMIN

NEHRU/PM....PANDIT MOTILAL NEHRU

B61
PANIKKAR K.M.,THE VOICE OF FREEDOM: SELECTED SPEECHES OF PANDIT MOTILAL NEHRU. INDIA UK CONSTN FINAN FORCES LEGIS DIPLOM TAX COLONIAL...POLICY MAJORIT ANTHOL 20 NEHRU/PM. PAGE 123 H2460
NAT/LISM ORD/FREE CHIEF NAT/G

NEIGH....NEIGHBORHOOD

N
KRADER L.,SOCIAL ORGANIZATION OF THE MONGOL-TURKIC PASTORAL NOMADS. SOCIETY FAM KIN NEIGH GP/REL MARRIAGE 16/20 MONGOLIA TURKIC MIGRATION. PAGE 88 H1763
BIO/SOC HABITAT CULTURE STRUCT

B18
BARRES M.,THE FAITH OF FRANCE (TRANS. BY ELISABETH MARBURY). FRANCE FAM MUNIC NEIGH POL/PAR SECT ALL/VALS 20. PAGE 11 H0227
TRADIT CULTURE WAR GP/REL

B28
YANG KUNG-SUN,THE BOOK OF LORD SHANG. LAW ECO/UNDEV LOC/G NAT/G NEIGH PLAN ECO/TAC LEGIT ATTIT SKILL ...CONCPT CON/ANAL WORK TOT/POP. PAGE 172 H3434
ASIA JURID

B31
HENNIG P.,GEOPOLITIK (2ND ED.). CULTURE MUNIC COLONIAL...CENSUS CHARTS 20. PAGE 70 H1398
GEOG HABITAT CREATE NEIGH

B35
DOUGLASS H.P.,THE PROTESTANT CHURCH AS A SOCIAL INSTITUTION. CULTURE FINAN NEIGH PROF/ORG OP/RES ADMIN...POLICY SOC/WK STAT BIBLIOG. PAGE 42 H0843
SECT PARTIC INGP/REL GP/REL

B42
REDFIELD R.,THE FOLK CULTURE OF YUCATAN. STRATA FAM KIN MUNIC SECT DISCRIM ISOLAT ANOMIE HEALTH ...BIBLIOG 20 MEXIC/AMER. PAGE 130 H2605
CULTURE NEIGH GP/COMP SOCIETY

B47
NIEBUHR R.,THE CHILDREN OF LIGHT AND THE CHILDREN OF DARKNESS: A VINDICATION OF DEMOCRACY AND CRITIQUE OF TRADITIONAL DEFENSE. UNIV STRUCT NAT/G SECT INGP/REL OWN PEACE ORD/FREE MARXISM ...IDEA/COMP GEN/LAWS 20 CHRISTIAN. PAGE 118 H2358
POPULISM DIPLOM NEIGH GP/REL

B49
SARGENT S.S.,CULTURE AND PERSONALITY. FUT UNIV SOCIETY FAM KIN NEIGH BIO/SOC DRIVE PERCEPT RIGID/FLEX LOVE RESPECT...PSY SOC CONCPT OBS TIME/SEQ TREND CON/ANAL CHARTS HYPO/EXP SIMUL TOT/POP. PAGE 138 H2754
CULTURE PERSON

B53
WAGLEY C.,AMAZON TOWN: A STUDY OF MAN IN THE TROPICS. BRAZIL L/A+17C STRATA STRUCT ECO/UNDEV AGRI EX/STRUC RACE/REL DISCRIM HABITAT WEALTH...OBS SOC/EXP 20. PAGE 164 H3285
SOC NEIGH CULTURE INGP/REL

B58
LERNER D.,THE PASSING OF TRADITIONAL SOCIETY: MODERNIZING THE MIDDLE EAST. IRAN ISLAM LEBANON SYRIA TURKEY UAR CULTURE INTELL STRATA KIN NAT/G NEIGH SECT EDU/PROP ATTIT PERSON...MYTH OBS 20. PAGE 95 H1888
ECO/UNDEV RIGID/FLEX

B58
MATOS J.,LAS ACTUALES COMMUNIDADES DE INDIGENAS: HUAROCHIRI EN 1955. PERU FAM NAT/G SECT EDU/PROP ADJUD GP/REL INGP/REL 20 INDIAN/AM. PAGE 105 H2091
STRUCT NEIGH KIN ECO/UNDEV

B59
EAENZA L.,COMMUNISMO E CATTOLICESIMO IN UNA PARROCHIA DI CAMPAGNA. ITALY CULTURE ELITES ECO/DEV AGRI KIN POL/PAR DOMIN LEGIT RIGID/FLEX...DECISION OBS IDEA/COMP 20 COM/PARTY CHURCH/STA. PAGE 44 H0878
ATTIT CATHISM NEIGH MARXISM

B60
HALBWACHS M.,POPULATION AND SOCIETY: INTRODUCTION TO SOCIAL MORPHOLOGY (TRANS. BY DUNCAN AND PFAUTZ). CULTURE SOCIETY AGRI INDUS HABITAT...CONCPT 20. PAGE 64 H1281
BIO/SOC GEOG NEIGH GP/COMP

B60
INTERNATIONAL AFRICAN INST,ETHNOGRAPHIC SURVEY OF AFRICA: WESTERN AFRICA: PEOPLES OF THE MIDDLE NIGER REGION, NORTHERN NIGERIA. AFR NIGER CULTURE ECO/UNDEV KIN NEIGH GOV/REL GP/REL ATTIT HEREDITY ...CHARTS BIBLIOG WORSHIP 20. PAGE 78 H1552
STRUCT GEOG HABITAT INGP/REL

L60
WHEELER G.,"RACIAL PROBLEMS IN SOVIET MUSLIM ASIA." COM CULTURE SOCIETY NEIGH SECT DOMIN EDU/PROP DISCRIM DISPL DRIVE PWR SOVEREIGN...CENSUS SAMP TREND 20 MUSLIM. PAGE 167 H3340
PERSON ATTIT USSR RACE/REL

S60
CROZIER B.,"FRANCE AND ALGERIA." ALGERIA EUR+WWI FRANCE FUT ISLAM ECO/UNDEV NEIGH CONSULT DELIB/GP ECO/TAC COLONIAL COERCE ATTIT...SOC INT CON/ANAL 20. PAGE 36 H0713
NAT/G FORCES GUERRILLA NAT/LISM

S60
GRIMSHAW A.D.,"URBAN RACIAL VIOLENCE IN THE UNITED STATES: CHANGING ECOLOGICAL CONSIDERATIONS." STRUCT MUNIC FORCES PARTIC DISCRIM ATTIT HABITAT ...IDEA/COMP 20 NEGRO. PAGE 61 H1228
CROWD RACE/REL GOV/COMP NEIGH

B61
BERKOWITZ L.,AGGRESSION: AS A SOCIAL PSYCHOLOGICAL ANALYSIS. UNIV CULTURE FACE/GP FAM KIN NEIGH EDU/PROP DISPL DRIVE HEALTH LOVE ORD/FREE...PSY SOC CONCPT OBS TREND. PAGE 15 H0305
SOCIETY COERCE WAR

B61
FIRTH R.,ELEMENTS OF SOCIAL ORGANIZATION (3RD ED.). STRATA STRUCT ECO/UNDEV NEIGH CHIEF INGP/REL ATTIT MORAL...PHIL/SCI GP/COMP WORSHIP SOC/INTEG 20. PAGE 50 H1009
SOC CULTURE SOCIETY KIN

B61
KEE R.,REFUGEE WORLD. AUSTRIA EUR+WWI GERMANY NEIGH EX/STRUC WORKER PROB/SOLV ECO/TAC RENT EDU/PROP INGP/REL COST LITERACY HABITAT 20 MIGRATION. PAGE 84 H1676
NAT/G GIVE WEALTH STRANGE

B61
VON MERING O.,A GRAMMAR OF HUMAN VALUES. WOR+45 CULTURE FACE/GP NEIGH CREATE EDU/PROP LEGIT ATTIT DRIVE PERSON ORD/FREE...PSY SOC METH/CNCPT OBS RECORD INT REC/INT STAND/INT QU CHARTS VAL/FREE. PAGE 164 H3275
SOCIETY MORAL

S61
LIEBERSON S.,"THE IMPACT OF RESIDENTIAL SEGREGATION ON ETHNIC ASSIMILATION" (BMR)" CULTURE MUNIC GP/REL RACE/REL DISCRIM...GEOG STAT CON/ANAL CHARTS SOC/INTEG 20 MIGRATION. PAGE 96 H1926
HABITAT ISOLAT NEIGH

B62
EDWARDS A.C.,THE OVIMBUNDU UNDER TWO SOVEREIGNTIES. CULTURE STRUCT FAM MARRIAGE HABITAT...SOC 19/20
KIN NEIGH

OVIMBUNDU. PAGE 45 H0891
SOCIETY CONTROL

B62
STATE AND LOCAL GOVERNMENT. MUNIC NAT/G NEIGH PRESS CONTROL CHOOSE REPRESENT...BIBLIOG 20. PAGE 104 H2076
PROVS LOC/G GOV/REL PWR

B62
VILAKAZI A.,ZULU TRANSFORMATIONS: A STUDY OF THE DYNAMICS OF SOCIAL CHANGE. AFR CULTURE ECO/UNDEV KIN NEIGH SEX...GEOG QU TREND CHARTS BIBLIOG 19/20. PAGE 163 H3254
MARRIAGE SECT SOC EDU/PROP

S62
ROTBERG R.,"THE RISE OF AFRICAN NATIONALISM: THE CASE OF EAST AND CENTRAL AFRICA." AFR CULTURE SOCIETY NEIGH DIPLOM DOMIN COLONIAL COERCE DISPL PERCEPT PWR SOVEREIGN...POLICY OBS/ENVIR TREND WORK 20. PAGE 135 H2690
ATTIT DRIVE NAT/LISM REV

B63
LETHBRIDGE H.J.,THE PEASANT AND THE COMMUNES. CHINA/COM COM USSR NEIGH PROB/SOLV ADJUST EFFICIENCY...POLICY METH/COMP NAT/COMP 20. PAGE 95 H1894
MARXISM ECO/TAC AGRI WORKER

B63
MARTINDALE D.,COMMUNITY, CHARACTER AND CIVILIZATION: STUDIES IN SOCIAL BEHAVIORISM. INTELL FAM NEIGH VOL/ASSN GP/REL NAT/LISM ATTIT PERSON ...CONCPT GP/COMP 20 BEHAVIORSM. PAGE 103 H2066
SOC METH/COMP CULTURE STRUCT

L63
JAY R.,"RELIGION AND POLITICS IN RURAL CENTRAL JAVA." S/ASIA SOCIETY NEIGH SECT PERSON HEALTH MORAL...SOC UNPLAN/INT TIME/SEQ JAVA VAL/FREE 20 WORSHIP. PAGE 80 H1594
CULTURE OBS

S63
NICHOLAS W.,"VILLAGE FACTIONS AND POLITICAL PARTIES IN RURAL WEST BENGAL." S/ASIA CULTURE STRATA FACE/GP KIN MUNIC DELIB/GP LEGIS DOMIN EDU/PROP COERCE CHOOSE ATTIT ALL/VALS...STAT TOT/POP VAL/FREE 20. PAGE 117 H2348
NEIGH POL/PAR

B64
ELKIN A.P.,THE AUSTRALIAN ABORIGINES - HOW TO UNDERSTAND THEM (4TH ED.). FAM NEIGH DEATH MARRIAGE ATTIT BIO/SOC HABITAT...PSY SOC MYTH WORSHIP AUSTRAL ABORIGINES. PAGE 45 H0908
CULTURE STRUCT SOCIETY KIN

B64
GREBLER L.,URBAN RENEWAL IN EUROPEAN COUNTRIES: ITS EMERGENCE AND POTENTIALS. EUR+WWI UK ECO/DEV LOC/G NEIGH CREATE ADMIN ATTIT...TREND NAT/COMP 20 URBAN/RNWL. PAGE 60 H1205
MUNIC PLAN CONSTRUC NAT/G

B64
THORNBURG M.W.,PEOPLE AND POLICY IN THE MIDDLE EAST. ISLAM ECO/UNDEV FAM KIN MUNIC NAT/G NEIGH POL/PAR SECT DELIB/GP LEGIS PLAN ECO/TAC DOMIN ADMIN ATTIT HEALTH RESPECT...SOC CONCPT METH/CNCPT OBS TIME/SEQ TOT/POP VAL/FREE. PAGE 154 H3088
TEC/DEV CULTURE

B64
VON GRUNEBAUM G.E.,MODERN ISLAM: THE SEARCH FOR CULTURAL IDENTITY. ACADEM NEIGH WRITING NAT/LISM ...HUM CONCPT 19/20 MUSLIM MID/EAST ARABS. PAGE 163 H3269
ISLAM CULTURE CREATE SECT

S64
SAYEED K.,"PATHAN REGIONALISM." ISLAM PAKISTAN S/ASIA CULTURE SOCIETY NAT/G NEIGH DIPLOM LEGIT COERCE CHOOSE ATTIT DISPL PERCEPT ALL/VALS SOVEREIGN...POLICY RELATIV SOC TIME/SEQ TOT/POP 20. PAGE 138 H2761
SECT NAT/LISM REGION

B65
ARENSBERG C.M.,CULTURE AND COMMUNITY. UNIV FACE/GP ACT/RES EDU/PROP LEAD REGION GP/REL PERS/REL HABITAT ALL/VALS...SOC CONCPT 20. PAGE 8 H0162
SOCIETY CULTURE NEIGH NEW/IDEA

B65
BOISSEVAIN J.,SAINTS AND FIREWORKS: RELIGION AND POLITICS IN RURAL MALTA. MALTA STRUCT FAM NEIGH POL/PAR REPRESENT INGP/REL CENTRAL...CHARTS BIBLIOG 20. PAGE 18 H0368
GP/REL NAT/G SECT MUNIC

B65
BURLING R.,HILL FARMS AND PADI FIELDS. BURMA S/ASIA THAILAND VIETNAM AGRI NEIGH SECT GP/REL NAT/LISM ORD/FREE 20 MID/EAST MIGRATION. PAGE 24 H0491
SOCIETY STRUCT CULTURE SOVEREIGN

B65
DUGGAR G.S.,RENEWAL OF TOWN AND VILLAGE I: A WORLD-WIDE SURVEY OF LOCAL GOVERNMENT EXPERIENCE. WOR+45 CONSTRUC INDUS CREATE BUDGET REGION GOV/REL...QU NAT/COMP 20 URBAN/RNWL. PAGE 43 H0859
MUNIC NEIGH PLAN ADMIN

B65
HAUSER P.M.,THE STUDY OF URBANIZATION. S/ASIA ECO/DEV ECO/UNDEV NEIGH ACT/RES GEOG. PAGE 68 H1359
CULTURE MUNIC SOC

B65
KLEIN J.,SAMPLES FROM ENGLISH CULTURES (2 VOLS.). UK STRATA FAM NEIGH WORKER ETIQUET ISOLAT AGE/C AGE/A HABITAT RIGID/FLEX...NET/THEORY CHARTS 20. PAGE 87 H1732
CULTURE INGP/REL ATTIT SOC

B65
LAMBIRI I.,SOCIAL CHANGE IN A GREEK COUNTRY TOWN. GREECE FAM PROB/SOLV ROUTINE TASK LEISURE INGP/REL CONSEN ORD/FREE...SOC INT QU CHARTS 20. PAGE 90 H1803
INDUS WORKER CULTURE NEIGH

B65
SPENCER P.,THE SAMBURU: A STUDY OF GERONTOCRACY IN A NOMADIC TRIBE. AFR SOCIETY ECO/UNDEV AGRI FAM NEIGH SECT GP/REL MARRIAGE WORSHIP 20 SAMBURU. PAGE 147 H2945
KIN STRUCT AGE/O CULTURE

S65
KEE W.S.,"CENTRAL CITY EXPENDITURES AND METROPOLITAN AREAS." PLAN BUDGET ECO/TAC TAX GP/REL WEALTH...CHARTS 20. PAGE 84 H1677
LOC/G MUNIC GOV/COMP NEIGH

B66
AHMED Z.,DUSK AND DAWN IN VILLAGE INDIA. INDIA S/ASIA UK CULTURE SOCIETY NAT/G DOMIN COLONIAL HABITAT SOVEREIGN...SOC DICTIONARY 20. PAGE 4 H0080
NEIGH ECO/UNDEV AGRI ADJUST

B66
HINTON W.,FANSHEN: A DOCUMENTARY OF REVOLUTION IN A CHINESE VILLAGE. ASIA ELITES MUNIC NAT/G POL/PAR SECT WORKER LEAD WAR PRIVIL PWR 20 MAO. PAGE 71 H1422
MARXISM REV NEIGH OWN

L67
CRIBBET J.E.,"SOME REFLECTIONS ON THE LAW OF LAND - A VIEW FROM SCANDINAVIA." DENMARK NETHERLAND NORWAY SWEDEN INDUS MUNIC NEIGH RACE/REL ATTIT HABITAT ...IDEA/COMP 20. PAGE 35 H0701
LAW PLAN CONTROL NAT/G

S67
BULLOUGH B.,"ALIENATION IN THE GHETTO." CULTURE NEIGH GP/REL INGP/REL ATTIT...PSY SOC SAMP. PAGE 23 H0471
DISCRIM ANOMIE ADJUST

S67
MALAN V.D.,"THE SILENT VILLAGE." KIN MUNIC NEIGH CHOOSE ISOLAT ROLE...SOC INDIAN/AM. PAGE 101 H2027
CULTURE STRUCT PREDICT

S67
WILSON J.Q.,"A GUIDE TO REAGAN COUNTRY* THE POLITICAL CULTURE OF SOUTHERN CALIFORNIA." NEIGH PROVS PARTIC CHOOSE ADJUST CONSEN PERSON CONSERVE CALIFORNIA REAGAN/RON. PAGE 169 H3379
CULTURE ATTIT MORAL

B82
RATZEL F.,ANTHROPO-GEOGRAPHIE. SEA AGRI NEIGH. PAGE 130 H2595
GEOG CULTURE HABITAT

B98
FORTES M.,AFRICAN POLITICAL SYSTEMS. ECO/UNDEV KIN LOC/G NEIGH POL/PAR SECT LEAD GP/REL ORD/FREE...SOC 20 NEGRO. PAGE 52 H1039
AFR CULTURE STRUCT

NELSON G.R. H2329

NEOLITHIC....NEOLITHIC PERIOD

NEPAL....SEE ALSO S/ASIA

N
US LIBRARY OF CONGRESS,SOUTHERN ASIA ACCESSIONS LIST. BURMA CEYLON INDIA NEPAL PAKISTAN S/ASIA THAILAND AGRI INDUS SCHOOL WORKER...ART/METH GEOG HEAL PHIL/SCI LING 20. PAGE 160 H3201
BIBLIOG/A SOCIETY CULTURE ECO/UNDEV

B59
WOOD H.B.,NEPAL BIBLIOGRAPHY. NEPAL S/ASIA NAT/G 20. PAGE 170 H3406
BIBLIOG CULTURE

B60
SALETORE B.A.,INDIA'S DIPLOMATIC RELATIONS WITH THE EAST. ASIA CEYLON INDIA NEPAL S/ASIA CULTURE 7/14 PERSIA. PAGE 137 H2740
DIPLOM NAT/COMP ETIQUET

B66
US DEPARTMENT OF THE ARMY,SOUTH ASIA: A STRATEGIC SURVEY (PAMPHLET NO. 550-3). AFGHANISTN INDIA NEPAL PAKISTAN ECO/UNDEV INT/ORG POL/PAR FORCES FOR/AID INT/TRADE LEAD WAR...POLICY SOC TREND 20. PAGE 160 H3195
BIBLIOG/A S/ASIA DIPLOM NAT/G

NESS G.D. H2330

NET/THEORY....NETWORK THEORY

B63
FAWCETT J.E.S.,THE BRITISH COMMONWEALTH IN INTERNATIONAL LAW. LAW INT/ORG NAT/G VOL/ASSN OP/RES DIPLOM ADJUD CENTRAL CONSEN...NET/THEORY CMN/WLTH TREATY. PAGE 49 H0977
INT/LAW STRUCT COLONIAL

B64
LEWIN P.,THE FOREIGN TRADE OF COMMUNIST CHINA* ITS IMPACT ON THE FREE WORLD. AFR EUR+WWI L/A+17C S/ASIA ECO/UNDEV CREATE FOR/AID...STAT NET/THEORY TREND CHARTS. PAGE 96 H1910
ASIA INT/TRADE NAT/COMP USSR

B65
KLEIN J.,SAMPLES FROM ENGLISH CULTURES (2 VOLS.). UK STRATA FAM NEIGH WORKER ETIQUET ISOLAT AGE/C AGE/A HABITAT RIGID/FLEX...NET/THEORY CHARTS 20. PAGE 87 H1732
CULTURE INGP/REL ATTIT SOC

S65
LEVI W.,"THE CONCEPT OF INTEGRATION IN RESEARCH ON PEACE." NAT/G VOL/ASSN DIPLOM TASK ADJUST NAT/LISM PEACE DRIVE LOVE...PSY NET/THEORY GEN/LAWS. PAGE 95 H1897 — CONCPT IDEA/COMP INT/ORG CENTRAL

S65
TRISKA J.F.,"SOVIET-AMERICAN RELATIONS* A MULTIPLE SYMMETRY MODEL." USA+45 USSR ACADEM ACT/RES EDU/PROP COERCE PERCEPT...NET/THEORY CHARTS NAT/COMP GEN/LAWS COLD/WAR. PAGE 157 H3132 — SIMUL EQUILIB DIPLOM

B66
FARRELL R.B.,APPROACHES TO COMPARATIVE AND INTERNATIONAL POLITICS. RUSSIA SOCIETY ACADEM GOV/REL GP/REL...METH/CNCPT NET/THEORY GOV/COMP HYPO/EXP SOC/EXP GEN/METH ANTHOL. PAGE 49 H0973 — DIPLOM NAT/COMP NAT/G

L66
ZOPPO C.E.,"NUCLEAR TECHNOLOGY, MULTIPOLARITY, AND INTERNATIONAL STABILITY." ASIA RUSSIA USA+45 STRUCT TOP/EX BAL/PWR DIPLOM DETER CIVMIL/REL NAT/COMP. PAGE 173 H3464 — NET/THEORY ORD/FREE DECISION NUC/PWR

S66
FELD W.,"NATIONAL ECONOMIC INTEREST GROUPS AND POLICY FORMATION IN THE EEC." NAT/G POL/PAR REGION CENTRAL SOVEREIGN...INT NET/THEORY EEC. PAGE 49 H0985 — LOBBY ELITES DECISION

S66
GALTUNG J.,"EAST-WEST INTERACTION PATTERNS." DIPLOM INT/TRADE...NET/THEORY CON/ANAL CHARTS NAT/COMP INDEX NATO COLD/WAR UN WARSAW/P. PAGE 55 H1090 — STAT HYPO/EXP

S67
RUCKER B.W.,"WHAT SOLUTIONS DO PEOPLE ENDORSE IN FREE PRESS-FAIR TRIAL DILEMMA?" LAW NAT/G CT/SYS ATTIT...NET/THEORY SAMP CHARTS IDEA/COMP METH 20. PAGE 136 H2710 — CONCPT PRESS ADJUD ORD/FREE

NETH/IND....NETHERLAND EAST INDIES (PRE-INDONESIA)

B45
US LIBRARY OF CONGRESS,NETHERLANDS EAST INDIES. INDONESIA LAW CULTURE AGRI INDUS SCHOOL COLONIAL HEALTH...GEOG JURID SOC 19/20 NETH/IND. PAGE 160 H3205 — BIBLIOG/A S/ASIA NAT/G

NETHERLAND....NETHERLANDS; SEE ALSO APPROPRIATE TIME/SPACE/ CULTURE INDEX

N
CARIBBEAN COMMISSION,CURRENT CARIBBEAN BIBLIOGRAPHY. FRANCE NETHERLAND UK CULTURE ECO/UNDEV PRESS LEAD ATTIT...GEOG SOC 20. PAGE 26 H0530 — BIBLIOG NAT/G L/A+17C DIPLOM

B00
HOBSON J.A.,THE WAR IN SOUTH AFRICA: ITS CAUSES AND EFFECTS. NETHERLAND SOUTH/AFR UK ELITES AGRI EXTR/IND POL/PAR DIPLOM PRESS RACE/REL ATTIT ORD/FREE SOVEREIGN...INT 19 NEGRO. PAGE 72 H1439 — WAR DOMIN POLICY NAT/G

B00
MARKHAM V.R.,SOUTH AFRICA, PAST AND PRESENT. NETHERLAND SOUTH/AFR CULTURE LEGIS EDU/PROP COLONIAL CHOOSE REPRESENT DISCRIM ATTIT...OBS TIME/SEQ 17/19 NEGRO BOER/WAR. PAGE 103 H2054 — WAR LEAD RACE/REL

B31
DEKAT A.D.A.,COLONIAL POLICY. S/ASIA CULTURE EX/STRUC ECO/TAC DOMIN ADMIN COLONIAL ROUTINE SOVEREIGN WEALTH...POLICY MGT RECORD KNO/TEST SAMP. PAGE 39 H0785 — DRIVE PWR INDONESIA NETHERLAND

B39
FURNIVALL J.S.,NETHERLANDS INDIA. INDIA NETHERLAND CULTURE INDUS NAT/G DIPLOM ADMIN WEALTH...POLICY CHARTS 17/20. PAGE 54 H1081 — COLONIAL ECO/UNDEV SOVEREIGN PLURISM

B51
WABEKE B.H.,A GUIDE TO DUTCH BIBLIOGRAPHIES. BELGIUM INDONESIA NETHERLAND DIPLOM INT/TRADE WAR NAT/LISM KNOWL...ART/METH HUM JURID CON/ANAL 14/20. PAGE 164 H3282 — BIBLIOG/A NAT/G CULTURE COLONIAL

B57
BUCK P.W.,CONTOL OF FOREIGN RELATIONS IN MODERN NATIONS. FRANCE L/A+17C NETHERLAND USSR WOR+45 INT/ORG TOP/EX BAL/PWR DOMIN EDU/PROP COERCE PEACE ATTIT...CONCPT TREND 20 CMN/WLTH. PAGE 23 H0465 — NAT/G PWR DIPLOM

B60
BAYER H.,WIRTSCHAFTSPROGNOSE UND WIRTSCHAFTSGESTALTUNG. GERMANY NETHERLAND MARKET PLAN CAP/ISM DEBATE...NAT/COMP 20. PAGE 12 H0242 — ECO/DEV ECO/UNDEV FINAN POLICY

B62
ROBINSON A.D.,DUTCH ORGANIZED AGRICULTURE IN INTERNATIONAL POLITICS, 1945-1960. EUR+WWI NETHERLAND STRUCT ECO/DEV NAT/G VOL/ASSN CONSULT DELIB/GP PLAN TEC/DEV INT/TRADE EDU/PROP ATTIT RIGID/FLEX ALL/VALS...NEW/IDEA TREND EEC 20. PAGE 132 H2648 — AGRI INT/ORG

B62
SELOSOEMARDJAN O.,SOCIAL CHANGES IN JOGJAKARTA. INDONESIA NETHERLAND ELITES STRATA STRUCT FAM POL/PAR CREATE DIPLOM INT/TRADE EDU/PROP ADMIN GOV/REL...SOC 20 JAVA CHINJAP. PAGE 141 H2825 — ECO/UNDEV CULTURE REV COLONIAL

B63
FARMER B.H.,CEYLON: A DIVIDED NATION. CEYLON INDIA NETHERLAND PORTUGAL UK ELITES POL/PAR COLONIAL ...SOC MYTH CHARTS GOV/COMP WORSHIP 20. PAGE 49 H0972 — DOMIN ORD/FREE ECO/UNDEV POLICY

B63
FRANZ G.,TEILUNG UND WIEDERVEREINIGUNG. GERMANY IRELAND ITALY NETHERLAND POLAND CULTURE BAL/PWR CHOOSE NAT/LISM ORD/FREE SOVEREIGN 19/20. PAGE 53 H1054 — DIPLOM WAR NAT/COMP ATTIT

B64
ARASARATNAM S.,CEYLON. CEYLON NETHERLAND PORTUGAL S/ASIA UK STRUCT ECO/UNDEV SECT DIPLOM DOMIN RACE/REL NAT/LISM 17/20 CMN/WLTH. PAGE 8 H0156 — COLONIAL NAT/G PROB/SOLV CULTURE

B65
CONRING E.,KIRCHE UND STAAT NACH DER LEHRE DER NIEDERLANDISCHEN CALVINISTEN IN DER ERSTEN HALFTE DES 17. JAHRHUNDERTS. NETHERLAND GP/REL...CONCPT 17 CHURCH/STA. PAGE 33 H0656 — SECT JURID NAT/G ORD/FREE

B65
EDELMAN M.,THE POLITICS OF WAGE-PRICE DECISIONS. GERMANY ITALY NETHERLAND UK INDUS LABOR POL/PAR PROB/SOLV BARGAIN PRICE ROUTINE BAL/PAY COST DEMAND 20. PAGE 44 H0888 — GOV/COMP CONTROL ECO/TAC PLAN

L67
CRIBBET J.E.,"SOME REFLECTIONS ON THE LAW OF LAND - A VIEW FROM SCANDINAVIA." DENMARK NETHERLAND NORWAY SWEDEN INDUS MUNIC NEIGH RACE/REL ATTIT HABITAT ...IDEA/COMP 20. PAGE 35 H0701 — LAW PLAN CONTROL NAT/G

S67
LEHMBRUCH G.,"WAHLREFORM UND POLITISCHES SYSTEM." NETHERLAND NAT/G LEGIS PARL/PROC...SOC 20. PAGE 93 H1864 — CHOOSE POL/PAR METH/CNCPT GP/COMP

N67
US HOUSE COMM SCI ASTRONAUT,GOVERNMENT, SCIENCE, AND INTERNATIONAL POLICY (PAMPHLET). INDIA NETHERLAND ECO/DEV ECO/UNDEV R+D ACADEM PLAN DIPLOM FOR/AID CONFER...PREDICT 20 CHINJAP. PAGE 160 H3198 — NAT/G POLICY CREATE TEC/DEV

NETWORK THEORY....SEE NET/THEORY

NEUBAUER D.E. H2331

NEUBURGER O. H2332,H2333,H2334,H2335

NEUMANN R.G. H2336

NEUMANN S. H2337,H2338,H2339,H2340

NEUMARK S.D. H2341

NEUSTADT I. H0342

NEUTRAL....POLITICAL NONALIGNMENT, LEGAL NEUTRALITY

B30
HULL W.I.,INDIA'S POLITICAL CRISIS. INDIA UK INT/ORG LABOR SECT DELIB/GP LEGIS DIPLOM NEUTRAL REGION CROWD GOV/REL MAJORITY ATTIT 20 NEHRU/J GANDHI/M COMMONWLTH. PAGE 75 H1492 — ORD/FREE NAT/G COLONIAL NAT/LISM

B36
RAPPARD W.E.,THE GOVERNMENT OF SWITZERLAND. SWITZERLND INT/ORG POL/PAR EX/STRUC DIPLOM NEUTRAL PARL/PROC REGION WAR HABITAT SOVEREIGN...NAT/COMP SOC/INTEG 20 LEAGUE/NAT WWI. PAGE 130 H2594 — CONSTN NAT/G CULTURE FEDERAL

B56
VON HARPE W.,DIE SOWJETUNION FINNLAND UND SKANDANAVIEN, 1945-1955. EUR+WWI FINLAND GERMANY USSR WAR INGP/REL ORD/FREE SOVEREIGN MARXISM ...POLICY GOV/COMP BIBLIOG 20 STALIN/J. PAGE 163 H3270 — DIPLOM COM NEUTRAL BAL/PWR

N57
JENNINGS W.I.,NATIONALISM, COLONIALISM, AND NEUTRALISM (PAMPHLET). ASIA INDIA S/ASIA UK INTELL ACADEM POL/PAR 20. PAGE 81 H1611 — NAT/LISM COLONIAL NEUTRAL ATTIT

B58
PALMER E.E.,THE COMMUNIST CHALLENGE. COM USA+45 USA-45 ECO/DEV ECO/UNDEV NEUTRAL ORD/FREE POPULISM ...CONCPT NAT/COMP ANTHOL 19/20 LENIN/VI STALIN/J MAO MARX/KARL COM/PARTY. PAGE 123 H2450 — MARXISM DIPLOM IDEA/COMP POLICY

B60
MINIFIE J.M.,PEACEMAKER OR POWDER-MONKEY. CANADA INT/ORG NAT/G FORCES LEAD WAR...PREDICT 20. PAGE 111 H2222 — DIPLOM POLICY NEUTRAL PEACE

B61
DUFFY J.,AFRICA SPEAKS. GHANA TOGO CULTURE ECO/UNDEV PROB/SOLV COLONIAL NEUTRAL DISCRIM NAT/LISM SOVEREIGN ALL/IDEOS...CONCPT ANTHOL SOC/INTEG 20 NEGRO THIRD/WRLD. PAGE 43 H0857 — AFR NAT/G FUT STRUCT

B62
BAULIN J.,THE ARAB ROLE IN AFRICA. AFR ALGERIA FUT ISLAM MOROCCO UAR COLONIAL NEUTRAL REV...SOC 20 TUNIS BOURGUIBA. PAGE 12 H0240 — NAT/LISM DIPLOM NAT/G SECT

B62
DUTOIT B.,LA NEUTRALITE SUISSE A L'HEURE EUROPEENNE. EUR+WWI MOD/EUR INT/ORG NAT/G VOL/ASSN PLAN BAL/PWR LEGIT NEUTRAL REGION PEACE ORD/FREE SOVEREIGN...CONCPT OBS TIME/SEQ TREND STERTYP VAL/FREE LEAGUE/NAT UN 20. PAGE 44 H0873 — ATTIT DIPLOM SWITZERLND

B63
BRECHER M.,THE NEW STATES OF ASIA. ASIA S/ASIA INT/ORG BAL/PWR COLONIAL NEUTRAL ORD/FREE PWR 20 UN. PAGE 20 H0407 — NAT/G ECO/UNDEV DIPLOM POLICY

B63
LYON P.,NEUTRALISM. ECO/UNDEV EDU/PROP COLONIAL ALL/IDEOS...IDEA/COMP 20 COLD/WAR UN. PAGE 99 H1985 — NAT/COMP NAT/LISM DIPLOM NEUTRAL

B64
GUTTERIDGE W.,MILITARY INSTITUTIONS AND POWER IN THE NEW STATES. WOR+45 INT/ORG FOR/AID NEUTRAL REV CIVMIL/REL ATTIT ROLE...GOV/COMP 20. PAGE 63 H1258 — FORCES DIPLOM ECO/UNDEV ELITES

B64
ROSENAU J.N.,INTERNATIONAL ASPECTS OF CIVIL STRIFE. CHINA/COM CUBA EUR+WWI USA+45 USSR BAL/PWR EDU/PROP NEUTRAL COERCE MORAL...NAT/COMP 20 COLD/WAR UN. PAGE 134 H2676 — POLICY DIPLOM REV WAR

B64
VOELKMANN K.,HERRSCHER VON MORGEN? BAL/PWR COLONIAL NEUTRAL REGION RACE/REL ALL/VALS SOVEREIGN...RECORD 20 COLD/WAR THIRD/WRLD. PAGE 163 H3259 — DIPLOM ECO/UNDEV CONTROL NAT/COMP

S64
LEVI W.,"INDIAN NEUTRALISM RECONSIDERED." ASIA CHINA/COM S/ASIA SOCIETY NAT/G ACT/RES LEGIT NEUTRAL COERCE ATTIT DRIVE PERCEPT RIGID/FLEX HEALTH LOVE PWR...DECISION RECORD TREND STERTYP 20. PAGE 95 H1896 — ORD/FREE CONCPT INDIA

S64
SMYTHE H.H.,"NEHRU AND INDIAN FOREIGN POLICY." S/ASIA ECO/UNDEV NAT/G POL/PAR CONSULT PLAN DIPLOM NEUTRAL COERCE ATTIT DRIVE PERSON MORAL ORD/FREE RESPECT...GEOG CONCPT TIME/SEQ TREND GEN/LAWS 20 NEHRU/J. PAGE 146 H2922 — TOP/EX BIOG INDIA

S64
VANDENBOSCH A.,"POWER BALANCE IN INDONESIA." S/ASIA USSR NAT/G TOP/EX BAL/PWR DOMIN NEUTRAL ORD/FREE PWR...POLICY TIME/SEQ GEN/LAWS 20 SUKARNO/A. PAGE 162 H3233 — FORCES TREND DIPLOM INDONESIA

B65
CRABB C.V. JR.,THE ELEPHANTS AND THE GRASS* A STUDY OF NONALIGNMENT. AFR ASIA INDIA S/ASIA USA+45 USSR BAL/PWR NEUTRAL ATTIT...TREND NAT/COMP COLD/WAR. PAGE 34 H0691 — ECO/UNDEV DIPLOM CONCPT

B65
O'BRIEN W.V.,THE NEW NATIONS IN INTERNATIONAL LAW AND DIPLOMACY* THE YEAR BOOK OF WORLD POLITY* VOLUME III. USA+45 ECO/UNDEV INT/ORG FORCES DIPLOM COLONIAL NEUTRAL REV NAT/LISM ATTIT RESPECT. PAGE 119 H2385 — INT/LAW CULTURE SOVEREIGN ANTHOL

B65
SMITH R.M.,CAMBODIA'S FOREIGN POLICY. ECO/UNDEV NAT/G NEUTRAL ORD/FREE COLD/WAR VAL/FREE. PAGE 146 H2917 — S/ASIA CAMBODIA DIPLOM

B65
WUORINEN J.H.,SCANDINAVIA. DENMARK FINLAND ICELAND NORWAY SWEDEN SOCIETY AGRI INDUS DELIB/GP DIPLOM INT/TRADE NEUTRAL...GEOG CHARTS BIBLIOG TREATY. PAGE 171 H3428 — NAT/G POL/PAR TREND POLICY

S65
BIRNBAUM K.,"SWEDEN'S NUCLEAR POLICY." WOR+45 POL/PAR CREATE TEC/DEV NEUTRAL RISK WAR ORD/FREE ...DECISION IDEA/COMP NAT/COMP TIME. PAGE 17 H0343 — SWEDEN NUC/PWR DIPLOM ARMS/CONT

C65
WUORINEN J.H.,"SCANDINAVIA." DENMARK FINLAND ICELAND NORWAY SWEDEN SOCIETY AGRI POL/PAR DELIB/GP DIPLOM INT/TRADE NEUTRAL WAR...CHARTS TREATY 20. PAGE 171 H3427 — BIBLIOG NAT/G POLICY

B66
DAENIKER G.,STRATEGIE DES KLEIN STAATS. SWITZERLND ACT/RES CREATE DIPLOM NEUTRAL DETER WAR WEAPON PWR SOVEREIGN...IDEA/COMP 20 COLD/WAR. PAGE 36 H0730 — NUC/PWR PLAN FORCES NAT/G

B66
DYCK H.V.,WEIMAR GERMANY AND SOVIET RUSSIA 1926-1933. EUR+WWI GERMANY UK USSR ECO/TAC INT/TRADE NEUTRAL WAR ATTIT 20 WEIMAR/REP TREATY. PAGE 44 H0877 — DIPLOM GOV/REL POLICY

B66
MCKAY V.,AFRICAN DIPLOMACY STUDIES IN THE DETERMINANTS OF FOREIGN POLICY. AFR SOUTH/AFR CULTURE NEUTRAL REGION SOVEREIGN...INT/LAW GOV/COMP ANTHOL 20. PAGE 107 H2138 — ECO/UNDEV RACE/REL CIVMIL/REL DIPLOM

S67
GRUNDY K.W.,"AFRICA IN THE WORLD ARENA." ECO/UNDEV BAL/PWR FOR/AID NEUTRAL REV NAT/LISM GOV/COMP. PAGE 62 H1240 — AFR DIPLOM INT/ORG COLONIAL

S67
ROSE S.,"ASIAN NATIONALISM* THE SECOND STAGE." ASIA COM ECO/UNDEV NAT/G PROB/SOLV DIPLOM FOR/AID DOMIN NEUTRAL REGION TASK...METH/COMP 20. PAGE 134 H2675 — NAT/LISM S/ASIA BAL/PWR COLONIAL

S67
SAVELYEV N.,"MONOPOLY DRIVE IN INDIA." INDIA INDUS NAT/G INT/TRADE NEUTRAL SANCTION GOV/REL CONSERVE ...MARXIST 20. PAGE 138 H2759 — ECO/UNDEV POL/PAR ECO/TAC CONTROL

S68
KANET R.E.,"RECENT SOVIET REASSESSMENT OF DEVELOPMENTS IN THE THIRD WORLD." ALGERIA GHANA INDONESIA USSR WOR+45 CONSTN ELITES INTELL STRUCT DOMIN CONTROL REV PWR MARXISM...IDEA/COMP METH 20 THIRD/WRLD. PAGE 83 H1653 — DIPLOM NEUTRAL NAT/G NAT/COMP

NEVADA....NEVADA

NEVITT A.A. H2342

NEW ECONOMICS....SEE NEW/ECONOM

NEW LIBERALISM....SEE NEW/LIB

NEW STATES....SEE ECO/UNDEV+GEOGRAPHIC AREA+COLONIAL+ NAT/LISM

NEW ZEALAND COMM OF ST SERVICE H2343

NEW/BRUNS....NEW BRUNSWICK, CANADA

B58
CUNNINGHAM W.B.,COMPULSORY CONCILIATION AND COLLECTIVE BARGAINING. CANADA NAT/G LEGIS ADJUD CT/SYS GP/REL...MGT 20 NEW/BRUNS STRIKE CASEBOOK. PAGE 36 H0722 — POLICY BARGAIN LABOR INDUS

NEW/DEAL....NEW DEAL OF F.D.R.'S ADMINISTRATION

B38
LAWLEY F.E.,THE GROWTH OF COLLECTIVE ECONOMY VOL. 2: INTERNATIONAL. WOR-45 AGRI INDUS EQUILIB OPTIMAL OWN WEALTH...NAT/COMP 19/20 NAZI NEW/DEAL MONOPOLY. PAGE 92 H1845 — ECO/TAC SOCISM NAT/LISM CONTROL

B66
KIRKENDALL R.S.,SOCIAL SCIENTISTS AND FARM POLITICS IN THE AGE OF ROOSEVELT. ACADEM PLAN ECO/TAC GIVE ADMIN CONTROL PRODUC...SOC 20 NEW/DEAL ROOSEVLT/F BURAGR/ECO. PAGE 86 H1722 — AGRI INTELL POLICY NAT/G

NEW/DELHI....NEW DELHI (UNCTAD MEETING OF DEVELOPED AND UNDERDEVELOPED NATIONS IN 1968)

NEW/ECO/MN....NEW ECONOMIC MECHANISM OF HUNGARY

NEW/ECONOM....NEW ECONOMICS

NEW/ENGLND....NEW ENGLAND

B39
MILLER P.,THE NEW ENGLAND MIND: THE SEVENTEENTH CENTURY. CULTURE DOMIN WRITING INGP/REL CONSEN MAJORITY PERCEPT KNOWL MORAL...CONCPT LING WORSHIP 17 NEW/ENGLND PROTESTANT. PAGE 111 H2214 — SECT REGION SOC ATTIT

NEW/FRONTR....NEW FRONTIER OF J.F.KENNEDY

NEW/GUINEA....NEW GUINEA

S21
MALINOWSKI B.,"THE PRIMITIVE ECONOMICS OF THE TROBRIAND ISLANDERS" (BMR)" CULTURE SOCIETY NAT/G CHIEF LEAD OWN...SOC MYTH WORSHIP 20 NEW/GUINEA TROBRIAND RESOURCE/N. PAGE 101 H2029 — ECO/UNDEV AGRI PRODUC STRUCT

B47
GITLOW A.L.,ECONOMICS OF THE MOUNT HAGEN TRIBES, NEW GUINEA. S/ASIA STRUCT AGRI FAM...GEOG MYTH 20 NEW/GUINEA. PAGE 57 H1137 — HABITAT ECO/UNDEV CULTURE KIN

B54
MALINOWSKI B.,MAGIC, SCIENCE AND RELIGION. AGRI KIN GP/REL ALL/VALS...MYTH OBS RECORD IDEA/COMP WORSHIP 20 NEW/GUINEA. PAGE 102 H2031 — CULTURE ATTIT SOC

B60
BURRIDGE K.,MAMBU: A MELANESIAN MILLENNIUM. ECO/UNDEV PROC/MFG FAM KIN CHIEF COLONIAL COERCE — S/ASIA SECT

GP/REL DRIVE WEALTH WORSHIP 20 NEW/GUINEA. PAGE 25 H0494 — CULTURE MYTH

B62

BERNOT R.M.,EXCESS AND RESTRAINT: SOCIAL CONTROL AMONG GUINEA MOUNTAIN PEOPLE. CULTURE FAM KIN CT/SYS COERCE WAR PERS/REL MARRIAGE HABITAT SEX ...MYTH 20 NEW/GUINEA. PAGE 16 H0314 — SOCIETY CONTROL STRUCT ADJUST

B64

LAWRENCE P.,ROAD BELONG CARGO: A STUDY OF CARGO MOVEMENT IN SOUTHERN MADANG DISTRICT, NEW GUINEA. S/ASIA CULTURE ECO/UNDEV PROC/MFG KIN CHIEF COLONIAL COERCE GP/REL DRIVE WEALTH WORSHIP 20 NEW/GUINEA. PAGE 92 H1846 — SOC SECT ALL/VALS MYTH

B65

LAWRENCE P.,GODS, GHOSTS, AND MEN IN MELANESIA: SOME RELIGIONS OF AUSTRALIAN NEW GUINEA AND THE NEW HEBRIDES. SOCIETY ECO/UNDEV FAM GP/REL INGP/REL HABITAT PERSON...GEOG SOC ANTHOL BIBLIOG WORSHIP 20 NEW/GUINEA. PAGE 92 H1847 — MYTH S/ASIA SECT CULTURE

B66

FISK E.K.,NEW GUINEA ON THE THRESHOLD; ASPECTS OF SOCIAL, POLITICAL, AND ECONOMIC DEVELOPMENT. AGRI NAT/G INT/TRADE ADMIN ADJUST LITERACY ROLE...CHARTS ANTHOL 20 NEW/GUINEA. PAGE 51 H1015 — ECO/UNDEV SOCIETY

NEW/HAMPSH....NEW HAMPSHIRE

NEW/HEBRID....NEW HEBRIDES

NEW/IDEA....NEW CONCEPT

NEW/JERSEY....NEW JERSEY

NEW/LEFT....THE NEW LEFT

NEW/LIB....NEW LIBERALISM

B40

MANNHEIM K.,MAN AND SOCIETY IN AN AGE OF RECONSTRUCTION. MOD/EUR CULTURE ECO/DEV PLAN TEC/DEV PERSON LAISSEZ NEW/LIB...NEW/IDEA IDEA/COMP BIBLIOG 19/20. PAGE 102 H2038 — CONCPT ATTIT SOCIETY TOTALISM

C41

WASSERMAN L.,"HANDBOOK OF POLITICAL "ISMS" CAP/ISM REPRESENT TOTALISM MARXISM NEW/LIB SOCISM...MAJORIT BIBLIOG 20. PAGE 166 H3313 — IDEA/COMP PHIL/SCI OWN NAT/G

B51

EUCKEN W.,THIS UNSUCCESSFUL AGE. GERMANY NAT/G WORKER TEC/DEV ECO/TAC ORD/FREE 20. PAGE 47 H0947 — ECO/DEV PLAN LAISSEZ NEW/LIB

C52

EBENSTEIN W.,"INTRODUCTION TO POLITICAL PHILOSOPHY." COM CONSTN INTELL CONTROL PERSON NEW/LIB SOCISM...PSY GEN/LAWS BIBLIOG/A. PAGE 44 H0883 — ALL/IDEOS PHIL/SCI IDEA/COMP NAT/G

C52

LEWIS B.W.,"BRITISH PLANNING AND NATIONALIZATION." UK INDUS SERV/IND LABOR NAT/G OP/RES TEC/DEV TAX WEALTH...CHARTS BIBLIOG 20. PAGE 96 H1912 — NEW/LIB ECO/DEV POL/PAR PLAN

B53

STOUT H.M.,BRITISH GOVERNMENT. UK FINAN LOC/G POL/PAR DELIB/GP DIPLOM ADMIN COLONIAL CHOOSE ORD/FREE...JURID BIBLIOG 20 COMMONWLTH. PAGE 150 H2990 — NAT/G PARL/PROC CONSTN NEW/LIB

N53

VITO F.,"RECENT DEVELOPMENTS IN THE THEORY OF DEMOCRATIC ADMIN" INTL POL SCI ASS'N CONFERENCE ON PUBLIC ADMINISTRATION... FRANCE ITALY UK REPRESENT EFFICIENCY NEW/LIB SOCISM...WELF/ST 20. PAGE 163 H3257 — GOV/COMP CONTROL EX/STRUC

S56

MACRAE D. JR.,"ROLL CALL VOTES AND LEADERSHIP." ACT/RES LEAD CHOOSE DRIVE CONSERVE NEW/LIB...STAT STYLE. PAGE 100 H2007 — POL/PAR GOV/COMP LEGIS SUPEGO

B59

JENKINS C.,POWER AT THE TOP: A CRITICAL SURVEY OF THE NATIONALIZED INDUSTRIES. UK POL/PAR CONTROL ...WELF/ST CHARTS 20 LABOR/PAR. PAGE 80 H1601 — NAT/G OWN INDUS NEW/LIB

B59

KELF-COHEN R.,NATIONALISATION IN BRITAIN: THE END OF DOGMA. EUR+WWI UK NAT/G POL/PAR WORKER ECO/TAC PARL/PROC WEALTH SOCISM...GOV/COMP 20. PAGE 84 H1683 — NEW/LIB ECO/DEV INDUS OWN

B60

PETERSON W.C.,THE WELFARE STATE IN FRANCE. EUR+WWI FRANCE FUT STRATA PROB/SOLV TAX GIVE RECEIVE INCOME ORD/FREE PWR...CHARTS 20. PAGE 125 H2496 — NEW/LIB ECO/TAC WEALTH NAT/G

B60

ROBERTSON D.,THE CONTROL OF INDUSTRY. UK MARKET LABOR WORKER PRICE CONTROL GP/REL COST DEMAND ORD/FREE WEALTH NEW/LIB SOCISM 20. PAGE 132 H2646 — INDUS FINAN NAT/G ECO/DEV

C60

EBENSTEIN W.,"MODERN POLITICAL THOUGHT (2ND ED.)" NAT/G CAP/ISM NAT/LISM PERSON ORD/FREE PWR ALL/IDEOS NEW/LIB SOCISM...TRADIT PSY BIBLIOG/A 18/20. PAGE 44 H0884 — IDEA/COMP PHIL/SCI CONCPT GEN/LAWS

B61

NARASIMHAN V.K.,THE PRESS, THE PUBLIC AND THE ADMINISTRATION (PAMPHLET). INDIA COM/IND CONTROL REPRESENT GOV/REL EFFICIENCY...ANTHOL 20. PAGE 116 H2312 — NAT/G ADMIN PRESS NEW/LIB

B63

BROGAN D.W.,POLITICAL PATTERNS IN TODAY'S WORLD. FRANCE USA+45 USSR WOR+45 CONSTN STRUCT PLAN DIPLOM ADMIN LEAD ROLE SUPEGO...PHIL/SCI 20. PAGE 21 H0429 — NAT/COMP NEW/LIB COM TOTALISM

B63

GRIMOND J.,THE LIBERAL CHALLENGE. UK SOCIETY INDUS POL/PAR LEGIS PLAN CAP/ISM DIPLOM EDU/PROP GOV/REL CONSERVE 20 PARLIAMENT REFORMERS. PAGE 61 H1227 — NAT/G NEW/LIB ECO/DEV POLICY

B63

HARTLEY A.,A STATE OF ENGLAND. UK ELITES SOCIETY ACADEM NAT/G SCHOOL INGP/REL CONSEN ORD/FREE NEW/LIB...POLICY 20. PAGE 67 H1349 — DIPLOM ATTIT INTELL ECO/DEV

B63

LAVROFF D.-G.,LES LIBERTES PUBLIQUES EN UNION SOVIETIQUE (REV. ED.). USSR NAT/G WORKER SANCTION CRIME MARXISM NEW/LIB...JURID BIBLIOG WORSHIP 20. PAGE 92 H1843 — ORD/FREE LAW ATTIT COM

B63

PELLING H.M.,A HISTORY OF BRITISH TRADE UNIONISM. UK ELITES ECO/DEV POL/PAR GP/REL PWR NEW/LIB 19/20. PAGE 124 H2485 — LABOR VOL/ASSN NAT/G

B64

COONDOO R.,THE DIVISION OF POWERS IN THE INDIAN CONSTITUTION. INDIA ECO/UNDEV FINAN TEC/DEV WAR CENTRAL EFFICIENCY NAT/LISM PWR WEALTH NEW/LIB ...BIBLIOG 18/20. PAGE 33 H0659 — CONSTN LEGIS WELF/ST GOV/COMP

B64

KRUEGER H.,ALLGEMEINE STAATSLEHRE. WOR+45 CONSTN SECT CHOOSE INGP/REL PWR NEW/LIB...JURID CLASSIF IDEA/COMP. PAGE 89 H1777 — NAT/G GOV/COMP SOCIETY

B64

MARSH D.C.,THE FUTURE OF THE WELFARE STATE. UK CONSTN NAT/G POL/PAR...POLICY WELF/ST 20. PAGE 103 H2058 — NEW/LIB ADMIN CONCPT INSPECT

B64

TAWNEY R.H.,EQUALITY. UK CULTURE STRATA ECO/TAC EDU/PROP REPRESENT OWN NEW/LIB...MAJORIT WELF/ST SOC 20. PAGE 153 H3051 — WEALTH STRUCT ELITES POPULISM

B65

PELLING H.,A SHORT HISTORY OF THE LABOUR PARTY (2ND ED.). UK NAT/G CHIEF PARL/PROC GP/REL INGP/REL 20 LABOR/PAR PARLIAMENT WILSON/H. PAGE 124 H2484 — POL/PAR NEW/LIB LEAD LABOR

B66

AIYAR S.P.,PERSPECTIVES ON THE WELFARE STATE. INDIA S/ASIA UK CONSTN ECO/UNDEV NAT/G INGP/REL CENTRAL NAT/LISM ATTIT...CONCPT ANTHOL BIBLIOG 20. PAGE 4 H0087 — NEW/LIB WELF/ST IDEA/COMP ADJUST

B67

ROELOFS H.M.,THE LANGUAGE OF MODERN POLITICS: AN INTRODUCTION TO THE STUDY OF GOVERNMENT. DIPLOM ADMIN MARXISM NEW/LIB...JURID CONCPT METH/COMP T 20. PAGE 133 H2657 — LEAD NAT/COMP PERS/REL NAT/G

B67

YAMAMURA K.,ECONOMIC POLICY IN POSTWAR JAPAN. ASIA FINAN POL/PAR DIPLOM LEAD NAT/LISM ATTIT NEW/LIB POPULISM 20 CHINJAP. PAGE 171 H3432 — ECO/DEV POLICY NAT/G TEC/DEV

S67

MARWICK A.,"THE LABOUR PARTY AND THE WELFARE STATE IN BRITAIN, 19001948." UK SOCIETY STRUCT ECO/DEV WORKER CREATE PRICE CHOOSE WEALTH NEW/LIB SOCISM ...POLICY HEAL 20 PARLIAMENT LABOR/PAR. PAGE 104 H2074 — POL/PAR RECEIVE LEGIS NAT/G

NEW/MEXICO....NEW MEXICO

NEW/YORK....NEW YORK STATE

NEW/ZEALND....NEW ZEALAND; SEE ALSO S/ASIA, COMMONWLTH

N

AUSTRALIAN NATIONAL RES COUN,AUSTRALIAN SOCIAL SCIENCE ABSTRACTS. NEW/ZEALND CULTURE SOCIETY LOC/G CT/SYS PARL/PROC...HEAL JURID PSY SOC 20 AUSTRAL. PAGE 9 H0181 — BIBLIOG/A POLICY NAT/G ADMIN

B42
CONOVER H.F.,NEW ZEALAND: A SELECTED LIST OF REFERENCES (PAMPHLET). NEW/ZEALND ECO/UNDEV AGRI INDUS LABOR NAT/G SCHOOL FORCES DIPLOM COLONIAL WAR ...HUM 20. PAGE 32 H0643
BIBLIOG/A S/ASIA CULTURE

B58
BRADY A.,DEMOCRACY IN THE DOMINIONS (3RD ED.). CANADA NEW/ZEALND SOUTH/AFR WOR+45 LAW EX/STRUC DOMIN COLONIAL PARL/PROC REPRESENT RACE/REL NAT/LISM WEALTH 20 AUSTRAL CMN/WLTH. PAGE 20 H0399
GOV/COMP POL/PAR POPULISM NAT/G

B62
CHAPMAN R.M.,NEW ZEALAND POLITICS IN ACTION: THE 1960 GENERAL ELECTION. NEW/ZEALND LEGIS EDU/PROP PRESS TV LEAD ATTIT...STAND/INT 20. PAGE 29 H0582
NAT/G CHOOSE POL/PAR

B62
NEW ZEALAND COMM OF ST SERVICE,THE STATE SERVICES IN NEW ZEALAND. NEW/ZEALND CONSULT EX/STRUC ACT/RES ...BIBLIOG 20. PAGE 117 H2343
ADMIN WORKER TEC/DEV NAT/G

S62
CORET A.,"LE STATUT DE L'ILE CHRISTMAS DE L'OCEAN INDIEN." FUT S/ASIA ECO/DEV ECO/UNDEV VOL/ASSN DELIB/GP PLAN...RELATIV OBS TIME/SEQ TREND AUSTRAL 20. PAGE 33 H0667
NAT/G INT/ORG NEW/ZEALND

B65
CAMERON W.J.,NEW ZEALAND. NEW/ZEALND S/ASIA DIPLOM INT/TRADE WRITING COLONIAL PARL/PROC...GEOG CMN/WLTH. PAGE 26 H0513
SOCIETY GP/REL STRUCT

B65
ROWAT D.C.,THE OMBUDSMAN: CITIZEN'S DEFENDER. DENMARK FINLAND NEW/ZEALND NORWAY SWEDEN CONSULT PROB/SOLV FEEDBACK PARTIC GP/REL...SOC CONCPT NEW/IDEA METH/COMP ANTHOL BIBLIOG 20. PAGE 135 H2701
INSPECT CONSTN NAT/G ADMIN

B66
EDWARDS C.D.,TRADE REGULATIONS OVERSEAS. IRELAND NEW/ZEALND SOUTH/AFR NAT/G CAP/ISM TARIFFS CONTROL ...POLICY JURID 20 EEC CHINJAP. PAGE 45 H0892
INT/TRADE DIPLOM INT/LAW ECO/TAC

S66
"RESEARCH WORK 1965-1966." NEW/ZEALND ELITES ACADEM LOC/G MUNIC POL/PAR PROVS DIPLOM COLONIAL...SOC 20 AUSTRAL. PAGE 2 H0047
BIBLIOG NAT/G CULTURE S/ASIA

B67
RAE D.,THE POLITICAL CONSEQUENCES OF ELECTORAL LAWS. EUR+WWI ICELAND ISRAEL NEW/ZEALND UK USA+45 ADJUD APPORT GP/REL MAJORITY...MATH STAT CENSUS CHARTS BIBLIOG 20 AUSTRAL. PAGE 129 H2579
POL/PAR CHOOSE NAT/COMP REPRESENT

S67
ANDERSON L.G.,"ADMINISTERING A GOVERNMENT SOCIAL SERVICE" NEW/ZEALND EX/STRUC TASK ROLE 20. PAGE 6 H0129
ADMIN NAT/G DELIB/GP SOC/WK

B95
SELIGMAN E.R.A.,ESSAYS IN TAXATION. NEW/ZEALND PRUSSIA UK USA-45 MARKET LOC/G CREATE PRICE CONTROL INCOME OWN WEALTH...GOV/COMP METH/COMP 19. PAGE 141 H2824
TAX TARIFFS INDUS NAT/G

NEWARK F.H. H2344

NEWARK/NJ....NEWARK, N.J.

NEWBURY C.W. H2345

NEWFNDLND....NEWFOUNDLAND, CANADA

NEWMAN J.H. H2346

NEWMAN R.P. H2347

NEWY/TIMES....NEW YORK TIMES

NICARAGUA....NICARAGUA; SEE ALSO L/A+17C

B47
DE NOIA J.,GUIDE TO OFFICIAL PUBLICATIONS OF THE OTHER AMERICAN REPUBLICS: NICARAGUA (VOL. XIV). NICARAGUA LAW LEGIS ADMIN CT/SYS...JURID 19/20. PAGE 38 H0765
BIBLIOG/A EDU/PROP NAT/G CONSTN

B65
RODRIGUEZ M.,CENTRAL AMERICA. COSTA/RICA GUATEMALA L/A+17C NICARAGUA DIPLOM COLONIAL REGION NAT/LISM ALL/IDEOS SOCISM...MAJORIT TIME/SEQ BIBLIOG 19/20. PAGE 133 H2656
CULTURE NAT/COMP NAT/G ECO/UNDEV

B67
OPERATIONS AND POLICY RESEARCH,NICARAGUA: ELECTION FACTBOOK: FEBRUARY 5, 1967 (PAMPHLET). NICARAGUA LAW NAT/G LEAD REPRESENT...STAT BIOG CHARTS 20. PAGE 121 H2423
POL/PAR CHOOSE PLAN ATTIT

S67
GRIEB K.J.,"THE UNITED STATES AND THE CENTRAL AMERICAN CONFEDERATION." COSTA/RICA EL/SALVADR GUATEMALA HONDURAS L/A+17C NICARAGUA NAT/G FORCES CONFER AGREE EXEC ARMS/CONT REV WAR PEACE ATTIT 20. PAGE 60 H1212
INT/ORG DIPLOM POLICY REGION

NICHOLAS W. H2348

NICHOLAS/I....CZAR NICHOLAS I

B61
MONAS S.,THE THIRD SECTION: POLICE AND SOCIETY IN RUSSIA UNDER NICHOLAS I. MOD/EUR RUSSIA ELITES STRUCT NAT/G EX/STRUC ADMIN CONTROL PWR CONSERVE ...DECISION 19 NICHOLAS/I. PAGE 112 H2238
ORD/FREE COM FORCES COERCE

NICHOLLS W.H. H2349

NICOL D. H2350

NICOLSON H. H2351,H2352,H2353,H2354

NICOLSON H.G. H2355

NICOLSON/A....SIR ARTHUR NICOLSON

NICULESCU B. H2356

NIEBUHR R. H2357,H2358,H2359,H2360

NIEBUHR/R....REINHOLD NIEBUHR

B61
LYFORD J.P.,THE AGREEABLE AUTOCRACIES. SOCIETY LABOR POL/PAR SECT DIPLOM CHOOSE...CONCPT 20 WHITE/T NIEBUHR/R. PAGE 99 H1982
ATTIT POPULISM PRESS NAT/G

B64
KARIEL H.S.,IN SEARCH OF AUTHORITY: TWENTIETH-CENTURY POLITICAL THOUGHT. WOR+45 WOR-45 NAT/G EX/STRUC TOTALISM DRIVE PWR...MGT PHIL/SCI GEN/LAWS 19/20 NIETZSCH/F FREUD/S WEBER/MAX NIEBUHR/R MARITAIN/J. PAGE 83 H1661
CONSTN CONCPT ORD/FREE IDEA/COMP

NIEBURG/HL....H.L. NIEBURG

NIEDERGANG M. H2361

NIETZSCH/F....FRIEDRICH NIETZSCHE

B63
STRAUSS L.,HISTORY OF POLITICAL PHILOSOPHY. LAW SOCIETY CAP/ISM MARXISM 19 AQUINAS/T BACON/F HEGEL/GWF MILL/JS NIETZSCH/F. PAGE 150 H2995
IDEA/COMP PHIL/SCI ANTHOL

B64
KARIEL H.S.,IN SEARCH OF AUTHORITY: TWENTIETH-CENTURY POLITICAL THOUGHT. WOR+45 WOR-45 NAT/G EX/STRUC TOTALISM DRIVE PWR...MGT PHIL/SCI GEN/LAWS 19/20 NIETZSCH/F FREUD/S WEBER/MAX NIEBUHR/R MARITAIN/J. PAGE 83 H1661
CONSTN CONCPT ORD/FREE IDEA/COMP

NIGER....SEE ALSO AFR

B60
CONOVER H.F.,OFFICIAL PUBLICATIONS OF FRENCH WEST AFRICA, 1946-1958. DAHOMEY IVORY/CST NIGER SENEGAL UPPER/VOLT CONSTN AGRI PRESS...CON/ANAL 20. PAGE 33 H0651
BIBLIOG COLONIAL NAT/G AFR

NIGERIA....SEE ALSO AFR

B00
MOCKLER-FERRYMAN A.,BRITISH WEST AFRICA. FRANCE GERMANY NIGER SIER/LEONE UK CULTURE DIPLOM WAR RACE/REL PRODUC PROFIT WEALTH...POLICY PREDICT 19. PAGE 112 H2232
AFR COLONIAL INT/TRADE CAP/ISM

B39
AKIGA,AKIGA'S STORY: THE TIV TRIBE AS SEEN BY ONE OF ITS MEMBERS. NIGERIA LAW STRUCT ECO/UNDEV FAM LEAD GP/REL MARRIAGE...LING WORSHIP 20. PAGE 4 H0089
KIN SECT SOC CULTURE

B53
MEAD M.,CULTURAL PATTERNS AND TECHNICAL CHANGE. BURMA GREECE NIGERIA ECO/UNDEV AGRI INDUS SCHOOL SECT CREATE FEEDBACK HABITAT...PSY METH/COMP BIBLIOG 20 UN. PAGE 108 H2152
HEALTH TEC/DEV CULTURE ADJUST

B55
INTERNATIONAL AFRICAN INST,ETHNOGRAPHIC SURVEY OF AFRICA: WESTERN AFRICA: PEOPLES OF THE NIGER-BENUE CONFLUENCE. AFR NIGER CULTURE ECO/UNDEV KIN GOV/REL GP/REL ATTIT HEREDITY...CHARTS BIBLIOG WORSHIP 20. PAGE 77 H1546
STRUCT GEOG HABITAT INGP/REL

B56
INTERNATIONAL AFRICAN INST,ETHNOGRAPHIC SURVEY OF AFRICA; WESTERN AFRICA: PAGAN PEOPLES OF CENTRAL AREA OF NORTHERN NIGERIA (VOL. XII). NIGERIA FAM KIN SECT ECO/TAC GOV/REL GP/REL ATTIT...LING CHARTS 20. PAGE 77 H1548
STRUCT INGP/REL HABITAT CULTURE

B56
PADMORE G.,PAN-AFRICANISM OR COMMUNISM. AFR FUT
POL/PAR

NIGERIA INTELL NAT/G COLONIAL FEDERAL ATTIT DRIVE PWR RESPECT WEALTH MARXISM...CONCPT AUD/VIS STERTYP 20. PAGE 122 H2440 — NAT/LISM

B57
INTERNATIONAL AFRICAN INST,ETHNOGRAPHIC SURVEY OF AFRICA: WESTERN AFRICA: THE BENIN KINGDOM. AFR NIGERIA CULTURE ECO/UNDEV KIN ECO/TAC GOV/REL AGE ATTIT HEREDITY...CHARTS BIBLIOG WORSHIP 20. PAGE 77 H1550 — STRUCT INGP/REL GEOG HABITAT

B58
CARTER G.M.,TRANSITION IN AFRICA; STUDIES IN POLITICAL ADAPTATION. AFR CENTRL/AFR GHANA NIGERIA CONSTN LOC/G POL/PAR ADMIN GP/REL FEDERAL...MAJORIT BIBLIOG 20. PAGE 27 H0543 — NAT/COMP PWR CONTROL NAT/G

B58
COLEMAN J.S.,NIGERIA: BACKGROUND TO NATIONALISM. AFR SOCIETY ECO/DEV KIN LOC/G POL/PAR TEC/DEV DOMIN ADMIN DRIVE PWR RESPECT...TRADIT SOC INT SAMP TIME/SEQ 20. PAGE 31 H0627 — NAT/G NAT/LISM NIGERIA

B59
CONOVER H.F.,NIGERIAN OFFICIAL PUBLICATIONS, 1869-1959: A GUIDE. NIGER CONSTN FINAN ACADEM SCHOOL FORCES PRESS ADMIN COLONIAL...HIST/WRIT 19/20. PAGE 33 H0650 — BIBLIOG NAT/G CON/ANAL

B60
INTERNATIONAL AFRICAN INST,ETHNOGRAPHIC SURVEY OF AFRICA: WESTERN AFRICA: PEOPLES OF THE MIDDLE NIGER REGION, NORTHERN NIGERIA. AFR NIGER CULTURE ECO/UNDEV KIN NEIGH GOV/REL GP/REL ATTIT HEREDITY ...CHARTS BIBLIOG WORSHIP 20. PAGE 78 H1552 — STRUCT GEOG HABITAT INGP/REL

B60
JEFFRIES C.,TRANSFER OF POWER: PROBLEMS OF THE PASSAGE TO SELFGOVERNMENT. CEYLON GHANA MALAYSIA NIGERIA UK INT/ORG CONSULT DELIB/GP LEGIS DIPLOM CONFER PARL/PROC 20. PAGE 80 H1595 — SOVEREIGN COLONIAL ORD/FREE NAT/G

B60
SMITH M.G.,GOVERNMENT IN ZAZZAU 1800-1950. NIGERIA UK CULTURE SOCIETY LOC/G ADMIN COLONIAL ...METH/CNCPT NEW/IDEA METH 19/20. PAGE 146 H2914 — REGION CONSTN KIN ECO/UNDEV

B60
THEOBOLD R.,THE NEW NATIONS OF WEST AFRICA. GHANA NIGERIA CULTURE INT/ORG ECO/TAC FOR/AID COLONIAL RACE/REL POPULISM...ANTHOL BIBLIOG 20 UN. PAGE 153 H3068 — AFR SOVEREIGN ECO/UNDEV DIPLOM

B62
BRETTON H.L.,POWER AND STABILITY IN NIGERIA: THE POLITICS OF DECOLONIZATION. AFR CONSTN INTELL ECO/UNDEV COM/IND KIN NAT/G POL/PAR PROVS VOL/ASSN LEGIS DOMIN EDU/PROP LEGIT EXEC ROUTINE CHOOSE NAT/LISM ATTIT PERCEPT ALL/VALS. PAGE 20 H0411 — CULTURE OBS NIGERIA

B62
TILMAN R.O.,THE NIGERIAN POLITICAL SXENE. NIGERIA DIPLOM COLONIAL PARTIC...POLICY SOC OBS PREDICT ANTHOL 20. PAGE 155 H3096 — NAT/G AFR ECO/UNDEV FEDERAL

B63
SKLAR R.L.,NIGERIAN POLITICAL PARTIES: POWER IN AN EMERGENT AFRICAN NATION. AFR EUR+WWI CULTURE STRATA NAT/G DELIB/GP EX/STRUC LEGIS DOMIN EDU/PROP ROUTINE CHOOSE ATTIT PERCEPT ORD/FREE PWR...SOC CONCPT OBS TOT/POP VAL/FREE. PAGE 145 H2898 — POL/PAR SOCIETY NAT/LISM NIGERIA

S63
DUDLEY B.J.,"THE NOMINATION OF PARLIAMENTARY CANDIDATES IN NORTHERN NIGERIA." AFR CONSTN CULTURE ELITES STRATA DELIB/GP LEGIS DOMIN EDU/PROP COERCE ATTIT SUPEGO PWR...STAT VAL/FREE 20. PAGE 43 H0854 — POL/PAR CHOOSE NIGERIA

B64
BROWN C.V.,GOVERNMENT AND BANKING IN WESTERN NIGERIA. AFR NIGERIA GOV/REL GP/REL...POLICY 20. PAGE 22 H0440 — ADMIN ECO/UNDEV FINAN NAT/G

B64
PHILLIPS C.S.,THE DEVELOPMENT OF NIGERIAN FOREIGN POLICY. AFR CONSTN CULTURE STRATA NAT/G LEGIS DOMIN LEGIT EXEC...RELATIV SOC TIME/SEQ TREND TOT/POP 20. PAGE 125 H2502 — CHOOSE POLICY DIPLOM NIGERIA

B64
WRAITH R.,CORRUPTION IN DEVELOPING COUNTRIES. NIGERIA UK LAW ELITES STRATA INDUS LOC/G NAT/G SECT FORCES EDU/PROP ADMIN PWR WEALTH 18/20. PAGE 171 H3414 — ECO/UNDEV CRIME SANCTION ATTIT

L64
MACKINTOSH J.P.,"NIGERIA'S EXTERNAL AFFAIRS." UK CULTURE ECO/UNDEV NAT/G VOL/ASSN EDU/PROP LEGIT ADMIN ATTIT ORD/FREE PWR 20. PAGE 100 H2002 — AFR DIPLOM NIGERIA

B65
BLITZ L.F.,THE POLITICS AND ADMINISTRATION OF NIGERIAN GOVERNMENT. NIGER CULTURE LOC/G LEGIS DIPLOM COLONIAL CT/SYS SOVEREIGN...GEOG SOC ANTHOL 20. PAGE 18 H0357 — NAT/G GOV/REL POL/PAR

B65
HARRIS R.L.,POLITICAL ORGANIZATION OF THE MBEMBE NIGERIA. AFR NIGERIA SOCIETY AGRI SECT WORKER PAY ...SOC WORSHIP 20 MBEMBE. PAGE 67 H1345 — STRUCT CHIEF CULTURE

B65
PROEHL P.O.,FOREIGN ENTERPRISE IN NIGERIA. NIGERIA FINAN LABOR NAT/G TAX 20. PAGE 128 H2562 — ECO/UNDEV ECO/TAC JURID CAP/ISM

B66
BASDEN G.T.,NIGER IBOS. NIGERIA STRUCT SECT CHIEF COLONIAL HABITAT...POLICY SOC MYTH OBS WORSHIP 20 IBO. PAGE 12 H0233 — CULTURE AFR SOCIETY

B66
CROWDER M.,A SHORT HISTORY OF NIGERIA. AFR NIGERIA UK ECO/UNDEV CHIEF INT/TRADE RACE/REL NAT/LISM ORD/FREE...GEOG SOC CHARTS BIBLIOG 14/20. PAGE 36 H0711 — COLONIAL NAT/G CULTURE

B66
FLINT J.E.,NIGERIA AND GHANA. AFR GHANA NIGERIA UK NAT/G DOMIN DISCRIM...CHARTS BIBLIOG/A 15/20 NEGRO MAPS. PAGE 51 H1026 — CULTURE COLONIAL NAT/LISM

B66
KASUNMU A.B.,NIGERIAN FAMILY LAW. NIGERIA KIN LEGIT ILLEGIT MARRIAGE AGE DRIVE HABITAT ALL/VALS...JURID IDEA/COMP T 20 ENGLSH/LAW. PAGE 83 H1667 — FAM LAW CULTURE AFR

B66
KEAY E.A.,THE NATIVE AND CUSTOMARY COURTS OF NIGERIA. NIGERIA CONSTN ELITES NAT/G TOP/EX PARTIC REGION...DECISION JURID 19/20. PAGE 84 H1673 — AFR ADJUD LAW

B66
US LIBRARY OF CONGRESS,NIGERIA: A GUIDE TO OFFICIAL PUBLICATIONS. CAMEROON NIGERIA UK DIPLOM...POLICY 19/20 UN LEAGUE/NAT. PAGE 161 H3215 — BIBLIOG ADMIN NAT/G COLONIAL

B66
ZOLBERG A.R.,CREATING POLITICAL ORDER. AFR CONGO/BRAZ GHANA NIGER KIN NAT/G DOMIN COLONIAL REGION CENTRAL NAT/LISM ATTIT PWR 20 CONGO/LEOP. PAGE 173 H3462 — SOVEREIGN ORD/FREE CONSTN POL/PAR

S66
MATTHEWS D.G.,"PRELUDE-COUP D'ETAT-MILITARY GOVERNMENT: A BIBLIOGRAPHICAL AND RESEARCH GUIDE TO NIGERIAN POL AND GOVT, JAN, 1965-66." AFR NIGER LAW CONSTN POL/PAR LEGIS CIVMIL/REL GOV/REL...STAT 20. PAGE 105 H2096 — BIBLIOG NAT/G ADMIN CHOOSE

B67
ARIKPO O.,THE DEVELOPMENT OF MODERN NIGERIA. AFR NIGERIA SOCIETY ECO/UNDEV KIN ADMIN FEDERAL NAT/LISM ORD/FREE WEALTH...POLICY GEOG BIBLIOG 19/20. PAGE 8 H0163 — NAT/G CULTURE CONSTN COLONIAL

B67
CURTIN P.D.,AFRICA REMEMBERED. NIGERIA SENEGAL CULTURE DIPLOM INT/TRADE GP/REL RACE/REL...RECORD ANTHOL 18/19 NEGRO. PAGE 36 H0727 — DOMIN ORD/FREE AFR DISCRIM

B67
WINTER E.H.,CONTEMPORARY CHANGE IN TRADITIONAL SOCIETIES: VOLUME I INTRODUCTION AND AFRICAN TRIBES. NIGERIA AGRI LOC/G NAT/G CREATE DOMIN COLONIAL CONTROL GP/REL PWR SOVEREIGN...SOC OBS 20 TANGANYIKA. PAGE 169 H3389 — SOCIETY AFR CONSERVE KIN

S67
VINCENT S.,"SHOULD BIAFRA SURVIVE?" NIGERIA ECO/UNDEV CHIEF FORCES ECO/TAC GP/REL DISCRIM PEACE ORD/FREE SOC/INTEG 20 BIAFRA IBO. PAGE 163 H3256 — AFR REV REGION NAT/G

S67
WILLIAMS F.R.A.,"FUNDAMENTAL RIGHTS AND THE PROSPECT FOR DEMOCRACY IN NIGERIA." FUT NIGERIA SOCIETY ECO/UNDEV LEGIS ADJUD CHOOSE 20. PAGE 168 H3366 — CONSTN LAW ORD/FREE NAT/G

L68
CURRENT HISTORY,"AFRICA, 1968." ETHIOPIA GHANA NIGERIA SOUTH/AFR CULTURE ECO/UNDEV KIN SECT CHIEF EX/STRUC WAR WEAPON CHOOSE CIVMIL/REL...GOV/COMP 20 AFRICA/E. PAGE 36 H0724 — RACE/REL NAT/LISM FORCES AFR

S68
CHAPMAN A.R.,"THE CIVIL WAR IN NIGERIA." AFR NIGERIA NAT/G PLAN ECO/TAC EDU/PROP COERCE WAR GOV/REL INGP/REL ORD/FREE PWR WEALTH SOC/INTEG 20 BIAFRA. PAGE 29 H0579 — REV RACE/REL

B99
KINGSLEY M.H.,WEST AFRICAN STUDIES. GHANA NIGERIA SIER/LEONE LAW EXTR/IND SECT DIPLOM INT/TRADE DOMIN RACE/REL OWN HEALTH...SOC 19. PAGE 86 H1717 — AFR HEREDITY COLONIAL CULTURE

NIH....NATIONAL INSTITUTE OF HEALTH

NIPA....NATIONAL INSTITUTE OF PUBLIC ADMINISTRATION

NIPPERDEY T. H2362

NIRRNHEIM O. H2363

NISEI....NISEI: JAPANESE AMERICANS

B49
GRODZINS M.,AMERICANS BETRAYED: POLITICS AND THE — DISCRIM

JAPANESE EXPANSION. PROVS COERCE CHOOSE GOV/REL GP/REL INGP/REL ATTIT ORD/FREE...DECISION CHARTS 20 NISEI. PAGE 61 H1230 — POLICY NAT/G WAR

NIXON/RM....PRESIDENT RICHARD M. NIXON

NJAMA K. H0225

NKRUMAH K. H2364

NKRUMAH/K....KWAME NKRUMAH

N
BROCKWAY A.F.,AFRICAN SOCIALISM. EUR+WWI GHANA ISLAM UAR ECO/UNDEV CAP/ISM INT/TRADE COLONIAL COERCE GOV/REL DISCRIM 20 NEGRO NKRUMAH/K NASSER/G. PAGE 21 H0423 — AFR SOCISM MARXISM

B66
AFRIFA A.A.,THE GHANA COUP. AFR GHANA ELITES NAT/G DIPLOM DOMIN 20 NKRUMAH/K. PAGE 4 H0076 — TOP/EX REV FORCES POL/PAR

NLC....NATIONAL LIBERATION COUNCIL IN GHANA

NLF....NATIONAL LIBERATION FRONT OF SOUTH VIETNAM

NLRB....NATIONAL LABOR RELATIONS BOARD

NOBECOURT R.G. H2365

NOBILITY....SEE ELITES

NOEL G.E. H2366

NOLTE E. H2367,H2368

NOLTING O.F. H2624

NOMAD M. H2369

NOMAD/MAX....MAX NOMAD

NOMADISM....SEE GEOG

NONALIGNED NATIONS....SEE THIRD/WRLD

NON-WHITE....SEE RACE/REL

NONVIOLENT....NONVIOLENCE (CONCEPT)

NORDEN A. H2370

NORDSKOG J.E. H2371

NORMS....SEE AVERAGE, ALSO APPROPRIATE VALUES AND DIMENSIONS OF GROUPS, STAT, LOG, ETC.

NORTH R.C. H2372,H2373

NORTH AFRICA....SEE AFRICA/N, ISLAM

NORTH ATLANTIC FREE TRADE AREA....SEE NAFTA

NORTH ATLANTIC TREATY ORGANIZATION....SEE NATO

NORTH KOREA....SEE KOREA/N

NORTH VIETNAM....SEE VIETNAM/N

NORTH/AMER....NORTH AMERICA, EXCLUSIVE OF CENTRAL AMERICA

NORTH/CAR....NORTH CAROLINA

NORTH/DAK....NORTH DAKOTA

NORTH/US....NORTHERN UNITED STATES

NORTHEDGE F.S. H2374

NORTHERN RHODESIA....SEE ZAMBIA

NORTHROP F.S.C. H2375,H2376

NORTHW/TER....NORTHWEST TERRITORIES, CANADA

NORTHWEST TERRITORIES, CANADA....SEE NORTHW/TER

NORTHWESTERN UNIVERSITY LIB H2377

NORTHWST/U....NORTHWESTERN UNIVERSITY

NORWAY....SEE ALSO APPROPRIATE TIME/SPACE/CULTURE INDEX

B23
LEES-SMITH H.B.,SECOND CHAMBERS IN THEORY AND PRACTICE. IRELAND NORWAY SOUTH/AFR UK LAW POL/PAR LEGIS CONTROL 20 CMN/WLTH. PAGE 93 H1858 — PARL/PROC DELIB/GP REPRESENT GP/COMP

B35
NORDSKOG J.E.,SOCIAL REFORM IN NORWAY. NORWAY INDUS NAT/G POL/PAR LEGIS ADJUD...SOC BIBLIOG SOC/INTEG 20. PAGE 119 H2371 — LABOR ADJUST

B53
ORFIELD L.B.,THE GROWTH OF SCANDINAVIAN LAW. DENMARK ICELAND NORWAY SWEDEN LAW DIPLOM...BIBLIOG 9/20. PAGE 121 H2426 — JURID CT/SYS NAT/G

B55
DUVERGER M.,THE POLITICAL ROLE OF WOMEN. FRANCE GERMANY/W NORWAY YUGOSLAVIA STRATA LOBBY AGE ATTIT ROLE...STAT SAMP CHARTS METH/COMP NAT/COMP HYPO/EXP FEMALE/SEX. PAGE 44 H0875 — SEX LEAD PARTIC CHOOSE

B55
RODNICK D.,THE NORWEGIANS: A STUDY IN NATIONAL CULTURE. NORWAY FAM INGP/REL PERS/REL AGE...PSY SOC SELF/OBS WORSHIP 20. PAGE 133 H2655 — CULTURE INT RECORD ATTIT

B59
FOX A.,THE POWER OF SMALL STATES: DIPLOMACY IN WORLD WAR TWO. EUR+WWI FINLAND NORWAY SPAIN SWEDEN TURKEY NAT/G TOP/EX DIPLOM PWR...HIST/WRIT 20. PAGE 52 H1044 — CONCPT STERTYP BAL/PWR

S59
LYNN D.B.,"THE EFFECTS OF FATHER-ABSENCE ON NORWEGIAN BOYS AND GIRLS." NORWAY CULTURE PERS/REL ADJUST DISPL LOVE...PSY CORREL STAT INT CON/ANAL CHARTS SOC/INTEG 20. PAGE 99 H1983 — SOC FAM AGE/C ANOMIE

L60
ROKKAN S.,"NORWAY AND THE UNITED STATES OF AMERICA." NORWAY CHOOSE...SOC STAND/INT SAMP CHARTS GP/COMP METH/COMP 20. PAGE 133 H2665 — STRUCT NAT/G PARTIC REPRESENT

B64
ANDREN N.,GOVERNMENT AND POLITICS IN THE NORDIC COUNTRIES: DENMARK, FINLAND, ICELAND, NORWAY, SWEDEN. DENMARK FINLAND ICELAND NORWAY SWEDEN POL/PAR CHIEF LEGIS ADMIN REGION REPRESENT ATTIT CONSERVE...CHARTS BIBLIOG/A 20. PAGE 7 H0137 — CONSTN NAT/G CULTURE GOV/COMP

B64
HALLER W.,DER SCHWEDISCHE JUSTITIEOMBUDSMAN. DENMARK FINLAND NORWAY SWEDEN LEGIS ADJUD CONTROL PERSON ORD/FREE...NAT/COMP 20 OMBUDSMAN. PAGE 64 H1288 — JURID PARL/PROC ADMIN CHIEF

B64
VALEN H.,POLITICAL PARTIES IN NORWAY. NORWAY ACADEM PARTIC ROUTINE INGP/REL KNOWL...QU 20. PAGE 161 H3220 — LOC/G POL/PAR PERSON

B65
ROWAT D.C.,THE OMBUDSMAN: CITIZEN'S DEFENDER. DENMARK FINLAND NEW/ZEALND NORWAY SWEDEN CONSULT PROB/SOLV FEEDBACK PARTIC GP/REL...SOC CONCPT NEW/IDEA METH/COMP ANTHOL BIBLIOG 20. PAGE 135 H2701 — INSPECT CONSTN NAT/G ADMIN

B65
WUORINEN J.H.,SCANDINAVIA. DENMARK FINLAND ICELAND NORWAY SWEDEN SOCIETY AGRI INDUS DELIB/GP DIPLOM INT/TRADE NEUTRAL...GEOG CHARTS BIBLIOG TREATY. PAGE 171 H3428 — NAT/G POL/PAR TREND POLICY

C65
WUORINEN J.H.,"SCANDINAVIA." DENMARK FINLAND ICELAND NORWAY SWEDEN SOCIETY AGRI POL/PAR DELIB/GP DIPLOM INT/TRADE NEUTRAL WAR...CHARTS TREATY 20. PAGE 171 H3427 — BIBLIOG NAT/G POLICY

B67
ANDERSON S.V.,THE NORDIC COUNCIL: A STUDY OF SCANDINAVIAN REGIONALISM. DENMARK FINLAND ICELAND NORWAY SWEDEN MARKET NAT/G VOL/ASSN CONSULT PARL/PROC ATTIT...TIME/SEQ BIBLIOG 20. PAGE 7 H0134 — INT/ORG REGION DIPLOM LEGIS

L67
CRIBBET J.E.,"SOME REFLECTIONS ON THE LAW OF LAND - A VIEW FROM SCANDINAVIA." DENMARK NETHERLAND NORWAY SWEDEN INDUS MUNIC NEIGH RACE/REL ATTIT HABITAT ...IDEA/COMP 20. PAGE 35 H0701 — LAW PLAN CONTROL NAT/G

L86
BURGESS J.W.,"THE RECENT CONSTITUTIONAL CRISIS IN NORWAY" MOD/EUR NORWAY SWEDEN LOC/G NAT/G CHIEF BAL/PWR NAT/LISM ORD/FREE 19. PAGE 24 H0481 — CONSTN SOVEREIGN GOV/REL

NOTTINGHAM J. H2678

NOVA/SCOT....NOVA SCOTIA, CANADA

B59
LEIGHTON A.H.,MY NAME IS LEGION; FOUNDATIONS FOR A THEORY OF MAN IN RELATION TO CULTURE (VOL. I). CULTURE STRANGE ANOMIE...SOC CONCPT METH/CNCPT CHARTS BIBLIOG METH 20 NOVA/SCOT. PAGE 93 H1867 — HEALTH PSY SOCIETY HABITAT

B63
LEIGHTON D.C.,THE CHARACTER OF DANGER (VOL. III). SOCIETY STRUCT STRANGE ANOMIE...SOC STAT CHARTS — HEALTH PSY

GP/COMP SOC/EXP SOC/INTEG 20 NOVA/SCOT. PAGE 94 H1868 — CULTURE

NOVE A. H2378

NOVOTNY/A....ANTONIN NOVOTNY

NRA....NATIONAL RECOVERY ADMINISTRATION

NSC....NATIONAL SECURITY COUNCIL

NSF....NATIONAL SCIENCE FOUNDATION

NSSF....NATIONAL SOCIAL SCIENCE FOUNDATION

NUC....NATIONAL UNITY COMMITTEE (TURKEY)

NUC/PWR....NUCLEAR POWER, INCLUDING NUCLEAR WEAPONS

N19
PROVISIONS SECTION OAU,ORGANIZATION OF AFRICAN UNITY: BASIC DOCUMENTS AND RESOLUTIONS (PAMPHLET). AFR CULTURE ECO/UNDEV DIPLOM ECO/TAC EDU/PROP COLONIAL ARMS/CONT NUC/PWR RACE/REL DISCRIM NAT/LISM 20 UN OAU. PAGE 128 H2564 — CONSTN EX/STRUC SOVEREIGN INT/ORG

B48
TOYNBEE A.J.,CIVILIZATION ON TRIAL. FUT WOR-45 NAT/G CREATE CAP/ISM DIPLOM NUC/PWR CHOOSE MARXISM ...GEOG CONCPT WORSHIP. PAGE 156 H3125 — SOCIETY TIME/SEQ NAT/COMP

B54
BUTZ O.,GERMANY: DILEMMA FOR AMERICAN POLICY. GERMANY USA+45 USA-45 USSR WOR+45 INT/ORG FORCES NUC/PWR EFFICIENCY PEACE PWR...GOV/COMP 20 COLD/WAR. PAGE 25 H0501 — DIPLOM NAT/G WAR POLICY

B56
ROBERTS H.L.,RUSSIA AND AMERICA. CHINA/COM S/ASIA USSR FORCES TEC/DEV FOR/AID NUC/PWR ALL/IDEOS ...MAJORIT TREND NAT/COMP 20 COLD/WAR UN NATO. PAGE 132 H2641 — DIPLOM INT/ORG BAL/PWR TOTALISM

B58
CROWE S.,THE LANDSCAPE OF POWER. UK CULTURE SERV/IND NAT/G CONSULT PARTIC NUC/PWR LEISURE...SOC EXHIBIT 20. PAGE 36 H0712 — HABITAT TEC/DEV PLAN CONTROL

B58
GARTHOFF R.L.,SOVIET STRATEGY IN THE NUCLEAR AGE. FUT USSR R+D INT/ORG NAT/G ACT/RES TEC/DEV DOMIN DETER WAR ATTIT PWR...RELATIV METH/CNCPT SELF/OBS TREND CON/ANAL STERTYP GEN/LAWS 20. PAGE 55 H1103 — COM FORCES BAL/PWR NUC/PWR

B59
STERNBERG F.,THE MILITARY AND INDUSTRIAL REVOLUTION OF OUR TIME. USA+45 USSR WOR+45 WORKER COMPUTER PLAN TEC/DEV NUC/PWR GP/REL...POLICY NAT/COMP 20. PAGE 149 H2981 — DIPLOM FORCES INDUS CIVMIL/REL

S60
KELLEY G.A.,"THE POLITICAL BACKGROUND OF THE FRENCH A-BOMB." EUR+WWI USSR FORCES TOP/EX TEC/DEV NUC/PWR ATTIT PWR...CONCPT OBS/ENVIR TREND 20. PAGE 84 H1686 — NAT/G RESPECT NAT/LISM FRANCE

B61
FULLER J.F.C.,THE CONDUCT OF WAR, 1789-1961. FRANCE RUSSIA SOCIETY NAT/G FORCES PROB/SOLV AGREE NUC/PWR WEAPON PEACE...SOC 18/20 TREATY COLD/WAR. PAGE 54 H1076 — WAR POLICY REV ROLE

B61
HARDT J.P.,THE COLD WAR ECONOMIC GAP. USA+45 USSR ECO/DEV FORCES INT/TRADE NUC/PWR PWR 20 COLD/WAR. PAGE 66 H1328 — DIPLOM ECO/TAC NAT/COMP POLICY

B61
KISSINGER H.A.,THE NECESSITY FOR CHOICE. FUT USA+45 ECO/UNDEV NAT/G PLAN BAL/PWR ECO/TAC ARMS/CONT DETER NUC/PWR ATTIT...POLICY CONCPT RECORD GEN/LAWS COLD/WAR 20. PAGE 87 H1728 — TOP/EX TREND DIPLOM

B61
SOKOL A.E.,SEAPOWER IN THE NUCLEAR AGE. USA+45 USSR DIST/IND FORCES INT/TRADE DETER WAR...POLICY NAT/COMP BIBLIOG COLD/WAR. PAGE 146 H2928 — SEA PWR WEAPON NUC/PWR

S61
SCHELLING T.C.,"NUCLEAR STRATEGY IN EUROPE." COM EUR+WWI USSR NAT/G FORCES NUC/PWR DRIVE ORD/FREE PWR...DECISION CONCPT OBS TREND HYPO/EXP 20. PAGE 139 H2784 — FUT COERCE ARMS/CONT WAR

B62
ABOSCH H.,THE MENACE OF THE MIRACLE: GERMANY FROM HITLER TO ADENAUER. EUR+WWI GERMANY/W CULTURE FORCES PRESS NUC/PWR WAR CHOOSE 20 HITLER/A ADENAUER/K. PAGE 3 H0057 — DIPLOM PEACE POLICY

B62
FRYKLUND R.,100 MILLION LIVES: MAXIMUM SURVIVAL IN A NUCLEAR WAR. USA+45 USSR CONTROL WEAPON ...IDEA/COMP NAT/COMP 20. PAGE 54 H1073 — NUC/PWR WAR PLAN DETER

B62
MORGENSTERN O.,STRATEGIE - HEUTE (2ND ED.). USA+45 USSR ECO/DEV DELIB/GP WAR PEACE ORD/FREE...GOV/COMP NAT/COMP 20 COLD/WAR NATO. PAGE 113 H2256 — NUC/PWR DIPLOM FORCES TEC/DEV

S62
STRACHEY J.,"COMMUNIST INTENTIONS." ASIA USSR YUGOSLAVIA INT/ORG NAT/G FORCES DOMIN EDU/PROP COERCE NUC/PWR NAT/LISM PEACE RIGID/FLEX PWR MARXISM...CONCPT MYTH OBS TIME/SEQ TREND COLD/WAR TOT/POP 20. PAGE 150 H2992 — COM ATTIT WAR

N62
US CONGRESS JT ATOM ENRGY COMM,PEACEFUL USES OF ATOMIC ENERGY, HEARING. USA+45 USSR TEC/DEV ATTIT RIGID/FLEX...TESTS CHARTS EXHIBIT METH/COMP 20 CONGRESS. PAGE 159 H3177 — NUC/PWR ACADEM SCHOOL NAT/COMP

B63
BROEKMEIJER M.W.,DEVELOPING COUNTRIES AND NATO. USSR FORCES DIPLOM NUC/PWR WAR PEACE TOTALISM 20 NATO. PAGE 21 H0427 — ECO/UNDEV FOR/AID ORD/FREE NAT/G

B63
US ATOMIC ENERGY COMMISSION,ATOMIC ENERGY IN THE SOVIET UNION: TRIP REPORT OF THE US ATOMIC ENERGY DELEGATION, MAY 1933. USSR R+D NAT/G CONSULT CREATE DIPLOM ADMIN ROUTINE EFFICIENCY PRODUC KNOWL SKILL ...NAT/COMP 20 AEC TRAVEL TREATY. PAGE 159 H3176 — METH/COMP OP/RES TEC/DEV NUC/PWR

S63
BECHHOEFER B.G.,"SOVIET ATTITUDE TOWARD DISARMAMENT." COM USSR NAT/G ACT/RES TEC/DEV NUC/PWR ATTIT DISPL RIGID/FLEX PWR...METH/CNCPT TREND GEN/LAWS COLD/WAR 20. PAGE 13 H0252 — FORCES EDU/PROP ARMS/CONT

B64
BELL C.,THE DEBATABLE ALLIANCE. COM UK USA+45 NAT/G FORCES PLAN BAL/PWR NUC/PWR WAR ATTIT...GOV/COMP 20. PAGE 13 H0263 — DIPLOM PWR PEACE POLICY

B64
BROWN N.,NUCLEAR WAR* THE IMPENDING STRATEGIC DEADLOCK. USA+45 USSR TEC/DEV BUDGET RISK ARMS/CONT NUC/PWR WEAPON COST BIO/SOC...GEOG IDEA/COMP NAT/COMP GAME NATO WARSAW/P. PAGE 22 H0448 — FORCES OP/RES WAR GEN/LAWS

B64
MILIBAND R.,THE SOCIALIST REGISTER: 1964. GERMANY/W ITALY UK LABOR POL/PAR ECO/TAC FOR/AID NUC/PWR ...POLICY SOCIALIST IDEA/COMP 20 MAO NASSER/G. PAGE 110 H2204 — MARXISM SOCISM CAP/ISM PROB/SOLV

B64
PITTMAN J.,PEACEFUL COEXISTENCE. USSR NAT/G NUC/PWR WAR ATTIT 20. PAGE 126 H2518 — DIPLOM PEACE POLICY FORCES

B64
WERNETTE J.P.,GOVERNMENT AND BUSINESS. LABOR CAP/ISM ECO/TAC INT/TRADE TAX ADMIN AUTOMAT NUC/PWR CIVMIL/REL DEMAND...MGT 20 MONOPOLY. PAGE 167 H3333 — NAT/G FINAN ECO/DEV CONTROL

S64
GOLDBERG A.,"THE MILITARY ORIGINS OF THE BRITISH NUCLEAR DETERRENT." EUR+WWI ECO/DEV NAT/G PLAN NUC/PWR ATTIT PWR...DECISION HIST/WRIT COLD/WAR 20. PAGE 58 H1156 — FORCES CONCPT DETER UK

S64
POWELL R.L.,"COMMUNIST CHINA'S MILITARY POTENTIAL." ASIA CHINA/COM NAT/G EX/STRUC EDU/PROP COERCE GUERRILLA NUC/PWR WAR...RECORD CON/ANAL 20. PAGE 128 H2551 — FORCES PWR

B65
GRETTON P.,MARITIME STRATEGY - A STUDY OF DEFENSE PROBLEMS. ASIA UK USSR DIPLOM COERCE DETER NUC/PWR WEAPON...CONCPT NAT/COMP 20. PAGE 60 H1211 — FORCES PLAN WAR SEA

B65
HALPERIN M.H.,COMMUNIST CHINA AND ARMS CONTROL. CHINA/COM FUT USA+45 CULTURE FORCES TEC/DEV ECO/TAC WAR PEACE ORD/FREE MARXISM 20 COLD/WAR. PAGE 64 H1292 — ATTIT POLICY ARMS/CONT NUC/PWR

B65
UN,SPACE ACTIVITIES AND RESOURCES: REVIEW OF UNITED NATION'S NATIONAL AND INTERNATIONAL PROGRAMS. INT/ORG LABOR PLAN TEC/DEV DIPLOM EFFICIENCY HEALTH ...GOV/COMP 20 UN. PAGE 158 H3155 — SPACE NUC/PWR FOR/AID PEACE

B65
US DEPARTMENT OF DEFENSE,US SECURITY ARMS CONTROL, AND DISARMAMENT 1961-1965 (PAMPHLET). CHINA/COM COM GERMANY/W ISRAEL SPACE USA+45 USSR WOR+45 FORCES EDU/PROP DETER EQUILIB PEACE ALL/VALS...GOV/COMP 20 NATO. PAGE 159 H3183 — BIBLIOG/A ARMS/CONT NUC/PWR DIPLOM

S65
BIRNBAUM K.,"SWEDEN'S NUCLEAR POLICY." WOR+45 POL/PAR CREATE TEC/DEV NEUTRAL RISK WAR ORD/FREE ...DECISION IDEA/COMP NAT/COMP TIME. PAGE 17 H0343 — SWEDEN NUC/PWR DIPLOM ARMS/CONT

S65
GRIFFITH S.B.,"COMMUNIST CHINA'S CAPACITY TO MAKE WAR." CHINA/COM COM NAT/G TOP/EX PLAN DOMIN COERCE NUC/PWR ATTIT RESPECT SKILL...CONCPT MYTH TIME/SEQ TREND COLD/WAR 20. PAGE 61 H1221 — FORCES PWR WEAPON ASIA

S65
LAULICHT J.,"PUBLIC OPINION AND FOREIGN POLICY DECISIONS." CANADA ELITES NAT/G FOR/AID LEAD NUC/PWR PERCEPT...INT QU CHARTS UN COLD/WAR. PAGE 92 H1839
DIPLOM ATTIT CON/ANAL SAMP

B66
DAENIKER G.,STRATEGIE DES KLEIN STAATS. SWITZERLND ACT/RES CREATE DIPLOM NEUTRAL DETER WAR WEAPON PWR SOVEREIGN...IDEA/COMP 20 COLD/WAR. PAGE 36 H0730
NUC/PWR PLAN FORCES NAT/G

B66
GRAHAM I.C.C.,PUBLICATIONS OF THE SOCIAL SCIENCE DEPARTMENT, THE RAND CORPORATION, 1948-1966. USSR WOR+45 NAT/G ARMS/CONT DETER WAR NAT/LISM...SOC GOV/COMP. PAGE 60 H1192
BIBLIOG DIPLOM NUC/PWR FORCES

B66
US DEPARTMENT OF THE ARMY,COMMUNIST CHINA: A STRATEGIC SURVEY: A BIBLIOGRAPHY (PAMPHLET NO. 20-67). CHINA/COM COM INDIA USSR NAT/G POL/PAR EX/STRUC FORCES NUC/PWR REV ATTIT...POLICY GEOG CHARTS. PAGE 160 H3194
BIBLIOG/A MARXISM S/ASIA DIPLOM

B66
ZABLOCKI C.J.,SINO-SOVIET RIVALRY. AFR ASIA CHINA/COM CUBA EUR+WWI L/A+17C USA+45 USSR WOR+45 POL/PAR FORCES COERCE NUC/PWR...GOV/COMP IDEA/COMP 20 MAO KHRUSH/N. PAGE 172 H3444
DIPLOM MARXISM COM

L66
ZOPPO C.E.,"NUCLEAR TECHNOLOGY, MULTIPOLARITY, AND INTERNATIONAL STABILITY." ASIA RUSSIA USA+45 STRUCT TOP/EX BAL/PWR DIPLOM DETER CIVMIL/REL NAT/COMP. PAGE 173 H3464
NET/THEORY ORD/FREE DECISION NUC/PWR

S66
QUESTER G.H.,"ON THE IDENTIFICATION OF REAL AND PRETENDED COMMUNIST MILITARY DOCTRINE." ASIA USSR DETER WAR ATTIT DRIVE HEALTH TIME/SEQ. PAGE 129 H2574
RATIONAL PERCEPT NUC/PWR NAT/COMP

B67
AMERICAN FRIENDS SERVICE COMM,IN PLACE OF WAR. NAT/G ACT/RES DIPLOM ADMIN NUC/PWR EFFICIENCY ...POLICY 20. PAGE 6 H0122
PEACE PACIFISM WAR DETER

B67
KAROL K.S.,CHINA, THE OTHER COMMUNISM (TRANS. BY TOM BAISTOW). CHINA/COM CULTURE INDUS FORCES DIPLOM EDU/PROP CONTROL EXEC NUC/PWR ATTIT...SOC CHARTS 20. PAGE 83 H1663
NAT/G POL/PAR MARXISM INGP/REL

B67
MCCLINTOCK R.,THE MEANING OF LIMITED WAR. FUT WOR+45 NAT/G FORCES GUERRILLA REV...POLICY SAMP/SIZ TREND NAT/COMP 45 COLD/WAR. PAGE 106 H2126
WAR NUC/PWR BAL/PWR DIPLOM

B67
POGANY A.H.,POLITICAL SCIENCE AND INTERNATIONAL RELATIONS, BOOKS RECOMMENDED FOR AMERICAN CATHOLIC COLLEGE LIBRARIES. INT/ORG LOC/G NAT/G FORCES BAL/PWR ECO/TAC NUC/PWR...CATH INT/LAW TREATY 20. PAGE 127 H2532
BIBLIOG DIPLOM

B67
REES D.,THE AGE OF CONTAINMENT. WOR+45 FORCES ARMS/CONT ATTIT PWR...CONCPT TREND METH/COMP BIBLIOG/A 20. PAGE 130 H2608
DIPLOM NUC/PWR MARXISM GOV/COMP

B67
ROWLAND J.,A HISTORY OF SINO-INDIAN RELATIONS; HOSTILE CO-EXISTENCE. ASIA CHINA/COM INDIA NAT/G NUC/PWR PWR WEALTH...GEOG BIBLIOG 13/20 COLD/WAR. PAGE 135 H2704
DIPLOM CENSUS IDEA/COMP

L67
ROBINSON T.W.,"A NATIONAL INTEREST ANALYSIS OF SINO-SOVIET RELATIONS." CHINA/COM USSR NAT/G NUC/PWR ATTIT PWR...CONCPT CHARTS 20. PAGE 132 H2650
MARXISM DIPLOM SOVEREIGN GEN/LAWS

S67
CHIU S.M.,"CHINA'S MILITARY POSTURE." CHINA/COM ELITES NAT/G POL/PAR TEC/DEV ECO/TAC DOMIN CONTROL LEAD REV MARXISM 20 MAO. PAGE 30 H0595
FORCES CIVMIL/REL NUC/PWR DIPLOM

S67
JAIN G.,"INDIA REJECTS THE POWER RACE* REALISM ABOUT NUCLEAR WEAPONS." FORCES PROB/SOLV FOR/AID ARMS/CONT COST PWR...GOV/COMP 20. PAGE 79 H1583
INDIA CHINA/COM NUC/PWR DIPLOM

S67
LALL B.G.,"GAPS IN THE ABM DEBATE." NAT/G DIPLOM DETER CIVMIL/REL 20. PAGE 90 H1798
NUC/PWR ARMS/CONT EX/STRUC FORCES

S67
MENDL W.,"FRENCH ATTITUDES ON DISARMAMENT." FRANCE CULTURE CHIEF FORCES DIPLOM LEAD WAR...TIME/SEQ 20 DEGAULLE/C. PAGE 109 H2175
NUC/PWR WEAPON ARMS/CONT POLICY

S67
NIEBUHR R.,"THE ETHICS OF WAR AND PEACE IN THE NUCLEAR AGE." VIETNAM INTELL CONFER CONTROL WAR GOV/REL PERS/REL ORD/FREE...POLICY INT GOV/COMP NAT/COMP 20 UN. PAGE 118 H2360
MORAL PEACE NUC/PWR DIPLOM

S67
OJHA I.C.,"CHINA'S CAUTIOUS AMERICAN POLICY." CHINA/COM VIETNAM NAT/G NUC/PWR PEACE 20. PAGE 121 H2411
DIPLOM POLICY WAR DECISION

S67
ROOT W.,"REPORT FROM PARIS - DE GAULLE: WHICH WAY TO THE FUTURE?" CANADA FRANCE ISLAM UK INT/ORG CHIEF CREATE AGREE CONTROL ARMS/CONT NUC/PWR EQUILIB PEACE PWR 20 DEGAULLE/C NATO. PAGE 134 H2670
POLICY DIPLOM NAT/G BAL/PWR

NUCLEAR POWER....SEE NUC/PWR

NUCLEAR WAR....SEE NUC/PWR+COERCE, WAR

NUGENT J.B. H2379

NUMELIN R. H2380

NUMERICAL INDICES....SEE INDEX

NUREMBERG....NUREMBERG WAR TRIALS

NYASALAND....SEE MALAWI

B65
WALKER A.A.,THE RHODESIAS AND NYASALAND: A GUIDE TO OFFICIAL PUBLICATIONS. RHODESIA UK OP/RES PLAN PROB/SOLV DIPLOM...POLICY SOC CON/ANAL 19/20 NYASALAND. PAGE 164 H3291
BIBLIOG NAT/G COLONIAL AFR

B67
WILLS A.J.,AN INTRODUCTION TO THE HISTORY OF CENTRAL AFRICA. RHODESIA ZAMBIA CULTURE SOCIETY ECO/UNDEV TEC/DEV DOMIN WAR ALL/VALS...POLICY TREND BIBLIOG T 14/20 NYASALAND. PAGE 169 H3375
AFR COLONIAL ORD/FREE

NYATURU....NYATURU, A TRIBE OF TANGANYIKA

NYC....NEW YORK CITY

NYE J. H2381

NYE J.S. H2382

NYERERE J.K. H2383

O

O'BRIEN F. H2384

O'BRIEN W.V. H2385,H2386

O'CONNELL J. H0684

O'CONNELL M.R. H2387

O'HEARN P.J.T. H2388

O'LEARY T.J. H2389

O'NEILL C.E. H2390

O'NEILL R.J. H2391

OAKESHOTT M. H2392

OAS....ORGANIZATION OF AMERICAN STATES; SEE ALSO INT/ORG, VOL/ASSN

B58
PAN AMERICAN UNION,REPERTORIO DE PUBLICACIONES PERIODICAS ACTUALES LATINO-AMERICANAS. CULTURE ECO/UNDEV ADMIN LEAD GOV/REL 20 OAS. PAGE 123 H2455
BIBLIOG L/A+17C NAT/G DIPLOM

B59
PANAMERICAN UNION,PUBLICATIONS: PAU AND OFFICIAL RECORDS OF THE OAS, IN ENGLISH, SPANISH, PORTUGUESE, AND FRENCH, 1958-59. NAT/G ATTIT...SOC 20 OAS. PAGE 123 H2456
BIBLIOG L/A+17C INT/LAW DIPLOM

S59
PLAZA G.,"FOR A REGIONAL MARKET IN LATIN AMERICA." FUT L/A+17C CULTURE INDUS NAT/G ECO/TAC INT/TRADE ATTIT WEALTH...NEW/IDEA TREND OAS 20. PAGE 126 H2527
MARKET INT/ORG REGION

S60
"THE EMERGING COMMON MARKETS IN LATIN AMERICA." FUT L/A+17C STRATA DIST/IND INDUS LABOR NAT/G LEGIS ECO/TAC ADMIN RIGID/FLEX HEALTH...NEW/IDEA TIME/SEQ OAS 20. PAGE 2 H0038
FINAN ECO/UNDEV INT/TRADE

S60
FITZGIBBON R.H.,"DICTATORSHIP AND DEMOCRACY IN LATIN AMERICA." FUT ECO/DEV ECO/UNDEV INT/ORG LOC/G NAT/G TOP/EX PLAN TEC/DEV ECO/TAC CHOOSE ATTIT DRIVE PERSON ALL/VALS OAS TOT/POP 20. PAGE 51 H1019
L/A+17C ACT/RES INT/TRADE

B61
GUEVARA E.,GUERRILLA WARFARE. L/A+17C ECO/UNDEV
FORCES

NAT/G POL/PAR VOL/ASSN PLAN DOMIN REV DRIVE PWR WEALTH...NEW/IDEA RECORD BIOG COLD/WAR MARX/KARL OAS 20. PAGE 62 H1247 COERCE GUERRILLA CUBA

S61
FITZGIBBON R.H.,"MEASUREMENT OF LATIN AMERICAN POLITICAL CHANGE." L/A+17C CONSTN CULTURE SOCIETY ECO/UNDEV NAT/G POL/PAR PUB/INST ACT/RES EDU/PROP PERCEPT KNOWL ORD/FREE SOVEREIGN...METH/CNCPT TREND OAS 20. PAGE 51 H1020 CHOOSE ATTIT

B62
DE MADARIAGA S.,L'AMERIQUE LATINE ENTRE L'OURS ET L'AIGLE. L/A+17C SOCIETY NAT/G ECO/TAC EDU/PROP REGION COERCE ATTIT ALL/VALS...MAJORIT TIME/SEQ STERTYP COLD/WAR OAS 20. PAGE 38 H0760 POL/PAR ECO/UNDEV

S62
HYDE D.,"COMMUNISM IN LATIN AMERICA." L/A+17C ECO/DEV NAT/G SECT EDU/PROP ATTIT ALL/VALS MARXISM ...SOC CONCPT TOT/POP COLD/WAR OAS 20. PAGE 76 H1515 COM POL/PAR REV

B63
RONNING C.N.,LAW AND POLITICS IN INTER-AMERICAN DIPLOMACY. L/A+17C ECO/UNDEV NAT/G CONSULT DELIB/GP CREATE CAP/ISM ECO/TAC LEGIT REGION RIGID/FLEX ...METH/CNCPT GEN/LAWS OAS 20. PAGE 133 H2668 VOL/ASSN ALL/VALS DIPLOM

S63
WELLS H.,"THE OAS AND THE DOMINICAN ELECTIONS." L/A+17C INT/ORG NAT/G POL/PAR TEC/DEV ECO/TAC EDU/PROP PERCEPT...TIME/SEQ OAS TOT/POP 20. PAGE 166 H3332 CONSULT CHOOSE DOMIN/REP

B65
AIR UNIVERSITY LIBRARY,LATIN AMERICA, SELECTED REFERENCES. ECO/UNDEV FORCES EDU/PROP MARXISM 20 OAS. PAGE 4 H0084 BIBLIOG L/A+17C NAT/G DIPLOM

B65
SLATER J.,A REVALUATION OF COLLECTIVE SECURITY* THE OAS IN ACTION. L/A+17C USA+45 NAT/G ADMIN COERCE ORD/FREE PWR...GOV/COMP IDEA/COMP GEN/LAWS OAS. PAGE 145 H2899 REGION INT/ORG FORCES

S65
PLANK J.N.,"THE CARIBBEAN* INTERVENTION, WHEN AND HOW." CUBA GUATEMALA HAITI PANAMA USA+45 VENEZUELA FORCES PROB/SOLV RISK COERCE...NAT/COMP OAS TIME. PAGE 126 H2521 SOVEREIGN MARXISM REV

B66
US DEPARTMENT OF STATE,RESEARCH ON THE AMERICAN REPUBLICS (EXTERNAL RESEARCH LIST NO 6-25). CULTURE SOCIETY POL/PAR DIPLOM EDU/PROP MARXISM WORSHIP 20 OAS. PAGE 159 H3189 BIBLIOG/A L/A+17C REGION NAT/G

B67
BURR R.N.,OUR TROUBLED HEMISPHERE: PERSPECTIVES ON UNITED STATES-LATIN AMERICAN RELATIONS. L/A+17C USA+45 USA-45 INT/ORG FOR/AID COLONIAL PWR 19/20 OAS. PAGE 25 H0493 DIPLOM NAT/COMP NAT/G POLICY

B67
PLANK J.,CUBA AND THE UNITED STATES: LONG RANGE PERSPECTIVES. CUBA L/A+17C USSR ECO/UNDEV NAT/G FORCES ECO/TAC INT/TRADE AGREE REV...PREDICT TREND ANTHOL 20 CASTRO/F COLD/WAR OAS. PAGE 126 H2520 DIPLOM

OATMAN M.E. H0348

OAU....ORGANIZATION FOR AFRICAN UNITY

N19
PROVISIONS SECTION OAU,ORGANIZATION OF AFRICAN UNITY: BASIC DOCUMENTS AND RESOLUTIONS (PAMPHLET). AFR CULTURE ECO/UNDEV DIPLOM ECO/TAC EDU/PROP COLONIAL ARMS/CONT NUC/PWR RACE/REL DISCRIM NAT/LISM 20 UN OAU. PAGE 128 H2564 CONSTN EX/STRUC SOVEREIGN INT/ORG

B65
NYE J.S. JR.,PAN-AFRICANISM AND EAST AFRICAN INTEGRATION. TANZANIA UGANDA STRUCT ECO/UNDEV NAT/G DIPLOM FEDERAL NAT/LISM...STAT SOC/EXP BIBLIOG EEC OAU. PAGE 119 H2382 REGION ATTIT GEN/LAWS AFR

L67
TOUVAL S.,"THE ORGANIZATION OF AFRICAN UNITY AND AFRICAN BORDERS." DEBATE REGION TASK REV ATTIT ORD/FREE...DECISION UN 20 OAU. PAGE 156 H3121 AFR NAT/G COLONIAL NAT/LISM

S67
ZARTMAN I.W.," NAT/G POL/PAR VOL/ASSN NAT/LISM ORD/FREE PWR...CONCPT NAT/COMP ORG/CHARTS OAU MAGHREB. PAGE 172 H3451 AFR ISLAM DIPLOM REGION

OAU PROVISIONS SECTION H2564

OBERLIN....OBERLIN, OHIO

OBESITY....SEE HEALTH, EATING

OBJECTIVE....OBJECTIVE, OBJECTIVITY

B56
WEBER M.,WIRTSCHAFT UND GESELLSCHAFT (2ND VOL.). STRUCT NAT/G POL/PAR LEAD PWR OBJECTIVE IDEA/COMP. PAGE 166 H3321 LEGIT JURID SOC

S60
WOLFINGER R.E.,"REPUTATION AND REALITY IN THE STUDY OF COMMUNITY POWER." STRUCT PROB/SOLV INGP/REL ATTIT OBJECTIVE...SOC METH/CNCPT PERS/COMP. PAGE 170 H3404 CULTURE MUNIC DOMIN PWR

B63
DE JOUVENEL B.,THE PURE THEORY OF POLITICS. NAT/G DIPLOM CONTROL GP/REL PERS/REL PERSON PWR OBJECTIVE CONCPT. PAGE 38 H0758 GEN/LAWS SOCIETY METH/CNCPT

B66
HATTICH M.,NATIONALBEWUSSTSEIN UND STAATSBEWUSSTSEIN IN DER PLURALISTISCHEN GESELLSCHAFT. GERMANY GP/REL ATTIT SOVEREIGN SOC/INTEG 20. PAGE 68 H1356 NAT/G NAT/LISM SOCIETY OBJECTIVE

S67
KROGER K.,"ZUR ENTWICKLUNG DER STAATSZWECKLEHRE IM 19 JAHRHUNDERT." GERMANY RATIONAL ATTIT...IDEA/COMP 19. PAGE 89 H1773 CONCPT NAT/G JURID OBJECTIVE

S68
HOOK S.,"THE ENLIGHTENMENT AND MARXISM." CULTURE SOCIETY RATIONAL ORD/FREE PLURISM SOCISM...CONCPT HIST/WRIT 18/19 MARX/KARL HEGEL/GWF ENLIGHTNMT. PAGE 73 H1462 IDEA/COMP MARXISM OBJECTIVE

OBLIGATION....SEE SUPEGO

OBS....OBSERVATION; SEE ALSO DIRECT OBSERVATION METHOD INDEX, P. XIV

B00
MARKHAM V.R.,SOUTH AFRICA, PAST AND PRESENT. NETHERLAND SOUTH/AFR CULTURE LEGIS EDU/PROP COLONIAL CHOOSE REPRESENT DISCRIM ATTIT...OBS TIME/SEQ 17/19 NEGRO BOER/WAR. PAGE 103 H2054 WAR LEAD RACE/REL

B00
VOLPICELLI Z.,RUSSIA ON THE PACIFIC AND THE SIBERIAN RAILWAY. MOD/EUR ECO/UNDEV INT/ORG FORCES PLAN DOMIN COLONIAL ROUTINE ATTIT ALL/VALS...OBS HIST/WRIT TIME/SEQ TREND CON/ANAL AUD/VIS CHARTS 18/19. PAGE 163 H3261 NAT/G ACT/RES RUSSIA

B04
REED W.A.,ETHNOLOGICAL SURVEY PUBLICATIONS (VOL. II). PHILIPPINE STRUCT INDUS SECT DEATH LEISURE HABITAT...AUD/VIS CHARTS WORSHIP 20 NABOLOI NEGRITO BATAK. PAGE 130 H2607 CULTURE SOCIETY SOC OBS

B05
PHILIPPINE ISLANDS BUREAU SCI,ETHNOLOGICAL SURVEY: THE BONTOC IGOROT. ECO/UNDEV AGRI FAM MARRIAGE HEALTH WEALTH...LING OBS AUD/VIS CHARTS WORSHIP 20 LUZON BONTOC. PAGE 125 H2500 CULTURE INGP/REL KIN STRUCT

B11
PHILLIPSON C.,THE INTERNATIONAL LAW AND CUSTOM OF ANCIENT GREECE AND ROME. MEDIT-7 UNIV INTELL SOCIETY STRUCT NAT/G LEGIS EXEC PERSON...CONCPT OBS CON/ANAL ROM/EMP. PAGE 125 H2504 INT/ORG LAW INT/LAW

B15
MICHELS R.,POLITICAL PARTIES. NAT/G BAL/PWR CHOOSE REPRESENT ATTIT SOCISM...PSY SOC CONCPT OBS 20 MONOPOLY. PAGE 110 H2198 POL/PAR CENTRAL LEAD PWR

B20
WEBB S.,INDUSTRIAL DEMOCRACY. UK PARTIC GP/REL ...SOC OBS RECORD CHARTS 18/20. PAGE 166 H3317 LABOR NAT/G VOL/ASSN MAJORIT

B21
STUART G.H.,FRENCH FOREIGN POLICY. CONSTN INT/ORG NAT/G POL/PAR EX/STRUC FORCES PLAN ECO/TAC DOMIN EDU/PROP ADJUD COERCE ATTIT DRIVE RIGID/FLEX ALL/VALS...POLICY OBS RECORD BIOG TIME/SEQ TREND. PAGE 150 H3000 MOD/EUR DIPLOM FRANCE

B29
ROBERTS S.H.,HISTORY OF FRENCH COLONIAL POLICY. AFR ASIA L/A+17C S/ASIA CULTURE ECO/DEV ECO/UNDEV FINAN NAT/G PLAN ECO/TAC DOMIN ROUTINE SOVEREIGN...OBS HIST/WRIT TREND CHARTS VAL/FREE 19/20. PAGE 132 H2642 INT/ORG ACT/RES FRANCE COLONIAL

B36
CULVER D.C.,METHODOLOGY OF SOCIAL SCIENCE RESEARCH: A BIBLIOGRAPHY. LAW CULTURE...CRIMLGY GEOG STAT OBS INT QU HIST/WRIT CHARTS 20. PAGE 36 H0719 BIBLIOG/A METH SOC

B37
PARSONS T.,THE STRUCTURE OF SOCIAL ACTION. UNIV INTELL SOCIETY INDUS MARKET ECO/TAC ROUTINE CHOOSE ALL/VALS...CONCPT OBS BIOG TREND GEN/LAWS 20. PAGE 124 H2471 CULTURE ATTIT CAP/ISM

B39
FIRTH R.,PRIMITIVE POLYNESIAN ECONOMY. SOCIETY DIST/IND SECT CHIEF CAP/ISM PRODUC WEALTH...SOC OBS METH WORSHIP 20 POLYNESIA. PAGE 50 H1007 ECO/UNDEV CULTURE AGRI ECO/TAC

B47
CROCKER W.R.,ON GOVERNING COLONIES: BEING AN OUTLINE OF THE REAL ISSUES AND A COMPARISON OF THE BRITISH, FRENCH, AND BELGIAN... AFR BELGIUM FRANCE COLONIAL POLICY GOV/COMP

UK CULTURE SOVEREIGN...OBS 20. PAGE 35 H0705 ADMIN

B47
JURJI E.J.,THE GREAT RELIGIONS OF THE MODERN WORLD. CULTURE INTELL SOCIETY INT/ORG CONSULT CHOOSE ATTIT DRIVE PERSON RIGID/FLEX...HUM CONCPT OBS BIOG HIST/WRIT TREND GEN/LAWS 20 WORSHIP. PAGE 82 H1643 UNIV SECT

B48
EDUARDO O.D.C.,THE NEGRO IN NORTHERN BRAZIL: A STUDY IN ACCULTURATION. BRAZIL ECO/UNDEV FAM SECT PAY REGION HABITAT CATHISM MYSTISM...GEOG OBS SOC/INTEG WORSHIP 20 NEGRO MARANHAO. PAGE 44 H0890 CULTURE ADJUST GP/REL

B48
FURNIVAL J.,COLONIAL POLICY AND PRACTICE A COMPARATIVE STUDY OF BURMA, AND NETHERLANDS INDIA. BURMA INDONESIA S/ASIA...GEOG OBS GOV/COMP METH/COMP 20. PAGE 54 H1080 COLONIAL NAT/LISM WEALTH SOVEREIGN

B48
MAUGHAM R.,NORTH AFRICAN NOTEBOOK. ALGERIA ISLAM LIBYA MOROCCO STRUCT ECO/UNDEV COLONIAL...SOC OBS AUD/VIS NAT/COMP WORSHIP 20 TUNIS. PAGE 105 H2102 SOCIETY RECORD NAT/LISM

S48
ALEXANDER L.,"WAR CRIMES, THEIR SOCIAL-PSYCHOLOGICAL ASPECTS." EUR+WWI GERMANY LAW CULTURE ELITES KIN POL/PAR PUB/INST FORCES DOMIN EDU/PROP COERCE CRIME ATTIT SUPEGO HEALTH MORAL PWR FASCISM ...PSY OBS TREND GEN/LAWS NAZI 20. PAGE 5 H0100 DRIVE WAR

B49
SARGENT S.S.,CULTURE AND PERSONALITY. FUT UNIV SOCIETY FAM KIN NEIGH BIO/SOC DRIVE PERCEPT RIGID/FLEX LOVE RESPECT...PSY SOC CONCPT OBS TIME/SEQ TREND CON/ANAL CHARTS HYPO/EXP SIMUL TOT/POP. PAGE 138 H2754 CULTURE PERSON

B50
CANTRIL H.,TENSIONS THAT CAUSE WAR. UNIV CULTURE R+D CREATE EDU/PROP DRIVE PERSON KNOWL ORD/FREE ...HUM PSY SOC OBS CENSUS TREND CON/ANAL SOC/EXP SIMUL GEN/METH ANTHOL COLD/WAR TOT/POP. PAGE 26 H0523 SOCIETY PHIL/SCI PEACE

B50
MACIVER R.M.,GREAT EXPRESSIONS OF HUMAN RIGHTS. LAW CONSTN CULTURE INTELL SOCIETY R+D INT/ORG ATTIT DRIVE...JURID OBS HIST/WRIT GEN/LAWS. PAGE 100 H1999 UNIV CONCPT

B50
ROHEIM G.,PSYCHOANALYSIS AND ANTHROPOLOGY. UNIV FAM PERS/REL ATTIT HABITAT...SOC OBS WORSHIP. PAGE 133 H2663 PSY BIOG CULTURE PERSON

B52
FORDE L.D.,HABITAT, ECONOMY AND SOCIETY. AFR L/A+17C S/ASIA STRUCT AGRI INGP/REL...GEOG OBS BIBLIOG 20. PAGE 52 H1037 SOC HABITAT CULTURE ECO/UNDEV

B52
ULAM A.B.,TITOISM AND THE COMINFORM. USSR WOR+45 STRUCT INT/ORG NAT/G ACT/RES PLAN EXEC ATTIT DRIVE ALL/VALS...CONCPT OBS VAL/FREE 20 COMINTERN TITO/MARSH. PAGE 157 H3149 COM POL/PAR TOTALISM YUGOSLAVIA

S52
EISENSTADT S.N.,"THE PROCESS OF ABSORPTION OF NEW IMMIGRANTS IN ISRAEL" (BMR)" ISRAEL CULTURE SCHOOL WORKER PARTIC DRIVE ORD/FREE...STAT OBS INT CHARTS SOC/INTEG 20 JEWS. PAGE 45 H0900 HABITAT ATTIT SAMP

S52
KECSKEMETI P.,"THE 'POLICY SCIENCES': ASPIRATION AND OUTLOOK." UNIV CULTURE INTELL SOCIETY STRUCT EDU/PROP ATTIT PERCEPT RIGID/FLEX KNOWL...PHIL/SCI METH/CNCPT OBS 20. PAGE 84 H1674 CREATE NEW/IDEA

B53
BIDNEY D.,THEORETICAL ANTHROPOLOGY. DRIVE ROLE ORD/FREE...CONCPT METH/CNCPT MYTH CLASSIF OBS IDEA/COMP METH/COMP BIBLIOG METH 20. PAGE 17 H0331 CULTURE SOC PSY PHIL/SCI

B53
LEITES N.,A STUDY OF BOLSHEVISM. WOR+45 WOR-45 ELITES SOCIETY INT/ORG NAT/G EX/STRUC EDU/PROP EXEC ROUTINE ATTIT MORAL MARXISM...CONCPT OBS VAL/FREE 20. PAGE 94 H1869 COM POL/PAR USSR TOTALISM

B53
WAGLEY C.,AMAZON TOWN: A STUDY OF MAN IN THE TROPICS. BRAZIL L/A+17C STRATA STRUCT ECO/UNDEV AGRI EX/STRUC RACE/REL DISCRIM HABITAT WEALTH...OBS SOC/EXP 20. PAGE 164 H3285 SOC NEIGH CULTURE INGP/REL

B54
FORDE C.D.,AFRICAN WORLDS. AFR CULTURE ROUTINE GP/REL PERS/REL ATTIT DRIVE ALL/VALS...OBS ANTHOL WORSHIP 20. PAGE 52 H1036 SOCIETY KIN SOC

B54
MALINOWSKI B.,MAGIC, SCIENCE AND RELIGION. AGRI KIN GP/REL ALL/VALS...MYTH OBS RECORD IDEA/COMP WORSHIP 20 NEW/GUINEA. PAGE 102 H2031 CULTURE ATTIT SOC

L54
FURNISS E.S.,"WEAKNESSES IN FRENCH FOREIGN POLICY-MAKING." EUR+WWI LEGIS LEGIT EXEC ATTIT RIGID/FLEX ORD/FREE...SOC CONCPT METH/CNCPT OBS 20. PAGE 54 H1078 NAT/G STRUCT DIPLOM FRANCE

B55
ALFIERI D.,DICTATORS FACE TO FACE. NAT/G TOP/EX DIPLOM EXEC COERCE ORD/FREE FASCISM...POLICY OBS 20 HITLER/A MUSSOLIN/B. PAGE 5 H0103 WAR CHIEF TOTALISM PERS/REL

B55
POLLOCK J.K.,GERMAN DEMOCRACY AT WORK. GERMANY/W LOC/G NAT/G DIPLOM PARL/PROC...OBS IDEA/COMP 20. PAGE 127 H2539 PARTIC POL/PAR CHOOSE EDU/PROP

L55
ROSTOW W.W.,"RUSSIA AND CHINA UNDER COMMUNISM." CHINA/COM USSR INTELL STRUCT INT/ORG NAT/G POL/PAR TOP/EX ACT/RES PLAN ADMIN ATTIT ALL/VALS MARXISM ...CONCPT OBS TIME/SEQ TREND GOV/COMP VAL/FREE 20. PAGE 134 H2689 COM ASIA

B56
GOFFMAN E.,THE PRESENTATION OF SELF IN EVERYDAY LIFE. CULTURE INGP/REL ATTIT DRIVE...SOC OBS RECORD 20. PAGE 58 H1154 PERS/COMP PERSON PERCEPT ROLE

B56
INTERNATIONAL AFRICAN INST,SOCIAL IMPLICATIONS OF INDUSTRIALIZATION AND URBANIZATION IN AFRICA SOUTH OF THE SAHARA. SOUTH/AFR INDUS LABOR MUNIC WORKER TEC/DEV...SOC OBS TREND ANTHOL 20. PAGE 77 H1549 AFR ECO/UNDEV ADJUST CULTURE

B56
MANNONI D.O.,PROSPERO AND CALIBAN: THE PSYCHOLOGY OF COLONIZATION. AFR EUR+WWI FAM KIN MUNIC SECT DOMIN ADMIN ATTIT DRIVE LOVE PWR RESPECT...PSY SOC CONCPT MYTH OBS DEEP/INT BIOG GEN/METH MALAGASY 20. PAGE 102 H2040 CULTURE COLONIAL

S56
KHAMA T.,"POLITICAL CHANGE IN AFRICAN SOCIETY." CONSTN SOCIETY LOC/G NAT/G POL/PAR EX/STRUC LEGIS LEGIT ADMIN CHOOSE REPRESENT NAT/LISM MORAL ORD/FREE PWR...CONCPT OBS TREND GEN/METH CMN/WLTH 17/20. PAGE 85 H1706 AFR ELITES

B57
ARON R.,L'UNIFICATION ECONOMIQUE DE L'EUROPE. EUR+WWI SWITZERLND UK INT/ORG NAT/G REGION NAT/LISM ORD/FREE PWR...CONCPT METH/CNCPT OBS TREND STERTYP GEN/LAWS EEC 20. PAGE 8 H0168 VOL/ASSN ECO/TAC

B57
KOENTJARANINGRAT R.,A PRELIMINARY DESCRIPTION OF THE JAVANESE KINSHIP SYSTEM. INDONESIA STRATA FAM INGP/REL ADJUST MARRIAGE AGE/C AGE/Y AGE/A PERSON ...OBS CHARTS DICTIONARY 20 JAVA. PAGE 87 H1736 KIN STRUCT ELITES CULTURE

B57
PIDDINGTON R.,AN INTRODUCTION TO SOCIAL ANTHROPOLOGY (VOL. II). SOCIETY STRUCT FAM INGP/REL ...OBS CHARTS. PAGE 125 H2507 CULTURE SOC TEC/DEV GEOG

S57
HAILEY,"TOMORROW IN AFRICA." CONSTN SOCIETY LOC/G NAT/G DOMIN ADJUD ADMIN GP/REL DISCRIM NAT/LISM ATTIT MORAL ORD/FREE...PSY SOC CONCPT OBS RECORD TREND GEN/LAWS CMN/WLTH 20. PAGE 64 H1277 AFR PERSON ELITES RACE/REL

S57
KILSON M.L.,"LAND AND POLITICS IN KENYA: AN ANALYSIS OF AFRICAN POLITICS IN A PLURAL SOCIETY." FUT LAW CULTURE KIN NAT/G ECO/TAC DOMIN REV NAT/LISM ORD/FREE PWR RESPECT SOVEREIGN WEALTH ...SOC OBS TREND WORK VAL/FREE CMN/WLTH 20. PAGE 86 H1710 AFR ECO/UNDEV

B58
KINTNER W.R.,ORGANIZING FOR CONFLICT: A PROPOSAL. USSR STRUCT NAT/G LEGIS ADMIN EXEC PEACE ORD/FREE PWR...CONCPT OBS TREND NAT/COMP VAL/FREE COLD/WAR 20. PAGE 86 H1719 USA+45 PLAN DIPLOM

B58
LERNER D.,THE PASSING OF TRADITIONAL SOCIETY: MODERNIZING THE MIDDLE EAST. IRAN ISLAM LEBANON SYRIA TURKEY UAR CULTURE INTELL STRATA KIN NAT/G NEIGH SECT EDU/PROP ATTIT PERSON...MYTH OBS 20. PAGE 95 H1888 ECO/UNDEV RIGID/FLEX

B58
STUBEL H.,THE MEWU FANTZU. CHINA/COM INDIA EDU/PROP ADJUD CRIME GP/REL OWN...OBS 20 TIBET. PAGE 150 H3001 CULTURE STRUCT SECT FAM

B58
VON FURER-HAIMEN E.,AN ANTHROPOLOGICAL BIBLIOGRAPHY OF SOUTH ASIA (VOL. I). STRATA STRUCT KIN SECT ACT/RES CREATE HABITAT...GEOG OBS 19/20. PAGE 163 H3267 BIBLIOG/A CULTURE S/ASIA SOC

B59
EAENZA L.,COMMUNISMO E CATTOLICESIMO IN UNA PARROCHIA DI CAMPAGNA. ITALY CULTURE ELITES ECO/DEV AGRI KIN POL/PAR DOMIN LEGIT RIGID/FLEX...DECISION OBS IDEA/COMP 20 COM/PARTY CHURCH/STA. PAGE 44 H0878 ATTIT CATHISM NEIGH MARXISM

B59
JACOBS N.,CULTURE FOR THE MILLIONS? INTELL SOCIETY NAT/G...POLICY SOC OBS ANTHOL 20. PAGE 79 H1579 CULTURE COM/IND PERF/ART

CONCPT

B59

LEE D.,FREEDOM AND CULTURE. WOR+45 WOR-45 FAM HABITAT PERSON LOVE MORAL...PSY SOC OBS NAT/COMP WORSHIP 20. PAGE 93 H1856
CULTURE SOCIETY CONCPT INGP/REL

B59

MEYER A.J.,MIDDLE EASTERN CAPITALISM: NINE ESSAYS. ISLAM CULTURE ECO/UNDEV INDUS MARKET NAT/G PLAN ATTIT RIGID/FLEX...STAT OBS TREND GEN/LAWS. PAGE 109 H2188
TEC/DEV ECO/TAC ANTHOL

B59

WRAITH R.E.,EAST AFRICAN CITIZEN. AFR GHANA UK AGRI INDUS LOC/G POL/PAR PROB/SOLV CONTROL REGION REPRESENT NAT/LISM PWR...OBS 20 AFRICA/E AFRICA/W. PAGE 171 H3415
ECO/UNDEV RACE/REL NAT/G NAT/COMP

S59

CHAPMAN B.,"THE FRENCH CONSEIL D'ETAT." FRANCE NAT/G CONSULT OP/RES PROB/SOLV PWR...OBS 20. PAGE 29 H0580
ADMIN LAW CT/SYS LEGIS

B60

COUGHLIN R.,DOUBLE IDENTITY: THE CHINESE AND MODERN THAILAND. CHINA/COM S/ASIA THAILAND ECO/UNDEV EXTR/IND FINAN INDUS KIN MUNIC NAT/G PROF/ORG SCHOOL SECT ATTIT DRIVE...CONCPT OBS 20. PAGE 34 H0676
ASIA FAM CULTURE

B60

THORD-GRAY I.,GRINGO REBEL. L/A+17C NAT/G CONTROL LEAD ATTIT...OBS 20 MEXIC/AMER. PAGE 154 H3087
REV FORCES CIVMIL/REL ORD/FREE

S60

JAFFEE A.J.,"POPULATION TRENDS AND CONTROLS IN UNDERDEVELOPED COUNTRIES." AFR FUT ISLAM L/A+17C S/ASIA CULTURE R+D FAM ACT/RES PLAN EDU/PROP BIO/SOC RIGID/FLEX HEALTH...SOC STAT OBS CHARTS 20. PAGE 79 H1582
ECO/UNDEV GEOG

S60

MAGATHAN W.,"SOME BASES OF WEST GERMAN MILITARY POLICY." EUR+WWI FUT INT/ORG TOP/EX ECO/TAC DOMIN DRIVE ORD/FREE PWR...TRADIT GEOG OBS TREND. PAGE 101 H2015
NAT/G FORCES GERMANY

S60

SPIRO H.J.,"NEW CONSTITUTIONAL FORMS IN AFRICA." FUT CULTURE SOCIETY ECO/UNDEV NAT/G POL/PAR VOL/ASSN EDU/PROP ATTIT DRIVE ORD/FREE PWR RESPECT ...POLICY CONCPT OBS TREND CON/ANAL STERTYP GEN/LAWS VAL/FREE. PAGE 148 H2950
AFR CONSTN FOR/AID NAT/LISM

S60

TIRYAKIAN E.A.,"APARTHEID AND POLITICS IN SOUTH AFRICA." SOUTH/AFR CULTURE STRATA ECO/DEV NAT/G POL/PAR ROUTINE CHOOSE GP/REL RACE/REL DISCRIM ATTIT ALL/VALS...CONCPT OBS TIME/SEQ VAL/FREE 20. PAGE 155 H3105
AFR DIPLOM

B61

BEDFORD S.,THE FACES OF JUSTICE: A TRAVELLER'S REPORT. AUSTRIA FRANCE GERMANY/W SWITZERLND UK UNIV WOR+45 WOR-45 CULTURE PARTIC GOV/REL MORAL...JURID OBS GOV/COMP 20. PAGE 13 H0257
CT/SYS ORD/FREE PERSON LAW

B61

BERKOWITZ L.,AGGRESSION: AS A SOCIAL PSYCHOLOGICAL ANALYSIS. UNIV CULTURE FACE/GP FAM KIN NEIGH EDU/PROP DISPL DRIVE HEALTH LOVE ORD/FREE...PSY SOC CONCPT OBS TREND. PAGE 15 H0305
SOCIETY COERCE WAR

B61

MARVICK D.,POLITICAL DECISION-MAKERS. INTELL STRATA NAT/G POL/PAR EX/STRUC LEGIS DOMIN EDU/PROP ATTIT PERSON PWR...PSY STAT OBS CONT/OBS STAND/INT UNPLAN/INT TIME/SEQ CHARTS STERTYP VAL/FREE. PAGE 104 H2073
TOP/EX BIOG ELITES

B61

VON MERING O.,A GRAMMAR OF HUMAN VALUES. WOR+45 CULTURE FACE/GP NEIGH CREATE EDU/PROP LEGIT ATTIT DRIVE PERSON ORD/FREE...PSY SOC METH/CNCPT OBS RECORD INT REC/INT STAND/INT QU CHARTS VAL/FREE. PAGE 164 H3275
SOCIETY MORAL

S61

MILLER E.,"LEGAL ASPECTS OF UN ACTION IN THE CONGO." AFR CULTURE ADMIN PEACE DRIVE RIGID/FLEX ORD/FREE...WELF/ST JURID OBS UN CONGO 20. PAGE 111 H2212
INT/ORG LEGIT

S61

SCHECHTMAN J.B.,"MINORITIES IN THE MIDDLE EAST." ISLAM INTELL SOCIETY STRATA KIN NAT/G VOL/ASSN EDU/PROP REGION GP/REL DISCRIM ATTIT BIO/SOC DISPL PERSON ALL/VALS...PSY SOC OBS SAMP GEN/LAWS 20. PAGE 139 H2776
SECT CULTURE RACE/REL

S61

SCHELLING T.C.,"NUCLEAR STRATEGY IN EUROPE." COM EUR+WWI USSR NAT/G FORCES NUC/PWR DRIVE ORD/FREE PWR...DECISION CONCPT OBS TREND HYPO/EXP 20. PAGE 139 H2784
FUT COERCE ARMS/CONT WAR

B62

ABRAHAM W.E.,THE MIND OF AFRICA. AFR SOCIETY STRATA KIN ECO/TAC DOMIN EDU/PROP LEGIT COERCE ATTIT ALL/VALS...MAJORIT SOC OBS HIST/WRIT TIME/SEQ TREND GHANA TOT/POP 20. PAGE 3 H0058
CULTURE SIMUL

B62

BRETTON H.L.,POWER AND STABILITY IN NIGERIA: THE POLITICS OF DECOLONIZATION. AFR CONSTN INTELL ECO/UNDEV COM/IND KIN NAT/G POL/PAR PROVS VOL/ASSN LEGIS DOMIN EDU/PROP LEGIT EXEC ROUTINE CHOOSE NAT/LISM ATTIT PERCEPT ALL/VALS. PAGE 20 H0411
CULTURE OBS NIGERIA

B62

DUTOIT B.,LA NEUTRALITE SUISSE A L'HEURE EUROPEENNE. EUR+WWI MOD/EUR INT/ORG NAT/G VOL/ASSN PLAN BAL/PWR LEGIT NEUTRAL REGION PEACE ORD/FREE SOVEREIGN...CONCPT OBS TIME/SEQ TREND STERTYP VAL/FREE LEAGUE/NAT UN 20. PAGE 44 H0873
ATTIT DIPLOM SWITZERLND

B62

EVANS-PRITCHARD E.E.,ESSAYS IN SOCIAL ANTHROPOLOGY. AFR KIN REGION INGP/REL DRIVE HABITAT...OBS METH 20 ZANDE. PAGE 48 H0954
SOCIETY CULTURE SOC STRUCT

B62

GUENA Y.,HISTORIQUE DE LA COMMUNAUTE. FUT ECO/UNDEV NAT/G PLAN EDU/PROP COLONIAL REGION NAT/LISM ALL/VALS SOVEREIGN...CONCPT OBS CHARTS 20. PAGE 62 H1244
AFR VOL/ASSN FOR/AID FRANCE

B62

INSTITUTE FOR STUDY OF USSR,YOUTH IN FERMENT. INTELL NAT/G PERF/ART POL/PAR SCHOOL VOL/ASSN FORCES EDU/PROP ATTIT DRIVE PERCEPT HEALTH KNOWL MORAL ORD/FREE RESPECT...SOC OBS HIST/WRIT VAL/FREE. PAGE 77 H1537
COM CULTURE USSR

B62

TILMAN R.O.,THE NIGERIAN POLITICAL SXENE. NIGERIA DIPLOM COLONIAL PARTIC...POLICY SOC OBS PREDICT ANTHOL 20. PAGE 155 H3096
NAT/G AFR ECO/UNDEV FEDERAL

B62

YOUNG G.,THE HILL TRIBES OF NORTHERN THAILAND. S/ASIA THAILAND FAM KIN LOC/G GP/REL HABITAT...GEOG LING OBS 20. PAGE 172 H3438
CULTURE STRUCT ECO/UNDEV SECT

L62

COHEN R.,"POWER IN COMPLEX SOCIETIES IN AFRICA." AFR KIN MUNIC POL/PAR DELIB/GP DOMIN ROUTINE ATTIT ALL/VALS...SOC STAT OBS INT QU CHARTS ANTHOL 20. PAGE 31 H0617
CULTURE STRATA ELITES

S62

CORET A.,"LE STATUT DE L'ILE CHRISTMAS DE L'OCEAN INDIEN." FUT S/ASIA ECO/DEV ECO/UNDEV VOL/ASSN DELIB/GP PLAN...RELATIV OBS TIME/SEQ TREND AUSTRAL 20. PAGE 33 H0667
NAT/G INT/ORG NEW/ZEALND

S62

IOVTCHOUK M.T.,"ON SOME THEORETICAL PRINCIPLES AND METHODS OF SOCIOLOGICAL INVESTIGATIONS (IN RUSSIAN)." FUT USA+45 STRATA R+D NAT/G POL/PAR TOP/EX ACT/RES PLAN ECO/TAC EDU/PROP ROUTINE ATTIT RIGID/FLEX MARXISM SOCISM...MARXIST METH/CNCPT OBS TREND NAT/COMP GEN/LAWS 20. PAGE 78 H1564
COM ECO/DEV CAP/ISM USSR

S62

SPRINGER H.W.,"FEDERATION IN THE CARIBBEAN: AN ATTEMPT THAT FAILED." L/A+17C ECO/UNDEV INT/ORG POL/PAR PROVS LEGIS CREATE PLAN LEGIT ADMIN FEDERAL ATTIT DRIVE PERSON ORD/FREE PWR...POLICY GEOG PSY CONCPT OBS CARIBBEAN CMN/WLTH 20. PAGE 148 H2955
VOL/ASSN NAT/G REGION

S62

STRACHEY J.,"COMMUNIST INTENTIONS." ASIA USSR YUGOSLAVIA INT/ORG NAT/G FORCES DOMIN EDU/PROP COERCE NUC/PWR NAT/LISM PEACE RIGID/FLEX PWR MARXISM...CONCPT MYTH OBS TIME/SEQ TREND COLD/WAR TOT/POP 20. PAGE 150 H2992
COM ATTIT WAR

B63

GEERTZ C.,PEDDLERS AND PRINCES: SOCIAL DEVELOPMENT AND ECONOMIC CHANGE IN TWO INDONESIAN TOWNS. S/ASIA CULTURE SOCIETY STRATA FACE/GP MUNIC CREATE TEC/DEV ECO/TAC ORD/FREE WEALTH...OBS INT CENSUS CHARTS WORK TOT/POP VAL/FREE 20. PAGE 55 H1106
ECO/UNDEV SOC ELITES INDONESIA

B63

HALPERIN M.H.,THE POLITICS OF SOCIAL CHANGE IN THE MIDDLE EAST AND NORTH AFRICA. ISLAM CULTURE ACT/RES REV ATTIT PERCEPT KNOWL...METH/CNCPT OBS TIME/SEQ GEN/METH TOT/POP VAL/FREE 20. PAGE 64 H1291
SOC TREND

B63

KOGAN N.,THE POLITICS OF ITALIAN FOREIGN POLICY. EUR+WWI LEGIS DOMIN LEGIT EXEC PWR RESPECT SKILL ...POLICY DECISION HUM SOC METH/CNCPT OBS INT CHARTS 20. PAGE 87 H1737
NAT/G ROUTINE DIPLOM ITALY

B63

LERNER R.,MEDIEVAL POLITICAL PHILOSOPHY. ISLAM MORAL PWR CATHISM...CATH CONCPT OBS IDEA/COMP ANTHOL 9/15 JEWS CHRISTIAN BACON/R AQUINAS/T. PAGE 95 H1890
KNOWL PHIL/SCI

B63

QUAISON-SACKEY A.,AFRICA UNBOUND: REFLECTIONS OF AN AFRICAN STATESMAN. ISLAM CULTURE INTELL INT/ORG POL/PAR TOP/EX DOMIN EDU/PROP LEGIT ATTIT PERSON ...CONCPT OBS TIME/SEQ CHARTS STERTYP 20 UN. PAGE 129 H2571
AFR BIOG

B63
RIVKIN A.,THE AFRICAN PRESENCE IN WORLD AFFAIRS. ECO/UNDEV AGRI INT/ORG LOC/G NAT/LISM...OBS PREDICT GOV/COMP 20. PAGE 132 H2635
AFR NAT/G DIPLOM BAL/PWR

B63
SKLAR R.L.,NIGERIAN POLITICAL PARTIES: POWER IN AN EMERGENT AFRICAN NATION. AFR EUR+WWI CULTURE STRATA NAT/G DELIB/GP EX/STRUC LEGIS DOMIN EDU/PROP ROUTINE CHOOSE ATTIT PERCEPT ORD/FREE PWR...SOC CONCPT OBS TOT/POP VAL/FREE. PAGE 145 H2898
POL/PAR SOCIETY NAT/LISM NIGERIA

B63
ULAM A.B.,THE NEW FACE OF SOVIET TOTALITARIANISM. FUT INTELL NAT/G POL/PAR EX/STRUC TOP/EX DIPLOM ECO/TAC DOMIN EDU/PROP LEGIT COERCE ATTIT RIGID/FLEX...OBS HIST/WRIT TREND TOT/POP VAL/FREE COLD/WAR. PAGE 158 H3150
COM PWR TOTALISM USSR

L63
CORWIN A.F.,"CONTEMPORARY MEXICAN ATTITUDES TOWARD POPULATION, POVERTY, AND PUBLIC OPINION." L/A+17C CULTURE SOCIETY ACT/RES ECO/TAC EDU/PROP PERSON HEALTH KNOWL...GEOG PHIL/SCI STAT OBS INT SAMP MEXIC/AMER VAL/FREE 20. PAGE 34 H0672
ATTIT QU

L63
JAY R.,"RELIGION AND POLITICS IN RURAL CENTRAL JAVA." S/ASIA SOCIETY NEIGH SECT PERSON HEALTH MORAL...SOC UNPLAN/INT TIME/SEQ JAVA VAL/FREE 20 WORSHIP. PAGE 80 H1594
CULTURE OBS

S63
AYAL E.B.,"VALUE SYSTEM AND ECONOMIC DEVELOPMENT IN JAPAN AND THAILAND." ASIA S/ASIA THAILAND CULTURE ECO/DEV CAP/ISM DOMIN NAT/LISM DRIVE RIGID/FLEX SOCISM...WELF/ST OBS TREND CON/ANAL GEN/LAWS 20 CHINJAP. PAGE 9 H0185
ECO/UNDEV ALL/VALS

S63
RUSTOW D.A.,"THE MILITARY IN MIDDLE EASTERN SOCIETY AND POLITICS." FUT ISLAM CONSTN SOCIETY FACE/GP NAT/G POL/PAR PROF/ORG CONSULT DOMIN ADMIN EXEC REGION COERCE NAT/LISM ATTIT DRIVE PERSON ORD/FREE PWR...POLICY CONCPT OBS STERTYP 20. PAGE 136 H2721
FORCES ELITES

B64
AGGER R.E.,THE RULERS AND THE RULED: POLITICAL POWER AND IMPOTENCE IN AMERICAN COMMUNITIES. CULTURE DOMIN CHOOSE ATTIT ALL/VALS...DECISION SOC CONCPT OBS QU CHARTS. PAGE 4 H0079
PWR STRUCT LOC/G MUNIC

B64
GLUCKMANN M.,CLOSED SYSTEMS AND OPEN MINDS: THE LIMITS OF NAIVETY IN SOCIAL ANTHROPOLOGY. AFR INDIA MUNIC...IDEA/COMP METH/COMP ANTHOL. PAGE 57 H1149
CULTURE OBS SOC

B64
HARRIS M.,THE NATURE OF CULTURAL THINGS. GP/REL PERS/REL DRIVE HABITAT PERSON ROLE...PHIL/SCI PSY SOC CHARTS BIBLIOG 20. PAGE 67 H1341
CULTURE OBS CLASSIF NEW/IDEA

B64
SCHNITGER F.M.,FORGOTTEN KINGDOMS IN SUMATRA. FAM SECT LEISURE HABITAT...OBS AUD/VIS WORSHIP 20 SUMATRA. PAGE 140 H2793
CULTURE AFR SOCIETY STRUCT

B64
SKINNER E.P.,THE MOSSI OF UPPER VOLTA: THE POLITICAL DEVELOPMENT OF A SUDANESE PEOPLE. AFR LAW AGRI FAM KIN POL/PAR PROVS SECT DELIB/GP EX/STRUC FORCES TOP/EX DOMIN EDU/PROP LEGIT CT/SYS COERCE CHOOSE ORD/FREE PWR WEALTH...SOC MYTH VAL/FREE. PAGE 145 H2897
CULTURE OBS UPPER/VOLT

B64
THORNBURG M.W.,PEOPLE AND POLICY IN THE MIDDLE EAST. ISLAM ECO/UNDEV FAM KIN MUNIC NAT/G NEIGH POL/PAR SECT DELIB/GP LEGIS PLAN ECO/TAC DOMIN ADMIN ATTIT HEALTH RESPECT...SOC CONCPT METH/CNCPT OBS TIME/SEQ TOT/POP VAL/FREE. PAGE 154 H3088
TEC/DEV CULTURE

B64
VON FURER-HAIMEN E.,AN ANTHROPOLOGICAL BIBLIOGRAPHY OF SOUTH ASIA (VOL. II). STRATA STRUCT KIN SECT ACT/RES CREATE HABITAT...GEOG OBS 20. PAGE 163 H3268
BIBLIOG/A CULTURE S/ASIA SOC

B64
WHITEFORD A.H.,TWO CITIES OF LATIN AMERICA: A COMPARATIVE DESCRIPTION OF SOCIAL CLASSES. L/A+17C CULTURE SOCIETY MUNIC DOMIN LEGIT ATTIT ALL/VALS ...STAT OBS VAL/FREE 20. PAGE 167 H3352
STRATA SOC

L64
BERELSON B.,"SAMPLE SURVEYS AND POPULATION CONTROL." ASIA FUT ISLAM L/A+17C CULTURE SOCIETY FAM NAT/G CONSULT PLAN EDU/PROP ATTIT DRIVE ALL/VALS...POLICY RELATIV HEAL PSY SOC CONCPT METH/CNCPT OBS OBS/ENVIR TOT/POP. PAGE 15 H0297
BIO/SOC SAMP

S64
MC WILLIAM M.,"THE WORLD BANK AND THE TRANSFER OF POWER IN KENYA." AFR ECO/UNDEV CONSULT ACT/RES TEC/DEV PERCEPT PWR SKILL WEALTH...CONCPT OBS TREND 20. PAGE 106 H2119
NAT/G ECO/TAC

S64
SCHEFFLER H.W.,"THE GENESIS AND REPRESSION OF CONFLICT: CHOISEUL ISLAND." S/ASIA LOC/G NAT/G FORCES LEGIS DIPLOM DOMIN LEGIT EXEC CHOOSE ATTIT RESPECT SKILL...POLICY JURID OBS TREND GEN/METH 20. PAGE 139 H2781
PWR COERCE WAR

B65
ADAM T.R.,GOVERNMENT AND POLITICS IN AFRICA SOUTH OF THE SAHARA. AFR EUR+WWI CONSTN CULTURE INTELL POL/PAR TOP/EX LEGIT REGION DRIVE...OBS TREND CMN/WLTH 20. PAGE 3 H0062
NAT/G TIME/SEQ RACE/REL COLONIAL

B65
BETTISON D.G.,THE PAPUA-GUINEA ELECTIONS 1964. S/ASIA CONSTN POL/PAR EDU/PROP PARTIC SUFF CENTRAL CONSEN...OBS CHARTS BIBLIOG 20. PAGE 16 H0324
NAT/G LEGIS CHOOSE REPRESENT

B65
DURKHEIM E.,THE ELEMENTARY FORMS OF THE RELIGIOUS LIFE. KIN PARTIC MORAL...PSY MYTH OBS IDEA/COMP METH WORSHIP 19/20. PAGE 43 H0870
SOC CULTURE CONCPT

B65
GHAI D.P.,PORTRAIT OF A MINORITY: ASIANS IN EAST AFRICA. S/ASIA TANZANIA UGANDA COLONIAL...SOC OBS PREDICT ANTHOL 20. PAGE 56 H1119
RACE/REL GP/REL CULTURE AFR

B65
INT. BANK RECONSTR. DEVELOP.,ECONOMIC DEVELOPMENT OF KUWAIT. ISLAM KUWAIT AGRI FINAN MARKET EX/STRUC TEC/DEV ECO/TAC ADMIN WEALTH...OBS CON/ANAL CHARTS 20. PAGE 77 H1541
INDUS NAT/G

B65
SIMMS R.P.,URBANIZATION IN WEST AFRICA; A REVIEW OF CURRENT LITERATURE. AFR PLAN TEC/DEV...SOC OBS NAT/COMP 20. PAGE 144 H2878
BIBLIOG/A MUNIC ECO/DEV ECO/UNDEV

B65
SIRISKAR V.M.,POLITICAL BEHAVIOR IN INDIA. INDIA SOCIETY MUNIC NAT/G PROVS ACT/RES SUFF...OBS CHARTS 20 POONA. PAGE 144 H2889
CHOOSE POL/PAR PWR ATTIT

S65
HUGHES T.L.,"SCHOLARS AND FOREIGN POLICY* VARIETIES OF RESEARCH EXPERIENCE." COM/IND DIPLOM ADMIN EXEC ROUTINE...MGT OBS CONGRESS PRESIDENT CAMELOT. PAGE 75 H1491
ACT/RES ACADEM CONTROL NAT/G

S65
SPAAK P.H.,"THE SEARCH FOR CONSENSUS: A NEW EFFORT TO BUILD EUROPE." FRANCE GERMANY ECO/DEV NAT/G CONSULT FORCES PLAN EDU/PROP REGION CONSEN ATTIT ...SOC METH/CNCPT OBS TREND EEC NATO WORK 20. PAGE 147 H2941
EUR+WWI INT/ORG

S65
THOMAS F.C. JR.,"THE PEACE CORPS IN MOROCCO." CULTURE MUNIC PROVS CREATE ROUTINE TASK ADJUST STRANGE...OBS PEACE/CORP. PAGE 154 H3077
MOROCCO FRANCE FOR/AID EDU/PROP

B66
BASDEN G.T.,NIGER IBOS. NIGERIA STRUCT SECT CHIEF COLONIAL HABITAT...POLICY SOC MYTH OBS WORSHIP 20 IBO. PAGE 12 H0233
CULTURE AFR SOCIETY

B66
DARLING M.,APPRENTICE TO POWER INDIA 1904-1908. INDIA LEAD GP/REL PERSON...GEOG 20. PAGE 37 H0742
OBS SOCIETY ADMIN NAT/G

B66
FRIEDRICH C.J.,REVOLUTION: NOMOS VIII. NAT/G SOCISM ...OBS TREND IDEA/COMP ANTHOL 18/20. PAGE 54 H1070
REV MARXISM CONCPT DIPLOM

B66
MERILLAT H.C.L.,LEGAL ADVISERS AND INTERNATIONAL ORGANIZATIONS. LAW NAT/G CONSULT OP/RES ADJUD SANCTION TASK CONSEN ORG/CHARTS. PAGE 109 H2178
INT/ORG INT/LAW CREATE OBS

B66
NEVITT A.A.,THE ECONOMIC PROBLEMS OF HOUSING. WOR+45 ECO/DEV ECO/UNDEV ACT/RES PROB/SOLV ECO/TAC RENT...OBS CHARTS 20. PAGE 117 H2342
HABITAT PROC/MFG DELIB/GP NAT/COMP

B66
WHITAKER A.P.,NATIONALISM IN CONTEMPORARY LATIN AMERICA. AGRI NAT/G WEALTH...POLICY SOC CONCPT OBS TREND 20. PAGE 167 H3344
NAT/LISM L/A+17C DIPLOM ECO/UNDEV

L66
HUNTINGTON S.P.,"POLITICAL MODERNIZATION* AMERICA VS EUROPE." EUR+WWI MOD/EUR UK USA+45 LAW ECO/UNDEV PWR SOVEREIGN CONSERVE LAISSEZ GOV/COMP. PAGE 75 H1505
STRUCT CREATE OBS

S66
HAIGH G.,"FIELD TRAINING IN HUMAN RELATIONS FOR THE PEACE CORPS." CONSULT CREATE EDU/PROP ADMIN TASK GP/REL ATTIT PERSON...PSY OBS SOC/EXP PEACE/CORP. PAGE 64 H1276
CULTURE PERS/REL FOR/AID ADJUST

S66
HEAPHEY J.,"THE ORGANIZATION OF EGYPT* INADEQUACIES OF A NONPOLITICAL MODEL FOR NATION-BUILDING." STRATA NAT/G CREATE PROB/SOLV ECO/TAC NAT/LISM
UAR ECO/UNDEV OBS

SOCISM RECORD. PAGE 69 H1377

S66
TURKEVICH J.,"SOVIET SCIENCE APPRAISED." USA+45 R+D ACADEM FORCES DIPLOM EDU/PROP WAR EFFICIENCY PEACE SKILL OBS. PAGE 157 H3137 — USSR TEC/DEV NAT/COMP ATTIT

B67
CARTER G.M.,SOUTH AFRICA'S TRANSKEI: THE POLITICS OF DOMESTIC COLONIALISM. SOUTH/AFR ECO/UNDEV AGRI NAT/G PROVS PLAN DOMIN REPRESENT ADJUST DISCRIM ...OBS BIBLIOG 20 BANTUSTANS TRANSKEI. PAGE 27 H0550 — STRATA GOV/REL COLONIAL POLICY

B67
CHANDRASEKHAR S.,ASIA'S POPULATION PROBLEMS. ASIA ECO/UNDEV PLAN AGE/C...OBS CHARTS BIBLIOG 18/20 AUSTRAL. PAGE 29 H0575 — PROB/SOLV NAT/COMP GEOG TREND

B67
SALISBURY H.E.,BEHIND THE LINES - HANOI. VIETNAM/N NAT/G GUERRILLA CIVMIL/REL NAT/LISM KNOWL 20. PAGE 137 H2741 — WAR PROB/SOLV DIPLOM OBS

B67
WINTER E.H.,CONTEMPORARY CHANGE IN TRADITIONAL SOCIETIES: VOLUME I INTRODUCTION AND AFRICAN TRIBES. NIGERIA AGRI LOC/G NAT/G CREATE DOMIN COLONIAL CONTROL GP/REL PWR SOVEREIGN...SOC OBS 20 TANGANYIKA. PAGE 169 H3389 — SOCIETY AFR CONSERVE KIN

L67
GALTUNG J.,"ON THE EFFECTS OF INTERNATIONAL ECONOMIC SANCTIONS, WITH EXAMPLES FROM THE CASE OF RHODESIA." NAT/G DIPLOM EDU/PROP ADJUST EFFICIENCY ATTIT MORAL...OBS CHARTS 20. PAGE 55 H1091 — SANCTION ECO/TAC INT/TRADE ECO/UNDEV

S67
HOPE M.,"THE RELUCTANT WAY: SELF-IMMOLATION IN VIETNAM." VIETNAM SOCIETY FAM KIN SECT DRIVE ALL/VALS...TRADIT OBS INT 20. PAGE 73 H1465 — CULTURE SUICIDE IDEA/COMP ATTIT

S67
KROLL M.,"POLITICAL LEADERSHIP AND ADMINISTRATIVE COMMUNICATIONS IN NEW NATION STATES* CASE STUDY OF TRINIDAD AND TOBAGO." L/A+17C TRINIDAD INTELL OP/RES DOMIN COLONIAL LEAD GP/REL CENTRAL EFFICIENCY...DECISION OBS METH/COMP 20. PAGE 89 H1774 — NAT/G ADMIN EDU/PROP CONTROL

OBS/ENVIR....SOCIAL MILIEU OF AND RESISTANCES TO OBSERVATIONS

C41
KLUCKHOHN C.,"PATTERNING AS EXEMPLIFIED IN NAVAHO CULTURE" IN EDWARD SAPIR, LANGUAGE, CULTURE, AND PERSONALITY (BMR)" KIN PERS/REL ATTIT PERSON...SOC CONCPT METH/CNCPT LING OBS/ENVIR CON/ANAL BIBLIOG SOC/INTEG 20 NAVAHO INDIAN/AM SAPIR/EDW. PAGE 87 H1733 — CULTURE INGP/REL STRUCT

B43
SERENI A.P.,THE ITALIAN CONCEPTION OF INTERNATIONAL LAW. EUR+WWI MOD/EUR INT/ORG NAT/G DOMIN COERCE ORD/FREE FASCISM...OBS/ENVIR TREND 20. PAGE 141 H2829 — LAW TIME/SEQ INT/LAW ITALY

C55
OLIVER D.L.,"A LEADER IN ACTION," IN D. A. OLIVER, SOLOMON ISLAND SOCIETY." S/ASIA SOCIETY STRUCT CONTROL TASK PWR...OBS/ENVIR WORSHIP 20. PAGE 121 H2413 — LEAD RESPECT CULTURE KIN

B59
WARNER W.L.,THE LIVING AND THE DEAD: A STUDY OF SYMBOLIC LIFE OF AMERICANS. INTELL KIN DEATH ALL/VALS ALL/IDEOS...CONCPT MYTH LING OBS/ENVIR CHARTS BIBLIOG WORSHIP 18/20. PAGE 165 H3311 — CULTURE SOC TIME/SEQ IDEA/COMP

B60
JAECKH A.,WELTSAAT; ERLEBTES UND ERSTREBTES. GERMANY WOR+45 WOR-45 PLAN WAR...POLICY OBS/ENVIR NAT/COMP PERS/COMP 20. PAGE 79 H1581 — BIOG NAT/G SELF/OBS DIPLOM

S60
KELLEY G.A.,"THE POLITICAL BACKGROUND OF THE FRENCH A-BOMB." EUR+WWI USSR FORCES TOP/EX TEC/DEV NUC/PWR ATTIT PWR...CONCPT OBS/ENVIR TREND 20. PAGE 84 H1686 — NAT/G RESPECT NAT/LISM FRANCE

S62
ROTBERG R.,"THE RISE OF AFRICAN NATIONALISM: THE CASE OF EAST AND CENTRAL AFRICA." AFR CULTURE SOCIETY NEIGH DIPLOM DOMIN COLONIAL COERCE DISPL PERCEPT PWR SOVEREIGN...POLICY OBS/ENVIR TREND WORK 20. PAGE 135 H2690 — ATTIT DRIVE NAT/LISM REV

B64
GRIFFITH W.,THE WELSH (2ND ED.). UK SOCIETY STRUCT SECT WRITING NAT/LISM...ART/METH MODAL OBS/ENVIR TREND SOC/INTEG WALES PURITAN MUSIC. PAGE 61 H1223 — CULTURE SOC LING

B64
MCCALL D.F.,AFRICA IN TIME PERSPECTIVE. AFR EXTR/IND KIN SECT CREATE PERS/REL HABITAT...GEOG METH/CNCPT LING BIBLIOG/A TIME 20. PAGE 106 H2124 — HIST/WRIT OBS/ENVIR CULTURE

L64
BERELSON B.,"SAMPLE SURVEYS AND POPULATION CONTROL." ASIA FUT ISLAM L/A+17C CULTURE SOCIETY FAM NAT/G CONSULT PLAN EDU/PROP ATTIT DRIVE ALL/VALS...POLICY RELATIV HEAL PSY SOC CONCPT METH/CNCPT OBS OBS/ENVIR TOT/POP. PAGE 15 H0297 — BIO/SOC SAMP

B65
ADENAUER K.,MEINE ERINNERUNGEN, 1945-53 (VOL. I), 1953-55 (VOL. II). EUR+WWI GERMANY CHIEF FORCES PROB/SOLV DIPLOM ARMS/CONT INGP/REL PEACE SOVEREIGN ...OBS/ENVIR RECORD 20. PAGE 3 H0069 — NAT/G BIOG SELF/OBS

B66
RADIN P.,THE METHOD AND THEORY OF ETHNOLOGY. CULTURE STRUCT BIO/SOC HABITAT...HUM OBS/ENVIR METH/COMP GEN/LAWS 20 HUMANISM. PAGE 129 H2578 — PHIL/SCI SOC METH SOCIETY

OBSCENITY....OBSCENITY

OBSERVATION....SEE DIRECT-OBSERVATION METHOD INDEX, P. XIV

OBSOLESCENCE, PLANNED....SEE OBSOLESCNC

OBSOLESCNC....OBSOLESCENCE, PLANNED

OBUKAR C. H2393

OCAM....SEE UAM

OCCUPATION....SEE WORKER

OCEANIA....OCEANIA: AUSTRALIA, NEW ZEALAND, MALAYSIA, MELANESIA, MICRONESIA, AND POLYNESIA

ODEGARD P.H. H2394

ODEGARD/P....PETER ODEGARD

ODINGA O. H2395

ODINGA/O....OGINGA ODINGA

B67
ODINGA O.,NOT YET UHURU. NAT/G POL/PAR PROB/SOLV COERCE REV WAR PERS/REL PERSON ORD/FREE...POLICY 20 ODINGA/O KENYATTA. PAGE 120 H2395 — ATTIT BIOG LEAD AFR

OECD H2396,H2397,H2398,H2399,H2400,H2401,H2402,H2427

OECD....ORGANIZATION FOR ECONOMIC COOPERATION AND DEVELOPMENT

B61
OECD,STATISTICS OF BALANCE OF PAYMENTS 1950-61. WOR+45 FINAN ECO/TAC INT/TRADE DEMAND WEALTH...STAT NAT/COMP 20 OEEC OECD. PAGE 120 H2396 — BAL/PAY ECO/DEV INT/ORG CHARTS

B64
OECD,DEVELOPMENT ASSISTANCE EFFORTS - POLICIES OF THE MEMBERS. AGRI INDUS BUDGET...GEOG NAT/COMP 20 OECD. PAGE 120 H2398 — INT/ORG FOR/AID ECO/UNDEV TEC/DEV

B65
OECD,MEDITERRANEAN REGIONAL PROJECT: TURKEY; EDUCATION AND DEVELOPMENT. FUT TURKEY SOCIETY STRATA FINAN NAT/G PROF/ORG PLAN PROB/SOLV ADMIN COST...STAT CHARTS 20 OECD. PAGE 120 H2399 — EDU/PROP ACADEM SCHOOL ECO/UNDEV

B65
OECD,THE MEDITERRANEAN REGIONAL PROJECT: ITALY; EDUCATION AND DEVELOPMENT. ITALY SOCIETY STRATA FINAN NAT/G PROF/ORG WORKER PLAN PROB/SOLV ADMIN ...STAT CHARTS METH 20 OECD. PAGE 120 H2400 — SCHOOL EDU/PROP ECO/UNDEV ACADEM

B65
OECD,THE MEDITERRANEAN REGIONAL PROJECT: GREECE; EDUCATION AND DEVELOPMENT. FUT GREECE SOCIETY AGRI FINAN NAT/G PROF/ORG WORKER PLAN PROB/SOLV ADMIN DEMAND ATTIT 20 OECD. PAGE 120 H2401 — EDU/PROP SCHOOL ACADEM ECO/UNDEV

B65
OECD,THE MEDITERRANEAN REGIONAL PROJECT: SPAIN; EDUCATION AND DEVELOPMENT. FUT SPAIN STRATA FINAN NAT/G WORKER PLAN PROB/SOLV ADMIN COST...POLICY STAT CHARTS 20 OECD. PAGE 120 H2402 — ECO/UNDEV EDU/PROP ACADEM SCHOOL

B65
ORG FOR ECO COOP AND DEVEL,THE MEDITERRANEAN REGIONAL PROJECT: AN EXPERIMENT IN PLANNING BY SIX COUNTRIES. FUT GREECE SPAIN TURKEY YUGOSLAVIA SOCIETY FINAN NAT/G PROF/ORG EDU/PROP ADMIN REGION COST...POLICY STAT CHARTS 20 OECD. PAGE 121 H2427 — PLAN ECO/UNDEV ACADEM SCHOOL

OECD DEVELOPMENT CENTRE H2403

OECD SEMINAR REGIONAL DEV H2404

OEEC....ORGANIZATION FOR EUROPEAN ECONOMIC COOPERATION; SEE ALSO VOL/ASSN, INT/ORG

GORDON L.,"THE ORGANIZATION FOR EUROPEAN ECONOMIC COOPERATION." EUR+WWI INDUS INT/ORG NAT/G CONSULT DELIB/GP ACT/RES CREATE PLAN TEC/DEV EDU/PROP LEGIT WEALTH OEEC 20. PAGE 59 H1178 — S56 VOL/ASSN ECO/DEV

ELKIN A.B.,"OEEC-ITS STRUCTURE AND POWERS." EUR+WWI CONSTN INDUS INT/ORG NAT/G VOL/ASSN DELIB/GP ACT/RES PLAN ORD/FREE WEALTH...CHARTS ORG/CHARTS OEEC 20. PAGE 45 H0907 — S58 ECO/DEV EX/STRUC

MURPHY J.C.,"SOME IMPLICATIONS OF EUROPE'S COMMON MARKET. IN (COOK P, ECONOMIC DEVELOPMENT AND INTERNATIONAL TRADE.." EUR+WWI ECO/DEV DIST/IND INDUS NAT/G PLAN ECO/TAC INT/TRADE WEALTH...STAT TREND OEEC TOT/POP 20 EEC. PAGE 115 H2298 — L59 MARKET INT/ORG REGION

HAAS E.B.,"CONSENSUS FORMATION IN THE COUNCIL OF EUROPE." EUR+WWI NAT/G DELIB/GP DIPLOM REGION CHOOSE PWR SOVEREIGN...RELATIV NEW/IDEA QUANT CHARTS INDEX TOT/POP OEEC 20 COUNCL/EUR. PAGE 63 H1265 — L60 POL/PAR INT/ORG STAT

OECD,STATISTICS OF BALANCE OF PAYMENTS 1950-61. WOR+45 FINAN ECO/TAC INT/TRADE DEMAND WEALTH...STAT NAT/COMP 20 OEEC OECD. PAGE 120 H2396 — B61 BAL/PAY ECO/DEV INT/ORG CHARTS

RAY J.,"THE EUROPEAN FREE-TRADE ASSOCIATION AND ITS IMPACT ON INDIA'S TRADE." EUR+WWI FRANCE GERMANY INDIA S/ASIA UK NAT/G VOL/ASSN PLAN INT/TRADE ROUTINE WEALTH...STAT CHARTS CMN/WLTH EEC OEEC 20 EFTA. PAGE 130 H2600 — S61 ECO/DEV ECO/TAC

MEADE J.E.,CASE STUDIES IN EUROPEAN ECONOMIC UNION. BELGIUM EUR+WWI LUXEMBOURG NAT/G INT/TRADE REGION ROUTINE WEALTH...METH/CNCPT STAT CHARTS ECSC TOT/POP OEEC EEC 20. PAGE 108 H2154 — B62 INT/ORG ECO/TAC

APPERT K.,"BERECHTIGE VORBEHALTE DER SCHWEIZERISCHEN ZUR INTEGRATION." EUR+WWI UK MARKET SERV/IND NAT/G PLAN RIGID/FLEX OEEC 20 EEC. PAGE 7 H0146 — S63 FINAN ATTIT SWITZERLND

OEO....OFFICE OF ECONOMIC OPPORTUNITY

OEP....OFFICE OF EMERGENCY PLANNING

OFFICE OF ECONOMIC OPPORTUNITY....SEE OEO

OFFICE OF EMERGENCY PLANNING....SEE OEP

OFFICE OF PRICE ADMINISTRATION....SEE OPA

OFFICE OF WAR INFORMATION....SEE OWI

OGBURN W.F. H2405

OGDEN F.D. H2407

OGILVIE C. H2408

OGILVY-WEBB M. H2409

OGOT B. H2410

OHIO....OHIO

OHLIN/HECK....OHLIN-HECKSCHER THEORY OF COMMODITY TRADE

OJHA I.C. H2411

OKELLO/J....JOHN OKELLO

OKINAWA....OKINAWA

OKLAHOMA....OKLAHOMA

OLAS....ORGANIZATION FOR LATIN AMERICAN SOLIDARITY

OLD LIBERAL....SEE OLD/LIB

OLD/LIB....OLD LIBERAL

BONAR J.,THEORIES OF POPULATION FROM RALEIGH TO ARTHUR YOUNG. CHRIST-17C MOD/EUR CULTURE SOCIETY R+D CREATE ATTIT PERCEPT RIGID/FLEX...OLD/LIB CONCPT NEW/IDEA TIME/SEQ IDEA/COMP STERTYP GEN/LAWS. PAGE 19 H0372 — B31 GEOG BIOG

HALL R.C.,"REPRESENTATION OF BIG BUSINESS IN THE HOUSE OF COMMONS." UK ECO/DEV INDUS PROF/ORG LEGIS CAP/ISM ECO/TAC LAISSEZ...POLICY OLD/LIB PLURIST MGT 20 HOUSE/CMNS. PAGE 64 H1287 — S38 LOBBY NAT/G

HAYEK F.A.,THE ROAD TO SERFDOM. NAT/G POL/PAR CREATE EDU/PROP ATTIT WEALTH LAISSEZ...OLD/LIB CONCPT TREND 20. PAGE 68 H1368 — B44 FUT PLAN ECO/TAC SOCISM

TANNENBAUM F.,"THE BALANCE OF POWER IN SOCIETY." UNIV STRUCT FAM NAT/G SECT PERS/REL EQUILIB UTOPIA DRIVE ALL/IDEOS...OLD/LIB CONCPT. PAGE 152 H3044 — S46 SOCIETY ALL/VALS GP/REL PEACE

ISAAC J.,ECONOMICS OF MIGRATION. MOD/EUR CULTURE STRATA STRUCT NAT/G COLONIAL WEALTH...OLD/LIB TREND TIME 19/20 EUROPE/W MIGRATION. PAGE 78 H1569 — B47 HABITAT SOC GEOG

BULLOCK A.,THE LIBERAL TRADITION FROM FOX TO KEYNES. UK CULTURE INTELL CREATE WRITING COLONIAL PERS/REL ATTIT ORD/FREE...POLICY OLD/LIB TRADIT CONCPT 18/20 CHURCHLL/W MILL/JS KEYNES/JM ASQUITH/HH. PAGE 23 H0469 — B57 ANTHOL DEBATE LAISSEZ

TINKER H.,INDIA AND PAKISTAN. INDIA PAKISTAN NAT/G POL/PAR...OLD/LIB TRADIT TREND CHARTS BIBLIOG 20. PAGE 155 H3102 — B62 ORD/FREE STRATA REPRESENT AUTHORIT

CARY J.,POWER IN MEN. NAT/G ORD/FREE...GEN/LAWS 20. PAGE 28 H0553 — B63 PHIL/SCI OLD/LIB LAISSEZ PWR

OLSON M. JR.,THE ECONOMICS OF WARTIME SHORTAGE. FRANCE GERMANY MOD/EUR UK AGRI PROB/SOLV ADMIN DEMAND WEALTH...POLICY OLD/LIB 17/20. PAGE 121 H2416 — B63 WAR ADJUST ECO/TAC NAT/COMP

HALEVY E.,THE ERA OF TYRANNIES (TRANS. BY R. K. WEBB). FRANCE MOD/EUR UK ECO/DEV LABOR NAT/G BAL/PWR FEDERAL ALL/VALS...OLD/LIB TREND 18/20 SAINTSIMON. PAGE 64 H1285 — B65 SOCISM CONCPT UTOPIA ORD/FREE

BURNHAM J.,THE WAR WE ARE IN, THE LAST DECADE AND THE NEXT. ASIA COM EUR+WWI S/ASIA WOR+45 ECO/UNDEV INT/ORG FORCES WAR...OLD/LIB TREND 20 COLD/WAR. PAGE 25 H0492 — B67 POLICY NAT/G DIPLOM NAT/COMP

SMITH A.,THE WEALTH OF NATIONS. UK STRUCT WORKER DIPLOM ECO/TAC OPTIMAL DRIVE PERSON ORD/FREE ...OLD/LIB GEN/LAWS 17/18. PAGE 145 H2905 — B76 WEALTH PRODUC INDUS LAISSEZ

TAINE H.A.,MODERN REGIME (2 VOLS.). FRANCE FAM REV CENTRAL MARRIAGE PWR...TREND 19 NAPOLEON/B. PAGE 152 H3037 — B90 STRUCT NAT/G OLD/LIB MORAL

OLD/STOR....CONVENTIONAL INFORMATION-STORAGE SYSTEMS

OLDMAN J.H. H2412

OLIGARCHY....SEE ELITES

OLIGOPOLY....SEE MONOPOLY

OLIN/MTHSN....OLIN MATHIESON

OLIVARES....OLIVARES, HEAD OF SPAIN DURING CATALAN REV., 1640

ELLIOT J.H.,THE REVOLT OF THE CATALANS. SPAIN LOC/G PROVS FORCES DIPLOM TASK WAR GOV/REL INGP/REL ...POLICY 17 OLIVARES. PAGE 45 H0909 — B63 REV NAT/G TOP/EX DOMIN

OLIVER D.L. H2413

OLIVER R. H2414

OLLE-LAPRUNE J. H2415

OLSON M. H2416

OMABOE E.N. H0342

OMAN C. H2417

OMBUDSMAN....OMBUDSMAN; DOMESTIC GRIEVANCE ORGAN

JUSTICE,THE CITIZEN AND THE ADMINISTRATION: THE REDRESS OF GRIEVANCES (PAMPHLET). EUR+WWI UK LAW CONSTN STRATA NAT/G CT/SYS PARTIC COERCE...NEW/IDEA IDEA/COMP 20 OMBUDSMAN. PAGE 82 H1644 — B61 INGP/REL CONSULT ADJUD REPRESENT

HALLER W.,DER SCHWEDISCHE JUSTITIEOMBUDSMAN. — B64 JURID

DENMARK FINLAND NORWAY SWEDEN LEGIS ADJUD CONTROL PERSON ORD/FREE...NAT/COMP 20 OMBUDSMAN. PAGE 64 H1288 — PARL/PROC ADMIN CHIEF

B66
ANDERSON S.V.,CANADIAN OMBUDSMAN PROPOSALS. CANADA LEGIS DEBATE PARL/PROC...MAJORIT JURID TIME/SEQ IDEA/COMP 20 OMBUDSMAN PARLIAMENT. PAGE 7 H0133 — NAT/G CREATE ADMIN POL/PAR

ONSLOW C. H2418

ONTARIO....ONTARIO, CANADA

ONUOHA B. H2419

OOSTEN F. H2420

OP/RES....OPERATIONS RESEARCH; SEE ALSO CREATE

B22
OGBURN W.F.,SOCIAL CHANGE WITH RESPECT TO CULTURE AND ORIGINAL NATURE. ACT/RES OP/RES CRIME GP/REL ANOMIE BIO/SOC PWR...PSY SOC TIME/SEQ METH SOC/INTEG. PAGE 120 H2405 — CULTURE CREATE TEC/DEV

B27
WILLOUGHBY W.F.,PRINCIPLES OF PUBLIC ADMINISTRATION WITH SPECIAL REFERENCE TO THE NATIONAL AND STATE GOVERNMENTS OF THE UNITED STATES. FINAN PROVS CHIEF CONSULT LEGIS CREATE BUDGET EXEC ROUTINE GOV/REL CENTRAL...MGT 20 BUR/BUDGET CONGRESS PRESIDENT. PAGE 169 H3373 — NAT/G EX/STRUC OP/RES ADMIN

B30
CANAWAY A.P.,THE FAILURE OF FEDERALISM IN AUSTRALIA. UK PROB/SOLV ADMIN EFFICIENCY ATTIT ...POLICY NAT/COMP 20 AUSTRAL. PAGE 26 H0518 — FEDERAL NAT/G CONSTN OP/RES

B35
DOUGLASS H.P.,THE PROTESTANT CHURCH AS A SOCIAL INSTITUTION. CULTURE FINAN NEIGH PROF/ORG OP/RES ADMIN...POLICY SOC/WK STAT BIBLIOG. PAGE 42 H0843 — SECT PARTIC INGP/REL GP/REL

B39
JENNINGS W.I.,PARLIAMENT. UK POL/PAR OP/RES BUDGET LEAD CHOOSE GP/REL...MGT 20 PARLIAMENT HOUSE/LORD HOUSE/CMNS. PAGE 80 H1609 — PARL/PROC LEGIS CONSTN NAT/G

B40
HERSKOVITS M.J.,THE ECONOMIC LIFE OF PRIMITIVE PEOPLES. INDUS OP/RES PLAN PROB/SOLV...BIBLIOG METH 20. PAGE 70 H1407 — CULTURE ECO/TAC ECO/UNDEV PRODUC

B41
COHEN E.W.,THE GROWTH OF THE BRITISH CIVIL SERVICE 1780-1939. UK NAT/G SENIOR ROUTINE GOV/REL...MGT METH/COMP BIBLIOG 18/20. PAGE 31 H0616 — OP/RES TIME/SEQ CENTRAL ADMIN

B50
LIPSET S.M.,AGRARIAN SOCIALISM. CANADA POL/PAR OP/RES ECO/TAC ADMIN ATTIT...TIME/SEQ NAT/COMP SOC/EXP 20 SASKATCH. PAGE 97 H1938 — SOCISM AGRI METH/COMP STRUCT

B52
SPICER E.H.,HUMAN PROBLEMS IN TECHNOLOGICAL CHANGE. ECO/UNDEV AGRI INDUS NAT/G ACT/RES LEAD GP/REL INGP/REL ROLE...INT METH 20 CASEBOOK. PAGE 147 H2947 — TEC/DEV CULTURE STRUCT OP/RES

C52
LEWIS B.W.,"BRITISH PLANNING AND NATIONALIZATION." UK INDUS SERV/IND LABOR NAT/G OP/RES TEC/DEV TAX WEALTH...CHARTS BIBLIOG 20. PAGE 96 H1912 — NEW/LIB ECO/DEV POL/PAR PLAN

N52
COORDINATING COMM DOC SOC SCI,INTERNATIONAL REPERTORY OF SOCIAL SCIENCE DOCUMENTATION CENTERS (PAMPHLET). ACT/RES OP/RES WRITING KNOWL...CON/ANAL METH. PAGE 33 H0661 — BIBLIOG/A R+D NAT/G INT/ORG

B53
APPLEBY P.H.,PUBLIC ADMINISTRATION IN INDIA: REPORT OF A SURVEY. INDIA LOC/G OP/RES ATTIT ORD/FREE 20. PAGE 7 H0147 — ADMIN NAT/G EX/STRUC GOV/REL

B53
KANTOR H.,A BIBLIOGRAPHY OF UNPUBLISHED DOCTORAL DISSERTATIONS AND MASTERS' THESES DEALING WITH GOVTS, POL, INT REL OF LAT AM. L/A+17C INT/ORG POL/PAR ACT/RES OP/RES CONFER ATTIT...INT/LAW PHIL/SCI 20. PAGE 83 H1656 — BIBLIOG ACADEM DIPLOM NAT/G

B59
JENNINGS W.I.,CABINET GOVERNMENT (3RD ED.). UK POL/PAR CHIEF BUDGET ADMIN CHOOSE GP/REL 20. PAGE 81 H1612 — DELIB/GP NAT/G CONSTN OP/RES

S59
CHAPMAN B.,"THE FRENCH CONSEIL D'ETAT." FRANCE NAT/G CONSULT OP/RES PROB/SOLV PWR...OBS 20. PAGE 29 H0580 — ADMIN LAW CT/SYS

LEGIS

B60
AUSTRUY J.,STRUCTURE ECONOMIQUE ET CIVILISATION: L'EGYPTE ET LE DESTIN ECONOMIQUE DE L'ISLAM. ISLAM UAR CREATE OP/RES ECO/TAC...SOC BIBLIOG 20 MUSLIM. PAGE 9 H0182 — ECO/UNDEV CULTURE STRUCT

B61
ETZIONI A.,COMPLEX ORGANIZATIONS: A SOCIOLOGICAL READER. CLIENT CULTURE STRATA CREATE OP/RES ADMIN ...POLICY METH/CNCPT BUREAUCRCY. PAGE 47 H0945 — VOL/ASSN STRUCT CLASSIF PROF/ORG

B61
YUAN TUNG-LI,A GUIDE TO DOCTORAL DISSERTATIONS BY CHINESE STUDENTS IN AMERICA, 1905-1960. ASIA CULTURE SOCIETY ECO/UNDEV NAT/G PROB/SOLV DIPLOM LEAD ATTIT...HUM SOC STAT 20. PAGE 172 H3442 — BIBLIOG ACADEM ACT/RES OP/RES

L61
KAUPER P.G.,"CHURCH AND STATE: COOPERATIVE SEPARATISM." NAT/G LEGIS OP/RES TAX EDU/PROP GP/REL TREND. PAGE 84 H1671 — SECT CONSTN LAW POLICY

S61
MACRIDIS R.C.,"INTEREST GROUPS IN COMPARATIVE ANALYSIS." CULTURE OP/RES LOBBY REPRESENT GP/REL AUTHORIT ORD/FREE PWR...POLICY DECISION METH/CNCPT CLASSIF. PAGE 101 H2010 — GP/COMP CONCPT PLURISM

B62
BINDER L.,IRAN: POLITICAL DEVELOPMENT IN A CHANGING SOCIETY. IRAN OP/RES REV GP/REL CENTRAL RATIONAL PWR...PHIL/SCI NAT/COMP GEN/LAWS 20. PAGE 17 H0337 — LEGIT NAT/G ADMIN STRUCT

B62
MEIER R.L.,A COMMUNICATIONS THEORY OF URBAN GROWTH. CULTURE ECO/DEV COMPUTER BUDGET UTIL KNOWL...SOC CONCPT METH 20 OPEN/SPACE. PAGE 108 H2164 — OP/RES COM/IND MUNIC CONTROL

B63
DEUTSCH K.W.,THE NERVES OF GOVERNMENT. NAT/G CREATE EDU/PROP CONTROL LEAD PWR...CONCPT GEN/LAWS 20. PAGE 40 H0799 — DECISION GAME SIMUL OP/RES

B63
DUE J.F.,STATE SALES TAX ADMINISTRATION. OP/RES BUDGET PAY ADMIN EXEC ROUTINE COST EFFICIENCY PROFIT...CHARTS METH/COMP 20. PAGE 43 H0855 — PROVS TAX STAT GOV/COMP

B63
FAWCETT J.E.S.,THE BRITISH COMMONWEALTH IN INTERNATIONAL LAW. LAW INT/ORG NAT/G VOL/ASSN OP/RES DIPLOM ADJUD CENTRAL CONSEN...NET/THEORY CMN/WLTH TREATY. PAGE 49 H0977 — INT/LAW STRUCT COLONIAL

B63
US ATOMIC ENERGY COMMISSION,ATOMIC ENERGY IN THE SOVIET UNION: TRIP REPORT OF THE US ATOMIC ENERGY DELEGATION, MAY 1933. USSR R+D NAT/G CONSULT CREATE DIPLOM ADMIN ROUTINE EFFICIENCY PRODUC KNOWL SKILL ...NAT/COMP 20 AEC TRAVEL TREATY. PAGE 159 H3176 — METH/COMP OP/RES TEC/DEV NUC/PWR

B64
BROWN N.,NUCLEAR WAR* THE IMPENDING STRATEGIC DEADLOCK. USA+45 USSR TEC/DEV BUDGET RISK ARMS/CONT NUC/PWR WEAPON COST BIO/SOC...GEOG IDEA/COMP NAT/COMP GAME NATO WARSAW/P. PAGE 22 H0448 — FORCES OP/RES WAR GEN/LAWS

B65
CARTER G.M.,POLITICS IN EUROPE. EUR+WWI FRANCE GERMANY/W UK USSR LAW CONSTN POL/PAR VOL/ASSN PRESS LOBBY PWR...ANTHOL SOC/INTEG EEC. PAGE 27 H0548 — GOV/COMP OP/RES ECO/DEV

B65
WALKER A.A.,THE RHODESIAS AND NYASALAND: A GUIDE TO OFFICIAL PUBLICATIONS. RHODESIA UK OP/RES PLAN PROB/SOLV DIPLOM...POLICY SOC CON/ANAL 19/20 NYASALAND. PAGE 164 H3291 — BIBLIOG NAT/G COLONIAL AFR

B65
WHITEMAN M.M.,DIGEST OF INTERNATIONAL LAW* VOLUME 5, DEPARTMENT OF STATE PUBLICATION 7873. USA+45 WOR+45 OP/RES...CONCPT CLASSIF RECORD IDEA/COMP. PAGE 167 H3353 — INT/LAW NAT/G NAT/COMP

S65
WHITE J.,"WEST GERMAN AID TO DEVELOPING COUNTRIES." INT/ORG OP/RES GIVE CENTRAL ATTIT DRIVE...STAT NAT/COMP COLD/WAR. PAGE 167 H3348 — GERMANY FOR/AID ECO/UNDEV CAP/ISM

S65
WOHLSTETTER R.,"CUBA AND PEARL HARBOR* HINDSIGHT AND FORESIGHT." USSR FORCES OP/RES TEC/DEV ATTIT PERCEPT...DECISION IDEA/COMP NAT/COMP STERTYP TIME. PAGE 170 H3395 — CUBA RISK WAR ACT/RES

B66
BHALERAO C.N.,PUBLIC SERVICE COMMISSIONS OF INDIA: A STUDY. INDIA SERV/IND EX/STRUC ROUTINE CHOOSE GOV/REL INGP/REL...KNO/TEST EXHIBIT 20. PAGE 16 H0326 — NAT/G OP/RES LOC/G ADMIN

B66
BROWN R.T.,TRANSPORT AND THE ECONOMIC INTEGRATION OF SOUTH AMERICA. L/A+17C ECO/UNDEV NAT/G OP/RES DIPLOM INT/TRADE REGION WEALTH...ECOMETRIC GEOG STAT LAFTA TIME. PAGE 22 H0449 — MARKET DIST/IND SIMUL

B66
BUTLER D.E.,THE BRITISH GENERAL ELECTION OF 1966. UK LOC/G NAT/G OP/RES CONFER CHOOSE MAJORITY ATTIT ...CHARTS TIME 20. PAGE 25 H0498 — POL/PAR REPRESENT GP/REL PERS/REL

B66
MERILLAT H.C.L.,LEGAL ADVISERS AND INTERNATIONAL ORGANIZATIONS. LAW NAT/G CONSULT OP/RES ADJUD SANCTION TASK CONSEN ORG/CHARTS. PAGE 109 H2178 — INT/ORG INT/LAW CREATE OBS

L66
"FEDERAL, STATE AND LOCAL GOVERNMENT PUBLICATIONS." ACADEM LOC/G NAT/G PROVS SCHOOL EFFICIENCY ...PHIL/SCI ANTHOL. PAGE 143 H2854 — BIBLIOG OP/RES METH

B67
ANDERSON C.W.,POLITICS AND ECONOMIC CHANGE IN LATIN AMERICA. L/A+17C INDUS NAT/G OP/RES ADMIN DEMAND ...POLICY STAT CHARTS NAT/COMP 20. PAGE 6 H0125 — ECO/UNDEV PROB/SOLV PLAN ECO/TAC

B67
COWLES M.,PERSPECTIVES IN THE EDUCATION OF DISADVANTAGED CHILDREN. CULTURE OP/RES PLAN PERS/REL ADJUST HABITAT PERCEPT KNOWL WEALTH ...SOC/WK IDEA/COMP ANTHOL 20. PAGE 34 H0686 — EDU/PROP AGE/C TEC/DEV SCHOOL

B67
GALBRAITH J.K.,THE NEW INDUSTRIAL STATE. INDUS LABOR LG/CO NAT/G POL/PAR SCHOOL OP/RES CAP/ISM EXEC TREND. PAGE 54 H1087 — TEC/DEV ECO/DEV SOCIETY MARKET

B67
VENKATESWARAN R.J.,CABINET GOVERNMENT IN INDIA. INDIA UK SOCIETY OP/RES COLONIAL LEAD EFFICIENCY ORD/FREE 20. PAGE 162 H3241 — DELIB/GP ADMIN CONSTN NAT/G

S67
BERLINER J.S.,"RUSSIA'S BUREAUCRATS - WHY THEY'RE REACTIONARY." USSR NAT/G OP/RES PROB/SOLV TEC/DEV CONTROL SANCTION EFFICIENCY DRIVE PERSON...TECHNIC SOC 20. PAGE 15 H0308 — CREATE ADMIN INDUS PRODUC

S67
COLLINS B.A.,"SOME NOTES ON PUBLIC SERVICE COMMISSIONS IN THE COMMONWEALTH CARIBBEAN." JAMAICA L/A+17C TRINIDAD UK NAT/G OP/RES DOMIN SENIOR COLONIAL CONTROL INGP/REL CENTRAL EFFICIENCY PWR ...DECISION 20. PAGE 31 H0631 — ADMIN EX/STRUC ECO/UNDEV CHOOSE

S67
KROLL M.,"POLITICAL LEADERSHIP AND ADMINISTRATIVE COMMUNICATIONS IN NEW NATION STATES* CASE STUDY OF TRINIDAD AND TOBAGO." L/A+17C TRINIDAD INTELL OP/RES DOMIN COLONIAL LEAD GP/REL CENTRAL EFFICIENCY...DECISION OBS METH/COMP 20. PAGE 89 H1774 — NAT/G ADMIN EDU/PROP CONTROL

S67
LEVCIK B.,"WAGES AND EMPLOYMENT PROBLEMS IN THE NEW SYSTEM OF PLANNED MANAGEMENT IN CZECHOSLOVAKIA." CZECHOSLVK EUR+WWI NAT/G OP/RES PLAN ADMIN ROUTINE INGP/REL CENTRAL EFFICIENCY PRODUC DECISION. PAGE 95 H1895 — MARXISM WORKER MGT PAY

S67
NUGENT J.B.,"ECONOMIC THOUGHT, INVESTMENT CRITERIA, AND DEVELOPMENT STRATEGIES IN GREECE* A POSTWAR SURVEY." GREECE AGRI INDUS INT/ORG NAT/G OP/RES DEMAND OPTIMAL PRODUC WEALTH 20 EEC. PAGE 119 H2379 — ECO/UNDEV PLAN FINAN

S68
LAPIERRE J.W.,"TRADITION ET MODERNITE A MADAGASCAR." ISLAM MADAGASCAR AGRI FINAN KIN NAT/G CREATE OP/RES GP/REL INGP/REL ATTIT CONSERVE...PSY 20. PAGE 91 H1813 — ECO/UNDEV FOR/AID CULTURE TEC/DEV

B96
SCHMOLLER G.,THE MERCANTILE SYSTEM AND ITS HISTORICAL SIGNIFICANCE: ILLUSTRATED CHIEFLY FROM PRUSSIAN HISTORY (TRANS.). PRUSSIA CULTURE INDUS KIN MUNIC NAT/G PROVS OP/RES ECO/TAC INT/TRADE SUPEGO PWR WEALTH 19 MERCANTLST. PAGE 139 H2790 — GEN/METH INGP/REL CONCPT

OPA....OFFICE OF PRICE ADMINISTRATION

OPEN/SPACE....OPEN SPACE - TOWN AND COUNTRY PLANNING

B62
MEIER R.L.,A COMMUNICATIONS THEORY OF URBAN GROWTH. CULTURE ECO/DEV COMPUTER BUDGET UTIL KNOWL...SOC CONCPT METH 20 OPEN/SPACE. PAGE 108 H2164 — OP/RES COM/IND MUNIC CONTROL

B64
CULLINGWORTH J.B.,TOWN AND COUNTRY PLANNING IN ENGLAND AND WALES. UK LAW SOCIETY CONSULT ACT/RES ADMIN ROUTINE LEISURE INGP/REL ADJUST PWR...GEOG 20 OPEN/SPACE URBAN/RNWL. PAGE 36 H0718 — MUNIC PLAN NAT/G PROB/SOLV

OPERATIONAL RESEARCH AND RELATED MANAGEMENT SCIENCE.... SEE OR/MS

OPERATIONS AND POLICY RESEARCH H2421,H2422,H2423

OPERATIONS RESEARCH....SEE OP/RES

OPINION TESTS AND POLLS....SEE KNO/TEST

OPPENHEIMER F. H2424

OPTIMAL....OPTIMALITY

B38
LAWLEY F.E.,THE GROWTH OF COLLECTIVE ECONOMY VOL. 1: NATIONAL. EUR+WWI AGRI INDUS NAT/G BARGAIN CAP/ISM ECO/TAC WAR OPTIMAL WEALTH...GOV/COMP METH/COMP 19/20 MONOPOLY. PAGE 92 H1844 — SOCISM PRICE CONTROL OWN

B38
LAWLEY F.E.,THE GROWTH OF COLLECTIVE ECONOMY VOL. 2: INTERNATIONAL. WOR-45 AGRI INDUS EQUILIB OPTIMAL OWN WEALTH...NAT/COMP 19/20 NAZI NEW/DEAL MONOPOLY. PAGE 92 H1845 — ECO/TAC SOCISM NAT/LISM CONTROL

B60
DIA M.,REFLEXIONS SUR L'ECONOMIE DE L'AFRIQUE NOIRE (REV. ED.). CULTURE ECO/UNDEV CREATE TEC/DEV DIPLOM INT/TRADE OPTIMAL ATTIT...POLICY 20. PAGE 41 H0816 — AFR ECO/TAC SOCISM PLAN

S62
MARTIN L.W.,"THE MARKET FOR STRATEGIC IDEAS IN BRITAIN: THE 'SANDYS ERA'" UK ARMS/CONT WAR GOV/REL OPTIMAL...POLICY DECISION GOV/COMP COLD/WAR CMN/WLTH. PAGE 103 H2063 — DIPLOM COERCE FORCES PWR

B64
BAUCHET P.,ECONOMIC PLANNING. FRANCE STRATA LG/CO CAP/ISM ADMIN PARL/PROC DEMAND OPTIMAL ATTIT PWR SOCISM...POLICY CHARTS 20. PAGE 12 H0238 — ECO/DEV NAT/G PLAN ECO/TAC

B64
INTERNATIONAL LABOUR OFFICE,EMPLOYMENT AND ECONOMIC GROWTH. ECO/DEV ECO/UNDEV NAT/G PLAN DIPLOM INT/TRADE CONTROL INCOME PRODUC WEALTH...STAT NAT/COMP 20 ILO. PAGE 78 H1558 — WORKER METH/COMP ECO/TAC OPTIMAL

B64
MARTINET G.,MARXISM OF OUR TIME: OR THE CONTRADICTIONS OF SOCIALISM. FRANCE NAT/G OPTIMAL RIGID/FLEX SOCISM...IDEA/COMP 20. PAGE 103 H2067 — MARXISM MARXIST PROB/SOLV CREATE

B65
HARBISON F.,MANPOWER AND EDUCATION. AFR CHINA/COM IRAN L/A+17C S/ASIA TEC/DEV ADJUST OPTIMAL SKILL ...ANTHOL 20. PAGE 66 H1325 — ECO/UNDEV EDU/PROP WORKER NAT/COMP

S67
NUGENT J.B.,"ECONOMIC THOUGHT, INVESTMENT CRITERIA, AND DEVELOPMENT STRATEGIES IN GREECE* A POSTWAR SURVEY." GREECE AGRI INDUS INT/ORG NAT/G OP/RES DEMAND OPTIMAL PRODUC WEALTH 20 EEC. PAGE 119 H2379 — ECO/UNDEV PLAN FINAN

B76
SMITH A.,THE WEALTH OF NATIONS. UK STRUCT WORKER DIPLOM ECO/TAC OPTIMAL DRIVE PERSON ORD/FREE ...OLD/LIB GEN/LAWS 17/18. PAGE 145 H2905 — WEALTH PRODUC INDUS LAISSEZ

OR/MS....OPERATIONAL RESEARCH AND RELATED MANAGEMENT SCIENCE

ORANGE FREE STATE....SEE ORANGE/STA

ORANGE/STA....ORANGE FREE STATE

B18
EYBERS G.W.,SELECT CONSTITUTIONAL DOCUMENTS ILLUSTRATING SOUTH AFRICAN HISTORY 1795-1910. SOUTH/AFR LOC/G LEGIS CT/SYS...JURID ANTHOL 18/20 NATAL CAPE/HOPE ORANGE/STA. PAGE 48 H0955 — CONSTN LAW NAT/G COLONIAL

ORD/FREE....SECURITY, ORDER, RESTRAINT, LIBERTY, FREEDOM

NSY
MACKENZIE K.R.,THE ENGLISH PARLIAMENT. UK POL/PAR CHIEF DIPLOM TAX TASK WAR AUTHORIT...POLICY TREND 12/20 PARLIAMENT. PAGE 100 H2000 — ORD/FREE LEGIS NAT/G

B00
HOBSON J.A.,THE WAR IN SOUTH AFRICA: ITS CAUSES AND EFFECTS. NETHERLAND SOUTH/AFR UK ELITES AGRI EXTR/IND POL/PAR DIPLOM PRESS RACE/REL ATTIT ORD/FREE SOVEREIGN...INT 19 NEGRO. PAGE 72 H1439 — WAR DOMIN POLICY NAT/G

B02
JELLINEK G.,LA DECLARATION DES DROITS DE L'HOMME ET DU CITOYEN (1895) (TRANSLATED FROM GERMAN BY G. FARDIS). FRANCE GERMANY USA-45 NAT/G SECT LEGIS 18. PAGE 80 H1598 — ORD/FREE CONCPT REV

B03
FAGUET E.,LE LIBERALISME. FRANCE PRESS ADJUD ADMIN DISCRIM CONSERVE SOCISM...TRADIT SOC LING WORSHIP PARLIAMENT. PAGE 48 H0960 — ORD/FREE EDU/PROP NAT/G LAW

B05
MACHIAVELLI N.,THE ART OF WAR. CHRIST-17C TOP/EX DRIVE ORD/FREE PWR SKILL...MGT CHARTS. PAGE 100 — NAT/G FORCES

H1993 — WAR, ITALY

C05
DUNNING W.A.,"HISTORY OF POLITICAL THEORIES FROM LUTHER TO MONTESQUIEU." LAW NAT/G SECT DIPLOM REV WAR ORD/FREE SOVEREIGN CONSERVE...TRADIT BIBLIOG 16/18. PAGE 43 H0867 — PHIL/SCI, CONCPT, GEN/LAWS

B08
LLOYD H.D.,THE SWISS DEMOCRACY. SWITZERLND INDUS NAT/G WORKER CHOOSE OWN ORD/FREE SOCISM...PLURIST 19/20 MONOPOLY. PAGE 97 H1944 — NAT/COMP, GOV/COMP, REPRESENT, POPULISM

C09
SCHAPIRO J.S.,"SOCIAL REFORM AND THE REFORMATION." CHRIST-17C GERMANY LAW CONSTN LG/CO NAT/G WORKER PROB/SOLV CT/SYS REV...BIBLIOG 16. PAGE 138 H2770 — ORD/FREE, SECT, ECO/TAC, BIOG

B10
MILL J.S.,UTILITARIANISM, LIBERTY, AND REPRESENTATIVE GOVERNMENT. CONTROL PERCEPT PERSON MORAL...CONCPT GEN/LAWS. PAGE 110 H2205 — HAPPINESS, ORD/FREE, REPRESENT, NAT/G

B11
HUXLEY T.H.,METHOD AND RESULTS: ESSAYS. EDU/PROP REPRESENT OWN PERSON PWR WEALTH...PSY IDEA/COMP GEN/LAWS. PAGE 76 H1514 — ORD/FREE, NAT/G, POPULISM, PLURIST

B12
SONOLET L.,L'AFRIQUE OCCIDENTALE FRANCAISE. FRANCE AGRI INDUS NAT/G SECT FORCES INT/TRADE EDU/PROP RACE/REL HEALTH ORD/FREE...CHARTS 19/20 NEGRO AFRICA/W. PAGE 147 H2933 — DOMIN, ADMIN, COLONIAL, AFR

B13
KROPOTKIN P.,THE CONQUEST OF BREAD. SOCIETY STRATA AGRI INDUS WORKER REV HAPPINESS INCOME PRODUC HEALTH MORAL ORD/FREE. PAGE 89 H1775 — ANARCH, SOCIALIST, OWN, AGREE

B14
CRAIG J.,ELEMENTS OF POLITICAL SCIENCE (3 VOLS.). CONSTN AGRI INDUS SCHOOL FORCES TAX CT/SYS SUFF MORAL WEALTH...CONCPT 19 CIVIL/LIB. PAGE 35 H0696 — PHIL/SCI, NAT/G, ORD/FREE

B14
FIGGIS J.N.,CHURCHES IN THE MODERN STATE (2ND ED.). LAW CHIEF BAL/PWR PWR...CONCPT CHURCH/STA POPE. PAGE 50 H0998 — SECT, NAT/G, SOCIETY, ORD/FREE

N16
MILTON J.,THE READIE AND EASY WAY TO ESTABLISH A FREE COMMONWEALTH. CONSTN LEGIS PARL/PROC CONSERVE ...MAJORIT 17. PAGE 111 H2219 — ORD/FREE, NAT/G, CHIEF, POPULISM

B17
VEBLEN T.B.,AN INQUIRY INTO THE NATURE OF PEACE AND THE TERMS OF ITS PERPETUATION. UNIV STRATA FINAN EDU/PROP PRICE COST DISCRIM NAT/LISM MORAL ORD/FREE PACIFIST 20 WORLDUNITY. PAGE 162 H3237 — PEACE, DIPLOM, WAR, NAT/G

N17
BURKE E.,THOUGHTS ON THE PROSPECT OF A REGICIDE PEACE (PAMPHLET). FRANCE UK SECT DOMIN MURDER PEACE ORD/FREE SOVEREIGN POPULISM...POLICY GOV/COMP IDEA/COMP 18 JACOBINISM COEXIST. PAGE 24 H0483 — REV, CHIEF, NAT/G, DIPLOM

N17
BURKE E.,THOUGHTS ON THE CAUSE OF THE PRESENT DISCONTENTS (PAMPHLET). MOD/EUR UK CONSTN CHIEF LEGIS DOMIN CONTROL EXEC REPRESENT POPULISM ...TRADIT NEW/IDEA METH/COMP 18 BURKE/EDM. PAGE 24 H0484 — ORD/FREE, REV, PARL/PROC, NAT/G

N17
BURKE E.,LETTER TO SIR HERCULES LANGRISHE (PAMPHLET). IRELAND UK NAT/G CHIEF DIPLOM DOMIN PARL/PROC COERCE ORD/FREE SOVEREIGN POPULISM ...TRADIT 18 BURKE/EDM. PAGE 24 H0485 — POLICY, COLONIAL, SECT

B18
YUKIO O.,THE VOICE OF JAPANESE DEMOCRACY, AN ESSAY ON CONSTITUTIONAL LOYALTY (TRANS BY J. E. BECKER). ASIA POL/PAR DELIB/GP EX/STRUC RIGID/FLEX ORD/FREE PWR...POLICY JURID METH/COMP 19/20 CHINJAP. PAGE 172 H3443 — CONSTN, MAJORIT, CHOOSE, NAT/G

B19
DE MAN H.,THE REMAKING OF A MIND. EUR+WWI NAT/G ECO/TAC REGION ORD/FREE SOCISM...BIOG 20 WWI EUROPE. PAGE 38 H0762 — PSY, WAR, SELF/OBS, PARTIC

B19
DUGUIT L.,LAW IN THE MODERN STATE (TRANS. BY FRIDA AND HAROLD LASKI). CONSTN SOCIETY STRUCT MORAL ORD/FREE SOVEREIGN 20. PAGE 43 H0860 — GEN/LAWS, CONCPT, NAT/G, LAW

N19
COUTROT A.,THE FIGHT OVER THE 1959 PRIVATE EDUCATION LAW IN FRANCE (PAMPHLET). FRANCE NAT/G SECT GIVE EDU/PROP GP/REL ATTIT RIGID/FLEX ORD/FREE 20 CHURCH/STA. PAGE 34 H0681 — SCHOOL, PARL/PROC, CATHISM, LAW

N19
FREEMAN H.A.,COERCION OF STATES IN FEDERAL UNIONS (PAMPHLET). WOR-45 DIPLOM CONTROL COERCE PEACE ORD/FREE...GOV/COMP METH/COMP NAT/COMP PACIFIST 20. PAGE 53 H1055 — FEDERAL, WAR, INT/ORG, PACIFISM

N19
HARTUNG F.,ENLIGHTENED DESPOTISM (PAMPHLET). ORD/FREE SOVEREIGN CONSERVE...PHIL/SCI FREDERICK ENLIGHTNMT. PAGE 67 H1350 — NAT/G, CHIEF, CONCPT, PWR

N19
MAO TSE-TUNG,ON SOME IMPORTANT PROBLEMS OF THE PARTY'S PRESENT POLICY. CHINA/COM CONSTN ELITES INTELL AGRI DOMIN EDU/PROP REV REPRESENT GP/REL OWN PEACE ORD/FREE 20 COM/PARTY. PAGE 102 H2044 — POLICY, NAT/G, CHIEF, LEGIT

N19
SENGHOR L.S.,AFRICAN SOCIALISM (PAMPHLET). AFR FRANCE MALI USSR ELITES ECO/UNDEV NAT/G DIPLOM DOMIN EDU/PROP ATTIT 20 NEGRO. PAGE 141 H2827 — SOCISM, MARXISM, ORD/FREE, NAT/LISM

N19
TEMPLE W.,AN ESSAY UPON THE ORIGINAL AND NATURE OF GOVERNMENT (PAMPHLET). CHRIST-17C UK FAM LOC/G LEGIT ORD/FREE CONSERVE 17. PAGE 153 H3060 — NAT/G, CONCPT, PWR, SOCIETY

N19
WEBB L.C.,CHURCH AND STATE IN ITALY: 1947-1957 (PAMPHLET). GERMANY ITALY CONSTN POL/PAR AGREE CONTROL PARTIC CHOOSE ATTIT ORD/FREE FASCISM MARXISM 20 CHURCH/STA MARITAIN/J SALO. PAGE 166 H3316 — SECT, CATHISM, NAT/G, GP/REL

B20
BOSANQUET B.,THE PHILOSOPHICAL THEORY OF THE STATE (3RD ED.). SECT LEGIS EDU/PROP ORD/FREE...POLICY SOC GOV/COMP IDEA/COMP NAT/COMP. PAGE 19 H0380 — GEN/LAWS, CONSTN, NAT/G

B20
COX H.,ECONOMIC LIBERTY. UNIV LAW INT/TRADE RATION TARIFFS RACE/REL SOCISM POLICY. PAGE 34 H0687 — NAT/G, ORD/FREE, ECO/TAC, PERSON

B20
HALDANE R.B.,BEFORE THE WAR. MOD/EUR SOCIETY INT/ORG NAT/G DELIB/GP PLAN DOMIN EDU/PROP LEGIT ADMIN COERCE ATTIT DRIVE MORAL ORD/FREE PWR...SOC CONCPT SELF/OBS RECORD BIOG TIME/SEQ. PAGE 64 H1282 — POLICY, DIPLOM, UK

B22
KRABBE H.,THE MODERN IDEA OF THE STATE. LAW CHIEF DIPLOM DOMIN ADMIN REPRESENT CENTRAL ORD/FREE ...NEW/IDEA GOV/COMP IDEA/COMP. PAGE 88 H1761 — SOVEREIGN, CONSTN, PHIL/SCI

B23
DELBRUCK H.,GOVERNMENT AND THE WILL OF THE PEOPLE (TRANS. BY ROY S. MACELWEE). MOD/EUR NAT/G CHOOSE REPRESENT...CONCPT 19/20. PAGE 39 H0788 — SOVEREIGN, ORD/FREE, MAJORITY, POL/PAR

B25
WEBSTER C.,THE FOREIGN POLICY OF CASTLEREAGH: 1815-1822. LAW NAT/G DELIB/GP TOP/EX BAL/PWR ORD/FREE PWR RESPECT 19. PAGE 166 H3322 — MOD/EUR, DIPLOM, UK

B26
FORTESCUE J.,THE GOVERNANCE OF ENGLAND (1471-76). UK LAW FINAN SECT LEGIS PROB/SOLV TAX DOMIN ADMIN GP/REL COST ORD/FREE PWR 14/15. PAGE 52 H1042 — CONSERVE, CONSTN, CHIEF, NAT/G

B26
HOCKING W.E.,PRESENT STATUS OF THE PHILOSOPHY OF LAW AND OF RIGHTS. UNIV CULTURE INTELL SOCIETY NAT/G CREATE LEGIT SANCTION ALL/VALS SOC/INTEG 18/20. PAGE 72 H1442 — JURID, PHIL/SCI, ORD/FREE

B26
MACIVER R.M.,THE MODERN STATE. POL/PAR ORD/FREE TIME/SEQ. PAGE 100 H1997 — NAT/G, CONCPT, JURID, SOVEREIGN

B26
SMITH T.V.,THE DEMOCRATIC WAY OF LIFE. UNIV SOCIETY NAT/G WORKER TASK CHOOSE ALL/VALS...IDEA/COMP WORSHIP. PAGE 146 H2919 — MAJORIT, CONCPT, ORD/FREE, LEAD

B27
BELLOC H.,THE SERVILE STATE (1912) (3RD ED.). PRUSSIA UK CULTURE STRATA INDUS NAT/G ECO/TAC CONTROL LEAD SUFF DISCRIM EQUILIB ORD/FREE WEALTH 20. PAGE 13 H0269 — WORKER, CAP/ISM, DOMIN, CATH

B27
JOHN OF SALISBURY,THE STATESMAN'S BOOK (1159) (TRANS. BY J. DICKINSON). DOMIN GP/REL MORAL ORD/FREE PWR CONSERVE...CATH CONCPT 12. PAGE 81 H1617 — NAT/G, SECT, CHIEF, LAW

B28
BUELL R.,THE NATIVE PROBLEM IN AFRICA. KIN LABOR LOC/G ECO/TAC ROUTINE ORD/FREE...REC/INT KNO/TEST CENSUS TREND CHARTS SOC/EXP STERTYP 20. PAGE 23 H0466 — AFR, CULTURE

B28
CORBETT P.E.,CANADA AND WORLD POLITICS. LAW CULTURE SOCIETY STRUCT MARKET INT/ORG FORCES ACT/RES PLAN ECO/TAC LEGIT ORD/FREE PWR RESPECT...SOC CONCPT TIME/SEQ TREND CMN/WLTH 20 LEAGUE/NAT. PAGE 33 H0662 — NAT/G, CANADA

B28
HOBBES T.,THE ELEMENTS OF LAW, NATURAL AND POLITIC (1650). STRATA NAT/G SECT CHIEF AGREE ATTIT ALL/VALS MORAL ORD/FREE POPULISM...POLICY CONCPT. PAGE 71 H1432
PERSON LAW SOVEREIGN CONSERVE

B28
MARSILIUS/PADUA,DEFENSOR PACIS (1324). CHRIST-17C CONSTN NAT/G DIPLOM DOMIN LEGIT CONTROL WAR PEACE ORD/FREE SOVEREIGN POPULISM 14 POPE. PAGE 103 H2059
CATH SECT GEN/LAWS

B29
CAM H.M.,BIBLIOGRAPHY OF ENGLISH CONSTITUTIONAL HISTORY (PAMPHLET). UK LAW LOC/G NAT/G POL/PAR SECT DELIB/GP ADJUD ORD/FREE 19/20 PARLIAMENT. PAGE 25 H0510
BIBLIOG/A CONSTN ADMIN PARL/PROC

B29
STURZO L.,THE INTERNATIONAL COMMUNITY AND THE RIGHT OF WAR (TRANS. BY BARBARA BARCLAY CARTER). CULTURE CREATE PROB/SOLV DIPLOM ADJUD CONTROL PEACE PERSON ORD/FREE...INT/LAW IDEA/COMP PACIFIST 20 LEAGUE/NAT. PAGE 150 H3003
INT/ORG PLAN WAR CONCPT

B30
BENTHAM J.,THE RATIONALE OF PUNISHMENT. UK LAW LOC/G NAT/G LEGIS CONTROL...JURID GEN/LAWS COURT/SYS 19. PAGE 14 H0289
CRIME SANCTION COERCE ORD/FREE

B30
BURLAMAQUI J.J.,PRINCIPLES OF NATURAL AND POLITIC LAW (2 VOLS.) (1747-51). EX/STRUC LEGIS AGREE CT/SYS CHOOSE ROLE SOVEREIGN 18 NATURL/LAW. PAGE 24 H0490
LAW NAT/G ORD/FREE CONCPT

B30
HATTERSLEY A.F.,A SHORT HISTORY OF DEMOCRACY. WOR-45 CONSTN NAT/G SECT DOMIN WAR CHOOSE ORD/FREE PWR...CONCPT GOV/COMP BIBLIOG ATHENS ROME. PAGE 68 H1355
REPRESENT MAJORIT POPULISM

B30
HULL W.I.,INDIA'S POLITICAL CRISIS. INDIA UK INT/ORG LABOR SECT DELIB/GP LEGIS DIPLOM NEUTRAL REGION CROWD GOV/REL MAJORITY ATTIT 20 NEHRU/J GANDHI/M COMMONWLTH. PAGE 75 H1492
ORD/FREE NAT/G COLONIAL NAT/LISM

B30
LASKI H.J.,LIBERTY IN THE MODERN STATE. UNIV SOCIETY STRATA CREATE BAL/PWR CONTROL RATIONAL ATTIT PWR 18/20. PAGE 91 H1828
CONCPT ORD/FREE NAT/G DOMIN

B30
OLDMAN J.H.,WHITE AND BLACK IN AFRICA. AFR STRUCT COLONIAL PARTIC DISCRIM ISOLAT PRIVIL 20 SMUTS/JAN NEGRO WHITE/SUP. PAGE 121 H2412
SOVEREIGN ORD/FREE RACE/REL NAT/G

B30
WILLOUGHBY W.W.,THE ETHICAL BASIS OF POLITICAL AUTHORITY. NAT/G LEGIS PARL/PROC INGP/REL UTOPIA ORD/FREE 16/20. PAGE 169 H3374
MORAL POLICY CONSTN

B31
MACIVER R.M.,SOCIETY: ITS STRUCTURE AND CHANGES. CULTURE STRATA FAM CROWD HABITAT ORD/FREE...PSY SOC CONCPT BIBLIOG 20. PAGE 100 H1998
STRUCT SOCIETY PERSON DRIVE

B32
BLUM L.,PEACE AND DISARMAMENT (TRANS. BY A. WERTH). NAT/G FORCES WORKER DIPLOM AGREE WAR ATTIT AUTHORIT ORD/FREE. PAGE 18 H0360
SOCIALIST PEACE INT/ORG ARMS/CONT

B32
LUNT D.C.,THE ROAD TO THE LAW. UK USA-45 LEGIS EDU/PROP OWN ORD/FREE...DECISION TIME/SEQ NAT/COMP 16/20 AUSTRAL ENGLSH/LAW COMMON/LAW. PAGE 99 H1980
ADJUD LAW JURID CT/SYS

B32
MARRARO H.R.,AMERICAN OPINION ON THE UNIFICATION OF ITALY. ITALY FORCES DIPLOM SOVEREIGN CATHISM CONSERVE...CONCPT NAT/COMP BIBLIOG 19. PAGE 103 H2056
ORD/FREE NAT/LISM REV CONSTN

S32
BEARD C.A.,"REPRESENTATIVE GOVERNMENT IN EVOLUTION" WOR-45 AGRI TEC/DEV DOMIN EFFICIENCY ORD/FREE CONSERVE...TIME/SEQ GOV/COMP IDEA/COMP GRECO/ROMN. PAGE 12 H0248
REPRESENT POPULISM NAT/G PWR

B33
BERDYAYEV N.,CHRISTIANITY AND CLASS WAR. UNIV SOCIETY WORKER CREATE PROB/SOLV ATTIT PERSON ORD/FREE...CONCPT CHRISTIAN. PAGE 15 H0296
SECT MARXISM STRATA GP/REL

B33
FERRERO G.,PEACE AND WAR (TRANS. BY BERTHA PRITCHARD). CULTURE FINAN SECT ATTIT SUPEGO MORAL ORD/FREE CONSERVE POPULISM SOCISM POLICY. PAGE 49 H0987
WAR PEACE DIPLOM PROB/SOLV

B35
DE TOCQUEVILLE A.,DEMOCRACY IN AMERICA (4 VOLS.) (TRANS. BY HENRY REEVE). CONSTN STRUCT LOC/G NAT/G POL/PAR PROVS ETIQUET CT/SYS MAJORITY ATTIT 18/19. PAGE 39 H0772
POPULISM MAJORIT ORD/FREE SOCIETY

B35
LASKI H.J.,THE STATE IN THEORY AND PRACTICE. ELITES ECO/TAC REPRESENT ORD/FREE PWR WEALTH POPULISM ...GOV/COMP GEN/LAWS 19/20. PAGE 92 H1829
CAP/ISM COERCE NAT/G FASCISM

B35
MARRIOTT J.A.,DICTATORSHIP AND DEMOCRACY. GERMANY GREECE UK CHIEF DIPLOM DOMIN LEGIT PEACE ORD/FREE CONSERVE...TREND ROME HITLER/A. PAGE 103 H2057
TOTALISM POPULISM PLURIST NAT/G

B35
PARETO V.,THE MIND AND SOCIETY (4 VOLS.). ELITES SECT ECO/TAC COERCE PERSON ORD/FREE PWR SOVEREIGN FASCISM POPULISM...TRADIT 19/20. PAGE 123 H2465
GEN/LAWS SOC PSY

B36
BELLOC H.,THE RESTORATION OF PROPERTY. UK STRATA NAT/G PROF/ORG DELIB/GP WORKER CREATE PROB/SOLV ECO/TAC PARTIC UTOPIA ORD/FREE SOCISM 20. PAGE 13 H0270
CONTROL MAJORIT CAP/ISM OWN

B36
HUBERMAN L.,MAN'S WORLDLY GOODS: THE STORY OF THE WEALTH OF NATIONS. CHRIST-17C EUR+WWI MOD/EUR SOCIETY DOMIN REV ORD/FREE...TIME/SEQ METH/COMP. PAGE 74 H1486
WEALTH CAP/ISM MARXISM CREATE

B36
MARITAIN J.,FREEDOM IN THE MODERN WORLD. CONSTN NAT/G SECT CAP/ISM MARXISM SOCISM...GOV/COMP IDEA/COMP 19/20 HUMANISM CHRISTIAN. PAGE 102 H2049
GEN/LAWS POLICY ORD/FREE

B36
SMITH T.V.,THE PROMISE OF AMERICAN POLITICS. USA-45 WOR-45 LAW CONSTN STRATA PARTIC FASCISM LAISSEZ MARXISM...MAJORIT METH/COMP 18/20 JEFFERSN/T LOCKE/JOHN BENTHAM/J. PAGE 146 H2920
CONCPT ORD/FREE IDEA/COMP NAT/COMP

B36
VICO G.B.,DIRITTO UNIVERSALE (1722) (VOL. 2, PARTS 1,2, AND 3, OF G.B. VICO, OPERE). UNIV DIPLOM AGREE WAR OWN KNOWL ORD/FREE SOVEREIGN DEITY. PAGE 162 H3249
JURID SECT CONCPT NAT/G

C36
MAZZINI J.,"FROM THE COUNCIL TO GOD" (1870) IN J. MAZZINI, ESSAYS." ITALY NAT/G EDU/PROP PARTIC ORD/FREE PWR SOVEREIGN 19 POPE CHRISTIAN DEITY. PAGE 106 H2112
CATHISM DOMIN NAT/LISM SUPEGO

B37
MARX K.,THE CIVIL WAR IN THE UNITED STATES. USA-45 WORKER DIPLOM INT/TRADE DOMIN RACE/REL ATTIT ...TREND 19. PAGE 104 H2078
WAR REV MARXIST ORD/FREE

B38
HEIMANN E.,COMMUNISM, FASCISM, OR DEMOCRACY? WOR-45 CONSTN SOCIETY STRATA AGRI CAP/ISM MORAL ORD/FREE ...MAJORIT METH/COMP NAT/COMP 19/20. PAGE 69 H1384
SOCISM MARXISM FASCISM PLURISM

B38
HOLDSWORTH W.S.,A HISTORY OF ENGLISH LAW; THE CENTURIES OF SETTLEMENT AND REFORM (VOL. X). INDIA UK CONSTN NAT/G CHIEF LEGIS ADMIN COLONIAL CT/SYS CHOOSE ORD/FREE PWR...JURID 18 PARLIAMENT COMMONWLTH COMMON/LAW. PAGE 72 H1451
LAW LOC/G EX/STRUC ADJUD

B39
BENES E.,INTERNATIONAL SECURITY. GERMANY UK NAT/G DELIB/GP PLAN BAL/PWR ATTIT ORD/FREE PWR LEAGUE/NAT 20 TREATY. PAGE 14 H0280
EUR+WWI INT/ORG WAR

B39
MARITAIN J.,SCHOLASTICISM AND POLITICS. CONSTN SOCIETY NAT/G INGP/REL PERSON CATHISM POPULISM 19/20 FREUD/S SCHOLASTIC CHURCH/STA CHRISTIAN. PAGE 103 H2050
SECT GEN/LAWS ORD/FREE

C39
BURKE E.,"ON THE REFORM OF THE REPRESENTATION IN THE HOUSE OF COMMONS" (1782) IN COLLECTED WORKS (VOL. 5)" UK ELITES STRATA NAT/G REPRESENT ORD/FREE PWR POPULISM...POLICY NEW/IDEA GEN/LAWS 18 BURKE/EDM. PAGE 24 H0486
TRADIT CONSTN PARL/PROC LEGIS

B40
HOBBES T.,BEHEMOTH (1668). UK CONSTN SECT DOMIN LEGIT UTIL ORD/FREE CATHISM...POLICY CONCPT GEN/LAWS 17 CHARLES/I CROMWELL/O PROTESTANT. PAGE 71 H1433
REV NAT/G CHIEF

B40
HUNTER R.,REVOLUTION: WHY, HOW, WHEN? NAT/G ECO/TAC EDU/PROP COERCE ORD/FREE FASCISM POPULISM SOCISM 18/20 HITLER/A LENIN/VI. PAGE 75 H1502
REV METH/COMP LEAD CONSTN

B40
MCILWAIN C.H.,CONSTITUTIONALISM, ANCIENT AND MODERN. CHRIST-17C MOD/EUR NAT/G CHIEF PROB/SOLV INSPECT AUTHORIT ORD/FREE PWR...TIME/SEQ ROMAN/REP. PAGE 107 H2134
CONSTN GEN/LAWS LAW

B40
SIMON Y.,NATURE AND FUNCTIONS OF AUTHORITY. UNIV SOCIETY NAT/G CHIEF CONCPT. PAGE 144 H2880
ORD/FREE DOMIN GEN/LAWS PERSON

B41
GREEN T.H.,PRINCIPLES OF PUBLIC ADMINISTRATION. UNIV CONSTN VOL/ASSN INGP/REL MORAL ORD/FREE ...GOV/COMP IDEA/COMP GEN/LAWS 20. PAGE 60 H1208
POLICY LAISSEZ MAJORIT

B42
BARKER E.,REFLECTIONS ON GOVERNMENT. EUR+WWI SOCIETY LEGIS EDU/PROP ADMIN LEAD PARTIC CHOOSE TOTALISM AUTHORIT ORD/FREE SOCISM 20. PAGE 11 H0218
NAT/G POPULISM ACT/RES GEN/LAWS

B42
CRAIG A.,ABOVE ALL LIBERTIES. FRANCE UK USA-45 LAW CONSTN CULTURE INTELL NAT/G SECT JUDGE...IDEA/COMP BIBLIOG 18/20. PAGE 35 H0692
ORD/FREE MORAL WRITING EDU/PROP

B42
FEFFERO G.,THE PRINCIPLES OF POWER (TRANS. BY T. JAECKEL). MOD/EUR CONSTN NAT/G CHIEF CONTROL REV WAR ORD/FREE CONSERVE FASCISM POPULISM...GEN/LAWS 18/20 EUROPE. PAGE 49 H0980
PWR LEGIT TRADIT ELITES

B42
FORTESCU J.,IN PRAISE OF ENGLISH LAW (1464) (TRANS. BY S.B. CHRIMES). UK ELITES CHIEF FORCES CT/SYS COERCE CRIME GOV/REL ILLEGIT...JURID GOV/COMP GEN/LAWS 15. PAGE 52 H1040
LAW CONSTN LEGIS ORD/FREE

B42
HEGEL G.W.F.,PHILOSOPHY OF RIGHT. UNIV FAM SECT CHIEF AGREE WAR MARRIAGE OWN ORD/FREE...POLICY CONCPT. PAGE 69 H1383
NAT/G LAW RATIONAL

B42
LA BOETIE E.,ANTI-DICTATOR (1548) (TRANS. BY H. KUNZ). CONSTN NAT/G CHIEF DOMIN LEGIT CONTROL POPULISM. PAGE 90 H1790
PWR ORD/FREE TOTALISM GEN/LAWS

C42
CRAIG A.,"ABOVE ALL LIBERTIES." FRANCE UK LAW CULTURE INTELL SECT ORD/FREE 18/20. PAGE 35 H0693
BIBLIOG/A EDU/PROP WRITING MORAL

B43
LASKI H.J.,REFLECTIONS ON THE REVOLUTIONS OF OUR TIME. COM USSR NAT/G WORKER UTOPIA ORD/FREE WEALTH MARXISM SOCISM 19/20. PAGE 92 H1830
CAP/ISM WELF/ST ECO/TAC POLICY

B43
MARITAIN J.,THE RIGHTS OF MAN AND NATURAL LAW. CONSTN NAT/G DOMIN LEGIT INGP/REL TOTALISM MORAL POPULISM WORSHIP 19/20 CIVIL/LIB CHURCH/STA NATURL/LAW. PAGE 103 H2051
PLURIST ORD/FREE GEN/LAWS

B43
MC DOWELL R.B.,IRISH PUBLIC OPINION, 1750-1800. IRELAND CONSTN VOL/ASSN WORKER ORD/FREE CATHISM CONSERVE...POLICY IDEA/COMP BIBLIOG 18/ PARLIAMENT. PAGE 106 H2118
ATTIT NAT/G DIPLOM REV

B43
SERENI A.P.,THE ITALIAN CONCEPTION OF INTERNATIONAL LAW. EUR+WWI MOD/EUR INT/ORG NAT/G DOMIN COERCE ORD/FREE FASCISM...OBS/ENVIR TREND 20. PAGE 141 H2829
LAW TIME/SEQ INT/LAW ITALY

C43
BENTHAM J.,"ON THE LIBERTY OF THE PRESS, AND PUBLIC DISCUSSION" IN J. BOWRING, ED., THE WORKS OF JEREMY BENTHAM." SPAIN UK LAW ELITES NAT/G LEGIS INSPECT LEGIT WRITING CONTROL PRIVIL TOTALISM AUTHORIT ...TRADIT 19 FREE/SPEE. PAGE 15 H0290
ORD/FREE PRESS CONFER CONSERVE

C43
BENTHAM J.,"PRINCIPLES OF INTERNATIONAL LAW" IN J. BOWRING, ED., THE WORKS OF JEREMY BENTHAM." UNIV NAT/G PLAN PROB/SOLV DIPLOM CONTROL SANCTION MORAL ORD/FREE PWR SOVEREIGN 19. PAGE 15 H0291
INT/LAW JURID WAR PEACE

B44
BERDYAEV N.,SLAVERY AND FREEDOM. NAT/G REV WAR NAT/LISM OWN AUTHORIT SEX CONSERVE SOCISM...TRADIT PHIL/SCI CIVIL/LIB. PAGE 15 H0295
ORD/FREE PERSON ELITES SOCIETY

B44
SUAREZ F.,A TREATISE ON LAWS AND GOD THE LAWGIVER (1612) IN SELECTIONS FROM THREE WORKS, VOL. II. FRANCE ITALY UK CULTURE NAT/G SECT CHIEF LEGIS DOMIN LEGIT CT/SYS ORD/FREE PWR WORSHIP 16/17. PAGE 150 H3004
LAW JURID GEN/LAWS CATH

B44
WOLFE D.M.,LEVELLER MANIFESTOES OF THE PURITAN REVOLUTION. UK CONSTN NAT/G SECT...CONCPT ANTHOL 17 LEVELLERS DECLAR/IND PURITAN LOCKE/JOHN. PAGE 170 H3400
POL/PAR REV ORD/FREE ATTIT

L44
HUXLEY J.,"THE FUTURE OF THE COLONIES." AFR SOCIETY NAT/G PLAN DOMIN COERCE ATTIT DRIVE ORD/FREE PWR WEALTH...TIME/SEQ TREND AUD/VIS CHARTS 20. PAGE 76 H1511
ECO/UNDEV FUT COLONIAL

C44
SUAREZ F.,"ON WAR" (1621) IN SELECTIONS FROM THREE WORKS, VOL. I." NAT/G SECT CHIEF DIPLOM LEGIT MORAL PWR...POLICY INT/LAW 17. PAGE 150 H3005
WAR REV ORD/FREE CATH

B45
CROCE B.,POLITICS AND MORALS. UNIV NAT/G ECO/TAC ORD/FREE MARXISM POPULISM SOCISM...REALPOL 15/20 HEGEL/GWF ROUSSEAU/J. PAGE 35 H0704
MORAL GEN/LAWS IDEA/COMP

C45
PAINE T.,"THE AGE OF REASON IN T. PAINE, THE COMPLETE WRITINGS OF THOMAS PAINE (VOL. 1) (1794-95)" CULTURE ACT/RES DOMIN UTOPIA ATTIT PERCEPT WORSHIP. PAGE 122 H2445
SECT KNOWL PHIL/SCI ORD/FREE

B46
BLUM L.,FOR ALL MANKIND (TRANS. BY W. PICKLES). FRANCE GERMANY USSR LAW SOCIETY STRUCT POL/PAR WORKER DIPLOM DOMIN CHOOSE ORD/FREE FASCISM 20. PAGE 18 H0361
POPULISM SOCIALIST NAT/G WAR

B46
GODWIN W.,ENQUIRY CONCERNING POLITICAL JUSTICE AND ITS INFLUENCE ON MORALS AND HAPPINESS (1793). UNIV SOCIETY NAT/G GP/REL INGP/REL HAPPINESS ALL/VALS CONCPT. PAGE 58 H1151
MORAL PERSON ORD/FREE

B46
MILL J.S.,ON LIBERTY. NAT/G LEGIT CONTROL PERS/REL PERCEPT...CONCPT 19. PAGE 110 H2206
ORD/FREE SOCIETY PERSON GEN/LAWS

S46
DE GRE G.,"FREEDOM AND SOCIAL STRUCTURE" (BMR)" UNIV SOCIETY DOMIN CONTROL TOTALISM PLURISM...SOC CHARTS. PAGE 38 H0753
ORD/FREE STRUCT CONCPT GP/REL

B47
BOWLE J.,WESTERN POLITICAL THOUGHT: AN HISTORICAL INTRODUCTION FROM THE ORIGINS TO ROUSSEAU. CONSTN NAT/G SECT CREATE RATIONAL ORD/FREE...SOC BIBLIOG/A. PAGE 19 H0391
ATTIT IDEA/COMP PHIL/SCI

B47
LOCKE J.,TWO TREATISES OF GOVERNMENT (1690). UK LAW SOCIETY LEGIS LEGIT AGREE REV OWN HEREDITY MORAL CONSERVE...POLICY MAJORIT 17 WILLIAM/3 NATURL/LAW. PAGE 97 H1946
CONCPT ORD/FREE NAT/G CONSEN

B47
MCILWAIN C.H.,CONSTITUTIONALISM: ANCIENT AND MODERN. USA+45 ROMAN/EMP LAW CHIEF LEGIS CT/SYS GP/REL ORD/FREE SOVEREIGN...POLICY TIME/SEQ ROMAN/REP EUROPE. PAGE 107 H2135
CONSTN NAT/G PARL/PROC GOV/COMP

B47
NIEBUHR R.,THE CHILDREN OF LIGHT AND THE CHILDREN OF DARKNESS: A VINDICATION OF DEMOCRACY AND CRITIQUE OF TRADITIONAL DEFENSE. UNIV STRUCT NAT/G SECT INGP/REL OWN PEACE ORD/FREE MARXISM ...IDEA/COMP GEN/LAWS 20 CHRISTIAN. PAGE 118 H2358
POPULISM DIPLOM NEIGH GP/REL

B48
LASKI H.S.,THE AMERICAN DEMOCRACY. CULTURE INDUS SECT WORKER DIPLOM EDU/PROP REPRESENT RACE/REL ORD/FREE PWR...NAT/COMP 18/20. PAGE 92 H1831
NAT/G LOC/G USA-45 POPULISM

B48
LAUTERBACH A.,ECONOMIC SECURITY AND INDIVIDUAL FREEDOM: CAN WE HAVE BOTH? COM EUR+WWI MOD/EUR UNIV WOR+45 CAP/ISM TOTALISM ALL/VALS...GOV/COMP BIBLIOG 20. PAGE 92 H1840
ORD/FREE ECO/DEV DECISION INGP/REL

B48
ROSSITER C.L.,CONSTITUTIONAL DICTATORSHIP; CRISIS GOVERNMENT IN THE MODERN DEMOCRACIES. FRANCE GERMANY UK USA-45 WOR-45 EX/STRUC BAL/PWR CONTROL COERCE WAR CENTRAL ORD/FREE...DECISION 19/20. PAGE 134 H2688
NAT/G AUTHORIT CONSTN TOTALISM

B48
TOWSTER J.,POLITICAL POWER IN THE USSR: 1917-1947. USSR CONSTN CULTURE ELITES CREATE PLAN COERCE CENTRAL ATTIT RIGID/FLEX ORD/FREE...BIBLIOG SOC/INTEG 20 LENIN/VI STALIN/J. PAGE 156 H3122
EX/STRUC NAT/G MARXISM PWR

B48
TURNER A.C.,FREE SPEECH AND BROADCASTING. UK USA+45 ORD/FREE NAT/COMP. PAGE 157 H3140
COM/IND NAT/G CONTROL METH/COMP

S48
ALMOND G.A.,"THE CHRISTIAN PARTIES OF WESTEN EUROPE." EUR+WWI NAT/G EDU/PROP LEGIT TOTALISM ORD/FREE PWR MARXISM...TREND CHARTS STERTYP GEN/LAWS COLD/WAR 20. PAGE 5 H0110
POL/PAR CATH SOCISM

B49
DE JOUVENEL B.,ON POWER: ITS NATURE AND THE HISTORY OF ITS GROWTH. SOCIETY CHIEF REV WAR ATTIT AUTHORIT ORD/FREE SOVEREIGN CONSERVE POPULISM CONCPT. PAGE 38 H0757
PWR NAT/G DOMIN CONTROL

B49
DENNING A.,FREEDOM UNDER THE LAW. MOD/EUR UK LAW SOCIETY CHIEF EX/STRUC LEGIS ADJUD CT/SYS PERS/REL PERSON 17/20 ENGLSH/LAW. PAGE 40 H0793
ORD/FREE JURID NAT/G

B49
GRODZINS M.,AMERICANS BETRAYED: POLITICS AND THE JAPANESE EXPANSION. PROVS COERCE CHOOSE GOV/REL GP/REL INGP/REL ATTIT ORD/FREE...DECISION CHARTS 20 NISEI. PAGE 61 H1230
DISCRIM POLICY NAT/G WAR

B49
SCHONS D.,BOOK CENSORSHIP IN NEW SPAIN (NEW WORLD STUDIES, BOOK II). SPAIN LAW CULTURE INSPECT ADJUD CT/SYS SANCTION GP/REL ORD/FREE 14/17. PAGE 140 H2797
CHRIST-17C EDU/PROP CONTROL PRESS

L49
BRECHT A.,"THE NEW GERMAN CONSTITUTION." GERMANY/W NAT/G CHIEF EX/STRUC LEGIS PROB/SOLV ADMIN REPRESENT TOTALISM ORD/FREE PLURISM...MAJORIT CHARTS 20. PAGE 20 H0409
CONSTN DIPLOM SOVEREIGN FEDERAL

B50
BERMAN H.J.,JUSTICE IN RUSSIA; AN INTERPRETATION OF SOVIET LAW. USSR LAW STRUCT LABOR FORCES AGREE GP/REL ORD/FREE SOCISM...TIME/SEQ 20. PAGE 15 H0309
JURID ADJUD MARXISM COERCE

B50
CANTRIL H.,TENSIONS THAT CAUSE WAR. UNIV CULTURE R+D CREATE EDU/PROP DRIVE PERSON KNOWL ORD/FREE ...HUM PSY SOC OBS CENSUS TREND CON/ANAL SOC/EXP SIMUL GEN/METH ANTHOL COLD/WAR TOT/POP. PAGE 26 H0523
SOCIETY PHIL/SCI PEACE

B50
DUCLOS P.,L'EVOLUTION DES RAPPORTS POLITIQUES DEPUIS 1750 (LIBERTE, INTEGRATION, UNITE). LAW INT/ORG FEDERAL TOTALISM ATTIT PWR...MAJORIT BIBLIOG 18/20 PARLIAMENT EUROPE. PAGE 43 H0852
ORD/FREE DIPLOM NAT/G GOV/COMP

B50
HOBBES T.,LEVIATHAN. UNIV CONSTN SOCIETY LOC/G NAT/G CONSULT TOP/EX DOMIN DRIVE PERSON PWR ...PHIL/SCI CONCPT SELF/OBS GEN/LAWS TOT/POP. PAGE 72 H1434
LAW ORD/FREE

B50
MACHIAVELLI N.,THE DISCOURSES (1516). NAT/G SECT FORCES DOMIN LEGIT CONTROL LEAD COERCE TOTALISM ORD/FREE. PAGE 100 H1995
PWR GEN/LAWS CHIEF

B50
ORTON W.A.,THE ECONOMIC ROLE OF THE STATE. INTELL ECO/UNDEV PLAN CONTROL PWR SOVEREIGN...POLICY 17/20. PAGE 122 H2431
ECO/DEV NAT/G ECO/TAC ORD/FREE

B50
SCHUMPETER J.A.,CAPITALISM, SOCIALISM, AND DEMOCRACY (3RD ED.). USA-45 USSR WOR+45 WOR-45 INTELL ECO/DEV ECO/UNDEV ECO/TAC WAR PRODUC ORD/FREE...MGT SOC 20 MARX/KARL. PAGE 140 H2804
SOCIALIST CAP/ISM MARXISM IDEA/COMP

B50
WHITE R.J.,THE CONSERVATIVE TRADITION. UK POL/PAR SUPEGO PWR RESPECT...POLICY ANTHOL 19. PAGE 167 H3350
CONSERVE CONCPT NAT/G ORD/FREE

B51
BISSAINTHE M.,DICTIONNAIRE DE BIBLIOGRAPHIE HAITIENNE. HAITI ELITES AGRI LEGIS DIPLOM INT/TRADE WRITING ORD/FREE CATHISM...ART/METH GEOG 19/20 NEGRO TREATY. PAGE 17 H0347
BIBLIOG L/A+17C SOCIETY NAT/G

B51
CARRINGTON C.E.,THE LIQUIDATION OF THE BRITISH EMPIRE. AFR NAT/G INT/TRADE COLONIAL RACE/REL ATTIT ORD/FREE...POLICY NAT/COMP 20 CMN/WLTH. PAGE 27 H0541
SOVEREIGN NAT/LISM DIPLOM GP/REL

B51
EUCKEN W.,THIS UNSUCCESSFUL AGE. GERMANY NAT/G WORKER TEC/DEV ECO/TAC ORD/FREE 20. PAGE 47 H0947
ECO/DEV PLAN LAISSEZ NEW/LIB

B51
HALEVY E.,IMPERIALISM AND THE RISE OF LABOR (2ND ED.). UK NAT/G POL/PAR TOP/EX ATTIT ORD/FREE PWR 19/20 PARLIAMENT LABOR/PAR. PAGE 64 H1284
COLONIAL LABOR POLICY WAR

B51
HUXLEY J.,FREEDOM AND CULTURE. UNIV LAW SOCIETY R+D ACADEM SCHOOL CREATE SANCTION ATTIT KNOWL...HUM ANTHOL 20. PAGE 76 H1512
CULTURE ORD/FREE PHIL/SCI IDEA/COMP

B51
MARX K.,THE EIGHTEENTH BRUMAIRE OF LOUIS BONAPARTE (1852). FRANCE STRATA FINAN INDUS LABOR CHIEF FORCES WORKER CAP/ISM ECO/TAC PARL/PROC ORD/FREE ...MARXIST 19. PAGE 104 H2080
REV MARXISM ELITES NAT/G

B51
YOUNG T.C.,NEAR EASTERN CULTURE AND SOCIETY. ISLAM ECO/UNDEV SECT WRITING ATTIT HABITAT ORD/FREE 20. PAGE 172 H3439
CULTURE STRUCT REGION DIPLOM

S51
MACRAE D.G.,"THE BOLSHEVIK IDEOLOGY; THE INTELLECTUAL AND EMOTIONAL FACTORS IN COMMUNIST AFFILIATION" (BMR)" COM LEAD REV ATTIT ORD/FREE ...SOC CON/ANAL 20 BOLSHEVISM. PAGE 100 H2008
MARXISM INTELL PHIL/SCI SECT

S51
NORTHROP F.S.C.,"ASIAN MENTALITY AND UNITED STATES FOREIGN POLICY." ASIA ISLAM USA+45 CULTURE SOCIETY SECT EDU/PROP LEGIT COERCE DRIVE MORAL ORD/FREE ...POLICY RELATIV TOT/POP 20. PAGE 119 H2376
S/ASIA ATTIT DIPLOM

B52
HIMMELFARB G.,LORD ACTON: A STUDY IN CONSCIENCE AND POLITICS. MOD/EUR NAT/G POL/PAR SECT LEGIS TOP/EX EDU/PROP ADMIN NAT/LISM ATTIT PERSON SUPEGO MORAL ORD/FREE...CONCPT PARLIAMENT 19 ACTON/LORD. PAGE 71 H1419
PWR BIOG

B52
ISAACS H.R.,AFRICA: NEW CRISES IN THE MAKING (PAMPHLET). EUR+WWI USA+45 ELITES ECO/UNDEV WAR DISCRIM NAT/LISM ATTIT...POLICY NEW/IDEA CHARTS GOV/COMP 20 NEGRO COLD/WAR. PAGE 78 H1570
COLONIAL AFR RACE/REL ORD/FREE

B52
JULIEN C.A.,L'AFRIQUE DU NORD EN MARCHE: NATIONALISMES MUSULMANS ET SOUVERAINETE FRANCAISE (2ND ED). AFR ALGERIA FRANCE ISLAM MOROCCO NAT/G CONTROL ORD/FREE...POLICY 19/20 TUNIS MUSLIM. PAGE 82 H1641
NAT/LISM COERCE DOMIN COLONIAL

B52
LOPEZ-AMO A.,LA MONARQUIA DE LA REFORMA SOCIAL. MOD/EUR SPAIN CONSTN NAT/G TASK EFFICIENCY CONSERVE ...ANARCH TRADIT SOC CONCPT IDEA/COMP 19/20. PAGE 98 H1967
MARXISM REV LEGIT ORD/FREE

B52
ROBBINS L.,THE THEORY OF ECONOMIC POLICY IN ENGLISH CLASSICAL POLITICAL ECONOMY. UK ECO/DEV WORKER PLAN CAP/ISM EDU/PROP CONTROL INCOME OWN HEALTH SOCISM ...POLICY 17/19. PAGE 132 H2639
ECO/TAC ORD/FREE IDEA/COMP NAT/G

S52
EISENSTADT S.N.,"THE PROCESS OF ABSORPTION OF NEW IMMIGRANTS IN ISRAEL" (BMR)" ISRAEL CULTURE SCHOOL WORKER PARTIC DRIVE ORD/FREE...STAT OBS INT CHARTS SOC/INTEG 20 JEWS. PAGE 45 H0900
HABITAT ATTIT SAMP

S52
SABINE G.H.,"THE TWO DEMOCRATIC TRADITIONS" (BMR)" FRANCE UK USA-45 NAT/G CONTROL CHOOSE ALL/IDEOS ...PHIL/SCI CONCPT IDEA/COMP 20. PAGE 136 H2727
ORD/FREE POPULISM INGP/REL NAT/COMP

B53
APPLEBY P.H.,PUBLIC ADMINISTRATION IN INDIA: REPORT OF A SURVEY. INDIA LOC/G OP/RES ATTIT ORD/FREE 20. PAGE 7 H0147
ADMIN NAT/G EX/STRUC GOV/REL

B53
BIDNEY D.,THEORETICAL ANTHROPOLOGY. DRIVE ROLE ORD/FREE...CONCPT METH/CNCPT MYTH CLASSIF OBS IDEA/COMP METH/COMP BIBLIOG METH 20. PAGE 17 H0331
CULTURE SOC PSY PHIL/SCI

B53
BUCHHEIM K.,GESCHICHTE DER CHRISTLICHEN PARTEIEN IN DEUTSCHLAND. GERMANY CREATE ATTIT SUPEGO ORD/FREE ...TIME/SEQ IDEA/COMP 19/20 CHRIS/DEM. PAGE 23 H0464
POL/PAR NAT/G

B53
HUNTER E.,BRAIN-WASHING IN RED CHINA. ASIA CHINA/COM CULTURE SOCIETY FORCES WAR TOTALISM ATTIT BIO/SOC DISPL DRIVE PERSON SUPEGO KNOWL ORD/FREE ...INT REC/INT COLD/WAR 20. PAGE 75 H1499
EDU/PROP COERCE

B53
KEESING F.M.,CULTURE CHANGE: AN ANALYSIS AND BIBLIOGRAPHY OF ANTHROPOLOGICAL SOURCES TO 1952. CULTURE STRUCT...TIME/SEQ 19/20. PAGE 84 H1679
BIBLIOG SOC CREATE ORD/FREE

B53
LIEBER F.,CIVIL LIBERTY AND SELF GOVERNMENT: VOLUME 2. NAT/G CONTROL CHOOSE PERSON PWR 19 CIVIL/LIB. PAGE 96 H1925
ORD/FREE SOVEREIGN CENTRAL CONCPT

B53
MARITAIN J.,L'HOMME ET L'ETAT. SECT DIPLOM GP/REL PEACE ORD/FREE...IDEA/COMP 17/20 CHURCH/STA NATURL/LAW. PAGE 103 H2052
CONCPT NAT/G SOVEREIGN COERCE

B53
NELSON G.R.,FREEDOM AND WELFARE: SOCIAL PATTERNS IN THE NORTHERN COUNTRIES OF EUROPE. EUR+WWI ECO/DEV NAT/G EDU/PROP LEGIT HEALTH ORD/FREE SKILL WEALTH ...STAT AUD/VIS SCANDINAV WORK TOT/POP 20. PAGE 116 H2329
PLAN ECO/TAC

B53
ROSCIO J.G.,OBRAS. L/A+17C SPAIN DIPLOM REV WAR NAT/LISM TOTALISM PWR SOVEREIGN 19. PAGE 134 H2671
ORD/FREE COLONIAL NAT/G PHIL/SCI

B53
STOUT H.M.,BRITISH GOVERNMENT. UK FINAN LOC/G POL/PAR DELIB/GP DIPLOM ADMIN COLONIAL CHOOSE ORD/FREE...JURID BIBLIOG 20 COMMONWLTH. PAGE 150 H2990
NAT/G PARL/PROC CONSTN NEW/LIB

L53
DEUTSCH K.W.,"THE GROWTH OF NATIONS: SOME RECURRENT PATTERNS OF POLITICAL AND SOCIAL INTEGRATION" (BMR)" UNIV CULTURE SOCIETY ECO/DEV ECO/UNDEV NAT/G CREATE GP/REL...CONCPT GEN/LAWS SOC/INTEG 11/20. PAGE 40 H0797
TREND NAT/LISM ORD/FREE

B54
BERGER M.,FREEDOM AND CONTROL IN MODERN SOCIETY. LABOR NAT/G VOL/ASSN AUTHORIT DRIVE PLURISM ...METH/CNCPT CLASSIF. PAGE 15 H0300
ORD/FREE CONTROL INGP/REL

B54
CAMPANELLA T.,A DISCOURSE TOUCHING THE SPANISH MONARCHY... (1640). SPAIN UNIV SEA STRATA FINAN SECT FORCES SUPEGO LOVE ORD/FREE...CONCPT 17.
CONSERVE CHIEF NAT/G

PAGE 26 H0514 — DIPLOM

B54

FRIEDRICH C.J.,TOTALITARIAN DICTATORSHIP AND AUTOCRACY. COM EUR+WWI GERMANY ITALY USSR INTELL ECO/DEV NAT/G POL/PAR FORCES TOP/EX ECO/TAC EDU/PROP LEGIT COERCE ATTIT ORD/FREE PWR FASCISM ...CONCPT TIME/SEQ GEN/LAWS NAZI 20. PAGE 53 H1068 — SOCIETY DOMIN TOTALISM

L54

FRIEDRICH C.J.,"TOTALITARIANISM." COM EUR+WWI NAT/G POL/PAR SECT FORCES PLAN ECO/TAC DOMIN EDU/PROP EXEC COERCE REV ORD/FREE PWR...SOC CONCPT NAZI 20. PAGE 53 H1067 — ATTIT TOTALISM

L54

FURNISS E.S.,"WEAKNESSES IN FRENCH FOREIGN POLICY-MAKING." EUR+WWI LEGIS LEGIT EXEC ATTIT RIGID/FLEX ORD/FREE...SOC CONCPT METH/CNCPT OBS 20. PAGE 54 H1078 — NAT/G STRUCT DIPLOM FRANCE

B55

ALFIERI D.,DICTATORS FACE TO FACE. NAT/G TOP/EX DIPLOM EXEC COERCE ORD/FREE FASCISM...POLICY OBS 20 HITLER/A MUSSOLIN/B. PAGE 5 H0103 — WAR CHIEF TOTALISM PERS/REL

B55

DE ARAGAO J.G.,LA JURIDICTION ADMINISTRATIVE AU BRESIL. BRAZIL ADJUD COLONIAL CT/SYS REV FEDERAL ORD/FREE...BIBLIOG 19/20. PAGE 37 H0749 — EX/STRUC ADMIN NAT/G

B55

FRANZ G.,KULTURKAMPF. AUSTRIA GERMANY PRUSSIA SWITZERLND POL/PAR DIPLOM GP/REL ATTIT ORD/FREE 18/19 CHURCH/STA. PAGE 53 H1053 — NAT/LISM CATHISM NAT/G REV

B55

INTERNATIONAL COMN JURISTS,JUSTICE ENSLAVED. COM CONSTN LABOR NAT/G CONTROL CHOOSE 20. PAGE 78 H1555 — SOCISM TOTALISM ORD/FREE COERCE

B55

LIPSCOMB J.F.,WHITE AFRICANS. SOCIETY STRUCT AGRI ECO/TAC ADJUD COLONIAL COERCE PERS/REL ADJUST. PAGE 97 H1937 — RACE/REL HABITAT ECO/UNDEV ORD/FREE

B55

POHLENZ M.,GRIECHISCHE FREIHEIT. GREECE DIPLOM WAR SUPEGO PWR RESPECT...IDEA/COMP. PAGE 127 H2533 — ORD/FREE CONCPT JURID NAT/G

B55

ROWE C.,VOLTAIRE AND THE STATE. FRANCE MOD/EUR BAL/PWR CONTROL TASK SUPEGO ORD/FREE PWR...CONCPT 18 VOLTAIRE. PAGE 135 H2702 — NAT/G DIPLOM NAT/LISM ATTIT

B55

SVARLIEN O.,AN INTRODUCTION TO THE LAW OF NATIONS. SEA AIR INT/ORG NAT/G CHIEF ADMIN AGREE WAR PRIVIL ORD/FREE SOVEREIGN...BIBLIOG 16/20. PAGE 151 H3012 — INT/LAW DIPLOM

B55

VERGNAUD P.,L'IDEE DE LA NATIONALITE ET DE LA LIBRE DISPOSITION DES PEUPLES DANS SES RAPPORTS AVEC L'IDEE DE L'ETAT. STRATA NAT/G EDU/PROP RACE/REL AUTHORIT FASCISM MARXISM MYTH. PAGE 162 H3243 — NAT/LISM DISCRIM ORD/FREE

C55

APTER D.E.,"THE GOLD COAST IN TRANSITION." AFR CONSTN LOC/G LEGIS DIPLOM COLONIAL CONTROL GOV/REL ...CHARTS BIBLIOG 20 CMN/WLTH. PAGE 7 H0150 — ORD/FREE REPRESENT PARL/PROC NAT/G

B56

CARRIL B.,PROBLEMAS DE LA REVOLUCION Y LA DEMOCRACIA. CONSTN FORCES DOMIN CONTROL TOTALISM PWR 20. PAGE 27 H0539 — REV ORD/FREE LEGIT NAT/G

B56

DOUGLAS W.O.,WE THE JUDGES. INDIA USA+45 USA-45 LAW NAT/G SECT LEGIS PRESS CRIME FEDERAL ORD/FREE ...POLICY GOV/COMP 19/20 WARRN/EARL MARSHALL/J SUPREME/CT. PAGE 42 H0841 — ADJUD CT/SYS CONSTN GOV/REL

B56

FIELD G.C.,POLITICAL THEORY. POL/PAR REPRESENT MORAL SOVEREIGN...JURID IDEA/COMP. PAGE 50 H0990 — CONCPT NAT/G ORD/FREE DIPLOM

B56

HATCH J.C.,NEW FROM AFRICA. AFR FUT UK NAT/G GUERRILLA ATTIT ORD/FREE PWR...AUD/VIS CHARTS 20. PAGE 68 H1354 — NAT/LISM COLONIAL RACE/REL

B56

KALLEN H.M.,CULTURAL PLURALISM AND THE AMERICAN IDEA. RACE/REL ADJUST PERSON ORD/FREE LAISSEZ ...PLURIST GEN/LAWS ANTHOL. PAGE 83 H1652 — PLURISM CULTURE GP/REL SECT

B56

KUPER L.,PASSIVE RESISTANCE IN SOUTH AFRICA. SOUTH/AFR LAW NAT/G POL/PAR VOL/ASSN DISCRIM ...POLICY SOC AUD/VIS 20. PAGE 89 H1782 — ORD/FREE RACE/REL ATTIT

B56

MUMFORD L.,THE TRANSFORMATIONS OF MAN. UNIV CULTURE INGP/REL HABITAT HEREDITY ALL/VALS ORD/FREE...MYTH TIME/SEQ TREND WORSHIP. PAGE 114 H2287 — IDEA/COMP PERSON CONCPT

B56

RIESENBERG P.N.,INALIENABILITY OF SOVEREIGNTY IN MEDIEVAL POLITICAL THOUGHT. CHRIST-17C INTELL NAT/G SECT CHIEF LEGIS SANCTION AUTHORIT ORD/FREE CONSERVE...IDEA/COMP BIBLIOG 12/16. PAGE 131 H2627 — SOVEREIGN ATTIT

B56

VON HARPE W.,DIE SOWJETUNION FINNLAND UND SKANDANAVIEN, 1945-1955. EUR+WWI FINLAND GERMANY USSR WAR INGP/REL ORD/FREE SOVEREIGN MARXISM ...POLICY GOV/COMP BIBLIOG 20 STALIN/J. PAGE 163 H3270 — DIPLOM COM NEUTRAL BAL/PWR

B56

WOLFF R.L.,THE BALKANS IN OUR TIME. ALBANIA FUT MOD/EUR USSR YUGOSLAVIA CULTURE INT/ORG SECT DIPLOM EDU/PROP COERCE WAR ORD/FREE...CHARTS 4/20 BALKANS COMINFORM. PAGE 170 H3403 — GEOG COM

S56

BLAU P.M.,"SOCIAL MOBILITY AND INTERPERSONAL RELATIONS" (BMR)" UNIV CULTURE STRUCT WORKER ANOMIE ...SOC SOC/INTEG 19/20. PAGE 18 H0355 — INGP/REL PERS/REL ORD/FREE STRATA

S56

KHAMA T.,"POLITICAL CHANGE IN AFRICAN SOCIETY." CONSTN SOCIETY LOC/G NAT/G POL/PAR EX/STRUC LEGIS LEGIT ADMIN CHOOSE REPRESENT NAT/LISM MORAL ORD/FREE PWR...CONCPT OBS TREND GEN/METH CMN/WLTH 17/20. PAGE 85 H1706 — AFR ELITES

B57

AMERICAN COUNCIL LEARNED SOC,GOVERNMENT UNDER LAW AND THE INDIVIDUAL. ASIA ISLAM USSR NAT/G...POLICY SOC NAT/COMP 20. PAGE 6 H0121 — SOCIETY ORD/FREE CONCPT IDEA/COMP

B57

ARON R.,L'UNIFICATION ECONOMIQUE DE L'EUROPE. EUR+WWI SWITZERLND UK INT/ORG NAT/G REGION NAT/LISM ORD/FREE PWR...CONCPT METH/CNCPT OBS TREND STERTYP GEN/LAWS EEC 20. PAGE 8 H0168 — VOL/ASSN ECO/TAC

B57

ARON R.,THE OPIUM OF THE INTELLECTUALS (TRANS. BY TERENCE KILMARTIN). FRANCE USSR WOR+45 CULTURE POL/PAR PLAN DOMIN EDU/PROP REV ATTIT ORD/FREE ...IDEA/COMP METH/COMP NAT/COMP 20 COM/PARTY. PAGE 8 H0169 — INTELL UTOPIA MYTH MARXISM

B57

BULLOCK A.,THE LIBERAL TRADITION FROM FOX TO KEYNES. UK CULTURE INTELL CREATE WRITING COLONIAL PERS/REL ATTIT ORD/FREE...POLICY OLD/LIB TRADIT CONCPT 18/20 CHURCHLL/W MILL/JS KEYNES/JM ASQUITH/HH. PAGE 23 H0469 — ANTHOL DEBATE LAISSEZ

B57

COLE G.D.H.,THE POST WAR CONDITIONS OF BRITAIN. EUR+WWI STRUCT NAT/G PLAN EDU/PROP LEGIT RIGID/FLEX ORD/FREE WEALTH...SOCIALIST WELF/ST STAT TREND CON/ANAL CHARTS PARLIAMENT WORK 20. PAGE 31 H0624 — ECO/DEV UK

B57

LONG H.A.,USURPERS - FOES OF FREE MAN. LAW NAT/G CHIEF LEGIS DOMIN ADJUD REPRESENT GOV/REL ORD/FREE LAISSEZ POPULISM...POLICY 18/20 SUPREME/CT ROOSEVLT/F CONGRESS CON/INTERP. PAGE 98 H1961 — CT/SYS CENTRAL FEDERAL CONSTN

B57

PLAYFAIR G.,THE OFFENDERS: THE CASE AGAINST LEGAL VENGEANCE. UNIV LAW SOCIETY NAT/G PROB/SOLV DEATH PERSON ORD/FREE...HEAL INT/LAW BIBLIOG 20 REFORMERS. PAGE 126 H2524 — CRIME TEC/DEV SANCTION CT/SYS

B57

REISS J.,GEORGE KENNANS POLITIK DER EINDAMMUNG. USSR NAT/G FORCES TOTALISM ATTIT ORD/FREE...POLICY 20 NATO TRUMAN/HS MARSHL/PLN KENNAN/G. PAGE 131 H2613 — DIPLOM DETER PEACE

B57

US SENATE SPEC COMM FOR AID,COMPILATION OF STUDIES AND SURVEYS. AFR ASIA L/A+17C USA+45 ECO/UNDEV AGRI INT/ORG CONSULT TEC/DEV CONFER TOTALISM...NAT/COMP 20 CONGRESS. PAGE 161 H3216 — FOR/AID DIPLOM ORD/FREE DELIB/GP

B57

US SENATE SPEC COMM FOR AID,HEARINGS BEFORE THE SPECIAL COMMITTEE TO STUDY THE FOREIGN AID PROGRAM. USA+45 USSR ECO/UNDEV INT/ORG FORCES WEAPON TOTALISM ATTIT SUPEGO...NAT/COMP CONGRESS. PAGE 161 H3217 — FOR/AID DIPLOM ORD/FREE TEC/DEV

B57

VON HIPPEL E.,GESCHICHTE DER STAATSPHILOSOPHIE (2 VOLS.). ASIA GREECE INDIA PRE/AMER UAR NAT/LISM ORD/FREE MARXISM. PAGE 164 H3272 — CULTURE CONCPT NAT/G

S57

COSER L.A.,"SOCIAL CONFLICT AND THE THEORY OF SOCIAL CHANGE." EUR+WWI CULTURE TEC/DEV PRODUC RIGID/FLEX SOC. PAGE 34 H0673 — GP/REL ROLE SOCIETY ORD/FREE

S57

HAILEY,"TOMORROW IN AFRICA." CONSTN SOCIETY LOC/G NAT/G DOMIN ADJUD ADMIN GP/REL DISCRIM NAT/LISM ATTIT MORAL ORD/FREE...PSY SOC CONCPT OBS RECORD TREND GEN/LAWS CMN/WLTH 20. PAGE 64 H1277 — AFR PERSON ELITES RACE/REL

S57
KILSON M.L.,"LAND AND POLITICS IN KENYA: AN ANALYSIS OF AFRICAN POLITICS IN A PLURAL SOCIETY." FUT LAW CULTURE KIN NAT/G ECO/TAC DOMIN REV NAT/LISM ORD/FREE PWR RESPECT SOVEREIGN WEALTH ...SOC OBS TREND WORK VAL/FREE CMN/WLTH 20. PAGE 86 H1710
AFR ECO/UNDEV

C57
WITTFOGEL K.A.,"ORIENTAL DESPOTISM: A COMPARATIVE STUDY OF TOTAL POWER." ASIA CULTURE STRATA NAT/G LEAD OWN ORD/FREE PWR...CONCPT TREND BIBLIOG 20. PAGE 170 H3393
TOTALISM HABITAT DOMIN ELITES

B58
ALMAGRO BASCH M.,ORIGEN Y FORMACION DEL PUEBLO HISPANO. PREHIST SPAIN REGION WAR RACE/REL HABITAT ORD/FREE...SOC SOC/INTEG 20. PAGE 5 H0109
CULTURE GP/REL ADJUST

B58
BUISSON L.,POTESTAS UND CARITAS. FRANCE GERMANY UK ORD/FREE...JURID IDEA/COMP NAT/COMP 12/16 POPE CHURCH/STA. PAGE 23 H0467
GP/REL PWR CATHISM NAT/G

B58
CRAIG G.A.,FROM BISMARCK TO ADENAUER: ASPECTS OF GERMAN STATECRAFT. GERMANY INTELL FORCES ECO/TAC CONFER COERCE WAR GP/REL ORD/FREE PWR CONSERVE 19/20 BISMARCK/O ADENAUER/K. PAGE 35 H0695
DIPLOM LEAD NAT/G

B58
DUNAYEVSKAYA R.,MARXISM AND FREEDOM: FROM 1776 UNTIL TODAY. COM USSR WORKER CAP/ISM DOMIN REV GP/REL TOTALISM ALL/VALS...MYTH BIOG IDEA/COMP 18/20 MARX/KARL LENIN/VI STALIN/J. PAGE 43 H0861
MARXISM CONCPT ORD/FREE

B58
FLORES X.,LA TRADICION CATOLICA Y EL FUTURO POLITICO DE ESPANA (PAMPHLET). SPAIN NAT/G ACT/RES LEAD GP/REL CATHISM 20 CHRISTIAN CHURCH/STA. PAGE 52 H1031
SECT POL/PAR ATTIT ORD/FREE

B58
GREAVES H.R.,THE FOUNDATIONS OF POLITICAL THEORY. WAR ATTIT SUPEGO ORD/FREE...IDEA/COMP SOC/INTEG. PAGE 60 H1203
CONCPT MORAL PERSON

B58
HAAS E.B.,THE UNITING OF EUROPE. EUR+WWI INT/ORG NAT/G POL/PAR TOP/EX ECO/TAC EDU/PROP LEGIT FEDERAL NAT/LISM DRIVE RIGID/FLEX ORD/FREE PWR PLURISM ...POLICY CONCPT INT GEN/LAWS ECSC EEC 20. PAGE 63 H1264
VOL/ASSN ECO/DEV

B58
HERRMANN K.,DAS STAATSDENKEN BEI LEIBNIZ. GP/REL ATTIT ORD/FREE...CONCPT IDEA/COMP 17 LEIBNITZ/G CHURCH/STA. PAGE 70 H1406
NAT/G JURID SECT EDU/PROP

B58
HSU U.T.,THE INVISIBLE CONFLICT. ASIA USSR ELITES NAT/G CONTROL LEAD COERCE REV WAR NAT/LISM ORD/FREE PWR 20 COM/PARTY ESPIONAGE. PAGE 74 H1485
MARXISM POL/PAR EDU/PROP FORCES

B58
INDIAN COUNCIL WORLD AFFAIRS,DEFENCE AND SECURITY IN THE INDIAN OCEAN AREA. INDIA S/ASIA CULTURE CONSULT DELIB/GP FORCES PROB/SOLV DIPLOM INT/TRADE 20 CMN/WLTH. PAGE 77 H1531
GEOG HABITAT ECO/UNDEV ORD/FREE

B58
KINTNER W.R.,ORGANIZING FOR CONFLICT: A PROPOSAL. USSR STRUCT NAT/G LEGIS ADMIN EXEC PEACE ORD/FREE PWR...CONCPT OBS TREND NAT/COMP VAL/FREE COLD/WAR 20. PAGE 86 H1719
USA+45 PLAN DIPLOM

B58
LAHBABI M.,LE GOUVERNEMENT MAROCAIN A L'AUBE DU XXE SIECLE. FRANCE MOROCCO CHIEF EX/STRUC LEGIS ORD/FREE PWR...JURID BIBLIOG 19/20. PAGE 90 H1797
NAT/G COLONIAL SOVEREIGN

B58
MEHNERT K.,DER SOWJETMENSCH. USSR NAT/G SECT EDU/PROP TOTALISM ORD/FREE 20. PAGE 108 H2161
SOCIETY ATTIT PERSON FAM

B58
PALMER E.E.,THE COMMUNIST CHALLENGE. COM USA+45 USA-45 ECO/DEV ECO/UNDEV NEUTRAL ORD/FREE POPULISM ...CONCPT NAT/COMP ANTHOL 19/20 LENIN/VI STALIN/J MAO MARX/KARL COM/PARTY. PAGE 123 H2450
MARXISM DIPLOM IDEA/COMP POLICY

S58
ELKIN A.B.,"OEEC-ITS STRUCTURE AND POWERS." EUR+WWI CONSTN INDUS INT/ORG NAT/G VOL/ASSN DELIB/GP ACT/RES PLAN ORD/FREE WEALTH...CHARTS ORG/CHARTS OEEC 20. PAGE 45 H0907
ECO/DEV EX/STRUC

S58
STAAR R.F.,"ELECTIONS IN COMMUNIST POLAND." EUR+WWI SOCIETY INT/ORG NAT/G POL/PAR LEGIS ACT/RES ECO/TAC EDU/PROP ADJUD ADMIN ROUTINE COERCE TOTALISM ATTIT ORD/FREE PWR 20. PAGE 148 H2963
COM CHOOSE POLAND

B59
CARPENTER G.W.,THE WAY IN AFRICA. AFR INDUS MUNIC DIPLOM DOMIN EDU/PROP COERCE DISCRIM NAT/LISM ORD/FREE 20 NEGRO CHRISTIAN. PAGE 27 H0535
CULTURE SECT ECO/UNDEV COLONIAL

B59
CHODOROV F.,THE RISE AND FALL OF SOCIETY. NAT/G CONTROL ORD/FREE...TIME/SEQ 20. PAGE 30 H0596
SOC INGP/REL ECO/DEV ATTIT

B59
EMME E.M.,THE IMPACT OF AIR POWER - NATIONAL SECURITY AND WORLD POLITICS. USA+45 USSR FORCES DIPLOM WEAPON PEACE TOTALISM...POLICY NAT/COMP 20 EUROPE. PAGE 46 H0921
DETER AIR WAR ORD/FREE

B59
GOPAL R.,INDIAN MUSLIMS: A POLITICAL HISTORY (1858-1947). INDIA ISLAM PAKISTAN NAT/G SECT LEGIS LEAD COERCE WAR REPRESENT ISOLAT ORD/FREE 19/20 HINDU MUSLIM. PAGE 59 H1175
COLONIAL GP/REL POL/PAR REGION

B59
INTERNATIONAL PRESS INSTITUTE,THE PRESS IN AUTHORITARIAN COUNTRIES. COM PORTUGAL SPAIN UAR USSR NAT/G DOMIN LEGIT ORD/FREE FASCISM SOCISM 20. PAGE 78 H1559
PRESS CONTROL TOTALISM EDU/PROP

B59
KIRCHHEIMER O.,GEGENWARTSPROBLEME DER ASYLGEWAHRUNG. DOMIN GP/REL ATTIT...NAT/COMP 20. PAGE 86 H1720
DIPLOM INT/LAW JURID ORD/FREE

B59
LEFEVRE R.,THE NATURE OF MAN AND HIS GOVERNMENT. EUR+WWI MOD/EUR CONSTN CULTURE MORAL MARXISM ...POLICY 18/20. PAGE 93 H1859
NAT/G TASK ORD/FREE ATTIT

B59
MAIER H.,REVOLUTION UND KIRCHE. FRANCE MOD/EUR SECT REV ORD/FREE...IDEA/COMP 18/19. PAGE 101 H2018
NAT/G CATHISM ATTIT POL/PAR

B59
MATHER F.C.,PUBLIC ORDER IN THE AGE OF THE CHARTISTS. UK CULTURE ADJUD CONTROL. PAGE 105 H2090
ORD/FREE FORCES COERCE CIVMIL/REL

B59
PARK R.L.,LEADERSHIP AND POLITICAL INSTITUTIONS IN INDIA. S/ASIA CULTURE ECO/UNDEV LOC/G MUNIC PROVS LEGIS PLAN ADMIN LEAD ORD/FREE WEALTH...GEOG SOC BIOG TOT/POP VAL/FREE 20. PAGE 123 H2468
NAT/G EXEC INDIA

B59
PAULSEN M.G.,LEGAL INSTITUTIONS TODAY AND TOMORROW. UK USA+45 NAT/G PROF/ORG PROVS ADMIN PARL/PROC ORD/FREE NAT/COMP. PAGE 124 H2477
JURID ADJUD JUDGE LEGIS

B59
SCHORN H.,DER RICHTER IM DRITTEN REICH; GESCHICHTE UND DOKUMENTE. GERMANY NAT/G LEGIT CT/SYS INGP/REL MORAL ORD/FREE RESPECT...JURID GP/COMP 20. PAGE 140 H2798
ADJUD JUDGE FASCISM

B59
SENGHOR L.S.,RAPPORT SUR LA DOCTRINE ET LA PROGRAMME DU PART I. FRANCE MALI CONSTN POL/PAR PLAN CHOOSE OWN ORD/FREE MARXISM...SOCIALIST 20 NEGRO. PAGE 141 H2828
ATTIT NAT/G AFR SOCISM

B59
SISSON C.H.,THE SPIRIT OF BRITISH ADMINISTRATION AND SOME EUROPEAN COMPARISONS. FRANCE GERMANY/W SWEDEN UK LAW EX/STRUC INGP/REL EFFICIENCY ORD/FREE ...DECISION 20. PAGE 144 H2890
GOV/COMP ADMIN ELITES ATTIT

B59
SZLUC T.,TWILIGHT OF THE TYRANTS. BRAZIL L/A+17C PERU VENEZUELA NAT/G FORCES CONTROL PERSON MORAL ORD/FREE PWR...CONCPT 20 ARGEN COLOMB. PAGE 151 H3028
TOTALISM CHIEF REV FASCISM

B59
VORSPAN A.,JUSTICE AND JUDAISM. FAM DIPLOM ECO/TAC EDU/PROP CRIME RACE/REL MARRIAGE ANOMIE ATTIT ORD/FREE...POLICY 20 UN. PAGE 164 H3279
SECT CULTURE ACT/RES GP/REL

B59
WILDNER H.,DIE TECHNIK DER DIPLOMATIE. TOP/EX ROLE ORD/FREE...INT/LAW JURID IDEA/COMP NAT/COMP 20. PAGE 168 H3364
DIPLOM POLICY DELIB/GP NAT/G

S59
JENKS C.W.,"THE CHALLENGE OF UNIVERSALITY." FUT UNIV CONSTN CULTURE CONSULT CREATE PLAN LEGIT ATTIT MORAL ORD/FREE RESPECT...MAJORIT JURID 20. PAGE 80 H1602
INT/ORG LAW PEACE INT/LAW

S59
LEVINE R.A.,"ANTI-EUROPEAN VIOLENCE IN AFRICA: A COMPARATIVE ANALYSIS." AFR CULTURE NAT/G DIPLOM EDU/PROP COLONIAL REGION COERCE ATTIT PWR...PSY CONCPT TIME/SEQ TREND HYPO/EXP SOC/EXP STERTYP GEN/METH COLD/WAR 20. PAGE 95 H1903
DRIVE ORD/FREE REV

S59
SILBERMAN L.,"CHANGE AND CONFLICT IN THE HORN OF AFRICA." EUR+WWI ITALY UK CULTURE FORCES ECO/TAC ADJUD COLONIAL ATTIT ORD/FREE PWR...DECISION METH/CNCPT HIST/WRIT SOMALI 20. PAGE 144 H2874
AFR TIME/SEQ

C59
COLLINS I.,"THE GOVERNMENT AND THE NEWSPAPER PRESS IN FRANCE, 1814-1881. FRANCE LAW ADMIN CT/SYS ...CON/ANAL BIBLIOG 19. PAGE 32 H0634
PRESS ORD/FREE NAT/G EDU/PROP

B60
JUNZ A.J.,PRESENT TRENDS IN AMERICAN NATIONAL GOVERNMENT. LEGIS DIPLOM ADMIN CT/SYS ORD/FREE ...CONCPT ANTHOL 20 CONGRESS PRESIDENT SUPREME/CT. PAGE 3 H0052
POL/PAR CHOOSE CONSTN NAT/G

B60
ALBI F.,TRATADO DE LOS MODOS DE GESTION DE LAS CORPORACIONES LOCALES. SPAIN FINAN NAT/G BUDGET CONTROL EXEC ROUTINE GOV/REL ORD/FREE SOVEREIGN ...MGT 20. PAGE 5 H0092
LOC/G LAW ADMIN MUNIC

B60
BANERJEE D.N.,OUR FUNDAMENTAL RIGHTS: THEIR NATURE AND EXTENT (AS JUDICIALLY DETERMINED). INDIA UK CULTURE STRATA NAT/G WORKER EDU/PROP CONTROL DISCRIM OWN...IDEA/COMP WORSHIP 20 REFORMERS COMMONWLTH. PAGE 10 H0207
CONSTN ORD/FREE LEGIS POLICY

B60
CASTBERG F.,FREEDOM OF SPEECH IN THE WEST. FRANCE GERMANY USA+45 USA-45 LAW CONSTN CHIEF PRESS DISCRIM...CONCPT 18/20. PAGE 28 H0558
ORD/FREE SANCTION ADJUD NAT/COMP

B60
CHATTERJI S.K.,AFRICANISM: THE AFRICAN PERSONALITY. KIN NAT/G SECT CREATE DIPLOM COLONIAL GP/REL ATTIT ORD/FREE...LING WORSHIP 20. PAGE 29 H0585
PERSON NAT/LISM AFR CULTURE

B60
EASTON S.C.,THE TWILIGHT OF EUROPEAN COLONIALISM. AFR S/ASIA CONSTN SOCIETY STRUCT ECO/UNDEV INDUS NAT/G FORCES ECO/TAC COLONIAL CT/SYS ATTIT KNOWL ORD/FREE PWR...SOCIALIST TIME/SEQ TREND CON/ANAL 20. PAGE 44 H0882
FINAN ADMIN

B60
GOODMAN E.,SOVIET DESIGN FOR A WORLD STATE. COM USSR NAT/G TOP/EX DIPLOM ECO/TAC DOMIN EDU/PROP COERCE REV ATTIT ORD/FREE...CON/ANAL 20. PAGE 59 H1171
PLAN PWR SOCISM TOTALISM

B60
GRAMPP W.D.,THE MANCHESTER SCHOOL OF ECONOMICS. UK LAW ECO/DEV COERCE ATTIT ORD/FREE LAISSEZ ...PHIL/SCI IDEA/COMP 19/20 MANCHESTER CORN/LAWS. PAGE 60 H1194
ECO/TAC VOL/ASSN LOBBY NAT/G

B60
HAYEK F.A.,THE CONSTITUTION OF LIBERTY. UNIV LAW CONSTN WORKER TAX EDU/PROP ADMIN CT/SYS COERCE DISCRIM...IDEA/COMP 20. PAGE 68 H1369
ORD/FREE CHOOSE NAT/G CONCPT

B60
JEFFRIES C.,TRANSFER OF POWER: PROBLEMS OF THE PASSAGE TO SELFGOVERNMENT. CEYLON GHANA MALAYSIA NIGERIA UK INT/ORG CONSULT DELIB/GP LEGIS DIPLOM CONFER PARL/PROC 20. PAGE 80 H1595
SOVEREIGN COLONIAL ORD/FREE NAT/G

B60
LINDSAY K.,EUROPEAN ASSEMBLIES: THE EXPERIMENTAL PERIOD 1949-1959. EUR+WWI ECO/DEV NAT/G POL/PAR LEGIS TOP/EX ACT/RES PLAN ECO/TAC DOMIN LEGIT ROUTINE ATTIT DRIVE ORD/FREE PWR SKILL...SOC CONCPT TREND CHARTS GEN/LAWS VAL/FREE. PAGE 97 H1932
VOL/ASSN INT/ORG REGION

B60
LISTER L.,EUROPE'S COAL AND STEEL COMMUNITY. FRANCE GERMANY STRUCT ECO/DEV EXTR/IND INDUS MARKET NAT/G DELIB/GP ECO/TAC INT/TRADE EDU/PROP ATTIT RIGID/FLEX ORD/FREE PWR WEALTH...CONCPT STAT TIME/SEQ CHARTS ECSC 20. PAGE 97 H1941
EUR+WWI INT/ORG REGION

B60
MACFARQUHAR R.,THE HUNDRED FLOWERS. ASIA NAT/G WORKER GP/REL ORD/FREE MARXISM 20 MAO. PAGE 100 H1991
DEBATE PRESS POL/PAR ATTIT

B60
MACRIDIS R.C.,THE DE GAULLE REPUBLIC: QUEST FOR UNITY. EUR+WWI NAT/G POL/PAR LEGIS LEGIT NAT/LISM ATTIT RIGID/FLEX ORD/FREE PWR...JURID CONCPT TIME/SEQ 20 DEGAULLE/C. PAGE 100 H2009
TOP/EX STRUCT FRANCE

B60
MATTHIAS E.,DAS ENDE DER PARTEIEN 1933. GERMANY NAT/G COERCE CHOOSE ORD/FREE PWR 20. PAGE 105 H2100
FASCISM POL/PAR DOMIN ATTIT

B60
MAYO H.B.,AN INTRODUCTION TO DEMOCRATIC THEORY. ORD/FREE...POLICY TIME/SEQ GOV/COMP STERTYP. PAGE 105 H2109
POPULISM CONCPT IDEA/COMP

B60
MOCTEZUMA A.P.,EL CONFLICTO RELIGIOSO DE 1926 (2ND ED.). L/A+17C LAW NAT/G LOBBY COERCE GP/REL ATTIT ...POLICY 20 MEXIC/AMER CHURCH/STA. PAGE 112 H2233
SECT ORD/FREE DISCRIM REV

B60
MOORE W.E.,LABOR COMMITMENT AND SOCIAL CHANGE IN DEVELOPING AREAS. SOCIETY STRATA ECO/UNDEV MARKET VOL/ASSN WORKER AUTHORIT SKILL...MGT NAT/COMP SOC/INTEG 20. PAGE 113 H2250
LABOR ORD/FREE ATTIT INDUS

B60
MORAES F.,THE REVOLT IN TIBET. ASIA CHINA/COM INDIA CULTURE CONTROL COERCE WAR TOTALISM...POLICY SOC WORSHIP 20 TIBET INTERVENT. PAGE 113 H2252
COLONIAL FORCES DIPLOM ORD/FREE

B60
MORRISON C.,THE POWERS THAT BE. NAT/G SUPEGO ...POLICY CONCPT IDEA/COMP WORSHIP 20 BIBLE. PAGE 113 H2265
HUM ORD/FREE

B60
PANIKKAR K.M.,THE STATE AND THE CITIZEN (2ND ED.). INDIA DOMIN ATTIT SUPEGO ORD/FREE WEALTH...GEOG CONCPT GP/COMP 20. PAGE 123 H2459
TEC/DEV POL/PAR NAT/G EDU/PROP

B60
PETERSON W.C.,THE WELFARE STATE IN FRANCE. EUR+WWI FRANCE FUT STRATA PROB/SOLV TAX GIVE RECEIVE INCOME ORD/FREE PWR...CHARTS 20. PAGE 125 H2496
NEW/LIB ECO/TAC WEALTH NAT/G

B60
PINTO F.B.M.,ENRIQUECIMENTO ILICITO NO EXERCICIO DE CARGOS PUBLICOS. BRAZIL L/A+17C USA+45 ELITES TRIBUTE CONTROL INGP/REL ORD/FREE PWR...NAT/COMP 20. PAGE 126 H2513
ADMIN NAT/G CRIME LAW

B60
ROBERTSON D.,THE CONTROL OF INDUSTRY. UK MARKET LABOR WORKER PRICE CONTROL GP/REL COST DEMAND ORD/FREE WEALTH NEW/LIB SOCISM 20. PAGE 132 H2646
INDUS FINAN NAT/G ECO/DEV

B60
SCHEIBER H.N.,THE WILSON ADMINISTRATION AND CIVIL LIBERTIES 1917-1921. LAW GOV/REL ATTIT 20 WILSON/W CIVIL/LIB. PAGE 139 H2782
ORD/FREE WAR NAT/G CONTROL

B60
STRACHEY J.,THE END OF EMPIRE. UK WOR+45 WOR-45 DIPLOM INT/TRADE DOMIN ADJUST ORD/FREE WEALTH ...SOCIALIST GOV/COMP TIME COMMONWLTH. PAGE 150 H2991
COLONIAL ECO/DEV BAL/PWR LAISSEZ

B60
THORD-GRAY I.,GRINGO REBEL. L/A+17C NAT/G CONTROL LEAD ATTIT...OBS 20 MEXIC/AMER. PAGE 154 H3087
REV FORCES CIVMIL/REL ORD/FREE

S60
CASSINELLI C.,"TOTALITARIANISM, IDEOLOGY AND PROPAGANDA." EUR+WWI CULTURE SOCIETY NAT/G DOMIN COERCE ORD/FREE FASCISM MARXISM...MARXIST CONCPT STERTYP GEN/LAWS TOT/POP 20. PAGE 28 H0554
ATTIT EDU/PROP TOTALISM

S60
EMERSON R.,"THE EROSION OF DEMOCRACY." AFR FUT LAW CULTURE INTELL SOCIETY ECO/UNDEV FAM LOC/G NAT/G FORCES PLAN TEC/DEV ECO/TAC ADMIN CT/SYS ATTIT ORD/FREE PWR...SOCIALIST SOC CONCPT STAND/INT TIME/SEQ WORK 20. PAGE 46 H0918
S/ASIA POL/PAR

S60
HALSEY A.H.,"THE CHANGING FUNCTIONS OF UNIVERSITIES IN ADVANCED INDUSTRIAL SOCIETIES." R+D EDU/PROP REPRESENT ROLE ORD/FREE PWR TREND. PAGE 65 H1298
ACADEM CREATE CULTURE ADJUST

S60
HOWARD M.,"BRITAIN'S DEFENSE: COMMITMENTS AND CAPABILITIES." EUR+WWI ECO/DEV NAT/G FORCES LEGIS PLAN DETER ORD/FREE WEALTH...POLICY CONCPT TIME/SEQ GEN/METH 20. PAGE 74 H1481
FUT PWR DIPLOM UK

S60
MAGATHAN W.,"SOME BASES OF WEST GERMAN MILITARY POLICY." EUR+WWI FUT INT/ORG TOP/EX ECO/TAC DOMIN DRIVE ORD/FREE PWR...TRADIT GEOG OBS TREND. PAGE 101 H2015
NAT/G FORCES GERMANY

S60
PERLMANN H.,"UPHEAVAL IN TURKEY." EUR+WWI ISLAM NAT/G FORCES TOP/EX LEGIT COERCE CHOOSE DRIVE ORD/FREE PWR...TIME/SEQ TOT/POP 20. PAGE 125 H2494
CONSTN TURKEY

S60
SPIRO H.J.,"NEW CONSTITUTIONAL FORMS IN AFRICA." FUT CULTURE SOCIETY ECO/UNDEV NAT/G POL/PAR VOL/ASSN EDU/PROP ATTIT DRIVE ORD/FREE PWR RESPECT ...POLICY CONCPT OBS TREND CON/ANAL STERTYP GEN/LAWS VAL/FREE. PAGE 148 H2950
AFR CONSTN FOR/AID NAT/LISM

S60
WYCKOFF T.,"THE ROLE OF THE MILITARY IN LATIN AMERICAN POLITICS." L/A+17C CONSTN CULTURE ECO/UNDEV POL/PAR FORCES LEGIS TOP/EX LEGIT GUERRILLA REV CHOOSE ORD/FREE PWR...TIME/SEQ VAL/FREE 20. PAGE 171 H3430
NAT/G COERCE TOTALISM

C60
EBENSTEIN W.,"MODERN POLITICAL THOUGHT (2ND ED.)" NAT/G CAP/ISM NAT/LISM PERSON ORD/FREE PWR ALL/IDEOS NEW/LIB SOCISM...TRADIT PSY BIBLIOG/A 18/20. PAGE 44 H0884
IDEA/COMP PHIL/SCI CONCPT GEN/LAWS

N60
RHODESIA-NYASA NATL ARCHIVES,A SELECT BIBLIOGRAPHY OF RECENT PUBLICATIONS CONCERNING THE FEDERATION OF
BIBLIOG ADMIN

RHODESIA AND NYASALAND (PAMPHLET). MALAWI RHODESIA LAW CULTURE STRUCT ECO/UNDEV LEGIS...GEOG 20. PAGE 131 H2620 — ORD/FREE NAT/G B61

AIYAR S.P.,FEDERALISM AND SOCIAL CHANGE. CANADA CULTURE STRUCT PLAN PROB/SOLV TEC/DEV ECO/TAC ORD/FREE...TIME/SEQ 18/20 AUSTRAL. PAGE 4 H0085 — FEDERAL NAT/G CENTRAL GOV/COMP B61

BEDFORD S.,THE FACES OF JUSTICE: A TRAVELLER'S REPORT. AUSTRIA FRANCE GERMANY/W SWITZERLND UK UNIV WOR+45 WOR-45 CULTURE PARTIC GOV/REL MORAL...JURID OBS GOV/COMP 20. PAGE 13 H0257 — CT/SYS ORD/FREE PERSON LAW B61

BELOFF M.,NEW DIMENSIONS IN FOREIGN POLICY: A STUDY IN BRITISH ADMINISTRATION. UK NAT/G ATTIT RIGID/FLEX ORD/FREE...GEN/LAWS EUR+WWI CMN/WLTH EEC 20. PAGE 14 H0271 — INT/ORG DIPLOM B61

BERKOWITZ L.,AGGRESSION: AS A SOCIAL PSYCHOLOGICAL ANALYSIS. UNIV CULTURE FACE/GP FAM KIN NEIGH EDU/PROP DISPL DRIVE HEALTH LOVE ORD/FREE...PSY SOC CONCPT OBS TREND. PAGE 15 H0305 — SOCIETY COERCE WAR B61

BONNEFOUS M.,EUROPE ET TIERS MONDE. EUR+WWI SOCIETY INT/ORG NAT/G VOL/ASSN ACT/RES TEC/DEV CAP/ISM ECO/TAC ATTIT ORD/FREE SOVEREIGN...POLICY CONCPT TREND 20. PAGE 19 H0373 — AFR ECO/UNDEV FOR/AID INT/TRADE B61

BOURDIEU P.,THE ALGERIANS (TRANS. BY A.C. ROSS; REV. ED.). ALGERIA ISLAM CULTURE MUNIC CAP/ISM COLONIAL GP/REL ORD/FREE SOVEREIGN 20. PAGE 19 H0385 — SOCIETY STRUCT ATTIT WAR B61

BROWN D.M.,THE NATIONALIST MOVEMENT. INDIA CULTURE STRATA REV MORAL ORD/FREE...BIBLIOG 20 HINDU. PAGE 22 H0443 — NAT/LISM LEAD CHIEF POL/PAR B61

CASSINELLI C.W.,THE POLITICS OF FREEDOM. FUT UNIV LAW POL/PAR CHOOSE ORD/FREE...POLICY CONCPT MYTH BIBLIOG. PAGE 28 H0555 — MAJORIT NAT/G PARL/PROC PARTIC B61

CATHERINE R.,LE FONCTIONNAIRE FRANCAIS. FRANCE NAT/G INGP/REL ATTIT MORAL ORD/FREE...T CIVIL/SERV. PAGE 28 H0559 — ADMIN GP/REL LEAD SUPEGO B61

CHAKRABARTI A.,NEHRU: HIS DEMOCRACY AND INDIA. ASIA INDIA UK CONSTN ECO/UNDEV SECT DIPLOM COLONIAL PEACE WEALTH...BIBLIOG 20 CONGRESS NEHRU/J GANDHI/M. PAGE 28 H0570 — ORD/FREE STRATA NAT/G CHIEF B61

COBBAN A.,ROUSSEAU AND THE MODERN STATE. SOCIETY DOMIN INGP/REL HAPPINESS ALL/VALS...CON/ANAL 18/20 ROUSSEAU/J. PAGE 30 H0611 — ORD/FREE ROLE NAT/G POLICY B61

DIA M.,THE AFRICAN NATIONS AND WORLD SOLIDARITY. ISLAM CULTURE ELITES ECO/DEV ECO/UNDEV INT/ORG NAT/G PLAN ECO/TAC INT/TRADE EDU/PROP NAT/LISM ATTIT DRIVE ORD/FREE WEALTH...SOCIALIST CONCPT CON/ANAL GEN/LAWS TOT/POP 20. PAGE 41 H0817 — AFR REGION SOCISM B61

DOOB L.W.,COMMUNICATION IN AFRICA: A SEARCH FOR BOUNDARIES. CULTURE SOCIETY EDU/PROP WRITING INGP/REL DRIVE ORD/FREE...ART/METH SOC LING BIBLIOG 20. PAGE 42 H0837 — AFR FEEDBACK PERCEPT PERS/REL B61

ERASMUS C.J.,MAN TAKES CONTROL: CULTURAL DEVELOPMENT AND AMERICAN AID. STRUCT OWN DRIVE PERCEPT...SOC 20 MEXIC/AMER. PAGE 47 H0937 — ORD/FREE CULTURE ECO/UNDEV TEC/DEV B61

ESTEVEZ A.,ASPECTOS ECONOMICO-FINANCIEROS DE LA CAMPANA SANMARITANA. L/A+17C SPAIN FINAN COLONIAL LEAD ROLE ORD/FREE WEALTH 19 SOUTH/AMER SAN/MARTIN. PAGE 47 H0942 — ECO/UNDEV REV BUDGET NAT/G B61

HADDAD J.A.,REVOLUCAO CUBANA E REVOLUCAO BRASILEIRA. BRAZIL CUBA L/A+17C STRATA AGRI WORKER EDU/PROP REGION...POLICY NAT/COMP 20. PAGE 63 H1272 — REV ORD/FREE DIPLOM ECO/UNDEV B61

HEMPSTONE S.,THE NEW AFRICA. AGRI INDUS KIN NAT/G COLONIAL MARXISM...SOC INT TREND NAT/COMP BIBLIOG/A 20. PAGE 69 H1392 — AFR ORD/FREE PERSON CULTURE B61

JAKOBSON M.,THE DIPLOMACY OF THE WINTER WAR. EUR+WWI FINLAND GERMANY USSR INT/ORG NAT/G PEACE TOTALISM PWR...POLICY CONCPT 20 TREATY. PAGE 79 H1588 — WAR ORD/FREE DIPLOM B61

KHALIQUZZAMAN C.,PATHWAY TO PAKISTAN. INDIA PAKISTAN UK SECT LEGIS CHOOSE RACE/REL ATTIT ORD/FREE 20 MUSLIM. PAGE 85 H1705 — GP/REL NAT/G COLONIAL SOVEREIGN B61

KHAN A.W.,INDIA WINS FREEDOM: THE OTHER SIDE. INDIA PAKISTAN CULTURE LEGIS DIPLOM PARL/PROC REV WAR NAT/LISM 20. PAGE 85 H1707 — SOVEREIGN GP/REL RACE/REL ORD/FREE B61

MACLEOD I.,NEVILLE CHAMBERLAIN. UK SOCIETY TOP/EX WAR PERSON ALL/VALS ORD/FREE PARLIAMENT 20 CHAMBRLN/N. PAGE 100 H2003 — BIOG NAT/G CREATE B61

MARX K.,THE COMMUNIST MANIFESTO. IN (MENDEL A. ESSENTIAL WORKS OF MARXISM, NEW YORK: BANTAM. FUT MOD/EUR CULTURE ECO/DEV ECO/UNDEV AGRI FINAN INDUS MARKET PROC/MFG LABOR MUNIC POL/PAR CONSULT FORCES CREATE PLAN ADMIN ATTIT DRIVE RIGID/FLEX ORD/FREE PWR RESPECT MARX/KARL WORK. PAGE 104 H2081 — COM NEW/IDEA CAP/ISM REV B61

MILLIKAW M.F.,THE EMERGING NATIONS: THEIR GROWTH AND UNITED STATES POLICY. FUT USA+45 WOR+45 WOR-45 NAT/G PLAN TEC/DEV BAL/PWR GOV/REL PEACE ORD/FREE 20. PAGE 111 H2216 — ECO/UNDEV POLICY DIPLOM FOR/AID B61

MONAS S.,THE THIRD SECTION: POLICE AND SOCIETY IN RUSSIA UNDER NICHOLAS I. MOD/EUR RUSSIA ELITES STRUCT NAT/G EX/STRUC ADMIN CONTROL PWR CONSERVE ...DECISION 19 NICHOLAS/I. PAGE 112 H2238 — ORD/FREE COM FORCES COERCE B61

NARAIN J.P.,SWARAJ FOR THE PEOPLE. INDIA CONSTN LOC/G MUNIC POL/PAR CHOOSE REPRESENT EFFICIENCY ATTIT PWR SOVEREIGN 20. PAGE 116 H2311 — NAT/G ORD/FREE EDU/PROP EX/STRUC B61

PANIKKAR K.M.,THE VOICE OF FREEDOM: SELECTED SPEECHES OF PANDIT MOTILAL NEHRU. INDIA UK CONSTN FINAN FORCES LEGIS DIPLOM TAX COLONIAL...POLICY MAJORIT ANTHOL 20 NEHRU/PM. PAGE 123 H2460 — NAT/LISM ORD/FREE CHIEF NAT/G B61

RAHNER H.,KIRCHE UND STAAT IM FRUHEN CHRISTENTUM. INGP/REL ORD/FREE PWR CATHISM...JURID 1/9 CHURCH/STA CHRISTIAN. PAGE 129 H2582 — NAT/G SECT ATTIT GP/REL B61

RAO K.V.,PARLIAMENTARY DEMOCRACY OF INDIA. INDIA EX/STRUC TOP/EX COLONIAL CT/SYS PARL/PROC ORD/FREE ...POLICY CONCPT TREND 20 PARLIAMENT. PAGE 130 H2592 — CONSTN ADJUD NAT/G FEDERAL B61

ROBERTSON A.H.,THE LAW OF INTERNATIONAL INSTITUTIONS IN EUROPE. EUR+WWI MOD/EUR INT/ORG NAT/G VOL/ASSN DELIB/GP...JURID TIME/SEQ TOT/POP 20 TREATY. PAGE 132 H2644 — RIGID/FLEX ORD/FREE B61

ROCHE J.P.,COURTS AND RIGHTS: THE AMERICAN JUDICIARY IN ACTION (2ND ED.). UK USA+45 USA-45 STRUCT TEC/DEV SANCTION PERS/REL RACE/REL ORD/FREE ...METH/CNCPT GOV/COMP METH/COMP T 13/20. PAGE 133 H2653 — JURID CT/SYS NAT/G PROVS B61

ROIG E.,MARTI, ANTIIMPERIALISTA. CUBA L/A+17C DIPLOM DOMIN COLONIAL CONTROL LEAD PWR SOVEREIGN ...PHIL/SCI 19 MARTI/JOSE INTERVENT. PAGE 133 H2664 — PERSON NAT/LISM ECO/UNDEV ORD/FREE B61

SANTHANAM K.,DEMOCRATIC PLANNING. INDIA AGRI FINAN LEGIS DIPLOM PARL/PROC ORD/FREE 20. PAGE 138 H2753 — PLAN NAT/G CONSTN POLICY B61

SCHECHTMAN J.B.,ON WINGS OF EAGLES: THE PLIGHT, EXODUS, AND HOMECOMING OF ORIENTAL JEWRY. ASIA ISLAM ISRAEL VOL/ASSN DIPLOM CONTROL ORD/FREE ...GEOG WORSHIP SOC/INTEG 20 JEWS ARABS MIGRATION. PAGE 139 H2777 — CULTURE HABITAT KIN SECT B61

SCHNAPPER B.,LA POLITIQUE ET LE COMMERCE FRANCAIS DANS LE GOLFE DE GUINEE DE 1838 A 1871. FRANCE GUINEA UK SEA EXTR/IND NAT/G DELIB/GP LEGIS ADMIN ORD/FREE...POLICY GEOG CENSUS CHARTS BIBLIOG 19. PAGE 139 H2791 — COLONIAL INT/TRADE DOMIN AFR B61

SEMINAR REPRESENTATIVE GOVT,AFRO-ASIAN ATTITUDES: SEMINAR ON REPRESENTATIVE GOVERNMENTSPUBLIC LIBERTIES IN STATES OF ASIA AND AFRICA, RHODES, 1958. AFR ASIA BURMA INDIA ISLAM UAR VIETNAM/S SOCIETY POL/PAR CHIEF EDU/PROP PRESS PERSON ...POLICY INT 20 TUNIS. PAGE 141 H2826 — CHOOSE ATTIT NAT/COMP ORD/FREE B61

VON MERING O.,A GRAMMAR OF HUMAN VALUES. WOR+45 CULTURE FACE/GP NEIGH CREATE EDU/PROP LEGIT ATTIT DRIVE PERSON ORD/FREE...PSY SOC METH/CNCPT OBS RECORD INT REC/INT STAND/INT QU CHARTS VAL/FREE. PAGE 164 H3275 — SOCIETY MORAL

S61
ELAZAR D.J.,"CHURCHES AS MOLDERS OF AMERICAN POLITICS." STRATA MUNIC EDU/PROP RACE/REL ORD/FREE SOC. PAGE 45 H0904 — SECT CULTURE REPRESENT LOC/G

S61
FITZGIBBON R.H.,"MEASUREMENT OF LATIN AMERICAN POLITICAL CHANGE." L/A+17C CONSTN CULTURE SOCIETY ECO/UNDEV NAT/G POL/PAR PUB/INST ACT/RES EDU/PROP PERCEPT KNOWL ORD/FREE SOVEREIGN...METH/CNCPT TREND OAS 20. PAGE 51 H1020 — CHOOSE ATTIT

S61
MACRIDIS R.C.,"INTEREST GROUPS IN COMPARATIVE ANALYSIS." CULTURE OP/RES LOBBY REPRESENT GP/REL AUTHORIT ORD/FREE PWR...POLICY DECISION METH/CNCPT CLASSIF. PAGE 101 H2010 — GP/COMP CONCPT PLURISM

S61
MILLER E.,"LEGAL ASPECTS OF UN ACTION IN THE CONGO." AFR CULTURE ADMIN PEACE DRIVE RIGID/FLEX ORD/FREE...WELF/ST JURID OBS UN CONGO 20. PAGE 111 H2212 — INT/ORG LEGIT

S61
PADELFORD N.J.,"POLITICS AND THE FUTURE OF ECOSOC." AFR S/ASIA ECO/UNDEV INDUS NAT/G DELIB/GP ACT/RES ORD/FREE WEALTH...CONCPT CHARTS UN 20 ECOSOC. PAGE 122 H2438 — INT/ORG TEC/DEV

S61
SCHELLING T.C.,"NUCLEAR STRATEGY IN EUROPE." COM EUR+WWI USSR NAT/G FORCES NUC/PWR DRIVE ORD/FREE PWR...DECISION CONCPT OBS TREND HYPO/EXP 20. PAGE 139 H2784 — FUT COERCE ARMS/CONT WAR

B62
BODIN J.,THE SIX BOOKES OF A COMMONWEALE (1576) (FACSIMILE REPRINT OF 1606 ENGLISH TRANSLATION). AUTHORIT ORD/FREE SOVEREIGN...TRADIT CONCPT. PAGE 18 H0364 — PWR CONSERVE CHIEF NAT/G

B62
BROWN B.E.,NEW DIRECTIONS IN COMPARATIVE POLITICS. AUSTRIA FRANCE GERMANY UK WOR+45 EX/STRUC LEGIS ORD/FREE 20. PAGE 22 H0439 — NAT/COMP METH POL/PAR FORCES

B62
CARY J.,THE CASE FOR AFRICAN FREEDOM AND OTHER WRITINGS ON AFRICA. AFR UK INDUS LOC/G NAT/G SECT INT/TRADE EDU/PROP GOV/REL RACE/REL ORD/FREE ...CONCPT ANTHOL 19/20. PAGE 27 H0552 — NAT/LISM COLONIAL TREND ECO/UNDEV

B62
DAVAR F.C.,IRAN AND INDIA THROUGH THE AGES. INDIA IRAN ELITES SECT CREATE ORD/FREE...LING BIBLIOG. PAGE 37 H0743 — NAT/COMP DIPLOM CULTURE

B62
DUTOIT B.,LA NEUTRALITE SUISSE A L'HEURE EUROPEENNE. EUR+WWI MOD/EUR INT/ORG NAT/G VOL/ASSN PLAN BAL/PWR LEGIT NEUTRAL REGION PEACE ORD/FREE SOVEREIGN...CONCPT OBS TIME/SEQ TREND STERTYP VAL/FREE LEAGUE/NAT UN 20. PAGE 44 H0873 — ATTIT DIPLOM SWITZERLND

B62
EBENSTEIN W.,TWO WAYS OF LIFE. USA+45 CULTURE ECO/DEV PLAN EDU/PROP CONTROL ORD/FREE...GOV/COMP IDEA/COMP T 20 MARX/KARL ENGELS/F LENIN/VI LOCKE/JOHN MILL/JS. PAGE 44 H0885 — MARXISM POPULISM ECO/TAC DIPLOM

B62
FINER S.E.,THE MAN ON HORSEBACK: ROLE OF THE MILITARY IN POLITICS. UNIV LAW CONSTN ELITES SOCIETY POL/PAR BAL/PWR DOMIN EDU/PROP LEGIT COERCE GUERRILLA REV WAR WEAPON DRIVE SUPEGO ORD/FREE PWR RESPECT...POLICY CONCPT GEN/METH. PAGE 50 H1003 — NAT/G FORCES TOTALISM

B62
GANJI M.,INTERNATIONAL PROTECTION OF HUMAN RIGHTS. WOR+45 CONSTN INT/TRADE CT/SYS SANCTION CRIME WAR RACE/REL...CHARTS IDEA/COMP NAT/COMP BIBLIOG 20 TREATY NEGRO LEAGUE/NAT UN CIVIL/LIB. PAGE 55 H1097 — ORD/FREE DISCRIM LEGIS DELIB/GP

B62
HOOK S.,THE PARADOXES OF FREEDOM. UNIV CONSTN INTELL LEGIS CONTROL REV CHOOSE SUPEGO...POLICY JURID IDEA/COMP 19/20 CIV/RIGHTS. PAGE 73 H1461 — CONCPT MAJORIT ORD/FREE ALL/VALS

B62
HUNKIN P.,ENSEIGNEMENT ET POLITIQUE EN FRANCE ET EN ANGLETERRE. FRANCE UK CONSTN ACADEM SECT CHIEF DELIB/GP PROB/SOLV CONTROL REV ORD/FREE CONSERVE ...BIBLIOG 18/20. PAGE 75 H1496 — EDU/PROP LEGIS IDEA/COMP NAT/G

B62
HUNTER G.,THE NEW SOCIETIES OF TROPICAL AFRICA. CULTURE INDUS KIN MUNIC WORKER INT/TRADE EDU/PROP ORD/FREE...INT TREND 20. PAGE 75 H1500 — AFR GOV/COMP ECO/UNDEV SOCIETY

B62
INSTITUTE FOR STUDY OF USSR,YOUTH IN FERMENT. INTELL NAT/G PERF/ART POL/PAR SCHOOL VOL/ASSN FORCES EDU/PROP ATTIT DRIVE PERCEPT HEALTH KNOWL MORAL ORD/FREE RESPECT...SOC OBS HIST/WRIT VAL/FREE. PAGE 77 H1537 — COM CULTURE USSR

B62
JENNINGS I.,PARTY POLITICS: THE STUFF OF POLITICS (VOL.III). UK NAT/G SECT CHIEF INT/TRADE RECEIVE COLONIAL GP/REL NAT/LISM ORD/FREE SOCISM 19/20 CHURCH/STA WHIG/PARTY. PAGE 80 H1607 — POL/PAR CONSTN PWR ALL/IDEOS

B62
JOHNSON J.J.,THE ROLE OF THE MILITARY IN UNDERDEVELOPED COUNTRIES. AFR BURMA INDONESIA ISLAM ISRAEL L/A+17C S/ASIA THAILAND CULTURE ECO/UNDEV KIN PROVS CONSULT ACT/RES COERCE REV DRIVE RIGID/FLEX ORD/FREE...RECORD ANTHOL 20. PAGE 81 H1622 — FORCES CONCPT

B62
KARNJAHAPRAKORN C.,MUNICIPAL GOVERNMENT IN THAILAND AS AN INSTITUTION AND PROCESS OF SELF-GOVERNMENT. THAILAND CULTURE FINAN EX/STRUC LEGIS PLAN CONTROL GOV/REL EFFICIENCY ATTIT...POLICY 20. PAGE 83 H1662 — LOC/G MUNIC ORD/FREE ADMIN

B62
LITT T.,FREIHEIT UND LEBENS ORDNUNG. COM NAT/G ATTIT KNOWL...POLICY 20. PAGE 97 H1942 — ORD/FREE MARXISM CONCPT IDEA/COMP

B62
MANSERGH N.,SOUTH AFRICA 1906-1961: THE PRICE OF MAGNANIMITY. SOUTH/AFR LEGIS LEGIT SUFF NAT/LISM ATTIT ORD/FREE 20 NEGRO 20. PAGE 102 H2041 — COLONIAL DISCRIM NAT/G

B62
MARTINDALE D.,SOCIAL LIFE AND CULTURAL CHANGE. GP/REL...PHIL/SCI SOC CONCPT. PAGE 103 H2065 — INTELL CULTURE ORD/FREE STRUCT

B62
MODELSKI G.,SEATO-SIX STUDIES. ASIA CHINA/COM INDIA S/ASIA INT/ORG NAT/G ECO/TAC DETER ATTIT ORD/FREE PWR...TIME/SEQ COLD/WAR TOT/POP 20 SEATO. PAGE 112 H2234 — MARKET ECO/UNDEV INT/TRADE

B62
MORGENSTERN O.,STRATEGIE - HEUTE (2ND ED.). USA+45 USSR ECO/DEV DELIB/GP WAR PEACE ORD/FREE...GOV/COMP NAT/COMP 20 COLD/WAR NATO. PAGE 113 H2256 — NUC/PWR DIPLOM FORCES TEC/DEV

B62
NOBECOURT R.G.,LES SECRETS DE LA PROPAGANDE EN FRANCE OCCUPEE. FRANCE ELITES NAT/G DIPLOM GP/REL NAT/LISM TOTALISM ORD/FREE 20 VICHY VICHY. PAGE 118 H2365 — METH/COMP EDU/PROP WAR CONTROL

B62
ROUSSEAU J.J.,THE SOCIAL CONTRACT. LAW CONSTN CHIEF DOMIN REPRESENT GP/REL ORD/FREE POPULISM...MAJORIT GOV/COMP 18. PAGE 135 H2700 — GEN/LAWS AGREE REV

B62
RUDE G.,WILKES AND LIBERTY. UK NAT/G POL/PAR REPRESENT ORD/FREE...SOC 18. PAGE 136 H2711 — PARL/PROC CHOOSE STRATA STRUCT

B62
STARR R.E.,POLAND 1944-1962: THE SOVIETIZATION OF A CAPTIVE PEOPLE. COM POLAND USSR POL/PAR SECT LEGIS DIPLOM DOMIN EDU/PROP CHOOSE ORD/FREE...POLICY CHARTS BIBLIOG 20. PAGE 149 H2973 — MARXISM NAT/G TOTALISM NAT/COMP

B62
TAYLOR D.,THE BRITISH IN AFRICA. UK CULTURE ECO/UNDEV INDUS DIPLOM INT/TRADE ADMIN WAR RACE/REL ORD/FREE SOVEREIGN...POLICY BIBLIOG 15/20 CMN/WLTH. PAGE 153 H3053 — AFR COLONIAL DOMIN

B62
TINKER H.,INDIA AND PAKISTAN. INDIA PAKISTAN NAT/G POL/PAR...OLD/LIB TRADIT TREND CHARTS BIBLIOG 20. PAGE 155 H3102 — ORD/FREE STRATA REPRESENT AUTHORIT

B62
VALERIANO N.D.,COUNTER-GUERRILLA OPERATIONS: THE PHILLIPINE EXPERIENCE. NAT/G CONSULT ACT/RES PLAN COERCE GUERRILLA ATTIT ORD/FREE PWR SKILL...GEOG NEW/IDEA TIME/SEQ CHARTS 20. PAGE 161 H3221 — S/ASIA FORCES PHILIPPINE

B62
WEHLER H.V.,SOZIALDEMOKRATIE UND NATIONALSTAAT. GERMANY POLAND USSR CULTURE SOCIETY STRUCT NAT/G POL/PAR DIPLOM ORD/FREE 19/20. PAGE 166 H3325 — NAT/LISM SOVEREIGN GP/REL ATTIT

B62
ZIESEL K.,DAS VERLORENE GEWISSEN. GERMANY/W NAT/G VOL/ASSN EDU/PROP PRESS SUPEGO...POLICY 20. PAGE 173 H3455 — MORAL PWR ORD/FREE RESPECT

S62
DUNN S.D.,"DIRECTED CULTURE CHANGE IN THE SOVIET UNION: SOME SOVIET STUDIES." SOCIETY ORD/FREE...SOC HIST/WRIT VAL/FREE 20. PAGE 43 H0866 — COM CULTURE USSR

S62
LANGER W.L.,"FAREWELL TO EMPIRE." EUR+WWI MOD/EUR NAT/G DIPLOM EDU/PROP COLONIAL ATTIT ORD/FREE PWR SOVEREIGN WEALTH...CONCPT TIME/SEQ GEN/LAWS TOT/POP VAL/FREE CMN/WLTH 20. PAGE 91 H1810 — DOMIN ECO/TAC NAT/LISM

S62
LEGUM C.,"THE DANGERS OF INDEPENDENCE" AFR UGANDA NAT/G DIPLOM DOMIN REGION CENTRAL ATTIT POPULISM 20. PAGE 93 H1862 — ORD/FREE SOVEREIGN NAT/LISM GOV/COMP

S62
MBOYA T.,"RELATIONS BETWEEN THE PRESS AND GOVERNMENT IN AFRICA." AFR DIPLOM EDU/PROP NAT/LISM ORD/FREE SOVEREIGN 20. PAGE 106 H2115
PRESS GP/REL ATTIT NAT/G

S62
MURACCIOLE L.,"LES CONSTITUTIONS DES ETATS AFRICAINS D'EXPRESSION FRANCAISE: LA CONSTITUTION DU 16 AVRIL 1962 DE LA REPUBLIQUE DU" AFR CHAD CHIEF LEGIS LEGIT COLONIAL EXEC ROUTINE ORD/FREE SOVEREIGN...SOC CONCPT 20. PAGE 115 H2291
NAT/G CONSTN

S62
PIQUEMAL M.,"LES PROBLEMES DES UNIONS D'ETATS EN AFRIQUE NOIRE." FRANCE SOCIETY INT/ORG NAT/G DELIB/GP PLAN LEGIT ADMIN COLONIAL ROUTINE ATTIT ORD/FREE PWR...GEOG METH/CNCPT 20. PAGE 126 H2515
AFR ECO/UNDEV REGION

S62
SPRINGER H.W.,"FEDERATION IN THE CARIBBEAN: AN ATTEMPT THAT FAILED." L/A+17C ECO/UNDEV INT/ORG POL/PAR PROVS LEGIS CREATE PLAN LEGIT ADMIN FEDERAL ATTIT DRIVE PERSON ORD/FREE PWR...POLICY GEOG PSY CONCPT OBS CARIBBEAN CMN/WLTH 20. PAGE 148 H2955
VOL/ASSN NAT/G REGION

C62
BACON F.,"OF SEDITIONS AND TROUBLES" (1625) IN F. BACON, ESSAYS." INDUS MARKET CHIEF ECO/TAC EDU/PROP CONTROL LEAD PEACE WEALTH 17 MACHIAVELL. PAGE 9 H0191
REV ORD/FREE NAT/G GEN/LAWS

B63
BADI J.,THE GOVERNMENT OF THE STATE OF ISRAEL: A CRITICAL ACCOUNT OF ITS PARLIAMENT, EXECUTIVE, AND JUDICIARY. ISRAEL ECO/DEV CHIEF DELIB/GP LEGIS DIPLOM CT/SYS INGP/REL PEACE ORD/FREE...BIBLIOG 20 PARLIAMENT ARABS MIGRATION. PAGE 10 H0193
NAT/G CONSTN EX/STRUC POL/PAR

B63
BARNETT A.D.,COMMUNIST STRATEGIES IN ASIA: A COMPARATIVE ANALYSIS OF GOVERNMENTS AND PARTIES. COM FUT S/ASIA CULTURE SOCIETY STRATA NAT/G DELIB/GP ACT/RES ECO/TAC EDU/PROP COERCE CHOOSE ATTIT RIGID/FLEX ORD/FREE PWR SKILL...SIMUL VAL/FREE 20. PAGE 11 H0223
ASIA POL/PAR DIPLOM USSR

B63
BIDNEY D.,THE CONCEPT OF FREEDOM IN ANTHROPOLOGY. UNIV CULTURE STRATA SECT CREATE NAT/LISM ...METH/COMP 20. PAGE 17 H0332
SOC PERSON ORD/FREE CONCPT

B63
BRECHER M.,THE NEW STATES OF ASIA. ASIA S/ASIA INT/ORG BAL/PWR COLONIAL NEUTRAL ORD/FREE PWR 20 UN. PAGE 20 H0407
NAT/G ECO/UNDEV DIPLOM POLICY

B63
BROEKMEIJER M.W.,DEVELOPING COUNTRIES AND NATO. USSR FORCES DIPLOM NUC/PWR WAR PEACE TOTALISM 20 NATO. PAGE 21 H0427
ECO/UNDEV FOR/AID ORD/FREE NAT/G

B63
BROOKES E.H.,POWER, LAW, RIGHT, AND LOVE: A STUDY IN POLITICAL VALUES. SOUTH/AFR NAT/G PERSON ...CONCPT IDEA/COMP 20. PAGE 21 H0432
PWR ORD/FREE JURID LOVE

B63
BRZEZINSKI Z.K.,AFRICA AND THE COMMUNIST WORLD. AFR ASIA COM CULTURE SOCIETY INT/ORG DELIB/GP ACT/RES ECO/TAC COERCE ORD/FREE PWR WEALTH...STAT TOT/POP VAL/FREE 20. PAGE 23 H0461
ATTIT EDU/PROP DIPLOM USSR

B63
CARTER G.M.,FIVE AFRICAN STATES: RESPONSES TO DIVERSITY. CONSTN CULTURE STRATA LEGIS PLAN ECO/TAC DOMIN EDU/PROP CT/SYS EXEC CHOOSE ATTIT HEALTH ORD/FREE PWR...TIME/SEQ TOT/POP VAL/FREE. PAGE 27 H0547
AFR SOCIETY

B63
CARY J.,POWER IN MEN. NAT/G ORD/FREE...GEN/LAWS 20. PAGE 28 H0553
PHIL/SCI OLD/LIB LAISSEZ PWR

B63
CONZE W.,DIE DEUTSCHE NATION. GERMANY NAT/G POL/PAR WAR ORD/FREE...TREND 8/20 NAZI. PAGE 33 H0657
NAT/LISM FASCISM ATTIT SOCIETY

B63
CRUICKSHANK M.,CHURCH AND STATE IN ENGLISH EDUCATION 1870 TO PRESENT. UK LEGIS TAX GIVE DOMIN LEGIT ORD/FREE 19/20 CHURCH/STA. PAGE 36 H0715
NAT/G SECT EDU/PROP GP/REL

B63
DE VRIES E.,SOCIAL ASPECTS OF ECONOMIC DEVELOPMENT IN LATIN AMERICA. CULTURE SOCIETY STRATA FINAN INDUS INT/ORG DELIB/GP ACT/RES ECO/TAC EDU/PROP ADMIN ATTIT SUPEGO HEALTH KNOWL ORD/FREE...SOC STAT TREND ANTHOL TOT/POP VAL/FREE. PAGE 39 H0777
L/A+17C ECO/UNDEV

B63
DECOTTIGNIES R.,LES NATIONALITES AFRICAINES. AFR NAT/G PROB/SOLV DIPLOM COLONIAL ORD/FREE...CHARTS GOV/COMP 20. PAGE 39 H0781
NAT/LISM JURID LEGIS

LAW

B63
FALL B.,THE TWO VIETNAMS. CULTURE SOCIETY ECO/UNDEV NAT/G TOP/EX ACT/RES PLAN ECO/TAC DOMIN EDU/PROP COERCE ATTIT DRIVE PERSON ORD/FREE PWR...SOC TIME/SEQ COLD/WAR 20. PAGE 48 H0965
S/ASIA BIOG VIETNAM

B63
FARMER B.H.,CEYLON: A DIVIDED NATION. CEYLON INDIA NETHERLAND PORTUGAL UK ELITES POL/PAR COLONIAL ...SOC MYTH CHARTS GOV/COMP WORSHIP 20. PAGE 49 H0972
DOMIN ORD/FREE ECO/UNDEV POLICY

B63
FIRST R.,SOUTH WEST AFRICA. SOUTH/AFR INT/ORG KIN NAT/G WORKER COLONIAL WAR...POLICY 20 UN TRUST/TERR AFRICA/SW. PAGE 50 H1006
DISCRIM ORD/FREE RACE/REL CONTROL

B63
FRANZ G.,TEILUNG UND WIEDERVEREINIGUNG. GERMANY IRELAND ITALY NETHERLAND POLAND CULTURE BAL/PWR CHOOSE NAT/LISM ORD/FREE SOVEREIGN 19/20. PAGE 53 H1054
DIPLOM WAR NAT/COMP ATTIT

B63
FRIEDRICH C.J.,MAN AND HIS GOVERNMENT: AN EMPIRICAL THEORY OF POLITICS. UNIV LOC/G NAT/G ADJUD REV INGP/REL DISCRIM PWR BIBLIOG. PAGE 53 H1069
PERSON ORD/FREE PARTIC CONTROL

B63
GEERTZ C.,PEDDLERS AND PRINCES: SOCIAL DEVELOPMENT AND ECONOMIC CHANGE IN TWO INDONESIAN TOWNS. S/ASIA CULTURE SOCIETY STRATA FACE/GP MUNIC CREATE TEC/DEV ECO/TAC ORD/FREE WEALTH...OBS INT CENSUS CHARTS WORK TOT/POP VAL/FREE 20. PAGE 55 H1106
ECO/UNDEV SOC ELITES INDONESIA

B63
GERSCHENKRON A.,THE STABILITY OF DICTATORSHIPS. NAT/G EDU/PROP TASK ATTIT PERSON...POLICY PSY SOC METH 19/20. PAGE 56 H1116
TOTALISM CONCPT CONTROL ORD/FREE

B63
GLADE W.P. JR.,THE POLITICAL ECONOMY OF MEXICO. FUT L/A+17C CULTURE SOCIETY AGRI INDUS DELIB/GP ACT/RES ECO/TAC ATTIT HEALTH ORD/FREE...STAT TIME/SEQ TREND MEXIC/AMER TOT/POP VAL/FREE 20. PAGE 57 H1138
FINAN ECO/UNDEV

B63
GLUCKMAN M.,ORDER AND REBELLION IN TRIBAL AFRICA. EUR+WWI LAW CULTURE STRATA KIN MUNIC DELIB/GP ACT/RES DOMIN EDU/PROP LEGIT ADMIN COERCE CHOOSE ATTIT PERSON ORD/FREE PWR...SOC CHARTS GEN/LAWS TOT/POP VAL/FREE. PAGE 57 H1147
AFR SOCIETY

B63
HARTLEY A.,A STATE OF ENGLAND. UK ELITES SOCIETY ACADEM NAT/G SCHOOL INGP/REL CONSEN ORD/FREE NEW/LIB...POLICY 20. PAGE 67 H1349
DIPLOM ATTIT INTELL ECO/DEV

B63
JENNINGS W.I.,DEMOCRACY IN AFRICA. UK CULTURE STRUCT ECO/UNDEV DIPLOM COLONIAL GP/REL ADJUST NAT/LISM ORD/FREE...GOV/COMP 20 THIRD/WRLD. PAGE 81 H1613
PROB/SOLV AFR CONSTN POPULISM

B63
JUDD P.,AFRICAN INDEPENDENCE: THE EXPLODING EMERGENCE OF THE NEW AFRICAN NATIONS. AFR UK LAW CONSTN CULTURE KIN DIPLOM ATTIT...CHARTS BIBLIOG 20 UN DEGAULLE/C NEGRO THIRD/WRLD. PAGE 82 H1640
ORD/FREE POLICY DOMIN LOC/G

B63
LAMB B.P.,INDIA: A WORLD IN TRANSITION. INDIA ECO/UNDEV SECT EDU/PROP COLONIAL HABITAT ORD/FREE ...GEOG CHARTS BIBLIOG SOC/INTEG 20. PAGE 90 H1799
POL/PAR NAT/G DIPLOM STRATA

B63
LAVROFF D.-G.,LES LIBERTES PUBLIQUES EN UNION SOVIETIQUE (REV. ED.). USSR NAT/G WORKER SANCTION CRIME MARXISM NEW/LIB...JURID BIBLIOG WORSHIP 20. PAGE 92 H1843
ORD/FREE LAW ATTIT COM

B63
MAIR L.,NEW NATIONS. AFR FAM MUNIC SECT DOMIN CHOOSE NAT/LISM ORD/FREE...SOC 19/20. PAGE 101 H2022
COLONIAL CULTURE TEC/DEV ECO/UNDEV

B63
MAYNE R.,THE COMMUNITY OF EUROPE. UK CONSTN NAT/G CONSULT DELIB/GP CREATE PLAN ECO/TAC LEGIT ADMIN ROUTINE ORD/FREE PWR WEALTH...CONCPT TIME/SEQ EEC EURATOM 20. PAGE 105 H2107
EUR+WWI INT/ORG REGION

B63
MULLER H.J.,FREEDOM IN THE WESTERN WORLD. PREHIST CULTURE SECT CREATE TEC/DEV DOMIN PWR WEALTH ...MAJORIT SOC CONCPT. PAGE 114 H2285
ORD/FREE TIME/SEQ SOCIETY

B63
NALBANDIAN L.,THE ARMENIAN REVOLUTIONARY MOVEMENT. MOD/EUR RUSSIA...IDEA/COMP NAT/COMP BIBLIOG 19 ARMENIA OTTOMAN. PAGE 115 H2306
NAT/LISM REV POL/PAR ORD/FREE

B63
PADELFORD N.J.,AFRICA AND WORLD ORDER. AFR COLONIAL SOVEREIGN...ANTHOL BIBLIOG 20 UN UNIFICA COMMONWLTH. PAGE 122 H2439
DIPLOM NAT/G ORD/FREE

B63
ROBERTSON A.H.,HUMAN RIGHTS IN EUROPE. CONSTN SOCIETY INT/ORG NAT/G VOL/ASSN DELIB/GP ACT/RES PLAN ADJUD REGION ROUTINE ATTIT LOVE ORD/FREE RESPECT...JURID SOC CONCPT SOC/EXP UN 20. PAGE 132 H2645
EUR+WWI PERSON

B63
RUITENBEER H.M.,THE DILEMMA OF ORGANIZATIONAL SOCIETY. CULTURE ECO/DEV MUNIC SECT TEC/DEV EDU/PROP NAT/LISM ORD/FREE...NAT/COMP 20 RIESMAN/D WHYTE/WF MERTON/R MEAD/MARG JASPERS/K. PAGE 136 H2716
PERSON ROLE ADMIN WORKER

B63
SILONE I.,THE SCHOOL FOR DICTATORS. EUR+WWI GERMANY ITALY SOCIETY NAT/G CHIEF EX/STRUC ATTIT MORAL PWR ...HIST/WRIT 20. PAGE 144 H2876
TOTALISM EDU/PROP ORD/FREE FASCISM

B63
SKLAR R.L.,NIGERIAN POLITICAL PARTIES: POWER IN AN EMERGENT AFRICAN NATION. AFR EUR+WWI CULTURE STRATA NAT/G DELIB/GP EX/STRUC LEGIS DOMIN EDU/PROP ROUTINE CHOOSE ATTIT PERCEPT ORD/FREE PWR...SOC CONCPT OBS TOT/POP VAL/FREE. PAGE 145 H2898
POL/PAR SOCIETY NAT/LISM NIGERIA

B63
VON DER MEHDEN F.R.,RELIGION AND NATIONALISM IN SOUTHEAST ASIA. BURMA PHILIPPINE S/ASIA INTELL SOCIETY DOMIN EDU/PROP LEGIT ATTIT MORAL ORD/FREE ...SOC CENSUS HIST/WRIT TOT/POP VAL/FREE 20 WORSHIP LONDON. PAGE 163 H3265
SECT CULTURE NAT/LISM

B63
WODDIS J.,AFRICA, THE WAY AHEAD. AFR FUT ELITES POL/PAR CAP/ISM DIPLOM DOMIN RACE/REL ATTIT ORD/FREE SOVEREIGN SOCISM 20 PANAF/FREE. PAGE 170 H3394
REV COLONIAL ECO/UNDEV NAT/G

L63
BOLGAR V.,"THE PUBLIC INTEREST: A JURISPRUDENTIAL AND COMPARATIVE OVERVIEW OF SYMPOSIUM ON FUNDAMENTAL CONCEPTS OF PUBLIC LAW" COM FRANCE GERMANY SWITZERLND LAW ADJUD ADMIN AGREE LAISSEZ ...JURID GEN/LAWS 20 EUROPE/E. PAGE 18 H0369
CONCPT ORD/FREE CONTROL NAT/COMP

L63
NASH M.,"PSYCHO-CULTURAL FACTORS IN ASIAN ECONOMIC GROWTH." ASIA ISLAM S/ASIA CULTURE ECO/UNDEV DELIB/GP EDU/PROP COERCE ATTIT PERSON HEALTH KNOWL ORD/FREE...PSY SOC STAT TREND ANTHOL VAL/FREE 20. PAGE 116 H2313
SOCIETY ECO/TAC

S63
DEUTSCHMANN P.J.,"THE MASS MEDIA IN AN UNDERDEVELOPED VILLAGE." L/A+17C EDU/PROP PERCEPT KNOWL ORD/FREE...SOC INT VAL/FREE 20. PAGE 40 H0809
COM/IND CULTURE

S63
GILLIN J.P.,"POSSIBLE CULTURAL MALADJUSTMENT IN MODERN LATIN AMERICA." ATTIT ORD/FREE...SOC TREND GEN/LAWS 20. PAGE 56 H1128
L/A+17C CULTURE

S63
GLUCKMAN M.,"CIVIL WAR AND THEORIES OF POWER IN BAROTSE-LAND: AFRICAN AND MEDIEVAL ANALOGIES." AFR CHRIST-17C LAW CONSTN CULTURE STRATA KIN DELIB/GP FORCES DOMIN LEGIT COERCE PERCEPT ORD/FREE...SOC INT TIME/SEQ GEN/LAWS VAL/FREE. PAGE 57 H1148
TOP/EX PWR WAR

S63
GROSSER A.,"FRANCE AND GERMANY IN THE ATLANTIC COMMUNITY." INT/ORG NAT/G TOP/EX DIPLOM REGION PEACE ATTIT ORD/FREE PWR...CONCPT RECORD TIME/SEQ GEN/LAWS VAL/FREE COLD/WAR 20. PAGE 62 H1234
EUR+WWI VOL/ASSN FRANCE GERMANY

S63
KOHN H.,"GERMANY IN WORLD POLITICS." EUR+WWI GERMANY GERMANY/W USSR NAT/G POL/PAR TOP/EX ATTIT ...CONCPT TREND GEN/LAWS 20 NATO ADENAUER/K. PAGE 87 H1746
ACT/RES ORD/FREE BAL/PWR

S63
MAZRUI A.A.,"ON THE CONCEPT 'WE ARE ALL AFRICANS'." AFR CULTURE KIN LOC/G NAT/G DOMIN EDU/PROP LEGIT ATTIT PERCEPT PERSON KNOWL ORD/FREE...TIME/SEQ TOT/POP 20. PAGE 106 H2110
PROVS INT/ORG NAT/LISM

S63
MBOYA T.,"AFRICAN SOCIALISM." ECO/UNDEV INT/ORG DIPLOM FOR/AID INT/TRADE REGION GP/REL ATTIT ORD/FREE EACM. PAGE 106 H2116
AFR SOCISM CULTURE NAT/LISM

S63
OGOT B.,"FROM CHIEF TO PRESIDENT." AFR SECT REGION NAT/LISM...SOC GOV/COMP NAT/COMP 20 PRESIDENT. PAGE 121 H2410
CHIEF CULTURE LEAD ORD/FREE

S63
ROGIN M.,"ROUSSEAU IN AFRICA." AFR MARXISM POPULISM SOCISM 20 ROUSSEAU/J. PAGE 133 H2661
IDEA/COMP CULTURE CONSTN ORD/FREE

S63
RUSTOW D.A.,"THE MILITARY IN MIDDLE EASTERN SOCIETY AND POLITICS." FUT ISLAM CONSTN SOCIETY FACE/GP NAT/G POL/PAR PROF/ORG CONSULT DOMIN ADMIN EXEC REGION COERCE NAT/LISM ATTIT DRIVE PERSON ORD/FREE PWR...POLICY CONCPT OBS STERTYP 20. PAGE 136 H2721
FORCES ELITES

S63
TILMAN R.O.,"MALAYSIA: THE PROBLEMS OF FEDERATION." ISLAM S/ASIA CONSTN PROVS SECT DELIB/GP DOMIN EDU/PROP LEGIT EXEC COERCE CHOOSE ATTIT HEALTH ORD/FREE PWR...STAT TOT/POP VAL/FREE 20. PAGE 155 H3097
NAT/G CULTURE MALAYSIA

B64
AGGARWALA R.C.,CONSTITUTIONAL HISTORY OF INDIA AND NATIONAL MOVEMENT INCLUDING COMPARATIVE STUDY OF MODERN INDIA CONSTITUTION. INDIA S/ASIA SECT VOL/ASSN EX/STRUC LEGIS COERCE REV INGP/REL ORD/FREE...SOC BIBLIOG 18/20 CMN/WLTH. PAGE 4 H0077
CONSTN COLONIAL DOMIN NAT/G

B64
ALVIM J.C.,A REVOLUCAO SEM RUMO. BRAZIL NAT/G BAL/PWR DIPLOM INT/TRADE PARTIC WEALTH...POLICY SOC SOC/INTEG 20. PAGE 6 H0118
REV CIVMIL/REL ECO/UNDEV ORD/FREE

B64
AVASTHI A.,ASPECTS OF ADMINISTRATION. INDIA UK USA+45 FINAN ACADEM DELIB/GP LEGIS RECEIVE PARL/PROC PRIVIL...NAT/COMP 20. PAGE 9 H0183
MGT ADMIN SOC/WK ORD/FREE

B64
BENDIX R.,NATION-BUILDING AND CITIZENSHIP: STUDIES OF OUR CHANGING SOCIAL ORDER. WOR+45 CULTURE LOC/G GOV/REL INGP/REL ORD/FREE PWR 20. PAGE 14 H0275
PARTIC NAT/COMP ADMIN AUTHORIT

B64
BRZEZINSKI Z.,POLITICAL POWER: USA/USSR. USA+45 USSR AGRI POL/PAR FORCES CREATE CHOOSE ATTIT ORD/FREE PWR MARXISM...MYTH 20 KENNEDY/JF. PAGE 23 H0457
NAT/G NAT/COMP POLICY LEAD

B64
BURKE F.G.,AFRICA'S QUEST FOR ORDER. AFR CULTURE KIN MUNIC NAT/G DIPLOM COLONIAL REV DISCRIM NAT/LISM AGE/Y 20. PAGE 24 H0488
ORD/FREE CONSEN RACE/REL LEAD

B64
COBBAN A.,ROUSSEAU AND THE MODERN STATE (2ND ED.). FRANCE PROB/SOLV NAT/LISM UTOPIA PERSON MORAL ...EPIST PHIL/SCI SOC IDEA/COMP 18 ROUSSEAU/J BURKE/EDM HOBBES/T HUME/D. PAGE 30 H0612
GEN/LAWS INGP/REL NAT/G ORD/FREE

B64
COWAN L.G.,THE DILEMMAS OF AFRICAN INDEPENDENCE. AFR INDUS NAT/G SECT DIPLOM ECO/TAC REGION MARXISM ...CHARTS BIBLIOG 20 MAPS. PAGE 34 H0683
ORD/FREE COLONIAL REV ECO/UNDEV

B64
CURTIN P.D.,THE IMAGE OF AFRICA: BRITISH IDEAS AND ACTION, 1780-1850. MOD/EUR SOCIETY FORCES ACT/RES DOMIN EDU/PROP COERCE ATTIT PERCEPT RIGID/FLEX SUPEGO HEALTH KNOWL MORAL ORD/FREE WEALTH...CONCPT WORK VAL/FREE. PAGE 36 H0726
AFR CULTURE UK DIPLOM

B64
DANIELS R.V.,RUSSIA. RUSSIA USSR STRUCT NAT/LISM TOTALISM ORD/FREE WEALTH...POLICY DECISION TREND. PAGE 37 H0740
MARXISM REV ECO/DEV DIPLOM

B64
DEL VAYO J.A.,CHINA TRIUMPHS. CHINA/COM CULTURE DIPLOM HEALTH 20. PAGE 39 H0787
MARXISM CREATE ORD/FREE POLICY

B64
GREAT BRITAIN CENTRAL OFF INF,CONSTITUTIONAL DEVELOPMENT IN THE COMMONWEALTH. VOL/ASSN PLAN DIPLOM COLONIAL INGP/REL NAT/LISM ORD/FREE PWR 17/20 CMN/WLTH. PAGE 60 H1202
REGION CONSTN NAT/G SOVEREIGN

B64
GROSSER A.,THE FEDERAL REPUBLIC OF GERMANY: A CONCISE HISTORY. GERMANY/W STRUCT MORAL ORD/FREE POPULISM SOCISM...SOC CONCPT 20. PAGE 62 H1235
NAT/G POL/PAR CHOOSE DIPLOM

B64
GROVES H.E.,THE CONSTITUTION OF MALAYSIA. MALAYSIA POL/PAR CHIEF CONSULT DELIB/GP CT/SYS PARL/PROC CHOOSE FEDERAL ORD/FREE 20. PAGE 62 H1238
CONSTN NAT/G LAW

B64
GUMPLOWICZ L.,RECHTSSTAAT UND SOZIALISMUS. STRATA ORD/FREE SOVEREIGN MARXISM...IDEA/COMP 16/20 KANT/I HOBBES/T. PAGE 62 H1251
JURID NAT/G SOCISM CONCPT

B64
HALLER W.,DER SCHWEDISCHE JUSTITIEOMBUDSMAN. DENMARK FINLAND NORWAY SWEDEN LEGIS ADJUD CONTROL PERSON ORD/FREE...NAT/COMP 20 OMBUDSMAN. PAGE 64 H1288
JURID PARL/PROC ADMIN CHIEF

B64
HILL C.R.,BANTUSTANS: THE FRAGMENTATION OF SOUTH AFRICA. AFR SOUTH/AFR ELITES SOCIETY KIN CONTROL DISCRIM ANOMIE ATTIT...POLICY CHARTS GOV/COMP 20 NEGRO BANTUSTANS TRANSKEI NATAL. PAGE 71 H1416
RACE/REL CULTURE LOC/G ORD/FREE

B64
HOROWITZ I.L.,REVOLUTION IN BRAZIL. BRAZIL L/A+17C ELITES STRATA NAT/G BAL/PWR PARTIC ATTIT 20. PAGE 74 H1473
ECO/UNDEV DIPLOM POLICY

ORD/FREE B64
INDIAN COMM PREVENTION CORRUPT,REPORT, 1964. INDIA NAT/G GOV/REL ATTIT ORD/FREE...CRIMLGY METH 20. PAGE 76 H1530 — CRIME ADMIN LEGIS LOC/G

B64
KARIEL H.S.,IN SEARCH OF AUTHORITY: TWENTIETH-CENTURY POLITICAL THOUGHT. WOR+45 WOR-45 NAT/G EX/STRUC TOTALISM DRIVE PWR...MGT PHIL/SCI GEN/LAWS 19/20 NIETZSCH/F FREUD/S WEBER/MAX NIEBUHR/R MARITAIN/J. PAGE 83 H1661 — CONSTN CONCPT ORD/FREE IDEA/COMP

B64
LEMARCHAND R.,POLITICAL AWAKENING IN THE BELGIAN CONGO. ECO/UNDEV VOL/ASSN DOMIN CHOOSE GP/REL INGP/REL DISCRIM ORD/FREE PWR...CHARTS 20 CONGO ARABS. PAGE 94 H1873 — NAT/LISM COLONIAL POL/PAR RACE/REL

B64
LIEVWEN E.,GENERALS VS PRESIDENTS: WEOMILITARISM IN LATIN AMERICA. L/A+17C FORCES DIPLOM FOR/AID LEAD ...NAT/COMP 20 PRESIDENT. PAGE 97 H1929 — CIVMIL/REL REV CONSERVE ORD/FREE

B64
MAUD J.,AID FOR DEVELOPING COUNTRIES. COM EUR+WWI UK INT/TRADE ORD/FREE...GOV/COMP 20. PAGE 105 H2101 — FOR/AID DIPLOM ECO/TAC ECO/UNDEV

B64
MBEKI G.,SOUTH AFRICA: THE PEASANT'S REVOLT. SOUTH/AFR POL/PAR COERCE REV NAT/LISM ORD/FREE SOVEREIGN 20 NEGRO. PAGE 106 H2114 — COLONIAL RACE/REL DISCRIM DOMIN

B64
NEWARK F.H.,NOTES ON IRISH LEGAL HISTORY (2ND ED.). IRELAND UK PARL/PROC ORD/FREE SOVEREIGN 12/20 ENGLSH/LAW. PAGE 117 H2344 — CT/SYS JURID ADJUD NAT/G

B64
PARANJAPE H.K.,THE FLIGHT OF TECHNICAL PERSONNEL IN PUBLIC UNDERTAKINGS. INDIA PAY DEMAND HAPPINESS ORD/FREE...MGT QU 20 MIGRATION. PAGE 123 H2464 — ADMIN NAT/G WORKER PLAN

B64
PIKE F.B.,THE CONFLICT BETWEEN CHURCH AND STATE IN LATIN AMERICA. L/A+17C CULTURE SOCIETY STRATA DOMIN EDU/PROP LEGIT COERCE ATTIT ORD/FREE PWR WEALTH ...CONCPT TIME/SEQ TREND VAL/FREE. PAGE 125 H2510 — SECT NAT/G

B64
RAISON T.,WHY CONSERVATIVE? UK FORCES DIPLOM ECO/TAC GIVE EDU/PROP ORD/FREE WEALTH LAISSEZ ...GOV/COMP 20 TORY/PARTY CONSRV/PAR. PAGE 129 H2583 — PLURISM CONSERVE POL/PAR NAT/G

B64
SKINNER E.P.,THE MOSSI OF UPPER VOLTA: THE POLITICAL DEVELOPMENT OF A SUDANESE PEOPLE. AFR LAW AGRI FAM KIN POL/PAR PROVS SECT DELIB/GP EX/STRUC FORCES TOP/EX DOMIN EDU/PROP LEGIT CT/SYS COERCE CHOOSE ORD/FREE PWR WEALTH...SOC MYTH VAL/FREE. PAGE 145 H2897 — CULTURE OBS UPPER/VOLT

B64
TINKER H.,BALLOT BOX AND BAYONET - PEOPLE AND GOVERNMENT IN EMERGENT ASIAN COUNTRIES. CEYLON INDIA INDONESIA PHILIPPINE POL/PAR ADMIN COLONIAL LEAD PARL/PROC CHOOSE CONSEN ORD/FREE SOVEREIGN PLURISM...GOV/COMP THIRD/WRLD. PAGE 155 H3104 — MYTH S/ASIA NAT/COMP NAT/LISM

B64
WAINHOUSE D.W.,REMNANTS OF EMPIRE: THE UNITED NATIONS AND THE END OF COLONIALISM. FUT PORTUGAL WOR+45 NAT/G CONSULT DOMIN LEGIT ADMIN ROUTINE ATTIT ORD/FREE...POLICY JURID RECORD INT TIME/SEQ UN CMN/WLTH 20. PAGE 164 H3287 — INT/ORG TREND COLONIAL

B64
WHEELER-BENNETT J.W.,THE NEMESIS OF POWER (2ND ED.). EUR+WWI GERMANY TOP/EX TEC/DEV ADMIN WAR PERS/REL RIGID/FLEX ROLE ORD/FREE PWR FASCISM 20 HITLER/A. PAGE 167 H3342 — FORCES NAT/G GP/REL STRUCT

B64
WILCOX W.A.,INDIA, PAKISTAN AND THE RISE OF CHINA. ASIA BURMA CEYLON CHINA/COM INDIA PAKISTAN S/ASIA NAT/G VOL/ASSN FORCES TOP/EX ACT/RES DOMIN REGION RIGID/FLEX ORD/FREE...POLICY GEN/LAWS COLD/WAR 20. PAGE 168 H3362 — CULTURE ATTIT DIPLOM

B64
ZOLLSCHAN G.K.,EXPLORATIONS IN SOCIAL CHANGE. SOCIETY STRATA STRUCT ECO/UNDEV EX/STRUC...PSY ANTHOL 20. PAGE 173 H3463 — ORD/FREE SIMUL CONCPT CULTURE

L64
MACKINTOSH J.P.,"NIGERIA'S EXTERNAL AFFAIRS." UK CULTURE ECO/UNDEV NAT/G VOL/ASSN EDU/PROP LEGIT ADMIN ATTIT ORD/FREE PWR 20. PAGE 100 H2002 — AFR DIPLOM NIGERIA

L64
SYMONDS R.,"REFLECTIONS IN LOCALISATION." AFR S/ASIA UK STRATA INT/ORG NAT/G SCHOOL EDU/PROP LEGIT KNOWL ORD/FREE PWR RESPECT CMN/WLTH 20. PAGE 151 H3023 — ADMIN MGT COLONIAL

S64
BRADLEY C.P.,"THE FORMATION OF MALAYSIA." INDIA S/ASIA POL/PAR VOL/ASSN TOP/EX LEGIT RACE/REL ORD/FREE 20. PAGE 20 H0398 — NAT/G CREATE COLONIAL MALAYSIA

S64
CLIGNET R.,"POTENTIAL ELITES IN GHANA AND THE IVORY COAST: A PRELIMINARY SURVEY." AFR CULTURE ELITES STRATA KIN NAT/G SECT DOMIN EXEC ORD/FREE RESPECT SKILL...POLICY RELATIV GP/COMP NAT/COMP 20. PAGE 30 H0605 — PWR LEGIT IVORY/CST GHANA

S64
ENNIS T.E.,"VIETNAM: LAND WITHOUT LAUGHTER." S/ASIA VIETNAM VIETNAM/S INTELL SOCIETY SECT FORCES DIPLOM LEGIT COERCE WAR ATTIT RIGID/FLEX ORD/FREE COLD/WAR 20. PAGE 46 H0929 — NAT/G TOP/EX GUERRILLA

S64
GRUNER E.,"PRENSA, PARTIDOS POLITICOS, Y GRUPOS DE PRESION EN SUIZA." EUR+WWI MOD/EUR NAT/G EDU/PROP LEGIT PRESS ATTIT KNOWL ORD/FREE...CONCPT STAT CON/ANAL CHARTS 20. PAGE 62 H1241 — POL/PAR SWITZERLND

S64
KANOUTE P.,"AFRICAN SOCIALISM." AFR CONSTN NAT/G COLONIAL ORD/FREE...GOV/COMP METH/COMP 20 EUROPE. PAGE 83 H1655 — SOCISM CULTURE STRUCT IDEA/COMP

S64
LEVI W.,"INDIAN NEUTRALISM RECONSIDERED." ASIA CHINA/COM S/ASIA SOCIETY NAT/G ACT/RES LEGIT NEUTRAL COERCE ATTIT DRIVE PERCEPT RIGID/FLEX HEALTH LOVE PWR...DECISION RECORD TREND STERTYP 20. PAGE 95 H1896 — ORD/FREE CONCPT INDIA

S64
LEWIS B.,"THE QUEST FOR FREEDOM--A SAD STORY OF THE MIDDLE EAST." ISLAM ISRAEL LEBANON TURKEY CULTURE NAT/G SECT LEGIS TOP/EX DOMIN EDU/PROP LEGIT ORD/FREE PWR RESPECT...POLICY TIME/SEQ VAL/FREE 20. PAGE 96 H1911 — CONSTN ATTIT NAT/LISM

S64
LOW D.A.,"LION RAMPANT." EUR+WWI MOD/EUR S/ASIA ECO/UNDEV NAT/G FORCES TEC/DEV ECO/TAC LEGIT ADMIN COLONIAL COERCE ORD/FREE RESPECT 19/20. PAGE 99 H1972 — AFR DOMIN DIPLOM UK

S64
MARTELLI G.,"PORTUGAL AND THE UNITED NATIONS." AFR EUR+WWI ELITES INT/ORG NAT/G PROVS PLAN DIPLOM ECO/TAC DOMIN COLONIAL RIGID/FLEX MORAL ORD/FREE PWR WEALTH...MYTH UN 20. PAGE 103 H2060 — ATTIT PORTUGAL

S64
RAMAZANI R.K.,"CHURCH AND STATE IN MODERNIZING SOCIETY: THE CASE OF IRAN." ISLAM CULTURE ORD/FREE PWR...TIME/SEQ VAL/FREE 17/20. PAGE 129 H2586 — SECT NAT/G ELITES IRAN

S64
RUDOLPH L.I.,"GENERALS AND POLITICIANS IN INDIA." INDIA S/ASIA CULTURE STRATA NAT/G LEGIS TOP/EX EDU/PROP ATTIT ORD/FREE PWR RESPECT SKILL...POLICY BIOG TIME/SEQ STERTYP VAL/FREE 20. PAGE 136 H2713 — FORCES COERCE

S64
SALVADORI M.,"EL CAPITALISMO EN LA EUROPA DE LA POSGUERRA." INT/ORG NAT/G POL/PAR PLAN ECO/TAC ATTIT ORD/FREE WEALTH...HIST/WRIT COLD/WAR EEC 20. PAGE 137 H2743 — EUR+WWI ECO/DEV CAP/ISM

S64
SMYTHE H.H.,"NEHRU AND INDIAN FOREIGN POLICY." S/ASIA ECO/UNDEV NAT/G POL/PAR CONSULT PLAN DIPLOM NEUTRAL COERCE ATTIT DRIVE PERSON MORAL ORD/FREE RESPECT...GEOG CONCPT TIME/SEQ TREND GEN/LAWS 20 NEHRU/J. PAGE 146 H2922 — TOP/EX BIOG INDIA

S64
TINKER H.,"POLITICS IN SOUTHEAST ASIA." INT/ORG NAT/G CREATE PLAN TEC/DEV GUERRILLA KNOWL ORD/FREE COLD/WAR. PAGE 155 H3103 — S/ASIA ACT/RES REGION

S64
VANDENBOSCH A.,"POWER BALANCE IN INDONESIA." S/ASIA USSR NAT/G TOP/EX BAL/PWR DOMIN NEUTRAL ORD/FREE PWR...POLICY TIME/SEQ GEN/LAWS 20 SUKARNO/A. PAGE 162 H3233 — FORCES TREND DIPLOM INDONESIA

B65
AIYAR S.P.,STUDIES IN INDIAN DEMOCRACY. INDIA STRATA ECO/UNDEV LABOR POL/PAR LEGIS DIPLOM LOBBY REGION CHOOSE ATTIT SOCISM...ANTHOL 20. PAGE 4 H0086 — ORD/FREE REPRESENT ADMIN NAT/G

B65
BERNDT R.M.,ABORIGINAL MAN IN AUSTRALIA. LAW DOMIN ADMIN COLONIAL MARRIAGE HABITAT ORD/FREE...LING CHARTS ANTHOL BIBLIOG WORSHIP 20 AUSTRAL ABORIGINES MUSIC ELKIN/AP. PAGE 16 H0312 — SOC CULTURE SOCIETY STRUCT

B65
BORTOLI G.,SOCIOLOGIE DU REFERENDUM DANS LA FRANCE MODERNE. FRANCE CONSTN EDU/PROP SUFF ATTIT ORD/FREE ...POLICY DECISION CHARTS BIBLIOG 20 DEGAULLE/C. PAGE 19 H0379 — LEGIS SOCIETY PWR NAT/G

B65
BROWNSON O.A.,THE AMERICAN REPUBLIC. NAT/G PROVS WAR GOV/REL PRIVIL ORD/FREE PWR ALL/IDEOS CONSERVE — CONSTN FEDERAL

...CONCPT 19 CIVIL/WAR. PAGE 22 H0452 SOVEREIGN

B65
BULMER-THOMAS I.,THE GROWTH OF THE BRITISH PARTY SYSTEM (VOL. II) 1924-1964. UK ECO/DEV BARGAIN WAR CHOOSE ATTIT ORD/FREE 20 LABOR/PAR CONSRV/PAR. PAGE 23 H0472 CHIEF POL/PAR PARL/PROC NAT/G

B65
BURLING R.,HILL FARMS AND PADI FIELDS. BURMA S/ASIA THAILAND VIETNAM AGRI NEIGH SECT GP/REL NAT/LISM ORD/FREE 20 MID/EAST MIGRATION. PAGE 24 H0491 SOCIETY STRUCT CULTURE SOVEREIGN

B65
CENTRAL GAZETTEERS UNIT,THE GAZETTEER OF INDIA (VOL. I). INDIA SOCIETY STRATA PLAN EDU/PROP NAT/LISM ORD/FREE WEALTH...GEOG LING CHARTS SOC/INTEG 20. PAGE 28 H0568 PRESS CULTURE SECT STRUCT

B65
CHARNAY J.P.,LE SUFFRAGE POLITIQUE EN FRANCE; ELECTIONS PARLEMENTAIRES, ELECTION PRESIDENTIELLE, REFERENDUMS. FRANCE CONSTN CHIEF DELIB/GP ECO/TAC EDU/PROP CRIME INGP/REL MORAL ORD/FREE PWR CATHISM 20 PARLIAMENT PRESIDENT. PAGE 29 H0584 CHOOSE SUFF NAT/G LEGIS

B65
CONRING E.,KIRCHE UND STAAT NACH DER LEHRE DER NIEDERLANDISCHEN CALVINISTEN IN DER ERSTEN HALFTE DES 17. JAHRHUNDERTS. NETHERLAND GP/REL...CONCPT 17 CHURCH/STA. PAGE 33 H0656 SECT JURID NAT/G ORD/FREE

B65
COX R.H.,THE STATE IN INTERNATIONAL RELATIONS. INT/ORG DIPLOM REV WAR PEACE MARXISM...CONCPT GOV/COMP. PAGE 34 H0690 SOVEREIGN NAT/G FASCISM ORD/FREE

B65
FAUST J.J.,A REVOLUCAO DEVORA SEUS PRESIDENTES. BRAZIL NAT/G POL/PAR LEAD CHOOSE CIVMIL/REL ORD/FREE 20 PRESIDENT. PAGE 49 H0976 PARTIC REV FORCES GP/REL

B65
GAJENDRAGADKAR P.B.,LAW, LIBERTY AND SOCIAL JUSTICE. INDIA CONSTN NAT/G SECT PLAN ECO/TAC PRESS POPULISM...SOC METH/COMP 20 HINDU. PAGE 54 H1086 ORD/FREE LAW ADJUD JURID

B65
GEWIRTH A.,POLITICAL PHILOSOPHY. UNIV SOCIETY NAT/G GP/REL INGP/REL CONSEN PWR...IDEA/COMP GEN/LAWS 17/19 HOBBES/T LOCKE/JOHN MARX/KARL MILL/JS ROUSSEAU/J. PAGE 56 H1118 ORD/FREE SOVEREIGN PHIL/SCI

B65
GILG P.,DIE ERNEUERUNG DES DEMOKRATISCHEN DENKENS IM WILHELMINISCHEN DEUTSCHLAND. GERMANY PARL/PROC CHOOSE REPRESENT...CONCPT 19/20 BISMARCK/O WILHELM/II. PAGE 56 H1126 POL/PAR ORD/FREE NAT/G

B65
GRIMAL H.,HISTOIRE DU COMMONWEALTH BRITANNIQUE. UK FINAN DOMIN ATTIT ORD/FREE...T 15/20 CMN/WLTH. PAGE 61 H1226 NAT/G COLONIAL DIPLOM INT/TRADE

B65
HALEVY E.,THE ERA OF TYRANNIES (TRANS. BY R. K. WEBB). FRANCE MOD/EUR UK ECO/DEV LABOR NAT/G BAL/PWR FEDERAL ALL/VALS...OLD/LIB TREND 18/20 SAINTSIMON. PAGE 64 H1285 SOCISM CONCPT UTOPIA ORD/FREE

B65
HALPERIN M.H.,COMMUNIST CHINA AND ARMS CONTROL. CHINA/COM FUT USA+45 CULTURE FORCES TEC/DEV ECO/TAC WAR PEACE ORD/FREE MARXISM 20 COLD/WAR. PAGE 64 H1292 ATTIT POLICY ARMS/CONT NUC/PWR

B65
HAMIL H.M.,DICTATORSHIP IN SPANISH AMERICA. NAT/G COERCE MORAL ORD/FREE...POLICY PSY SOC ANTHOL 18/20. PAGE 65 H1300 TOTALISM CHIEF L/A+17C FASCISM

B65
IANNI O.,ESTADO E CAPITALISMO. L/A+17C FINAN TEC/DEV ECO/TAC ORD/FREE WEALTH POLICY. PAGE 76 H1518 ECO/UNDEV STRUCT INDUS NAT/G

B65
KOUSOULAS D.G.,REVOLUTION AND DEFEAT; THE STORY OF THE GREEK COMMUNIST PARTY. GREECE INT/ORG EX/STRUC DIPLOM FOR/AID EDU/PROP PARL/PROC ADJUST ATTIT 20 COM/PARTY. PAGE 88 H1759 REV MARXISM POL/PAR ORD/FREE

B65
LAMBIRI I.,SOCIAL CHANGE IN A GREEK COUNTRY TOWN. GREECE FAM PROB/SOLV ROUTINE TASK LEISURE INGP/REL CONSEN ORD/FREE...SOC INT QU CHARTS 20. PAGE 90 H1803 INDUS WORKER CULTURE NEIGH

B65
MENON K.P.S.,MANY WORLDS. INDIA BAL/PWR CAP/ISM COLONIAL REV ORD/FREE PWR MARXISM...POLICY 20 COLD/WAR. PAGE 109 H2176 BIOG DIPLOM NAT/G

B65
MOORE W.E.,THE IMPACT OF INDUSTRY. CULTURE STRUCT ORD/FREE...TREND 20. PAGE 113 H2251 INDUS MGT TEC/DEV ECO/UNDEV

B65
MURDOCK G.P.,CULTURE AND SOCIETY. SOCIETY STRATA STRUCT SECT CREATE CONTROL ORD/FREE...GP/COMP ANTHOL 20. PAGE 115 H2294 CULTURE PHIL/SCI METH IDEA/COMP

B65
NEWBURY C.W.,BRITISH POLICY TOWARDS WEST AFRICA: SELECT DOCUMENTS 1786-1874. AFR UK INT/TRADE DOMIN ADMIN COLONIAL CT/SYS COERCE ORD/FREE...BIBLIOG/A 18/19. PAGE 117 H2345 DIPLOM POLICY NAT/G WRITING

B65
PADELFORD N.,THE UNITED NATIONS IN THE BALANCE* ACCOMPLISHMENTS AND PROSPECTS. NAT/G VOL/ASSN DIPLOM ADMIN COLONIAL CT/SYS REGION WAR ORD/FREE ...ANTHOL UN. PAGE 122 H2437 INT/ORG CONTROL

B65
PEASLEE A.J.,CONSTITUTIONS OF NATIONS* THIRD REVISED EDITION (VOLUME I* AFRICA). LAW EX/STRUC LEGIS TOP/EX LEGIT CT/SYS ROUTINE ORD/FREE PWR SOVEREIGN...CON/ANAL CHARTS. PAGE 124 H2481 AFR CHOOSE CONSTN NAT/G

B65
RUBINSTEIN A.Z.,THE CHALLENGE OF POLITICS: IDEAS AND ISSUES (2ND ED.). UNIV ELITES SOCIETY EX/STRUC BAL/PWR PARL/PROC AUTHORIT...DECISION ANTHOL 20. PAGE 136 H2709 NAT/G DIPLOM GP/REL ORD/FREE

B65
SLATER J.,A REVALUATION OF COLLECTIVE SECURITY* THE OAS IN ACTION. L/A+17C USA+45 NAT/G ADMIN COERCE ORD/FREE PWR...GOV/COMP IDEA/COMP GEN/LAWS OAS. PAGE 145 H2899 REGION INT/ORG FORCES

B65
SMITH R.M.,CAMBODIA'S FOREIGN POLICY. ECO/UNDEV NAT/G NEUTRAL ORD/FREE COLD/WAR VAL/FREE. PAGE 146 H2917 S/ASIA CAMBODIA DIPLOM

B65
STEINER K.,LOCAL GOVERNMENT IN JAPAN. CONSTN CULTURE NAT/G ADMIN CHOOSE...SOC STAT 20 CHINJAP. PAGE 149 H2976 LOC/G SOCIETY JURID ORD/FREE

B65
TUTSCH H.E.,FACETS OF ARAB NATIONALISM. ISLAM ISRAEL CULTURE STRUCT SECT RIGID/FLEX ORD/FREE MARXISM SOCISM 20. PAGE 157 H3143 ECO/UNDEV NAT/LISM TEC/DEV SOCIETY

L65
HOUN F.S.,"THE COMMUNIST MONOLITH VERSUS THE CHINESE TRADITION." CULTURE INTELL SOCIETY STRUCT DOMIN GP/REL ORD/FREE CONSERVE PLURISM...GOV/COMP WORSHIP. PAGE 74 H1479 ASIA MARXISM TOTALISM

L65
SHARMA S.P.,"THE INDIA-CHINA BORDER DISPUTE: AN INDIAN PERSPECTIVE." ASIA CHINA/COM S/ASIA NAT/G LEGIT CT/SYS NAT/LISM DRIVE MORAL ORD/FREE PWR 20. PAGE 142 H2850 LAW ATTIT SOVEREIGN INDIA

S65
BIRNBAUM K.,"SWEDEN'S NUCLEAR POLICY." WOR+45 POL/PAR CREATE TEC/DEV NEUTRAL RISK WAR ORD/FREE ...DECISION IDEA/COMP NAT/COMP TIME. PAGE 17 H0343 SWEDEN NUC/PWR DIPLOM ARMS/CONT

S65
GORDON M.,"THE SETTING FOR EUROPEAN ARMS CONTROLS* POLITICAL AND STRATEGIC CHOICES OF EUROPEAN ELITES." FRANCE GERMANY UK USA+45 USSR ARMS/CONT DETER ATTIT ORD/FREE...SAMP NAT/COMP NATO. PAGE 59 H1179 REC/INT ELITES RISK WAR

S65
PLISCHKE E.,"INTEGRATING BERLIN AND THE FEDERAL REPUBLIC OF GERMANY." EUR+WWI GERMANY/W LEGIS TEC/DEV DOMIN ORD/FREE PWR...JURID 20 BERLIN. PAGE 126 H2528 DIPLOM NAT/G MUNIC

S65
STAAR R.F.,"RETROGRESSION IN POLAND." COM USSR AGRI INDUS NAT/G CREATE EDU/PROP TOTALISM RIGID/FLEX ORD/FREE PWR SOCISM...RECORD CHARTS 20. PAGE 148 H2965 TOP/EX ECO/TAC POLAND

S65
VUCINICH W.S.,"WHITHER RUMANIA." COM USSR YUGOSLAVIA NAT/G VOL/ASSN DELIB/GP TOP/EX LEGIT NAT/LISM TOTALISM ATTIT DRIVE RIGID/FLEX ORD/FREE WEALTH SOCISM...TIME/SEQ TREND 20. PAGE 164 H3281 ECO/DEV CREATE ROMANIA

C65
BORTOLI G.,"SOCIOLOGIE DU REFERENDUM DANS LA FRANCE MODERNE." FRANCE CONSTN NAT/G EDU/PROP SUFF ATTIT ORD/FREE...POLICY DECISION SOC CHARTS 20. PAGE 19 H0378 BIBLIOG LEGIS SOCIETY PWR

B66
ARCHER P.,FREEDOM AT STAKE. UK LAW NAT/G LEGIS JUDGE CRIME MORAL...CONCPT 20 CIVIL/LIB. PAGE 8 H0159 ORD/FREE NAT/COMP POLICY

B66
BARNETT D.L.,MAU MAU FROM WITHIN. AFR UK POL/PAR LEAD GUERRILLA AUTHORIT ORD/FREE...SOC BIOG 20 NEGRO MAU/MAU. PAGE 11 H0225 REV CULTURE NAT/G

B66
BIRKHEAD G.S.,ADMINISTRATIVE PROBLEMS IN PAKISTAN. PAKISTAN AGRI FINAN INDUS LG/CO ECO/TAC CONTROL PWR ADMIN NAT/G

...CHARTS ANTHOL 20. PAGE 17 H0340
ORD/FREE ECO/UNDEV

B66
CAUTE D.,THE LEFT IN EUROPE SINCE 1789. EUR+WWI MOD/EUR NAT/G POL/PAR REV...TIME/SEQ GEN/LAWS BIBLIOG 18/20. PAGE 28 H0564
ALL/IDEOS ORD/FREE CONCPT STRATA

B66
CROWDER M.,A SHORT HISTORY OF NIGERIA. AFR NIGERIA UK ECO/UNDEV CHIEF INT/TRADE RACE/REL NAT/LISM ORD/FREE...GEOG SOC CHARTS BIBLIOG 14/20. PAGE 36 H0711
COLONIAL NAT/G CULTURE

B66
DALLIN A.,POLITICS IN THE SOVIET UNION: 7 CASES. COM USSR LAW POL/PAR CHIEF FORCES WRITING CONTROL PARL/PROC CIVMIL/REL TOTALISM...ANTHOL 20 KHRUSH/N STALIN/J CASEBOOK COM/PARTY. PAGE 37 H0736
MARXISM DOMIN ORD/FREE GOV/REL

B66
DE TOCQUEVILLE A,DEMOCRACY IN AMERICA (1834-1840) (2 VOLS. IN I; TRANS. BY G. LAWRENCE). FRANCE CULTURE STRATA POL/PAR CT/SYS REPRESENT FEDERAL ORD/FREE SOVEREIGN...MAJORIT TREND GEN/LAWS 18/19. PAGE 39 H0773
POPULISM USA-45 CONSTN NAT/COMP

B66
FORD P.,CARDINAL MORAN AND THE A. L. P. NAT/G POL/PAR SECT DELIB/GP LOBBY REV CHOOSE ORD/FREE MARXISM 19/20 AUSTRAL PROTESTANT LABOR/PAR. PAGE 52 H1035
CATHISM SOCISM LABOR SOCIETY

B66
FUCHS W.P.,STAAT UND KIRCHE IM WANDEL DER JAHRHUNDERTE. EUR+WWI MOD/EUR UK REV...JURID CONCPT 4/20 EUROPE CHRISTIAN CHURCH/STA. PAGE 54 H1074
SECT NAT/G ORD/FREE GP/REL

B66
GARCON M.,LETTRE OUVERTE A LA JUSTICE. FRANCE NAT/G PROB/SOLV PAY EFFICIENCY MORAL 20. PAGE 55 H1100
ORD/FREE ADJUD CT/SYS

B66
GERARD-LIBOIS J.,KATANGA SECESSION. INT/ORG FORCES DIPLOM ADMIN CONTROL WAR CHOOSE PWR...CHARTS 20 KATANGA TSHOMBE/M UN. PAGE 56 H1114
NAT/G REGION ORD/FREE REV

B66
HERMANN F.G.,DER KAMPF GEGEN RELIGION UND KIRCHE IN DER SOWJETISCHEN BESATZUNGSZONE DEUTSCHLANDS. GERMANY/E EDU/PROP ATTIT PERSON MORAL MARXISM 20 LENIN/VI STALIN/J KHRUSH/N. PAGE 70 H1400
SECT ORD/FREE GP/REL NAT/G

B66
HEYMANN F.G.,POLAND AND CZECHOSLOVAKIA. COM CZECHOSLVK POLAND...CHARTS BIBLIOG/A 9/20. PAGE 70 H1413
CULTURE NAT/LISM ORD/FREE WAR

B66
HIDAYATULLAH M.,DEMOCRACY IN INDIA AND THE JUDICIAL PROCESS. INDIA EX/STRUC LEGIS LEAD GOV/REL ATTIT ORD/FREE...MAJORIT CONCPT 20 NEHRU/J. PAGE 71 H1415
NAT/G CT/SYS CONSTN JURID

B66
JOHNSON N.,PARLIAMENT AND ADMINISTRATION: THE ESTIMATES COMMITTEE 1945-65. FUT UK NAT/G EX/STRUC PLAN BUDGET ORD/FREE...T 20 PARLIAMENT HOUSE/CMNS. PAGE 81 H1625
LEGIS ADMIN FINAN DELIB/GP

B66
KAUNDA K.,ZAMBIA: INDEPENDENCE AND BEYOND: THE SPEECHES OF KENNETH KAUNDA. AFR FUT ZAMBIA SOCIETY ECO/UNDEV NAT/G PROB/SOLV ECO/TAC ADMIN RACE/REL SOVEREIGN 20. PAGE 84 H1670
ORD/FREE COLONIAL CONSTN LEAD

B66
KAZAMIAS A.M.,EDUCATION AND QUEST FOR MODERNITY IN TURKEY. ISLAM SOCIETY SECT NAT/LISM ATTIT ORD/FREE SOVEREIGN TURKS. PAGE 84 H1672
NAT/G EDU/PROP STRATA CULTURE

B66
LOCKE J.,THE SECOND TREATISE OF GOVERNMENT: AN ESSAY CONCERNING THE TRUE ORIGINAL EXTENT AND END OF CIVIL GOVERNMENT (3RD ED.). CONSTN SOCIETY CONTROL OWN...PHIL/SCI 17 NATURL/LAW. PAGE 97 H1947
NAT/G PWR GEN/LAWS ORD/FREE

B66
NAMBOODIRIPAD E.M.,ECONOMICS AND POLITICS OF INDIA'S SOCIALIST PATTERN. INDIA STRATA AGRI INDUS NAT/G PRICE ORD/FREE SOVEREIGN 20. PAGE 115 H2307
ECO/UNDEV PLAN SOCISM CAP/ISM

B66
NIEDERGANG M.,LA REVOLUTION DE SAINT-DOMINGUE. DOMIN/REP INT/ORG NAT/G CONTROL LEAD GP/REL ORD/FREE MARXISM 20. PAGE 118 H2361
REV FORCES DIPLOM

B66
RICHERT F.,DIE NATIONALE WELLE. GERMANY GERMANY/W PARL/PROC ORD/FREE FASCISM...TREND 19/20. PAGE 131 H2622
POL/PAR ATTIT NAT/LISM NAT/G

B66
RINGHOFER K.,STRUKTURPROBLEME DES RECHTES. AUSTRIA ATTIT ORD/FREE...IDEA/COMP 20. PAGE 132 H2630
JURID PROVS NAT/G NAT/LISM

B66
RISTIC D.N.,YUGOSLAVIA'S REVOLUTION OF 1941. EUR+WWI YUGOSLAVIA NAT/G WAR ORD/FREE...RECORD BIBLIOG 20 HITLER/A TREATY. PAGE 132 H2633
REV ATTIT FASCISM DIPLOM

B66
ROOS H.,A HISTORY OF MODERN POLAND FROM THE FOUNDATION OF THE STATE IN THE FIRST WORLD WAR TO THE PRESENT DAY. EUR+WWI POLAND INTELL SOCIETY ECO/TAC LEAD REV ATTIT ORD/FREE MARXISM...BIBLIOG 20 WWI PARTITION. PAGE 133 H2669
NAT/G WAR DIPLOM

B66
ROSNER J.,DER FASCHISMUS. AUSTRIA GERMANY ITALY STRATA NAT/G POL/PAR COERCE RACE/REL TOTALISM ATTIT AUTHORIT...IDEA/COMP 20 NAZI ANTI/SEMIT. PAGE 134 H2684
NAT/LISM FASCISM ORD/FREE WAR

B66
SETTON K.M.,GREAT PROBLEMS IN EUROPEAN CIVILIZATION. CHRIST-17C EUR+WWI MOD/EUR SECT GP/REL ALL/VALS ORD/FREE ALL/IDEOS...TREND ANTHOL T CHRISTIAN RENAISSAN PROTESTANT. PAGE 142 H2835
CULTURE CONCPT IDEA/COMP

B66
SRINIVAS M.N.,SOCIAL CHANGE IN MODERN INDIA. INDIA CULTURE SOCIETY STRUCT SECT TEC/DEV...METH/CNCPT SELF/OBS WORSHIP 20. PAGE 148 H2961
ORD/FREE STRATA SOC ECO/UNDEV

B66
SWEET E.C.,CIVIL LIBERTIES IN AMERICA. LAW CONSTN NAT/G PRESS CT/SYS DISCRIM ATTIT WORSHIP 20 CIVIL/LIB. PAGE 151 H3018
ADJUD ORD/FREE SUFF COERCE

B66
TYSON G.,NEHRU: THE YEARS OF POWER. INDIA UK STRATA ECO/UNDEV FINAN SECT TASK WAR ORD/FREE MARXISM ...POLICY BIBLIOG 20 NEHRU/J. PAGE 157 H3145
CHIEF PWR DIPLOM NAT/G

B66
WEBER J.,EOTVOS UND DIE UNGARISCHE NATIONALITATENFRAGE. HUNGARY CULTURE SOCIETY REV ORD/FREE SOVEREIGN...BIOG 19. PAGE 166 H3318
NAT/LISM GP/REL ATTIT CONCPT

B66
ZEINE Z.N.,THE EMERGENCE OF ARAB NATIONALISM (REV. ED.). TURKEY UK NAT/G SECT TEC/DEV LEAD REV WAR AGE/Y ROLE ORD/FREE...TRADIT CHARTS BIBLIOG 20 ARABS OTTOMAN. PAGE 173 H3453
ISLAM NAT/LISM DIPLOM

B66
ZINKIN T.,CHALLENGES IN INDIA. INDIA PAKISTAN LAW AGRI FINAN INDUS TOP/EX TEC/DEV CONTROL ROUTINE ORD/FREE PWR 20 NEHRU/J SHASTRI/LB CIVIL/SERV. PAGE 173 H3458
NAT/G ECO/TAC POLICY ADMIN

B66
ZOLBERG A.R.,CREATING POLITICAL ORDER. AFR CONGO/BRAZ GHANA NIGER KIN NAT/G DOMIN COLONIAL REGION CENTRAL NAT/LISM ATTIT PWR 20 CONGO/LEOP. PAGE 173 H3462
SOVEREIGN ORD/FREE CONSTN POL/PAR

L66
ZOPPO C.E.,"NUCLEAR TECHNOLOGY, MULTIPOLARITY, AND INTERNATIONAL STABILITY." ASIA RUSSIA USA+45 STRUCT TOP/EX BAL/PWR DIPLOM DETER CIVMIL/REL NAT/COMP. PAGE 173 H3464
NET/THEORY ORD/FREE DECISION NUC/PWR

S66
BLANC N.,"SPAIN: LEARNING THROUGH STRUGGLE" SPAIN STRATA STRUCT SECT FORCES PROB/SOLV AGE/Y ATTIT ORD/FREE PWR WEALTH MARXISM SOCISM 19/20 FRANCO/F SUCCESSION. PAGE 18 H0352
NAT/G FUT SOCIALIST TOTALISM

S66
ROTHCHILD D.,"THE LIMITS OF FEDERALISM: AN EXAMINATION OF POLITICAL INSTITUTIONAL TRANSFER IN AFRICA." AFR CONSTN CULTURE ELITES ECO/UNDEV KIN PROB/SOLV ADMIN ORD/FREE PWR...POLICY 20. PAGE 135 H2695
FEDERAL NAT/G NAT/LISM COLONIAL

C66
ROSENBERG C.G. JR.,"THE MYTH OF "MAU-MAU:" NATIONALISM IN KENYA." AFR CULTURE NAT/G POL/PAR COERCE REV RACE/REL ATTIT ORD/FREE SOVEREIGN...MYTH BIBLIOG 20. PAGE 134 H2678
NAT/LISM COLONIAL MAJORIT LEAD

B67
ARIKPO O.,THE DEVELOPMENT OF MODERN NIGERIA. AFR NIGERIA SOCIETY ECO/UNDEV KIN ADMIN FEDERAL NAT/LISM ORD/FREE WEALTH...POLICY GEOG BIBLIOG 19/20. PAGE 8 H0163
NAT/G CULTURE CONSTN COLONIAL

B67
BAIN C.A.,VIETNAM: THE ROOTS OF CONFLICT. FRANCE S/ASIA USSR VIETNAM POL/PAR SECT FORCES COLONIAL NAT/LISM PEACE ORD/FREE MARXISM...GEOG CHARTS 4/20. PAGE 10 H0202
NAT/G WAR CULTURE

B67
BUNN R.F.,POLITICS AND CIVIL LIBERTIES IN EUROPE: FOUR CASE STUDIES. FRANCE GERMANY/W UK USSR NAT/G PRESS CRIME CROWD PRIVIL ATTIT 20. PAGE 24 H0476
ORD/FREE CONSTN NAT/COMP LAW

B67
CHILCOTE R.H.,PORTUGUESE AFRICA. PORTUGAL CULTURE SOCIETY ECO/UNDEV DOMIN NAT/LISM...TREND IDEA/COMP NAT/COMP BIBLIOG 15/20. PAGE 29 H0589
AFR COLONIAL ORD/FREE

PROB/SOLV

B67
CURTIN P.D.,AFRICA REMEMBERED. NIGERIA SENEGAL CULTURE DIPLOM INT/TRADE GP/REL RACE/REL...RECORD ANTHOL 18/19 NEGRO. PAGE 36 H0727 DOMIN ORD/FREE AFR DISCRIM

B67
EVANS R.H.,COEXISTENCE: COMMUNISM AND ITS PRACTICE IN BOLOGNA, 1945-1965. ITALY CAP/ISM ADMIN CHOOSE PEACE ORD/FREE...SOC STAT DEEP/INT SAMP CHARTS BIBLIOG 20. PAGE 48 H0952 MARXISM CULTURE MUNIC POL/PAR

B67
FANON F.,TOWARD THE AFRICAN REVOLUTION. AFR FRANCE CULTURE ELITES LEAD REV GP/REL ORD/FREE SOVEREIGN 20. PAGE 49 H0969 COLONIAL DOMIN ECO/UNDEV RACE/REL

B67
FISHEL L.H. JR.,THE NEGRO AMERICAN: A DOCUMENTARY HISTORY. SOCIETY NAT/G ROLE...POLICY ANTHOL 15/20 NEGRO. PAGE 51 H1013 ORD/FREE DISCRIM RACE/REL STRATA

B67
LENG S.C.,JUSTICE IN COMMUNIST CHINA: A SURVEY OF THE JUDICIAL SYSTEM OF THE CHINESE PEOPLE'S REPUBLIC. CHINA/COM LAW CONSTN LOC/G NAT/G PROF/ORG CONSULT FORCES ADMIN CRIME ORD/FREE...BIBLIOG 20 MAO. PAGE 94 H1877 CT/SYS ADJUD JURID MARXISM

B67
NESS G.D.,BUREAUCRACY AND RURAL DEVELOPMENT IN MALAYSIA. MALAYSIA UK SOCIETY FINAN INDUS WORKER TEC/DEV ECO/TAC COLONIAL EQUILIB ORD/FREE...STAT CHARTS 20. PAGE 117 H2330 ECO/UNDEV PLAN NAT/G ADMIN

B67
NYERERE J.K.,FREEDOM AND UNITY/UHURU NA UMOJA: A SELECTION FROM WRITINGS AND SPEECHES, 1952-65. TANZANIA ELITES ECO/UNDEV INT/ORG NAT/G CREATE DIPLOM COLONIAL REGION RACE/REL...ANTHOL 20. PAGE 119 H2383 SOVEREIGN AFR TREND ORD/FREE

B67
ODINGA O.,NOT YET UHURU. NAT/G POL/PAR PROB/SOLV COERCE REV WAR PERS/REL PERSON ORD/FREE...POLICY 20 ODINGA/O KENYATTA. PAGE 120 H2395 ATTIT BIOG LEAD AFR

B67
PATAI R.,GOLDEN RIVER TO GOLDEN ROAD: SOCIETY, CULTURE, AND CHANGE IN THE MIDDLE EAST (2ND ED.). ELITES FAM KIN TEC/DEV MARRIAGE NAT/LISM SEX ORD/FREE...TREND GP/COMP WORSHIP 20. PAGE 124 H2476 CULTURE SOCIETY ISLAM STRUCT

B67
PIKE F.B.,FREEDOM AND REFORM IN LATIN AMERICA. BRAZIL URUGUAY CONSTN CULTURE SECT DIPLOM EDU/PROP PARTIC DRIVE ALL/VALS CATHISM...GEOG ANTHOL BIBLIOG REFORMERS BOLIV. PAGE 126 H2511 L/A+17C ORD/FREE ECO/UNDEV REV

B67
POMEROY W.J.,HALF A CENTURY OF SOCIALISM. USSR LAW AGRI INDUS NAT/G CREATE DIPLOM EDU/PROP PERSON ORD/FREE WEALTH...POLICY TREND 20. PAGE 127 H2541 SOCISM MARXISM COM SOCIETY

B67
ROSENTHAL A.H.,THE SOCIAL PROGRAMS OF SWEDEN. SWEDEN USA+45 FINAN NAT/G PLAN PROB/SOLV INSPECT ORD/FREE...POLICY HEAL SOC CHARTS NAT/COMP 20. PAGE 134 H2681 GIVE SOC/WK WEALTH METH/COMP

B67
VENKATESWARAN R.J.,CABINET GOVERNMENT IN INDIA. INDIA UK SOCIETY OP/RES COLONIAL LEAD EFFICIENCY ORD/FREE 20. PAGE 162 H3241 DELIB/GP ADMIN CONSTN NAT/G

B67
WILLS A.J.,AN INTRODUCTION TO THE HISTORY OF CENTRAL AFRICA. RHODESIA ZAMBIA CULTURE SOCIETY ECO/UNDEV TEC/DEV DOMIN WAR ALL/VALS...POLICY TREND BIBLIOG T 14/20 NYASALAND. PAGE 169 H3375 AFR COLONIAL ORD/FREE

L67
AUSTIN D.A.,"POLITICAL CONFLICT IN AFRICA." CONSTN NAT/G CREATE ADMIN COLONIAL ORD/FREE MARXISM POPULISM SOCISM...NAT/COMP ANTHOL 20. PAGE 9 H0180 ANOMIE AFR POL/PAR

L67
TOUVAL S.,"THE ORGANIZATION OF AFRICAN UNITY AND AFRICAN BORDERS." DEBATE REGION TASK REV ATTIT ORD/FREE...DECISION UN 20 OAU. PAGE 156 H3121 AFR NAT/G COLONIAL NAT/LISM

S67
ABDEL-MALEK A.,"THE CRISIS IN NASSER'S EGYPT." ISLAM UAR STRUCT POL/PAR EX/STRUC CREATE PLAN WAR ATTIT ORD/FREE PWR...POLICY DECISION 20. PAGE 3 H0054 FORCES LEAD PROB/SOLV NAT/G

S67
ADOKO A.,"THE CONSTITUTION OF UGANDA." AFR UGANDA LOC/G CHIEF FORCES LEGIS ADJUD EXEC CHOOSE NAT/LISM ...IDEA/COMP 20. PAGE 4 H0072 NAT/G CONSTN ORD/FREE LAW

S67
BATOR V.,"ONE WAR* TWO VIETNAMS." S/ASIA VIETNAM DIPLOM SUFF ATTIT ORD/FREE 20. PAGE 12 H0236 WAR BAL/PWR NAT/G

STRUCT

S67
BEVEL D.N.,"JOURNEY TO NORTH VIETNAM." VIETNAM/N CONSTN NAT/G FORCES PROB/SOLV DEATH CIVMIL/REL PEACE MORAL...ANTHOL 20 NEGRO. PAGE 16 H0325 ATTIT DIPLOM ORD/FREE WAR

S67
BRADLEY A.W.,"CONSTITUTION-MAKING IN UGANDA." UGANDA LAW CHIEF DELIB/GP LEGIS ADMIN EXEC PARL/PROC RACE/REL ORD/FREE...GOV/COMP 20. PAGE 20 H0397 NAT/G CREATE CONSTN FEDERAL

S67
DANA MONTANO S.M.,"APLICACIONES CONCRETAS DE LAS RESOLUCIONES Y RECOMENDACIONES DE LAS CONFERENCIAS INTERAMERICANAS DE ABOGADOS" L/A+17C NAT/G PROVS GOV/REL PERCEPT 20 ARGEN. PAGE 37 H0739 JURID CT/SYS ORD/FREE BAL/PWR

S67
GRANT C.H.,"RURAL LOCAL GOVERNMENT IN GUYANA AND BRITISH HONDURAS." GUYANA HONDURAS L/A+17C AGRI NAT/G EX/STRUC ACT/RES REGION GOV/REL EFFICIENCY ORD/FREE 20. PAGE 60 H1196 ECO/UNDEV LOC/G ADMIN MUNIC

S67
HALPERN B.,"THE ORIGINS OF THE CRISIS." ISLAM ISRAEL INT/ORG FORCES WEAPON PEACE ORD/FREE TREATY 20 UN. PAGE 65 H1296 WAR NAT/G DIPLOM

S67
KASFIR N.,"THE UGANDA CONSTITUENT ASSEMBLY DEBATE." UGANDA REPRESENT FEDERAL ORD/FREE POPULISM...POLICY DECISION 20. PAGE 83 H1665 CONSTN CONFER LAW NAT/G

S67
MATTHEWS R.O.,"THE SUEZ CANAL DISPUTE* A CASE STUDY IN PEACEFUL SETTLEMENT." FRANCE ISRAEL UAR UK NAT/G CONTROL LEAD COERCE WAR NAT/LISM ROLE ORD/FREE PWR ...INT/LAW UN 20. PAGE 105 H2099 PEACE DIPLOM ADJUD

S67
MAYANJA A.,"THE GOVERNMENT'S PROPOSALS ON THE NEW CONSTITUTION." AFR UGANDA LAW CHIEF LEGIS ADJUD REPRESENT FEDERAL PWR 20. PAGE 105 H2105 CONSTN CONFER ORD/FREE NAT/G

S67
MCCLEERY W.,"AN INTERVIEW WITH J. DOUGLAS BROWN ON THE 'WAY' OF VIETNAM" COM VIETNAM INTELL ECO/DEV ACADEM NAT/G COERCE PERSON SUPEGO ORD/FREE 20. PAGE 106 H2125 ATTIT WAR COLONIAL MARXISM

S67
MOZINGO D.,"CONTAINMENT IN ASIA RECONSIDERED." NAT/G DIPLOM REV PEACE ORD/FREE 20. PAGE 114 H2275 ATTIT CONTROL NAT/LISM EFFICIENCY

S67
NIEBUHR R.,"THE ETHICS OF WAR AND PEACE IN THE NUCLEAR AGE." VIETNAM INTELL CONFER CONTROL WAR GOV/REL PERS/REL ORD/FREE...POLICY INT GOV/COMP NAT/COMP 20 UN. PAGE 118 H2360 MORAL PEACE NUC/PWR DIPLOM

S67
RENFIELD R.L.,"A POLICY FOR VIETNAM." COM VIETNAM NAT/G POL/PAR VOL/ASSN CHIEF DIPLOM EDU/PROP DETER REPRESENT ATTIT ORD/FREE 20. PAGE 131 H2615 WAR POLICY PLAN COERCE

S67
RUCKER B.W.,"WHAT SOLUTIONS DO PEOPLE ENDORSE IN FREE PRESS-FAIR TRIAL DILEMMA?" LAW NAT/G CT/SYS ATTIT...NET/THEORY SAMP CHARTS IDEA/COMP METH 20. PAGE 136 H2710 CONCPT PRESS ADJUD ORD/FREE

S67
SNELLEN I.T.,"APARTHEID* CHECKS AND CHANGES." SOUTH/AFR NAT/G PROB/SOLV COLONIAL REGION TASK GP/REL RACE/REL EFFICIENCY PRIVIL ORD/FREE 20. PAGE 146 H2923 DISCRIM NAT/LISM EQUILIB CONTROL

S67
SPINELLI A.,"EUROPEAN UNION IN THE RESISTANCE." NAT/G BAL/PWR DIPLOM CONFER REGION TOTALISM ORD/FREE POLICY. PAGE 147 H2948 NAT/LISM FEDERAL EUR+WWI INT/ORG

S67
SUNG C.H.,"POLITICAL DIAGNOSIS OF KOREAN SOCIETY* A SURVEY OF MILITARY AND CIVILIAN VALUES." KOREA/S ECO/UNDEV NAT/G CIVMIL/REL...QU SAMP GP/COMP. PAGE 151 H3009 ELITES FORCES ATTIT ORD/FREE

S67
TAYLOR P.B. JR.,"PROGRESS IN VENEZUELA." L/A+17C VENEZUELA AGRI INDUS LG/CO NAT/G SML/CO CHOOSE ...POLICY 20. PAGE 153 H3057 ECO/UNDEV ECO/TAC POL/PAR ORD/FREE

S67
VINCENT S.,"SHOULD BIAFRA SURVIVE?" NIGERIA ECO/UNDEV CHIEF FORCES ECO/TAC GP/REL DISCRIM PEACE ORD/FREE SOC/INTEG 20 BIAFRA IBO. PAGE 163 H3256 AFR REV REGION NAT/G

S67
WHITE J.W.,"MASS MOVEMENTS AND DEMOCRACY: SOKAGAKKAI IN JAPANESE POLITICS." NAT/G GP/REL ALL/VALS ORD/FREE WORSHIP 20 CHINJAP. PAGE 167 H3349 SECT PWR ATTIT POL/PAR

S67
WILLIAMS F.R.A.,"FUNDAMENTAL RIGHTS AND THE PROSPECT FOR DEMOCRACY IN NIGERIA." FUT NIGERIA SOCIETY ECO/UNDEV LEGIS ADJUD CHOOSE 20. PAGE 168 H3366
CONSTN LAW ORD/FREE NAT/G

S67
ZARTMAN I.W.," NAT/G POL/PAR VOL/ASSN NAT/LISM ORD/FREE PWR...CONCPT NAT/COMP ORG/CHARTS OAU MAGHREB. PAGE 172 H3451
AFR ISLAM DIPLOM REGION

B68
DE SPINOZA B.,TRACTATUS THEOLOGICO-POLITICUS (TRANS. BY R. WILLIS). UNIV CHIEF DOMIN PWR WORSHIP. PAGE 38 H0771
SECT NAT/G ORD/FREE

B68
PROUDHON J.P.,IDEE GENERALE DE LA REVOLUTION AU XIXE SIECLE (1851). FRANCE UNIV NAT/G CREATE AGREE UTOPIA ORD/FREE...ANARCH 19. PAGE 128 H2563
REV SOCIETY WORKER LABOR

S68
BOSSCHERE G D.E.,"A L'EST DU NOUVEAU." CZECHOSLVK HUNGARY POLAND ROMANIA YUGOSLAVIA AGRI CREATE ECO/TAC COERCE GP/REL ATTIT MARXISM SOCISM 20. PAGE 19 H0382
ORD/FREE COM NAT/G DIPLOM

S68
CHAPMAN A.R.,"THE CIVIL WAR IN NIGERIA." AFR NIGERIA NAT/G PLAN ECO/TAC EDU/PROP COERCE WAR GOV/REL INGP/REL ORD/FREE PWR WEALTH SOC/INTEG 20 BIAFRA. PAGE 29 H0579
REV RACE/REL

S68
DEUTSCHER I.,"GERMANY AND MARXISM." FUT GERMANY/W NAT/G...MARXIST TREND 20. PAGE 40 H0808
SOCISM ORD/FREE POPULISM POL/PAR

S68
HOOK S.,"THE ENLIGHTENMENT AND MARXISM." CULTURE SOCIETY RATIONAL ORD/FREE PLURISM SOCISM...CONCPT HIST/WRIT 18/19 MARX/KARL HEGEL/GWF ENLIGHTNMT. PAGE 73 H1462
IDEA/COMP MARXISM OBJECTIVE

B73
STEPHEN J.F.,LIBERTY, EQUALITY, FRATERNITY. UNIV SOCIETY NAT/G LEGIS DOMIN AGREE PERS/REL ATTIT MORAL...IDEA/COMP 19 MILL/JS. PAGE 149 H2978
ORD/FREE CONCPT COERCE SECT

B76
SMITH A.,THE WEALTH OF NATIONS. UK STRUCT WORKER DIPLOM ECO/TAC OPTIMAL DRIVE PERSON ORD/FREE ...OLD/LIB GEN/LAWS 17/18. PAGE 145 H2905
WEALTH PRODUC INDUS LAISSEZ

C80
ARNOLD M.,"EQUALITY" IN MIXED ESSAYS." MOD/EUR UK ELITES STRATA NAT/G...CONCPT IDEA/COMP NAT/COMP SOC/INTEG 19. PAGE 8 H0167
ORD/FREE UTOPIA SOCIETY STRUCT

N80
MILL J.S.,"AN ESSAY ON GOVERNMENT" (PAMPHLET). ELITES NAT/G CHIEF OWN ORD/FREE PWR WEALTH GEN/LAWS. PAGE 110 H2207
CONSTN POPULISM REPRESENT UTIL

B82
MACDONALD D.,AFRICANA; OR, THE HEART OF HEATHEN AFRICA, VOL. II: MISSION LIFE. SOCIETY STRATA KIN CREATE EDU/PROP ADMIN COERCE LITERACY HEALTH...MYTH WORSHIP 19 LIVNGSTN/D MISSION NEGRO. PAGE 100 H1990
SECT AFR CULTURE ORD/FREE

C82
MILL J.S.,"CIVILIZATION" IN DISSERTATIONS AND DISCUSSIONS." MOD/EUR UK ECO/DEV CONTROL MORAL ORD/FREE PWR...SOC IDEA/COMP 19. PAGE 110 H2208
SOCIETY NAT/G STRUCT CONCPT

B84
ENGELS F.,THE ORIGIN OF THE FAMILY, PRIVATE PROPERTY, AND THE STATE (TRANS. BY E. UNTERMANN). UNIV ELITES SOCIETY CAP/ISM ECO/TAC MARRIAGE ORD/FREE POPULISM...MARXIST SOC ENGELS. PAGE 46 H0926
FAM OWN WEALTH SOCISM

B85
BLISS P.,OF SOVEREIGNTY. NAT/G PROVS GOV/REL PRIVIL ORD/FREE PWR CONSERVE...CONCPT 19. PAGE 18 H0356
CONSTN SOVEREIGN FEDERAL

L86
BURGESS J.W.,"THE RECENT CONSTITUTIONAL CRISIS IN NORWAY" MOD/EUR NORWAY SWEDEN LOC/G NAT/G CHIEF BAL/PWR NAT/LISM ORD/FREE 19. PAGE 24 H0481
CONSTN SOVEREIGN GOV/REL

B90
BURKE E.,REFLECTIONS ON THE REVOLUTION IN FRANCE. FRANCE UK NAT/G DOMIN LEGIT PEACE PWR SOVEREIGN CONSERVE...POLICY GEN/LAWS 18. PAGE 24 H0487
REV ORD/FREE CHIEF TRADIT

B91
BENTHAM J.,A FRAGMENT ON GOVERNMENT (1776). CONSTN MUNIC NAT/G SECT AGREE HAPPINESS UTIL MORAL ORD/FREE...JURID CONCPT. PAGE 15 H0292
SOVEREIGN LAW DOMIN

B91
MILL J.S.,SOCIALISM (1859). MOD/EUR AGRI INDUS NAT/G REV INCOME PRODUC ORD/FREE POPULISM SOCISM ...GOV/COMP METH/COMP 19. PAGE 110 H2209
WEALTH SOCIALIST ECO/TAC OWN

B91
PAINE T.,RIGHTS OF MAN. FRANCE MOD/EUR CONSTN NAT/G CHIEF DOMIN LEGIT SOVEREIGN...MAJORIT IDEA/COMP 18 BURKE/EDM CIVIL/LIB. PAGE 122 H2446
GEN/LAWS ORD/FREE REV AGREE

B94
BENOIST C.,LA POLITIQUE. FRANCE LAW SOCIETY STRUCT POL/PAR PARL/PROC GP/REL ATTIT PWR 19/20. PAGE 14 H0283
NAT/G REPRESENT ORD/FREE

B95
HAMMOND B.E.,THE POLITICAL INSTITUTIONS OF THE ANCIENT GREEKS. GREECE MUNIC PROVS COERCE WAR ORD/FREE ARISTOTLE. PAGE 65 H1307
GOV/COMP NAT/G IDEA/COMP CONCPT

B96
DE VATTEL E.,THE LAW OF NATIONS. AGRI FINAN CHIEF DIPLOM INT/TRADE AGREE OWN ALL/VALS MORAL ORD/FREE SOVEREIGN...GEN/LAWS 18 NATURL/LAW WOLFF/C. PAGE 39 H0774
LAW CONCPT NAT/G INT/LAW

B96
ESMEIN A.,ELEMENTS DE DROIT CONSTITUTIONNEL. FRANCE UK CHIEF EX/STRUC LEGIS ADJUD CT/SYS PARL/PROC REV GOV/REL ORD/FREE...JURID METH/COMP 18/19. PAGE 47 H0940
LAW CONSTN NAT/G CONCPT

B98
FORTES M.,AFRICAN POLITICAL SYSTEMS. ECO/UNDEV KIN LOC/G NEIGH POL/PAR SECT LEAD GP/REL ORD/FREE...SOC 20 NEGRO. PAGE 52 H1039
AFR CULTURE STRUCT

B99
LECKY W.E.H.,DEMOCRACY AND LIBERTY (2 VOLS.). LAW CONSTN STRATA POL/PAR SECT WORKER DIPLOM ADJUD REPRESENT NAT/LISM CONSERVE. PAGE 93 H1851
LEGIS NAT/G POPULISM ORD/FREE

ORDER....SEE ORD/FREE

ORDONNEAU P. H2425

OREGON....OREGON

ORFIELD L.B. H2426

ORG/CHARTS....ORGANIZATIONAL CHARTS, BLUEPRINTS

ORGANIZATION FOR AFRICAN UNITY....SEE OAU

ORGANIZATION FOR ECONOMIC COOPERATION AND DEVELOPMENT.... SEE OECD

ORGANIZATION FOR EUROPEAN ECONOMIC COOPERATION....SEE OEEC

ORGANIZATION FOR LATIN AMERICAN SOLIDARITY....SEE OLAS

ORGANIZATION OF AFRICAN STATES.... SEE AFR/STATES

ORGANIZATION OF AMERICAN STATES....SEE OAS

ORGANIZATION, INTERNATIONAL....SEE INT/ORG

ORGANIZATION, LABOR....SEE LABOR

ORGANIZATION, POLITICAL....SEE POL/PAR

ORGANIZATION, PROFESSIONAL....SEE PROF/ORG

ORGANIZATION, VOLUNTARY....SEE VOL/ASSN

ORGANIZATIONAL BEHAVIOR, NONEXECUTIVE....SEE ADMIN

ORGANIZATIONAL CHARTS....SEE ORG/CHARTS

ORGANSKI A.F.K. H2428

ORNES G.E. H2429

ORTEGA Y GASSET J. H2430

ORTHO/GK....GREEK ORTHODOX CHURCH

ORTHO/RUSS....RUSSIAN ORTHODOX CATHOLIC

B37
BERDYAEV N.,THE ORIGIN OF RUSSIAN COMMUNISM. MOD/EUR RUSSIA USSR INTELL SECT REV...ANARCH HUM 19/20 ORTHO/RUSS COM/PARTY CHRISTIAN. PAGE 15 H0294
MARXISM NAT/LISM CULTURE ATTIT

B53
CURTISS J.S.,THE RUSSIAN CHURCH AND THE SOVIET STATE 1917-1950. COM USSR CONTROL LEAD REV MARXISM ...POLICY BIBLIOG 20 CHURCH/STA ORTHO/RUSS. PAGE 36 H0728
GP/REL NAT/G SECT PWR

ORTHODOX EASTERN CHURCH....SEE ORTHO/GK

ORTON W.A. H2431

ORWELL/G....GEORGE ORWELL

OSHOGBO....OSHOGBO, WEST AFRICA

B65
KUPER H.,URBANIZATION AND MIGRATION IN WEST AFRICA. UPPER/VOLT CULTURE ECO/UNDEV WORKER REGION GOV/REL ...LING ANTHOL SOC/INTEG 20 AFRICA/W OSHOGBO MOSSI MIGRATION. PAGE 89 H1781 — AFR HABITAT MUNIC GEOG

OSSIPOV G. H1564

OSTRY S. H3409

OTERO L.M. H2432

OTTENBERG P. H2433

OTTENBERG S. H2433

OTTOMAN....OTTOMAN EMPIRE

L56
EISENTADT S.N.,"POLITICAL STRUGGLE IN BUREAUCRATIC SOCIETIES" ASIA CULTURE ADJUD SANCTION PWR BUREAUCRCY OTTOMAN BYZANTINE. PAGE 45 H0901 — ADMIN CHIEF CONTROL ROUTINE

B58
SHAW S.J.,THE FINANCIAL AND ADMINISTRATIVE ORGANIZATION AND DEVELOPMENT OF OTTOMAN EGYPT 1517-1798. UAR LOC/G FORCES BUDGET INT/TRADE TAX EATING INCOME WEALTH...CHARTS BIBLIOG 16/18 OTTOMAN NAPOLEON/B. PAGE 143 H2853 — FINAN ADMIN GOV/REL CULTURE

B63
NALBANDIAN L.,THE ARMENIAN REVOLUTIONARY MOVEMENT. MOD/EUR RUSSIA...IDEA/COMP NAT/COMP BIBLIOG 19 ARMENIA OTTOMAN. PAGE 115 H2306 — NAT/LISM REV POL/PAR ORD/FREE

B66
ZEINE Z.N.,THE EMERGENCE OF ARAB NATIONALISM (REV. ED.). TURKEY UK NAT/G SECT TEC/DEV LEAD REV WAR AGE/Y ROLE ORD/FREE...TRADIT CHARTS BIBLIOG 20 ARABS OTTOMAN. PAGE 173 H3453 — ISLAM NAT/LISM DIPLOM

OUTER SPACE....SEE SPACE

OUTER/MONG....OUTER MONGOLIA

OVERSEAS DEVELOPMENT INSTITUTE....SEE OVRSEA/DEV

OVERSEAS DEVELOPMENT INSTIT H2434

OVERSTREET G.D. H2435

OVIMBUNDU....OVIMBUNDU PEOPLES OF ANGOLA

B62
EDWARDS A.C.,THE OVIMBUNDU UNDER TWO SOVEREIGNTIES. CULTURE STRUCT FAM MARRIAGE HABITAT...SOC 19/20 OVIMBUNDU. PAGE 45 H0891 — KIN NEIGH SOCIETY CONTROL

OVRSEA/DEV....OVERSEAS DEVELOPMENT INSTITUTE

OWEN G. H2436

OWEN/RBT....ROBERT OWEN

OWI....OFFICE OF WAR INFORMATION

OWN....OWNERSHIP, OWNER

B03
GRIFFIN A.P.C.,SELECT LIST OF REFERENCES ON GOVERNMENT OWNERSHIP OF RAILROADS (PAMPHLET). MOD/EUR NAT/G ADMIN...MGT GOV/COMP 19/20. PAGE 61 H1217 — BIBLIOG/A SOCISM OWN DIST/IND

B08
LLOYD H.D.,THE SWISS DEMOCRACY. SWITZERLND INDUS NAT/G WORKER CHOOSE OWN ORD/FREE SOCISM...PLURIST 19/20 MONOPOLY. PAGE 97 H1944 — NAT/COMP GOV/COMP REPRESENT POPULISM

B09
JUSTINIAN,THE DIGEST (DIGESTA CORPUS JURIS CIVILIS) (2 VOLS.) (TRANS. BY C. H. MONRO). ROMAN/EMP LAW FAM LOC/G LEGIS EDU/PROP CONTROL MARRIAGE OWN ROLE CIVIL/LAW. PAGE 82 H1645 — JURID CT/SYS NAT/G STRATA

B11
HUXLEY T.H.,METHOD AND RESULTS: ESSAYS. EDU/PROP REPRESENT OWN PERSON PWR WEALTH...PSY IDEA/COMP GEN/LAWS. PAGE 76 H1514 — ORD/FREE NAT/G POPULISM PLURIST

B13
KROPOTKIN P.,THE CONQUEST OF BREAD. SOCIETY STRATA AGRI INDUS WORKER REV HAPPINESS INCOME PRODUC HEALTH MORAL ORD/FREE. PAGE 89 H1775 — ANARCH SOCIALIST OWN AGREE

B14
OPPENHEIMER F.,THE STATE. FUT SOCIETY STRATA STRUCT WORKER CAP/ISM WAR GP/REL SOCISM...SOC NAT/COMP SOC/INTEG. PAGE 121 H2424 — ELITES OWN DOMIN NAT/G

B17
DE VICTORIA F.,DE INDIS ET DE JURE BELLI (1557) IN F. DE VICTORIA, DE INDIS ET DE JURE BELLI REFLECTIONES. UNIV NAT/G SECT CHIEF PARTIC COERCE PEACE MORAL...POLICY 16 INDIAN/AM CHRISTIAN CONSCN/OBJ. PAGE 39 H0775 — WAR INT/LAW OWN

N19
MAO TSE-TUNG,ON SOME IMPORTANT PROBLEMS OF THE PARTY'S PRESENT POLICY. CHINA/COM CONSTN ELITES INTELL AGRI DOMIN EDU/PROP REV REPRESENT GP/REL OWN PEACE ORD/FREE 20 COM/PARTY. PAGE 102 H2044 — POLICY NAT/G CHIEF LEGIT

B20
MALTHUS T.R.,PRINCIPLES OF POLITICAL ECONOMY. UK AGRI INDUS MARKET NAT/G DIPLOM PRICE CONTROL BAL/PAY COST OWN PWR LAISSEZ 18/19. PAGE 102 H2034 — GEN/LAWS DEMAND WEALTH

S21
MALINOWSKI B.,"THE PRIMITIVE ECONOMICS OF THE TROBRIAND ISLANDERS" (BMR)" CULTURE SOCIETY NAT/G CHIEF LEAD OWN...SOC MYTH WORSHIP 20 NEW/GUINEA TROBRIAND RESOURCE/N. PAGE 101 H2029 — ECO/UNDEV AGRI PRODUC STRUCT

B26
TAWNEY R.H.,RELIGION AND THE RISE OF CAPITALISM. UK CULTURE NAT/G TEC/DEV OWN LAISSEZ...POLICY SOC TIME/SEQ 16/19. PAGE 153 H3050 — SECT WEALTH INDUS CAP/ISM

B32
LUNT D.C.,THE ROAD TO THE LAW. UK USA-45 LEGIS EDU/PROP OWN ORD/FREE...DECISION TIME/SEQ NAT/COMP 16/20 AUSTRAL ENGLSH/LAW COMMON/LAW. PAGE 99 H1980 — ADJUD LAW JURID CT/SYS

B33
TANNENBAUM F.,PEACE BY REVOLUTION. ECO/UNDEV AGRI SECT WORKER DIPLOM EDU/PROP DISCRIM OWN WEALTH POPULISM 17/20 MEXIC/AMER INDIAN/AM. PAGE 152 H3043 — CULTURE COLONIAL RACE/REL REV

B35
MORE T.,UTOPIA (1516) (TRANS. BY R. ROBYNSON). LAW CULTURE SOCIETY STRUCT FAM SECT EDU/PROP WAR OWN UTIL KNOWL WEALTH 16. PAGE 113 H2253 — UTOPIA NAT/G ECO/TAC GEN/LAWS

B36
BELLOC H.,THE RESTORATION OF PROPERTY. UK STRATA NAT/G PROF/ORG DELIB/GP WORKER CREATE PROB/SOLV ECO/TAC PARTIC UTOPIA ORD/FREE SOCISM 20. PAGE 13 H0270 — CONTROL MAJORIT CAP/ISM OWN

B36
VICO G.B.,DIRITTO UNIVERSALE (1722) (VOL. 2, PARTS 1,2, AND 3, OF G.B. VICO, OPERE). UNIV DIPLOM AGREE WAR OWN KNOWL ORD/FREE SOVEREIGN DEITY. PAGE 162 H3249 — JURID SECT CONCPT NAT/G

B38
LAWLEY F.E.,THE GROWTH OF COLLECTIVE ECONOMY VOL. 1: NATIONAL. EUR+WWI AGRI INDUS NAT/G BARGAIN CAP/ISM ECO/TAC WAR OPTIMAL WEALTH...GOV/COMP METH/COMP 19/20 MONOPOLY. PAGE 92 H1844 — SOCISM PRICE CONTROL OWN

B38
LAWLEY F.E.,THE GROWTH OF COLLECTIVE ECONOMY VOL. 2: INTERNATIONAL. WOR-45 AGRI INDUS EQUILIB OPTIMAL OWN WEALTH...NAT/COMP 19/20 NAZI NEW/DEAL MONOPOLY. PAGE 92 H1845 — ECO/TAC SOCISM NAT/LISM CONTROL

B38
MARX K.,THE GERMAN IDEOLOGY, PARTS 1 AND 3 (1846). MOD/EUR LAW STRATA WORKER DOMIN REV UTOPIA SOCISM 19 MARX/KARL. PAGE 104 H2079 — MARXIST OWN PRODUC ECO/TAC

C41
WASSERMAN L.,"HANDBOOK OF POLITICAL "ISMS" CAP/ISM REPRESENT TOTALISM MARXISM NEW/LIB SOCISM...MAJORIT BIBLIOG 20. PAGE 166 H3313 — IDEA/COMP PHIL/SCI OWN NAT/G

B42
HEGEL G.W.F.,PHILOSOPHY OF RIGHT. UNIV FAM SECT CHIEF AGREE WAR MARRIAGE OWN ORD/FREE...POLICY CONCPT. PAGE 69 H1383 — NAT/G LAW RATIONAL

B44
BERDYAEV N.,SLAVERY AND FREEDOM. NAT/G REV WAR NAT/LISM OWN AUTHORIT SEX CONSERVE SOCISM...TRADIT PHIL/SCI CIVIL/LIB. PAGE 15 H0295 — ORD/FREE PERSON ELITES SOCIETY

B47
LOCKE J.,TWO TREATISES OF GOVERNMENT (1690). UK LAW SOCIETY LEGIS LEGIT AGREE REV OWN HEREDITY MORAL CONSERVE...POLICY MAJORIT 17 WILLIAM/3 NATURL/LAW. PAGE 97 H1946 — CONCPT ORD/FREE NAT/G CONSEN

B47
NIEBUHR R.,THE CHILDREN OF LIGHT AND THE CHILDREN OF DARKNESS: A VINDICATION OF DEMOCRACY AND CRITIQUE OF TRADITIONAL DEFENSE. UNIV STRUCT NAT/G — POPULISM DIPLOM NEIGH

SECT INGP/REL OWN PEACE ORD/FREE MARXISM GP/REL
...IDEA/COMP GEN/LAWS 20 CHRISTIAN. PAGE 118 H2358

B52
ROBBINS L.,THE THEORY OF ECONOMIC POLICY IN ENGLISH ECO/TAC
CLASSICAL POLITICAL ECONOMY. UK ECO/DEV WORKER PLAN ORD/FREE
CAP/ISM EDU/PROP CONTROL INCOME OWN HEALTH SOCISM IDEA/COMP
...POLICY 17/19. PAGE 132 H2639 NAT/G

B54
FRIEDMAN W.,THE PUBLIC CORPORATION: A COMPARATIVE LAW
SYMPOSIUM (UNIVERSITY OF TORONTO SCHOOL OF LAW SOCISM
COMPARATIVE LAW SERIES, VOL. I). SWEDEN USA+45 LG/CO
INDUS INT/ORG NAT/G REGION CENTRAL FEDERAL...POLICY OWN
JURID IDEA/COMP NAT/COMP ANTHOL 20 COMMONWLTH
MONOPOLY EUROPE. PAGE 53 H1065

B55
CHARMATZ J.P.,COMPARATIVE STUDIES IN COMMUNITY MARRIAGE
PROPERTY LAW. FRANCE USA+45...JURID GOV/COMP ANTHOL LAW
20. PAGE 29 H0583 OWN
MUNIC

B55
SMITH G.,A CONSTITUTIONAL AND LEGAL HISTORY OF CONSTN
ENGLAND. UK ELITES NAT/G LEGIS ADJUD OWN HABITAT PARTIC
POPULISM...JURID 20 ENGLSH/LAW. PAGE 145 H2909 LAW
CT/SYS

S55
GOODENOUGH W.H.,"A PROBLEM IN MALAYO-POLYNESIAN KIN
SOCIAL ORGANIZATION" (BMR)" MALAYSIA S/ASIA CULTURE STRUCT
AGRI PROB/SOLV OWN HABITAT...SOC 20 20 POLYNESIA. FAM
PAGE 58 H1170 ECO/UNDEV

C57
WITTFOGEL K.A.,"ORIENTAL DESPOTISM: A COMPARATIVE TOTALISM
STUDY OF TOTAL POWER." ASIA CULTURE STRATA NAT/G HABITAT
LEAD OWN ORD/FREE PWR...CONCPT TREND BIBLIOG 20. DOMIN
PAGE 170 H3393 ELITES

B58
PAYNO M.,LA REFORMA SOCIAL EN ESPANA Y MEXICO. SECT
SPAIN ECO/TAC TAX LOBBY COERCE REV OWN CATHISM NAT/G
19/20 MEXIC/AMER. PAGE 124 H2479 LAW
ELITES

B58
STUBEL H.,THE MEWU FANTZU. CHINA/COM INDIA EDU/PROP CULTURE
ADJUD CRIME GP/REL OWN...OBS 20 TIBET. PAGE 150 STRUCT
H3001 SECT
FAM

B59
GINSBURG M.,LAW AND OPINION IN ENGLAND. UK CULTURE JURID
KIN LABOR LEGIS EDU/PROP ADMIN CT/SYS CRIME OWN POLICY
HEALTH...ANTHOL 20 ENGLSH/LAW. PAGE 56 H1132 ECO/TAC

B59
HANSON A.H.,THE STRUCTURE AND CONTROL OF STATE NAT/G
ENTERPRISES IN TURKEY. TURKEY LAW ADMIN GOV/REL LG/CO
EFFICIENCY...CHARTS 20. PAGE 66 H1319 OWN
CONTROL

B59
JENKINS C.,POWER AT THE TOP: A CRITICAL SURVEY OF NAT/G
THE NATIONALIZED INDUSTRIES. UK POL/PAR CONTROL OWN
...WELF/ST CHARTS 20 LABOR/PAR. PAGE 80 H1601 INDUS
NEW/LIB

B59
KELF-COHEN R.,NATIONALISATION IN BRITAIN: THE END NEW/LIB
OF DOGMA. EUR+WWI UK NAT/G POL/PAR WORKER ECO/TAC ECO/DEV
PARL/PROC WEALTH SOCISM...GOV/COMP 20. PAGE 84 INDUS
H1683 OWN

B59
SENGHOR L.S.,RAPPORT SUR LA DOCTRINE ET LA ATTIT
PROGRAMME DU PART I. FRANCE MALI CONSTN POL/PAR NAT/G
PLAN CHOOSE OWN ORD/FREE MARXISM...SOCIALIST 20 AFR
NEGRO. PAGE 141 H2828 SOCISM

B60
BANERJEE D.N.,OUR FUNDAMENTAL RIGHTS: THEIR NATURE CONSTN
AND EXTENT (AS JUDICIALLY DETERMINED). INDIA UK ORD/FREE
CULTURE STRATA NAT/G WORKER EDU/PROP CONTROL LEGIS
DISCRIM OWN...IDEA/COMP WORSHIP 20 REFORMERS POLICY
COMMONWLTH. PAGE 10 H0207

B60
BHAMBHRI C.P.,PARLIAMENTARY CONTROL OVER STATE NAT/G
ENTERPRISE IN INDIA. INDIA DELIB/GP ADMIN CONTROL OWN
INGP/REL EFFICIENCY 20 PARLIAMENT. PAGE 16 H0327 INDUS
PARL/PROC

B60
WEINER H.E.,BRITISH LABOR AND PUBLIC OWNERSHIP. UK LABOR
SERV/IND LG/CO WORKER CONTROL OWN 20. PAGE 166 NAT/G
H3327 INDUS
ATTIT

B61
ERASMUS C.J.,MAN TAKES CONTROL: CULTURAL ORD/FREE
DEVELOPMENT AND AMERICAN AID. STRUCT OWN DRIVE CULTURE
PERCEPT...SOC 20 MEXIC/AMER. PAGE 47 H0937 ECO/UNDEV
TEC/DEV

B61
LAHAYE R.,LES ENTREPRISES PUBLIQUES AU MAROC. NAT/G
FRANCE MOROCCO LAW DIST/IND EXTR/IND FINAN CONSULT INDUS
PLAN TEC/DEV ADMIN AGREE CONTROL OWN...POLICY 20. ECO/UNDEV
PAGE 90 H1796 ECO/TAC

B61
SHARMA T.R.,THE WORKING OF STATE ENTERPRISES IN NAT/G
INDIA. INDIA DELIB/GP LEGIS WORKER BUDGET PRICE INDUS
CONTROL GP/REL OWN ATTIT...MGT CHARTS 20. PAGE 142 ADMIN
H2851 SOCISM

B62
GRZYBOWSKI K.,SOVIET LEGAL INSTITUTIONS. USA+45 ADJUD
USSR ECO/DEV NAT/G EDU/PROP CONTROL CT/SYS CRIME LAW
OWN ATTIT PWR SOCISM...NAT/COMP 20. PAGE 62 H1242 JURID

B62
MACPHERSON C.B.,THE POLITICAL THEORY OF POSSESSIVE PHIL/SCI
INDIVIDUALISM. UK MARKET NAT/G PERS/REL RATIONAL OWN
...IDEA/COMP 17/19 LOCKE/JOHN. PAGE 100 H2006

B62
SMITH M.G.,KINSHIP AND COMMUNITY IN CARRIACOU. CULTURE
WEST/IND STRATA AGRI FAM SECT WORKER MARRIAGE OWN HABITAT
HEREDITY WEALTH...SOC 18/20. PAGE 146 H2915 KIN
STRUCT

B63
ELWIN V.,A NEW DEAL FOR TRIBAL INDIA. INDIA AGRI ECO/UNDEV
COM/IND INDUS KIN TEC/DEV TAX EDU/PROP OWN HEALTH CULTURE
20. PAGE 46 H0912 CONSTN
SOC/WK

B63
FURTADO C.,THE ECONOMIC GROWTH OF BRAZIL: A SURVEY ECO/UNDEV
FROM COLONIAL TO MODERN TIMES. L/A+17C AGRI TEC/DEV
DIST/IND EXTR/IND INDUS WORKER COLONIAL RACE/REL LABOR
OWN GOV/COMP. PAGE 54 H1082 DOMIN

B63
MARX K.,THE POVERTY OF PHILOSOPHY (1847). SOCIETY MARXIST
STRATA INDUS WORKER OWN UTOPIA SOCISM...GEN/LAWS PRODUC
MARX/KARL. PAGE 104 H2082

B63
SHANKS M.,THE LESSONS OF PUBLIC ENTERPRISE. UK SOCISM
LEGIS WORKER ECO/TAC ADMIN PARL/PROC GOV/REL ATTIT OWN
...POLICY MGT METH/COMP NAT/COMP ANTHOL 20 NAT/G
PARLIAMENT. PAGE 142 H2840 INDUS

B63
SPRING D.,THE ENGLISH LANDED ESTATE IN THE STRATA
NINETEENTH CENTURY: ITS ADMINISTRATION. UK ELITES PERS/REL
STRUCT AGRI NAT/G GP/REL OWN PWR WEALTH...BIBLIOG MGT
19 HOUSE/LORD. PAGE 148 H2954

B63
THOMPSON F.M.L.,ENGLISH LANDED SOCIETY IN THE STRATA
NINETEENTH CENTURY. UK STRUCT MUNIC NAT/G CONTROL PWR
WAR GP/REL OWN WEALTH...BIBLIOG 18/20. PAGE 154 ELITES
H3081 GOV/REL

B64
BEATTIE J.,OTHER CULTURES. UNIV LAW FAM POL/PAR METH/CNCPT
SECT ADJUD OWN ALL/VALS WEALTH...SOC NAT/COMP CULTURE
SOC/INTEG 20. PAGE 13 H0251 STRUCT

B64
FROMM E.,MARX'S CONCEPT OF MAN. LABOR OWN PERSON INGP/REL
...HUM IDEA/COMP GEN/LAWS 17 MARX/KARL EUROPE CONCPT
SPINOZA/B GOETHE/J HEGEL/GWF. PAGE 54 H1072 MARXISM
SOCISM

B64
HAAR C.M.,LAW AND LAND: ANGLO-AMERICAN PLANNING LAW
PRACTICE. UK USA+45 NAT/G TEC/DEV BUDGET CT/SYS PLAN
INGP/REL EFFICIENCY OWN...JURID 20. PAGE 63 H1263 MUNIC
NAT/COMP

B64
HALE O.J.,THE CAPTIVE PRESS IN THE THIRD REICH. COM/IND
GERMANY CULTURE LG/CO NAT/G POL/PAR PLAN DOMIN TASK PRESS
CENTRAL OWN TOTALISM PWR...BIBLIOG 20 HITLER/A NAZI CONTROL
AMMAN/MAX. PAGE 64 H1283 FASCISM

B64
MORGAN L.H.,ANCIENT SOCIETY (1877). SOCIETY FAM OWN KIN
...INT QU GEN/LAWS SOC/INTEG. PAGE 113 H2255 MARRIAGE
CULTURE

B64
SZLADITS C.,BIBLIOGRAPHY ON FOREIGN AND COMPARATIVE BIBLIOG/A
LAW: BOOKS AND ARTICLES IN ENGLISH (SUPPLEMENT JURID
1962). FINAN INDUS JUDGE LICENSE ADMIN CT/SYS ADJUD
PARL/PROC OWN...INT/LAW CLASSIF METH/COMP NAT/COMP LAW
20. PAGE 151 H3027

B64
TAWNEY R.H.,EQUALITY. UK CULTURE STRATA ECO/TAC WEALTH
EDU/PROP REPRESENT OWN NEW/LIB...MAJORIT WELF/ST STRUCT
SOC 20. PAGE 153 H3051 ELITES
POPULISM

B65
BARRY E.E.,NATIONALISATION IN BRITISH POLITICS: THE NAT/G
HISTORICAL BACKGROUND. UK AGRI DIST/IND EXTR/IND OWN
LABOR LG/CO ATTIT CONSERVE SOCISM 19/20 LABOR/PAR. INDUS
PAGE 12 H0231 POL/PAR

B65
ONUOHA B.,THE ELEMENTS OF AFRICAN SOCIALISM. AFR SOCISM
FINAN SECT TEC/DEV FOR/AID GP/REL OWN LAISSEZ ECO/UNDEV
MARXISM...CONCPT BIBLIOG 20. PAGE 121 H2419 NAT/G
EX/STRUC

B65
SHEPHERD W.G.,ECONOMIC PERFORMANCE UNDER PUBLIC PROC/MFG
OWNERSHIP: BRITISH FUEL AND POWER. UK BUDGET GP/REL NAT/G
...METH/CNCPT CHARTS BIBLIOG 20. PAGE 143 H2858 OWN
FINAN

B65
SWIFT M.G.,MALAY PEASANT SOCIETY IN JELEBU. STRUCT

MALAYSIA FAM INT/TRADE ADJUD OWN WEALTH...SOC WORSHIP 20. PAGE 151 H3020 — ECO/UNDEV CULTURE SOCIETY

B66
HINTON W.,FANSHEN: A DOCUMENTARY OF REVOLUTION IN A CHINESE VILLAGE. ASIA ELITES MUNIC NAT/G POL/PAR SECT WORKER LEAD WAR PRIVIL PWR 20 MAO. PAGE 71 H1422 — MARXISM REV NEIGH OWN

B66
LOCKE J.,THE SECOND TREATISE OF GOVERNMENT: AN ESSAY CONCERNING THE TRUE ORIGINAL EXTENT AND END OF CIVIL GOVERNMENT (3RD ED.). CONSTN SOCIETY CONTROL OWN...PHIL/SCI 17 NATURL/LAW. PAGE 97 H1947 — NAT/G PWR GEN/LAWS ORD/FREE

B66
TIVEY L.J.,NATIONALISATION IN BRITISH INDUSTRY. UK LEGIS PARL/PROC GP/REL OWN ATTIT SOCISM 20. PAGE 156 H3109 — NAT/G INDUS CONTROL LG/CO

B67
JAIN R.K.,MANAGEMENT OF STATE ENTERPRISES. INDIA SOCIETY FINAN WORKER BUDGET ADMIN CONTROL OWN 20. PAGE 79 H1584 — NAT/G SOCISM INDUS MGT

L67
LARKIN E.,"ECONOMIC GROWTH, CAPITAL INVESTMENT, AND THE ROMAN CATHOLIC CHURCH IN NINETEENTH-CENTURY IRELAND." IRELAND AGRI DIST/IND NAT/G GIVE OWN CATHISM...CHARTS 19. PAGE 91 H1823 — FINAN SECT WEALTH ECO/UNDEV

S67
BRANCO R.,"LAND REFORM* THE ANSWER TO LATIN AMERICA'S AGRICULTURAL DEVELOPMENT?" L/A+17C NAT/G PLAN TEC/DEV BUDGET RENT EFFICIENCY 20. PAGE 20 H0404 — ECO/UNDEV AGRI TAX OWN

S67
BURGHART A.,"CATHOLIC SOCIAL THOUGHT IN AUSTRIA." AUSTRIA EUR+WWI NAT/G PAY PERS/REL OWN MARXISM SOCISM...SOC 20. PAGE 24 H0482 — CATHISM ATTIT TREND SOCIETY

S67
CARIAS B.,"EL CONTROL DE LAS EMPRESAS PUBLICAS POR GRUPOS DE INTERESES DE LA COMUNIDAD." FRANCE UK VENEZUELA INDUS NAT/G CONTROL OWN PWR...DECISION NAT/COMP 20. PAGE 26 H0529 — WORKER REPRESENT MGT SOCISM

S67
CARR E.H.,"REVOLUTION FROM ABOVE." USSR STRATA FINAN INDUS NAT/G DOMIN LEAD GP/REL INGP/REL OWN PRODUC PWR 20 STALIN/J. PAGE 27 H0538 — AGRI POLICY COM EFFICIENCY

S67
CATTELL D.T.,"A NEO-MARXIST THEORY OF COMPARATIVE ANALYSIS." USSR STRATA INSPECT DOMIN CONTROL COERCE OWN TOTALISM PWR...FASCIST HYPO/EXP METH 20. PAGE 28 H0561 — GOV/COMP MARXISM SIMUL CLASSIF

S67
JENCKS C.E.,"SOCIAL STATUS OF COAL MINERS IN BRITAIN SINCE NATIONALIZATION." UK STRATA STRUCT LABOR RECEIVE GP/REL INCOME OWN ATTIT HABITAT...MGT T 20. PAGE 80 H1600 — EXTR/IND WORKER CONTROL NAT/G

S67
NATSAGDORJ A.S.,"THE ECONOMIC BASIS OF FEUDALISM IN MONGOLIA." ASIA COM USSR OWN WEALTH CONSERVE...SOC 20 MONGOLIA. PAGE 116 H2324 — ECO/TAC AGRI NAT/COMP MARXISM

B75
MAINE H.S.,LECTURES ON THE EARLY HISTORY OF INSTITUTIONS. IRELAND UK CONSTN ELITES STRUCT FAM KIN CHIEF LEGIS CT/SYS OWN SOVEREIGN...CONCPT 16 BENTHAM/J BREHON ROMAN/LAW. PAGE 101 H2021 — CULTURE LAW INGP/REL

N80
MILL J.S.,"AN ESSAY ON GOVERNMENT" (PAMPHLET). ELITES NAT/G CHIEF OWN ORD/FREE PWR WEALTH GEN/LAWS. PAGE 110 H2207 — CONSTN POPULISM REPRESENT UTIL

B84
ENGELS F.,THE ORIGIN OF THE FAMILY, PRIVATE PROPERTY, AND THE STATE (TRANS. BY E. UNTERMANN). UNIV ELITES SOCIETY CAP/ISM ECO/TAC MARRIAGE ORD/FREE POPULISM...MARXIST SOC ENGELS. PAGE 46 H0926 — FAM OWN WEALTH SOCISM

B91
MILL J.S.,SOCIALISM (1859). MOD/EUR AGRI INDUS NAT/G REV INCOME PRODUC ORD/FREE POPULISM SOCISM ...GOV/COMP METH/COMP 19. PAGE 110 H2209 — WEALTH SOCIALIST ECO/TAC OWN

B95
SELIGMAN E.R.A.,ESSAYS IN TAXATION. NEW/ZEALND PRUSSIA UK USA-45 MARKET LOC/G CREATE PRICE CONTROL INCOME OWN WEALTH...GOV/COMP METH/COMP 19. PAGE 141 H2824 — TAX TARIFFS INDUS NAT/G

B96
DE VATTEL E.,THE LAW OF NATIONS. AGRI FINAN CHIEF DIPLOM INT/TRADE AGREE OWN ALL/VALS MORAL ORD/FREE SOVEREIGN...GEN/LAWS 18 NATURL/LAW WOLFF/C. PAGE 39 H0774 — LAW CONCPT NAT/G INT/LAW

B99
KINGSLEY M.H.,WEST AFRICAN STUDIES. GHANA NIGERIA SIER/LEONE LAW EXTR/IND SECT DIPLOM INT/TRADE DOMIN RACE/REL OWN HEALTH...SOC 19. PAGE 86 H1717 — AFR HEREDITY COLONIAL CULTURE

OXFORD/GRP....OXFORD GROUP

P

PACIFIC/IS....PACIFIC ISLANDS: US TRUST TERRITORY OF THE PACIFIC ISLANDS - CAROLINE ISLANDS, MARSHALL ISLANDS, AND MARIANA ISLANDS

PACIFISM....SEE ALSO ARMS/CONT, PEACE

N19
FREEMAN H.A.,COERCION OF STATES IN FEDERAL UNIONS (PAMPHLET). WOR-45 DIPLOM CONTROL COERCE PEACE ORD/FREE...GOV/COMP METH/COMP NAT/COMP PACIFIST 20. PAGE 53 H1055 — FEDERAL WAR INT/ORG PACIFISM

B55
VIGON J.,TEORIA DEL MILITARISMO. NAT/G DIPLOM COLONIAL COERCE GUERRILLA CIVMIL/REL NAT/LISM MORAL ALL/IDEOS PACIFISM 18/20. PAGE 163 H3253 — FORCES PHIL/SCI WAR POLICY

B67
AMERICAN FRIENDS SERVICE COMM,IN PLACE OF WAR. NAT/G ACT/RES DIPLOM ADMIN NUC/PWR EFFICIENCY ...POLICY 20. PAGE 6 H0122 — PEACE PACIFISM WAR DETER

B67
ZINN H.,VIETNAM THE LOGIC OF WITHDRAWAL. VIETNAM/S NAT/G DIPLOM DEATH MORAL 20. PAGE 173 H3459 — WAR COST PACIFISM ATTIT

PACIFIST....PACIFIST; SEE ALSO PEACE

B17
VEBLEN T.B.,AN INQUIRY INTO THE NATURE OF PEACE AND THE TERMS OF ITS PERPETUATION. UNIV STRATA FINAN EDU/PROP PRICE COST DISCRIM NAT/LISM MORAL ORD/FREE PACIFIST 20 WORLDUNITY. PAGE 162 H3237 — PEACE DIPLOM WAR NAT/G

N19
FREEMAN H.A.,COERCION OF STATES IN FEDERAL UNIONS (PAMPHLET). WOR-45 DIPLOM CONTROL COERCE PEACE ORD/FREE...GOV/COMP METH/COMP NAT/COMP PACIFIST 20. PAGE 53 H1055 — FEDERAL WAR INT/ORG PACIFISM

B29
STURZO L.,THE INTERNATIONAL COMMUNITY AND THE RIGHT OF WAR (TRANS. BY BARBARA BARCLAY CARTER). CULTURE CREATE PROB/SOLV DIPLOM ADJUD CONTROL PEACE PERSON ORD/FREE...INT/LAW IDEA/COMP PACIFIST 20 LEAGUE/NAT. PAGE 150 H3003 — INT/ORG PLAN WAR CONCPT

B65
NORDEN A.,WAR AND NAZI CRIMINALS IN WEST GERMANY: STATE, ECONOMY, ADMINISTRATION, ARMY, JUSTICE, SCIENCE. GERMANY GERMANY/W MOD/EUR ECO/DEV ACADEM EX/STRUC FORCES DOMIN ADMIN CT/SYS...POLICY MAJORIT PACIFIST 20. PAGE 119 H2370 — FASCIST WAR NAT/G TOP/EX

B67
ROSENBLUTH G.,THE CANADIAN ECONOMY AND DISARMAMENT. CANADA FUT ECO/DEV INDUS R+D DELIB/GP DIPLOM ECO/TAC CIVMIL/REL PEACE...POLICY BIBLIOG PACIFIST 20. PAGE 134 H2679 — ARMS/CONT STAT PLAN NAT/G

PADELFORD N.J. H2437,H2438,H2439

PADMORE G. H2440

PADOVER S.K. H3084

PAGE C.H. H0300

PAGE S.W. H2441

PAGINSKY P. H2442

PAI G.A. H2443

PAIKERT G.C. H2444

PAIN....SEE HEALTH

PAINE T. H2445,H2446

PAK H. H2447

PAKISTAN....SEE ALSO S/ASIA

N
US LIBRARY OF CONGRESS,SOUTHERN ASIA ACCESSIONS LIST. BURMA CEYLON INDIA NEPAL PAKISTAN S/ASIA THAILAND AGRI INDUS SCHOOL WORKER...ART/METH GEOG HEAL PHIL/SCI LING 20. PAGE 160 H3201 — BIBLIOG/A SOCIETY CULTURE ECO/UNDEV

B51
GHANI A.R.,PAKISTAN: A SELECT BIBLIOGRAPHY. — BIBLIOG

PAKISTAN S/ASIA CULTURE...GEOG 20. PAGE 56 H1120
AGRI INDUS

B51
JENNINGS I.,THE COMMONWEALTH IN ASIA. CEYLON INDIA PAKISTAN CULTURE STRATA NAT/G LEGIS DIPLOM COLONIAL ATTIT...DECISION 20 CMN/WLTH. PAGE 80 H1604
CONSTN INT/ORG POLICY PLAN

B51
JENNINGS S.I.,THE COMMONWEALTH IN ASIA. CEYLON INDIA PAKISTAN S/ASIA UK CONSTN CULTURE SOCIETY STRATA STRUCT NAT/G POL/PAR EDU/PROP LEAD WAR 20 CMN/WLTH. PAGE 80 H1608
NAT/LISM REGION COLONIAL DIPLOM

B53
ELAHI K.N.,A GUIDE TO WORKS OF REFERENCE PUBLISHED IN PAKISTAN (PAMPHLET). PAKISTAN DIPLOM COLONIAL LEAD. PAGE 45 H0903
BIBLIOG S/ASIA NAT/G

B56
JENNINGS W.I.,THE APPROACH TO SELF-GOVERNMENT. CEYLON INDIA PAKISTAN S/ASIA UK SOCIETY POL/PAR DELIB/GP LEGIS ECO/TAC EDU/PROP ADMIN EXEC CHOOSE ATTIT ALL/VALS...JURID CONCPT GEN/METH TOT/POP 20. PAGE 81 H1610
NAT/G CONSTN COLONIAL

B56
WILSON P.,GOVERNMENT AND POLITICS OF INDIA AND PAKISTAN: 1885-1955; A BIBLIOGRAPHY OF WORKS IN WESTERN LANGUAGES. INDIA PAKISTAN CONSTN LOC/G POL/PAR FORCES DIPLOM ADMIN WAR CHOOSE...BIOG CON/ANAL 19/20. PAGE 169 H3380
BIBLIOG COLONIAL NAT/G S/ASIA

B57
CENTRAL ASIAN RESEARCH CENTRE,BIBLIOGRAPHY OF RECENT SOVIET SOURCE MATERIAL ON SOVIET CENTRAL ASIA AND THE BORDERLANDS. AFGHANISTN INDIA PAKISTAN UAR USSR ECO/UNDEV AGRI EXTR/IND INDUS ACADEM ADMIN ...HEAL HUM LING CON/ANAL 20. PAGE 28 H0567
BIBLIOG/A COM CULTURE NAT/G

B57
SHEIKH N.A.,SOME ASPECTS OF THE CONSTITUTION AND THE ECONOMICS OF ISLAM. PAKISTAN CULTURE AGRI FINAN LABOR NAT/G SECT INT/TRADE 20 MUSLIM. PAGE 143 H2855
ISLAM POLICY ECO/TAC CONSTN

B57
WILSON P.,SOUTH ASIA; A SELECTED BIBLIOGRAPHY ON INDIA, PAKISTAN, CEYLON (PAMPHLET). CEYLON INDIA PAKISTAN LAW ECO/UNDEV PLAN DIPLOM 20. PAGE 169 H3381
BIBLIOG S/ASIA CULTURE NAT/G

B59
GOPAL R.,INDIAN MUSLIMS: A POLITICAL HISTORY (1858-1947). INDIA ISLAM PAKISTAN NAT/G SECT LEGIS LEAD COERCE WAR REPRESENT ISOLAT ORD/FREE 19/20 HINDU MUSLIM. PAGE 59 H1175
COLONIAL GP/REL POL/PAR REGION

B59
MADHOK B.,POLITICAL TRENDS IN INDIA. INDIA PAKISTAN UK STRATA ECO/UNDEV POL/PAR LEGIS CAP/ISM DIPLOM COLONIAL CHOOSE MARXISM...SOC TREND 20 GANDHI/M NEHRU/J. PAGE 101 H2014
GEOG NAT/G

B60
ABERNATHY G.L.,PAKISTAN: A SELECTED, ANNOTATED BIBLIOGRAPHY (2ND ED., PAMPHLET). PAKISTAN CULTURE LEAD 20. PAGE 3 H0056
BIBLIOG/A SOC

B61
BINDER L.,RELIGION AND POLITICS IN PAKISTAN. ISLAM PAKISTAN NAT/G SECT LEGIS CREATE CHOOSE GP/REL ...MAJORIT TRADIT 20. PAGE 17 H0336
CONSTN CONFER NAT/LISM POL/PAR

B61
KHALIQUZZAMAN C.,PATHWAY TO PAKISTAN. INDIA PAKISTAN UK SECT LEGIS CHOOSE RACE/REL ATTIT ORD/FREE 20 MUSLIM. PAGE 85 H1705
GP/REL NAT/G COLONIAL SOVEREIGN

B61
KHAN A.W.,INDIA WINS FREEDOM: THE OTHER SIDE. INDIA PAKISTAN CULTURE LEGIS DIPLOM PARL/PROC REV WAR NAT/LISM 20. PAGE 85 H1707
SOVEREIGN GP/REL RACE/REL ORD/FREE

B62
GALENSON W.,LABOR IN DEVELOPING COUNTRIES. BRAZIL INDONESIA ISRAEL PAKISTAN TURKEY AGRI INDUS WORKER PAY PRICE GP/REL WEALTH...MGT CHARTS METH/COMP NAT/COMP 20. PAGE 54 H1088
LABOR ECO/UNDEV BARGAIN POL/PAR

B62
INAYATULLAH,BUREAUCRACY AND DEVELOPMENT IN PAKISTAN. PAKISTAN ECO/UNDEV EDU/PROP CONFER ...ANTHOL DICTIONARY 20 BUREAUCRCY. PAGE 76 H1526
EX/STRUC ADMIN NAT/G LOC/G

B62
MANSUR F.,PROCESS OF INDEPENDENCE. GHANA INDIA INDONESIA PAKISTAN CONSTN ELITES INTELL STRUCT ACADEM NAT/G REV PWR 20. PAGE 102 H2043
NAT/COMP POL/PAR SOVEREIGN COLONIAL

B62
TINKER H.,INDIA AND PAKISTAN. INDIA PAKISTAN NAT/G POL/PAR...OLD/LIB TRADIT TREND CHARTS BIBLIOG 20. PAGE 155 H3102
ORD/FREE STRATA REPRESENT AUTHORIT

B62
ZINKIN T.,REPORTING INDIA. INDIA PAKISTAN WOR+45 SOCIETY SECT FORCES EDU/PROP CROWD DISCRIM NAT/LISM
STRATA COLONIAL

MARXISM...POLICY 20. PAGE 173 H3457
BAL/PWR CONTROL

B63
HAQ M.,THE STRATEGY OF ECONOMIC PLANNING. PAKISTAN AGRI FINAN INDUS NAT/G FOR/AID TAX CONTROL REGION PRODUC...POLICY CHARTS 20. PAGE 66 H1324
ECO/TAC ECO/UNDEV PLAN PROB/SOLV

B63
KAHIN G.M.,MAJOR GOVERNMENTS OF ASIA (2ND ED.). ASIA INDIA INDONESIA PAKISTAN S/ASIA DIPLOM...SOC 20 CHINJAP. PAGE 83 H1650
GOV/COMP POL/PAR ELITES

B63
LIVINGSTON W.S.,FEDERALISM IN THE COMMONWEALTH - A BIBLIOGRAPHICAL COMMENTARY. CANADA INDIA PAKISTAN UK STRUCT LOC/G NAT/G POL/PAR...NAT/COMP 20 AUSTRAL. PAGE 97 H1943
BIBLIOG JURID FEDERAL CONSTN

B63
WEINER M.,POLITICAL CHANGE IN SOUTH ASIA. CEYLON INDIA PAKISTAN S/ASIA CULTURE ELITES ECO/UNDEV EX/STRUC ADMIN CONTROL CHOOSE CONSERVE...GOV/COMP ANTHOL 20. PAGE 166 H3328
NAT/G CONSTN TEC/DEV

B63
WILCOX W.A.,PAKISTAN; THE CONSOLIDATION OF A NATION. INDIA PAKISTAN CONSTN SECT PROB/SOLV COLONIAL PARTIC GP/REL FEDERAL...POLICY 19/20. PAGE 168 H3361
NAT/LISM ECO/UNDEV DIPLOM STRUCT

B64
DE SMITH S.A.,THE NEW COMMONWEALTH AND ITS CONSTITUTIONS. AFR CYPRUS PAKISTAN S/ASIA INT/ORG NAT/G LEGIS LEGIT RIGID/FLEX PWR...CONCPT TIME/SEQ CMN/WLTH 20. PAGE 38 H0770
EX/STRUC CONSTN SOVEREIGN

B64
GOODNOW H.F.,THE CIVIL SERVICE OF PAKISTAN: BUREAUCRACY IN A NEW NATION. INDIA PAKISTAN S/ASIA ECO/UNDEV PROVS CHIEF PARTIC CHOOSE EFFICIENCY PWR ...BIBLIOG 20. PAGE 59 H1173
ADMIN GOV/REL LAW NAT/G

B64
MAHAR J.M.,INDIA: A CRITICAL BIBLIOGRAPHY. INDIA PAKISTAN CULTURE ECO/UNDEV LOC/G POL/PAR SECT PROB/SOLV DIPLOM ADMIN COLONIAL PARL/PROC ATTIT 20. PAGE 101 H2016
BIBLIOG/A S/ASIA NAT/G LEAD

B64
WILCOX W.A.,INDIA, PAKISTAN AND THE RISE OF CHINA. ASIA BURMA CEYLON CHINA/COM INDIA PAKISTAN S/ASIA NAT/G VOL/ASSN FORCES TOP/EX ACT/RES DOMIN REGION RIGID/FLEX ORD/FREE...POLICY GEN/LAWS COLD/WAR 20. PAGE 168 H3362
CULTURE ATTIT DIPLOM

S64
"FURTHER READING." INDIA PAKISTAN SECT WAR PEACE ATTIT...POLICY 20. PAGE 2 H0044
BIBLIOG GP/REL DIPLOM NAT/G

S64
SAYEED K.,"PATHAN REGIONALISM." ISLAM PAKISTAN S/ASIA CULTURE SOCIETY NAT/G NEIGH DIPLOM LEGIT COERCE CHOOSE ATTIT DISPL PERCEPT ALL/VALS SOVEREIGN...POLICY RELATIV SOC TIME/SEQ TOT/POP 20. PAGE 138 H2761
SECT NAT/LISM REGION

B65
NATIONAL BOOK CENTRE PAKISTAN,BOOKS ON PAKISTAN: A BIBLIOGRAPHY. PAKISTAN CULTURE DIPLOM ADMIN ATTIT ...MAJORIT SOC CONCPT 20. PAGE 116 H2319
BIBLIOG CONSTN S/ASIA NAT/G

B65
ONSLOW C.,ASIAN ECONOMIC DEVELOPMENT. BURMA CEYLON INDIA MALAYSIA PAKISTAN S/ASIA AGRI INDUS MARKET PROB/SOLV CAP/ISM FOR/AID INT/TRADE DEMAND WEALTH ...POLICY ANTHOL 20. PAGE 121 H2418
ECO/UNDEV ECO/TAC PLAN NAT/G

B65
QURESHI I.H.,THE STRUGGLE FOR PAKISTAN. INDIA PAKISTAN UK CULTURE LEGIS DIPLOM EDU/PROP COLONIAL ATTIT SOVEREIGN 19/20 MUSLIM. PAGE 129 H2576
GP/REL RACE/REL WAR SECT

B65
SCHULER E.A.,THE PAKISTAN ACADEMIES FOR RURAL DEVELOPMENT COMILLA AND PESHAWAR 1959-1964. PAKISTAN S/ASIA SOCIETY STRUCT AGRI NAT/G TEC/DEV EDU/PROP 20. PAGE 140 H2801
BIBLIOG PLAN ECO/TAC ECO/UNDEV

S65
ASHFORD D.E.,"BUREAUCRATS AND CITIZENS." MOROCCO PAKISTAN PARTIC 20 TUNIS. PAGE 9 H0172
GOV/COMP ADMIN EX/STRUC ROLE

B66
BIRKHEAD G.S.,ADMINISTRATIVE PROBLEMS IN PAKISTAN. PAKISTAN AGRI FINAN INDUS LG/CO ECO/TAC CONTROL PWR ...CHARTS ANTHOL 20. PAGE 17 H0340
ADMIN NAT/G ORD/FREE ECO/UNDEV

B66
BRAIBANTI R.,ASIAN BUREAUCRATIC SYSTEMS EMERGENT FROM THE BRITISH IMPERIAL TRADITION. BURMA CEYLON INDIA PAKISTAN UK ELITES ECO/UNDEV NAT/G...MGT SOC CHARTS ANTHOL 19/20. PAGE 20 H0401
GOV/COMP COLONIAL ADMIN S/ASIA

B66
BRAIBANTI R.,RESEARCH ON THE BUREAUCRACY OF PAKISTAN. PAKISTAN LAW CULTURE INTELL ACADEM LOC/G
HABITAT NAT/G

SECT PRESS CT/SYS...LING CHARTS 20 BUREAUCRCY. PAGE 20 H0402 ADMIN CONSTN

B66
MASON E.S.,ECONOMIC DEVELOPMENT IN INDIA AND PAKISTAN. INDIA PAKISTAN AGRI FINAN PLAN BUDGET INT/TRADE WEALTH...POLICY STAT TREND CHARTS 20. PAGE 104 H2086 NAT/COMP ECO/UNDEV ECO/TAC FOR/AID

B66
US DEPARTMENT OF THE ARMY,SOUTH ASIA: A STRATEGIC SURVEY (PAMPHLET NO. 550-3). AFGHANISTN INDIA NEPAL PAKISTAN ECO/UNDEV INT/ORG POL/PAR FORCES FOR/AID INT/TRADE LEAD WAR...POLICY SOC TREND 20. PAGE 160 H3195 BIBLIOG/A S/ASIA DIPLOM NAT/G

B66
WINKS R.W.,THE HISTORIOGRAPHY OF THE BRITISH EMPIRE-COMMONWEALTH. CANADA INDIA PAKISTAN UK CULTURE SOCIETY STRUCT POL/PAR...CONCPT NAT/COMP 20 AUSTRAL. PAGE 169 H3386 HIST/WRIT TREND IDEA/COMP METH/COMP

B66
ZINKIN T.,CHALLENGES IN INDIA. INDIA PAKISTAN LAW AGRI FINAN INDUS TOP/EX TEC/DEV CONTROL ROUTINE ORD/FREE PWR 20 NEHRU/J SHASTRI/LB CIVIL/SERV. PAGE 173 H3458 NAT/G ECO/TAC POLICY ADMIN

S66
MANSERGH N.,"THE PARTITION OF INDIA IN RETROSPECT." INDIA PAKISTAN S/ASIA UK DIPLOM COLONIAL GP/REL PWR 20. PAGE 102 H2042 NAT/G PARL/PROC POLICY POL/PAR

B67
ASHFORD D.E.,NATIONAL DEVELOPMENT AND LOCAL REFORM: POLITICAL PARTICIPATION IN MOROCCO, TUNISIA, AND PAKISTAN. MOROCCO PAKISTAN CULTURE PROB/SOLV ATTIT ...POLICY SOC METH/COMP NAT/COMP BIBLIOG 20 TUNIS. PAGE 9 H0173 PARTIC ECO/UNDEV ADJUST NAT/G

B67
MUHAMMAD A.C.,THE EMERGENCE OF PAKISTAN. PAKISTAN S/ASIA CONSTN ECO/UNDEV NAT/G CONTROL NAT/LISM 20. PAGE 114 H2281 DIPLOM COLONIAL SECT PROB/SOLV

B67
PAPANEK G.F.,PAKISTAN'S DEVELOPMENT: SOCIAL GOALS AND PRIVATE INCENTIVES. PAKISTAN INDUS NAT/G PROB/SOLV CONTROL EFFICIENCY SOCISM...CHARTS 20. PAGE 123 H2463 ECO/UNDEV PLAN CAP/ISM ECO/TAC

PAKISTAN/E....EAST PAKISTAN

PALACIOS A.L. H2448

PALESTINE....PALESTINE (PRE-1948 ISRAEL); SEE ALSO ISRAEL

PALMER E.E. H2449,H2450

PALMER N.D. H2451,H2452

PALMER R.R. H2453

PAN S. H2454

PAN AFRICAN FREEDOM MOVEMENT....SEE PANAF/FREE

PAN AMERICAN UNION H2455,H2456

PANAF/FREE....PAN AFRICAN FREEDOM MOVEMENT

B62
AMERICAN SOCIETY AFR CULTURE,PAN-AFRICANISM RECONSIDERED. AFR SOCIETY STRUCT SCHOOL CAP/ISM EDU/PROP...ART/METH NEW/IDEA PREDICT ANTHOL 20 PANAF/FREE NEGRO. PAGE 6 H0123 DIPLOM FEDERAL NAT/LISM CULTURE

B63
WODDIS J.,AFRICA, THE WAY AHEAD. AFR FUT ELITES POL/PAR CAP/ISM DIPLOM DOMIN RACE/REL ATTIT ORD/FREE SOVEREIGN SOCISM 20 PANAF/FREE. PAGE 170 H3394 REV COLONIAL ECO/UNDEV NAT/G

PANAFR/ISM....PAN-AFRICANISM

PANAMA CANAL ZONE....SEE CANAL/ZONE

PANAMA....PANAMA

B40
BROWN A.D.,PANAMA CANAL AND PANAMA CANAL ZONE: A SELECTED LIST OF REFERENCES. PANAMA NAT/G SCHOOL DIPLOM HEALTH...GEOG SOC 20 CANAL/ZONE. PAGE 22 H0436 BIBLIOG/A ECO/UNDEV

B47
DE NOIA J.,GUIDE TO OFFICIAL PUBLICATIONS OF THE OTHER AMERICAN REPUBLICS: PANAMA (VOL. XV). PANAMA LAW LEGIS EDU/PROP CT/SYS 20. PAGE 38 H0766 BIBLIOG/A CONSTN ADMIN NAT/G

B60
DE HERRERA C.D.,LISTA BIBLIOGRAFICA DE LOS TRABAJOS DE GRADUACION Y TESIS PRESENTADOS EN LA UNIVERSIDAD, 1939-1960. PANAMA DIPLOM LEAD...SOC 20. PAGE 38 H0754 BIBLIOG L/A+17C NAT/G ACADEM

B64
MUSEUM FUR VOLKERKUNDE WIEN,ZENTRALAMERIKA MEXIKO VOLKER UND KULTUREN. COSTA/RICA GUATEMALA L/A+17C PANAMA SECT WAR GP/REL SOVEREIGN...ART/METH 20 CENTRAL/AM MEXIC/AMER. PAGE 115 H2300 SOCIETY STRUCT CULTURE AGRI

S65
PLANK J.N.,"THE CARIBBEAN* INTERVENTION, WHEN AND HOW." CUBA GUATEMALA HAITI PANAMA USA+45 VENEZUELA FORCES PROB/SOLV RISK COERCE...NAT/COMP OAS TIME. PAGE 126 H2521 SOVEREIGN MARXISM REV

B66
HOYT E.C.,NATIONAL POLICY AND INTERNATIONAL LAW* CASE STUDIES FROM AMERICAN CANAL POLICY* MONOGRAPH NO. 1 -- 1966-1967. PANAMA UK ELITES BAL/PWR EFFICIENCY...CLASSIF NAT/COMP SOC/EXP COLOMB TREATY. PAGE 74 H1483 INT/LAW USA-45 DIPLOM PWR

PANIKKAR K.M. H2457,H2458,H2459,H2460,H2461

PAN-AFRICANISM....SEE PANAFR/ISM

PANJAB, PANJABI PEOPLE....SEE PUNJAB

PANJABI K.L. H2462

PAPANEK G.F. H2463

PAPUA....PAPUA

L95
BELSHAW C.S.,"IN SEARCH OF WEALTH; STUDY OF EMERGENCE OF COMMERCIAL OPERA TIONS IN MELANESIAN SOCIETY OF SOUTHEASTERN PAPUA." S/ASIA CULTURE KIN ECO/TAC DEMAND INCOME 20 MELANESIA PAPUA. PAGE 14 H0272 INT/TRADE ECO/UNDEV METH/COMP SOCIETY

PARAGUAY....SEE ALSO L/A+17C

B62
PASTOR R.S.,A STATEMENT OF THE LAWS OF PARAGUAY IN MATTERS AFFECTING BUSINESS (2ND ED.). PARAGUAY INDUS FAM LABOR LG/CO NAT/G LEGIS TAX CONTROL MARRIAGE 20. PAGE 124 H2474 FINAN ECO/UNDEV LAW CONSTN

B67
PENDLE G.,PARAGUAY: A RIVERSIDE NATION (3RD ED.). PARAGUAY CHIEF ISOLAT...HUM CHARTS BIBLIOG 16/20. PAGE 124 H2487 CULTURE GEOG ECO/UNDEV

PARANJAPE H.K. H2464

PARETO V. H2465,H2466

PARETO/V....VILFREDO PARETO

PARGELLIS S. H0865

PARIS....PARIS, FRANCE

B30
MASON E.S.,THE PARIS COMMUNE: AN EPISODE IN THE HISTORY OF THE SOCIALIST MOVEMENT. FRANCE MOD/EUR ELITES SOCIETY STRATA ECO/DEV WORKER EDU/PROP CHOOSE INGP/REL SOCISM 19 MARX/KARL PARIS. PAGE 104 H2085 NAT/G REV MARXISM

PARISH H.C. H2087

PARK A.G. H2467

PARK R.L. H2468

PARK/R....ROBERT PARK

S49
HUGHES E.C.,"SOCIAL CHANGE AND STATUS PROTEST: AN ESSAY ON THE MARGINAL MAN" (BMR)" EUR+WWI UK USA+45 CULTURE SOCIETY STRUCT RACE/REL...SOC NAT/COMP SOC/INTEG 19/20 NEGRO PARK/R. PAGE 74 H1490 STRATA ATTIT DISCRIM

PARKER/H....HENRY PARKER

PARKFOREST....PARK FOREST, ILLINOIS

PARL/PROC....PARLIAMENTARY PROCESSES; SEE ALSO LEGIS

N
AUSTRALIAN NATIONAL RES COUN,AUSTRALIAN SOCIAL SCIENCE ABSTRACTS. NEW/ZEALND CULTURE SOCIETY LOC/G CT/SYS PARL/PROC...HEAL JURID PSY SOC 20 AUSTRAL. PAGE 9 H0181 BIBLIOG/A POLICY NAT/G ADMIN

B10
MCILWAIN C.H.,THE HIGH COURT OF PARLIAMENT AND ITS SUPREMACY B1910 1878 408. UK EX/STRUC PARL/PROC GOV/REL INGP/REL PRIVIL 12/20 PARLIAMENT ENGLSH/LAW. PAGE 107 H2132
LAW LEGIS CONSTN NAT/G

B10
TEMPERLEY H.W.V.,SENATES AND UPPER CHAMBERS; THEIR USE AND FUNCTION IN THE MODERN STATE... UK WOR-45 CONSTN NAT/G POL/PAR PROVS SECT COLONIAL LEAD CHOOSE REPRESENT PWR...BIBLIOG 19/20 PARLIAMENT SENATE CMN/WLTH HOUSE/LORD. PAGE 153 H3059
PARL/PROC NAT/COMP LEGIS EX/STRUC

N16
MILTON J.,THE READIE AND EASY WAY TO ESTABLISH A FREE COMMONWEALTH. CONSTN LEGIS PARL/PROC CONSERVE ...MAJORIT 17. PAGE 111 H2219
ORD/FREE NAT/G CHIEF POPULISM

B17
HARLOW R.V.,THE HISTORY OF LEGISLATIVE METHODS IN THE PERIOD BEFORE 1825. USA-45 EX/STRUC ADMIN COLONIAL LEAD PARL/PROC ROUTINE...GP/COMP GOV/COMP HOUSE/REP. PAGE 66 H1333
LEGIS DELIB/GP PROVS POL/PAR

N17
BURKE E.,THOUGHTS ON THE CAUSE OF THE PRESENT DISCONTENTS (PAMPHLET). MOD/EUR UK CONSTN CHIEF LEGIS DOMIN CONTROL EXEC REPRESENT POPULISM ...TRADIT NEW/IDEA METH/COMP 18 BURKE/EDM. PAGE 24 H0484
ORD/FREE REV PARL/PROC NAT/G

N17
BURKE E.,LETTER TO SIR HERCULES LANGRISHE (PAMPHLET). IRELAND UK NAT/G CHIEF DIPLOM DOMIN PARL/PROC COERCE ORD/FREE SOVEREIGN POPULISM ...TRADIT 18 BURKE/EDM. PAGE 24 H0485
POLICY COLONIAL SECT

N19
ADMINISTRATIVE STAFF COLLEGE,THE ACCOUNTABILITY OF GOVERNMENT DEPARTMENTS (PAMPHLET) (REV. ED.). UK CONSTN FINAN NAT/G CONSULT ADMIN INGP/REL CONSEN PRIVIL 20 PARLIAMENT. PAGE 3 H0070
PARL/PROC ELITES SANCTION PROB/SOLV

N19
COUTROT A.,THE FIGHT OVER THE 1959 PRIVATE EDUCATION LAW IN FRANCE (PAMPHLET). FRANCE NAT/G SECT GIVE EDU/PROP GP/REL ATTIT RIGID/FLEX ORD/FREE 20 CHURCH/STA. PAGE 34 H0681
SCHOOL PARL/PROC CATHISM LAW

N19
TREVELYAN G.M.,THE TWO-PARTY SYSTEM IN ENGLISH POLITICAL HISTORY (PAMPHLET). UK CHIEF LEGIS COLONIAL EXEC REV CHOOSE 17/19. PAGE 157 H3131
PARL/PROC POL/PAR NAT/G PWR

B23
FINER H.,REPRESENTATIVE GOVERNMENT AND A PARLIAMENT OF INDUSTRY. A STUDY OF THE GERMAN FEDERAL ECONOMIC COUNCIL. GERMANY UK CONSTN INDUS PARL/PROC ...NAT/COMP 20. PAGE 50 H1002
DELIB/GP ECO/TAC WAR REV

B23
LEES-SMITH H.B.,SECOND CHAMBERS IN THEORY AND PRACTICE. IRELAND NORWAY SOUTH/AFR UK LAW POL/PAR LEGIS CONTROL 20 CMN/WLTH. PAGE 93 H1858
PARL/PROC DELIB/GP REPRESENT GP/COMP

B23
ROBERT H.M.,PARLIAMENTARY LAW. POL/PAR LEGIS PARTIC CHOOSE REPRESENT GP/REL. PAGE 132 H2640
PARL/PROC DELIB/GP NAT/G JURID

B26
POLLARD A.F.,THE EVOLUTION OF PARLIAMENT. UK CONSTN POL/PAR EX/STRUC GOV/REL INGP/REL PRIVIL RIGID/FLEX ...TIME/SEQ 11/20 CMN/WLTH PARLIAMENT. PAGE 127 H2536
LEGIS PARL/PROC NAT/G

B27
GOOCH G.P.,ENGLISH DEMOCRATIC IDEAS IN THE SEVENTEENTH CENTURY (2ND ED.). UK LAW SECT FORCES DIPLOM LEAD PARL/PROC REV ATTIT AUTHORIT...ANARCH CONCPT 17 PARLIAMENT CMN/WLTH REFORMERS. PAGE 58 H1167
IDEA/COMP MAJORIT EX/STRUC CONSERVE

B29
CAM H.M.,BIBLIOGRAPHY OF ENGLISH CONSTITUTIONAL HISTORY (PAMPHLET). UK LAW LOC/G NAT/G POL/PAR SECT DELIB/GP ADJUD ORD/FREE 19/20 PARLIAMENT. PAGE 25 H0510
BIBLIOG/A CONSTN ADMIN PARL/PROC

B30
WILLOUGHBY W.W.,THE ETHICAL BASIS OF POLITICAL AUTHORITY. NAT/G LEGIS PARL/PROC INGP/REL UTOPIA ORD/FREE 16/20. PAGE 169 H3374
MORAL POLICY CONSTN

B32
GREAT BRIT COMM MINISTERS PWR,REPORT. UK LAW CONSTN CONSULT LEGIS PARL/PROC SANCTION SOVEREIGN ...DECISION JURID 20 PARLIAMENT. PAGE 60 H1201
EX/STRUC NAT/G PWR CONTROL

B32
MCKISACK M.,THE PARLIAMENTARY REPRESENTATION OF THE ENGLISH BOROUGHS DURING THE MIDDLE AGES. UK CONSTN CULTURE ELITES EX/STRUC TAX PAY ADJUD PARL/PROC APPORT FEDERAL...POLICY 13/15 PARLIAMENT. PAGE 107 H2139
NAT/G MUNIC LEGIS CHOOSE

L34
GOSNELL H.F.,"BRITISH ROYAL COMMISSIONS OF INQUIRY" UK CONSTN LEGIS PRESS ADMIN PARL/PROC...DECISION 20 PARLIAMENT. PAGE 59 H1184
DELIB/GP INSPECT POLICY NAT/G

B35
TAKEUCHI T.,WAR AND DIPLOMACY IN THE JAPANESE EMPIRE. ASIA ELITES STRATA NAT/G SECT LEGIS ACT/RES PLAN LEGIT PARL/PROC ROUTINE WAR...MGT BIOG CHINJAP TOT/POP 19/20 CHINJAP. PAGE 152 H3038
EXEC STRUCT

B36
CLARKE M.V.,MEDIEVAL REPRESENTATION AND CONSENT. IRELAND UK REPRESENT SUFF. PAGE 30 H0603
PARL/PROC LEGIS NAT/G

B36
CLOKIE H.M.,THE ORIGIN AND NATURE OF CONSTITUTIONAL GOVERNMENT. UK NAT/G POL/PAR CONSULT LEGIS ...GOV/COMP 14/20 CABINET PARLIAMENT. PAGE 30 H0606
CONCPT CONSTN PARL/PROC

B36
RAPPARD W.E.,THE GOVERNMENT OF SWITZERLAND. SWITZERLND INT/ORG POL/PAR EX/STRUC DIPLOM NEUTRAL PARL/PROC REGION WAR HABITAT SOVEREIGN...NAT/COMP SOC/INTEG 20 LEAGUE/NAT WWI. PAGE 130 H2594
CONSTN NAT/G CULTURE FEDERAL

B38
DUNHAM W.H. JR.,COMPLAINT AND REFORM IN ENGLAND 1436-1714. UK LAW ACADEM NAT/G POL/PAR SCHOOL PRESS COLONIAL PARL/PROC MORAL...SOC/WK ANTHOL 15/18 HAKLUYT/R COWPER/W. PAGE 43 H0865
ATTIT SOCIETY SECT

B38
HOLDSWORTH W.S.,A HISTORY OF ENGLISH LAW; THE CENTURIES OF SETTLEMENT AND REFORM (VOL. XI). UK CONSTN NAT/G EX/STRUC DIPLOM ADJUD CT/SYS LEAD CRIME ATTIT...INT/LAW JURID 18 CMN/WLTH PARLIAMENT ENGLSH/LAW. PAGE 73 H1452
LAW COLONIAL LEGIS PARL/PROC

B39
JENNINGS W.I.,PARLIAMENT. UK POL/PAR OP/RES BUDGET LEAD CHOOSE GP/REL...MGT 20 PARLIAMENT HOUSE/LORD HOUSE/CMNS. PAGE 80 H1609
PARL/PROC LEGIS CONSTN NAT/G

C39
BURKE E.,"ON THE REFORM OF THE REPRESENTATION IN THE HOUSE OF COMMONS" (1782) IN COLLECTED WORKS (VOL. 5)" UK ELITES STRATA NAT/G REPRESENT ORD/FREE PWR POPULISM...POLICY NEW/IDEA GEN/LAWS 18 BURKE/EDM. PAGE 24 H0486
TRADIT CONSTN PARL/PROC LEGIS

B41
CROTHERS G.D.,THE GERMAN ELECTIONS OF 1907. GERMANY NAT/G EDU/PROP COLONIAL ATTIT. PAGE 35 H0709
CHOOSE PARL/PROC NAT/LISM POL/PAR

S43
PRICE D.K.,"THE PARLIAMENTARY AND PRESIDENTIAL SYSTEMS" (BMR)" USA-45 NAT/G EX/STRUC PARL/PROC GOV/REL PWR 20 PRESIDENT CONGRESS PARLIAMENT. PAGE 128 H2561
LEGIS REPRESENT ADMIN GOV/COMP

N45
INDIA QUARTERLY, A JOURNAL OF INTERNATIONAL AFFAIRS. INDIA LAW CONSTN ECO/UNDEV INT/ORG POL/PAR COLONIAL LEAD PARL/PROC WAR ATTIT...SOC 20 CMN/WLTH. PAGE 2 H0033
BIBLIOG/A S/ASIA DIPLOM NAT/G

S45
SPENCER R.C.,"PARTY GOVERNMENT AND THE SWEDISH RISKDAG." SWEDEN CHOOSE MAJORITY. PAGE 147 H2946
GOV/COMP NAT/G POL/PAR PARL/PROC

B47
MCILWAIN C.H.,CONSTITUTIONALISM: ANCIENT AND MODERN. USA+45 ROMAN/EMP LAW CHIEF LEGIS CT/SYS GP/REL ORD/FREE SOVEREIGN...POLICY TIME/SEQ ROMAN/REP EUROPE. PAGE 107 H2135
CONSTN NAT/G PARL/PROC GOV/COMP

B48
NEUBURGER O.,GUIDE TO OFFICIAL PUBLICATIONS OF THE OTHER AMERICAN REPUBLICS: VENEZUELA (VOL. XIX). VENEZUELA FINAN LEGIS PLAN BUDGET DIPLOM CT/SYS PARL/PROC 19/20. PAGE 117 H2335
BIBLIOG/A NAT/G CONSTN LAW

B50
WADE E.C.S.,CONSTITUTIONAL LAW; AN OUTLINE OF THE LAW AND PRACTICE OF THE CONSTITUTION. UK LEGIS DOMIN ADMIN GP/REL 16/20 CMN/WLTH PARLIAMENT ENGLSH/LAW. PAGE 164 H3283
CONSTN NAT/G PARL/PROC LAW

B51
MARX K.,THE EIGHTEENTH BRUMAIRE OF LOUIS BONAPARTE (1852). FRANCE STRATA FINAN INDUS LABOR CHIEF FORCES WORKER CAP/ISM ECO/TAC PARL/PROC ORD/FREE ...MARXIST 19. PAGE 104 H2080
REV MARXISM ELITES NAT/G

B53
STOUT H.M.,BRITISH GOVERNMENT. UK FINAN LOC/G POL/PAR DELIB/GP DIPLOM ADMIN COLONIAL CHOOSE ORD/FREE...JURID BIBLIOG 20 COMMONWLTH. PAGE 150 H2990
NAT/G PARL/PROC CONSTN NEW/LIB

B54
JENNINGS I.,THE QUEEN'S GOVERNMENT. UK POL/PAR DELIB/GP ADJUD ADMIN CT/SYS PARL/PROC REPRESENT CONSERVE 13/20 PARLIAMENT. PAGE 80 H1605
NAT/G CONSTN LEGIS CHIEF

B54
MORRISON H.,GOVERNMENT AND PARLIAMENT. UK NAT/G PARLIAMENT. PAGE 113 H2266
GOV/REL EX/STRUC LEGIS

PARL/PROC

C54
LANDAU J.M.,"PARLIAMENTS AND PARTIES IN EGYPT." UAR NAT/G SECT CONSULT LEGIS TOP/EX PROB/SOLV ADMIN COLONIAL...GEN/LAWS BIBLIOG 19/20. PAGE 90 H1804
ISLAM NAT/LISM PARL/PROC POL/PAR

B55
BRACHER K.D.,DIE AUFLOSUNG DER WEIMARER REPUBLIK. EUR+WWI GERMANY...TIME/SEQ 20. PAGE 20 H0395
TOTALISM NAT/G POL/PAR PARL/PROC

B55
GALLOWAY G.B.,CONGRESS AND PARLIAMENT: THEIR ORGANIZATION AND OPERATION IN THE US AND THE UK: PLANNING PAMPHLET NO. 93. POL/PAR EX/STRUC DEBATE CONTROL LEAD ROUTINE EFFICIENCY PWR...POLICY CONGRESS PARLIAMENT. PAGE 54 H1089
DELIB/GP LEGIS PARL/PROC GOV/COMP

B55
POLLOCK J.K.,GERMAN DEMOCRACY AT WORK. GERMANY/W LOC/G NAT/G DIPLOM PARL/PROC...OBS IDEA/COMP 20. PAGE 127 H2539
PARTIC POL/PAR CHOOSE EDU/PROP

C55
APTER D.E.,"THE GOLD COAST IN TRANSITION." AFR CONSTN LOC/G LEGIS DIPLOM COLONIAL CONTROL GOV/REL ...CHARTS BIBLIOG 20 CMN/WLTH. PAGE 7 H0150
ORD/FREE REPRESENT PARL/PROC NAT/G

B56
EMDEN C.S.,THE PEOPLE AND THE CONSTITUTION (2ND ED.). UK LEGIS POPULISM 17/20 PARLIAMENT. PAGE 46 H0916
CONSTN PARL/PROC NAT/G LAW

B56
HERNANDEZ URBINA A.,LOS PARTIDOS Y LA CRISIS DEL APRA. PERU NAT/G LEAD LOBBY CHOOSE SOCISM...POLICY DECISION 20 COM/PARTY APRA CONGRESS. PAGE 70 H1402
POL/PAR PARTIC PARL/PROC GP/REL

B56
WEBER M.,STAATSSOZIOLOGIE. STRUCT LEGIT ADMIN PARL/PROC SUPEGO CONSERVE JURID. PAGE 166 H3320
SOC NAT/G POL/PAR LEAD

S56
EPSTEIN L.D.,"COHESION OF BRITISH PARLIAMENTARY PARTIES." UK STRUCT ADMIN ROUTINE INGP/REL PWR ...GP/COMP PARLIAMENT. PAGE 47 H0935
NAT/G PARL/PROC POL/PAR

N56
US HOUSE COMM FOREIGN AFFAIRS,REPORT OF THE SPECIAL STUDY MISSION TO AFRICA, SOUTH AND EAST OF THE SAHARA (PAMPHLET). AFR SOUTH/AFR USA+45 STRUCT INT/TRADE PARL/PROC NAT/LISM ATTIT ALL/VALS HEALTH ...POLICY 20 CONGRESS. PAGE 160 H3197
FOR/AID COLONIAL ECO/UNDEV DIPLOM

B57
MEINECKE F.,MACHIAVELLISM. CHRIST-17C FRANCE GERMANY ITALY MOD/EUR BAL/PWR PARL/PROC TOTALISM ...PHIL/SCI 15/20 MACHIAVELL. PAGE 108 H2166
NAT/LISM NAT/G PWR

B57
POPLAI S.L.,NATIONAL POLITICS AND 1957 ELECTIONS IN INDIA. INDIA BARGAIN PARL/PROC CONSEN NAT/LISM PWR WEALTH 20. PAGE 127 H2543
POL/PAR CHOOSE POLICY NAT/G

C57
MORRIS-JONES W.H.,"PARLIAMENT IN INDIA." INDIA CONSTN LEGIS CONFER COLONIAL CHOOSE PRIVIL ATTIT ...GOV/COMP BIBLIOG 20. PAGE 113 H2264
PARL/PROC EX/STRUC NAT/G POL/PAR

B58
BRADY A.,DEMOCRACY IN THE DOMINIONS (3RD ED.). CANADA NEW/ZEALND SOUTH/AFR WOR+45 LAW EX/STRUC DOMIN COLONIAL PARL/PROC REPRESENT RACE/REL NAT/LISM WEALTH 20 AUSTRAL CMN/WLTH. PAGE 20 H0399
GOV/COMP POL/PAR POPULISM NAT/G

B58
EUSDEN J.D.,PURITANS, LAWYERS, AND POLITICS IN EARLY SEVENTEENTH-CENTURY ENGLAND. UK CT/SYS PARL/PROC RATIONAL PWR SOVEREIGN...IDEA/COMP BIBLIOG 17 PURITAN COMMON/LAW. PAGE 48 H0951
GP/REL SECT NAT/G LAW

B58
HANSARD SOCIETY PARL GOVT,WHAT ARE THE PROBLEMS OF PARLIAMENTARY GOVERNMENT IN WEST AFRICA? PROB/SOLV DIPLOM GP/REL 20 PARLIAMENT AFRICA/W. PAGE 66 H1317
PARL/PROC POL/PAR AFR NAT/G

S58
SCHUMM S.,"INTEREST REPRESENTATION IN FRANCE AND GERMANY." EUR+WWI FRANCE GERMANY INSPECT PARL/PROC REPRESENT 20 WEIMAR/REP. PAGE 140 H2803
LOBBY DELIB/GP NAT/G

C58
GOLAY J.F.,"THE FOUNDING OF THE FEDERAL REPUBLIC OF GERMANY." GERMANY/W CONSTN EX/STRUC DIPLOM ADMIN CHOOSE...DECISION BIBLIOG 20. PAGE 58 H1155
FEDERAL NAT/G PARL/PROC POL/PAR

C58
WILDING N.,"AN ENCYCLOPEDIA OF PARLIAMENT." UK LAW CONSTN CHIEF PROB/SOLV DIPLOM DEBATE WAR INGP/REL PRIVIL...BIBLIOG DICTIONARY 13/20 CMN/WLTH PARLIAMENT. PAGE 168 H3363
PARL/PROC POL/PAR NAT/G ADMIN

B59
BUNDESMIN FUR VERTRIEBENE,ZEITTAFEL DER VORGESCHICHTE UND DES ABLAUFS DER VERTREIBUNG SOWIE DER UNTERBRINGUNG UND EINGLIEDERUNG DER (2 VOLS.). GERMANY/E GERMANY/W NAT/G PROVS PROB/SOLV DIPLOM PARL/PROC ATTIT...BIBLIOG SOC/INTEG 20 MIGRATION PARLIAMENT. PAGE 24 H0475
JURID GP/REL INT/LAW

B59
KELF-COHEN R.,NATIONALISATION IN BRITAIN: THE END OF DOGMA. EUR+WWI UK NAT/G POL/PAR WORKER ECO/TAC PARL/PROC WEALTH SOCISM...GOV/COMP 20. PAGE 84 H1683
NEW/LIB ECO/DEV INDUS OWN

B59
LEITES N.,ON THE GAME OF POLITICS IN FRANCE. ALGERIA FRANCE CONSTN SECT VOL/ASSN ECO/TAC INT/TRADE PARL/PROC WAR SOCISM 20 DEGAULLE/C EEC. PAGE 94 H1871
POL/PAR NAT/G LEGIS IDEA/COMP

B59
PAULSEN M.G.,LEGAL INSTITUTIONS TODAY AND TOMORROW. UK USA+45 NAT/G PROF/ORG PROVS ADMIN PARL/PROC ORD/FREE NAT/COMP. PAGE 124 H2477
JURID ADJUD JUDGE LEGIS

B59
SQUIBB G.D.,THE HIGH COURT OF CHIVALRY. UK NAT/G FORCES ADJUD WAR 14/20 PARLIAMENT ENGLSH/LAW. PAGE 148 H2959
CT/SYS PARL/PROC JURID

B60
BHAMBHRI C.P.,PARLIAMENTARY CONTROL OVER STATE ENTERPRISE IN INDIA. INDIA DELIB/GP ADMIN CONTROL INGP/REL EFFICIENCY 20 PARLIAMENT. PAGE 16 H0327
NAT/G OWN INDUS PARL/PROC

B60
BREDVOLD L.I.,THE PHILOSOPHY OF EDMUND BURKE. POL/PAR PARL/PROC REPRESENT CONSERVE...JURID 18 BURKE/EDM. PAGE 20 H0410
PHIL/SCI NAT/G CONCPT

B60
CONOVER H.F.,OFFICIAL PUBLICATIONS OF SOMALILAND, 1941-1959: A GUIDE. SOMALIA AGRI FINAN INT/ORG SCHOOL INT/TRADE PRESS CONFER COLONIAL PARL/PROC 20 CONGRESS. PAGE 33 H0652
BIBLIOG NAT/G CON/ANAL

B60
JEFFRIES C.,TRANSFER OF POWER: PROBLEMS OF THE PASSAGE TO SELFGOVERNMENT. CEYLON GHANA MALAYSIA NIGERIA UK INT/ORG CONSULT DELIB/GP LEGIS DIPLOM CONFER PARL/PROC 20. PAGE 80 H1595
SOVEREIGN COLONIAL ORD/FREE NAT/G

B60
JHA C.,INDIAN GOVERNMENT AND POLITICS. INDIA SERV/IND POL/PAR PROVS LEGIS CT/SYS CHOOSE GOV/REL FEDERAL 20. PAGE 81 H1616
NAT/G PARL/PROC CONSTN ADJUST

B60
US LIBRARY OF CONGRESS,INDEX TO LATIN AMERICAN LEGISLATION: 1950-1960 (2 VOLS.). NAT/G DELIB/GP ADMIN PARL/PROC 20. PAGE 161 H3211
BIBLIOG/A LEGIS L/A+17C JURID

B61
CASSINELLI C.W.,THE POLITICS OF FREEDOM. FUT UNIV LAW POL/PAR CHOOSE ORD/FREE...POLICY CONCPT MYTH BIBLIOG. PAGE 28 H0555
MAJORIT NAT/G PARL/PROC PARTIC

B61
DRAGNICH A.N.,MAJOR EUROPEAN GOVERNMENTS. FRANCE GERMANY/W UK USSR LOC/G EX/STRUC CT/SYS PARL/PROC ATTIT MARXISM...JURID MGT NAT/COMP 19/20. PAGE 42 H0846
NAT/G LEGIS CONSTN POL/PAR

B61
HARE T.,A TREATISE ON THE ELECTION OF REPRESENTATIVES, PARLIAMENTARY AND MUNICIPAL. UK CONSTN NAT/G PARL/PROC CHOOSE ATTIT...MAJORIT 18/19 PARLIAMENT. PAGE 66 H1330
LEGIS GOV/REL CONSEN REPRESENT

B61
KHAN A.W.,INDIA WINS FREEDOM: THE OTHER SIDE. INDIA PAKISTAN CULTURE LEGIS DIPLOM PARL/PROC REV WAR NAT/LISM 20. PAGE 85 H1707
SOVEREIGN GP/REL RACE/REL ORD/FREE

B61
MILIBAND R.,PARLIAMENTARY SOCIALISM. EUR+WWI UK EXEC LEAD PARL/PROC GP/REL...POLICY 20 PARLIAMENT LABOR/PAR. PAGE 110 H2203
POL/PAR NAT/G PWR SOCISM

B61
MUNGER E.S.,AFRICAN FIELD REPORTS 1952-1961. SOUTH/AFR SOCIETY ECO/UNDEV NAT/G POL/PAR COLONIAL EXEC PARL/PROC GUERRILLA RACE/REL ALL/IDEOS...SOC AUD/VIS 20. PAGE 114 H2288
AFR DISCRIM RECORD

B61
NIPPERDEY T.,DIE ORGANISATION DER DEUTSCHEN PARTEIEN VOR 1918. GERMANY CONSTN STRUCT TEC/DEV CHOOSE ADJUST ATTIT...CONCPT TIME/SEQ 19/20. PAGE 118 H2362
POL/PAR PARL/PROC NAT/G

B61
RAO K.V.,PARLIAMENTARY DEMOCRACY OF INDIA. INDIA EX/STRUC TOP/EX COLONIAL CT/SYS PARL/PROC ORD/FREE ...POLICY CONCPT TREND 20 PARLIAMENT. PAGE 130 H2592
CONSTN ADJUD NAT/G FEDERAL

B61
SANTHANAM K.,DEMOCRATIC PLANNING. INDIA AGRI FINAN LEGIS DIPLOM PARL/PROC ORD/FREE 20. PAGE 138 H2753
PLAN NAT/G CONSTN POLICY

B61
TREVE W.,DEUTSCHE PARTEIPROGRAMME 1861-1961. GERMANY GERMANY/W DELIB/GP CONFER CHOOSE REPRESENT 19/20. PAGE 157 H3130
POL/PAR NAT/G LEGIS PARL/PROC

B61
WILLSON F.M.G.,ADMINISTRATORS IN ACTION. UK MARKET TEC/DEV PARL/PROC 20. PAGE 169 H3376
ADMIN NAT/G CONSTN

S61
LOEWENBERG G.,"PARLIAMENTARISM IN WESTERN GERMANY: THE FUNCTIONING OF THE BUNDESTAG" (BMR)" GERMANY/W NAT/G POL/PAR CHIEF LEAD 20 PARLIAMENT. PAGE 98 H1952
LEGIS CHOOSE CONSTN PARL/PROC

C61
LAPONCE J.A.,"THE GOVERNMENT OF THE FIFTH REPUBLIC." FRANCE CHIEF LEGIS PARL/PROC CHOOSE ...CHARTS GP/COMP IDEA/COMP BIBLIOG/A 20. PAGE 91 H1814
POL/PAR NAT/G CONSTN DOMIN

C61
MOODIE G.C.,"THE GOVERNMENT OF GREAT BRITAIN." UK LAW STRUCT LOC/G POL/PAR DIPLOM RECEIVE ADMIN COLONIAL CHOOSE...BIBLIOG 20 PARLIAMENT. PAGE 112 H2247
NAT/G SOCIETY PARL/PROC GOV/COMP

B62
ANDREWS W.G.,EUROPEAN POLITICAL INSTITUTIONS. FRANCE GERMANY UK USSR TOP/EX LEAD PARL/PROC CHOOSE 20. PAGE 7 H0139
NAT/COMP POL/PAR EX/STRUC LEGIS

B62
BROWN S.D.,STUDIES ON ASIA, 1962. ASIA BURMA INDIA ISLAM ISRAEL S/ASIA ECO/UNDEV POL/PAR SECT ECO/TAC ...ANTHOL 20 CHINJAP. PAGE 22 H0450
PWR PARL/PROC

B62
KASTARI P.,LA PRESIDENCE DE LA REPUBLIQUE EN FINLANDE. FINLAND CONSTN NAT/G POL/PAR LEGIS LEGIT ATTIT...JURID CONCPT 20 PRESIDENT. PAGE 83 H1666
PARL/PROC CHIEF PWR DECISION

B62
RUDE G.,WILKES AND LIBERTY. UK NAT/G POL/PAR REPRESENT ORD/FREE...SOC 18. PAGE 136 H2711
PARL/PROC CHOOSE STRATA STRUCT

B62
SCALAPINO R.A.,PARTIES AND POLITICS IN CONTEMPORARY JAPAN. EX/STRUC DIPLOM CHOOSE NAT/LISM ATTIT ...POLICY 20 CHINJAP. PAGE 138 H2762
POL/PAR PARL/PROC ELITES DECISION

S62
ROSE R.,"THE POLITICAL IDEALS OF ENGLISH PARTY ACTIVISTS" (BMR)" UK PARL/PROC PARTIC ATTIT ROLE ...SAMP/SIZ CHARTS 20. PAGE 134 H2673
POL/PAR LOBBY REPRESENT NAT/G

B63
MERKL P.H.,THE ORIGIN OF THE WEST GERMAN REPUBLIC. GERMANY/W WOR+45 POL/PAR DIPLOM LEAD LOBBY REPRESENT GP/REL NAT/LISM 20. PAGE 109 H2179
CONSTN PARL/PROC CONTROL BAL/PWR

B63
RICHARDSON H.G.,THE ADMINISTRATION OF IRELAND 1172-1377. IRELAND CONSTN EX/STRUC LEGIS JUDGE CT/SYS PARL/PROC...CHARTS BIBLIOG 12/14. PAGE 131 H2621
ADMIN NAT/G PWR

B63
SHANKS M.,THE LESSONS OF PUBLIC ENTERPRISE. UK LEGIS WORKER ECO/TAC ADMIN PARL/PROC GOV/REL ATTIT ...POLICY MGT METH/COMP NAT/COMP ANTHOL 20 PARLIAMENT. PAGE 142 H2840
SOCISM OWN NAT/G INDUS

B63
WHEARE K.C.,LEGISLATURES. POL/PAR DELIB/GP WAR PEACE CONCPT. PAGE 167 H3338
LEGIS PARL/PROC JURID GOV/COMP

S63
LAMBERT D.,"LA TRANSPOSITION DU REGIME PRESIDENTIEL HORS DES ETATSUNIS; LE CAS DE L'AMERIQUE LATINE." NAT/G EX/STRUC LEGIS PARL/PROC PWR 18/20 PRESIDENT CENTRAL/AM SOUTH/AMER. PAGE 90 H1800
DELIB/GP CHIEF L/A+17C GOV/REL

B64
ALDEFER H.F.,A BIBLIOGRAPHY OF AFRICAN GOVERNMENT: 1950-1964. ALGERIA GUINEA LIBERIA UAR ECO/UNDEV POL/PAR LEGIS COLONIAL LEAD PARL/PROC NAT/LISM 20. PAGE 5 H0098
BIBLIOG AFR LOC/G NAT/G

B64
AVASTHI A.,ASPECTS OF ADMINISTRATION. INDIA UK USA+45 FINAN ACADEM DELIB/GP LEGIS RECEIVE PARL/PROC PRIVIL...NAT/COMP 20. PAGE 9 H0183
MGT ADMIN SOC/WK ORD/FREE

B64
BAGEHOT W.,THE ENGLISH CONSTITUTION. UK CHIEF CONSULT LEGIS BAL/PWR PWR...BIBLIOG 18/19 PARLIAMENT. PAGE 10 H0198
CONSTN PARL/PROC NAT/G CONCPT

B64
BAUCHET P.,ECONOMIC PLANNING. FRANCE STRATA LG/CO CAP/ISM ADMIN PARL/PROC DEMAND OPTIMAL ATTIT PWR SOCISM...POLICY CHARTS 20. PAGE 12 H0238
ECO/DEV NAT/G PLAN ECO/TAC

B64
DOWNIE R.S.,GOVERNMENT ACTION AND MORALITY: SOME PRINCIPLES AND CONCEPTS OF LIBERAL-DEMOCRACY. UK PARL/PROC ATTIT ROLE...MAJORIT DECISION CONCPT 20. PAGE 42 H0845
NAT/G MORAL POLICY GEN/LAWS

B64
FORBES A.H.,CURRENT RESEARCH IN BRITISH STUDIES. UK CONSTN CULTURE POL/PAR SECT DIPLOM ADMIN...JURID BIOG WORSHIP 20. PAGE 52 H1034
BIBLIOG PERSON NAT/G PARL/PROC

B64
GESELLSCHAFT RECHTSVERGLEICH,BIBLIOGRAPHIE DES DEUTSCHEN RECHTS (BIBLIOGRAPHY OF GERMAN LAW, TRANS. BY COURTLAND PETERSON). GERMANY FINAN INDUS LABOR SECT FORCES CT/SYS PARL/PROC CRIME...INT/LAW SOC NAT/COMP 20. PAGE 56 H1117
BIBLIOG/A JURID CONSTN ADMIN

B64
GROVES H.E.,THE CONSTITUTION OF MALAYSIA. MALAYSIA POL/PAR CHIEF CONSULT DELIB/GP CT/SYS PARL/PROC CHOOSE FEDERAL ORD/FREE 20. PAGE 62 H1238
CONSTN NAT/G LAW

B64
HALLER W.,DER SCHWEDISCHE JUSTITIEOMBUDSMAN. DENMARK FINLAND NORWAY SWEDEN LEGIS ADJUD CONTROL PERSON ORD/FREE...NAT/COMP 20 OMBUDSMAN. PAGE 64 H1288
JURID PARL/PROC ADMIN CHIEF

B64
HOPKINSON T.,SOUTH AFRICA. SOUTH/AFR UK NAT/G POL/PAR LEGIS ECO/TAC PARL/PROC WAR...JURID AUD/VIS 19/20. PAGE 73 H1467
SOCIETY RACE/REL DISCRIM

B64
KAACK H.,DIE PARTEIEN IN DER VERFASSUNGSWIRKLICHKEIT DER BUNDESREPUBLIK. GERMANY/W ADMIN PARL/PROC CHOOSE...JURID 20. PAGE 82 H1646
POL/PAR PROVS NAT/G

B64
LEDERMAN W.R.,THE COURTS AND THE CANDIAN CONSTITUTION. CANADA PARL/PROC...POLICY JURID GOV/COMP ANTHOL 19/20 SUPREME/CT PARLIAMENT. PAGE 93 H1854
CONSTN CT/SYS LEGIS LAW

B64
MAHAR J.M.,INDIA: A CRITICAL BIBLIOGRAPHY. INDIA PAKISTAN CULTURE ECO/UNDEV LOC/G POL/PAR SECT PROB/SOLV DIPLOM ADMIN COLONIAL PARL/PROC ATTIT 20. PAGE 101 H2016
BIBLIOG/A S/ASIA NAT/G LEAD

B64
NEWARK F.H.,NOTES ON IRISH LEGAL HISTORY (2ND ED.). IRELAND UK PARL/PROC ORD/FREE SOVEREIGN 12/20 ENGLSH/LAW. PAGE 117 H2344
CT/SYS JURID ADJUD NAT/G

B64
NICOL D.,AFRICA - A SUBJECTIVE VIEW. AFR INT/ORG PLAN ADMIN COLONIAL PARL/PROC PARTIC REGION GOV/REL LITERACY ATTIT...BIBLIOG 20 CIVIL/SERV. PAGE 118 H2350
NAT/G LEAD CULTURE ACADEM

B64
O'HEARN P.J.T.,PEACE, ORDER AND GOOD GOVERNMENT; A NEW CONSTITUTION FOR CANADA. CANADA EX/STRUC LEGIS CT/SYS PARL/PROC...BIBLIOG 20. PAGE 120 H2388
NAT/G CONSTN LAW CREATE

B64
QUIGG P.W.,AFRICA: A FOREIGN AFFAIRS READER. AFR FRANCE PORTUGAL UK DIPLOM LEAD PARL/PROC MARXISM ...MAJORIT METH/CNCPT GOV/COMP IDEA/COMP ANTHOL 19/20. PAGE 129 H2575
COLONIAL SOVEREIGN NAT/LISM RACE/REL

B64
SIEKANOWICZ P.,LEGAL SOURCES AND BIBLIOGRAPHY OF POLAND. COM POLAND CONSTN NAT/G PARL/PROC SANCTION CRIME MARXISM 16/20. PAGE 143 H2870
BIBLIOG ADJUD LAW JURID

B64
SZLADITS C.,BIBLIOGRAPHY ON FOREIGN AND COMPARATIVE LAW: BOOKS AND ARTICLES IN ENGLISH (SUPPLEMENT 1962). FINAN INDUS JUDGE LICENSE ADMIN CT/SYS PARL/PROC OWN...INT/LAW CLASSIF METH/COMP NAT/COMP 20. PAGE 151 H3027
BIBLIOG/A JURID ADJUD LAW

B64
TINKER H.,BALLOT BOX AND BAYONET - PEOPLE AND GOVERNMENT IN EMERGENT ASIAN COUNTRIES. CEYLON INDIA INDONESIA PHILIPPINE POL/PAR ADMIN COLONIAL LEAD PARL/PROC CHOOSE CONSEN ORD/FREE SOVEREIGN PLURISM...GOV/COMP THIRD/WRLD. PAGE 155 H3104
MYTH S/ASIA NAT/COMP NAT/LISM

S64
GIROD R.,"LE SYSTEME DES PARTIS EN SUISSE." CONSTN LOC/G DELIB/GP FEDERAL ALL/VALS. PAGE 57 H1136
POL/PAR LEGIS NAT/G PARL/PROC

B65
BULMER-THOMAS I.,THE GROWTH OF THE BRITISH PARTY SYSTEM (VOL. II) 1924-1964. UK ECO/DEV BARGAIN WAR
CHIEF POL/PAR

CHOOSE ATTIT ORD/FREE 20 LABOR/PAR CONSRV/PAR. PAGE 23 H0472 — PARL/PROC NAT/G

B65
CAMERON W.J.,NEW ZEALAND. NEW/ZEALND S/ASIA DIPLOM INT/TRADE WRITING COLONIAL PARL/PROC...GEOG CMN/WLTH. PAGE 26 H0513 — SOCIETY GP/REL STRUCT

B65
CARTER G.M.,GOVERNMENT AND POLITICS IN THE TWENTIETH CENTURY (REV. ED.). WOR+45 NAT/G POL/PAR LEGIS DIPLOM LEAD PARL/PROC CHOOSE TOTALISM 20. PAGE 27 H0549 — GOV/COMP ECO/UNDEV ALL/IDEOS ECO/DEV

B65
GEORGE M.,THE WARPED VISION. EUR+WWI UK NAT/G POL/PAR LEGIS PARL/PROC SANCTION COERCE WAR GOV/REL PEACE RESPECT 20 CONSRV/PAR. PAGE 56 H1113 — LEAD ATTIT DIPLOM POLICY

B65
GILG P.,DIE ERNEUERUNG DES DEMOKRATISCHEN DENKENS IM WILHELMINISCHEN DEUTSCHLAND. GERMANY PARL/PROC CHOOSE REPRESENT...CONCPT 19/20 BISMARCK/O WILHELM/II. PAGE 56 H1126 — POL/PAR ORD/FREE NAT/G

B65
KOUSOULAS D.G.,REVOLUTION AND DEFEAT; THE STORY OF THE GREEK COMMUNIST PARTY. GREECE INT/ORG EX/STRUC DIPLOM FOR/AID EDU/PROP PARL/PROC ADJUST ATTIT 20 COM/PARTY. PAGE 88 H1759 — REV MARXISM POL/PAR ORD/FREE

B65
NAMIER L.B.,THE STRUCTURE OF POLITICS AT THE ACCESSION OF GEORGE III. UK LOC/G TOP/EX COLONIAL LEAD PARTIC REV CHOOSE REPRESENT GOV/REL PERSON SOVEREIGN...GOV/COMP 18 PARLIAMENT. PAGE 115 H2309 — PARL/PROC LEGIS NAT/G POL/PAR

B65
PELLING H.,A SHORT HISTORY OF THE LABOUR PARTY (2ND ED.). UK NAT/G CHIEF PARL/PROC GP/REL INGP/REL 20 LABOR/PAR PARLIAMENT WILSON/H. PAGE 124 H2484 — POL/PAR NEW/LIB LEAD LABOR

B65
PYLEE M.V.,CONSTITUTIONAL GOVERNMENT IN INDIA (2ND REV. ED.). INDIA POL/PAR EX/STRUC DIPLOM COLONIAL CT/SYS PARL/PROC PRIVIL...JURID 16/20. PAGE 128 H2569 — CONSTN NAT/G PROVS FEDERAL

B65
RUBINSTEIN A.Z.,THE CHALLENGE OF POLITICS: IDEAS AND ISSUES (2ND ED.). UNIV ELITES SOCIETY EX/STRUC BAL/PWR PARL/PROC AUTHORIT...DECISION ANTHOL 20. PAGE 136 H2709 — NAT/G DIPLOM GP/REL ORD/FREE

B65
SAKAI R.K.,STUDIES ON ASIA, 1965. INDIA KOREA S/ASIA USA+45 CONSTN KIN SECT PARTIC SUFF NAT/LISM ...POLICY SOC 19/20 CHINJAP. PAGE 137 H2737 — PARL/PROC ASIA

B65
SHARMA S.A.,PARLIAMENTARY GOVERNMENT IN INDIA. INDIA FINAN LOC/G PROVS DELIB/GP PLAN ADMIN CT/SYS FEDERAL...JURID 20. PAGE 142 H2849 — NAT/G CONSTN PARL/PROC LEGIS

B66
AGGARWALA R.N.,FINANCIAL COMMITTEES OF THE INDIAN PARLIAMENT: A STUDY IN PARLIAMENTARY CONTROL OVER PUBLIC EXPENDITURE. INDIA FINAN NAT/G ROLE...CHARTS METH/COMP METH 20 PARLIAMENT. PAGE 4 H0078 — PARL/PROC BUDGET CONTROL DELIB/GP

B66
ANDERSON S.V.,CANADIAN OMBUDSMAN PROPOSALS. CANADA LEGIS DEBATE PARL/PROC...MAJORIT JURID TIME/SEQ IDEA/COMP 20 OMBUDSMAN PARLIAMENT. PAGE 7 H0133 — NAT/G CREATE ADMIN POL/PAR

B66
CHAPMAN B.,THE PROFESSION OF GOVERNMENT: THE PUBLIC SERVICE IN EUROPE. CONSTN NAT/G POL/PAR EX/STRUC LEGIS TOP/EX PROB/SOLV DEBATE EXEC PARL/PROC PARTIC 20. PAGE 29 H0581 — BIBLIOG ADMIN EUR+WWI GOV/COMP

B66
DALLIN A.,POLITICS IN THE SOVIET UNION: 7 CASES. COM USSR LAW POL/PAR CHIEF FORCES WRITING CONTROL PARL/PROC CIVMIL/REL TOTALISM...ANTHOL 20 KHRUSH/N STALIN/J CASEBOOK COM/PARTY. PAGE 37 H0736 — MARXISM DOMIN ORD/FREE GOV/REL

B66
DEXTER N.C.,GUIDE TO CONTEMPORARY POLITICS. EUR+WWI UK PARL/PROC GP/REL KNOWL...POLICY MAJORIT IDEA/COMP 20. PAGE 41 H0815 — POL/PAR CONCPT NAT/G

B66
GRAHAM B.D.,THE FORMATION OF THE AUSTRALIAN COUNTRY PARTIES. CANADA USA+45 USA-45 SOCIETY PLAN ECO/TAC ...NAT/COMP 20 AUSTRAL. PAGE 59 H1190 — POL/PAR AGRI REGION PARL/PROC

B66
INTERPARLIAMENTARY UNION,PARLIAMENTS: COMPARATIVE STUDY ON STRUCTURE AND FUNCTIONING OF REPRESENTATIVE INSTITUTIONS IN FIFTY-FIVE COUNTRIES. WOR+45 POL/PAR DELIB/GP BUDGET ADMIN CONTROL CHOOSE. PAGE 78 H1560 — PARL/PROC LEGIS GOV/COMP EX/STRUC

B66
LEROY P.,L'ORGANIZATION CONSTITUTIONNELLE ET LES CRISES. FRANCE NAT/G ADJUD CONTROL PARL/PROC WAR ...POLICY BIBLIOG 20. PAGE 95 H1892 — CONSTN PWR EXEC LEGIS

B66
LOVEDAY P.,PARLIAMENT FACTIONS AND PARTIES: THE FIRST THIRTY YEARS OF RESPONSIBLE GOVERNMENT IN NEW SOUTH WALES, 1856-1889. PROVS LEAD PARL/PROC PARTIC GP/REL INGP/REL MAJORITY PWR...GP/COMP 19 AUSTRAL. PAGE 99 H1970 — POL/PAR ELITES NAT/G LEGIS

B66
POLE J.R.,POLITICAL REPRESENTATION IN ENGLAND AND THE ORIGINS OF THE AMERICAN REPUBLIC. UK USA-45 CONSTN ELITES NAT/G POL/PAR LEGIS PARL/PROC ...MAJORIT 17/19. PAGE 127 H2534 — REPRESENT GOV/COMP

B66
RICHERT F.,DIE NATIONALE WELLE. GERMANY GERMANY/W PARL/PROC ORD/FREE FASCISM...TREND 19/20. PAGE 131 H2622 — POL/PAR ATTIT NAT/LISM NAT/G

B66
TIVEY L.J.,NATIONALISATION IN BRITISH INDUSTRY. UK LEGIS PARL/PROC GP/REL OWN ATTIT SOCISM 20. PAGE 156 H3109 — NAT/G INDUS CONTROL LG/CO

S66
MANSERGH N.,"THE PARTITION OF INDIA IN RETROSPECT." INDIA PAKISTAN S/ASIA UK DIPLOM COLONIAL GP/REL PWR 20. PAGE 102 H2042 — NAT/G PARL/PROC POLICY POL/PAR

B67
ANDERSON O.,A LIBERAL STATE AT WAR. MOD/EUR UK LAW CULTURE STRUCT ECO/DEV NAT/G DIPLOM PARL/PROC GP/REL ALL/VALS...CONCPT 19. PAGE 7 H0131 — WAR FORCES

B67
ANDERSON S.V.,THE NORDIC COUNCIL: A STUDY OF SCANDINAVIAN REGIONALISM. DENMARK FINLAND ICELAND NORWAY SWEDEN MARKET NAT/G VOL/ASSN CONSULT PARL/PROC ATTIT...TIME/SEQ BIBLIOG 20. PAGE 7 H0134 — INT/ORG REGION DIPLOM LEGIS

B67
BROWN L.N.,FRENCH ADMINISTRATIVE LAW. FRANCE UK CONSTN NAT/G LEGIS DOMIN CONTROL EXEC PARL/PROC PWR ...JURID METH/COMP GEN/METH. PAGE 22 H0447 — EX/STRUC LAW IDEA/COMP CT/SYS

B67
KORNBERG A.,CANADIAN LEGISLATIVE BEHAVIOR: A STUDY OF THE 25TH PARLIAMENT. CANADA NAT/G POL/PAR PARL/PROC CHOOSE INGP/REL ADJUST ANOMIE RIGID/FLEX ...SOC STAND/INT CHARTS SOC/EXP 20 PARLIAMENT. PAGE 88 H1756 — ATTIT LEGIS ROLE

B67
MORRIS A.J.A.,PARLIAMENTARY DEMOCRACY IN THE NINETEENTH CENTURY. UK INDUS LOC/G NAT/G POL/PAR CONSULT LEGIS INT/TRADE ADMIN CHOOSE SUFF SOVEREIGN 19 PARLIAMENT. PAGE 113 H2261 — TIME/SEQ CONSTN PARL/PROC POPULISM

B67
SCHWARTZ B.,THE ROOTS OF FREEDOM: A CONSTITUTIONAL HISTORY OF ENGLAND. UK LAW POL/PAR DELIB/GP LEGIS REV REPRESENT...JURID BIBLIOG/A 13/20. PAGE 140 H2809 — CONSTN PARL/PROC NAT/G

B67
WALTZ K.N.,FOREIGN POLICY AND DEMOCRATIC POLITICS: THE AMERICAN AND BRITISH EXPERIENCE. FRANCE UK USA+45 PARL/PROC GOV/REL CONSERVE...DECISION 20. PAGE 165 H3298 — POLICY DIPLOM NAT/G GOV/COMP

S67
BAIKALOV A.,"EMERGENCY LEGISLATION IN WEST GERMANY." GERMANY/W LABOR NAT/G POL/PAR SANCTION ...MARXIST 20. PAGE 10 H0199 — LAW TOTALISM LEGIS PARL/PROC

S67
BRADLEY A.W.,"CONSTITUTION-MAKING IN UGANDA." UGANDA LAW CHIEF DELIB/GP LEGIS ADMIN EXEC PARL/PROC RACE/REL ORD/FREE...GOV/COMP 20. PAGE 20 H0397 — NAT/G CREATE CONSTN FEDERAL

S67
LEGRES A.,"LES FONCTIONS D'UN PARLEMENT MODERNE." FRANCE DEBATE PARL/PROC SANCTION ATTIT PWR 20 PARLIAMENT. PAGE 93 H1860 — NAT/G LAW LEGIS CHOOSE

S67
LEHMBRUCH G.,"WAHLREFORM UND POLITISCHES SYSTEM." NETHERLAND NAT/G LEGIS PARL/PROC...SOC 20. PAGE 93 H1864 — CHOOSE POL/PAR METH/CNCPT GP/COMP

S67
STRAFFORD P.,"FRENCH ELECTIONS." FRANCE NAT/G CHIEF LEGIS BAL/PWR ECO/TAC PARL/PROC PARTIC ATTIT 20. PAGE 150 H2993 — POL/PAR SOCISM CENTRAL MARXISM

S67
WHITE W.L.,"THE TREASURY BOARD AND PARLIAMENT." CANADA CONSTN CONSULT LEGIS LEAD PARL/PROC GP/REL ...DECISION 20. PAGE 167 H3351 — FINAN DELIB/GP NAT/G ADMIN

S67
YEFROMEV A.,"THE TRUE FACE OF THE WEST GERMAN NATIONAL-DEMOCRATS." GERMANY/W NAT/G DOMIN LEAD SANCTION WAR ATTIT PERSON...MARXIST 20. PAGE 172 H3436 — POL/PAR TOTALISM PARL/PROC DIPLOM

B79
BRODERICK G.C.,POLITICAL STUDIES. IRELAND UK ROMAN/EMP LAW ACADEM LOC/G NAT/G DIPLOM PARL/PROC SUFF GP/REL LAISSEZ...ANTHOL. PAGE 21 H0424 — CONSTN COLONIAL

B87
KINNEAR J.B.,PRINCIPLES OF CIVIL GOVERNMENT. MOD/EUR USA-45 CONSTN LOC/G EX/STRUC ADMIN PARL/PROC RACE/REL...CONCPT 18/19. PAGE 86 H1718 — POL/PAR NAT/G GOV/COMP REPRESENT

B91
SIDGWICK H.,THE ELEMENTS OF POLITICS. LOC/G NAT/G LEGIS DIPLOM ADJUD CONTROL EXEC PARL/PROC REPRESENT GOV/REL SOVEREIGN ALL/IDEOS 19 MILL/JS BENTHAM/J. PAGE 143 H2868 — POLICY LAW CONCPT

B94
BENOIST C.,LA POLITIQUE. FRANCE LAW SOCIETY STRUCT POL/PAR PARL/PROC GP/REL ATTIT PWR 19/20. PAGE 14 H0283 — NAT/G REPRESENT ORD/FREE

B96
ESMEIN A.,ELEMENTS DE DROIT CONSTITUTIONNEL. FRANCE UK CHIEF EX/STRUC LEGIS ADJUD CT/SYS PARL/PROC REV GOV/REL ORD/FREE...JURID METH/COMP 18/19. PAGE 47 H0940 — LAW CONSTN NAT/G CONCPT

B96
LOWELL A.L.,GOVERNMENTS AND PARTIES IN CONTINENTAL EUROPE (VOL. I). MOD/EUR LOC/G NAT/G SECT CHIEF LEGIS PARL/PROC GOV/REL...POLICY 19. PAGE 99 H1973 — POL/PAR GOV/COMP CONSTN EX/STRUC

B96
LOWELL A.L.,GOVERNMENTS AND PARTIES IN CONTINENTAL EUROPE, VOL. II. AUSTRIA GERMANY HUNGARY MOD/EUR SWITZERLND SOCIETY EX/STRUC LEGIS DIPLOM AGREE LEAD PARL/PROC PWR...POLICY 19. PAGE 99 H1974 — POL/PAR NAT/G GOV/REL ELITES

PARLIAMENTARY PROCESSES....SEE PARL/PROC

PARLIAMENT....PARLIAMENT (ALL NATIONS); SEE ALSO LEGIS

N
CANADIAN GOVERNMENT PUBLICATIONS (1955-). CANADA AGRI FINAN LABOR FORCES INT/TRADE HEALTH...JURID 20 PARLIAMENT. PAGE 1 H0003 — BIBLIOG/A NAT/G DIPLOM INT/ORG

NSY
MACKENZIE K.R.,THE ENGLISH PARLIAMENT. UK POL/PAR CHIEF DIPLOM TAX TASK WAR AUTHORIT...POLICY TREND 12/20 PARLIAMENT. PAGE 100 H2000 — ORD/FREE LEGIS NAT/G

B02
SEELEY J.R.,THE EXPANSION OF ENGLAND. MOD/EUR S/ASIA UK CULTURE NAT/G FORCES PLAN DOMIN EDU/PROP COLONIAL ROUTINE ATTIT ALL/VALS SOVEREIGN...CONCPT HIST/WRIT PARLIAMENT 18 CMN/WLTH. PAGE 141 H2819 — INT/ORG ACT/RES CAP/ISM INDIA

B03
FAGUET E.,LE LIBERALISME. FRANCE PRESS ADJUD ADMIN DISCRIM CONSERVE SOCISM...TRADIT SOC LING WORSHIP PARLIAMENT. PAGE 48 H0960 — ORD/FREE EDU/PROP NAT/G LAW

B10
MCILWAIN C.H.,THE HIGH COURT OF PARLIAMENT AND ITS SUPREMACY B1910 1878 408. UK EX/STRUC PARL/PROC GOV/REL INGP/REL PRIVIL 12/20 PARLIAMENT ENGLSH/LAW. PAGE 107 H2132 — LAW LEGIS CONSTN NAT/G

B10
TEMPERLEY H.W.V.,SENATES AND UPPER CHAMBERS; THEIR USE AND FUNCTION IN THE MODERN STATE... UK WOR-45 CONSTN NAT/G POL/PAR PROVS SECT COLONIAL LEAD CHOOSE REPRESENT PWR...BIBLIOG 19/20 PARLIAMENT SENATE CMN/WLTH HOUSE/LORD. PAGE 153 H3059 — PARL/PROC NAT/COMP LEGIS EX/STRUC

B13
BARDOUX J.,L'ANGLETERRE RADICALE; ESSAI DE LA PSYCHOLOGIE SOCIALE (1906-1913). UK CONSTN NAT/G WORKER CREATE BUDGET ECO/TAC ATTIT...POLICY 20 PARLIAMENT LABOR/PAR STRIKE NAVY. PAGE 11 H0215 — POL/PAR CHOOSE COLONIAL LEGIS

N19
ADMINISTRATIVE STAFF COLLEGE,THE ACCOUNTABILITY OF GOVERNMENT DEPARTMENTS (PAMPHLET) (REV. ED.). UK CONSTN FINAN NAT/G CONSULT ADMIN INGP/REL CONSEN PRIVIL 20 PARLIAMENT. PAGE 3 H0070 — PARL/PROC ELITES SANCTION PROB/SOLV

B24
BAGEHOT W.,THE ENGLISH CONSTITUTION AND OTHER POLITICAL ESSAYS. UK DELIB/GP BAL/PWR ADMIN CONTROL EXEC ROUTINE CONSERVE...METH PARLIAMENT 19/20. PAGE 10 H0197 — NAT/G STRUCT CONCPT

B24
HOLDSWORTH W.S.,A HISTORY OF ENGLISH LAW; THE COMMON LAW AND ITS RIVALS (VOL. IV). UK SEA AGRI CHIEF ADJUD CONTROL CRIME GOV/REL...INT/LAW JURID NAT/COMP 16/17 PARLIAMENT COMMON/LAW CANON/LAW ENGLSH/LAW. PAGE 72 H1449 — LAW LEGIS CT/SYS CONSTN

B25
TEMPERLEY H.,THE FOREIGN POLICY OF CANNING: 1822-1827. MOD/EUR NAT/G TOP/EX EDU/PROP ROUTINE ATTIT RIGID/FLEX SUPEGO PWR SKILL...TIME/SEQ PARLIAMENT 20. PAGE 153 H3058 — PERSON DIPLOM UK BIOG

B26
POLLARD A.F.,THE EVOLUTION OF PARLIAMENT. UK CONSTN POL/PAR EX/STRUC GOV/REL INGP/REL PRIVIL RIGID/FLEX ...TIME/SEQ 11/20 CMN/WLTH PARLIAMENT. PAGE 127 H2536 — LEGIS PARL/PROC NAT/G

B27
FLOURNOY F.,PARLIAMENT AND WAR. MOD/EUR UK NAT/G FORCES LEGIS TOP/EX DIPLOM LEGIT DEBATE ATTIT RIGID/FLEX PWR...DECISION TIME/SEQ PARLIAMENT 19/20. PAGE 52 H1032 — COERCE WAR

B27
GOOCH G.P.,ENGLISH DEMOCRATIC IDEAS IN THE SEVENTEENTH CENTURY (2ND ED.). UK LAW SECT FORCES DIPLOM LEAD PARL/PROC REV ATTIT AUTHORIT...ANARCH CONCPT 17 PARLIAMENT CMN/WLTH REFORMERS. PAGE 58 H1167 — IDEA/COMP MAJORIT EX/STRUC CONSERVE

C28
SCHNEIDER H.W.,"MAKING THE FASCIST STATE." ITALY CULTURE LABOR DIPLOM REV WAR NAT/LISM TOTALISM ATTIT DRIVE SOCISM...BIBLIOG PARLIAMENT 20. PAGE 140 H2792 — FASCISM POLICY POL/PAR

B29
CAM H.M.,BIBLIOGRAPHY OF ENGLISH CONSTITUTIONAL HISTORY (PAMPHLET). UK LAW LOC/G NAT/G POL/PAR SECT DELIB/GP ADJUD ORD/FREE 19/20 PARLIAMENT. PAGE 25 H0510 — BIBLIOG/A CONSTN ADMIN PARL/PROC

B32
GREAT BRIT COMM MINISTERS PWR,REPORT. UK LAW CONSTN CONSULT LEGIS PARL/PROC SANCTION SOVEREIGN ...DECISION JURID 20 PARLIAMENT. PAGE 60 H1201 — EX/STRUC NAT/G PWR CONTROL

B32
MCKISACK M.,THE PARLIAMENTARY REPRESENTATION OF THE ENGLISH BOROUGHS DURING THE MIDDLE AGES. UK CONSTN CULTURE ELITES EX/STRUC TAX PAY ADJUD PARL/PROC APPORT FEDERAL...POLICY 13/15 PARLIAMENT. PAGE 107 H2139 — NAT/G MUNIC LEGIS CHOOSE

L34
GOSNELL H.F.,"BRITISH ROYAL COMMISSIONS OF INQUIRY" UK CONSTN LEGIS PRESS ADMIN PARL/PROC...DECISION 20 PARLIAMENT. PAGE 59 H1184 — DELIB/GP INSPECT POLICY NAT/G

B36
CLOKIE H.M.,THE ORIGIN AND NATURE OF CONSTITUTIONAL GOVERNMENT. UK NAT/G POL/PAR CONSULT LEGIS ...GOV/COMP 14/20 CABINET PARLIAMENT. PAGE 30 H0606 — CONCPT CONSTN PARL/PROC

B38
HOLDSWORTH W.S.,A HISTORY OF ENGLISH LAW; THE CENTURIES OF SETTLEMENT AND REFORM (VOL. X). INDIA UK CONSTN NAT/G CHIEF LEGIS ADMIN COLONIAL CT/SYS CHOOSE ORD/FREE PWR...JURID 18 PARLIAMENT COMMONWLTH COMMON/LAW. PAGE 72 H1451 — LAW LOC/G EX/STRUC ADJUD

B38
HOLDSWORTH W.S.,A HISTORY OF ENGLISH LAW; THE CENTURIES OF SETTLEMENT AND REFORM (VOL. XI). UK CONSTN NAT/G EX/STRUC DIPLOM ADJUD CT/SYS LEAD CRIME ATTIT...INT/LAW JURID 18 CMN/WLTH PARLIAMENT ENGLSH/LAW. PAGE 73 H1452 — LAW COLONIAL LEGIS PARL/PROC

B39
JENNINGS W.I.,PARLIAMENT. UK POL/PAR OP/RES BUDGET LEAD CHOOSE GP/REL...MGT 20 PARLIAMENT HOUSE/LORD HOUSE/CMNS. PAGE 80 H1609 — PARL/PROC LEGIS CONSTN NAT/G

B43
MC DOWELL R.B.,IRISH PUBLIC OPINION, 1750-1800. IRELAND CONSTN VOL/ASSN WORKER ORD/FREE CATHISM CONSERVE...POLICY IDEA/COMP BIBLIOG 18/ PARLIAMENT. PAGE 106 H2118 — ATTIT NAT/G DIPLOM REV

S43
PRICE D.K.,"THE PARLIAMENTARY AND PRESIDENTIAL SYSTEMS" (BMR)" USA-45 NAT/G EX/STRUC PARL/PROC GOV/REL PWR 20 PRESIDENT CONGRESS PARLIAMENT. PAGE 128 H2561 — LEGIS REPRESENT ADMIN GOV/COMP

B50
DUCLOS P.,L'EVOLUTION DES RAPPORTS POLITIQUES DEPUIS 1750 (LIBERTE, INTEGRATION, UNITE). LAW INT/ORG FEDERAL TOTALISM ATTIT PWR...MAJORIT BIBLIOG 18/20 PARLIAMENT EUROPE. PAGE 43 H0852 — ORD/FREE DIPLOM NAT/G GOV/COMP

B50
LYONS F.S.L.,THE IRISH PARLIAMENTARY PARTY, 1890-1910: STUDIES IN IRISH HISTORY (VOL. 4). IRELAND DELIB/GP LEGIS PAY EDU/PROP ADMIN GP/REL ATTIT...BIBLIOG 19/20 PARLIAMENT PARNELL/CS DIRECT/NAT. PAGE 99 H1986 — POL/PAR CHOOSE NAT/G POLICY

B50
WADE E.C.S.,CONSTITUTIONAL LAW; AN OUTLINE OF THE LAW AND PRACTICE OF THE CONSTITUTION. UK LEGIS DOMIN ADMIN GP/REL 16/20 CMN/WLTH PARLIAMENT ENGLSH/LAW. PAGE 164 H3283 — CONSTN NAT/G PARL/PROC LAW

B51
HALEVY E.,IMPERIALISM AND THE RISE OF LABOR (2ND ED.). UK NAT/G POL/PAR TOP/EX ATTIT ORD/FREE PWR 19/20 PARLIAMENT LABOR/PAR. PAGE 64 H1284 — COLONIAL LABOR POLICY WAR

B52
HIMMELFARB G.,LORD ACTON: A STUDY IN CONSCIENCE AND POLITICS. MOD/EUR NAT/G POL/PAR SECT LEGIS TOP/EX EDU/PROP ADMIN NAT/LISM ATTIT PERSON SUPEGO MORAL — PWR BIOG

ORD/FREE...CONCPT PARLIAMENT 19 ACTON/LORD. PAGE 71 H1419

C53
BULNER-THOMAS I.,"THE PARTY SYSTEM IN GREAT BRITAIN." UK CONSTN SECT PRESS CONFER GP/REL ATTIT ...POLICY TREND BIBLIOG 19/20 PARLIAMENT. PAGE 23 H0473
NAT/G POL/PAR ADMIN ROUTINE

B54
JENNINGS I.,THE QUEEN'S GOVERNMENT. UK POL/PAR DELIB/GP ADJUD ADMIN CT/SYS PARL/PROC REPRESENT CONSERVE 13/20 PARLIAMENT. PAGE 80 H1605
NAT/G CONSTN LEGIS CHIEF

B54
MORRISON H.,GOVERNMENT AND PARLIAMENT. UK NAT/G PARLIAMENT. PAGE 113 H2266
GOV/REL EX/STRUC LEGIS PARL/PROC

B55
GALLOWAY G.B.,CONGRESS AND PARLIAMENT: THEIR ORGANIZATION AND OPERATION IN THE US AND THE UK: PLANNING PAMPHLET NO. 93. POL/PAR EX/STRUC DEBATE CONTROL LEAD ROUTINE EFFICIENCY PWR...POLICY CONGRESS PARLIAMENT. PAGE 54 H1089
DELIB/GP LEGIS PARL/PROC GOV/COMP

B56
EMDEN C.S.,THE PEOPLE AND THE CONSTITUTION (2ND ED.). UK LEGIS POPULISM 17/20 PARLIAMENT. PAGE 46 H0916
CONSTN PARL/PROC NAT/G LAW

S56
EPSTEIN L.D.,"COHESION OF BRITISH PARLIAMENTARY PARTIES." UK STRUCT ADMIN ROUTINE INGP/REL PWR ...GP/COMP PARLIAMENT. PAGE 47 H0935
NAT/G PARL/PROC POL/PAR

B57
COLE G.D.H.,THE POST WAR CONDITIONS OF BRITAIN. EUR+WWI STRUCT NAT/G PLAN EDU/PROP LEGIT RIGID/FLEX ORD/FREE WEALTH...SOCIALIST WELF/ST STAT TREND CON/ANAL CHARTS PARLIAMENT WORK 20. PAGE 31 H0624
ECO/DEV UK

B58
HANSARD SOCIETY PARL GOVT,WHAT ARE THE PROBLEMS OF PARLIAMENTARY GOVERNMENT IN WEST AFRICA? PROB/SOLV DIPLOM GP/REL 20 PARLIAMENT AFRICA/W. PAGE 66 H1317
PARL/PROC POL/PAR AFR NAT/G

C58
WILDING N.,"AN ENCYCLOPEDIA OF PARLIAMENT." UK LAW CONSTN CHIEF PROB/SOLV DIPLOM DEBATE WAR INGP/REL PRIVIL...BIBLIOG DICTIONARY 13/20 CMN/WLTH PARLIAMENT. PAGE 168 H3363
PARL/PROC POL/PAR NAT/G ADMIN

B59
BUNDESMIN FUR VERTRIEBENE,ZEITTAFEL DER VORGESCHICHTE UND DES ABLAUFS DER VERTREIBUNG SOWIE DER UNTERBRINGUNG UND EINGLIEDERUNG DER (2 VOLS.). GERMANY/E GERMANY/W NAT/G PROVS PROB/SOLV DIPLOM PARL/PROC ATTIT...BIBLIOG SOC/INTEG 20 MIGRATION PARLIAMENT. PAGE 24 H0475
JURID GP/REL INT/LAW

B59
SQUIBB G.D.,THE HIGH COURT OF CHIVALRY. UK NAT/G FORCES ADJUD WAR 14/20 PARLIAMENT ENGLSH/LAW. PAGE 148 H2959
CT/SYS PARL/PROC JURID

B60
BHAMBHRI C.P.,PARLIAMENTARY CONTROL OVER STATE ENTERPRISE IN INDIA. INDIA DELIB/GP ADMIN CONTROL INGP/REL EFFICIENCY 20 PARLIAMENT. PAGE 16 H0327
NAT/G OWN INDUS PARL/PROC

B60
KERSELL J.E.,PARLIAMENTARY SUPERVISION OF DELEGATED LEGISLATION. UK EFFICIENCY PWR...POLICY CHARTS BIBLIOG METH 20 PARLIAMENT. PAGE 85 H1699
LEGIS CONTROL NAT/G EX/STRUC

B60
LASKIN B.,CANADIAN CONSTITUTIONAL LAW: TEXT AND NOTES ON DISTRIBUTION OF LEGISLATIVE POWER (2ND ED.). CANADA LOC/G ECO/TAC TAX CONTROL CT/SYS CRIME FEDERAL PWR...JURID 20 PARLIAMENT. PAGE 92 H1832
CONSTN NAT/G LAW LEGIS

B61
GUIZOT F.P.G.,HISTORY OF THE ORIGIN OF REPRESENTATIVE GOVERNMENT IN EUROPE. CHRIST-17C FRANCE MOD/EUR SPAIN UK LAW CHIEF FORCES POPULISM ...MAJORIT TIME/SEQ GOV/COMP NAT/COMP 4/19 PARLIAMENT. PAGE 62 H1250
LEGIS REPRESENT CONSTN NAT/G

B61
HARE T.,A TREATISE ON THE ELECTION OF REPRESENTATIVES, PARLIAMENTARY AND MUNICIPAL. UK CONSTN NAT/G PARL/PROC CHOOSE ATTIT...MAJORIT 18/19 PARLIAMENT. PAGE 66 H1330
LEGIS GOV/REL CONSEN REPRESENT

B61
MACLEOD I.,NEVILLE CHAMBERLAIN. UK SOCIETY TOP/EX WAR PERSON ALL/VALS ORD/FREE PARLIAMENT 20 CHAMBRLN/N. PAGE 100 H2003
BIOG NAT/G CREATE

B61
MILIBAND R.,PARLIAMENTARY SOCIALISM. EUR+WWI UK EXEC LEAD PARL/PROC GP/REL...POLICY 20 PARLIAMENT LABOR/PAR. PAGE 110 H2203
POL/PAR NAT/G PWR SOCISM

B61
RAO K.V.,PARLIAMENTARY DEMOCRACY OF INDIA. INDIA EX/STRUC TOP/EX COLONIAL CT/SYS PARL/PROC ORD/FREE ...POLICY CONCPT TREND 20 PARLIAMENT. PAGE 130 H2592
CONSTN ADJUD NAT/G FEDERAL

S61
LOEWENBERG G.,"PARLIAMENTARISM IN WESTERN GERMANY: THE FUNCTIONING OF THE BUNDESTAG" (BMR)" GERMANY/W NAT/G POL/PAR CHIEF LEAD 20 PARLIAMENT. PAGE 98 H1952
LEGIS CHOOSE CONSTN PARL/PROC

C61
MOODIE G.C.,"THE GOVERNMENT OF GREAT BRITAIN." UK LAW STRUCT LOC/G POL/PAR DIPLOM RECEIVE ADMIN COLONIAL CHOOSE...BIBLIOG 20 PARLIAMENT. PAGE 112 H2247
NAT/G SOCIETY PARL/PROC GOV/COMP

B62
HANSON A.H.,MANAGERIAL PROBLEMS IN PUBLIC ENTERPRISE. INDIA DELIB/GP GP/REL INGP/REL EFFICIENCY 20 PARLIAMENT. PAGE 66 H1320
MGT NAT/G INDUS PROB/SOLV

S62
THOMPSON D.,"THE UNITED KINGDOM AND THE TREATY OF ROME." EUR+WWI INT/ORG NAT/G DELIB/GP LEGIS INT/TRADE RIGID/FLEX...CONCPT EEC PARLIAMENT CMN/WLTH 20. PAGE 154 H3079
ADJUD JURID

B63
ARAZI A.,LE SYSTEME ELECTORAL ISRAELIEN. ISRAEL NAT/G ADMIN ALL/VALS PARLIAMENT. PAGE 8 H0158
LEGIS CHOOSE POL/PAR

B63
BADI J.,THE GOVERNMENT OF THE STATE OF ISRAEL: A CRITICAL ACCOUNT OF ITS PARLIAMENT, EXECUTIVE, AND JUDICIARY. ISRAEL ECO/DEV CHIEF DELIB/GP LEGIS DIPLOM CT/SYS INGP/REL PEACE ORD/FREE...BIBLIOG 20 PARLIAMENT ARABS MIGRATION. PAGE 10 H0193
NAT/G CONSTN EX/STRUC POL/PAR

B63
GRIMOND J.,THE LIBERAL CHALLENGE. UK SOCIETY INDUS POL/PAR LEGIS PLAN CAP/ISM DIPLOM EDU/PROP GOV/REL CONSERVE 20 PARLIAMENT REFORMERS. PAGE 61 H1227
NAT/G NEW/LIB ECO/DEV POLICY

B63
SHANKS M.,THE LESSONS OF PUBLIC ENTERPRISE. UK LEGIS WORKER ECO/TAC ADMIN PARL/PROC GOV/REL ATTIT ...POLICY MGT METH/COMP NAT/COMP ANTHOL 20 PARLIAMENT. PAGE 142 H2840
SOCISM OWN NAT/G INDUS

S63
EMERI C.,"LES FORCES POLITIQUES AU PARLEMENT" EUR+WWI FRANCE ELITES DELIB/GP TOP/EX LEGIT ATTIT ...SOC 20 PARLIAMENT. PAGE 46 H0917
POL/PAR LEGIS PWR NAT/G

B64
BAGEHOT W.,THE ENGLISH CONSTITUTION. UK CHIEF CONSULT LEGIS BAL/PWR PWR...BIBLIOG 18/19 PARLIAMENT. PAGE 10 H0198
CONSTN PARL/PROC NAT/G CONCPT

B64
LEDERMAN W.R.,THE COURTS AND THE CANDIAN CONSTITUTION. CANADA PARL/PROC...POLICY JURID GOV/COMP ANTHOL 19/20 SUPREME/CT PARLIAMENT. PAGE 93 H1854
CONSTN CT/SYS LEGIS LAW

B65
CHARNAY J.P.,LE SUFFRAGE POLITIQUE EN FRANCE; ELECTIONS PARLEMENTAIRES, ELECTION PRESIDENTIELLE, REFERENDUMS. FRANCE CONSTN CHIEF DELIB/GP ECO/TAC EDU/PROP CRIME INGP/REL MORAL ORD/FREE PWR CATHISM 20 PARLIAMENT PRESIDENT. PAGE 29 H0584
CHOOSE SUFF NAT/G LEGIS

B65
CHRIMES S.B.,ENGLISH CONSTITUTIONAL HISTORY (3RD ED.). UK CHIEF CONSULT DELIB/GP LEGIS CT/SYS 15/20 COMMON/LAW PARLIAMENT. PAGE 30 H0598
CONSTN BAL/PWR NAT/G

B65
NAMIER L.B.,THE STRUCTURE OF POLITICS AT THE ACCESSION OF GEORGE III. UK LOC/G TOP/EX COLONIAL LEAD PARTIC REV CHOOSE REPRESENT GOV/REL PERSON SOVEREIGN...GOV/COMP 18 PARLIAMENT. PAGE 115 H2309
PARL/PROC LEGIS NAT/G POL/PAR

B65
O'CONNELL M.R.,IRISH POLITICS AND SOCIAL CONFLICT IN THE AGE OF THE AMERICAN REVOLUTION. FRANCE IRELAND MOD/EUR STRATA SECT LEGIS DIPLOM INT/TRADE DOMIN REV WAR...BIBLIOG 18 PARLIAMENT. PAGE 119 H2387
CATHISM ATTIT NAT/G DELIB/GP

B65
PELLING H.,A SHORT HISTORY OF THE LABOUR PARTY (2ND ED.). UK NAT/G CHIEF PARL/PROC GP/REL INGP/REL 20 LABOR/PAR PARLIAMENT WILSON/H. PAGE 124 H2484
POL/PAR NEW/LIB LEAD LABOR

B66
ADAMS J.C.,THE GOVERNMENT OF REPUBLICAN ITALY (2ND ED.). ITALY LOC/G POL/PAR DELIB/GP LEGIS WORKER ADMIN CT/SYS FASCISM...CHARTS BIBLIOG 20 PARLIAMENT. PAGE 3 H0064
NAT/G CHOOSE EX/STRUC CONSTN

B66
AGGARWALA R.N.,FINANCIAL COMMITTEES OF THE INDIAN PARLIAMENT: A STUDY IN PARLIAMENTARY CONTROL OVER PUBLIC EXPENDITURE. INDIA FINAN NAT/G ROLE...CHARTS METH/COMP METH 20 PARLIAMENT. PAGE 4 H0078
PARL/PROC BUDGET CONTROL DELIB/GP

B66
ANDERSON S.V.,CANADIAN OMBUDSMAN PROPOSALS. CANADA LEGIS DEBATE PARL/PROC...MAJORIT JURID TIME/SEQ
NAT/G CREATE

IDEA/COMP 20 OMBUDSMAN PARLIAMENT. PAGE 7 H0133 — ADMIN POL/PAR

B66
FINER S.E.,ANONYMOUS EMPIRE: STUDY OF THE LOBBY IN GREAT BRITAIN. UK CONSTN LABOR POL/PAR SECT DOMIN EDU/PROP PRESS CHOOSE...CONCPT CHARTS 20 PARLIAMENT. PAGE 50 H1004 — LOBBY NAT/G LEGIS PWR

B66
FRANK E.,LAWMAKERS IN A CHANGING WORLD. FRANCE UK USSR WOR+45 PARTIC EFFICIENCY ROLE ALL/IDEOS ...CHARTS ANTHOL PARLIAMENT 20 UN COLD/WAR. PAGE 52 H1049 — GOV/COMP LEGIS NAT/G DIPLOM

B66
HOLDSWORTH W.S.,A HISTORY OF ENGLISH LAW; THE CENTURIES OF SETTLEMENT AND REFORM (VOL. XVI). UK LOC/G NAT/G EX/STRUC LEGIS CT/SYS LEAD ATTIT ...POLICY DECISION JURID IDEA/COMP 18 PARLIAMENT. PAGE 73 H1454 — BIOG PERSON PROF/ORG LAW

B66
JOHNSON N.,PARLIAMENT AND ADMINISTRATION: THE ESTIMATES COMMITTEE 1945-65. FUT UK NAT/G EX/STRUC PLAN BUDGET ORD/FREE...T 20 PARLIAMENT HOUSE/CMNS. PAGE 81 H1625 — LEGIS ADMIN FINAN DELIB/GP

B66
NOEL G.E.,THE NEW BRITAIN AND HAROLD WILSON: INTERIM REPORT, 1966 GENERAL ELECTION. UK POL/PAR CONSULT PROB/SOLV BUDGET DIPLOM ECO/TAC LEAD CHOOSE ATTIT 20 WILSON/H PARLIAMENT. PAGE 118 H2366 — BIOG PERSON NAT/G CHIEF

B67
CANTOR N.F.,THE ENGLISH TRADITION* TWENTIETH-CENTURY VIEWS OF ENGLISH HISTORY (2VOLS.). UK STRATA NAT/G SECT WAR...POLICY GOV/COMP IDEA/COMP ANTHOL T PARLIAMENT CMN/WLTH. PAGE 26 H0522 — CT/SYS LAW POL/PAR

B67
KORNBERG A.,CANADIAN LEGISLATIVE BEHAVIOR: A STUDY OF THE 25TH PARLIAMENT. CANADA NAT/G POL/PAR PARL/PROC CHOOSE INGP/REL ADJUST ANOMIE RIGID/FLEX ...SOC STAND/INT CHARTS SOC/EXP 20 PARLIAMENT. PAGE 88 H1756 — ATTIT LEGIS ROLE

B67
MORRIS A.J.A.,PARLIAMENTARY DEMOCRACY IN THE NINETEENTH CENTURY. UK INDUS LOC/G NAT/G POL/PAR CONSULT LEGIS INT/TRADE ADMIN CHOOSE SUFF SOVEREIGN 19 PARLIAMENT. PAGE 113 H2261 — TIME/SEQ CONSTN PARL/PROC POPULISM

S67
ADNITT F.W.,"THE RISE OF ENGLISH RADICALISM -- PART 2." UK NAT/G WORKER INCOME WEALTH...BIOG 19 PARLIAMENT. PAGE 4 H0071 — LEGIS LOBBY

S67
DERRICK P.,"THE WHITE PAPER ON INCOMES." EUR+WWI UK LAW LABOR NAT/G PLAN PROB/SOLV GP/REL...GOV/COMP PARLIAMENT. PAGE 40 H0794 — INCOME POL/PAR POLICY

S67
LEGRES A.,"LES FONCTIONS D'UN PARLEMENT MODERNE." FRANCE DEBATE PARL/PROC SANCTION ATTIT PWR 20 PARLIAMENT. PAGE 93 H1860 — NAT/G LAW LEGIS CHOOSE

S67
MARWICK A.,"THE LABOUR PARTY AND THE WELFARE STATE IN BRITAIN, 19001948." UK SOCIETY STRUCT ECO/DEV WORKER CREATE PRICE CHOOSE WEALTH NEW/LIB SOCISM ...POLICY HEAL 20 PARLIAMENT LABOR/PAR. PAGE 104 H2074 — POL/PAR RECEIVE LEGIS NAT/G

PARNELL/CS....CHARLES STEWART PARNELL

B50
LYONS F.S.L.,THE IRISH PARLIAMENTARY PARTY, 1890-1910: STUDIES IN IRISH HISTORY (VOL. 4). IRELAND DELIB/GP LEGIS PAY EDU/PROP ADMIN GP/REL ATTIT...BIBLIOG 19/20 PARLIAMENT PARNELL/CS DIRECT/NAT. PAGE 99 H1986 — POL/PAR CHOOSE NAT/G POLICY

PAROLE....SEE PUB/INST, ROUTINE, CRIME

PARRINDER G. H2469

PARRIS H.W. H2470

PARSONS T. H2471,H2472

PARSONS/T....TALCOTT PARSONS

PARTH/SASS....PARTHO-SASSANIAN EMPIRE

B63
JAIRAZBHOY R.A.,FOREIGN INFLUENCE IN ANCIENT INDIA. INDIA ELITES SECT DIPLOM EDU/PROP COLONIAL REGION GP/REL...ART/METH LING WORSHIP +/14 GRECO/ROMN MESOPOTAM PERSIA PARTH/SASS. PAGE 79 H1587 — CULTURE SOCIETY COERCE DOMIN

PARTIC....PARTICIPATION; CIVIC ACTIVITY AND NONACTIVITY

N
SCHADERA I.,SELECT BIBLIOGRAPHY OF SOUTH AFRICAN NATIVE LIFE AND PROBLEMS. SOUTH/AFR LAW CULTURE ECO/UNDEV COLONIAL PARTIC...POLICY LING 20. PAGE 138 H2768 — BIBLIOG/A SOC AFR STRUCT

N
CIVIL SERVICE JOURNAL. PARTIC INGP/REL PERS/REL ...MGT BIBLIOG/A 20. PAGE 1 H0015 — ADMIN NAT/G SERV/IND WORKER

B09
LOBINGIER C.S.,THE PEOPLE'S LAW OR POPULAR PARTICIPATION IN LAW-MAKING. FRANCE SWITZERLND UK LOC/G NAT/G PROVS LEGIS SUFF MAJORITY PWR POPULISM ...GOV/COMP BIBLIOG 19. PAGE 97 H1945 — CONSTN LAW PARTIC

B17
DE VICTORIA F.,DE INDIS ET DE JURE BELLI (1557) IN F. DE VICTORIA, DE INDIS ET DE JURE BELLI REFLECTIONES. UNIV NAT/G SECT CHIEF PARTIC COERCE PEACE MORAL...POLICY 16 INDIAN/AM CHRISTIAN CONSCN/OBJ. PAGE 39 H0775 — WAR INT/LAW OWN

B19
DE MAN H.,THE REMAKING OF A MIND. EUR+WWI NAT/G ECO/TAC REGION ORD/FREE SOCISM...BIOG 20 WWI EUROPE. PAGE 38 H0762 — PSY WAR SELF/OBS PARTIC

N19
GRIFFITH W.,THE PUBLIC SERVICE (PAMPHLET). UK LAW LOC/G NAT/G PARTIC CHOOSE DRIVE ROLE SKILL...CHARTS 20 CIVIL/SERV. PAGE 61 H1222 — ADMIN EFFICIENCY EDU/PROP GOV/REL

N19
HANNA A.J.,EUROPEAN RULE IN AFRICA (PAMPHLET). BELGIUM FRANCE MOD/EUR UK WOR+45 WOR-45 ECO/UNDEV NAT/G PARTIC SOVEREIGN...NAT/COMP 19/20. PAGE 66 H1314 — DIPLOM COLONIAL AFR NAT/LISM

N19
LIEBKNECHT W.P.C.,SOCIALISM (2 PTS.; 1875, 1894) (PAMPHLET). WORKER CAP/ISM EDU/PROP WEALTH POPULISM. PAGE 97 H1927 — ECO/TAC STRATA SOCIALIST PARTIC

N19
WEBB L.C.,CHURCH AND STATE IN ITALY: 1947-1957 (PAMPHLET). GERMANY ITALY CONSTN POL/PAR AGREE CONTROL PARTIC CHOOSE ATTIT ORD/FREE FASCISM MARXISM 20 CHURCH/STA MARITAIN/J SALO. PAGE 166 H3316 — SECT CATHISM NAT/G GP/REL

B20
WEBB S.,INDUSTRIAL DEMOCRACY. UK PARTIC GP/REL ...SOC OBS RECORD CHARTS 18/20. PAGE 166 H3317 — LABOR NAT/G VOL/ASSN MAJORIT

B21
KREY A.C.,THE FIRST CRUSADE. CHRIST-17C SOCIETY STRATA NAT/G SECT FORCES WORKER WRITING LEAD ATTIT ...CHARTS 11 CHRISTIAN CRUSADES. PAGE 88 H1767 — WAR CATH DIPLOM PARTIC

B23
ROBERT H.M.,PARLIAMENTARY LAW. POL/PAR LEGIS PARTIC CHOOSE REPRESENT GP/REL. PAGE 132 H2640 — PARL/PROC DELIB/GP NAT/G JURID

B30
OLDMAN J.H.,WHITE AND BLACK IN AFRICA. AFR STRUCT COLONIAL PARTIC DISCRIM ISOLAT PRIVIL 20 SMUTS/JAN NEGRO WHITE/SUP. PAGE 121 H2412 — SOVEREIGN ORD/FREE RACE/REL NAT/G

B35
DOUGLASS H.P.,THE PROTESTANT CHURCH AS A SOCIAL INSTITUTION. CULTURE FINAN NEIGH PROF/ORG OP/RES ADMIN...POLICY SOC/WK STAT BIBLIOG. PAGE 42 H0843 — SECT PARTIC INGP/REL GP/REL

B36
BELLOC H.,THE RESTORATION OF PROPERTY. UK STRATA NAT/G PROF/ORG DELIB/GP WORKER CREATE PROB/SOLV ECO/TAC PARTIC UTOPIA ORD/FREE SOCISM 20. PAGE 13 H0270 — CONTROL MAJORIT CAP/ISM OWN

B36
SMITH T.V.,THE PROMISE OF AMERICAN POLITICS. USA-45 WOR-45 LAW CONSTN STRATA PARTIC FASCISM LAISSEZ MARXISM...MAJORIT METH/COMP 18/20 JEFFERSN/T LOCKE/JOHN BENTHAM/J. PAGE 146 H2920 — CONCPT ORD/FREE IDEA/COMP NAT/COMP

C36
MAZZINI J.,"FROM THE COUNCIL TO GOD" (1870) IN J. MAZZINI, ESSAYS." ITALY NAT/G EDU/PROP PARTIC ORD/FREE PWR SOVEREIGN 19 POPE CHRISTIAN DEITY. PAGE 106 H2112 — CATHISM DOMIN NAT/LISM SUPEGO

B37
TINGSTEN H.,POLITICAL BEHAVIOR. EUR+WWI STRATA NAT/G POL/PAR ACT/RES AGE...TREND CHARTS 20 FEMALE/SEX. PAGE 155 H3100 — CHOOSE ATTIT PARTIC

S38
MERTON R.K.,"SOCIAL STRUCTURE AND ANOMIE" (BMR)" UNIV CULTURE STRATA CREATE PARTIC ATTIT BIO/SOC PERSON...SOC CONCPT 20. PAGE 109 H2186 — SOCIETY STRUCT ANOMIE DRIVE

B40
MCHENRY D.E.,HIS MAJESTY'S OPPOSITION: STRUCTURE AND PROBLEMS OF THE BRITISH LABOUR PARTY 1931-1938. — POL/PAR MGT

UK FINAN LABOR LOC/G DELIB/GP LEGIS EDU/PROP LEAD PARTIC CHOOSE GP/REL SOCISM...TREND 20 LABOR/PAR. PAGE 107 H2130
NAT/G POLICY

B42
BARKER E.,REFLECTIONS ON GOVERNMENT. EUR+WWI SOCIETY LEGIS EDU/PROP ADMIN LEAD PARTIC CHOOSE TOTALISM AUTHORIT ORD/FREE SOCISM 20. PAGE 11 H0218
NAT/G POPULISM ACT/RES GEN/LAWS

B45
DITTMANN,DAS POLITISCHE DEUTSCHLAND VOR HITLER. GERMANY LOC/G PROVS...CHARTS GP/COMP 20. PAGE 41 H0827
POL/PAR NAT/G PARTIC

B45
HORN O.B.,BRITISH PUBLIC OPINION AND THE FIRST PARTITION OF POLAND. POLAND UK LEGIS PRESS RUMOR CONTROL PARTIC NAT/LISM SOVEREIGN 18/19. PAGE 73 H1469
DIPLOM POLICY ATTIT NAT/G

B47
HERSKOVITS M.U.,MAN AND HIS WORK. UNIV SECT TEC/DEV PARTIC...PHIL/SCI LING AUD/VIS BIBLIOG. PAGE 70 H1409
SOC CULTURE INGP/REL HABITAT

B48
HARRIS G.M.,COMPARATIVE LOCAL GOVERNMENT. FINAN CHOOSE ALL/VALS. PAGE 67 H1339
PARTIC GOV/REL LOC/G GOV/COMP

B49
SAUVY A.,LE POUVOIR ET L'OPINION. FRANCE STRATA NAT/G PERCEPT...POLICY PSY 20. PAGE 138 H2758
EDU/PROP MYTH PARTIC ATTIT

B49
VIERECK P.,CONSERVATISM REVISITED: THE REVOLT AGAINST REVOLT 1815-1949. EUR+WWI ELITES NAT/G FORCES PARTIC GOV/REL NAT/LISM...MAJORIT CONCPT GOV/COMP METTRNCH/K. PAGE 163 H3251
CONSERVE MARXISM REALPOL

B50
HOOKER R.,OF THE LAWS OF ECCLESIASTICAL POLITY (1594) (ABR. BY J. S. MARSHALL). UK UNIV CHIEF PARTIC MORAL...JURID GEN/LAWS WORSHIP 16. PAGE 73 H1463
SECT CONCPT LAW NAT/G

S52
EISENSTADT S.N.,"THE PROCESS OF ABSORPTION OF NEW IMMIGRANTS IN ISRAEL" (BMR)" ISRAEL CULTURE SCHOOL WORKER PARTIC DRIVE ORD/FREE...STAT OBS INT CHARTS SOC/INTEG 20 JEWS. PAGE 45 H0900
HABITAT ATTIT SAMP

S53
DRUCKER P.F.,"THE EMPLOYEE SOCIETY." STRUCT BAL/PWR PARTIC REPRESENT PWR...DECISION CONCPT. PAGE 42 H0849
LABOR MGT WORKER CULTURE

B54
HAMSON C.J.,EXECUTIVE DISCRETION AND JUDICIAL CONTROL; AN ASPECT OF THE FRENCH CONSEIL D'ETAT. EUR+WWI FRANCE MOD/EUR UK NAT/G EX/STRUC PARTIC CONSERVE...JURID BIBLIOG/A 18/20 SUPREME/CT. PAGE 65 H1310
ELITES ADJUD NAT/COMP

B55
DUVERGER M.,THE POLITICAL ROLE OF WOMEN. FRANCE GERMANY/W NORWAY YUGOSLAVIA STRATA LOBBY AGE ATTIT ROLE...STAT SAMP CHARTS METH/COMP NAT/COMP HYPO/EXP FEMALE/SEX. PAGE 44 H0875
SEX LEAD PARTIC CHOOSE

B55
POLLOCK J.K.,GERMAN DEMOCRACY AT WORK. GERMANY/W LOC/G NAT/G DIPLOM PARL/PROC...OBS IDEA/COMP 20. PAGE 127 H2539
PARTIC POL/PAR CHOOSE EDU/PROP

B55
SMITH G.,A CONSTITUTIONAL AND LEGAL HISTORY OF ENGLAND. UK ELITES NAT/G LEGIS ADJUD OWN HABITAT POPULISM...JURID 20 ENGLSH/LAW. PAGE 145 H2909
CONSTN PARTIC LAW CT/SYS

B56
HERNANDEZ URBINA A.,LOS PARTIDOS Y LA CRISIS DEL APRA. PERU NAT/G LEAD LOBBY CHOOSE SOCISM...POLICY DECISION 20 COM/PARTY APRA CONGRESS. PAGE 70 H1402
POL/PAR PARTIC PARL/PROC GP/REL

L56
EPSTEIN L.D.,"BRITISH MASS PARTIES IN COMPARISON WITH AMERICAN PARTIES" UK USA+45 STRATA ECO/DEV LABOR...CON/ANAL 20. PAGE 47 H0936
POL/PAR NAT/COMP PARTIC CHOOSE

B57
TAYLOR J.V.,CHRISTIANITY AND POLITICS IN AFRICA. AFR CONTROL PARTIC GP/REL RACE/REL ATTIT...POLICY BIBLIOG/A WORSHIP 20. PAGE 153 H3055
SECT NAT/G NAT/LISM

L57
LIPSET S.M.,"POLITICAL SOCIOLOGY." NAT/G POL/PAR ECO/TAC PARTIC CHOOSE PWR...BIBLIOG/A 20. PAGE 97 H1939
SOC ALL/IDEOS ACADEM

B58
COWAN L.G.,LOCAL GOVERNMENT IN WEST AFRICA. AFR FRANCE UK CULTURE KIN POL/PAR CHIEF LEGIS CREATE ADMIN PARTIC GOV/REL GP/REL...METH/COMP 20. PAGE 34 H0682
LOC/G COLONIAL SOVEREIGN REPRESENT

B58
CROWE S.,THE LANDSCAPE OF POWER. UK CULTURE SERV/IND NAT/G CONSULT PARTIC NUC/PWR LEISURE...SOC EXHIBIT 20. PAGE 36 H0712
HABITAT TEC/DEV PLAN CONTROL

B58
OGDEN F.D.,THE POLL TAX IN THE SOUTH. USA+45 USA-45 CONSTN ADJUD ADMIN PARTIC CRIME...TIME/SEQ GOV/COMP METH/COMP 18/20 SOUTH/US. PAGE 120 H2407
TAX CHOOSE RACE/REL DISCRIM

B58
PALMER E.E.,"POLITICAL MAN" IN E. PALMER, PROBLEMS IN DEMOCRATIC CITIZENSHIP. LOC/G NAT/G LEGIS PRESS CHOOSE REPRESENT GP/REL...DECISION SOC IDEA/COMP ANTHOL 20. PAGE 123 H2449
PARTIC POL/PAR EDU/PROP MAJORIT

B59
BARRON R.,PARTIES AND POLITICS IN MODERN FRANCE. FRANCE LOC/G DELIB/GP LEGIS TOP/EX EDU/PROP LEGIT TV FEEDBACK 20. PAGE 12 H0230
POL/PAR ALL/IDEOS CHOOSE PARTIC

S59
GABLE R.W.,"CULTURE AND ADMINISTRATION IN IRAN." IRAN EXEC PARTIC REPRESENT PWR. PAGE 54 H1085
ADMIN CULTURE EX/STRUC INGP/REL

S59
LEYS C.,"MODELS, THEORIES, AND THE THEORY OF POLITICAL PARTIES" CANADA LIECHTENST UK LOC/G NAT/G PARTIC REPRESENT GP/REL CONSEN EQUILIB MAJORITY ...NEW/IDEA MATH CHARTS 20. PAGE 96 H1919
POL/PAR CHOOSE METH/CNCPT SIMUL

B60
NICHOLLS W.H.,SOUTHERN TRADITION AND REGIONAL PROGRESS. STRATA STRUCT SCHOOL WORKER PARTIC REGION RACE/REL CONSEN ATTIT...SOC METH/CNCPT 19/20 SOUTH/US TVA. PAGE 118 H2349
RIGID/FLEX CONSERVE AGRI CULTURE

L60
ROKKAN S.,"NORWAY AND THE UNITED STATES OF AMERICA." NORWAY CHOOSE...SOC STAND/INT SAMP CHARTS GP/COMP METH/COMP 20. PAGE 133 H2665
STRUCT NAT/G PARTIC REPRESENT

S60
GRIMSHAW A.D.,"URBAN RACIAL VIOLENCE IN THE UNITED STATES: CHANGING ECOLOGICAL CONSIDERATIONS." STRUCT MUNIC FORCES PARTIC DISCRIM ATTIT HABITAT ...IDEA/COMP 20 NEGRO. PAGE 61 H1228
CROWD RACE/REL GOV/COMP NEIGH

B61
BEDFORD S.,THE FACES OF JUSTICE: A TRAVELLER'S REPORT. AUSTRIA FRANCE GERMANY/W SWITZERLND UK UNIV WOR+45 WOR-45 CULTURE PARTIC GOV/REL MORAL...JURID OBS GOV/COMP 20. PAGE 13 H0257
CT/SYS ORD/FREE PERSON LAW

B61
CASSINELLI C.W.,THE POLITICS OF FREEDOM. FUT UNIV LAW POL/PAR CHOOSE ORD/FREE...POLICY CONCPT MYTH BIBLIOG. PAGE 28 H0555
MAJORIT NAT/G PARL/PROC PARTIC

B61
JUSTICE,THE CITIZEN AND THE ADMINISTRATION: THE REDRESS OF GRIEVANCES (PAMPHLET). EUR+WWI UK LAW CONSTN STRATA NAT/G CT/SYS PARTIC COERCE...NEW/IDEA IDEA/COMP 20 OMBUDSMAN. PAGE 82 H1644
INGP/REL CONSULT ADJUD REPRESENT

B61
LENIN V.I.,WHAT IS TO BE DONE? (1902). RUSSIA LABOR NAT/G POL/PAR WORKER CAP/ISM ECO/TAC ADMIN PARTIC ...MARXIST IDEA/COMP GEN/LAWS 19/20. PAGE 94 H1881
EDU/PROP PRESS MARXISM METH/COMP

B62
HABERMAS J.,STRUKTURWANDEL DER OFFENTLICHKEIT. NAT/G EDU/PROP PRESS LEAD PARTIC PWR 20. PAGE 63 H1268
ATTIT CONCPT DOMIN

B62
TILMAN R.O.,THE NIGERIAN POLITICAL SXENE. NIGERIA DIPLOM COLONIAL PARTIC...POLICY SOC OBS PREDICT ANTHOL 20. PAGE 155 H3096
NAT/G AFR ECO/UNDEV FEDERAL

S62
ROSE R.,"THE POLITICAL IDEALS OF ENGLISH PARTY ACTIVISTS" (BMR)" UK PARL/PROC PARTIC ATTIT ROLE ...SAMP/SIZ CHARTS 20. PAGE 134 H2673
POL/PAR LOBBY REPRESENT NAT/G

B63
ALMOND G.A.,THE CIVIC CULTURE: POLITICAL ATTITUDES AND DEMOCRACY IN FIVE NATIONS. GERMANY/W ITALY UK USA+45 SOCIETY STRUCT PARTIC...SOC DEEP/INT SAMP 20 MEXIC/AMER. PAGE 6 H0113
POPULISM CULTURE NAT/COMP ATTIT

B63
BELFRAGE C.,THE MAN AT THE DOOR WITH THE GUN. CUBA L/A+17C NAT/G LEAD PARTIC GP/REL PWR...POLICY 20 CASTRO/F. PAGE 13 H0261
REGION ECO/UNDEV STRUCT ATTIT

B63
BERLIN I.,KARL MARX, HIS LIFE AND ENVIRONMENT (3RD ED.). MOD/EUR USSR INTELL EDU/PROP PARTIC REV ATTIT 19 MARX/KARL. PAGE 15 H0307
BIOG PERSON MARXISM CONCPT

B63
CROSS C.,THE FASCISTS IN BRITAIN. UK ELITES LABOR
POL/PAR

NAT/G DOMIN PARTIC DISCRIM TOTALISM ATTIT...STERTYP 20. PAGE 35 H0708
FASCISM RACE/REL LEAD

B63
FRIEDRICH C.J.,MAN AND HIS GOVERNMENT: AN EMPIRICAL THEORY OF POLITICS. UNIV LOC/G NAT/G ADJUD REV INGP/REL DISCRIM PWR BIBLIOG. PAGE 53 H1069
PERSON ORD/FREE PARTIC CONTROL

B63
REYNOLDS B.,MAGIC, DIVINATION AND WITCHCRAFT AMONG THE BAROTSE OF NORTHERN RHODESIA. RHODESIA CULTURE KIN CREATE LEGIT PARTIC DEATH DREAM STRANGE HABITAT PERSON...AUD/VIS WORSHIP 20. PAGE 131 H2619
AFR SOC MYTH SECT

B63
SCHUMAN S.I.,LEGAL POSITIVISM: ITS SCOPE AND LIMITATIONS. CONSTN NAT/G DIPLOM PARTIC UTOPIA ...POLICY DECISION PHIL/SCI CONCPT 20. PAGE 140 H2802
GEN/METH LAW METH/COMP

B63
WILCOX W.A.,PAKISTAN; THE CONSOLIDATION OF A NATION. INDIA PAKISTAN CONSTN SECT PROB/SOLV COLONIAL PARTIC GP/REL FEDERAL...POLICY 19/20. PAGE 168 H3361
NAT/LISM ECO/UNDEV DIPLOM STRUCT

B64
ALVIM J.C.,A REVOLUCAO SEM RUMO. BRAZIL NAT/G BAL/PWR DIPLOM INT/TRADE PARTIC WEALTH...POLICY SOC SOC/INTEG 20. PAGE 6 H0118
REV CIVMIL/REL ECO/UNDEV ORD/FREE

B64
BENDIX R.,NATION-BUILDING AND CITIZENSHIP: STUDIES OF OUR CHANGING SOCIAL ORDER. WOR+45 CULTURE LOC/G GOV/REL INGP/REL ORD/FREE PWR 20. PAGE 14 H0275
PARTIC NAT/COMP ADMIN AUTHORIT

B64
DOOLIN D.J.,COMMUNIST CHINA: THE POLITICS OF STUDENT OPPOSITION. CHINA/COM ELITES STRATA ACADEM NAT/G WRITING CT/SYS LEAD PARTIC COERCE TOTALISM 20. PAGE 42 H0838
MARXISM DEBATE AGE/Y PWR

B64
GOODNOW H.F.,THE CIVIL SERVICE OF PAKISTAN: BUREAUCRACY IN A NEW NATION. INDIA PAKISTAN S/ASIA ECO/UNDEV PROVS CHIEF PARTIC CHOOSE EFFICIENCY PWR ...BIBLIOG 20. PAGE 59 H1173
ADMIN GOV/REL LAW NAT/G

B64
HOROWITZ I.L.,REVOLUTION IN BRAZIL. BRAZIL L/A+17C ELITES STRATA NAT/G BAL/PWR PARTIC ATTIT 20. PAGE 74 H1473
ECO/UNDEV DIPLOM POLICY ORD/FREE

B64
MORGENTHAU R.S.,POLITICAL PARTIES IN FRENCH-SPEAKING WEST AFRICA. AFR FRANCE GUINEA IVORY/CST MALI SENEGAL CONSTN LEGIS CREATE PLAN LOBBY PARTIC GP/REL...POLICY BIBLIOG 20. PAGE 113 H2257
POL/PAR NAT/G SOVEREIGN COLONIAL

B64
NICOL D.,AFRICA - A SUBJECTIVE VIEW. AFR INT/ORG PLAN ADMIN COLONIAL PARL/PROC PARTIC REGION GOV/REL LITERACY ATTIT...BIBLIOG 20 CIVIL/SERV. PAGE 118 H2350
NAT/G LEAD CULTURE ACADEM

B64
RIDLEY F.,PUBLIC ADMINISTRATION IN FRANCE. FRANCE UK EX/STRUC CONTROL PARTIC EFFICIENCY 20. PAGE 131 H2625
ADMIN REPRESENT GOV/COMP PWR

B64
VALEN H.,POLITICAL PARTIES IN NORWAY. NORWAY ACADEM PARTIC ROUTINE INGP/REL KNOWL...QU 20. PAGE 161 H3220
LOC/G POL/PAR PERSON

S64
UNRUH J.M.,"SCIENTIFIC INPUTS TO LEGISLATIVE DECISION-MAKING (SUPPLEMENT)" USA+45 ACADEM NAT/G PROVS GOV/REL GOV/COMP. PAGE 159 H3171
CREATE DECISION LEGIS PARTIC

B65
BETTISON D.G.,THE PAPUA-GUINEA ELECTIONS 1964. S/ASIA CONSTN POL/PAR EDU/PROP PARTIC SUFF CENTRAL CONSEN...OBS CHARTS BIBLIOG 20. PAGE 16 H0324
NAT/G LEGIS CHOOSE REPRESENT

B65
DURKHEIM E.,THE ELEMENTARY FORMS OF THE RELIGIOUS LIFE. KIN PARTIC MORAL...PSY MYTH OBS IDEA/COMP METH WORSHIP 19/20. PAGE 43 H0870
SOC CULTURE CONCPT

B65
EASTON D.,A SYSTEM ANALYSIS OF POLITICAL LIFE. UNIV STRUCT NAT/G FEEDBACK PARTIC PERS/REL EFFICIENCY ...TREND CHARTS METH/COMP 20. PAGE 44 H0881
SIMUL POLICY GEN/METH

B65
FAUST J.J.,A REVOLUCAO DEVORA SEUS PRESIDENTES. BRAZIL NAT/G POL/PAR LEAD CHOOSE CIVMIL/REL ORD/FREE 20 PRESIDENT. PAGE 49 H0976
PARTIC REV FORCES GP/REL

B65
GINIEWSKI P.,THE TWO FACES OF APARTHEID. AFR SOUTH/AFR STRATA AGRI INDUS COLONIAL PARTIC SOVEREIGN...CONCPT GOV/COMP NAT/COMP 19/20 NEGRO. PAGE 56 H1131
DISCRIM NAT/G RACE/REL STRUCT

B65
HADWIGER D.F.,PRESSURES AND PROTEST. NAT/G LEGIS PLAN LEAD PARTIC ROUTINE ATTIT POLICY. PAGE 63 H1273
AGRI GP/REL LOBBY CHOOSE

B65
JACOB H.,POLITICS IN THE AMERICAN STATES; A COMPARATIVE ANALYSIS. USA+45 POL/PAR CHIEF LEGIS TAX EDU/PROP CONTROL CT/SYS LOBBY PARTIC...DECISION CHARTS 20. PAGE 79 H1578
PROVS GOV/COMP PWR

B65
LANDE C.H.,LEADERS, FACTIONS, AND PARTIES. PHILIPPINE CONSTN LOC/G NAT/G PARTIC...CHARTS BIBLIOG 20. PAGE 90 H1806
LEAD POL/PAR POLICY

B65
MCWHINNEY E.,JUDICIAL REVIEW IN THE ENGLISH-SPEAKING WORLD (3RD ED.). CANADA UK WOR+45 LEGIS CONTROL EXEC PARTIC...JURID 20 AUSTRAL. PAGE 108 H2151
GOV/COMP CT/SYS ADJUD CONSTN

B65
NAMIER L.B.,THE STRUCTURE OF POLITICS AT THE ACCESSION OF GEORGE III. UK LOC/G TOP/EX COLONIAL LEAD PARTIC REV CHOOSE REPRESENT GOV/REL PERSON SOVEREIGN...GOV/COMP 18 PARLIAMENT. PAGE 115 H2309
PARL/PROC LEGIS NAT/G POL/PAR

B65
OBUKAR C.,THE MODERN AFRICAN. AGRI INDUS WORKER CAP/ISM EDU/PROP PARTIC RACE/REL NAT/LISM ALL/VALS MARXISM...SOC IDEA/COMP 20. PAGE 120 H2393
AFR ECO/UNDEV CULTURE SOVEREIGN

B65
ROWAT D.C.,THE OMBUDSMAN: CITIZEN'S DEFENDER. DENMARK FINLAND NEW/ZEALND NORWAY SWEDEN CONSULT PROB/SOLV FEEDBACK PARTIC GP/REL...SOC CONCPT NEW/IDEA METH/COMP ANTHOL BIBLIOG 20. PAGE 135 H2701
INSPECT CONSTN NAT/G ADMIN

B65
SAKAI R.K.,STUDIES ON ASIA, 1965. INDIA KOREA S/ASIA USA+45 CONSTN KIN SECT PARTIC SUFF NAT/LISM ...POLICY SOC 19/20 CHINJAP. PAGE 137 H2737
PARL/PROC ASIA

B65
WARD W.E.,GOVERNMENT IN WEST AFRICA. WOR+45 POL/PAR EX/STRUC PLAN PARTIC GP/REL SOVEREIGN 20 AFRICA/W. PAGE 165 H3308
GOV/COMP CONSTN COLONIAL ECO/UNDEV

S65
ASHFORD D.E.,"BUREAUCRATS AND CITIZENS." MOROCCO PAKISTAN PARTIC 20 TUNIS. PAGE 9 H0172
GOV/COMP ADMIN EX/STRUC ROLE

S65
GANGAL S.C.,"SURVEY OF RECENT RESEARCH: INDIA AND THE COMMONWEALTH" INDIA UK NAT/G INT/TRADE PARTIC GOV/REL ROLE 20 CMN/WLTH. PAGE 55 H1095
BIBLIOG POLICY REGION DIPLOM

N65
MOTE M.E.,SOVIET LOCAL AND REPUBLIC ELECTIONS. COM USSR NAT/G PLAN PARTIC GOV/REL TOTALISM PWR ...CHARTS 20. PAGE 114 H2270
CHOOSE ADMIN CONTROL LOC/G

B66
CHAPMAN B.,THE PROFESSION OF GOVERNMENT: THE PUBLIC SERVICE IN EUROPE. CONSTN NAT/G POL/PAR EX/STRUC LEGIS TOP/EX PROB/SOLV DEBATE EXEC PARL/PROC PARTIC 20. PAGE 29 H0581
BIBLIOG ADMIN EUR+WWI GOV/COMP

B66
DAHL R.A.,POLITICAL OPPOSITIONS IN WESTERN DEMOCRACIES. EUR+WWI USA+45 USA-45 SOCIETY STRATA ECO/DEV NAT/G LEGIS REPRESENT...TREND NAT/COMP ANTHOL 20. PAGE 37 H0732
POL/PAR CHOOSE PARTIC PLURISM

B66
FRANK E.,LAWMAKERS IN A CHANGING WORLD. FRANCE UK USSR WOR+45 PARTIC EFFICIENCY ROLE ALL/IDEOS ...CHARTS ANTHOL PARLIAMENT 20 UN COLD/WAR. PAGE 52 H1049
GOV/COMP LEGIS NAT/G DIPLOM

B66
KEAY E.A.,THE NATIVE AND CUSTOMARY COURTS OF NIGERIA. NIGERIA CONSTN ELITES NAT/G TOP/EX PARTIC REGION...DECISION JURID 19/20. PAGE 84 H1673
AFR ADJUD LAW

B66
LOVEDAY P.,PARLIAMENT FACTIONS AND PARTIES: THE FIRST THIRTY YEARS OF RESPONSIBLE GOVERNMENT IN NEW SOUTH WALES, 1856-1889. PROVS LEAD PARL/PROC PARTIC GP/REL INGP/REL MAJORITY PWR...GP/COMP 19 AUSTRAL. PAGE 99 H1970
POL/PAR ELITES NAT/G LEGIS

B66
MAC DONALD H.M.,THE INTELLECTUAL IN POLITICS. GERMANY PERU SWEDEN UK USSR NAT/G CONSULT PLAN EDU/PROP TASK INGP/REL EFFICIENCY RATIONAL ALL/VALS 20. PAGE 99 H1987
ALL/IDEOS INTELL POL/PAR PARTIC

B66
MATTHEWS R.,AFRICAN POWDER KEG: REVOLT AND DISSENT IN SIX EMERGENT NATIONS. AFR ALGERIA DAHOMEY GABON GHANA MALAWI GAMBLE LEAD PARTIC REV DRIVE...BIOG TREND GOV/COMP 20. PAGE 105 H2098
ELITES ECO/UNDEV TOP/EX CONTROL

B66
SWARTZ M.J.,POLITICAL ANTHROPOLOGY. WOR+45 POL/PAR
PARTIC

ACT/RES REV GP/REL DRIVE...SOC CONCPT TIME/SEQ GP/COMP ANTHOL WORSHIP 20. PAGE 151 H3013 — RIGID/FLEX LOC/G CREATE

B66
SYMONDS R.,THE BRITISH AND THEIR SUCCESSORS. AFR CEYLON INDIA UK SCHOOL FORCES EDU/PROP ADMIN PARTIC ...NAT/COMP BIBLIOG 20 AFRICA/W AFRICA/E. PAGE 151 H3024 — NAT/G ECO/UNDEV POLICY COLONIAL

S66
COWAN L.G.,"THE MILITARY AND AFRICAN POLITICS." AFR FUT NAT/G POL/PAR PARTIC REV 20. PAGE 34 H0685 — CIVMIL/REL FORCES PWR LEAD

B67
ASHFORD D.E.,NATIONAL DEVELOPMENT AND LOCAL REFORM: POLITICAL PARTICIPATION IN MOROCCO, TUNISIA, AND PAKISTAN. MOROCCO PAKISTAN CULTURE PROB/SOLV ATTIT ...POLICY SOC METH/COMP NAT/COMP BIBLIOG 20 TUNIS. PAGE 9 H0173 — PARTIC ECO/UNDEV ADJUST NAT/G

B67
ERDMAN H.L.,THE SWATANTRA PARTY AND INDIAN CONSERVATISM. INDIA S/ASIA SOCIETY STRATA LOC/G NAT/G LEAD PARTIC GP/REL ATTIT...CONCPT GP/COMP BIBLIOG 20 SWATANTRA. PAGE 47 H0938 — POL/PAR CONSERVE CHOOSE POLICY

B67
KING M.L. JR.,WHERE DO WE GO FROM HERE: CHAOS OR COMMUNITY? MUNIC NAT/G PARTIC INGP/REL ALL/VALS ...POLICY CONCPT BIOG 20. PAGE 86 H1715 — RACE/REL DISCRIM STRUCT PWR

B67
PIKE F.B.,FREEDOM AND REFORM IN LATIN AMERICA. BRAZIL URUGUAY CONSTN CULTURE SECT DIPLOM EDU/PROP PARTIC DRIVE ALL/VALS CATHISM...GEOG ANTHOL BIBLIOG REFORMERS BOLIV. PAGE 126 H2511 — L/A+17C ORD/FREE ECO/UNDEV REV

L67
GLAZER M.,"LAS ACTITUDES Y ACTIVIDADES POLITICAS DE LOS ESTUDIANTES DE LA UNIVERSIDAD DE CHILE." CHILE NAT/G POL/PAR EDU/PROP LOBBY ATTIT 20. PAGE 57 H1141 — ACADEM AGE/Y PARTIC ELITES

L67
TABORSKY E.,"THE COMMUNIST PARTIES OF THE 'THIRD WORLD' IN SOVIET STRATEGY." AFR ASIA L/A+17C USSR INTELL NAT/G WORKER PLAN CONTROL LEAD PARTIC REV ...GOV/COMP 20 COM/PARTY THIRD/WRLD. PAGE 152 H3032 — POL/PAR MARXISM ECO/UNDEV DIPLOM

S67
ALTBACH P.,"STUDENT POLITICS." GP/REL ATTIT ROLE PWR 20. PAGE 6 H0116 — INTELL PARTIC UTIL NAT/G

S67
CAMERON R.,"SOME LESSONS OF HISTORY FOR DEVELOPING NATIONS." WOR+45 WOR-45 FINAN NAT/G WORKER EDU/PROP PARTIC ROLE...DECISION METH/COMP 18/20. PAGE 25 H0511 — ECO/UNDEV NAT/COMP POLICY CONCPT

S67
DEWHURST A.,"THE WAGE MOVEMENT IN CANADA." CANADA AGRI NAT/G PARTIC COST PRODUC PROFIT 20. PAGE 41 H0811 — WORKER MARXIST INDUS LABOR

S67
DRYDEN S.,"LOCAL GOVERNMENT IN TANZANIA PART II" TANZANIA LAW NAT/G POL/PAR CONTROL PARTIC REPRESENT ...DECISION 20. PAGE 42 H0850 — LOC/G GOV/REL ADMIN STRUCT

S67
LAQUEUR W.,"BONN IS NOT WEIMAR* REFLECTIONS ON THE RADICAL RIGHT IN GER MANY." CULTURE LOC/G NAT/G PARTIC CHOOSE. PAGE 91 H1822 — GERMANY/W FASCISM NAT/LISM

S67
NEALE R.S.,"WORKING CLASS WOMEN AND WOMEN'S SUFFRAGE." UK LAW CONSTN LABOR NAT/G DELIB/GP LEGIS WORKER PAY PARTIC CHOOSE 19 FEMALE/SEX. PAGE 116 H2326 — STRATA SEX SUFF DISCRIM

S67
PAK H.,"CHINA'S MILITIA AND MAO TSE-TUNG'S 'PEOPLE'S WAR'." CHINA/COM SOCIETY POL/PAR EX/STRUC PROB/SOLV PARTIC COERCE WAR CIVMIL/REL ATTIT DRIVE MARXISM...METH/COMP 20 MAO. PAGE 122 H2447 — FORCES NAT/G WORKER CHIEF

S67
STRAFFORD P.,"FRENCH ELECTIONS." FRANCE NAT/G CHIEF LEGIS BAL/PWR ECO/TAC PARL/PROC PARTIC ATTIT 20. PAGE 150 H2993 — POL/PAR SOCISM CENTRAL MARXISM

S67
WILSON J.Q.,"A GUIDE TO REAGAN COUNTRY* THE POLITICAL CULTURE OF SOUTHERN CALIFORNIA." NEIGH PROVS PARTIC CHOOSE ADJUST CONSEN PERSON CONSERVE CALIFORNIA REAGAN/RON. PAGE 169 H3379 — CULTURE ATTIT MORAL

B76
TAINE H.A.,THE ANCIENT REGIME. FRANCE STRATA FORCES PARTIC EQUILIB WEALTH CONSERVE POPULISM...GOV/COMP SOC/INTEG 18/19. PAGE 152 H3035 — NAT/G GOV/REL TAX REV

PARTIES, POLITICAL....SEE POL/PAR

PARTITION....PARTITIONS AND PARTITIONING - DIVISION OF AN EXISTING POLITICAL-GEOGRAPHICAL ENTITY INTO TWO OR MORE AUTONOMOUS ZONES

B66
ROOS H.,A HISTORY OF MODERN POLAND FROM THE FOUNDATION OF THE STATE IN THE FIRST WORLD WAR TO THE PRESENT DAY. EUR+WWI POLAND INTELL SOCIETY ECO/TAC LEAD REV ATTIT ORD/FREE MARXISM...BIBLIOG 20 WWI PARTITION. PAGE 133 H2669 — NAT/G WAR DIPLOM

PASSIN H. H2473

PASSPORT....SEE LICENSE, TRAVEL

PASTOR R.S. H2474

PATAI R. H2475,H2476

PATENT....PATENT

PATENT/OFF....U.S. PATENT OFFICE

PATHAN....PATHAN PEOPLE (PAKISTAN, AFGHANISTAN)

PATHET/LAO....PATHET LAO

PATRIOTISM....SEE NAT/LISM

PAULING/L....LINUS PAULING

PAULLIN O. H1055

PAULSEN M.G. H2477

PAUW B.A. H2478

PAY....EARNINGS; SEE ALSO INCOME

N19
BUSINESS ECONOMISTS' GROUP,INCOME POLICIES (PAMPHLET). UK INDUS LABOR TOP/EX PAY COST PRODUC ...ECOMETRIC GOV/COMP SIMUL ANTHOL 20. PAGE 25 H0497 — INCOME WORKER WEALTH POLICY

N19
FIKS M.,PUBLIC ADMINISTRATION IN ISRAEL (PAMPHLET). ISRAEL SCHOOL EX/STRUC BUDGET PAY INGP/REL ...DECISION 20 CIVIL/SERV. PAGE 50 H0999 — EDU/PROP NAT/G ADMIN WORKER

N19
INTERNATIONAL LABOUR OFFICE,EMPLOYMENT, UNEMPLOYMENT AND LABOUR FORCE STATISTICS (PAMPHLET). EUR+WWI STRATA AGRI INDUS NAT/G PROB/SOLV PAY AGE SEX...SAMP NAT/COMP METH 20 ILO. PAGE 78 H1557 — WORKER LABOR STAT ECO/DEV

B32
MCKISACK M.,THE PARLIAMENTARY REPRESENTATION OF THE ENGLISH BOROUGHS DURING THE MIDDLE AGES. UK CONSTN CULTURE ELITES EX/STRUC TAX PAY ADJUD PARL/PROC APPORT FEDERAL...POLICY 13/15 PARLIAMENT. PAGE 107 H2139 — NAT/G MUNIC LEGIS CHOOSE

B39
MARQUAND H.A.,ORGANIZED LABOUR IN FOUR CONTINENTS. EUR+WWI USA-45 INDUS NAT/G PAY GP/REL TOTALISM ATTIT WEALTH ALL/IDEOS...TREND NAT/COMP 20 ILO AFL/CIO EUROPE CHINJAP MEXIC/AMER. PAGE 103 H2055 — LABOR WORKER CONCPT ANTHOL

B40
WUNDERLICH F.,LABOR UNDER GERMAN DEMOCRACY, ARBITRATION 1918-1933. GERMANY NAT/G PAY REPAR ADJUD CT/SYS GP/REL...MAJORIT 20. PAGE 171 H3426 — LABOR WORKER INDUS BARGAIN

B48
EDUARDO O.D.C.,THE NEGRO IN NORTHERN BRAZIL: A STUDY IN ACCULTURATION. BRAZIL ECO/UNDEV FAM SECT PAY REGION HABITAT CATHISM MYSTISM...GEOG OBS SOC/INTEG WORSHIP 20 NEGRO MARANHAO. PAGE 44 H0890 — CULTURE ADJUST GP/REL

B50
LYONS F.S.L.,THE IRISH PARLIAMENTARY PARTY, 1890-1910: STUDIES IN IRISH HISTORY (VOL. 4). IRELAND DELIB/GP LEGIS PAY EDU/PROP ADMIN GP/REL ATTIT...BIBLIOG 19/20 PARLIAMENT PARNELL/CS DIRECT/NAT. PAGE 99 H1986 — POL/PAR CHOOSE NAT/G POLICY

B59
ROSOLIO D.,TEN YEARS OF THE CIVIL SERVICE IN ISRAEL (1948-1958) (PAMPHLET). ISRAEL NAT/G RECEIVE 20. PAGE 134 H2685 — ADMIN WORKER GOV/REL PAY

B60
KENEN P.B.,BRITISH MONETARY POLICY AND THE BALANCE OF PAYMENTS 1951-57. UK PLAN BUDGET ECO/TAC INT/TRADE PAY PRICE COST ATTIT 20. PAGE 84 H1687 — BAL/PAY PROB/SOLV FINAN NAT/G

B61
AYLMER G.,THE KING'S SERVANTS. UK ELITES CHIEF PAY CT/SYS WEALTH 17 CROMWELL/O CHARLES/I. PAGE 9 H0187 — ADMIN ROUTINE EX/STRUC

NAT/G

B61
ROSE D.L.,THE VIETNAMESE CIVIL SERVICE. VIETNAM CONSULT DELIB/GP GIVE PAY EDU/PROP COLONIAL GOV/REL UTIL...CHARTS 20. PAGE 134 H2672
ADMIN EFFICIENCY STAT NAT/G

B62
GALENSON W.,LABOR IN DEVELOPING COUNTRIES. BRAZIL INDONESIA ISRAEL PAKISTAN TURKEY AGRI INDUS WORKER PAY PRICE GP/REL WEALTH...MGT CHARTS METH/COMP NAT/COMP 20. PAGE 54 H1088
LABOR ECO/UNDEV BARGAIN POL/PAR

B62
WOODS H.D.,LABOUR POLICY AND LABOUR ECONOMICS IN CANADA. CANADA FUT NAT/G VOL/ASSN WORKER BARGAIN ECO/TAC PAY CONFER GP/REL 20. PAGE 170 H3409
LABOR POLICY INDUS ECO/DEV

B63
DUE J.F.,STATE SALES TAX ADMINISTRATION. OP/RES BUDGET PAY ADMIN EXEC ROUTINE COST EFFICIENCY PROFIT...CHARTS METH/COMP 20. PAGE 43 H0855
PROVS TAX STAT GOV/COMP

B63
GUIMARAES A.P.,INFLACAO E MONOPOLIO NO BRASIL. BRAZIL FINAN NAT/G PLAN PAY...METH/COMP 20. PAGE 62 H1248
ECO/UNDEV PRICE INT/TRADE BAL/PAY

B64
PARANJAPE H.K.,THE FLIGHT OF TECHNICAL PERSONNEL IN PUBLIC UNDERTAKINGS. INDIA PAY DEMAND HAPPINESS ORD/FREE...MGT QU 20 MIGRATION. PAGE 123 H2464
ADMIN NAT/G WORKER PLAN

B65
HARRIS R.L.,POLITICAL ORGANIZATION OF THE MBEMBE NIGERIA. AFR NIGERIA SOCIETY AGRI SECT WORKER PAY ...SOC WORSHIP 20 MBEMBE. PAGE 67 H1345
STRUCT CHIEF CULTURE

B66
BRODERSEN A.,THE SOVIET WORKER: LABOR AND GOVERNMENT IN SOVIET SOCIETY. USSR STRUCT INDUS LABOR PLAN PAY INGP/REL PRODUC...POLICY GEN/LAWS BIBLIOG 20 STALIN/J LENIN/VI BOLSHEVISM KHRUSH/N. PAGE 21 H0425
WORKER ROLE NAT/G MARXISM

B66
GARCON M.,LETTRE OUVERTE A LA JUSTICE. FRANCE NAT/G PROB/SOLV PAY EFFICIENCY MORAL 20. PAGE 55 H1100
ORD/FREE ADJUD CT/SYS

B66
PLATE H.,PARTEIFINANZIERUNG UND GRUNDESETZ. GERMANY NAT/G PLAN GIVE PAY INCOME WEALTH...JURID 20. PAGE 126 H2522
POL/PAR CONSTN FINAN

B67
HAWTREY R.,INCOMES AND MONEY. EUR+WWI FUT UK LABOR WORKER INT/TRADE TAX PAY BAL/PAY COST WEALTH 20. PAGE 68 H1363
FINAN NAT/G POLICY ECO/DEV

S67
BURGHART A.,"CATHOLIC SOCIAL THOUGHT IN AUSTRIA." AUSTRIA EUR+WWI NAT/G PAY PERS/REL OWN MARXISM SOCISM...SOC 20. PAGE 24 H0482
CATHISM ATTIT TREND SOCIETY

S67
LEVCIK B.,"WAGES AND EMPLOYMENT PROBLEMS IN THE NEW SYSTEM OF PLANNED MANAGEMENT IN CZECHOSLOVAKIA." CZECHOSLVK EUR+WWI NAT/G OP/RES PLAN ADMIN ROUTINE INGP/REL CENTRAL EFFICIENCY PRODUC DECISION. PAGE 95 H1895
MARXISM WORKER MGT PAY

S67
NEALE R.S.,"WORKING CLASS WOMEN AND WOMEN'S SUFFRAGE." UK LAW CONSTN LABOR NAT/G DELIB/GP LEGIS WORKER PAY PARTIC CHOOSE 19 FEMALE/SEX. PAGE 116 H2326
STRATA SEX SUFF DISCRIM

PAYNO M. H2479

PAZ O. H2480

PEACE CORPS....SEE PEACE/CORP

PEACE OF WESTPHALIA....SEE WESTPHALIA

PEACE....SEE ALSO ORD/FREE

B06
SUMNER W.G.,FOLKWAYS: STUDY OF THE SOCIOLOGICAL IMPORTANCE OF USAGES, MANNERS, CUSTOMS, MORES, AND MORALS. STRUCT KIN ETIQUET ROUTINE MURDER MARRIAGE PEACE SEX ALL/VALS WEALTH BIBLIOG. PAGE 150 H3008
CULTURE SOC SANCTION MORAL

B15
FARIES J.C.,THE RISE OF INTERNATIONALISM. ASIA MOD/EUR NAT/G VOL/ASSN DELIB/GP BAL/PWR EDU/PROP ARMS/CONT RIGID/FLEX TREND. PAGE 49 H0971
INT/ORG DIPLOM PEACE

B17
DE VICTORIA F.,DE INDIS ET DE JURE BELLI (1557) IN F. DE VICTORIA, DE INDIS ET DE JURE BELLI REFLECTIONES. UNIV NAT/G SECT CHIEF PARTIC COERCE PEACE MORAL...POLICY 16 INDIAN/AM CHRISTIAN CONSCN/OBJ. PAGE 39 H0775
WAR INT/LAW OWN

B17
VEBLEN T.B.,AN INQUIRY INTO THE NATURE OF PEACE AND THE TERMS OF ITS PERPETUATION. UNIV STRATA FINAN EDU/PROP PRICE COST DISCRIM NAT/LISM MORAL ORD/FREE PACIFIST 20 WORLDUNITY. PAGE 162 H3237
PEACE DIPLOM WAR NAT/G

N17
BURKE E.,THOUGHTS ON THE PROSPECT OF A REGICIDE PEACE (PAMPHLET). FRANCE UK SECT DOMIN MURDER PEACE ORD/FREE SOVEREIGN POPULISM...POLICY GOV/COMP IDEA/COMP 18 JACOBINISM COEXIST. PAGE 24 H0483
REV CHIEF NAT/G DIPLOM

B19
ROUSSEAU J.J.,A LASTING PEACE. INT/ORG NAT/G CHIEF DIPLOM DETER WAR POLICY. PAGE 135 H2697
PLAN PEACE UTIL

N19
BENTHAM J.,A PLAN FOR AN UNIVERSAL AND PERPETUAL PEACE (1838) (PAMPHLET). NAT/G FORCES BAL/PWR INT/TRADE ADMIN AGREE CT/SYS ARMS/CONT SOVEREIGN WEALTH GEN/LAWS. PAGE 14 H0288
INT/ORG INT/LAW PEACE COLONIAL

N19
FREEMAN H.A.,COERCION OF STATES IN FEDERAL UNIONS (PAMPHLET). WOR-45 DIPLOM CONTROL COERCE PEACE ORD/FREE...GOV/COMP METH/COMP NAT/COMP PACIFIST 20. PAGE 53 H1055
FEDERAL WAR INT/ORG PACIFISM

N19
MAO TSE-TUNG,ON SOME IMPORTANT PROBLEMS OF THE PARTY'S PRESENT POLICY. CHINA/COM CONSTN ELITES INTELL AGRI DOMIN EDU/PROP REV REPRESENT GP/REL OWN PEACE ORD/FREE 20 COM/PARTY. PAGE 102 H2044
POLICY NAT/G CHIEF LEGIT

N19
MASSEY V.,CANADIANS AND THEIR COMMONWEALTH: THE ROMANES LECTURE DELIVERED IN THE SHELDONIAN THEATRE JUNE 1, 1961 (PAMPHLET). CANADA UK CULTURE ECO/DEV REPRESENT NAT/LISM PEACE PWR CONSERVE 20 CMN/WLTH. PAGE 104 H2088
ATTIT DIPLOM NAT/G SOVEREIGN

B21
BALFOUR A.J.,ESSAYS SPECULATIVE AND POLITICAL. SEA CULTURE CREATE WAR NAT/LISM PEACE LOVE...ART/METH INT/LAW CONCPT ANTHOL 20 JEWS. PAGE 10 H0204
PHIL/SCI SOCIETY DIPLOM

B28
MARSILIUS/PADUA,DEFENSOR PACIS (1324). CHRIST-17C CONSTN NAT/G DIPLOM DOMIN LEGIT CONTROL WAR PEACE ORD/FREE SOVEREIGN POPULISM 14 POPE. PAGE 103 H2059
CATH SECT GEN/LAWS

B29
LANGER W.L.,THE FRANCO-RUSSIAN ALLIANCE: 1890-1894. FRANCE MOD/EUR UK USSR NAT/G CHIEF FORCES BAL/PWR AGREE WAR PEACE PWR...TIME/SEQ TREATY 19 BISMARCK/O. PAGE 91 H1809
DIPLOM

B29
STURZO L.,THE INTERNATIONAL COMMUNITY AND THE RIGHT OF WAR (TRANS. BY BARBARA BARCLAY CARTER). CULTURE CREATE PROB/SOLV DIPLOM ADJUD CONTROL PEACE PERSON ORD/FREE...INT/LAW IDEA/COMP PACIFIST 20 LEAGUE/NAT. PAGE 150 H3003
INT/ORG PLAN WAR CONCPT

B32
BLUM L.,PEACE AND DISARMAMENT (TRANS. BY A. WERTH). NAT/G FORCES WORKER DIPLOM AGREE WAR ATTIT AUTHORIT ORD/FREE. PAGE 18 H0360
SOCIALIST PEACE INT/ORG ARMS/CONT

B32
THIBAUDET A.,LES IDEES POLITIQUES DE LA FRANCE. FRANCE NAT/G SECT PRESS REV NAT/LISM PEACE ATTIT ...PSY 19/20 JACOBINISM JAURES/JL. PAGE 154 H3070
IDEA/COMP ALL/IDEOS CATHISM

B33
DAHLIN E.,FRENCH AND GERMAN PUBLIC OPINION ON DECLARED WAR AIMS 1914-1918. BELGIUM FRANCE GERMANY NAT/G POL/PAR DIPLOM COERCE REV WAR PEACE 20 WWI WILSON/W. PAGE 37 H0733
ATTIT EDU/PROP DOMIN NAT/COMP

B33
FERRERO G.,PEACE AND WAR (TRANS. BY BERTHA PRITCHARD). CULTURE FINAN SECT ATTIT SUPEGO MORAL ORD/FREE CONSERVE POPULISM SOCISM POLICY. PAGE 49 H0987
WAR PEACE DIPLOM PROB/SOLV

B35
MARRIOTT J.A.,DICTATORSHIP AND DEMOCRACY. GERMANY GREECE UK CHIEF DIPLOM DOMIN LEGIT PEACE ORD/FREE CONSERVE...TREND ROME HITLER/A. PAGE 103 H2057
TOTALISM POPULISM PLURIST NAT/G

B37
CARLYLE T.,THE FRENCH REVOLUTION (2 VOLS.). FRANCE CONSTN NAT/G FORCES COERCE MURDER PEACE MORAL POPULISM...TIME/SEQ IDEA/COMP GEN/LAWS 18. PAGE 26 H0532
REV CHIEF TRADIT

B38
SAINT-PIERRE C.I.,SCHEME FOR LASTING PEACE (TRANS. BY H. BELLOT). INDUS NAT/G CHIEF FORCES INT/TRADE CT/SYS WAR PWR SOVEREIGN WEALTH...POLICY 18. PAGE 137 H2732
INT/ORG PEACE AGREE INT/LAW

B40
BROGAN D.W.,THE DEVELOPMENT OF MODERN FRANCE (1870-1939). FRANCE GERMANY UK USSR CONSTN CHIEF LEGIS DIPLOM AGREE COLONIAL WAR NAT/LISM PEACE SOCISM 19/20 TREATY. PAGE 21 H0428
MOD/EUR NAT/G

C43
BENTHAM J.,"PRINCIPLES OF INTERNATIONAL LAW" IN J. BOWRING, ED., THE WORKS OF JEREMY BENTHAM." UNIV
INT/LAW JURID

NAT/G PLAN PROB/SOLV DIPLOM CONTROL SANCTION MORAL ORD/FREE PWR SOVEREIGN 19. PAGE 15 H0291
WAR PEACE

B46
ALLEN J.S.,WORLD MONOPOLY AND PEACE. GERMANY UK USSR FINAN INDUS LG/CO DOMIN CONTROL PEACE PWR WEALTH SOCISM...NAT/COMP 20 MONOPOLY. PAGE 5 H0105
CAP/ISM DIPLOM WAR COLONIAL

S46
TANNENBAUM F.,"THE BALANCE OF POWER IN SOCIETY." UNIV STRUCT FAM NAT/G SECT PERS/REL EQUILIB UTOPIA DRIVE ALL/IDEOS...OLD/LIB CONCPT. PAGE 152 H3044
SOCIETY ALL/VALS GP/REL PEACE

B47
NIEBUHR R.,THE CHILDREN OF LIGHT AND THE CHILDREN OF DARKNESS: A VINDICATION OF DEMOCRACY AND CRITIQUE OF TRADITIONAL DEFENSE. UNIV STRUCT NAT/G SECT INGP/REL OWN PEACE ORD/FREE MARXISM ...IDEA/COMP GEN/LAWS 20 CHRISTIAN. PAGE 118 H2358
POPULISM DIPLOM NEIGH GP/REL

B48
JONES H.D.,UNESCO: A SELECTED LIST OF REFERENCES. CULTURE CREATE PEACE ATTIT DRIVE 20 UNESCO UN. PAGE 82 H1631
BIBLIOG/A INT/ORG DIPLOM EDU/PROP

B50
CANTRIL H.,TENSIONS THAT CAUSE WAR. UNIV CULTURE R+D CREATE EDU/PROP DRIVE PERSON KNOWL ORD/FREE ...HUM PSY SOC OBS CENSUS TREND CON/ANAL SOC/EXP SIMUL GEN/METH ANTHOL COLD/WAR TOT/POP. PAGE 26 H0523
SOCIETY PHIL/SCI PEACE

C50
NUMELIN R.,"THE BEGINNINGS OF DIPLOMACY." INT/TRADE WAR GP/REL PEACE STRANGE ATTIT...INT/LAW CONCPT BIBLIOG. PAGE 119 H2380
DIPLOM KIN CULTURE LAW

B51
LOOS W.A.,RELIGIOUS FAITH AND WORLD CULTURE. INTELL SOCIETY SECT EDU/PROP ROUTINE ATTIT PERSON ALL/VALS MORAL...CONCPT GEN/LAWS VAL/FREE. PAGE 98 H1964
UNIV CULTURE PEACE

B53
COBLENTZ S.A.,FROM ARROW TO ATOM BOMB: THE PSYCHOLOGICAL HISTORY OF WAR. PREHIST CULTURE CROWD PEACE DRIVE MORAL PWR...GP/COMP IDEA/COMP. PAGE 31 H0613
WAR PSY SOCIETY

B53
MARITAIN J.,L'HOMME ET L'ETAT. SECT DIPLOM GP/REL PEACE ORD/FREE...IDEA/COMP 17/20 CHURCH/STA NATURL/LAW. PAGE 103 H2052
CONCPT NAT/G SOVEREIGN COERCE

B54
BUTZ O.,GERMANY: DILEMMA FOR AMERICAN POLICY. GERMANY USA+45 USA-45 USSR WOR+45 INT/ORG FORCES NUC/PWR EFFICIENCY PEACE PWR...GOV/COMP 20 COLD/WAR. PAGE 25 H0501
DIPLOM NAT/G WAR POLICY

B55
INSTITUTE POLITISCHE WISSEN,POLITISCHE LITERATUR (3 VOLS.). INT/ORG LEAD WAR PEACE...CONCPT TREND NAT/COMP 20. PAGE 77 H1540
BIBLIOG/A NAT/G DIPLOM POLICY

B55
KHADDURI M.,WAR AND PEACE IN THE LAW OF ISLAM. CONSTN CULTURE SOCIETY STRATA NAT/G PROVS SECT FORCES TOP/EX CREATE DOMIN EDU/PROP ADJUD COERCE ATTIT RIGID/FLEX ALL/VALS...CONCPT TIME/SEQ TOT/POP VAL/FREE. PAGE 85 H1702
ISLAM JURID PEACE WAR

B55
MAZZINI J.,THE DUTIES OF MAN. MOD/EUR LAW SOCIETY FAM NAT/G POL/PAR SECT VOL/ASSN EX/STRUC ACT/RES CREATE REV PEACE ATTIT ALL/VALS...GEN/LAWS WORK 19. PAGE 106 H2113
SUPEGO CONCPT NAT/LISM

B55
TAN C.C.,THE BOXER CATASTROPHE. ASIA UK USSR ELITES POL/PAR VOL/ASSN FORCES PROB/SOLV DIPLOM ADMIN COLONIAL NAT/LISM PEACE TREATY 19/20 BOXER/REBL. PAGE 152 H3040
REV NAT/G WAR

B57
BUCK P.W.,CONTOL OF FOREIGN RELATIONS IN MODERN NATIONS. FRANCE L/A+17C NETHERLAND USSR WOR+45 INT/ORG TOP/EX BAL/PWR DOMIN EDU/PROP COERCE PEACE ATTIT...CONCPT TREND 20 CMN/WLTH. PAGE 23 H0465
NAT/G PWR DIPLOM

B57
REISS J.,GEORGE KENNANS POLITIK DER EINDAMMUNG. USSR NAT/G FORCES TOTALISM ATTIT ORD/FREE...POLICY 20 NATO TRUMAN/HS MARSHL/PLN KENNAN/G. PAGE 131 H2613
DIPLOM DETER PEACE

B58
CHANG H.,WITHIN THE FOUR SEAS. ASIA WAR MORAL MARXISM...IDEA/COMP NAT/COMP 20 CONFUCIUS. PAGE 29 H0577
PEACE DIPLOM KNOWL CULTURE

B58
KINTNER W.R.,ORGANIZING FOR CONFLICT: A PROPOSAL. USSR STRUCT NAT/G LEGIS ADMIN EXEC PEACE ORD/FREE PWR...CONCPT OBS TREND NAT/COMP VAL/FREE COLD/WAR 20. PAGE 86 H1719
USA+45 PLAN DIPLOM

B59
EMME E.M.,THE IMPACT OF AIR POWER - NATIONAL SECURITY AND WORLD POLITICS. USA+45 USSR FORCES DIPLOM WEAPON PEACE TOTALISM...POLICY NAT/COMP 20 EUROPE. PAGE 46 H0921
DETER AIR WAR ORD/FREE

B59
THOMAS D.H.,GUIDE TO THE DIPLOMATIC ARCHIVES OF WESTERN EUROPE. EUR+WWI ELITES INT/ORG NAT/G BAL/PWR INT/TRADE PEACE. PAGE 154 H3076
BIBLIOG DIPLOM CONFER

S59
JENKS C.W.,"THE CHALLENGE OF UNIVERSALITY." FUT UNIV CONSTN CULTURE CONSULT CREATE PLAN LEGIT ATTIT MORAL ORD/FREE RESPECT...MAJORIT JURID 20. PAGE 80 H1602
INT/ORG LAW PEACE INT/LAW

B60
ALBRECHT-CARRIE R.,FRANCE, EUROPE AND THE TWO WORLD WARS. EUR+WWI FRANCE GERMANY MOD/EUR UK ECO/DEV NAT/G FORCES BAL/PWR DOMIN ARMS/CONT PEACE PWR 20 TREATY EUROPE. PAGE 5 H0096
DIPLOM WAR

B60
FURNIA A.H.,THE DIPLOMACY OF APPEASEMENT: ANGLO-FRENCH RELATIONS AND THE PRELUDE TO WORLD WAR II 1931-1938. FRANCE GERMANY UK ELITES NAT/G DELIB/GP FORCES WAR PEACE RIGID/FLEX 20. PAGE 54 H1077
DIPLOM BAL/PWR COERCE

B60
MINIFIE J.M.,PEACEMAKER OR POWDER-MONKEY. CANADA INT/ORG NAT/G FORCES LEAD WAR...PREDICT 20. PAGE 111 H2222
DIPLOM POLICY NEUTRAL PEACE

B60
SETHE P.,SCHICKSALSSTUNDEN DER WELTGESCHICHTE (6TH ED.). NAT/G BAL/PWR DOMIN REV PWR...NAT/COMP 16/20. PAGE 141 H2831
DIPLOM WAR PEACE

B60
SOUTH AFRICAN CONGRESS OF DEM,FACE THE FUTURE. SOUTH/AFR ELITES LEGIS ADMIN REGION COERCE PEACE ATTIT 20. PAGE 147 H2938
RACE/REL DISCRIM CONSTN NAT/G

C60
COX R.H.,"LOCKE ON WAR AND PEACE." UK DIPLOM DOMIN PWR...BIOG IDEA/COMP BIBLIOG 18. PAGE 34 H0689
CONCPT NAT/G PEACE WAR

B61
CHAKRABARTI A.,NEHRU: HIS DEMOCRACY AND INDIA. ASIA INDIA UK CONSTN ECO/UNDEV SECT DIPLOM COLONIAL PEACE WEALTH...BIBLIOG 20 CONGRESS NEHRU/J GANDHI/M. PAGE 28 H0570
ORD/FREE STRATA NAT/G CHIEF

B61
FULLER J.F.C.,THE CONDUCT OF WAR, 1789-1961. FRANCE RUSSIA SOCIETY NAT/G FORCES PROB/SOLV AGREE NUC/PWR WEAPON PEACE...SOC 18/20 TREATY COLD/WAR. PAGE 54 H1076
WAR POLICY REV ROLE

B61
JAKOBSON M.,THE DIPLOMACY OF THE WINTER WAR. EUR+WWI FINLAND GERMANY USSR INT/ORG NAT/G PEACE TOTALISM PWR...POLICY CONCPT 20 TREATY. PAGE 79 H1588
WAR ORD/FREE DIPLOM

B61
MILLIKAW M.F.,THE EMERGING NATIONS: THEIR GROWTH AND UNITED STATES POLICY. FUT USA+45 WOR+45 WOR-45 NAT/G PLAN TEC/DEV BAL/PWR GOV/REL PEACE ORD/FREE 20. PAGE 111 H2216
ECO/UNDEV POLICY DIPLOM FOR/AID

B61
PECKERT J.,DIE GROSSEN UND DIE KLEINEN MAECHTE. COM GERMANY/W ECO/DEV ECO/UNDEV NAT/G WAR RACE/REL PEACE...POLICY GP/COMP GOV/COMP 20 COLD/WAR. PAGE 124 H2482
DIPLOM ECO/TAC BAL/PWR

S61
MILLER E.,"LEGAL ASPECTS OF UN ACTION IN THE CONGO." AFR CULTURE ADMIN PEACE DRIVE RIGID/FLEX ORD/FREE...WELF/ST JURID OBS UN CONGO 20. PAGE 111 H2212
INT/ORG LEGIT

B62
ABOSCH H.,THE MENACE OF THE MIRACLE: GERMANY FROM HITLER TO ADENAUER. EUR+WWI GERMANY/W CULTURE FORCES PRESS NUC/PWR WAR CHOOSE 20 HITLER/A ADENAUER/K. PAGE 3 H0057
DIPLOM PEACE POLICY

B62
BAFFREY S.A.,THE RED MYTH: A HISTORY OF COMMUNISM FROM MARX TO KHRUSHCHEV. USSR NAT/G CHIEF CAP/ISM DIPLOM EDU/PROP REV WAR PEACE TOTALISM...POLICY 20 STALIN/J KHRUSH/N. PAGE 10 H0195
CONCPT MARXISM TV

B62
CALVOCORESSI P.,WORLD ORDER AND NEW STATES: PROBLEMS OF KEEPING THE PEACE. AFR EUR+WWI S/ASIA ELITES NAT/G ECO/TAC FOR/AID EDU/PROP COERCE ATTIT DRIVE ALL/VALS...GEN/LAWS COLD/WAR 20 UN. PAGE 25 H0509
INT/ORG PEACE

B62
DUTOIT B.,LA NEUTRALITE SUISSE A L'HEURE EUROPEENNE. EUR+WWI MOD/EUR INT/ORG NAT/G VOL/ASSN PLAN BAL/PWR LEGIT NEUTRAL REGION PEACE ORD/FREE SOVEREIGN...CONCPT OBS TIME/SEQ TREND STERTYP VAL/FREE LEAGUE/NAT UN 20. PAGE 44 H0873
ATTIT DIPLOM SWITZERLND

B62
JACKSON W.A.D.,RUSSO-CHINESE BORDERLANDS. ASIA COM USSR NAT/G PROVS EX/STRUC FORCES DOMIN COERCE PEACE
GEOG DIPLOM

ATTIT PWR SOVEREIGN WEALTH...CONCPT TREND CHARTS STERTYP VAL/FREE. PAGE 79 H1576
RUSSIA

B62
MORGENSTERN O.,STRATEGIE - HEUTE (2ND ED.). USA+45 USSR ECO/DEV DELIB/GP WAR PEACE ORD/FREE...GOV/COMP NAT/COMP 20 COLD/WAR NATO. PAGE 113 H2256
NUC/PWR DIPLOM FORCES TEC/DEV

S62
STRACHEY J.,"COMMUNIST INTENTIONS." ASIA USSR YUGOSLAVIA INT/ORG NAT/G FORCES DOMIN EDU/PROP COERCE NUC/PWR NAT/LISM PEACE RIGID/FLEX PWR MARXISM...CONCPT MYTH OBS TIME/SEQ TREND COLD/WAR TOT/POP 20. PAGE 150 H2992
COM ATTIT WAR

C62
BACON F.,"OF SEDITIONS AND TROUBLES" (1625) IN F. BACON, ESSAYS." INDUS MARKET CHIEF ECO/TAC EDU/PROP CONTROL LEAD PEACE WEALTH 17 MACHIAVELL. PAGE 9 H0191
REV ORD/FREE NAT/G GEN/LAWS

B63
BADI J.,THE GOVERNMENT OF THE STATE OF ISRAEL: A CRITICAL ACCOUNT OF ITS PARLIAMENT, EXECUTIVE, AND JUDICIARY. ISRAEL ECO/DEV CHIEF DELIB/GP LEGIS DIPLOM CT/SYS INGP/REL PEACE ORD/FREE...BIBLIOG 20 PARLIAMENT ARABS MIGRATION. PAGE 10 H0193
NAT/G CONSTN EX/STRUC POL/PAR

B63
BROEKMEIJER M.W.,DEVELOPING COUNTRIES AND NATO. USSR FORCES DIPLOM NUC/PWR WAR PEACE TOTALISM 20 NATO. PAGE 21 H0427
ECO/UNDEV FOR/AID ORD/FREE NAT/G

B63
HAMM H.,ALBANIA - CHINA'S BEACHHEAD IN EUROPE. ALBANIA CHINA/COM USSR YUGOSLAVIA ELITES SOCIETY POL/PAR DELIB/GP FORCES ECO/TAC COERCE ISOLAT PEACE MARXISM...IDEA/COMP 20 MAO. PAGE 65 H1304
DIPLOM REV NAT/G POLICY

B63
KATEB G.,UTOPIA AND ITS ENEMIES. CULTURE STRATA ECO/DEV INDUS REV MORAL...PSY IDEA/COMP 19/20. PAGE 84 H1668
UTOPIA SOCIETY PHIL/SCI PEACE

B63
LARSON A.,A WARLESS WORLD. FUT CULTURE NAT/G VOL/ASSN FORCES CREATE DOMIN PEACE ALL/VALS...HUM STERTYP 20. PAGE 91 H1824
SOCIETY CONCPT ARMS/CONT

B63
WHEARE K.C.,LEGISLATURES. POL/PAR DELIB/GP WAR PEACE CONCPT. PAGE 167 H3338
LEGIS PARL/PROC JURID GOV/COMP

S63
GROSSER A.,"FRANCE AND GERMANY IN THE ATLANTIC COMMUNITY." INT/ORG NAT/G TOP/EX DIPLOM REGION PEACE ATTIT ORD/FREE PWR...CONCPT RECORD TIME/SEQ GEN/LAWS VAL/FREE COLD/WAR 20. PAGE 62 H1234
EUR+WWI VOL/ASSN FRANCE GERMANY

S63
TANG P.S.H.,"SINO-SOVIET TENSIONS." ASIA CHINA/COM COM CUBA KOREA/N VIETNAM/N NAT/G VOL/ASSN DELIB/GP PEACE PERCEPT PWR...METH/CNCPT MYTH RECORD TREND GEN/LAWS 20. PAGE 152 H3041
ACT/RES EDU/PROP REV

B64
BELL C.,THE DEBATABLE ALLIANCE. COM UK USA+45 NAT/G FORCES PLAN BAL/PWR NUC/PWR WAR ATTIT...GOV/COMP 20. PAGE 13 H0263
DIPLOM PWR PEACE POLICY

B64
PITTMAN J.,PEACEFUL COEXISTENCE. USSR NAT/G NUC/PWR WAR ATTIT 20. PAGE 126 H2518
DIPLOM PEACE POLICY FORCES

B64
SEGAL R.,SANCTIONS AGAINST SOUTH AFRICA. AFR SOUTH/AFR NAT/G INT/TRADE RACE/REL PEACE PWR ...INT/LAW ANTHOL 20 UN. PAGE 141 H2821
SANCTION DISCRIM ECO/TAC POLICY

B64
UNESCO,WORLD COMMUNICATIONS: PRESS, RADIO, TELEVISION, FILM (4TH ED.). WOR+45 DIPLOM TV PEACE ...NAT/COMP SOC/INTEG 20 FILM. PAGE 158 H3163
COM/IND EDU/PROP PRESS TEC/DEV

B64
WRIGHT Q.,A STUDY OF WAR. LAW NAT/G PROB/SOLV BAL/PWR NAT/LISM PEACE ATTIT SOVEREIGN...CENSUS SOC/INTEG. PAGE 171 H3421
WAR CONCPT DIPLOM CONTROL

S64
"FURTHER READING." INDIA PAKISTAN SECT WAR PEACE ATTIT...POLICY 20. PAGE 2 H0044
BIBLIOG GP/REL DIPLOM NAT/G

S64
HIRAI N.,"SHINTO AND INTERNATIONAL PROBLEMS." SOCIETY NAT/G PLAN EDU/PROP RACE/REL PEACE ATTIT PERCEPT LOVE MORAL...HUM MYTH RECORD SAMP TREND STERTYP TOT/POP 20 UN CHINJAP SHINTO. PAGE 71 H1423
ASIA SECT

S64
LERNER W.,"THE HISTORICAL ORIGINS OF THE SOVIET DOCTRINE OF PEACEFUL COEXISTENCE." COM USSR INT/ORG
EDU/PROP DIPLOM

NAT/G VOL/ASSN PLAN PEACE ATTIT RIGID/FLEX PWR MARXISM...TIME/SEQ COLD/WAR 20. PAGE 95 H1891

S64
ZARTMAN I.W.,"LES RELATIONS ENTRE LA FRANCE ET L'ALGERIA DEPUIS LES ACCORDS D'EVIAN." EUR+WWI FUT ISLAM CULTURE AGRI EXTR/IND FINAN INDUS POL/PAR DIPLOM ECO/TAC FOR/AID PEACE ATTIT DRIVE ALL/VALS ...TIME/SEQ VAL/FREE 20. PAGE 172 H3450
ECO/UNDEV ALGERIA FRANCE

B65
ADENAUER K.,MEINE ERINNERUNGEN, 1945-53 (VOL. I), 1953-55 (VOL. II). EUR+WWI GERMANY CHIEF FORCES PROB/SOLV DIPLOM ARMS/CONT INGP/REL PEACE SOVEREIGN ...OBS/ENVIR RECORD 20. PAGE 3 H0069
NAT/G BIOG SELF/OBS

B65
COX R.H.,THE STATE IN INTERNATIONAL RELATIONS. INT/ORG DIPLOM REV WAR PEACE MARXISM...CONCPT GOV/COMP. PAGE 34 H0690
SOVEREIGN NAT/G FASCISM ORD/FREE

B65
DOLCI D.,A NEW WORLD IN THE MAKING. GHANA SENEGAL USSR YUGOSLAVIA CULTURE INT/ORG PLAN EDU/PROP GP/REL PEACE MORAL...GEOG SOC 20 COLD/WAR. PAGE 42 H0834
SOCIETY ALL/VALS DRIVE PERSON

B65
GEORGE M.,THE WARPED VISION. EUR+WWI UK NAT/G POL/PAR LEGIS PARL/PROC SANCTION COERCE WAR GOV/REL PEACE RESPECT 20 CONSRV/PAR. PAGE 56 H1113
LEAD ATTIT DIPLOM POLICY

B65
GRAHAM G.S.,THE POLITICS OF NAVAL SUPREMACY; STUDIES IN BRITISH MARITIME ASCENDANCY. UK SEA NAT/G BAL/PWR LEAD WAR WEAPON PEACE...POLICY 18/19 COMMONWLTH. PAGE 60 H1191
FORCES PWR COLONIAL DIPLOM

B65
HALPERIN M.H.,COMMUNIST CHINA AND ARMS CONTROL. CHINA/COM FUT USA+45 CULTURE FORCES TEC/DEV ECO/TAC WAR PEACE ORD/FREE MARXISM 20 COLD/WAR. PAGE 64 H1292
ATTIT POLICY ARMS/CONT NUC/PWR

B65
LARUS J.,COMPARATIVE WORLD POLITICS. ASIA INDIA WOR+45 WOR-45 BAL/PWR WAR PEACE RATIONAL MORAL PWR ...REALPOL INT/LAW MUSLIM. PAGE 91 H1825
GOV/COMP IDEA/COMP DIPLOM NAT/COMP

B65
MCSHERRY J.E.,RUSSIA AND THE UNITED STATES UNDER EISENHOWER, KHRUSHCHEV, AND KENNEDY. USSR EX/STRUC TOP/EX PRESS WAR...POLICY TREND 20. PAGE 108 H2150
DIPLOM CHIEF NAT/G PEACE

B65
O'BRIEN F.,CRISIS IN WORLD COMMUNISM* MARXISM IN SEARCH OF EFFICIENCY. COM ECO/DEV PLAN INT/TRADE WAR ADJUST PEACE...STAT TIME/SEQ GOV/COMP NAT/COMP COLD/WAR. PAGE 119 H2384
MARXISM USSR DRIVE EFFICIENCY

B65
UN,SPACE ACTIVITIES AND RESOURCES: REVIEW OF UNITED NATION'S NATIONAL AND INTERNATIONAL PROGRAMS. INT/ORG LABOR PLAN TEC/DEV DIPLOM EFFICIENCY HEALTH ...GOV/COMP 20 UN. PAGE 158 H3155
SPACE NUC/PWR FOR/AID PEACE

B65
US DEPARTMENT OF DEFENSE,US SECURITY ARMS CONTROL, AND DISARMAMENT 1961-1965 (PAMPHLET). CHINA/COM COM GERMANY/W ISRAEL SPACE USA+45 USSR WOR+45 FORCES EDU/PROP DETER EQUILIB PEACE ALL/VALS...GOV/COMP 20 NATO. PAGE 159 H3183
BIBLIOG/A ARMS/CONT NUC/PWR DIPLOM

B65
WOLFE B.D.,MARXISM; ONE HUNDRED YEARS IN THE LIFE OF A DOCTRINE. USSR WAR NAT/LISM PEACE TOTALISM ...MAJORIT 20 MARX/KARL. PAGE 170 H3399
MARXISM LEAD ATTIT

S65
LEVI W.,"THE CONCEPT OF INTEGRATION IN RESEARCH ON PEACE." NAT/G VOL/ASSN DIPLOM TASK ADJUST NAT/LISM PEACE DRIVE LOVE...PSY NET/THEORY GEN/LAWS. PAGE 95 H1897
CONCPT IDEA/COMP INT/ORG CENTRAL

S65
STAROBIN J.R.,"COMMUNISM IN WESTERN EUROPE." FRANCE GERMANY ITALY USA+45 USSR ECO/DEV FEDERAL PEACE ATTIT DRIVE PWR TREND. PAGE 149 H2972
MARXISM EUR+WWI POL/PAR NAT/COMP

B66
MAICHEL K.,CATALOG OF SOVIET AND RUSSIAN NEWSPAPERS AT THE HOOVER INSTITUTION OF WAR, REVOLUTION AND PEACE. USSR NAT/G EDU/PROP LEAD REV WAR PEACE ATTIT 19/20. PAGE 101 H2017
BIBLIOG/A PRESS COM MARXISM

B66
MARTIN L.W.,DIPLOMACY IN MODERN EUROPEAN HISTORY. EUR+WWI MOD/EUR INT/ORG NAT/G EX/STRUC ROUTINE WAR PEACE TOTALISM PWR 15/20 COLD/WAR EUROPE/W. PAGE 103 H2064
DIPLOM POLICY

B66
SOBEL L.A.,SOUTH VIETNAM: US-COMMUNIST CONFRONTATION IN SOUTHEAST ASIA 1961-65. VIETNAM FOR/AID CROWD DETER REV PEACE...GEOG 20 INTERVENT DIEM COLD/WAR. PAGE 146 H2926
WAR TIME/SEQ FORCES NAT/G

B66
STADLER K.R.,THE BIRTH OF THE AUSTRIAN REPUBLIC, 1918-1921. AUSTRIA PLAN TASK PEACE...POLICY
NAT/G DIPLOM

DECISION 20. PAGE 148 H2966 — WAR DELIB/GP

B66
THOMPSON J.M.,RUSSIA, BOLSHEVISM, AND THE VERSAILLES PEACE. RUSSIA USSR INT/ORG NAT/G DELIB/GP AGREE REV WAR PWR 20 TREATY VERSAILLES BOLSHEVISM. PAGE 154 H3083 — DIPLOM PEACE MARXISM

B66
THORNTON M.J.,NAZISM, 1918-1945. GERMANY INT/ORG DIPLOM REV PEACE FASCISM...CONCPT 20 HITLER/A WEIMAR/REP NAZI. PAGE 155 H3089 — TOTALISM POL/PAR NAT/G WAR

B66
WEINSTEIN F.B.,VIETNAM'S UNHELD ELECTIONS: THE FAILURE TO CARRY OUT THE 1956 REUNIFICATION ELECTIONS... (MONOGRAPH). VIETNAM/S VIETNAM/N LEGIT CONFER ADJUD WAR PEACE 20 TREATY GENEVA/CON UNIFICA. PAGE 166 H3330 — AGREE NAT/G CHOOSE DIPLOM

S66
TURKEVICH J.,"SOVIET SCIENCE APPRAISED." USA+45 R+D ACADEM FORCES DIPLOM EDU/PROP WAR EFFICIENCY PEACE SKILL OBS. PAGE 157 H3137 — USSR TEC/DEV NAT/COMP ATTIT

B67
AMERICAN FRIENDS SERVICE COMM,IN PLACE OF WAR. NAT/G ACT/RES DIPLOM ADMIN NUC/PWR EFFICIENCY ...POLICY 20. PAGE 6 H0122 — PEACE PACIFISM WAR DETER

B67
BAIN C.A.,VIETNAM: THE ROOTS OF CONFLICT. FRANCE S/ASIA USSR VIETNAM POL/PAR SECT FORCES COLONIAL NAT/LISM PEACE ORD/FREE MARXISM...GEOG CHARTS 4/20. PAGE 10 H0202 — NAT/G WAR CULTURE

B67
BOHANNAN P.,LAW AND WARFARE. CULTURE CT/SYS COERCE REV PEACE...JURID SOC CONCPT ANTHOL 20. PAGE 18 H0367 — METH/COMP ADJUD WAR LAW

B67
EVANS R.H.,COEXISTENCE: COMMUNISM AND ITS PRACTICE IN BOLOGNA, 1945-1965. ITALY CAP/ISM ADMIN CHOOSE PEACE ORD/FREE...SOC STAT DEEP/INT SAMP CHARTS BIBLIOG 20. PAGE 48 H0952 — MARXISM CULTURE MUNIC POL/PAR

B67
FAY S.B.,THE ORIGINS OF THE WORLD WAR (2ND REV. ED. 2 VOLS.). NAT/G FORCES DIPLOM CONFER LEAD PEACE ...REALPOL GOV/COMP 19/20. PAGE 49 H0978 — MOD/EUR WAR REGION INT/ORG

B67
PLANCK C.R.,THE CHANGING STATUS OF GERMAN REUNIFICATION IN WESTERN DIPLOMACY, 1955-1966. GERMANY DELIB/GP PLAN PEACE...TREND 20 KENNEDY/JF DEGAULLE/C. PAGE 126 H2519 — NAT/G DIPLOM CENTRAL

B67
RAMUNDO B.A.,PEACEFUL COEXISTENCE: INTERNATIONAL LAW IN THE BUILDING OF COMMUNISM. USSR INT/ORG DIPLOM COLONIAL ARMS/CONT ROLE SOVEREIGN...POLICY METH/COMP NAT/COMP BIBLIOG. PAGE 129 H2588 — INT/LAW PEACE MARXISM METH/CNCPT

B67
ROSENBLUTH G.,THE CANADIAN ECONOMY AND DISARMAMENT. CANADA FUT ECO/DEV INDUS R+D DELIB/GP DIPLOM ECO/TAC CIVMIL/REL PEACE...POLICY BIBLIOG PACIFIST 20. PAGE 134 H2679 — ARMS/CONT STAT PLAN NAT/G

S67
BEVEL D.N.,"JOURNEY TO NORTH VIETNAM." VIETNAM/N CONSTN NAT/G FORCES PROB/SOLV DEATH CIVMIL/REL PEACE MORAL...ANTHOL 20 NEGRO. PAGE 16 H0325 — ATTIT DIPLOM ORD/FREE WAR

S67
GRIEB K.J.,"THE UNITED STATES AND THE CENTRAL AMERICAN CONFEDERATION." COSTA/RICA EL/SALVADR GUATEMALA HONDURAS L/A+17C NICARAGUA NAT/G FORCES CONFER AGREE EXEC ARMS/CONT REV WAR PEACE ATTIT 20. PAGE 60 H1212 — INT/ORG DIPLOM POLICY REGION

S67
HALPERN B.,"THE ORIGINS OF THE CRISIS." ISLAM ISRAEL INT/ORG FORCES WEAPON PEACE ORD/FREE TREATY 20 UN. PAGE 65 H1296 — WAR NAT/G DIPLOM

S67
MATTHEWS R.O.,"THE SUEZ CANAL DISPUTE* A CASE STUDY IN PEACEFUL SETTLEMENT." FRANCE ISRAEL UAR UK NAT/G CONTROL LEAD COERCE WAR NAT/LISM ROLE ORD/FREE PWR ...INT/LAW UN 20. PAGE 105 H2099 — PEACE DIPLOM ADJUD

S67
MOZINGO D.,"CONTAINMENT IN ASIA RECONSIDERED." NAT/G DIPLOM REV PEACE ORD/FREE 20. PAGE 114 H2275 — ATTIT CONTROL NAT/LISM EFFICIENCY

S67
NAHUMI M.,"THE POWERS IN THE MIDDLE EAST CONFLICT." ISLAM ISRAEL JORDAN UAR NAT/G PEACE ATTIT 20 JEWS. PAGE 115 H2304 — DIPLOM WAR NAT/LISM

S67
NIEBUHR R.,"THE ETHICS OF WAR AND PEACE IN THE NUCLEAR AGE." VIETNAM INTELL CONFER CONTROL WAR GOV/REL PERS/REL ORD/FREE...POLICY INT GOV/COMP NAT/COMP 20 UN. PAGE 118 H2360 — MORAL PEACE NUC/PWR DIPLOM

S67
OJHA I.C.,"CHINA'S CAUTIOUS AMERICAN POLICY." CHINA/COM VIETNAM NAT/G NUC/PWR PEACE 20. PAGE 121 H2411 — DIPLOM POLICY WAR DECISION

S67
RONNING C.,"NANKING: 1950." ASIA CANADA CHINA/COM NAT/G PLAN ECO/TAC REV ADJUST 20. PAGE 133 H2667 — DIPLOM ROLE PEACE

S67
ROOT W.,"REPORT FROM PARIS - DE GAULLE: WHICH WAY TO THE FUTURE?" CANADA FRANCE ISLAM UK INT/ORG CHIEF CREATE AGREE CONTROL ARMS/CONT NUC/PWR EQUILIB PEACE PWR 20 DEGAULLE/C NATO. PAGE 134 H2670 — POLICY DIPLOM NAT/G BAL/PWR

S67
VINCENT S.,"SHOULD BIAFRA SURVIVE?" NIGERIA ECO/UNDEV CHIEF FORCES ECO/TAC GP/REL DISCRIM PEACE ORD/FREE SOC/INTEG 20 BIAFRA IBO. PAGE 163 H3256 — AFR REV REGION NAT/G

C67
GEHLEN M.P.,"THE POLITICS OF COEXISTENCE: SOVIET METHODS AND MOTIVES." COM USSR NAT/G INT/TRADE EDU/PROP ARMS/CONT DETER KNOWL...CHARTS IDEA/COMP 20 COLD/WAR. PAGE 55 H1108 — BIBLIOG PEACE DIPLOM MARXISM

B90
BURKE E.,REFLECTIONS ON THE REVOLUTION IN FRANCE. FRANCE UK NAT/G DOMIN LEGIT PEACE PWR SOVEREIGN CONSERVE...POLICY GEN/LAWS 18. PAGE 24 H0487 — REV ORD/FREE CHIEF TRADIT

PEACE/CORP....PEACE CORPS

S65
THOMAS F.C. JR.,"THE PEACE CORPS IN MOROCCO." CULTURE MUNIC PROVS CREATE ROUTINE TASK ADJUST STRANGE...OBS PEACE/CORP. PAGE 154 H3077 — MOROCCO FRANCE FOR/AID EDU/PROP

S66
HAIGH G.,"FIELD TRAINING IN HUMAN RELATIONS FOR THE PEACE CORPS." CONSULT CREATE EDU/PROP ADMIN TASK GP/REL ATTIT PERSON...PSY OBS SOC/EXP PEACE/CORP. PAGE 64 H1276 — CULTURE PERS/REL FOR/AID ADJUST

PEACEFUL COEXISTENCE....SEE PEACE+COLD/WAR

PEARSON/L....LESTER PEARSON

B65
GWYN R.J.,THE SHAPE OF SCANDAL: A STUDY OF A GOVERNMENT IN CRISIS. CANADA LEGIS ADJUD CT/SYS SANCTION CMN/WLTH 20 PEARSON/L. PAGE 63 H1260 — ELITES NAT/G CRIME

PEASLEE A.J. H2481

PEASNT/WAR....PEASANT WAR (1525)

PECKERT J. H2482

PELCOVITS N.A. H2483

PELLING H.M. H2484,H2485

PELZER K.J. H2486

PENDLE G. H2487

PENN/WM....WILLIAM PENN

PENNSYLVAN....PENNSYLVANIA

PENOLOGY....SEE CRIME

PENTAGON....PENTAGON

PENTONY D.E. H2488

PERAZA SARAUSA F. H2489,H2490

PERCEPT....PERCEPTION AND COGNITION

B10
MILL J.S.,UTILITARIANISM, LIBERTY, AND REPRESENTATIVE GOVERNMENT. CONTROL PERCEPT PERSON MORAL...CONCPT GEN/LAWS. PAGE 110 H2205 — HAPPINESS ORD/FREE REPRESENT NAT/G

B31
BONAR J.,THEORIES OF POPULATION FROM RALEIGH TO ARTHUR YOUNG. CHRIST-17C MOD/EUR CULTURE SOCIETY R+D CREATE ATTIT PERCEPT RIGID/FLEX...OLD/LIB CONCPT NEW/IDEA TIME/SEQ IDEA/COMP STERTYP — GEOG BIOG

GEN/LAWS. PAGE 19 H0372 CONCPT SOC

B38
JESSOP T.E.,A BIBLIOGRAPHY OF DAVID HUME AND OF SCOTTISH PHILOSOPHY FROM FRANCIS HUTCHESON TO LORD BALFOUR. UK INTELL NAT/G ATTIT...CONCPT 17/20 HUME/D CMN/WLTH. PAGE 81 H1615
BIBLIOG EPIST PERCEPT BIOG

B39
MILLER P.,THE NEW ENGLAND MIND: THE SEVENTEENTH CENTURY. CULTURE DOMIN WRITING INGP/REL CONSEN MAJORITY PERCEPT KNOWL MORAL...CONCPT LING WORSHIP 17 NEW/ENGLND PROTESTANT. PAGE 111 H2214
SECT REGION SOC ATTIT

S41
ABEL T.,"THE ELEMENT OF DECISION IN THE PATTERN OF WAR." EUR+WWI FUT NAT/G TOP/EX DIPLOM ROUTINE COERCE DISPL PERCEPT PWR...SOC METH/CNCPT HIST/WRIT TREND GEN/LAWS 20. PAGE 3 H0055
TEC/DEV FORCES WAR

B44
KNORR K.E.,BRITISH COLONIAL THEORIES 1570-1850. NAT/G DELIB/GP ECO/TAC PERCEPT PWR...WELF/ST METH/CNCPT CONT/OBS TIME/SEQ SIMUL TOT/POP 20. PAGE 87 H1734
ACT/RES DOMIN COLONIAL

C45
PAINE T.,"THE AGE OF REASON IN T. PAINE, THE COMPLETE WRITINGS OF THOMAS PAINE (VOL. 1) (1794-95)" CULTURE ACT/RES DOMIN UTOPIA ATTIT PERCEPT WORSHIP. PAGE 122 H2445
SECT KNOWL PHIL/SCI ORD/FREE

B46
MILL J.S.,ON LIBERTY. NAT/G LEGIT CONTROL PERS/REL PERCEPT...CONCPT 19. PAGE 110 H2206
ORD/FREE SOCIETY PERSON GEN/LAWS

B49
SARGENT S.S.,CULTURE AND PERSONALITY. FUT UNIV SOCIETY FAM KIN NEIGH BIO/SOC DRIVE PERCEPT RIGID/FLEX LOVE RESPECT...PSY SOC CONCPT OBS TIME/SEQ TREND CON/ANAL CHARTS HYPO/EXP SIMUL TOT/POP. PAGE 138 H2754
CULTURE PERSON

B49
SAUVY A.,LE POUVOIR ET L'OPINION. FRANCE STRATA NAT/G PERCEPT...POLICY PSY 20. PAGE 138 H2758
EDU/PROP MYTH PARTIC ATTIT

S51
GOULD J.,"THE KOMSOMOL AND THE HITLER JUGEND." COM EUR+WWI GERMANY SOCIETY NAT/G POL/PAR SCHOOL TOTALISM DRIVE PERCEPT KNOWL FASCISM...SOC NAZI TOT/POP 20. PAGE 59 H1185
EDU/PROP CON/ANAL SOCISM

B52
CALLOT E.,LA SOCIETE ET SON ENVIRONNEMENT: ESSAI SUR LES PRINCIPES DES SCIENCES SOCIALES. GP/REL ADJUST CONSEN ISOLAT HABITAT PERCEPT PERSON ...BIBLIOG SOC/INTEG 20. PAGE 25 H0507
SOCIETY PHIL/SCI CULTURE

S52
KECSKEMETI P.,"THE 'POLICY SCIENCES': ASPIRATION AND OUTLOOK." UNIV CULTURE INTELL SOCIETY STRUCT EDU/PROP ATTIT PERCEPT RIGID/FLEX KNOWL...PHIL/SCI METH/CNCPT OBS 20. PAGE 84 H1674
CREATE NEW/IDEA

B53
MEYER P.,THE JEWS IN THE SOVIET SATELLITES. CZECHOSLVK POLAND SOCIETY STRATA NAT/G BAL/PWR ECO/TAC EDU/PROP LEGIT ADMIN COERCE ATTIT DISPL PERCEPT HEALTH PWR RESPECT WEALTH...METH/CNCPT JEWS VAL/FREE NAZI 20. PAGE 110 H2192
COM SECT TOTALISM USSR

B54
SCHRAMM W.,THE PROCESS AND EFFECTS OF MASS COMMUNICATION. CULTURE INTELL SOCIETY COM/IND DRIVE PERCEPT PERSON RIGID/FLEX KNOWL...PSY SOC CONCPT CHARTS. PAGE 140 H2800
ATTIT EDU/PROP

B56
DEUTSCH K.W.,AN INTERDISCIPLINARY BIBLIOGRAPHY ON NATIONALISM, 1935-1953. CULTURE SOCIETY SECT ATTIT HABITAT HEREDITY PERCEPT ROLE WEALTH...METH/CNCPT LING 20. PAGE 40 H0798
BIBLIOG/A NAT/LISM COLONIAL ADJUST

B56
GOFFMAN E.,THE PRESENTATION OF SELF IN EVERYDAY LIFE. CULTURE INGP/REL ATTIT DRIVE...SOC OBS RECORD 20. PAGE 58 H1154
PERS/COMP PERSON PERCEPT ROLE

B56
MYERS F.M.,THE WARFARE OF DEMOCRATIC IDEALS. SECT KNOWL MORAL CATHISM...TRADIT CONCPT 20. PAGE 115 H2302
POPULISM CHOOSE REPRESENT PERCEPT

B56
READ M.,EDUCATION AND SOCIAL CHANGE IN TROPICAL AREAS. AFR L/A+17C SOCIETY LITERACY PERCEPT PERSON WEALTH...HEAL PHIL/SCI SOC 20. PAGE 130 H2603
EDU/PROP HABITAT DRIVE CULTURE

S57
SPROUT H.,"ENVIRONMENTAL FACTORS IN THE STUDY OF INTERNATIONAL POLITICS." UNIV SOCIETY ECO/DEV NAT/G DELIB/GP TOP/EX ROUTINE ATTIT PERCEPT...POLICY GEOG CONCPT MYTH TIME/SEQ. PAGE 148 H2957
DECISION GEN/LAWS DIPLOM

B58
HENLE P.,LANGUAGE, THOUGHT AND CULTURE. CULTURE GP/REL PERCEPT...PSY TREND ANTHOL 20. PAGE 70 H1397
LING RATIONAL

B58
STEINBERG C.S.,THE MASS COMMUNICATORS: PUBLIC RELATIONS, PUBLIC OPINION, AND MASS MEDIA. CULTURE CONSULT ACT/RES FEEDBACK DISPL WEALTH 20. PAGE 149 H2975
EDU/PROP ATTIT COM/IND PERCEPT

B60
ALMOND G.A.,THE POLITICS OF THE DEVELOPING AREAS. AFR ISLAM L/A+17C S/ASIA SOCIETY ECO/UNDEV NAT/G ADMIN PERCEPT KNOWL SOVEREIGN...CONCPT GEN/LAWS 20. PAGE 6 H0112
EX/STRUC ATTIT NAT/LISM

B60
BARBU Z.,PROBLEMS OF HISTORICAL PSYCHOLOGY. GREECE MEDIT-7 UK CULTURE TEC/DEV ADJUST RATIONAL ATTIT PERCEPT...METH/CNCPT NEW/IDEA TIME/SEQ GEN/METH. PAGE 11 H0214
PERSON PSY HIST/WRIT IDEA/COMP

B60
SCANLON D.G.,INTERNATIONAL EDUCATION: A DOCUMENTARY HISTORY. ADMIN CONTROL ATTIT PERCEPT...BIOG ANTHOL METH 20. PAGE 138 H2765
EDU/PROP INT/ORG NAT/COMP DIPLOM

S60
NORTH R.C.,"DIE DISKREPANZ ZWISCHEN REALITAT UND WUNSCHBILD ALS INNENPOLITISCHER FAKTOR." ASIA CHINA/COM COM FUT ECO/UNDEV NAT/G PLAN DOMIN ADMIN COERCE PERCEPT...SOC MYTH GEN/METH WORK TOT/POP 20. PAGE 119 H2373
SOCIETY ECO/TAC

B61
DOOB L.W.,COMMUNICATION IN AFRICA: A SEARCH FOR BOUNDARIES. CULTURE SOCIETY EDU/PROP WRITING INGP/REL DRIVE ORD/FREE...ART/METH SOC LING BIBLIOG 20. PAGE 42 H0837
AFR FEEDBACK PERCEPT PERS/REL

B61
ERASMUS C.J.,MAN TAKES CONTROL: CULTURAL DEVELOPMENT AND AMERICAN AID. STRUCT OWN DRIVE PERCEPT...SOC 20 MEXIC/AMER. PAGE 47 H0937
ORD/FREE CULTURE ECO/UNDEV TEC/DEV

B61
LUNDBERG G.A.,CAN SCIENCE SAVE US. UNIV CULTURE INTELL SOCIETY ECO/DEV R+D PLAN EDU/PROP ROUTINE CHOOSE ATTIT PERCEPT ALL/VALS...TREND 20. PAGE 99 H1979
ACT/RES CONCPT TOTALISM

S61
FITZGIBBON R.H.,"MEASUREMENT OF LATIN AMERICAN POLITICAL CHANGE." L/A+17C CONSTN CULTURE SOCIETY ECO/UNDEV NAT/G POL/PAR PUB/INST ACT/RES EDU/PROP PERCEPT KNOWL ORD/FREE SOVEREIGN...METH/CNCPT TREND OAS 20. PAGE 51 H1020
CHOOSE ATTIT

S61
SCHAPIRO L.,"SOVIET GOVERNMENT TODAY." COM EUR+WWI INT/ORG POL/PAR VOL/ASSN ACT/RES PLAN PERCEPT ...CONCPT TREND TOT/POP VAL/FREE 20. PAGE 139 H2773
NAT/G TOTALISM USSR

B62
BRETTON H.L.,POWER AND STABILITY IN NIGERIA: THE POLITICS OF DECOLONIZATION. AFR CONSTN INTELL ECO/UNDEV COM/IND KIN NAT/G POL/PAR PROVS VOL/ASSN LEGIS DOMIN EDU/PROP LEGIT EXEC ROUTINE CHOOSE NAT/LISM ATTIT PERCEPT ALL/VALS. PAGE 20 H0411
CULTURE OBS NIGERIA

B62
HAY S.N.,SOUTHEAST ASIAN HISTORY: A BIBLIOGRAPHICAL GUIDE. STRATA KIN NAT/G REGION GUERRILLA REV WAR ADJUST HABITAT PERCEPT ALL/IDEOS...CHARTS 5/20. PAGE 68 H1365
BIBLIOG/A S/ASIA CULTURE

B62
INSTITUTE FOR STUDY OF USSR,YOUTH IN FERMENT. INTELL NAT/G PERF/ART POL/PAR SCHOOL VOL/ASSN FORCES EDU/PROP ATTIT DRIVE PERCEPT HEALTH KNOWL MORAL ORD/FREE RESPECT...SOC OBS HIST/WRIT VAL/FREE. PAGE 77 H1537
COM CULTURE USSR

B62
KRECH D.,INDIVIDUAL IN SOCIETY; A TEXTBOOK OF SOCIAL PSYCHOLOGY. UNIV CULTURE LEAD INGP/REL ATTIT DRIVE PERCEPT ROLE...PHIL/SCI BIBLIOG T. PAGE 88 H1765
PSY SOC SOCIETY PERS/REL

B62
KRUGLAK T.E.,THE TWO FACES OF TASS. COM COM/IND NAT/G ACT/RES PLAN PRESS PERCEPT PERSON KNOWL 20. PAGE 89 H1778
PUB/INST EDU/PROP USSR

S62
LONDON K.,"SINO-SOVIET RELATIONS IN THE CONTEXT OF THE 'WORLD SOCIALIST SYSTEM'." ASIA CHINA/COM COM USSR INT/ORG NAT/G TOP/EX BAL/PWR DIPLOM DOMIN ATTIT PERCEPT RIGID/FLEX PWR MARXISM...METH/CNCPT TREND 20. PAGE 98 H1957
DELIB/GP CONCPT SOCISM

S62
MONNIER J.P.,"LA SUCCESSION D'ETATS EN MATIERE DE RESPONSABILITE INTERNATIONALE." UNIV CONSTN INTELL SOCIETY ADJUD ROUTINE PERCEPT SUPEGO...GEN/LAWS TOT/POP 20. PAGE 112 H2240
NAT/G JURID INT/LAW

S62
ROTBERG R.,"THE RISE OF AFRICAN NATIONALISM: THE CASE OF EAST AND CENTRAL AFRICA." AFR CULTURE SOCIETY NEIGH DIPLOM DOMIN COLONIAL COERCE DISPL PERCEPT PWR SOVEREIGN...POLICY OBS/ENVIR TREND WORK 20. PAGE 135 H2690
ATTIT DRIVE NAT/LISM REV

S62
VIGNES D.,"L'AUTORITE DES TRAITES INTERNATIONAUX EN DROIT INTERNE." EUR+WWI UNIV LAW CONSTN INTELL NAT/G POL/PAR DIPLOM ATTIT PERCEPT ALL/VALS ...POLICY INT/LAW JURID CONCPT TIME/SEQ 20 TREATY. PAGE 163 H3252 STRUCT LEGIT FRANCE

B63
HALPERIN M.H.,THE POLITICS OF SOCIAL CHANGE IN THE MIDDLE EAST AND NORTH AFRICA. ISLAM CULTURE ACT/RES REV ATTIT PERCEPT KNOWL...METH/CNCPT OBS TIME/SEQ GEN/METH TOT/POP VAL/FREE 20. PAGE 64 H1291 SOC TREND

B63
KRAEHE E.,METTERNICH'S GERMAN POLICY: THE CONTEST WITH NAPOLEON, 1799-1814, VOL. 1. FRANCE MOD/EUR NAT/G CONSULT TOP/EX PLAN BAL/PWR DOMIN COERCE ATTIT DRIVE PERCEPT PERSON SKILL...CONCPT RECORD TIME/SEQ TREND 18/19. PAGE 88 H1764 BIOG GERMANY DIPLOM

B63
SKLAR R.L.,NIGERIAN POLITICAL PARTIES: POWER IN AN EMERGENT AFRICAN NATION. AFR EUR+WWI CULTURE STRATA NAT/G DELIB/GP EX/STRUC LEGIS DOMIN EDU/PROP ROUTINE CHOOSE ATTIT PERCEPT ORD/FREE PWR...SOC CONCPT OBS TOT/POP VAL/FREE. PAGE 145 H2898 POL/PAR SOCIETY NAT/LISM NIGERIA

S63
ARASTEH R.,"THE ROLE OF INTELLECTUALS IN ADMINISTRATIVE DEVELOPMENT AND SOCIAL CHANGE IN MODERN IRAN." ISLAM CULTURE NAT/G CONSULT ACT/RES EDU/PROP EXEC ATTIT BIO/SOC PERCEPT SUPEGO ALL/VALS ...POLICY MGT PSY SOC CONCPT 20. PAGE 8 H0157 INTELL ADMIN IRAN

S63
DEUTSCHMANN P.J.,"THE MASS MEDIA IN AN UNDERDEVELOPED VILLAGE." L/A+17C EDU/PROP PERCEPT KNOWL ORD/FREE...SOC INT VAL/FREE 20. PAGE 40 H0809 COM/IND CULTURE

S63
GLUCKMAN M.,"CIVIL WAR AND THEORIES OF POWER IN BAROTSE-LAND: AFRICAN AND MEDIEVAL ANALOGIES." AFR CHRIST-17C LAW CONSTN CULTURE STRATA KIN DELIB/GP FORCES DOMIN LEGIT COERCE PERCEPT ORD/FREE...SOC INT TIME/SEQ GEN/LAWS VAL/FREE. PAGE 57 H1148 TOP/EX PWR WAR

S63
MAZRUI A.A.,"ON THE CONCEPT 'WE ARE ALL AFRICANS'." AFR CULTURE KIN LOC/G NAT/G DOMIN EDU/PROP LEGIT ATTIT PERCEPT PERSON KNOWL ORD/FREE...TIME/SEQ TOT/POP 20. PAGE 106 H2110 PROVS INT/ORG NAT/LISM

S63
ROUGEMONT D.,"LES NOUVELLES CHANCES DE L'EUROPE." EUR+WWI FUT ECO/DEV INT/ORG NAT/G ACT/RES PLAN TEC/DEV EDU/PROP ADMIN COLONIAL FEDERAL ATTIT PWR SKILL...TREND 20. PAGE 135 H2696 ECO/UNDEV PERCEPT

S63
TANG P.S.H.,"SINO-SOVIET TENSIONS." ASIA CHINA/COM COM CUBA KOREA/N VIETNAM/N NAT/G VOL/ASSN DELIB/GP PEACE PERCEPT PWR...METH/CNCPT MYTH RECORD TREND GEN/LAWS 20. PAGE 152 H3041 ACT/RES EDU/PROP REV

S63
WEISSBERG G.,"MAPS AS EVIDENCE IN INTERNATIONAL BOUNDARY DISPUTES: A REAPPRAISAL." CHINA/COM EUR+WWI INDIA MOD/EUR S/ASIA INT/ORG NAT/G LEGIT PERCEPT...JURID CHARTS 20. PAGE 166 H3331 LAW GEOG SOVEREIGN

S63
WELLS H.,"THE OAS AND THE DOMINICAN ELECTIONS." L/A+17C INT/ORG NAT/G POL/PAR TEC/DEV ECO/TAC EDU/PROP PERCEPT...TIME/SEQ OAS TOT/POP 20. PAGE 166 H3332 CONSULT CHOOSE DOMIN/REP

B64
CURTIN P.D.,THE IMAGE OF AFRICA: BRITISH IDEAS AND ACTION, 1780-1850. MOD/EUR SOCIETY FORCES ACT/RES DOMIN EDU/PROP COERCE ATTIT PERCEPT RIGID/FLEX SUPEGO HEALTH KNOWL MORAL ORD/FREE WEALTH...CONCPT WORK VAL/FREE. PAGE 36 H0726 AFR CULTURE UK DIPLOM

B64
JOSEPHSON E.,MAN ALONE: ALIENATION IN MODERN SOCIETY. WOR+45 ECO/DEV WORKER WAR LEISURE RACE/REL ANOMIE ATTIT PERCEPT PERSON ALL/VALS...ANTHOL 20. PAGE 82 H1636 STRANGE CULTURE SOCIETY ADJUST

B64
NORTHROP F.S.,CROSS-CULTURAL UNDERSTANDING: EPISTEMOLOGY IN ANTHROPOLOGY. BURMA GREECE THAILAND HABITAT PERCEPT PERSON...PHIL/SCI SOC METH 20 MEXIC/AMER CHINJAP. PAGE 119 H2375 EPIST PSY CULTURE CONCPT

B64
THORNTON T.P.,THE THIRD WORLD IN SOVIET PERSPECTIVE: STUDIES BY SOVIET WRITERS ON THE DEVELOPING AREAS. AFR L/A+17C S/ASIA STRATA AGRI INDUS MARKET NAT/G POL/PAR ECO/TAC COLONIAL PERCEPT PWR WEALTH...MARXIST STAT CHARTS WORK MARX/KARL 20. PAGE 155 H3090 ECO/UNDEV ACT/RES USSR DIPLOM

L64
FINDLATER R.,"US." EUR+WWI GERMANY USSR SOCIETY FACE/GP EDU/PROP PERCEPT PERSON ALL/VALS...PSY SOC CONCPT SELF/OBS SAMP TREND 20. PAGE 50 H1001 CULTURE ATTIT UK

S64
COLEMAN J.S.,"COLLECTIVE DECISIONS." CULTURE ATTIT PERCEPT PWR SOC. PAGE 31 H0628 DECISION INGP/REL PERSON METH/COMP

S64
HIRAI N.,"SHINTO AND INTERNATIONAL PROBLEMS." SOCIETY NAT/G PLAN EDU/PROP RACE/REL PEACE ATTIT PERCEPT LOVE MORAL...HUM MYTH RECORD SAMP TREND STERTYP TOT/POP 20 UN CHINJAP SHINTO. PAGE 71 H1423 ASIA SECT

S64
JOHNSON K.F.,"CAUSAL FACTORS IN LATIN AMERICAN POLITICAL INSTABILITY." CULTURE NAT/G VOL/ASSN EX/STRUC FORCES EDU/PROP LEGIT ADMIN COERCE REV ATTIT KNOWL PWR...STYLE RECORD CHARTS WORK 20. PAGE 81 H1624 L/A+17C PERCEPT ELITES

S64
LANGERHANS H.,"NEHRU'S BITTERNESS." FUT INDIA S/ASIA CONSTN CULTURE ECO/UNDEV ECO/TAC DOMIN EDU/PROP ATTIT PERCEPT PERSON...POLICY 20 NEHRU/J. PAGE 91 H1811 ECO/DEV BIOG

S64
LEVI W.,"INDIAN NEUTRALISM RECONSIDERED." ASIA CHINA/COM S/ASIA SOCIETY NAT/G ACT/RES LEGIT NEUTRAL COERCE ATTIT DRIVE PERCEPT RIGID/FLEX HEALTH LOVE PWR...DECISION RECORD TREND STERTYP 20. PAGE 95 H1896 ORD/FREE CONCPT INDIA

S64
MC WILLIAM M.,"THE WORLD BANK AND THE TRANSFER OF POWER IN KENYA." AFR ECO/UNDEV CONSULT ACT/RES TEC/DEV PERCEPT PWR SKILL WEALTH...CONCPT OBS TREND 20. PAGE 106 H2119 NAT/G ECO/TAC

S64
NASH M.,"SOCIAL PREREQUISITES TO ECONOMIC GROWTH IN LATIN AMERICA AND SOUTHEAST ASIA." L/A+17C S/ASIA CULTURE SOCIETY ECO/UNDEV AGRI INDUS NAT/G PLAN TEC/DEV EDU/PROP ROUTINE ALL/VALS...POLICY RELATIV SOC NAT/COMP WORK TOT/POP 20. PAGE 116 H2314 ECO/DEV PERCEPT

S64
SAYEED K.,"PATHAN REGIONALISM." ISLAM PAKISTAN S/ASIA CULTURE SOCIETY NAT/G NEIGH DIPLOM LEGIT COERCE CHOOSE ATTIT DISPL PERCEPT ALL/VALS SOVEREIGN...POLICY RELATIV SOC TIME/SEQ TOT/POP 20. PAGE 138 H2761 SECT NAT/LISM REGION

B65
COSTA H DE L.A.,THE BACKGROUND OF NATIONALISM AND OTHER ESSAYS. ASIA PHILIPPINE ATTIT PERCEPT CATHISM ...ANTHOL 20. PAGE 34 H0674 NAT/LISM CULTURE ANOMIE NAT/G

B65
HYMES D.,THE USE OF COMPUTERS IN ANTHROPOLOGY. CULTURE PROF/ORG CONSULT CREATE EFFICIENCY PERCEPT ...CLASSIF LING CON/ANAL COMPUT/IR METH/COMP ANTHOL 20. PAGE 76 H1517 METH COMPUTER TEC/DEV SOC

B65
JANSEN M.B.,CHANGING JAPANESE ATTITUDES TOWARD MODERNIZATION. ASIA CHINA/COM S/ASIA INTELL SOCIETY KIN NAT/G SECT PERCEPT RIGID/FLEX...SOC CONCPT TIME/SEQ TREND TOT/POP 19/20 CHINJAP. PAGE 80 H1591 TEC/DEV ATTIT INDIA

S65
COOPER P.,"THE DEVELOPMENT OF THE CONCEPT OF WAR." UK COERCE ATTIT PERCEPT PERSON...STAT CHARTS CHINJAP. PAGE 33 H0660 CULTURE WAR SAMP STAND/INT

S65
LAULICHT J.,"PUBLIC OPINION AND FOREIGN POLICY DECISIONS." CANADA ELITES NAT/G FOR/AID LEAD NUC/PWR PERCEPT...INT QU CHARTS UN COLD/WAR. PAGE 92 H1839 DIPLOM ATTIT CON/ANAL SAMP

S65
MARK M.,"MUST WE FIGHT SOCIAL REVOLUTIONS OF THE LEFT?" L/A+17C USA+45 ECO/UNDEV DIPLOM ADJUST PERCEPT...IDEA/COMP NAT/COMP. PAGE 103 H2053 NAT/LISM REV MARXISM CREATE

S65
TRISKA J.F.,"SOVIET-AMERICAN RELATIONS* A MULTIPLE SYMMETRY MODEL." USA+45 USSR ACADEM ACT/RES EDU/PROP COERCE PERCEPT...NET/THEORY CHARTS NAT/COMP GEN/LAWS COLD/WAR. PAGE 157 H3132 SIMUL EQUILIB DIPLOM

S65
WATT D.C.,"RESTRICTIONS ON RESEARCH* THE FIFTY-YEAR RULE AND BRITISH FOREIGN POLICY." ACADEM PERCEPT ...HIST/WRIT NAT/COMP TIME. PAGE 166 H3315 UK USA+45 DIPLOM

S65
WEDGE B.,"PSYCHOLOGICAL FACTORS IN SOVIET DISARMAMENT NEGOTIATION." USA+45 CONFER ATTIT PERCEPT PERSON...PSY NAT/COMP. PAGE 166 H3324 USSR DIPLOM ARMS/CONT

S65
WOHLSTETTER R.,"CUBA AND PEARL HARBOR* HINDSIGHT AND FORESIGHT." USSR FORCES OP/RES TEC/DEV ATTIT PERCEPT...DECISION IDEA/COMP NAT/COMP STERTYP TIME. PAGE 170 H3395 CUBA RISK WAR ACT/RES

S65
WOLF C. JR.,"THE POLITICAL EFFECTS OF SOME MILITARY PROGRAMS* SOME INDICATIONS FROM LATIN AMERICA." ELITES STRATA BUDGET FOR/AID WEAPON ATTIT PERCEPT PWR...REGRESS SYS/QU CHARTS NAT/COMP. PAGE 170 H3397 L/A+17C FORCES CIVMIL/REL PROBABIL

S65
WRIGHT Q.,"THE ESCALATION OF INTERNATIONAL CONFLICTS." WOR+45 WOR-45 FORCES DIPLOM RISK COST WAR PERCEPT

ATTIT ALL/VALS...INT/LAW QUANT STAT NAT/COMP. PAGE 171 H3422 PREDICT MATH

B66
BERELSON B.,READER IN PUBLIC OPINION AND COMMUNICATION (2ND ED.). UNIV NAT/G PRESS GP/REL PERS/REL PERCEPT RIGID/FLEX...MAJORIT QUANT METH/COMP ANTHOL BIBLIOG 20. PAGE 15 H0298 EDU/PROP ATTIT CONCPT COM/IND

S66
GILBERT S.P.,"WARS OF LIBERATION AND SOVIET MILITARY AID POLICY." ASIA INDIA INDONESIA UAR USA+45 STRATA WAR PERCEPT MARXISM...STAT NAT/COMP. PAGE 56 H1124 USSR FOR/AID WEAPON DRIVE

S66
QUESTER G.H.,"ON THE IDENTIFICATION OF REAL AND PRETENDED COMMUNIST MILITARY DOCTRINE." ASIA USSR DETER WAR ATTIT DRIVE HEALTH TIME/SEQ. PAGE 129 H2574 RATIONAL PERCEPT NUC/PWR NAT/COMP

S66
SCHWARTZ M.,"THE 1964 PRESIDENTIAL ELECTIONS THROUGH SOVIET EYES." ASIA POL/PAR DIPLOM ATTIT MARXISM...NAT/COMP COLD/WAR. PAGE 140 H2811 USSR USA+45 PERCEPT

S66
SMITH D.D.,"MODAL ATTITUDE CLUSTERS* A SUPPLEMENT FOR THE STUDY OF NATIONAL CHARACTER." CULTURE NAT/G PERCEPT...SOC NEW/IDEA MODAL RECORD GEN/METH. PAGE 145 H2906 ATTIT PERSON PSY CONCPT

B67
COWLES M.,PERSPECTIVES IN THE EDUCATION OF DISADVANTAGED CHILDREN. CULTURE OP/RES PLAN PERS/REL ADJUST HABITAT PERCEPT KNOWL WEALTH ...SOC/WK IDEA/COMP ANTHOL 20. PAGE 34 H0686 EDU/PROP AGE/C TEC/DEV SCHOOL

B67
LAMBERT W.E.,CHILDREN'S VIEWS OF FOREIGN PEOPLES: A CROSS-NATIONAL STUDY. UNIV CULTURE EDU/PROP RACE/REL ATTIT PERCEPT ROLE...STAT STAND/INT CHARTS GP/COMP NAT/COMP. PAGE 90 H1802 AGE/C STRANGE GP/REL STERTYP

S67
DANA MONTANO S.M.,"APLICACIONES CONCRETAS DE LAS RESOLUCIONES Y RECOMENDACIONES DE LAS CONFERENCIAS INTERAMERICANAS DE ABOGADOS" L/A+17C NAT/G PROVS GOV/REL PERCEPT 20 ARGEN. PAGE 37 H0739 JURID CT/SYS ORD/FREE BAL/PWR

S67
KRISTOF L.K.D.,"THE STATE-IDEA, THE NATIONAL IDEA AND THE IMAGE OF THE FATHERLAND." CONSTN CULTURE INTELL SOCIETY WORKER TASK DRIVE HABITAT...MYTH GOV/COMP IDEA/COMP. PAGE 89 H1769 GEOG CONCPT NAT/G PERCEPT

S67
SZALAY L.B.,"SOVIET DOMESTIC PROPAGANDA AND LIBERALIZATION." COM USSR SOCIETY COM/IND NAT/G POL/PAR EX/STRUC TEC/DEV LEAD ATTIT ROLE MARXISM ...METH/COMP 20. PAGE 151 H3026 EDU/PROP TOTALISM PERSON PERCEPT

PERCEPTION....SEE PERCEPT

PERCY/CHAS....CHARLES PERCY

PEREZ ORTIZ R. H2491

PERF/ART....PERFORMING ARTS

B12
HEINSIUS W.,ALLGEMEINES BUCHER-LEXICON ODER VOLLSTANDIGES ALPHABETISCHES VERZEICHNIS ALLER VON 1700 BIS ZU ENDE...(1892). GERMANY PERF/ART...HUM SOC 18/19. PAGE 69 H1387 BIBLIOG POLICY ATTIT NAT/G

B42
BARNES H.E.,SOCIAL INSTITUTIONS IN AN ERA OF WORLD UPHEAVAL. INDUS FAM NAT/G PERF/ART SECT AUTOMAT PERSON MORAL...PREDICT 20. PAGE 11 H0221 SOCIETY CULTURE TECHRACY TREND

B50
COUNCIL BRITISH NATIONAL BIB,BRITISH NATIONAL BIBLIOGRAPHY. UK AGRI CONSTRUC PERF/ART POL/PAR SECT CREATE INT/TRADE LEAD...HUM JURID PHIL/SCI 20. PAGE 34 H0677 BIBLIOG/A NAT/G TEC/DEV DIPLOM

B59
JACOBS N.,CULTURE FOR THE MILLIONS? INTELL SOCIETY NAT/G...POLICY SOC OBS ANTHOL 20. PAGE 79 H1579 CULTURE COM/IND PERF/ART CONCPT

B61
FREYRE G.,THE PORTUGUESE AND THE TROPICS. L/A+17C PORTUGAL SOCIETY PERF/ART ADMIN TASK GP/REL ...ART/METH CONCPT SOC/INTEG 20. PAGE 53 H1060 COLONIAL METH PLAN CULTURE

B62
BRUMBERG A.,RUSSIA UNDER KHRUSHCHEV. FUT USSR SOCIETY ECO/DEV AGRI PERF/ART WORKER PWR...SOC ANTHOL 20 KHRUSH/N. PAGE 22 H0453 COM MARXISM NAT/G CHIEF

B62
INSTITUTE FOR STUDY OF USSR,YOUTH IN FERMENT. INTELL NAT/G PERF/ART POL/PAR SCHOOL VOL/ASSN FORCES EDU/PROP ATTIT DRIVE PERCEPT HEALTH KNOWL MORAL ORD/FREE RESPECT...SOC OBS HIST/WRIT VAL/FREE. PAGE 77 H1537 COM CULTURE USSR

B63
SAKAI R.K.,STUDIES ON ASIA, 1963. ASIA INDIA ISRAEL S/ASIA USA+45 PERF/ART POL/PAR SECT REGION NAT/LISM ...SOC LING TREND ANTHOL 19/20 CHINJAP. PAGE 137 H2735 PWR CULTURE

B64
CAUTE D.,COMMUNISM AND THE FRENCH INTELLECTUALS, 1914-1960. COM EUR+WWI MOD/EUR NAT/G PERF/ART PROF/ORG CREATE EDU/PROP ATTIT PERSON KNOWL MARXISM ...SOC TIME/SEQ MARX/KARL 20 MALRAUX/A GIDE/A SARTRE/J. PAGE 28 H0563 POL/PAR INTELL

S64
SOLOVEYTCHIK G.,"BOOKS ON RUSSIA." USSR ELITES NAT/G PERF/ART REV GOV/REL MARXISM...AUD/VIS 20. PAGE 147 H2929 BIBLIOG/A COM CULTURE

B65
JOHNSON P.,KHRUSHCHEV AND THE ARTS: POLITICS OF SOVIET CULTURE, 1962-1964. COM USSR NAT/G PERF/ART CONFER DEBATE GP/REL PERS/REL UTIL ATTIT DRIVE 20 KHRUSH/N. PAGE 81 H1626 CULTURE MARXISM POLICY CHIEF

PERFORMING ARTS....SEE PERF/ART; ALSO ART/METH

PERKINS D. H2492

PERKINS D.H. H1292,H2493

PERKINS H.C. H2451

PERLMANN H. H2494

PERON/JUAN....JUAN PERON

B57
HERNANDEZ-ARREGU J.,IMPERIALISMO Y CULTURA (LA POLITICA EN LA INTELIGENCIA ARGENTINA). L/A+17C CULTURE ELITES WRITING COLONIAL CROWD ATTIT FASCISM MARXISM SOCISM...BIOG IDEA/COMP 20 ARGEN PERON/JUAN COM/PARTY. PAGE 70 H1403 INTELL CREATE ART/METH HUM

PERS/COMP....COMPARISON OF PERSONS

S31
HEINBERG J.G.,"THE PERSONNEL OF FRENCH CABINETS, 1871-1930." FRANCE STRATA CHIEF CHOOSE REPRESENT MAJORITY...STAT QU CENSUS TREND CHARTS PERS/COMP 19/20 CHAMBR/DEP. PAGE 69 H1386 ELITES NAT/G DELIB/GP TOP/EX

S49
DEXTER L.A.,"A DIALOGUE ON THE SOCIAL PSYCHOLOGY OF COLONIALISM AND ON CERTAIN PUERTO RICAN PROFESSIONAL PERSONALITY PATTERNS." L/A+17C PUERT/RICO STRATA STRUCT DOMIN ISOLAT DRIVE ...NAT/COMP PERS/COMP HYPO/EXP 20 JEWS NEGRO. PAGE 41 H0813 COLONIAL SOC PSY PERSON

B56
GOFFMAN E.,THE PRESENTATION OF SELF IN EVERYDAY LIFE. CULTURE INGP/REL ATTIT DRIVE...SOC OBS RECORD 20. PAGE 58 H1154 PERS/COMP PERSON PERCEPT ROLE

B57
NARAIN D.,HINDU CHARACTER (A FEW GLIMPSES). INDIA DIPLOM SUICIDE PERS/REL ATTIT...PSY NAT/COMP PERS/COMP BIBLIOG WORSHIP 20 HINDU. PAGE 116 H2310 PERSON STERTYP SUPEGO SECT

B59
FAYERWEATHER J.,THE EXECUTIVE OVERSEAS: ADMINISTRATIVE ATTITUDES AND RELATIONSHIPS IN A FOREIGN CULTURE. USA+45 WOR+45 CULTURE LG/CO SML/CO ATTIT...MGT PERS/COMP 20 MEXIC/AMER. PAGE 49 H0979 INT/TRADE TOP/EX NAT/COMP PERS/REL

B60
JAECKH A.,WELTSAAT; ERLEBTES UND ERSTREBTES. GERMANY WOR+45 WOR-45 PLAN WAR...POLICY OBS/ENVIR NAT/COMP PERS/COMP 20. PAGE 79 H1581 BIOG NAT/G SELF/OBS DIPLOM

S60
WOLFINGER R.E.,"REPUTATION AND REALITY IN THE STUDY OF COMMUNITY POWER." STRUCT PROB/SOLV INGP/REL ATTIT OBJECTIVE...SOC METH/CNCPT PERS/COMP. PAGE 170 H3404 CULTURE MUNIC DOMIN PWR

B63
MCNEAL R.H.,THE BOLSHEVIK TRADITION: LENIN, STALIN, KHRUSHCHEV. USSR NAT/G SUPEGO CONSERVE...IDEA/COMP GEN/LAWS 20 LENIN/VI STALIN/J KHRUSH/N. PAGE 107 H2145 INTELL BIOG PERS/COMP

B65
GOPAL S.,BRITISH POLICY IN INDIA 1858-1905. INDIA UK ELITES CHIEF DELIB/GP ECO/TAC GP/REL DISCRIM ATTIT...IDEA/COMP NAT/COMP PERS/COMP BIBLIOG/A 19/20. PAGE 59 H1176 COLONIAL ADMIN POL/PAR ECO/UNDEV

B66
MERRITT R.L.,COMPARING NATIONS* THE USE OF QUANTITATIVE DATA IN CROSSNATIONAL RESEARCH. ACADEM DIPLOM GP/REL...PHIL/SCI STAT TREND GP/COMP PERS/COMP GEN/METH ANTHOL BIBLIOG INDEX. PAGE 109 H2184 NAT/COMP MATH COMPUT/IR QUANT

L67
PICKERING J.F.,"RECRUITMENT TO THE ADMINISTRATIVE PERS/COMP
CLASS, 1960-1964: PART 2" UK STRATA NAT/G WORKER ADMIN
...STAT CHARTS 20. PAGE 125 H2505 KNO/TEST
EDU/PROP

S67
ADAMS R.N.,"ETHICS AND THE SOCIAL ANTHROPOLOGIST IN L/A+17C
LATIN AMERICA." USA+45 INTELL PROB/SOLV ECO/TAC POLICY
LEAD...DECISION SOC NAT/COMP PERS/COMP. PAGE 3 ECO/UNDEV
H0066 CONSULT

S68
LAVRIN J.,"THE TWO WORLDS." RUSSIA USSR SOCIETY NAT/COMP
STRUCT NAT/G DIPLOM ATTIT PERSON MARXISM...GEOG SOC NAT/LISM
IDEA/COMP PERS/COMP 18/20. PAGE 92 H1842 CULTURE

PERS/REL....RELATIONS BETWEEN PERSONS AND INTERPERSONAL COMMUNICATION

N
CIVIL SERVICE JOURNAL. PARTIC INGP/REL PERS/REL ADMIN
...MGT BIBLIOG/A 20. PAGE 1 H0015 NAT/G
SERV/IND
WORKER

N
PRESSE UNIVERSITAIRES,ANNEE SOCIOLOGIQUE. EUR+WWI BIBLIOG
FRANCE MOD/EUR FAM ACT/RES WAR INGP/REL PERS/REL SOC
CONSEN DRIVE MORAL...CON/ANAL 19/20. PAGE 128 H2557 CULTURE
SOCIETY

B32
NIEBUHR R.,MORAL MAN AND IMMORAL SOCIETY* A STUDY MORAL
IN ETHICS AND POLITICS. UNIV CULTURE SOCIETY STRUCT PWR
DIPLOM GOV/REL GP/REL PERS/REL...TREND IDEA/COMP.
PAGE 118 H2357

B37
HORNEY K.,THE NEUROTIC PERSONALITY OF OUR TIME. PSY
SOCIETY PERS/REL ADJUST HAPPINESS ANOMIE ATTIT PERSON
DRIVE SEX LOVE PWR CONCPT. PAGE 74 H1472 STRANGE
CULTURE

S39
LASSWELL H.D.,"PERSON, PERSONALITY, GROUP, CULTURE" PERSON
(BMR)" UNIV CREATE EDU/PROP...EPIST CONCPT LING GP/REL
METH. PAGE 92 H1833 CULTURE
PERS/REL

C41
KLUCKHOHN C.,"PATTERNING AS EXEMPLIFIED IN NAVAHO CULTURE
CULTURE" IN EDWARD SAPIR, LANGUAGE, CULTURE, AND INGP/REL
PERSONALITY (BMR)" KIN PERS/REL ATTIT PERSON...SOC STRUCT
CONCPT METH/CNCPT LING OBS/ENVIR CON/ANAL BIBLIOG
SOC/INTEG 20 NAVAHO INDIAN/AM SAPIR/EDW. PAGE 87
H1733

B45
VENABLE V.,HUMAN NATURE: THE MARXIAN VIEW. UNIV PERSON
STRATA CAP/ISM REV GP/REL PERS/REL PRODUC KNOWL MARXISM
...PHIL/SCI CONCPT IDEA/COMP 19 MARX/KARL ENGELS/F. WORKER
PAGE 162 H3240 UTOPIA

B46
MILL J.S.,ON LIBERTY. NAT/G LEGIT CONTROL PERS/REL ORD/FREE
PERCEPT...CONCPT 19. PAGE 110 H2206 SOCIETY
PERSON
GEN/LAWS

S46
TANNENBAUM F.,"THE BALANCE OF POWER IN SOCIETY." SOCIETY
UNIV STRUCT FAM NAT/G SECT PERS/REL EQUILIB UTOPIA ALL/VALS
DRIVE ALL/IDEOS...OLD/LIB CONCPT. PAGE 152 H3044 GP/REL
PEACE

B48
WOLFE B.D.,THREE WHO MADE A REVOLUTION. USSR CONSTN BIOG
NAT/G CAP/ISM EDU/PROP CONTROL WAR GP/REL INGP/REL REV
PERS/REL ROLE 20 STALIN/J LENIN/VI TROTSKY/L LEAD
BOLSHEVISM. PAGE 170 H3398 MARXISM

L48
SHILS E.A.,"COHESION AND DISINTEGRATION IN THE EDU/PROP
WEHRMACHT IN WORLD WAR II." GERMANY STRUCT DOMIN DRIVE
WAR INGP/REL ISOLAT NAT/LISM ATTIT AUTHORIT SUPEGO PERS/REL
RESPECT...PSY CON/ANAL 20 NAZI. PAGE 143 H2862 FORCES

B49
DENNING A.,FREEDOM UNDER THE LAW. MOD/EUR UK LAW ORD/FREE
SOCIETY CHIEF EX/STRUC LEGIS ADJUD CT/SYS PERS/REL JURID
PERSON 17/20 ENGLSH/LAW. PAGE 40 H0793 NAT/G

B50
ROHEIM G.,PSYCHOANALYSIS AND ANTHROPOLOGY. UNIV FAM PSY
PERS/REL ATTIT HABITAT...SOC OBS WORSHIP. PAGE 133 BIOG
H2663 CULTURE
PERSON

B51
BERNATZIK H.A.,THE SPIRITS OF THE YELLOW LEAVES. SOC
BURMA LAOS S/ASIA THAILAND VIETNAM SOCIETY AGRI KIN
COLONIAL LEISURE GP/REL PERS/REL ISOLAT AGE HABITAT ECO/UNDEV
SEX WORSHIP 20. PAGE 16 H0310 CULTURE

B54
FORDE C.D.,AFRICAN WORLDS. AFR CULTURE ROUTINE SOCIETY
GP/REL PERS/REL ATTIT DRIVE ALL/VALS...OBS ANTHOL KIN
WORSHIP 20. PAGE 52 H1036 SOC

B54
TITIEV M.,THE SCIENCE OF MAN. LAW STRATA KIN GP/REL SOC
PERS/REL HABITAT HEREDITY KNOWL...LING CHARTS PSY
BIBLIOG WORSHIP. PAGE 155 H3107 CULTURE

B55
ALFIERI D.,DICTATORS FACE TO FACE. NAT/G TOP/EX WAR
DIPLOM EXEC COERCE ORD/FREE FASCISM...POLICY OBS 20 CHIEF
HITLER/A MUSSOLIN/B. PAGE 5 H0103 TOTALISM
PERS/REL

B55
LIPSCOMB J.F.,WHITE AFRICANS. SOCIETY STRUCT AGRI RACE/REL
ECO/TAC ADJUD COLONIAL COERCE PERS/REL ADJUST. HABITAT
PAGE 97 H1937 ECO/UNDEV
ORD/FREE

B55
RODNICK D.,THE NORWEGIANS: A STUDY IN NATIONAL CULTURE
CULTURE. NORWAY FAM INGP/REL PERS/REL AGE...PSY SOC INT
SELF/OBS WORSHIP 20. PAGE 133 H2655 RECORD
ATTIT

B56
GLUCKMAN M.,CUSTOM AND CONFLICT IN AFRICA. AFR FAM CULTURE
KIN NAT/G DOMIN DISCRIM DRIVE MORAL PWR...SOC CREATE
BIBLIOG WORSHIP 20. PAGE 57 H1145 PERS/REL
GP/COMP

S56
BLAU P.M.,"SOCIAL MOBILITY AND INTERPERSONAL INGP/REL
RELATIONS" (BMR)" UNIV CULTURE STRUCT WORKER ANOMIE PERS/REL
...SOC SOC/INTEG 19/20. PAGE 18 H0355 ORD/FREE
STRATA

B57
BULLOCK A.,THE LIBERAL TRADITION FROM FOX TO ANTHOL
KEYNES. UK CULTURE INTELL CREATE WRITING COLONIAL DEBATE
PERS/REL ATTIT ORD/FREE...POLICY OLD/LIB TRADIT LAISSEZ
CONCPT 18/20 CHURCHLL/W MILL/JS KEYNES/JM
ASQUITH/HH. PAGE 23 H0469

B57
MUELLER-DEHAM A.,HUMAN RELATIONS AND POWER; SOCIO- GEN/LAWS
POLITICAL ANALYSIS AND SYNTHESIS. CONSTN SOCIETY PERS/REL
NAT/G POL/PAR PROVS LEGIS POPULISM...SOC NEW/IDEA. PWR
PAGE 114 H2280 CONCPT

B57
NARAIN D.,HINDU CHARACTER (A FEW GLIMPSES). INDIA PERSON
DIPLOM SUICIDE PERS/REL ATTIT...PSY NAT/COMP STERTYP
PERS/COMP BIBLIOG WORSHIP 20 HINDU. PAGE 116 H2310 SUPEGO
SECT

S57
DEXTER L.A.,"A SOCIAL THEORY OF MENTAL DEFICIENCY." SOC
CULTURE PUB/INST PROB/SOLV CRIME PERS/REL STRANGE PSY
PERSON SUPEGO SKILL...EPIST SOC/WK HYPO/EXP. HEALTH
PAGE 41 H0814 ROLE

B58
DWARKADAS R.,ROLE OF HIGHER CIVIL SERVICE IN INDIA. ADMIN
INDIA ECO/UNDEV LEGIS PROB/SOLV GP/REL PERS/REL NAT/G
...POLICY WELF/ST DECISION ORG/CHARTS BIBLIOG 20 ROLE
CIVIL/SERV INTRVN/ECO. PAGE 44 H0876 PLAN

B58
GLUCKMAN M.,ANALYSIS OF A SOCIAL SITUATION IN CULTURE
MODERN ZULULAND. AFR PERS/REL ADJUST DISCRIM RACE/REL
EQUILIB NAT/LISM...SOC RECORD AUD/VIS 20 ZULULAND. STRUCT
PAGE 57 H1146 GP/REL

B59
FAYERWEATHER J.,THE EXECUTIVE OVERSEAS: INT/TRADE
ADMINISTRATIVE ATTITUDES AND RELATIONSHIPS IN A TOP/EX
FOREIGN CULTURE. USA+45 WOR+45 CULTURE LG/CO SML/CO NAT/COMP
ATTIT...MGT PERS/COMP 20 MEXIC/AMER. PAGE 49 H0979 PERS/REL

S59
LYNN D.B.,"THE EFFECTS OF FATHER-ABSENCE ON SOC
NORWEGIAN BOYS AND GIRLS." NORWAY CULTURE PERS/REL FAM
ADJUST DISPL LOVE...PSY CORREL STAT INT CON/ANAL AGE/C
CHARTS SOC/INTEG 20. PAGE 99 H1983 ANOMIE

B60
BEATTIE J.,BUNYORO, AN AFRICAN KINGDOM. UGANDA CULTURE
STRATA INGP/REL PERS/REL...SOC BIBLIOG 19/20. ELITES
PAGE 13 H0250 SECT
KIN

B60
MANIS J.G.,MAN AND SOCIETY. STRATA LEAD INGP/REL SOC
PERS/REL ATTIT PWR...PSY ANTHOL T SOC/INTEG SOCIETY
MARX/KARL MILL/JS FREUD/S CHURCHLL/W SPENCER/H STRUCT
RUSSELL/B. PAGE 102 H2036 CULTURE

B61
DOOB L.W.,COMMUNICATION IN AFRICA: A SEARCH FOR AFR
BOUNDARIES. CULTURE SOCIETY EDU/PROP WRITING FEEDBACK
INGP/REL DRIVE ORD/FREE...ART/METH SOC LING BIBLIOG PERCEPT
20. PAGE 42 H0837 PERS/REL

B61
PAZ O.,THE LABYRINTH OF SOLITUDE; LIFE AND THOUGHT CULTURE
IN MEXICO (TRANS. BY LYSANDER KEMP). INTELL PERSON
COLONIAL REV...PSY SOC TIME/SEQ 16/20 MEXIC/AMER. PERS/REL
PAGE 124 H2480 SOCIETY

B61
ROCHE J.P.,COURTS AND RIGHTS: THE AMERICAN JURID
JUDICIARY IN ACTION (2ND ED.). UK USA+45 USA-45 CT/SYS
STRUCT TEC/DEV SANCTION PERS/REL RACE/REL ORD/FREE NAT/G
...METH/CNCPT GOV/COMP METH/COMP T 13/20. PAGE 133 PROVS
H2653

L61
EZELLPH,"THE HISPANIC AGRICULTURATION OF THE GILA CULTURE
RIVER PIMAS." FAM TEC/DEV PERS/REL ADJUST...GEOG SOC

MYTH CHARTS BIBLIOG WORSHIP 17/20. PAGE 48 H0956
AGRI DRIVE

B62
BERNOT R.M.,EXCESS AND RESTRAINT: SOCIAL CONTROL AMONG GUINEA MOUNTAIN PEOPLE. CULTURE FAM KIN CT/SYS COERCE WAR PERS/REL MARRIAGE HABITAT SEX ...MYTH 20 NEW/GUINEA. PAGE 16 H0314
SOCIETY CONTROL STRUCT ADJUST

B62
FALKENBERG J.,KIN AND TOTEM; GROUP RELATIONS OF AUSTRALIAN ABORIGINES IN THE PORT KEATS DISTRICT. SOCIETY STRATA STRUCT GP/REL PERS/REL MARRIAGE AGE ATTIT SEX...SOC STAT CHARTS AUSTRAL ABORIGINES. PAGE 48 H0964
KIN INGP/REL CULTURE FAM

B62
KRECH D.,INDIVIDUAL IN SOCIETY; A TEXTBOOK OF SOCIAL PSYCHOLOGY. UNIV CULTURE LEAD INGP/REL ATTIT DRIVE PERCEPT ROLE...PHIL/SCI BIBLIOG T. PAGE 88 H1765
PSY SOC SOCIETY PERS/REL

B62
MACPHERSON C.B.,THE POLITICAL THEORY OF POSSESSIVE INDIVIDUALISM. UK MARKET NAT/G PERS/REL RATIONAL ...IDEA/COMP 17/19 LOCKE/JOHN. PAGE 100 H2006
PHIL/SCI OWN

B62
MALINOWSKI B.,SEX, CULTURE, AND MYTH. UNIV SOCIETY FAM PERS/REL MARRIAGE RATIONAL HABITAT PERSON SUPEGO MORAL WORSHIP 20. PAGE 102 H2032
MYTH SECT SEX CULTURE

B63
AZEVEDO T.,SOCIAL CHANGE IN BRAZIL. BRAZIL ECO/DEV COM/IND FAM NAT/G SECT GP/REL PERS/REL...CONCPT WORSHIP 20. PAGE 9 H0188
TEC/DEV STRUCT SOC CULTURE

B63
DE JOUVENEL B.,THE PURE THEORY OF POLITICS. NAT/G DIPLOM CONTROL GP/REL PERS/REL PERSON PWR OBJECTIVE CONCPT. PAGE 38 H0758
GEN/LAWS SOCIETY METH/CNCPT

B63
EICH H.,THE UNLOVED GERMANS. EUR+WWI GERMANY PERS/REL RACE/REL DISCRIM HABITAT SUPEGO FASCISM ...PSY SOC AUD/VIS 19/20 JEWS. PAGE 45 H0898
STERTYP PERSON CULTURE ATTIT

B63
SPRING D.,THE ENGLISH LANDED ESTATE IN THE NINETEENTH CENTURY: ITS ADMINISTRATION. UK ELITES STRUCT AGRI NAT/G GP/REL OWN PWR WEALTH...BIBLIOG 19 HOUSE/LORD. PAGE 148 H2954
STRATA PERS/REL MGT

C63
HSU F.L.,"COHESION AND DIVISION IN THE AMERICAN WORLD" HSU FL. CLAN, CASTE, AND CLUB." CULTURE EDU/PROP CONFER SANCTION PERSON...PSY GP/COMP. PAGE 74 H1484
PERS/REL AGE/Y ADJUST VOL/ASSN

B64
ETZIONI A.,MODERN ORGANIZATIONS. CLIENT STRUCT DOMIN CONTROL LEAD PERS/REL AUTHORIT...CLASSIF BUREAUCRCY. PAGE 47 H0946
MGT ADMIN PLAN CULTURE

B64
GREEN M.M.,IBO VILLAGE AFFAIRS. AFR FORCES PERS/REL ADJUST ISOLAT ATTIT HABITAT PERSON ALL/VALS...JURID RECORD SOC/INTEG 20 IBO. PAGE 60 H1207
MUNIC CULTURE ECO/UNDEV SOC

B64
HARRIS M.,THE NATURE OF CULTURAL THINGS. GP/REL PERS/REL DRIVE HABITAT PERSON ROLE...PHIL/SCI PSY SOC CHARTS BIBLIOG 20. PAGE 67 H1341
CULTURE OBS CLASSIF NEW/IDEA

B64
LATORRE A.,UNIVERSIDAD Y SOCIEDAD. SPAIN EDU/PROP LEAD GP/REL PERS/REL ATTIT KNOWL. PAGE 92 H1837
ACADEM CULTURE ROLE INTELL

B64
MCCALL D.F.,AFRICA IN TIME PERSPECTIVE. AFR EXTR/IND KIN SECT CREATE PERS/REL HABITAT...GEOG METH/CNCPT LING BIBLIOG/A TIME 20. PAGE 106 H2124
HIST/WRIT OBS/ENVIR CULTURE

B64
MEAD M.,CONTINUITIES IN CULTURAL EVOLUTION. FACE/GP KIN ACT/RES EDU/PROP GP/REL INGP/REL DRIVE HEREDITY ROLE...TIME/SEQ TREND METH SOC/INTEG 20. PAGE 108 H2153
CULTURE SOC PERS/REL

B64
RIES J.C.,THE MANAGEMENT OF DEFENSE: ORGANIZATION AND CONTROL OF THE US ARMED SERVICES. PROF/ORG DELIB/GP EX/STRUC LEGIS GOV/REL PERS/REL CENTRAL RATIONAL PWR...POLICY TREND GOV/COMP BIBLIOG. PAGE 131 H2626
FORCES ACT/RES DECISION CONTROL

B64
WHEELER-BENNETT J.W.,THE NEMESIS OF POWER (2ND ED.). EUR+WWI GERMANY TOP/EX TEC/DEV ADMIN WAR PERS/REL RIGID/FLEX ROLE ORD/FREE PWR FASCISM 20 HITLER/A. PAGE 167 H3342
FORCES NAT/G GP/REL STRUCT

B65
ADENAUER K.,MEMOIRS 1945-53. EUR+WWI GERMANY/W ECO/DEV CHIEF FORCES ECO/TAC WAR GOV/REL PWR SOVEREIGN 20 NATO ADENAUER/K. PAGE 3 H0068
BIOG DIPLOM NAT/G PERS/REL

B65
ARENSBERG C.M.,CULTURE AND COMMUNITY. UNIV FACE/GP ACT/RES EDU/PROP LEAD REGION GP/REL PERS/REL HABITAT ALL/VALS...SOC CONCPT 20. PAGE 8 H0162
SOCIETY CULTURE NEIGH NEW/IDEA

B65
BETEILLE A.,CASTE, CLASS, AND POWER. INDIA MUNIC SECT REGION GP/REL PERS/REL ATTIT HABITAT RIGID/FLEX...SOC 20. PAGE 16 H0323
STRATA CULTURE PWR STRUCT

B65
EASTON D.,A SYSTEM ANALYSIS OF POLITICAL LIFE. UNIV STRUCT NAT/G FEEDBACK PARTIC PERS/REL EFFICIENCY ...TREND CHARTS METH/COMP 20. PAGE 44 H0881
SIMUL POLICY GEN/METH

B65
HART B.H.L.,THE MEMOIRS OF CAPTAIN LIDDELL HART (VOL. I). UK NAT/G PLAN TEC/DEV DIPLOM ADMIN WEAPON GOV/REL PERS/REL ATTIT PWR FASCISM...POLICY 20. PAGE 67 H1348
FORCES BIOG LEAD WAR

B65
JOHNSON P.,KHRUSHCHEV AND THE ARTS: POLITICS OF SOVIET CULTURE, 1962-1964. COM USSR NAT/G PERF/ART CONFER DEBATE GP/REL PERS/REL UTIL ATTIT DRIVE 20 KHRUSH/N. PAGE 81 H1626
CULTURE MARXISM POLICY CHIEF

B66
AIR FORCE ACADEMY ASSEMBLY,CULTURAL AFFAIRS AND FOREIGN RELATIONS. NAT/G VOL/ASSN ALL/VALS. PAGE 4 H0083
CULTURE SOCIETY PERS/REL DIPLOM

B66
BERELSON B.,READER IN PUBLIC OPINION AND COMMUNICATION (2ND ED.). UNIV NAT/G PRESS GP/REL PERS/REL PERCEPT RIGID/FLEX...MAJORIT QUANT METH/COMP ANTHOL BIBLIOG 20. PAGE 15 H0298
EDU/PROP ATTIT CONCPT COM/IND

B66
BUTLER D.E.,THE BRITISH GENERAL ELECTION OF 1966. UK LOC/G NAT/G OP/RES CONFER CHOOSE MAJORITY ATTIT ...CHARTS TIME 20. PAGE 25 H0498
POL/PAR REPRESENT GP/REL PERS/REL

B66
KEITH G.,THE FADING COLOUR BAR. AFR CENTRL/AFR UK ZAMBIA CULTURE SCHOOL EDU/PROP PERS/REL DISCRIM AGE ...AUD/VIS NAT/COMP SOC/INTEG 20 NEGRO. PAGE 84 H1682
RACE/REL STRUCT ATTIT NAT/G

B66
RAEFF M.,ORIGINS OF THE RUSSIAN INTELLIGENTSIA: THE EIGHTEENTH-CENTURY NOBILITY. RUSSIA FAM NAT/G EDU/PROP ADMIN PERS/REL ATTIT...HUM BIOG 18. PAGE 129 H2580
INTELL ELITES STRATA CONSERVE

S66
HAIGH G.,"FIELD TRAINING IN HUMAN RELATIONS FOR THE PEACE CORPS." CONSULT CREATE EDU/PROP ADMIN TASK GP/REL ATTIT PERSON...PSY OBS SOC/EXP PEACE/CORP. PAGE 64 H1276
CULTURE PERS/REL FOR/AID ADJUST

B67
COWLES M.,PERSPECTIVES IN THE EDUCATION OF DISADVANTAGED CHILDREN. CULTURE OP/RES PLAN PERS/REL ADJUST HABITAT PERCEPT KNOWL WEALTH ...SOC/WK IDEA/COMP ANTHOL 20. PAGE 34 H0686
EDU/PROP AGE/C TEC/DEV SCHOOL

B67
FANON F.,BLACK SKIN, WHITE MASKS: THE EXPERIENCES OF A BLACK MAN IN A WHITE WORLD. CULTURE COLONIAL HAPPINESS ISOLAT STRANGE ATTIT HABITAT RIGID/FLEX SEX...BIOG STERTYP SOC/INTEG 20 NEGRO. PAGE 49 H0970
DISCRIM PERS/REL RACE/REL PSY

B67
GELLHORN W.,OMBUDSMEN AND OTHERS: CITIZENS' PROTECTORS IN NINE COUNTRIES. WOR+45 LAW CONSTN LEGIS INSPECT ADJUD ADMIN CONTROL CT/SYS CHOOSE PERS/REL...STAT CHARTS 20. PAGE 55 H1109
NAT/COMP REPRESENT INGP/REL PROB/SOLV

B67
MUNGER E.S.,AFRIKANER AND AFRICAN NATIONALISM: SOUTH AFRICAN PARALLELS AND PARAMETERS. SOUTH/AFR WOR+45 CULTURE ELITES STRUCT NAT/G PROB/SOLV DOMIN CONTROL PERS/REL NAT/LISM...SOC 20. PAGE 115 H2289
AFR RACE/REL

B67
ODINGA O.,NOT YET UHURU. NAT/G POL/PAR PROB/SOLV COERCE REV WAR PERS/REL PERSON ORD/FREE...POLICY 20 ODINGA/O KENYATTA. PAGE 120 H2395
ATTIT BIOG LEAD AFR

B67
ROELOFS H.M.,THE LANGUAGE OF MODERN POLITICS: AN INTRODUCTION TO THE STUDY OF GOVERNMENT. DIPLOM ADMIN MARXISM NEW/LIB...JURID CONCPT METH/COMP T 20. PAGE 133 H2657
LEAD NAT/COMP PERS/REL NAT/G

S67
BURGHART A.,"CATHOLIC SOCIAL THOUGHT IN AUSTRIA." AUSTRIA EUR+WWI NAT/G PAY PERS/REL OWN MARXISM SOCISM...SOC 20. PAGE 24 H0482
CATHISM ATTIT TREND SOCIETY

S67
CROCKETT D.G.,"THE MP AND HIS CONSTITUENTS." UK POL/PAR...DECISION 20. PAGE 35 H0706
EXEC NAT/G PERS/REL REPRESENT

S67
MALLORY J.R.,"THE MINISTER'S OFFICE STAFF* AN UNREFORMED PART OF PUBLIC SERVICE." CONSTN ELITES STRATA NAT/G PROB/SOLV TASK CHOOSE PERS/REL EFFICIENCY...DECISION 20. PAGE 102 H2033
CANADA ADMIN EX/STRUC STRUCT

S67
NIEBUHR R.,"THE ETHICS OF WAR AND PEACE IN THE NUCLEAR AGE." VIETNAM INTELL CONFER CONTROL WAR GOV/REL PERS/REL ORD/FREE...POLICY INT GOV/COMP NAT/COMP 20 UN. PAGE 118 H2360
MORAL PEACE NUC/PWR DIPLOM

S67
SCOTT J.W.,"SOURCES OF SOCIAL CHANGE IN COMMUNITY, FAMILY, AND FERTILITY IN A PUERTO RICAN TOWN." PUERT/RICO CULTURE STRUCT ECO/UNDEV INDUS PERS/REL ROLE...SOC STAND/INT. PAGE 141 H2815
FAM MARRIAGE LITERACY ATTIT

B73
STEPHEN J.F.,LIBERTY, EQUALITY, FRATERNITY. UNIV SOCIETY NAT/G LEGIS DOMIN AGREE PERS/REL ATTIT MORAL...IDEA/COMP 19 MILL/JS. PAGE 149 H2978
ORD/FREE CONCPT COERCE SECT

PERS/TEST....PERSONALITY TESTS

PERSHAD A. H2460

PERSIA....PERSIA: ANCIENT IRAN

B58
SALETORE B.A.,INDIA'S DIPLOMATIC RELATIONS WITH THE WEST. GREECE INDIA CULTURE ETIQUET...IDEA/COMP 3 ROM/EMP PERSIA. PAGE 137 H2739
DIPLOM CONCPT INT/TRADE

B60
SALETORE B.A.,INDIA'S DIPLOMATIC RELATIONS WITH THE EAST. ASIA CEYLON INDIA NEPAL S/ASIA CULTURE 7/14 PERSIA. PAGE 137 H2740
DIPLOM NAT/COMP ETIQUET

B61
VON EICKSTEDT E.,TURKEN, KURDEN UND IRANER SEIT DEM ALTERTUM. IRAN TURKEY GP/REL BIO/SOC HABITAT...PSY 20 PERSIA. PAGE 163 H3266
CULTURE SOC SOCIETY STRUCT

B63
JAIRAZBHOY R.A.,FOREIGN INFLUENCE IN ANCIENT INDIA. INDIA ELITES SECT DIPLOM EDU/PROP COLONIAL REGION GP/REL...ART/METH LING WORSHIP +/14 GRECO/ROMN MESOPOTAM PERSIA PARTH/SASS. PAGE 79 H1587
CULTURE SOCIETY COERCE DOMIN

PERSON....PERSONALITY AND HUMAN NATURE

N
BIBLIOTECH NACIONAL,CATALOGO BREVE DE LA BIBLIOTECA AMERICANA DE JT MEDINA (2 VOLS.). CHILE NAT/G PERSON HUM. PAGE 16 H0330
BIBLIOG/A CHARTS L/A+17C

N
INTERNATIONAL BIBLIOGRAPHIE DER DEUTSCHEN ZEITSCHRIFTENLITERATUR. EUR+WWI GERMANY MOD/EUR ECO/DEV POL/PAR LEAD WAR NAT/LISM ATTIT...EPIST PHIL/SCI 19/20. PAGE 1 H0004
BIBLIOG/A NAT/G PERSON CULTURE

N
PUBLISHERS' TRADE LIST ANNUAL. LAW POL/PAR ADMIN PERSON ALL/IDEOS...HUM SOC 19/20. PAGE 1 H0020
BIBLIOG NAT/G DIPLOM POLICY

N
SUBJECT GUIDE TO BOOKS IN PRINT: AN INDEX TO THE PUBLISHERS' TRADE LIST ANNUAL. UNIV LAW LOC/G DIPLOM WRITING ADMIN LEAD PERSON...MGT SOC. PAGE 2 H0024
BIBLIOG ECO/DEV POL/PAR NAT/G

N
DEUTSCHE BUCHEREI,DEUTSCHES BUCHERVERZEICHNIS. GERMANY LAW CULTURE POL/PAR ADMIN LEAD ATTIT PERSON ...SOC 20. PAGE 40 H0805
BIBLIOG NAT/G DIPLOM ECO/DEV

B00
OMAN C.,A HISTORY OF THE ART OF WAR: THE MIDDLE AGES FROM THE FOURTH TO THE FOURTEENTH CENTURY. CHRIST-17C MEDIT-7 CULTURE SOCIETY INT/ORG ROUTINE PERSON...CONT/OBS HIST/WRIT CHARTS VAL/FREE. PAGE 121 H2417
FORCES SKILL WAR

B10
MILL J.S.,UTILITARIANISM, LIBERTY, AND REPRESENTATIVE GOVERNMENT. CONTROL PERCEPT PERSON MORAL...CONCPT GEN/LAWS. PAGE 110 H2205
HAPPINESS ORD/FREE REPRESENT NAT/G

B11
HUXLEY T.H.,METHOD AND RESULTS: ESSAYS. EDU/PROP REPRESENT OWN PERSON PWR WEALTH...PSY IDEA/COMP GEN/LAWS. PAGE 76 H1514
ORD/FREE NAT/G POPULISM PLURIST

B11
PHILLIPSON C.,THE INTERNATIONAL LAW AND CUSTOM OF ANCIENT GREECE AND ROME. MEDIT-7 UNIV INTELL SOCIETY STRUCT NAT/G LEGIS EXEC PERSON...CONCPT OBS CON/ANAL ROM/EMP. PAGE 125 H2504
INT/ORG LAW INT/LAW

N13
H T.,GRUNDZUGE DES CHINESISCHEN VOLKSCHARACTERS. ASIA CULTURE SOCIETY...HUM 19/20. PAGE 63 H1262
ATTIT PERSON

ART/METH LING

B16
PUFENDORF S.,LAW OF NATURE AND OF NATIONS (ABRIDGED). UNIV LAW NAT/G DIPLOM AGREE WAR PERSON ALL/VALS PWR...POLICY 18 DEITY NATURL/LAW. PAGE 128 H2565
CONCPT INT/LAW SECT MORAL

B20
COX H.,ECONOMIC LIBERTY. UNIV LAW INT/TRADE RATION TARIFFS RACE/REL SOCISM POLICY. PAGE 34 H0687
NAT/G ORD/FREE ECO/TAC PERSON

B21
WALLAS G.,HUMAN NATURE IN POLITICS (3RD ED.). UNIV NAT/G LEAD CHOOSE REPRESENT GP/REL NAT/LISM RATIONAL BIO/SOC HEREDITY ALL/VALS MAJORIT. PAGE 165 H3293
PSY DRIVE PERSON

B25
TEMPERLEY H.,THE FOREIGN POLICY OF CANNING: 1822-1827. MOD/EUR NAT/G TOP/EX EDU/PROP ROUTINE ATTIT RIGID/FLEX SUPEGO PWR SKILL...TIME/SEQ PARLIAMENT 20. PAGE 153 H3058
PERSON DIPLOM UK BIOG

B28
HOBBES T.,THE ELEMENTS OF LAW, NATURAL AND POLITIC (1650). STRATA NAT/G SECT CHIEF AGREE ATTIT ALL/VALS MORAL ORD/FREE POPULISM...POLICY CONCPT. PAGE 71 H1432
PERSON LAW SOVEREIGN CONSERVE

B29
STURZO L.,THE INTERNATIONAL COMMUNITY AND THE RIGHT OF WAR (TRANS. BY BARBARA BARCLAY CARTER). CULTURE CREATE PROB/SOLV DIPLOM ADJUD CONTROL PEACE PERSON ORD/FREE...INT/LAW IDEA/COMP PACIFIST 20 LEAGUE/NAT. PAGE 150 H3003
INT/ORG PLAN WAR CONCPT

B31
MACIVER R.M.,SOCIETY: ITS STRUCTURE AND CHANGES. CULTURE STRATA FAM CROWD HABITAT ORD/FREE...PSY SOC CONCPT BIBLIOG 20. PAGE 100 H1998
STRUCT SOCIETY PERSON DRIVE

B33
BERDYAYEV N.,CHRISTIANITY AND CLASS WAR. UNIV SOCIETY WORKER CREATE PROB/SOLV ATTIT PERSON ORD/FREE...CONCPT CHRISTIAN. PAGE 15 H0296
SECT MARXISM STRATA GP/REL

B34
BENEDICT R.,PATTERNS OF CULTURE. S/ASIA FAM KIN PERSON RESPECT...CONCPT SELF/OBS. PAGE 14 H0278
CULTURE SOC

B35
AQUINAS T.,ON THE GOVERNANCE OF RULERS (1265-66). UNIV SOCIETY STRATA FAM HABITAT PERSON ALL/VALS PWR SOVEREIGN CONSERVE...POLICY BIBLE. PAGE 8 H0155
CATH NAT/G CHIEF SUPEGO

B35
PARETO V.,THE MIND AND SOCIETY (4 VOLS.). ELITES SECT ECO/TAC COERCE PERSON ORD/FREE PWR SOVEREIGN FASCISM POPULISM...TRADIT 19/20. PAGE 123 H2465
GEN/LAWS SOC PSY

B37
HORNEY K.,THE NEUROTIC PERSONALITY OF OUR TIME. SOCIETY PERS/REL ADJUST HAPPINESS ANOMIE ATTIT DRIVE SEX LOVE PWR CONCPT. PAGE 74 H1472
PSY PERSON STRANGE CULTURE

B38
DEL TORO J.,A BIBLIOGRAPHY OF THE COLLECTIVE BIOGRAPHY OF SPANISH AMERICA. ELITES NAT/G WRITING LEAD PERSON 19/20. PAGE 39 H0786
BIBLIOG/A L/A+17C BIOG

B38
POUND R.,THE FORMATIVE ERA OF AMERICAN LAW. CULTURE NAT/G PROVS LEGIS ADJUD CT/SYS PERSON SOVEREIGN ...POLICY IDEA/COMP GEN/LAWS 18/19. PAGE 127 H2548
CONSTN LAW CREATE JURID

B38
RAWLINSON H.G.,INDIA: A SHORT CULTURAL HISTORY. INDIA LAW STRATA FORCES INT/TRADE ADMIN COLONIAL PERSON...GEOG HUM BIBLIOG WORSHIP 20. PAGE 130 H2598
CULTURE SECT MYTH ART/METH

S38
MERTON R.K.,"SOCIAL STRUCTURE AND ANOMIE" (BMR)" UNIV CULTURE STRATA CREATE PARTIC ATTIT BIO/SOC PERSON...SOC CONCPT 20. PAGE 109 H2186
SOCIETY STRUCT ANOMIE DRIVE

B39
MARITAIN J.,SCHOLASTICISM AND POLITICS. CONSTN SOCIETY NAT/G INGP/REL PERSON CATHISM POPULISM 19/20 FREUD/S SCHOLASTIC CHURCH/STA CHRISTIAN. PAGE 103 H2050
SECT GEN/LAWS ORD/FREE

S39
LASSWELL H.D.,"PERSON, PERSONALITY, GROUP, CULTURE" (BMR)" UNIV CREATE EDU/PROP...EPIST CONCPT LING METH. PAGE 92 H1833
PERSON GP/REL CULTURE PERS/REL

B40
LEDERER E.,STATE OF THE MASSES. GERMANY ITALY SOCIETY NAT/G ECO/TAC EDU/PROP LEAD TOTALISM ...SOCIALIST PSY 20. PAGE 93 H1852
CROWD FASCISM AUTHORIT PERSON

B40
MANNHEIM K.,MAN AND SOCIETY IN AN AGE OF
CONCPT

RECONSTRUCTION. MOD/EUR CULTURE ECO/DEV PLAN TEC/DEV PERSON LAISSEZ NEW/LIB...NEW/IDEA IDEA/COMP BIBLIOG 19/20. PAGE 102 H2038
ATTIT SOCIETY TOTALISM

B40
SIMON Y.,NATURE AND FUNCTIONS OF AUTHORITY. UNIV SOCIETY NAT/G CHIEF CONCPT. PAGE 144 H2880
ORD/FREE DOMIN GEN/LAWS PERSON

B40
TONNIES F.,FUNDAMENTAL CONCEPTS OF SOCIOLOGY (1887) (TRANS. BY C. LOOMIS). LAW STRATA STRUCT FAM MUNIC NAT/G DOMIN LEGIT SANCTION COERCE CRIME PERSON 19. PAGE 156 H3115
CULTURE SOCIETY GEN/LAWS SOC

C41
KLUCKHOHN C.,"PATTERNING AS EXEMPLIFIED IN NAVAHO CULTURE" IN EDWARD SAPIR, LANGUAGE, CULTURE, AND PERSONALITY (BMR)" KIN PERS/REL ATTIT PERSON...SOC CONCPT METH/CNCPT LING OBS/ENVIR CON/ANAL BIBLIOG SOC/INTEG 20 NAVAHO INDIAN/AM SAPIR/EDW. PAGE 87 H1733
CULTURE INGP/REL STRUCT

B42
BARNES H.E.,SOCIAL INSTITUTIONS IN AN ERA OF WORLD UPHEAVAL. INDUS FAM NAT/G PERF/ART SECT AUTOMAT PERSON MORAL...PREDICT 20. PAGE 11 H0221
SOCIETY CULTURE TECHRACY TREND

B44
BERDYAEV N.,SLAVERY AND FREEDOM. NAT/G REV WAR NAT/LISM OWN AUTHORIT SEX CONSERVE SOCISM...TRADIT PHIL/SCI CIVIL/LIB. PAGE 15 H0295
ORD/FREE PERSON ELITES SOCIETY

B45
HUNTINGTON E.,MAINSPRINGS OF CIVILIZATION. UNIV CULTURE SOCIETY BIO/SOC PERSON KNOWL SKILL...PSY RECORD HIST/WRIT TREND CHARTS TOT/POP. PAGE 75 H1504
SOC GEOG

B45
LINTON R.,THE CULTURAL BACKGROUND OF PERSONALITY. UNIV PERSON ALL/VALS...SOC CONCPT TIME/SEQ GEN/METH TOT/POP VAL/FREE. PAGE 97 H1935
CULTURE ATTIT

B45
MCBRYDE F.W.,CULTURAL AND HISTORICAL GEOGRAPHY OF SOUTHWEST GUATEMALA. GUATEMALA AGRI KIN PERSON ...GEOG AUD/VIS CHARTS 20. PAGE 106 H2123
HABITAT ISOLAT CULTURE ECO/UNDEV

B45
VENABLE V.,HUMAN NATURE: THE MARXIAN VIEW. UNIV STRATA CAP/ISM REV GP/REL PERS/REL PRODUC KNOWL ...PHIL/SCI CONCPT IDEA/COMP 19 MARX/KARL ENGELS/F. PAGE 162 H3240
PERSON MARXISM WORKER UTOPIA

B46
GODWIN W.,ENQUIRY CONCERNING POLITICAL JUSTICE AND ITS INFLUENCE ON MORALS AND HAPPINESS (1793). UNIV SOCIETY NAT/G GP/REL INGP/REL HAPPINESS ALL/VALS CONCPT. PAGE 58 H1151
MORAL PERSON ORD/FREE

B46
MILL J.S.,ON LIBERTY. NAT/G LEGIT CONTROL PERS/REL PERCEPT...CONCPT 19. PAGE 110 H2206
ORD/FREE SOCIETY PERSON GEN/LAWS

B46
NICOLSON H.,THE CONGRESS OF VIENNA. MOD/EUR NAT/G FORCES BAL/PWR DOMIN LEGIT COERCE PERSON PWR ...RECORD TIME/SEQ STERTYP 19 CONG/VIENN. PAGE 118 H2353
CONCPT POLICY DIPLOM

B47
JURJI E.J.,THE GREAT RELIGIONS OF THE MODERN WORLD. CULTURE INTELL SOCIETY INT/ORG CONSULT CHOOSE ATTIT DRIVE PERSON RIGID/FLEX...HUM CONCPT OBS BIOG HIST/WRIT TREND GEN/LAWS 20 WORSHIP. PAGE 82 H1643
UNIV SECT

B49
DENNING A.,FREEDOM UNDER THE LAW. MOD/EUR UK LAW SOCIETY CHIEF EX/STRUC LEGIS ADJUD CT/SYS PERS/REL PERSON 17/20 ENGLSH/LAW. PAGE 40 H0793
ORD/FREE JURID NAT/G

B49
GORER G.,THE PEOPLE OF GREAT RUSSIA: A PSYCHOLOGICAL STUDY. RUSSIA USSR NAT/G DIPLOM LEAD AGE/C ANOMIE ATTIT DRIVE...POLICY 20. PAGE 59 H1182
ISOLAT PERSON PSY SOCIETY

B49
SARGENT S.S.,CULTURE AND PERSONALITY. FUT UNIV SOCIETY FAM KIN NEIGH BIO/SOC DRIVE PERCEPT RIGID/FLEX LOVE RESPECT...PSY SOC CONCPT OBS TIME/SEQ TREND CON/ANAL CHARTS HYPO/EXP SIMUL TOT/POP. PAGE 138 H2754
CULTURE PERSON

S49
DEXTER L.A.,"A DIALOGUE ON THE SOCIAL PSYCHOLOGY OF COLONIALISM AND ON CERTAIN PUERTO RICAN PROFESSIONAL PERSONALITY PATTERNS." L/A+17C PUERT/RICO STRATA STRUCT DOMIN ISOLAT DRIVE ...NAT/COMP PERS/COMP HYPO/EXP 20 JEWS NEGRO. PAGE 41 H0813
COLONIAL SOC PSY PERSON

C49
SCHAPIRO J.S.,"LIBERALISM AND THE CHALLENGE OF FASCISM." FRANCE UK STRATA PERSON...CONCPT BIOG IDEA/COMP BIBLIOG 18/20. PAGE 139 H2771
FASCISM LAISSEZ ATTIT

B50
CANTRIL H.,TENSIONS THAT CAUSE WAR. UNIV CULTURE R+D CREATE EDU/PROP DRIVE PERSON KNOWL ORD/FREE ...HUM PSY SOC OBS CENSUS TREND CON/ANAL SOC/EXP SIMUL GEN/METH ANTHOL COLD/WAR TOT/POP. PAGE 26 H0523
SOCIETY PHIL/SCI PEACE

B50
CARR E.H.,STUDIES IN REVOLUTION. CREATE WAR PERSON ALL/IDEOS MARXISM SOCISM...PHIL/SCI METH/COMP ANTHOL 18/20 SAINTSIMON MARX/KARL PROUDHON/P LASSALLE/F PLEKHNV/GV. PAGE 27 H0537
REV IDEA/COMP COERCE BIOG

B50
HOBBES T.,LEVIATHAN. UNIV CONSTN SOCIETY LOC/G NAT/G CONSULT TOP/EX DOMIN DRIVE PERSON PWR ...PHIL/SCI CONCPT SELF/OBS GEN/LAWS TOT/POP. PAGE 72 H1434
LAW ORD/FREE

B50
ROHEIM G.,PSYCHOANALYSIS AND ANTHROPOLOGY. UNIV FAM PERS/REL ATTIT HABITAT...SOC OBS WORSHIP. PAGE 133 H2663
PSY BIOG CULTURE PERSON

C50
ROUSSEAU J.J.,"DISCOURSE ON THE ORIGIN OF INEQUALITY" (1755) IN THE SOCIAL CONTRACT AND DISCOURSES." UNIV NAT/G PLAN BAL/PWR HAPPINESS UTOPIA BIO/SOC HEREDITY MORAL...WELF/ST CONCPT. PAGE 135 H2698
SOCIETY STRUCT PERSON GEN/LAWS

B51
LEMERT E.M.,SOCIAL PATHOLOGY. CULTURE BIO/SOC PERSON SEX 20 PROSTITUTN. PAGE 94 H1876
SOC ANOMIE CONCPT CRIME

B51
LOOS W.A.,RELIGIOUS FAITH AND WORLD CULTURE. INTELL SOCIETY SECT EDU/PROP ROUTINE ATTIT PERSON ALL/VALS MORAL...CONCPT GEN/LAWS VAL/FREE. PAGE 98 H1964
UNIV CULTURE PEACE

B51
MUMFORD L.,THE CONDUCT OF LIFE. UNIV SOCIETY CREATE ...TECHNIC METH/CNCPT TIME/SEQ TREND GEN/LAWS BIBLIOG/A. PAGE 114 H2286
ALL/VALS CULTURE PERSON CONCPT

B51
PARSONS T.,TOWARD A GENERAL THEORY OF ACTION. CULTURE PERSON...PSY SIMUL ANTHOL SOC/INTEG 20. PAGE 124 H2472
SOC PHIL/SCI DRIVE ACT/RES

B51
WEBSTER C.,THE FOREIGN POLICY OF PALMERSTON - 1830 TO 1841. MOD/EUR UK LAW CONSTN INTELL SOCIETY STRUCT NAT/G FORCES TOP/EX CREATE BAL/PWR PWR 19. PAGE 166 H3323
ADMIN PERSON DIPLOM

B52
CALLOT E.,LA SOCIETE ET SON ENVIRONNEMENT: ESSAI SUR LES PRINCIPES DES SCIENCES SOCIALES. GP/REL ADJUST CONSEN ISOLAT HABITAT PERCEPT PERSON ...BIBLIOG SOC/INTEG 20. PAGE 25 H0507
SOCIETY PHIL/SCI CULTURE

B52
HIMMELFARB G.,LORD ACTON: A STUDY IN CONSCIENCE AND POLITICS. MOD/EUR NAT/G POL/PAR SECT LEGIS TOP/EX EDU/PROP ADMIN NAT/LISM ATTIT PERSON SUPEGO MORAL ORD/FREE...CONCPT PARLIAMENT 19 ACTON/LORD. PAGE 71 H1419
PWR BIOG

C52
EBENSTEIN W.,"INTRODUCTION TO POLITICAL PHILOSOPHY." COM CONSTN INTELL CONTROL PERSON NEW/LIB SOCISM...PSY GEN/LAWS BIBLIOG/A. PAGE 44 H0883
ALL/IDEOS PHIL/SCI IDEA/COMP NAT/G

B53
HUNTER E.,BRAIN-WASHING IN RED CHINA. ASIA CHINA/COM CULTURE SOCIETY FORCES WAR TOTALISM ATTIT BIO/SOC DISPL DRIVE PERSON SUPEGO KNOWL ORD/FREE ...INT REC/INT COLD/WAR 20. PAGE 75 H1499
EDU/PROP COERCE

B53
LENZ F.,DIE BEWEGUNGEN DER GROSSEN MACHTE. USA+45 USA-45 USSR SOCIETY STRATA STRUCT NAT/G PERSON MARXISM...CONCPT IDEA/COMP NAT/COMP 18/20. PAGE 94 H1883
BAL/PWR TREND DIPLOM HIST/WRIT

B53
LIEBER F.,CIVIL LIBERTY AND SELF GOVERNMENT: VOLUME 2. NAT/G CONTROL CHOOSE PERSON PWR 19 CIVIL/LIB. PAGE 96 H1925
ORD/FREE SOVEREIGN CENTRAL CONCPT

B53
REDFIELD R.,THE PRIMITIVE WORLD AND ITS TRANSFORMATIONS. UNIV CULTURE ATTIT MORAL...CONCPT TREND. PAGE 130 H2606
SOC CREATE PERSON SOCIETY

S53
ROGOFF N.,"SOCIAL STRATIFICATION IN FRANCE AND IN THE UNITED STATES" (BMR)" FRANCE USA+45 WORKER ADJUST PERSON...SOC 20. PAGE 133 H2662
STRUCT STRATA ATTIT NAT/COMP

B54
MATTHEWS D.R.,THE SOCIAL BACKGROUND OF POLITICAL DECISION-MAKERS. CULTURE SOCIETY STRATA FAM EX/STRUC LEAD ATTIT BIO/SOC DRIVE PERSON ALL/VALS
DECISION BIOG SOC

HIST/WRIT. PAGE 105 H2097

B54
SCHRAMM W.,THE PROCESS AND EFFECTS OF MASS COMMUNICATION. CULTURE INTELL SOCIETY COM/IND DRIVE PERCEPT PERSON RIGID/FLEX KNOWL...PSY SOC CONCPT CHARTS. PAGE 140 H2800
ATTIT EDU/PROP

B54
SPENCER H.,SOCIAL STATICS. MOD/EUR UNIV SOCIETY ECO/DEV NAT/G ACT/RES PLAN EDU/PROP PERSON...POLICY CONCPT. PAGE 147 H2944
MORAL ECO/TAC

B55
APTER D.E.,THE GOLD COAST IN TRANSITION. FUT CONSTN CULTURE SOCIETY ECO/UNDEV FAM KIN LOC/G NAT/G POL/PAR LEGIS TOP/EX EDU/PROP LEGIT ADMIN ATTIT PERSON PWR...CONCPT STAT INT CENSUS TOT/POP VAL/FREE. PAGE 7 H0149
AFR SOVEREIGN

S55
GLADSTONE A.E.,"THE POSSIBILITY OF PREDICTING REACTIONS TO INTERNATIONAL EVENTS." UNIV SOCIETY NAT/G FORCES CREATE EDU/PROP COERCE WAR ATTIT PERSON KNOWL PWR SKILL...METH/CNCPT NEW/IDEA ORG/CHARTS. PAGE 57 H1139
PHIL/SCI CONCPT

B56
BECKER H.,MAN IN RECIPROCITY: INTRODUCTORY LECTURES ON CULTURE, SOCIETY, AND PERSONALITY. LAW FAM SECT REGION GP/REL ADJUST ATTIT PERSON...BIBLIOG 20. PAGE 13 H0253
CULTURE STRUCT SOC PSY

B56
GOFFMAN E.,THE PRESENTATION OF SELF IN EVERYDAY LIFE. CULTURE INGP/REL ATTIT DRIVE...SOC OBS RECORD 20. PAGE 58 H1154
PERS/COMP PERSON PERCEPT ROLE

B56
KALLEN H.M.,CULTURAL PLURALISM AND THE AMERICAN IDEA. RACE/REL ADJUST PERSON ORD/FREE LAISSEZ ...PLURIST GEN/LAWS ANTHOL. PAGE 83 H1652
PLURISM CULTURE GP/REL SECT

B56
MUMFORD L.,THE TRANSFORMATIONS OF MAN. UNIV CULTURE INGP/REL HABITAT HEREDITY ALL/VALS ORD/FREE...MYTH TIME/SEQ TREND WORSHIP. PAGE 114 H2287
IDEA/COMP PERSON CONCPT

B56
READ M.,EDUCATION AND SOCIAL CHANGE IN TROPICAL AREAS. AFR L/A+17C SOCIETY LITERACY PERCEPT PERSON WEALTH...HEAL PHIL/SCI SOC 20. PAGE 130 H2603
EDU/PROP HABITAT DRIVE CULTURE

B56
SHAPIRO H.L.,MAN, CULTURE, AND SOCIETY. STRUCT FAM SECT GP/REL INGP/REL...ART/METH GEOG PSY LING ANTHOL BIBLIOG. PAGE 142 H2842
CULTURE PERSON SOC

B56
SMEDLEY A.,THE GREAT ROAD: THE LIFE AND TIMES OF CHU TEH. ASIA USSR NAT/G POL/PAR DIPLOM COERCE GUERRILLA CIVMIL/REL NAT/LISM PERSON SKILL MARXISM ...BIOG 20 CHINJAP MAO. PAGE 145 H2903
REV WAR FORCES

B56
WEIL E.,PHILOSOPHIE POLITIQUE. UNIV CULTURE RATIONAL PERSON ROLE. PAGE 166 H3326
SOCIETY NAT/G MORAL

B57
KOENTJARANINGRAT R.,A PRELIMINARY DESCRIPTION OF THE JAVANESE KINSHIP SYSTEM. INDONESIA STRATA FAM INGP/REL ADJUST MARRIAGE AGE/C AGE/Y AGE/A PERSON ...OBS CHARTS DICTIONARY 20 JAVA. PAGE 87 H1736
KIN STRUCT ELITES CULTURE

B57
LAQUER W.Z.,COMMUNISM AND NATIONALISM IN THE MIDDLE EAST. ELITES INTELL STRATA NAT/G POL/PAR SECT VOL/ASSN TOP/EX DOMIN LEGIT REGION COERCE ATTIT PERSON PWR...CONCPT HIST/WRIT TIME/SEQ TREND GEN/LAWS VAL/FREE. PAGE 91 H1817
ISLAM NAT/LISM

B57
MENDIETTA Y NUNE L.,THEORIE DES GROUPEMENT SOCIAUX SUIVI D'UNE ETUDE SUR LE DROIT SOCIAL. ELITES FAM KIN NAT/G PROB/SOLV CROWD ISOLAT ATTIT PERSON ...JURID CONCPT SOC/INTEG. PAGE 109 H2174
SOC STRATA STRUCT DISCRIM

B57
NARAIN D.,HINDU CHARACTER (A FEW GLIMPSES). INDIA DIPLOM SUICIDE PERS/REL ATTIT...PSY NAT/COMP PERS/COMP BIBLIOG WORSHIP 20 HINDU. PAGE 116 H2310
PERSON STERTYP SUPEGO SECT

B57
PLAYFAIR G.,THE OFFENDERS: THE CASE AGAINST LEGAL VENGEANCE. UNIV LAW SOCIETY NAT/G PROB/SOLV DEATH PERSON ORD/FREE...HEAL INT/LAW BIBLIOG 20 REFORMERS. PAGE 126 H2524
CRIME TEC/DEV SANCTION CT/SYS

B57
ROSS R.,THE FABRIC OF SOCIETY. STRATA GP/REL PERSON ...CONCPT METH T 20. PAGE 134 H2687
SOC PHIL/SCI CULTURE STRUCT

S57
DEXTER L.A.,"A SOCIAL THEORY OF MENTAL DEFICIENCY." CULTURE PUB/INST PROB/SOLV CRIME PERS/REL STRANGE PERSON SUPEGO SKILL...EPIST SOC/WK HYPO/EXP. PAGE 41 H0814
SOC PSY HEALTH ROLE

S57
HAILEY,"TOMORROW IN AFRICA." CONSTN SOCIETY LOC/G NAT/G DOMIN ADJUD ADMIN GP/REL DISCRIM NAT/LISM ATTIT MORAL ORD/FREE...PSY SOC CONCPT OBS RECORD TREND GEN/LAWS CMN/WLTH 20. PAGE 64 H1277
AFR PERSON ELITES RACE/REL

B58
GREAVES H.R.,THE FOUNDATIONS OF POLITICAL THEORY. WAR ATTIT SUPEGO ORD/FREE...IDEA/COMP SOC/INTEG. PAGE 60 H1203
CONCPT MORAL PERSON

B58
HAYCRAFT J.,BABEL IN SPAIN. SPAIN ATTIT...RELATIV 20. PAGE 68 H1367
CULTURE PERSON BIOG GEOG

B58
LERNER D.,THE PASSING OF TRADITIONAL SOCIETY: MODERNIZING THE MIDDLE EAST. IRAN ISLAM LEBANON SYRIA TURKEY UAR CULTURE INTELL STRATA KIN NAT/G NEIGH SECT EDU/PROP ATTIT PERSON...MYTH OBS 20. PAGE 95 H1888
ECO/UNDEV RIGID/FLEX

B58
MEHNERT K.,DER SOWJETMENSCH. USSR NAT/G SECT EDU/PROP TOTALISM ORD/FREE 20. PAGE 108 H2161
SOCIETY ATTIT PERSON FAM

B58
ORNES G.E.,TRUJILLO: LITTLE CAESAR OF THE CARIBBEAN. DOMIN/REP FAM NAT/G FORCES BUDGET CRIME REV PERSON 20 TRUJILLO/R. PAGE 122 H2429
BIOG PWR TOTALISM CHIEF

B58
ORTEGA Y GASSET J.,MAN AND CRISIS. SECT CREATE PERSON CONSERVE...GEN/LAWS RENAISSAN. PAGE 122 H2430
PHIL/SCI CULTURE CONCPT

B59
DUNHAM H.W.,SOCIOLOGICAL THEORY AND MENTAL DISORDER. UNIV SOCIETY STRATA HABITAT PERSON...GEOG CHARTS SOC/EXP TIME. PAGE 43 H0864
HEALTH SOC PSY CULTURE

B59
GOLDSCHMIDT W.,UNDERSTANDING HUMAN SOCIETY. SOCIETY CREATE ATTIT...GEOG PHIL/SCI CONCPT GP/COMP. PAGE 58 H1159
CULTURE STRUCT TEC/DEV PERSON

B59
GOLDWIN R.A.,READINGS IN RUSSIAN FOREIGN POLICY. HUNGARY USSR YUGOSLAVIA ELITES INT/ORG NAT/G REV WAR NAT/LISM PERSON SOCISM...CHARTS 20 MAPS BOLSHEVISM. PAGE 58 H1160
COM MARXISM DIPLOM POLICY

B59
HONINGMAN J.J.,THE WORLD OF MAN. CHRIST-17C MEDIT-7 PRE/AMER PREHIST CREATE INGP/REL BIO/SOC HABITAT ...PSY SOC BIBLIOG. PAGE 73 H1460
CULTURE METH PERSON STRUCT

B59
LEE D.,FREEDOM AND CULTURE. WOR+45 WOR-45 FAM HABITAT PERSON LOVE MORAL...PSY SOC OBS NAT/COMP WORSHIP 20. PAGE 93 H1856
CULTURE SOCIETY CONCPT INGP/REL

B59
PAGE S.W.,LENIN AND WORLD REVOLUTION. COM USSR NAT/G DOMIN COERCE CROWD UTOPIA ATTIT AUTHORIT DRIVE PWR...CONCPT MYTH 19/20 LENIN/VI MARX/KARL. PAGE 122 H2441
REV PERSON MARXISM BIOG

B59
SITHOLE N.,AFRICAN NATIONALISM. UNIV CULTURE SECT ADMIN COLONIAL CHOOSE. PAGE 145 H2892
RACE/REL AFR NAT/LISM PERSON

B59
SZLUC T.,TWILIGHT OF THE TYRANTS. BRAZIL L/A+17C PERU VENEZUELA NAT/G FORCES CONTROL PERSON MORAL ORD/FREE PWR...CONCPT 20 ARGEN COLOMB. PAGE 151 H3028
TOTALISM CHIEF REV FASCISM

S59
MCNEIL E.B.,"PSYCHOLOGY AND AGGRESSION." CULTURE SOCIETY ACT/RES DISPL PERSON HEALTH. PAGE 107 H2146
DRIVE PSY

S59
SCOTT W.A.,"EMPIRICAL ASSESSMENT OF VALUES AND IDEOLOGIES." CULTURE SOCIETY SECT CREATE DRIVE PERSON MORAL PWR...SOC METH/CNCPT STAT CONT/OBS DEEP/INT DEEP/QU CHARTS VAL/FREE. PAGE 141 H2817
ATTIT PSY

B60
BARBU Z.,PROBLEMS OF HISTORICAL PSYCHOLOGY. GREECE MEDIT-7 UK CULTURE TEC/DEV ADJUST RATIONAL ATTIT PERCEPT...METH/CNCPT NEW/IDEA TIME/SEQ GEN/METH. PAGE 11 H0214
PERSON PSY HIST/WRIT IDEA/COMP

B60
CHATTERJI S.K.,AFRICANISM: THE AFRICAN PERSONALITY. KIN NAT/G SECT CREATE DIPLOM COLONIAL GP/REL ATTIT ORD/FREE...LING WORSHIP 20. PAGE 29 H0585
PERSON NAT/LISM AFR CULTURE

B60
DICHTER E.,THE STRATEGY OF DESIRE. UNIV CULTURE ACT/RES ATTIT DRIVE 20. PAGE 41 H0821
EDU/PROP PSY CONSULT

PERSON

B60
GENTILE G.,GENESIS AND STRUCTURE OF SOCIETY (TRANS. BY H.S. HARRIS). NAT/G SECT ATTIT SUPEGO...JURID 20. PAGE 56 H1111
SOCIETY STRUCT PERSON

B60
HAMADY S.,TEMPERAMENT AND CHARACTER OF THE ARABS. FAM NAT/G SECT DIPLOM NAT/LISM...POLICY 20 ARABS. PAGE 65 H1299
NAT/COMP PERSON CULTURE ISLAM

B60
MINER H.M.,OASIS AND CASBAH: ALGERIAN CULTURE AND PERSONALITY IN CHANGE. ALGERIA FRANCE SOCIETY MUNIC COLONIAL ATTIT...INT PROJ/TEST CHARTS 20. PAGE 111 H2221
GP/COMP PERSON CULTURE ADJUST

B60
NAKAMURA H.,THE WAYS OF THINKING OF EASTERN PEOPLES. ASIA INDIA PERSON...HUM SOC LING LOG WORSHIP CHINJAP. PAGE 115 H2305
CULTURE SECT ATTIT

B60
SHIRER W.L.,THE RISE AND FALL OF THE THIRD REICH: A HISTORY OF NAZI GERMANY. EUR+WWI CULTURE ECO/DEV INDUS NAT/G POL/PAR FORCES PLAN TEC/DEV ECO/TAC COERCE ATTIT DRIVE PERSON PWR...MYSTIC PSY SOC MYTH STAT CHARTS EXHIBIT WORK VAL/FREE. PAGE 143 H2864
STRUCT GERMANY TOTALISM

B60
VON KOENIGSWALD H.,SIE SUCHEN ZUFLUCHT. GERMANY/E NAT/G PLAN ECO/TAC SOCISM...GEOG CENSUS 20 BERLIN. PAGE 164 H3273
GP/REL COERCE DOMIN PERSON

B60
RUDD J.,TABOO, A STUDY OF MALAGASY CUSTOMS AND BELIEFS. MADAGASCAR LAW FAM CONTROL CRIME PERSON ...CONCPT 20. PAGE 173 H3466
CULTURE DOMIN SECT SANCTION

L60
WHEELER G.,"RACIAL PROBLEMS IN SOVIET MUSLIM ASIA." COM CULTURE SOCIETY NEIGH SECT DOMIN EDU/PROP DISCRIM DISPL DRIVE PWR SOVEREIGN...CENSUS SAMP TREND 20 MUSLIM. PAGE 167 H3340
PERSON ATTIT USSR RACE/REL

S60
ARENDT H.,"SOCIETY AND CULTURE." FUT CULTURE INTELL STRATA EDU/PROP ATTIT PERSON KNOWL...ART/METH HUM 20. PAGE 8 H0161
SOCIETY CREATE

S60
FITZGIBBON R.H.,"DICTATORSHIP AND DEMOCRACY IN LATIN AMERICA." FUT ECO/DEV ECO/UNDEV INT/ORG LOC/G NAT/G TOP/EX PLAN TEC/DEV ECO/TAC CHOOSE ATTIT DRIVE PERSON ALL/VALS OAS TOT/POP 20. PAGE 51 H1019
L/A+17C ACT/RES INT/TRADE

S60
LEVINE R.A.,"THE INTERNALIZATION OF POLITICAL VALUES IN STATELESS SOCIETIES." AFR FAM KIN LOC/G PROVS JUDGE PERSON RIGID/FLEX...DECISION SOC TIME/SEQ 20. PAGE 95 H1904
CULTURE ATTIT

S60
TURNER R.H.,"SPONSORED AND CONTEST MOBILITY IN THE SCHOOL SYSTEM." UK USA+45 ELITES STRATA ACADEM FACE/GP EDU/PROP CONTROL INGP/REL ADJUST ATTIT PERSON...METH/COMP 20. PAGE 157 H3142
AGE/Y NAT/COMP SCHOOL STRUCT

C60
BOGARDUS E.S.,"THE DEVELOPMENT OF SOCIAL THOUGHT." SOCIETY PERSON KNOWL...EPIST CONCPT BIBLIOG T. PAGE 18 H0365
INTELL CULTURE IDEA/COMP GP/COMP

C60
EBENSTEIN W.,"MODERN POLITICAL THOUGHT (2ND ED.)" NAT/G CAP/ISM NAT/LISM PERSON ORD/FREE PWR ALL/IDEOS NEW/LIB SOCISM...TRADIT PSY BIBLIOG/A 18/20. PAGE 44 H0884
IDEA/COMP PHIL/SCI CONCPT GEN/LAWS

B61
BEDFORD S.,THE FACES OF JUSTICE: A TRAVELLER'S REPORT. AUSTRIA FRANCE GERMANY/W SWITZERLND UK UNIV WOR+45 WOR-45 CULTURE PARTIC GOV/REL MORAL...JURID OBS GOV/COMP 20. PAGE 13 H0257
CT/SYS ORD/FREE PERSON LAW

B61
BULLOCK A.,HITLER: A STUDY IN TYRANNY. EUR+WWI GERMANY SOCIETY STRUCT NAT/G POL/PAR FORCES CREATE DOMIN EDU/PROP EXEC COERCE WAR NAT/LISM DISPL DRIVE PERSON PWR...PSY NAZI 20 HITLER/A. PAGE 23 H0470
ATTIT BIOG TOTALISM

B61
HEMPSTONE S.,THE NEW AFRICA. AGRI INDUS KIN NAT/G COLONIAL MARXISM...SOC INT TREND NAT/COMP BIBLIOG/A 20. PAGE 69 H1392
AFR ORD/FREE PERSON CULTURE

B61
MACLEOD I.,NEVILLE CHAMBERLAIN. UK SOCIETY TOP/EX WAR PERSON ALL/VALS ORD/FREE PARLIAMENT 20 CHAMBRLN/N. PAGE 100 H2003
BIOG NAT/G CREATE

B61
MARVICK D.,POLITICAL DECISION-MAKERS. INTELL STRATA NAT/G POL/PAR EX/STRUC LEGIS DOMIN EDU/PROP ATTIT PERSON PWR...PSY STAT OBS CONT/OBS STAND/INT UNPLAN/INT TIME/SEQ CHARTS STERTYP VAL/FREE. PAGE 104 H2073
TOP/EX BIOG ELITES

B61
PAZ O.,THE LABYRINTH OF SOLITUDE; LIFE AND THOUGHT IN MEXICO (TRANS. BY LYSANDER KEMP). INTELL COLONIAL REV...PSY SOC TIME/SEQ 16/20 MEXIC/AMER. PAGE 124 H2480
CULTURE PERSON PERS/REL SOCIETY

B61
ROIG E.,MARTI, ANTIIMPERIALISTA. CUBA L/A+17C DIPLOM DOMIN COLONIAL CONTROL LEAD PWR SOVEREIGN ...PHIL/SCI 19 MARTI/JOSE INTERVENT. PAGE 133 H2664
PERSON NAT/LISM ECO/UNDEV ORD/FREE

B61
SEMINAR REPRESENTATIVE GOVT,AFRO-ASIAN ATTITUDES: SEMINAR ON REPRESENTATIVE GOVERNMENTSPUBLIC LIBERTIES IN STATES OF ASIA AND AFRICA, RHODES, 1958. AFR ASIA BURMA INDIA ISLAM UAR VIETNAM/S SOCIETY POL/PAR CHIEF EDU/PROP PRESS PERSON ...POLICY INT 20 TUNIS. PAGE 141 H2826
CHOOSE ATTIT NAT/COMP ORD/FREE

B61
VON MERING O.,A GRAMMAR OF HUMAN VALUES. WOR+45 CULTURE FACE/GP NEIGH CREATE EDU/PROP LEGIT ATTIT DRIVE PERSON ORD/FREE...PSY SOC METH/CNCPT OBS RECORD INT REC/INT STAND/INT QU CHARTS VAL/FREE. PAGE 164 H3275
SOCIETY MORAL

S61
SCHECHTMAN J.B.,"MINORITIES IN THE MIDDLE EAST." ISLAM INTELL SOCIETY STRATA KIN NAT/G VOL/ASSN EDU/PROP REGION GP/REL DISCRIM ATTIT BIO/SOC DISPL PERSON ALL/VALS...PSY SOC OBS SAMP GEN/LAWS 20. PAGE 139 H2776
SECT CULTURE RACE/REL

S61
ZAGORIA D.S.,"THE FUTURE OF SINO-SOVIET RELATIONS." CHINA/COM INT/ORG NAT/G POL/PAR VOL/ASSN ACT/RES PLAN PERSON...METH/CNCPT TIME/SEQ TOT/POP VAL/FREE 20 MAO KHRUSH/N. PAGE 172 H3445
ASIA COM TOTALISM USSR

B62
BERGER M.,THE ARAB WORLD TODAY. CULTURE FAM INT/ORG NAT/G SECT FORCES ECO/TAC NAT/LISM HABITAT...CHARTS BIBLIOG 20 ARABS. PAGE 15 H0301
ISLAM PERSON STRUCT SOCIETY

B62
BUSIA K.A.,THE CHALLENGE OF AFRICA. CULTURE KIN MUNIC NAT/G POL/PAR SCHOOL DELIB/GP PLAN ECO/TAC DOMIN EDU/PROP TOTALISM ATTIT PERSON ALL/VALS SOVEREIGN...SOC CONCPT STERTYP TOT/POP VAL/FREE 20. PAGE 25 H0496
AFR ECO/UNDEV NAT/LISM

B62
HO PING-TI,THE LADDER OF SUCCESS IN IMPERIAL CHINA: ASPECTS OF SOCIAL MOBILITY, 1368-1911. INTELL STRATA FAM KIN MUNIC NAT/G PROVS SCHOOL DELIB/GP DOMIN EDU/PROP ADMIN ROUTINE PERSON ALL/VALS...SOC STAT BIOG HIST/WRIT TIME/SEQ VAL/FREE. PAGE 71 H1431
ASIA CULTURE

B62
KRUGLAK T.E.,THE TWO FACES OF TASS. COM COM/IND NAT/G ACT/RES PLAN PRESS PERCEPT PERSON KNOWL 20. PAGE 89 H1778
PUB/INST EDU/PROP USSR

B62
LEGUM C.,PAN-AFRICANISM: A SHORT POLITICAL GUIDE. ISLAM CULTURE INTELL ECO/DEV NAT/G POL/PAR DELIB/GP PLAN EDU/PROP FEDERAL NAT/LISM ATTIT DRIVE PERSON ...RECORD TIME/SEQ CHARTS STERTYP 20. PAGE 93 H1861
AFR CONCPT

B62
MALINOWSKI B.,SEX, CULTURE, AND MYTH. UNIV SOCIETY FAM PERS/REL MARRIAGE RATIONAL HABITAT PERSON SUPEGO MORAL WORSHIP 20. PAGE 102 H2032
MYTH SECT SEX CULTURE

B62
OLLE-LAPRUNE J.,LA STABILITE DES MINISTRES SOUS LA TROISIEME REPUBLIQUE, 1879-1940. FRANCE CONSTN POL/PAR LEAD WAR INGP/REL RIGID/FLEX PWR...POLICY CHARTS 19/20. PAGE 121 H2415
LEGIS NAT/G ADMIN PERSON

S62
MU FU-SHENG,"THE WILTING OF THE HUNDRED FLOWERS: FREE THOUGHT IN CHINA TODAY." ASIA CHINA/COM CULTURE FAM NAT/G EDU/PROP REV TOTALISM ATTIT PERSON RESPECT...GEOG INT UNPLAN/INT COLD/WAR 20. PAGE 114 H2278
INTELL ELITES

S62
SPRINGER H.W.,"FEDERATION IN THE CARIBBEAN: AN ATTEMPT THAT FAILED." L/A+17C ECO/UNDEV INT/ORG POL/PAR PROVS LEGIS CREATE PLAN LEGIT ADMIN FEDERAL ATTIT DRIVE PERSON ORD/FREE PWR...POLICY GEOG PSY CONCPT OBS CARIBBEAN CMN/WLTH 20. PAGE 148 H2955
VOL/ASSN NAT/G REGION

B63
BERLIN I.,KARL MARX, HIS LIFE AND ENVIRONMENT (3RD ED.). MOD/EUR USSR INTELL EDU/PROP PARTIC REV ATTIT 19 MARX/KARL. PAGE 15 H0307
BIOG PERSON MARXISM CONCPT

B63
BIDNEY D.,THE CONCEPT OF FREEDOM IN ANTHROPOLOGY. UNIV CULTURE STRATA SECT CREATE NAT/LISM ...METH/COMP 20. PAGE 17 H0332
SOC PERSON ORD/FREE CONCPT

B63
BROOKES E.H.,POWER, LAW, RIGHT, AND LOVE: A STUDY IN POLITICAL VALUES. SOUTH/AFR NAT/G PERSON ...CONCPT IDEA/COMP 20. PAGE 21 H0432
PWR ORD/FREE JURID LOVE

B63
DE JOUVENEL B.,THE PURE THEORY OF POLITICS. NAT/G DIPLOM CONTROL GP/REL PERS/REL PERSON PWR OBJECTIVE CONCPT. PAGE 38 H0758 — GEN/LAWS SOCIETY METH/CNCPT

B63
EICH H.,THE UNLOVED GERMANS. EUR+WWI GERMANY PERS/REL RACE/REL DISCRIM HABITAT SUPEGO FASCISM ...PSY SOC AUD/VIS 19/20 JEWS. PAGE 45 H0898 — STERTYP PERSON CULTURE ATTIT

B63
ELIAS T.O.,GOVERNMENT AND POLITICS IN AFRICA. CONSTN CULTURE SOCIETY NAT/G POL/PAR DIPLOM REPRESENT PERSON...SOC TREND BIBLIOG 4/20. PAGE 45 H0906 — AFR NAT/LISM COLONIAL LAW

B63
FALL B.,THE TWO VIETNAMS. CULTURE SOCIETY ECO/UNDEV NAT/G TOP/EX ACT/RES PLAN ECO/TAC DOMIN EDU/PROP COERCE ATTIT DRIVE PERSON ORD/FREE PWR...SOC TIME/SEQ COLD/WAR 20. PAGE 48 H0965 — S/ASIA BIOG VIETNAM

B63
FRIEDRICH C.J.,MAN AND HIS GOVERNMENT: AN EMPIRICAL THEORY OF POLITICS. UNIV LOC/G NAT/G ADJUD REV INGP/REL DISCRIM PWR BIBLIOG. PAGE 53 H1069 — PERSON ORD/FREE PARTIC CONTROL

B63
GERSCHENKRON A.,THE STABILITY OF DICTATORSHIPS. NAT/G EDU/PROP TASK ATTIT PERSON...POLICY PSY SOC METH 19/20. PAGE 56 H1116 — TOTALISM CONCPT CONTROL ORD/FREE

B63
GLUCKMAN M.,ORDER AND REBELLION IN TRIBAL AFRICA. EUR+WWI LAW CULTURE STRATA KIN MUNIC DELIB/GP ACT/RES DOMIN EDU/PROP LEGIT ADMIN COERCE CHOOSE ATTIT PERSON ORD/FREE PWR...SOC CHARTS GEN/LAWS TOT/POP VAL/FREE. PAGE 57 H1147 — AFR SOCIETY

B63
KRAEHE E.,METTERNICH'S GERMAN POLICY: THE CONTEST WITH NAPOLEON, 1799-1814, VOL. 1. FRANCE MOD/EUR NAT/G CONSULT TOP/EX PLAN BAL/PWR DOMIN COERCE ATTIT DRIVE PERCEPT PERSON SKILL...CONCPT RECORD TIME/SEQ TREND 18/19. PAGE 88 H1764 — BIOG GERMANY DIPLOM

B63
MARTINDALE D.,COMMUNITY, CHARACTER AND CIVILIZATION: STUDIES IN SOCIAL BEHAVIORISM. INTELL FAM NEIGH VOL/ASSN GP/REL NAT/LISM ATTIT PERSON ...CONCPT GP/COMP 20 BEHAVIORSM. PAGE 103 H2066 — SOC METH/COMP CULTURE STRUCT

B63
MONTAGUE J.B. JR.,CLASS AND NATIONALITY; ENGLISH AND AMERICAN STUDIES. UK USA+45 ELITES STRUCT WORKER ATTIT PWR...SOC CHARTS SOC/EXP 20. PAGE 112 H2243 — STRATA NAT/LISM PERSON NAT/COMP

B63
QUAISON-SACKEY A.,AFRICA UNBOUND: REFLECTIONS OF AN AFRICAN STATESMAN. ISLAM CULTURE INTELL INT/ORG POL/PAR TOP/EX DOMIN EDU/PROP LEGIT ATTIT PERSON ...CONCPT OBS TIME/SEQ CHARTS STERTYP 20 UN. PAGE 129 H2571 — AFR BIOG

B63
REYNOLDS B.,MAGIC, DIVINATION AND WITCHCRAFT AMONG THE BAROTSE OF NORTHERN RHODESIA. RHODESIA CULTURE KIN CREATE LEGIT PARTIC DEATH DREAM STRANGE HABITAT PERSON...AUD/VIS WORSHIP 20. PAGE 131 H2619 — AFR SOC MYTH SECT

B63
ROBERTSON A.H.,HUMAN RIGHTS IN EUROPE. CONSTN SOCIETY INT/ORG NAT/G VOL/ASSN DELIB/GP ACT/RES PLAN ADJUD REGION ROUTINE ATTIT LOVE ORD/FREE RESPECT...JURID SOC CONCPT SOC/EXP UN 20. PAGE 132 H2645 — EUR+WWI PERSON

B63
RUITENBEER H.M.,THE DILEMMA OF ORGANIZATIONAL SOCIETY. CULTURE ECO/DEV MUNIC SECT TEC/DEV EDU/PROP NAT/LISM ORD/FREE...NAT/COMP 20 RIESMAN/D WHYTE/WF MERTON/R MEAD/MARG JASPERS/K. PAGE 136 H2716 — PERSON ROLE ADMIN WORKER

L63
CORWIN A.F.,"CONTEMPORARY MEXICAN ATTITUDES TOWARD POPULATION, POVERTY, AND PUBLIC OPINION." L/A+17C CULTURE SOCIETY ACT/RES ECO/TAC EDU/PROP PERSON HEALTH KNOWL...GEOG PHIL/SCI STAT OBS INT SAMP MEXIC/AMER VAL/FREE 20. PAGE 34 H0672 — ATTIT QU

L63
FREUND G.,"ADENAUER AND THE FUTURE OF GERMANY." EUR+WWI FUT GERMANY/W FORCES LEGIT ADMIN ROUTINE ATTIT DRIVE PERSON PWR...POLICY TIME/SEQ TREND VAL/FREE 20 ADENAUER/K. PAGE 53 H1058 — NAT/G BIOG DIPLOM GERMANY

L63
JAY R.,"RELIGION AND POLITICS IN RURAL CENTRAL JAVA." S/ASIA SOCIETY NEIGH SECT PERSON HEALTH MORAL...SOC UNPLAN/INT TIME/SEQ JAVA VAL/FREE 20 WORSHIP. PAGE 80 H1594 — CULTURE OBS

L63
NASH M.,"PSYCHO-CULTURAL FACTORS IN ASIAN ECONOMIC GROWTH." ASIA ISLAM S/ASIA CULTURE ECO/UNDEV DELIB/GP EDU/PROP COERCE ATTIT PERSON HEALTH KNOWL ORD/FREE...PSY SOC STAT TREND ANTHOL VAL/FREE 20. PAGE 116 H2313 — SOCIETY ECO/TAC

S63
ANTHON C.G.,"THE END OF THE ADENAUER ERA." EUR+WWI GERMANY/W CONSTN EX/STRUC CREATE DIPLOM LEGIT ATTIT PERSON ALL/VALS...RECORD 20 ADENAUER/K. PAGE 7 H0144 — NAT/G TOP/EX BAL/PWR GERMANY

S63
MAZRUI A.A.,"ON THE CONCEPT 'WE ARE ALL AFRICANS'." AFR CULTURE KIN LOC/G NAT/G DOMIN EDU/PROP LEGIT ATTIT PERCEPT PERSON KNOWL ORD/FREE...TIME/SEQ TOT/POP 20. PAGE 106 H2110 — PROVS INT/ORG NAT/LISM

S63
RINTELEN F.,"L'HOMME EUROPEEN." EUR+WWI FUT CULTURE INTELL SECT EDU/PROP ATTIT ALL/VALS...HUM SOC METH/CNCPT TREND GEN/LAWS 20 WORSHIP. PAGE 132 H2631 — SOCIETY PERSON

S63
RUSTOW D.A.,"THE MILITARY IN MIDDLE EASTERN SOCIETY AND POLITICS." FUT ISLAM CONSTN SOCIETY FACE/GP NAT/G POL/PAR PROF/ORG CONSULT DOMIN ADMIN EXEC REGION COERCE NAT/LISM ATTIT DRIVE PERSON ORD/FREE PWR...POLICY CONCPT OBS STERTYP 20. PAGE 136 H2721 — FORCES ELITES

C63
HSU F.L.,"COHESION AND DIVISION IN THE AMERICAN WORLD" HSU FL. CLAN, CASTE, AND CLUB." CULTURE EDU/PROP CONFER SANCTION PERSON...PSY GP/COMP. PAGE 74 H1484 — PERS/REL AGE/Y ADJUST VOL/ASSN

B64
BRIGHT J.R.,RESEARCH, DEVELOPMENT AND TECHNOLOGICAL INNOVATION. CULTURE R+D CREATE PLAN PROB/SOLV AUTOMAT RISK PERSON...DECISION CONCPT PREDICT BIBLIOG. PAGE 21 H0419 — TEC/DEV NEW/IDEA INDUS MGT

B64
CAUTE D.,COMMUNISM AND THE FRENCH INTELLECTUALS, 1914-1960. COM EUR+WWI MOD/EUR NAT/G PERF/ART PROF/ORG CREATE EDU/PROP ATTIT PERSON KNOWL MARXISM ...SOC TIME/SEQ MARX/KARL 20 MALRAUX/A GIDE/A SARTRE/J. PAGE 28 H0563 — POL/PAR INTELL

B64
COBBAN A.,ROUSSEAU AND THE MODERN STATE (2ND ED.). FRANCE PROB/SOLV NAT/LISM UTOPIA PERSON MORAL ...EPIST PHIL/SCI SOC IDEA/COMP 18 ROUSSEAU/J BURKE/EDM HOBBES/T HUME/D. PAGE 30 H0612 — GEN/LAWS INGP/REL NAT/G ORD/FREE

B64
FISCHER L.,THE LIFE OF LENIN. USSR LEAD REV WAR ...SOC 19/20 LENIN/VI COM/PARTY BOLSHEVISM. PAGE 51 H1011 — BIOG MARXISM PERSON CHIEF

B64
FORBES A.H.,CURRENT RESEARCH IN BRITISH STUDIES. UK CONSTN CULTURE POL/PAR SECT DIPLOM ADMIN...JURID BIOG WORSHIP 20. PAGE 52 H1034 — BIBLIOG PERSON NAT/G PARL/PROC

B64
FROMM E.,MARX'S CONCEPT OF MAN. LABOR OWN PERSON ...HUM IDEA/COMP GEN/LAWS 17 MARX/KARL EUROPE SPINOZA/B GOETHE/J HEGEL/GWF. PAGE 54 H1072 — INGP/REL CONCPT MARXISM SOCISM

B64
GREEN M.M.,IBO VILLAGE AFFAIRS. AFR FORCES PERS/REL ADJUST ISOLAT ATTIT HABITAT PERSON ALL/VALS...JURID RECORD SOC/INTEG 20 IBO. PAGE 60 H1207 — MUNIC CULTURE ECO/UNDEV SOC

B64
GRIFFITH W.E.,THE SINO-SOVIET RIFT. ASIA CHINA/COM COM CUBA USSR YUGOSLAVIA NAT/G POL/PAR VOL/ASSN DELIB/GP FORCES TOP/EX DIPLOM EDU/PROP DRIVE PERSON PWR...TREND 20 TREATY. PAGE 61 H1224 — ATTIT TIME/SEQ BAL/PWR SOCISM

B64
HALLER W.,DER SCHWEDISCHE JUSTITIEOMBUDSMAN. DENMARK FINLAND NORWAY SWEDEN LEGIS ADJUD CONTROL PERSON ORD/FREE...NAT/COMP 20 OMBUDSMAN. PAGE 64 H1288 — JURID PARL/PROC ADMIN CHIEF

B64
HARRIS M.,THE NATURE OF CULTURAL THINGS. GP/REL PERS/REL DRIVE HABITAT PERSON ROLE...PHIL/SCI PSY SOC CHARTS BIBLIOG 20. PAGE 67 H1341 — CULTURE OBS CLASSIF NEW/IDEA

B64
JOSEPHSON E.,MAN ALONE: ALIENATION IN MODERN SOCIETY. WOR+45 ECO/DEV WORKER WAR LEISURE RACE/REL ANOMIE ATTIT PERCEPT PERSON ALL/VALS...ANTHOL 20. PAGE 82 H1636 — STRANGE CULTURE SOCIETY ADJUST

B64
NORTHROP F.S.,CROSS-CULTURAL UNDERSTANDING: EPISTEMOLOGY IN ANTHROPOLOGY. BURMA GREECE THAILAND HABITAT PERCEPT PERSON...PHIL/SCI SOC METH 20 MEXIC/AMER CHINJAP. PAGE 119 H2375 — EPIST PSY CULTURE CONCPT

B64
REMAK J.,THE GENTLE CRITIC: THEODOR FONTANE AND GERMAN POLITICS, 1848-1898. GERMANY PRUSSIA CULTURE ELITES BAL/PWR DIPLOM WRITING GOV/REL...HUM BIOG 19 BISMARCK/O JUNKER FONTANE/T. PAGE 131 H2614 — PERSON SOCIETY WORKER CHIEF

B64
TAYLOR E.,RICHER BY ASIA. S/ASIA CULTURE VOL/ASSN ACT/RES ATTIT DISPL PERSON ALL/VALS...INT/LAW MYTH SELF/OBS 20. PAGE 153 H3054 — SOCIETY RIGID/FLEX INDIA

B64
VALEN H.,POLITICAL PARTIES IN NORWAY. NORWAY ACADEM PARTIC ROUTINE INGP/REL KNOWL...QU 20. PAGE 161 H3220
LOC/G POL/PAR PERSON

L64
FINDLATER R.,"US." EUR+WWI GERMANY USSR SOCIETY FACE/GP EDU/PROP PERCEPT PERSON ALL/VALS...PSY SOC CONCPT SELF/OBS SAMP TREND 20. PAGE 50 H1001
CULTURE ATTIT UK

S64
COLEMAN J.S.,"COLLECTIVE DECISIONS." CULTURE ATTIT PERCEPT PWR SOC. PAGE 31 H0628
DECISION INGP/REL PERSON METH/COMP

S64
CROZIER B.,"POUVOIR ET ORGANISATION." SOCIETY NAT/G DOMIN...PSY SOC CONCPT TOT/POP VAL/FREE 20. PAGE 36 H0714
PERSON PWR DIPLOM

S64
LANGERHANS H.,"NEHRU'S BITTERNESS." FUT INDIA S/ASIA CONSTN CULTURE ECO/UNDEV ECO/TAC DOMIN EDU/PROP ATTIT PERCEPT PERSON...POLICY 20 NEHRU/J. PAGE 91 H1811
ECO/DEV BIOG

S64
SMYTHE H.H.,"NEHRU AND INDIAN FOREIGN POLICY." S/ASIA ECO/UNDEV NAT/G POL/PAR CONSULT PLAN DIPLOM NEUTRAL COERCE ATTIT DRIVE PERSON MORAL ORD/FREE RESPECT...GEOG CONCPT TIME/SEQ TREND GEN/LAWS 20 NEHRU/J. PAGE 146 H2922
TOP/EX BIOG INDIA

C64
HARRIS M.,"THE NATURE OF CULTURAL THINGS." GP/REL DRIVE HABITAT PERSON ROLE...PHIL/SCI 20. PAGE 67 H1340
BIBLIOG CULTURE PSY SOC

B65
ACHTERBERG E.,BERLINER HOCHFINANZ - KAISER, FURSTEN, MILLIONARE UM 1900. GERMANY NAT/G EDU/PROP PERSON...MGT 19/20. PAGE 3 H0060
FINAN MUNIC BIOG ECO/TAC

B65
DOLCI D.,A NEW WORLD IN THE MAKING. GHANA SENEGAL USSR YUGOSLAVIA CULTURE INT/ORG PLAN EDU/PROP GP/REL PEACE MORAL...GEOG SOC 20 COLD/WAR. PAGE 42 H0834
SOCIETY ALL/VALS DRIVE PERSON

B65
EDINGER L.J.,KURT SCHUMACHER: A STUDY IN PERSONALITY AND POLITICAL BEHAVIOR. EUR+WWI GERMANY NAT/G DRIVE ROLE PWR SOCISM...BIBLIOG 20 SOC/DEMPAR SCHUMCHR/K. PAGE 44 H0889
TOP/EX LEAD PERSON BIOG

B65
GOETHE J.W.,GOETHE UBER DIE DEUTSCHEN. GERMANY CULTURE...NAT/COMP 18/19 GOETHE/J. PAGE 58 H1152
ATTIT PERSON SOCIETY

B65
GOLEMBIEWSKI R.T.,MEN, MANAGEMENT, AND MORALITY; TOWARD A NEW ORGANIZATIONAL ETHIC. CONSTN EX/STRUC CREATE ADMIN CONTROL INGP/REL PERSON SUPEGO MORAL PWR...GOV/COMP METH/COMP 20 BUREAUCRCY. PAGE 58 H1161
LG/CO MGT PROB/SOLV

B65
LAWRENCE P.,GODS, GHOSTS, AND MEN IN MELANESIA: SOME RELIGIONS OF AUSTRALIAN NEW GUINEA AND THE NEW HEBRIDES. SOCIETY ECO/UNDEV FAM GP/REL INGP/REL HABITAT PERSON...GEOG SOC ANTHOL BIBLIOG WORSHIP 20 NEW/GUINEA. PAGE 92 H1847
MYTH S/ASIA SECT CULTURE

B65
NAMIER L.B.,THE STRUCTURE OF POLITICS AT THE ACCESSION OF GEORGE III. UK LOC/G TOP/EX COLONIAL LEAD PARTIC REV CHOOSE REPRESENT GOV/REL PERSON SOVEREIGN...GOV/COMP 18 PARLIAMENT. PAGE 115 H2309
PARL/PROC LEGIS NAT/G POL/PAR

B65
ROSENBERG A.,DEMOCRACY AND SOCIALISM. COM EUR+WWI FRANCE MOD/EUR STRUCT INT/ORG NAT/G POL/PAR TOP/EX EDU/PROP COERCE PERSON PWR FASCISM MARXISM...CONCPT TIME/SEQ MARX/KARL 19/20. PAGE 134 H2677
ATTIT

B65
VON STACKELBERG K.,ALLE KRETER LUGEN VORURTEILE UBER MENSCHEN UND VOLKER. DIPLOM DOMIN RUMOR NAT/LISM PERSON KNOWL...SOC QU BIBLIOG 20. PAGE 164 H3277
NAT/COMP ATTIT EDU/PROP SAMP

B65
ZIOCK H.,SIND DIE DEUTSCHEN WIRKLICH SO? GERMANY SOCIETY...NAT/COMP ANTHOL 19/20. PAGE 173 H3460
PERSON ATTIT CULTURE STRUCT

S65
COOPER P.,"THE DEVELOPMENT OF THE CONCEPT OF WAR." UK COERCE ATTIT PERCEPT PERSON...STAT CHARTS CHINJAP. PAGE 33 H0660
CULTURE WAR SAMP STAND/INT

S65
WEDGE B.,"PSYCHOLOGICAL FACTORS IN SOVIET DISARMAMENT NEGOTIATION." USA+45 CONFER ATTIT PERCEPT PERSON...PSY NAT/COMP. PAGE 166 H3324
USSR DIPLOM ARMS/CONT

C65
COLEMAN J.S.,"EDUCATION AND POLITICAL DEVELOPMENT." COM CULTURE INTELL STRUCT SCHOOL PERSON SOVEREIGN ...POLICY ANTHOL BIBLIOG/A METH 20. PAGE 31 H0629
ECO/UNDEV NAT/LISM EDU/PROP TEC/DEV

B66
DARLING M.,APPRENTICE TO POWER INDIA 1904-1908. INDIA LEAD GP/REL PERSON...GEOG 20. PAGE 37 H0742
OBS SOCIETY ADMIN NAT/G

B66
DEUTSCHER I.,STALIN: A POLITICAL BIOGRAPHY. EUR+WWI USSR POL/PAR FORCES DIPLOM ADMIN LEAD REV WAR TOTALISM PERSON 20 STALIN/J ROOSEVLT/F LENIN/VI HITLER/A. PAGE 40 H0807
BIOG MARXISM TOP/EX PWR

B66
HERMANN F.G.,DER KAMPF GEGEN RELIGION UND KIRCHE IN DER SOWJETISCHEN BESATZUNGSZONE DEUTSCHLANDS. GERMANY/E EDU/PROP ATTIT PERSON MORAL MARXISM 20 LENIN/VI STALIN/J KHRUSH/N. PAGE 70 H1400
SECT ORD/FREE GP/REL NAT/G

B66
HOLDSWORTH W.S.,A HISTORY OF ENGLISH LAW; THE CENTURIES OF SETTLEMENT AND REFORM (VOL. XVI). UK LOC/G NAT/G EX/STRUC LEGIS CT/SYS LEAD ATTIT ...POLICY DECISION JURID IDEA/COMP 18 PARLIAMENT. PAGE 73 H1454
BIOG PERSON PROF/ORG LAW

B66
KEIL S.,SEXUALITAT - ERKENNTNISSE UND MASS-STABE. CULTURE DOMIN MARRIAGE AGE/Y AGE/A PERSON SUPEGO PLURISM 17/20. PAGE 84 H1681
SEX ATTIT STRUCT SOCIETY

B66
NOEL G.E.,THE NEW BRITAIN AND HAROLD WILSON: INTERIM REPORT, 1966 GENERAL ELECTION. UK POL/PAR CONSULT PROB/SOLV BUDGET DIPLOM ECO/TAC LEAD CHOOSE ATTIT 20 WILSON/H PARLIAMENT. PAGE 118 H2366
BIOG PERSON NAT/G CHIEF

B66
SPEARS E.L.,TWO MEN WHO SAVED FRANCE: PETAIN AND DE GAULLE. FRANCE CONSTN FORCES DIPLOM WAR PERSON 20 WWI PETAIN/HP DEGAULLE/C. PAGE 147 H2942
BIOG LEAD CHIEF NAT/G

B66
TSURUMI K.,ADULT SOCIALIZATION AND SOCIAL CHANGE: JAPAN BEFORE AND AFTER DEFEAT IN WORLD WAR II. FAM DEATH SUPEGO...PSY SOC 20 CHINJAP. PAGE 157 H3133
SOCIETY AGE/A WAR PERSON

B66
VON ARSENIEW W.,DIE GEISTIGEN SCHICKSALE DES RUSSISCHEN VOLKES. RUSSIA USSR SOCIETY STRUCT NAT/G SECT CHIEF REV 19/20. PAGE 163 H3262
ATTIT PERSON CULTURE DRIVE

S66
HAIGH G.,"FIELD TRAINING IN HUMAN RELATIONS FOR THE PEACE CORPS." CONSULT CREATE EDU/PROP ADMIN TASK GP/REL ATTIT PERSON...PSY OBS SOC/EXP PEACE/CORP. PAGE 64 H1276
CULTURE PERS/REL FOR/AID ADJUST

S66
SMITH D.D.,"MODAL ATTITUDE CLUSTERS* A SUPPLEMENT FOR THE STUDY OF NATIONAL CHARACTER." CULTURE NAT/G PERCEPT...SOC NEW/IDEA MODAL RECORD GEN/METH. PAGE 145 H2906
ATTIT PERSON PSY CONCPT

B67
DAVIDSON E.,THE TRIAL OF THE GERMANS* NUREMBERG* 1946-48. EUR+WWI GERMANY CULTURE NAT/G LEAD PERSON HEALTH...CRIMLGY PSY SOC BIOG JEWS. PAGE 37 H0745
FASCISM ADJUD TOTALISM WAR

B67
ODINGA O.,NOT YET UHURU. NAT/G POL/PAR PROB/SOLV COERCE REV WAR PERS/REL PERSON ORD/FREE...POLICY 20 ODINGA/O KENYATTA. PAGE 120 H2395
ATTIT BIOG LEAD AFR

B67
POMEROY W.J.,HALF A CENTURY OF SOCIALISM. USSR LAW AGRI INDUS NAT/G CREATE DIPLOM EDU/PROP PERSON ORD/FREE WEALTH...POLICY TREND 20. PAGE 127 H2541
SOCISM MARXISM COM SOCIETY

B67
WARD L.,LESTER WARD AND THE WELFARE STATE. SOCIETY NAT/G CREATE RECEIVE EQUILIB UTOPIA HABITAT HEREDITY PERSON...POLICY SOC BIOG 19/20 WARD/LEST. PAGE 165 H3303
ALL/VALS NEW/IDEA WELF/ST CONCPT

L67
GRAUBARD S.R.,"TOWARD THE YEAR 2000: WORK IN PROGRESS." FUT ACADEM SECT DELIB/GP DIPLOM EDU/PROP AGE/Y PERSON ROLE...PSY ANTHOL. PAGE 60 H1199
PREDICT PROB/SOLV SOCIETY CULTURE

S67
BELGION M.,"THE CASE FOR REHABILITATING MARSHAL PETAIN." EUR+WWI FRANCE NAT/G DIPLOM ATTIT PERSON MORAL PETAIN/HP. PAGE 13 H0262
WAR FORCES LEAD

S67
BERLINER J.S.,"RUSSIA'S BUREAUCRATS - WHY THEY'RE REACTIONARY." USSR NAT/G OP/RES PROB/SOLV TEC/DEV CONTROL SANCTION EFFICIENCY DRIVE PERSON...TECHNIC SOC 20. PAGE 15 H0308
CREATE ADMIN INDUS PRODUC

S67
MCCLEERY W.,"AN INTERVIEW WITH J. DOUGLAS BROWN ON THE 'WAY' OF VIETNAM" COM VIETNAM INTELL ECO/DEV ACADEM NAT/G COERCE PERSON SUPEGO ORD/FREE 20.
ATTIT WAR COLONIAL

PAGE 106 H2125 MARXISM

S67
RAUM O.,"THE MODERN LEADERSHIP GROUP AMONG THE SOUTH AFRICAN XHOSA." SOUTH/AFR SOCIETY SECT EX/STRUC REPRESENT GP/REL INGP/REL PERSON ...METH/COMP 17/20 XHOSA NEGRO. PAGE 130 H2596 RACE/REL KIN LEAD CULTURE

S67
RIESMAN D.,"SOME QUESTIONS ABOUT THE STUDY OF AMERICAN CHARACTER IN THE TWENTIETH CENTURY." STRATA PRESS PERSON RIGID/FLEX SOC. PAGE 131 H2628 CULTURE ATTIT DRIVE GEN/LAWS

S67
SZALAY L.B.,"SOVIET DOMESTIC PROPAGANDA AND LIBERALIZATION." COM USSR SOCIETY COM/IND NAT/G POL/PAR EX/STRUC TEC/DEV LEAD ATTIT ROLE MARXISM ...METH/COMP 20. PAGE 151 H3026 EDU/PROP TOTALISM PERSON PERCEPT

S67
WILSON J.Q.,"A GUIDE TO REAGAN COUNTRY* THE POLITICAL CULTURE OF SOUTHERN CALIFORNIA." NEIGH PROVS PARTIC CHOOSE ADJUST CONSEN PERSON CONSERVE CALIFORNIA REAGAN/RON. PAGE 169 H3379 CULTURE ATTIT MORAL

S67
YEFROMEV A.,"THE TRUE FACE OF THE WEST GERMAN NATIONAL-DEMOCRATS." GERMANY/W NAT/G DOMIN LEAD SANCTION WAR ATTIT PERSON...MARXIST 20. PAGE 172 H3436 POL/PAR TOTALISM PARL/PROC DIPLOM

L68
CURRENT HISTORY,"DE GAULLE'S FRANCE." FRANCE MOD/EUR WOR+45 INDUS MARKET INT/ORG BUDGET DIPLOM AUTHORIT DRIVE...GOV/COMP IDEA/COMP 20 DEGAULLE/C EEC. PAGE 36 H0723 INT/TRADE PERSON LEAD NAT/LISM

S68
LAVRIN J.,"THE TWO WORLDS." RUSSIA USSR SOCIETY STRUCT NAT/G DIPLOM ATTIT PERSON MARXISM...GEOG SOC IDEA/COMP PERS/COMP 18/20. PAGE 92 H1842 NAT/COMP NAT/LISM CULTURE

B70
BOSSUET J.B.,"POLITIQUE TIREE DE L'ECRITURE SAINTE" (1679-1709) IN J.B. BOSSUET, OEVRES DE BOSSUET. NAT/G GP/REL AUTHORIT HEREDITY PERSON ALL/VALS SOVEREIGN 18 BIBLE DEITY CHRISTIAN. PAGE 19 H0383 TRADIT CHIEF SECT CONCPT

B76
SMITH A.,THE WEALTH OF NATIONS. UK STRUCT WORKER DIPLOM ECO/TAC OPTIMAL DRIVE PERSON ORD/FREE ...OLD/LIB GEN/LAWS 17/18. PAGE 145 H2905 WEALTH PRODUC INDUS LAISSEZ

B85
BLUNTSCHLI J.K.,THE THEORY OF THE STATE. GERMANY CONSTN INGP/REL NAT/LISM PERSON SOVEREIGN CONSERVE ...SOC. PAGE 18 H0362 CONCPT LEGIS NAT/G

B96
KROPOTKIN P.,L'ANARCHIE. NAT/G VOL/ASSN REV MORAL WEALTH...POLICY 19. PAGE 89 H1776 SOCIETY ANARCH PERSON CONCPT

PERSONAL RELATIONS....SEE PERS/REL

PERSONALITY....SEE PERSON, ALSO PERSONALITY INDEX, P. XIII

PERSONALITY TESTS....SEE PERS/TEST

PERSUASION....SEE LOBBY, EDU/PROP

PERU....SEE ALSO L/A+17C

N19
OPERATIONS AND POLICY RESEARCH,PERU ELECTION MEMORANDA (PAMPHLET). L/A+17C PERU POL/PAR LEGIS EXEC APPORT REPRESENT 20. PAGE 121 H2421 CHOOSE CONSTN SUFF NAT/G

B48
DE NOIA J.,GUIDE TO OFFICIAL PUBLICATIONS OF OTHER AMERICAN REPUBLICS: PERU (VOL. XVII). PERU LAW LEGIS ADMIN CT/SYS...JURID 19/20. PAGE 38 H0767 BIBLIOG/A CONSTN NAT/G EDU/PROP

B56
HERNANDEZ URBINA A.,LOS PARTIDOS Y LA CRISIS DEL APRA. PERU NAT/G LEAD LOBBY CHOOSE SOCISM...POLICY DECISION 20 COM/PARTY APRA CONGRESS. PAGE 70 H1402 POL/PAR PARTIC PARL/PROC GP/REL

B58
MATOS J.,LAS ACTUALES COMMUNIDADES DE INDIGENAS: HUAROCHIRI EN 1955. PERU FAM NAT/G SECT EDU/PROP ADJUD GP/REL INGP/REL 20 INDIAN/AM. PAGE 105 H2091 STRUCT NEIGH KIN ECO/UNDEV

B59
SZLUC T.,TWILIGHT OF THE TYRANTS. BRAZIL L/A+17C PERU VENEZUELA NAT/G FORCES CONTROL PERSON MORAL ORD/FREE PWR...CONCPT 20 ARGEN COLOMB. PAGE 151 H3028 TOTALISM CHIEF REV FASCISM

S61
RANDALL F.B.,"COMMUNISM IN THE HIGH ANDES." L/A+17C PERU USSR SOCIETY PLAN EDU/PROP TOTALISM ATTIT RIGID/FLEX PWR WEALTH...HUM CONCPT GEN/LAWS 20 BOLIV EQUADOR. PAGE 129 H2589 CULTURE DRIVE

B66
MAC DONALD H.M.,THE INTELLECTUAL IN POLITICS. GERMANY PERU SWEDEN UK USSR NAT/G CONSULT PLAN EDU/PROP TASK INGP/REL EFFICIENCY RATIONAL ALL/VALS 20. PAGE 99 H1987 ALL/IDEOS INTELL POL/PAR PARTIC

S67
PETRAS J.,"GUERRILLA MOVEMENTS IN LATIN AMERICA - I." GUATEMALA PERU VENEZUELA NAT/G COLONIAL LEAD ATTIT PWR...TIME/SEQ METH/COMP 20 COLOMB. PAGE 125 H2497 GUERRILLA REV L/A+17C MARXISM

PETAIN/HP....H.P. PETAIN

B66
SPEARS E.L.,TWO MEN WHO SAVED FRANCE: PETAIN AND DE GAULLE. FRANCE CONSTN FORCES DIPLOM WAR PERSON 20 WWI PETAIN/HP DEGAULLE/C. PAGE 147 H2942 BIOG LEAD CHIEF NAT/G

S67
BELGION M.,"THE CASE FOR REHABILITATING MARSHAL PETAIN." EUR+WWI FRANCE NAT/G DIPLOM ATTIT PERSON MORAL PETAIN/HP. PAGE 13 H0262 WAR FORCES LEAD

PETERS....PETERS V. NEW YORK

PETERSON W.C. H2496

PETRAS J. H2497

PETTIT L.K. H0094

PHADINIS U. H2498

PHELPS E.S. H2499

PHIL/SCI....SCIENTIFIC METHOD AND PHILOSOPHY OF SCIENCE

B
DEUTSCHE BIBLIOTH FRANKF A M,DEUTSCHE BIBLIOGRAPHIE. EUR+WWI GERMANY ECO/DEV FORCES DIPLOM LEAD...POLICY PHIL/SCI SOC 20. PAGE 40 H0802 BIBLIOG LAW ADMIN NAT/G

N
AMERICAN POLITICAL SCIENCE REVIEW. USA+45 USA-45 WOR+45 WOR-45 INT/ORG ADMIN...INT/LAW PHIL/SCI CONCPT METH 20 UN. PAGE 1 H0001 BIBLIOG/A DIPLOM NAT/G GOV/COMP

N
INTERNATIONAL BIBLIOGRAPHIE DER DEUTSCHEN ZEITSCHRIFTENLITERATUR. EUR+WWI GERMANY MOD/EUR ECO/DEV POL/PAR LEAD WAR NAT/LISM ATTIT...EPIST PHIL/SCI 19/20. PAGE 1 H0004 BIBLIOG/A NAT/G PERSON CULTURE

N
JOURNAL OF ASIAN STUDIES. CULTURE ECO/DEV SECT DIPLOM EDU/PROP WAR NAT/LISM...PHIL/SCI SOC 20. PAGE 1 H0005 BIBLIOG ASIA S/ASIA NAT/G

N
MIDDLE EAST JOURNAL. CULTURE SECT DIPLOM LEAD GOV/REL ATTIT...POLICY PHIL/SCI SOC LING BIOG 20. PAGE 1 H0007 BIBLIOG ISLAM NAT/G ECO/UNDEV

N
NEUE POLITISCHE LITERATUR. AFR ASIA EUR+WWI GERMANY RUSSIA SOCIETY ECO/DEV ECO/UNDEV PLAN PROB/SOLV LEAD MARXISM...PHIL/SCI CONCPT 20. PAGE 1 H0008 BIBLIOG DIPLOM COM NAT/G

N
BIBLIOGRAPHIE DE LA PHILOSOPHIE. LAW CULTURE SECT EDU/PROP MORAL...HUM METH/CNCPT 20. PAGE 1 H0012 BIBLIOG/A PHIL/SCI CONCPT LOG

N
DEUTSCHE BUCHEREI,DEUTSCHE NATIONALBIBLIOGRAPHIE. GERMANY ECO/DEV DIPLOM AGE/Y ATTIT...PHIL/SCI SOC 20. PAGE 40 H0803 BIBLIOG NAT/G LEAD POLICY

N
MIDDLE EAST INSTITUTE,CURRENT RESEARCH ON THE MIDDLE EAST....PHIL/SCI PSY SOC LING 20. PAGE 110 H2201 BIBLIOG R+D ISLAM NAT/G

N
US LIBRARY OF CONGRESS,SOUTHERN ASIA ACCESSIONS LIST. BURMA CEYLON INDIA NEPAL PAKISTAN S/ASIA THAILAND AGRI INDUS SCHOOL WORKER...ART/METH GEOG HEAL PHIL/SCI LING 20. PAGE 160 H3201 BIBLIOG/A SOCIETY CULTURE ECO/UNDEV

B01
BRYCE J.,STUDIES IN HISTORY AND JURISPRUDENCE (2 VOLS.). ICELAND SOUTH/AFR UK LAW PROB/SOLV SOVEREIGN...PHIL/SCI NAT/COMP ROME/ANC ROMAN/LAW. PAGE 23 H0455 IDEA/COMP CONSTN JURID

C05
DUNNING W.A.,"HISTORY OF POLITICAL THEORIES FROM LUTHER TO MONTESQUIEU." LAW NAT/G SECT DIPLOM REV WAR ORD/FREE SOVEREIGN CONSERVE...TRADIT BIBLIOG PHIL/SCI CONCPT GEN/LAWS

16/18. PAGE 43 H0867

B14
CRAIG J.,ELEMENTS OF POLITICAL SCIENCE (3 VOLS.). CONSTN AGRI INDUS SCHOOL FORCES TAX CT/SYS SUFF MORAL WEALTH...CONCPT 19 CIVIL/LIB. PAGE 35 H0696 PHIL/SCI NAT/G ORD/FREE

N19
HARTUNG F.,ENLIGHTENED DESPOTISM (PAMPHLET). ORD/FREE SOVEREIGN CONSERVE...PHIL/SCI FREDERICK ENLIGHTNMT. PAGE 67 H1350 NAT/G CHIEF CONCPT PWR

B20
COLE G.D.H.,SOCIAL THEORY. CULTURE LOC/G SECT REGION REPRESENT ATTIT DRIVE...PSY SOC BIBLIOG. PAGE 31 H0621 CONCPT NAT/G PHIL/SCI

C20
BLACHLY F.F.,"THE GOVERNMENT AND ADMINISTRATION OF GERMANY." GERMANY CONSTN LOC/G PROVS DELIB/GP EX/STRUC FORCES LEGIS TOP/EX CT/SYS...BIBLIOG/A 19/20. PAGE 17 H0348 NAT/G GOV/REL ADMIN PHIL/SCI

C20
DUNNING W.A.,"A HISTORY OF POLITICAL THINKERS FROM ROUSSEAU TO SPENCER." NAT/G REV NAT/LISM UTIL CONSERVE MARXISM POPULISM...JURID BIBLIOG 18/19. PAGE 43 H0868 IDEA/COMP PHIL/SCI CONCPT GEN/LAWS

B21
BALFOUR A.J.,ESSAYS SPECULATIVE AND POLITICAL. SEA CULTURE CREATE WAR NAT/LISM PEACE LOVE...ART/METH INT/LAW CONCPT ANTHOL 20 JEWS. PAGE 10 H0204 PHIL/SCI SOCIETY DIPLOM

B22
KRABBE H.,THE MODERN IDEA OF THE STATE. LAW CHIEF DIPLOM DOMIN ADMIN REPRESENT CENTRAL ORD/FREE ...NEW/IDEA GOV/COMP IDEA/COMP. PAGE 88 H1761 SOVEREIGN CONSTN PHIL/SCI

B23
POUND R.,INTERPRETATIONS OF LEGAL HISTORY. CULTURE ...PHIL/SCI NEW/IDEA CLASSIF SIMUL GEN/LAWS 19/20. PAGE 127 H2547 LAW IDEA/COMP JURID

B24
SHIROKOGOROFF S.M.,ETHNICAL UNIT AND MILIEU. GP/REL ...PHIL/SCI SOC MATH METH. PAGE 143 H2865 IDEA/COMP HABITAT CULTURE SOCIETY

B26
HOCKING W.E.,PRESENT STATUS OF THE PHILOSOPHY OF LAW AND OF RIGHTS. UNIV CULTURE INTELL SOCIETY NAT/G CREATE LEGIT SANCTION ALL/VALS SOC/INTEG 18/20. PAGE 72 H1442 JURID PHIL/SCI ORD/FREE

B28
BARKER E.,POLITICAL THOUGHT IN ENGLAND: FROM HERBERT SPENCER TO THE PRESENT DAY. UK ALL/IDEOS ...PHIL/SCI 19/20 SPENCER/H GREEN/TH BENTHAM/J MAITLAND/F. PAGE 11 H0217 INTELL GEN/LAWS IDEA/COMP

B36
BATTAGLIA F.,LINEAMENTI DI STORIA DELLE DOCTRINE POLITICHE CON APPENDICI BIBLIOGRAFICHE. ITALY PROB/SOLV LEAD 20. PAGE 12 H0237 BIBLIOG PHIL/SCI CONCPT NAT/G

S38
LUNDBERG G.A.,"THE CONCEPT OF LAW IN THE SOCIAL SCIENCES"(BMR)" CULTURE INTELL SOCIETY STRUCT CREATE...NEW/IDEA 20. PAGE 99 H1978 EPIST GEN/LAWS CONCPT PHIL/SCI

B40
THE GUIDE TO CATHOLIC LITERATURE, 1888-1940. ALL/VALS...POLICY MYSTIC HUM PHIL/SCI 19/20. PAGE 2 H0032 BIBLIOG/A CATHISM DIPLOM CULTURE

S40
GURVITCH G.,"MAJOR PROBLEMS OF THE SOCIOLOGY OF LAW." CULTURE SANCTION KNOWL MORAL...POLICY EPIST JURID WORSHIP. PAGE 63 H1255 SOC LAW PHIL/SCI

B41
GRISMER R.,A NEW BIBLIOGRAPHY OF THE LITERATURES OF SPAIN AND SPANISH AMERICA. CHRIST-17C MOD/EUR PRE/AMER SPAIN CULTURE DIPLOM EDU/PROP...ART/METH GEOG HUM PHIL/SCI 20. PAGE 61 H1229 BIBLIOG LAW NAT/G ECO/UNDEV

C41
WASSERMAN L.,"HANDBOOK OF POLITICAL "ISMS" CAP/ISM REPRESENT TOTALISM MARXISM NEW/LIB SOCISM...MAJORIT BIBLIOG 20. PAGE 166 H3313 IDEA/COMP PHIL/SCI OWN NAT/G

B43
LENIN V.I.,STATE AND REVOLUTION. USSR CAP/ISM ...ANARCH MARXIST PHIL/SCI IDEA/COMP 20. PAGE 94 H1878 SOCIETY NAT/G REV MARXISM

B44
BERDYAEV N.,SLAVERY AND FREEDOM. NAT/G REV WAR NAT/LISM OWN AUTHORIT SEX CONSERVE SOCISM...TRADIT PHIL/SCI CIVIL/LIB. PAGE 15 H0295 ORD/FREE PERSON ELITES SOCIETY

B45
MERRIAM C.E.,SYSTEMATIC POLITICS. FUT POL/PAR DELIB/GP DIPLOM ADJUD ADMIN LEAD CHOOSE ATTIT...MGT PHIL/SCI TREND. PAGE 109 H2183 NAT/G METH/CNCPT CREATE

B45
PERAZA SARAUSA F.,BIBLIOGRAFIAS CUBANAS. CUBA CULTURE ECO/UNDEV AGRI EDU/PROP PRESS CIVMIL/REL ...POLICY GEOG PHIL/SCI BIOG 19/20. PAGE 125 H2489 BIBLIOG/A L/A+17C NAT/G DIPLOM

B45
VENABLE V.,HUMAN NATURE: THE MARXIAN VIEW. UNIV STRATA CAP/ISM REV GP/REL PERS/REL PRODUC KNOWL ...PHIL/SCI CONCPT IDEA/COMP 19 MARX/KARL ENGELS/F. PAGE 162 H3240 PERSON MARXISM WORKER UTOPIA

C45
PAINE T.,"THE AGE OF REASON IN T. PAINE, THE COMPLETE WRITINGS OF THOMAS PAINE (VOL. 1) (1794-95)" CULTURE ACT/RES DOMIN UTOPIA ATTIT PERCEPT WORSHIP. PAGE 122 H2445 SECT KNOWL PHIL/SCI ORD/FREE

B46
CASSIRER E.,THE MYTH OF THE STATE. WOR-45 SOCIETY RACE/REL RATIONAL PWR FASCISM...PHIL/SCI PSY LING TREND HEGEL/GWF MACHIAVELL. PAGE 28 H0557 MYTH CONCPT NAT/G IDEA/COMP

B46
FEIBLEMAN J.,THE THEORY OF HUMAN CULTURE. UNIV CONSTN SOCIETY...CONCPT CLASSIF TIME/SEQ. PAGE 49 H0981 GEN/LAWS CULTURE SOC PHIL/SCI

B47
BEHAR D.,BIBLIOGRAFIA HISPANOAMERICANA. LIBROS ANTIGUOS Y MODERNOS REFERENTES A AMERICA Y ESPANA. PORTUGAL SPAIN CONSTN NAT/G SECT CREATE REV WAR GOV/REL...ART/METH GEOG PHIL/SCI LING 20 ARGEN. PAGE 13 H0260 BIBLIOG L/A+17C CULTURE

B47
BOWLE J.,WESTERN POLITICAL THOUGHT: AN HISTORICAL INTRODUCTION FROM THE ORIGINS TO ROUSSEAU. CONSTN NAT/G SECT CREATE RATIONAL ORD/FREE...SOC BIBLIOG/A. PAGE 19 H0391 ATTIT IDEA/COMP PHIL/SCI

B47
HERSKOVITS M.U.,MAN AND HIS WORK. UNIV SECT TEC/DEV PARTIC...PHIL/SCI LING AUD/VIS BIBLIOG. PAGE 70 H1409 SOC CULTURE INGP/REL HABITAT

B48
FLOREN LOZANO L.,BIBLIOGRAFIA DE LA BIBLIOGRAFIA DOMINICANA. DOMIN/REP NAT/G DIPLOM EDU/PROP CIVMIL/REL...POLICY ART/METH GEOG PHIL/SCI HIST/WRIT 20. PAGE 51 H1027 BIBLIOG/A BIOG L/A+17C CULTURE

B48
GRIFFITH E.S.,RESEARCH IN POLITICAL SCIENCE: THE WORK OF PANELS OF RESEARCH COMMITTEE, APSA. WOR+45 WOR-45 COM/IND R+D FORCES ACT/RES WAR...GOV/COMP ANTHOL 20. PAGE 61 H1220 BIBLIOG PHIL/SCI DIPLOM JURID

B49
HEADLAM-MORLEY,BIBLIOGRAPHY IN POLITICS FOR THE HONOUR SCHOOL OF PHILOSOPHY, POLITICS AND ECONOMICS (PAMPHLET). UK CONSTN LABOR MUNIC DIPLOM ADMIN 19/20. PAGE 69 H1375 BIBLIOG NAT/G PHIL/SCI GOV/REL

B50
CANTRIL H.,TENSIONS THAT CAUSE WAR. UNIV CULTURE R+D CREATE EDU/PROP DRIVE PERSON KNOWL ORD/FREE ...HUM PSY SOC OBS CENSUS TREND CON/ANAL SOC/EXP SIMUL GEN/METH ANTHOL COLD/WAR TOT/POP. PAGE 26 H0523 SOCIETY PHIL/SCI PEACE

B50
CARR E.H.,STUDIES IN REVOLUTION. CREATE WAR PERSON ALL/IDEOS MARXISM SOCISM...PHIL/SCI METH/COMP ANTHOL 18/20 SAINTSIMON MARX/KARL PROUDHON/P LASSALLE/F PLEKHNV/GV. PAGE 27 H0537 REV IDEA/COMP COERCE BIOG

B50
COUNCIL BRITISH NATIONAL BIB,BRITISH NATIONAL BIBLIOGRAPHY. UK AGRI CONSTRUC PERF/ART POL/PAR SECT CREATE INT/TRADE LEAD...HUM JURID PHIL/SCI 20. PAGE 34 H0677 BIBLIOG/A NAT/G TEC/DEV DIPLOM

B50
GOFF F.R.,FIFTEENTH CENTURY BOOKS IN THE LIBRARY OF CONGRESS. CHRIST-17C GERMANY ITALY CULTURE INTELL SECT CREATE...PHIL/SCI CONCPT CLASSIF BIOG TIME/SEQ 15. PAGE 58 H1153 BIBLIOG KNOWL HUM

B50
HOBBES T.,LEVIATHAN. UNIV CONSTN SOCIETY LOC/G NAT/G CONSULT TOP/EX DOMIN DRIVE PERSON PWR ...PHIL/SCI CONCPT SELF/OBS GEN/LAWS TOT/POP. PAGE 72 H1434 LAW ORD/FREE

B50
WILBUR C.M.,CHINESE SOURCES ON THE HISTORY OF THE CHINESE COMMUNIST MOVEMENT (PAMPHLET). CHINA/COM ECO/UNDEV PROVS FORCES WAR...PHIL/SCI 20. PAGE 168 H3360 BIBLIOG/A MARXISM REV NAT/G

B51
HUXLEY J.,FREEDOM AND CULTURE. UNIV LAW SOCIETY R+D ACADEM SCHOOL CREATE SANCTION ATTIT KNOWL...HUM ANTHOL 20. PAGE 76 H1512 CULTURE ORD/FREE PHIL/SCI IDEA/COMP

B51
PARSONS T.,TOWARD A GENERAL THEORY OF ACTION. CULTURE PERSON...PSY SIMUL ANTHOL SOC/INTEG 20. PAGE 124 H2472 SOC PHIL/SCI DRIVE ACT/RES

S51
MACRAE D.G.,"THE BOLSHEVIK IDEOLOGY; THE INTELLECTUAL AND EMOTIONAL FACTORS IN COMMUNIST AFFILIATION" (BMR)" COM LEAD REV ATTIT ORD/FREE ...SOC CON/ANAL 20 BOLSHEVISM. PAGE 100 H2008
MARXISM INTELL PHIL/SCI SECT

B52
APPADORAI A.,THE SUBSTANCE OF POLITICS (6TH ED.). EX/STRUC LEGIS DIPLOM CT/SYS CHOOSE FASCISM MARXISM SOCISM...BIBLIOG T. PAGE 7 H0145
PHIL/SCI NAT/G

B52
CALLOT E.,LA SOCIETE ET SON ENVIRONNEMENT: ESSAI SUR LES PRINCIPES DES SCIENCES SOCIALES. GP/REL ADJUST CONSEN ISOLAT HABITAT PERCEPT PERSON ...BIBLIOG SOC/INTEG 20. PAGE 25 H0507
SOCIETY PHIL/SCI CULTURE

B52
TAX S.,HERITAGE OF CONQUEST. L/A+17C ECO/UNDEV LOC/G WEALTH...POLICY ANTHOL WORSHIP 20 MEXIC/AMER CENTRAL/AM. PAGE 153 H3052
PHIL/SCI CULTURE SOCIETY

S52
KECSKEMETI P.,"THE 'POLICY SCIENCES': ASPIRATION AND OUTLOOK." UNIV CULTURE INTELL SOCIETY STRUCT EDU/PROP ATTIT PERCEPT RIGID/FLEX KNOWL...PHIL/SCI METH/CNCPT OBS 20. PAGE 84 H1674
CREATE NEW/IDEA

S52
SABINE G.H.,"THE TWO DEMOCRATIC TRADITIONS" (BMR)" FRANCE UK USA-45 NAT/G CONTROL CHOOSE ALL/IDEOS ...PHIL/SCI CONCPT IDEA/COMP 20. PAGE 136 H2727
ORD/FREE POPULISM INGP/REL NAT/COMP

C52
EBENSTEIN W.,"INTRODUCTION TO POLITICAL PHILOSOPHY." COM CONSTN INTELL CONTROL PERSON NEW/LIB SOCISM...PSY GEN/LAWS BIBLIOG/A. PAGE 44 H0883
ALL/IDEOS PHIL/SCI IDEA/COMP NAT/G

B53
BIDNEY D.,THEORETICAL ANTHROPOLOGY. DRIVE ROLE ORD/FREE...CONCPT METH/CNCPT MYTH CLASSIF OBS IDEA/COMP METH/COMP BIBLIOG METH 20. PAGE 17 H0331
CULTURE SOC PSY PHIL/SCI

B53
KANTOR H.,A BIBLIOGRAPHY OF UNPUBLISHED DOCTORAL DISSERTATIONS AND MASTERS' THESES DEALING WITH GOVTS, POL, INT REL OF LAT AM. L/A+17C INT/ORG POL/PAR ACT/RES OP/RES CONFER ATTIT...INT/LAW PHIL/SCI 20. PAGE 83 H1656
BIBLIOG ACADEM DIPLOM NAT/G

B53
MAXIMOFF G.P.,THE POLITICAL PHILOSOPHY OF BAKUNIN: SCIENTIFIC ANARCHISM. STRUCT INGP/REL FEDERAL MARXISM...ANARCH BIOG 19 BAKUNIN. PAGE 105 H2104
SOCIETY PHIL/SCI NAT/G IDEA/COMP

B53
ROSCIO J.G.,OBRAS. L/A+17C SPAIN DIPLOM REV WAR NAT/LISM TOTALISM PWR SOVEREIGN 19. PAGE 134 H2671
ORD/FREE COLONIAL NAT/G PHIL/SCI

B54
GIRALSO JARAMLLO G.,BIBLIOGRAFIA DE BIBLIOGRAFIAS COLOMBIANAS. L/A+17C ACADEM SECT CREATE EDU/PROP ...ART/METH GEOG LING TREND 20 COLOMB. PAGE 57 H1135
BIBLIOG/A CULTURE PHIL/SCI ECO/UNDEV

B54
LENIN V.I.,SELECTED WORKS (12 VOLS.). USSR INTELL SOCIETY STRATA STRUCT NAT/G POL/PAR WORKER CAP/ISM REV WAR...MARXIST PHIL/SCI 20 MARX/KARL LENIN/VI. PAGE 94 H1880
COM MARXISM

B54
SPROTT W.J.H.,SCIENCE AND SOCIAL ACTION. STRUCT ACT/RES CRIME GP/REL INGP/REL ANOMIE...PSY SOC/INTEG 19/20. PAGE 148 H2956
SOC CULTURE PHIL/SCI

B55
MAYO H.B.,DEMOCRACY AND MARXISM. COM USSR STRATA NAT/G WORKER ECO/TAC REV MORAL...PHIL/SCI HIST/WRIT IDEA/COMP WORSHIP 20 MARX/KARL LENIN/VI STALIN/J TROTSKY/L. PAGE 105 H2108
MARXISM CAP/ISM

B55
MOHL R.V.,DIE GESCHICHTE UND LITERATUR DER STAATSWISSENSCHAFTEN (3 VOLS.). LAW NAT/G...JURID METH/COMP METH. PAGE 112 H2236
PHIL/SCI MOD/EUR

B55
VIGON J.,TEORIA DEL MILITARISMO. NAT/G DIPLOM COLONIAL COERCE GUERRILLA CIVMIL/REL NAT/LISM MORAL ALL/IDEOS PACIFISM 18/20. PAGE 163 H3253
FORCES PHIL/SCI WAR POLICY

S55
GLADSTONE A.E.,"THE POSSIBILITY OF PREDICTING REACTIONS TO INTERNATIONAL EVENTS." UNIV SOCIETY NAT/G FORCES CREATE EDU/PROP COERCE WAR ATTIT PERSON KNOWL PWR SKILL...METH/CNCPT NEW/IDEA ORG/CHARTS. PAGE 57 H1139
PHIL/SCI CONCPT

B56
CEPEDA U.A.,EN TORNO AL CONCEPTO DEL ESTADO EN LOS REYES CATHOLICOS. SPAIN SOCIETY STRUCT SECT LEGIT WAR ATTIT WORSHIP 15/17. PAGE 28 H0569
NAT/G PHIL/SCI CHIEF PWR

B56
DRIVER H.E.,AN INTEGRATION OF FUNCTIONAL, EVOLUTIONARY AND HISTORICAL THEORY BY MEANS OF CORRELATIONS. INGP/REL BIO/SOC HABITAT...PHIL/SCI GEN/LAWS. PAGE 42 H0847
CULTURE METH SOC CORREL

B56
EVANS-PRITCHARD E.E.,THE INSTITUTIONS OF PRIMITIVE SOCIETY. LAW SOCIETY KIN ACT/RES CREATE ALL/VALS ...ART/METH SOC METH/CNCPT WORSHIP 20. PAGE 48 H0953
STRUCT PHIL/SCI CULTURE CONCPT

B56
READ M.,EDUCATION AND SOCIAL CHANGE IN TROPICAL AREAS. AFR L/A+17C SOCIETY LITERACY PERCEPT PERSON WEALTH...HEAL PHIL/SCI SOC 20. PAGE 130 H2603
EDU/PROP HABITAT DRIVE CULTURE

B56
VUCINICH A.,THE SOVIET ACADEMY OF SCIENCES. USSR STRUCT ACADEM NAT/G EDU/PROP ADMIN LEAD ROLE ...BIBLIOG 20 ACADEM/SCI. PAGE 164 H3280
PHIL/SCI CREATE INTELL PROF/ORG

S56
ALMOND G.A.,"COMPARATIVE POLITICAL SYSTEMS" (BMR)" WOR+45 WOR-45 PROB/SOLV DIPLOM EFFICIENCY ...PHIL/SCI SOC METH 17/20. PAGE 5 H0111
GOV/COMP CONCPT ALL/IDEOS NAT/COMP

B57
LOUCKS W.N.,COMPARATIVE ECONOMIC SYSTEMS (5TH ED.). COM UK USSR INDUS POL/PAR PLAN CAP/ISM TOTALISM MARXISM...PHIL/SCI BIBLIOG 19/20. PAGE 99 H1969
NAT/COMP IDEA/COMP SOCISM

B57
MEINECKE F.,MACHIAVELLISM. CHRIST-17C FRANCE GERMANY ITALY MOD/EUR BAL/PWR PARL/PROC TOTALISM ...PHIL/SCI 15/20 MACHIAVELL. PAGE 108 H2166
NAT/LISM NAT/G PWR

B57
ROSS R.,THE FABRIC OF SOCIETY. STRATA GP/REL PERSON ...CONCPT METH T 20. PAGE 134 H2687
SOC PHIL/SCI CULTURE STRUCT

S57
NEUMANN S.,"COMPARATIVE POLITICS: A HALF CENTURY APPRAISAL" USA+45 USA-45...SOC TIME/SEQ TREND NAT/COMP METH 20. PAGE 117 H2339
PHIL/SCI GOV/COMP GEN/METH

B58
BAGBY P.,CULTURE AND HISTORY....PHIL/SCI CONCPT LING LOG IDEA/COMP GEN/LAWS BIBLIOG 20. PAGE 10 H0196
HIST/WRIT CULTURE GP/COMP NAT/COMP

B58
LEPOINTE G.,ELEMENTS DE BIBLIOGRAPHIE SUR L'HISTOIRE DES INSTITUTIONS ET DES FAITS SOCIAUX, 987-1875. FRANCE SOCIETY NAT/G PROVS SECT ...PHIL/SCI 19/20. PAGE 94 H1887
BIBLIOG LAW

B58
MECRENSKY E.,SCIENTIFIC MANPOWER IN EUROPE. WOR+45 EDU/PROP GOV/REL SKILL...TECHNIC PHIL/SCI INT CHARTS BIBLIOG 20. PAGE 108 H2157
ECO/TAC TEC/DEV METH/COMP NAT/COMP

B58
ORTEGA Y GASSET J.,MAN AND CRISIS. SECT CREATE PERSON CONSERVE...GEN/LAWS RENAISSAN. PAGE 122 H2430
PHIL/SCI CULTURE CONCPT

B59
GOLDSCHMIDT W.,UNDERSTANDING HUMAN SOCIETY. SOCIETY CREATE ATTIT...GEOG PHIL/SCI CONCPT GP/COMP. PAGE 58 H1159
CULTURE STRUCT TEC/DEV PERSON

B59
SANCHEZ A.L.,EL CONCEPTO DEL ESTADO EN EL PENSAMIENTO ESPANOL DEL SIGLO XVI. SPAIN LEGIS JUDGE BAL/PWR LEGIT EXEC WAR PWR...MAJORIT 16. PAGE 137 H2747
NAT/G PHIL/SCI LAW SOVEREIGN

B60
BREDVOLD L.I.,THE PHILOSOPHY OF EDMUND BURKE. POL/PAR PARL/PROC REPRESENT CONSERVE...JURID 18 BURKE/EDM. PAGE 20 H0410
PHIL/SCI NAT/G CONCPT

B60
FRANCIS R.G.,THE PREDICTIVE PROCESS. PLAN MARXISM ...DECISION SOC CONCPT NAT/COMP 19/20. PAGE 52 H1047
PREDICT PHIL/SCI TREND

B60
GRAMPP W.D.,THE MANCHESTER SCHOOL OF ECONOMICS. UK LAW ECO/DEV COERCE ATTIT ORD/FREE LAISSEZ ...PHIL/SCI IDEA/COMP 19/20 MANCHESTER CORN/LAWS. PAGE 60 H1194
ECO/TAC VOL/ASSN LOBBY NAT/G

B60
KOHN H.,PAN-SLAVISM: ITS HISTORY AND IDEOLOGY. COM CZECHOSLVK EUR+WWI MOD/EUR USSR YUGOSLAVIA CULTURE ELITES INTELL KIN NAT/G EDU/PROP DRIVE SOVEREIGN ...HUM PHIL/SCI MYTH HIST/WRIT 19/20. PAGE 87 H1745
ATTIT CONCPT NAT/LISM

B60
MEYRIAT J.,LA SCIENCE POLITIQUE EN FRANCE, 1945-1958; BIBLIOGRAPHIES FRANCAISES DE SCIENCES SOCIALES (VOL. I). EUR+WWI FRANCE POL/PAR DIPLOM ADMIN CHOOSE ATTIT...IDEA/COMP METH/COMP NAT/COMP 20. PAGE 110 H2193
BIBLIOG/A NAT/G CONCPT PHIL/SCI

C60
EBENSTEIN W.,"MODERN POLITICAL THOUGHT (2ND ED.)" NAT/G CAP/ISM NAT/LISM PERSON ORD/FREE PWR ALL/IDEOS NEW/LIB SOCISM...TRADIT PSY BIBLIOG/A
IDEA/COMP PHIL/SCI CONCPT

18/20. PAGE 44 H0884 GEN/LAWS

B61
FIELD H.,ANCIENT AND MODERN MAN IN SOUTHWESTERN ASIA: II. CULTURE SOCIETY...CLASSIF MATH GP/COMP NAT/COMP 20. PAGE 50 H0992 STAT CHARTS PHIL/SCI RECORD

B61
FIRTH R.,ELEMENTS OF SOCIAL ORGANIZATION (3RD ED.). STRATA STRUCT ECO/UNDEV NEIGH CHIEF INGP/REL ATTIT MORAL...PHIL/SCI GP/COMP WORSHIP SOC/INTEG 20. PAGE 50 H1009 SOC CULTURE SOCIETY KIN

B61
ROIG E.,MARTI, ANTIIMPERIALISTA. CUBA L/A+17C DIPLOM DOMIN COLONIAL CONTROL LEAD PWR SOVEREIGN ...PHIL/SCI 19 MARTI/JOSE INTERVENT. PAGE 133 H2664 PERSON NAT/LISM ECO/UNDEV ORD/FREE

B61
TACHAKKYO K.,BIBLIOGRAPHY OF KOREAN STUDIES: A BIBLIOGRAPHICAL GUIDE TO KOREAN PUBLICATIONS ON KOREAN STUDIES APPEARING 1945-1958. KOREA LAW...HUM JURID PHIL/SCI LING 19/20. PAGE 152 H3033 BIBLIOG/A SOCIETY CULTURE WAR

B61
WARD R.E.,JAPANESE POLITICAL SCIENCE: A GUIDE TO JAPANESE REFERENCE AND RESEARCH MATERIALS (2ND ED.). LAW CONSTN STRATA NAT/G POL/PAR DELIB/GP LEGIS ADMIN CHOOSE GP/REL...INT/LAW 19/20 CHINJAP. PAGE 165 H3306 BIBLIOG/A PHIL/SCI

B61
ZIMMERMAN I.,A GUIDE TO CURRENT LATIN AMERICAN PERIODICALS: HUMANITIES AND SOCIAL SCIENCES. LABOR SECT EDU/PROP...GEOG HUM SOC LING STAT NAT/COMP 20. PAGE 173 H3456 BIBLIOG/A DIPLOM L/A+17C PHIL/SCI

B62
BELL D.,THE END OF IDEOLOGY (REV. ED.). USA+45 USA-45 ELITES STRATA LABOR CREATE CRIME PWR MARXISM ...PHIL/SCI METH/COMP 20 EUROPE. PAGE 13 H0265 CROWD CAP/ISM SOCISM IDEA/COMP

B62
BINDER L.,IRAN: POLITICAL DEVELOPMENT IN A CHANGING SOCIETY. IRAN OP/RES REV GP/REL CENTRAL RATIONAL PWR...PHIL/SCI NAT/COMP GEN/LAWS 20. PAGE 17 H0337 LEGIT NAT/G ADMIN STRUCT

B62
KRECH D.,INDIVIDUAL IN SOCIETY; A TEXTBOOK OF SOCIAL PSYCHOLOGY. UNIV CULTURE LEAD INGP/REL ATTIT DRIVE PERCEPT ROLE...PHIL/SCI BIBLIOG T. PAGE 88 H1765 PSY SOC SOCIETY PERS/REL

B62
MACPHERSON C.B.,THE POLITICAL THEORY OF POSSESSIVE INDIVIDUALISM. UK MARKET NAT/G PERS/REL RATIONAL ...IDEA/COMP 17/19 LOCKE/JOHN. PAGE 100 H2006 PHIL/SCI OWN

B62
MARTINDALE D.,SOCIAL LIFE AND CULTURAL CHANGE. GP/REL...PHIL/SCI SOC CONCPT. PAGE 103 H2065 INTELL CULTURE ORD/FREE STRUCT

B62
MEYER A.G.,LENINISM. USSR STRUCT NAT/G CAP/ISM LEAD WAR PWR SOVEREIGN...BIBLIOG 20 LENIN/VI. PAGE 109 H2187 POL/PAR REV MARXISM PHIL/SCI

B62
MILLER J.D.B.,THE NATURE OF POLITICS. NAT/G DOMIN LEGIT LEAD...CONCPT METH. PAGE 111 H2213 METH/COMP IDEA/COMP PHIL/SCI

B62
ROSENZWEIG F.,HEGEL UND DER STAAT. GERMANY SOCIETY FAM POL/PAR NAT/LISM...BIOG 19. PAGE 134 H2682 JURID NAT/G CONCPT PHIL/SCI

B63
BROGAN D.W.,POLITICAL PATTERNS IN TODAY'S WORLD. FRANCE USA+45 USSR WOR+45 CONSTN STRUCT PLAN DIPLOM ADMIN LEAD ROLE SUPEGO...PHIL/SCI 20. PAGE 21 H0429 NAT/COMP NEW/LIB COM TOTALISM

B63
CARY J.,POWER IN MEN. NAT/G ORD/FREE...GEN/LAWS 20. PAGE 28 H0553 PHIL/SCI OLD/LIB LAISSEZ PWR

B63
ENKE S.,ECONOMICS FOR DEVELOPMENT. AGRI TEC/DEV CAP/ISM DIPLOM ECO/TAC TAX ATTIT DRIVE HABITAT WEALTH...GOV/COMP BIBLIOG 20. PAGE 46 H0928 ECO/UNDEV PHIL/SCI CON/ANAL

B63
KATEB G.,UTOPIA AND ITS ENEMIES. CULTURE STRATA ECO/DEV INDUS REV MORAL...PSY IDEA/COMP 19/20. PAGE 84 H1668 UTOPIA SOCIETY PHIL/SCI PEACE

B63
KROEBER A.L.,ANTHROPOLOGY: BIOLOGY AND RACE. UNIV CULTURE HABITAT...PSY 20. PAGE 89 H1772 SOC PHIL/SCI RACE/REL INGP/REL

B63
LERNER R.,MEDIEVAL POLITICAL PHILOSOPHY. ISLAM MORAL PWR CATHISM...CATH CONCPT OBS IDEA/COMP ANTHOL 9/15 JEWS CHRISTIAN BACON/R AQUINAS/T. PAGE 95 H1890 KNOWL PHIL/SCI

B63
SCHELER M.,SCHRIFTEN ZUR SOZIOLOGIE UND WELTANSCHAUUNGSLEHRE (GESAMMELTE WERKE, BAND 6; 2ND ED.). SECT ALL/IDEOS...SOC CONCPT GP/COMP NAT/COMP 20. PAGE 139 H2783 SOCIETY IDEA/COMP PHIL/SCI

B63
SCHUMAN S.I.,LEGAL POSITIVISM: ITS SCOPE AND LIMITATIONS. CONSTN NAT/G DIPLOM PARTIC UTOPIA ...POLICY DECISION PHIL/SCI CONCPT 20. PAGE 140 H2802 GEN/METH LAW METH/COMP

B63
STRAUSS L.,HISTORY OF POLITICAL PHILOSOPHY. LAW SOCIETY CAP/ISM MARXISM 19 AQUINAS/T BACON/F HEGEL/GWF MILL/JS NIETZSCH/F. PAGE 150 H2995 IDEA/COMP PHIL/SCI ANTHOL

L63
CORWIN A.F.,"CONTEMPORARY MEXICAN ATTITUDES TOWARD POPULATION, POVERTY, AND PUBLIC OPINION." L/A+17C CULTURE SOCIETY ACT/RES ECO/TAC EDU/PROP PERSON HEALTH KNOWL...GEOG PHIL/SCI STAT OBS INT SAMP MEXIC/AMER VAL/FREE 20. PAGE 34 H0672 ATTIT QU

B64
COBBAN A.,ROUSSEAU AND THE MODERN STATE (2ND ED.). FRANCE PROB/SOLV NAT/LISM UTOPIA PERSON MORAL ...EPIST PHIL/SCI SOC IDEA/COMP 18 ROUSSEAU/J BURKE/EDM HOBBES/T HUME/D. PAGE 30 H0612 GEN/LAWS INGP/REL NAT/G ORD/FREE

B64
HARRIS M.,THE NATURE OF CULTURAL THINGS. GP/REL PERS/REL DRIVE HABITAT PERSON ROLE...PHIL/SCI PSY SOC CHARTS BIBLIOG 20. PAGE 67 H1341 CULTURE OBS CLASSIF NEW/IDEA

B64
JARVIE I.C.,THE REVOLUTION IN ANTHROPOLOGY. UNIV CULTURE SOCIETY SECT...MYTH 20 POPPER/K. PAGE 80 H1592 SOC TREND PHIL/SCI METH

B64
KARIEL H.S.,IN SEARCH OF AUTHORITY: TWENTIETH-CENTURY POLITICAL THOUGHT. WOR+45 WOR-45 NAT/G EX/STRUC TOTALISM DRIVE PWR...MGT PHIL/SCI GEN/LAWS 19/20 NIETZSCH/F FREUD/S WEBER/MAX NIEBUHR/R MARITAIN/J. PAGE 83 H1661 CONSTN CONCPT ORD/FREE IDEA/COMP

B64
MINAR D.W.,IDEAS AND POLITICS: THE AMERICAN EXPERIENCE. SECT CHIEF LEGIS CREATE ADJUD EXEC REV PWR...PHIL/SCI CONCPT IDEA/COMP 18/20 HAMILTON/A JEFFERSN/T DECLAR/IND JACKSON/A PRESIDENT. PAGE 111 H2220 CONSTN NAT/G FEDERAL

B64
NORTHROP F.S.,CROSS-CULTURAL UNDERSTANDING: EPISTEMOLOGY IN ANTHROPOLOGY. BURMA GREECE THAILAND HABITAT PERCEPT PERSON...PHIL/SCI SOC METH 20 MEXIC/AMER CHINJAP. PAGE 119 H2375 EPIST PSY CULTURE CONCPT

B64
TODD W.B.,A BIBLIOGRAPHY OF EDMUND BURKE. MOD/EUR UK NAT/G EDU/PROP ATTIT...HUM 18 BURKE/EDM. PAGE 156 H3110 BIBLIOG/A PHIL/SCI WRITING CONCPT

C64
HARRIS M.,"THE NATURE OF CULTURAL THINGS." GP/REL DRIVE HABITAT PERSON ROLE...PHIL/SCI 20. PAGE 67 H1340 BIBLIOG CULTURE PSY SOC

B65
GEWIRTH A.,POLITICAL PHILOSOPHY. UNIV SOCIETY NAT/G GP/REL INGP/REL CONSEN PWR...IDEA/COMP GEN/LAWS 17/19 HOBBES/T LOCKE/JOHN MARX/KARL MILL/JS ROUSSEAU/J. PAGE 56 H1118 ORD/FREE SOVEREIGN PHIL/SCI

B65
GOULD J.,PENGUIN SURVEY OF THE SOCIAL SCIENCES* 1965. CULTURE SOCIETY R+D FAM KIN MUNIC ACT/RES DIPLOM SKILL. PAGE 59 H1186 SOC PHIL/SCI USSR UK

B65
MURDOCK G.P.,CULTURE AND SOCIETY. SOCIETY STRATA STRUCT SECT CREATE CONTROL ORD/FREE...GP/COMP ANTHOL 20. PAGE 115 H2294 CULTURE PHIL/SCI METH IDEA/COMP

B65
SLOTKIN J.S.,READINGS IN EARLY ANTHROPOLOGY. INTELL SECT CREATE ATTIT KNOWL...HUM PHIL/SCI PSY LING 1/18. PAGE 145 H2902 SOC CULTURE GP/COMP

B65
ULLMANN W.,A HISTORY OF POLITICAL THOUGHT: THE MIDDLE AGES. CHRIST-17C LOC/G NAT/G CENTRAL PWR ...PHIL/SCI LOG BIBLIOG 6/15. PAGE 158 H3153 IDEA/COMP SOVEREIGN SECT LAW

C65
STERN F.,"THE POLITICS OF CULTURAL DESPAIR." NAT/LISM...IDEA/COMP BIBLIOG 19/20. PAGE 149 H2979 CULTURE PHIL/SCI CONSERVE TOTALISM

B66
CAPELL A.,STUDIES IN SOCIO-LINGUISTICS. CULTURE LING

ADJUST...CLASSIF IDEA/COMP SOC/EXP BIBLIOG 20. PAGE 26 H0525 — SOC PHIL/SCI CORREL

B66
GURR T.,NEW ERROR-COMPENSATED MEASURES FOR COMPARING NATIONS* SOME CORRELATES OF CIVIL VIOLENCE. WOR+45 SOCIETY REV ISOLAT...PHIL/SCI SOC QUANT TESTS SAMP/SIZ HYPO/EXP. PAGE 63 H1254 — NAT/COMP INDEX COERCE NEW/IDEA

B66
HACKETT J.,L'ECONOMIE BRITANNIQUE: PROBLEMES ET PERSPECTIVES. FRANCE UK LABOR MUNIC NAT/G EX/STRUC PROB/SOLV BAL/PAY INCOME RIGID/FLEX...MGT PHIL/SCI CHARTS 20. PAGE 63 H1271 — ECO/DEV FINAN ECO/TAC PLAN

B66
HOPKINS J.F.K.,ARABIC PERIODICAL LITERATURE, 1961. ISLAM LAW CULTURE SECT...GEOG HEAL PHIL/SCI PSY SOC 20. PAGE 73 H1466 — BIBLIOG/A NAT/LISM TEC/DEV INDUS

B66
LENSKI G.E.,POWER AND PRIVILEGE: A THEORY OF SOCIAL STRATIFICATION. SWEDEN UK UNIV USSR CULTURE ECO/UNDEV PRIVIL PWR...PHIL/SCI CONCPT CHARTS IDEA/COMP HYPO/EXP METH MARX/KARL. PAGE 94 H1882 — SOC STRATA STRUCT SOCIETY

B66
LOCKE J.,THE SECOND TREATISE OF GOVERNMENT: AN ESSAY CONCERNING THE TRUE ORIGINAL EXTENT AND END OF CIVIL GOVERNMENT (3RD ED.). CONSTN SOCIETY CONTROL OWN...PHIL/SCI 17 NATURL/LAW. PAGE 97 H1947 — NAT/G PWR GEN/LAWS ORD/FREE

B66
MADAN G.R.,ECONOMIC THINKING IN INDIA. INDIA ECO/UNDEV AGRI FINAN INDUS LABOR PLAN CAP/ISM INT/TRADE MARXISM SOCISM...POLICY 1/20. PAGE 101 H2013 — ECO/TAC PHIL/SCI NAT/G POL/PAR

B66
MERRITT R.L.,COMPARING NATIONS* THE USE OF QUANTITATIVE DATA IN CROSSNATIONAL RESEARCH. ACADEM DIPLOM GP/REL...PHIL/SCI STAT TREND GP/COMP PERS/COMP GEN/METH ANTHOL BIBLIOG INDEX. PAGE 109 H2184 — NAT/COMP MATH COMPUT/IR QUANT

B66
RADIN P.,THE METHOD AND THEORY OF ETHNOLOGY. CULTURE STRUCT BIO/SOC HABITAT...HUM OBS/ENVIR METH/COMP GEN/LAWS 20 HUMANISM. PAGE 129 H2578 — PHIL/SCI SOC METH SOCIETY

B66
SOROKIN P.A.,SOCIOLOGICAL THEORIES OF TODAY. SOCIETY STRUCT FAM SECT GP/REL ADJUST...PHIL/SCI PSY TREND METH/COMP 20. PAGE 147 H2935 — SOC CULTURE METH/CNCPT EPIST

L66
"FEDERAL, STATE AND LOCAL GOVERNMENT PUBLICATIONS." ACADEM LOC/G NAT/G PROVS SCHOOL EFFICIENCY ...PHIL/SCI ANTHOL. PAGE 143 H2854 — BIBLIOG OP/RES METH

B67
DEGLER C.N.,THE AGE OF THE ECONOMIC REVOLUTION 1876-1900. USA-45 AGRI MUNIC POL/PAR SECT ECO/TAC CHOOSE...PHIL/SCI CHARTS NAT/COMP 19 NEGRO. PAGE 39 H0782 — INDUS SOCIETY ECO/DEV TEC/DEV

B67
NATIONAL SCIENCE FOUNDATION,DIRECTORY OF SELECTED RESEARCH INSTITUTES IN EASTERN EUROPE. BULGARIA CZECHOSLVK HUNGARY POLAND ROMANIA INTELL ACADEM NAT/G ACT/RES 20. PAGE 116 H2323 — INDEX R+D COM PHIL/SCI

B67
UNESCO,PRINCIPLES AND PROBLEMS OF NATIONAL SCIENCE POLICIES. WOR+45 ECO/DEV ECO/UNDEV R+D INT/ORG PROB/SOLV CONFER...PHIL/SCI CHARTS 20 UNESCO UN. PAGE 158 H3165 — NAT/COMP POLICY TEC/DEV CREATE

B83
AMOS S.,THE SCIENCE OF POLITICS. MOD/EUR CONSTN LOC/G NAT/G EX/STRUC LEGIS DIPLOM...METH/COMP 19/20. PAGE 6 H0124 — NEW/IDEA PHIL/SCI CONCPT

PHILADELPH....PHILADELPHIA, PENNSYLVANIA

B99
DU BOIS W.E.B.,THE PHILADELPHIA NEGRO: A SOCIAL STUDY. CULTURE STRATA KIN CRIME SUFF ADJUST DISCRIM ISOLAT HABITAT HEREDITY ALL/VALS SOC/INTEG 17/19 NEGRO PHILADELPH. PAGE 42 H0851 — INGP/REL RACE/REL SOC CENSUS

PHILANTHROPY....SEE GIVE+WEALTH

PHILIP A. H2055

PHILIP/J....JOHN PHILIP

B63
MAC MILLAN W.M.,BANTU, BOER, AND BRITON: THE MAKING OF THE SOUTH AFRICAN NATIVE PROBLEM. SOUTH/AFR UK LAW KIN NAT/G SECT LEGIS COLONIAL ISOLAT ATTIT ...BIOG 18/20 BANTU NEGRO PHILIP/J MISSION. PAGE 100 H1989 — AFR RACE/REL ELITES

PHILIPPINE ISLANDS BUREAU SCI H2500

PHILIPPINE STUDIES PROGRAM H2501

PHILIPPINE....PHILIPPINES; SEE ALSO S/ASIA

B04
REED W.A.,ETHNOLOGICAL SURVEY PUBLICATIONS (VOL. II). PHILIPPINE STRUCT INDUS SECT DEATH LEISURE HABITAT...AUD/VIS CHARTS WORSHIP 20 NABOLOI NEGRITO BATAK. PAGE 130 H2607 — CULTURE SOCIETY SOC OBS

B49
PELZER K.J.,SELECTED BIBLIOGRAPHY ON THE GEOGRAPHY OF SOUTHEAST ASIA (3 VOLS., 1949-1956). PHILIPPINE CULTURE...SOC 20 MALAYA. PAGE 124 H2486 — BIBLIOG S/ASIA GEOG

B55
UN ECONOMIC COMN ASIA & FAR E,ECONOMIC SURVEY OF ASIA AND THE FAR EAST, 1954. AFGHANISTN CEYLON INDIA PHILIPPINE S/ASIA ECO/DEV FINAN INDUS INT/TRADE PRODUC WEALTH...STAT CHARTS 20 CHINJAP. PAGE 158 H3158 — ECO/UNDEV PRICE NAT/COMP ASIA

B56
EGGAN F.,SELECTED BIBLIOGRAPHY OF THE PHILIPPINES. PHILIPPINE ATTIT...SOC NAT/COMP 20. PAGE 45 H0896 — BIBLIOG/A ASIA CULTURE SOCIETY

B56
PHILIPPINE STUDIES PROGRAM,SELECTED BIBLIOGRAPHY ON THE PHILIPPINES, TOPICALLY ARRANGED AND ANNOTATED. PHILIPPINE SECT DIPLOM COLONIAL LEAD...SOC 18/20. PAGE 125 H2501 — BIBLIOG/A S/ASIA NAT/G ECO/UNDEV

B60
WOLF C.,FOREIGN AID: THEORY AND PRACTICE IN SOUTHERN ASIA. CEYLON INDONESIA PHILIPPINE S/ASIA CULTURE STRATA ECO/UNDEV PLAN EDU/PROP ATTIT ...METH/CNCPT MATH QUANT STAT CONT/OBS TIME/SEQ SIMUL TOT/POP 20. PAGE 170 H3396 — ACT/RES ECO/TAC FOR/AID

B62
KEESING F.M.,THE ETHNOHISTORY OF NORTHERN LUZON. PHILIPPINE ECO/UNDEV FAM SECT CHIEF REGION GP/REL HABITAT...GEOG LING BIBLIOG WORSHIP 20. PAGE 84 H1680 — CULTURE SOC KIN

B62
VALERIANO N.D.,COUNTER-GUERRILLA OPERATIONS: THE PHILLIPINE EXPERIENCE. NAT/G CONSULT ACT/RES PLAN COERCE GUERRILLA ATTIT ORD/FREE PWR SKILL...GEOG NEW/IDEA TIME/SEQ CHARTS 20. PAGE 161 H3221 — S/ASIA FORCES PHILIPPINE

B63
STIFEL L.D.,THE TEXTILE INDUSTRY - A CASE STUDY OF INDUSTRIAL DEVELOPMENT IN THE PHILIPPINES (PAPER). PHILIPPINE WORKER CAP/ISM INT/TRADE TARIFFS RECEIVE PRICE ADMIN COST EFFICIENCY WEALTH...BIBLIOG 20. PAGE 149 H2986 — S/ASIA ECO/UNDEV PROC/MFG NAT/G

B63
VON DER MEHDEN F.R.,RELIGION AND NATIONALISM IN SOUTHEAST ASIA. BURMA PHILIPPINE S/ASIA INTELL SOCIETY DOMIN EDU/PROP LEGIT ATTIT MORAL ORD/FREE ...SOC CENSUS HIST/WRIT TOT/POP VAL/FREE 20 WORSHIP LONDON. PAGE 163 H3265 — SECT CULTURE NAT/LISM

B64
TINKER H.,BALLOT BOX AND BAYONET - PEOPLE AND GOVERNMENT IN EMERGENT ASIAN COUNTRIES. CEYLON INDIA INDONESIA PHILIPPINE POL/PAR ADMIN COLONIAL LEAD PARL/PROC CHOOSE CONSEN ORD/FREE SOVEREIGN PLURISM...GOV/COMP THIRD/WRLD. PAGE 155 H3104 — MYTH S/ASIA NAT/COMP NAT/LISM

B65
COSTA H DE L.A.,THE BACKGROUND OF NATIONALISM AND OTHER ESSAYS. ASIA PHILIPPINE ATTIT PERCEPT CATHISM ...ANTHOL 20. PAGE 34 H0674 — NAT/LISM CULTURE ANOMIE NAT/G

B65
FILIPINIANA BOOK GUILD,THE COLONIZATION AND CONQUEST OF THE PHILIPPINES BY SPAIN. PHILIPPINE SPAIN ELITES AGRI KIN CHIEF DOMIN CONTROL ATTIT PWR ...ANTHOL WORSHIP 16. PAGE 50 H1000 — COLONIAL COERCE CULTURE WAR

B65
LANDE C.H.,LEADERS, FACTIONS, AND PARTIES. PHILIPPINE CONSTN LOC/G NAT/G PARTIC...CHARTS BIBLIOG 20. PAGE 90 H1806 — LEAD POL/PAR POLICY

S65
SANDERS R.,"MASS SUPPORT AND COMMUNIST INSURRECTION." GREECE MALAYSIA PHILIPPINE VIETNAM STRUCT ECO/UNDEV POL/PAR FORCES CREATE REV ...GP/COMP IDEA/COMP. PAGE 138 H2751 — GUERRILLA MARXISM GOV/COMP

B66
FARWELL G.,MASK OF ASIA: THE PHILIPPINES. PHILIPPINE SECT DIPLOM ATTIT...SOC RECORD PREDICT BIBLIOG 20. PAGE 49 H0974 — S/ASIA CULTURE

PHILIPPINES....SEE PHILIPPINE; S/ASIA

PHILLIP/IV....PHILLIP IV OF SPAIN

PHILLIPS C.S. H2502

PHILLIPS G.G. H3283

PHILLIPS O.H. H2503

PHILLIPS/F....F. PHILLIPS - POLICE CHIEF, N.Y.C.

PHILLIPSON C. H2504

PHILOSOPHR....PHILOSOPHER

PHILOSOPHY....SEE GEN/LAWS. PHILOSOPHY OF SCIENCE....SEE PHIL/SCI

PHILOSOPHY OF SCIENCE....SEE PHIL/SCI

PHOTOGRAPHS....SEE AUD/VIS

PHS....PUBLIC HEALTH SERVICE

PICKERING J.F. H2505

PICKLES D. H2506

PIDDINGTON R. H2507

PIERCE R.A. H2508,H2509

PIERCE/F....PRESIDENT FRANKLIN PIERCE

PIGOU/AC....ARTHUR CECIL PIGOU

PIKE F.B. H2510,H2511

PINCUS/J....JOHN PINCUS

PINNICK A.W. H2512

PINTO F.B.M. H2513

PIPES R. H2514

PIQUEMAL M. H2515

PISTRAK L. H2516

PITCHER G.M. H2517

PITTMAN J. H2518

PITTMAN M. H2518

PITTSBURGH....PITTSBURGH, PENNSYLVANIA

PLAN....PLANNING

N
NEUE POLITISCHE LITERATUR. AFR ASIA EUR+WWI GERMANY RUSSIA SOCIETY ECO/DEV ECO/UNDEV PLAN PROB/SOLV LEAD MARXISM...PHIL/SCI CONCPT 20. PAGE 1 H0008
BIBLIOG DIPLOM COM NAT/G

N
INDIA: A REFERENCE ANNUAL. INDIA CULTURE COM/IND R+D FORCES PLAN RECEIVE EDU/PROP HEALTH...STAT CHARTS BIBLIOG 20. PAGE 1 H0017
CONSTN LABOR INT/ORG

N
US CONSOLATE GENERAL HONG KONG,REVIEW OF THE HONG KONG CHINESE PRESS. ECO/UNDEV LOC/G NAT/G PLAN DIPLOM EDU/PROP LEAD GP/REL MARXISM...POLICY INDEX 20. PAGE 159 H3178
BIBLIOG/A ASIA PRESS ATTIT

N
US CONSULATE GENERAL HONG KONG,CURRENT BACKGROUND. CHINA/COM ECO/UNDEV LOC/G NAT/G PLAN DIPLOM EDU/PROP LEAD REV ATTIT...POLICY INDEX 20. PAGE 159 H3179
BIBLIOG/A MARXIST ASIA PRESS

N
US CONSULATE GENERAL HONG KONG,SURVEY OF CHINA MAINLAND PRESS. CHINA/COM ECO/UNDEV LOC/G NAT/G PLAN DIPLOM EDU/PROP LEAD REV ATTIT...POLICY INDEX 20. PAGE 159 H3181
BIBLIOG/A MARXIST ASIA PRESS

N
US CONSULATE GENERAL HONG KONG,US CONSULATE GENERAL, HONG KONG, PRESS SUMMARIES. CHINA/COM ECO/UNDEV LOC/G NAT/G PLAN DIPLOM EDU/PROP LEAD REV ATTIT...POLICY INDEX 20. PAGE 159 H3182
BIBLIOG/A MARXIST ASIA PRESS

N
US LIBRARY OF CONGRESS,ACCESSIONS LIST - INDIA. INDIA CULTURE AGRI LOC/G POL/PAR PLAN PROB/SOLV TEC/DEV DIPLOM EDU/PROP LEAD GP/REL ATTIT 20. PAGE 160 H3199
BIBLIOG S/ASIA ECO/UNDEV NAT/G

N
US LIBRARY OF CONGRESS,ACCESSIONS LIST -- ISRAEL. ISRAEL CULTURE ECO/UNDEV POL/PAR PLAN PROB/SOLV TEC/DEV DIPLOM EDU/PROP LEAD WAR ATTIT 20 JEWS. PAGE 160 H3200
BIBLIOG ISLAM NAT/G GP/REL

NCO
CARRINGTON C.E.,THE COMMONWEALTH IN AFRICA (PAMPHLET). UK STRUCT NAT/G COLONIAL REPRESENT GOV/REL RACE/REL NAT/LISM...MAJORIT 20 EEC NEGRO COLD/WAR. PAGE 27 H0540
ECO/UNDEV AFR DIPLOM PLAN

B00
DE JOMINI A.H.,THE ART OF WAR. MOD/EUR NAT/G BAL/PWR DIPLOM DOMIN EXEC ROUTINE COERCE DRIVE PWR SKILL...POLICY CONCPT CHARTS STERTYP 19. PAGE 38 H0755
PLAN FORCES WAR WEAPON

B00
VOLPICELLI Z.,RUSSIA ON THE PACIFIC AND THE SIBERIAN RAILWAY. MOD/EUR ECO/UNDEV INT/ORG FORCES PLAN DOMIN COLONIAL ROUTINE ATTIT ALL/VALS...OBS HIST/WRIT TIME/SEQ TREND CON/ANAL AUD/VIS CHARTS 18/19. PAGE 163 H3261
NAT/G ACT/RES RUSSIA

B02
SEELEY J.R.,THE EXPANSION OF ENGLAND. MOD/EUR S/ASIA UK CULTURE NAT/G FORCES PLAN DOMIN EDU/PROP COLONIAL ROUTINE ATTIT ALL/VALS SOVEREIGN...CONCPT HIST/WRIT PARLIAMENT 18 CMN/WLTH. PAGE 141 H2819
INT/ORG ACT/RES CAP/ISM INDIA

B19
ROUSSEAU J.J.,A LASTING PEACE. INT/ORG NAT/G CHIEF DIPLOM DETER WAR POLICY. PAGE 135 H2697
PLAN PEACE UTIL

N19
ANDERSON J.,THE ORGANIZATION OF ECONOMIC STUDIES IN RELATION TO THE PROBLEMS OF GOVERNMENT (PAMPHLET). UK FINAN INDUS DELIB/GP PLAN PROB/SOLV ADMIN 20. PAGE 6 H0128
ECO/TAC ACT/RES NAT/G CENTRAL

N19
CANADA CIVIL SERV COMM,THE ANALYSIS OF ORGANIZATION IN THE GOVERNMENT OF CANADA (PAMPHLET). CANADA CONSTN EX/STRUC LEGIS TOP/EX CREATE PLAN CONTROL GP/REL 20. PAGE 26 H0517
NAT/G MGT ADMIN DELIB/GP

N19
GORWALA A.D.,THE ADMINISTRATIVE JUNGLE (PAMPHLET). INDIA NAT/G LEGIS ECO/TAC CONTROL GOV/REL ...METH/COMP 20. PAGE 59 H1183
ADMIN POLICY PLAN ECO/UNDEV

N19
HACKETT J.,ECONOMIC PLANNING IN FRANCE; ITS RELATION TO THE POLICIES OF THE DEVELOPED COUNTRIES OF WESTERN EUROPE (PAMPHLET). EUR+WWI FRANCE ECO/DEV PROB/SOLV CONTROL...POLICY 20 EUROPE/W. PAGE 63 H1270
ECO/TAC NAT/G PLAN INSPECT

N19
HAJDA J.,THE COLD WAR VIEWED AS A SOCIOLOGICAL PROBLEM (PAMPHLET). COM CZECHOSLVK EUR+WWI SOCIETY PLAN EDU/PROP CONTROL TASK ATTIT MARXISM...POLICY 20 COLD/WAR MIGRATION. PAGE 64 H1280
DIPLOM LEAD PWR NAT/G

N19
OPERATIONS AND POLICY RESEARCH,URUGUAY: ELECTION FACTBOOK: NOVEMBER 27, 1966 (PAMPHLET). URUGUAY LAW NAT/G LEAD REPRESENT...STAT BIOG CHARTS 20. PAGE 121 H2422
POL/PAR CHOOSE PLAN ATTIT

N19
STEUBER F.A.,THE CONTRIBUTION OF SWITZERLAND TO THE ECONOMIC AND SOCIAL DEVELOPMENT OF LOW-INCOME COUNTRIES (PAMPHLET). SWITZERLND FINAN NAT/G VOL/ASSN INT/TRADE DRIVE...CHARTS 20. PAGE 149 H2982
FOR/AID ECO/UNDEV PLAN DIPLOM

N19
WILSON T.,FINANCIAL ASSISTANCE WITH REGIONAL DEVELOPMENT (PAMPHLET). CANADA INDUS NAT/G PLAN TAX CONTROL COST EFFICIENCY...POLICY CHARTS 20. PAGE 169 H3382
FINAN ECO/TAC REGION GOV/REL

B20
HALDANE R.B.,BEFORE THE WAR. MOD/EUR SOCIETY INT/ORG NAT/G DELIB/GP PLAN DOMIN EDU/PROP LEGIT ADMIN COERCE ATTIT DRIVE MORAL ORD/FREE PWR...SOC CONCPT SELF/OBS RECORD BIOG TIME/SEQ. PAGE 64 H1282
POLICY DIPLOM UK

B21
STUART G.H.,FRENCH FOREIGN POLICY. CONSTN INT/ORG NAT/G POL/PAR EX/STRUC FORCES PLAN ECO/TAC DOMIN EDU/PROP ADJUD COERCE ATTIT DRIVE RIGID/FLEX ALL/VALS...POLICY OBS RECORD BIOG TIME/SEQ TREND. PAGE 150 H3000
MOD/EUR DIPLOM FRANCE

B26
MCPHEE A.,THE ECONOMIC REVOLUTION IN BRITISH WEST AFRICA. AFR UK CULTURE DIST/IND FINAN INDUS PLAN GP/REL RACE/REL 20 AFRICA/W. PAGE 107 H2148
ECO/UNDEV INT/TRADE COLONIAL GEOG

B28
CORBETT P.E.,CANADA AND WORLD POLITICS. LAW CULTURE SOCIETY STRUCT MARKET INT/ORG FORCES ACT/RES PLAN ECO/TAC LEGIT ORD/FREE PWR RESPECT...SOC CONCPT TIME/SEQ TREND CMN/WLTH 20 LEAGUE/NAT. PAGE 33 H0662
NAT/G CANADA

B28
YANG KUNG-SUN,THE BOOK OF LORD SHANG. LAW ECO/UNDEV LOC/G NAT/G NEIGH PLAN ECO/TAC LEGIT ATTIT SKILL ...CONCPT CON/ANAL WORK TOT/POP. PAGE 172 H3434
ASIA JURID

B29
ROBERTS S.H.,HISTORY OF FRENCH COLONIAL POLICY. AFR ASIA L/A+17C S/ASIA CULTURE ECO/DEV ECO/UNDEV FINAN NAT/G PLAN ECO/TAC DOMIN ROUTINE SOVEREIGN...OBS HIST/WRIT TREND CHARTS VAL/FREE 19/20. PAGE 132 H2642
INT/ORG ACT/RES FRANCE COLONIAL

B29
STURZO L.,THE INTERNATIONAL COMMUNITY AND THE RIGHT
INT/ORG

OF WAR (TRANS. BY BARBARA BARCLAY CARTER). CULTURE CREATE PROB/SOLV DIPLOM ADJUD CONTROL PEACE PERSON ORD/FREE...INT/LAW IDEA/COMP PACIFIST 20 LEAGUE/NAT. PAGE 150 H3003 — PLAN WAR CONCPT

B34
RIDLEY C.E.,THE CITY-MANAGER PROFESSION. CHIEF PLAN ADMIN CONTROL ROUTINE CHOOSE...TECHNIC CHARTS GOV/COMP BIBLIOG 20. PAGE 131 H2624 — MUNIC EX/STRUC LOC/G EXEC

B35
TAKEUCHI T.,WAR AND DIPLOMACY IN THE JAPANESE EMPIRE. ASIA ELITES STRATA NAT/G SECT LEGIS ACT/RES PLAN LEGIT PARL/PROC ROUTINE WAR...MGT BIOG CHINJAP TOT/POP 19/20 CHINJAP. PAGE 152 H3038 — EXEC STRUCT

B37
BOURNE H.E.,THE WORLD WAR: A LIST OF THE MORE IMPORTANT BOOKS PUBLISHED BEFORE 1937 (PAMPHLET). EUR+WWI NAT/G DIPLOM ATTIT SOC. PAGE 19 H0386 — BIBLIOG/A WAR FORCES PLAN

B38
HARPER S.N.,THE GOVERNMENT OF THE SOVIET UNION. COM USSR LAW CONSTN ECO/DEV PLAN TEC/DEV DIPLOM INT/TRADE ADMIN REV NAT/LISM...POLICY 20. PAGE 67 H1337 — MARXISM NAT/G LEAD POL/PAR

B39
BENES E.,INTERNATIONAL SECURITY. GERMANY UK NAT/G DELIB/GP PLAN BAL/PWR ATTIT ORD/FREE PWR LEAGUE/NAT 20 TREATY. PAGE 14 H0280 — EUR+WWI INT/ORG WAR

B39
DEWEY J.,FREEDOM AND CULTURE. FUT CONSTN CULTURE INTELL NAT/G CONSULT PLAN CHOOSE ATTIT...CONCPT GEN/METH 20. PAGE 40 H0810 — SOCIETY CREATE

B39
HITLER A.,MEIN KAMPF. EUR+WWI FUT MOD/EUR STRUCT INT/ORG LABOR NAT/G POL/PAR FORCES CREATE PLAN BAL/PWR DIPLOM ECO/TAC DOMIN EDU/PROP ADMIN COERCE ATTIT...SOCIALIST BIOG TREND NAZI. PAGE 71 H1428 — PWR NEW/IDEA WAR

B39
TAGGART F.J.,ROME AND CHINA. MEDIT-7 INT/ORG NAT/G FORCES LEGIS TOP/EX PLAN PWR SOVEREIGN...CHARTS TOT/POP ROM/EMP. PAGE 152 H3034 — ASIA WAR

S39
COLE G.D.H.,"NAZI ECONOMICS: HOW DO THEY MANAGE IT?" GERMANY FORCES WORKER BUDGET INT/TRADE ROUTINE COERCE WAR 20 HITLER/A NAZI. PAGE 31 H0622 — FASCISM ECO/TAC ATTIT PLAN

B40
HERSKOVITS M.J.,THE ECONOMIC LIFE OF PRIMITIVE PEOPLES. INDUS OP/RES PLAN PROB/SOLV...BIBLIOG METH 20. PAGE 70 H1407 — CULTURE ECO/TAC ECO/UNDEV PRODUC

B40
MANNHEIM K.,MAN AND SOCIETY IN AN AGE OF RECONSTRUCTION. MOD/EUR CULTURE ECO/DEV PLAN TEC/DEV PERSON LAISSEZ NEW/LIB...NEW/IDEA IDEA/COMP BIBLIOG 19/20. PAGE 102 H2038 — CONCPT ATTIT SOCIETY TOTALISM

B40
WOLFERS A.,BRITAIN AND FRANCE BETWEEN TWO WORLD WARS. FRANCE UK INT/ORG NAT/G PLAN BARGAIN ECO/TAC AGREE ISOLAT ALL/IDEOS...DECISION GEOG 20 TREATY VERSAILLES INTERVENT. PAGE 170 H3402 — DIPLOM WAR POLICY

B41
HITLER A.,MEIN KAMPF (UNABR. ENG. VERSION) (1925). GERMANY CONSTN TEC/DEV RACE/REL NAT/LISM TOTALISM SOVEREIGN...BIOG 20 HITLER/A TREATY. PAGE 71 H1429 — EDU/PROP WAR PLAN FASCISM

B43
EARLE E.M.,MAKERS OF MODERN STRATEGY: MILITARY THOUGHT FROM MACHIAVELLI TO HITLER. EUR+WWI MOD/EUR NAT/G ACT/RES BAL/PWR DOMIN COERCE ATTIT DRIVE RIGID/FLEX ALL/VALS...METH/CNCPT BIOG 16/20. PAGE 44 H0879 — PLAN FORCES WAR

B43
GRIERSON P.,BOOKS ON SOVIET RUSSIA 1917-42: A BIBLIOGRAPHY AND A GUIDE TO READING. USSR CULTURE ELITES NAT/G PLAN DIPLOM REV...GEOG 20. PAGE 61 H1213 — BIBLIOG/A COM MARXISM LEAD

C43
BENTHAM J.,"PRINCIPLES OF INTERNATIONAL LAW" IN J. BOWRING, ED., THE WORKS OF JEREMY BENTHAM." UNIV NAT/G PLAN PROB/SOLV DIPLOM CONTROL SANCTION MORAL ORD/FREE PWR SOVEREIGN 19. PAGE 15 H0291 — INT/LAW JURID WAR PEACE

B44
HAYEK F.A.,THE ROAD TO SERFDOM. NAT/G POL/PAR CREATE EDU/PROP ATTIT WEALTH LAISSEZ...OLD/LIB CONCPT TREND 20. PAGE 68 H1368 — FUT PLAN ECO/TAC SOCISM

L44
HUXLEY J.,"THE FUTURE OF THE COLONIES." AFR SOCIETY NAT/G PLAN DOMIN COERCE ATTIT DRIVE ORD/FREE PWR WEALTH...TIME/SEQ TREND AUD/VIS CHARTS 20. PAGE 76 H1511 — ECO/UNDEV FUT COLONIAL

B48
LINEBARGER P.,PSYCHOLOGICAL WARFARE. NAT/G PLAN DIPLOM DOMIN ATTIT...POLICY CONCPT EXHIBIT 20 WWI. PAGE 97 H1933 — EDU/PROP PSY WAR COM/IND

B48
NEUBURGER O.,GUIDE TO OFFICIAL PUBLICATIONS OF THE OTHER AMERICAN REPUBLICS: VENEZUELA (VOL. XIX). VENEZUELA FINAN LEGIS PLAN BUDGET DIPLOM CT/SYS PARL/PROC 19/20. PAGE 117 H2335 — BIBLIOG/A NAT/G CONSTN LAW

B48
ROSENFARB J.,FREEDOM AND THE ADMINISTRATIVE STATE. NAT/G ROUTINE EFFICIENCY PRODUC RATIONAL UTIL ...TECHNIC WELF/ST MGT 20 BUREAUCRCY. PAGE 134 H2680 — ECO/DEV INDUS PLAN WEALTH

B48
TOWSTER J.,POLITICAL POWER IN THE USSR: 1917-1947. USSR CONSTN CULTURE ELITES CREATE PLAN COERCE CENTRAL ATTIT RIGID/FLEX ORD/FREE...BIBLIOG SOC/INTEG 20 LENIN/VI STALIN/J. PAGE 156 H3122 — EX/STRUC NAT/G MARXISM PWR

B49
SINGER K.,THE IDEA OF CONFLICT. UNIV INTELL INT/ORG NAT/G PLAN ROUTINE ATTIT DRIVE ALL/VALS...POLICY CONCPT TIME/SEQ. PAGE 144 H2882 — ACT/RES SOC

S49
STEINMETZ H.,"THE PROBLEMS OF THE LANDRAT: A STUDY OF COUNTY GOVERNMENT IN THE US ZONE OF GERMANY." GERMANY/W USA+45 INDUS PLAN DIPLOM EDU/PROP CONTROL WAR GOV/REL FEDERAL WEALTH PLURISM...GOV/COMP 20 LANDRAT. PAGE 149 H2977 — LOC/G COLONIAL MGT TOP/EX

B50
ORTON W.A.,THE ECONOMIC ROLE OF THE STATE. INTELL ECO/UNDEV PLAN CONTROL PWR SOVEREIGN...POLICY 17/20. PAGE 122 H2431 — ECO/DEV NAT/G ECO/TAC ORD/FREE

B50
US DEPARTMENT OF STATE,DOCUMENTS ON GERMAN FOREIGN POLICY, 1918-1945 (13 VOLS.). EUR+WWI GERMANY NAT/G PLAN DIPLOM DOMIN EDU/PROP CONTROL NAT/LISM ...ANTHOL 20. PAGE 159 H3186 — BIBLIOG/A WAR POLICY FASCIST

C50
ROUSSEAU J.J.,"DISCOURSE ON THE ORIGIN OF INEQUALITY" (1755) IN THE SOCIAL CONTRACT AND DISCOURSES." UNIV NAT/G PLAN BAL/PWR HAPPINESS UTOPIA BIO/SOC HEREDITY MORAL...WELF/ST CONCPT. PAGE 135 H2698 — SOCIETY STRUCT PERSON GEN/LAWS

B51
BORKENAU F.,EUROPEAN COMMUNISM. COM EUR+WWI GERMANY SPAIN USSR INT/ORG PLAN REV WAR ATTIT 20 STALIN/J HITLER/A. PAGE 19 H0376 — MARXISM POLICY DIPLOM NAT/G

B51
EUCKEN W.,THIS UNSUCCESSFUL AGE. GERMANY NAT/G WORKER TEC/DEV ECO/TAC ORD/FREE 20. PAGE 47 H0947 — ECO/DEV PLAN LAISSEZ NEW/LIB

B51
JENNINGS I.,THE COMMONWEALTH IN ASIA. CEYLON INDIA PAKISTAN CULTURE STRATA NAT/G LEGIS DIPLOM COLONIAL ATTIT...DECISION 20 CMN/WLTH. PAGE 80 H1604 — CONSTN INT/ORG POLICY PLAN

B52
LEYS W.,ETHICS FOR POLICY DECISIONS. INTELL NAT/G CONSULT PLAN DOMIN EDU/PROP LEGIT COERCE KNOWL MORAL PWR...HUM GEN/LAWS. PAGE 96 H1920 — ACT/RES POLICY

B52
ROBBINS L.,THE THEORY OF ECONOMIC POLICY IN ENGLISH CLASSICAL POLITICAL ECONOMY. UK ECO/DEV WORKER PLAN CAP/ISM EDU/PROP CONTROL INCOME OWN HEALTH SOCISM ...POLICY 17/19. PAGE 132 H2639 — ECO/TAC ORD/FREE IDEA/COMP NAT/G

B52
ULAM A.B.,TITOISM AND THE COMINFORM. USSR WOR+45 STRUCT INT/ORG NAT/G ACT/RES PLAN EXEC ATTIT DRIVE ALL/VALS...CONCPT OBS VAL/FREE 20 COMINTERN TITO/MARSH. PAGE 157 H3149 — COM POL/PAR TOTALISM YUGOSLAVIA

B52
WALTERS F.P.,A HISTORY OF THE LEAGUE OF NATIONS. EUR+WWI CONSTN NAT/G LEGIS TOP/EX ACT/RES PLAN EDU/PROP LEGIT ROUTINE ATTIT...TREND LEAGUE/NAT 20 CHINJAP. PAGE 165 H3297 — INT/ORG TIME/SEQ NAT/LISM

S52
MCDOUGAL M.S.,"THE COMPARATIVE STUDY OF LAW FOR POLICY PURPOSES." FUT NAT/G POL/PAR CONSULT ADJUD PWR SOVEREIGN...METH/CNCPT IDEA/COMP SIMUL 20. PAGE 106 H2129 — PLAN JURID NAT/LISM

C52
LEWIS B.W.,"BRITISH PLANNING AND NATIONALIZATION." UK INDUS SERV/IND LABOR NAT/G OP/RES TEC/DEV TAX WEALTH...CHARTS BIBLIOG 20. PAGE 96 H1912 — NEW/LIB ECO/DEV POL/PAR PLAN

B53
LEITES N.,A STUDY OF BOLSHEVISM. ELITES STRATA INT/ORG LOC/G POL/PAR WORKER EDU/PROP REV TOTALISM UTOPIA PWR...CONCPT 20 BOLSHEVISM. PAGE 94 H1870 — MARXISM PLAN COM

B53
NELSON G.R.,FREEDOM AND WELFARE: SOCIAL PATTERNS IN THE NORTHERN COUNTRIES OF EUROPE. EUR+WWI ECO/DEV NAT/G EDU/PROP LEGIT HEALTH ORD/FREE SKILL WEALTH ...STAT AUD/VIS SCANDINAV WORK TOT/POP 20. PAGE 116 H2329 — PLAN ECO/TAC

B53
SWEEZY P.M.,THE PRESENT AS HISTORY. NAT/G PLAN COLONIAL ATTIT...POLICY SOCIALIST 19/20. PAGE 151 H3019
ECO/DEV CAP/ISM SOCISM ECO/TAC

B54
BINANI G.D.,INDIA AT A GLANCE (REV. ED.). INDIA COM/IND FINAN INDUS LABOR PROVS SCHOOL PLAN DIPLOM INT/TRADE ADMIN...JURID 20. PAGE 17 H0335
INDEX CON/ANAL NAT/G ECO/UNDEV

B54
GERMANY FOREIGN MINISTRY,DOCUMENTS ON GERMAN FOREIGN POLICY 1918-1945, SERIES C (1933-1937) VOLS. I-V. GERMANY MOD/EUR FORCES PLAN ECO/TAC ...FASCIST CHARTS ANTHOL 20. PAGE 56 H1115
NAT/G DIPLOM POLICY

B54
GRAYSON H.,ECONOMIC PLANNING UNDER FREE ENTERPRISE. CANADA FUT UK DELIB/GP BUDGET CONFER CONTROL ...POLICY DECISION 20. PAGE 60 H1200
PLAN ECO/TAC NAT/COMP NAT/G

B54
SPENCER H.,SOCIAL STATICS. MOD/EUR UNIV SOCIETY ECO/DEV NAT/G ACT/RES PLAN EDU/PROP PERSON...POLICY CONCPT. PAGE 147 H2944
MORAL ECO/TAC

L54
FRIEDRICH C.J.,"TOTALITARIANISM." COM EUR+WWI NAT/G POL/PAR SECT FORCES PLAN ECO/TAC DOMIN EDU/PROP EXEC COERCE REV ORD/FREE PWR...SOC CONCPT NAZI 20. PAGE 53 H1067
ATTIT TOTALISM

S54
DODD S.C.,"THE SCIENTIFIC MEASUREMENT OF FITNESS FOR SELF-GOVERNMENT." FUT CONSTN ECO/UNDEV INT/ORG PLAN PWR...CONCPT QUANT CON/ANAL SOC/EXP UN LEAGUE/NAT 20. PAGE 41 H0830
NAT/G STAT SOVEREIGN

C54
GUINS G.C.,"SOVIET LAW AND SOVIET SOCIETY." COM USSR STRATA FAM NAT/G WORKER DOMIN RACE/REL ...BIBLIOG 20. PAGE 62 H1249
LAW STRUCT PLAN

B55
RUSTOW D.A.,THE POLITICS OF COMPROMISE. SWEDEN LABOR EX/STRUC LEGIS PLAN REPRESENT SOCISM...SOC 19/20. PAGE 136 H2720
POL/PAR NAT/G POLICY ECO/TAC

B55
TOYNBEE A.,THE REALIGNMENT OF EUROPE. COM GREECE ITALY NAT/G BAL/PWR ECO/TAC EDU/PROP REV SOVEREIGN ...SOC TIME/SEQ TREND COLD/WAR 20. PAGE 156 H3123
EUR+WWI PLAN USSR

L55
ROSTOW W.W.,"RUSSIA AND CHINA UNDER COMMUNISM." CHINA/COM USSR INTELL STRUCT INT/ORG NAT/G POL/PAR TOP/EX ACT/RES PLAN ADMIN ATTIT ALL/VALS MARXISM ...CONCPT OBS TIME/SEQ TREND GOV/COMP VAL/FREE 20. PAGE 134 H2689
COM ASIA

C55
GRASSMUCK G.L.,"A MANUAL OF LEBANESE ADMINISTRATION." LEBANON PLAN...CHARTS BIBLIOG/A 20. PAGE 60 H1198
ADMIN NAT/G ISLAM EX/STRUC

S56
GORDON L.,"THE ORGANIZATION FOR EUROPEAN ECONOMIC COOPERATION." EUR+WWI INDUS INT/ORG NAT/G CONSULT DELIB/GP ACT/RES CREATE PLAN TEC/DEV EDU/PROP LEGIT WEALTH OEEC 20. PAGE 59 H1178
VOL/ASSN ECO/DEV

B57
ARON R.,THE OPIUM OF THE INTELLECTUALS (TRANS. BY TERENCE KILMARTIN). FRANCE USSR WOR+45 CULTURE POL/PAR PLAN DOMIN EDU/PROP REV ATTIT ORD/FREE ...IDEA/COMP METH/COMP NAT/COMP 20 COM/PARTY. PAGE 8 H0169
INTELL UTOPIA MYTH MARXISM

B57
CHANDRA S.,PARTIES AND POLITICS AT THE MUGHAL COURT: 1707-1740. INDIA CULTURE EX/STRUC CREATE PLAN PWR...BIBLIOG/A 18. PAGE 29 H0574
POL/PAR ELITES NAT/G

B57
COLE G.D.H.,THE POST WAR CONDITIONS OF BRITAIN. EUR+WWI STRUCT NAT/G PLAN EDU/PROP LEGIT RIGID/FLEX ORD/FREE WEALTH...SOCIALIST WELF/ST STAT TREND CON/ANAL CHARTS PARLIAMENT WORK 20. PAGE 31 H0624
ECO/DEV UK

B57
HOUN F.W.,CENTRAL GOVERNMENT OF CHINA, 1912-1928. ASIA CONSTN CHIEF LEGIS CONTROL PWR...BIBLIOG 20. PAGE 74 H1480
POL/PAR ATTIT NAT/G PLAN

B57
LOUCKS W.N.,COMPARATIVE ECONOMIC SYSTEMS (5TH ED.). COM UK USSR INDUS POL/PAR PLAN CAP/ISM TOTALISM MARXISM...PHIL/SCI BIBLIOG 19/20. PAGE 99 H1969
NAT/COMP IDEA/COMP SOCISM

B57
WILSON P.,SOUTH ASIA; A SELECTED BIBLIOGRAPHY ON INDIA, PAKISTAN, CEYLON (PAMPHLET). CEYLON INDIA PAKISTAN LAW ECO/UNDEV PLAN DIPLOM 20. PAGE 169 H3381
BIBLIOG S/ASIA CULTURE NAT/G

S57
LEWIS E.G.,"PARLIAMENTARY CONTROL OF NATIONALIZED INDUSTRY IN FRANCE." FRANCE NAT/G DELIB/GP ACT/RES PLAN PROB/SOLV ECO/TAC DOMIN CENTRAL. PAGE 96 H1914
PWR LEGIS INDUS CONTROL

B58
LIST OF PUBLICATIONS (PERIODICAL OR AD HOC) ISSUED BY VARIOUS MINISTRIES OF THE GOVERNMENT OF INDIA (3RD ED.). INDIA ECO/UNDEV PLAN...POLICY MGT 20. PAGE 2 H0037
BIBLIOG NAT/G ADMIN

B58
CROWE S.,THE LANDSCAPE OF POWER. UK CULTURE SERV/IND NAT/G CONSULT PARTIC NUC/PWR LEISURE...SOC EXHIBIT 20. PAGE 36 H0712
HABITAT TEC/DEV PLAN CONTROL

B58
DUCLOUX L.,FROM BLACKMAIL TO TREASON. FRANCE PLAN DIPLOM EDU/PROP PRESS RUMOR NAT/LISM...CRIMLGY 20. PAGE 43 H0853
COERCE CRIME NAT/G PWR

B58
DWARKADAS R.,ROLE OF HIGHER CIVIL SERVICE IN INDIA. INDIA ECO/UNDEV LEGIS PROB/SOLV GP/REL PERS/REL ...POLICY WELF/ST DECISION ORG/CHARTS BIBLIOG 20 CIVIL/SERV INTRVN/ECO. PAGE 44 H0876
ADMIN NAT/G ROLE PLAN

B58
HANCE W.A.,AFRICAN ECONOMIC DEVELOPMENT. AGRI DIST/IND INDUS R+D ACT/RES PLAN CAP/ISM FOR/AID ...GOV/COMP BIBLIOG 20. PAGE 65 H1312
AFR ECO/UNDEV PROB/SOLV TEC/DEV

B58
JACOBSSON P.,SOME MONETARY PROBLEMS, INTERNATIONAL AND NATIONAL. WOR+45 WOR-45 ECO/DEV FORCES WORKER PROB/SOLV DIPLOM INT/TRADE...ANTHOL 20. PAGE 79 H1580
FINAN PLAN ECO/TAC NAT/COMP

B58
KINTNER W.R.,ORGANIZING FOR CONFLICT: A PROPOSAL. USSR STRUCT NAT/G LEGIS ADMIN EXEC PEACE ORD/FREE PWR...CONCPT OBS TREND NAT/COMP VAL/FREE COLD/WAR 20. PAGE 86 H1719
USA+45 PLAN DIPLOM

B58
NICULESCU B.,COLONIAL PLANNING: A COMPARATIVE STUDY. AFR AGRI LOC/G MUNIC NAT/G DELIB/GP COLONIAL 20. PAGE 118 H2356
PLAN ECO/UNDEV TEC/DEV NAT/COMP

B58
SCOTT D.J.R.,RUSSIAN POLITICAL INSTITUTIONS. RUSSIA USSR CONSTN AGRI DELIB/GP PLAN EDU/PROP CONTROL CHOOSE EFFICIENCY ATTIT MARXISM...BIBLIOG/A 13/20. PAGE 141 H2813
NAT/G POL/PAR ADMIN DECISION

S58
ELKIN A.B.,"OEEC-ITS STRUCTURE AND POWERS." EUR+WWI CONSTN INDUS INT/ORG NAT/G VOL/ASSN DELIB/GP ACT/RES PLAN ORD/FREE WEALTH...CHARTS ORG/CHARTS OEEC 20. PAGE 45 H0907
ECO/DEV EX/STRUC

S58
EULAV H.,"HD LASSWELL'S DEVELOPMENTAL ANALYSIS." FUT CULTURE TOP/EX PLAN CHOOSE SUPEGO PWR...TREND HYPO/EXP SIMUL GEN/METH VAL/FREE 20 LASSWELL/H. PAGE 47 H0948
CONCPT NEW/IDEA ELITES

S58
GARCEAU O.,"INTEREST GROUP THEORY IN POLITICAL RESEARCH." ELITES NAT/G PLAN LEAD REPRESENT INGP/REL POLICY. PAGE 55 H1098
GP/COMP GP/REL LOBBY PLURISM

B59
CUCCORESE H.J.,HISTORIA DE LA CONVERSION DEL PAPEL MONEDA EN BUENOS AIRES, 1861-1867. LAW LOC/G NAT/G ATTIT...POLICY BIBLIOG 19 ARGEN BUENOS/AIR GOLD/STAND. PAGE 36 H0717
FINAN PLAN LEGIS

B59
ETSCHMANN R.,DIE WAHRUNGS- UND DEVISENPOLITIK DES OSTBLOCKS UND IHRE AUSWIRKUNGEN AUF DIE WIRTSCHAFTSBEZIEHUNGEN ZWISCHEN OST U WEST. BULGARIA CZECHOSLVK HUNGARY POLAND USSR MARKET NAT/G PLAN DIPLOM...NAT/COMP 20. PAGE 47 H0943
ECO/TAC FINAN POLICY INT/TRADE

B59
GUDIN E.,INFLACAO (2ND ED.). INDUS NAT/G PLAN ECO/TAC CONTROL COST 20. PAGE 62 H1243
ECO/UNDEV INT/TRADE BAL/PAY FINAN

B59
MEYER A.J.,MIDDLE EASTERN CAPITALISM: NINE ESSAYS. ISLAM CULTURE ECO/UNDEV INDUS MARKET NAT/G PLAN ATTIT RIGID/FLEX...STAT OBS TREND GEN/LAWS. PAGE 109 H2188
TEC/DEV ECO/TAC ANTHOL

B59
PARK R.L.,LEADERSHIP AND POLITICAL INSTITUTIONS IN INDIA. S/ASIA CULTURE ECO/UNDEV LOC/G MUNIC PROVS LEGIS PLAN ADMIN LEAD ORD/FREE WEALTH...GEOG SOC BIOG TOT/POP VAL/FREE 20. PAGE 123 H2468
NAT/G EXEC INDIA

B59
SENGHOR L.S.,RAPPORT SUR LA DOCTRINE ET LA PROGRAMME DU PART I. FRANCE MALI CONSTN POL/PAR PLAN CHOOSE OWN ORD/FREE MARXISM...SOCIALIST 20 NEGRO. PAGE 141 H2828
ATTIT NAT/G AFR SOCISM

B59
STERNBERG F.,THE MILITARY AND INDUSTRIAL REVOLUTION OF OUR TIME. USA+45 USSR WOR+45 WORKER COMPUTER PLAN TEC/DEV NUC/PWR GP/REL...POLICY NAT/COMP 20.
DIPLOM FORCES INDUS

PAGE 149 H2981 CIVMIL/REL

L59
JANIS I.L.,"DECISIONAL CONFLICT: A THEORETICAL ANALYSIS." INTELL NAT/G POL/PAR DELIB/GP LEGIS TOP/EX PLAN...DECISION CONGRESS NAZI 20 WWI. PAGE 80 H1590
ACT/RES PSY DIPLOM

L59
MURPHY J.C.,"SOME IMPLICATIONS OF EUROPE'S COMMON MARKET. IN (COOK P, ECONOMIC DEVELOPMENT AND INTERNATIONAL TRADE.." EUR+WWI ECO/DEV DIST/IND INDUS NAT/G PLAN ECO/TAC INT/TRADE WEALTH...STAT TREND OEEC TOT/POP 20 EEC. PAGE 115 H2298
MARKET INT/ORG REGION

S59
JENKS C.W.,"THE CHALLENGE OF UNIVERSALITY." FUT UNIV CONSTN CULTURE CONSULT CREATE PLAN LEGIT ATTIT MORAL ORD/FREE RESPECT...MAJORIT JURID 20. PAGE 80 H1602
INT/ORG LAW PEACE INT/LAW

S59
WARBURG J.P.,"THE CENTRAL EUROPEAN CRISIS: A PROPOSAL FOR WESTERN INITIATIVE." EUR+WWI INT/ORG NAT/G LEGIT DETER WAR...CONCPT BER/BLOC UN 20. PAGE 165 H3302
PLAN GERMANY

S59
ZAUBERMAN A.,"SOVIET BLOC ECONOMIC INTEGRATION." COM CULTURE INTELL ECO/DEV INDUS TOP/EX ACT/RES PLAN ECO/TAC INT/TRADE ROUTINE CHOOSE ATTIT ...TIME/SEQ 20. PAGE 172 H3452
MARKET INT/ORG USSR TOTALISM

B60
BAYER H.,WIRTSCHAFTSPROGNOSE UND WIRTSCHAFTSGESTALTUNG. GERMANY NETHERLAND MARKET PLAN CAP/ISM DEBATE...NAT/COMP 20. PAGE 12 H0242
ECO/DEV ECO/UNDEV FINAN POLICY

B60
BOMBACH G.,STABILE PREISE IN WACHSENDER WIRTSCHAFT: DAS INFLATIONSPROBLEM. BARGAIN CAP/ISM PRICE COST ...NAT/COMP 20 GOLD/STAND. PAGE 19 H0371
ECO/UNDEV PLAN FINAN ECO/TAC

B60
CARTER G.M.,INDEPENDENCE FOR AFRICA. AFR FUT SOCIETY STRATA ECO/DEV POL/PAR DELIB/GP PLAN DOMIN EDU/PROP COLONIAL REGION ATTIT DRIVE SOVEREIGN ...RECORD INT TIME/SEQ CHARTS 20. PAGE 27 H0544
NAT/G PWR NAT/LISM

B60
DIA M.,REFLEXIONS SUR L'ECONOMIE DE L'AFRIQUE NOIRE (REV. ED.). CULTURE ECO/UNDEV CREATE TEC/DEV DIPLOM INT/TRADE OPTIMAL ATTIT...POLICY 20. PAGE 41 H0816
AFR ECO/TAC SOCISM PLAN

B60
FRANCIS R.G.,THE PREDICTIVE PROCESS. PLAN MARXISM ...DECISION SOC CONCPT NAT/COMP 19/20. PAGE 52 H1047
PREDICT PHIL/SCI TREND

B60
GONZALEZ NAVARRO M.,LA COLONIZACION EN MEXICO, 1877-1910. AGRI NAT/G PLAN PROB/SOLV INCOME ...POLICY JURID CENSUS 19/20 MEXIC/AMER MIGRATION. PAGE 58 H1164
ECO/UNDEV GEOG HABITAT COLONIAL

B60
GOODMAN E.,SOVIET DESIGN FOR A WORLD STATE. COM USSR NAT/G TOP/EX DIPLOM ECO/TAC DOMIN EDU/PROP COERCE REV ATTIT ORD/FREE...CON/ANAL 20. PAGE 59 H1171
PLAN PWR SOCISM TOTALISM

B60
HARRISON S.S.,INDIA: THE MOST DANGEROUS DECADES. INDIA CONSTN STRATA POL/PAR SECT PLAN ADMIN CHOOSE GP/REL TOTALISM MARXISM...LING 20 NEHRU/J. PAGE 67 H1347
CULTURE ECO/UNDEV PROB/SOLV REGION

B60
JAECKH A.,WELTSAAT; ERLEBTES UND ERSTREBTES. GERMANY WOR+45 WOR-45 PLAN WAR...POLICY OBS/ENVIR NAT/COMP PERS/COMP 20. PAGE 79 H1581
BIOG NAT/G SELF/OBS DIPLOM

B60
KENEN P.B.,BRITISH MONETARY POLICY AND THE BALANCE OF PAYMENTS 1951-57. UK PLAN BUDGET ECO/TAC INT/TRADE PAY PRICE COST ATTIT 20. PAGE 84 H1687
BAL/PAY PROB/SOLV FINAN NAT/G

B60
LEYDER J.,BIBLIOGRAPHIE DE L'ENSEIGNEMENT SUPERIEUR ET DE LA RECHERCHE SCIENTIFIQUE EN AFRIQUE INTERTROPICALE (2 VOLS.). AFR CULTURE ECO/UNDEV AGRI PLAN EDU/PROP ADMIN COLONIAL...GEOG SOC/INTEG 20 NEGRO. PAGE 96 H1918
BIBLIOG/A ACT/RES ACADEM R+D

B60
LINDSAY K.,EUROPEAN ASSEMBLIES: THE EXPERIMENTAL PERIOD 1949-1959. EUR+WWI ECO/DEV NAT/G POL/PAR LEGIS TOP/EX ACT/RES PLAN ECO/TAC DOMIN LEGIT ROUTINE ATTIT DRIVE ORD/FREE PWR SKILL...SOC CONCPT TREND CHARTS GEN/LAWS VAL/FREE. PAGE 97 H1932
VOL/ASSN INT/ORG REGION

B60
MCCLOSKY H.,THE SOVIET DICTATORSHIP. FUT CONSTN CULTURE INTELL SOCIETY POL/PAR SECT VOL/ASSN FORCES PLAN TEC/DEV DOMIN EDU/PROP COERCE PWR MARXISM ...POLICY CONCPT MYTH STERTYP 20. PAGE 106 H2127
COM NAT/G TOTALISM USSR

B60
NEALE A.D.,THE FLOW OF RESOURCES FROM RICH TO POOR. WOR+45 ECO/DEV ECO/UNDEV FINAN INDUS NAT/G PLAN EFFICIENCY WEALTH...POLICY NAT/COMP 20 RESOURCE/N. PAGE 116 H2325
FOR/AID DIPLOM METH/CNCPT

B60
SHIRER W.L.,THE RISE AND FALL OF THE THIRD REICH: A HISTORY OF NAZI GERMANY. EUR+WWI CULTURE ECO/DEV INDUS NAT/G POL/PAR FORCES PLAN TEC/DEV ECO/TAC COERCE ATTIT DRIVE PERSON PWR...MYSTIC PSY SOC MYTH STAT CHARTS EXHIBIT WORK VAL/FREE. PAGE 143 H2864
STRUCT GERMANY TOTALISM

B60
VON KOENIGSWALD H.,SIE SUCHEN ZUFLUCHT. GERMANY/E NAT/G PLAN ECO/TAC SOCISM...GEOG CENSUS 20 BERLIN. PAGE 164 H3273
GP/REL COERCE DOMIN PERSON

B60
WOLF C.,FOREIGN AID: THEORY AND PRACTICE IN SOUTHERN ASIA. CEYLON INDONESIA PHILIPPINE S/ASIA CULTURE STRATA ECO/UNDEV PLAN EDU/PROP ATTIT ...METH/CNCPT MATH QUANT STAT CONT/OBS TIME/SEQ SIMUL TOT/POP 20. PAGE 170 H3396
ACT/RES ECO/TAC FOR/AID

S60
BERG E.J.,"ECONOMIC BASIS OF POLITICAL CHOICE IN FRENCH WEST AFRICA." FRANCE ECO/UNDEV AGRI INDUS NAT/G PLAN LEGIT COLONIAL REGION ATTIT PWR WEALTH ...CONCPT 20. PAGE 15 H0299
AFR ECO/TAC

S60
COOK R.C.,"THE WORLD'S GREAT CITIES: EVOLUTION OR DEVOLUTION?" WOR+45 WOR-45 ECO/DEV ECO/UNDEV ACT/RES PROB/SOLV...GEOG TREND CHARTS NAT/COMP BIBLIOG 20. PAGE 33 H0658
MUNIC HABITAT PLAN CENSUS

S60
EMERSON R.,"THE EROSION OF DEMOCRACY." AFR FUT LAW CULTURE INTELL SOCIETY ECO/UNDEV FAM LOC/G NAT/G FORCES PLAN TEC/DEV ECO/TAC ADMIN CT/SYS ATTIT ORD/FREE PWR...SOCIALIST SOC CONCPT STAND/INT TIME/SEQ WORK 20. PAGE 46 H0918
S/ASIA POL/PAR

S60
FITZGIBBON R.H.,"DICTATORSHIP AND DEMOCRACY IN LATIN AMERICA." FUT ECO/DEV ECO/UNDEV INT/ORG LOC/G NAT/G TOP/EX PLAN TEC/DEV ECO/TAC CHOOSE ATTIT DRIVE PERSON ALL/VALS OAS TOT/POP 20. PAGE 51 H1019
L/A+17C ACT/RES INT/TRADE

S60
FRANKEL S.H.,"ECONOMIC ASPECTS OF POLITICAL INDEPENDENCE IN AFRICA." AFR FUT SOCIETY ECO/UNDEV COM/IND FINAN LEGIS PLAN TEC/DEV CAP/ISM ECO/TAC INT/TRADE ADMIN ATTIT DRIVE RIGID/FLEX PWR WEALTH ...MGT NEW/IDEA MATH TIME/SEQ VAL/FREE 20. PAGE 53 H1052
NAT/G FOR/AID

S60
GROSSMAN G.,"SOVIET GROWTH: ROUTINE, INERTIA, AND PRESSURE." COM STRATA NAT/G DELIB/GP PLAN TEC/DEV ECO/TAC EDU/PROP ADMIN ROUTINE DRIVE WEALTH COLD/WAR 20. PAGE 62 H1236
POL/PAR ECO/DEV USSR

S60
HOWARD M.,"BRITAIN'S DEFENSE: COMMITMENTS AND CAPABILITIES." EUR+WWI ECO/DEV NAT/G FORCES LEGIS PLAN DETER ORD/FREE WEALTH...POLICY CONCPT TIME/SEQ GEN/METH 20. PAGE 74 H1481
FUT PWR DIPLOM UK

S60
JAFFEE A.J.,"POPULATION TRENDS AND CONTROLS IN UNDERDEVELOPED COUNTRIES." AFR FUT ISLAM L/A+17C S/ASIA CULTURE R+D FAM ACT/RES PLAN EDU/PROP BIO/SOC RIGID/FLEX HEALTH...SOC STAT OBS CHARTS 20. PAGE 79 H1582
ECO/UNDEV GEOG

S60
NORTH R.C.,"DIE DISKREPANZ ZWISCHEN REALITAT UND WUNSCHBILD ALS INNENPOLITISCHER FAKTOR." ASIA CHINA/COM COM FUT ECO/UNDEV NAT/G PLAN DOMIN ADMIN COERCE PERCEPT...SOC MYTH GEN/METH WORK TOT/POP 20. PAGE 119 H2373
SOCIETY ECO/TAC

S60
RIVKIN A.,"AFRICAN ECONOMIC DEVELOPMENT: ADVANCED TECHNOLOGY AND THE STAGES OF GROWTH." CULTURE ECO/UNDEV AGRI COM/IND EXTR/IND PLAN ECO/TAC ATTIT DRIVE RIGID/FLEX SKILL WEALTH...MGT SOC GEN/LAWS WORK TOT/POP 20. PAGE 132 H2634
AFR TEC/DEV FOR/AID

S60
SHILS E.,"THE INTELLECTUALS IN THE POLITICAL DEVELOPMENT OF THE NEW STATES." AFR ASIA S/ASIA ELITES LOC/G NAT/G CONSULT EX/STRUC CREATE PLAN ECO/TAC DOMIN LEGIT DRIVE PWR...TRADIT CONCPT STERTYP GEN/LAWS 20. PAGE 143 H2861
POL/PAR INTELL NAT/LISM

S60
WOLFE T.W.,"KHRUSHCHEV'S DISARMAMENT STRATEGY." COM NAT/G TOP/EX PLAN BAL/PWR DIPLOM ARMS/CONT COERCE ATTIT...POLICY CONCPT RECORD TREND CON/ANAL COLD/WAR 20 KHRUSH/N. PAGE 170 H3401
PWR GEN/LAWS USSR

B61
AIYAR S.P.,FEDERALISM AND SOCIAL CHANGE. CANADA CULTURE STRUCT PLAN PROB/SOLV TEC/DEV ECO/TAC ORD/FREE...TIME/SEQ 18/20 AUSTRAL. PAGE 4 H0085
FEDERAL NAT/G CENTRAL GOV/COMP

B61
BREWIS T.N.,CANADIAN ECONOMIC POLICY. CANADA BUDGET CAP/ISM INT/TRADE RATION TARIFFS TAX PRICE CONTROL ROUTINE FEDERAL INCOME PRODUC 20 GOLD/STAND. PAGE 20 H0412
ECO/DEV ECO/TAC NAT/G PLAN

B61
DIA M.,THE AFRICAN NATIONS AND WORLD SOLIDARITY. ISLAM CULTURE ELITES ECO/DEV ECO/UNDEV INT/ORG NAT/G PLAN ECO/TAC INT/TRADE EDU/PROP NAT/LISM ATTIT DRIVE ORD/FREE WEALTH...SOCIALIST CONCPT CON/ANAL GEN/LAWS TOT/POP 20. PAGE 41 H0817
AFR REGION SOCISM

B61
DONNISON F.S.V.,CIVIL AFFAIRS AND MILITARY GOVERNMENT NORTH-WEST EUROPE 1944-1946. EUR+WWI FRANCE GERMANY UK USSR LOC/G PROVS PLAN PROB/SOLV BAL/PWR ECO/TAC CONTROL PWR...CHARTS 20. PAGE 42 H0836
NAT/G WAR FORCES CIVMIL/REL

B61
FREYRE G.,THE PORTUGUESE AND THE TROPICS. L/A+17C PORTUGAL SOCIETY PERF/ART ADMIN TASK GP/REL ...ART/METH CONCPT SOC/INTEG 20. PAGE 53 H1060
COLONIAL METH PLAN CULTURE

B61
GUEVARA E.,GUERRILLA WARFARE. L/A+17C ECO/UNDEV NAT/G POL/PAR VOL/ASSN PLAN DOMIN REV DRIVE PWR WEALTH...NEW/IDEA RECORD BIOG COLD/WAR MARX/KARL OAS 20. PAGE 62 H1247
FORCES COERCE GUERRILLA CUBA

B61
INDIAN NATIONAL CONGRESS,SOUVENIR, 66TH SESSION. INDIA S/ASIA CONSTN CULTURE LEGIS CREATE TEC/DEV LEAD TASK...GEOG CHARTS 20. PAGE 77 H1533
CONFER PLAN NAT/G POLICY

B61
KISSINGER H.A.,THE NECESSITY FOR CHOICE. FUT USA+45 ECO/UNDEV NAT/G PLAN BAL/PWR ECO/TAC ARMS/CONT DETER NUC/PWR ATTIT...POLICY CONCPT RECORD GEN/LAWS COLD/WAR 20. PAGE 87 H1728
TOP/EX TREND DIPLOM

B61
LAHAYE R.,LES ENTREPRISES PUBLIQUES AU MAROC. FRANCE MOROCCO LAW DIST/IND EXTR/IND FINAN CONSULT PLAN TEC/DEV ADMIN AGREE CONTROL OWN...POLICY 20. PAGE 90 H1796
NAT/G INDUS ECO/UNDEV ECO/TAC

B61
LUNDBERG G.A.,CAN SCIENCE SAVE US. UNIV CULTURE INTELL SOCIETY ECO/DEV R+D PLAN EDU/PROP ROUTINE CHOOSE ATTIT PERCEPT ALL/VALS...TREND 20. PAGE 99 H1979
ACT/RES CONCPT TOTALISM

B61
MARX K.,THE COMMUNIST MANIFESTO. IN (MENDEL A. ESSENTIAL WORKS OF MARXISM, NEW YORK: BANTAM. FUT MOD/EUR CULTURE ECO/DEV ECO/UNDEV AGRI FINAN INDUS MARKET PROC/MFG LABOR MUNIC POL/PAR CONSULT FORCES CREATE PLAN ADMIN ATTIT DRIVE RIGID/FLEX ORD/FREE PWR RESPECT MARX/KARL WORK. PAGE 104 H2081
COM NEW/IDEA CAP/ISM REV

B61
MAYNE A.,DESIGNING AND ADMINISTERING A REGIONAL ECONOMIC DEVELOPMENT PLAN WITH SPECIFIC REFERENCE TO PUERTO RICO (PAMPHLET). PUERT/RICO SOCIETY NAT/G DELIB/GP REGION...DECISION 20. PAGE 105 H2106
ECO/UNDEV PLAN CREATE ADMIN

B61
MERRIAM A.,CONGO: BACKGROUND OF CONFLICT. AFR FUT KIN MUNIC NAT/G POL/PAR PROVS DELIB/GP PLAN DOMIN COERCE ATTIT...TIME/SEQ CHARTS CONGO 20. PAGE 109 H2182
CHOOSE GUERRILLA

B61
MILLIKAW M.F.,THE EMERGING NATIONS: THEIR GROWTH AND UNITED STATES POLICY. FUT USA+45 WOR+45 WOR-45 NAT/G PLAN TEC/DEV BAL/PWR GOV/REL PEACE ORD/FREE 20. PAGE 111 H2216
ECO/UNDEV POLICY DIPLOM FOR/AID

B61
NATIONAL BANK OF LIBYA,INFLATION IN LIBYA (PAMPHLET). LIBYA SOCIETY NAT/G PLAN INT/TRADE ...STAT CHARTS 20 GOLD/STAND. PAGE 116 H2318
ECO/TAC ECO/UNDEV FINAN BUDGET

B61
NICOLSON H.G.,THE OLD DIPLOMACY AND THE NEW. NAT/G PLAN PROB/SOLV...METH 20. PAGE 118 H2355
DIPLOM POLICY INT/ORG

B61
NOVE A.,THE SOVIET ECONOMY. USSR ECO/DEV FINAN NAT/G ECO/TAC PRICE ADMIN EFFICIENCY MARXISM ...TREND BIBLIOG 20. PAGE 119 H2378
PLAN PRODUC POLICY

B61
SANTHANAM K.,DEMOCRATIC PLANNING. INDIA AGRI FINAN LEGIS DIPLOM PARL/PROC ORD/FREE 20. PAGE 138 H2753
PLAN NAT/G CONSTN POLICY

B61
STAHL W.,EDUCATION FOR DEMOCRACY IN WEST GERMANY: ACHIEVEMENT SHORTCOMINGS - PROSPECTS. GERMANY/W SOCIETY NAT/G FORCES PLAN PROB/SOLV PRESS ALL/VALS ...POLICY MAJORIT CONCPT ANTHOL 20. PAGE 148 H2967
EDU/PROP POPULISM AGE/Y ADJUST

S61
RANDALL F.B.,"COMMUNISM IN THE HIGH ANDES." L/A+17C PERU USSR SOCIETY PLAN EDU/PROP TOTALISM ATTIT RIGID/FLEX PWR WEALTH...HUM CONCPT GEN/LAWS 20 BOLIV EQUADOR. PAGE 129 H2589
CULTURE DRIVE

S61
RAY J.,"THE EUROPEAN FREE-TRADE ASSOCIATION AND ITS IMPACT ON INDIA'S TRADE." EUR+WWI FRANCE GERMANY INDIA S/ASIA UK NAT/G VOL/ASSN PLAN INT/TRADE ROUTINE WEALTH...STAT CHARTS CMN/WLTH EEC OEEC 20 EFTA. PAGE 130 H2600
ECO/DEV ECO/TAC

S61
SCHAPIRO L.,"SOVIET GOVERNMENT TODAY." COM EUR+WWI INT/ORG POL/PAR VOL/ASSN ACT/RES PLAN PERCEPT ...CONCPT TREND TOT/POP VAL/FREE 20. PAGE 139 H2773
NAT/G TOTALISM USSR

S61
TOMASIC D.,"POLITICAL LEADERSHIP IN CONTEMPORARY POLAND." COM EUR+WWI GERMANY NAT/G POL/PAR SECT DELIB/GP PLAN ECO/TAC DOMIN EDU/PROP PWR MARXISM ...MARXIST GEOG MGT CONCPT TIME/SEQ STERTYP 20. PAGE 156 H3111
SOCIETY ROUTINE USSR POLAND

S61
VALLET R.,"IRAN: KEY TO THE MIDDLE EAST." COM IRAQ ISLAM KUWAIT LEBANON SAUDI/ARAB TURKEY ELITES SOCIETY INDUS PROC/MFG POL/PAR TOP/EX PLAN BAL/PWR DIPLOM ECO/TAC ALL/VALS...TREND CENTO 20. PAGE 161 H3224
NAT/G ECO/UNDEV IRAN

S61
ZAGORIA D.S.,"THE FUTURE OF SINO-SOVIET RELATIONS." CHINA/COM INT/ORG NAT/G POL/PAR VOL/ASSN ACT/RES PLAN PERSON...METH/CNCPT TIME/SEQ TOT/POP VAL/FREE 20 MAO KHRUSH/N. PAGE 172 H3445
ASIA COM TOTALISM USSR

B62
THREE PRELIMINARY BIBLIOGRAPHIES OF WORKS RELATED TO THE SOCIAL SCIENCES IN LATIN AMERICA. BRAZIL CULTURE SOCIETY NAT/G PLAN PROB/SOLV...PSY 20 MEXIC/AMER. PAGE 2 H0040
BIBLIOG L/A+17C SOC AGRI

B62
BARNETT A.D.,COMMUNIST CHINA IN PERSPECTIVE. CHINA/COM FUT CULTURE ECO/UNDEV TEC/DEV CONTROL 20. PAGE 11 H0222
REV MARXISM TREND PLAN

B62
BUSIA K.A.,THE CHALLENGE OF AFRICA. CULTURE KIN MUNIC NAT/G POL/PAR SCHOOL DELIB/GP PLAN ECO/TAC DOMIN EDU/PROP TOTALISM ATTIT PERSON ALL/VALS SOVEREIGN...SOC CONCPT STERTYP TOT/POP VAL/FREE 20. PAGE 25 H0496
AFR ECO/UNDEV NAT/LISM

B62
CARTER G.M.,AFRICAN ONE-PARTY STATES. ISLAM IVORY/CST LIBERIA CONSTN CULTURE SOCIETY POL/PAR PLAN DOMIN EDU/PROP EXEC REGION CHOOSE ATTIT ALL/VALS...CONCPT TIME/SEQ CHARTS VAL/FREE 20 TANGANYIKA. PAGE 27 H0545
AFR NAT/LISM

B62
COUNCIL ON WORLD TENSIONS,RESTLESS NATIONS. WOR+45 STRUCT INT/ORG NAT/G PLAN ECO/TAC...NAT/COMP ANTHOL 20. PAGE 34 H0678
ECO/UNDEV POLICY DIPLOM TASK

B62
DUROSELLE J.B.,LES NOUVEAUX ETATS DANS LES RELATIONS INTERNATIONALES. AFR CHINA/COM FRANCE MOROCCO S/ASIA USSR ECO/UNDEV INT/ORG PLAN ECO/TAC EDU/PROP ATTIT DRIVE...TREND TOT/POP TUNIS 20. PAGE 44 H0872
NAT/G CONSTN DIPLOM

B62
DUTOIT B.,LA NEUTRALITE SUISSE A L'HEURE EUROPEENNE. EUR+WWI MOD/EUR INT/ORG NAT/G VOL/ASSN PLAN BAL/PWR LEGIT NEUTRAL REGION PEACE ORD/FREE SOVEREIGN...CONCPT OBS TIME/SEQ TREND STERTYP VAL/FREE LEAGUE/NAT UN 20. PAGE 44 H0873
ATTIT DIPLOM SWITZERLND

B62
EBENSTEIN W.,TWO WAYS OF LIFE. USA+45 CULTURE ECO/DEV PLAN EDU/PROP CONTROL ORD/FREE...GOV/COMP IDEA/COMP T 20 MARX/KARL ENGELS/F LENIN/VI LOCKE/JOHN MILL/JS. PAGE 44 H0885
MARXISM POPULISM ECO/TAC DIPLOM

B62
FRYKLUND R.,100 MILLION LIVES: MAXIMUM SURVIVAL IN A NUCLEAR WAR. USA+45 USSR CONTROL WEAPON ...IDEA/COMP NAT/COMP 20. PAGE 54 H1073
NUC/PWR WAR PLAN DETER

B62
GOURE L.,CIVIL DEFENSE IN THE SOVIET UNION. COM USA+45 USSR MUNIC NAT/G DETER ATTIT MARXISM ...NAT/COMP 20 CIV/DEFENS. PAGE 59 H1188
PLAN FORCES WAR COERCE

B62
GUENA Y.,HISTORIQUE DE LA COMMUNAUTE. FUT ECO/UNDEV NAT/G PLAN EDU/PROP COLONIAL REGION NAT/LISM ALL/VALS SOVEREIGN...CONCPT OBS CHARTS 20. PAGE 62 H1244
AFR VOL/ASSN FOR/AID FRANCE

B62
HATCH J.,AFRICA TODAY-AND TOMORROW: AN OUTLINE OF BASIC FACTS AND MAJOR PROBLEMS. AFR FUT ISLAM STRATA ECO/UNDEV INT/ORG NAT/G POL/PAR DELIB/GP TOP/EX EDU/PROP LEGIT CHOOSE ATTIT...TIME/SEQ TOT/POP COLD/WAR 20. PAGE 67 H1353
PLAN CONSTN NAT/LISM

B62
KARNJAHAPRAKORN C.,MUNICIPAL GOVERNMENT IN THAILAND AS AN INSTITUTION AND PROCESS OF SELF-GOVERNMENT. THAILAND CULTURE FINAN EX/STRUC LEGIS PLAN CONTROL GOV/REL EFFICIENCY ATTIT...POLICY 20. PAGE 83 H1662
LOC/G MUNIC ORD/FREE ADMIN

B62
KRUGLAK T.E.,THE TWO FACES OF TASS. COM COM/IND NAT/G ACT/RES PLAN PRESS PERCEPT PERSON KNOWL 20.
PUB/INST EDU/PROP

PAGE 89 H1778 USSR

B62
LAQUEUR W.,THE FUTURE OF COMMUNIST SOCIETY. CHINA/COM USSR LAW ECO/DEV NAT/G POL/PAR PLAN PROB/SOLV DIPLOM LEAD...POLICY CONCPT IDEA/COMP ANTHOL 20. PAGE 91 H1820 MARXISM COM FUT SOCIETY

B62
LEGUM C.,PAN-AFRICANISM: A SHORT POLITICAL GUIDE. ISLAM CULTURE INTELL ECO/DEV NAT/G POL/PAR DELIB/GP PLAN EDU/PROP FEDERAL NAT/LISM ATTIT DRIVE PERSON ...RECORD TIME/SEQ CHARTS STERTYP 20. PAGE 93 H1861 AFR CONCPT

B62
MEHNERT K.,SOVIET MAN AND HIS WORLD. COM USSR INTELL FAM WORKER PLAN EDU/PROP REV PRODUC MARXISM ...SOC TREND SOC/INTEG 20 LENIN/VI STALIN/J KHRUSH/N. PAGE 108 H2162 SOCIETY CULTURE ECO/DEV

B62
MELADY T.,THE WHITE MAN'S FUTURE IN BLACK AFRICA. FUT CULTURE SOCIETY NAT/G POL/PAR PLAN ECO/TAC DOMIN EDU/PROP LEGIT COLONIAL RACE/REL ATTIT DRIVE ALL/VALS...PSY SOC CONCPT TIME/SEQ TOT/POP VAL/FREE 20. PAGE 108 H2167 AFR STRATA ELITES

B62
MOUSSA P.,THE UNDERPRIVILEGED NATIONS. FINAN INT/ORG PLAN PROB/SOLV CAP/ISM GIVE TASK WEALTH ...POLICY SOC 20. PAGE 114 H2273 ECO/UNDEV NAT/G DIPLOM FOR/AID

B62
RANNEY A.,THE DOCTRINE OF RESPONSIBLE PARTY GOVERNMENT. USA+45 USA-45 CONSTN PLAN CHOOSE ...MAJORIT GOV/COMP IDEA/COMP 20. PAGE 130 H2591 POL/PAR POLICY REPRESENT NAT/G

B62
ROBINSON A.D.,DUTCH ORGANIZED AGRICULTURE IN INTERNATIONAL POLITICS, 1945-1960. EUR+WWI NETHERLAND STRUCT ECO/DEV NAT/G VOL/ASSN CONSULT DELIB/GP PLAN TEC/DEV INT/TRADE EDU/PROP ATTIT RIGID/FLEX ALL/VALS...NEW/IDEA TREND EEC 20. PAGE 132 H2648 AGRI INT/ORG

B62
UNECA LIBRARY,BOOKS ON AFRICA IN THE UNECA LIBRARY. WOR+45 AGRI INT/ORG NAT/G PLAN WRITING REGION...SOC STAT UN. PAGE 158 H3160 BIBLIOG AFR ECO/UNDEV TEC/DEV

B62
UNECA LIBRARY,NEW ACQUISITIONS IN THE UNECA LIBRARY. LAW NAT/G PLAN PROB/SOLV TEC/DEV ADMIN REGION...GEOG SOC 20 UN. PAGE 158 H3161 BIBLIOG AFR ECO/UNDEV INT/ORG

B62
VALERIANO N.D.,COUNTER-GUERRILLA OPERATIONS: THE PHILLIPINE EXPERIENCE. NAT/G CONSULT ACT/RES PLAN COERCE GUERRILLA ATTIT ORD/FREE PWR SKILL...GEOG NEW/IDEA TIME/SEQ CHARTS 20. PAGE 161 H3221 S/ASIA FORCES PHILIPPINE

B62
WALSTON H.,AGRICULTURE UNDER COMMUNISM. CHINA/COM COM PROB/SOLV HAPPINESS RIGID/FLEX...POLICY METH/COMP 20. PAGE 165 H3295 AGRI MARXISM PLAN CREATE

S62
ANSPRENGER F.,"NATIONALISM, COMMUNISM, AND THE UNCOMMITTED NATIONS: AMERICAN PROFILES." FUT ISLAM CULTURE SOCIETY ECO/UNDEV NAT/G POL/PAR PLAN ECO/TAC EDU/PROP COERCE CHOOSE ALL/VALS MARXISM SOCISM...SOC CONCPT BIOG TREND 20. PAGE 7 H0142 AFR COM NAT/LISM

S62
CORET A.,"LE STATUT DE L'ILE CHRISTMAS DE L'OCEAN INDIEN." FUT S/ASIA ECO/DEV ECO/UNDEV VOL/ASSN DELIB/GP PLAN...RELATIV OBS TIME/SEQ TREND AUSTRAL 20. PAGE 33 H0667 NAT/G INT/ORG NEW/ZEALND

S62
CROAN M.,"POLYCENTRISM: COMMUNIST INTERNATIONAL RELATIONS." ASIA STRUCT INT/ORG NAT/G POL/PAR CONSULT PLAN DOMIN EDU/PROP COERCE ATTIT RIGID/FLEX SOCISM...POLICY CONCPT TREND CON/ANAL GEN/LAWS MARX/KARL. PAGE 35 H0703 COM CREATE DIPLOM NAT/LISM

S62
GUETZKOW H.,"THE POTENTIAL OF CASE STUDY IN ANALYZING INTERNATIONAL CONFLICT." EUR+WWI FUT GERMANY INTELL SOCIETY STRUCT INT/ORG LOC/G NAT/G CONSULT CREATE PLAN CHOOSE ATTIT RIGID/FLEX ...POLICY SAAR 20. PAGE 62 H1246 EDU/PROP METH/CNCPT COERCE FRANCE

S62
IOVTCHOUK M.T.,"ON SOME THEORETICAL PRINCIPLES AND METHODS OF SOCIOLOGICAL INVESTIGATIONS (IN RUSSIAN)." FUT USA+45 STRATA R+D NAT/G POL/PAR TOP/EX ACT/RES PLAN ECO/TAC EDU/PROP ROUTINE ATTIT RIGID/FLEX MARXISM SOCISM...MARXIST METH/CNCPT OBS TREND NAT/COMP GEN/LAWS 20. PAGE 78 H1564 COM ECO/DEV CAP/ISM USSR

S62
KOLARZ W.,"THE IMPACT OF COMMUNISM ON WEST AFRICA." AFR FUT SOCIETY INT/ORG NAT/G CREATE PLAN DOMIN EDU/PROP COERCE NAT/LISM ATTIT RIGID/FLEX SOCISM ...POLICY CONCPT TREND MARX/KARL 20. PAGE 88 H1751 COM POL/PAR COLONIAL

S62
MARIAS J.,"A PROGRAM FOR EUROPE." EUR+WWI INT/ORG NAT/G PLAN DIPLOM DOMIN PWR...STERTYP TOT/POP 20. PAGE 102 H2048 VOL/ASSN CREATE REGION

S62
PIQUEMAL M.,"LES PROBLEMES DES UNIONS D'ETATS EN AFRIQUE NOIRE." FRANCE SOCIETY INT/ORG NAT/G DELIB/GP PLAN LEGIT ADMIN COLONIAL ROUTINE ATTIT ORD/FREE PWR...GEOG METH/CNCPT 20. PAGE 126 H2515 AFR ECO/UNDEV REGION

S62
PISTRAK L.,"SOVIET VIEWS ON AFRICA." AFR COM FUT ISLAM USSR INTELL STRUCT KIN POL/PAR PLAN EDU/PROP RIGID/FLEX PWR MARXISM...TIME/SEQ WORK TOT/POP 20. PAGE 126 H2516 NAT/G ATTIT SOCISM

S62
SARKISYANZ E.,"NATIONALISM, CAPITALISM, AND THE UNCOMMITED NATIONS: MARXISM AND ASIAN CULTURAL TRADITIONS." ASIA BURMA CHINA/COM COM CULTURE SOCIETY NAT/G POL/PAR PLAN DOMIN EDU/PROP COLONIAL COERCE ATTIT RIGID/FLEX...CONCPT TREND MARX/KARL 20 TIBET BUDDHISM. PAGE 138 H2755 S/ASIA SECT NAT/LISM CAP/ISM

S62
SHATTEN F.,"POLYCENTRISM: AFRICA: NATIONALISM AND COMMUNISM." ASIA COM FUT ISLAM CULTURE SOCIETY ECO/UNDEV NAT/G PLAN DOMIN COLONIAL COERCE CHOOSE RIGID/FLEX ALL/VALS MARXISM...CONCPT TREND 20. PAGE 143 H2852 AFR ATTIT NAT/LISM SOCISM

S62
SPRINGER H.W.,"FEDERATION IN THE CARIBBEAN: AN ATTEMPT THAT FAILED." L/A+17C ECO/UNDEV INT/ORG POL/PAR PROVS LEGIS CREATE PLAN LEGIT ADMIN FEDERAL ATTIT DRIVE PERSON ORD/FREE PWR...POLICY GEOG PSY CONCPT OBS CARIBBEAN CMN/WLTH 20. PAGE 148 H2955 VOL/ASSN NAT/G REGION

S62
WALTER E.,"VERS UNE CLASSIFICATION SCIENTIFIQUE DE LA SOCIOLOGIA." UNIV CULTURE INTELL SOCIETY R+D ACT/RES LEGIT ROUTINE ATTIT KNOWL...JURID MGT TREND GEN/LAWS 20. PAGE 165 H3296 PLAN CONCPT

B63
BERGSON A.,ECONOMIC TRENDS IN THE SOVIET UNION. USSR ECO/UNDEV AGRI NAT/G FORCES PLAN TEC/DEV INT/TRADE BAL/PAY...POLICY ANTHOL 20. PAGE 15 H0302 ECO/DEV NAT/COMP INDUS LABOR

B63
BROGAN D.W.,POLITICAL PATTERNS IN TODAY'S WORLD. FRANCE USA+45 USSR WOR+45 CONSTN STRUCT PLAN DIPLOM ADMIN LEAD ROLE SUPEGO...PHIL/SCI 20. PAGE 21 H0429 NAT/COMP NEW/LIB COM TOTALISM

B63
CARTER G.M.,FIVE AFRICAN STATES: RESPONSES TO DIVERSITY. CONSTN CULTURE STRATA LEGIS PLAN ECO/TAC DOMIN EDU/PROP CT/SYS EXEC CHOOSE ATTIT HEALTH ORD/FREE PWR...TIME/SEQ TOT/POP VAL/FREE. PAGE 27 H0547 AFR SOCIETY

B63
COLUMBIA U SCHOOL OF LAW,PUBLIC INTERNATIONAL DEVELOPMENT FINANCING IN SENEGAL. SENEGAL FINAN DELIB/GP GIVE EFFICIENCY...CHARTS GOV/COMP ANTHOL 20. PAGE 32 H0636 FOR/AID PLAN RECEIVE ECO/UNDEV

B63
CREMEANS C.,THE ARABS AND THE WORLD: NASSER'S ARAB NATIONALIST POLICY. FUT ISLAM UAR USA+45 SOCIETY STRATA NAT/G POL/PAR PLAN DIPLOM EDU/PROP LEGIT DRIVE ALL/VALS...INT TIME/SEQ CHARTS 20 NASSER/G. PAGE 35 H0700 TOP/EX ATTIT REGION NAT/LISM

B63
DALAND R.T.,PERSPECTIVES OF BRAZILIAN PUBLIC ADMINISTRATION (VOL. I). BRAZIL LAW ECO/UNDEV SCHOOL CHIEF TEC/DEV CONFER CONTROL GP/REL ATTIT ROLE PWR...ANTHOL 20. PAGE 37 H0735 ADMIN NAT/G PLAN GOV/REL

B63
FALL B.,THE TWO VIETNAMS. CULTURE SOCIETY ECO/UNDEV NAT/G TOP/EX ACT/RES PLAN ECO/TAC DOMIN EDU/PROP COERCE ATTIT DRIVE PERSON ORD/FREE PWR...SOC TIME/SEQ COLD/WAR 20. PAGE 48 H0965 S/ASIA BIOG VIETNAM

B63
FRANKEL J.,THE MAKING OF FOREIGN POLICY: AN ANALYSIS OF DECISION-MAKING. CHINA/COM EUR+WWI USA+45 ELITES INTELL FORCES LEGIS PLAN ATTIT ALL/VALS MORAL CONSERVE...GOV/COMP 20 PRESIDENT UN TREATY. PAGE 53 H1051 POLICY DECISION PROB/SOLV DIPLOM

B63
GRIMOND J.,THE LIBERAL CHALLENGE. UK SOCIETY INDUS POL/PAR LEGIS PLAN CAP/ISM DIPLOM EDU/PROP GOV/REL CONSERVE 20 PARLIAMENT REFORMERS. PAGE 61 H1227 NAT/G NEW/LIB ECO/DEV POLICY

B63
GUIMARAES A.P.,INFLACAO E MONOPOLIO NO BRASIL. BRAZIL FINAN NAT/G PLAN PAY...METH/COMP 20. PAGE 62 H1248 ECO/UNDEV PRICE INT/TRADE BAL/PAY

B63
HAQ M.,THE STRATEGY OF ECONOMIC PLANNING. PAKISTAN AGRI FINAN INDUS NAT/G FOR/AID TAX CONTROL REGION PRODUC...POLICY CHARTS 20. PAGE 66 H1324 ECO/TAC ECO/UNDEV PLAN PROB/SOLV

B63
INDIAN INSTITUTE PUBLIC ADMIN,CASES IN INDIAN DECISION

ADMINISTRATION. INDIA AGRI NAT/G PROB/SOLV TEC/DEV ECO/TAC ADMIN...ANTHOL METH 20. PAGE 77 H1532 — PLAN MGT ECO/UNDEV

B63
INTERNATIONAL ASSOCIATION RES,AFRICAN STUDIES IN INCOME AND WEALTH. AFR NAT/G PROB/SOLV DEMAND INCOME...ECOMETRIC METH/COMP 20. PAGE 78 H1553 — WEALTH PLAN ECO/UNDEV BUDGET

B63
ISSAWI C.,EGYPT IN REVOLUTION: AN ECONOMIC ANALYSIS. ISLAM STRUCT ECO/UNDEV AGRI FINAN INDUS PLAN EXEC REV NAT/LISM ATTIT RIGID/FLEX WEALTH SOCISM...STAT WORK 20. PAGE 79 H1573 — NAT/G UAR

B63
KLEIMAN R.,ATLANTIC CRISIS; AMERICAN DIPLOMACY CONFRONTS A RESURGENT EUROPE. EUR+WWI USA+45 ECO/DEV AGRI NAT/G CHIEF FORCES PLAN LEAD ATTIT ...CONCPT 20 NATO KENNEDY/JF DEGAULLE/C EEC JOHNSON/LB. PAGE 87 H1731 — DIPLOM REGION POLICY

B63
KRAEHE E.,METTERNICH'S GERMAN POLICY: THE CONTEST WITH NAPOLEON, 1799-1814, VOL. 1. FRANCE MOD/EUR NAT/G CONSULT TOP/EX PLAN BAL/PWR DOMIN COERCE ATTIT DRIVE PERCEPT PERSON SKILL...CONCPT RECORD TIME/SEQ TREND 18/19. PAGE 88 H1764 — BIOG GERMANY DIPLOM

B63
KURZMAN D.,SUBVERSION OF THE INNOCENTS: PATTERNS OF COMMUNIST PENETRATION OF AFRICA, THE MIDDLE EAST AND AFRICA. AFR ASIA ISLAM S/ASIA CULTURE NAT/G FORCES PLAN EDU/PROP ADMIN ATTIT...CONCPT INT UNPLAN/INT TIME/SEQ. PAGE 89 H1785 — COM COERCE

B63
MAYNE R.,THE COMMUNITY OF EUROPE. UK CONSTN NAT/G CONSULT DELIB/GP CREATE PLAN ECO/TAC LEGIT ADMIN ROUTINE ORD/FREE PWR WEALTH...CONCPT TIME/SEQ EEC EURATOM 20. PAGE 105 H2107 — EUR+WWI INT/ORG REGION

B63
NKRUMAH K.,AFRICA MUST UNITE. AFR FUT GHANA CONSTN CULTURE SOCIETY NAT/G POL/PAR DELIB/GP TOP/EX PLAN DOMIN EDU/PROP ATTIT DRIVE...TIME/SEQ CHARTS TOT/POP 20. PAGE 118 H2364 — CONCPT GEN/LAWS REGION

B63
OECD,FOOD AID: ITS ROLE IN ECONOMIC DEVELOPMENT. FINAN NAT/G PLAN DIPLOM GIVE TASK WEALTH ...METH/COMP METH 20. PAGE 120 H2397 — ECO/UNDEV FOR/AID INT/ORG POLICY

B63
ROBERTSON A.H.,HUMAN RIGHTS IN EUROPE. CONSTN SOCIETY INT/ORG NAT/G VOL/ASSN DELIB/GP ACT/RES PLAN ADJUD REGION ROUTINE ATTIT LOVE ORD/FREE RESPECT...JURID SOC CONCPT SOC/EXP UN 20. PAGE 132 H2645 — EUR+WWI PERSON

B63
SCHECHTMAN J.B.,THE REFUGEE IN THE WORLD: DISPLACEMENT AND INTEGRATION. AFR ASIA EUR+WWI ISLAM L/A+17C S/ASIA CULTURE STRATA LOC/G EX/STRUC PLAN ECO/TAC ROUTINE...CONCPT TIME/SEQ VAL/FREE 20. PAGE 139 H2779 — INT/ORG SOC

B63
SWEARER H.R.,CONTEMPORARY COMMUNISM: THEORY AND PRACTICE. COM USSR SOCIETY ECO/DEV POL/PAR FORCES PLAN ADMIN LEAD NAT/LISM...POLICY ANTHOL 20 LENIN/VI COM/PARTY. PAGE 151 H3015 — MARXISM CONCPT DIPLOM NAT/G

B63
THUCYDIDES,THE PELOPONESIAN WARS. MEDIT-7 CULTURE INT/ORG NAT/G FORCES TOP/EX PLAN ROUTINE PWR ...CONCPT. PAGE 155 H3091 — ATTIT COERCE WAR

B63
UN SECRETARY GENERAL,PLANNING FOR ECONOMIC DEVELOPMENT. ECO/UNDEV FINAN BUDGET INT/TRADE TARIFFS TAX ADMIN 20 UN. PAGE 158 H3159 — PLAN ECO/TAC MGT NAT/COMP

B63
VIARD R.,LA FIN DE L'EMPIRE COLONIAL FRANCAIS. AFR FUT S/ASIA ECO/UNDEV NAT/G CONSULT PLAN ECO/TAC EDU/PROP REGION NAT/LISM ALL/VALS...CONCPT TIME/SEQ TREND VAL/FREE 20. PAGE 162 H3248 — VOL/ASSN COLONIAL FRANCE

B63
WALKER A.A.,OFFICIAL PUBLICATIONS OF SIERRA LEONE AND GAMBIA. GAMBIA SIER/LEONE UK LAW CONSTN LEGIS PLAN BUDGET DIPLOM...SOC SAMP CON/ANAL 20. PAGE 164 H3290 — BIBLIOG NAT/G COLONIAL ADMIN

B63
ZARTMAN I.W.,GOVERNMENT AND POLITICS IN NORTHERN AFRICA. AFR ALGERIA ISLAM LIBYA MOROCCO UAR ELITES SOCIETY PLAN ECO/TAC DOMIN EDU/PROP LEGIT ATTIT ...GEOG CONCPT TIME/SEQ 20 TUNIS. PAGE 172 H3448 — CULTURE DRIVE NAT/LISM

L63
MICHAEL F.,"KHRUSHCHEV'S DISLOYAL OPPOSITION: STRUCTURAL CHANGE AND POWER STRUGGLE IN COMMUNIST BLOC." ASIA CHINA/COM FUT NAT/G POL/PAR CONSULT PLAN DOMIN ATTIT...POLICY CONCPT TREND MARX/KARL 20 KHRUSH/N. PAGE 110 H2195 — COM STRUCT NAT/LISM USSR

S63
APPERT K.,"BERECHTIGE VORBEHALTE DER SCHWEIZERISCHEN ZUR INTEGRATION." EUR+WWI UK MARKET SERV/IND NAT/G PLAN RIGID/FLEX OEEC 20 EEC. PAGE 7 H0146 — FINAN ATTIT SWITZERLND

S63
HALPERN A.M.,"THE EMERGENCE OF AN ASIAN COMMUNIST BLOC." ASIA CHINA/COM COM FUT KOREA/N S/ASIA VIETNAM/N STRATA NAT/G DELIB/GP FORCES TOP/EX PLAN BAL/PWR COERCE DETER PWR COLD/WAR WORK 20. PAGE 65 H1295 — POL/PAR EDU/PROP DIPLOM

S63
HOSKINS H.L.,"ARAB SOCIALISM IN THE UAR." ISLAM USSR AGRI INDUS NAT/G TOP/EX CREATE DIPLOM EDU/PROP DRIVE KNOWL PWR SOCISM...POLICY CONCPT TREND SUEZ 20. PAGE 74 H1478 — ECO/DEV PLAN UAR

S63
POPPINO R.E.,"IMBALANCE IN BRAZIL." L/A+17C NAT/G TOP/EX PLAN DIPLOM LEGIT DRIVE WEALTH...CON/ANAL LAFTA 20. PAGE 127 H2544 — POL/PAR ECO/TAC BRAZIL

S63
ROUGEMONT D.,"LES NOUVELLES CHANCES DE L'EUROPE." EUR+WWI FUT ECO/DEV INT/ORG NAT/G ACT/RES PLAN TEC/DEV EDU/PROP ADMIN COLONIAL FEDERAL ATTIT PWR SKILL...TREND 20. PAGE 135 H2696 — ECO/UNDEV PERCEPT

S63
SOEMARDJORN S.,"SOME SOCIAL AND CULTURAL IMPLICATIONS OF INDONESIA'S PLANNED AND UNPLANNED DEVELOPMENT." EUR+WWI FUT MOD/EUR S/ASIA CONSTN SOCIETY DELIB/GP ACT/RES PLAN ECO/TAC EDU/PROP COERCE ATTIT ALL/VALS...TIME/SEQ 20. PAGE 146 H2927 — ECO/UNDEV CULTURE INDONESIA

B64
BAUCHET P.,ECONOMIC PLANNING. FRANCE STRATA LG/CO CAP/ISM ADMIN PARL/PROC DEMAND OPTIMAL ATTIT PWR SOCISM...POLICY CHARTS 20. PAGE 12 H0238 — ECO/DEV NAT/G PLAN ECO/TAC

B64
BELL C.,THE DEBATABLE ALLIANCE. COM UK USA+45 NAT/G FORCES PLAN BAL/PWR NUC/PWR WAR ATTIT...GOV/COMP 20. PAGE 13 H0263 — DIPLOM PWR PEACE POLICY

B64
BINDER L.,THE IDEOLOGICAL REVOLUTION IN THE MIDDLE EAST. ISLAM STRUCT INT/ORG KIN SECT EX/STRUC TOP/EX PLAN ATTIT DRIVE RIGID/FLEX PWR...MYTH TOT/POP 20. PAGE 17 H0338 — POL/PAR NAT/G NAT/LISM

B64
BRIGHT J.R.,RESEARCH, DEVELOPMENT AND TECHNOLOGICAL INNOVATION. CULTURE R+D CREATE PLAN PROB/SOLV AUTOMAT RISK PERSON...DECISION CONCPT PREDICT BIBLIOG. PAGE 21 H0419 — TEC/DEV NEW/IDEA INDUS MGT

B64
CULLINGWORTH J.B.,TOWN AND COUNTRY PLANNING IN ENGLAND AND WALES. UK LAW SOCIETY CONSULT ACT/RES ADMIN ROUTINE LEISURE INGP/REL ADJUST PWR...GEOG 20 OPEN/SPACE URBAN/RNWL. PAGE 36 H0718 — MUNIC PLAN NAT/G PROB/SOLV

B64
ETZIONI A.,MODERN ORGANIZATIONS. CLIENT STRUCT DOMIN CONTROL LEAD PERS/REL AUTHORIT...CLASSIF BUREAUCRCY. PAGE 47 H0946 — MGT ADMIN PLAN CULTURE

B64
FLORENCE P.S.,ECONOMICS AND SOCIOLOGY OF INDUSTRY; A REALISTIC ANALYSIS OF DEVELOPMENT. ECO/UNDEV LG/CO NAT/G PLAN...GEOG MGT BIBLIOG 20. PAGE 51 H1029 — INDUS SOC ADMIN

B64
FRIEDLAND W.H.,AFRICAN SOCIALISM. ECO/UNDEV MARKET LABOR NAT/G POL/PAR PLAN CAP/ISM ECO/TAC EDU/PROP CHOOSE ATTIT DRIVE PWR WEALTH...POLICY CONCPT RECORD STERTYP 20. PAGE 53 H1063 — AFR SOCISM

B64
GILLY A.,INSIDE THE CUBAN REVOLUTION. CUBA AGRI INDUS LABOR CREATE DIPLOM...METH/COMP 20. PAGE 56 H1129 — REV PLAN MARXISM ECO/UNDEV

B64
GREAT BRITAIN CENTRAL OFF INF,CONSTITUTIONAL DEVELOPMENT IN THE COMMONWEALTH. VOL/ASSN PLAN DIPLOM COLONIAL INGP/REL NAT/LISM ORD/FREE PWR 17/20 CMN/WLTH. PAGE 60 H1202 — REGION CONSTN NAT/G SOVEREIGN

B64
GREBLER L.,URBAN RENEWAL IN EUROPEAN COUNTRIES: ITS EMERGENCE AND POTENTIALS. EUR+WWI UK ECO/DEV LOC/G NEIGH CREATE ADMIN ATTIT...TREND NAT/COMP 20 URBAN/RNWL. PAGE 60 H1205 — MUNIC PLAN CONSTRUC NAT/G

B64
HAAR C.M.,LAW AND LAND: ANGLO-AMERICAN PLANNING PRACTICE. UK USA+45 NAT/G TEC/DEV BUDGET CT/SYS INGP/REL EFFICIENCY OWN...JURID 20. PAGE 63 H1263 — LAW PLAN MUNIC NAT/COMP

B64
HALE O.J.,THE CAPTIVE PRESS IN THE THIRD REICH. GERMANY CULTURE LG/CO NAT/G POL/PAR PLAN DOMIN TASK CENTRAL OWN TOTALISM PWR...BIBLIOG 20 HITLER/A NAZI AMMAN/MAX. PAGE 64 H1283 — COM/IND PRESS CONTROL FASCISM

B64
HARBISON F.H.,EDUCATION, MANPOWER, AND ECONOMIC GROWTH. WOR+45 ECO/DEV ECO/UNDEV ACADEM LABOR — PLAN TEC/DEV

SCHOOL WORKER UTIL...IDEA/COMP NAT/COMP. PAGE 66 H1326 — EDU/PROP SKILL

B64

HERSKOVITS M.J.,ECONOMIC TRANSITION IN AFRICA. FUT INT/ORG NAT/G WORKER PROB/SOLV TEC/DEV INT/TRADE EQUILIB INCOME...ANTHOL 20. PAGE 70 H1408 — AFR ECO/UNDEV PLAN ADMIN

B64

INTERNATIONAL LABOUR OFFICE,EMPLOYMENT AND ECONOMIC GROWTH. ECO/DEV ECO/UNDEV NAT/G PLAN DIPLOM INT/TRADE CONTROL INCOME PRODUC WEALTH...STAT NAT/COMP 20 ILO. PAGE 78 H1558 — WORKER METH/COMP ECO/TAC OPTIMAL

B64

INTL CONF ON POPULATION,POPULATION DYNAMICS: INTERNATIONAL ACTION AND TRAINING PROGRAMS. INDIA KOREA L/A+17C TAIWAN USA+45 WOR+45 FAM PLAN CONFER ...NEW/IDEA ANTHOL 20 CHINJAP BIRTH/CON. PAGE 78 H1561 — NAT/COMP CONTROL ATTIT EDU/PROP

B64

JUCKER-FLEETWOOD E.,MONEY AND FINANCE IN AFRICA. ISLAM ECO/UNDEV SERV/IND NAT/G EX/STRUC PLAN ECO/TAC ROUTINE WEALTH...MGT TOT/POP 20. PAGE 82 H1639 — AFR FINAN

B64

KELLER J.W.,GERMANY, THE WALL AND BERLIN. EUR+WWI ECO/DEV NAT/G VOL/ASSN FORCES PLAN ECO/TAC EDU/PROP COERCE...POLICY CONCPT INT TREND COLD/WAR BER/BLOC 20 BERLIN. PAGE 84 H1685 — ATTIT ALL/VALS DIPLOM GERMANY

B64

LEBRUN J.,BIBLIOGRAPHIE DE LA FERTILITE DES SOLS ET ELEMENTS DE SOCIOLOGIE RURALE EN AFRIQUE AU SUD DU SAHARA. AFR PLAN TEC/DEV EFFICIENCY PRODUC...GEOG SOC NAT/COMP 20. PAGE 93 H1850 — BIBLIOG/A ECO/UNDEV HABITAT AGRI

B64

MELADY T.,FACES OF AFRICA. AFR FUT ISLAM NAT/G POL/PAR SCHOOL DELIB/GP PLAN ECO/TAC EDU/PROP ATTIT ALL/VALS...CHARTS TOT/POP VAL/FREE 20. PAGE 108 H2168 — ECO/UNDEV TREND NAT/LISM

B64

MORGENTHAU R.S.,POLITICAL PARTIES IN FRENCH-SPEAKING WEST AFRICA. AFR FRANCE GUINEA IVORY/CST MALI SENEGAL CONSTN LEGIS CREATE PLAN LOBBY PARTIC GP/REL...POLICY BIBLIOG 20. PAGE 113 H2257 — POL/PAR NAT/G SOVEREIGN COLONIAL

B64

NICOL D.,AFRICA - A SUBJECTIVE VIEW. AFR INT/ORG PLAN ADMIN COLONIAL PARL/PROC PARTIC REGION GOV/REL LITERACY ATTIT...BIBLIOG 20 CIVIL/SERV. PAGE 118 H2350 — NAT/G LEAD CULTURE ACADEM

B64

OECD SEMINAR REGIONAL DEV,REGIONAL DEVELOPMENT IN ISRAEL. ISRAEL STRUCT ECO/UNDEV NAT/G REGION...GEOG 20. PAGE 120 H2404 — ADMIN PROVS PLAN METH/COMP

B64

PARANJAPE H.K.,THE FLIGHT OF TECHNICAL PERSONNEL IN PUBLIC UNDERTAKINGS. INDIA PAY DEMAND HAPPINESS ORD/FREE...MGT QU 20 MIGRATION. PAGE 123 H2464 — ADMIN NAT/G WORKER PLAN

B64

PINNICK A.W.,COUNTRY PLANNERS IN ACTION. UK FINAN SERV/IND NAT/G CONSULT DELIB/GP PRICE CONTROL ROUTINE LEISURE AGE/C...GEOG 20 URBAN/RNWL. PAGE 126 H2512 — MUNIC PLAN INDUS ATTIT

B64

POWELSON J.P.,LATIN AMERICA: TODAY'S ECONOMIC AND SOCIAL REVOLUTION. L/A+17C INTELL SOCIETY STRUCT AGRI INDUS NAT/G DIPLOM ECO/TAC REV...POLICY 20. PAGE 128 H2552 — ECO/UNDEV WEALTH ADJUST PLAN

B64

RAPHAEL M.,PENSIONS AND PUBLIC SERVANTS. UK NAT/G PLAN INGP/REL COST EFFICIENCY ATTIT...POLICY 17/20 CIVIL/SERV. PAGE 130 H2593 — RECEIVE ADMIN INCOME AGE/O

B64

ROBERTS HL,FOREIGN AFFAIRS BIBLIOGRAPHY, 1952-1962. ECO/DEV SECT PLAN FOR/AID INT/TRADE ARMS/CONT NAT/LISM ATTIT...INT/LAW GOV/COMP IDEA/COMP 20. PAGE 132 H2643 — BIBLIOG/A DIPLOM INT/ORG WAR

B64

THAILAND NATIONAL ECO DEV,THE NATIONAL ECONOMIC DEVELOPMENT PLAN: 1961-66: SECOND PHASE 1964-66. THAILAND AGRI FINAN BUDGET EFFICIENCY INCOME...STAT CHARTS 20. PAGE 153 H3065 — ECO/UNDEV ECO/TAC PLAN NAT/G

B64

THORNBURG M.W.,PEOPLE AND POLICY IN THE MIDDLE EAST. ISLAM ECO/UNDEV FAM KIN MUNIC NAT/G NEIGH POL/PAR SECT DELIB/GP LEGIS PLAN ECO/TAC DOMIN ADMIN ATTIT HEALTH RESPECT...SOC CONCPT METH/CNCPT OBS TIME/SEQ TOT/POP VAL/FREE. PAGE 154 H3088 — TEC/DEV CULTURE

B64

WILSON T.,POLICIES FOR REGIONAL DEVELOPMENT. CANADA UK FINAN INDUS NAT/G BUDGET TAX GIVE COST ...NAT/COMP 20. PAGE 169 H3383 — REGION PLAN ECO/DEV ECO/TAC

L64

BERELSON B.,"SAMPLE SURVEYS AND POPULATION CONTROL." ASIA FUT ISLAM L/A+17C CULTURE SOCIETY FAM NAT/G CONSULT PLAN EDU/PROP ATTIT DRIVE ALL/VALS...POLICY RELATIV HEAL PSY SOC CONCPT METH/CNCPT OBS OBS/ENVIR TOT/POP. PAGE 15 H0297 — BIO/SOC SAMP

L64

HAAS E.B.,"ECONOMICS AND DIFFERENTIAL PATTERNS OF POLITICAL INTEGRATION: PROJECTIONS ABOUT UNITY IN LATIN AMERICA." SOCIETY NAT/G DELIB/GP ACT/RES CREATE PLAN ECO/TAC REGION ROUTINE ATTIT DRIVE PWR WEALTH...CONCPT TREND CHARTS LAFTA 20. PAGE 63 H1266 — L/A+17C INT/ORG MARKET

S64

CLIFFE L.,"TANGANYIKA'S TWO YEARS OF INDEPENDENCE." AFR INDUS MARKET NAT/G POL/PAR DELIB/GP CREATE ECO/TAC LEGIT DRIVE ALL/VALS...METH/CNCPT RECORD 20 TANGANYIKA. PAGE 30 H0604 — ECO/UNDEV PLAN

S64

GARMARNIKOW M.,"INFLUENCE-BUYING IN WEST AFRICA." COM FUT USSR INTELL NAT/G PLAN TEC/DEV ECO/TAC DOMIN EDU/PROP REGION NAT/LISM ATTIT DRIVE ALL/VALS SOVEREIGN...POLICY PSY SOC CONCPT TREND STERTYP WORK COLD/WAR 20. PAGE 55 H1102 — AFR ECO/UNDEV FOR/AID SOCISM

S64

GOLDBERG A.,"THE MILITARY ORIGINS OF THE BRITISH NUCLEAR DETERRENT." EUR+WWI ECO/DEV NAT/G PLAN NUC/PWR ATTIT PWR...DECISION HIST/WRIT COLD/WAR 20. PAGE 58 H1156 — FORCES CONCPT DETER UK

S64

HIRAI N.,"SHINTO AND INTERNATIONAL PROBLEMS." SOCIETY NAT/G PLAN EDU/PROP RACE/REL PEACE ATTIT PERCEPT LOVE MORAL...HUM MYTH RECORD SAMP TREND STERTYP TOT/POP 20 UN CHINJAP SHINTO. PAGE 71 H1423 — ASIA SECT

S64

LERNER W.,"THE HISTORICAL ORIGINS OF THE SOVIET DOCTRINE OF PEACEFUL COEXISTENCE." COM USSR INT/ORG NAT/G VOL/ASSN PLAN PEACE ATTIT RIGID/FLEX PWR MARXISM...TIME/SEQ COLD/WAR 20. PAGE 95 H1891 — EDU/PROP DIPLOM

S64

MARES V.E.,"EAST EUROPE'S SECOND CHANCE." COM EUR+WWI HUNGARY ROMANIA USSR YUGOSLAVIA ECO/UNDEV NAT/G TOP/EX CREATE PLAN TEC/DEV REGION NAT/LISM RIGID/FLEX PWR...CONCPT STAT COMECON 20. PAGE 102 H2047 — VOL/ASSN ECO/TAC

S64

MARTELLI G.,"PORTUGAL AND THE UNITED NATIONS." AFR EUR+WWI ELITES INT/ORG NAT/G PROVS PLAN DIPLOM ECO/TAC DOMIN COLONIAL RIGID/FLEX MORAL ORD/FREE PWR WEALTH...MYTH UN 20. PAGE 103 H2060 — ATTIT PORTUGAL

S64

NASH M.,"SOCIAL PREREQUISITES TO ECONOMIC GROWTH IN LATIN AMERICA AND SOUTHEAST ASIA." L/A+17C S/ASIA CULTURE SOCIETY ECO/UNDEV AGRI INDUS NAT/G PLAN TEC/DEV EDU/PROP ROUTINE ALL/VALS...POLICY RELATIV SOC NAT/COMP WORK TOT/POP 20. PAGE 116 H2314 — ECO/DEV PERCEPT

S64

NEEDHAM T.,"SCIENCE AND SOCIETY IN EAST AND WEST." INTELL STRATA R+D LOC/G NAT/G PROVS CONSULT ACT/RES CREATE PLAN TEC/DEV EDU/PROP ADMIN ATTIT ALL/VALS ...POLICY RELATIV MGT CONCPT NEW/IDEA TIME/SEQ WORK WORK. PAGE 116 H2327 — ASIA STRUCT

S64

SAAB H.,"THE ARAB SEARCH FOR A FEDERAL UNION." SOCIETY INT/ORG NAT/G DELIB/GP FORCES ACT/RES TEC/DEV ECO/TAC DOMIN LEGIT REGION ROUTINE ATTIT DRIVE RIGID/FLEX ALL/VALS...SOC CONCPT NEW/IDEA TIME/SEQ TREND. PAGE 136 H2726 — ISLAM PLAN

S64

SALVADORI M.,"EL CAPITALISMO EN LA EUROPA DE LA POSGUERRA." INT/ORG NAT/G POL/PAR PLAN ECO/TAC ATTIT ORD/FREE WEALTH...HIST/WRIT COLD/WAR EEC 20. PAGE 137 H2743 — EUR+WWI ECO/DEV CAP/ISM

S64

SMYTHE H.H.,"NEHRU AND INDIAN FOREIGN POLICY." S/ASIA ECO/UNDEV NAT/G POL/PAR CONSULT PLAN DIPLOM NEUTRAL COERCE ATTIT DRIVE PERSON MORAL ORD/FREE RESPECT...GEOG CONCPT TIME/SEQ TREND GEN/LAWS 20 NEHRU/J. PAGE 146 H2922 — TOP/EX BIOG INDIA

S64

TINKER H.,"POLITICS IN SOUTHEAST ASIA." INT/ORG NAT/G CREATE PLAN TEC/DEV GUERRILLA KNOWL ORD/FREE COLD/WAR. PAGE 155 H3103 — S/ASIA ACT/RES REGION

N64

KENYA MINISTRY ECO PLAN DEV,AFRICAN SOCIALISM AND ITS APPLICATION TO PLANNING IN KENYA (PAMPHLET). AFR AGRI INDUS WORKER TAX COLONIAL WEALTH 20. PAGE 85 H1691 — NAT/G SOCISM PLAN ECO/UNDEV

B65

APPLEMAN P.,THE SILENT EXPLOSION. WOR+45 ECO/DEV ECO/UNDEV PLAN HEALTH ALL/IDEOS CATHISM...POLICY STAT RECORD GP/COMP IDEA/COMP NAT/COMP 20 BIRTH/CON COM/PARTY. PAGE 7 H0148 — GEOG CENSUS AGRI BIO/SOC

B65

CAMPBELL G.A.,THE CIVIL SERVICE IN BRITAIN (2ND ED.). UK DELIB/GP FORCES WORKER CREATE PLAN ...POLICY AUD/VIS 19/20 CIVIL/SERV. PAGE 26 H0515 — ADMIN LEGIS NAT/G FINAN

B65
CENTRAL GAZETTEERS UNIT,THE GAZETTEER OF INDIA (VOL. I). INDIA SOCIETY STRATA PLAN EDU/PROP NAT/LISM ORD/FREE WEALTH...GEOG LING CHARTS SOC/INTEG 20. PAGE 28 H0568
PRESS CULTURE SECT STRUCT

B65
DOLCI D.,A NEW WORLD IN THE MAKING. GHANA SENEGAL USSR YUGOSLAVIA CULTURE INT/ORG PLAN EDU/PROP GP/REL PEACE MORAL...GEOG SOC 20 COLD/WAR. PAGE 42 H0834
SOCIETY ALL/VALS DRIVE PERSON

B65
DUGGAR G.S.,RENEWAL OF TOWN AND VILLAGE I: A WORLD-WIDE SURVEY OF LOCAL GOVERNMENT EXPERIENCE. WOR+45 CONSTRUC INDUS CREATE BUDGET REGION GOV/REL...QU NAT/COMP 20 URBAN/RNWL. PAGE 43 H0859
MUNIC NEIGH PLAN ADMIN

B65
EDELMAN M.,THE POLITICS OF WAGE-PRICE DECISIONS. GERMANY ITALY NETHERLAND UK INDUS LABOR POL/PAR PROB/SOLV BARGAIN PRICE ROUTINE BAL/PAY COST DEMAND 20. PAGE 44 H0888
GOV/COMP CONTROL ECO/TAC PLAN

B65
EUROPEAN FREE TRADE ASSN,REGIONAL DEVELOPMENT POLICIES IN EFTA. ECO/UNDEV INT/ORG PLAN REGION ...POLICY GEOG EFTA. PAGE 48 H0950
EUR+WWI ECO/DEV NAT/COMP INT/TRADE

B65
FORM W.H.,INDUSTRIAL RELATIONS AND SOCIAL CHANGE IN LATIN AMERICA. L/A+17C AGRI LABOR NAT/G PLAN PROB/SOLV DIPLOM...MGT SOC ANTHOL BIBLIOG/A METH 20. PAGE 52 H1038
INDUS GP/REL NAT/COMP ECO/UNDEV

B65
GAJENDRAGADKAR P.B.,LAW, LIBERTY AND SOCIAL JUSTICE. INDIA CONSTN NAT/G SECT PLAN ECO/TAC PRESS POPULISM...SOC METH/COMP 20 HINDU. PAGE 54 H1086
ORD/FREE LAW ADJUD JURID

B65
GRETTON P.,MARITIME STRATEGY - A STUDY OF DEFENSE PROBLEMS. ASIA UK USSR DIPLOM COERCE DETER NUC/PWR WEAPON...CONCPT NAT/COMP 20. PAGE 60 H1211
FORCES PLAN WAR SEA

B65
HADWIGER D.F.,PRESSURES AND PROTEST. NAT/G LEGIS PLAN LEAD PARTIC ROUTINE ATTIT POLICY. PAGE 63 H1273
AGRI GP/REL LOBBY CHOOSE

B65
HART B.H.L.,THE MEMOIRS OF CAPTAIN LIDDELL HART (VOL. I). UK NAT/G PLAN TEC/DEV DIPLOM ADMIN WEAPON GOV/REL PERS/REL ATTIT PWR FASCISM...POLICY 20. PAGE 67 H1348
FORCES BIOG LEAD WAR

B65
HERBST J.,THE GERMAN HISTORICAL SCHOOL IN AMERICAN SCHOLARSHIP; A STUDY IN THE TRANSFER OF CULTURE. GERMANY USA+45 INTELL SOCIETY ACADEM PLAN ATTIT IDEA/COMP. PAGE 70 H1399
CULTURE NAT/COMP HIST/WRIT

B65
HONDURAS CONSEJO NAC DE ECO,PLAN NACIONAL DE DESARROLLO ECONOMICO Y SOCIAL DE HONDURAS 1965-69. HONDURAS AGRI INDUS BAL/PAY INCOME 20. PAGE 73 H1459
ECO/UNDEV NAT/G PLAN POLICY

B65
JASNY H.,KHRUSHCHEV'S CROP POLICY. USSR ECO/DEV PLAN MARXISM...STAT 20 KHRUSH/N RESOURCE/N. PAGE 80 H1593
AGRI NAT/G POLICY ECO/TAC

B65
MEAGHER R.F.,PUBLIC INTERNATIONAL DEVELOPMENT FINANCING IN SUDAN. SUDAN FINAN DELIB/GP GIVE ...CHARTS GOV/COMP 20. PAGE 108 H2155
FOR/AID PLAN RECEIVE ECO/UNDEV

B65
MEIER R.L.,DEVELOPMENTAL PLANNING. PUERT/RICO INDUS PUB/INST SCHOOL CREATE ECO/TAC FOR/AID...NAT/COMP 20. PAGE 108 H2165
PLAN ECO/UNDEV GOV/COMP TEC/DEV

B65
MERKL P.H.,GERMANY: YESTERDAY AND TOMORROW. GERMANY POL/PAR PLAN DIPLOM LEAD FEDERAL 19/20. PAGE 109 H2181
NAT/G FUT

B65
O'BRIEN F.,CRISIS IN WORLD COMMUNISM* MARXISM IN SEARCH OF EFFICIENCY. COM ECO/DEV PLAN INT/TRADE WAR ADJUST PEACE...STAT TIME/SEQ GOV/COMP NAT/COMP COLD/WAR. PAGE 119 H2384
MARXISM USSR DRIVE EFFICIENCY

B65
OECD,MEDITERRANEAN REGIONAL PROJECT: TURKEY; EDUCATION AND DEVELOPMENT. FUT TURKEY SOCIETY STRATA FINAN NAT/G PROF/ORG PLAN PROB/SOLV ADMIN COST...STAT CHARTS 20 OECD. PAGE 120 H2399
EDU/PROP ACADEM SCHOOL ECO/UNDEV

B65
OECD,THE MEDITERRANEAN REGIONAL PROJECT: ITALY; EDUCATION AND DEVELOPMENT. ITALY SOCIETY STRATA FINAN NAT/G PROF/ORG WORKER PLAN PROB/SOLV ADMIN ...STAT CHARTS METH 20 OECD. PAGE 120 H2400
SCHOOL EDU/PROP ECO/UNDEV ACADEM

B65
OECD,THE MEDITERRANEAN REGIONAL PROJECT: GREECE; EDUCATION AND DEVELOPMENT. FUT GREECE SOCIETY AGRI FINAN NAT/G PROF/ORG WORKER PLAN PROB/SOLV ADMIN DEMAND ATTIT 20 OECD. PAGE 120 H2401
EDU/PROP SCHOOL ACADEM ECO/UNDEV

B65
OECD,THE MEDITERRANEAN REGIONAL PROJECT: SPAIN; EDUCATION AND DEVELOPMENT. FUT SPAIN STRATA FINAN NAT/G WORKER PLAN PROB/SOLV ADMIN COST...POLICY STAT CHARTS 20 OECD. PAGE 120 H2402
ECO/UNDEV EDU/PROP ACADEM SCHOOL

B65
ONSLOW C.,ASIAN ECONOMIC DEVELOPMENT. BURMA CEYLON INDIA MALAYSIA PAKISTAN S/ASIA AGRI INDUS MARKET PROB/SOLV CAP/ISM FOR/AID INT/TRADE DEMAND WEALTH ...POLICY ANTHOL 20. PAGE 121 H2418
ECO/UNDEV ECO/TAC PLAN NAT/G

B65
ORG FOR ECO COOP AND DEVEL,THE MEDITERRANEAN REGIONAL PROJECT: AN EXPERIMENT IN PLANNING BY SIX COUNTRIES. FUT GREECE SPAIN TURKEY YUGOSLAVIA SOCIETY FINAN NAT/G PROF/ORG EDU/PROP ADMIN REGION COST...POLICY STAT CHARTS 20 OECD. PAGE 121 H2427
PLAN ECO/UNDEV ACADEM SCHOOL

B65
PARRIS H.W.,GOVERNMENT AND THE RAILWAYS IN NINETEENTH-CENTURY BRITAIN. UK DELIB/GP CONTROL LEAD CENTRAL 19 RAILROAD. PAGE 124 H2470
DIST/IND NAT/G PLAN GP/REL

B65
RANDALL F.B.,STALIN'S RUSSIA. USSR STRUCT AGRI NAT/G PLAN DIPLOM WAR TOTALISM MARXISM...BIBLIOG/A 19/20 STALIN/J. PAGE 129 H2590
BIOG INDUS ECO/DEV

B65
SCHULER E.A.,THE PAKISTAN ACADEMIES FOR RURAL DEVELOPMENT COMILLA AND PESHAWAR 1959-1964. PAKISTAN S/ASIA SOCIETY STRUCT AGRI NAT/G TEC/DEV EDU/PROP 20. PAGE 140 H2801
BIBLIOG PLAN ECO/TAC ECO/UNDEV

B65
SHARMA S.A.,PARLIAMENTARY GOVERNMENT IN INDIA. INDIA FINAN LOC/G PROVS DELIB/GP PLAN ADMIN CT/SYS FEDERAL...JURID 20. PAGE 142 H2849
NAT/G CONSTN PARL/PROC LEGIS

B65
SIMMS R.P.,URBANIZATION IN WEST AFRICA; A REVIEW OF CURRENT LITERATURE. AFR PLAN TEC/DEV...SOC OBS NAT/COMP 20. PAGE 144 H2878
BIBLIOG/A MUNIC ECO/DEV ECO/UNDEV

B65
UN,SPACE ACTIVITIES AND RESOURCES: REVIEW OF UNITED NATION'S NATIONAL AND INTERNATIONAL PROGRAMS. INT/ORG LABOR PLAN TEC/DEV DIPLOM EFFICIENCY HEALTH ...GOV/COMP 20 UN. PAGE 158 H3155
SPACE NUC/PWR FOR/AID PEACE

B65
VERMOT-GAUCHY M.,L'EDUCATION NATIONALE DANS LA FRANCE DE 1975. FRANCE FUT CULTURE ELITES R+D SCHOOL PLAN EDU/PROP EFFICIENCY...POLICY PREDICT CHARTS INDEX 20. PAGE 162 H3245
ACADEM CREATE TREND INTELL

B65
WALKER A.A.,THE RHODESIAS AND NYASALAND: A GUIDE TO OFFICIAL PUBLICATIONS. RHODESIA UK OP/RES PLAN PROB/SOLV DIPLOM...POLICY SOC CON/ANAL 19/20 NYASALAND. PAGE 164 H3291
BIBLIOG NAT/G COLONIAL AFR

B65
WARD W.E.,GOVERNMENT IN WEST AFRICA. WOR+45 POL/PAR EX/STRUC PLAN PARTIC GP/REL SOVEREIGN 20 AFRICA/W. PAGE 165 H3308
GOV/COMP CONSTN COLONIAL ECO/UNDEV

S65
GRIFFITH S.B.,"COMMUNIST CHINA'S CAPACITY TO MAKE WAR." CHINA/COM COM NAT/G TOP/EX PLAN DOMIN COERCE NUC/PWR ATTIT RESPECT SKILL...CONCPT MYTH TIME/SEQ TREND COLD/WAR 20. PAGE 61 H1221
FORCES PWR WEAPON ASIA

S65
KEE W.S.,"CENTRAL CITY EXPENDITURES AND METROPOLITAN AREAS." PLAN BUDGET ECO/TAC TAX GP/REL WEALTH...CHARTS 20. PAGE 84 H1677
LOC/G MUNIC GOV/COMP NEIGH

S65
PRABHAKAR P.,"SURVEY OF RESEARCH AND SOURCE MATERIALS; THE SINO-INDIAN BORDER DISPUTE." CHINA/COM INDIA LAW NAT/G PLAN BAL/PWR WAR...POLICY 20 COLD/WAR. PAGE 128 H2553
BIBLIOG ASIA S/ASIA DIPLOM

S65
SPAAK P.H.,"THE SEARCH FOR CONSENSUS: A NEW EFFORT TO BUILD EUROPE." FRANCE GERMANY ECO/DEV NAT/G CONSULT FORCES PLAN EDU/PROP REGION CONSEN ATTIT ...SOC METH/CNCPT OBS TREND EEC NATO WORK 20. PAGE 147 H2941
EUR+WWI INT/ORG

S65
TABORSKY E.,"CHANGE IN CZECHOSLOVAKIA." COM USSR ELITES INTELL AGRI INDUS NAT/G DELIB/GP EX/STRUC ECO/TAC TOTALISM ATTIT RIGID/FLEX SOCISM...MGT CONCPT TREND 20. PAGE 152 H3031
ECO/DEV PLAN CZECHOSLVK

S65
VAN DEN BERG M.,"SOME METHODOLOGICAL ASPECTS OF SOUTH AFRICA'S FIRST E.D.P." SOUTH/AFR NAT/G CREATE TEC/DEV CAP/ISM INCOME PRODUC...CON/ANAL CHARTS 20. PAGE 161 H3226
ECO/DEV PLAN METH STAT

N65
MOTE M.E.,SOVIET LOCAL AND REPUBLIC ELECTIONS. COM
CHOOSE

USSR NAT/G PLAN PARTIC GOV/REL TOTALISM PWR ...CHARTS 20. PAGE 114 H2270
ADMIN CONTROL LOC/G

B66
AMER ENTERPRISE INST PUB POL,SIGNIFICANT ISSUES IN ECONOMIC AID TO DEVELOPING COUNTRIES. FINAN INT/ORG NAT/G PLAN PROB/SOLV GIVE TASK WEALTH...DECISION 20. PAGE 6 H0119
ECO/UNDEV FOR/AID DIPLOM POLICY

B66
ASHRAF A.,THE CITY GOVERNMENT OF CALCUTTA: A STUDY OF INERTIA. INDIA ELITES INDUS NAT/G EX/STRUC ACT/RES PLAN PROB/SOLV LEAD HABITAT...BIBLIOG 20 CALCUTTA. PAGE 9 H0175
LOC/G MUNIC ADMIN ECO/UNDEV

B66
BIRMINGHAM W.,A STUDY OF CONTEMPORARY GHANA VOL I: THE ECONOMY OF GHANA. AFR GHANA PLAN...POLICY STAT CHARTS ANTHOL BIBLIOG 20. PAGE 17 H0342
ECO/UNDEV ECO/TAC NAT/G PRODUC

B66
BRODERSEN A.,THE SOVIET WORKER: LABOR AND GOVERNMENT IN SOVIET SOCIETY. USSR STRUCT INDUS LABOR PLAN PAY INGP/REL PRODUC...POLICY GEN/LAWS BIBLIOG 20 STALIN/J LENIN/VI BOLSHEVISM KHRUSH/N. PAGE 21 H0425
WORKER ROLE NAT/G MARXISM

B66
BROWN L.C.,STATE AND SOCIETY IN INDEPENDENT NORTH AFRICA. ALGERIA LIBYA MOROCCO AGRI INDUS INT/ORG POL/PAR SECT PLAN DIPLOM COLONIAL...LING NAT/COMP ANTHOL BIBLIOG 20 TUNIS MUSLIM. PAGE 22 H0446
NAT/G SOCIETY CULTURE ECO/UNDEV

B66
COLE A.B.,SOCIALIST PARTIES IN POSTWAR JAPAN. STRATA AGRI LABOR PLAN DIPLOM ECO/TAC AGREE LEAD CHOOSE ATTIT...CHARTS 20 CHINJAP SOC/DEMPAR. PAGE 31 H0620
POL/PAR POLICY SOCISM NAT/G

B66
DAENIKER G.,STRATEGIE DES KLEIN STAATS. SWITZERLND ACT/RES CREATE DIPLOM NEUTRAL DETER WAR WEAPON PWR SOVEREIGN...IDEA/COMP 20 COLD/WAR. PAGE 36 H0730
NUC/PWR PLAN FORCES NAT/G

B66
DOBB M.,SOVIET ECONOMIC DEVELOPMENT SINCE 1917. USSR ECO/DEV ECO/UNDEV LABOR NAT/G TEC/DEV ECO/TAC ROUTINE PRODUC MARXISM 20. PAGE 41 H0829
PLAN INDUS WORKER

B66
FOX K.A.,THE THEORY OF QUANTITATIVE ECONOMIC POLICY WITH APPLICATIONS TO ECONOMIC GROWTH AND STABILIZATION. ECO/DEV AGRI NAT/G PLAN ADMIN RISK ...DECISION IDEA/COMP SIMUL T. PAGE 52 H1045
ECO/TAC ECOMETRIC EQUILIB GEN/LAWS

B66
GLAZER M.,THE FEDERAL GOVERNMENT AND THE UNIVERSITY. CHILE PROB/SOLV DIPLOM GIVE ADMIN WAR ...POLICY SOC 20. PAGE 57 H1140
BIBLIOG/A NAT/G PLAN ACADEM

B66
GRAHAM B.D.,THE FORMATION OF THE AUSTRALIAN COUNTRY PARTIES. CANADA USA+45 USA-45 SOCIETY PLAN ECO/TAC ...NAT/COMP 20 AUSTRAL. PAGE 59 H1190
POL/PAR AGRI REGION PARL/PROC

B66
HACKETT J.,L'ECONOMIE BRITANNIQUE: PROBLEMES ET PERSPECTIVES. FRANCE UK LABOR MUNIC NAT/G EX/STRUC PROB/SOLV BAL/PAY INCOME RIGID/FLEX...MGT PHIL/SCI CHARTS 20. PAGE 63 H1271
ECO/DEV FINAN ECO/TAC PLAN

B66
HANSON J.W.,EDUCATION AND THE DEVELOPMENT OF NATIONS. DIPLOM TASK ADJUST EFFICIENCY...POLICY ANTHOL 20. PAGE 66 H1322
ECO/UNDEV EDU/PROP NAT/G PLAN

B66
IOWA STATE U CTR AGRI AND ECO,RESEARCH AND EDUCATION FOR REGIONAL AND AREA DEVELOPMENT. FUT LAW CULTURE R+D LOC/G PLAN KNOWL...POLICY CHARTS ANTHOL 20. PAGE 78 H1565
REGION ACT/RES ECO/TAC INDUS

B66
JOHNSON N.,PARLIAMENT AND ADMINISTRATION: THE ESTIMATES COMMITTEE 1945-65. FUT UK NAT/G EX/STRUC PLAN BUDGET ORD/FREE...T 20 PARLIAMENT HOUSE/CMNS. PAGE 81 H1625
LEGIS ADMIN FINAN DELIB/GP

B66
KIRDAR U.,THE STRUCTURE OF UNITED NATIONS ECONOMIC AID TO UNDERDEVELOPED COUNTRIES. AGRI FINAN INDUS NAT/G EX/STRUC PLAN GIVE TASK...POLICY 20 UN. PAGE 86 H1721
INT/ORG FOR/AID ECO/UNDEV ADMIN

B66
KIRKENDALL R.S.,SOCIAL SCIENTISTS AND FARM POLITICS IN THE AGE OF ROOSEVELT. ACADEM PLAN ECO/TAC GIVE ADMIN CONTROL PRODUC...SOC 20 NEW/DEAL ROOSEVLT/F BURAGR/ECO. PAGE 86 H1722
AGRI INTELL POLICY NAT/G

B66
KOMIYA R.,POSTWAR ECONOMIC GROWTH IN JAPAN. ELITES NAT/G EX/STRUC TEC/DEV BUDGET DIPLOM CONTROL BAL/PAY PRODUC...BIBLIOG 20 CHINJAP. PAGE 88 H1754
ECO/DEV POLICY PLAN ADJUST

B66
MAC DONALD H.M.,THE INTELLECTUAL IN POLITICS. GERMANY PERU SWEDEN UK USSR NAT/G CONSULT PLAN EDU/PROP TASK INGP/REL EFFICIENCY RATIONAL ALL/VALS 20. PAGE 99 H1987
ALL/IDEOS INTELL POL/PAR PARTIC

B66
MADAN G.R.,ECONOMIC THINKING IN INDIA. INDIA ECO/UNDEV AGRI FINAN INDUS LABOR PLAN CAP/ISM INT/TRADE MARXISM SOCISM...POLICY 1/20. PAGE 101 H2013
ECO/TAC PHIL/SCI NAT/G POL/PAR

B66
MASON E.S.,ECONOMIC DEVELOPMENT IN INDIA AND PAKISTAN. INDIA PAKISTAN AGRI FINAN PLAN BUDGET INT/TRADE WEALTH...POLICY STAT TREND CHARTS 20. PAGE 104 H2086
NAT/COMP ECO/UNDEV ECO/TAC FOR/AID

B66
NAMBOODIRIPAD E.M.,ECONOMICS AND POLITICS OF INDIA'S SOCIALIST PATTERN. INDIA STRATA AGRI INDUS NAT/G PRICE ORD/FREE SOVEREIGN 20. PAGE 115 H2307
ECO/UNDEV PLAN SOCISM CAP/ISM

B66
OECD DEVELOPMENT CENTRE,CATALOGUE OF SOCIAL AND ECONOMIC DEVELOPMENT INSTITUTES AND PROGRAMMES* RESEARCH. ACT/RES PLAN TEC/DEV EDU/PROP...SOC GP/COMP NAT/COMP. PAGE 120 H2403
ECO/UNDEV ECO/DEV R+D ACADEM

B66
PLATE H.,PARTEIFINANZIERUNG UND GRUNDESETZ. GERMANY NAT/G PLAN GIVE PAY INCOME WEALTH...JURID 20. PAGE 126 H2522
POL/PAR CONSTN FINAN

B66
SAINDERICHIN P.,HISTORIE SECRETE D'UNE ELECTION, DECEMBER 5-19, 1965. FRANCE NAT/G DELIB/GP LEGIS PLAN EDU/PROP TV SOCISM...MARXIST 20 DEGAULLE/C. PAGE 137 H2731
CHOOSE CHIEF PROB/SOLV POL/PAR

B66
SMITH H.E.,READINGS IN ECONOMIC DEVELOPMENT AND ADMINISTRATION IN TANZANIA. TANZANIA FINAN INDUS LABOR NAT/G PLAN PROB/SOLV INT/TRADE COLONIAL REGION...ANTHOL BIBLIOG 20 AFRICA/E. PAGE 146 H2910
TEC/DEV ADMIN GOV/REL

B66
SPULBER N.,THE STATE AND ECONOMIC DEVELOPMENT IN EASTERN EUROPE. BULGARIA COM CZECHOSLVK HUNGARY POLAND YUGOSLAVIA CULTURE PLAN CAP/ISM INT/TRADE CONTROL...POLICY CHARTS METH/COMP BIBLIOG/A 19/20. PAGE 148 H2958
ECO/DEV ECO/UNDEV NAT/G TOTALISM

B66
STADLER K.R.,THE BIRTH OF THE AUSTRIAN REPUBLIC, 1918-1921. AUSTRIA PLAN TASK PEACE...POLICY DECISION 20. PAGE 148 H2966
NAT/G DIPLOM WAR DELIB/GP

B66
WEINSTEIN B.,GABON: NATION-BUILDING ON THE OGOOUE. AFR GABON WOR+45 CULTURE SOCIETY PLAN DIPLOM COLONIAL INGP/REL ANOMIE HABITAT SUPEGO 20. PAGE 166 H3329
ECO/UNDEV GP/REL LEAD NAT/G

S66
"FURTHER READING." INDIA LOC/G NAT/G PLAN ADMIN WEALTH...GEOG SOC CONCPT CENSUS 20. PAGE 2 H0049
BIBLIOG ECO/UNDEV TEC/DEV PROVS

S66
ADAMS T.W.,"THE FIRST REPUBLIC OF CYPRUS: A REVIEW OF AN UNWORKABLE CONSTITUTION." CYPRUS FUT PLAN NAT/LISM POPULISM 20. PAGE 3 H0067
CONSTN NAT/G PROB/SOLV

S66
MALENBAUM W.,"GOVERNMENT, ENTREPRENEURSHIP, AND ECONOMIC GROWTH IN POOR LANDS." ELITES ECO/UNDEV INDUS CREATE DRIVE. PAGE 101 H2028
ECO/TAC PLAN CONSERVE NAT/G

B67
ANDERSON C.W.,POLITICS AND ECONOMIC CHANGE IN LATIN AMERICA. L/A+17C INDUS NAT/G OP/RES ADMIN DEMAND ...POLICY STAT CHARTS NAT/COMP 20. PAGE 6 H0125
ECO/UNDEV PROB/SOLV PLAN ECO/TAC

B67
BADGLEY R.F.,DOCTORS' STRIKE; MEDICAL CARE AND CONFLICT IN SASKATCHEWAN. CANADA NAT/G PROF/ORG GP/REL ADJUST ATTIT...HEAL SOC 20. PAGE 10 H0192
HEALTH PLAN LABOR BARGAIN

B67
CARTER G.M.,SOUTH AFRICA'S TRANSKEI: THE POLITICS OF DOMESTIC COLONIALISM. SOUTH/AFR ECO/UNDEV AGRI NAT/G PROVS PLAN DOMIN REPRESENT ADJUST DISCRIM ...OBS BIBLIOG 20 BANTUSTANS TRANSKEI. PAGE 27 H0550
STRATA GOV/REL COLONIAL POLICY

B67
CHANDRASEKHAR S.,ASIA'S POPULATION PROBLEMS. ASIA ECO/UNDEV PLAN AGE/C...OBS CHARTS BIBLIOG 18/20 AUSTRAL. PAGE 29 H0575
PROB/SOLV NAT/COMP GEOG TREND

B67
COWLES M.,PERSPECTIVES IN THE EDUCATION OF DISADVANTAGED CHILDREN. CULTURE OP/RES PLAN PERS/REL ADJUST HABITAT PERCEPT KNOWL WEALTH ...SOC/WK IDEA/COMP ANTHOL 20. PAGE 34 H0686
EDU/PROP AGE/C TEC/DEV SCHOOL

B67
GILL R.T.,ECONOMIC DEVELOPMENT: PAST AND PRESENT (2ND ED.). ASIA INDIA USA+45 USA-45 WOR+45 WOR-45 DEMAND EFFICIENCY NAT/LISM WEALTH...GOV/COMP
ECO/DEV ECO/UNDEV PLAN

METH/COMP 18/20. PAGE 56 H1127 — PROB/SOLV

B67
GROSS B.M.,ACTION UNDER PLANNING: THE GUIDANCE OF ECONOMIC DEVELOPMENT. STRUCT R+D NAT/G ACT/RES HABITAT...DECISION 20. PAGE 62 H1232 — ECO/UNDEV PLAN ADMIN MGT

B67
HILSMAN R.,TO MOVE A NATION: THE POLITICS OF FOREIGN POLICY IN THE ADMINISTRATION OF JOHN F. KENNEDY. CHINA/COM COM USSR VIETNAM NAT/G DELIB/GP FORCES PLAN PROB/SOLV BAL/PWR COLONIAL EXEC REV PWR 20 KENNEDY/JF PRESIDENT. PAGE 71 H1418 — CHIEF DIPLOM

B67
HOLLERMAN L.,JAPAN'S DEPENDENCE ON THE WORLD ECONOMY. INDUS MARKET LABOR NAT/G DIPLOM 20 CHINJAP. PAGE 73 H1457 — PLAN ECO/DEV ECO/TAC INT/TRADE

B67
JOUVENEL B D.E.,THE ART OF CONJECTURE. FUT CONSULT EX/STRUC CHOOSE GOV/REL ALL/VALS. PAGE 82 H1638 — PREDICT DELIB/GP PLAN NAT/G

B67
MEHDI M.T.,PEACE IN THE MIDDLE EAST. ISRAEL SOCIETY NAT/G PLAN EDU/PROP NAT/LISM DRIVE...IDEA/COMP 20 JEWS. PAGE 108 H2160 — ISLAM DIPLOM GP/REL COERCE

B67
MOORE J.R.,THE ECONOMIC IMPACT OF THE TVA. AGRI INDUS PLAN BARGAIN CONTROL REGION GOV/REL DEMAND EFFICIENCY SOCISM 20 TVA. PAGE 112 H2249 — ECO/UNDEV ECO/DEV NAT/G CREATE

B67
NESS G.D.,BUREAUCRACY AND RURAL DEVELOPMENT IN MALAYSIA. MALAYSIA UK SOCIETY FINAN INDUS WORKER TEC/DEV ECO/TAC COLONIAL EQUILIB ORD/FREE...STAT CHARTS 20. PAGE 117 H2330 — ECO/UNDEV PLAN NAT/G ADMIN

B67
OPERATIONS AND POLICY RESEARCH,NICARAGUA: ELECTION FACTBOOK: FEBRUARY 5, 1967 (PAMPHLET). NICARAGUA LAW NAT/G LEAD REPRESENT...STAT BIOG CHARTS 20. PAGE 121 H2423 — POL/PAR CHOOSE PLAN ATTIT

B67
PAPANEK G.F.,PAKISTAN'S DEVELOPMENT: SOCIAL GOALS AND PRIVATE INCENTIVES. PAKISTAN INDUS NAT/G PROB/SOLV CONTROL EFFICIENCY SOCISM...CHARTS 20. PAGE 123 H2463 — ECO/UNDEV PLAN CAP/ISM ECO/TAC

B67
PLANCK C.R.,THE CHANGING STATUS OF GERMAN REUNIFICATION IN WESTERN DIPLOMACY, 1955-1966. GERMANY DELIB/GP PLAN PEACE...TREND 20 KENNEDY/JF DEGAULLE/C. PAGE 126 H2519 — NAT/G DIPLOM CENTRAL

B67
PLISCHKE E.,CONDUCT OF AMERICAN DIPLOMACY (3RD REV. ED.). INT/ORG NAT/G PROB/SOLV FOR/AID...CHARTS BIBLIOG T 20 DEPT/STATE. PAGE 126 H2529 — DIPLOM RATIONAL PLAN

B67
POSNER M.V.,ITALIAN PUBLIC ENTERPRISE. ITALY ECO/DEV FINAN INDUS CREATE ECO/TAC ADMIN CONTROL EFFICIENCY PRODUC...TREND CHARTS 20. PAGE 127 H2545 — NAT/G PLAN CAP/ISM SOCISM

B67
ROSENBLUTH G.,THE CANADIAN ECONOMY AND DISARMAMENT. CANADA FUT ECO/DEV INDUS R+D DELIB/GP DIPLOM ECO/TAC CIVMIL/REL PEACE...POLICY BIBLIOG PACIFIST 20. PAGE 134 H2679 — ARMS/CONT STAT PLAN NAT/G

B67
ROSENTHAL A.H.,THE SOCIAL PROGRAMS OF SWEDEN. SWEDEN USA+45 FINAN NAT/G PLAN PROB/SOLV INSPECT ORD/FREE...POLICY HEAL SOC CHARTS NAT/COMP 20. PAGE 134 H2681 — GIVE SOC/WK WEALTH METH/COMP

B67
SCHUTZ W.W.,RETHINKING GERMAN POLICY; NEW APPROACHES TO REUNIFICATION. GERMANY USSR PLAN CONFER...POLICY 20. PAGE 140 H2806 — REGION NAT/G DIPLOM PROB/SOLV

B67
SHAPIRO P.S.,COMMUNICATIONS OR TRANSPORT: DECISION-MAKING IN DEVELOPING COUNTRIES. WOR+45 NAT/G PLAN ALL/IDEOS MARXISM...NAT/COMP GEN/LAWS. PAGE 142 H2844 — BUDGET COM/IND DECISION ECO/DEV

B67
THOMAN R.S.,GEOGRAPHY OF INTERNATIONAL TRADE. WOR+45 ECO/DEV ECO/UNDEV INT/ORG LG/CO PLAN BAL/PAY ...STAT CHARTS NAT/COMP 20. PAGE 154 H3075 — INT/TRADE GEOG ECO/TAC DIPLOM

B67
TREADGOLD D.W.,SOVIET AND CHINESE COMMUNISM* SIMILARITIES AND DIFFERENCES. CHINA/COM COM NAT/G PLAN DIPLOM CENTRAL PWR MARXISM...POLICY 20. PAGE 156 H3128 — CULTURE NAT/LISM

B67
VALI F.A.,THE QUEST FOR A UNITED GERMANY. GERMANY PROB/SOLV DIPLOM ADJUST...BIBLIOG 20. PAGE 161 H3222 — NAT/G ATTIT PLAN CENTRAL

B67
WOODRUFF W.,IMPACT OF WESTERN MAN. ECO/DEV INDUS CREATE PLAN PROB/SOLV COLONIAL GOV/REL...CHARTS GOV/COMP BIBLIOG 18/20. PAGE 170 H3407 — EUR+WWI MOD/EUR CAP/ISM

B67
ZALESKI E.,PLANNING REFORMS IN THE SOVIET UNION 1962-1966. COM USSR NAT/G CONFER CONTROL EFFICIENCY MARXISM...POLICY DECISION 20. PAGE 172 H3446 — ECO/DEV PLAN ADMIN CENTRAL

L67
BERNSTEIN T.P.,"LEADERSHIP AND MASS MOBILIZATION IN THE SOVIET AND CHINESE COLLECTIVISATION CAMPAIGNS OF 1929-30, 1955-56: COMPARISON." CHINA/COM USSR WORKER CONTROL COERCE PRODUC ATTIT...NAT/COMP 20. PAGE 16 H0317 — FEDERAL PLAN AGRI NAT/G

L67
CRIBBET J.E.,"SOME REFLECTIONS ON THE LAW OF LAND - A VIEW FROM SCANDINAVIA." DENMARK NETHERLAND NORWAY SWEDEN INDUS MUNIC NEIGH RACE/REL ATTIT HABITAT ...IDEA/COMP 20. PAGE 35 H0701 — LAW PLAN CONTROL NAT/G

L67
RUTH J.M.,"THE ADMINISTRATION OF WATER RESOURCES IN GUATEMALA." GUATEMALA L/A+17C DIST/IND LOC/G NAT/G EX/STRUC ADMIN GOV/REL DEMAND EQUILIB WEALTH...GEOG MGT 20. PAGE 136 H2723 — EFFICIENCY ECO/UNDEV PLAN ACT/RES

L67
TABORSKY E.,"THE COMMUNIST PARTIES OF THE 'THIRD WORLD' IN SOVIET STRATEGY." AFR ASIA L/A+17C USSR INTELL NAT/G WORKER PLAN CONTROL LEAD PARTIC REV ...GOV/COMP 20 COM/PARTY THIRD/WRLD. PAGE 152 H3032 — POL/PAR MARXISM ECO/UNDEV DIPLOM

S67
"PROTEST AGAINST SOVIET INDUSTRIALIZATION ILLS IN LITHUANIA* A MEMORANDUM." USSR LITHUANIA NAT/G PROVS COST GEOG. PAGE 2 H0050 — INDUS COLONIAL NAT/LISM PLAN

S67
ABDEL-MALEK A.,"THE CRISIS IN NASSER'S EGYPT." ISLAM UAR STRUCT POL/PAR EX/STRUC CREATE PLAN WAR ATTIT ORD/FREE PWR...POLICY DECISION 20. PAGE 3 H0054 — FORCES LEAD PROB/SOLV NAT/G

S67
BAER W.,"THE INFLATION CONTROVERSY IN LATIN AMERICA: SURVEY." L/A+17C ECO/UNDEV AGRI FINAN INDUS PLAN PROB/SOLV TEC/DEV...BIBLIOG/A 20. PAGE 10 H0194 — NAT/G BAL/PAY ECO/TAC BUDGET

S67
BELLER I.,"ECONOMIC POLICY AND THE DEMANDS OF LABOR." PLAN TAX GIVE PRICE WAR COST PRODUC WEALTH. PAGE 13 H0268 — NAT/G ECO/TAC SOC/WK INCOME

S67
BRANCO R.,"LAND REFORM* THE ANSWER TO LATIN AMERICA'S AGRICULTURAL DEVELOPMENT?" L/A+17C NAT/G PLAN TEC/DEV BUDGET RENT EFFICIENCY 20. PAGE 20 H0404 — ECO/UNDEV AGRI TAX OWN

S67
BUTTINGER J.,"VIETNAM* FRAUD OF THE 'OTHER WAR'." VIETNAM/S ELITES STRUCT AGRI NAT/G FOR/AID RENT TREND. PAGE 25 H0499 — PLAN WEALTH REV ECO/UNDEV

S67
CHU-YUAN CHENG,"THE CULTURAL REVOLUTION AND CHINA'S ECONOMY." CHINA/COM AGRI DIST/IND INDUS MARKET NAT/G WORKER PLAN INT/TRADE DOMIN DEMAND PRODUC ...CHARTS 20 MAO. PAGE 30 H0600 — ECO/DEV ECO/TAC REV SOCISM

S67
DERRICK P.,"THE WHITE PAPER ON INCOMES." EUR+WWI UK LAW LABOR NAT/G PLAN PROB/SOLV GP/REL...GOV/COMP PARLIAMENT. PAGE 40 H0794 — INCOME POL/PAR POLICY

S67
DESHPANDE A.M.,"FEDERAL-STATE FISCAL RELATIONS IN INDIA" (REVIEW ARTICLE)" GERMANY USSR DELIB/GP PLAN BUDGET ECO/TAC INCOME 20 SOC/DEMPAR SOC/REVPAR. PAGE 40 H0795 — FINAN NAT/G GOV/REL TAX

S67
DIAMANT A.,"EUROPEAN MODELS OF BUREAUCRACY AND DEVELOPMENT." EX/STRUC PLAN ADMIN CONTROL ROUTINE GOV/REL CENTRAL...DECISION TIME/SEQ CHARTS. PAGE 41 H0818 — NAT/G EQUILIB ACT/RES NAT/COMP

S67
GLOBERSON A.,"SOCIAL GROWTH IN THE DEVELOPING COUNTRIES." CULTURE SOCIETY CONSULT PROB/SOLV SOC. PAGE 57 H1144 — ECO/UNDEV FOR/AID EDU/PROP PLAN

S67
GREGORY R.,"THE MINISTER'S LINE: OR, THE M4 COMES TO BERKSHIRE. PART I." UK CONSTN DIST/IND LEGIS TOP/EX PLAN ADJUD...GEOG 20. PAGE 60 H1210 — DECISION CONSTRUC NAT/G DELIB/GP

S67
HARBRON J.D.,"UNIFICATION IN CANADA: FAIT ACCOMPLI" CANADA STRATA NAT/G DELIB/GP BUDGET GP/REL 20 NAVY. PAGE 66 H1327 — INGP/REL FORCES PLAN ATTIT

S67
HASSAN M.F.,"THE SECOND FOUR-YEAR PLAN OF — ECO/UNDEV

VENEZUELA." L/A+17C VENEZUELA AGRI INDUS NAT/G PLAN RATION CONTROL HABITAT...MATH STAT 20. PAGE 67 H1352 — FINAN BUDGET PROB/SOLV

S67
LEVCIK B.,"WAGES AND EMPLOYMENT PROBLEMS IN THE NEW SYSTEM OF PLANNED MANAGEMENT IN CZECHOSLOVAKIA." CZECHOSLVK EUR+WWI NAT/G OP/RES PLAN ADMIN ROUTINE INGP/REL CENTRAL EFFICIENCY PRODUC DECISION. PAGE 95 H1895 — MARXISM WORKER MGT PAY

S67
LICHFIELD N.,"THE EVALUATION OF CAPITAL INVESTMENT PROJECTS IN TOWN CENTRE REDEVELOPMENT." UK CONSTRUC MUNIC CONSULT COST...METH/CNCPT IDEA/COMP 20. PAGE 96 H1923 — PLAN ECO/TAC NAT/G DECISION

S67
LOFCHIE M.F.,"OKELLO'S REVOLUTION." TANZANIA NAT/G POL/PAR FORCES PLAN CONTROL 20. PAGE 98 H1954 — AFR REV LEAD CHIEF

S67
NUGENT J.B.,"ECONOMIC THOUGHT, INVESTMENT CRITERIA, AND DEVELOPMENT STRATEGIES IN GREECE* A POSTWAR SURVEY." GREECE AGRI INDUS INT/ORG NAT/G OP/RES DEMAND OPTIMAL PRODUC WEALTH 20 EEC. PAGE 119 H2379 — ECO/UNDEV PLAN FINAN

S67
PAI G.A.,"TAXATION AND PLANNING IN INDIA: A BIRDS-EYE VIEW." INDIA ELITES NAT/G LEGIS BUDGET CONTROL LOBBY INCOME...STAT CHARTS 20. PAGE 122 H2443 — TAX PLAN WEALTH STRATA

S67
PERKINS D.H.,"ECONOMIC GROWTH IN CHINA AND THE CULTURAL REVOLUTION(1960APRIL 1967)" CHINA/COM FUT AGRI INDUS PLAN LEAD MARXISM...CHARTS 20 MAO. PAGE 125 H2493 — ECO/TAC CULTURE REV ECO/UNDEV

S67
PLUMPTRE A.F.W.,"PERSPECTIVE ON OUR AID TO OTHERS." CANADA CREATE 20. PAGE 127 H2530 — FOR/AID DIPLOM NAT/G PLAN

S67
RENFIELD R.L.,"A POLICY FOR VIETNAM." COM VIETNAM NAT/G POL/PAR VOL/ASSN CHIEF DIPLOM EDU/PROP DETER REPRESENT ATTIT ORD/FREE 20. PAGE 131 H2615 — WAR POLICY PLAN COERCE

S67
RICHMAN B.M.,"CAPITALISTS & MANAGERS IN COMMUNIST CHINA." ASIA CHINA/COM ECO/UNDEV NAT/G CONSULT EX/STRUC PLAN EFFICIENCY PRODUC WEALTH MARXISM ...MGT CHARTS 20. PAGE 131 H2623 — CAP/ISM INDUS

S67
RONNING C.,"NANKING: 1950." ASIA CANADA CHINA/COM NAT/G PLAN ECO/TAC REV ADJUST 20. PAGE 133 H2667 — DIPLOM ROLE PEACE

S67
SINGH B.,"ITALIAN EXPERIENCE IN REGIONAL ECONOMIC DEVELOPMENT AND LESSONS FOR OTHER COUNTRIES." EUR+WWI ITALY INDUS NAT/G ACT/RES REGION GP/REL EFFICIENCY EQUILIB PRODUC WEALTH. PAGE 144 H2884 — ECO/UNDEV PLAN ECO/TAC CONTROL

S67
SLOAN P.,"FIFTY YEARS OF SOVIET RULE." USSR INDUS EDU/PROP EFFICIENCY PRODUC HEALTH KNOWL MORAL WEALTH MARXISM...POLICY 20. PAGE 145 H2900 — CREATE NAT/G PLAN INSPECT

S67
SMITH J.E.,"RED PRUSSIANISM OF THE GERMAN DEMOCRATIC REPUBLIC." GERMANY/E INTELL TOP/EX WORKER PLAN DIPLOM PRODUC ATTIT WEALTH MARXISM. PAGE 146 H2912 — NAT/G TOTALISM INDUS NAT/LISM

S67
TIVEY L.,"THE POLITICAL CONSEQUENCES OF ECONOMIC PLANNING." UK CONSTN INDUS ACT/RES ADMIN CONTROL LOBBY REPRESENT EFFICIENCY SUPEGO SOVEREIGN ...DECISION 20. PAGE 155 H3108 — PLAN POLICY NAT/G

S67
WILPERT C.,"A LOOK IN THE MIRROR AND OVER THE WALL." GERMANY POL/PAR...KNO/TEST COLD/WAR. PAGE 169 H3378 — NAT/G PLAN DIPLOM ATTIT

N67
US HOUSE COMM SCI ASTRONAUT,GOVERNMENT, SCIENCE, AND INTERNATIONAL POLICY (PAMPHLET). INDIA NETHERLAND ECO/DEV ECO/UNDEV R+D ACADEM PLAN DIPLOM FOR/AID CONFER...PREDICT 20 CHINJAP. PAGE 160 H3198 — NAT/G POLICY CREATE TEC/DEV

S68
CHAPMAN A.R.,"THE CIVIL WAR IN NIGERIA." AFR NIGERIA NAT/G PLAN ECO/TAC EDU/PROP COERCE WAR GOV/REL INGP/REL ORD/FREE PWR WEALTH SOC/INTEG 20 BIAFRA. PAGE 29 H0579 — REV RACE/REL

S68
GUZZARDI W.,"THE DECLINE OF THE STERLING CLUB." UK WOR+45 NAT/G PLAN DIPLOM INT/TRADE AGREE CONSEN EQUILIB SOVEREIGN...POLICY NEW/IDEA 20 COMMONWLTH GOLD/STAND. PAGE 63 H1259 — FINAN ECO/TAC WEALTH NAT/COMP

PLAN/UNIT....PLANNED UNIT DEVELOPMENT

PLANCK C.R. H2519

PLANK J.N. H2520,H2521

PLATE H. H2522

PLATO H2523

PLATO....PLATO

C52
HUME D.,"IDEA OF A PERFECT COMMONWEALTH" IN D. HUME, POLITICAL DISCOURSES (1752)" UK NAT/G DOMIN GP/REL CONSERVE...POLICY CONCPT GEN/LAWS 18 MORE/THOM PLATO. PAGE 75 H1494 — CONSTN CHIEF SOCIETY GOV/COMP

PLAYFAIR G. H2524

PLAYFAIR R.L. H2525,H2526

PLAZA G. H2527

PLEKHNV/GV....G.V. PLEKHANOV

B50
CARR E.H.,STUDIES IN REVOLUTION. CREATE WAR PERSON ALL/IDEOS MARXISM SOCISM...PHIL/SCI METH/COMP ANTHOL 18/20 SAINTSIMON MARX/KARL PROUDHON/P LASSALLE/F PLEKHNV/GV. PAGE 27 H0537 — REV IDEA/COMP COERCE BIOG

PLISCHKE E. H2528,H2529

PLUMMER C. H1042

PLUMPTRE A.F.W. H2530

PLUNKITT/G....G.W. PLUNKITT, TAMMANY BOSS

PLURALISM....SEE PLURISM, PLURIST

PLURISM....PLURALISM, SOCIO-POLITICAL ORDER OF AUTONOMOUS GROUPS

C28
WARD P.W.,"SOVEREIGNTY: A STUDY OF A CONTEMPORARY POLITICAL NOTION." CONSTN NAT/G DIPLOM REPRESENT PLURISM...IDEA/COMP BIBLIOG. PAGE 165 H3304 — SOVEREIGN CONCPT NAT/LISM

C31
MOGI S.,"THE PROBLEM OF FEDERALISM: A STUDY IN THE HISTORY OF POLITICAL THEORY." CONSTN COLONIAL NAT/LISM SOVEREIGN LAISSEZ PLURISM 18/20. PAGE 112 H2235 — FEDERAL CONCPT NAT/G

B38
HEIMANN E.,COMMUNISM, FASCISM, OR DEMOCRACY? WOR-45 CONSTN SOCIETY STRATA AGRI CAP/ISM MORAL ORD/FREE ...MAJORIT METH/COMP NAT/COMP 19/20. PAGE 69 H1384 — SOCISM MARXISM FASCISM PLURISM

B39
FURNIVALL J.S.,NETHERLANDS INDIA. INDIA NETHERLAND CULTURE INDUS NAT/G DIPLOM ADMIN WEALTH...POLICY CHARTS 17/20. PAGE 54 H1081 — COLONIAL ECO/UNDEV SOVEREIGN PLURISM

S46
DE GRE G.,"FREEDOM AND SOCIAL STRUCTURE" (BMR)" UNIV SOCIETY DOMIN CONTROL TOTALISM PLURISM...SOC CHARTS. PAGE 38 H0753 — ORD/FREE STRUCT CONCPT GP/REL

L49
BRECHT A.,"THE NEW GERMAN CONSTITUTION." GERMANY/W NAT/G CHIEF EX/STRUC LEGIS PROB/SOLV ADMIN REPRESENT TOTALISM ORD/FREE PLURISM...MAJORIT CHARTS 20. PAGE 20 H0409 — CONSTN DIPLOM SOVEREIGN FEDERAL

S49
STEINMETZ H.,"THE PROBLEMS OF THE LANDRAT: A STUDY OF COUNTY GOVERNMENT IN THE US ZONE OF GERMANY." GERMANY/W USA+45 INDUS PLAN DIPLOM EDU/PROP CONTROL WAR GOV/REL FEDERAL WEALTH PLURISM...GOV/COMP 20 LANDRAT. PAGE 149 H2977 — LOC/G COLONIAL MGT TOP/EX

B54
BERGER M.,FREEDOM AND CONTROL IN MODERN SOCIETY. LABOR NAT/G VOL/ASSN AUTHORIT DRIVE PLURISM ...METH/CNCPT CLASSIF. PAGE 15 H0300 — ORD/FREE CONTROL INGP/REL

B56
KALLEN H.M.,CULTURAL PLURALISM AND THE AMERICAN IDEA. RACE/REL ADJUST PERSON ORD/FREE LAISSEZ ...PLURIST GEN/LAWS ANTHOL. PAGE 83 H1652 — PLURISM CULTURE GP/REL SECT

B58
HAAS E.B.,THE UNITING OF EUROPE. EUR+WWI INT/ORG NAT/G POL/PAR TOP/EX ECO/TAC EDU/PROP LEGIT FEDERAL NAT/LISM DRIVE RIGID/FLEX ORD/FREE PWR PLURISM ...POLICY CONCPT INT GEN/LAWS ECSC EEC 20. PAGE 63 H1264 — VOL/ASSN ECO/DEV

B58
HERMENS F.A.,THE REPRESENTATIVE REPUBLIC. USA-45 PLURISM GOV/COMP. PAGE 70 H1401
POL/PAR CHOOSE REPRESENT

S58
GARCEAU O.,"INTEREST GROUP THEORY IN POLITICAL RESEARCH." ELITES NAT/G PLAN LEAD REPRESENT INGP/REL POLICY. PAGE 55 H1098
GP/COMP GP/REL LOBBY PLURISM

B59
DAHRENDORF R.,CLASS AND CLASS CONFLICT IN INDUSTRIAL SOCIETY. LABOR NAT/G COERCE ROLE PLURISM ...POLICY MGT CONCPT CLASSIF. PAGE 37 H0734
VOL/ASSN STRUCT SOC GP/REL

B59
MILLER A.S.,PRIVATE GOVERNMENTS AND THE CONSTITUTION (PAMPHLET). LAW LABOR NAT/G ROLE PWR PLURISM...POLICY DECISION. PAGE 111 H2211
FEDERAL CONSTN VOL/ASSN CONSEN

C59
KORNHAUSER W.,"THE POLITICS OF MASS SOCIETY." COM CULTURE ELITES INTELL STRATA POL/PAR ATTIT...SOC CHARTS GEN/LAWS BIBLIOG 20. PAGE 88 H1757
CROWD PLURISM CONSTN SOCIETY

S61
EHRMANN H.W.,"FRENCH BUREAUCRACY AND ORGANIZED INTERESTS" (BMR)" FRANCE NAT/G DELIB/GP ROUTINE ...INT 20 BUREAUCRCY CIVIL/SERV. PAGE 45 H0897
ADMIN DECISION PLURISM LOBBY

S61
MACRIDIS R.C.,"INTEREST GROUPS IN COMPARATIVE ANALYSIS." CULTURE OP/RES LOBBY REPRESENT GP/REL AUTHORIT ORD/FREE PWR...POLICY DECISION METH/CNCPT CLASSIF. PAGE 101 H2010
GP/COMP CONCPT PLURISM

B64
AKZIN B.,STATE AND NATION. UNIV ECO/UNDEV DIPLOM RACE/REL NAT/LISM ATTIT PLURISM...CONCPT IDEA/COMP 20. PAGE 4 H0090
GP/REL NAT/G KIN

B64
HORNE D.,THE LUCKY COUNTRY: AUSTRALIA TODAY. UK CULTURE STRATA ATTIT PWR PLURISM...GOV/COMP 20 AUSTRAL. PAGE 73 H1471
RACE/REL DIPLOM NAT/G STRUCT

B64
RAISON T.,WHY CONSERVATIVE? UK FORCES DIPLOM ECO/TAC GIVE EDU/PROP ORD/FREE WEALTH LAISSEZ ...GOV/COMP 20 TORY/PARTY CONSRV/PAR. PAGE 129 H2583
PLURISM CONSERVE POL/PAR NAT/G

B64
TINKER H.,BALLOT BOX AND BAYONET - PEOPLE AND GOVERNMENT IN EMERGENT ASIAN COUNTRIES. CEYLON INDIA INDONESIA PHILIPPINE POL/PAR ADMIN COLONIAL LEAD PARL/PROC CHOOSE CONSEN ORD/FREE SOVEREIGN PLURISM...GOV/COMP THIRD/WRLD. PAGE 155 H3104
MYTH S/ASIA NAT/COMP NAT/LISM

L65
HOUN F.S.,"THE COMMUNIST MONOLITH VERSUS THE CHINESE TRADITION." CULTURE INTELL SOCIETY STRUCT DOMIN GP/REL ORD/FREE CONSERVE PLURISM...GOV/COMP WORSHIP. PAGE 74 H1479
ASIA MARXISM TOTALISM

B66
BEER S.H.,BRITISH POLITICS IN THE COLLECTIVIST AGE. UK NAT/G CONTROL CHOOSE GP/REL ATTIT PWR PLURISM ...MAJORIT WELF/ST 16/20. PAGE 13 H0258
POL/PAR SOCISM TRADIT GP/COMP

B66
DAHL R.A.,POLITICAL OPPOSITIONS IN WESTERN DEMOCRACIES. EUR+WWI USA+45 USA-45 SOCIETY STRATA ECO/DEV NAT/G LEGIS REPRESENT...TREND NAT/COMP ANTHOL 20. PAGE 37 H0732
POL/PAR CHOOSE PARTIC PLURISM

B66
KEIL S.,SEXUALITAT - ERKENNTNISSE UND MASS-STABE. CULTURE DOMIN MARRIAGE AGE/Y AGE/A PERSON SUPEGO PLURISM 17/20. PAGE 84 H1681
SEX ATTIT STRUCT SOCIETY

S67
ALBINSKI H.S.,"POLITICS AND BICULTURISM IN CANADA: THE FLAG DEBATE." CANADA SOCIETY NAT/G PROVS DELIB/GP DEBATE REGION SOVEREIGN PLURISM...POLICY SOC/INTEG 20. PAGE 5 H0093
NAT/LISM GP/REL POL/PAR CULTURE

S67
JANICKE M.,"MONOPOLISMUS UND PLURALISMUS IM KOMMUNISTISCHEN HERRSCHAFTSSYSTEM" COM CZECHOSLVK USSR YUGOSLAVIA SOCIETY CONTROL RIGID/FLEX...CONCPT NAT/COMP 20. PAGE 79 H1589
TOTALISM POL/PAR ATTIT PLURISM

S67
MURVAR V.,"MAX WEBER'S CONCEPT OF HEIROCRACY: A STUDY IN THE TYPOLOGY OF CHURCH-STATE RELATIONS" UNIV INGP/REL ATTIT PLURISM...SOC CONCPT 20 WEBER/MAX. PAGE 115 H2299
SECT NAT/G GP/REL STRUCT

S68
HOOK S.,"THE ENLIGHTENMENT AND MARXISM." CULTURE SOCIETY RATIONAL ORD/FREE PLURISM SOCISM...CONCPT HIST/WRIT 18/19 MARX/KARL HEGEL/GWF ENLIGHTNMT. PAGE 73 H1462
IDEA/COMP MARXISM OBJECTIVE

PLURIST....PLURALIST

B08
LLOYD H.D.,THE SWISS DEMOCRACY. SWITZERLND INDUS NAT/G WORKER CHOOSE OWN ORD/FREE SOCISM...PLURIST 19/20 MONOPOLY. PAGE 97 H1944
NAT/COMP GOV/COMP REPRESENT POPULISM

B11
HUXLEY T.H.,METHOD AND RESULTS: ESSAYS. EDU/PROP REPRESENT OWN PERSON PWR WEALTH...PSY IDEA/COMP GEN/LAWS. PAGE 76 H1514
ORD/FREE NAT/G POPULISM PLURIST

B35
MARRIOTT J.A.,DICTATORSHIP AND DEMOCRACY. GERMANY GREECE UK CHIEF DIPLOM DOMIN LEGIT PEACE ORD/FREE CONSERVE...TREND ROME HITLER/A. PAGE 103 H2057
TOTALISM POPULISM PLURIST NAT/G

S38
HALL R.C.,"REPRESENTATION OF BIG BUSINESS IN THE HOUSE OF COMMONS." UK ECO/DEV INDUS PROF/ORG LEGIS CAP/ISM ECO/TAC LAISSEZ...POLICY OLD/LIB PLURIST MGT 20 HOUSE/CMNS. PAGE 64 H1287
LOBBY NAT/G

B43
MARITAIN J.,THE RIGHTS OF MAN AND NATURAL LAW. CONSTN NAT/G DOMIN LEGIT INGP/REL TOTALISM MORAL POPULISM WORSHIP 19/20 CIVIL/LIB CHURCH/STA NATURL/LAW. PAGE 103 H2051
PLURIST ORD/FREE GEN/LAWS

B56
KALLEN H.M.,CULTURAL PLURALISM AND THE AMERICAN IDEA. RACE/REL ADJUST PERSON ORD/FREE LAISSEZ ...PLURIST GEN/LAWS ANTHOL. PAGE 83 H1652
PLURISM CULTURE GP/REL SECT

POBEDONOSTSEV K.P. H2531

POGANY A.H. H2532

POGANY H.L. H2532

POHLENZ M. H2533

POL....POLITICAL AND POWER PROCESS

POL/PAR....POLITICAL PARTIES

N
INTERNATIONAL BIBLIOGRAPHIE DER DEUTSCHEN ZEITSCHRIFTENLITERATUR. EUR+WWI GERMANY MOD/EUR ECO/DEV POL/PAR LEAD WAR NAT/LISM ATTIT...EPIST PHIL/SCI 19/20. PAGE 1 H0004
BIBLIOG/A NAT/G PERSON CULTURE

N
PEKING REVIEW. CHINA/COM CULTURE AGRI INDUS DIPLOM EDU/PROP GUERRILLA ATTIT MARXISM...BIBLIOG 20. PAGE 1 H0009
MARXIST NAT/G POL/PAR PRESS

N
CHINA QUARTERLY. COM AGRI INDUS ACADEM POL/PAR INT/TRADE CONFER GOV/REL...TIME/SEQ CON/ANAL INDEX 20. PAGE 1 H0014
BIBLIOG/A ASIA DIPLOM POLICY

N
HANDBOOK OF LATIN AMERICAN STUDIES. LAW CULTURE ECO/UNDEV POL/PAR ADMIN LEAD...SOC 20. PAGE 1 H0016
BIBLIOG/A L/A+17C NAT/G DIPLOM

N
PUBLISHERS' TRADE LIST ANNUAL. LAW POL/PAR ADMIN PERSON ALL/IDEOS...HUM SOC 19/20. PAGE 1 H0020
BIBLIOG NAT/G DIPLOM POLICY

N
SUBJECT GUIDE TO BOOKS IN PRINT: AN INDEX TO THE PUBLISHERS' TRADE LIST ANNUAL. UNIV LAW LOC/G DIPLOM WRITING ADMIN LEAD PERSON...MGT SOC. PAGE 2 H0024
BIBLIOG ECO/DEV POL/PAR NAT/G

N
NEUE POLITISCHE LITERATUR; BERICHTE UBER DAS INTERNATIONALE SCHRIFTTUM ZUR POLITIK. WOR+45 LAW CONSTN POL/PAR ADMIN LEAD GOV/REL...POLICY IDEA/COMP. PAGE 2 H0027
BIBLIOG/A DIPLOM NAT/G NAT/COMP

N
CORNELL UNIVERSITY LIBRARY,SOUTHEAST ASIA ACCESSIONS LIST. LAW SOCIETY STRUCT ECO/UNDEV POL/PAR TEC/DEV DIPLOM LEAD REGION. PAGE 34 H0671
BIBLIOG S/ASIA NAT/G CULTURE

N
DEUTSCHE BUCHEREI,DEUTSCHES BUCHERVERZEICHNIS. GERMANY LAW CULTURE POL/PAR ADMIN LEAD ATTIT PERSON ...SOC 20. PAGE 40 H0805
BIBLIOG NAT/G DIPLOM ECO/DEV

N
EUROPA PUBLICATIONS LIMITED,THE EUROPA YEAR BOOK. CONSTN FINAN INDUS POL/PAR DIPLOM TV CT/SYS...STAT BIOG CHARTS WORSHIP 20. PAGE 47 H0949
BIBLIOG NAT/G PRESS INT/ORG

N
INSTITUTE OF HISPANIC STUDIES,HISPANIC AMERICAN REPORT. EUR+WWI SPAIN LAW CONSTN ECO/UNDEV POL/PAR
BIBLIOG/A L/A+17C

EX/STRUC LEGIS LEAD...HUM SOC 20. PAGE 77 H1538
NAT/G
DIPLOM

N
KYRIAK T.E.,CHINA: A BIBLIOGRAPHY. ASIA CHINA/COM AGRI FINAN INDUS NAT/G INT/TRADE PRESS...SOC 20. PAGE 90 H1789
BIBLIOG/A
MARXISM
TOP/EX
POL/PAR

N
US LIBRARY OF CONGRESS,ACCESSIONS LIST - INDIA. INDIA CULTURE AGRI LOC/G POL/PAR PLAN PROB/SOLV TEC/DEV DIPLOM EDU/PROP LEAD GP/REL ATTIT 20. PAGE 160 H3199
BIBLIOG
S/ASIA
ECO/UNDEV
NAT/G

N
US LIBRARY OF CONGRESS,ACCESSIONS LIST -- ISRAEL. ISRAEL CULTURE ECO/UNDEV POL/PAR PLAN PROB/SOLV TEC/DEV DIPLOM EDU/PROP LEAD WAR ATTIT 20 JEWS. PAGE 160 H3200
BIBLIOG
ISLAM
NAT/G
GP/REL

NSY
MACKENZIE K.R.,THE ENGLISH PARLIAMENT. UK POL/PAR CHIEF DIPLOM TAX TASK WAR AUTHORIT...POLICY TREND 12/20 PARLIAMENT. PAGE 100 H2000
ORD/FREE
LEGIS
NAT/G

B00
HOBSON J.A.,THE WAR IN SOUTH AFRICA: ITS CAUSES AND EFFECTS. NETHERLAND SOUTH/AFR UK ELITES AGRI EXTR/IND POL/PAR DIPLOM PRESS RACE/REL ATTIT ORD/FREE SOVEREIGN...INT 19 NEGRO. PAGE 72 H1439
WAR
DOMIN
POLICY
NAT/G

B10
TEMPERLEY H.W.V.,SENATES AND UPPER CHAMBERS; THEIR USE AND FUNCTION IN THE MODERN STATE... UK WOR-45 CONSTN NAT/G POL/PAR PROVS SECT COLONIAL LEAD CHOOSE REPRESENT PWR...BIBLIOG 19/20 PARLIAMENT SENATE CMN/WLTH HOUSE/LORD. PAGE 153 H3059
PARL/PROC
NAT/COMP
LEGIS
EX/STRUC

B13
BARDOUX J.,L'ANGLETERRE RADICALE; ESSAI DE LA PSYCHOLOGIE SOCIALE (1906-1913). UK CONSTN NAT/G WORKER CREATE BUDGET ECO/TAC ATTIT...POLICY 20 PARLIAMENT LABOR/PAR STRIKE NAVY. PAGE 11 H0215
POL/PAR
CHOOSE
COLONIAL
LEGIS

B13
SIEGFRIED A.,TABLEAU POLITIQUE DE LA FRANCE DE L'OUEST SOUS LA TROISIEME REPUBLIQUE. FRANCE STRATA STRUCT NAT/G POL/PAR PROVS REGION GOV/REL ATTIT PWR ...TREND TIME 19. PAGE 143 H2869
SOC
GEOG
SOCIETY

B15
MICHELS R.,POLITICAL PARTIES. NAT/G BAL/PWR CHOOSE REPRESENT ATTIT SOCISM...PSY SOC CONCPT OBS 20 MONOPOLY. PAGE 110 H2198
POL/PAR
CENTRAL
LEAD
PWR

B17
HARLOW R.V.,THE HISTORY OF LEGISLATIVE METHODS IN THE PERIOD BEFORE 1825. USA-45 EX/STRUC ADMIN COLONIAL LEAD PARL/PROC ROUTINE...GP/COMP GOV/COMP HOUSE/REP. PAGE 66 H1333
LEGIS
DELIB/GP
PROVS
POL/PAR

B18
BARRES M.,THE FAITH OF FRANCE (TRANS. BY ELISABETH MARBURY). FRANCE FAM MUNIC NEIGH POL/PAR SECT ALL/VALS 20. PAGE 11 H0227
TRADIT
CULTURE
WAR
GP/REL

B18
YUKIO O.,THE VOICE OF JAPANESE DEMOCRACY, AN ESSAY ON CONSTITUTIONAL LOYALTY (TRANS BY J. E. BECKER). ASIA POL/PAR DELIB/GP EX/STRUC RIGID/FLEX ORD/FREE PWR...POLICY JURID METH/COMP 19/20 CHINJAP. PAGE 172 H3443
CONSTN
MAJORIT
CHOOSE
NAT/G

B19
NATHAN M.,THE SOUTH AFRICAN COMMONWEALTH: CONSTITUTION, PROBLEMS, SOCIAL CONDITIONS. SOUTH/AFR UK CULTURE INDUS EX/STRUC LEGIS BUDGET EDU/PROP ADMIN CT/SYS GP/REL RACE/REL...LING 19/20 CMN/WLTH. PAGE 116 H2317
CONSTN
NAT/G
POL/PAR
SOCIETY

N19
BRIMMELL G.H.,COMMUNISM IN SOUTHEAST ASIA (PAMPHLET). BURMA CAMBODIA COM INDIA INDONESIA LAOS MOD/EUR NAT/G POL/PAR FORCES CAP/ISM CONTROL WEALTH ...MYTH 20. PAGE 21 H0420
MARXISM
S/ASIA
REV
ECO/UNDEV

N19
MEZERIK A.G.,APARTHEID IN THE REPUBLIC OF SOUTH AFRICA (PAMPHLET). DIPLOM DOMIN CONTROL COERCE REPRESENT CONSEN ATTIT. PAGE 110 H2194
DISCRIM
RACE/REL
POL/PAR
POLICY

N19
OPERATIONS AND POLICY RESEARCH,PERU ELECTION MEMORANDA (PAMPHLET). L/A+17C PERU POL/PAR LEGIS EXEC APPORT REPRESENT 20. PAGE 121 H2421
CHOOSE
CONSTN
SUFF
NAT/G

N19
OPERATIONS AND POLICY RESEARCH,URUGUAY: ELECTION FACTBOOK: NOVEMBER 27, 1966 (PAMPHLET). URUGUAY LAW NAT/G LEAD REPRESENT...STAT BIOG CHARTS 20. PAGE 121 H2422
POL/PAR
CHOOSE
PLAN
ATTIT

N19
ROWE J.W.,THE ARGENTINE ELECTIONS OF 1963 (PAMPHLET). L/A+17C LOC/G NAT/G LEGIS REPRESENT 20 ARGEN. PAGE 135 H2703
CHOOSE
CONSTN
APPORT
POL/PAR

N19
TREVELYAN G.M.,THE TWO-PARTY SYSTEM IN ENGLISH POLITICAL HISTORY (PAMPHLET). UK CHIEF LEGIS COLONIAL EXEC REV CHOOSE 17/19. PAGE 157 H3131
PARL/PROC
POL/PAR
NAT/G
PWR

N19
WEBB L.C.,CHURCH AND STATE IN ITALY: 1947-1957 (PAMPHLET). GERMANY ITALY CONSTN POL/PAR AGREE CONTROL PARTIC CHOOSE ATTIT ORD/FREE FASCISM MARXISM 20 CHURCH/STA MARITAIN/J SALO. PAGE 166 H3316
SECT
CATHISM
NAT/G
GP/REL

B21
BERGSTRASSER L.,GESCHICHTE DER POLITISCHEN PARTEIEN. GERMANY MOD/EUR NAT/G PRESS PWR ...TIME/SEQ 17/20. PAGE 15 H0303
POL/PAR
LAISSEZ
CONSERVE

B21
STUART G.H.,FRENCH FOREIGN POLICY. CONSTN INT/ORG NAT/G POL/PAR EX/STRUC FORCES PLAN ECO/TAC DOMIN EDU/PROP ADJUD COERCE ATTIT DRIVE RIGID/FLEX ALL/VALS...POLICY OBS RECORD BIOG TIME/SEQ TREND. PAGE 150 H3000
MOD/EUR
DIPLOM
FRANCE

B23
DELBRUCK H.,GOVERNMENT AND THE WILL OF THE PEOPLE (TRANS. BY ROY S. MACELWEE). MOD/EUR NAT/G CHOOSE REPRESENT...CONCPT 19/20. PAGE 39 H0788
SOVEREIGN
ORD/FREE
MAJORITY
POL/PAR

B23
FRANK T.,A HISTORY OF ROME. MEDIT-7 INTELL SOCIETY LOC/G NAT/G POL/PAR FORCES LEGIS DOMIN LEGIT ALL/VALS...POLICY CONCPT TIME/SEQ GEN/LAWS ROM/EMP ROM/EMP. PAGE 53 H1050
EXEC
STRUCT
ELITES

B23
LEES-SMITH H.B.,SECOND CHAMBERS IN THEORY AND PRACTICE. IRELAND NORWAY SOUTH/AFR UK LAW POL/PAR LEGIS CONTROL 20 CMN/WLTH. PAGE 93 H1858
PARL/PROC
DELIB/GP
REPRESENT
GP/COMP

B23
ROBERT H.M.,PARLIAMENTARY LAW. POL/PAR LEGIS PARTIC CHOOSE REPRESENT GP/REL. PAGE 132 H2640
PARL/PROC
DELIB/GP
NAT/G
JURID

B24
MARTIN B.K.,THE TRIUMPH OF LORD PALMERSTON. MOD/EUR RUSSIA TURKEY UK NAT/G DELIB/GP 19. PAGE 103 H2061
ATTIT
WAR
POL/PAR
POLICY

B26
MACIVER R.M.,THE MODERN STATE. POL/PAR ORD/FREE TIME/SEQ. PAGE 100 H1997
NAT/G
CONCPT
JURID
SOVEREIGN

B26
POLLARD A.F.,THE EVOLUTION OF PARLIAMENT. UK CONSTN POL/PAR EX/STRUC GOV/REL INGP/REL PRIVIL RIGID/FLEX ...TIME/SEQ 11/20 CMN/WLTH PARLIAMENT. PAGE 127 H2536
LEGIS
PARL/PROC
NAT/G

S27
MICHELS R.,"SOME REFLECTIONS ON THE SOCIOLOGICAL CHARACTER OF POLITICAL PARTIES" (BMR)" WOR-45 STRATA MAJORITY DRIVE...GOV/COMP 20. PAGE 110 H2199
POL/PAR
PWR
LEAD
CONCPT

B28
FYFE H.,THE BRITISH LIBERAL PARTY. UK SECT ADMIN LEAD CHOOSE GP/REL PWR SOCISM...MAJORIT TIME/SEQ 19/20 LIB/PARTY CONSRV/PAR. PAGE 54 H1084
POL/PAR
NAT/G
REPRESENT
POPULISM

C28
SCHNEIDER H.W.,"MAKING THE FASCIST STATE." ITALY CULTURE LABOR DIPLOM REV WAR NAT/LISM TOTALISM ATTIT DRIVE SOCISM...BIBLIOG PARLIAMENT 20. PAGE 140 H2792
FASCISM
POLICY
POL/PAR

B29
CAM H.M.,BIBLIOGRAPHY OF ENGLISH CONSTITUTIONAL HISTORY (PAMPHLET). UK LAW LOC/G NAT/G POL/PAR SECT DELIB/GP ADJUD ORD/FREE 19/20 PARLIAMENT. PAGE 25 H0510
BIBLIOG/A
CONSTN
ADMIN
PARL/PROC

B33
DAHLIN E.,FRENCH AND GERMAN PUBLIC OPINION ON DECLARED WAR AIMS 1914-1918. BELGIUM FRANCE GERMANY NAT/G POL/PAR DIPLOM COERCE REV WAR PEACE 20 WWI WILSON/W. PAGE 37 H0733
ATTIT
EDU/PROP
DOMIN
NAT/COMP

B33
MOSS W.,POLITICAL PARTIES IN THE IRISH FREE STATE. IRELAND UK LAW FINAN LABOR DELIB/GP TOP/EX TARIFFS EDU/PROP...CHARTS GP/COMP 20. PAGE 113 H2269
POL/PAR
NAT/G
CHOOSE
POLICY

C33
MURET C.T.,"FRENCH ROYALIST DOCTRINES SINCE THE REVOLUTION." FRANCE CONSTN NAT/G SECT ADMIN LEAD SOVEREIGN...POLICY BIOG IDEA/COMP BIBLIOG 18/20. PAGE 115 H2295
POL/PAR
ATTIT
INTELL
CONSERVE

B34
STALIN J.,PROBLEMS OF LENINISM. USSR STRATA INDUS LOC/G POL/PAR ECO/TAC CONTROL TOTALISM PWR SOCISM LENIN/VI STALIN/J. PAGE 148 H2968
MARXISM
REV
ELITES
NAT/G

B35
DE TOCQUEVILLE A.,DEMOCRACY IN AMERICA (4 VOLS.)
POPULISM

(TRANS. BY HENRY REEVE). CONSTN STRUCT LOC/G NAT/G POL/PAR PROVS ETIQUET CT/SYS MAJORITY ATTIT 18/19. PAGE 39 H0772 MAJORIT ORD/FREE SOCIETY

B35
NORDSKOG J.E.,SOCIAL REFORM IN NORWAY. NORWAY INDUS NAT/G POL/PAR LEGIS ADJUD...SOC BIBLIOG SOC/INTEG 20. PAGE 119 H2371 LABOR ADJUST

B36
CLOKIE H.M.,THE ORIGIN AND NATURE OF CONSTITUTIONAL GOVERNMENT. UK NAT/G POL/PAR CONSULT LEGIS ...GOV/COMP 14/20 CABINET PARLIAMENT. PAGE 30 H0606 CONCPT CONSTN PARL/PROC

B36
LAPRADE W.T.,PUBLIC OPINION AND POLITICS IN EIGHTEENTH CENTURY ENGLAND. UK CULTURE POL/PAR CHIEF TOP/EX LEAD REV NAT/LISM PWR 18 PROTESTANT PROTESTANT CHURCH/STA. PAGE 91 H1815 POLICY ELITES ATTIT TIME/SEQ

B36
RAPPARD W.E.,THE GOVERNMENT OF SWITZERLAND. SWITZERLND INT/ORG POL/PAR EX/STRUC DIPLOM NEUTRAL PARL/PROC REGION WAR HABITAT SOVEREIGN...NAT/COMP SOC/INTEG 20 LEAGUE/NAT WWI. PAGE 130 H2594 CONSTN NAT/G CULTURE FEDERAL

B37
BORGESE G.A.,GOLIATH: THE MARCH OF FASCISM. GERMANY ITALY LAW POL/PAR SECT DIPLOM SOCISM...JURID MYTH 20 DANTE MACHIAVELL MUSSOLIN/B. PAGE 19 H0375 POLICY NAT/LISM FASCISM NAT/G

B37
CLOKIE H.M.,ROYAL COMMISSIONS OF INQUIRY; THE SIGNIFICANCE OF INVESTIGATIONS IN BRITISH POLITICS. UK POL/PAR CONFER ROUTINE...POLICY DECISION TIME/SEQ 16/20. PAGE 30 H0607 NAT/G DELIB/GP INSPECT

B37
TINGSTEN H.,POLITICAL BEHAVIOR. EUR+WWI STRATA NAT/G POL/PAR ACT/RES AGE...TREND CHARTS 20 FEMALE/SEX. PAGE 155 H3100 CHOOSE ATTIT PARTIC

B38
DAVIES E.,"NATIONAL" CAPITALISM: THE GOVERNMENT'S RECORD AS PROTECTOR OF PRIVATE MONOPOLY. UK ELITES SOCIETY STRATA POL/PAR WORKER PROB/SOLV CONTROL SOCISM 20 MONOPOLY LABOR/PAR CHAMBRLN/N. PAGE 37 H0747 CAP/ISM NAT/G INDUS POLICY

B38
DUNHAM W.H. JR.,COMPLAINT AND REFORM IN ENGLAND 1436-1714. UK LAW ACADEM NAT/G POL/PAR SCHOOL PRESS COLONIAL PARL/PROC MORAL...SOC/WK ANTHOL 15/18 HAKLUYT/R COWPER/W. PAGE 43 H0865 ATTIT SOCIETY SECT

B38
HARPER S.N.,THE GOVERNMENT OF THE SOVIET UNION. COM USSR LAW CONSTN ECO/DEV PLAN TEC/DEV DIPLOM INT/TRADE ADMIN REV NAT/LISM...POLICY 20. PAGE 67 H1337 MARXISM NAT/G LEAD POL/PAR

B38
IIZAWA S.,POLITICS AND POLITICAL PARTIES IN JAPAN. ELITES VOL/ASSN CHOOSE SUFF CIVMIL/REL GP/REL 19/20 CHINJAP. PAGE 76 H1522 POL/PAR REPRESENT FORCES NAT/G

B39
ANDERSON P.R.,THE BACKGROUND OF ANTI-ENGLISH FEELING IN GERMANY, 1890-1902. GERMANY MOD/EUR UK NAT/G POL/PAR TOP/EX WAR...IDEA/COMP 19/20. PAGE 7 H0132 DIPLOM EDU/PROP ATTIT COLONIAL

B39
HITLER A.,MEIN KAMPF. EUR+WWI FUT MOD/EUR STRUCT INT/ORG LABOR NAT/G POL/PAR FORCES CREATE PLAN BAL/PWR DIPLOM ECO/TAC DOMIN EDU/PROP ADMIN COERCE ATTIT...SOCIALIST BIOG TREND NAZI. PAGE 71 H1428 PWR NEW/IDEA WAR

B39
JENNINGS W.I.,PARLIAMENT. UK POL/PAR OP/RES BUDGET LEAD CHOOSE GP/REL...MGT 20 PARLIAMENT HOUSE/LORD HOUSE/CMNS. PAGE 80 H1609 PARL/PROC LEGIS CONSTN NAT/G

B39
SCHOCKEL E.,DAS POLITISCHE PLAKAT. EUR+WWI GERMANY NAT/G PWR FASCISM EXHIBIT. PAGE 140 H2794 EDU/PROP ATTIT DOMIN POL/PAR

C39
REISCHAUER R.,"JAPAN'S GOVERNMENT--POLITICS." CONSTN STRATA POL/PAR FORCES LEGIS DIPLOM ADMIN EXEC CENTRAL...POLICY BIBLIOG 20 CHINJAP. PAGE 131 H2610 NAT/G S/ASIA CONCPT ROUTINE

B40
MCHENRY D.E.,HIS MAJESTY'S OPPOSITION: STRUCTURE AND PROBLEMS OF THE BRITISH LABOUR PARTY 1931-1938. UK FINAN LABOR LOC/G DELIB/GP LEGIS EDU/PROP LEAD PARTIC CHOOSE GP/REL SOCISM...TREND 20 LABOR/PAR. PAGE 107 H2130 POL/PAR MGT NAT/G POLICY

S40
FAHS C.B.,"POLITICAL GROUPS IN THE JAPANESE HOUSE OF PEERS." ELITES NAT/G ADMIN GP/REL...TREND CHINJAP. PAGE 48 H0961 ROUTINE POL/PAR LEGIS

B41
CROTHERS G.D.,THE GERMAN ELECTIONS OF 1907. GERMANY NAT/G EDU/PROP COLONIAL ATTIT. PAGE 35 H0709 CHOOSE PARL/PROC NAT/LISM POL/PAR

B41
PALMER R.R.,TWELVE WHO RULED. MOD/EUR ELITES STRUCT NAT/G POL/PAR DELIB/GP DOMIN ATTIT SUPEGO PWR ...POLICY CONCPT 18. PAGE 123 H2453 TOP/EX BIOG REV FRANCE

B42
BAYNES N.H.,INTELLECTUAL LIBERTY AND TOTALITARIAN CLAIMS. EUR+WWI GERMANY ITALY INTELL POL/PAR CIVMIL/REL NAT/LISM SOCISM CONCPT. PAGE 12 H0245 KNOWL FASCISM EDU/PROP ACADEM

B42
JOSHI P.S.,THE TYRANNY OF COLOUR. INDIA SOUTH/AFR UK ECO/UNDEV NAT/G POL/PAR DIPLOM ECO/TAC WAR ...POLICY 19/20. PAGE 82 H1637 COLONIAL DISCRIM RACE/REL

B42
NEUBURGER O.,OFFICIAL PUBLICATIONS OF PRESENT-DAY GERMANY: GOVERNMENT, CORPORATE ORGANIZATIONS, AND NATIONAL SOCIALIST PARTY. GERMANY CONSTN COM/IND POL/PAR EDU/PROP PRESS 20 NAZI. PAGE 117 H2332 BIBLIOG/A FASCISM NAT/G ADMIN

B44
HAYEK F.A.,THE ROAD TO SERFDOM. NAT/G POL/PAR CREATE EDU/PROP ATTIT WEALTH LAISSEZ...OLD/LIB CONCPT TREND 20. PAGE 68 H1368 FUT PLAN ECO/TAC SOCISM

B44
SHELBY C.,LATIN AMERICAN PERIODICALS CURRENTLY RECEIVED IN THE LIBRARY OF CONGRESS AND IN LIBRARY OF DEPARTMENT OF AGRICULTURE. SOCIETY AGRI INDUS LABOR POL/PAR INT/TRADE...GEOG SOC 20. PAGE 143 H2856 BIBLIOG ECO/UNDEV CULTURE L/A+17C

B44
WOLFE D.M.,LEVELLER MANIFESTOES OF THE PURITAN REVOLUTION. UK CONSTN NAT/G SECT...CONCPT ANTHOL 17 LEVELLERS DECLAR/IND PURITAN LOCKE/JOHN. PAGE 170 H3400 POL/PAR REV ORD/FREE ATTIT

N45
INDIA QUARTERLY, A JOURNAL OF INTERNATIONAL AFFAIRS. INDIA LAW CONSTN ECO/UNDEV INT/ORG POL/PAR COLONIAL LEAD PARL/PROC WAR ATTIT...SOC 20 CMN/WLTH. PAGE 2 H0033 BIBLIOG/A S/ASIA DIPLOM NAT/G

B45
CLAGETT H.L.,COMMUNIST CHINA: RUTHLESS ENEMY OR PAPER TIGER (PAMPHLET). CHINA/COM ECO/UNDEV AGRI INDUS NAT/G POL/PAR ECO/TAC INT/TRADE GUERRILLA ATTIT...CHARTS NAT/COMP ORG/CHARTS 20. PAGE 30 H0602 BIBLIOG/A MARXISM DIPLOM COERCE

B45
CONOVER H.F.,THE GOVERNMENTS OF THE MAJOR FOREIGN POWERS: A BIBLIOGRAPHY. FRANCE GERMANY ITALY UK USSR CONSTN LOC/G POL/PAR EX/STRUC FORCES ADMIN CT/SYS CIVMIL/REL TOTALISM...POLICY 19/20. PAGE 32 H0645 BIBLIOG NAT/G DIPLOM

B45
CONOVER H.F.,ITALY: ECONOMICS, POLITICS AND MILITARY AFFAIRS, 1940-1945. ITALY ELITES NAT/G POL/PAR EX/STRUC TOP/EX DIPLOM DOMIN CONTROL COERCE WAR CIVMIL/REL EFFICIENCY 20. PAGE 32 H0646 BIBLIOG TOTALISM FORCES

B45
DITTMANN,DAS POLITISCHE DEUTSCHLAND VOR HITLER. GERMANY LOC/G PROVS...CHARTS GP/COMP 20. PAGE 41 H0827 POL/PAR NAT/G PARTIC

B45
MERRIAM C.E.,SYSTEMATIC POLITICS. FUT POL/PAR DELIB/GP DIPLOM ADJUD ADMIN LEAD CHOOSE ATTIT...MGT PHIL/SCI TREND. PAGE 109 H2183 NAT/G METH/CNCPT CREATE

S45
SPENCER R.C.,"PARTY GOVERNMENT AND THE SWEDISH RISKDAG." SWEDEN CHOOSE MAJORITY. PAGE 147 H2946 GOV/COMP NAT/G POL/PAR PARL/PROC

B46
BLUM L.,FOR ALL MANKIND (TRANS. BY W. PICKLES). FRANCE GERMANY USSR LAW SOCIETY STRUCT POL/PAR WORKER DIPLOM DOMIN CHOOSE ORD/FREE FASCISM 20. PAGE 18 H0361 POPULISM SOCIALIST NAT/G WAR

N47
CANNON J.P.,AMERICAN STALINISM AND ANTI-STALINISM PAMPHLET). NAT/G WORKER DOMIN EDU/PROP REV GP/REL ...MARXIST CONCPT 20 STALIN/J TROTSKY/L. PAGE 26 H0521 LABOR MARXISM CAP/ISM POL/PAR

B48
WRIGHT G.,THE RESHAPING OF FRENCH DEMOCRACY. FRANCE NAT/G POL/PAR SECT LEAD CHOOSE GP/REL INGP/REL MARXISM SOCISM...CHARTS BIBLIOG 20 DEGAULLE/C. PAGE 171 H3418 CONSTN POPULISM CREATE LEGIS

S48
ALEXANDER L.,"WAR CRIMES, THEIR SOCIAL-PSYCHOLOGICAL ASPECTS." EUR+WWI GERMANY LAW CULTURE ELITES KIN POL/PAR PUB/INST FORCES DOMIN EDU/PROP COERCE CRIME ATTIT SUPEGO HEALTH MORAL PWR FASCISM ...PSY OBS TREND GEN/LAWS NAZI 20. PAGE 5 H0100 DRIVE WAR

S48
ALMOND G.A.,"THE CHRISTIAN PARTIES OF WESTEN EUROPE." EUR+WWI NAT/G EDU/PROP LEGIT TOTALISM ORD/FREE PWR MARXISM...TREND CHARTS STERTYP GEN/LAWS COLD/WAR 20. PAGE 5 H0110 POL/PAR CATH SOCISM

B49
HINDEN R.,EMPIRE AND AFTER. UK POL/PAR BAL/PWR DIPLOM INT/TRADE WAR NAT/LISM PWR 17/20. PAGE 71 H1420
NAT/G COLONIAL ATTIT POLICY

S49
BOUSCAREN A.T.,"THE EUROPEAN CHRISTIAN DEMOCRATS" EUR+WWI NAT/G LEGIS 19/20 CHRIS/DEM EUROPE. PAGE 19 H0387
REPRESENT POL/PAR

C49
YANAGA C.,"JAPAN SINCE PERRY." S/ASIA CULTURE ECO/DEV FORCES WAR 19/20 CHINJAP. PAGE 172 H3433
DIPLOM POL/PAR CIVMIL/REL NAT/LISM

B50
ALBRECHT-CARRIE R.,ITALY FROM NAPOLEON TO MUSSOLINI. GERMANY ITALY SPAIN SOCIETY ECO/DEV POL/PAR LEGIS AGREE CONTROL WAR NAT/LISM TOTALISM PWR SOCISM...SOC 19/20 TREATY. PAGE 5 H0095
FASCISM NAT/G

B50
COUNCIL BRITISH NATIONAL BIB,BRITISH NATIONAL BIBLIOGRAPHY. UK AGRI CONSTRUC PERF/ART POL/PAR SECT CREATE INT/TRADE LEAD...HUM JURID PHIL/SCI 20. PAGE 34 H0677
BIBLIOG/A NAT/G TEC/DEV DIPLOM

B50
GATZKE H.W.,GERMANY'S DRIVE TO THE WEST. BELGIUM GERMANY MOD/EUR AGRI INDUS POL/PAR FORCES DOMIN AGREE CONTROL REGION COERCE 20 TREATY WWI. PAGE 55 H1104
WAR POLICY NAT/G DIPLOM

B50
KANN R.A.,THE MULTINATIONAL EMPIRE (2 VOLS.). AUSTRIA CZECHOSLVK GERMANY HUNGARY CULTURE NAT/G POL/PAR PROVS REGION REV FEDERAL...GEOG TREND CHARTS IDEA/COMP NAT/COMP 19/20. PAGE 83 H1654
NAT/LISM MOD/EUR

B50
LIPSET S.M.,AGRARIAN SOCIALISM. CANADA POL/PAR OP/RES ECO/TAC ADMIN ATTIT...TIME/SEQ NAT/COMP SOC/EXP 20 SASKATCH. PAGE 97 H1938
SOCISM AGRI METH/COMP STRUCT

B50
LYONS F.S.L.,THE IRISH PARLIAMENTARY PARTY, 1890-1910: STUDIES IN IRISH HISTORY (VOL. 4). IRELAND DELIB/GP LEGIS PAY EDU/PROP ADMIN GP/REL ATTIT...BIBLIOG 19/20 PARLIAMENT PARNELL/CS DIRECT/NAT. PAGE 99 H1986
POL/PAR CHOOSE NAT/G POLICY

B50
MCHENRY D.E.,THE THIRD FORCE IN CANADA: THE COOPERATIVE COMMONWEALTH FEDERATION, 1932-1948. CANADA EX/STRUC LEGIS REPRESENT 20 LABOR/PAR. PAGE 107 H2131
POL/PAR ADMIN CHOOSE POLICY

B50
TRAGER F.N.,MARXISM IN SOUTHEAST ASIA. BURMA INDONESIA THAILAND VIETNAM CULTURE SOCIETY NAT/G VOL/ASSN EXEC ROUTINE COERCE ATTIT RIGID/FLEX PWR ...METH/CNCPT TIME/SEQ STERTYP GEN/LAWS MARX/KARL VAL/FREE COLD/WAR NAM 20. PAGE 156 H3126
S/ASIA POL/PAR REV

B50
WHITE R.J.,THE CONSERVATIVE TRADITION. UK POL/PAR SUPEGO PWR RESPECT...POLICY ANTHOL 19. PAGE 167 H3350
CONSERVE CONCPT NAT/G ORD/FREE

C50
STOKES W.S.,"HONDURAS: AN AREA STUDY IN GOVERNMENT." HONDURAS NAT/G POL/PAR COLONIAL CT/SYS ROUTINE CHOOSE REPRESENT...GEOG RECORD BIBLIOG 19/20. PAGE 149 H2988
CONSTN LAW L/A+17C ADMIN

B51
CHRISTENSEN A.N.,THE EVOLUTION OF LATIN AMERICAN GOVERNMENT: A BOOK OF READINGS. ECO/UNDEV INDUS LOC/G POL/PAR EX/STRUC LEGIS FOR/AID CT/SYS ...SOC/WK 20 SOUTH/AMER. PAGE 30 H0599
NAT/G CONSTN DIPLOM L/A+17C

B51
HALEVY E.,IMPERIALISM AND THE RISE OF LABOR (2ND ED.). UK NAT/G POL/PAR TOP/EX ATTIT ORD/FREE PWR 19/20 PARLIAMENT LABOR/PAR. PAGE 64 H1284
COLONIAL LABOR POLICY WAR

B51
JENNINGS S.I.,THE COMMONWEALTH IN ASIA. CEYLON INDIA PAKISTAN S/ASIA UK CONSTN CULTURE SOCIETY STRATA STRUCT NAT/G POL/PAR EDU/PROP LEAD WAR 20 CMN/WLTH. PAGE 80 H1608
NAT/LISM REGION COLONIAL DIPLOM

B51
MEYER E.W.,POLITICAL PARTIES IN WESTERN GERMANY (PAMPHLET). GERMANY/W MUNIC NAT/G GOV/REL ALL/IDEOS 20 UNIFICA BERLIN. PAGE 109 H2190
POL/PAR LOBBY CHOOSE CONSTN

B51
US LIBRARY OF CONGRESS,EAST EUROPEAN ACCESSIONS LIST (VOL. I). POL/PAR DIPLOM ADMIN LEAD 20. PAGE 160 H3207
BIBLIOG/A COM SOCIETY NAT/G

S51
GOULD J.,"THE KOMSOMOL AND THE HITLER JUGEND." COM EUR+WWI GERMANY SOCIETY NAT/G POL/PAR SCHOOL TOTALISM DRIVE PERCEPT KNOWL FASCISM...SOC NAZI TOT/POP 20. PAGE 59 H1185
EDU/PROP CON/ANAL SOCISM

N51
MEYER E.W.,POLITICAL PARTIES IN WESTERN GERMANY (PAMPHLET). EUR+WWI GERMANY/W PRESS LEAD CHOOSE REPRESENT ATTIT 20. PAGE 109 H2189
BIBLIOG POL/PAR NAT/G VOL/ASSN

B52
BAILEY S.D.,THE BRITISH PARTY SYSTEM. UK LEGIS ...POLICY GP/COMP ANTHOL 11/20. PAGE 10 H0200
POL/PAR LOC/G NAT/G DELIB/GP

B52
BENTHAM A.,HANDBOOK OF POLITICAL FALLACIES. FUT MOD/EUR LAW INTELL LOC/G MUNIC NAT/G DELIB/GP LEGIS CREATE EDU/PROP CT/SYS ATTIT RIGID/FLEX KNOWL PWR ...RELATIV PSY SOC CONCPT SELF/OBS TREND STERTYP TOT/POP. PAGE 14 H0286
POL/PAR

B52
HIMMELFARB G.,LORD ACTON: A STUDY IN CONSCIENCE AND POLITICS. MOD/EUR NAT/G POL/PAR SECT LEGIS TOP/EX EDU/PROP ADMIN NAT/LISM ATTIT PERSON SUPEGO MORAL ORD/FREE...CONCPT PARLIAMENT 19 ACTON/LORD. PAGE 71 H1419
PWR BIOG

B52
SPENCER F.A.,WAR AND POSTWAR GREECE: AN ANALYSIS BASED ON GREEK WRITINGS. GREECE SOCIETY NAT/G POL/PAR FORCES CREATE DIPLOM LEAD MARXISM...SOC 20. PAGE 147 H2943
BIBLIOG/A WAR REV

B52
ULAM A.B.,TITOISM AND THE COMINFORM. USSR WOR+45 STRUCT INT/ORG NAT/G ACT/RES PLAN EXEC ATTIT DRIVE ALL/VALS...CONCPT OBS VAL/FREE 20 COMINTERN TITO/MARSH. PAGE 157 H3149
COM POL/PAR TOTALISM YUGOSLAVIA

S52
MCDOUGAL M.S.,"THE COMPARATIVE STUDY OF LAW FOR POLICY PURPOSES." FUT NAT/G POL/PAR CONSULT ADJUD PWR SOVEREIGN...METH/CNCPT IDEA/COMP SIMUL 20. PAGE 106 H2129
PLAN JURID NAT/LISM

C52
LEWIS B.W.,"BRITISH PLANNING AND NATIONALIZATION." UK INDUS SERV/IND LABOR NAT/G OP/RES TEC/DEV TAX WEALTH...CHARTS BIBLIOG 20. PAGE 96 H1912
NEW/LIB ECO/DEV POL/PAR PLAN

B53
BARZEL R.,DIE DEUTSCHEN PARTEIEN. GERMANY MARXISM SOCISM...CONCPT IDEA/COMP 19/20 SOC/DEMPAR CHRIS/DEM. PAGE 12 H0232
POL/PAR NAT/G LAISSEZ

B53
BUCHHEIM K.,GESCHICHTE DER CHRISTLICHEN PARTEIEN IN DEUTSCHLAND. GERMANY CREATE ATTIT SUPEGO ORD/FREE ...TIME/SEQ IDEA/COMP 19/20 CHRIS/DEM. PAGE 23 H0464
POL/PAR NAT/G

B53
KANTOR H.,A BIBLIOGRAPHY OF UNPUBLISHED DOCTORAL DISSERTATIONS AND MASTERS' THESES DEALING WITH GOVTS, POL, INT REL OF LAT AM. L/A+17C INT/ORG POL/PAR ACT/RES OP/RES CONFER ATTIT...INT/LAW PHIL/SCI 20. PAGE 83 H1656
BIBLIOG ACADEM DIPLOM NAT/G

B53
LEITES N.,A STUDY OF BOLSHEVISM. WOR+45 WOR-45 ELITES SOCIETY INT/ORG NAT/G EX/STRUC EDU/PROP EXEC ROUTINE ATTIT MORAL MARXISM...CONCPT OBS VAL/FREE 20. PAGE 94 H1869
COM POL/PAR USSR TOTALISM

B53
LEITES N.,A STUDY OF BOLSHEVISM. ELITES STRATA INT/ORG LOC/G POL/PAR WORKER EDU/PROP REV TOTALISM UTOPIA PWR...CONCPT 20 BOLSHEVISM. PAGE 94 H1870
MARXISM PLAN COM

B53
SHIRATO I.,JAPANESE SOURCES ON THE HISTORY OF THE CHINESE COMMUNIST MOVEMENT (PAMPHLET). CHINA/COM USSR CONSTRUC NAT/G POL/PAR FORCES DIPLOM DOMIN EDU/PROP CONTROL WAR TOTALISM SOCISM 20. PAGE 143 H2863
BIBLIOG/A MARXISM ECO/UNDEV

B53
STOUT H.M.,BRITISH GOVERNMENT. UK FINAN LOC/G POL/PAR DELIB/GP DIPLOM ADMIN COLONIAL CHOOSE ORD/FREE...JURID BIBLIOG 20 COMMONWLTH. PAGE 150 H2990
NAT/G PARL/PROC CONSTN NEW/LIB

C53
BULNER-THOMAS I.,"THE PARTY SYSTEM IN GREAT BRITAIN." UK CONSTN SECT PRESS CONFER GP/REL ATTIT ...POLICY TREND BIBLIOG 19/20 PARLIAMENT. PAGE 23 H0473
NAT/G POL/PAR ADMIN ROUTINE

B54
EPSTEIN L.D.,BRITAIN - UNEASY ALLY. KOREA UK USA+45 NAT/G POL/PAR ECO/TAC FOR/AID INT/TRADE WAR LABOR/PAR CONSRV/PAR. PAGE 47 H0934
DIPLOM ATTIT POLICY NAT/COMP

B54
FRIEDRICH C.J.,TOTALITARIAN DICTATORSHIP AND AUTOCRACY. COM EUR+WWI GERMANY ITALY USSR INTELL ECO/DEV NAT/G POL/PAR FORCES TOP/EX ECO/TAC EDU/PROP LEGIT COERCE ATTIT ORD/FREE PWR FASCISM ...CONCPT TIME/SEQ GEN/LAWS NAZI 20. PAGE 53 H1068
SOCIETY DOMIN TOTALISM

B54
JENNINGS I.,THE QUEEN'S GOVERNMENT. UK POL/PAR DELIB/GP ADJUD ADMIN CT/SYS PARL/PROC REPRESENT
NAT/G CONSTN

CONSERVE 13/20 PARLIAMENT. PAGE 80 H1605
LEGIS CHIEF

B54
LENIN V.I.,SELECTED WORKS (12 VOLS.). USSR INTELL SOCIETY STRATA STRUCT NAT/G POL/PAR WORKER CAP/ISM REV WAR...MARXIST PHIL/SCI 20 MARX/KARL LENIN/VI. PAGE 94 H1880
COM MARXISM

L54
FRIEDRICH C.J.,"TOTALITARIANISM." COM EUR+WWI NAT/G POL/PAR SECT FORCES PLAN ECO/TAC DOMIN EDU/PROP EXEC COERCE REV ORD/FREE PWR...SOC CONCPT NAZI 20. PAGE 53 H1067
ATTIT TOTALISM

C54
DE GRAZIA A.,"THE COMPARATIVE SURVEY OF EUROPEAN-AMERICAN POLITICAL BEHAV IOR; A RESEARCH PROSPECTUS (PAPER)" EUR+WWI FRANCE GERMANY SPAIN UK USA+45 WOR+45 STRATA POL/PAR DIPLOM EDU/PROP COLONIAL LEAD WAR NAT/LISM CONCPT. PAGE 37 H0752
BIBLIOG R+D METH NAT/COMP

C54
HAMMER E.J.,"THE STRUGGLE FOR INDOCHINA." COM VIETNAM POL/PAR REV CENTRAL NAT/LISM ATTIT...POLICY CHARTS BIBLIOG 20. PAGE 65 H1305
WAR COLONIAL S/ASIA NAT/G

C54
LANDAU J.M.,"PARLIAMENTS AND PARTIES IN EGYPT." UAR NAT/G SECT CONSULT LEGIS TOP/EX PROB/SOLV ADMIN COLONIAL...GEN/LAWS BIBLIOG 19/20. PAGE 90 H1804
ISLAM NAT/LISM PARL/PROC POL/PAR

B55
APTER D.E.,THE GOLD COAST IN TRANSITION. FUT CONSTN CULTURE SOCIETY ECO/UNDEV FAM KIN LOC/G NAT/G POL/PAR LEGIS TOP/EX EDU/PROP LEGIT ADMIN ATTIT PERSON PWR...CONCPT STAT INT CENSUS TOT/POP VAL/FREE. PAGE 7 H0149
AFR SOVEREIGN

B55
BRACHER K.D.,DIE AUFLOSUNG DER WEIMARER REPUBLIK. EUR+WWI GERMANY...TIME/SEQ 20. PAGE 20 H0395
TOTALISM NAT/G POL/PAR PARL/PROC

B55
FLECHTHEIM O.K.,DIE DEUTSCHEN PARTEIEN SEIT 1945. GERMANY/W CONSTN STRUCT FINAN ATTIT 20. PAGE 51 H1022
POL/PAR NAT/G GP/COMP

B55
FRANZ G.,KULTURKAMPF. AUSTRIA GERMANY PRUSSIA SWITZERLND POL/PAR DIPLOM GP/REL ATTIT ORD/FREE 18/19 CHURCH/STA. PAGE 53 H1053
NAT/LISM CATHISM NAT/G REV

B55
GALLOWAY G.B.,CONGRESS AND PARLIAMENT: THEIR ORGANIZATION AND OPERATION IN THE US AND THE UK: PLANNING PAMPHLET NO. 93. POL/PAR EX/STRUC DEBATE CONTROL LEAD ROUTINE EFFICIENCY PWR...POLICY CONGRESS PARLIAMENT. PAGE 54 H1089
DELIB/GP LEGIS PARL/PROC GOV/COMP

B55
HEYDTE A F.,SOZIOLOGIE DER DEUTSCHEN PARTEIEN. GERMANY/W CONSTN ELITES CHOOSE 20. PAGE 70 H1412
POL/PAR SOC STRUCT NAT/G

B55
MAZZINI J.,THE DUTIES OF MAN. MOD/EUR LAW SOCIETY FAM NAT/G POL/PAR SECT VOL/ASSN EX/STRUC ACT/RES CREATE REV PEACE ATTIT ALL/VALS...GEN/LAWS WORK 19. PAGE 106 H2113
SUPEGO CONCPT NAT/LISM

B55
NAMIER L.,PERSONALITIES AND POWERS. EUR+WWI MOD/EUR NAT/G POL/PAR TOP/EX EDU/PROP KNOWL...GEOG 17/20. PAGE 115 H2308
TIME/SEQ DIPLOM UK

B55
POLLOCK J.K.,GERMAN DEMOCRACY AT WORK. GERMANY/W LOC/G NAT/G DIPLOM PARL/PROC...OBS IDEA/COMP 20. PAGE 127 H2539
PARTIC POL/PAR CHOOSE EDU/PROP

B55
RUSTOW D.A.,THE POLITICS OF COMPROMISE. SWEDEN LABOR EX/STRUC LEGIS PLAN REPRESENT SOCISM...SOC 19/20. PAGE 136 H2720
POL/PAR NAT/G POLICY ECO/TAC

B55
TAN C.C.,THE BOXER CATASTROPHE. ASIA UK USSR ELITES POL/PAR VOL/ASSN FORCES PROB/SOLV DIPLOM ADMIN COLONIAL NAT/LISM PEACE TREATY 19/20 BOXER/REBL. PAGE 152 H3040
REV NAT/G WAR

B55
WOYTINSKY W.S.,WORLD COMMERCE AND GOVERNMENTS: TRENDS AND OUTLOOK. WOR+45 FINAN POL/PAR DIPLOM ECO/TAC FOR/AID DOMIN WAR CHOOSE...CHARTS BIBLIOG 20 LEAGUE/NAT UN ILO. PAGE 171 H3413
INT/TRADE DIST/IND NAT/COMP NAT/G

L55
ROSTOW W.W.,"RUSSIA AND CHINA UNDER COMMUNISM." CHINA/COM USSR INTELL STRUCT INT/ORG NAT/G POL/PAR TOP/EX ACT/RES PLAN ADMIN ATTIT ALL/VALS MARXISM ...CONCPT OBS TIME/SEQ TREND GOV/COMP VAL/FREE 20. PAGE 134 H2689
COM ASIA

B56
FIELD G.C.,POLITICAL THEORY. POL/PAR REPRESENT
CONCPT

MORAL SOVEREIGN...JURID IDEA/COMP. PAGE 50 H0990
NAT/G ORD/FREE DIPLOM

B56
HERNANDEZ URBINA A.,LOS PARTIDOS Y LA CRISIS DEL APRA. PERU NAT/G LEAD LOBBY CHOOSE SOCISM...POLICY DECISION 20 COM/PARTY APRA CONGRESS. PAGE 70 H1402
POL/PAR PARTIC PARL/PROC GP/REL

B56
JENNINGS W.I.,THE APPROACH TO SELF-GOVERNMENT. CEYLON INDIA PAKISTAN S/ASIA UK SOCIETY POL/PAR DELIB/GP LEGIS ECO/TAC EDU/PROP ADMIN EXEC CHOOSE ATTIT ALL/VALS...JURID CONCPT GEN/METH TOT/POP 20. PAGE 81 H1610
NAT/G CONSTN COLONIAL

B56
KUPER L.,PASSIVE RESISTANCE IN SOUTH AFRICA. SOUTH/AFR LAW NAT/G POL/PAR VOL/ASSN DISCRIM ...POLICY SOC AUD/VIS 20. PAGE 89 H1782
ORD/FREE RACE/REL ATTIT

B56
PADMORE G.,PAN-AFRICANISM OR COMMUNISM. AFR FUT NIGERIA INTELL NAT/G COLONIAL FEDERAL ATTIT DRIVE PWR RESPECT WEALTH MARXISM...CONCPT AUD/VIS STERTYP 20. PAGE 122 H2440
POL/PAR NAT/LISM

B56
SMEDLEY A.,THE GREAT ROAD: THE LIFE AND TIMES OF CHU TEH. ASIA USSR NAT/G POL/PAR DIPLOM COERCE GUERRILLA CIVMIL/REL NAT/LISM PERSON SKILL MARXISM ...BIOG 20 CHINJAP MAO. PAGE 145 H2903
REV WAR FORCES

B56
VON BECKERATH E.,HANDWORTERBUCH DER SOCIALWISSENSCHAFTEN (II VOLS.). EUR+WWI GERMANY POL/PAR WORKER DIPLOM LEAD CHOOSE SUFF WEALTH...SOC 20. PAGE 163 H3263
BIBLIOG INT/TRADE NAT/G ECO/DEV

B56
WEBER M.,STAATSSOZIOLOGIE. STRUCT LEGIT ADMIN PARL/PROC SUPEGO CONSERVE JURID. PAGE 166 H3320
SOC NAT/G POL/PAR LEAD

B56
WEBER M.,WIRTSCHAFT UND GESELLSCHAFT (2ND VOL.). STRUCT NAT/G POL/PAR LEAD PWR OBJECTIVE IDEA/COMP. PAGE 166 H3321
LEGIT JURID SOC

B56
WHITAKER A.P.,ARGENTINE UPHEAVAL. STRUCT FORCES DIPLOM COERCE PWR 20 ARGEN. PAGE 167 H3343
REV POL/PAR STRATA NAT/G

B56
WILSON P.,GOVERNMENT AND POLITICS OF INDIA AND PAKISTAN: 1885-1955; A BIBLIOGRAPHY OF WORKS IN WESTERN LANGUAGES. INDIA PAKISTAN CONSTN LOC/G POL/PAR FORCES DIPLOM ADMIN WAR CHOOSE...BIOG CON/ANAL 19/20. PAGE 169 H3380
BIBLIOG COLONIAL NAT/G S/ASIA

L56
EPSTEIN L.D.,"BRITISH MASS PARTIES IN COMPARISON WITH AMERICAN PARTIES" UK USA+45 STRATA ECO/DEV LABOR...CON/ANAL 20. PAGE 47 H0936
POL/PAR NAT/COMP PARTIC CHOOSE

S56
EPSTEIN L.D.,"COHESION OF BRITISH PARLIAMENTARY PARTIES." UK STRUCT ADMIN ROUTINE INGP/REL PWR ...GP/COMP PARLIAMENT. PAGE 47 H0935
NAT/G PARL/PROC POL/PAR

S56
KHAMA T.,"POLITICAL CHANGE IN AFRICAN SOCIETY." CONSTN SOCIETY LOC/G NAT/G POL/PAR EX/STRUC LEGIS LEGIT ADMIN CHOOSE REPRESENT NAT/LISM MORAL ORD/FREE PWR...CONCPT OBS TREND GEN/METH CMN/WLTH 17/20. PAGE 85 H1706
AFR ELITES

S56
MACRAE D. JR.,"ROLL CALL VOTES AND LEADERSHIP." ACT/RES LEAD CHOOSE DRIVE CONSERVE NEW/LIB...STAT STYLE. PAGE 100 H2007
POL/PAR GOV/COMP LEGIS SUPEGO

C56
FALL B.B.,"THE VIET-MINH REGIME." VIETNAM LAW ECO/UNDEV POL/PAR FORCES DOMIN WAR ATTIT MARXISM ...BIOG PREDICT BIBLIOG/A 20. PAGE 48 H0967
NAT/G ADMIN EX/STRUC LEAD

C56
NEUMANN S.,"MODERN POLITICAL PARTIES: APPROACHES TO COMPARATIVE POLITIC. FRANCE UK EX/STRUC DOMIN ADMIN LEAD REPRESENT TOTALISM ATTIT...POLICY TREND METH/COMP ANTHOL BIBLIOG/A 20 CMN/WLTH. PAGE 117 H2338
POL/PAR GOV/COMP ELITES MAJORIT

B57
ARON R.,THE OPIUM OF THE INTELLECTUALS (TRANS. BY TERENCE KILMARTIN). FRANCE USSR WOR+45 CULTURE POL/PAR PLAN DOMIN EDU/PROP REV ATTIT ORD/FREE ...IDEA/COMP METH/COMP NAT/COMP 20 COM/PARTY. PAGE 8 H0169
INTELL UTOPIA MYTH MARXISM

B57
CHANDRA S.,PARTIES AND POLITICS AT THE MUGHAL COURT: 1707-1740. INDIA CULTURE EX/STRUC CREATE PLAN PWR...BIBLIOG/A 18. PAGE 29 H0574
POL/PAR ELITES NAT/G

B57
HAMMOND B.,BANKS AND POLITICS IN AMERICA FROM THE
FINAN

REVOLUTION TO THE CIVIL WAR. CANADA USA-45 STRATA ...NAT/COMP 18/19. PAGE 65 H1306
PWR POL/PAR NAT/G

B57
HODGKIN T.,NATIONALISM IN COLONIAL AFRICA. STRATA STRUCT MUNIC NAT/G POL/PAR LEGIS ATTIT SOVEREIGN ...POLICY TREND BIBLIOG 20. PAGE 72 H1444
AFR COLONIAL NAT/LISM DIPLOM

B57
HOUN F.W.,CENTRAL GOVERNMENT OF CHINA, 1912-1928. ASIA CONSTN CHIEF LEGIS CONTROL PWR...BIBLIOG 20. PAGE 74 H1480
POL/PAR ATTIT NAT/G PLAN

B57
IKE N.,JAPANESE POLITICS. INTELL STRUCT AGRI INDUS FAM KIN LABOR PRESS CHOOSE ATTIT...DECISION BIBLIOG 19/20 CHINJAP. PAGE 76 H1523
NAT/G ADMIN POL/PAR CULTURE

B57
KENNEDY M.D.,A SHORT HISTORY OF COMMUNISM IN ASIA. ASIA BURMA INDIA S/ASIA THAILAND NAT/G POL/PAR LEAD REV WAR MARXISM SOCISM...POLICY 20 CHINJAP. PAGE 85 H1688
DIPLOM NAT/LISM TOTALISM COERCE

B57
LAQUER W.Z.,COMMUNISM AND NATIONALISM IN THE MIDDLE EAST. ELITES INTELL STRATA NAT/G POL/PAR SECT VOL/ASSN TOP/EX DOMIN LEGIT REGION COERCE ATTIT PERSON PWR...CONCPT HIST/WRIT TIME/SEQ TREND GEN/LAWS VAL/FREE. PAGE 91 H1817
ISLAM NAT/LISM

B57
LOUCKS W.N.,COMPARATIVE ECONOMIC SYSTEMS (5TH ED.). COM UK USSR INDUS POL/PAR PLAN CAP/ISM TOTALISM MARXISM...PHIL/SCI BIBLIOG 19/20. PAGE 99 H1969
NAT/COMP IDEA/COMP SOCISM

B57
MUELLER-DEHAM A.,HUMAN RELATIONS AND POWER; SOCIO-POLITICAL ANALYSIS AND SYNTHESIS. CONSTN SOCIETY NAT/G POL/PAR PROVS LEGIS POPULISM...SOC NEW/IDEA. PAGE 114 H2280
GEN/LAWS PERS/REL PWR CONCPT

B57
POPLAI S.L.,NATIONAL POLITICS AND 1957 ELECTIONS IN INDIA. INDIA BARGAIN PARL/PROC CONSEN NAT/LISM PWR WEALTH 20. PAGE 127 H2543
POL/PAR CHOOSE POLICY NAT/G

B57
ROBERTSON H.M.,SOUTH AFRICA, ECONOMIC AND POLITICAL ASPECTS. SOUTH/AFR CONSTN CULTURE POL/PAR LEGIS DIPLOM DOMIN COLONIAL...SOC BIBLIOG 19/20. PAGE 132 H2647
RACE/REL ECO/UNDEV ECO/TAC DISCRIM

B57
SCHLESINGER J.A.,HOW THEY BECAME GOVERNOR; A STUDY OF COMPARATIVE STATE POLITICS, 1870-1950. USA+45 USA-45 LAW POL/PAR LEGIS EDU/PROP REGION...STAT TREND CHARTS TIME 19/20 GOVERNOR. PAGE 139 H2788
PROVS CHIEF GOV/COMP CHOOSE

B57
TOMASIC D.A.,NATIONAL COMMUNISM AND SOVIET STRATEGY. UK USSR YUGOSLAVIA NAT/G POL/PAR CHIEF CREATE DOMIN REV WAR PWR...BIOG TREND 20 TITO/MARSH STALIN/J. PAGE 156 H3112
COM NAT/LISM MARXISM DIPLOM

L57
BENDIX R.,"POLITICAL SOCIOLOGY." CULTURE INTELL LABOR POL/PAR SECT LEGIS EDU/PROP ADMIN CHOOSE CIVMIL/REL ATTIT...IDEA/COMP 20. PAGE 14 H0274
BIBLIOG/A ACT/RES SOC

L57
LIPSET S.M.,"POLITICAL SOCIOLOGY." NAT/G POL/PAR ECO/TAC PARTIC CHOOSE PWR...BIBLIOG/A 20. PAGE 97 H1939
SOC ALL/IDEOS ACADEM

C57
MORRIS-JONES W.H.,"PARLIAMENT IN INDIA." INDIA CONSTN LEGIS CONFER COLONIAL CHOOSE PRIVIL ATTIT ...GOV/COMP BIBLIOG 20. PAGE 113 H2264
PARL/PROC EX/STRUC NAT/G POL/PAR

N57
JENNINGS W.I.,NATIONALISM, COLONIALISM, AND NEUTRALISM (PAMPHLET). ASIA INDIA S/ASIA UK INTELL ACADEM POL/PAR 20. PAGE 81 H1611
NAT/LISM COLONIAL NEUTRAL ATTIT

B58
BRADY A.,DEMOCRACY IN THE DOMINIONS (3RD ED.). CANADA NEW/ZEALND SOUTH/AFR WOR+45 LAW EX/STRUC DOMIN COLONIAL PARL/PROC REPRESENT RACE/REL NAT/LISM WEALTH 20 AUSTRAL CMN/WLTH. PAGE 20 H0399
GOV/COMP POL/PAR POPULISM NAT/G

B58
CAMPBELL P.,FRENCH ELECTORAL SYSTEMS AND ELECTIONS SINCE 1789 (2ND ED.). FRANCE NAT/G EX/STRUC PWR ...CHARTS 18/20. PAGE 26 H0516
REPRESENT CHOOSE POL/PAR SUFF

B58
CARTER G.M.,TRANSITION IN AFRICA; STUDIES IN POLITICAL ADAPTATION. AFR CENTRL/AFR GHANA NIGERIA CONSTN LOC/G POL/PAR ADMIN GP/REL FEDERAL...MAJORIT BIBLIOG 20. PAGE 27 H0543
NAT/COMP PWR CONTROL NAT/G

B58
COLEMAN J.S.,NIGERIA: BACKGROUND TO NATIONALISM. AFR SOCIETY ECO/DEV KIN LOC/G POL/PAR TEC/DEV DOMIN ADMIN DRIVE PWR RESPECT...TRADIT SOC INT SAMP TIME/SEQ 20. PAGE 31 H0627
NAT/G NAT/LISM NIGERIA

B58
COWAN L.G.,LOCAL GOVERNMENT IN WEST AFRICA. AFR FRANCE UK CULTURE KIN POL/PAR CHIEF LEGIS CREATE ADMIN PARTIC GOV/REL GP/REL...METH/COMP 20. PAGE 34 H0682
LOC/G COLONIAL SOVEREIGN REPRESENT

B58
FLORES X.,LA TRADICION CATOLICA Y EL FUTURO POLITICO DE ESPANA (PAMPHLET). SPAIN NAT/G ACT/RES LEAD GP/REL CATHISM 20 CHRISTIAN CHURCH/STA. PAGE 52 H1031
SECT POL/PAR ATTIT ORD/FREE

B58
HAAS E.B.,THE UNITING OF EUROPE. EUR+WWI INT/ORG NAT/G POL/PAR TOP/EX ECO/TAC EDU/PROP LEGIT FEDERAL NAT/LISM DRIVE RIGID/FLEX ORD/FREE PWR PLURISM ...POLICY CONCPT INT GEN/LAWS ECSC EEC 20. PAGE 63 H1264
VOL/ASSN ECO/DEV

B58
HANSARD SOCIETY PARL GOVT,WHAT ARE THE PROBLEMS OF PARLIAMENTARY GOVERNMENT IN WEST AFRICA? PROB/SOLV DIPLOM GP/REL 20 PARLIAMENT AFRICA/W. PAGE 66 H1317
PARL/PROC POL/PAR AFR NAT/G

B58
HERMENS F.A.,THE REPRESENTATIVE REPUBLIC. USA-45 PLURISM GOV/COMP. PAGE 70 H1401
POL/PAR CHOOSE REPRESENT

B58
HSU U.T.,THE INVISIBLE CONFLICT. ASIA USSR ELITES NAT/G CONTROL LEAD COERCE REV WAR NAT/LISM ORD/FREE PWR 20 COM/PARTY ESPIONAGE. PAGE 74 H1485
MARXISM POL/PAR EDU/PROP FORCES

B58
PALMER E.E.,"POLITICAL MAN" IN E. PALMER, PROBLEMS IN DEMOCRATIC CITIZENSHIP. LOC/G NAT/G LEGIS PRESS CHOOSE REPRESENT GP/REL...DECISION SOC IDEA/COMP ANTHOL 20. PAGE 123 H2449
PARTIC POL/PAR EDU/PROP MAJORIT

B58
SCHOEPS H.J.,KONSERVATIVE ERNEUERUNG IDEEN ZUR DEUTSCHEN POLITIK. GERMANY ELITES SOCIETY ACADEM CHOOSE SOCISM 19/20. PAGE 140 H2796
POL/PAR IDEA/COMP CONSERVE NAT/G

B58
SCOTT D.J.R.,RUSSIAN POLITICAL INSTITUTIONS. RUSSIA USSR CONSTN AGRI DELIB/GP PLAN EDU/PROP CONTROL CHOOSE EFFICIENCY ATTIT MARXISM...BIBLIOG/A 13/20. PAGE 141 H2813
NAT/G POL/PAR ADMIN DECISION

B58
WIGGIN L.M.,THE FACTION OF COUSINS: A POLITICAL ACCOUNT OF THE GRENVILLES, 1733-1763. UK STRUCT KIN NAT/G INGP/REL...CONCPT BIOG BIBLIOG/A 18 GRENVILLES. PAGE 168 H3357
FAM POL/PAR PWR

B58
WILMERDING L. JR.,THE ELECTORAL COLLEGE. CONSTN NAT/G POL/PAR DELIB/GP LEGIS PROB/SOLV CONFER EXEC LEAD APPORT REPRESENT. PAGE 169 H3377
CHOOSE DECISION ACT/RES

S58
APTER D.E.,"A COMPARATIVE METHOD FOR THE STUDY OF POLITICS" (BMR)" UNIV SOCIETY STRATA NAT/G POL/PAR ...CHARTS SIMUL 20. PAGE 8 H0151
SOC METH METH/COMP

S58
PYE L.W.,"THE NON-WESTERN POLITICAL PROCESS" (BMR)" AFR ASIA ISLAM S/ASIA DIPLOM ADMIN LEAD LOBBY ROUTINE CONSEN...DECISION 20. PAGE 128 H2567
CULTURE POL/PAR NAT/G LOC/G

S58
STAAR R.F.,"ELECTIONS IN COMMUNIST POLAND." EUR+WWI SOCIETY INT/ORG NAT/G POL/PAR LEGIS ACT/RES ECO/TAC EDU/PROP ADJUD ADMIN ROUTINE COERCE TOTALISM ATTIT ORD/FREE PWR 20. PAGE 148 H2963
COM CHOOSE POLAND

C58
GOLAY J.F.,"THE FOUNDING OF THE FEDERAL REPUBLIC OF GERMANY." GERMANY/W CONSTN EX/STRUC DIPLOM ADMIN CHOOSE...DECISION BIBLIOG 20. PAGE 58 H1155
FEDERAL NAT/G PARL/PROC POL/PAR

C58
WILDING N.,"AN ENCYCLOPEDIA OF PARLIAMENT." UK LAW CONSTN CHIEF PROB/SOLV DIPLOM DEBATE WAR INGP/REL PRIVIL...BIBLIOG DICTIONARY 13/20 CMN/WLTH PARLIAMENT. PAGE 168 H3363
PARL/PROC POL/PAR NAT/G ADMIN

B59
BARRON R.,PARTIES AND POLITICS IN MODERN FRANCE. FRANCE LOC/G DELIB/GP LEGIS TOP/EX EDU/PROP LEGIT TV FEEDBACK 20. PAGE 12 H0230
POL/PAR ALL/IDEOS CHOOSE PARTIC

B59
BROWN D.F.,THE GROWTH OF DEMOCRATIC GOVERNMENT. WOR+45 BARGAIN EDU/PROP LOBBY APPORT CHOOSE 20. PAGE 22 H0441
GOV/COMP LEGIS POL/PAR CHIEF

B59
CAREW-HUNT R.C.,BOOKS ON COMMUNISM. NAT/G POL/PAR DIPLOM REV...BIOG 19/20. PAGE 26 H0528
BIBLIOG/A MARXISM COM ASIA

B59
EAENZA L.,COMMUNISMO E CATTOLICESIMO IN UNA PARROCHIA DI CAMPAGNA, ITALY CULTURE ELITES ECO/DEV
ATTIT CATHISM

AGRI KIN POL/PAR DOMIN LEGIT RIGID/FLEX...DECISION OBS IDEA/COMP 20 COM/PARTY CHURCH/STA. PAGE 44 H0878 NEIGH MARXISM

B59
EPSTEIN F.T.,EAST GERMANY: A SELECTED BIBLIOGRAPHY (PAMPHLET). COM GERMANY/E LAW AGRI FINAN INDUS LABOR POL/PAR EDU/PROP ADMIN AGE/Y 20. PAGE 47 H0932 BIBLIOG/A INTELL MARXISM NAT/G

B59
GOPAL R.,INDIAN MUSLIMS: A POLITICAL HISTORY (1858-1947). INDIA ISLAM PAKISTAN NAT/G SECT LEGIS LEAD COERCE WAR REPRESENT ISOLAT ORD/FREE 19/20 HINDU MUSLIM. PAGE 59 H1175 COLONIAL GP/REL POL/PAR REGION

B59
JENKINS C.,POWER AT THE TOP: A CRITICAL SURVEY OF THE NATIONALIZED INDUSTRIES. UK POL/PAR CONTROL ...WELF/ST CHARTS 20 LABOR/PAR. PAGE 80 H1601 NAT/G OWN INDUS NEW/LIB

B59
JENNINGS W.I.,CABINET GOVERNMENT (3RD ED.). UK POL/PAR CHIEF BUDGET ADMIN CHOOSE GP/REL 20. PAGE 81 H1612 DELIB/GP NAT/G CONSTN OP/RES

B59
KELF-COHEN R.,NATIONALISATION IN BRITAIN: THE END OF DOGMA. EUR+WWI UK NAT/G POL/PAR WORKER ECO/TAC PARL/PROC WEALTH SOCISM...GOV/COMP 20. PAGE 84 H1683 NEW/LIB ECO/DEV INDUS OWN

B59
LEITES N.,ON THE GAME OF POLITICS IN FRANCE. ALGERIA FRANCE CONSTN SECT VOL/ASSN ECO/TAC INT/TRADE PARL/PROC WAR SOCISM 20 DEGAULLE/C EEC. PAGE 94 H1871 POL/PAR NAT/G LEGIS IDEA/COMP

B59
MADHOK B.,POLITICAL TRENDS IN INDIA. INDIA PAKISTAN UK STRATA ECO/UNDEV POL/PAR LEGIS CAP/ISM DIPLOM COLONIAL CHOOSE MARXISM...SOC TREND 20 GANDHI/M NEHRU/J. PAGE 101 H2014 GEOG NAT/G

B59
MAIER H.,REVOLUTION UND KIRCHE. FRANCE MOD/EUR SECT REV ORD/FREE...IDEA/COMP 18/19. PAGE 101 H2018 NAT/G CATHISM ATTIT POL/PAR

B59
MARTZ J.D.,CENTRAL AMERICA: THE CRISIS AND THE CHALLENGE. L/A+17C POL/PAR CHIEF CHOOSE SOVEREIGN ...BIOG TREND BIBLIOG 20 CENTRAL/AM. PAGE 104 H2071 NAT/G GOV/REL DIPLOM GOV/COMP

B59
OVERSTREET G.D.,COMMUNISM IN INDIA. INDIA S/ASIA CONSTN INT/ORG LEAD GP/REL...CHARTS BIBLIOG 20. PAGE 122 H2435 MARXISM NAT/LISM POL/PAR WAR

B59
PANIKKAR K.M.,THE AFRO-ASIAN STATES AND THEIR PROBLEMS. COM CULTURE KIN POL/PAR SECT DIPLOM EDU/PROP COLONIAL SOVEREIGN...TECHNIC GOV/COMP 20. PAGE 123 H2458 AFR S/ASIA ECO/UNDEV

B59
SENGHOR L.S.,RAPPORT SUR LA DOCTRINE ET LA PROGRAMME DU PART I. FRANCE MALI CONSTN POL/PAR PLAN CHOOSE OWN ORD/FREE MARXISM...SOCIALIST 20 NEGRO. PAGE 141 H2828 ATTIT NAT/G AFR SOCISM

B59
VERNEY D.V.,PUBLIC ENTERPRISE IN SWEDEN. FUT SWEDEN UK INDUS POL/PAR LEGIS PROB/SOLV CAP/ISM INT/TRADE CONTROL SOCISM...MGT CONCPT NAT/COMP 20 SOCDEM/PAR CIVIL/SERV. PAGE 162 H3246 ECO/DEV POLICY LG/CO NAT/G

B59
WRAITH R.E.,EAST AFRICAN CITIZEN. AFR GHANA UK AGRI INDUS LOC/G POL/PAR PROB/SOLV CONTROL REGION REPRESENT NAT/LISM PWR...OBS 20 AFRICA/E AFRICA/W. PAGE 171 H3415 ECO/UNDEV RACE/REL NAT/G NAT/COMP

L59
JANIS I.L.,"DECISIONAL CONFLICT: A THEORETICAL ANALYSIS." INTELL NAT/G POL/PAR DELIB/GP LEGIS TOP/EX PLAN...DECISION CONGRESS NAZI 20 WWI. PAGE 80 H1590 ACT/RES PSY DIPLOM

S59
LEYS C.,"MODELS, THEORIES, AND THE THEORY OF POLITICAL PARTIES" CANADA LIECHTENST UK LOC/G NAT/G PARTIC REPRESENT GP/REL CONSEN EQUILIB MAJORITY ...NEW/IDEA MATH CHARTS 20. PAGE 96 H1919 POL/PAR CHOOSE METH/CNCPT SIMUL

S59
MENDELSON W.,"JUDICIAL REVIEW AND PARTY POLITICS" (BMR)" UK USA+45 USA-45 NAT/G LEGIS PROB/SOLV EDU/PROP ADJUD EFFICIENCY...POLICY NAT/COMP 19/20 AUSTRAL SUPREME/CT. PAGE 109 H2171 CT/SYS POL/PAR BAL/PWR JURID

S59
SKILLING H.G.,"COMMUNISM: NATIONAL OR INTERNATIONAL." CHINA/COM USSR YUGOSLAVIA NAT/G POL/PAR VOL/ASSN DOMIN REGION COERCE ATTIT PWR MARXISM SOCISM...CONCPT TOT/POP 20 TITO/MARSH. PAGE 145 H2894 COM TREND

C59
KARPAT K.H.,"TURKEY'S POLITICS: THE TRANSITION TO A MULTI-PARTY SYSTEM." COM TURKEY CULTURE ECO/UNDEV SECT TEC/DEV NAT/LISM ATTIT...SOC CON/ANAL BIBLIOG 20. PAGE 83 H1664 POL/PAR NAT/G

C59
KORNHAUSER W.,"THE POLITICS OF MASS SOCIETY." COM CULTURE ELITES INTELL STRATA POL/PAR ATTIT...SOC CHARTS GEN/LAWS BIBLIOG 20. PAGE 88 H1757 CROWD PLURISM CONSTN SOCIETY

B60
JUNZ A.J.,PRESENT TRENDS IN AMERICAN NATIONAL GOVERNMENT. LEGIS DIPLOM ADMIN CT/SYS ORD/FREE ...CONCPT ANTHOL 20 CONGRESS PRESIDENT SUPREME/CT. PAGE 3 H0052 POL/PAR CHOOSE CONSTN NAT/G

B60
AYEARST M.,THE BRITISH WEST INDIES: THE SEARCH FOR SELF-GOVERNMENT. FUT WEST/IND LOC/G POL/PAR EX/STRUC LEGIS CHOOSE FEDERAL...NAT/COMP BIBLIOG 17/20. PAGE 9 H0186 CONSTN COLONIAL REPRESENT NAT/G

B60
BREDVOLD L.I.,THE PHILOSOPHY OF EDMUND BURKE. POL/PAR PARL/PROC REPRESENT CONSERVE...JURID 18 BURKE/EDM. PAGE 20 H0410 PHIL/SCI NAT/G CONCPT

B60
CARTER G.M.,INDEPENDENCE FOR AFRICA. AFR FUT SOCIETY STRATA ECO/DEV POL/PAR DELIB/GP PLAN DOMIN EDU/PROP COLONIAL REGION ATTIT DRIVE SOVEREIGN ...RECORD INT TIME/SEQ CHARTS 20. PAGE 27 H0544 NAT/G PWR NAT/LISM

B60
HARRISON S.S.,INDIA: THE MOST DANGEROUS DECADES. INDIA CONSTN STRATA POL/PAR SECT PLAN ADMIN CHOOSE GP/REL TOTALISM MARXISM...LING 20 NEHRU/J. PAGE 67 H1347 CULTURE ECO/UNDEV PROB/SOLV REGION

B60
JEMOLO A.C.,CHURCH AND STATE IN ITALY 1850-1950 (TRANS. BY DAVID MOORE). ITALY CONSTN STRATA WAR FASCISM SOCISM...TIME/SEQ 19/20 CHURCH/STA CHRIS/DEM. PAGE 80 H1599 GP/REL NAT/G CATHISM POL/PAR

B60
JHA C.,INDIAN GOVERNMENT AND POLITICS. INDIA SERV/IND POL/PAR PROVS LEGIS CT/SYS CHOOSE GOV/REL FEDERAL 20. PAGE 81 H1616 NAT/G PARL/PROC CONSTN ADJUST

B60
JOHNSON H.M.,SOCIOLOGY: A SYSTEMATIC INTRODUCTION. MARKET FAM LABOR POL/PAR CHOOSE DISCRIM MARRIAGE ALL/IDEOS...BIBLIOG T WORSHIP. PAGE 81 H1620 SOC SOCIETY CULTURE GEN/LAWS

B60
LA PONCE J.A.,THE PROTECTION OF MINORITIES. WOR+45 WOR-45 NAT/G POL/PAR SUFF...INT/LAW CLASSIF GP/COMP GOV/COMP BIBLIOG 17/20 CIVIL/LIB CIV/RIGHTS. PAGE 90 H1793 INGP/REL DOMIN SOCIETY RACE/REL

B60
LINDSAY K.,EUROPEAN ASSEMBLIES: THE EXPERIMENTAL PERIOD 1949-1959. EUR+WWI ECO/DEV NAT/G POL/PAR LEGIS TOP/EX ACT/RES PLAN ECO/TAC DOMIN LEGIT ROUTINE ATTIT DRIVE ORD/FREE PWR SKILL...SOC CONCPT TREND CHARTS GEN/LAWS VAL/FREE. PAGE 97 H1932 VOL/ASSN INT/ORG REGION

B60
LOMBARDO TOLEDANO V,EL NEONAZISMO; SUS CHARACTERISTICAS Y PELIGROS. GERMANY/W POL/PAR COLONIAL LEAD LOBBY ATTIT 20 NAZI. PAGE 98 H1956 NAT/G FASCISM POLICY DIPLOM

B60
MACFARQUHAR R.,THE HUNDRED FLOWERS. ASIA NAT/G WORKER GP/REL ORD/FREE MARXISM 20 MAO. PAGE 100 H1991 DEBATE PRESS POL/PAR ATTIT

B60
MACRIDIS R.C.,THE DE GAULLE REPUBLIC: QUEST FOR UNITY. EUR+WWI NAT/G POL/PAR LEGIS LEGIT NAT/LISM ATTIT RIGID/FLEX ORD/FREE PWR...JURID CONCPT TIME/SEQ 20 DEGAULLE/C. PAGE 100 H2009 TOP/EX STRUCT FRANCE

B60
MATTHIAS E.,DAS ENDE DER PARTEIEN 1933. GERMANY NAT/G COERCE CHOOSE ORD/FREE PWR 20. PAGE 105 H2100 FASCISM POL/PAR DOMIN ATTIT

B60
MC CLELLAN G.S.,INDIA. CHINA/COM INDIA CONSTN ELITES STRATA AGRI POL/PAR FOR/AID ARMS/CONT REV MARXISM...CENSUS BIBLIOG 20 COLD/WAR GANDHI/M NEHRU/J. PAGE 106 H2117 DIPLOM NAT/G SOCIETY ECO/UNDEV

B60
MCCLOSKY H.,THE SOVIET DICTATORSHIP. FUT CONSTN CULTURE INTELL SOCIETY POL/PAR SECT VOL/ASSN FORCES PLAN TEC/DEV DOMIN EDU/PROP COERCE PWR MARXISM ...POLICY CONCPT MYTH STERTYP 20. PAGE 106 H2127 COM NAT/G TOTALISM USSR

B60
MEYRIAT J.,LA SCIENCE POLITIQUE EN FRANCE, 1945-1958; BIBLIOGRAPHIES FRANCAISES DE SCIENCES SOCIALES (VOL. I). EUR+WWI FRANCE POL/PAR DIPLOM ADMIN CHOOSE ATTIT...IDEA/COMP METH/COMP NAT/COMP 20. PAGE 110 H2193 BIBLIOG/A NAT/G CONCPT PHIL/SCI

B60
MORRIS I.,NATIONALISM AND THE RIGHT WING IN JAPAN: POL/PAR

A STUDY OF POST WAR TRENDS. ASIA ELITES NAT/G DELIB/GP FORCES TOP/EX CHOOSE ATTIT...INT GEN/LAWS CONGRESS 20 CHINJAP. PAGE 113 H2262 TREND NAT/LISM

B60
PANIKKAR K.M.,THE STATE AND THE CITIZEN (2ND ED.). INDIA DOMIN ATTIT SUPEGO ORD/FREE WEALTH...GEOG CONCPT GP/COMP 20. PAGE 123 H2459 TEC/DEV POL/PAR NAT/G EDU/PROP

B60
ROSKAM K.L.,APARTHEID AND DISCRIMINATION. SOUTH/AFR SOCIETY STRUCT NAT/G POL/PAR GP/REL ISOLAT ...BIBLIOG 20. PAGE 134 H2683 DISCRIM RACE/REL CULTURE POLICY

B60
ROY N.C.,THE CIVIL SERVICE IN INDIA. INDIA POL/PAR ECO/TAC INCOME...JURID MGT 20 CIVIL/SERV. PAGE 135 H2705 ADMIN NAT/G DELIB/GP CONFER

B60
SCHAPIRO L.,THE COMMUNIST PARTY OF THE SOVIET UNION. COM LAW SOCIETY STRATA STRUCT ECO/DEV LABOR NAT/G POL/PAR CREATE DOMIN EDU/PROP COERCE TOTALISM MARXISM...POLICY CONCPT MYTH TIME/SEQ WORK TOT/POP 20 LENIN/VI STALIN/J. PAGE 139 H2772 INTELL PWR USSR

B60
SHIRER W.L.,THE RISE AND FALL OF THE THIRD REICH: A HISTORY OF NAZI GERMANY. EUR+WWI CULTURE ECO/DEV INDUS NAT/G POL/PAR FORCES PLAN TEC/DEV ECO/TAC COERCE ATTIT DRIVE PERSON PWR...MYSTIC PSY SOC MYTH STAT CHARTS EXHIBIT WORK VAL/FREE. PAGE 143 H2864 STRUCT GERMANY TOTALISM

B60
STOLPER W.F.,GERMANY BETWEEN EAST AND WEST: THE ECONOMICS OF COMPETITIVE COEXISTENCE. FUT GERMANY/E GERMANY/W WOR+45 FINAN POL/PAR BUDGET ECO/TAC FOR/AID INT/TRADE...STAT CHARTS METH/COMP 20 COLD/WAR. PAGE 150 H2989 ECO/DEV DIPLOM GOV/COMP BAL/PWR

B60
WORLEY P.,ASIA TODAY (REV. ED.) (PAMPHLET). COM ECO/UNDEV AGRI FINAN INDUS POL/PAR FOR/AID ADMIN MARXISM 20. PAGE 170 H3411 BIBLIOG/A ASIA DIPLOM NAT/G

B60
ZENKOVSKY S.A.,PAN-TURKISM AND ISLAM IN RUSSIA. ASIA RUSSIA USSR CULTURE POL/PAR DOMIN REV GP/REL MARXISM...LING GP/COMP BIBLIOG 19/20 TURKIC. PAGE 173 H3454 SECT NAT/LISM COM ISLAM

L60
HAAS E.B.,"CONSENSUS FORMATION IN THE COUNCIL OF EUROPE." EUR+WWI NAT/G DELIB/GP DIPLOM REGION CHOOSE PWR SOVEREIGN...RELATIV NEW/IDEA QUANT CHARTS INDEX TOT/POP OEEC 20 COUNCL/EUR. PAGE 63 H1265 POL/PAR INT/ORG STAT

L60
KAPLAN M.A.,"COMMUNIST COUP IN CZECHOSLOVAKIA." COM EUR+WWI INTELL LABOR LOC/G NAT/G POL/PAR FORCES EDU/PROP EXEC MARXISM...TIME/SEQ HYPO/EXP 20. PAGE 83 H1659 STRUCT COERCE CZECHOSLVK

S60
APTER D.E.,"THE ROLE OF TRADITIONALISM IN THE POLITICAL MODERNIZATION OF GHANA AND UGANDA" (BMR)" AFR GHANA UGANDA CULTURE NAT/G POL/PAR NAT/LISM ...CON/ANAL 20. PAGE 8 H0152 CONSERVE ADMIN GOV/COMP PROB/SOLV

S60
BRZEZINSKI Z.K.,"PATTERNS AND LIMITS OF THE SINO-SOVIET DISPUTE." ASIA CHINA/COM COM FUT STRATA NAT/G EX/STRUC FORCES BAL/PWR DIPLOM ECO/TAC DOMIN EDU/PROP ADMIN COERCE WAR ATTIT RIGID/FLEX ...GEN/LAWS VAL/FREE 20. PAGE 23 H0459 POL/PAR PWR REV USSR

S60
EMERSON R.,"THE EROSION OF DEMOCRACY." AFR FUT LAW CULTURE INTELL SOCIETY ECO/UNDEV FAM LOC/G NAT/G FORCES PLAN TEC/DEV ECO/TAC ADMIN CT/SYS ATTIT ORD/FREE PWR...SOCIALIST SOC CONCPT STAND/INT TIME/SEQ WORK 20. PAGE 46 H0918 S/ASIA POL/PAR

S60
GROSSMAN G.,"SOVIET GROWTH: ROUTINE, INERTIA, AND PRESSURE." COM STRATA NAT/G DELIB/GP PLAN TEC/DEV ECO/TAC EDU/PROP ADMIN ROUTINE DRIVE WEALTH COLD/WAR 20. PAGE 62 H1236 POL/PAR ECO/DEV USSR

S60
NORTHEDGE F.S.,"BRITISH FOREIGN POLICY AND THE PARTY SYSTEM." EUR+WWI FUT INT/ORG NAT/G EDU/PROP ATTIT PWR...POLICY CONCPT MYTH TIME/SEQ TREND 20 UN. PAGE 119 H2374 POL/PAR CHOOSE DIPLOM UK

S60
SHILS E.,"THE INTELLECTUALS IN THE POLITICAL DEVELOPMENT OF THE NEW STATES." AFR ASIA S/ASIA ELITES LOC/G NAT/G CONSULT EX/STRUC CREATE PLAN ECO/TAC DOMIN LEGIT DRIVE PWR...TRADIT CONCPT STERTYP GEN/LAWS 20. PAGE 143 H2861 POL/PAR INTELL NAT/LISM

S60
SPIRO H.J.,"NEW CONSTITUTIONAL FORMS IN AFRICA." FUT CULTURE SOCIETY ECO/UNDEV NAT/G POL/PAR VOL/ASSN EDU/PROP ATTIT DRIVE ORD/FREE PWR RESPECT ...POLICY CONCPT OBS TREND CON/ANAL STERTYP GEN/LAWS VAL/FREE. PAGE 148 H2950 AFR CONSTN FOR/AID NAT/LISM

S60
TAUBER K.,"ASPECTS OF NATIONALIST-COMMUNIST COLLABORATION IN POSTWAR GERMANY." COM EUR+WWI USSR NAT/G VOL/ASSN ATTIT DRIVE PWR...TIME/SEQ COLD/WAR TOT/POP 20. PAGE 152 H3049 POL/PAR EDU/PROP GERMANY

S60
TIRYAKIAN E.A.,"APARTHEID AND POLITICS IN SOUTH AFRICA." SOUTH/AFR CULTURE STRATA ECO/DEV NAT/G POL/PAR ROUTINE CHOOSE GP/REL RACE/REL DISCRIM ATTIT ALL/VALS...CONCPT OBS TIME/SEQ VAL/FREE 20. PAGE 155 H3105 AFR DIPLOM

S60
WYCKOFF T.,"THE ROLE OF THE MILITARY IN LATIN AMERICAN POLITICS." L/A+17C CONSTN CULTURE ECO/UNDEV POL/PAR FORCES LEGIS TOP/EX LEGIT GUERRILLA REV CHOOSE ORD/FREE PWR...TIME/SEQ VAL/FREE 20. PAGE 171 H3430 NAT/G COERCE TOTALISM

C60
HAZARD J.N.,"THE SOVIET SYSTEM OF GOVERNMENT." USSR SOCIETY INDUS NAT/G POL/PAR DIPLOM CT/SYS...JURID CHARTS BIBLIOG/A 20. PAGE 69 H1373 COM NAT/COMP STRUCT ADMIN

C60
WRIGGINS W.H.,"CEYLON: DILEMMAS OF A NEW NATION." ASIA CEYLON CONSTN STRUCT POL/PAR SECT FORCES DIPLOM GOV/REL NAT/LISM...CHARTS BIBLIOG 20. PAGE 171 H3417 PROB/SOLV NAT/G ECO/UNDEV

B61
APTER D.E.,THE POLITICAL KINGDOM IN UGANDA. UGANDA CULTURE ECO/UNDEV AGRI KIN SECT TOP/EX REGION ATTIT HABITAT CONSERVE...GEOG AUD/VIS 20. PAGE 8 H0153 NAT/LISM POL/PAR COLONIAL ECO/TAC

B61
BIEBUYCK D.,CONGO TRIBES AND PARTIES. AFR CONGO/BRAZ CONSTN NAT/G COLONIAL CHOOSE FEDERAL 20 CONGO/LEOP. PAGE 17 H0333 KIN POL/PAR GP/REL SOVEREIGN

B61
BINDER L.,RELIGION AND POLITICS IN PAKISTAN. ISLAM PAKISTAN NAT/G SECT LEGIS CREATE CHOOSE GP/REL ...MAJORIT TRADIT 20. PAGE 17 H0336 CONSTN CONFER NAT/LISM POL/PAR

B61
BISHOP D.G.,THE ADMINISTRATION OF BRITISH FOREIGN RELATIONS. EUR+WWI MOD/EUR INT/ORG NAT/G POL/PAR DELIB/GP LEGIS TOP/EX ECO/TAC DOMIN EDU/PROP ADMIN COERCE 20. PAGE 17 H0344 ROUTINE PWR DIPLOM UK

B61
BROWN D.M.,THE NATIONALIST MOVEMENT. INDIA CULTURE STRATA REV MORAL ORD/FREE...BIBLIOG 20 HINDU. PAGE 22 H0443 NAT/LISM LEAD CHIEF POL/PAR

B61
BULLOCK A.,HITLER: A STUDY IN TYRANNY. EUR+WWI GERMANY SOCIETY STRUCT NAT/G POL/PAR FORCES CREATE DOMIN EDU/PROP EXEC COERCE WAR NAT/LISM DISPL DRIVE PERSON PWR...PSY NAZI 20 HITLER/A. PAGE 23 H0470 ATTIT BIOG TOTALISM

B61
BURDEAU G.,O PODER EXECUTIVO NA FRANCA. EUR+WWI FRANCE CONSTN DELIB/GP LEGIT ADMIN ATTIT ALL/VALS CONCPT. PAGE 24 H0478 TOP/EX POL/PAR NAT/G LEGIS

B61
BURDETTE F.L.,POLITICAL SCIENCE: A SELECTED BIBLIOGRAPHY OF BOOKS IN PRINT, WITH ANNOTATIONS (PAMPHLET). LAW LOC/G NAT/G POL/PAR PROVS DIPLOM EDU/PROP ADMIN CHOOSE ATTIT 20. PAGE 24 H0479 BIBLIOG/A GOV/COMP CONCPT ROUTINE

B61
BURKS R.V.,THE DYNAMICS OF COMMUNISM IN EASTERN EUROPE. COM YUGOSLAVIA POL/PAR RACE/REL ISOLAT ...CORREL CON/ANAL CHARTS GP/COMP DICTIONARY 20 EUROPE/E SLAV/MACED. PAGE 24 H0489 MARXISM STRUCT WORKER REPRESENT

B61
CARNELL F.,THE POLITICS OF THE NEW STATES: A SELECT ANNOTATED BIBLIOGRAPHY WITH SPECIAL REFERENCE TO THE COMMONWEALTH. CONSTN ELITES LABOR NAT/G POL/PAR EX/STRUC DIPLOM ADJUD ADMIN...GOV/COMP 20 COMMONWLTH. PAGE 27 H0534 BIBLIOG/A AFR ASIA COLONIAL

B61
CASSINELLI C.W.,THE POLITICS OF FREEDOM. FUT UNIV LAW POL/PAR CHOOSE ORD/FREE...POLICY CONCPT MYTH BIBLIOG. PAGE 28 H0555 MAJORIT NAT/G PARL/PROC PARTIC

B61
CONQUEST R.,POWER AND POLICY IN THE USSR. USSR NAT/G POL/PAR DIPLOM MARXISM 20. PAGE 33 H0655 COM HIST/WRIT GOV/REL PWR

B61
DRAGNICH A.N.,MAJOR EUROPEAN GOVERNMENTS. FRANCE GERMANY/W UK USSR LOC/G EX/STRUC CT/SYS PARL/PROC ATTIT MARXISM...JURID MGT NAT/COMP 19/20. PAGE 42 H0846 NAT/G LEGIS CONSTN POL/PAR

B61
GUEVARA E.,GUERRILLA WARFARE. L/A+17C ECO/UNDEV NAT/G POL/PAR VOL/ASSN PLAN DOMIN REV DRIVE PWR FORCES COERCE

WEALTH...NEW/IDEA RECORD BIOG COLD/WAR MARX/KARL OAS 20. PAGE 62 H1247 — GUERRILLA CUBA

B61
HISTORICAL RESEARCH INSTITUTE,A SHORT BIBLIOGRAPHY OF INDO-MUSLIM HISTORY. INDIA S/ASIA DIPLOM EDU/PROP COLONIAL LEAD NAT/LISM ATTIT...BIOG 19/20. PAGE 71 H1427 — BIBLIOG NAT/G SECT POL/PAR

B61
JENNINGS I.,PARTY POLITICS: THE GROWTH OF PARTIES (VOL. II). UK SOCIETY NAT/G LEGIS ATTIT 18/20 LABOR/PAR LIB/PARTY CONSRV/PAR. PAGE 80 H1606 — CHOOSE POL/PAR PWR POLICY

B61
LA PONCE J.A.,THE GOVERNMENT OF THE FIFTH REPUBLIC: FRENCH POLITICAL PARTIES AND THE CONSTITUTION. ALGERIA FRANCE LAW NAT/G DELIB/GP LEGIS ECO/TAC MARXISM SOCISM...CHARTS BIBLIOG/A 20 DEGAULLE/C. PAGE 90 H1794 — PWR POL/PAR CONSTN CHIEF

B61
LENIN V.I.,WHAT IS TO BE DONE? (1902). RUSSIA LABOR NAT/G POL/PAR WORKER CAP/ISM ECO/TAC ADMIN PARTIC ...MARXIST IDEA/COMP GEN/LAWS 19/20. PAGE 94 H1881 — EDU/PROP PRESS MARXISM METH/COMP

B61
LEVIN L.A.,BIBLIOGRAFIIA BIBLIOGRAFII PROIZVEDENII K. MARKSA, F. ENGELSA, V.I. LENINA. COM USSR NAT/G POL/PAR WORKER LEAD REV ATTIT...POLICY IDEA/COMP 20 MARX/KARL LENIN/VI ENGELS. PAGE 95 H1899 — BIBLIOG/A MARXISM MARXIST CONCPT

B61
LYFORD J.P.,THE AGREEABLE AUTOCRACIES. SOCIETY LABOR POL/PAR SECT DIPLOM CHOOSE...CONCPT 20 WHITE/T NIEBUHR/R. PAGE 99 H1982 — ATTIT POPULISM PRESS NAT/G

B61
MARVICK D.,POLITICAL DECISION-MAKERS. INTELL STRATA NAT/G POL/PAR EX/STRUC LEGIS DOMIN EDU/PROP ATTIT PERSON PWR...PSY STAT OBS CONT/OBS STAND/INT UNPLAN/INT TIME/SEQ CHARTS STERTYP VAL/FREE. PAGE 104 H2073 — TOP/EX BIOG ELITES

B61
MARX K.,THE COMMUNIST MANIFESTO. IN (MENDEL A. ESSENTIAL WORKS OF MARXISM, NEW YORK: BANTAM. FUT MOD/EUR CULTURE ECO/DEV ECO/UNDEV AGRI FINAN INDUS MARKET PROC/MFG LABOR MUNIC POL/PAR CONSULT FORCES CREATE PLAN ADMIN ATTIT DRIVE RIGID/FLEX ORD/FREE PWR RESPECT MARX/KARL WORK. PAGE 104 H2081 — COM NEW/IDEA CAP/ISM REV

B61
MERRIAM A.,CONGO: BACKGROUND OF CONFLICT. AFR FUT KIN MUNIC NAT/G POL/PAR PROVS DELIB/GP PLAN DOMIN COERCE ATTIT...TIME/SEQ CHARTS CONGO 20. PAGE 109 H2182 — CHOOSE GUERRILLA

B61
MILIBAND R.,PARLIAMENTARY SOCIALISM. EUR+WWI UK EXEC LEAD PARL/PROC GP/REL...POLICY 20 PARLIAMENT LABOR/PAR. PAGE 110 H2203 — POL/PAR NAT/G PWR SOCISM

B61
MOLLAU G.,INTERNATIONAL COMMUNISM AND WORLD REVOLUTION: HISTORY AND METHODS. RUSSIA USSR INT/ORG NAT/G POL/PAR VOL/ASSN FORCES BAL/PWR DIPLOM EXEC REGION WAR ATTIT PWR MARXISM...CONCPT TIME/SEQ COLD/WAR 19/20. PAGE 112 H2237 — COM REV

B61
MUNGER E.S.,AFRICAN FIELD REPORTS 1952-1961. SOUTH/AFR SOCIETY ECO/UNDEV NAT/G POL/PAR COLONIAL EXEC PARL/PROC GUERRILLA RACE/REL ALL/IDEOS...SOC AUD/VIS 20. PAGE 114 H2288 — AFR DISCRIM RECORD

B61
NARAIN J.P.,SWARAJ FOR THE PEOPLE. INDIA CONSTN LOC/G MUNIC POL/PAR CHOOSE REPRESENT EFFICIENCY ATTIT PWR SOVEREIGN 20. PAGE 116 H2311 — NAT/G ORD/FREE EDU/PROP EX/STRUC

B61
NIPPERDEY T.,DIE ORGANISATION DER DEUTSCHEN PARTEIEN VOR 1918. GERMANY CONSTN STRUCT TEC/DEV CHOOSE ADJUST ATTIT...CONCPT TIME/SEQ 19/20. PAGE 118 H2362 — POL/PAR PARL/PROC NAT/G

B61
PALMER N.D.,THE INDIAN POLITICAL SYSTEM. INDIA ECO/UNDEV SECT CHIEF COLONIAL CHOOSE ALL/IDEOS SOCISM...CHARTS BIBLIOG/A 20. PAGE 123 H2452 — NAT/LISM POL/PAR NAT/G DIPLOM

B61
PANIKKAR K.M.,REVOLUTION IN AFRICA. AFR GUINEA ECO/UNDEV POL/PAR DIPLOM COLONIAL EXEC LEAD SOVEREIGN...CHARTS 20. PAGE 123 H2461 — NAT/LISM NAT/G CHIEF

B61
REISKY-DUBNIC V.,COMMUNIST PROPAGANDA METHODS. CULTURE POL/PAR VOL/ASSN ATTIT...CONCPT TOT/POP. PAGE 131 H2611 — COM EDU/PROP TOTALISM

B61
SCHWARTZ H.,THE RED PHOENIX: RUSSIA SINCE WORLD WAR II. USA+45 WOR+45 ELITES POL/PAR TEC/DEV ECO/TAC MARXISM. PAGE 140 H2810 — DIPLOM NAT/G ECO/DEV

B61
SEMINAR REPRESENTATIVE GOVT,AFRO-ASIAN ATTITUDES: SEMINAR ON REPRESENTATIVE GOVERNMENTSPUBLIC LIBERTIES IN STATES OF ASIA AND AFRICA, RHODES, 1958. AFR ASIA BURMA INDIA ISLAM UAR VIETNAM/S SOCIETY POL/PAR CHIEF EDU/PROP PRESS PERSON ...POLICY INT 20 TUNIS. PAGE 141 H2826 — CHOOSE ATTIT NAT/COMP ORD/FREE

B61
SETON-WATSON H.,FROM LENIN TO KHRUSHCHEV: THE HISTORY OF WORLD COMMUNISM. ASIA COM EUR+WWI ISLAM S/ASIA ECO/DEV ECO/UNDEV NAT/G POL/PAR DIPLOM ECO/TAC EDU/PROP COERCE GUERRILLA ATTIT DRIVE WORK TOT/POP NAZI 20. PAGE 141 H2832 — PWR REV USSR

B61
SPOONER F.P.,SOUTH AFRICAN PREDICAMENT. FUT SOUTH/AFR INDUS POL/PAR RACE/REL INCOME...CHARTS 20 NEGRO. PAGE 148 H2953 — ECO/DEV DISCRIM ECO/TAC POLICY

B61
TREVE W.,DEUTSCHE PARTEIPROGRAMME 1861-1961. GERMANY GERMANY/W DELIB/GP CONFER CHOOSE REPRESENT 19/20. PAGE 157 H3130 — POL/PAR NAT/G LEGIS PARL/PROC

B61
WARD R.E.,JAPANESE POLITICAL SCIENCE: A GUIDE TO JAPANESE REFERENCE AND RESEARCH MATERIALS (2ND ED.). LAW CONSTN STRATA NAT/G POL/PAR DELIB/GP LEGIS ADMIN CHOOSE GP/REL...INT/LAW 19/20 CHINJAP. PAGE 165 H3306 — BIBLIOG/A PHIL/SCI

B61
WEST F.J.,POLITICAL ADVANCEMENT IN THE SOUTH PACIFIC. CONSTN CULTURE POL/PAR LEGIS DOMIN ADMIN CHOOSE SOVEREIGN VAL/FREE 20 FIJI TAHITI SAMOA. PAGE 167 H3335 — S/ASIA LOC/G COLONIAL

S61
DOGAN M.,"LES OFFICIERS DANS LA CARRIERE POLITIQUE DE MARECHAL MACMAHON AU GENERAL DE GAULLE." EUR+WWI FRANCE MOD/EUR ELITES STRATA POL/PAR LEGIT ATTIT ALL/VALS...SOC CONCPT 19/20. PAGE 42 H0833 — PROF/ORG FORCES NAT/G DELIB/GP

S61
FITZGIBBON R.H.,"MEASUREMENT OF LATIN AMERICAN POLITICAL CHANGE." L/A+17C CONSTN CULTURE SOCIETY ECO/UNDEV NAT/G POL/PAR PUB/INST ACT/RES EDU/PROP PERCEPT KNOWL ORD/FREE SOVEREIGN...METH/CNCPT TREND OAS 20. PAGE 51 H1020 — CHOOSE ATTIT

S61
LOEWENBERG G.,"PARLIAMENTARISM IN WESTERN GERMANY: THE FUNCTIONING OF THE BUNDESTAG" (BMR)" GERMANY/W NAT/G POL/PAR CHIEF LEAD 20 PARLIAMENT. PAGE 98 H1952 — LEGIS CHOOSE CONSTN PARL/PROC

S61
NEEDLER M.C.,"THE POLITICAL DEVELOPMENT OF MEXICO." STRUCT NAT/G ADMIN RIGID/FLEX...TIME/SEQ TREND MEXIC/AMER TOT/POP VAL/FREE 19/20. PAGE 116 H2328 — L/A+17C POL/PAR

S61
SCHAPIRO L.,"SOVIET GOVERNMENT TODAY." COM EUR+WWI INT/ORG POL/PAR VOL/ASSN ACT/RES PLAN PERCEPT ...CONCPT TREND TOT/POP VAL/FREE 20. PAGE 139 H2773 — NAT/G TOTALISM USSR

S61
TOMASIC D.,"POLITICAL LEADERSHIP IN CONTEMPORARY POLAND." COM EUR+WWI GERMANY NAT/G POL/PAR SECT DELIB/GP PLAN ECO/TAC DOMIN EDU/PROP PWR MARXISM ...MARXIST GEOG MGT CONCPT TIME/SEQ STERTYP 20. PAGE 156 H3111 — SOCIETY ROUTINE USSR POLAND

S61
VALLET R.,"IRAN: KEY TO THE MIDDLE EAST." COM IRAQ ISLAM KUWAIT LEBANON SAUDI/ARAB TURKEY ELITES SOCIETY INDUS PROC/MFG POL/PAR TOP/EX PLAN BAL/PWR DIPLOM ECO/TAC ALL/VALS...TREND CENTO 20. PAGE 161 H3224 — NAT/G ECO/UNDEV IRAN

S61
ZAGORIA D.S.,"THE FUTURE OF SINO-SOVIET RELATIONS." CHINA/COM INT/ORG NAT/G POL/PAR VOL/ASSN ACT/RES PLAN PERSON...METH/CNCPT TIME/SEQ TOT/POP VAL/FREE 20 MAO KHRUSH/N. PAGE 172 H3445 — ASIA COM TOTALISM USSR

C61
LAPONCE J.A.,"THE GOVERNMENT OF THE FIFTH REPUBLIC." FRANCE CHIEF LEGIS PARL/PROC CHOOSE ...CHARTS GP/COMP IDEA/COMP BIBLIOG/A 20. PAGE 91 H1814 — POL/PAR NAT/G CONSTN DOMIN

C61
MOODIE G.C.,"THE GOVERNMENT OF GREAT BRITAIN." UK LAW STRUCT LOC/G POL/PAR DIPLOM RECEIVE ADMIN COLONIAL CHOOSE...BIBLIOG 20 PARLIAMENT. PAGE 112 H2247 — NAT/G SOCIETY PARL/PROC GOV/COMP

B62
ANDREWS W.G.,EUROPEAN POLITICAL INSTITUTIONS. FRANCE GERMANY UK USSR TOP/EX LEAD PARL/PROC CHOOSE 20. PAGE 7 H0139 — NAT/COMP POL/PAR EX/STRUC LEGIS

B62
ANDREWS W.G.,FRENCH POLITICS AND ALGERIA: THE PROCESS OF POLICY FORMATION 1954-1962. ALGERIA FRANCE CONSTN ELITES POL/PAR CHIEF DELIB/GP LEGIS DIPLOM PRESS CHOOSE 20. PAGE 7 H0140 — GOV/COMP EXEC COLONIAL

B62
ARNE S.,LE PRESIDENT DU CONSEIL DES MINISTRES SOUS LA IV REPUBLIQUE. EUR+WWI FRANCE LEGIT PWR...BIOG — DELIB/GP POL/PAR

CHARTS. PAGE 8 H0165 NAT/G LEGIS

B62
BRETTON H.L.,POWER AND STABILITY IN NIGERIA: THE POLITICS OF DECOLONIZATION. AFR CONSTN INTELL ECO/UNDEV COM/IND KIN NAT/G POL/PAR PROVS VOL/ASSN LEGIS DOMIN EDU/PROP LEGIT EXEC ROUTINE CHOOSE NAT/LISM ATTIT PERCEPT ALL/VALS. PAGE 20 H0411 CULTURE OBS NIGERIA

B62
BROWN B.E.,NEW DIRECTIONS IN COMPARATIVE POLITICS. AUSTRIA FRANCE GERMANY UK WOR+45 EX/STRUC LEGIS ORD/FREE 20. PAGE 22 H0439 NAT/COMP METH POL/PAR FORCES

B62
BROWN S.D.,STUDIES ON ASIA, 1962. ASIA BURMA INDIA ISLAM ISRAEL S/ASIA ECO/UNDEV POL/PAR SECT ECO/TAC ...ANTHOL 20 CHINJAP. PAGE 22 H0450 PWR PARL/PROC

B62
BUSIA K.A.,THE CHALLENGE OF AFRICA. CULTURE KIN MUNIC NAT/G POL/PAR SCHOOL DELIB/GP PLAN ECO/TAC DOMIN EDU/PROP TOTALISM ATTIT PERSON ALL/VALS SOVEREIGN...SOC CONCPT STERTYP TOT/POP VAL/FREE 20. PAGE 25 H0496 AFR ECO/UNDEV NAT/LISM

B62
CARTER G.M.,AFRICAN ONE-PARTY STATES. ISLAM IVORY/CST LIBERIA CONSTN CULTURE SOCIETY POL/PAR PLAN DOMIN EDU/PROP EXEC REGION CHOOSE ATTIT ALL/VALS...CONCPT TIME/SEQ CHARTS VAL/FREE 20 TANGANYIKA. PAGE 27 H0545 AFR NAT/LISM

B62
CARTER G.M.,THE GOVERNMENT OF THE SOVIET UNION. USSR CULTURE LOC/G DIPLOM ECO/TAC ADJUD CT/SYS LEAD WEALTH...CHARTS T 20 COM/PARTY. PAGE 27 H0546 NAT/G MARXISM POL/PAR EX/STRUC

B62
CHAPMAN R.M.,NEW ZEALAND POLITICS IN ACTION: THE 1960 GENERAL ELECTION. NEW/ZEALND LEGIS EDU/PROP PRESS TV LEAD ATTIT...STAND/INT 20. PAGE 29 H0582 NAT/G CHOOSE POL/PAR

B62
DE MADARIAGA S.,L'AMERIQUE LATINE ENTRE L'OURS ET L'AIGLE. L/A+17C SOCIETY NAT/G ECO/TAC EDU/PROP REGION COERCE ATTIT ALL/VALS...MAJORIT TIME/SEQ STERTYP COLD/WAR OAS 20. PAGE 38 H0760 POL/PAR ECO/UNDEV

B62
FEIT E.,SOUTH AFRICA, THE DYNAMICS OF THE AFRICAN NATIONAL CONGRESS. AFR SOUTH/AFR LAW INTELL STRATA KIN NAT/G POL/PAR ECO/TAC DOMIN RISK COERCE 20 NEGRO. PAGE 49 H0984 RACE/REL ELITES CONTROL STRUCT

B62
FINER S.E.,THE MAN ON HORSEBACK: ROLE OF THE MILITARY IN POLITICS. UNIV LAW CONSTN ELITES SOCIETY POL/PAR BAL/PWR DOMIN EDU/PROP LEGIT COERCE GUERRILLA REV WAR WEAPON DRIVE SUPEGO ORD/FREE PWR RESPECT...POLICY CONCPT GEN/METH. PAGE 50 H1003 NAT/G FORCES TOTALISM

B62
GALENSON W.,LABOR IN DEVELOPING COUNTRIES. BRAZIL INDONESIA ISRAEL PAKISTAN TURKEY AGRI INDUS WORKER PAY PRICE GP/REL WEALTH...MGT CHARTS METH/COMP NAT/COMP 20. PAGE 54 H1088 LABOR ECO/UNDEV BARGAIN POL/PAR

B62
HATCH J.,AFRICA TODAY-AND TOMORROW: AN OUTLINE OF BASIC FACTS AND MAJOR PROBLEMS. AFR FUT ISLAM STRATA ECO/UNDEV INT/ORG NAT/G POL/PAR DELIB/GP TOP/EX EDU/PROP LEGIT CHOOSE ATTIT...TIME/SEQ TOT/POP COLD/WAR 20. PAGE 67 H1353 PLAN CONSTN NAT/LISM

B62
INSTITUTE FOR STUDY OF USSR,YOUTH IN FERMENT. INTELL NAT/G PERF/ART POL/PAR SCHOOL VOL/ASSN FORCES EDU/PROP ATTIT DRIVE PERCEPT HEALTH KNOWL MORAL ORD/FREE RESPECT...SOC OBS HIST/WRIT VAL/FREE. PAGE 77 H1537 COM CULTURE USSR

B62
JENNINGS I.,PARTY POLITICS: THE STUFF OF POLITICS (VOL.III). UK NAT/G SECT CHIEF INT/TRADE RECEIVE COLONIAL GP/REL NAT/LISM ORD/FREE SOCISM 19/20 CHURCH/STA WHIG/PARTY. PAGE 80 H1607 POL/PAR CONSTN PWR ALL/IDEOS

B62
KASTARI P.,LA PRESIDENCE DE LA REPUBLIQUE EN FINLANDE. FINLAND CONSTN NAT/G POL/PAR LEGIS LEGIT ATTIT...JURID CONCPT 20 PRESIDENT. PAGE 83 H1666 PARL/PROC CHIEF PWR DECISION

B62
LAQUEUR W.,THE FUTURE OF COMMUNIST SOCIETY. CHINA/COM USSR LAW ECO/DEV NAT/G POL/PAR PLAN PROB/SOLV DIPLOM LEAD...POLICY CONCPT IDEA/COMP ANTHOL 20. PAGE 91 H1820 MARXISM COM FUT SOCIETY

B62
LEGUM C.,PAN-AFRICANISM: A SHORT POLITICAL GUIDE. ISLAM CULTURE INTELL ECO/DEV NAT/G POL/PAR DELIB/GP PLAN EDU/PROP FEDERAL NAT/LISM ATTIT DRIVE PERSON ...RECORD TIME/SEQ CHARTS STERTYP 20. PAGE 93 H1861 AFR CONCPT

B62
MANSUR F.,PROCESS OF INDEPENDENCE. GHANA INDIA INDONESIA PAKISTAN CONSTN ELITES INTELL STRUCT ACADEM NAT/G REV PWR 20. PAGE 102 H2043 NAT/COMP POL/PAR SOVEREIGN COLONIAL

B62
MELADY T.,THE WHITE MAN'S FUTURE IN BLACK AFRICA. FUT CULTURE SOCIETY NAT/G POL/PAR PLAN ECO/TAC DOMIN EDU/PROP LEGIT COLONIAL RACE/REL ATTIT DRIVE ALL/VALS...PSY SOC CONCPT TIME/SEQ TOT/POP VAL/FREE 20. PAGE 108 H2167 AFR STRATA ELITES

B62
MEYER A.G.,LENINISM. USSR STRUCT NAT/G CAP/ISM LEAD WAR PWR SOVEREIGN...BIBLIOG 20 LENIN/VI. PAGE 109 H2187 POL/PAR REV MARXISM PHIL/SCI

B62
OLLE-LAPRUNE J.,LA STABILITE DES MINISTRES SOUS LA TROISIEME REPUBLIQUE, 1879-1940. FRANCE CONSTN POL/PAR LEAD WAR INGP/REL RIGID/FLEX PWR...POLICY CHARTS 19/20. PAGE 121 H2415 LEGIS NAT/G ADMIN PERSON

B62
RANNEY A.,THE DOCTRINE OF RESPONSIBLE PARTY GOVERNMENT. USA+45 USA-45 CONSTN PLAN CHOOSE ...MAJORIT GOV/COMP IDEA/COMP 20. PAGE 130 H2591 POL/PAR POLICY REPRESENT NAT/G

B62
ROSENZWEIG F.,HEGEL UND DER STAAT. GERMANY SOCIETY FAM POL/PAR NAT/LISM...BIOG 19. PAGE 134 H2682 JURID NAT/G CONCPT PHIL/SCI

B62
RUDE G.,WILKES AND LIBERTY. UK NAT/G POL/PAR REPRESENT ORD/FREE...SOC 18. PAGE 136 H2711 PARL/PROC CHOOSE STRATA STRUCT

B62
SCALAPINO R.A.,PARTIES AND POLITICS IN CONTEMPORARY JAPAN. EX/STRUC DIPLOM CHOOSE NAT/LISM ATTIT ...POLICY 20 CHINJAP. PAGE 138 H2762 POL/PAR PARL/PROC ELITES DECISION

B62
SCHIEDER T.,THE STATE AND SOCIETY IN OUR TIMES (TRANS. BY C.A.M. SYM). SOCIETY NAT/G POL/PAR REV GP/REL ALL/IDEOS 19/20. PAGE 139 H2786 STRUCT PWR HIST/WRIT

B62
SCHMIDT-VOLKMAR E.,DER KULTURKAMPF IN DEUTSCHLAND 1871-1890. GERMANY PRUSSIA SOCIETY STRUCT SECT DIPLOM GP/REL NAT/LISM 19 CHURCH/STA BISMARCK/O. PAGE 139 H2789 POL/PAR CATHISM ATTIT NAT/G

B62
SELOSOEMARDJAN O.,SOCIAL CHANGES IN JOGJAKARTA. INDONESIA NETHERLAND ELITES STRATA STRUCT FAM POL/PAR CREATE DIPLOM INT/TRADE EDU/PROP ADMIN GOV/REL...SOC 20 JAVA CHINJAP. PAGE 141 H2825 ECO/UNDEV CULTURE REV COLONIAL

B62
SILBERMAN B.S.,JAPAN AND KOREA; A CRITICAL BIBLIOGRAPHY. KOREA LAW STRATA STRUCT AGRI INDUS NAT/G POL/PAR SECT...HUM LING IDEA/COMP 5/20 CHINJAP. PAGE 144 H2872 BIBLIOG/A CULTURE S/ASIA

B62
STARR R.E.,POLAND 1944-1962: THE SOVIETIZATION OF A CAPTIVE PEOPLE. COM POLAND USSR POL/PAR SECT LEGIS DIPLOM DOMIN EDU/PROP CHOOSE ORD/FREE...POLICY CHARTS BIBLIOG 20. PAGE 149 H2973 MARXISM NAT/G TOTALISM NAT/COMP

B62
TATZ C.M.,SHADOW AND SUBSTANCE IN SOUTH AFRICA. SOUTH/AFR AGRI NAT/G POL/PAR DOMIN GP/REL ATTIT PWR 20. PAGE 152 H3048 RACE/REL REPRESENT DISCRIM LEGIS

B62
TINKER H.,INDIA AND PAKISTAN. INDIA PAKISTAN NAT/G POL/PAR...OLD/LIB TRADIT TREND CHARTS BIBLIOG 20. PAGE 155 H3102 ORD/FREE STRATA REPRESENT AUTHORIT

B62
VAN RENSBURG P.,GUILTY LAND: THE HISTORY OF APARTHEID. SOUTH/AFR NAT/G POL/PAR DOMIN CHOOSE ...SOC 19/20 NEGRO. PAGE 162 H3231 RACE/REL DISCRIM NAT/LISM POLICY

B62
WEHLER H.V.,SOZIALDEMOKRATIE UND NATIONALSTAAT. GERMANY POLAND USSR CULTURE SOCIETY STRUCT NAT/G POL/PAR DIPLOM ORD/FREE 19/20. PAGE 166 H3325 NAT/LISM SOVEREIGN GP/REL ATTIT

B62
WHITING K.R.,THE SOVIET UNION TODAY: A CONCISE HANDBOOK. USSR ELITES AGRI INDUS POL/PAR FORCES DIPLOM EDU/PROP LEAD...GEOG TREND 19/20. PAGE 168 H3354 NAT/G ATTIT MARXISM POLICY

L62
COHEN R.,"POWER IN COMPLEX SOCIETIES IN AFRICA." AFR KIN MUNIC POL/PAR DELIB/GP DOMIN ROUTINE ATTIT ALL/VALS...SOC STAT OBS INT QU CHARTS ANTHOL 20. PAGE 31 H0617 CULTURE STRATA ELITES

S62
ANSPRENGER F.,"NATIONALISM, COMMUNISM, AND THE UNCOMMITTED NATIONS: AMERICAN PROFILES." FUT ISLAM CULTURE SOCIETY ECO/UNDEV NAT/G POL/PAR PLAN ECO/TAC EDU/PROP COERCE CHOOSE ALL/VALS MARXISM SOCISM...SOC CONCPT BIOG TREND 20. PAGE 7 H0142 AFR COM NAT/LISM

S62
CROAN M.,"POLYCENTRISM: COMMUNIST INTERNATIONAL RELATIONS." ASIA STRUCT INT/ORG NAT/G POL/PAR CONSULT PLAN DOMIN EDU/PROP COERCE ATTIT RIGID/FLEX SOCISM...POLICY CONCPT TREND CON/ANAL GEN/LAWS MARX/KARL. PAGE 35 H0703
COM CREATE DIPLOM NAT/LISM

S62
HYDE D.,"COMMUNISM IN LATIN AMERICA." L/A+17C ECO/DEV NAT/G SECT EDU/PROP ATTIT ALL/VALS MARXISM ...SOC CONCPT TOT/POP COLD/WAR OAS 20. PAGE 76 H1515
COM POL/PAR REV

S62
IOVTCHOUK M.T.,"ON SOME THEORETICAL PRINCIPLES AND METHODS OF SOCIOLOGICAL INVESTIGATIONS (IN RUSSIAN)." FUT USA+45 STRATA R+D NAT/G POL/PAR TOP/EX ACT/RES PLAN ECO/TAC EDU/PROP ROUTINE ATTIT RIGID/FLEX MARXISM SOCISM...MARXIST METH/CNCPT OBS TREND NAT/COMP GEN/LAWS 20. PAGE 78 H1564
COM ECO/DEV CAP/ISM USSR

S62
KOLARZ W.,"THE IMPACT OF COMMUNISM ON WEST AFRICA." AFR FUT SOCIETY INT/ORG NAT/G CREATE PLAN DOMIN EDU/PROP COERCE NAT/LISM ATTIT RIGID/FLEX SOCISM ...POLICY CONCPT TREND MARX/KARL 20. PAGE 88 H1751
COM POL/PAR COLONIAL

S62
PISTRAK L.,"SOVIET VIEWS ON AFRICA." AFR COM FUT ISLAM USSR INTELL STRUCT KIN POL/PAR PLAN EDU/PROP RIGID/FLEX PWR MARXISM...TIME/SEQ WORK TOT/POP 20. PAGE 126 H2516
NAT/G ATTIT SOCISM

S62
ROSE R.,"THE POLITICAL IDEALS OF ENGLISH PARTY ACTIVISTS" (BMR)" UK PARL/PROC PARTIC ATTIT ROLE ...SAMP/SIZ CHARTS 20. PAGE 134 H2673
POL/PAR LOBBY REPRESENT NAT/G

S62
SARKISYANZ E.,"NATIONALISM, CAPITALISM, AND THE UNCOMMITED NATIONS: MARXISM AND ASIAN CULTURAL TRADITIONS." ASIA BURMA CHINA/COM COM CULTURE SOCIETY NAT/G POL/PAR PLAN DOMIN EDU/PROP COLONIAL COERCE ATTIT RIGID/FLEX...CONCPT TREND MARX/KARL 20 TIBET BUDDHISM. PAGE 138 H2755
S/ASIA SECT NAT/LISM CAP/ISM

S62
SPRINGER H.W.,"FEDERATION IN THE CARIBBEAN: AN ATTEMPT THAT FAILED." L/A+17C ECO/UNDEV INT/ORG POL/PAR PROVS LEGIS CREATE PLAN LEGIT ADMIN FEDERAL ATTIT DRIVE PERSON ORD/FREE PWR...POLICY GEOG PSY CONCPT OBS CARIBBEAN CMN/WLTH 20. PAGE 148 H2955
VOL/ASSN NAT/G REGION

S62
VIGNES D.,"L'AUTORITE DES TRAITES INTERNATIONAUX EN DROIT INTERNE." EUR+WWI UNIV LAW CONSTN INTELL NAT/G POL/PAR DIPLOM ATTIT PERCEPT ALL/VALS ...POLICY INT/LAW JURID CONCPT TIME/SEQ 20 TREATY. PAGE 163 H3252
STRUCT LEGIT FRANCE

B63
ADRIAN C.R.,GOVERNING OVER FIFTY STATES AND THEIR COMMUNITIES. USA+45 CONSTN FINAN MUNIC NAT/G POL/PAR EX/STRUC LEGIS ADMIN CONTROL CT/SYS ...CHARTS 20. PAGE 4 H0073
PROVS LOC/G GOV/REL GOV/COMP

B63
ARAZI A.,LE SYSTEME ELECTORAL ISRAELIEN. ISRAEL NAT/G ADMIN ALL/VALS PARLIAMENT. PAGE 8 H0158
LEGIS CHOOSE POL/PAR

B63
BADI J.,THE GOVERNMENT OF THE STATE OF ISRAEL: A CRITICAL ACCOUNT OF ITS PARLIAMENT, EXECUTIVE, AND JUDICIARY. ISRAEL ECO/DEV CHIEF DELIB/GP LEGIS DIPLOM CT/SYS INGP/REL PEACE ORD/FREE...BIBLIOG 20 PARLIAMENT ARABS MIGRATION. PAGE 10 H0193
NAT/G CONSTN EX/STRUC POL/PAR

B63
BARNETT A.D.,COMMUNIST STRATEGIES IN ASIA: A COMPARATIVE ANALYSIS OF GOVERNMENTS AND PARTIES. COM FUT S/ASIA CULTURE SOCIETY STRATA NAT/G DELIB/GP ACT/RES ECO/TAC EDU/PROP COERCE CHOOSE ATTIT RIGID/FLEX ORD/FREE PWR SKILL...SIMUL VAL/FREE 20. PAGE 11 H0223
ASIA POL/PAR DIPLOM USSR

B63
BLONDEL J.,VOTERS, PARTIES, AND LEADERS. UK ELITES LOC/G NAT/G PROVS ACT/RES DOMIN REPRESENT GP/REL INGP/REL...SOC BIBLIOG 20. PAGE 18 H0358
POL/PAR STRATA LEGIS ADMIN

B63
BORKENAU F.,THE SPANISH COCKPIT. SPAIN ELITES STRATA POL/PAR ACT/RES CROWD WAR GP/REL INGP/REL ...SOC NAT/COMP 20. PAGE 19 H0377
REV CONSERVE SOCISM FORCES

B63
CHOU S.H.,THE CHINESE INFLATION 1937-1949. ASIA SOCIETY POL/PAR FOR/AID INT/TRADE BAL/PAY WEALTH MARXISM...STAT CHARTS 20 COM/PARTY GOLD/STAND. PAGE 30 H0597
FINAN ECO/TAC BUDGET NAT/G

B63
CONZE W.,DIE DEUTSCHE NATION. GERMANY NAT/G POL/PAR WAR ORD/FREE...TREND 8/20 NAZI. PAGE 33 H0657
NAT/LISM FASCISM ATTIT SOCIETY

B63
CRANKSHAW E.,THE NEW COLD WAR: MOSCOW V. PEKIN. CHINA/COM USSR INTELL POL/PAR DELIB/GP CAP/ISM COERCE REV NAT/LISM TOTALISM DRIVE...POLICY IDEA/COMP 20 KHRUSH/N. PAGE 35 H0698
ATTIT DIPLOM NAT/COMP MARXISM

B63
CREMEANS C.,THE ARABS AND THE WORLD: NASSER'S ARAB NATIONALIST POLICY. FUT ISLAM UAR USA+45 SOCIETY STRATA NAT/G POL/PAR PLAN DIPLOM EDU/PROP LEGIT DRIVE ALL/VALS...INT TIME/SEQ CHARTS 20 NASSER/G. PAGE 35 H0700
TOP/EX ATTIT REGION NAT/LISM

B63
CROSS C.,THE FASCISTS IN BRITAIN. UK ELITES LABOR NAT/G DOMIN PARTIC DISCRIM TOTALISM ATTIT...STERTYP 20. PAGE 35 H0708
POL/PAR FASCISM RACE/REL LEAD

B63
ECKSTEIN H.,COMPARATIVE POLITICS. POL/PAR LEGIS CT/SYS CHOOSE TOTALISM PWR POPULISM...METH/COMP GEN/METH ANTHOL BIBLIOG 20. PAGE 44 H0886
NAT/COMP CONSTN REPRESENT NAT/G

B63
ELIAS T.O.,GOVERNMENT AND POLITICS IN AFRICA. CONSTN CULTURE SOCIETY NAT/G POL/PAR DIPLOM REPRESENT PERSON...SOC TREND BIBLIOG 4/20. PAGE 45 H0906
AFR NAT/LISM COLONIAL LAW

B63
FABER K.,DIE NATIONALISTISCHE PUBLIZISTIK DEUTSCHLANDS VON 1866 BIS 1871 (2 VOLS.). EUR+WWI GERMANY DIPLOM EDU/PROP 19. PAGE 48 H0957
BIBLIOG/A NAT/G NAT/LISM POL/PAR

B63
FARMER B.H.,CEYLON: A DIVIDED NATION. CEYLON INDIA NETHERLAND PORTUGAL UK ELITES POL/PAR COLONIAL ...SOC MYTH CHARTS GOV/COMP WORSHIP 20. PAGE 49 H0972
DOMIN ORD/FREE ECO/UNDEV POLICY

B63
FLECHTHEIM O.K.,DOKUMENTE ZUR PARTEIPOLITISCHEN ENTWICKLUNG IN DEUTSCHLAND SEIT 1945 (2 VOLS.). EUR+WWI GERMANY/W...CONCPT ANTHOL 20. PAGE 51 H1023
POL/PAR ELITES NAT/G TIME/SEQ

B63
GRIMOND J.,THE LIBERAL CHALLENGE. UK SOCIETY INDUS POL/PAR LEGIS PLAN CAP/ISM DIPLOM EDU/PROP GOV/REL CONSERVE 20 PARLIAMENT REFORMERS. PAGE 61 H1227
NAT/G NEW/LIB ECO/DEV POLICY

B63
HAMM H.,ALBANIA - CHINA'S BEACHHEAD IN EUROPE. ALBANIA CHINA/COM USSR YUGOSLAVIA ELITES SOCIETY POL/PAR DELIB/GP FORCES ECO/TAC COERCE ISOLAT PEACE MARXISM...IDEA/COMP 20 MAO. PAGE 65 H1304
DIPLOM REV NAT/G POLICY

B63
HUGHES A.J.,EAST AFRICA: THE SEARCH FOR UNITY- KENYA, TANGANYIKA, UGANDA, AND ZANZIBAR. TANZANIA UGANDA CONSTN POL/PAR SECT CHIEF DELIB/GP LEGIS WAR CHOOSE NAT/LISM MARXISM...POLICY CHARTS 20 NEGRO UN. PAGE 74 H1488
NAT/G DOMIN LOC/G AFR

B63
HYDE D.,THE PEACEFUL ASSAULT. COM UAR USSR ECO/DEV ECO/UNDEV NAT/G POL/PAR CAP/ISM PWR 20. PAGE 76 H1516
MARXISM CONTROL ECO/TAC DIPLOM

B63
JACOB H.,GERMAN ADMINISTRATION SINCE BISMARCK: CENTRAL AUTHORITY VERSUS LOCAL AUTONOMY. GERMANY GERMANY/W LAW POL/PAR CONTROL CENTRAL TOTALISM FASCISM...MAJORIT DECISION STAT CHARTS GOV/COMP 19/20 BISMARCK/O HITLER/A WEIMAR/REP. PAGE 79 H1577
ADMIN NAT/G LOC/G POLICY

B63
JUNOD V.,HANDBOOK OF AFRICA. AFR ISLAM CONSTN SOCIETY NAT/G POL/PAR...GEOG SOC STAT CHARTS WORK 20. PAGE 82 H1642
ECO/UNDEV REGION

B63
KAHIN G.M.,MAJOR GOVERNMENTS OF ASIA (2ND ED.). ASIA INDIA INDONESIA PAKISTAN S/ASIA DIPLOM...SOC 20 CHINJAP. PAGE 83 H1650
GOV/COMP POL/PAR ELITES

B63
KHADDURI M.,MODERN LIBYA: A STUDY IN POLITICAL DEVELOPMENT. EUR+WWI ISLAM LIBYA ELITES INT/ORG POL/PAR FORCES DIPLOM FOR/AID DOMIN EDU/PROP LEGIT NAT/LISM DRIVE RIGID/FLEX SKILL...CONCPT TIME/SEQ TREND 20. PAGE 85 H1704
NAT/G STRUCT

B63
LAMB B.P.,INDIA: A WORLD IN TRANSITION. INDIA ECO/UNDEV SECT EDU/PROP COLONIAL HABITAT ORD/FREE ...GEOG CHARTS BIBLIOG SOC/INTEG 20. PAGE 90 H1799
POL/PAR NAT/G DIPLOM STRATA

B63
LEWIN J.,POLITICS AND LAW IN SOUTH AFRICA. SOUTH/AFR UK POL/PAR BAL/PWR ECO/TAC COLONIAL CONTROL GP/REL DISCRIM PWR 20 NEGRO. PAGE 96 H1909
NAT/LISM POLICY LAW RACE/REL

B63
LIVINGSTON W.S.,FEDERALISM IN THE COMMONWEALTH - A BIBLIOGRAPHICAL COMMENTARY. CANADA INDIA PAKISTAN UK STRUCT LOC/G NAT/G POL/PAR...NAT/COMP 20 AUSTRAL. PAGE 97 H1943
BIBLIOG JURID FEDERAL CONSTN

B63
MERKL P.H.,THE ORIGIN OF THE WEST GERMAN REPUBLIC. GERMANY/W WOR+45 POL/PAR DIPLOM LEAD LOBBY REPRESENT GP/REL NAT/LISM 20. PAGE 109 H2179
CONSTN PARL/PROC CONTROL BAL/PWR

B63
MOSELY P.E.,THE SOVIET UNION, 1922-1962: A FOREIGN AFFAIRS READER. ASIA POLAND USSR CULTURE INTELL AGRI POL/PAR WORKER INT/TRADE DOMIN WAR NAT/LISM MARXISM SOCISM 20 KHRUSH/N. PAGE 113 H2267
PWR POLICY DIPLOM

B63
NALBANDIAN L.,THE ARMENIAN REVOLUTIONARY MOVEMENT. MOD/EUR RUSSIA...IDEA/COMP NAT/COMP BIBLIOG 19 ARMENIA OTTOMAN. PAGE 115 H2306
NAT/LISM REV POL/PAR ORD/FREE

B63
NKRUMAH K.,AFRICA MUST UNITE. AFR FUT GHANA CONSTN CULTURE SOCIETY NAT/G POL/PAR DELIB/GP TOP/EX PLAN DOMIN EDU/PROP ATTIT DRIVE...TIME/SEQ CHARTS TOT/POP 20. PAGE 118 H2364
CONCPT GEN/LAWS REGION

B63
PELLING H.M.,A HISTORY OF BRITISH TRADE UNIONISM. UK ELITES ECO/DEV POL/PAR GP/REL PWR NEW/LIB 19/20. PAGE 124 H2485
LABOR VOL/ASSN NAT/G

B63
QUAISON-SACKEY A.,AFRICA UNBOUND: REFLECTIONS OF AN AFRICAN STATESMAN. ISLAM CULTURE INTELL INT/ORG POL/PAR TOP/EX DOMIN EDU/PROP LEGIT ATTIT PERSON ...CONCPT OBS TIME/SEQ CHARTS STERTYP 20 UN. PAGE 129 H2571
AFR BIOG

B63
SAKAI R.K.,STUDIES ON ASIA, 1963. ASIA INDIA ISRAEL S/ASIA USA+45 PERF/ART POL/PAR SECT REGION NAT/LISM ...SOC LING TREND ANTHOL 19/20 CHINJAP. PAGE 137 H2735
PWR CULTURE

B63
SKLAR R.L.,NIGERIAN POLITICAL PARTIES: POWER IN AN EMERGENT AFRICAN NATION. AFR EUR+WWI CULTURE STRATA NAT/G DELIB/GP EX/STRUC LEGIS DOMIN EDU/PROP ROUTINE CHOOSE ATTIT PERCEPT ORD/FREE PWR...SOC CONCPT OBS TOT/POP VAL/FREE. PAGE 145 H2898
POL/PAR SOCIETY NAT/LISM NIGERIA

B63
STEVENS G.G.,EGYPT YESTERDAY AND TODAY. CONSTN ECO/UNDEV AGRI INDUS NAT/G POL/PAR FORCES ECO/TAC EDU/PROP COERCE WAR NAT/LISM DRIVE ALL/VALS ...TIME/SEQ WORK SUEZ 20. PAGE 149 H2983
ISLAM TOP/EX REV UAR

B63
SWEARER H.R.,CONTEMPORARY COMMUNISM: THEORY AND PRACTICE. COM USSR SOCIETY ECO/DEV POL/PAR FORCES PLAN ADMIN LEAD NAT/LISM...POLICY ANTHOL 20 LENIN/VI COM/PARTY. PAGE 151 H3015
MARXISM CONCPT DIPLOM NAT/G

B63
THORBURN H.G.,PARTY POLITICS IN CANADA. CANADA ELITES STRUCT INDUS PWR 20. PAGE 154 H3086
POL/PAR CONCPT NAT/G PROVS

B63
ULAM A.B.,THE NEW FACE OF SOVIET TOTALITARIANISM. FUT INTELL NAT/G POL/PAR EX/STRUC TOP/EX DIPLOM ECO/TAC DOMIN EDU/PROP LEGIT COERCE ATTIT RIGID/FLEX...OBS HIST/WRIT TREND TOT/POP VAL/FREE COLD/WAR. PAGE 158 H3150
COM PWR TOTALISM USSR

B63
WHEARE K.C.,LEGISLATURES. POL/PAR DELIB/GP WAR PEACE CONCPT. PAGE 167 H3338
LEGIS PARL/PROC JURID GOV/COMP

B63
WODDIS J.,AFRICA, THE WAY AHEAD. AFR FUT ELITES POL/PAR CAP/ISM DIPLOM DOMIN RACE/REL ATTIT ORD/FREE SOVEREIGN SOCISM 20 PANAF/FREE. PAGE 170 H3394
REV COLONIAL ECO/UNDEV NAT/G

L63
MICHAEL F.,"KHRUSHCHEV'S DISLOYAL OPPOSITION: STRUCTURAL CHANGE AND POWER STRUGGLE IN COMMUNIST BLOC." ASIA CHINA/COM FUT NAT/G POL/PAR CONSULT PLAN DOMIN ATTIT...POLICY CONCPT TREND MARX/KARL 20 KHRUSH/N. PAGE 110 H2195
COM STRUCT NAT/LISM USSR

L63
ROSE R.,"COMPARATIVE STUDIES IN POLITICAL FINANCE: A SYMPOSIUM." ASIA EUR+WWI S/ASIA LAW CULTURE DELIB/GP LEGIS ACT/RES ECO/TAC EDU/PROP CHOOSE ATTIT RIGID/FLEX SUPEGO PWR SKILL WEALTH...STAT ANTHOL VAL/FREE. PAGE 134 H2674
FINAN POL/PAR

S63
CRUTCHER J.,"PAN AFRICANISM: AFRICAN ODYSSEY." AFR NAT/G POL/PAR PROF/ORG VOL/ASSN TOP/EX CREATE REGION RACE/REL ALL/VALS...CONCPT TIME/SEQ TREND CON/ANAL 20. PAGE 36 H0716
PROVS DELIB/GP COLONIAL

S63
DUDLEY B.J.,"THE NOMINATION OF PARLIAMENTARY CANDIDATES IN NORTHERN NIGERIA." AFR CONSTN CULTURE ELITES STRATA DELIB/GP LEGIS DOMIN EDU/PROP COERCE ATTIT SUPEGO PWR...STAT VAL/FREE 20. PAGE 43 H0854
POL/PAR CHOOSE NIGERIA

S63
EMERI C.,"LES FORCES POLITIQUES AU PARLEMENT" EUR+WWI FRANCE ELITES DELIB/GP TOP/EX LEGIT ATTIT ...SOC 20 PARLIAMENT. PAGE 46 H0917
POL/PAR LEGIS PWR NAT/G

S63
HALPERN A.M.,"THE EMERGENCE OF AN ASIAN COMMUNIST BLOC." ASIA CHINA/COM COM FUT KOREA/N S/ASIA VIETNAM/N STRATA NAT/G DELIB/GP FORCES TOP/EX PLAN BAL/PWR COERCE DETER PWR COLD/WAR WORK 20. PAGE 65 H1295
POL/PAR EDU/PROP DIPLOM

S63
HARRIS R.L.,"COMMUNISM AND ASIA: ILLUSIONS AND MISCONCEPTIONS." ASIA COM FUT S/ASIA ECO/UNDEV AGRI NAT/G POL/PAR EX/STRUC EDU/PROP COERCE ATTIT MARXISM COLD/WAR TOT/POP 20. PAGE 67 H1344
PWR GUERRILLA

S63
HINDLEY D.,"FOREIGN AID TO INDONESIA AND ITS POLITICAL IMPLICATIONS." INDONESIA POL/PAR ATTIT SOVEREIGN...CHARTS 20. PAGE 71 H1421
FOR/AID NAT/G WEALTH ECO/TAC

S63
KOHN H.,"GERMANY IN WORLD POLITICS." EUR+WWI GERMANY GERMANY/W USSR NAT/G POL/PAR TOP/EX ATTIT ...CONCPT TREND GEN/LAWS 20 NATO ADENAUER/K. PAGE 87 H1746
ACT/RES ORD/FREE BAL/PWR

S63
LEE J.M.,"PARLIAMENT IN REPUBLICAN GHANA." AFR CONSTN CULTURE SOCIETY STRATA POL/PAR DELIB/GP TOP/EX DOMIN EDU/PROP LEGIT COERCE CHOOSE ATTIT ALL/VALS...CONCPT STAT TIME/SEQ VAL/FREE 20. PAGE 93 H1857
LEGIS GHANA

S63
NICHOLAS W.,"VILLAGE FACTIONS AND POLITICAL PARTIES IN RURAL WEST BENGAL." S/ASIA CULTURE STRATA FACE/GP KIN MUNIC DELIB/GP LEGIS DOMIN EDU/PROP COERCE CHOOSE ATTIT ALL/VALS...STAT TOT/POP VAL/FREE 20. PAGE 117 H2348
NEIGH POL/PAR

S63
NYE J.,"TANGANYIKA'S SELF-HELP." TANZANIA NAT/G GIVE COST EFFICIENCY NAT/LISM 20. PAGE 119 H2381
ECO/TAC POL/PAR ECO/UNDEV WORKER

S63
POPPINO R.E.,"IMBALANCE IN BRAZIL." L/A+17C NAT/G TOP/EX PLAN DIPLOM LEGIT DRIVE WEALTH...CON/ANAL LAFTA 20. PAGE 127 H2544
POL/PAR ECO/TAC BRAZIL

S63
RUSTOW D.A.,"THE MILITARY IN MIDDLE EASTERN SOCIETY AND POLITICS." FUT ISLAM CONSTN SOCIETY FACE/GP NAT/G POL/PAR PROF/ORG CONSULT DOMIN ADMIN EXEC REGION COERCE NAT/LISM ATTIT DRIVE PERSON ORD/FREE PWR...POLICY CONCPT OBS STERTYP 20. PAGE 136 H2721
FORCES ELITES

S63
WELLS H.,"THE OAS AND THE DOMINICAN ELECTIONS." L/A+17C INT/ORG NAT/G POL/PAR TEC/DEV ECO/TAC EDU/PROP PERCEPT...TIME/SEQ OAS TOT/POP 20. PAGE 166 H3332
CONSULT CHOOSE DOMIN/REP

S63
ZOLBERG A.R.,"MASS PARTIES AND NATIONAL INTEGRATION: THE CASE OF THE IVORY COAST" (BMR)" AFR IVORY/CST CONSTN VOL/ASSN DIPLOM LEAD GP/REL INGP/REL 20. PAGE 173 H3461
POL/PAR ECO/UNDEV NAT/G ADJUST

B64
AFRO ASIAN SOLIDARITY AGAINST IMPERIALISM. AFR ISLAM S/ASIA ECO/UNDEV NAT/G POL/PAR TOP/EX PRESS ...INT ANTHOL 20 CHOU/ENLAI. PAGE 2 H0043
MARXISM DIPLOM EDU/PROP CHIEF

B64
ALDEFER H.F.,A BIBLIOGRAPHY OF AFRICAN GOVERNMENT: 1950-1964. ALGERIA GUINEA LIBERIA UAR ECO/UNDEV POL/PAR LEGIS COLONIAL LEAD PARL/PROC NAT/LISM 20. PAGE 5 H0098
BIBLIOG AFR LOC/G NAT/G

B64
ANDREN N.,GOVERNMENT AND POLITICS IN THE NORDIC COUNTRIES: DENMARK, FINLAND, ICELAND, NORWAY, SWEDEN. DENMARK FINLAND ICELAND NORWAY SWEDEN POL/PAR CHIEF LEGIS ADMIN REGION REPRESENT ATTIT CONSERVE...CHARTS BIBLIOG/A 20. PAGE 7 H0137
CONSTN NAT/G CULTURE GOV/COMP

B64
BEATTIE J.,OTHER CULTURES. UNIV LAW FAM POL/PAR SECT ADJUD OWN ALL/VALS WEALTH...SOC NAT/COMP SOC/INTEG 20. PAGE 13 H0251
METH/CNCPT CULTURE STRUCT

B64
BERRINGTON H.,HOW NATIONS ARE GOVERNED. FRANCE WOR+45 ECO/UNDEV INT/ORG POL/PAR CHOOSE TOTALISM KNOWL...MAJORIT T 20 UN COMMONWLTH THIRD/WRLD. PAGE 16 H0320
NAT/G GOV/COMP ECO/DEV CONSTN

B64
BINDER L.,THE IDEOLOGICAL REVOLUTION IN THE MIDDLE EAST. ISLAM STRUCT INT/ORG KIN SECT EX/STRUC TOP/EX PLAN ATTIT DRIVE RIGID/FLEX PWR...MYTH TOT/POP 20. PAGE 17 H0338
POL/PAR NAT/G NAT/LISM

B64
BRZEZINSKI Z.,POLITICAL POWER: USA/USSR. USA+45 USSR AGRI POL/PAR FORCES CREATE CHOOSE ATTIT ORD/FREE PWR MARXISM...MYTH 20 KENNEDY/JF. PAGE 23 H0457
NAT/G NAT/COMP POLICY LEAD

B64
CAUTE D.,COMMUNISM AND THE FRENCH INTELLECTUALS, 1914-1960. COM EUR+WWI MOD/EUR NAT/G PERF/ART PROF/ORG CREATE EDU/PROP ATTIT PERSON KNOWL MARXISM ...SOC TIME/SEQ MARX/KARL 20 MALRAUX/A GIDE/A SARTRE/J. PAGE 28 H0563
POL/PAR INTELL

B64
CLUBB O.E. JR.,TWENTIETH CENTURY CHINA. ASIA CHINA/COM INTELL NAT/G POL/PAR VOL/ASSN ACT/RES EDU/PROP COERCE REV PWR...TIME/SEQ 20. PAGE 30 H0608
TOP/EX DRIVE

B64
FAINSOD M.,HOW RUSSIA IS RULED (REV. ED.). RUSSIA USSR AGRI PROC/MFG LABOR POL/PAR EX/STRUC CONTROL PWR...POLICY BIBLIOG 19/20 KHRUSH/N COM/PARTY. PAGE 48 H0963
NAT/G REV MARXISM

B64
FORBES A.H.,CURRENT RESEARCH IN BRITISH STUDIES. UK CONSTN CULTURE POL/PAR SECT DIPLOM ADMIN...JURID BIOG WORSHIP 20. PAGE 52 H1034
BIBLIOG PERSON NAT/G PARL/PROC

B64
FRIEDLAND W.H.,AFRICAN SOCIALISM. ECO/UNDEV MARKET LABOR NAT/G POL/PAR PLAN CAP/ISM ECO/TAC EDU/PROP CHOOSE ATTIT DRIVE PWR WEALTH...POLICY CONCPT RECORD STERTYP 20. PAGE 53 H1063
AFR SOCISM

B64
GRIFFITH W.E.,THE SINO-SOVIET RIFT. ASIA CHINA/COM COM CUBA USSR YUGOSLAVIA NAT/G POL/PAR VOL/ASSN DELIB/GP FORCES TOP/EX DIPLOM EDU/PROP DRIVE PERSON PWR...TREND 20 TREATY. PAGE 61 H1224
ATTIT TIME/SEQ BAL/PWR SOCISM

B64
GRIFFITH W.E.,COMMUNISM IN EUROPE (2 VOLS.). CZECHOSLVK USSR WOR+45 WOR-45 YUGOSLAVIA INGP/REL MARXISM SOCISM...ANTHOL 20 EUROPE/E. PAGE 61 H1225
COM POL/PAR DIPLOM GOV/COMP

B64
GROSSER A.,THE FEDERAL REPUBLIC OF GERMANY: A CONCISE HISTORY. GERMANY/W STRUCT MORAL ORD/FREE POPULISM SOCISM...SOC CONCPT 20. PAGE 62 H1235
NAT/G POL/PAR CHOOSE DIPLOM

B64
GROVES H.E.,THE CONSTITUTION OF MALAYSIA. MALAYSIA POL/PAR CHIEF CONSULT DELIB/GP CT/SYS PARL/PROC CHOOSE FEDERAL ORD/FREE 20. PAGE 62 H1238
CONSTN NAT/G LAW

B64
HALE O.J.,THE CAPTIVE PRESS IN THE THIRD REICH. GERMANY CULTURE LG/CO NAT/G POL/PAR PLAN DOMIN TASK CENTRAL OWN TOTALISM PWR...BIBLIOG 20 HITLER/A NAZI AMMAN/MAX. PAGE 64 H1283
COM/IND PRESS CONTROL FASCISM

B64
HALPERIN S.W.,MUSSOLINI AND ITALIAN FASCISM. ITALY NAT/G POL/PAR SECT ECO/TAC LEAD PWR SOCISM...POLICY 20 MUSSOLIN/B. PAGE 64 H1294
FASCISM NAT/LISM EDU/PROP CHIEF

B64
HANNA W.J.,POLITICS IN BLACK AFRICA: A SELECTIVE BIBLIOGRAPHY OF RELEVANT PERIODICAL LITERATURE. AFR LAW LOC/G MUNIC NAT/G POL/PAR LOBBY CHOOSE RACE/REL SOVEREIGN 20. PAGE 66 H1315
BIBLIOG NAT/LISM COLONIAL

B64
HOLDSWORTH W.S.,A HISTORY OF ENGLISH LAW; THE CENTURIES OF DEVELOPMENT AND REFORM (VOL. XIV). UK CONSTN LOC/G NAT/G POL/PAR CHIEF EX/STRUC ADJUD COLONIAL ATTIT...INT/LAW JURID 18/19 TORY/PARTY COMMONWLTH WHIG/PARTY COMMON/LAW. PAGE 73 H1453
LAW LEGIS LEAD CT/SYS

B64
HOPKINSON T.,SOUTH AFRICA. SOUTH/AFR UK NAT/G POL/PAR LEGIS ECO/TAC PARL/PROC WAR...JURID AUD/VIS 19/20. PAGE 73 H1467
SOCIETY RACE/REL DISCRIM

B64
IMAZ J.L.,LOS QUE MANDAN. INDUS LABOR NAT/G POL/PAR PROVS SECT CHIEF TOP/EX CONTROL 20 ARGEN. PAGE 76 H1524
LEAD FORCES ELITES ATTIT

B64
KAACK H.,DIE PARTEIEN IN DER VERFASSUNGSWIRKLICHKEIT DER BUNDESREPUBLIK. GERMANY/W ADMIN PARL/PROC CHOOSE...JURID 20. PAGE 82 H1646
POL/PAR PROVS NAT/G

B64
KOLARZ W.,BOOKS ON COMMUNISM. USSR WOR+45 CULTURE NAT/G POL/PAR DIPLOM LEAD...CONCPT GOV/COMP IDEA/COMP. PAGE 88 H1752
BIBLIOG/A SOCIETY COM MARXISM

B64
LEMARCHAND R.,POLITICAL AWAKENING IN THE BELGIAN CONGO. ECO/UNDEV VOL/ASSN DOMIN CHOOSE GP/REL INGP/REL DISCRIM ORD/FREE PWR...CHARTS 20 CONGO ARABS. PAGE 94 H1873
NAT/LISM COLONIAL POL/PAR RACE/REL

B64
LIGGETT E.,BRITISH POLITICAL ISSUES: VOLUME 1. UK LAW CONSTN LOC/G NAT/G ADJUD 20. PAGE 97 H1930
POL/PAR GOV/REL CT/SYS DIPLOM

B64
MAHAR J.M.,INDIA: A CRITICAL BIBLIOGRAPHY. INDIA PAKISTAN CULTURE ECO/UNDEV LOC/G POL/PAR SECT PROB/SOLV DIPLOM ADMIN COLONIAL PARL/PROC ATTIT 20. PAGE 101 H2016
BIBLIOG/A S/ASIA NAT/G LEAD

B64
MAIER J.,POLITICS OF CHANGE IN LATIN AMERICA. BRAZIL L/A+17C STRATA INT/ORG NAT/G POL/PAR FOR/AID REV 20. PAGE 101 H2019
SOCIETY NAT/LISM DIPLOM REGION

B64
MARSH D.C.,THE FUTURE OF THE WELFARE STATE. UK CONSTN NAT/G POL/PAR...POLICY WELF/ST 20. PAGE 103 H2058
NEW/LIB ADMIN CONCPT INSPECT

B64
MBEKI G.,SOUTH AFRICA: THE PEASANT'S REVOLT. SOUTH/AFR POL/PAR COERCE REV NAT/LISM ORD/FREE SOVEREIGN 20 NEGRO. PAGE 106 H2114
COLONIAL RACE/REL DISCRIM DOMIN

B64
MELADY T.,FACES OF AFRICA. AFR FUT ISLAM NAT/G POL/PAR SCHOOL DELIB/GP PLAN ECO/TAC EDU/PROP ATTIT ALL/VALS...CHARTS TOT/POP VAL/FREE 20. PAGE 108 H2168
ECO/UNDEV TREND NAT/LISM

B64
MILIBAND R.,THE SOCIALIST REGISTER: 1964. GERMANY/W ITALY UK LABOR POL/PAR ECO/TAC FOR/AID NUC/PWR ...POLICY SOCIALIST IDEA/COMP 20 MAO NASSER/G. PAGE 110 H2204
MARXISM SOCISM CAP/ISM PROB/SOLV

B64
MORGAN H.W.,AMERICAN SOCIALISM 1900-1960. USA+45 USA-45 INTELL AGRI LABOR WORKER BARGAIN ECO/TAC GP/REL RACE/REL 20 NEGRO MIGRATION GOLD/STAND. PAGE 113 H2254
SOCISM POL/PAR ECO/DEV STRATA

B64
MORGENTHAU R.S.,POLITICAL PARTIES IN FRENCH-SPEAKING WEST AFRICA. AFR FRANCE GUINEA IVORY/CST MALI SENEGAL CONSTN LEGIS CREATE PLAN LOBBY PARTIC GP/REL...POLICY BIBLIOG 20. PAGE 113 H2257
POL/PAR NAT/G SOVEREIGN COLONIAL

B64
RAISON T.,WHY CONSERVATIVE? UK FORCES DIPLOM ECO/TAC GIVE EDU/PROP ORD/FREE WEALTH LAISSEZ ...GOV/COMP 20 TORY/PARTY CONSRV/PAR. PAGE 129 H2583
PLURISM CONSERVE POL/PAR NAT/G

B64
RESHETAR J.S. JR.,A CONCISE HISTORY OF THE COMMUNIST PARTY OF THE SOVIET UNION (REV. ED.). COM USSR NAT/G EXEC 19/20 LENIN/VI STALIN/J KHRUSH/N. PAGE 131 H2618
CHIEF POL/PAR MARXISM PWR

B64
SAKAI R.K.,STUDIES ON ASIA, 1964. ASIA CHINA/COM ISRAEL MALAYSIA S/ASIA USA+45 USSR ECO/UNDEV FAM POL/PAR SECT CONSULT NAT/LISM...POLICY SOC 20 CHINJAP. PAGE 137 H2736
PWR DIPLOM

B64
SKINNER E.P.,THE MOSSI OF UPPER VOLTA: THE POLITICAL DEVELOPMENT OF A SUDANESE PEOPLE. AFR LAW AGRI FAM KIN POL/PAR PROVS SECT DELIB/GP EX/STRUC FORCES TOP/EX DOMIN EDU/PROP LEGIT CT/SYS COERCE CHOOSE ORD/FREE PWR WEALTH...SOC MYTH VAL/FREE. PAGE 145 H2897
CULTURE OBS UPPER/VOLT

B64
THORNBURG M.W.,PEOPLE AND POLICY IN THE MIDDLE EAST. ISLAM ECO/UNDEV FAM KIN MUNIC NAT/G NEIGH POL/PAR SECT DELIB/GP LEGIS PLAN ECO/TAC DOMIN ADMIN ATTIT HEALTH RESPECT...SOC CONCPT METH/CNCPT OBS TIME/SEQ TOT/POP VAL/FREE. PAGE 154 H3088
TEC/DEV CULTURE

B64
THORNTON T.P.,THE THIRD WORLD IN SOVIET PERSPECTIVE: STUDIES BY SOVIET WRITERS ON THE DEVELOPING AREAS. AFR L/A+17C S/ASIA STRATA AGRI INDUS MARKET NAT/G POL/PAR ECO/TAC COLONIAL PERCEPT PWR WEALTH...MARXIST STAT CHARTS WORK MARX/KARL 20. PAGE 155 H3090
ECO/UNDEV ACT/RES USSR DIPLOM

B64
TINKER H.,BALLOT BOX AND BAYONET - PEOPLE AND GOVERNMENT IN EMERGENT ASIAN COUNTRIES. CEYLON INDIA INDONESIA PHILIPPINE POL/PAR ADMIN COLONIAL LEAD PARL/PROC CHOOSE CONSEN ORD/FREE SOVEREIGN PLURISM...GOV/COMP THIRD/WRLD. PAGE 155 H3104
MYTH S/ASIA NAT/COMP NAT/LISM

B64
UTECHIN S.V.,RUSSIAN POLITICAL THOUGHT: A CONCISE HISTORY. RUSSIA USSR INTELL STRATA POL/PAR SECT LEGIS EDU/PROP REV WAR MARXISM...ANARCH BIBLIOG 9/20 REFORMERS SLAVS. PAGE 161 H3218
IDEA/COMP ATTIT ALL/IDEOS NAT/G

B64
VALEN H.,POLITICAL PARTIES IN NORWAY. NORWAY ACADEM PARTIC ROUTINE INGP/REL KNOWL...QU 20. PAGE 161 H3220
LOC/G POL/PAR PERSON

B64
WARD R.E.,POLITICAL MODERNIZATION IN JAPAN AND TURKEY. ASIA ISLAM S/ASIA CONSTN CULTURE STRATA COM/IND POL/PAR FORCES ACT/RES ECO/TAC DOMIN EDU/PROP LEGIT ADMIN CHOOSE ATTIT ALL/VALS...STAT TIME/SEQ VAL/FREE CHINJAP. PAGE 165 H3307
SOCIETY TURKEY

B64
WHEARE K.C.,FEDERAL GOVERNMENT (4TH ED.). WOR+45 WOR-45 POL/PAR LEGIS BAL/PWR CT/SYS...POLICY JURID CONCPT GOV/COMP 17/20. PAGE 167 H3339 FEDERAL CONSTN EX/STRUC NAT/COMP

B64
WRIGHT G.,RURAL REVOLUTION IN FRANCE: THE PEASANTRY IN THE TWENTIETH CENTURY. EUR+WWI MOD/EUR LAW CULTURE AGRI POL/PAR DELIB/GP LEGIS ECO/TAC EDU/PROP COERCE CHOOSE ATTIT RIGID/FLEX HEALTH ...STAT CENSUS CHARTS VAL/FREE 20. PAGE 171 H3419 PWR STRATA FRANCE REV

B64
ZARTMAN I.W.,MOROCCO: PROBLEMS OF NEW POWER. ISLAM CULTURE ECO/UNDEV AGRI POL/PAR SCHOOL FORCES ADMIN ...CONCPT STAT INT CENSUS TIME/SEQ CHARTS WORK VAL/FREE 20. PAGE 172 H3449 CHOOSE MOROCCO DELIB/GP DECISION

L64
ROTBERG R.,"THE FEDERATION MOVEMENT IN BRITISH EAST AND CENTRAL AFRICA." AFR RHODESIA UGANDA ECO/UNDEV NAT/G POL/PAR FORCES DOMIN LEGIT ADMIN COERCE ATTIT ...CONCPT TREND 20 TANGANYIKA. PAGE 135 H2691 VOL/ASSN PWR REGION

S64
BRADLEY C.P.,"THE FORMATION OF MALAYSIA." INDIA S/ASIA POL/PAR VOL/ASSN TOP/EX LEGIT RACE/REL ORD/FREE 20. PAGE 20 H0398 NAT/G CREATE COLONIAL MALAYSIA

S64
CATTELL D.T.,"SOVIET POLICIES IN LATIN AMERICA." COM CUBA L/A+17C USSR SOCIETY NAT/G POL/PAR FORCES CREATE ECO/TAC EDU/PROP REGION REV RIGID/FLEX ...GEN/LAWS COLD/WAR 20. PAGE 28 H0560 DRIVE PWR

S64
CLIFFE L.,"TANGANYIKA'S TWO YEARS OF INDEPENDENCE." AFR INDUS MARKET NAT/G POL/PAR DELIB/GP CREATE ECO/TAC LEGIT DRIVE ALL/VALS...METH/CNCPT RECORD 20 TANGANYIKA. PAGE 30 H0604 ECO/UNDEV PLAN

S64
GIROD R.,"LE SYSTEME DES PARTIS EN SUISSE." CONSTN LOC/G DELIB/GP FEDERAL ALL/VALS. PAGE 57 H1136 POL/PAR LEGIS NAT/G PARL/PROC

S64
GRUNER E.,"PRENSA, PARTIDOS POLITICOS, Y GRUPOS DE PRESION EN SUIZA." EUR+WWI MOD/EUR NAT/G EDU/PROP LEGIT PRESS ATTIT KNOWL ORD/FREE...CONCPT STAT CON/ANAL CHARTS 20. PAGE 62 H1241 POL/PAR SWITZERLND

S64
HORECKY P.L.,"LIBRARY OF CONGRESS PUBLICATIONS IN AID OF USSR AND EAST EUROPEAN RESEARCH." BULGARIA CZECHOSLVK POLAND USSR YUGOSLAVIA NAT/G POL/PAR DIPLOM ADMIN GOV/REL...CLASSIF 20. PAGE 73 H1468 BIBLIOG/A COM MARXISM

S64
LANGER P.F.,"JAPAN'S RELATIONS WITH CHINA." ASIA CHINA/COM KOREA S/ASIA ECO/DEV NAT/G POL/PAR EDU/PROP ATTIT ALL/VALS...METH/CNCPT TIME/SEQ TREND 20 CHINJAP. PAGE 91 H1808 RIGID/FLEX ECO/TAC

S64
MERKL P.H.,"EUROPEAN ASSEMBLY PARTIES AND NATIONAL DELEGATIONS." INT/ORG DELIB/GP DOMIN EDU/PROP LEGIT CHOOSE PWR...STAT VAL/FREE 20. PAGE 109 H2180 EUR+WWI POL/PAR REGION

S64
PRELOT M.,"LA INFLUENCIA POLITICA Y ELECTORAL DE LA PRENSA EN LA FRANCIA ACTUAL." EUR+WWI SOCIETY NAT/G POL/PAR PROF/ORG PRESS ATTIT PWR...CONCPT 20. PAGE 128 H2556 EDU/PROP FRANCE

S64
SALVADORI M.,"EL CAPITALISMO EN LA EUROPA DE LA POSGUERRA." INT/ORG NAT/G POL/PAR PLAN ECO/TAC ATTIT ORD/FREE WEALTH...HIST/WRIT COLD/WAR EEC 20. PAGE 137 H2743 EUR+WWI ECO/DEV CAP/ISM

S64
SMYTHE H.H.,"NEHRU AND INDIAN FOREIGN POLICY." S/ASIA ECO/UNDEV NAT/G POL/PAR CONSULT PLAN DIPLOM NEUTRAL COERCE ATTIT DRIVE PERSON MORAL ORD/FREE RESPECT...GEOG CONCPT TIME/SEQ TREND GEN/LAWS 20 NEHRU/J. PAGE 146 H2922 TOP/EX BIOG INDIA

S64
SWEARER H.R.,"AFTER KHRUSHCHEV: WHAT NEXT." COM FUT USSR CONSTN ELITES NAT/G POL/PAR CHIEF DELIB/GP LEGIS DOMIN LEAD...RECORD TREND STERTYP GEN/METH 20. PAGE 151 H3016 EX/STRUC PWR

S64
ZARTMAN I.W.,"LES RELATIONS ENTRE LA FRANCE ET L'ALGERIA DEPUIS LES ACCORDS D'EVIAN." EUR+WWI FUT ISLAM CULTURE AGRI EXTR/IND FINAN INDUS POL/PAR DIPLOM ECO/TAC FOR/AID PEACE ATTIT DRIVE ALL/VALS ...TIME/SEQ VAL/FREE 20. PAGE 172 H3450 ECO/UNDEV ALGERIA FRANCE

C64
SCOTT R.E.,"MEXICAN GOVERNMENT IN TRANSITION (REV ED)" CULTURE STRUCT POL/PAR CHIEF ADMIN LOBBY REV CHOOSE GP/REL DRIVE...BIBLIOG METH 20 MEXIC/AMER. PAGE 141 H2816 NAT/G L/A+17C ROUTINE CONSTN

B65
ADAM T.R.,GOVERNMENT AND POLITICS IN AFRICA SOUTH OF THE SAHARA. AFR EUR+WWI CONSTN CULTURE INTELL POL/PAR TOP/EX LEGIT REGION DRIVE...OBS TREND CMN/WLTH 20. PAGE 3 H0062 NAT/G TIME/SEQ RACE/REL COLONIAL

B65
AIYAR S.P.,STUDIES IN INDIAN DEMOCRACY. INDIA STRATA ECO/UNDEV LABOR POL/PAR LEGIS DIPLOM LOBBY REGION CHOOSE ATTIT SOCISM...ANTHOL 20. PAGE 4 H0086 ORD/FREE REPRESENT ADMIN NAT/G

B65
ALEXANDER R.J.,ORGANIZED LABOR IN LATIN AMERICA. L/A+17C INT/ORG LEGIS WORKER TEC/DEV BARGAIN INT/TRADE REV...NAT/COMP BIBLIOG 20. PAGE 5 H0102 LABOR POL/PAR ECO/UNDEV POLICY

B65
APTER D.E.,THE POLITICS OF MODERNIZATION. AFR L/A+17C CULTURE NAT/G POL/PAR ADMIN COLONIAL NAT/LISM ATTIT RIGID/FLEX PWR...SOC CONCPT. PAGE 8 H0154 ECO/UNDEV GEN/LAWS STRATA CREATE

B65
BARRY E.E.,NATIONALISATION IN BRITISH POLITICS: THE HISTORICAL BACKGROUND. UK AGRI DIST/IND EXTR/IND LABOR LG/CO ATTIT CONSERVE SOCISM 19/20 LABOR/PAR. PAGE 12 H0231 NAT/G OWN INDUS POL/PAR

B65
BETTISON D.G.,THE PAPUA-GUINEA ELECTIONS 1964. S/ASIA CONSTN POL/PAR EDU/PROP PARTIC SUFF CENTRAL CONSEN...OBS CHARTS BIBLIOG 20. PAGE 16 H0324 NAT/G LEGIS CHOOSE REPRESENT

B65
BLITZ L.F.,THE POLITICS AND ADMINISTRATION OF NIGERIAN GOVERNMENT. NIGER CULTURE LOC/G LEGIS DIPLOM COLONIAL CT/SYS SOVEREIGN...GEOG SOC ANTHOL 20. PAGE 18 H0357 NAT/G GOV/REL POL/PAR

B65
BOISSEVAIN J.,SAINTS AND FIREWORKS: RELIGION AND POLITICS IN RURAL MALTA. MALTA STRUCT FAM NEIGH POL/PAR REPRESENT INGP/REL CENTRAL...CHARTS BIBLIOG 20. PAGE 18 H0368 GP/REL NAT/G SECT MUNIC

B65
BRASS P.R.,FACTIONAL POLITICS IN AN INDIAN STATE: THE CONGRESS PARTY IN UTTAR PRADESH. INDIA UK CONSTN CULTURE ECO/UNDEV LOC/G DOMIN COLONIAL CROWD GP/REL ADJUST CENTRAL RIGID/FLEX SOVEREIGN 20 UTTAR/PRAD CONGRESS/P. PAGE 20 H0406 POL/PAR PROVS LEGIS CHOOSE

B65
BULMER-THOMAS I.,THE GROWTH OF THE BRITISH PARTY SYSTEM (VOL. II) 1924-1964. UK ECO/DEV BARGAIN WAR CHOOSE ATTIT ORD/FREE 20 LABOR/PAR CONSRV/PAR. PAGE 23 H0472 CHIEF POL/PAR PARL/PROC NAT/G

B65
CARTER G.M.,POLITICS IN EUROPE. EUR+WWI FRANCE GERMANY/W UK USSR LAW CONSTN POL/PAR VOL/ASSN PRESS LOBBY PWR...ANTHOL SOC/INTEG EEC. PAGE 27 H0548 GOV/COMP OP/RES ECO/DEV

B65
CARTER G.M.,GOVERNMENT AND POLITICS IN THE TWENTIETH CENTURY (REV. ED.). WOR+45 NAT/G POL/PAR LEGIS DIPLOM LEAD PARL/PROC CHOOSE TOTALISM 20. PAGE 27 H0549 GOV/COMP ECO/UNDEV ALL/IDEOS ECO/DEV

B65
CHANDA A.,FEDERALISM IN INDIA. INDIA UK ELITES FINAN NAT/G POL/PAR EX/STRUC LEGIS DIPLOM TAX GOV/REL POPULISM...POLICY 20. PAGE 28 H0572 CONSTN CENTRAL FEDERAL

B65
CHEN T.H.,THE CHINESE COMMUNIST REGIME: A DOCUMENTARY STUDY (2 VOLS.). CHINA/COM LAW CONSTN ELITES ECO/UNDEV LEGIS ECO/TAC ADMIN CONTROL PWR ...SOC 20. PAGE 29 H0587 MARXISM POL/PAR NAT/G

B65
COLLINS H.,KARL MARX AND THE BRITISH LABOR MOVEMENT, YEARS OF THE FIRST INTERNATIONAL. EUR+WWI MOD/EUR UK STRATA INDUS NAT/G POL/PAR SOCISM ...CONCPT 19/20 MARX/KARL. PAGE 32 H0633 MARXISM LABOR INT/ORG WORKER

B65
COWAN L.G.,EDUCATION AND NATION-BUILDING IN AFRICA. AFR CULTURE ECO/UNDEV POL/PAR ACT/RES LEAD SOVEREIGN...METH/COMP ANTHOL BIBLIOG 20. PAGE 34 H0684 EDU/PROP COLONIAL ACADEM NAT/LISM

B65
EDELMAN M.,THE POLITICS OF WAGE-PRICE DECISIONS. GERMANY ITALY NETHERLAND UK INDUS LABOR POL/PAR PROB/SOLV BARGAIN PRICE ROUTINE BAL/PAY COST DEMAND 20. PAGE 44 H0888 GOV/COMP CONTROL ECO/TAC PLAN

B65
FAUST J.J.,A REVOLUCAO DEVORA SEUS PRESIDENTES. BRAZIL NAT/G POL/PAR LEAD CHOOSE CIVMIL/REL ORD/FREE 20 PRESIDENT. PAGE 49 H0976 PARTIC REV FORCES GP/REL

B65
FREY F.W.,THE TURKISH POLITICAL ELITE. TURKEY CULTURE INTELL NAT/G EX/STRUC CHOOSE ATTIT PWR ...METH/CNCPT CHARTS WORSHIP 20. PAGE 53 H1059 ELITES SOCIETY POL/PAR

B65
GEORGE M.,THE WARPED VISION. EUR+WWI UK NAT/G POL/PAR LEGIS PARL/PROC SANCTION COERCE WAR GOV/REL PEACE RESPECT 20 CONSRV/PAR. PAGE 56 H1113 LEAD ATTIT DIPLOM POLICY

B65
GILG P.,DIE ERNEUERUNG DES DEMOKRATISCHEN DENKENS POL/PAR

IM WILHELMINISCHEN DEUTSCHLAND. GERMANY PARL/PROC ORD/FREE
CHOOSE REPRESENT...CONCPT 19/20 BISMARCK/O NAT/G
WILHELM/II. PAGE 56 H1126

B65
GOPAL S.,BRITISH POLICY IN INDIA 1858-1905. INDIA COLONIAL
UK ELITES CHIEF DELIB/GP ECO/TAC GP/REL DISCRIM ADMIN
ATTIT...IDEA/COMP NAT/COMP PERS/COMP BIBLIOG/A POL/PAR
19/20. PAGE 59 H1176 ECO/UNDEV

B65
GREGG J.L.,POLITICAL PARTIES AND PARTY SYSTEMS IN LEAD
GUATEMALA, 1944-1963. GUATEMALA L/A+17C EX/STRUC POL/PAR
FORCES CREATE CONTROL REV CHOOSE PWR...TREND NAT/G
IDEA/COMP 20. PAGE 60 H1209 CHIEF

B65
HARMON R.B.,POLITICAL SCIENCE: A BIBLIOGRAPHICAL BIBLIOG
GUIDE TO THE LITERATURE. WOR+45 WOR-45 R+D INT/ORG POL/PAR
LOC/G NAT/G DIPLOM ADMIN...CONCPT METH. PAGE 67 LAW
H1334 GOV/COMP

B65
INST INTL DES CIVILISATION DIF,THE CONSTITUTIONS CONSTN
AND ADMINISTRATIVE INSTITUTIONS OF THE NEW STATES. ADMIN
AFR ISLAM S/ASIA NAT/G POL/PAR DELIB/GP EX/STRUC ADJUD
CONFER EFFICIENCY NAT/LISM...JURID SOC 20. PAGE 77 ECO/UNDEV
H1535

B65
JACKSON G.,THE SPANISH REPUBLIC AND THE CIVIL WAR, ATTIT
1931-1939. EUR+WWI INTELL STRUCT COM/IND NAT/G GUERRILLA
POL/PAR LEGIS EDU/PROP EXEC COERCE NAT/LISM DRIVE SPAIN
PWR...INT TIME/SEQ TOT/POP 20. PAGE 79 H1574

B65
JACOB H.,POLITICS IN THE AMERICAN STATES; A PROVS
COMPARATIVE ANALYSIS. USA+45 POL/PAR CHIEF LEGIS GOV/COMP
TAX EDU/PROP CONTROL CT/SYS LOBBY PARTIC...DECISION PWR
CHARTS 20. PAGE 79 H1578

B65
JONAS E.,DIE VOLKSKONSERVATIVEN 1928-1933. GERMANY POL/PAR
EX/STRUC...CONCPT TIME/SEQ 20 HITLER/A. PAGE 82 NAT/G
H1628 GP/REL

B65
KOHN H.,AFRICAN NATIONALISM IN THE TWENTIETH NAT/LISM
CENTURY. AFR NAT/G POL/PAR COLONIAL REGION DISCRIM CULTURE
SOVEREIGN 20. PAGE 87 H1747 ATTIT

B65
KOUSOULAS D.G.,REVOLUTION AND DEFEAT; THE STORY OF REV
THE GREEK COMMUNIST PARTY. GREECE INT/ORG EX/STRUC MARXISM
DIPLOM FOR/AID EDU/PROP PARL/PROC ADJUST ATTIT 20 POL/PAR
COM/PARTY. PAGE 88 H1759 ORD/FREE

B65
KUPER L.,AN AFRICAN BOURGEOISIE. SOUTH/AFR LAW RACE/REL
INTELL NAT/G POL/PAR VOL/ASSN DISCRIM...POLICY 20. SOC
PAGE 89 H1783 STRUCT

B65
LANDE C.H.,LEADERS, FACTIONS, AND PARTIES. LEAD
PHILIPPINE CONSTN LOC/G NAT/G PARTIC...CHARTS POL/PAR
BIBLIOG 20. PAGE 90 H1806 POLICY

B65
LEWIS W.A.,POLITICS IN WEST AFRICA. AFR BAL/PWR POL/PAR
DIPLOM REPRESENT...POLICY 20. PAGE 96 H1916 ELITES
NAT/G
ECO/UNDEV

B65
MEHROTRA S.R.,INDIA AND THE COMMONWEALTH 1885-1929. DIPLOM
INDIA UK INT/ORG VOL/ASSN GP/REL ATTIT...POLICY NAT/G
BIBLIOG 19/20 CMN/WLTH. PAGE 108 H2163 POL/PAR
NAT/LISM

B65
MERKL P.H.,GERMANY: YESTERDAY AND TOMORROW. GERMANY NAT/G
POL/PAR PLAN DIPLOM LEAD FEDERAL 19/20. PAGE 109 FUT
H2181

B65
MOORE C.H.,TUNISIA SINCE INDEPENDENCE. ELITES LOC/G NAT/G
POL/PAR ADMIN COLONIAL CONTROL EXEC GOV/REL EX/STRUC
TOTALISM MARXISM...INT 20 TUNIS. PAGE 112 H2248 SOCISM

B65
NAMIER L.B.,THE STRUCTURE OF POLITICS AT THE PARL/PROC
ACCESSION OF GEORGE III. UK LOC/G TOP/EX COLONIAL LEGIS
LEAD PARTIC REV CHOOSE REPRESENT GOV/REL PERSON NAT/G
SOVEREIGN...GOV/COMP 18 PARLIAMENT. PAGE 115 H2309 POL/PAR

B65
ORGANSKI A.F.K.,THE STAGES OF POLITICAL ECO/DEV
DEVELOPMENT. STRATA AGRI INDUS NAT/G POL/PAR ECO/UNDEV
COLONIAL PWR WEALTH...CLASSIF TIME/SEQ. PAGE 121 GEN/LAWS
H2428 CREATE

B65
PELLING H.,A SHORT HISTORY OF THE LABOUR PARTY (2ND POL/PAR
ED.). UK NAT/G CHIEF PARL/PROC GP/REL INGP/REL 20 NEW/LIB
LABOR/PAR PARLIAMENT WILSON/H. PAGE 124 H2484 LEAD
LABOR

B65
PYLEE M.V.,CONSTITUTIONAL GOVERNMENT IN INDIA (2ND CONSTN
REV. ED.). INDIA POL/PAR EX/STRUC DIPLOM COLONIAL NAT/G
CT/SYS PARL/PROC PRIVIL...JURID 16/20. PAGE 128 PROVS
H2569 FEDERAL

B65
ROSENBERG A.,DEMOCRACY AND SOCIALISM. COM EUR+WWI ATTIT
FRANCE MOD/EUR STRUCT INT/ORG NAT/G POL/PAR TOP/EX
EDU/PROP COERCE PERSON PWR FASCISM MARXISM...CONCPT
TIME/SEQ MARX/KARL 19/20. PAGE 134 H2677

B65
SABLE M.H.,MASTER DIRECTORY FOR LATIN AMERICA. AGRI INDEX
COM/IND FINAN R+D ACADEM LABOR NAT/G POL/PAR L/A+17C
VOL/ASSN INT/TRADE EDU/PROP 20. PAGE 136 H2728 INT/ORG
DIPLOM

B65
SALVADORI M.,ITALY. AUSTRIA FRANCE GERMANY ITALY NAT/LISM
SPAIN CULTURE NAT/G POL/PAR DIPLOM WAR FASCISM CATHISM
LAISSEZ MARXISM...TIME/SEQ CHARTS BIBLIOG/A. SOCIETY
PAGE 137 H2744

B65
SCALAPINO R.A.,THE COMMUNIST REVOLUTION IN ASIA* ASIA
TACTICS, GOALS, AND ACHIEVEMENTS. INDIA INTELL S/ASIA
POL/PAR FORCES DOMIN EDU/PROP LEGIT COERCE REV MARXISM
ATTIT CHINJAP. PAGE 138 H2763 NAT/COMP

B65
SIRISKAR V.M.,POLITICAL BEHAVIOR IN INDIA. INDIA CHOOSE
SOCIETY MUNIC NAT/G PROVS ACT/RES SUFF...OBS CHARTS POL/PAR
20 POONA. PAGE 144 H2889 PWR
ATTIT

B65
STERN F.,THE POLITICS OF CULTURAL DESPAIR. EUR+WWI CULTURE
GERMANY POL/PAR SECT RACE/REL STRANGE TOTALISM ATTIT
...ART/METH MYTH BIBLIOG 20 JEWS. PAGE 149 H2980 NAT/LISM
FASCISM

B65
ULAM A.,THE BOLSHEVIKS. COM USSR NAT/G CHIEF SOCISM
ECO/TAC ADMIN LEAD WAR POPULISM...POLICY 19/20 POL/PAR
LENIN/VI BOLSHEVISM. PAGE 157 H3148 TOP/EX
REV

B65
VATCHER W.H. JR.,WHITE LAAGER: THE RISE OF NAT/LISM
AFRIKANER NATIONALISM. AFR SOUTH/AFR CULTURE POL/PAR
TOTALISM 20. PAGE 162 H3235 RACE/REL
DISCRIM

B65
WARD W.E.,GOVERNMENT IN WEST AFRICA. WOR+45 POL/PAR GOV/COMP
EX/STRUC PLAN PARTIC GP/REL SOVEREIGN 20 AFRICA/W. CONSTN
PAGE 165 H3308 COLONIAL
ECO/UNDEV

B65
WUORINEN J.H.,SCANDINAVIA. DENMARK FINLAND ICELAND NAT/G
NORWAY SWEDEN SOCIETY AGRI INDUS DELIB/GP DIPLOM POL/PAR
INT/TRADE NEUTRAL...GEOG CHARTS BIBLIOG TREATY. TREND
PAGE 171 H3428 POLICY

L65
MATTHEWS D.G.,"A CURRENT BIBLIOGRAPHY ON ETHIOPIAN BIBLIOG/A
AFFAIRS: A SELECT BIBLIOGRAPHY FROM 1950-1964." ADMIN
ETHIOPIA LAW CULTURE ECO/UNDEV INDUS LABOR SECT POL/PAR
FORCES DIPLOM CIVMIL/REL RACE/REL...LING STAT 20. NAT/G
PAGE 105 H2093

L65
MATTHEWS D.G.,"A CURRENT BIBLIOGRAPHY ON SUDANESE BIBLIOG
AFFAIRS; A SELECT BIBLIOGRAPHY FROM 1960-1964." ECO/UNDEV
SUDAN LAW CULTURE AGRI FINAN INDUS LABOR POL/PAR NAT/G
TEC/DEV FOR/AID RACE/REL LITERACY...LING 20. DIPLOM
PAGE 105 H2094

L65
SCHAFFER B.B.,"THE CONCEPT OF PREPARATION* SOME ECO/UNDEV
QUESTIONS ABOUT THE TRANSFER OF SYSTEMS OF UK
GOVERNMENT." AFR ASIA CANADA ELITES NAT/G POL/PAR RECORD
COLONIAL RIGID/FLEX IDEA/COMP. PAGE 138 H2769

S65
BIRNBAUM K.,"SWEDEN'S NUCLEAR POLICY." WOR+45 SWEDEN
POL/PAR CREATE TEC/DEV NEUTRAL RISK WAR ORD/FREE NUC/PWR
...DECISION IDEA/COMP NAT/COMP TIME. PAGE 17 H0343 DIPLOM
ARMS/CONT

S65
CAIRNS J.C.,"FRANCE, DECEMBER 1965: END OF THE CHOOSE
ELECTIVE MONARACHY" EUR+WWI FRANCE FUT CONSTN NAT/G
SOCIETY CHIEF BAL/PWR ATTIT ALL/IDEOS 20 DEGAULLE/C POL/PAR
PRESIDENT. PAGE 25 H0505 PWR

S65
SANDERS R.,"MASS SUPPORT AND COMMUNIST GUERRILLA
INSURRECTION." GREECE MALAYSIA PHILIPPINE VIETNAM MARXISM
STRUCT ECO/UNDEV POL/PAR FORCES CREATE REV GOV/COMP
...GP/COMP IDEA/COMP. PAGE 138 H2751

S65
STAROBIN J.R.,"COMMUNISM IN WESTERN EUROPE." FRANCE MARXISM
GERMANY ITALY USA+45 USSR ECO/DEV FEDERAL PEACE EUR+WWI
ATTIT DRIVE PWR TREND. PAGE 149 H2972 POL/PAR
NAT/COMP

C65
NEUMANN S.,"PERMANENT REVOLUTION: TOTALITARIANISM TOTALISM
IN THE AGE OF INTERNA TIONAL CIVIL WAR (2ND ED.)" REV
EUR+WWI ELITES POL/PAR DOMIN EDU/PROP LEAD CROWD FASCISM
REPRESENT...MAJORIT GOV/COMP BIBLIOG 20. PAGE 117 STRUCT
H2340

C65
WUORINEN J.H.,"SCANDINAVIA." DENMARK FINLAND BIBLIOG
ICELAND NORWAY SWEDEN SOCIETY AGRI POL/PAR DELIB/GP NAT/G
DIPLOM INT/TRADE NEUTRAL WAR...CHARTS TREATY 20. POLICY
PAGE 171 H3427

B66
ADAMS J.C.,THE GOVERNMENT OF REPUBLICAN ITALY (2ND ED.). ITALY LOC/G POL/PAR DELIB/GP LEGIS WORKER ADMIN CT/SYS FASCISM...CHARTS BIBLIOG 20 PARLIAMENT. PAGE 3 H0064
NAT/G CHOOSE EX/STRUC CONSTN

B66
AFRIFA A.A.,THE GHANA COUP. AFR GHANA ELITES NAT/G DIPLOM DOMIN 20 NKRUMAH/K. PAGE 4 H0076
TOP/EX REV FORCES POL/PAR

B66
ANDERSON S.V.,CANADIAN OMBUDSMAN PROPOSALS. CANADA LEGIS DEBATE PARL/PROC...MAJORIT JURID TIME/SEQ IDEA/COMP 20 OMBUDSMAN PARLIAMENT. PAGE 7 H0133
NAT/G CREATE ADMIN POL/PAR

B66
BARNETT D.L.,MAU MAU FROM WITHIN. AFR UK POL/PAR LEAD GUERRILLA AUTHORIT ORD/FREE...SOC BIOG 20 NEGRO MAU/MAU. PAGE 11 H0225
REV CULTURE NAT/G

B66
BEER S.H.,BRITISH POLITICS IN THE COLLECTIVIST AGE. UK NAT/G CONTROL CHOOSE GP/REL ATTIT PWR PLURISM ...MAJORIT WELF/ST 16/20. PAGE 13 H0258
POL/PAR SOCISM TRADIT GP/COMP

B66
BRECHER M.,SUCCESSION IN INDIA. INDIA USA+45 CONSTN AGRI POL/PAR PROVS SECT DELIB/GP FORCES PROB/SOLV ECO/TAC PWR...LING 20 CONGRESS NEHRU/J. PAGE 20 H0408
CHIEF DECISION CHOOSE

B66
BROWN J.F.,THE NEW EASTERN EUROPE. ALBANIA BULGARIA HUNGARY POLAND ROMANIA CULTURE AGRI POL/PAR WAR NAT/LISM MARXISM...CHARTS BIBLIOG 20. PAGE 22 H0444
DIPLOM COM NAT/G ECO/UNDEV

B66
BROWN L.C.,STATE AND SOCIETY IN INDEPENDENT NORTH AFRICA. ALGERIA LIBYA MOROCCO AGRI INDUS INT/ORG POL/PAR SECT PLAN DIPLOM COLONIAL...LING NAT/COMP ANTHOL BIBLIOG 20 TUNIS MUSLIM. PAGE 22 H0446
NAT/G SOCIETY CULTURE ECO/UNDEV

B66
BUTLER D.E.,THE BRITISH GENERAL ELECTION OF 1966. UK LOC/G NAT/G OP/RES CONFER CHOOSE MAJORITY ATTIT ...CHARTS TIME 20. PAGE 25 H0498
POL/PAR REPRESENT GP/REL PERS/REL

B66
CAUTE D.,THE LEFT IN EUROPE SINCE 1789. EUR+WWI MOD/EUR NAT/G POL/PAR REV...TIME/SEQ GEN/LAWS BIBLIOG 18/20. PAGE 28 H0564
ALL/IDEOS ORD/FREE CONCPT STRATA

B66
CHAPMAN B.,THE PROFESSION OF GOVERNMENT: THE PUBLIC SERVICE IN EUROPE. CONSTN NAT/G POL/PAR EX/STRUC LEGIS TOP/EX PROB/SOLV DEBATE EXEC PARL/PROC PARTIC 20. PAGE 29 H0581
BIBLIOG ADMIN EUR+WWI GOV/COMP

B66
COLE A.B.,SOCIALIST PARTIES IN POSTWAR JAPAN. STRATA AGRI LABOR PLAN DIPLOM ECO/TAC AGREE LEAD CHOOSE ATTIT...CHARTS 20 CHINJAP SOC/DEMPAR. PAGE 31 H0620
POL/PAR POLICY SOCISM NAT/G

B66
DAHL R.A.,POLITICAL OPPOSITIONS IN WESTERN DEMOCRACIES. EUR+WWI USA+45 USA-45 SOCIETY STRATA ECO/DEV NAT/G LEGIS REPRESENT...TREND NAT/COMP ANTHOL 20. PAGE 37 H0732
POL/PAR CHOOSE PARTIC PLURISM

B66
DALLIN A.,POLITICS IN THE SOVIET UNION: 7 CASES. COM USSR LAW POL/PAR CHIEF FORCES WRITING CONTROL PARL/PROC CIVMIL/REL TOTALISM...ANTHOL 20 KHRUSH/N STALIN/J CASEBOOK COM/PARTY. PAGE 37 H0736
MARXISM DOMIN ORD/FREE GOV/REL

B66
DE TOCQUEVILLE A,DEMOCRACY IN AMERICA (1834-1840) (2 VOLS. IN I; TRANS. BY G. LAWRENCE). FRANCE CULTURE STRATA POL/PAR CT/SYS REPRESENT FEDERAL ORD/FREE SOVEREIGN...MAJORIT TREND GEN/LAWS 18/19. PAGE 39 H0773
POPULISM USA-45 CONSTN NAT/COMP

B66
DE VORE B.B.,LAND AND LIBERTY; A HISTORY OF THE MEXICAN REVOLUTION. CONSTN INTELL NAT/G CONTROL LEAD CHOOSE TOTALISM AUTHORIT...BIBLIOG 19/20 MEXIC/AMER DIAZ/P LIB/PARTY MAGON/F MADERO/F. PAGE 39 H0776
REV CHIEF POL/PAR

B66
DEUTSCHE INST ZEITGESCHICHTE,DIE WESTDEUTSCHEN PARTEIEN: 1945-1965. GERMANY/W CHOOSE PWR ...TIME/SEQ 20. PAGE 40 H0806
POL/PAR CONCPT NAT/G PROVS

B66
DEUTSCHER I.,STALIN: A POLITICAL BIOGRAPHY. EUR+WWI USSR POL/PAR FORCES DIPLOM ADMIN LEAD REV WAR TOTALISM PERSON 20 STALIN/J ROOSEVLT/F LENIN/VI HITLER/A. PAGE 40 H0807
BIOG MARXISM TOP/EX PWR

B66
DEXTER N.C.,GUIDE TO CONTEMPORARY POLITICS. EUR+WWI UK PARL/PROC GP/REL KNOWL...POLICY MAJORIT IDEA/COMP 20. PAGE 41 H0815
POL/PAR CONCPT NAT/G

B66
DODGE D.,AFRICAN POLITICS IN PERSPECTIVE. ELITES POL/PAR PROB/SOLV LEAD...POLICY 20 THIRD/WRLD. PAGE 41 H0831
AFR NAT/G COLONIAL SOVEREIGN

B66
EPSTEIN F.T.,THE AMERICAN BIBLIOGRAPHY OF RUSSIAN AND EAST EUROPEAN STUDIES FOR 1964. USSR LOC/G NAT/G POL/PAR FORCES ADMIN ARMS/CONT...JURID CONCPT 20 UN. PAGE 47 H0933
BIBLIOG COM MARXISM DIPLOM

B66
FINER S.E.,ANONYMOUS EMPIRE: STUDY OF THE LOBBY IN GREAT BRITAIN. UK CONSTN LABOR POL/PAR SECT DOMIN EDU/PROP PRESS CHOOSE...CONCPT CHARTS 20 PARLIAMENT. PAGE 50 H1004
LOBBY NAT/G LEGIS PWR

B66
FORD P.,CARDINAL MORAN AND THE A. L. P. NAT/G POL/PAR SECT DELIB/GP LOBBY REV CHOOSE ORD/FREE MARXISM 19/20 AUSTRAL PROTESTANT LABOR/PAR. PAGE 52 H1035
CATHISM SOCISM LABOR SOCIETY

B66
GRAHAM B.D.,THE FORMATION OF THE AUSTRALIAN COUNTRY PARTIES. CANADA USA+45 USA-45 SOCIETY PLAN ECO/TAC ...NAT/COMP 20 AUSTRAL. PAGE 59 H1190
POL/PAR AGRI REGION PARL/PROC

B66
GUNN G.E.,THE POLITICAL HISTORY OF NEWFOUNDLAND 1832-1864. CANADA FINAN LEGIS CHOOSE REPRESENT ...CHARTS 19. PAGE 62 H1252
POL/PAR NAT/G CONSTN

B66
HARMON R.B.,SOURCES AND PROBLEMS OF BIBLIOGRAPHY IN POLITICAL SCIENCE (PAMPHLET). INT/ORG LOC/G MUNIC POL/PAR ADMIN GOV/REL ALL/IDEOS...JURID MGT CONCPT 19/20. PAGE 67 H1335
BIBLIOG DIPLOM INT/LAW NAT/G

B66
HENKYS R.,DEUTSCHLAND UND DIE OSTLICHEN NACHBARN. GERMANY POLAND NAT/G POL/PAR INGP/REL ATTIT 20 MIGRATION. PAGE 70 H1396
GP/REL JURID INT/LAW DIPLOM

B66
HINTON W.,FANSHEN: A DOCUMENTARY OF REVOLUTION IN A CHINESE VILLAGE. ASIA ELITES MUNIC NAT/G POL/PAR SECT WORKER LEAD WAR PRIVIL PWR 20 MAO. PAGE 71 H1422
MARXISM REV NEIGH OWN

B66
INSTITUTE COMP STUDY POL SYS,DOMINICAN REPUBLIC ELECTION FACT BOOK. DOMIN/REP LAW LEGIS REPRESENT ...JURID CHARTS 20. PAGE 77 H1536
SUFF CHOOSE POL/PAR NAT/G

B66
INTERPARLIAMENTARY UNION,PARLIAMENTS: COMPARATIVE STUDY ON STRUCTURE AND FUNCTIONING OF REPRESENTATIVE INSTITUTIONS IN FIFTY-FIVE COUNTRIES. WOR+45 POL/PAR DELIB/GP BUDGET ADMIN CONTROL CHOOSE. PAGE 78 H1560
PARL/PROC LEGIS GOV/COMP EX/STRUC

B66
LEIBLER I.,SOVIET JEWRY AND HUMAN RIGHTS. USSR INTELL NAT/G DOMIN ATTIT 20 AUSTRAL JEWS. PAGE 93 H1865
DISCRIM RACE/REL MARXISM POL/PAR

B66
LONDON DAILY TELEGRAPH,ELECTION '66: GALLUP ANALYSIS OF THE VOTING RESULTS. UK LEGIS COMPUTER ATTIT...QU SAMP CHARTS 20 LABOR/PAR HOUSE/CMNS. PAGE 98 H1959
STAT CHOOSE REPRESENT POL/PAR

B66
LOVEDAY P.,PARLIAMENT FACTIONS AND PARTIES: THE FIRST THIRTY YEARS OF RESPONSIBLE GOVERNMENT IN NEW SOUTH WALES, 1856-1889. PROVS LEAD PARL/PROC PARTIC GP/REL INGP/REL MAJORITY PWR...GP/COMP 19 AUSTRAL. PAGE 99 H1970
POL/PAR ELITES NAT/G LEGIS

B66
MAC DONALD H.M.,THE INTELLECTUAL IN POLITICS. GERMANY PERU SWEDEN UK USSR NAT/G CONSULT PLAN EDU/PROP TASK INGP/REL EFFICIENCY RATIONAL ALL/VALS 20. PAGE 99 H1987
ALL/IDEOS INTELL POL/PAR PARTIC

B66
MADAN G.R.,ECONOMIC THINKING IN INDIA. INDIA ECO/UNDEV AGRI FINAN INDUS LABOR PLAN CAP/ISM INT/TRADE MARXISM SOCISM...POLICY 1/20. PAGE 101 H2013
ECO/TAC PHIL/SCI NAT/G POL/PAR

B66
NEUMANN R.G.,THE GOVERNMENT OF THE GERMAN FEDERAL REPUBLIC. EUR+WWI GERMANY/W LOC/G EX/STRUC LEGIS CT/SYS INGP/REL PWR...BIBLIOG 20 ADENAUER/K. PAGE 117 H2336
NAT/G POL/PAR DIPLOM CONSTN

B66
NOEL G.E.,THE NEW BRITAIN AND HAROLD WILSON: INTERIM REPORT, 1966 GENERAL ELECTION. UK POL/PAR CONSULT PROB/SOLV BUDGET DIPLOM ECO/TAC LEAD CHOOSE ATTIT 20 WILSON/H PARLIAMENT. PAGE 118 H2366
BIOG PERSON NAT/G CHIEF

B66
NOLTE E.,THREE FACES OF FASCISM. FRANCE GERMANY DOMIN LEGIT COERCE CROWD REV WAR GP/REL RACE/REL SOVEREIGN...GOV/COMP IDEA/COMP 19/20 HITLER/A MUSSOLIN/B MARX/KARL. PAGE 118 H2368
FASCISM TOTALISM NAT/G POL/PAR

B66
O'NEILL R.J.,THE GERMAN ARMY AND THE NAZI PARTY, 1933-1939. GERMANY ELITES NAT/G EDU/PROP CONTROL LEAD COERCE WAR...POLICY INT TIME/SEQ BIBLIOG 20 HITLER/A NAZI. PAGE 120 H2391
CIVMIL/REL FORCES FASCISM POL/PAR

B66
PLATE H.,PARTEIFINANZIERUNG UND GRUNDESETZ. GERMANY NAT/G PLAN GIVE PAY INCOME WEALTH...JURID 20. PAGE 126 H2522
POL/PAR CONSTN FINAN

B66
POLE J.R.,POLITICAL REPRESENTATION IN ENGLAND AND THE ORIGINS OF THE AMERICAN REPUBLIC. UK USA-45 CONSTN ELITES NAT/G POL/PAR LEGIS PARL/PROC ...MAJORIT 17/19. PAGE 127 H2534
REPRESENT GOV/COMP

B66
RICHERT F.,DIE NATIONALE WELLE. GERMANY GERMANY/W PARL/PROC ORD/FREE FASCISM...TREND 19/20. PAGE 131 H2622
POL/PAR ATTIT NAT/LISM NAT/G

B66
RIZK C.,LE REGIME POLITIQUE LIBANAIS. ISLAM LEBANON STRUCT POL/PAR SECT LOBBY GP/REL 20 ARABS MUSLIM CHRISTIAN. PAGE 132 H2637
ECO/UNDEV NAT/G CULTURE

B66
ROGGER H.,THE EUROPEAN RIGHT. EUR+WWI CONSERVE ...ANTHOL BIBLIOG 20. PAGE 133 H2660
NAT/COMP POL/PAR IDEA/COMP TRADIT

B66
ROSNER J.,DER FASCHISMUS. AUSTRIA GERMANY ITALY STRATA NAT/G POL/PAR COERCE RACE/REL TOTALISM ATTIT AUTHORIT...IDEA/COMP 20 NAZI ANTI/SEMIT. PAGE 134 H2684
NAT/LISM FASCISM ORD/FREE WAR

B66
ROSS A.M.,INDUSTRIAL RELATIONS AND ECONOMIC DEVELOPMENT. POL/PAR LEGIS WORKER BARGAIN PRICE EXEC LOBBY INCOME PWR...DECISION ANTHOL BIBLIOG 20. PAGE 134 H2686
ECO/UNDEV LABOR NAT/G GP/REL

B66
SAINDERICHIN P.,HISTORIE SECRETE D'UNE ELECTION, DECEMBER 5-19, 1965. FRANCE NAT/G DELIB/GP LEGIS PLAN EDU/PROP TV SOCISM...MARXIST 20 DEGAULLE/C. PAGE 137 H2731
CHOOSE CHIEF PROB/SOLV POL/PAR

B66
SAKAI R.K.,STUDIES ON ASIA, 1966. CEYLON INDIA USA-45 INDUS POL/PAR DIPLOM ECO/TAC MARXISM ...POLICY 19/20 CHINJAP. PAGE 137 H2738
SECT ECO/UNDEV

B66
SCHURMANN F.,IDEOLOGY AND ORGANIZATION IN COMMUNIST CHINA. CHINA/COM LOC/G MUNIC POL/PAR ECO/TAC CONTROL ATTIT...MGT STERTYP 20 COM/PARTY. PAGE 140 H2805
MARXISM STRUCT ADMIN NAT/G

B66
SHARMA B.M.,THE REPUBLIC OF INDIA; CONSTITUTION AND GOVERNMENT. INDIA POL/PAR LEGIS EFFICIENCY ...TIME/SEQ GOV/COMP 20. PAGE 142 H2846
PROVS NAT/G CONSTN

B66
SILBERMAN B.S.,MODERN JAPANESE LEADERSHIP; TRANSITION AND CHANGE. NAT/G POL/PAR CHIEF ADMIN REPRESENT GP/REL ADJUST RIGID/FLEX...SOC METH/COMP ANTHOL 19/20 CHINJAP CHRISTIAN. PAGE 144 H2873
LEAD CULTURE ELITES MUNIC

B66
SWARTZ M.J.,POLITICAL ANTHROPOLOGY. WOR+45 POL/PAR ACT/RES REV GP/REL DRIVE...SOC CONCPT TIME/SEQ GP/COMP ANTHOL WORSHIP 20. PAGE 151 H3013
PARTIC RIGID/FLEX LOC/G CREATE

B66
THORNTON M.J.,NAZISM, 1918-1945. GERMANY INT/ORG DIPLOM REV PEACE FASCISM...CONCPT 20 HITLER/A WEIMAR/REP NAZI. PAGE 155 H3089
TOTALISM POL/PAR NAT/G WAR

B66
TORMIN W.,GESCHICHTE DER DEUTSCHEN PARTEIEN SEIT 1848. GERMANY CHOOSE PWR...CONCPT 19/20 WEIMAR/REP. PAGE 156 H3116
POL/PAR CONSTN NAT/G TOTALISM

B66
US DEPARTMENT OF STATE,RESEARCH ON AFRICA (EXTERNAL RESEARCH LIST NO 5-25). LAW CULTURE ECO/UNDEV POL/PAR DIPLOM EDU/PROP LEAD REGION MARXISM...GEOG LING WORSHIP 20. PAGE 159 H3188
BIBLIOG/A ASIA S/ASIA NAT/G

B66
US DEPARTMENT OF STATE,RESEARCH ON THE AMERICAN REPUBLICS (EXTERNAL RESEARCH LIST NO 6-25). CULTURE SOCIETY POL/PAR DIPLOM EDU/PROP MARXISM WORSHIP 20 OAS. PAGE 159 H3189
BIBLIOG/A L/A+17C REGION NAT/G

B66
US DEPARTMENT OF STATE,RESEARCH ON THE MIDDLE EAST (EXTERNAL RESEARCH LIST NO 4-25). GREECE ISRAEL SYRIA UAR YEMEN CULTURE SOCIETY POL/PAR SECT DIPLOM EDU/PROP WAR NAT/LISM...GEOG GOV/COMP 20. PAGE 160 H3190
BIBLIOG/A ISLAM NAT/G REGION

B66
US DEPARTMENT OF STATE,RESEARCH ON WESTERN EUROPE, GREAT BRITAIN, AND CANADA (EXTERNAL RESEARCH LIST NO 3-25). CANADA GERMANY/W UK LAW CULTURE NAT/G POL/PAR FORCES EDU/PROP REGION MARXISM...GEOG SOC WORSHIP 20 CMN/WLTH. PAGE 160 H3192
BIBLIOG/A EUR+WWI DIPLOM

B66
US DEPARTMENT OF THE ARMY,COMMUNIST CHINA: A STRATEGIC SURVEY: A BIBLIOGRAPHY (PAMPHLET NO. 20-67). CHINA/COM COM INDIA USSR NAT/G POL/PAR EX/STRUC FORCES NUC/PWR REV ATTIT...POLICY GEOG CHARTS. PAGE 160 H3194
BIBLIOG/A MARXISM S/ASIA DIPLOM

B66
US DEPARTMENT OF THE ARMY,SOUTH ASIA: A STRATEGIC SURVEY (PAMPHLET NO. 550-3). AFGHANISTN INDIA NEPAL PAKISTAN ECO/UNDEV INT/ORG POL/PAR FORCES FOR/AID INT/TRADE LEAD WAR...POLICY SOC TREND 20. PAGE 160 H3195
BIBLIOG/A S/ASIA DIPLOM NAT/G

B66
WINKS R.W.,THE HISTORIOGRAPHY OF THE BRITISH EMPIRE-COMMONWEALTH. CANADA INDIA PAKISTAN UK CULTURE SOCIETY STRUCT POL/PAR...CONCPT NAT/COMP 20 AUSTRAL. PAGE 169 H3386
HIST/WRIT TREND IDEA/COMP METH/COMP

B66
WUEST J.J.,NEW SOURCE BOOK IN MAJOR EUROPEAN GOVERNMENTS. CHRIST-17C EUR+WWI FRANCE GERMANY ITALY MOD/EUR UK USSR LOC/G POL/PAR CHIEF EX/STRUC CHOOSE CONSERVE MARXISM...JURID T 13/20. PAGE 171 H3425
NAT/G CONSTN LEGIS

B66
ZABLOCKI C.J.,SINO-SOVIET RIVALRY. AFR ASIA CHINA/COM CUBA EUR+WWI L/A+17C USA+45 USSR WOR+45 POL/PAR FORCES COERCE NUC/PWR...GOV/COMP IDEA/COMP 20 MAO KHRUSH/N. PAGE 172 H3444
DIPLOM MARXISM COM

B66
ZOLBERG A.R.,CREATING POLITICAL ORDER. AFR CONGO/BRAZ GHANA NIGER KIN NAT/G DOMIN COLONIAL REGION CENTRAL NAT/LISM ATTIT PWR 20 CONGO/LEOP. PAGE 173 H3462
SOVEREIGN ORD/FREE CONSTN POL/PAR

L66
MCAUSLAN J.P.W.,"CONSTITUTIONAL INNOVATION AND POLITICAL STABILITY IN TANZANIA: A PRELIMINARY ASSESSMENT." AFR TANZANIA ELITES CHIEF EX/STRUC RIGID/FLEX PWR 20 PRESIDENT BUREAUCRCY. PAGE 106 H2122
CONSTN NAT/G EXEC POL/PAR

S66
"RESEARCH WORK 1965-1966." NEW/ZEALND ELITES ACADEM LOC/G MUNIC POL/PAR PROVS DIPLOM COLONIAL...SOC 20 AUSTRAL. PAGE 2 H0047
BIBLIOG NAT/G CULTURE S/ASIA

S66
COWAN L.G.,"THE MILITARY AND AFRICAN POLITICS." AFR FUT NAT/G POL/PAR PARTIC REV 20. PAGE 34 H0685
CIVMIL/REL FORCES PWR LEAD

S66
FELD W.,"NATIONAL ECONOMIC INTEREST GROUPS AND POLICY FORMATION IN THE EEC." NAT/G POL/PAR REGION CENTRAL SOVEREIGN...INT NET/THEORY EEC. PAGE 49 H0985
LOBBY ELITES DECISION

S66
GAMER R.E.,"URGENT SINGAPORE, PATIENT MALAYSIA." MALAYSIA S/ASIA ECO/UNDEV POL/PAR CHIEF TARIFFS TAX CONTROL LEAD REGION PWR 20 SINGAPORE. PAGE 55 H1094
DIPLOM NAT/G POLICY ECO/TAC

S66
MANSERGH N.,"THE PARTITION OF INDIA IN RETROSPECT." INDIA PAKISTAN S/ASIA UK DIPLOM COLONIAL GP/REL PWR 20. PAGE 102 H2042
NAT/G PARL/PROC POLICY POL/PAR

S66
MATTHEWS D.G.,"ETHIOPIAN OUTLINE: A BIBLIOGRAPHIC RESEARCH GUIDE." ETHIOPIA LAW STRUCT ECO/UNDEV AGRI LABOR SECT CHIEF DELIB/GP EX/STRUC ADMIN...LING ORG/CHARTS 20. PAGE 105 H2095
BIBLIOG NAT/G DIPLOM POL/PAR

S66
MATTHEWS D.G.,"PRELUDE-COUP D'ETAT-MILITARY GOVERNMENT: A BIBLIOGRAPHICAL AND RESEARCH GUIDE TO NIGERIAN POL AND GOVT, JAN, 1965-66." AFR NIGER LAW CONSTN POL/PAR LEGIS CIVMIL/REL GOV/REL...STAT 20. PAGE 105 H2096
BIBLIOG NAT/G ADMIN CHOOSE

S66
SCHWARTZ M.,"THE 1964 PRESIDENTIAL ELECTIONS THROUGH SOVIET EYES." ASIA POL/PAR DIPLOM ATTIT MARXISM...NAT/COMP COLD/WAR. PAGE 140 H2811
USSR USA+45 PERCEPT

S66
SNOW P.G.,"A SCALOGRAM ANALYSIS OF POLITICAL DEVELOPMENT." STRATA ECO/UNDEV POL/PAR REGION ALL/VALS PWR...SOC CHARTS. PAGE 146 H2924
L/A+17C NAT/COMP TESTS CLASSIF

S66
STRAYER J.R.,"PROBLEMS OF DICTATORSHIP* THE RUSSIAN EXPERIENCE." ASIA MOD/EUR ELITES STRATA POL/PAR CREATE NAT/LISM MARXISM...GOV/COMP NAT/COMP. PAGE 150 H2997
NAT/G GEN/LAWS USSR TOTALISM

C66
ROSENBERG C.G. JR.,"THE MYTH OF "MAU-MAU:" NATIONALISM IN KENYA." AFR CULTURE NAT/G POL/PAR COERCE REV RACE/REL ATTIT ORD/FREE SOVEREIGN...MYTH BIBLIOG 20. PAGE 134 H2678
NAT/LISM COLONIAL MAJORIT LEAD

B67
ALBINSKI H.S.,EUROPEAN POLITICAL PROCESSES: ESSAYS AND READINGS. EUR+WWI FRANCE GERMANY MOD/EUR UK ELITES POL/PAR PWR...CHARTS ANTHOL 18/20. PAGE 5 H0094
NAT/COMP POLICY IDEA/COMP

B67
ANDERSON E.N.,POLITICAL INSTITUTIONS AND SOCIAL CHANGE IN CONTINENTAL EUROPE IN THE NINETEENTH CENTURY. MOD/EUR LAW CONSTN SOCIETY POL/PAR TEC/DEV LEAD REV ATTIT...BIBLIOG 19. PAGE 6 H0127
NAT/G NAT/COMP METH/COMP INDUS

B67
ANDERSON T.,RUSSIAN POLITICAL THOUGHT; AN INTRODUCTION. USSR NAT/G POL/PAR CHIEF MARXISM ...TIME/SEQ BIBLIOG 9/20. PAGE 7 H0135
TREND CONSTN ATTIT

B67
BAIN C.A.,VIETNAM: THE ROOTS OF CONFLICT. FRANCE S/ASIA USSR VIETNAM POL/PAR SECT FORCES COLONIAL NAT/LISM PEACE ORD/FREE MARXISM...GEOG CHARTS 4/20. PAGE 10 H0202
NAT/G WAR CULTURE

B67
BROMKE A.,POLAND'S POLITICS: IDEALISM VS. REALISM. COM GERMANY POLAND RUSSIA USSR POL/PAR CATHISM ...BIBLIOG 19/20. PAGE 21 H0431
NAT/G DIPLOM MARXISM

B67
BRZEZINSKI Z.K.,IDEOLOGY AND POWER IN SOVIET POLITICS. USSR NAT/G POL/PAR PWR...GEN/LAWS 19/20. PAGE 23 H0462
DIPLOM EX/STRUC MARXISM

B67
CANTOR N.F.,THE ENGLISH TRADITION* TWENTIETH-CENTURY VIEWS OF ENGLISH HISTORY (2VOLS.). UK STRATA NAT/G SECT WAR...POLICY GOV/COMP IDEA/COMP ANTHOL T PARLIAMENT CMN/WLTH. PAGE 26 H0522
CT/SYS LAW POL/PAR

B67
DEGLER C.N.,THE AGE OF THE ECONOMIC REVOLUTION 1876-1900. USA-45 AGRI MUNIC POL/PAR SECT ECO/TAC CHOOSE...PHIL/SCI CHARTS NAT/COMP 19 NEGRO. PAGE 39 H0782
INDUS SOCIETY ECO/DEV TEC/DEV

B67
DIX R.H.,COLOMBIA: THE POLITICAL DIMENSIONS OF CHANGE. ELITES POL/PAR DOMIN REV...AUD/VIS 20 COLOMB. PAGE 41 H0828
L/A+17C NAT/G TEC/DEV LEAD

B67
ERDMAN H.L.,THE SWATANTRA PARTY AND INDIAN CONSERVATISM. INDIA S/ASIA SOCIETY STRATA LOC/G NAT/G LEAD PARTIC GP/REL ATTIT...CONCPT GP/COMP BIBLIOG 20 SWATANTRA. PAGE 47 H0938
POL/PAR CONSERVE CHOOSE POLICY

B67
EVANS R.H.,COEXISTENCE: COMMUNISM AND ITS PRACTICE IN BOLOGNA, 1945-1965. ITALY CAP/ISM ADMIN CHOOSE PEACE ORD/FREE...SOC STAT DEEP/INT SAMP CHARTS BIBLIOG 20. PAGE 48 H0952
MARXISM CULTURE MUNIC POL/PAR

B67
GALBRAITH J.K.,THE NEW INDUSTRIAL STATE. INDUS LABOR LG/CO NAT/G POL/PAR SCHOOL OP/RES CAP/ISM EXEC TREND. PAGE 54 H1087
TEC/DEV ECO/DEV SOCIETY MARKET

B67
HANRIEDER W.F.,WEST GERMAN FOREIGN POLICY 1949-1963: INTERNATIONAL PRESSURE AND DOMESTIC RESPONSE. EUR+WWI GERMANY/W POL/PAR LOBBY CONSEN 20. PAGE 66 H1316
DIPLOM POLICY NAT/G ATTIT

B67
KAROL K.S.,CHINA, THE OTHER COMMUNISM (TRANS. BY TOM BAISTOW). CHINA/COM CULTURE INDUS FORCES DIPLOM EDU/PROP CONTROL EXEC NUC/PWR ATTIT...SOC CHARTS 20. PAGE 83 H1663
NAT/G POL/PAR MARXISM INGP/REL

B67
KOLKOWICZ R.,THE SOVIET MILITARY AND THE COMMUNIST PARTY. COM USSR ELITES NAT/G CREATE CIVMIL/REL GP/REL...TREND BIBLIOG/A 20 COM/PARTY. PAGE 88 H1753
MARXISM CONSTN FORCES POL/PAR

B67
KORNBERG A.,CANADIAN LEGISLATIVE BEHAVIOR: A STUDY OF THE 25TH PARLIAMENT. CANADA NAT/G POL/PAR PARL/PROC CHOOSE INGP/REL ADJUST ANOMIE RIGID/FLEX ...SOC STAND/INT CHARTS SOC/EXP 20 PARLIAMENT. PAGE 88 H1756
ATTIT LEGIS ROLE

B67
MORRIS A.J.A.,PARLIAMENTARY DEMOCRACY IN THE NINETEENTH CENTURY. UK INDUS LOC/G NAT/G POL/PAR CONSULT LEGIS INT/TRADE ADMIN CHOOSE SUFF SOVEREIGN 19 PARLIAMENT. PAGE 113 H2261
TIME/SEQ CONSTN PARL/PROC POPULISM

B67
ODINGA O.,NOT YET UHURU. NAT/G POL/PAR PROB/SOLV COERCE REV WAR PERS/REL PERSON ORD/FREE...POLICY 20 ODINGA/O KENYATTA. PAGE 120 H2395
ATTIT BIOG LEAD AFR

B67
OPERATIONS AND POLICY RESEARCH,NICARAGUA: ELECTION FACTBOOK: FEBRUARY 5, 1967 (PAMPHLET). NICARAGUA LAW NAT/G LEAD REPRESENT...STAT BIOG CHARTS 20. PAGE 121 H2423
POL/PAR CHOOSE PLAN ATTIT

B67
PYE L.W.,SOUTHEAST ASIA'S POLITICAL SYSTEMS. ASIA S/ASIA STRUCT ECO/UNDEV EX/STRUC CAP/ISM DIPLOM ALL/IDEOS...TREND CHARTS. PAGE 128 H2568
NAT/G POL/PAR GOV/COMP

B67
RAE D.,THE POLITICAL CONSEQUENCES OF ELECTORAL LAWS. EUR+WWI ICELAND ISRAEL NEW/ZEALND UK USA+45 ADJUD APPORT GP/REL MAJORITY...MATH STAT CENSUS CHARTS BIBLIOG 20 AUSTRAL. PAGE 129 H2579
POL/PAR CHOOSE NAT/COMP REPRESENT

B67
RUDMAN H.C.,THE SCHOOL AND STATE IN THE USSR. COM USSR ACADEM LABOR LOC/G PUB/INST EDU/PROP GP/REL ROLE...POLICY DECISION MGT CHARTS 20. PAGE 136 H2712
SCHOOL ADMIN NAT/G POL/PAR

B67
RUSTOW D.A.,A WORLD OF NATIONS; PROBLEMS OF POLITICAL MODERNIZATION. CONSTN NAT/G POL/PAR FORCES DIPLOM LEAD AUTHORIT...CHARTS IDEA/COMP 20. PAGE 136 H2722
PROB/SOLV ECO/UNDEV CONCPT NAT/COMP

B67
RYDER A.J.,THE GERMAN REVOLUTION OF 1918; A STUDY OF GERMAN SOCIALISM IN WAR AND REVOLT. GERMANY NAT/G POL/PAR GP/REL...BIBLIOG 20. PAGE 136 H2724
SOCISM WAR REV INGP/REL

B67
SCHECTER J.,THE NEW FACE OF BUDDHA: BUDDHISM AND POLITICAL POWER IN SOUTHEAST ASIA. S/ASIA NAT/G POL/PAR NAT/LISM ATTIT MARXISM...BIBLIOG 20. PAGE 139 H2780
SECT POLICY PWR LEAD

B67
SCHWARTZ B.,THE ROOTS OF FREEDOM: A CONSTITUTIONAL HISTORY OF ENGLAND. UK LAW POL/PAR DELIB/GP LEGIS REV REPRESENT...JURID BIBLIOG/A 13/20. PAGE 140 H2809
CONSTN PARL/PROC NAT/G

B67
SCHWARTZ M.A.,PUBLIC OPINION AND CANADIAN IDENTITY. CANADA SOCIETY LOC/G DIPLOM ADMIN LEAD REGION GP/REL SAMP. PAGE 141 H2812
ATTIT NAT/G NAT/LISM POL/PAR

B67
SETON-WATSON H.,THE RUSSIAN EMPIRE, 1801-1917. COM RUSSIA STRATA ECO/DEV AGRI INDUS POL/PAR DIPLOM NAT/LISM MARXISM...IDEA/COMP BIBLIOG 19/20 MARX/KARL. PAGE 142 H2834
SOCIETY NAT/G LEAD POLICY

B67
TOMPKINS S.R.,THE TRIUMPH OF BOLSHEVISM: REVOLUTION OR REACTION? USSR WORKER PRESS WEALTH MARXISM POPULISM...BIOG TREND IDEA/COMP BIBLIOG 19/20 LENIN/VI. PAGE 156 H3113
REV NAT/G POL/PAR NAT/LISM

B67
UNIVERSAL REFERENCE SYSTEM,COMPARATIVE GOVERNMENT AND CULTURES (VOLUME X). WOR+45 WOR-45 NAT/G POL/PAR ATTIT...CON/ANAL COMPUT/IR IDEA/COMP GEN/METH. PAGE 158 H3168
BIBLIOG/A GOV/COMP CULTURE NAT/COMP

B67
WARREN S.,THE AMERICAN PRESIDENT. POL/PAR FORCES LEGIS DIPLOM ECO/TAC ADMIN EXEC PWR...ANTHOL 18/20 ROOSEVLT/F KENNEDY/JF JOHNSON/LB TRUMAN/HS WILSON/W. PAGE 165 H3312
CHIEF LEAD NAT/G CONSTN

B67
WISEMAN H.V.,BRITAIN AND THE COMMONWEALTH. EUR+WWI FUT UK ECO/DEV POL/PAR TEC/DEV INT/TRADE LEAD ROLE SOVEREIGN...SOC TREND 20 CMN/WLTH. PAGE 169 H3391
INT/ORG DIPLOM NAT/G NAT/COMP

B67
YAMAMURA K.,ECONOMIC POLICY IN POSTWAR JAPAN. ASIA FINAN POL/PAR DIPLOM LEAD NAT/LISM ATTIT NEW/LIB POPULISM 20 CHINJAP. PAGE 171 H3432
ECO/DEV POLICY NAT/G TEC/DEV

L67
AUSTIN D.A.,"POLITICAL CONFLICT IN AFRICA." CONSTN NAT/G CREATE ADMIN COLONIAL ORD/FREE MARXISM POPULISM SOCISM...NAT/COMP ANTHOL 20. PAGE 9 H0180
ANOMIE AFR POL/PAR

L67
EGBERT D.D.,"THE IDEA OF 'AVANT-GARDE' IN ART AND POLITICS." USSR CULTURE INTELL POL/PAR CREATE EDU/PROP CONTROL REV ANOMIE DRIVE ROLE...IDEA/COMP 20. PAGE 45 H0895
ART/METH COM ATTIT

L67
GLAZER M.,"LAS ACTITUDES Y ACTIVIDADES POLITICAS DE LOS ESTUDIANTES DE LA UNIVERSIDAD DE CHILE." CHILE NAT/G POL/PAR EDU/PROP LOBBY ATTIT 20. PAGE 57 H1141
ACADEM AGE/Y PARTIC ELITES

L67
ISRAEL J.,"THE RED GUARDS IN HISTORICAL PERSPECTIVE: CONTINUITY AND CHANGE IN THE CHINESE YOUTH MOVEMENT." CHINA/COM FUT POL/PAR CONTROL REV GP/REL 20. PAGE 79 H1572
AGE/Y LOBBY MARXISM NAT/G

L67
SCALAPINO R.A.,"A SURVEY OF ASIA IN 1966." ASIA S/ASIA CONSTN SOCIETY POL/PAR CHIEF WAR...ANTHOL 20. PAGE 138 H2764
DIPLOM

L67
TABORSKY E.,"THE COMMUNIST PARTIES OF THE 'THIRD WORLD' IN SOVIET STRATEGY." AFR ASIA L/A+17C USSR INTELL NAT/G WORKER PLAN CONTROL LEAD PARTIC REV ...GOV/COMP 20 COM/PARTY THIRD/WRLD. PAGE 152 H3032
POL/PAR MARXISM ECO/UNDEV DIPLOM

L67
TAMBIAH S.J.,"THE POLITICS OF LANGUAGE IN INDIA AND
POL/PAR

CEYLON." CEYLON INDIA NAT/G DOMIN ADMIN...SOC 20. PAGE 152 H3039
LING NAT/LISM REGION

L67
VAN DER KROEF J.M.,"INDONESIA: THE BATTLE OF THE 'OLD' AND THE 'NEW ORDER'." INDONESIA ISLAM ELITES POL/PAR DOMIN INGP/REL NAT/LISM PWR...IDEA/COMP 20. PAGE 161 H3229
FORCES MARXISM NAT/G BAL/PWR

S67
ABDEL-MALEK A.,"THE CRISIS IN NASSER'S EGYPT." ISLAM UAR STRUCT POL/PAR EX/STRUC CREATE PLAN WAR ATTIT ORD/FREE PWR...POLICY DECISION 20. PAGE 3 H0054
FORCES LEAD PROB/SOLV NAT/G

S67
AKE C.,"POLITICAL INTEGRATION AND POLITICAL STABILITY." ELITES POL/PAR LEAD ADJUST EFFICIENCY ATTIT AUTHORIT DRIVE...CONCPT 20. PAGE 4 H0088
CULTURE NAT/G CONTROL GP/REL

S67
ALBINSKI H.S.,"POLITICS AND BICULTURISM IN CANADA: THE FLAG DEBATE." CANADA SOCIETY NAT/G PROVS DELIB/GP DEBATE REGION SOVEREIGN PLURISM...POLICY SOC/INTEG 20. PAGE 5 H0093
NAT/LISM GP/REL POL/PAR CULTURE

S67
ALEXANDER A.,"CANADA'S PARLIAMENTARY SECRETARIES: THEIR POLITICAL AND CONSTITUTIONAL POSITION." CANADA UK NAT/G POL/PAR GOV/REL...GOV/COMP 20. PAGE 5 H0099
CONSTN ADMIN EX/STRUC DELIB/GP

S67
BAIKALOV A.,"EMERGENCY LEGISLATION IN WEST GERMANY." GERMANY/W LABOR NAT/G POL/PAR SANCTION ...MARXIST 20. PAGE 10 H0199
LAW TOTALISM LEGIS PARL/PROC

S67
CHIU S.M.,"CHINA'S MILITARY POSTURE." CHINA/COM ELITES NAT/G POL/PAR TEC/DEV ECO/TAC DOMIN CONTROL LEAD REV MARXISM 20 MAO. PAGE 30 H0595
FORCES CIVMIL/REL NUC/PWR DIPLOM

S67
COHEN A.,"REVOLUTION IN ARGENTINA?" L/A+17C NAT/G POL/PAR CHIEF PROB/SOLV ECO/TAC 20 ARGEN. PAGE 31 H0615
REV ECO/UNDEV CONTROL BIOG

S67
CROCKETT D.G.,"THE MP AND HIS CONSTITUENTS." UK POL/PAR...DECISION 20. PAGE 35 H0706
EXEC NAT/G PERS/REL REPRESENT

S67
DERRICK P.,"THE WHITE PAPER ON INCOMES." EUR+WWI UK LAW LABOR NAT/G PLAN PROB/SOLV GP/REL...GOV/COMP PARLIAMENT. PAGE 40 H0794
INCOME POL/PAR POLICY

S67
DRYDEN S.,"LOCAL GOVERNMENT IN TANZANIA PART II" TANZANIA LAW NAT/G POL/PAR CONTROL PARTIC REPRESENT ...DECISION 20. PAGE 42 H0850
LOC/G GOV/REL ADMIN STRUCT

S67
ELLISON H.J.,"THE SOCIALIST REVOLUTIONARIES." USSR ECO/UNDEV NAT/G INGP/REL EFFICIENCY ATTIT PWR MARXISM...CONCPT IDEA/COMP 20 SOC/REVPAR. PAGE 46 H0911
POL/PAR REV AGRI

S67
FUSARO A.,"THE EFFECT OF PROPORTIONAL REPRESENTATION ON VOTING IN THE AUSTRALIAN SENATE." S/ASIA CONSTN POL/PAR CONTROL GP/REL PWR...CHARTS 20 AUSTRAL HOUSE/REP SENATE. PAGE 54 H1083
LEGIS CHOOSE REPRESENT NAT/G

S67
GOODSELL J.N.,"BALAGUER'S DOMINICAN REPUBLIC." DOMIN/REP FUT L/A+17C POL/PAR PROB/SOLV ECO/TAC 20. PAGE 59 H1174
ECO/UNDEV CHIEF POLICY NAT/G

S67
GRAHAM R.,"BRAZIL'S DILEMMA." BRAZIL FUT L/A+17C NAT/G CHIEF PROB/SOLV ECO/TAC PWR 20. PAGE 60 H1193
ECO/UNDEV CONSTN POL/PAR POLICY

S67
HANSON A.H.,"INDIA AFTER THE ELECTIONS." INDIA ECO/UNDEV LEGIS TEC/DEV FOR/AID GP/REL FEDERAL ATTIT 20. PAGE 66 H1321
NAT/G POL/PAR REGION CENTRAL

S67
HEATH D.B.,"BOLIVIA UNDER BARRIENTOS." L/A+17C NAT/G CHIEF DIPLOM ECO/TAC...POLICY 20 BOLIV. PAGE 69 H1379
ECO/UNDEV POL/PAR REV CONSTN

S67
IDENBURG P.J.,"POLITICAL STRUCTURAL DEVELOPMENT IN TROPICAL AFRICA." UK ECO/UNDEV KIN POL/PAR CHIEF EX/STRUC CREATE COLONIAL CONTROL REPRESENT RACE/REL ...MAJORIT TREND 20. PAGE 76 H1521
AFR CONSTN NAT/G GOV/COMP

S67
JANICKE M.,"MONOPOLISMUS UND PLURALISMUS IM KOMMUNISTISCHEN HERRSCHAFTSSYSTEM" COM CZECHOSLVK USSR YUGOSLAVIA SOCIETY CONTROL RIGID/FLEX...CONCPT NAT/COMP 20. PAGE 79 H1589
TOTALISM POL/PAR ATTIT PLURISM

S67
LEHMBRUCH G.,"WAHLREFORM UND POLITISCHES SYSTEM." NETHERLAND NAT/G LEGIS PARL/PROC...SOC 20. PAGE 93 H1864
CHOOSE POL/PAR METH/CNCPT GP/COMP

S67
LOFCHIE M.F.,"OKELLO'S REVOLUTION." TANZANIA NAT/G POL/PAR FORCES PLAN CONTROL 20. PAGE 98 H1954
AFR REV LEAD CHIEF

S67
MARWICK A.,"THE LABOUR PARTY AND THE WELFARE STATE IN BRITAIN, 19001948." UK SOCIETY STRUCT ECO/DEV WORKER CREATE PRICE CHOOSE WEALTH NEW/LIB SOCISM ...POLICY HEAL 20 PARLIAMENT LABOR/PAR. PAGE 104 H2074
POL/PAR RECEIVE LEGIS NAT/G

S67
MOZINGO D.,"CHINA AND INDONESIA." CHINA/COM INDONESIA POL/PAR 20. PAGE 114 H2276
MARXISM CONTROL DIPLOM NAT/G

S67
NEUBAUER D.E.,"SOME CONDITIONS OF DEMOCRACY." ECO/DEV COM/IND DIST/IND POL/PAR EDU/PROP REPRESENT ...SOC STAT NAT/COMP 20. PAGE 117 H2331
NAT/G CHOOSE MAJORIT ECO/UNDEV

S67
PAK H.,"CHINA'S MILITIA AND MAO TSE-TUNG'S 'PEOPLE'S WAR'." CHINA/COM SOCIETY POL/PAR EX/STRUC PROB/SOLV PARTIC COERCE WAR CIVMIL/REL ATTIT DRIVE MARXISM...METH/COMP 20 MAO. PAGE 122 H2447
FORCES NAT/G WORKER CHIEF

S67
RENFIELD R.L.,"A POLICY FOR VIETNAM." COM VIETNAM NAT/G POL/PAR VOL/ASSN CHIEF DIPLOM EDU/PROP DETER REPRESENT ATTIT ORD/FREE 20. PAGE 131 H2615
WAR POLICY PLAN COERCE

S67
SAVELYEV N.,"MONOPOLY DRIVE IN INDIA." INDIA INDUS NAT/G INT/TRADE NEUTRAL SANCTION GOV/REL CONSERVE ...MARXIST 20. PAGE 138 H2759
ECO/UNDEV POL/PAR ECO/TAC CONTROL

S67
SAVER W.,"NATIONAL SOCIALISM: TOTALITARIANISM OR FASCISM?" GERMANY STRUCT POL/PAR PROB/SOLV MARXISM ...SOC CONCPT HIST/WRIT IDEA/COMP 20 HITLER/A COLD/WAR. PAGE 138 H2760
SOCISM NAT/G TOTALISM FASCISM

S67
SHELDON C.H.,"PUBLIC OPINION AND HIGH COURTS: COMMUNIST PARTY CASES IN FOUR CONSTITUTIONAL SYSTEMS." CANADA GERMANY/W WOR+45 POL/PAR MARXISM ...METH/COMP NAT/COMP 20 AUSTRAL. PAGE 143 H2857
ATTIT CT/SYS CONSTN DECISION

S67
SHIGEO N.,"THE GREAT CULTURAL REVOLUTION." ASIA ECO/UNDEV AGRI NAT/G CHIEF ECO/TAC EDU/PROP CONTROL LEAD PWR 20 MAO. PAGE 143 H2860
CREATE REV CULTURE POL/PAR

S67
SIPPEL D.,"INDIENS UNSICHERE ZUKUNFT." INDIA CULTURE ACADEM POL/PAR LEGIS COLONIAL CHOOSE SOVEREIGN...JURID 20. PAGE 144 H2888
SOCIETY STRUCT ECO/UNDEV NAT/G

S67
SOARES G.,"SOCIO-ECONOMIC VARIABLES AND VOTING FOR THE RADICAL LEFT: CHILE 1952." CHILE INDUS NAT/G WORKER ADJUST STRANGE ANOMIE WEALTH...METH/CNCPT CORREL 20. PAGE 146 H2925
STRATA POL/PAR CHOOSE STAT

S67
SOMMER T.,"BONN CHANGES COURSE." GERMANY/W NAT/G POL/PAR PROB/SOLV NAT/LISM 20 NATO BERLIN/BLO. PAGE 147 H2932
DIPLOM BAL/PWR INT/ORG

S67
SPITTMANN I.,"EAST GERMANY: THE SWINGING PENDULUM." COM GERMANY/E NAT/G EFFICIENCY MARXISM 20. PAGE 148 H2952
PRODUC POL/PAR WEALTH ATTIT

S67
STRAFFORD P.,"FRENCH ELECTIONS." FRANCE NAT/G CHIEF LEGIS BAL/PWR ECO/TAC PARL/PROC PARTIC ATTIT 20. PAGE 150 H2993
POL/PAR SOCISM CENTRAL MARXISM

S67
SZALAY L.B.,"SOVIET DOMESTIC PROPAGANDA AND LIBERALIZATION." COM USSR SOCIETY COM/IND NAT/G POL/PAR EX/STRUC TEC/DEV LEAD ATTIT ROLE MARXISM ...METH/COMP 20. PAGE 151 H3026
EDU/PROP TOTALISM PERSON PERCEPT

S67
TAYLOR P.B. JR.,"PROGRESS IN VENEZUELA." L/A+17C VENEZUELA AGRI INDUS LG/CO NAT/G SML/CO CHOOSE ...POLICY 20. PAGE 153 H3057
ECO/UNDEV ECO/TAC POL/PAR ORD/FREE

S67
THEROUX P.,"HATING THE ASIANS." TANZANIA UGANDA CONSTN INDUS NAT/G POL/PAR WORKER ECO/TAC HABITAT LOVE...POLICY GEOG 20 MIGRATION. PAGE 154 H3069
AFR RACE/REL SOVEREIGN ATTIT

S67
WHITE J.W.,"MASS MOVEMENTS AND DEMOCRACY: SOKAGAKKAI IN JAPANESE POLITICS." NAT/G GP/REL ALL/VALS ORD/FREE WORSHIP 20 CHINJAP. PAGE 167 H3349
SECT PWR ATTIT POL/PAR

S67
WILLIAMS P.M.,"THE FRENCH GENERAL ELECTION OF MARCH 1967." FRANCE INDUS WORKER NAT/LISM PWR SOCISM 20. PAGE 168 H3368
POL/PAR NAT/G ATTIT CHOOSE

S67
WILPERT C.,"A LOOK IN THE MIRROR AND OVER THE WALL." GERMANY POL/PAR...KNO/TEST COLD/WAR. PAGE 169 H3378
NAT/G PLAN DIPLOM ATTIT

S67
YEFROMEV A.,"THE TRUE FACE OF THE WEST GERMAN NATIONAL-DEMOCRATS." GERMANY/W NAT/G DOMIN LEAD SANCTION WAR ATTIT PERSON...MARXIST 20. PAGE 172 H3436
POL/PAR TOTALISM PARL/PROC DIPLOM

S67
ZARTMAN I.W.," NAT/G POL/PAR VOL/ASSN NAT/LISM ORD/FREE PWR...CONCPT NAT/COMP ORG/CHARTS OAU MAGHREB. PAGE 172 H3451
AFR ISLAM DIPLOM REGION

C67
LING D.L.,"TUNISIA: FROM PROTECTORATE TO REPUBLIC." CULTURE NAT/G POL/PAR CHIEF DIPLOM COERCE WAR PWR ...BIBLIOG 19/20 TUNIS. PAGE 97 H1934
AFR NAT/LISM COLONIAL PROB/SOLV

S68
DEUTSCHER I.,"GERMANY AND MARXISM." FUT GERMANY/W NAT/G...MARXIST TREND 20. PAGE 40 H0808
SOCISM ORD/FREE POPULISM POL/PAR

B85
TAINE H.A.,THE FRENCH REVOLUTION (3 VOLS.) (TRANS. BY J. DURAND). FRANCE MOD/EUR SOCIETY STRATA POL/PAR ECO/TAC DOMIN EDU/PROP GP/REL PWR ...GOV/COMP IDEA/COMP 18. PAGE 152 H3036
REV NAT/G EX/STRUC LEAD

B87
KINNEAR J.B.,PRINCIPLES OF CIVIL GOVERNMENT. MOD/EUR USA-45 CONSTN LOC/G EX/STRUC ADMIN PARL/PROC RACE/REL...CONCPT 18/19. PAGE 86 H1718
POL/PAR NAT/G GOV/COMP REPRESENT

B94
BENOIST C.,LA POLITIQUE. FRANCE LAW SOCIETY STRUCT POL/PAR PARL/PROC GP/REL ATTIT PWR 19/20. PAGE 14 H0283
NAT/G REPRESENT ORD/FREE

B96
LOWELL A.L.,GOVERNMENTS AND PARTIES IN CONTINENTAL EUROPE (VOL. I). MOD/EUR LOC/G NAT/G SECT CHIEF LEGIS PARL/PROC GOV/REL...POLICY 19. PAGE 99 H1973
POL/PAR GOV/COMP CONSTN EX/STRUC

B96
LOWELL A.L.,GOVERNMENTS AND PARTIES IN CONTINENTAL EUROPE, VOL. II. AUSTRIA GERMANY HUNGARY MOD/EUR SWITZERLND SOCIETY EX/STRUC LEGIS DIPLOM AGREE LEAD PARL/PROC PWR...POLICY 19. PAGE 99 H1974
POL/PAR NAT/G GOV/REL ELITES

B98
FORTES M.,AFRICAN POLITICAL SYSTEMS. ECO/UNDEV KIN LOC/G NEIGH POL/PAR SECT LEAD GP/REL ORD/FREE...SOC 20 NEGRO. PAGE 52 H1039
AFR CULTURE STRUCT

B99
LECKY W.E.H.,DEMOCRACY AND LIBERTY (2 VOLS.). LAW CONSTN STRATA POL/PAR SECT WORKER DIPLOM ADJUD REPRESENT NAT/LISM CONSERVE. PAGE 93 H1851
LEGIS NAT/G POPULISM ORD/FREE

POLAND....SEE ALSO COM

B13
DIE REKLAME IHRE KUNST UND WISSENSCHAFT. GERMANY POLAND SWITZERLND USA+45 TEC/DEV CAP/ISM DEMAND ...ART/METH EXHIBIT METH/COMP ANTHOL 20. PAGE 135 H2707
EDU/PROP MARKET NAT/COMP ATTIT

B18
KERNER R.J.,SLAVIC EUROPE: A SELECTED BIBLIOGRAPHY IN THE WESTERN EUROPEAN LANGUAGES. BULGARIA CZECHOSLVK GERMANY/E POLAND RUSSIA YUGOSLAVIA NAT/G DIPLOM MARXISM...LING 19/20. PAGE 85 H1695
BIBLIOG SOCIETY CULTURE COM

N19
TABORSKY E.,CONFORMITY UNDER COMMUNISM (PAMPHLET). CZECHOSLVK HUNGARY POLAND SCHOOL DOMIN PRESS ...TREND GOV/COMP 20. PAGE 152 H3030
COM CONTROL EDU/PROP NAT/G

B45
HORN O.B.,BRITISH PUBLIC OPINION AND THE FIRST PARTITION OF POLAND. POLAND UK LEGIS PRESS RUMOR CONTROL PARTIC NAT/LISM SOVEREIGN 18/19. PAGE 73 H1469
DIPLOM POLICY ATTIT NAT/G

B53
MEYER P.,THE JEWS IN THE SOVIET SATELLITES. CZECHOSLVK POLAND SOCIETY STRATA NAT/G BAL/PWR ECO/TAC EDU/PROP LEGIT ADMIN COERCE ATTIT DISPL PERCEPT HEALTH PWR RESPECT WEALTH...METH/CNCPT JEWS VAL/FREE NAZI 20. PAGE 110 H2192
COM SECT TOTALISM USSR

B55
MID-EUROPEAN LAW PROJECT,CHURCH AND STATE BEHIND THE IRON CURTAIN. COM CZECHOSLVK HUNGARY POLAND USSR CULTURE SECT EDU/PROP GOV/REL CATHISM...CHARTS ANTHOL BIBLIOG WORSHIP 20 CHURCH/STA. PAGE 110 H2202
LAW MARXISM POLICY

S58
STAAR R.F.,"ELECTIONS IN COMMUNIST POLAND." EUR+WWI SOCIETY INT/ORG NAT/G POL/PAR LEGIS ACT/RES ECO/TAC EDU/PROP ADJUD ADMIN ROUTINE COERCE TOTALISM ATTIT ORD/FREE PWR 20. PAGE 148 H2963
COM CHOOSE POLAND

B59
ETSCHMANN R.,DIE WAHRUNGS- UND DEVISENPOLITIK DES OSTBLOCKS UND IHRE AUSWIRKUNGEN AUF DIE WIRTSCHAFTSBEZIEHUNGEN ZWISCHEN OST U WEST. BULGARIA CZECHOSLVK HUNGARY POLAND USSR MARKET NAT/G PLAN DIPLOM...NAT/COMP 20. PAGE 47 H0943
ECO/TAC FINAN POLICY INT/TRADE

S61
TOMASIC D.,"POLITICAL LEADERSHIP IN CONTEMPORARY POLAND." COM EUR+WWI GERMANY NAT/G POL/PAR SECT DELIB/GP PLAN ECO/TAC DOMIN EDU/PROP PWR MARXISM ...MARXIST GEOG MGT CONCPT TIME/SEQ STERTYP 20. PAGE 156 H3111
SOCIETY ROUTINE USSR POLAND

B62
SCHECHTMAN J.B.,POSTWAR POPULATION TRANSFERS IN EUROPE: 1945-1955. COM CZECHOSLVK GERMANY POLAND USSR CULTURE SOCIETY PROB/SOLV AGREE NAT/LISM...SOC STAT TREND CHARTS METH/COMP 20 MIGRATION. PAGE 139 H2778
GEOG CENSUS EUR+WWI HABITAT

B62
STARR R.E.,POLAND 1944-1962: THE SOVIETIZATION OF A CAPTIVE PEOPLE. COM POLAND USSR POL/PAR SECT LEGIS DIPLOM DOMIN EDU/PROP CHOOSE ORD/FREE...POLICY CHARTS BIBLIOG 20. PAGE 149 H2973
MARXISM NAT/G TOTALISM NAT/COMP

B62
WEHLER H.V.,SOZIALDEMOKRATIE UND NATIONALSTAAT. GERMANY POLAND USSR CULTURE SOCIETY STRUCT NAT/G POL/PAR DIPLOM ORD/FREE 19/20. PAGE 166 H3325
NAT/LISM SOVEREIGN GP/REL ATTIT

B63
FRANZ G.,TEILUNG UND WIEDERVEREINIGUNG. GERMANY IRELAND ITALY NETHERLAND POLAND CULTURE BAL/PWR CHOOSE NAT/LISM ORD/FREE SOVEREIGN 19/20. PAGE 53 H1054
DIPLOM WAR NAT/COMP ATTIT

B63
MOSELY P.E.,THE SOVIET UNION, 1922-1962: A FOREIGN AFFAIRS READER. ASIA POLAND USSR CULTURE INTELL AGRI POL/PAR WORKER INT/TRADE DOMIN WAR NAT/LISM MARXISM SOCISM 20 KHRUSH/N. PAGE 113 H2267
PWR POLICY DIPLOM

B64
SIEKANOWICZ P.,LEGAL SOURCES AND BIBLIOGRAPHY OF POLAND. COM POLAND CONSTN NAT/G PARL/PROC SANCTION CRIME MARXISM 16/20. PAGE 143 H2870
BIBLIOG ADJUD LAW JURID

S64
HORECKY P.L.,"LIBRARY OF CONGRESS PUBLICATIONS IN AID OF USSR AND EAST EUROPEAN RESEARCH." BULGARIA CZECHOSLVK POLAND USSR YUGOSLAVIA NAT/G POL/PAR DIPLOM ADMIN GOV/REL...CLASSIF 20. PAGE 73 H1468
BIBLIOG/A COM MARXISM

B65
ALTON T.P.,POLISH NATIONAL INCOME AND PRODUCT IN 1954, 1955, AND 1956. POLAND FINAN EX/STRUC ECO/TAC PRICE COST WEALTH 20. PAGE 6 H0117
COM INDUS NAT/G ECO/DEV

S65
STAAR R.F.,"RETROGRESSION IN POLAND." COM USSR AGRI INDUS NAT/G CREATE EDU/PROP TOTALISM RIGID/FLEX ORD/FREE PWR SOCISM...RECORD CHARTS 20. PAGE 148 H2965
TOP/EX ECO/TAC POLAND

B66
BROWN J.F.,THE NEW EASTERN EUROPE. ALBANIA BULGARIA HUNGARY POLAND ROMANIA CULTURE AGRI POL/PAR WAR NAT/LISM MARXISM...CHARTS BIBLIOG 20. PAGE 22 H0444
DIPLOM COM NAT/G ECO/UNDEV

B66
HENKYS R.,DEUTSCHLAND UND DIE OSTLICHEN NACHBARN. GERMANY POLAND NAT/G POL/PAR INGP/REL ATTIT 20 MIGRATION. PAGE 70 H1396
GP/REL JURID INT/LAW DIPLOM

B66
HEYMANN F.G.,POLAND AND CZECHOSLOVAKIA. COM CZECHOSLVK POLAND...CHARTS BIBLIOG/A 9/20. PAGE 70 H1413
CULTURE NAT/LISM ORD/FREE WAR

B66
JACKSON G.D.,COMINTERN AND PEASANT IN EAST EUROPE 1919-1930. BULGARIA COM CZECHOSLVK EUR+WWI POLAND ROMANIA YUGOSLAVIA STRATA AGRI VOL/ASSN DIPLOM CONTROL CROWD WEALTH...POLICY NAT/COMP 20. PAGE 79 H1575
MARXISM ECO/UNDEV WORKER INT/ORG

B66
ROOS H.,A HISTORY OF MODERN POLAND FROM THE FOUNDATION OF THE STATE IN THE FIRST WORLD WAR TO THE PRESENT DAY. EUR+WWI POLAND INTELL SOCIETY ECO/TAC LEAD REV ATTIT ORD/FREE MARXISM...BIBLIOG
NAT/G WAR DIPLOM

20 WWI PARTITION. PAGE 133 H2669

B66
SPULBER N.,THE STATE AND ECONOMIC DEVELOPMENT IN EASTERN EUROPE. BULGARIA COM CZECHOSLVK HUNGARY POLAND YUGOSLAVIA CULTURE PLAN CAP/ISM INT/TRADE CONTROL...POLICY CHARTS METH/COMP BIBLIOG/A 19/20. PAGE 148 H2958 — ECO/DEV ECO/UNDEV NAT/G TOTALISM

B67
BROMKE A.,POLAND'S POLITICS: IDEALISM VS. REALISM. COM GERMANY POLAND RUSSIA USSR POL/PAR CATHISM ...BIBLIOG 19/20. PAGE 21 H0431 — NAT/G DIPLOM MARXISM

B67
BRZEZINSKI Z.K.,THE SOVIET BLOC: UNITY AND CONFLICT (2ND ED., REV., ENLARGED). COM POLAND USSR INTELL CHIEF EX/STRUC CONTROL EXEC GOV/REL PWR MARXISM ...TREND IDEA/COMP 20 LENIN/VI MARX/KARL STALIN/J. PAGE 23 H0463 — NAT/G DIPLOM

B67
NATIONAL SCIENCE FOUNDATION,DIRECTORY OF SELECTED RESEARCH INSTITUTES IN EASTERN EUROPE. BULGARIA CZECHOSLVK HUNGARY POLAND ROMANIA INTELL ACADEM NAT/G ACT/RES 20. PAGE 116 H2323 — INDEX R+D COM PHIL/SCI

S67
SEIDLER G.L.,"MARXIST LEGAL THOUGHT IN POLAND." POLAND SOCIETY R+D LOC/G NAT/G ACT/RES ADJUD CT/SYS SUPEGO PWR...SOC TREND 20 MARX/KARL. PAGE 141 H2822 — MARXISM LAW CONCPT EFFICIENCY

S68
BOSSCHERE G D.E.,"A L'EST DU NOUVEAU." CZECHOSLVK HUNGARY POLAND ROMANIA YUGOSLAVIA AGRI CREATE ECO/TAC COERCE GP/REL ATTIT MARXISM SOCISM 20. PAGE 19 H0382 — ORD/FREE COM NAT/G DIPLOM

POLE J.R. H2534

POLI J. H2731

POLICE....SEE FORCES

POLICY....ETHICS OF PUBLIC POLICIES

POLIT/ACTN....POLITICAL ACTION COMMITTEE

POLITBURO....POLITBURO (U.S.S.R.)

POLITICAL FINANCING....SEE POL+FINAN

POLITICAL MACHINE....SEE POL+ADMIN

POLITICAL MOVEMENT....SEE IDEOLOGICAL TOPIC INDEX

POLITICAL ORGANIZATION....SEE POL/PAR

POLITICAL PROCESS....SEE LEGIS

POLITICAL SYSTEMS....SEE IDEOLOGICAL TOPIC INDEX

POLITICAL SYSTEMS THEORY....SEE GEN/LAWS+NET/THEORY

POLITICAL THEORY....SEE IDEOLOGICAL TOPIC INDEX

POLITICS....SEE POL

POLK W.R. H2535

POLK/JAMES....PRESIDENT JAMES POLK

POLLACK/N....NORMAN POLLACK

POLLARD A.F. H2536

POLLOCK F. H2537,H2538

POLLOCK J.K. H2539

POLLUTION....AIR OR WATER POLLUTION

POLSKY N. H2540

POLYNESIA....POLYNESIA

B39
FIRTH R.,PRIMITIVE POLYNESIAN ECONOMY. SOCIETY DIST/IND SECT CHIEF CAP/ISM PRODUC WEALTH...SOC OBS METH WORSHIP 20 POLYNESIA. PAGE 50 H1007 — ECO/UNDEV CULTURE AGRI ECO/TAC

S55
GOODENOUGH W.H.,"A PROBLEM IN MALAYO-POLYNESIAN SOCIAL ORGANIZATION" (BMR)" MALAYSIA S/ASIA CULTURE AGRI PROB/SOLV OWN HABITAT...SOC 20 20 POLYNESIA. PAGE 58 H1170 — KIN STRUCT FAM ECO/UNDEV

B61
FIRTH R.,HISTORY AND TRADITIONS OF TIKOPIA. S/ASIA KIN SECT RUMOR WAR...MYTH WORSHIP 20 POLYNESIA. PAGE 50 H1008 — CULTURE STRUCT HUM

POMEROY W.J. H2541

PONOMARYOV B. H2542

POONA....POONA, INDIA

B65
SIRISKAR V.M.,POLITICAL BEHAVIOR IN INDIA. INDIA SOCIETY MUNIC NAT/G PROVS ACT/RES SUFF...OBS CHARTS 20 POONA. PAGE 144 H2889 — CHOOSE POL/PAR PWR ATTIT

POPE....POPE

B14
FIGGIS J.N.,CHURCHES IN THE MODERN STATE (2ND ED.). LAW CHIEF BAL/PWR PWR...CONCPT CHURCH/STA POPE. PAGE 50 H0998 — SECT NAT/G SOCIETY ORD/FREE

B28
MARSILIUS/PADUA,DEFENSOR PACIS (1324). CHRIST-17C CONSTN NAT/G DIPLOM DOMIN LEGIT CONTROL WAR PEACE ORD/FREE SOVEREIGN POPULISM 14 POPE. PAGE 103 H2059 — CATH SECT GEN/LAWS

C36
MAZZINI J.,"FROM THE COUNCIL TO GOD" (1870) IN J. MAZZINI, ESSAYS." ITALY NAT/G EDU/PROP PARTIC ORD/FREE PWR SOVEREIGN 19 POPE CHRISTIAN DEITY. PAGE 106 H2112 — CATHISM DOMIN NAT/LISM SUPEGO

B57
KANTOROWICZ E.,THE KING'S TWO BODIES; A STUDY IN MEDIEVAL POLITICAL THEOLOGY. UK LAW CONSTN NAT/G CT/SYS...ART/METH HUM CONCPT MYTH TIME/SEQ BIBLIOG 4/17 ELIZABTH/I POPE CHURCH/STA. PAGE 83 H1657 — JURID SECT CHIEF SOVEREIGN

B58
BUISSON L.,POTESTAS UND CARITAS. FRANCE GERMANY UK ORD/FREE...JURID IDEA/COMP NAT/COMP 12/16 POPE CHURCH/STA. PAGE 23 H0467 — GP/REL PWR CATHISM NAT/G

B61
ULLMAN W.,PRINCIPLES OF GOVERNMENT AND POLITICS IN THE MIDDLE AGES. LAW CONSTN DOMIN EDU/PROP LEGIT TOTALISM SOVEREIGN POPULISM...POLICY GOV/COMP IDEA/COMP 12/16 POPE KING CHURCH/STA. PAGE 158 H3152 — SECT CHIEF NAT/G LEGIS

B82
CUNNINGHAM W.,THE GROWTH OF ENGLISH INDUSTRY AND COMMERCE. FUT UK FINAN NAT/G CAP/ISM...POLICY 20 MERCANTLST CHRISTIAN POPE. PAGE 36 H0721 — INDUS INT/TRADE SML/CO CONSERVE

POPLAI S.L. H2543

POPPER/K....KARL POPPER

B64
JARVIE I.C.,THE REVOLUTION IN ANTHROPOLOGY. UNIV CULTURE SOCIETY SECT...MYTH 20 POPPER/K. PAGE 80 H1592 — SOC TREND PHIL/SCI METH

POPPINO R.E. H2544

POPULATION....SEE GEOG, CENSUS

POPULISM....MAJORITARIANISM

B08
LLOYD H.D.,THE SWISS DEMOCRACY. SWITZERLND INDUS NAT/G WORKER CHOOSE OWN ORD/FREE SOCISM...PLURIST 19/20 MONOPOLY. PAGE 97 H1944 — NAT/COMP GOV/COMP REPRESENT POPULISM

B09
LOBINGIER C.S.,THE PEOPLE'S LAW OR POPULAR PARTICIPATION IN LAW-MAKING. FRANCE SWITZERLND UK LOC/G NAT/G PROVS LEGIS SUFF MAJORITY PWR POPULISM ...GOV/COMP BIBLIOG 19. PAGE 97 H1945 — CONSTN LAW PARTIC

B11
HUXLEY T.H.,METHOD AND RESULTS: ESSAYS. EDU/PROP REPRESENT OWN PERSON PWR WEALTH...PSY IDEA/COMP GEN/LAWS. PAGE 76 H1514 — ORD/FREE NAT/G POPULISM PLURIST

N16
MILTON J.,THE READIE AND EASY WAY TO ESTABLISH A FREE COMMONWEALTH. CONSTN LEGIS PARL/PROC CONSERVE ...MAJORIT 17. PAGE 111 H2219 — ORD/FREE NAT/G CHIEF POPULISM

N17
BURKE E.,THOUGHTS ON THE PROSPECT OF A REGICIDE PEACE (PAMPHLET). FRANCE UK SECT DOMIN MURDER PEACE ORD/FREE SOVEREIGN POPULISM...POLICY GOV/COMP IDEA/COMP 18 JACOBINISM COEXIST. PAGE 24 H0483 — REV CHIEF NAT/G DIPLOM

N17
BURKE E.,THOUGHTS ON THE CAUSE OF THE PRESENT DISCONTENTS (PAMPHLET). MOD/EUR UK CONSTN CHIEF LEGIS DOMIN CONTROL EXEC REPRESENT POPULISM ...TRADIT NEW/IDEA METH/COMP 18 BURKE/EDM. PAGE 24 H0484
ORD/FREE REV PARL/PROC NAT/G

N17
BURKE E.,LETTER TO SIR HERCULES LANGRISHE (PAMPHLET). IRELAND UK NAT/G CHIEF DIPLOM DOMIN PARL/PROC COERCE ORD/FREE SOVEREIGN POPULISM ...TRADIT 18 BURKE/EDM. PAGE 24 H0485
POLICY COLONIAL SECT

N19
LIEBKNECHT W.P.C.,SOCIALISM (2 PTS.; 1875, 1894) (PAMPHLET). WORKER CAP/ISM EDU/PROP WEALTH POPULISM. PAGE 97 H1927
ECO/TAC STRATA SOCIALIST PARTIC

C20
DUNNING W.A.,"A HISTORY OF POLITICAL THINKERS FROM ROUSSEAU TO SPENCER." NAT/G REV NAT/LISM UTIL CONSERVE MARXISM POPULISM...JURID BIBLIOG 18/19. PAGE 43 H0868
IDEA/COMP PHIL/SCI CONCPT GEN/LAWS

B28
FYFE H.,THE BRITISH LIBERAL PARTY. UK SECT ADMIN LEAD CHOOSE GP/REL PWR SOCISM...MAJORIT TIME/SEQ 19/20 LIB/PARTY CONSRV/PAR. PAGE 54 H1084
POL/PAR NAT/G REPRESENT POPULISM

B28
HOBBES T.,THE ELEMENTS OF LAW, NATURAL AND POLITIC (1650). STRATA NAT/G SECT CHIEF AGREE ATTIT ALL/VALS MORAL ORD/FREE POPULISM...POLICY CONCPT. PAGE 71 H1432
PERSON LAW SOVEREIGN CONSERVE

B28
MARSILIUS/PADUA,DEFENSOR PACIS (1324). CHRIST-17C CONSTN NAT/G DIPLOM DOMIN LEGIT CONTROL WAR PEACE ORD/FREE SOVEREIGN POPULISM 14 POPE. PAGE 103 H2059
CATH SECT GEN/LAWS

B30
HATTERSLEY A.F.,A SHORT HISTORY OF DEMOCRACY. WOR-45 CONSTN NAT/G SECT DOMIN WAR CHOOSE ORD/FREE PWR...CONCPT GOV/COMP BIBLIOG ATHENS ROME. PAGE 68 H1355
REPRESENT MAJORIT POPULISM

S32
BEARD C.A.,"REPRESENTATIVE GOVERNMENT IN EVOLUTION" WOR-45 AGRI TEC/DEV DOMIN EFFICIENCY ORD/FREE CONSERVE...TIME/SEQ GOV/COMP IDEA/COMP GRECO/ROMN. PAGE 12 H0248
REPRESENT POPULISM NAT/G PWR

B33
FERRERO G.,PEACE AND WAR (TRANS. BY BERTHA PRITCHARD). CULTURE FINAN SECT ATTIT SUPEGO MORAL ORD/FREE CONSERVE POPULISM SOCISM POLICY. PAGE 49 H0987
WAR PEACE DIPLOM PROB/SOLV

B33
TANNENBAUM F.,PEACE BY REVOLUTION. ECO/UNDEV AGRI SECT WORKER DIPLOM EDU/PROP DISCRIM OWN WEALTH POPULISM 17/20 MEXIC/AMER INDIAN/AM. PAGE 152 H3043
CULTURE COLONIAL RACE/REL REV

B35
DE TOCQUEVILLE A.,DEMOCRACY IN AMERICA (4 VOLS.) (TRANS. BY HENRY REEVE). CONSTN STRUCT LOC/G NAT/G POL/PAR PROVS ETIQUET CT/SYS MAJORITY ATTIT 18/19. PAGE 39 H0772
POPULISM MAJORIT ORD/FREE SOCIETY

B35
LASKI H.J.,THE STATE IN THEORY AND PRACTICE. ELITES ECO/TAC REPRESENT ORD/FREE PWR WEALTH POPULISM ...GOV/COMP GEN/LAWS 19/20. PAGE 92 H1829
CAP/ISM COERCE NAT/G FASCISM

B35
MARRIOTT J.A.,DICTATORSHIP AND DEMOCRACY. GERMANY GREECE UK CHIEF DIPLOM DOMIN LEGIT PEACE ORD/FREE CONSERVE...TREND ROME HITLER/A. PAGE 103 H2057
TOTALISM POPULISM PLURIST NAT/G

B35
PARETO V.,THE MIND AND SOCIETY (4 VOLS.). ELITES SECT ECO/TAC COERCE PERSON ORD/FREE PWR SOVEREIGN FASCISM POPULISM...TRADIT 19/20. PAGE 123 H2465
GEN/LAWS SOC PSY

B37
CARLYLE T.,THE FRENCH REVOLUTION (2 VOLS.). FRANCE CONSTN NAT/G FORCES COERCE MURDER PEACE MORAL POPULISM...TIME/SEQ IDEA/COMP GEN/LAWS 18. PAGE 26 H0532
REV CHIEF TRADIT

B38
REICH N.,LABOR RELATIONS IN REPUBLICAN GERMANY. GERMANY CONSTN ECO/DEV INDUS NAT/G ADMIN CONTROL GP/REL FASCISM POPULISM 20 WEIMAR/REP. PAGE 130 H2609
WORKER MGT LABOR BARGAIN

B39
MARITAIN J.,SCHOLASTICISM AND POLITICS. CONSTN SOCIETY NAT/G INGP/REL PERSON CATHISM POPULISM 19/20 FREUD/S SCHOLASTIC CHURCH/STA CHRISTIAN. PAGE 103 H2050
SECT GEN/LAWS ORD/FREE

B39
OAKESHOTT M.,THE SOCIAL AND POLITICAL DOCTRINES OF CONTEMPORARY EUROPE. EUR+WWI RATIONAL CATHISM FASCISM MARXISM POPULISM...POLICY ANTHOL 20 NAZI. PAGE 120 H2392
IDEA/COMP GOV/COMP ALL/IDEOS NAT/G

C39
BURKE E.,"ON THE REFORM OF THE REPRESENTATION IN THE HOUSE OF COMMONS" (1782) IN COLLECTED WORKS (VOL. 5)" UK ELITES STRATA NAT/G REPRESENT ORD/FREE PWR POPULISM...POLICY NEW/IDEA GEN/LAWS 18 BURKE/EDM. PAGE 24 H0486
TRADIT CONSTN PARL/PROC LEGIS

B40
HUNTER R.,REVOLUTION: WHY, HOW, WHEN? NAT/G ECO/TAC EDU/PROP COERCE ORD/FREE FASCISM POPULISM SOCISM 18/20 HITLER/A LENIN/VI. PAGE 75 H1502
REV METH/COMP LEAD CONSTN

S41
DENNERY E.,"DEMOCRACY AND THE FRENCH ARMY." FRANCE NAT/G EX/STRUC LEAD REV ROLE 18/20. PAGE 40 H0792
FORCES POPULISM STRATA CIVMIL/REL

B42
BARKER E.,REFLECTIONS ON GOVERNMENT. EUR+WWI SOCIETY LEGIS EDU/PROP ADMIN LEAD PARTIC CHOOSE TOTALISM AUTHORIT ORD/FREE SOCISM 20. PAGE 11 H0218
NAT/G POPULISM ACT/RES GEN/LAWS

B42
FEFFERO G.,THE PRINCIPLES OF POWER (TRANS. BY T. JAECKEL). MOD/EUR CONSTN NAT/G CHIEF CONTROL REV WAR ORD/FREE CONSERVE FASCISM POPULISM...GEN/LAWS 18/20 EUROPE. PAGE 49 H0980
PWR LEGIT TRADIT ELITES

B42
LA BOETIE E.,ANTI-DICTATOR (1548) (TRANS. BY H. KUNZ). CONSTN NAT/G CHIEF DOMIN LEGIT CONTROL POPULISM. PAGE 90 H1790
PWR ORD/FREE TOTALISM GEN/LAWS

B43
LENIN V.I.,LEFT WING COMMUNISM: AN INFANTILE DISORDER (1920). GERMANY MOD/EUR USSR STRUCT CHIEF DOMIN EDU/PROP LEGIT LEAD REPRESENT POPULISM ...METH/COMP 19 LENIN/VI COM/PARTY MENSHEVIK. PAGE 94 H1879
COM MARXISM NAT/G REV

B43
MARITAIN J.,THE RIGHTS OF MAN AND NATURAL LAW. CONSTN NAT/G DOMIN LEGIT INGP/REL TOTALISM MORAL POPULISM WORSHIP 19/20 CIVIL/LIB CHURCH/STA NATURL/LAW. PAGE 103 H2051
PLURIST ORD/FREE GEN/LAWS

B45
CROCE B.,POLITICS AND MORALS. UNIV NAT/G ECO/TAC ORD/FREE MARXISM POPULISM SOCISM...REALPOL 15/20 HEGEL/GWF ROUSSEAU/J. PAGE 35 H0704
MORAL GEN/LAWS IDEA/COMP

B46
BLUM L.,FOR ALL MANKIND (TRANS. BY W. PICKLES). FRANCE GERMANY USSR LAW SOCIETY STRUCT POL/PAR WORKER DIPLOM DOMIN CHOOSE ORD/FREE FASCISM 20. PAGE 18 H0361
POPULISM SOCIALIST NAT/G WAR

B47
NIEBUHR R.,THE CHILDREN OF LIGHT AND THE CHILDREN OF DARKNESS: A VINDICATION OF DEMOCRACY AND CRITIQUE OF TRADITIONAL DEFENSE. UNIV STRUCT NAT/G SECT INGP/REL OWN PEACE ORD/FREE MARXISM ...IDEA/COMP GEN/LAWS 20 CHRISTIAN. PAGE 118 H2358
POPULISM DIPLOM NEIGH GP/REL

B48
LASKI H.S.,THE AMERICAN DEMOCRACY. CULTURE INDUS SECT WORKER DIPLOM EDU/PROP REPRESENT RACE/REL ORD/FREE PWR...NAT/COMP 18/20. PAGE 92 H1831
NAT/G LOC/G USA-45 POPULISM

B48
WRIGHT G.,THE RESHAPING OF FRENCH DEMOCRACY. FRANCE NAT/G POL/PAR SECT LEAD CHOOSE GP/REL INGP/REL MARXISM SOCISM...CHARTS BIBLIOG 20 DEGAULLE/C. PAGE 171 H3418
CONSTN POPULISM CREATE LEGIS

B49
DE JOUVENEL B.,ON POWER: ITS NATURE AND THE HISTORY OF ITS GROWTH. SOCIETY CHIEF REV WAR ATTIT AUTHORIT ORD/FREE SOVEREIGN CONSERVE POPULISM CONCPT. PAGE 38 H0757
PWR NAT/G DOMIN CONTROL

B49
MAO TSE-TUNG,NEW DEMOCRACY. CHINA/COM NAT/G DIPLOM ECO/TAC EDU/PROP REV...CONCPT METH SOC/INTEG 20. PAGE 102 H2045
SOCISM MARXISM POPULISM CULTURE

B49
ROGERS C.B.,THE SPIRIT OF REVOLUTION IN 1789: A STUDY OF PUBLIC OPINION ...AT THE BEGINNING OF THE FRENCH REVOLUTION. FRANCE CULTURE ELITES EDU/PROP COERCE CROWD...BIBLIOG 18 MUSIC. PAGE 133 H2658
ATTIT POPULISM REV CREATE

B50
HALLOWELL J.H.,MAIN CURRENTS IN MODERN POLITICAL THOUGHT. CONSTN SECT LEGIS...MAJORIT CONCPT 17/20 MARX/KARL MILL/JS HOBBES/T LENIN/VI. PAGE 64 H1290
IDEA/COMP POPULISM SOCISM

B52
MONTAGU A.,MAN'S MOST DANGEROUS MYTH: THE FALLACY OF RACE. LAW PROB/SOLV WAR HABITAT POPULISM...PSY CONCPT CHARTS BIBLIOG NEGRO JEWS. PAGE 112 H2242
DISCRIM MYTH CULTURE RACE/REL

S52
SABINE G.H.,"THE TWO DEMOCRATIC TRADITIONS" (BMR)" FRANCE UK USA-45 NAT/G CONTROL CHOOSE ALL/IDEOS ...PHIL/SCI CONCPT IDEA/COMP 20. PAGE 136 H2727
ORD/FREE POPULISM INGP/REL NAT/COMP

B55
SMITH G.,A CONSTITUTIONAL AND LEGAL HISTORY OF
CONSTN

ENGLAND. UK ELITES NAT/G LEGIS ADJUD OWN HABITAT POPULISM...JURID 20 ENGLSH/LAW. PAGE 145 H2909
PARTIC LAW CT/SYS

B55
WHEARE K.C.,GOVERNMENT BY COMMITTEE; AN ESSAY ON THE BRITISH CONSTITUTION. UK NAT/G LEGIS INSPECT CONFER ADJUD ADMIN CONTROL TASK EFFICIENCY ROLE POPULISM 20. PAGE 167 H3337
DELIB/GP CONSTN LEAD GP/COMP

C55
SANTAYANA G.,"REASON IN SOCIETY" IN G. SANTAYANA, THE LIFE OF REASON." INDUS FAM NAT/G WAR GP/REL HAPPINESS PRODUC LOVE WEALTH CONSERVE POPULISM CONCPT. PAGE 138 H2752
RATIONAL SOCIETY CULTURE ATTIT

B56
EMDEN C.S.,THE PEOPLE AND THE CONSTITUTION (2ND ED.). UK LEGIS POPULISM 17/20 PARLIAMENT. PAGE 46 H0916
CONSTN PARL/PROC NAT/G LAW

B56
MYERS F.M.,THE WARFARE OF DEMOCRATIC IDEALS. SECT KNOWL MORAL CATHISM...TRADIT CONCPT 20. PAGE 115 H2302
POPULISM CHOOSE REPRESENT PERCEPT

B57
LONG H.A.,USURPERS - FOES OF FREE MAN. LAW NAT/G CHIEF LEGIS DOMIN ADJUD REPRESENT GOV/REL ORD/FREE LAISSEZ POPULISM...POLICY 18/20 SUPREME/CT ROOSEVLT/F CONGRESS CON/INTERP. PAGE 98 H1961
CT/SYS CENTRAL FEDERAL CONSTN

B57
MUELLER-DEHAM A.,HUMAN RELATIONS AND POWER; SOCIO-POLITICAL ANALYSIS AND SYNTHESIS. CONSTN SOCIETY NAT/G POL/PAR PROVS LEGIS POPULISM...SOC NEW/IDEA. PAGE 114 H2280
GEN/LAWS PERS/REL PWR CONCPT

B58
ARON R.,SOCIOLOGIE DES SOCIETES INDUSTRIELLES: ESQUISSE D'UNE THEORIE DES REGIMES POLITIQUES. FRANCE SOCIETY NAT/G PROB/SOLV ATTIT RIGID/FLEX MARXISM POPULISM...POLICY SOC T 20 MARX/KARL TOCQUEVILL. PAGE 8 H0170
TOTALISM INDUS CONSTN GOV/COMP

B58
BRADY A.,DEMOCRACY IN THE DOMINIONS (3RD ED.). CANADA NEW/ZEALND SOUTH/AFR WOR+45 LAW EX/STRUC DOMIN COLONIAL PARL/PROC REPRESENT RACE/REL NAT/LISM WEALTH 20 AUSTRAL CMN/WLTH. PAGE 20 H0399
GOV/COMP POL/PAR POPULISM NAT/G

B58
PALMER E.E.,THE COMMUNIST CHALLENGE. COM USA+45 USA-45 ECO/DEV ECO/UNDEV NEUTRAL ORD/FREE POPULISM ...CONCPT NAT/COMP ANTHOL 19/20 LENIN/VI STALIN/J MAO MARX/KARL COM/PARTY. PAGE 123 H2450
MARXISM DIPLOM IDEA/COMP POLICY

B58
STRONG C.F.,MODERN POLITICAL CONSTITUTIONS. LAW CHIEF DELIB/GP EX/STRUC LEGIS ADJUD CHOOSE FEDERAL POPULISM...CONCPT BIBLIOG 20 UN. PAGE 150 H2998
CONSTN IDEA/COMP NAT/G

B60
MAYO H.B.,AN INTRODUCTION TO DEMOCRATIC THEORY. ORD/FREE...POLICY TIME/SEQ GOV/COMP STERTYP. PAGE 105 H2109
POPULISM CONCPT IDEA/COMP

B60
THEOBOLD R.,THE NEW NATIONS OF WEST AFRICA. GHANA NIGERIA CULTURE INT/ORG ECO/TAC FOR/AID COLONIAL RACE/REL POPULISM...ANTHOL BIBLIOG 20 UN. PAGE 153 H3068
AFR SOVEREIGN ECO/UNDEV DIPLOM

B60
WILLIAMS L.E.,OVERSEAS CHINESE NATIONALISM: THE GENESIS OF THE PAN-CHINESE MOVEMENT IN INDONESIA, 1900-1916. ASIA COM INDONESIA AGRI INT/ORG LOC/G DIPLOM EDU/PROP HABITAT PWR POPULISM...GEOG LING CENSUS 20. PAGE 168 H3367
NAT/LISM GP/REL DECISION NAT/G

B61
GUIZOT F.P.G.,HISTORY OF THE ORIGIN OF REPRESENTATIVE GOVERNMENT IN EUROPE. CHRIST-17C FRANCE MOD/EUR SPAIN UK LAW CHIEF FORCES POPULISM ...MAJORIT TIME/SEQ GOV/COMP NAT/COMP 4/19 PARLIAMENT. PAGE 62 H1250
LEGIS REPRESENT CONSTN NAT/G

B61
LICHTHEIM G.,MARXISM. GERMANY SOCIETY WORKER CAP/ISM ECO/TAC NAT/LISM POPULISM...TIME/SEQ GOV/COMP NAT/COMP 18/20 COM/PARTY. PAGE 96 H1924
MARXISM SOCISM IDEA/COMP CULTURE

B61
LYFORD J.P.,THE AGREEABLE AUTOCRACIES. SOCIETY LABOR POL/PAR SECT DIPLOM CHOOSE...CONCPT 20 WHITE/T NIEBUHR/R. PAGE 99 H1982
ATTIT POPULISM PRESS NAT/G

B61
STAHL W.,EDUCATION FOR DEMOCRACY IN WEST GERMANY: ACHIEVEMENT SHORTCOMINGS - PROSPECTS. GERMANY/W SOCIETY NAT/G FORCES PLAN PROB/SOLV PRESS ALL/VALS ...POLICY MAJORIT CONCPT ANTHOL 20. PAGE 148 H2967
EDU/PROP POPULISM AGE/Y ADJUST

B61
ULLMAN W.,PRINCIPLES OF GOVERNMENT AND POLITICS IN THE MIDDLE AGES. LAW CONSTN DOMIN EDU/PROP LEGIT TOTALISM SOVEREIGN POPULISM...POLICY GOV/COMP IDEA/COMP 12/16 POPE KING CHURCH/STA. PAGE 158 H3152
SECT CHIEF NAT/G LEGIS

B62
EBENSTEIN W.,TWO WAYS OF LIFE. USA+45 CULTURE ECO/DEV PLAN EDU/PROP CONTROL ORD/FREE...GOV/COMP IDEA/COMP T 20 MARX/KARL ENGELS/F LENIN/VI LOCKE/JOHN MILL/JS. PAGE 44 H0885
MARXISM POPULISM ECO/TAC DIPLOM

B62
KINDERSLEY R.,THE FIRST RUSSIAN REVISIONISTS. COM USSR LAW ELITES INTELL NAT/G LEGIS ECO/TAC EDU/PROP CONTROL LEAD GP/REL SOCISM 19/20 MARX/KARL BOLSHEVISM. PAGE 86 H1712
CONSTN MARXISM POPULISM BIOG

B62
ROUSSEAU J.J.,THE SOCIAL CONTRACT. LAW CONSTN CHIEF DOMIN REPRESENT GP/REL ORD/FREE POPULISM...MAJORIT GOV/COMP 18. PAGE 135 H2700
GEN/LAWS AGREE REV

S62
LEGUM C.,"THE DANGERS OF INDEPENDENCE" AFR UGANDA NAT/G DIPLOM DOMIN REGION CENTRAL ATTIT POPULISM 20. PAGE 93 H1862
ORD/FREE SOVEREIGN NAT/LISM GOV/COMP

B63
ALMOND G.A.,THE CIVIC CULTURE: POLITICAL ATTITUDES AND DEMOCRACY IN FIVE NATIONS. GERMANY/W ITALY UK USA+45 SOCIETY STRUCT PARTIC...SOC DEEP/INT SAMP 20 MEXIC/AMER. PAGE 6 H0113
POPULISM CULTURE NAT/COMP ATTIT

B63
ECKSTEIN H.,COMPARATIVE POLITICS. POL/PAR LEGIS CT/SYS CHOOSE TOTALISM PWR POPULISM...METH/COMP GEN/METH ANTHOL BIBLIOG 20. PAGE 44 H0886
NAT/COMP CONSTN REPRESENT NAT/G

B63
JENNINGS W.I.,DEMOCRACY IN AFRICA. UK CULTURE STRUCT ECO/UNDEV DIPLOM COLONIAL GP/REL ADJUST NAT/LISM ORD/FREE...GOV/COMP 20 THIRD/WRLD. PAGE 81 H1613
PROB/SOLV AFR CONSTN POPULISM

S63
ROGIN M.,"ROUSSEAU IN AFRICA." AFR MARXISM POPULISM SOCISM 20 ROUSSEAU/J. PAGE 133 H2661
IDEA/COMP CULTURE CONSTN ORD/FREE

B64
GROSSER A.,THE FEDERAL REPUBLIC OF GERMANY: A CONCISE HISTORY. GERMANY/W STRUCT MORAL ORD/FREE POPULISM SOCISM...SOC CONCPT 20. PAGE 62 H1235
NAT/G POL/PAR CHOOSE DIPLOM

B64
TAWNEY R.H.,EQUALITY. UK CULTURE STRATA ECO/TAC EDU/PROP REPRESENT OWN NEW/LIB...MAJORIT WELF/ST SOC 20. PAGE 153 H3051
WEALTH STRUCT ELITES POPULISM

B65
CHANDA A.,FEDERALISM IN INDIA. INDIA UK ELITES FINAN NAT/G POL/PAR EX/STRUC LEGIS DIPLOM TAX GOV/REL POPULISM...POLICY 20. PAGE 28 H0572
CONSTN CENTRAL FEDERAL

B65
FAGG J.E.,CUBA, HAITI, AND THE DOMINICAN REPUBLIC. CUBA DOMIN/REP HAITI L/A+17C NAT/G DIPLOM ECO/TAC DOMIN CHOOSE AUTHORIT ROLE SOVEREIGN POPULISM 17/20. PAGE 48 H0959
COLONIAL ECO/UNDEV REV GOV/COMP

B65
GAJENDRAGADKAR P.B.,LAW, LIBERTY AND SOCIAL JUSTICE. INDIA CONSTN NAT/G SECT PLAN ECO/TAC PRESS POPULISM...SOC METH/COMP 20 HINDU. PAGE 54 H1086
ORD/FREE LAW ADJUD JURID

B65
THE STATE AND ECONOMIC ENTERPRISE IN JAPAN; ESSAYS IN THE POLITICAL ECONOMY OF GROWTH. AGRI INDUS DRIVE POPULISM...CHARTS NAT/COMP ANTHOL 19/20 CHINJAP. PAGE 98 H1949
ECO/UNDEV ECO/DEV CAP/ISM ECO/TAC

B65
MONTESQUIEU C DE S.,CONSIDERATIONS ON THE CAUSES OF THE GREATNESS OF THE ROMANS AND THEIR DECLINE (1748 TRANS. BY D. LOWENTHAL). ROMAN/EMP SECT CHIEF EX/STRUC FORCES LEGIS DOMIN WAR POPULISM...POLICY REALPOL ROME/ANC. PAGE 112 H2244
NAT/G PWR COLONIAL MORAL

B65
TINGSTEN H.,THE PROBLEM OF DEMOCRACY. ELITES SOCIETY STRATA NAT/G CONSEN TOTALISM WELF/ST. PAGE 155 H3101
IDEA/COMP GOV/COMP POPULISM SOCISM

B65
ULAM A.,THE BOLSHEVIKS. COM USSR NAT/G CHIEF ECO/TAC ADMIN LEAD WAR POPULISM...POLICY 19/20 LENIN/VI BOLSHEVISM. PAGE 157 H3148
SOCISM POL/PAR TOP/EX REV

B66
BRACKMAN A.C.,SOUTHEAST ASIA'S SECOND FRONT: THE POWER STRUGGLE IN THE MALAY ARCHIPELAGO. CHINA/COM INDONESIA MALAYSIA ECO/UNDEV INT/ORG NAT/G FORCES DIPLOM EDU/PROP REGION COERCE GUERRILLA AUTHORIT POPULISM...MAJORIT 20 KENNEDY/JF SEATO. PAGE 20 H0396
S/ASIA MARXISM REV

B66
DE TOCQUEVILLE A,DEMOCRACY IN AMERICA (1834-1840) (2 VOLS. IN I; TRANS. BY G. LAWRENCE). FRANCE CULTURE STRATA POL/PAR CT/SYS REPRESENT FEDERAL ORD/FREE SOVEREIGN...MAJORIT TREND GEN/LAWS 18/19.
POPULISM USA-45 CONSTN NAT/COMP

PAGE 39 H0773

S66
ADAMS T.W.,"THE FIRST REPUBLIC OF CYPRUS: A REVIEW OF AN UNWORKABLE CONSTITUTION." CYPRUS FUT PLAN NAT/LISM POPULISM 20. PAGE 3 H0067
CONSTN NAT/G PROB/SOLV

S66
MCLENNAN B.N.,"EVOLUTION OF CONCEPTS OF REPRESENTATION IN INDONESIA" INDONESIA...CONCPT IDEA/COMP METH 20. PAGE 107 H2143
REPRESENT NAT/G POPULISM PWR

B67
MCLAUGHLIN M.R.,RELIGIOUS EDUCATION AND THE STATE: DEMOCRACY FINDS A WAY. CANADA EUR+WWI GP/REL POPULISM...CATH NAT/COMP 20 AUSTRAL. PAGE 107 H2141
SECT NAT/G EDU/PROP POLICY

B67
MENDEL A.P.,POLITICAL MEMOIRS 1905-1917 BY PAUL MILIUKOV (TRANS. BY CARL GOLDBERG). USSR AGRI DIPLOM ECO/TAC POPULISM...MAJORIT 20. PAGE 109 H2170
BIOG LEAD NAT/G CONSTN

B67
MORRIS A.J.A.,PARLIAMENTARY DEMOCRACY IN THE NINETEENTH CENTURY. UK INDUS LOC/G NAT/G POL/PAR CONSULT LEGIS INT/TRADE ADMIN CHOOSE SUFF SOVEREIGN 19 PARLIAMENT. PAGE 113 H2261
TIME/SEQ CONSTN PARL/PROC POPULISM

B67
TOMPKINS S.R.,THE TRIUMPH OF BOLSHEVISM: REVOLUTION OR REACTION? USSR WORKER PRESS WEALTH MARXISM POPULISM...BIOG TREND IDEA/COMP BIBLIOG 19/20 LENIN/VI. PAGE 156 H3113
REV NAT/G POL/PAR NAT/LISM

B67
YAMAMURA K.,ECONOMIC POLICY IN POSTWAR JAPAN. ASIA FINAN POL/PAR DIPLOM LEAD NAT/LISM ATTIT NEW/LIB POPULISM 20 CHINJAP. PAGE 171 H3432
ECO/DEV POLICY NAT/G TEC/DEV

L67
AUSTIN D.A.,"POLITICAL CONFLICT IN AFRICA." CONSTN NAT/G CREATE ADMIN COLONIAL ORD/FREE MARXISM POPULISM SOCISM...NAT/COMP ANTHOL 20. PAGE 9 H0180
ANOMIE AFR POL/PAR

S67
KASFIR N.,"THE UGANDA CONSTITUENT ASSEMBLY DEBATE." UGANDA REPRESENT FEDERAL ORD/FREE POPULISM...POLICY DECISION 20. PAGE 83 H1665
CONSTN CONFER LAW NAT/G

S67
MANGLAPUS R.S.,"ASIAN REVOLUTION AND AMERICAN IDEOLOGY." USA+45 SOCIETY CAP/ISM DIPLOM ADJUST CENTRAL...NAT/COMP 20. PAGE 102 H2035
REV POPULISM ATTIT ASIA

S67
SOLT L.F.,"PURITANISM, CAPITALISM, DEMOCRACY, AND THE NEW SCIENCE." NAT/G GP/REL CONSERVE...IDEA/COMP GEN/LAWS. PAGE 147 H2931
SECT CAP/ISM RATIONAL POPULISM

S68
DEUTSCHER I.,"GERMANY AND MARXISM." FUT GERMANY/W NAT/G...MARXIST TREND 20. PAGE 40 H0808
SOCISM ORD/FREE POPULISM POL/PAR

B76
TAINE H.A.,THE ANCIENT REGIME. FRANCE STRATA FORCES PARTIC EQUILIB WEALTH CONSERVE POPULISM...GOV/COMP SOC/INTEG 18/19. PAGE 152 H3035
NAT/G GOV/REL TAX REV

N80
MILL J.S.,"AN ESSAY ON GOVERNMENT" (PAMPHLET). ELITES NAT/G CHIEF OWN ORD/FREE PWR WEALTH GEN/LAWS. PAGE 110 H2207
CONSTN POPULISM REPRESENT UTIL

B84
ENGELS F.,THE ORIGIN OF THE FAMILY, PRIVATE PROPERTY, AND THE STATE (TRANS. BY E. UNTERMANN). UNIV ELITES SOCIETY CAP/ISM ECO/TAC MARRIAGE ORD/FREE POPULISM...MARXIST SOC ENGELS. PAGE 46 H0926
FAM OWN WEALTH SOCISM

B87
ADAMS J.,A DEFENSE OF THE CONSTITUTIONS OF GOVERNMENT OF THE UNITED STATES OF AMERICA. USA-45 STRATA CHIEF EX/STRUC LEGIS CT/SYS CONSERVE POPULISM...CONCPT CON/ANAL GOV/COMP. PAGE 3 H0063
CONSTN BAL/PWR PWR NAT/G

B91
MILL J.S.,SOCIALISM (1859). MOD/EUR AGRI INDUS NAT/G REV INCOME PRODUC ORD/FREE POPULISM SOCISM ...GOV/COMP METH/COMP 19. PAGE 110 H2209
WEALTH SOCIALIST ECO/TAC OWN

B99
LECKY W.E.H.,DEMOCRACY AND LIBERTY (2 VOLS.). LAW CONSTN STRATA POL/PAR SECT WORKER DIPLOM ADJUD REPRESENT NAT/LISM CONSERVE. PAGE 93 H1851
LEGIS NAT/G POPULISM ORD/FREE

PORTUGAL....SEE ALSO APPROPRIATE TIME/SPACE/CULTURE INDEX

B17
DOS SANTOS M.,BIBLIOGRAPHIA GERAL, A DESCRIPCAO BIBLIOGRAFICA DE LIVROS TANTO DE AUTORES PORTUGUEZES COMO BRASILEIROS... BRAZIL PORTUGAL NAT/G LEAD GP/REL 15/20. PAGE 42 H0840
BIBLIOG/A L/A+17C DIPLOM COLONIAL

B47
BEHAR D.,BIBLIOGRAFIA HISPANOAMERICANA. LIBROS ANTIGUOS Y MODERNOS REFERENTES A AMERICA Y ESPANA. PORTUGAL SPAIN CONSTN NAT/G SECT CREATE REV WAR GOV/REL...ART/METH GEOG PHIL/SCI LING 20 ARGEN. PAGE 13 H0260
BIBLIOG L/A+17C CULTURE

B50
FIGANIERE J.C.,BIBLIOTHECA HISTORICA PORTUGUEZA. BRAZIL PORTUGAL SECT ADMIN. PAGE 50 H0997
BIBLIOG NAT/G DIPLOM COLONIAL

B57
RUMEU DE ARMAS A.,ESPANA EEN EL AFRICA ATLANTICA. AFR CHRIST-17C PORTUGAL SPAIN DIPLOM ECO/TAC CONTROL 14/16 AFRICA/W. PAGE 136 H2717
NAT/G COLONIAL CHIEF PWR

B59
INTERNATIONAL PRESS INSTITUTE,THE PRESS IN AUTHORITARIAN COUNTRIES. COM PORTUGAL SPAIN UAR USSR NAT/G DOMIN LEGIT ORD/FREE FASCISM SOCISM 20. PAGE 78 H1559
PRESS CONTROL TOTALISM EDU/PROP

B61
FREYRE G.,THE PORTUGUESE AND THE TROPICS. L/A+17C PORTUGAL SOCIETY PERF/ART ADMIN TASK GP/REL ...ART/METH CONCPT SOC/INTEG 20. PAGE 53 H1060
COLONIAL METH PLAN CULTURE

B63
DEBRAY P.,LE PORTUGAL ENTRE DEUX REVOLUTIONS. EUR+WWI PORTUGAL CONSTN LEGIT ADMIN ATTIT ALL/VALS ...DECISION CONCPT 20 SALAZAR/A. PAGE 39 H0779
NAT/G DELIB/GP TOP/EX

B63
FARMER B.H.,CEYLON: A DIVIDED NATION. CEYLON INDIA NETHERLAND PORTUGAL UK ELITES POL/PAR COLONIAL ...SOC MYTH CHARTS GOV/COMP WORSHIP 20. PAGE 49 H0972
DOMIN ORD/FREE ECO/UNDEV POLICY

B64
ARASARATNAM S.,CEYLON. CEYLON NETHERLAND PORTUGAL S/ASIA UK STRUCT ECO/UNDEV SECT DIPLOM DOMIN RACE/REL NAT/LISM 17/20 CMN/WLTH. PAGE 8 H0156
COLONIAL NAT/G PROB/SOLV CULTURE

B64
QUIGG P.W.,AFRICA: A FOREIGN AFFAIRS READER. AFR FRANCE PORTUGAL UK DIPLOM LEAD PARL/PROC MARXISM ...MAJORIT METH/CNCPT GOV/COMP IDEA/COMP ANTHOL 19/20. PAGE 129 H2575
COLONIAL SOVEREIGN NAT/LISM RACE/REL

B64
WAINHOUSE D.W.,REMNANTS OF EMPIRE: THE UNITED NATIONS AND THE END OF COLONIALISM. FUT PORTUGAL WOR+45 NAT/G CONSULT DOMIN LEGIT ADMIN ROUTINE ATTIT ORD/FREE...POLICY JURID RECORD INT TIME/SEQ UN CMN/WLTH 20. PAGE 164 H3287
INT/ORG TREND COLONIAL

S64
MARTELLI G.,"PORTUGAL AND THE UNITED NATIONS." AFR EUR+WWI ELITES INT/ORG NAT/G PROVS PLAN DIPLOM ECO/TAC DOMIN COLONIAL RIGID/FLEX MORAL ORD/FREE PWR WEALTH...MYTH UN 20. PAGE 103 H2060
ATTIT PORTUGAL

B65
HAVIGHURST R.J.,SOCIETY AND EDUCATION IN BRAZIL. BRAZIL PORTUGAL ECO/UNDEV INDUS NAT/G CREATE INSPECT COLONIAL ADJUST DEMAND LITERACY...CENSUS TREND CHARTS 16/20. PAGE 68 H1362
SCHOOL ACADEM ACT/RES CULTURE

B65
HISPANIC SOCIETY OF AMERICA,CATALOGUE (10 VOLS.). PORTUGAL PRE/AMER SPAIN NAT/G ADMIN...POLICY SOC 15/20. PAGE 71 H1426
BIBLIOG L/A+17C COLONIAL DIPLOM

B66
BIRMINGHAM D.,TRADE AND CONFLICT IN ANGOLA. PORTUGAL CULTURE FORCES DIPLOM GP/REL PROFIT HABITAT NAT/COMP. PAGE 17 H0341
WAR INT/TRADE ECO/UNDEV COLONIAL

B67
CHILCOTE R.H.,PORTUGUESE AFRICA. PORTUGAL CULTURE SOCIETY ECO/UNDEV DOMIN NAT/LISM...TREND IDEA/COMP NAT/COMP BIBLIOG 15/20. PAGE 29 H0589
AFR COLONIAL ORD/FREE PROB/SOLV

S67
HAMMOND R.J.,"RACE ATTITUDES AND POLICIES IN PORTUGUESE AFRICA IN THE NINETEENTH AND TWENTIETH CENTURIES." AFR PORTUGAL NAT/G SECT EDU/PROP COLONIAL ATTIT RIGID/FLEX SEX MORAL RESPECT 19/20 NEGRO. PAGE 65 H1309
POLICY RACE/REL DISCRIM SOCIETY

POSNER M.V. H2545

POSTAL/SYS....POSTAL SYSTEMS

B08
THE GOVERNMENT OF SOUTH AFRICA (VOL. II). SOUTH/AFR STRATA EXTR/IND EX/STRUC TOP/EX BUDGET ADJUD ADMIN CT/SYS PRODUC...CORREL CENSUS 19 RAILROAD CIVIL/SERV POSTAL/SYS. PAGE 2 H0030
CONSTN FINAN LEGIS NAT/G

POSTOFFICE....POST OFFICE DEPARTMENT

POTAPOV L.P. H1900

POTSDAM....POTSDAM

POULLIER J.P. H0791

POUND R. H2546,H2547,H2548

POUND/ROS....ROSCOE POUND

POVERTY....SEE WEALTH, INCOME

POVRTY/WAR....WAR ON POVERTY; SEE ALSO GREAT/SOC, JOHNSN/LB

POWELL D. H2549

POWELL J.D. H2550

POWELL R.L. H2551

POWELL/AC....ADAM CLAYTON POWELL

POWELSON J.P. H2552

POWER....SEE PWR

PPBS....PLANNING-PROGRAMMING-BUDGETING SYSTEM

PRABHAKAR P. H2553

PRAGMATICS....SEE LOG

PRASAD B. H2554

PRATT I.A. H2555

PRE/AMER....PRE-EUROPEAN AMERICAS

B41
GRISMER R.,A NEW BIBLIOGRAPHY OF THE LITERATURES OF SPAIN AND SPANISH AMERICA. CHRIST-17C MOD/EUR PRE/AMER SPAIN CULTURE DIPLOM EDU/PROP...ART/METH GEOG HUM PHIL/SCI 20. PAGE 61 H1229
BIBLIOG LAW NAT/G ECO/UNDEV

B42
PAGINSKY P.,GERMAN WORKS RELATING TO AMERICA, 1493-1800; A LIST COMPILED FROM THE COLLECTIONS OF THE NEW YORK PUBLIC LIBRARY. GERMANY PRE/AMER CULTURE COLONIAL ATTIT...POLICY SOC 15/19. PAGE 122 H2442
BIBLIOG/A NAT/G L/A+17C DIPLOM

B57
VON HIPPEL E.,GESCHICHTE DER STAATSPHILOSOPHIE (2 VOLS.). ASIA GREECE INDIA PRE/AMER UAR NAT/LISM ORD/FREE MARXISM. PAGE 164 H3272
CULTURE CONCPT NAT/G

B59
HONINGMAN J.J.,THE WORLD OF MAN. CHRIST-17C MEDIT-7 PRE/AMER PREHIST CREATE INGP/REL BIO/SOC HABITAT ...PSY SOC BIBLIOG. PAGE 73 H1460
CULTURE METH PERSON STRUCT

B61
ACOSTA SAIGNES M.,ESTUDIOS DE ETNOLOGIA ANTIGUA DE VENEZUELA (2ND ED.). PRE/AMER VENEZUELA...ART/METH SOC BIBLIOG INDIAN/AM. PAGE 3 H0061
CULTURE STRUCT GP/REL HABITAT

B62
DIAZ J.S.,MANUAL DE BIBLIOGRAFIA DE LA LITERATURA ESPANOLA. PRE/AMER SPAIN ECO/UNDEV DIPLOM LEAD ATTIT...SOC 15/20. PAGE 41 H0820
BIBLIOG L/A+17C NAT/G COLONIAL

B63
PRICE A.G.,THE WESTERN INVASIONS OF THE PACIFIC AND ITS CONTINENTS. ASIA PRE/AMER S/ASIA ECO/UNDEV KIN NAT/G SECT FORCES DOMIN HEALTH...SOC 16/20. PAGE 128 H2560
COLONIAL CULTURE GEOG HABITAT

B64
BEDERMAN S.H.,THE ETHNOLOGICAL CONTRIBUTIONS OF JOHN LEDYARD (PAMPHLET). ASIA PRE/AMER S/ASIA...SOC 18 LEDYARD/J KAMCHATKA TAHITI TARTARS INDIAN/AM. PAGE 13 H0256
CULTURE BIOG METH/CNCPT STRUCT

B64
HARRIS M.,PATTERNS OF RACE IN THE AMERICAS. BRAZIL L/A+17C STRATA ECO/UNDEV AGRI KIN MUNIC SECT COLONIAL RACE/REL...SOC SOC/INTEG 17/20 NEGRO INDIAN/AM. PAGE 67 H1342
STRUCT PRE/AMER CULTURE SOCIETY

B65
HISPANIC SOCIETY OF AMERICA,CATALOGUE (10 VOLS.). PORTUGAL PRE/AMER SPAIN NAT/G ADMIN...POLICY SOC 15/20. PAGE 71 H1426
BIBLIOG L/A+17C COLONIAL DIPLOM

B66
MASUR G.,NATIONALISM IN LATIN AMERICA* DIVERSITY AND UNITY. CHRIST-17C PRE/AMER ELITES ECO/UNDEV CREATE DIPLOM INT/TRADE COLONIAL REV SOVEREIGN SOC. PAGE 105 H2089
L/A+17C NAT/LISM CULTURE

PRE/US/AM....PRE-1776 UNITED STATES (THE COLONIES)

PREDICT....PREDICTION OF FUTURE EVENTS, SEE ALSO FUT

B00
MOCKLER-FERRYMAN A.,BRITISH WEST AFRICA. FRANCE GERMANY NIGER SIER/LEONE UK CULTURE DIPLOM WAR RACE/REL PRODUC PROFIT WEALTH...POLICY PREDICT 19. PAGE 112 H2232
AFR COLONIAL INT/TRADE CAP/ISM

B42
BARNES H.E.,SOCIAL INSTITUTIONS IN AN ERA OF WORLD UPHEAVAL. INDUS FAM NAT/G PERF/ART SECT AUTOMAT PERSON MORAL...PREDICT 20. PAGE 11 H0221
SOCIETY CULTURE TECHRACY TREND

B53
SQUIRES J.D.,BRITISH PROPAGANDA AT HOME AND IN THE UNITED STATES FROM 1914 TO 1917. UK NAT/G PROB/SOLV DOMIN PRESS EFFICIENCY...PSY PREDICT 20 WWI INTERVENT PSY/WAR. PAGE 148 H2960
EDU/PROP CONTROL WAR DIPLOM

C56
FALL B.B.,"THE VIET-MINH REGIME." VIETNAM LAW ECO/UNDEV POL/PAR FORCES DOMIN WAR ATTIT MARXISM ...BIOG PREDICT BIBLIOG/A 20. PAGE 48 H0967
NAT/G ADMIN EX/STRUC LEAD

L58
BELL D.,"TEN THEORIES IN SEARCH OF REALITY: THE PREDICTION OF SOVIET BEHAVIOR IN THE SOCIAL SCIENCES" (BMR)" COM USSR...POLICY SOC METH/COMP 20. PAGE 13 H0264
MARXISM PREDICT IDEA/COMP

B60
FRANCIS R.G.,THE PREDICTIVE PROCESS. PLAN MARXISM ...DECISION SOC CONCPT NAT/COMP 19/20. PAGE 52 H1047
PREDICT PHIL/SCI TREND

B60
KERR C.,INDUSTRIALISM AND INDUSTRIAL MAN. CULTURE SOCIETY ECO/UNDEV NAT/G ADMIN PRODUC WEALTH ...PREDICT TREND NAT/COMP 19/20. PAGE 85 H1697
WORKER MGT ECO/DEV INDUS

B60
MINIFIE J.M.,PEACEMAKER OR POWDER-MONKEY. CANADA INT/ORG NAT/G FORCES LEAD WAR...PREDICT 20. PAGE 111 H2222
DIPLOM POLICY NEUTRAL PEACE

B62
AMERICAN SOCIETY AFR CULTURE,PAN-AFRICANISM RECONSIDERED. AFR SOCIETY STRUCT SCHOOL CAP/ISM EDU/PROP...ART/METH NEW/IDEA PREDICT ANTHOL 20 PANAF/FREE NEGRO. PAGE 6 H0123
DIPLOM FEDERAL NAT/LISM CULTURE

B62
TILMAN R.O.,THE NIGERIAN POLITICAL SXENE. NIGERIA DIPLOM COLONIAL PARTIC...POLICY SOC OBS PREDICT ANTHOL 20. PAGE 155 H3096
NAT/G AFR ECO/UNDEV FEDERAL

B63
RIVKIN A.,THE AFRICAN PRESENCE IN WORLD AFFAIRS. ECO/UNDEV AGRI INT/ORG LOC/G NAT/LISM...OBS PREDICT GOV/COMP 20. PAGE 132 H2635
AFR NAT/G DIPLOM BAL/PWR

B64
BRIGHT J.R.,RESEARCH, DEVELOPMENT AND TECHNOLOGICAL INNOVATION. CULTURE R+D CREATE PLAN PROB/SOLV AUTOMAT RISK PERSON...DECISION CONCPT PREDICT BIBLIOG. PAGE 21 H0419
TEC/DEV NEW/IDEA INDUS MGT

B64
SANDEE J.,EUROPE'S FUTURE CONSUMPTION. EUR+WWI FUT EDU/PROP...IDEA/COMP NAT/COMP ANTHOL 20 EUROPE. PAGE 137 H2750
MARKET ECO/DEV PREDICT PRICE

B65
GHAI D.P.,PORTRAIT OF A MINORITY: ASIANS IN EAST AFRICA. S/ASIA TANZANIA UGANDA COLONIAL...SOC OBS PREDICT ANTHOL 20. PAGE 56 H1119
RACE/REL GP/REL CULTURE AFR

B65
VERMOT-GAUCHY M.,L'EDUCATION NATIONALE DANS LA FRANCE DE 1975. FRANCE FUT CULTURE ELITES R+D SCHOOL PLAN EDU/PROP EFFICIENCY...POLICY PREDICT CHARTS INDEX 20. PAGE 162 H3245
ACADEM CREATE TREND INTELL

S65
WRIGHT Q.,"THE ESCALATION OF INTERNATIONAL CONFLICTS." WOR+45 WOR-45 FORCES DIPLOM RISK COST ATTIT ALL/VALS...INT/LAW QUANT STAT NAT/COMP. PAGE 171 H3422
WAR PERCEPT PREDICT MATH

B66
BLACK C.E.,THE DYNAMICS OF MODERNIZATION: A STUDY IN COMPARATIVE HISTORY. STRUCT ECO/DEV ECO/UNDEV NAT/G DIPLOM LEAD REV...PREDICT TIME/SEQ TREND SOC/INTEG 17/20. PAGE 17 H0350
SOCIETY SOC NAT/COMP

B66
FARWELL G.,MASK OF ASIA: THE PHILIPPINES. PHILIPPINE SECT DIPLOM ATTIT...SOC RECORD PREDICT BIBLIOG 20. PAGE 49 H0974
S/ASIA CULTURE

B66
UN ECONOMIC AND SOCIAL COUNCIL,WORLD POPULATION PROSPECTS AS ASSESSED IN 1963. FUT WOR+45 DEATH AGE ...TREND CHARTS UN. PAGE 158 H3157
PREDICT CENSUS GEOG

NAT/COMP

S66
KAPIL R.L.,"ON THE CONFLICT POTENTIAL OF INHERITED BOUNDARIES IN AFRICA." MOD/EUR MOROCCO UAR EX/STRUC DIPLOM LEGIT REGION ADJUST...RECORD NAT/COMP GEN/LAWS. PAGE 83 H1658
AFR COLONIAL PREDICT GEOG

B67
JOUVENEL B D.E.,THE ART OF CONJECTURE. FUT CONSULT EX/STRUC CHOOSE GOV/REL ALL/VALS. PAGE 82 H1638
PREDICT DELIB/GP PLAN NAT/G

B67
PLANK J.,CUBA AND THE UNITED STATES: LONG RANGE PERSPECTIVES. CUBA L/A+17C USSR ECO/UNDEV NAT/G FORCES ECO/TAC INT/TRADE AGREE REV...PREDICT TREND ANTHOL 20 CASTRO/F COLD/WAR OAS. PAGE 126 H2520
DIPLOM

B67
SPIRO H.S.,PATTERNS OF AFRICAN DEVLOPMENT: FIVE COMPARISONS. STRUCT ECO/UNDEV NAT/G CONSERVE SOCISM ...PREDICT NAT/COMP 20 CHINJAP. PAGE 148 H2951
AFR CONSTN NAT/LISM TREND

L67
GRAUBARD S.R.,"TOWARD THE YEAR 2000: WORK IN PROGRESS." FUT ACADEM SECT DELIB/GP DIPLOM EDU/PROP AGE/Y PERSON ROLE...PSY ANTHOL. PAGE 60 H1199
PREDICT PROB/SOLV SOCIETY CULTURE

S67
FINLAY D.J.,"THE GHANA COUP...ONE YEAR LATER." GHANA FORCES FOR/AID PRESS CONTROL CIVMIL/REL NAT/LISM AUTHORIT PWR...PREDICT 20. PAGE 50 H1005
REV NAT/G ATTIT ECO/UNDEV

S67
MALAN V.D.,"THE SILENT VILLAGE." KIN MUNIC NEIGH CHOOSE ISOLAT ROLE...SOC INDIAN/AM. PAGE 101 H2027
CULTURE STRUCT PREDICT

S67
SMITH J.E.,"THE RED PRUSSIANISM OF THE GERMAN DEMOCRATIC REPUBLIC." GERMANY/E INTELL NAT/G SECT CHIEF...PREDICT TIME/SEQ 20. PAGE 146 H2913
MARXISM NAT/LISM GOV/COMP EDU/PROP

N67
US HOUSE COMM SCI ASTRONAUT,GOVERNMENT, SCIENCE, AND INTERNATIONAL POLICY (PAMPHLET). INDIA NETHERLAND ECO/DEV ECO/UNDEV R+D ACADEM PLAN DIPLOM FOR/AID CONFER...PREDICT 20 CHINJAP. PAGE 160 H3198
NAT/G POLICY CREATE TEC/DEV

PREDICTION....SEE PREDICT, FUT

PREFECT....PREFECTS AND PREFECTORALISM

B63
FRIED R.C.,THE ITALIAN PREFECTS. ITALY STRATA ECO/DEV NAT/LISM ALL/IDEOS...TREND CHARTS METH/COMP BIBLIOG 17/20 PREFECT. PAGE 53 H1061
ADMIN NAT/G EFFICIENCY

PREHIST....PREHISTORIC SOCIETY, PRIOR TO 3000 B.C.

B31
KROEBER A.L.,SOURCE BOOK IN ANTHROPOLOGY. PREHIST SECT RACE/REL...LING GP/COMP ANTHOL. PAGE 89 H1770
SOC HEREDITY CULTURE ALL/VALS

B53
COBLENTZ S.A.,FROM ARROW TO ATOM BOMB: THE PSYCHOLOGICAL HISTORY OF WAR. PREHIST CULTURE CROWD PEACE DRIVE MORAL PWR...GP/COMP IDEA/COMP. PAGE 31 H0613
WAR PSY SOCIETY

B56
LEVIN M.G.,THE PEOPLES OF SIBERIA. PREHIST ECO/UNDEV KIN SECT HABITAT...CLASSIF AUD/VIS WORSHIP 20 SIBERIA. PAGE 95 H1900
CULTURE SOCIETY ASIA

B58
ALMAGRO BASCH M.,ORIGEN Y FORMACION DEL PUEBLO HISPANO. PREHIST SPAIN REGION WAR RACE/REL HABITAT ORD/FREE...SOC SOC/INTEG 20. PAGE 5 H0109
CULTURE GP/REL ADJUST

B59
HONINGMAN J.J.,THE WORLD OF MAN. CHRIST-17C MEDIT-7 PRE/AMER PREHIST CREATE INGP/REL BIO/SOC HABITAT ...PSY SOC BIBLIOG. PAGE 73 H1460
CULTURE METH PERSON STRUCT

B63
MULLER H.J.,FREEDOM IN THE WESTERN WORLD. PREHIST CULTURE SECT CREATE TEC/DEV DOMIN PWR WEALTH ...MAJORIT SOC CONCPT. PAGE 114 H2285
ORD/FREE TIME/SEQ SOCIETY

B63
STUCKI C.W.,AMERICAN DOCTORAL DISSERTATIONS ON ASIA 1933-62 (A PAPER). PREHIST INDUS NAT/G GOV/REL ALL/IDEOS...ART/METH GEOG SOC LING 20. PAGE 150 H3002
BIBLIOG ASIA SOCIETY S/ASIA

B64
KIDD K.E.,BRIEF BIBLIOGRAPHY OF ONTARIO ANTHROPOLOGY (PAMPHLET). CANADA PREHIST HABITAT ...MYTH WORSHIP. PAGE 86 H1708
BIBLIOG SOC LING CULTURE

PREHISTORIC SOCIETY....SEE PREHIST

PREJUDICE....SEE DISCRIM

PRELOT M. H2556

PREOBRAZHENSKY E. H0468

PRESIDENT....PRESIDENCY (ALL NATIONS); SEE ALSO CHIEF

B27
WILLOUGHBY W.F.,PRINCIPLES OF PUBLIC ADMINISTRATION WITH SPECIAL REFERENCE TO THE NATIONAL AND STATE GOVERNMENTS OF THE UNITED STATES. FINAN PROVS CHIEF CONSULT LEGIS CREATE BUDGET EXEC ROUTINE GOV/REL CENTRAL...MGT 20 BUR/BUDGET CONGRESS PRESIDENT. PAGE 169 H3373
NAT/G EX/STRUC OP/RES ADMIN

S43
PRICE D.K.,"THE PARLIAMENTARY AND PRESIDENTIAL SYSTEMS" (BMR)" USA-45 NAT/G EX/STRUC PARL/PROC GOV/REL PWR 20 PRESIDENT CONGRESS PARLIAMENT. PAGE 128 H2561
LEGIS REPRESENT ADMIN GOV/COMP

B47
MARX F.M.,THE PRESIDENT AND HIS STAFF SERVICES PUBLIC ADMINISTRATION SERVICES NUMBER 98 (PAMPHLET). FINAN ADMIN CT/SYS REPRESENT PWR 20 PRESIDENT. PAGE 104 H2075
CONSTN CHIEF NAT/G EX/STRUC

B60
JUNZ A.J.,PRESENT TRENDS IN AMERICAN NATIONAL GOVERNMENT. LEGIS DIPLOM ADMIN CT/SYS ORD/FREE ...CONCPT ANTHOL 20 CONGRESS PRESIDENT SUPREME/CT. PAGE 3 H0052
POL/PAR CHOOSE CONSTN NAT/G

B62
KASTARI P.,LA PRESIDENCE DE LA REPUBLIQUE EN FINLANDE. FINLAND CONSTN NAT/G POL/PAR LEGIS LEGIT ATTIT...JURID CONCPT 20 PRESIDENT. PAGE 83 H1666
PARL/PROC CHIEF PWR DECISION

B63
FRANKEL J.,THE MAKING OF FOREIGN POLICY: AN ANALYSIS OF DECISION-MAKING. CHINA/COM EUR+WWI USA+45 ELITES INTELL FORCES LEGIS PLAN ATTIT ALL/VALS MORAL CONSERVE...GOV/COMP 20 PRESIDENT UN TREATY. PAGE 53 H1051
POLICY DECISION PROB/SOLV DIPLOM

S63
LAMBERT D.,"LA TRANSPOSITION DU REGIME PRESIDENTIEL HORS DES ETATSUNIS: LE CAS DE L'AMERIQUE LATINE." NAT/G EX/STRUC LEGIS PARL/PROC PWR 18/20 PRESIDENT CENTRAL/AM SOUTH/AMER. PAGE 90 H1800
DELIB/GP CHIEF L/A+17C GOV/REL

S63
OGOT B.,"FROM CHIEF TO PRESIDENT." AFR SECT REGION NAT/LISM...SOC GOV/COMP NAT/COMP 20 PRESIDENT. PAGE 121 H2410
CHIEF CULTURE LEAD ORD/FREE

B64
LIEVWEN E.,GENERALS VS PRESIDENTS: WEOMILITARISM IN LATIN AMERICA. L/A+17C FORCES DIPLOM FOR/AID LEAD ...NAT/COMP 20 PRESIDENT. PAGE 97 H1929
CIVMIL/REL REV CONSERVE ORD/FREE

B64
MINAR D.W.,IDEAS AND POLITICS: THE AMERICAN EXPERIENCE. SECT CHIEF LEGIS CREATE ADJUD EXEC REV PWR...PHIL/SCI CONCPT IDEA/COMP 18/20 HAMILTON/A JEFFERSN/T DECLAR/IND JACKSON/A PRESIDENT. PAGE 111 H2220
CONSTN NAT/G FEDERAL

B64
PERKINS D.,THE AMERICAN DEMOCRACY: ITS RISE TO POWER. ASIA USSR LAW CULTURE FINAN EDU/PROP COLONIAL CHOOSE...POLICY CHARTS BIBLIOG WORSHIP PRESIDENT 15/20 NEGRO. PAGE 125 H2492
LOC/G ECO/TAC WAR DIPLOM

B64
US HOUSE COMM BANKING-CURR,INTERNATIONAL DEVELOPMENT ASSOCIATION ACT AMENDMENT. CHINA/COM USA+45 USSR FINAN FORCES LEGIS DIPLOM CONFER EFFICIENCY...CHARTS GOV/COMP 20 PRESIDENT CONGRESS INTL/DEV. PAGE 160 H3196
BAL/PAY FOR/AID RECORD ECO/TAC

B65
CHARNAY J.P.,LE SUFFRAGE POLITIQUE EN FRANCE; ELECTIONS PARLEMENTAIRES, ELECTION PRESIDENTIELLE, REFERENDUMS. FRANCE CONSTN CHIEF DELIB/GP ECO/TAC EDU/PROP CRIME INGP/REL MORAL ORD/FREE PWR CATHISM 20 PARLIAMENT PRESIDENT. PAGE 29 H0584
CHOOSE SUFF NAT/G LEGIS

B65
FAUST J.J.,A REVOLUCAO DEVORA SEUS PRESIDENTES. BRAZIL NAT/G POL/PAR LEAD CHOOSE CIVMIL/REL ORD/FREE 20 PRESIDENT. PAGE 49 H0976
PARTIC REV FORCES GP/REL

S65
CAIRNS J.C.,"FRANCE, DECEMBER 1965: END OF THE ELECTIVE MONARACHY" EUR+WWI FRANCE FUT CONSTN SOCIETY CHIEF BAL/PWR ATTIT ALL/IDEOS 20 DEGAULLE/C PRESIDENT. PAGE 25 H0505
CHOOSE NAT/G POL/PAR PWR

S65
HUGHES T.L.,"SCHOLARS AND FOREIGN POLICY* VARIETIES OF RESEARCH EXPERIENCE." COM/IND DIPLOM ADMIN EXEC ROUTINE...MGT OBS CONGRESS PRESIDENT CAMELOT. PAGE 75 H1491
ACT/RES ACADEM CONTROL NAT/G

L66
MCAUSLAN J.P.W.,"CONSTITUTIONAL INNOVATION AND
CONSTN

POLITICAL STABILITY IN TANZANIA: A PRELIMINARY ASSESSMENT." AFR TANZANIA ELITES CHIEF EX/STRUC RIGID/FLEX PWR 20 PRESIDENT BUREAUCRCY. PAGE 106 H2122 — NAT/G EXEC POL/PAR

B67

HILSMAN R.,TO MOVE A NATION: THE POLITICS OF FOREIGN POLICY IN THE ADMINISTRATION OF JOHN F. KENNEDY. CHINA/COM COM USSR VIETNAM NAT/G DELIB/GP FORCES PLAN PROB/SOLV BAL/PWR COLONIAL EXEC REV PWR 20 KENNEDY/JF PRESIDENT. PAGE 71 H1418 — CHIEF DIPLOM

PRESS....PRESS, OPERATIONS OF ALL PRINTED MEDIA, EXCEPT FILM AND TV (Q.V.), JOURNALISM; SEE ALSO COM/IND

N

TOTEMEYER G.,SOUTH AFRICA; SOUTHWEST AFRICA: A BIBLIOGRAPHY, 1945-1963. AFR SOUTH/AFR PRESS...SOC 20. PAGE 157 H3134 — BIBLIOG CULTURE NAT/G EDU/PROP

N

PEKING REVIEW. CHINA/COM CULTURE AGRI INDUS DIPLOM EDU/PROP GUERRILLA ATTIT MARXISM...BIBLIOG 20. PAGE 1 H0009 — MARXIST NAT/G POL/PAR PRESS

N

AFRICAN RESEARCH BULLETIN. AFR CULTURE NAT/G COLONIAL...SOC 20. PAGE 1 H0010 — BIBLIOG/A DIPLOM PRESS

N

DAILY SUMMARY OF THE JAPANESE PRESS. NAT/G DIPLOM LEAD 20 CHINJAP. PAGE 1 H0013 — BIBLIOG PRESS ASIA ATTIT

N

LONDON TIMES OFFICIAL INDEX. UK LAW ECO/DEV NAT/G DIPLOM LEAD ATTIT 20. PAGE 1 H0018 — BIBLIOG INDEX PRESS WRITING

N

"PROLOG",DIGEST OF THE SOVIET UKRANIAN PRESS. USSR LAW AGRI INDUS PROVS SCHOOL DIPLOM GOV/REL ATTIT ...HUM LING 20. PAGE 3 H0053 — BIBLIOG/A NAT/G PRESS COM

N

CARIBBEAN COMMISSION,CURRENT CARIBBEAN BIBLIOGRAPHY. FRANCE NETHERLAND UK CULTURE ECO/UNDEV PRESS LEAD ATTIT...GEOG SOC 20. PAGE 26 H0530 — BIBLIOG NAT/G L/A+17C DIPLOM

N

EUROPA PUBLICATIONS LIMITED,THE EUROPA YEAR BOOK. CONSTN FINAN INDUS POL/PAR DIPLOM TV CT/SYS...STAT BIOG CHARTS WORSHIP 20. PAGE 47 H0949 — BIBLIOG NAT/G PRESS INT/ORG

N

KYRIAK T.E.,CHINA: A BIBLIOGRAPHY. ASIA CHINA/COM AGRI FINAN INDUS NAT/G INT/TRADE PRESS...SOC 20. PAGE 90 H1789 — BIBLIOG/A MARXISM TOP/EX POL/PAR

N

SOUTH AFRICA STATE LIBRARY,SOUTH AFRICAN NATIONAL BIBLIOGRAPHY, SANB. SOUTH/AFR LAW NAT/G EDU/PROP ...MGT PSY SOC 20. PAGE 147 H2937 — BIBLIOG PRESS WRITING

N

US CONSOLATE GENERAL HONG KONG,REVIEW OF THE HONG KONG CHINESE PRESS. ECO/UNDEV LOC/G NAT/G PLAN DIPLOM EDU/PROP LEAD GP/REL MARXISM...POLICY INDEX 20. PAGE 159 H3178 — BIBLIOG/A ASIA PRESS ATTIT

N

US CONSULATE GENERAL HONG KONG,CURRENT BACKGROUND. CHINA/COM ECO/UNDEV LOC/G NAT/G PLAN DIPLOM EDU/PROP LEAD REV ATTIT...POLICY INDEX 20. PAGE 159 H3179 — BIBLIOG/A MARXIST ASIA PRESS

N

US CONSULATE GENERAL HONG KONG,EXTRACTS FROM CHINA MAINLAND MAGAZINES. ASIA CHINA/COM ECO/UNDEV NAT/G CHIEF LEAD ATTIT...MARXIST INDEX 20. PAGE 159 H3180 — BIBLIOG MARXISM PRESS

N

US CONSULATE GENERAL HONG KONG,SURVEY OF CHINA MAINLAND PRESS. CHINA/COM ECO/UNDEV LOC/G NAT/G PLAN DIPLOM EDU/PROP LEAD REV ATTIT...POLICY INDEX 20. PAGE 159 H3181 — BIBLIOG/A MARXIST ASIA PRESS

N

US CONSULATE GENERAL HONG KONG,US CONSULATE GENERAL, HONG KONG, PRESS SUMMARIES. CHINA/COM ECO/UNDEV LOC/G NAT/G PLAN DIPLOM EDU/PROP LEAD REV ATTIT...POLICY INDEX 20. PAGE 159 H3182 — BIBLIOG/A MARXIST ASIA PRESS

B00

HOBSON J.A.,THE WAR IN SOUTH AFRICA: ITS CAUSES AND EFFECTS. NETHERLAND SOUTH/AFR UK ELITES AGRI EXTR/IND POL/PAR DIPLOM PRESS RACE/REL ATTIT ORD/FREE SOVEREIGN...INT 19 NEGRO. PAGE 72 H1439 — WAR DOMIN POLICY NAT/G

B03

FAGUET E.,LE LIBERALISME. FRANCE PRESS ADJUD ADMIN DISCRIM CONSERVE SOCISM...TRADIT SOC LING WORSHIP PARLIAMENT. PAGE 48 H0960 — ORD/FREE EDU/PROP NAT/G LAW

B08

NIRRNHEIM O.,DAS ERSTE JAHR DES MINISTERIUMS BISMARCK UND DIE OEFFENTLICHE MEINUNG (HEIDELBERGER ABHANDLUNGEN, 20. HEFT). GERMANY MOD/EUR LEGIS DIPLOM EDU/PROP INGP/REL...BIOG GOV/COMP IDEA/COMP BIBLIOG 19 BISMARCK/O. PAGE 118 H2363 — CHIEF PRESS NAT/G ATTIT

N19

TABORSKY E.,CONFORMITY UNDER COMMUNISM (PAMPHLET). CZECHOSLVK HUNGARY POLAND SCHOOL DOMIN PRESS ...TREND GOV/COMP 20. PAGE 152 H3030 — COM CONTROL EDU/PROP NAT/G

B21

BERGSTRASSER L.,GESCHICHTE DER POLITISCHEN PARTEIEN. GERMANY MOD/EUR NAT/G PRESS PWR ...TIME/SEQ 17/20. PAGE 15 H0303 — POL/PAR LAISSEZ CONSERVE

B22

TONNIES F.,KRITIK DER OFFENTLICHEN MEINUNG. FRANCE UK CULTURE COM/IND DOMIN PRESS RUMOR ROLE NAT/COMP. PAGE 156 H3114 — SOCIETY SOC ATTIT

B23

KADEN E.H.,DER POLITISCHE CHARAKTER DER FRANZOSISCHEN KULTURPROPAGANDA AM RHEIN. FRANCE MOD/EUR DOMIN PRESS...GEOG METH/COMP 20. PAGE 82 H1648 — EDU/PROP ATTIT DIPLOM NAT/G

B27

CHILDS J.B.,AN ACCOUNT OF GOVERNMENT DOCUMENT BIBLIOGRAPHY IN THE UNITED STATES AND ELSEWHERE (A PAPER). LOC/G PRESS CENTRAL KNOWL...METH 19/20 LEAGUE/NAT. PAGE 29 H0590 — BIBLIOG/A CON/ANAL NAT/G

B28

CHILDS J.B.,FOREIGN GOVERNMENT PUBLICATIONS (PAMPHLET). LEGIS DIPLOM 19/20. PAGE 29 H0591 — BIBLIOG PRESS NAT/G

B29

LEITZ F.,DIE PUBLIZITAT DER AKTIENGESELLSCHAFT. BELGIUM FRANCE GERMANY UK FINAN PRESS GP/REL PROFIT KNOWL 20. PAGE 94 H1872 — LG/CO JURID ECO/TAC NAT/COMP

B31

DUFFIELD M.,KING LEGION. NAT/G PROVS SECT LEGIS EDU/PROP PRESS GP/REL AGE/Y MARXISM POLICY. PAGE 43 H0856 — SUPEGO FORCES VOL/ASSN LOBBY

B32

THIBAUDET A.,LES IDEES POLITIQUES DE LA FRANCE. FRANCE NAT/G SECT PRESS REV NAT/LISM PEACE ATTIT ...PSY 19/20 JACOBINISM JAURES/JL. PAGE 154 H3070 — IDEA/COMP ALL/IDEOS CATHISM

B33

PUBLIC OPINION AND WORLD POLITICS. UNIV LAW CULTURE NAT/G PRESS REV GP/REL...MAJORIT METH/COMP ANTHOL 20. PAGE 171 H3420 — DIPLOM EDU/PROP ATTIT MAJORITY

B34

GONZALEZ PALENCIA A,ESTUDIO HISTORICO SOBRE LA CENSURA GUBERNATIVA EN ESPANA 1800-1833. NAT/G COERCE INGP/REL ATTIT AUTHORIT KNOWL...POLICY JURID 19. PAGE 58 H1165 — LEGIT EDU/PROP PRESS CONTROL

L34

GOSNELL H.F.,"BRITISH ROYAL COMMISSIONS OF INQUIRY" UK CONSTN LEGIS PRESS ADMIN PARL/PROC...DECISION 20 PARLIAMENT. PAGE 59 H1184 — DELIB/GP INSPECT POLICY NAT/G

B36

WANDERSCHECK H.,WELTKRIEG UND PROPAGANDA. GERMANY MOD/EUR UK COM/IND NAT/G DOMIN PRESS ATTIT...POLICY 20 HITLER/A. PAGE 165 H3299 — EDU/PROP PSY WAR KNOWL

B37

MUNZENBERG W.,PROPAGANDA ALS WAFFE. COM/IND PRESS COERCE WAR...PSY 20. PAGE 115 H2290 — EDU/PROP DOMIN NAT/G LEAD

B38

DUNHAM W.H. JR.,COMPLAINT AND REFORM IN ENGLAND 1436-1714. UK LAW ACADEM NAT/G POL/PAR SCHOOL PRESS COLONIAL PARL/PROC MORAL...SOC/WK ANTHOL 15/18 HAKLUYT/R COWPER/W. PAGE 43 H0865 — ATTIT SOCIETY SECT

B40

WANDERSCHECK H.,FRANKREICHS PROPAGANDA GEGEN DEUTSCHLAND. FRANCE GERMANY MOD/EUR UK NAT/G DIPLOM WAR 20 JEWS. PAGE 165 H3300 — EDU/PROP ATTIT DOMIN PRESS

B41

BAUMANN G.,GRUNDLAGEN UND PRAXIS DER INTERNATIONALEN PROPAGANDA. FRANCE GERMANY UK CULTURE COM/IND PRESS PWR...PSY METH/COMP 20. PAGE 12 H0241 — EDU/PROP DOMIN ATTIT DIPLOM

B42

NEUBURGER O.,OFFICIAL PUBLICATIONS OF PRESENT-DAY GERMANY: GOVERNMENT, CORPORATE ORGANIZATIONS, AND NATIONAL SOCIALIST PARTY. GERMANY CONSTN COM/IND POL/PAR EDU/PROP PRESS 20 NAZI. PAGE 117 H2332 — BIBLIOG/A FASCISM NAT/G ADMIN

C43

BENTHAM J.,"ON THE LIBERTY OF THE PRESS, AND PUBLIC DISCUSSION" IN J. BOWRING, ED., THE WORKS OF JEREMY BENTHAM." SPAIN UK LAW ELITES NAT/G LEGIS INSPECT — ORD/FREE PRESS CONFER

LEGIT WRITING CONTROL PRIVIL TOTALISM AUTHORIT ...TRADIT 19 FREE/SPEE. PAGE 15 H0290
CONSERVE

B45
HORN O.B.,BRITISH PUBLIC OPINION AND THE FIRST PARTITION OF POLAND. POLAND UK LEGIS PRESS RUMOR CONTROL PARTIC NAT/LISM SOVEREIGN 18/19. PAGE 73 H1469
DIPLOM POLICY ATTIT NAT/G

B45
PERAZA SARAUSA F.,BIBLIOGRAFIAS CUBANAS. CUBA CULTURE ECO/UNDEV AGRI EDU/PROP PRESS CIVMIL/REL ...POLICY GEOG PHIL/SCI BIOG 19/20. PAGE 125 H2489
BIBLIOG/A L/A+17C NAT/G DIPLOM

B47
NEUBURGER O.,GUIDE TO OFFICIAL PUBLICATIONS OF THE OTHER AMERICAN REPUBLICS: HAITI (VOL. XII). HAITI LAW FINAN LEGIS PRESS...JURID 20. PAGE 117 H2334
BIBLIOG/A CONSTN NAT/G EDU/PROP

B49
SCHONS D.,BOOK CENSORSHIP IN NEW SPAIN (NEW WORLD STUDIES, BOOK II). SPAIN LAW CULTURE INSPECT ADJUD CT/SYS SANCTION GP/REL ORD/FREE 14/17. PAGE 140 H2797
CHRIST-17C EDU/PROP CONTROL PRESS

B50
IRION F.C.,PUBLIC OPINION AND PROPAGANDA. STRUCT COM/IND FAM SECT COERCE 20 FILM. PAGE 78 H1568
EDU/PROP ATTIT NAT/G PRESS

B50
WARD R.E.,A GUIDE TO JAPANESE REFERENCE AND RESEARCH MATERIALS IN THE FIELD OF POLITICAL SCIENCE. LAW CONSTN LOC/G PRESS ADMIN...SOC CON/ANAL METH 19/20 CHINJAP. PAGE 165 H3305
BIBLIOG/A ASIA NAT/G

N51
MEYER E.W.,POLITICAL PARTIES IN WESTERN GERMANY (PAMPHLET). EUR+WWI GERMANY/W PRESS LEAD CHOOSE REPRESENT ATTIT 20. PAGE 109 H2189
BIBLIOG POL/PAR NAT/G VOL/ASSN

B52
SCHATTSCHNEIDER E.E.,A GUIDE TO THE STUDY OF PUBLIC AFFAIRS. LAW LOC/G NAT/G LEGIS BUDGET PRESS ADMIN LOBBY...JURID CHARTS 20. PAGE 139 H2775
ACT/RES INTELL ACADEM METH/COMP

B53
SQUIRES J.D.,BRITISH PROPAGANDA AT HOME AND IN THE UNITED STATES FROM 1914 TO 1917. UK NAT/G PROB/SOLV DOMIN PRESS EFFICIENCY...PSY PREDICT 20 WWI INTERVENT PSY/WAR. PAGE 148 H2960
EDU/PROP CONTROL WAR DIPLOM

C53
BULNER-THOMAS I.,"THE PARTY SYSTEM IN GREAT BRITAIN." UK CONSTN SECT PRESS CONFER GP/REL ATTIT ...POLICY TREND BIBLIOG 19/20 PARLIAMENT. PAGE 23 H0473
NAT/G POL/PAR ADMIN ROUTINE

B54
US LIBRARY OF CONGRESS,RESEARCH AND INFORMATION ON AFRICA: CONTINUING SOURCES. ISLAM ECO/UNDEV AGRI INDUS R+D ACADEM NAT/G INT/TRADE...SOC 20. PAGE 161 H3210
BIBLIOG/A AFR PRESS COM/IND

B56
DOUGLAS W.O.,WE THE JUDGES. INDIA USA+45 USA-45 LAW NAT/G SECT LEGIS PRESS CRIME FEDERAL ORD/FREE ...POLICY GOV/COMP 19/20 WARRN/EARL MARSHALL/J SUPREME/CT. PAGE 42 H0841
ADJUD CT/SYS CONSTN GOV/REL

B57
IKE N.,JAPANESE POLITICS. INTELL STRUCT AGRI INDUS FAM KIN LABOR PRESS CHOOSE ATTIT...DECISION BIBLIOG 19/20 CHINJAP. PAGE 76 H1523
NAT/G ADMIN POL/PAR CULTURE

B58
DUCLOUX L.,FROM BLACKMAIL TO TREASON. FRANCE PLAN DIPLOM EDU/PROP PRESS RUMOR NAT/LISM...CRIMLGY 20. PAGE 43 H0853
COERCE CRIME NAT/G PWR

B58
PALMER E.E.,"POLITICAL MAN" IN E. PALMER, PROBLEMS IN DEMOCRATIC CITIZENSHIP. LOC/G NAT/G LEGIS PRESS CHOOSE REPRESENT GP/REL...DECISION SOC IDEA/COMP ANTHOL 20. PAGE 123 H2449
PARTIC POL/PAR EDU/PROP MAJORIT

B59
CONOVER H.F.,NIGERIAN OFFICIAL PUBLICATIONS, 1869-1959: A GUIDE. NIGER CONSTN FINAN ACADEM SCHOOL FORCES PRESS ADMIN COLONIAL...HIST/WRIT 19/20. PAGE 33 H0650
BIBLIOG NAT/G CON/ANAL

B59
INTERNATIONAL PRESS INSTITUTE,THE PRESS IN AUTHORITARIAN COUNTRIES. COM PORTUGAL SPAIN UAR USSR NAT/G DOMIN LEGIT ORD/FREE FASCISM SOCISM 20. PAGE 78 H1559
PRESS CONTROL TOTALISM EDU/PROP

B59
LOPEZ M.M.,CATALOGOS DE PUBLICACIONES PERIODICAS MEXICANAS. L/A+17C CULTURE NAT/G DIPLOM 20 MEXIC/AMER. PAGE 98 H1965
BIBLIOG PRESS CON/ANAL

C59
COLLINS I.,"THE GOVERNMENT AND THE NEWSPAPER PRESS IN FRANCE, 1814-1881. FRANCE LAW ADMIN CT/SYS ...CON/ANAL BIBLIOG 19. PAGE 32 H0634
PRESS ORD/FREE NAT/G EDU/PROP

B60
CASTBERG F.,FREEDOM OF SPEECH IN THE WEST. FRANCE GERMANY USA+45 USA-45 LAW CONSTN CHIEF PRESS DISCRIM...CONCPT 18/20. PAGE 28 H0558
ORD/FREE SANCTION ADJUD NAT/COMP

B60
CONOVER H.F.,OFFICIAL PUBLICATIONS OF FRENCH WEST AFRICA, 1946-1958. DAHOMEY IVORY/CST NIGER SENEGAL UPPER/VOLT CONSTN AGRI PRESS...CON/ANAL 20. PAGE 33 H0651
BIBLIOG COLONIAL NAT/G AFR

B60
CONOVER H.F.,OFFICIAL PUBLICATIONS OF SOMALILAND, 1941-1959: A GUIDE. SOMALIA AGRI FINAN INT/ORG SCHOOL INT/TRADE PRESS CONFER COLONIAL PARL/PROC 20 CONGRESS. PAGE 33 H0652
BIBLIOG NAT/G CON/ANAL

B60
EMERY E.,INTRODUCTION TO MASS COMMUNICATIONS. ACADEM PROF/ORG SCHOOL ACT/RES EDU/PROP ATTIT ...CONCPT BIBLIOG/A. PAGE 46 H0920
COM/IND PRESS CON/ANAL CULTURE

B60
HAUSER O.,PREUSSISCHE STAATSRASON UND NATIONALER GEDANKE. PRUSSIA SOCIETY PRESS ADMIN...CONCPT 19/20. PAGE 68 H1358
NAT/LISM NAT/G ATTIT PROVS

B60
MACFARQUHAR R.,THE HUNDRED FLOWERS. ASIA NAT/G WORKER GP/REL ORD/FREE MARXISM 20 MAO. PAGE 100 H1991
DEBATE PRESS POL/PAR ATTIT

B61
BROUGHTON M.,PRESS AND POLITICS OF SOUTH AFRICA. SOUTH/AFR NAT/G COLONIAL GP/REL ADJUST 20. PAGE 22 H0435
NAT/LISM PRESS PWR CULTURE

B61
LENIN V.I.,WHAT IS TO BE DONE? (1902). RUSSIA LABOR NAT/G POL/PAR WORKER CAP/ISM ECO/TAC ADMIN PARTIC ...MARXIST IDEA/COMP GEN/LAWS 19/20. PAGE 94 H1881
EDU/PROP PRESS MARXISM METH/COMP

B61
LYFORD J.P.,THE AGREEABLE AUTOCRACIES. SOCIETY LABOR POL/PAR SECT DIPLOM CHOOSE...CONCPT 20 WHITE/T NIEBUHR/R. PAGE 99 H1982
ATTIT POPULISM PRESS NAT/G

B61
NARASIMHAN V.K.,THE PRESS, THE PUBLIC AND THE ADMINISTRATION (PAMPHLET). INDIA COM/IND CONTROL REPRESENT GOV/REL EFFICIENCY...ANTHOL 20. PAGE 116 H2312
NAT/G ADMIN PRESS NEW/LIB

B61
SEMINAR REPRESENTATIVE GOVT,AFRO-ASIAN ATTITUDES: SEMINAR ON REPRESENTATIVE GOVERNMENTSPUBLIC LIBERTIES IN STATES OF ASIA AND AFRICA, RHODES, 1958. AFR ASIA BURMA INDIA ISLAM UAR VIETNAM/S SOCIETY POL/PAR CHIEF EDU/PROP PRESS PERSON ...POLICY INT 20 TUNIS. PAGE 141 H2826
CHOOSE ATTIT NAT/COMP ORD/FREE

B61
STAHL W.,EDUCATION FOR DEMOCRACY IN WEST GERMANY: ACHIEVEMENT SHORTCOMINGS - PROSPECTS. GERMANY/W SOCIETY NAT/G FORCES PLAN PROB/SOLV PRESS ALL/VALS ...POLICY MAJORIT CONCPT ANTHOL 20. PAGE 148 H2967
EDU/PROP POPULISM AGE/Y ADJUST

B62
ABOSCH H.,THE MENACE OF THE MIRACLE: GERMANY FROM HITLER TO ADENAUER. EUR+WWI GERMANY/W CULTURE FORCES PRESS NUC/PWR WAR CHOOSE 20 HITLER/A ADENAUER/K. PAGE 3 H0057
DIPLOM PEACE POLICY

B62
ANDREWS W.G.,FRENCH POLITICS AND ALGERIA: THE PROCESS OF POLICY FORMATION 1954-1962. ALGERIA FRANCE CONSTN ELITES POL/PAR CHIEF DELIB/GP LEGIS DIPLOM PRESS CHOOSE 20. PAGE 7 H0140
GOV/COMP EXEC COLONIAL

B62
CHAPMAN R.M.,NEW ZEALAND POLITICS IN ACTION: THE 1960 GENERAL ELECTION. NEW/ZEALND LEGIS EDU/PROP PRESS TV LEAD ATTIT...STAND/INT 20. PAGE 29 H0582
NAT/G CHOOSE POL/PAR

B62
HABERMAS J.,STRUKTURWANDEL DER OFFENTLICHKEIT. NAT/G EDU/PROP PRESS LEAD PARTIC PWR 20. PAGE 63 H1268
ATTIT CONCPT DOMIN

B62
HANAK H.,GREAT BRITAIN AND AUSTRIA-HUNGARY DURING THE FIRST WORLD WAR: A STUDY IN THE FORMATION OF PUBLIC OPINION. CZECHOSLVK UK NAT/G GIVE DOMIN EDU/PROP CONSERVE...BIBLIOG 20 AUST/HUNG WWI. PAGE 65 H1311
WAR DIPLOM ATTIT PRESS

B62
KRUGLAK T.E.,THE TWO FACES OF TASS. COM COM/IND NAT/G ACT/RES PLAN PRESS PERCEPT PERSON KNOWL 20. PAGE 89 H1778
PUB/INST EDU/PROP USSR

B62
STATE AND LOCAL GOVERNMENT. MUNIC NAT/G NEIGH PRESS CONTROL CHOOSE REPRESENT...BIBLIOG 20. PAGE 104 H2076
PROVS LOC/G GOV/REL PWR

B62
ZIESEL K.,DAS VERLORENE GEWISSEN. GERMANY/W NAT/G VOL/ASSN EDU/PROP PRESS SUPEGO...POLICY 20. PAGE 173 H3455
MORAL PWR ORD/FREE RESPECT

S62
MBOYA T.,"RELATIONS BETWEEN THE PRESS AND GOVERNMENT IN AFRICA." AFR DIPLOM EDU/PROP NAT/LISM ORD/FREE SOVEREIGN 20. PAGE 106 H2115
PRESS GP/REL ATTIT NAT/G

B63
CHEN N.-.R.,THE ECONOMY OF MAINLAND CHINA, 1949-1963: A BIBLIOGRAPHY OF MATERIALS IN ENGLISH. CHINA/COM ECO/UNDEV PRESS 20. PAGE 29 H0586
BIBLIOG MARXISM NAT/G ASIA

B64
AFRO ASIAN SOLIDARITY AGAINST IMPERIALISM. AFR ISLAM S/ASIA ECO/UNDEV NAT/G POL/PAR TOP/EX PRESS ...INT ANTHOL 20 CHOU/ENLAI. PAGE 2 H0043
MARXISM DIPLOM EDU/PROP CHIEF

B64
BEARDSLEY R.K.,STUDIES ON ECONOMIC LIFE IN JAPAN (OCCASIONAL PAPERS NO. 8). INDUS FAM HABITAT...GEOG GOV/COMP 20 CHINJAP. PAGE 12 H0249
WEALTH PRESS PRODUC INCOME

B64
HALE O.J.,THE CAPTIVE PRESS IN THE THIRD REICH. GERMANY CULTURE LG/CO NAT/G POL/PAR PLAN DOMIN TASK CENTRAL OWN TOTALISM PWR...BIBLIOG 20 HITLER/A NAZI AMMAN/MAX. PAGE 64 H1283
COM/IND PRESS CONTROL FASCISM

B64
MUSSO AMBROSI L.A.,BIBLIOGRAFIA DE BIBLIOGRAFIAS URUGUAYAS. URUGUAY DIPLOM ADMIN ATTIT...SOC 20. PAGE 115 H2301
BIBLIOG NAT/G L/A+17C PRESS

B64
PERAZA SARAUSA F.,DIRECTORIO DE REVISTAS Y PERIODICOS DE CUBA. CUBA L/A+17C NAT/G ATTIT 20. PAGE 125 H2490
BIBLIOG/A PRESS SERV/IND LEAD

B64
UNESCO,WORLD COMMUNICATIONS: PRESS, RADIO, TELEVISION, FILM (4TH ED.). WOR+45 DIPLOM TV PEACE ...NAT/COMP SOC/INTEG 20 FILM. PAGE 158 H3163
COM/IND EDU/PROP PRESS TEC/DEV

S64
GRUNER E.,"PRENSA, PARTIDOS POLITICOS, Y GRUPOS DE PRESION EN SUIZA." EUR+WWI MOD/EUR NAT/G EDU/PROP LEGIT PRESS ATTIT KNOWL ORD/FREE...CONCPT STAT CON/ANAL CHARTS 20. PAGE 62 H1241
POL/PAR SWITZERLND

S64
PRELOT M.,"LA INFLUENCIA POLITICA Y ELECTORAL DE LA PRENSA EN LA FRANCIA ACTUAL." EUR+WWI SOCIETY NAT/G POL/PAR PROF/ORG PRESS ATTIT PWR...CONCPT 20. PAGE 128 H2556
EDU/PROP FRANCE

B65
CARTER G.M.,POLITICS IN EUROPE. EUR+WWI FRANCE GERMANY/W UK USSR LAW CONSTN POL/PAR VOL/ASSN PRESS LOBBY PWR...ANTHOL SOC/INTEG EEC. PAGE 27 H0548
GOV/COMP OP/RES ECO/DEV

B65
CENTRAL GAZETTEERS UNIT,THE GAZETTEER OF INDIA (VOL. I). INDIA SOCIETY STRATA PLAN EDU/PROP NAT/LISM ORD/FREE WEALTH...GEOG LING CHARTS SOC/INTEG 20. PAGE 28 H0568
PRESS CULTURE SECT STRUCT

B65
GAJENDRAGADKAR P.B.,LAW, LIBERTY AND SOCIAL JUSTICE. INDIA CONSTN NAT/G SECT PLAN ECO/TAC PRESS POPULISM...SOC METH/COMP 20 HINDU. PAGE 54 H1086
ORD/FREE LAW ADJUD JURID

B65
MCSHERRY J.E.,RUSSIA AND THE UNITED STATES UNDER EISENHOWER, KHRUSHCHEV, AND KENNEDY. USSR EX/STRUC TOP/EX PRESS WAR...POLICY TREND 20. PAGE 108 H2150
DIPLOM CHIEF NAT/G PEACE

B65
POBEDONOSTSEV K.P.,REFLECTIONS OF A RUSSIAN STATESMAN. RUSSIA LAW ELITES EDU/PROP PRESS ADJUD MARRIAGE ATTIT PWR...MAJORIT TRADIT 19 CHURCH/STA. PAGE 127 H2531
TOTALISM POLICY CONSTN NAT/G

B66
BERELSON B.,READER IN PUBLIC OPINION AND COMMUNICATION (2ND ED.). UNIV NAT/G PRESS GP/REL PERS/REL PERCEPT RIGID/FLEX...MAJORIT QUANT METH/COMP ANTHOL BIBLIOG 20. PAGE 15 H0298
EDU/PROP ATTIT CONCPT COM/IND

B66
BRAIBANTI R.,RESEARCH ON THE BUREAUCRACY OF PAKISTAN. PAKISTAN LAW CULTURE INTELL ACADEM LOC/G SECT PRESS CT/SYS...LING CHARTS 20 BUREAUCRCY. PAGE 20 H0402
HABITAT NAT/G ADMIN CONSTN

B66
FINER S.E.,ANONYMOUS EMPIRE: STUDY OF THE LOBBY IN GREAT BRITAIN. UK CONSTN LABOR POL/PAR SECT DOMIN EDU/PROP PRESS CHOOSE...CONCPT CHARTS 20 PARLIAMENT. PAGE 50 H1004
LOBBY NAT/G LEGIS PWR

B66
MAICHEL K.,CATALOG OF SOVIET AND RUSSIAN NEWSPAPERS AT THE HOOVER INSTITUTION OF WAR, REVOLUTION AND PEACE. USSR NAT/G EDU/PROP LEAD REV WAR PEACE ATTIT 19/20. PAGE 101 H2017
BIBLIOG/A PRESS COM MARXISM

B66
SWEET E.C.,CIVIL LIBERTIES IN AMERICA. LAW CONSTN NAT/G PRESS CT/SYS DISCRIM ATTIT WORSHIP 20 CIVIL/LIB. PAGE 151 H3018
ADJUD ORD/FREE SUFF COERCE

C66
WINT G.,"ASIA: A HANDBOOK." ASIA S/ASIA INDUS LABOR SECT PRESS RACE/REL MARXISM...STAT CHARTS BIBLIOG 20. PAGE 169 H3388
ECO/UNDEV DIPLOM NAT/G SOCIETY

B67
BUNN R.F.,POLITICS AND CIVIL LIBERTIES IN EUROPE: FOUR CASE STUDIES. FRANCE GERMANY/W UK USSR NAT/G PRESS CRIME CROWD PRIVIL ATTIT 20. PAGE 24 H0476
ORD/FREE CONSTN NAT/COMP LAW

B67
MICKIEWICZ E.P.,SOVIET POLITICAL SCHOOLS: THE COMMUNIST PARTY ADULT INSTRUCTION SYSTEM. COM USSR INTELL SCHOOL WORKER CREATE PRESS ADMIN CONTROL ATTIT KNOWL...PROG/TEAC SOC/INTEG 20 COM/PARTY. PAGE 110 H2200
NAT/G EDU/PROP AGE/A MARXISM

B67
POLSKY N.,HUSTLERS, BEATS, AND OTHERS. FACE/GP PRESS CRIME ADJUST ANOMIE DRIVE WEALTH...PSY SOC 20. PAGE 127 H2540
CULTURE CRIMLGY NEW/IDEA STRUCT

B67
TOMPKINS S.R.,THE TRIUMPH OF BOLSHEVISM: REVOLUTION OR REACTION? USSR WORKER PRESS WEALTH MARXISM POPULISM...BIOG TREND IDEA/COMP BIBLIOG 19/20 LENIN/VI. PAGE 156 H3113
REV NAT/G POL/PAR NAT/LISM

S67
FINLAY D.J.,"THE GHANA COUP...ONE YEAR LATER." GHANA FORCES FOR/AID PRESS CONTROL CIVMIL/REL NAT/LISM AUTHORIT PWR...PREDICT 20. PAGE 50 H1005
REV NAT/G ATTIT ECO/UNDEV

S67
FRANCIS M.J.,"THE US PRESS AND CASTRO: A STUDY IN DECLINING RELATIONS." COM DIPLOM WAR TOTALISM ATTIT SOCISM...POLICY IDEA/COMP 20. PAGE 52 H1046
PRESS LEAD REV NAT/G

S67
LANE J.P.,"FUNCTIONS OF MASS MEDIA IN BRAZIL'S 1964 CRISIS." BRAZIL NAT/G FORCES TOP/EX PRESS TV ATTIT PWR...METH/CNCPT 20. PAGE 90 H1807
CIVMIL/REL REV COM/IND EDU/PROP

S67
READ J.S.,"CENSORED." UGANDA CONSTN INTELL SOCIETY NAT/G DIPLOM PRESS WRITING ADJUD ADMIN COLONIAL RISK...IDEA/COMP 20. PAGE 130 H2602
EDU/PROP AFR CREATE

S67
RIESMAN D.,"SOME QUESTIONS ABOUT THE STUDY OF AMERICAN CHARACTER IN THE TWENTIETH CENTURY." STRATA PRESS PERSON RIGID/FLEX SOC. PAGE 131 H2628
CULTURE ATTIT DRIVE GEN/LAWS

S67
RUCKER B.W.,"WHAT SOLUTIONS DO PEOPLE ENDORSE IN FREE PRESS-FAIR TRIAL DILEMMA?" LAW NAT/G CT/SYS ATTIT...NET/THEORY SAMP CHARTS IDEA/COMP METH 20. PAGE 136 H2710
CONCPT PRESS ADJUD ORD/FREE

S68
SHAPIRO J.P.,"SOVIET HISTORIOGRAPHY AND THE MOSCOW TRIALS: AFTER THIRTY YEARS." USSR NAT/G LEGIT PRESS CONTROL LEAD ATTIT MARXISM...NEW/IDEA METH 20 TROTSKY/L STALIN/J KHRUSH/N. PAGE 142 H2843
HIST/WRIT EDU/PROP SANCTION ADJUD

PRESSE UNIVERSITAIRES H2557

PRESSURE GROUPS....SEE LOBBY

PRESTHUS R.V. H2558

PREVITE-ORTON C.W. H2559

PRICE A.G. H2560

PRICE D.K. H2561

PRICE F.W. H1863

PRICE CONTROL....SEE PRICE, COST, PLAN, RATION

PRICE....SEE ALSO COST

B17
VEBLEN T.B.,AN INQUIRY INTO THE NATURE OF PEACE AND THE TERMS OF ITS PERPETUATION. UNIV STRATA FINAN EDU/PROP PRICE COST DISCRIM NAT/LISM MORAL ORD/FREE PACIFIST 20 WORLDUNITY. PAGE 162 H3237
PEACE DIPLOM WAR NAT/G

B20
MALTHUS T.R.,PRINCIPLES OF POLITICAL ECONOMY. UK AGRI INDUS MARKET NAT/G DIPLOM PRICE CONTROL BAL/PAY COST OWN PWR LAISSEZ 18/19. PAGE 102 H2034
GEN/LAWS DEMAND WEALTH

B38
LAWLEY F.E.,THE GROWTH OF COLLECTIVE ECONOMY VOL. 1: NATIONAL. EUR+WWI AGRI INDUS NAT/G BARGAIN CAP/ISM ECO/TAC WAR OPTIMAL WEALTH...GOV/COMP METH/COMP 19/20 MONOPOLY. PAGE 92 H1844 SOCISM PRICE CONTROL OWN

C54
BERLE A.A. JR.,"THE 20TH CENTURY CAPITALIST REVOLUTION." ECO/DEV NAT/G DIPLOM PRICE CONTROL ATTIT...BIBLIOG/A 20. PAGE 15 H0306 LG/CO CAP/ISM MGT PWR

B55
UN ECONOMIC COMN ASIA & FAR E,ECONOMIC SURVEY OF ASIA AND THE FAR EAST, 1954. AFGHANISTN CEYLON INDIA PHILIPPINE S/ASIA ECO/DEV FINAN INDUS INT/TRADE PRODUC WEALTH...STAT CHARTS 20 CHINJAP. PAGE 158 H3158 ECO/UNDEV PRICE NAT/COMP ASIA

B57
NEUMARK S.D.,ECONOMIC INFLUENCES ON THE SOUTH AFRICAN FRONTIER, 1652-1836. SOUTH/AFR SEA AGRI NAT/G FORCES WORKER DIPLOM INT/TRADE PRICE DEMAND PRODUC...STAT CHARTS 17/19 FRONTIER. PAGE 117 H2341 COLONIAL ECO/UNDEV ECO/TAC MARKET

B58
AVRAMOVIC D.,POSTWAR GROWTH IN INTERNATIONAL INDEBTEDNESS. WOR+45 AGRI INDUS CAP/ISM PRICE INCOME...NAT/COMP 20 GOLD/STAND SILVER. PAGE 9 H0184 INT/TRADE FINAN COST BAL/PAY

B60
BOMBACH G.,STABILE PREISE IN WACHSENDER WIRTSCHAFT: DAS INFLATIONSPROBLEM. BARGAIN CAP/ISM PRICE COST ...NAT/COMP 20 GOLD/STAND. PAGE 19 H0371 ECO/UNDEV PLAN FINAN ECO/TAC

B60
KENEN P.B.,BRITISH MONETARY POLICY AND THE BALANCE OF PAYMENTS 1951-57. UK PLAN BUDGET ECO/TAC INT/TRADE PAY PRICE COST ATTIT 20. PAGE 84 H1687 BAL/PAY PROB/SOLV FINAN NAT/G

B60
ROBERTSON D.,THE CONTROL OF INDUSTRY. UK MARKET LABOR WORKER PRICE CONTROL GP/REL COST DEMAND ORD/FREE WEALTH NEW/LIB SOCISM 20. PAGE 132 H2646 INDUS FINAN NAT/G ECO/DEV

B61
BREWIS T.N.,CANADIAN ECONOMIC POLICY. CANADA BUDGET CAP/ISM INT/TRADE RATION TARIFFS TAX PRICE CONTROL ROUTINE FEDERAL INCOME PRODUC 20 GOLD/STAND. PAGE 20 H0412 ECO/DEV ECO/TAC NAT/G PLAN

B61
HAUSER M.,DIE URSACHEN DER FRANZOSISCHEN INFLATION IN DEN JAHREN 1946-1952. FRANCE INDUS NAT/G BUDGET DIPLOM ECO/TAC FOR/AID COST MONEY 20 GOLD/STAND. PAGE 68 H1357 ECO/DEV FINAN PRICE

B61
NOVE A.,THE SOVIET ECONOMY. USSR ECO/DEV FINAN NAT/G ECO/TAC PRICE ADMIN EFFICIENCY MARXISM ...TREND BIBLIOG 20. PAGE 119 H2378 PLAN PRODUC POLICY

B61
SHARMA T.R.,THE WORKING OF STATE ENTERPRISES IN INDIA. INDIA DELIB/GP LEGIS WORKER BUDGET PRICE CONTROL GP/REL OWN ATTIT...MGT CHARTS 20. PAGE 142 H2851 NAT/G INDUS ADMIN SOCISM

B62
GALENSON W.,LABOR IN DEVELOPING COUNTRIES. BRAZIL INDONESIA ISRAEL PAKISTAN TURKEY AGRI INDUS WORKER PAY PRICE GP/REL WEALTH...MGT CHARTS METH/COMP NAT/COMP 20. PAGE 54 H1088 LABOR ECO/UNDEV BARGAIN POL/PAR

B62
MICHAELY M.,CONCENTRATION IN INTERNATIONAL TRADE. ECO/DEV ECO/UNDEV PRICE INCOME...CHARTS NAT/COMP 20. PAGE 110 H2197 INT/TRADE MARKET FINAN GEOG

B63
AHN L.A.,FUNFZIG JAHRE ZWISCHEN INFLATION UND DEFLATION. GERMANY DIPLOM PRICE...CONCPT 20 GOLD/STAND. PAGE 4 H0081 FINAN CAP/ISM NAT/COMP ECO/TAC

B63
BANERJI A.K.,INDIA'S BALANCE OF PAYMENTS. INDIA NAT/G PRICE BAL/PAY COST INCOME 20. PAGE 10 H0208 INT/TRADE DIPLOM FINAN BUDGET

B63
GUIMARAES A.P.,INFLACAO E MONOPOLIO NO BRASIL. BRAZIL FINAN NAT/G PLAN PAY...METH/COMP 20. PAGE 62 H1248 ECO/UNDEV PRICE INT/TRADE BAL/PAY

B63
SELF P.,THE STATE AND THE FARMER. UK ECO/DEV MARKET WORKER PRICE CONTROL GP/REL...WELF/ST 20 DEPT/AGRI. PAGE 141 H2823 AGRI NAT/G ADMIN VOL/ASSN

B63
STIFEL L.D.,THE TEXTILE INDUSTRY - A CASE STUDY OF INDUSTRIAL DEVELOPMENT IN THE PHILIPPINES (PAPER). PHILIPPINE WORKER CAP/ISM INT/TRADE TARIFFS RECEIVE PRICE ADMIN COST EFFICIENCY WEALTH...BIBLIOG 20. PAGE 149 H2986 S/ASIA ECO/UNDEV PROC/MFG NAT/G

N63
LEDERER W.,THE BALANCE ON FOREIGN TRANSACTIONS: PROBLEMS OF DEFINITION AND MEASUREMENT (PAMPHLET). USA+45 BUDGET DIPLOM ECO/TAC PRICE GOV/REL...POLICY STAT NAT/COMP METH 20. PAGE 93 H1853 FINAN BAL/PAY INT/TRADE ECO/DEV

B64
BROWN W.M.,THE EXTERNAL LIQUIDITY OF AN ADVANCED COUNTRY. CANADA FRANCE GERMANY/W SWEDEN UK USA+45 ECO/DEV DIPLOM PRICE...CONCPT STAT NAT/COMP 20. PAGE 22 H0451 FINAN INT/TRADE COST INCOME

B64
PINNICK A.W.,COUNTRY PLANNERS IN ACTION. UK FINAN SERV/IND NAT/G CONSULT DELIB/GP PRICE CONTROL ROUTINE LEISURE AGE/C...GEOG 20 URBAN/RNWL. PAGE 126 H2512 MUNIC PLAN INDUS ATTIT

B64
SANDEE J.,EUROPE'S FUTURE CONSUMPTION. EUR+WWI FUT EDU/PROP...IDEA/COMP NAT/COMP ANTHOL 20 EUROPE. PAGE 137 H2750 MARKET ECO/DEV PREDICT PRICE

B64
URQUIDI V.L.,THE CHALLENGE OF DEVELOPMENT IN LATIN AMERICA. L/A+17C FINAN INT/ORG TEC/DEV DIPLOM INT/TRADE PRICE REGION PRODUC...CHARTS 20. PAGE 159 H3175 ECO/UNDEV ECO/TAC NAT/G TREND

B65
ALTON T.P.,POLISH NATIONAL INCOME AND PRODUCT IN 1954, 1955, AND 1956. POLAND FINAN EX/STRUC ECO/TAC PRICE COST WEALTH 20. PAGE 6 H0117 COM INDUS NAT/G ECO/DEV

B65
CHAO K.,THE RATE AND PATTERN OF INDUSTRIAL GROWTH IN COMMUNIST CHINA. CHINA/COM ECO/UNDEV TEC/DEV PRICE...NAT/COMP BIBLIOG 20. PAGE 29 H0578 INDUS INDEX STAT PRODUC

B65
EDELMAN M.,THE POLITICS OF WAGE-PRICE DECISIONS. GERMANY ITALY NETHERLAND UK INDUS LABOR POL/PAR PROB/SOLV BARGAIN PRICE ROUTINE BAL/PAY COST DEMAND 20. PAGE 44 H0888 GOV/COMP CONTROL ECO/TAC PLAN

B65
HAEFELE E.T.,GOVERNMENT CONTROLS ON TRANSPORT. AFR RHODESIA TANZANIA DIPLOM ECO/TAC TARIFFS PRICE ADJUD CONTROL REGION EFFICIENCY...POLICY 20 CONGO. PAGE 64 H1274 ECO/UNDEV DIST/IND FINAN NAT/G

B65
TEW B.,WEALTH AND INCOME. UK BUDGET INT/TRADE PRICE BAL/PAY DEMAND...CHARTS GOV/COMP 20 AUSTRAL. PAGE 153 H3064 FINAN ECO/DEV WEALTH INCOME

B65
YOUNG A.N.,CHINA'S WARTIME FINANCE AND INFLATION. ASIA AGRI INDUS NAT/G ECO/TAC CONFER PRICE WAR COST 20. PAGE 172 H3437 FINAN FOR/AID TAX BUDGET

B66
NAMBOODIRIPAD E.M.,ECONOMICS AND POLITICS OF INDIA'S SOCIALIST PATTERN. INDIA STRATA AGRI INDUS NAT/G PRICE ORD/FREE SOVEREIGN 20. PAGE 115 H2307 ECO/UNDEV PLAN SOCISM CAP/ISM

B66
ROSS A.M.,INDUSTRIAL RELATIONS AND ECONOMIC DEVELOPMENT. POL/PAR LEGIS WORKER BARGAIN PRICE EXEC LOBBY INCOME PWR...DECISION ANTHOL BIBLIOG 20. PAGE 134 H2686 ECO/UNDEV LABOR NAT/G GP/REL

B67
DENISON E.F.,WHY GROWTH RATES DIFFER; POSTWAR EXPERIENCE IN NINE WESTERN COUNTRIES. WOR+45 FINAN WORKER TEC/DEV EDU/PROP PRICE PRODUC WEALTH ...ECOMETRIC STAT CHARTS BIBLIOG. PAGE 40 H0791 METH NAT/COMP ECO/DEV ECO/TAC

B67
RUEFF J.,BALANCE OF PAYMENTS. WOR+45 FINAN TEC/DEV DIPLOM TARIFFS PRICE CONTROL...POLICY CONCPT IDEA/COMP. PAGE 136 H2715 INT/TRADE BAL/PAY ECO/TAC NAT/COMP

L67
KELLEHER G.W.,"THE COMMON MARKET ANTITRUST LAWS: THE FIRST TEN YEARS." EUR+WWI INDUS PRICE ADJUD AGREE CONTROL PROFIT...POLICY 20 EEC. PAGE 84 H1684 INT/ORG INT/TRADE MARKET NAT/G

S67
BELLER I.,"ECONOMIC POLICY AND THE DEMANDS OF LABOR." PLAN TAX GIVE PRICE WAR COST PRODUC WEALTH. PAGE 13 H0268 NAT/G ECO/TAC SOC/WK INCOME

S67
MARWICK A.,"THE LABOUR PARTY AND THE WELFARE STATE IN BRITAIN, 19001948." UK SOCIETY STRUCT ECO/DEV WORKER CREATE PRICE CHOOSE WEALTH NEW/LIB SOCISM ...POLICY HEAL 20 PARLIAMENT LABOR/PAR. PAGE 104 H2074 POL/PAR RECEIVE LEGIS NAT/G

B95
SELIGMAN E.R.A.,ESSAYS IN TAXATION. NEW/ZEALND PRUSSIA UK USA-45 MARKET LOC/G CREATE PRICE CONTROL INCOME OWN WEALTH...GOV/COMP METH/COMP 19. PAGE 141 H2824 TAX TARIFFS INDUS NAT/G

PRICING....SEE PRICE, ECO

PRIESTLEY F.E.L. H1151

PRIMARIES....ELECTORAL PRIMARIES

PRIME/MIN....PRIME MINISTER

PRINCETN/U....PRINCETON UNIVERSITY

PRISON....PRISONS; SEE ALSO PUB/INST

PRIVACY....PRIVACY AND ITS INVASION

PRIVIL....PRIVILEGED, AS CONDITION

B10
MCILWAIN C.H.,THE HIGH COURT OF PARLIAMENT AND ITS SUPREMACY B1910 1878 408. UK EX/STRUC PARL/PROC GOV/REL INGP/REL PRIVIL 12/20 PARLIAMENT ENGLSH/LAW. PAGE 107 H2132
LAW LEGIS CONSTN NAT/G

N19
ADMINISTRATIVE STAFF COLLEGE,THE ACCOUNTABILITY OF GOVERNMENT DEPARTMENTS (PAMPHLET) (REV. ED.). UK CONSTN FINAN NAT/G CONSULT ADMIN INGP/REL CONSEN PRIVIL 20 PARLIAMENT. PAGE 3 H0070
PARL/PROC ELITES SANCTION PROB/SOLV

B26
POLLARD A.F.,THE EVOLUTION OF PARLIAMENT. UK CONSTN POL/PAR EX/STRUC GOV/REL INGP/REL PRIVIL RIGID/FLEX ...TIME/SEQ 11/20 CMN/WLTH PARLIAMENT. PAGE 127 H2536
LEGIS PARL/PROC NAT/G

B30
OLDMAN J.H.,WHITE AND BLACK IN AFRICA. AFR STRUCT COLONIAL PARTIC DISCRIM ISOLAT PRIVIL 20 SMUTS/JAN NEGRO WHITE/SUP. PAGE 121 H2412
SOVEREIGN ORD/FREE RACE/REL NAT/G

B39
MCILWAIN C.H.,CONSTITUTIONALISM AND THE CHANGING WORLD. UK USA-45 LEGIS PRIVIL AUTHORIT SOVEREIGN ...GOV/COMP 15/20 MAGNA/CART HOUSE/CMNS. PAGE 107 H2133
CONSTN POLICY JURID

B41
GILMORE M.P.,ARGUMENT FROM ROMAN LAW IN POLITICAL THOUGHT, 1200-1600. INTELL LICENSE CONTROL CT/SYS GOV/REL PRIVIL PWR...IDEA/COMP BIBLIOG 13/16. PAGE 56 H1130
JURID LAW CONCPT NAT/G

C43
BENTHAM J.,"ON THE LIBERTY OF THE PRESS, AND PUBLIC DISCUSSION" IN J. BOWRING, ED., THE WORKS OF JEREMY BENTHAM." SPAIN UK LAW ELITES NAT/G LEGIS INSPECT LEGIT WRITING CONTROL PRIVIL TOTALISM AUTHORIT ...TRADIT 19 FREE/SPEE. PAGE 15 H0290
ORD/FREE PRESS CONFER CONSERVE

B55
SVARLIEN O.,AN INTRODUCTION TO THE LAW OF NATIONS. SEA AIR INT/ORG NAT/G CHIEF ADMIN AGREE WAR PRIVIL ORD/FREE SOVEREIGN...BIBLIOG 16/20. PAGE 151 H3012
INT/LAW DIPLOM

C57
MORRIS-JONES W.H.,"PARLIAMENT IN INDIA." INDIA CONSTN LEGIS CONFER COLONIAL CHOOSE PRIVIL ATTIT ...GOV/COMP BIBLIOG 20. PAGE 113 H2264
PARL/PROC EX/STRUC NAT/G POL/PAR

C58
WILDING N.,"AN ENCYCLOPEDIA OF PARLIAMENT." UK LAW CONSTN CHIEF PROB/SOLV DIPLOM DEBATE WAR INGP/REL PRIVIL...BIBLIOG DICTIONARY 13/20 CMN/WLTH PARLIAMENT. PAGE 168 H3363
PARL/PROC POL/PAR NAT/G ADMIN

B61
ALSTON P.L.,STATE EDUCATION AND SOCIAL CHANGE IN THE RUSSIAN EMPIRE 1871-1914 (PAPER). RUSSIA ELITES PROF/ORG EDU/PROP CONTROL PRIVIL AGE/Y...BIBLIOG 19/20. PAGE 6 H0115
SCHOOL SOCIETY NAT/G GP/REL

B64
AVASTHI A.,ASPECTS OF ADMINISTRATION. INDIA UK USA+45 FINAN ACADEM DELIB/GP LEGIS RECEIVE PARL/PROC PRIVIL...NAT/COMP 20. PAGE 9 H0183
MGT ADMIN SOC/WK ORD/FREE

B65
BROWNSON O.A.,THE AMERICAN REPUBLIC. NAT/G PROVS WAR GOV/REL PRIVIL ORD/FREE PWR ALL/IDEOS CONSERVE ...CONCPT 19 CIVIL/WAR. PAGE 22 H0452
CONSTN FEDERAL SOVEREIGN

B65
PYLEE M.V.,CONSTITUTIONAL GOVERNMENT IN INDIA (2ND REV. ED.). INDIA POL/PAR EX/STRUC DIPLOM COLONIAL CT/SYS PARL/PROC PRIVIL...JURID 16/20. PAGE 128 H2569
CONSTN NAT/G PROVS FEDERAL

B66
DOUMA J.,BIBLIOGRAPHY ON THE INTERNATIONAL COURT INCLUDING THE PERMANENT COURT, 1918-1964. WOR+45 WOR-45 DELIB/GP WAR PRIVIL...JURID NAT/COMP 20 UN LEAGUE/NAT. PAGE 42 H0844
BIBLIOG/A INT/ORG CT/SYS DIPLOM

B66
HINTON W.,FANSHEN: A DOCUMENTARY OF REVOLUTION IN A CHINESE VILLAGE. ASIA ELITES MUNIC NAT/G POL/PAR SECT WORKER LEAD WAR PRIVIL PWR 20 MAO. PAGE 71 H1422
MARXISM REV NEIGH OWN

B66
LENSKI G.E.,POWER AND PRIVILEGE: A THEORY OF SOCIAL STRATIFICATION. SWEDEN UK UNIV USSR CULTURE ECO/UNDEV PRIVIL PWR...PHIL/SCI CONCPT CHARTS IDEA/COMP HYPO/EXP METH MARX/KARL. PAGE 94 H1882
SOC STRATA STRUCT SOCIETY

B67
BUNN R.F.,POLITICS AND CIVIL LIBERTIES IN EUROPE: FOUR CASE STUDIES. FRANCE GERMANY/W UK USSR NAT/G PRESS CRIME CROWD PRIVIL ATTIT 20. PAGE 24 H0476
ORD/FREE CONSTN NAT/COMP LAW

S67
AMERASINGHE C.F.,"SOME LEGAL PROBLEMS OF STATE TRADING IN SOUTHEAST ASIA." PROB/SOLV ADJUD CONTROL CT/SYS GP/REL 20. PAGE 6 H0120
INT/TRADE NAT/G INT/LAW PRIVIL

S67
SCOVILLE W.J.,"GOVERNMENT REGULATION AND GROWTH IN THE FRENCH PAPER INDUSTRY DURING THE EIGHTEENTH CENTURY." FRANCE MOD/EUR FINAN CAP/ISM TAX ADMIN CONTROL PRIVIL LAISSEZ...POLICY 18. PAGE 141 H2818
NAT/G PROC/MFG ECO/DEV INGP/REL

S67
SNELLEN I.T.,"APARTHEID* CHECKS AND CHANGES." SOUTH/AFR NAT/G PROB/SOLV COLONIAL REGION TASK GP/REL RACE/REL EFFICIENCY PRIVIL ORD/FREE 20. PAGE 146 H2923
DISCRIM NAT/LISM EQUILIB CONTROL

S67
SUBRAMANIAM V.,"REPRESENTATIVE BUREAUCRACY: A REASSESSMENT." USA+45 ELITES LOC/G NAT/G ADMIN GOV/REL PRIVIL DRIVE ROLE...POLICY CENSUS 20 CIVIL/SERV BUREAUCRCY. PAGE 150 H3006
STRATA GP/REL MGT GOV/COMP

B85
BLISS P.,OF SOVEREIGNTY. NAT/G PROVS GOV/REL PRIVIL ORD/FREE PWR CONSERVE...CONCPT 19. PAGE 18 H0356
CONSTN SOVEREIGN FEDERAL

PRIVILEGE....SEE PRIVIL

PROB/SOLV....PROBLEM SOLVING

N
BULLETIN ANALYTIQUE DE DOCUMENTATION POLITIQUE, ECONOMIQUE, ET SOCIAL CONTEMPORAIRE. FRANCE WOR+45 SOCIETY ECO/DEV ECO/UNDEV INT/ORG LOC/G PROB/SOLV FOR/AID LEAD REGION SOC. PAGE 1 H0002
BIBLIOG/A DIPLOM NAT/COMP NAT/G

N
NEUE POLITISCHE LITERATUR. AFR ASIA EUR+WWI GERMANY RUSSIA SOCIETY ECO/DEV ECO/UNDEV PLAN PROB/SOLV LEAD MARXISM...PHIL/SCI CONCPT 20. PAGE 1 H0008
BIBLIOG DIPLOM COM NAT/G

N
PUBLISHERS' CIRCULAR, THE OFFICIAL ORGAN OF THE PUBLISHERS' ASSOCIATION OF GREAT BRITAIN AND IRELAND. EUR+WWI MOD/EUR UK LAW PROB/SOLV DIPLOM COLONIAL ATTIT...HUM 19/20 CMN/WLTH. PAGE 1 H0019
BIBLIOG NAT/G WRITING LEAD

N
US LIBRARY OF CONGRESS,ACCESSIONS LIST - INDIA. INDIA CULTURE AGRI LOC/G POL/PAR PLAN PROB/SOLV TEC/DEV DIPLOM EDU/PROP LEAD GP/REL ATTIT 20. PAGE 160 H3199
BIBLIOG S/ASIA ECO/UNDEV NAT/G

N
US LIBRARY OF CONGRESS,ACCESSIONS LIST -- ISRAEL. ISRAEL CULTURE ECO/UNDEV POL/PAR PLAN PROB/SOLV TEC/DEV DIPLOM EDU/PROP LEAD WAR ATTIT 20 JEWS. PAGE 160 H3200
BIBLIOG ISLAM NAT/G GP/REL

B01
BRYCE J.,STUDIES IN HISTORY AND JURISPRUDENCE (2 VOLS.). ICELAND SOUTH/AFR UK LAW PROB/SOLV SOVEREIGN...PHIL/SCI NAT/COMP ROME/ANC ROMAN/LAW. PAGE 23 H0455
IDEA/COMP CONSTN JURID

C09
SCHAPIRO J.S.,"SOCIAL REFORM AND THE REFORMATION." CHRIST-17C GERMANY LAW CONSTN LG/CO NAT/G WORKER PROB/SOLV CT/SYS REV...BIBLIOG 16. PAGE 138 H2770
ORD/FREE SECT ECO/TAC BIOG

N19
ADMINISTRATIVE STAFF COLLEGE,THE ACCOUNTABILITY OF GOVERNMENT DEPARTMENTS (PAMPHLET) (REV. ED.). UK CONSTN FINAN NAT/G CONSULT ADMIN INGP/REL CONSEN PRIVIL 20 PARLIAMENT. PAGE 3 H0070
PARL/PROC ELITES SANCTION PROB/SOLV

N19
ANDERSON J.,THE ORGANIZATION OF ECONOMIC STUDIES IN RELATION TO THE PROBLEMS OF GOVERNMENT (PAMPHLET). UK FINAN INDUS DELIB/GP PLAN PROB/SOLV ADMIN 20. PAGE 6 H0128
ECO/TAC ACT/RES NAT/G CENTRAL

N19
HACKETT J.,ECONOMIC PLANNING IN FRANCE; ITS RELATION TO THE POLICIES OF THE DEVELOPED COUNTRIES OF WESTERN EUROPE (PAMPHLET). EUR+WWI FRANCE ECO/DEV PROB/SOLV CONTROL...POLICY 20 EUROPE/W. PAGE 63 H1270
ECO/TAC NAT/G PLAN INSPECT

N19
INTERNATIONAL LABOUR OFFICE,EMPLOYMENT, UNEMPLOYMENT AND LABOUR FORCE STATISTICS (PAMPHLET). EUR+WWI STRATA AGRI INDUS NAT/G PROB/SOLV PAY AGE SEX...SAMP NAT/COMP METH 20 ILO. PAGE 78 H1557
WORKER LABOR STAT ECO/DEV

N19
SOUTH AFRICA COMMISSION ON FUT,INTERIM AND FINAL REPORTS ON FUTURE FORM OF GOVERNMENT IN THE SOUTH-WEST AFRICAN PROTECTORATE (PAMPHLET). SOUTH/AFR NAT/G FORCES CONFER COLONIAL CONTROL 20 AFRICA/SW. PAGE 147 H2936
CONSTN REPRESENT ADMIN PROB/SOLV

B26
FORTESCUE J.,THE GOVERNANCE OF ENGLAND (1471-76). UK LAW FINAN SECT LEGIS PROB/SOLV TAX DOMIN ADMIN GP/REL COST ORD/FREE PWR 14/15. PAGE 52 H1042
CONSERVE CONSTN CHIEF NAT/G

B29
STURZO L.,THE INTERNATIONAL COMMUNITY AND THE RIGHT OF WAR (TRANS. BY BARBARA BARCLAY CARTER). CULTURE CREATE PROB/SOLV DIPLOM ADJUD CONTROL PEACE PERSON ORD/FREE...INT/LAW IDEA/COMP PACIFIST 20 LEAGUE/NAT. PAGE 150 H3003
INT/ORG PLAN WAR CONCPT

B30
CANAWAY A.P.,THE FAILURE OF FEDERALISM IN AUSTRALIA. UK PROB/SOLV ADMIN EFFICIENCY ATTIT ...POLICY NAT/COMP 20 AUSTRAL. PAGE 26 H0518
FEDERAL NAT/G CONSTN OP/RES

B30
SMUTS J.C.,AFRICA AND SOME WORLD PROBLEMS. RHODESIA SOUTH/AFR CULTURE ECO/UNDEV INDUS INT/ORG SECT PROB/SOLV REGION GOV/REL DISCRIM ATTIT 19/20 LEAGUE/NAT LIVNGSTN/D NEGRO. PAGE 146 H2921
LEGIS AFR COLONIAL RACE/REL

B31
CROOK W.H.,THE GENERAL STRIKE: A STUDY OF LABOR'S TRAGIC WEAPON IN THEORY AND PRACTICE. BELGIUM FRANCE SWEDEN UK WOR-45 PROB/SOLV ECO/TAC DOMIN PWR ...POLICY TIME/SEQ NAT/COMP GEN/LAWS 19/20 STRIKE. PAGE 35 H0707
LABOR WORKER LG/CO BARGAIN

B31
LORWIN L.L.,ADVISORY ECONOMIC COUNCILS. EUR+WWI FRANCE GERMANY PROB/SOLV INGP/REL...CLASSIF GP/COMP. PAGE 99 H1968
CONSULT DELIB/GP ECO/TAC NAT/G

B33
BERDYAYEV N.,CHRISTIANITY AND CLASS WAR. UNIV SOCIETY WORKER CREATE PROB/SOLV ATTIT PERSON ORD/FREE...CONCPT CHRISTIAN. PAGE 15 H0296
SECT MARXISM STRATA GP/REL

B33
ENSOR R.C.K.,COURTS AND JUDGES IN FRANCE, GERMANY, AND ENGLAND. FRANCE GERMANY UK LAW PROB/SOLV ADMIN ROUTINE CRIME ROLE...METH/COMP 20 CIVIL/LAW. PAGE 46 H0930
CT/SYS EX/STRUC ADJUD NAT/COMP

B33
FERRERO G.,PEACE AND WAR (TRANS. BY BERTHA PRITCHARD). CULTURE FINAN SECT ATTIT SUPEGO MORAL ORD/FREE CONSERVE POPULISM SOCISM POLICY. PAGE 49 H0987
WAR PEACE DIPLOM PROB/SOLV

B35
RAM J.,THE SCIENCE OF LEGAL JUDGMENT: A TREATISE... UK CONSTN NAT/G LEGIS CREATE PROB/SOLV AGREE CT/SYS ...INT/LAW CONCPT 19 ENGLSH/LAW CANON/LAW CIVIL/LAW CTS/WESTM. PAGE 129 H2584
LAW JURID EX/STRUC ADJUD

B36
BATTAGLIA F.,LINEAMENTI DI STORIA DELLE DOCTRINE POLITICHE CON APPENDICI BIBLIOGRAFICHE. ITALY PROB/SOLV LEAD 20. PAGE 12 H0237
BIBLIOG PHIL/SCI CONCPT NAT/G

B36
BELLOC H.,THE RESTORATION OF PROPERTY. UK STRATA NAT/G PROF/ORG DELIB/GP WORKER CREATE PROB/SOLV ECO/TAC PARTIC UTOPIA ORD/FREE SOCISM 20. PAGE 13 H0270
CONTROL MAJORIT CAP/ISM OWN

B36
PREVITE-ORTON C.W.,THE CAMBRIDGE MEDIEVAL HISTORY (8 VOLS.). CHRIST-17C NAT/G PROB/SOLV TEC/DEV LEAD ...POLICY CONCPT WORSHIP. PAGE 128 H2559
BIBLIOG IDEA/COMP TREND

B37
VON HAYEK F.A.,MONETARY NATIONALISM AND INTERNATIONAL STABILITY. WOR-45 ECO/DEV NAT/G PROB/SOLV INT/TRADE...POLICY CONCPT METH/COMP NAT/COMP 20. PAGE 163 H3271
ECO/TAC FINAN DIPLOM NAT/LISM

B38
DAVIES E.,"NATIONAL" CAPITALISM: THE GOVERNMENT'S RECORD AS PROTECTOR OF PRIVATE MONOPOLY. UK ELITES SOCIETY STRATA POL/PAR WORKER PROB/SOLV CONTROL SOCISM 20 MONOPOLY LABOR/PAR CHAMBRLN/N. PAGE 37 H0747
CAP/ISM NAT/G INDUS POLICY

B39
SIEYES E.J.,LES DISCOURS DE SIEYES DANS LES DEBATS CONSTITUTIONNELS DE L'AN III (2 ET 18 THERMIDOR). FRANCE LAW NAT/G PROB/SOLV BAL/PWR GOV/REL 18 JURY. PAGE 144 H2871
CONSTN ADJUD LEGIS EX/STRUC

B40
HERSKOVITS M.J.,THE ECONOMIC LIFE OF PRIMITIVE PEOPLES. INDUS OP/RES PLAN PROB/SOLV...BIBLIOG METH 20. PAGE 70 H1407
CULTURE ECO/TAC ECO/UNDEV PRODUC

B40
MCILWAIN C.H.,CONSTITUTIONALISM, ANCIENT AND MODERN. CHRIST-17C MOD/EUR NAT/G CHIEF PROB/SOLV INSPECT AUTHORIT ORD/FREE PWR...TIME/SEQ ROMAN/REP. PAGE 107 H2134
CONSTN GEN/LAWS LAW

C43
BENTHAM J.,"PRINCIPLES OF INTERNATIONAL LAW" IN J. BOWRING, ED., THE WORKS OF JEREMY BENTHAM." UNIV NAT/G PLAN PROB/SOLV DIPLOM CONTROL SANCTION MORAL ORD/FREE PWR SOVEREIGN 19. PAGE 15 H0291
INT/LAW JURID WAR PEACE

B44
KRIS E.,GERMAN RADIO PROPAGANDA: REPORT ON HOME BROADCASTS DURING THE WAR. EUR+WWI GERMANY CULTURE CONSULT PROB/SOLV FEEDBACK TASK INGP/REL DRIVE PWR FASCISM...CON/ANAL METH/COMP 20. PAGE 89 H1768
EDU/PROP DOMIN ACT/RES ATTIT

B46
DAVIES E.,NATIONAL ENTERPRISE: THE DEVELOPMENT OF THE PUBLIC CORPORATION. UK LG/CO EX/STRUC WORKER PROB/SOLV COST ATTIT SOCISM 20. PAGE 37 H0748
ADMIN NAT/G CONTROL INDUS

L49
BRECHT A.,"THE NEW GERMAN CONSTITUTION." GERMANY/W NAT/G CHIEF EX/STRUC LEGIS PROB/SOLV ADMIN REPRESENT TOTALISM ORD/FREE PLURISM...MAJORIT CHARTS 20. PAGE 20 H0409
CONSTN DIPLOM SOVEREIGN FEDERAL

B52
MONTAGU A.,MAN'S MOST DANGEROUS MYTH: THE FALLACY OF RACE. LAW PROB/SOLV WAR HABITAT POPULISM...PSY CONCPT CHARTS BIBLIOG NEGRO JEWS. PAGE 112 H2242
DISCRIM MYTH CULTURE RACE/REL

B52
US DEPARTMENT OF STATE,RESEARCH ON EASTERN EUROPE (EXCLUDING USSR). EUR+WWI LAW ECO/DEV NAT/G PROB/SOLV DIPLOM ADMIN LEAD MARXISM...TREND 19/20. PAGE 159 H3187
BIBLIOG R+D ACT/RES COM

B53
SQUIRES J.D.,BRITISH PROPAGANDA AT HOME AND IN THE UNITED STATES FROM 1914 TO 1917. UK NAT/G PROB/SOLV DOMIN PRESS EFFICIENCY...PSY PREDICT 20 WWI INTERVENT PSY/WAR. PAGE 148 H2960
EDU/PROP CONTROL WAR DIPLOM

B54
SCHWARTZ B.,FRENCH ADMINISTRATIVE LAW AND THE COMMON-LAW WORLD. FRANCE CULTURE LOC/G NAT/G PROVS DELIB/GP EX/STRUC LEGIS PROB/SOLV CT/SYS EXEC GOV/REL...IDEA/COMP ENGLSH/LAW. PAGE 140 H2808
JURID LAW METH/COMP ADJUD

C54
LANDAU J.M.,"PARLIAMENTS AND PARTIES IN EGYPT." UAR NAT/G SECT CONSULT LEGIS TOP/EX PROB/SOLV ADMIN COLONIAL...GEN/LAWS BIBLIOG 19/20. PAGE 90 H1804
ISLAM NAT/LISM PARL/PROC POL/PAR

B55
FOGARTY M.P.,ECONOMIC CONTROL. FUT UK ECO/DEV FINAN CONSULT INT/TRADE...CHARTS BIBLIOG/A 20. PAGE 52 H1033
ECO/TAC NAT/G CONTROL PROB/SOLV

B55
HELANDER S.,DAS AUTARKIEPROBLEM IN DER WELTWIRTSCHAFT. PROB/SOLV BAL/PWR BARGAIN CAP/ISM ECO/TAC SOVEREIGN 20. PAGE 69 H1388
NAT/COMP COLONIAL DIPLOM

B55
QUAN K.L.,INTRODUCTION TO ASIA: A SELECTIVE GUIDE TO BACKGROUND READING. ECO/UNDEV NAT/G PROB/SOLV DIPLOM ATTIT 20. PAGE 129 H2572
BIBLIOG/A S/ASIA CULTURE ASIA

B55
TAN C.C.,THE BOXER CATASTROPHE. ASIA UK USSR ELITES POL/PAR VOL/ASSN FORCES PROB/SOLV DIPLOM ADMIN COLONIAL NAT/LISM PEACE TREATY 19/20 BOXER/REBL. PAGE 152 H3040
REV NAT/G WAR

B55
THOMPSON V.,MINORITY PROBLEMS IN SOUTHEAST ASIA. CAMBODIA CHINA/COM LAOS S/ASIA KIN NAT/G SECT PROB/SOLV EDU/PROP REGION GP/REL RACE/REL MARXISM ...SOC 20 BUDDHISM UN. PAGE 154 H3085
INGP/REL GEOG DIPLOM STRUCT

S55
GOODENOUGH W.H.,"A PROBLEM IN MALAYO-POLYNESIAN SOCIAL ORGANIZATION" (BMR)" MALAYSIA S/ASIA CULTURE AGRI PROB/SOLV OWN HABITAT...SOC 20 20 POLYNESIA. PAGE 58 H1170
KIN STRUCT FAM ECO/UNDEV

S56
ALMOND G.A.,"COMPARATIVE POLITICAL SYSTEMS" (BMR)" WOR+45 WOR-45 PROB/SOLV DIPLOM EFFICIENCY ...PHIL/SCI SOC METH 17/20. PAGE 5 H0111
GOV/COMP CONCPT ALL/IDEOS NAT/COMP

B57
CONOVER H.F.,NORTH AND NORTHEAST AFRICA; A SELECTED ANNOTATED LIST OF WRITINGS. ALGERIA MOROCCO SUDAN UAR CULTURE INT/ORG PROB/SOLV ADJUD NAT/LISM PWR WEALTH...SOC 20 UN. PAGE 32 H0649
BIBLIOG/A DIPLOM AFR ECO/UNDEV

B57
MENDIETTA Y NUNE L.,THEORIE DES GROUPEMENT SOCIAUX SUIVI D'UNE ETUDE SUR LE DROIT SOCIAL. ELITES FAM KIN NAT/G PROB/SOLV CROWD ISOLAT ATTIT PERSON ...JURID CONCPT SOC/INTEG. PAGE 109 H2174
SOC STRATA STRUCT DISCRIM

B57
PLAYFAIR G.,THE OFFENDERS: THE CASE AGAINST LEGAL VENGEANCE. UNIV LAW SOCIETY NAT/G PROB/SOLV DEATH PERSON ORD/FREE...HEAL INT/LAW BIBLIOG 20 REFORMERS. PAGE 126 H2524
CRIME TEC/DEV SANCTION CT/SYS

S57
DEXTER L.A.,"A SOCIAL THEORY OF MENTAL DEFICIENCY." CULTURE PUB/INST PROB/SOLV CRIME PERS/REL STRANGE PERSON SUPEGO SKILL...EPIST SOC/WK HYPO/EXP. PAGE 41 H0814
SOC PSY HEALTH ROLE

S57
LEWIS E.G.,"PARLIAMENTARY CONTROL OF NATIONALIZED INDUSTRY IN FRANCE." FRANCE NAT/G DELIB/GP ACT/RES PLAN PROB/SOLV ECO/TAC DOMIN CENTRAL. PAGE 96 H1914
PWR LEGIS INDUS CONTROL

B58
ARON R.,SOCIOLOGIE DES SOCIETES INDUSTRIELLES: ESQUISSE D'UNE THEORIE DES REGIMES POLITIQUES. FRANCE SOCIETY NAT/G PROB/SOLV ATTIT RIGID/FLEX MARXISM POPULISM...POLICY SOC T 20 MARX/KARL TOCQUEVILL. PAGE 8 H0170
TOTALISM INDUS CONSTN GOV/COMP

B58
DWARKADAS R.,ROLE OF HIGHER CIVIL SERVICE IN INDIA. INDIA ECO/UNDEV LEGIS PROB/SOLV GP/REL PERS/REL ...POLICY WELF/ST DECISION ORG/CHARTS BIBLIOG 20 CIVIL/SERV INTRVN/ECO. PAGE 44 H0876
ADMIN NAT/G ROLE PLAN

B58
HANCE W.A.,AFRICAN ECONOMIC DEVELOPMENT. AGRI DIST/IND INDUS R+D ACT/RES PLAN CAP/ISM FOR/AID ...GOV/COMP BIBLIOG 20. PAGE 65 H1312
AFR ECO/UNDEV PROB/SOLV TEC/DEV

B58
HANSARD SOCIETY PARL GOVT,WHAT ARE THE PROBLEMS OF PARLIAMENTARY GOVERNMENT IN WEST AFRICA? PROB/SOLV DIPLOM GP/REL 20 PARLIAMENT AFRICA/W. PAGE 66 H1317
PARL/PROC POL/PAR AFR NAT/G

B58
INDIAN COUNCIL WORLD AFFAIRS,DEFENCE AND SECURITY IN THE INDIAN OCEAN AREA. INDIA S/ASIA CULTURE CONSULT DELIB/GP FORCES PROB/SOLV DIPLOM INT/TRADE 20 CMN/WLTH. PAGE 77 H1531
GEOG HABITAT ECO/UNDEV ORD/FREE

B58
JACOBSSON P.,SOME MONETARY PROBLEMS, INTERNATIONAL AND NATIONAL. WOR+45 WOR-45 ECO/DEV FORCES WORKER PROB/SOLV DIPLOM INT/TRADE...ANTHOL 20. PAGE 79 H1580
FINAN PLAN ECO/TAC NAT/COMP

B58
LOWER A.R.M.,EVOLVING CANADIAN FEDERALISM. CANADA WEST/IND CONSTN PROB/SOLV COLONIAL REGION NAT/LISM ...ANTHOL 20. PAGE 99 H1976
FEDERAL NAT/G DIPLOM RACE/REL

B58
TILLION G.,ALGERIA: THE REALITIES. ALGERIA FRANCE ISLAM CULTURE STRATA PROB/SOLV DOMIN REV NAT/LISM WEALTH MARXISM...GEOG 20. PAGE 155 H3094
ECO/UNDEV SOC COLONIAL DIPLOM

B58
VARG P.A.,MISSIONARIES, CHINESE, AND DIPLOMATS: THE AMERICAN PROTESTANT MISSIONARY MOVEMENT IN CHINA, 1890-1952. ASIA ECO/UNDEV NAT/G PROB/SOLV CAP/ISM EDU/PROP COLONIAL NAT/LISM ATTIT MARXISM...NAT/COMP STERTYP 20 CHINJAP PROTESTANT MISSION. PAGE 162 H3234
CULTURE DIPLOM SECT

B58
WILMERDING L. JR.,THE ELECTORAL COLLEGE. CONSTN NAT/G POL/PAR DELIB/GP LEGIS PROB/SOLV CONFER EXEC LEAD APPORT REPRESENT. PAGE 169 H3377
CHOOSE DECISION ACT/RES

C58
GINSBURG N.,"MALAYA." MALAYSIA PROB/SOLV REGION NAT/LISM KNOWL WEALTH...GEOG SOC CHARTS BIBLIOG 20. PAGE 57 H1133
COM/IND ECO/UNDEV CULTURE NAT/G

C58
WILDING N.,"AN ENCYCLOPEDIA OF PARLIAMENT." UK LAW CONSTN CHIEF PROB/SOLV DIPLOM DEBATE WAR INGP/REL PRIVIL...BIBLIOG DICTIONARY 13/20 CMN/WLTH PARLIAMENT. PAGE 168 H3363
PARL/PROC POL/PAR NAT/G ADMIN

B59
BUNDESMIN FUR VERTRIEBENE,ZEITTAFEL DER VORGESCHICHTE UND DES ABLAUFS DER VERTREIBUNG SOWIE DER UNTERBRINGUNG UND EINGLIEDERUNG DER (2 VOLS.). GERMANY/E GERMANY/W NAT/G PROVS PROB/SOLV DIPLOM PARL/PROC ATTIT...BIBLIOG SOC/INTEG 20 MIGRATION PARLIAMENT. PAGE 24 H0475
JURID GP/REL INT/LAW

B59
VERNEY D.V.,PUBLIC ENTERPRISE IN SWEDEN. FUT SWEDEN UK INDUS POL/PAR LEGIS PROB/SOLV CAP/ISM INT/TRADE CONTROL SOCISM...MGT CONCPT NAT/COMP 20 SOCDEM/PAR CIVIL/SERV. PAGE 162 H3246
ECO/DEV POLICY LG/CO NAT/G

B59
WRAITH R.E.,EAST AFRICAN CITIZEN. AFR GHANA UK AGRI INDUS LOC/G POL/PAR PROB/SOLV CONTROL REGION REPRESENT NAT/LISM PWR...OBS 20 AFRICA/E AFRICA/W. PAGE 171 H3415
ECO/UNDEV RACE/REL NAT/G NAT/COMP

S59
CHAPMAN B.,"THE FRENCH CONSEIL D'ETAT." FRANCE NAT/G CONSULT OP/RES PROB/SOLV PWR...OBS 20. PAGE 29 H0580
ADMIN LAW CT/SYS LEGIS

S59
DUNCAN O.D.,"CULTURAL, BEHAVIORAL, AND ECOLOGICAL PERSPECTIVES IN THE STUDY OF SOCIAL ORGANIZATION" (BMR)" UNIV STRATA EX/STRUC PROB/SOLV ADMIN ATTIT SOC/INTEG 20 BUREAUCRCY. PAGE 43 H0862
CULTURE METH/COMP SOCIETY HABITAT

S59
MENDELSON W.,"JUDICIAL REVIEW AND PARTY POLITICS" (BMR)" UK USA+45 USA-45 NAT/G LEGIS PROB/SOLV EDU/PROP ADJUD EFFICIENCY...POLICY NAT/COMP 19/20 AUSTRAL SUPREME/CT. PAGE 109 H2171
CT/SYS POL/PAR BAL/PWR JURID

B60
FEIS H.,BETWEEN WAR AND PEACE: THE POTSDAM CONFERENCE. EUR+WWI NAT/G DELIB/GP PROB/SOLV REPAR WAR CIVMIL/REL...BIBLIOG 20. PAGE 49 H0983
DIPLOM CONFER BAL/PWR

B60
GONZALEZ NAVARRO M.,LA COLONIZACION EN MEXICO, 1877-1910. AGRI NAT/G PLAN PROB/SOLV INCOME ...POLICY JURID CENSUS 19/20 MEXIC/AMER MIGRATION. PAGE 58 H1164
ECO/UNDEV GEOG HABITAT COLONIAL

B60
HARRISON S.S.,INDIA: THE MOST DANGEROUS DECADES. INDIA CONSTN STRATA POL/PAR SECT PLAN ADMIN CHOOSE GP/REL TOTALISM MARXISM...LING 20 NEHRU/J. PAGE 67 H1347
CULTURE ECO/UNDEV PROB/SOLV REGION

B60
KENEN P.B.,BRITISH MONETARY POLICY AND THE BALANCE OF PAYMENTS 1951-57. UK PLAN BUDGET ECO/TAC INT/TRADE PAY PRICE COST ATTIT 20. PAGE 84 H1687
BAL/PAY PROB/SOLV FINAN NAT/G

B60
PETERSON W.C.,THE WELFARE STATE IN FRANCE. EUR+WWI FRANCE FUT STRATA PROB/SOLV TAX GIVE RECEIVE INCOME ORD/FREE PWR...CHARTS 20. PAGE 125 H2496
NEW/LIB ECO/TAC WEALTH NAT/G

S60
APTER D.E.,"THE ROLE OF TRADITIONALISM IN THE POLITICAL MODERNIZATION OF GHANA AND UGANDA" (BMR)" AFR GHANA UGANDA CULTURE NAT/G POL/PAR NAT/LISM ...CON/ANAL 20. PAGE 8 H0152
CONSERVE ADMIN GOV/COMP PROB/SOLV

S60
BANFIELD E.C.,"THE POLITICAL IMPLICATIONS OF METROPOLITAN GROWTH" (BMR)" UK USA+45 LOC/G PROB/SOLV ADMIN GP/REL...METH/COMP NAT/COMP 20. PAGE 10 H0209
TASK MUNIC GOV/COMP CENSUS

S60
COOK R.C.,"THE WORLD'S GREAT CITIES: EVOLUTION OR DEVOLUTION?" WOR+45 WOR-45 ECO/DEV ECO/UNDEV ACT/RES PROB/SOLV...GEOG TREND CHARTS NAT/COMP BIBLIOG 20. PAGE 33 H0658
MUNIC HABITAT PLAN CENSUS

S60
WOLFINGER R.E.,"REPUTATION AND REALITY IN THE STUDY OF COMMUNITY POWER." STRUCT PROB/SOLV INGP/REL ATTIT OBJECTIVE...SOC METH/CNCPT PERS/COMP. PAGE 170 H3404
CULTURE MUNIC DOMIN PWR

C60
HAZARD J.N.,"SETTLING DISPUTES IN SOVIET SOCIETY: THE FORMATIVE YEARS OF LEGAL INSTITUTIONS." USSR NAT/G PROF/ORG PROB/SOLV CONTROL CT/SYS ROUTINE REV CENTRAL...JURID BIBLIOG 20. PAGE 68 H1372
ADJUD LAW COM POLICY

C60
WRIGGINS W.H.,"CEYLON: DILEMMAS OF A NEW NATION." ASIA CEYLON CONSTN STRUCT POL/PAR SECT FORCES DIPLOM GOV/REL NAT/LISM...CHARTS BIBLIOG 20. PAGE 171 H3417
PROB/SOLV NAT/G ECO/UNDEV

B61
AIYAR S.P.,FEDERALISM AND SOCIAL CHANGE. CANADA CULTURE STRUCT PLAN PROB/SOLV TEC/DEV ECO/TAC ORD/FREE...TIME/SEQ 18/20 AUSTRAL. PAGE 4 H0085
FEDERAL NAT/G CENTRAL GOV/COMP

B61
DELEFORTRIE-SOU N.,LES DIRIGEANTS DE L'INDUSTRIE FRANCAISE. FRANCE CULTURE ELITES PROB/SOLV ...DECISION STAT CHARTS 20. PAGE 39 H0789
INDUS STRATA TOP/EX LEAD

B61
DONNISON F.S.V.,CIVIL AFFAIRS AND MILITARY GOVERNMENT NORTH-WEST EUROPE 1944-1946. EUR+WWI FRANCE GERMANY UK USSR LOC/G PROVS PLAN PROB/SOLV BAL/PWR ECO/TAC CONTROL PWR...CHARTS 20. PAGE 42 H0836
NAT/G WAR FORCES CIVMIL/REL

B61
DUFFY J.,AFRICA SPEAKS. GHANA TOGO CULTURE ECO/UNDEV PROB/SOLV COLONIAL NEUTRAL DISCRIM NAT/LISM SOVEREIGN ALL/IDEOS...CONCPT ANTHOL SOC/INTEG 20 NEGRO THIRD/WRLD. PAGE 43 H0857
AFR NAT/G FUT STRUCT

B61
FULLER J.F.C.,THE CONDUCT OF WAR, 1789-1961. FRANCE RUSSIA SOCIETY NAT/G FORCES PROB/SOLV AGREE NUC/PWR WEAPON PEACE...SOC 18/20 TREATY COLD/WAR. PAGE 54 H1076
WAR POLICY REV ROLE

B61
KEE R.,REFUGEE WORLD. AUSTRIA EUR+WWI GERMANY NEIGH EX/STRUC WORKER PROB/SOLV ECO/TAC RENT EDU/PROP INGP/REL COST LITERACY HABITAT 20 MIGRATION. PAGE 84 H1676
NAT/G GIVE WEALTH STRANGE

B61
NEWMAN R.P.,RECOGNITION OF COMMUNIST CHINA? A STUDY IN ARGUMENT. CHINA/COM NAT/G PROB/SOLV RATIONAL
MARXISM ATTIT

...INT/LAW LOG IDEA/COMP BIBLIOG 20. PAGE 117 H2347 DIPLOM POLICY

B61
NICOLSON H.G.,THE OLD DIPLOMACY AND THE NEW. NAT/G PLAN PROB/SOLV...METH 20. PAGE 118 H2355
DIPLOM POLICY INT/ORG

B61
STAHL W.,EDUCATION FOR DEMOCRACY IN WEST GERMANY: ACHIEVEMENT SHORTCOMINGS - PROSPECTS. GERMANY/W SOCIETY NAT/G FORCES PLAN PROB/SOLV PRESS ALL/VALS ...POLICY MAJORIT CONCPT ANTHOL 20. PAGE 148 H2967
EDU/PROP POPULISM AGE/Y ADJUST

B61
YUAN TUNG-LI,A GUIDE TO DOCTORAL DISSERTATIONS BY CHINESE STUDENTS IN AMERICA, 1905-1960. ASIA CULTURE SOCIETY ECO/UNDEV NAT/G PROB/SOLV DIPLOM LEAD ATTIT...HUM SOC STAT 20. PAGE 172 H3442
BIBLIOG ACADEM ACT/RES OP/RES

S61
HOSELITZ B.F.,"ECONOMIC DEVELOPMENT AND POLITICAL STABILITY IN INDIA" INDIA NAT/G GP/REL...POLICY 20. PAGE 74 H1475
ECO/UNDEV GEN/LAWS PROB/SOLV

S61
TUCKER R.C.,"TOWARDS A COMPARATIVE POLITICS OF MOVEMENT-REGIMES" (BMR)" USSR CONSTN NAT/G CREATE PROB/SOLV DIPLOM DOMIN REV...GP/COMP IDEA/COMP METH 20 STALIN/J BOLSHEVISM. PAGE 157 H3135
MARXISM POLICY GEN/LAWS PWR

B62
THREE PRELIMINARY BIBLIOGRAPHIES OF WORKS RELATED TO THE SOCIAL SCIENCES IN LATIN AMERICA. BRAZIL CULTURE SOCIETY NAT/G PLAN PROB/SOLV...PSY 20 MEXIC/AMER. PAGE 2 H0040
BIBLIOG L/A+17C SOC AGRI

B62
ESCUELA SUPERIOR DE ADMIN PUBL,INFORME DEL SEMINARIO SOBRE SERVICIO CIVIL O CARRERA ADMINISTRATIVA. L/A+17C ELITES STRATA CONFER CONTROL GOV/REL INGP/REL SUPEGO 20 CENTRAL/AM CIVIL/SERV. PAGE 47 H0939
ADMIN NAT/G PROB/SOLV ATTIT

B62
HANSON A.H.,MANAGERIAL PROBLEMS IN PUBLIC ENTERPRISE. INDIA DELIB/GP GP/REL INGP/REL EFFICIENCY 20 PARLIAMENT. PAGE 66 H1320
MGT NAT/G INDUS PROB/SOLV

B62
HUNKIN P.,ENSEIGNEMENT ET POLITIQUE EN FRANCE ET EN ANGLETERRE. FRANCE UK CONSTN ACADEM SECT CHIEF DELIB/GP PROB/SOLV CONTROL REV ORD/FREE CONSERVE ...BIBLIOG 18/20. PAGE 75 H1496
EDU/PROP LEGIS IDEA/COMP NAT/G

B62
LAQUEUR W.,THE FUTURE OF COMMUNIST SOCIETY. CHINA/COM USSR LAW ECO/DEV NAT/G POL/PAR PLAN PROB/SOLV DIPLOM LEAD...POLICY CONCPT IDEA/COMP ANTHOL 20. PAGE 91 H1820
MARXISM COM FUT SOCIETY

B62
LOWENSTEIN A.K.,BRUTAL MANDATE: A JOURNEY TO SOUTH WEST AFRICA. CULTURE INT/ORG NAT/G DIPLOM...GEOG 20 UN AFRICA/SW. PAGE 99 H1975
AFR POLICY RACE/REL PROB/SOLV

B62
MEGGITT M.J.,DESERT PEOPLE. ECO/UNDEV KIN CREATE PROB/SOLV CONTROL DRIVE ROLE...GEOG SOC MYTH CHARTS BIBLIOG 20 AUSTRAL. PAGE 108 H2159
ADJUST CULTURE INGP/REL HABITAT

B62
MOUSSA P.,THE UNDERPRIVILEGED NATIONS. FINAN INT/ORG PLAN PROB/SOLV CAP/ISM GIVE TASK WEALTH ...POLICY SOC 20. PAGE 114 H2273
ECO/UNDEV NAT/G DIPLOM FOR/AID

B62
SCHECHTMAN J.B.,POSTWAR POPULATION TRANSFERS IN EUROPE: 1945-1955. COM CZECHOSLVK GERMANY POLAND USSR CULTURE SOCIETY PROB/SOLV AGREE NAT/LISM...SOC STAT TREND CHARTS METH/COMP 20 MIGRATION. PAGE 139 H2778
GEOG CENSUS EUR+WWI HABITAT

B62
UNECA LIBRARY,NEW ACQUISITIONS IN THE UNECA LIBRARY. LAW NAT/G PLAN PROB/SOLV TEC/DEV ADMIN REGION...GEOG SOC 20 UN. PAGE 158 H3161
BIBLIOG AFR ECO/UNDEV INT/ORG

B62
WALSTON H.,AGRICULTURE UNDER COMMUNISM. CHINA/COM COM PROB/SOLV HAPPINESS RIGID/FLEX...POLICY METH/COMP 20. PAGE 165 H3295
AGRI MARXISM PLAN CREATE

C62
BACON F.,"OF EMPIRE" (1612) IN F. BACON, ESSAYS." ELITES NAT/G PROB/SOLV DIPLOM ADMIN CONTROL WEALTH 16/17 KING. PAGE 9 H0190
PWR CHIEF DOMIN GEN/LAWS

B63
DECOTTIGNIES R.,LES NATIONALITES AFRICAINES. AFR NAT/G PROB/SOLV DIPLOM COLONIAL ORD/FREE...CHARTS GOV/COMP 20. PAGE 39 H0781
NAT/LISM JURID LEGIS LAW

B63
FRANKEL J.,THE MAKING OF FOREIGN POLICY: AN ANALYSIS OF DECISION-MAKING. CHINA/COM EUR+WWI USA+45 ELITES INTELL FORCES LEGIS PLAN ATTIT ALL/VALS MORAL CONSERVE...GOV/COMP 20 PRESIDENT UN TREATY. PAGE 53 H1051
POLICY DECISION PROB/SOLV DIPLOM

B63
HAQ M.,THE STRATEGY OF ECONOMIC PLANNING. PAKISTAN AGRI FINAN INDUS NAT/G FOR/AID TAX CONTROL REGION PRODUC...POLICY CHARTS 20. PAGE 66 H1324
ECO/TAC ECO/UNDEV PLAN PROB/SOLV

B63
INDIAN INSTITUTE PUBLIC ADMIN,CASES IN INDIAN ADMINISTRATION. INDIA AGRI NAT/G PROB/SOLV TEC/DEV ECO/TAC ADMIN...ANTHOL METH 20. PAGE 77 H1532
DECISION PLAN MGT ECO/UNDEV

B63
INTERNATIONAL ASSOCIATION RES,AFRICAN STUDIES IN INCOME AND WEALTH. AFR NAT/G PROB/SOLV DEMAND INCOME...ECOMETRIC METH/COMP 20. PAGE 78 H1553
WEALTH PLAN ECO/UNDEV BUDGET

B63
JENNINGS W.I.,DEMOCRACY IN AFRICA. UK CULTURE STRUCT ECO/UNDEV DIPLOM COLONIAL GP/REL ADJUST NAT/LISM ORD/FREE...GOV/COMP 20 THIRD/WRLD. PAGE 81 H1613
PROB/SOLV AFR CONSTN POPULISM

B63
LETHBRIDGE H.J.,THE PEASANT AND THE COMMUNES. CHINA/COM COM USSR NEIGH PROB/SOLV ADJUST EFFICIENCY...POLICY METH/COMP NAT/COMP 20. PAGE 95 H1894
MARXISM ECO/TAC AGRI WORKER

B63
OLSON M. JR.,THE ECONOMICS OF WARTIME SHORTAGE. FRANCE GERMANY MOD/EUR UK AGRI PROB/SOLV ADMIN DEMAND WEALTH...POLICY OLD/LIB 17/20. PAGE 121 H2416
WAR ADJUST ECO/TAC NAT/COMP

B63
SINGH H.L.,PROBLEMS AND POLICIES OF THE BRITISH IN INDIA, 1885-1898. INDIA UK NAT/G FORCES LEGIS PROB/SOLV CONTROL RACE/REL ADJUST DISCRIM NAT/LISM RIGID/FLEX...MGT 19 CIVIL/SERV. PAGE 144 H2885
COLONIAL PWR POLICY ADMIN

B63
WILCOX W.A.,PAKISTAN; THE CONSOLIDATION OF A NATION. INDIA PAKISTAN CONSTN SECT PROB/SOLV COLONIAL PARTIC GP/REL FEDERAL...POLICY 19/20. PAGE 168 H3361
NAT/LISM ECO/UNDEV DIPLOM STRUCT

B64
ARASARATNAM S.,CEYLON. CEYLON NETHERLAND PORTUGAL S/ASIA UK STRUCT ECO/UNDEV SECT DIPLOM DOMIN RACE/REL NAT/LISM 17/20 CMN/WLTH. PAGE 8 H0156
COLONIAL NAT/G PROB/SOLV CULTURE

B64
BELL W.,JAMAICAN LEADERS: POLITICAL ATTITUDES IN A NEW NATION. JAMAICA STRUCT ACT/RES CREATE PROB/SOLV DIPLOM COLONIAL LEAD...QU 20. PAGE 13 H0267
NAT/LISM ATTIT DRIVE SOVEREIGN

B64
BERNDT R.M.,THE WORLD OF THE FIRST AUSTRALIANS. S/ASIA ECO/UNDEV WORKER PROB/SOLV EFFICIENCY ROLE ...SOC MYTH WORSHIP AUSTRAL ABORIGINES. PAGE 16 H0311
CULTURE KIN STRUCT DRIVE

B64
BRIGHT J.R.,RESEARCH, DEVELOPMENT AND TECHNOLOGICAL INNOVATION. CULTURE R+D CREATE PLAN PROB/SOLV AUTOMAT RISK PERSON...DECISION CONCPT PREDICT BIBLIOG. PAGE 21 H0419
TEC/DEV NEW/IDEA INDUS MGT

B64
COBBAN A.,ROUSSEAU AND THE MODERN STATE (2ND ED.). FRANCE PROB/SOLV NAT/LISM UTOPIA PERSON MORAL ...EPIST PHIL/SCI SOC IDEA/COMP 18 ROUSSEAU/J BURKE/EDM HOBBES/T HUME/D. PAGE 30 H0612
GEN/LAWS INGP/REL NAT/G ORD/FREE

B64
COLLINS B.E.,A SOCIAL PSYCHOLOGY OF GROUP PROCESSES FOR DECISION-MAKING. PROB/SOLV ROUTINE...SOC CHARTS HYPO/EXP. PAGE 32 H0632
FACE/GP DECISION NAT/G INDUS

B64
CULLINGWORTH J.B.,TOWN AND COUNTRY PLANNING IN ENGLAND AND WALES. UK LAW SOCIETY CONSULT ACT/RES ADMIN ROUTINE LEISURE INGP/REL ADJUST PWR...GEOG 20 OPEN/SPACE URBAN/RNWL. PAGE 36 H0718
MUNIC PLAN NAT/G PROB/SOLV

B64
DICKEY J.S.,THE UNITED STATES AND CANADA. CANADA USA+45...SOC 20. PAGE 41 H0822
DIPLOM TREND GOV/COMP PROB/SOLV

B64
HERSKOVITS M.J.,ECONOMIC TRANSITION IN AFRICA. FUT INT/ORG NAT/G WORKER PROB/SOLV TEC/DEV INT/TRADE EQUILIB INCOME...ANTHOL 20. PAGE 70 H1408
AFR ECO/UNDEV PLAN ADMIN

B64
MAHAR J.M.,INDIA: A CRITICAL BIBLIOGRAPHY. INDIA PAKISTAN CULTURE ECO/UNDEV LOC/G POL/PAR SECT PROB/SOLV DIPLOM ADMIN COLONIAL PARL/PROC ATTIT 20. PAGE 101 H2016
BIBLIOG/A S/ASIA NAT/G LEAD

B64
MARTINET G.,MARXISM OF OUR TIME: OR THE CONTRADICTIONS OF SOCIALISM. FRANCE NAT/G OPTIMAL RIGID/FLEX SOCISM...IDEA/COMP 20. PAGE 103 H2067
MARXISM MARXIST PROB/SOLV

CREATE

B64
MILIBAND R.,THE SOCIALIST REGISTER: 1964. GERMANY/W ITALY UK LABOR POL/PAR ECO/TAC FOR/AID NUC/PWR ...POLICY SOCIALIST IDEA/COMP 20 MAO NASSER/G. PAGE 110 H2204
MARXISM SOCISM CAP/ISM PROB/SOLV

B64
MOUMOUNI A.,L'EDUCATION EN AFRIQUE. UNIV CULTURE ELITES INTELL EDU/PROP ADMIN COLONIAL...LING TREND BIBLIOG 20. PAGE 114 H2271
SCHOOL AFR PROB/SOLV

B64
WALDMAN E.,THE GOOSE STEP IS VERBOTEN: THE GERMAN ARMY TODAY. GERMANY/W LAW CONSTN LEGIS PROB/SOLV DOMIN CONTROL CIVMIL/REL GOV/REL INGP/REL ATTIT ...DEEP/QU 20. PAGE 164 H3289
SOC FORCES NAT/G

B64
WRIGHT Q.,A STUDY OF WAR. LAW NAT/G PROB/SOLV BAL/PWR NAT/LISM PEACE ATTIT SOVEREIGN...CENSUS SOC/INTEG. PAGE 171 H3421
WAR CONCPT DIPLOM CONTROL

S64
EISTER A.W.,"PERSPECTIVE ON FUNCTIONS OF RELIGION IN A DEVELOPING COUNTRY: ISLAM IN PAKISTAN." ISLAM CULTURE MUNIC ACT/RES CREATE PROB/SOLV TEC/DEV WORSHIP. PAGE 45 H0902
ATTIT SECT ECO/DEV

B65
ADENAUER K.,MEINE ERINNERUNGEN, 1945-53 (VOL. I), 1953-55 (VOL. II). EUR+WWI GERMANY CHIEF FORCES PROB/SOLV DIPLOM ARMS/CONT INGP/REL PEACE SOVEREIGN ...OBS/ENVIR RECORD 20. PAGE 3 H0069
NAT/G BIOG SELF/OBS

B65
BENTWICH J.S.,EDUCATION IN ISRAEL. ISRAEL CULTURE STRATA PROB/SOLV TEC/DEV ADJUST ALL/VALS 20 JEWS. PAGE 15 H0293
SECT EDU/PROP ACADEM SCHOOL

B65
CRAMER J.F.,CONTEMPORARY EDUCATION: A COMPARATIVE STUDY OF NATIONAL SYSTEMS (2ND ED.). CHINA/COM EUR+WWI INDIA USA+45 FINAN PROB/SOLV ADMIN CONTROL ATTIT...IDEA/COMP METH/COMP 20 CHINJAP. PAGE 35 H0697
EDU/PROP NAT/COMP SCHOOL ACADEM

B65
EDELMAN M.,THE POLITICS OF WAGE-PRICE DECISIONS. GERMANY ITALY NETHERLAND UK INDUS LABOR POL/PAR PROB/SOLV BARGAIN PRICE ROUTINE BAL/PAY COST DEMAND 20. PAGE 44 H0888
GOV/COMP CONTROL ECO/TAC PLAN

B65
FORM W.H.,INDUSTRIAL RELATIONS AND SOCIAL CHANGE IN LATIN AMERICA. L/A+17C AGRI LABOR NAT/G PLAN PROB/SOLV DIPLOM...MGT SOC ANTHOL BIBLIOG/A METH 20. PAGE 52 H1038
INDUS GP/REL NAT/COMP ECO/UNDEV

B65
GOLEMBIEWSKI R.T.,MEN, MANAGEMENT, AND MORALITY; TOWARD A NEW ORGANIZATIONAL ETHIC. CONSTN EX/STRUC CREATE ADMIN CONTROL INGP/REL PERSON SUPEGO MORAL PWR...GOV/COMP METH/COMP 20 BUREAUCRCY. PAGE 58 H1161
LG/CO MGT PROB/SOLV

B65
HALEVY E.,THE ERA OF TYRANNIES (TRANS. BY R. K. WEBB). WOR-45 ECO/DEV PROB/SOLV CONTROL COERCE REV WAR TOTALISM 20. PAGE 64 H1286
SOCISM IDEA/COMP DOMIN

B65
HANSER C.J.,GUIDE TO DECISION: ROYAL COMMISSION. UK INTELL EXTR/IND SCHOOL PROB/SOLV EXEC ROUTINE CHOOSE GOV/REL GP/REL HEALTH...CHARTS 20. PAGE 66 H1318
NAT/G DELIB/GP EX/STRUC PWR

B65
HESS A.G.,CHASING THE DRAGON: A REPORT ON DRUG ADDICTION IN HONG KONG. ASIA CULTURE PROB/SOLV TRIBUTE...POLICY PSY SOC CLASSIF STAT 17/20 HONG/KONG. PAGE 70 H1411
BIO/SOC CRIME SOCIETY LAW

B65
JAIN S.C.,THE STATE AND AGRICULTURE. INDIA S/ASIA ECO/UNDEV PROB/SOLV CAP/ISM MARXISM SOCISM 20. PAGE 79 H1586
NAT/G POLICY AGRI ECO/TAC

B65
LAMBIRI I.,SOCIAL CHANGE IN A GREEK COUNTRY TOWN. GREECE FAM PROB/SOLV ROUTINE TASK LEISURE INGP/REL CONSEN ORD/FREE...SOC INT QU CHARTS 20. PAGE 90 H1803
INDUS WORKER CULTURE NEIGH

B65
OECD,MEDITERRANEAN REGIONAL PROJECT: TURKEY; EDUCATION AND DEVELOPMENT. FUT TURKEY SOCIETY STRATA FINAN NAT/G PROF/ORG PLAN PROB/SOLV ADMIN COST...STAT CHARTS 20 OECD. PAGE 120 H2399
EDU/PROP ACADEM SCHOOL ECO/UNDEV

B65
OECD,THE MEDITERRANEAN REGIONAL PROJECT: ITALY; EDUCATION AND DEVELOPMENT. ITALY SOCIETY STRATA FINAN NAT/G PROF/ORG WORKER PLAN PROB/SOLV ADMIN ...STAT CHARTS METH 20 OECD. PAGE 120 H2400
SCHOOL EDU/PROP ECO/UNDEV ACADEM

B65
OECD,THE MEDITERRANEAN REGIONAL PROJECT: GREECE; EDUCATION AND DEVELOPMENT. FUT GREECE SOCIETY AGRI FINAN NAT/G PROF/ORG WORKER PLAN PROB/SOLV ADMIN DEMAND ATTIT 20 OECD. PAGE 120 H2401
EDU/PROP SCHOOL ACADEM ECO/UNDEV

B65
OECD,THE MEDITERRANEAN REGIONAL PROJECT: SPAIN; EDUCATION AND DEVELOPMENT. FUT SPAIN STRATA FINAN NAT/G WORKER PLAN PROB/SOLV ADMIN COST...POLICY STAT CHARTS 20 OECD. PAGE 120 H2402
ECO/UNDEV EDU/PROP ACADEM SCHOOL

B65
ONSLOW C.,ASIAN ECONOMIC DEVELOPMENT. BURMA CEYLON INDIA MALAYSIA PAKISTAN S/ASIA AGRI INDUS MARKET PROB/SOLV CAP/ISM FOR/AID INT/TRADE DEMAND WEALTH ...POLICY ANTHOL 20. PAGE 121 H2418
ECO/UNDEV ECO/TAC PLAN NAT/G

B65
ROWAT D.C.,THE OMBUDSMAN: CITIZEN'S DEFENDER. DENMARK FINLAND NEW/ZEALND NORWAY SWEDEN CONSULT PROB/SOLV FEEDBACK PARTIC GP/REL...SOC CONCPT NEW/IDEA METH/COMP ANTHOL BIBLIOG 20. PAGE 135 H2701
INSPECT CONSTN NAT/G ADMIN

B65
WALKER A.A.,THE RHODESIAS AND NYASALAND: A GUIDE TO OFFICIAL PUBLICATIONS. RHODESIA UK OP/RES PLAN PROB/SOLV DIPLOM...POLICY SOC CON/ANAL 19/20 NYASALAND. PAGE 164 H3291
BIBLIOG NAT/G COLONIAL AFR

S65
PLANK J.N.,"THE CARIBBEAN* INTERVENTION, WHEN AND HOW." CUBA GUATEMALA HAITI PANAMA USA+45 VENEZUELA FORCES PROB/SOLV RISK COERCE...NAT/COMP OAS TIME. PAGE 126 H2521
SOVEREIGN MARXISM REV

B66
AMER ENTERPRISE INST PUB POL,SIGNIFICANT ISSUES IN ECONOMIC AID TO DEVELOPING COUNTRIES. FINAN INT/ORG NAT/G PLAN PROB/SOLV GIVE TASK WEALTH...DECISION 20. PAGE 6 H0119
ECO/UNDEV FOR/AID DIPLOM POLICY

B66
ASHRAF A.,THE CITY GOVERNMENT OF CALCUTTA: A STUDY OF INERTIA. INDIA ELITES INDUS NAT/G EX/STRUC ACT/RES PLAN PROB/SOLV LEAD HABITAT...BIBLIOG 20 CALCUTTA. PAGE 9 H0175
LOC/G MUNIC ADMIN ECO/UNDEV

B66
BRECHER M.,SUCCESSION IN INDIA. INDIA USA+45 CONSTN AGRI POL/PAR PROVS SECT DELIB/GP FORCES PROB/SOLV ECO/TAC PWR...LING 20 CONGRESS NEHRU/J. PAGE 20 H0408
CHIEF DECISION CHOOSE

B66
CHAPMAN B.,THE PROFESSION OF GOVERNMENT: THE PUBLIC SERVICE IN EUROPE. CONSTN NAT/G POL/PAR EX/STRUC LEGIS TOP/EX PROB/SOLV DEBATE EXEC PARL/PROC PARTIC 20. PAGE 29 H0581
BIBLIOG ADMIN EUR+WWI GOV/COMP

B66
DIAMOND S.,THE TRANSFORMATION OF EAST AFRICA. NAT/G SCHOOL CREATE PROB/SOLV COLONIAL REGION RACE/REL FEDERAL...SOC ANTHOL WORSHIP 20 AFRICA/E. PAGE 41 H0819
CULTURE AFR TEC/DEV INDUS

B66
DODGE D.,AFRICAN POLITICS IN PERSPECTIVE. ELITES POL/PAR PROB/SOLV LEAD...POLICY 20 THIRD/WRLD. PAGE 41 H0831
AFR NAT/G COLONIAL SOVEREIGN

B66
GARCON M.,LETTRE OUVERTE A LA JUSTICE. FRANCE NAT/G PROB/SOLV PAY EFFICIENCY MORAL 20. PAGE 55 H1100
ORD/FREE ADJUD CT/SYS

B66
GHOSH P.K.,THE CONSTITUTION OF INDIA: HOW IT HAS BEEN FRAMED. INDIA LOC/G DELIB/GP EX/STRUC PROB/SOLV BUDGET INT/TRADE CT/SYS CHOOSE...LING 20. PAGE 56 H1121
CONSTN NAT/G LEGIS FEDERAL

B66
GLAZER M.,THE FEDERAL GOVERNMENT AND THE UNIVERSITY. CHILE PROB/SOLV DIPLOM GIVE ADMIN WAR ...POLICY SOC 20. PAGE 57 H1140
BIBLIOG/A NAT/G PLAN ACADEM

B66
HACKETT J.,L'ECONOMIE BRITANNIQUE: PROBLEMES ET PERSPECTIVES. FRANCE UK LABOR MUNIC NAT/G EX/STRUC PROB/SOLV BAL/PAY INCOME RIGID/FLEX...MGT PHIL/SCI CHARTS 20. PAGE 63 H1271
ECO/DEV FINAN ECO/TAC PLAN

B66
KAUNDA K.,ZAMBIA: INDEPENDENCE AND BEYOND: THE SPEECHES OF KENNETH KAUNDA. AFR FUT ZAMBIA SOCIETY ECO/UNDEV NAT/G PROB/SOLV ECO/TAC ADMIN RACE/REL SOVEREIGN 20. PAGE 84 H1670
ORD/FREE COLONIAL CONSTN LEAD

B66
NEVITT A.A.,THE ECONOMIC PROBLEMS OF HOUSING. WOR+45 ECO/DEV ECO/UNDEV ACT/RES PROB/SOLV ECO/TAC RENT...OBS CHARTS 20. PAGE 117 H2342
HABITAT PROC/MFG DELIB/GP NAT/COMP

B66
NOEL G.E.,THE NEW BRITAIN AND HAROLD WILSON: INTERIM REPORT, 1966 GENERAL ELECTION. UK POL/PAR CONSULT PROB/SOLV BUDGET DIPLOM ECO/TAC LEAD CHOOSE ATTIT 20 WILSON/H PARLIAMENT. PAGE 118 H2366
BIOG PERSON NAT/G CHIEF

B66
OWEN G.,INDUSTRY IN THE UNITED STATES. UK USA+45 NAT/G WEALTH...DECISION NAT/COMP 20. PAGE 122 H2436
METH/COMP INDUS MGT PROB/SOLV

B66
SAINDERICHIN P.,HISTORIE SECRETE D'UNE ELECTION, DECEMBER 5-19, 1965. FRANCE NAT/G DELIB/GP LEGIS PLAN EDU/PROP TV SOCISM...MARXIST 20 DEGAULLE/C. PAGE 137 H2731 — CHOOSE CHIEF PROB/SOLV POL/PAR

B66
SMITH H.E.,READINGS IN ECONOMIC DEVELOPMENT AND ADMINISTRATION IN TANZANIA. TANZANIA FINAN INDUS LABOR NAT/G PLAN PROB/SOLV INT/TRADE COLONIAL REGION...ANTHOL BIBLIOG 20 AFRICA/E. PAGE 146 H2910 — TEC/DEV ADMIN GOV/REL

B66
THOMPSON J.H.,MODERNIZATION OF THE ARAB WORLD. FUT ISRAEL STRUCT ECO/UNDEV DIPLOM INGP/REL ATTIT ...CENSUS ANTHOL 20 ARABS. PAGE 154 H3082 — ADJUST ISLAM PROB/SOLV NAT/COMP

B66
WILLNER A.R.,THE NEOTRADITIONAL ACCOMMODATION TO POLITICAL INDEPENDENCE* THE CASE OF INDONESIA * RESEARCH MONOGRAPH NO. 26. CULTURE ECO/UNDEV CREATE PROB/SOLV FOR/AID LEGIT COLONIAL EFFICIENCY NAT/LISM ALL/VALS SOC. PAGE 168 H3371 — INDONESIA CONSERVE ELITES ADMIN

S66
ADAMS T.W.,"THE FIRST REPUBLIC OF CYPRUS: A REVIEW OF AN UNWORKABLE CONSTITUTION." CYPRUS FUT PLAN NAT/LISM POPULISM 20. PAGE 3 H0067 — CONSTN NAT/G PROB/SOLV

S66
BLANC N.,"SPAIN: LEARNING THROUGH STRUGGLE" SPAIN STRATA STRUCT SECT FORCES PROB/SOLV AGE/Y ATTIT ORD/FREE PWR WEALTH MARXISM SOCISM 19/20 FRANCO/F SUCCESSION. PAGE 18 H0352 — NAT/G FUT SOCIALIST TOTALISM

S66
FLEMING W.G.,"AUTHORITY, EFFICIENCY, AND ROLE STRESS: PROBLEMS IN THE DEVELOPMENT OF EAST AFRICAN BUREAUCRACIES." AFR UGANDA STRUCT PROB/SOLV ROUTINE INGP/REL ROLE...MGT SOC GP/COMP GOV/COMP 20 TANGANYIKA AFRICA/E. PAGE 51 H1024 — DOMIN EFFICIENCY COLONIAL ADMIN

S66
HEAPHEY J.,"THE ORGANIZATION OF EGYPT* INADEQUACIES OF A NONPOLITICAL MODEL FOR NATION-BUILDING." STRATA NAT/G CREATE PROB/SOLV ECO/TAC NAT/LISM SOCISM RECORD. PAGE 69 H1377 — UAR ECO/UNDEV OBS

S66
ROTHCHILD D.,"THE LIMITS OF FEDERALISM: AN EXAMINATION OF POLITICAL INSTITUTIONAL TRANSFER IN AFRICA." AFR CONSTN CULTURE ELITES ECO/UNDEV KIN PROB/SOLV ADMIN ORD/FREE PWR...POLICY 20. PAGE 135 H2695 — FEDERAL NAT/G NAT/LISM COLONIAL

S66
SCHOENBRON D.,"VIETNAM* THE CASE FOR EXTRICATION." NAT/G FORCES PROB/SOLV DIPLOM COLONIAL CONTROL COERCE...CONCPT 20. PAGE 140 H2795 — VIETNAM WAR GUERRILLA

B67
ANDERSON C.W.,POLITICS AND ECONOMIC CHANGE IN LATIN AMERICA. L/A+17C INDUS NAT/G OP/RES ADMIN DEMAND ...POLICY STAT CHARTS NAT/COMP 20. PAGE 6 H0125 — ECO/UNDEV PROB/SOLV PLAN ECO/TAC

B67
ASHFORD D.E.,NATIONAL DEVELOPMENT AND LOCAL REFORM: POLITICAL PARTICIPATION IN MOROCCO, TUNISIA, AND PAKISTAN. MOROCCO PAKISTAN CULTURE PROB/SOLV ATTIT ...POLICY SOC METH/COMP NAT/COMP BIBLIOG 20 TUNIS. PAGE 9 H0173 — PARTIC ECO/UNDEV ADJUST NAT/G

B67
CHANDRASEKHAR S.,ASIA'S POPULATION PROBLEMS. ASIA ECO/UNDEV PLAN AGE/C...OBS CHARTS BIBLIOG 18/20 AUSTRAL. PAGE 29 H0575 — PROB/SOLV NAT/COMP GEOG TREND

B67
CHILCOTE R.H.,PORTUGUESE AFRICA. PORTUGAL CULTURE SOCIETY ECO/UNDEV DOMIN NAT/LISM...TREND IDEA/COMP NAT/COMP BIBLIOG 15/20. PAGE 29 H0589 — AFR COLONIAL ORD/FREE PROB/SOLV

B67
FIELD M.G.,SOVIET SOCIALIZED MEDICINE. USSR FINAN R+D PROB/SOLV ADMIN SOCISM...MGT SOC CONCPT 20. PAGE 50 H0993 — PUB/INST HEALTH NAT/G MARXISM

B67
GELLHORN W.,OMBUDSMEN AND OTHERS: CITIZENS' PROTECTORS IN NINE COUNTRIES. WOR+45 LAW CONSTN LEGIS INSPECT ADJUD ADMIN CONTROL CT/SYS CHOOSE PERS/REL...STAT CHARTS 20. PAGE 55 H1109 — NAT/COMP REPRESENT INGP/REL PROB/SOLV

B67
GILL R.T.,ECONOMIC DEVELOPMENT: PAST AND PRESENT (2ND ED.). ASIA INDIA USA+45 USA-45 WOR+45 WOR-45 DEMAND EFFICIENCY NAT/LISM WEALTH...GOV/COMP METH/COMP 18/20. PAGE 56 H1127 — ECO/DEV ECO/UNDEV PLAN PROB/SOLV

B67
HILSMAN R.,TO MOVE A NATION: THE POLITICS OF FOREIGN POLICY IN THE ADMINISTRATION OF JOHN F. KENNEDY. CHINA/COM COM USSR VIETNAM NAT/G DELIB/GP FORCES PLAN PROB/SOLV BAL/PWR COLONIAL EXEC REV PWR 20 KENNEDY/JF PRESIDENT. PAGE 71 H1418 — CHIEF DIPLOM

B67
HODGKINSON R.G.,THE ORIGINS OF THE NATIONAL HEALTH SERVICE: THE MEDICAL SERVICES OF THE NEW POOR LAW, 1834-1871. UK INDUS MUNIC WORKER PROB/SOLV EFFICIENCY ATTIT HEALTH WEALTH SOCISM...JURID SOC/WK 19/20. PAGE 72 H1445 — HEAL NAT/G POLICY LAW

B67
MUHAMMAD A.C.,THE EMERGENCE OF PAKISTAN. PAKISTAN S/ASIA CONSTN ECO/UNDEV NAT/G CONTROL NAT/LISM 20. PAGE 114 H2281 — DIPLOM COLONIAL SECT PROB/SOLV

B67
MUNGER E.S.,AFRIKANER AND AFRICAN NATIONALISM: SOUTH AFRICAN PARALLELS AND PARAMETERS. SOUTH/AFR WOR+45 CULTURE ELITES STRUCT NAT/G PROB/SOLV DOMIN CONTROL PERS/REL NAT/LISM...SOC 20. PAGE 115 H2289 — AFR RACE/REL

B67
ODINGA O.,NOT YET UHURU. NAT/G POL/PAR PROB/SOLV COERCE REV WAR PERS/REL PERSON ORD/FREE...POLICY 20 ODINGA/O KENYATTA. PAGE 120 H2395 — ATTIT BIOG LEAD AFR

B67
PAPANEK G.F.,PAKISTAN'S DEVELOPMENT: SOCIAL GOALS AND PRIVATE INCENTIVES. PAKISTAN INDUS NAT/G PROB/SOLV CONTROL EFFICIENCY SOCISM...CHARTS 20. PAGE 123 H2463 — ECO/UNDEV PLAN CAP/ISM ECO/TAC

B67
PLISCHKE E.,CONDUCT OF AMERICAN DIPLOMACY (3RD REV. ED.). INT/ORG NAT/G PROB/SOLV FOR/AID...CHARTS BIBLIOG T 20 DEPT/STATE. PAGE 126 H2529 — DIPLOM RATIONAL PLAN

B67
ROSENTHAL A.H.,THE SOCIAL PROGRAMS OF SWEDEN. SWEDEN USA+45 FINAN NAT/G PLAN PROB/SOLV INSPECT ORD/FREE...POLICY HEAL SOC CHARTS NAT/COMP 20. PAGE 134 H2681 — GIVE SOC/WK WEALTH METH/COMP

B67
RUSTOW D.A.,A WORLD OF NATIONS; PROBLEMS OF POLITICAL MODERNIZATION. CONSTN NAT/G POL/PAR FORCES DIPLOM LEAD AUTHORIT...CHARTS IDEA/COMP 20. PAGE 136 H2722 — PROB/SOLV ECO/UNDEV CONCPT NAT/COMP

B67
SALISBURY H.E.,BEHIND THE LINES - HANOI. VIETNAM/N NAT/G GUERRILLA CIVMIL/REL NAT/LISM KNOWL 20. PAGE 137 H2741 — WAR PROB/SOLV DIPLOM OBS

B67
SCHUTZ W.W.,RETHINKING GERMAN POLICY; NEW APPROACHES TO REUNIFICATION. GERMANY USSR PLAN CONFER...POLICY 20. PAGE 140 H2806 — REGION NAT/G DIPLOM PROB/SOLV

B67
THOMPSON E.T.,PERSPECTIVES ON THE SOUTH: AGENDA FOR RESEARCH. CULTURE ECO/UNDEV SECT GP/REL EFFICIENCY ALL/VALS...HUM SOC CONCPT LING 20 NEGRO. PAGE 154 H3080 — PROB/SOLV IDEA/COMP REGION ACT/RES

B67
UNESCO,PRINCIPLES AND PROBLEMS OF NATIONAL SCIENCE POLICIES. WOR+45 ECO/DEV ECO/UNDEV R+D INT/ORG PROB/SOLV CONFER...PHIL/SCI CHARTS 20 UNESCO UN. PAGE 158 H3165 — NAT/COMP POLICY TEC/DEV CREATE

B67
VALI F.A.,THE QUEST FOR A UNITED GERMANY. GERMANY PROB/SOLV DIPLOM ADJUST...BIBLIOG 20. PAGE 161 H3222 — NAT/G ATTIT PLAN CENTRAL

B67
WOODRUFF W.,IMPACT OF WESTERN MAN. ECO/DEV INDUS CREATE PLAN PROB/SOLV COLONIAL GOV/REL...CHARTS GOV/COMP BIBLIOG 18/20. PAGE 170 H3407 — EUR+WWI MOD/EUR CAP/ISM

L67
GRAUBARD S.R.,"TOWARD THE YEAR 2000: WORK IN PROGRESS." FUT ACADEM SECT DELIB/GP DIPLOM EDU/PROP AGE/Y PERSON ROLE...PSY ANTHOL. PAGE 60 H1199 — PREDICT PROB/SOLV SOCIETY CULTURE

L67
WAELBROECK M.,"THE APPLICATION OF EEC LAW BY NATIONAL COURTS." EUR+WWI INT/ORG CT/SYS...JURID EEC TREATY. PAGE 164 H3284 — INT/LAW NAT/G LAW PROB/SOLV

S67
ABDEL-MALEK A.,"THE CRISIS IN NASSER'S EGYPT." ISLAM UAR STRUCT POL/PAR EX/STRUC CREATE PLAN WAR ATTIT ORD/FREE PWR...POLICY DECISION 20. PAGE 3 H0054 — FORCES LEAD PROB/SOLV NAT/G

S67
ADAMS R.N.,"ETHICS AND THE SOCIAL ANTHROPOLOGIST IN LATIN AMERICA." USA+45 INTELL PROB/SOLV ECO/TAC LEAD...DECISION SOC NAT/COMP PERS/COMP. PAGE 3 H0066 — L/A+17C POLICY ECO/UNDEV CONSULT

S67
AMERASINGHE C.F.,"SOME LEGAL PROBLEMS OF STATE TRADING IN SOUTHEAST ASIA." PROB/SOLV ADJUD CONTROL CT/SYS GP/REL 20. PAGE 6 H0120 — INT/TRADE NAT/G INT/LAW PRIVIL

S67
BAER W.,"THE INFLATION CONTROVERSY IN LATIN AMERICA: SURVEY." L/A+17C ECO/UNDEV AGRI FINAN INDUS PLAN PROB/SOLV TEC/DEV...BIBLIOG/A 20. PAGE 10 H0194 — NAT/G BAL/PAY ECO/TAC BUDGET

S67
BERLINER J.S.,"RUSSIA'S BUREAUCRATS - WHY THEY'RE REACTIONARY." USSR NAT/G OP/RES PROB/SOLV TEC/DEV CONTROL SANCTION EFFICIENCY DRIVE PERSON...TECHNIC SOC 20. PAGE 15 H0308
CREATE ADMIN INDUS PRODUC

S67
BEVEL D.N.,"JOURNEY TO NORTH VIETNAM." VIETNAM/N CONSTN NAT/G FORCES PROB/SOLV DEATH CIVMIL/REL PEACE MORAL...ANTHOL 20 NEGRO. PAGE 16 H0325
ATTIT DIPLOM ORD/FREE WAR

S67
COHEN A.,"REVOLUTION IN ARGENTINA?" L/A+17C NAT/G POL/PAR CHIEF PROB/SOLV ECO/TAC 20 ARGEN. PAGE 31 H0615
REV ECO/UNDEV CONTROL BIOG

S67
CRITTENDEN J.,"DIMENSIONS OF MODERNIZATION IN THE AMERICAN STATES." USA+45 STRUCT MUNIC PROB/SOLV CONTROL LITERACY HABITAT...CONCPT METH/CNCPT CORREL CONT/OBS CENSUS 20. PAGE 35 H0702
PROVS GOV/COMP STAT ECO/DEV

S67
DERRICK P.,"THE WHITE PAPER ON INCOMES." EUR+WWI UK LAW LABOR NAT/G PLAN PROB/SOLV GP/REL...GOV/COMP PARLIAMENT. PAGE 40 H0794
INCOME POL/PAR POLICY

S67
DOERN G.B.,"THE ROYAL COMMISSIONS IN THE GENERAL POLICY PROCESS AND IN FEDERAL-PROVINCIAL RELATIONS." CANADA CONSTN ACADEM PROVS CONSULT DELIB/GP LEGIS ACT/RES PROB/SOLV CONFER CONTROL EFFICIENCY...METH/COMP 20 SENATE ROYAL/COMM. PAGE 42 H0832
R+D EX/STRUC GOV/REL NAT/G

S67
EPSTEIN E.H.,"NATIONAL IDENTITY AND THE LANGUAGE ISSUE IN PUERTO RICO." PUERT/RICO CULTURE STRUCT NAT/G PROB/SOLV SKILL...JURID STAT METH/COMP 20. PAGE 47 H0931
EDU/PROP SCHOOL LING NAT/LISM

S67
GAMARNIKOW M.,"THE NEW ROLE OF PRIVATE ENTERPRISE." ECO/DEV INDUS NAT/G SML/CO CREATE PROB/SOLV MARXISM ...POLICY TREND IDEA/COMP 20. PAGE 55 H1092
ECO/TAC ATTIT CAP/ISM COM

S67
GLOBERSON A.,"SOCIAL GROWTH IN THE DEVELOPING COUNTRIES." CULTURE SOCIETY CONSULT PROB/SOLV SOC. PAGE 57 H1144
ECO/UNDEV FOR/AID EDU/PROP PLAN

S67
GOODSELL J.N.,"BALAGUER'S DOMINICAN REPUBLIC." DOMIN/REP FUT L/A+17C POL/PAR PROB/SOLV ECO/TAC 20. PAGE 59 H1174
ECO/UNDEV CHIEF POLICY NAT/G

S67
GRAHAM R.,"BRAZIL'S DILEMMA." BRAZIL FUT L/A+17C NAT/G CHIEF PROB/SOLV ECO/TAC PWR 20. PAGE 60 H1193
ECO/UNDEV CONSTN POL/PAR POLICY

S67
HASSAN M.F.,"THE SECOND FOUR-YEAR PLAN OF VENEZUELA." L/A+17C VENEZUELA AGRI INDUS NAT/G PLAN RATION CONTROL HABITAT...MATH STAT 20. PAGE 67 H1352
ECO/UNDEV FINAN BUDGET PROB/SOLV

S67
JAIN G.,"INDIA REJECTS THE POWER RACE* REALISM ABOUT NUCLEAR WEAPONS." FORCES PROB/SOLV FOR/AID ARMS/CONT COST PWR...GOV/COMP 20. PAGE 79 H1583
INDIA CHINA/COM NUC/PWR DIPLOM

S67
KYLE K.,"BACKGROUND TO THE CRISIS" ISLAM ISRAEL UAR UK USSR NAT/G PROB/SOLV LEGIT CONTROL REGION STRANGE MORAL 20 JEWS. PAGE 89 H1787
DIPLOM POLICY SOVEREIGN COERCE

S67
LEVI W.,"THE ELITIST NATURE OF NEW ASIA'S FOREIGN POLICY." CULTURE ECO/UNDEV NAT/G PROB/SOLV EDU/PROP COLONIAL CONTROL REGION NAT/LISM...NAT/COMP 20. PAGE 95 H1898
POLICY ELITES DIPLOM CREATE

S67
MALLORY J.R.,"THE MINISTER'S OFFICE STAFF* AN UNREFORMED PART OF PUBLIC SERVICE." CONSTN ELITES STRATA NAT/G PROB/SOLV TASK CHOOSE PERS/REL EFFICIENCY...DECISION 20. PAGE 102 H2033
CANADA ADMIN EX/STRUC STRUCT

S67
NIEBUHR R.,"THE SOCIAL MYTHS IN THE COLD WAR." USA+45 USSR VIETNAM PROB/SOLV BAL/PWR ARMS/CONT NAT/LISM PWR ALL/IDEOS CONCPT. PAGE 118 H2359
MYTH DIPLOM GOV/COMP

S67
PAK H.,"CHINA'S MILITIA AND MAO TSE-TUNG'S 'PEOPLE'S WAR'." CHINA/COM SOCIETY POL/PAR EX/STRUC PROB/SOLV PARTIC COERCE WAR CIVMIL/REL ATTIT DRIVE MARXISM...METH/COMP 20 MAO. PAGE 122 H2447
FORCES NAT/G WORKER CHIEF

S67
ROSE S.,"ASIAN NATIONALISM* THE SECOND STAGE." ASIA COM ECO/UNDEV NAT/G PROB/SOLV DIPLOM FOR/AID DOMIN NEUTRAL REGION TASK...METH/COMP 20. PAGE 134 H2675
NAT/LISM S/ASIA BAL/PWR COLONIAL

S67
SALYZYN V.,"FEDERAL-PROVINCIAL TAX SHARING SCHEMES." CANADA LOC/G PROB/SOLV TEC/DEV BUDGET GOV/REL EFFICIENCY 20. PAGE 137 H2746
PROVS TAX MUNIC NAT/G

S67
SAVER W.,"NATIONAL SOCIALISM: TOTALITARIANISM OR FASCISM?" GERMANY STRUCT POL/PAR PROB/SOLV MARXISM ...SOC CONCPT HIST/WRIT IDEA/COMP 20 HITLER/A COLD/WAR. PAGE 138 H2760
SOCISM NAT/G TOTALISM FASCISM

S67
SCHACHTER G.,"REGIONAL DEVELOPMENT IN THE ITALIAN DUAL ECONOMY" ITALY AGRI INDUS MARKET WORKER ECO/TAC CONTROL INCOME PRODUC 20. PAGE 138 H2767
REGION ECO/UNDEV NAT/G PROB/SOLV

S67
SMITH J.E.,"THE GERMAN DEMOCRATIC REPUBLIC AND THE WEST." GERMANY/E ECO/DEV NAT/G PROB/SOLV CONTROL REV TOTALISM...GOV/COMP 20. PAGE 146 H2911
DIPLOM PWR MARXISM

S67
SNELLEN I.T.,"APARTHEID* CHECKS AND CHANGES." SOUTH/AFR NAT/G PROB/SOLV COLONIAL REGION TASK GP/REL RACE/REL EFFICIENCY PRIVIL ORD/FREE 20. PAGE 146 H2923
DISCRIM NAT/LISM EQUILIB CONTROL

S67
SOMMER T.,"BONN CHANGES COURSE." GERMANY/W NAT/G POL/PAR PROB/SOLV NAT/LISM 20 NATO BERLIN/BLO. PAGE 147 H2932
DIPLOM BAL/PWR INT/ORG

C67
LING D.L.,"TUNISIA: FROM PROTECTORATE TO REPUBLIC." CULTURE NAT/G POL/PAR CHIEF DIPLOM COERCE WAR PWR ...BIBLIOG 19/20 TUNIS. PAGE 97 H1934
AFR NAT/LISM COLONIAL PROB/SOLV

PROBABIL....PROBABILITY; SEE ALSO GAMBLE

S57
MARCH J.C.,"PARTY LEGISLATIVE REPRESENTATION AS A FUNCTION OF ELECTION RESULTS." DRIVE...PROBABIL REGRESS STYLE CHARTS HYPO/EXP SIMUL. PAGE 102 H2046
REPRESENT GOV/COMP LEGIS CHOOSE

S65
WOLF C. JR.,"THE POLITICAL EFFECTS OF SOME MILITARY PROGRAMS* SOME INDICATIONS FROM LATIN AMERICA." ELITES STRATA BUDGET FOR/AID WEAPON ATTIT PERCEPT PWR...REGRESS SYS/QU CHARTS NAT/COMP. PAGE 170 H3397
L/A+17C FORCES CIVMIL/REL PROBABIL

PROBABILITY....SEE PROBABIL

PROBLEM SOLVING....SEE PROB/SOLV

PROC/MFG....PROCESSING OR MANUFACTURING INDUSTRIES

B55
RESHETAR J.S.,PROBLEMS OF ANALYZING AND PREDICTING SOVIET BEHAVIOR. USSR CULTURE ECO/DEV AGRI DIST/IND EXTR/IND PROC/MFG NAT/G SECT TOP/EX ACT/RES ADMIN PWR WEALTH...SOC METH TOT/POP VAL/FREE 20. PAGE 131 H2617
COM ATTIT

B60
BURRIDGE K.,MAMBU: A MELANESIAN MILLENNIUM. ECO/UNDEV PROC/MFG FAM KIN CHIEF COLONIAL COERCE GP/REL DRIVE WEALTH WORSHIP 20 NEW/GUINEA. PAGE 25 H0494
S/ASIA SECT CULTURE MYTH

B61
MARX K.,THE COMMUNIST MANIFESTO. IN (MENDEL A. ESSENTIAL WORKS OF MARXISM, NEW YORK: BANTAM. FUT MOD/EUR CULTURE ECO/DEV ECO/UNDEV AGRI FINAN INDUS MARKET PROC/MFG LABOR MUNIC POL/PAR CONSULT FORCES CREATE PLAN ADMIN ATTIT DRIVE RIGID/FLEX ORD/FREE PWR RESPECT MARX/KARL WORK. PAGE 104 H2081
COM NEW/IDEA CAP/ISM REV

S61
VALLET R.,"IRAN: KEY TO THE MIDDLE EAST." COM IRAQ ISLAM KUWAIT LEBANON SAUDI/ARAB TURKEY ELITES SOCIETY INDUS PROC/MFG POL/PAR TOP/EX PLAN BAL/PWR DIPLOM ECO/TAC ALL/VALS...TREND CENTO 20. PAGE 161 H3224
NAT/G ECO/UNDEV IRAN

B62
GREEN L.P.,DEVELOPMENT IN AFRICA. AFR CENTRL/AFR GHANA RHODESIA SOUTH/AFR AGRI PROC/MFG INT/TRADE DEMAND NAT/LISM PRODUC WEALTH...GEOG METH/CNCPT CHARTS BIBLIOG 20. PAGE 60 H1206
CULTURE ECO/UNDEV GOV/REL TREND

B63
STIFEL L.D.,THE TEXTILE INDUSTRY - A CASE STUDY OF INDUSTRIAL DEVELOPMENT IN THE PHILIPPINES (PAPER). PHILIPPINE WORKER CAP/ISM INT/TRADE TARIFFS RECEIVE PRICE ADMIN COST EFFICIENCY WEALTH...BIBLIOG 20. PAGE 149 H2986
S/ASIA ECO/UNDEV PROC/MFG NAT/G

B64
FAINSOD M.,HOW RUSSIA IS RULED (REV. ED.). RUSSIA USSR AGRI PROC/MFG LABOR POL/PAR EX/STRUC CONTROL PWR...POLICY BIBLIOG 19/20 KHRUSH/N COM/PARTY. PAGE 48 H0963
NAT/G REV MARXISM

B64
LAWRENCE P.,ROAD BELONG CARGO: A STUDY OF CARGO
SOC

MOVEMENT IN SOUTHERN MADANG DISTRICT, NEW GUINEA. S/ASIA CULTURE ECO/UNDEV PROC/MFG KIN CHIEF COLONIAL COERCE GP/REL DRIVE WEALTH WORSHIP 20 NEW/GUINEA. PAGE 92 H1846 — SECT ALL/VALS MYTH

B64
RAMAZANI R.K.,THE MIDDLE EAST AND THE EUROPEAN COMMON MARKET. EUR+WWI ISLAM ECO/DEV EXTR/IND MARKET PROC/MFG INT/ORG NAT/G TEC/DEV ECO/TAC REGION DRIVE WEALTH...STAT CHARTS EEC TOT/POP 20. PAGE 129 H2587 — ECO/UNDEV ATTIT INT/TRADE

B65
SHEPHERD W.G.,ECONOMIC PERFORMANCE UNDER PUBLIC OWNERSHIP: BRITISH FUEL AND POWER. UK BUDGET GP/REL ...METH/CNCPT CHARTS BIBLIOG 20. PAGE 143 H2858 — PROC/MFG NAT/G OWN FINAN

B66
NEVITT A.A.,THE ECONOMIC PROBLEMS OF HOUSING. WOR+45 ECO/DEV ECO/UNDEV ACT/RES PROB/SOLV ECO/TAC RENT...OBS CHARTS 20. PAGE 117 H2342 — HABITAT PROC/MFG DELIB/GP NAT/COMP

S67
ALPANDER G.G.,"ENTREPRENEURS AND PRIVATE ENTERPRISE IN TURKEY." TURKEY INDUS PROC/MFG EDU/PROP ATTIT DRIVE WEALTH...GEOG MGT SOC STAT TREND CHARTS 20. PAGE 6 H0114 — ECO/UNDEV LG/CO NAT/G POLICY

S67
SCOVILLE W.J.,"GOVERNMENT REGULATION AND GROWTH IN THE FRENCH PAPER INDUSTRY DURING THE EIGHTEENTH CENTURY." FRANCE MOD/EUR FINAN CAP/ISM TAX ADMIN CONTROL PRIVIL LAISSEZ...POLICY 18. PAGE 141 H2818 — NAT/G PROC/MFG ECO/DEV INGP/REL

PROCEDURAL SYSTEMS....SEE ROUTINE, ALSO PROCESSES AND PRACTICES INDEX

PROCESSING OR MANUFACTURING INDUSTRY....SEE PROC/MFG

PRODUC....PRODUCTIVITY; SEE ALSO PLAN

B00
MOCKLER-FERRYMAN A.,BRITISH WEST AFRICA. FRANCE GERMANY NIGER SIER/LEONE UK CULTURE DIPLOM WAR RACE/REL PRODUC PROFIT WEALTH...POLICY PREDICT 19. PAGE 112 H2232 — AFR COLONIAL INT/TRADE CAP/ISM

B08
THE GOVERNMENT OF SOUTH AFRICA (VOL. II). SOUTH/AFR STRATA EXTR/IND EX/STRUC TOP/EX BUDGET ADJUD ADMIN CT/SYS PRODUC...CORREL CENSUS 19 RAILROAD CIVIL/SERV POSTAL/SYS. PAGE 2 H0030 — CONSTN FINAN LEGIS NAT/G

B13
KROPOTKIN P.,THE CONQUEST OF BREAD. SOCIETY STRATA AGRI INDUS WORKER REV HAPPINESS INCOME PRODUC HEALTH MORAL ORD/FREE. PAGE 89 H1775 — ANARCH SOCIALIST OWN AGREE

N19
BUSINESS ECONOMISTS' GROUP,INCOME POLICIES (PAMPHLET). UK INDUS LABOR TOP/EX PAY COST PRODUC ...ECOMETRIC GOV/COMP SIMUL ANTHOL 20. PAGE 25 H0497 — INCOME WORKER WEALTH POLICY

S21
MALINOWSKI B.,"THE PRIMITIVE ECONOMICS OF THE TROBRIAND ISLANDERS" (BMR)" CULTURE SOCIETY NAT/G CHIEF LEAD OWN...SOC MYTH WORSHIP 20 NEW/GUINEA TROBRIAND RESOURCE/N. PAGE 101 H2029 — ECO/UNDEV AGRI PRODUC STRUCT

B38
MARX K.,THE GERMAN IDEOLOGY, PARTS 1 AND 3 (1846). MOD/EUR LAW STRATA WORKER DOMIN REV UTOPIA SOCISM 19 MARX/KARL. PAGE 104 H2079 — MARXIST OWN PRODUC ECO/TAC

B39
FIRTH R.,PRIMITIVE POLYNESIAN ECONOMY. SOCIETY DIST/IND SECT CHIEF CAP/ISM PRODUC WEALTH...SOC OBS METH WORSHIP 20 POLYNESIA. PAGE 50 H1007 — ECO/UNDEV CULTURE AGRI ECO/TAC

B40
HERSKOVITS M.J.,THE ECONOMIC LIFE OF PRIMITIVE PEOPLES. INDUS OP/RES PLAN PROB/SOLV...BIBLIOG METH 20. PAGE 70 H1407 — CULTURE ECO/TAC ECO/UNDEV PRODUC

B45
VENABLE V.,HUMAN NATURE: THE MARXIAN VIEW. UNIV STRATA CAP/ISM REV GP/REL PERS/REL PRODUC KNOWL ...PHIL/SCI CONCPT IDEA/COMP 19 MARX/KARL ENGELS/F. PAGE 162 H3240 — PERSON MARXISM WORKER UTOPIA

B48
MINISTERE FINANCES ET ECO,BULLETIN BIBLIOGRAPHIQUE. AFR EUR+WWI FRANCE CULTURE STRUCT FINAN NAT/G ACT/RES INT/TRADE ADMIN REGION PRODUC STAT. PAGE 111 H2224 — BIBLIOG/A ECO/UNDEV TEC/DEV COLONIAL

B48
ROSENFARB J.,FREEDOM AND THE ADMINISTRATIVE STATE. NAT/G ROUTINE EFFICIENCY PRODUC RATIONAL UTIL ...TECHNIC WELF/ST MGT 20 BUREAUCRCY. PAGE 134 H2680 — ECO/DEV INDUS PLAN WEALTH

B48
WHITE C.L.,HUMAN GEOGRAPHY: AN ECOLOGICAL STUDY OF GEOGRAPHY. UNIV SEA CULTURE AGRI EXTR/IND RACE/REL PRODUC...CHARTS HYPO/EXP SIMUL GEN/LAWS T. PAGE 167 H3345 — SOC HABITAT GEOG SOCIETY

B50
SCHUMPETER J.A.,CAPITALISM, SOCIALISM, AND DEMOCRACY (3RD ED.). USA-45 USSR WOR+45 WOR-45 INTELL ECO/DEV ECO/UNDEV ECO/TAC WAR PRODUC ORD/FREE...MGT SOC 20 MARX/KARL. PAGE 140 H2804 — SOCIALIST CAP/ISM MARXISM IDEA/COMP

B55
UN ECONOMIC COMN ASIA & FAR E,ECONOMIC SURVEY OF ASIA AND THE FAR EAST, 1954. AFGHANISTN CEYLON INDIA PHILIPPINE S/ASIA ECO/DEV FINAN INDUS INT/TRADE PRODUC WEALTH...STAT CHARTS 20 CHINJAP. PAGE 158 H3158 — ECO/UNDEV PRICE NAT/COMP ASIA

C55
SANTAYANA G.,"REASON IN SOCIETY" IN G. SANTAYANA, THE LIFE OF REASON." INDUS FAM NAT/G WAR GP/REL HAPPINESS PRODUC LOVE WEALTH CONSERVE POPULISM CONCPT. PAGE 138 H2752 — RATIONAL SOCIETY CULTURE ATTIT

B57
NEUMARK S.D.,ECONOMIC INFLUENCES ON THE SOUTH AFRICAN FRONTIER, 1652-1836. SOUTH/AFR SEA AGRI NAT/G FORCES WORKER DIPLOM INT/TRADE PRICE DEMAND PRODUC...STAT CHARTS 17/19 FRONTIER. PAGE 117 H2341 — COLONIAL ECO/UNDEV ECO/TAC MARKET

B57
PALACIOS A.L.,PETROLEO, MONOPOLIOS, Y LATIFUNDIOS. L/A+17C EXTR/IND NAT/G TEC/DEV ECO/TAC CONTROL PRODUC 20 ARGEN MONOPOLY RESOURCE/N. PAGE 123 H2448 — ECO/UNDEV NAT/LISM INDUS AGRI

S57
COSER L.A.,"SOCIAL CONFLICT AND THE THEORY OF SOCIAL CHANGE." EUR+WWI CULTURE TEC/DEV PRODUC RIGID/FLEX SOC. PAGE 34 H0673 — GP/REL ROLE SOCIETY ORD/FREE

S58
LOCKWOOD W.W.,"THE SOCIALISTIC SOCIETY: INDIA AND JAPAN." INDIA ECO/DEV ECO/UNDEV INDUS NAT/G CONTROL LEAD PRODUC WEALTH 20 CHINJAP. PAGE 98 H1948 — ECO/TAC NAT/COMP FINAN SOCISM

B60
KERR C.,INDUSTRIALISM AND INDUSTRIAL MAN. CULTURE SOCIETY ECO/UNDEV NAT/G ADMIN PRODUC WEALTH ...PREDICT TREND NAT/COMP 19/20. PAGE 85 H1697 — WORKER MGT ECO/DEV INDUS

B61
BREWIS T.N.,CANADIAN ECONOMIC POLICY. CANADA BUDGET CAP/ISM INT/TRADE RATION TARIFFS TAX PRICE CONTROL ROUTINE FEDERAL INCOME PRODUC 20 GOLD/STAND. PAGE 20 H0412 — ECO/DEV ECO/TAC NAT/G PLAN

B61
NOVE A.,THE SOVIET ECONOMY. USSR ECO/DEV FINAN NAT/G ECO/TAC PRICE ADMIN EFFICIENCY MARXISM ...TREND BIBLIOG 20. PAGE 119 H2378 — PLAN PRODUC POLICY

B61
STARK H.,SOCIAL AND ECONOMIC FRONTIERS IN LATIN AMERICA (2ND ED.). CUBA FUT CULTURE AGRI INDUS ECO/TAC PRODUC ATTIT MARXISM...NAT/COMP BIBLIOG T 20. PAGE 149 H2971 — L/A+17C SOCIETY DIPLOM ECO/UNDEV

B62
GREEN L.P.,DEVELOPMENT IN AFRICA. AFR CENTRL/AFR GHANA RHODESIA SOUTH/AFR AGRI PROC/MFG INT/TRADE DEMAND NAT/LISM PRODUC WEALTH...GEOG METH/CNCPT CHARTS BIBLIOG 20. PAGE 60 H1206 — CULTURE ECO/UNDEV GOV/REL TREND

B62
MARTINS A.F.,REVOLUCAO BRANCA NO CAMPO. L/A+17C SERV/IND DEMAND EFFICIENCY PRODUC...POLICY METH/COMP. PAGE 104 H2070 — AGRI ECO/UNDEV TEC/DEV NAT/COMP

B62
MEHNERT K.,SOVIET MAN AND HIS WORLD. COM USSR INTELL FAM WORKER PLAN EDU/PROP REV PRODUC MARXISM ...SOC TREND SOC/INTEG 20 LENIN/VI STALIN/J KHRUSH/N. PAGE 108 H2162 — SOCIETY CULTURE ECO/DEV

B63
HAQ M.,THE STRATEGY OF ECONOMIC PLANNING. PAKISTAN AGRI FINAN INDUS NAT/G FOR/AID TAX CONTROL REGION PRODUC...POLICY CHARTS 20. PAGE 66 H1324 — ECO/TAC ECO/UNDEV PLAN PROB/SOLV

B63
MARX K.,THE POVERTY OF PHILOSOPHY (1847). SOCIETY STRATA INDUS WORKER OWN UTOPIA SOCISM...GEN/LAWS MARX/KARL. PAGE 104 H2082 — MARXIST PRODUC

B63
US ATOMIC ENERGY COMMISSION,ATOMIC ENERGY IN THE SOVIET UNION: TRIP REPORT OF THE US ATOMIC ENERGY DELEGATION, MAY 1933. USSR R+D NAT/G CONSULT CREATE DIPLOM ADMIN ROUTINE EFFICIENCY PRODUC KNOWL SKILL ...NAT/COMP 20 AEC TRAVEL TREATY. PAGE 159 H3176 — METH/COMP OP/RES TEC/DEV NUC/PWR

B64
BEARDSLEY R.K.,STUDIES ON ECONOMIC LIFE IN JAPAN (OCCASIONAL PAPERS NO. 8). INDUS FAM HABITAT...GEOG GOV/COMP 20 CHINJAP. PAGE 12 H0249 — WEALTH PRESS PRODUC INCOME

B64
INTERNATIONAL LABOUR OFFICE,EMPLOYMENT AND ECONOMIC GROWTH. ECO/DEV ECO/UNDEV NAT/G PLAN DIPLOM INT/TRADE CONTROL INCOME PRODUC WEALTH...STAT — WORKER METH/COMP ECO/TAC

NAT/COMP 20 ILO. PAGE 78 H1558 — OPTIMAL

B64
LEBRUN J.,BIBLIOGRAPHIE DE LA FERTILITE DES SOLS ET ELEMENTS DE SOCIOLOGIE RURALE EN AFRIQUE AU SUD DU SAHARA. AFR PLAN TEC/DEV EFFICIENCY PRODUC...GEOG SOC NAT/COMP 20. PAGE 93 H1850 — BIBLIOG/A ECO/UNDEV HABITAT AGRI

B64
SOLOW R.M.,THE NATURE AND SOURCES OF UNEMPLOYMENT IN THE UNITED STATES (PAMPHLET). USA+45 INDUS LABOR TEC/DEV ECO/TAC SKILL WEALTH...TREND NAT/COMP 20. PAGE 147 H2930 — ECO/DEV WORKER STAT PRODUC

B64
URQUIDI V.L.,THE CHALLENGE OF DEVELOPMENT IN LATIN AMERICA. L/A+17C FINAN INT/ORG TEC/DEV DIPLOM INT/TRADE PRICE REGION PRODUC...CHARTS 20. PAGE 159 H3175 — ECO/UNDEV ECO/TAC NAT/G TREND

B65
CHAO K.,THE RATE AND PATTERN OF INDUSTRIAL GROWTH IN COMMUNIST CHINA. CHINA/COM ECO/UNDEV TEC/DEV PRICE...NAT/COMP BIBLIOG 20. PAGE 29 H0578 — INDUS INDEX STAT PRODUC

B65
HERRICK B.H.,URBAN MIGRATION AND ECONOMIC DEVELOPMENT IN CHILE. CHILE AGRI INDUS LABOR NAT/G CENTRAL PRODUC...STAT SAMP CHARTS BIBLIOG/A 20 MIGRATION. PAGE 70 H1404 — HABITAT GEOG MUNIC ECO/UNDEV

B65
MAIR L.,AN INTRODUCTION TO SOCIAL ANTHROPOLOGY. LAW STRATA FINAN FAM KIN SECT INT/TRADE RACE/REL ADJUST PRODUC...T 20. PAGE 101 H2023 — SOC STRUCT CULTURE SOCIETY

S65
POWELL J.D.,"MILITARY ASSISTANCE AND MILITARISM IN LATIN AMERICA." USA+45 INT/ORG NAT/G CONTROL REGION PRODUC WEALTH...CLASSIF STAT NAT/COMP CONGRESS. PAGE 128 H2550 — L/A+17C FORCES FOR/AID PWR

S65
VAN DEN BERG M.,"SOME METHODOLOGICAL ASPECTS OF SOUTH AFRICA'S FIRST E.D.P." SOUTH/AFR NAT/G CREATE TEC/DEV CAP/ISM INCOME PRODUC...CON/ANAL CHARTS 20. PAGE 161 H3226 — ECO/DEV PLAN METH STAT

B66
BIRMINGHAM W.,A STUDY OF CONTEMPORARY GHANA VOL I: THE ECONOMY OF GHANA. AFR GHANA PLAN...POLICY STAT CHARTS ANTHOL BIBLIOG 20. PAGE 17 H0342 — ECO/UNDEV ECO/TAC NAT/G PRODUC

B66
BRODERSEN A.,THE SOVIET WORKER: LABOR AND GOVERNMENT IN SOVIET SOCIETY. USSR STRUCT INDUS LABOR PLAN PAY INGP/REL PRODUC...POLICY GEN/LAWS BIBLIOG 20 STALIN/J LENIN/VI BOLSHEVISM KHRUSH/N. PAGE 21 H0425 — WORKER ROLE NAT/G MARXISM

B66
DOBB M.,SOVIET ECONOMIC DEVELOPMENT SINCE 1917. USSR ECO/DEV ECO/UNDEV LABOR NAT/G TEC/DEV ECO/TAC ROUTINE PRODUC MARXISM 20. PAGE 41 H0829 — PLAN INDUS WORKER

B66
KIRKENDALL R.S.,SOCIAL SCIENTISTS AND FARM POLITICS IN THE AGE OF ROOSEVELT. ACADEM PLAN ECO/TAC GIVE ADMIN CONTROL PRODUC...SOC 20 NEW/DEAL ROOSEVLT/F BURAGR/ECO. PAGE 86 H1722 — AGRI INTELL POLICY NAT/G

B66
KOMIYA R.,POSTWAR ECONOMIC GROWTH IN JAPAN. ELITES NAT/G EX/STRUC TEC/DEV BUDGET DIPLOM CONTROL BAL/PAY PRODUC...BIBLIOG 20 CHINJAP. PAGE 88 H1754 — ECO/DEV POLICY PLAN ADJUST

B66
KUZNETS S.,MODERN ECONOMIC GROWTH. WOR+45 WOR-45 ECO/DEV ECO/UNDEV AGRI FINAN INDUS TEC/DEV EFFICIENCY INCOME...NAT/COMP 19/20. PAGE 89 H1786 — TIME/SEQ WEALTH PRODUC

S66
BENOIT J.,"WORLD DEFENSE EXPENDITURES." WOR+45 WEAPON COST PRODUC. PAGE 14 H0284 — FORCES STAT NAT/COMP BUDGET

B67
DENISON E.F.,WHY GROWTH RATES DIFFER; POSTWAR EXPERIENCE IN NINE WESTERN COUNTRIES. WOR+45 FINAN WORKER TEC/DEV EDU/PROP PRICE PRODUC WEALTH ...ECOMETRIC STAT CHARTS BIBLIOG. PAGE 40 H0791 — METH NAT/COMP ECO/DEV ECO/TAC

B67
POSNER M.V.,ITALIAN PUBLIC ENTERPRISE. ITALY ECO/DEV FINAN INDUS CREATE ECO/TAC ADMIN CONTROL EFFICIENCY PRODUC...TREND CHARTS 20. PAGE 127 H2545 — NAT/G PLAN CAP/ISM SOCISM

L67
BERNSTEIN T.P.,"LEADERSHIP AND MASS MOBILIZATION IN THE SOVIET AND CHINESE COLLECTIVISATION CAMPAIGNS OF 1929-30, 1955-56: COMPARISON." CHINA/COM USSR WORKER CONTROL COERCE PRODUC ATTIT...NAT/COMP 20. PAGE 16 H0317 — FEDERAL PLAN AGRI NAT/G

S67
BELLER I.,"ECONOMIC POLICY AND THE DEMANDS OF LABOR." PLAN TAX GIVE PRICE WAR COST PRODUC WEALTH. PAGE 13 H0268 — NAT/G ECO/TAC SOC/WK INCOME

S67
BERLINER J.S.,"RUSSIA'S BUREAUCRATS - WHY THEY'RE REACTIONARY." USSR NAT/G OP/RES PROB/SOLV TEC/DEV CONTROL SANCTION EFFICIENCY DRIVE PERSON...TECHNIC SOC 20. PAGE 15 H0308 — CREATE ADMIN INDUS PRODUC

S67
CARR E.H.,"REVOLUTION FROM ABOVE." USSR STRATA FINAN INDUS NAT/G DOMIN LEAD GP/REL INGP/REL OWN PRODUC PWR 20 STALIN/J. PAGE 27 H0538 — AGRI POLICY COM EFFICIENCY

S67
CHU-YUAN CHENG,"THE CULTURAL REVOLUTION AND CHINA'S ECONOMY." CHINA/COM AGRI DIST/IND INDUS MARKET NAT/G WORKER PLAN INT/TRADE DOMIN DEMAND PRODUC ...CHARTS 20 MAO. PAGE 30 H0600 — ECO/DEV ECO/TAC REV SOCISM

S67
DENISON E.F.,"SOURCES OF GROWTH IN NINE WESTERN COUNTRIES." WORKER TEC/DEV COST PRODUC...TREND NAT/COMP. PAGE 39 H0790 — INCOME NAT/G EUR+WWI ECO/DEV

S67
DEWHURST A.,"THE WAGE MOVEMENT IN CANADA." CANADA AGRI NAT/G PARTIC COST PRODUC PROFIT 20. PAGE 41 H0811 — WORKER MARXIST INDUS LABOR

S67
LEVCIK B.,"WAGES AND EMPLOYMENT PROBLEMS IN THE NEW SYSTEM OF PLANNED MANAGEMENT IN CZECHOSLOVAKIA." CZECHOSLVK EUR+WWI NAT/G OP/RES PLAN ADMIN ROUTINE INGP/REL CENTRAL EFFICIENCY PRODUC DECISION. PAGE 95 H1895 — MARXISM WORKER MGT PAY

S67
NUGENT J.B.,"ECONOMIC THOUGHT, INVESTMENT CRITERIA, AND DEVELOPMENT STRATEGIES IN GREECE* A POSTWAR SURVEY." GREECE AGRI INDUS INT/ORG NAT/G OP/RES DEMAND OPTIMAL PRODUC WEALTH 20 EEC. PAGE 119 H2379 — ECO/UNDEV PLAN FINAN

S67
RICHMAN B.M.,"CAPITALISTS & MANAGERS IN COMMUNIST CHINA." ASIA CHINA/COM ECO/UNDEV NAT/G CONSULT EX/STRUC PLAN EFFICIENCY PRODUC WEALTH MARXISM ...MGT CHARTS 20. PAGE 131 H2623 — CAP/ISM INDUS

S67
SCHACHTER G.,"REGIONAL DEVELOPMENT IN THE ITALIAN DUAL ECONOMY" ITALY AGRI INDUS MARKET WORKER ECO/TAC CONTROL INCOME PRODUC 20. PAGE 138 H2767 — REGION ECO/UNDEV NAT/G PROB/SOLV

S67
SINGH B.,"ITALIAN EXPERIENCE IN REGIONAL ECONOMIC DEVELOPMENT AND LESSONS FOR OTHER COUNTRIES." EUR+WWI ITALY INDUS NAT/G ACT/RES REGION GP/REL EFFICIENCY EQUILIB PRODUC WEALTH. PAGE 144 H2884 — ECO/UNDEV PLAN ECO/TAC CONTROL

S67
SLOAN P.,"FIFTY YEARS OF SOVIET RULE." USSR INDUS EDU/PROP EFFICIENCY PRODUC HEALTH KNOWL MORAL WEALTH MARXISM...POLICY 20. PAGE 145 H2900 — CREATE NAT/G PLAN INSPECT

S67
SMITH J.E.,"RED PRUSSIANISM OF THE GERMAN DEMOCRATIC REPUBLIC." GERMANY/E INTELL TOP/EX WORKER PLAN DIPLOM PRODUC ATTIT WEALTH MARXISM. PAGE 146 H2912 — NAT/G TOTALISM INDUS NAT/LISM

S67
SPITTMANN I.,"EAST GERMANY: THE SWINGING PENDULUM." COM GERMANY/E NAT/G EFFICIENCY MARXISM 20. PAGE 148 H2952 — PRODUC POL/PAR WEALTH ATTIT

B76
SMITH A.,THE WEALTH OF NATIONS. UK STRUCT WORKER DIPLOM ECO/TAC OPTIMAL DRIVE PERSON ORD/FREE ...OLD/LIB GEN/LAWS 17/18. PAGE 145 H2905 — WEALTH PRODUC INDUS LAISSEZ

B91
MILL J.S.,SOCIALISM (1859). MOD/EUR AGRI INDUS NAT/G REV INCOME PRODUC ORD/FREE POPULISM SOCISM ...GOV/COMP METH/COMP 19. PAGE 110 H2209 — WEALTH SOCIALIST ECO/TAC OWN

PRODUCTIVITY....SEE PRODUC

PROEHL P.O. H2562

PROF/ORG....PROFESSIONAL ORGANIZATIONS

B27
WEBER M.,GENERAL ECONOMIC HISTORY. CHRIST-17C MOD/EUR STRUCT AGRI EXTR/IND FINAN INDUS MARKET FAM MUNIC NAT/G PROF/ORG SECT ECO/TAC 8/20. PAGE 166 H3319 — ECO/DEV CAP/ISM

B35
DOUGLASS H.P.,THE PROTESTANT CHURCH AS A SOCIAL INSTITUTION. CULTURE FINAN NEIGH PROF/ORG OP/RES ADMIN...POLICY SOC/WK STAT BIBLIOG. PAGE 42 H0843 — SECT PARTIC INGP/REL GP/REL

B36
BELLOC H.,THE RESTORATION OF PROPERTY. UK STRATA NAT/G PROF/ORG DELIB/GP WORKER CREATE PROB/SOLV — CONTROL MAJORIT

ECO/TAC PARTIC UTOPIA ORD/FREE SOCISM 20. PAGE 13 H0270 — CAP/ISM OWN

S38

HALL R.C.,"REPRESENTATION OF BIG BUSINESS IN THE HOUSE OF COMMONS." UK ECO/DEV INDUS PROF/ORG LEGIS CAP/ISM ECO/TAC LAISSEZ...POLICY OLD/LIB PLURIST MGT 20 HOUSE/CMNS. PAGE 64 H1287 — LOBBY NAT/G

S39

HECKSCHER G.,"GROUP ORGANIZATION IN SWEDEN." SWEDEN STRATA ECO/DEV AGRI INDUS LABOR NAT/G PROF/ORG ECO/TAC CENTRAL SOCISM...MGT 19/20. PAGE 69 H1382 — LAISSEZ SOC

B56

VUCINICH A.,THE SOVIET ACADEMY OF SCIENCES. USSR STRUCT ACADEM NAT/G EDU/PROP ADMIN LEAD ROLE ...BIBLIOG 20 ACADEM/SCI. PAGE 164 H3280 — PHIL/SCI CREATE INTELL PROF/ORG

B58

INDIA (REPUBLIC) PARLIAMENT,CLASSIFIED LIST OF PUBLIC UNDERTAKINGS AND OTHER BODIES IN INDIA. INDIA ACADEM LG/CO CONSULT LEGIT CONFER GOV/REL 20. PAGE 76 H1528 — NAT/G LEGIS LICENSE PROF/ORG

B59

PAULSEN M.G.,LEGAL INSTITUTIONS TODAY AND TOMORROW. UK USA+45 NAT/G PROF/ORG PROVS ADMIN PARL/PROC ORD/FREE NAT/COMP. PAGE 124 H2477 — JURID ADJUD JUDGE LEGIS

B60

COUGHLIN R.,DOUBLE IDENTITY: THE CHINESE AND MODERN THAILAND. CHINA/COM S/ASIA THAILAND ECO/UNDEV EXTR/IND FINAN INDUS KIN MUNIC NAT/G PROF/ORG SCHOOL SECT ATTIT DRIVE...CONCPT OBS 20. PAGE 34 H0676 — ASIA FAM CULTURE

B60

EMERY E.,INTRODUCTION TO MASS COMMUNICATIONS. ACADEM PROF/ORG SCHOOL ACT/RES EDU/PROP ATTIT ...CONCPT BIBLIOG/A. PAGE 46 H0920 — COM/IND PRESS CON/ANAL CULTURE

S60

TAYLOR M.G.,"THE ROLE OF THE MEDICAL PROFESSION IN THE FORMULATION AND EXECUTION OF PUBLIC POLICY" (BMR)" CANADA NAT/G CONSULT ADMIN REPRESENT GP/REL ROLE SOVEREIGN...DECISION 20 CMA. PAGE 153 H3056 — PROF/ORG HEALTH LOBBY POLICY

C60

HAZARD J.N.,"SETTLING DISPUTES IN SOVIET SOCIETY: THE FORMATIVE YEARS OF LEGAL INSTITUTIONS." USSR NAT/G PROF/ORG PROB/SOLV CONTROL CT/SYS ROUTINE REV CENTRAL...JURID BIBLIOG 20. PAGE 68 H1372 — ADJUD LAW COM POLICY

B61

ALSTON P.L.,STATE EDUCATION AND SOCIAL CHANGE IN THE RUSSIAN EMPIRE 1871-1914 (PAPER). RUSSIA ELITES PROF/ORG EDU/PROP CONTROL PRIVIL AGE/Y...BIBLIOG 19/20. PAGE 6 H0115 — SCHOOL SOCIETY NAT/G GP/REL

B61

ETZIONI A.,COMPLEX ORGANIZATIONS: A SOCIOLOGICAL READER. CLIENT CULTURE STRATA CREATE OP/RES ADMIN ...POLICY METH/CNCPT BUREAUCRCY. PAGE 47 H0945 — VOL/ASSN STRUCT CLASSIF PROF/ORG

S61

DOGAN M.,"LES OFFICIERS DANS LA CARRIERE POLITIQUE DE MARECHAL MACMAHON AU GENERAL DE GAULLE." EUR+WWI FRANCE MOD/EUR ELITES STRATA POL/PAR LEGIT ATTIT ALL/VALS...SOC CONCPT 19/20. PAGE 42 H0833 — PROF/ORG FORCES NAT/G DELIB/GP

S63

CRUTCHER J.,"PAN AFRICANISM: AFRICAN ODYSSEY." AFR NAT/G POL/PAR PROF/ORG VOL/ASSN TOP/EX CREATE REGION RACE/REL ALL/VALS...CONCPT TIME/SEQ TREND CON/ANAL 20. PAGE 36 H0716 — PROVS DELIB/GP COLONIAL

S63

RUSTOW D.A.,"THE MILITARY IN MIDDLE EASTERN SOCIETY AND POLITICS." FUT ISLAM CONSTN SOCIETY FACE/GP NAT/G POL/PAR PROF/ORG CONSULT DOMIN ADMIN EXEC REGION COERCE NAT/LISM ATTIT DRIVE PERSON ORD/FREE PWR...POLICY CONCPT OBS STERTYP 20. PAGE 136 H2721 — FORCES ELITES

B64

CAUTE D.,COMMUNISM AND THE FRENCH INTELLECTUALS, 1914-1960. COM EUR+WWI MOD/EUR NAT/G PERF/ART PROF/ORG CREATE EDU/PROP ATTIT PERSON KNOWL MARXISM ...SOC TIME/SEQ MARX/KARL 20 MALRAUX/A GIDE/A SARTRE/J. PAGE 28 H0563 — POL/PAR INTELL

B64

RIES J.C.,THE MANAGEMENT OF DEFENSE: ORGANIZATION AND CONTROL OF THE US ARMED SERVICES. PROF/ORG DELIB/GP EX/STRUC LEGIS GOV/REL PERS/REL CENTRAL RATIONAL PWR...POLICY TREND GOV/COMP BIBLIOG. PAGE 131 H2626 — FORCES ACT/RES DECISION CONTROL

S64

ADAMS R.,"POLITICS AND SOCIAL ANTHROPOLOGY IN SPANISH AMERICA." FUT CULTURE SOCIETY NAT/G PROF/ORG EDU/PROP ATTIT RIGID/FLEX ALL/VALS ...POLICY GEOG METH/CNCPT MYTH TREND VAL/FREE 20. PAGE 3 H0065 — L/A+17C SOC

S64

PRELOT M.,"LA INFLUENCIA POLITICA Y ELECTORAL DE LA PRENSA EN LA FRANCIA ACTUAL." EUR+WWI SOCIETY NAT/G POL/PAR PROF/ORG PRESS ATTIT PWR...CONCPT 20. PAGE 128 H2556 — EDU/PROP FRANCE

B65

HYMES D.,THE USE OF COMPUTERS IN ANTHROPOLOGY. CULTURE PROF/ORG CONSULT CREATE EFFICIENCY PERCEPT ...CLASSIF LING CON/ANAL COMPUT/IR METH/COMP ANTHOL 20. PAGE 76 H1517 — METH COMPUTER TEC/DEV SOC

B65

NATIONAL REFERRAL CENTER SCI,A DIRECTORY OF INFORMATION RESOURCES IN THE UNITED STATES; SOCIAL SCIENCES. USA+45 PROF/ORG...PSY SOC 20. PAGE 116 H2322 — INDEX R+D ACADEM ACT/RES

B65

OECD,MEDITERRANEAN REGIONAL PROJECT: TURKEY; EDUCATION AND DEVELOPMENT. FUT TURKEY SOCIETY STRATA FINAN NAT/G PROF/ORG PLAN PROB/SOLV ADMIN COST...STAT CHARTS 20 OECD. PAGE 120 H2399 — EDU/PROP ACADEM SCHOOL ECO/UNDEV

B65

OECD,THE MEDITERRANEAN REGIONAL PROJECT: ITALY; EDUCATION AND DEVELOPMENT. ITALY SOCIETY STRATA FINAN NAT/G PROF/ORG WORKER PLAN PROB/SOLV ADMIN ...STAT CHARTS METH 20 OECD. PAGE 120 H2400 — SCHOOL EDU/PROP ECO/UNDEV ACADEM

B65

OECD,THE MEDITERRANEAN REGIONAL PROJECT: GREECE; EDUCATION AND DEVELOPMENT. FUT GREECE SOCIETY AGRI FINAN NAT/G PROF/ORG WORKER PLAN PROB/SOLV ADMIN DEMAND ATTIT 20 OECD. PAGE 120 H2401 — EDU/PROP SCHOOL ACADEM ECO/UNDEV

B65

ORG FOR ECO COOP AND DEVEL,THE MEDITERRANEAN REGIONAL PROJECT: AN EXPERIMENT IN PLANNING BY SIX COUNTRIES. FUT GREECE SPAIN TURKEY YUGOSLAVIA SOCIETY FINAN NAT/G PROF/ORG EDU/PROP ADMIN REGION COST...POLICY STAT CHARTS 20 OECD. PAGE 121 H2427 — PLAN ECO/UNDEV ACADEM SCHOOL

B65

RENNER K.,MENSCH UND GESELLSCHAFT - GRUNDRISS EINER SOZIOLOGIE (2ND ED.). STRATA FAM LABOR PROF/ORG WAR ...JURID CLASSIF 20. PAGE 131 H2616 — SOC STRUCT NAT/G SOCIETY

B65

SHRIMALI K.L.,EDUCATION IN CHANGING INDIA. INDIA CULTURE DIPLOM FOR/AID GP/REL RACE/REL ATTIT SOC/INTEG 20 UNESCO CMN/WLTH. PAGE 143 H2866 — EDU/PROP PROF/ORG ACADEM

B66

BECKER J.,BESSARABIEN UND SEIN DEUTSCHTUM. ROMANIA USSR STRUCT INDUS PROF/ORG SECT GP/REL INGP/REL 15/20 BESSARABIA. PAGE 13 H0254 — PROVS CULTURE SOCIETY

B66

HOLDSWORTH W.S.,A HISTORY OF ENGLISH LAW; THE CENTURIES OF SETTLEMENT AND REFORM (VOL. XVI). UK LOC/G NAT/G EX/STRUC LEGIS CT/SYS LEAD ATTIT ...POLICY DECISION JURID IDEA/COMP 18 PARLIAMENT. PAGE 73 H1454 — BIOG PERSON PROF/ORG LAW

S66

LODGE G.C.,"REVOLUTION IN LATIN AMERICA." USA+45 ELITES INDUS LABOR PROF/ORG SECT TEC/DEV CAP/ISM SKILL MARXISM...POLICY NAT/COMP. PAGE 98 H1950 — ATTIT REV L/A+17C IDEA/COMP

B67

BADGLEY R.F.,DOCTORS' STRIKE; MEDICAL CARE AND CONFLICT IN SASKATCHEWAN. CANADA NAT/G PROF/ORG GP/REL ADJUST ATTIT...HEAL SOC 20. PAGE 10 H0192 — HEALTH PLAN LABOR BARGAIN

B67

LENG S.C.,JUSTICE IN COMMUNIST CHINA: A SURVEY OF THE JUDICIAL SYSTEM OF THE CHINESE PEOPLE'S REPUBLIC. CHINA/COM LAW CONSTN LOC/G NAT/G PROF/ORG CONSULT FORCES ADMIN CRIME ORD/FREE...BIBLIOG 20 MAO. PAGE 94 H1877 — CT/SYS ADJUD JURID MARXISM

S67

HUNTINGTON S.P.,"INTRODUCTION: SOCIAL SCIENCE AND VIETNAM." VIETNAM CULTURE 20. PAGE 75 H1506 — ACADEM KNOWL PROF/ORG SOCIETY

PROFESSIONAL ORGANIZATION....SEE PROF/ORG

PROFIT

B00

MOCKLER-FERRYMAN A.,BRITISH WEST AFRICA. FRANCE GERMANY NIGER SIER/LEONE UK CULTURE DIPLOM WAR RACE/REL PRODUC PROFIT WEALTH...POLICY PREDICT 19. PAGE 112 H2232 — AFR COLONIAL INT/TRADE CAP/ISM

B29

LEITZ F.,DIE PUBLIZITAT DER AKTIENGESELLSCHAFT. BELGIUM FRANCE GERMANY UK FINAN PRESS GP/REL PROFIT KNOWL 20. PAGE 94 H1872 — LG/CO JURID ECO/TAC NAT/COMP

B63

DUE J.F.,STATE SALES TAX ADMINISTRATION. OP/RES BUDGET PAY ADMIN EXEC ROUTINE COST EFFICIENCY PROFIT...CHARTS METH/COMP 20. PAGE 43 H0855 — PROVS TAX STAT GOV/COMP

S65

GOLDMAN M.I.,"A BALANCE SHEET OF SOVIET FOREIGN AID." USA+45 ECO/UNDEV BAL/PWR ECO/TAC RENT GIVE EDU/PROP CONTROL COST PROFIT GEN/METH. PAGE 58 H1158 — USSR FOR/AID NAT/COMP EFFICIENCY

B66
BIRMINGHAM D.,TRADE AND CONFLICT IN ANGOLA. PORTUGAL CULTURE FORCES DIPLOM GP/REL PROFIT HABITAT NAT/COMP. PAGE 17 H0341 — WAR INT/TRADE ECO/UNDEV COLONIAL

L67
KELLEHER G.W.,"THE COMMON MARKET ANTITRUST LAWS: THE FIRST TEN YEARS." EUR+WWI INDUS PRICE ADJUD AGREE CONTROL PROFIT...POLICY 20 EEC. PAGE 84 H1684 — INT/ORG INT/TRADE MARKET NAT/G

S67
DEWHURST A.,"THE WAGE MOVEMENT IN CANADA." CANADA AGRI NAT/G PARTIC COST PRODUC PROFIT 20. PAGE 41 H0811 — WORKER MARXIST INDUS LABOR

PROFUMO/J....JOHN PROFUMO, THE PROFUMO AFFAIR

PROG/TEAC....PROGRAMMED INSTRUCTION

B67
MICKIEWICZ E.P.,SOVIET POLITICAL SCHOOLS: THE COMMUNIST PARTY ADULT INSTRUCTION SYSTEM. COM USSR INTELL SCHOOL WORKER CREATE PRESS ADMIN CONTROL ATTIT KNOWL...PROG/TEAC SOC/INTEG 20 COM/PARTY. PAGE 110 H2200 — NAT/G EDU/PROP AGE/A MARXISM

PROGRAMMED INSTRUCTION....SEE PROG/TEAC

PROGRAMMING....SEE COMPUTER

PROGRSV/M....PROGRESSIVE MOVEMENT (ALL NATIONS)

PROJ/TEST....PROJECTIVE TESTS

B60
MINER H.M.,OASIS AND CASBAH: ALGERIAN CULTURE AND PERSONALITY IN CHANGE. ALGERIA FRANCE SOCIETY MUNIC COLONIAL ATTIT...INT PROJ/TEST CHARTS 20. PAGE 111 H2221 — GP/COMP PERSON CULTURE ADJUST

PROJECTION....SEE DISPL
PROLOG H0053
PROPAGANDA....SEE EDU/PROP

PROPERTY TAX....SEE PROPERTY/TX

PROPERTY/TX....PROPERTY TAX

PROSTITUTN....SEE ALSO SEX + CRIME

B51
LEMERT E.M.,SOCIAL PATHOLOGY. CULTURE BIO/SOC PERSON SEX 20 PROSTITUTN. PAGE 94 H1876 — SOC ANOMIE CONCPT CRIME

PROTECTIONISM....SEE PROTECTNSM

PROTECTNSM....PROTECTIONISM

PROTEST....SEE COERCE

PROTESTANT....PROTESTANTS, PROTESTANTISM

B17
DE MAISTRE J.,DU PAPE (1817). FRANCE LAW SOCIETY SECT DOMIN REV HAPPINESS PWR SOVEREIGN 18/19 PROTESTANT. PAGE 38 H0761 — CATH CHIEF LEGIT NAT/G

B36
LAPRADE W.T.,PUBLIC OPINION AND POLITICS IN EIGHTEENTH CENTURY ENGLAND. UK CULTURE POL/PAR CHIEF TOP/EX LEAD REV NAT/LISM PWR 18 PROTESTANT PROTESTANT CHURCH/STA. PAGE 91 H1815 — POLICY ELITES ATTIT TIME/SEQ

B36
LAPRADE W.T.,PUBLIC OPINION AND POLITICS IN EIGHTEENTH CENTURY ENGLAND. UK CULTURE POL/PAR CHIEF TOP/EX LEAD REV NAT/LISM PWR 18 PROTESTANT PROTESTANT CHURCH/STA. PAGE 91 H1815 — POLICY ELITES ATTIT TIME/SEQ

B39
MILLER P.,THE NEW ENGLAND MIND: THE SEVENTEENTH CENTURY. CULTURE DOMIN WRITING INGP/REL CONSEN MAJORITY PERCEPT KNOWL MORAL...CONCPT LING WORSHIP 17 NEW/ENGLND PROTESTANT. PAGE 111 H2214 — SECT REGION SOC ATTIT

B40
HOBBES T.,BEHEMOTH (1668). UK CONSTN SECT DOMIN LEGIT UTIL ORD/FREE CATHISM...POLICY CONCPT GEN/LAWS 17 CHARLES/I CROMWELL/O PROTESTANT. PAGE 71 H1433 — REV NAT/G CHIEF

B49
HAUSER R.,AUTORITAT UND MACHT. SOCIETY SECT PWR CATHISM...JURID CONCPT 16/20 PROTESTANT LUTHER/M CALVIN/J CHURCH/STA. PAGE 68 H1360 — SOVEREIGN NAT/G LEGIT

B58
VARG P.A.,MISSIONARIES, CHINESE, AND DIPLOMATS: THE AMERICAN PROTESTANT MISSIONARY MOVEMENT IN CHINA, 1890-1952. ASIA ECO/UNDEV NAT/G PROB/SOLV CAP/ISM EDU/PROP COLONIAL NAT/LISM ATTIT MARXISM...NAT/COMP STERTYP 20 CHINJAP PROTESTANT MISSION. PAGE 162 H3234 — CULTURE DIPLOM SECT

B63
FRITZ H.E.,THE MOVEMENT FOR INDIAN ASSIMILATION, 1860-1890. SECT FORCES GP/REL RACE/REL DISCRIM FEDERAL CATHISM...BIBLIOG 19 INDIAN/AM PROTESTANT GRANT/US. PAGE 54 H1071 — CULTURE NAT/G ECO/TAC ATTIT

B66
FORD P.,CARDINAL MORAN AND THE A. L. P. NAT/G POL/PAR SECT DELIB/GP LOBBY REV CHOOSE ORD/FREE MARXISM 19/20 AUSTRAL PROTESTANT LABOR/PAR. PAGE 52 H1035 — CATHISM SOCISM LABOR SOCIETY

B66
SETTON K.M.,GREAT PROBLEMS IN EUROPEAN CIVILIZATION. CHRIST-17C EUR+WWI MOD/EUR SECT GP/REL ALL/VALS ORD/FREE ALL/IDEOS...TREND ANTHOL T CHRISTIAN RENAISSAN PROTESTANT. PAGE 142 H2835 — CULTURE CONCPT IDEA/COMP

S67
RAMA C.M.,"PASADO Y PRESENTE DE LA RELIGION EN AMERICA LATINA." L/A+17C ELITES SOCIETY STRATA MARXISM...STAT WORSHIP PROTESTANT. PAGE 129 H2585 — SECT CATHISM STRUCT NAT/COMP

PROUDHON J.P. H2563

PROUDHON/P....PIERRE JOSEPH PROUDHON

B50
CARR E.H.,STUDIES IN REVOLUTION. CREATE WAR PERSON ALL/IDEOS MARXISM SOCISM...PHIL/SCI METH/COMP ANTHOL 18/20 SAINTSIMON MARX/KARL PROUDHON/P LASSALLE/F PLEKHNV/GV. PAGE 27 H0537 — REV IDEA/COMP COERCE BIOG

PROVISIONS SECTION OAU H2564

PROVS....STATE AND PROVINCES

N
"PROLOG",DIGEST OF THE SOVIET UKRANIAN PRESS. USSR LAW AGRI INDUS PROVS SCHOOL DIPLOM GOV/REL ATTIT ...HUM LING 20. PAGE 3 H0053 — BIBLIOG/A NAT/G PRESS COM

B09
LOBINGIER C.S.,THE PEOPLE'S LAW OR POPULAR PARTICIPATION IN LAW-MAKING. FRANCE SWITZERLND UK LOC/G NAT/G PROVS LEGIS SUFF MAJORITY PWR POPULISM ...GOV/COMP BIBLIOG 19. PAGE 97 H1945 — CONSTN LAW PARTIC

B10
TEMPERLEY H.W.V.,SENATES AND UPPER CHAMBERS; THEIR USE AND FUNCTION IN THE MODERN STATE... UK WOR-45 CONSTN NAT/G POL/PAR PROVS SECT COLONIAL LEAD CHOOSE REPRESENT PWR...BIBLIOG 19/20 PARLIAMENT SENATE CMN/WLTH HOUSE/LORD. PAGE 153 H3059 — PARL/PROC NAT/COMP LEGIS EX/STRUC

B13
SIEGFRIED A.,TABLEAU POLITIQUE DE LA FRANCE DE L'OUEST SOUS LA TROISIEME REPUBLIQUE. FRANCE STRATA STRUCT NAT/G POL/PAR PROVS REGION GOV/REL ATTIT PWR ...TREND TIME 19. PAGE 143 H2869 — SOC GEOG SOCIETY

B17
HARLOW R.V.,THE HISTORY OF LEGISLATIVE METHODS IN THE PERIOD BEFORE 1825. USA-45 EX/STRUC ADMIN COLONIAL LEAD PARL/PROC ROUTINE...GP/COMP GOV/COMP HOUSE/REP. PAGE 66 H1333 — LEGIS DELIB/GP PROVS POL/PAR

C20
BLACHLY F.F.,"THE GOVERNMENT AND ADMINISTRATION OF GERMANY." GERMANY CONSTN LOC/G PROVS DELIB/GP EX/STRUC FORCES LEGIS TOP/EX CT/SYS...BIBLIOG/A 19/20. PAGE 17 H0348 — NAT/G GOV/REL ADMIN PHIL/SCI

B25
WILLIAMS B.,THE SELBORNE MEMORANDUM. AFR FUT SOUTH/AFR UK NAT/G BUDGET DIPLOM REGION GOV/REL SOVEREIGN...POLICY CHARTS 20 UNIFICA SELBORNE/W. PAGE 168 H3365 — COLONIAL PROVS

B27
PANIKKAR K.M.,INDIAN STATES AND THE GOVERNMENT OF INDIA. INDIA UK CONSTN CONTROL TASK GP/REL SOVEREIGN WEALTH...TREND BIBLIOG 19. PAGE 123 H2457 — GOV/COMP COLONIAL BAL/PWR PROVS

B27
WILLOUGHBY W.F.,PRINCIPLES OF PUBLIC ADMINISTRATION WITH SPECIAL REFERENCE TO THE NATIONAL AND STATE GOVERNMENTS OF THE UNITED STATES. FINAN PROVS CHIEF CONSULT LEGIS CREATE BUDGET EXEC ROUTINE GOV/REL CENTRAL...MGT 20 BUR/BUDGET CONGRESS PRESIDENT. PAGE 169 H3373 — NAT/G EX/STRUC OP/RES ADMIN

B30
BYNKERSHOEK C.,QUAESTIONUM JURIS PUBLICI LIBRI DUO. CHRIST-17C MOD/EUR CONSTN ELITES SOCIETY NAT/G PROVS EX/STRUC FORCES TOP/EX BAL/PWR DIPLOM ATTIT MORAL...TRADIT CONCPT. PAGE 25 H0502 — INT/ORG LAW NAT/LISM INT/LAW

B31
DUFFIELD M.,KING LEGION. NAT/G PROVS SECT LEGIS EDU/PROP PRESS GP/REL AGE/Y MARXISM POLICY. PAGE 43 — SUPEGO FORCES

H0856
VOL/ASSN LOBBY

B35
DE TOCQUEVILLE A.,DEMOCRACY IN AMERICA (4 VOLS.) (TRANS. BY HENRY REEVE). CONSTN STRUCT LOC/G NAT/G POL/PAR PROVS ETIQUET CT/SYS MAJORITY ATTIT 18/19. PAGE 39 H0772
POPULISM MAJORIT ORD/FREE SOCIETY

B38
POUND R.,THE FORMATIVE ERA OF AMERICAN LAW. CULTURE NAT/G PROVS LEGIS ADJUD CT/SYS PERSON SOVEREIGN ...POLICY IDEA/COMP GEN/LAWS 18/19. PAGE 127 H2548
CONSTN LAW CREATE JURID

B39
ANDERSON W.,LOCAL GOVERNMENT IN EUROPE. FRANCE GERMANY ITALY UK USSR MUNIC PROVS ADMIN GOV/REL CENTRAL SOVEREIGN 20. PAGE 7 H0136
GOV/COMP NAT/COMP LOC/G CONSTN

B44
GYORGY A.,GEOPOLITICS: THE NEW GERMAN SCIENCE. EUR+WWI GERMANY STRATA NAT/G PROVS DOMIN EDU/PROP ATTIT DRIVE FASCISM...GEOG NAZI 20. PAGE 63 H1261
PWR LEGIT WAR

B45
DITTMANN,DAS POLITISCHE DEUTSCHLAND VOR HITLER. GERMANY LOC/G PROVS...CHARTS GP/COMP 20. PAGE 41 H0827
POL/PAR NAT/G PARTIC

B49
GRODZINS M.,AMERICANS BETRAYED: POLITICS AND THE JAPANESE EXPANSION. PROVS COERCE CHOOSE GOV/REL GP/REL INGP/REL ATTIT ORD/FREE...DECISION CHARTS 20 NISEI. PAGE 61 H1230
DISCRIM POLICY NAT/G WAR

B50
KANN R.A.,THE MULTINATIONAL EMPIRE (2 VOLS.). AUSTRIA CZECHOSLVK GERMANY HUNGARY CULTURE NAT/G POL/PAR PROVS REGION REV FEDERAL...GEOG TREND CHARTS IDEA/COMP NAT/COMP 19/20. PAGE 83 H1654
NAT/LISM MOD/EUR

B50
WILBUR C.M.,CHINESE SOURCES ON THE HISTORY OF THE CHINESE COMMUNIST MOVEMENT (PAMPHLET). CHINA/COM ECO/UNDEV PROVS FORCES WAR...PHIL/SCI 20. PAGE 168 H3360
BIBLIOG/A MARXISM REV NAT/G

B54
BINANI G.D.,INDIA AT A GLANCE (REV. ED.). INDIA COM/IND FINAN INDUS LABOR PROVS SCHOOL PLAN DIPLOM INT/TRADE ADMIN...JURID 20. PAGE 17 H0335
INDEX CON/ANAL NAT/G ECO/UNDEV

B54
SCHWARTZ B.,FRENCH ADMINISTRATIVE LAW AND THE COMMON-LAW WORLD. FRANCE CULTURE LOC/G NAT/G PROVS DELIB/GP EX/STRUC LEGIS PROB/SOLV CT/SYS EXEC GOV/REL...IDEA/COMP ENGLSH/LAW. PAGE 140 H2808
JURID LAW METH/COMP ADJUD

B55
KHADDURI M.,WAR AND PEACE IN THE LAW OF ISLAM. CONSTN CULTURE SOCIETY STRATA NAT/G PROVS SECT FORCES TOP/EX CREATE DOMIN EDU/PROP ADJUD COERCE ATTIT RIGID/FLEX ALL/VALS...CONCPT TIME/SEQ TOT/POP VAL/FREE. PAGE 85 H1702
ISLAM JURID PEACE WAR

B57
ALEXANDER L.M.,WORLD POLITICAL PATTERNS. NAT/G PROVS CAP/ISM DIPLOM COLONIAL NAT/LISM...POLICY GEOG CHARTS METH/COMP NAT/COMP 20. PAGE 5 H0101
CONTROL METH GOV/COMP

B57
BOUSTEDT O.,REGIONALE STRUKTUR- UND WIRTSCHAFTSFORSCHUNG. WOR+45 WOR-45 MUNIC PROVS STAT. PAGE 19 H0388
GEOG CONCPT NAT/COMP

B57
MUELLER-DEHAM A.,HUMAN RELATIONS AND POWER; SOCIO-POLITICAL ANALYSIS AND SYNTHESIS. CONSTN SOCIETY NAT/G POL/PAR PROVS LEGIS POPULISM...SOC NEW/IDEA. PAGE 114 H2280
GEN/LAWS PERS/REL PWR CONCPT

B57
SCHLESINGER J.A.,HOW THEY BECAME GOVERNOR; A STUDY OF COMPARATIVE STATE POLITICS, 1870-1950. USA+45 USA-45 LAW POL/PAR LEGIS EDU/PROP REGION...STAT TREND CHARTS TIME 19/20 GOVERNOR. PAGE 139 H2788
PROVS CHIEF GOV/COMP CHOOSE

B58
LEPOINTE G.,ELEMENTS DE BIBLIOGRAPHIE SUR L'HISTOIRE DES INSTITUTIONS ET DES FAITS SOCIAUX, 987-1875. FRANCE SOCIETY NAT/G PROVS SECT ...PHIL/SCI 19/20. PAGE 94 H1887
BIBLIOG LAW

B59
BUNDESMIN FUR VERTRIEBENE,ZEITTAFEL DER VORGESCHICHTE UND DES ABLAUFS DER VERTREIBUNG SOWIE DER UNTERBRINGUNG UND EINGLIEDERUNG DER (2 VOLS.). GERMANY/E GERMANY/W NAT/G PROVS PROB/SOLV DIPLOM PARL/PROC ATTIT...BIBLIOG SOC/INTEG 20 MIGRATION PARLIAMENT. PAGE 24 H0475
JURID GP/REL INT/LAW

B59
HEMMERLE J.,SUDETENDEUTSCHE BIBLIOGRAPHIE 1949-1953. CZECHOSLVK GERMANY SOCIETY STRUCT SECT ...GEOG JURID 20. PAGE 69 H1391
BIBLIOG PROVS GP/REL CULTURE

B59
HENDERSON G.P.,REFERENCE MANUAL OF DIRECTORIES (16 VOLS.). MUNIC PROVS GOV/REL 20. PAGE 70 H1394
BIBLIOG/A NAT/COMP NAT/G INDUS

B59
LEMBERG E.,DIE VERTRIEBENEN IN WESTDEUTSCHLAND (3 VOLS.). GERMANY/W CULTURE STRUCT AGRI PROVS ADMIN ...JURID 20 MIGRATION. PAGE 94 H1875
GP/REL INGP/REL SOCIETY

B59
PARK R.L.,LEADERSHIP AND POLITICAL INSTITUTIONS IN INDIA. S/ASIA CULTURE ECO/UNDEV LOC/G MUNIC PROVS LEGIS PLAN ADMIN LEAD ORD/FREE WEALTH...GEOG SOC BIOG TOT/POP VAL/FREE 20. PAGE 123 H2468
NAT/G EXEC INDIA

B59
PAULSEN M.G.,LEGAL INSTITUTIONS TODAY AND TOMORROW. UK USA+45 NAT/G PROF/ORG PROVS ADMIN PARL/PROC ORD/FREE NAT/COMP. PAGE 124 H2477
JURID ADJUD JUDGE LEGIS

B59
ROCHE J.,LA COLONISATION ALLEMANDE ET LE RIO GRANDE DO SUL. BRAZIL L/A+17C NAT/G PROVS INGP/REL RACE/REL DISCRIM HABITAT...GEOG SOC/INTEG 19/20 MIGRATION. PAGE 133 H2652
ECO/UNDEV GP/REL ATTIT

B59
SISSONS C.B.,CHURCH AND STATE IN CANADIAN EDUCATION: AN HISTORICAL STUDY. CANADA ACADEM NAT/G SCHOOL LEGIS REGION MAJORITY...MAJORIT WORSHIP 18/20 CHURCH/STA. PAGE 145 H2891
SECT EDU/PROP PROVS GP/REL

B60
HAUSER O.,PREUSSISCHE STAATSRASON UND NATIONALER GEDANKE. PRUSSIA SOCIETY PRESS ADMIN...CONCPT 19/20. PAGE 68 H1358
NAT/LISM NAT/G ATTIT PROVS

B60
HUGHES C.C.,PEOPLE OF COVE AND WOODLOT; COMMUNITIES FROM THE VIEWPOINT OF SOCIAL PSYCHIATRY. CULTURE FAM PROVS HABITAT...PSY QU SAMP/SIZ CHARTS BIBLIOG 20. PAGE 74 H1489
GEOG SOCIETY STRUCT HEALTH

B60
JHA C.,INDIAN GOVERNMENT AND POLITICS. INDIA SERV/IND POL/PAR PROVS LEGIS CT/SYS CHOOSE GOV/REL FEDERAL 20. PAGE 81 H1616
NAT/G PARL/PROC CONSTN ADJUST

B60
PRASAD B.,THE ORIGINS OF PROVINCIAL AUTONOMY. INDIA UK FINAN LOC/G FORCES LEGIS CONTROL CT/SYS PWR ...JURID 19/20. PAGE 128 H2554
CENTRAL PROVS COLONIAL NAT/G

S60
GINSBURGS G.,"PEKING-LHASA-NEW DELHI." CHINA/COM FUT INDIA S/ASIA KIN NAT/G PROVS SECT FORCES BAL/PWR ECO/TAC DOMIN EDU/PROP LEGIT ADMIN REGION GUERRILLA PWR...TREND TIBET 20. PAGE 57 H1134
ASIA COERCE DIPLOM

S60
LEVINE R.A.,"THE INTERNALIZATION OF POLITICAL VALUES IN STATELESS SOCIETIES." AFR FAM KIN LOC/G PROVS JUDGE PERSON RIGID/FLEX...DECISION SOC TIME/SEQ 20. PAGE 95 H1904
CULTURE ATTIT

B61
BURDETTE F.L.,POLITICAL SCIENCE: A SELECTED BIBLIOGRAPHY OF BOOKS IN PRINT, WITH ANNOTATIONS (PAMPHLET). LAW LOC/G NAT/G POL/PAR PROVS DIPLOM EDU/PROP ADMIN CHOOSE ATTIT 20. PAGE 24 H0479
BIBLIOG/A GOV/COMP CONCPT ROUTINE

B61
DONNISON F.S.V.,CIVIL AFFAIRS AND MILITARY GOVERNMENT NORTH-WEST EUROPE 1944-1946. EUR+WWI FRANCE GERMANY UK USSR LOC/G PROVS PLAN PROB/SOLV BAL/PWR ECO/TAC CONTROL PWR...CHARTS 20. PAGE 42 H0836
NAT/G WAR FORCES CIVMIL/REL

B61
MARTINEZ RIOS J.,BIBLIOGRAFIA ANTROPOLOGICA Y SOCIOLOGICA DEL ESTADO DE OAXACA. WRITING...LING 12/20 INDIAN/AM MEXIC/AMER. PAGE 103 H2069
BIBLIOG SOC PROVS CULTURE

B61
MERRIAM A.,CONGO: BACKGROUND OF CONFLICT. AFR FUT KIN MUNIC NAT/G POL/PAR PROVS DELIB/GP PLAN DOMIN COERCE ATTIT...TIME/SEQ CHARTS CONGO 20. PAGE 109 H2182
CHOOSE GUERRILLA

B61
ROCHE J.P.,COURTS AND RIGHTS: THE AMERICAN JUDICIARY IN ACTION (2ND ED.). UK USA+45 USA-45 STRUCT TEC/DEV SANCTION PERS/REL RACE/REL ORD/FREE ...METH/CNCPT GOV/COMP METH/COMP T 13/20. PAGE 133 H2653
JURID CT/SYS NAT/G PROVS

B62
BRETTON H.L.,POWER AND STABILITY IN NIGERIA: THE POLITICS OF DECOLONIZATION. AFR CONSTN INTELL ECO/UNDEV COM/IND KIN NAT/G POL/PAR PROVS VOL/ASSN LEGIS DOMIN EDU/PROP LEGIT EXEC ROUTINE CHOOSE NAT/LISM ATTIT PERCEPT ALL/VALS. PAGE 20 H0411
CULTURE OBS NIGERIA

B62
HO PING-TI,THE LADDER OF SUCCESS IN IMPERIAL CHINA: ASPECTS OF SOCIAL MOBILITY, 1368-1911. INTELL STRATA FAM KIN MUNIC NAT/G PROVS SCHOOL DELIB/GP DOMIN EDU/PROP ADMIN ROUTINE PERSON ALL/VALS...SOC STAT BIOG HIST/WRIT TIME/SEQ VAL/FREE. PAGE 71 H1431
ASIA CULTURE

B62
JACKSON W.A.D.,RUSSO-CHINESE BORDERLANDS. ASIA COM
GEOG

USSR NAT/G PROVS EX/STRUC FORCES DOMIN COERCE PEACE ATTIT PWR SOVEREIGN WEALTH...CONCPT TREND CHARTS STERTYP VAL/FREE. PAGE 79 H1576 DIPLOM RUSSIA

B62
JOHNSON J.J.,THE ROLE OF THE MILITARY IN UNDERDEVELOPED COUNTRIES. AFR BURMA INDONESIA ISLAM ISRAEL L/A+17C S/ASIA THAILAND CULTURE ECO/UNDEV KIN PROVS CONSULT ACT/RES COERCE REV DRIVE RIGID/FLEX ORD/FREE...RECORD ANTHOL 20. PAGE 81 H1622 FORCES CONCPT

B62
STATE AND LOCAL GOVERNMENT. MUNIC NAT/G NEIGH PRESS CONTROL CHOOSE REPRESENT...BIBLIOG 20. PAGE 104 H2076 PROVS LOC/G GOV/REL PWR

B62
MUKERJI S.N.,ADMINISTRATION OF EDUCATION IN INDIA. ACADEM LOC/G PROVS ROUTINE...POLICY STAT CHARTS 20. PAGE 114 H2282 SCHOOL ADMIN NAT/G EDU/PROP

S62
SPRINGER H.W.,"FEDERATION IN THE CARIBBEAN: AN ATTEMPT THAT FAILED." L/A+17C ECO/UNDEV INT/ORG POL/PAR PROVS LEGIS CREATE PLAN LEGIT ADMIN FEDERAL ATTIT DRIVE PERSON ORD/FREE PWR...POLICY GEOG PSY CONCPT OBS CARIBBEAN CMN/WLTH 20. PAGE 148 H2955 VOL/ASSN NAT/G REGION

B63
ADRIAN C.R.,GOVERNING OVER FIFTY STATES AND THEIR COMMUNITIES. USA+45 CONSTN FINAN MUNIC NAT/G POL/PAR EX/STRUC LEGIS ADMIN CONTROL CT/SYS ...CHARTS 20. PAGE 4 H0073 PROVS LOC/G GOV/REL GOV/COMP

B63
BLONDEL J.,VOTERS, PARTIES, AND LEADERS. UK ELITES LOC/G NAT/G PROVS ACT/RES DOMIN REPRESENT GP/REL INGP/REL...SOC BIBLIOG 20. PAGE 18 H0358 POL/PAR STRATA LEGIS ADMIN

B63
DUE J.F.,STATE SALES TAX ADMINISTRATION. OP/RES BUDGET PAY ADMIN EXEC ROUTINE COST EFFICIENCY PROFIT...CHARTS METH/COMP 20. PAGE 43 H0855 PROVS TAX STAT GOV/COMP

B63
ELLIOT J.H.,THE REVOLT OF THE CATALANS. SPAIN LOC/G PROVS FORCES DIPLOM TASK WAR GOV/REL INGP/REL ...POLICY 17 OLIVARES. PAGE 45 H0909 REV NAT/G TOP/EX DOMIN

B63
HAILEY L.,THE REPUBLIC OF SOUTH AFRICA AND THE HIGH COMMISSION TERRITORIES. AFR SOUTH/AFR UK INT/ORG NAT/G PROVS RACE/REL SOVEREIGN...CHARTS 19/20 COMMONWLTH. PAGE 64 H1278 COLONIAL DIPLOM ATTIT

B63
LEONARD T.J.,THE FEDERAL SYSTEM OF INDIA. INDIA MUNIC NAT/G PROVS ADMIN SOVEREIGN...IDEA/COMP 20. PAGE 94 H1885 FEDERAL MGT NAT/COMP METH/COMP

B63
THORBURN H.G.,PARTY POLITICS IN CANADA. CANADA ELITES STRUCT INDUS PWR 20. PAGE 154 H3086 POL/PAR CONCPT NAT/G PROVS

B63
TOUVAL S.,SOMALI NATIONALISM: INTERNATIONAL POLITICS AND THE DRIVE FOR UNITY IN THE HORN OF AFRICA. AFR CULTURE PROVS LEGIS EDU/PROP REGION COERCE ATTIT...MYTH UNPLAN/INT TIME/SEQ SOMALI VAL/FREE 20. PAGE 156 H3118 SOCIETY EXEC NAT/LISM

S63
CRUTCHER J.,"PAN AFRICANISM: AFRICAN ODYSSEY." AFR NAT/G POL/PAR PROF/ORG VOL/ASSN TOP/EX CREATE REGION RACE/REL ALL/VALS...CONCPT TIME/SEQ TREND CON/ANAL 20. PAGE 36 H0716 PROVS DELIB/GP COLONIAL

S63
MAZRUI A.A.,"ON THE CONCEPT 'WE ARE ALL AFRICANS'." AFR CULTURE KIN LOC/G NAT/G DOMIN EDU/PROP LEGIT ATTIT PERCEPT PERSON KNOWL ORD/FREE...TIME/SEQ TOT/POP 20. PAGE 106 H2110 PROVS INT/ORG NAT/LISM

S63
TILMAN R.O.,"MALAYSIA: THE PROBLEMS OF FEDERATION." ISLAM S/ASIA CONSTN PROVS SECT DELIB/GP DOMIN EDU/PROP LEGIT EXEC COERCE CHOOSE ATTIT HEALTH ORD/FREE PWR...STAT TOT/POP VAL/FREE 20. PAGE 155 H3097 NAT/G CULTURE MALAYSIA

B64
FREISEN J.,STAAT UND KATHOLISCHE KIRCHE IN DEN DEUTSCHEN BUNDESSTAATEN (2 VOLS.). GERMANY LAW FAM NAT/G EDU/PROP GP/REL MARRIAGE WEALTH 19/20 CHURCH/STA. PAGE 53 H1056 SECT CATHISM JURID PROVS

B64
GOODNOW H.F.,THE CIVIL SERVICE OF PAKISTAN: BUREAUCRACY IN A NEW NATION. INDIA PAKISTAN S/ASIA ECO/UNDEV PROVS CHIEF PARTIC CHOOSE EFFICIENCY PWR ...BIBLIOG 20. PAGE 59 H1173 ADMIN GOV/REL LAW NAT/G

B64
HEIMSATH C.H.,INDIAN NATIONALISM AND HINDU SOCIAL REFORM. S/ASIA LAW CULTURE SOCIETY STRATA PROVS VOL/ASSN DELIB/GP LEGIS TOP/EX DOMIN EDU/PROP LEGIT ATTIT ALL/VALS...POLICY SOC TIME/SEQ STERTYP VAL/FREE 19/20. PAGE 69 H1385 SECT NAT/G

B64
IMAZ J.L.,LOS QUE MANDAN. INDUS LABOR NAT/G POL/PAR PROVS SECT CHIEF TOP/EX CONTROL 20 ARGEN. PAGE 76 H1524 LEAD FORCES ELITES ATTIT

B64
KAACK H.,DIE PARTEIEN IN DER VERFASSUNGSWIRKLICHKEIT DER BUNDESREPUBLIK. GERMANY/W ADMIN PARL/PROC CHOOSE...JURID 20. PAGE 82 H1646 POL/PAR PROVS NAT/G

B64
OECD SEMINAR REGIONAL DEV,REGIONAL DEVELOPMENT IN ISRAEL. ISRAEL STRUCT ECO/UNDEV NAT/G REGION...GEOG 20. PAGE 120 H2404 ADMIN PROVS PLAN METH/COMP

B64
SKINNER E.P.,THE MOSSI OF UPPER VOLTA: THE POLITICAL DEVELOPMENT OF A SUDANESE PEOPLE. AFR LAW AGRI FAM KIN POL/PAR PROVS SECT DELIB/GP EX/STRUC FORCES TOP/EX DOMIN EDU/PROP LEGIT CT/SYS COERCE CHOOSE ORD/FREE PWR WEALTH...SOC MYTH VAL/FREE. PAGE 145 H2897 CULTURE OBS UPPER/VOLT

S64
MARTELLI G.,"PORTUGAL AND THE UNITED NATIONS." AFR EUR+WWI ELITES INT/ORG NAT/G PROVS PLAN DIPLOM ECO/TAC DOMIN COLONIAL RIGID/FLEX MORAL ORD/FREE PWR WEALTH...MYTH UN 20. PAGE 103 H2060 ATTIT PORTUGAL

S64
NEEDHAM T.,"SCIENCE AND SOCIETY IN EAST AND WEST." INTELL STRATA R+D LOC/G NAT/G PROVS CONSULT ACT/RES CREATE PLAN TEC/DEV EDU/PROP ADMIN ATTIT ALL/VALS ...POLICY RELATIV MGT CONCPT NEW/IDEA TIME/SEQ WORK WORK. PAGE 116 H2327 ASIA STRUCT

S64
UNRUH J.M.,"SCIENTIFIC INPUTS TO LEGISLATIVE DECISION-MAKING (SUPPLEMENT)" USA+45 ACADEM NAT/G PROVS GOV/REL GOV/COMP. PAGE 159 H3171 CREATE DECISION LEGIS PARTIC

B65
BRASS P.R.,FACTIONAL POLITICS IN AN INDIAN STATE: THE CONGRESS PARTY IN UTTAR PRADESH. INDIA UK CONSTN CULTURE ECO/UNDEV LOC/G DOMIN COLONIAL CROWD GP/REL ADJUST CENTRAL RIGID/FLEX SOVEREIGN 20 UTTAR/PRAD CONGRESS/P. PAGE 20 H0406 POL/PAR PROVS LEGIS CHOOSE

B65
BROCK C.,A GUIDE TO LIBRARY RESOURCES FOR POLITICAL SCIENCE STUDENTS AT THE UNIVERSITY OF NORTH CAROLINA (PAMPHLET). USA+45 WOR+45 PROVS ATTIT MARXISM...POLICY NAT/COMP UN. PAGE 21 H0422 BIBLIOG/A DIPLOM NAT/G INT/ORG

B65
BROWNSON O.A.,THE AMERICAN REPUBLIC. NAT/G PROVS WAR GOV/REL PRIVIL ORD/FREE PWR ALL/IDEOS CONSERVE ...CONCPT 19 CIVIL/WAR. PAGE 22 H0452 CONSTN FEDERAL SOVEREIGN

B65
JACOB H.,POLITICS IN THE AMERICAN STATES; A COMPARATIVE ANALYSIS. USA+45 POL/PAR CHIEF LEGIS TAX EDU/PROP CONTROL CT/SYS LOBBY PARTIC...DECISION CHARTS 20. PAGE 79 H1578 PROVS GOV/COMP PWR

B65
KAAS L.,DIE GEISTLICHE GERICHTSBARKEIT DER KATHOLISCHEN KIRCHE IN PREUSSEN (2 VOLS.). PRUSSIA CONSTN NAT/G PROVS SECT ADJUD ADMIN ATTIT 16/20. PAGE 82 H1647 JURID CATHISM GP/REL CT/SYS

B65
PYLEE M.V.,CONSTITUTIONAL GOVERNMENT IN INDIA (2ND REV. ED.). INDIA POL/PAR EX/STRUC DIPLOM COLONIAL CT/SYS PARL/PROC PRIVIL...JURID 16/20. PAGE 128 H2569 CONSTN NAT/G PROVS FEDERAL

B65
SHARMA S.A.,PARLIAMENTARY GOVERNMENT IN INDIA. INDIA FINAN LOC/G PROVS DELIB/GP PLAN ADMIN CT/SYS FEDERAL...JURID 20. PAGE 142 H2849 NAT/G CONSTN PARL/PROC LEGIS

B65
SIRISKAR V.M.,POLITICAL BEHAVIOR IN INDIA. INDIA SOCIETY MUNIC NAT/G PROVS ACT/RES SUFF...OBS CHARTS 20 POONA. PAGE 144 H2889 CHOOSE POL/PAR PWR ATTIT

S65
THOMAS F.C. JR.,"THE PEACE CORPS IN MOROCCO." CULTURE MUNIC PROVS CREATE ROUTINE TASK ADJUST STRANGE...OBS PEACE/CORP. PAGE 154 H3077 MOROCCO FRANCE FOR/AID EDU/PROP

B66
BECKER J.,BESSARABIEN UND SEIN DEUTSCHTUM. ROMANIA USSR STRUCT INDUS PROF/ORG SECT GP/REL INGP/REL 15/20 BESSARABIA. PAGE 13 H0254 PROVS CULTURE SOCIETY

B66
BRECHER M.,SUCCESSION IN INDIA. INDIA USA+45 CONSTN AGRI POL/PAR PROVS SECT DELIB/GP FORCES PROB/SOLV ECO/TAC PWR...LING 20 CONGRESS NEHRU/J. PAGE 20 H0408 CHIEF DECISION CHOOSE

B66
DEUTSCHE INST ZEITGESCHICHTE,DIE WESTDEUTSCHEN PARTEIEN: 1945-1965. GERMANY/W CHOOSE PWR ...TIME/SEQ 20. PAGE 40 H0806 — POL/PAR CONCPT NAT/G PROVS

B66
DUNCOMBE H.S.,COUNTY GOVERNMENT IN AMERICA. USA+45 FINAN MUNIC ADMIN ROUTINE GOV/REL...GOV/COMP 20. PAGE 43 H0863 — LOC/G PROVS CT/SYS TOP/EX

B66
HOWE R.W.,BLACK AFRICA: FROM PRE-HISTORY TO THE EVE OF THE COLONIAL ERA. ECO/UNDEV KIN PROVS SECT INT/TRADE EDU/PROP COLONIAL...BIBLIOG WORSHIP. PAGE 74 H1482 — AFR CULTURE SOC

B66
LOVEDAY P.,PARLIAMENT FACTIONS AND PARTIES: THE FIRST THIRTY YEARS OF RESPONSIBLE GOVERNMENT IN NEW SOUTH WALES, 1856-1889. PROVS LEAD PARL/PROC PARTIC GP/REL INGP/REL MAJORITY PWR...GP/COMP 19 AUSTRAL. PAGE 99 H1970 — POL/PAR ELITES NAT/G LEGIS

B66
O'NEILL C.E.,CHURCH AND STATE IN FRENCH COLONIAL LOUISIANA: POLICY AND POLITICS TO 1732. PROVS VOL/ASSN DELIB/GP ADJUD ADMIN GP/REL ATTIT DRIVE ...POLICY BIBLIOG 17/18 LOUISIANA CHURCH/STA. PAGE 120 H2390 — COLONIAL NAT/G SECT PWR

B66
RINGHOFER K.,STRUKTURPROBLEME DES RECHTES. AUSTRIA ATTIT ORD/FREE...IDEA/COMP 20. PAGE 132 H2630 — JURID PROVS NAT/G NAT/LISM

B66
SASTRI K.V.S.,FEDERAL-STATE FISCAL RELATIONS IN INDIA: A STUDY OF THE FINANCE COMMISSION AND TECHNIQUES OF FINANCIAL ADJUSTMENT. INDIA PROVS DELIB/GP GOV/REL FEDERAL...MATH CHARTS 20. PAGE 138 H2756 — TAX BUDGET FINAN NAT/G

B66
SHARMA B.M.,THE REPUBLIC OF INDIA; CONSTITUTION AND GOVERNMENT. INDIA POL/PAR LEGIS EFFICIENCY ...TIME/SEQ GOV/COMP 20. PAGE 142 H2846 — PROVS NAT/G CONSTN

L66
"FEDERAL, STATE AND LOCAL GOVERNMENT PUBLICATIONS." ACADEM LOC/G NAT/G PROVS SCHOOL EFFICIENCY ...PHIL/SCI ANTHOL. PAGE 143 H2854 — BIBLIOG OP/RES METH

S66
"RESEARCH WORK 1965-1966." NEW/ZEALND ELITES ACADEM LOC/G MUNIC POL/PAR PROVS DIPLOM COLONIAL...SOC 20 AUSTRAL. PAGE 2 H0047 — BIBLIOG NAT/G CULTURE S/ASIA

S66
"FURTHER READING." INDIA LOC/G NAT/G PLAN ADMIN WEALTH...GEOG SOC CONCPT CENSUS 20. PAGE 2 H0049 — BIBLIOG ECO/UNDEV TEC/DEV PROVS

B67
CARTER G.M.,SOUTH AFRICA'S TRANSKEI: THE POLITICS OF DOMESTIC COLONIALISM. SOUTH/AFR ECO/UNDEV AGRI NAT/G PROVS PLAN DOMIN REPRESENT ADJUST DISCRIM ...OBS BIBLIOG 20 BANTUSTANS TRANSKEI. PAGE 27 H0550 — STRATA GOV/REL COLONIAL POLICY

B67
FISHER M.,PROVINCES AND PROVINCIAL CAPITALS OF THE WORLD. WOR+45 PROVS REGION. PAGE 51 H1014 — GEOG NAT/G NAT/COMP STAT

L67
MCALLISTER J.T. JR.,"THE POSSIBILITIES FOR DIPLOMACY IN SOUTHEAST ASIA." LAOS VIETNAM INT/ORG NAT/G PROVS BAL/PWR DOMIN AGREE COLONIAL WAR PWR 17/20 TREATY. PAGE 106 H2121 — DIPLOM S/ASIA

L67
WILBER L.A.,"THE GOVERNMENTAL STRUCTURE OF MISSISSIPPI: ITS STRENGTHS AND WEAKNESSES." AGRI LOC/G SCHOOL EX/STRUC LEGIS TOP/EX BUDGET CT/SYS APPORT RACE/REL...GOV/COMP 20 MISSISSIPP. PAGE 168 H3359 — CONSTN PROVS STAT CON/ANAL

S67
"PROTEST AGAINST SOVIET INDUSTRIALIZATION ILLS IN LITHUANIA* A MEMORANDUM." USSR LITHUANIA NAT/G PROVS COST GEOG. PAGE 2 H0050 — INDUS COLONIAL NAT/LISM PLAN

S67
ALBINSKI H.S.,"POLITICS AND BICULTURISM IN CANADA: THE FLAG DEBATE." CANADA SOCIETY NAT/G PROVS DELIB/GP DEBATE REGION SOVEREIGN PLURISM...POLICY SOC/INTEG 20. PAGE 5 H0093 — NAT/LISM GP/REL POL/PAR CULTURE

S67
CRITTENDEN J.,"DIMENSIONS OF MODERNIZATION IN THE AMERICAN STATES." USA+45 STRUCT MUNIC PROB/SOLV CONTROL LITERACY HABITAT...CONCPT METH/CNCPT CORREL CONT/OBS CENSUS 20. PAGE 35 H0702 — PROVS GOV/COMP STAT ECO/DEV

S67
DANA MONTANO S.M.,"APLICACIONES CONCRETAS DE LAS RESOLUCIONES Y RECOMENDACIONES DE LAS CONFERENCIAS INTERAMERICANAS DE ABOGADOS" L/A+17C NAT/G PROVS GOV/REL PERCEPT 20 ARGEN. PAGE 37 H0739 — JURID CT/SYS ORD/FREE BAL/PWR

S67
DOERN G.B.,"THE ROYAL COMMISSIONS IN THE GENERAL POLICY PROCESS AND IN FEDERAL-PROVINCIAL RELATIONS." CANADA CONSTN ACADEM PROVS CONSULT DELIB/GP LEGIS ACT/RES PROB/SOLV CONFER CONTROL EFFICIENCY...METH/COMP 20 SENATE ROYAL/COMM. PAGE 42 H0832 — R+D EX/STRUC GOV/REL NAT/G

S67
SALYZYN V.,"FEDERAL-PROVINCIAL TAX SHARING SCHEMES." CANADA LOC/G PROB/SOLV TEC/DEV BUDGET GOV/REL EFFICIENCY 20. PAGE 137 H2746 — PROVS TAX MUNIC NAT/G

S67
SHARKANSKY I.,"ECONOMIC AND POLITICAL CORRELATES OF STATE GOVERNMENT EXPENDITURE: GENERAL TENDENCIES AND DEVIANT CASES." USA+45 LOC/G NAT/G TAX GIVE INCOME...CENSUS CHARTS. PAGE 142 H2845 — PROVS BUDGET GOV/COMP

S67
WILSON J.Q.,"A GUIDE TO REAGAN COUNTRY* THE POLITICAL CULTURE OF SOUTHERN CALIFORNIA." NEIGH PROVS PARTIC CHOOSE ADJUST CONSEN PERSON CONSERVE CALIFORNIA REAGAN/RON. PAGE 169 H3379 — CULTURE ATTIT MORAL

B85
BLISS P.,OF SOVEREIGNTY. NAT/G PROVS GOV/REL PRIVIL ORD/FREE PWR CONSERVE...CONCPT 19. PAGE 18 H0356 — CONSTN SOVEREIGN FEDERAL

B95
HAMMOND B.E.,THE POLITICAL INSTITUTIONS OF THE ANCIENT GREEKS. GREECE MUNIC PROVS COERCE WAR ORD/FREE ARISTOTLE. PAGE 65 H1307 — GOV/COMP NAT/G IDEA/COMP CONCPT

B96
SCHMOLLER G.,THE MERCANTILE SYSTEM AND ITS HISTORICAL SIGNIFICANCE: ILLUSTRATED CHIEFLY FROM PRUSSIAN HISTORY (TRANS.). PRUSSIA CULTURE INDUS KIN MUNIC NAT/G PROVS OP/RES ECO/TAC INT/TRADE SUPEGO PWR WEALTH 19 MERCANTLST. PAGE 139 H2790 — GEN/METH INGP/REL CONCPT

PRUITT/DG....DEAN G. PRUITT

PRUSSIA....PRUSSIA

B22
FICHTE J.G.,ADDRESSES TO THE GERMAN NATION. GERMANY PRUSSIA ELITES NAT/G SECT CREATE INT/TRADE HEREDITY ...ART/METH LING 19 FRANK/PARL. PAGE 50 H0989 — NAT/LISM CULTURE EDU/PROP REGION

B27
BELLOC H.,THE SERVILE STATE (1912) (3RD ED.). PRUSSIA UK CULTURE STRATA INDUS NAT/G ECO/TAC CONTROL LEAD SUFF DISCRIM EQUILIB ORD/FREE WEALTH 20. PAGE 13 H0269 — WORKER CAP/ISM DOMIN CATH

B52
SKALWEIT S.,FRANKREICH UND FRIEDRICH DER GROSSE. FRANCE GERMANY PRUSSIA NAT/G DOMIN WAR 18 FREDERICK. PAGE 145 H2893 — ATTIT EDU/PROP DIPLOM SOC

B55
CRAIG G.A.,THE POLITICS OF THE PRUSSIAN ARMY 1640-1945. CHRIST-17C EUR+WWI MOD/EUR PRUSSIA STRUCT DIPLOM ADMIN REV WAR...SOC BIBLIOG 17/20. PAGE 35 H0694 — FORCES NAT/G ROLE CHIEF

B55
FRANZ G.,KULTURKAMPF. AUSTRIA GERMANY PRUSSIA SWITZERLND POL/PAR DIPLOM GP/REL ATTIT ORD/FREE 18/19 CHURCH/STA. PAGE 53 H1053 — NAT/LISM CATHISM NAT/G REV

B60
HAUSER O.,PREUSSISCHE STAATSRASON UND NATIONALER GEDANKE. PRUSSIA SOCIETY PRESS ADMIN...CONCPT 19/20. PAGE 68 H1358 — NAT/LISM NAT/G ATTIT PROVS

B62
SCHMIDT-VOLKMAR E.,DER KULTURKAMPF IN DEUTSCHLAND 1871-1890. GERMANY PRUSSIA SOCIETY STRUCT SECT DIPLOM GP/REL NAT/LISM 19 CHURCH/STA BISMARCK/O. PAGE 139 H2789 — POL/PAR CATHISM ATTIT NAT/G

B64
REMAK J.,THE GENTLE CRITIC: THEODOR FONTANE AND GERMAN POLITICS, 1848-1898. GERMANY PRUSSIA CULTURE ELITES BAL/PWR DIPLOM WRITING GOV/REL...HUM BIOG 19 BISMARCK/O JUNKER FONTANE/T. PAGE 131 H2614 — PERSON SOCIETY WORKER CHIEF

B65
KAAS L.,DIE GEISTLICHE GERICHTSBARKEIT DER KATHOLISCHEN KIRCHE IN PREUSSEN (2 VOLS.). PRUSSIA CONSTN NAT/G PROVS SECT ADJUD ADMIN ATTIT 16/20. PAGE 82 H1647 — JURID CATHISM GP/REL CT/SYS

B95
SELIGMAN E.R.A.,ESSAYS IN TAXATION. NEW/ZEALND PRUSSIA UK USA-45 MARKET LOC/G CREATE PRICE CONTROL INCOME OWN WEALTH...GOV/COMP METH/COMP 19. PAGE 141 H2824 — TAX TARIFFS INDUS NAT/G

B96
SCHMOLLER G.,THE MERCANTILE SYSTEM AND ITS — GEN/METH

HISTORICAL SIGNIFICANCE: ILLUSTRATED CHIEFLY FROM PRUSSIAN HISTORY (TRANS.). PRUSSIA CULTURE INDUS KIN MUNIC NAT/G PROVS OP/RES ECO/TAC INT/TRADE SUPEGO PWR WEALTH 19 MERCANTLST. PAGE 139 H2790
INGP/REL CONCPT

PSY....PSYCHOLOGY

N
ACAD RUMANIAN SCI DOC CTR,RUMANIAN SCIENTIFIC ABSTRACTS: SOCIAL SCIENCES. ROMANIA FINAN HABITAT ...ART/METH GEOG HUM JURID PSY 20. PAGE 3 H0059
BIBLIOG/A CULTURE LING LAW

N
AUSTRALIAN NATIONAL RES COUN,AUSTRALIAN SOCIAL SCIENCE ABSTRACTS. NEW/ZEALND CULTURE SOCIETY LOC/G CT/SYS PARL/PROC...HEAL JURID PSY SOC 20 AUSTRAL. PAGE 9 H0181
BIBLIOG/A POLICY NAT/G ADMIN

N
MIDDLE EAST INSTITUTE,CURRENT RESEARCH ON THE MIDDLE EAST....PHIL/SCI PSY SOC LING 20. PAGE 110 H2201
BIBLIOG R+D ISLAM NAT/G

N
SOUTH AFRICA STATE LIBRARY,SOUTH AFRICAN NATIONAL BIBLIOGRAPHY, SANB. SOUTH/AFR LAW NAT/G EDU/PROP ...MGT PSY SOC 20. PAGE 147 H2937
BIBLIOG PRESS WRITING

B11
HUXLEY T.H.,METHOD AND RESULTS: ESSAYS. EDU/PROP REPRESENT OWN PERSON PWR WEALTH...PSY IDEA/COMP GEN/LAWS. PAGE 76 H1514
ORD/FREE NAT/G POPULISM PLURIST

B15
MICHELS R.,POLITICAL PARTIES. NAT/G BAL/PWR CHOOSE REPRESENT ATTIT SOCISM...PSY SOC CONCPT OBS 20 MONOPOLY. PAGE 110 H2198
POL/PAR CENTRAL LEAD PWR

B19
DE MAN H.,THE REMAKING OF A MIND. EUR+WWI NAT/G ECO/TAC REGION ORD/FREE SOCISM...BIOG 20 WWI EUROPE. PAGE 38 H0762
PSY WAR SELF/OBS PARTIC

B20
COLE G.D.H.,SOCIAL THEORY. CULTURE LOC/G SECT REGION REPRESENT ATTIT DRIVE...PSY SOC BIBLIOG. PAGE 31 H0621
CONCPT NAT/G PHIL/SCI

B20
MACIVER R.M.,COMMUNITY: A SOCIOLOGICAL STUDY; BEING AN ATTEMPT TO SET OUT THE FUNDAMENTAL LAWS OF SOCIAL LIFE. UNIV STRUCT NAT/G CONTROL WAR BIO/SOC ...PSY SOC CONCPT GEN/LAWS. PAGE 100 H1996
REGION SOCIETY GP/REL

B21
WALLAS G.,HUMAN NATURE IN POLITICS (3RD ED.). UNIV NAT/G LEAD CHOOSE REPRESENT GP/REL NAT/LISM RATIONAL BIO/SOC HEREDITY ALL/VALS MAJORIT. PAGE 165 H3293
PSY DRIVE PERSON

B22
OGBURN W.F.,SOCIAL CHANGE WITH RESPECT TO CULTURE AND ORIGINAL NATURE. ACT/RES OP/RES CRIME GP/REL ANOMIE BIO/SOC PWR...PSY SOC TIME/SEQ METH SOC/INTEG. PAGE 120 H2405
CULTURE CREATE TEC/DEV

B26
MALINOWSKI B.,CRIME AND CUSTOM IN SAVAGE SOCIETY. SOCIETY FAM SECT LEGIT SANCTION MARRIAGE MYSTISM ...PSY SOC 19/20 MELANESIA CANON/LAW. PAGE 102 H2030
LAW CULTURE CRIME ADJUD

B28
SOROKIN P.,CONTEMPORARY SOCIOLOGICAL THEORIES. MOD/EUR UNIV SOCIETY R+D SCHOOL ECO/TAC EDU/PROP ROUTINE ATTIT DRIVE...PSY CONCPT TIME/SEQ TREND GEN/LAWS 20. PAGE 147 H2934
CULTURE SOC WAR

B29
DAVIE M.R.,THE EVOLUTION OF WAR. CULTURE KIN COERCE WAR ATTIT DRIVE...PSY SOC TIME/SEQ TREND GEN/LAWS. PAGE 37 H0746
FORCES STERTYP

B31
MACIVER R.M.,SOCIETY: ITS STRUCTURE AND CHANGES. CULTURE STRATA FAM CROWD HABITAT ORD/FREE...PSY SOC CONCPT BIBLIOG 20. PAGE 100 H1998
STRUCT SOCIETY PERSON DRIVE

B32
THIBAUDET A.,LES IDEES POLITIQUES DE LA FRANCE. FRANCE NAT/G SECT PRESS REV NAT/LISM PEACE ATTIT ...PSY 19/20 JACOBINISM JAURES/JL. PAGE 154 H3070
IDEA/COMP ALL/IDEOS CATHISM

B33
MANNHEIM E.,DIE TRAGER DER OFFENTLICHEN MEINUNG. ADJUST ATTIT...PSY 19/20. PAGE 102 H2037
SOC CULTURE CONCPT INDUS

B35
PARETO V.,THE MIND AND SOCIETY (4 VOLS.). ELITES SECT ECO/TAC COERCE PERSON ORD/FREE PWR SOVEREIGN FASCISM POPULISM...TRADIT 19/20. PAGE 123 H2465
GEN/LAWS SOC PSY

B36
WANDERSCHECK H.,WELTKRIEG UND PROPAGANDA. GERMANY MOD/EUR UK COM/IND NAT/G DOMIN PRESS ATTIT...POLICY 20 HITLER/A. PAGE 165 H3299
EDU/PROP PSY WAR KNOWL

B37
HORNEY K.,THE NEUROTIC PERSONALITY OF OUR TIME. SOCIETY PERS/REL ADJUST HAPPINESS ANOMIE ATTIT DRIVE SEX LOVE PWR CONCPT. PAGE 74 H1472
PSY PERSON STRANGE CULTURE

B37
MUNZENBERG W.,PROPAGANDA ALS WAFFE. COM/IND PRESS COERCE WAR...PSY 20. PAGE 115 H2290
EDU/PROP DOMIN NAT/G LEAD

B40
LEDERER E.,STATE OF THE MASSES. GERMANY ITALY SOCIETY NAT/G ECO/TAC EDU/PROP LEAD TOTALISM ...SOCIALIST PSY 20. PAGE 93 H1852
CROWD FASCISM AUTHORIT PERSON

B40
ZWEIG F.,THE WORKER IN AN AFFLUENT SOCIETY: FAMILY LIFE AND INDUSTRY. UK STRATA LG/CO ECO/TAC LEISURE INGP/REL HAPPINESS HEALTH...PSY SOC/WK INT CHARTS WORSHIP 20 FEMALE/SEX. PAGE 173 H3465
MARRIAGE ATTIT FINAN CULTURE

B41
BAUMANN G.,GRUNDLAGEN UND PRAXIS DER INTERNATIONALEN PROPAGANDA. FRANCE GERMANY UK CULTURE COM/IND PRESS PWR...PSY METH/COMP 20. PAGE 12 H0241
EDU/PROP DOMIN ATTIT DIPLOM

B45
HUNTINGTON E.,MAINSPRINGS OF CIVILIZATION. UNIV CULTURE SOCIETY BIO/SOC PERSON KNOWL SKILL...PSY RECORD HIST/WRIT TREND CHARTS TOT/POP. PAGE 75 H1504
SOC GEOG

B46
CASSIRER E.,THE MYTH OF THE STATE. WOR-45 SOCIETY RACE/REL RATIONAL PWR FASCISM...PHIL/SCI PSY LING TREND HEGEL/GWF MACHIAVELL. PAGE 28 H0557
MYTH CONCPT NAT/G IDEA/COMP

B48
LINEBARGER P.,PSYCHOLOGICAL WARFARE. NAT/G PLAN DIPLOM DOMIN ATTIT...POLICY CONCPT EXHIBIT 20 WWI. PAGE 97 H1933
EDU/PROP PSY WAR COM/IND

L48
SHILS E.A.,"COHESION AND DISINTEGRATION IN THE WEHRMACHT IN WORLD WAR II." GERMANY STRUCT DOMIN WAR INGP/REL ISOLAT NAT/LISM ATTIT AUTHORIT SUPEGO RESPECT...PSY CON/ANAL 20 NAZI. PAGE 143 H2862
EDU/PROP DRIVE PERS/REL FORCES

S48
ALEXANDER L.,"WAR CRIMES, THEIR SOCIAL-PSYCHOLOGICAL ASPECTS." EUR+WWI GERMANY LAW CULTURE ELITES KIN POL/PAR PUB/INST FORCES DOMIN EDU/PROP COERCE CRIME ATTIT SUPEGO HEALTH MORAL PWR FASCISM ...PSY OBS TREND GEN/LAWS NAZI 20. PAGE 5 H0100
DRIVE WAR

B49
GORER G.,THE PEOPLE OF GREAT RUSSIA: A PSYCHOLOGICAL STUDY. RUSSIA USSR NAT/G DIPLOM LEAD AGE/C ANOMIE ATTIT DRIVE...POLICY 20. PAGE 59 H1182
ISOLAT PERSON PSY SOCIETY

B49
SARGENT S.S.,CULTURE AND PERSONALITY. FUT UNIV SOCIETY FAM KIN NEIGH BIO/SOC DRIVE PERCEPT RIGID/FLEX LOVE RESPECT...PSY SOC CONCPT OBS TIME/SEQ TREND CON/ANAL CHARTS HYPO/EXP SIMUL TOT/POP. PAGE 138 H2754
CULTURE PERSON

B49
SAUVY A.,LE POUVOIR ET L'OPINION. FRANCE STRATA NAT/G PERCEPT...POLICY PSY 20. PAGE 138 H2758
EDU/PROP MYTH PARTIC ATTIT

S49
DEXTER L.A.,"A DIALOGUE ON THE SOCIAL PSYCHOLOGY OF COLONIALISM AND ON CERTAIN PUERTO RICAN PROFESSIONAL PERSONALITY PATTERNS." L/A+17C PUERT/RICO STRATA STRUCT DOMIN ISOLAT DRIVE ...NAT/COMP PERS/COMP HYPO/EXP 20 JEWS NEGRO. PAGE 41 H0813
COLONIAL SOC PSY PERSON

S49
MACKENZIE R.D.,"ECOLOGY, HUMAN." UNIV CULTURE ECO/DEV ECO/UNDEV ATTIT...POLICY GEOG PSY CONCPT METH/CNCPT CONT/OBS TREND GEN/LAWS. PAGE 100 H2001
SOCIETY BIO/SOC

B50
CANTRIL H.,TENSIONS THAT CAUSE WAR. UNIV CULTURE R+D CREATE EDU/PROP DRIVE PERSON KNOWL ORD/FREE ...HUM PSY SOC OBS CENSUS TREND CON/ANAL SOC/EXP SIMUL GEN/METH ANTHOL COLD/WAR TOT/POP. PAGE 26 H0523
SOCIETY PHIL/SCI PEACE

B50
ROHEIM G.,PSYCHOANALYSIS AND ANTHROPOLOGY. UNIV FAM PERS/REL ATTIT HABITAT...SOC OBS WORSHIP. PAGE 133 H2663
PSY BIOG CULTURE PERSON

B51
PARSONS T.,TOWARD A GENERAL THEORY OF ACTION. CULTURE PERSON...PSY SIMUL ANTHOL SOC/INTEG 20. PAGE 124 H2472
SOC PHIL/SCI DRIVE ACT/RES

B52
BENTHAM A.,HANDBOOK OF POLITICAL FALLACIES. FUT MOD/EUR LAW INTELL LOC/G MUNIC NAT/G DELIB/GP LEGIS CREATE EDU/PROP CT/SYS ATTIT RIGID/FLEX KNOWL PWR ...RELATIV PSY SOC CONCPT SELF/OBS TREND STERTYP TOT/POP. PAGE 14 H0286 — POL/PAR

B52
KROEBER A.L.,THE NATURE OF CULTURE. UNIV STRATA FAM KIN SECT...PSY GP/COMP 16/20 INDIAN/AM. PAGE 89 H1771 — CULTURE SOCIETY CONCPT STRUCT

B52
LEVY M.,THE STRUCTURE OF SOCIETY. CULTURE STRATA DRIVE KNOWL...PSY CONCPT METH/CNCPT NEW/IDEA STYLE GEN/LAWS. PAGE 95 H1907 — SOCIETY SOC

B52
MONTAGU A.,MAN'S MOST DANGEROUS MYTH: THE FALLACY OF RACE. LAW PROB/SOLV WAR HABITAT POPULISM...PSY CONCPT CHARTS BIBLIOG NEGRO JEWS. PAGE 112 H2242 — DISCRIM MYTH CULTURE RACE/REL

C52
EBENSTEIN W.,"INTRODUCTION TO POLITICAL PHILOSOPHY." COM CONSTN INTELL CONTROL PERSON NEW/LIB SOCISM...PSY GEN/LAWS BIBLIOG/A. PAGE 44 H0883 — ALL/IDEOS PHIL/SCI IDEA/COMP NAT/G

B53
BENDIX R.,CLASS, STATUS AND POWER: A READER IN SOCIAL STRATIFICATION. USA+45 SOCIETY ACT/RES DOMIN ATTIT RIGID/FLEX...PSY SOC CONCPT METH/COMP NAT/COMP 20. PAGE 14 H0273 — STRATA PWR STRUCT ROLE

B53
BIDNEY D.,THEORETICAL ANTHROPOLOGY. DRIVE ROLE ORD/FREE...CONCPT METH/CNCPT MYTH CLASSIF OBS IDEA/COMP METH/COMP BIBLIOG METH 20. PAGE 17 H0331 — CULTURE SOC PSY PHIL/SCI

B53
COBLENTZ S.A.,FROM ARROW TO ATOM BOMB: THE PSYCHOLOGICAL HISTORY OF WAR. PREHIST CULTURE CROWD PEACE DRIVE MORAL PWR...GP/COMP IDEA/COMP. PAGE 31 H0613 — WAR PSY SOCIETY

B53
MEAD M.,CULTURAL PATTERNS AND TECHNICAL CHANGE. BURMA GREECE NIGERIA ECO/UNDEV AGRI INDUS SCHOOL SECT CREATE FEEDBACK HABITAT...PSY METH/COMP BIBLIOG 20 UN. PAGE 108 H2152 — HEALTH TEC/DEV CULTURE ADJUST

B53
SQUIRES J.D.,BRITISH PROPAGANDA AT HOME AND IN THE UNITED STATES FROM 1914 TO 1917. UK NAT/G PROB/SOLV DOMIN PRESS EFFICIENCY...PSY PREDICT 20 WWI INTERVENT PSY/WAR. PAGE 148 H2960 — EDU/PROP CONTROL WAR DIPLOM

B54
SCHRAMM W.,THE PROCESS AND EFFECTS OF MASS COMMUNICATION. CULTURE INTELL SOCIETY COM/IND DRIVE PERCEPT PERSON RIGID/FLEX KNOWL...PSY SOC CONCPT CHARTS. PAGE 140 H2800 — ATTIT EDU/PROP

B54
SPROTT W.J.H.,SCIENCE AND SOCIAL ACTION. STRUCT ACT/RES CRIME GP/REL INGP/REL ANOMIE...PSY SOC/INTEG 19/20. PAGE 148 H2956 — SOC CULTURE PHIL/SCI

B54
TITIEV M.,THE SCIENCE OF MAN. LAW STRATA KIN GP/REL PERS/REL HABITAT HEREDITY KNOWL...LING CHARTS BIBLIOG WORSHIP. PAGE 155 H3107 — SOC PSY CULTURE

S54
BALANDIER G.,"SOCIOLOGIE DE LA COLONISATION ET RELATIONS ENTRE SOCIETES GLOBALES." AFR SOCIETY ECO/UNDEV KIN DOMIN EDU/PROP RIGID/FLEX PWR...PSY CONCPT TREND TOT/POP. PAGE 10 H0203 — CULTURE SOC COLONIAL

B55
RODNICK D.,THE NORWEGIANS: A STUDY IN NATIONAL CULTURE. NORWAY FAM INGP/REL PERS/REL AGE...PSY SOC SELF/OBS WORSHIP 20. PAGE 133 H2655 — CULTURE INT RECORD ATTIT

B56
BECKER H.,MAN IN RECIPROCITY: INTRODUCTORY LECTURES ON CULTURE, SOCIETY, AND PERSONALITY. LAW FAM SECT REGION GP/REL ADJUST ATTIT PERSON...BIBLIOG 20. PAGE 13 H0253 — CULTURE STRUCT SOC PSY

B56
MANNONI D.O.,PROSPERO AND CALIBAN: THE PSYCHOLOGY OF COLONIZATION. AFR EUR+WWI FAM KIN MUNIC SECT DOMIN ADMIN ATTIT DRIVE LOVE PWR RESPECT...PSY SOC CONCPT MYTH OBS DEEP/INT BIOG GEN/METH MALAGASY 20. PAGE 102 H2040 — CULTURE COLONIAL

B56
SHAPIRO H.L.,MAN, CULTURE, AND SOCIETY. STRUCT FAM SECT GP/REL INGP/REL...ART/METH GEOG PSY LING ANTHOL BIBLIOG. PAGE 142 H2842 — CULTURE PERSON SOC

B57
NARAIN D.,HINDU CHARACTER (A FEW GLIMPSES). INDIA DIPLOM SUICIDE PERS/REL ATTIT...PSY NAT/COMP PERS/COMP BIBLIOG WORSHIP 20 HINDU. PAGE 116 H2310 — PERSON STERTYP SUPEGO SECT

S57
DEXTER L.A.,"A SOCIAL THEORY OF MENTAL DEFICIENCY." CULTURE PUB/INST PROB/SOLV CRIME PERS/REL STRANGE PERSON SUPEGO SKILL...EPIST SOC/WK HYPO/EXP. PAGE 41 H0814 — SOC PSY HEALTH ROLE

S57
HAILEY,"TOMORROW IN AFRICA." CONSTN SOCIETY LOC/G NAT/G DOMIN ADJUD ADMIN GP/REL DISCRIM NAT/LISM ATTIT MORAL ORD/FREE...PSY SOC CONCPT OBS RECORD TREND GEN/LAWS CMN/WLTH 20. PAGE 64 H1277 — AFR PERSON ELITES RACE/REL

B58
GURVITCH G.,TRAITE DE SOCIOLOGIE (2 VOLS.). FRANCE CULTURE INDUS GP/REL INGP/REL...PSY BIBLIOG 20. PAGE 63 H1256 — ANTHOL SOC METH/COMP METH/CNCPT

B58
HENLE P.,LANGUAGE, THOUGHT AND CULTURE. CULTURE GP/REL PERCEPT...PSY TREND ANTHOL 20. PAGE 70 H1397 — LING RATIONAL CONCPT SOC

B58
SCOTT J.P.,AGGRESSION. CULTURE FAM SCHOOL ATTIT DISPL HEALTH...SOC CONCPT NEW/IDEA CHARTS LAB/EXP. PAGE 141 H2814 — DRIVE PSY WAR

B58
WARNER W.L.,A BLACK CIVILIZATION - A SOCIAL STUDY OF AN AUSTRALIAN TRIBE. SOCIETY FAM MARRIAGE...PSY SOC MYTH CHARTS 20 AUSTRAL MAPS MURNGIN RITUAL. PAGE 165 H3310 — CULTURE KIN STRUCT DEATH

B59
DUNHAM H.W.,SOCIOLOGICAL THEORY AND MENTAL DISORDER. UNIV SOCIETY STRATA HABITAT PERSON...GEOG CHARTS SOC/EXP TIME. PAGE 43 H0864 — HEALTH SOC PSY CULTURE

B59
HOBSBAWM E.J.,PRIMITIVE REBELS; STUDIES IN ARCHAIC FORMS OF SOCIAL MOVEMENT IN THE 19TH AND 20TH CENTURIES. ITALY SPAIN CULTURE VOL/ASSN RISK CROWD GP/REL INGP/REL ISOLAT TOTALISM...PSY SOC 18/20. PAGE 72 H1438 — SOCIETY CRIME REV GUERRILLA

B59
HONINGMAN J.J.,THE WORLD OF MAN. CHRIST-17C MEDIT-7 PRE/AMER PREHIST CREATE INGP/REL BIO/SOC HABITAT ...PSY SOC BIBLIOG. PAGE 73 H1460 — CULTURE METH PERSON STRUCT

B59
LEE D.,FREEDOM AND CULTURE. WOR+45 WOR-45 FAM HABITAT PERSON LOVE MORAL...PSY SOC OBS NAT/COMP WORSHIP 20. PAGE 93 H1856 — CULTURE SOCIETY CONCPT INGP/REL

B59
LEIGHTON A.H.,MY NAME IS LEGION: FOUNDATIONS FOR A THEORY OF MAN IN RELATION TO CULTURE (VOL. I). CULTURE STRANGE ANOMIE...SOC CONCPT METH/CNCPT CHARTS BIBLIOG METH 20 NOVA/SCOT. PAGE 93 H1867 — HEALTH PSY SOCIETY HABITAT

L59
JANIS I.L.,"DECISIONAL CONFLICT: A THEORETICAL ANALYSIS." INTELL NAT/G POL/PAR DELIB/GP LEGIS TOP/EX PLAN...DECISION CONGRESS NAZI 20 WWI. PAGE 80 H1590 — ACT/RES PSY DIPLOM

S59
LEVINE R.A.,"ANTI-EUROPEAN VIOLENCE IN AFRICA: A COMPARATIVE ANALYSIS." AFR CULTURE NAT/G DIPLOM EDU/PROP COLONIAL REGION COERCE ATTIT PWR...PSY CONCPT TIME/SEQ TREND HYPO/EXP SOC/EXP STERTYP GEN/METH COLD/WAR 20. PAGE 95 H1903 — DRIVE ORD/FREE REV

S59
LYNN D.B.,"THE EFFECTS OF FATHER-ABSENCE ON NORWEGIAN BOYS AND GIRLS." NORWAY CULTURE PERS/REL ADJUST DISPL LOVE...PSY CORREL STAT INT CON/ANAL CHARTS SOC/INTEG 20. PAGE 99 H1983 — SOC FAM AGE/C ANOMIE

S59
MCNEIL E.B.,"PSYCHOLOGY AND AGGRESSION." CULTURE SOCIETY ACT/RES DISPL PERSON HEALTH. PAGE 107 H2146 — DRIVE PSY

S59
SCOTT W.A.,"EMPIRICAL ASSESSMENT OF VALUES AND IDEOLOGIES." CULTURE SOCIETY SECT CREATE DRIVE PERSON MORAL PWR...SOC METH/CNCPT STAT CONT/OBS DEEP/INT DEEP/QU CHARTS VAL/FREE. PAGE 141 H2817 — ATTIT PSY

C59
EASTON D.,"POLITICAL ANTHROPOLOGY" IN BIENNIAL REVIEW OF ANTHROPOLOGY" UNIV LAW CULTURE ELITES SOCIETY CREATE...PSY CONCPT GP/COMP GEN/METH 20. PAGE 44 H0880 — SOC BIBLIOG/A NEW/IDEA

B60
BARBU Z.,PROBLEMS OF HISTORICAL PSYCHOLOGY. GREECE MEDIT-7 UK CULTURE TEC/DEV ADJUST RATIONAL ATTIT PERCEPT...METH/CNCPT NEW/IDEA TIME/SEQ GEN/METH. PAGE 11 H0214 — PERSON PSY HIST/WRIT IDEA/COMP

B60
DICHTER E.,THE STRATEGY OF DESIRE. UNIV CULTURE ACT/RES ATTIT DRIVE 20. PAGE 41 H0821 — EDU/PROP PSY CONSULT PERSON

B60
HUGHES C.C.,PEOPLE OF COVE AND WOODLOT; COMMUNITIES FROM THE VIEWPOINT OF SOCIAL PSYCHIATRY. CULTURE FAM PROVS HABITAT...PSY QU SAMP/SIZ CHARTS BIBLIOG 20. PAGE 74 H1489 — GEOG SOCIETY STRUCT HEALTH

B60
MANIS J.G.,MAN AND SOCIETY. STRATA LEAD INGP/REL PERS/REL ATTIT PWR...PSY ANTHOL T SOC/INTEG MARX/KARL MILL/JS FREUD/S CHURCHLL/W SPENCER/H RUSSELL/B. PAGE 102 H2036
SOC SOCIETY STRUCT CULTURE

B60
SHIRER W.L.,THE RISE AND FALL OF THE THIRD REICH: A HISTORY OF NAZI GERMANY. EUR+WWI CULTURE ECO/DEV INDUS NAT/G POL/PAR FORCES PLAN TEC/DEV ECO/TAC COERCE ATTIT DRIVE PERSON PWR...MYSTIC PSY SOC MYTH STAT CHARTS EXHIBIT WORK VAL/FREE. PAGE 143 H2864
STRUCT GERMANY TOTALISM

C60
EBENSTEIN W.,"MODERN POLITICAL THOUGHT (2ND ED.)" NAT/G CAP/ISM NAT/LISM PERSON ORD/FREE PWR ALL/IDEOS NEW/LIB SOCISM...TRADIT PSY BIBLIOG/A 18/20. PAGE 44 H0884
IDEA/COMP PHIL/SCI CONCPT GEN/LAWS

B61
BERKOWITZ L.,AGGRESSION: AS A SOCIAL PSYCHOLOGICAL ANALYSIS. UNIV CULTURE FACE/GP FAM KIN NEIGH EDU/PROP DISPL DRIVE HEALTH LOVE ORD/FREE...PSY SOC CONCPT OBS TREND. PAGE 15 H0305
SOCIETY COERCE WAR

B61
BULLOCK A.,HITLER: A STUDY IN TYRANNY. EUR+WWI GERMANY SOCIETY STRUCT NAT/G POL/PAR FORCES CREATE DOMIN EDU/PROP EXEC COERCE WAR NAT/LISM DISPL DRIVE PERSON PWR...PSY NAZI 20 HITLER/A. PAGE 23 H0470
ATTIT BIOG TOTALISM

B61
MARVICK D.,POLITICAL DECISION-MAKERS. INTELL STRATA NAT/G POL/PAR EX/STRUC LEGIS DOMIN EDU/PROP ATTIT PERSON PWR...PSY STAT OBS CONT/OBS STAND/INT UNPLAN/INT TIME/SEQ CHARTS STERTYP VAL/FREE. PAGE 104 H2073
TOP/EX BIOG ELITES

B61
PAZ O.,THE LABYRINTH OF SOLITUDE; LIFE AND THOUGHT IN MEXICO (TRANS. BY LYSANDER KEMP). INTELL COLONIAL REV...PSY SOC TIME/SEQ 16/20 MEXIC/AMER. PAGE 124 H2480
CULTURE PERSON PERS/REL SOCIETY

B61
VON EICKSTEDT E.,TURKEN, KURDEN UND IRANER SEIT DEM ALTERTUM. IRAN TURKEY GP/REL BIO/SOC HABITAT...PSY 20 PERSIA. PAGE 163 H3266
CULTURE SOC SOCIETY STRUCT

B61
VON MERING O.,A GRAMMAR OF HUMAN VALUES. WOR+45 CULTURE FACE/GP NEIGH CREATE EDU/PROP LEGIT ATTIT DRIVE PERSON ORD/FREE...PSY SOC METH/CNCPT OBS RECORD INT REC/INT STAND/INT QU CHARTS VAL/FREE. PAGE 164 H3275
SOCIETY MORAL

S61
SCHECHTMAN J.B.,"MINORITIES IN THE MIDDLE EAST." ISLAM INTELL SOCIETY STRATA KIN NAT/G VOL/ASSN EDU/PROP REGION GP/REL DISCRIM ATTIT BIO/SOC DISPL PERSON ALL/VALS...PSY SOC OBS SAMP GEN/LAWS 20. PAGE 139 H2776
SECT CULTURE RACE/REL

B62
THREE PRELIMINARY BIBLIOGRAPHIES OF WORKS RELATED TO THE SOCIAL SCIENCES IN LATIN AMERICA. BRAZIL CULTURE SOCIETY NAT/G PLAN PROB/SOLV...PSY 20 MEXIC/AMER. PAGE 2 H0040
BIBLIOG L/A+17C SOC AGRI

B62
KRECH D.,INDIVIDUAL IN SOCIETY; A TEXTBOOK OF SOCIAL PSYCHOLOGY. UNIV CULTURE LEAD INGP/REL ATTIT DRIVE PERCEPT ROLE...PHIL/SCI BIBLIOG T. PAGE 88 H1765
PSY SOC SOCIETY PERS/REL

B62
MELADY T.,THE WHITE MAN'S FUTURE IN BLACK AFRICA. FUT CULTURE SOCIETY NAT/G POL/PAR PLAN ECO/TAC DOMIN EDU/PROP LEGIT COLONIAL RACE/REL ATTIT DRIVE ALL/VALS...PSY SOC CONCPT TIME/SEQ TOT/POP VAL/FREE 20. PAGE 108 H2167
AFR STRATA ELITES

B62
YU LIEN YEN CHIU,INDEX TO THE CLASSIFIED FILES ON COMMUNIST CHINA. CHINA/COM CULTURE ECO/UNDEV CIVMIL/REL PWR WEALTH MARXISM...PSY SOC METH 20. PAGE 172 H3440
BIBLIOG INDEX COM

L62
NOLTE E.,"ZUR PHANOMENOLOGIE DES FASCHIMUS." EUR+WWI GERMANY ITALY TURKEY INTELL NAT/G CHIEF CONSULT FORCES CREATE DOMIN EDU/PROP COERCE WAR CHOOSE DRIVE FASCISM...PSY CONCPT MYTH GEN/METH LEAGUE/NAT NAZI 20. PAGE 118 H2367
ATTIT PWR

S62
SPRINGER H.W.,"FEDERATION IN THE CARIBBEAN: AN ATTEMPT THAT FAILED." L/A+17C ECO/UNDEV INT/ORG POL/PAR PROVS LEGIS CREATE PLAN LEGIT ADMIN FEDERAL ATTIT DRIVE PERSON ORD/FREE PWR...POLICY GEOG PSY CONCPT OBS CARIBBEAN CMN/WLTH 20. PAGE 148 H2955
VOL/ASSN NAT/G REGION

B63
CONFERENCE ABORIGINAL STUDIES,AUSTRALIAN ABORIGINAL STUDIES. ECO/UNDEV INT/TRADE COLONIAL ADJUST HABITAT HEREDITY...GEOG PSY LING SOC/EXP ANTHOL WORSHIP 20 AUSTRAL ABORIGINES. PAGE 32 H0638
SOC SOCIETY CULTURE STRUCT

B63
EICH H.,THE UNLOVED GERMANS. EUR+WWI GERMANY PERS/REL RACE/REL DISCRIM HABITAT SUPEGO FASCISM ...PSY SOC AUD/VIS 19/20 JEWS. PAGE 45 H0898
STERTYP PERSON CULTURE

ATTIT

B63
GERSCHENKRON A.,THE STABILITY OF DICTATORSHIPS. NAT/G EDU/PROP TASK ATTIT PERSON...POLICY PSY SOC METH 19/20. PAGE 56 H1116
TOTALISM CONCPT CONTROL ORD/FREE

B63
KATEB G.,UTOPIA AND ITS ENEMIES. CULTURE STRATA ECO/DEV INDUS REV MORAL...PSY IDEA/COMP 19/20. PAGE 84 H1668
UTOPIA SOCIETY PHIL/SCI PEACE

B63
KROEBER A.L.,ANTHROPOLOGY: BIOLOGY AND RACE. UNIV CULTURE HABITAT...PSY 20. PAGE 89 H1772
SOC PHIL/SCI RACE/REL INGP/REL

B63
LEIGHTON D.C.,THE CHARACTER OF DANGER (VOL. III). SOCIETY STRUCT STRANGE ANOMIE...SOC STAT CHARTS GP/COMP SOC/EXP SOC/INTEG 20 NOVA/SCOT. PAGE 94 H1868
HEALTH PSY CULTURE

B63
TUCKER R.C.,THE SOVIET POLITICAL MIND. COM INTELL NAT/G TOP/EX EDU/PROP ADMIN COERCE TOTALISM ATTIT PWR MARXISM...PSY MYTH HYPO/EXP 20. PAGE 157 H3136
STRUCT RIGID/FLEX ELITES USSR

L63
NASH M.,"PSYCHO-CULTURAL FACTORS IN ASIAN ECONOMIC GROWTH." ASIA ISLAM S/ASIA CULTURE ECO/UNDEV DELIB/GP EDU/PROP COERCE ATTIT PERSON HEALTH KNOWL ORD/FREE...PSY SOC STAT TREND ANTHOL VAL/FREE 20. PAGE 116 H2313
SOCIETY ECO/TAC

S63
ARASTEH R.,"THE ROLE OF INTELLECTUALS IN ADMINISTRATIVE DEVELOPMENT AND SOCIAL CHANGE IN MODERN IRAN." ISLAM CULTURE NAT/G CONSULT ACT/RES EDU/PROP EXEC ATTIT BIO/SOC PERCEPT SUPEGO ALL/VALS ...POLICY MGT PSY SOC CONCPT 20. PAGE 8 H0157
INTELL ADMIN IRAN

C63
BECKHAM R.S.,"A BASIC LIST OF BOOKS AND PERIODICALS FOR COLLEGE LIBRARIES." UNIV GP/REL...PSY SOC. PAGE 13 H0255
BIBLIOG SOCIETY CULTURE KNOWL

C63
HSU F.L.,"COHESION AND DIVISION IN THE AMERICAN WORLD" HSU FL. CLAN, CASTE, AND CLUB." CULTURE EDU/PROP CONFER SANCTION PERSON...PSY GP/COMP. PAGE 74 H1484
PERS/REL AGE/Y ADJUST VOL/ASSN

B64
ELKIN A.P.,THE AUSTRALIAN ABORIGINES - HOW TO UNDERSTAND THEM (4TH ED.). FAM NEIGH DEATH MARRIAGE ATTIT BIO/SOC HABITAT...PSY SOC MYTH WORSHIP AUSTRAL ABORIGINES. PAGE 45 H0908
CULTURE STRUCT SOCIETY KIN

B64
HARRIS M.,THE NATURE OF CULTURAL THINGS. GP/REL PERS/REL DRIVE HABITAT PERSON ROLE...PHIL/SCI PSY SOC CHARTS BIBLIOG 20. PAGE 67 H1341
CULTURE OBS CLASSIF NEW/IDEA

B64
NORTHROP F.S.,CROSS-CULTURAL UNDERSTANDING: EPISTEMOLOGY IN ANTHROPOLOGY. BURMA GREECE THAILAND HABITAT PERCEPT PERSON...PHIL/SCI SOC METH 20 MEXIC/AMER CHINJAP. PAGE 119 H2375
EPIST PSY CULTURE CONCPT

B64
ON CULTURE AND SOCIAL CHANGE. FAM NAT/G ACT/RES ECO/TAC RACE/REL...PSY TIME/SEQ TREND IDEA/COMP METH/COMP ANTHOL BIBLIOG 20. PAGE 120 H2406
CULTURE TEC/DEV STRUCT CREATE

B64
ZOLLSCHAN G.K.,EXPLORATIONS IN SOCIAL CHANGE. SOCIETY STRATA STRUCT ECO/UNDEV EX/STRUC...PSY ANTHOL 20. PAGE 173 H3463
ORD/FREE SIMUL CONCPT CULTURE

L64
BERELSON B.,"SAMPLE SURVEYS AND POPULATION CONTROL." ASIA FUT ISLAM L/A+17C CULTURE SOCIETY FAM NAT/G CONSULT PLAN EDU/PROP ATTIT DRIVE ALL/VALS...POLICY RELATIV HEAL PSY SOC CONCPT METH/CNCPT OBS OBS/ENVIR TOT/POP. PAGE 15 H0297
BIO/SOC SAMP

L64
FINDLATER R.,"US." EUR+WWI GERMANY USSR SOCIETY FACE/GP EDU/PROP PERCEPT PERSON ALL/VALS...PSY SOC CONCPT SELF/OBS SAMP TREND 20. PAGE 50 H1001
CULTURE ATTIT UK

S64
CROZIER B.,"POUVOIR ET ORGANISATION." SOCIETY NAT/G DOMIN...PSY SOC CONCPT TOT/POP VAL/FREE 20. PAGE 36 H0714
PERSON PWR DIPLOM

S64
GARMARNIKOW M.,"INFLUENCE-BUYING IN WEST AFRICA." COM FUT USSR INTELL NAT/G PLAN TEC/DEV ECO/TAC DOMIN EDU/PROP REGION NAT/LISM ATTIT DRIVE ALL/VALS SOVEREIGN...POLICY PSY SOC CONCPT TREND STERTYP WORK COLD/WAR 20. PAGE 55 H1102
AFR ECO/UNDEV FOR/AID SOCISM

C64
HARRIS M.,"THE NATURE OF CULTURAL THINGS." GP/REL DRIVE HABITAT PERSON ROLE...PHIL/SCI 20. PAGE 67
BIBLIOG CULTURE

H1340 PSY SOC

B65
BRAMSTED E.K.,GOEBBELS AND NATIONAL SOCIALIST PROPAGANDA, 1925-1945. EUR+WWI GERMANY UK USSR NAT/G FORCES WAR FASCISM...TIME/SEQ 20 GOEBBELS/J NAZI. PAGE 20 H0403 EDU/PROP PSY COM/IND

B65
DURKHEIM E.,THE ELEMENTARY FORMS OF THE RELIGIOUS LIFE. KIN PARTIC MORAL...PSY MYTH OBS IDEA/COMP METH WORSHIP 19/20. PAGE 43 H0870 SOC CULTURE CONCPT

B65
HAMIL H.M.,DICTATORSHIP IN SPANISH AMERICA. NAT/G COERCE MORAL ORD/FREE...POLICY PSY SOC ANTHOL 18/20. PAGE 65 H1300 TOTALISM CHIEF L/A+17C FASCISM

B65
HESS A.G.,CHASING THE DRAGON: A REPORT ON DRUG ADDICTION IN HONG KONG. ASIA CULTURE PROB/SOLV TRIBUTE...POLICY PSY SOC CLASSIF STAT 17/20 HONG/KONG. PAGE 70 H1411 BIO/SOC CRIME SOCIETY LAW

B65
NATIONAL REFERRAL CENTER SCI,A DIRECTORY OF INFORMATION RESOURCES IN THE UNITED STATES; SOCIAL SCIENCES. USA+45 PROF/ORG...PSY SOC 20. PAGE 116 H2322 INDEX R+D ACADEM ACT/RES

B65
SLOTKIN J.S.,READINGS IN EARLY ANTHROPOLOGY. INTELL SECT CREATE ATTIT KNOWL...HUM PHIL/SCI PSY LING 1/18. PAGE 145 H2902 SOC CULTURE GP/COMP

S65
LEVI W.,"THE CONCEPT OF INTEGRATION IN RESEARCH ON PEACE." NAT/G VOL/ASSN DIPLOM TASK ADJUST NAT/LISM PEACE DRIVE LOVE...PSY NET/THEORY GEN/LAWS. PAGE 95 H1897 CONCPT IDEA/COMP INT/ORG CENTRAL

S65
WEDGE B.,"PSYCHOLOGICAL FACTORS IN SOVIET DISARMAMENT NEGOTIATION." USA+45 CONFER ATTIT PERCEPT PERSON...PSY NAT/COMP. PAGE 166 H3324 USSR DIPLOM ARMS/CONT

B66
HOPKINS J.F.K.,ARABIC PERIODICAL LITERATURE, 1961. ISLAM LAW CULTURE SECT...GEOG HEAL PHIL/SCI PSY SOC 20. PAGE 73 H1466 BIBLIOG/A NAT/LISM TEC/DEV INDUS

B66
KIRKLAND E.C.,A BIBLIOGRAPHY OF SOUTH ASIAN FOLKLORE. WRITING HABITAT ALL/VALS MYSTISM ...ART/METH GEOG PSY SOC MYTH WORSHIP 13/20. PAGE 86 H1723 BIBLIOG S/ASIA CULTURE CREATE

B66
SMELSER N.J.,SOCIAL STRUCTURE AND MOBILITY IN ECONOMIC DEVELOPMENT. CULTURE SOCIETY CONFER...PSY SOC CHARTS METH/COMP NAT/COMP ANTHOL METH 20. PAGE 145 H2904 STRUCT STRATA ECO/UNDEV ECO/DEV

B66
SOROKIN P.A.,SOCIOLOGICAL THEORIES OF TODAY. SOCIETY STRUCT FAM SECT GP/REL ADJUST...PHIL/SCI PSY TREND METH/COMP 20. PAGE 147 H2935 SOC CULTURE METH/CNCPT EPIST

B66
TSURUMI K.,ADULT SOCIALIZATION AND SOCIAL CHANGE: JAPAN BEFORE AND AFTER DEFEAT IN WORLD WAR II. FAM DEATH SUPEGO...PSY SOC 20 CHINJAP. PAGE 157 H3133 SOCIETY AGE/A WAR PERSON

S66
HAIGH G.,"FIELD TRAINING IN HUMAN RELATIONS FOR THE PEACE CORPS." CONSULT CREATE EDU/PROP ADMIN TASK GP/REL ATTIT PERSON...PSY OBS SOC/EXP PEACE/CORP. PAGE 64 H1276 CULTURE PERS/REL FOR/AID ADJUST

S66
SMITH D.D.,"MODAL ATTITUDE CLUSTERS* A SUPPLEMENT FOR THE STUDY OF NATIONAL CHARACTER." CULTURE NAT/G PERCEPT...SOC NEW/IDEA MODAL RECORD GEN/METH. PAGE 145 H2906 ATTIT PERSON PSY CONCPT

C66
DEUTSCH K.W.,"NATIONALISM AND SOCIAL COMMUNICATION." CULTURE INGP/REL ATTIT PWR...PSY SOC CONCPT LING IDEA/COMP 20. PAGE 40 H0800 BIBLIOG NAT/LISM GEN/LAWS

B67
DAVIDSON E.,THE TRIAL OF THE GERMANS* NUREMBERG* 1946-48. EUR+WWI GERMANY CULTURE NAT/G LEAD PERSON HEALTH...CRIMLGY PSY SOC BIOG JEWS. PAGE 37 H0745 FASCISM ADJUD TOTALISM WAR

B67
FANON F.,BLACK SKIN, WHITE MASKS: THE EXPERIENCES OF A BLACK MAN IN A WHITE WORLD. CULTURE COLONIAL HAPPINESS ISOLAT STRANGE ATTIT HABITAT RIGID/FLEX SEX...BIOG STERTYP SOC/INTEG 20 NEGRO. PAGE 49 H0970 DISCRIM PERS/REL RACE/REL PSY

B67
POLSKY N.,HUSTLERS, BEATS, AND OTHERS. FACE/GP PRESS CRIME ADJUST ANOMIE DRIVE WEALTH...PSY SOC 20. PAGE 127 H2540 CULTURE CRIMLGY NEW/IDEA STRUCT

L67
GRAUBARD S.R.,"TOWARD THE YEAR 2000: WORK IN PROGRESS." FUT ACADEM SECT DELIB/GP DIPLOM EDU/PROP AGE/Y PERSON ROLE...PSY ANTHOL. PAGE 60 H1199 PREDICT PROB/SOLV SOCIETY CULTURE

S67
BULLOUGH B.,"ALIENATION IN THE GHETTO." CULTURE NEIGH GP/REL INGP/REL ATTIT...PSY SOC SAMP. PAGE 23 H0471 DISCRIM ANOMIE ADJUST

S68
LAPIERRE J.W.,"TRADITION ET MODERNITE A MADAGASCAR." ISLAM MADAGASCAR AGRI FINAN KIN NAT/G CREATE OP/RES GP/REL INGP/REL ATTIT CONSERVE...PSY 20. PAGE 91 H1813 ECO/UNDEV FOR/AID CULTURE TEC/DEV

PSY/WAR....PSYCHOLOGICAL WARFARE; SEE ALSO PSY + EDU/PROP + WAR

B53
SQUIRES J.D.,BRITISH PROPAGANDA AT HOME AND IN THE UNITED STATES FROM 1914 TO 1917. UK NAT/G PROB/SOLV DOMIN PRESS EFFICIENCY...PSY PREDICT 20 WWI INTERVENT PSY/WAR. PAGE 148 H2960 EDU/PROP CONTROL WAR DIPLOM

PSYCHIATRY....SEE PSY

PSYCHOANALYSIS....SEE BIOG, PSY

PSYCHO-DRAMA....SEE SELF/OBS

PSYCHOLOGICAL WARFARE....SEE PSY+EDU/PROP+WAR

PSYCHOLOGY....SEE PSY

PUB/INST....MENTAL, CORRECTIONAL, AND OTHER HABITATIONAL INSTITUTIONS

B37
UNION OF SOUTH AFRICA,REPORT CONCERNING ADMINISTRATION OF SOUTH WEST AFRICA (6 VOLS.). SOUTH/AFR INDUS PUB/INST FORCES LEGIS BUDGET DIPLOM EDU/PROP ADJUD CT/SYS...GEOG CHARTS 20 AFRICA/SW LEAGUE/NAT. PAGE 158 H3166 NAT/G ADMIN COLONIAL CONSTN

B39
BARNES H.E.,SOCIETY IN TRANSITION: PROBLEMS OF A CHANGING ERA. USA-45 INDUS MUNIC PUB/INST EDU/PROP CRIME RACE/REL...SOC MYTH NAT/COMP. PAGE 11 H0220 SOCIETY CULTURE TECHRACY TEC/DEV

S48
ALEXANDER L.,"WAR CRIMES, THEIR SOCIAL-PSYCHOLOGICAL ASPECTS." EUR+WWI GERMANY LAW CULTURE ELITES KIN POL/PAR PUB/INST FORCES DOMIN EDU/PROP COERCE CRIME ATTIT SUPEGO HEALTH MORAL PWR FASCISM ...PSY OBS TREND GEN/LAWS NAZI 20. PAGE 5 H0100 DRIVE WAR

S57
DEXTER L.A.,"A SOCIAL THEORY OF MENTAL DEFICIENCY." CULTURE PUB/INST PROB/SOLV CRIME PERS/REL STRANGE PERSON SUPEGO SKILL...EPIST SOC/WK HYPO/EXP. PAGE 41 H0814 SOC PSY HEALTH ROLE

S61
FITZGIBBON R.H.,"MEASUREMENT OF LATIN AMERICAN POLITICAL CHANGE." L/A+17C CONSTN CULTURE SOCIETY ECO/UNDEV NAT/G POL/PAR PUB/INST ACT/RES EDU/PROP PERCEPT KNOWL ORD/FREE SOVEREIGN...METH/CNCPT TREND OAS 20. PAGE 51 H1020 CHOOSE ATTIT

B62
KRUGLAK T.E.,THE TWO FACES OF TASS. COM COM/IND NAT/G ACT/RES PLAN PRESS PERCEPT PERSON KNOWL 20. PAGE 89 H1778 PUB/INST EDU/PROP USSR

B65
CHANDLER M.J.,A GUIDE TO RECORDS IN BARBADOS. WEST/IND PUB/INST SCHOOL SECT...HIST/WRIT 20. PAGE 28 H0573 BIBLIOG LOC/G L/A+17C NAT/G

B65
MEIER R.L.,DEVELOPMENTAL PLANNING. PUERT/RICO INDUS PUB/INST SCHOOL CREATE ECO/TAC FOR/AID...NAT/COMP 20. PAGE 108 H2165 PLAN ECO/UNDEV GOV/COMP TEC/DEV

B67
BODENHEIMER E.,TREATISE ON JUSTICE. INT/ORG NAT/G PUB/INST ACT/RES RISK CRIME INGP/REL DISCRIM DRIVE LAISSEZ 20. PAGE 18 H0363 ALL/VALS STRUCT JURID CONCPT

B67
FIELD M.G.,SOVIET SOCIALIZED MEDICINE. USSR FINAN R+D PROB/SOLV ADMIN SOCISM...MGT SOC CONCPT 20. PAGE 50 H0993 PUB/INST HEALTH NAT/G MARXISM

B67
RUDMAN H.C.,THE SCHOOL AND STATE IN THE USSR. COM USSR ACADEM LABOR LOC/G PUB/INST EDU/PROP GP/REL ROLE...POLICY DECISION MGT CHARTS 20. PAGE 136 H2712 SCHOOL ADMIN NAT/G POL/PAR

PUB/TRANS....PUBLIC TRANSPORTATION

PUBL/WORKS....PUBLIC WORKS

PUBLIC ADMINISTRATION....SEE ADMIN, NAT/G

PUBLIC HEALTH SERVICE....SEE PHS

PUBLIC OPINION....SEE ATTIT

PUBLIC POLICY....SEE NAT/G+PLAN

PUBLIC RELATIONS....SEE NAT/G+RELATIONS INDEX

PUBLIC WORKS....SEE PUBL/WORKS

PUBLIC/EDU....PUBLIC EDUCATION ASSOCIATION

PUBLIC/REL....PUBLIC RELATIONS; SEE ALSO NAT/G + RELATIONS INDEX

PUBLIC/USE....PUBLIC USE

PUEBLO....PUEBLO INCIDENT; SEE ALSO KOREA/N

PUERT/RICN....PUERTO RICAN

PUERT/RICO....PUERTO RICO; SEE ALSO L/A+17C

B01
GRIFFIN A.P.C.,A LIST OF BOOKS ON PORTO RICO. PUERT/RICO CULTURE LOC/G...GEOG MGT 19/20. PAGE 61 H1215 — BIBLIOG/A SOCIETY COLONIAL ADMIN

S49
DEXTER L.A.,"A DIALOGUE ON THE SOCIAL PSYCHOLOGY OF COLONIALISM AND ON CERTAIN PUERTO RICAN PROFESSIONAL PERSONALITY PATTERNS." L/A+17C PUERT/RICO STRATA STRUCT DOMIN ISOLAT DRIVE ...NAT/COMP PERS/COMP HYPO/EXP 20 JEWS NEGRO. PAGE 41 H0813 — COLONIAL SOC PSY PERSON

B61
MAYNE A.,DESIGNING AND ADMINISTERING A REGIONAL ECONOMIC DEVELOPMENT PLAN WITH SPECIFIC REFERENCE TO PUERTO RICO (PAMPHLET). PUERT/RICO SOCIETY NAT/G DELIB/GP REGION...DECISION 20. PAGE 105 H2106 — ECO/UNDEV PLAN CREATE ADMIN

B65
MEIER R.L.,DEVELOPMENTAL PLANNING. PUERT/RICO INDUS PUB/INST SCHOOL CREATE ECO/TAC FOR/AID...NAT/COMP 20. PAGE 108 H2165 — PLAN ECO/UNDEV GOV/COMP TEC/DEV

S67
EPSTEIN E.H.,"NATIONAL IDENTITY AND THE LANGUAGE ISSUE IN PUERTO RICO." PUERT/RICO CULTURE STRUCT NAT/G PROB/SOLV SKILL...JURID STAT METH/COMP 20. PAGE 47 H0931 — EDU/PROP SCHOOL LING NAT/LISM

S67
SCOTT J.W.,"SOURCES OF SOCIAL CHANGE IN COMMUNITY, FAMILY, AND FERTILITY IN A PUERTO RICAN TOWN." PUERT/RICO CULTURE STRUCT ECO/UNDEV INDUS PERS/REL ROLE...SOC STAND/INT. PAGE 141 H2815 — FAM MARRIAGE LITERACY ATTIT

PUERTO RICANS....SEE PUERT/RICN

PUFENDORF S. H2565

PULLMAN....PULLMAN, ILLINOIS

PUNDEEF M.V. H2566

PUNISHMENT....SEE ADJUD, LAW, LEGIT, SANCTION

PUNJAB....THE PUNJAB AND ITS PEOPLES

PUNTA DEL ESTE....SEE PUNTA/ESTE

PUNTA/ESTE....PUNTA DEL ESTE

PURGE....PURGES

PURHAM/M....MARGERY PURHAM

PURITAN....PURITANS

B44
WOLFE D.M.,LEVELLER MANIFESTOES OF THE PURITAN REVOLUTION. UK CONSTN NAT/G SECT...CONCPT ANTHOL 17 LEVELLERS DECLAR/IND PURITAN LOCKE/JOHN. PAGE 170 H3400 — POL/PAR REV ORD/FREE ATTIT

B58
EUSDEN J.D.,PURITANS, LAWYERS, AND POLITICS IN EARLY SEVENTEENTH-CENTURY ENGLAND. UK CT/SYS PARL/PROC RATIONAL PWR SOVEREIGN...IDEA/COMP BIBLIOG 17 PURITAN COMMON/LAW. PAGE 48 H0951 — GP/REL SECT NAT/G LAW

B64
GRIFFITH W.,THE WELSH (2ND ED.). UK SOCIETY STRUCT SECT WRITING NAT/LISM...ART/METH MODAL OBS/ENVIR TREND SOC/INTEG WALES PURITAN MUSIC. PAGE 61 H1223 — CULTURE SOC LING

PWR....POWER, PARTICIPATION IN DECISION-MAKING

B00
BENEDETTI V.,STUDIES IN DIPLOMACY. BELGIUM FRANCE GERMANY MOD/EUR CONSTN NAT/G CONSULT TOP/EX DOMIN EDU/PROP COERCE ATTIT...CONCPT INT BIOG TREND 19. PAGE 14 H0276 — PWR GEN/LAWS DIPLOM

B00
DE JOMINI A.H.,THE ART OF WAR. MOD/EUR NAT/G BAL/PWR DIPLOM DOMIN EXEC ROUTINE COERCE DRIVE PWR SKILL...POLICY CONCPT CHARTS STERTYP 19. PAGE 38 H0755 — PLAN FORCES WAR WEAPON

B04
DANTE ALIGHIERI,DE MONARCHIA (CA .1310). CHRIST-17C ITALY DOMIN LEGIT ATTIT PWR...CATH CONCPT TIME/SEQ. PAGE 37 H0741 — SECT NAT/G SOVEREIGN

B05
MACHIAVELLI N.,THE ART OF WAR. CHRIST-17C TOP/EX DRIVE ORD/FREE PWR SKILL...MGT CHARTS. PAGE 100 H1993 — NAT/G FORCES WAR ITALY

B09
LOBINGIER C.S.,THE PEOPLE'S LAW OR POPULAR PARTICIPATION IN LAW-MAKING. FRANCE SWITZERLND UK LOC/G NAT/G PROVS LEGIS SUFF MAJORITY PWR POPULISM ...GOV/COMP BIBLIOG 19. PAGE 97 H1945 — CONSTN LAW PARTIC

B10
TEMPERLEY H.W.V.,SENATES AND UPPER CHAMBERS; THEIR USE AND FUNCTION IN THE MODERN STATE... UK WOR-45 CONSTN NAT/G POL/PAR PROVS SECT COLONIAL LEAD CHOOSE REPRESENT PWR...BIBLIOG 19/20 PARLIAMENT SENATE CMN/WLTH HOUSE/LORD. PAGE 153 H3059 — PARL/PROC NAT/COMP LEGIS EX/STRUC

B11
HUXLEY T.H.,METHOD AND RESULTS: ESSAYS. EDU/PROP REPRESENT OWN PERSON PWR WEALTH...PSY IDEA/COMP GEN/LAWS. PAGE 76 H1514 — ORD/FREE NAT/G POPULISM PLURIST

B12
HARIOU M.,LA SOUVERAINTE NATIONALE. EX/STRUC FORCES LEGIS CHOOSE PWR JURID. PAGE 66 H1331 — SOVEREIGN CONCPT NAT/G REPRESENT

B13
SIEGFRIED A.,TABLEAU POLITIQUE DE LA FRANCE DE L'OUEST SOUS LA TROISIEME REPUBLIQUE. FRANCE STRATA STRUCT NAT/G POL/PAR PROVS REGION GOV/REL ATTIT PWR ...TREND TIME 19. PAGE 143 H2869 — SOC GEOG SOCIETY

B14
BERHARDI F.,GERMANY AND THE NEXT WAR. MOD/EUR NAT/G SCHOOL FORCES ACT/RES DOMIN EDU/PROP SUPEGO PWR ...TIME/SEQ STERTYP TOT/POP 20 WWI. PAGE 15 H0304 — DRIVE COERCE WAR GERMANY

B14
BERNHARDI F.,ON THE WAR OF TODAY. MOD/EUR INT/ORG NAT/G TOP/EX PWR CHARTS. PAGE 16 H0313 — FORCES SKILL WAR

B14
FIGGIS J.N.,CHURCHES IN THE MODERN STATE (2ND ED.). LAW CHIEF BAL/PWR PWR...CONCPT CHURCH/STA POPE. PAGE 50 H0998 — SECT NAT/G SOCIETY ORD/FREE

B15
MICHELS R.,POLITICAL PARTIES. NAT/G BAL/PWR CHOOSE REPRESENT ATTIT SOCISM...PSY SOC CONCPT OBS 20 MONOPOLY. PAGE 110 H2198 — POL/PAR CENTRAL LEAD PWR

B16
PUFENDORF S.,LAW OF NATURE AND OF NATIONS (ABRIDGED). UNIV LAW NAT/G DIPLOM AGREE WAR PERSON ALL/VALS PWR...POLICY 18 DEITY NATURL/LAW. PAGE 128 H2565 — CONCPT INT/LAW SECT MORAL

B16
TREITSCHKE H.,POLITICS. UNIV SOCIETY STRATA NAT/G EX/STRUC LEGIS DOMIN EDU/PROP ATTIT PWR RESPECT ...CONCPT TIME/SEQ GEN/LAWS TOT/POP 20. PAGE 157 H3129 — EXEC ELITES GERMANY

B17
DE MAISTRE J.,DU PAPE (1817). FRANCE LAW SOCIETY SECT DOMIN REV HAPPINESS PWR SOVEREIGN 18/19 PROTESTANT. PAGE 38 H0761 — CATH CHIEF LEGIT NAT/G

B18
WILSON W.,THE STATE: ELEMENTS OF HISTORICAL AND PRACTICAL POLITICS. FRANCE GERMANY ITALY UK USSR CONSTN EX/STRUC LEGIS CT/SYS WAR PWR...POLICY GOV/COMP 20. PAGE 169 H3385 — NAT/G JURID CONCPT NAT/COMP

B18
YUKIO O.,THE VOICE OF JAPANESE DEMOCRACY, AN ESSAY ON CONSTITUTIONAL LOYALTY (TRANS BY J. E. BECKER). ASIA POL/PAR DELIB/GP EX/STRUC RIGID/FLEX ORD/FREE PWR...POLICY JURID METH/COMP 19/20 CHINJAP. PAGE 172 H3443 — CONSTN MAJORIT CHOOSE NAT/G

N19
HAJDA J.,THE COLD WAR VIEWED AS A SOCIOLOGICAL PROBLEM (PAMPHLET). COM CZECHOSLVK EUR+WWI SOCIETY PLAN EDU/PROP CONTROL TASK ATTIT MARXISM...POLICY 20 COLD/WAR MIGRATION. PAGE 64 H1280 — DIPLOM LEAD PWR NAT/G

N19
HARTUNG F.,ENLIGHTENED DESPOTISM (PAMPHLET). ORD/FREE SOVEREIGN CONSERVE...PHIL/SCI FREDERICK ENLIGHTNMT. PAGE 67 H1350
NAT/G CHIEF CONCPT PWR

N19
MASSEY V.,CANADIANS AND THEIR COMMONWEALTH: THE ROMANES LECTURE DELIVERED IN THE SHELDONIAN THEATRE JUNE 1, 1961 (PAMPHLET). CANADA UK CULTURE ECO/DEV REPRESENT NAT/LISM PEACE PWR CONSERVE 20 CMN/WLTH. PAGE 104 H2088
ATTIT DIPLOM NAT/G SOVEREIGN

N19
POUND R.,ORGANIZATION OF THE COURTS (PAMPHLET). MOD/EUR UK USA-45 ADJUD PWR...GOV/COMP 10/20 EUROPE. PAGE 127 H2546
CT/SYS JURID STRUCT ADMIN

N19
TEMPLE W.,AN ESSAY UPON THE ORIGINAL AND NATURE OF GOVERNMENT (PAMPHLET). CHRIST-17C UK FAM LOC/G LEGIT ORD/FREE CONSERVE 17. PAGE 153 H3060
NAT/G CONCPT PWR SOCIETY

N19
TREVELYAN G.M.,THE TWO-PARTY SYSTEM IN ENGLISH POLITICAL HISTORY (PAMPHLET). UK CHIEF LEGIS COLONIAL EXEC REV CHOOSE 17/19. PAGE 157 H3131
PARL/PROC POL/PAR NAT/G PWR

B20
HALDANE R.B.,BEFORE THE WAR. MOD/EUR SOCIETY INT/ORG NAT/G DELIB/GP PLAN DOMIN EDU/PROP LEGIT ADMIN COERCE ATTIT DRIVE MORAL ORD/FREE PWR...SOC CONCPT SELF/OBS RECORD BIOG TIME/SEQ. PAGE 64 H1282
POLICY DIPLOM UK

B20
MALTHUS T.R.,PRINCIPLES OF POLITICAL ECONOMY. UK AGRI INDUS MARKET NAT/G DIPLOM PRICE CONTROL BAL/PAY COST OWN PWR LAISSEZ 18/19. PAGE 102 H2034
GEN/LAWS DEMAND WEALTH

B21
BERGSTRASSER L.,GESCHICHTE DER POLITISCHEN PARTEIEN. GERMANY MOD/EUR NAT/G PRESS PWR ...TIME/SEQ 17/20. PAGE 15 H0303
POL/PAR LAISSEZ CONSERVE

B22
OGBURN W.F.,SOCIAL CHANGE WITH RESPECT TO CULTURE AND ORIGINAL NATURE. ACT/RES OP/RES CRIME GP/REL ANOMIE BIO/SOC PWR...PSY SOC TIME/SEQ METH SOC/INTEG. PAGE 120 H2405
CULTURE CREATE TEC/DEV

B22
URE P.N.,THE ORIGIN OF TYRANNY. MEDIT-7 FINAN INDUS CHIEF FORCES ECO/TAC WEALTH. PAGE 159 H3174
AUTHORIT PWR NAT/G MARKET

B25
MAURRAS C.,ENQUETE SUR LA MONARCHIE (1909). FRANCE CONTROL REPRESENT DISCRIM HEREDITY PWR CONSERVE 20 BUREAUCRCY. PAGE 105 H2103
TRADIT AUTHORIT NAT/G CHIEF

B25
TEMPERLEY H.,THE FOREIGN POLICY OF CANNING: 1822-1827. MOD/EUR NAT/G TOP/EX EDU/PROP ROUTINE ATTIT RIGID/FLEX SUPEGO PWR SKILL...TIME/SEQ PARLIAMENT 20. PAGE 153 H3058
PERSON DIPLOM UK BIOG

B25
WEBSTER C.,THE FOREIGN POLICY OF CASTLEREAGH: 1815-1822. LAW NAT/G DELIB/GP TOP/EX BAL/PWR ORD/FREE PWR RESPECT 19. PAGE 166 H3322
MOD/EUR DIPLOM UK

B26
FORTESCUE J.,THE GOVERNANCE OF ENGLAND (1471-76). UK LAW FINAN SECT LEGIS PROB/SOLV TAX DOMIN ADMIN GP/REL COST ORD/FREE PWR 14/15. PAGE 52 H1042
CONSERVE CONSTN CHIEF NAT/G

B26
MCIVER R.M.,THE MODERN STATE. UNIV LAW AUTHORIT SOVEREIGN IDEA/COMP. PAGE 107 H2136
GEN/LAWS CONSTN NAT/G PWR

B27
EDWARDS L.P.,THE NATURAL HISTORY OF REVOLUTION. UNIV NAT/G VOL/ASSN COERCE DRIVE WEALTH...TREND GEN/LAWS. PAGE 45 H0893
PWR GUERRILLA REV

B27
FLOURNOY F.,PARLIAMENT AND WAR. MOD/EUR UK NAT/G FORCES LEGIS TOP/EX DIPLOM LEGIT DEBATE ATTIT RIGID/FLEX PWR...DECISION TIME/SEQ PARLIAMENT 19/20. PAGE 52 H1032
COERCE WAR

B27
JOHN OF SALISBURY,THE STATESMAN'S BOOK (1159) (TRANS. BY J. DICKINSON). DOMIN GP/REL MORAL ORD/FREE PWR CONSERVE...CATH CONCPT 12. PAGE 81 H1617
NAT/G SECT CHIEF LAW

S27
MICHELS R.,"SOME REFLECTIONS ON THE SOCIOLOGICAL CHARACTER OF POLITICAL PARTIES" (BMR)" WOR-45 STRATA MAJORITY DRIVE...GOV/COMP 20. PAGE 110 H2199
POL/PAR PWR LEAD CONCPT

B28
CORBETT P.E.,CANADA AND WORLD POLITICS. LAW CULTURE SOCIETY STRUCT MARKET INT/ORG FORCES ACT/RES PLAN ECO/TAC LEGIT ORD/FREE PWR RESPECT...SOC CONCPT TIME/SEQ TREND CMN/WLTH 20 LEAGUE/NAT. PAGE 33 H0662
NAT/G CANADA

B28
FYFE H.,THE BRITISH LIBERAL PARTY. UK SECT ADMIN LEAD CHOOSE GP/REL PWR SOCISM...MAJORIT TIME/SEQ 19/20 LIB/PARTY CONSRV/PAR. PAGE 54 H1084
POL/PAR NAT/G REPRESENT POPULISM

B28
HURST C.,GREAT BRITAIN AND THE DOMINIONS. EUR+WWI CULTURE ECO/DEV INT/ORG NAT/G DIPLOM ECO/TAC COLONIAL ATTIT PWR SOVEREIGN...TIME/SEQ GEN/LAWS TOT/POP VAL/FREE 20 CMN/WLTH. PAGE 75 H1508
VOL/ASSN DOMIN UK

B29
LANGER W.L.,THE FRANCO-RUSSIAN ALLIANCE: 1890-1894. FRANCE MOD/EUR UK USSR NAT/G CHIEF FORCES BAL/PWR AGREE WAR PEACE PWR...TIME/SEQ TREATY 19 BISMARCK/O. PAGE 91 H1809
DIPLOM

B30
HATTERSLEY A.F.,A SHORT HISTORY OF DEMOCRACY. WOR-45 CONSTN NAT/G SECT DOMIN WAR CHOOSE ORD/FREE PWR...CONCPT GOV/COMP BIBLIOG ATHENS ROME. PAGE 68 H1355
REPRESENT MAJORIT POPULISM

B30
LASKI H.J.,LIBERTY IN THE MODERN STATE. UNIV SOCIETY STRATA CREATE BAL/PWR CONTROL RATIONAL ATTIT PWR 18/20. PAGE 91 H1828
CONCPT ORD/FREE NAT/G DOMIN

B31
CROOK W.H.,THE GENERAL STRIKE: A STUDY OF LABOR'S TRAGIC WEAPON IN THEORY AND PRACTICE. BELGIUM FRANCE SWEDEN UK WOR-45 PROB/SOLV ECO/TAC DOMIN PWR ...POLICY TIME/SEQ NAT/COMP GEN/LAWS 19/20 STRIKE. PAGE 35 H0707
LABOR WORKER LG/CO BARGAIN

B31
DEKAT A.D.A.,COLONIAL POLICY. S/ASIA CULTURE EX/STRUC ECO/TAC DOMIN ADMIN COLONIAL ROUTINE SOVEREIGN WEALTH...POLICY MGT RECORD KNO/TEST SAMP. PAGE 39 H0785
DRIVE PWR INDONESIA NETHERLAND

B32
GREAT BRIT COMM MINISTERS PWR,REPORT. UK LAW CONSTN CONSULT LEGIS PARL/PROC SANCTION SOVEREIGN ...DECISION JURID 20 PARLIAMENT. PAGE 60 H1201
EX/STRUC NAT/G PWR CONTROL

B32
NIEBUHR R.,MORAL MAN AND IMMORAL SOCIETY* A STUDY IN ETHICS AND POLITICS. UNIV CULTURE SOCIETY STRUCT DIPLOM GOV/REL GP/REL PERS/REL...TREND IDEA/COMP. PAGE 118 H2357
MORAL PWR

S32
BEARD C.A.,"THE TEUTONIC ORIGINS OF REPRESENTATIVE GOVERNMENT" UK ROMAN/EMP TAX COERCE PWR IDEA/COMP. PAGE 12 H0247
REPRESENT NAT/G

S32
BEARD C.A.,"REPRESENTATIVE GOVERNMENT IN EVOLUTION" WOR-45 AGRI TEC/DEV DOMIN EFFICIENCY ORD/FREE CONSERVE...TIME/SEQ GOV/COMP IDEA/COMP GRECO/ROMN. PAGE 12 H0248
REPRESENT POPULISM NAT/G PWR

B34
STALIN J.,PROBLEMS OF LENINISM. USSR STRATA INDUS LOC/G POL/PAR ECO/TAC CONTROL TOTALISM PWR SOCISM LENIN/VI STALIN/J. PAGE 148 H2968
MARXISM REV ELITES NAT/G

B35
AQUINAS T.,ON THE GOVERNANCE OF RULERS (1265-66). UNIV SOCIETY STRATA FAM HABITAT PERSON ALL/VALS PWR SOVEREIGN CONSERVE...POLICY BIBLE. PAGE 8 H0155
CATH NAT/G CHIEF SUPEGO

B35
LASKI H.J.,THE STATE IN THEORY AND PRACTICE. ELITES ECO/TAC REPRESENT ORD/FREE PWR WEALTH POPULISM ...GOV/COMP GEN/LAWS 19/20. PAGE 92 H1829
CAP/ISM COERCE NAT/G FASCISM

B35
PARETO V.,THE MIND AND SOCIETY (4 VOLS.). ELITES SECT ECO/TAC COERCE PERSON ORD/FREE PWR SOVEREIGN FASCISM POPULISM...TRADIT 19/20. PAGE 123 H2465
GEN/LAWS SOC PSY

B36
LAPRADE W.T.,PUBLIC OPINION AND POLITICS IN EIGHTEENTH CENTURY ENGLAND. UK CULTURE POL/PAR CHIEF TOP/EX LEAD REV NAT/LISM PWR 18 PROTESTANT PROTESTANT CHURCH/STA. PAGE 91 H1815
POLICY ELITES ATTIT TIME/SEQ

C36
MAZZINI J.,"FROM THE COUNCIL TO GOD" (1870) IN J. MAZZINI, ESSAYS." ITALY NAT/G EDU/PROP PARTIC ORD/FREE PWR SOVEREIGN 19 POPE CHRISTIAN DEITY. PAGE 106 H2112
CATHISM DOMIN NAT/LISM SUPEGO

B37
HAMILTON W.H.,THE POWER TO GOVERN. ECO/DEV FINAN INDUS ECO/TAC INT/TRADE TARIFFS TAX CONTROL CT/SYS WAR COST PWR 18/20 SUPREME/CT. PAGE 65 H1303
LING CONSTN NAT/G POLICY

B37
HORNEY K.,THE NEUROTIC PERSONALITY OF OUR TIME. SOCIETY PERS/REL ADJUST HAPPINESS ANOMIE ATTIT DRIVE SEX LOVE PWR CONCPT. PAGE 74 H1472
PSY PERSON STRANGE CULTURE

L37
NICOLSON H.,"THE MEANING OF PRESTIGE." EUR+WWI MOD/EUR UK CULTURE SOCIETY NAT/G DIPLOM DOMIN LEGIT ATTIT DRIVE PWR...METH/CNCPT RECORD TIME/SEQ GEN/METH CMN/WLTH TOT/POP 20. PAGE 118 H2351
CONCPT STERTYP

B38
HOLDSWORTH W.S.,A HISTORY OF ENGLISH LAW; THE CENTURIES OF SETTLEMENT AND REFORM (VOL. X). INDIA UK CONSTN NAT/G CHIEF LEGIS ADMIN COLONIAL CT/SYS CHOOSE ORD/FREE PWR...JURID 18 PARLIAMENT COMMONWLTH COMMON/LAW. PAGE 72 H1451
LAW LOC/G EX/STRUC ADJUD

B38
SAINT-PIERRE C.I.,SCHEME FOR LASTING PEACE (TRANS. BY H. BELLOT). INDUS NAT/G CHIEF FORCES INT/TRADE CT/SYS WAR PWR SOVEREIGN WEALTH...POLICY 18. PAGE 137 H2732
INT/ORG PEACE AGREE INT/LAW

B39
BENES E.,INTERNATIONAL SECURITY. GERMANY UK NAT/G DELIB/GP PLAN BAL/PWR ATTIT ORD/FREE PWR LEAGUE/NAT 20 TREATY. PAGE 14 H0280
EUR+WWI INT/ORG WAR

B39
BENES E.,DEMOCRACY TODAY AND TOMORROW. EUR+WWI SOCIETY ECO/DEV DELIB/GP ECO/TAC REGION ATTIT PWR FASCISM...CONCPT LEAGUE/NAT 20. PAGE 14 H0281
NAT/G LEGIT NAT/LISM

B39
ENGELS F.,HERRN EUGEN DUHRING'S REVOLUTION IN SCIENCE (1878). CULTURE STRATA STRUCT FAM SECT ECO/TAC REV WAR SOCISM...MARXIST 19. PAGE 46 H0925
PWR SOCIETY WEALTH GEN/LAWS

B39
HITLER A.,MEIN KAMPF. EUR+WWI FUT MOD/EUR STRUCT INT/ORG LABOR NAT/G POL/PAR FORCES CREATE PLAN BAL/PWR DIPLOM ECO/TAC DOMIN EDU/PROP ADMIN COERCE ATTIT...SOCIALIST BIOG TREND NAZI. PAGE 71 H1428
PWR NEW/IDEA WAR

B39
KOHN H.,REVOLUTIONS AND DICTATORSHIPS. COM EUR+WWI ISLAM MOD/EUR NAT/G CHIEF FORCES WAR CIVMIL/REL PWR MARXISM 18/20. PAGE 87 H1739
NAT/LISM TOTALISM REV FASCISM

B39
SCHOCKEL E.,DAS POLITISCHE PLAKAT. EUR+WWI GERMANY NAT/G PWR FASCISM EXHIBIT. PAGE 140 H2794
EDU/PROP ATTIT DOMIN POL/PAR

B39
TAGGART F.J.,ROME AND CHINA. MEDIT-7 INT/ORG NAT/G FORCES LEGIS TOP/EX PLAN PWR SOVEREIGN...CHARTS TOT/POP ROM/EMP. PAGE 152 H3034
ASIA WAR

C39
BURKE E.,"ON THE REFORM OF THE REPRESENTATION IN THE HOUSE OF COMMONS" (1782) IN COLLECTED WORKS (VOL. 5)" UK ELITES STRATA NAT/G REPRESENT ORD/FREE PWR POPULISM...POLICY NEW/IDEA GEN/LAWS 18 BURKE/EDM. PAGE 24 H0486
TRADIT CONSTN PARL/PROC LEGIS

B40
MCILWAIN C.H.,CONSTITUTIONALISM, ANCIENT AND MODERN. CHRIST-17C MOD/EUR NAT/G CHIEF PROB/SOLV INSPECT AUTHORIT ORD/FREE PWR...TIME/SEQ ROMAN/REP. PAGE 107 H2134
CONSTN GEN/LAWS LAW

S40
BROMAGE A.W.,"THE VOCATIONAL SENATE IN IRELAND" EUR+WWI IRELAND. PAGE 21 H0430
PWR NAT/G REPRESENT LEGIS

B41
BAUMANN G.,GRUNDLAGEN UND PRAXIS DER INTERNATIONALEN PROPAGANDA. FRANCE GERMANY UK CULTURE COM/IND PRESS PWR...PSY METH/COMP 20. PAGE 12 H0241
EDU/PROP DOMIN ATTIT DIPLOM

B41
GILMORE M.P.,ARGUMENT FROM ROMAN LAW IN POLITICAL THOUGHT, 1200-1600. INTELL LICENSE CONTROL CT/SYS GOV/REL PRIVIL PWR...IDEA/COMP BIBLIOG 13/16. PAGE 56 H1130
JURID LAW CONCPT NAT/G

B41
HAUSHOFER K.,WEHR-GEOPOLITIK. EUR+WWI GERMANY MOD/EUR NAT/G ACT/RES BAL/PWR PWR...STAT TIME/SEQ CHARTS NAZI 20. PAGE 68 H1361
FORCES GEOG WAR

B41
PALMER R.R.,TWELVE WHO RULED. MOD/EUR ELITES STRUCT NAT/G POL/PAR DELIB/GP DOMIN ATTIT SUPEGO PWR ...POLICY CONCPT 18. PAGE 123 H2453
TOP/EX BIOG REV FRANCE

S41
ABEL T.,"THE ELEMENT OF DECISION IN THE PATTERN OF WAR." EUR+WWI FUT NAT/G TOP/EX DIPLOM ROUTINE COERCE DISPL PERCEPT PWR...SOC METH/CNCPT HIST/WRIT TREND GEN/LAWS 20. PAGE 3 H0055
TEC/DEV FORCES WAR

B42
FEFFERO G.,THE PRINCIPLES OF POWER (TRANS. BY T. JAECKEL). MOD/EUR CONSTN NAT/G CHIEF CONTROL REV WAR ORD/FREE CONSERVE FASCISM POPULISM...GEN/LAWS 18/20 EUROPE. PAGE 49 H0980
PWR LEGIT TRADIT ELITES

B42
LA BOETIE E.,ANTI-DICTATOR (1548) (TRANS. BY H. KUNZ). CONSTN NAT/G CHIEF DOMIN LEGIT CONTROL POPULISM. PAGE 90 H1790
PWR ORD/FREE TOTALISM GEN/LAWS

B42
SINGTON D.,THE GOEBBELS EXPERIMENT. GERMANY MOD/EUR NAT/G EX/STRUC FORCES CONTROL ROUTINE WAR TOTALISM PWR...ART/METH HUM 20 NAZI GOEBBELS/J. PAGE 144 H2886
FASCISM EDU/PROP ATTIT COM/IND

S43
PRICE D.K.,"THE PARLIAMENTARY AND PRESIDENTIAL SYSTEMS" (BMR)" USA-45 NAT/G EX/STRUC PARL/PROC GOV/REL PWR 20 PRESIDENT CONGRESS PARLIAMENT. PAGE 128 H2561
LEGIS REPRESENT ADMIN GOV/COMP

C43
BENTHAM J.,"PRINCIPLES OF INTERNATIONAL LAW" IN J. BOWRING, ED., THE WORKS OF JEREMY BENTHAM." UNIV NAT/G PLAN PROB/SOLV DIPLOM CONTROL SANCTION MORAL ORD/FREE PWR SOVEREIGN 19. PAGE 15 H0291
INT/LAW JURID WAR PEACE

B44
GYORGY A.,GEOPOLITICS: THE NEW GERMAN SCIENCE. EUR+WWI GERMANY STRATA NAT/G PROVS DOMIN EDU/PROP ATTIT DRIVE FASCISM...GEOG NAZI 20. PAGE 63 H1261
PWR LEGIT WAR

B44
KNORR K.E.,BRITISH COLONIAL THEORIES 1570-1850. NAT/G DELIB/GP ECO/TAC PERCEPT PWR...WELF/ST METH/CNCPT CONT/OBS TIME/SEQ SIMUL TOT/POP 20. PAGE 87 H1734
ACT/RES DOMIN COLONIAL

B44
KRIS E.,GERMAN RADIO PROPAGANDA: REPORT ON HOME BROADCASTS DURING THE WAR. EUR+WWI GERMANY CULTURE CONSULT PROB/SOLV FEEDBACK TASK INGP/REL DRIVE PWR FASCISM...CON/ANAL METH/COMP 20. PAGE 89 H1768
EDU/PROP DOMIN ACT/RES ATTIT

B44
SUAREZ F.,A TREATISE ON LAWS AND GOD THE LAWGIVER (1612) IN SELECTIONS FROM THREE WORKS, VOL. II. FRANCE ITALY UK CULTURE NAT/G SECT CHIEF LEGIS DOMIN LEGIT CT/SYS ORD/FREE PWR WORSHIP 16/17. PAGE 150 H3004
LAW JURID GEN/LAWS CATH

L44
HUXLEY J.,"THE FUTURE OF THE COLONIES." AFR SOCIETY NAT/G PLAN DOMIN COERCE ATTIT DRIVE ORD/FREE PWR WEALTH...TIME/SEQ TREND AUD/VIS CHARTS 20. PAGE 76 H1511
ECO/UNDEV FUT COLONIAL

C44
SUAREZ F.,"ON WAR" (1621) IN SELECTIONS FROM THREE WORKS, VOL. I." NAT/G SECT CHIEF DIPLOM LEGIT MORAL PWR...POLICY INT/LAW 17. PAGE 150 H3005
WAR REV ORD/FREE CATH

B46
ALLEN J.S.,WORLD MONOPOLY AND PEACE. GERMANY UK USSR FINAN INDUS LG/CO DOMIN CONTROL PEACE PWR WEALTH SOCISM...NAT/COMP 20 MONOPOLY. PAGE 5 H0105
CAP/ISM DIPLOM WAR COLONIAL

B46
CASSIRER E.,THE MYTH OF THE STATE. WOR-45 SOCIETY RACE/REL RATIONAL PWR FASCISM...PHIL/SCI PSY LING TREND HEGEL/GWF MACHIAVELL. PAGE 28 H0557
MYTH CONCPT NAT/G IDEA/COMP

B46
NICOLSON H.,THE CONGRESS OF VIENNA. MOD/EUR NAT/G FORCES BAL/PWR DOMIN LEGIT COERCE PERSON PWR ...RECORD TIME/SEQ STERTYP 19 CONG/VIENN. PAGE 118 H2353
CONCPT POLICY DIPLOM

B47
MARX F.M.,THE PRESIDENT AND HIS STAFF SERVICES PUBLIC ADMINISTRATION SERVICES NUMBER 98 (PAMPHLET). FINAN ADMIN CT/SYS REPRESENT PWR 20 PRESIDENT. PAGE 104 H2075
CONSTN CHIEF NAT/G EX/STRUC

B48
CLYDE P.H.,THE FAR EAST: A HISTORY OF THE IMPACT OF THE WEST ON EASTERN ASIA. CHINA/COM CULTURE INT/TRADE DOMIN COLONIAL WAR PWR...CHARTS BIBLIOG 19/20 CHINJAP. PAGE 30 H0609
DIPLOM ASIA

B48
LASKI H.S.,THE AMERICAN DEMOCRACY. CULTURE INDUS SECT WORKER DIPLOM EDU/PROP REPRESENT RACE/REL ORD/FREE PWR...NAT/COMP 18/20. PAGE 92 H1831
NAT/G LOC/G USA-45 POPULISM

B48
TOWSTER J.,POLITICAL POWER IN THE USSR: 1917-1947. USSR CONSTN CULTURE ELITES CREATE PLAN COERCE CENTRAL ATTIT RIGID/FLEX ORD/FREE...BIBLIOG SOC/INTEG 20 LENIN/VI STALIN/J. PAGE 156 H3122
EX/STRUC NAT/G MARXISM PWR

S48
ALEXANDER L.,"WAR CRIMES, THEIR SOCIAL-PSYCHOLOGICAL ASPECTS." EUR+WWI GERMANY LAW CULTURE ELITES KIN POL/PAR PUB/INST FORCES DOMIN EDU/PROP COERCE CRIME ATTIT SUPEGO HEALTH MORAL PWR FASCISM ...PSY OBS TREND GEN/LAWS NAZI 20. PAGE 5 H0100
DRIVE WAR

S48
ALMOND G.A.,"THE CHRISTIAN PARTIES OF WESTEN EUROPE." EUR+WWI NAT/G EDU/PROP LEGIT TOTALISM ORD/FREE PWR MARXISM...TREND CHARTS STERTYP GEN/LAWS COLD/WAR 20. PAGE 5 H0110
POL/PAR CATH SOCISM

B49
DE JOUVENEL B.,ON POWER: ITS NATURE AND THE HISTORY OF ITS GROWTH. SOCIETY CHIEF REV WAR ATTIT AUTHORIT
PWR NAT/G

ORD/FREE SOVEREIGN CONSERVE POPULISM CONCPT. PAGE 38 H0757 DOMIN CONTROL

B49
HAUSER R.,AUTORITAT UND MACHT. SOCIETY SECT PWR CATHISM...JURID CONCPT 16/20 PROTESTANT LUTHER/M CALVIN/J CHURCH/STA. PAGE 68 H1360 SOVEREIGN NAT/G LEGIT

B49
HINDEN R.,EMPIRE AND AFTER. UK POL/PAR BAL/PWR DIPLOM INT/TRADE WAR NAT/LISM PWR 17/20. PAGE 71 H1420 NAT/G COLONIAL ATTIT POLICY

B49
LASSWELL H.D.,LANGUAGE OF POLITICS. COM NAT/G ACT/RES ATTIT PWR...STAT RECORD CON/ANAL GEN/METH 20. PAGE 92 H1834 EDU/PROP METH/CNCPT

B49
SCHWARTZ B.,LAW AND THE EXECUTIVE IN BRITAIN: A COMPARATIVE STUDY. UK USA+45 LAW EX/STRUC PWR ...GOV/COMP 20. PAGE 140 H2807 ADMIN EXEC CONTROL REPRESENT

B49
WORMUTH F.D.,THE ORIGINS OF MODERN CONSTITUTIONALISM. GREECE UK LEGIS CREATE TEC/DEV BAL/PWR DOMIN ADJUD REV WAR PWR...JURID ROMAN/REP CROMWELL/O. PAGE 170 H3412 NAT/G CONSTN LAW

B50
ALBRECHT-CARRIE R.,ITALY FROM NAPOLEON TO MUSSOLINI. GERMANY ITALY SPAIN SOCIETY ECO/DEV POL/PAR LEGIS AGREE CONTROL WAR NAT/LISM TOTALISM PWR SOCISM...SOC 19/20 TREATY. PAGE 5 H0095 FASCISM NAT/G

B50
CORNELL U DEPT ASIAN STUDIES,SOUTHEAST ASIA PROGRAM DATA PAPER. BURMA CAMBODIA INDONESIA MALAYSIA VIETNAM SOCIETY STRUCT NAT/G SECT DIPLOM FOR/AID PWR WEALTH...SOC 20. PAGE 33 H0670 BIBLIOG/A CULTURE S/ASIA ECO/UNDEV

B50
DUCLOS P.,L'EVOLUTION DES RAPPORTS POLITIQUES DEPUIS 1750 (LIBERTE, INTEGRATION, UNITE). LAW INT/ORG FEDERAL TOTALISM ATTIT PWR...MAJORIT BIBLIOG 18/20 PARLIAMENT EUROPE. PAGE 43 H0852 ORD/FREE DIPLOM NAT/G GOV/COMP

B50
GLEASON J.H.,THE GENESIS OF RUSSOPHOBIA IN GREAT BRITAIN: A STUDY OF THE INTERACTION OF POLICY AND OPINION. ASIA RUSSIA UK NAT/G AGREE CONTROL REV WAR LOVE PWR TREATY 19. PAGE 57 H1142 DIPLOM POLICY DOMIN COLONIAL

B50
HOBBES T.,LEVIATHAN. UNIV CONSTN SOCIETY LOC/G NAT/G CONSULT TOP/EX DOMIN DRIVE PERSON PWR ...PHIL/SCI CONCPT SELF/OBS GEN/LAWS TOT/POP. PAGE 72 H1434 LAW ORD/FREE

B50
MACHIAVELLI N.,THE DISCOURSES (1516). NAT/G SECT FORCES DOMIN LEGIT CONTROL LEAD COERCE TOTALISM ORD/FREE. PAGE 100 H1995 PWR GEN/LAWS CHIEF

B50
ORTON W.A.,THE ECONOMIC ROLE OF THE STATE. INTELL ECO/UNDEV PLAN CONTROL PWR SOVEREIGN...POLICY 17/20. PAGE 122 H2431 ECO/DEV NAT/G ECO/TAC ORD/FREE

B50
TRAGER F.N.,MARXISM IN SOUTHEAST ASIA. BURMA INDONESIA THAILAND VIETNAM CULTURE SOCIETY NAT/G VOL/ASSN EXEC ROUTINE COERCE ATTIT RIGID/FLEX PWR ...METH/CNCPT TIME/SEQ STERTYP GEN/LAWS MARX/KARL VAL/FREE COLD/WAR NAM 20. PAGE 156 H3126 S/ASIA POL/PAR REV

B50
WHITE R.J.,THE CONSERVATIVE TRADITION. UK POL/PAR SUPEGO PWR RESPECT...POLICY ANTHOL 19. PAGE 167 H3350 CONSERVE CONCPT NAT/G ORD/FREE

B51
HALEVY E.,IMPERIALISM AND THE RISE OF LABOR (2ND ED.). UK NAT/G POL/PAR TOP/EX ATTIT ORD/FREE PWR 19/20 PARLIAMENT LABOR/PAR. PAGE 64 H1284 COLONIAL LABOR POLICY WAR

B51
WEBSTER C.,THE FOREIGN POLICY OF PALMERSTON - 1830 TO 1841. MOD/EUR UK LAW CONSTN INTELL SOCIETY STRUCT NAT/G FORCES TOP/EX CREATE BAL/PWR PWR 19. PAGE 166 H3323 ADMIN PERSON DIPLOM

B51
WHEARE K.C.,MODERN CONSTITUTIONS (HOME UNIVERSITY LIBRARY). UNIV LAW NAT/G LEGIS...CONCPT TREND BIBLIOG. PAGE 167 H3336 CONSTN CLASSIF PWR CREATE

B52
BENTHAM A.,HANDBOOK OF POLITICAL FALLACIES. FUT MOD/EUR LAW INTELL LOC/G MUNIC NAT/G DELIB/GP LEGIS CREATE EDU/PROP CT/SYS ATTIT RIGID/FLEX KNOWL PWR ...RELATIV PSY SOC CONCPT SELF/OBS TREND STERTYP TOT/POP. PAGE 14 H0286 POL/PAR

B52
HIMMELFARB G.,LORD ACTON: A STUDY IN CONSCIENCE AND POLITICS. MOD/EUR NAT/G POL/PAR SECT LEGIS TOP/EX EDU/PROP ADMIN NAT/LISM ATTIT PERSON SUPEGO MORAL ORD/FREE...CONCPT PARLIAMENT 19 ACTON/LORD. PAGE 71 H1419 PWR BIOG

B52
KOLARZ W.,RUSSIA AND HER COLONIES. COM RUSSIA LAW CULTURE ECO/DEV KIN LOC/G SECT TEC/DEV ECO/TAC EDU/PROP REGION COERCE ATTIT PWR SOVEREIGN...SOC TIME/SEQ CON/ANAL VAL/FREE 19/20. PAGE 88 H1749 NAT/G DOMIN USSR COLONIAL

B52
LEYS W.,ETHICS FOR POLICY DECISIONS. INTELL NAT/G CONSULT PLAN DOMIN EDU/PROP LEGIT COERCE KNOWL MORAL PWR...HUM GEN/LAWS. PAGE 96 H1920 ACT/RES POLICY

B52
THOM J.M.,GUIDE TO RESEARCH MATERIAL IN POLITICAL SCIENCE (PAMPHLET). ELITES LOC/G MUNIC NAT/G LEGIS DIPLOM ADJUD CIVMIL/REL GOV/REL PWR MGT. PAGE 154 H3074 BIBLIOG/A KNOWL

S52
MCDOUGAL M.S.,"THE COMPARATIVE STUDY OF LAW FOR POLICY PURPOSES." FUT NAT/G POL/PAR CONSULT ADJUD PWR SOVEREIGN...METH/CNCPT IDEA/COMP SIMUL 20. PAGE 106 H2129 PLAN JURID NAT/LISM

S52
MUEHLMANN W.E.,"L'IDEE NATIONALE ALLEMANDE ET L'IDEE NATIONALE FRANCAISE." EUR+WWI MOD/EUR SOCIETY KIN NAT/G PWR RESPECT...SOC CONCPT TIME/SEQ GEN/LAWS 19/20. PAGE 114 H2279 CULTURE ATTIT FRANCE GERMANY

B53
BENDIX R.,CLASS, STATUS AND POWER: A READER IN SOCIAL STRATIFICATION. USA+45 SOCIETY ACT/RES DOMIN ATTIT RIGID/FLEX...PSY SOC CONCPT METH/COMP NAT/COMP 20. PAGE 14 H0273 STRATA PWR STRUCT ROLE

B53
COBLENTZ S.A.,FROM ARROW TO ATOM BOMB: THE PSYCHOLOGICAL HISTORY OF WAR. PREHIST CULTURE CROWD PEACE DRIVE MORAL PWR...GP/COMP IDEA/COMP. PAGE 31 H0613 WAR PSY SOCIETY

B53
CURTISS J.S.,THE RUSSIAN CHURCH AND THE SOVIET STATE 1917-1950. COM USSR CONTROL LEAD REV MARXISM ...POLICY BIBLIOG 20 CHURCH/STA ORTHO/RUSS. PAGE 36 H0728 GP/REL NAT/G SECT PWR

B53
LEITES N.,A STUDY OF BOLSHEVISM. ELITES STRATA INT/ORG LOC/G POL/PAR WORKER EDU/PROP REV TOTALISM UTOPIA PWR...CONCPT 20 BOLSHEVISM. PAGE 94 H1870 MARXISM PLAN COM

B53
LIEBER F.,CIVIL LIBERTY AND SELF GOVERNMENT: VOLUME 2. NAT/G CONTROL CHOOSE PERSON PWR 19 CIVIL/LIB. PAGE 96 H1925 ORD/FREE SOVEREIGN CENTRAL CONCPT

B53
MEYER P.,THE JEWS IN THE SOVIET SATELLITES. CZECHOSLVK POLAND SOCIETY STRATA NAT/G BAL/PWR ECO/TAC EDU/PROP LEGIT ADMIN COERCE ATTIT DISPL PERCEPT HEALTH PWR RESPECT WEALTH...METH/CNCPT JEWS VAL/FREE NAZI 20. PAGE 110 H2192 COM SECT TOTALISM USSR

B53
ROSCIO J.G.,OBRAS. L/A+17C SPAIN DIPLOM REV WAR NAT/LISM TOTALISM PWR SOVEREIGN 19. PAGE 134 H2671 ORD/FREE COLONIAL NAT/G PHIL/SCI

S53
DRUCKER P.F.,"THE EMPLOYEE SOCIETY." STRUCT BAL/PWR PARTIC REPRESENT PWR...DECISION CONCPT. PAGE 42 H0849 LABOR MGT WORKER CULTURE

C53
DORWART R.A.,"THE ADMINISTRATIVE REFORMS OF FREDRICK WILLIAM I OF PRUSSIA. GERMANY MOD/EUR CHIEF CONTROL PWR...BIBLIOG 16/18. PAGE 42 H0839 ADMIN NAT/G CENTRAL GOV/REL

B54
BUTZ O.,GERMANY: DILEMMA FOR AMERICAN POLICY. GERMANY USA+45 USA-45 USSR WOR+45 INT/ORG FORCES NUC/PWR EFFICIENCY PEACE PWR...GOV/COMP 20 COLD/WAR. PAGE 25 H0501 DIPLOM NAT/G WAR POLICY

B54
FRIEDRICH C.J.,TOTALITARIAN DICTATORSHIP AND AUTOCRACY. COM EUR+WWI GERMANY ITALY USSR INTELL ECO/DEV NAT/G POL/PAR FORCES TOP/EX ECO/TAC EDU/PROP LEGIT COERCE ATTIT ORD/FREE PWR FASCISM ...CONCPT TIME/SEQ GEN/LAWS NAZI 20. PAGE 53 H1068 SOCIETY DOMIN TOTALISM

B54
GATZKE H.W.,STRESEMANN AND THE REARMAMENT OF GERMANY. EUR+WWI GERMANY USSR FINAN NAT/G ECO/TAC ATTIT...BIOG METH 20 STRESEMN/G. PAGE 55 H1105 FORCES INDUS PWR

B54
HAZARD B.H. JR.,KOREAN STUDIES GUIDE. KOREA CONSTN CULTURE AGRI FAM SECT CREATE WAR NAT/LISM HABITAT PWR...CHARTS 14/20. PAGE 68 H1371 BIBLIOG/A ELITES GP/REL

B54
PARRINDER G.,AFRICAN TRADITIONAL RELIGION. AFR SOCIETY EDU/PROP GP/REL PWR...SOC CONCPT IDEA/COMP WORSHIP 20 DEITY. PAGE 124 H2469 SECT MYTH ATTIT CULTURE

B54
SALVEMINI G.,PRELUDE TO WORLD WAR II. ITALY MOD/EUR WAR

INT/ORG BAL/PWR EDU/PROP CONTROL TOTALISM...TREND NAT/COMP BIBLIOG 19 HITLER/A LEAGUE/NAT MUSSOLIN/B. PAGE 137 H2745 FASCISM LEAD PWR

L54
FRIEDRICH C.J.,"TOTALITARIANISM." COM EUR+WWI NAT/G POL/PAR SECT FORCES PLAN ECO/TAC DOMIN EDU/PROP EXEC COERCE REV ORD/FREE PWR...SOC CONCPT NAZI 20. PAGE 53 H1067 ATTIT TOTALISM

S54
BALANDIER G.,"SOCIOLOGIE DE LA COLONISATION ET RELATIONS ENTRE SOCIETES GLOBALES." AFR SOCIETY ECO/UNDEV KIN DOMIN EDU/PROP RIGID/FLEX PWR...PSY CONCPT TREND TOT/POP. PAGE 10 H0203 CULTURE SOC COLONIAL

S54
DODD S.C.,"THE SCIENTIFIC MEASUREMENT OF FITNESS FOR SELF-GOVERNMENT." FUT CONSTN ECO/UNDEV INT/ORG PLAN PWR...CONCPT QUANT CON/ANAL SOC/EXP UN LEAGUE/NAT 20. PAGE 41 H0830 NAT/G STAT SOVEREIGN

C54
BERLE A.A. JR.,"THE 20TH CENTURY CAPITALIST REVOLUTION." ECO/DEV NAT/G DIPLOM PRICE CONTROL ATTIT...BIBLIOG/A 20. PAGE 15 H0306 LG/CO CAP/ISM MGT PWR

B55
APTER D.E.,THE GOLD COAST IN TRANSITION. FUT CONSTN CULTURE SOCIETY ECO/UNDEV FAM KIN LOC/G NAT/G POL/PAR LEGIS TOP/EX EDU/PROP LEGIT ADMIN ATTIT PERSON PWR...CONCPT STAT INT CENSUS TOT/POP VAL/FREE. PAGE 7 H0149 AFR SOVEREIGN

B55
GALLOWAY G.B.,CONGRESS AND PARLIAMENT: THEIR ORGANIZATION AND OPERATION IN THE US AND THE UK: PLANNING PAMPHLET NO. 93. POL/PAR EX/STRUC DEBATE CONTROL LEAD ROUTINE EFFICIENCY PWR...POLICY CONGRESS PARLIAMENT. PAGE 54 H1089 DELIB/GP LEGIS PARL/PROC GOV/COMP

B55
KOHN H.,THE MIND OF MODERN RUSSIA. COM MOD/EUR USSR SOCIETY NAT/G SECT FORCES TOP/EX COERCE TOTALISM DRIVE RIGID/FLEX PWR SOVEREIGN...CONCPT TIME/SEQ WORK. PAGE 87 H1742 INTELL GEN/LAWS SOCISM RUSSIA

B55
POHLENZ M.,GRIECHISCHE FREIHEIT. GREECE DIPLOM WAR SUPEGO PWR RESPECT...IDEA/COMP. PAGE 127 H2533 ORD/FREE CONCPT JURID NAT/G

B55
RESHETAR J.S.,PROBLEMS OF ANALYZING AND PREDICTING SOVIET BEHAVIOR. USSR CULTURE ECO/DEV AGRI DIST/IND EXTR/IND PROC/MFG NAT/G SECT TOP/EX ACT/RES ADMIN PWR WEALTH...SOC METH TOT/POP VAL/FREE 20. PAGE 131 H2617 COM ATTIT

B55
ROWE C.,VOLTAIRE AND THE STATE. FRANCE MOD/EUR BAL/PWR CONTROL TASK SUPEGO ORD/FREE PWR...CONCPT 18 VOLTAIRE. PAGE 135 H2702 NAT/G DIPLOM NAT/LISM ATTIT

B55
SHAFER B.C.,NATIONALISM: MYTH AND REALITY. FRANCE UK USA+45 USA-45 CULTURE SOCIETY STRUCT ECO/DEV WAR PWR...NAT/COMP BIBLIOG 18/20. PAGE 142 H2837 NAT/LISM MYTH NAT/G CONCPT

S55
BENN S.I.,"THE USES OF 'SOVEREIGNTY'." UNIV NAT/G LEGIS DIPLOM COERCE...METH/CNCPT GEN/LAWS. PAGE 14 H0282 SOVEREIGN IDEA/COMP CONCPT PWR

S55
GLADSTONE A.E.,"THE POSSIBILITY OF PREDICTING REACTIONS TO INTERNATIONAL EVENTS." UNIV SOCIETY NAT/G FORCES CREATE EDU/PROP COERCE WAR ATTIT PERSON KNOWL PWR SKILL...METH/CNCPT NEW/IDEA ORG/CHARTS. PAGE 57 H1139 PHIL/SCI CONCPT

C55
OLIVER D.L.,"A LEADER IN ACTION," IN D. A. OLIVER, SOLOMON ISLAND SOCIETY." S/ASIA SOCIETY STRUCT CONTROL TASK PWR...OBS/ENVIR WORSHIP 20. PAGE 121 H2413 LEAD RESPECT CULTURE KIN

B56
CARRIL B.,PROBLEMAS DE LA REVOLUCION Y LA DEMOCRACIA. CONSTN FORCES DOMIN CONTROL TOTALISM PWR 20. PAGE 27 H0539 REV ORD/FREE LEGIT NAT/G

B56
CEPEDA U.A.,EN TORNO AL CONCEPTO DEL ESTADO EN LOS REYES CATHOLICOS. SPAIN SOCIETY STRUCT SECT LEGIT WAR ATTIT WORSHIP 15/17. PAGE 28 H0569 NAT/G PHIL/SCI CHIEF PWR

B56
GLUCKMAN M.,CUSTOM AND CONFLICT IN AFRICA. AFR FAM KIN NAT/G DOMIN DISCRIM DRIVE MORAL PWR...SOC BIBLIOG WORSHIP 20. PAGE 57 H1145 CULTURE CREATE PERS/REL GP/COMP

B56
HATCH J.C.,NEW FROM AFRICA. AFR FUT UK NAT/G GUERRILLA ATTIT ORD/FREE PWR...AUD/VIS CHARTS 20. PAGE 68 H1354 NAT/LISM COLONIAL RACE/REL

B56
MANNONI D.O.,PROSPERO AND CALIBAN: THE PSYCHOLOGY OF COLONIZATION. AFR EUR+WWI FAM KIN MUNIC SECT DOMIN ADMIN ATTIT DRIVE LOVE PWR RESPECT...PSY SOC CONCPT MYTH OBS DEEP/INT BIOG GEN/METH MALAGASY 20. PAGE 102 H2040 CULTURE COLONIAL

B56
PADMORE G.,PAN-AFRICANISM OR COMMUNISM. AFR FUT NIGERIA INTELL NAT/G COLONIAL FEDERAL ATTIT DRIVE PWR RESPECT WEALTH MARXISM...CONCPT AUD/VIS STERTYP 20. PAGE 122 H2440 POL/PAR NAT/LISM

B56
SPINKA M.,THE CHURCH IN SOVIET RUSSIA. USSR CONTROL LEAD TASK COERCE 20. PAGE 147 H2949 GP/REL NAT/G SECT PWR

B56
WEBER M.,WIRTSCHAFT UND GESELLSCHAFT (2ND VOL.). STRUCT NAT/G POL/PAR LEAD PWR OBJECTIVE IDEA/COMP. PAGE 166 H3321 LEGIT JURID SOC

B56
WHITAKER A.P.,ARGENTINE UPHEAVAL. STRUCT FORCES DIPLOM COERCE PWR 20 ARGEN. PAGE 167 H3343 REV POL/PAR STRATA NAT/G

L56
EISENTADT S.N.,"POLITICAL STRUGGLE IN BUREAUCRATIC SOCIETIES" ASIA CULTURE ADJUD SANCTION PWR BUREAUCRCY OTTOMAN BYZANTINE. PAGE 45 H0901 ADMIN CHIEF CONTROL ROUTINE

S56
EPSTEIN L.D.,"COHESION OF BRITISH PARLIAMENTARY PARTIES." UK STRUCT ADMIN ROUTINE INGP/REL PWR ...GP/COMP PARLIAMENT. PAGE 47 H0935 NAT/G PARL/PROC POL/PAR

S56
KHAMA T.,"POLITICAL CHANGE IN AFRICAN SOCIETY." CONSTN SOCIETY LOC/G NAT/G POL/PAR EX/STRUC LEGIS LEGIT ADMIN CHOOSE REPRESENT NAT/LISM MORAL ORD/FREE PWR...CONCPT OBS TREND GEN/METH CMN/WLTH 17/20. PAGE 85 H1706 AFR ELITES

B57
ARON R.,L'UNIFICATION ECONOMIQUE DE L'EUROPE. EUR+WWI SWITZERLND UK INT/ORG NAT/G REGION NAT/LISM ORD/FREE PWR...CONCPT METH/CNCPT OBS TREND STERTYP GEN/LAWS EEC 20. PAGE 8 H0168 VOL/ASSN ECO/TAC

B57
BUCK P.W.,CONTOL OF FOREIGN RELATIONS IN MODERN NATIONS. FRANCE L/A+17C NETHERLAND USSR WOR+45 INT/ORG TOP/EX BAL/PWR DOMIN EDU/PROP COERCE PEACE ATTIT...CONCPT TREND 20 CMN/WLTH. PAGE 23 H0465 NAT/G PWR DIPLOM

B57
CHANDRA S.,PARTIES AND POLITICS AT THE MUGHAL COURT: 1707-1740. INDIA CULTURE EX/STRUC CREATE PLAN PWR...BIBLIOG/A 18. PAGE 29 H0574 POL/PAR ELITES NAT/G

B57
CONOVER H.F.,NORTH AND NORTHEAST AFRICA; A SELECTED ANNOTATED LIST OF WRITINGS. ALGERIA MOROCCO SUDAN UAR CULTURE INT/ORG PROB/SOLV ADJUD NAT/LISM PWR WEALTH...SOC 20 UN. PAGE 32 H0649 BIBLIOG/A DIPLOM AFR ECO/UNDEV

B57
HAMMOND B.,BANKS AND POLITICS IN AMERICA FROM THE REVOLUTION TO THE CIVIL WAR. CANADA USA-45 STRATA ...NAT/COMP 18/19. PAGE 65 H1306 FINAN PWR POL/PAR NAT/G

B57
HOUN F.W.,CENTRAL GOVERNMENT OF CHINA, 1912-1928. ASIA CONSTN CHIEF LEGIS CONTROL PWR...BIBLIOG 20. PAGE 74 H1480 POL/PAR ATTIT NAT/G PLAN

B57
LAQUER W.Z.,COMMUNISM AND NATIONALISM IN THE MIDDLE EAST. ELITES INTELL STRATA NAT/G POL/PAR SECT VOL/ASSN TOP/EX DOMIN LEGIT REGION COERCE ATTIT PERSON PWR...CONCPT HIST/WRIT TIME/SEQ TREND GEN/LAWS VAL/FREE. PAGE 91 H1817 ISLAM NAT/LISM

B57
MEINECKE F.,MACHIAVELLISM. CHRIST-17C FRANCE GERMANY ITALY MOD/EUR BAL/PWR PARL/PROC TOTALISM ...PHIL/SCI 15/20 MACHIAVELL. PAGE 108 H2166 NAT/LISM NAT/G PWR

B57
MUELLER-DEHAM A.,HUMAN RELATIONS AND POWER; SOCIO-POLITICAL ANALYSIS AND SYNTHESIS. CONSTN SOCIETY NAT/G POL/PAR PROVS LEGIS POPULISM...SOC NEW/IDEA. PAGE 114 H2280 GEN/LAWS PERS/REL PWR CONCPT

B57
PALMER N.D.,INTERNATIONAL RELATIONS. WOR+45 INT/ORG NAT/G ECO/TAC EDU/PROP COLONIAL WAR PWR SOVEREIGN ...POLICY T 20 TREATY. PAGE 123 H2451 DIPLOM BAL/PWR NAT/COMP

B57
POPLAI S.L.,NATIONAL POLITICS AND 1957 ELECTIONS IN INDIA. INDIA BARGAIN PARL/PROC CONSEN NAT/LISM PWR WEALTH 20. PAGE 127 H2543 POL/PAR CHOOSE POLICY NAT/G

B57
RUMEU DE ARMAS A.,ESPANA EEN EL AFRICA ATLANTICA. AFR CHRIST-17C PORTUGAL SPAIN DIPLOM ECO/TAC NAT/G COLONIAL

CONTROL 14/16 AFRICA/W. PAGE 136 H2717 CHIEF PWR

B57
TOMASIC D.A.,NATIONAL COMMUNISM AND SOVIET STRATEGY. UK USSR YUGOSLAVIA NAT/G POL/PAR CHIEF CREATE DOMIN REV WAR PWR...BIOG TREND 20 TITO/MARSH STALIN/J. PAGE 156 H3112 COM NAT/LISM MARXISM DIPLOM

L57
LIPSET S.M.,"POLITICAL SOCIOLOGY." NAT/G POL/PAR ECO/TAC PARTIC CHOOSE PWR...BIBLIOG/A 20. PAGE 97 H1939 SOC ALL/IDEOS ACADEM

S57
KILSON M.L.,"LAND AND POLITICS IN KENYA: AN ANALYSIS OF AFRICAN POLITICS IN A PLURAL SOCIETY." FUT LAW CULTURE KIN NAT/G ECO/TAC DOMIN REV NAT/LISM ORD/FREE PWR RESPECT SOVEREIGN WEALTH ...SOC OBS TREND WORK VAL/FREE CMN/WLTH 20. PAGE 86 H1710 AFR ECO/UNDEV

S57
LEWIS E.G.,"PARLIAMENTARY CONTROL OF NATIONALIZED INDUSTRY IN FRANCE." FRANCE NAT/G DELIB/GP ACT/RES PLAN PROB/SOLV ECO/TAC DOMIN CENTRAL. PAGE 96 H1914 PWR LEGIS INDUS CONTROL

C57
WITTFOGEL K.A.,"ORIENTAL DESPOTISM: A COMPARATIVE STUDY OF TOTAL POWER." ASIA CULTURE STRATA NAT/G LEAD OWN ORD/FREE PWR...CONCPT TREND BIBLIOG 20. PAGE 170 H3393 TOTALISM HABITAT DOMIN ELITES

B58
BUISSON L.,POTESTAS UND CARITAS. FRANCE GERMANY UK ORD/FREE...JURID IDEA/COMP NAT/COMP 12/16 POPE CHURCH/STA. PAGE 23 H0467 GP/REL PWR CATHISM NAT/G

B58
CAMPBELL P.,FRENCH ELECTORAL SYSTEMS AND ELECTIONS SINCE 1789 (2ND ED.). FRANCE NAT/G EX/STRUC PWR ...CHARTS 18/20. PAGE 26 H0516 REPRESENT CHOOSE POL/PAR SUFF

B58
CARTER G.M.,TRANSITION IN AFRICA; STUDIES IN POLITICAL ADAPTATION. AFR CENTRL/AFR GHANA NIGERIA CONSTN LOC/G POL/PAR ADMIN GP/REL FEDERAL...MAJORIT BIBLIOG 20. PAGE 27 H0543 NAT/COMP PWR CONTROL NAT/G

B58
COLEMAN J.S.,NIGERIA: BACKGROUND TO NATIONALISM. AFR SOCIETY ECO/DEV KIN LOC/G POL/PAR TEC/DEV DOMIN ADMIN DRIVE PWR RESPECT...TRADIT SOC INT SAMP TIME/SEQ 20. PAGE 31 H0627 NAT/G NAT/LISM NIGERIA

B58
CRAIG G.A.,FROM BISMARCK TO ADENAUER: ASPECTS OF GERMAN STATECRAFT. GERMANY INTELL FORCES ECO/TAC CONFER COERCE WAR GP/REL ORD/FREE PWR CONSERVE 19/20 BISMARCK/O ADENAUER/K. PAGE 35 H0695 DIPLOM LEAD NAT/G

B58
DUCLOUX L.,FROM BLACKMAIL TO TREASON. FRANCE PLAN DIPLOM EDU/PROP PRESS RUMOR NAT/LISM...CRIMLGY 20. PAGE 43 H0853 COERCE CRIME NAT/G PWR

B58
EMMET D.M.,FUNCTION, PURPOSE AND POWERS. SECT ATTIT MORAL PWR...CONCPT MYTH. PAGE 46 H0923 SOC CULTURE ALL/VALS GEN/LAWS

B58
EUSDEN J.D.,PURITANS, LAWYERS, AND POLITICS IN EARLY SEVENTEENTH-CENTURY ENGLAND. UK CT/SYS PARL/PROC RATIONAL PWR SOVEREIGN...IDEA/COMP BIBLIOG 17 PURITAN COMMON/LAW. PAGE 48 H0951 GP/REL SECT NAT/G LAW

B58
GARTHOFF R.L.,SOVIET STRATEGY IN THE NUCLEAR AGE. FUT USSR R+D INT/ORG NAT/G ACT/RES TEC/DEV DOMIN DETER WAR ATTIT PWR...RELATIV METH/CNCPT SELF/OBS TREND CON/ANAL STERTYP GEN/LAWS 20. PAGE 55 H1103 COM FORCES BAL/PWR NUC/PWR

B58
HAAS E.B.,THE UNITING OF EUROPE. EUR+WWI INT/ORG NAT/G POL/PAR TOP/EX ECO/TAC EDU/PROP LEGIT FEDERAL NAT/LISM DRIVE RIGID/FLEX ORD/FREE PWR PLURISM ...POLICY CONCPT INT GEN/LAWS ECSC EEC 20. PAGE 63 H1264 VOL/ASSN ECO/DEV

B58
HSU U.T.,THE INVISIBLE CONFLICT. ASIA USSR ELITES NAT/G CONTROL LEAD COERCE REV WAR NAT/LISM ORD/FREE PWR 20 COM/PARTY ESPIONAGE. PAGE 74 H1485 MARXISM POL/PAR EDU/PROP FORCES

B58
KINTNER W.R.,ORGANIZING FOR CONFLICT: A PROPOSAL. USSR STRUCT NAT/G LEGIS ADMIN EXEC PEACE ORD/FREE PWR...CONCPT OBS TREND NAT/COMP VAL/FREE COLD/WAR 20. PAGE 86 H1719 USA+45 PLAN DIPLOM

B58
LAHBABI M.,LE GOUVERNEMENT MAROCAIN A L'AUBE DU XXE SIECLE. FRANCE MOROCCO CHIEF EX/STRUC LEGIS ORD/FREE PWR...JURID BIBLIOG 19/20. PAGE 90 H1797 NAT/G COLONIAL SOVEREIGN

B58
LAQUER W.Z.,THE MIDDLE EAST IN TRANSITION. COM USSR ECO/UNDEV NAT/G VOL/ASSN EDU/PROP EXEC ATTIT DRIVE PWR MARXISM COLD/WAR TOT/POP 20. PAGE 91 H1818 ISLAM TREND NAT/LISM

B58
ORNES G.E.,TRUJILLO: LITTLE CAESAR OF THE CARIBBEAN. DOMIN/REP FAM NAT/G FORCES BUDGET CRIME REV PERSON 20 TRUJILLO/R. PAGE 122 H2429 BIOG PWR TOTALISM CHIEF

B58
WIGGIN L.M.,THE FACTION OF COUSINS: A POLITICAL ACCOUNT OF THE GRENVILLES, 1733-1763. UK STRUCT KIN NAT/G INGP/REL...CONCPT BIOG BIBLIOG/A 18 GRENVILLES. PAGE 168 H3357 FAM POL/PAR PWR

S58
EULAV H.,"HD LASSWELL'S DEVELOPMENTAL ANALYSIS." FUT CULTURE TOP/EX PLAN CHOOSE SUPEGO PWR...TREND HYPO/EXP SIMUL GEN/METH VAL/FREE 20 LASSWELL/H. PAGE 47 H0948 CONCPT NEW/IDEA ELITES

S58
MAIR L.P.,"REPRESENTATIVE LOCAL GOVERNMENT AS A PROBLEM IN SOCIAL CHANGE." ECO/UNDEV KIN LOC/G NAT/G SCHOOL JUDGE ADMIN ROUTINE REPRESENT RIGID/FLEX RESPECT...CONCPT STERTYP CMN/WLTH 20. PAGE 101 H2025 AFR PWR ELITES

S58
STAAR R.F.,"ELECTIONS IN COMMUNIST POLAND." EUR+WWI SOCIETY INT/ORG NAT/G POL/PAR LEGIS ACT/RES ECO/TAC EDU/PROP ADJUD ADMIN ROUTINE COERCE TOTALISM ATTIT ORD/FREE PWR 20. PAGE 148 H2963 COM CHOOSE POLAND

C58
MORRALL J.B.,"POLITICAL THOUGHT IN MEDIEVAL TIMES." LAW NAT/G SECT DOMIN ATTIT PWR...BIOG HIST/WRIT BIBLIOG. PAGE 113 H2260 CHRIST-17C CONCPT

B59
BLOOMFIELD L.P.,WESTERN EUROPE AND THE UN - TRENDS AND PROSPECTS. EUR+WWI BAL/PWR DIPLOM ECO/TAC COLONIAL ATTIT PWR...POLICY 20 UN EUROPE/W. PAGE 18 H0359 INT/ORG TREND FUT NAT/G

B59
FOX A.,THE POWER OF SMALL STATES: DIPLOMACY IN WORLD WAR TWO. EUR+WWI FINLAND NORWAY SPAIN SWEDEN TURKEY NAT/G TOP/EX DIPLOM PWR...HIST/WRIT 20. PAGE 52 H1044 CONCPT STERTYP BAL/PWR

B59
HENDEL S.,THE SOVIET CRUCIBLE. USSR LEAD COERCE NAT/LISM UTOPIA PWR...POLICY CONCPT ANTHOL 20 STALIN/J LENIN/VI MARX/KARL BOLSHEVIK. PAGE 70 H1393 COM MARXISM REV TOTALISM

B59
LAQUER W.Z.,THE SOVIET UNION AND THE MIDDLE EAST. COM UAR USSR ECO/UNDEV NAT/G VOL/ASSN ECO/TAC EDU/PROP COLONIAL EXEC PWR...TIME/SEQ TREND COLD/WAR 20. PAGE 91 H1819 ISLAM DRIVE FOR/AID NAT/LISM

B59
MILLER A.S.,PRIVATE GOVERNMENTS AND THE CONSTITUTION (PAMPHLET). LAW LABOR NAT/G ROLE PWR PLURISM...POLICY DECISION. PAGE 111 H2211 FEDERAL CONSTN VOL/ASSN CONSEN

B59
PAGE S.W.,LENIN AND WORLD REVOLUTION. COM USSR NAT/G DOMIN COERCE CROWD UTOPIA ATTIT AUTHORIT DRIVE PWR...CONCPT MYTH 19/20 LENIN/VI MARX/KARL. PAGE 122 H2441 REV PERSON MARXISM BIOG

B59
SANCHEZ A.L.,EL CONCEPTO DEL ESTADO EN EL PENSAMIENTO ESPANOL DEL SIGLO XVI. SPAIN LEGIS JUDGE BAL/PWR LEGIT EXEC WAR PWR...MAJORIT 16. PAGE 137 H2747 NAT/G PHIL/SCI LAW SOVEREIGN

B59
SZLUC T.,TWILIGHT OF THE TYRANTS. BRAZIL L/A+17C PERU VENEZUELA NAT/G FORCES CONTROL PERSON MORAL ORD/FREE PWR...CONCPT 20 ARGEN COLOMB. PAGE 151 H3028 TOTALISM CHIEF REV FASCISM

B59
WRAITH R.E.,EAST AFRICAN CITIZEN. AFR GHANA UK AGRI INDUS LOC/G POL/PAR PROB/SOLV CONTROL REGION REPRESENT NAT/LISM PWR...OBS 20 AFRICA/E AFRICA/W. PAGE 171 H3415 ECO/UNDEV RACE/REL NAT/G NAT/COMP

S59
CHAPMAN B.,"THE FRENCH CONSEIL D'ETAT." FRANCE NAT/G CONSULT OP/RES PROB/SOLV PWR...OBS 20. PAGE 29 H0580 ADMIN LAW CT/SYS LEGIS

S59
GABLE R.W.,"CULTURE AND ADMINISTRATION IN IRAN." IRAN EXEC PARTIC REPRESENT PWR. PAGE 54 H1085 ADMIN CULTURE EX/STRUC INGP/REL

S59
LABEDZ L.,"IDEOLOGY: THE FOURTH STAGE." COM USSR NAT/G TOP/EX LEGIT ATTIT PWR MARXISM...METH/CNCPT HIST/WRIT STERTYP TOT/POP 20. PAGE 90 H1795 CONCPT GEN/LAWS

S59
LEVINE R.A.,"ANTI-EUROPEAN VIOLENCE IN AFRICA: A COMPARATIVE ANALYSIS." AFR CULTURE NAT/G DIPLOM EDU/PROP COLONIAL REGION COERCE ATTIT PWR...PSY CONCPT TIME/SEQ TREND HYPO/EXP SOC/EXP STERTYP GEN/METH COLD/WAR 20. PAGE 95 H1903 DRIVE ORD/FREE REV

S59
SCOTT W.A.,"EMPIRICAL ASSESSMENT OF VALUES AND IDEOLOGIES." CULTURE SOCIETY SECT CREATE DRIVE PERSON MORAL PWR...SOC METH/CNCPT STAT CONT/OBS DEEP/INT DEEP/QU CHARTS VAL/FREE. PAGE 141 H2817 ATTIT PSY

S59
SILBERMAN L.,"CHANGE AND CONFLICT IN THE HORN OF AFRICA." EUR+WWI ITALY UK CULTURE FORCES ECO/TAC ADJUD COLONIAL ATTIT ORD/FREE PWR...DECISION METH/CNCPT HIST/WRIT SOMALI 20. PAGE 144 H2874 AFR TIME/SEQ

S59
SKILLING H.G.,"COMMUNISM: NATIONAL OR INTERNATIONAL." CHINA/COM USSR YUGOSLAVIA NAT/G POL/PAR VOL/ASSN DOMIN REGION COERCE ATTIT PWR MARXISM SOCISM...CONCPT TOT/POP 20 TITO/MARSH. PAGE 145 H2894 COM TREND

B60
ALBRECHT-CARRIE R.,FRANCE, EUROPE AND THE TWO WORLD WARS. EUR+WWI FRANCE GERMANY MOD/EUR UK ECO/DEV NAT/G FORCES BAL/PWR DOMIN ARMS/CONT PEACE PWR 20 TREATY EUROPE. PAGE 5 H0096 DIPLOM WAR

B60
BRZEZINSKI Z.K.,THE SOVIET BLOC-UNITY AND CONFLICT. COM USSR CONSTN DOMIN ADMIN TOTALISM PWR...SOC MYTH RECORD TREND STERTYP GEN/LAWS GEN/METH TOT/POP 20. PAGE 23 H0458 ATTIT EDU/PROP

B60
CARTER G.M.,INDEPENDENCE FOR AFRICA. AFR FUT SOCIETY STRATA ECO/DEV POL/PAR DELIB/GP PLAN DOMIN EDU/PROP COLONIAL REGION ATTIT DRIVE SOVEREIGN ...RECORD INT TIME/SEQ CHARTS 20. PAGE 27 H0544 NAT/G PWR NAT/LISM

B60
EASTON S.C.,THE TWILIGHT OF EUROPEAN COLONIALISM. AFR S/ASIA CONSTN SOCIETY STRUCT ECO/UNDEV INDUS NAT/G FORCES ECO/TAC COLONIAL CT/SYS ATTIT KNOWL ORD/FREE PWR...SOCIALIST TIME/SEQ TREND CON/ANAL 20. PAGE 44 H0882 FINAN ADMIN

B60
FISCHER L.,THE SOVIETS IN WORLD AFFAIRS. CHINA/COM COM EUR+WWI USSR INT/ORG CONFER LEAD ARMS/CONT REV PWR...CHARTS 20 TREATY VERSAILLES. PAGE 51 H1010 DIPLOM NAT/G POLICY MARXISM

B60
FURNISS E.S.,FRANCE, TROUBLED ALLY. EUR+WWI FUT CULTURE SOCIETY BAL/PWR ADMIN ATTIT DRIVE PWR ...TREND TOT/POP 20 DEGAULLE/C. PAGE 54 H1079 NAT/G FRANCE

B60
GOODMAN E.,SOVIET DESIGN FOR A WORLD STATE. COM USSR NAT/G TOP/EX DIPLOM ECO/TAC DOMIN EDU/PROP COERCE REV ATTIT ORD/FREE...CON/ANAL 20. PAGE 59 H1171 PLAN PWR SOCISM TOTALISM

B60
KERSELL J.E.,PARLIAMENTARY SUPERVISION OF DELEGATED LEGISLATION. UK EFFICIENCY PWR...POLICY CHARTS BIBLIOG METH 20 PARLIAMENT. PAGE 85 H1699 LEGIS CONTROL NAT/G EX/STRUC

B60
LASKIN B.,CANADIAN CONSTITUTIONAL LAW: TEXT AND NOTES ON DISTRIBUTION OF LEGISLATIVE POWER (2ND ED.). CANADA LOC/G ECO/TAC TAX CONTROL CT/SYS CRIME FEDERAL PWR...JURID 20 PARLIAMENT. PAGE 92 H1832 CONSTN NAT/G LAW LEGIS

B60
LINDSAY K.,EUROPEAN ASSEMBLIES: THE EXPERIMENTAL PERIOD 1949-1959. EUR+WWI ECO/DEV NAT/G POL/PAR LEGIS TOP/EX ACT/RES PLAN ECO/TAC DOMIN LEGIT ROUTINE ATTIT DRIVE ORD/FREE PWR SKILL...SOC CONCPT TREND CHARTS GEN/LAWS VAL/FREE. PAGE 97 H1932 VOL/ASSN INT/ORG REGION

B60
LISTER L.,EUROPE'S COAL AND STEEL COMMUNITY. FRANCE GERMANY STRUCT ECO/DEV EXTR/IND INDUS MARKET NAT/G DELIB/GP ECO/TAC INT/TRADE EDU/PROP ATTIT RIGID/FLEX ORD/FREE PWR WEALTH...CONCPT STAT TIME/SEQ CHARTS ECSC 20. PAGE 97 H1941 EUR+WWI INT/ORG REGION

B60
MACRIDIS R.C.,THE DE GAULLE REPUBLIC: QUEST FOR UNITY. EUR+WWI NAT/G POL/PAR LEGIS LEGIT NAT/LISM ATTIT RIGID/FLEX ORD/FREE PWR...JURID CONCPT TIME/SEQ 20 DEGAULLE/C. PAGE 100 H2009 TOP/EX STRUCT FRANCE

B60
MANIS J.G.,MAN AND SOCIETY. STRATA LEAD INGP/REL PERS/REL ATTIT PWR...PSY ANTHOL T SOC/INTEG MARX/KARL MILL/JS FREUD/S CHURCHLL/W SPENCER/H RUSSELL/B. PAGE 102 H2036 SOC SOCIETY STRUCT CULTURE

B60
MATTHIAS E.,DAS ENDE DER PARTEIEN 1933. GERMANY NAT/G COERCE CHOOSE ORD/FREE PWR 20. PAGE 105 H2100 FASCISM POL/PAR DOMIN ATTIT

B60
MCCLOSKY H.,THE SOVIET DICTATORSHIP. FUT CONSTN CULTURE INTELL SOCIETY POL/PAR SECT VOL/ASSN FORCES PLAN TEC/DEV DOMIN EDU/PROP COERCE PWR MARXISM ...POLICY CONCPT MYTH STERTYP 20. PAGE 106 H2127 COM NAT/G TOTALISM USSR

B60
PETERSON W.C.,THE WELFARE STATE IN FRANCE. EUR+WWI FRANCE FUT STRATA PROB/SOLV TAX GIVE RECEIVE INCOME ORD/FREE PWR...CHARTS 20. PAGE 125 H2496 NEW/LIB ECO/TAC WEALTH NAT/G

B60
PINTO F.B.M.,ENRIQUECIMENTO ILICITO NO EXERCICIO DE CARGOS PUBLICOS. BRAZIL L/A+17C USA+45 ELITES TRIBUTE CONTROL INGP/REL ORD/FREE PWR...NAT/COMP 20. PAGE 126 H2513 ADMIN NAT/G CRIME LAW

B60
PRASAD B.,THE ORIGINS OF PROVINCIAL AUTONOMY. INDIA UK FINAN LOC/G FORCES LEGIS CONTROL CT/SYS PWR ...JURID 19/20. PAGE 128 H2554 CENTRAL PROVS COLONIAL NAT/G

B60
SCHAPIRO L.,THE COMMUNIST PARTY OF THE SOVIET UNION. COM LAW SOCIETY STRATA STRUCT ECO/DEV LABOR NAT/G POL/PAR CREATE DOMIN EDU/PROP COERCE TOTALISM MARXISM...POLICY CONCPT MYTH TIME/SEQ WORK TOT/POP 20 LENIN/VI STALIN/J. PAGE 139 H2772 INTELL PWR USSR

B60
SETHE P.,SCHICKSALSSTUNDEN DER WELTGESCHICHTE (6TH ED.). NAT/G BAL/PWR DOMIN REV PWR...NAT/COMP 16/20. PAGE 141 H2831 DIPLOM WAR PEACE

B60
SHIRER W.L.,THE RISE AND FALL OF THE THIRD REICH: A HISTORY OF NAZI GERMANY. EUR+WWI CULTURE ECO/DEV INDUS NAT/G POL/PAR FORCES PLAN TEC/DEV ECO/TAC COERCE ATTIT DRIVE PERSON PWR...MYSTIC PSY SOC MYTH STAT CHARTS EXHIBIT WORK VAL/FREE. PAGE 143 H2864 STRUCT GERMANY TOTALISM

B60
WILLIAMS L.E.,OVERSEAS CHINESE NATIONALISM: THE GENESIS OF THE PAN-CHINESE MOVEMENT IN INDONESIA, 1900-1916. ASIA COM INDONESIA AGRI INT/ORG LOC/G DIPLOM EDU/PROP HABITAT PWR POPULISM...GEOG LING CENSUS 20. PAGE 168 H3367 NAT/LISM GP/REL DECISION NAT/G

L60
HAAS E.B.,"CONSENSUS FORMATION IN THE COUNCIL OF EUROPE." EUR+WWI NAT/G DELIB/GP DIPLOM REGION CHOOSE PWR SOVEREIGN...RELATIV NEW/IDEA QUANT CHARTS INDEX TOT/POP OEEC 20 COUNCL/EUR. PAGE 63 H1265 POL/PAR INT/ORG STAT

L60
WHEELER G.,"RACIAL PROBLEMS IN SOVIET MUSLIM ASIA." COM CULTURE SOCIETY NEIGH SECT DOMIN EDU/PROP DISCRIM DISPL DRIVE PWR SOVEREIGN...CENSUS SAMP TREND 20 MUSLIM. PAGE 167 H3340 PERSON ATTIT USSR RACE/REL

S60
BERG E.J.,"ECONOMIC BASIS OF POLITICAL CHOICE IN FRENCH WEST AFRICA." FRANCE ECO/UNDEV AGRI INDUS NAT/G PLAN LEGIT COLONIAL REGION ATTIT PWR WEALTH ...CONCPT 20. PAGE 15 H0299 AFR ECO/TAC

S60
BRZEZINSKI Z.K.,"PATTERNS AND LIMITS OF THE SINO-SOVIET DISPUTE." ASIA CHINA/COM COM FUT STRATA NAT/G EX/STRUC FORCES BAL/PWR DIPLOM ECO/TAC DOMIN EDU/PROP ADMIN COERCE WAR ATTIT RIGID/FLEX ...GEN/LAWS VAL/FREE 20. PAGE 23 H0459 POL/PAR PWR REV USSR

S60
EMERSON R.,"THE EROSION OF DEMOCRACY." AFR FUT LAW CULTURE INTELL SOCIETY ECO/UNDEV FAM LOC/G NAT/G FORCES PLAN TEC/DEV ECO/TAC ADMIN CT/SYS ATTIT ORD/FREE PWR...SOCIALIST SOC CONCPT STAND/INT TIME/SEQ WORK 20. PAGE 46 H0918 S/ASIA POL/PAR

S60
FRANKEL S.H.,"ECONOMIC ASPECTS OF POLITICAL INDEPENDENCE IN AFRICA." AFR FUT SOCIETY ECO/UNDEV COM/IND FINAN LEGIS PLAN TEC/DEV CAP/ISM ECO/TAC INT/TRADE ADMIN ATTIT DRIVE RIGID/FLEX PWR WEALTH ...MGT NEW/IDEA MATH TIME/SEQ VAL/FREE 20. PAGE 53 H1052 NAT/G FOR/AID

S60
GINSBURGS G.,"PEKING-LHASA-NEW DELHI." CHINA/COM FUT INDIA S/ASIA KIN NAT/G PROVS SECT FORCES BAL/PWR ECO/TAC DOMIN EDU/PROP LEGIT ADMIN REGION GUERRILLA PWR...TREND TIBET 20. PAGE 57 H1134 ASIA COERCE DIPLOM

S60
HALSEY A.H.,"THE CHANGING FUNCTIONS OF UNIVERSITIES IN ADVANCED INDUSTRIAL SOCIETIES." R+D EDU/PROP REPRESENT ROLE ORD/FREE PWR TREND. PAGE 65 H1298 ACADEM CREATE CULTURE ADJUST

S60
HOWARD M.,"BRITAIN'S DEFENSE: COMMITMENTS AND CAPABILITIES." EUR+WWI ECO/DEV NAT/G FORCES LEGIS PLAN DETER ORD/FREE WEALTH...POLICY CONCPT TIME/SEQ GEN/METH 20. PAGE 74 H1481 FUT PWR DIPLOM UK

S60
KELLEY G.A.,"THE POLITICAL BACKGROUND OF THE FRENCH A-BOMB." EUR+WWI USSR FORCES TOP/EX TEC/DEV NUC/PWR ATTIT PWR...CONCPT OBS/ENVIR TREND 20. PAGE 84 H1686 NAT/G RESPECT NAT/LISM FRANCE

S60
MAGATHAN W.,"SOME BASES OF WEST GERMAN MILITARY POLICY." EUR+WWI FUT INT/ORG TOP/EX ECO/TAC DOMIN DRIVE ORD/FREE PWR...TRADIT GEOG OBS TREND. PAGE 101 H2015 NAT/G FORCES GERMANY

S60
NORTH R.C.,"THE NEW EXPANSIONISM." ASIA CHINA/COM ATTIT

FUT INDIA CULTURE SOCIETY NAT/G TOP/EX DOMIN COERCE PWR MARXISM...CONCPT TIME/SEQ TREND GEN/LAWS COLD/WAR 20 MAO. PAGE 119 H2372 — DRIVE NAT/LISM

S60
NORTHEDGE F.S.,"BRITISH FOREIGN POLICY AND THE PARTY SYSTEM." EUR+WWI FUT INT/ORG NAT/G EDU/PROP ATTIT PWR...POLICY CONCPT MYTH TIME/SEQ TREND 20 UN. PAGE 119 H2374 — POL/PAR CHOOSE DIPLOM UK

S60
PERLMANN H.,"UPHEAVAL IN TURKEY." EUR+WWI ISLAM NAT/G FORCES TOP/EX LEGIT COERCE CHOOSE DRIVE ORD/FREE PWR...TIME/SEQ TOT/POP 20. PAGE 125 H2494 — CONSTN TURKEY

S60
SHILS E.,"THE INTELLECTUALS IN THE POLITICAL DEVELOPMENT OF THE NEW STATES." AFR ASIA S/ASIA ELITES LOC/G NAT/G CONSULT EX/STRUC CREATE PLAN ECO/TAC DOMIN LEGIT DRIVE PWR...TRADIT CONCPT STERTYP GEN/LAWS 20. PAGE 143 H2861 — POL/PAR INTELL NAT/LISM

S60
SPIRO H.J.,"NEW CONSTITUTIONAL FORMS IN AFRICA." FUT CULTURE SOCIETY ECO/UNDEV NAT/G POL/PAR VOL/ASSN EDU/PROP ATTIT DRIVE ORD/FREE PWR RESPECT ...POLICY CONCPT OBS TREND CON/ANAL STERTYP GEN/LAWS VAL/FREE. PAGE 148 H2950 — AFR CONSTN FOR/AID NAT/LISM

S60
TAUBER K.,"ASPECTS OF NATIONALIST-COMMUNIST COLLABORATION IN POSTWAR GERMANY." COM EUR+WWI USSR NAT/G VOL/ASSN ATTIT DRIVE PWR...TIME/SEQ COLD/WAR TOT/POP 20. PAGE 152 H3049 — POL/PAR EDU/PROP GERMANY

S60
WOLFE T.W.,"KHRUSHCHEV'S DISARMAMENT STRATEGY." COM NAT/G TOP/EX PLAN BAL/PWR DIPLOM ARMS/CONT COERCE ATTIT...POLICY CONCPT RECORD TREND CON/ANAL COLD/WAR 20 KHRUSH/N. PAGE 170 H3401 — PWR GEN/LAWS USSR

S60
WOLFINGER R.E.,"REPUTATION AND REALITY IN THE STUDY OF COMMUNITY POWER." STRUCT PROB/SOLV INGP/REL ATTIT OBJECTIVE...SOC METH/CNCPT PERS/COMP. PAGE 170 H3404 — CULTURE MUNIC DOMIN PWR

S60
WYCKOFF T.,"THE ROLE OF THE MILITARY IN LATIN AMERICAN POLITICS." L/A+17C CONSTN CULTURE ECO/UNDEV POL/PAR FORCES LEGIS TOP/EX LEGIT GUERRILLA REV CHOOSE ORD/FREE PWR...TIME/SEQ VAL/FREE 20. PAGE 171 H3430 — NAT/G COERCE TOTALISM

C60
COX R.H.,"LOCKE ON WAR AND PEACE." UK DIPLOM DOMIN PWR...BIOG IDEA/COMP BIBLIOG 18. PAGE 34 H0689 — CONCPT NAT/G PEACE WAR

C60
EBENSTEIN W.,"MODERN POLITICAL THOUGHT (2ND ED.)" NAT/G CAP/ISM NAT/LISM PERSON ORD/FREE PWR ALL/IDEOS NEW/LIB SOCISM...TRADIT PSY BIBLIOG/A 18/20. PAGE 44 H0884 — IDEA/COMP PHIL/SCI CONCPT GEN/LAWS

B61
BISHOP D.G.,THE ADMINISTRATION OF BRITISH FOREIGN RELATIONS. EUR+WWI MOD/EUR INT/ORG NAT/G POL/PAR DELIB/GP LEGIS TOP/EX ECO/TAC DOMIN EDU/PROP ADMIN COERCE 20. PAGE 17 H0344 — ROUTINE PWR DIPLOM UK

B61
BROUGHTON M.,PRESS AND POLITICS OF SOUTH AFRICA. SOUTH/AFR NAT/G COLONIAL GP/REL ADJUST 20. PAGE 22 H0435 — NAT/LISM PRESS PWR CULTURE

B61
BULLOCK A.,HITLER: A STUDY IN TYRANNY. EUR+WWI GERMANY SOCIETY STRUCT NAT/G POL/PAR FORCES CREATE DOMIN EDU/PROP EXEC COERCE WAR NAT/LISM DISPL DRIVE PERSON PWR...PSY NAZI 20 HITLER/A. PAGE 23 H0470 — ATTIT BIOG TOTALISM

B61
CONQUEST R.,POWER AND POLICY IN THE USSR. USSR NAT/G POL/PAR DIPLOM MARXISM 20. PAGE 33 H0655 — COM HIST/WRIT GOV/REL PWR

B61
DALLIN D.J.,SOVIET FOREIGN POLICY AFTER STALIN. ASIA CHINA/COM EUR+WWI GERMANY IRAN UK YUGOSLAVIA INT/ORG NAT/G VOL/ASSN FORCES TOP/EX BAL/PWR DOMIN EDU/PROP COERCE ATTIT PWR 20. PAGE 37 H0737 — COM DIPLOM USSR

B61
DONNISON F.S.V.,CIVIL AFFAIRS AND MILITARY GOVERNMENT NORTH-WEST EUROPE 1944-1946. EUR+WWI FRANCE GERMANY UK USSR LOC/G PROVS PLAN PROB/SOLV BAL/PWR ECO/TAC CONTROL PWR...CHARTS 20. PAGE 42 H0836 — NAT/G WAR FORCES CIVMIL/REL

B61
GUEVARA E.,GUERRILLA WARFARE. L/A+17C ECO/UNDEV NAT/G POL/PAR VOL/ASSN PLAN DOMIN REV DRIVE PWR WEALTH...NEW/IDEA RECORD BIOG COLD/WAR MARX/KARL OAS 20. PAGE 62 H1247 — FORCES COERCE GUERRILLA CUBA

B61
HARDT J.P.,THE COLD WAR ECONOMIC GAP. USA+45 USSR ECO/DEV FORCES INT/TRADE NUC/PWR PWR 20 COLD/WAR. PAGE 66 H1328 — DIPLOM ECO/TAC NAT/COMP POLICY

B61
JAKOBSON M.,THE DIPLOMACY OF THE WINTER WAR. EUR+WWI FINLAND GERMANY USSR INT/ORG NAT/G PEACE TOTALISM PWR...POLICY CONCPT 20 TREATY. PAGE 79 H1588 — WAR ORD/FREE DIPLOM

B61
JENNINGS I.,PARTY POLITICS: THE GROWTH OF PARTIES (VOL. II). UK SOCIETY NAT/G LEGIS ATTIT 18/20 LABOR/PAR LIB/PARTY CONSRV/PAR. PAGE 80 H1606 — CHOOSE POL/PAR PWR POLICY

B61
KEREKES T.,THE ARAB MIDDLE EAST AND MUSLIM AFRICA. ISLAM SOCIETY ECO/UNDEV SECT VOL/ASSN TOP/EX REGION ATTIT PWR...GEOG CONCPT TIME/SEQ GEN/LAWS 20. PAGE 85 H1694 — NAT/G TREND NAT/LISM

B61
LA PONCE J.A.,THE GOVERNMENT OF THE FIFTH REPUBLIC: FRENCH POLITICAL PARTIES AND THE CONSTITUTION. ALGERIA FRANCE LAW NAT/G DELIB/GP LEGIS ECO/TAC MARXISM SOCISM...CHARTS BIBLIOG/A 20 DEGAULLE/C. PAGE 90 H1794 — PWR POL/PAR CONSTN CHIEF

B61
MARVICK D.,POLITICAL DECISION-MAKERS. INTELL STRATA NAT/G POL/PAR EX/STRUC LEGIS DOMIN EDU/PROP ATTIT PERSON PWR...PSY STAT OBS CONT/OBS STAND/INT UNPLAN/INT TIME/SEQ CHARTS STERTYP VAL/FREE. PAGE 104 H2073 — TOP/EX BIOG ELITES

B61
MARX K.,THE COMMUNIST MANIFESTO. IN (MENDEL A. ESSENTIAL WORKS OF MARXISM, NEW YORK: BANTAM. FUT MOD/EUR CULTURE ECO/DEV ECO/UNDEV AGRI FINAN INDUS MARKET PROC/MFG LABOR MUNIC POL/PAR CONSULT FORCES CREATE PLAN ADMIN ATTIT DRIVE RIGID/FLEX ORD/FREE PWR RESPECT MARX/KARL WORK. PAGE 104 H2081 — COM NEW/IDEA CAP/ISM REV

B61
MILIBAND R.,PARLIAMENTARY SOCIALISM. EUR+WWI UK EXEC LEAD PARL/PROC GP/REL...POLICY 20 PARLIAMENT LABOR/PAR. PAGE 110 H2203 — POL/PAR NAT/G PWR SOCISM

B61
MOLLAU G.,INTERNATIONAL COMMUNISM AND WORLD REVOLUTION: HISTORY AND METHODS. RUSSIA USSR INT/ORG NAT/G POL/PAR VOL/ASSN FORCES BAL/PWR DIPLOM EXEC REGION WAR ATTIT PWR MARXISM...CONCPT TIME/SEQ COLD/WAR 19/20. PAGE 112 H2237 — COM REV

B61
MONAS S.,THE THIRD SECTION: POLICE AND SOCIETY IN RUSSIA UNDER NICHOLAS I. MOD/EUR RUSSIA ELITES STRUCT NAT/G EX/STRUC ADMIN CONTROL PWR CONSERVE ...DECISION 19 NICHOLAS/I. PAGE 112 H2238 — ORD/FREE COM FORCES COERCE

B61
NARAIN J.P.,SWARAJ FOR THE PEOPLE. INDIA CONSTN LOC/G MUNIC POL/PAR CHOOSE REPRESENT EFFICIENCY ATTIT PWR SOVEREIGN 20. PAGE 116 H2311 — NAT/G ORD/FREE EDU/PROP EX/STRUC

B61
RAHNER H.,KIRCHE UND STAAT IM FRUHEN CHRISTENTUM. INGP/REL ORD/FREE PWR CATHISM...JURID 1/9 CHURCH/STA CHRISTIAN. PAGE 129 H2582 — NAT/G SECT ATTIT GP/REL

B61
ROIG E.,MARTI, ANTIIMPERIALISTA. CUBA L/A+17C DIPLOM DOMIN COLONIAL CONTROL LEAD PWR SOVEREIGN ...PHIL/SCI 19 MARTI/JOSE INTERVENT. PAGE 133 H2664 — PERSON NAT/LISM ECO/UNDEV ORD/FREE

B61
SAFRAN M.,EGYPT IN SEARCH OF POLITICAL COMMUNITY: AN ANALYSIS OF THE INTELLECTUAL AND POLITICAL EVOLUTION OF EGYPT, 1804-1952. ISLAM NAT/G SECT EDU/PROP COERCE ATTIT DRIVE KNOWL PWR...TIME/SEQ 20. PAGE 137 H2729 — INTELL NAT/LISM UAR

B61
SETON-WATSON H.,FROM LENIN TO KHRUSHCHEV: THE HISTORY OF WORLD COMMUNISM. ASIA COM EUR+WWI ISLAM S/ASIA ECO/DEV ECO/UNDEV NAT/G POL/PAR DIPLOM ECO/TAC EDU/PROP COERCE GUERRILLA ATTIT DRIVE WORK TOT/POP NAZI 20. PAGE 141 H2832 — PWR REV USSR

B61
SOKOL A.E.,SEAPOWER IN THE NUCLEAR AGE. USA+45 USSR DIST/IND FORCES INT/TRADE DETER WAR...POLICY NAT/COMP BIBLIOG COLD/WAR. PAGE 146 H2928 — SEA PWR WEAPON NUC/PWR

S61
ANDERSON O.,"ECONOMIC WARFARE IN THE CRIMEAN WAR." EUR+WWI MOD/EUR NAT/G ACT/RES WAR DRIVE PWR 19/20. PAGE 6 H0130 — ECO/TAC UK RUSSIA

S61
BRZEZINSKI Z.K.,"THE ORGANIZATION OF THE COMMUNIST CAMP." COM CZECHOSLVK COM/IND NAT/G DELIB/GP INT/TRADE DOMIN EDU/PROP EXEC ROUTINE COERCE ATTIT PWR...MGT CONCPT TIME/SEQ CHARTS VAL/FREE 20 TREATY. PAGE 23 H0460 — VOL/ASSN DIPLOM USSR

S61
MACRIDIS R.C.,"INTEREST GROUPS IN COMPARATIVE ANALYSIS." CULTURE OP/RES LOBBY REPRESENT GP/REL AUTHORIT ORD/FREE PWR...POLICY DECISION METH/CNCPT — GP/COMP CONCPT PLURISM

CLASSIF. PAGE 101 H2010

S61
RANDALL F.B.,"COMMUNISM IN THE HIGH ANDES." L/A+17C PERU USSR SOCIETY PLAN EDU/PROP TOTALISM ATTIT RIGID/FLEX PWR WEALTH...HUM CONCPT GEN/LAWS 20 BOLIV EQUADOR. PAGE 129 H2589
CULTURE DRIVE

S61
SCHELLING T.C.,"NUCLEAR STRATEGY IN EUROPE." COM EUR+WWI USSR NAT/G FORCES NUC/PWR DRIVE ORD/FREE PWR...DECISION CONCPT OBS TREND HYPO/EXP 20. PAGE 139 H2784
FUT COERCE ARMS/CONT WAR

S61
TANHAM B.K.,"COMMUNIST REVOLUTIONARY WARFARE: THE VIETMINH IN INDOCHINA." EUR+WWI S/ASIA VIETNAM NAT/G EDU/PROP LEGIT GUERRILLA ATTIT PWR...CONCPT GEN/LAWS 20. PAGE 152 H3042
FORCES ECO/TAC WAR FRANCE

S61
TOMASIC D.,"POLITICAL LEADERSHIP IN CONTEMPORARY POLAND." COM EUR+WWI GERMANY NAT/G POL/PAR SECT DELIB/GP PLAN ECO/TAC DOMIN EDU/PROP PWR MARXISM ...MARXIST GEOG MGT CONCPT TIME/SEQ STERTYP 20. PAGE 156 H3111
SOCIETY ROUTINE USSR POLAND

S61
TUCKER R.C.,"TOWARDS A COMPARATIVE POLITICS OF MOVEMENT-REGIMES" (BMR)" USSR CONSTN NAT/G CREATE PROB/SOLV DIPLOM DOMIN REV...GP/COMP IDEA/COMP METH 20 STALIN/J BOLSHEVISM. PAGE 157 H3135
MARXISM POLICY GEN/LAWS PWR

B62
ARNE S.,LE PRESIDENT DU CONSEIL DES MINISTRES SOUS LA IV REPUBLIQUE. EUR+WWI FRANCE LEGIT PWR...BIOG CHARTS. PAGE 8 H0165
DELIB/GP POL/PAR NAT/G LEGIS

B62
BELL D.,THE END OF IDEOLOGY (REV. ED.). USA+45 USA-45 ELITES STRATA LABOR CREATE CRIME PWR MARXISM ...PHIL/SCI METH/COMP 20 EUROPE. PAGE 13 H0265
CROWD CAP/ISM SOCISM IDEA/COMP

B62
BINDER L.,IRAN: POLITICAL DEVELOPMENT IN A CHANGING SOCIETY. IRAN OP/RES REV GP/REL CENTRAL RATIONAL PWR...PHIL/SCI NAT/COMP GEN/LAWS 20. PAGE 17 H0337
LEGIT NAT/G ADMIN STRUCT

B62
BODIN J.,THE SIX BOOKES OF A COMMONWEALE (1576) (FACSIMILE REPRINT OF 1606 ENGLISH TRANSLATION). AUTHORIT ORD/FREE SOVEREIGN...TRADIT CONCPT. PAGE 18 H0364
PWR CONSERVE CHIEF NAT/G

B62
BROWN S.D.,STUDIES ON ASIA, 1962. ASIA BURMA INDIA ISLAM ISRAEL S/ASIA ECO/UNDEV POL/PAR SECT ECO/TAC ...ANTHOL 20 CHINJAP. PAGE 22 H0450
PWR PARL/PROC

B62
BRUMBERG A.,RUSSIA UNDER KHRUSHCHEV. FUT USSR SOCIETY ECO/DEV AGRI PERF/ART WORKER PWR...SOC ANTHOL 20 KHRUSH/N. PAGE 22 H0453
COM MARXISM NAT/G CHIEF

B62
DEHIO L.,THE PRECARIOUS BALANCE: FOUR CENTURIES OF THE EUROPEAN POWER STRUGGLE. FRANCE GERMANY SPAIN NAT/G DOMIN PWR...GOV/COMP 8/20. PAGE 39 H0784
BAL/PWR WAR DIPLOM COERCE

B62
FINER S.E.,THE MAN ON HORSEBACK: ROLE OF THE MILITARY IN POLITICS. UNIV LAW CONSTN ELITES SOCIETY POL/PAR BAL/PWR DOMIN EDU/PROP LEGIT COERCE GUERRILLA REV WAR WEAPON DRIVE SUPEGO ORD/FREE PWR RESPECT...POLICY CONCPT GEN/METH. PAGE 50 H1003
NAT/G FORCES TOTALISM

B62
GRZYBOWSKI K.,SOVIET LEGAL INSTITUTIONS. USA+45 USSR ECO/DEV NAT/G EDU/PROP CONTROL CT/SYS CRIME OWN ATTIT PWR SOCISM...NAT/COMP 20. PAGE 62 H1242
ADJUD LAW JURID

B62
HABERMAS J.,STRUKTURWANDEL DER OFFENTLICHKEIT. NAT/G EDU/PROP PRESS LEAD PARTIC PWR 20. PAGE 63 H1268
ATTIT CONCPT DOMIN

B62
JACKSON W.A.D.,RUSSO-CHINESE BORDERLANDS. ASIA COM USSR NAT/G PROVS EX/STRUC FORCES DOMIN COERCE PEACE ATTIT PWR SOVEREIGN WEALTH...CONCPT TREND CHARTS STERTYP VAL/FREE. PAGE 79 H1576
GEOG DIPLOM RUSSIA

B62
JENNINGS I.,PARTY POLITICS: THE STUFF OF POLITICS (VOL.III). UK NAT/G SECT CHIEF INT/TRADE RECEIVE COLONIAL GP/REL NAT/LISM ORD/FREE SOCISM 19/20 CHURCH/STA WHIG/PARTY. PAGE 80 H1607
POL/PAR CONSTN PWR ALL/IDEOS

B62
KASTARI P.,LA PRESIDENCE DE LA REPUBLIQUE EN FINLANDE. FINLAND CONSTN NAT/G POL/PAR LEGIS LEGIT ATTIT...JURID CONCPT 20 PRESIDENT. PAGE 83 H1666
PARL/PROC CHIEF PWR DECISION

B62
LAQUEUR W.,POLYCENTRISM. CHINA/COM COM USSR WOR+45 INT/ORG NAT/G ECO/TAC DOMIN LEAD ATTIT PWR SOVEREIGN...ANTHOL 20. PAGE 91 H1821
MARXISM DIPLOM BAL/PWR POLICY

B62
MANSUR F.,PROCESS OF INDEPENDENCE. GHANA INDIA INDONESIA PAKISTAN CONSTN ELITES INTELL STRUCT ACADEM NAT/G REV PWR 20. PAGE 102 H2043
NAT/COMP POL/PAR SOVEREIGN COLONIAL

B62
STATE AND LOCAL GOVERNMENT. MUNIC NAT/G NEIGH PRESS CONTROL CHOOSE REPRESENT...BIBLIOG 20. PAGE 104 H2076
PROVS LOC/G GOV/REL PWR

B62
MEYER A.G.,LENINISM. USSR STRUCT NAT/G CAP/ISM LEAD WAR PWR SOVEREIGN...BIBLIOG 20 LENIN/VI. PAGE 109 H2187
POL/PAR REV MARXISM PHIL/SCI

B62
MODELSKI G.,SEATO-SIX STUDIES. ASIA CHINA/COM INDIA S/ASIA INT/ORG NAT/G ECO/TAC DETER ATTIT ORD/FREE PWR...TIME/SEQ COLD/WAR TOT/POP 20 SEATO. PAGE 112 H2234
MARKET ECO/UNDEV INT/TRADE

B62
OLLE-LAPRUNE J.,LA STABILITE DES MINISTRES SOUS LA TROISIEME REPUBLIQUE, 1879-1940. FRANCE CONSTN POL/PAR LEAD WAR INGP/REL RIGID/FLEX PWR...POLICY CHARTS 19/20. PAGE 121 H2415
LEGIS NAT/G ADMIN PERSON

B62
PENTONY D.E.,RED WORLD IN TUMULT: COMMUNIST FOREIGN POLICIES. CHINA/COM COM NAT/G EDU/PROP COERCE ATTIT PWR RESPECT...SOC CHARTS 20. PAGE 124 H2488
ECO/UNDEV DOMIN USSR ASIA

B62
PHILLIPS O.H.,CONSTITUTIONAL AND ADMINISTRATIVE LAW (3RD ED.). UK INT/ORG LOC/G CHIEF EX/STRUC LEGIS BAL/PWR ADJUD COLONIAL CT/SYS PWR...CHARTS 20. PAGE 125 H2503
JURID ADMIN CONSTN NAT/G

B62
SCHIEDER T.,THE STATE AND SOCIETY IN OUR TIMES (TRANS. BY C.A.M. SYM). SOCIETY NAT/G POL/PAR REV GP/REL ALL/IDEOS 19/20. PAGE 139 H2786
STRUCT PWR HIST/WRIT

B62
TATZ C.M.,SHADOW AND SUBSTANCE IN SOUTH AFRICA. SOUTH/AFR AGRI NAT/G POL/PAR DOMIN GP/REL ATTIT PWR 20. PAGE 152 H3048
RACE/REL REPRESENT DISCRIM LEGIS

B62
VALERIANO N.D.,COUNTER-GUERRILLA OPERATIONS: THE PHILLIPINE EXPERIENCE. NAT/G CONSULT ACT/RES PLAN COERCE GUERRILLA ATTIT ORD/FREE PWR SKILL...GEOG NEW/IDEA TIME/SEQ CHARTS 20. PAGE 161 H3221
S/ASIA FORCES PHILIPPINE

B62
YU LIEN YEN CHIU,INDEX TO THE CLASSIFIED FILES ON COMMUNIST CHINA. CHINA/COM CULTURE ECO/UNDEV CIVMIL/REL PWR WEALTH MARXISM...PSY SOC METH 20. PAGE 172 H3440
BIBLIOG INDEX COM

B62
ZIESEL K.,DAS VERLORENE GEWISSEN. GERMANY/W NAT/G VOL/ASSN EDU/PROP PRESS SUPEGO...POLICY 20. PAGE 173 H3455
MORAL PWR ORD/FREE RESPECT

L62
NOLTE E.,"ZUR PHANOMENOLOGIE DES FASCHIMUS." EUR+WWI GERMANY ITALY TURKEY INTELL NAT/G CHIEF CONSULT FORCES CREATE DOMIN EDU/PROP COERCE WAR CHOOSE DRIVE FASCISM...PSY CONCPT MYTH GEN/METH LEAGUE/NAT NAZI 20. PAGE 118 H2367
ATTIT PWR

S62
BELL W.,"EQUALITY AND ATTITUDES OF ELITES IN JAMAICA" L/A+17C STRATA PWR WEALTH...SOC QU TREND. PAGE 13 H0266
ELITES FUT SOCIETY CULTURE

S62
LANGER W.L.,"FAREWELL TO EMPIRE." EUR+WWI MOD/EUR NAT/G DIPLOM EDU/PROP COLONIAL ATTIT ORD/FREE PWR SOVEREIGN WEALTH...CONCPT TIME/SEQ GEN/LAWS TOT/POP VAL/FREE CMN/WLTH 20. PAGE 91 H1810
DOMIN ECO/TAC NAT/LISM

S62
LONDON K.,"SINO-SOVIET RELATIONS IN THE CONTEXT OF THE 'WORLD SOCIALIST SYSTEM'." ASIA CHINA/COM COM USSR INT/ORG NAT/G TOP/EX BAL/PWR DIPLOM DOMIN ATTIT PERCEPT RIGID/FLEX PWR MARXISM...METH/CNCPT TREND 20. PAGE 98 H1957
DELIB/GP CONCPT SOCISM

S62
MARIAS J.,"A PROGRAM FOR EUROPE." EUR+WWI INT/ORG NAT/G PLAN DIPLOM DOMIN PWR...STERTYP TOT/POP 20. PAGE 102 H2048
VOL/ASSN CREATE REGION

S62
MARTIN L.W.,"THE MARKET FOR STRATEGIC IDEAS IN BRITAIN: THE 'SANDYS ERA'" UK ARMS/CONT WAR GOV/REL OPTIMAL...POLICY DECISION GOV/COMP COLD/WAR CMN/WLTH. PAGE 103 H2063
DIPLOM COERCE FORCES PWR

S62
PASSIN H.,"THE SOURCES OF PROTEST IN JAPAN." CULTURE SOCIETY EDU/PROP COERCE NAT/LISM DISPL DRIVE PWR RESPECT...POLICY SOC TREND 20 CHINJAP. PAGE 124 H2473
ASIA ATTIT REV

S62
PIQUEMAL M.,"LES PROBLEMES DES UNIONS D'ETATS EN AFRIQUE NOIRE." FRANCE SOCIETY INT/ORG NAT/G DELIB/GP PLAN LEGIT ADMIN COLONIAL ROUTINE ATTIT ORD/FREE PWR...GEOG METH/CNCPT 20. PAGE 126 H2515 — AFR ECO/UNDEV REGION

S62
PISTRAK L.,"SOVIET VIEWS ON AFRICA." AFR COM FUT ISLAM USSR INTELL STRUCT KIN POL/PAR PLAN EDU/PROP RIGID/FLEX PWR MARXISM...TIME/SEQ WORK TOT/POP 20. PAGE 126 H2516 — NAT/G ATTIT SOCISM

S62
ROTBERG R.,"THE RISE OF AFRICAN NATIONALISM: THE CASE OF EAST AND CENTRAL AFRICA." AFR CULTURE SOCIETY NEIGH DIPLOM DOMIN COLONIAL COERCE DISPL PERCEPT PWR SOVEREIGN...POLICY OBS/ENVIR TREND WORK 20. PAGE 135 H2690 — ATTIT DRIVE NAT/LISM REV

S62
SPRINGER H.W.,"FEDERATION IN THE CARIBBEAN: AN ATTEMPT THAT FAILED." L/A+17C ECO/UNDEV INT/ORG POL/PAR PROVS LEGIS CREATE PLAN LEGIT ADMIN FEDERAL ATTIT DRIVE PERSON ORD/FREE PWR...POLICY GEOG PSY CONCPT OBS CARIBBEAN CMN/WLTH 20. PAGE 148 H2955 — VOL/ASSN NAT/G REGION

S62
STRACHEY J.,"COMMUNIST INTENTIONS." ASIA USSR YUGOSLAVIA INT/ORG NAT/G FORCES DOMIN EDU/PROP COERCE NUC/PWR NAT/LISM PEACE RIGID/FLEX PWR MARXISM...CONCPT MYTH OBS TIME/SEQ TREND COLD/WAR TOT/POP 20. PAGE 150 H2992 — COM ATTIT WAR

C62
BACON F.,"OF EMPIRE" (1612) IN F. BACON, ESSAYS." ELITES NAT/G PROB/SOLV DIPLOM ADMIN CONTROL WEALTH 16/17 KING. PAGE 9 H0190 — PWR CHIEF DOMIN GEN/LAWS

B63
ATTIA G.E.D.,LES FORCES ARMEES DES NATIONS UNIES EN COREE ET AU MOYENORIENT. KOREA CONSTN NAT/G DELIB/GP LEGIS PWR...IDEA/COMP NAT/COMP BIBLIOG UN SUEZ. PAGE 9 H0177 — FORCES INT/LAW

B63
BARNETT A.D.,COMMUNIST STRATEGIES IN ASIA: A COMPARATIVE ANALYSIS OF GOVERNMENTS AND PARTIES. COM FUT S/ASIA CULTURE SOCIETY STRATA NAT/G DELIB/GP ACT/RES ECO/TAC EDU/PROP COERCE CHOOSE ATTIT RIGID/FLEX ORD/FREE PWR SKILL...SIMUL VAL/FREE 20. PAGE 11 H0223 — ASIA POL/PAR DIPLOM USSR

B63
BELFRAGE C.,THE MAN AT THE DOOR WITH THE GUN. CUBA L/A+17C NAT/G LEAD PARTIC GP/REL PWR...POLICY 20 CASTRO/F. PAGE 13 H0261 — REGION ECO/UNDEV STRUCT ATTIT

B63
BIALEK R.W.,CATHOLIC POLITICS: A HISTORY BASED ON ECUADOR. ECUADOR SPAIN CULTURE STRUCT CONTROL REV PWR...BIBLIOG WORSHIP 18/20. PAGE 16 H0329 — COLONIAL CATHISM GOV/REL HABITAT

B63
BRECHER M.,THE NEW STATES OF ASIA. ASIA S/ASIA INT/ORG BAL/PWR COLONIAL NEUTRAL ORD/FREE PWR 20 UN. PAGE 20 H0407 — NAT/G ECO/UNDEV DIPLOM POLICY

B63
BROOKES E.H.,POWER, LAW, RIGHT, AND LOVE: A STUDY IN POLITICAL VALUES. SOUTH/AFR NAT/G PERSON ...CONCPT IDEA/COMP 20. PAGE 21 H0432 — PWR ORD/FREE JURID LOVE

B63
BRZEZINSKI Z.K.,AFRICA AND THE COMMUNIST WORLD. AFR ASIA COM CULTURE SOCIETY INT/ORG DELIB/GP ACT/RES ECO/TAC COERCE ORD/FREE PWR WEALTH...STAT TOT/POP VAL/FREE 20. PAGE 23 H0461 — ATTIT EDU/PROP DIPLOM USSR

B63
CARTER G.M.,FIVE AFRICAN STATES: RESPONSES TO DIVERSITY. CONSTN CULTURE STRATA LEGIS PLAN ECO/TAC DOMIN EDU/PROP CT/SYS EXEC CHOOSE ATTIT HEALTH ORD/FREE PWR...TIME/SEQ TOT/POP VAL/FREE. PAGE 27 H0547 — AFR SOCIETY

B63
CARY J.,POWER IN MEN. NAT/G ORD/FREE...GEN/LAWS 20. PAGE 28 H0553 — PHIL/SCI OLD/LIB LAISSEZ PWR

B63
DALAND R.T.,PERSPECTIVES OF BRAZILIAN PUBLIC ADMINISTRATION (VOL. I). BRAZIL LAW ECO/UNDEV SCHOOL CHIEF TEC/DEV CONFER CONTROL GP/REL ATTIT ROLE PWR...ANTHOL 20. PAGE 37 H0735 — ADMIN NAT/G PLAN GOV/REL

B63
DE JOUVENEL B.,THE PURE THEORY OF POLITICS. NAT/G DIPLOM CONTROL GP/REL PERS/REL PERSON PWR OBJECTIVE CONCPT. PAGE 38 H0758 — GEN/LAWS SOCIETY METH/CNCPT

B63
DEUTSCH K.W.,THE NERVES OF GOVERNMENT. NAT/G CREATE EDU/PROP CONTROL LEAD PWR...CONCPT GEN/LAWS 20. PAGE 40 H0799 — DECISION GAME SIMUL OP/RES

B63
ECKSTEIN H.,COMPARATIVE POLITICS. POL/PAR LEGIS CT/SYS CHOOSE TOTALISM PWR POPULISM...METH/COMP GEN/METH ANTHOL BIBLIOG 20. PAGE 44 H0886 — NAT/COMP CONSTN REPRESENT NAT/G

B63
FALL B.,THE TWO VIETNAMS. CULTURE SOCIETY ECO/UNDEV NAT/G TOP/EX ACT/RES PLAN ECO/TAC DOMIN EDU/PROP COERCE ATTIT DRIVE PERSON ORD/FREE PWR...SOC TIME/SEQ COLD/WAR 20. PAGE 48 H0965 — S/ASIA BIOG VIETNAM

B63
FRIEDRICH C.J.,MAN AND HIS GOVERNMENT: AN EMPIRICAL THEORY OF POLITICS. UNIV LOC/G NAT/G ADJUD REV INGP/REL DISCRIM PWR BIBLIOG. PAGE 53 H1069 — PERSON ORD/FREE PARTIC CONTROL

B63
GLUCKMAN M.,ORDER AND REBELLION IN TRIBAL AFRICA. EUR+WWI LAW CULTURE STRATA KIN MUNIC DELIB/GP ACT/RES DOMIN EDU/PROP LEGIT ADMIN COERCE CHOOSE ATTIT PERSON ORD/FREE PWR...SOC CHARTS GEN/LAWS TOT/POP VAL/FREE. PAGE 57 H1147 — AFR SOCIETY

B63
HYDE D.,THE PEACEFUL ASSAULT. COM UAR USSR ECO/DEV ECO/UNDEV NAT/G POL/PAR CAP/ISM PWR 20. PAGE 76 H1516 — MARXISM CONTROL ECO/TAC DIPLOM

B63
KOGAN N.,THE POLITICS OF ITALIAN FOREIGN POLICY. EUR+WWI LEGIS DOMIN LEGIT EXEC PWR RESPECT SKILL ...POLICY DECISION HUM SOC METH/CNCPT OBS INT CHARTS 20. PAGE 87 H1737 — NAT/G ROUTINE DIPLOM ITALY

B63
LERNER R.,MEDIEVAL POLITICAL PHILOSOPHY. ISLAM MORAL PWR CATHISM...CATH CONCPT OBS IDEA/COMP ANTHOL 9/15 JEWS CHRISTIAN BACON/R AQUINAS/T. PAGE 95 H1890 — KNOWL PHIL/SCI

B63
LEWIN J.,POLITICS AND LAW IN SOUTH AFRICA. SOUTH/AFR UK POL/PAR BAL/PWR ECO/TAC COLONIAL CONTROL GP/REL DISCRIM PWR 20 NEGRO. PAGE 96 H1909 — NAT/LISM POLICY LAW RACE/REL

B63
MAYNE R.,THE COMMUNITY OF EUROPE. UK CONSTN NAT/G CONSULT DELIB/GP CREATE PLAN ECO/TAC LEGIT ADMIN ROUTINE ORD/FREE PWR WEALTH...CONCPT TIME/SEQ EEC EURATOM 20. PAGE 105 H2107 — EUR+WWI INT/ORG REGION

B63
MONGER G.W.,THE END OF ISOLATION. FRANCE MOD/EUR RUSSIA UK NAT/G LEGIS TOP/EX GOV/REL PWR 20 TREATY CHINJAP. PAGE 112 H2239 — DIPLOM POLICY WAR

B63
MONTAGUE J.B. JR.,CLASS AND NATIONALITY; ENGLISH AND AMERICAN STUDIES. UK USA+45 ELITES STRUCT WORKER ATTIT PWR...SOC CHARTS SOC/EXP 20. PAGE 112 H2243 — STRATA NAT/LISM PERSON NAT/COMP

B63
MOSELY P.E.,THE SOVIET UNION, 1922-1962: A FOREIGN AFFAIRS READER. ASIA POLAND USSR CULTURE INTELL AGRI POL/PAR WORKER INT/TRADE DOMIN WAR NAT/LISM MARXISM SOCISM 20 KHRUSH/N. PAGE 113 H2267 — PWR POLICY DIPLOM

B63
MULLER H.J.,FREEDOM IN THE WESTERN WORLD. PREHIST CULTURE SECT CREATE TEC/DEV DOMIN PWR WEALTH ...MAJORIT SOC CONCPT. PAGE 114 H2285 — ORD/FREE TIME/SEQ SOCIETY

B63
OTERO L.M.,HONDURAS. HONDURAS SPAIN STRUCT SECT COLONIAL REV WAR ATTIT PWR...GEOG WORSHIP 16/20. PAGE 122 H2432 — NAT/G SOCIETY NAT/LISM ECO/UNDEV

B63
PELLING H.M.,A HISTORY OF BRITISH TRADE UNIONISM. UK ELITES ECO/DEV POL/PAR GP/REL PWR NEW/LIB 19/20. PAGE 124 H2485 — LABOR VOL/ASSN NAT/G

B63
RICHARDSON H.G.,THE ADMINISTRATION OF IRELAND 1172-1377. IRELAND CONSTN EX/STRUC LEGIS JUDGE CT/SYS PARL/PROC...CHARTS BIBLIOG 12/14. PAGE 131 H2621 — ADMIN NAT/G PWR

B63
SAKAI R.K.,STUDIES ON ASIA, 1963. ASIA INDIA ISRAEL S/ASIA USA+45 PERF/ART POL/PAR SECT REGION NAT/LISM ...SOC LING TREND ANTHOL 19/20 CHINJAP. PAGE 137 H2735 — PWR CULTURE

B63
SHANNON R.T.,GLADSTONE AND THE BULGARIAN AGITATION OF 1876. BULGARIA TURKEY UK DIPLOM COERCE REV ATTIT 19 GLADSTON/W DISRAELI/B. PAGE 142 H2841 — EDU/PROP NAT/G PWR CONSEN

B63
SILONE I.,THE SCHOOL FOR DICTATORS. EUR+WWI GERMANY ITALY SOCIETY NAT/G CHIEF EX/STRUC ATTIT MORAL PWR ...HIST/WRIT 20. PAGE 144 H2876 — TOTALISM EDU/PROP ORD/FREE FASCISM

B63
SINGH H.L.,PROBLEMS AND POLICIES OF THE BRITISH IN INDIA, 1885-1898. INDIA UK NAT/G FORCES LEGIS — COLONIAL PWR

PROB/SOLV CONTROL RACE/REL ADJUST DISCRIM NAT/LISM RIGID/FLEX...MGT 19 CIVIL/SERV. PAGE 144 H2885 POLICY ADMIN

B63
SKLAR R.L.,NIGERIAN POLITICAL PARTIES: POWER IN AN EMERGENT AFRICAN NATION. AFR EUR+WWI CULTURE STRATA NAT/G DELIB/GP EX/STRUC LEGIS DOMIN EDU/PROP ROUTINE CHOOSE ATTIT PERCEPT ORD/FREE PWR...SOC CONCPT OBS TOT/POP VAL/FREE. PAGE 145 H2898 POL/PAR SOCIETY NAT/LISM NIGERIA

B63
SPRING D.,THE ENGLISH LANDED ESTATE IN THE NINETEENTH CENTURY: ITS ADMINISTRATION. UK ELITES STRUCT AGRI NAT/G GP/REL OWN PWR WEALTH...BIBLIOG 19 HOUSE/LORD. PAGE 148 H2954 STRATA PERS/REL MGT

B63
THOMPSON F.M.L.,ENGLISH LANDED SOCIETY IN THE NINETEENTH CENTURY. UK STRUCT MUNIC NAT/G CONTROL WAR GP/REL OWN WEALTH...BIBLIOG 18/20. PAGE 154 H3081 STRATA PWR ELITES GOV/REL

B63
THORBURN H.G.,PARTY POLITICS IN CANADA. CANADA ELITES STRUCT INDUS PWR 20. PAGE 154 H3086 POL/PAR CONCPT NAT/G PROVS

B63
THUCYDIDES,THE PELOPONESIAN WARS. MEDIT-7 CULTURE INT/ORG NAT/G FORCES TOP/EX PLAN ROUTINE PWR ...CONCPT. PAGE 155 H3091 ATTIT COERCE WAR

B63
TUCKER R.C.,THE SOVIET POLITICAL MIND. COM INTELL NAT/G TOP/EX EDU/PROP ADMIN COERCE TOTALISM ATTIT PWR MARXISM...PSY MYTH HYPO/EXP 20. PAGE 157 H3136 STRUCT RIGID/FLEX ELITES USSR

B63
ULAM A.B.,THE NEW FACE OF SOVIET TOTALITARIANISM. FUT INTELL NAT/G POL/PAR EX/STRUC TOP/EX DIPLOM ECO/TAC DOMIN EDU/PROP LEGIT COERCE ATTIT RIGID/FLEX...OBS HIST/WRIT TREND TOT/POP VAL/FREE COLD/WAR. PAGE 158 H3150 COM PWR TOTALISM USSR

L63
FREUND G.,"ADENAUER AND THE FUTURE OF GERMANY." EUR+WWI FUT GERMANY/W FORCES LEGIT ADMIN ROUTINE ATTIT DRIVE PERSON PWR...POLICY TIME/SEQ TREND VAL/FREE 20 ADENAUER/K. PAGE 53 H1058 NAT/G BIOG DIPLOM GERMANY

L63
ROSE R.,"COMPARATIVE STUDIES IN POLITICAL FINANCE: A SYMPOSIUM." ASIA EUR+WWI S/ASIA LAW CULTURE DELIB/GP LEGIS ACT/RES ECO/TAC EDU/PROP CHOOSE ATTIT RIGID/FLEX SUPEGO PWR SKILL WEALTH...STAT ANTHOL VAL/FREE. PAGE 134 H2674 FINAN POL/PAR

L63
ZARTMAN I.W.,"THE SAHARA--BRIDGE OR BARRIER." ISLAM CULTURE SOCIETY NAT/G DELIB/GP DOMIN EDU/PROP LEGIT ATTIT...HIST/WRIT TIME/SEQ CHARTS TOT/POP VAL/FREE 20. PAGE 172 H3447 INT/ORG PWR NAT/LISM

S63
BANFIELD J.,"FEDERATION IN EAST-AFRICA." AFR UGANDA ELITES INT/ORG NAT/G VOL/ASSN LEGIS ECO/TAC FEDERAL ATTIT SOVEREIGN TOT/POP 20 TANGANYIKA. PAGE 10 H0210 EX/STRUC PWR REGION

S63
BECHHOEFER B.G.,"SOVIET ATTITUDE TOWARD DISARMAMENT." COM USSR NAT/G ACT/RES TEC/DEV NUC/PWR ATTIT DISPL RIGID/FLEX PWR...METH/CNCPT TREND GEN/LAWS COLD/WAR 20. PAGE 13 H0252 FORCES EDU/PROP ARMS/CONT

S63
BILL J.A.,"THE SOCIAL AND ECONOMIC FOUNDATIONS OF POWER IN CONTEMPORARY IRAN." ISLAM CULTURE NAT/G ECO/TAC DOMIN COERCE ATTIT PWR WEALTH...TREND VAL/FREE 20. PAGE 17 H0334 SOCIETY STRATA IRAN

S63
DUDLEY B.J.,"THE NOMINATION OF PARLIAMENTARY CANDIDATES IN NORTHERN NIGERIA." AFR CONSTN CULTURE ELITES STRATA DELIB/GP LEGIS DOMIN EDU/PROP COERCE ATTIT SUPEGO PWR...STAT VAL/FREE 20. PAGE 43 H0854 POL/PAR CHOOSE NIGERIA

S63
DUTT V.P.,"CHINA: JEALOUS NEIGHBOR." ASIA CHINA/COM INDIA S/ASIA NAT/G TOP/EX DOMIN COERCE REV ATTIT ...POLICY COLD/WAR 20. PAGE 44 H0874 FORCES PWR DIPLOM

S63
EMERI C.,"LES FORCES POLITIQUES AU PARLEMENT" EUR+WWI FRANCE ELITES DELIB/GP TOP/EX LEGIT ATTIT ...SOC 20 PARLIAMENT. PAGE 46 H0917 POL/PAR LEGIS PWR NAT/G

S63
GLUCKMAN M.,"CIVIL WAR AND THEORIES OF POWER IN BAROTSE-LAND: AFRICAN AND MEDIEVAL ANALOGIES." AFR CHRIST-17C LAW CONSTN CULTURE STRATA KIN DELIB/GP FORCES DOMIN LEGIT COERCE PERCEPT ORD/FREE...SOC INT TIME/SEQ GEN/LAWS VAL/FREE. PAGE 57 H1148 TOP/EX PWR WAR

S63
GROSSER A.,"FRANCE AND GERMANY IN THE ATLANTIC COMMUNITY." INT/ORG NAT/G TOP/EX DIPLOM REGION PEACE ATTIT ORD/FREE PWR...CONCPT RECORD TIME/SEQ GEN/LAWS VAL/FREE COLD/WAR 20. PAGE 62 H1234 EUR+WWI VOL/ASSN FRANCE GERMANY

S63
HALPERN A.M.,"THE EMERGENCE OF AN ASIAN COMMUNIST BLOC." ASIA CHINA/COM COM FUT KOREA/N S/ASIA VIETNAM/N STRATA NAT/G DELIB/GP FORCES TOP/EX PLAN BAL/PWR COERCE DETER PWR COLD/WAR WORK 20. PAGE 65 H1295 POL/PAR EDU/PROP DIPLOM

S63
HARRIS R.L.,"COMMUNISM AND ASIA: ILLUSIONS AND MISCONCEPTIONS." ASIA COM FUT S/ASIA ECO/UNDEV AGRI NAT/G POL/PAR EX/STRUC EDU/PROP COERCE ATTIT MARXISM COLD/WAR TOT/POP 20. PAGE 67 H1344 PWR GUERRILLA

S63
HOSKINS H.L.,"ARAB SOCIALISM IN THE UAR." ISLAM USSR AGRI INDUS NAT/G TOP/EX CREATE DIPLOM EDU/PROP DRIVE KNOWL PWR SOCISM...POLICY CONCPT TREND SUEZ 20. PAGE 74 H1478 ECO/DEV PLAN UAR

S63
HUREWITZ J.C.,"LEBANESE DEMOCRACY IN ITS INTERNATIONAL SETTING." FRANCE ISLAM UK LOC/G NAT/G SECT DOMIN EDU/PROP EXEC ATTIT PWR...TIME/SEQ 20. PAGE 75 H1507 STRUCT LEBANON

S63
LAMBERT D.,"LA TRANSPOSITION DU REGIME PRESIDENTIEL HORS DES ETATSUNIS; LE CAS DE L'AMERIQUE LATINE." NAT/G EX/STRUC LEGIS PARL/PROC PWR 18/20 PRESIDENT CENTRAL/AM SOUTH/AMER. PAGE 90 H1800 DELIB/GP CHIEF L/A+17C GOV/REL

S63
MONROE A.D.,"BRITAIN AND THE EUROPEAN COMMUNITY." EUR+WWI FRANCE NAT/G DELIB/GP TOP/EX ECO/TAC DOMIN PWR...POLICY RECORD GEN/LAWS EEC EFTA 20 EFTA CMN/WLTH. PAGE 112 H2241 VOL/ASSN ATTIT UK

S63
ROUGEMONT D.,"LES NOUVELLES CHANCES DE L'EUROPE." EUR+WWI FUT ECO/DEV INT/ORG NAT/G ACT/RES PLAN TEC/DEV EDU/PROP ADMIN COLONIAL FEDERAL ATTIT PWR SKILL...TREND 20. PAGE 135 H2696 ECO/UNDEV PERCEPT

S63
RUSTOW D.A.,"THE MILITARY IN MIDDLE EASTERN SOCIETY AND POLITICS." FUT ISLAM CONSTN SOCIETY FACE/GP NAT/G POL/PAR PROF/ORG CONSULT DOMIN ADMIN EXEC REGION COERCE NAT/LISM ATTIT DRIVE PERSON ORD/FREE PWR...POLICY CONCPT OBS STERTYP 20. PAGE 136 H2721 FORCES ELITES

S63
TANG P.S.H.,"SINO-SOVIET TENSIONS." ASIA CHINA/COM COM CUBA KOREA/N VIETNAM/N NAT/G VOL/ASSN DELIB/GP PEACE PERCEPT PWR...METH/CNCPT MYTH RECORD TREND GEN/LAWS 20. PAGE 152 H3041 ACT/RES EDU/PROP REV

S63
TILMAN R.O.,"MALAYSIA: THE PROBLEMS OF FEDERATION." ISLAM S/ASIA CONSTN PROVS SECT DELIB/GP DOMIN EDU/PROP LEGIT EXEC COERCE CHOOSE ATTIT HEALTH ORD/FREE PWR...STAT TOT/POP VAL/FREE 20. PAGE 155 H3097 NAT/G CULTURE MALAYSIA

C63
ATTIA G.E.O.,"LES FORCES ARMEES DES NATIONS UNIES EN COREE ET AU MOYENORIENT." KOREA CONSTN DELIB/GP LEGIS PWR...IDEA/COMP NAT/COMP BIBLIOG UN SUEZ. PAGE 9 H0178 FORCES NAT/G INT/LAW

B64
AGGER R.E.,THE RULERS AND THE RULED: POLITICAL POWER AND IMPOTENCE IN AMERICAN COMMUNITIES. CULTURE DOMIN CHOOSE ATTIT ALL/VALS...DECISION SOC CONCPT OBS QU CHARTS. PAGE 4 H0079 PWR STRUCT LOC/G MUNIC

B64
BAGEHOT W.,THE ENGLISH CONSTITUTION. UK CHIEF CONSULT LEGIS BAL/PWR PWR...BIBLIOG 18/19 PARLIAMENT. PAGE 10 H0198 CONSTN PARL/PROC NAT/G CONCPT

B64
BAUCHET P.,ECONOMIC PLANNING. FRANCE STRATA LG/CO CAP/ISM ADMIN PARL/PROC DEMAND OPTIMAL ATTIT PWR SOCISM...POLICY CHARTS 20. PAGE 12 H0238 ECO/DEV NAT/G PLAN ECO/TAC

B64
BELL C.,THE DEBATABLE ALLIANCE. COM UK USA+45 NAT/G FORCES PLAN BAL/PWR NUC/PWR WAR ATTIT...GOV/COMP 20. PAGE 13 H0263 DIPLOM PWR PEACE POLICY

B64
BENDIX R.,NATION-BUILDING AND CITIZENSHIP: STUDIES OF OUR CHANGING SOCIAL ORDER. WOR+45 CULTURE LOC/G GOV/REL INGP/REL ORD/FREE PWR 20. PAGE 14 H0275 PARTIC NAT/COMP ADMIN AUTHORIT

B64
BINDER L.,THE IDEOLOGICAL REVOLUTION IN THE MIDDLE EAST. ISLAM STRUCT INT/ORG KIN SECT EX/STRUC TOP/EX PLAN ATTIT DRIVE RIGID/FLEX PWR...MYTH TOT/POP 20. PAGE 17 H0338 POL/PAR NAT/G NAT/LISM

B64
BRZEZINSKI Z.,POLITICAL POWER: USA/USSR. USA+45 USSR AGRI POL/PAR FORCES CREATE CHOOSE ATTIT ORD/FREE PWR MARXISM...MYTH 20 KENNEDY/JF. PAGE 23 H0457 NAT/G NAT/COMP POLICY LEAD

B64
CLUBB O.E. JR.,TWENTIETH CENTURY CHINA. ASIA CHINA/COM INTELL NAT/G POL/PAR VOL/ASSN ACT/RES EDU/PROP COERCE REV PWR...TIME/SEQ 20. PAGE 30 H0608 TOP/EX DRIVE

B64
COONDOO R.,THE DIVISION OF POWERS IN THE INDIAN CONSTITUTION. INDIA ECO/UNDEV FINAN TEC/DEV WAR CENTRAL EFFICIENCY NAT/LISM PWR WEALTH NEW/LIB ...BIBLIOG 18/20. PAGE 33 H0659
CONSTN LEGIS WELF/ST GOV/COMP

B64
CULLINGWORTH J.B.,TOWN AND COUNTRY PLANNING IN ENGLAND AND WALES. UK LAW SOCIETY CONSULT ACT/RES ADMIN ROUTINE LEISURE INGP/REL ADJUST PWR...GEOG 20 OPEN/SPACE URBAN/RNWL. PAGE 36 H0718
MUNIC PLAN NAT/G PROB/SOLV

B64
DE SMITH S.A.,THE NEW COMMONWEALTH AND ITS CONSTITUTIONS. AFR CYPRUS PAKISTAN S/ASIA INT/ORG NAT/G LEGIS LEGIT RIGID/FLEX PWR...CONCPT TIME/SEQ CMN/WLTH 20. PAGE 38 H0770
EX/STRUC CONSTN SOVEREIGN

B64
DOOLIN D.J.,COMMUNIST CHINA: THE POLITICS OF STUDENT OPPOSITION. CHINA/COM ELITES STRATA ACADEM NAT/G WRITING CT/SYS LEAD PARTIC COERCE TOTALISM 20. PAGE 42 H0838
MARXISM DEBATE AGE/Y PWR

B64
FAINSOD M.,HOW RUSSIA IS RULED (REV. ED.). RUSSIA USSR AGRI PROC/MFG LABOR POL/PAR EX/STRUC CONTROL PWR...POLICY BIBLIOG 19/20 KHRUSH/N COM/PARTY. PAGE 48 H0963
NAT/G REV MARXISM

B64
FRIEDLAND W.H.,AFRICAN SOCIALISM. ECO/UNDEV MARKET LABOR NAT/G POL/PAR PLAN CAP/ISM ECO/TAC EDU/PROP CHOOSE ATTIT DRIVE PWR WEALTH...POLICY CONCPT RECORD STERTYP 20. PAGE 53 H1063
AFR SOCISM

B64
GOODNOW H.F.,THE CIVIL SERVICE OF PAKISTAN: BUREAUCRACY IN A NEW NATION. INDIA PAKISTAN S/ASIA ECO/UNDEV PROVS CHIEF PARTIC CHOOSE EFFICIENCY PWR ...BIBLIOG 20. PAGE 59 H1173
ADMIN GOV/REL LAW NAT/G

B64
GREAT BRITAIN CENTRAL OFF INF,CONSTITUTIONAL DEVELOPMENT IN THE COMMONWEALTH. VOL/ASSN PLAN DIPLOM COLONIAL INGP/REL NAT/LISM ORD/FREE PWR 17/20 CMN/WLTH. PAGE 60 H1202
REGION CONSTN NAT/G SOVEREIGN

B64
GRIFFITH W.E.,THE SINO-SOVIET RIFT. ASIA CHINA/COM COM CUBA USSR YUGOSLAVIA NAT/G POL/PAR VOL/ASSN DELIB/GP FORCES TOP/EX DIPLOM EDU/PROP DRIVE PERSON PWR...TREND 20 TREATY. PAGE 61 H1224
ATTIT TIME/SEQ BAL/PWR SOCISM

B64
HALE O.J.,THE CAPTIVE PRESS IN THE THIRD REICH. GERMANY CULTURE LG/CO NAT/G POL/PAR PLAN DOMIN TASK CENTRAL OWN TOTALISM PWR...BIBLIOG 20 HITLER/A NAZI AMMAN/MAX. PAGE 64 H1283
COM/IND PRESS CONTROL FASCISM

B64
HALPERIN S.W.,MUSSOLINI AND ITALIAN FASCISM. ITALY NAT/G POL/PAR SECT ECO/TAC LEAD PWR SOCISM...POLICY 20 MUSSOLIN/B. PAGE 64 H1294
FASCISM NAT/LISM EDU/PROP CHIEF

B64
HELMREICH E.,A FREE CHURCH IN A FREE STATE? FRANCE GERMANY ITALY SECT LEAD PWR CATHISM...POLICY ANTHOL WORSHIP 19/20 CHURCH/STA. PAGE 69 H1389
GP/REL NAT/G

B64
HORNE D.,THE LUCKY COUNTRY: AUSTRALIA TODAY. UK CULTURE STRATA ATTIT PWR PLURISM...GOV/COMP 20 AUSTRAL. PAGE 73 H1471
RACE/REL DIPLOM NAT/G STRUCT

B64
KARIEL H.S.,IN SEARCH OF AUTHORITY: TWENTIETH-CENTURY POLITICAL THOUGHT. WOR+45 WOR-45 NAT/G EX/STRUC TOTALISM DRIVE PWR...MGT PHIL/SCI GEN/LAWS 19/20 NIETZSCH/F FREUD/S WEBER/MAX NIEBUHR/R MARITAIN/J. PAGE 83 H1661
CONSTN CONCPT ORD/FREE IDEA/COMP

B64
KRUEGER H.,ALLGEMEINE STAATSLEHRE. WOR+45 CONSTN SECT CHOOSE INGP/REL PWR NEW/LIB...JURID CLASSIF IDEA/COMP. PAGE 89 H1777
NAT/G GOV/COMP SOCIETY

B64
LEMARCHAND R.,POLITICAL AWAKENING IN THE BELGIAN CONGO. ECO/UNDEV VOL/ASSN DOMIN CHOOSE GP/REL INGP/REL DISCRIM ORD/FREE PWR...CHARTS 20 CONGO ARABS. PAGE 94 H1873
NAT/LISM COLONIAL POL/PAR RACE/REL

B64
MINAR D.W.,IDEAS AND POLITICS: THE AMERICAN EXPERIENCE. SECT CHIEF LEGIS CREATE ADJUD EXEC REV PWR...PHIL/SCI CONCPT IDEA/COMP 18/20 HAMILTON/A JEFFERSN/T DECLAR/IND JACKSON/A PRESIDENT. PAGE 111 H2220
CONSTN NAT/G FEDERAL

B64
PIKE F.B.,THE CONFLICT BETWEEN CHURCH AND STATE IN LATIN AMERICA. L/A+17C CULTURE SOCIETY STRATA DOMIN EDU/PROP LEGIT COERCE ATTIT ORD/FREE PWR WEALTH ...CONCPT TIME/SEQ TREND VAL/FREE. PAGE 125 H2510
SECT NAT/G

B64
RESHETAR J.S. JR.,A CONCISE HISTORY OF THE COMMUNIST PARTY OF THE SOVIET UNION (REV. ED.). COM USSR NAT/G EXEC 19/20 LENIN/VI STALIN/J KHRUSH/N. PAGE 131 H2618
CHIEF POL/PAR MARXISM PWR

B64
RIDLEY F.,PUBLIC ADMINISTRATION IN FRANCE. FRANCE UK EX/STRUC CONTROL PARTIC EFFICIENCY 20. PAGE 131 H2625
ADMIN REPRESENT GOV/COMP PWR

B64
RIES J.C.,THE MANAGEMENT OF DEFENSE: ORGANIZATION AND CONTROL OF THE US ARMED SERVICES. PROF/ORG DELIB/GP EX/STRUC LEGIS GOV/REL PERS/REL CENTRAL RATIONAL PWR...POLICY TREND GOV/COMP BIBLIOG. PAGE 131 H2626
FORCES ACT/RES DECISION CONTROL

B64
SAKAI R.K.,STUDIES ON ASIA, 1964. ASIA CHINA/COM ISRAEL MALAYSIA S/ASIA USA+45 USSR ECO/UNDEV FAM POL/PAR SECT CONSULT NAT/LISM...POLICY SOC 20 CHINJAP. PAGE 137 H2736
PWR DIPLOM

B64
SEGAL R.,SANCTIONS AGAINST SOUTH AFRICA. AFR SOUTH/AFR NAT/G INT/TRADE RACE/REL PEACE PWR ...INT/LAW ANTHOL 20 UN. PAGE 141 H2821
SANCTION DISCRIM ECO/TAC POLICY

B64
SINGER M.R.,THE EMERGING ELITE: A STUDY OF POLITICAL LEADERSHIP IN CEYLON. S/ASIA ECO/UNDEV AGRI KIN NAT/G SECT EX/STRUC LEGIT ATTIT PWR RESPECT...SOC STAT CHARTS 20. PAGE 144 H2883
TOP/EX STRATA NAT/LISM CEYLON

B64
SKINNER E.P.,THE MOSSI OF UPPER VOLTA: THE POLITICAL DEVELOPMENT OF A SUDANESE PEOPLE. AFR LAW AGRI FAM KIN POL/PAR PROVS SECT DELIB/GP EX/STRUC FORCES TOP/EX DOMIN EDU/PROP LEGIT CT/SYS COERCE CHOOSE ORD/FREE PWR WEALTH...SOC MYTH VAL/FREE. PAGE 145 H2897
CULTURE OBS UPPER/VOLT

B64
TEPASKE J.J.,EXPLOSIVE FORCES IN LATIN AMERICA. CULTURE INTELL ECO/UNDEV INT/ORG NAT/G SECT FORCES ECO/TAC EDU/PROP PWR WEALTH SOC. PAGE 153 H3063
L/A+17C RIGID/FLEX FOR/AID USSR

B64
THORNTON T.P.,THE THIRD WORLD IN SOVIET PERSPECTIVE: STUDIES BY SOVIET WRITERS ON THE DEVELOPING AREAS. AFR L/A+17C S/ASIA STRATA AGRI INDUS MARKET NAT/G POL/PAR ECO/TAC COLONIAL PERCEPT PWR WEALTH...MARXIST STAT CHARTS WORK MARX/KARL 20. PAGE 155 H3090
ECO/UNDEV ACT/RES USSR DIPLOM

B64
TIERNEY B.,THE CRISIS OF CHURCH AND STATE 1050-1300. DOMIN EDU/PROP CONTROL PWR CONSERVE 11/14. PAGE 155 H3092
SECT NAT/G GP/REL

B64
WALLBANK T.W.,DOCUMENTS ON MODERN AFRICA. NAT/G COLONIAL GP/REL ATTIT PWR...BIBLIOG 19/20. PAGE 165 H3294
AFR NAT/LISM ECO/UNDEV DIPLOM

B64
WHEELER-BENNETT J.W.,THE NEMESIS OF POWER (2ND ED.). EUR+WWI GERMANY TOP/EX TEC/DEV ADMIN WAR PERS/REL RIGID/FLEX ROLE ORD/FREE PWR FASCISM 20 HITLER/A. PAGE 167 H3342
FORCES NAT/G GP/REL STRUCT

B64
WHITE D.S.,SEEDS OF DISCORD. EUR+WWI FRANCE NAT/G VOL/ASSN FORCES DIPLOM DOMIN NAT/LISM DISPL RIGID/FLEX PWR...RECORD INT BIOG 20 DEGAULLE/C ROOSEVLT/F CHURCHLL/W HULL. PAGE 167 H3347
TOP/EX ATTIT

B64
WRAITH R.,CORRUPTION IN DEVELOPING COUNTRIES. NIGERIA UK LAW ELITES STRATA INDUS LOC/G NAT/G SECT FORCES EDU/PROP ADMIN PWR WEALTH 18/20. PAGE 171 H3414
ECO/UNDEV CRIME SANCTION ATTIT

B64
WRIGHT G.,RURAL REVOLUTION IN FRANCE: THE PEASANTRY IN THE TWENTIETH CENTURY. EUR+WWI MOD/EUR LAW CULTURE AGRI POL/PAR DELIB/GP LEGIS ECO/TAC EDU/PROP COERCE CHOOSE ATTIT RIGID/FLEX HEALTH ...STAT CENSUS CHARTS VAL/FREE 20. PAGE 171 H3419
PWR STRATA FRANCE REV

L64
HAAS E.B.,"ECONOMICS AND DIFFERENTIAL PATTERNS OF POLITICAL INTEGRATION: PROJECTIONS ABOUT UNITY IN LATIN AMERICA." SOCIETY NAT/G DELIB/GP ACT/RES CREATE PLAN ECO/TAC REGION ROUTINE ATTIT DRIVE PWR WEALTH...CONCPT TREND CHARTS LAFTA 20. PAGE 63 H1266
L/A+17C INT/ORG MARKET

L64
MACKINTOSH J.P.,"NIGERIA'S EXTERNAL AFFAIRS." UK CULTURE ECO/UNDEV NAT/G VOL/ASSN EDU/PROP LEGIT ADMIN ATTIT ORD/FREE PWR 20. PAGE 100 H2002
AFR DIPLOM NIGERIA

L64
ROTBERG R.,"THE FEDERATION MOVEMENT IN BRITISH EAST AND CENTRAL AFRICA." AFR RHODESIA UGANDA ECO/UNDEV NAT/G POL/PAR FORCES DOMIN LEGIT ADMIN COERCE ATTIT ...CONCPT TREND 20 TANGANYIKA. PAGE 135 H2691
VOL/ASSN PWR REGION

L64
SYMONDS R.,"REFLECTIONS IN LOCALISATION." AFR S/ASIA UK STRATA INT/ORG NAT/G SCHOOL EDU/PROP LEGIT KNOWL ORD/FREE PWR RESPECT CMN/WLTH 20. PAGE 151 H3023
ADMIN MGT COLONIAL

S64
BARIETY J.,"LA POLITIQUE EXTERIEURE ALLEMANDE DANS L'HIVER 1939-1940." COM FINLAND GERMANY ISLAM ITALY USSR NAT/G FORCES ECO/TAC DOMIN EDU/PROP COERCE WAR PWR WEALTH...HIST/WRIT NAZI TOT/POP VAL/FREE 20. PAGE 11 H0216 EUR+WWI DIPLOM

S64
BENSON M.,"SOUTH AFRICA AND WORLD OPINION." AFR SOUTH/AFR INTELL SOCIETY TOP/EX ECO/TAC DOMIN COERCE DISCRIM ATTIT PWR WEALTH...POLICY RECORD 20. PAGE 14 H0285 NAT/G RIGID/FLEX RACE/REL

S64
CATTELL D.T.,"SOVIET POLICIES IN LATIN AMERICA." COM CUBA L/A+17C USSR SOCIETY NAT/G POL/PAR FORCES CREATE ECO/TAC EDU/PROP REGION REV RIGID/FLEX ...GEN/LAWS COLD/WAR 20. PAGE 28 H0560 DRIVE PWR

S64
CLIGNET R.,"POTENTIAL ELITES IN GHANA AND THE IVORY COAST: A PRELIMINARY SURVEY." AFR CULTURE ELITES STRATA KIN NAT/G SECT DOMIN EXEC ORD/FREE RESPECT SKILL...POLICY RELATIV GP/COMP NAT/COMP 20. PAGE 30 H0605 PWR LEGIT IVORY/CST GHANA

S64
COLEMAN J.S.,"COLLECTIVE DECISIONS." CULTURE ATTIT PERCEPT PWR SOC. PAGE 31 H0628 DECISION INGP/REL PERSON METH/COMP

S64
CROZIER B.,"POUVOIR ET ORGANISATION." SOCIETY NAT/G DOMIN...PSY SOC CONCPT TOT/POP VAL/FREE 20. PAGE 36 H0714 PERSON PWR DIPLOM

S64
DE GAULLE C.,"FRENCH WORLD VIEW." AFR ASIA CHINA/COM EUR+WWI ISLAM ECO/UNDEV INT/ORG NAT/G VOL/ASSN ACT/RES DIPLOM ECO/TAC EDU/PROP ATTIT DRIVE WEALTH 20. PAGE 37 H0751 TOP/EX PWR FOR/AID FRANCE

S64
GOLDBERG A.,"THE MILITARY ORIGINS OF THE BRITISH NUCLEAR DETERRENT." EUR+WWI ECO/DEV NAT/G PLAN NUC/PWR ATTIT PWR...DECISION HIST/WRIT COLD/WAR 20. PAGE 58 H1156 FORCES CONCPT DETER UK

S64
GROSS J.A.,"WHITEHALL AND THE COMMONWEALTH." EUR+WWI MOD/EUR INT/ORG NAT/G CONSULT DELIB/GP LEGIS DOMIN ADMIN COLONIAL ROUTINE PWR CMN/WLTH 19/20. PAGE 62 H1233 EX/STRUC ATTIT TREND

S64
JOHNSON K.F.,"CAUSAL FACTORS IN LATIN AMERICAN POLITICAL INSTABILITY." CULTURE NAT/G VOL/ASSN EX/STRUC FORCES EDU/PROP LEGIT ADMIN COERCE REV ATTIT KNOWL PWR...STYLE RECORD CHARTS WORK 20. PAGE 81 H1624 L/A+17C PERCEPT ELITES

S64
KOVNER M.,"THE SINO-SOVIET DISPUTE: COMMUNISM AT THE CROSSROADS." ASIA CHINA/COM COM USSR ECO/UNDEV NAT/G TOP/EX CREATE BAL/PWR DOMIN EDU/PROP PWR ...CONCPT COMECON 20. PAGE 88 H1760 ATTIT TREND

S64
LERNER W.,"THE HISTORICAL ORIGINS OF THE SOVIET DOCTRINE OF PEACEFUL COEXISTENCE." COM USSR INT/ORG NAT/G VOL/ASSN PLAN PEACE ATTIT RIGID/FLEX PWR MARXISM...TIME/SEQ COLD/WAR 20. PAGE 95 H1891 EDU/PROP DIPLOM

S64
LEVI W.,"INDIAN NEUTRALISM RECONSIDERED." ASIA CHINA/COM S/ASIA SOCIETY NAT/G ACT/RES LEGIT NEUTRAL COERCE ATTIT DRIVE PERCEPT RIGID/FLEX HEALTH LOVE PWR...DECISION RECORD TREND STERTYP 20. PAGE 95 H1896 ORD/FREE CONCPT INDIA

S64
LEWIS B.,"THE QUEST FOR FREEDOM--A SAD STORY OF THE MIDDLE EAST." ISLAM ISRAEL LEBANON TURKEY CULTURE NAT/G SECT LEGIS TOP/EX DOMIN EDU/PROP LEGIT ORD/FREE PWR RESPECT...POLICY TIME/SEQ VAL/FREE 20. PAGE 96 H1911 CONSTN ATTIT NAT/LISM

S64
MARES V.E.,"EAST EUROPE'S SECOND CHANCE." COM EUR+WWI HUNGARY ROMANIA USSR YUGOSLAVIA ECO/UNDEV NAT/G TOP/EX CREATE PLAN TEC/DEV REGION NAT/LISM RIGID/FLEX PWR...CONCPT STAT COMECON 20. PAGE 102 H2047 VOL/ASSN ECO/TAC

S64
MARTELLI G.,"PORTUGAL AND THE UNITED NATIONS." AFR EUR+WWI ELITES INT/ORG NAT/G PROVS PLAN DIPLOM ECO/TAC DOMIN COLONIAL RIGID/FLEX MORAL ORD/FREE PWR WEALTH...MYTH UN 20. PAGE 103 H2060 ATTIT PORTUGAL

S64
MC WILLIAM M.,"THE WORLD BANK AND THE TRANSFER OF POWER IN KENYA." AFR ECO/UNDEV CONSULT ACT/RES TEC/DEV PERCEPT PWR SKILL WEALTH...CONCPT OBS TREND 20. PAGE 106 H2119 NAT/G ECO/TAC

S64
MERKL P.H.,"EUROPEAN ASSEMBLY PARTIES AND NATIONAL DELEGATIONS." INT/ORG DELIB/GP DOMIN EDU/PROP LEGIT CHOOSE PWR...STAT VAL/FREE 20. PAGE 109 H2180 EUR+WWI POL/PAR REGION

S64
MOZINGO D.P.,"CHINA'S RELATIONS WITH HER ASIAN NEIGHBORS." ASIA CHINA/COM S/ASIA VIETNAM NAT/G DELIB/GP FORCES CREATE DOMIN EDU/PROP REV RIGID/FLEX PWR...TIME/SEQ GEN/LAWS COLD/WAR 20. PAGE 114 H2277 VOL/ASSN POLICY DIPLOM

S64
POWELL R.L.,"COMMUNIST CHINA'S MILITARY POTENTIAL." ASIA CHINA/COM NAT/G EX/STRUC EDU/PROP COERCE GUERRILLA NUC/PWR WAR...RECORD CON/ANAL 20. PAGE 128 H2551 FORCES PWR

S64
PRELOT M.,"LA INFLUENCIA POLITICA Y ELECTORAL DE LA PRENSA EN LA FRANCIA ACTUAL." EUR+WWI SOCIETY NAT/G POL/PAR PROF/ORG PRESS ATTIT PWR...CONCPT 20. PAGE 128 H2556 EDU/PROP FRANCE

S64
RAMAZANI R.K.,"CHURCH AND STATE IN MODERNIZING SOCIETY: THE CASE OF IRAN." ISLAM CULTURE ORD/FREE PWR...TIME/SEQ VAL/FREE 17/20. PAGE 129 H2586 SECT NAT/G ELITES IRAN

S64
REISS I.,"LE DECLENCHEMENT DE LA PREMIERE GUERRE MONDIALE." GERMANY RUSSIA NAT/G FORCES DOMIN EDU/PROP COERCE RIGID/FLEX PWR SOVEREIGN...RELATIV HIST/WRIT TOT/POP AUST/HUNG SERBIA 20. PAGE 131 H2612 MOD/EUR BAL/PWR DIPLOM WAR

S64
RUDOLPH L.I.,"GENERALS AND POLITICIANS IN INDIA." INDIA S/ASIA CULTURE STRATA NAT/G LEGIS TOP/EX EDU/PROP ATTIT ORD/FREE PWR RESPECT SKILL...POLICY BIOG TIME/SEQ STERTYP VAL/FREE 20. PAGE 136 H2713 FORCES COERCE

S64
SCHEFFLER H.W.,"THE GENESIS AND REPRESSION OF CONFLICT: CHOISEUL ISLAND." S/ASIA LOC/G NAT/G FORCES LEGIS DIPLOM DOMIN LEGIT EXEC CHOOSE ATTIT RESPECT SKILL...POLICY JURID OBS TREND GEN/METH 20. PAGE 139 H2781 PWR COERCE WAR

S64
SWEARER H.R.,"AFTER KHRUSHCHEV: WHAT NEXT." COM FUT USSR CONSTN ELITES NAT/G POL/PAR CHIEF DELIB/GP LEGIS DOMIN LEAD...RECORD TREND STERTYP GEN/METH 20. PAGE 151 H3016 EX/STRUC PWR

S64
TOYNBEE A.,"BRITAIN AND THE ARABS: THE NEED FOR A NEW START." NAT/G CREATE COLONIAL ATTIT RIGID/FLEX MORAL PWR...POLICY HIST/WRIT 20. PAGE 156 H3124 ISLAM ECO/TAC DIPLOM UK

S64
VANDENBOSCH A.,"POWER BALANCE IN INDONESIA." S/ASIA USSR NAT/G TOP/EX BAL/PWR DOMIN NEUTRAL ORD/FREE PWR...POLICY TIME/SEQ GEN/LAWS 20 SUKARNO/A. PAGE 162 H3233 FORCES TREND DIPLOM INDONESIA

B65
ADENAUER K.,MEMOIRS 1945-53. EUR+WWI GERMANY/W ECO/DEV CHIEF FORCES ECO/TAC WAR GOV/REL PWR SOVEREIGN 20 NATO ADENAUER/K. PAGE 3 H0068 BIOG DIPLOM NAT/G PERS/REL

B65
APTER D.E.,THE POLITICS OF MODERNIZATION. AFR L/A+17C CULTURE NAT/G POL/PAR ADMIN COLONIAL NAT/LISM ATTIT RIGID/FLEX PWR...SOC CONCPT. PAGE 8 H0154 ECO/UNDEV GEN/LAWS STRATA CREATE

B65
BETEILLE A.,CASTE, CLASS, AND POWER. INDIA MUNIC SECT REGION GP/REL PERS/REL ATTIT HABITAT RIGID/FLEX...SOC 20. PAGE 16 H0323 STRATA CULTURE PWR STRUCT

B65
BORTOLI G.,SOCIOLOGIE DU REFERENDUM DANS LA FRANCE MODERNE. FRANCE CONSTN EDU/PROP SUFF ATTIT ORD/FREE ...POLICY DECISION CHARTS BIBLIOG 20 DEGAULLE/C. PAGE 19 H0379 LEGIS SOCIETY PWR NAT/G

B65
BROWNSON O.A.,THE AMERICAN REPUBLIC. NAT/G PROVS WAR GOV/REL PRIVIL ORD/FREE PWR ALL/IDEOS CONSERVE ...CONCPT 19 CIVIL/WAR. PAGE 22 H0452 CONSTN FEDERAL SOVEREIGN

B65
CALLEO D.P.,EUROPE'S FUTURE: THE GRAND ALTERNATIVES. UK INT/ORG DIPLOM PWR SOVEREIGN ...CONCPT IDEA/COMP NAT/COMP BIBLIOG 20 EEC EUROPE DEGAULLE/C NATO. PAGE 25 H0506 FUT EUR+WWI FEDERAL NAT/LISM

B65
CARTER G.M.,POLITICS IN EUROPE. EUR+WWI FRANCE GERMANY/W UK USSR LAW CONSTN POL/PAR VOL/ASSN PRESS LOBBY PWR...ANTHOL SOC/INTEG EEC. PAGE 27 H0548 GOV/COMP OP/RES ECO/DEV

B65
CHARNAY J.P.,LE SUFFRAGE POLITIQUE EN FRANCE; ELECTIONS PARLEMENTAIRES, ELECTION PRESIDENTIELLE, REFERENDUMS. FRANCE CONSTN CHIEF DELIB/GP ECO/TAC EDU/PROP CRIME INGP/REL MORAL ORD/FREE PWR CATHISM 20 PARLIAMENT PRESIDENT. PAGE 29 H0584 CHOOSE SUFF NAT/G LEGIS

B65
CHEN T.H.,THE CHINESE COMMUNIST REGIME: A DOCUMENTARY STUDY (2 VOLS.). CHINA/COM LAW CONSTN ELITES ECO/UNDEV LEGIS ECO/TAC ADMIN CONTROL PWR ...SOC 20. PAGE 29 H0587 MARXISM POL/PAR NAT/G

B65
DAHL R.A.,MODERN POLITICAL ANALYSIS. UNIV COERCE ...MAJORIT DECISION METH. PAGE 36 H0731
CONCPT GOV/COMP PWR

B65
EDINGER L.J.,KURT SCHUMACHER: A STUDY IN PERSONALITY AND POLITICAL BEHAVIOR. EUR+WWI GERMANY NAT/G DRIVE ROLE PWR SOCISM...BIBLIOG 20 SOC/DEMPAR SCHUMCHR/K. PAGE 44 H0889
TOP/EX LEAD PERSON BIOG

B65
FILIPINIANA BOOK GUILD,THE COLONIZATION AND CONQUEST OF THE PHILIPPINES BY SPAIN. PHILIPPINE SPAIN ELITES AGRI KIN CHIEF DOMIN CONTROL ATTIT PWR ...ANTHOL WORSHIP 16. PAGE 50 H1000
COLONIAL COERCE CULTURE WAR

B65
FREY F.W.,THE TURKISH POLITICAL ELITE. TURKEY CULTURE INTELL NAT/G EX/STRUC CHOOSE ATTIT PWR ...METH/CNCPT CHARTS WORSHIP 20. PAGE 53 H1059
ELITES SOCIETY POL/PAR

B65
GEWIRTH A.,POLITICAL PHILOSOPHY. UNIV SOCIETY NAT/G GP/REL INGP/REL CONSEN PWR...IDEA/COMP GEN/LAWS 17/19 HOBBES/T LOCKE/JOHN MARX/KARL MILL/JS ROUSSEAU/J. PAGE 56 H1118
ORD/FREE SOVEREIGN PHIL/SCI

B65
GOLEMBIEWSKI R.T.,MEN, MANAGEMENT, AND MORALITY; TOWARD A NEW ORGANIZATIONAL ETHIC. CONSTN EX/STRUC CREATE ADMIN CONTROL INGP/REL PERSON SUPEGO MORAL PWR...GOV/COMP METH/COMP 20 BUREAUCRCY. PAGE 58 H1161
LG/CO MGT PROB/SOLV

B65
GRAHAM G.S.,THE POLITICS OF NAVAL SUPREMACY; STUDIES IN BRITISH MARITIME ASCENDANCY. UK SEA NAT/G BAL/PWR LEAD WAR WEAPON PEACE...POLICY 18/19 COMMONWLTH. PAGE 60 H1191
FORCES PWR COLONIAL DIPLOM

B65
GREGG J.L.,POLITICAL PARTIES AND PARTY SYSTEMS IN GUATEMALA, 1944-1963. GUATEMALA L/A+17C EX/STRUC FORCES CREATE CONTROL REV CHOOSE PWR...TREND IDEA/COMP 20. PAGE 60 H1209
LEAD POL/PAR NAT/G CHIEF

B65
HANSER C.J.,GUIDE TO DECISION: ROYAL COMMISSION. UK INTELL EXTR/IND SCHOOL PROB/SOLV EXEC ROUTINE CHOOSE GOV/REL GP/REL HEALTH...CHARTS 20. PAGE 66 H1318
NAT/G DELIB/GP EX/STRUC PWR

B65
HART B.H.L.,THE MEMOIRS OF CAPTAIN LIDDELL HART (VOL. I). UK NAT/G PLAN TEC/DEV DIPLOM ADMIN WEAPON GOV/REL PERS/REL ATTIT PWR FASCISM...POLICY 20. PAGE 67 H1348
FORCES BIOG LEAD WAR

B65
JACKSON G.,THE SPANISH REPUBLIC AND THE CIVIL WAR, 1931-1939. EUR+WWI INTELL STRUCT COM/IND NAT/G POL/PAR LEGIS EDU/PROP EXEC COERCE NAT/LISM DRIVE PWR...INT TIME/SEQ TOT/POP 20. PAGE 79 H1574
ATTIT GUERRILLA SPAIN

B65
JACOB H.,POLITICS IN THE AMERICAN STATES; A COMPARATIVE ANALYSIS. USA+45 POL/PAR CHIEF LEGIS TAX EDU/PROP CONTROL CT/SYS LOBBY PARTIC...DECISION CHARTS 20. PAGE 79 H1578
PROVS GOV/COMP PWR

B65
LARUS J.,COMPARATIVE WORLD POLITICS. ASIA INDIA WOR+45 WOR-45 BAL/PWR WAR PEACE RATIONAL MORAL PWR ...REALPOL INT/LAW MUSLIM. PAGE 91 H1825
GOV/COMP IDEA/COMP DIPLOM NAT/COMP

B65
MENON K.P.S.,MANY WORLDS. INDIA BAL/PWR CAP/ISM COLONIAL REV ORD/FREE PWR MARXISM...POLICY 20 COLD/WAR. PAGE 109 H2176
BIOG DIPLOM NAT/G

B65
MONTESQUIEU C DE S.,CONSIDERATIONS ON THE CAUSES OF THE GREATNESS OF THE ROMANS AND THEIR DECLINE (1748 TRANS. BY D. LOWENTHAL). ROMAN/EMP SECT CHIEF EX/STRUC FORCES LEGIS DOMIN WAR POPULISM...POLICY REALPOL ROME/ANC. PAGE 112 H2244
NAT/G PWR COLONIAL MORAL

B65
ORGANSKI A.F.K.,THE STAGES OF POLITICAL DEVELOPMENT. STRATA AGRI INDUS NAT/G POL/PAR COLONIAL PWR WEALTH...CLASSIF TIME/SEQ. PAGE 121 H2428
ECO/DEV ECO/UNDEV GEN/LAWS CREATE

B65
PEASLEE A.J.,CONSTITUTIONS OF NATIONS* THIRD REVISED EDITION (VOLUME I* AFRICA). LAW EX/STRUC LEGIS TOP/EX LEGIT CT/SYS ROUTINE ORD/FREE PWR SOVEREIGN...CON/ANAL CHARTS. PAGE 124 H2481
AFR CHOOSE CONSTN NAT/G

B65
POBEDONOSTSEV K.P.,REFLECTIONS OF A RUSSIAN STATESMAN. RUSSIA LAW ELITES EDU/PROP PRESS ADJUD MARRIAGE ATTIT PWR...MAJORIT TRADIT 19 CHURCH/STA. PAGE 127 H2531
TOTALISM POLICY CONSTN NAT/G

B65
ROSENBERG A.,DEMOCRACY AND SOCIALISM. COM EUR+WWI FRANCE MOD/EUR STRUCT INT/ORG NAT/G POL/PAR TOP/EX EDU/PROP COERCE PERSON PWR FASCISM MARXISM...CONCPT TIME/SEQ MARX/KARL 19/20. PAGE 134 H2677
ATTIT

B65
ROTBERG R.I.,A POLITICAL HISTORY OF TROPICAL AFRICA. EX/STRUC DIPLOM INT/TRADE DOMIN ADMIN RACE/REL NAT/LISM PWR SOVEREIGN...GEOG TIME/SEQ BIBLIOG 1/20. PAGE 135 H2692
AFR CULTURE COLONIAL

B65
SIRISKAR V.M.,POLITICAL BEHAVIOR IN INDIA. INDIA SOCIETY MUNIC NAT/G PROVS ACT/RES SUFF...OBS CHARTS 20 POONA. PAGE 144 H2889
CHOOSE POL/PAR PWR ATTIT

B65
SLATER J.,A REVALUATION OF COLLECTIVE SECURITY* THE OAS IN ACTION. L/A+17C USA+45 NAT/G ADMIN COERCE ORD/FREE PWR...GOV/COMP IDEA/COMP GEN/LAWS OAS. PAGE 145 H2899
REGION INT/ORG FORCES

B65
ULLMANN W.,A HISTORY OF POLITICAL THOUGHT: THE MIDDLE AGES. CHRIST-17C LOC/G NAT/G CENTRAL PWR ...PHIL/SCI LOG BIBLIOG 6/15. PAGE 158 H3153
IDEA/COMP SOVEREIGN SECT LAW

L65
LASSWELL H.D.,"THE POLICY SCIENCES OF DEVELOPMENT." CULTURE SOCIETY EX/STRUC CREATE ADMIN ATTIT KNOWL ...SOC CONCPT SIMUL GEN/METH. PAGE 92 H1835
PWR METH/CNCPT DIPLOM

L65
SHARMA S.P.,"THE INDIA-CHINA BORDER DISPUTE: AN INDIAN PERSPECTIVE." ASIA CHINA/COM S/ASIA NAT/G LEGIT CT/SYS NAT/LISM DRIVE MORAL ORD/FREE PWR 20. PAGE 142 H2850
LAW ATTIT SOVEREIGN INDIA

S65
CAIRNS J.C.,"FRANCE, DECEMBER 1965: END OF THE ELECTIVE MONARACHY" EUR+WWI FRANCE FUT CONSTN SOCIETY CHIEF BAL/PWR ATTIT ALL/IDEOS 20 DEGAULLE/C PRESIDENT. PAGE 25 H0505
CHOOSE NAT/G POL/PAR PWR

S65
GRIFFITH S.B.,"COMMUNIST CHINA'S CAPACITY TO MAKE WAR." CHINA/COM COM NAT/G TOP/EX PLAN DOMIN COERCE NUC/PWR ATTIT RESPECT SKILL...CONCPT MYTH TIME/SEQ TREND COLD/WAR 20. PAGE 61 H1221
FORCES PWR WEAPON ASIA

S65
HAYTER T.,"FRENCH AID TO AFRICA* ITS SCOPE AND ACHIEVEMENTS." CULTURE ECO/TAC INT/TRADE ADMIN REGION CENTRAL FEDERAL LOVE PWR SOVEREIGN EEC. PAGE 68 H1370
AFR FRANCE FOR/AID COLONIAL

S65
JENSEN L.,"MILITARY CAPABILITIES AND BARGAINING BEHAVIOR." USA+45 USSR ARMS/CONT DETER COST ATTIT ...METH/CNCPT STAT SYS/QU CON/ANAL CHARTS NAT/COMP. PAGE 81 H1614
DIPLOM DRIVE PWR STERTYP

S65
MCALISTER L.N.,"CHANGING CONCEPTS OF THE ROLE OF THE MILITARY IN LATIN AMERICA." CULTURE NAT/G CREATE REGION NAT/LISM ATTIT SOVEREIGN...NAT/COMP GEN/LAWS. PAGE 106 H2120
L/A+17C FORCES IDEA/COMP PWR

S65
PLISCHKE E.,"INTEGRATING BERLIN AND THE FEDERAL REPUBLIC OF GERMANY." EUR+WWI GERMANY/W LEGIS TEC/DEV DOMIN ORD/FREE PWR...JURID 20 BERLIN. PAGE 126 H2528
DIPLOM NAT/G MUNIC

S65
POWELL J.D.,"MILITARY ASSISTANCE AND MILITARISM IN LATIN AMERICA." USA+45 INT/ORG NAT/G CONTROL REGION PRODUC WEALTH...CLASSIF STAT NAT/COMP CONGRESS. PAGE 128 H2550
L/A+17C FORCES FOR/AID PWR

S65
STAAR R.F.,"RETROGRESSION IN POLAND." COM USSR AGRI INDUS NAT/G CREATE EDU/PROP TOTALISM RIGID/FLEX ORD/FREE PWR SOCISM...RECORD CHARTS 20. PAGE 148 H2965
TOP/EX ECO/TAC POLAND

S65
STAROBIN J.R.,"COMMUNISM IN WESTERN EUROPE." FRANCE GERMANY ITALY USA+45 USSR ECO/DEV FEDERAL PEACE ATTIT DRIVE PWR TREND. PAGE 149 H2972
MARXISM EUR+WWI POL/PAR NAT/COMP

S65
TENDLER J.D.,"TECHNOLOGY AND ECONOMIC DEVELOPMENT* THE CASE OF HYDRO VS THERMAL POWER." CONSTRUC DIST/IND CREATE TEC/DEV INT/TRADE CENTRAL PWR SKILL WEALTH...MGT NAT/COMP ARGEN. PAGE 153 H3061
BRAZIL INDUS ECO/UNDEV

S65
WOLF C. JR.,"THE POLITICAL EFFECTS OF SOME MILITARY PROGRAMS* SOME INDICATIONS FROM LATIN AMERICA." ELITES STRATA BUDGET FOR/AID WEAPON ATTIT PERCEPT PWR...REGRESS SYS/QU CHARTS NAT/COMP. PAGE 170 H3397
L/A+17C FORCES CIVMIL/REL PROBABIL

C65
BORTOLI G.,"SOCIOLOGIE DU REFERENDUM DANS LA FRANCE MODERNE." FRANCE CONSTN NAT/G EDU/PROP SUFF ATTIT ORD/FREE...POLICY DECISION SOC CHARTS 20. PAGE 19 H0378
BIBLIOG LEGIS SOCIETY PWR

N65
MOTE M.E.,SOVIET LOCAL AND REPUBLIC ELECTIONS. COM USSR NAT/G PLAN PARTIC GOV/REL TOTALISM PWR ...CHARTS 20. PAGE 114 H2270
CHOOSE ADMIN CONTROL LOC/G

B66
BEER S.H.,BRITISH POLITICS IN THE COLLECTIVIST AGE. UK NAT/G CONTROL CHOOSE GP/REL ATTIT PWR PLURISM
POL/PAR SOCISM

...MAJORIT WELF/ST 16/20. PAGE 13 H0258 TRADIT GP/COMP

B66
BIRKHEAD G.S.,ADMINISTRATIVE PROBLEMS IN PAKISTAN. PAKISTAN AGRI FINAN INDUS LG/CO ECO/TAC CONTROL PWR ...CHARTS ANTHOL 20. PAGE 17 H0340 ADMIN NAT/G ORD/FREE ECO/UNDEV

B66
BRECHER M.,SUCCESSION IN INDIA. INDIA USA+45 CONSTN AGRI POL/PAR PROVS SECT DELIB/GP FORCES PROB/SOLV ECO/TAC PWR...LING 20 CONGRESS NEHRU/J. PAGE 20 H0408 CHIEF DECISION CHOOSE

B66
DAENIKER G.,STRATEGIE DES KLEIN STAATS. SWITZERLND ACT/RES CREATE DIPLOM NEUTRAL DETER WAR WEAPON PWR SOVEREIGN...IDEA/COMP 20 COLD/WAR. PAGE 36 H0730 NUC/PWR PLAN FORCES NAT/G

B66
DEUTSCHE INST ZEITGESCHICHTE,DIE WESTDEUTSCHEN PARTEIEN: 1945-1965. GERMANY/W CHOOSE PWR ...TIME/SEQ 20. PAGE 40 H0806 POL/PAR CONCPT NAT/G PROVS

B66
DEUTSCHER I.,STALIN: A POLITICAL BIOGRAPHY. EUR+WWI USSR POL/PAR FORCES DIPLOM ADMIN LEAD REV WAR TOTALISM PERSON 20 STALIN/J ROOSEVLT/F LENIN/VI HITLER/A. PAGE 40 H0807 BIOG MARXISM TOP/EX PWR

B66
FAGEN R.R.,POLITICS AND COMMUNICATION. WOR+45 ECO/DEV NAT/G CONTROL ATTIT 20. PAGE 48 H0958 COM/IND GOV/COMP PWR EDU/PROP

B66
FINER S.E.,ANONYMOUS EMPIRE: STUDY OF THE LOBBY IN GREAT BRITAIN. UK CONSTN LABOR POL/PAR SECT DOMIN EDU/PROP PRESS CHOOSE...CONCPT CHARTS 20 PARLIAMENT. PAGE 50 H1004 LOBBY NAT/G LEGIS PWR

B66
FRIED R.C.,COMPARATIVE POLITICAL INSTITUTIONS. USSR EX/STRUC FORCES LEGIS JUDGE CONTROL REPRESENT ALL/IDEOS 20 CONGRESS BUREAUCRCY. PAGE 53 H1062 NAT/G PWR EFFICIENCY GOV/COMP

B66
GERARD-LIBOIS J.,KATANGA SECESSION. INT/ORG FORCES DIPLOM ADMIN CONTROL WAR CHOOSE PWR...CHARTS 20 KATANGA TSHOMBE/M UN. PAGE 56 H1114 NAT/G REGION ORD/FREE REV

B66
HAMILTON W.B.,A DECADE OF THE COMMONWEALTH, 1955-1964. UK LAW ELITES FINAN FOR/AID CONFER COLONIAL PWR...GEOG CHARTS ANTHOL 20 CMN/WLTH UN. PAGE 65 H1302 INT/ORG INGP/REL DIPLOM NAT/G

B66
HAY P.,FEDERALISM AND SUPRANATIONAL ORGANIZATIONS: PATTERNS FOR NEW LEGAL STRUCTURES. EUR+WWI LAW NAT/G VOL/ASSN DIPLOM PWR...NAT/COMP TREATY EEC. PAGE 68 H1364 SOVEREIGN FEDERAL INT/ORG INT/LAW

B66
HINTON W.,FANSHEN: A DOCUMENTARY OF REVOLUTION IN A CHINESE VILLAGE. ASIA ELITES MUNIC NAT/G POL/PAR SECT WORKER LEAD WAR PRIVIL PWR 20 MAO. PAGE 71 H1422 MARXISM REV NEIGH OWN

B66
HOYT E.C.,NATIONAL POLICY AND INTERNATIONAL LAW* CASE STUDIES FROM AMERICAN CANAL POLICY* MONOGRAPH NO. 1 -- 1966-1967. PANAMA UK ELITES BAL/PWR EFFICIENCY...CLASSIF NAT/COMP SOC/EXP COLOMB TREATY. PAGE 74 H1483 INT/LAW USA-45 DIPLOM PWR

B66
LENSKI G.E.,POWER AND PRIVILEGE: A THEORY OF SOCIAL STRATIFICATION. SWEDEN UK UNIV USSR CULTURE ECO/UNDEV PRIVIL PWR...PHIL/SCI CONCPT CHARTS IDEA/COMP HYPO/EXP METH MARX/KARL. PAGE 94 H1882 SOC STRATA STRUCT SOCIETY

B66
LEROY P.,L'ORGANIZATION CONSTITUTIONNELLE ET LES CRISES. FRANCE NAT/G ADJUD CONTROL PARL/PROC WAR ...POLICY BIBLIOG 20. PAGE 95 H1892 CONSTN PWR EXEC LEGIS

B66
LOCKE J.,THE SECOND TREATISE OF GOVERNMENT: AN ESSAY CONCERNING THE TRUE ORIGINAL EXTENT AND END OF CIVIL GOVERNMENT (3RD ED.). CONSTN SOCIETY CONTROL OWN...PHIL/SCI 17 NATURL/LAW. PAGE 97 H1947 NAT/G PWR GEN/LAWS ORD/FREE

B66
LONDON K.,EASTERN EUROPE IN TRANSITION. CHINA/COM USSR DOMIN COLONIAL CENTRAL RIGID/FLEX PWR...SOC ANTHOL 20. PAGE 98 H1958 SOVEREIGN COM NAT/LISM DIPLOM

B66
LOVEDAY P.,PARLIAMENT FACTIONS AND PARTIES: THE FIRST THIRTY YEARS OF RESPONSIBLE GOVERNMENT IN NEW SOUTH WALES, 1856-1889. PROVS LEAD PARL/PROC PARTIC GP/REL INGP/REL MAJORITY PWR...GP/COMP 19 AUSTRAL. PAGE 99 H1970 POL/PAR ELITES NAT/G LEGIS

B66
MARTIN L.W.,DIPLOMACY IN MODERN EUROPEAN HISTORY. EUR+WWI MOD/EUR INT/ORG NAT/G EX/STRUC ROUTINE WAR PEACE TOTALISM PWR 15/20 COLD/WAR EUROPE/W. PAGE 103 H2064 DIPLOM POLICY

B66
NEUMANN R.G.,THE GOVERNMENT OF THE GERMAN FEDERAL REPUBLIC. EUR+WWI GERMANY/W LOC/G EX/STRUC LEGIS CT/SYS INGP/REL PWR...BIBLIOG 20 ADENAUER/K. PAGE 117 H2336 NAT/G POL/PAR DIPLOM CONSTN

B66
O'NEILL C.E.,CHURCH AND STATE IN FRENCH COLONIAL LOUISIANA: POLICY AND POLITICS TO 1732. PROVS VOL/ASSN DELIB/GP ADJUD ADMIN GP/REL ATTIT DRIVE ...POLICY BIBLIOG 17/18 LOUISIANA CHURCH/STA. PAGE 120 H2390 COLONIAL NAT/G SECT PWR

B66
ODEGARD P.H.,POLITICAL POWER AND SOCIAL CHANGE. UNIV NAT/G CREATE ALL/IDEOS...POLICY GEOG SOC CENSUS TREND. PAGE 120 H2394 PWR TEC/DEV IDEA/COMP

B66
ROSS A.M.,INDUSTRIAL RELATIONS AND ECONOMIC DEVELOPMENT. POL/PAR LEGIS WORKER BARGAIN PRICE EXEC LOBBY INCOME PWR...DECISION ANTHOL BIBLIOG 20. PAGE 134 H2686 ECO/UNDEV LABOR NAT/G GP/REL

B66
THOMPSON J.M.,RUSSIA, BOLSHEVISM, AND THE VERSAILLES PEACE. RUSSIA USSR INT/ORG NAT/G DELIB/GP AGREE REV WAR PWR 20 TREATY VERSAILLES BOLSHEVISM. PAGE 154 H3083 DIPLOM PEACE MARXISM

B66
TORMIN W.,GESCHICHTE DER DEUTSCHEN PARTEIEN SEIT 1848. GERMANY CHOOSE PWR...CONCPT 19/20 WEIMAR/REP. PAGE 156 H3116 POL/PAR CONSTN NAT/G TOTALISM

B66
TYSON G.,NEHRU: THE YEARS OF POWER. INDIA UK STRATA ECO/UNDEV FINAN SECT TASK WAR ORD/FREE MARXISM ...POLICY BIBLIOG 20 NEHRU/J. PAGE 157 H3145 CHIEF PWR DIPLOM NAT/G

B66
VIEN N.C.,SEEKING THE TRUTH. VIETNAM DELIB/GP DOMIN RISK MARXISM 20 KY/NGUYEN. PAGE 162 H3250 NAT/G COLONIAL PWR SOVEREIGN

B66
ZINKIN T.,CHALLENGES IN INDIA. INDIA PAKISTAN LAW AGRI FINAN INDUS TOP/EX TEC/DEV CONTROL ROUTINE ORD/FREE PWR 20 NEHRU/J SHASTRI/LB CIVIL/SERV. PAGE 173 H3458 NAT/G ECO/TAC POLICY ADMIN

B66
ZOLBERG A.R.,CREATING POLITICAL ORDER. AFR CONGO/BRAZ GHANA NIGER KIN NAT/G DOMIN COLONIAL REGION CENTRAL NAT/LISM ATTIT PWR 20 CONGO/LEOP. PAGE 173 H3462 SOVEREIGN ORD/FREE CONSTN POL/PAR

L66
HUNTINGTON S.P.,"POLITICAL MODERNIZATION* AMERICA VS EUROPE." EUR+WWI MOD/EUR UK USA+45 LAW ECO/UNDEV PWR SOVEREIGN CONSERVE LAISSEZ GOV/COMP. PAGE 75 H1505 STRUCT CREATE OBS

L66
LEMARCHAND R.,"SOCIAL CHANGE AND POLITICAL MODERNISATION IN BURUNDI." AFR BURUNDI STRATA CHIEF EX/STRUC RIGID/FLEX PWR...SOC 20. PAGE 94 H1874 NAT/G STRUCT ELITES CONSERVE

L66
MCAUSLAN J.P.W.,"CONSTITUTIONAL INNOVATION AND POLITICAL STABILITY IN TANZANIA: A PRELIMINARY ASSESSMENT." AFR TANZANIA ELITES CHIEF EX/STRUC RIGID/FLEX PWR 20 PRESIDENT BUREAUCRCY. PAGE 106 H2122 CONSTN NAT/G EXEC POL/PAR

S66
BLANC N.,"SPAIN: LEARNING THROUGH STRUGGLE" SPAIN STRATA STRUCT SECT FORCES PROB/SOLV AGE/Y ATTIT ORD/FREE PWR WEALTH MARXISM SOCISM 19/20 FRANCO/F SUCCESSION. PAGE 18 H0352 NAT/G FUT SOCIALIST TOTALISM

S66
COWAN L.G.,"THE MILITARY AND AFRICAN POLITICS." AFR FUT NAT/G POL/PAR PARTIC REV 20. PAGE 34 H0685 CIVMIL/REL FORCES PWR LEAD

S66
DETTER I.,"THE PROBLEM OF UNEQUAL TREATIES." CONSTN NAT/G LEGIS COLONIAL COERCE PWR...GEOG UN TIME TREATY. PAGE 40 H0796 SOVEREIGN DOMIN INT/LAW ECO/UNDEV

S66
GAMER R.E.,"URGENT SINGAPORE, PATIENT MALAYSIA." MALAYSIA S/ASIA ECO/UNDEV POL/PAR CHIEF TARIFFS TAX CONTROL LEAD REGION PWR 20 SINGAPORE. PAGE 55 H1094 DIPLOM NAT/G POLICY ECO/TAC

S66
MANSERGH N.,"THE PARTITION OF INDIA IN RETROSPECT." INDIA PAKISTAN S/ASIA UK DIPLOM COLONIAL GP/REL PWR 20. PAGE 102 H2042 NAT/G PARL/PROC POLICY POL/PAR

S66
MCLENNAN B.N.,"EVOLUTION OF CONCEPTS OF REPRESENT

REPRESENTATION IN INDONESIA" INDONESIA...CONCPT IDEA/COMP METH 20. PAGE 107 H2143 NAT/G POPULISM PWR

S66
MERRITT R.L.,"SELECTED ARTICLES AND DOCUMENTS ON COMPARATIVE GOVERNMENT AND CROSS-NATIONAL RESEARCH." AFR ASIA EUR+WWI L/A+17C MOD/EUR ELITES R+D ACT/RES DIPLOM PWR...SOC CONCPT 18/20. PAGE 109 H2185 BIBLIOG GOV/COMP NAT/G GOV/REL

S66
ROTHCHILD D.,"THE LIMITS OF FEDERALISM: AN EXAMINATION OF POLITICAL INSTITUTIONAL TRANSFER IN AFRICA." AFR CONSTN CULTURE ELITES ECO/UNDEV KIN PROB/SOLV ADMIN ORD/FREE PWR...POLICY 20. PAGE 135 H2695 FEDERAL NAT/G NAT/LISM COLONIAL

S66
SKILLING H.G.,"THE RUMANIAN NATIONAL COURSE." COM EUR+WWI ROMANIA NAT/G ECO/TAC PWR 20. PAGE 145 H2896 NAT/LISM POLICY DIPLOM MARXISM

S66
SNOW P.G.,"A SCALOGRAM ANALYSIS OF POLITICAL DEVELOPMENT." STRATA ECO/UNDEV POL/PAR REGION ALL/VALS PWR...SOC CHARTS. PAGE 146 H2924 L/A+17C NAT/COMP TESTS CLASSIF

C66
DEUTSCH K.W.,"NATIONALISM AND SOCIAL COMMUNICATION." CULTURE INGP/REL ATTIT PWR...PSY SOC CONCPT LING IDEA/COMP 20. PAGE 40 H0800 BIBLIOG NAT/LISM GEN/LAWS

B67
ALBINSKI H.S.,EUROPEAN POLITICAL PROCESSES: ESSAYS AND READINGS. EUR+WWI FRANCE GERMANY MOD/EUR UK ELITES POL/PAR PWR...CHARTS ANTHOL 18/20. PAGE 5 H0094 NAT/COMP POLICY IDEA/COMP

B67
BANKWITZ P.C.,MAXINE WEYGAND AND CIVIL-MILITARY RELATIONS IN MODERN FRANCE. FRANCE LEAD WAR PWR ...INT BIBLIOG 20. PAGE 11 H0212 CIVMIL/REL FORCES NAT/G TOP/EX

B67
BROWN L.N.,FRENCH ADMINISTRATIVE LAW. FRANCE UK CONSTN NAT/G LEGIS DOMIN CONTROL EXEC PARL/PROC PWR ...JURID METH/COMP GEN/METH. PAGE 22 H0447 EX/STRUC LAW IDEA/COMP CT/SYS

B67
BRZEZINSKI Z.K.,IDEOLOGY AND POWER IN SOVIET POLITICS. USSR NAT/G POL/PAR PWR...GEN/LAWS 19/20. PAGE 23 H0462 DIPLOM EX/STRUC MARXISM

B67
BRZEZINSKI Z.K.,THE SOVIET BLOC: UNITY AND CONFLICT (2ND ED., REV., ENLARGED). COM POLAND USSR INTELL CHIEF EX/STRUC CONTROL EXEC GOV/REL PWR MARXISM ...TREND IDEA/COMP 20 LENIN/VI MARX/KARL STALIN/J. PAGE 23 H0463 NAT/G DIPLOM

B67
BURR R.N.,OUR TROUBLED HEMISPHERE: PERSPECTIVES ON UNITED STATES-LATIN AMERICAN RELATIONS. L/A+17C USA+45 USA-45 INT/ORG FOR/AID COLONIAL PWR 19/20 OAS. PAGE 25 H0493 DIPLOM NAT/COMP NAT/G POLICY

B67
CORDIER A.W.,COLUMBIA ESSAYS IN INTERNATIONAL AFFAIRS. ASIA CHINA/COM FRANCE S/ASIA SPAIN UAR ECO/UNDEV LOC/G ECO/TAC GUERRILLA PWR...BIOG ANTHOL 18/20 MAU/MAU. PAGE 33 H0663 NAT/G DIPLOM MARXISM POLICY

B67
HILSMAN R.,TO MOVE A NATION: THE POLITICS OF FOREIGN POLICY IN THE ADMINISTRATION OF JOHN F. KENNEDY. CHINA/COM COM USSR VIETNAM NAT/G DELIB/GP FORCES PLAN PROB/SOLV BAL/PWR COLONIAL EXEC REV PWR 20 KENNEDY/JF PRESIDENT. PAGE 71 H1418 CHIEF DIPLOM

B67
HUTCHINS F.G.,THE ILLUSION OF PERMANENCE: BRITISH IMPERIALISM IN INDIA. INDIA UK CULTURE STRUCT NAT/G REV GP/REL RACE/REL ADJUST DISCRIM ATTIT MORAL PWR SOC/INTEG 18/20. PAGE 75 H1509 COLONIAL CONTROL SOVEREIGN CONSERVE

B67
KENNETT L.,THE FRENCH ARMIES IN THE SEVEN YEARS' WAR. FRANCE NAT/G CONTROL LEAD WAR CIVMIL/REL EFFICIENCY ATTIT PWR SKILL CONSERVE 18. PAGE 85 H1690 FORCES CHIEF METH/COMP

B67
KING M.L. JR.,WHERE DO WE GO FROM HERE: CHAOS OR COMMUNITY? MUNIC NAT/G PARTIC INGP/REL ALL/VALS ...POLICY CONCPT BIOG 20. PAGE 86 H1715 RACE/REL DISCRIM STRUCT PWR

B67
MCNELLY T.,SOURCES IN MODERN EAST ASIAN HISTORY AND POLITICS. KOREA VIETNAM CULTURE DIPLOM COLONIAL REV WAR PWR ALL/IDEOS MARXISM...ANTHOL 20 CHINJAP. PAGE 107 H2147 NAT/COMP ASIA S/ASIA SOCIETY

B67
MENARD O.D.,THE ARMY AND THE FIFTH REPUBLIC. ALGERIA FRANCE VIETNAM ELITES STRATA COLONIAL CONTROL LOBBY WAR CIVMIL/REL ROLE PWR...POLICY 20 DEGAULLE/C. PAGE 108 H2169 FORCES ATTIT NAT/G

B67
REES D.,THE AGE OF CONTAINMENT. WOR+45 FORCES ARMS/CONT ATTIT PWR...CONCPT TREND METH/COMP BIBLIOG/A 20. PAGE 130 H2608 DIPLOM NUC/PWR MARXISM GOV/COMP

B67
ROWLAND J.,A HISTORY OF SINO-INDIAN RELATIONS; HOSTILE CO-EXISTENCE. ASIA CHINA/COM INDIA NAT/G NUC/PWR PWR WEALTH...GEOG BIBLIOG 13/20 COLD/WAR. PAGE 135 H2704 DIPLOM CENSUS IDEA/COMP

B67
SCHECTER J.,THE NEW FACE OF BUDDHA: BUDDHISM AND POLITICAL POWER IN SOUTHEAST ASIA. S/ASIA NAT/G POL/PAR NAT/LISM ATTIT MARXISM...BIBLIOG 20. PAGE 139 H2780 SECT POLICY PWR LEAD

B67
TREADGOLD D.W.,SOVIET AND CHINESE COMMUNISM* SIMILARITIES AND DIFFERENCES. CHINA/COM COM NAT/G PLAN DIPLOM CENTRAL PWR MARXISM...POLICY 20. PAGE 156 H3128 CULTURE NAT/LISM

B67
WARREN S.,THE AMERICAN PRESIDENT. POL/PAR FORCES LEGIS DIPLOM ECO/TAC ADMIN EXEC PWR...ANTHOL 18/20 ROOSEVLT/F KENNEDY/JF JOHNSON/LB TRUMAN/HS WILSON/W. PAGE 165 H3312 CHIEF LEAD NAT/G CONSTN

B67
WINTER E.H.,CONTEMPORARY CHANGE IN TRADITIONAL SOCIETIES: VOLUME I INTRODUCTION AND AFRICAN TRIBES. NIGERIA AGRI LOC/G NAT/G CREATE DOMIN COLONIAL CONTROL GP/REL PWR SOVEREIGN...SOC OBS 20 TANGANYIKA. PAGE 169 H3389 SOCIETY AFR CONSERVE KIN

L67
BRIDGHAM P.,"MAO'S "CULTURAL REVOLUTION"* ORIGIN AND DEVELOPMENT." NAT/G LEAD CIVMIL/REL NAT/LISM TOTALISM ATTIT DRIVE PWR MARXISM 20. PAGE 21 H0413 CHINA/COM CULTURE REV CROWD

L67
MCALLISTER J.T. JR.,"THE POSSIBILITIES FOR DIPLOMACY IN SOUTHEAST ASIA." LAOS VIETNAM INT/ORG NAT/G PROVS BAL/PWR DOMIN AGREE COLONIAL WAR PWR 17/20 TREATY. PAGE 106 H2121 DIPLOM S/ASIA

L67
ROBINSON T.W.,"A NATIONAL INTEREST ANALYSIS OF SINO-SOVIET RELATIONS." CHINA/COM USSR NAT/G NUC/PWR ATTIT PWR...CONCPT CHARTS 20. PAGE 132 H2650 MARXISM DIPLOM SOVEREIGN GEN/LAWS

L67
SEGAL A.,"THE INTEGRATION OF DEVELOPING COUNTRIES: SOME THOUGHTS ON EAST AFRICA AND CENTRAL AMERICA." AFR L/A+17C INT/ORG NAT/G VOL/ASSN FOR/AID INT/TRADE EQUILIB NAT/LISM PWR 20. PAGE 141 H2820 ECO/UNDEV DIPLOM REGION

L67
VAN DER KROEF J.M.,"INDONESIA: THE BATTLE OF THE 'OLD' AND THE 'NEW ORDER'." INDONESIA ISLAM ELITES POL/PAR DOMIN INGP/REL NAT/LISM PWR...IDEA/COMP 20. PAGE 161 H3229 FORCES MARXISM NAT/G BAL/PWR

S67
ABDEL-MALEK A.,"THE CRISIS IN NASSER'S EGYPT." ISLAM UAR STRUCT POL/PAR EX/STRUC CREATE PLAN WAR ATTIT ORD/FREE PWR...POLICY DECISION 20. PAGE 3 H0054 FORCES LEAD PROB/SOLV NAT/G

S67
ALTBACH P.,"STUDENT POLITICS." GP/REL ATTIT ROLE PWR 20. PAGE 6 H0116 INTELL PARTIC UTIL NAT/G

S67
CARIAS B.,"EL CONTROL DE LAS EMPRESAS PUBLICAS POR GRUPOS DE INTERESES DE LA COMUNIDAD." FRANCE UK VENEZUELA INDUS NAT/G CONTROL OWN PWR...DECISION NAT/COMP 20. PAGE 26 H0529 WORKER REPRESENT MGT SOCISM

S67
CARR E.H.,"REVOLUTION FROM ABOVE." USSR STRATA FINAN INDUS NAT/G DOMIN LEAD GP/REL INGP/REL OWN PRODUC PWR 20 STALIN/J. PAGE 27 H0538 AGRI POLICY COM EFFICIENCY

S67
CATTELL D.T.,"A NEO-MARXIST THEORY OF COMPARATIVE ANALYSIS." USSR STRATA INSPECT DOMIN CONTROL COERCE OWN TOTALISM PWR...FASCIST HYPO/EXP METH 20. PAGE 28 H0561 GOV/COMP MARXISM SIMUL CLASSIF

S67
COLLINS B.A.,"SOME NOTES ON PUBLIC SERVICE COMMISSIONS IN THE COMMONWEALTH CARIBBEAN." JAMAICA L/A+17C TRINIDAD UK NAT/G OP/RES DOMIN SENIOR COLONIAL CONTROL INGP/REL CENTRAL EFFICIENCY PWR ...DECISION 20. PAGE 31 H0631 ADMIN EX/STRUC ECO/UNDEV CHOOSE

S67
ELLISON H.J.,"THE SOCIALIST REVOLUTIONARIES." USSR ECO/UNDEV NAT/G INGP/REL EFFICIENCY ATTIT PWR MARXISM...CONCPT IDEA/COMP 20 SOC/REVPAR. PAGE 46 H0911 POL/PAR REV AGRI

S67
FINLAY D.J.,"THE GHANA COUP...ONE YEAR LATER." GHANA FORCES FOR/AID PRESS CONTROL CIVMIL/REL NAT/LISM AUTHORIT PWR...PREDICT 20. PAGE 50 H1005 REV NAT/G ATTIT

ECO/UNDEV

S67
FUSARO A.,"THE EFFECT OF PROPORTIONAL REPRESENTATION ON VOTING IN THE AUSTRALIAN SENATE." S/ASIA CONSTN POL/PAR CONTROL GP/REL PWR...CHARTS 20 AUSTRAL HOUSE/REP SENATE. PAGE 54 H1083
LEGIS CHOOSE REPRESENT NAT/G

S67
GRAHAM R.,"BRAZIL'S DILEMMA." BRAZIL FUT L/A+17C NAT/G CHIEF PROB/SOLV ECO/TAC PWR 20. PAGE 60 H1193
ECO/UNDEV CONSTN POL/PAR POLICY

S67
HOFMANN W.,"THE PUBLIC INTEREST PRESSURE GROUP: THE CASE OF THE DEUTSCHE STADTETAG." GERMANY GERMANY/W CONSTN STRUCT NAT/G CENTRAL FEDERAL PWR...TIME/SEQ 20. PAGE 72 H1447
LOC/G VOL/ASSN LOBBY ADMIN

S67
JAIN G.,"INDIA REJECTS THE POWER RACE* REALISM ABOUT NUCLEAR WEAPONS." FORCES PROB/SOLV FOR/AID ARMS/CONT COST PWR...GOV/COMP 20. PAGE 79 H1583
INDIA CHINA/COM NUC/PWR DIPLOM

S67
KOHN W.S.G.,"THE SOVEREIGNTY OF LIECHTENSTEIN." LIECHTENST SWITZERLND USSR CONSTN DEBATE WAR CONSERVE 18/20 UN. PAGE 88 H1748
SOVEREIGN NAT/G PWR DIPLOM

S67
LANE J.P.,"FUNCTIONS OF MASS MEDIA IN BRAZIL'S 1964 CRISIS." BRAZIL NAT/G FORCES TOP/EX PRESS TV ATTIT PWR...METH/CNCPT 20. PAGE 90 H1807
CIVMIL/REL REV COM/IND EDU/PROP

S67
LEGRES A.,"LES FONCTIONS D'UN PARLEMENT MODERNE." FRANCE DEBATE PARL/PROC SANCTION ATTIT PWR 20 PARLIAMENT. PAGE 93 H1860
NAT/G LAW LEGIS CHOOSE

S67
LOGERECI A.,"ALBANIA AND CHINA* THE INCONGRUOUS ALLIANCE." NAT/LISM PWR...GOV/COMP 20. PAGE 98 H1955
ALBANIA CHINA/COM DIPLOM MARXISM

S67
MATTHEWS R.O.,"THE SUEZ CANAL DISPUTE* A CASE STUDY IN PEACEFUL SETTLEMENT." FRANCE ISRAEL UAR UK NAT/G CONTROL LEAD COERCE WAR NAT/LISM ROLE ORD/FREE PWR ...INT/LAW UN 20. PAGE 105 H2099
PEACE DIPLOM ADJUD

S67
MAYANJA A.,"THE GOVERNMENT'S PROPOSALS ON THE NEW CONSTITUTION." AFR UGANDA LAW CHIEF LEGIS ADJUD REPRESENT FEDERAL PWR 20. PAGE 105 H2105
CONSTN CONFER ORD/FREE NAT/G

S67
NIEBUHR R.,"THE SOCIAL MYTHS IN THE COLD WAR." USA+45 USSR VIETNAM PROB/SOLV BAL/PWR ARMS/CONT NAT/LISM PWR ALL/IDEOS CONCPT. PAGE 118 H2359
MYTH DIPLOM GOV/COMP

S67
PETRAS J.,"GUERRILLA MOVEMENTS IN LATIN AMERICA - I." GUATEMALA PERU VENEZUELA NAT/G COLONIAL LEAD ATTIT PWR...TIME/SEQ METH/COMP 20 COLOMB. PAGE 125 H2497
GUERRILLA REV L/A+17C MARXISM

S67
ROOT W.,"REPORT FROM PARIS - DE GAULLE: WHICH WAY TO THE FUTURE?" CANADA FRANCE ISLAM UK INT/ORG CHIEF CREATE AGREE CONTROL ARMS/CONT NUC/PWR EQUILIB PEACE PWR 20 DEGAULLE/C NATO. PAGE 134 H2670
POLICY DIPLOM NAT/G BAL/PWR

S67
SEIDLER G.L.,"MARXIST LEGAL THOUGHT IN POLAND." POLAND SOCIETY R+D LOC/G NAT/G ACT/RES ADJUD CT/SYS SUPEGO PWR...SOC TREND 20 MARX/KARL. PAGE 141 H2822
MARXISM LAW CONCPT EFFICIENCY

S67
SHIGEO N.,"THE GREAT CULTURAL REVOLUTION." ASIA ECO/UNDEV AGRI NAT/G CHIEF ECO/TAC EDU/PROP CONTROL LEAD PWR 20 MAO. PAGE 143 H2860
CREATE REV CULTURE POL/PAR

S67
SMITH J.E.,"THE GERMAN DEMOCRATIC REPUBLIC AND THE WEST." GERMANY/E ECO/DEV NAT/G PROB/SOLV CONTROL REV TOTALISM...GOV/COMP 20. PAGE 146 H2911
DIPLOM PWR MARXISM

S67
THIEN T.T.,"VIETNAM: A CASE OF SOCIAL ALIENATION." VIETNAM AGRI FORCES FOR/AID ADMIN REPRESENT INGP/REL PWR 19/20. PAGE 154 H3071
NAT/G ELITES WORKER STRANGE

S67
WHITE J.W.,"MASS MOVEMENTS AND DEMOCRACY: SOKAGAKKAI IN JAPANESE POLITICS." NAT/G GP/REL ALL/VALS ORD/FREE WORSHIP 20 CHINJAP. PAGE 167 H3349
SECT PWR ATTIT POL/PAR

S67
WILLIAMS P.M.,"THE FRENCH GENERAL ELECTION OF MARCH 1967." FRANCE INDUS WORKER NAT/LISM PWR SOCISM 20. PAGE 168 H3368
POL/PAR NAT/G ATTIT CHOOSE

S67
WRAITH R.E.,"ADMINISTRATIVE CHANGE IN THE NEW AFRICA." AFR LG/CO ADJUD INGP/REL PWR...RECORD GP/COMP 20. PAGE 171 H3416
ADMIN NAT/G LOC/G ECO/UNDEV

S67
ZARTMAN I.W.," NAT/G POL/PAR VOL/ASSN NAT/LISM ORD/FREE PWR...CONCPT NAT/COMP ORG/CHARTS OAU MAGHREB. PAGE 172 H3451
AFR ISLAM DIPLOM REGION

C67
LING D.L.,"TUNISIA: FROM PROTECTORATE TO REPUBLIC." CULTURE NAT/G POL/PAR CHIEF DIPLOM COERCE WAR PWR ...BIBLIOG 19/20 TUNIS. PAGE 97 H1934
AFR NAT/LISM COLONIAL PROB/SOLV

B68
DE SPINOZA B.,TRACTATUS THEOLOGICO-POLITICUS (TRANS. BY R. WILLIS). UNIV CHIEF DOMIN PWR WORSHIP. PAGE 38 H0771
SECT NAT/G ORD/FREE

S68
CHAPMAN A.R.,"THE CIVIL WAR IN NIGERIA." AFR NIGERIA NAT/G PLAN ECO/TAC EDU/PROP COERCE WAR GOV/REL INGP/REL ORD/FREE PWR WEALTH SOC/INTEG 20 BIAFRA. PAGE 29 H0579
REV RACE/REL

S68
KANET R.E.,"RECENT SOVIET REASSESSMENT OF DEVELOPMENTS IN THE THIRD WORLD." ALGERIA GHANA INDONESIA USSR WOR+45 CONSTN ELITES INTELL STRUCT DOMIN CONTROL REV PWR MARXISM...IDEA/COMP METH 20 THIRD/WRLD. PAGE 83 H1653
DIPLOM NEUTRAL NAT/G NAT/COMP

N80
MILL J.S.,"AN ESSAY ON GOVERNMENT" (PAMPHLET). ELITES NAT/G CHIEF OWN ORD/FREE PWR WEALTH GEN/LAWS. PAGE 110 H2207
CONSTN POPULISM REPRESENT UTIL

C82
MILL J.S.,"CIVILIZATION" IN DISSERTATIONS AND DISCUSSIONS." MOD/EUR UK ECO/DEV CONTROL MORAL ORD/FREE PWR...SOC IDEA/COMP 19. PAGE 110 H2208
SOCIETY NAT/G STRUCT CONCPT

B85
BLISS P.,OF SOVEREIGNTY. NAT/G PROVS GOV/REL PRIVIL ORD/FREE PWR CONSERVE...CONCPT 19. PAGE 18 H0356
CONSTN SOVEREIGN FEDERAL

B85
TAINE H.A.,THE FRENCH REVOLUTION (3 VOLS.) (TRANS. BY J. DURAND). FRANCE MOD/EUR SOCIETY STRATA POL/PAR ECO/TAC DOMIN EDU/PROP GP/REL PWR ...GOV/COMP IDEA/COMP 18. PAGE 152 H3036
REV NAT/G EX/STRUC LEAD

B87
ADAMS J.,A DEFENSE OF THE CONSTITUTIONS OF GOVERNMENT OF THE UNITED STATES OF AMERICA. USA-45 STRATA CHIEF EX/STRUC LEGIS CT/SYS CONSERVE POPULISM...CONCPT CON/ANAL GOV/COMP. PAGE 3 H0063
CONSTN BAL/PWR PWR NAT/G

B90
BURKE E.,REFLECTIONS ON THE REVOLUTION IN FRANCE. FRANCE UK NAT/G DOMIN LEGIT PEACE PWR SOVEREIGN CONSERVE...POLICY GEN/LAWS 18. PAGE 24 H0487
REV ORD/FREE CHIEF TRADIT

B90
TAINE H.A.,MODERN REGIME (2 VOLS.). FRANCE FAM REV CENTRAL MARRIAGE PWR...TREND 19 NAPOLEON/B. PAGE 152 H3037
STRUCT NAT/G OLD/LIB MORAL

B94
BENOIST C.,LA POLITIQUE. FRANCE LAW SOCIETY STRUCT POL/PAR PARL/PROC GP/REL ATTIT PWR 19/20. PAGE 14 H0283
NAT/G REPRESENT ORD/FREE

B96
LOWELL A.L.,GOVERNMENTS AND PARTIES IN CONTINENTAL EUROPE, VOL. II. AUSTRIA GERMANY HUNGARY MOD/EUR SWITZERLND SOCIETY EX/STRUC LEGIS DIPLOM AGREE LEAD PARL/PROC PWR...POLICY 19. PAGE 99 H1974
POL/PAR NAT/G GOV/REL ELITES

B96
MARX K.,REVOLUTION AND COUNTER-REVOLUTION. GERMANY CONSTN ELITES INDUS NAT/G DIPLOM ECO/TAC WEALTH. PAGE 104 H2083
MARXIST REV PWR STRATA

B96
SCHMOLLER G.,THE MERCANTILE SYSTEM AND ITS HISTORICAL SIGNIFICANCE: ILLUSTRATED CHIEFLY FROM PRUSSIAN HISTORY (TRANS.). PRUSSIA CULTURE INDUS KIN MUNIC NAT/G PROVS OP/RES ECO/TAC INT/TRADE SUPEGO PWR WEALTH 19 MERCANTLST. PAGE 139 H2790
GEN/METH INGP/REL CONCPT

PYE L.W. H2567,H2568

PYLEE M.V. H2569

PYRAH G.B. H2570

Q

QU....QUESTIONNAIRES; SEE ALSO QUESTIONNAIRES INDEX, P. XIV

S31
HEINBERG J.G.,"THE PERSONNEL OF FRENCH CABINETS, 1871-1930." FRANCE STRATA CHIEF CHOOSE REPRESENT
ELITES NAT/G

MAJORITY...STAT QU CENSUS TREND CHARTS PERS/COMP 19/20 CHAMBR/DEP. PAGE 69 H1386 — DELIB/GP TOP/EX

B36
CULVER D.C.,METHODOLOGY OF SOCIAL SCIENCE RESEARCH: A BIBLIOGRAPHY. LAW CULTURE...CRIMLGY GEOG STAT OBS INT QU HIST/WRIT CHARTS 20. PAGE 36 H0719 — BIBLIOG/A METH SOC

B53
MURPHY G.,IN THE MINDS OF MEN: THE STUDY OF HUMAN BEHAVIOR AND SOCIAL TENSIONS IN INDIA. FUT S/ASIA FAM INT/ORG NAT/G DIPLOM EDU/PROP GP/REL ATTIT RIGID/FLEX ALL/VALS...SOC QU UNESCO 20. PAGE 115 H2297 — SECT STRATA INDIA

S53
BAUER R.A.,"WORD-OF-MOUTH COMMUNICATION IN THE SOVIET UNION." COM INTELL SOCIETY LABOR ATTIT KNOWL ...INT QU SAMP CHARTS 20. PAGE 12 H0239 — CULTURE USSR

B60
HUGHES C.C.,PEOPLE OF COVE AND WOODLOT; COMMUNITIES FROM THE VIEWPOINT OF SOCIAL PSYCHIATRY. CULTURE FAM PROVS HABITAT...PSY QU SAMP/SIZ CHARTS BIBLIOG 20. PAGE 74 H1489 — GEOG SOCIETY STRUCT HEALTH

B61
VON MERING O.,A GRAMMAR OF HUMAN VALUES. WOR+45 CULTURE FACE/GP NEIGH CREATE EDU/PROP LEGIT ATTIT DRIVE PERSON ORD/FREE...PSY SOC METH/CNCPT OBS RECORD INT REC/INT STAND/INT QU CHARTS VAL/FREE. PAGE 164 H3275 — SOCIETY MORAL

B62
VILAKAZI A.,ZULU TRANSFORMATIONS: A STUDY OF THE DYNAMICS OF SOCIAL CHANGE. AFR CULTURE ECO/UNDEV KIN NEIGH SEX...GEOG QU TREND CHARTS BIBLIOG 19/20. PAGE 163 H3254 — MARRIAGE SECT SOC EDU/PROP

L62
COHEN R.,"POWER IN COMPLEX SOCIETIES IN AFRICA." AFR KIN MUNIC POL/PAR DELIB/GP DOMIN ROUTINE ATTIT ALL/VALS...SOC STAT OBS INT QU CHARTS ANTHOL 20. PAGE 31 H0617 — CULTURE STRATA ELITES

S62
BELL W.,"EQUALITY AND ATTITUDES OF ELITES IN JAMAICA" L/A+17C STRATA PWR WEALTH...SOC QU TREND. PAGE 13 H0266 — ELITES FUT SOCIETY CULTURE

L63
CORWIN A.F.,"CONTEMPORARY MEXICAN ATTITUDES TOWARD POPULATION, POVERTY, AND PUBLIC OPINION." L/A+17C CULTURE SOCIETY ACT/RES ECO/TAC EDU/PROP PERSON HEALTH KNOWL...GEOG PHIL/SCI STAT OBS INT SAMP MEXIC/AMER VAL/FREE 20. PAGE 34 H0672 — ATTIT QU

B64
AGGER R.E.,THE RULERS AND THE RULED: POLITICAL POWER AND IMPOTENCE IN AMERICAN COMMUNITIES. CULTURE DOMIN CHOOSE ATTIT ALL/VALS...DECISION SOC CONCPT OBS QU CHARTS. PAGE 4 H0079 — PWR STRUCT LOC/G MUNIC

B64
BELL W.,JAMAICAN LEADERS: POLITICAL ATTITUDES IN A NEW NATION. JAMAICA STRUCT ACT/RES CREATE PROB/SOLV DIPLOM COLONIAL LEAD...QU 20. PAGE 13 H0267 — NAT/LISM ATTIT DRIVE SOVEREIGN

B64
MORGAN L.H.,ANCIENT SOCIETY (1877). SOCIETY FAM OWN ...INT QU GEN/LAWS SOC/INTEG. PAGE 113 H2255 — KIN MARRIAGE CULTURE

B64
PARANJAPE H.K.,THE FLIGHT OF TECHNICAL PERSONNEL IN PUBLIC UNDERTAKINGS. INDIA PAY DEMAND HAPPINESS ORD/FREE...MGT QU 20 MIGRATION. PAGE 123 H2464 — ADMIN NAT/G WORKER PLAN

B64
VALEN H.,POLITICAL PARTIES IN NORWAY. NORWAY ACADEM PARTIC ROUTINE INGP/REL KNOWL...QU 20. PAGE 161 H3220 — LOC/G POL/PAR PERSON

S64
LEWIS R.,"OPINION SURVEYING IN KOREA." ASIA FUT KOREA LEGIS EDU/PROP EXEC ALL/VALS...POLICY CONCPT MYTH TESTS CON/ANAL GEN/METH TOT/POP VAL/FREE 20. PAGE 96 H1915 — NAT/G QU

B65
DUGGAR G.S.,RENEWAL OF TOWN AND VILLAGE I: A WORLD-WIDE SURVEY OF LOCAL GOVERNMENT EXPERIENCE. WOR+45 CONSTRUC INDUS CREATE BUDGET REGION GOV/REL...QU NAT/COMP 20 URBAN/RNWL. PAGE 43 H0859 — MUNIC NEIGH PLAN ADMIN

B65
LAMBIRI I.,SOCIAL CHANGE IN A GREEK COUNTRY TOWN. GREECE FAM PROB/SOLV ROUTINE TASK LEISURE INGP/REL CONSEN ORD/FREE...SOC INT QU CHARTS 20. PAGE 90 H1803 — INDUS WORKER CULTURE NEIGH

B65
VON STACKELBERG K.,ALLE KRETER LUGEN VORURTEILE UBER MENSCHEN UND VOLKER. DIPLOM DOMIN RUMOR NAT/LISM PERSON KNOWL...SOC QU BIBLIOG 20. PAGE 164 H3277 — NAT/COMP ATTIT EDU/PROP SAMP

S65
LAULICHT J.,"PUBLIC OPINION AND FOREIGN POLICY DECISIONS." CANADA ELITES NAT/G FOR/AID LEAD NUC/PWR PERCEPT...INT QU CHARTS UN COLD/WAR. PAGE 92 H1839 — DIPLOM ATTIT CON/ANAL SAMP

B66
LONDON DAILY TELEGRAPH,ELECTION '66: GALLUP ANALYSIS OF THE VOTING RESULTS. UK LEGIS COMPUTER ATTIT...QU SAMP CHARTS 20 LABOR/PAR HOUSE/CMNS. PAGE 98 H1959 — STAT CHOOSE REPRESENT POL/PAR

B66
VOGT E.Z.,PEOPLE OF RIMROCK. STRATA STRUCT KIN SECT GP/REL HABITAT ALL/VALS...GEOG INT QU 20 TEXAS NAVAHO MORMON SPAN/AMER ZUNI. PAGE 163 H3260 — CULTURE GP/COMP SOC SOCIETY

S67
BHATNAGAR J.K.,"THE VALUES AND ATTITUDES OF SOME INDIAN AND BRITISH STUDENTS." INDIA UK ECO/UNDEV LEGIT COLONIAL GP/REL SOVEREIGN...QU 20. PAGE 16 H0328 — NAT/COMP ATTIT EDU/PROP ACADEM

S67
SUNG C.H.,"POLITICAL DIAGNOSIS OF KOREAN SOCIETY* A SURVEY OF MILITARY AND CIVILIAN VALUES." KOREA/S ECO/UNDEV NAT/G CIVMIL/REL...QU SAMP GP/COMP. PAGE 151 H3009 — ELITES FORCES ATTIT ORD/FREE

QĀ'IMAH BI-AL-KUTUB WA-AL-MARAJI' 'AN AL-JAZĪRAH AL-'ARABIYAH
QĀ'IMAH BI-AL-KUTUB WA-AL-MARAJI' 'AN TŪNIS
QUAISON-SACKEY A. H2571

QUAKER....QUAKER

QUAN K.L. H2572

QUANT....QUANTIFICATION

S54
DODD S.C.,"THE SCIENTIFIC MEASUREMENT OF FITNESS FOR SELF-GOVERNMENT." FUT CONSTN ECO/UNDEV INT/ORG PLAN PWR...CONCPT QUANT CON/ANAL SOC/EXP UN LEAGUE/NAT 20. PAGE 41 H0830 — NAT/G STAT SOVEREIGN

B60
WOLF C.,FOREIGN AID: THEORY AND PRACTICE IN SOUTHERN ASIA. CEYLON INDONESIA PHILIPPINE S/ASIA CULTURE STRATA ECO/UNDEV PLAN EDU/PROP ATTIT ...METH/CNCPT MATH QUANT STAT CONT/OBS TIME/SEQ SIMUL TOT/POP 20. PAGE 170 H3396 — ACT/RES ECO/TAC FOR/AID

L60
HAAS E.B.,"CONSENSUS FORMATION IN THE COUNCIL OF EUROPE." EUR+WWI NAT/G DELIB/GP DIPLOM REGION CHOOSE PWR SOVEREIGN...RELATIV NEW/IDEA QUANT CHARTS INDEX TOT/POP OEEC 20 COUNCL/EUR. PAGE 63 H1265 — POL/PAR INT/ORG STAT

N63
RUMMEL R.J.,A FOREIGN CONFLICT BEHAVIOR CODE SHEET. ACT/RES DIPLOM...NEW/IDEA CHARTS NAT/COMP. PAGE 136 H2718 — QUANT WAR CLASSIF SIMUL

B65
TILLY C.,MEASURING POLITICAL UPHEAVAL* RESEARCH MONOGRAPH NO. 19. FRANCE INDUS NAT/G FORCES WORKER ...GEOG RECORD EXHIBIT GEN/METH BIBLIOG INDEX. PAGE 155 H3095 — CLASSIF QUANT COERCE REV

S65
WRIGHT Q.,"THE ESCALATION OF INTERNATIONAL CONFLICTS." WOR+45 WOR-45 FORCES DIPLOM RISK COST ATTIT ALL/VALS...INT/LAW QUANT STAT NAT/COMP. PAGE 171 H3422 — WAR PERCEPT PREDICT MATH

B66
BERELSON B.,READER IN PUBLIC OPINION AND COMMUNICATION (2ND ED.). UNIV NAT/G PRESS GP/REL PERS/REL PERCEPT RIGID/FLEX...MAJORIT QUANT METH/COMP ANTHOL BIBLIOG 20. PAGE 15 H0298 — EDU/PROP ATTIT CONCPT COM/IND

B66
GURR T.,NEW ERROR-COMPENSATED MEASURES FOR COMPARING NATIONS* SOME CORRELATES OF CIVIL VIOLENCE. WOR+45 SOCIETY REV ISOLAT...PHIL/SCI SOC QUANT TESTS SAMP/SIZ HYPO/EXP. PAGE 63 H1254 — NAT/COMP INDEX COERCE NEW/IDEA

B66
MERRITT R.L.,COMPARING NATIONS* THE USE OF QUANTITATIVE DATA IN CROSSNATIONAL RESEARCH. ACADEM DIPLOM GP/REL...PHIL/SCI STAT TREND GP/COMP PERS/COMP GEN/METH ANTHOL BIBLIOG INDEX. PAGE 109 H2184 — NAT/COMP MATH COMPUT/IR QUANT

QUANTIFICATION....SEE QUANT

QUANTITATIVE CONTENT ANALYSIS....SEE CON/ANAL

QUARLES B. H1013

QUEBEC....QUEBEC, CANADA

QUERARD J.M. H2573

QUESTER G.H. H2574

QUESTIONNAIRES....SEE QU

QUIGG P.W. H2575

QURESHI I.H. H2576

R

R+D....RESEARCH AND DEVELOPMENT GROUP

N
INDIA: A REFERENCE ANNUAL. INDIA CULTURE COM/IND R+D FORCES PLAN RECEIVE EDU/PROP HEALTH...STAT CHARTS BIBLIOG 20. PAGE 1 H0017
CONSTN LABOR INT/ORG

N
CARNEGIE ENDOWMENT,CURRENT RESEARCH IN INTERNATIONAL AFFAIRS: SELECTED BIBLIOGRAPHY OF WORK IN PROGRESS BY PRIVATE RESEARCH AGENCIES. WOR+45 NAT/G ACT/RES GOV/COMP. PAGE 27 H0533
BIBLIOG/A DIPLOM R+D

N
MIDDLE EAST INSTITUTE,CURRENT RESEARCH ON THE MIDDLE EAST....PHIL/SCI PSY SOC LING 20. PAGE 110 H2201
BIBLIOG R+D ISLAM NAT/G

B28
SOROKIN P.,CONTEMPORARY SOCIOLOGICAL THEORIES. MOD/EUR UNIV SOCIETY R+D SCHOOL ECO/TAC EDU/PROP ROUTINE ATTIT DRIVE...PSY CONCPT TIME/SEQ TREND GEN/LAWS 20. PAGE 147 H2934
CULTURE SOC WAR

B31
BONAR J.,THEORIES OF POPULATION FROM RALEIGH TO ARTHUR YOUNG. CHRIST-17C MOD/EUR CULTURE SOCIETY R+D CREATE ATTIT PERCEPT RIGID/FLEX...OLD/LIB CONCPT NEW/IDEA TIME/SEQ IDEA/COMP STERTYP GEN/LAWS. PAGE 19 H0372
GEOG BIOG

B48
GRIFFITH E.S.,RESEARCH IN POLITICAL SCIENCE: THE WORK OF PANELS OF RESEARCH COMMITTEE, APSA. WOR+45 WOR-45 COM/IND R+D FORCES ACT/RES WAR...GOV/COMP ANTHOL 20. PAGE 61 H1220
BIBLIOG PHIL/SCI DIPLOM JURID

B50
CANTRIL H.,TENSIONS THAT CAUSE WAR. UNIV CULTURE R+D CREATE EDU/PROP DRIVE PERSON KNOWL ORD/FREE ...HUM PSY SOC OBS CENSUS TREND CON/ANAL SOC/EXP SIMUL GEN/METH ANTHOL COLD/WAR TOT/POP. PAGE 26 H0523
SOCIETY PHIL/SCI PEACE

B50
MACIVER R.M.,GREAT EXPRESSIONS OF HUMAN RIGHTS. LAW CONSTN CULTURE INTELL SOCIETY R+D INT/ORG ATTIT DRIVE...JURID OBS HIST/WRIT GEN/LAWS. PAGE 100 H1999
UNIV CONCPT

B51
HUXLEY J.,FREEDOM AND CULTURE. UNIV LAW SOCIETY R+D ACADEM SCHOOL CREATE SANCTION ATTIT KNOWL...HUM ANTHOL 20. PAGE 76 H1512
CULTURE ORD/FREE PHIL/SCI IDEA/COMP

B51
MORLEY C.,GUIDE TO RESEARCH IN RUSSIAN HISTORY. USSR MARXISM...BIOG HIST/WRIT ANTHOL DICTIONARY. PAGE 113 H2259
BIBLIOG/A R+D NAT/G COM

B52
US DEPARTMENT OF STATE,RESEARCH ON EASTERN EUROPE (EXCLUDING USSR). EUR+WWI LAW ECO/DEV NAT/G PROB/SOLV DIPLOM ADMIN LEAD MARXISM...TREND 19/20. PAGE 159 H3187
BIBLIOG R+D ACT/RES COM

N52
COORDINATING COMM DOC SOC SCI,INTERNATIONAL REPERTORY OF SOCIAL SCIENCE DOCUMENTATION CENTERS (PAMPHLET). ACT/RES OP/RES WRITING KNOWL...CON/ANAL METH. PAGE 33 H0661
BIBLIOG/A R+D NAT/G INT/ORG

B54
US LIBRARY OF CONGRESS,RESEARCH AND INFORMATION ON AFRICA: CONTINUING SOURCES. ISLAM ECO/UNDEV AGRI INDUS R+D ACADEM NAT/G INT/TRADE...SOC 20. PAGE 161 H3210
BIBLIOG/A AFR PRESS COM/IND

S54
MIT CENTER INTERNATIONAL STU,"A PLAN OF RESEARCH IN INTERNATIONAL COMMUNICATION: A REPORT." UNIV CULTURE INTELL SOCIETY ACT/RES ALL/VALS...CONCPT METH/CNCPT. PAGE 111 H2227
R+D STYLE

C54
DE GRAZIA A.,"THE COMPARATIVE SURVEY OF EUROPEAN-AMERICAN POLITICAL BEHAV IOR; A RESEARCH PROSPECTUS (PAPER)" EUR+WWI FRANCE GERMANY SPAIN UK USA+45 WOR+45 STRATA POL/PAR DIPLOM EDU/PROP COLONIAL LEAD WAR NAT/LISM CONCPT. PAGE 37 H0752
BIBLIOG R+D METH NAT/COMP

B55
BAILEY S.K.,RESEARCH FRONTIERS IN POLITICS AND GOVERNMENT. CONSTN LEGIS ADMIN REV CHOOSE...CONCPT IDEA/COMP GAME ANTHOL 20. PAGE 10 H0201
R+D METH NAT/G

B58
GARTHOFF R.L.,SOVIET STRATEGY IN THE NUCLEAR AGE. FUT USSR R+D INT/ORG NAT/G ACT/RES TEC/DEV DOMIN DETER WAR ATTIT PWR...RELATIV METH/CNCPT SELF/OBS TREND CON/ANAL STERTYP GEN/LAWS 20. PAGE 55 H1103
COM FORCES BAL/PWR NUC/PWR

B58
HANCE W.A.,AFRICAN ECONOMIC DEVELOPMENT. AGRI DIST/IND INDUS R+D ACT/RES PLAN CAP/ISM FOR/AID ...GOV/COMP BIBLIOG 20. PAGE 65 H1312
AFR ECO/UNDEV PROB/SOLV TEC/DEV

B59
ELDRIDGE H.T.,THE MATERIALS OF DEMOGRAPHY: A SELECTED AND ANNOTATED BIBLIOGRAPHY. R+D DEATH ...SAMP METH/COMP NAT/COMP 20. PAGE 45 H0905
BIBLIOG/A GEOG STAT TREND

B60
LEYDER J.,BIBLIOGRAPHIE DE L'ENSEIGNEMENT SUPERIEUR ET DE LA RECHERCHE SCIENTIFIQUE EN AFRIQUE INTERTROPICALE (2 VOLS.). AFR CULTURE ECO/UNDEV AGRI PLAN EDU/PROP ADMIN COLONIAL...GEOG SOC/INTEG 20 NEGRO. PAGE 96 H1918
BIBLIOG/A ACT/RES ACADEM R+D

S60
HALSEY A.H.,"THE CHANGING FUNCTIONS OF UNIVERSITIES IN ADVANCED INDUSTRIAL SOCIETIES." R+D EDU/PROP REPRESENT ROLE ORD/FREE PWR TREND. PAGE 65 H1298
ACADEM CREATE CULTURE ADJUST

S60
JAFFEE A.J.,"POPULATION TRENDS AND CONTROLS IN UNDERDEVELOPED COUNTRIES." AFR FUT ISLAM L/A+17C S/ASIA CULTURE R+D FAM ACT/RES PLAN EDU/PROP BIO/SOC RIGID/FLEX HEALTH...SOC STAT OBS CHARTS 20. PAGE 79 H1582
ECO/UNDEV GEOG

B61
LUNDBERG G.A.,CAN SCIENCE SAVE US. UNIV CULTURE INTELL SOCIETY ECO/DEV R+D PLAN EDU/PROP ROUTINE CHOOSE ATTIT PERCEPT ALL/VALS...TREND 20. PAGE 99 H1979
ACT/RES CONCPT TOTALISM

L62
"AMERICAN BEHAVIORAL SCIENTIST." USSR LAW NAT/G ...SOC 20 UN. PAGE 2 H0039
BIBLIOG AFR R+D

S62
IOVTCHOUK M.T.,"ON SOME THEORETICAL PRINCIPLES AND METHODS OF SOCIOLOGICAL INVESTIGATIONS (IN RUSSIAN)." FUT USA+45 STRATA R+D NAT/G POL/PAR TOP/EX ACT/RES PLAN ECO/TAC EDU/PROP ROUTINE ATTIT RIGID/FLEX MARXISM SOCISM...MARXIST METH/CNCPT OBS TREND NAT/COMP GEN/LAWS 20. PAGE 78 H1564
COM ECO/DEV CAP/ISM USSR

S62
WALTER E.,"VERS UNE CLASSIFICATION SCIENTIFIQUE DE LA SOCIOLOGIA." UNIV CULTURE INTELL SOCIETY R+D ACT/RES LEGIT ROUTINE ATTIT KNOWL...JURID MGT TREND GEN/LAWS 20. PAGE 165 H3296
PLAN CONCPT

B63
US ATOMIC ENERGY COMMISSION,ATOMIC ENERGY IN THE SOVIET UNION: TRIP REPORT OF THE US ATOMIC ENERGY DELEGATION, MAY 1933. USSR R+D NAT/G CONSULT CREATE DIPLOM ADMIN ROUTINE EFFICIENCY PRODUC KNOWL SKILL ...NAT/COMP 20 AEC TRAVEL TREATY. PAGE 159 H3176
METH/COMP OP/RES TEC/DEV NUC/PWR

B64
BRIGHT J.R.,RESEARCH, DEVELOPMENT AND TECHNOLOGICAL INNOVATION. CULTURE R+D CREATE PLAN PROB/SOLV AUTOMAT RISK PERSON...DECISION CONCPT PREDICT BIBLIOG. PAGE 21 H0419
TEC/DEV NEW/IDEA INDUS MGT

S64
NEEDHAM T.,"SCIENCE AND SOCIETY IN EAST AND WEST." INTELL STRATA R+D LOC/G NAT/G PROVS CONSULT ACT/RES CREATE PLAN TEC/DEV EDU/PROP ADMIN ATTIT ALL/VALS ...POLICY RELATIV MGT CONCPT NEW/IDEA TIME/SEQ WORK WORK. PAGE 116 H2327
ASIA STRUCT

B65
CHENG C.-Y.,SCIENTIFIC AND ENGINEERING MANPOWER IN COMMUNIST CHINA, 1949-1963. CHINA/COM USSR ELITES ECO/DEV R+D ACADEM LABOR NAT/G EDU/PROP CONTROL UTIL...POLICY BIBLIOG 20. PAGE 29 H0588
WORKER CONSULT MARXISM BIOG

B65
GOULD J.,PENGUIN SURVEY OF THE SOCIAL SCIENCES* 1965. CULTURE SOCIETY R+D FAM KIN MUNIC ACT/RES DIPLOM SKILL. PAGE 59 H1186
SOC PHIL/SCI USSR UK

B65
HARMON R.B.,POLITICAL SCIENCE: A BIBLIOGRAPHICAL GUIDE TO THE LITERATURE. WOR+45 WOR-45 R+D INT/ORG LOC/G NAT/G DIPLOM ADMIN...CONCPT METH. PAGE 67 H1334
BIBLIOG POL/PAR LAW GOV/COMP

B65
NATIONAL REFERRAL CENTER SCI,A DIRECTORY OF INFORMATION RESOURCES IN THE UNITED STATES; SOCIAL SCIENCES. USA+45 PROF/ORG...PSY SOC 20. PAGE 116 H2322
INDEX R+D ACADEM ACT/RES

B65
SABLE M.H.,MASTER DIRECTORY FOR LATIN AMERICA. AGRI COM/IND FINAN R+D ACADEM LABOR NAT/G POL/PAR VOL/ASSN INT/TRADE EDU/PROP 20. PAGE 136 H2728
INDEX L/A+17C INT/ORG DIPLOM

B65
VERMOT-GAUCHY M.,L'EDUCATION NATIONALE DANS LA FRANCE DE 1975. FRANCE FUT CULTURE ELITES R+D SCHOOL PLAN EDU/PROP EFFICIENCY...POLICY PREDICT CHARTS INDEX 20. PAGE 162 H3245
ACADEM CREATE TREND INTELL

B66
IOWA STATE U CTR AGRI AND ECO,RESEARCH AND EDUCATION FOR REGIONAL AND AREA DEVELOPMENT. FUT LAW CULTURE R+D LOC/G PLAN KNOWL...POLICY CHARTS ANTHOL 20. PAGE 78 H1565
REGION ACT/RES ECO/TAC INDUS

B66
OECD DEVELOPMENT CENTRE,CATALOGUE OF SOCIAL AND ECONOMIC DEVELOPMENT INSTITUTES AND PROGRAMMES* RESEARCH. ACT/RES PLAN TEC/DEV EDU/PROP...SOC GP/COMP NAT/COMP. PAGE 120 H2403
ECO/UNDEV ECO/DEV R+D ACADEM

S66
MERRITT R.L.,"SELECTED ARTICLES AND DOCUMENTS ON COMPARATIVE GOVERNMENT AND CROSS-NATIONAL RESEARCH." AFR ASIA EUR+WWI L/A+17C MOD/EUR ELITES R+D ACT/RES DIPLOM PWR...SOC CONCPT 18/20. PAGE 109 H2185
BIBLIOG GOV/COMP NAT/G GOV/REL

S66
TURKEVICH J.,"SOVIET SCIENCE APPRAISED." USA+45 R+D ACADEM FORCES DIPLOM EDU/PROP WAR EFFICIENCY PEACE SKILL OBS. PAGE 157 H3137
USSR TEC/DEV NAT/COMP ATTIT

B67
FIELD M.G.,SOVIET SOCIALIZED MEDICINE. USSR FINAN R+D PROB/SOLV ADMIN SOCISM...MGT SOC CONCPT 20. PAGE 50 H0993
PUB/INST HEALTH NAT/G MARXISM

B67
GROSS B.M.,ACTION UNDER PLANNING: THE GUIDANCE OF ECONOMIC DEVELOPMENT. STRUCT R+D NAT/G ACT/RES HABITAT...DECISION 20. PAGE 62 H1232
ECO/UNDEV PLAN ADMIN MGT

B67
NATIONAL SCIENCE FOUNDATION,DIRECTORY OF SELECTED RESEARCH INSTITUTES IN EASTERN EUROPE. BULGARIA CZECHOSLVK HUNGARY POLAND ROMANIA INTELL ACADEM NAT/G ACT/RES 20. PAGE 116 H2323
INDEX R+D COM PHIL/SCI

B67
ROSENBLUTH G.,THE CANADIAN ECONOMY AND DISARMAMENT. CANADA FUT ECO/DEV INDUS R+D DELIB/GP DIPLOM ECO/TAC CIVMIL/REL PEACE...POLICY BIBLIOG PACIFIST 20. PAGE 134 H2679
ARMS/CONT STAT PLAN NAT/G

B67
UNESCO,PRINCIPLES AND PROBLEMS OF NATIONAL SCIENCE POLICIES. WOR+45 ECO/DEV ECO/UNDEV R+D INT/ORG PROB/SOLV CONFER...PHIL/SCI CHARTS 20 UNESCO UN. PAGE 158 H3165
NAT/COMP POLICY TEC/DEV CREATE

L67
LATIN AMERICAN STUDIES ASSN,"RESEARCH ON EDUCATION IN LATIN AMERICA." L/A+17C NAT/G HABITAT...GOV/COMP ANTHOL 20. PAGE 92 H1836
EDU/PROP SCHOOL ACADEM R+D

S67
DOERN G.B.,"THE ROYAL COMMISSIONS IN THE GENERAL POLICY PROCESS AND IN FEDERAL-PROVINCIAL RELATIONS." CANADA CONSTN ACADEM PROVS CONSULT DELIB/GP LEGIS ACT/RES PROB/SOLV CONFER CONTROL EFFICIENCY...METH/COMP 20 SENATE ROYAL/COMM. PAGE 42 H0832
R+D EX/STRUC GOV/REL NAT/G

S67
SEIDLER G.L.,"MARXIST LEGAL THOUGHT IN POLAND." POLAND SOCIETY R+D LOC/G NAT/G ACT/RES ADJUD CT/SYS SUPEGO PWR...SOC TREND 20 MARX/KARL. PAGE 141 H2822
MARXISM LAW CONCPT EFFICIENCY

N67
US HOUSE COMM SCI ASTRONAUT,GOVERNMENT, SCIENCE, AND INTERNATIONAL POLICY (PAMPHLET). INDIA NETHERLAND ECO/DEV ECO/UNDEV R+D ACADEM PLAN DIPLOM FOR/AID CONFER...PREDICT 20 CHINJAP. PAGE 160 H3198
NAT/G POLICY CREATE TEC/DEV

RACE....SEE RACE/REL, KIN

RACE/REL....RACE RELATIONS; SEE ALSO DISCRIM, ISOLAT, KIN

N
HOOVER INSTITUTION,UNITED STATES AND CANADIAN PUBLICATIONS ON AFRICA. CULTURE ECO/UNDEV AGRI TEC/DEV EDU/PROP COLONIAL RACE/REL NAT/LISM ATTIT HEALTH...SOC SOC/WK 20. PAGE 73 H1464
BIBLIOG DIPLOM NAT/G AFR

N
NORTHWESTERN UNIVERSITY LIB,JOINT ACQUISITIONS LIST OF AFRICANA. AFR SOCIETY STRUCT EDU/PROP COLONIAL GP/REL RACE/REL NAT/LISM SOVEREIGN...SOC 20. PAGE 119 H2377
BIBLIOG CULTURE ECO/UNDEV INDUS

NCO
CARRINGTON C.E.,THE COMMONWEALTH IN AFRICA (PAMPHLET). UK STRUCT NAT/G COLONIAL REPRESENT GOV/REL RACE/REL NAT/LISM...MAJORIT 20 EEC NEGRO COLD/WAR. PAGE 27 H0540
ECO/UNDEV AFR DIPLOM PLAN

B00
HOBSON J.A.,THE WAR IN SOUTH AFRICA: ITS CAUSES AND EFFECTS. NETHERLAND SOUTH/AFR UK ELITES AGRI EXTR/IND POL/PAR DIPLOM PRESS RACE/REL ATTIT ORD/FREE SOVEREIGN...INT 19 NEGRO. PAGE 72 H1439
WAR DOMIN POLICY NAT/G

B00
MARKHAM V.R.,SOUTH AFRICA, PAST AND PRESENT. NETHERLAND SOUTH/AFR CULTURE LEGIS EDU/PROP COLONIAL CHOOSE REPRESENT DISCRIM ATTIT...OBS TIME/SEQ 17/19 NEGRO BOER/WAR. PAGE 103 H2054
WAR LEAD RACE/REL

B00
MOCKLER-FERRYMAN A.,BRITISH WEST AFRICA. FRANCE GERMANY NIGER SIER/LEONE UK CULTURE DIPLOM WAR
AFR COLONIAL

RACE/REL PRODUC PROFIT WEALTH...POLICY PREDICT 19. PAGE 112 H2232
INT/TRADE CAP/ISM

C06
MONTGOMERY H.,"A DICTIONARY OF POLITICAL PHRASES AND ILLUSIONS WITH A SHORT BIBLIOGRAPHY." EUR+WWI MOD/EUR UK AGRI LABOR LOC/G NAT/G COLONIAL CHOOSE RACE/REL. PAGE 112 H2245
BIBLIOG DICTIONARY POLICY DIPLOM

B10
MENDELSSOHN S.,SOUTH AFRICAN BIBLIOGRAPHY (2 VOLS.). SOUTH/AFR EXTR/IND LABOR SECT DIPLOM INT/TRADE COLONIAL RACE/REL DISCRIM...GEOG 20. PAGE 109 H2172
BIBLIOG/A AFR NAT/G NAT/LISM

B10
MENDELSSOHN S.,MENDELSSOHN'S SOUTH AFRICA BIBLIOGRAPHY (VOL. I). SOUTH/AFR RACE/REL...GEOG JURID 19/20. PAGE 109 H2173
BIBLIOG/A CULTURE

B12
SONOLET L.,L'AFRIQUE OCCIDENTALE FRANCAISE. FRANCE AGRI INDUS NAT/G SECT FORCES INT/TRADE EDU/PROP RACE/REL HEALTH ORD/FREE...CHARTS 19/20 NEGRO AFRICA/W. PAGE 147 H2933
DOMIN ADMIN COLONIAL AFR

B19
NATHAN M.,THE SOUTH AFRICAN COMMONWEALTH: CONSTITUTION, PROBLEMS, SOCIAL CONDITIONS. SOUTH/AFR UK CULTURE INDUS EX/STRUC LEGIS BUDGET EDU/PROP ADMIN CT/SYS GP/REL RACE/REL...LING 19/20 CMN/WLTH. PAGE 116 H2317
CONSTN NAT/G POL/PAR SOCIETY

N19
MEZERIK A.G.,APARTHEID IN THE REPUBLIC OF SOUTH AFRICA (PAMPHLET). DIPLOM DOMIN CONTROL COERCE REPRESENT CONSEN ATTIT. PAGE 110 H2194
DISCRIM RACE/REL POL/PAR POLICY

N19
PROVISIONS SECTION OAU,ORGANIZATION OF AFRICAN UNITY: BASIC DOCUMENTS AND RESOLUTIONS (PAMPHLET). AFR CULTURE ECO/UNDEV DIPLOM ECO/TAC EDU/PROP COLONIAL ARMS/CONT NUC/PWR RACE/REL DISCRIM NAT/LISM 20 UN OAU. PAGE 128 H2564
CONSTN EX/STRUC SOVEREIGN INT/ORG

B20
COX H.,ECONOMIC LIBERTY. UNIV LAW INT/TRADE RATION TARIFFS RACE/REL SOCISM POLICY. PAGE 34 H0687
NAT/G ORD/FREE ECO/TAC PERSON

B23
WILLOUGHBY W.C.,RACE PROBLEMS IN THE NEW AFRICA: A STUDY OF THE RELATION OF BANTU AND BRITONS IN THOSE PARTS OF BANTU AFRICA... AFR STRUCT SECT DOMIN EDU/PROP GP/REL ATTIT WORSHIP 20 BANTU EUROPE MISSION CHRISTIAN. PAGE 168 H3372
KIN COLONIAL RACE/REL CULTURE

B24
WALKER F.D.,AFRICA AND HER PEOPLES. ISLAM STRUCT FAM SECT EDU/PROP INGP/REL RACE/REL HABITAT...GEOG SOC IDEA/COMP WORSHIP 20 NEGRO. PAGE 164 H3292
CULTURE AFR GP/COMP KIN

B26
MCPHEE A.,THE ECONOMIC REVOLUTION IN BRITISH WEST AFRICA. AFR UK CULTURE DIST/IND FINAN INDUS PLAN GP/REL RACE/REL 20 AFRICA/W. PAGE 107 H2148
ECO/UNDEV INT/TRADE COLONIAL GEOG

B27
SMITH E.W.,THE GOLDEN STOOL: SOME ASPECTS OF THE CONFLICT OF CULTURES IN AFRICA. AFR FINAN INDUS SECT INT/TRADE COERCE CHOOSE RACE/REL ATTIT...GEOG LING 20 NEGRO. PAGE 145 H2907
COLONIAL CULTURE GP/REL EDU/PROP

B30
OLDMAN J.H.,WHITE AND BLACK IN AFRICA. AFR STRUCT COLONIAL PARTIC DISCRIM ISOLAT PRIVIL 20 SMUTS/JAN NEGRO WHITE/SUP. PAGE 121 H2412
SOVEREIGN ORD/FREE RACE/REL NAT/G

B30
SMUTS J.C.,AFRICA AND SOME WORLD PROBLEMS. RHODESIA SOUTH/AFR CULTURE ECO/UNDEV INDUS INT/ORG SECT PROB/SOLV REGION GOV/REL DISCRIM ATTIT 19/20 LEAGUE/NAT LIVNGSTN/D NEGRO. PAGE 146 H2921
LEGIS AFR COLONIAL RACE/REL

B31
KROEBER A.L.,SOURCE BOOK IN ANTHROPOLOGY. PREHIST SECT RACE/REL...LING GP/COMP ANTHOL. PAGE 89 H1770
SOC HEREDITY CULTURE ALL/VALS

B33
TANNENBAUM F.,PEACE BY REVOLUTION. ECO/UNDEV AGRI SECT WORKER DIPLOM EDU/PROP DISCRIM OWN WEALTH POPULISM 17/20 MEXIC/AMER INDIAN/AM. PAGE 152 H3043
CULTURE COLONIAL RACE/REL REV

B37
MARX K.,THE CIVIL WAR IN THE UNITED STATES. USA-45 WORKER DIPLOM INT/TRADE DOMIN RACE/REL ATTIT ...TREND 19. PAGE 104 H2078
WAR REV MARXIST ORD/FREE

B38
CARVALHO C.M.,GEOGRAPHIA HUMANA; POLITICA E ECONOMICA (3RD ED.). BRAZIL CULTURE AGRI INDUS DIPLOM COLONIAL GP/REL RACE/REL...LING 20 RESOURCE/N. PAGE 27 H0551
GEOG HABITAT

B39
BARNES H.E.,SOCIETY IN TRANSITION: PROBLEMS OF A
SOCIETY

CHANGING ERA. USA-45 INDUS MUNIC PUB/INST EDU/PROP CRIME RACE/REL...SOC MYTH NAT/COMP. PAGE 11 H0220
CULTURE TECHRACY TEC/DEV

HILL R.L.,A BIBLIOGRAPHY OF THE ANGLO-EGYPTIAN SUDAN FROM THE EARLIEST TIMES TO 1937. AFR ETHIOPIA SUDAN UAR LAW COM/IND SECT RACE/REL...GEOG HEAL SOC LING 19/20 NEGRO. PAGE 71 H1417
B39 BIBLIOG CULTURE NAT/COMP GP/COMP

HITLER A.,MEIN KAMPF (UNABR. ENG. VERSION) (1925). GERMANY CONSTN TEC/DEV RACE/REL NAT/LISM TOTALISM SOVEREIGN...BIOG 20 HITLER/A TREATY. PAGE 71 H1429
B41 EDU/PROP WAR PLAN FASCISM

JOSHI P.S.,THE TYRANNY OF COLOUR. INDIA SOUTH/AFR UK ECO/UNDEV NAT/G POL/PAR DIPLOM ECO/TAC WAR ...POLICY 19/20. PAGE 82 H1637
B42 COLONIAL DISCRIM RACE/REL

VAN VALKENBURG S.,"ELEMENTS OF POLITICAL GEOGRAPHY." FRANCE COM/IND INDUS NAT/G SECT RACE/REL...LING TREND GEN/LAWS BIBLIOG 20. PAGE 162 H3232
C44 GEOG DIPLOM COLONIAL

WOOLBERT R.G.,FOREIGN AFFAIRS BIBLIOGRAPHY, 1932-1942. INT/ORG SECT INT/TRADE COLONIAL RACE/REL NAT/LISM...GEOG INT/LAW GOV/COMP IDEA/COMP 20. PAGE 170 H3410
B45 BIBLIOG/A DIPLOM WAR

CASSIRER E.,THE MYTH OF THE STATE. WOR-45 SOCIETY RACE/REL RATIONAL PWR FASCISM...PHIL/SCI PSY LING TREND HEGEL/GWF MACHIAVELL. PAGE 28 H0557
B46 MYTH CONCPT NAT/G IDEA/COMP

HUTTON J.,THE CONSTITUTION OF THE UNION OF SOUTH AFRICA: BIBLIOGRAPHY (PAMPHLET). SOUTH/AFR MUNIC DIPLOM RACE/REL 20. PAGE 75 H1510
B46 BIBLIOG CONSTN NAT/G LOC/G

COX O.C.,CASTE, CLASS, AND RACE. INDIA WOR+45 WOR-45 SECT TEC/DEV MARRIAGE ROLE MARXISM...MAJORIT NAT/COMP SOC/INTEG 20 NEGRO HINDU. PAGE 34 H0688
B48 RACE/REL STRUCT STRATA DISCRIM

LASKI H.S.,THE AMERICAN DEMOCRACY. CULTURE INDUS SECT WORKER DIPLOM EDU/PROP REPRESENT RACE/REL ORD/FREE PWR...NAT/COMP 18/20. PAGE 92 H1831
B48 NAT/G LOC/G USA-45 POPULISM

WHITE C.L.,HUMAN GEOGRAPHY: AN ECOLOGICAL STUDY OF GEOGRAPHY. UNIV SEA CULTURE AGRI EXTR/IND RACE/REL PRODUC...CHARTS HYPO/EXP SIMUL GEN/LAWS T. PAGE 167 H3345
B48 SOC HABITAT GEOG SOCIETY

HUGHES E.C.,"SOCIAL CHANGE AND STATUS PROTEST: AN ESSAY ON THE MARGINAL MAN" (BMR)" EUR+WWI UK USA+45 CULTURE SOCIETY STRUCT RACE/REL...SOC NAT/COMP SOC/INTEG 19/20 NEGRO PARK/R. PAGE 74 H1490
S49 STRATA ATTIT DISCRIM

CARRINGTON C.E.,THE LIQUIDATION OF THE BRITISH EMPIRE. AFR NAT/G INT/TRADE COLONIAL RACE/REL ATTIT ORD/FREE...POLICY NAT/COMP 20 CMN/WLTH. PAGE 27 H0541
B51 SOVEREIGN NAT/LISM DIPLOM GP/REL

ISAACS H.R.,AFRICA: NEW CRISES IN THE MAKING (PAMPHLET). EUR+WWI USA+45 ELITES ECO/UNDEV WAR DISCRIM NAT/LISM ATTIT...POLICY NEW/IDEA CHARTS GOV/COMP 20 NEGRO COLD/WAR. PAGE 78 H1570
B52 COLONIAL AFR RACE/REL ORD/FREE

MONTAGU A.,MAN'S MOST DANGEROUS MYTH: THE FALLACY OF RACE. LAW PROB/SOLV WAR HABITAT POPULISM...PSY CONCPT CHARTS BIBLIOG NEGRO JEWS. PAGE 112 H2242
B52 DISCRIM MYTH CULTURE RACE/REL

DAVIDSON B.,THE NEW WEST AFRICA: PROBLEMS OF INDEPENDENCE. UK AGRI TEC/DEV DIPLOM GP/REL RACE/REL SOVEREIGN...ANTHOL 20 AFRICA/W. PAGE 37 H0744
B53 AFR COLONIAL ECO/UNDEV NAT/G

WAGLEY C.,AMAZON TOWN: A STUDY OF MAN IN THE TROPICS. BRAZIL L/A+17C STRATA STRUCT ECO/UNDEV AGRI EX/STRUC RACE/REL DISCRIM HABITAT WEALTH...OBS SOC/EXP 20. PAGE 164 H3285
B53 SOC NEIGH CULTURE INGP/REL

KOLARZ W.,THE PEOPLES OF THE SOVIET FAR EAST. RUSSIA USSR STRUCT LEAD ISOLAT NAT/LISM...CHARTS 20. PAGE 88 H1750
B54 COLONIAL RACE/REL ADJUST CULTURE

GUINS G.C.,"SOVIET LAW AND SOVIET SOCIETY." COM USSR STRATA FAM NAT/G WORKER DOMIN RACE/REL ...BIBLIOG 20. PAGE 62 H1249
C54 LAW STRUCT PLAN

KRUSE H.,DAS STAATSANGEHORIGKEITSRECHT DER ARABISCHEN STAATEN. ISLAM JORDAN LIBYA SYRIA UAR NAT/G SECT RACE/REL...INT/LAW 6/20 TREATY. PAGE 89 H1779
B55 JURID NAT/LISM DIPLOM GP/REL

LIPSCOMB J.F.,WHITE AFRICANS. SOCIETY STRUCT AGRI ECO/TAC ADJUD COLONIAL COERCE PERS/REL ADJUST. PAGE 97 H1937
B55 RACE/REL HABITAT ECO/UNDEV ORD/FREE

PYRAH G.B.,IMPERIAL POLICY AND SOUTH AFRICA 1902-1910. SOUTH/AFR UK NAT/G WAR DISCRIM...CONCPT CHARTS BIBLIOG/A 19/20 CMN/WLTH. PAGE 129 H2570
B55 DIPLOM COLONIAL POLICY RACE/REL

THOMPSON V.,MINORITY PROBLEMS IN SOUTHEAST ASIA. CAMBODIA CHINA/COM LAOS S/ASIA KIN NAT/G SECT PROB/SOLV EDU/PROP REGION GP/REL RACE/REL MARXISM ...SOC 20 BUDDHISM UN. PAGE 154 H3085
B55 INGP/REL GEOG DIPLOM STRUCT

VERGNAUD P.,L'IDEE DE LA NATIONALITE ET DE LA LIBRE DISPOSITION DES PEUPLES DANS SES RAPPORTS AVEC L'IDEE DE L'ETAT. STRATA NAT/G EDU/PROP RACE/REL AUTHORIT FASCISM MARXISM MYTH. PAGE 162 H3243
B55 NAT/LISM DISCRIM ORD/FREE

HATCH J.C.,NEW FROM AFRICA. AFR FUT UK NAT/G GUERRILLA ATTIT ORD/FREE PWR...AUD/VIS CHARTS 20. PAGE 68 H1354
B56 NAT/LISM COLONIAL RACE/REL

IRIKURA J.K.,SOUTHEAST ASIA: SELECTED ANNOTATED BIBLIOGRAPHY OF JAPANESE PUBLICATIONS. CULTURE ADMIN RACE/REL 20 CHINJAP. PAGE 78 H1567
B56 BIBLIOG/A S/ASIA DIPLOM

KALLEN H.M.,CULTURAL PLURALISM AND THE AMERICAN IDEA. RACE/REL ADJUST PERSON ORD/FREE LAISSEZ ...PLURIST GEN/LAWS ANTHOL. PAGE 83 H1652
B56 PLURISM CULTURE GP/REL SECT

KUPER L.,PASSIVE RESISTANCE IN SOUTH AFRICA. SOUTH/AFR LAW NAT/G POL/PAR VOL/ASSN DISCRIM ...POLICY SOC AUD/VIS 20. PAGE 89 H1782
B56 ORD/FREE RACE/REL ATTIT

VIANNA F.J.,EVOLUCAO DE POVO BRASILEIRO (4TH ED.). BRAZIL TEC/DEV COLONIAL GP/REL ATTIT SOVEREIGN ...SOC SOC/INTEG 15/20. PAGE 162 H3247
B56 STRUCT RACE/REL NAT/G

BYRNES R.F.,BIBLIOGRAPHY OF AMERICAN PUBLICATIONS ON EAST CENTRAL EUROPE, 1945-1957 (VOL. XXII). SECT DIPLOM EDU/PROP RACE/REL...ART/METH GEOG JURID SOC LING 20 JEWS. PAGE 25 H0503
B57 BIBLIOG/A COM MARXISM NAT/G

ROBERTSON H.M.,SOUTH AFRICA, ECONOMIC AND POLITICAL ASPECTS. SOUTH/AFR CONSTN CULTURE POL/PAR LEGIS DIPLOM DOMIN COLONIAL...SOC BIBLIOG 19/20. PAGE 132 H2647
B57 RACE/REL ECO/UNDEV ECO/TAC DISCRIM

TAYLOR J.V.,CHRISTIANITY AND POLITICS IN AFRICA. AFR CONTROL PARTIC GP/REL RACE/REL ATTIT...POLICY BIBLIOG/A WORSHIP 20. PAGE 153 H3055
B57 SECT NAT/G NAT/LISM

HAILEY,"TOMORROW IN AFRICA." CONSTN SOCIETY LOC/G NAT/G DOMIN ADJUD ADMIN GP/REL DISCRIM NAT/LISM ATTIT MORAL ORD/FREE...PSY SOC CONCPT OBS RECORD TREND GEN/LAWS CMN/WLTH 20. PAGE 64 H1277
S57 AFR PERSON ELITES RACE/REL

ALMAGRO BASCH M.,ORIGEN Y FORMACION DEL PUEBLO HISPANO. PREHIST SPAIN REGION WAR RACE/REL HABITAT ORD/FREE...SOC SOC/INTEG 20. PAGE 5 H0109
B58 CULTURE GP/REL ADJUST

BRADY A.,DEMOCRACY IN THE DOMINIONS (3RD ED.). CANADA NEW/ZEALND SOUTH/AFR WOR+45 LAW EX/STRUC DOMIN COLONIAL PARL/PROC REPRESENT RACE/REL NAT/LISM WEALTH 20 AUSTRAL CMN/WLTH. PAGE 20 H0399
B58 GOV/COMP POL/PAR POPULISM NAT/G

GLUCKMAN M.,ANALYSIS OF A SOCIAL SITUATION IN MODERN ZULULAND. AFR PERS/REL ADJUST DISCRIM EQUILIB NAT/LISM...SOC RECORD AUD/VIS 20 ZULULAND. PAGE 57 H1146
B58 CULTURE RACE/REL STRUCT GP/REL

LOWER A.R.M.,EVOLVING CANADIAN FEDERALISM. CANADA WEST/IND CONSTN PROB/SOLV COLONIAL REGION NAT/LISM ...ANTHOL 20. PAGE 99 H1976
B58 FEDERAL NAT/G DIPLOM RACE/REL

OGDEN F.D.,THE POLL TAX IN THE SOUTH. USA+45 USA-45 CONSTN ADJUD ADMIN PARTIC CRIME...TIME/SEQ GOV/COMP METH/COMP 18/20 SOUTH/US. PAGE 120 H2407
B58 TAX CHOOSE RACE/REL DISCRIM

KITTLER G.D.,EQUATORIAL AFRICA: THE NEW WORLD OF TOMORROW. CENTRL/AFR INDUS KIN SECT CHIEF EDU/PROP CHOOSE HEALTH...GEOG WORSHIP 20. PAGE 87 H1730
B59 RACE/REL AFR ECO/UNDEV CULTURE

ROCHE J.,LA COLONISATION ALLEMANDE ET LE RIO GRANDE DO SUL. BRAZIL L/A+17C NAT/G PROVS INGP/REL RACE/REL DISCRIM HABITAT...GEOG SOC/INTEG 19/20 MIGRATION. PAGE 133 H2652
B59 ECO/UNDEV GP/REL ATTIT

SITHOLE N.,AFRICAN NATIONALISM. UNIV CULTURE SECT
B59 RACE/REL

ADMIN COLONIAL CHOOSE. PAGE 145 H2892
AFR NAT/LISM PERSON

B59
VITTACHIT,EMERGENCY '58. CEYLON UK STRUCT NAT/G FORCES ADJUD CRIME REV NAT/LISM 20. PAGE 163 H3258
RACE/REL DISCRIM DIPLOM SOVEREIGN

B59
VORSPAN A.,JUSTICE AND JUDAISM. FAM DIPLOM ECO/TAC EDU/PROP CRIME RACE/REL MARRIAGE ANOMIE ATTIT ORD/FREE...POLICY 20 UN. PAGE 164 H3279
SECT CULTURE ACT/RES GP/REL

B59
WRAITH R.E.,EAST AFRICAN CITIZEN. AFR GHANA UK AGRI INDUS LOC/G POL/PAR PROB/SOLV CONTROL REGION REPRESENT NAT/LISM PWR...OBS 20 AFRICA/E AFRICA/W. PAGE 171 H3415
ECO/UNDEV RACE/REL NAT/G NAT/COMP

B60
KEPHART C.,RACES OF MAN. GP/REL HABITAT...LING SOC/INTEG 20 MIGRATION MISCEGEN. PAGE 85 H1692
CULTURE RACE/REL HEREDITY GEOG

B60
LA PONCE J.A.,THE PROTECTION OF MINORITIES. WOR+45 WOR-45 NAT/G POL/PAR SUFF...INT/LAW CLASSIF GP/COMP GOV/COMP BIBLIOG 17/20 CIVIL/LIB CIV/RIGHTS. PAGE 90 H1793
INGP/REL DOMIN SOCIETY RACE/REL

B60
NICHOLLS W.H.,SOUTHERN TRADITION AND REGIONAL PROGRESS. STRATA STRUCT SCHOOL WORKER PARTIC REGION RACE/REL CONSEN ATTIT...SOC METH/CNCPT 19/20 SOUTH/US TVA. PAGE 118 H2349
RIGID/FLEX CONSERVE AGRI CULTURE

B60
ROSKAM K.L.,APARTHEID AND DISCRIMINATION. SOUTH/AFR SOCIETY STRUCT NAT/G POL/PAR GP/REL ISOLAT ...BIBLIOG 20. PAGE 134 H2683
DISCRIM RACE/REL CULTURE POLICY

B60
SOUTH AFRICAN CONGRESS OF DEM,FACE THE FUTURE. SOUTH/AFR ELITES LEGIS ADMIN REGION COERCE PEACE ATTIT 20. PAGE 147 H2938
RACE/REL DISCRIM CONSTN NAT/G

B60
THE AFRICA 1960 COMMITTEE,MANDATE IN TRUST; THE PROBLEM OF SOUTH WEST AFRICA. GERMANY STRUCT REGION SANCTION CHOOSE DISCRIM...INT/LAW 20 AFRICA/SW UN LEAGUE/NAT TRUST/TERR. PAGE 153 H3066
NAT/G DIPLOM COLONIAL RACE/REL

B60
THEOBOLD R.,THE NEW NATIONS OF WEST AFRICA. GHANA NIGERIA CULTURE INT/ORG ECO/TAC FOR/AID COLONIAL RACE/REL POPULISM...ANTHOL BIBLIOG 20 UN. PAGE 153 H3068
AFR SOVEREIGN ECO/UNDEV DIPLOM

L60
WHEELER G.,"RACIAL PROBLEMS IN SOVIET MUSLIM ASIA." COM CULTURE SOCIETY NEIGH SECT DOMIN EDU/PROP DISCRIM DISPL DRIVE PWR SOVEREIGN...CENSUS SAMP TREND 20 MUSLIM. PAGE 167 H3340
PERSON ATTIT USSR RACE/REL

S60
BERREMAN G.D.,"CASTE IN INDIA AND THE UNITED STATES" (BMR)" INDIA USA+45 CULTURE SOCIETY STRUCT SECT GP/REL DISCRIM HEREDITY...SOC STERTYP 20 NEGRO HINDU. PAGE 16 H0318
STRATA RACE/REL NAT/COMP ATTIT

S60
GRIMSHAW A.D.,"URBAN RACIAL VIOLENCE IN THE UNITED STATES: CHANGING ECOLOGICAL CONSIDERATIONS." STRUCT MUNIC FORCES PARTIC DISCRIM ATTIT HABITAT ...IDEA/COMP 20 NEGRO. PAGE 61 H1228
CROWD RACE/REL GOV/COMP NEIGH

S60
TIRYAKIAN E.A.,"APARTHEID AND POLITICS IN SOUTH AFRICA." SOUTH/AFR CULTURE STRATA ECO/DEV NAT/G POL/PAR ROUTINE CHOOSE GP/REL RACE/REL DISCRIM ATTIT ALL/VALS...CONCPT OBS TIME/SEQ VAL/FREE 20. PAGE 155 H3105
AFR DIPLOM

C60
FITZSIMMONS T.,"USSR: ITS PEOPLE, ITS SOCIETY, ITS CULTURE." USSR FAM SECT DIPLOM EDU/PROP ADMIN RACE/REL ATTIT...POLICY CHARTS BIBLIOG 20. PAGE 51 H1021
CULTURE STRUCT SOCIETY COM

C60
SMITH T.E.,"ELECTIONS IN DEVELOPING COUNTRIES: A STUDY OF ELECTORAL PROCEDURES USED IN TOPICAL AFRICA, SOUTH-EAST ASIA..." AFR S/ASIA UK ROUTINE GOV/REL RACE/REL...GOV/COMP BIBLIOG 20. PAGE 146 H2918
ECO/UNDEV CHOOSE REPRESENT ADMIN

B61
ALLIGHAN G.,VERWOERD - THE END. SOUTH/AFR TOP/EX DIPLOM COLONIAL DISCRIM TOTALISM ATTIT AUTHORIT ...BIOG 20 NEGRO VERWOERD/H. PAGE 5 H0107
CONTROL CHIEF RACE/REL NAT/G

B61
BURKS R.V.,THE DYNAMICS OF COMMUNISM IN EASTERN EUROPE. COM YUGOSLAVIA POL/PAR RACE/REL ISOLAT ...CORREL CON/ANAL CHARTS GP/COMP DICTIONARY 20 EUROPE/E SLAV/MACED. PAGE 24 H0489
MARXISM STRUCT WORKER REPRESENT

B61
KHALIQUZZAMAN C.,PATHWAY TO PAKISTAN. INDIA PAKISTAN UK SECT LEGIS CHOOSE RACE/REL ATTIT ORD/FREE 20 MUSLIM. PAGE 85 H1705
GP/REL NAT/G COLONIAL SOVEREIGN

B61
KHAN A.W.,INDIA WINS FREEDOM: THE OTHER SIDE. INDIA PAKISTAN CULTURE LEGIS DIPLOM PARL/PROC REV WAR NAT/LISM 20. PAGE 85 H1707
SOVEREIGN GP/REL RACE/REL ORD/FREE

B61
MACLURE M.,AFRICA: THE POLITICAL PATTERN. SOUTH/AFR CULTURE LEGIS DIPLOM COLONIAL RACE/REL 20. PAGE 100 H2005
AFR POLICY NAT/G

B61
MUNGER E.S.,AFRICAN FIELD REPORTS 1952-1961. SOUTH/AFR SOCIETY ECO/UNDEV NAT/G POL/PAR COLONIAL EXEC PARL/PROC GUERRILLA RACE/REL ALL/IDEOS...SOC AUD/VIS 20. PAGE 114 H2288
AFR DISCRIM RECORD

B61
PECKERT J.,DIE GROSSEN UND DIE KLEINEN MAECHTE. COM GERMANY/W ECO/DEV ECO/UNDEV NAT/G WAR RACE/REL PEACE...POLICY GP/COMP GOV/COMP 20 COLD/WAR. PAGE 124 H2482
DIPLOM ECO/TAC BAL/PWR

B61
ROCHE J.P.,COURTS AND RIGHTS: THE AMERICAN JUDICIARY IN ACTION (2ND ED.). UK USA+45 USA-45 STRUCT TEC/DEV SANCTION PERS/REL RACE/REL ORD/FREE ...METH/CNCPT GOV/COMP METH/COMP T 13/20. PAGE 133 H2653
JURID CT/SYS NAT/G PROVS

B61
SCHIEDER T.,DOCUMENTS ON THE EXPULSION OF THE GERMANS FROM EASTERN-CENTRAL-EUROPE (VOL. II/III). COM EUR+WWI GERMANY HUNGARY ROMANIA USSR DIPLOM RACE/REL 20 MIGRATION. PAGE 139 H2785
GEOG CULTURE

B61
SPOONER F.P.,SOUTH AFRICAN PREDICAMENT. FUT SOUTH/AFR INDUS POL/PAR RACE/REL INCOME...CHARTS 20 NEGRO. PAGE 148 H2953
ECO/DEV DISCRIM ECO/TAC POLICY

B61
TURNBULL C.M.,THE FOREST PEOPLE. EATING GP/REL INGP/REL RACE/REL ISOLAT HABITAT HEREDITY...GEOG SOC LING DICTIONARY WORSHIP 20 CONGO NEGRO BA/MBUTI. PAGE 157 H3138
AFR CULTURE KIN RECORD

S61
ELAZAR D.J.,"CHURCHES AS MOLDERS OF AMERICAN POLITICS." STRATA MUNIC EDU/PROP RACE/REL ORD/FREE SOC. PAGE 45 H0904
SECT CULTURE REPRESENT LOC/G

S61
LIEBERSON S.,"THE IMPACT OF RESIDENTIAL SEGREGATION ON ETHNIC ASSIMILATION" (BMR)" CULTURE MUNIC GP/REL RACE/REL DISCRIM...GEOG STAT CON/ANAL CHARTS SOC/INTEG 20 MIGRATION. PAGE 96 H1926
HABITAT ISOLAT NEIGH

S61
SCHECHTMAN J.B.,"MINORITIES IN THE MIDDLE EAST." ISLAM INTELL SOCIETY STRATA KIN NAT/G VOL/ASSN EDU/PROP REGION GP/REL DISCRIM ATTIT BIO/SOC DISPL PERSON ALL/VALS...PSY SOC OBS SAMP GEN/LAWS 20. PAGE 139 H2776
SECT CULTURE RACE/REL

B62
CARY J.,THE CASE FOR AFRICAN FREEDOM AND OTHER WRITINGS ON AFRICA. AFR UK INDUS LOC/G NAT/G SECT INT/TRADE EDU/PROP GOV/REL RACE/REL ORD/FREE ...CONCPT ANTHOL 19/20. PAGE 27 H0552
NAT/LISM COLONIAL TREND ECO/UNDEV

B62
DEBUYST F.,LAS CLASES SOCIALES EN AMERICA LATINA. L/A+17C SOCIETY STRUCT WORKER EDU/PROP RACE/REL ATTIT HABITAT ROLE...GEOG SOC NAT/COMP SOC/INTEG 20. PAGE 39 H0780
STRATA GP/REL WEALTH

B62
FEIT E.,SOUTH AFRICA, THE DYNAMICS OF THE AFRICAN NATIONAL CONGRESS. AFR SOUTH/AFR LAW INTELL STRATA KIN NAT/G POL/PAR ECO/TAC DOMIN RISK COERCE 20 NEGRO. PAGE 49 H0984
RACE/REL ELITES CONTROL STRUCT

B62
GANJI M.,INTERNATIONAL PROTECTION OF HUMAN RIGHTS. WOR+45 CONSTN INT/TRADE CT/SYS SANCTION CRIME WAR RACE/REL...CHARTS IDEA/COMP NAT/COMP BIBLIOG 20 TREATY NEGRO LEAGUE/NAT UN CIVIL/LIB. PAGE 55 H1097
ORD/FREE DISCRIM LEGIS DELIB/GP

B62
HARRINGTON M.,THE OTHER AMERICA: POVERTY IN THE UNITED STATES. WORKER CREATE REPRESENT RACE/REL AGE/O DRIVE POLICY. PAGE 67 H1338
WEALTH WELF/ST INCOME CULTURE

B62
LOWENSTEIN A.K.,BRUTAL MANDATE: A JOURNEY TO SOUTH WEST AFRICA. CULTURE INT/ORG NAT/G DIPLOM...GEOG 20 UN AFRICA/SW. PAGE 99 H1975
AFR POLICY RACE/REL PROB/SOLV

B62
MANNING H.T.,THE REVOLT OF FRENCH CANADA 1800-1835. CANADA UK CULTURE GOV/REL RACE/REL...BIBLIOG 19. PAGE 102 H2039
NAT/LISM COLONIAL GEOG

B62
MELADY T.,THE WHITE MAN'S FUTURE IN BLACK AFRICA. FUT CULTURE SOCIETY NAT/G POL/PAR PLAN ECO/TAC DOMIN EDU/PROP LEGIT COLONIAL RACE/REL ATTIT DRIVE ALL/VALS...PSY SOC CONCPT TIME/SEQ TOT/POP VAL/FREE 20. PAGE 108 H2167
AFR STRATA ELITES

B62
TATZ C.M.,SHADOW AND SUBSTANCE IN SOUTH AFRICA. SOUTH/AFR AGRI NAT/G POL/PAR DOMIN GP/REL ATTIT PWR 20. PAGE 152 H3048
RACE/REL REPRESENT DISCRIM LEGIS

B62
TAYLOR D.,THE BRITISH IN AFRICA. UK CULTURE ECO/UNDEV INDUS DIPLOM INT/TRADE ADMIN WAR RACE/REL ORD/FREE SOVEREIGN...POLICY BIBLIOG 15/20 CMN/WLTH. PAGE 153 H3053
AFR COLONIAL DOMIN

B62
VAN RENSBURG P.,GUILTY LAND: THE HISTORY OF APARTHEID. SOUTH/AFR NAT/G POL/PAR DOMIN CHOOSE ...SOC 19/20 NEGRO. PAGE 162 H3231
RACE/REL DISCRIM NAT/LISM POLICY

B63
CROSS C.,THE FASCISTS IN BRITAIN. UK ELITES LABOR NAT/G DOMIN PARTIC DISCRIM TOTALISM ATTIT...STERTYP 20. PAGE 35 H0708
POL/PAR FASCISM RACE/REL LEAD

B63
EICH H.,THE UNLOVED GERMANS. EUR+WWI GERMANY PERS/REL RACE/REL DISCRIM HABITAT SUPEGO FASCISM ...PSY SOC AUD/VIS 19/20 JEWS. PAGE 45 H0898
STERTYP PERSON CULTURE ATTIT

B63
FIRST R.,SOUTH WEST AFRICA. SOUTH/AFR INT/ORG KIN NAT/G WORKER COLONIAL WAR...POLICY 20 UN TRUST/TERR AFRICA/SW. PAGE 50 H1006
DISCRIM ORD/FREE RACE/REL CONTROL

B63
FRITZ H.E.,THE MOVEMENT FOR INDIAN ASSIMILATION, 1860-1890. SECT FORCES GP/REL RACE/REL DISCRIM FEDERAL CATHISM...BIBLIOG 19 INDIAN/AM PROTESTANT GRANT/US. PAGE 54 H1071
CULTURE NAT/G ECO/TAC ATTIT

B63
FURTADO C.,THE ECONOMIC GROWTH OF BRAZIL: A SURVEY FROM COLONIAL TO MODERN TIMES. L/A+17C AGRI DIST/IND EXTR/IND INDUS WORKER COLONIAL RACE/REL OWN GOV/COMP. PAGE 54 H1082
ECO/UNDEV TEC/DEV LABOR DOMIN

B63
HAILEY L.,THE REPUBLIC OF SOUTH AFRICA AND THE HIGH COMMISSION TERRITORIES. AFR SOUTH/AFR UK INT/ORG NAT/G PROVS RACE/REL SOVEREIGN...CHARTS 19/20 COMMONWLTH. PAGE 64 H1278
COLONIAL DIPLOM ATTIT

B63
KROEBER A.L.,ANTHROPOLOGY: BIOLOGY AND RACE. UNIV CULTURE HABITAT...PSY 20. PAGE 89 H1772
SOC PHIL/SCI RACE/REL INGP/REL

B63
LEWIN J.,POLITICS AND LAW IN SOUTH AFRICA. SOUTH/AFR UK POL/PAR BAL/PWR ECO/TAC COLONIAL CONTROL GP/REL DISCRIM PWR 20 NEGRO. PAGE 96 H1909
NAT/LISM POLICY LAW RACE/REL

B63
MAC MILLAN W.M.,BANTU, BOER, AND BRITON: THE MAKING OF THE SOUTH AFRICAN NATIVE PROBLEM. SOUTH/AFR UK LAW KIN NAT/G SECT LEGIS COLONIAL ISOLAT ATTIT ...BIOG 18/20 BANTU NEGRO PHILIP/J MISSION. PAGE 100 H1989
AFR RACE/REL ELITES

B63
SETON-WATSON H.,THE NEW IMPERIALISM. COM EUR+WWI MOD/EUR ECO/UNDEV NAT/G FORCES DIPLOM DOMIN EDU/PROP LEGIT COLONIAL EXEC COERCE GP/REL RACE/REL DISCRIM ATTIT...TIME/SEQ 20. PAGE 142 H2833
ECO/TAC RUSSIA USSR

B63
SILVERT K.H.,EXPECTANT PEOPLES: NATIONALISM AND DEVELOPMENT. CULTURE STRATA SECT LEAD REGION RACE/REL ALL/IDEOS...GEN/LAWS SOC/INTEG 20. PAGE 144 H2877
NAT/LISM ECO/UNDEV ALL/VALS

B63
SINGH H.L.,PROBLEMS AND POLICIES OF THE BRITISH IN INDIA, 1885-1898. INDIA UK NAT/G FORCES LEGIS PROB/SOLV CONTROL RACE/REL ADJUST DISCRIM NAT/LISM RIGID/FLEX...MGT 19 CIVIL/SERV. PAGE 144 H2885
COLONIAL PWR POLICY ADMIN

B63
WODDIS J.,AFRICA, THE WAY AHEAD. AFR FUT ELITES POL/PAR CAP/ISM DIPLOM DOMIN RACE/REL ATTIT ORD/FREE SOVEREIGN SOCISM 20 PANAF/FREE. PAGE 170 H3394
REV COLONIAL ECO/UNDEV NAT/G

S63
CRUTCHER J.,"PAN AFRICANISM: AFRICAN ODYSSEY." AFR NAT/G POL/PAR PROF/ORG VOL/ASSN TOP/EX CREATE REGION RACE/REL ALL/VALS...CONCPT TIME/SEQ TREND CON/ANAL 20. PAGE 36 H0716
PROVS DELIB/GP COLONIAL

B64
AKZIN B.,STATE AND NATION. UNIV ECO/UNDEV DIPLOM RACE/REL NAT/LISM ATTIT PLURISM...CONCPT IDEA/COMP 20. PAGE 4 H0090
GP/REL NAT/G KIN

B64
ARASARATNAM S.,CEYLON. CEYLON NETHERLAND PORTUGAL S/ASIA UK STRUCT ECO/UNDEV SECT DIPLOM DOMIN RACE/REL NAT/LISM 17/20 CMN/WLTH. PAGE 8 H0156
COLONIAL NAT/G PROB/SOLV CULTURE

B64
BUNTING B.P.,THE RISE OF THE SOUTH AFRICAN REICH. SOUTH/AFR INT/ORG NAT/G FORCES DIPLOM CONTROL WAR TOTALISM ATTIT...GOV/COMP 19/20. PAGE 24 H0477
RACE/REL DISCRIM NAT/LISM TREND

B64
BURKE F.G.,AFRICA'S QUEST FOR ORDER. AFR CULTURE KIN MUNIC NAT/G DIPLOM COLONIAL REV DISCRIM NAT/LISM AGE/Y 20. PAGE 24 H0488
ORD/FREE CONSEN RACE/REL LEAD

B64
HANNA W.J.,POLITICS IN BLACK AFRICA: A SELECTIVE BIBLIOGRAPHY OF RELEVANT PERIODICAL LITERATURE. AFR LAW LOC/G MUNIC NAT/G POL/PAR LOBBY CHOOSE RACE/REL SOVEREIGN 20. PAGE 66 H1315
BIBLIOG NAT/LISM COLONIAL

B64
HARRIS M.,PATTERNS OF RACE IN THE AMERICAS. BRAZIL L/A+17C STRATA ECO/UNDEV AGRI KIN MUNIC SECT COLONIAL RACE/REL...SOC SOC/INTEG 17/20 NEGRO INDIAN/AM. PAGE 67 H1342
STRUCT PRE/AMER CULTURE SOCIETY

B64
HILL C.R.,BANTUSTANS: THE FRAGMENTATION OF SOUTH AFRICA. AFR SOUTH/AFR ELITES SOCIETY KIN CONTROL DISCRIM ANOMIE ATTIT...POLICY CHARTS GOV/COMP 20 NEGRO BANTUSTANS TRANSKEI NATAL. PAGE 71 H1416
RACE/REL CULTURE LOC/G ORD/FREE

B64
HOPKINSON T.,SOUTH AFRICA. SOUTH/AFR UK NAT/G POL/PAR LEGIS ECO/TAC PARL/PROC WAR...JURID AUD/VIS 19/20. PAGE 73 H1467
SOCIETY RACE/REL DISCRIM

B64
HORNE D.,THE LUCKY COUNTRY: AUSTRALIA TODAY. UK CULTURE STRATA ATTIT PWR PLURISM...GOV/COMP 20 AUSTRAL. PAGE 73 H1471
RACE/REL DIPLOM NAT/G STRUCT

B64
JOSEPHSON E.,MAN ALONE: ALIENATION IN MODERN SOCIETY. WOR+45 ECO/DEV WORKER WAR LEISURE RACE/REL ANOMIE ATTIT PERCEPT PERSON ALL/VALS...ANTHOL 20. PAGE 82 H1636
STRANGE CULTURE SOCIETY ADJUST

B64
KITCHEN H.,A HANDBOOK OF AFRICAN AFFAIRS. ECO/UNDEV CREATE DIPLOM COLONIAL RACE/REL...ART/METH GEOG CHARTS 20. PAGE 87 H1729
AFR NAT/G INT/ORG FORCES

B64
LEMARCHAND R.,POLITICAL AWAKENING IN THE BELGIAN CONGO. ECO/UNDEV VOL/ASSN DOMIN CHOOSE GP/REL INGP/REL DISCRIM ORD/FREE PWR...CHARTS 20 CONGO ARABS. PAGE 94 H1873
NAT/LISM COLONIAL POL/PAR RACE/REL

B64
MATTHEWS D.G.,A CURRENT VIEW OF AFRICANA (PAMPHLET). CULTURE ECO/UNDEV DIPLOM RACE/REL ATTIT 20. PAGE 105 H2092
BIBLIOG/A AFR NAT/G NAT/LISM

B64
MBEKI G.,SOUTH AFRICA: THE PEASANT'S REVOLT. SOUTH/AFR POL/PAR COERCE REV NAT/LISM ORD/FREE SOVEREIGN 20 NEGRO. PAGE 106 H2114
COLONIAL RACE/REL DISCRIM DOMIN

B64
MORGAN H.W.,AMERICAN SOCIALISM 1900-1960. USA+45 USA-45 INTELL AGRI LABOR WORKER BARGAIN ECO/TAC GP/REL RACE/REL 20 NEGRO MIGRATION GOLD/STAND. PAGE 113 H2254
SOCISM POL/PAR ECO/DEV STRATA

B64
ON CULTURE AND SOCIAL CHANGE. FAM NAT/G ACT/RES ECO/TAC RACE/REL...PSY TIME/SEQ TREND IDEA/COMP METH/COMP ANTHOL BIBLIOG 20. PAGE 120 H2406
CULTURE TEC/DEV STRUCT CREATE

B64
QUIGG P.W.,AFRICA: A FOREIGN AFFAIRS READER. AFR FRANCE PORTUGAL UK DIPLOM LEAD PARL/PROC MARXISM ...MAJORIT METH/CNCPT GOV/COMP IDEA/COMP ANTHOL 19/20. PAGE 129 H2575
COLONIAL SOVEREIGN NAT/LISM RACE/REL

B64
SEGAL R.,SANCTIONS AGAINST SOUTH AFRICA. AFR SOUTH/AFR NAT/G INT/TRADE RACE/REL PEACE PWR ...INT/LAW ANTHOL 20 UN. PAGE 141 H2821
SANCTION DISCRIM ECO/TAC POLICY

B64
VOELKMANN K.,HERRSCHER VON MORGEN? BAL/PWR COLONIAL NEUTRAL REGION RACE/REL ALL/VALS SOVEREIGN...RECORD 20 COLD/WAR THIRD/WRLD. PAGE 163 H3259
DIPLOM ECO/UNDEV CONTROL NAT/COMP

S64
BENSON M.,"SOUTH AFRICA AND WORLD OPINION." AFR SOUTH/AFR INTELL SOCIETY TOP/EX ECO/TAC DOMIN COERCE DISCRIM ATTIT PWR WEALTH...POLICY RECORD 20. PAGE 14 H0285
NAT/G RIGID/FLEX RACE/REL

S64
BRADLEY C.P.,"THE FORMATION OF MALAYSIA." INDIA
NAT/G

S/ASIA POL/PAR VOL/ASSN TOP/EX LEGIT RACE/REL ORD/FREE 20. PAGE 20 H0398 CREATE COLONIAL MALAYSIA

S64
HIRAI N.,"SHINTO AND INTERNATIONAL PROBLEMS." SOCIETY NAT/G PLAN EDU/PROP RACE/REL PEACE ATTIT PERCEPT LOVE MORAL...HUM MYTH RECORD SAMP TREND STERTYP TOT/POP 20 UN CHINJAP SHINTO. PAGE 71 H1423 ASIA SECT

B65
ADAM T.R.,GOVERNMENT AND POLITICS IN AFRICA SOUTH OF THE SAHARA. AFR EUR+WWI CONSTN CULTURE INTELL POL/PAR TOP/EX LEGIT REGION DRIVE...OBS TREND CMN/WLTH 20. PAGE 3 H0062 NAT/G TIME/SEQ RACE/REL COLONIAL

B65
GHAI D.P.,PORTRAIT OF A MINORITY: ASIANS IN EAST AFRICA. S/ASIA TANZANIA UGANDA COLONIAL...SOC OBS PREDICT ANTHOL 20. PAGE 56 H1119 RACE/REL GP/REL CULTURE AFR

B65
GINIEWSKI P.,THE TWO FACES OF APARTHEID. AFR SOUTH/AFR STRATA AGRI INDUS COLONIAL PARTIC SOVEREIGN...CONCPT GOV/COMP NAT/COMP 19/20 NEGRO. PAGE 56 H1131 DISCRIM NAT/G RACE/REL STRUCT

B65
KUPER L.,AN AFRICAN BOURGEOISIE. SOUTH/AFR LAW INTELL NAT/G POL/PAR VOL/ASSN DISCRIM...POLICY 20. PAGE 89 H1783 RACE/REL SOC STRUCT

B65
MAIR L.,AN INTRODUCTION TO SOCIAL ANTHROPOLOGY. LAW STRATA FINAN FAM KIN SECT INT/TRADE RACE/REL ADJUST PRODUC...T 20. PAGE 101 H2023 SOC STRUCT CULTURE SOCIETY

B65
MEYER F.S.,THE AFRICAN NETTLE. SOUTH/AFR NAT/LISM SOVEREIGN...ANTHOL 20 EUROPE. PAGE 110 H2191 AFR COLONIAL RACE/REL ECO/UNDEV

B65
OBUKAR C.,THE MODERN AFRICAN. AGRI INDUS WORKER CAP/ISM EDU/PROP PARTIC RACE/REL NAT/LISM ALL/VALS MARXISM...SOC IDEA/COMP 20. PAGE 120 H2393 AFR ECO/UNDEV CULTURE SOVEREIGN

B65
PANJABI K.L.,THE CIVIL SERVANT IN INDIA. INDIA UK NAT/G CONSULT EX/STRUC REGION GP/REL RACE/REL 20. PAGE 123 H2462 ADMIN WORKER BIOG COLONIAL

B65
QURESHI I.H.,THE STRUGGLE FOR PAKISTAN. INDIA PAKISTAN UK CULTURE LEGIS DIPLOM EDU/PROP COLONIAL ATTIT SOVEREIGN 19/20 MUSLIM. PAGE 129 H2576 GP/REL RACE/REL WAR SECT

B65
ROTBERG R.I.,A POLITICAL HISTORY OF TROPICAL AFRICA. EX/STRUC DIPLOM INT/TRADE DOMIN ADMIN RACE/REL NAT/LISM PWR SOVEREIGN...GEOG TIME/SEQ BIBLIOG 1/20. PAGE 135 H2692 AFR CULTURE COLONIAL

B65
SHRIMALI K.L.,EDUCATION IN CHANGING INDIA. INDIA CULTURE DIPLOM FOR/AID GP/REL RACE/REL ATTIT SOC/INTEG 20 UNESCO CMN/WLTH. PAGE 143 H2866 EDU/PROP PROF/ORG ACADEM

B65
STERN F.,THE POLITICS OF CULTURAL DESPAIR. EUR+WWI GERMANY POL/PAR SECT RACE/REL STRANGE TOTALISM ...ART/METH MYTH BIBLIOG 20 JEWS. PAGE 149 H2980 CULTURE ATTIT NAT/LISM FASCISM

B65
VAN DEN BERGHE P.L.,SOUTH AFRICA: A STUDY IN CONFLICT. AFR CULTURE SOCIETY STRATA STRUCT COERCE SEGREGAT. PAGE 161 H3227 DOMIN RACE/REL DISCRIM

B65
VAN DEN BERGHE P.L.,AFRICA: SOCIAL PROBLEMS OF CHANGE AND CONFLICT. ELITES STRATA ECO/UNDEV KIN MUNIC DIPLOM GP/REL RACE/REL NAT/LISM...ANTHOL BIBLIOG 20. PAGE 161 H3228 SOC CULTURE AFR STRUCT

B65
VATCHER W.H. JR.,WHITE LAAGER: THE RISE OF AFRIKANER NATIONALISM. AFR SOUTH/AFR CULTURE TOTALISM 20. PAGE 162 H3235 NAT/LISM POL/PAR RACE/REL DISCRIM

L65
MATTHEWS D.G.,"A CURRENT BIBLIOGRAPHY ON ETHIOPIAN AFFAIRS: A SELECT BIBLIOGRAPHY FROM 1950-1964." ETHIOPIA LAW CULTURE ECO/UNDEV INDUS LABOR SECT FORCES DIPLOM CIVMIL/REL RACE/REL...LING STAT 20. PAGE 105 H2093 BIBLIOG/A ADMIN POL/PAR NAT/G

L65
MATTHEWS D.G.,"A CURRENT BIBLIOGRAPHY ON SUDANESE AFFAIRS; A SELECT BIBLIOGRAPHY FROM 1960-1964." SUDAN LAW CULTURE AGRI FINAN INDUS LABOR POL/PAR TEC/DEV FOR/AID RACE/REL LITERACY...LING 20. PAGE 105 H2094 BIBLIOG ECO/UNDEV NAT/G DIPLOM

S65
MULLER A.L.,"SOME NON-ECONOMIC DETERMINANTS OF THE ECONOMIC STATUS OF ASIANS IN AFRICA." AFR SOUTH/AFR CULTURE 20. PAGE 114 H2283 DISCRIM RACE/REL LABOR

SECT

B66
CADY J.F.,THAILAND, BURMA, LAOS AND CAMBODIA. FRANCE UK CULTURE NAT/G DOMIN GP/REL RACE/REL HABITAT...GEOG TREND CHINJAP BUDDHISM. PAGE 25 H0504 S/ASIA COLONIAL REGION SECT

B66
CROWDER M.,A SHORT HISTORY OF NIGERIA. AFR NIGERIA UK ECO/UNDEV CHIEF INT/TRADE RACE/REL NAT/LISM ORD/FREE...GEOG SOC CHARTS BIBLIOG 14/20. PAGE 36 H0711 COLONIAL NAT/G CULTURE

B66
DIAMOND S.,THE TRANSFORMATION OF EAST AFRICA. NAT/G SCHOOL CREATE PROB/SOLV COLONIAL REGION RACE/REL FEDERAL...SOC ANTHOL WORSHIP 20 AFRICA/E. PAGE 41 H0819 CULTURE AFR TEC/DEV INDUS

B66
KAUNDA K.,ZAMBIA: INDEPENDENCE AND BEYOND: THE SPEECHES OF KENNETH KAUNDA. AFR FUT ZAMBIA SOCIETY ECO/UNDEV NAT/G PROB/SOLV ECO/TAC ADMIN RACE/REL SOVEREIGN 20. PAGE 84 H1670 ORD/FREE COLONIAL CONSTN LEAD

B66
KEITH G.,THE FADING COLOUR BAR. AFR CENTRL/AFR UK ZAMBIA CULTURE SCHOOL EDU/PROP PERS/REL DISCRIM AGE ...AUD/VIS NAT/COMP SOC/INTEG 20 NEGRO. PAGE 84 H1682 RACE/REL STRUCT ATTIT NAT/G

B66
KEYES J.G.,A BIBLIOGRAPHY OF WESTERN LANGUAGE PUBLICATIONS CONCERNING NORTH VIETNAM IN THE CORNELL LIBRARY. VIETNAM/N NAT/G FORCES TEC/DEV DIPLOM LEAD RACE/REL...GEOG SOC 20. PAGE 85 H1700 BIBLIOG/A CULTURE ECO/UNDEV S/ASIA

B66
LEIBLER I.,SOVIET JEWRY AND HUMAN RIGHTS. USSR INTELL NAT/G DOMIN ATTIT 20 AUSTRAL JEWS. PAGE 93 H1865 DISCRIM RACE/REL MARXISM POL/PAR

B66
MCKAY V.,AFRICAN DIPLOMACY STUDIES IN THE DETERMINANTS OF FOREIGN POLICY. AFR SOUTH/AFR CULTURE NEUTRAL REGION SOVEREIGN...INT/LAW GOV/COMP ANTHOL 20. PAGE 107 H2138 ECO/UNDEV RACE/REL CIVMIL/REL DIPLOM

B66
MULLER C.F.J.,A SELECT BIBLIOGRAPHY OF SOUTH AFRICAN HISTORY; A GUIDE FOR HISTORICAL RESEARCH. SOUTH/AFR UK LAW CONSTN SOCIETY STRUCT AGRI SECT DIPLOM COLONIAL LEAD RACE/REL...POLICY 17/20 NEGRO. PAGE 114 H2284 BIBLIOG AFR NAT/G

B66
NOLTE E.,THREE FACES OF FASCISM. FRANCE GERMANY DOMIN LEGIT COERCE CROWD REV WAR GP/REL RACE/REL SOVEREIGN...GOV/COMP IDEA/COMP 19/20 HITLER/A MUSSOLIN/B MARX/KARL. PAGE 118 H2368 FASCISM TOTALISM NAT/G POL/PAR

B66
ROSNER J.,DER FASCHISMUS. AUSTRIA GERMANY ITALY STRATA NAT/G POL/PAR COERCE RACE/REL TOTALISM ATTIT AUTHORIT...IDEA/COMP 20 NAZI ANTI/SEMIT. PAGE 134 H2684 NAT/LISM FASCISM ORD/FREE WAR

C66
ROSENBERG C.G. JR.,"THE MYTH OF "MAU-MAU:" NATIONALISM IN KENYA." AFR CULTURE NAT/G POL/PAR COERCE REV RACE/REL ATTIT ORD/FREE SOVEREIGN...MYTH BIBLIOG 20. PAGE 134 H2678 NAT/LISM COLONIAL MAJORIT LEAD

C66
WINT G.,"ASIA: A HANDBOOK." ASIA S/ASIA INDUS LABOR SECT PRESS RACE/REL MARXISM...STAT CHARTS BIBLIOG 20. PAGE 169 H3388 ECO/UNDEV DIPLOM NAT/G SOCIETY

B67
CURTIN P.D.,AFRICA REMEMBERED. NIGERIA SENEGAL CULTURE DIPLOM INT/TRADE GP/REL RACE/REL...RECORD ANTHOL 18/19 NEGRO. PAGE 36 H0727 DOMIN ORD/FREE AFR DISCRIM

B67
FALL B.B.,HO CHI MINH ON REVOLUTION: SELECTED WRITINGS, 1920-66. COM VIETNAM ELITES NAT/G COERCE GUERRILLA RACE/REL MARXISM...MARXIST ANTHOL 20. PAGE 48 H0968 REV COLONIAL ECO/UNDEV S/ASIA

B67
FANON F.,TOWARD THE AFRICAN REVOLUTION. AFR FRANCE CULTURE ELITES LEAD REV GP/REL ORD/FREE SOVEREIGN 20. PAGE 49 H0969 COLONIAL DOMIN ECO/UNDEV RACE/REL

B67
FANON F.,BLACK SKIN, WHITE MASKS: THE EXPERIENCES OF A BLACK MAN IN A WHITE WORLD. CULTURE COLONIAL HAPPINESS ISOLAT STRANGE ATTIT HABITAT RIGID/FLEX SEX...BIOG STERTYP SOC/INTEG 20 NEGRO. PAGE 49 H0970 DISCRIM PERS/REL RACE/REL PSY

B67
FISHEL L.H. JR.,THE NEGRO AMERICAN: A DOCUMENTARY HISTORY. SOCIETY NAT/G ROLE...POLICY ANTHOL 15/20 NEGRO. PAGE 51 H1013 ORD/FREE DISCRIM RACE/REL STRATA

B67
HUTCHINS F.G.,THE ILLUSION OF PERMANENCE: BRITISH IMPERIALISM IN INDIA. INDIA UK CULTURE STRUCT NAT/G COLONIAL CONTROL

REV GP/REL RACE/REL ADJUST DISCRIM ATTIT MORAL PWR SOC/INTEG 18/20. PAGE 75 H1509 — SOVEREIGN CONSERVE

B67
KING M.L. JR.,WHERE DO WE GO FROM HERE: CHAOS OR COMMUNITY? MUNIC NAT/G PARTIC INGP/REL ALL/VALS ...POLICY CONCPT BIOG 20. PAGE 86 H1715 — RACE/REL DISCRIM STRUCT PWR

B67
LAMBERT W.E.,CHILDREN'S VIEWS OF FOREIGN PEOPLES: A CROSS-NATIONAL STUDY. UNIV CULTURE EDU/PROP RACE/REL ATTIT PERCEPT ROLE...STAT STAND/INT CHARTS GP/COMP NAT/COMP. PAGE 90 H1802 — AGE/C STRANGE GP/REL STERTYP

B67
MAZRUI A.A.,THE ANGLO-AFRICAN COMMONWEALTH; POLITICAL FRICTION AND CULTURAL FUSION. AFR INT/ORG VOL/ASSN CHIEF GP/REL INGP/REL RACE/REL NAT/LISM 20 CMN/WLTH EEC. PAGE 106 H2111 — COLONIAL SOVEREIGN DIPLOM CULTURE

B67
MUNGER E.S.,AFRIKANER AND AFRICAN NATIONALISM: SOUTH AFRICAN PARALLELS AND PARAMETERS. SOUTH/AFR WOR+45 CULTURE ELITES STRUCT NAT/G PROB/SOLV DOMIN CONTROL PERS/REL NAT/LISM...SOC 20. PAGE 115 H2289 — AFR RACE/REL

B67
NYERERE J.K.,FREEDOM AND UNITY/UHURU NA UMOJA: A SELECTION FROM WRITINGS AND SPEECHES, 1952-65. TANZANIA ELITES ECO/UNDEV INT/ORG NAT/G CREATE DIPLOM COLONIAL REGION RACE/REL...ANTHOL 20. PAGE 119 H2383 — SOVEREIGN AFR TREND ORD/FREE

B67
OLIVER R.,AFRICA SINCE 1800. AFR ISLAM CULTURE ECO/UNDEV SECT DOMIN RACE/REL DISCRIM SOVEREIGN 19/20. PAGE 121 H2414 — DIPLOM COLONIAL REGION

B67
THOMAS P.,DOWN THESE MEAN STREETS. GP/REL RACE/REL ADJUST...SOC SELF/OBS 20. PAGE 154 H3078 — DISCRIM KIN CULTURE BIOG

L67
CRIBBET J.E.,"SOME REFLECTIONS ON THE LAW OF LAND - A VIEW FROM SCANDINAVIA." DENMARK NETHERLAND NORWAY SWEDEN INDUS MUNIC NEIGH RACE/REL ATTIT HABITAT ...IDEA/COMP 20. PAGE 35 H0701 — LAW PLAN CONTROL NAT/G

L67
UNESCO,"APARTHEID." SOUTH/AFR STRUCT KIN SCHOOL SECT WORKER DOMIN EDU/PROP REGION RACE/REL ISOLAT 20. PAGE 158 H3164 — DISCRIM CULTURE COERCE COLONIAL

L67
WILBER L.A.,"THE GOVERNMENTAL STRUCTURE OF MISSISSIPPI: ITS STRENGTHS AND WEAKNESSES." AGRI LOC/G SCHOOL EX/STRUC LEGIS TOP/EX BUDGET CT/SYS APPORT RACE/REL...GOV/COMP 20 MISSISSIPP. PAGE 168 H3359 — CONSTN PROVS STAT CON/ANAL

S67
BRADLEY A.W.,"CONSTITUTION-MAKING IN UGANDA." UGANDA LAW CHIEF DELIB/GP LEGIS ADMIN EXEC PARL/PROC RACE/REL ORD/FREE...GOV/COMP 20. PAGE 20 H0397 — NAT/G CREATE CONSTN FEDERAL

S67
HAMMOND R.J.,"RACE ATTITUDES AND POLICIES IN PORTUGUESE AFRICA IN THE NINETEENTH AND TWENTIETH CENTURIES." AFR PORTUGAL NAT/G SECT EDU/PROP COLONIAL ATTIT RIGID/FLEX SEX MORAL RESPECT 19/20 NEGRO. PAGE 65 H1309 — POLICY RACE/REL DISCRIM SOCIETY

S67
IDENBURG P.J.,"POLITICAL STRUCTURAL DEVELOPMENT IN TROPICAL AFRICA." UK ECO/UNDEV KIN POL/PAR CHIEF EX/STRUC CREATE COLONIAL CONTROL REPRESENT RACE/REL ...MAJORIT TREND 20. PAGE 76 H1521 — AFR CONSTN NAT/G GOV/COMP

S67
RAUM O.,"THE MODERN LEADERSHIP GROUP AMONG THE SOUTH AFRICAN XHOSA." SOUTH/AFR SOCIETY SECT EX/STRUC REPRESENT GP/REL INGP/REL PERSON ...METH/COMP 17/20 XHOSA NEGRO. PAGE 130 H2596 — RACE/REL KIN LEAD CULTURE

S67
ROTBERG R.I.,"COLONIALISM AND AFTER: THE POLITICAL LITERATURE OF CENTRAL AFRICA - A BIBLIOGRAPHIC ESSAY." AFR CHIEF EX/STRUC REV INGP/REL RACE/REL SOVEREIGN 20. PAGE 135 H2693 — BIBLIOG/A COLONIAL DIPLOM NAT/G

S67
SNELLEN I.T.,"APARTHEID* CHECKS AND CHANGES." SOUTH/AFR NAT/G PROB/SOLV COLONIAL REGION TASK GP/REL RACE/REL EFFICIENCY PRIVIL ORD/FREE 20. PAGE 146 H2923 — DISCRIM NAT/LISM EQUILIB CONTROL

S67
THEROUX P.,"HATING THE ASIANS." TANZANIA UGANDA CONSTN INDUS NAT/G POL/PAR WORKER ECO/TAC HABITAT LOVE...POLICY GEOG 20 MIGRATION. PAGE 154 H3069 — AFR RACE/REL SOVEREIGN ATTIT

L68
CURRENT HISTORY,"AFRICA, 1968." ETHIOPIA GHANA NIGERIA SOUTH/AFR CULTURE ECO/UNDEV KIN SECT CHIEF EX/STRUC WAR WEAPON CHOOSE CIVMIL/REL...GOV/COMP 20 AFRICA/E. PAGE 36 H0724 — RACE/REL NAT/LISM FORCES AFR

S68
CHAPMAN A.R.,"THE CIVIL WAR IN NIGERIA." AFR NIGERIA NAT/G PLAN ECO/TAC EDU/PROP COERCE WAR GOV/REL INGP/REL ORD/FREE PWR WEALTH SOC/INTEG 20 BIAFRA. PAGE 29 H0579 — REV RACE/REL

S68
DUGARD J.,"THE REVOCATION OF THE MANDATE FOR SOUTH WEST AFRICA." SOUTH/AFR WOR+45 STRATA NAT/G DELIB/GP DIPLOM ADJUD SANCTION CHOOSE RACE/REL ...POLICY NAT/COMP 20 AFRICA/SW UN TRUST/TERR LEAGUE/NAT. PAGE 43 H0858 — AFR INT/ORG DISCRIM COLONIAL

S68
LAWRIE G.,"WHAT WILL CHANGE SOUTH AFRICA?" AFR SOUTH/AFR ELITES DOMIN CONTROL REPRESENT...TIME/SEQ TREND 20. PAGE 93 H1848 — RACE/REL DIPLOM NAT/G POLICY

B87
KINNEAR J.B.,PRINCIPLES OF CIVIL GOVERNMENT. MOD/EUR USA-45 CONSTN LOC/G EX/STRUC ADMIN PARL/PROC RACE/REL...CONCPT 18/19. PAGE 86 H1718 — POL/PAR NAT/G GOV/COMP REPRESENT

B99
DU BOIS W.E.B.,THE PHILADELPHIA NEGRO: A SOCIAL STUDY. CULTURE STRATA KIN CRIME SUFF ADJUST DISCRIM ISOLAT HABITAT HEREDITY ALL/VALS SOC/INTEG 17/19 NEGRO PHILADELPH. PAGE 42 H0851 — INGP/REL RACE/REL SOC CENSUS

B99
KINGSLEY M.H.,WEST AFRICAN STUDIES. GHANA NIGERIA SIER/LEONE LAW EXTR/IND SECT DIPLOM INT/TRADE DOMIN RACE/REL OWN HEALTH...SOC 19. PAGE 86 H1717 — AFR HEREDITY COLONIAL CULTURE

RADCLIFFE-BROWN A.R. H2577

RADIN P. H2578

RAE D. H2579

RAEFF M. H2580

RAF....ROYAL AIR FORCE

RAGANOV V. H0199

RAGHAVAN M.D. H2581

RAHMAN/TA....TUNKU ABDUL RAHMAN

RAHNER H. H2582

RAILROAD....RAILROADS AND RAILWAY SYSTEMS

B05
GRIFFIN A.P.C.,LIST OF BOOKS ON RAILROADS IN FOREIGN COUNTRIES. MOD/EUR ECO/DEV NAT/G CONTROL SOCISM...JURID 19/20 RAILROAD. PAGE 61 H1219 — BIBLIOG/A SERV/IND ADMIN DIST/IND

B08
THE GOVERNMENT OF SOUTH AFRICA (VOL. II). SOUTH/AFR STRATA EXTR/IND EX/STRUC TOP/EX BUDGET ADJUD ADMIN CT/SYS PRODUC...CORREL CENSUS 19 RAILROAD CIVIL/SERV POSTAL/SYS. PAGE 2 H0030 — CONSTN FINAN LEGIS NAT/G

B65
PARRIS H.W.,GOVERNMENT AND THE RAILWAYS IN NINETEENTH-CENTURY BRITAIN. UK DELIB/GP CONTROL LEAD CENTRAL 19 RAILROAD. PAGE 124 H2470 — DIST/IND NAT/G PLAN GP/REL

RAISON T. H2583

RAJARATAM/S....S. RAJARATAM

RAJASTHAN....RAJASTHAN

RAM J. H2584

RAMA C.M. H2585

RAMA RAO T.V. H0335

RAMAZANI R.K. H2586,H2587

RAMUNDO B.A. H2588

RANDALL F.B. H2589,H2590

RANDALL L. H2589

RANDOMNESS....SEE PROB/SOLV

RANKE/L....LEOPOLD VON RANKE

RANKING SYSTEMS....SEE SENIOR

RANKOVIC/A....ALEXANDER RANKOVIC, YUGOSLAVIA'S FORMER VICE PRESIDENT

RANNEY A. H2591

RANZ H. H0388

RAO K.V. H2592

RAPHAEL M. H2593

RAPPARD W.E. H2594

RATION....RATIONING

B20
COX H.,ECONOMIC LIBERTY. UNIV LAW INT/TRADE RATION TARIFFS RACE/REL SOCISM POLICY. PAGE 34 H0687
NAT/G ORD/FREE ECO/TAC PERSON

B39
VAN BILJON F.J.,STATE INTERFERENCE IN SOUTH AFRICA. SOUTH/AFR ECO/UNDEV AGRI INDUS WORKER RATION WEALTH ...JURID 20. PAGE 161 H3225
ECO/TAC POLICY INT/TRADE NAT/G

B61
BREWIS T.N.,CANADIAN ECONOMIC POLICY. CANADA BUDGET CAP/ISM INT/TRADE RATION TARIFFS TAX PRICE CONTROL ROUTINE FEDERAL INCOME PRODUC 20 GOLD/STAND. PAGE 20 H0412
ECO/DEV ECO/TAC NAT/G PLAN

B67
DALTON G.,TRIBAL AND PEASANT ECONOMIES. SOCIETY FINAN FAM INT/TRADE RATION ADJUST WEALTH...CHARTS ANTHOL BIBLIOG T. PAGE 37 H0738
SOC ECO/UNDEV NAT/COMP

S67
HASSAN M.F.,"THE SECOND FOUR-YEAR PLAN OF VENEZUELA." L/A+17C VENEZUELA AGRI INDUS NAT/G PLAN RATION CONTROL HABITAT...MATH STAT 20. PAGE 67 H1352
ECO/UNDEV FINAN BUDGET PROB/SOLV

RATIONAL....RATIONALITY

B21
WALLAS G.,HUMAN NATURE IN POLITICS (3RD ED.). UNIV NAT/G LEAD CHOOSE REPRESENT GP/REL NAT/LISM RATIONAL BIO/SOC HEREDITY ALL/VALS MAJORIT. PAGE 165 H3293
PSY DRIVE PERSON

B30
LASKI H.J.,LIBERTY IN THE MODERN STATE. UNIV SOCIETY STRATA CREATE BAL/PWR CONTROL RATIONAL ATTIT PWR 18/20. PAGE 91 H1828
CONCPT ORD/FREE NAT/G DOMIN

B39
OAKESHOTT M.,THE SOCIAL AND POLITICAL DOCTRINES OF CONTEMPORARY EUROPE. EUR+WWI RATIONAL CATHISM FASCISM MARXISM POPULISM...POLICY ANTHOL 20 NAZI. PAGE 120 H2392
IDEA/COMP GOV/COMP ALL/IDEOS NAT/G

B42
HEGEL G.W.F.,PHILOSOPHY OF RIGHT. UNIV FAM SECT CHIEF AGREE WAR MARRIAGE OWN ORD/FREE...POLICY CONCPT. PAGE 69 H1383
NAT/G LAW RATIONAL

B46
CASSIRER E.,THE MYTH OF THE STATE. WOR-45 SOCIETY RACE/REL RATIONAL PWR FASCISM...PHIL/SCI PSY LING TREND HEGEL/GWF MACHIAVELL. PAGE 28 H0557
MYTH CONCPT NAT/G IDEA/COMP

B47
BOWLE J.,WESTERN POLITICAL THOUGHT: AN HISTORICAL INTRODUCTION FROM THE ORIGINS TO ROUSSEAU. CONSTN NAT/G SECT CREATE RATIONAL ORD/FREE...SOC BIBLIOG/A. PAGE 19 H0391
ATTIT IDEA/COMP PHIL/SCI

B48
ROSENFARB J.,FREEDOM AND THE ADMINISTRATIVE STATE. NAT/G ROUTINE EFFICIENCY PRODUC RATIONAL UTIL ...TECHNIC WELF/ST MGT 20 BUREAUCRCY. PAGE 134 H2680
ECO/DEV INDUS PLAN WEALTH

C51
HAMMOND M.,"CITY-STATE AND WORLD STATE." CONSTN INTELL LOC/G LEGIT CENTRAL RATIONAL BIBLIOG. PAGE 65 H1308
NAT/G ATTIT REGION MEDIT-7

B55
FRIEDMAN G.,INDUSTRIAL SOCIETY: THE EMERGENCE OF THE HUMAN PROBLEMS OF AUTOMATION. UNIV CULTURE ECO/DEV TEC/DEV INGP/REL HAPPINESS RATIONAL UTOPIA ROLE...HUM SOC TIME/SEQ 20. PAGE 53 H1064
AUTOMAT ADJUST ALL/VALS CONCPT

C55
SANTAYANA G.,"REASON IN SOCIETY" IN G. SANTAYANA, THE LIFE OF REASON." INDUS FAM NAT/G WAR GP/REL HAPPINESS PRODUC LOVE WEALTH CONSERVE POPULISM CONCPT. PAGE 138 H2752
RATIONAL SOCIETY CULTURE ATTIT

B56
WEIL E.,PHILOSOPHIE POLITIQUE. UNIV CULTURE RATIONAL PERSON ROLE. PAGE 166 H3326
SOCIETY NAT/G MORAL

B58
EUSDEN J.D.,PURITANS, LAWYERS, AND POLITICS IN EARLY SEVENTEENTH-CENTURY ENGLAND. UK CT/SYS PARL/PROC RATIONAL PWR SOVEREIGN...IDEA/COMP BIBLIOG 17 PURITAN COMMON/LAW. PAGE 48 H0951
GP/REL SECT NAT/G LAW

B58
HENLE P.,LANGUAGE, THOUGHT AND CULTURE. CULTURE GP/REL PERCEPT...PSY TREND ANTHOL 20. PAGE 70 H1397
LING RATIONAL CONCPT SOC

B60
BARBU Z.,PROBLEMS OF HISTORICAL PSYCHOLOGY. GREECE MEDIT-7 UK CULTURE TEC/DEV ADJUST RATIONAL ATTIT PERCEPT...METH/CNCPT NEW/IDEA TIME/SEQ GEN/METH. PAGE 11 H0214
PERSON PSY HIST/WRIT IDEA/COMP

B61
NEWMAN R.P.,RECOGNITION OF COMMUNIST CHINA? A STUDY IN ARGUMENT. CHINA/COM NAT/G PROB/SOLV RATIONAL ...INT/LAW LOG IDEA/COMP BIBLIOG 20. PAGE 117 H2347
MARXISM ATTIT DIPLOM POLICY

B62
BINDER L.,IRAN: POLITICAL DEVELOPMENT IN A CHANGING SOCIETY. IRAN OP/RES REV GP/REL CENTRAL RATIONAL PWR...PHIL/SCI NAT/COMP GEN/LAWS 20. PAGE 17 H0337
LEGIT NAT/G ADMIN STRUCT

B62
MACPHERSON C.B.,THE POLITICAL THEORY OF POSSESSIVE INDIVIDUALISM. UK MARKET NAT/G PERS/REL RATIONAL ...IDEA/COMP 17/19 LOCKE/JOHN. PAGE 100 H2006
PHIL/SCI OWN

B62
MALINOWSKI B.,SEX, CULTURE, AND MYTH. UNIV SOCIETY FAM PERS/REL MARRIAGE RATIONAL HABITAT PERSON SUPEGO MORAL WORSHIP 20. PAGE 102 H2032
MYTH SECT SEX CULTURE

B64
RIES J.C.,THE MANAGEMENT OF DEFENSE: ORGANIZATION AND CONTROL OF THE US ARMED SERVICES. PROF/ORG DELIB/GP EX/STRUC LEGIS GOV/REL PERS/REL CENTRAL RATIONAL PWR...POLICY TREND GOV/COMP BIBLIOG. PAGE 131 H2626
FORCES ACT/RES DECISION CONTROL

B65
LARUS J.,COMPARATIVE WORLD POLITICS. ASIA INDIA WOR+45 WOR-45 BAL/PWR WAR PEACE RATIONAL MORAL PWR ...REALPOL INT/LAW MUSLIM. PAGE 91 H1825
GOV/COMP IDEA/COMP DIPLOM NAT/COMP

B66
MAC DONALD H.M.,THE INTELLECTUAL IN POLITICS. GERMANY PERU SWEDEN UK USSR NAT/G CONSULT PLAN EDU/PROP TASK INGP/REL EFFICIENCY RATIONAL ALL/VALS 20. PAGE 99 H1987
ALL/IDEOS INTELL POL/PAR PARTIC

S66
QUESTER G.H.,"ON THE IDENTIFICATION OF REAL AND PRETENDED COMMUNIST MILITARY DOCTRINE." ASIA USSR DETER WAR ATTIT DRIVE HEALTH TIME/SEQ. PAGE 129 H2574
RATIONAL PERCEPT NUC/PWR NAT/COMP

B67
PLISCHKE E.,CONDUCT OF AMERICAN DIPLOMACY (3RD REV. ED.). INT/ORG NAT/G PROB/SOLV FOR/AID...CHARTS BIBLIOG T 20 DEPT/STATE. PAGE 126 H2529
DIPLOM RATIONAL PLAN

S67
KROGER K.,"ZUR ENTWICKLUNG DER STAATSZWECKLEHRE IM 19 JAHRHUNDERT." GERMANY RATIONAL ATTIT...IDEA/COMP 19. PAGE 89 H1773
CONCPT NAT/G JURID OBJECTIVE

S67
SOLT L.F.,"PURITANISM, CAPITALISM, DEMOCRACY, AND THE NEW SCIENCE." NAT/G GP/REL CONSERVE...IDEA/COMP GEN/LAWS. PAGE 147 H2931
SECT CAP/ISM RATIONAL POPULISM

S68
HOOK S.,"THE ENLIGHTENMENT AND MARXISM." CULTURE SOCIETY RATIONAL ORD/FREE PLURISM SOCISM...CONCPT HIST/WRIT 18/19 MARX/KARL HEGEL/GWF ENLIGHTNMT. PAGE 73 H1462
IDEA/COMP MARXISM OBJECTIVE

RATZEL F. H2595

RAUM O. H2596

RAVKIN A. H2597

RAWLINSON H.G. H2598

RAY A. H2599

RAY J. H2600

RAYNER E.G. H0815

RAZAFIMBAHINY J. H2601

READ J.S. H2602

READ M. H2603

REAGAN/RON....RONALD REAGAN

S67
WILSON J.Q.,"A GUIDE TO REAGAN COUNTRY* THE POLITICAL CULTURE OF SOUTHERN CALIFORNIA." NEIGH PROVS PARTIC CHOOSE ADJUST CONSEN PERSON CONSERVE
CULTURE ATTIT MORAL

CALIFORNIA REAGAN/RON. PAGE 169 H3379

REALPOL....REALPOLITIK, PRACTICAL POLITICS

B45
CROCE B.,POLITICS AND MORALS. UNIV NAT/G ECO/TAC ORD/FREE MARXISM POPULISM SOCISM...REALPOL 15/20 HEGEL/GWF ROUSSEAU/J. PAGE 35 H0704 — MORAL GEN/LAWS IDEA/COMP

B49
VIERECK P.,CONSERVATISM REVISITED: THE REVOLT AGAINST REVOLT 1815-1949. EUR+WWI ELITES NAT/G FORCES PARTIC GOV/REL NAT/LISM...MAJORIT CONCPT GOV/COMP METTRNCH/K. PAGE 163 H3251 — CONSERVE MARXISM REALPOL

B65
LARUS J.,COMPARATIVE WORLD POLITICS. ASIA INDIA WOR+45 WOR-45 BAL/PWR WAR PEACE RATIONAL MORAL PWR ...REALPOL INT/LAW MUSLIM. PAGE 91 H1825 — GOV/COMP IDEA/COMP DIPLOM NAT/COMP

B65
MONTESQUIEU C DE S.,CONSIDERATIONS ON THE CAUSES OF THE GREATNESS OF THE ROMANS AND THEIR DECLINE (1748 TRANS. BY D. LOWENTHAL). ROMAN/EMP SECT CHIEF EX/STRUC FORCES LEGIS DOMIN WAR POPULISM...POLICY REALPOL ROME/ANC. PAGE 112 H2244 — NAT/G PWR COLONIAL MORAL

B67
FAY S.B.,THE ORIGINS OF THE WORLD WAR (2ND REV. ED. 2 VOLS.). NAT/G FORCES DIPLOM CONFER LEAD PEACE ...REALPOL GOV/COMP 19/20. PAGE 49 H0978 — MOD/EUR WAR REGION INT/ORG

S67
HEASMAN D.J.,"THE GIBRALTAR AFFAIR." SPAIN UK NAT/G BAL/PWR CONSEN NAT/LISM ATTIT...REALPOL 20. PAGE 69 H1378 — DIPLOM COLONIAL REGION

REALPOLITIK....SEE REALPOL

REAMAN G.E. H2604

REC/INT....RECORDING OF INTERVIEWS

B28
BUELL R.,THE NATIVE PROBLEM IN AFRICA. KIN LABOR LOC/G ECO/TAC ROUTINE ORD/FREE...REC/INT KNO/TEST CENSUS TREND CHARTS SOC/EXP STERTYP 20. PAGE 23 H0466 — AFR CULTURE

B53
HUNTER E.,BRAIN-WASHING IN RED CHINA. ASIA CHINA/COM CULTURE SOCIETY FORCES WAR TOTALISM ATTIT BIO/SOC DISPL DRIVE PERSON SUPEGO KNOWL ORD/FREE ...INT REC/INT COLD/WAR 20. PAGE 75 H1499 — EDU/PROP COERCE

B61
VON MERING O.,A GRAMMAR OF HUMAN VALUES. WOR+45 CULTURE FACE/GP NEIGH CREATE EDU/PROP LEGIT ATTIT DRIVE PERSON ORD/FREE...PSY SOC METH/CNCPT OBS RECORD INT REC/INT STAND/INT QU CHARTS VAL/FREE. PAGE 164 H3275 — SOCIETY MORAL

S65
GORDON M.,"THE SETTING FOR EUROPEAN ARMS CONTROLS* POLITICAL AND STRATEGIC CHOICES OF EUROPEAN ELITES." FRANCE GERMANY UK USA+45 USSR ARMS/CONT DETER ATTIT ORD/FREE...SAMP NAT/COMP NATO. PAGE 59 H1179 — REC/INT ELITES RISK WAR

RECALL....RECALL PROCEDURE

RECEIVE....RECEIVING (IN WELFARE SENSE)

N
INDIA: A REFERENCE ANNUAL. INDIA CULTURE COM/IND R+D FORCES PLAN RECEIVE EDU/PROP HEALTH...STAT CHARTS BIBLIOG 20. PAGE 1 H0017 — CONSTN LABOR INT/ORG

B59
ROSOLIO D.,TEN YEARS OF THE CIVIL SERVICE IN ISRAEL (1948-1958) (PAMPHLET). ISRAEL NAT/G RECEIVE 20. PAGE 134 H2685 — ADMIN WORKER GOV/REL PAY

B60
PETERSON W.C.,THE WELFARE STATE IN FRANCE. EUR+WWI FRANCE FUT STRATA PROB/SOLV TAX GIVE RECEIVE INCOME ORD/FREE PWR...CHARTS 20. PAGE 125 H2496 — NEW/LIB ECO/TAC WEALTH NAT/G

C61
MOODIE G.C.,"THE GOVERNMENT OF GREAT BRITAIN." UK LAW STRUCT LOC/G POL/PAR DIPLOM RECEIVE ADMIN COLONIAL CHOOSE...BIBLIOG 20 PARLIAMENT. PAGE 112 H2247 — NAT/G SOCIETY PARL/PROC GOV/COMP

B62
JENNINGS I.,PARTY POLITICS: THE STUFF OF POLITICS (VOL.III). UK NAT/G SECT CHIEF INT/TRADE RECEIVE COLONIAL GP/REL NAT/LISM ORD/FREE SOCISM 19/20 CHURCH/STA WHIG/PARTY. PAGE 80 H1607 — POL/PAR CONSTN PWR ALL/IDEOS

B63
COLUMBIA U SCHOOL OF LAW,PUBLIC INTERNATIONAL DEVELOPMENT FINANCING IN SENEGAL. SENEGAL FINAN DELIB/GP GIVE EFFICIENCY...CHARTS GOV/COMP ANTHOL 20. PAGE 32 H0636 — FOR/AID PLAN RECEIVE ECO/UNDEV

B63
STIFEL L.D.,THE TEXTILE INDUSTRY - A CASE STUDY OF INDUSTRIAL DEVELOPMENT IN THE PHILIPPINES (PAPER). PHILIPPINE WORKER CAP/ISM INT/TRADE TARIFFS RECEIVE PRICE ADMIN COST EFFICIENCY WEALTH...BIBLIOG 20. PAGE 149 H2986 — S/ASIA ECO/UNDEV PROC/MFG NAT/G

B64
AVASTHI A.,ASPECTS OF ADMINISTRATION. INDIA UK USA+45 FINAN ACADEM DELIB/GP LEGIS RECEIVE PARL/PROC PRIVIL...NAT/COMP 20. PAGE 9 H0183 — MGT ADMIN SOC/WK ORD/FREE

B64
RAPHAEL M.,PENSIONS AND PUBLIC SERVANTS. UK NAT/G PLAN INGP/REL COST EFFICIENCY ATTIT...POLICY 17/20 CIVIL/SERV. PAGE 130 H2593 — RECEIVE ADMIN INCOME AGE/O

B65
MEAGHER R.F.,PUBLIC INTERNATIONAL DEVELOPMENT FINANCING IN SUDAN. SUDAN FINAN DELIB/GP GIVE ...CHARTS GOV/COMP 20. PAGE 108 H2155 — FOR/AID PLAN RECEIVE ECO/UNDEV

B66
BUKHARIN N.,THE ABC OF COMMUNISM: A POPULAR EXPLANATION OF THE PROGRAM OF THE COMMUNIST PARTY OF RUSSIA. USSR STRATA SECT FORCES WORKER CAP/ISM RECEIVE EDU/PROP NAT/LISM TOTALISM 20. PAGE 23 H0468 — MARXISM CONCPT POLICY REV

B67
WARD L.,LESTER WARD AND THE WELFARE STATE. SOCIETY NAT/G CREATE RECEIVE EQUILIB UTOPIA HABITAT HEREDITY PERSON...POLICY SOC BIOG 19/20 WARD/LEST. PAGE 165 H3303 — ALL/VALS NEW/IDEA WELF/ST CONCPT

S67
JENCKS C.E.,"SOCIAL STATUS OF COAL MINERS IN BRITAIN SINCE NATIONALIZATION." UK STRATA STRUCT LABOR RECEIVE GP/REL INCOME OWN ATTIT HABITAT...MGT T 20. PAGE 80 H1600 — EXTR/IND WORKER CONTROL NAT/G

S67
MARWICK A.,"THE LABOUR PARTY AND THE WELFARE STATE IN BRITAIN, 19001948." UK SOCIETY STRUCT ECO/DEV WORKER CREATE PRICE CHOOSE WEALTH NEW/LIB SOCISM ...POLICY HEAL 20 PARLIAMENT LABOR/PAR. PAGE 104 H2074 — POL/PAR RECEIVE LEGIS NAT/G

RECIFE....RECIFE, BRAZIL

RECIPROCITY....SEE SANCTION

RECONSTRUCTION PERIOD....SEE CIVIL/WAR

RECORD....RECORDING OF DIRECT OBSERVATIONS

B20
HALDANE R.B.,BEFORE THE WAR. MOD/EUR SOCIETY INT/ORG NAT/G DELIB/GP PLAN DOMIN EDU/PROP LEGIT ADMIN COERCE ATTIT DRIVE MORAL ORD/FREE PWR...SOC CONCPT SELF/OBS RECORD BIOG TIME/SEQ. PAGE 64 H1282 — POLICY DIPLOM UK

B20
WEBB S.,INDUSTRIAL DEMOCRACY. UK PARTIC GP/REL ...SOC OBS RECORD CHARTS 18/20. PAGE 166 H3317 — LABOR NAT/G VOL/ASSN MAJORIT

B21
STUART G.H.,FRENCH FOREIGN POLICY. CONSTN INT/ORG NAT/G POL/PAR EX/STRUC FORCES PLAN ECO/TAC DOMIN EDU/PROP ADJUD COERCE ATTIT DRIVE RIGID/FLEX ALL/VALS...POLICY OBS RECORD BIOG TIME/SEQ TREND. PAGE 150 H3000 — MOD/EUR DIPLOM FRANCE

B31
DEKAT A.D.A.,COLONIAL POLICY. S/ASIA CULTURE EX/STRUC ECO/TAC DOMIN ADMIN COLONIAL ROUTINE SOVEREIGN WEALTH...POLICY MGT RECORD KNO/TEST SAMP. PAGE 39 H0785 — DRIVE PWR INDONESIA NETHERLAND

L37
NICOLSON H.,"THE MEANING OF PRESTIGE." EUR+WWI MOD/EUR UK CULTURE SOCIETY NAT/G DIPLOM DOMIN LEGIT ATTIT DRIVE PWR...METH/CNCPT RECORD TIME/SEQ GEN/METH CMN/WLTH TOT/POP 20. PAGE 118 H2351 — CONCPT STERTYP

B40
JORDAN W.K.,THE DEVELOPMENT OF RELIGIOUS TOLERATION IN ENGLAND. CHRIST-17C CULTURE SOCIETY LEGIT ATTIT RESPECT...POLICY CONCPT RECORD TIME/SEQ STERTYP GEN/LAWS TOT/POP 16/17. PAGE 82 H1635 — SECT UK

B41
HAYAKAWA S.I.,LANGUAGE IN ACTION. CULTURE INTELL SOCIETY KNOWL...METH/CNCPT LING LOG RECORD STERTYP GEN/METH TOT/POP 20. PAGE 68 H1366 — EDU/PROP SOC

B45
HUNTINGTON E.,MAINSPRINGS OF CIVILIZATION. UNIV CULTURE SOCIETY BIO/SOC PERSON KNOWL SKILL...PSY RECORD HIST/WRIT TREND CHARTS TOT/POP. PAGE 75 H1504 — SOC GEOG

B46
NICOLSON H.,THE CONGRESS OF VIENNA. MOD/EUR NAT/G FORCES BAL/PWR DOMIN LEGIT COERCE PERSON PWR ...RECORD TIME/SEQ STERTYP 19 CONG/VIENN. PAGE 118 — CONCPT POLICY DIPLOM

H2353

B48
MAUGHAM R.,NORTH AFRICAN NOTEBOOK. ALGERIA ISLAM LIBYA MOROCCO STRUCT ECO/UNDEV COLONIAL...SOC OBS AUD/VIS NAT/COMP WORSHIP 20 TUNIS. PAGE 105 H2102 SOCIETY RECORD NAT/LISM

B49
LASSWELL H.D.,LANGUAGE OF POLITICS. COM NAT/G ACT/RES ATTIT PWR...STAT RECORD CON/ANAL GEN/METH 20. PAGE 92 H1834 EDU/PROP METH/CNCPT

C50
STOKES W.S.,"HONDURAS: AN AREA STUDY IN GOVERNMENT." HONDURAS NAT/G POL/PAR COLONIAL CT/SYS ROUTINE CHOOSE REPRESENT...GEOG RECORD BIBLIOG 19/20. PAGE 149 H2988 CONSTN LAW L/A+17C ADMIN

B54
MALINOWSKI B.,MAGIC, SCIENCE AND RELIGION. AGRI KIN GP/REL ALL/VALS...MYTH OBS RECORD IDEA/COMP WORSHIP 20 NEW/GUINEA. PAGE 102 H2031 CULTURE ATTIT SOC

B55
RODNICK D.,THE NORWEGIANS: A STUDY IN NATIONAL CULTURE. NORWAY FAM INGP/REL PERS/REL AGE...PSY SOC SELF/OBS WORSHIP 20. PAGE 133 H2655 CULTURE INT RECORD ATTIT

B56
GOFFMAN E.,THE PRESENTATION OF SELF IN EVERYDAY LIFE. CULTURE INGP/REL ATTIT DRIVE...SOC OBS RECORD 20. PAGE 58 H1154 PERS/COMP PERSON PERCEPT ROLE

S57
HAILEY,"TOMORROW IN AFRICA." CONSTN SOCIETY LOC/G NAT/G DOMIN ADJUD ADMIN GP/REL DISCRIM NAT/LISM ATTIT MORAL ORD/FREE...PSY SOC CONCPT OBS RECORD TREND GEN/LAWS CMN/WLTH 20. PAGE 64 H1277 AFR PERSON ELITES RACE/REL

B58
GLUCKMAN M.,ANALYSIS OF A SOCIAL SITUATION IN MODERN ZULULAND. AFR PERS/REL ADJUST DISCRIM EQUILIB NAT/LISM...SOC RECORD AUD/VIS 20 ZULULAND. PAGE 57 H1146 CULTURE RACE/REL STRUCT GP/REL

B60
BRZEZINSKI Z.K.,THE SOVIET BLOC-UNITY AND CONFLICT. COM USSR CONSTN DOMIN ADMIN TOTALISM PWR...SOC MYTH RECORD TREND STERTYP GEN/LAWS GEN/METH TOT/POP 20. PAGE 23 H0458 ATTIT EDU/PROP

B60
CARTER G.M.,INDEPENDENCE FOR AFRICA. AFR FUT SOCIETY STRATA ECO/DEV POL/PAR DELIB/GP PLAN DOMIN EDU/PROP COLONIAL REGION ATTIT DRIVE SOVEREIGN ...RECORD INT TIME/SEQ CHARTS 20. PAGE 27 H0544 NAT/G PWR NAT/LISM

S60
WOLFE T.W.,"KHRUSHCHEV'S DISARMAMENT STRATEGY." COM NAT/G TOP/EX PLAN BAL/PWR DIPLOM ARMS/CONT COERCE ATTIT...POLICY CONCPT RECORD TREND CON/ANAL COLD/WAR 20 KHRUSH/N. PAGE 170 H3401 PWR GEN/LAWS USSR

B61
FIELD H.,ANCIENT AND MODERN MAN IN SOUTHWESTERN ASIA: II. CULTURE SOCIETY...CLASSIF MATH GP/COMP NAT/COMP 20. PAGE 50 H0992 STAT CHARTS PHIL/SCI RECORD

B61
GOULD S.H.,SCIENCES IN COMMUNIST CHINA. CHINA/COM FUT INDUS NAT/G TOTALISM...RECORD TOT/POP 20. PAGE 59 H1187 ASIA TEC/DEV

B61
GUEVARA E.,GUERRILLA WARFARE. L/A+17C ECO/UNDEV NAT/G POL/PAR VOL/ASSN PLAN DOMIN REV DRIVE PWR WEALTH...NEW/IDEA RECORD BIOG COLD/WAR MARX/KARL OAS 20. PAGE 62 H1247 FORCES COERCE GUERRILLA CUBA

B61
KISSINGER H.A.,THE NECESSITY FOR CHOICE. FUT USA+45 ECO/UNDEV NAT/G PLAN BAL/PWR ECO/TAC ARMS/CONT DETER NUC/PWR ATTIT...POLICY CONCPT RECORD GEN/LAWS COLD/WAR 20. PAGE 87 H1728 TOP/EX TREND DIPLOM

B61
MUNGER E.S.,AFRICAN FIELD REPORTS 1952-1961. SOUTH/AFR SOCIETY ECO/UNDEV NAT/G POL/PAR COLONIAL EXEC PARL/PROC GUERRILLA RACE/REL ALL/IDEOS...SOC AUD/VIS 20. PAGE 114 H2288 AFR DISCRIM RECORD

B61
TURNBULL C.M.,THE FOREST PEOPLE. EATING GP/REL INGP/REL RACE/REL ISOLAT HABITAT HEREDITY...GEOG SOC LING DICTIONARY WORSHIP 20 CONGO NEGRO BA/MBUTI. PAGE 157 H3138 AFR CULTURE KIN RECORD

B61
VON MERING O.,A GRAMMAR OF HUMAN VALUES. WOR+45 CULTURE FACE/GP NEIGH CREATE EDU/PROP LEGIT ATTIT DRIVE PERSON ORD/FREE...PSY SOC METH/CNCPT OBS RECORD INT REC/INT STAND/INT QU CHARTS VAL/FREE. PAGE 164 H3275 SOCIETY MORAL

B62
JOHNSON J.J.,THE ROLE OF THE MILITARY IN UNDERDEVELOPED COUNTRIES. AFR BURMA INDONESIA ISLAM ISRAEL L/A+17C S/ASIA THAILAND CULTURE ECO/UNDEV KIN PROVS CONSULT ACT/RES COERCE REV DRIVE RIGID/FLEX ORD/FREE...RECORD ANTHOL 20. PAGE 81 H1622 FORCES CONCPT

B62
LEGUM C.,PAN-AFRICANISM: A SHORT POLITICAL GUIDE. ISLAM CULTURE INTELL ECO/DEV NAT/G POL/PAR DELIB/GP PLAN EDU/PROP FEDERAL NAT/LISM ATTIT DRIVE PERSON ...RECORD TIME/SEQ CHARTS STERTYP 20. PAGE 93 H1861 AFR CONCPT

B63
KRAEHE E.,METTERNICH'S GERMAN POLICY: THE CONTEST WITH NAPOLEON, 1799-1814, VOL. 1. FRANCE MOD/EUR NAT/G CONSULT TOP/EX PLAN BAL/PWR DOMIN COERCE ATTIT DRIVE PERCEPT PERSON SKILL...CONCPT RECORD TIME/SEQ TREND 18/19. PAGE 88 H1764 BIOG GERMANY DIPLOM

B63
STIRNIMANN H.,NGUNI UND GNONI; EINE KULTURGESCHICHTLICHE STUDIE (ACTA ETHNOLOGICA ET LINGUISTICA, NUMBER 6). AFR MALAWI SOUTH/AFR FORCES HABITAT...RECORD CHARTS BIBLIOG WORSHIP 19/20 NATAL. PAGE 149 H2987 CULTURE GP/COMP SOCIETY

S63
ANTHON C.G.,"THE END OF THE ADENAUER ERA." EUR+WWI GERMANY/W CONSTN EX/STRUC CREATE DIPLOM LEGIT ATTIT PERSON ALL/VALS...RECORD 20 ADENAUER/K. PAGE 7 H0144 NAT/G TOP/EX BAL/PWR GERMANY

S63
GROSSER A.,"FRANCE AND GERMANY IN THE ATLANTIC COMMUNITY." INT/ORG NAT/G TOP/EX DIPLOM REGION PEACE ATTIT ORD/FREE PWR...CONCPT RECORD TIME/SEQ GEN/LAWS VAL/FREE COLD/WAR 20. PAGE 62 H1234 EUR+WWI VOL/ASSN FRANCE GERMANY

S63
MONROE A.D.,"BRITAIN AND THE EUROPEAN COMMUNITY." EUR+WWI FRANCE NAT/G DELIB/GP TOP/EX ECO/TAC DOMIN PWR...POLICY RECORD GEN/LAWS EEC EFTA 20 EFTA CMN/WLTH. PAGE 112 H2241 VOL/ASSN ATTIT UK

S63
STAAR R.F.,"HOW STRONG IS THE SOVIET BLOC." COM USSR ECO/DEV NAT/G DELIB/GP ECO/TAC RIGID/FLEX ...CONCPT RECORD CHARTS 20. PAGE 148 H2964 FORCES MYTH TOTALISM

S63
TANG P.S.H.,"SINO-SOVIET TENSIONS." ASIA CHINA/COM COM CUBA KOREA/N VIETNAM/N NAT/G VOL/ASSN DELIB/GP PEACE PERCEPT PWR...METH/CNCPT MYTH RECORD TREND GEN/LAWS 20. PAGE 152 H3041 ACT/RES EDU/PROP REV

B64
FRANCK T.M.,EAST AFRICAN UNITY THROUGH LAW. MALAWI TANZANIA UGANDA UK ZAMBIA CONSTN INT/ORG NAT/G ADMIN ROUTINE TASK NAT/LISM ATTIT SOVEREIGN ...RECORD IDEA/COMP NAT/COMP. PAGE 52 H1048 AFR FEDERAL REGION INT/LAW

B64
FRIEDLAND W.H.,AFRICAN SOCIALISM. ECO/UNDEV MARKET LABOR NAT/G POL/PAR PLAN CAP/ISM ECO/TAC EDU/PROP CHOOSE ATTIT DRIVE PWR WEALTH...POLICY CONCPT RECORD STERTYP 20. PAGE 53 H1063 AFR SOCISM

B64
GREEN M.M.,IBO VILLAGE AFFAIRS. AFR FORCES PERS/REL ADJUST ISOLAT ATTIT HABITAT PERSON ALL/VALS...JURID RECORD SOC/INTEG 20 IBO. PAGE 60 H1207 MUNIC CULTURE ECO/UNDEV SOC

B64
US HOUSE COMM BANKING-CURR,INTERNATIONAL DEVELOPMENT ASSOCIATION ACT AMENDMENT. CHINA/COM USA+45 USSR FINAN FORCES LEGIS DIPLOM CONFER EFFICIENCY...CHARTS GOV/COMP 20 PRESIDENT CONGRESS INTL/DEV. PAGE 160 H3196 BAL/PAY FOR/AID RECORD ECO/TAC

B64
VOELKMANN K.,HERRSCHER VON MORGEN? BAL/PWR COLONIAL NEUTRAL REGION RACE/REL ALL/VALS SOVEREIGN...RECORD 20 COLD/WAR THIRD/WRLD. PAGE 163 H3259 DIPLOM ECO/UNDEV CONTROL NAT/COMP

B64
WAINHOUSE D.W.,REMNANTS OF EMPIRE: THE UNITED NATIONS AND THE END OF COLONIALISM. FUT PORTUGAL WOR+45 NAT/G CONSULT DOMIN LEGIT ADMIN ROUTINE ATTIT ORD/FREE...POLICY JURID RECORD INT TIME/SEQ UN CMN/WLTH 20. PAGE 164 H3287 INT/ORG TREND COLONIAL

B64
WHITE D.S.,SEEDS OF DISCORD. EUR+WWI FRANCE NAT/G VOL/ASSN FORCES DIPLOM DOMIN NAT/LISM DISPL RIGID/FLEX PWR...RECORD INT BIOG 20 DEGAULLE/C ROOSEVLT/F CHURCHLL/W HULL. PAGE 167 H3347 TOP/EX ATTIT

S64
BENSON M.,"SOUTH AFRICA AND WORLD OPINION." AFR SOUTH/AFR INTELL SOCIETY TOP/EX ECO/TAC DOMIN COERCE DISCRIM ATTIT PWR WEALTH...POLICY RECORD 20. PAGE 14 H0285 NAT/G RIGID/FLEX RACE/REL

S64
CLIFFE L.,"TANGANYIKA'S TWO YEARS OF INDEPENDENCE." AFR INDUS MARKET NAT/G POL/PAR DELIB/GP CREATE ECO/TAC LEGIT DRIVE ALL/VALS...METH/CNCPT RECORD 20 TANGANYIKA. PAGE 30 H0604 ECO/UNDEV PLAN

S64
HIRAI N.,"SHINTO AND INTERNATIONAL PROBLEMS." SOCIETY NAT/G PLAN EDU/PROP RACE/REL PEACE ATTIT PERCEPT LOVE MORAL...HUM MYTH RECORD SAMP TREND STERTYP TOT/POP 20 UN CHINJAP SHINTO. PAGE 71 H1423 ASIA SECT

S64
JOHNSON K.F.,"CAUSAL FACTORS IN LATIN AMERICAN POLITICAL INSTABILITY." CULTURE NAT/G VOL/ASSN L/A+17C PERCEPT

EX/STRUC FORCES EDU/PROP LEGIT ADMIN COERCE REV ATTIT KNOWL PWR...STYLE RECORD CHARTS WORK 20. PAGE 81 H1624 — ELITES

S64
LEVI W.,"INDIAN NEUTRALISM RECONSIDERED." ASIA CHINA/COM S/ASIA SOCIETY NAT/G ACT/RES LEGIT NEUTRAL COERCE ATTIT DRIVE PERCEPT RIGID/FLEX HEALTH LOVE PWR...DECISION RECORD TREND STERTYP 20. PAGE 95 H1896 — ORD/FREE CONCPT INDIA

S64
POWELL R.L.,"COMMUNIST CHINA'S MILITARY POTENTIAL." ASIA CHINA/COM NAT/G EX/STRUC EDU/PROP COERCE GUERRILLA NUC/PWR WAR...RECORD CON/ANAL 20. PAGE 128 H2551 — FORCES PWR

S64
SWEARER H.R.,"AFTER KHRUSHCHEV: WHAT NEXT." COM FUT USSR CONSTN ELITES NAT/G POL/PAR CHIEF DELIB/GP LEGIS DOMIN LEAD...RECORD TREND STERTYP GEN/METH 20. PAGE 151 H3016 — EX/STRUC PWR

S64
TOUVAL S.,"THE SOMALI REPUBLIC." AFR ISLAM SOMALIA FAM KIN NAT/G CREATE FOR/AID LEGIT ATTIT ALL/VALS ...RECORD TREND 20. PAGE 156 H3119 — ECO/UNDEV RIGID/FLEX

B65
ADENAUER K.,MEINE ERINNERUNGEN, 1945-53 (VOL. I), 1953-55 (VOL. II). EUR+WWI GERMANY CHIEF FORCES PROB/SOLV DIPLOM ARMS/CONT INGP/REL PEACE SOVEREIGN ...OBS/ENVIR RECORD 20. PAGE 3 H0069 — NAT/G BIOG SELF/OBS

B65
APPLEMAN P.,THE SILENT EXPLOSION. WOR+45 ECO/DEV ECO/UNDEV PLAN HEALTH ALL/IDEOS CATHISM...POLICY STAT RECORD GP/COMP IDEA/COMP NAT/COMP 20 BIRTH/CON COM/PARTY. PAGE 7 H0148 — GEOG CENSUS AGRI BIO/SOC

B65
TILLY C.,MEASURING POLITICAL UPHEAVAL* RESEARCH MONOGRAPH NO. 19. FRANCE INDUS NAT/G FORCES WORKER ...GEOG RECORD EXHIBIT GEN/METH BIBLIOG INDEX. PAGE 155 H3095 — CLASSIF QUANT COERCE REV

B65
WHITEMAN M.M.,DIGEST OF INTERNATIONAL LAW* VOLUME 5, DEPARTMENT OF STATE PUBLICATION 7873. USA+45 WOR+45 OP/RES...CONCPT CLASSIF RECORD IDEA/COMP. PAGE 167 H3353 — INT/LAW NAT/G NAT/COMP

L65
SCHAFFER B.B.,"THE CONCEPT OF PREPARATION* SOME QUESTIONS ABOUT THE TRANSFER OF SYSTEMS OF GOVERNMENT." AFR ASIA CANADA ELITES NAT/G POL/PAR COLONIAL RIGID/FLEX IDEA/COMP. PAGE 138 H2769 — ECO/UNDEV UK RECORD

S65
BRANDENBURG F.,"THE RELEVANCE OF MEXICAN EXPERIENCE TO LATIN AMERICAN DEVELOPMENT." BRAZIL CHILE VENEZUELA STRUCT ECO/UNDEV AGRI CREATE ECO/TAC ...STAT RECORD MEXIC/AMER ARGEN COLOMB. PAGE 20 H0405 — L/A+17C GOV/COMP

S65
STAAR R.F.,"RETROGRESSION IN POLAND." COM USSR AGRI INDUS NAT/G CREATE EDU/PROP TOTALISM RIGID/FLEX ORD/FREE PWR SOCISM...RECORD CHARTS 20. PAGE 148 H2965 — TOP/EX ECO/TAC POLAND

B66
ELLIS A.B.,THE EWE-SPEAKING PEOPLES OF THE SLAVE COAST OF WEST AFRICA. AFR FORCES ADJUST...LING RECORD GP/COMP WORSHIP 20 AFRICA/W DEITY. PAGE 45 H0910 — MYTH CULTURE HABITAT

B66
FARWELL G.,MASK OF ASIA: THE PHILIPPINES. PHILIPPINE SECT DIPLOM ATTIT...SOC RECORD PREDICT BIBLIOG 20. PAGE 49 H0974 — S/ASIA CULTURE

B66
RISTIC D.N.,YUGOSLAVIA'S REVOLUTION OF 1941. EUR+WWI YUGOSLAVIA NAT/G WAR ORD/FREE...RECORD BIBLIOG 20 HITLER/A TREATY. PAGE 132 H2633 — REV ATTIT FASCISM DIPLOM

L66
KRENZ F.E.,"THE REFUGEE AS A SUBJECT OF INTERNATIONAL LAW." FUT LAW NAT/G CREATE ADJUD ISOLAT STRANGE...RECORD UN. PAGE 88 H1766 — INT/LAW DISCRIM NEW/IDEA

S66
HEAPHEY J.,"THE ORGANIZATION OF EGYPT* INADEQUACIES OF A NONPOLITICAL MODEL FOR NATION-BUILDING." STRATA NAT/G CREATE PROB/SOLV ECO/TAC NAT/LISM SOCISM RECORD. PAGE 69 H1377 — UAR ECO/UNDEV OBS

S66
KAPIL R.L.,"ON THE CONFLICT POTENTIAL OF INHERITED BOUNDARIES IN AFRICA." MOD/EUR MOROCCO UAR EX/STRUC DIPLOM LEGIT REGION ADJUST...RECORD NAT/COMP GEN/LAWS. PAGE 83 H1658 — AFR COLONIAL PREDICT GEOG

S66
SMITH D.D.,"MODAL ATTITUDE CLUSTERS* A SUPPLEMENT FOR THE STUDY OF NATIONAL CHARACTER." CULTURE NAT/G PERCEPT...SOC NEW/IDEA MODAL RECORD GEN/METH. PAGE 145 H2906 — ATTIT PERSON PSY CONCPT

S66
TOUVAL S.,"AFRICA'S FRONTIERS* REACTIONS TO A COLONIAL LEGACY." L/A+17C CONFER ADJUD COLONIAL APPORT CONSEN NAT/LISM RESPECT...RECORD NAT/COMP. PAGE 156 H3120 — AFR GEOG SOVEREIGN WAR

B67
CURTIN P.D.,AFRICA REMEMBERED. NIGERIA SENEGAL CULTURE DIPLOM INT/TRADE GP/REL RACE/REL...RECORD ANTHOL 18/19 NEGRO. PAGE 36 H0727 — DOMIN ORD/FREE AFR DISCRIM

S67
WRAITH R.E.,"ADMINISTRATIVE CHANGE IN THE NEW AFRICA." AFR LG/CO ADJUD INGP/REL PWR...RECORD GP/COMP 20. PAGE 171 H3416 — ADMIN NAT/G LOC/G ECO/UNDEV

RECORDING OF INTERVIEWS....SEE REC/INT

RECORDS....SEE OLD/STOR

RECTITUDE....SEE MORAL

RED/GUARD....RED GUARD

REDFIELD R. H2605,H2606

REDFIELD/R....ROBERT REDFIELD

C60
HOSELITZ B.,"THE ROLE OF CITIES IN THE ECONOMIC GROWTH OF UNDERDEVELOPED COUNTRIES" IN "SOCIOLOGICAL ASPECTS OF ECONOMIC GROWTH"(BMR). CULTURE LOC/G ACT/RES...SOC IDEA/COMP METH/COMP METH 14/20 REDFIELD/R. PAGE 74 H1474 — METH/CNCPT MUNIC TEC/DEV ECO/UNDEV

REED W.A. H2607

REED/STAN....JUSTICE STANLEY REED

REES D. H2608

REFERENDUM....REFERENDUM; SEE ALSO PARTIC

REFORMERS....REFORMERS

B14
LEVINE L.,SYNDICALISM IN FRANCE (2ND ED.). FRANCE LAW SOCIETY ECO/DEV NAT/G ECO/TAC LEAD ATTIT ...POLICY CONCPT STAT BIBLIOG 18/20 REFORMERS. PAGE 95 H1902 — LABOR INDUS SOCISM REV

B27
GOOCH G.P.,ENGLISH DEMOCRATIC IDEAS IN THE SEVENTEENTH CENTURY (2ND ED.). UK LAW SECT FORCES DIPLOM LEAD PARL/PROC REV ATTIT AUTHORIT...ANARCH CONCPT 17 PARLIAMENT CMN/WLTH REFORMERS. PAGE 58 H1167 — IDEA/COMP MAJORIT EX/STRUC CONSERVE

B57
PLAYFAIR G.,THE OFFENDERS: THE CASE AGAINST LEGAL VENGEANCE. UNIV LAW SOCIETY NAT/G PROB/SOLV DEATH PERSON ORD/FREE...HEAL INT/LAW BIBLIOG 20 REFORMERS. PAGE 126 H2524 — CRIME TEC/DEV SANCTION CT/SYS

B60
BANERJEE D.N.,OUR FUNDAMENTAL RIGHTS: THEIR NATURE AND EXTENT (AS JUDICIALLY DETERMINED). INDIA UK CULTURE STRATA NAT/G WORKER EDU/PROP CONTROL DISCRIM OWN...IDEA/COMP WORSHIP 20 REFORMERS COMMONWLTH. PAGE 10 H0207 — CONSTN ORD/FREE LEGIS POLICY

B63
GRIMOND J.,THE LIBERAL CHALLENGE. UK SOCIETY INDUS POL/PAR LEGIS PLAN CAP/ISM DIPLOM EDU/PROP GOV/REL CONSERVE 20 PARLIAMENT REFORMERS. PAGE 61 H1227 — NAT/G NEW/LIB ECO/DEV POLICY

B64
UTECHIN S.V.,RUSSIAN POLITICAL THOUGHT: A CONCISE HISTORY. RUSSIA USSR INTELL STRATA POL/PAR SECT LEGIS EDU/PROP REV WAR MARXISM...ANARCH BIBLIOG 9/20 REFORMERS SLAVS. PAGE 161 H3218 — IDEA/COMP ATTIT ALL/IDEOS NAT/G

B64
WERTHEIM W.F.,EAST-WEST PARALLELS. INDONESIA S/ASIA NAT/G SECT...TIME/SEQ METH REFORMERS S/EASTASIA. PAGE 167 H3334 — SOC ECO/UNDEV CULTURE NAT/LISM

B67
PIKE F.B.,FREEDOM AND REFORM IN LATIN AMERICA. BRAZIL URUGUAY CONSTN CULTURE SECT DIPLOM EDU/PROP PARTIC DRIVE ALL/VALS CATHISM...GEOG ANTHOL BIBLIOG REFORMERS BOLIV. PAGE 126 H2511 — L/A+17C ORD/FREE ECO/UNDEV REV

REGION....REGIONALISM

N
BULLETIN ANALYTIQUE DE DOCUMENTATION POLITIQUE, ECONOMIQUE, ET SOCIAL CONTEMPORAIRE. FRANCE WOR+45 SOCIETY ECO/DEV ECO/UNDEV INT/ORG LOC/G PROB/SOLV FOR/AID LEAD REGION SOC. PAGE 1 H0002 — BIBLIOG/A DIPLOM NAT/COMP NAT/G

N
AFRICAN BIBLIOGRAPHIC CENTER,A CURRENT BIBLIOGRAPHY ON AFRICAN AFFAIRS. LAW CULTURE ECO/UNDEV LABOR SECT DIPLOM FOR/AID COLONIAL NAT/LISM...LING 20. PAGE 4 H0075 — BIBLIOG/A AFR NAT/G REGION

N
ASIA FOUNDATION,LIBRARY NOTES. LAW CONSTN CULTURE SOCIETY ECO/UNDEV INT/ORG NAT/G COLONIAL LEAD REGION NAT/LISM ATTIT 20 UN. PAGE 9 H0176
BIBLIOG/A ASIA S/ASIA DIPLOM

N
CORNELL UNIVERSITY LIBRARY,SOUTHEAST ASIA ACCESSIONS LIST. LAW SOCIETY STRUCT ECO/UNDEV POL/PAR TEC/DEV DIPLOM LEAD REGION. PAGE 34 H0671
BIBLIOG S/ASIA NAT/G CULTURE

B13
SIEGFRIED A.,TABLEAU POLITIQUE DE LA FRANCE DE L'OUEST SOUS LA TROISIEME REPUBLIQUE. FRANCE STRATA STRUCT NAT/G POL/PAR PROVS REGION GOV/REL ATTIT PWR ...TREND TIME 19. PAGE 143 H2869
SOC GEOG SOCIETY

B19
DE MAN H.,THE REMAKING OF A MIND. EUR+WWI NAT/G ECO/TAC REGION ORD/FREE SOCISM...BIOG 20 WWI EUROPE. PAGE 38 H0762
PSY WAR SELF/OBS PARTIC

N19
WILSON T.,FINANCIAL ASSISTANCE WITH REGIONAL DEVELOPMENT (PAMPHLET). CANADA INDUS NAT/G PLAN TAX CONTROL COST EFFICIENCY...POLICY CHARTS 20. PAGE 169 H3382
FINAN ECO/TAC REGION GOV/REL

B20
COLE G.D.H.,SOCIAL THEORY. CULTURE LOC/G SECT REGION REPRESENT ATTIT DRIVE...PSY SOC BIBLIOG. PAGE 31 H0621
CONCPT NAT/G PHIL/SCI

B20
MACIVER R.M.,COMMUNITY: A SOCIOLOGICAL STUDY; BEING AN ATTEMPT TO SET OUT THE FUNDAMENTAL LAWS OF SOCIAL LIFE. UNIV STRUCT NAT/G CONTROL WAR BIO/SOC ...PSY SOC CONCPT GEN/LAWS. PAGE 100 H1996
REGION SOCIETY GP/REL

B22
FICHTE J.G.,ADDRESSES TO THE GERMAN NATION. GERMANY PRUSSIA ELITES NAT/G SECT CREATE INT/TRADE HEREDITY ...ART/METH LING 19 FRANK/PARL. PAGE 50 H0989
NAT/LISM CULTURE EDU/PROP REGION

B25
WILLIAMS B.,THE SELBORNE MEMORANDUM. AFR FUT SOUTH/AFR UK NAT/G BUDGET DIPLOM REGION GOV/REL SOVEREIGN...POLICY CHARTS 20 UNIFICA SELBORNE/W. PAGE 168 H3365
COLONIAL PROVS

B30
HULL W.I.,INDIA'S POLITICAL CRISIS. INDIA UK INT/ORG LABOR SECT DELIB/GP LEGIS DIPLOM NEUTRAL REGION CROWD GOV/REL MAJORITY ATTIT 20 NEHRU/J GANDHI/M COMMONWLTH. PAGE 75 H1492
ORD/FREE NAT/G COLONIAL NAT/LISM

B30
SMUTS J.C.,AFRICA AND SOME WORLD PROBLEMS. RHODESIA SOUTH/AFR CULTURE ECO/UNDEV INDUS INT/ORG SECT PROB/SOLV REGION GOV/REL DISCRIM ATTIT 19/20 LEAGUE/NAT LIVNGSTN/D NEGRO. PAGE 146 H2921
LEGIS AFR COLONIAL RACE/REL

B36
RAPPARD W.E.,THE GOVERNMENT OF SWITZERLAND. SWITZERLND INT/ORG POL/PAR EX/STRUC DIPLOM NEUTRAL PARL/PROC REGION WAR HABITAT SOVEREIGN...NAT/COMP SOC/INTEG 20 LEAGUE/NAT WWI. PAGE 130 H2594
CONSTN NAT/G CULTURE FEDERAL

B39
BENES E.,DEMOCRACY TODAY AND TOMORROW. EUR+WWI SOCIETY ECO/DEV DELIB/GP ECO/TAC REGION ATTIT PWR FASCISM...CONCPT LEAGUE/NAT 20. PAGE 14 H0281
NAT/G LEGIT NAT/LISM

B39
MILLER P.,THE NEW ENGLAND MIND: THE SEVENTEENTH CENTURY. CULTURE DOMIN WRITING INGP/REL CONSEN MAJORITY PERCEPT KNOWL MORAL...CONCPT LING WORSHIP 17 NEW/ENGLND PROTESTANT. PAGE 111 H2214
SECT REGION SOC ATTIT

B44
KOHN H.,THE IDEA OF NATIONALISM. UNIV SOCIETY KIN CREATE REGION CENTRAL SOVEREIGN. PAGE 87 H1740
NAT/LISM CONCPT NAT/G GP/REL

B48
EDUARDO O.D.C.,THE NEGRO IN NORTHERN BRAZIL: A STUDY IN ACCULTURATION. BRAZIL ECO/UNDEV FAM SECT PAY REGION HABITAT CATHISM MYSTISM...GEOG OBS SOC/INTEG WORSHIP 20 NEGRO MARANHAO. PAGE 44 H0890
CULTURE ADJUST GP/REL

B48
MINISTERE FINANCES ET ECO,BULLETIN BIBLIOGRAPHIQUE. AFR EUR+WWI FRANCE CULTURE STRUCT FINAN NAT/G ACT/RES INT/TRADE ADMIN REGION PRODUC STAT. PAGE 111 H2224
BIBLIOG/A ECO/UNDEV TEC/DEV COLONIAL

B50
GATZKE H.W.,GERMANY'S DRIVE TO THE WEST. BELGIUM GERMANY MOD/EUR AGRI INDUS POL/PAR FORCES DOMIN AGREE CONTROL REGION COERCE 20 TREATY WWI. PAGE 55 H1104
WAR POLICY NAT/G DIPLOM

B50
KANN R.A.,THE MULTINATIONAL EMPIRE (2 VOLS.). AUSTRIA CZECHOSLVK GERMANY HUNGARY CULTURE NAT/G POL/PAR PROVS REGION REV FEDERAL...GEOG TREND CHARTS IDEA/COMP NAT/COMP 19/20. PAGE 83 H1654
NAT/LISM MOD/EUR

B51
JENNINGS S.I.,THE COMMONWEALTH IN ASIA. CEYLON INDIA PAKISTAN S/ASIA UK CONSTN CULTURE SOCIETY STRATA STRUCT NAT/G POL/PAR EDU/PROP LEAD WAR 20 CMN/WLTH. PAGE 80 H1608
NAT/LISM REGION COLONIAL DIPLOM

B51
YOUNG T.C.,NEAR EASTERN CULTURE AND SOCIETY. ISLAM ECO/UNDEV SECT WRITING ATTIT HABITAT ORD/FREE 20. PAGE 172 H3439
CULTURE STRUCT REGION DIPLOM

C51
HAMMOND M.,"CITY-STATE AND WORLD STATE." CONSTN INTELL LOC/G LEGIT CENTRAL RATIONAL BIBLIOG. PAGE 65 H1308
NAT/G ATTIT REGION MEDIT-7

B52
KOLARZ W.,RUSSIA AND HER COLONIES. COM RUSSIA LAW CULTURE ECO/DEV KIN LOC/G SECT TEC/DEV ECO/TAC EDU/PROP REGION COERCE ATTIT PWR SOVEREIGN...SOC TIME/SEQ CON/ANAL VAL/FREE 19/20. PAGE 88 H1749
NAT/G DOMIN USSR COLONIAL

B54
FRIEDMAN W.,THE PUBLIC CORPORATION: A COMPARATIVE SYMPOSIUM (UNIVERSITY OF TORONTO SCHOOL OF LAW COMPARATIVE LAW SERIES, VOL. I). SWEDEN USA+45 INDUS INT/ORG NAT/G REGION CENTRAL FEDERAL...POLICY JURID IDEA/COMP NAT/COMP 20 COMMONWLTH MONOPOLY EUROPE. PAGE 53 H1065
LAW SOCISM LG/CO OWN

B55
THOMPSON V.,MINORITY PROBLEMS IN SOUTHEAST ASIA. CAMBODIA CHINA/COM LAOS S/ASIA KIN NAT/G SECT PROB/SOLV EDU/PROP REGION GP/REL RACE/REL MARXISM ...SOC 20 BUDDHISM UN. PAGE 154 H3085
INGP/REL GEOG DIPLOM STRUCT

S55
DE SMITH S.A.,"CONSTITUTIONAL MONARCHY IN BURGANDA." AFR UGANDA UK STRUCT CHIEF REGION INGP/REL ADJUST NAT/LISM SOVEREIGN CONSERVE ...POLICY 19/20 BURGANDA. PAGE 38 H0769
NAT/G DIPLOM CONSTN COLONIAL

B56
BECKER H.,MAN IN RECIPROCITY: INTRODUCTORY LECTURES ON CULTURE, SOCIETY, AND PERSONALITY. LAW FAM SECT REGION GP/REL ADJUST ATTIT PERSON...BIBLIOG 20. PAGE 13 H0253
CULTURE STRUCT SOC PSY

B57
ARON R.,L'UNIFICATION ECONOMIQUE DE L'EUROPE. EUR+WWI SWITZERLND UK INT/ORG NAT/G REGION NAT/LISM ORD/FREE PWR...CONCPT METH/CNCPT OBS TREND STERTYP GEN/LAWS EEC 20. PAGE 8 H0168
VOL/ASSN ECO/TAC

B57
INTERNATIONAL AFRICAN INST,ETHNOGRAPHIC SURVEY OF AFRICA: WESTERN AFRICA: THE WOLOF OF SENEGAMBIA. AFR SENEGAL CULTURE ECO/UNDEV FAM KIN REGION ...CHARTS GP/COMP BIBLIOG WORSHIP 20. PAGE 78 H1551
STRUCT GEOG HABITAT INGP/REL

B57
KOHN H.,AMERICAN NATIONALISM. EUR+WWI USA+45 USA-45 COLONIAL REGION 18/20. PAGE 87 H1744
NAT/LISM NAT/COMP FEDERAL DIPLOM

B57
LAQUER W.Z.,COMMUNISM AND NATIONALISM IN THE MIDDLE EAST. ELITES INTELL STRATA NAT/G POL/PAR SECT VOL/ASSN TOP/EX DOMIN LEGIT REGION COERCE ATTIT PERSON PWR...CONCPT HIST/WRIT TIME/SEQ TREND GEN/LAWS VAL/FREE. PAGE 91 H1817
ISLAM NAT/LISM

B57
SCHLESINGER J.A.,HOW THEY BECAME GOVERNOR; A STUDY OF COMPARATIVE STATE POLITICS, 1870-1950. USA+45 USA-45 LAW POL/PAR LEGIS EDU/PROP REGION...STAT TREND CHARTS TIME 19/20 GOVERNOR. PAGE 139 H2788
PROVS CHIEF GOV/COMP CHOOSE

B58
ALMAGRO BASCH M.,ORIGEN Y FORMACION DEL PUEBLO HISPANO. PREHIST SPAIN REGION WAR RACE/REL HABITAT ORD/FREE...SOC SOC/INTEG 20. PAGE 5 H0109
CULTURE GP/REL ADJUST

B58
INTERNATIONAL ECONOMIC ASSN,ECONOMICS OF INTERNATIONAL MIGRATION. WOR+45 WOR-45 ECO/UNDEV FINAN NAT/G REGION...NAT/COMP METH 20. PAGE 78 H1556
CENSUS GEOG DIPLOM ECO/TAC

B58
LOWER A.R.M.,EVOLVING CANADIAN FEDERALISM. CANADA WEST/IND CONSTN PROB/SOLV COLONIAL REGION NAT/LISM ...ANTHOL 20. PAGE 99 H1976
FEDERAL NAT/G DIPLOM RACE/REL

C58
FIFIELD R.H.,"THE DIPLOMACY OF SOUTHEAST ASIA: 1945-1958." INT/ORG NAT/G COLONIAL REGION...CHARTS BIBLIOG 20 UN. PAGE 50 H0996
S/ASIA DIPLOM NAT/LISM

C58
GINSBURG N.,"MALAYA." MALAYSIA PROB/SOLV REGION NAT/LISM KNOWL WEALTH...GEOG SOC CHARTS BIBLIOG 20. PAGE 57 H1133
COM/IND ECO/UNDEV CULTURE NAT/G

B59
GOPAL R.,INDIAN MUSLIMS: A POLITICAL HISTORY (1858-1947). INDIA ISLAM PAKISTAN NAT/G SECT LEGIS LEAD COERCE WAR REPRESENT ISOLAT ORD/FREE 19/20 HINDU MUSLIM. PAGE 59 H1175
COLONIAL GP/REL POL/PAR REGION

B59
SISSONS C.B.,CHURCH AND STATE IN CANADIAN EDUCATION: AN HISTORICAL STUDY. CANADA ACADEM NAT/G
SECT EDU/PROP

SCHOOL LEGIS REGION MAJORITY...MAJORIT WORSHIP 18/20 CHURCH/STA. PAGE 145 H2891 PROVS GP/REL

B59
WRAITH R.E.,EAST AFRICAN CITIZEN. AFR GHANA UK AGRI INDUS LOC/G POL/PAR PROB/SOLV CONTROL REGION REPRESENT NAT/LISM PWR...OBS 20 AFRICA/E AFRICA/W. PAGE 171 H3415 ECO/UNDEV RACE/REL NAT/G NAT/COMP

L59
MURPHY J.C.,"SOME IMPLICATIONS OF EUROPE'S COMMON MARKET. IN (COOK P, ECONOMIC DEVELOPMENT AND INTERNATIONAL TRADE.," EUR+WWI ECO/DEV DIST/IND INDUS NAT/G PLAN ECO/TAC INT/TRADE WEALTH...STAT TREND OEEC TOT/POP 20 EEC. PAGE 115 H2298 MARKET INT/ORG REGION

S59
LEVINE R.A.,"ANTI-EUROPEAN VIOLENCE IN AFRICA: A COMPARATIVE ANALYSIS." AFR CULTURE NAT/G DIPLOM EDU/PROP COLONIAL REGION COERCE ATTIT PWR...PSY CONCPT TIME/SEQ TREND HYPO/EXP SOC/EXP STERTYP GEN/METH COLD/WAR 20. PAGE 95 H1903 DRIVE ORD/FREE REV

S59
PLAZA G.,"FOR A REGIONAL MARKET IN LATIN AMERICA." FUT L/A+17C CULTURE INDUS NAT/G ECO/TAC INT/TRADE ATTIT WEALTH...NEW/IDEA TREND OAS 20. PAGE 126 H2527 MARKET INT/ORG REGION

S59
SKILLING H.G.,"COMMUNISM: NATIONAL OR INTERNATIONAL." CHINA/COM USSR YUGOSLAVIA NAT/G POL/PAR VOL/ASSN DOMIN REGION COERCE ATTIT PWR MARXISM SOCISM...CONCPT TOT/POP 20 TITO/MARSH. PAGE 145 H2894 COM TREND

B60
CARTER G.M.,INDEPENDENCE FOR AFRICA. AFR FUT SOCIETY STRATA ECO/DEV POL/PAR DELIB/GP PLAN DOMIN EDU/PROP COLONIAL REGION ATTIT DRIVE SOVEREIGN ...RECORD INT TIME/SEQ CHARTS 20. PAGE 27 H0544 NAT/G PWR NAT/LISM

B60
HARRISON S.S.,INDIA: THE MOST DANGEROUS DECADES. INDIA CONSTN STRATA POL/PAR SECT PLAN ADMIN CHOOSE GP/REL TOTALISM MARXISM...LING 20 NEHRU/J. PAGE 67 H1347 CULTURE ECO/UNDEV PROB/SOLV REGION

B60
LINDSAY K.,EUROPEAN ASSEMBLIES: THE EXPERIMENTAL PERIOD 1949-1959. EUR+WWI ECO/DEV NAT/G POL/PAR LEGIS TOP/EX ACT/RES PLAN ECO/TAC DOMIN LEGIT ROUTINE ATTIT DRIVE ORD/FREE PWR SKILL...SOC CONCPT TREND CHARTS GEN/LAWS VAL/FREE. PAGE 97 H1932 VOL/ASSN INT/ORG REGION

B60
LISTER L.,EUROPE'S COAL AND STEEL COMMUNITY. FRANCE GERMANY STRUCT ECO/DEV EXTR/IND INDUS MARKET NAT/G DELIB/GP ECO/TAC INT/TRADE EDU/PROP ATTIT RIGID/FLEX ORD/FREE PWR WEALTH...CONCPT STAT TIME/SEQ CHARTS ECSC 20. PAGE 97 H1941 EUR+WWI INT/ORG REGION

B60
NICHOLLS W.H.,SOUTHERN TRADITION AND REGIONAL PROGRESS. STRATA STRUCT SOCIETY WORKER PARTIC REGION RACE/REL CONSEN ATTIT...SOC METH/CNCPT 19/20 SOUTH/US TVA. PAGE 118 H2349 RIGID/FLEX CONSERVE AGRI CULTURE

B60
SMITH M.G.,GOVERNMENT IN ZAZZAU 1800-1950. NIGERIA UK CULTURE SOCIETY LOC/G ADMIN COLONIAL ...METH/CNCPT NEW/IDEA METH 19/20. PAGE 146 H2914 REGION CONSTN KIN ECO/UNDEV

B60
SOUTH AFRICAN CONGRESS OF DEM,FACE THE FUTURE. SOUTH/AFR ELITES LEGIS ADMIN REGION COERCE PEACE ATTIT 20. PAGE 147 H2938 RACE/REL DISCRIM CONSTN NAT/G

B60
THE AFRICA 1960 COMMITTEE,MANDATE IN TRUST; THE PROBLEM OF SOUTH WEST AFRICA. GERMANY STRUCT REGION SANCTION CHOOSE DISCRIM...INT/LAW 20 AFRICA/SW UN LEAGUE/NAT TRUST/TERR. PAGE 153 H3066 NAT/G DIPLOM COLONIAL RACE/REL

L60
HAAS E.B.,"CONSENSUS FORMATION IN THE COUNCIL OF EUROPE." EUR+WWI NAT/G DELIB/GP DIPLOM REGION CHOOSE PWR SOVEREIGN...RELATIV NEW/IDEA QUANT CHARTS INDEX TOT/POP OEEC 20 COUNCL/EUR. PAGE 63 H1265 POL/PAR INT/ORG STAT

S60
BERG E.J.,"ECONOMIC BASIS OF POLITICAL CHOICE IN FRENCH WEST AFRICA." FRANCE ECO/UNDEV AGRI INDUS NAT/G PLAN LEGIT COLONIAL REGION ATTIT PWR WEALTH ...CONCPT 20. PAGE 15 H0299 AFR ECO/TAC

S60
GINSBURGS G.,"PEKING-LHASA-NEW DELHI." CHINA/COM FUT INDIA S/ASIA KIN NAT/G PROVS SECT FORCES BAL/PWR ECO/TAC DOMIN EDU/PROP LEGIT ADMIN REGION GUERRILLA PWR...TREND TIBET 20. PAGE 57 H1134 ASIA COERCE DIPLOM

S60
MURPHEY R.,"ECONOMIC CONFLICTS IN SOUTH ASIA." ASIA CULTURE INTELL ECO/TAC REGION ATTIT DRIVE KNOWL ...METH/CNCPT TIME/SEQ STERTYP TOT/POP VAL/FREE 20. PAGE 115 H2296 S/ASIA ECO/UNDEV

B61
ANSPRENGER F.,POLITIK IM SCHWARZEN AFRIKA. FRANCE NAT/G DIPLOM REGION REV NAT/LISM...CHARTS BIBLIOG 19/20. PAGE 7 H0141 AFR COLONIAL SOVEREIGN

B61
APTER D.E.,THE POLITICAL KINGDOM IN UGANDA. UGANDA CULTURE ECO/UNDEV AGRI KIN SECT TOP/EX REGION ATTIT HABITAT CONSERVE...GEOG AUD/VIS 20. PAGE 8 H0153 NAT/LISM POL/PAR COLONIAL ECO/TAC

B61
DIA M.,THE AFRICAN NATIONS AND WORLD SOLIDARITY. ISLAM CULTURE ELITES ECO/DEV ECO/UNDEV INT/ORG NAT/G PLAN ECO/TAC INT/TRADE EDU/PROP NAT/LISM ATTIT DRIVE ORD/FREE WEALTH...SOCIALIST CONCPT CON/ANAL GEN/LAWS TOT/POP 20. PAGE 41 H0817 AFR REGION SOCISM

B61
HADDAD J.A.,REVOLUCAO CUBANA E REVOLUCAO BRASILEIRA. BRAZIL CUBA L/A+17C STRATA AGRI WORKER EDU/PROP REGION...POLICY NAT/COMP 20. PAGE 63 H1272 REV ORD/FREE DIPLOM ECO/UNDEV

B61
HOLDSWORTH M.,SOVIET AFRICAN STUDIES 1918-1959. USSR ACADEM NAT/G DIPLOM REGION KNOWL 20. PAGE 72 H1448 BIBLIOG/A AFR HABITAT NAT/COMP

B61
KEREKES T.,THE ARAB MIDDLE EAST AND MUSLIM AFRICA. ISLAM SOCIETY ECO/UNDEV SECT VOL/ASSN TOP/EX REGION ATTIT PWR...GEOG CONCPT TIME/SEQ GEN/LAWS 20. PAGE 85 H1694 NAT/G TREND NAT/LISM

B61
MAYNE A.,DESIGNING AND ADMINISTERING A REGIONAL ECONOMIC DEVELOPMENT PLAN WITH SPECIFIC REFERENCE TO PUERTO RICO (PAMPHLET). PUERT/RICO SOCIETY NAT/G DELIB/GP REGION...DECISION 20. PAGE 105 H2106 ECO/UNDEV PLAN CREATE ADMIN

B61
MOLLAU G.,INTERNATIONAL COMMUNISM AND WORLD REVOLUTION: HISTORY AND METHODS. RUSSIA USSR INT/ORG NAT/G POL/PAR VOL/ASSN FORCES BAL/PWR DIPLOM EXEC REGION WAR ATTIT PWR MARXISM...CONCPT TIME/SEQ COLD/WAR 19/20. PAGE 112 H2237 COM REV

B61
RYDINGS H.A.,THE BIBLIOGRAPHIES OF WEST AFRICA (PAMPHLET). ECO/UNDEV NAT/G COLONIAL REGION ATTIT 20. PAGE 136 H2725 BIBLIOG/A AFR NAT/COMP

S61
SCHECHTMAN J.B.,"MINORITIES IN THE MIDDLE EAST." ISLAM INTELL SOCIETY STRATA KIN NAT/G VOL/ASSN EDU/PROP REGION GP/REL DISCRIM ATTIT BIO/SOC DISPL PERSON ALL/VALS...PSY SOC OBS SAMP GEN/LAWS 20. PAGE 139 H2776 SECT CULTURE RACE/REL

B62
CARTER G.M.,AFRICAN ONE-PARTY STATES. ISLAM IVORY/CST LIBERIA CONSTN CULTURE SOCIETY POL/PAR PLAN DOMIN EDU/PROP EXEC REGION CHOOSE ATTIT ALL/VALS...CONCPT TIME/SEQ CHARTS VAL/FREE 20 TANGANYIKA. PAGE 27 H0545 AFR NAT/LISM

B62
DE MADARIAGA S.,L'AMERIQUE LATINE ENTRE L'OURS ET L'AIGLE. L/A+17C SOCIETY NAT/G ECO/TAC EDU/PROP REGION COERCE ATTIT ALL/VALS...MAJORIT TIME/SEQ STERTYP COLD/WAR OAS 20. PAGE 38 H0760 POL/PAR ECO/UNDEV

B62
DUTOIT B.,LA NEUTRALITE SUISSE A L'HEURE EUROPEENNE. EUR+WWI MOD/EUR INT/ORG NAT/G VOL/ASSN PLAN BAL/PWR LEGIT NEUTRAL REGION PEACE ORD/FREE SOVEREIGN...CONCPT OBS TIME/SEQ TREND STERTYP VAL/FREE LEAGUE/NAT UN 20. PAGE 44 H0873 ATTIT DIPLOM SWITZERLND

B62
EVANS-PRITCHARD E.E.,ESSAYS IN SOCIAL ANTHROPOLOGY. AFR KIN REGION INGP/REL DRIVE HABITAT...OBS METH 20 ZANDE. PAGE 48 H0954 SOCIETY CULTURE SOC STRUCT

B62
GUENA Y.,HISTORIQUE DE LA COMMUNAUTE. FUT ECO/UNDEV NAT/G PLAN EDU/PROP COLONIAL REGION NAT/LISM ALL/VALS SOVEREIGN...CONCPT OBS CHARTS 20. PAGE 62 H1244 AFR VOL/ASSN FOR/AID FRANCE

B62
HAY S.N.,SOUTHEAST ASIAN HISTORY: A BIBLIOGRAPHICAL GUIDE. STRATA KIN NAT/G REGION GUERRILLA REV WAR ADJUST HABITAT PERCEPT ALL/IDEOS...CHARTS 5/20. PAGE 68 H1365 BIBLIOG/A S/ASIA CULTURE

B62
KEESING F.M.,THE ETHNOHISTORY OF NORTHERN LUZON. PHILIPPINE ECO/UNDEV FAM SECT CHIEF REGION GP/REL HABITAT...GEOG LING BIBLIOG WORSHIP 20. PAGE 84 H1680 CULTURE SOC KIN

B62
MEADE J.E.,CASE STUDIES IN EUROPEAN ECONOMIC UNION. BELGIUM EUR+WWI LUXEMBOURG NAT/G INT/TRADE REGION ROUTINE WEALTH...METH/CNCPT STAT CHARTS ECSC TOT/POP OEEC EEC 20. PAGE 108 H2154 INT/ORG ECO/TAC

B62
UNECA LIBRARY,BOOKS ON AFRICA IN THE UNECA LIBRARY. WOR+45 AGRI INT/ORG NAT/G PLAN WRITING REGION...SOC STAT UN. PAGE 158 H3160 BIBLIOG AFR ECO/UNDEV TEC/DEV

B62
UNECA LIBRARY,NEW ACQUISITIONS IN THE UNECA LIBRARY. LAW NAT/G PLAN PROB/SOLV TEC/DEV ADMIN REGION...GEOG SOC 20 UN. PAGE 158 H3161
BIBLIOG AFR ECO/UNDEV INT/ORG

S62
LEGUM C.,"THE DANGERS OF INDEPENDENCE" AFR UGANDA NAT/G DIPLOM DOMIN REGION CENTRAL ATTIT POPULISM 20. PAGE 93 H1862
ORD/FREE SOVEREIGN NAT/LISM GOV/COMP

S62
MARIAS J.,"A PROGRAM FOR EUROPE." EUR+WWI INT/ORG NAT/G PLAN DIPLOM DOMIN PWR...STERTYP TOT/POP 20. PAGE 102 H2048
VOL/ASSN CREATE REGION

S62
PIQUEMAL M.,"LES PROBLEMES DES UNIONS D'ETATS EN AFRIQUE NOIRE." FRANCE SOCIETY INT/ORG NAT/G DELIB/GP PLAN LEGIT ADMIN COLONIAL ROUTINE ATTIT ORD/FREE PWR...GEOG METH/CNCPT 20. PAGE 126 H2515
AFR ECO/UNDEV REGION

S62
SPRINGER H.W.,"FEDERATION IN THE CARIBBEAN: AN ATTEMPT THAT FAILED." L/A+17C ECO/UNDEV INT/ORG POL/PAR PROVS LEGIS CREATE PLAN LEGIT ADMIN FEDERAL ATTIT DRIVE PERSON ORD/FREE PWR...POLICY GEOG PSY CONCPT OBS CARIBBEAN CMN/WLTH 20. PAGE 148 H2955
VOL/ASSN NAT/G REGION

B63
BELFRAGE C.,THE MAN AT THE DOOR WITH THE GUN. CUBA L/A+17C NAT/G LEAD PARTIC GP/REL PWR...POLICY 20 CASTRO/F. PAGE 13 H0261
REGION ECO/UNDEV STRUCT ATTIT

B63
CANELAS O.A.,RADIOGRAFIA DE LA ALIANZA PARA EL ATRASO. L/A+17C USA+45 ECO/TAC DOMIN COLONIAL NAT/LISM...SOCIALIST NAT/COMP 20. PAGE 26 H0519
REV DIPLOM ECO/UNDEV REGION

B63
CREMEANS C.,THE ARABS AND THE WORLD: NASSER'S ARAB NATIONALIST POLICY. FUT ISLAM UAR USA+45 SOCIETY STRATA NAT/G POL/PAR PLAN DIPLOM EDU/PROP LEGIT DRIVE ALL/VALS...INT TIME/SEQ CHARTS 20 NASSER/G. PAGE 35 H0700
TOP/EX ATTIT REGION NAT/LISM

B63
HAQ M.,THE STRATEGY OF ECONOMIC PLANNING. PAKISTAN AGRI FINAN INDUS NAT/G FOR/AID TAX CONTROL REGION PRODUC...POLICY CHARTS 20. PAGE 66 H1324
ECO/TAC ECO/UNDEV PLAN PROB/SOLV

B63
HARDY M.J.L.,BLOOD FEUDS AND THE PAYMENT OF BLOOD MONEY IN THE MIDDLE EAST. ISLAM SOCIETY SECT REGION SANCTION COERCE DEATH MURDER 7/20 ARABS. PAGE 66 H1329
KIN TRIBUTE LAW CULTURE

B63
JAIRAZBHOY R.A.,FOREIGN INFLUENCE IN ANCIENT INDIA. INDIA ELITES SECT DIPLOM EDU/PROP COLONIAL REGION GP/REL...ART/METH LING WORSHIP +/14 GRECO/ROMN MESOPOTAM PERSIA PARTH/SASS. PAGE 79 H1587
CULTURE SOCIETY COERCE DOMIN

B63
JUNOD V.,HANDBOOK OF AFRICA. AFR ISLAM CONSTN SOCIETY NAT/G POL/PAR...GEOG SOC STAT CHARTS WORK 20. PAGE 82 H1642
ECO/UNDEV REGION

B63
KLEIMAN R.,ATLANTIC CRISIS; AMERICAN DIPLOMACY CONFRONTS A RESURGENT EUROPE. EUR+WWI USA+45 ECO/DEV AGRI NAT/G CHIEF FORCES PLAN LEAD ATTIT ...CONCPT 20 NATO KENNEDY/JF DEGAULLE/C EEC JOHNSON/LB. PAGE 87 H1731
DIPLOM REGION POLICY

B63
MAYNE R.,THE COMMUNITY OF EUROPE. UK CONSTN NAT/G CONSULT DELIB/GP CREATE PLAN ECO/TAC LEGIT ADMIN ROUTINE ORD/FREE PWR WEALTH...CONCPT TIME/SEQ EEC EURATOM 20. PAGE 105 H2107
EUR+WWI INT/ORG REGION

B63
NKRUMAH K.,AFRICA MUST UNITE. AFR FUT GHANA CONSTN CULTURE SOCIETY NAT/G POL/PAR DELIB/GP TOP/EX PLAN DOMIN EDU/PROP ATTIT DRIVE...TIME/SEQ CHARTS TOT/POP 20. PAGE 118 H2364
CONCPT GEN/LAWS REGION

B63
ROBERTSON A.H.,HUMAN RIGHTS IN EUROPE. CONSTN SOCIETY INT/ORG NAT/G VOL/ASSN DELIB/GP ACT/RES PLAN ADJUD REGION ROUTINE ATTIT LOVE ORD/FREE RESPECT...JURID SOC CONCPT SOC/EXP UN 20. PAGE 132 H2645
EUR+WWI PERSON

B63
RONNING C.N.,LAW AND POLITICS IN INTER-AMERICAN DIPLOMACY. L/A+17C ECO/UNDEV NAT/G CONSULT DELIB/GP CREATE CAP/ISM ECO/TAC LEGIT REGION RIGID/FLEX ...METH/CNCPT GEN/LAWS OAS 20. PAGE 133 H2668
VOL/ASSN ALL/VALS DIPLOM

B63
SAKAI R.K.,STUDIES ON ASIA, 1963. ASIA INDIA ISRAEL S/ASIA USA+45 PERF/ART POL/PAR SECT REGION NAT/LISM ...SOC LING TREND ANTHOL 19/20 CHINJAP. PAGE 137 H2735
PWR CULTURE

B63
SILVERT K.H.,EXPECTANT PEOPLES: NATIONALISM AND DEVELOPMENT. CULTURE STRATA SECT LEAD REGION RACE/REL ALL/IDEOS...GEN/LAWS SOC/INTEG 20. PAGE 144 H2877
NAT/LISM ECO/UNDEV ALL/VALS

B63
TOUVAL S.,SOMALI NATIONALISM: INTERNATIONAL POLITICS AND THE DRIVE FOR UNITY IN THE HORN OF AFRICA. AFR CULTURE PROVS LEGIS EDU/PROP REGION COERCE ATTIT...MYTH UNPLAN/INT TIME/SEQ SOMALI VAL/FREE 20. PAGE 156 H3118
SOCIETY EXEC NAT/LISM

B63
VIARD R.,LA FIN DE L'EMPIRE COLONIAL FRANCAIS. AFR FUT S/ASIA ECO/UNDEV NAT/G CONSULT PLAN ECO/TAC EDU/PROP REGION NAT/LISM ALL/VALS...CONCPT TIME/SEQ TREND VAL/FREE 20. PAGE 162 H3248
VOL/ASSN COLONIAL FRANCE

S63
BANFIELD J.,"FEDERATION IN EAST-AFRICA." AFR UGANDA ELITES INT/ORG NAT/G VOL/ASSN LEGIS ECO/TAC FEDERAL ATTIT SOVEREIGN TOT/POP 20 TANGANYIKA. PAGE 10 H0210
EX/STRUC PWR REGION

S63
CRUTCHER J.,"PAN AFRICANISM: AFRICAN ODYSSEY." AFR NAT/G POL/PAR PROF/ORG VOL/ASSN TOP/EX CREATE REGION RACE/REL ALL/VALS...CONCPT TIME/SEQ TREND CON/ANAL 20. PAGE 36 H0716
PROVS DELIB/GP COLONIAL

S63
GROSSER A.,"FRANCE AND GERMANY IN THE ATLANTIC COMMUNITY." INT/ORG NAT/G TOP/EX DIPLOM REGION PEACE ATTIT ORD/FREE PWR...CONCPT RECORD TIME/SEQ GEN/LAWS VAL/FREE COLD/WAR 20. PAGE 62 H1234
EUR+WWI VOL/ASSN FRANCE GERMANY

S63
LERNER D.,"WILL EUROPEAN UNION BRING ABOUT MERGED NATIONAL GOALS." EUR+WWI FRANCE GERMANY UK ECO/DEV NAT/G VOL/ASSN DELIB/GP BAL/PWR ECO/TAC NAT/LISM EEC 20 DEGAULLE/C. PAGE 95 H1889
ATTIT STERTYP ELITES REGION

S63
MBOYA T.,"AFRICAN SOCIALISM." ECO/UNDEV INT/ORG DIPLOM FOR/AID INT/TRADE REGION GP/REL ATTIT ORD/FREE EACM. PAGE 106 H2116
AFR SOCISM CULTURE NAT/LISM

S63
MORISON D.,"AFRICAN STUDIES IN THE SOVIET UNION." AFR COM CULTURE INTELL REGION ATTIT KNOWL...HUM TREND 20. PAGE 113 H2258
EDU/PROP USSR

S63
OGOT B.,"FROM CHIEF TO PRESIDENT." AFR SECT REGION NAT/LISM...SOC GOV/COMP NAT/COMP 20 PRESIDENT. PAGE 121 H2410
CHIEF CULTURE LEAD ORD/FREE

S63
RUSTOW D.A.,"THE MILITARY IN MIDDLE EASTERN SOCIETY AND POLITICS." FUT ISLAM CONSTN SOCIETY FACE/GP NAT/G POL/PAR PROF/ORG CONSULT DOMIN ADMIN EXEC REGION COERCE NAT/LISM ATTIT DRIVE PERSON ORD/FREE PWR...POLICY CONCPT OBS STERTYP 20. PAGE 136 H2721
FORCES ELITES

N63
LIBRARY HUNGARIAN ACADEMY SCI,HUNGARIAN PUBLICATIONS ON ASIA AND AFRICA, 1950-1962: A SELECTED BIBLIOGRAPHY (PAMPHLET). AFR ASIA HUNGARY S/ASIA ECO/UNDEV NAT/G EDU/PROP ATTIT 20 UNESCO. PAGE 96 H1922
BIBLIOG REGION DIPLOM WRITING

B64
ANDREN N.,GOVERNMENT AND POLITICS IN THE NORDIC COUNTRIES: DENMARK, FINLAND, ICELAND, NORWAY, SWEDEN. DENMARK FINLAND ICELAND NORWAY SWEDEN POL/PAR CHIEF LEGIS ADMIN REGION REPRESENT ATTIT CONSERVE...CHARTS BIBLIOG/A 20. PAGE 7 H0137
CONSTN NAT/G CULTURE GOV/COMP

B64
BUTWELL R.,SOUTHEAST ASIA TODAY - AND TOMORROW. NAT/G COLONIAL LEAD REGION WAR CHOOSE WEALTH MARXISM 20. PAGE 25 H0500
S/ASIA DIPLOM ECO/UNDEV NAT/LISM

B64
COWAN L.G.,THE DILEMMAS OF AFRICAN INDEPENDENCE. AFR INDUS NAT/G SECT DIPLOM ECO/TAC REGION MARXISM ...CHARTS BIBLIOG 20 MAPS. PAGE 34 H0683
ORD/FREE COLONIAL REV ECO/UNDEV

B64
FRANCK T.M.,EAST AFRICAN UNITY THROUGH LAW. MALAWI TANZANIA UGANDA UK ZAMBIA CONSTN INT/ORG NAT/G ADMIN ROUTINE TASK NAT/LISM ATTIT SOVEREIGN ...RECORD IDEA/COMP NAT/COMP. PAGE 52 H1048
AFR FEDERAL REGION INT/LAW

B64
GREAT BRITAIN CENTRAL OFF INF,CONSTITUTIONAL DEVELOPMENT IN THE COMMONWEALTH. VOL/ASSN PLAN DIPLOM COLONIAL INGP/REL NAT/LISM ORD/FREE PWR 17/20 CMN/WLTH. PAGE 60 H1202
REGION CONSTN NAT/G SOVEREIGN

B64
KIS T.I.,LES PAYS DE L'EUROPE DE L'EST: LEURS RAPPORTS MUTUELS ET LE PROBLEME DE LEUR INTEGRATION DANS L'ORBITE DE L'USSR. EUR+WWI RUSSIA USSR INT/ORG NAT/G REV ATTIT...JURID SOC BIBLIOG WARSAW/P COMECON EUROPE/E. PAGE 86 H1727
DIPLOM COM MARXISM REGION

B64
MAIER J.,POLITICS OF CHANGE IN LATIN AMERICA. BRAZIL L/A+17C STRATA INT/ORG NAT/G POL/PAR FOR/AID REV 20. PAGE 101 H2019
SOCIETY NAT/LISM DIPLOM REGION

B64
NICOL D.,AFRICA - A SUBJECTIVE VIEW. AFR INT/ORG PLAN ADMIN COLONIAL PARL/PROC PARTIC REGION GOV/REL LITERACY ATTIT...BIBLIOG 20 CIVIL/SERV. PAGE 118 H2350
NAT/G LEAD CULTURE ACADEM

B64
OECD SEMINAR REGIONAL DEV,REGIONAL DEVELOPMENT IN ISRAEL. ISRAEL STRUCT ECO/UNDEV NAT/G REGION...GEOG 20. PAGE 120 H2404
ADMIN PROVS PLAN METH/COMP

B64
RAMAZANI R.K.,THE MIDDLE EAST AND THE EUROPEAN COMMON MARKET. EUR+WWI ISLAM ECO/DEV EXTR/IND MARKET PROC/MFG INT/ORG NAT/G TEC/DEV ECO/TAC REGION DRIVE WEALTH...STAT CHARTS EEC TOT/POP 20. PAGE 129 H2587
ECO/UNDEV ATTIT INT/TRADE

B64
URQUIDI V.L.,THE CHALLENGE OF DEVELOPMENT IN LATIN AMERICA. L/A+17C FINAN INT/ORG TEC/DEV DIPLOM INT/TRADE PRICE REGION PRODUC...CHARTS 20. PAGE 159 H3175
ECO/UNDEV ECO/TAC NAT/G TREND

B64
VOELKMANN K.,HERRSCHER VON MORGEN? BAL/PWR COLONIAL NEUTRAL REGION RACE/REL ALL/VALS SOVEREIGN...RECORD 20 COLD/WAR THIRD/WRLD. PAGE 163 H3259
DIPLOM ECO/UNDEV CONTROL NAT/COMP

B64
WILCOX W.A.,INDIA, PAKISTAN AND THE RISE OF CHINA. ASIA BURMA CEYLON CHINA/COM INDIA PAKISTAN S/ASIA NAT/G VOL/ASSN FORCES TOP/EX ACT/RES DOMIN REGION RIGID/FLEX ORD/FREE...POLICY GEN/LAWS COLD/WAR 20. PAGE 168 H3362
CULTURE ATTIT DIPLOM

B64
WILSON T.,POLICIES FOR REGIONAL DEVELOPMENT. CANADA UK FINAN INDUS NAT/G BUDGET TAX GIVE COST ...NAT/COMP 20. PAGE 169 H3383
REGION PLAN ECO/DEV ECO/TAC

L64
HAAS E.B.,"ECONOMICS AND DIFFERENTIAL PATTERNS OF POLITICAL INTEGRATION: PROJECTIONS ABOUT UNITY IN LATIN AMERICA." SOCIETY NAT/G DELIB/GP ACT/RES CREATE PLAN ECO/TAC REGION ROUTINE ATTIT DRIVE PWR WEALTH...CONCPT TREND CHARTS LAFTA 20. PAGE 63 H1266
L/A+17C INT/ORG MARKET

L64
ROTBERG R.,"THE FEDERATION MOVEMENT IN BRITISH EAST AND CENTRAL AFRICA." AFR RHODESIA UGANDA ECO/UNDEV NAT/G POL/PAR FORCES DOMIN LEGIT ADMIN COERCE ATTIT ...CONCPT TREND 20 TANGANYIKA. PAGE 135 H2691
VOL/ASSN PWR REGION

S64
CATTELL D.T.,"SOVIET POLICIES IN LATIN AMERICA." COM CUBA L/A+17C USSR SOCIETY NAT/G POL/PAR FORCES CREATE ECO/TAC EDU/PROP REGION REV RIGID/FLEX ...GEN/LAWS COLD/WAR 20. PAGE 28 H0560
DRIVE PWR

S64
GARMARNIKOW M.,"INFLUENCE-BUYING IN WEST AFRICA." COM FUT USSR INTELL NAT/G PLAN TEC/DEV ECO/TAC DOMIN EDU/PROP REGION NAT/LISM ATTIT DRIVE ALL/VALS SOVEREIGN...POLICY PSY SOC CONCPT TREND STERTYP WORK COLD/WAR 20. PAGE 55 H1102
AFR ECO/UNDEV FOR/AID SOCISM

S64
MARES V.E.,"EAST EUROPE'S SECOND CHANCE." COM EUR+WWI HUNGARY ROMANIA USSR YUGOSLAVIA ECO/UNDEV NAT/G TOP/EX CREATE PLAN TEC/DEV REGION NAT/LISM RIGID/FLEX PWR...CONCPT STAT COMECON 20. PAGE 102 H2047
VOL/ASSN ECO/TAC

S64
MERKL P.H.,"EUROPEAN ASSEMBLY PARTIES AND NATIONAL DELEGATIONS." INT/ORG DELIB/GP DOMIN EDU/PROP LEGIT CHOOSE PWR...STAT VAL/FREE 20. PAGE 109 H2180
EUR+WWI POL/PAR REGION

S64
SAAB H.,"THE ARAB SEARCH FOR A FEDERAL UNION." SOCIETY INT/ORG NAT/G DELIB/GP FORCES ACT/RES TEC/DEV ECO/TAC DOMIN LEGIT REGION ROUTINE ATTIT DRIVE RIGID/FLEX ALL/VALS...SOC CONCPT NEW/IDEA TIME/SEQ TREND. PAGE 136 H2726
ISLAM PLAN

S64
SAYEED K.,"PATHAN REGIONALISM." ISLAM PAKISTAN S/ASIA CULTURE SOCIETY NAT/G NEIGH DIPLOM LEGIT COERCE CHOOSE ATTIT DISPL PERCEPT ALL/VALS SOVEREIGN...POLICY RELATIV SOC TIME/SEQ TOT/POP 20. PAGE 138 H2761
SECT NAT/LISM REGION

S64
TINKER H.,"POLITICS IN SOUTHEAST ASIA." INT/ORG NAT/G CREATE PLAN TEC/DEV GUERRILLA KNOWL ORD/FREE COLD/WAR. PAGE 155 H3103
S/ASIA ACT/RES REGION

B65
ADAM T.R.,GOVERNMENT AND POLITICS IN AFRICA SOUTH OF THE SAHARA. AFR EUR+WWI CONSTN CULTURE INTELL POL/PAR TOP/EX LEGIT REGION DRIVE...OBS TREND CMN/WLTH 20. PAGE 3 H0062
NAT/G TIME/SEQ RACE/REL COLONIAL

B65
AIYAR S.P.,STUDIES IN INDIAN DEMOCRACY. INDIA STRATA ECO/UNDEV LABOR POL/PAR LEGIS DIPLOM LOBBY REGION CHOOSE ATTIT SOCISM...ANTHOL 20. PAGE 4 H0086
ORD/FREE REPRESENT ADMIN NAT/G

B65
ARENSBERG C.M.,CULTURE AND COMMUNITY. UNIV FACE/GP ACT/RES EDU/PROP LEAD REGION GP/REL PERS/REL HABITAT ALL/VALS...SOC CONCPT 20. PAGE 8 H0162
SOCIETY CULTURE NEIGH NEW/IDEA

B65
BETEILLE A.,CASTE, CLASS, AND POWER. INDIA MUNIC SECT REGION GP/REL PERS/REL ATTIT HABITAT RIGID/FLEX...SOC 20. PAGE 16 H0323
STRATA CULTURE PWR STRUCT

B65
DUGGAR G.S.,RENEWAL OF TOWN AND VILLAGE I: A WORLD-WIDE SURVEY OF LOCAL GOVERNMENT EXPERIENCE. WOR+45 CONSTRUC INDUS CREATE BUDGET REGION GOV/REL...QU NAT/COMP 20 URBAN/RNWL. PAGE 43 H0859
MUNIC NEIGH PLAN ADMIN

B65
EUROPEAN FREE TRADE ASSN,REGIONAL DEVELOPMENT POLICIES IN EFTA. ECO/UNDEV INT/ORG PLAN REGION ...POLICY GEOG EFTA. PAGE 48 H0950
EUR+WWI ECO/DEV NAT/COMP INT/TRADE

B65
FOSTER P.,EDUCATION AND SOCIAL CHANGE IN GHANA. GHANA CULTURE STRUCT ECO/UNDEV TEC/DEV REGION EFFICIENCY LITERACY ALL/VALS SOVEREIGN...STAT METH/COMP 19/20 GOLD/COAST. PAGE 52 H1043
SCHOOL CREATE SOCIETY

B65
HAEFELE E.T.,GOVERNMENT CONTROLS ON TRANSPORT. AFR RHODESIA TANZANIA DIPLOM ECO/TAC TARIFFS PRICE ADJUD CONTROL REGION EFFICIENCY...POLICY 20 CONGO. PAGE 64 H1274
ECO/UNDEV DIST/IND FINAN NAT/G

B65
KOHN H.,AFRICAN NATIONALISM IN THE TWENTIETH CENTURY. AFR NAT/G POL/PAR COLONIAL REGION DISCRIM SOVEREIGN 20. PAGE 87 H1747
NAT/LISM CULTURE ATTIT

B65
KUPER H.,URBANIZATION AND MIGRATION IN WEST AFRICA. UPPER/VOLT CULTURE ECO/UNDEV WORKER REGION GOV/REL ...LING ANTHOL SOC/INTEG 20 AFRICA/W OSHOGBO MOSSI MIGRATION. PAGE 89 H1781
AFR HABITAT MUNIC GEOG

B65
NYE J.S. JR.,PAN-AFRICANISM AND EAST AFRICAN INTEGRATION. TANZANIA UGANDA STRUCT ECO/UNDEV NAT/G DIPLOM FEDERAL NAT/LISM...STAT SOC/EXP BIBLIOG EEC OAU. PAGE 119 H2382
REGION ATTIT GEN/LAWS AFR

B65
ORG FOR ECO COOP AND DEVEL,THE MEDITERRANEAN REGIONAL PROJECT: AN EXPERIMENT IN PLANNING BY SIX COUNTRIES. FUT GREECE SPAIN TURKEY YUGOSLAVIA SOCIETY FINAN NAT/G PROF/ORG EDU/PROP ADMIN REGION COST...POLICY STAT CHARTS 20 OECD. PAGE 121 H2427
PLAN ECO/UNDEV ACADEM SCHOOL

B65
PADELFORD N.,THE UNITED NATIONS IN THE BALANCE* ACCOMPLISHMENTS AND PROSPECTS. NAT/G VOL/ASSN DIPLOM ADMIN COLONIAL CT/SYS REGION WAR ORD/FREE ...ANTHOL UN. PAGE 122 H2437
INT/ORG CONTROL

B65
PANJABI K.L.,THE CIVIL SERVANT IN INDIA. INDIA UK NAT/G CONSULT EX/STRUC REGION GP/REL RACE/REL 20. PAGE 123 H2462
ADMIN WORKER BIOG COLONIAL

B65
POLK W.R.,THE UNITED STATES AND THE ARAB WORLD. USA+45 ECO/UNDEV EXTR/IND SECT WAR NAT/LISM ATTIT ...NAT/COMP COLD/WAR. PAGE 127 H2535
ISLAM REGION CULTURE DIPLOM

B65
RODRIGUEZ M.,CENTRAL AMERICA. COSTA/RICA GUATEMALA L/A+17C NICARAGUA DIPLOM COLONIAL REGION NAT/LISM ALL/IDEOS SOCISM...MAJORIT TIME/SEQ BIBLIOG 19/20. PAGE 133 H2656
CULTURE NAT/COMP NAT/G ECO/UNDEV

B65
SLATER J.,A REVALUATION OF COLLECTIVE SECURITY* THE OAS IN ACTION. L/A+17C USA+45 NAT/G ADMIN COERCE ORD/FREE PWR...GOV/COMP IDEA/COMP GEN/LAWS OAS. PAGE 145 H2899
REGION INT/ORG FORCES

B65
WURFEL S.W.,FOREIGN ENTERPRISE IN COLOMBIA. FINAN LABOR NAT/G ECO/TAC TAX REGION 20 COLOMB. PAGE 171 H3429
ECO/UNDEV INT/TRADE JURID CAP/ISM

L65
WIONCZEK M.,"LATIN AMERICA FREE TRADE ASSOCIATION." AGRI DIST/IND FINAN INDUS INT/ORG LABOR NAT/G TEC/DEV ECO/TAC HEALTH SKILL WEALTH...POLICY RELATIV MGT LAFTA 20. PAGE 169 H3390
L/A+17C MARKET REGION

S65
GANGAL S.C.,"SURVEY OF RECENT RESEARCH: INDIA AND THE COMMONWEALTH" INDIA UK NAT/G INT/TRADE PARTIC GOV/REL ROLE 20 CMN/WLTH. PAGE 55 H1095
BIBLIOG POLICY REGION DIPLOM

S65
HAYTER T.,"FRENCH AID TO AFRICA* ITS SCOPE AND ACHIEVEMENTS." CULTURE ECO/TAC INT/TRADE ADMIN REGION CENTRAL FEDERAL LOVE PWR SOVEREIGN EEC. PAGE 68 H1370
AFR FRANCE FOR/AID COLONIAL

S65
KINDLEBERGER C.P.,"MASS MIGRATION, THEN AND NOW." LAW ECO/DEV ECO/UNDEV INDUS LABOR INT/TRADE FEEDBACK REGION RIGID/FLEX...SOC NAT/COMP EEC. PAGE 86 H1714
EUR+WWI USA-45 WORKER IDEA/COMP

S65
MCALISTER L.N.,"CHANGING CONCEPTS OF THE ROLE OF THE MILITARY IN LATIN AMERICA." CULTURE NAT/G CREATE REGION NAT/LISM ATTIT SOVEREIGN...NAT/COMP GEN/LAWS. PAGE 106 H2120
L/A+17C FORCES IDEA/COMP PWR

S65
POWELL J.D.,"MILITARY ASSISTANCE AND MILITARISM IN LATIN AMERICA." USA+45 INT/ORG NAT/G CONTROL REGION PRODUC WEALTH...CLASSIF STAT NAT/COMP CONGRESS. PAGE 128 H2550
L/A+17C FORCES FOR/AID PWR

S65
SPAAK P.H.,"THE SEARCH FOR CONSENSUS: A NEW EFFORT TO BUILD EUROPE." FRANCE GERMANY ECO/DEV NAT/G CONSULT FORCES PLAN EDU/PROP REGION CONSEN ATTIT ...SOC METH/CNCPT OBS TREND EEC NATO WORK 20. PAGE 147 H2941
EUR+WWI INT/ORG

B66
BRACKMAN A.C.,SOUTHEAST ASIA'S SECOND FRONT: THE POWER STRUGGLE IN THE MALAY ARCHIPELAGO. CHINA/COM INDONESIA MALAYSIA ECO/UNDEV INT/ORG NAT/G FORCES DIPLOM EDU/PROP REGION COERCE GUERRILLA AUTHORIT POPULISM...MAJORIT 20 KENNEDY/JF SEATO. PAGE 20 H0396
S/ASIA MARXISM REV

B66
BROWN R.T.,TRANSPORT AND THE ECONOMIC INTEGRATION OF SOUTH AMERICA. L/A+17C ECO/UNDEV NAT/G OP/RES DIPLOM INT/TRADE REGION WEALTH...ECOMETRIC GEOG STAT LAFTA TIME. PAGE 22 H0449
MARKET DIST/IND SIMUL

B66
CADY J.F.,THAILAND, BURMA, LAOS AND CAMBODIA. FRANCE UK CULTURE NAT/G DOMIN GP/REL RACE/REL HABITAT...GEOG TREND CHINJAP BUDDHISM. PAGE 25 H0504
S/ASIA COLONIAL REGION SECT

B66
CHANG,THE PARTY AND THE NATIONAL QUESTION IN CHINA (TRANS. BY GEORGE MOSELEY). CHINA/COM CULTURE CONTROL NAT/LISM...CHARTS BIBLIOG/A 20. PAGE 29 H0576
GP/REL REGION ISOLAT MARXISM

B66
DIAMOND S.,THE TRANSFORMATION OF EAST AFRICA. NAT/G SCHOOL CREATE PROB/SOLV COLONIAL REGION RACE/REL FEDERAL...SOC ANTHOL WORSHIP 20 AFRICA/E. PAGE 41 H0819
CULTURE AFR TEC/DEV INDUS

B66
FITZGERALD C.P.,A CONCISE HISTORY OF EAST ASIA. ASIA KOREA S/ASIA INT/TRADE REGION MARXISM 20 CHINJAP. PAGE 51 H1017
ECO/UNDEV COLONIAL CULTURE

B66
GERARD-LIBOIS J.,KATANGA SECESSION. INT/ORG FORCES DIPLOM ADMIN CONTROL WAR CHOOSE PWR...CHARTS 20 KATANGA TSHOMBE/M UN. PAGE 56 H1114
NAT/G REGION ORD/FREE REV

B66
GORDON B.K.,THE DIMENSIONS OF CONFLICT IN SOUTHEAST ASIA. S/ASIA FORCES ADJUD REGION...CHARTS 20. PAGE 59 H1177
DIPLOM NAT/COMP INT/ORG VOL/ASSN

B66
GRAHAM B.D.,THE FORMATION OF THE AUSTRALIAN COUNTRY PARTIES. CANADA USA+45 USA-45 SOCIETY PLAN ECO/TAC ...NAT/COMP 20 AUSTRAL. PAGE 59 H1190
POL/PAR AGRI REGION PARL/PROC

B66
IOWA STATE U CTR AGRI AND ECO,RESEARCH AND EDUCATION FOR REGIONAL AND AREA DEVELOPMENT. FUT LAW CULTURE R+D LOC/G PLAN KNOWL...POLICY CHARTS ANTHOL 20. PAGE 78 H1565
REGION ACT/RES ECO/TAC INDUS

B66
KEAY E.A.,THE NATIVE AND CUSTOMARY COURTS OF NIGERIA. NIGERIA CONSTN ELITES NAT/G TOP/EX PARTIC REGION...DECISION JURID 19/20. PAGE 84 H1673
AFR ADJUD LAW

B66
MCKAY V.,AFRICAN DIPLOMACY STUDIES IN THE DETERMINANTS OF FOREIGN POLICY. AFR SOUTH/AFR CULTURE NEUTRAL REGION SOVEREIGN...INT/LAW GOV/COMP ANTHOL 20. PAGE 107 H2138
ECO/UNDEV RACE/REL CIVMIL/REL DIPLOM

B66
SCHRAM S.,MAO TSE-TUNG. ASIA CHINA/COM CONTROL REGION ATTIT...POLICY IDEA/COMP 20 MAO. PAGE 140 H2799
BIOG MARXISM TOP/EX GUERRILLA

B66
SMITH H.E.,READINGS IN ECONOMIC DEVELOPMENT AND ADMINISTRATION IN TANZANIA. TANZANIA FINAN INDUS LABOR NAT/G PLAN PROB/SOLV INT/TRADE COLONIAL REGION...ANTHOL BIBLIOG 20 AFRICA/E. PAGE 146 H2910
TEC/DEV ADMIN GOV/REL

B66
US DEPARTMENT OF STATE,RESEARCH ON AFRICA (EXTERNAL RESEARCH LIST NO 5-25). LAW CULTURE ECO/UNDEV POL/PAR DIPLOM EDU/PROP LEAD REGION MARXISM...GEOG LING WORSHIP 20. PAGE 159 H3188
BIBLIOG/A ASIA S/ASIA NAT/G

B66
US DEPARTMENT OF STATE,RESEARCH ON THE AMERICAN REPUBLICS (EXTERNAL RESEARCH LIST NO 6-25). CULTURE SOCIETY POL/PAR DIPLOM EDU/PROP MARXISM WORSHIP 20 OAS. PAGE 159 H3189
BIBLIOG/A L/A+17C REGION NAT/G

B66
US DEPARTMENT OF STATE,RESEARCH ON THE MIDDLE EAST (EXTERNAL RESEARCH LIST NO 4-25). GREECE ISRAEL SYRIA UAR YEMEN CULTURE SOCIETY POL/PAR SECT DIPLOM EDU/PROP WAR NAT/LISM...GEOG GOV/COMP 20. PAGE 160 H3190
BIBLIOG/A ISLAM NAT/G REGION

B66
US DEPARTMENT OF STATE,RESEARCH ON THE USSR AND EASTERN EUROPE (EXTERNAL RESEARCH LIST NO 1-25). USSR LAW CULTURE SOCIETY NAT/G TEC/DEV DIPLOM EDU/PROP REGION...GEOG LING. PAGE 160 H3191
BIBLIOG/A EUR+WWI COM MARXISM

B66
US DEPARTMENT OF STATE,RESEARCH ON WESTERN EUROPE, GREAT BRITAIN, AND CANADA (EXTERNAL RESEARCH LIST NO 3-25). CANADA GERMANY/W UK LAW CULTURE NAT/G POL/PAR FORCES EDU/PROP REGION MARXISM...GEOG SOC WORSHIP 20 CMN/WLTH. PAGE 160 H3192
BIBLIOG/A EUR+WWI DIPLOM

B66
ZOLBERG A.R.,CREATING POLITICAL ORDER. AFR CONGO/BRAZ GHANA NIGER KIN NAT/G DOMIN COLONIAL REGION CENTRAL NAT/LISM ATTIT PWR 20 CONGO/LEOP. PAGE 173 H3462
SOVEREIGN ORD/FREE CONSTN POL/PAR

S66
FELD W.,"NATIONAL ECONOMIC INTEREST GROUPS AND POLICY FORMATION IN THE EEC." NAT/G POL/PAR REGION CENTRAL SOVEREIGN...INT NET/THEORY EEC. PAGE 49 H0985
LOBBY ELITES DECISION

S66
GAMER R.E.,"URGENT SINGAPORE, PATIENT MALAYSIA." MALAYSIA S/ASIA ECO/UNDEV POL/PAR CHIEF TARIFFS TAX CONTROL LEAD REGION PWR 20 SINGAPORE. PAGE 55 H1094
DIPLOM NAT/G POLICY ECO/TAC

S66
KAPIL R.L.,"ON THE CONFLICT POTENTIAL OF INHERITED BOUNDARIES IN AFRICA." MOD/EUR MOROCCO UAR EX/STRUC DIPLOM LEGIT REGION ADJUST...RECORD NAT/COMP GEN/LAWS. PAGE 83 H1658
AFR COLONIAL PREDICT GEOG

S66
SNOW P.G.,"A SCALOGRAM ANALYSIS OF POLITICAL DEVELOPMENT." STRATA ECO/UNDEV POL/PAR REGION ALL/VALS PWR...SOC CHARTS. PAGE 146 H2924
L/A+17C NAT/COMP TESTS CLASSIF

B67
ANDERSON S.V.,THE NORDIC COUNCIL: A STUDY OF SCANDINAVIAN REGIONALISM. DENMARK FINLAND ICELAND NORWAY SWEDEN MARKET NAT/G VOL/ASSN CONSULT PARL/PROC ATTIT...TIME/SEQ BIBLIOG 20. PAGE 7 H0134
INT/ORG REGION DIPLOM LEGIS

B67
FAY S.B.,THE ORIGINS OF THE WORLD WAR (2ND REV. ED. 2 VOLS.). NAT/G FORCES DIPLOM CONFER LEAD PEACE ...REALPOL GOV/COMP 19/20. PAGE 49 H0978
MOD/EUR WAR REGION INT/ORG

B67
FISHER M.,PROVINCES AND PROVINCIAL CAPITALS OF THE WORLD. WOR+45 PROVS REGION. PAGE 51 H1014
GEOG NAT/G NAT/COMP STAT

B67
MOORE J.R.,THE ECONOMIC IMPACT OF THE TVA. AGRI INDUS PLAN BARGAIN CONTROL REGION GOV/REL DEMAND EFFICIENCY SOCISM 20 TVA. PAGE 112 H2249
ECO/UNDEV ECO/DEV NAT/G CREATE

B67
NYERERE J.K.,FREEDOM AND UNITY/UHURU NA UMOJA: A SELECTION FROM WRITINGS AND SPEECHES, 1952-65. TANZANIA ELITES ECO/UNDEV INT/ORG NAT/G CREATE DIPLOM COLONIAL REGION RACE/REL...ANTHOL 20. PAGE 119 H2383
SOVEREIGN AFR TREND ORD/FREE

B67
OLIVER R.,AFRICA SINCE 1800. AFR ISLAM CULTURE ECO/UNDEV SECT DOMIN RACE/REL DISCRIM SOVEREIGN 19/20. PAGE 121 H2414
DIPLOM COLONIAL REGION

B67
SCHUTZ W.W.,RETHINKING GERMAN POLICY; NEW APPROACHES TO REUNIFICATION. GERMANY USSR PLAN CONFER...POLICY 20. PAGE 140 H2806
REGION NAT/G DIPLOM PROB/SOLV

B67
SCHWARTZ M.A.,PUBLIC OPINION AND CANADIAN IDENTITY. CANADA SOCIETY LOC/G DIPLOM ADMIN LEAD REGION GP/REL SAMP. PAGE 141 H2812
ATTIT NAT/G NAT/LISM POL/PAR

B67
THOMPSON E.T.,PERSPECTIVES ON THE SOUTH: AGENDA FOR RESEARCH. CULTURE ECO/UNDEV SECT GP/REL EFFICIENCY ALL/VALS...HUM SOC CONCPT LING 20 NEGRO. PAGE 154 H3080
PROB/SOLV IDEA/COMP REGION ACT/RES

L67
HOSHII I.,"JAPAN'S STAKE IN ASIA." ASIA S/ASIA CAP/ISM ECO/TAC ROLE...GEOG 20 CHINJAP. PAGE 74 H1477
DIPLOM REGION NAT/G

INT/ORG

L67
SEGAL A.,"THE INTEGRATION OF DEVELOPING COUNTRIES: SOME THOUGHTS ON EAST AFRICA AND CENTRAL AMERICA." AFR L/A+17C INT/ORG NAT/G VOL/ASSN FOR/AID INT/TRADE EQUILIB NAT/LISM PWR 20. PAGE 141 H2820
ECO/UNDEV DIPLOM REGION

L67
TAMBIAH S.J.,"THE POLITICS OF LANGUAGE IN INDIA AND CEYLON." CEYLON INDIA NAT/G DOMIN ADMIN...SOC 20. PAGE 152 H3039
POL/PAR LING NAT/LISM REGION

L67
TOUVAL S.,"THE ORGANIZATION OF AFRICAN UNITY AND AFRICAN BORDERS." DEBATE REGION TASK REV ATTIT ORD/FREE...DECISION UN 20 OAU. PAGE 156 H3121
AFR NAT/G COLONIAL NAT/LISM

L67
UNESCO,"APARTHEID." SOUTH/AFR STRUCT KIN SCHOOL SECT WORKER DOMIN EDU/PROP REGION RACE/REL ISOLAT 20. PAGE 158 H3164
DISCRIM CULTURE COERCE COLONIAL

S67
ALBINSKI H.S.,"POLITICS AND BICULTURISM IN CANADA: THE FLAG DEBATE." CANADA SOCIETY NAT/G PROVS DELIB/GP DEBATE REGION SOVEREIGN PLURISM...POLICY SOC/INTEG 20. PAGE 5 H0093
NAT/LISM GP/REL POL/PAR CULTURE

S67
COHEN R.,"ANTHROPOLOGY AND POLITICAL SCIENCE: COURTSHIP OR MARRIAGE?" CULTURE STRATA STRUCT MUNIC REGION UTOPIA...NEW/IDEA TREND IDEA/COMP METH/COMP 20. PAGE 31 H0618
SOC INGP/REL AFR

S67
GRANT C.H.,"RURAL LOCAL GOVERNMENT IN GUYANA AND BRITISH HONDURAS." GUYANA HONDURAS L/A+17C AGRI NAT/G EX/STRUC ACT/RES REGION GOV/REL EFFICIENCY ORD/FREE 20. PAGE 60 H1196
ECO/UNDEV LOC/G ADMIN MUNIC

S67
GRIEB K.J.,"THE UNITED STATES AND THE CENTRAL AMERICAN CONFEDERATION." COSTA/RICA EL/SALVADR GUATEMALA HONDURAS L/A+17C NICARAGUA NAT/G FORCES CONFER AGREE EXEC ARMS/CONT REV WAR PEACE ATTIT 20. PAGE 60 H1212
INT/ORG DIPLOM POLICY REGION

S67
HANSON A.H.,"INDIA AFTER THE ELECTIONS." INDIA ECO/UNDEV LEGIS TEC/DEV FOR/AID GP/REL FEDERAL ATTIT 20. PAGE 66 H1321
NAT/G POL/PAR REGION CENTRAL

S67
HEASMAN D.J.,"THE GIBRALTAR AFFAIR." SPAIN UK NAT/G BAL/PWR CONSEN NAT/LISM ATTIT...REALPOL 20. PAGE 69 H1378
DIPLOM COLONIAL REGION

S67
HEBAL J.J.,"APPROACHES TO REGIONAL AND METROPOLITAN GOVERNMENTS IN THE UNITED STATES AND CANADA." CANADA FUT USA+45 MUNIC...TREND 20. PAGE 69 H1380
ADMIN REGION LOC/G NAT/COMP

S67
KYLE K.,"BACKGROUND TO THE CRISIS" ISLAM ISRAEL UAR UK USSR NAT/G PROB/SOLV LEGIT CONTROL REGION STRANGE MORAL 20 JEWS. PAGE 89 H1787
DIPLOM POLICY SOVEREIGN COERCE

S67
LEVI W.,"THE ELITIST NATURE OF NEW ASIA'S FOREIGN POLICY." CULTURE ECO/UNDEV NAT/G PROB/SOLV EDU/PROP COLONIAL CONTROL REGION NAT/LISM...NAT/COMP 20. PAGE 95 H1898
POLICY ELITES DIPLOM CREATE

S67
ROSE S.,"ASIAN NATIONALISM* THE SECOND STAGE." ASIA COM ECO/UNDEV NAT/G PROB/SOLV DIPLOM FOR/AID DOMIN NEUTRAL REGION TASK...METH/COMP 20. PAGE 134 H2675
NAT/LISM S/ASIA BAL/PWR COLONIAL

S67
SCHACHTER G.,"REGIONAL DEVELOPMENT IN THE ITALIAN DUAL ECONOMY" ITALY AGRI INDUS MARKET WORKER ECO/TAC CONTROL INCOME PRODUC 20. PAGE 138 H2767
REGION ECO/UNDEV NAT/G PROB/SOLV

S67
SINGH B.,"ITALIAN EXPERIENCE IN REGIONAL ECONOMIC DEVELOPMENT AND LESSONS FOR OTHER COUNTRIES." EUR+WWI ITALY INDUS NAT/G ACT/RES REGION GP/REL EFFICIENCY EQUILIB PRODUC WEALTH. PAGE 144 H2884
ECO/UNDEV PLAN ECO/TAC CONTROL

S67
SNELLEN I.T.,"APARTHEID* CHECKS AND CHANGES." SOUTH/AFR NAT/G PROB/SOLV COLONIAL REGION TASK GP/REL RACE/REL EFFICIENCY PRIVIL ORD/FREE 20. PAGE 146 H2923
DISCRIM NAT/LISM EQUILIB CONTROL

S67
SPINELLI A.,"EUROPEAN UNION IN THE RESISTANCE." NAT/G BAL/PWR DIPLOM CONFER REGION TOTALISM ORD/FREE POLICY. PAGE 147 H2948
NAT/LISM FEDERAL EUR+WWI INT/ORG

S67
VINCENT S.,"SHOULD BIAFRA SURVIVE?" NIGERIA ECO/UNDEV CHIEF FORCES ECO/TAC GP/REL DISCRIM PEACE ORD/FREE SOC/INTEG 20 BIAFRA IBO. PAGE 163 H3256
AFR REV REGION NAT/G

S67
ZARTMAN I.W.," NAT/G POL/PAR VOL/ASSN NAT/LISM ORD/FREE PWR...CONCPT NAT/COMP ORG/CHARTS OAU MAGHREB. PAGE 172 H3451
AFR ISLAM DIPLOM REGION

S68
DOUGLAS-HOME C.,"A MISTAKEN POLICY IN ADEN." YEMEN CULTURE ECO/UNDEV INDUS FORCES WORKER DIPLOM ECO/TAC CONTROL 20 ADEN. PAGE 42 H0842
SOVEREIGN COLONIAL POLICY REGION

S68
LUKASZEWSKI J.,"WESTERN INTEGRATION AND THE PEOPLE'S DEMOCRACIES." USSR ELITES ECO/DEV NAT/G VOL/ASSN INT/TRADE AGREE REV FEDERAL WEALTH SOCISM ...NAT/COMP SOC/INTEG 20 EEC. PAGE 99 H1977
DIPLOM INT/ORG COM REGION

REGRESS....REGRESSION ANALYSIS; SEE ALSO CON/ANAL

S57
MARCH J.C.,"PARTY LEGISLATIVE REPRESENTATION AS A FUNCTION OF ELECTION RESULTS." DRIVE...PROBABIL REGRESS STYLE CHARTS HYPO/EXP SIMUL. PAGE 102 H2046
REPRESENT GOV/COMP LEGIS CHOOSE

S65
WOLF C. JR.,"THE POLITICAL EFFECTS OF SOME MILITARY PROGRAMS* SOME INDICATIONS FROM LATIN AMERICA." ELITES STRATA BUDGET FOR/AID WEAPON ATTIT PERCEPT PWR...REGRESS SYS/QU CHARTS NAT/COMP. PAGE 170 H3397
L/A+17C FORCES CIVMIL/REL PROBABIL

REGRESSION ANALYSIS....SEE REGRESS

REHABILITATION....SEE REHABILITN

REHABILITN....REHABILITATION

REICH N. H2609

REISCHAUER R. H2610

REISCHAUER R.D. H3082

REISKY-DUBNIC V. H2611

REISS I. H2612

REISS J. H2613

RELATIONS AMONG GROUPS....SEE GP/REL

RELATISM....RELATIVISM

RELATIV....RELATIVITY

S51
NORTHROP F.S.C.,"ASIAN MENTALITY AND UNITED STATES FOREIGN POLICY." ASIA ISLAM USA+45 CULTURE SOCIETY SECT EDU/PROP LEGIT COERCE DRIVE MORAL ORD/FREE ...POLICY RELATIV TOT/POP 20. PAGE 119 H2376
S/ASIA ATTIT DIPLOM

B52
BENTHAM A.,HANDBOOK OF POLITICAL FALLACIES. FUT MOD/EUR LAW INTELL LOC/G MUNIC NAT/G DELIB/GP LEGIS CREATE EDU/PROP CT/SYS ATTIT RIGID/FLEX KNOWL PWR ...RELATIV PSY SOC CONCPT SELF/OBS TREND STERTYP TOT/POP. PAGE 14 H0286
POL/PAR

B57
DEAN V.M.,THE NATURE OF THE NON-WESTERN WORLD. AFR ASIA L/A+17C S/ASIA CULTURE SOCIETY STRATA ECO/DEV DIPLOM ECO/TAC FOR/AID ATTIT DRIVE ALL/VALS ...RELATIV SOC CONCPT TIME/SEQ TREND TOT/POP 20. PAGE 39 H0778
ECO/UNDEV STERTYP NAT/LISM

B58
GARTHOFF R.L.,SOVIET STRATEGY IN THE NUCLEAR AGE. FUT USSR R+D INT/ORG NAT/G ACT/RES TEC/DEV DOMIN DETER WAR ATTIT PWR...RELATIV METH/CNCPT SELF/OBS TREND CON/ANAL STERTYP GEN/LAWS 20. PAGE 55 H1103
COM FORCES BAL/PWR NUC/PWR

B58
HAYCRAFT J.,BABEL IN SPAIN. SPAIN ATTIT...RELATIV 20. PAGE 68 H1367
CULTURE PERSON BIOG GEOG

L60
HAAS E.B.,"CONSENSUS FORMATION IN THE COUNCIL OF EUROPE." EUR+WWI NAT/G DELIB/GP DIPLOM REGION CHOOSE PWR SOVEREIGN...RELATIV NEW/IDEA QUANT CHARTS INDEX TOT/POP OEEC 20 COUNCL/EUR. PAGE 63 H1265
POL/PAR INT/ORG STAT

S62
CORET A.,"LE STATUT DE L'ILE CHRISTMAS DE L'OCEAN INDIEN." FUT S/ASIA ECO/DEV ECO/UNDEV VOL/ASSN DELIB/GP PLAN...RELATIV OBS TIME/SEQ TREND AUSTRAL 20. PAGE 33 H0667
NAT/G INT/ORG NEW/ZEALND

B64
LI C.M.,INDUSTRIAL DEVELOPMENT IN COMMUNIST CHINA. CHINA/COM ECO/DEV ECO/UNDEV AGRI FINAN INDUS MARKET LABOR NAT/G ECO/TAC INT/TRADE EXEC ALL/VALS
ASIA TEC/DEV

...POLICY RELATIV TREND WORK TOT/POP VAL/FREE 20. PAGE 96 H1921

B64
PHILLIPS C.S.,THE DEVELOPMENT OF NIGERIAN FOREIGN POLICY. AFR CONSTN CULTURE STRATA NAT/G LEGIS DOMIN LEGIT EXEC...RELATIV SOC TIME/SEQ TREND TOT/POP 20. PAGE 125 H2502
CHOOSE POLICY DIPLOM NIGERIA

B64
PIPES R.,THE FORMATION OF THE SOVIET UNION. EUR+WWI MOD/EUR STRUCT ECO/UNDEV NAT/G LEGIS DOMIN LEGIT CT/SYS EXEC COERCE ALL/VALS...POLICY RELATIV HIST/WRIT TIME/SEQ TOT/POP 19/20. PAGE 126 H2514
COM USSR RUSSIA

L64
BERELSON B.,"SAMPLE SURVEYS AND POPULATION CONTROL." ASIA FUT ISLAM L/A+17C CULTURE SOCIETY FAM NAT/G CONSULT PLAN EDU/PROP ATTIT DRIVE ALL/VALS...POLICY RELATIV HEAL PSY SOC CONCPT METH/CNCPT OBS OBS/ENVIR TOT/POP. PAGE 15 H0297
BIO/SOC SAMP

S64
CLIGNET R.,"POTENTIAL ELITES IN GHANA AND THE IVORY COAST: A PRELIMINARY SURVEY." AFR CULTURE ELITES STRATA KIN NAT/G SECT DOMIN EXEC ORD/FREE RESPECT SKILL...POLICY RELATIV GP/COMP NAT/COMP 20. PAGE 30 H0605
PWR LEGIT IVORY/CST GHANA

S64
CROUZET F.,"WARS, BLOCKADE, AND ECONOMIC CHANGE IN EUROPE, 1792-1815." UK INDUS NAT/G TEC/DEV ECO/TAC WEALTH...POLICY RELATIV HIST/WRIT TIME/SEQ 18/19. PAGE 35 H0710
MOD/EUR MARKET

S64
NASH M.,"SOCIAL PREREQUISITES TO ECONOMIC GROWTH IN LATIN AMERICA AND SOUTHEAST ASIA." L/A+17C S/ASIA CULTURE SOCIETY ECO/UNDEV AGRI INDUS NAT/G PLAN TEC/DEV EDU/PROP ROUTINE ALL/VALS...POLICY RELATIV SOC NAT/COMP WORK TOT/POP 20. PAGE 116 H2314
ECO/DEV PERCEPT

S64
NEEDHAM T.,"SCIENCE AND SOCIETY IN EAST AND WEST." INTELL STRATA R+D LOC/G NAT/G PROVS CONSULT ACT/RES CREATE PLAN TEC/DEV EDU/PROP ADMIN ATTIT ALL/VALS ...POLICY RELATIV MGT CONCPT NEW/IDEA TIME/SEQ WORK WORK. PAGE 116 H2327
ASIA STRUCT

S64
REISS I.,"LE DECLENCHEMENT DE LA PREMIERE GUERRE MONDIALE." GERMANY RUSSIA NAT/G FORCES DOMIN EDU/PROP COERCE RIGID/FLEX PWR SOVEREIGN...RELATIV HIST/WRIT TOT/POP AUST/HUNG SERBIA 20. PAGE 131 H2612
MOD/EUR BAL/PWR DIPLOM WAR

S64
SAYEED K.,"PATHAN REGIONALISM." ISLAM PAKISTAN S/ASIA CULTURE SOCIETY NAT/G NEIGH DIPLOM LEGIT COERCE CHOOSE ATTIT DISPL PERCEPT ALL/VALS SOVEREIGN...POLICY RELATIV SOC TIME/SEQ TOT/POP 20. PAGE 138 H2761
SECT NAT/LISM REGION

L65
WIONCZEK M.,"LATIN AMERICA FREE TRADE ASSOCIATION." AGRI DIST/IND FINAN INDUS INT/ORG LABOR NAT/G TEC/DEV ECO/TAC HEALTH SKILL WEALTH...POLICY RELATIV MGT LAFTA 20. PAGE 169 H3390
L/A+17C MARKET REGION

RELATIVISM....SEE RELATISM, RELATIV

RELATIVITY....SEE RELATIV

RELIABILITY....SEE METH/CNCPT

RELIGION....SEE SECT, WORSHIP

RELIGIOUS GROUP....SEE SECT

REMAK J. H2614

RENAISSAN....RENAISSANCE

B58
ORTEGA Y GASSET J.,MAN AND CRISIS. SECT CREATE PERSON CONSERVE...GEN/LAWS RENAISSAN. PAGE 122 H2430
PHIL/SCI CULTURE CONCPT

B66
SETTON K.M.,GREAT PROBLEMS IN EUROPEAN CIVILIZATION. CHRIST-17C EUR+WWI MOD/EUR SECT GP/REL ALL/VALS ORD/FREE ALL/IDEOS...TREND ANTHOL T CHRISTIAN RENAISSAN PROTESTANT. PAGE 142 H2835
CULTURE CONCPT IDEA/COMP

RENFIELD R.L. H2615

RENNER G.T. H3345

RENNER K. H2616

RENT....RENTING

B61
KEE R.,REFUGEE WORLD. AUSTRIA EUR+WWI GERMANY NEIGH EX/STRUC WORKER PROB/SOLV ECO/TAC RENT EDU/PROP INGP/REL COST LITERACY HABITAT 20 MIGRATION. PAGE 84 H1676
NAT/G GIVE WEALTH STRANGE

S65
GOLDMAN M.I.,"A BALANCE SHEET OF SOVIET FOREIGN AID." USA+45 ECO/UNDEV BAL/PWR ECO/TAC RENT GIVE EDU/PROP CONTROL COST PROFIT GEN/METH. PAGE 58 H1158
USSR FOR/AID NAT/COMP EFFICIENCY

B66
NEVITT A.A.,THE ECONOMIC PROBLEMS OF HOUSING. WOR+45 ECO/DEV ECO/UNDEV ACT/RES PROB/SOLV ECO/TAC RENT...OBS CHARTS 20. PAGE 117 H2342
HABITAT PROC/MFG DELIB/GP NAT/COMP

S67
BRANCO R.,"LAND REFORM* THE ANSWER TO LATIN AMERICA'S AGRICULTURAL DEVELOPMENT?" L/A+17C NAT/G PLAN TEC/DEV BUDGET RENT EFFICIENCY 20. PAGE 20 H0404
ECO/UNDEV AGRI TAX OWN

S67
BUTTINGER J.,"VIETNAM* FRAUD OF THE 'OTHER WAR'." VIETNAM/S ELITES STRUCT AGRI NAT/G FOR/AID RENT TREND. PAGE 25 H0499
PLAN WEALTH REV ECO/UNDEV

REP/CONVEN....REPUBLICAN (PARTY - U.S.) NATIONAL CONVENTION

REPAR....REPARATIONS; SEE ALSO INT/REL, SANCTION

B40
WUNDERLICH F.,LABOR UNDER GERMAN DEMOCRACY, ARBITRATION 1918-1933. GERMANY NAT/G PAY REPAR ADJUD CT/SYS GP/REL...MAJORIT 20. PAGE 171 H3426
LABOR WORKER INDUS BARGAIN

B60
FEIS H.,BETWEEN WAR AND PEACE: THE POTSDAM CONFERENCE. EUR+WWI NAT/G DELIB/GP PROB/SOLV REPAR WAR CIVMIL/REL...BIBLIOG 20. PAGE 49 H0983
DIPLOM CONFER BAL/PWR

B65
BRIDGMAN J.,GERMAN AFRICA: A SELECT ANNOTATED BIBLIOGRAPHY. AFR AGRI DIPLOM REPAR WAR FASCISM 20. PAGE 21 H0414
BIBLIOG/A COLONIAL NAT/G EDU/PROP

REPARATIONS....SEE REPAR

REPRESENT....REPRESENTATION; SEE ALSO LEGIS

NC0
CARRINGTON C.E.,THE COMMONWEALTH IN AFRICA (PAMPHLET). UK STRUCT NAT/G COLONIAL REPRESENT GOV/REL RACE/REL NAT/LISM...MAJORIT 20 EEC NEGRO COLD/WAR. PAGE 27 H0540
ECO/UNDEV AFR DIPLOM PLAN

B00
MARKHAM V.R.,SOUTH AFRICA, PAST AND PRESENT. NETHERLAND SOUTH/AFR CULTURE LEGIS EDU/PROP COLONIAL CHOOSE REPRESENT DISCRIM ATTIT...OBS TIME/SEQ 17/19 NEGRO BOER/WAR. PAGE 103 H2054
WAR LEAD RACE/REL

B08
LLOYD H.D.,THE SWISS DEMOCRACY. SWITZERLND INDUS NAT/G WORKER CHOOSE OWN ORD/FREE SOCISM...PLURIST 19/20 MONOPOLY. PAGE 97 H1944
NAT/COMP GOV/COMP REPRESENT POPULISM

B10
MILL J.S.,UTILITARIANISM, LIBERTY, AND REPRESENTATIVE GOVERNMENT. CONTROL PERCEPT PERSON MORAL...CONCPT GEN/LAWS. PAGE 110 H2205
HAPPINESS ORD/FREE REPRESENT NAT/G

B10
TEMPERLEY H.W.V.,SENATES AND UPPER CHAMBERS; THEIR USE AND FUNCTION IN THE MODERN STATE... UK WOR-45 CONSTN NAT/G POL/PAR PROVS SECT COLONIAL LEAD CHOOSE REPRESENT PWR...BIBLIOG 19/20 PARLIAMENT SENATE CMN/WLTH HOUSE/LORD. PAGE 153 H3059
PARL/PROC NAT/COMP LEGIS EX/STRUC

B11
HUXLEY T.H.,METHOD AND RESULTS: ESSAYS. EDU/PROP REPRESENT OWN PERSON PWR WEALTH...PSY IDEA/COMP GEN/LAWS. PAGE 76 H1514
ORD/FREE NAT/G POPULISM PLURIST

B12
HARIOU M.,LA SOUVERAINTE NATIONALE. EX/STRUC FORCES LEGIS CHOOSE PWR JURID. PAGE 66 H1331
SOVEREIGN CONCPT NAT/G REPRESENT

B15
MICHELS R.,POLITICAL PARTIES. NAT/G BAL/PWR CHOOSE REPRESENT ATTIT SOCISM...PSY SOC CONCPT OBS 20 MONOPOLY. PAGE 110 H2198
POL/PAR CENTRAL LEAD PWR

N17
BURKE E.,THOUGHTS ON THE CAUSE OF THE PRESENT DISCONTENTS (PAMPHLET). MOD/EUR UK CONSTN CHIEF LEGIS DOMIN CONTROL EXEC REPRESENT POPULISM ...TRADIT NEW/IDEA METH/COMP 18 BURKE/EDM. PAGE 24 H0484
ORD/FREE REV PARL/PROC NAT/G

N19
MAO TSE-TUNG,ON SOME IMPORTANT PROBLEMS OF THE PARTY'S PRESENT POLICY. CHINA/COM CONSTN ELITES INTELL AGRI DOMIN EDU/PROP REV REPRESENT GP/REL OWN PEACE ORD/FREE 20 COM/PARTY. PAGE 102 H2044
POLICY NAT/G CHIEF LEGIT

N19
MASSEY V.,CANADIANS AND THEIR COMMONWEALTH: THE ROMANES LECTURE DELIVERED IN THE SHELDONIAN THEATRE JUNE 1, 1961 (PAMPHLET). CANADA UK CULTURE ECO/DEV REPRESENT NAT/LISM PEACE PWR CONSERVE 20 CMN/WLTH. PAGE 104 H2088
ATTIT DIPLOM NAT/G SOVEREIGN

N19
MEZERIK A.G.,APARTHEID IN THE REPUBLIC OF SOUTH AFRICA (PAMPHLET). DIPLOM DOMIN CONTROL COERCE REPRESENT CONSEN ATTIT. PAGE 110 H2194
DISCRIM RACE/REL POL/PAR POLICY

N19
OPERATIONS AND POLICY RESEARCH,PERU ELECTION MEMORANDA (PAMPHLET). L/A+17C PERU POL/PAR LEGIS EXEC APPORT REPRESENT 20. PAGE 121 H2421
CHOOSE CONSTN SUFF NAT/G

N19
OPERATIONS AND POLICY RESEARCH,URUGUAY: ELECTION FACTBOOK: NOVEMBER 27, 1966 (PAMPHLET). URUGUAY LAW NAT/G LEAD REPRESENT...STAT BIOG CHARTS 20. PAGE 121 H2422
POL/PAR CHOOSE PLAN ATTIT

N19
ROWE J.W.,THE ARGENTINE ELECTIONS OF 1963 (PAMPHLET). L/A+17C LOC/G NAT/G LEGIS REPRESENT 20 ARGEN. PAGE 135 H2703
CHOOSE CONSTN APPORT POL/PAR

N19
SOUTH AFRICA COMMISSION ON FUT,INTERIM AND FINAL REPORTS ON FUTURE FORM OF GOVERNMENT IN THE SOUTH-WEST AFRICAN PROTECTORATE (PAMPHLET). SOUTH/AFR NAT/G FORCES CONFER COLONIAL CONTROL 20 AFRICA/SW. PAGE 147 H2936
CONSTN REPRESENT ADMIN PROB/SOLV

B20
COLE G.D.H.,SOCIAL THEORY. CULTURE LOC/G SECT REGION REPRESENT ATTIT DRIVE...PSY SOC BIBLIOG. PAGE 31 H0621
CONCPT NAT/G PHIL/SCI

B21
WALLAS G.,HUMAN NATURE IN POLITICS (3RD ED.). UNIV NAT/G LEAD CHOOSE REPRESENT GP/REL NAT/LISM RATIONAL BIO/SOC HEREDITY ALL/VALS MAJORIT. PAGE 165 H3293
PSY DRIVE PERSON

B22
KRABBE H.,THE MODERN IDEA OF THE STATE. LAW CHIEF DIPLOM DOMIN ADMIN REPRESENT CENTRAL ORD/FREE ...NEW/IDEA GOV/COMP IDEA/COMP. PAGE 88 H1761
SOVEREIGN CONSTN PHIL/SCI

B23
DELBRUCK H.,GOVERNMENT AND THE WILL OF THE PEOPLE (TRANS. BY ROY S. MACELWEE). MOD/EUR NAT/G CHOOSE REPRESENT...CONCPT 19/20. PAGE 39 H0788
SOVEREIGN ORD/FREE MAJORITY POL/PAR

B23
LEES-SMITH H.B.,SECOND CHAMBERS IN THEORY AND PRACTICE. IRELAND NORWAY SOUTH/AFR UK LAW POL/PAR LEGIS CONTROL 20 CMN/WLTH. PAGE 93 H1858
PARL/PROC DELIB/GP REPRESENT GP/COMP

B23
ROBERT H.M.,PARLIAMENTARY LAW. POL/PAR LEGIS PARTIC CHOOSE REPRESENT GP/REL. PAGE 132 H2640
PARL/PROC DELIB/GP NAT/G JURID

B25
MAURRAS C.,ENQUETE SUR LA MONARCHIE (1909). FRANCE CONTROL REPRESENT DISCRIM HEREDITY PWR CONSERVE 20 BUREAUCRCY. PAGE 105 H2103
TRADIT AUTHORIT NAT/G CHIEF

B28
FYFE H.,THE BRITISH LIBERAL PARTY. UK SECT ADMIN LEAD CHOOSE GP/REL PWR SOCISM...MAJORIT TIME/SEQ 19/20 LIB/PARTY CONSRV/PAR. PAGE 54 H1084
POL/PAR NAT/G REPRESENT POPULISM

C28
WARD P.W.,"SOVEREIGNTY: A STUDY OF A CONTEMPORARY POLITICAL NOTION." CONSTN NAT/G DIPLOM REPRESENT PLURISM...IDEA/COMP BIBLIOG. PAGE 165 H3304
SOVEREIGN CONCPT NAT/LISM

B30
HATTERSLEY A.F.,A SHORT HISTORY OF DEMOCRACY. WOR-45 CONSTN NAT/G SECT DOMIN WAR CHOOSE ORD/FREE PWR...CONCPT GOV/COMP BIBLIOG ATHENS ROME. PAGE 68 H1355
REPRESENT MAJORIT POPULISM

S31
HEINBERG J.G.,"THE PERSONNEL OF FRENCH CABINETS, 1871-1930." FRANCE STRATA CHIEF CHOOSE REPRESENT MAJORITY...STAT QU CENSUS TREND CHARTS PERS/COMP 19/20 CHAMBR/DEP. PAGE 69 H1386
ELITES NAT/G DELIB/GP TOP/EX

C31
MACLEOD W.C.,"THE ORIGIN AND HISTORY OF POLITICS." UNIV CULTURE NAT/G REPRESENT...SOC CONCPT TREND BIBLIOG. PAGE 100 H2004
METH STRUCT SOCIETY

S32
BEARD C.A.,"THE TEUTONIC ORIGINS OF REPRESENTATIVE GOVERNMENT" UK ROMAN/EMP TAX COERCE PWR IDEA/COMP. PAGE 12 H0247
REPRESENT NAT/G

S32
BEARD C.A.,"REPRESENTATIVE GOVERNMENT IN EVOLUTION" WOR-45 AGRI TEC/DEV DOMIN EFFICIENCY ORD/FREE CONSERVE...TIME/SEQ GOV/COMP IDEA/COMP GRECO/ROMN. PAGE 12 H0248
REPRESENT POPULISM NAT/G PWR

B34
LIPPMANN W.,THE METHOD OF FREEDOM. SOCIETY INDUS LABOR LOBBY WAR REPRESENT...POLICY IDEA/COMP METH/COMP 19/20. PAGE 97 H1936
CONCPT MAJORIT NAT/G

B35
LASKI H.J.,THE STATE IN THEORY AND PRACTICE. ELITES ECO/TAC REPRESENT ORD/FREE PWR WEALTH POPULISM ...GOV/COMP GEN/LAWS 19/20. PAGE 92 H1829
CAP/ISM COERCE NAT/G FASCISM

B36
CLARKE M.V.,MEDIEVAL REPRESENTATION AND CONSENT. IRELAND UK REPRESENT SUFF. PAGE 30 H0603
PARL/PROC LEGIS NAT/G

B38
IIZAWA S.,POLITICS AND POLITICAL PARTIES IN JAPAN. ELITES VOL/ASSN CHOOSE SUFF CIVMIL/REL GP/REL 19/20 CHINJAP. PAGE 76 H1522
POL/PAR REPRESENT FORCES NAT/G

C39
BURKE E.,"ON THE REFORM OF THE REPRESENTATION IN THE HOUSE OF COMMONS" (1782) IN COLLECTED WORKS (VOL. 5)" UK ELITES STRATA NAT/G REPRESENT ORD/FREE PWR POPULISM...POLICY NEW/IDEA GEN/LAWS 18 BURKE/EDM. PAGE 24 H0486
TRADIT CONSTN PARL/PROC LEGIS

S40
BROMAGE A.W.,"THE VOCATIONAL SENATE IN IRELAND" EUR+WWI IRELAND. PAGE 21 H0430
PWR NAT/G REPRESENT LEGIS

C41
WASSERMAN L.,"HANDBOOK OF POLITICAL "ISMS" CAP/ISM REPRESENT TOTALISM MARXISM NEW/LIB SOCISM...MAJORIT BIBLIOG 20. PAGE 166 H3313
IDEA/COMP PHIL/SCI OWN NAT/G

B42
NEUMANN S.,PERMANENT REVOLUTION: THE TOTAL STATE IN A WORLD AT WAR. COM EUR+WWI GERMANY USSR EX/STRUC DIPLOM CONTROL COERCE REPRESENT MARXISM...SOC GOV/COMP BIBLIOG 20 HITLER/A STALIN/J. PAGE 117 H2337
FASCISM TOTALISM DOMIN EDU/PROP

B43
LENIN V.I.,LEFT WING COMMUNISM: AN INFANTILE DISORDER (1920). GERMANY MOD/EUR USSR STRUCT CHIEF DOMIN EDU/PROP LEGIT LEAD REPRESENT POPULISM ...METH/COMP 19 LENIN/VI COM/PARTY MENSHEVIK. PAGE 94 H1879
COM MARXISM NAT/G REV

S43
PRICE D.K.,"THE PARLIAMENTARY AND PRESIDENTIAL SYSTEMS" (BMR)" USA-45 NAT/G EX/STRUC PARL/PROC GOV/REL PWR 20 PRESIDENT CONGRESS PARLIAMENT. PAGE 128 H2561
LEGIS REPRESENT ADMIN GOV/COMP

B44
BARKER E.,THE DEVELOPMENT OF PUBLIC SERVICES IN WESTERN WUROPE: 1660-1930. FRANCE GERMANY UK SCHOOL CONTROL REPRESENT ROLE...WELF/ST 17/20. PAGE 11 H0219
GOV/COMP ADMIN EX/STRUC

B47
MARX F.M.,THE PRESIDENT AND HIS STAFF SERVICES PUBLIC ADMINISTRATION SERVICES NUMBER 98 (PAMPHLET). FINAN ADMIN CT/SYS REPRESENT PWR 20 PRESIDENT. PAGE 104 H2075
CONSTN CHIEF NAT/G EX/STRUC

B48
LASKI H.S.,THE AMERICAN DEMOCRACY. CULTURE INDUS SECT WORKER DIPLOM EDU/PROP REPRESENT RACE/REL ORD/FREE PWR...NAT/COMP 18/20. PAGE 92 H1831
NAT/G LOC/G USA-45 POPULISM

B49
SCHWARTZ B.,LAW AND THE EXECUTIVE IN BRITAIN: A COMPARATIVE STUDY. UK USA+45 LAW EX/STRUC PWR ...GOV/COMP 20. PAGE 140 H2807
ADMIN EXEC CONTROL REPRESENT

L49
BRECHT A.,"THE NEW GERMAN CONSTITUTION." GERMANY/W NAT/G CHIEF EX/STRUC LEGIS PROB/SOLV ADMIN REPRESENT TOTALISM ORD/FREE PLURISM...MAJORIT CHARTS 20. PAGE 20 H0409
CONSTN DIPLOM SOVEREIGN FEDERAL

S49
BOUSCAREN A.T.,"THE EUROPEAN CHRISTIAN DEMOCRATS" EUR+WWI NAT/G LEGIS 19/20 CHRIS/DEM EUROPE. PAGE 19 H0387
REPRESENT POL/PAR

B50
MCHENRY D.E.,THE THIRD FORCE IN CANADA: THE COOPERATIVE COMMONWEALTH FEDERATION, 1932-1948. CANADA EX/STRUC LEGIS REPRESENT 20 LABOR/PAR. PAGE 107 H2131
POL/PAR ADMIN CHOOSE POLICY

C50
STOKES W.S.,"HONDURAS: AN AREA STUDY IN GOVERNMENT." HONDURAS NAT/G POL/PAR COLONIAL CT/SYS ROUTINE CHOOSE REPRESENT...GEOG RECORD BIBLIOG 19/20. PAGE 149 H2988
CONSTN LAW L/A+17C ADMIN

N51
MEYER E.W.,POLITICAL PARTIES IN WESTERN GERMANY (PAMPHLET). EUR+WWI GERMANY/W PRESS LEAD CHOOSE REPRESENT ATTIT 20. PAGE 109 H2189
BIBLIOG POL/PAR NAT/G VOL/ASSN

S53
DRUCKER P.F.,"THE EMPLOYEE SOCIETY." STRUCT BAL/PWR PARTIC REPRESENT PWR...DECISION CONCPT. PAGE 42 H0849 — LABOR MGT WORKER CULTURE

N53
VITO F.,"RECENT DEVELOPMENTS IN THE THEORY OF DEMOCRATIC ADMIN" INTL POL SCI ASS'N CONFERENCE ON PUBLIC ADMINISTRATION... FRANCE ITALY UK REPRESENT EFFICIENCY NEW/LIB SOCISM...WELF/ST 20. PAGE 163 H3257 — GOV/COMP CONTROL EX/STRUC

B54
JENNINGS I.,THE QUEEN'S GOVERNMENT. UK POL/PAR DELIB/GP ADJUD ADMIN CT/SYS PARL/PROC REPRESENT CONSERVE 13/20 PARLIAMENT. PAGE 80 H1605 — NAT/G CONSTN LEGIS CHIEF

S54
COLE T.,"LESSONS FROM RECENT EUROPEAN EXPERIENCE." EUR+WWI EX/STRUC 20. PAGE 31 H0626 — GOV/COMP ADMIN REPRESENT

B55
RUSTOW D.A.,THE POLITICS OF COMPROMISE. SWEDEN LABOR EX/STRUC LEGIS PLAN REPRESENT SOCISM...SOC 19/20. PAGE 136 H2720 — POL/PAR NAT/G POLICY ECO/TAC

C55
APTER D.E.,"THE GOLD COAST IN TRANSITION." AFR CONSTN LOC/G LEGIS DIPLOM COLONIAL CONTROL GOV/REL ...CHARTS BIBLIOG 20 CMN/WLTH. PAGE 7 H0150 — ORD/FREE REPRESENT PARL/PROC NAT/G

B56
FIELD G.C.,POLITICAL THEORY. POL/PAR REPRESENT MORAL SOVEREIGN...JURID IDEA/COMP. PAGE 50 H0990 — CONCPT NAT/G ORD/FREE DIPLOM

B56
MYERS F.M.,THE WARFARE OF DEMOCRATIC IDEALS. SECT KNOWL MORAL CATHISM...TRADIT CONCPT 20. PAGE 115 H2302 — POPULISM CHOOSE REPRESENT PERCEPT

S56
KHAMA T.,"POLITICAL CHANGE IN AFRICAN SOCIETY." CONSTN SOCIETY LOC/G NAT/G POL/PAR EX/STRUC LEGIS LEGIT ADMIN CHOOSE REPRESENT NAT/LISM MORAL ORD/FREE PWR...CONCPT OBS TREND GEN/METH CMN/WLTH 17/20. PAGE 85 H1706 — AFR ELITES

C56
NEUMANN S.,"MODERN POLITICAL PARTIES: APPROACHES TO COMPARATIVE POLITIC. FRANCE UK EX/STRUC DOMIN ADMIN LEAD REPRESENT TOTALISM ATTIT...POLICY TREND METH/COMP ANTHOL BIBLIOG/A 20 CMN/WLTH. PAGE 117 H2338 — POL/PAR GOV/COMP ELITES MAJORIT

B57
LONG H.A.,USURPERS - FOES OF FREE MAN. LAW NAT/G CHIEF LEGIS DOMIN ADJUD REPRESENT GOV/REL ORD/FREE LAISSEZ POPULISM...POLICY 18/20 SUPREME/CT ROOSEVLT/F CONGRESS CON/INTERP. PAGE 98 H1961 — CT/SYS CENTRAL FEDERAL CONSTN

S57
MARCH J.C.,"PARTY LEGISLATIVE REPRESENTATION AS A FUNCTION OF ELECTION RESULTS." DRIVE...PROBABIL REGRESS STYLE CHARTS HYPO/EXP SIMUL. PAGE 102 H2046 — REPRESENT GOV/COMP LEGIS CHOOSE

B58
BRADY A.,DEMOCRACY IN THE DOMINIONS (3RD ED.). CANADA NEW/ZEALND SOUTH/AFR WOR+45 LAW EX/STRUC DOMIN COLONIAL PARL/PROC REPRESENT RACE/REL NAT/LISM WEALTH 20 AUSTRAL CMN/WLTH. PAGE 20 H0399 — GOV/COMP POL/PAR POPULISM NAT/G

B58
CAMPBELL P.,FRENCH ELECTORAL SYSTEMS AND ELECTIONS SINCE 1789 (2ND ED.). FRANCE NAT/G EX/STRUC PWR ...CHARTS 18/20. PAGE 26 H0516 — REPRESENT CHOOSE POL/PAR SUFF

B58
COWAN L.G.,LOCAL GOVERNMENT IN WEST AFRICA. AFR FRANCE UK CULTURE KIN POL/PAR CHIEF LEGIS CREATE ADMIN PARTIC GOV/REL GP/REL...METH/COMP 20. PAGE 34 H0682 — LOC/G COLONIAL SOVEREIGN REPRESENT

B58
HERMENS F.A.,THE REPRESENTATIVE REPUBLIC. USA-45 PLURISM GOV/COMP. PAGE 70 H1401 — POL/PAR CHOOSE REPRESENT

B58
PALMER E.E.,"POLITICAL MAN" IN E. PALMER, PROBLEMS IN DEMOCRATIC CITIZENSHIP. LOC/G NAT/G LEGIS PRESS CHOOSE REPRESENT GP/REL...DECISION SOC IDEA/COMP ANTHOL 20. PAGE 123 H2449 — PARTIC POL/PAR EDU/PROP MAJORIT

B58
WILMERDING L. JR.,THE ELECTORAL COLLEGE. CONSTN NAT/G POL/PAR DELIB/GP LEGIS PROB/SOLV CONFER EXEC LEAD APPORT REPRESENT. PAGE 169 H3377 — CHOOSE DECISION ACT/RES

S58
GARCEAU O.,"INTEREST GROUP THEORY IN POLITICAL RESEARCH." ELITES NAT/G PLAN LEAD REPRESENT INGP/REL POLICY. PAGE 55 H1098 — GP/COMP GP/REL LOBBY PLURISM

S58
GUSFIELD J.R.,"EQUALITARIANISM AND BUREAUCRATIC RECRUITMENT." UK USA+45 USA-45 EX/STRUC 19/20. PAGE 63 H1257 — GOV/COMP REPRESENT TOP/EX ELITES

S58
MAIR L.P.,"REPRESENTATIVE LOCAL GOVERNMENT AS A PROBLEM IN SOCIAL CHANGE." ECO/UNDEV KIN LOC/G NAT/G SCHOOL JUDGE ADMIN ROUTINE REPRESENT RIGID/FLEX RESPECT...CONCPT STERTYP CMN/WLTH 20. PAGE 101 H2025 — AFR PWR ELITES

S58
SCHUMM S.,"INTEREST REPRESENTATION IN FRANCE AND GERMANY." EUR+WWI FRANCE GERMANY INSPECT PARL/PROC REPRESENT 20 WEIMAR/REP. PAGE 140 H2803 — LOBBY DELIB/GP NAT/G

B59
GOPAL R.,INDIAN MUSLIMS: A POLITICAL HISTORY (1858-1947). INDIA ISLAM PAKISTAN NAT/G SECT LEGIS LEAD COERCE WAR REPRESENT ISOLAT ORD/FREE 19/20 HINDU MUSLIM. PAGE 59 H1175 — COLONIAL GP/REL POL/PAR REGION

B59
WRAITH R.E.,EAST AFRICAN CITIZEN. AFR GHANA UK AGRI INDUS LOC/G POL/PAR PROB/SOLV CONTROL REGION REPRESENT NAT/LISM PWR...OBS 20 AFRICA/E AFRICA/W. PAGE 171 H3415 — ECO/UNDEV RACE/REL NAT/G NAT/COMP

S59
GABLE R.W.,"CULTURE AND ADMINISTRATION IN IRAN." IRAN EXEC PARTIC REPRESENT PWR. PAGE 54 H1085 — ADMIN CULTURE EX/STRUC INGP/REL

S59
LEYS C.,"MODELS, THEORIES, AND THE THEORY OF POLITICAL PARTIES" CANADA LIECHTENST UK LOC/G NAT/G PARTIC REPRESENT GP/REL CONSEN EQUILIB MAJORITY ...NEW/IDEA MATH CHARTS 20. PAGE 96 H1919 — POL/PAR CHOOSE METH/CNCPT SIMUL

B60
AYEARST M.,THE BRITISH WEST INDIES: THE SEARCH FOR SELF-GOVERNMENT. FUT WEST/IND LOC/G POL/PAR EX/STRUC LEGIS CHOOSE FEDERAL...NAT/COMP BIBLIOG 17/20. PAGE 9 H0186 — CONSTN COLONIAL REPRESENT NAT/G

B60
BREDVOLD L.I.,THE PHILOSOPHY OF EDMUND BURKE. POL/PAR PARL/PROC REPRESENT CONSERVE...JURID 18 BURKE/EDM. PAGE 20 H0410 — PHIL/SCI NAT/G CONCPT

L60
ROKKAN S.,"NORWAY AND THE UNITED STATES OF AMERICA." NORWAY CHOOSE...SOC STAND/INT SAMP CHARTS GP/COMP METH/COMP 20. PAGE 133 H2665 — STRUCT NAT/G PARTIC REPRESENT

S60
HALSEY A.H.,"THE CHANGING FUNCTIONS OF UNIVERSITIES IN ADVANCED INDUSTRIAL SOCIETIES." R+D EDU/PROP REPRESENT ROLE ORD/FREE PWR TREND. PAGE 65 H1298 — ACADEM CREATE CULTURE ADJUST

S60
TAYLOR M.G.,"THE ROLE OF THE MEDICAL PROFESSION IN THE FORMULATION AND EXECUTION OF PUBLIC POLICY" (BMR)" CANADA NAT/G CONSULT ADMIN REPRESENT GP/REL ROLE SOVEREIGN...DECISION 20 CMA. PAGE 153 H3056 — PROF/ORG HEALTH LOBBY POLICY

C60
SMITH T.E.,"ELECTIONS IN DEVELOPING COUNTRIES: A STUDY OF ELECTORAL PROCEDURES USED IN TOPICAL AFRICA, SOUTH-EAST ASIA..." AFR S/ASIA UK ROUTINE GOV/REL RACE/REL...GOV/COMP BIBLIOG 20. PAGE 146 H2918 — ECO/UNDEV CHOOSE REPRESENT ADMIN

B61
BURKS R.V.,THE DYNAMICS OF COMMUNISM IN EASTERN EUROPE. COM YUGOSLAVIA POL/PAR RACE/REL ISOLAT ...CORREL CON/ANAL CHARTS GP/COMP DICTIONARY 20 EUROPE/E SLAV/MACED. PAGE 24 H0489 — MARXISM STRUCT WORKER REPRESENT

B61
GUIZOT F.P.G.,HISTORY OF THE ORIGIN OF REPRESENTATIVE GOVERNMENT IN EUROPE. CHRIST-17C FRANCE MOD/EUR SPAIN UK LAW CHIEF FORCES POPULISM ...MAJORIT TIME/SEQ GOV/COMP NAT/COMP 4/19 PARLIAMENT. PAGE 62 H1250 — LEGIS REPRESENT CONSTN NAT/G

B61
HALPERIN S.,THE POLITICAL WORLD OF AMERICAN ZIONISM. ISRAEL FINAN LABOR VOL/ASSN GIVE LOBBY REPRESENT GP/REL ATTIT POLICY. PAGE 64 H1293 — CULTURE SECT EDU/PROP DELIB/GP

B61
HARE T.,A TREATISE ON THE ELECTION OF REPRESENTATIVES, PARLIAMENTARY AND MUNICIPAL. UK CONSTN NAT/G PARL/PROC CHOOSE ATTIT...MAJORIT 18/19 PARLIAMENT. PAGE 66 H1330 — LEGIS GOV/REL CONSEN REPRESENT

B61
JUSTICE,THE CITIZEN AND THE ADMINISTRATION: THE REDRESS OF GRIEVANCES (PAMPHLET). EUR+WWI UK LAW CONSTN STRATA NAT/G CT/SYS PARTIC COERCE...NEW/IDEA IDEA/COMP 20 OMBUDSMAN. PAGE 82 H1644 — INGP/REL CONSULT ADJUD REPRESENT

B61
NARAIN J.P.,SWARAJ FOR THE PEOPLE. INDIA CONSTN LOC/G MUNIC POL/PAR CHOOSE REPRESENT EFFICIENCY ATTIT PWR SOVEREIGN 20. PAGE 116 H2311 — NAT/G ORD/FREE EDU/PROP EX/STRUC

B61
NARASIMHAN V.K.,THE PRESS, THE PUBLIC AND THE ADMINISTRATION (PAMPHLET). INDIA COM/IND CONTROL REPRESENT GOV/REL EFFICIENCY...ANTHOL 20. PAGE 116 H2312
NAT/G ADMIN PRESS NEW/LIB

B61
TREVE W.,DEUTSCHE PARTEIPROGRAMME 1861-1961. GERMANY GERMANY/W DELIB/GP CONFER CHOOSE REPRESENT 19/20. PAGE 157 H3130
POL/PAR NAT/G LEGIS PARL/PROC

S61
ELAZAR D.J.,"CHURCHES AS MOLDERS OF AMERICAN POLITICS." STRATA MUNIC EDU/PROP RACE/REL ORD/FREE SOC. PAGE 45 H0904
SECT CULTURE REPRESENT LOC/G

S61
MACRIDIS R.C.,"INTEREST GROUPS IN COMPARATIVE ANALYSIS." CULTURE OP/RES LOBBY REPRESENT GP/REL AUTHORIT ORD/FREE PWR...POLICY DECISION METH/CNCPT CLASSIF. PAGE 101 H2010
GP/COMP CONCPT PLURISM

B62
HARRINGTON M.,THE OTHER AMERICA: POVERTY IN THE UNITED STATES. WORKER CREATE REPRESENT RACE/REL AGE/O DRIVE POLICY. PAGE 67 H1338
WEALTH WELF/ST INCOME CULTURE

B62
STATE AND LOCAL GOVERNMENT. MUNIC NAT/G NEIGH PRESS CONTROL CHOOSE REPRESENT...BIBLIOG 20. PAGE 104 H2076
PROVS LOC/G GOV/REL PWR

B62
RANNEY A.,THE DOCTRINE OF RESPONSIBLE PARTY GOVERNMENT. USA+45 USA-45 CONSTN PLAN CHOOSE ...MAJORIT GOV/COMP IDEA/COMP 20. PAGE 130 H2591
POL/PAR POLICY REPRESENT NAT/G

B62
ROUSSEAU J.J.,THE SOCIAL CONTRACT. LAW CONSTN CHIEF DOMIN REPRESENT GP/REL ORD/FREE POPULISM...MAJORIT GOV/COMP 18. PAGE 135 H2700
GEN/LAWS AGREE REV

B62
RUDE G.,WILKES AND LIBERTY. UK NAT/G POL/PAR REPRESENT ORD/FREE...SOC 18. PAGE 136 H2711
PARL/PROC CHOOSE STRATA STRUCT

B62
TATZ C.M.,SHADOW AND SUBSTANCE IN SOUTH AFRICA. SOUTH/AFR AGRI NAT/G POL/PAR DOMIN GP/REL ATTIT PWR 20. PAGE 152 H3048
RACE/REL REPRESENT DISCRIM LEGIS

B62
TINKER H.,INDIA AND PAKISTAN. INDIA PAKISTAN NAT/G POL/PAR...OLD/LIB TRADIT TREND CHARTS BIBLIOG 20. PAGE 155 H3102
ORD/FREE STRATA REPRESENT AUTHORIT

S62
BRAIBANTI R.,"REFLECTIONS ON BUREAUCRATIC CORRPUTION." LAW REPRESENT 20. PAGE 20 H0400
CONTROL MORAL ADMIN GOV/COMP

S62
ROSE R.,"THE POLITICAL IDEALS OF ENGLISH PARTY ACTIVISTS" (BMR)" UK PARL/PROC PARTIC ATTIT ROLE ...SAMP/SIZ CHARTS 20. PAGE 134 H2673
POL/PAR LOBBY REPRESENT NAT/G

B63
BLONDEL J.,VOTERS, PARTIES, AND LEADERS. UK ELITES LOC/G NAT/G PROVS ACT/RES DOMIN REPRESENT GP/REL INGP/REL...SOC BIBLIOG 20. PAGE 18 H0358
POL/PAR STRATA LEGIS ADMIN

B63
ECKSTEIN H.,COMPARATIVE POLITICS. POL/PAR LEGIS CT/SYS CHOOSE TOTALISM PWR POPULISM...METH/COMP GEN/METH ANTHOL BIBLIOG 20. PAGE 44 H0886
NAT/COMP CONSTN REPRESENT NAT/G

B63
ELIAS T.O.,GOVERNMENT AND POLITICS IN AFRICA. CONSTN CULTURE SOCIETY NAT/G POL/PAR DIPLOM REPRESENT PERSON...SOC TREND BIBLIOG 4/20. PAGE 45 H0906
AFR NAT/LISM COLONIAL LAW

B63
MERKL P.H.,THE ORIGIN OF THE WEST GERMAN REPUBLIC. GERMANY/W WOR+45 POL/PAR DIPLOM LEAD LOBBY REPRESENT GP/REL NAT/LISM 20. PAGE 109 H2179
CONSTN PARL/PROC CONTROL BAL/PWR

B64
ANDREN N.,GOVERNMENT AND POLITICS IN THE NORDIC COUNTRIES: DENMARK, FINLAND, ICELAND, NORWAY, SWEDEN. DENMARK FINLAND ICELAND NORWAY SWEDEN POL/PAR CHIEF LEGIS ADMIN REGION REPRESENT ATTIT CONSERVE...CHARTS BIBLIOG/A 20. PAGE 7 H0137
CONSTN NAT/G CULTURE GOV/COMP

B64
RIDLEY F.,PUBLIC ADMINISTRATION IN FRANCE. FRANCE UK EX/STRUC CONTROL PARTIC EFFICIENCY 20. PAGE 131 H2625
ADMIN REPRESENT GOV/COMP PWR

B64
TAWNEY R.H.,EQUALITY. UK CULTURE STRATA ECO/TAC EDU/PROP REPRESENT OWN NEW/LIB...MAJORIT WELF/ST SOC 20. PAGE 153 H3051
WEALTH STRUCT ELITES POPULISM

B65
AIYAR S.P.,STUDIES IN INDIAN DEMOCRACY. INDIA STRATA ECO/UNDEV LABOR POL/PAR LEGIS DIPLOM LOBBY REGION CHOOSE ATTIT SOCISM...ANTHOL 20. PAGE 4 H0086
ORD/FREE REPRESENT ADMIN NAT/G

B65
ALLEN W.S.,THE NAZI SEIZURE OF POWER. GERMANY NAT/G CHIEF LEAD COERCE CHOOSE REPRESENT GOV/REL AUTHORIT ...DECISION 20 HITLER/A NAZI. PAGE 5 H0106
MUNIC FASCISM TOTALISM LOC/G

B65
BETTISON D.G.,THE PAPUA-GUINEA ELECTIONS 1964. S/ASIA CONSTN POL/PAR EDU/PROP PARTIC SUFF CENTRAL CONSEN...OBS CHARTS BIBLIOG 20. PAGE 16 H0324
NAT/G LEGIS CHOOSE REPRESENT

B65
BOISSEVAIN J.,SAINTS AND FIREWORKS: RELIGION AND POLITICS IN RURAL MALTA. MALTA STRUCT FAM NEIGH POL/PAR REPRESENT INGP/REL CENTRAL...CHARTS BIBLIOG 20. PAGE 18 H0368
GP/REL NAT/G SECT MUNIC

B65
GILG P.,DIE ERNEUERUNG DES DEMOKRATISCHEN DENKENS IM WILHELMINISCHEN DEUTSCHLAND. GERMANY PARL/PROC CHOOSE REPRESENT...CONCPT 19/20 BISMARCK/O WILHELM/II. PAGE 56 H1126
POL/PAR ORD/FREE NAT/G

B65
LEWIS W.A.,POLITICS IN WEST AFRICA. AFR BAL/PWR DIPLOM REPRESENT...POLICY 20. PAGE 96 H1916
POL/PAR ELITES NAT/G ECO/UNDEV

B65
NAMIER L.B.,THE STRUCTURE OF POLITICS AT THE ACCESSION OF GEORGE III. UK LOC/G TOP/EX COLONIAL LEAD PARTIC REV CHOOSE REPRESENT GOV/REL PERSON SOVEREIGN...GOV/COMP 18 PARLIAMENT. PAGE 115 H2309
PARL/PROC LEGIS NAT/G POL/PAR

C65
NEUMANN S.,"PERMANENT REVOLUTION: TOTALITARIANISM IN THE AGE OF INTERNA TIONAL CIVIL WAR (2ND ED.)" EUR+WWI ELITES POL/PAR DOMIN EDU/PROP LEAD CROWD REPRESENT...MAJORIT GOV/COMP BIBLIOG 20. PAGE 117 H2340
TOTALISM REV FASCISM STRUCT

B66
BUTLER D.E.,THE BRITISH GENERAL ELECTION OF 1966. UK LOC/G NAT/G OP/RES CONFER CHOOSE MAJORITY ATTIT ...CHARTS TIME 20. PAGE 25 H0498
POL/PAR REPRESENT GP/REL PERS/REL

B66
DAHL R.A.,POLITICAL OPPOSITIONS IN WESTERN DEMOCRACIES. EUR+WWI USA+45 USA-45 SOCIETY STRATA ECO/DEV NAT/G LEGIS REPRESENT...TREND NAT/COMP ANTHOL 20. PAGE 37 H0732
POL/PAR CHOOSE PARTIC PLURISM

B66
DE TOCQUEVILLE A,DEMOCRACY IN AMERICA (1834-1840) (2 VOLS. IN I; TRANS. BY G. LAWRENCE). FRANCE CULTURE STRATA POL/PAR CT/SYS REPRESENT FEDERAL ORD/FREE SOVEREIGN...MAJORIT TREND GEN/LAWS 18/19. PAGE 39 H0773
POPULISM USA-45 CONSTN NAT/COMP

B66
FRIED R.C.,COMPARATIVE POLITICAL INSTITUTIONS. USSR EX/STRUC FORCES LEGIS JUDGE CONTROL REPRESENT ALL/IDEOS 20 CONGRESS BUREAUCRCY. PAGE 53 H1062
NAT/G PWR EFFICIENCY GOV/COMP

B66
GUNN G.E.,THE POLITICAL HISTORY OF NEWFOUNDLAND 1832-1864. CANADA FINAN LEGIS CHOOSE REPRESENT ...CHARTS 19. PAGE 62 H1252
POL/PAR NAT/G CONSTN

B66
INSTITUTE COMP STUDY POL SYS,DOMINICAN REPUBLIC ELECTION FACT BOOK. DOMIN/REP LAW LEGIS REPRESENT ...JURID CHARTS 20. PAGE 77 H1536
SUFF CHOOSE POL/PAR NAT/G

B66
LONDON DAILY TELEGRAPH,ELECTION '66: GALLUP ANALYSIS OF THE VOTING RESULTS. UK LEGIS COMPUTER ATTIT...QU SAMP CHARTS 20 LABOR/PAR HOUSE/CMNS. PAGE 98 H1959
STAT CHOOSE REPRESENT POL/PAR

B66
POLE J.R.,POLITICAL REPRESENTATION IN ENGLAND AND THE ORIGINS OF THE AMERICAN REPUBLIC. UK USA-45 CONSTN ELITES NAT/G POL/PAR LEGIS PARL/PROC ...MAJORIT 17/19. PAGE 127 H2534
REPRESENT GOV/COMP

B66
SILBERMAN B.S.,MODERN JAPANESE LEADERSHIP; TRANSITION AND CHANGE. NAT/G POL/PAR CHIEF ADMIN REPRESENT GP/REL ADJUST RIGID/FLEX...SOC METH/COMP ANTHOL 19/20 CHINJAP CHRISTIAN. PAGE 144 H2873
LEAD CULTURE ELITES MUNIC

S66
MCLENNAN B.N.,"EVOLUTION OF CONCEPTS OF REPRESENTATION IN INDONESIA" INDONESIA...CONCPT IDEA/COMP METH 20. PAGE 107 H2143
REPRESENT NAT/G POPULISM PWR

B67
CARTER G.M.,SOUTH AFRICA'S TRANSKEI: THE POLITICS OF DOMESTIC COLONIALISM. SOUTH/AFR ECO/UNDEV AGRI NAT/G PROVS PLAN DOMIN REPRESENT ADJUST DISCRIM ...OBS BIBLIOG 20 BANTUSTANS TRANSKEI. PAGE 27 H0550 — STRATA GOV/REL COLONIAL POLICY

B67
GELLHORN W.,OMBUDSMEN AND OTHERS: CITIZENS' PROTECTORS IN NINE COUNTRIES. WOR+45 LAW CONSTN LEGIS INSPECT ADJUD ADMIN CONTROL CT/SYS CHOOSE PERS/REL...STAT CHARTS 20. PAGE 55 H1109 — NAT/COMP REPRESENT INGP/REL PROB/SOLV

B67
OPERATIONS AND POLICY RESEARCH,NICARAGUA: ELECTION FACTBOOK: FEBRUARY 5, 1967 (PAMPHLET). NICARAGUA LAW NAT/G LEAD REPRESENT...STAT BIOG CHARTS 20. PAGE 121 H2423 — POL/PAR CHOOSE PLAN ATTIT

B67
RAE D.,THE POLITICAL CONSEQUENCES OF ELECTORAL LAWS. EUR+WWI ICELAND ISRAEL NEW/ZEALND UK USA+45 ADJUD APPORT GP/REL MAJORITY...MATH STAT CENSUS CHARTS BIBLIOG 20 AUSTRAL. PAGE 129 H2579 — POL/PAR CHOOSE NAT/COMP REPRESENT

B67
SCHWARTZ B.,THE ROOTS OF FREEDOM: A CONSTITUTIONAL HISTORY OF ENGLAND. UK LAW POL/PAR DELIB/GP LEGIS REV REPRESENT...JURID BIBLIOG/A 13/20. PAGE 140 H2809 — CONSTN PARL/PROC NAT/G

S67
CARIAS B.,"EL CONTROL DE LAS EMPRESAS PUBLICAS POR GRUPOS DE INTERESES DE LA COMUNIDAD." FRANCE UK VENEZUELA INDUS NAT/G CONTROL OWN PWR...DECISION NAT/COMP 20. PAGE 26 H0529 — WORKER REPRESENT MGT SOCISM

S67
CROCKETT D.G.,"THE MP AND HIS CONSTITUENTS." UK POL/PAR...DECISION 20. PAGE 35 H0706 — EXEC NAT/G PERS/REL REPRESENT

S67
DRYDEN S.,"LOCAL GOVERNMENT IN TANZANIA PART II" TANZANIA LAW NAT/G POL/PAR CONTROL PARTIC REPRESENT ...DECISION 20. PAGE 42 H0850 — LOC/G GOV/REL ADMIN STRUCT

S67
FUSARO A.,"THE EFFECT OF PROPORTIONAL REPRESENTATION ON VOTING IN THE AUSTRALIAN SENATE." S/ASIA CONSTN POL/PAR CONTROL GP/REL PWR...CHARTS 20 AUSTRAL HOUSE/REP SENATE. PAGE 54 H1083 — LEGIS CHOOSE REPRESENT NAT/G

S67
IDENBURG P.J.,"POLITICAL STRUCTURAL DEVELOPMENT IN TROPICAL AFRICA." UK ECO/UNDEV KIN POL/PAR CHIEF EX/STRUC CREATE COLONIAL CONTROL REPRESENT RACE/REL ...MAJORIT TREND 20. PAGE 76 H1521 — AFR CONSTN NAT/G GOV/COMP

S67
KASFIR N.,"THE UGANDA CONSTITUENT ASSEMBLY DEBATE." UGANDA REPRESENT FEDERAL ORD/FREE POPULISM...POLICY DECISION 20. PAGE 83 H1665 — CONSTN CONFER LAW NAT/G

S67
MAYANJA A.,"THE GOVERNMENT'S PROPOSALS ON THE NEW CONSTITUTION." AFR UGANDA LAW CHIEF LEGIS ADJUD REPRESENT FEDERAL PWR 20. PAGE 105 H2105 — CONSTN CONFER ORD/FREE NAT/G

S67
NEUBAUER D.E.,"SOME CONDITIONS OF DEMOCRACY." ECO/DEV COM/IND DIST/IND POL/PAR EDU/PROP REPRESENT ...SOC STAT NAT/COMP 20. PAGE 117 H2331 — NAT/G CHOOSE MAJORIT ECO/UNDEV

S67
RAUM O.,"THE MODERN LEADERSHIP GROUP AMONG THE SOUTH AFRICAN XHOSA." SOUTH/AFR SOCIETY SECT EX/STRUC REPRESENT GP/REL INGP/REL PERSON ...METH/COMP 17/20 XHOSA NEGRO. PAGE 130 H2596 — RACE/REL KIN LEAD CULTURE

S67
RENFIELD R.L.,"A POLICY FOR VIETNAM." COM VIETNAM NAT/G POL/PAR VOL/ASSN CHIEF DIPLOM EDU/PROP DETER REPRESENT ATTIT ORD/FREE 20. PAGE 131 H2615 — WAR POLICY PLAN COERCE

S67
THIEN T.T.,"VIETNAM: A CASE OF SOCIAL ALIENATION." VIETNAM AGRI FORCES FOR/AID ADMIN REPRESENT INGP/REL PWR 19/20. PAGE 154 H3071 — NAT/G ELITES WORKER STRANGE

S67
TIVEY L.,"THE POLITICAL CONSEQUENCES OF ECONOMIC PLANNING." UK CONSTN INDUS ACT/RES ADMIN CONTROL LOBBY REPRESENT EFFICIENCY SUPEGO SOVEREIGN ...DECISION 20. PAGE 155 H3108 — PLAN POLICY NAT/G

S68
LAWRIE G.,"WHAT WILL CHANGE SOUTH AFRICA?" AFR SOUTH/AFR ELITES DOMIN CONTROL REPRESENT...TIME/SEQ TREND 20. PAGE 93 H1848 — RACE/REL DIPLOM NAT/G POLICY

N80
MILL J.S.,"AN ESSAY ON GOVERNMENT" (PAMPHLET). ELITES NAT/G CHIEF OWN ORD/FREE PWR WEALTH GEN/LAWS. PAGE 110 H2207 — CONSTN POPULISM REPRESENT UTIL

B87
KINNEAR J.B.,PRINCIPLES OF CIVIL GOVERNMENT. MOD/EUR USA-45 CONSTN LOC/G EX/STRUC ADMIN PARL/PROC RACE/REL...CONCPT 18/19. PAGE 86 H1718 — POL/PAR NAT/G GOV/COMP REPRESENT

B91
SIDGWICK H.,THE ELEMENTS OF POLITICS. LOC/G NAT/G LEGIS DIPLOM ADJUD CONTROL EXEC PARL/PROC REPRESENT GOV/REL SOVEREIGN ALL/IDEOS 19 MILL/JS BENTHAM/J. PAGE 143 H2868 — POLICY LAW CONCPT

B94
BENOIST C.,LA POLITIQUE. FRANCE LAW SOCIETY STRUCT POL/PAR PARL/PROC GP/REL ATTIT PWR 19/20. PAGE 14 H0283 — NAT/G REPRESENT ORD/FREE

B99
LECKY W.E.H.,DEMOCRACY AND LIBERTY (2 VOLS.). LAW CONSTN STRATA POL/PAR SECT WORKER DIPLOM ADJUD REPRESENT NAT/LISM CONSERVE. PAGE 93 H1851 — LEGIS NAT/G POPULISM ORD/FREE

REPUBLIC OF CHINA....SEE TAIWAN

REPUBLICAN....REPUBLICAN PARTY (ALL NATIONS)

RESEARCH....SEE ACT/RES, OP/RES, R+D, CREATE

RESEARCH AND DEVELOPMENT GROUP....SEE R+D

RESERVE SYSTEM, FEDERAL....SEE FED/RESERV

RESHETAR J.S. H2617,H2618

RESIST/INT....SOCIAL RESISTANCE TO INTERVIEWS

RESOURCE/N....NATURAL RESOURCES

B16
CALVERT A.F.,SOUTHWEST AFRICA 1884-1914 (2ND ED.). GERMANY EXTR/IND NAT/G FORCES...GEOG AUD/VIS CHARTS 19/20 RESOURCE/N AFRICA/SW. PAGE 25 H0508 — COLONIAL ECO/UNDEV AFR

S21
MALINOWSKI B.,"THE PRIMITIVE ECONOMICS OF THE TROBRIAND ISLANDERS" (BMR)" CULTURE SOCIETY NAT/G CHIEF LEAD OWN...SOC MYTH WORSHIP 20 NEW/GUINEA TROBRIAND RESOURCE/N. PAGE 101 H2029 — ECO/UNDEV AGRI PRODUC STRUCT

B38
CARVALHO C.M.,GEOGRAPHIA HUMANA; POLITICA E ECONOMICA (3RD ED.). BRAZIL CULTURE AGRI INDUS DIPLOM COLONIAL GP/REL RACE/REL...LING 20 RESOURCE/N. PAGE 27 H0551 — GEOG HABITAT

B54
WILLIAMSON H.F.,ECONOMIC DEVELOPMENT - PRINCIPLES AND PATTERNS. INDIA KOREA CULTURE ECO/DEV ECO/UNDEV TEC/DEV...CENSUS NAT/COMP 20 CHINJAP MEXIC/AMER RESOURCE/N. PAGE 168 H3369 — ECO/TAC GEOG LABOR

B57
PALACIOS A.L.,PETROLEO, MONOPOLIOS, Y LATIFUNDIOS. L/A+17C EXTR/IND NAT/G TEC/DEV ECO/TAC CONTROL PRODUC 20 ARGEN MONOPOLY RESOURCE/N. PAGE 123 H2448 — ECO/UNDEV NAT/LISM INDUS AGRI

B60
NEALE A.D.,THE FLOW OF RESOURCES FROM RICH TO POOR. WOR+45 ECO/DEV ECO/UNDEV FINAN INDUS NAT/G PLAN EFFICIENCY WEALTH...POLICY NAT/COMP 20 RESOURCE/N. PAGE 116 H2325 — FOR/AID DIPLOM METH/CNCPT

B65
JASNY H.,KHRUSHCHEV'S CROP POLICY. USSR ECO/DEV PLAN MARXISM...STAT 20 KHRUSH/N RESOURCE/N. PAGE 80 H1593 — AGRI NAT/G POLICY ECO/TAC

RESPECT....RESPECT, SOCIAL CLASS, STRATIFICATION (CONTEMPT)

B16
TREITSCHKE H.,POLITICS. UNIV SOCIETY STRATA NAT/G EX/STRUC LEGIS DOMIN EDU/PROP ATTIT PWR RESPECT ...CONCPT TIME/SEQ GEN/LAWS TOT/POP 20. PAGE 157 H3129 — EXEC ELITES GERMANY

B17
BARRES M.,THE UNDYING SPIRIT OF FRANCE (TRANS. BY M. CORWIN). FRANCE DOMIN LEAD DEATH ATTIT RESPECT ...NAT/COMP 20 WWI. PAGE 11 H0226 — NAT/LISM FORCES WAR CULTURE

N19
BARRES M.,"THE WAR AND THE SPIRIT OF YOUTH" (PAMPHLET). FRANCE FORCES DOMIN LEAD DEATH AGE/Y ATTIT RESPECT...FASCIST 20 WWI. PAGE 11 H0228 — WAR NAT/LISM CULTURE MYSTIC

B25
WEBSTER C.,THE FOREIGN POLICY OF CASTLEREAGH: 1815-1822. LAW NAT/G DELIB/GP TOP/EX BAL/PWR ORD/FREE PWR RESPECT 19. PAGE 166 H3322 — MOD/EUR DIPLOM UK

B28
CORBETT P.E.,CANADA AND WORLD POLITICS. LAW CULTURE SOCIETY STRUCT MARKET INT/ORG FORCES ACT/RES PLAN ECO/TAC LEGIT ORD/FREE PWR RESPECT...SOC CONCPT — NAT/G CANADA

TIME/SEQ TREND CMN/WLTH 20 LEAGUE/NAT. PAGE 33
H0662

B28
HOLDSWORTH W.S.,THE HISTORIANS OF ANGLO-AMERICAN LAW. UK USA-45 INTELL LEGIS RESPECT...BIOG NAT/COMP 17/20 COMMON/LAW. PAGE 72 H1450
HIST/WRIT LAW JURID

B34
BENEDICT R.,PATTERNS OF CULTURE. S/ASIA FAM KIN PERSON RESPECT...CONCPT SELF/OBS. PAGE 14 H0278
CULTURE SOC

B40
JORDAN W.K.,THE DEVELOPMENT OF RELIGIOUS TOLERATION IN ENGLAND. CHRIST-17C CULTURE SOCIETY LEGIT ATTIT RESPECT...POLICY CONCPT RECORD TIME/SEQ STERTYP GEN/LAWS TOT/POP 16/17. PAGE 82 H1635
SECT UK

B45
WARNER W.L.,THE SOCIAL SYSTEM OF AMERICAN ETHNIC GROUPS. STRATA FAM EDU/PROP ATTIT HABITAT RESPECT CLASSIF. PAGE 165 H3309
CULTURE VOL/ASSN SECT GP/COMP

L48
SHILS E.A.,"COHESION AND DISINTEGRATION IN THE WEHRMACHT IN WORLD WAR II." GERMANY STRUCT DOMIN WAR INGP/REL ISOLAT NAT/LISM ATTIT AUTHORIT SUPEGO RESPECT...PSY CON/ANAL 20 NAZI. PAGE 143 H2862
EDU/PROP DRIVE PERS/REL FORCES

B49
SARGENT S.S.,CULTURE AND PERSONALITY. FUT UNIV SOCIETY FAM KIN NEIGH BIO/SOC DRIVE PERCEPT RIGID/FLEX LOVE RESPECT...PSY SOC CONCPT OBS TIME/SEQ TREND CON/ANAL CHARTS HYPO/EXP SIMUL TOT/POP. PAGE 138 H2754
CULTURE PERSON

B50
WHITE R.J.,THE CONSERVATIVE TRADITION. UK POL/PAR SUPEGO PWR RESPECT...POLICY ANTHOL 19. PAGE 167 H3350
CONSERVE CONCPT NAT/G ORD/FREE

S52
MUEHLMANN W.E.,"L'IDEE NATIONALE ALLEMANDE ET L'IDEE NATIONALE FRANCAISE." EUR+WWI MOD/EUR SOCIETY KIN NAT/G PWR RESPECT...SOC CONCPT TIME/SEQ GEN/LAWS 19/20. PAGE 114 H2279
CULTURE ATTIT FRANCE GERMANY

B53
MEYER P.,THE JEWS IN THE SOVIET SATELLITES. CZECHOSLVK POLAND SOCIETY STRATA NAT/G BAL/PWR ECO/TAC EDU/PROP LEGIT ADMIN COERCE ATTIT DISPL PERCEPT HEALTH PWR RESPECT WEALTH...METH/CNCPT JEWS VAL/FREE NAZI 20. PAGE 110 H2192
COM SECT TOTALISM USSR

B55
POHLENZ M.,GRIECHISCHE FREIHEIT. GREECE DIPLOM WAR SUPEGO PWR RESPECT...IDEA/COMP. PAGE 127 H2533
ORD/FREE CONCPT JURID NAT/G

C55
OLIVER D.L.,"A LEADER IN ACTION," IN D. A. OLIVER, SOLOMON ISLAND SOCIETY." S/ASIA SOCIETY STRUCT CONTROL TASK PWR...OBS/ENVIR WORSHIP 20. PAGE 121 H2413
LEAD RESPECT CULTURE KIN

B56
MANNONI D.O.,PROSPERO AND CALIBAN: THE PSYCHOLOGY OF COLONIZATION. AFR EUR+WWI FAM KIN MUNIC SECT DOMIN ADMIN ATTIT DRIVE LOVE PWR RESPECT...PSY SOC CONCPT MYTH OBS DEEP/INT BIOG GEN/METH MALAGASY 20. PAGE 102 H2040
CULTURE COLONIAL

B56
PADMORE G.,PAN-AFRICANISM OR COMMUNISM. AFR FUT NIGERIA INTELL NAT/G COLONIAL FEDERAL ATTIT DRIVE PWR RESPECT WEALTH MARXISM...CONCPT AUD/VIS STERTYP 20. PAGE 122 H2440
POL/PAR NAT/LISM

S57
KILSON M.L.,"LAND AND POLITICS IN KENYA: AN ANALYSIS OF AFRICAN POLITICS IN A PLURAL SOCIETY." FUT LAW CULTURE KIN NAT/G ECO/TAC DOMIN REV NAT/LISM ORD/FREE PWR RESPECT SOVEREIGN WEALTH ...SOC OBS TREND WORK VAL/FREE CMN/WLTH 20. PAGE 86 H1710
AFR ECO/UNDEV

B58
COLEMAN J.S.,NIGERIA: BACKGROUND TO NATIONALISM. AFR SOCIETY ECO/DEV KIN LOC/G POL/PAR TEC/DEV DOMIN ADMIN DRIVE PWR RESPECT...TRADIT SOC INT SAMP TIME/SEQ 20. PAGE 31 H0627
NAT/G NAT/LISM NIGERIA

S58
MAIR L.P.,"REPRESENTATIVE LOCAL GOVERNMENT AS A PROBLEM IN SOCIAL CHANGE." ECO/UNDEV KIN LOC/G NAT/G SCHOOL JUDGE ADMIN ROUTINE REPRESENT RIGID/FLEX RESPECT...CONCPT STERTYP CMN/WLTH 20. PAGE 101 H2025
AFR PWR ELITES

B59
SCHORN H.,DER RICHTER IM DRITTEN REICH; GESCHICHTE UND DOKUMENTE. GERMANY NAT/G LEGIT CT/SYS INGP/REL MORAL ORD/FREE RESPECT...JURID GP/COMP 20. PAGE 140 H2798
ADJUD JUDGE FASCISM

S59
JENKS C.W.,"THE CHALLENGE OF UNIVERSALITY." FUT UNIV CONSTN CULTURE CONSULT CREATE PLAN LEGIT ATTIT MORAL ORD/FREE RESPECT...MAJORIT JURID 20. PAGE 80 H1602
INT/ORG LAW PEACE INT/LAW

S60
KELLEY G.A.,"THE POLITICAL BACKGROUND OF THE FRENCH A-BOMB." EUR+WWI USSR FORCES TOP/EX TEC/DEV NUC/PWR ATTIT PWR...CONCPT OBS/ENVIR TREND 20. PAGE 84 H1686
NAT/G RESPECT NAT/LISM FRANCE

S60
SPIRO H.J.,"NEW CONSTITUTIONAL FORMS IN AFRICA." FUT CULTURE SOCIETY ECO/UNDEV NAT/G POL/PAR VOL/ASSN EDU/PROP ATTIT DRIVE ORD/FREE PWR RESPECT ...POLICY CONCPT OBS TREND CON/ANAL STERTYP GEN/LAWS VAL/FREE. PAGE 148 H2950
AFR CONSTN FOR/AID NAT/LISM

B61
MARX K.,THE COMMUNIST MANIFESTO. IN (MENDEL A. ESSENTIAL WORKS OF MARXISM, NEW YORK: BANTAM. FUT MOD/EUR CULTURE ECO/DEV ECO/UNDEV AGRI FINAN INDUS MARKET PROC/MFG LABOR MUNIC POL/PAR CONSULT FORCES CREATE PLAN ADMIN ATTIT DRIVE RIGID/FLEX ORD/FREE PWR RESPECT MARX/KARL WORK. PAGE 104 H2081
COM NEW/IDEA CAP/ISM REV

B62
FINER S.E.,THE MAN ON HORSEBACK: ROLE OF THE MILITARY IN POLITICS. UNIV LAW CONSTN ELITES SOCIETY POL/PAR BAL/PWR DOMIN EDU/PROP LEGIT COERCE GUERRILLA REV WAR WEAPON DRIVE SUPEGO ORD/FREE PWR RESPECT...POLICY CONCPT GEN/METH. PAGE 50 H1003
NAT/G FORCES TOTALISM

B62
INSTITUTE FOR STUDY OF USSR,YOUTH IN FERMENT. INTELL NAT/G PERF/ART POL/PAR SCHOOL VOL/ASSN FORCES EDU/PROP ATTIT DRIVE PERCEPT HEALTH KNOWL MORAL ORD/FREE RESPECT...SOC OBS HIST/WRIT VAL/FREE. PAGE 77 H1537
COM CULTURE USSR

B62
PAIKERT G.C.,THE GERMAN EXODUS. EUR+WWI GERMANY/W LAW CULTURE SOCIETY STRUCT INDUS NAT/LISM RESPECT SOVEREIGN...CHARTS BIBLIOG SOC/INTEG 20 MIGRATION. PAGE 122 H2444
INGP/REL STRANGE GEOG GP/REL

B62
PENTONY D.E.,RED WORLD IN TUMULT: COMMUNIST FOREIGN POLICIES. CHINA/COM COM NAT/G EDU/PROP COERCE ATTIT PWR RESPECT...SOC CHARTS 20. PAGE 124 H2488
ECO/UNDEV DOMIN USSR ASIA

B62
ZIESEL K.,DAS VERLORENE GEWISSEN. GERMANY/W NAT/G VOL/ASSN EDU/PROP PRESS SUPEGO...POLICY 20. PAGE 173 H3455
MORAL PWR ORD/FREE RESPECT

S62
MU FU-SHENG,"THE WILTING OF THE HUNDRED FLOWERS: FREE THOUGHT IN CHINA TODAY." ASIA CHINA/COM CULTURE FAM NAT/G EDU/PROP REV TOTALISM ATTIT PERSON RESPECT...GEOG INT UNPLAN/INT COLD/WAR 20. PAGE 114 H2278
INTELL ELITES

S62
PASSIN H.,"THE SOURCES OF PROTEST IN JAPAN." CULTURE SOCIETY EDU/PROP COERCE NAT/LISM DISPL DRIVE PWR RESPECT...POLICY SOC TREND 20 CHINJAP. PAGE 124 H2473
ASIA ATTIT REV

B63
KOGAN N.,THE POLITICS OF ITALIAN FOREIGN POLICY. EUR+WWI LEGIS DOMIN LEGIT EXEC PWR RESPECT SKILL ...POLICY DECISION HUM SOC METH/CNCPT OBS INT CHARTS 20. PAGE 87 H1737
NAT/G ROUTINE DIPLOM ITALY

B63
ROBERTSON A.H.,HUMAN RIGHTS IN EUROPE. CONSTN SOCIETY INT/ORG NAT/G VOL/ASSN DELIB/GP ACT/RES PLAN ADJUD REGION ROUTINE ATTIT LOVE ORD/FREE RESPECT...JURID SOC CONCPT SOC/EXP UN 20. PAGE 132 H2645
EUR+WWI PERSON

B64
SINGER M.R.,THE EMERGING ELITE: A STUDY OF POLITICAL LEADERSHIP IN CEYLON. S/ASIA ECO/UNDEV AGRI KIN NAT/G SECT EX/STRUC LEGIT ATTIT PWR RESPECT...SOC STAT CHARTS 20. PAGE 144 H2883
TOP/EX STRATA NAT/LISM CEYLON

B64
THORNBURG M.W.,PEOPLE AND POLICY IN THE MIDDLE EAST. ISLAM ECO/UNDEV FAM KIN MUNIC NAT/G NEIGH POL/PAR SECT DELIB/GP LEGIS PLAN ECO/TAC DOMIN ADMIN ATTIT HEALTH RESPECT...SOC CONCPT METH/CNCPT OBS TIME/SEQ TOT/POP VAL/FREE. PAGE 154 H3088
TEC/DEV CULTURE

L64
SYMONDS R.,"REFLECTIONS IN LOCALISATION." AFR S/ASIA UK STRATA INT/ORG NAT/G SCHOOL EDU/PROP LEGIT KNOWL ORD/FREE PWR RESPECT CMN/WLTH 20. PAGE 151 H3023
ADMIN MGT COLONIAL

S64
CLIGNET R.,"POTENTIAL ELITES IN GHANA AND THE IVORY COAST: A PRELIMINARY SURVEY." AFR CULTURE ELITES STRATA KIN NAT/G SECT DOMIN EXEC ORD/FREE RESPECT SKILL...POLICY RELATIV GP/COMP NAT/COMP 20. PAGE 30 H0605
PWR LEGIT IVORY/CST GHANA

S64
LEWIS B.,"THE QUEST FOR FREEDOM--A SAD STORY OF THE MIDDLE EAST." ISLAM ISRAEL LEBANON TURKEY CULTURE NAT/G SECT LEGIS TOP/EX DOMIN EDU/PROP LEGIT ORD/FREE PWR RESPECT...POLICY TIME/SEQ VAL/FREE 20. PAGE 96 H1911
CONSTN ATTIT NAT/LISM

S64
LOW D.A.,"LION RAMPANT." EUR+WWI MOD/EUR S/ASIA ECO/UNDEV NAT/G FORCES TEC/DEV ECO/TAC LEGIT ADMIN COLONIAL COERCE ORD/FREE RESPECT 19/20. PAGE 99 H1972
AFR DOMIN DIPLOM UK

S64
RUDOLPH L.I.,"GENERALS AND POLITICIANS IN INDIA." INDIA S/ASIA CULTURE STRATA NAT/G LEGIS TOP/EX EDU/PROP ATTIT ORD/FREE PWR RESPECT SKILL...POLICY BIOG TIME/SEQ STERTYP VAL/FREE 20. PAGE 136 H2713
FORCES COERCE

S64
SCHEFFLER H.W.,"THE GENESIS AND REPRESSION OF CONFLICT: CHOISEUL ISLAND." S/ASIA LOC/G NAT/G FORCES LEGIS DIPLOM DOMIN LEGIT EXEC CHOOSE ATTIT RESPECT SKILL...POLICY JURID OBS TREND GEN/METH 20. PAGE 139 H2781
PWR COERCE WAR

S64
SMYTHE H.H.,"NEHRU AND INDIAN FOREIGN POLICY." S/ASIA ECO/UNDEV NAT/G POL/PAR CONSULT PLAN DIPLOM NEUTRAL COERCE ATTIT DRIVE PERSON MORAL ORD/FREE RESPECT...GEOG CONCPT TIME/SEQ TREND GEN/LAWS 20 NEHRU/J. PAGE 146 H2922
TOP/EX BIOG INDIA

B65
GEORGE M.,THE WARPED VISION. EUR+WWI UK NAT/G POL/PAR LEGIS PARL/PROC SANCTION COERCE WAR GOV/REL PEACE RESPECT 20 CONSRV/PAR. PAGE 56 H1113
LEAD ATTIT DIPLOM POLICY

B65
O'BRIEN W.V.,THE NEW NATIONS IN INTERNATIONAL LAW AND DIPLOMACY* THE YEAR BOOK OF WORLD POLITY* VOLUME III. USA+45 ECO/UNDEV INT/ORG FORCES DIPLOM COLONIAL NEUTRAL REV NAT/LISM ATTIT RESPECT. PAGE 119 H2385
INT/LAW CULTURE SOVEREIGN ANTHOL

S65
GRIFFITH S.B.,"COMMUNIST CHINA'S CAPACITY TO MAKE WAR." CHINA/COM COM NAT/G TOP/EX PLAN DOMIN COERCE NUC/PWR ATTIT RESPECT SKILL...CONCPT MYTH TIME/SEQ TREND COLD/WAR 20. PAGE 61 H1221
FORCES PWR WEAPON ASIA

S66
TOUVAL S.,"AFRICA'S FRONTIERS* REACTIONS TO A COLONIAL LEGACY." L/A+17C CONFER ADJUD COLONIAL APPORT CONSEN NAT/LISM RESPECT...RECORD NAT/COMP. PAGE 156 H3120
AFR GEOG SOVEREIGN WAR

S67
BASKIN D.B.,"NATIONALITY DOCTRINE AND ANTI-SEMITISM IN THE USSR." USSR CULTURE STRATA ISOLAT MAJORITY ATTIT RIGID/FLEX RESPECT...GP/COMP JEWS. PAGE 12 H0234
NAT/LISM MARXISM GP/REL DISCRIM

S67
HAMMOND R.J.,"RACE ATTITUDES AND POLICIES IN PORTUGUESE AFRICA IN THE NINETEENTH AND TWENTIETH CENTURIES." AFR PORTUGAL NAT/G SECT EDU/PROP COLONIAL ATTIT RIGID/FLEX SEX MORAL RESPECT 19/20 NEGRO. PAGE 65 H1309
POLICY RACE/REL DISCRIM SOCIETY

RESPONSIBILITY....SEE SUPEGO, RESPECT

RESPONSIVENESS....SEE RIGID/FLEX

RESTRAINT....SEE ORD/FREE

RETAILING....SEE MARKET

RETIREMENT....SEE SENIOR, ADMIN

REUTHER/W....WALTER REUTHER

REV....REVOLUTION; SEE ALSO WAR

N
US CONSULATE GENERAL HONG KONG,CURRENT BACKGROUND. CHINA/COM ECO/UNDEV LOC/G NAT/G PLAN DIPLOM EDU/PROP LEAD REV ATTIT...POLICY INDEX 20. PAGE 159 H3179
BIBLIOG/A MARXIST ASIA PRESS

N
US CONSULATE GENERAL HONG KONG,SURVEY OF CHINA MAINLAND PRESS. CHINA/COM ECO/UNDEV LOC/G NAT/G PLAN DIPLOM EDU/PROP LEAD REV ATTIT...POLICY INDEX 20. PAGE 159 H3181
BIBLIOG/A MARXIST ASIA PRESS

N
US CONSULATE GENERAL HONG KONG,US CONSULATE GENERAL, HONG KONG, PRESS SUMMARIES. CHINA/COM ECO/UNDEV LOC/G NAT/G PLAN DIPLOM EDU/PROP LEAD REV ATTIT...POLICY INDEX 20. PAGE 159 H3182
BIBLIOG/A MARXIST ASIA PRESS

B02
JELLINEK G.,LA DECLARATION DES DROITS DE L'HOMME ET DU CITOYEN (1895) (TRANSLATED FROM GERMAN BY G. FARDIS). FRANCE GERMANY USA-45 NAT/G SECT LEGIS 18. PAGE 80 H1598
ORD/FREE CONCPT REV

C05
DUNNING W.A.,"HISTORY OF POLITICAL THEORIES FROM LUTHER TO MONTESQUIEU." LAW NAT/G SECT DIPLOM REV WAR ORD/FREE SOVEREIGN CONSERVE...TRADIT BIBLIOG 16/18. PAGE 43 H0867
PHIL/SCI CONCPT GEN/LAWS

C09
SCHAPIRO J.S.,"SOCIAL REFORM AND THE REFORMATION." CHRIST-17C GERMANY LAW CONSTN LG/CO NAT/G WORKER PROB/SOLV CT/SYS REV...BIBLIOG 16. PAGE 138 H2770
ORD/FREE SECT ECO/TAC BIOG

B13
KROPOTKIN P.,THE CONQUEST OF BREAD. SOCIETY STRATA AGRI INDUS WORKER REV HAPPINESS INCOME PRODUC HEALTH MORAL ORD/FREE. PAGE 89 H1775
ANARCH SOCIALIST OWN AGREE

B14
LEVINE L.,SYNDICALISM IN FRANCE (2ND ED.). FRANCE LAW SOCIETY ECO/DEV NAT/G ECO/TAC LEAD ATTIT ...POLICY CONCPT STAT BIBLIOG 18/20 REFORMERS. PAGE 95 H1902
LABOR INDUS SOCISM REV

B17
DE MAISTRE J.,DU PAPE (1817). FRANCE LAW SOCIETY SECT DOMIN REV HAPPINESS PWR SOVEREIGN 18/19 PROTESTANT. PAGE 38 H0761
CATH CHIEF LEGIT NAT/G

N17
BURKE E.,THOUGHTS ON THE PROSPECT OF A REGICIDE PEACE (PAMPHLET). FRANCE UK SECT DOMIN MURDER PEACE ORD/FREE SOVEREIGN POPULISM...POLICY GOV/COMP IDEA/COMP 18 JACOBINISM COEXIST. PAGE 24 H0483
REV CHIEF NAT/G DIPLOM

N17
BURKE E.,THOUGHTS ON THE CAUSE OF THE PRESENT DISCONTENTS (PAMPHLET). MOD/EUR UK CONSTN CHIEF LEGIS DOMIN CONTROL EXEC REPRESENT POPULISM ...TRADIT NEW/IDEA METH/COMP 18 BURKE/EDM. PAGE 24 H0484
ORD/FREE REV PARL/PROC NAT/G

N19
BRIMMELL G.H.,COMMUNISM IN SOUTHEAST ASIA (PAMPHLET). BURMA CAMBODIA COM INDIA INDONESIA LAOS MOD/EUR NAT/G POL/PAR FORCES CAP/ISM CONTROL WEALTH ...MYTH 20. PAGE 21 H0420
MARXISM S/ASIA REV ECO/UNDEV

N19
MAO TSE-TUNG,ON SOME IMPORTANT PROBLEMS OF THE PARTY'S PRESENT POLICY. CHINA/COM CONSTN ELITES INTELL AGRI DOMIN EDU/PROP REV REPRESENT GP/REL OWN PEACE ORD/FREE 20 COM/PARTY. PAGE 102 H2044
POLICY NAT/G CHIEF LEGIT

N19
TREVELYAN G.M.,THE TWO-PARTY SYSTEM IN ENGLISH POLITICAL HISTORY (PAMPHLET). UK CHIEF LEGIS COLONIAL EXEC REV CHOOSE 17/19. PAGE 157 H3131
PARL/PROC POL/PAR NAT/G PWR

C20
DUNNING W.A.,"A HISTORY OF POLITICAL THINKERS FROM ROUSSEAU TO SPENCER." NAT/G REV NAT/LISM UTIL CONSERVE MARXISM POPULISM...JURID BIBLIOG 18/19. PAGE 43 H0868
IDEA/COMP PHIL/SCI CONCPT GEN/LAWS

B23
FINER H.,REPRESENTATIVE GOVERNMENT AND A PARLIAMENT OF INDUSTRY. A STUDY OF THE GERMAN FEDERAL ECONOMIC COUNCIL. GERMANY UK CONSTN INDUS PARL/PROC ...NAT/COMP 20. PAGE 50 H1002
DELIB/GP ECO/TAC WAR REV

B27
EDWARDS L.P.,THE NATURAL HISTORY OF REVOLUTION. UNIV NAT/G VOL/ASSN COERCE DRIVE WEALTH...TREND GEN/LAWS. PAGE 45 H0893
PWR GUERRILLA REV

B27
ENGELS F.,THE PEASANT WAR IN GERMANY (1850). GERMANY MOD/EUR AGRI WORKER LEAD COERCE INGP/REL ...TREND 16/19. PAGE 46 H0924
WAR STRATA REV MARXIST

B27
GOOCH G.P.,ENGLISH DEMOCRATIC IDEAS IN THE SEVENTEENTH CENTURY (2ND ED.). UK LAW SECT FORCES DIPLOM LEAD PARL/PROC REV ATTIT AUTHORIT...ANARCH CONCPT 17 PARLIAMENT CMN/WLTH REFORMERS. PAGE 58 H1167
IDEA/COMP MAJORIT EX/STRUC CONSERVE

C28
SCHNEIDER H.W.,"MAKING THE FASCIST STATE." ITALY CULTURE LABOR DIPLOM REV WAR NAT/LISM TOTALISM ATTIT DRIVE SOCISM...BIBLIOG PARLIAMENT 20. PAGE 140 H2792
FASCISM POLICY POL/PAR

B29
DE REPARAZ G.,GEOGRAFIA Y POLITICA. CHILE SPAIN USSR NAT/G DIPLOM REV MARXISM...POLICY 19/20. PAGE 38 H0768
GEOG MOD/EUR

B30
MASON E.S.,THE PARIS COMMUNE: AN EPISODE IN THE HISTORY OF THE SOCIALIST MOVEMENT. FRANCE MOD/EUR ELITES SOCIETY STRATA ECO/DEV WORKER EDU/PROP CHOOSE INGP/REL SOCISM 19 MARX/KARL PARIS. PAGE 104 H2085
NAT/G REV MARXISM

B32
MARRARO H.R.,AMERICAN OPINION ON THE UNIFICATION OF ITALY. ITALY FORCES DIPLOM SOVEREIGN CATHISM CONSERVE...CONCPT NAT/COMP BIBLIOG 19. PAGE 103 H2056
ORD/FREE NAT/LISM REV CONSTN

B32
THIBAUDET A.,LES IDEES POLITIQUES DE LA FRANCE. FRANCE NAT/G SECT PRESS REV NAT/LISM PEACE ATTIT ...PSY 19/20 JACOBINISM JAURES/JL. PAGE 154 H3070
IDEA/COMP ALL/IDEOS CATHISM

B33
DAHLIN E.,FRENCH AND GERMAN PUBLIC OPINION ON DECLARED WAR AIMS 1914-1918. BELGIUM FRANCE GERMANY
ATTIT EDU/PROP

NAT/G POL/PAR DIPLOM COERCE REV WAR PEACE 20 WWI WILSON/W. PAGE 37 H0733 — DOMIN NAT/COMP

B33
TANNENBAUM F.,PEACE BY REVOLUTION. ECO/UNDEV AGRI SECT WORKER DIPLOM EDU/PROP DISCRIM OWN WEALTH POPULISM 17/20 MEXIC/AMER INDIAN/AM. PAGE 152 H3043 — CULTURE COLONIAL RACE/REL REV

B33
PUBLIC OPINION AND WORLD POLITICS. UNIV LAW CULTURE NAT/G PRESS REV GP/REL...MAJORIT METH/COMP ANTHOL 20. PAGE 171 H3420 — DIPLOM EDU/PROP ATTIT MAJORITY

B34
MARX K.,THE CLASS STRUGGLES IN FRANCE. FRANCE INDUS WORKER CONSERVE...TREND GEN/LAWS 19. PAGE 104 H2077 — MARXIST STRATA REV INT/TRADE

B34
STALIN J.,PROBLEMS OF LENINISM. USSR STRATA INDUS LOC/G POL/PAR ECO/TAC CONTROL TOTALISM PWR SOCISM LENIN/VI STALIN/J. PAGE 148 H2968 — MARXISM REV ELITES NAT/G

B36
BOYCE A.N.,EUROPE AND SOUTH AFRICA. FRANCE GERMANY ITALY SOUTH/AFR UK INDUS NAT/G CONTROL REV WAR NAT/LISM...CONCPT HIST/WRIT 20. PAGE 20 H0392 — COLONIAL GOV/COMP NAT/COMP DIPLOM

B36
HUBERMAN L.,MAN'S WORLDLY GOODS: THE STORY OF THE WEALTH OF NATIONS. CHRIST-17C EUR+WWI MOD/EUR SOCIETY DOMIN REV ORD/FREE...TIME/SEQ METH/COMP. PAGE 74 H1486 — WEALTH CAP/ISM MARXISM CREATE

B36
LAPRADE W.T.,PUBLIC OPINION AND POLITICS IN EIGHTEENTH CENTURY ENGLAND. UK CULTURE POL/PAR CHIEF TOP/EX LEAD REV NAT/LISM PWR 18 PROTESTANT PROTESTANT CHURCH/STA. PAGE 91 H1815 — POLICY ELITES ATTIT TIME/SEQ

B37
BERDYAEV N.,THE ORIGIN OF RUSSIAN COMMUNISM. MOD/EUR RUSSIA USSR INTELL SECT REV...ANARCH HUM 19/20 ORTHO/RUSS COM/PARTY CHRISTIAN. PAGE 15 H0294 — MARXISM NAT/LISM CULTURE ATTIT

B37
CARLYLE T.,THE FRENCH REVOLUTION (2 VOLS.). FRANCE CONSTN NAT/G FORCES COERCE MURDER PEACE MORAL POPULISM...TIME/SEQ IDEA/COMP GEN/LAWS 18. PAGE 26 H0532 — REV CHIEF TRADIT

B37
MARX K.,THE CIVIL WAR IN THE UNITED STATES. USA-45 WORKER DIPLOM INT/TRADE DOMIN RACE/REL ATTIT ...TREND 19. PAGE 104 H2078 — WAR REV MARXIST ORD/FREE

B38
HARPER S.N.,THE GOVERNMENT OF THE SOVIET UNION. COM USSR LAW CONSTN ECO/DEV PLAN TEC/DEV DIPLOM INT/TRADE ADMIN REV NAT/LISM...POLICY 20. PAGE 67 H1337 — MARXISM NAT/G LEAD POL/PAR

B38
MARX K.,THE GERMAN IDEOLOGY, PARTS 1 AND 3 (1846). MOD/EUR LAW STRATA WORKER DOMIN REV UTOPIA SOCISM 19 MARX/KARL. PAGE 104 H2079 — MARXIST OWN PRODUC ECO/TAC

B39
ENGELS F.,HERRN EUGEN DUHRING'S REVOLUTION IN SCIENCE (1878). CULTURE STRATA STRUCT FAM SECT ECO/TAC REV WAR SOCISM...MARXIST 19. PAGE 46 H0925 — PWR SOCIETY WEALTH GEN/LAWS

B39
KOHN H.,REVOLUTIONS AND DICTATORSHIPS. COM EUR+WWI ISLAM MOD/EUR NAT/G CHIEF FORCES WAR CIVMIL/REL PWR MARXISM 18/20. PAGE 87 H1739 — NAT/LISM TOTALISM REV FASCISM

B40
HOBBES T.,BEHEMOTH (1668). UK CONSTN SECT DOMIN LEGIT UTIL ORD/FREE CATHISM...POLICY CONCPT GEN/LAWS 17 CHARLES/I CROMWELL/O PROTESTANT. PAGE 71 H1433 — REV NAT/G CHIEF

B40
HUNTER R.,REVOLUTION: WHY, HOW, WHEN? NAT/G ECO/TAC EDU/PROP COERCE ORD/FREE FASCISM POPULISM SOCISM 18/20 HITLER/A LENIN/VI. PAGE 75 H1502 — REV METH/COMP LEAD CONSTN

B41
PALMER R.R.,TWELVE WHO RULED. MOD/EUR ELITES STRUCT NAT/G POL/PAR DELIB/GP DOMIN ATTIT SUPEGO PWR ...POLICY CONCPT 18. PAGE 123 H2453 — TOP/EX BIOG REV FRANCE

S41
DENNERY E.,"DEMOCRACY AND THE FRENCH ARMY." FRANCE NAT/G EX/STRUC LEAD REV ROLE 18/20. PAGE 40 H0792 — FORCES POPULISM STRATA CIVMIL/REL

B42
FEFFERO G.,THE PRINCIPLES OF POWER (TRANS. BY T. JAECKEL). MOD/EUR CONSTN NAT/G CHIEF CONTROL REV WAR ORD/FREE CONSERVE FASCISM POPULISM...GEN/LAWS 18/20 EUROPE. PAGE 49 H0980 — PWR LEGIT TRADIT ELITES

B43
GRIERSON P.,BOOKS ON SOVIET RUSSIA 1917-42: A BIBLIOGRAPHY AND A GUIDE TO READING. USSR CULTURE ELITES NAT/G PLAN DIPLOM REV...GEOG 20. PAGE 61 H1213 — BIBLIOG/A COM MARXISM LEAD

B43
LENIN V.I.,STATE AND REVOLUTION. USSR CAP/ISM ...ANARCH MARXIST PHIL/SCI IDEA/COMP 20. PAGE 94 H1878 — SOCIETY NAT/G REV MARXISM

B43
LENIN V.I.,LEFT WING COMMUNISM: AN INFANTILE DISORDER (1920). GERMANY MOD/EUR USSR STRUCT CHIEF DOMIN EDU/PROP LEGIT LEAD REPRESENT POPULISM ...METH/COMP 19 LENIN/VI COM/PARTY MENSHEVIK. PAGE 94 H1879 — COM MARXISM NAT/G REV

B43
MC DOWELL R.B.,IRISH PUBLIC OPINION, 1750-1800. IRELAND CONSTN VOL/ASSN WORKER ORD/FREE CATHISM CONSERVE...POLICY IDEA/COMP BIBLIOG 18/ PARLIAMENT. PAGE 106 H2118 — ATTIT NAT/G DIPLOM REV

B44
BERDYAEV N.,SLAVERY AND FREEDOM. NAT/G REV WAR NAT/LISM OWN AUTHORIT SEX CONSERVE SOCISM...TRADIT PHIL/SCI CIVIL/LIB. PAGE 15 H0295 — ORD/FREE PERSON ELITES SOCIETY

B44
WOLFE D.M.,LEVELLER MANIFESTOES OF THE PURITAN REVOLUTION. UK CONSTN NAT/G SECT...CONCPT ANTHOL 17 LEVELLERS DECLAR/IND PURITAN LOCKE/JOHN. PAGE 170 H3400 — POL/PAR REV ORD/FREE ATTIT

C44
SUAREZ F.,"ON WAR" (1621) IN SELECTIONS FROM THREE WORKS, VOL. I." NAT/G SECT CHIEF DIPLOM LEGIT MORAL PWR...POLICY INT/LAW 17. PAGE 150 H3005 — WAR REV ORD/FREE CATH

B45
VENABLE V.,HUMAN NATURE: THE MARXIAN VIEW. UNIV STRATA CAP/ISM REV GP/REL PERS/REL PRODUC KNOWL ...PHIL/SCI CONCPT IDEA/COMP 19 MARX/KARL ENGELS/F. PAGE 162 H3240 — PERSON MARXISM WORKER UTOPIA

B47
BEHAR D.,BIBLIOGRAFIA HISPANOAMERICANA. LIBROS ANTIGUOS Y MODERNOS REFERENTES A AMERICA Y ESPANA. PORTUGAL SPAIN CONSTN NAT/G SECT CREATE REV WAR GOV/REL...ART/METH GEOG PHIL/SCI LING 20 ARGEN. PAGE 13 H0260 — BIBLIOG L/A+17C CULTURE

B47
LOCKE J.,TWO TREATISES OF GOVERNMENT (1690). UK LAW SOCIETY LEGIS LEGIT AGREE REV OWN HEREDITY MORAL CONSERVE...POLICY MAJORIT 17 WILLIAM/3 NATURL/LAW. PAGE 97 H1946 — CONCPT ORD/FREE NAT/G CONSEN

N47
CANNON J.P.,AMERICAN STALINISM AND ANTI-STALINISM (PAMPHLET). NAT/G WORKER DOMIN EDU/PROP REV GP/REL ...MARXIST CONCPT 20 STALIN/J TROTSKY/L. PAGE 26 H0521 — LABOR MARXISM CAP/ISM POL/PAR

B48
WOLFE B.D.,THREE WHO MADE A REVOLUTION. USSR CONSTN NAT/G CAP/ISM EDU/PROP CONTROL WAR GP/REL INGP/REL PERS/REL ROLE 20 STALIN/J LENIN/VI TROTSKY/L BOLSHEVISM. PAGE 170 H3398 — BIOG REV LEAD MARXISM

B49
DE JOUVENEL B.,ON POWER: ITS NATURE AND THE HISTORY OF ITS GROWTH. SOCIETY CHIEF REV WAR ATTIT AUTHORIT ORD/FREE SOVEREIGN CONSERVE POPULISM CONCPT. PAGE 38 H0757 — PWR NAT/G DOMIN CONTROL

B49
MAO TSE-TUNG,NEW DEMOCRACY. CHINA/COM NAT/G DIPLOM ECO/TAC EDU/PROP REV...CONCPT METH SOC/INTEG 20. PAGE 102 H2045 — SOCISM MARXISM POPULISM CULTURE

B49
ROGERS C.B.,THE SPIRIT OF REVOLUTION IN 1789: A STUDY OF PUBLIC OPINION ...AT THE BEGINNING OF THE FRENCH REVOLUTION. FRANCE CULTURE ELITES EDU/PROP COERCE CROWD...BIBLIOG 18 MUSIC. PAGE 133 H2658 — ATTIT POPULISM REV CREATE

B49
WORMUTH F.D.,THE ORIGINS OF MODERN CONSTITUTIONALISM. GREECE UK LEGIS CREATE TEC/DEV BAL/PWR DOMIN ADJUD REV WAR PWR...JURID ROMAN/REP CROMWELL/O. PAGE 170 H3412 — NAT/G CONSTN LAW

B50
CARR E.H.,STUDIES IN REVOLUTION. CREATE WAR PERSON ALL/IDEOS MARXISM SOCISM...PHIL/SCI METH/COMP ANTHOL 18/20 SAINTSIMON MARX/KARL PROUDHON/P LASSALLE/F PLEKHNV/GV. PAGE 27 H0537 — REV IDEA/COMP COERCE BIOG

B50
GLEASON J.H.,THE GENESIS OF RUSSOPHOBIA IN GREAT BRITAIN: A STUDY OF THE INTERACTION OF POLICY AND OPINION. ASIA RUSSIA UK NAT/G AGREE CONTROL REV WAR LOVE PWR TREATY 19. PAGE 57 H1142 — DIPLOM POLICY DOMIN COLONIAL

B50
KANN R.A.,THE MULTINATIONAL EMPIRE (2 VOLS.). AUSTRIA CZECHOSLVK GERMANY HUNGARY CULTURE NAT/G — NAT/LISM MOD/EUR

POL/PAR PROVS REGION REV FEDERAL...GEOG TREND CHARTS IDEA/COMP NAT/COMP 19/20. PAGE 83 H1654

B50
TRAGER F.N.,MARXISM IN SOUTHEAST ASIA. BURMA INDONESIA THAILAND VIETNAM CULTURE SOCIETY NAT/G VOL/ASSN EXEC ROUTINE COERCE ATTIT RIGID/FLEX PWR ...METH/CNCPT TIME/SEQ STERTYP GEN/LAWS MARX/KARL VAL/FREE COLD/WAR NAM 20. PAGE 156 H3126
S/ASIA POL/PAR REV

B50
WILBUR C.M.,CHINESE SOURCES ON THE HISTORY OF THE CHINESE COMMUNIST MOVEMENT (PAMPHLET). CHINA/COM ECO/UNDEV PROVS FORCES WAR...PHIL/SCI 20. PAGE 168 H3360
BIBLIOG/A MARXISM REV NAT/G

B51
BORKENAU F.,EUROPEAN COMMUNISM. COM EUR+WWI GERMANY SPAIN USSR INT/ORG PLAN REV WAR ATTIT 20 STALIN/J HITLER/A. PAGE 19 H0376
MARXISM POLICY DIPLOM NAT/G

B51
MARX K.,THE EIGHTEENTH BRUMAIRE OF LOUIS BONAPARTE (1852). FRANCE STRATA FINAN INDUS LABOR CHIEF FORCES WORKER CAP/ISM ECO/TAC PARL/PROC ORD/FREE ...MARXIST 19. PAGE 104 H2080
REV MARXISM ELITES NAT/G

S51
MACRAE D.G.,"THE BOLSHEVIK IDEOLOGY; THE INTELLECTUAL AND EMOTIONAL FACTORS IN COMMUNIST AFFILIATION" (BMR)" COM LEAD REV ATTIT ORD/FREE ...SOC CON/ANAL 20 BOLSHEVISM. PAGE 100 H2008
MARXISM INTELL PHIL/SCI SECT

C51
BEST H.,"THE SOVIET STATE AND ITS INCEPTION." USSR CULTURE INDUS DIPLOM WEALTH...GEOG SOC BIBLIOG 20. PAGE 16 H0322
COM GEN/METH REV MARXISM

B52
LOPEZ-AMO A.,LA MONARQUIA DE LA REFORMA SOCIAL. MOD/EUR SPAIN CONSTN NAT/G TASK EFFICIENCY CONSERVE ...ANARCH TRADIT SOC CONCPT IDEA/COMP 19/20. PAGE 98 H1967
MARXISM REV LEGIT ORD/FREE

B52
SPENCER F.A.,WAR AND POSTWAR GREECE: AN ANALYSIS BASED ON GREEK WRITINGS. GREECE SOCIETY NAT/G POL/PAR FORCES CREATE DIPLOM LEAD MARXISM...SOC 20. PAGE 147 H2943
BIBLIOG/A WAR REV

B53
CURTISS J.S.,THE RUSSIAN CHURCH AND THE SOVIET STATE 1917-1950. COM USSR CONTROL LEAD REV MARXISM ...POLICY BIBLIOG 20 CHURCH/STA ORTHO/RUSS. PAGE 36 H0728
GP/REL NAT/G SECT PWR

B53
LEITES N.,A STUDY OF BOLSHEVISM. ELITES STRATA INT/ORG LOC/G POL/PAR WORKER EDU/PROP REV TOTALISM UTOPIA PWR...CONCPT 20 BOLSHEVISM. PAGE 94 H1870
MARXISM PLAN COM

B53
ROSCIO J.G.,OBRAS. L/A+17C SPAIN DIPLOM REV WAR NAT/LISM TOTALISM PWR SOVEREIGN 19. PAGE 134 H2671
ORD/FREE COLONIAL NAT/G PHIL/SCI

B54
LENIN V.I.,SELECTED WORKS (12 VOLS.). USSR INTELL SOCIETY STRATA STRUCT NAT/G POL/PAR WORKER CAP/ISM REV WAR...MARXIST PHIL/SCI 20 MARX/KARL LENIN/VI. PAGE 94 H1880
COM MARXISM

L54
FRIEDRICH C.J.,"TOTALITARIANISM." COM EUR+WWI NAT/G POL/PAR SECT FORCES PLAN ECO/TAC DOMIN EDU/PROP EXEC COERCE REV ORD/FREE PWR...SOC CONCPT NAZI 20. PAGE 53 H1067
ATTIT TOTALISM

C54
HAMMER E.J.,"THE STRUGGLE FOR INDOCHINA." COM VIETNAM POL/PAR REV CENTRAL NAT/LISM ATTIT...POLICY CHARTS BIBLIOG 20. PAGE 65 H1305
WAR COLONIAL S/ASIA NAT/G

B55
BAILEY S.K.,RESEARCH FRONTIERS IN POLITICS AND GOVERNMENT. CONSTN LEGIS ADMIN REV CHOOSE...CONCPT IDEA/COMP GAME ANTHOL 20. PAGE 10 H0201
R+D METH NAT/G

B55
CRAIG G.A.,THE POLITICS OF THE PRUSSIAN ARMY 1640-1945. CHRIST-17C EUR+WWI MOD/EUR PRUSSIA STRUCT DIPLOM ADMIN REV WAR...SOC BIBLIOG 17/20. PAGE 35 H0694
FORCES NAT/G ROLE CHIEF

B55
DE ARAGAO J.G.,LA JURIDICTION ADMINISTRATIVE AU BRESIL. BRAZIL ADJUD COLONIAL CT/SYS REV FEDERAL ORD/FREE...BIBLIOG 19/20. PAGE 37 H0749
EX/STRUC ADMIN NAT/G

B55
FRANZ G.,KULTURKAMPF. AUSTRIA GERMANY PRUSSIA SWITZERLND POL/PAR DIPLOM GP/REL ATTIT ORD/FREE 18/19 CHURCH/STA. PAGE 53 H1053
NAT/LISM CATHISM NAT/G REV

B55
KOHN H.,NATIONALISM: ITS MEANING AND HISTORY. GP/REL INGP/REL ATTIT...CONCPT NAT/COMP 16/20 MACHIAVELL. PAGE 87 H1743
NAT/LISM DIPLOM FASCISM REV

B55
MAYO H.B.,DEMOCRACY AND MARXISM. COM USSR STRATA NAT/G WORKER ECO/TAC REV MORAL...PHIL/SCI HIST/WRIT IDEA/COMP WORSHIP 20 MARX/KARL LENIN/VI STALIN/J TROTSKY/L. PAGE 105 H2108
MARXISM CAP/ISM

B55
MAZZINI J.,THE DUTIES OF MAN. MOD/EUR LAW SOCIETY FAM NAT/G POL/PAR SECT VOL/ASSN EX/STRUC ACT/RES CREATE REV PEACE ATTIT ALL/VALS...GEN/LAWS WORK 19. PAGE 106 H2113
SUPEGO CONCPT NAT/LISM

B55
TAN C.C.,THE BOXER CATASTROPHE. ASIA UK USSR ELITES POL/PAR VOL/ASSN FORCES PROB/SOLV DIPLOM ADMIN COLONIAL NAT/LISM PEACE TREATY 19/20 BOXER/REBL. PAGE 152 H3040
REV NAT/G WAR

B55
TOYNBEE A.,THE REALIGNMENT OF EUROPE. COM GREECE ITALY NAT/G BAL/PWR ECO/TAC EDU/PROP REV SOVEREIGN ...SOC TIME/SEQ TREND COLD/WAR 20. PAGE 156 H3123
EUR+WWI PLAN USSR

B56
CARRIL B.,PROBLEMAS DE LA REVOLUCION Y LA DEMOCRACIA. CONSTN FORCES DOMIN CONTROL TOTALISM PWR 20. PAGE 27 H0539
REV ORD/FREE LEGIT NAT/G

B56
SMEDLEY A.,THE GREAT ROAD: THE LIFE AND TIMES OF CHU TEH. ASIA USSR NAT/G POL/PAR DIPLOM COERCE GUERRILLA CIVMIL/REL NAT/LISM PERSON SKILL MARXISM ...BIOG 20 CHINJAP MAO. PAGE 145 H2903
REV WAR FORCES

B56
WHITAKER A.P.,ARGENTINE UPHEAVAL. STRUCT FORCES DIPLOM COERCE PWR 20 ARGEN. PAGE 167 H3343
REV POL/PAR STRATA NAT/G

B57
ARON R.,THE OPIUM OF THE INTELLECTUALS (TRANS. BY TERENCE KILMARTIN). FRANCE USSR WOR+45 CULTURE POL/PAR PLAN DOMIN EDU/PROP REV ATTIT ORD/FREE ...IDEA/COMP METH/COMP NAT/COMP 20 COM/PARTY. PAGE 8 H0169
INTELL UTOPIA MYTH MARXISM

B57
KENNEDY M.D.,A SHORT HISTORY OF COMMUNISM IN ASIA. ASIA BURMA INDIA S/ASIA THAILAND NAT/G POL/PAR LEAD REV WAR MARXISM SOCISM...POLICY 20 CHINJAP. PAGE 85 H1688
DIPLOM NAT/LISM TOTALISM COERCE

B57
PARK A.G.,BOLSHEVISM IN TURKESTAN 1917-1927. COM RUSSIA USSR CULTURE AGRI SECT DOMIN GP/REL INGP/REL NAT/LISM...BIBLIOG 20 TURKESTAN. PAGE 123 H2467
REV POLICY MARXISM ISLAM

B57
TOMASIC D.A.,NATIONAL COMMUNISM AND SOVIET STRATEGY. UK USSR YUGOSLAVIA NAT/G POL/PAR CHIEF CREATE DOMIN REV WAR PWR...BIOG TREND 20 TITO/MARSH STALIN/J. PAGE 156 H3112
COM NAT/LISM MARXISM DIPLOM

S57
KILSON M.L.,"LAND AND POLITICS IN KENYA: AN ANALYSIS OF AFRICAN POLITICS IN A PLURAL SOCIETY." FUT LAW CULTURE KIN NAT/G ECO/TAC DOMIN REV NAT/LISM ORD/FREE PWR RESPECT SOVEREIGN WEALTH ...SOC OBS TREND WORK VAL/FREE CMN/WLTH 20. PAGE 86 H1710
AFR ECO/UNDEV

B58
DUNAYEVSKAYA R.,MARXISM AND FREEDOM: FROM 1776 UNTIL TODAY. COM USSR WORKER CAP/ISM DOMIN REV GP/REL TOTALISM ALL/VALS...MYTH BIOG IDEA/COMP 18/20 MARX/KARL LENIN/VI STALIN/J. PAGE 43 H0861
MARXISM CONCPT ORD/FREE

B58
HSU U.T.,THE INVISIBLE CONFLICT. ASIA USSR ELITES NAT/G CONTROL LEAD COERCE REV WAR NAT/LISM ORD/FREE PWR 20 COM/PARTY ESPIONAGE. PAGE 74 H1485
MARXISM POL/PAR EDU/PROP FORCES

B58
JOHNSON J.J.,POLITICAL CHANGE IN LATIN AMERICA: THE EMERGENCE OF THE MIDDLE SECTORS. INTELL STRATA STRUCT ECO/UNDEV MUNIC TEC/DEV LEAD REV...DECISION TREND GOV/COMP BIBLIOG/A 20. PAGE 81 H1621
L/A+17C ELITES GP/REL DOMIN

B58
ORNES G.E.,TRUJILLO: LITTLE CAESAR OF THE CARIBBEAN. DOMIN/REP FAM NAT/G FORCES BUDGET CRIME REV PERSON 20 TRUJILLO/R. PAGE 122 H2429
BIOG PWR TOTALISM CHIEF

B58
PAYNO M.,LA REFORMA SOCIAL EN ESPANA Y MEXICO. SPAIN ECO/TAC TAX LOBBY COERCE REV OWN CATHISM 19/20 MEXIC/AMER. PAGE 124 H2479
SECT NAT/G LAW ELITES

B58
TILLION G.,ALGERIA: THE REALITIES. ALGERIA FRANCE ISLAM CULTURE STRATA PROB/SOLV DOMIN REV NAT/LISM WEALTH MARXISM...GEOG 20. PAGE 155 H3094
ECO/UNDEV SOC COLONIAL DIPLOM

B59
CAREW-HUNT R.C.,BOOKS ON COMMUNISM. NAT/G POL/PAR DIPLOM REV...BIOG 19/20. PAGE 26 H0528
BIBLIOG/A MARXISM COM

ASIA

B59
GOLDWIN R.A.,READINGS IN RUSSIAN FOREIGN POLICY. HUNGARY USSR YUGOSLAVIA ELITES INT/ORG NAT/G REV WAR NAT/LISM PERSON SOCISM...CHARTS 20 MAPS BOLSHEVISM. PAGE 58 H1160
COM MARXISM DIPLOM POLICY

B59
HENDEL S.,THE SOVIET CRUCIBLE. USSR LEAD COERCE NAT/LISM UTOPIA PWR...POLICY CONCPT ANTHOL 20 STALIN/J LENIN/VI MARX/KARL BOLSHEVIK. PAGE 70 H1393
COM MARXISM REV TOTALISM

B59
HOBSBAWM E.J.,PRIMITIVE REBELS; STUDIES IN ARCHAIC FORMS OF SOCIAL MOVEMENT IN THE 19TH AND 20TH CENTURIES. ITALY SPAIN CULTURE VOL/ASSN RISK CROWD GP/REL INGP/REL ISOLAT TOTALISM...PSY SOC 18/20. PAGE 72 H1438
SOCIETY CRIME REV GUERRILLA

B59
LANDAUER C.,EUROPEAN SOCIALISM (2 VOLS.). COM EUR+WWI MOD/EUR INTELL INDUS REV WAR...MAJORIT IDEA/COMP BIBLIOG 19/20 HITLER/A. PAGE 90 H1805
SOCISM NAT/COMP LABOR MARXISM

B59
MAIER H.,REVOLUTION UND KIRCHE. FRANCE MOD/EUR SECT REV ORD/FREE...IDEA/COMP 18/19. PAGE 101 H2018
NAT/G CATHISM ATTIT POL/PAR

B59
PAGE S.W.,LENIN AND WORLD REVOLUTION. COM USSR NAT/G DOMIN COERCE CROWD UTOPIA ATTIT AUTHORIT DRIVE PWR...CONCPT MYTH 19/20 LENIN/VI MARX/KARL. PAGE 122 H2441
REV PERSON MARXISM BIOG

B59
SZLUC T.,TWILIGHT OF THE TYRANTS. BRAZIL L/A+17C PERU VENEZUELA NAT/G FORCES CONTROL PERSON MORAL ORD/FREE PWR...CONCPT 20 ARGEN COLOMB. PAGE 151 H3028
TOTALISM CHIEF REV FASCISM

B59
VITTACHIT,EMERGENCY '58. CEYLON UK STRUCT NAT/G FORCES ADJUD CRIME REV NAT/LISM 20. PAGE 163 H3258
RACE/REL DISCRIM DIPLOM SOVEREIGN

S59
LEVINE R.A.,"ANTI-EUROPEAN VIOLENCE IN AFRICA: A COMPARATIVE ANALYSIS." AFR CULTURE NAT/G DIPLOM EDU/PROP COLONIAL REGION COERCE ATTIT PWR...PSY CONCPT TIME/SEQ TREND HYPO/EXP SOC/EXP STERTYP GEN/METH COLD/WAR 20. PAGE 95 H1903
DRIVE ORD/FREE REV

S59
MECHAM J.L.,"LATIN AMERICAN CONSTITUTIONS: NOMINAL AND REAL" (BMR)" L/A+17C REV...CON/ANAL NAT/COMP 20. PAGE 108 H2156
CONSTN CHOOSE CONCPT NAT/G

B60
FISCHER L.,THE SOVIETS IN WORLD AFFAIRS. CHINA/COM COM EUR+WWI USSR INT/ORG CONFER LEAD ARMS/CONT REV PWR...CHARTS 20 TREATY VERSAILLES. PAGE 51 H1010
DIPLOM NAT/G POLICY MARXISM

B60
GOODMAN E.,SOVIET DESIGN FOR A WORLD STATE. COM USSR NAT/G TOP/EX DIPLOM ECO/TAC DOMIN EDU/PROP COERCE REV ATTIT ORD/FREE...CON/ANAL 20. PAGE 59 H1171
PLAN PWR SOCISM TOTALISM

B60
MC CLELLAN G.S.,INDIA. CHINA/COM INDIA CONSTN ELITES STRATA AGRI POL/PAR FOR/AID ARMS/CONT REV MARXISM...CENSUS BIBLIOG 20 COLD/WAR GANDHI/M NEHRU/J. PAGE 106 H2117
DIPLOM NAT/G SOCIETY ECO/UNDEV

B60
MOCTEZUMA A.P.,EL CONFLICTO RELIGIOSO DE 1926 (2ND ED.). L/A+17C LAW NAT/G LOBBY COERCE GP/REL ATTIT ...POLICY 20 MEXIC/AMER CHURCH/STA. PAGE 112 H2233
SECT ORD/FREE DISCRIM REV

B60
PIERCE R.A.,RUSSIAN CENTRAL ASIA, 1867-1917. ASIA RUSSIA CULTURE AGRI INDUS EDU/PROP REV NAT/LISM ...CHARTS BIBLIOG 19/20 BOLSHEVISM INTERVENT. PAGE 125 H2509
COLONIAL DOMIN ADMIN ECO/UNDEV

B60
SETHE P.,SCHICKSALSSTUNDEN DER WELTGESCHICHTE (6TH ED.). NAT/G BAL/PWR DOMIN REV PWR...NAT/COMP 16/20. PAGE 141 H2831
DIPLOM WAR PEACE

B60
SZTARAY Z.,BIBLIOGRAPHY ON HUNGARY. HUNGARY MOD/EUR CULTURE INDUS SECT DIPLOM REV...ART/METH SOC LING 18/20. PAGE 151 H3029
BIBLIOG NAT/G COM MARXISM

B60
THORD-GRAY I.,GRINGO REBEL. L/A+17C NAT/G CONTROL LEAD ATTIT...OBS 20 MEXIC/AMER. PAGE 154 H3087
REV FORCES CIVMIL/REL ORD/FREE

B60
ZENKOVSKY S.A.,PAN-TURKISM AND ISLAM IN RUSSIA. ASIA RUSSIA USSR CULTURE POL/PAR DOMIN REV GP/REL MARXISM...LING GP/COMP BIBLIOG 19/20 TURKIC. PAGE 173 H3454
SECT NAT/LISM COM ISLAM

S60
BRZEZINSKI Z.K.,"PATTERNS AND LIMITS OF THE SINO-SOVIET DISPUTE." ASIA CHINA/COM COM FUT STRATA NAT/G EX/STRUC FORCES BAL/PWR DIPLOM ECO/TAC DOMIN EDU/PROP ADMIN COERCE WAR ATTIT RIGID/FLEX ...GEN/LAWS VAL/FREE 20. PAGE 23 H0459
POL/PAR PWR REV USSR

S60
WYCKOFF T.,"THE ROLE OF THE MILITARY IN LATIN AMERICAN POLITICS." L/A+17C CONSTN CULTURE ECO/UNDEV POL/PAR FORCES LEGIS TOP/EX LEGIT GUERRILLA REV CHOOSE ORD/FREE PWR...TIME/SEQ VAL/FREE 20. PAGE 171 H3430
NAT/G COERCE TOTALISM

C60
HAZARD J.N.,"SETTLING DISPUTES IN SOVIET SOCIETY: THE FORMATIVE YEARS OF LEGAL INSTITUTIONS." USSR NAT/G PROF/ORG PROB/SOLV CONTROL CT/SYS ROUTINE REV CENTRAL...JURID BIBLIOG 20. PAGE 68 H1372
ADJUD LAW COM POLICY

B61
ANSPRENGER F.,POLITIK IM SCHWARZEN AFRIKA. FRANCE NAT/G DIPLOM REGION REV NAT/LISM...CHARTS BIBLIOG 19/20. PAGE 7 H0141
AFR COLONIAL SOVEREIGN

B61
ASHLEY M.P.,GREAT BRITAIN TO 1688: A MODERN HISTORY. UK NAT/G CHIEF LEAD REV WAR...POLICY BIBLIOG 1/17. PAGE 9 H0174
DOMIN CONSERVE

B61
BROWN D.M.,THE NATIONALIST MOVEMENT. INDIA CULTURE STRATA REV MORAL ORD/FREE...BIBLIOG 20 HINDU. PAGE 22 H0443
NAT/LISM LEAD CHIEF POL/PAR

B61
ESTEVEZ A.,ASPECTOS ECONOMICO-FINANCIEROS DE LA CAMPANA SANMARITANA. L/A+17C SPAIN FINAN COLONIAL LEAD ROLE ORD/FREE WEALTH 19 SOUTH/AMER SAN/MARTIN. PAGE 47 H0942
ECO/UNDEV REV BUDGET NAT/G

B61
FULLER J.F.C.,THE CONDUCT OF WAR, 1789-1961. FRANCE RUSSIA SOCIETY NAT/G FORCES PROB/SOLV AGREE NUC/PWR WEAPON PEACE...SOC 18/20 TREATY COLD/WAR. PAGE 54 H1076
WAR POLICY REV ROLE

B61
GUEVARA E.,GUERRILLA WARFARE. L/A+17C ECO/UNDEV NAT/G POL/PAR VOL/ASSN PLAN DOMIN REV DRIVE PWR WEALTH...NEW/IDEA RECORD BIOG COLD/WAR MARX/KARL OAS 20. PAGE 62 H1247
FORCES COERCE GUERRILLA CUBA

B61
HADDAD J.A.,REVOLUCAO CUBANA E REVOLUCAO BRASILEIRA. BRAZIL CUBA L/A+17C STRATA AGRI WORKER EDU/PROP REGION...POLICY NAT/COMP 20. PAGE 63 H1272
REV ORD/FREE DIPLOM ECO/UNDEV

B61
KEDOURIE E.,NATIONALISM (REV. ED.). MOD/EUR SOVEREIGN...CONCPT 19/20. PAGE 84 H1675
NAT/LISM NAT/G CREATE REV

B61
KHAN A.W.,INDIA WINS FREEDOM: THE OTHER SIDE. INDIA PAKISTAN CULTURE LEGIS DIPLOM PARL/PROC REV WAR NAT/LISM 20. PAGE 85 H1707
SOVEREIGN GP/REL RACE/REL ORD/FREE

B61
LEVIN L.A.,BIBLIOGRAFIIA BIBLIOGRAFII PROIZVEDENII K. MARKSA, F. ENGELSA, V.I. LENINA. COM USSR NAT/G POL/PAR WORKER LEAD REV ATTIT...POLICY IDEA/COMP 20 MARX/KARL LENIN/VI ENGELS. PAGE 95 H1899
BIBLIOG/A MARXISM MARXIST CONCPT

B61
MARX K.,THE COMMUNIST MANIFESTO. IN (MENDEL A. ESSENTIAL WORKS OF MARXISM, NEW YORK: BANTAM. FUT MOD/EUR CULTURE ECO/DEV ECO/UNDEV AGRI FINAN INDUS MARKET PROC/MFG LABOR MUNIC POL/PAR CONSULT FORCES CREATE PLAN ADMIN ATTIT DRIVE RIGID/FLEX ORD/FREE PWR RESPECT MARX/KARL WORK. PAGE 104 H2081
COM NEW/IDEA CAP/ISM REV

B61
MOLLAU G.,INTERNATIONAL COMMUNISM AND WORLD REVOLUTION: HISTORY AND METHODS. RUSSIA USSR INT/ORG NAT/G POL/PAR VOL/ASSN FORCES BAL/PWR DIPLOM EXEC REGION WAR ATTIT PWR MARXISM...CONCPT TIME/SEQ COLD/WAR 19/20. PAGE 112 H2237
COM REV

B61
PAZ O.,THE LABYRINTH OF SOLITUDE; LIFE AND THOUGHT IN MEXICO (TRANS. BY LYSANDER KEMP). INTELL COLONIAL REV...PSY SOC TIME/SEQ 16/20 MEXIC/AMER. PAGE 124 H2480
CULTURE PERSON PERS/REL SOCIETY

B61
SETON-WATSON H.,FROM LENIN TO KHRUSHCHEV: THE HISTORY OF WORLD COMMUNISM. ASIA COM EUR+WWI ISLAM S/ASIA ECO/DEV ECO/UNDEV NAT/G POL/PAR DIPLOM ECO/TAC EDU/PROP COERCE GUERRILLA ATTIT DRIVE WORK TOT/POP NAZI 20. PAGE 141 H2832
PWR REV USSR

S61
TUCKER R.C.,"TOWARDS A COMPARATIVE POLITICS OF MOVEMENT-REGIMES" (BMR)" USSR CONSTN NAT/G CREATE PROB/SOLV DIPLOM DOMIN REV...GP/COMP IDEA/COMP METH 20 STALIN/J BOLSHEVISM. PAGE 157 H3135
MARXISM POLICY GEN/LAWS PWR

B62
BAFFREY S.A.,THE RED MYTH: A HISTORY OF COMMUNISM FROM MARX TO KHRUSHCHEV. USSR NAT/G CHIEF CAP/ISM DIPLOM EDU/PROP REV WAR PEACE TOTALISM...POLICY 20 STALIN/J KHRUSH/N. PAGE 10 H0195
CONCPT MARXISM TV

B62
BARNETT A.D.,COMMUNIST CHINA IN PERSPECTIVE. CHINA/COM FUT CULTURE ECO/UNDEV TEC/DEV CONTROL 20. PAGE 11 H0222
REV MARXISM TREND PLAN

B62
BAULIN J.,THE ARAB ROLE IN AFRICA. AFR ALGERIA FUT ISLAM MOROCCO UAR COLONIAL NEUTRAL REV...SOC 20 TUNIS BOURGUIBA. PAGE 12 H0240
NAT/LISM DIPLOM NAT/G SECT

B62
BINDER L.,IRAN: POLITICAL DEVELOPMENT IN A CHANGING SOCIETY. IRAN OP/RES REV GP/REL CENTRAL RATIONAL PWR...PHIL/SCI NAT/COMP GEN/LAWS 20. PAGE 17 H0337
LEGIT NAT/G ADMIN STRUCT

B62
FINER S.E.,THE MAN ON HORSEBACK: ROLE OF THE MILITARY IN POLITICS. UNIV LAW CONSTN ELITES SOCIETY POL/PAR BAL/PWR DOMIN EDU/PROP LEGIT COERCE GUERRILLA REV WAR WEAPON DRIVE SUPEGO ORD/FREE PWR RESPECT...POLICY CONCPT GEN/METH. PAGE 50 H1003
NAT/G FORCES TOTALISM

B62
HAIM S.G.,ARAB NATIONALISM. ISLAM CONSTN GP/REL ...ANTHOL BIBLIOG JEWS 20 MID/EAST ARABS. PAGE 64 H1279
NAT/LISM REV SECT DIPLOM

B62
HAY S.N.,SOUTHEAST ASIAN HISTORY: A BIBLIOGRAPHICAL GUIDE. STRATA KIN NAT/G REGION GUERRILLA REV WAR ADJUST HABITAT PERCEPT ALL/IDEOS...CHARTS 5/20. PAGE 68 H1365
BIBLIOG/A S/ASIA CULTURE

B62
HOOK S.,THE PARADOXES OF FREEDOM. UNIV CONSTN INTELL LEGIS CONTROL REV CHOOSE SUPEGO...POLICY JURID IDEA/COMP 19/20 CIV/RIGHTS. PAGE 73 H1461
CONCPT MAJORIT ORD/FREE ALL/VALS

B62
HUNKIN P.,ENSEIGNEMENT ET POLITIQUE EN FRANCE ET EN ANGLETERRE. FRANCE UK CONSTN ACADEM SECT CHIEF DELIB/GP PROB/SOLV CONTROL REV ORD/FREE CONSERVE ...BIBLIOG 18/20. PAGE 75 H1496
EDU/PROP LEGIS IDEA/COMP NAT/G

B62
JOHNSON J.J.,THE ROLE OF THE MILITARY IN UNDERDEVELOPED COUNTRIES. AFR BURMA INDONESIA ISLAM ISRAEL L/A+17C S/ASIA THAILAND CULTURE ECO/UNDEV KIN PROVS CONSULT ACT/RES COERCE REV DRIVE RIGID/FLEX ORD/FREE...RECORD ANTHOL 20. PAGE 81 H1622
FORCES CONCPT

B62
MANSUR F.,PROCESS OF INDEPENDENCE. GHANA INDIA INDONESIA PAKISTAN CONSTN ELITES INTELL STRUCT ACADEM NAT/G REV PWR 20. PAGE 102 H2043
NAT/COMP POL/PAR SOVEREIGN COLONIAL

B62
MEHNERT K.,SOVIET MAN AND HIS WORLD. COM USSR INTELL FAM WORKER PLAN EDU/PROP REV PRODUC MARXISM ...SOC TREND SOC/INTEG 20 LENIN/VI STALIN/J KHRUSH/N. PAGE 108 H2162
SOCIETY CULTURE ECO/DEV

B62
MEYER A.G.,LENINISM. USSR STRUCT NAT/G CAP/ISM LEAD WAR PWR SOVEREIGN...BIBLIOG 20 LENIN/VI. PAGE 109 H2187
POL/PAR REV MARXISM PHIL/SCI

B62
ROUSSEAU J.J.,THE SOCIAL CONTRACT. LAW CONSTN CHIEF DOMIN REPRESENT GP/REL ORD/FREE POPULISM...MAJORIT GOV/COMP 18. PAGE 135 H2700
GEN/LAWS AGREE REV

B62
SCHIEDER T.,THE STATE AND SOCIETY IN OUR TIMES (TRANS. BY C.A.M. SYM). SOCIETY NAT/G POL/PAR REV GP/REL ALL/IDEOS 19/20. PAGE 139 H2786
STRUCT PWR HIST/WRIT

B62
SELOSOEMARDJAN O.,SOCIAL CHANGES IN JOGJAKARTA. INDONESIA NETHERLAND ELITES STRATA STRUCT FAM POL/PAR CREATE DIPLOM INT/TRADE EDU/PROP ADMIN GOV/REL...SOC 20 JAVA CHINJAP. PAGE 141 H2825
ECO/UNDEV CULTURE REV COLONIAL

S62
HYDE D.,"COMMUNISM IN LATIN AMERICA." L/A+17C ECO/DEV NAT/G SECT EDU/PROP ATTIT ALL/VALS MARXISM ...SOC CONCPT TOT/POP COLD/WAR OAS 20. PAGE 76 H1515
COM POL/PAR REV

S62
MU FU-SHENG,"THE WILTING OF THE HUNDRED FLOWERS: FREE THOUGHT IN CHINA TODAY." ASIA CHINA/COM CULTURE FAM NAT/G EDU/PROP REV TOTALISM ATTIT PERSON RESPECT...GEOG INT UNPLAN/INT COLD/WAR 20. PAGE 114 H2278
INTELL ELITES

S62
PASSIN H.,"THE SOURCES OF PROTEST IN JAPAN." CULTURE SOCIETY EDU/PROP COERCE NAT/LISM DISPL DRIVE PWR RESPECT...POLICY SOC TREND 20 CHINJAP. PAGE 124 H2473
ASIA ATTIT REV

S62
ROTBERG R.,"THE RISE OF AFRICAN NATIONALISM: THE CASE OF EAST AND CENTRAL AFRICA." AFR CULTURE SOCIETY NEIGH DIPLOM DOMIN COLONIAL COERCE DISPL PERCEPT PWR SOVEREIGN...POLICY OBS/ENVIR TREND WORK 20. PAGE 135 H2690
ATTIT DRIVE NAT/LISM REV

C62
BACON F.,"OF SEDITIONS AND TROUBLES" (1625) IN F. BACON, ESSAYS." INDUS MARKET CHIEF ECO/TAC EDU/PROP CONTROL LEAD PEACE WEALTH 17 MACHIAVELL. PAGE 9 H0191
REV ORD/FREE NAT/G GEN/LAWS

B63
BERLIN I.,KARL MARX, HIS LIFE AND ENVIRONMENT (3RD ED.). MOD/EUR USSR INTELL EDU/PROP PARTIC REV ATTIT 19 MARX/KARL. PAGE 15 H0307
BIOG PERSON MARXISM CONCPT

B63
BIALEK R.W.,CATHOLIC POLITICS: A HISTORY BASED ON ECUADOR. ECUADOR SPAIN CULTURE STRUCT CONTROL REV PWR...BIBLIOG WORSHIP 18/20. PAGE 16 H0329
COLONIAL CATHISM GOV/REL HABITAT

B63
BORKENAU F.,THE SPANISH COCKPIT. SPAIN ELITES STRATA POL/PAR ACT/RES CROWD WAR GP/REL INGP/REL ...SOC NAT/COMP 20. PAGE 19 H0377
REV CONSERVE SOCISM FORCES

B63
CANELAS O.A.,RADIOGRAFIA DE LA ALIANZA PARA EL ATRASO. L/A+17C USA+45 ECO/TAC DOMIN COLONIAL NAT/LISM...SOCIALIST NAT/COMP 20. PAGE 26 H0519
REV DIPLOM ECO/UNDEV REGION

B63
CRANKSHAW E.,THE NEW COLD WAR: MOSCOW V. PEKIN. CHINA/COM USSR INTELL POL/PAR DELIB/GP CAP/ISM COERCE REV NAT/LISM TOTALISM DRIVE...POLICY IDEA/COMP 20 KHRUSH/N. PAGE 35 H0698
ATTIT DIPLOM NAT/COMP MARXISM

B63
ELLIOT J.H.,THE REVOLT OF THE CATALANS. SPAIN LOC/G PROVS FORCES DIPLOM TASK WAR GOV/REL INGP/REL ...POLICY 17 OLIVARES. PAGE 45 H0909
REV NAT/G TOP/EX DOMIN

B63
FRIEDRICH C.J.,MAN AND HIS GOVERNMENT: AN EMPIRICAL THEORY OF POLITICS. UNIV LOC/G NAT/G ADJUD REV INGP/REL DISCRIM PWR BIBLIOG. PAGE 53 H1069
PERSON ORD/FREE PARTIC CONTROL

B63
GEERTZ C.,OLD SOCIETIES AND NEW STATES: THE QUEST FOR MODERNITY IN ASIA AND AFRICA. AFR ASIA LAW CULTURE SECT EDU/PROP REV...GOV/COMP NAT/COMP 20. PAGE 55 H1107
ECO/UNDEV TEC/DEV NAT/LISM SOVEREIGN

B63
HALPERIN M.H.,THE POLITICS OF SOCIAL CHANGE IN THE MIDDLE EAST AND NORTH AFRICA. ISLAM CULTURE ACT/RES REV ATTIT PERCEPT KNOWL...METH/CNCPT OBS TIME/SEQ GEN/METH TOT/POP VAL/FREE 20. PAGE 64 H1291
SOC TREND

B63
HAMM H.,ALBANIA - CHINA'S BEACHHEAD IN EUROPE. ALBANIA CHINA/COM USSR YUGOSLAVIA ELITES SOCIETY POL/PAR DELIB/GP FORCES ECO/TAC COERCE ISOLAT PEACE MARXISM...IDEA/COMP 20 MAO. PAGE 65 H1304
DIPLOM REV NAT/G POLICY

B63
ISSAWI C.,EGYPT IN REVOLUTION: AN ECONOMIC ANALYSIS. ISLAM STRUCT ECO/UNDEV AGRI FINAN INDUS PLAN EXEC REV NAT/LISM ATTIT RIGID/FLEX WEALTH SOCISM...STAT WORK 20. PAGE 79 H1573
NAT/G UAR

B63
KATEB G.,UTOPIA AND ITS ENEMIES. CULTURE STRATA ECO/DEV INDUS REV MORAL...PSY IDEA/COMP 19/20. PAGE 84 H1668
UTOPIA SOCIETY PHIL/SCI PEACE

B63
LEE C.,THE POLITICS OF KOREAN NATIONALISM. KOREA S/ASIA DIPLOM REV WAR 14/20 CHINJAP. PAGE 93 H1855
NAT/LISM SOVEREIGN COLONIAL

B63
NALBANDIAN L.,THE ARMENIAN REVOLUTIONARY MOVEMENT. MOD/EUR RUSSIA...IDEA/COMP NAT/COMP BIBLIOG 19 ARMENIA OTTOMAN. PAGE 115 H2306
NAT/LISM REV POL/PAR ORD/FREE

B63
OTERO L.M.,HONDURAS. HONDURAS SPAIN STRUCT SECT COLONIAL REV WAR ATTIT PWR...GEOG WORSHIP 16/20. PAGE 122 H2432
NAT/G SOCIETY NAT/LISM ECO/UNDEV

B63
SHANNON R.T.,GLADSTONE AND THE BULGARIAN AGITATION OF 1876. BULGARIA TURKEY UK DIPLOM COERCE REV ATTIT 19 GLADSTON/W DISRAELI/B. PAGE 142 H2841
EDU/PROP NAT/G PWR CONSEN

B63
STEVENS G.G.,EGYPT YESTERDAY AND TODAY. CONSTN ECO/UNDEV AGRI INDUS NAT/G POL/PAR FORCES ECO/TAC EDU/PROP COERCE WAR NAT/LISM DRIVE ALL/VALS ...TIME/SEQ WORK SUEZ 20. PAGE 149 H2983
ISLAM TOP/EX REV UAR

B63
WODDIS J.,AFRICA, THE WAY AHEAD. AFR FUT ELITES POL/PAR CAP/ISM DIPLOM DOMIN RACE/REL ATTIT ORD/FREE SOVEREIGN SOCISM 20 PANAF/FREE. PAGE 170 H3394
REV COLONIAL ECO/UNDEV NAT/G

S63
DUTT V.P.,"CHINA: JEALOUS NEIGHBOR." ASIA CHINA/COM INDIA S/ASIA NAT/G TOP/EX DOMIN COERCE REV ATTIT ...POLICY COLD/WAR 20. PAGE 44 H0874
FORCES PWR DIPLOM

S63
TANG P.S.H.,"SINO-SOVIET TENSIONS." ASIA CHINA/COM COM CUBA KOREA/N VIETNAM/N NAT/G VOL/ASSN DELIB/GP PEACE PERCEPT PWR...METH/CNCPT MYTH RECORD TREND GEN/LAWS 20. PAGE 152 H3041
ACT/RES EDU/PROP REV

B64
AGGARWALA R.C.,CONSTITUTIONAL HISTORY OF INDIA AND NATIONAL MOVEMENT INCLUDING COMPARATIVE STUDY OF MODERN INDIA CONSTITUTION. INDIA S/ASIA SECT VOL/ASSN EX/STRUC LEGIS COERCE REV INGP/REL ORD/FREE...SOC BIBLIOG 18/20 CMN/WLTH. PAGE 4 H0077
CONSTN COLONIAL DOMIN NAT/G

B64
ALVIM J.C.,A REVOLUCAO SEM RUMO. BRAZIL NAT/G BAL/PWR DIPLOM INT/TRADE PARTIC WEALTH...POLICY SOC SOC/INTEG 20. PAGE 6 H0118
REV CIVMIL/REL ECO/UNDEV ORD/FREE

B64
BURKE F.G.,AFRICA'S QUEST FOR ORDER. AFR CULTURE KIN MUNIC NAT/G DIPLOM COLONIAL REV DISCRIM NAT/LISM AGE/Y 20. PAGE 24 H0488
ORD/FREE CONSEN RACE/REL LEAD

B64
CLUBB O.E. JR.,TWENTIETH CENTURY CHINA. ASIA CHINA/COM INTELL NAT/G POL/PAR VOL/ASSN ACT/RES EDU/PROP COERCE REV PWR...TIME/SEQ 20. PAGE 30 H0608
TOP/EX DRIVE

B64
COWAN L.G.,THE DILEMMAS OF AFRICAN INDEPENDENCE. AFR INDUS NAT/G SECT DIPLOM ECO/TAC REGION MARXISM ...CHARTS BIBLIOG 20 MAPS. PAGE 34 H0683
ORD/FREE COLONIAL REV ECO/UNDEV

B64
DANIELS R.V.,RUSSIA. RUSSIA USSR STRUCT NAT/LISM TOTALISM ORD/FREE WEALTH...POLICY DECISION TREND. PAGE 37 H0740
MARXISM REV ECO/DEV DIPLOM

B64
FAINSOD M.,HOW RUSSIA IS RULED (REV. ED.). RUSSIA USSR AGRI PROC/MFG LABOR POL/PAR EX/STRUC CONTROL PWR...POLICY BIBLIOG 19/20 KHRUSH/N COM/PARTY. PAGE 48 H0963
NAT/G REV MARXISM

B64
FALL B.,STREET WITHOUT JOY. FRANCE USA+45 DIPLOM ECO/TAC FOR/AID GUERRILLA REV WEAPON...TREND 20. PAGE 48 H0966
WAR S/ASIA FORCES COERCE

B64
FISCHER L.,THE LIFE OF LENIN. USSR LEAD REV WAR ...SOC 19/20 LENIN/VI COM/PARTY BOLSHEVISM. PAGE 51 H1011
BIOG MARXISM PERSON CHIEF

B64
GILLY A.,INSIDE THE CUBAN REVOLUTION. CUBA AGRI INDUS LABOR CREATE DIPLOM...METH/COMP 20. PAGE 56 H1129
REV PLAN MARXISM ECO/UNDEV

B64
GUTTERIDGE W.,MILITARY INSTITUTIONS AND POWER IN THE NEW STATES. WOR+45 INT/ORG FOR/AID NEUTRAL REV CIVMIL/REL ATTIT ROLE...GOV/COMP 20. PAGE 63 H1258
FORCES DIPLOM ECO/UNDEV ELITES

B64
KIS T.I.,LES PAYS DE L'EUROPE DE L'EST: LEURS RAPPORTS MUTUELS ET LE PROBLEME DE LEUR INTEGRATION DANS L'ORBITE DE L'USSR. EUR+WWI RUSSIA USSR INT/ORG NAT/G REV ATTIT...JURID SOC BIBLIOG WARSAW/P COMECON EUROPE/E. PAGE 86 H1727
DIPLOM COM MARXISM REGION

B64
LIEVWEN E.,GENERALS VS PRESIDENTS: WEOMILITARISM IN LATIN AMERICA. L/A+17C FORCES DIPLOM FOR/AID LEAD ...NAT/COMP 20 PRESIDENT. PAGE 97 H1929
CIVMIL/REL REV CONSERVE ORD/FREE

B64
MAIER J.,POLITICS OF CHANGE IN LATIN AMERICA. BRAZIL L/A+17C STRATA INT/ORG NAT/G POL/PAR FOR/AID REV 20. PAGE 101 H2019
SOCIETY NAT/LISM DIPLOM REGION

B64
MARTINEZ J.R.,THREE CASES OF COMMUNISM: CUBA, BRAZIL, AND MEXICO. BRAZIL CUBA L/A+17C CONSTN NAT/G DIPLOM ECO/TAC GP/REL INGP/REL...GP/COMP BIBLIOG 20 MEXIC/AMER COM/PARTY. PAGE 103 H2068
MARXISM BIOG REV NAT/COMP

B64
MBEKI G.,SOUTH AFRICA: THE PEASANT'S REVOLT. SOUTH/AFR POL/PAR COERCE REV NAT/LISM ORD/FREE SOVEREIGN 20 NEGRO. PAGE 106 H2114
COLONIAL RACE/REL DISCRIM DOMIN

B64
MINAR D.W.,IDEAS AND POLITICS: THE AMERICAN EXPERIENCE. SECT CHIEF LEGIS CREATE ADJUD EXEC REV PWR...PHIL/SCI CONCPT IDEA/COMP 18/20 HAMILTON/A JEFFERSN/T DECLAR/IND JACKSON/A PRESIDENT. PAGE 111 H2220
CONSTN NAT/G FEDERAL

B64
POWELSON J.P.,LATIN AMERICA: TODAY'S ECONOMIC AND SOCIAL REVOLUTION. L/A+17C INTELL SOCIETY STRUCT AGRI INDUS NAT/G DIPLOM ECO/TAC REV...POLICY 20. PAGE 128 H2552
ECO/UNDEV WEALTH ADJUST PLAN

B64
ROSENAU J.N.,INTERNATIONAL ASPECTS OF CIVIL STRIFE. CHINA/COM CUBA EUR+WWI USA+45 USSR BAL/PWR EDU/PROP NEUTRAL COERCE MORAL...NAT/COMP 20 COLD/WAR UN. PAGE 134 H2676
POLICY DIPLOM REV WAR

B64
SANCHEZ J.M.,REFORM AND REACTION. SPAIN STRATA NAT/LISM TOTALISM 20. PAGE 137 H2749
NAT/G SECT GP/REL REV

B64
UTECHIN S.V.,RUSSIAN POLITICAL THOUGHT: A CONCISE HISTORY. RUSSIA USSR INTELL STRATA POL/PAR SECT LEGIS EDU/PROP REV WAR MARXISM...ANARCH BIBLIOG 9/20 REFORMERS SLAVS. PAGE 161 H3218
IDEA/COMP ATTIT ALL/IDEOS NAT/G

B64
VON STEIN L.J.,THE HISTORY OF THE SOCIAL MOVEMENT IN FRANCE, 1789-1850 (TRANS. BY K. MENGELBERG). COM FRANCE MOD/EUR NAT/G EX/STRUC INGP/REL ALL/IDEOS CONSERVE MARXISM...SOC BIBLIOG 18/19. PAGE 164 H3278
REV STRATA

B64
WRIGHT G.,RURAL REVOLUTION IN FRANCE: THE PEASANTRY IN THE TWENTIETH CENTURY. EUR+WWI MOD/EUR LAW CULTURE AGRI POL/PAR DELIB/GP LEGIS ECO/TAC EDU/PROP COERCE CHOOSE ATTIT RIGID/FLEX HEALTH ...STAT CENSUS CHARTS VAL/FREE 20. PAGE 171 H3419
PWR STRATA FRANCE REV

S64
CATTELL D.T.,"SOVIET POLICIES IN LATIN AMERICA." COM CUBA L/A+17C USSR SOCIETY NAT/G POL/PAR FORCES CREATE ECO/TAC EDU/PROP REGION REV RIGID/FLEX ...GEN/LAWS COLD/WAR 20. PAGE 28 H0560
DRIVE PWR

S64
JOHNSON K.F.,"CAUSAL FACTORS IN LATIN AMERICAN POLITICAL INSTABILITY." CULTURE NAT/G VOL/ASSN EX/STRUC FORCES EDU/PROP LEGIT ADMIN COERCE REV ATTIT KNOWL PWR...STYLE RECORD CHARTS WORK 20. PAGE 81 H1624
L/A+17C PERCEPT ELITES

S64
MOZINGO D.P.,"CHINA'S RELATIONS WITH HER ASIAN NEIGHBORS." ASIA CHINA/COM S/ASIA VIETNAM NAT/G DELIB/GP FORCES CREATE DOMIN EDU/PROP REV RIGID/FLEX PWR...TIME/SEQ GEN/LAWS COLD/WAR 20. PAGE 114 H2277
VOL/ASSN POLICY DIPLOM

S64
SOLOVEYTCHIK G.,"BOOKS ON RUSSIA." USSR ELITES NAT/G PERF/ART REV GOV/REL MARXISM...AUD/VIS 20. PAGE 147 H2929
BIBLIOG/A COM CULTURE

C64
SCOTT R.E.,"MEXICAN GOVERNMENT IN TRANSITION (REV ED)" CULTURE STRUCT POL/PAR CHIEF ADMIN LOBBY REV CHOOSE GP/REL DRIVE...BIBLIOG METH 20 MEXIC/AMER. PAGE 141 H2816
NAT/G L/A+17C ROUTINE CONSTN

B65
ALEXANDER R.J.,ORGANIZED LABOR IN LATIN AMERICA. L/A+17C INT/ORG LEGIS WORKER TEC/DEV BARGAIN INT/TRADE REV...NAT/COMP BIBLIOG 20. PAGE 5 H0102
LABOR POL/PAR ECO/UNDEV POLICY

B65
COX R.H.,THE STATE IN INTERNATIONAL RELATIONS. INT/ORG DIPLOM REV WAR PEACE MARXISM...CONCPT GOV/COMP. PAGE 34 H0690
SOVEREIGN NAT/G FASCISM ORD/FREE

B65
FAGG J.E.,CUBA, HAITI, AND THE DOMINICAN REPUBLIC. CUBA DOMIN/REP HAITI L/A+17C NAT/G DIPLOM ECO/TAC DOMIN CHOOSE AUTHORIT ROLE SOVEREIGN POPULISM 17/20. PAGE 48 H0959
COLONIAL ECO/UNDEV REV GOV/COMP

B65
FAUST J.J.,A REVOLUCAO DEVORA SEUS PRESIDENTES. BRAZIL NAT/G POL/PAR LEAD CHOOSE CIVMIL/REL ORD/FREE 20 PRESIDENT. PAGE 49 H0976
PARTIC REV FORCES GP/REL

B65
GODECHOT J.,FRANCE AND THE ATLANTIC REVOLUTION OF THE EIGHTEENTH CENTURY 1770-1799. FRANCE CULTURE SOCIETY...GEOG 18. PAGE 57 H1150
MOD/EUR NAT/G REV ECO/UNDEV

B65
GREGG J.L.,POLITICAL PARTIES AND PARTY SYSTEMS IN GUATEMALA, 1944-1963. GUATEMALA L/A+17C EX/STRUC FORCES CREATE CONTROL REV CHOOSE PWR...TREND IDEA/COMP 20. PAGE 60 H1209
LEAD POL/PAR NAT/G CHIEF

B65
HALEVY E.,THE ERA OF TYRANNIES (TRANS. BY R. K.
SOCISM

WEBB). WOR-45 ECO/DEV PROB/SOLV CONTROL COERCE REV WAR TOTALISM 20. PAGE 64 H1286 IDEA/COMP DOMIN

B65
KOUSOULAS D.G.,REVOLUTION AND DEFEAT; THE STORY OF THE GREEK COMMUNIST PARTY. GREECE INT/ORG EX/STRUC DIPLOM FOR/AID EDU/PROP PARL/PROC ADJUST ATTIT 20 COM/PARTY. PAGE 88 H1759 REV MARXISM POL/PAR ORD/FREE

B65
MENON K.P.S.,MANY WORLDS. INDIA BAL/PWR CAP/ISM COLONIAL REV ORD/FREE PWR MARXISM...POLICY 20 COLD/WAR. PAGE 109 H2176 BIOG DIPLOM NAT/G

B65
NAMIER L.B.,THE STRUCTURE OF POLITICS AT THE ACCESSION OF GEORGE III. UK LOC/G TOP/EX COLONIAL LEAD PARTIC REV CHOOSE REPRESENT GOV/REL PERSON SOVEREIGN...GOV/COMP 18 PARLIAMENT. PAGE 115 H2309 PARL/PROC LEGIS NAT/G POL/PAR

B65
O'BRIEN W.V.,THE NEW NATIONS IN INTERNATIONAL LAW AND DIPLOMACY* THE YEAR BOOK OF WORLD POLITY* VOLUME III. USA+45 ECO/UNDEV INT/ORG FORCES DIPLOM COLONIAL NEUTRAL REV NAT/LISM ATTIT RESPECT. PAGE 119 H2385 INT/LAW CULTURE SOVEREIGN ANTHOL

B65
O'CONNELL M.R.,IRISH POLITICS AND SOCIAL CONFLICT IN THE AGE OF THE AMERICAN REVOLUTION. FRANCE IRELAND MOD/EUR STRATA SECT LEGIS DIPLOM INT/TRADE DOMIN REV WAR...BIBLIOG 18 PARLIAMENT. PAGE 119 H2387 CATHISM ATTIT NAT/G DELIB/GP

B65
ROMEIN J.,THE ASIAN CENTURY. ASIA COM S/ASIA DIPLOM COLONIAL TIME 20. PAGE 133 H2666 REV NAT/LISM CULTURE MARXISM

B65
SCALAPINO R.A.,THE COMMUNIST REVOLUTION IN ASIA* TACTICS, GOALS, AND ACHIEVEMENTS. INDIA INTELL POL/PAR FORCES DOMIN EDU/PROP LEGIT COERCE REV ATTIT CHINJAP. PAGE 138 H2763 ASIA S/ASIA MARXISM NAT/COMP

B65
TILLY C.,MEASURING POLITICAL UPHEAVAL* RESEARCH MONOGRAPH NO. 19. FRANCE INDUS NAT/G FORCES WORKER ...GEOG RECORD EXHIBIT GEN/METH BIBLIOG INDEX. PAGE 155 H3095 CLASSIF QUANT COERCE REV

B65
ULAM A.,THE BOLSHEVIKS. COM USSR NAT/G CHIEF ECO/TAC ADMIN LEAD WAR POPULISM...POLICY 19/20 LENIN/VI BOLSHEVISM. PAGE 157 H3148 SOCISM POL/PAR TOP/EX REV

S65
MARK M.,"MUST WE FIGHT SOCIAL REVOLUTIONS OF THE LEFT?" L/A+17C USA+45 ECO/UNDEV DIPLOM ADJUST PERCEPT...IDEA/COMP NAT/COMP. PAGE 103 H2053 NAT/LISM REV MARXISM CREATE

S65
PLANK J.N.,"THE CARIBBEAN* INTERVENTION, WHEN AND HOW." CUBA GUATEMALA HAITI PANAMA USA+45 VENEZUELA FORCES PROB/SOLV RISK COERCE...NAT/COMP OAS TIME. PAGE 126 H2521 SOVEREIGN MARXISM REV

S65
SANDERS R.,"MASS SUPPORT AND COMMUNIST INSURRECTION." GREECE MALAYSIA PHILIPPINE VIETNAM STRUCT ECO/UNDEV POL/PAR FORCES CREATE REV ...GP/COMP IDEA/COMP. PAGE 138 H2751 GUERRILLA MARXISM GOV/COMP

C65
NEUMANN S.,"PERMANENT REVOLUTION: TOTALITARIANISM IN THE AGE OF INTERNA TIONAL CIVIL WAR (2ND ED.)" EUR+WWI ELITES POL/PAR DOMIN EDU/PROP LEAD CROWD REPRESENT...MAJORIT GOV/COMP BIBLIOG 20. PAGE 117 H2340 TOTALISM REV FASCISM STRUCT

B66
AFRIFA A.A.,THE GHANA COUP. AFR GHANA ELITES NAT/G DIPLOM DOMIN 20 NKRUMAH/K. PAGE 4 H0076 TOP/EX REV FORCES POL/PAR

B66
BARNETT D.L.,MAU MAU FROM WITHIN. AFR UK POL/PAR LEAD GUERRILLA AUTHORIT ORD/FREE...SOC BIOG 20 NEGRO MAU/MAU. PAGE 11 H0225 REV CULTURE NAT/G

B66
BLACK C.E.,THE DYNAMICS OF MODERNIZATION: A STUDY IN COMPARATIVE HISTORY. STRUCT ECO/DEV ECO/UNDEV NAT/G DIPLOM LEAD REV...PREDICT TIME/SEQ TREND SOC/INTEG 17/20. PAGE 17 H0350 SOCIETY SOC NAT/COMP

B66
BRACKMAN A.C.,SOUTHEAST ASIA'S SECOND FRONT: THE POWER STRUGGLE IN THE MALAY ARCHIPELAGO. CHINA/COM INDONESIA MALAYSIA ECO/UNDEV INT/ORG NAT/G FORCES DIPLOM EDU/PROP REGION COERCE GUERRILLA AUTHORIT POPULISM...MAJORIT 20 KENNEDY/JF SEATO. PAGE 20 H0396 S/ASIA MARXISM REV

B66
BUKHARIN N.,THE ABC OF COMMUNISM: A POPULAR EXPLANATION OF THE PROGRAM OF THE COMMUNIST PARTY OF RUSSIA. USSR STRATA SECT FORCES WORKER CAP/ISM RECEIVE EDU/PROP NAT/LISM TOTALISM 20. PAGE 23 H0468 MARXISM CONCPT POLICY REV

B66
CAUTE D.,THE LEFT IN EUROPE SINCE 1789. EUR+WWI MOD/EUR NAT/G POL/PAR REV...TIME/SEQ GEN/LAWS BIBLIOG 18/20. PAGE 28 H0564 ALL/IDEOS ORD/FREE CONCPT STRATA

B66
COEDES G.,THE MAKING OF SOUTH EAST ASIA. BURMA CAMBODIA LAOS S/ASIA THAILAND VIETNAM REV WAR CIVMIL/REL...GEOG 6/13. PAGE 31 H0614 CULTURE FORCES DOMIN

B66
DE VORE B.B.,LAND AND LIBERTY; A HISTORY OF THE MEXICAN REVOLUTION. CONSTN INTELL NAT/G CONTROL LEAD CHOOSE TOTALISM AUTHORIT...BIBLIOG 19/20 MEXIC/AMER DIAZ/P LIB/PARTY MAGON/F MADERO/F. PAGE 39 H0776 REV CHIEF POL/PAR

B66
DEUTSCHER I.,STALIN: A POLITICAL BIOGRAPHY. EUR+WWI USSR POL/PAR FORCES DIPLOM ADMIN LEAD REV WAR TOTALISM PERSON 20 STALIN/J ROOSEVLT/F LENIN/VI HITLER/A. PAGE 40 H0807 BIOG MARXISM TOP/EX PWR

B66
FIELDHOUSE D.K.,THE COLONIAL EMPIRES: A COMPARATIVE SURVEY FROM THE 18TH CENTURY. UK WOR-45 REV HABITAT 17/18. PAGE 50 H0994 NAT/COMP COLONIAL NAT/G DOMIN

B66
FITZGERALD C.P.,THE BIRTH OF COMMUNIST CHINA (2ND ED.). ASIA CHINA/COM STRUCT BAL/PWR DIPLOM ECO/TAC INT/TRADE WEALTH 20. PAGE 51 H1018 REV MARXISM ECO/UNDEV

B66
FORD P.,CARDINAL MORAN AND THE A. L. P. NAT/G POL/PAR SECT DELIB/GP LOBBY REV CHOOSE ORD/FREE MARXISM 19/20 AUSTRAL PROTESTANT LABOR/PAR. PAGE 52 H1035 CATHISM SOCISM LABOR SOCIETY

B66
FRIEDRICH C.J.,REVOLUTION: NOMOS VIII. NAT/G SOCISM ...OBS TREND IDEA/COMP ANTHOL 18/20. PAGE 54 H1070 REV MARXISM CONCPT DIPLOM

B66
FUCHS W.P.,STAAT UND KIRCHE IM WANDEL DER JAHRHUNDERTE. EUR+WWI MOD/EUR UK REV...JURID CONCPT 4/20 EUROPE CHRISTIAN CHURCH/STA. PAGE 54 H1074 SECT NAT/G ORD/FREE GP/REL

B66
GERARD-LIBOIS J.,KATANGA SECESSION. INT/ORG FORCES DIPLOM ADMIN CONTROL WAR CHOOSE PWR...CHARTS 20 KATANGA TSHOMBE/M UN. PAGE 56 H1114 NAT/G REGION ORD/FREE REV

B66
GURR T.,NEW ERROR-COMPENSATED MEASURES FOR COMPARING NATIONS* SOME CORRELATES OF CIVIL VIOLENCE. WOR+45 SOCIETY REV ISOLAT...PHIL/SCI SOC QUANT TESTS SAMP/SIZ HYPO/EXP. PAGE 63 H1254 NAT/COMP INDEX COERCE NEW/IDEA

B66
HINTON W.,FANSHEN: A DOCUMENTARY OF REVOLUTION IN A CHINESE VILLAGE. ASIA ELITES MUNIC NAT/G POL/PAR SECT WORKER LEAD WAR PRIVIL PWR 20 MAO. PAGE 71 H1422 MARXISM REV NEIGH OWN

B66
MACFARQUHAR R.,CHINA UNDER MAO: POLITICS TAKES COMMAND. CHINA/COM COM AGRI INDUS CHIEF FORCES DIPLOM INT/TRADE EDU/PROP TASK REV ADJUST...ANTHOL 20 MAO. PAGE 100 H1992 ECO/UNDEV TEC/DEV ECO/TAC ADMIN

B66
MAICHEL K.,CATALOG OF SOVIET AND RUSSIAN NEWSPAPERS AT THE HOOVER INSTITUTION OF WAR, REVOLUTION AND PEACE. USSR NAT/G EDU/PROP LEAD REV WAR PEACE ATTIT 19/20. PAGE 101 H2017 BIBLIOG/A PRESS COM MARXISM

B66
MASUR G.,NATIONALISM IN LATIN AMERICA* DIVERSITY AND UNITY. CHRIST-17C PRE/AMER ELITES ECO/UNDEV CREATE DIPLOM INT/TRADE COLONIAL REV SOVEREIGN SOC. PAGE 105 H2089 L/A+17C NAT/LISM CULTURE

B66
MATTHEWS R.,AFRICAN POWDER KEG: REVOLT AND DISSENT IN SIX EMERGENT NATIONS. AFR ALGERIA DAHOMEY GABON GHANA MALAWI GAMBLE LEAD PARTIC REV DRIVE...BIOG TREND GOV/COMP 20. PAGE 105 H2098 ELITES ECO/UNDEV TOP/EX CONTROL

B66
NIEDERGANG M.,LA REVOLUTION DE SAINT-DOMINGUE. DOMIN/REP INT/ORG NAT/G CONTROL LEAD GP/REL ORD/FREE MARXISM 20. PAGE 118 H2361 REV FORCES DIPLOM

B66
NOLTE E.,THREE FACES OF FASCISM. FRANCE GERMANY DOMIN LEGIT COERCE CROWD REV WAR GP/REL RACE/REL SOVEREIGN...GOV/COMP IDEA/COMP 19/20 HITLER/A MUSSOLIN/B MARX/KARL. PAGE 118 H2368 FASCISM TOTALISM NAT/G POL/PAR

B66
RISTIC D.N.,YUGOSLAVIA'S REVOLUTION OF 1941. EUR+WWI YUGOSLAVIA NAT/G WAR ORD/FREE...RECORD BIBLIOG 20 HITLER/A TREATY. PAGE 132 H2633 REV ATTIT FASCISM DIPLOM

B66
ROOS H.,A HISTORY OF MODERN POLAND FROM THE FOUNDATION OF THE STATE IN THE FIRST WORLD WAR TO NAT/G WAR

THE PRESENT DAY. EUR+WWI POLAND INTELL SOCIETY ECO/TAC LEAD REV ATTIT ORD/FREE MARXISM...BIBLIOG 20 WWI PARTITION. PAGE 133 H2669 — DIPLOM

B66
SCHATTEN F.,COMMUNISM IN AFRICA. AFR GHANA GUINEA MALI CULTURE ECO/UNDEV LABOR SECT ECO/TAC EDU/PROP REV 20. PAGE 139 H2774 — COLONIAL NAT/LISM MARXISM DIPLOM

B66
SOBEL L.A.,SOUTH VIETNAM: US-COMMUNIST CONFRONTATION IN SOUTHEAST ASIA 1961-65. VIETNAM FOR/AID CROWD DETER REV PEACE...GEOG 20 INTERVENT DIEM COLD/WAR. PAGE 146 H2926 — WAR TIME/SEQ FORCES NAT/G

B66
SWARTZ M.J.,POLITICAL ANTHROPOLOGY. WOR+45 POL/PAR ACT/RES REV GP/REL DRIVE...SOC CONCPT TIME/SEQ GP/COMP ANTHOL WORSHIP 20. PAGE 151 H3013 — PARTIC RIGID/FLEX LOC/G CREATE

B66
THOMPSON J.M.,RUSSIA, BOLSHEVISM, AND THE VERSAILLES PEACE. RUSSIA USSR INT/ORG NAT/G DELIB/GP AGREE REV WAR PWR 20 TREATY VERSAILLES BOLSHEVISM. PAGE 154 H3083 — DIPLOM PEACE MARXISM

B66
THORNTON M.J.,NAZISM, 1918-1945. GERMANY INT/ORG DIPLOM REV PEACE FASCISM...CONCPT 20 HITLER/A WEIMAR/REP NAZI. PAGE 155 H3089 — TOTALISM POL/PAR NAT/G WAR

B66
US DEPARTMENT OF THE ARMY,COMMUNIST CHINA: A STRATEGIC SURVEY: A BIBLIOGRAPHY (PAMPHLET NO. 20-67). CHINA/COM COM INDIA USSR NAT/G POL/PAR EX/STRUC FORCES NUC/PWR REV ATTIT...POLICY GEOG CHARTS. PAGE 160 H3194 — BIBLIOG/A MARXISM S/ASIA DIPLOM

B66
VON ARSENIEW W.,DIE GEISTIGEN SCHICKSALE DES RUSSISCHEN VOLKES. RUSSIA USSR SOCIETY STRUCT NAT/G SECT CHIEF REV 19/20. PAGE 163 H3262 — ATTIT PERSON CULTURE DRIVE

B66
WEBER J.,EOTVOS UND DIE UNGARISCHE NATIONALITATENFRAGE. HUNGARY CULTURE SOCIETY REV ORD/FREE SOVEREIGN...BIOG 19. PAGE 166 H3318 — NAT/LISM GP/REL ATTIT CONCPT

B66
WHEELER G.,THE PEOPLES OF SOVIET CENTRAL ASIA: A BACKGROUND BOOK. ISLAM USSR STRATA STRUCT FORCES REV WAR HABITAT 7/20. PAGE 167 H3341 — COLONIAL DOMIN CULTURE ADJUST

B66
ZEINE Z.N.,THE EMERGENCE OF ARAB NATIONALISM (REV. ED.). TURKEY UK NAT/G SECT ECO/TAC LEAD REV WAR AGE/Y ROLE ORD/FREE...TRADIT CHARTS BIBLIOG 20 ARABS OTTOMAN. PAGE 173 H3453 — ISLAM NAT/LISM DIPLOM

S66
COWAN L.G.,"THE MILITARY AND AFRICAN POLITICS." AFR FUT NAT/G POL/PAR PARTIC REV 20. PAGE 34 H0685 — CIVMIL/REL FORCES PWR LEAD

S66
LODGE G.C.,"REVOLUTION IN LATIN AMERICA." USA+45 ELITES INDUS LABOR PROF/ORG SECT TEC/DEV CAP/ISM SKILL MARXISM...POLICY NAT/COMP. PAGE 98 H1950 — ATTIT REV L/A+17C IDEA/COMP

C66
ROSENBERG C.G. JR.,"THE MYTH OF "MAU-MAU:" NATIONALISM IN KENYA." AFR CULTURE NAT/G POL/PAR COERCE REV RACE/REL ATTIT ORD/FREE SOVEREIGN...MYTH BIBLIOG 20. PAGE 134 H2678 — NAT/LISM COLONIAL MAJORIT LEAD

B67
ALLWORTH E.,CENTRAL ASIA: A CENTURY OF RUSSIAN RULE. USSR INTELL SOCIETY AGRI INDUS COLONIAL REV WAR NAT/LISM...ART/METH GEOG LING 19/20. PAGE 5 H0108 — ASIA CULTURE NAT/G

B67
ANDERSON E.N.,POLITICAL INSTITUTIONS AND SOCIAL CHANGE IN CONTINENTAL EUROPE IN THE NINETEENTH CENTURY. MOD/EUR LAW CONSTN SOCIETY POL/PAR TEC/DEV LEAD REV ATTIT...BIBLIOG 19. PAGE 6 H0127 — NAT/G NAT/COMP METH/COMP INDUS

B67
BOHANNAN P.,LAW AND WARFARE. CULTURE CT/SYS COERCE REV PEACE...JURID SOC CONCPT ANTHOL 20. PAGE 18 H0367 — METH/COMP ADJUD WAR LAW

B67
DIX R.H.,COLOMBIA: THE POLITICAL DIMENSIONS OF CHANGE. ELITES POL/PAR DOMIN REV...AUD/VIS 20 COLOMB. PAGE 41 H0828 — L/A+17C NAT/G TEC/DEV LEAD

B67
FALL B.B.,HO CHI MINH ON REVOLUTION: SELECTED WRITINGS, 1920-66. COM VIETNAM ELITES NAT/G COERCE GUERRILLA RACE/REL MARXISM...MARXIST ANTHOL 20. PAGE 48 H0968 — REV COLONIAL ECO/UNDEV S/ASIA

B67
FANON F.,TOWARD THE AFRICAN REVOLUTION. AFR FRANCE CULTURE ELITES LEAD REV GP/REL ORD/FREE SOVEREIGN 20. PAGE 49 H0969 — COLONIAL DOMIN ECO/UNDEV RACE/REL

B67
HILSMAN R.,TO MOVE A NATION: THE POLITICS OF FOREIGN POLICY IN THE ADMINISTRATION OF JOHN F. KENNEDY. CHINA/COM COM USSR VIETNAM NAT/G DELIB/GP FORCES PLAN PROB/SOLV BAL/PWR COLONIAL EXEC REV PWR 20 KENNEDY/JF PRESIDENT. PAGE 71 H1418 — CHIEF DIPLOM

B67
HUTCHINS F.G.,THE ILLUSION OF PERMANENCE: BRITISH IMPERIALISM IN INDIA. INDIA UK CULTURE STRUCT NAT/G REV GP/REL RACE/REL ADJUST DISCRIM ATTIT MORAL PWR SOC/INTEG 18/20. PAGE 75 H1509 — COLONIAL CONTROL SOVEREIGN CONSERVE

B67
LAQUER W.,THE FATE OF THE REVOLUTION: INTERPRETATIONS OF SOVIET HISTORY. RUSSIA NAT/G MARXISM...BIBLIOG 20 STALIN/J. PAGE 91 H1816 — REV KNOWL HIST/WRIT IDEA/COMP

B67
MCCLINTOCK R.,THE MEANING OF LIMITED WAR. FUT WOR+45 NAT/G FORCES GUERRILLA REV...POLICY SAMP/SIZ TREND NAT/COMP 45 COLD/WAR. PAGE 106 H2126 — WAR NUC/PWR BAL/PWR DIPLOM

B67
MCNELLY T.,SOURCES IN MODERN EAST ASIAN HISTORY AND POLITICS. KOREA VIETNAM CULTURE DIPLOM COLONIAL REV WAR PWR ALL/IDEOS MARXISM...ANTHOL 20 CHINJAP. PAGE 107 H2147 — NAT/COMP ASIA S/ASIA SOCIETY

B67
ODINGA O.,NOT YET UHURU. NAT/G POL/PAR PROB/SOLV COERCE REV WAR PERS/REL PERSON ORD/FREE...POLICY 20 ODINGA/O KENYATTA. PAGE 120 H2395 — ATTIT BIOG LEAD AFR

B67
PIKE F.B.,FREEDOM AND REFORM IN LATIN AMERICA. BRAZIL URUGUAY CONSTN CULTURE SECT DIPLOM EDU/PROP PARTIC DRIVE ALL/VALS CATHISM...GEOG ANTHOL BIBLIOG REFORMERS BOLIV. PAGE 126 H2511 — L/A+17C ORD/FREE ECO/UNDEV REV

B67
PLANK J.,CUBA AND THE UNITED STATES: LONG RANGE PERSPECTIVES. CUBA L/A+17C USSR ECO/UNDEV NAT/G FORCES ECO/TAC INT/TRADE AGREE REV...PREDICT TREND ANTHOL 20 CASTRO/F COLD/WAR OAS. PAGE 126 H2520 — DIPLOM

B67
RYDER A.J.,THE GERMAN REVOLUTION OF 1918; A STUDY OF GERMAN SOCIALISM IN WAR AND REVOLT. GERMANY NAT/G POL/PAR GP/REL...BIBLIOG 20. PAGE 136 H2724 — SOCISM WAR REV INGP/REL

B67
SCHWARTZ B.,THE ROOTS OF FREEDOM: A CONSTITUTIONAL HISTORY OF ENGLAND. UK LAW POL/PAR DELIB/GP LEGIS REV REPRESENT...JURID BIBLIOG/A 13/20. PAGE 140 H2809 — CONSTN PARL/PROC NAT/G

B67
TOMPKINS S.R.,THE TRIUMPH OF BOLSHEVISM: REVOLUTION OR REACTION? USSR WORKER PRESS WEALTH MARXISM POPULISM...BIOG TREND IDEA/COMP BIBLIOG 19/20 LENIN/VI. PAGE 156 H3113 — REV NAT/G POL/PAR NAT/LISM

B67
WIENER F.B.,CIVILIANS UNDER MILITARY JUSTICE; THE BRITISH PRACTICE SINCE 1689 ESPECIALLY IN NORTH AMERICA. UK USA-45 LAW CONSTN CRIME REV...DECISION CHARTS NAT/COMP BIBLIOG 17/20. PAGE 168 H3356 — CT/SYS FORCES ADJUD

L67
BRIDGHAM P.,"MAO'S "CULTURAL REVOLUTION"* ORIGIN AND DEVELOPMENT." NAT/G LEAD CIVMIL/REL NAT/LISM TOTALISM ATTIT DRIVE PWR MARXISM 20. PAGE 21 H0413 — CHINA/COM CULTURE REV CROWD

L67
EGBERT D.D.,"THE IDEA OF 'AVANT-GARDE' IN ART AND POLITICS." USSR CULTURE INTELL POL/PAR CREATE EDU/PROP CONTROL REV ANOMIE DRIVE ROLE...IDEA/COMP 20. PAGE 45 H0895 — ART/METH COM ATTIT

L67
ISRAEL J.,"THE RED GUARDS IN HISTORICAL PERSPECTIVE: CONTINUITY AND CHANGE IN THE CHINESE YOUTH MOVEMENT." CHINA/COM FUT POL/PAR CONTROL REV GP/REL 20. PAGE 79 H1572 — AGE/Y LOBBY MARXISM NAT/G

L67
TABORSKY E.,"THE COMMUNIST PARTIES OF THE 'THIRD WORLD' IN SOVIET STRATEGY." AFR ASIA L/A+17C USSR INTELL NAT/G WORKER PLAN CONTROL LEAD PARTIC REV ...GOV/COMP 20 COM/PARTY THIRD/WRLD. PAGE 152 H3032 — POL/PAR MARXISM ECO/UNDEV DIPLOM

L67
TOUVAL S.,"THE ORGANIZATION OF AFRICAN UNITY AND AFRICAN BORDERS." DEBATE REGION TASK REV ATTIT ORD/FREE...DECISION UN 20 OAU. PAGE 156 H3121 — AFR NAT/G COLONIAL NAT/LISM

S67
BASOV V.,"THE DEVELOPMENT OF PUBLIC EDUCATION AND THE BUDGET." USSR NAT/G CONTROL REV COST AGE...STAT 20. PAGE 12 H0235 — BUDGET GIVE EDU/PROP SCHOOL

S67
BUTTINGER J.,"VIETNAM* FRAUD OF THE 'OTHER WAR'." — PLAN

VIETNAM/S ELITES STRUCT AGRI NAT/G FOR/AID RENT TREND. PAGE 25 H0499
WEALTH REV ECO/UNDEV

S67
CHIU S.M.,"CHINA'S MILITARY POSTURE." CHINA/COM ELITES NAT/G POL/PAR TEC/DEV ECO/TAC DOMIN CONTROL LEAD REV MARXISM 20 MAO. PAGE 30 H0595
FORCES CIVMIL/REL NUC/PWR DIPLOM

S67
CHU-YUAN CHENG,"THE CULTURAL REVOLUTION AND CHINA'S ECONOMY." CHINA/COM AGRI DIST/IND INDUS MARKET NAT/G WORKER PLAN INT/TRADE DOMIN DEMAND PRODUC ...CHARTS 20 MAO. PAGE 30 H0600
ECO/DEV ECO/TAC REV SOCISM

S67
COHEN A.,"REVOLUTION IN ARGENTINA?" L/A+17C NAT/G POL/PAR CHIEF PROB/SOLV ECO/TAC 20 ARGEN. PAGE 31 H0615
REV ECO/UNDEV CONTROL BIOG

S67
ELLISON H.J.,"THE SOCIALIST REVOLUTIONARIES." USSR ECO/UNDEV NAT/G INGP/REL EFFICIENCY ATTIT PWR MARXISM...CONCPT IDEA/COMP 20 SOC/REVPAR. PAGE 46 H0911
POL/PAR REV AGRI

S67
FINLAY D.J.,"THE GHANA COUP...ONE YEAR LATER." GHANA FORCES FOR/AID PRESS CONTROL CIVMIL/REL NAT/LISM AUTHORIT PWR...PREDICT 20. PAGE 50 H1005
REV NAT/G ATTIT ECO/UNDEV

S67
FRANCIS M.J.,"THE US PRESS AND CASTRO: A STUDY IN DECLINING RELATIONS." COM DIPLOM WAR TOTALISM ATTIT SOCISM...POLICY IDEA/COMP 20. PAGE 52 H1046
PRESS LEAD REV NAT/G

S67
GONZALEZ M.P.,"CUBA, UNA REVOLUCION EN MARCHA." CUBA L/A+17C USA+45 VIETNAM ECO/UNDEV FORCES DIPLOM DOMIN...POLICY MARXIST NAT/COMP CASTRO/F. PAGE 58 H1163
REV NAT/G COLONIAL SOVEREIGN

S67
GRIEB K.J.,"THE UNITED STATES AND THE CENTRAL AMERICAN CONFEDERATION." COSTA/RICA EL/SALVADR GUATEMALA HONDURAS L/A+17C NICARAGUA NAT/G FORCES CONFER AGREE EXEC ARMS/CONT REV WAR PEACE ATTIT 20. PAGE 60 H1212
INT/ORG DIPLOM POLICY REGION

S67
GRUNDY K.W.,"AFRICA IN THE WORLD ARENA." ECO/UNDEV BAL/PWR FOR/AID NEUTRAL REV NAT/LISM GOV/COMP. PAGE 62 H1240
AFR DIPLOM INT/ORG COLONIAL

S67
HEATH D.B.,"BOLIVIA UNDER BARRIENTOS." L/A+17C NAT/G CHIEF DIPLOM ECO/TAC...POLICY 20 BOLIV. PAGE 69 H1379
ECO/UNDEV POL/PAR REV CONSTN

S67
JOINER C.A.,"THE UBIQUITY OF THE ADMINISTRATIVE ROLE IN COUNTERINSURGENC. VIETNAM/S SOCIETY STRUCT NAT/G GP/REL EFFICIENCY 20. PAGE 81 H1627
ADMIN POLICY REV ATTIT

S67
LANE J.P.,"FUNCTIONS OF MASS MEDIA IN BRAZIL'S 1964 CRISIS." BRAZIL NAT/G FORCES TOP/EX PRESS TV ATTIT PWR...METH/CNCPT 20. PAGE 90 H1807
CIVMIL/REL REV COM/IND EDU/PROP

S67
LOFCHIE M.F.,"OKELLO'S REVOLUTION." TANZANIA NAT/G POL/PAR FORCES PLAN CONTROL 20. PAGE 98 H1954
AFR REV LEAD CHIEF

S67
MANGLAPUS R.S.,"ASIAN REVOLUTION AND AMERICAN IDEOLOGY." USA+45 SOCIETY CAP/ISM DIPLOM ADJUST CENTRAL...NAT/COMP 20. PAGE 102 H2035
REV POPULISM ATTIT ASIA

S67
MOZINGO D.,"CONTAINMENT IN ASIA RECONSIDERED." NAT/G DIPLOM REV PEACE ORD/FREE 20. PAGE 114 H2275
ATTIT CONTROL NAT/LISM EFFICIENCY

S67
PERKINS D.H.,"ECONOMIC GROWTH IN CHINA AND THE CULTURAL REVOLUTION(1960APRIL 1967)" CHINA/COM FUT AGRI INDUS PLAN LEAD MARXISM...CHARTS 20 MAO. PAGE 125 H2493
ECO/TAC CULTURE REV ECO/UNDEV

S67
PETRAS J.,"GUERRILLA MOVEMENTS IN LATIN AMERICA - I." GUATEMALA PERU VENEZUELA NAT/G COLONIAL LEAD ATTIT PWR...TIME/SEQ METH/COMP 20 COLOMB. PAGE 125 H2497
GUERRILLA REV L/A+17C MARXISM

S67
RONNING C.,"NANKING: 1950." ASIA CANADA CHINA/COM NAT/G PLAN ECO/TAC REV ADJUST 20. PAGE 133 H2667
DIPLOM ROLE PEACE

S67
ROTBERG R.I.,"COLONIALISM AND AFTER: THE POLITICAL LITERATURE OF CENTRAL AFRICA - A BIBLIOGRAPHIC ESSAY." AFR CHIEF EX/STRUC REV INGP/REL RACE/REL SOVEREIGN 20. PAGE 135 H2693
BIBLIOG/A COLONIAL DIPLOM NAT/G

S67
SHIGEO N.,"THE GREAT CULTURAL REVOLUTION." ASIA ECO/UNDEV AGRI NAT/G CHIEF ECO/TAC EDU/PROP CONTROL LEAD PWR 20 MAO. PAGE 143 H2860
CREATE REV CULTURE POL/PAR

S67
SMITH J.E.,"THE GERMAN DEMOCRATIC REPUBLIC AND THE WEST." GERMANY/E ECO/DEV NAT/G PROB/SOLV CONTROL REV TOTALISM...GOV/COMP 20. PAGE 146 H2911
DIPLOM PWR MARXISM

S67
SULLIVAN J.H.,"THE PRESS AND POLITICS IN INDONESIA." INDONESIA NAT/G WRITING REV...TREND GOV/COMP 20. PAGE 150 H3007
CIVMIL/REL KNOWL TOTALISM

S67
TANTER R.,"A THEORY OF REVOLUTION." ASIA CUBA L/A+17C S/ASIA SOCIETY NAT/G ADJUST...CONCPT CHARTS. PAGE 152 H3046
REV ECO/UNDEV EDU/PROP METH/COMP

S67
VINCENT S.,"SHOULD BIAFRA SURVIVE?" NIGERIA ECO/UNDEV CHIEF FORCES ECO/TAC GP/REL DISCRIM PEACE ORD/FREE SOC/INTEG 20 BIAFRA IBO. PAGE 163 H3256
AFR REV REGION NAT/G

S67
VON LAUE T.H.,"WESTERNIZATION, REVOLUTION AND THE SEARCH FOR A BASIS OF AUTHORITY - RUSSIA IN 1917." USSR ELITES INTELL ECO/UNDEV NAT/G WORKER ECO/TAC TAX ADMIN LEAD AUTHORIT 20 LENIN/VI. PAGE 164 H3274
MARXISM REV COM DOMIN

B68
PROUDHON J.P.,IDEE GENERALE DE LA REVOLUTION AU XIXE SIECLE (1851). FRANCE UNIV NAT/G CREATE AGREE UTOPIA ORD/FREE...ANARCH 19. PAGE 128 H2563
REV SOCIETY WORKER LABOR

S68
CHAPMAN A.R.,"THE CIVIL WAR IN NIGERIA." AFR NIGERIA NAT/G PLAN ECO/TAC EDU/PROP COERCE WAR GOV/REL INGP/REL ORD/FREE PWR WEALTH SOC/INTEG 20 BIAFRA. PAGE 29 H0579
REV RACE/REL

S68
KANET R.E.,"RECENT SOVIET REASSESSMENT OF DEVELOPMENTS IN THE THIRD WORLD." ALGERIA GHANA INDONESIA USSR WOR+45 CONSTN ELITES INTELL STRUCT DOMIN CONTROL REV PWR MARXISM...IDEA/COMP METH 20 THIRD/WRLD. PAGE 83 H1653
DIPLOM NEUTRAL NAT/G NAT/COMP

S68
LUKASZEWSKI J.,"WESTERN INTEGRATION AND THE PEOPLE'S DEMOCRACIES." USSR ELITES ECO/DEV NAT/G VOL/ASSN INT/TRADE AGREE REV FEDERAL WEALTH SOCISM ...NAT/COMP SOC/INTEG 20 EEC. PAGE 99 H1977
DIPLOM INT/ORG COM REGION

B76
TAINE H.A.,THE ANCIENT REGIME. FRANCE STRATA FORCES PARTIC EQUILIB WEALTH CONSERVE POPULISM...GOV/COMP SOC/INTEG 18/19. PAGE 152 H3035
NAT/G GOV/REL TAX REV

B85
TAINE H.A.,THE FRENCH REVOLUTION (3 VOLS.) (TRANS. BY J. DURAND). FRANCE MOD/EUR SOCIETY STRATA POL/PAR ECO/TAC DOMIN EDU/PROP GP/REL PWR ...GOV/COMP IDEA/COMP 18. PAGE 152 H3036
REV NAT/G EX/STRUC LEAD

B89
FERNEUIL T.,LES PRINCIPES DE 1789 ET LA SCIENCE SOCIALE. FRANCE NAT/G REV ATTIT...CONCPT TREND IDEA/COMP 18/19. PAGE 49 H0986
CONSTN POLICY LAW

B90
BURKE E.,REFLECTIONS ON THE REVOLUTION IN FRANCE. FRANCE UK NAT/G DOMIN LEGIT PEACE PWR SOVEREIGN CONSERVE...POLICY GEN/LAWS 18. PAGE 24 H0487
REV ORD/FREE CHIEF TRADIT

B90
TAINE H.A.,MODERN REGIME (2 VOLS.). FRANCE FAM REV CENTRAL MARRIAGE PWR...TREND 19 NAPOLEON/B. PAGE 152 H3037
STRUCT NAT/G OLD/LIB MORAL

B91
MILL J.S.,SOCIALISM (1859). MOD/EUR AGRI INDUS NAT/G REV INCOME PRODUC ORD/FREE POPULISM SOCISM ...GOV/COMP METH/COMP 19. PAGE 110 H2209
WEALTH SOCIALIST ECO/TAC OWN

B91
PAINE T.,RIGHTS OF MAN. FRANCE MOD/EUR CONSTN NAT/G CHIEF DOMIN LEGIT SOVEREIGN...MAJORIT IDEA/COMP 18 BURKE/EDM CIVIL/LIB. PAGE 122 H2446
GEN/LAWS ORD/FREE REV AGREE

B96
ESMEIN A.,ELEMENTS DE DROIT CONSTITUTIONNEL. FRANCE UK CHIEF EX/STRUC LEGIS ADJUD CT/SYS PARL/PROC REV GOV/REL ORD/FREE...JURID METH/COMP 18/19. PAGE 47 H0940
LAW CONSTN NAT/G CONCPT

B96
KROPOTKIN P.,L'ANARCHIE. NAT/G VOL/ASSN REV MORAL WEALTH...POLICY 19. PAGE 89 H1776
SOCIETY ANARCH PERSON CONCPT

B96
MARX K.,REVOLUTION AND COUNTER-REVOLUTION. GERMANY CONSTN ELITES INDUS NAT/G DIPLOM ECO/TAC WEALTH. PAGE 104 H2083 — MARXIST REV PWR STRATA

REVOLUTION....SEE REV

REWARD....SEE SANCTION

REYNOLDS B. H2619

RHODE/ISL....RHODE ISLAND

RHODES/C....CECIL RHODES

RHODESIA....SEE ALSO AFR

B30
SMUTS J.C.,AFRICA AND SOME WORLD PROBLEMS. RHODESIA SOUTH/AFR CULTURE ECO/UNDEV INDUS INT/ORG SECT PROB/SOLV REGION GOV/REL DISCRIM ATTIT 19/20 LEAGUE/NAT LIVNGSTN/D NEGRO. PAGE 146 H2921 — LEGIS AFR COLONIAL RACE/REL

B34
LOVELL R.I.,THE STRUGGLE FOR SOUTH AFRICA, 1875-1899. GERMANY RHODESIA SOUTH/AFR UK NAT/G ECO/TAC HABITAT WEALTH...POLICY 19. PAGE 99 H1971 — COLONIAL DIPLOM WAR GP/REL

B51
INTERNATIONAL AFRICAN INST,ETHNOGRAPHIC SURVEY OF AFRICA: WEST CENTRAL AFRICA (VOLS. I-III, 1951-1953). AFR RHODESIA CULTURE ECO/UNDEV HEREDITY ...GEOG SOC CHARTS BIBLIOG WORSHIP 20 CONGO/LEOP. PAGE 77 H1543 — STRUCT KIN INGP/REL HABITAT

N60
RHODESIA-NYASA NATL ARCHIVES,A SELECT BIBLIOGRAPHY OF RECENT PUBLICATIONS CONCERNING THE FEDERATION OF RHODESIA AND NYASALAND (PAMPHLET). MALAWI RHODESIA LAW CULTURE STRUCT ECO/UNDEV LEGIS...GEOG 20. PAGE 131 H2620 — BIBLIOG ADMIN ORD/FREE NAT/G

B61
JONES R.,AFRICA BIBLIOGRAPHY SERIES: SOUTH EAST CENTRAL AFRICA AND MADAGASCAR. AFR MADAGASCAR RHODESIA SECT BIO/SOC...JURID NAT/COMP 20. PAGE 82 H1633 — BIBLIOG/A SOC CULTURE LING

B62
GREEN L.P.,DEVELOPMENT IN AFRICA. AFR CENTRL/AFR GHANA RHODESIA SOUTH/AFR AGRI PROC/MFG INT/TRADE DEMAND NAT/LISM PRODUC WEALTH...GEOG METH/CNCPT CHARTS BIBLIOG 20. PAGE 60 H1206 — CULTURE ECO/UNDEV GOV/REL TREND

B63
REYNOLDS B.,MAGIC, DIVINATION AND WITCHCRAFT AMONG THE BAROTSE OF NORTHERN RHODESIA. RHODESIA CULTURE KIN CREATE LEGIT PARTIC DEATH DREAM STRANGE HABITAT PERSON...AUD/VIS WORSHIP 20. PAGE 131 H2619 — AFR SOC MYTH SECT

L64
ROTBERG R.,"THE FEDERATION MOVEMENT IN BRITISH EAST AND CENTRAL AFRICA." AFR RHODESIA UGANDA ECO/UNDEV NAT/G POL/PAR FORCES DOMIN LEGIT ADMIN COERCE ATTIT ...CONCPT TREND 20 TANGANYIKA. PAGE 135 H2691 — VOL/ASSN PWR REGION

B65
HAEFELE E.T.,GOVERNMENT CONTROLS ON TRANSPORT. AFR RHODESIA TANZANIA DIPLOM ECO/TAC TARIFFS PRICE ADJUD CONTROL REGION EFFICIENCY...POLICY 20 CONGO. PAGE 64 H1274 — ECO/UNDEV DIST/IND FINAN NAT/G

B65
WALKER A.A.,THE RHODESIAS AND NYASALAND: A GUIDE TO OFFICIAL PUBLICATIONS. RHODESIA UK OP/RES PLAN PROB/SOLV DIPLOM...POLICY SOC CON/ANAL 19/20 NYASALAND. PAGE 164 H3291 — BIBLIOG NAT/G COLONIAL AFR

B67
WILLS A.J.,AN INTRODUCTION TO THE HISTORY OF CENTRAL AFRICA. RHODESIA ZAMBIA CULTURE SOCIETY ECO/UNDEV TEC/DEV DOMIN WAR ALL/VALS...POLICY TREND BIBLIOG T 14/20 NYASALAND. PAGE 169 H3375 — AFR COLONIAL ORD/FREE

RHODESIA-NYASA NATL ARCHIVES H2620

RICARDO/D....DAVID RICARDO

RICHARD/H....HENRY RICHARD (WELSH POLITICIAN - 19TH CENTURY)

RICHARDSON H.G. H2621

RICHARDSON S.S. H1673

RICHERT F. H2622

RICHMAN B.M. H2623

RICKMAN J. H1182

RIDLEY C.E. H2624

RIDLEY F. H2625

RIES J.C. H2626

RIESENBERG P.N. H2627

RIESMAN D. H2628,H2629

RIESMAN E.T. H2629

RIESMAN/D....DAVID RIESMAN

B63
RUITENBEER H.M.,THE DILEMMA OF ORGANIZATIONAL SOCIETY. CULTURE ECO/DEV MUNIC SECT TEC/DEV EDU/PROP NAT/LISM ORD/FREE...NAT/COMP 20 RIESMAN/D WHYTE/WF MERTON/R MEAD/MARG JASPERS/K. PAGE 136 H2716 — PERSON ROLE ADMIN WORKER

RIGGS/FRED....FRED W. RIGGS

RIGHTS/MAN....RIGHTS OF MAN

RIGID/FLEX....DEGREE OF RESPONSIVENESS TO NEW IDEAS, METHODS, AND PEOPLE

B15
FARIES J.C.,THE RISE OF INTERNATIONALISM. ASIA MOD/EUR NAT/G VOL/ASSN DELIB/GP BAL/PWR EDU/PROP ARMS/CONT RIGID/FLEX TREND. PAGE 49 H0971 — INT/ORG DIPLOM PEACE

B18
YUKIO O.,THE VOICE OF JAPANESE DEMOCRACY, AN ESSAY ON CONSTITUTIONAL LOYALTY (TRANS BY J. E. BECKER). ASIA POL/PAR DELIB/GP EX/STRUC RIGID/FLEX ORD/FREE PWR...POLICY JURID METH/COMP 19/20 CHINJAP. PAGE 172 H3443 — CONSTN MAJORIT CHOOSE NAT/G

N19
COUTROT A.,THE FIGHT OVER THE 1959 PRIVATE EDUCATION LAW IN FRANCE (PAMPHLET). FRANCE NAT/G SECT GIVE EDU/PROP GP/REL ATTIT RIGID/FLEX ORD/FREE 20 CHURCH/STA. PAGE 34 H0681 — SCHOOL PARL/PROC CATHISM LAW

B21
STUART G.H.,FRENCH FOREIGN POLICY. CONSTN INT/ORG NAT/G POL/PAR EX/STRUC FORCES PLAN ECO/TAC DOMIN EDU/PROP ADJUD COERCE ATTIT DRIVE RIGID/FLEX ALL/VALS...POLICY OBS RECORD BIOG TIME/SEQ TREND. PAGE 150 H3000 — MOD/EUR DIPLOM FRANCE

B25
TEMPERLEY H.,THE FOREIGN POLICY OF CANNING: 1822-1827. MOD/EUR NAT/G TOP/EX EDU/PROP ROUTINE ATTIT RIGID/FLEX SUPEGO PWR SKILL...TIME/SEQ PARLIAMENT 20. PAGE 153 H3058 — PERSON DIPLOM UK BIOG

B26
POLLARD A.F.,THE EVOLUTION OF PARLIAMENT. UK CONSTN POL/PAR EX/STRUC GOV/REL INGP/REL PRIVIL RIGID/FLEX ...TIME/SEQ 11/20 CMN/WLTH PARLIAMENT. PAGE 127 H2536 — LEGIS PARL/PROC NAT/G

B27
FLOURNOY F.,PARLIAMENT AND WAR. MOD/EUR UK NAT/G FORCES LEGIS TOP/EX DIPLOM LEGIT DEBATE ATTIT RIGID/FLEX PWR...DECISION TIME/SEQ PARLIAMENT 19/20. PAGE 52 H1032 — COERCE WAR

B31
BONAR J.,THEORIES OF POPULATION FROM RALEIGH TO ARTHUR YOUNG. CHRIST-17C MOD/EUR CULTURE SOCIETY R+D CREATE ATTIT PERCEPT RIGID/FLEX...OLD/LIB CONCPT NEW/IDEA TIME/SEQ IDEA/COMP STERTYP GEN/LAWS. PAGE 19 H0372 — GEOG BIOG

B39
NICOLSON H.,CURZON: THE LAST PHASE, 1919-1925. UK NAT/G DELIB/GP TOP/EX ROUTINE WAR RIGID/FLEX ...METH/CNCPT 20 CURZON/GN. PAGE 118 H2352 — POLICY DIPLOM BIOG

B43
EARLE E.M.,MAKERS OF MODERN STRATEGY: MILITARY THOUGHT FROM MACHIAVELLI TO HITLER. EUR+WWI MOD/EUR NAT/G ACT/RES BAL/PWR DOMIN COERCE ATTIT DRIVE RIGID/FLEX ALL/VALS...METH/CNCPT BIOG 16/20. PAGE 44 H0879 — PLAN FORCES WAR

B45
LASKER B.,ASIA ON THE MOVE. ASIA BURMA S/ASIA THAILAND USSR ECO/UNDEV FAM KIN WAR NAT/LISM ATTIT ...GEOG CENSUS TREND AUSTRAL 20. PAGE 91 H1826 — CULTURE RIGID/FLEX

B47
JURJI E.J.,THE GREAT RELIGIONS OF THE MODERN WORLD. CULTURE INTELL SOCIETY INT/ORG CONSULT CHOOSE ATTIT DRIVE PERSON RIGID/FLEX...HUM CONCPT OBS BIOG HIST/WRIT TREND GEN/LAWS 20 WORSHIP. PAGE 82 H1643 — UNIV SECT

B48
TOWSTER J.,POLITICAL POWER IN THE USSR: 1917-1947. USSR CONSTN CULTURE ELITES CREATE PLAN COERCE CENTRAL ATTIT RIGID/FLEX ORD/FREE...BIBLIOG SOC/INTEG 20 LENIN/VI STALIN/J. PAGE 156 H3122 — EX/STRUC NAT/G MARXISM PWR

B49
SARGENT S.S.,CULTURE AND PERSONALITY. FUT UNIV SOCIETY FAM KIN NEIGH BIO/SOC DRIVE PERCEPT RIGID/FLEX LOVE RESPECT...PSY SOC CONCPT OBS TIME/SEQ TREND CON/ANAL CHARTS HYPO/EXP SIMUL TOT/POP. PAGE 138 H2754 — CULTURE PERSON

B50
TRAGER F.N.,MARXISM IN SOUTHEAST ASIA. BURMA S/ASIA
INDONESIA THAILAND VIETNAM CULTURE SOCIETY NAT/G POL/PAR
VOL/ASSN EXEC ROUTINE COERCE ATTIT RIGID/FLEX PWR REV
...METH/CNCPT TIME/SEQ STERTYP GEN/LAWS MARX/KARL
VAL/FREE COLD/WAR NAM 20. PAGE 156 H3126

B52
BENTHAM A.,HANDBOOK OF POLITICAL FALLACIES. FUT POL/PAR
MOD/EUR LAW INTELL LOC/G MUNIC NAT/G DELIB/GP LEGIS
CREATE EDU/PROP CT/SYS ATTIT RIGID/FLEX KNOWL PWR
...RELATIV PSY SOC CONCPT SELF/OBS TREND STERTYP
TOT/POP. PAGE 14 H0286

S52
KECSKEMETI P.,"THE 'POLICY SCIENCES': ASPIRATION CREATE
AND OUTLOOK." UNIV CULTURE INTELL SOCIETY STRUCT NEW/IDEA
EDU/PROP ATTIT PERCEPT RIGID/FLEX KNOWL...PHIL/SCI
METH/CNCPT OBS 20. PAGE 84 H1674

B53
BENDIX R.,CLASS, STATUS AND POWER: A READER IN STRATA
SOCIAL STRATIFICATION. USA+45 SOCIETY ACT/RES DOMIN PWR
ATTIT RIGID/FLEX...PSY SOC CONCPT METH/COMP STRUCT
NAT/COMP 20. PAGE 14 H0273 ROLE

B53
MURPHY G.,IN THE MINDS OF MEN: THE STUDY OF HUMAN SECT
BEHAVIOR AND SOCIAL TENSIONS IN INDIA. FUT S/ASIA STRATA
FAM INT/ORG NAT/G DIPLOM EDU/PROP GP/REL ATTIT INDIA
RIGID/FLEX ALL/VALS...SOC QU UNESCO 20. PAGE 115
H2297

B54
SCHRAMM W.,THE PROCESS AND EFFECTS OF MASS ATTIT
COMMUNICATION. CULTURE INTELL SOCIETY COM/IND DRIVE EDU/PROP
PERCEPT PERSON RIGID/FLEX KNOWL...PSY SOC CONCPT
CHARTS. PAGE 140 H2800

L54
FURNISS E.S.,"WEAKNESSES IN FRENCH FOREIGN POLICY- NAT/G
MAKING." EUR+WWI LEGIS LEGIT EXEC ATTIT RIGID/FLEX STRUCT
ORD/FREE...SOC CONCPT METH/CNCPT OBS 20. PAGE 54 DIPLOM
H1078 FRANCE

S54
BALANDIER G.,"SOCIOLOGIE DE LA COLONISATION ET CULTURE
RELATIONS ENTRE SOCIETES GLOBALES." AFR SOCIETY SOC
ECO/UNDEV KIN DOMIN EDU/PROP RIGID/FLEX PWR...PSY COLONIAL
CONCPT TREND TOT/POP. PAGE 10 H0203

B55
KHADDURI M.,WAR AND PEACE IN THE LAW OF ISLAM. ISLAM
CONSTN CULTURE SOCIETY STRATA NAT/G PROVS SECT JURID
FORCES TOP/EX CREATE DOMIN EDU/PROP ADJUD COERCE PEACE
ATTIT RIGID/FLEX ALL/VALS...CONCPT TIME/SEQ TOT/POP WAR
VAL/FREE. PAGE 85 H1702

B55
KOHN H.,THE MIND OF MODERN RUSSIA. COM MOD/EUR USSR INTELL
SOCIETY NAT/G SECT FORCES TOP/EX COERCE TOTALISM GEN/LAWS
DRIVE RIGID/FLEX PWR SOVEREIGN...CONCPT TIME/SEQ SOCISM
WORK. PAGE 87 H1742 RUSSIA

B57
COLE G.D.H.,THE POST WAR CONDITIONS OF BRITAIN. ECO/DEV
EUR+WWI STRUCT NAT/G PLAN EDU/PROP LEGIT RIGID/FLEX UK
ORD/FREE WEALTH...SOCIALIST WELF/ST STAT TREND
CON/ANAL CHARTS PARLIAMENT WORK 20. PAGE 31 H0624

S57
COSER L.A.,"SOCIAL CONFLICT AND THE THEORY OF GP/REL
SOCIAL CHANGE." EUR+WWI CULTURE TEC/DEV PRODUC ROLE
RIGID/FLEX SOC. PAGE 34 H0673 SOCIETY
ORD/FREE

B58
ARON R.,SOCIOLOGIE DES SOCIETES INDUSTRIELLES: TOTALISM
ESQUISSE D'UNE THEORIE DES REGIMES POLITIQUES. INDUS
FRANCE SOCIETY NAT/G PROB/SOLV ATTIT RIGID/FLEX CONSTN
MARXISM POPULISM...POLICY SOC T 20 MARX/KARL GOV/COMP
TOCQUEVILL. PAGE 8 H0170

B58
HAAS E.B.,THE UNITING OF EUROPE. EUR+WWI INT/ORG VOL/ASSN
NAT/G POL/PAR TOP/EX ECO/TAC EDU/PROP LEGIT FEDERAL ECO/DEV
NAT/LISM DRIVE RIGID/FLEX ORD/FREE PWR PLURISM
...POLICY CONCPT INT GEN/LAWS ECSC EEC 20. PAGE 63
H1264

B58
LERNER D.,THE PASSING OF TRADITIONAL SOCIETY: ECO/UNDEV
MODERNIZING THE MIDDLE EAST. IRAN ISLAM LEBANON RIGID/FLEX
SYRIA TURKEY UAR CULTURE INTELL STRATA KIN NAT/G
NEIGH SECT EDU/PROP ATTIT PERSON...MYTH OBS 20.
PAGE 95 H1888

S58
MAIR L.P.,"REPRESENTATIVE LOCAL GOVERNMENT AS A AFR
PROBLEM IN SOCIAL CHANGE." ECO/UNDEV KIN LOC/G PWR
NAT/G SCHOOL JUDGE ADMIN ROUTINE REPRESENT ELITES
RIGID/FLEX RESPECT...CONCPT STERTYP CMN/WLTH 20.
PAGE 101 H2025

B59
EAENZA L.,COMMUNISMO E CATTOLICESIMO IN UNA ATTIT
PARROCHIA DI CAMPAGNA. ITALY CULTURE ELITES ECO/DEV CATHISM
AGRI KIN POL/PAR DOMIN LEGIT RIGID/FLEX...DECISION NEIGH
OBS IDEA/COMP 20 COM/PARTY CHURCH/STA. PAGE 44 MARXISM
H0878

B59
MEYER A.J.,MIDDLE EASTERN CAPITALISM: NINE ESSAYS. TEC/DEV
ISLAM CULTURE ECO/UNDEV INDUS MARKET NAT/G PLAN ECO/TAC
ATTIT RIGID/FLEX...STAT OBS TREND GEN/LAWS. ANTHOL
PAGE 109 H2188

B60
BLACK C.E.,THE TRANSFORMATION OF RUSSIAN SOCIETY. CULTURE
COM MOD/EUR RUSSIA SOCIETY EDU/PROP COERCE ALL/VALS RIGID/FLEX
19/20. PAGE 17 H0349 USSR

B60
FURNIA A.H.,THE DIPLOMACY OF APPEASEMENT: ANGLO- DIPLOM
FRENCH RELATIONS AND THE PRELUDE TO WORLD WAR II BAL/PWR
1931-1938. FRANCE GERMANY UK ELITES NAT/G DELIB/GP COERCE
FORCES WAR PEACE RIGID/FLEX 20. PAGE 54 H1077

B60
LISTER L.,EUROPE'S COAL AND STEEL COMMUNITY. FRANCE EUR+WWI
GERMANY STRUCT ECO/DEV EXTR/IND INDUS MARKET NAT/G INT/ORG
DELIB/GP ECO/TAC INT/TRADE EDU/PROP ATTIT REGION
RIGID/FLEX ORD/FREE PWR WEALTH...CONCPT STAT
TIME/SEQ CHARTS ECSC 20. PAGE 97 H1941

B60
MACRIDIS R.C.,THE DE GAULLE REPUBLIC: QUEST FOR TOP/EX
UNITY. EUR+WWI NAT/G POL/PAR LEGIS LEGIT NAT/LISM STRUCT
ATTIT RIGID/FLEX ORD/FREE PWR...JURID CONCPT FRANCE
TIME/SEQ 20 DEGAULLE/C. PAGE 100 H2009

B60
NICHOLLS W.H.,SOUTHERN TRADITION AND REGIONAL RIGID/FLEX
PROGRESS. STRATA STRUCT SCHOOL WORKER PARTIC REGION CONSERVE
RACE/REL CONSEN ATTIT...SOC METH/CNCPT 19/20 AGRI
SOUTH/US TVA. PAGE 118 H2349 CULTURE

S60
"THE EMERGING COMMON MARKETS IN LATIN AMERICA." FUT FINAN
L/A+17C STRATA DIST/IND INDUS LABOR NAT/G LEGIS ECO/UNDEV
ECO/TAC ADMIN RIGID/FLEX HEALTH...NEW/IDEA TIME/SEQ INT/TRADE
OAS 20. PAGE 2 H0038

S60
BRZEZINSKI Z.K.,"PATTERNS AND LIMITS OF THE SINO- POL/PAR
SOVIET DISPUTE." ASIA CHINA/COM COM FUT STRATA PWR
NAT/G EX/STRUC FORCES BAL/PWR DIPLOM ECO/TAC DOMIN REV
EDU/PROP ADMIN COERCE WAR ATTIT RIGID/FLEX USSR
...GEN/LAWS VAL/FREE 20. PAGE 23 H0459

S60
FRANKEL S.H.,"ECONOMIC ASPECTS OF POLITICAL NAT/G
INDEPENDENCE IN AFRICA." AFR FUT SOCIETY ECO/UNDEV FOR/AID
COM/IND FINAN LEGIS PLAN TEC/DEV CAP/ISM ECO/TAC
INT/TRADE ADMIN ATTIT DRIVE RIGID/FLEX PWR WEALTH
...MGT NEW/IDEA MATH TIME/SEQ VAL/FREE 20. PAGE 53
H1052

S60
JAFFEE A.J.,"POPULATION TRENDS AND CONTROLS IN ECO/UNDEV
UNDERDEVELOPED COUNTRIES." AFR FUT ISLAM L/A+17C GEOG
S/ASIA CULTURE R+D FAM ACT/RES PLAN EDU/PROP
BIO/SOC RIGID/FLEX HEALTH...SOC STAT OBS CHARTS 20.
PAGE 79 H1582

S60
LEVINE R.A.,"THE INTERNALIZATION OF POLITICAL CULTURE
VALUES IN STATELESS SOCIETIES." AFR FAM KIN LOC/G ATTIT
PROVS JUDGE PERSON RIGID/FLEX...DECISION SOC
TIME/SEQ 20. PAGE 95 H1904

S60
RIVKIN A.,"AFRICAN ECONOMIC DEVELOPMENT: ADVANCED AFR
TECHNOLOGY AND THE STAGES OF GROWTH." CULTURE TEC/DEV
ECO/UNDEV AGRI COM/IND EXTR/IND PLAN ECO/TAC ATTIT FOR/AID
DRIVE RIGID/FLEX SKILL WEALTH...MGT SOC GEN/LAWS
WORK TOT/POP 20. PAGE 132 H2634

B61
BELOFF M.,NEW DIMENSIONS IN FOREIGN POLICY: A STUDY INT/ORG
IN BRITISH ADMINISTRATION. UK NAT/G ATTIT DIPLOM
RIGID/FLEX ORD/FREE...GEN/LAWS EUR+WWI CMN/WLTH EEC
20. PAGE 14 H0271

B61
MARX K.,THE COMMUNIST MANIFESTO. IN (MENDEL A. COM
ESSENTIAL WORKS OF MARXISM, NEW YORK: BANTAM. FUT NEW/IDEA
MOD/EUR CULTURE ECO/DEV ECO/UNDEV AGRI FINAN INDUS CAP/ISM
MARKET PROC/MFG LABOR MUNIC POL/PAR CONSULT FORCES REV
CREATE PLAN ADMIN ATTIT DRIVE RIGID/FLEX ORD/FREE
PWR RESPECT MARX/KARL WORK. PAGE 104 H2081

B61
ROBERTSON A.H.,THE LAW OF INTERNATIONAL RIGID/FLEX
INSTITUTIONS IN EUROPE. EUR+WWI MOD/EUR INT/ORG ORD/FREE
NAT/G VOL/ASSN DELIB/GP...JURID TIME/SEQ TOT/POP 20
TREATY. PAGE 132 H2644

S61
MILLER E.,"LEGAL ASPECTS OF UN ACTION IN THE INT/ORG
CONGO." AFR CULTURE ADMIN PEACE DRIVE RIGID/FLEX LEGIT
ORD/FREE...WELF/ST JURID OBS UN CONGO 20. PAGE 111
H2212

S61
NEEDLER M.C.,"THE POLITICAL DEVELOPMENT OF MEXICO." L/A+17C
STRUCT NAT/G ADMIN RIGID/FLEX...TIME/SEQ TREND POL/PAR
MEXIC/AMER TOT/POP VAL/FREE 19/20. PAGE 116 H2328

S61
RANDALL F.B.,"COMMUNISM IN THE HIGH ANDES." L/A+17C CULTURE
PERU USSR SOCIETY PLAN EDU/PROP TOTALISM ATTIT DRIVE
RIGID/FLEX PWR WEALTH...HUM CONCPT GEN/LAWS 20
BOLIV EQUADOR. PAGE 129 H2589

B62
CHAKRAVARTI P.C.,INDIA'S CHINA POLICY. ASIA RIGID/FLEX

CHINA/COM S/ASIA CULTURE NAT/G TOP/EX ACT/RES EDU/PROP DRIVE ALL/VALS...MYTH 20. PAGE 28 H0571
TREND INDIA

B62
JOHNSON J.J.,THE ROLE OF THE MILITARY IN UNDERDEVELOPED COUNTRIES. AFR BURMA INDONESIA ISLAM ISRAEL L/A+17C S/ASIA THAILAND CULTURE ECO/UNDEV KIN PROVS CONSULT ACT/RES COERCE REV DRIVE RIGID/FLEX ORD/FREE...RECORD ANTHOL 20. PAGE 81 H1622
FORCES CONCPT

B62
OLLE-LAPRUNE J.,LA STABILITE DES MINISTRES SOUS LA TROISIEME REPUBLIQUE, 1879-1940. FRANCE CONSTN POL/PAR LEAD WAR INGP/REL RIGID/FLEX PWR...POLICY CHARTS 19/20. PAGE 121 H2415
LEGIS NAT/G ADMIN PERSON

B62
ROBINSON A.D.,DUTCH ORGANIZED AGRICULTURE IN INTERNATIONAL POLITICS, 1945-1960. EUR+WWI NETHERLAND STRUCT ECO/DEV NAT/G VOL/ASSN CONSULT DELIB/GP PLAN TEC/DEV INT/TRADE EDU/PROP ATTIT RIGID/FLEX ALL/VALS...NEW/IDEA TREND EEC 20. PAGE 132 H2648
AGRI INT/ORG

B62
WALSTON H.,AGRICULTURE UNDER COMMUNISM. CHINA/COM COM PROB/SOLV HAPPINESS RIGID/FLEX...POLICY METH/COMP 20. PAGE 165 H3295
AGRI MARXISM PLAN CREATE

S62
CROAN M.,"POLYCENTRISM: COMMUNIST INTERNATIONAL RELATIONS." ASIA STRUCT INT/ORG NAT/G POL/PAR CONSULT PLAN DOMIN EDU/PROP COERCE ATTIT RIGID/FLEX SOCISM...POLICY CONCPT TREND CON/ANAL GEN/LAWS MARX/KARL. PAGE 35 H0703
COM CREATE DIPLOM NAT/LISM

S62
GUETZKOW H.,"THE POTENTIAL OF CASE STUDY IN ANALYZING INTERNATIONAL CONFLICT." EUR+WWI FUT GERMANY INTELL SOCIETY STRUCT INT/ORG LOC/G NAT/G CONSULT CREATE PLAN CHOOSE ATTIT RIGID/FLEX ...POLICY SAAR 20. PAGE 62 H1246
EDU/PROP METH/CNCPT COERCE FRANCE

S62
IOVTCHOUK M.T.,"ON SOME THEORETICAL PRINCIPLES AND METHODS OF SOCIOLOGICAL INVESTIGATIONS (IN RUSSIAN)." FUT USA+45 STRATA R+D NAT/G POL/PAR TOP/EX ACT/RES PLAN ECO/TAC EDU/PROP ROUTINE ATTIT RIGID/FLEX MARXISM SOCISM...MARXIST METH/CNCPT OBS TREND NAT/COMP GEN/LAWS 20. PAGE 78 H1564
COM ECO/DEV CAP/ISM USSR

S62
KOLARZ W.,"THE IMPACT OF COMMUNISM ON WEST AFRICA." AFR FUT SOCIETY INT/ORG NAT/G CREATE PLAN DOMIN EDU/PROP COERCE NAT/LISM ATTIT RIGID/FLEX SOCISM ...POLICY CONCPT TREND MARX/KARL 20. PAGE 88 H1751
COM POL/PAR COLONIAL

S62
LONDON K.,"SINO-SOVIET RELATIONS IN THE CONTEXT OF THE 'WORLD SOCIALIST SYSTEM'." ASIA CHINA/COM COM USSR INT/ORG NAT/G TOP/EX BAL/PWR DIPLOM DOMIN ATTIT PERCEPT RIGID/FLEX PWR MARXISM...METH/CNCPT TREND 20. PAGE 98 H1957
DELIB/GP CONCPT SOCISM

S62
MOUSKHELY M.,"LA NAISSANCE DES ETATS EN DROIT INTERNATIONAL PUBLIC." UNIV SOCIETY INT/ORG VOL/ASSN LEGIT ATTIT RIGID/FLEX...JURID TIME/SEQ 20. PAGE 114 H2272
NAT/G STRUCT INT/LAW

S62
PISTRAK L.,"SOVIET VIEWS ON AFRICA." AFR COM FUT ISLAM USSR INTELL STRUCT KIN POL/PAR PLAN EDU/PROP RIGID/FLEX PWR MARXISM...TIME/SEQ WORK TOT/POP 20. PAGE 126 H2516
NAT/G ATTIT SOCISM

S62
SARKISYANZ E.,"NATIONALISM, CAPITALISM, AND THE UNCOMMITED NATIONS: MARXISM AND ASIAN CULTURAL TRADITIONS." ASIA BURMA CHINA/COM COM CULTURE SOCIETY NAT/G POL/PAR PLAN DOMIN EDU/PROP COLONIAL COERCE ATTIT RIGID/FLEX...CONCPT TREND MARX/KARL 20 TIBET BUDDHISM. PAGE 138 H2755
S/ASIA SECT NAT/LISM CAP/ISM

S62
SHATTEN F.,"POLYCENTRISM: AFRICA: NATIONALISM AND COMMUNISM." ASIA COM FUT ISLAM CULTURE SOCIETY ECO/UNDEV NAT/G PLAN DOMIN COLONIAL COERCE CHOOSE RIGID/FLEX ALL/VALS MARXISM...CONCPT TREND 20. PAGE 143 H2852
AFR ATTIT NAT/LISM SOCISM

S62
STRACHEY J.,"COMMUNIST INTENTIONS." ASIA USSR YUGOSLAVIA INT/ORG NAT/G FORCES DOMIN EDU/PROP COERCE NUC/PWR NAT/LISM PEACE RIGID/FLEX PWR MARXISM...CONCPT MYTH OBS TIME/SEQ TREND COLD/WAR TOT/POP 20. PAGE 150 H2992
COM ATTIT WAR

S62
THOMPSON D.,"THE UNITED KINGDOM AND THE TREATY OF ROME." EUR+WWI INT/ORG NAT/G DELIB/GP LEGIS INT/TRADE RIGID/FLEX...CONCPT EEC PARLIAMENT CMN/WLTH 20. PAGE 154 H3079
ADJUD JURID

N62
US CONGRESS JT ATOM ENRGY COMM,PEACEFUL USES OF ATOMIC ENERGY, HEARING. USA+45 USSR TEC/DEV ATTIT RIGID/FLEX...TESTS CHARTS EXHIBIT METH/COMP 20 CONGRESS. PAGE 159 H3177
NUC/PWR ACADEM SCHOOL NAT/COMP

B63
BARNETT A.D.,COMMUNIST STRATEGIES IN ASIA: A COMPARATIVE ANALYSIS OF GOVERNMENTS AND PARTIES. COM FUT S/ASIA CULTURE SOCIETY STRATA NAT/G DELIB/GP ACT/RES ECO/TAC EDU/PROP COERCE CHOOSE ATTIT RIGID/FLEX ORD/FREE PWR SKILL...SIMUL VAL/FREE 20. PAGE 11 H0223
ASIA POL/PAR DIPLOM USSR

B63
ISSAWI C.,EGYPT IN REVOLUTION: AN ECONOMIC ANALYSIS. ISLAM STRUCT ECO/UNDEV AGRI FINAN INDUS PLAN EXEC REV NAT/LISM ATTIT RIGID/FLEX WEALTH SOCISM...STAT WORK 20. PAGE 79 H1573
NAT/G UAR

B63
JELAVICH C.,THE BALKANS IN TRANSITION: ESSAYS ON THE DEVELOPMENT OF BALKAN LIFE AND POLITICS SINCE THE EIGHTEENTH CENTURY. COM GREECE TURKEY ECO/UNDEV NAT/G SECT ATTIT...GEOG SOC CONCPT TIME/SEQ ANTHOL 18/20. PAGE 80 H1596
CULTURE RIGID/FLEX

B63
KHADDURI M.,MODERN LIBYA: A STUDY IN POLITICAL DEVELOPMENT. EUR+WWI ISLAM LIBYA ELITES INT/ORG POL/PAR FORCES DIPLOM FOR/AID DOMIN EDU/PROP LEGIT NAT/LISM DRIVE RIGID/FLEX SKILL...CONCPT TIME/SEQ TREND 20. PAGE 85 H1704
NAT/G STRUCT

B63
RONNING C.N.,LAW AND POLITICS IN INTER-AMERICAN DIPLOMACY. L/A+17C ECO/UNDEV NAT/G CONSULT DELIB/GP CREATE CAP/ISM ECO/TAC LEGIT REGION RIGID/FLEX ...METH/CNCPT GEN/LAWS OAS 20. PAGE 133 H2668
VOL/ASSN ALL/VALS DIPLOM

B63
SINGH H.L.,PROBLEMS AND POLICIES OF THE BRITISH IN INDIA, 1885-1898. INDIA UK NAT/G FORCES LEGIS PROB/SOLV CONTROL RACE/REL ADJUST DISCRIM NAT/LISM RIGID/FLEX...MGT 19 CIVIL/SERV. PAGE 144 H2885
COLONIAL PWR POLICY ADMIN

B63
TUCKER R.C.,THE SOVIET POLITICAL MIND. COM INTELL NAT/G TOP/EX EDU/PROP ADMIN COERCE TOTALISM ATTIT PWR MARXISM...PSY MYTH HYPO/EXP 20. PAGE 157 H3136
STRUCT RIGID/FLEX ELITES USSR

B63
ULAM A.B.,THE NEW FACE OF SOVIET TOTALITARIANISM. FUT INTELL NAT/G POL/PAR EX/STRUC TOP/EX DIPLOM ECO/TAC DOMIN EDU/PROP LEGIT COERCE ATTIT RIGID/FLEX...OBS HIST/WRIT TREND TOT/POP VAL/FREE COLD/WAR. PAGE 158 H3150
COM PWR TOTALISM USSR

L63
ROSE R.,"COMPARATIVE STUDIES IN POLITICAL FINANCE: A SYMPOSIUM." ASIA EUR+WWI S/ASIA LAW CULTURE DELIB/GP LEGIS ACT/RES ECO/TAC EDU/PROP CHOOSE ATTIT RIGID/FLEX SUPEGO PWR SKILL WEALTH...STAT ANTHOL VAL/FREE. PAGE 134 H2674
FINAN POL/PAR

S63
APPERT K.,"BERECHTIGE VORBEHALTE DER SCHWEIZERISCHEN ZUR INTEGRATION." EUR+WWI UK MARKET SERV/IND NAT/G PLAN RIGID/FLEX OEEC 20 EEC. PAGE 7 H0146
FINAN ATTIT SWITZERLND

S63
AYAL E.B.,"VALUE SYSTEM AND ECONOMIC DEVELOPMENT IN JAPAN AND THAILAND." ASIA S/ASIA THAILAND CULTURE ECO/DEV CAP/ISM DOMIN NAT/LISM DRIVE RIGID/FLEX SOCISM...WELF/ST OBS TREND CON/ANAL GEN/LAWS 20 CHINJAP. PAGE 9 H0185
ECO/UNDEV ALL/VALS

S63
BECHHOEFER B.G.,"SOVIET ATTITUDE TOWARD DISARMAMENT." COM USSR NAT/G ACT/RES TEC/DEV NUC/PWR ATTIT DISPL RIGID/FLEX PWR...METH/CNCPT TREND GEN/LAWS COLD/WAR 20. PAGE 13 H0252
FORCES EDU/PROP ARMS/CONT

S63
LOPEZIBOR J.,"L'EUROPE, FORME DE VIE." CHRIST-17C EUR+WWI FUT MOD/EUR SOCIETY INT/ORG SECT EDU/PROP ATTIT RIGID/FLEX ALL/VALS...POLICY HUM SOC TIME/SEQ TREND GEN/LAWS. PAGE 98 H1966
NAT/G CULTURE

S63
STAAR R.F.,"HOW STRONG IS THE SOVIET BLOC." COM USSR ECO/DEV NAT/G DELIB/GP ECO/TAC RIGID/FLEX ...CONCPT RECORD CHARTS 20. PAGE 148 H2964
FORCES MYTH TOTALISM

B64
BINDER L.,THE IDEOLOGICAL REVOLUTION IN THE MIDDLE EAST. ISLAM STRUCT INT/ORG KIN SECT EX/STRUC TOP/EX PLAN ATTIT DRIVE RIGID/FLEX PWR...MYTH TOT/POP 20. PAGE 17 H0338
POL/PAR NAT/G NAT/LISM

B64
CURTIN P.D.,THE IMAGE OF AFRICA: BRITISH IDEAS AND ACTION, 1780-1850. MOD/EUR SOCIETY FORCES ACT/RES DOMIN EDU/PROP COERCE ATTIT PERCEPT RIGID/FLEX SUPEGO HEALTH KNOWL MORAL ORD/FREE WEALTH...CONCPT WORK VAL/FREE. PAGE 36 H0726
AFR CULTURE UK DIPLOM

B64
DE SMITH S.A.,THE NEW COMMONWEALTH AND ITS CONSTITUTIONS. AFR CYPRUS PAKISTAN S/ASIA INT/ORG NAT/G LEGIS LEGIT RIGID/FLEX PWR...CONCPT TIME/SEQ CMN/WLTH 20. PAGE 38 H0770
EX/STRUC CONSTN SOVEREIGN

B64
MARTINET G.,MARXISM OF OUR TIME: OR THE CONTRADICTIONS OF SOCIALISM. FRANCE NAT/G OPTIMAL RIGID/FLEX SOCISM...IDEA/COMP 20. PAGE 103 H2067
MARXISM MARXIST PROB/SOLV

CREATE

B64
TAYLOR E.,RICHER BY ASIA. S/ASIA CULTURE VOL/ASSN ACT/RES ATTIT DISPL PERSON ALL/VALS...INT/LAW MYTH SELF/OBS 20. PAGE 153 H3054
SOCIETY RIGID/FLEX INDIA

B64
TEPASKE J.J.,EXPLOSIVE FORCES IN LATIN AMERICA. CULTURE INTELL ECO/UNDEV INT/ORG NAT/G SECT FORCES ECO/TAC EDU/PROP PWR WEALTH SOC. PAGE 153 H3063
L/A+17C RIGID/FLEX FOR/AID USSR

B64
WHEELER-BENNETT J.W.,THE NEMESIS OF POWER (2ND ED.). EUR+WWI GERMANY TOP/EX TEC/DEV ADMIN WAR PERS/REL RIGID/FLEX ROLE ORD/FREE PWR FASCISM 20 HITLER/A. PAGE 167 H3342
FORCES NAT/G GP/REL STRUCT

B64
WHITE D.S.,SEEDS OF DISCORD. EUR+WWI FRANCE NAT/G VOL/ASSN FORCES DIPLOM DOMIN NAT/LISM DISPL RIGID/FLEX PWR...RECORD INT BIOG 20 DEGAULLE/C ROOSEVLT/F CHURCHLL/W HULL. PAGE 167 H3347
TOP/EX ATTIT

B64
WILCOX W.A.,INDIA, PAKISTAN AND THE RISE OF CHINA. ASIA BURMA CEYLON CHINA/COM INDIA PAKISTAN S/ASIA NAT/G VOL/ASSN FORCES TOP/EX ACT/RES DOMIN REGION RIGID/FLEX ORD/FREE...POLICY GEN/LAWS COLD/WAR 20. PAGE 168 H3362
CULTURE ATTIT DIPLOM

B64
WRIGHT G.,RURAL REVOLUTION IN FRANCE: THE PEASANTRY IN THE TWENTIETH CENTURY. EUR+WWI MOD/EUR LAW CULTURE AGRI POL/PAR DELIB/GP LEGIS ECO/TAC EDU/PROP COERCE CHOOSE ATTIT RIGID/FLEX HEALTH ...STAT CENSUS CHARTS VAL/FREE 20. PAGE 171 H3419
PWR STRATA FRANCE REV

S64
ADAMS R.,"POLITICS AND SOCIAL ANTHROPOLOGY IN SPANISH AMERICA." FUT CULTURE SOCIETY NAT/G PROF/ORG EDU/PROP ATTIT RIGID/FLEX ALL/VALS ...POLICY GEOG METH/CNCPT MYTH TREND VAL/FREE 20. PAGE 3 H0065
L/A+17C SOC

S64
BENSON M.,"SOUTH AFRICA AND WORLD OPINION." AFR SOUTH/AFR INTELL SOCIETY TOP/EX ECO/TAC DOMIN COERCE DISCRIM ATTIT PWR WEALTH...POLICY RECORD 20. PAGE 14 H0285
NAT/G RIGID/FLEX RACE/REL

S64
CATTELL D.T.,"SOVIET POLICIES IN LATIN AMERICA." COM CUBA L/A+17C USSR SOCIETY NAT/G POL/PAR FORCES CREATE ECO/TAC EDU/PROP REGION REV RIGID/FLEX ...GEN/LAWS COLD/WAR 20. PAGE 28 H0560
DRIVE PWR

S64
ENNIS T.E.,"VIETNAM: LAND WITHOUT LAUGHTER." S/ASIA VIETNAM VIETNAM/S INTELL SOCIETY SECT FORCES DIPLOM LEGIT COERCE WAR ATTIT RIGID/FLEX ORD/FREE COLD/WAR 20. PAGE 46 H0929
NAT/G TOP/EX GUERRILLA

S64
LANGER P.F.,"JAPAN'S RELATIONS WITH CHINA." ASIA CHINA/COM KOREA S/ASIA ECO/DEV NAT/G POL/PAR EDU/PROP ATTIT ALL/VALS...METH/CNCPT TIME/SEQ TREND 20 CHINJAP. PAGE 91 H1808
RIGID/FLEX ECO/TAC

S64
LERNER W.,"THE HISTORICAL ORIGINS OF THE SOVIET DOCTRINE OF PEACEFUL COEXISTENCE." COM USSR INT/ORG NAT/G VOL/ASSN PLAN PEACE ATTIT RIGID/FLEX PWR MARXISM...TIME/SEQ COLD/WAR 20. PAGE 95 H1891
EDU/PROP DIPLOM

S64
LEVI W.,"INDIAN NEUTRALISM RECONSIDERED." ASIA CHINA/COM S/ASIA SOCIETY NAT/G ACT/RES LEGIT NEUTRAL COERCE ATTIT DRIVE PERCEPT RIGID/FLEX HEALTH LOVE PWR...DECISION RECORD TREND STERTYP 20. PAGE 95 H1896
ORD/FREE CONCPT INDIA

S64
MARES V.E.,"EAST EUROPE'S SECOND CHANCE." COM EUR+WWI HUNGARY ROMANIA USSR YUGOSLAVIA ECO/UNDEV NAT/G TOP/EX CREATE PLAN TEC/DEV REGION NAT/LISM RIGID/FLEX PWR...CONCPT STAT COMECON 20. PAGE 102 H2047
VOL/ASSN ECO/TAC

S64
MARTELLI G.,"PORTUGAL AND THE UNITED NATIONS." AFR EUR+WWI ELITES INT/ORG NAT/G PROVS PLAN DIPLOM ECO/TAC DOMIN COLONIAL RIGID/FLEX MORAL ORD/FREE PWR WEALTH...MYTH UN 20. PAGE 103 H2060
ATTIT PORTUGAL

S64
MOZINGO D.P.,"CHINA'S RELATIONS WITH HER ASIAN NEIGHBORS." ASIA CHINA/COM S/ASIA VIETNAM NAT/G DELIB/GP FORCES CREATE DOMIN EDU/PROP REV RIGID/FLEX PWR...TIME/SEQ GEN/LAWS COLD/WAR 20. PAGE 114 H2277
VOL/ASSN POLICY DIPLOM

S64
REISS I.,"LE DECLENCHEMENT DE LA PREMIERE GUERRE MONDIALE." GERMANY RUSSIA NAT/G FORCES DOMIN EDU/PROP COERCE RIGID/FLEX PWR SOVEREIGN...RELATIV HIST/WRIT TOT/POP AUST/HUNG SERBIA 20. PAGE 131 H2612
MOD/EUR BAL/PWR DIPLOM WAR

S64
SAAB H.,"THE ARAB SEARCH FOR A FEDERAL UNION." SOCIETY INT/ORG NAT/G DELIB/GP FORCES ACT/RES TEC/DEV ECO/TAC DOMIN LEGIT REGION ROUTINE ATTIT DRIVE RIGID/FLEX ALL/VALS...SOC CONCPT NEW/IDEA TIME/SEQ TREND. PAGE 136 H2726
ISLAM PLAN

S64
TOUVAL S.,"THE SOMALI REPUBLIC." AFR ISLAM SOMALIA FAM KIN NAT/G CREATE FOR/AID LEGIT ATTIT ALL/VALS ...RECORD TREND 20. PAGE 156 H3119
ECO/UNDEV RIGID/FLEX

S64
TOYNBEE A.,"BRITAIN AND THE ARABS: THE NEED FOR A NEW START." NAT/G CREATE COLONIAL ATTIT RIGID/FLEX MORAL PWR...POLICY HIST/WRIT 20. PAGE 156 H3124
ISLAM ECO/TAC DIPLOM UK

B65
APTER D.E.,THE POLITICS OF MODERNIZATION. AFR L/A+17C CULTURE NAT/G POL/PAR ADMIN COLONIAL NAT/LISM ATTIT RIGID/FLEX PWR...SOC CONCPT. PAGE 8 H0154
ECO/UNDEV GEN/LAWS STRATA CREATE

B65
BETEILLE A.,CASTE, CLASS, AND POWER. INDIA MUNIC SECT REGION GP/REL PERS/REL ATTIT HABITAT RIGID/FLEX...SOC 20. PAGE 16 H0323
STRATA CULTURE PWR STRUCT

B65
BRASS P.R.,FACTIONAL POLITICS IN AN INDIAN STATE: THE CONGRESS PARTY IN UTTAR PRADESH. INDIA UK CONSTN CULTURE ECO/UNDEV LOC/G DOMIN COLONIAL CROWD GP/REL ADJUST CENTRAL RIGID/FLEX SOVEREIGN 20 UTTAR/PRAD CONGRESS/P. PAGE 20 H0406
POL/PAR PROVS LEGIS CHOOSE

B65
JANSEN M.B.,CHANGING JAPANESE ATTITUDES TOWARD MODERNIZATION. ASIA CHINA/COM S/ASIA INTELL SOCIETY KIN NAT/G SECT PERCEPT RIGID/FLEX...SOC CONCPT TIME/SEQ TREND TOT/POP 19/20 CHINJAP. PAGE 80 H1591
TEC/DEV ATTIT INDIA

B65
KLEIN J.,SAMPLES FROM ENGLISH CULTURES (2 VOLS.). UK STRATA FAM NEIGH WORKER ETIQUET ISOLAT AGE/C AGE/A HABITAT RIGID/FLEX...NET/THEORY CHARTS 20. PAGE 87 H1732
CULTURE INGP/REL ATTIT SOC

B65
TUTSCH H.E.,FACETS OF ARAB NATIONALISM. ISLAM ISRAEL CULTURE STRUCT SECT RIGID/FLEX ORD/FREE MARXISM SOCISM 20. PAGE 157 H3143
ECO/UNDEV NAT/LISM TEC/DEV SOCIETY

L65
SCHAFFER B.B.,"THE CONCEPT OF PREPARATION* SOME QUESTIONS ABOUT THE TRANSFER OF SYSTEMS OF GOVERNMENT." AFR ASIA CANADA ELITES NAT/G POL/PAR COLONIAL RIGID/FLEX IDEA/COMP. PAGE 138 H2769
ECO/UNDEV UK RECORD

S65
HELMREICH E.C.,"KADAR'S HUNGARY." COM EUR+WWI HUNGARY USSR INTELL ECO/DEV AGRI INT/ORG TOP/EX DOMIN ALL/VALS WORK COLD/WAR 20. PAGE 69 H1390
NAT/G RIGID/FLEX TOTALISM

S65
KINDLEBERGER C.P.,"MASS MIGRATION, THEN AND NOW." LAW ECO/DEV ECO/UNDEV INDUS LABOR INT/TRADE FEEDBACK REGION RIGID/FLEX...SOC NAT/COMP EEC. PAGE 86 H1714
EUR+WWI USA-45 WORKER IDEA/COMP

S65
ROGGER H.,"EAST GERMANY: STABLE OR IMMOBILE." COM EUR+WWI GERMANY/E NAT/G INT/TRADE DOMIN EDU/PROP COERCE TOTALISM COLD/WAR 20. PAGE 133 H2659
TOP/EX RIGID/FLEX GERMANY

S65
RUBINSTEIN A.Z.,"YUGOSLAVIA'S OPENING SOCIETY." COM USSR INTELL NAT/G LEGIS TOP/EX LEGIT CT/SYS RIGID/FLEX ALL/VALS SOCISM...HUM TIME/SEQ TREND 20. PAGE 135 H2708
CONSTN EX/STRUC YUGOSLAVIA

S65
STAAR R.F.,"RETROGRESSION IN POLAND." COM USSR AGRI INDUS NAT/G CREATE EDU/PROP TOTALISM RIGID/FLEX ORD/FREE PWR SOCISM...RECORD CHARTS 20. PAGE 148 H2965
TOP/EX ECO/TAC POLAND

S65
TABORSKY E.,"CHANGE IN CZECHOSLOVAKIA." COM USSR ELITES INTELL AGRI INDUS NAT/G DELIB/GP EX/STRUC ECO/TAC TOTALISM ATTIT RIGID/FLEX SOCISM...MGT CONCPT TREND 20. PAGE 152 H3031
ECO/DEV PLAN CZECHOSLVK

S65
VUCINICH W.S.,"WHITHER RUMANIA." COM USSR YUGOSLAVIA NAT/G VOL/ASSN DELIB/GP TOP/EX LEGIT NAT/LISM TOTALISM ATTIT DRIVE RIGID/FLEX ORD/FREE WEALTH SOCISM...TIME/SEQ TREND 20. PAGE 164 H3281
ECO/DEV CREATE ROMANIA

B66
BERELSON B.,READER IN PUBLIC OPINION AND COMMUNICATION (2ND ED.). UNIV NAT/G PRESS GP/REL PERS/REL PERCEPT RIGID/FLEX...MAJORIT QUANT METH/COMP ANTHOL BIBLIOG 20. PAGE 15 H0298
EDU/PROP ATTIT CONCPT COM/IND

B66
HACKETT J.,L'ECONOMIE BRITANNIQUE: PROBLEMES ET PERSPECTIVES. FRANCE UK LABOR MUNIC NAT/G EX/STRUC PROB/SOLV BAL/PAY INCOME RIGID/FLEX...MGT PHIL/SCI CHARTS 20. PAGE 63 H1271
ECO/DEV FINAN ECO/TAC PLAN

B66
LONDON K.,EASTERN EUROPE IN TRANSITION. CHINA/COM USSR DOMIN COLONIAL CENTRAL RIGID/FLEX PWR...SOC ANTHOL 20. PAGE 98 H1958
SOVEREIGN COM NAT/LISM DIPLOM

B66
SILBERMAN B.S.,MODERN JAPANESE LEADERSHIP; TRANSITION AND CHANGE. NAT/G POL/PAR CHIEF ADMIN REPRESENT GP/REL ADJUST RIGID/FLEX...SOC METH/COMP ANTHOL 19/20 CHINJAP CHRISTIAN. PAGE 144 H2873
LEAD CULTURE ELITES MUNIC

B66
SWARTZ M.J.,POLITICAL ANTHROPOLOGY. WOR+45 POL/PAR ACT/RES REV GP/REL DRIVE...SOC CONCPT TIME/SEQ GP/COMP ANTHOL WORSHIP 20. PAGE 151 H3013
PARTIC RIGID/FLEX LOC/G CREATE

L66
LEMARCHAND R.,"SOCIAL CHANGE AND POLITICAL MODERNISATION IN BURUNDI." AFR BURUNDI STRATA CHIEF EX/STRUC RIGID/FLEX PWR...SOC 20. PAGE 94 H1874
NAT/G STRUCT ELITES CONSERVE

L66
MCAUSLAN J.P.W.,"CONSTITUTIONAL INNOVATION AND POLITICAL STABILITY IN TANZANIA: A PRELIMINARY ASSESSMENT." AFR TANZANIA ELITES CHIEF EX/STRUC RIGID/FLEX PWR 20 PRESIDENT BUREAUCRCY. PAGE 106 H2122
CONSTN NAT/G EXEC POL/PAR

S66
MCLANE C.B.,"SOVIET DOCTRINE AND THE MILITARY COUPS IN AFRICA." ALGERIA GHANA COLONIAL NAT/LISM RIGID/FLEX SOVEREIGN MARXISM...DECISION NAT/COMP. PAGE 107 H2140
USSR ATTIT AFR FORCES

B67
FANON F.,BLACK SKIN, WHITE MASKS: THE EXPERIENCES OF A BLACK MAN IN A WHITE WORLD. CULTURE COLONIAL HAPPINESS ISOLAT STRANGE ATTIT HABITAT RIGID/FLEX SEX...BIOG STERTYP SOC/INTEG 20 NEGRO. PAGE 49 H0970
DISCRIM PERS/REL RACE/REL PSY

B67
KORNBERG A.,CANADIAN LEGISLATIVE BEHAVIOR: A STUDY OF THE 25TH PARLIAMENT. CANADA NAT/G POL/PAR PARL/PROC CHOOSE INGP/REL ADJUST ANOMIE RIGID/FLEX ...SOC STAND/INT CHARTS SOC/EXP 20 PARLIAMENT. PAGE 88 H1756
ATTIT LEGIS ROLE

B67
NASH M.,MACHINE AGE MAYA. GUATEMALA L/A+17C STRUCT AGRI WORKER CREATE INCOME ATTIT RIGID/FLEX ROLE ...IDEA/COMP SOC/EXP WORSHIP 20 INDIAN/AM. PAGE 116 H2315
INDUS CULTURE SOC MUNIC

S67
BASKIN D.B.,"NATIONALITY DOCTRINE AND ANTI-SEMITISM IN THE USSR." USSR CULTURE STRATA ISOLAT MAJORITY ATTIT RIGID/FLEX RESPECT...GP/COMP JEWS. PAGE 12 H0234
NAT/LISM MARXISM GP/REL DISCRIM

S67
GLENN N.D.,"RURAL-URBAN DIFFERENCES IN REPORTED ATTITUDES AND BEHAVIOR" STRATA GP/REL CONSEN HABITAT RIGID/FLEX SAMP. PAGE 57 H1143
CULTURE ATTIT KIN CHARTS

S67
HAMMOND R.J.,"RACE ATTITUDES AND POLICIES IN PORTUGUESE AFRICA IN THE NINETEENTH AND TWENTIETH CENTURIES." AFR PORTUGAL NAT/G SECT EDU/PROP COLONIAL ATTIT RIGID/FLEX SEX MORAL RESPECT 19/20 NEGRO. PAGE 65 H1309
POLICY RACE/REL DISCRIM SOCIETY

S67
JANICKE M.,"MONOPOLISMUS UND PLURALISMUS IM KOMMUNISTISCHEN HERRSCHAFTSSYSTEM" COM CZECHOSLVK USSR YUGOSLAVIA SOCIETY CONTROL RIGID/FLEX...CONCPT NAT/COMP 20. PAGE 79 H1589
TOTALISM POL/PAR ATTIT PLURISM

S67
RIESMAN D.,"SOME QUESTIONS ABOUT THE STUDY OF AMERICAN CHARACTER IN THE TWENTIETH CENTURY." STRATA PRESS PERSON RIGID/FLEX SOC. PAGE 131 H2628
CULTURE ATTIT DRIVE GEN/LAWS

S67
SYRKIN M.,"THE RIGHT TO BE ORDINARY." ISLAM ISRAEL NAT/G COERCE NAT/LISM RIGID/FLEX 20. PAGE 151 H3025
SOVEREIGN WAR FORCES DIPLOM

RINGHOFER K. H2630

RINTELEN F. H2631

RIO/PACT....RIO PACT

RIOT....RIOTS; SEE ALSO CROWD

RIPLEY W.Z. H2632

RISK....SEE ALSO GAMBLE

B37
THOMPSON J.W.,SECRET DIPLOMACY: A RECORD OF ESPIONAGE AND DOUBLE-DEALING: 1500-1815. CHRIST-17C MOD/EUR NAT/G WRITING RISK MORAL...ANTHOL BIBLIOG 16/19 ESPIONAGE. PAGE 154 H3084
DIPLOM CRIME

B59
HOBSBAWM E.J.,PRIMITIVE REBELS; STUDIES IN ARCHAIC FORMS OF SOCIAL MOVEMENT IN THE 19TH AND 20TH CENTURIES. ITALY SPAIN CULTURE VOL/ASSN RISK CROWD GP/REL INGP/REL ISOLAT TOTALISM...PSY SOC 18/20. PAGE 72 H1438
SOCIETY CRIME REV GUERRILLA

B62
FEIT E.,SOUTH AFRICA, THE DYNAMICS OF THE AFRICAN NATIONAL CONGRESS. AFR SOUTH/AFR LAW INTELL STRATA KIN NAT/G POL/PAR ECO/TAC DOMIN RISK COERCE 20 NEGRO. PAGE 49 H0984
RACE/REL ELITES CONTROL STRUCT

B64
BRIGHT J.R.,RESEARCH, DEVELOPMENT AND TECHNOLOGICAL INNOVATION. CULTURE R+D CREATE PLAN PROB/SOLV AUTOMAT RISK PERSON...DECISION CONCPT PREDICT BIBLIOG. PAGE 21 H0419
TEC/DEV NEW/IDEA INDUS MGT

B64
BROWN N.,NUCLEAR WAR* THE IMPENDING STRATEGIC DEADLOCK. USA+45 USSR TEC/DEV BUDGET RISK ARMS/CONT NUC/PWR WEAPON COST BIO/SOC...GEOG IDEA/COMP NAT/COMP GAME NATO WARSAW/P. PAGE 22 H0448
FORCES OP/RES WAR GEN/LAWS

S65
BIRNBAUM K.,"SWEDEN'S NUCLEAR POLICY." WOR+45 POL/PAR CREATE TEC/DEV NEUTRAL RISK WAR ORD/FREE ...DECISION IDEA/COMP NAT/COMP TIME. PAGE 17 H0343
SWEDEN NUC/PWR DIPLOM ARMS/CONT

S65
GORDON M.,"THE SETTING FOR EUROPEAN ARMS CONTROLS* POLITICAL AND STRATEGIC CHOICES OF EUROPEAN ELITES." FRANCE GERMANY UK USA+45 USSR ARMS/CONT DETER ATTIT ORD/FREE...SAMP NAT/COMP NATO. PAGE 59 H1179
REC/INT ELITES RISK WAR

S65
PLANK J.N.,"THE CARIBBEAN* INTERVENTION, WHEN AND HOW." CUBA GUATEMALA HAITI PANAMA USA+45 VENEZUELA FORCES PROB/SOLV RISK COERCE...NAT/COMP OAS TIME. PAGE 126 H2521
SOVEREIGN MARXISM REV

S65
WOHLSTETTER R.,"CUBA AND PEARL HARBOR* HINDSIGHT AND FORESIGHT." USSR FORCES OP/RES TEC/DEV ATTIT PERCEPT...DECISION IDEA/COMP NAT/COMP STERTYP TIME. PAGE 170 H3395
CUBA RISK WAR ACT/RES

S65
WRIGHT Q.,"THE ESCALATION OF INTERNATIONAL CONFLICTS." WOR+45 WOR-45 FORCES DIPLOM RISK COST ATTIT ALL/VALS...INT/LAW QUANT STAT NAT/COMP. PAGE 171 H3422
WAR PERCEPT PREDICT MATH

B66
FOX K.A.,THE THEORY OF QUANTITATIVE ECONOMIC POLICY WITH APPLICATIONS TO ECONOMIC GROWTH AND STABILIZATION. ECO/DEV AGRI NAT/G PLAN ADMIN RISK ...DECISION IDEA/COMP SIMUL T. PAGE 52 H1045
ECO/TAC ECOMETRIC EQUILIB GEN/LAWS

B66
VIEN N.C.,SEEKING THE TRUTH. VIETNAM DELIB/GP DOMIN RISK MARXISM 20 KY/NGUYEN. PAGE 162 H3250
NAT/G COLONIAL PWR SOVEREIGN

B67
BODENHEIMER E.,TREATISE ON JUSTICE. INT/ORG NAT/G PUB/INST ACT/RES RISK CRIME INGP/REL DISCRIM DRIVE LAISSEZ 20. PAGE 18 H0363
ALL/VALS STRUCT JURID CONCPT

S67
READ J.S.,"CENSORED." UGANDA CONSTN INTELL SOCIETY NAT/G DIPLOM PRESS WRITING ADJUD ADMIN COLONIAL RISK...IDEA/COMP 20. PAGE 130 H2602
EDU/PROP AFR CREATE

RISTIC D.N. H2633

RITCHIE/JM....JESS M. RITCHIE

RITSCHL/H....HANS RITSCHL

RITUAL....RITUALS AND SYMBOLIC CEREMONIES; SEE ALSO WORSHIP, SECT

B27
HOCART A.M.,KINGSHIP. UNIV CULTURE EX/STRUC TRIBUTE ROUTINE CHOOSE ROLE SOVEREIGN RITUAL 20 KING. PAGE 72 H1441
CHIEF MYTH IDEA/COMP

B35
GORER G.,AFRICA DANCES: A BOOK ABOUT WEST AFRICAN NEGROES. STRUCT LOC/G SECT FORCES TAX ADMIN COLONIAL...ART/METH MYTH WORSHIP 20 NEGRO AFRICA/W CHRISTIAN RITUAL. PAGE 59 H1181
AFR ATTIT CULTURE SOCIETY

B58
WARNER W.L.,A BLACK CIVILIZATION - A SOCIAL STUDY OF AN AUSTRALIAN TRIBE. SOCIETY FAM MARRIAGE...PSY SOC MYTH CHARTS 20 AUSTRAL MAPS MURNGIN RITUAL. PAGE 165 H3310
CULTURE KIN STRUCT DEATH

B66
HAHN C.H.L.,THE NATIVE TRIBES OF SOUTH WEST AFRICA. LAW FAM SECT HABITAT SKILL...SOC AUD/VIS WORSHIP RITUAL 20 AFRICA/SW. PAGE 64 H1275
CULTURE SOCIETY STRUCT AFR

RIVKIN A. H2634,H2635

RIVLIN B. H2636

RIZK C. H2637

RKFDV....REICHSKOMMISSARIAT FUR DIE FESTIGUNG DEUTSCHEN VOLKSTUMS

RKO....R.K.O.

ROBBINS J.J. H2638

ROBBINS L. H2639

ROBERT H.M. H2640

ROBERTS H.L. H2215,H2641

ROBERTS S.H. H2642

ROBERTS CF J.R. H1133

ROBERTS HL H2643

ROBERTSON A.H. H2644,H2645

ROBERTSON D. H2646

ROBERTSON H.M. H2647

ROBESPR/M....MAXIMILIAN FRANCOIS ROBESPIERRE

ROBINSN/JH....JAMES HARVEY ROBINSON

ROBINSON A.D. H2648

ROBINSON E.A.G. H2649

ROBINSON J.W. H0607

ROBINSON K. H1302

ROBINSON T.W. H2650

ROBINSON W.C. H2651

ROBINSON/H....HENRY ROBINSON

ROCHE J. H2652

ROCHE J.P. H2653

ROCHET W. H2654

RODBRTUS/C....CARL RODBERTUS

RODNICK D. H2655

RODRIGUEZ M. H2656

ROELOFS H.M. H2657

ROGERS C.B. H2658

ROGERS E.S. H1708

ROGGER H. H2659,H2660

ROGIN M. H2661

ROGOFF N. H2662

ROHEIM G. H2663

ROIG E. H2664

ROKKAN S. H2184,H2665

ROLE....ROLE, REFERENCE GROUP, CROSS-PRESSURES

B09
JUSTINIAN,THE DIGEST (DIGESTA CORPUS JURIS CIVILIS) (2 VOLS.) (TRANS. BY C. H. MONRO). ROMAN/EMP LAW FAM LOC/G LEGIS EDU/PROP CONTROL MARRIAGE OWN ROLE CIVIL/LAW. PAGE 82 H1645 — JURID CT/SYS NAT/G STRATA

N19
GRIFFITH W.,THE PUBLIC SERVICE (PAMPHLET). UK LAW LOC/G NAT/G PARTIC CHOOSE DRIVE ROLE SKILL...CHARTS 20 CIVIL/SERV. PAGE 61 H1222 — ADMIN EFFICIENCY EDU/PROP GOV/REL

B22
TONNIES F.,KRITIK DER OFFENTLICHEN MEINUNG. FRANCE UK CULTURE COM/IND DOMIN PRESS RUMOR ROLE NAT/COMP. PAGE 156 H3114 — SOCIETY SOC ATTIT

B27
HOCART A.M.,KINGSHIP. UNIV CULTURE EX/STRUC TRIBUTE ROUTINE CHOOSE ROLE SOVEREIGN RITUAL 20 KING. PAGE 72 H1441 — CHIEF MYTH IDEA/COMP

B30
BURLAMAQUI J.J.,PRINCIPLES OF NATURAL AND POLITIC LAW (2 VOLS.) (1747-51). EX/STRUC LEGIS AGREE CT/SYS CHOOSE ROLE SOVEREIGN 18 NATURL/LAW. PAGE 24 H0490 — LAW NAT/G ORD/FREE CONCPT

B33
ENSOR R.C.K.,COURTS AND JUDGES IN FRANCE, GERMANY, AND ENGLAND. FRANCE GERMANY UK LAW PROB/SOLV ADMIN ROUTINE CRIME ROLE...METH/COMP 20 CIVIL/LAW. PAGE 46 H0930 — CT/SYS EX/STRUC ADJUD NAT/COMP

C34
BENEDICT R.,"RITUAL" IN ERA SELIGMAN, ENCYCLOPEDIA OF THE SOCIAL SCIENCES." GP/REL...SOC STYLE IDEA/COMP WORSHIP. PAGE 14 H0279 — CULTURE ROUTINE ROLE STRUCT

S41
DENNERY E.,"DEMOCRACY AND THE FRENCH ARMY." FRANCE NAT/G EX/STRUC LEAD REV ROLE 18/20. PAGE 40 H0792 — FORCES POPULISM STRATA CIVMIL/REL

B44
BARKER E.,THE DEVELOPMENT OF PUBLIC SERVICES IN WESTERN WUROPE: 1660-1930. FRANCE GERMANY UK SCHOOL CONTROL REPRESENT ROLE...WELF/ST 17/20. PAGE 11 H0219 — GOV/COMP ADMIN EX/STRUC

B48
COX O.C.,CASTE, CLASS, AND RACE. INDIA WOR+45 WOR-45 SECT TEC/DEV MARRIAGE ROLE MARXISM...MAJORIT NAT/COMP SOC/INTEG 20 NEGRO HINDU. PAGE 34 H0688 — RACE/REL STRUCT STRATA DISCRIM

B48
WOLFE B.D.,THREE WHO MADE A REVOLUTION. USSR CONSTN NAT/G CAP/ISM EDU/PROP CONTROL WAR GP/REL INGP/REL PERS/REL ROLE 20 STALIN/J LENIN/VI TROTSKY/L BOLSHEVISM. PAGE 170 H3398 — BIOG REV LEAD MARXISM

B52
SPICER E.H.,HUMAN PROBLEMS IN TECHNOLOGICAL CHANGE. ECO/UNDEV AGRI INDUS NAT/G ACT/RES LEAD GP/REL INGP/REL ROLE...INT METH 20 CASEBOOK. PAGE 147 H2947 — TEC/DEV CULTURE STRUCT OP/RES

B53
BENDIX R.,CLASS, STATUS AND POWER: A READER IN SOCIAL STRATIFICATION. USA+45 SOCIETY ACT/RES DOMIN ATTIT RIGID/FLEX...PSY SOC CONCPT METH/COMP NAT/COMP 20. PAGE 14 H0273 — STRATA PWR STRUCT ROLE

B53
BIDNEY D.,THEORETICAL ANTHROPOLOGY. DRIVE ROLE ORD/FREE...CONCPT METH/CNCPT MYTH CLASSIF OBS IDEA/COMP METH/COMP BIBLIOG METH 20. PAGE 17 H0331 — CULTURE SOC PSY PHIL/SCI

B55
CRAIG G.A.,THE POLITICS OF THE PRUSSIAN ARMY 1640-1945. CHRIST-17C EUR+WWI MOD/EUR PRUSSIA STRUCT DIPLOM ADMIN REV WAR...SOC BIBLIOG 17/20. PAGE 35 H0694 — FORCES NAT/G ROLE CHIEF

B55
DUVERGER M.,THE POLITICAL ROLE OF WOMEN. FRANCE GERMANY/W NORWAY YUGOSLAVIA STRATA LOBBY AGE ATTIT ROLE...STAT SAMP CHARTS METH/COMP NAT/COMP HYPO/EXP FEMALE/SEX. PAGE 44 H0875 — SEX LEAD PARTIC CHOOSE

B55
FRIEDMAN G.,INDUSTRIAL SOCIETY: THE EMERGENCE OF THE HUMAN PROBLEMS OF AUTOMATION. UNIV CULTURE ECO/DEV TEC/DEV INGP/REL HAPPINESS RATIONAL UTOPIA ROLE...HUM SOC TIME/SEQ 20. PAGE 53 H1064 — AUTOMAT ADJUST ALL/VALS CONCPT

B55
WHEARE K.C.,GOVERNMENT BY COMMITTEE: AN ESSAY ON THE BRITISH CONSTITUTION. UK NAT/G LEGIS INSPECT CONFER ADJUD ADMIN CONTROL TASK EFFICIENCY ROLE POPULISM 20. PAGE 167 H3337 — DELIB/GP CONSTN LEAD GP/COMP

B56
DEUTSCH K.W.,AN INTERDISCIPLINARY BIBLIOGRAPHY ON NATIONALISM, 1935-1953. CULTURE SOCIETY SECT ATTIT HABITAT HEREDITY PERCEPT ROLE WEALTH...METH/CNCPT LING 20. PAGE 40 H0798 — BIBLIOG/A NAT/LISM COLONIAL ADJUST

B56
GOFFMAN E.,THE PRESENTATION OF SELF IN EVERYDAY LIFE. CULTURE INGP/REL ATTIT DRIVE...SOC OBS RECORD 20. PAGE 58 H1154 — PERS/COMP PERSON PERCEPT ROLE

B56
VUCINICH A.,THE SOVIET ACADEMY OF SCIENCES. USSR STRUCT ACADEM NAT/G EDU/PROP ADMIN LEAD ROLE ...BIBLIOG 20 ACADEM/SCI. PAGE 164 H3280 — PHIL/SCI CREATE INTELL PROF/ORG

B56
WEIL E.,PHILOSOPHIE POLITIQUE. UNIV CULTURE RATIONAL PERSON ROLE. PAGE 166 H3326 — SOCIETY NAT/G MORAL

B57
SCARROW H.A.,THE HIGHER PUBLIC SERVICE OF THE COMMONWEALTH OF AUSTRALIA. LAW SENIOR LOBBY ROLE 20 AUSTRAL CIVIL/SERV COMMONWLTH. PAGE 138 H2766 — ADMIN NAT/G EX/STRUC GOV/COMP

S57
COSER L.A.,"SOCIAL CONFLICT AND THE THEORY OF — GP/REL

SOCIAL CHANGE." EUR+WWI CULTURE TEC/DEV PRODUC RIGID/FLEX SOC. PAGE 34 H0673
ROLE SOCIETY ORD/FREE

S57
DEXTER L.A.,"A SOCIAL THEORY OF MENTAL DEFICIENCY." CULTURE PUB/INST PROB/SOLV CRIME PERS/REL STRANGE PERSON SUPEGO SKILL...EPIST SOC/WK HYPO/EXP. PAGE 41 H0814
SOC PSY HEALTH ROLE

B58
DWARKADAS R.,ROLE OF HIGHER CIVIL SERVICE IN INDIA. INDIA ECO/UNDEV LEGIS PROB/SOLV GP/REL PERS/REL ...POLICY WELF/ST DECISION ORG/CHARTS BIBLIOG 20 CIVIL/SERV INTRVN/ECO. PAGE 44 H0876
ADMIN NAT/G ROLE PLAN

B59
DAHRENDORF R.,CLASS AND CLASS CONFLICT IN INDUSTRIAL SOCIETY. LABOR NAT/G COERCE ROLE PLURISM ...POLICY MGT CONCPT CLASSIF. PAGE 37 H0734
VOL/ASSN STRUCT SOC GP/REL

B59
MILLER A.S.,PRIVATE GOVERNMENTS AND THE CONSTITUTION (PAMPHLET). LAW LABOR NAT/G ROLE PWR PLURISM...POLICY DECISION. PAGE 111 H2211
FEDERAL CONSTN VOL/ASSN CONSEN

B59
WILDNER H.,DIE TECHNIK DER DIPLOMATIE. TOP/EX ROLE ORD/FREE...INT/LAW JURID IDEA/COMP NAT/COMP 20. PAGE 168 H3364
DIPLOM POLICY DELIB/GP NAT/G

S60
HALSEY A.H.,"THE CHANGING FUNCTIONS OF UNIVERSITIES IN ADVANCED INDUSTRIAL SOCIETIES." R+D EDU/PROP REPRESENT ROLE ORD/FREE PWR TREND. PAGE 65 H1298
ACADEM CREATE CULTURE ADJUST

S60
TAYLOR M.G.,"THE ROLE OF THE MEDICAL PROFESSION IN THE FORMULATION AND EXECUTION OF PUBLIC POLICY" (BMR)" CANADA NAT/G CONSULT ADMIN REPRESENT GP/REL ROLE SOVEREIGN...DECISION 20 CMA. PAGE 153 H3056
PROF/ORG HEALTH LOBBY POLICY

B61
COBBAN A.,ROUSSEAU AND THE MODERN STATE. SOCIETY DOMIN INGP/REL HAPPINESS ALL/VALS...CON/ANAL 18/20 ROUSSEAU/J. PAGE 30 H0611
ORD/FREE ROLE NAT/G POLICY

B61
ESTEBAN J.C.,IMPERIALISMO Y DESARROLLO ECONOMICO. L/A+17C FINAN INDUS NAT/G ECO/TAC CONTROL ROLE. PAGE 47 H0941
ECO/UNDEV NAT/LISM DIPLOM BAL/PAY

B61
ESTEVEZ A.,ASPECTOS ECONOMICO-FINANCIEROS DE LA CAMPANA SANMARITANA. L/A+17C SPAIN FINAN COLONIAL LEAD ROLE ORD/FREE WEALTH 19 SOUTH/AMER SAN/MARTIN. PAGE 47 H0942
ECO/UNDEV REV BUDGET NAT/G

B61
FULLER J.F.C.,THE CONDUCT OF WAR, 1789-1961. FRANCE RUSSIA SOCIETY NAT/G FORCES PROB/SOLV AGREE NUC/PWR WEAPON PEACE...SOC 18/20 TREATY COLD/WAR. PAGE 54 H1076
WAR POLICY REV ROLE

B61
HUNT E.F.,SOCIAL SCIENCE. DIPLOM ECO/TAC ROUTINE GP/REL DEMAND DISCRIM EFFICIENCY HABITAT ALL/IDEOS ...SOC T 20. PAGE 75 H1497
CULTURE ADJUST STRATA ROLE

B62
DEBUYST F.,LAS CLASES SOCIALES EN AMERICA LATINA. L/A+17C SOCIETY STRUCT WORKER EDU/PROP RACE/REL ATTIT HABITAT ROLE...GEOG SOC NAT/COMP SOC/INTEG 20. PAGE 39 H0780
STRATA GP/REL WEALTH

B62
KRECH D.,INDIVIDUAL IN SOCIETY; A TEXTBOOK OF SOCIAL PSYCHOLOGY. UNIV CULTURE LEAD INGP/REL ATTIT DRIVE PERCEPT ROLE...PHIL/SCI BIBLIOG T. PAGE 88 H1765
PSY SOC SOCIETY PERS/REL

B62
MEGGITT M.J.,DESERT PEOPLE. ECO/UNDEV KIN CREATE PROB/SOLV CONTROL DRIVE ROLE...GEOG SOC MYTH CHARTS BIBLIOG 20 AUSTRAL. PAGE 108 H2159
ADJUST CULTURE INGP/REL HABITAT

S62
ROSE R.,"THE POLITICAL IDEALS OF ENGLISH PARTY ACTIVISTS" (BMR)" UK PARL/PROC PARTIC ATTIT ROLE ...SAMP/SIZ CHARTS 20. PAGE 134 H2673
POL/PAR LOBBY REPRESENT NAT/G

B63
BROGAN D.W.,POLITICAL PATTERNS IN TODAY'S WORLD. FRANCE USA+45 USSR WOR+45 CONSTN STRUCT PLAN DIPLOM ADMIN LEAD ROLE SUPEGO...PHIL/SCI 20. PAGE 21 H0429
NAT/COMP NEW/LIB COM TOTALISM

B63
DALAND R.T.,PERSPECTIVES OF BRAZILIAN PUBLIC ADMINISTRATION (VOL. I). BRAZIL LAW ECO/UNDEV SCHOOL CHIEF TEC/DEV CONFER CONTROL GP/REL ATTIT ROLE PWR...ANTHOL 20. PAGE 37 H0735
ADMIN NAT/G PLAN GOV/REL

B63
MENZEL J.M.,THE CHINESE CIVIL SERVICE: CAREER OPEN TO TALENT? ASIA ROUTINE INGP/REL DISCRIM ATTIT ROLE KNOWL ANTHOL. PAGE 109 H2177
ADMIN NAT/G DECISION ELITES

B63
RUITENBEER H.M.,THE DILEMMA OF ORGANIZATIONAL SOCIETY. CULTURE ECO/DEV MUNIC SECT TEC/DEV EDU/PROP NAT/LISM ORD/FREE...NAT/COMP 20 RIESMAN/D WHYTE/WF MERTON/R MEAD/MARG JASPERS/K. PAGE 136 H2716
PERSON ROLE ADMIN WORKER

B63
TINDALE N.B.,ABORIGINAL AUSTRALIANS. KIN CREATE ROLE...SOC MYTH TREND 20 AUSTRAL ABORIGINES MIGRATION. PAGE 155 H3099
CULTURE DRIVE ECO/UNDEV HABITAT

B64
BERNDT R.M.,THE WORLD OF THE FIRST AUSTRALIANS. S/ASIA ECO/UNDEV WORKER PROB/SOLV EFFICIENCY ROLE ...SOC MYTH WORSHIP AUSTRAL ABORIGINES. PAGE 16 H0311
CULTURE KIN STRUCT DRIVE

B64
DOWNIE R.S.,GOVERNMENT ACTION AND MORALITY: SOME PRINCIPLES AND CONCEPTS OF LIBERAL-DEMOCRACY. UK PARL/PROC ATTIT ROLE...MAJORIT DECISION CONCPT 20. PAGE 42 H0845
NAT/G MORAL POLICY GEN/LAWS

B64
GUTTERIDGE W.,MILITARY INSTITUTIONS AND POWER IN THE NEW STATES. WOR+45 INT/ORG FOR/AID NEUTRAL REV CIVMIL/REL ATTIT ROLE...GOV/COMP 20. PAGE 63 H1258
FORCES DIPLOM ECO/UNDEV ELITES

B64
HARRIS M.,THE NATURE OF CULTURAL THINGS. GP/REL PERS/REL DRIVE HABITAT PERSON ROLE...PHIL/SCI PSY SOC CHARTS BIBLIOG 20. PAGE 67 H1341
CULTURE OBS CLASSIF NEW/IDEA

B64
LATORRE A.,UNIVERSIDAD Y SOCIEDAD. SPAIN EDU/PROP LEAD GP/REL PERS/REL ATTIT KNOWL. PAGE 92 H1837
ACADEM CULTURE ROLE INTELL

B64
MEAD M.,CONTINUITIES IN CULTURAL EVOLUTION. FACE/GP KIN ACT/RES EDU/PROP GP/REL INGP/REL DRIVE HEREDITY ROLE...TIME/SEQ TREND METH SOC/INTEG 20. PAGE 108 H2153
CULTURE SOC PERS/REL

B64
WHEELER-BENNETT J.W.,THE NEMESIS OF POWER (2ND ED.). EUR+WWI GERMANY TOP/EX TEC/DEV ADMIN WAR PERS/REL RIGID/FLEX ROLE ORD/FREE PWR FASCISM 20 HITLER/A. PAGE 167 H3342
FORCES NAT/G GP/REL STRUCT

C64
HARRIS M.,"THE NATURE OF CULTURAL THINGS." GP/REL DRIVE HABITAT PERSON ROLE...PHIL/SCI 20. PAGE 67 H1340
BIBLIOG CULTURE PSY SOC

B65
EDINGER L.J.,KURT SCHUMACHER: A STUDY IN PERSONALITY AND POLITICAL BEHAVIOR. EUR+WWI GERMANY NAT/G DRIVE ROLE PWR SOCISM...BIBLIOG 20 SOC/DEMPAR SCHUMCHR/K. PAGE 44 H0889
TOP/EX LEAD PERSON BIOG

B65
FAGG J.E.,CUBA, HAITI, AND THE DOMINICAN REPUBLIC. CUBA DOMIN/REP HAITI L/A+17C NAT/G DIPLOM ECO/TAC DOMIN CHOOSE AUTHORIT ROLE SOVEREIGN POPULISM 17/20. PAGE 48 H0959
COLONIAL ECO/UNDEV REV GOV/COMP

S65
ASHFORD D.E.,"BUREAUCRATS AND CITIZENS." MOROCCO PAKISTAN PARTIC 20 TUNIS. PAGE 9 H0172
GOV/COMP ADMIN EX/STRUC ROLE

S65
GANGAL S.C.,"SURVEY OF RECENT RESEARCH: INDIA AND THE COMMONWEALTH" INDIA UK NAT/G INT/TRADE PARTIC GOV/REL ROLE 20 CMN/WLTH. PAGE 55 H1095
BIBLIOG POLICY REGION DIPLOM

B66
AGGARWALA R.N.,FINANCIAL COMMITTEES OF THE INDIAN PARLIAMENT: A STUDY IN PARLIAMENTARY CONTROL OVER PUBLIC EXPENDITURE. INDIA FINAN NAT/G ROLE...CHARTS METH/COMP METH 20 PARLIAMENT. PAGE 4 H0078
PARL/PROC BUDGET CONTROL DELIB/GP

B66
BRODERSEN A.,THE SOVIET WORKER: LABOR AND GOVERNMENT IN SOVIET SOCIETY. USSR STRUCT INDUS LABOR PLAN PAY INGP/REL PRODUC...POLICY GEN/LAWS BIBLIOG 20 STALIN/J LENIN/VI BOLSHEVISM KHRUSH/N. PAGE 21 H0425
WORKER ROLE NAT/G MARXISM

B66
FISK E.K.,NEW GUINEA ON THE THRESHOLD; ASPECTS OF SOCIAL, POLITICAL, AND ECONOMIC DEVELOPMENT. AGRI NAT/G INT/TRADE ADMIN ADJUST LITERACY ROLE...CHARTS ANTHOL 20 NEW/GUINEA. PAGE 51 H1015
ECO/UNDEV SOCIETY

B66
FRANK E.,LAWMAKERS IN A CHANGING WORLD. FRANCE UK USSR WOR+45 PARTIC EFFICIENCY ROLE ALL/IDEOS ...CHARTS ANTHOL PARLIAMENT 20 UN COLD/WAR. PAGE 52 H1049
GOV/COMP LEGIS NAT/G DIPLOM

B66
WANG Y.C.,CHINESE INTELLECTUALS AND THE WEST
INTELL

1872-1949. ASIA ELITES LEAD STRANGE ROLE MARXISM ...CHARTS 19/20. PAGE 165 H3301 EDU/PROP CULTURE SOCIETY
B66

ZEINE Z.N.,THE EMERGENCE OF ARAB NATIONALISM (REV. ED.). TURKEY UK NAT/G SECT TEC/DEV LEAD REV WAR AGE/Y ROLE ORD/FREE...TRADIT CHARTS BIBLIOG 20 ARABS OTTOMAN. PAGE 173 H3453 ISLAM NAT/LISM DIPLOM
S66

FLEMING W.G.,"AUTHORITY, EFFICIENCY, AND ROLE STRESS: PROBLEMS IN THE DEVELOPMENT OF EAST AFRICAN BUREAUCRACIES." AFR UGANDA STRUCT PROB/SOLV ROUTINE INGP/REL ROLE...MGT SOC GP/COMP GOV/COMP 20 TANGANYIKA AFRICA/E. PAGE 51 H1024 DOMIN EFFICIENCY COLONIAL ADMIN
B67

FISHEL L.H. JR.,THE NEGRO AMERICAN: A DOCUMENTARY HISTORY. SOCIETY NAT/G ROLE...POLICY ANTHOL 15/20 NEGRO. PAGE 51 H1013 ORD/FREE DISCRIM RACE/REL STRATA
B67

KORNBERG A.,CANADIAN LEGISLATIVE BEHAVIOR: A STUDY OF THE 25TH PARLIAMENT. CANADA NAT/G POL/PAR PARL/PROC CHOOSE INGP/REL ADJUST ANOMIE RIGID/FLEX ...SOC STAND/INT CHARTS SOC/EXP 20 PARLIAMENT. PAGE 88 H1756 ATTIT LEGIS ROLE
B67

LAMBERT W.E.,CHILDREN'S VIEWS OF FOREIGN PEOPLES: A CROSS-NATIONAL STUDY. UNIV CULTURE EDU/PROP RACE/REL ATTIT PERCEPT ROLE...STAT STAND/INT CHARTS GP/COMP NAT/COMP. PAGE 90 H1802 AGE/C STRANGE GP/REL STERTYP
B67

MENARD O.D.,THE ARMY AND THE FIFTH REPUBLIC. ALGERIA FRANCE VIETNAM ELITES STRATA COLONIAL CONTROL LOBBY WAR CIVMIL/REL ROLE PWR...POLICY 20 DEGAULLE/C. PAGE 108 H2169 FORCES ATTIT NAT/G
B67

NASH M.,MACHINE AGE MAYA. GUATEMALA L/A+17C STRUCT AGRI WORKER CREATE INCOME ATTIT RIGID/FLEX ROLE ...IDEA/COMP SOC/EXP WORSHIP 20 INDIAN/AM. PAGE 116 H2315 INDUS CULTURE SOC MUNIC
B67

RAMUNDO B.A.,PEACEFUL COEXISTENCE: INTERNATIONAL LAW IN THE BUILDING OF COMMUNISM. USSR INT/ORG DIPLOM COLONIAL ARMS/CONT ROLE SOVEREIGN...POLICY METH/COMP NAT/COMP BIBLIOG. PAGE 129 H2588 INT/LAW PEACE MARXISM METH/CNCPT
B67

RUDMAN H.C.,THE SCHOOL AND STATE IN THE USSR. COM USSR ACADEM LABOR LOC/G PUB/INST EDU/PROP GP/REL ROLE...POLICY DECISION MGT CHARTS 20. PAGE 136 H2712 SCHOOL ADMIN NAT/G POL/PAR
B67

WISEMAN H.V.,BRITAIN AND THE COMMONWEALTH. EUR+WWI FUT UK ECO/DEV POL/PAR TEC/DEV INT/TRADE LEAD ROLE SOVEREIGN...SOC TREND 20 CMN/WLTH. PAGE 169 H3391 INT/ORG DIPLOM NAT/G NAT/COMP
L67

EGBERT D.D.,"THE IDEA OF 'AVANT-GARDE' IN ART AND POLITICS." USSR CULTURE INTELL POL/PAR CREATE EDU/PROP CONTROL REV ANOMIE DRIVE ROLE...IDEA/COMP 20. PAGE 45 H0895 ART/METH COM ATTIT
L67

GRAUBARD S.R.,"TOWARD THE YEAR 2000: WORK IN PROGRESS." FUT ACADEM SECT DELIB/GP DIPLOM EDU/PROP AGE/Y PERSON ROLE...PSY ANTHOL. PAGE 60 H1199 PREDICT PROB/SOLV SOCIETY CULTURE
L67

HOSHII I.,"JAPAN'S STAKE IN ASIA." ASIA S/ASIA CAP/ISM ECO/TAC ROLE...GEOG 20 CHINJAP. PAGE 74 H1477 DIPLOM REGION NAT/G INT/ORG
S67

ALTBACH P.,"STUDENT POLITICS." GP/REL ATTIT ROLE PWR 20. PAGE 6 H0116 INTELL PARTIC UTIL NAT/G
S67

ANDERSON L.G.,"ADMINISTERING A GOVERNMENT SOCIAL SERVICE" NEW/ZEALND EX/STRUC TASK ROLE 20. PAGE 6 H0129 ADMIN NAT/G DELIB/GP SOC/WK
S67

CAMERON R.,"SOME LESSONS OF HISTORY FOR DEVELOPING NATIONS." WOR+45 WOR-45 FINAN NAT/G WORKER EDU/PROP PARTIC ROLE...DECISION METH/COMP 18/20. PAGE 25 H0511 ECO/UNDEV NAT/COMP POLICY CONCPT
S67

KNOWLES A.F.,"NOTES ON A CANADIAN MASS MEDIA POLICY." CANADA TV CONTROL ROLE...METH/COMP 20. PAGE 87 H1735 EDU/PROP COM/IND NAT/G POLICY
S67

MALAN V.D.,"THE SILENT VILLAGE." KIN MUNIC NEIGH CHOOSE ISOLAT ROLE...SOC INDIAN/AM. PAGE 101 H2027 CULTURE STRUCT PREDICT
S67

MATTHEWS R.O.,"THE SUEZ CANAL DISPUTE* A CASE STUDY IN PEACEFUL SETTLEMENT." FRANCE ISRAEL UAR UK NAT/G CONTROL LEAD COERCE WAR NAT/LISM ROLE ORD/FREE PWR ...INT/LAW UN 20. PAGE 105 H2099 PEACE DIPLOM ADJUD
S67

RONNING C.,"NANKING: 1950." ASIA CANADA CHINA/COM NAT/G PLAN ECO/TAC REV ADJUST 20. PAGE 133 H2667 DIPLOM ROLE PEACE
S67

SCOTT J.W.,"SOURCES OF SOCIAL CHANGE IN COMMUNITY, FAMILY, AND FERTILITY IN A PUERTO RICAN TOWN." PUERT/RICO CULTURE STRUCT ECO/UNDEV INDUS PERS/REL ROLE...SOC STAND/INT. PAGE 141 H2815 FAM MARRIAGE LITERACY ATTIT
S67

SUBRAMANIAM V.,"REPRESENTATIVE BUREAUCRACY: A REASSESSMENT." USA+45 ELITES LOC/G NAT/G ADMIN GOV/REL PRIVIL DRIVE ROLE...POLICY CENSUS 20 CIVIL/SERV BUREAUCRCY. PAGE 150 H3006 STRATA GP/REL MGT GOV/COMP
S67

SZALAY L.B.,"SOVIET DOMESTIC PROPAGANDA AND LIBERALIZATION." COM USSR SOCIETY COM/IND NAT/G POL/PAR EX/STRUC TEC/DEV LEAD ATTIT ROLE MARXISM ...METH/COMP 20. PAGE 151 H3026 EDU/PROP TOTALISM PERSON PERCEPT

ROMAN CATHOLIC....SEE CATH, CATHISM

ROMAN/EMP....ROMAN EMPIRE

N

BURY J.B.,THE CAMBRIDGE ANCIENT HISTORY (12 VOLS.). MEDIT-7 DIPLOM COLONIAL WAR...HUM EGYPT/ANC ROME/EMP BABYLONIA GREECE/ANC. PAGE 25 H0495 BIBLIOG/A SOCIETY CULTURE NAT/G
B09

JUSTINIAN,THE DIGEST (DIGESTA CORPUS JURIS CIVILIS) (2 VOLS.) (TRANS. BY C. H. MONRO). ROMAN/EMP LAW FAM LOC/G LEGIS EDU/PROP CONTROL MARRIAGE OWN ROLE CIVIL/LAW. PAGE 82 H1645 JURID CT/SYS NAT/G STRATA
B11

PHILLIPSON C.,THE INTERNATIONAL LAW AND CUSTOM OF ANCIENT GREECE AND ROME. MEDIT-7 UNIV INTELL SOCIETY STRUCT NAT/G LEGIS EXEC PERSON...CONCPT OBS CON/ANAL ROM/EMP. PAGE 125 H2504 INT/ORG LAW INT/LAW
B23

FRANK T.,A HISTORY OF ROME. MEDIT-7 INTELL SOCIETY LOC/G NAT/G POL/PAR FORCES LEGIS DOMIN LEGIT ALL/VALS...POLICY CONCPT TIME/SEQ GEN/LAWS ROM/EMP ROM/EMP. PAGE 53 H1050 EXEC STRUCT ELITES
B23

GRANT C.F.,STUDIES IN NORTH AFRICA. ALGERIA MOROCCO ROMAN/EMP CULTURE STRUCT NAT/G DIPLOM WAR ...NAT/COMP TUNIS EUROPE. PAGE 60 H1195 ISLAM SECT DOMIN COLONIAL
S32

BEARD C.A.,"THE TEUTONIC ORIGINS OF REPRESENTATIVE GOVERNMENT" UK ROMAN/EMP TAX COERCE PWR IDEA/COMP. PAGE 12 H0247 REPRESENT NAT/G
B39

TAGGART F.J.,ROME AND CHINA. MEDIT-7 INT/ORG NAT/G FORCES LEGIS TOP/EX PLAN PWR SOVEREIGN...CHARTS TOT/POP ROM/EMP. PAGE 152 H3034 ASIA WAR
B47

MCILWAIN C.H.,CONSTITUTIONALISM: ANCIENT AND MODERN. USA+45 ROMAN/EMP LAW CHIEF LEGIS CT/SYS GP/REL ORD/FREE SOVEREIGN...POLICY TIME/SEQ ROMAN/REP EUROPE. PAGE 107 H2135 CONSTN NAT/G PARL/PROC GOV/COMP
B58

SALETORE B.A.,INDIA'S DIPLOMATIC RELATIONS WITH THE WEST. GREECE INDIA CULTURE ETIQUET...IDEA/COMP 3 ROM/EMP PERSIA. PAGE 137 H2739 DIPLOM CONCPT INT/TRADE
B58

SYME R.,COLONIAL ELITES: ROME, SPAIN, AND THE AMERICAS. CHRIST-17C MOD/EUR SPAIN UK USA-45 CULTURE NAT/G CHIEF TOP/EX...GOV/COMP IDEA/COMP NAT/COMP ROM/EMP GIBBON/EDW TOYNBEE/A. PAGE 151 H3022 COLONIAL ELITES DOMIN
B62

TYSKEVIC S.,DIE EINHEIT DER KIRCHE UND BYZANZ (TRANS. BY F.K. LIESNER). ROMAN/EMP ADJUD GP/REL 1/17 CHRISTIAN BYZANTINE. PAGE 157 H3144 SECT NAT/G CATHISM ATTIT
B65

MONTESQUIEU C DE S.,CONSIDERATIONS ON THE CAUSES OF THE GREATNESS OF THE ROMANS AND THEIR DECLINE (1748 TRANS. BY D. LOWENTHAL). ROMAN/EMP SECT CHIEF EX/STRUC FORCES LEGIS DOMIN WAR POPULISM...POLICY REALPOL ROME/ANC. PAGE 112 H2244 NAT/G PWR COLONIAL MORAL
B66

COLEMAN-NORTON P.R.,ROMAN STATE AND CHRISTIAN CHURCH: A COLLECTION OF LEGAL DOCUMENTS TO A.D. 535 (3 VOLS.). CHRIST-17C ROMAN/EMP...ANTHOL DICTIONARY 6 CHRISTIAN CHURCH/STA. PAGE 31 H0630 GP/REL NAT/G SECT LAW
B66

FEINE H.E.,REICH UND KIRCHE. CHRIST-17C MOD/EUR JURID

ROMAN/EMP LAW CHOOSE ATTIT 10/19 CHURCH/STA ROMAN/LAW. PAGE 49 H0982 — SECT NAT/G GP/REL

B79
BRODERICK G.C.,POLITICAL STUDIES. IRELAND UK ROMAN/EMP LAW ACADEM LOC/G NAT/G DIPLOM PARL/PROC SUFF GP/REL LAISSEZ...ANTHOL. PAGE 21 H0424 — CONSTN COLONIAL

ROMAN/LAW....ROMAN LAW

B01
BRYCE J.,STUDIES IN HISTORY AND JURISPRUDENCE (2 VOLS.). ICELAND SOUTH/AFR UK LAW PROB/SOLV SOVEREIGN...PHIL/SCI NAT/COMP ROME/ANC ROMAN/LAW. PAGE 23 H0455 — IDEA/COMP CONSTN JURID

B66
FEINE H.E.,REICH UND KIRCHE. CHRIST-17C MOD/EUR ROMAN/EMP LAW CHOOSE ATTIT 10/19 CHURCH/STA ROMAN/LAW. PAGE 49 H0982 — JURID SECT NAT/G GP/REL

B75
MAINE H.S.,LECTURES ON THE EARLY HISTORY OF INSTITUTIONS. IRELAND UK CONSTN ELITES STRUCT FAM KIN CHIEF LEGIS CT/SYS OWN SOVEREIGN...CONCPT 16 BENTHAM/J BREHON ROMAN/LAW. PAGE 101 H2021 — CULTURE LAW INGP/REL

ROMAN/REP....ROMAN REPUBLIC

B40
MCILWAIN C.H.,CONSTITUTIONALISM, ANCIENT AND MODERN. CHRIST-17C MOD/EUR NAT/G CHIEF PROB/SOLV INSPECT AUTHORIT ORD/FREE PWR...TIME/SEQ ROMAN/REP. PAGE 107 H2134 — CONSTN GEN/LAWS LAW

B47
MCILWAIN C.H.,CONSTITUTIONALISM: ANCIENT AND MODERN. USA+45 ROMAN/EMP LAW CHIEF LEGIS CT/SYS GP/REL ORD/FREE SOVEREIGN...POLICY TIME/SEQ ROMAN/REP EUROPE. PAGE 107 H2135 — CONSTN NAT/G PARL/PROC GOV/COMP

B49
WORMUTH F.D.,THE ORIGINS OF MODERN CONSTITUTIONALISM. GREECE UK LEGIS CREATE TEC/DEV BAL/PWR DOMIN ADJUD REV WAR PWR...JURID ROMAN/REP CROMWELL/O. PAGE 170 H3412 — NAT/G CONSTN LAW

ROMANIA....SEE ALSO COM

N
ACAD RUMANIAN SCI DOC CTR,RUMANIAN SCIENTIFIC ABSTRACTS: SOCIAL SCIENCES. ROMANIA FINAN HABITAT ...ART/METH GEOG HUM JURID PSY 20. PAGE 3 H0059 — BIBLIOG/A CULTURE LING LAW

B61
SCHIEDER T.,DOCUMENTS ON THE EXPULSION OF THE GERMANS FROM EASTERN-CENTRAL-EUROPE (VOL. II/III). COM EUR+WWI GERMANY HUNGARY ROMANIA USSR DIPLOM RACE/REL 20 MIGRATION. PAGE 139 H2785 — GEOG CULTURE

B63
FISCHER-GALATI S.A.,RUMANIA; A BIBLIOGRAPHIC GUIDE (PAMPHLET). ROMANIA INTELL ECO/DEV LABOR SECT WEALTH...GEOG SOC/WK LING 20. PAGE 51 H1012 — BIBLIOG/A NAT/G COM LAW

S64
MARES V.E.,"EAST EUROPE'S SECOND CHANCE." COM EUR+WWI HUNGARY ROMANIA USSR YUGOSLAVIA ECO/UNDEV NAT/G TOP/EX CREATE PLAN TEC/DEV REGION NAT/LISM RIGID/FLEX PWR...CONCPT STAT COMECON 20. PAGE 102 H2047 — VOL/ASSN ECO/TAC

B65
JELAVICH C.,THE BALKANS. ALBANIA BULGARIA GREECE ROMANIA YUGOSLAVIA ECO/UNDEV WAR SOVEREIGN MARXISM 6/20. PAGE 80 H1597 — NAT/LISM NAT/G

S65
VUCINICH W.S.,"WHITHER RUMANIA." COM USSR YUGOSLAVIA NAT/G VOL/ASSN DELIB/GP TOP/EX LEGIT NAT/LISM TOTALISM ATTIT DRIVE RIGID/FLEX ORD/FREE WEALTH SOCISM...TIME/SEQ TREND 20. PAGE 164 H3281 — ECO/DEV CREATE ROMANIA

B66
BECKER J.,BESSARABIEN UND SEIN DEUTSCHTUM. ROMANIA USSR STRUCT INDUS PROF/ORG SECT GP/REL INGP/REL 15/20 BESSARABIA. PAGE 13 H0254 — PROVS CULTURE SOCIETY

B66
BROWN J.F.,THE NEW EASTERN EUROPE. ALBANIA BULGARIA HUNGARY POLAND ROMANIA CULTURE AGRI POL/PAR WAR NAT/LISM MARXISM...CHARTS BIBLIOG 20. PAGE 22 H0444 — DIPLOM COM NAT/G ECO/UNDEV

B66
JACKSON G.D.,COMINTERN AND PEASANT IN EAST EUROPE 1919-1930. BULGARIA COM CZECHOSLVK EUR+WWI POLAND ROMANIA YUGOSLAVIA STRATA AGRI VOL/ASSN DIPLOM CONTROL CROWD WEALTH...POLICY NAT/COMP 20. PAGE 79 H1575 — MARXISM ECO/UNDEV WORKER INT/ORG

S66
SKILLING H.G.,"THE RUMANIAN NATIONAL COURSE." COM EUR+WWI ROMANIA NAT/G ECO/TAC PWR 20. PAGE 145 H2896 — NAT/LISM POLICY DIPLOM MARXISM

B67
NATIONAL SCIENCE FOUNDATION,DIRECTORY OF SELECTED RESEARCH INSTITUTES IN EASTERN EUROPE. BULGARIA CZECHOSLVK HUNGARY POLAND ROMANIA INTELL ACADEM NAT/G ACT/RES 20. PAGE 116 H2323 — INDEX R+D COM PHIL/SCI

S68
BOSSCHERE G D.E.,"A L'EST DU NOUVEAU." CZECHOSLVK HUNGARY POLAND ROMANIA YUGOSLAVIA AGRI CREATE ECO/TAC COERCE GP/REL ATTIT MARXISM SOCISM 20. PAGE 19 H0382 — ORD/FREE COM NAT/G DIPLOM

ROME....ROME

B30
HATTERSLEY A.F.,A SHORT HISTORY OF DEMOCRACY. WOR-45 CONSTN NAT/G SECT DOMIN WAR CHOOSE ORD/FREE PWR...CONCPT GOV/COMP BIBLIOG ATHENS ROME. PAGE 68 H1355 — REPRESENT MAJORIT POPULISM

B35
MARRIOTT J.A.,DICTATORSHIP AND DEMOCRACY. GERMANY GREECE UK CHIEF DIPLOM DOMIN LEGIT PEACE ORD/FREE CONSERVE...TREND ROME HITLER/A. PAGE 103 H2057 — TOTALISM POPULISM PLURIST NAT/G

ROME/ANC....ANCIENT ROME; SEE ALSO ROMAN/EMP, ROMAN/REP

B01
BRYCE J.,STUDIES IN HISTORY AND JURISPRUDENCE (2 VOLS.). ICELAND SOUTH/AFR UK LAW PROB/SOLV SOVEREIGN...PHIL/SCI NAT/COMP ROME/ANC ROMAN/LAW. PAGE 23 H0455 — IDEA/COMP CONSTN JURID

B65
MONTESQUIEU C DE S.,CONSIDERATIONS ON THE CAUSES OF THE GREATNESS OF THE ROMANS AND THEIR DECLINE (1748 TRANS. BY D. LOWENTHAL). ROMAN/EMP SECT CHIEF EX/STRUC FORCES LEGIS DOMIN WAR POPULISM...POLICY REALPOL ROME/ANC. PAGE 112 H2244 — NAT/G PWR COLONIAL MORAL

ROMEIN J. H2666

ROMNEY/GEO....GEORGE ROMNEY

RONNING C. H2667

RONNING C.N. H2668

ROOS H. H2669

ROOSEVLT/F....PRESIDENT FRANKLIN D. ROOSEVELT

B57
LONG H.A.,USURPERS - FOES OF FREE MAN. LAW NAT/G CHIEF LEGIS DOMIN ADJUD REPRESENT GOV/REL ORD/FREE LAISSEZ POPULISM...POLICY 18/20 SUPREME/CT ROOSEVLT/F CONGRESS CON/INTERP. PAGE 98 H1961 — CT/SYS CENTRAL FEDERAL CONSTN

B64
WHITE D.S.,SEEDS OF DISCORD. EUR+WWI FRANCE NAT/G VOL/ASSN FORCES DIPLOM DOMIN NAT/LISM DISPL RIGID/FLEX PWR...RECORD INT BIOG 20 DEGAULLE/C ROOSEVLT/F CHURCHLL/W HULL. PAGE 167 H3347 — TOP/EX ATTIT

B66
DEUTSCHER I.,STALIN: A POLITICAL BIOGRAPHY. EUR+WWI USSR POL/PAR FORCES DIPLOM ADMIN LEAD REV WAR TOTALISM PERSON 20 STALIN/J ROOSEVLT/F LENIN/VI HITLER/A. PAGE 40 H0807 — BIOG MARXISM TOP/EX PWR

B66
KIRKENDALL R.S.,SOCIAL SCIENTISTS AND FARM POLITICS IN THE AGE OF ROOSEVELT. ACADEM PLAN ECO/TAC GIVE ADMIN CONTROL PRODUC...SOC 20 NEW/DEAL ROOSEVLT/F BURAGR/ECO. PAGE 86 H1722 — AGRI INTELL POLICY NAT/G

B67
WARREN S.,THE AMERICAN PRESIDENT. POL/PAR FORCES LEGIS DIPLOM ECO/TAC ADMIN EXEC PWR...ANTHOL 18/20 ROOSEVLT/F KENNEDY/JF JOHNSON/LB TRUMAN/HS WILSON/W. PAGE 165 H3312 — CHIEF LEAD NAT/G CONSTN

ROOSEVLT/T....PRESIDENT THEODORE ROOSEVELT

ROOT W. H2670

ROSBERG C.E. H1063

ROSCIO J.G. H2671

ROSE D.L. H2672

ROSE R. H2673,H2674

ROSE S. H2675

ROSENAU J.N. H2676

ROSENBERG A. H2677

ROSENBERG C.G. H2678

ROSENBLUTH G. H2679

ROSENFARB J. H2680

ROSENTHAL A.H. H2681

ROSENZWEIG F. H2682

ROSKAM K.L. H2683

ROSNER J. H2684

ROSOLIO D. H2685

ROSS A.M. H2686

ROSS E. H1570

ROSS R. H2687

ROSS R.G. H0410

ROSS/EH....EDWARD H. ROSS

ROSSITER C.L. H2688

ROSSMOOR....ROSSMOOR LEISURE WORLD, SEAL BEACH, CAL.

ROSTOW W.W. H2689

ROTBERG R.I. H2690,H2691,H2692,H2693

ROTH A.R. H2694

ROTHCHILD D. H2695

ROUGEMONT D. H2696

ROUSSEAU J.J. H2697,H2698,H2699,H2700

ROUSSEAU/J....JEAN JACQUES ROUSSEAU

B45
CROCE B.,POLITICS AND MORALS. UNIV NAT/G ECO/TAC ORD/FREE MARXISM POPULISM SOCISM...REALPOL 15/20 HEGEL/GWF ROUSSEAU/J. PAGE 35 H0704 — MORAL / GEN/LAWS / IDEA/COMP

B61
COBBAN A.,ROUSSEAU AND THE MODERN STATE. SOCIETY DOMIN INGP/REL HAPPINESS ALL/VALS...CON/ANAL 18/20 ROUSSEAU/J. PAGE 30 H0611 — ORD/FREE / ROLE / NAT/G / POLICY

S63
ROGIN M.,"ROUSSEAU IN AFRICA." AFR MARXISM POPULISM SOCISM 20 ROUSSEAU/J. PAGE 133 H2661 — IDEA/COMP / CULTURE / CONSTN / ORD/FREE

B64
COBBAN A.,ROUSSEAU AND THE MODERN STATE (2ND ED.). FRANCE PROB/SOLV NAT/LISM UTOPIA PERSON MORAL ...EPIST PHIL/SCI SOC IDEA/COMP 18 ROUSSEAU/J BURKE/EDM HOBBES/T HUME/D. PAGE 30 H0612 — GEN/LAWS / INGP/REL / NAT/G / ORD/FREE

B65
GEWIRTH A.,POLITICAL PHILOSOPHY. UNIV SOCIETY NAT/G GP/REL INGP/REL CONSEN PWR...IDEA/COMP GEN/LAWS 17/19 HOBBES/T LOCKE/JOHN MARX/KARL MILL/JS ROUSSEAU/J. PAGE 56 H1118 — ORD/FREE / SOVEREIGN / PHIL/SCI

ROUTINE....PROCEDURAL AND WORK SYSTEMS

N
REVUE FRANCAISE DE SCIENCE POLITIQUE. FRANCE UK ...BIBLIOG/A 20. PAGE 1 H0021 — NAT/G / DIPLOM / CONCPT / ROUTINE

B00
DE JOMINI A.H.,THE ART OF WAR. MOD/EUR NAT/G BAL/PWR DIPLOM DOMIN EXEC ROUTINE COERCE DRIVE PWR SKILL...POLICY CONCPT CHARTS STERTYP 19. PAGE 38 H0755 — PLAN / FORCES / WAR / WEAPON

B00
MAINE H.S.,ANCIENT LAW. MEDIT-7 CULTURE SOCIETY KIN SECT LEGIS LEGIT ROUTINE...JURID HIST/WRIT CON/ANAL TOT/POP VAL/FREE. PAGE 101 H2020 — FAM / LAW

B00
OMAN C.,A HISTORY OF THE ART OF WAR: THE MIDDLE AGES FROM THE FOURTH TO THE FOURTEENTH CENTURY. CHRIST-17C MEDIT-7 CULTURE SOCIETY INT/ORG ROUTINE PERSON...CONT/OBS HIST/WRIT CHARTS VAL/FREE. PAGE 121 H2417 — FORCES / SKILL / WAR

B00
VOLPICELLI Z.,RUSSIA ON THE PACIFIC AND THE SIBERIAN RAILWAY. MOD/EUR ECO/UNDEV INT/ORG FORCES PLAN DOMIN COLONIAL ROUTINE ATTIT ALL/VALS...OBS HIST/WRIT TIME/SEQ TREND CON/ANAL AUD/VIS CHARTS 18/19. PAGE 163 H3261 — NAT/G / ACT/RES / RUSSIA

B02
SEELEY J.R.,THE EXPANSION OF ENGLAND. MOD/EUR S/ASIA UK CULTURE NAT/G FORCES PLAN DOMIN EDU/PROP COLONIAL ROUTINE ATTIT ALL/VALS SOVEREIGN...CONCPT HIST/WRIT PARLIAMENT 18 CMN/WLTH. PAGE 141 H2819 — INT/ORG / ACT/RES / CAP/ISM / INDIA

B06
SUMNER W.G.,FOLKWAYS: STUDY OF THE SOCIOLOGICAL IMPORTANCE OF USAGES, MANNERS, CUSTOMS, MORES, AND MORALS. STRUCT KIN ETIQUET ROUTINE MURDER MARRIAGE PEACE SEX ALL/VALS WEALTH BIBLIOG. PAGE 150 H3008 — CULTURE / SOC / SANCTION / MORAL

B17
HARLOW R.V.,THE HISTORY OF LEGISLATIVE METHODS IN THE PERIOD BEFORE 1825. USA-45 EX/STRUC ADMIN COLONIAL LEAD PARL/PROC ROUTINE...GP/COMP GOV/COMP HOUSE/REP. PAGE 66 H1333 — LEGIS / DELIB/GP / PROVS / POL/PAR

B24
BAGEHOT W.,THE ENGLISH CONSTITUTION AND OTHER POLITICAL ESSAYS. UK DELIB/GP BAL/PWR ADMIN CONTROL EXEC ROUTINE CONSERVE...METH PARLIAMENT 19/20. PAGE 10 H0197 — NAT/G / STRUCT / CONCPT

B25
TEMPERLEY H.,THE FOREIGN POLICY OF CANNING: 1822-1827. MOD/EUR NAT/G TOP/EX EDU/PROP ROUTINE ATTIT RIGID/FLEX SUPEGO PWR SKILL...TIME/SEQ PARLIAMENT 20. PAGE 153 H3058 — PERSON / DIPLOM / UK / BIOG

B27
HOCART A.M.,KINGSHIP. UNIV CULTURE EX/STRUC TRIBUTE ROUTINE CHOOSE ROLE SOVEREIGN RITUAL 20 KING. PAGE 72 H1441 — CHIEF / MYTH / IDEA/COMP

B27
WILLOUGHBY W.F.,PRINCIPLES OF PUBLIC ADMINISTRATION WITH SPECIAL REFERENCE TO THE NATIONAL AND STATE GOVERNMENTS OF THE UNITED STATES. FINAN PROVS CHIEF CONSULT LEGIS CREATE BUDGET EXEC ROUTINE GOV/REL CENTRAL...MGT 20 BUR/BUDGET CONGRESS PRESIDENT. PAGE 169 H3373 — NAT/G / EX/STRUC / OP/RES / ADMIN

B28
BUELL R.,THE NATIVE PROBLEM IN AFRICA. KIN LABOR LOC/G ECO/TAC ROUTINE ORD/FREE...REC/INT KNO/TEST CENSUS TREND CHARTS SOC/EXP STERTYP 20. PAGE 23 H0466 — AFR / CULTURE

B28
SOROKIN P.,CONTEMPORARY SOCIOLOGICAL THEORIES. MOD/EUR UNIV SOCIETY R+D SCHOOL ECO/TAC EDU/PROP ROUTINE ATTIT DRIVE...PSY CONCPT TIME/SEQ TREND GEN/LAWS 20. PAGE 147 H2934 — CULTURE / SOC / WAR

B29
ROBERTS S.H.,HISTORY OF FRENCH COLONIAL POLICY. AFR ASIA L/A+17C S/ASIA CULTURE ECO/DEV ECO/UNDEV FINAN NAT/G PLAN ECO/TAC DOMIN ROUTINE SOVEREIGN...OBS HIST/WRIT TREND CHARTS VAL/FREE 19/20. PAGE 132 H2642 — INT/ORG / ACT/RES / FRANCE / COLONIAL

B31
DEKAT A.D.A.,COLONIAL POLICY. S/ASIA CULTURE EX/STRUC ECO/TAC DOMIN ADMIN COLONIAL ROUTINE SOVEREIGN WEALTH...POLICY MGT RECORD KNO/TEST SAMP. PAGE 39 H0785 — DRIVE / PWR / INDONESIA / NETHERLAND

B33
ENSOR R.C.K.,COURTS AND JUDGES IN FRANCE, GERMANY, AND ENGLAND. FRANCE GERMANY UK LAW PROB/SOLV ADMIN ROUTINE CRIME ROLE...METH/COMP 20 CIVIL/LAW. PAGE 46 H0930 — CT/SYS / EX/STRUC / ADJUD / NAT/COMP

B34
RIDLEY C.E.,THE CITY-MANAGER PROFESSION. CHIEF PLAN ADMIN CONTROL ROUTINE CHOOSE...TECHNIC CHARTS GOV/COMP BIBLIOG 20. PAGE 131 H2624 — MUNIC / EX/STRUC / LOC/G / EXEC

C34
BENEDICT R.,"RITUAL" IN ERA SELIGMAN, ENCYCLOPEDIA OF THE SOCIAL SCIENCES." GP/REL...SOC STYLE IDEA/COMP WORSHIP. PAGE 14 H0279 — CULTURE / ROUTINE / ROLE / STRUCT

B35
TAKEUCHI T.,WAR AND DIPLOMACY IN THE JAPANESE EMPIRE. ASIA ELITES STRATA NAT/G SECT LEGIS ACT/RES PLAN LEGIT PARL/PROC ROUTINE WAR...MGT BIOG CHINJAP TOT/POP 19/20 CHINJAP. PAGE 152 H3038 — EXEC / STRUCT

B37
CLOKIE H.M.,ROYAL COMMISSIONS OF INQUIRY; THE SIGNIFICANCE OF INVESTIGATIONS IN BRITISH POLITICS. UK POL/PAR CONFER ROUTINE...POLICY DECISION TIME/SEQ 16/20. PAGE 30 H0607 — NAT/G / DELIB/GP / INSPECT

B37
PARSONS T.,THE STRUCTURE OF SOCIAL ACTION. UNIV INTELL SOCIETY INDUS MARKET ECO/TAC ROUTINE CHOOSE ALL/VALS...CONCPT OBS BIOG TREND GEN/LAWS 20. PAGE 124 H2471 — CULTURE / ATTIT / CAP/ISM

B39
NICOLSON H.,CURZON: THE LAST PHASE, 1919-1925. UK NAT/G DELIB/GP TOP/EX ROUTINE WAR RIGID/FLEX ...METH/CNCPT 20 CURZON/GN. PAGE 118 H2352
POLICY DIPLOM BIOG

S39
COLE G.D.H.,"NAZI ECONOMICS: HOW DO THEY MANAGE IT?" GERMANY FORCES WORKER BUDGET INT/TRADE ROUTINE COERCE WAR 20 HITLER/A NAZI. PAGE 31 H0622
FASCISM ECO/TAC ATTIT PLAN

C39
REISCHAUER R.,"JAPAN'S GOVERNMENT--POLITICS." CONSTN STRATA POL/PAR FORCES LEGIS DIPLOM ADMIN EXEC CENTRAL...POLICY BIBLIOG 20 CHINJAP. PAGE 131 H2610
NAT/G S/ASIA CONCPT ROUTINE

S40
FAHS C.B.,"POLITICAL GROUPS IN THE JAPANESE HOUSE OF PEERS." ELITES NAT/G ADMIN GP/REL...TREND CHINJAP. PAGE 48 H0961
ROUTINE POL/PAR LEGIS

B41
COHEN E.W.,THE GROWTH OF THE BRITISH CIVIL SERVICE 1780-1939. UK NAT/G SENIOR ROUTINE GOV/REL...MGT METH/COMP BIBLIOG 18/20. PAGE 31 H0616
OP/RES TIME/SEQ CENTRAL ADMIN

S41
ABEL T.,"THE ELEMENT OF DECISION IN THE PATTERN OF WAR." EUR+WWI FUT NAT/G TOP/EX DIPLOM ROUTINE COERCE DISPL PERCEPT PWR...SOC METH/CNCPT HIST/WRIT TREND GEN/LAWS 20. PAGE 3 H0055
TEC/DEV FORCES WAR

B42
SINGTON D.,THE GOEBBELS EXPERIMENT. GERMANY MOD/EUR NAT/G EX/STRUC FORCES CONTROL ROUTINE WAR TOTALISM PWR...ART/METH HUM 20 NAZI GOEBBELS/J. PAGE 144 H2886
FASCISM EDU/PROP ATTIT COM/IND

B48
ROSENFARB J.,FREEDOM AND THE ADMINISTRATIVE STATE. NAT/G ROUTINE EFFICIENCY PRODUC RATIONAL UTIL ...TECHNIC WELF/ST MGT 20 BUREAUCRCY. PAGE 134 H2680
ECO/DEV INDUS PLAN WEALTH

B49
SINGER K.,THE IDEA OF CONFLICT. UNIV INTELL INT/ORG NAT/G PLAN ROUTINE ATTIT DRIVE ALL/VALS...POLICY CONCPT TIME/SEQ. PAGE 144 H2882
ACT/RES SOC

B50
TRAGER F.N.,MARXISM IN SOUTHEAST ASIA. BURMA INDONESIA THAILAND VIETNAM CULTURE SOCIETY NAT/G VOL/ASSN EXEC ROUTINE COERCE ATTIT RIGID/FLEX PWR ...METH/CNCPT TIME/SEQ STERTYP GEN/LAWS MARX/KARL VAL/FREE COLD/WAR NAM 20. PAGE 156 H3126
S/ASIA POL/PAR REV

C50
STOKES W.S.,"HONDURAS: AN AREA STUDY IN GOVERNMENT." HONDURAS NAT/G POL/PAR COLONIAL CT/SYS ROUTINE CHOOSE REPRESENT...GEOG RECORD BIBLIOG 19/20. PAGE 149 H2988
CONSTN LAW L/A+17C ADMIN

B51
LOOS W.A.,RELIGIOUS FAITH AND WORLD CULTURE. INTELL SOCIETY SECT EDU/PROP ROUTINE ATTIT PERSON ALL/VALS MORAL...CONCPT GEN/LAWS VAL/FREE. PAGE 98 H1964
UNIV CULTURE PEACE

B52
WALTERS F.P.,A HISTORY OF THE LEAGUE OF NATIONS. EUR+WWI CONSTN NAT/G LEGIS TOP/EX ACT/RES PLAN EDU/PROP LEGIT ROUTINE ATTIT...TREND LEAGUE/NAT 20 CHINJAP. PAGE 165 H3297
INT/ORG TIME/SEQ NAT/LISM

B53
LEITES N.,A STUDY OF BOLSHEVISM. WOR+45 WOR-45 ELITES SOCIETY INT/ORG NAT/G EX/STRUC EDU/PROP EXEC ROUTINE ATTIT MORAL MARXISM...CONCPT OBS VAL/FREE 20. PAGE 94 H1869
COM POL/PAR USSR TOTALISM

C53
BULNER-THOMAS I.,"THE PARTY SYSTEM IN GREAT BRITAIN." UK CONSTN SECT PRESS CONFER GP/REL ATTIT ...POLICY TREND BIBLIOG 19/20 PARLIAMENT. PAGE 23 H0473
NAT/G POL/PAR ADMIN ROUTINE

B54
FORDE C.D.,AFRICAN WORLDS. AFR CULTURE ROUTINE GP/REL PERS/REL ATTIT DRIVE ALL/VALS...OBS ANTHOL WORSHIP 20. PAGE 52 H1036
SOCIETY KIN SOC

B55
GALLOWAY G.B.,CONGRESS AND PARLIAMENT: THEIR ORGANIZATION AND OPERATION IN THE US AND THE UK: PLANNING PAMPHLET NO. 93. POL/PAR EX/STRUC DEBATE CONTROL LEAD ROUTINE EFFICIENCY PWR...POLICY CONGRESS PARLIAMENT. PAGE 54 H1089
DELIB/GP LEGIS PARL/PROC GOV/COMP

B56
SYKES G.M.,CRIME AND SOCIETY. LAW STRATA STRUCT ACT/RES ROUTINE ANOMIE WEALTH...POLICY SOC/INTEG 20. PAGE 151 H3021
CRIMLGY CRIME CULTURE INGP/REL

L56
EISENTADT S.N.,"POLITICAL STRUGGLE IN BUREAUCRATIC SOCIETIES" ASIA CULTURE ADJUD SANCTION PWR BUREAUCRCY OTTOMAN BYZANTINE. PAGE 45 H0901
ADMIN CHIEF CONTROL ROUTINE

S56
EPSTEIN L.D.,"COHESION OF BRITISH PARLIAMENTARY PARTIES." UK STRUCT ADMIN ROUTINE INGP/REL PWR ...GP/COMP PARLIAMENT. PAGE 47 H0935
NAT/G PARL/PROC POL/PAR

S57
HODGETTS J.E.,"THE CIVIL SERVICE AND POLICY FORMATION." CANADA NAT/G EX/STRUC ROUTINE GOV/REL 20. PAGE 72 H1443
ADMIN DECISION EFFICIENCY POLICY

S57
SPROUT H.,"ENVIRONMENTAL FACTORS IN THE STUDY OF INTERNATIONAL POLITICS." UNIV SOCIETY ECO/DEV NAT/G DELIB/GP TOP/EX ROUTINE ATTIT PERCEPT...POLICY GEOG CONCPT MYTH TIME/SEQ. PAGE 148 H2957
DECISION GEN/LAWS DIPLOM

S58
MAIR L.P.,"REPRESENTATIVE LOCAL GOVERNMENT AS A PROBLEM IN SOCIAL CHANGE." ECO/UNDEV KIN LOC/G NAT/G SCHOOL JUDGE ADMIN ROUTINE REPRESENT RIGID/FLEX RESPECT...CONCPT STERTYP CMN/WLTH 20. PAGE 101 H2025
AFR PWR ELITES

S58
PYE L.W.,"THE NON-WESTERN POLITICAL PROCESS" (BMR)" AFR ASIA ISLAM S/ASIA DIPLOM ADMIN LEAD LOBBY ROUTINE CONSEN...DECISION 20. PAGE 128 H2567
CULTURE POL/PAR NAT/G LOC/G

S58
STAAR R.F.,"ELECTIONS IN COMMUNIST POLAND." EUR+WWI SOCIETY INT/ORG NAT/G POL/PAR LEGIS ACT/RES ECO/TAC EDU/PROP ADJUD ADMIN ROUTINE COERCE TOTALISM ATTIT ORD/FREE PWR 20. PAGE 148 H2963
COM CHOOSE POLAND

S59
ZAUBERMAN A.,"SOVIET BLOC ECONOMIC INTEGRATION." COM CULTURE INTELL ECO/DEV INDUS TOP/EX ACT/RES PLAN ECO/TAC INT/TRADE ROUTINE CHOOSE ATTIT ...TIME/SEQ 20. PAGE 172 H3452
MARKET INT/ORG USSR TOTALISM

B60
ALBI F.,TRATADO DE LOS MODOS DE GESTION DE LAS CORPORACIONES LOCALES. SPAIN FINAN NAT/G BUDGET CONTROL EXEC ROUTINE GOV/REL ORD/FREE SOVEREIGN ...MGT 20. PAGE 5 H0092
LOC/G LAW ADMIN MUNIC

B60
LINDSAY K.,EUROPEAN ASSEMBLIES: THE EXPERIMENTAL PERIOD 1949-1959. EUR+WWI ECO/DEV NAT/G POL/PAR LEGIS TOP/EX ACT/RES PLAN ECO/TAC DOMIN LEGIT ROUTINE ATTIT DRIVE ORD/FREE PWR SKILL...SOC CONCPT TREND CHARTS GEN/LAWS VAL/FREE. PAGE 97 H1932
VOL/ASSN INT/ORG REGION

S60
GROSSMAN G.,"SOVIET GROWTH: ROUTINE, INERTIA, AND PRESSURE." COM STRATA NAT/G DELIB/GP PLAN TEC/DEV ECO/TAC EDU/PROP ADMIN ROUTINE DRIVE WEALTH COLD/WAR 20. PAGE 62 H1236
POL/PAR ECO/DEV USSR

S60
TIRYAKIAN E.A.,"APARTHEID AND POLITICS IN SOUTH AFRICA." SOUTH/AFR CULTURE STRATA ECO/DEV NAT/G POL/PAR ROUTINE CHOOSE GP/REL RACE/REL DISCRIM ATTIT ALL/VALS...CONCPT OBS TIME/SEQ VAL/FREE 20. PAGE 155 H3105
AFR DIPLOM

C60
HAZARD J.N.,"SETTLING DISPUTES IN SOVIET SOCIETY: THE FORMATIVE YEARS OF LEGAL INSTITUTIONS." USSR NAT/G PROF/ORG PROB/SOLV CONTROL CT/SYS ROUTINE REV CENTRAL...JURID BIBLIOG 20. PAGE 68 H1372
ADJUD LAW COM POLICY

C60
SMITH T.E.,"ELECTIONS IN DEVELOPING COUNTRIES: A STUDY OF ELECTORAL PROCEDURES USED IN TOPICAL AFRICA, SOUTH-EAST ASIA..." AFR S/ASIA UK ROUTINE GOV/REL RACE/REL...GOV/COMP BIBLIOG 20. PAGE 146 H2918
ECO/UNDEV CHOOSE REPRESENT ADMIN

B61
AYLMER G.,THE KING'S SERVANTS. UK ELITES CHIEF PAY CT/SYS WEALTH 17 CROMWELL/O CHARLES/I. PAGE 9 H0187
ADMIN ROUTINE EX/STRUC NAT/G

B61
BISHOP D.G.,THE ADMINISTRATION OF BRITISH FOREIGN RELATIONS. EUR+WWI MOD/EUR INT/ORG NAT/G POL/PAR DELIB/GP LEGIS TOP/EX ECO/TAC DOMIN EDU/PROP ADMIN COERCE 20. PAGE 17 H0344
ROUTINE PWR DIPLOM UK

B61
BREWIS T.N.,CANADIAN ECONOMIC POLICY. CANADA BUDGET CAP/ISM INT/TRADE RATION TARIFFS TAX PRICE CONTROL ROUTINE FEDERAL INCOME PRODUC 20 GOLD/STAND. PAGE 20 H0412
ECO/DEV ECO/TAC NAT/G PLAN

B61
BURDETTE F.L.,POLITICAL SCIENCE: A SELECTED BIBLIOGRAPHY OF BOOKS IN PRINT, WITH ANNOTATIONS (PAMPHLET). LAW LOC/G NAT/G POL/PAR PROVS DIPLOM EDU/PROP ADMIN CHOOSE ATTIT 20. PAGE 24 H0479
BIBLIOG/A GOV/COMP CONCPT ROUTINE

B61
HICKS U.K.,DEVELOPMENT FROM BELOW. UK INDUS ADMIN COLONIAL ROUTINE GOV/REL...POLICY METH/CNCPT CHARTS 19/20 CMN/WLTH. PAGE 71 H1414
ECO/UNDEV LOC/G GOV/COMP METH/COMP

B61
HUNT E.F.,SOCIAL SCIENCE. DIPLOM ECO/TAC ROUTINE GP/REL DEMAND DISCRIM EFFICIENCY HABITAT ALL/IDEOS ...SOC T 20. PAGE 75 H1497
CULTURE ADJUST STRATA ROLE

B61
LUNDBERG G.A.,CAN SCIENCE SAVE US. UNIV CULTURE
ACT/RES

INTELL SOCIETY ECO/DEV R+D PLAN EDU/PROP ROUTINE CHOOSE ATTIT PERCEPT ALL/VALS...TREND 20. PAGE 99 H1979
CONCPT TOTALISM

S61
BRZEZINSKI Z.K.,"THE ORGANIZATION OF THE COMMUNIST CAMP." COM CZECHOSLVK COM/IND NAT/G DELIB/GP INT/TRADE DOMIN EDU/PROP EXEC ROUTINE COERCE ATTIT PWR...MGT CONCPT TIME/SEQ CHARTS VAL/FREE 20 TREATY. PAGE 23 H0460
VOL/ASSN DIPLOM USSR

S61
EHRMANN H.W.,"FRENCH BUREAUCRACY AND ORGANIZED INTERESTS" (BMR)" FRANCE NAT/G DELIB/GP ROUTINE ...INT 20 BUREAUCRCY CIVIL/SERV. PAGE 45 H0897
ADMIN DECISION PLURISM LOBBY

S61
RAY J.,"THE EUROPEAN FREE-TRADE ASSOCIATION AND ITS IMPACT ON INDIA'S TRADE." EUR+WWI FRANCE GERMANY INDIA S/ASIA UK NAT/G VOL/ASSN PLAN INT/TRADE ROUTINE WEALTH...STAT CHARTS CMN/WLTH EEC OEEC 20 EFTA. PAGE 130 H2600
ECO/DEV ECO/TAC

S61
TOMASIC D.,"POLITICAL LEADERSHIP IN CONTEMPORARY POLAND." COM EUR+WWI GERMANY NAT/G POL/PAR SECT DELIB/GP PLAN ECO/TAC DOMIN EDU/PROP PWR MARXISM ...MARXIST GEOG MGT CONCPT TIME/SEQ STERTYP 20. PAGE 156 H3111
SOCIETY ROUTINE USSR POLAND

B62
BRETTON H.L.,POWER AND STABILITY IN NIGERIA: THE POLITICS OF DECOLONIZATION. AFR CONSTN INTELL ECO/UNDEV COM/IND KIN NAT/G POL/PAR PROVS VOL/ASSN LEGIS DOMIN EDU/PROP LEGIT EXEC ROUTINE CHOOSE NAT/LISM ATTIT PERCEPT ALL/VALS. PAGE 20 H0411
CULTURE OBS NIGERIA

B62
HO PING-TI,THE LADDER OF SUCCESS IN IMPERIAL CHINA: ASPECTS OF SOCIAL MOBILITY, 1368-1911. INTELL STRATA FAM KIN MUNIC NAT/G PROVS SCHOOL DELIB/GP DOMIN EDU/PROP ADMIN ROUTINE PERSON ALL/VALS...SOC STAT BIOG HIST/WRIT TIME/SEQ VAL/FREE. PAGE 71 H1431
ASIA CULTURE

B62
MEADE J.E.,CASE STUDIES IN EUROPEAN ECONOMIC UNION. BELGIUM EUR+WWI LUXEMBOURG NAT/G INT/TRADE REGION ROUTINE WEALTH...METH/CNCPT STAT CHARTS ECSC TOT/POP OEEC EEC 20. PAGE 108 H2154
INT/ORG ECO/TAC

B62
MUKERJI S.N.,ADMINISTRATION OF EDUCATION IN INDIA. ACADEM LOC/G PROVS ROUTINE...POLICY STAT CHARTS 20. PAGE 114 H2282
SCHOOL ADMIN NAT/G EDU/PROP

L62
COHEN R.,"POWER IN COMPLEX SOCIETIES IN AFRICA." AFR KIN MUNIC POL/PAR DELIB/GP DOMIN ROUTINE ATTIT ALL/VALS...SOC STAT OBS INT QU CHARTS ANTHOL 20. PAGE 31 H0617
CULTURE STRATA ELITES

L62
MURACCIOLE L.,"LA BANQUE CENTRALE DES ETATS DE L'AFRIQUE DE L'OUEST." AFR LAW ECO/UNDEV INT/ORG NAT/G CONSULT ECO/TAC ROUTINE...CHARTS 20. PAGE 115 H2292
ISLAM FINAN INT/TRADE

S62
IOVTCHOUK M.T.,"ON SOME THEORETICAL PRINCIPLES AND METHODS OF SOCIOLOGICAL INVESTIGATIONS (IN RUSSIAN)." FUT USA+45 STRATA R+D NAT/G POL/PAR TOP/EX ACT/RES PLAN ECO/TAC EDU/PROP ROUTINE ATTIT RIGID/FLEX MARXISM SOCISM...MARXIST METH/CNCPT OBS TREND NAT/COMP GEN/LAWS 20. PAGE 78 H1564
COM ECO/DEV CAP/ISM USSR

S62
MONNIER J.P.,"LA SUCCESSION D'ETATS EN MATIERE DE RESPONSABILITE INTERNATIONALE." UNIV CONSTN INTELL SOCIETY ADJUD ROUTINE PERCEPT SUPEGO...GEN/LAWS TOT/POP 20. PAGE 112 H2240
NAT/G JURID INT/LAW

S62
MURACCIOLE L.,"LES CONSTITUTIONS DES ETATS AFRICAINS D'EXPRESSION FRANCAISE: LA CONSTITUTION DU 16 AVRIL 1962 DE LA REPUBLIQUE DU" AFR CHAD CHIEF LEGIS LEGIT COLONIAL EXEC ROUTINE ORD/FREE SOVEREIGN...SOC CONCPT 20. PAGE 115 H2291
NAT/G CONSTN

S62
PIQUEMAL M.,"LES PROBLEMES DES UNIONS D'ETATS EN AFRIQUE NOIRE." FRANCE SOCIETY INT/ORG NAT/G DELIB/GP PLAN LEGIT ADMIN COLONIAL ROUTINE ATTIT ORD/FREE PWR...GEOG METH/CNCPT 20. PAGE 126 H2515
AFR ECO/UNDEV REGION

S62
WALTER E.,"VERS UNE CLASSIFICATION SCIENTIFIQUE DE LA SOCIOLOGIA." UNIV CULTURE INTELL SOCIETY R+D ACT/RES LEGIT ROUTINE ATTIT KNOWL...JURID MGT TREND GEN/LAWS 20. PAGE 165 H3296
PLAN CONCPT

B63
DUE J.F.,STATE SALES TAX ADMINISTRATION. OP/RES BUDGET PAY ADMIN EXEC ROUTINE COST EFFICIENCY PROFIT...CHARTS METH/COMP 20. PAGE 43 H0855
PROVS TAX STAT GOV/COMP

B63
KOGAN N.,THE POLITICS OF ITALIAN FOREIGN POLICY. EUR+WWI LEGIS DOMIN LEGIT EXEC PWR RESPECT SKILL ...POLICY DECISION HUM SOC METH/CNCPT OBS INT CHARTS 20. PAGE 87 H1737
NAT/G ROUTINE DIPLOM ITALY

B63
MAYNE R.,THE COMMUNITY OF EUROPE. UK CONSTN NAT/G CONSULT DELIB/GP CREATE PLAN ECO/TAC LEGIT ADMIN ROUTINE ORD/FREE PWR WEALTH...CONCPT TIME/SEQ EEC EURATOM 20. PAGE 105 H2107
EUR+WWI INT/ORG REGION

B63
MENZEL J.M.,THE CHINESE CIVIL SERVICE: CAREER OPEN TO TALENT? ASIA ROUTINE INGP/REL DISCRIM ATTIT ROLE KNOWL ANTHOL. PAGE 109 H2177
ADMIN NAT/G DECISION ELITES

B63
ROBERTSON A.H.,HUMAN RIGHTS IN EUROPE. CONSTN SOCIETY INT/ORG NAT/G VOL/ASSN DELIB/GP ACT/RES PLAN ADJUD REGION ROUTINE ATTIT LOVE ORD/FREE RESPECT...JURID SOC CONCPT SOC/EXP UN 20. PAGE 132 H2645
EUR+WWI PERSON

B63
SCHECHTMAN J.B.,THE REFUGEE IN THE WORLD: DISPLACEMENT AND INTEGRATION. AFR ASIA EUR+WWI ISLAM L/A+17C S/ASIA CULTURE STRATA LOC/G EX/STRUC PLAN ECO/TAC ROUTINE...CONCPT TIME/SEQ VAL/FREE 20. PAGE 139 H2779
INT/ORG SOC

B63
SKLAR R.L.,NIGERIAN POLITICAL PARTIES: POWER IN AN EMERGENT AFRICAN NATION. AFR EUR+WWI CULTURE STRATA NAT/G DELIB/GP EX/STRUC LEGIS DOMIN EDU/PROP ROUTINE CHOOSE ATTIT PERCEPT ORD/FREE PWR...SOC CONCPT OBS TOT/POP VAL/FREE. PAGE 145 H2898
POL/PAR SOCIETY NAT/LISM NIGERIA

B63
THUCYDIDES,THE PELOPONESIAN WARS. MEDIT-7 CULTURE INT/ORG NAT/G FORCES TOP/EX PLAN ROUTINE PWR ...CONCPT. PAGE 155 H3091
ATTIT COERCE WAR

B63
US ATOMIC ENERGY COMMISSION,ATOMIC ENERGY IN THE SOVIET UNION: TRIP REPORT OF THE US ATOMIC ENERGY DELEGATION, MAY 1933. USSR R+D NAT/G CONSULT CREATE DIPLOM ADMIN ROUTINE EFFICIENCY PRODUC KNOWL SKILL ...NAT/COMP 20 AEC TRAVEL TREATY. PAGE 159 H3176
METH/COMP OP/RES TEC/DEV NUC/PWR

L63
FREUND G.,"ADENAUER AND THE FUTURE OF GERMANY." EUR+WWI FUT GERMANY/W FORCES LEGIT ADMIN ROUTINE ATTIT DRIVE PERSON PWR...POLICY TIME/SEQ TREND VAL/FREE 20 ADENAUER/K. PAGE 53 H1058
NAT/G BIOG DIPLOM GERMANY

B64
COLLINS B.E.,A SOCIAL PSYCHOLOGY OF GROUP PROCESSES FOR DECISION-MAKING. PROB/SOLV ROUTINE...SOC CHARTS HYPO/EXP. PAGE 32 H0632
FACE/GP DECISION NAT/G INDUS

B64
CULLINGWORTH J.B.,TOWN AND COUNTRY PLANNING IN ENGLAND AND WALES. UK LAW SOCIETY CONSULT ACT/RES ADMIN ROUTINE LEISURE INGP/REL ADJUST PWR...GEOG 20 OPEN/SPACE URBAN/RNWL. PAGE 36 H0718
MUNIC PLAN NAT/G PROB/SOLV

B64
FRANCK T.M.,EAST AFRICAN UNITY THROUGH LAW. MALAWI TANZANIA UGANDA UK ZAMBIA CONSTN INT/ORG NAT/G ADMIN ROUTINE TASK NAT/LISM ATTIT SOVEREIGN ...RECORD IDEA/COMP NAT/COMP. PAGE 52 H1048
AFR FEDERAL REGION INT/LAW

B64
JUCKER-FLEETWOOD E.,MONEY AND FINANCE IN AFRICA. ISLAM ECO/UNDEV SERV/IND NAT/G EX/STRUC PLAN ECO/TAC ROUTINE WEALTH...MGT TOT/POP 20. PAGE 82 H1639
AFR FINAN

B64
PINNICK A.W.,COUNTRY PLANNERS IN ACTION. UK FINAN SERV/IND NAT/G CONSULT DELIB/GP PRICE CONTROL ROUTINE LEISURE AGE/C...GEOG 20 URBAN/RNWL. PAGE 126 H2512
MUNIC PLAN INDUS ATTIT

B64
VALEN H.,POLITICAL PARTIES IN NORWAY. NORWAY ACADEM PARTIC ROUTINE INGP/REL KNOWL...QU 20. PAGE 161 H3220
LOC/G POL/PAR PERSON

B64
WAINHOUSE D.W.,REMNANTS OF EMPIRE: THE UNITED NATIONS AND THE END OF COLONIALISM. FUT PORTUGAL WOR+45 NAT/G CONSULT DOMIN LEGIT ADMIN ROUTINE ATTIT ORD/FREE...POLICY JURID RECORD INT TIME/SEQ UN CMN/WLTH 20. PAGE 164 H3287
INT/ORG TREND COLONIAL

L64
HAAS E.B.,"ECONOMICS AND DIFFERENTIAL PATTERNS OF POLITICAL INTEGRATION: PROJECTIONS ABOUT UNITY IN LATIN AMERICA." SOCIETY NAT/G DELIB/GP ACT/RES CREATE PLAN ECO/TAC REGION ROUTINE ATTIT DRIVE PWR WEALTH...CONCPT TREND CHARTS LAFTA 20. PAGE 63 H1266
L/A+17C INT/ORG MARKET

S64
GROSS J.A.,"WHITEHALL AND THE COMMONWEALTH." EUR+WWI MOD/EUR INT/ORG NAT/G CONSULT DELIB/GP LEGIS DOMIN ADMIN COLONIAL ROUTINE PWR CMN/WLTH 19/20. PAGE 62 H1233
EX/STRUC ATTIT TREND

S64
NASH M.,"SOCIAL PREREQUISITES TO ECONOMIC GROWTH IN LATIN AMERICA AND SOUTHEAST ASIA." L/A+17C S/ASIA CULTURE SOCIETY ECO/UNDEV AGRI INDUS NAT/G PLAN TEC/DEV EDU/PROP ROUTINE ALL/VALS...POLICY RELATIV
ECO/DEV PERCEPT

SOC NAT/COMP WORK TOT/POP 20. PAGE 116 H2314

S64
SAAB H.,"THE ARAB SEARCH FOR A FEDERAL UNION." SOCIETY INT/ORG NAT/G DELIB/GP FORCES ACT/RES TEC/DEV ECO/TAC DOMIN LEGIT REGION ROUTINE ATTIT DRIVE RIGID/FLEX ALL/VALS...SOC CONCPT NEW/IDEA TIME/SEQ TREND. PAGE 136 H2726 — ISLAM PLAN

C64
SCOTT R.E.,"MEXICAN GOVERNMENT IN TRANSITION (REV ED)" CULTURE STRUCT POL/PAR CHIEF ADMIN LOBBY REV CHOOSE GP/REL DRIVE...BIBLIOG METH 20 MEXIC/AMER. PAGE 141 H2816 — NAT/G L/A+17C ROUTINE CONSTN

B65
EDELMAN M.,THE POLITICS OF WAGE-PRICE DECISIONS. GERMANY ITALY NETHERLAND UK INDUS LABOR POL/PAR PROB/SOLV BARGAIN PRICE ROUTINE BAL/PAY COST DEMAND 20. PAGE 44 H0888 — GOV/COMP CONTROL ECO/TAC PLAN

B65
HADWIGER D.F.,PRESSURES AND PROTEST. NAT/G LEGIS PLAN LEAD PARTIC ROUTINE ATTIT POLICY. PAGE 63 H1273 — AGRI GP/REL LOBBY CHOOSE

B65
HANSER C.J.,GUIDE TO DECISION: ROYAL COMMISSION. UK INTELL EXTR/IND SCHOOL PROB/SOLV EXEC ROUTINE CHOOSE GOV/REL GP/REL HEALTH...CHARTS 20. PAGE 66 H1318 — NAT/G DELIB/GP EX/STRUC PWR

B65
LAMBIRI I.,SOCIAL CHANGE IN A GREEK COUNTRY TOWN. GREECE FAM PROB/SOLV ROUTINE TASK LEISURE INGP/REL CONSEN ORD/FREE...SOC INT QU CHARTS 20. PAGE 90 H1803 — INDUS WORKER CULTURE NEIGH

B65
PEASLEE A.J.,CONSTITUTIONS OF NATIONS* THIRD REVISED EDITION (VOLUME I* AFRICA). LAW EX/STRUC LEGIS TOP/EX LEGIT CT/SYS ROUTINE ORD/FREE PWR SOVEREIGN...CON/ANAL CHARTS. PAGE 124 H2481 — AFR CHOOSE CONSTN NAT/G

S65
HUGHES T.L.,"SCHOLARS AND FOREIGN POLICY* VARIETIES OF RESEARCH EXPERIENCE." COM/IND DIPLOM ADMIN EXEC ROUTINE...MGT OBS CONGRESS PRESIDENT CAMELOT. PAGE 75 H1491 — ACT/RES ACADEM CONTROL NAT/G

S65
THOMAS F.C. JR.,"THE PEACE CORPS IN MOROCCO." CULTURE MUNIC PROVS CREATE ROUTINE TASK ADJUST STRANGE...OBS PEACE/CORP. PAGE 154 H3077 — MOROCCO FRANCE FOR/AID EDU/PROP

B66
BHALERAO C.N.,PUBLIC SERVICE COMMISSIONS OF INDIA: A STUDY. INDIA SERV/IND EX/STRUC ROUTINE CHOOSE GOV/REL INGP/REL...KNO/TEST EXHIBIT 20. PAGE 16 H0326 — NAT/G OP/RES LOC/G ADMIN

B66
DOBB M.,SOVIET ECONOMIC DEVELOPMENT SINCE 1917. USSR ECO/DEV ECO/UNDEV LABOR NAT/G TEC/DEV ECO/TAC ROUTINE PRODUC MARXISM 20. PAGE 41 H0829 — PLAN INDUS WORKER

B66
DUNCOMBE H.S.,COUNTY GOVERNMENT IN AMERICA. USA+45 FINAN MUNIC ADMIN ROUTINE GOV/REL...GOV/COMP 20. PAGE 43 H0863 — LOC/G PROVS CT/SYS TOP/EX

B66
MARTIN L.W.,DIPLOMACY IN MODERN EUROPEAN HISTORY. EUR+WWI MOD/EUR INT/ORG NAT/G EX/STRUC ROUTINE WAR PEACE TOTALISM PWR 15/20 COLD/WAR EUROPE/W. PAGE 103 H2064 — DIPLOM POLICY

B66
ZINKIN T.,CHALLENGES IN INDIA. INDIA PAKISTAN LAW AGRI FINAN INDUS TOP/EX TEC/DEV CONTROL ROUTINE ORD/FREE PWR 20 NEHRU/J SHASTRI/LB CIVIL/SERV. PAGE 173 H3458 — NAT/G ECO/TAC POLICY ADMIN

S66
FLEMING W.G.,"AUTHORITY, EFFICIENCY, AND ROLE STRESS: PROBLEMS IN THE DEVELOPMENT OF EAST AFRICAN BUREAUCRACIES." AFR UGANDA STRUCT PROB/SOLV ROUTINE INGP/REL ROLE...MGT SOC GP/COMP GOV/COMP 20 TANGANYIKA AFRICA/E. PAGE 51 H1024 — DOMIN EFFICIENCY COLONIAL ADMIN

S67
DIAMANT A.,"EUROPEAN MODELS OF BUREAUCRACY AND DEVELOPMENT." EX/STRUC PLAN ADMIN CONTROL ROUTINE GOV/REL CENTRAL...DECISION TIME/SEQ CHARTS. PAGE 41 H0818 — NAT/G EQUILIB ACT/RES NAT/COMP

S67
LEVCIK B.,"WAGES AND EMPLOYMENT PROBLEMS IN THE NEW SYSTEM OF PLANNED MANAGEMENT IN CZECHOSLOVAKIA." CZECHOSLVK EUR+WWI NAT/G OP/RES PLAN ADMIN ROUTINE INGP/REL CENTRAL EFFICIENCY PRODUC DECISION. PAGE 95 H1895 — MARXISM WORKER MGT PAY

ROWAT D.C. H2701

ROWE C. H2702

ROWE J.W. H2703

ROWLAND J. H2704

ROY N.C. H2705

ROY/MN....M.N. ROY

ROYAL AIR FORCE....SEE RAF

ROYAL GEOGRAPHICAL SOCIETY H2706

ROYAL/COMM....ROYAL COMMISSION (CANADA)

S67
DOERN G.B.,"THE ROYAL COMMISSIONS IN THE GENERAL POLICY PROCESS AND IN FEDERAL-PROVINCIAL RELATIONS." CANADA CONSTN ACADEM PROVS CONSULT DELIB/GP LEGIS ACT/RES PROB/SOLV CONFER CONTROL EFFICIENCY...METH/COMP 20 SENATE ROYAL/COMM. PAGE 42 H0832 — R+D EX/STRUC GOV/REL NAT/G

RUBINSTEIN A.Z. H2708,H2709

RUCKER B.W. H2710

RUDE G. H2711

RUDMAN H.C. H2712

RUDOLPH L.I. H2713

RUDOLPH S. H2713

RUDY Z. H2714

RUEF/ABE....ABRAHAM RUEF

RUEFF J. H2715

RUITENBEER H.M. H2716

RULE J. H3095

RULES/COMM....RULES COMMITTEES OF CONGRESS

RUMEU DE ARMAS A. H2717

RUMMEL R.J. H2718

RUMOR....SEE ALSO PERS/REL

B22
TONNIES F.,KRITIK DER OFFENTLICHEN MEINUNG. FRANCE UK CULTURE COM/IND DOMIN PRESS RUMOR ROLE NAT/COMP. PAGE 156 H3114 — SOCIETY SOC ATTIT

B45
HORN O.B.,BRITISH PUBLIC OPINION AND THE FIRST PARTITION OF POLAND. POLAND UK LEGIS PRESS RUMOR CONTROL PARTIC NAT/LISM SOVEREIGN 18/19. PAGE 73 H1469 — DIPLOM POLICY ATTIT NAT/G

B56
DE JONG L.,THE GERMAN FIFTH COLUMN IN THE SECOND WORLD WAR. EUR+WWI GERMANY NAT/G DIPLOM ATTIT FASCISM...MYTH 20 NAZI. PAGE 38 H0756 — EDU/PROP WAR RUMOR

B58
DUCLOUX L.,FROM BLACKMAIL TO TREASON. FRANCE PLAN DIPLOM EDU/PROP PRESS RUMOR NAT/LISM...CRIMLGY 20. PAGE 43 H0853 — COERCE CRIME NAT/G PWR

B61
FIRTH R.,HISTORY AND TRADITIONS OF TIKOPIA. S/ASIA KIN SECT RUMOR WAR...MYTH WORSHIP 20 POLYNESIA. PAGE 50 H1008 — CULTURE STRUCT HUM

B65
VON STACKELBERG K.,ALLE KRETER LUGEN VORURTEILE UBER MENSCHEN UND VOLKER. DIPLOM DOMIN RUMOR NAT/LISM PERSON KNOWL...SOC QU BIBLIOG 20. PAGE 164 H3277 — NAT/COMP ATTIT EDU/PROP SAMP

RURAL....RURAL AREAS, PEOPLE, ETC.

RUSK/DEAN....DEAN RUSK

RUSKIN/J....JOHN RUSKIN

RUSSELL/B....BERTRAND RUSSELL

B60
MANIS J.G.,MAN AND SOCIETY. STRATA LEAD INGP/REL PERS/REL ATTIT PWR...PSY ANTHOL T SOC/INTEG MARX/KARL MILL/JS FREUD/S CHURCHLL/W SPENCER/H RUSSELL/B. PAGE 102 H2036 — SOC SOCIETY STRUCT CULTURE

RUSSETT B.M. H2719

RUSSIA....PRE-REVOLUTIONARY RUSSIA; SEE ALSO APPROPRIATE TIME/SPACE/CULTURE INDEX

N
NEUE POLITISCHE LITERATUR. AFR ASIA EUR+WWI GERMANY RUSSIA SOCIETY ECO/DEV ECO/UNDEV PLAN PROB/SOLV LEAD MARXISM...PHIL/SCI CONCPT 20. PAGE 1 H0008
BIBLIOG DIPLOM COM NAT/G

B00
VOLPICELLI Z.,RUSSIA ON THE PACIFIC AND THE SIBERIAN RAILWAY. MOD/EUR ECO/UNDEV INT/ORG FORCES PLAN DOMIN COLONIAL ROUTINE ATTIT ALL/VALS...OBS HIST/WRIT TIME/SEQ TREND CON/ANAL AUD/VIS CHARTS 18/19. PAGE 163 H3261
NAT/G ACT/RES RUSSIA

B18
KERNER R.J.,SLAVIC EUROPE: A SELECTED BIBLIOGRAPHY IN THE WESTERN EUROPEAN LANGUAGES. BULGARIA CZECHOSLVK GERMANY/E POLAND RUSSIA YUGOSLAVIA NAT/G DIPLOM MARXISM...LING 19/20. PAGE 85 H1695
BIBLIOG SOCIETY CULTURE COM

B24
MARTIN B.K.,THE TRIUMPH OF LORD PALMERSTON. MOD/EUR RUSSIA TURKEY UK NAT/G DELIB/GP 19. PAGE 103 H2061
ATTIT WAR POL/PAR POLICY

B37
BERDYAEV N.,THE ORIGIN OF RUSSIAN COMMUNISM. MOD/EUR RUSSIA USSR INTELL SECT REV...ANARCH HUM 19/20 ORTHO/RUSS COM/PARTY CHRISTIAN. PAGE 15 H0294
MARXISM NAT/LISM CULTURE ATTIT

B39
KERNER R.J.,NORTHEAST ASIA: A SELECTED BIBLIOGRAPHY (2 VOLS.). KOREA RUSSIA NAT/G DIPLOM...GEOG 19/20 CHINJAP. PAGE 85 H1696
BIBLIOG ASIA SOCIETY CULTURE

B49
GORER G.,THE PEOPLE OF GREAT RUSSIA: A PSYCHOLOGICAL STUDY. RUSSIA USSR NAT/G DIPLOM LEAD AGE/C ANOMIE ATTIT DRIVE...POLICY 20. PAGE 59 H1182
ISOLAT PERSON PSY SOCIETY

B50
GLEASON J.H.,THE GENESIS OF RUSSOPHOBIA IN GREAT BRITAIN: A STUDY OF THE INTERACTION OF POLICY AND OPINION. ASIA RUSSIA UK NAT/G AGREE CONTROL REV WAR LOVE PWR TREATY 19. PAGE 57 H1142
DIPLOM POLICY DOMIN COLONIAL

B52
KOLARZ W.,RUSSIA AND HER COLONIES. COM RUSSIA LAW CULTURE ECO/DEV KIN LOC/G SECT TEC/DEV ECO/TAC EDU/PROP REGION COERCE ATTIT PWR SOVEREIGN...SOC TIME/SEQ CON/ANAL VAL/FREE 19/20. PAGE 88 H1749
NAT/G DOMIN USSR COLONIAL

B54
KOLARZ W.,THE PEOPLES OF THE SOVIET FAR EAST. RUSSIA USSR STRUCT LEAD ISOLAT NAT/LISM...CHARTS 20. PAGE 88 H1750
COLONIAL RACE/REL ADJUST CULTURE

B55
KOHN H.,THE MIND OF MODERN RUSSIA. COM MOD/EUR USSR SOCIETY NAT/G SECT FORCES TOP/EX COERCE TOTALISM DRIVE RIGID/FLEX PWR SOVEREIGN...CONCPT TIME/SEQ WORK. PAGE 87 H1742
INTELL GEN/LAWS SOCISM RUSSIA

B57
PARK A.G.,BOLSHEVISM IN TURKESTAN 1917-1927. COM RUSSIA USSR CULTURE AGRI SECT DOMIN GP/REL INGP/REL NAT/LISM...BIBLIOG 20 TURKESTAN. PAGE 123 H2467
REV POLICY MARXISM ISLAM

B58
SCOTT D.J.R.,RUSSIAN POLITICAL INSTITUTIONS. RUSSIA USSR CONSTN AGRI DELIB/GP PLAN EDU/PROP CONTROL CHOOSE EFFICIENCY ATTIT MARXISM...BIBLIOG/A 13/20. PAGE 141 H2813
NAT/G POL/PAR ADMIN DECISION

B60
BLACK C.E.,THE TRANSFORMATION OF RUSSIAN SOCIETY. COM MOD/EUR RUSSIA SOCIETY EDU/PROP COERCE ALL/VALS 19/20. PAGE 17 H0349
CULTURE RIGID/FLEX USSR

B60
PIERCE R.A.,RUSSIAN CENTRAL ASIA, 1867-1917. ASIA RUSSIA CULTURE AGRI INDUS EDU/PROP REV NAT/LISM ...CHARTS BIBLIOG 19/20 BOLSHEVISM INTERVENT. PAGE 125 H2509
COLONIAL DOMIN ADMIN ECO/UNDEV

B60
ZENKOVSKY S.A.,PAN-TURKISM AND ISLAM IN RUSSIA. ASIA RUSSIA USSR CULTURE POL/PAR DOMIN REV GP/REL MARXISM...LING GP/COMP BIBLIOG 19/20 TURKIC. PAGE 173 H3454
SECT NAT/LISM COM ISLAM

B61
ALSTON P.L.,STATE EDUCATION AND SOCIAL CHANGE IN THE RUSSIAN EMPIRE 1871-1914 (PAPER). RUSSIA ELITES PROF/ORG EDU/PROP CONTROL PRIVIL AGE/Y...BIBLIOG 19/20. PAGE 6 H0115
SCHOOL SOCIETY NAT/G GP/REL

B61
FULLER J.F.C.,THE CONDUCT OF WAR, 1789-1961. FRANCE RUSSIA SOCIETY NAT/G FORCES PROB/SOLV AGREE NUC/PWR WEAPON PEACE...SOC 18/20 TREATY COLD/WAR. PAGE 54 H1076
WAR POLICY REV ROLE

B61
LENIN V.I.,WHAT IS TO BE DONE? (1902). RUSSIA LABOR NAT/G POL/PAR WORKER CAP/ISM ECO/TAC ADMIN PARTIC ...MARXIST IDEA/COMP GEN/LAWS 19/20. PAGE 94 H1881
EDU/PROP PRESS MARXISM METH/COMP

B61
MOLLAU G.,INTERNATIONAL COMMUNISM AND WORLD REVOLUTION: HISTORY AND METHODS. RUSSIA USSR INT/ORG NAT/G POL/PAR VOL/ASSN FORCES BAL/PWR DIPLOM EXEC REGION WAR ATTIT PWR MARXISM...CONCPT TIME/SEQ COLD/WAR 19/20. PAGE 112 H2237
COM REV

B61
MONAS S.,THE THIRD SECTION: POLICE AND SOCIETY IN RUSSIA UNDER NICHOLAS I. MOD/EUR RUSSIA ELITES STRUCT NAT/G EX/STRUC ADMIN CONTROL PWR CONSERVE ...DECISION 19 NICHOLAS/I. PAGE 112 H2238
ORD/FREE COM FORCES COERCE

S61
ANDERSON O.,"ECONOMIC WARFARE IN THE CRIMEAN WAR." EUR+WWI MOD/EUR NAT/G ACT/RES WAR DRIVE PWR 19/20. PAGE 6 H0130
ECO/TAC UK RUSSIA

B62
JACKSON W.A.D.,RUSSO-CHINESE BORDERLANDS. ASIA COM USSR NAT/G PROVS EX/STRUC FORCES DOMIN COERCE PEACE ATTIT PWR SOVEREIGN WEALTH...CONCPT TREND CHARTS STERTYP VAL/FREE. PAGE 79 H1576
GEOG DIPLOM RUSSIA

B63
MONGER G.W.,THE END OF ISOLATION. FRANCE MOD/EUR RUSSIA UK NAT/G LEGIS TOP/EX GOV/REL PWR 20 TREATY CHINJAP. PAGE 112 H2239
DIPLOM POLICY WAR

B63
NALBANDIAN L.,THE ARMENIAN REVOLUTIONARY MOVEMENT. MOD/EUR RUSSIA...IDEA/COMP NAT/COMP BIBLIOG 19 ARMENIA OTTOMAN. PAGE 115 H2306
NAT/LISM REV POL/PAR ORD/FREE

B63
SETON-WATSON H.,THE NEW IMPERIALISM. COM EUR+WWI MOD/EUR ECO/UNDEV NAT/G FORCES DIPLOM DOMIN EDU/PROP LEGIT COLONIAL EXEC COERCE GP/REL RACE/REL DISCRIM ATTIT...TIME/SEQ 20. PAGE 142 H2833
ECO/TAC RUSSIA USSR

B64
DANIELS R.V.,RUSSIA. RUSSIA USSR STRUCT NAT/LISM TOTALISM ORD/FREE WEALTH...POLICY DECISION TREND. PAGE 37 H0740
MARXISM REV ECO/DEV DIPLOM

B64
FAINSOD M.,HOW RUSSIA IS RULED (REV. ED.). RUSSIA USSR AGRI PROC/MFG LABOR POL/PAR EX/STRUC CONTROL PWR...POLICY BIBLIOG 19/20 KHRUSH/N COM/PARTY. PAGE 48 H0963
NAT/G REV MARXISM

B64
KIS T.I.,LES PAYS DE L'EUROPE DE L'EST: LEURS RAPPORTS MUTUELS ET LE PROBLEME DE LEUR INTEGRATION DANS L'ORBITE DE L'USSR. EUR+WWI RUSSIA USSR INT/ORG NAT/G REV ATTIT...JURID SOC BIBLIOG WARSAW/P COMECON EUROPE/E. PAGE 86 H1727
DIPLOM COM MARXISM REGION

B64
PIPES R.,THE FORMATION OF THE SOVIET UNION. EUR+WWI MOD/EUR STRUCT ECO/UNDEV NAT/G LEGIS DOMIN LEGIT CT/SYS EXEC COERCE ALL/VALS...POLICY RELATIV HIST/WRIT TIME/SEQ TOT/POP 19/20. PAGE 126 H2514
COM USSR RUSSIA

B64
UTECHIN S.V.,RUSSIAN POLITICAL THOUGHT: A CONCISE HISTORY. RUSSIA USSR INTELL STRATA POL/PAR SECT LEGIS EDU/PROP REV WAR MARXISM...ANARCH BIBLIOG 9/20 REFORMERS SLAVS. PAGE 161 H3218
IDEA/COMP ATTIT ALL/IDEOS NAT/G

S64
REISS I.,"LE DECLENCHEMENT DE LA PREMIERE GUERRE MONDIALE." GERMANY RUSSIA NAT/G FORCES DOMIN EDU/PROP COERCE RIGID/FLEX PWR SOVEREIGN...RELATIV HIST/WRIT TOT/POP AUST/HUNG SERBIA 20. PAGE 131 H2612
MOD/EUR BAL/PWR DIPLOM WAR

B65
POBEDONOSTSEV K.P.,REFLECTIONS OF A RUSSIAN STATESMAN. RUSSIA LAW ELITES EDU/PROP PRESS ADJUD MARRIAGE ATTIT PWR...MAJORIT TRADIT 19 CHURCH/STA. PAGE 127 H2531
TOTALISM POLICY CONSTN NAT/G

B66
FARRELL R.B.,APPROACHES TO COMPARATIVE AND INTERNATIONAL POLITICS. RUSSIA SOCIETY ACADEM GOV/REL GP/REL...METH/CNCPT NET/THEORY GOV/COMP HYPO/EXP SOC/EXP GEN/METH ANTHOL. PAGE 49 H0973
DIPLOM NAT/COMP NAT/G

B66
RAEFF M.,ORIGINS OF THE RUSSIAN INTELLIGENTSIA: THE EIGHTEENTH-CENTURY NOBILITY. RUSSIA FAM NAT/G EDU/PROP ADMIN PERS/REL ATTIT...HUM BIOG 18. PAGE 129 H2580
INTELL ELITES STRATA CONSERVE

B66
THOMPSON J.M.,RUSSIA, BOLSHEVISM, AND THE VERSAILLES PEACE. RUSSIA USSR INT/ORG NAT/G DELIB/GP AGREE REV WAR PWR 20 TREATY VERSAILLES BOLSHEVISM. PAGE 154 H3083
DIPLOM PEACE MARXISM

B66
VON ARSENIEW W.,DIE GEISTIGEN SCHICKSALE DES RUSSISCHEN VOLKES. RUSSIA USSR SOCIETY STRUCT NAT/G SECT CHIEF REV 19/20. PAGE 163 H3262
ATTIT PERSON CULTURE DRIVE

L66
ZOPPO C.E.,"NUCLEAR TECHNOLOGY, MULTIPOLARITY, AND INTERNATIONAL STABILITY." ASIA RUSSIA USA+45 STRUCT TOP/EX BAL/PWR DIPLOM DETER CIVMIL/REL NAT/COMP. PAGE 173 H3464
NET/THEORY ORD/FREE DECISION NUC/PWR

B67
BROMKE A.,POLAND'S POLITICS: IDEALISM VS. REALISM. COM GERMANY POLAND RUSSIA USSR POL/PAR CATHISM ...BIBLIOG 19/20. PAGE 21 H0431
NAT/G DIPLOM MARXISM

B67
LAQUER W.,THE FATE OF THE REVOLUTION: INTERPRETATIONS OF SOVIET HISTORY. RUSSIA NAT/G MARXISM...BIBLIOG 20 STALIN/J. PAGE 91 H1816
REV KNOWL HIST/WRIT IDEA/COMP

B67
SETON-WATSON H.,THE RUSSIAN EMPIRE, 1801-1917. COM RUSSIA STRATA ECO/DEV AGRI INDUS POL/PAR DIPLOM NAT/LISM MARXISM...IDEA/COMP BIBLIOG 19/20 MARX/KARL. PAGE 142 H2834
SOCIETY NAT/G LEAD POLICY

S68
LAVRIN J.,"THE TWO WORLDS." RUSSIA USSR SOCIETY STRUCT NAT/G DIPLOM ATTIT PERSON MARXISM...GEOG SOC IDEA/COMP PERS/COMP 18/20. PAGE 92 H1842
NAT/COMP NAT/LISM CULTURE

RUSTOW D.A. H2720,H2721,H2722

RUTH J.M. H2723
RUUD J. H3466
RWANDA....SEE ALSO AFR

RYDER A.J. H2724

RYDINGS H.A. H2725

RYUKYUS....RYUKYU ISLANDS

S

S/AFR....SOUTH AFRICA, SEE ALSO AFR

S/ASIA....SOUTHEAST ASIA; SEE ALSO APPROPRIATE NATIONS

N
JOURNAL OF ASIAN STUDIES. CULTURE ECO/DEV SECT DIPLOM EDU/PROP WAR NAT/LISM...PHIL/SCI SOC 20. PAGE 1 H0005
BIBLIOG ASIA S/ASIA NAT/G

N
ASIA FOUNDATION,LIBRARY NOTES. LAW CONSTN CULTURE SOCIETY ECO/UNDEV INT/ORG NAT/G COLONIAL LEAD REGION NAT/LISM ATTIT 20 UN. PAGE 9 H0176
BIBLIOG/A ASIA S/ASIA DIPLOM

N
CORNELL UNIVERSITY LIBRARY,SOUTHEAST ASIA ACCESSIONS LIST. LAW SOCIETY STRUCT ECO/UNDEV POL/PAR TEC/DEV DIPLOM LEAD REGION. PAGE 34 H0671
BIBLIOG S/ASIA NAT/G CULTURE

N
INADA S.,INTRODUCTION TO SCIENTIFIC WORKS IN HUMANITIES AND SOCIAL SCIENCES PUBLISHED IN JAPAN. LAW CULTURE ACADEM EDU/PROP...ART/METH HUM 20 CHINJAP. PAGE 76 H1525
BIBLIOG/A NAT/G SOC S/ASIA

N
KYRIAK T.E.,ASIAN DEVELOPMENTS: A BIBLIOGRAPHY. INDONESIA KOREA/N VIETNAM/N CULTURE SOCIETY ECO/UNDEV NAT/G DIPLOM...SOC TREND 20 MONGOLIA. PAGE 90 H1788
BIBLIOG/A ALL/IDEOS S/ASIA ASIA

N
US LIBRARY OF CONGRESS,ACCESSIONS LIST - INDIA. INDIA CULTURE AGRI LOC/G POL/PAR PLAN PROB/SOLV TEC/DEV DIPLOM EDU/PROP LEAD GP/REL ATTIT 20. PAGE 160 H3199
BIBLIOG S/ASIA ECO/UNDEV NAT/G

N
US LIBRARY OF CONGRESS,SOUTHERN ASIA ACCESSIONS LIST. BURMA CEYLON INDIA NEPAL PAKISTAN S/ASIA THAILAND AGRI INDUS SCHOOL WORKER...ART/METH GEOG HEAL PHIL/SCI LING 20. PAGE 160 H3201
BIBLIOG/A SOCIETY CULTURE ECO/UNDEV

B02
SEELEY J.R.,THE EXPANSION OF ENGLAND. MOD/EUR S/ASIA UK CULTURE NAT/G FORCES PLAN DOMIN EDU/PROP COLONIAL ROUTINE ATTIT ALL/VALS SOVEREIGN...CONCPT HIST/WRIT PARLIAMENT 18 CMN/WLTH. PAGE 141 H2819
INT/ORG ACT/RES CAP/ISM INDIA

B12
CORDIER H.,BIBLIOTHECA INDOSINICA: DICTIONAIRE BIBLIOGRAPHIQUE DES OUVRAGES RELATIFS A LA PENINSULE INDOCHINOISE. BURMA LAOS MALAYSIA S/ASIA THAILAND VIETNAM SECT...LING 20. PAGE 33 H0665
BIBLIOG/A GEOG NAT/G

N19
BRIMMELL G.H.,COMMUNISM IN SOUTHEAST ASIA (PAMPHLET). BURMA CAMBODIA COM INDIA INDONESIA LAOS MOD/EUR NAT/G POL/PAR FORCES CAP/ISM CONTROL WEALTH ...MYTH 20. PAGE 21 H0420
MARXISM S/ASIA REV ECO/UNDEV

N19
GOODMAN G.K.,IMPERIAL JAPAN AND ASIA: A REASSESSMENT (PAMPHLET). ASIA S/ASIA ECO/DEV FORCES LEAD WAR NAT/LISM ATTIT...DECISION CONCPT BIBLIOG 19/20 CHINJAP. PAGE 59 H1172
DIPLOM NAT/G POLICY COLONIAL

B29
ROBERTS S.H.,HISTORY OF FRENCH COLONIAL POLICY. AFR ASIA L/A+17C S/ASIA CULTURE ECO/DEV ECO/UNDEV FINAN NAT/G PLAN ECO/TAC DOMIN ROUTINE SOVEREIGN...OBS HIST/WRIT TREND CHARTS VAL/FREE 19/20. PAGE 132 H2642
INT/ORG ACT/RES FRANCE COLONIAL

B31
DEKAT A.D.A.,COLONIAL POLICY. S/ASIA CULTURE EX/STRUC ECO/TAC DOMIN ADMIN COLONIAL ROUTINE SOVEREIGN WEALTH...POLICY MGT RECORD KNO/TEST SAMP. PAGE 39 H0785
DRIVE PWR INDONESIA NETHERLAND

B34
BENEDICT R.,PATTERNS OF CULTURE. S/ASIA FAM KIN PERSON RESPECT...CONCPT SELF/OBS. PAGE 14 H0278
CULTURE SOC

C39
REISCHAUER R.,"JAPAN'S GOVERNMENT--POLITICS." CONSTN STRATA POL/PAR FORCES LEGIS DIPLOM ADMIN EXEC CENTRAL...POLICY BIBLIOG 20 CHINJAP. PAGE 131 H2610
NAT/G S/ASIA CONCPT ROUTINE

B42
CONOVER H.F.,THE NETHERLANDS EAST INDIES: A SELECTED LIST OF REFERENCES. ECO/UNDEV AGRI EXTR/IND LABOR SCHOOL SECT INT/TRADE COLONIAL HEALTH...GEOG 19/20. PAGE 32 H0642
BIBLIOG S/ASIA CULTURE

B42
CONOVER H.F.,NEW ZEALAND: A SELECTED LIST OF REFERENCES (PAMPHLET). NEW/ZEALND ECO/UNDEV AGRI INDUS LABOR NAT/G SCHOOL FORCES DIPLOM COLONIAL WAR ...HUM 20. PAGE 32 H0643
BIBLIOG/A S/ASIA CULTURE

N45
INDIA QUARTERLY, A JOURNAL OF INTERNATIONAL AFFAIRS. INDIA LAW CONSTN ECO/UNDEV INT/ORG POL/PAR COLONIAL LEAD PARL/PROC WAR ATTIT...SOC 20 CMN/WLTH. PAGE 2 H0033
BIBLIOG/A S/ASIA DIPLOM NAT/G

B45
HARVARD WIDENER LIBRARY,INDOCHINA: A SELECTED LIST OF REFERENCES. CAMBODIA FRANCE S/ASIA VIETNAM COLONIAL...POLICY 19/20. PAGE 67 H1351
BIBLIOG/A ACADEM DIPLOM NAT/G

B45
LASKER B.,ASIA ON THE MOVE. ASIA BURMA S/ASIA THAILAND USSR ECO/UNDEV FAM KIN WAR NAT/LISM ATTIT ...GEOG CENSUS TREND AUSTRAL 20. PAGE 91 H1826
CULTURE RIGID/FLEX

B45
US LIBRARY OF CONGRESS,NETHERLANDS EAST INDIES. INDONESIA LAW CULTURE AGRI INDUS SCHOOL COLONIAL HEALTH...GEOG JURID SOC 19/20 NETH/IND. PAGE 160 H3205
BIBLIOG/A S/ASIA NAT/G

N46
HOBBS C.C.,SOUTHEAST ASIA, 1935-45: A SELECTED LIST OF REFERENCE BOOKS (PAMPHLET). S/ASIA AGRI INDUS NAT/G SECT DIPLOM WAR...ART/METH GEOG SOC LING 20. PAGE 72 H1435
BIBLIOG/A CULTURE HABITAT

B47
GITLOW A.L.,ECONOMICS OF THE MOUNT HAGEN TRIBES, NEW GUINEA. S/ASIA STRUCT AGRI FAM...GEOG MYTH 20 NEW/GUINEA. PAGE 57 H1137
HABITAT ECO/UNDEV CULTURE KIN

B48
FURNIVAL J.,COLONIAL POLICY AND PRACTICE A COMPARATIVE STUDY OF BURMA, AND NETHERLANDS INDIA. BURMA INDONESIA S/ASIA...GEOG OBS GOV/COMP METH/COMP 20. PAGE 54 H1080
COLONIAL NAT/LISM WEALTH SOVEREIGN

B49
PELZER K.J.,SELECTED BIBLIOGRAPHY ON THE GEOGRAPHY OF SOUTHEAST ASIA (3 VOLS., 1949-1956). PHILIPPINE CULTURE...SOC 20 MALAYA. PAGE 124 H2486
BIBLIOG S/ASIA GEOG

C49
YANAGA C.,"JAPAN SINCE PERRY." S/ASIA CULTURE ECO/DEV FORCES WAR 19/20 CHINJAP. PAGE 172 H3433
DIPLOM POL/PAR CIVMIL/REL NAT/LISM

B50
CORNELL U DEPT ASIAN STUDIES,SOUTHEAST ASIA PROGRAM DATA PAPER. BURMA CAMBODIA INDONESIA MALAYSIA VIETNAM SOCIETY STRUCT NAT/G SECT DIPLOM FOR/AID PWR WEALTH...SOC 20. PAGE 33 H0670
BIBLIOG/A CULTURE S/ASIA ECO/UNDEV

B50
EMBREE J.F.,BIBLIOGRAPHY OF THE PEOPLES AND CULTURES OF MAINLAND SOUTHEAST ASIA. CAMBODIA LAOS THAILAND VIETNAM LAW...GEOG HUM SOC MYTH LING CHARTS WORSHIP 20. PAGE 46 H0915
BIBLIOG/A CULTURE S/ASIA

B50
HOBBS C.C.,INDOCHINA, A BIBLIOGRAPHY OF THE LAND AND PEOPLE. VIETNAM CULTURE AGRI INDUS NAT/G SECT ...ART/METH GEOG SOC LING 20. PAGE 72 H1436
BIBLIOG/A S/ASIA COLONIAL ECO/UNDEV

B50
TRAGER F.N.,MARXISM IN SOUTHEAST ASIA. BURMA INDONESIA THAILAND VIETNAM CULTURE SOCIETY NAT/G VOL/ASSN EXEC ROUTINE COERCE ATTIT RIGID/FLEX PWR ...METH/CNCPT TIME/SEQ STERTYP GEN/LAWS MARX/KARL VAL/FREE COLD/WAR NAM 20. PAGE 156 H3126
S/ASIA POL/PAR REV

B51
BERNATZIK H.A.,THE SPIRITS OF THE YELLOW LEAVES. BURMA LAOS S/ASIA THAILAND VIETNAM SOCIETY AGRI COLONIAL LEISURE GP/REL PERS/REL ISOLAT AGE HABITAT SEX WORSHIP 20. PAGE 16 H0310
SOC KIN ECO/UNDEV CULTURE

B51
GHANI A.R.,PAKISTAN: A SELECT BIBLIOGRAPHY. PAKISTAN S/ASIA CULTURE...GEOG 20. PAGE 56 H1120
BIBLIOG AGRI INDUS

B51
JENNINGS S.I.,THE COMMONWEALTH IN ASIA. CEYLON INDIA PAKISTAN S/ASIA UK CONSTN CULTURE SOCIETY STRATA STRUCT NAT/G POL/PAR EDU/PROP LEAD WAR 20 CMN/WLTH. PAGE 80 H1608
NAT/LISM REGION COLONIAL DIPLOM

S51
NORTHROP F.S.C.,"ASIAN MENTALITY AND UNITED STATES FOREIGN POLICY." ASIA ISLAM USA+45 CULTURE SOCIETY SECT EDU/PROP LEGIT COERCE DRIVE MORAL ORD/FREE ...POLICY RELATIV TOT/POP 20. PAGE 119 H2376
S/ASIA ATTIT DIPLOM

B52
FORDE L.D.,HABITAT, ECONOMY AND SOCIETY. AFR L/A+17C S/ASIA STRUCT AGRI INGP/REL...GEOG OBS BIBLIOG 20. PAGE 52 H1037
SOC HABITAT CULTURE ECO/UNDEV

B53
ELAHI K.N.,A GUIDE TO WORKS OF REFERENCE PUBLISHED IN PAKISTAN (PAMPHLET). PAKISTAN DIPLOM COLONIAL LEAD. PAGE 45 H0903
BIBLIOG S/ASIA NAT/G

B53
MIT CENTER INTERNATIONAL STU,BIBLIOGRAPHY OF THE ECONOMIC AND POLITICAL DEVELOPMENT OF INDONESIA. INDONESIA STRUCT NAT/G COLONIAL LEAD...STAT 20. PAGE 111 H2226
BIBLIOG ECO/UNDEV TEC/DEV S/ASIA

B53
MURPHY G.,IN THE MINDS OF MEN: THE STUDY OF HUMAN BEHAVIOR AND SOCIAL TENSIONS IN INDIA. FUT S/ASIA FAM INT/ORG NAT/G DIPLOM EDU/PROP GP/REL ATTIT RIGID/FLEX ALL/VALS...SOC QU UNESCO 20. PAGE 115 H2297
SECT STRATA INDIA

C54
HAMMER E.J.,"THE STRUGGLE FOR INDOCHINA." COM VIETNAM POL/PAR REV CENTRAL NAT/LISM ATTIT...POLICY CHARTS BIBLIOG 20. PAGE 65 H1305
WAR COLONIAL S/ASIA NAT/G

B55
QUAN K.L.,INTRODUCTION TO ASIA: A SELECTIVE GUIDE TO BACKGROUND READING. ECO/UNDEV NAT/G PROB/SOLV DIPLOM ATTIT 20. PAGE 129 H2572
BIBLIOG/A S/ASIA CULTURE ASIA

B55
THOMPSON V.,MINORITY PROBLEMS IN SOUTHEAST ASIA. CAMBODIA CHINA/COM LAOS S/ASIA KIN NAT/G SECT PROB/SOLV EDU/PROP REGION GP/REL RACE/REL MARXISM ...SOC 20 BUDDHISM UN. PAGE 154 H3085
INGP/REL GEOG DIPLOM STRUCT

B55
UN ECONOMIC COMN ASIA & FAR E,ECONOMIC SURVEY OF ASIA AND THE FAR EAST, 1954. AFGHANISTN CEYLON INDIA PHILIPPINE S/ASIA ECO/DEV FINAN INDUS INT/TRADE PRODUC WEALTH...STAT CHARTS 20 CHINJAP. PAGE 158 H3158
ECO/UNDEV PRICE NAT/COMP ASIA

S55
GOODENOUGH W.H.,"A PROBLEM IN MALAYO-POLYNESIAN SOCIAL ORGANIZATION" (BMR)" MALAYSIA S/ASIA CULTURE AGRI PROB/SOLV OWN HABITAT...SOC 20 20 POLYNESIA. PAGE 58 H1170
KIN STRUCT FAM ECO/UNDEV

C55
OLIVER D.L.,"A LEADER IN ACTION," IN D. A. OLIVER, SOLOMON ISLAND SOCIETY." S/ASIA SOCIETY STRUCT CONTROL TASK PWR...OBS/ENVIR WORSHIP 20. PAGE 121 H2413
LEAD RESPECT CULTURE KIN

B56
IRIKURA J.K.,SOUTHEAST ASIA: SELECTED ANNOTATED BIBLIOGRAPHY OF JAPANESE PUBLICATIONS. CULTURE ADMIN RACE/REL 20 CHINJAP. PAGE 78 H1567
BIBLIOG/A S/ASIA DIPLOM

B56
JENNINGS W.I.,THE APPROACH TO SELF-GOVERNMENT. CEYLON INDIA PAKISTAN S/ASIA UK SOCIETY POL/PAR DELIB/GP LEGIS ECO/TAC EDU/PROP ADMIN EXEC CHOOSE ATTIT ALL/VALS...JURID CONCPT GEN/METH TOT/POP 20. PAGE 81 H1610
NAT/G CONSTN COLONIAL

B56
PHILIPPINE STUDIES PROGRAM,SELECTED BIBLIOGRAPHY ON THE PHILIPPINES, TOPICALLY ARRANGED AND ANNOTATED. PHILIPPINE SECT DIPLOM COLONIAL LEAD...SOC 18/20. PAGE 125 H2501
BIBLIOG/A S/ASIA NAT/G ECO/UNDEV

B56
ROBERTS H.L.,RUSSIA AND AMERICA. CHINA/COM S/ASIA USSR FORCES TEC/DEV FOR/AID NUC/PWR ALL/IDEOS ...MAJORIT TREND NAT/COMP 20 COLD/WAR UN NATO. PAGE 132 H2641
DIPLOM INT/ORG BAL/PWR TOTALISM

B56
TRAGER F.N.,ANNOTATED BIBLIOGRAPHY OF BURMA. BURMA STRUCT NAT/G...GEOG JURID MGT SOC 20. PAGE 156 H3127
BIBLIOG/A S/ASIA CULTURE SOCIETY

B56
WILSON P.,GOVERNMENT AND POLITICS OF INDIA AND PAKISTAN: 1885-1955; A BIBLIOGRAPHY OF WORKS IN WESTERN LANGUAGES. INDIA PAKISTAN CONSTN LOC/G POL/PAR FORCES DIPLOM ADMIN WAR CHOOSE...BIOG CON/ANAL 19/20. PAGE 169 H3380
BIBLIOG COLONIAL NAT/G S/ASIA

B57
DEAN V.M.,THE NATURE OF THE NON-WESTERN WORLD. AFR ASIA L/A+17C S/ASIA CULTURE SOCIETY STRATA ECO/DEV DIPLOM ECO/TAC FOR/AID ATTIT DRIVE ALL/VALS ...RELATIV SOC CONCPT TIME/SEQ TREND TOT/POP 20. PAGE 39 H0778
ECO/UNDEV STERTYP NAT/LISM

B57
KENNEDY M.D.,A SHORT HISTORY OF COMMUNISM IN ASIA. ASIA BURMA INDIA S/ASIA THAILAND NAT/G POL/PAR LEAD REV WAR MARXISM SOCISM...POLICY 20 CHINJAP. PAGE 85 H1688
DIPLOM NAT/LISM TOTALISM COERCE

B57
SOUTH PACIFIC COMMISSION,INDEX OF SOCIAL SCIENCE RESEARCH THESES ON THE SOUTH PACIFIC. S/ASIA ACADEM ADMIN COLONIAL...SOC 20. PAGE 147 H2939
BIBLIOG/A ACT/RES SECT CULTURE

B57
WILSON P.,SOUTH ASIA; A SELECTED BIBLIOGRAPHY ON INDIA, PAKISTAN, CEYLON (PAMPHLET). CEYLON INDIA PAKISTAN LAW ECO/UNDEV PLAN DIPLOM 20. PAGE 169 H3381
BIBLIOG S/ASIA CULTURE NAT/G

N57
JENNINGS W.I.,NATIONALISM, COLONIALISM, AND NEUTRALISM (PAMPHLET). ASIA INDIA S/ASIA UK INTELL ACADEM POL/PAR 20. PAGE 81 H1611
NAT/LISM COLONIAL NEUTRAL ATTIT

B58
INDIAN COUNCIL WORLD AFFAIRS,DEFENCE AND SECURITY IN THE INDIAN OCEAN AREA. INDIA S/ASIA CULTURE CONSULT DELIB/GP FORCES PROB/SOLV DIPLOM INT/TRADE 20 CMN/WLTH. PAGE 77 H1531
GEOG HABITAT ECO/UNDEV ORD/FREE

B58
MASON J.B.,THAILAND BIBLIOGRAPHY. S/ASIA THAILAND CULTURE EDU/PROP ADMIN...GEOG SOC LING 20. PAGE 104 H2087
BIBLIOG/A ECO/UNDEV DIPLOM NAT/G

B58
VON FURER-HAIMEN E.,AN ANTHROPOLOGICAL BIBLIOGRAPHY OF SOUTH ASIA (VOL. I). STRATA STRUCT KIN SECT ACT/RES CREATE HABITAT...GEOG OBS 19/20. PAGE 163 H3267
BIBLIOG/A CULTURE S/ASIA SOC

S58
PYE L.W.,"THE NON-WESTERN POLITICAL PROCESS" (BMR)" AFR ASIA ISLAM S/ASIA DIPLOM ADMIN LEAD LOBBY ROUTINE CONSEN...DECISION 20. PAGE 128 H2567
CULTURE POL/PAR NAT/G LOC/G

C58
BLANCHARD W.,"THAILAND." THAILAND CULTURE AGRI FINAN INDUS FAM LABOR INT/TRADE ATTIT...GEOG HEAL SOC BIBLIOG 20. PAGE 18 H0354
NAT/G DIPLOM ECO/UNDEV S/ASIA

C58
FIFIELD R.H.,"THE DIPLOMACY OF SOUTHEAST ASIA: 1945-1958." INT/ORG NAT/G COLONIAL REGION...CHARTS BIBLIOG 20 UN. PAGE 50 H0996
S/ASIA DIPLOM NAT/LISM

B59
OVERSTREET G.D.,COMMUNISM IN INDIA. INDIA S/ASIA CONSTN INT/ORG LEAD GP/REL...CHARTS BIBLIOG 20. PAGE 122 H2435
MARXISM NAT/LISM POL/PAR WAR

B59
PANIKKAR K.M.,THE AFRO-ASIAN STATES AND THEIR PROBLEMS. COM CULTURE KIN POL/PAR SECT DIPLOM EDU/PROP COLONIAL SOVEREIGN...TECHNIC GOV/COMP 20. PAGE 123 H2458
AFR S/ASIA ECO/UNDEV

B59
PARK R.L.,LEADERSHIP AND POLITICAL INSTITUTIONS IN INDIA. S/ASIA CULTURE ECO/UNDEV LOC/G MUNIC PROVS LEGIS PLAN ADMIN LEAD ORD/FREE WEALTH...GEOG SOC BIOG TOT/POP VAL/FREE 20. PAGE 123 H2468
NAT/G EXEC INDIA

B59
VINACKE H.M.,A HISTORY OF THE FAR EAST IN MODERN TIMES (6TH ED.). KOREA S/ASIA USSR CONSTN CULTURE STRATA ECO/UNDEV NAT/G CHIEF FOR/AID INT/TRADE GP/REL...SOC NAT/COMP 19/20 CHINJAP. PAGE 163 H3255
STRUCT ASIA

B59
WOOD H.B.,NEPAL BIBLIOGRAPHY. NEPAL S/ASIA NAT/G 20. PAGE 170 H3406
BIBLIOG CULTURE

B60
ALMOND G.A.,THE POLITICS OF THE DEVELOPING AREAS. AFR ISLAM L/A+17C S/ASIA SOCIETY ECO/UNDEV NAT/G ADMIN PERCEPT KNOWL SOVEREIGN...CONCPT GEN/LAWS 20. PAGE 6 H0112
EX/STRUC ATTIT NAT/LISM

B60
BURRIDGE K.,MAMBU: A MELANESIAN MILLENNIUM. ECO/UNDEV PROC/MFG FAM KIN CHIEF COLONIAL COERCE GP/REL DRIVE WEALTH WORSHIP 20 NEW/GUINEA. PAGE 25 H0494
S/ASIA SECT CULTURE MYTH

B60
COUGHLIN R.,DOUBLE IDENTITY: THE CHINESE AND MODERN THAILAND. CHINA/COM S/ASIA THAILAND ECO/UNDEV EXTR/IND FINAN INDUS KIN MUNIC NAT/G PROF/ORG SCHOOL SECT ATTIT DRIVE...CONCPT OBS 20. PAGE 34 H0676
ASIA FAM CULTURE

B60
EASTON S.C.,THE TWILIGHT OF EUROPEAN COLONIALISM. AFR S/ASIA CONSTN SOCIETY STRUCT ECO/UNDEV INDUS NAT/G FORCES ECO/TAC COLONIAL CT/SYS ATTIT KNOWL ORD/FREE PWR...SOCIALIST TIME/SEQ TREND CON/ANAL 20. PAGE 44 H0882
FINAN ADMIN

B60
EMERSON R.,FROM EMPIRE TO NATION: THE RISE TO SELF-ASSERTION OF ASIAN AND AFRICAN PEOPLES. S/ASIA CULTURE NAT/G SECT DIPLOM ATTIT SOVEREIGN MARXISM ...POLICY BIBLIOG 19/20. PAGE 46 H0919 NAT/LISM COLONIAL AFR ASIA

B60
SAKAI R.K.,STUDIES ON ASIA, 1960. ASIA CHINA/COM S/ASIA COM/IND ECO/TAC...ANTHOL 17/20 MALAYA. PAGE 137 H2733 ECO/UNDEV SOC

B60
SALETORE B.A.,INDIA'S DIPLOMATIC RELATIONS WITH THE EAST. ASIA CEYLON INDIA NEPAL S/ASIA CULTURE 7/14 PERSIA. PAGE 137 H2740 DIPLOM NAT/COMP ETIQUET

B60
WOLF C.,FOREIGN AID: THEORY AND PRACTICE IN SOUTHERN ASIA. CEYLON INDONESIA PHILIPPINE S/ASIA CULTURE STRATA ECO/UNDEV PLAN EDU/PROP ATTIT ...METH/CNCPT MATH QUANT STAT CONT/OBS TIME/SEQ SIMUL TOT/POP 20. PAGE 170 H3396 ACT/RES ECO/TAC FOR/AID

S60
EMERSON R.,"THE EROSION OF DEMOCRACY." AFR FUT LAW CULTURE INTELL SOCIETY ECO/UNDEV FAM LOC/G NAT/G FORCES PLAN TEC/DEV ECO/TAC ADMIN CT/SYS ATTIT ORD/FREE PWR...SOCIALIST SOC CONCPT STAND/INT TIME/SEQ WORK 20. PAGE 46 H0918 S/ASIA POL/PAR

S60
GINSBURGS G.,"PEKING-LHASA-NEW DELHI." CHINA/COM FUT INDIA S/ASIA KIN NAT/G PROVS SECT FORCES BAL/PWR ECO/TAC DOMIN EDU/PROP LEGIT ADMIN REGION GUERRILLA PWR...TREND TIBET 20. PAGE 57 H1134 ASIA COERCE DIPLOM

S60
JAFFEE A.J.,"POPULATION TRENDS AND CONTROLS IN UNDERDEVELOPED COUNTRIES." AFR FUT ISLAM L/A+17C S/ASIA CULTURE R+D FAM ACT/RES PLAN EDU/PROP BIO/SOC RIGID/FLEX HEALTH...SOC STAT OBS CHARTS 20. PAGE 79 H1582 ECO/UNDEV GEOG

S60
KEYFITZ N.,"WESTERN PERSPECTIVES AND ASIAN PROBLEMS." ASIA EUR+WWI S/ASIA SOCIETY FOR/AID ...POLICY SOC CONCPT STERTYP WORK TOT/POP 20. PAGE 85 H1701 CULTURE ATTIT

S60
MURPHEY R.,"ECONOMIC CONFLICTS IN SOUTH ASIA." ASIA CULTURE INTELL ECO/TAC REGION ATTIT DRIVE KNOWL ...METH/CNCPT TIME/SEQ STERTYP TOT/POP VAL/FREE 20. PAGE 115 H2296 S/ASIA ECO/UNDEV

S60
SHILS E.,"THE INTELLECTUALS IN THE POLITICAL DEVELOPMENT OF THE NEW STATES." AFR ASIA S/ASIA ELITES LOC/G NAT/G CONSULT EX/STRUC CREATE PLAN ECO/TAC DOMIN LEGIT DRIVE PWR...TRADIT CONCPT STERTYP GEN/LAWS 20. PAGE 143 H2861 POL/PAR INTELL NAT/LISM

C60
SMITH T.E.,"ELECTIONS IN DEVELOPING COUNTRIES: A STUDY OF ELECTORAL PROCEDURES USED IN TOPICAL AFRICA, SOUTH-EAST ASIA..." AFR S/ASIA UK ROUTINE GOV/REL RACE/REL...GOV/COMP BIBLIOG 20. PAGE 146 H2918 ECO/UNDEV CHOOSE REPRESENT ADMIN

B61
BEARCE G.D.,BRITISH ATTITUDES TOWARDS INDIA 1784-1858. INDIA S/ASIA UK SECT ECO/TAC...POLICY HUM 18/19. PAGE 12 H0246 COLONIAL ATTIT ALL/IDEOS NAT/G

B61
COHN B.S.,DEVELOPMENT AND IMPACT OF BRITISH ADMINISTRATION IN INDIA: A BIBLIOGRAPHIC ESSAY. INDIA UK ECO/UNDEV NAT/G DOMIN...POLICY MGT SOC 19/20. PAGE 31 H0619 BIBLIOG/A COLONIAL S/ASIA ADMIN

B61
FIRTH R.,HISTORY AND TRADITIONS OF TIKOPIA. S/ASIA KIN SECT RUMOR WAR...MYTH WORSHIP 20 POLYNESIA. PAGE 50 H1008 CULTURE STRUCT HUM

B61
HISTORICAL RESEARCH INSTITUTE,A SHORT BIBLIOGRAPHY OF INDO-MUSLIM HISTORY. INDIA S/ASIA DIPLOM EDU/PROP COLONIAL LEAD NAT/LISM ATTIT...BIOG 19/20. PAGE 71 H1427 BIBLIOG NAT/G SECT POL/PAR

B61
INDIAN NATIONAL CONGRESS,SOUVENIR, 66TH SESSION. INDIA S/ASIA CONSTN CULTURE LEGIS CREATE TEC/DEV LEAD TASK...GEOG CHARTS 20. PAGE 77 H1533 CONFER PLAN NAT/G POLICY

B61
SAKAI R.K.,STUDIES ON ASIA, 1961. ASIA BURMA INDIA S/ASIA FINAN ECO/TAC NAT/LISM SOCISM...POLICY ANTHOL 19/20 CHINJAP. PAGE 137 H2734 ECO/UNDEV SECT

B61
SETON-WATSON H.,FROM LENIN TO KHRUSHCHEV: THE HISTORY OF WORLD COMMUNISM. ASIA COM EUR+WWI ISLAM S/ASIA ECO/DEV ECO/UNDEV NAT/G POL/PAR DIPLOM ECO/TAC EDU/PROP COERCE GUERRILLA ATTIT DRIVE WORK TOT/POP NAZI 20. PAGE 141 H2832 PWR REV USSR

B61
WEST F.J.,POLITICAL ADVANCEMENT IN THE SOUTH PACIFIC. CONSTN CULTURE POL/PAR LEGIS DOMIN ADMIN CHOOSE SOVEREIGN VAL/FREE 20 FIJI TAHITI SAMOA. PAGE 167 H3335 S/ASIA LOC/G COLONIAL

S61
PADELFORD N.J.,"POLITICS AND THE FUTURE OF ECOSOC." AFR S/ASIA ECO/UNDEV INDUS NAT/G DELIB/GP ACT/RES ORD/FREE WEALTH...CONCPT CHARTS UN 20 ECOSOC. PAGE 122 H2438 INT/ORG TEC/DEV

S61
RAY J.,"THE EUROPEAN FREE-TRADE ASSOCIATION AND ITS IMPACT ON INDIA'S TRADE." EUR+WWI FRANCE GERMANY INDIA S/ASIA UK NAT/G VOL/ASSN PLAN INT/TRADE ROUTINE WEALTH...STAT CHARTS CMN/WLTH EEC OEEC 20 EFTA. PAGE 130 H2600 ECO/DEV ECO/TAC

S61
TANHAM B.K.,"COMMUNIST REVOLUTIONARY WARFARE: THE VIETMINH IN INDOCHINA." EUR+WWI S/ASIA VIETNAM NAT/G EDU/PROP LEGIT GUERRILLA ATTIT PWR...CONCPT GEN/LAWS 20. PAGE 152 H3042 FORCES ECO/TAC WAR FRANCE

B62
BROWN S.D.,STUDIES ON ASIA, 1962. ASIA BURMA INDIA ISLAM ISRAEL S/ASIA ECO/UNDEV POL/PAR SECT ECO/TAC ...ANTHOL 20 CHINJAP. PAGE 22 H0450 PWR PARL/PROC

B62
CALVOCORESSI P.,WORLD ORDER AND NEW STATES: PROBLEMS OF KEEPING THE PEACE. AFR EUR+WWI S/ASIA ELITES NAT/G ECO/TAC FOR/AID EDU/PROP COERCE ATTIT DRIVE ALL/VALS...GEN/LAWS COLD/WAR 20 UN. PAGE 25 H0509 INT/ORG PEACE

B62
CHAKRAVARTI P.C.,INDIA'S CHINA POLICY. ASIA CHINA/COM S/ASIA CULTURE NAT/G TOP/EX ACT/RES EDU/PROP DRIVE ALL/VALS...MYTH 20. PAGE 28 H0571 RIGID/FLEX TREND INDIA

B62
DILLING A.R.,ABORIGINE CULTURE HISTORY - A SURVEY OF PUBLICATIONS 1954-1957. GUINEA...SOC CHARTS NAT/COMP BIBLIOG/A AUSTRAL ABORIGINES. PAGE 41 H0825 S/ASIA HIST/WRIT CULTURE KIN

B62
DUROSELLE J.B.,LES NOUVEAUX ETATS DANS LES RELATIONS INTERNATIONALES. AFR CHINA/COM FRANCE MOROCCO S/ASIA USSR ECO/UNDEV INT/ORG PLAN ECO/TAC EDU/PROP ATTIT DRIVE...TREND TOT/POP TUNIS 20. PAGE 44 H0872 NAT/G CONSTN DIPLOM

B62
HAY S.N.,SOUTHEAST ASIAN HISTORY: A BIBLIOGRAPHICAL GUIDE. STRATA KIN NAT/G REGION GUERRILLA REV WAR ADJUST HABITAT PERCEPT ALL/IDEOS...CHARTS 5/20. PAGE 68 H1365 BIBLIOG/A S/ASIA CULTURE

B62
JOHNSON J.J.,THE ROLE OF THE MILITARY IN UNDERDEVELOPED COUNTRIES. AFR BURMA INDONESIA ISLAM ISRAEL L/A+17C S/ASIA THAILAND CULTURE ECO/UNDEV KIN PROVS CONSULT ACT/RES COERCE REV DRIVE RIGID/FLEX ORD/FREE...RECORD ANTHOL 20. PAGE 81 H1622 FORCES CONCPT

B62
KENNEDY R.,BIBLIOGRAPHY OF INDONESIAN PEOPLES AND CULTURES (2ND REV. ED.). INDONESIA STRUCT ECO/UNDEV SCHOOL EDU/PROP COLONIAL...GEOG SOC LING NAT/COMP 20. PAGE 85 H1689 BIBLIOG S/ASIA CULTURE KIN

B62
MODELSKI G.,SEATO-SIX STUDIES. ASIA CHINA/COM INDIA S/ASIA INT/ORG NAT/G ECO/TAC DETER ATTIT ORD/FREE PWR...TIME/SEQ COLD/WAR TOT/POP 20 SEATO. PAGE 112 H2234 MARKET ECO/UNDEV INT/TRADE

B62
SILBERMAN B.S.,JAPAN AND KOREA; A CRITICAL BIBLIOGRAPHY. KOREA LAW STRATA STRUCT AGRI INDUS NAT/G POL/PAR SECT...HUM LING IDEA/COMP 5/20 CHINJAP. PAGE 144 H2872 BIBLIOG/A CULTURE S/ASIA

B62
US DEPARTMENT OF THE ARMY,GUIDE TO JAPANESE MONOGRAPHS AND JAPANESE STUDIES ON MANCHURIA: 1945-1960. CHINA/COM NAT/G DIPLOM LEAD COERCE WAR ...CHARTS 19/20 CHINJAP. PAGE 160 H3193 BIBLIOG/A FORCES ASIA S/ASIA

B62
VALERIANO N.D.,COUNTER-GUERRILLA OPERATIONS: THE PHILLIPINE EXPERIENCE. NAT/G CONSULT ACT/RES PLAN COERCE GUERRILLA ATTIT ORD/FREE PWR SKILL...GEOG NEW/IDEA TIME/SEQ CHARTS 20. PAGE 161 H3221 S/ASIA FORCES PHILIPPINE

B62
YOUNG G.,THE HILL TRIBES OF NORTHERN THAILAND. S/ASIA THAILAND FAM KIN LOC/G GP/REL HABITAT...GEOG LING OBS 20. PAGE 172 H3438 CULTURE STRUCT ECO/UNDEV SECT

L62
CORET A.,"L'INDEPENDANCE DU SAMOA OCCIDENTAL." S/ASIA LAW INT/ORG EXEC ALL/VALS SAMOA UN 20. PAGE 33 H0668 NAT/G STRUCT SOVEREIGN

S62
CORET A.,"LE STATUT DE L'ILE CHRISTMAS DE L'OCEAN INDIEN." FUT S/ASIA ECO/DEV ECO/UNDEV VOL/ASSN DELIB/GP PLAN...RELATIV OBS TIME/SEQ TREND AUSTRAL 20. PAGE 33 H0667 NAT/G INT/ORG NEW/ZEALND

S62
SARKISYANZ E.,"NATIONALISM, CAPITALISM, AND THE UNCOMMITED NATIONS: MARXISM AND ASIAN CULTURAL S/ASIA SECT

TRADITIONS." ASIA BURMA CHINA/COM COM CULTURE SOCIETY NAT/G POL/PAR PLAN DOMIN EDU/PROP COLONIAL COERCE ATTIT RIGID/FLEX...CONCPT TREND MARX/KARL 20 TIBET BUDDHISM. PAGE 138 H2755 NAT/LISM CAP/ISM

B63
BARNETT A.D.,COMMUNIST STRATEGIES IN ASIA: A COMPARATIVE ANALYSIS OF GOVERNMENTS AND PARTIES. COM FUT S/ASIA CULTURE SOCIETY STRATA NAT/G DELIB/GP ACT/RES ECO/TAC EDU/PROP COERCE CHOOSE ATTIT RIGID/FLEX ORD/FREE PWR SKILL...SIMUL VAL/FREE 20. PAGE 11 H0223 ASIA POL/PAR DIPLOM USSR

B63
BRECHER M.,THE NEW STATES OF ASIA. ASIA S/ASIA INT/ORG BAL/PWR COLONIAL NEUTRAL ORD/FREE PWR 20 UN. PAGE 20 H0407 NAT/G ECO/UNDEV DIPLOM POLICY

B63
FALL B.,THE TWO VIETNAMS. CULTURE SOCIETY ECO/UNDEV NAT/G TOP/EX ACT/RES PLAN ECO/TAC DOMIN EDU/PROP COERCE ATTIT DRIVE PERSON ORD/FREE PWR...SOC TIME/SEQ COLD/WAR 20. PAGE 48 H0965 S/ASIA BIOG VIETNAM

B63
GEERTZ C.,PEDDLERS AND PRINCES: SOCIAL DEVELOPMENT AND ECONOMIC CHANGE IN TWO INDONESIAN TOWNS. S/ASIA CULTURE SOCIETY STRATA FACE/GP MUNIC CREATE TEC/DEV ECO/TAC ORD/FREE WEALTH...OBS INT CENSUS CHARTS WORK TOT/POP VAL/FREE 20. PAGE 55 H1106 ECO/UNDEV SOC ELITES INDONESIA

B63
KAHIN G.M.,MAJOR GOVERNMENTS OF ASIA (2ND ED.). ASIA INDIA INDONESIA PAKISTAN S/ASIA DIPLOM...SOC 20 CHINJAP. PAGE 83 H1650 GOV/COMP POL/PAR ELITES

B63
KAPP W.K.,HINDU CULTURE: ECONOMIC DEVELOPMENT AND ECONOMIC PLANNING IN INDIA. INDIA S/ASIA CULTURE ECO/TAC EDU/PROP ADMIN ALL/VALS...POLICY MGT TIME/SEQ VAL/FREE 20. PAGE 83 H1660 SECT ECO/UNDEV

B63
KURZMAN D.,SUBVERSION OF THE INNOCENTS: PATTERNS OF COMMUNIST PENETRATION OF AFRICA, THE MIDDLE EAST AND AFRICA. AFR ASIA ISLAM S/ASIA CULTURE NAT/G FORCES PLAN EDU/PROP ADMIN ATTIT...CONCPT INT UNPLAN/INT TIME/SEQ. PAGE 89 H1785 COM COERCE

B63
LEE C.,THE POLITICS OF KOREAN NATIONALISM. KOREA S/ASIA DIPLOM REV WAR 14/20 CHINJAP. PAGE 93 H1855 NAT/LISM SOVEREIGN COLONIAL

B63
NATIONAL OFF STATE GOVT THAI,STATISTICAL BIBLIOGRAPHY: AN ANNOTATED BIBLIOGRAPHY OF THAI GOVERNMENTAL STATISTICAL PUBLICATIONS. THAILAND AGRI 20. PAGE 116 H2321 BIBLIOG/A STAT NAT/G S/ASIA

B63
PRICE A.G.,THE WESTERN INVASIONS OF THE PACIFIC AND ITS CONTINENTS. ASIA PRE/AMER S/ASIA ECO/UNDEV KIN NAT/G SECT FORCES DOMIN HEALTH...SOC 16/20. PAGE 128 H2560 COLONIAL CULTURE GEOG HABITAT

B63
SAKAI R.K.,STUDIES ON ASIA, 1963. ASIA INDIA ISRAEL S/ASIA USA+45 PERF/ART POL/PAR SECT REGION NAT/LISM ...SOC LING TREND ANTHOL 19/20 CHINJAP. PAGE 137 H2735 PWR CULTURE

B63
SCHECHTMAN J.B.,THE REFUGEE IN THE WORLD: DISPLACEMENT AND INTEGRATION. AFR ASIA EUR+WWI ISLAM L/A+17C S/ASIA CULTURE STRATA LOC/G EX/STRUC PLAN ECO/TAC ROUTINE...CONCPT TIME/SEQ VAL/FREE 20. PAGE 139 H2779 INT/ORG SOC

B63
STIFEL L.D.,THE TEXTILE INDUSTRY - A CASE STUDY OF INDUSTRIAL DEVELOPMENT IN THE PHILIPPINES (PAPER). PHILIPPINE WORKER CAP/ISM INT/TRADE TARIFFS RECEIVE PRICE ADMIN COST EFFICIENCY WEALTH...BIBLIOG 20. PAGE 149 H2986 S/ASIA ECO/UNDEV PROC/MFG NAT/G

B63
STUCKI C.W.,AMERICAN DOCTORAL DISSERTATIONS ON ASIA 1933-62 (A PAPER). PREHIST INDUS NAT/G GOV/REL ALL/IDEOS...ART/METH GEOG SOC LING 20. PAGE 150 H3002 BIBLIOG ASIA SOCIETY S/ASIA

B63
VIARD R.,LA FIN DE L'EMPIRE COLONIAL FRANCAIS. AFR FUT S/ASIA ECO/UNDEV NAT/G CONSULT PLAN ECO/TAC EDU/PROP REGION NAT/LISM ALL/VALS...CONCPT TIME/SEQ TREND VAL/FREE 20. PAGE 162 H3248 VOL/ASSN COLONIAL FRANCE

B63
VON DER MEHDEN F.R.,RELIGION AND NATIONALISM IN SOUTHEAST ASIA. BURMA PHILIPPINE S/ASIA INTELL SOCIETY DOMIN EDU/PROP LEGIT ATTIT MORAL ORD/FREE ...SOC CENSUS HIST/WRIT TOT/POP VAL/FREE 20 WORSHIP LONDON. PAGE 163 H3265 SECT CULTURE NAT/LISM

B63
WEINER M.,POLITICAL CHANGE IN SOUTH ASIA. CEYLON INDIA PAKISTAN S/ASIA CULTURE ELITES ECO/UNDEV EX/STRUC ADMIN CONTROL CHOOSE CONSERVE...GOV/COMP ANTHOL 20. PAGE 166 H3328 NAT/G CONSTN TEC/DEV

L63
JAY R.,"RELIGION AND POLITICS IN RURAL CENTRAL JAVA." S/ASIA SOCIETY NEIGH SECT PERSON HEALTH MORAL...SOC UNPLAN/INT TIME/SEQ JAVA VAL/FREE 20 WORSHIP. PAGE 80 H1594 CULTURE OBS

L63
NASH M.,"PSYCHO-CULTURAL FACTORS IN ASIAN ECONOMIC GROWTH." ASIA ISLAM S/ASIA CULTURE ECO/UNDEV DELIB/GP EDU/PROP COERCE ATTIT PERSON HEALTH KNOWL ORD/FREE...PSY SOC STAT TREND ANTHOL VAL/FREE 20. PAGE 116 H2313 SOCIETY ECO/TAC

L63
ROSE R.,"COMPARATIVE STUDIES IN POLITICAL FINANCE: A SYMPOSIUM." ASIA EUR+WWI S/ASIA LAW CULTURE DELIB/GP LEGIS ACT/RES ECO/TAC EDU/PROP CHOOSE ATTIT RIGID/FLEX SUPEGO PWR SKILL WEALTH...STAT ANTHOL VAL/FREE. PAGE 134 H2674 FINAN POL/PAR

S63
AYAL E.B.,"VALUE SYSTEM AND ECONOMIC DEVELOPMENT IN JAPAN AND THAILAND." ASIA S/ASIA THAILAND CULTURE ECO/DEV CAP/ISM DOMIN NAT/LISM DRIVE RIGID/FLEX SOCISM...WELF/ST OBS TREND CON/ANAL GEN/LAWS 20 CHINJAP. PAGE 9 H0185 ECO/UNDEV ALL/VALS

S63
DUTT V.P.,"CHINA: JEALOUS NEIGHBOR." ASIA CHINA/COM INDIA S/ASIA NAT/G TOP/EX DOMIN COERCE REV ATTIT ...POLICY COLD/WAR 20. PAGE 44 H0874 FORCES PWR DIPLOM

S63
HALPERN A.M.,"THE EMERGENCE OF AN ASIAN COMMUNIST BLOC." ASIA CHINA/COM COM FUT KOREA/N S/ASIA VIETNAM/N STRATA NAT/G DELIB/GP FORCES TOP/EX PLAN BAL/PWR COERCE DETER PWR COLD/WAR WORK 20. PAGE 65 H1295 POL/PAR EDU/PROP DIPLOM

S63
HARRIS R.L.,"A COMPARATIVE ANALYSIS OF THE ADMINISTRATIVE SYSTEMS OF CANADA AND CEYLON." S/ASIA CULTURE SOCIETY STRATA TOP/EX ACT/RES DOMIN EDU/PROP LEGIT COERCE ATTIT SUPEGO ALL/VALS...MGT CHARTS GEN/LAWS VAL/FREE 20. PAGE 67 H1343 DELIB/GP EX/STRUC CANADA CEYLON

S63
HARRIS R.L.,"COMMUNISM AND ASIA: ILLUSIONS AND MISCONCEPTIONS." ASIA COM FUT S/ASIA ECO/UNDEV AGRI NAT/G POL/PAR EX/STRUC EDU/PROP COERCE ATTIT MARXISM COLD/WAR TOT/POP 20. PAGE 67 H1344 PWR GUERRILLA

S63
NICHOLAS W.,"VILLAGE FACTIONS AND POLITICAL PARTIES IN RURAL WEST BENGAL." S/ASIA CULTURE STRATA FACE/GP KIN MUNIC DELIB/GP LEGIS DOMIN EDU/PROP COERCE CHOOSE ATTIT ALL/VALS...STAT TOT/POP VAL/FREE 20. PAGE 117 H2348 NEIGH POL/PAR

S63
SOEMARDJORN S.,"SOME SOCIAL AND CULTURAL IMPLICATIONS OF INDONESIA'S PLANNED AND UNPLANNED DEVELOPMENT." EUR+WWI FUT MOD/EUR S/ASIA CONSTN SOCIETY DELIB/GP ACT/RES PLAN ECO/TAC EDU/PROP COERCE ATTIT ALL/VALS...TIME/SEQ 20. PAGE 146 H2927 ECO/UNDEV CULTURE INDONESIA

S63
TILMAN R.O.,"MALAYSIA: THE PROBLEMS OF FEDERATION." ISLAM S/ASIA CONSTN PROVS SECT DELIB/GP DOMIN EDU/PROP LEGIT EXEC COERCE CHOOSE ATTIT HEALTH ORD/FREE PWR...STAT TOT/POP VAL/FREE 20. PAGE 155 H3097 NAT/G CULTURE MALAYSIA

S63
WEISSBERG G.,"MAPS AS EVIDENCE IN INTERNATIONAL BOUNDARY DISPUTES: A REAPPRAISAL." CHINA/COM EUR+WWI INDIA MOD/EUR S/ASIA INT/ORG NAT/G LEGIT PERCEPT...JURID CHARTS 20. PAGE 166 H3331 LAW GEOG SOVEREIGN

N63
LIBRARY HUNGARIAN ACADEMY SCI,HUNGARIAN PUBLICATIONS ON ASIA AND AFRICA, 1950-1962: A SELECTED BIBLIOGRAPHY (PAMPHLET). AFR ASIA HUNGARY S/ASIA ECO/UNDEV NAT/G EDU/PROP ATTIT 20 UNESCO. PAGE 96 H1922 BIBLIOG REGION DIPLOM WRITING

B64
AFRO ASIAN SOLIDARITY AGAINST IMPERIALISM. AFR ISLAM S/ASIA ECO/UNDEV NAT/G POL/PAR TOP/EX PRESS ...INT ANTHOL 20 CHOU/ENLAI. PAGE 2 H0043 MARXISM DIPLOM EDU/PROP CHIEF

B64
AGGARWALA R.C.,CONSTITUTIONAL HISTORY OF INDIA AND NATIONAL MOVEMENT INCLUDING COMPARATIVE STUDY OF MODERN INDIA CONSTITUTION. INDIA S/ASIA SECT VOL/ASSN EX/STRUC LEGIS COERCE REV INGP/REL ORD/FREE...SOC BIBLIOG 18/20 CMN/WLTH. PAGE 4 H0077 CONSTN COLONIAL DOMIN NAT/G

B64
ARASARATNAM S.,CEYLON. CEYLON NETHERLAND PORTUGAL S/ASIA UK STRUCT ECO/UNDEV SECT DIPLOM DOMIN RACE/REL NAT/LISM 17/20 CMN/WLTH. PAGE 8 H0156 COLONIAL NAT/G PROB/SOLV CULTURE

B64
BEDERMAN S.H.,THE ETHNOLOGICAL CONTRIBUTIONS OF JOHN LEDYARD (PAMPHLET). ASIA PRE/AMER S/ASIA...SOC 18 LEDYARD/J KAMCHATKA TAHITI TARTARS INDIAN/AM. PAGE 13 H0256 CULTURE BIOG METH/CNCPT STRUCT

B64
BERNDT R.M.,THE WORLD OF THE FIRST AUSTRALIANS. S/ASIA ECO/UNDEV WORKER PROB/SOLV EFFICIENCY ROLE ...SOC MYTH WORSHIP AUSTRAL ABORIGINES. PAGE 16 CULTURE KIN STRUCT

H0311 DRIVE

B64
BUTWELL R.,SOUTHEAST ASIA TODAY - AND TOMORROW. NAT/G COLONIAL LEAD REGION WAR CHOOSE WEALTH MARXISM 20. PAGE 25 H0500
S/ASIA DIPLOM ECO/UNDEV NAT/LISM

B64
DE SMITH S.A.,THE NEW COMMONWEALTH AND ITS CONSTITUTIONS. AFR CYPRUS PAKISTAN S/ASIA INT/ORG NAT/G LEGIS LEGIT RIGID/FLEX PWR...CONCPT TIME/SEQ CMN/WLTH 20. PAGE 38 H0770
EX/STRUC CONSTN SOVEREIGN

B64
EMBREE A.T.,A GUIDE TO PAPERBACKS ON ASIA; SELECTED AND ANNOTATED (PAMPHLET). CULTURE SOCIETY ECO/UNDEV SECT DIPLOM COLONIAL MARXISM...SOC 20. PAGE 46 H0913
BIBLIOG/A ASIA S/ASIA NAT/G

B64
FALL B.,STREET WITHOUT JOY. FRANCE USA+45 DIPLOM ECO/TAC FOR/AID GUERRILLA REV WEAPON...TREND 20. PAGE 48 H0966
WAR S/ASIA FORCES COERCE

B64
GOODNOW H.F.,THE CIVIL SERVICE OF PAKISTAN: BUREAUCRACY IN A NEW NATION. INDIA PAKISTAN S/ASIA ECO/UNDEV PROVS CHIEF PARTIC CHOOSE EFFICIENCY PWR ...BIBLIOG 20. PAGE 59 H1173
ADMIN GOV/REL LAW NAT/G

B64
HEIMSATH C.H.,INDIAN NATIONALISM AND HINDU SOCIAL REFORM. S/ASIA LAW CULTURE SOCIETY STRATA PROVS VOL/ASSN DELIB/GP LEGIS TOP/EX DOMIN EDU/PROP LEGIT ATTIT ALL/VALS...POLICY SOC TIME/SEQ STERTYP VAL/FREE 19/20. PAGE 69 H1385
SECT NAT/G

B64
HOBBS C.C.,SOUTHEAST ASIA: AN ANNOTATED BIBLIOGRAPHY OF SELECTED REFERENCES IN WESTERN LANGUAGES (REV. ED.). CAMBODIA INDONESIA LAOS THAILAND VIETNAM CONSTN NAT/G...SOC WORSHIP 20. PAGE 72 H1437
BIBLIOG/A S/ASIA CULTURE SOCIETY

B64
LAWRENCE P.,ROAD BELONG CARGO: A STUDY OF CARGO MOVEMENT IN SOUTHERN MADANG DISTRICT, NEW GUINEA. S/ASIA CULTURE ECO/UNDEV PROC/MFG KIN CHIEF COLONIAL COERCE GP/REL DRIVE WEALTH WORSHIP 20 NEW/GUINEA. PAGE 92 H1846
SOC SECT ALL/VALS MYTH

B64
LEWIN P.,THE FOREIGN TRADE OF COMMUNIST CHINA* ITS IMPACT ON THE FREE WORLD. AFR EUR+WWI L/A+17C S/ASIA ECO/UNDEV CREATE FOR/AID...STAT NET/THEORY TREND CHARTS. PAGE 96 H1910
ASIA INT/TRADE NAT/COMP USSR

B64
MAHAR J.M.,INDIA: A CRITICAL BIBLIOGRAPHY. INDIA PAKISTAN CULTURE ECO/UNDEV LOC/G POL/PAR SECT PROB/SOLV DIPLOM ADMIN COLONIAL PARL/PROC ATTIT 20. PAGE 101 H2016
BIBLIOG/A S/ASIA NAT/G LEAD

B64
RAGHAVAN M.D.,INDIA IN CEYLONESE HISTORY, SOCIETY AND CULTURE. CEYLON INDIA S/ASIA LAW SOCIETY INT/TRADE ATTIT...ART/METH JURID SOC LING 20. PAGE 129 H2581
DIPLOM CULTURE SECT STRUCT

B64
SAKAI R.K.,STUDIES ON ASIA, 1964. ASIA CHINA/COM ISRAEL MALAYSIA S/ASIA USA+45 USSR ECO/UNDEV FAM POL/PAR SECT CONSULT NAT/LISM...POLICY SOC 20 CHINJAP. PAGE 137 H2736
PWR DIPLOM

B64
SINAI I.R.,THE CHALLENGE OF MODERNISATION* THE WEST'S IMPACT ON THE NON-WESTERN WORLD. EUR+WWI CULTURE ELITES SECT CONSERVE SOCISM...GP/COMP IDEA/COMP NAT/COMP GEN/LAWS. PAGE 144 H2881
ASIA S/ASIA ECO/UNDEV CREATE

B64
SINGER M.R.,THE EMERGING ELITE: A STUDY OF POLITICAL LEADERSHIP IN CEYLON. S/ASIA ECO/UNDEV AGRI KIN NAT/G SECT EX/STRUC LEGIT ATTIT PWR RESPECT...SOC STAT CHARTS 20. PAGE 144 H2883
TOP/EX STRATA NAT/LISM CEYLON

B64
TAYLOR E.,RICHER BY ASIA. S/ASIA CULTURE VOL/ASSN ACT/RES ATTIT DISPL PERSON ALL/VALS...INT/LAW MYTH SELF/OBS 20. PAGE 153 H3054
SOCIETY RIGID/FLEX INDIA

B64
THORNTON T.P.,THE THIRD WORLD IN SOVIET PERSPECTIVE: STUDIES BY SOVIET WRITERS ON THE DEVELOPING AREAS. AFR L/A+17C S/ASIA STRATA AGRI INDUS MARKET NAT/G POL/PAR ECO/TAC COLONIAL PERCEPT PWR WEALTH...MARXIST STAT CHARTS WORK MARX/KARL 20. PAGE 155 H3090
ECO/UNDEV ACT/RES USSR DIPLOM

B64
TILMAN R.O.,BUREAUCRATIC TRANSITION IN MALAYA. MALAYSIA S/ASIA UK NAT/G EX/STRUC DIPLOM...CHARTS BIBLIOG 20. PAGE 155 H3098
ADMIN COLONIAL SOVEREIGN EFFICIENCY

B64
TINKER H.,BALLOT BOX AND BAYONET - PEOPLE AND GOVERNMENT IN EMERGENT ASIAN COUNTRIES. CEYLON INDIA INDONESIA PHILIPPINE POL/PAR ADMIN COLONIAL LEAD PARL/PROC CHOOSE CONSEN ORD/FREE SOVEREIGN PLURISM...GOV/COMP THIRD/WRLD. PAGE 155 H3104
MYTH S/ASIA NAT/COMP NAT/LISM

B64
US LIBRARY OF CONGRESS,SOUTHEAST ASIA. CULTURE ...SOC STAT 20. PAGE 161 H3213
BIBLIOG/A S/ASIA ECO/UNDEV NAT/G

B64
VON FURER-HAIMEN E.,AN ANTHROPOLOGICAL BIBLIOGRAPHY OF SOUTH ASIA (VOL. II). STRATA STRUCT KIN SECT ACT/RES CREATE HABITAT...GEOG OBS 20. PAGE 163 H3268
BIBLIOG/A CULTURE S/ASIA SOC

B64
WARD R.E.,POLITICAL MODERNIZATION IN JAPAN AND TURKEY. ASIA ISLAM S/ASIA CONSTN CULTURE STRATA COM/IND POL/PAR FORCES ACT/RES ECO/TAC DOMIN EDU/PROP LEGIT ADMIN CHOOSE ATTIT ALL/VALS...STAT TIME/SEQ VAL/FREE CHINJAP. PAGE 165 H3307
SOCIETY TURKEY

B64
WERTHEIM W.F.,EAST-WEST PARALLELS. INDONESIA S/ASIA NAT/G SECT...TIME/SEQ METH REFORMERS S/EASTASIA. PAGE 167 H3334
SOC ECO/UNDEV CULTURE NAT/LISM

B64
WILCOX W.A.,INDIA, PAKISTAN AND THE RISE OF CHINA. ASIA BURMA CEYLON CHINA/COM INDIA PAKISTAN S/ASIA NAT/G VOL/ASSN FORCES TOP/EX ACT/RES DOMIN REGION RIGID/FLEX ORD/FREE...POLICY GEN/LAWS COLD/WAR 20. PAGE 168 H3362
CULTURE ATTIT DIPLOM

L64
SYMONDS R.,"REFLECTIONS IN LOCALISATION." AFR S/ASIA UK STRATA INT/ORG NAT/G SCHOOL EDU/PROP LEGIT KNOWL ORD/FREE PWR RESPECT CMN/WLTH 20. PAGE 151 H3023
ADMIN MGT COLONIAL

S64
"FURTHER READING." INDIA ATTIT...POLICY 20 NEHRU/J. PAGE 2 H0042
BIBLIOG S/ASIA CHIEF NAT/G

S64
BRADLEY C.P.,"THE FORMATION OF MALAYSIA." INDIA S/ASIA POL/PAR VOL/ASSN TOP/EX LEGIT RACE/REL ORD/FREE 20. PAGE 20 H0398
NAT/G CREATE COLONIAL MALAYSIA

S64
ENNIS T.E.,"VIETNAM: LAND WITHOUT LAUGHTER." S/ASIA VIETNAM VIETNAM/S INTELL SOCIETY SECT FORCES DIPLOM LEGIT COERCE WAR ATTIT RIGID/FLEX ORD/FREE COLD/WAR 20. PAGE 46 H0929
NAT/G TOP/EX GUERRILLA

S64
LANGER P.F.,"JAPAN'S RELATIONS WITH CHINA." ASIA CHINA/COM KOREA S/ASIA ECO/DEV NAT/G POL/PAR EDU/PROP ATTIT ALL/VALS...METH/CNCPT TIME/SEQ TREND 20 CHINJAP. PAGE 91 H1808
RIGID/FLEX ECO/TAC

S64
LANGERHANS H.,"NEHRU'S BITTERNESS." FUT INDIA S/ASIA CONSTN CULTURE ECO/UNDEV ECO/TAC DOMIN EDU/PROP ATTIT PERCEPT PERSON...POLICY 20 NEHRU/J. PAGE 91 H1811
ECO/DEV BIOG

S64
LEVI W.,"INDIAN NEUTRALISM RECONSIDERED." ASIA CHINA/COM S/ASIA SOCIETY NAT/G ACT/RES LEGIT NEUTRAL COERCE ATTIT DRIVE PERCEPT RIGID/FLEX HEALTH LOVE PWR...DECISION RECORD TREND STERTYP 20. PAGE 95 H1896
ORD/FREE CONCPT INDIA

S64
LOW D.A.,"LION RAMPANT." EUR+WWI MOD/EUR S/ASIA ECO/UNDEV NAT/G FORCES TEC/DEV ECO/TAC LEGIT ADMIN COLONIAL COERCE ORD/FREE RESPECT 19/20. PAGE 99 H1972
AFR DOMIN DIPLOM UK

S64
MOZINGO D.P.,"CHINA'S RELATIONS WITH HER ASIAN NEIGHBORS." ASIA CHINA/COM S/ASIA VIETNAM NAT/G DELIB/GP FORCES CREATE DOMIN EDU/PROP REV RIGID/FLEX PWR...TIME/SEQ GEN/LAWS COLD/WAR 20. PAGE 114 H2277
VOL/ASSN POLICY DIPLOM

S64
NASH M.,"SOCIAL PREREQUISITES TO ECONOMIC GROWTH IN LATIN AMERICA AND SOUTHEAST ASIA." L/A+17C S/ASIA CULTURE SOCIETY ECO/UNDEV AGRI INDUS NAT/G PLAN TEC/DEV EDU/PROP ROUTINE ALL/VALS...POLICY RELATIV SOC NAT/COMP WORK TOT/POP 20. PAGE 116 H2314
ECO/DEV PERCEPT

S64
RUDOLPH L.I.,"GENERALS AND POLITICIANS IN INDIA." INDIA S/ASIA CULTURE STRATA NAT/G LEGIS TOP/EX EDU/PROP ATTIT ORD/FREE PWR RESPECT SKILL...POLICY BIOG TIME/SEQ STERTYP VAL/FREE 20. PAGE 136 H2713
FORCES COERCE

S64
SAYEED K.,"PATHAN REGIONALISM." ISLAM PAKISTAN S/ASIA CULTURE SOCIETY NAT/G NEIGH DIPLOM LEGIT COERCE CHOOSE ATTIT DISPL PERCEPT ALL/VALS SOVEREIGN...POLICY RELATIV SOC TIME/SEQ TOT/POP 20. PAGE 138 H2761
SECT NAT/LISM REGION

S64
SCHEFFLER H.W.,"THE GENESIS AND REPRESSION OF CONFLICT: CHOISEUL ISLAND." S/ASIA LOC/G NAT/G FORCES LEGIS DIPLOM DOMIN LEGIT EXEC CHOOSE ATTIT RESPECT SKILL...POLICY JURID OBS TREND GEN/METH 20.
PWR COERCE WAR

PAGE 139 H2781

S64
SMYTHE H.H.,"NEHRU AND INDIAN FOREIGN POLICY." S/ASIA ECO/UNDEV NAT/G POL/PAR CONSULT PLAN DIPLOM NEUTRAL COERCE ATTIT DRIVE PERSON MORAL ORD/FREE RESPECT...GEOG CONCPT TIME/SEQ TREND GEN/LAWS 20 NEHRU/J. PAGE 146 H2922
TOP/EX BIOG INDIA

S64
TINKER H.,"POLITICS IN SOUTHEAST ASIA." INT/ORG NAT/G CREATE PLAN TEC/DEV GUERRILLA KNOWL ORD/FREE COLD/WAR. PAGE 155 H3103
S/ASIA ACT/RES REGION

S64
VANDENBOSCH A.,"POWER BALANCE IN INDONESIA." S/ASIA USSR NAT/G TOP/EX BAL/PWR DOMIN NEUTRAL ORD/FREE PWR...POLICY TIME/SEQ GEN/LAWS 20 SUKARNO/A. PAGE 162 H3233
FORCES TREND DIPLOM INDONESIA

B65
BETTISON D.G.,THE PAPUA-GUINEA ELECTIONS 1964. S/ASIA CONSTN POL/PAR EDU/PROP PARTIC SUFF CENTRAL CONSEN...OBS CHARTS BIBLIOG 20. PAGE 16 H0324
NAT/G LEGIS CHOOSE REPRESENT

B65
BURLING R.,HILL FARMS AND PADI FIELDS. BURMA S/ASIA THAILAND VIETNAM AGRI NEIGH SECT GP/REL NAT/LISM ORD/FREE 20 MID/EAST MIGRATION. PAGE 24 H0491
SOCIETY STRUCT CULTURE SOVEREIGN

B65
CAMERON W.J.,NEW ZEALAND. NEW/ZEALND S/ASIA DIPLOM INT/TRADE WRITING COLONIAL PARL/PROC...GEOG CMN/WLTH. PAGE 26 H0513
SOCIETY GP/REL STRUCT

B65
CRABB C.V. JR.,THE ELEPHANTS AND THE GRASS* A STUDY OF NONALIGNMENT. AFR ASIA INDIA S/ASIA USA+45 USSR BAL/PWR NEUTRAL ATTIT...TREND NAT/COMP COLD/WAR. PAGE 34 H0691
ECO/UNDEV DIPLOM CONCPT

B65
GHAI D.P.,PORTRAIT OF A MINORITY: ASIANS IN EAST AFRICA. S/ASIA TANZANIA UGANDA COLONIAL...SOC OBS PREDICT ANTHOL 20. PAGE 56 H1119
RACE/REL GP/REL CULTURE AFR

B65
HARBISON F.,MANPOWER AND EDUCATION. AFR CHINA/COM IRAN L/A+17C S/ASIA TEC/DEV ADJUST OPTIMAL SKILL ...ANTHOL 20. PAGE 66 H1325
ECO/UNDEV EDU/PROP WORKER NAT/COMP

B65
HAUSER P.M.,THE STUDY OF URBANIZATION. S/ASIA ECO/DEV ECO/UNDEV NEIGH ACT/RES GEOG. PAGE 68 H1359
CULTURE MUNIC SOC

B65
INST INTL DES CIVILISATION DIF,THE CONSTITUTIONS AND ADMINISTRATIVE INSTITUTIONS OF THE NEW STATES. AFR ISLAM S/ASIA NAT/G POL/PAR DELIB/GP EX/STRUC CONFER EFFICIENCY NAT/LISM...JURID SOC 20. PAGE 77 H1535
CONSTN ADMIN ADJUD ECO/UNDEV

B65
JAIN S.C.,THE STATE AND AGRICULTURE. INDIA S/ASIA ECO/UNDEV PROB/SOLV CAP/ISM MARXISM SOCISM 20. PAGE 79 H1586
NAT/G POLICY AGRI ECO/TAC

B65
JANSEN M.B.,CHANGING JAPANESE ATTITUDES TOWARD MODERNIZATION. ASIA CHINA/COM S/ASIA INTELL SOCIETY KIN NAT/G SECT PERCEPT RIGID/FLEX...SOC CONCPT TIME/SEQ TREND TOT/POP 19/20 CHINJAP. PAGE 80 H1591
TEC/DEV ATTIT INDIA

B65
LAWRENCE P.,GODS, GHOSTS, AND MEN IN MELANESIA: SOME RELIGIONS OF AUSTRALIAN NEW GUINEA AND THE NEW HEBRIDES. SOCIETY ECO/UNDEV FAM GP/REL INGP/REL HABITAT PERSON...GEOG SOC ANTHOL BIBLIOG WORSHIP 20 NEW/GUINEA. PAGE 92 H1847
MYTH S/ASIA SECT CULTURE

B65
NATIONAL BOOK CENTRE PAKISTAN,BOOKS ON PAKISTAN: A BIBLIOGRAPHY. PAKISTAN CULTURE DIPLOM ADMIN ATTIT ...MAJORIT SOC CONCPT 20. PAGE 116 H2319
BIBLIOG CONSTN S/ASIA NAT/G

B65
ONSLOW C.,ASIAN ECONOMIC DEVELOPMENT. BURMA CEYLON INDIA MALAYSIA PAKISTAN S/ASIA AGRI INDUS MARKET PROB/SOLV CAP/ISM FOR/AID INT/TRADE DEMAND WEALTH ...POLICY ANTHOL 20. PAGE 121 H2418
ECO/UNDEV ECO/TAC PLAN NAT/G

B65
ROMEIN J.,THE ASIAN CENTURY. ASIA COM S/ASIA DIPLOM COLONIAL TIME 20. PAGE 133 H2666
REV NAT/LISM CULTURE MARXISM

B65
SAKAI R.K.,STUDIES ON ASIA, 1965. INDIA KOREA S/ASIA USA+45 CONSTN KIN SECT PARTIC SUFF NAT/LISM ...POLICY SOC 19/20 CHINJAP. PAGE 137 H2737
PARL/PROC ASIA

B65
SCALAPINO R.A.,THE COMMUNIST REVOLUTION IN ASIA* TACTICS, GOALS, AND ACHIEVEMENTS. INDIA INTELL POL/PAR FORCES DOMIN EDU/PROP LEGIT COERCE REV ATTIT CHINJAP. PAGE 138 H2763
ASIA S/ASIA MARXISM NAT/COMP

B65
SCHULER E.A.,THE PAKISTAN ACADEMIES FOR RURAL DEVELOPMENT COMILLA AND PESHAWAR 1959-1964. PAKISTAN S/ASIA SOCIETY STRUCT AGRI NAT/G TEC/DEV EDU/PROP 20. PAGE 140 H2801
BIBLIOG PLAN ECO/TAC ECO/UNDEV

B65
SMITH R.M.,CAMBODIA'S FOREIGN POLICY. ECO/UNDEV NAT/G NEUTRAL ORD/FREE COLD/WAR VAL/FREE. PAGE 146 H2917
S/ASIA CAMBODIA DIPLOM

B65
VON RENESSE E.A.,UNVOLLENDETE DEMOKRATIEN. AFR ISLAM S/ASIA SOCIETY ACT/RES COLONIAL...JURID CHARTS BIBLIOG METH 13/20. PAGE 164 H3276
ECO/UNDEV NAT/COMP SOVEREIGN

B65
WAINWRIGHT M.D.,A GUIDE TO WESTERN MANUSCRIPTS AND DOCUMENTS IN THE BRITISH ISLES RELATING TO SOUTH AND SOUTHEAST ASIA. UK CULTURE...SOC 15/20. PAGE 164 H3288
BIBLIOG S/ASIA WRITING

L65
SHARMA S.P.,"THE INDIA-CHINA BORDER DISPUTE: AN INDIAN PERSPECTIVE." ASIA CHINA/COM S/ASIA NAT/G LEGIT CT/SYS NAT/LISM DRIVE MORAL ORD/FREE PWR 20. PAGE 142 H2850
LAW ATTIT SOVEREIGN INDIA

S65
PRABHAKAR P.,"SURVEY OF RESEARCH AND SOURCE MATERIALS; THE SINO-INDIAN BORDER DISPUTE." CHINA/COM INDIA LAW NAT/G PLAN BAL/PWR WAR...POLICY 20 COLD/WAR. PAGE 128 H2553
BIBLIOG ASIA S/ASIA DIPLOM

B66
AHMED Z.,DUSK AND DAWN IN VILLAGE INDIA. INDIA S/ASIA UK CULTURE SOCIETY NAT/G DOMIN COLONIAL HABITAT SOVEREIGN...SOC DICTIONARY 20. PAGE 4 H0080
NEIGH ECO/UNDEV AGRI ADJUST

B66
AIYAR S.P.,PERSPECTIVES ON THE WELFARE STATE. INDIA S/ASIA UK CONSTN ECO/UNDEV NAT/G INGP/REL CENTRAL NAT/LISM ATTIT...CONCPT ANTHOL BIBLIOG 20. PAGE 4 H0087
NEW/LIB WELF/ST IDEA/COMP ADJUST

B66
BRACKMAN A.C.,SOUTHEAST ASIA'S SECOND FRONT: THE POWER STRUGGLE IN THE MALAY ARCHIPELAGO. CHINA/COM INDONESIA MALAYSIA ECO/UNDEV INT/ORG NAT/G FORCES DIPLOM EDU/PROP REGION COERCE GUERRILLA AUTHORIT POPULISM...MAJORIT 20 KENNEDY/JF SEATO. PAGE 20 H0396
S/ASIA MARXISM REV

B66
BRAIBANTI R.,ASIAN BUREAUCRATIC SYSTEMS EMERGENT FROM THE BRITISH IMPERIAL TRADITION. BURMA CEYLON INDIA PAKISTAN UK ELITES ECO/UNDEV NAT/G...MGT SOC CHARTS ANTHOL 19/20. PAGE 20 H0401
GOV/COMP COLONIAL ADMIN S/ASIA

B66
CADY J.F.,THAILAND, BURMA, LAOS AND CAMBODIA. FRANCE UK CULTURE NAT/G DOMIN GP/REL RACE/REL HABITAT...GEOG TREND CHINJAP BUDDHISM. PAGE 25 H0504
S/ASIA COLONIAL REGION SECT

B66
COEDES G.,THE MAKING OF SOUTH EAST ASIA. BURMA CAMBODIA LAOS S/ASIA THAILAND VIETNAM REV WAR CIVMIL/REL...GEOG 6/13. PAGE 31 H0614
CULTURE FORCES DOMIN

B66
EMBREE A.T.,ASIA: A GUIDE TO BASIC BOOKS (PAMPHLET). ECO/UNDEV SECT FORCES DIPLOM ALL/IDEOS ...SOC 20. PAGE 46 H0914
BIBLIOG/A ASIA S/ASIA NAT/G

B66
FARWELL G.,MASK OF ASIA: THE PHILIPPINES. PHILIPPINE SECT DIPLOM ATTIT...SOC RECORD PREDICT BIBLIOG 20. PAGE 49 H0974
S/ASIA CULTURE

B66
FITZGERALD C.P.,A CONCISE HISTORY OF EAST ASIA. ASIA KOREA S/ASIA INT/TRADE REGION MARXISM 20 CHINJAP. PAGE 51 H1017
ECO/UNDEV COLONIAL CULTURE

B66
GORDON B.K.,THE DIMENSIONS OF CONFLICT IN SOUTHEAST ASIA. S/ASIA FORCES ADJUD REGION...CHARTS 20. PAGE 59 H1177
DIPLOM NAT/COMP INT/ORG VOL/ASSN

B66
HARRISON B.,SOUTH-EAST ASIA: A SHORT HISTORY (3RD ED.). ECO/UNDEV INDUS NAT/G SECT BAL/PWR NAT/LISM ...SOC 15/20 S/EASTASIA. PAGE 67 H1346
COLONIAL S/ASIA CULTURE

B66
KEYES J.G.,A BIBLIOGRAPHY OF WESTERN LANGUAGE PUBLICATIONS CONCERNING NORTH VIETNAM IN THE CORNELL LIBRARY. VIETNAM/N NAT/G FORCES TEC/DEV DIPLOM LEAD RACE/REL...GEOG SOC 20. PAGE 85 H1700
BIBLIOG/A CULTURE ECO/UNDEV S/ASIA

B66
KIRKLAND E.C.,A BIBLIOGRAPHY OF SOUTH ASIAN FOLKLORE. WRITING HABITAT ALL/VALS MYSTISM ...ART/METH GEOG PSY SOC MYTH WORSHIP 13/20. PAGE 86 H1723
BIBLIOG S/ASIA CULTURE CREATE

B66
LEIGH M.B.,CHECK LIST OF HOLDINGS ON BORNEO IN THE CORNELL UNIVERSITY LIBRARIES (PAMPHLET). BORNEO MALAYSIA LAW CONSTN GP/REL SOC. PAGE 93 H1866
BIBLIOG S/ASIA DIPLOM NAT/G

B66
US DEPARTMENT OF STATE,RESEARCH ON AFRICA (EXTERNAL RESEARCH LIST NO 5-25). LAW CULTURE ECO/UNDEV POL/PAR DIPLOM EDU/PROP LEAD REGION MARXISM...GEOG LING WORSHIP 20. PAGE 159 H3188 — BIBLIOG/A ASIA S/ASIA NAT/G

B66
US DEPARTMENT OF THE ARMY,COMMUNIST CHINA: A STRATEGIC SURVEY: A BIBLIOGRAPHY (PAMPHLET NO. 20-67). CHINA/COM COM INDIA USSR NAT/G POL/PAR EX/STRUC FORCES NUC/PWR REV ATTIT...POLICY GEOG CHARTS. PAGE 160 H3194 — BIBLIOG/A MARXISM S/ASIA DIPLOM

B66
US DEPARTMENT OF THE ARMY,SOUTH ASIA: A STRATEGIC SURVEY (PAMPHLET NO. 550-3). AFGHANISTN INDIA NEPAL PAKISTAN ECO/UNDEV INT/ORG POL/PAR FORCES FOR/AID INT/TRADE LEAD WAR...POLICY SOC TREND 20. PAGE 160 H3195 — BIBLIOG/A S/ASIA DIPLOM NAT/G

S66
"RESEARCH WORK 1965-1966." NEW/ZEALND ELITES ACADEM LOC/G MUNIC POL/PAR PROVS DIPLOM COLONIAL...SOC 20 AUSTRAL. PAGE 2 H0047 — BIBLIOG NAT/G CULTURE S/ASIA

S66
GAMER R.E.,"URGENT SINGAPORE, PATIENT MALAYSIA." MALAYSIA S/ASIA ECO/UNDEV POL/PAR CHIEF TARIFFS TAX CONTROL LEAD REGION PWR 20 SINGAPORE. PAGE 55 H1094 — DIPLOM NAT/G POLICY ECO/TAC

S66
MANSERGH N.,"THE PARTITION OF INDIA IN RETROSPECT." INDIA PAKISTAN S/ASIA UK DIPLOM COLONIAL GP/REL PWR 20. PAGE 102 H2042 — NAT/G PARL/PROC POLICY POL/PAR

C66
WINT G.,"ASIA: A HANDBOOK." ASIA S/ASIA INDUS LABOR SECT PRESS RACE/REL MARXISM...STAT CHARTS BIBLIOG 20. PAGE 169 H3388 — ECO/UNDEV DIPLOM NAT/G SOCIETY

B67
BAIN C.A.,VIETNAM: THE ROOTS OF CONFLICT. FRANCE S/ASIA USSR VIETNAM POL/PAR SECT FORCES COLONIAL NAT/LISM PEACE ORD/FREE MARXISM...GEOG CHARTS 4/20. PAGE 10 H0202 — NAT/G WAR CULTURE

B67
BURNHAM J.,THE WAR WE ARE IN, THE LAST DECADE AND THE NEXT. ASIA COM EUR+WWI S/ASIA WOR+45 ECO/UNDEV INT/ORG FORCES WAR...OLD/LIB TREND 20 COLD/WAR. PAGE 25 H0492 — POLICY NAT/G DIPLOM NAT/COMP

B67
CORDIER A.W.,COLUMBIA ESSAYS IN INTERNATIONAL AFFAIRS. ASIA CHINA/COM FRANCE S/ASIA SPAIN UAR ECO/UNDEV LOC/G ECO/TAC GUERRILLA PWR...BIOG ANTHOL 18/20 MAU/MAU. PAGE 33 H0663 — NAT/G DIPLOM MARXISM POLICY

B67
ERDMAN H.L.,THE SWATANTRA PARTY AND INDIAN CONSERVATISM. INDIA S/ASIA SOCIETY STRATA LOC/G NAT/G LEAD PARTIC GP/REL ATTIT...CONCPT GP/COMP BIBLIOG 20 SWATANTRA. PAGE 47 H0938 — POL/PAR CONSERVE CHOOSE POLICY

B67
FALL B.B.,HO CHI MINH ON REVOLUTION: SELECTED WRITINGS, 1920-66. COM VIETNAM ELITES NAT/G COERCE GUERRILLA RACE/REL MARXISM...MARXIST ANTHOL 20. PAGE 48 H0968 — REV COLONIAL ECO/UNDEV S/ASIA

B67
MCNELLY T.,SOURCES IN MODERN EAST ASIAN HISTORY AND POLITICS. KOREA VIETNAM CULTURE DIPLOM COLONIAL REV WAR PWR ALL/IDEOS MARXISM...ANTHOL 20 CHINJAP. PAGE 107 H2147 — NAT/COMP ASIA S/ASIA SOCIETY

B67
MUHAMMAD A.C.,THE EMERGENCE OF PAKISTAN. PAKISTAN S/ASIA CONSTN ECO/UNDEV NAT/G CONTROL NAT/LISM 20. PAGE 114 H2281 — DIPLOM COLONIAL SECT PROB/SOLV

B67
PYE L.W.,SOUTHEAST ASIA'S POLITICAL SYSTEMS. ASIA S/ASIA STRUCT ECO/UNDEV EX/STRUC CAP/ISM DIPLOM ALL/IDEOS...TREND CHARTS. PAGE 128 H2568 — NAT/G POL/PAR GOV/COMP

B67
SCHECTER J.,THE NEW FACE OF BUDDHA: BUDDHISM AND POLITICAL POWER IN SOUTHEAST ASIA. S/ASIA NAT/G POL/PAR NAT/LISM ATTIT MARXISM...BIBLIOG 20. PAGE 139 H2780 — SECT POLICY PWR LEAD

L67
HOSHII I.,"JAPAN'S STAKE IN ASIA." ASIA S/ASIA CAP/ISM ECO/TAC ROLE...GEOG 20 CHINJAP. PAGE 74 H1477 — DIPLOM REGION NAT/G INT/ORG

L67
MCALLISTER J.T. JR.,"THE POSSIBILITIES FOR DIPLOMACY IN SOUTHEAST ASIA." LAOS VIETNAM INT/ORG NAT/G PROVS BAL/PWR DOMIN AGREE COLONIAL WAR PWR 17/20 TREATY. PAGE 106 H2121 — DIPLOM S/ASIA

L67
SCALAPINO R.A.,"A SURVEY OF ASIA IN 1966." ASIA S/ASIA CONSTN SOCIETY POL/PAR CHIEF WAR...ANTHOL 20. PAGE 138 H2764 — DIPLOM

S67
BATOR V.,"ONE WAR* TWO VIETNAMS." S/ASIA VIETNAM DIPLOM SUFF ATTIT ORD/FREE 20. PAGE 12 H0236 — WAR BAL/PWR NAT/G STRUCT

S67
FUSARO A.,"THE EFFECT OF PROPORTIONAL REPRESENTATION ON VOTING IN THE AUSTRALIAN SENATE." S/ASIA CONSTN POL/PAR CONTROL GP/REL PWR...CHARTS 20 AUSTRAL HOUSE/REP SENATE. PAGE 54 H1083 — LEGIS CHOOSE REPRESENT NAT/G

S67
ROSE S.,"ASIAN NATIONALISM* THE SECOND STAGE." ASIA COM ECO/UNDEV NAT/G PROB/SOLV DIPLOM FOR/AID DOMIN NEUTRAL REGION TASK...METH/COMP 20. PAGE 134 H2675 — NAT/LISM S/ASIA BAL/PWR COLONIAL

S67
TANTER R.,"A THEORY OF REVOLUTION." ASIA CUBA L/A+17C S/ASIA SOCIETY NAT/G ADJUST...CONCPT CHARTS. PAGE 152 H3046 — REV ECO/UNDEV EDU/PROP METH/COMP

L95
BELSHAW C.S.,"IN SEARCH OF WEALTH; STUDY OF EMERGENCE OF COMMERCIAL OPERA TIONS IN MELANESIAN SOCIETY OF SOUTHEASTERN PAPUA." S/ASIA CULTURE KIN ECO/TAC DEMAND INCOME 20 MELANESIA PAPUA. PAGE 14 H0272 — INT/TRADE ECO/UNDEV METH/COMP SOCIETY

S/EASTASIA....SOUTHEAST ASIA: CAMBODIA, LAOS, NORTH AND SOUTH VIETNAM, AND THAILAND

B64
WERTHEIM W.F.,EAST-WEST PARALLELS. INDONESIA S/ASIA NAT/G SECT...TIME/SEQ METH REFORMERS S/EASTASIA. PAGE 167 H3334 — SOC ECO/UNDEV CULTURE NAT/LISM

B66
HARRISON B.,SOUTH-EAST ASIA: A SHORT HISTORY (3RD ED.). ECO/UNDEV INDUS NAT/G SECT BAL/PWR NAT/LISM ...SOC 15/20 S/EASTASIA. PAGE 67 H1346 — COLONIAL S/ASIA CULTURE

SAAB H. H2726

SAAR....SAAR VALLEY, GERMANY

S62
GUETZKOW H.,"THE POTENTIAL OF CASE STUDY IN ANALYZING INTERNATIONAL CONFLICT." EUR+WWI FUT GERMANY INTELL SOCIETY STRUCT INT/ORG LOC/G NAT/G CONSULT CREATE PLAN CHOOSE ATTIT RIGID/FLEX ...POLICY SAAR 20. PAGE 62 H1246 — EDU/PROP METH/CNCPT COERCE FRANCE

SABAH....SABAH, MALAYSIA

SABBATINO....SABBATINO CASE

SABINE G.H. H2727

SABLE M.H. H2728

SABRAN B. H0779

SAFRAN M. H2729

SAHARA....SAHARA, AFRICA

B58
BRIGGS L.C.,THE LIVING RACES OF THE SAHARA. STRATA AGRI KIN INT/TRADE HABITAT...GEOG AUD/VIS CHARTS BIBLIOG 20 SAHARA MIGRATION. PAGE 21 H0417 — STRUCT SOCIETY SOC CULTURE

SAHLINS M.D. H2730

SAINDERICHIN P. H2731

SAINT AUGUSTINE....SEE AUGUSTINE

SAINT/PIER....JACQUES SAINT-PIERRE

SAINT-PIERRE C.I. H2732

SAINTSIMON....COMTE DE SAINT-SIMON

B50
CARR E.H.,STUDIES IN REVOLUTION. CREATE WAR PERSON ALL/IDEOS MARXISM SOCISM...PHIL/SCI METH/COMP ANTHOL 18/20 SAINTSIMON MARX/KARL PROUDHON/P LASSALLE/F PLEKHNV/GV. PAGE 27 H0537 — REV IDEA/COMP COERCE BIOG

B65
HALEVY E.,THE ERA OF TYRANNIES (TRANS. BY R. K. WEBB). FRANCE MOD/EUR UK ECO/DEV LABOR NAT/G BAL/PWR FEDERAL ALL/VALS...OLD/LIB TREND 18/20 SAINTSIMON. PAGE 64 H1285 — SOCISM CONCPT UTOPIA ORD/FREE

SAKAI R.K. H2733,H2734,H2735,H2736,H2737,H2738

SALARY....SEE WORKER, WEALTH, ROUTINE

SALARY INFORMATION RETRIEVAL SYSTEM....SEE SIRS

SALAZAR/A....ANTONIO DE OLIVERA SALAZAR

B63
DEBRAY P.,LE PORTUGAL ENTRE DEUX REVOLUTIONS. EUR+WWI PORTUGAL CONSTN LEGIT ADMIN ATTIT ALL/VALS ...DECISION CONCPT 20 SALAZAR/A. PAGE 39 H0779
NAT/G DELIB/GP TOP/EX

SALERA V. H0927

SALETORE B.A. H2739,H2740

SALIBI K. H1198

SALIENCE....SALIENCE

SALINGER/P....PIERRE SALINGER

SALISBURY H.E. H2741

SALKEVER L.R. H2742

SALO....SALO REPUBLIC

N19
WEBB L.C.,CHURCH AND STATE IN ITALY: 1947-1957 (PAMPHLET). GERMANY ITALY CONSTN POL/PAR AGREE CONTROL PARTIC CHOOSE ATTIT ORD/FREE FASCISM MARXISM 20 CHURCH/STA MARITAIN/J SALO. PAGE 166 H3316
SECT CATHISM NAT/G GP/REL

SALVADORI M. H2743,H2744

SALVEMINI G. H2745

SALYZYN V. H2746

SAMBURU....SAMBURU TRIBE OF EAST AFRICA

B65
SPENCER P.,THE SAMBURU: A STUDY OF GERONTOCRACY IN A NOMADIC TRIBE. AFR SOCIETY ECO/UNDEV AGRI FAM NEIGH SECT GP/REL MARRIAGE WORSHIP 20 SAMBURU. PAGE 147 H2945
KIN STRUCT AGE/O CULTURE

SAMOA....SEE ALSO WEST/SAMOA

B61
WEST F.J.,POLITICAL ADVANCEMENT IN THE SOUTH PACIFIC. CONSTN CULTURE POL/PAR LEGIS DOMIN ADMIN CHOOSE SOVEREIGN VAL/FREE 20 FIJI TAHITI SAMOA. PAGE 167 H3335
S/ASIA LOC/G COLONIAL

L62
CORET A.,"L'INDEPENDANCE DU SAMOA OCCIDENTAL." S/ASIA LAW INT/ORG EXEC ALL/VALS SAMOA UN 20. PAGE 33 H0668
NAT/G STRUCT SOVEREIGN

SAMP....SAMPLE SURVEY

N19
INTERNATIONAL LABOUR OFFICE,EMPLOYMENT, UNEMPLOYMENT AND LABOUR FORCE STATISTICS (PAMPHLET). EUR+WWI STRATA AGRI INDUS NAT/G PROB/SOLV PAY AGE SEX...SAMP NAT/COMP METH 20 ILO. PAGE 78 H1557
WORKER LABOR STAT ECO/DEV

B31
DEKAT A.D.A.,COLONIAL POLICY. S/ASIA CULTURE EX/STRUC ECO/TAC DOMIN ADMIN COLONIAL ROUTINE SOVEREIGN WEALTH...POLICY MGT RECORD KNO/TEST SAMP. PAGE 39 H0785
DRIVE PWR INDONESIA NETHERLAND

S52
EISENSTADT S.N.,"THE PROCESS OF ABSORPTION OF NEW IMMIGRANTS IN ISRAEL" (BMR)" ISRAEL CULTURE SCHOOL WORKER PARTIC DRIVE ORD/FREE...STAT OBS INT CHARTS SOC/INTEG 20 JEWS. PAGE 45 H0900
HABITAT ATTIT SAMP

S53
BAUER R.A.,"WORD-OF-MOUTH COMMUNICATION IN THE SOVIET UNION." COM INTELL SOCIETY LABOR ATTIT KNOWL ...INT QU SAMP CHARTS 20. PAGE 12 H0239
CULTURE USSR

B55
DUVERGER M.,THE POLITICAL ROLE OF WOMEN. FRANCE GERMANY/W NORWAY YUGOSLAVIA STRATA LOBBY AGE ATTIT ROLE...STAT SAMP CHARTS METH/COMP NAT/COMP HYPO/EXP FEMALE/SEX. PAGE 44 H0875
SEX LEAD PARTIC CHOOSE

B58
COLEMAN J.S.,NIGERIA: BACKGROUND TO NATIONALISM. AFR SOCIETY ECO/DEV KIN LOC/G POL/PAR TEC/DEV DOMIN ADMIN DRIVE PWR RESPECT...TRADIT SOC INT SAMP TIME/SEQ 20. PAGE 31 H0627
NAT/G NAT/LISM NIGERIA

B59
ELDRIDGE H.T.,THE MATERIALS OF DEMOGRAPHY: A SELECTED AND ANNOTATED BIBLIOGRAPHY. R+D DEATH ...SAMP METH/COMP NAT/COMP 20. PAGE 45 H0905
BIBLIOG/A GEOG STAT TREND

B59
SVALASTOGA K.,PRESTIGE, CLASS, AND MOBILITY. DENMARK UK EDU/PROP INCOME WEALTH...SOC SAMP 20. PAGE 151 H3010
NAT/COMP STRATA STRUCT ELITES

L60
ROKKAN S.,"NORWAY AND THE UNITED STATES OF AMERICA." NORWAY CHOOSE...SOC STAND/INT SAMP CHARTS GP/COMP METH/COMP 20. PAGE 133 H2665
STRUCT NAT/G PARTIC REPRESENT

L60
WHEELER G.,"RACIAL PROBLEMS IN SOVIET MUSLIM ASIA." COM CULTURE SOCIETY NEIGH SECT DOMIN EDU/PROP DISCRIM DISPL DRIVE PWR SOVEREIGN...CENSUS SAMP TREND 20 MUSLIM. PAGE 167 H3340
PERSON ATTIT USSR RACE/REL

B61
EMMET C.,THE VANISHING SWASTIKA. GERMANY/W ELITES CRIME WAR...SAMP 20. PAGE 46 H0922
FASCISM ATTIT AGE/Y NAT/G

S61
SCHECHTMAN J.B.,"MINORITIES IN THE MIDDLE EAST." ISLAM INTELL SOCIETY STRATA KIN NAT/G VOL/ASSN EDU/PROP REGION GP/REL DISCRIM ATTIT BIO/SOC DISPL PERSON ALL/VALS...PSY SOC OBS SAMP GEN/LAWS 20. PAGE 139 H2776
SECT CULTURE RACE/REL

B63
ALMOND G.A.,THE CIVIC CULTURE: POLITICAL ATTITUDES AND DEMOCRACY IN FIVE NATIONS. GERMANY/W ITALY UK USA+45 SOCIETY STRUCT PARTIC...SOC DEEP/INT SAMP 20 MEXIC/AMER. PAGE 6 H0113
POPULISM CULTURE NAT/COMP ATTIT

B63
WALKER A.A.,OFFICIAL PUBLICATIONS OF SIERRA LEONE AND GAMBIA. GAMBIA SIER/LEONE UK LAW CONSTN LEGIS PLAN BUDGET DIPLOM...SOC SAMP CON/ANAL 20. PAGE 164 H3290
BIBLIOG NAT/G COLONIAL ADMIN

L63
CORWIN A.F.,"CONTEMPORARY MEXICAN ATTITUDES TOWARD POPULATION, POVERTY, AND PUBLIC OPINION." L/A+17C CULTURE SOCIETY ACT/RES ECO/TAC EDU/PROP PERSON HEALTH KNOWL...GEOG PHIL/SCI STAT OBS INT SAMP MEXIC/AMER VAL/FREE 20. PAGE 34 H0672
ATTIT QU

L64
BERELSON B.,"SAMPLE SURVEYS AND POPULATION CONTROL." ASIA FUT ISLAM L/A+17C CULTURE SOCIETY FAM NAT/G CONSULT PLAN EDU/PROP ATTIT DRIVE ALL/VALS...POLICY RELATIV HEAL PSY SOC CONCPT METH/CNCPT OBS OBS/ENVIR TOT/POP. PAGE 15 H0297
BIO/SOC SAMP

L64
FINDLATER R.,"US." EUR+WWI GERMANY USSR SOCIETY FACE/GP EDU/PROP PERCEPT PERSON ALL/VALS...PSY SOC CONCPT SELF/OBS SAMP TREND 20. PAGE 50 H1001
CULTURE ATTIT UK

S64
HIRAI N.,"SHINTO AND INTERNATIONAL PROBLEMS." SOCIETY NAT/G PLAN EDU/PROP RACE/REL PEACE ATTIT PERCEPT LOVE MORAL...HUM MYTH RECORD SAMP TREND STERTYP TOT/POP 20 UN CHINJAP SHINTO. PAGE 71 H1423
ASIA SECT

B65
HERRICK B.H.,URBAN MIGRATION AND ECONOMIC DEVELOPMENT IN CHILE. CHILE AGRI INDUS LABOR NAT/G CENTRAL PRODUC...STAT SAMP CHARTS BIBLIOG/A 20 MIGRATION. PAGE 70 H1404
HABITAT GEOG MUNIC ECO/UNDEV

B65
VON STACKELBERG K.,ALLE KRETER LUGEN VORURTEILE UBER MENSCHEN UND VOLKER. DIPLOM DOMIN RUMOR NAT/LISM PERSON KNOWL...SOC QU BIBLIOG 20. PAGE 164 H3277
NAT/COMP ATTIT EDU/PROP SAMP

S65
COOPER P.,"THE DEVELOPMENT OF THE CONCEPT OF WAR." UK COERCE ATTIT PERCEPT PERSON...STAT CHARTS CHINJAP. PAGE 33 H0660
CULTURE WAR SAMP STAND/INT

S65
GORDON M.,"THE SETTING FOR EUROPEAN ARMS CONTROLS* POLITICAL AND STRATEGIC CHOICES OF EUROPEAN ELITES." FRANCE GERMANY UK USA+45 USSR ARMS/CONT DETER ATTIT ORD/FREE...SAMP NAT/COMP NATO. PAGE 59 H1179
REC/INT ELITES RISK WAR

S65
LAULICHT J.,"PUBLIC OPINION AND FOREIGN POLICY DECISIONS." CANADA ELITES NAT/G FOR/AID LEAD NUC/PWR PERCEPT...INT QU CHARTS UN COLD/WAR. PAGE 92 H1839
DIPLOM ATTIT CON/ANAL SAMP

B66
LONDON DAILY TELEGRAPH,ELECTION '66: GALLUP ANALYSIS OF THE VOTING RESULTS. UK LEGIS COMPUTER ATTIT...QU SAMP CHARTS 20 LABOR/PAR HOUSE/CMNS. PAGE 98 H1959
STAT CHOOSE REPRESENT POL/PAR

B67
EVANS R.H.,COEXISTENCE: COMMUNISM AND ITS PRACTICE IN BOLOGNA, 1945-1965. ITALY CAP/ISM ADMIN CHOOSE PEACE ORD/FREE...SOC STAT DEEP/INT SAMP CHARTS BIBLIOG 20. PAGE 48 H0952
MARXISM CULTURE MUNIC POL/PAR

B67
SCHWARTZ M.A.,PUBLIC OPINION AND CANADIAN IDENTITY.
ATTIT

CANADA SOCIETY LOC/G DIPLOM ADMIN LEAD REGION GP/REL SAMP. PAGE 141 H2812 — NAT/G NAT/LISM POL/PAR

S67
BULLOUGH B.,"ALIENATION IN THE GHETTO." CULTURE NEIGH GP/REL INGP/REL ATTIT...PSY SOC SAMP. PAGE 23 H0471 — DISCRIM ANOMIE ADJUST

S67
GLENN N.D.,"RURAL-URBAN DIFFERENCES IN REPORTED ATTITUDES AND BEHAVIOR" STRATA GP/REL CONSEN HABITAT RIGID/FLEX SAMP. PAGE 57 H1143 — CULTURE ATTIT KIN CHARTS

S67
RUCKER B.W.,"WHAT SOLUTIONS DO PEOPLE ENDORSE IN FREE PRESS-FAIR TRIAL DILEMMA?" LAW NAT/G CT/SYS ATTIT...NET/THEORY SAMP CHARTS IDEA/COMP METH 20. PAGE 136 H2710 — CONCPT PRESS ADJUD ORD/FREE

S67
SUNG C.H.,"POLITICAL DIAGNOSIS OF KOREAN SOCIETY* A SURVEY OF MILITARY AND CIVILIAN VALUES." KOREA/S ECO/UNDEV NAT/G CIVMIL/REL...QU SAMP GP/COMP. PAGE 151 H3009 — ELITES FORCES ATTIT ORD/FREE

SAMP/SIZ....SIZES AND TECHNIQUES OF SAMPLING

B60
HUGHES C.C.,PEOPLE OF COVE AND WOODLOT; COMMUNITIES FROM THE VIEWPOINT OF SOCIAL PSYCHIATRY. CULTURE FAM PROVS HABITAT...PSY QU SAMP/SIZ CHARTS BIBLIOG 20. PAGE 74 H1489 — GEOG SOCIETY STRUCT HEALTH

S62
ROSE R.,"THE POLITICAL IDEALS OF ENGLISH PARTY ACTIVISTS" (BMR)" UK PARL/PROC PARTIC ATTIT ROLE ...SAMP/SIZ CHARTS 20. PAGE 134 H2673 — POL/PAR LOBBY REPRESENT NAT/G

B66
GURR T.,NEW ERROR-COMPENSATED MEASURES FOR COMPARING NATIONS* SOME CORRELATES OF CIVIL VIOLENCE. WOR+45 SOCIETY REV ISOLAT...PHIL/SCI SOC QUANT TESTS SAMP/SIZ HYPO/EXP. PAGE 63 H1254 — NAT/COMP INDEX COERCE NEW/IDEA

B67
MCCLINTOCK R.,THE MEANING OF LIMITED WAR. FUT WOR+45 NAT/G FORCES GUERRILLA REV...POLICY SAMP/SIZ TREND NAT/COMP 45 COLD/WAR. PAGE 106 H2126 — WAR NUC/PWR BAL/PWR DIPLOM

SAMPLE....SEE SAMP

SAMPLE AND SAMPLING....SEE UNIVERSES AND SAMPLING INDEX, P. XIV

SAMUEL CLEMENS....SEE TWAIN/MARK

SAMUELSN/P....PAUL SAMUELSON

SAN/FRAN....SAN FRANCISCO

SAN/MARINO....SAN MARINO

SAN/MARTIN....JOSE DE SAN MARTIN

B31
KIRKPATRICK F.A.,A HISTORY OF THE ARGENTINE REPUBLIC. SPAIN UK CONSTN SOCIETY ECO/UNDEV EX/STRUC DIPLOM FOR/AID LEAD WAR ATTIT...BIOG CHARTS 16/20 ARGEN SAN/MARTIN. PAGE 86 H1724 — NAT/G L/A+17C COLONIAL

B61
ESTEVEZ A.,ASPECTOS ECONOMICO-FINANCIEROS DE LA CAMPANA SANMARITANA. L/A+17C SPAIN FINAN COLONIAL LEAD ROLE ORD/FREE WEALTH 19 SOUTH/AMER SAN/MARTIN. PAGE 47 H0942 — ECO/UNDEV REV BUDGET NAT/G

SAN/QUENTN....SAN QUENTIN PRISON

SANCHEZ A.L. H2747

SANCHEZ J.D. H2748

SANCHEZ J.M. H2749

SANCTION....SANCTION OF LAW AND SEMI-LEGAL PRIVATE ASSOCIATIONS AND SOCIAL GROUPS

B06
SUMNER W.G.,FOLKWAYS: STUDY OF THE SOCIOLOGICAL IMPORTANCE OF USAGES, MANNERS, CUSTOMS, MORES, AND MORALS. STRUCT KIN ETIQUET ROUTINE MURDER MARRIAGE PEACE SEX ALL/VALS WEALTH BIBLIOG. PAGE 150 H3008 — CULTURE SOC SANCTION MORAL

N19
ADMINISTRATIVE STAFF COLLEGE,THE ACCOUNTABILITY OF GOVERNMENT DEPARTMENTS (PAMPHLET) (REV. ED.). UK CONSTN FINAN NAT/G CONSULT ADMIN INGP/REL CONSEN PRIVIL 20 PARLIAMENT. PAGE 3 H0070 — PARL/PROC ELITES SANCTION PROB/SOLV

B26
HOCKING W.E.,PRESENT STATUS OF THE PHILOSOPHY OF LAW AND OF RIGHTS. UNIV CULTURE INTELL SOCIETY NAT/G CREATE LEGIT SANCTION ALL/VALS SOC/INTEG 18/20. PAGE 72 H1442 — JURID PHIL/SCI ORD/FREE

B26
MALINOWSKI B.,CRIME AND CUSTOM IN SAVAGE SOCIETY. SOCIETY FAM SECT LEGIT SANCTION MARRIAGE MYSTISM ...PSY SOC 19/20 MELANESIA CANON/LAW. PAGE 102 H2030 — LAW CULTURE CRIME ADJUD

B30
BENTHAM J.,THE RATIONALE OF PUNISHMENT. UK LAW LOC/G NAT/G LEGIS CONTROL...JURID GEN/LAWS COURT/SYS 19. PAGE 14 H0289 — CRIME SANCTION COERCE ORD/FREE

B32
GREAT BRIT COMM MINISTERS PWR,REPORT. UK LAW CONSTN CONSULT LEGIS PARL/PROC SANCTION SOVEREIGN ...DECISION JURID 20 PARLIAMENT. PAGE 60 H1201 — EX/STRUC NAT/G PWR CONTROL

B40
TONNIES F.,FUNDAMENTAL CONCEPTS OF SOCIOLOGY (1887) (TRANS. BY C. LOOMIS). LAW STRATA STRUCT FAM MUNIC NAT/G DOMIN LEGIT SANCTION COERCE CRIME PERSON 19. PAGE 156 H3115 — CULTURE SOCIETY GEN/LAWS SOC

S40
GURVITCH G.,"MAJOR PROBLEMS OF THE SOCIOLOGY OF LAW." CULTURE SANCTION KNOWL MORAL...POLICY EPIST JURID WORSHIP. PAGE 63 H1255 — SOC LAW PHIL/SCI

C43
BENTHAM J.,"PRINCIPLES OF INTERNATIONAL LAW" IN J. BOWRING, ED., THE WORKS OF JEREMY BENTHAM." UNIV NAT/G PLAN PROB/SOLV DIPLOM CONTROL SANCTION MORAL ORD/FREE PWR SOVEREIGN 19. PAGE 15 H0291 — INT/LAW JURID WAR PEACE

B49
SCHONS D.,BOOK CENSORSHIP IN NEW SPAIN (NEW WORLD STUDIES, BOOK II). SPAIN LAW CULTURE INSPECT ADJUD CT/SYS SANCTION GP/REL ORD/FREE 14/17. PAGE 140 H2797 — CHRIST-17C EDU/PROP CONTROL PRESS

B51
HUXLEY J.,FREEDOM AND CULTURE. UNIV LAW SOCIETY R+D ACADEM SCHOOL CREATE SANCTION ATTIT KNOWL...HUM ANTHOL 20. PAGE 76 H1512 — CULTURE ORD/FREE PHIL/SCI IDEA/COMP

B55
KHADDURI M.,LAW IN THE MIDDLE EAST. LAW CONSTN ACADEM FAM EDU/PROP CT/SYS SANCTION CRIME...INT/LAW GOV/COMP ANTHOL 6/20 MID/EAST. PAGE 85 H1703 — ADJUD JURID ISLAM

B56
RIESENBERG P.N.,INALIENABILITY OF SOVEREIGNTY IN MEDIEVAL POLITICAL THOUGHT. CHRIST-17C INTELL NAT/G SECT CHIEF LEGIS SANCTION AUTHORIT ORD/FREE CONSERVE...IDEA/COMP BIBLIOG 12/16. PAGE 131 H2627 — SOVEREIGN ATTIT

L56
EISENTADT S.N.,"POLITICAL STRUGGLE IN BUREAUCRATIC SOCIETIES" ASIA CULTURE ADJUD SANCTION PWR BUREAUCRCY OTTOMAN BYZANTINE. PAGE 45 H0901 — ADMIN CHIEF CONTROL ROUTINE

B57
PLAYFAIR G.,THE OFFENDERS: THE CASE AGAINST LEGAL VENGEANCE. UNIV LAW SOCIETY NAT/G PROB/SOLV DEATH PERSON ORD/FREE...HEAL INT/LAW BIBLIOG 20 REFORMERS. PAGE 126 H2524 — CRIME TEC/DEV SANCTION CT/SYS

B60
CASTBERG F.,FREEDOM OF SPEECH IN THE WEST. FRANCE GERMANY USA+45 USA-45 LAW CONSTN CHIEF PRESS DISCRIM...CONCPT 18/20. PAGE 28 H0558 — ORD/FREE SANCTION ADJUD NAT/COMP

B60
THE AFRICA 1960 COMMITTEE,MANDATE IN TRUST; THE PROBLEM OF SOUTH WEST AFRICA. GERMANY STRUCT REGION SANCTION CHOOSE DISCRIM...INT/LAW 20 AFRICA/SW UN LEAGUE/NAT TRUST/TERR. PAGE 153 H3066 — NAT/G DIPLOM COLONIAL RACE/REL

B60
RUDD J.,TABOO, A STUDY OF MALAGASY CUSTOMS AND BELIEFS. MADAGASCAR LAW FAM CONTROL CRIME PERSON ...CONCPT 20. PAGE 173 H3466 — CULTURE DOMIN SECT SANCTION

B61
ROCHE J.P.,COURTS AND RIGHTS: THE AMERICAN JUDICIARY IN ACTION (2ND ED.). UK USA+45 USA-45 STRUCT TEC/DEV SANCTION PERS/REL RACE/REL ORD/FREE ...METH/CNCPT GOV/COMP METH/COMP T 13/20. PAGE 133 H2653 — JURID CT/SYS NAT/G PROVS

B62
GANJI M.,INTERNATIONAL PROTECTION OF HUMAN RIGHTS. WOR+45 CONSTN INT/TRADE CT/SYS SANCTION CRIME WAR RACE/REL...CHARTS IDEA/COMP NAT/COMP BIBLIOG 20 TREATY NEGRO LEAGUE/NAT UN CIVIL/LIB. PAGE 55 H1097 — ORD/FREE DISCRIM LEGIS DELIB/GP

B63
HARDY M.J.L.,BLOOD FEUDS AND THE PAYMENT OF BLOOD MONEY IN THE MIDDLE EAST. ISLAM SOCIETY SECT REGION SANCTION COERCE DEATH MURDER 7/20 ARABS. PAGE 66 H1329 — KIN TRIBUTE LAW CULTURE

B63
LAVROFF D.-G.,LES LIBERTES PUBLIQUES EN UNION SOVIETIQUE (REV. ED.). USSR NAT/G WORKER SANCTION CRIME MARXISM NEW/LIB...JURID BIBLIOG WORSHIP 20. PAGE 92 H1843 — ORD/FREE LAW ATTIT COM

C63
HSU F.L.,"COHESION AND DIVISION IN THE AMERICAN WORLD" HSU FL. CLAN, CASTE, AND CLUB." CULTURE EDU/PROP CONFER SANCTION PERSON...PSY GP/COMP. PAGE 74 H1484 — PERS/REL AGE/Y ADJUST VOL/ASSN

B64
SEGAL R.,SANCTIONS AGAINST SOUTH AFRICA. AFR SOUTH/AFR NAT/G INT/TRADE RACE/REL PEACE PWR ...INT/LAW ANTHOL 20 UN. PAGE 141 H2821 — SANCTION DISCRIM ECO/TAC POLICY

B64
SIEKANOWICZ P.,LEGAL SOURCES AND BIBLIOGRAPHY OF POLAND. COM POLAND CONSTN NAT/G PARL/PROC SANCTION CRIME MARXISM 16/20. PAGE 143 H2870 — BIBLIOG ADJUD LAW JURID

B64
WRAITH R.,CORRUPTION IN DEVELOPING COUNTRIES. NIGERIA UK LAW ELITES STRATA INDUS LOC/G NAT/G SECT FORCES EDU/PROP ADMIN PWR WEALTH 18/20. PAGE 171 H3414 — ECO/UNDEV CRIME SANCTION ATTIT

B65
GEORGE M.,THE WARPED VISION. EUR+WWI UK NAT/G POL/PAR LEGIS PARL/PROC SANCTION COERCE WAR GOV/REL PEACE RESPECT 20 CONSRV/PAR. PAGE 56 H1113 — LEAD ATTIT DIPLOM POLICY

B65
GWYN R.J.,THE SHAPE OF SCANDAL: A STUDY OF A GOVERNMENT IN CRISIS. CANADA LEGIS ADJUD CT/SYS SANCTION CMN/WLTH 20 PEARSON/L. PAGE 63 H1260 — ELITES NAT/G CRIME

B66
MERILLAT H.C.L.,LEGAL ADVISERS AND INTERNATIONAL ORGANIZATIONS. LAW NAT/G CONSULT OP/RES ADJUD SANCTION TASK CONSEN ORG/CHARTS. PAGE 109 H2178 — INT/ORG INT/LAW CREATE OBS

L67
GALTUNG J.,"ON THE EFFECTS OF INTERNATIONAL ECONOMIC SANCTIONS, WITH EXAMPLES FROM THE CASE OF RHODESIA." NAT/G DIPLOM EDU/PROP ADJUST EFFICIENCY ATTIT MORAL...OBS CHARTS 20. PAGE 55 H1091 — SANCTION ECO/TAC INT/TRADE ECO/UNDEV

S67
BAIKALOV A.,"EMERGENCY LEGISLATION IN WEST GERMANY." GERMANY/W LABOR NAT/G POL/PAR SANCTION ...MARXIST 20. PAGE 10 H0199 — LAW TOTALISM LEGIS PARL/PROC

S67
BERLINER J.S.,"RUSSIA'S BUREAUCRATS - WHY THEY'RE REACTIONARY." USSR NAT/G OP/RES PROB/SOLV TEC/DEV CONTROL SANCTION EFFICIENCY DRIVE PERSON...TECHNIC SOC 20. PAGE 15 H0308 — CREATE ADMIN INDUS PRODUC

S67
LEGRES A.,"LES FONCTIONS D'UN PARLEMENT MODERNE." FRANCE DEBATE PARL/PROC SANCTION ATTIT PWR 20 PARLIAMENT. PAGE 93 H1860 — NAT/G LAW LEGIS CHOOSE

S67
SAVELYEV N.,"MONOPOLY DRIVE IN INDIA." INDIA INDUS NAT/G INT/TRADE NEUTRAL SANCTION GOV/REL CONSERVE ...MARXIST 20. PAGE 138 H2759 — ECO/UNDEV POL/PAR ECO/TAC CONTROL

S67
YEFROMEV A.,"THE TRUE FACE OF THE WEST GERMAN NATIONAL-DEMOCRATS." GERMANY/W NAT/G DOMIN LEAD SANCTION WAR ATTIT PERSON...MARXIST 20. PAGE 172 H3436 — POL/PAR TOTALISM PARL/PROC DIPLOM

S68
DUGARD J.,"THE REVOCATION OF THE MANDATE FOR SOUTH WEST AFRICA." SOUTH/AFR WOR+45 STRATA NAT/G DELIB/GP DIPLOM ADJUD SANCTION CHOOSE RACE/REL ...POLICY NAT/COMP 20 AFRICA/SW UN TRUST/TERR LEAGUE/NAT. PAGE 43 H0858 — AFR INT/ORG DISCRIM COLONIAL

S68
SHAPIRO J.P.,"SOVIET HISTORIOGRAPHY AND THE MOSCOW TRIALS: AFTER THIRTY YEARS." USSR NAT/G LEGIT PRESS CONTROL LEAD ATTIT MARXISM...NEW/IDEA METH 20 TROTSKY/L STALIN/J KHRUSH/N. PAGE 142 H2843 — HIST/WRIT EDU/PROP SANCTION ADJUD

B98
POLLOCK F.,THE HISTORY OF ENGLISH LAW BEFORE THE TIME OF EDWARD I (2 VOLS, 2ND ED.). UK CULTURE LOC/G LEGIS LICENSE AGREE CONTROL CT/SYS SANCTION CRIME...TIME/SEQ 13 COMMON/LAW CANON/LAW. PAGE 127 H2538 — LAW ADJUD JURID

SANDEE J. H2750

SANDERS R. H2751

SANTAYAN/G....GEORGE SANTAYANA

SANTAYANA G. H2752

SANTHANAM K. H2753

SAO/PAULO....SAO PAULO, BRAZIL

SAPIR/EDW....EDWARD SAPIR

C41
KLUCKHOHN C.,"PATTERNING AS EXEMPLIFIED IN NAVAHO CULTURE" IN EDWARD SAPIR, LANGUAGE, CULTURE, AND PERSONALITY (BMR)" KIN PERS/REL ATTIT PERSON...SOC CONCPT METH/CNCPT LING OBS/ENVIR CON/ANAL BIBLIOG SOC/INTEG 20 NAVAHO INDIAN/AM SAPIR/EDW. PAGE 87 H1733 — CULTURE INGP/REL STRUCT

SARAWAK....SARAWAK, MALAYSIA

SARGENT S.S. H2754

SARKISYANZ E. H2755

SARTRE/J....JEAN-PAUL SARTRE

B64
CAUTE D.,COMMUNISM AND THE FRENCH INTELLECTUALS, 1914-1960. COM EUR+WWI MOD/EUR NAT/G PERF/ART PROF/ORG CREATE EDU/PROP ATTIT PERSON KNOWL MARXISM ...SOC TIME/SEQ MARX/KARL 20 MALRAUX/A GIDE/A SARTRE/J. PAGE 28 H0563 — POL/PAR INTELL

SARVODAYA....SARVODAYA - GANDHIAN SOCIALIST POLITICAL IDEAL OF UNIVERSAL MATERIAL AND SPIRITUAL WELFARE; SEE ALSO GANDHI/M

SASKATCH....SASKATCHEWAN, CANADA

B50
LIPSET S.M.,AGRARIAN SOCIALISM. CANADA POL/PAR OP/RES ECO/TAC ADMIN ATTIT...TIME/SEQ NAT/COMP SOC/EXP 20 SASKATCH. PAGE 97 H1938 — SOCISM AGRI METH/COMP STRUCT

SASKATCHEWAN, CANADA...SEE SASKATCH

SASTRI K.V.S. H2756

SATELLITE....SPACE SATELLITES

SATISFACTION....SEE HAPPINESS

SAUDI/ARAB....SAUDI ARABIA; SEE ALSO ISLAM

B58
MACRO E.,BIBLIOGRAPHY OF THE ARABIAN PENINSULA (PAMPHLET). KUWAIT SAUDI/ARAB YEMEN COLONIAL...GEOG 19/20. PAGE 101 H2012 — BIBLIOG ISLAM CULTURE NAT/G

S61
VALLET R.,"IRAN: KEY TO THE MIDDLE EAST." COM IRAQ ISLAM KUWAIT LEBANON SAUDI/ARAB TURKEY ELITES SOCIETY INDUS PROC/MFG POL/PAR TOP/EX PLAN BAL/PWR DIPLOM ECO/TAC ALL/VALS...TREND CENTO 20. PAGE 161 H3224 — NAT/G ECO/UNDEV IRAN

B63
UAR MINISTRY OF CULTURE,A BIBLIOGRAPHICAL LIST OF ARABIAN PENINSULA. ISLAM SAUDI/ARAB YEMEN FINAN NAT/G DIPLOM 19/20. PAGE 157 H3147 — BIBLIOG GEOG INDUS SECT

SAUVAGET J. H2757

SAUVY A. H2758

SAVELYEV N. H2759

SAUER W. H2760

SAVILLE J. H2204

SAVORY R.M. H3355

SAWREY W.L. H1983

SAX/JOSEPH....JOSEPH SAX

SAY/EMIL....EMIL SAY

SAYEED K. H2761

SAYLES G.O. H2621

SBA....SMALL BUSINESS ADMINISTRATION

SCALAPINO R.A. H2762,H2763,H2764

SCALES....SEE TESTS AND SCALES INDEX, P. XIV

SCANDINAV....SCANDINAVIAN COUNTRIES

B53
NELSON G.R.,FREEDOM AND WELFARE: SOCIAL PATTERNS IN THE NORTHERN COUNTRIES OF EUROPE. EUR+WWI ECO/DEV NAT/G EDU/PROP LEGIT HEALTH ORD/FREE SKILL WEALTH — PLAN ECO/TAC

...STAT AUD/VIS SCANDINAV WORK TOT/POP 20. PAGE 116 H2329

SCANLON D.G. H0684,H2765

SCANLON/H....HUGH SCANLON

SCARROW H.A. H2766

SCHACHTER G. H2767

SCHADERA I. H2768

SCHAFFER B.B. H2769

SCHAPIRO J.S. H2770,H2771

SCHAPIRO L. H2772,H2773

SCHATTEN F. H2774

SCHATTSCHNEIDER E.E. H2775

SCHECHTMAN J.B. H2776,H2777,H2778,H2779

SCHECTER J. H2780

SCHEFFLER H.W. H2781

SCHEIBER H.N. H2782

SCHELER M. H2783

SCHELLING T.C. H2784

SCHEURER/K....AUGUSTE SCHEURER-KESTNER

SCHEURER-KESTNER, AUGUSTE....SEE SCHEURER/K

SCHIEDER T. H2785,H2786

SCHINDLR/P....PAULINE SCHINDLER

SCHIZO....SCHIZOPHRENIA

SCHLESINGER J.A. H2788

SCHMIDT-VOLKMAR E. H2789

SCHMITTER P.C. H1266

SCHMOLLER G. H2790

SCHNAPPER B. H2791

SCHNEIDER H.W. H2792

SCHNITGER F.M. H2793

SCHNORE L.F. H0862,H1359

SCHOCKEL E. H2794

SCHOENBRUN D. H2795

SCHOEPS H.J. H2796

SCHOLASTIC....SCHOLASTICISM (MEDIEVAL)

B39
MARITAIN J.,SCHOLASTICISM AND POLITICS. CONSTN SOCIETY NAT/G INGP/REL PERSON CATHISM POPULISM 19/20 FREUD/S SCHOLASTIC CHURCH/STA CHRISTIAN. PAGE 103 H2050
SECT
GEN/LAWS
ORD/FREE

SCHONS D. H2797

SCHOOL....SCHOOLS, EXCEPT UNIVERSITIES

N
"PROLOG",DIGEST OF THE SOVIET UKRANIAN PRESS. USSR LAW AGRI INDUS PROVS SCHOOL DIPLOM GOV/REL ATTIT ...HUM LING 20. PAGE 3 H0053
BIBLIOG/A
NAT/G
PRESS
COM

N
US LIBRARY OF CONGRESS,SOUTHERN ASIA ACCESSIONS LIST. BURMA CEYLON INDIA NEPAL PAKISTAN S/ASIA THAILAND AGRI INDUS SCHOOL WORKER...ART/METH GEOG HEAL PHIL/SCI LING 20. PAGE 160 H3201
BIBLIOG/A
SOCIETY
CULTURE
ECO/UNDEV

B14
BERHARDI F.,GERMANY AND THE NEXT WAR. MOD/EUR NAT/G SCHOOL FORCES ACT/RES DOMIN EDU/PROP SUPEGO PWR ...TIME/SEQ STERTYP TOT/POP 20 WWI. PAGE 15 H0304
DRIVE
COERCE
WAR
GERMANY

B14
CRAIG J.,ELEMENTS OF POLITICAL SCIENCE (3 VOLS.). CONSTN AGRI INDUS SCHOOL FORCES TAX CT/SYS SUFF MORAL WEALTH...CONCPT 19 CIVIL/LIB. PAGE 35 H0696
PHIL/SCI
NAT/G
ORD/FREE

N19
COUTROT A.,THE FIGHT OVER THE 1959 PRIVATE EDUCATION LAW IN FRANCE (PAMPHLET). FRANCE NAT/G SECT GIVE EDU/PROP GP/REL ATTIT RIGID/FLEX ORD/FREE 20 CHURCH/STA. PAGE 34 H0681
SCHOOL
PARL/PROC
CATHISM
LAW

N19
FIKS M.,PUBLIC ADMINISTRATION IN ISRAEL (PAMPHLET). ISRAEL SCHOOL EX/STRUC BUDGET PAY INGP/REL ...DECISION 20 CIVIL/SERV. PAGE 50 H0999
EDU/PROP
NAT/G
ADMIN
WORKER

N19
SALKEVER L.R.,SUB-SAHARA AFRICA (PAMPHLET). AFR USSR EXTR/IND NAT/G SCHOOL DIPLOM COLONIAL WEALTH ...GEOG CHARTS 16/20. PAGE 137 H2742
ECO/UNDEV
TEC/DEV
TASK
INT/TRADE

N19
TABORSKY E.,CONFORMITY UNDER COMMUNISM (PAMPHLET). CZECHOSLVK HUNGARY POLAND SCHOOL DOMIN PRESS ...TREND GOV/COMP 20. PAGE 152 H3030
COM
CONTROL
EDU/PROP
NAT/G

B28
SOROKIN P.,CONTEMPORARY SOCIOLOGICAL THEORIES. MOD/EUR UNIV SOCIETY R+D SCHOOL ECO/TAC EDU/PROP ROUTINE ATTIT DRIVE...PSY CONCPT TIME/SEQ TREND GEN/LAWS 20. PAGE 147 H2934
CULTURE
SOC
WAR

B38
DUNHAM W.H. JR.,COMPLAINT AND REFORM IN ENGLAND 1436-1714. UK LAW ACADEM NAT/G POL/PAR SCHOOL PRESS COLONIAL PARL/PROC MORAL...SOC/WK ANTHOL 15/18 HAKLUYT/R COWPER/W. PAGE 43 H0865
ATTIT
SOCIETY
SECT

B40
BROWN A.D.,PANAMA CANAL AND PANAMA CANAL ZONE: A SELECTED LIST OF REFERENCES. PANAMA NAT/G SCHOOL DIPLOM HEALTH...GEOG SOC 20 CANAL/ZONE. PAGE 22 H0436
BIBLIOG/A
ECO/UNDEV

B42
BLANCHARD L.R.,MARTINIQUE: A SELECTED LIST OF REFERENCES (PAMPHLET). WEST/IND AGRI LOC/G SCHOOL ...ART/METH GEOG JURID CHARTS 20. PAGE 18 H0353
BIBLIOG/A
SOCIETY
CULTURE
COLONIAL

B42
CONOVER H.F.,THE NETHERLANDS EAST INDIES: A SELECTED LIST OF REFERENCES. ECO/UNDEV AGRI EXTR/IND LABOR SCHOOL SECT INT/TRADE COLONIAL HEALTH...GEOG 19/20. PAGE 32 H0642
BIBLIOG
S/ASIA
CULTURE

B42
CONOVER H.F.,NEW ZEALAND: A SELECTED LIST OF REFERENCES (PAMPHLET). NEW/ZEALND ECO/UNDEV AGRI INDUS LABOR NAT/G SCHOOL FORCES DIPLOM COLONIAL WAR ...HUM 20. PAGE 32 H0643
BIBLIOG/A
S/ASIA
CULTURE

B44
BARKER E.,THE DEVELOPMENT OF PUBLIC SERVICES IN WESTERN WUROPE: 1660-1930. FRANCE GERMANY UK SCHOOL CONTROL REPRESENT ROLE...WELF/ST 17/20. PAGE 11 H0219
GOV/COMP
ADMIN
EX/STRUC

B45
US LIBRARY OF CONGRESS,NETHERLANDS EAST INDIES. INDONESIA LAW CULTURE AGRI INDUS SCHOOL COLONIAL HEALTH...GEOG JURID SOC 19/20 NETH/IND. PAGE 160 H3205
BIBLIOG/A
S/ASIA
NAT/G

B51
HUXLEY J.,FREEDOM AND CULTURE. UNIV LAW SOCIETY R+D ACADEM SCHOOL CREATE SANCTION ATTIT KNOWL...HUM ANTHOL 20. PAGE 76 H1512
CULTURE
ORD/FREE
PHIL/SCI
IDEA/COMP

S51
GOULD J.,"THE KOMSOMOL AND THE HITLER JUGEND." COM EUR+WWI GERMANY SOCIETY NAT/G POL/PAR SCHOOL TOTALISM DRIVE PERCEPT KNOWL FASCISM...SOC NAZI TOT/POP 20. PAGE 59 H1185
EDU/PROP
CON/ANAL
SOCISM

S52
EISENSTADT S.N.,"THE PROCESS OF ABSORPTION OF NEW IMMIGRANTS IN ISRAEL" (BMR)" ISRAEL CULTURE SCHOOL WORKER PARTIC DRIVE ORD/FREE...STAT OBS INT CHARTS SOC/INTEG 20 JEWS. PAGE 45 H0900
HABITAT
ATTIT
SAMP

B53
MEAD M.,CULTURAL PATTERNS AND TECHNICAL CHANGE. BURMA GREECE NIGERIA ECO/UNDEV AGRI INDUS SCHOOL SECT CREATE FEEDBACK HABITAT...PSY METH/COMP BIBLIOG 20 UN. PAGE 108 H2152
HEALTH
TEC/DEV
CULTURE
ADJUST

B54
BINANI G.D.,INDIA AT A GLANCE (REV. ED.). INDIA COM/IND FINAN INDUS LABOR PROVS SCHOOL PLAN DIPLOM INT/TRADE ADMIN...JURID 20. PAGE 17 H0335
INDEX
CON/ANAL
NAT/G
ECO/UNDEV

B55
SHUMSKY A.,THE CLASH OF CULTURES IN ISRAEL: A PROBLEM FOR EDUCATION. ISRAEL CULTURE INTELL NAT/G ACT/RES DISCRIM AGE/Y...BIBLIOG 20 JEWS. PAGE 143 H2867
GP/REL
EDU/PROP
SCHOOL
AGE/C

B58
SCOTT J.P.,AGGRESSION. CULTURE FAM SCHOOL ATTIT DISPL HEALTH...SOC CONCPT NEW/IDEA CHARTS LAB/EXP. PAGE 141 H2814
DRIVE
PSY
WAR

S58
MAIR L.P.,"REPRESENTATIVE LOCAL GOVERNMENT AS A PROBLEM IN SOCIAL CHANGE." ECO/UNDEV KIN LOC/G NAT/G SCHOOL JUDGE ADMIN ROUTINE REPRESENT RIGID/FLEX RESPECT...CONCPT STERTYP CMN/WLTH 20. PAGE 101 H2025
AFR PWR ELITES

B59
CONOVER H.F.,NIGERIAN OFFICIAL PUBLICATIONS, 1869-1959: A GUIDE. NIGER CONSTN FINAN ACADEM SCHOOL FORCES PRESS ADMIN COLONIAL...HIST/WRIT 19/20. PAGE 33 H0650
BIBLIOG NAT/G CON/ANAL

B59
SISSONS C.B.,CHURCH AND STATE IN CANADIAN EDUCATION: AN HISTORICAL STUDY. CANADA ACADEM NAT/G SCHOOL LEGIS REGION MAJORITY...MAJORIT WORSHIP 18/20 CHURCH/STA. PAGE 145 H2891
SECT EDU/PROP PROVS GP/REL

B60
CONOVER H.F.,OFFICIAL PUBLICATIONS OF SOMALILAND, 1941-1959: A GUIDE. SOMALIA AGRI FINAN INT/ORG SCHOOL INT/TRADE PRESS CONFER COLONIAL PARL/PROC 20 CONGRESS. PAGE 33 H0652
BIBLIOG NAT/G CON/ANAL

B60
COUGHLIN R.,DOUBLE IDENTITY: THE CHINESE AND MODERN THAILAND. CHINA/COM S/ASIA THAILAND ECO/UNDEV EXTR/IND FINAN INDUS KIN MUNIC NAT/G PROF/ORG SCHOOL SECT ATTIT DRIVE...CONCPT OBS 20. PAGE 34 H0676
ASIA FAM CULTURE

B60
EMERY E.,INTRODUCTION TO MASS COMMUNICATIONS. ACADEM PROF/ORG SCHOOL ACT/RES EDU/PROP ATTIT ...CONCPT BIBLIOG/A. PAGE 46 H0920
COM/IND PRESS CON/ANAL CULTURE

B60
NICHOLLS W.H.,SOUTHERN TRADITION AND REGIONAL PROGRESS. STRATA STRUCT SCHOOL WORKER PARTIC REGION RACE/REL CONSEN ATTIT...SOC METH/CNCPT 19/20 SOUTH/US TVA. PAGE 118 H2349
RIGID/FLEX CONSERVE AGRI CULTURE

S60
TURNER R.H.,"SPONSORED AND CONTEST MOBILITY IN THE SCHOOL SYSTEM." UK USA+45 ELITES STRATA ACADEM FACE/GP EDU/PROP CONTROL INGP/REL ADJUST ATTIT PERSON...METH/COMP 20. PAGE 157 H3142
AGE/Y NAT/COMP SCHOOL STRUCT

B61
ALSTON P.L.,STATE EDUCATION AND SOCIAL CHANGE IN THE RUSSIAN EMPIRE 1871-1914 (PAPER). RUSSIA ELITES PROF/ORG EDU/PROP CONTROL PRIVIL AGE/Y...BIBLIOG 19/20. PAGE 6 H0115
SCHOOL SOCIETY NAT/G GP/REL

B62
AMERICAN SOCIETY AFR CULTURE,PAN-AFRICANISM RECONSIDERED. AFR SOCIETY STRUCT SCHOOL CAP/ISM EDU/PROP...ART/METH NEW/IDEA PREDICT ANTHOL 20 PANAF/FREE NEGRO. PAGE 6 H0123
DIPLOM FEDERAL NAT/LISM CULTURE

B62
BUSIA K.A.,THE CHALLENGE OF AFRICA. CULTURE KIN MUNIC NAT/G POL/PAR SCHOOL DELIB/GP PLAN ECO/TAC DOMIN EDU/PROP TOTALISM ATTIT PERSON ALL/VALS SOVEREIGN...SOC CONCPT STERTYP TOT/POP VAL/FREE 20. PAGE 25 H0496
AFR ECO/UNDEV NAT/LISM

B62
HO PING-TI,THE LADDER OF SUCCESS IN IMPERIAL CHINA: ASPECTS OF SOCIAL MOBILITY, 1368-1911. INTELL STRATA FAM KIN MUNIC NAT/G PROVS SCHOOL DELIB/GP DOMIN EDU/PROP ADMIN ROUTINE PERSON ALL/VALS...SOC STAT BIOG HIST/WRIT TIME/SEQ VAL/FREE. PAGE 71 H1431
ASIA CULTURE

B62
INSTITUTE FOR STUDY OF USSR,YOUTH IN FERMENT. INTELL NAT/G PERF/ART POL/PAR SCHOOL VOL/ASSN FORCES EDU/PROP ATTIT DRIVE PERCEPT HEALTH KNOWL MORAL ORD/FREE RESPECT...SOC OBS HIST/WRIT VAL/FREE. PAGE 77 H1537
COM CULTURE USSR

B62
KENNEDY R.,BIBLIOGRAPHY OF INDONESIAN PEOPLES AND CULTURES (2ND REV. ED.). INDONESIA STRUCT ECO/UNDEV SCHOOL EDU/PROP COLONIAL...GEOG SOC LING NAT/COMP 20. PAGE 85 H1689
BIBLIOG S/ASIA CULTURE KIN

B62
MUKERJI S.N.,ADMINISTRATION OF EDUCATION IN INDIA. ACADEM LOC/G PROVS ROUTINE...POLICY STAT CHARTS 20. PAGE 114 H2282
SCHOOL ADMIN NAT/G EDU/PROP

N62
US CONGRESS JT ATOM ENRGY COMM,PEACEFUL USES OF ATOMIC ENERGY, HEARING. USA+45 USSR TEC/DEV ATTIT RIGID/FLEX...TESTS CHARTS EXHIBIT METH/COMP 20 CONGRESS. PAGE 159 H3177
NUC/PWR ACADEM SCHOOL NAT/COMP

B63
BRITISH AID. UK AGRI DIST/IND INDUS SCHOOL TEC/DEV INT/TRADE COLONIAL DEMAND...TREND CHARTS 20. PAGE 2 H0041
FOR/AID ECO/UNDEV NAT/G FINAN

B63
DALAND R.T.,PERSPECTIVES OF BRAZILIAN PUBLIC ADMINISTRATION (VOL. I). BRAZIL LAW ECO/UNDEV SCHOOL CHIEF TEC/DEV CONFER CONTROL GP/REL ATTIT ROLE PWR...ANTHOL 20. PAGE 37 H0735
ADMIN NAT/G PLAN GOV/REL

B63
GOURNAY B.,PUBLIC ADMINISTRATION. FRANCE LAW CONSTN AGRI FINAN LABOR SCHOOL EX/STRUC CHOOSE...MGT METH/COMP 20. PAGE 59 H1189
BIBLIOG/A ADMIN NAT/G LOC/G

B63
HARTLEY A.,A STATE OF ENGLAND. UK ELITES SOCIETY ACADEM NAT/G SCHOOL INGP/REL CONSEN ORD/FREE NEW/LIB...POLICY 20. PAGE 67 H1349
DIPLOM ATTIT INTELL ECO/DEV

B63
WAGLEY C.,INTRODUCTION TO BRAZIL. BRAZIL L/A+17C FAM KIN SCHOOL SECT ATTIT WEALTH...GEOG SOC. PAGE 164 H3286
ECO/UNDEV ELITES HABITAT STRATA

B63
WILSON U.,EDUCATION AND CHANGING WEST AFRICAN CULTURE. AFR MOD/EUR UK CULTURE ECO/UNDEV MUNIC CONSULT 19/20 CMN/WLTH AFRICA/W. PAGE 169 H3384
COLONIAL POLICY SCHOOL

B64
HARBISON F.H.,EDUCATION, MANPOWER, AND ECONOMIC GROWTH. WOR+45 ECO/DEV ECO/UNDEV ACADEM LABOR SCHOOL WORKER UTIL...IDEA/COMP NAT/COMP. PAGE 66 H1326
PLAN TEC/DEV EDU/PROP SKILL

B64
MELADY T.,FACES OF AFRICA. AFR FUT ISLAM NAT/G POL/PAR SCHOOL DELIB/GP PLAN ECO/TAC EDU/PROP ATTIT ALL/VALS...CHARTS TOT/POP VAL/FREE 20. PAGE 108 H2168
ECO/UNDEV TREND NAT/LISM

B64
MOUMOUNI A.,L'EDUCATION EN AFRIQUE. UNIV CULTURE ELITES INTELL EDU/PROP ADMIN COLONIAL...LING TREND BIBLIOG 20. PAGE 114 H2271
SCHOOL AFR PROB/SOLV

B64
ZARTMAN I.W.,MOROCCO: PROBLEMS OF NEW POWER. ISLAM CULTURE ECO/UNDEV AGRI POL/PAR SCHOOL FORCES ADMIN ...CONCPT STAT INT CENSUS TIME/SEQ CHARTS WORK VAL/FREE 20. PAGE 172 H3449
CHOOSE MOROCCO DELIB/GP DECISION

L64
SYMONDS R.,"REFLECTIONS IN LOCALISATION." AFR S/ASIA UK STRATA INT/ORG NAT/G SCHOOL EDU/PROP LEGIT KNOWL ORD/FREE PWR RESPECT CMN/WLTH 20. PAGE 151 H3023
ADMIN MGT COLONIAL

B65
BENTWICH J.S.,EDUCATION IN ISRAEL. ISRAEL CULTURE STRATA PROB/SOLV TEC/DEV ADJUST ALL/VALS 20 JEWS. PAGE 15 H0293
SECT EDU/PROP ACADEM SCHOOL

B65
CHANDLER M.J.,A GUIDE TO RECORDS IN BARBADOS. WEST/IND PUB/INST SCHOOL SECT...HIST/WRIT 20. PAGE 28 H0573
BIBLIOG LOC/G L/A+17C NAT/G

B65
CRAMER J.F.,CONTEMPORARY EDUCATION: A COMPARATIVE STUDY OF NATIONAL SYSTEMS (2ND ED.). CHINA/COM EUR+WWI INDIA USA+45 FINAN PROB/SOLV ADMIN CONTROL ATTIT...IDEA/COMP METH/COMP 20 CHINJAP. PAGE 35 H0697
EDU/PROP NAT/COMP SCHOOL ACADEM

B65
FOSTER P.,EDUCATION AND SOCIAL CHANGE IN GHANA. GHANA CULTURE STRUCT ECO/UNDEV TEC/DEV REGION EFFICIENCY LITERACY ALL/VALS SOVEREIGN...STAT METH/COMP 19/20 GOLD/COAST. PAGE 52 H1043
SCHOOL CREATE SOCIETY

B65
HANSER C.J.,GUIDE TO DECISION: ROYAL COMMISSION. UK INTELL EXTR/IND SCHOOL PROB/SOLV EXEC ROUTINE CHOOSE GOV/REL GP/REL HEALTH...CHARTS 20. PAGE 66 H1318
NAT/G DELIB/GP EX/STRUC PWR

B65
HAPGOOD D.,AFRICA: FROM INDEPENDENCE TO TOMARROW. AFR GUINEA SENEGAL CULTURE ELITES ECO/UNDEV AGRI SCHOOL FOR/AID COLONIAL MARXISM...TREND 20. PAGE 66 H1323
ECO/TAC SOCIETY NAT/G

B65
HAVIGHURST R.J.,SOCIETY AND EDUCATION IN BRAZIL. BRAZIL PORTUGAL ECO/UNDEV INDUS NAT/G CREATE INSPECT COLONIAL ADJUST DEMAND LITERACY...CENSUS TREND CHARTS 16/20. PAGE 68 H1362
SCHOOL ACADEM ACT/RES CULTURE

B65
MEIER R.L.,DEVELOPMENTAL PLANNING. PUERT/RICO INDUS PUB/INST SCHOOL CREATE ECO/TAC FOR/AID...NAT/COMP 20. PAGE 108 H2165
PLAN ECO/UNDEV GOV/COMP TEC/DEV

B65
OECD,MEDITERRANEAN REGIONAL PROJECT: TURKEY; EDUCATION AND DEVELOPMENT. FUT TURKEY SOCIETY STRATA FINAN NAT/G PROF/ORG PLAN PROB/SOLV ADMIN COST...STAT CHARTS 20 OECD. PAGE 120 H2399
EDU/PROP ACADEM SCHOOL ECO/UNDEV

B65
OECD,THE MEDITERRANEAN REGIONAL PROJECT: ITALY; EDUCATION AND DEVELOPMENT. ITALY SOCIETY STRATA FINAN NAT/G PROF/ORG WORKER PLAN PROB/SOLV ADMIN ...STAT CHARTS METH 20 OECD. PAGE 120 H2400
SCHOOL EDU/PROP ECO/UNDEV ACADEM

B65
OECD,THE MEDITERRANEAN REGIONAL PROJECT: GREECE;
EDU/PROP

EDUCATION AND DEVELOPMENT. FUT GREECE SOCIETY AGRI FINAN NAT/G PROF/ORG WORKER PLAN PROB/SOLV ADMIN DEMAND ATTIT 20 OECD. PAGE 120 H2401 — SCHOOL ACADEM ECO/UNDEV

B65
OECD,THE MEDITERRANEAN REGIONAL PROJECT: SPAIN; EDUCATION AND DEVELOPMENT. FUT SPAIN STRATA FINAN NAT/G WORKER PLAN PROB/SOLV ADMIN COST...POLICY STAT CHARTS 20 OECD. PAGE 120 H2402 — ECO/UNDEV EDU/PROP ACADEM SCHOOL

B65
ORG FOR ECO COOP AND DEVEL,THE MEDITERRANEAN REGIONAL PROJECT: AN EXPERIMENT IN PLANNING BY SIX COUNTRIES. FUT GREECE SPAIN TURKEY YUGOSLAVIA SOCIETY FINAN NAT/G PROF/ORG EDU/PROP ADMIN REGION COST...POLICY STAT CHARTS 20 OECD. PAGE 121 H2427 — PLAN ECO/UNDEV ACADEM SCHOOL

B65
VERMOT-GAUCHY M.,L'EDUCATION NATIONALE DANS LA FRANCE DE 1975. FRANCE FUT CULTURE ELITES R+D SCHOOL PLAN EDU/PROP EFFICIENCY...POLICY PREDICT CHARTS INDEX 20. PAGE 162 H3245 — ACADEM CREATE TREND INTELL

S65
"FURTHER READING." INDIA NAT/G ADMIN 20. PAGE 2 H0045 — BIBLIOG EDU/PROP SCHOOL ACADEM

C65
COLEMAN J.S.,"EDUCATION AND POLITICAL DEVELOPMENT." COM CULTURE INTELL STRUCT SCHOOL PERSON SOVEREIGN ...POLICY ANTHOL BIBLIOG/A METH 20. PAGE 31 H0629 — ECO/UNDEV NAT/LISM EDU/PROP TEC/DEV

B66
BARRETT J.,THAT BETTER COUNTRY: RELIGIOUS ASPECT OF LIFE IN EASTERN AUSTRALIA, 1835-1850. LAW ECO/UNDEV SCHOOL TEC/DEV EDU/PROP CONTROL HABITAT MORAL WORSHIP 19 AUSTRAL CHURCH/STA. PAGE 11 H0229 — SECT CULTURE GOV/REL

B66
DIAMOND S.,THE TRANSFORMATION OF EAST AFRICA. NAT/G SCHOOL CREATE PROB/SOLV COLONIAL REGION RACE/REL FEDERAL...SOC ANTHOL WORSHIP 20 AFRICA/E. PAGE 41 H0819 — CULTURE AFR TEC/DEV INDUS

B66
KEITH G.,THE FADING COLOUR BAR. AFR CENTRL/AFR UK ZAMBIA CULTURE SCHOOL EDU/PROP PERS/REL DISCRIM AGE ...AUD/VIS NAT/COMP SOC/INTEG 20 NEGRO. PAGE 84 H1682 — RACE/REL STRUCT ATTIT NAT/G

B66
SYMONDS R.,THE BRITISH AND THEIR SUCCESSORS. AFR CEYLON INDIA UK SCHOOL FORCES EDU/PROP ADMIN PARTIC ...NAT/COMP BIBLIOG 20 AFRICA/W AFRICA/E. PAGE 151 H3024 — NAT/G ECO/UNDEV POLICY COLONIAL

L66
"FEDERAL, STATE AND LOCAL GOVERNMENT PUBLICATIONS." ACADEM LOC/G NAT/G PROVS SCHOOL EFFICIENCY ...PHIL/SCI ANTHOL. PAGE 143 H2854 — BIBLIOG OP/RES METH

B67
COWLES M.,PERSPECTIVES IN THE EDUCATION OF DISADVANTAGED CHILDREN. CULTURE OP/RES PLAN PERS/REL ADJUST HABITAT PERCEPT KNOWL WEALTH ...SOC/WK IDEA/COMP ANTHOL 20. PAGE 34 H0686 — EDU/PROP AGE/C TEC/DEV SCHOOL

B67
GALBRAITH J.K.,THE NEW INDUSTRIAL STATE. INDUS LABOR LG/CO NAT/G POL/PAR SCHOOL OP/RES CAP/ISM EXEC TREND. PAGE 54 H1087 — TEC/DEV ECO/DEV SOCIETY MARKET

B67
MICKIEWICZ E.P.,SOVIET POLITICAL SCHOOLS: THE COMMUNIST PARTY ADULT INSTRUCTION SYSTEM. COM USSR INTELL SCHOOL WORKER CREATE PRESS ADMIN CONTROL ATTIT KNOWL...PROG/TEAC SOC/INTEG 20 COM/PARTY. PAGE 110 H2200 — NAT/G EDU/PROP AGE/A MARXISM

B67
RUDMAN H.C.,THE SCHOOL AND STATE IN THE USSR. COM USSR ACADEM LABOR LOC/G PUB/INST EDU/PROP GP/REL ROLE...POLICY DECISION MGT CHARTS 20. PAGE 136 H2712 — SCHOOL ADMIN NAT/G POL/PAR

L67
LATIN AMERICAN STUDIES ASSN,"RESEARCH ON EDUCATION IN LATIN AMERICA." L/A+17C NAT/G HABITAT...GOV/COMP ANTHOL 20. PAGE 92 H1836 — EDU/PROP SCHOOL ACADEM R+D

L67
UNESCO,"APARTHEID." SOUTH/AFR STRUCT KIN SCHOOL SECT WORKER DOMIN EDU/PROP REGION RACE/REL ISOLAT 20. PAGE 158 H3164 — DISCRIM CULTURE COERCE COLONIAL

L67
WILBER L.A.,"THE GOVERNMENTAL STRUCTURE OF MISSISSIPPI: ITS STRENGTHS AND WEAKNESSES." AGRI LOC/G SCHOOL EX/STRUC LEGIS TOP/EX BUDGET CT/SYS APPORT RACE/REL...GOV/COMP 20 MISSISSIPP. PAGE 168 H3359 — CONSTN PROVS STAT CON/ANAL

S67
BASOV V.,"THE DEVELOPMENT OF PUBLIC EDUCATION AND THE BUDGET." USSR NAT/G CONTROL REV COST AGE...STAT 20. PAGE 12 H0235 — BUDGET GIVE EDU/PROP SCHOOL

S67
EPSTEIN E.H.,"NATIONAL IDENTITY AND THE LANGUAGE ISSUE IN PUERTO RICO." PUERT/RICO CULTURE STRUCT NAT/G PROB/SOLV SKILL...JURID STAT METH/COMP 20. PAGE 47 H0931 — EDU/PROP SCHOOL LING NAT/LISM

SCHORN H. H2798

SCHRAM S. H2799

SCHRAMM W. H2800

SCHULER E.A. H2801

SCHUMAN S.I. H2802

SCHUMCHR/K....KURT SCHUMACHER

B65
EDINGER L.J.,KURT SCHUMACHER: A STUDY IN PERSONALITY AND POLITICAL BEHAVIOR. EUR+WWI GERMANY NAT/G DRIVE ROLE PWR SOCISM...BIBLIOG 20 SOC/DEMPAR SCHUMCHR/K. PAGE 44 H0889 — TOP/EX LEAD PERSON BIOG

SCHUMM S. H2803

SCHUMPETER J.A. H2804

SCHUMPTR/J....JOSEPH SCHUMPETER

SCHURMANN F. H2805

SCHUTZ W.W. H2806

SCHWARTZ B. H2807,H2808,H2809

SCHWARTZ H. H2810

SCHWARTZ M.A. H2811,H2812

SCHWINN....ARNOLD, SCHWINN + COMPANY

SCI/ADVSRY....SCIENCE ADVISORY COMMISSION

SCIENCE....SEE PHIL/SCI, CREATE

SCIENCE ADVISORY COMMISSION....SEE SCI/ADVSRY

SCIENTIFIC METHOD....SEE PHIL/SCI

SCOT/YARD....SCOTLAND YARD - LONDON POLICE HEADQUARTERS AND DETECTIVE BUREAU

B66
HOEVELER H.J.,INTERNATIONALE BEKAMPFUNG DES VERBRECHENS. AUSTRIA SWITZERLND WOR+45 INT/ORG CONTROL BIO/SOC...METH/COMP NAT/COMP 20 MAFIA SCOT/YARD FBI. PAGE 72 H1446 — CRIMLGY CRIME DIPLOM INT/LAW

SCOTLAND....SCOTLAND

SCOTT A. H0412

SCOTT D.J.R. H2813

SCOTT F.R. H1976

SCOTT G.B. H0775

SCOTT J.P. H2814

SCOTT J.W. H2815

SCOTT R.E. H2816

SCOTT W.A. H2817

SCOVILLE W.J. H2818

SCREENING AND SELECTION....SEE CHOOSE, SAMP

SDR....SPECIAL DRAWING RIGHTS

SDS....STUDENTS FOR A DEMOCRATIC SOCIETY

SEA....LOCALE OF SUBJECT ACTIVITY IS AQUATIC

B12
BRUNHES J.,LA GEOGRAPHIE HUMAINE: ESSAI DE CLASSIFICATION POSITIVE PRINCIPES ET EXEMPLES (2ND ED.). UNIV SEA AGRI EXTR/IND DRIVE...SOC CHARTS 20. PAGE 23 H0454 — GEOG HABITAT CULTURE

B21
BALFOUR A.J.,ESSAYS SPECULATIVE AND POLITICAL. SEA — PHIL/SCI

CULTURE CREATE WAR NAT/LISM PEACE LOVE...ART/METH INT/LAW CONCPT ANTHOL 20 JEWS. PAGE 10 H0204 — SOCIETY DIPLOM

B24
HOLDSWORTH W.S.,A HISTORY OF ENGLISH LAW; THE COMMON LAW AND ITS RIVALS (VOL. IV). UK SEA AGRI CHIEF ADJUD CONTROL CRIME GOV/REL...INT/LAW JURID NAT/COMP 16/17 PARLIAMENT COMMON/LAW CANON/LAW ENGLSH/LAW. PAGE 72 H1449 — LAW LEGIS CT/SYS CONSTN

B48
WHITE C.L.,HUMAN GEOGRAPHY: AN ECOLOGICAL STUDY OF GEOGRAPHY. UNIV SEA CULTURE AGRI EXTR/IND RACE/REL PRODUC...CHARTS HYPO/EXP SIMUL GEN/LAWS T. PAGE 167 H3345 — SOC HABITAT GEOG SOCIETY

B54
CAMPANELLA T.,A DISCOURSE TOUCHING THE SPANISH MONARCHY... (1640). SPAIN UNIV SEA STRATA FINAN SECT FORCES SUPEGO LOVE ORD/FREE...CONCPT 17. PAGE 26 H0514 — CONSERVE CHIEF NAT/G DIPLOM

B55
SVARLIEN O.,AN INTRODUCTION TO THE LAW OF NATIONS. SEA AIR INT/ORG NAT/G CHIEF ADMIN AGREE WAR PRIVIL ORD/FREE SOVEREIGN...BIBLIOG 16/20. PAGE 151 H3012 — INT/LAW DIPLOM

B57
NEUMARK S.D.,ECONOMIC INFLUENCES ON THE SOUTH AFRICAN FRONTIER, 1652-1836. SOUTH/AFR SEA AGRI NAT/G FORCES WORKER DIPLOM INT/TRADE PRICE DEMAND PRODUC...STAT CHARTS 17/19 FRONTIER. PAGE 117 H2341 — COLONIAL ECO/UNDEV ECO/TAC MARKET

B61
SCHNAPPER B.,LA POLITIQUE ET LE COMMERCE FRANCAIS DANS LE GOLFE DE GUINEE DE 1838 A 1871. FRANCE GUINEA UK SEA EXTR/IND NAT/G DELIB/GP LEGIS ADMIN ORD/FREE...POLICY GEOG CENSUS CHARTS BIBLIOG 19. PAGE 139 H2791 — COLONIAL INT/TRADE DOMIN AFR

B61
SOKOL A.E.,SEAPOWER IN THE NUCLEAR AGE. USA+45 USSR DIST/IND FORCES INT/TRADE DETER WAR...POLICY NAT/COMP BIBLIOG COLD/WAR. PAGE 146 H2928 — SEA PWR WEAPON NUC/PWR

B62
HENDERSON W.O.,THE GENESIS OF THE COMMON MARKET. EUR+WWI FRANCE MOD/EUR UK SEA COM/IND EXTR/IND COLONIAL DISCRIM...TIME/SEQ CHARTS BIBLIOG 18/20 EEC TREATY. PAGE 70 H1395 — ECO/DEV INT/TRADE DIPLOM

B65
GRAHAM G.S.,THE POLITICS OF NAVAL SUPREMACY; STUDIES IN BRITISH MARITIME ASCENDANCY. UK SEA NAT/G BAL/PWR LEAD WAR WEAPON PEACE...POLICY 18/19 COMMONWLTH. PAGE 60 H1191 — FORCES PWR COLONIAL DIPLOM

B65
GRETTON P.,MARITIME STRATEGY - A STUDY OF DEFENSE PROBLEMS. ASIA UK USSR DIPLOM COERCE DETER NUC/PWR WEAPON...CONCPT NAT/COMP 20. PAGE 60 H1211 — FORCES PLAN WAR SEA

B82
RATZEL F.,ANTHROPO-GEOGRAPHIE. SEA AGRI NEIGH. PAGE 130 H2595 — GEOG CULTURE HABITAT

SEARCH FOR EDUCATION, ELEVATION, AND KNOWLEDGE....SEE SEEK

SEATO....SOUTH EAST ASIA TREATY ORGANIZATION; SEE ALSO INT/ORG, VOL/ASSN, FORCES, DETER

B62
MODELSKI G.,SEATO-SIX STUDIES. ASIA CHINA/COM INDIA S/ASIA INT/ORG NAT/G ECO/TAC DETER ATTIT ORD/FREE PWR...TIME/SEQ COLD/WAR TOT/POP 20 SEATO. PAGE 112 H2234 — MARKET ECO/UNDEV INT/TRADE

B66
BRACKMAN A.C.,SOUTHEAST ASIA'S SECOND FRONT: THE POWER STRUGGLE IN THE MALAY ARCHIPELAGO. CHINA/COM INDONESIA MALAYSIA ECO/UNDEV INT/ORG NAT/G FORCES DIPLOM EDU/PROP REGION COERCE GUERRILLA AUTHORIT POPULISM...MAJORIT 20 KENNEDY/JF SEATO. PAGE 20 H0396 — S/ASIA MARXISM REV

SEATTLE....SEATTLE, WASHINGTON

SEC/EXCHNG....SECURITY EXCHANGE COMMISSION

SEC/REFORM....SECOND REFORM ACT OF 1867 (U.K.)

SEC/STATE....U.S. SECRETARY OF STATE

SECOND REFORM ACT OF 1867 (U.K.)....SEE SEC/REFORM

SECRETARY OF STATE (U.S.)....SEE SEC/STATE

SECT....CHURCH, SECT, RELIGIOUS GROUP

N
JOURNAL OF ASIAN STUDIES. CULTURE ECO/DEV SECT DIPLOM EDU/PROP WAR NAT/LISM...PHIL/SCI SOC 20. PAGE 1 H0005 — BIBLIOG ASIA S/ASIA NAT/G

N
MIDDLE EAST JOURNAL. CULTURE SECT DIPLOM LEAD GOV/REL ATTIT...POLICY PHIL/SCI SOC LING BIOG 20. PAGE 1 H0007 — BIBLIOG ISLAM NAT/G ECO/UNDEV

N
BIBLIOGRAPHIE DE LA PHILOSOPHIE. LAW CULTURE SECT EDU/PROP MORAL...HUM METH/CNCPT 20. PAGE 1 H0012 — BIBLIOG/A PHIL/SCI CONCPT LOG

N
THE STATESMAN'S YEARBOOK; STATISTICAL AND HISTORICAL ANNUAL OF THE STATES OF THE WORLD. WOR+45 WOR-45 COM/IND FINAN INDUS SECT FORCES TEC/DEV EDU/PROP...GEOG BIBLIOG 19/20. PAGE 1 H0023 — NAT/COMP GOV/COMP STAT CONSTN

N
AFRICAN BIBLIOGRAPHIC CENTER,A CURRENT BIBLIOGRAPHY ON AFRICAN AFFAIRS. LAW CULTURE ECO/UNDEV LABOR SECT DIPLOM FOR/AID COLONIAL NAT/LISM...LING 20. PAGE 4 H0075 — BIBLIOG/A AFR NAT/G REGION

N
CORDIER H.,BIBLIOTECA SINICA. SOCIETY STRUCT SECT DIPLOM COLONIAL...GEOG SOC CON/ANAL. PAGE 33 H0664 — BIBLIOG/A NAT/G CULTURE ASIA

B00
MAINE H.S.,ANCIENT LAW. MEDIT-7 CULTURE SOCIETY KIN SECT LEGIS LEGIT ROUTINE...JURID HIST/WRIT CON/ANAL TOT/POP VAL/FREE. PAGE 101 H2020 — FAM LAW

B02
JELLINEK G.,LA DECLARATION DES DROITS DE L'HOMME ET DU CITOYEN (1895) (TRANSLATED FROM GERMAN BY G. FARDIS). FRANCE GERMANY USA-45 NAT/G SECT LEGIS 18. PAGE 80 H1598 — ORD/FREE CONCPT REV

B04
DANTE ALIGHIERI,DE MONARCHIA (CA .1310). CHRIST-17C ITALY DOMIN LEGIT ATTIT PWR...CATH CONCPT TIME/SEQ. PAGE 37 H0741 — SECT NAT/G SOVEREIGN

B04
REED W.A.,ETHNOLOGICAL SURVEY PUBLICATIONS (VOL. II). PHILIPPINE STRUCT INDUS SECT DEATH LEISURE HABITAT...AUD/VIS CHARTS WORSHIP 20 NABOLOI NEGRITO BATAK. PAGE 130 H2607 — CULTURE SOCIETY SOC OBS

C05
DUNNING W.A.,"HISTORY OF POLITICAL THEORIES FROM LUTHER TO MONTESQUIEU." LAW NAT/G SECT DIPLOM REV WAR ORD/FREE SOVEREIGN CONSERVE...TRADIT BIBLIOG 16/18. PAGE 43 H0867 — PHIL/SCI CONCPT GEN/LAWS

C09
SCHAPIRO J.S.,"SOCIAL REFORM AND THE REFORMATION." CHRIST-17C GERMANY LAW CONSTN LG/CO NAT/G WORKER PROB/SOLV CT/SYS REV...BIBLIOG 16. PAGE 138 H2770 — ORD/FREE SECT ECO/TAC BIOG

B10
MENDELSSOHN S.,SOUTH AFRICAN BIBLIOGRAPHY (2 VOLS.). SOUTH/AFR EXTR/IND LABOR SECT DIPLOM INT/TRADE COLONIAL RACE/REL DISCRIM...GEOG 20. PAGE 109 H2172 — BIBLIOG/A AFR NAT/G NAT/LISM

B10
TEMPERLEY H.W.V.,SENATES AND UPPER CHAMBERS; THEIR USE AND FUNCTION IN THE MODERN STATE... UK WOR-45 CONSTN NAT/G POL/PAR PROVS SECT COLONIAL LEAD CHOOSE REPRESENT PWR...BIBLIOG 19/20 PARLIAMENT SENATE CMN/WLTH HOUSE/LORD. PAGE 153 H3059 — PARL/PROC NAT/COMP LEGIS EX/STRUC

B12
CORDIER H.,BIBLIOTHECA INDOSINICA: DICTIONAIRE BIBLIOGRAPHIQUE DES OUVRAGES RELATIFS A LA PENINSULE INDOCHINOISE. BURMA LAOS MALAYSIA S/ASIA THAILAND VIETNAM SECT...LING 20. PAGE 33 H0665 — BIBLIOG/A GEOG NAT/G

B12
SONOLET L.,L'AFRIQUE OCCIDENTALE FRANCAISE. FRANCE AGRI INDUS NAT/G SECT FORCES INT/TRADE EDU/PROP RACE/REL HEALTH ORD/FREE...CHARTS 19/20 NEGRO AFRICA/W. PAGE 147 H2933 — DOMIN ADMIN COLONIAL AFR

B14
FIGGIS J.N.,CHURCHES IN THE MODERN STATE (2ND ED.). LAW CHIEF BAL/PWR PWR...CONCPT CHURCH/STA POPE. PAGE 50 H0998 — SECT NAT/G SOCIETY ORD/FREE

B16
PUFENDORF S.,LAW OF NATURE AND OF NATIONS (ABRIDGED). UNIV LAW NAT/G DIPLOM AGREE WAR PERSON ALL/VALS PWR...POLICY 18 DEITY NATURL/LAW. PAGE 128 H2565 — CONCPT INT/LAW SECT MORAL

B17
DE MAISTRE J.,DU PAPE (1817). FRANCE LAW SOCIETY SECT DOMIN REV HAPPINESS PWR SOVEREIGN 18/19 PROTESTANT. PAGE 38 H0761 — CATH CHIEF LEGIT NAT/G

B17
DE VICTORIA F.,DE INDIS ET DE JURE BELLI (1557) IN F. DE VICTORIA, DE INDIS ET DE JURE BELLI REFLECTIONES. UNIV NAT/G SECT CHIEF PARTIC COERCE PEACE MORAL...POLICY 16 INDIAN/AM CHRISTIAN CONSCN/OBJ. PAGE 39 H0775 — WAR INT/LAW OWN

N17
BURKE E.,THOUGHTS ON THE PROSPECT OF A REGICIDE PEACE (PAMPHLET). FRANCE UK SECT DOMIN MURDER PEACE ORD/FREE SOVEREIGN POPULISM...POLICY GOV/COMP IDEA/COMP 18 JACOBINISM COEXIST. PAGE 24 H0483
REV CHIEF NAT/G DIPLOM

N17
BURKE E.,LETTER TO SIR HERCULES LANGRISHE (PAMPHLET). IRELAND UK NAT/G CHIEF DIPLOM DOMIN PARL/PROC COERCE ORD/FREE SOVEREIGN POPULISM ...TRADIT 18 BURKE/EDM. PAGE 24 H0485
POLICY COLONIAL SECT

B18
BARRES M.,THE FAITH OF FRANCE (TRANS. BY ELISABETH MARBURY). FRANCE FAM MUNIC NEIGH POL/PAR SECT ALL/VALS 20. PAGE 11 H0227
TRADIT CULTURE WAR GP/REL

N19
COUTROT A.,THE FIGHT OVER THE 1959 PRIVATE EDUCATION LAW IN FRANCE (PAMPHLET). FRANCE NAT/G SECT GIVE EDU/PROP GP/REL ATTIT RIGID/FLEX ORD/FREE 20 CHURCH/STA. PAGE 34 H0681
SCHOOL PARL/PROC CATHISM LAW

N19
WEBB L.C.,CHURCH AND STATE IN ITALY: 1947-1957 (PAMPHLET). GERMANY ITALY CONSTN POL/PAR AGREE CONTROL PARTIC CHOOSE ATTIT ORD/FREE FASCISM MARXISM 20 CHURCH/STA MARITAIN/J SALO. PAGE 166 H3316
SECT CATHISM NAT/G GP/REL

B20
BOSANQUET B.,THE PHILOSOPHICAL THEORY OF THE STATE (3RD ED.). SECT LEGIS EDU/PROP ORD/FREE...POLICY SOC GOV/COMP IDEA/COMP NAT/COMP. PAGE 19 H0380
GEN/LAWS CONSTN NAT/G

B20
COLE G.D.H.,SOCIAL THEORY. CULTURE LOC/G SECT REGION REPRESENT ATTIT DRIVE...PSY SOC BIBLIOG. PAGE 31 H0621
CONCPT NAT/G PHIL/SCI

B21
KREY A.C.,THE FIRST CRUSADE. CHRIST-17C SOCIETY STRATA NAT/G SECT FORCES WORKER WRITING LEAD ATTIT ...CHARTS 11 CHRISTIAN CRUSADES. PAGE 88 H1767
WAR CATH DIPLOM PARTIC

B22
FICHTE J.G.,ADDRESSES TO THE GERMAN NATION. GERMANY PRUSSIA ELITES NAT/G SECT CREATE INT/TRADE HEREDITY ...ART/METH LING 19 FRANK/PARL. PAGE 50 H0989
NAT/LISM CULTURE EDU/PROP REGION

B23
GRANT C.F.,STUDIES IN NORTH AFRICA. ALGERIA MOROCCO ROMAN/EMP CULTURE STRUCT NAT/G DIPLOM WAR ...NAT/COMP TUNIS EUROPE. PAGE 60 H1195
ISLAM SECT DOMIN COLONIAL

B23
WILLOUGHBY W.C.,RACE PROBLEMS IN THE NEW AFRICA: A STUDY OF THE RELATION OF BANTU AND BRITONS IN THOSE PARTS OF BANTU AFRICA... AFR STRUCT SECT DOMIN EDU/PROP GP/REL ATTIT WORSHIP 20 BANTU EUROPE MISSION CHRISTIAN. PAGE 168 H3372
KIN COLONIAL RACE/REL CULTURE

B24
WALKER F.D.,AFRICA AND HER PEOPLES. ISLAM STRUCT FAM SECT EDU/PROP INGP/REL RACE/REL HABITAT...GEOG SOC IDEA/COMP WORSHIP 20 NEGRO. PAGE 164 H3292
CULTURE AFR GP/COMP KIN

B26
FORTESCUE J.,THE GOVERNANCE OF ENGLAND (1471-76). UK LAW FINAN SECT LEGIS PROB/SOLV TAX DOMIN ADMIN GP/REL COST ORD/FREE PWR 14/15. PAGE 52 H1042
CONSERVE CONSTN CHIEF NAT/G

B26
MALINOWSKI B.,CRIME AND CUSTOM IN SAVAGE SOCIETY. SOCIETY FAM SECT LEGIT SANCTION MARRIAGE MYSTISM ...PSY SOC 19/20 MELANESIA CANON/LAW. PAGE 102 H2030
LAW CULTURE CRIME ADJUD

B26
TAWNEY R.H.,RELIGION AND THE RISE OF CAPITALISM. UK CULTURE NAT/G TEC/DEV OWN LAISSEZ...POLICY SOC TIME/SEQ 16/19. PAGE 153 H3050
SECT WEALTH INDUS CAP/ISM

B27
GOOCH G.P.,ENGLISH DEMOCRATIC IDEAS IN THE SEVENTEENTH CENTURY (2ND ED.). UK LAW SECT FORCES DIPLOM LEAD PARL/PROC REV ATTIT AUTHORIT...ANARCH CONCPT 17 PARLIAMENT CMN/WLTH REFORMERS. PAGE 58 H1167
IDEA/COMP MAJORIT EX/STRUC CONSERVE

B27
JOHN OF SALISBURY,THE STATESMAN'S BOOK (1159) (TRANS. BY J. DICKINSON). DOMIN GP/REL MORAL ORD/FREE PWR CONSERVE...CATH CONCPT 12. PAGE 81 H1617
NAT/G SECT CHIEF LAW

B27
SMITH E.W.,THE GOLDEN STOOL: SOME ASPECTS OF THE CONFLICT OF CULTURES IN AFRICA. AFR FINAN INDUS SECT INT/TRADE COERCE CHOOSE RACE/REL ATTIT...GEOG LING 20 NEGRO. PAGE 145 H2907
COLONIAL CULTURE GP/REL EDU/PROP

B27
WEBER M.,GENERAL ECONOMIC HISTORY. CHRIST-17C MOD/EUR STRUCT AGRI EXTR/IND FINAN INDUS MARKET FAM MUNIC NAT/G PROF/ORG SECT ECO/TAC 8/20. PAGE 166 H3319
ECO/DEV CAP/ISM

B28
FYFE H.,THE BRITISH LIBERAL PARTY. UK SECT ADMIN LEAD CHOOSE GP/REL PWR SOCISM...MAJORIT TIME/SEQ 19/20 LIB/PARTY CONSRV/PAR. PAGE 54 H1084
POL/PAR NAT/G REPRESENT POPULISM

B28
HOBBES T.,THE ELEMENTS OF LAW, NATURAL AND POLITIC (1650). STRATA NAT/G SECT CHIEF AGREE ATTIT ALL/VALS MORAL ORD/FREE POPULISM...POLICY CONCPT. PAGE 71 H1432
PERSON LAW SOVEREIGN CONSERVE

B28
MARSILIUS/PADUA,DEFENSOR PACIS (1324). CHRIST-17C CONSTN NAT/G DIPLOM DOMIN LEGIT CONTROL WAR PEACE ORD/FREE SOVEREIGN POPULISM 14 POPE. PAGE 103 H2059
CATH SECT GEN/LAWS

B29
CAM H.M.,BIBLIOGRAPHY OF ENGLISH CONSTITUTIONAL HISTORY (PAMPHLET). UK LAW LOC/G NAT/G POL/PAR SECT DELIB/GP ADJUD ORD/FREE 19/20 PARLIAMENT. PAGE 25 H0510
BIBLIOG/A CONSTN ADMIN PARL/PROC

B30
HATTERSLEY A.F.,A SHORT HISTORY OF DEMOCRACY. WOR-45 CONSTN NAT/G SECT DOMIN WAR CHOOSE ORD/FREE PWR...CONCPT GOV/COMP BIBLIOG ATHENS ROME. PAGE 68 H1355
REPRESENT MAJORIT POPULISM

B30
HULL W.I.,INDIA'S POLITICAL CRISIS. INDIA UK INT/ORG LABOR SECT DELIB/GP LEGIS DIPLOM NEUTRAL REGION CROWD GOV/REL MAJORITY ATTIT 20 NEHRU/J GANDHI/M COMMONWLTH. PAGE 75 H1492
ORD/FREE NAT/G COLONIAL NAT/LISM

B30
SMUTS J.C.,AFRICA AND SOME WORLD PROBLEMS. RHODESIA SOUTH/AFR CULTURE ECO/UNDEV INDUS INT/ORG SECT PROB/SOLV REGION GOV/REL DISCRIM ATTIT 19/20 LEAGUE/NAT LIVNGSTN/D NEGRO. PAGE 146 H2921
LEGIS AFR COLONIAL RACE/REL

B31
DUFFIELD M.,KING LEGION. NAT/G PROVS SECT LEGIS EDU/PROP PRESS GP/REL AGE/Y MARXISM POLICY. PAGE 43 H0856
SUPEGO FORCES VOL/ASSN LOBBY

B31
KROEBER A.L.,SOURCE BOOK IN ANTHROPOLOGY. PREHIST SECT RACE/REL...LING GP/COMP ANTHOL. PAGE 89 H1770
SOC HEREDITY CULTURE ALL/VALS

B32
BRYCE J.,THE HOLY ROMAN EMPIRE. GERMANY ITALY MOD/EUR CULTURE SOCIETY STRUCT INT/ORG NAT/G SECT DIPLOM DOMIN WAR SUPEGO ALL/VALS SOVEREIGN...GEOG SOC TIME/SEQ CHARTS STERTYP. PAGE 23 H0456
CHRIST-17C NAT/LISM

B32
THIBAUDET A.,LES IDEES POLITIQUES DE LA FRANCE. FRANCE NAT/G SECT PRESS REV NAT/LISM PEACE ATTIT ...PSY 19/20 JACOBINISM JAURES/JL. PAGE 154 H3070
IDEA/COMP ALL/IDEOS CATHISM

B33
BERDYAYEV N.,CHRISTIANITY AND CLASS WAR. UNIV SOCIETY WORKER CREATE PROB/SOLV ATTIT PERSON ORD/FREE...CONCPT CHRISTIAN. PAGE 15 H0296
SECT MARXISM STRATA GP/REL

B33
FERRERO G.,PEACE AND WAR (TRANS. BY BERTHA PRITCHARD). CULTURE FINAN SECT ATTIT SUPEGO MORAL ORD/FREE CONSERVE POPULISM SOCISM POLICY. PAGE 49 H0987
WAR PEACE DIPLOM PROB/SOLV

B33
TANNENBAUM F.,PEACE BY REVOLUTION. ECO/UNDEV AGRI SECT WORKER DIPLOM EDU/PROP DISCRIM OWN WEALTH POPULISM 17/20 MEXIC/AMER INDIAN/AM. PAGE 152 H3043
CULTURE COLONIAL RACE/REL REV

C33
MURET C.T.,"FRENCH ROYALIST DOCTRINES SINCE THE REVOLUTION." FRANCE CONSTN NAT/G SECT ADMIN LEAD SOVEREIGN...POLICY BIOG IDEA/COMP BIBLIOG 18/20. PAGE 115 H2295
POL/PAR ATTIT INTELL CONSERVE

B34
DE CENIVAL P.,BIBLIOGRAPHIE MAROCAINE: 1923-1933. FRANCE MOROCCO SECT ADMIN LEAD GP/REL ATTIT...LING 20. PAGE 37 H0750
BIBLIOG/A ISLAM NAT/G COLONIAL

B35
DOUGLASS H.P.,THE PROTESTANT CHURCH AS A SOCIAL INSTITUTION. CULTURE FINAN NEIGH PROF/ORG OP/RES ADMIN...POLICY SOC/WK STAT BIBLIOG. PAGE 42 H0843
SECT PARTIC INGP/REL GP/REL

B35
GORER G.,AFRICA DANCES: A BOOK ABOUT WEST AFRICAN NEGROES. STRUCT LOC/G SECT FORCES TAX ADMIN COLONIAL...ART/METH MYTH WORSHIP 20 NEGRO AFRICA/W CHRISTIAN RITUAL. PAGE 59 H1181
AFR ATTIT CULTURE SOCIETY

B35
MORE T.,UTOPIA (1516) (TRANS. BY R. ROBYNSON). LAW CULTURE SOCIETY STRUCT FAM SECT EDU/PROP WAR OWN UTIL KNOWL WEALTH 16. PAGE 113 H2253
UTOPIA NAT/G ECO/TAC GEN/LAWS

B35
PARETO V.,THE MIND AND SOCIETY (4 VOLS.). ELITES SECT ECO/TAC COERCE PERSON ORD/FREE PWR SOVEREIGN
GEN/LAWS SOC

FASCISM POPULISM...TRADIT 19/20. PAGE 123 H2465 PSY

B35
TAKEUCHI T.,WAR AND DIPLOMACY IN THE JAPANESE EMPIRE. ASIA ELITES STRATA NAT/G SECT LEGIS ACT/RES PLAN LEGIT PARL/PROC ROUTINE WAR...MGT BIOG CHINJAP TOT/POP 19/20 CHINJAP. PAGE 152 H3038 EXEC STRUCT

B36
MARITAIN J.,FREEDOM IN THE MODERN WORLD. CONSTN NAT/G SECT CAP/ISM MARXISM SOCISM...GOV/COMP IDEA/COMP 19/20 HUMANISM CHRISTIAN. PAGE 102 H2049 GEN/LAWS POLICY ORD/FREE

B36
VICO G.B.,DIRITTO UNIVERSALE (1722) (VOL. 2, PARTS 1,2, AND 3, OF G.B. VICO, OPERE). UNIV DIPLOM AGREE WAR OWN KNOWL ORD/FREE SOVEREIGN DEITY. PAGE 162 H3249 JURID SECT CONCPT NAT/G

B37
BERDYAEV N.,THE ORIGIN OF RUSSIAN COMMUNISM. MOD/EUR RUSSIA USSR INTELL SECT REV...ANARCH HUM 19/20 ORTHO/RUSS COM/PARTY CHRISTIAN. PAGE 15 H0294 MARXISM NAT/LISM CULTURE ATTIT

B37
BORGESE G.A.,GOLIATH: THE MARCH OF FASCISM. GERMANY ITALY LAW POL/PAR SECT DIPLOM SOCISM...JURID MYTH 20 DANTE MACHIAVELL MUSSOLIN/B. PAGE 19 H0375 POLICY NAT/LISM FASCISM NAT/G

B38
COUPLAND R.,EAST AFRICA AND ITS INVADERS. AFR ISLAM STRATA SECT FORCES DIPLOM TRIBUTE CONTROL DISCRIM NAT/LISM 19 AFRICA/E EUROPE MISSION. PAGE 34 H0680 CULTURE ELITES COLONIAL MARKET

B38
DUNHAM W.H. JR.,COMPLAINT AND REFORM IN ENGLAND 1436-1714. UK LAW ACADEM NAT/G POL/PAR SCHOOL PRESS COLONIAL PARL/PROC MORAL...SOC/WK ANTHOL 15/18 HAKLUYT/R COWPER/W. PAGE 43 H0865 ATTIT SOCIETY SECT

B38
RAWLINSON H.G.,INDIA: A SHORT CULTURAL HISTORY. INDIA LAW STRATA FORCES INT/TRADE ADMIN COLONIAL PERSON...GEOG HUM BIBLIOG WORSHIP 20. PAGE 130 H2598 CULTURE SECT MYTH ART/METH

B39
AKIGA,AKIGA'S STORY: THE TIV TRIBE AS SEEN BY ONE OF ITS MEMBERS. NIGERIA LAW STRUCT ECO/UNDEV FAM LEAD GP/REL MARRIAGE...LING WORSHIP 20. PAGE 4 H0089 KIN SECT SOC CULTURE

B39
ENGELS F.,HERRN EUGEN DUHRING'S REVOLUTION IN SCIENCE (1878). CULTURE STRATA STRUCT FAM SECT ECO/TAC REV WAR SOCISM...MARXIST 19. PAGE 46 H0925 PWR SOCIETY WEALTH GEN/LAWS

B39
FIRTH R.,PRIMITIVE POLYNESIAN ECONOMY. SOCIETY DIST/IND SECT CHIEF CAP/ISM PRODUC WEALTH...SOC OBS METH WORSHIP 20 POLYNESIA. PAGE 50 H1007 ECO/UNDEV CULTURE AGRI ECO/TAC

B39
HILL R.L.,A BIBLIOGRAPHY OF THE ANGLO-EGYPTIAN SUDAN FROM THE EARLIEST TIMES TO 1937. AFR ETHIOPIA SUDAN UAR LAW COM/IND SECT RACE/REL...GEOG HEAL SOC LING 19/20 NEGRO. PAGE 71 H1417 BIBLIOG CULTURE NAT/COMP GP/COMP

B39
MARITAIN J.,SCHOLASTICISM AND POLITICS. CONSTN SOCIETY NAT/G INGP/REL PERSON CATHISM POPULISM 19/20 FREUD/S SCHOLASTIC CHURCH/STA CHRISTIAN. PAGE 103 H2050 SECT GEN/LAWS ORD/FREE

B39
MILLER P.,THE NEW ENGLAND MIND: THE SEVENTEENTH CENTURY. CULTURE DOMIN WRITING INGP/REL CONSEN MAJORITY PERCEPT KNOWL MORAL...CONCPT LING WORSHIP 17 NEW/ENGLND PROTESTANT. PAGE 111 H2214 SECT REGION SOC ATTIT

B40
HOBBES T.,BEHEMOTH (1668). UK CONSTN SECT DOMIN LEGIT UTIL ORD/FREE CATHISM...POLICY CONCPT GEN/LAWS 17 CHARLES/I CROMWELL/O PROTESTANT. PAGE 71 H1433 REV NAT/G CHIEF

B40
JORDAN W.K.,THE DEVELOPMENT OF RELIGIOUS TOLERATION IN ENGLAND. CHRIST-17C CULTURE SOCIETY LEGIT ATTIT RESPECT...POLICY CONCPT RECORD TIME/SEQ STERTYP GEN/LAWS TOT/POP 16/17. PAGE 82 H1635 SECT UK

B41
KEESING F.M.,THE SOUTH SEAS IN THE MODERN WORLD. INDONESIA STRUCT FAM SECT EDU/PROP LEAD INCOME WEALTH...HEAL SOC 20. PAGE 84 H1678 CULTURE ECO/UNDEV GOV/COMP DIPLOM

B42
BARNES H.E.,SOCIAL INSTITUTIONS IN AN ERA OF WORLD UPHEAVAL. INDUS FAM NAT/G PERF/ART SECT AUTOMAT PERSON MORAL...PREDICT 20. PAGE 11 H0221 SOCIETY CULTURE TECHRACY TREND

B42
CONOVER H.F.,FRENCH COLONIES IN AFRICA: A LIST OF REFERENCES. ALGERIA FRANCE MOROCCO SOMALIA SUDAN CULTURE AGRI LOC/G SECT FORCES DIPLOM INT/TRADE NAT/LISM HEALTH...CON/ANAL 20. PAGE 32 H0641 BIBLIOG AFR ECO/UNDEV COLONIAL

B42
CONOVER H.F.,THE NETHERLANDS EAST INDIES: A SELECTED LIST OF REFERENCES. ECO/UNDEV AGRI EXTR/IND LABOR SCHOOL SECT INT/TRADE COLONIAL HEALTH...GEOG 19/20. PAGE 32 H0642 BIBLIOG S/ASIA CULTURE

B42
CRAIG A.,ABOVE ALL LIBERTIES. FRANCE UK USA-45 LAW CONSTN CULTURE INTELL NAT/G SECT JUDGE...IDEA/COMP BIBLIOG 18/20. PAGE 35 H0692 ORD/FREE MORAL WRITING EDU/PROP

B42
HEGEL G.W.F.,PHILOSOPHY OF RIGHT. UNIV FAM SECT CHIEF AGREE WAR MARRIAGE OWN ORD/FREE...POLICY CONCPT. PAGE 69 H1383 NAT/G LAW RATIONAL

B42
REDFIELD R.,THE FOLK CULTURE OF YUCATAN. STRATA FAM KIN MUNIC SECT DISCRIM ISOLAT ANOMIE HEALTH ...BIBLIOG 20 MEXIC/AMER. PAGE 130 H2605 CULTURE NEIGH GP/COMP SOCIETY

C42
CRAIG A.,"ABOVE ALL LIBERTIES." FRANCE UK LAW CULTURE INTELL SECT ORD/FREE 18/20. PAGE 35 H0693 BIBLIOG/A EDU/PROP WRITING MORAL

B43
BROWN A.D.,GREECE: SELECTED LIST OF REFERENCES. GREECE ECO/UNDEV AGRI FINAN INDUS LABOR SECT TEC/DEV INT/TRADE LEAD...SOC 20. PAGE 22 H0438 BIBLIOG/A WAR DIPLOM NAT/G

B44
CASSIRER E.,AN ESSAY ON MAN: AN INTRODUCTION TO A PHILOSOPHY OF HUMAN CULTURE. UNIV SECT CREATE EDU/PROP ATTIT KNOWL...HUM CONCPT MYTH TOT/POP. PAGE 28 H0556 CULTURE SOC

B44
SUAREZ F.,A TREATISE ON LAWS AND GOD THE LAWGIVER (1612) IN SELECTIONS FROM THREE WORKS, VOL. II. FRANCE ITALY UK CULTURE NAT/G SECT CHIEF LEGIS DOMIN LEGIT CT/SYS ORD/FREE PWR WORSHIP 16/17. PAGE 150 H3004 LAW JURID GEN/LAWS CATH

B44
US LIBRARY OF CONGRESS,RUSSIA: A CHECK LIST PRELIMINARY TO A BASIC BIBLIOGRAPHY OF MATERIALS IN THE RUSSIAN LANGUAGE. COM USSR CULTURE EDU/PROP MARXISM...ART/METH HUM LING 19/20. PAGE 160 H3204 BIBLIOG LAW SECT

B44
WOLFE D.M.,LEVELLER MANIFESTOES OF THE PURITAN REVOLUTION. UK CONSTN NAT/G SECT...CONCPT ANTHOL 17 LEVELLERS DECLAR/IND PURITAN LOCKE/JOHN. PAGE 170 H3400 POL/PAR REV ORD/FREE ATTIT

C44
SUAREZ F.,"ON WAR" (1621) IN SELECTIONS FROM THREE WORKS, VOL. I." NAT/G SECT CHIEF DIPLOM LEGIT MORAL PWR...POLICY INT/LAW 17. PAGE 150 H3005 WAR REV ORD/FREE CATH

C44
VAN VALKENBURG S.,"ELEMENTS OF POLITICAL GEOGRAPHY." FRANCE COM/IND INDUS NAT/G SECT RACE/REL...LING TREND GEN/LAWS BIBLIOG 20. PAGE 162 H3232 GEOG DIPLOM COLONIAL

B45
CONOVER H.F.,THE NAZI STATE: WAR CRIMES AND WAR CRIMINALS. GERMANY CULTURE NAT/G SECT FORCES DIPLOM INT/TRADE EDU/PROP...INT/LAW BIOG HIST/WRIT TIME/SEQ 20. PAGE 32 H0647 BIBLIOG WAR CRIME

B45
WARNER W.L.,THE SOCIAL SYSTEM OF AMERICAN ETHNIC GROUPS. STRATA FAM EDU/PROP ATTIT HABITAT RESPECT CLASSIF. PAGE 165 H3309 CULTURE VOL/ASSN SECT GP/COMP

B45
WOOLBERT R.G.,FOREIGN AFFAIRS BIBLIOGRAPHY, 1932-1942. INT/ORG SECT INT/TRADE COLONIAL RACE/REL NAT/LISM...GEOG INT/LAW GOV/COMP IDEA/COMP 20. PAGE 170 H3410 BIBLIOG/A DIPLOM WAR

C45
PAINE T.,"THE AGE OF REASON IN T. PAINE, THE COMPLETE WRITINGS OF THOMAS PAINE (VOL. 1) (1794-95)" CULTURE ACT/RES DOMIN UTOPIA ATTIT PERCEPT WORSHIP. PAGE 122 H2445 SECT KNOWL PHIL/SCI ORD/FREE

S46
TANNENBAUM F.,"THE BALANCE OF POWER IN SOCIETY." UNIV STRUCT FAM NAT/G SECT PERS/REL EQUILIB UTOPIA DRIVE ALL/IDEOS...OLD/LIB CONCPT. PAGE 152 H3044 SOCIETY ALL/VALS GP/REL PEACE

N46
HOBBS C.C.,SOUTHEAST ASIA, 1935-45: A SELECTED LIST OF REFERENCE BOOKS (PAMPHLET). S/ASIA AGRI INDUS NAT/G SECT DIPLOM WAR...ART/METH GEOG SOC LING 20. PAGE 72 H1435 BIBLIOG/A CULTURE HABITAT

B47
BEHAR D.,BIBLIOGRAFIA HISPANOAMERICANA. LIBROS ANTIGUOS Y MODERNOS REFERENTES A AMERICA Y ESPANA. PORTUGAL SPAIN CONSTN NAT/G SECT CREATE REV WAR GOV/REL...ART/METH GEOG PHIL/SCI LING 20 ARGEN. PAGE 13 H0260 BIBLIOG L/A+17C CULTURE

BOWLE J.,WESTERN POLITICAL THOUGHT: AN HISTORICAL INTRODUCTION FROM THE ORIGINS TO ROUSSEAU. CONSTN NAT/G SECT CREATE RATIONAL ORD/FREE...SOC BIBLIOG/A. PAGE 19 H0391 — B47 — ATTIT IDEA/COMP PHIL/SCI

HERSKOVITS M.U.,MAN AND HIS WORK. UNIV SECT TEC/DEV PARTIC...PHIL/SCI LING AUD/VIS BIBLIOG. PAGE 70 H1409 — B47 — SOC CULTURE INGP/REL HABITAT

JURJI E.J.,THE GREAT RELIGIONS OF THE MODERN WORLD. CULTURE INTELL SOCIETY INT/ORG CONSULT CHOOSE ATTIT DRIVE PERSON RIGID/FLEX...HUM CONCPT OBS BIOG HIST/WRIT TREND GEN/LAWS 20 WORSHIP. PAGE 82 H1643 — B47 — UNIV SECT

NIEBUHR R.,THE CHILDREN OF LIGHT AND THE CHILDREN OF DARKNESS: A VINDICATION OF DEMOCRACY AND CRITIQUE OF TRADITIONAL DEFENSE. UNIV STRUCT NAT/G SECT INGP/REL OWN PEACE ORD/FREE MARXISM ...IDEA/COMP GEN/LAWS 20 CHRISTIAN. PAGE 118 H2358 — B47 — POPULISM DIPLOM NEIGH GP/REL

COX O.C.,CASTE, CLASS, AND RACE. INDIA WOR+45 WOR-45 SECT TEC/DEV MARRIAGE ROLE MARXISM...MAJORIT NAT/COMP SOC/INTEG 20 NEGRO HINDU. PAGE 34 H0688 — B48 — RACE/REL STRUCT STRATA DISCRIM

EDUARDO O.D.C.,THE NEGRO IN NORTHERN BRAZIL: A STUDY IN ACCULTURATION. BRAZIL ECO/UNDEV FAM SECT PAY REGION HABITAT CATHISM MYSTISM...GEOG OBS SOC/INTEG WORSHIP 20 NEGRO MARANHAO. PAGE 44 H0890 — B48 — CULTURE ADJUST GP/REL

LASKI H.S.,THE AMERICAN DEMOCRACY. CULTURE INDUS SECT WORKER DIPLOM EDU/PROP REPRESENT RACE/REL ORD/FREE PWR...NAT/COMP 18/20. PAGE 92 H1831 — B48 — NAT/G LOC/G USA-45 POPULISM

WRIGHT G.,THE RESHAPING OF FRENCH DEMOCRACY. FRANCE NAT/G POL/PAR SECT LEAD CHOOSE GP/REL INGP/REL MARXISM SOCISM...CHARTS BIBLIOG 20 DEGAULLE/C. PAGE 171 H3418 — B48 — CONSTN POPULISM CREATE LEGIS

HAUSER R.,AUTORITAT UND MACHT. SOCIETY SECT PWR CATHISM...JURID CONCPT 16/20 PROTESTANT LUTHER/M CALVIN/J CHURCH/STA. PAGE 68 H1360 — B49 — SOVEREIGN NAT/G LEGIT

HOLLERAN M.P.,CHURCH AND STATE IN GUATEMALA. GUATEMALA LAW STRUCT CATHISM...SOC SOC/INTEG 17/20 CHURCH/STA. PAGE 73 H1456 — B49 — SECT NAT/G GP/REL CULTURE

CORNELL U DEPT ASIAN STUDIES,SOUTHEAST ASIA PROGRAM DATA PAPER. BURMA CAMBODIA INDONESIA MALAYSIA VIETNAM SOCIETY STRUCT NAT/G SECT DIPLOM FOR/AID PWR WEALTH...SOC 20. PAGE 33 H0670 — B50 — BIBLIOG/A CULTURE S/ASIA ECO/UNDEV

COUNCIL BRITISH NATIONAL BIB,BRITISH NATIONAL BIBLIOGRAPHY. UK AGRI CONSTRUC PERF/ART POL/PAR SECT CREATE INT/TRADE LEAD...HUM JURID PHIL/SCI 20. PAGE 34 H0677 — B50 — BIBLIOG/A NAT/G TEC/DEV DIPLOM

FIGANIERE J.C.,BIBLIOTHECA HISTORICA PORTUGUEZA. BRAZIL PORTUGAL SECT ADMIN. PAGE 50 H0997 — B50 — BIBLIOG NAT/G DIPLOM COLONIAL

GOFF F.R.,FIFTEENTH CENTURY BOOKS IN THE LIBRARY OF CONGRESS. CHRIST-17C GERMANY ITALY CULTURE INTELL SECT CREATE...PHIL/SCI CONCPT CLASSIF BIOG TIME/SEQ 15. PAGE 58 H1153 — B50 — BIBLIOG KNOWL HUM

HALLOWELL J.H.,MAIN CURRENTS IN MODERN POLITICAL THOUGHT. CONSTN SECT LEGIS...MAJORIT CONCPT 17/20 MARX/KARL MILL/JS HOBBES/T LENIN/VI. PAGE 64 H1290 — B50 — IDEA/COMP POPULISM SOCISM

HARLEY G.W.,MASKS AS AGENTS OF SOCIAL CONTROL IN NORTHEAST LIBERIA. AFR LIBERIA LAW CULTURE ADJUST CONSEN MORAL...GEOG SOC WORSHIP 20. PAGE 66 H1332 — B50 — CONTROL ECO/UNDEV SECT CHIEF

HOBBS C.C.,INDOCHINA, A BIBLIOGRAPHY OF THE LAND AND PEOPLE. VIETNAM CULTURE AGRI INDUS NAT/G SECT ...ART/METH GEOG SOC LING 20. PAGE 72 H1436 — B50 — BIBLIOG/A S/ASIA COLONIAL ECO/UNDEV

HOOKER R.,OF THE LAWS OF ECCLESIASTICAL POLITY (1594) (ABR. BY J. S. MARSHALL). UK UNIV CHIEF PARTIC MORAL...JURID GEN/LAWS WORSHIP 16. PAGE 73 H1463 — B50 — SECT CONCPT LAW NAT/G

IRION F.C.,PUBLIC OPINION AND PROPAGANDA. STRUCT COM/IND FAM SECT COERCE 20 FILM. PAGE 78 H1568 — B50 — EDU/PROP ATTIT NAT/G PRESS

JONES H.D.,KOREA, AN ANNOTATED BIBLIOGRAPHY OF PUBLICATIONS IN WESTERN LANGUAGES. KOREA CULTURE MUNIC SECT FORCES DIPLOM HEALTH WEALTH...ART/METH GEOG SOC LING 20. PAGE 82 H1632 — B50 — BIBLIOG/A ASIA NAT/G ECO/UNDEV

MACHIAVELLI N.,THE DISCOURSES (1516). NAT/G SECT FORCES DOMIN LEGIT CONTROL LEAD COERCE TOTALISM ORD/FREE. PAGE 100 H1995 — B50 — PWR GEN/LAWS CHIEF

SMITH E.W.,AFRICAN IDEAS OF GOD. ATTIT...CONCPT MYTH IDEA/COMP ANTHOL BIBLIOG. PAGE 145 H2908 — B50 — SOC AFR CULTURE SECT

LOOS W.A.,RELIGIOUS FAITH AND WORLD CULTURE. INTELL SOCIETY SECT EDU/PROP ROUTINE ATTIT PERSON ALL/VALS MORAL...CONCPT GEN/LAWS VAL/FREE. PAGE 98 H1964 — B51 — UNIV CULTURE PEACE

YOUNG T.C.,NEAR EASTERN CULTURE AND SOCIETY. ISLAM ECO/UNDEV SECT WRITING ATTIT HABITAT ORD/FREE 20. PAGE 172 H3439 — B51 — CULTURE STRUCT REGION DIPLOM

MACRAE D.G.,"THE BOLSHEVIK IDEOLOGY; THE INTELLECTUAL AND EMOTIONAL FACTORS IN COMMUNIST AFFILIATION" (BMR)" COM LEAD REV ATTIT ORD/FREE ...SOC CON/ANAL 20 BOLSHEVISM. PAGE 100 H2008 — S51 — MARXISM INTELL PHIL/SCI SECT

NORTHROP F.S.C.,"ASIAN MENTALITY AND UNITED STATES FOREIGN POLICY." ASIA ISLAM USA+45 CULTURE SOCIETY SECT EDU/PROP LEGIT COERCE DRIVE MORAL ORD/FREE ...POLICY RELATIV TOT/POP 20. PAGE 119 H2376 — S51 — S/ASIA ATTIT DIPLOM

ETTINGHAUSEN R.,SELECTED AND ANNOTATED BIBLIOGRAPHY OF BOOKS AND PERIODICALS IN WESTERN LANGUAGES DEALING WITH NEAR AND MIDDLE EAST. LAW CULTURE SECT ...ART/METH GEOG SOC. PAGE 47 H0944 — B52 — BIBLIOG/A ISLAM MEDIT-7

HIMMELFARB G.,LORD ACTON: A STUDY IN CONSCIENCE AND POLITICS. MOD/EUR NAT/G POL/PAR SECT LEGIS TOP/EX EDU/PROP ADMIN NAT/LISM ATTIT PERSON SUPEGO MORAL ORD/FREE...CONCPT PARLIAMENT 19 ACTON/LORD. PAGE 71 H1419 — B52 — PWR BIOG

KOLARZ W.,RUSSIA AND HER COLONIES. COM RUSSIA LAW CULTURE ECO/DEV KIN LOC/G SECT TEC/DEV ECO/TAC EDU/PROP REGION COERCE ATTIT PWR SOVEREIGN...SOC TIME/SEQ CON/ANAL VAL/FREE 19/20. PAGE 88 H1749 — B52 — NAT/G DOMIN USSR COLONIAL

KROEBER A.L.,THE NATURE OF CULTURE. UNIV STRATA FAM KIN SECT...PSY GP/COMP 16/20 INDIAN/AM. PAGE 89 H1771 — B52 — CULTURE SOCIETY CONCPT STRUCT

BROWN D.M.,THE WHITE UMBRELLA: INDIAN POLITICAL THOUGHT FROM MANU TO GANDHI. INDIA LAW NAT/G SECT WRITING NAT/LISM...ANTHOL BIBLIOG 20 HINDU GANDHI/M MANU. PAGE 22 H0442 — B53 — CONCPT DOMIN CONSERVE

CURTISS J.S.,THE RUSSIAN CHURCH AND THE SOVIET STATE 1917-1950. COM USSR CONTROL LEAD REV MARXISM ...POLICY BIBLIOG 20 CHURCH/STA ORTHO/RUSS. PAGE 36 H0728 — B53 — GP/REL NAT/G SECT PWR

MARITAIN J.,L'HOMME ET L'ETAT. SECT DIPLOM GP/REL PEACE ORD/FREE...IDEA/COMP 17/20 CHURCH/STA NATURL/LAW. PAGE 103 H2052 — B53 — CONCPT NAT/G SOVEREIGN COERCE

MEAD M.,CULTURAL PATTERNS AND TECHNICAL CHANGE. BURMA GREECE NIGERIA ECO/UNDEV AGRI INDUS SCHOOL SECT CREATE FEEDBACK HABITAT...PSY METH/COMP BIBLIOG 20 UN. PAGE 108 H2152 — B53 — HEALTH TEC/DEV CULTURE ADJUST

MEYER P.,THE JEWS IN THE SOVIET SATELLITES. CZECHOSLVK POLAND SOCIETY STRATA NAT/G BAL/PWR ECO/TAC EDU/PROP LEGIT ADMIN COERCE ATTIT DISPL PERCEPT HEALTH PWR RESPECT WEALTH...METH/CNCPT JEWS VAL/FREE NAZI 20. PAGE 110 H2192 — B53 — COM SECT TOTALISM USSR

MURPHY G.,IN THE MINDS OF MEN: THE STUDY OF HUMAN BEHAVIOR AND SOCIAL TENSIONS IN INDIA. FUT S/ASIA FAM INT/ORG NAT/G DIPLOM EDU/PROP GP/REL ATTIT RIGID/FLEX ALL/VALS...SOC QU UNESCO 20. PAGE 115 H2297 — B53 — SECT STRATA INDIA

BULNER-THOMAS I.,"THE PARTY SYSTEM IN GREAT BRITAIN." UK CONSTN SECT PRESS CONFER GP/REL ATTIT ...POLICY TREND BIBLIOG 19/20 PARLIAMENT. PAGE 23 H0473 — C53 — NAT/G POL/PAR ADMIN ROUTINE

CAMPANELLA T.,A DISCOURSE TOUCHING THE SPANISH MONARCHY... (1640). SPAIN UNIV SEA STRATA FINAN SECT FORCES SUPEGO LOVE ORD/FREE...CONCPT 17. PAGE 26 H0514 — B54 — CONSERVE CHIEF NAT/G DIPLOM

GIRALSO JARAMLLO G.,BIBLIOGRAFIA DE BIBLIOGRAFIAS — B54 — BIBLIOG/A

COLOMBIANAS. L/A+17C ACADEM SECT CREATE EDU/PROP ...ART/METH GEOG LING TREND 20 COLOMB. PAGE 57 H1135 — CULTURE PHIL/SCI ECO/UNDEV

B54
HAZARD B.H. JR.,KOREAN STUDIES GUIDE. KOREA CONSTN CULTURE AGRI FAM SECT CREATE WAR NAT/LISM HABITAT PWR...CHARTS 14/20. PAGE 68 H1371 — BIBLIOG/A ELITES GP/REL

B54
LEWIS E.,MEDIEVAL POLITICAL IDEAS. LAW CULTURE SOCIETY ECO/UNDEV NAT/G SECT GOV/REL ATTIT ...BIBLIOG/A T 11/15. PAGE 96 H1913 — CHRIST-17C IDEA/COMP INTELL CONCPT

B54
PARRINDER G.,AFRICAN TRADITIONAL RELIGION. AFR SOCIETY EDU/PROP GP/REL PWR...SOC CONCPT IDEA/COMP WORSHIP 20 DEITY. PAGE 124 H2469 — SECT MYTH ATTIT CULTURE

L54
FRIEDRICH C.J.,"TOTALITARIANISM." COM EUR+WWI NAT/G POL/PAR SECT FORCES PLAN ECO/TAC DOMIN EDU/PROP EXEC COERCE REV ORD/FREE PWR...SOC CONCPT NAZI 20. PAGE 53 H1067 — ATTIT TOTALISM

C54
LANDAU J.M.,"PARLIAMENTS AND PARTIES IN EGYPT." UAR NAT/G SECT CONSULT LEGIS TOP/EX PROB/SOLV ADMIN COLONIAL...GEN/LAWS BIBLIOG 19/20. PAGE 90 H1804 — ISLAM NAT/LISM PARL/PROC POL/PAR

B55
BENEDICT B.,A SHORT ANNOTATED BIBLIOGRAPHY RELATING TO THE SOCIOLOGY OF MUSLIM PEOPLES. NAT/G...SOC 20. PAGE 14 H0277 — BIBLIOG/A ISLAM SECT CULTURE

B55
KHADDURI M.,WAR AND PEACE IN THE LAW OF ISLAM. CONSTN CULTURE SOCIETY STRATA NAT/G PROVS SECT FORCES TOP/EX CREATE DOMIN EDU/PROP ADJUD COERCE ATTIT RIGID/FLEX ALL/VALS...CONCPT TIME/SEQ TOT/POP VAL/FREE. PAGE 85 H1702 — ISLAM JURID PEACE WAR

B55
KOHN H.,THE MIND OF MODERN RUSSIA. COM MOD/EUR USSR SOCIETY NAT/G SECT FORCES TOP/EX COERCE TOTALISM DRIVE RIGID/FLEX PWR SOVEREIGN...CONCPT TIME/SEQ WORK. PAGE 87 H1742 — INTELL GEN/LAWS SOCISM RUSSIA

B55
KRUSE H.,DAS STAATSANGEHORIGKEITSRECHT DER ARABISCHEN STAATEN. ISLAM JORDAN LIBYA SYRIA UAR NAT/G SECT RACE/REL...INT/LAW 6/20 TREATY. PAGE 89 H1779 — JURID NAT/LISM DIPLOM GP/REL

B55
MAZZINI J.,THE DUTIES OF MAN. MOD/EUR LAW SOCIETY FAM NAT/G POL/PAR SECT VOL/ASSN EX/STRUC ACT/RES CREATE REV PEACE ATTIT ALL/VALS...GEN/LAWS WORK 19. PAGE 106 H2113 — SUPEGO CONCPT NAT/LISM

B55
MID-EUROPEAN LAW PROJECT,CHURCH AND STATE BEHIND THE IRON CURTAIN. COM CZECHOSLVK HUNGARY POLAND USSR CULTURE SECT EDU/PROP GOV/REL CATHISM...CHARTS ANTHOL BIBLIOG WORSHIP 20 CHURCH/STA. PAGE 110 H2202 — LAW MARXISM POLICY

B55
RESHETAR J.S.,PROBLEMS OF ANALYZING AND PREDICTING SOVIET BEHAVIOR. USSR CULTURE ECO/DEV AGRI DIST/IND EXTR/IND PROC/MFG NAT/G SECT TOP/EX ACT/RES ADMIN PWR WEALTH...SOC METH TOT/POP VAL/FREE 20. PAGE 131 H2617 — COM ATTIT

B55
STEWARD J.H.,THEORY OF CULTURE CHANGE; THE METHODOLOGY OF MULTILINEAR EVOLUTION. SOCIETY KIN SECT GP/REL INGP/REL...BIBLIOG SOC/INTEG 20. PAGE 149 H2984 — CULTURE CONCPT METH/COMP HABITAT

B55
THOMPSON V.,MINORITY PROBLEMS IN SOUTHEAST ASIA. CAMBODIA CHINA/COM LAOS S/ASIA KIN NAT/G SECT PROB/SOLV EDU/PROP REGION GP/REL RACE/REL MARXISM ...SOC 20 BUDDHISM UN. PAGE 154 H3085 — INGP/REL GEOG DIPLOM STRUCT

B55
WRONG D.H.,AMERICAN AND CANADIAN VIEWPOINTS. CANADA USA+45 CONSTN STRATA FAM SECT WORKER ECO/TAC EDU/PROP ADJUD MARRIAGE...IDEA/COMP 20. PAGE 171 H3424 — DIPLOM ATTIT NAT/COMP CULTURE

B56
BECKER H.,MAN IN RECIPROCITY: INTRODUCTORY LECTURES ON CULTURE, SOCIETY, AND PERSONALITY. LAW FAM SECT REGION GP/REL ADJUST ATTIT PERSON...BIBLIOG 20. PAGE 13 H0253 — CULTURE STRUCT SOC PSY

B56
CEPEDA U.A.,EN TORNO AL CONCEPTO DEL ESTADO EN LOS REYES CATHOLICOS. SPAIN SOCIETY STRUCT SECT LEGIT WAR ATTIT WORSHIP 15/17. PAGE 28 H0569 — NAT/G PHIL/SCI CHIEF PWR

B56
DEUTSCH K.W.,AN INTERDISCIPLINARY BIBLIOGRAPHY ON NATIONALISM, 1935-1953. CULTURE SOCIETY SECT ATTIT HABITAT HEREDITY PERCEPT ROLE WEALTH...METH/CNCPT LING 20. PAGE 40 H0798 — BIBLIOG/A NAT/LISM COLONIAL ADJUST

B56
DOUGLAS W.O.,WE THE JUDGES. INDIA USA+45 USA-45 LAW NAT/G SECT LEGIS PRESS CRIME FEDERAL ORD/FREE ...POLICY GOV/COMP 19/20 WARRN/EARL MARSHALL/J SUPREME/CT. PAGE 42 H0841 — ADJUD CT/SYS CONSTN GOV/REL

B56
INTERNATIONAL AFRICAN INST,ETHNOGRAPHIC SURVEY OF AFRICA: WESTERN AFRICA: PAGAN PEOPLES OF CENTRAL AREA OF NORTHERN NIGERIA (VOL. XII). NIGERIA FAM KIN SECT ECO/TAC GOV/REL GP/REL ATTIT...LING CHARTS 20. PAGE 77 H1548 — STRUCT INGP/REL HABITAT CULTURE

B56
KALLEN H.M.,CULTURAL PLURALISM AND THE AMERICAN IDEA. RACE/REL ADJUST PERSON ORD/FREE LAISSEZ ...PLURIST GEN/LAWS ANTHOL. PAGE 83 H1652 — PLURISM CULTURE GP/REL SECT

B56
LEVIN M.G.,THE PEOPLES OF SIBERIA. PREHIST ECO/UNDEV KIN SECT HABITAT...CLASSIF AUD/VIS WORSHIP 20 SIBERIA. PAGE 95 H1900 — CULTURE SOCIETY ASIA

B56
MANNONI D.O.,PROSPERO AND CALIBAN: THE PSYCHOLOGY OF COLONIZATION. AFR EUR+WWI FAM KIN MUNIC SECT DOMIN ADMIN ATTIT DRIVE LOVE PWR RESPECT...PSY SOC CONCPT MYTH OBS DEEP/INT BIOG GEN/METH MALAGASY 20. PAGE 102 H2040 — CULTURE COLONIAL

B56
MYERS F.M.,THE WARFARE OF DEMOCRATIC IDEALS. SECT KNOWL MORAL CATHISM...TRADIT CONCPT 20. PAGE 115 H2302 — POPULISM CHOOSE REPRESENT PERCEPT

B56
PHILIPPINE STUDIES PROGRAM,SELECTED BIBLIOGRAPHY ON THE PHILIPPINES, TOPICALLY ARRANGED AND ANNOTATED. PHILIPPINE SECT DIPLOM COLONIAL LEAD...SOC 18/20. PAGE 125 H2501 — BIBLIOG/A S/ASIA NAT/G ECO/UNDEV

B56
RIESENBERG P.N.,INALIENABILITY OF SOVEREIGNTY IN MEDIEVAL POLITICAL THOUGHT. CHRIST-17C INTELL NAT/G SECT CHIEF LEGIS SANCTION AUTHORIT ORD/FREE CONSERVE...IDEA/COMP BIBLIOG 12/16. PAGE 131 H2627 — SOVEREIGN ATTIT

B56
SHAPIRO H.L.,MAN, CULTURE, AND SOCIETY. STRUCT FAM SECT GP/REL INGP/REL...ART/METH GEOG PSY LING ANTHOL BIBLIOG. PAGE 142 H2842 — CULTURE PERSON SOC

B56
SPINKA M.,THE CHURCH IN SOVIET RUSSIA. USSR CONTROL LEAD TASK COERCE 20. PAGE 147 H2949 — GP/REL NAT/G SECT PWR

B56
WOLFF R.L.,THE BALKANS IN OUR TIME. ALBANIA FUT MOD/EUR USSR YUGOSLAVIA CULTURE INT/ORG SECT DIPLOM EDU/PROP COERCE WAR ORD/FREE...CHARTS 4/20 BALKANS COMINFORM. PAGE 170 H3403 — GEOG COM

B57
BYRNES R.F.,BIBLIOGRAPHY OF AMERICAN PUBLICATIONS ON EAST CENTRAL EUROPE, 1945-1957 (VOL. XXII). SECT DIPLOM EDU/PROP RACE/REL...ART/METH GEOG JURID SOC LING 20 JEWS. PAGE 25 H0503 — BIBLIOG/A COM MARXISM NAT/G

B57
KANTOROWICZ E.,THE KING'S TWO BODIES; A STUDY IN MEDIEVAL POLITICAL THEOLOGY. UK LAW CONSTN NAT/G CT/SYS...ART/METH HUM CONCPT MYTH TIME/SEQ BIBLIOG 4/17 ELIZABTH/I POPE CHURCH/STA. PAGE 83 H1657 — JURID SECT CHIEF SOVEREIGN

B57
LAQUER W.Z.,COMMUNISM AND NATIONALISM IN THE MIDDLE EAST. ELITES INTELL STRATA NAT/G POL/PAR SECT VOL/ASSN TOP/EX DOMIN LEGIT REGION COERCE ATTIT PERSON PWR...CONCPT HIST/WRIT TIME/SEQ TREND GEN/LAWS VAL/FREE. PAGE 91 H1817 — ISLAM NAT/LISM

B57
LOOMIS C.P.,RURAL SOCIOLOGY. CULTURE KIN NAT/G SECT VOL/ASSN ACT/RES EDU/PROP HEALTH. PAGE 98 H1963 — SOC AGRI METH T

B57
MOYER K.E.,FROM IRAN TO MORROCCO; FROM TURKEY TO THE SUDAN: A SELECTED AND ANNOTATED BIBLIOGRAPHY OF NORTH AFRICA AND NEAR EAST... ISLAM DIPLOM EDU/PROP 20. PAGE 114 H2274 — BIBLIOG/A ECO/UNDEV SECT NAT/G

B57
NARAIN D.,HINDU CHARACTER (A FEW GLIMPSES). INDIA DIPLOM SUICIDE PERS/REL ATTIT...PSY NAT/COMP PERS/COMP BIBLIOG WORSHIP 20 HINDU. PAGE 116 H2310 — PERSON STERTYP SUPEGO SECT

B57
PARK A.G.,BOLSHEVISM IN TURKESTAN 1917-1927. COM RUSSIA USSR CULTURE AGRI SECT DOMIN GP/REL INGP/REL NAT/LISM...BIBLIOG 20 TURKESTAN. PAGE 123 H2467 — REV POLICY MARXISM ISLAM

B57
REAMAN G.E.,THE TRAIL OF THE BLACK WALNUT. CANADA AGRI COLONIAL...CHARTS BIBLIOG 18 GERMANS/PA. PAGE 130 H2604 — STRANGE SECT CULTURE

B57
SHEIKH N.A.,SOME ASPECTS OF THE CONSTITUTION AND THE ECONOMICS OF ISLAM. PAKISTAN CULTURE AGRI FINAN LABOR NAT/G SECT INT/TRADE 20 MUSLIM. PAGE 143 H2855
ISLAM POLICY ECO/TAC CONSTN

B57
SOUTH PACIFIC COMMISSION,INDEX OF SOCIAL SCIENCE RESEARCH THESES ON THE SOUTH PACIFIC. S/ASIA ACADEM ADMIN COLONIAL...SOC 20. PAGE 147 H2939
BIBLIOG/A ACT/RES SECT CULTURE

B57
TAYLOR J.V.,CHRISTIANITY AND POLITICS IN AFRICA. AFR CONTROL PARTIC GP/REL RACE/REL ATTIT...POLICY BIBLIOG/A WORSHIP 20. PAGE 153 H3055
SECT NAT/G NAT/LISM

L57
BENDIX R.,"POLITICAL SOCIOLOGY." CULTURE INTELL LABOR POL/PAR SECT LEGIS EDU/PROP ADMIN CHOOSE CIVMIL/REL ATTIT...IDEA/COMP 20. PAGE 14 H0274
BIBLIOG/A ACT/RES SOC

B58
EMMET D.M.,FUNCTION, PURPOSE AND POWERS. SECT ATTIT MORAL PWR...CONCPT MYTH. PAGE 46 H0923
SOC CULTURE ALL/VALS GEN/LAWS

B58
EUSDEN J.D.,PURITANS, LAWYERS, AND POLITICS IN EARLY SEVENTEENTH-CENTURY ENGLAND. UK CT/SYS PARL/PROC RATIONAL PWR SOVEREIGN...IDEA/COMP BIBLIOG 17 PURITAN COMMON/LAW. PAGE 48 H0951
GP/REL SECT NAT/G LAW

B58
FLORES X.,LA TRADICION CATOLICA Y EL FUTURO POLITICO DE ESPANA (PAMPHLET). SPAIN NAT/G ACT/RES LEAD GP/REL CATHISM 20 CHRISTIAN CHURCH/STA. PAGE 52 H1031
SECT POL/PAR ATTIT ORD/FREE

B58
HERRMANN K.,DAS STAATSDENKEN BEI LEIBNIZ. GP/REL ATTIT ORD/FREE...CONCPT IDEA/COMP 17 LEIBNITZ/G CHURCH/STA. PAGE 70 H1406
NAT/G JURID SECT EDU/PROP

B58
KURL S.,ESTONIA: A SELECTED BIBLIOGRAPHY. USSR ESTONIA LAW INTELL SECT...ART/METH GEOG HUM SOC 20. PAGE 89 H1784
BIBLIOG CULTURE NAT/G

B58
LEPOINTE G.,ELEMENTS DE BIBLIOGRAPHIE SUR L'HISTOIRE DES INSTITUTIONS ET DES FAITS SOCIAUX, 987-1875. FRANCE SOCIETY NAT/G PROVS SECT ...PHIL/SCI 19/20. PAGE 94 H1887
BIBLIOG LAW

B58
LERNER D.,THE PASSING OF TRADITIONAL SOCIETY: MODERNIZING THE MIDDLE EAST. IRAN ISLAM LEBANON SYRIA TURKEY UAR CULTURE INTELL STRATA KIN NAT/G NEIGH SECT EDU/PROP ATTIT PERSON...MYTH OBS 20. PAGE 95 H1888
ECO/UNDEV RIGID/FLEX

B58
MATOS J.,LAS ACTUALES COMMUNIDADES DE INDIGENAS: HUAROCHIRI EN 1955. PERU FAM NAT/G SECT EDU/PROP ADJUD GP/REL INGP/REL 20 INDIAN/AM. PAGE 105 H2091
STRUCT NEIGH KIN ECO/UNDEV

B58
MEHNERT K.,DER SOWJETMENSCH. USSR NAT/G SECT EDU/PROP TOTALISM ORD/FREE 20. PAGE 108 H2161
SOCIETY ATTIT PERSON FAM

B58
ORTEGA Y GASSET J.,MAN AND CRISIS. SECT CREATE PERSON CONSERVE...GEN/LAWS RENAISSAN. PAGE 122 H2430
PHIL/SCI CULTURE CONCPT

B58
PAYNO M.,LA REFORMA SOCIAL EN ESPANA Y MEXICO. SPAIN ECO/TAC TAX LOBBY COERCE REV OWN CATHISM 19/20 MEXIC/AMER. PAGE 124 H2479
SECT NAT/G LAW ELITES

B58
STUBEL H.,THE MEWU FANTZU. CHINA/COM INDIA EDU/PROP ADJUD CRIME GP/REL OWN...OBS 20 TIBET. PAGE 150 H3001
CULTURE STRUCT SECT FAM

B58
VARG P.A.,MISSIONARIES, CHINESE, AND DIPLOMATS: THE AMERICAN PROTESTANT MISSIONARY MOVEMENT IN CHINA, 1890-1952. ASIA ECO/UNDEV NAT/G PROB/SOLV CAP/ISM EDU/PROP COLONIAL NAT/LISM ATTIT MARXISM...NAT/COMP STERTYP 20 CHINJAP PROTESTANT MISSION. PAGE 162 H3234
CULTURE DIPLOM SECT

B58
VON FURER-HAIMEN E.,AN ANTHROPOLOGICAL BIBLIOGRAPHY OF SOUTH ASIA (VOL. I). STRATA STRUCT KIN SECT ACT/RES CREATE HABITAT...GEOG OBS 19/20. PAGE 163 H3267
BIBLIOG/A CULTURE S/ASIA SOC

B58
YUAN TUNG-LI,CHINA IN WESTERN LITERATURE. SECT DIPLOM...ART/METH GEOG JURID SOC BIOG CON/ANAL. PAGE 172 H3441
BIBLIOG ASIA CULTURE HUM

C58
MORRALL J.B.,"POLITICAL THOUGHT IN MEDIEVAL TIMES." LAW NAT/G SECT DOMIN ATTIT PWR...BIOG HIST/WRIT BIBLIOG. PAGE 113 H2260
CHRIST-17C CONCPT

B59
BROSE O.J.,CHURCH AND PARLIAMENT: THE RESHAPING OF THE CHURCH OF ENGLAND 1828-1860. UK SOCIETY TEC/DEV ATTIT LAISSEZ...BIBLIOG 19 CHURCH/STA. PAGE 22 H0434
SECT LEGIS GP/REL NAT/G

B59
CARPENTER G.W.,THE WAY IN AFRICA. AFR INDUS MUNIC DIPLOM DOMIN EDU/PROP COERCE DISCRIM NAT/LISM ORD/FREE 20 NEGRO CHRISTIAN. PAGE 27 H0535
CULTURE SECT ECO/UNDEV COLONIAL

B59
GOPAL R.,INDIAN MUSLIMS: A POLITICAL HISTORY (1858-1947). INDIA ISLAM PAKISTAN NAT/G SECT LEGIS LEAD COERCE WAR REPRESENT ISOLAT ORD/FREE 19/20 HINDU MUSLIM. PAGE 59 H1175
COLONIAL GP/REL POL/PAR REGION

B59
HEMMERLE J.,SUDETENDEUTSCHE BIBLIOGRAPHIE 1949-1953. CZECHOSLVK GERMANY SOCIETY STRUCT SECT ...GEOG JURID 20. PAGE 69 H1391
BIBLIOG PROVS GP/REL CULTURE

B59
KITTLER G.D.,EQUATORIAL AFRICA: THE NEW WORLD OF TOMORROW. CENTRL/AFR INDUS KIN SECT CHIEF EDU/PROP CHOOSE HEALTH...GEOG WORSHIP 20. PAGE 87 H1730
RACE/REL AFR ECO/UNDEV CULTURE

B59
LEITES N.,ON THE GAME OF POLITICS IN FRANCE. ALGERIA FRANCE CONSTN SECT VOL/ASSN ECO/TAC INT/TRADE PARL/PROC WAR SOCISM 20 DEGAULLE/C EEC. PAGE 94 H1871
POL/PAR NAT/G LEGIS IDEA/COMP

B59
MAIER H.,REVOLUTION UND KIRCHE. FRANCE MOD/EUR SECT REV ORD/FREE...IDEA/COMP 18/19. PAGE 101 H2018
NAT/G CATHISM ATTIT POL/PAR

B59
PANIKKAR K.M.,THE AFRO-ASIAN STATES AND THEIR PROBLEMS. COM CULTURE KIN POL/PAR SECT DIPLOM EDU/PROP COLONIAL SOVEREIGN...TECHNIC GOV/COMP 20. PAGE 123 H2458
AFR S/ASIA ECO/UNDEV

B59
SHARMA R.S.,ASPECTS OF POLITICAL IDEAS AND INSTITUTIONS IN ANCIENT INDIA. INDIA SOCIETY STRUCT FAM VOL/ASSN TAX DOMIN...CONCPT HIST/WRIT 7. PAGE 142 H2848
CULTURE JURID DELIB/GP SECT

B59
SISSONS C.B.,CHURCH AND STATE IN CANADIAN EDUCATION: AN HISTORICAL STUDY. CANADA ACADEM NAT/G SCHOOL LEGIS REGION MAJORITY...MAJORIT WORSHIP 18/20 CHURCH/STA. PAGE 145 H2891
SECT EDU/PROP PROVS GP/REL

B59
SITHOLE N.,AFRICAN NATIONALISM. UNIV CULTURE SECT ADMIN COLONIAL CHOOSE. PAGE 145 H2892
RACE/REL AFR NAT/LISM PERSON

B59
VORSPAN A.,JUSTICE AND JUDAISM. FAM DIPLOM ECO/TAC EDU/PROP CRIME RACE/REL MARRIAGE ANOMIE ATTIT ORD/FREE...POLICY 20 UN. PAGE 164 H3279
SECT CULTURE ACT/RES GP/REL

S59
SCOTT W.A.,"EMPIRICAL ASSESSMENT OF VALUES AND IDEOLOGIES." CULTURE SOCIETY SECT CREATE DRIVE PERSON MORAL PWR...SOC METH/CNCPT STAT CONT/OBS DEEP/INT DEEP/QU CHARTS VAL/FREE. PAGE 141 H2817
ATTIT PSY

C59
KARPAT K.H.,"TURKEY'S POLITICS: THE TRANSITION TO A MULTI-PARTY SYSTEM." COM TURKEY CULTURE ECO/UNDEV SECT TEC/DEV NAT/LISM ATTIT...SOC CON/ANAL BIBLIOG 20. PAGE 83 H1664
POL/PAR NAT/G

B60
BEATTIE J.,BUNYORO, AN AFRICAN KINGDOM. UGANDA STRATA INGP/REL PERS/REL...SOC BIBLIOG 19/20. PAGE 13 H0250
CULTURE ELITES SECT KIN

B60
BOZEMAN A.B.,POLITICS AND CULTURE IN INTERNATIONAL HISTORY. WOR-45 STRUCT SECT...SOC TIME/SEQ NAT/COMP BIBLIOG. PAGE 20 H0393
CULTURE DIPLOM GOV/COMP ALL/IDEOS

B60
BURRIDGE K.,MAMBU: A MELANESIAN MILLENNIUM. ECO/UNDEV PROC/MFG FAM KIN CHIEF COLONIAL COERCE GP/REL DRIVE WEALTH WORSHIP 20 NEW/GUINEA. PAGE 25 H0494
S/ASIA SECT CULTURE MYTH

B60
CHATTERJI S.K.,AFRICANISM: THE AFRICAN PERSONALITY. KIN NAT/G SECT CREATE DIPLOM COLONIAL GP/REL ATTIT ORD/FREE...LING WORSHIP 20. PAGE 29 H0585
PERSON NAT/LISM AFR CULTURE

B60
COUGHLIN R.,DOUBLE IDENTITY: THE CHINESE AND MODERN THAILAND. CHINA/COM S/ASIA THAILAND ECO/UNDEV EXTR/IND FINAN INDUS KIN MUNIC NAT/G PROF/ORG
ASIA FAM CULTURE

SCHOOL SECT ATTIT DRIVE...CONCPT OBS 20. PAGE 34
H0676

B60
EMERSON R.,FROM EMPIRE TO NATION: THE RISE TO SELF-ASSERTION OF ASIAN AND AFRICAN PEOPLES. S/ASIA CULTURE NAT/G SECT DIPLOM ATTIT SOVEREIGN MARXISM ...POLICY BIBLIOG 19/20. PAGE 46 H0919
NAT/LISM COLONIAL AFR ASIA

B60
GENTILE G.,GENESIS AND STRUCTURE OF SOCIETY (TRANS. BY H.S. HARRIS). NAT/G SECT ATTIT SUPEGO...JURID 20. PAGE 56 H1111
SOCIETY STRUCT PERSON

B60
HAMADY S.,TEMPERAMENT AND CHARACTER OF THE ARABS. FAM NAT/G SECT DIPLOM NAT/LISM...POLICY 20 ARABS. PAGE 65 H1299
NAT/COMP PERSON CULTURE ISLAM

B60
HARRISON S.S.,INDIA: THE MOST DANGEROUS DECADES. INDIA CONSTN STRATA POL/PAR SECT PLAN ADMIN CHOOSE GP/REL TOTALISM MARXISM...LING 20 NEHRU/J. PAGE 67 H1347
CULTURE ECO/UNDEV PROB/SOLV REGION

B60
MCCLOSKY H.,THE SOVIET DICTATORSHIP. FUT CONSTN CULTURE INTELL SOCIETY POL/PAR SECT VOL/ASSN FORCES PLAN TEC/DEV DOMIN EDU/PROP COERCE PWR MARXISM ...POLICY CONCPT MYTH STERTYP 20. PAGE 106 H2127
COM NAT/G TOTALISM USSR

B60
MOCTEZUMA A.P.,EL CONFLICTO RELIGIOSO DE 1926 (2ND ED.). L/A+17C LAW NAT/G LOBBY COERCE GP/REL ATTIT ...POLICY 20 MEXIC/AMER CHURCH/STA. PAGE 112 H2233
SECT ORD/FREE DISCRIM REV

B60
NAKAMURA H.,THE WAYS OF THINKING OF EASTERN PEOPLES. ASIA INDIA PERSON...HUM SOC LING LOG WORSHIP CHINJAP. PAGE 115 H2305
CULTURE SECT ATTIT

B60
SZTARAY Z.,BIBLIOGRAPHY ON HUNGARY. HUNGARY MOD/EUR CULTURE INDUS SECT DIPLOM REV...ART/METH SOC LING 18/20. PAGE 151 H3029
BIBLIOG NAT/G COM MARXISM

B60
ZENKOVSKY S.A.,PAN-TURKISM AND ISLAM IN RUSSIA. ASIA RUSSIA USSR CULTURE POL/PAR DOMIN REV GP/REL MARXISM...LING GP/COMP BIBLIOG 19/20 TURKIC. PAGE 173 H3454
SECT NAT/LISM COM ISLAM

B60
RUDD J.,TABOO, A STUDY OF MALAGASY CUSTOMS AND BELIEFS. MADAGASCAR LAW FAM CONTROL CRIME PERSON ...CONCPT 20. PAGE 173 H3466
CULTURE DOMIN SECT SANCTION

L60
WHEELER G.,"RACIAL PROBLEMS IN SOVIET MUSLIM ASIA." COM CULTURE SOCIETY NEIGH SECT DOMIN EDU/PROP DISCRIM DISPL DRIVE PWR SOVEREIGN...CENSUS SAMP TREND 20 MUSLIM. PAGE 167 H3340
PERSON ATTIT USSR RACE/REL

S60
BERREMAN G.D.,"CASTE IN INDIA AND THE UNITED STATES" (BMR)" INDIA USA+45 CULTURE SOCIETY STRUCT SECT GP/REL DISCRIM HEREDITY...SOC STERTYP 20 NEGRO HINDU. PAGE 16 H0318
STRATA RACE/REL NAT/COMP ATTIT

S60
GINSBURGS G.,"PEKING-LHASA-NEW DELHI." CHINA/COM FUT INDIA S/ASIA KIN NAT/G PROVS SECT FORCES BAL/PWR ECO/TAC DOMIN EDU/PROP LEGIT ADMIN REGION GUERRILLA PWR...TREND TIBET 20. PAGE 57 H1134
ASIA COERCE DIPLOM

C60
FITZSIMMONS T.,"USSR: ITS PEOPLE, ITS SOCIETY, ITS CULTURE." USSR FAM SECT DIPLOM EDU/PROP ADMIN RACE/REL ATTIT...POLICY CHARTS BIBLIOG 20. PAGE 51 H1021
CULTURE STRUCT SOCIETY COM

C60
WRIGGINS W.H.,"CEYLON: DILEMMAS OF A NEW NATION." ASIA CEYLON CONSTN STRUCT POL/PAR SECT FORCES DIPLOM GOV/REL NAT/LISM...CHARTS BIBLIOG 20. PAGE 171 H3417
PROB/SOLV NAT/G ECO/UNDEV

B61
APTER D.E.,THE POLITICAL KINGDOM IN UGANDA. UGANDA CULTURE ECO/UNDEV AGRI KIN SECT TOP/EX REGION ATTIT HABITAT CONSERVE...GEOG AUD/VIS 20. PAGE 8 H0153
NAT/LISM POL/PAR COLONIAL ECO/TAC

B61
BEARCE G.D.,BRITISH ATTITUDES TOWARDS INDIA 1784-1858. INDIA S/ASIA UK SECT ECO/TAC...POLICY HUM 18/19. PAGE 12 H0246
COLONIAL ATTIT ALL/IDEOS NAT/G

B61
BINDER L.,RELIGION AND POLITICS IN PAKISTAN. ISLAM PAKISTAN NAT/G SECT LEGIS CREATE CHOOSE GP/REL ...MAJORIT TRADIT 20. PAGE 17 H0336
CONSTN CONFER NAT/LISM POL/PAR

B61
CHAKRABARTI A.,NEHRU: HIS DEMOCRACY AND INDIA. ASIA INDIA UK CONSTN ECO/UNDEV SECT DIPLOM COLONIAL PEACE WEALTH...BIBLIOG 20 CONGRESS NEHRU/J GANDHI/M. PAGE 28 H0570
ORD/FREE STRATA NAT/G CHIEF

B61
FIRTH R.,HISTORY AND TRADITIONS OF TIKOPIA. S/ASIA KIN SECT RUMOR WAR...MYTH WORSHIP 20 POLYNESIA. PAGE 50 H1008
CULTURE STRUCT HUM

B61
HALPERIN S.,THE POLITICAL WORLD OF AMERICAN ZIONISM. ISRAEL FINAN LABOR VOL/ASSN GIVE LOBBY REPRESENT GP/REL ATTIT POLICY. PAGE 64 H1293
CULTURE SECT EDU/PROP DELIB/GP

B61
HISTORICAL RESEARCH INSTITUTE,A SHORT BIBLIOGRAPHY OF INDO-MUSLIM HISTORY. INDIA S/ASIA DIPLOM EDU/PROP COLONIAL LEAD NAT/LISM ATTIT...BIOG 19/20. PAGE 71 H1427
BIBLIOG NAT/G SECT POL/PAR

B61
JONES R.,AFRICA BIBLIOGRAPHY SERIES: SOUTH EAST CENTRAL AFRICA AND MADAGASCAR. AFR MADAGASCAR RHODESIA SECT BIO/SOC...JURID NAT/COMP 20. PAGE 82 H1633
BIBLIOG/A SOC CULTURE LING

B61
KEREKES T.,THE ARAB MIDDLE EAST AND MUSLIM AFRICA. ISLAM SOCIETY ECO/UNDEV SECT VOL/ASSN TOP/EX REGION ATTIT PWR...GEOG CONCPT TIME/SEQ GEN/LAWS 20. PAGE 85 H1694
NAT/G TREND NAT/LISM

B61
KHALIQUZZAMAN C.,PATHWAY TO PAKISTAN. INDIA PAKISTAN UK SECT LEGIS CHOOSE RACE/REL ATTIT ORD/FREE 20 MUSLIM. PAGE 85 H1705
GP/REL NAT/G COLONIAL SOVEREIGN

B61
LYFORD J.P.,THE AGREEABLE AUTOCRACIES. SOCIETY LABOR POL/PAR SECT DIPLOM CHOOSE...CONCPT 20 WHITE/T NIEBUHR/R. PAGE 99 H1982
ATTIT POPULISM PRESS NAT/G

B61
PALMER N.D.,THE INDIAN POLITICAL SYSTEM. INDIA ECO/UNDEV SECT CHIEF COLONIAL CHOOSE ALL/IDEOS SOCISM...CHARTS BIBLIOG/A 20. PAGE 123 H2452
NAT/LISM POL/PAR NAT/G DIPLOM

B61
RAHNER H.,KIRCHE UND STAAT IM FRUHEN CHRISTENTUM. INGP/REL ORD/FREE PWR CATHISM...JURID 1/9 CHURCH/STA CHRISTIAN. PAGE 129 H2582
NAT/G SECT ATTIT GP/REL

B61
SAFRAN M.,EGYPT IN SEARCH OF POLITICAL COMMUNITY: AN ANALYSIS OF THE INTELLECTUAL AND POLITICAL EVOLUTION OF EGYPT, 1804-1952. ISLAM NAT/G SECT EDU/PROP COERCE ATTIT DRIVE KNOWL PWR...TIME/SEQ 20. PAGE 137 H2729
INTELL NAT/LISM UAR

B61
SAKAI R.K.,STUDIES ON ASIA, 1961. ASIA BURMA INDIA S/ASIA FINAN ECO/TAC NAT/LISM SOCISM...POLICY ANTHOL 19/20 CHINJAP. PAGE 137 H2734
ECO/UNDEV SECT

B61
SCHECHTMAN J.B.,ON WINGS OF EAGLES: THE PLIGHT, EXODUS, AND HOMECOMING OF ORIENTAL JEWRY. ASIA ISLAM ISRAEL VOL/ASSN DIPLOM CONTROL ORD/FREE ...GEOG WORSHIP SOC/INTEG 20 JEWS ARABS MIGRATION. PAGE 139 H2777
CULTURE HABITAT KIN SECT

B61
SHIELS W.E.,KING AND CHURCH: THE RISE AND FALL OF THE PATRONATO REAL. SPAIN INGP/REL...CONCPT WORSHIP 16/19 CHURCH/STA MISSION. PAGE 143 H2859
SECT NAT/G CHIEF POLICY

B61
UAR MINISTRY OF CULTURE,A BIBLIOGRAPHICAL LIST OF TUNISIA. ISLAM CULTURE NAT/G EDU/PROP COLONIAL ...GEOG 19/20 TUNIS. PAGE 157 H3146
BIBLIOG DIPLOM SECT

B61
ULLMAN W.,PRINCIPLES OF GOVERNMENT AND POLITICS IN THE MIDDLE AGES. LAW CONSTN DOMIN EDU/PROP LEGIT TOTALISM SOVEREIGN POPULISM...POLICY GOV/COMP IDEA/COMP 12/16 POPE KING CHURCH/STA. PAGE 158 H3152
SECT CHIEF NAT/G LEGIS

B61
ZIMMERMAN I.,A GUIDE TO CURRENT LATIN AMERICAN PERIODICALS: HUMANITIES AND SOCIAL SCIENCES. LABOR SECT EDU/PROP...GEOG HUM SOC LING STAT NAT/COMP 20. PAGE 173 H3456
BIBLIOG/A DIPLOM L/A+17C PHIL/SCI

L61
KAUPER P.G.,"CHURCH AND STATE: COOPERATIVE SEPARATISM." NAT/G LEGIS OP/RES TAX EDU/PROP GP/REL TREND. PAGE 84 H1671
SECT CONSTN LAW POLICY

S61
ELAZAR D.J.,"CHURCHES AS MOLDERS OF AMERICAN POLITICS." STRATA MUNIC EDU/PROP RACE/REL ORD/FREE SOC. PAGE 45 H0904
SECT CULTURE REPRESENT LOC/G

S61
SCHECHTMAN J.B.,"MINORITIES IN THE MIDDLE EAST." ISLAM INTELL SOCIETY STRATA KIN NAT/G VOL/ASSN EDU/PROP REGION GP/REL DISCRIM ATTIT BIO/SOC DISPL PERSON ALL/VALS...PSY SOC OBS SAMP GEN/LAWS 20. PAGE 139 H2776
SECT CULTURE RACE/REL

S61
TOMASIC D.,"POLITICAL LEADERSHIP IN CONTEMPORARY POLAND." COM EUR+WWI GERMANY NAT/G POL/PAR SECT DELIB/GP PLAN ECO/TAC DOMIN EDU/PROP PWR MARXISM ...MARXIST GEOG MGT CONCPT TIME/SEQ STERTYP 20. PAGE 156 H3111
SOCIETY ROUTINE USSR POLAND

B62
BAULIN J.,THE ARAB ROLE IN AFRICA. AFR ALGERIA FUT ISLAM MOROCCO UAR COLONIAL NEUTRAL REV...SOC 20 TUNIS BOURGUIBA. PAGE 12 H0240
NAT/LISM DIPLOM NAT/G SECT

B62
BERGER M.,THE ARAB WORLD TODAY. CULTURE FAM INT/ORG NAT/G SECT FORCES ECO/TAC NAT/LISM HABITAT...CHARTS BIBLIOG 20 ARABS. PAGE 15 H0301
ISLAM PERSON STRUCT SOCIETY

B62
BROWN S.D.,STUDIES ON ASIA, 1962. ASIA BURMA INDIA ISLAM ISRAEL S/ASIA ECO/UNDEV POL/PAR SECT ECO/TAC ...ANTHOL 20 CHINJAP. PAGE 22 H0450
PWR PARL/PROC

B62
CARY J.,THE CASE FOR AFRICAN FREEDOM AND OTHER WRITINGS ON AFRICA. AFR UK INDUS LOC/G NAT/G SECT INT/TRADE EDU/PROP GOV/REL RACE/REL ORD/FREE ...CONCPT ANTHOL 19/20. PAGE 27 H0552
NAT/LISM COLONIAL TREND ECO/UNDEV

B62
DAVAR F.C.,IRAN AND INDIA THROUGH THE AGES. INDIA IRAN ELITES SECT CREATE ORD/FREE...LING BIBLIOG. PAGE 37 H0743
NAT/COMP DIPLOM CULTURE

B62
HAIM S.G.,ARAB NATIONALISM. ISLAM CONSTN GP/REL ...ANTHOL BIBLIOG JEWS 20 MID/EAST ARABS. PAGE 64 H1279
NAT/LISM REV SECT DIPLOM

B62
HUNKIN P.,ENSEIGNEMENT ET POLITIQUE EN FRANCE ET EN ANGLETERRE. FRANCE UK CONSTN ACADEM SECT CHIEF DELIB/GP PROB/SOLV CONTROL REV ORD/FREE CONSERVE ...BIBLIOG 18/20. PAGE 75 H1496
EDU/PROP LEGIS IDEA/COMP NAT/G

B62
JENNINGS I.,PARTY POLITICS: THE STUFF OF POLITICS (VOL.III). UK NAT/G SECT CHIEF INT/TRADE RECEIVE COLONIAL GP/REL NAT/LISM ORD/FREE SOCISM 19/20 CHURCH/STA WHIG/PARTY. PAGE 80 H1607
POL/PAR CONSTN PWR ALL/IDEOS

B62
KEESING F.M.,THE ETHNOHISTORY OF NORTHERN LUZON. PHILIPPINE ECO/UNDEV FAM SECT CHIEF REGION GP/REL HABITAT...GEOG LING BIBLIOG WORSHIP 20. PAGE 84 H1680
CULTURE SOC KIN

B62
KIDDER F.E.,THESES ON PAN AMERICAN TOPICS. LAW CULTURE NAT/G SECT DIPLOM HEALTH...ART/METH GEOG SOC 13/20. PAGE 86 H1709
BIBLIOG CHRIST-17C L/A+17C SOCIETY

B62
KOSAMBI D.D.,MYTH AND REALITY. INDIA AGRI KIN SECT HABITAT...SOC 20. PAGE 88 H1758
CULTURE SOCIETY MYTH ATTIT

B62
MALINOWSKI B.,SEX, CULTURE, AND MYTH. UNIV SOCIETY FAM PERS/REL MARRIAGE RATIONAL HABITAT PERSON SUPEGO MORAL WORSHIP 20. PAGE 102 H2032
MYTH SECT SEX CULTURE

B62
RUDY Z.,ETHNOSOZIOLOGIE SOWJETISCHER VOLKER. USSR SOCIETY STRUCT FAM SECT GP/REL ATTIT...SOC SOC/INTEG 20. PAGE 136 H2714
MYTH CULTURE KIN

B62
SCHMIDT-VOLKMAR E.,DER KULTURKAMPF IN DEUTSCHLAND 1871-1890. GERMANY PRUSSIA SOCIETY STRUCT SECT DIPLOM GP/REL NAT/LISM 19 CHURCH/STA BISMARCK/O. PAGE 139 H2789
POL/PAR CATHISM ATTIT NAT/G

B62
SILBERMAN B.S.,JAPAN AND KOREA; A CRITICAL BIBLIOGRAPHY. KOREA LAW STRATA STRUCT AGRI INDUS NAT/G POL/PAR SECT...HUM LING IDEA/COMP 5/20 CHINJAP. PAGE 144 H2872
BIBLIOG/A CULTURE S/ASIA

B62
SMITH M.G.,KINSHIP AND COMMUNITY IN CARRIACOU. WEST/IND STRATA AGRI FAM SECT WORKER MARRIAGE OWN HEREDITY WEALTH...SOC 18/20. PAGE 146 H2915
CULTURE HABITAT KIN STRUCT

B62
STARR R.E.,POLAND 1944-1962: THE SOVIETIZATION OF A CAPTIVE PEOPLE. COM POLAND USSR POL/PAR SECT LEGIS DIPLOM DOMIN EDU/PROP CHOOSE ORD/FREE...POLICY CHARTS BIBLIOG 20. PAGE 149 H2973
MARXISM NAT/G TOTALISM NAT/COMP

B62
THIERRY S.S.,LE VATICAN SECRET. CHRIST-17C EUR+WWI MOD/EUR VATICAN NAT/G SECT DELIB/GP DOMIN LEGIT SOVEREIGN. PAGE 154 H3072
ADMIN EX/STRUC CATHISM DECISION

B62
TURNBULL C.M.,THE LONELY AFRICAN. AFR MUNIC SECT ANOMIE ALL/VALS...DECISION 20. PAGE 157 H3139
CULTURE ISOLAT KIN TRADIT

B62
TYSKEVIC S.,DIE EINHEIT DER KIRCHE UND BYZANZ (TRANS. BY F.K. LIESNER). ROMAN/EMP ADJUD GP/REL 1/17 CHRISTIAN BYZANTINE. PAGE 157 H3144
SECT NAT/G CATHISM ATTIT

B62
UMENDRAS H.,LES SOCIETESRFRANCAISES; BIBLIOGRAPHIES FRANCAISES DE SCIENCE SOCIALES (VOL. III). FRANCE SECT WORKER 20. PAGE 158 H3154
BIBLIOG/A AGRI MUNIC CULTURE

B62
US LIBRARY OF CONGRESS,A LIST OF AMERICAN DOCTORAL DISSERTATIONS ON AFRICA. SOCIETY SECT DIPLOM EDU/PROP ADMIN...GEOG 19/20. PAGE 161 H3212
BIBLIOG AFR ACADEM CULTURE

B62
VILAKAZI A.,ZULU TRANSFORMATIONS: A STUDY OF THE DYNAMICS OF SOCIAL CHANGE. AFR CULTURE ECO/UNDEV KIN NEIGH SEX...GEOG QU TREND CHARTS BIBLIOG 19/20. PAGE 163 H3254
MARRIAGE SECT SOC EDU/PROP

B62
YOUNG G.,THE HILL TRIBES OF NORTHERN THAILAND. S/ASIA THAILAND FAM KIN LOC/G GP/REL HABITAT...GEOG LING OBS 20. PAGE 172 H3438
CULTURE STRUCT ECO/UNDEV SECT

B62
ZINKIN T.,REPORTING INDIA. INDIA PAKISTAN WOR+45 SOCIETY SECT FORCES EDU/PROP CROWD DISCRIM NAT/LISM MARXISM...POLICY 20. PAGE 173 H3457
STRATA COLONIAL BAL/PWR CONTROL

S62
HYDE D.,"COMMUNISM IN LATIN AMERICA." L/A+17C ECO/DEV NAT/G SECT EDU/PROP ATTIT ALL/VALS MARXISM ...SOC CONCPT TOT/POP COLD/WAR OAS 20. PAGE 76 H1515
COM POL/PAR REV

S62
SARKISYANZ E.,"NATIONALISM, CAPITALISM, AND THE UNCOMMITED NATIONS: MARXISM AND ASIAN CULTURAL TRADITIONS." ASIA BURMA CHINA/COM COM CULTURE SOCIETY NAT/G POL/PAR PLAN DOMIN EDU/PROP COLONIAL COERCE ATTIT RIGID/FLEX...CONCPT TREND MARX/KARL 20 TIBET BUDDHISM. PAGE 138 H2755
S/ASIA SECT NAT/LISM CAP/ISM

B63
AZEVEDO T.,SOCIAL CHANGE IN BRAZIL. BRAZIL ECO/DEV COM/IND FAM NAT/G SECT GP/REL PERS/REL...CONCPT WORSHIP 20. PAGE 9 H0188
TEC/DEV STRUCT SOC CULTURE

B63
BERREMAN G.D.,HINDUS OF THE HIMALAYAS. INDIA STRATA STRUCT KIN MUNIC 20 HINDU. PAGE 16 H0319
CULTURE SECT GP/REL ECO/UNDEV

B63
BIDNEY D.,THE CONCEPT OF FREEDOM IN ANTHROPOLOGY. UNIV CULTURE STRATA SECT CREATE NAT/LISM ...METH/COMP 20. PAGE 17 H0332
SOC PERSON ORD/FREE CONCPT

B63
CONOVER H.F.,AFRICA SOUTH OF THE SAHARA. CULTURE SECT TEC/DEV...ART/METH GEOG SOC. PAGE 33 H0654
BIBLIOG/A AFR CON/ANAL

B63
CRUICKSHANK M.,CHURCH AND STATE IN ENGLISH EDUCATION 1870 TO PRESENT. UK LEGIS TAX GIVE DOMIN LEGIT ORD/FREE 19/20 CHURCH/STA. PAGE 36 H0715
NAT/G SECT EDU/PROP GP/REL

B63
FISCHER-GALATI S.A.,RUMANIA; A BIBLIOGRAPHIC GUIDE (PAMPHLET). ROMANIA INTELL ECO/DEV LABOR SECT WEALTH...GEOG SOC/WK LING 20. PAGE 51 H1012
BIBLIOG/A NAT/G COM LAW

B63
FRITZ H.E.,THE MOVEMENT FOR INDIAN ASSIMILATION, 1860-1890. SECT FORCES GP/REL RACE/REL DISCRIM FEDERAL CATHISM...BIBLIOG 19 INDIAN/AM PROTESTANT GRANT/US. PAGE 54 H1071
CULTURE NAT/G ECO/TAC ATTIT

B63
GEERTZ C.,OLD SOCIETIES AND NEW STATES: THE QUEST FOR MODERNITY IN ASIA AND AFRICA. AFR ASIA LAW CULTURE SECT EDU/PROP REV...GOV/COMP NAT/COMP 20. PAGE 55 H1107
ECO/UNDEV TEC/DEV NAT/LISM SOVEREIGN

B63
HARDY M.J.L.,BLOOD FEUDS AND THE PAYMENT OF BLOOD MONEY IN THE MIDDLE EAST. ISLAM SOCIETY SECT REGION SANCTION COERCE DEATH MURDER 7/20 ARABS. PAGE 66 H1329
KIN TRIBUTE LAW CULTURE

B63
HUGHES A.J.,EAST AFRICA: THE SEARCH FOR UNITY- KENYA, TANGANYIKA, UGANDA, AND ZANZIBAR. TANZANIA UGANDA CONSTN POL/PAR SECT CHIEF DELIB/GP LEGIS WAR CHOOSE NAT/LISM MARXISM...POLICY CHARTS 20 NEGRO UN. PAGE 74 H1488
NAT/G DOMIN LOC/G AFR

B63
JAIRAZBHOY R.A.,FOREIGN INFLUENCE IN ANCIENT INDIA.
CULTURE

INDIA ELITES SECT DIPLOM EDU/PROP COLONIAL REGION GP/REL...ART/METH LING WORSHIP +/14 GRECO/ROMN MESOPOTAM PERSIA PARTH/SASS. PAGE 79 H1587 SOCIETY COERCE DOMIN

B63
JELAVICH C.,THE BALKANS IN TRANSITION: ESSAYS ON THE DEVELOPMENT OF BALKAN LIFE AND POLITICS SINCE THE EIGHTEENTH CENTURY. COM GREECE TURKEY ECO/UNDEV NAT/G SECT ATTIT...GEOG SOC CONCPT TIME/SEQ ANTHOL 18/20. PAGE 80 H1596 CULTURE RIGID/FLEX

B63
KAPP W.K.,HINDU CULTURE: ECONOMIC DEVELOPMENT AND ECONOMIC PLANNING IN INDIA. INDIA S/ASIA CULTURE ECO/TAC EDU/PROP ADMIN ALL/VALS...POLICY MGT TIME/SEQ VAL/FREE 20. PAGE 83 H1660 SECT ECO/UNDEV

B63
LAMB B.P.,INDIA: A WORLD IN TRANSITION. INDIA ECO/UNDEV SECT EDU/PROP COLONIAL HABITAT ORD/FREE ...GEOG CHARTS BIBLIOG SOC/INTEG 20. PAGE 90 H1799 POL/PAR NAT/G DIPLOM STRATA

B63
MAC MILLAN W.M.,BANTU, BOER, AND BRITON: THE MAKING OF THE SOUTH AFRICAN NATIVE PROBLEM. SOUTH/AFR UK LAW KIN NAT/G SECT LEGIS COLONIAL ISOLAT ATTIT ...BIOG 18/20 BANTU NEGRO PHILIP/J MISSION. PAGE 100 H1989 AFR RACE/REL ELITES

B63
MAIR L.,NEW NATIONS. AFR FAM MUNIC SECT DOMIN CHOOSE NAT/LISM ORD/FREE...SOC 19/20. PAGE 101 H2022 COLONIAL CULTURE TEC/DEV ECO/UNDEV

B63
MULLER H.J.,FREEDOM IN THE WESTERN WORLD. PREHIST CULTURE SECT CREATE TEC/DEV DOMIN PWR WEALTH ...MAJORIT SOC CONCPT. PAGE 114 H2285 ORD/FREE TIME/SEQ SOCIETY

B63
OTERO L.M.,HONDURAS. HONDURAS SPAIN STRUCT SECT COLONIAL REV WAR ATTIT PWR...GEOG WORSHIP 16/20. PAGE 122 H2432 NAT/G SOCIETY NAT/LISM ECO/UNDEV

B63
PAUW B.A.,THE SECOND GENERATION. SOUTH/AFR INDUS FAM LABOR SECT EDU/PROP MARRIAGE ATTIT...SOC 20. PAGE 124 H2478 KIN CULTURE STRUCT SOCIETY

B63
PRICE A.G.,THE WESTERN INVASIONS OF THE PACIFIC AND ITS CONTINENTS. ASIA PRE/AMER S/ASIA ECO/UNDEV KIN NAT/G SECT FORCES DOMIN HEALTH...SOC 16/20. PAGE 128 H2560 COLONIAL CULTURE GEOG HABITAT

B63
REYNOLDS B.,MAGIC, DIVINATION AND WITCHCRAFT AMONG THE BAROTSE OF NORTHERN RHODESIA. RHODESIA CULTURE KIN CREATE LEGIT PARTIC DEATH DREAM STRANGE HABITAT PERSON...AUD/VIS WORSHIP 20. PAGE 131 H2619 AFR SOC MYTH SECT

B63
RUITENBEER H.M.,THE DILEMMA OF ORGANIZATIONAL SOCIETY. CULTURE ECO/DEV MUNIC SECT TEC/DEV EDU/PROP NAT/LISM ORD/FREE...NAT/COMP 20 RIESMAN/D WHYTE/WF MERTON/R MEAD/MARG JASPERS/K. PAGE 136 H2716 PERSON ROLE ADMIN WORKER

B63
SAKAI R.K.,STUDIES ON ASIA, 1963. ASIA INDIA ISRAEL S/ASIA USA+45 PERF/ART POL/PAR SECT REGION NAT/LISM ...SOC LING TREND ANTHOL 19/20 CHINJAP. PAGE 137 H2735 PWR CULTURE

B63
SCHELER M.,SCHRIFTEN ZUR SOZIOLOGIE UND WELTANSCHAUUNGSLEHRE (GESAMMELTE WERKE, BAND 6; 2ND ED.). SECT ALL/IDEOS...SOC CONCPT GP/COMP NAT/COMP 20. PAGE 139 H2783 SOCIETY IDEA/COMP PHIL/SCI

B63
SILVERT K.H.,EXPECTANT PEOPLES: NATIONALISM AND DEVELOPMENT. CULTURE STRATA SECT LEAD REGION RACE/REL ALL/IDEOS...GEN/LAWS SOC/INTEG 20. PAGE 144 H2877 NAT/LISM ECO/UNDEV ALL/VALS

B63
UAR MINISTRY OF CULTURE,A BIBLIOGRAPHICAL LIST OF ARABIAN PENINSULA. ISLAM SAUDI/ARAB YEMEN FINAN NAT/G DIPLOM 19/20. PAGE 157 H3147 BIBLIOG GEOG INDUS SECT

B63
VON DER MEHDEN F.R.,RELIGION AND NATIONALISM IN SOUTHEAST ASIA. BURMA PHILIPPINE S/ASIA INTELL SOCIETY DOMIN EDU/PROP LEGIT ATTIT MORAL ORD/FREE ...SOC CENSUS HIST/WRIT TOT/POP VAL/FREE 20 WORSHIP LONDON. PAGE 163 H3265 SECT CULTURE NAT/LISM

B63
WAGLEY C.,INTRODUCTION TO BRAZIL. BRAZIL L/A+17C FAM KIN SCHOOL SECT ATTIT WEALTH...GEOG SOC. PAGE 164 H3286 ECO/UNDEV ELITES HABITAT STRATA

B63
WILCOX W.A.,PAKISTAN; THE CONSOLIDATION OF A NATION. INDIA PAKISTAN CONSTN SECT PROB/SOLV COLONIAL PARTIC GP/REL FEDERAL...POLICY 19/20. PAGE 168 H3361 NAT/LISM ECO/UNDEV DIPLOM STRUCT

L63
JAY R.,"RELIGION AND POLITICS IN RURAL CENTRAL JAVA." S/ASIA SOCIETY NEIGH SECT PERSON HEALTH MORAL...SOC UNPLAN/INT TIME/SEQ JAVA VAL/FREE 20 WORSHIP. PAGE 80 H1594 CULTURE OBS

S63
HUREWITZ J.C.,"LEBANESE DEMOCRACY IN ITS INTERNATIONAL SETTING." FRANCE ISLAM UK LOC/G NAT/G SECT DOMIN EDU/PROP EXEC ATTIT PWR...TIME/SEQ 20. PAGE 75 H1507 STRUCT LEBANON

S63
LOPEZIBOR J.,"L'EUROPE, FORME DE VIE." CHRIST-17C EUR+WWI FUT MOD/EUR SOCIETY INT/ORG SECT EDU/PROP ATTIT RIGID/FLEX ALL/VALS...POLICY HUM SOC TIME/SEQ TREND GEN/LAWS. PAGE 98 H1966 NAT/G CULTURE

S63
OGOT B.,"FROM CHIEF TO PRESIDENT." AFR SECT REGION NAT/LISM...SOC GOV/COMP NAT/COMP 20 PRESIDENT. PAGE 121 H2410 CHIEF CULTURE LEAD ORD/FREE

S63
RINTELEN F.,"L'HOMME EUROPEEN." EUR+WWI FUT CULTURE INTELL SECT EDU/PROP ATTIT ALL/VALS...HUM SOC METH/CNCPT TREND GEN/LAWS 20 WORSHIP. PAGE 132 H2631 SOCIETY PERSON

S63
TILMAN R.O.,"MALAYSIA: THE PROBLEMS OF FEDERATION." ISLAM S/ASIA CONSTN PROVS SECT DELIB/GP DOMIN EDU/PROP LEGIT EXEC COERCE CHOOSE ATTIT HEALTH ORD/FREE PWR...STAT TOT/POP VAL/FREE 20. PAGE 155 H3097 NAT/G CULTURE MALAYSIA

B64
AGGARWALA R.C.,CONSTITUTIONAL HISTORY OF INDIA AND NATIONAL MOVEMENT INCLUDING COMPARATIVE STUDY OF MODERN INDIA CONSTITUTION. INDIA S/ASIA SECT VOL/ASSN EX/STRUC LEGIS COERCE REV INGP/REL ORD/FREE...SOC BIBLIOG 18/20 CMN/WLTH. PAGE 4 H0077 CONSTN COLONIAL DOMIN NAT/G

B64
ANDREWS D.H.,LATIN AMERICA: A BIBLIOGRAPHY OF PAPERBACK BOOKS. SECT INT/TRADE EDU/PROP WAR GOV/REL ADJUST NAT/LISM ATTIT...ART/METH LING BIOG 20. PAGE 7 H0138 BIBLIOG L/A+17C CULTURE NAT/G

B64
ARASARATNAM S.,CEYLON. CEYLON NETHERLAND PORTUGAL S/ASIA UK STRUCT ECO/UNDEV SECT DIPLOM DOMIN RACE/REL NAT/LISM 17/20 CMN/WLTH. PAGE 8 H0156 COLONIAL NAT/G PROB/SOLV CULTURE

B64
BEATTIE J.,OTHER CULTURES. UNIV LAW FAM POL/PAR SECT ADJUD OWN ALL/VALS WEALTH...SOC NAT/COMP SOC/INTEG 20. PAGE 13 H0251 METH/CNCPT CULTURE STRUCT

B64
BINDER L.,THE IDEOLOGICAL REVOLUTION IN THE MIDDLE EAST. ISLAM STRUCT INT/ORG KIN SECT EX/STRUC TOP/EX PLAN ATTIT DRIVE RIGID/FLEX PWR...MYTH TOT/POP 20. PAGE 17 H0338 POL/PAR NAT/G NAT/LISM

B64
COWAN L.G.,THE DILEMMAS OF AFRICAN INDEPENDENCE. AFR INDUS NAT/G SECT DIPLOM ECO/TAC REGION MARXISM ...CHARTS BIBLIOG 20 MAPS. PAGE 34 H0683 ORD/FREE COLONIAL REV ECO/UNDEV

B64
EMBREE A.T.,A GUIDE TO PAPERBACKS ON ASIA; SELECTED AND ANNOTATED (PAMPHLET). CULTURE SOCIETY ECO/UNDEV SECT DIPLOM COLONIAL MARXISM...SOC 20. PAGE 46 H0913 BIBLIOG/A ASIA S/ASIA NAT/G

B64
FORBES A.H.,CURRENT RESEARCH IN BRITISH STUDIES. UK CONSTN CULTURE POL/PAR SECT DIPLOM ADMIN...JURID BIOG WORSHIP 20. PAGE 52 H1034 BIBLIOG PERSON NAT/G PARL/PROC

B64
FREISEN J.,STAAT UND KATHOLISCHE KIRCHE IN DEN DEUTSCHEN BUNDESSTAATEN (2 VOLS.). GERMANY LAW FAM NAT/G EDU/PROP GP/REL MARRIAGE WEALTH 19/20 CHURCH/STA. PAGE 53 H1056 SECT CATHISM JURID PROVS

B64
GESELLSCHAFT RECHTSVERGLEICH,BIBLIOGRAPHIE DES DEUTSCHEN RECHTS (BIBLIOGRAPHY OF GERMAN LAW, TRANS. BY COURTLAND PETERSON). GERMANY FINAN INDUS LABOR SECT FORCES CT/SYS PARL/PROC CRIME...INT/LAW SOC NAT/COMP 20. PAGE 56 H1117 BIBLIOG/A JURID CONSTN ADMIN

B64
GRIFFITH W.,THE WELSH (2ND ED.). UK SOCIETY STRUCT SECT WRITING NAT/LISM...ART/METH MODAL OBS/ENVIR TREND SOC/INTEG WALES PURITAN MUSIC. PAGE 61 H1223 CULTURE SOC LING

B64
HALPERIN S.W.,MUSSOLINI AND ITALIAN FASCISM. ITALY NAT/G POL/PAR SECT ECO/TAC LEAD PWR SOCISM...POLICY 20 MUSSOLIN/B. PAGE 64 H1294 FASCISM NAT/LISM EDU/PROP CHIEF

B64
HAMILTON W.B.,THE TRANSFER OF INSTITUTIONS. CANADA INDIA UK LAW AGRI LABOR SECT COLONIAL 18/20. PAGE 65 H1301 NAT/COMP ECO/UNDEV EDU/PROP CULTURE

B64
HARRIS M.,PATTERNS OF RACE IN THE AMERICAS. BRAZIL L/A+17C STRATA ECO/UNDEV AGRI KIN MUNIC SECT COLONIAL RACE/REL...SOC SOC/INTEG 17/20 NEGRO INDIAN/AM. PAGE 67 H1342 — STRUCT PRE/AMER CULTURE SOCIETY

B64
HEIMSATH C.H.,INDIAN NATIONALISM AND HINDU SOCIAL REFORM. S/ASIA LAW CULTURE SOCIETY STRATA PROVS VOL/ASSN DELIB/GP LEGIS TOP/EX DOMIN EDU/PROP LEGIT ATTIT ALL/VALS...POLICY SOC TIME/SEQ STERTYP VAL/FREE 19/20. PAGE 69 H1385 — SECT NAT/G

B64
HELMREICH E.,A FREE CHURCH IN A FREE STATE? FRANCE GERMANY ITALY SECT LEAD PWR CATHISM...POLICY ANTHOL WORSHIP 19/20 CHURCH/STA. PAGE 69 H1389 — GP/REL NAT/G

B64
HUXLEY M.,FAREWILL TO EDEN. SOCIETY ACT/RES EDU/PROP HEALTH...SOC AUD/VIS. PAGE 76 H1513 — ECO/UNDEV SECT CULTURE ADJUST

B64
IMAZ J.L.,LOS QUE MANDAN. INDUS LABOR NAT/G POL/PAR PROVS SECT CHIEF TOP/EX CONTROL 20 ARGEN. PAGE 76 H1524 — LEAD FORCES ELITES ATTIT

B64
JARVIE I.C.,THE REVOLUTION IN ANTHROPOLOGY. UNIV CULTURE SOCIETY SECT...MYTH 20 POPPER/K. PAGE 80 H1592 — SOC TREND PHIL/SCI METH

B64
KAUFMANN R.,MILLENARISME ET ACCULTURATION. SOCIETY DOMIN COLONIAL NAT/LISM ATTIT...SOC BIBLIOG 20 JEHOVA/WIT SEVENTHDAY. PAGE 84 H1669 — AFR SECT MYTH CULTURE

B64
KRUEGER H.,ALLGEMEINE STAATSLEHRE. WOR+45 CONSTN SECT CHOOSE INGP/REL PWR NEW/LIB...JURID CLASSIF IDEA/COMP. PAGE 89 H1777 — NAT/G GOV/COMP SOCIETY

B64
LAWRENCE P.,ROAD BELONG CARGO: A STUDY OF CARGO MOVEMENT IN SOUTHERN MADANG DISTRICT, NEW GUINEA. S/ASIA CULTURE ECO/UNDEV PROC/MFG KIN CHIEF COLONIAL COERCE GP/REL DRIVE WEALTH WORSHIP 20 NEW/GUINEA. PAGE 92 H1846 — SOC SECT ALL/VALS MYTH

B64
MAHAR J.M.,INDIA: A CRITICAL BIBLIOGRAPHY. INDIA PAKISTAN CULTURE ECO/UNDEV LOC/G POL/PAR SECT PROB/SOLV DIPLOM ADMIN COLONIAL PARL/PROC ATTIT 20. PAGE 101 H2016 — BIBLIOG/A S/ASIA NAT/G LEAD

B64
MCCALL D.F.,AFRICA IN TIME PERSPECTIVE. AFR EXTR/IND KIN SECT CREATE PERS/REL HABITAT...GEOG METH/CNCPT LING BIBLIOG/A TIME 20. PAGE 106 H2124 — HIST/WRIT OBS/ENVIR CULTURE

B64
MINAR D.W.,IDEAS AND POLITICS: THE AMERICAN EXPERIENCE. SECT CHIEF LEGIS CREATE ADJUD EXEC REV PWR...PHIL/SCI CONCPT IDEA/COMP 18/20 HAMILTON/A JEFFERSN/T DECLAR/IND JACKSON/A PRESIDENT. PAGE 111 H2220 — CONSTN NAT/G FEDERAL

B64
MUSEUM FUR VOLKERKUNDE WIEN,ZENTRALAMERIKA MEXIKO VOLKER UND KULTUREN. COSTA/RICA GUATEMALA L/A+17C PANAMA SECT WAR GP/REL SOVEREIGN...ART/METH 20 CENTRAL/AM MEXIC/AMER. PAGE 115 H2300 — SOCIETY STRUCT CULTURE AGRI

B64
NATIONAL BOOK LEAGUE,THE COMMONWEALTH IN BOOKS: AN ANNOTATED LIST. CANADA UK LOC/G SECT ADMIN...SOC BIOG 20 CMN/WLTH. PAGE 116 H2320 — BIBLIOG/A JURID NAT/G

B64
PIKE F.B.,THE CONFLICT BETWEEN CHURCH AND STATE IN LATIN AMERICA. L/A+17C CULTURE SOCIETY STRATA DOMIN EDU/PROP LEGIT COERCE ATTIT ORD/FREE PWR WEALTH ...CONCPT TIME/SEQ TREND VAL/FREE. PAGE 125 H2510 — SECT NAT/G

B64
RAGHAVAN M.D.,INDIA IN CEYLONESE HISTORY, SOCIETY AND CULTURE. CEYLON INDIA S/ASIA LAW SOCIETY INT/TRADE ATTIT...ART/METH JURID SOC LING 20. PAGE 129 H2581 — DIPLOM CULTURE SECT STRUCT

B64
ROBERTS HL,FOREIGN AFFAIRS BIBLIOGRAPHY, 1952-1962. ECO/DEV SECT PLAN FOR/AID INT/TRADE ARMS/CONT NAT/LISM ATTIT...INT/LAW GOV/COMP IDEA/COMP 20. PAGE 132 H2643 — BIBLIOG/A DIPLOM INT/ORG WAR

B64
SAKAI R.K.,STUDIES ON ASIA, 1964. ASIA CHINA/COM ISRAEL MALAYSIA S/ASIA USA+45 USSR ECO/UNDEV FAM POL/PAR SECT CONSULT NAT/LISM...POLICY SOC 20 CHINJAP. PAGE 137 H2736 — PWR DIPLOM

B64
SANCHEZ J.M.,REFORM AND REACTION. SPAIN STRATA NAT/LISM TOTALISM 20. PAGE 137 H2749 — NAT/G SECT GP/REL REV

B64
SCHNITGER F.M.,FORGOTTEN KINGDOMS IN SUMATRA. FAM SECT LEISURE HABITAT...OBS AUD/VIS WORSHIP 20 SUMATRA. PAGE 140 H2793 — CULTURE AFR SOCIETY STRUCT

B64
SINAI I.R.,THE CHALLENGE OF MODERNISATION* THE WEST'S IMPACT ON THE NON-WESTERN WORLD. EUR+WWI CULTURE ELITES SECT CONSERVE SOCISM...GP/COMP IDEA/COMP NAT/COMP GEN/LAWS. PAGE 144 H2881 — ASIA S/ASIA ECO/UNDEV CREATE

B64
SINGER M.R.,THE EMERGING ELITE: A STUDY OF POLITICAL LEADERSHIP IN CEYLON. S/ASIA ECO/UNDEV AGRI KIN NAT/G SECT EX/STRUC LEGIT ATTIT PWR RESPECT...SOC STAT CHARTS 20. PAGE 144 H2883 — TOP/EX STRATA NAT/LISM CEYLON

B64
SKINNER E.P.,THE MOSSI OF UPPER VOLTA: THE POLITICAL DEVELOPMENT OF A SUDANESE PEOPLE. AFR LAW AGRI FAM KIN POL/PAR PROVS SECT DELIB/GP EX/STRUC FORCES TOP/EX DOMIN EDU/PROP LEGIT CT/SYS COERCE CHOOSE ORD/FREE PWR WEALTH...SOC MYTH VAL/FREE. PAGE 145 H2897 — CULTURE OBS UPPER/VOLT

B64
TEPASKE J.J.,EXPLOSIVE FORCES IN LATIN AMERICA. CULTURE INTELL ECO/UNDEV INT/ORG NAT/G SECT FORCES ECO/TAC EDU/PROP PWR WEALTH SOC. PAGE 153 H3063 — L/A+17C RIGID/FLEX FOR/AID USSR

B64
THORNBURG M.W.,PEOPLE AND POLICY IN THE MIDDLE EAST. ISLAM ECO/UNDEV FAM KIN MUNIC NAT/G NEIGH POL/PAR SECT DELIB/GP LEGIS PLAN ECO/TAC DOMIN ADMIN ATTIT HEALTH RESPECT...SOC CONCPT METH/CNCPT OBS TIME/SEQ TOT/POP VAL/FREE. PAGE 154 H3088 — TEC/DEV CULTURE

B64
TIERNEY B.,THE CRISIS OF CHURCH AND STATE 1050-1300. DOMIN EDU/PROP CONTROL PWR CONSERVE 11/14. PAGE 155 H3092 — SECT NAT/G GP/REL

B64
UTECHIN S.V.,RUSSIAN POLITICAL THOUGHT: A CONCISE HISTORY. RUSSIA USSR INTELL STRATA POL/PAR SECT LEGIS EDU/PROP REV WAR MARXISM...ANARCH BIBLIOG 9/20 REFORMERS SLAVS. PAGE 161 H3218 — IDEA/COMP ATTIT ALL/IDEOS NAT/G

B64
VON FURER-HAIMEN E.,AN ANTHROPOLOGICAL BIBLIOGRAPHY OF SOUTH ASIA (VOL. II). STRATA STRUCT KIN SECT ACT/RES CREATE HABITAT...GEOG OBS 20. PAGE 163 H3268 — BIBLIOG/A CULTURE S/ASIA SOC

B64
VON GRUNEBAUM G.E.,MODERN ISLAM: THE SEARCH FOR CULTURAL IDENTITY. ACADEM NEIGH WRITING NAT/LISM ...HUM CONCPT 19/20 MUSLIM MID/EAST ARABS. PAGE 163 H3269 — ISLAM CULTURE CREATE SECT

B64
WERTHEIM W.F.,EAST-WEST PARALLELS. INDONESIA S/ASIA NAT/G SECT...TIME/SEQ METH REFORMERS S/EASTASIA. PAGE 167 H3334 — SOC ECO/UNDEV CULTURE NAT/LISM

B64
WICKENS G.M.,PERSIA IN ISLAMIC TIMES: A PRACTICAL BIBLIOGRAPHY OF ITS HISTORY, CULTURE AND LANGUAGE (PAMPHLET). IRAN ISLAM SECT. PAGE 168 H3355 — BIBLIOG CULTURE LING

B64
WRAITH R.,CORRUPTION IN DEVELOPING COUNTRIES. NIGERIA UK LAW ELITES STRATA INDUS LOC/G NAT/G SECT FORCES EDU/PROP ADMIN PWR WEALTH 18/20. PAGE 171 H3414 — ECO/UNDEV CRIME SANCTION ATTIT

S64
"FURTHER READING." INDIA PAKISTAN SECT WAR PEACE ATTIT...POLICY 20. PAGE 2 H0044 — BIBLIOG GP/REL DIPLOM NAT/G

S64
CLIGNET R.,"POTENTIAL ELITES IN GHANA AND THE IVORY COAST: A PRELIMINARY SURVEY." AFR CULTURE ELITES STRATA KIN NAT/G SECT DOMIN EXEC ORD/FREE RESPECT SKILL...POLICY RELATIV GP/COMP NAT/COMP 20. PAGE 30 H0605 — PWR LEGIT IVORY/CST GHANA

S64
EISTER A.W.,"PERSPECTIVE ON FUNCTIONS OF RELIGION IN A DEVELOPING COUNTRY: ISLAM IN PAKISTAN." ISLAM CULTURE MUNIC ACT/RES CREATE PROB/SOLV TEC/DEV WORSHIP. PAGE 45 H0902 — ATTIT SECT ECO/DEV

S64
ENNIS T.E.,"VIETNAM: LAND WITHOUT LAUGHTER." S/ASIA VIETNAM VIETNAM/S INTELL SOCIETY SECT FORCES DIPLOM LEGIT COERCE WAR ATTIT RIGID/FLEX ORD/FREE COLD/WAR 20. PAGE 46 H0929 — NAT/G TOP/EX GUERRILLA

S64
HIRAI N.,"SHINTO AND INTERNATIONAL PROBLEMS." SOCIETY NAT/G PLAN EDU/PROP RACE/REL PEACE ATTIT PERCEPT LOVE MORAL...HUM MYTH RECORD SAMP TREND STERTYP TOT/POP 20 UN CHINJAP SHINTO. PAGE 71 H1423 — ASIA SECT

S64
LEWIS B.,"THE QUEST FOR FREEDOM--A SAD STORY OF THE MIDDLE EAST." ISLAM ISRAEL LEBANON TURKEY CULTURE NAT/G SECT LEGIS TOP/EX DOMIN EDU/PROP LEGIT ORD/FREE PWR RESPECT...POLICY TIME/SEQ VAL/FREE 20. PAGE 96 H1911 — CONSTN ATTIT NAT/LISM

S64
RAMAZANI R.K.,"CHURCH AND STATE IN MODERNIZING SOCIETY: THE CASE OF IRAN." ISLAM CULTURE ORD/FREE PWR...TIME/SEQ VAL/FREE 17/20. PAGE 129 H2586
SECT NAT/G ELITES IRAN

S64
SAYEED K.,"PATHAN REGIONALISM." ISLAM PAKISTAN S/ASIA CULTURE SOCIETY NAT/G NEIGH DIPLOM LEGIT COERCE CHOOSE ATTIT DISPL PERCEPT ALL/VALS SOVEREIGN...POLICY RELATIV SOC TIME/SEQ TOT/POP 20. PAGE 138 H2761
SECT NAT/LISM REGION

B65
BENTWICH J.S.,EDUCATION IN ISRAEL. ISRAEL CULTURE STRATA PROB/SOLV TEC/DEV ADJUST ALL/VALS 20 JEWS. PAGE 15 H0293
SECT EDU/PROP ACADEM SCHOOL

B65
BETEILLE A.,CASTE, CLASS, AND POWER. INDIA MUNIC SECT REGION GP/REL PERS/REL ATTIT HABITAT RIGID/FLEX...SOC 20. PAGE 16 H0323
STRATA CULTURE PWR STRUCT

B65
BOISSEVAIN J.,SAINTS AND FIREWORKS: RELIGION AND POLITICS IN RURAL MALTA. MALTA STRUCT FAM NEIGH POL/PAR REPRESENT INGP/REL CENTRAL...CHARTS BIBLIOG 20. PAGE 18 H0368
GP/REL NAT/G SECT MUNIC

B65
BURLING R.,HILL FARMS AND PADI FIELDS. BURMA S/ASIA THAILAND VIETNAM AGRI NEIGH SECT GP/REL NAT/LISM ORD/FREE 20 MID/EAST MIGRATION. PAGE 24 H0491
SOCIETY STRUCT CULTURE SOVEREIGN

B65
CENTRAL GAZETTEERS UNIT,THE GAZETTEER OF INDIA (VOL. I). INDIA SOCIETY STRATA PLAN EDU/PROP NAT/LISM ORD/FREE WEALTH...GEOG LING CHARTS SOC/INTEG 20. PAGE 28 H0568
PRESS CULTURE SECT STRUCT

B65
CHANDLER M.J.,A GUIDE TO RECORDS IN BARBADOS. WEST/IND PUB/INST SCHOOL SECT...HIST/WRIT 20. PAGE 28 H0573
BIBLIOG LOC/G L/A+17C NAT/G

B65
CONRING E.,KIRCHE UND STAAT NACH DER LEHRE DER NIEDERLANDISCHEN CALVINISTEN IN DER ERSTEN HALFTE DES 17. JAHRHUNDERTS. NETHERLAND GP/REL...CONCPT 17 CHURCH/STA. PAGE 33 H0656
SECT JURID NAT/G ORD/FREE

B65
GAJENDRAGADKAR P.B.,LAW, LIBERTY AND SOCIAL JUSTICE. INDIA CONSTN NAT/G SECT PLAN ECO/TAC PRESS POPULISM...SOC METH/COMP 20 HINDU. PAGE 54 H1086
ORD/FREE LAW ADJUD JURID

B65
HARRIS R.L.,POLITICAL ORGANIZATION OF THE MBEMBE NIGERIA. AFR NIGERIA SOCIETY AGRI SECT WORKER PAY ...SOC WORSHIP 20 MBEMBE. PAGE 67 H1345
STRUCT CHIEF CULTURE

B65
HORNE A.J.,THE COMMONWEALTH TODAY. AFR ASIA CANADA UK STRUCT ECO/UNDEV NAT/G SECT GP/REL 20 AUSTRAL CMN/WLTH. PAGE 73 H1470
BIBLIOG/A SOCIETY CULTURE

B65
HUNT G.L.,CALVINISM AND THE POLITICAL ORDER. NAT/G LEAD...POLICY IDEA/COMP ANTHOL WORSHIP 20. PAGE 75 H1498
SECT CONCPT

B65
JANSEN M.B.,CHANGING JAPANESE ATTITUDES TOWARD MODERNIZATION. ASIA CHINA/COM S/ASIA INTELL SOCIETY KIN NAT/G SECT PERCEPT RIGID/FLEX...SOC CONCPT TIME/SEQ TREND TOT/POP 19/20 CHINJAP. PAGE 80 H1591
TEC/DEV ATTIT INDIA

B65
KAAS L.,DIE GEISTLICHE GERICHTSBARKEIT DER KATHOLISCHEN KIRCHE IN PREUSSEN (2 VOLS.). PRUSSIA CONSTN NAT/G PROVS SECT ADJUD ADMIN ATTIT 16/20. PAGE 82 H1647
JURID CATHISM GP/REL CT/SYS

B65
LAWRENCE P.,GODS, GHOSTS, AND MEN IN MELANESIA: SOME RELIGIONS OF AUSTRALIAN NEW GUINEA AND THE NEW HEBRIDES. SOCIETY ECO/UNDEV FAM GP/REL INGP/REL HABITAT PERSON...GEOG SOC ANTHOL BIBLIOG WORSHIP 20 NEW/GUINEA. PAGE 92 H1847
MYTH S/ASIA SECT CULTURE

B65
MAIR L.,AN INTRODUCTION TO SOCIAL ANTHROPOLOGY. LAW STRATA FINAN FAM KIN SECT INT/TRADE RACE/REL ADJUST PRODUC...T 20. PAGE 101 H2023
SOC STRUCT CULTURE SOCIETY

B65
MONTESQUIEU C DE S.,CONSIDERATIONS ON THE CAUSES OF THE GREATNESS OF THE ROMANS AND THEIR DECLINE (1748 TRANS. BY D. LOWENTHAL). ROMAN/EMP SECT CHIEF EX/STRUC FORCES LEGIS DOMIN WAR POPULISM...POLICY REALPOL ROME/ANC. PAGE 112 H2244
NAT/G PWR COLONIAL MORAL

B65
MURDOCK G.P.,CULTURE AND SOCIETY. SOCIETY STRATA STRUCT SECT CREATE CONTROL ORD/FREE...GP/COMP ANTHOL 20. PAGE 115 H2294
CULTURE PHIL/SCI METH IDEA/COMP

B65
O'CONNELL M.R.,IRISH POLITICS AND SOCIAL CONFLICT IN THE AGE OF THE AMERICAN REVOLUTION. FRANCE IRELAND MOD/EUR STRATA SECT LEGIS DIPLOM INT/TRADE DOMIN REV WAR...BIBLIOG 18 PARLIAMENT. PAGE 119 H2387
CATHISM ATTIT NAT/G DELIB/GP

B65
ONUOHA B.,THE ELEMENTS OF AFRICAN SOCIALISM. AFR FINAN SECT TEC/DEV FOR/AID GP/REL OWN LAISSEZ MARXISM...CONCPT BIBLIOG 20. PAGE 121 H2419
SOCISM ECO/UNDEV NAT/G EX/STRUC

B65
POLK W.R.,THE UNITED STATES AND THE ARAB WORLD. USA+45 ECO/UNDEV EXTR/IND SECT WAR NAT/LISM ATTIT ...NAT/COMP COLD/WAR. PAGE 127 H2535
ISLAM REGION CULTURE DIPLOM

B65
QURESHI I.H.,THE STRUGGLE FOR PAKISTAN. INDIA PAKISTAN UK CULTURE LEGIS DIPLOM EDU/PROP COLONIAL ATTIT SOVEREIGN 19/20 MUSLIM. PAGE 129 H2576
GP/REL RACE/REL WAR SECT

B65
SAKAI R.K.,STUDIES ON ASIA, 1965. INDIA KOREA S/ASIA USA+45 CONSTN KIN SECT PARTIC SUFF NAT/LISM ...POLICY SOC 19/20 CHINJAP. PAGE 137 H2737
PARL/PROC ASIA

B65
SLOTKIN J.S.,READINGS IN EARLY ANTHROPOLOGY. INTELL SECT CREATE ATTIT KNOWL...HUM PHIL/SCI PSY LING 1/18. PAGE 145 H2902
SOC CULTURE GP/COMP

B65
SPENCER P.,THE SAMBURU: A STUDY OF GERONTOCRACY IN A NOMADIC TRIBE. AFR SOCIETY ECO/UNDEV AGRI FAM NEIGH SECT GP/REL MARRIAGE WORSHIP 20 SAMBURU. PAGE 147 H2945
KIN STRUCT AGE/O CULTURE

B65
STERN F.,THE POLITICS OF CULTURAL DESPAIR. EUR+WWI GERMANY POL/PAR SECT RACE/REL STRANGE TOTALISM ...ART/METH MYTH BIBLIOG 20 JEWS. PAGE 149 H2980
CULTURE ATTIT NAT/LISM FASCISM

B65
TUTSCH H.E.,FACETS OF ARAB NATIONALISM. ISLAM ISRAEL CULTURE STRUCT SECT RIGID/FLEX ORD/FREE MARXISM SOCISM 20. PAGE 157 H3143
ECO/UNDEV NAT/LISM TEC/DEV SOCIETY

B65
ULLMANN W.,A HISTORY OF POLITICAL THOUGHT: THE MIDDLE AGES. CHRIST-17C LOC/G NAT/G CENTRAL PWR ...PHIL/SCI LOG BIBLIOG 6/15. PAGE 158 H3153
IDEA/COMP SOVEREIGN SECT LAW

B65
US LIBRARY OF CONGRESS,RARE BOOKS DIVISION: GUIDE TO ITS COLLECTION AND SERVICES. LOC/G SECT WAR. PAGE 161 H3214
BIBLIOG/A NAT/G DIPLOM

B65
WOLPERT S.,INDIA. INDIA UK ECO/UNDEV DIPLOM GP/REL WEALTH 20 NEHRU/J. PAGE 170 H3405
CULTURE COLONIAL NAT/LISM SECT

L65
MATTHEWS D.G.,"A CURRENT BIBLIOGRAPHY ON ETHIOPIAN AFFAIRS: A SELECT BIBLIOGRAPHY FROM 1950-1964." ETHIOPIA LAW CULTURE ECO/UNDEV INDUS LABOR SECT FORCES DIPLOM CIVMIL/REL RACE/REL...LING STAT 20. PAGE 105 H2093
BIBLIOG/A ADMIN POL/PAR NAT/G

S65
MULLER A.L.,"SOME NON-ECONOMIC DETERMINANTS OF THE ECONOMIC STATUS OF ASIANS IN AFRICA." AFR SOUTH/AFR CULTURE 20. PAGE 114 H2283
DISCRIM RACE/REL LABOR SECT

B66
BARRETT J.,THAT BETTER COUNTRY: RELIGIOUS ASPECT OF LIFE IN EASTERN AUSTRALIA, 1835-1850. LAW ECO/UNDEV SCHOOL TEC/DEV EDU/PROP CONTROL HABITAT MORAL WORSHIP 19 AUSTRAL CHURCH/STA. PAGE 11 H0229
SECT CULTURE GOV/REL

B66
BASDEN G.T.,NIGER IBOS. NIGERIA STRUCT SECT CHIEF COLONIAL HABITAT...POLICY SOC MYTH OBS WORSHIP 20 IBO. PAGE 12 H0233
CULTURE AFR SOCIETY

B66
BECKER J.,BESSARABIEN UND SEIN DEUTSCHTUM. ROMANIA USSR STRUCT INDUS PROF/ORG SECT GP/REL INGP/REL 15/20 BESSARABIA. PAGE 13 H0254
PROVS CULTURE SOCIETY

B66
BRAIBANTI R.,RESEARCH ON THE BUREAUCRACY OF PAKISTAN. PAKISTAN LAW CULTURE INTELL ACADEM LOC/G SECT PRESS CT/SYS...LING CHARTS 20 BUREAUCRCY. PAGE 20 H0402
HABITAT NAT/G ADMIN CONSTN

B66
BRECHER M.,SUCCESSION IN INDIA. INDIA USA+45 CONSTN AGRI POL/PAR PROVS SECT DELIB/GP FORCES PROB/SOLV ECO/TAC PWR...LING 20 CONGRESS NEHRU/J. PAGE 20 H0408
CHIEF DECISION CHOOSE

B66
BROWN L.C.,STATE AND SOCIETY IN INDEPENDENT NORTH AFRICA. ALGERIA LIBYA MOROCCO AGRI INDUS INT/ORG POL/PAR SECT PLAN DIPLOM COLONIAL...LING NAT/COMP
NAT/G SOCIETY CULTURE

ANTHOL BIBLIOG 20 TUNIS MUSLIM. PAGE 22 H0446 ECO/UNDEV

B66
BUKHARIN N.,THE ABC OF COMMUNISM: A POPULAR EXPLANATION OF THE PROGRAM OF THE COMMUNIST PARTY OF RUSSIA. USSR STRATA SECT FORCES WORKER CAP/ISM RECEIVE EDU/PROP NAT/LISM TOTALISM 20. PAGE 23 H0468 MARXISM CONCPT POLICY REV

B66
CADY J.F.,THAILAND, BURMA, LAOS AND CAMBODIA. FRANCE UK CULTURE NAT/G DOMIN GP/REL RACE/REL HABITAT...GEOG TREND CHINJAP BUDDHISM. PAGE 25 H0504 S/ASIA COLONIAL REGION SECT

B66
COLEMAN-NORTON P.R.,ROMAN STATE AND CHRISTIAN CHURCH: A COLLECTION OF LEGAL DOCUMENTS TO A.D. 535 (3 VOLS.). CHRIST-17C ROMAN/EMP...ANTHOL DICTIONARY 6 CHRISTIAN CHURCH/STA. PAGE 31 H0630 GP/REL NAT/G SECT LAW

B66
EMBREE A.T.,ASIA: A GUIDE TO BASIC BOOKS (PAMPHLET). ECO/UNDEV SECT FORCES DIPLOM ALL/IDEOS ...SOC 20. PAGE 46 H0914 BIBLIOG/A ASIA S/ASIA NAT/G

B66
FARWELL G.,MASK OF ASIA: THE PHILIPPINES. PHILIPPINE SECT DIPLOM ATTIT...SOC RECORD PREDICT BIBLIOG 20. PAGE 49 H0974 S/ASIA CULTURE

B66
FEINE H.E.,REICH UND KIRCHE. CHRIST-17C MOD/EUR ROMAN/EMP LAW CHOOSE ATTIT 10/19 CHURCH/STA ROMAN/LAW. PAGE 49 H0982 JURID SECT NAT/G GP/REL

B66
FINER S.E.,ANONYMOUS EMPIRE: STUDY OF THE LOBBY IN GREAT BRITAIN. UK CONSTN LABOR POL/PAR SECT DOMIN EDU/PROP PRESS CHOOSE...CONCPT CHARTS 20 PARLIAMENT. PAGE 50 H1004 LOBBY NAT/G LEGIS PWR

B66
FORD P.,CARDINAL MORAN AND THE A. L. P. NAT/G POL/PAR SECT DELIB/GP LOBBY REV CHOOSE ORD/FREE MARXISM 19/20 AUSTRAL PROTESTANT LABOR/PAR. PAGE 52 H1035 CATHISM SOCISM LABOR SOCIETY

B66
FUCHS W.P.,STAAT UND KIRCHE IM WANDEL DER JAHRHUNDERTE. EUR+WWI MOD/EUR UK REV...JURID CONCPT 4/20 EUROPE CHRISTIAN CHURCH/STA. PAGE 54 H1074 SECT NAT/G ORD/FREE GP/REL

B66
HAHN C.H.L.,THE NATIVE TRIBES OF SOUTH WEST AFRICA. LAW FAM SECT HABITAT SKILL...SOC AUD/VIS WORSHIP RITUAL 20 AFRICA/SW. PAGE 64 H1275 CULTURE SOCIETY STRUCT AFR

B66
HARRISON B.,SOUTH-EAST ASIA: A SHORT HISTORY (3RD ED.). ECO/UNDEV INDUS NAT/G SECT BAL/PWR NAT/LISM ...SOC 15/20 S/EASTASIA. PAGE 67 H1346 COLONIAL S/ASIA CULTURE

B66
HERMANN F.G.,DER KAMPF GEGEN RELIGION UND KIRCHE IN DER SOWJETISCHEN BESATZUNGSZONE DEUTSCHLANDS. GERMANY/E EDU/PROP ATTIT PERSON MORAL MARXISM 20 LENIN/VI STALIN/J KHRUSH/N. PAGE 70 H1400 SECT ORD/FREE GP/REL NAT/G

B66
HINTON W.,FANSHEN: A DOCUMENTARY OF REVOLUTION IN A CHINESE VILLAGE. ASIA ELITES MUNIC NAT/G POL/PAR SECT WORKER LEAD WAR PRIVIL PWR 20 MAO. PAGE 71 H1422 MARXISM REV NEIGH OWN

B66
HOPKINS J.F.K.,ARABIC PERIODICAL LITERATURE, 1961. ISLAM LAW CULTURE SECT...GEOG HEAL PHIL/SCI PSY SOC 20. PAGE 73 H1466 BIBLIOG/A NAT/LISM TEC/DEV INDUS

B66
HOWE R.W.,BLACK AFRICA: FROM PRE-HISTORY TO THE EVE OF THE COLONIAL ERA. ECO/UNDEV KIN PROVS SECT INT/TRADE EDU/PROP COLONIAL...BIBLIOG WORSHIP. PAGE 74 H1482 AFR CULTURE SOC

B66
IBRAHIM-HILMY,THE LITERATURE OF EGYPT AND THE SOUDAN: FROM THE EARLIEST TIMES TO THE YEAR 1885 INCLUSIVE (2 VOLS.). MEDIT-7 SUDAN UAR LAW SOCIETY SECT ATTIT EGYPT/ANC. PAGE 76 H1520 BIBLIOG CULTURE ISLAM NAT/G

B66
JONES D.H.,AFRICA BIBLIOGRAPHY SERIES: EAST AFRICA. AFR UGANDA SECT BIO/SOC...JURID NAT/COMP 20. PAGE 82 H1630 BIBLIOG/A SOC CULTURE LING

B66
KAZAMIAS A.M.,EDUCATION AND QUEST FOR MODERNITY IN TURKEY. ISLAM SOCIETY SECT NAT/LISM ATTIT ORD/FREE SOVEREIGN TURKS. PAGE 84 H1672 NAT/G EDU/PROP STRATA CULTURE

B66
KERR M.H.,ISLAMIC REFORM: THE POLITICAL AND LEGAL THEORIES OF MUHAMMAD 'ABDUH AND RASHID RIDA. NAT/G SECT LEAD SOVEREIGN CONSERVE...JURID BIBLIOG WORSHIP 20. PAGE 85 H1698 LAW CONCPT ISLAM

B66
LEYBURN J.G.,THE HAITIAN PEOPLE (REV. ED.). HAITI SOCIETY FAM SECT DOMIN COLONIAL MARRIAGE...SOC CHARTS BIBLIOG/A 18/10. PAGE 96 H1917 STRUCT STRATA INGP/REL CULTURE

B66
MULLER C.F.J.,A SELECT BIBLIOGRAPHY OF SOUTH AFRICAN HISTORY; A GUIDE FOR HISTORICAL RESEARCH. SOUTH/AFR UK LAW CONSTN SOCIETY STRUCT AGRI SECT DIPLOM COLONIAL LEAD RACE/REL...POLICY 17/20 NEGRO. PAGE 114 H2284 BIBLIOG AFR NAT/G

B66
O'NEILL C.E.,CHURCH AND STATE IN FRENCH COLONIAL LOUISIANA: POLICY AND POLITICS TO 1732. PROVS VOL/ASSN DELIB/GP ADJUD ADMIN GP/REL ATTIT DRIVE ...POLICY BIBLIOG 17/18 LOUISIANA CHURCH/STA. PAGE 120 H2390 COLONIAL NAT/G SECT PWR

B66
RIZK C.,LE REGIME POLITIQUE LIBANAIS. ISLAM LEBANON STRUCT POL/PAR SECT LOBBY GP/REL 20 ARABS MUSLIM CHRISTIAN. PAGE 132 H2637 ECO/UNDEV NAT/G CULTURE

B66
SAKAI R.K.,STUDIES ON ASIA, 1966. CEYLON INDIA USA-45 INDUS POL/PAR DIPLOM ECO/TAC MARXISM ...POLICY 19/20 CHINJAP. PAGE 137 H2738 SECT ECO/UNDEV

B66
SCHATTEN F.,COMMUNISM IN AFRICA. AFR GHANA GUINEA MALI CULTURE ECO/UNDEV LABOR SECT ECO/TAC EDU/PROP REV 20. PAGE 139 H2774 COLONIAL NAT/LISM MARXISM DIPLOM

B66
SETTON K.M.,GREAT PROBLEMS IN EUROPEAN CIVILIZATION. CHRIST-17C EUR+WWI MOD/EUR SECT GP/REL ALL/VALS ORD/FREE ALL/IDEOS...TREND ANTHOL T CHRISTIAN RENAISSAN PROTESTANT. PAGE 142 H2835 CULTURE CONCPT IDEA/COMP

B66
SOROKIN P.A.,SOCIOLOGICAL THEORIES OF TODAY. SOCIETY STRUCT FAM SECT GP/REL ADJUST...PHIL/SCI PSY TREND METH/COMP 20. PAGE 147 H2935 SOC CULTURE METH/CNCPT EPIST

B66
SRINIVAS M.N.,SOCIAL CHANGE IN MODERN INDIA. INDIA CULTURE SOCIETY STRUCT SECT TEC/DEV...METH/CNCPT SELF/OBS WORSHIP 20. PAGE 148 H2961 ORD/FREE STRATA SOC ECO/UNDEV

B66
TYSON G.,NEHRU: THE YEARS OF POWER. INDIA UK STRATA ECO/UNDEV FINAN SECT TASK WAR ORD/FREE MARXISM ...POLICY BIBLIOG 20 NEHRU/J. PAGE 157 H3145 CHIEF PWR DIPLOM NAT/G

B66
US DEPARTMENT OF STATE,RESEARCH ON THE MIDDLE EAST (EXTERNAL RESEARCH LIST NO 4-25). GREECE ISRAEL SYRIA UAR YEMEN CULTURE SOCIETY POL/PAR SECT DIPLOM EDU/PROP WAR NAT/LISM...GEOG GOV/COMP 20. PAGE 160 H3190 BIBLIOG/A ISLAM NAT/G REGION

B66
VOGT E.Z.,PEOPLE OF RIMROCK. STRATA STRUCT KIN SECT GP/REL HABITAT ALL/VALS...GEOG INT QU 20 TEXAS NAVAHO MORMON SPAN/AMER ZUNI. PAGE 163 H3260 CULTURE GP/COMP SOC SOCIETY

B66
VON ARSENIEW W.,DIE GEISTIGEN SCHICKSALE DES RUSSISCHEN VOLKES. RUSSIA USSR SOCIETY STRUCT NAT/G SECT CHIEF REV 19/20. PAGE 163 H3262 ATTIT PERSON CULTURE DRIVE

B66
ZEINE Z.N.,THE EMERGENCE OF ARAB NATIONALISM (REV. ED.). TURKEY UK NAT/G SECT TEC/DEV LEAD REV WAR AGE/Y ROLE ORD/FREE...TRADIT CHARTS BIBLIOG 20 ARABS OTTOMAN. PAGE 173 H3453 ISLAM NAT/LISM DIPLOM

S66
BLANC N.,"SPAIN: LEARNING THROUGH STRUGGLE" SPAIN STRATA STRUCT SECT FORCES PROB/SOLV AGE/Y ATTIT ORD/FREE PWR WEALTH MARXISM SOCISM 19/20 FRANCO/F SUCCESSION. PAGE 18 H0352 NAT/G FUT SOCIALIST TOTALISM

S66
LODGE G.C.,"REVOLUTION IN LATIN AMERICA." USA+45 ELITES INDUS LABOR PROF/ORG SECT TEC/DEV CAP/ISM SKILL MARXISM...POLICY NAT/COMP. PAGE 98 H1950 ATTIT REV L/A+17C IDEA/COMP

S66
MATTHEWS D.G.,"ETHIOPIAN OUTLINE: A BIBLIOGRAPHIC RESEARCH GUIDE." ETHIOPIA LAW STRUCT ECO/UNDEV AGRI LABOR SECT CHIEF DELIB/GP EX/STRUC ADMIN...LING ORG/CHARTS 20. PAGE 105 H2095 BIBLIOG NAT/G DIPLOM POL/PAR

C66
WINT G.,"ASIA: A HANDBOOK." ASIA S/ASIA INDUS LABOR SECT PRESS RACE/REL MARXISM...STAT CHARTS BIBLIOG 20. PAGE 169 H3388 ECO/UNDEV DIPLOM NAT/G SOCIETY

B67
ALBA V.,THE MEXICANS; THE MAKING OF A NATION. SOCIETY ECO/UNDEV AGRI INDUS SECT STRANGE ATTIT ...GEOG 20 MEXIC/AMER. PAGE 4 H0091 CONSTN NAT/G CULTURE ANOMIE

B67
BAIN C.A.,VIETNAM: THE ROOTS OF CONFLICT. FRANCE S/ASIA USSR VIETNAM POL/PAR SECT FORCES COLONIAL NAT/LISM PEACE ORD/FREE MARXISM...GEOG CHARTS 4/20. PAGE 10 H0202
NAT/G WAR CULTURE

B67
CANTOR N.F.,THE ENGLISH TRADITION* TWENTIETH-CENTURY VIEWS OF ENGLISH HISTORY (2VOLS.). UK STRATA NAT/G SECT WAR...POLICY GOV/COMP IDEA/COMP ANTHOL T PARLIAMENT CMN/WLTH. PAGE 26 H0522
CT/SYS LAW POL/PAR

B67
DEGLER C.N.,THE AGE OF THE ECONOMIC REVOLUTION 1876-1900. USA-45 AGRI MUNIC POL/PAR SECT ECO/TAC CHOOSE...PHIL/SCI CHARTS NAT/COMP 19 NEGRO. PAGE 39 H0782
INDUS SOCIETY ECO/DEV TEC/DEV

B67
MCLAUGHLIN M.R.,RELIGIOUS EDUCATION AND THE STATE: DEMOCRACY FINDS A WAY. CANADA EUR+WWI GP/REL POPULISM...CATH NAT/COMP 20 AUSTRAL. PAGE 107 H2141
SECT NAT/G EDU/PROP POLICY

B67
MUHAMMAD A.C.,THE EMERGENCE OF PAKISTAN. PAKISTAN S/ASIA CONSTN ECO/UNDEV NAT/G CONTROL NAT/LISM 20. PAGE 114 H2281
DIPLOM COLONIAL SECT PROB/SOLV

B67
OLIVER R.,AFRICA SINCE 1800. AFR ISLAM CULTURE ECO/UNDEV SECT DOMIN RACE/REL DISCRIM SOVEREIGN 19/20. PAGE 121 H2414
DIPLOM COLONIAL REGION

B67
PIKE F.B.,FREEDOM AND REFORM IN LATIN AMERICA. BRAZIL URUGUAY CONSTN CULTURE SECT DIPLOM EDU/PROP PARTIC DRIVE ALL/VALS CATHISM...GEOG ANTHOL BIBLIOG REFORMERS BOLIV. PAGE 126 H2511
L/A+17C ORD/FREE ECO/UNDEV REV

B67
SCHECTER J.,THE NEW FACE OF BUDDHA: BUDDHISM AND POLITICAL POWER IN SOUTHEAST ASIA. S/ASIA NAT/G POL/PAR NAT/LISM ATTIT MARXISM...BIBLIOG 20. PAGE 139 H2780
SECT POLICY PWR LEAD

B67
SHAKABPA T.W.D.,TIBET: A POLITICAL HISTORY. CHINA/COM UK CHIEF LEAD...INT BIBLIOG 20 TIBET. PAGE 142 H2839
DIPLOM SECT NAT/G

B67
THOMPSON E.T.,PERSPECTIVES ON THE SOUTH: AGENDA FOR RESEARCH. CULTURE ECO/UNDEV SECT GP/REL EFFICIENCY ALL/VALS...HUM SOC CONCPT LING 20 NEGRO. PAGE 154 H3080
PROB/SOLV IDEA/COMP REGION ACT/RES

L67
GOOD E.M.,"CAPITAL PUNISHMENT AND ITS ALTERNATIVES IN ANCIENT NEAR EASTERN LAW." SOCIETY SECT INGP/REL CONSEN ATTIT SEX MORAL...CRIMLGY GP/COMP. PAGE 58 H1168
MEDIT-7 LAW JURID CULTURE

L67
GRAUBARD S.R.,"TOWARD THE YEAR 2000: WORK IN PROGRESS." FUT ACADEM SECT DELIB/GP DIPLOM EDU/PROP AGE/Y PERSON ROLE...PSY ANTHOL. PAGE 60 H1199
PREDICT PROB/SOLV SOCIETY CULTURE

L67
LARKIN E.,"ECONOMIC GROWTH, CAPITAL INVESTMENT, AND THE ROMAN CATHOLIC CHURCH IN NINETEENTH-CENTURY IRELAND." IRELAND AGRI DIST/IND NAT/G GIVE OWN CATHISM...CHARTS 19. PAGE 91 H1823
FINAN SECT WEALTH ECO/UNDEV

L67
UNESCO,"APARTHEID." SOUTH/AFR STRUCT KIN SCHOOL SECT WORKER DOMIN EDU/PROP REGION RACE/REL ISOLAT 20. PAGE 158 H3164
DISCRIM CULTURE COERCE COLONIAL

S67
HAMMOND R.J.,"RACE ATTITUDES AND POLICIES IN PORTUGUESE AFRICA IN THE NINETEENTH AND TWENTIETH CENTURIES." AFR PORTUGAL NAT/G SECT EDU/PROP COLONIAL ATTIT RIGID/FLEX SEX MORAL RESPECT 19/20 NEGRO. PAGE 65 H1309
POLICY RACE/REL DISCRIM SOCIETY

S67
HOPE M.,"THE RELUCTANT WAY: SELF-IMMOLATION IN VIETNAM." VIETNAM SOCIETY FAM KIN SECT DRIVE ALL/VALS...TRADIT OBS INT 20. PAGE 73 H1465
CULTURE SUICIDE IDEA/COMP ATTIT

S67
MURVAR V.,"MAX WEBER'S CONCEPT OF HEIROCRACY: A STUDY IN THE TYPOLOGY OF CHURCH-STATE RELATIONS" UNIV INGP/REL ATTIT PLURISM...SOC CONCPT 20 WEBER/MAX. PAGE 115 H2299
SECT NAT/G GP/REL STRUCT

S67
POWELL D.,"THE EFFECTIVENESS OF SOVIET ANTI-RELIGIOUS PROPAGANDA." USSR NAT/G DOMIN LEGIT NAT/LISM 20. PAGE 127 H2549
EDU/PROP ATTIT SECT CONTROL

S67
RAMA C.M.,"PASADO Y PRESENTE DE LA RELIGION EN AMERICA LATINA." L/A+17C ELITES SOCIETY STRATA MARXISM...STAT WORSHIP PROTESTANT. PAGE 129 H2585
SECT CATHISM STRUCT NAT/COMP

S67
RAUM O.,"THE MODERN LEADERSHIP GROUP AMONG THE SOUTH AFRICAN XHOSA." SOUTH/AFR SOCIETY SECT EX/STRUC REPRESENT GP/REL INGP/REL PERSON ...METH/COMP 17/20 XHOSA NEGRO. PAGE 130 H2596
RACE/REL KIN LEAD CULTURE

S67
SMITH J.E.,"THE RED PRUSSIANISM OF THE GERMAN DEMOCRATIC REPUBLIC." GERMANY/E INTELL NAT/G SECT CHIEF...PREDICT TIME/SEQ 20. PAGE 146 H2913
MARXISM NAT/LISM GOV/COMP EDU/PROP

S67
SOLT L.F.,"PURITANISM, CAPITALISM, DEMOCRACY, AND THE NEW SCIENCE." NAT/G GP/REL CONSERVE...IDEA/COMP GEN/LAWS. PAGE 147 H2931
SECT CAP/ISM RATIONAL POPULISM

S67
WHITE J.W.,"MASS MOVEMENTS AND DEMOCRACY: SOKAGAKKAI IN JAPANESE POLITICS." NAT/G GP/REL ALL/VALS ORD/FREE WORSHIP 20 CHINJAP. PAGE 167 H3349
SECT PWR ATTIT POL/PAR

B68
DE SPINOZA B.,TRACTATUS THEOLOGICO-POLITICUS (TRANS. BY R. WILLIS). UNIV CHIEF DOMIN PWR WORSHIP. PAGE 38 H0771
SECT NAT/G ORD/FREE

L68
CURRENT HISTORY,"AFRICA, 1968." ETHIOPIA GHANA NIGERIA SOUTH/AFR CULTURE ECO/UNDEV KIN SECT CHIEF EX/STRUC WAR WEAPON CHOOSE CIVMIL/REL...GOV/COMP 20 AFRICA/E. PAGE 36 H0724
RACE/REL NAT/LISM FORCES AFR

B70
BOSSUET J.B.,"POLITIQUE TIREE DE L'ECRITURE SAINTE" (1679-1709) IN J.B. BOSSUET, OEVRES DE BOSSUET. NAT/G GP/REL AUTHORIT HEREDITY PERSON ALL/VALS SOVEREIGN 18 BIBLE DEITY CHRISTIAN. PAGE 19 H0383
TRADIT CHIEF SECT CONCPT

B73
STEPHEN J.F.,LIBERTY, EQUALITY, FRATERNITY. UNIV SOCIETY NAT/G LEGIS DOMIN AGREE PERS/REL ATTIT MORAL...IDEA/COMP 19 MILL/JS. PAGE 149 H2978
ORD/FREE CONCPT COERCE SECT

B75
NEWMAN J.H.,A LETTER ADDRESSED TO THE DUKE OF NORFOLK ON THE OCCASION OF MR. GLADSTONE'S RECENT EXPOSTULATION. NAT/G SECT CHIEF LEGIS CONTROL LEAD GP/REL SUPEGO SOC/INTEG WORSHIP 19 ENGLAND. PAGE 117 H2346
POLICY DOMIN SOVEREIGN CATHISM

B82
MACDONALD D.,AFRICANA; OR, THE HEART OF HEATHEN AFRICA, VOL. II: MISSION LIFE. SOCIETY STRATA KIN CREATE EDU/PROP ADMIN COERCE LITERACY HEALTH...MYTH WORSHIP 19 LIVNGSTN/D MISSION NEGRO. PAGE 100 H1990
SECT AFR CULTURE ORD/FREE

B86
MAS LATRIE L.,RELATIONS ET COMMERCE DE L'AFRIQUE SEPTENTRIONALE OU MAGREB AVEC LES NATIONS CHRETIENNES AU MOYEN AGE. CULTURE CHIEF FORCES WAR ...SOC CENSUS TREATY 10/16. PAGE 104 H2084
ISLAM SECT DIPLOM INT/TRADE

C89
PLAYFAIR R.L.,"A BIBLIOGRAPHY OF ALGERIA." ALGERIA CULTURE ECO/UNDEV DIST/IND EXTR/IND FINAN SECT CRIME 16/19. PAGE 126 H2525
BIBLIOG/A ISLAM GEOG

B91
BENTHAM J.,A FRAGMENT ON GOVERNMENT (1776). CONSTN MUNIC NAT/G SECT AGREE HAPPINESS UTIL MORAL ORD/FREE...JURID CONCPT. PAGE 15 H0292
SOVEREIGN LAW DOMIN

B96
LOWELL A.L.,GOVERNMENTS AND PARTIES IN CONTINENTAL EUROPE (VOL. I). MOD/EUR LOC/G NAT/G SECT CHIEF LEGIS PARL/PROC GOV/REL...POLICY 19. PAGE 99 H1973
POL/PAR GOV/COMP CONSTN EX/STRUC

B97
JENKS E.J.,LAW AND POLITICS IN THE MIDDLE AGES. CHRIST-17C CULTURE STRUCT KIN NAT/G SECT CT/SYS GP/REL...CLASSIF CHARTS IDEA/COMP BIBLIOG 8/16. PAGE 80 H1603
LAW SOCIETY ADJUST

B98
FORTES M.,AFRICAN POLITICAL SYSTEMS. ECO/UNDEV KIN LOC/G NEIGH POL/PAR SECT LEAD GP/REL ORD/FREE...SOC 20 NEGRO. PAGE 52 H1039
AFR CULTURE STRUCT

B99
KINGSLEY M.H.,WEST AFRICAN STUDIES. GHANA NIGERIA SIER/LEONE LAW EXTR/IND SECT DIPLOM INT/TRADE DOMIN RACE/REL OWN HEALTH...SOC 19. PAGE 86 H1717
AFR HEREDITY COLONIAL CULTURE

B99
LECKY W.E.H.,DEMOCRACY AND LIBERTY (2 VOLS.). LAW CONSTN STRATA POL/PAR SECT WORKER DIPLOM ADJUD REPRESENT NAT/LISM CONSERVE. PAGE 93 H1851
LEGIS NAT/G POPULISM ORD/FREE

B99
RIPLEY W.Z.,A SELECTED BIBLIOGRAPHY OF THE ANTHROPOLOGY AND ETHNOLOGY OF EUROPE. SOCIETY STRATA STRUCT KIN SECT VOL/ASSN GP/REL INGP/REL HABITAT...GEOG 19. PAGE 132 H2632
BIBLIOG/A MOD/EUR SOC CULTURE

SECUR/COUN....UNITED NATIONS SECURITY COUNCIL

SECUR/PROG....SECURITY PROGRAM

SECURITIES....SEE FINAN

SECURITY....SEE ORD/FREE

SECURITY COUNCIL....SEE UN+DELIB/GP+PWR

SECURITY EXCHANGE COMMISSION....SEE SEC/EXCHNG

SECURITY PROGRAM....SEE SECUR/PROG

SEDITION....SEDITION

SEEK....SEARCH FOR EDUCATION, ELEVATION, AND KNOWLEDGE

SEELEY J.R. H2819

SEGAL A. H2820

SEGAL R. H2821

SEGREGAT....SEGREGATION

B65
VAN DEN BERGHE P.L.,SOUTH AFRICA: A STUDY IN CONFLICT. AFR CULTURE SOCIETY STRATA STRUCT COERCE SEGREGAT. PAGE 161 H3227 — DOMIN RACE/REL DISCRIM

SEGREGATION....SEE NEGRO, SOUTH/US, RACE/REL, SOC/INTEG, CIV/RIGHTS, DISCRIM, MISCEGEN, ISOLAT, SCHOOL, STRANGE, ANOMIE,SEGREGAT

SEIDLER G.L. H2822

SELASSIE/H....HAILE SELASSIE

SELBORNE/W....WILLIAM SELBORNE

B25
WILLIAMS B.,THE SELBORNE MEMORANDUM. AFR FUT SOUTH/AFR UK NAT/G BUDGET DIPLOM REGION GOV/REL SOVEREIGN...POLICY CHARTS 20 UNIFICA SELBORNE/W. PAGE 168 H3365 — COLONIAL PROVS

SELEC/SERV....SELECTIVE SERVICE

SELF P. H2823

SELF/OBS....SELF/OBSERVATION

B19
DE MAN H.,THE REMAKING OF A MIND. EUR+WWI NAT/G ECO/TAC REGION ORD/FREE SOCISM...BIOG 20 WWI EUROPE. PAGE 38 H0762 — PSY WAR SELF/OBS PARTIC

B20
HALDANE R.B.,BEFORE THE WAR. MOD/EUR SOCIETY INT/ORG NAT/G DELIB/GP PLAN DOMIN EDU/PROP LEGIT ADMIN COERCE ATTIT DRIVE MORAL ORD/FREE PWR...SOC CONCPT SELF/OBS RECORD BIOG TIME/SEQ. PAGE 64 H1282 — POLICY DIPLOM UK

B34
BENEDICT R.,PATTERNS OF CULTURE. S/ASIA FAM KIN PERSON RESPECT...CONCPT SELF/OBS. PAGE 14 H0278 — CULTURE SOC

B50
HOBBES T.,LEVIATHAN. UNIV CONSTN SOCIETY LOC/G NAT/G CONSULT TOP/EX DOMIN DRIVE PERSON PWR ...PHIL/SCI CONCPT SELF/OBS GEN/LAWS TOT/POP. PAGE 72 H1434 — LAW ORD/FREE

B52
BENTHAM A.,HANDBOOK OF POLITICAL FALLACIES. FUT MOD/EUR LAW INTELL LOC/G MUNIC NAT/G DELIB/GP LEGIS CREATE EDU/PROP CT/SYS ATTIT RIGID/FLEX KNOWL PWR ...RELATIV PSY SOC CONCPT SELF/OBS TREND STERTYP TOT/POP. PAGE 14 H0286 — POL/PAR

B55
RODNICK D.,THE NORWEGIANS: A STUDY IN NATIONAL CULTURE. NORWAY FAM INGP/REL PERS/REL AGE...PSY SOC SELF/OBS WORSHIP 20. PAGE 133 H2655 — CULTURE INT RECORD ATTIT

B58
GARTHOFF R.L.,SOVIET STRATEGY IN THE NUCLEAR AGE. FUT USSR R+D INT/ORG NAT/G ACT/RES TEC/DEV DOMIN DETER WAR ATTIT PWR...RELATIV METH/CNCPT SELF/OBS TREND CON/ANAL STERTYP GEN/LAWS 20. PAGE 55 H1103 — COM FORCES BAL/PWR NUC/PWR

B60
BRIGGS L.C.,TRIBES OF THE SAHARA. AFR MOROCCO STRATA AGRI GP/REL HEALTH...GEOG SOC MYTH LING BIBLIOG 13/20 ARABS. PAGE 21 H0418 — CULTURE HABITAT KIN SELF/OBS

B60
JAECKH A.,WELTSAAT; ERLEBTES UND ERSTREBTES. GERMANY WOR+45 WOR-45 PLAN WAR...POLICY OBS/ENVIR NAT/COMP PERS/COMP 20. PAGE 79 H1581 — BIOG NAT/G SELF/OBS DIPLOM

B64
TAYLOR E.,RICHER BY ASIA. S/ASIA CULTURE VOL/ASSN ACT/RES ATTIT DISPL PERSON ALL/VALS...INT/LAW MYTH SELF/OBS 20. PAGE 153 H3054 — SOCIETY RIGID/FLEX INDIA

L64
FINDLATER R.,"US." EUR+WWI GERMANY USSR SOCIETY FACE/GP EDU/PROP PERCEPT PERSON ALL/VALS...PSY SOC CONCPT SELF/OBS SAMP TREND 20. PAGE 50 H1001 — CULTURE ATTIT UK

B65
ADENAUER K.,MEINE ERINNERUNGEN, 1945-53 (VOL. I), 1953-55 (VOL. II). EUR+WWI GERMANY CHIEF FORCES PROB/SOLV DIPLOM ARMS/CONT INGP/REL PEACE SOVEREIGN ...OBS/ENVIR RECORD 20. PAGE 3 H0069 — NAT/G BIOG SELF/OBS

B66
SRINIVAS M.N.,SOCIAL CHANGE IN MODERN INDIA. INDIA CULTURE SOCIETY STRUCT SECT TEC/DEV...METH/CNCPT SELF/OBS WORSHIP 20. PAGE 148 H2961 — ORD/FREE STRATA SOC ECO/UNDEV

B67
THOMAS P.,DOWN THESE MEAN STREETS. GP/REL RACE/REL ADJUST...SOC SELF/OBS 20. PAGE 154 H3078 — DISCRIM KIN CULTURE BIOG

SELIGMAN E.R.A. H2824

SELOSOEMARDJAN O. H2825

SEMANTICS...SEE LOG

SEMINAR REPRESENTATIVE GOVT H2826

SEN/SPACE....UNITED STATES SENATE SPECIAL COMMITTEE ON SPACE ASTRONAUTICS

SENATE SPECIAL COMMITTEE ON SPACE ASTRONAUTICS....SEE SEN/SPACE

SENATE....SENATE (ALL NATIONS); SEE ALSO CONGRESS, LEGIS

B10
TEMPERLEY H.W.V.,SENATES AND UPPER CHAMBERS; THEIR USE AND FUNCTION IN THE MODERN STATE... UK WOR-45 CONSTN NAT/G POL/PAR PROVS SECT COLONIAL LEAD CHOOSE REPRESENT PWR...BIBLIOG 19/20 PARLIAMENT SENATE CMN/WLTH HOUSE/LORD. PAGE 153 H3059 — PARL/PROC NAT/COMP LEGIS EX/STRUC

S67
DOERN G.B.,"THE ROYAL COMMISSIONS IN THE GENERAL POLICY PROCESS AND IN FEDERAL-PROVINCIAL RELATIONS." CANADA CONSTN ACADEM PROVS CONSULT DELIB/GP LEGIS ACT/RES PROB/SOLV CONFER CONTROL EFFICIENCY...METH/COMP 20 SENATE ROYAL/COMM. PAGE 42 H0832 — R+D EX/STRUC GOV/REL NAT/G

S67
FUSARO A.,"THE EFFECT OF PROPORTIONAL REPRESENTATION ON VOTING IN THE AUSTRALIAN SENATE." S/ASIA CONSTN POL/PAR CONTROL GP/REL PWR...CHARTS 20 AUSTRAL HOUSE/REP SENATE. PAGE 54 H1083 — LEGIS CHOOSE REPRESENT NAT/G

SENEGAL....SEE ALSO AFR

B57
INTERNATIONAL AFRICAN INST,ETHNOGRAPHIC SURVEY OF AFRICA: WESTERN AFRICA: THE WOLOF OF SENEGAMBIA. AFR SENEGAL CULTURE ECO/UNDEV FAM KIN REGION ...CHARTS GP/COMP BIBLIOG WORSHIP 20. PAGE 78 H1551 — STRUCT GEOG HABITAT INGP/REL

B60
CONOVER H.F.,OFFICIAL PUBLICATIONS OF FRENCH WEST AFRICA, 1946-1958. DAHOMEY IVORY/CST NIGER SENEGAL UPPER/VOLT CONSTN AGRI PRESS...CON/ANAL 20. PAGE 33 H0651 — BIBLIOG COLONIAL NAT/G AFR

B63
COLUMBIA U SCHOOL OF LAW,PUBLIC INTERNATIONAL DEVELOPMENT FINANCING IN SENEGAL. SENEGAL FINAN DELIB/GP GIVE EFFICIENCY...CHARTS GOV/COMP ANTHOL 20. PAGE 32 H0636 — FOR/AID PLAN RECEIVE ECO/UNDEV

B64
MORGENTHAU R.S.,POLITICAL PARTIES IN FRENCH-SPEAKING WEST AFRICA. AFR FRANCE GUINEA IVORY/CST MALI SENEGAL CONSTN LEGIS CREATE PLAN LOBBY PARTIC GP/REL...POLICY BIBLIOG 20. PAGE 113 H2257 — POL/PAR NAT/G SOVEREIGN COLONIAL

B65
DOLCI D.,A NEW WORLD IN THE MAKING. GHANA SENEGAL USSR YUGOSLAVIA CULTURE INT/ORG PLAN EDU/PROP GP/REL PEACE MORAL...GEOG SOC 20 COLD/WAR. PAGE 42 H0834 — SOCIETY ALL/VALS DRIVE PERSON

B65
HAPGOOD D.,AFRICA: FROM INDEPENDENCE TO TOMARROW. AFR GUINEA SENEGAL CULTURE ELITES ECO/UNDEV AGRI SCHOOL FOR/AID COLONIAL MARXISM...TREND 20. PAGE 66 H1323 — ECO/TAC SOCIETY NAT/G

B67
CURTIN P.D.,AFRICA REMEMBERED. NIGERIA SENEGAL CULTURE DIPLOM INT/TRADE GP/REL RACE/REL...RECORD ANTHOL 18/19 NEGRO. PAGE 36 H0727 — DOMIN ORD/FREE AFR DISCRIM

SENGHOR L.S. H2827,H2828

SENGUPTA J.K. H1045

SENIOR....SENIORITY; SEE ALSO ADMIN, ROUTINE

B41
COHEN E.W.,THE GROWTH OF THE BRITISH CIVIL SERVICE 1780-1939. UK NAT/G SENIOR ROUTINE GOV/REL...MGT METH/COMP BIBLIOG 18/20. PAGE 31 H0616 — OP/RES TIME/SEQ CENTRAL ADMIN

B57
SCARROW H.A.,THE HIGHER PUBLIC SERVICE OF THE COMMONWEALTH OF AUSTRALIA. LAW SENIOR LOBBY ROLE 20 AUSTRAL CIVIL/SERV COMMONWLTH. PAGE 138 H2766 — ADMIN NAT/G EX/STRUC GOV/COMP

S67
COLLINS B.A.,"SOME NOTES ON PUBLIC SERVICE COMMISSIONS IN THE COMMONWEALTH CARIBBEAN." JAMAICA L/A+17C TRINIDAD UK NAT/G OP/RES DOMIN SENIOR COLONIAL CONTROL INGP/REL CENTRAL EFFICIENCY PWR ...DECISION 20. PAGE 31 H0631 — ADMIN EX/STRUC ECO/UNDEV CHOOSE

SEPARATION....SEE ISOLAT, DISCRIM, RACE/REL

SERBIA....SERBIA

S64
REISS I.,"LE DECLENCHEMENT DE LA PREMIERE GUERRE MONDIALE." GERMANY RUSSIA NAT/G FORCES DOMIN EDU/PROP COERCE RIGID/FLEX PWR SOVEREIGN...RELATIV HIST/WRIT TOT/POP AUST/HUNG SERBIA 20. PAGE 131 H2612 — MOD/EUR BAL/PWR DIPLOM WAR

SERENI A.P. H2829

SERRANO MOSCOSO E. H2830

SERV/IND....SERVICE INDUSTRY

N
CIVIL SERVICE JOURNAL. PARTIC INGP/REL PERS/REL ...MGT BIBLIOG/A 20. PAGE 1 H0015 — ADMIN NAT/G SERV/IND WORKER

B05
GRIFFIN A.P.C.,LIST OF BOOKS ON RAILROADS IN FOREIGN COUNTRIES. MOD/EUR ECO/DEV NAT/G CONTROL SOCISM...JURID 19/20 RAILROAD. PAGE 61 H1219 — BIBLIOG/A SERV/IND ADMIN DIST/IND

C52
LEWIS B.W.,"BRITISH PLANNING AND NATIONALIZATION." UK INDUS SERV/IND LABOR NAT/G OP/RES TEC/DEV TAX WEALTH...CHARTS BIBLIOG 20. PAGE 96 H1912 — NEW/LIB ECO/DEV POL/PAR PLAN

B58
CROWE S.,THE LANDSCAPE OF POWER. UK CULTURE SERV/IND NAT/G CONSULT PARTIC NUC/PWR LEISURE...SOC EXHIBIT 20. PAGE 36 H0712 — HABITAT TEC/DEV PLAN CONTROL

B60
JHA C.,INDIAN GOVERNMENT AND POLITICS. INDIA SERV/IND POL/PAR PROVS LEGIS CT/SYS CHOOSE GOV/REL FEDERAL 20. PAGE 81 H1616 — NAT/G PARL/PROC CONSTN ADJUST

B60
WEINER H.E.,BRITISH LABOR AND PUBLIC OWNERSHIP. UK SERV/IND LG/CO WORKER CONTROL OWN 20. PAGE 166 H3327 — LABOR NAT/G INDUS ATTIT

B62
MARTINS A.F.,REVOLUCAO BRANCA NO CAMPO. L/A+17C SERV/IND DEMAND EFFICIENCY PRODUC...POLICY METH/COMP. PAGE 104 H2070 — AGRI ECO/UNDEV TEC/DEV NAT/COMP

S63
APPERT K.,"BERECHTIGE VORBEHALTE DER SCHWEIZERISCHEN ZUR INTEGRATION." EUR+WWI UK MARKET SERV/IND NAT/G PLAN RIGID/FLEX OEEC 20 EEC. PAGE 7 H0146 — FINAN ATTIT SWITZERLND

B64
JUCKER-FLEETWOOD E.,MONEY AND FINANCE IN AFRICA. ISLAM ECO/UNDEV SERV/IND NAT/G EX/STRUC PLAN ECO/TAC ROUTINE WEALTH...MGT TOT/POP 20. PAGE 82 H1639 — AFR FINAN

B64
PERAZA SARAUSA F.,DIRECTORIO DE REVISTAS Y PERIODICOS DE CUBA. CUBA L/A+17C NAT/G ATTIT 20. PAGE 125 H2490 — BIBLIOG/A PRESS SERV/IND LEAD

B64
PINNICK A.W.,COUNTRY PLANNERS IN ACTION. UK FINAN SERV/IND NAT/G CONSULT DELIB/GP PRICE CONTROL ROUTINE LEISURE AGE/C...GEOG 20 URBAN/RNWL. PAGE 126 H2512 — MUNIC PLAN INDUS ATTIT

B66
BHALERAO C.N.,PUBLIC SERVICE COMMISSIONS OF INDIA: A STUDY. INDIA SERV/IND EX/STRUC ROUTINE CHOOSE GOV/REL INGP/REL...KNO/TEST EXHIBIT 20. PAGE 16 H0326 — NAT/G OP/RES LOC/G ADMIN

L67
WRIGHT W.R.,"FOREIGN-OWNED RAILWAYS IN ARGENTINA: A CASE STUDY OF ECONOMIC NATIONALISM." L/A+17C UK ECO/UNDEV SERV/IND LG/CO NAT/G TEC/DEV BAL/PWR EQUILIB ARGEN. PAGE 171 H3423 — NAT/LISM CAP/ISM ECO/TAC COLONIAL

SERVAN/JJ....JEAN JACQUES SERVAN-SCHREIBER

SERVAN-SCHREIBER, JEAN-JACQUES....SEE SERVAN/JJ

SERVICE E.R. H2730

SERVICE INDUSTRY....SEE SERV/IND

SET THEORY....SEE CLASSIF

SETHE P. H2831

SETON-WATSON H. H2832,H2833,H2834

SETTON K.M. H2835

SEVENTHDAY....SEVENTH DAY ADVENTISTS

B64
KAUFMANN R.,MILLENARISME ET ACCULTURATION. SOCIETY DOMIN COLONIAL NAT/LISM ATTIT...SOC BIBLIOG 20 JEHOVA/WIT SEVENTHDAY. PAGE 84 H1669 — AFR SECT MYTH CULTURE

SEX DIFFERENCES....SEE SEX

SEX....SEE ALSO BIO/SOC

B06
SUMNER W.G.,FOLKWAYS: STUDY OF THE SOCIOLOGICAL IMPORTANCE OF USAGES, MANNERS, CUSTOMS, MORES, AND MORALS. STRUCT KIN ETIQUET ROUTINE MURDER MARRIAGE PEACE SEX ALL/VALS WEALTH BIBLIOG. PAGE 150 H3008 — CULTURE SOC SANCTION MORAL

N19
INTERNATIONAL LABOUR OFFICE,EMPLOYMENT, UNEMPLOYMENT AND LABOUR FORCE STATISTICS (PAMPHLET). EUR+WWI STRATA AGRI INDUS NAT/G PROB/SOLV PAY AGE SEX...SAMP NAT/COMP METH 20 ILO. PAGE 78 H1557 — WORKER LABOR STAT ECO/DEV

B37
HORNEY K.,THE NEUROTIC PERSONALITY OF OUR TIME. SOCIETY PERS/REL ADJUST HAPPINESS ANOMIE ATTIT DRIVE SEX LOVE PWR CONCPT. PAGE 74 H1472 — PSY PERSON STRANGE CULTURE

B44
BERDYAEV N.,SLAVERY AND FREEDOM. NAT/G REV WAR NAT/LISM OWN AUTHORIT SEX CONSERVE SOCISM...TRADIT PHIL/SCI CIVIL/LIB. PAGE 15 H0295 — ORD/FREE PERSON ELITES SOCIETY

B51
BERNATZIK H.A.,THE SPIRITS OF THE YELLOW LEAVES. BURMA LAOS S/ASIA THAILAND VIETNAM SOCIETY AGRI COLONIAL LEISURE GP/REL PERS/REL ISOLAT AGE HABITAT SEX WORSHIP 20. PAGE 16 H0310 — SOC KIN ECO/UNDEV CULTURE

B51
LEMERT E.M.,SOCIAL PATHOLOGY. CULTURE BIO/SOC PERSON SEX 20 PROSTITUTN. PAGE 94 H1876 — SOC ANOMIE CONCPT CRIME

B55
DUVERGER M.,THE POLITICAL ROLE OF WOMEN. FRANCE GERMANY/W NORWAY YUGOSLAVIA STRATA LOBBY AGE ATTIT ROLE...STAT SAMP CHARTS METH/COMP NAT/COMP HYPO/EXP FEMALE/SEX. PAGE 44 H0875 — SEX LEAD PARTIC CHOOSE

B61
BLAKE J.,FAMILY STRUCTURE IN JAMAICA. JAMAICA CULTURE SOCIETY ACT/RES CONTROL MARRIAGE AGE ...POLICY SOC BIBLIOG 20. PAGE 18 H0351 — FAM SEX STRUCT ATTIT

B61
VAN GULIK R.H.,SEXUAL LIFE IN ANCIENT CHINA. ASIA LEISURE...CHARTS. PAGE 161 H3230 — SEX CULTURE MARRIAGE LOVE

B62
BERNOT R.M.,EXCESS AND RESTRAINT: SOCIAL CONTROL AMONG GUINEA MOUNTAIN PEOPLE. CULTURE FAM KIN CT/SYS COERCE WAR PERS/REL MARRIAGE HABITAT SEX ...MYTH 20 NEW/GUINEA. PAGE 16 H0314 — SOCIETY CONTROL STRUCT ADJUST

B62
FALKENBERG J.,KIN AND TOTEM; GROUP RELATIONS OF AUSTRALIAN ABORIGINES IN THE PORT KEATS DISTRICT. SOCIETY STRATA STRUCT GP/REL PERS/REL MARRIAGE AGE ATTIT SEX...SOC STAT CHARTS AUSTRAL ABORIGINES. PAGE 48 H0964 — KIN INGP/REL CULTURE FAM

B62
MALINOWSKI B.,SEX, CULTURE, AND MYTH. UNIV SOCIETY FAM PERS/REL MARRIAGE RATIONAL HABITAT PERSON SUPEGO MORAL WORSHIP 20. PAGE 102 H2032 — MYTH SECT SEX CULTURE

B62
VILAKAZI A.,ZULU TRANSFORMATIONS: A STUDY OF THE DYNAMICS OF SOCIAL CHANGE. AFR CULTURE ECO/UNDEV KIN NEIGH SEX...GEOG QU TREND CHARTS BIBLIOG 19/20. PAGE 163 H3254
MARRIAGE SECT SOC EDU/PROP

B63
GOODE W.J.,WORLD REVOLUTION AND FAMILY PATTERNS. AFR CHINA/COM INDIA UAR CREATE ADJUST ATTIT SEX ...SOC 20 CHINJAP. PAGE 58 H1169
FAM NAT/COMP CULTURE MARRIAGE

B66
KEIL S.,SEXUALITAT - ERKENNTNISSE UND MASS-STABE. CULTURE DOMIN MARRIAGE AGE/Y AGE/A PERSON SUPEGO PLURISM 17/20. PAGE 84 H1681
SEX ATTIT STRUCT SOCIETY

B67
FANON F.,BLACK SKIN, WHITE MASKS: THE EXPERIENCES OF A BLACK MAN IN A WHITE WORLD. CULTURE COLONIAL HAPPINESS ISOLAT STRANGE ATTIT HABITAT RIGID/FLEX SEX...BIOG STERTYP SOC/INTEG 20 NEGRO. PAGE 49 H0970
DISCRIM PERS/REL RACE/REL PSY

B67
PATAI R.,GOLDEN RIVER TO GOLDEN ROAD: SOCIETY, CULTURE, AND CHANGE IN THE MIDDLE EAST (2ND ED.). ELITES FAM KIN TEC/DEV MARRIAGE NAT/LISM SEX ORD/FREE...TREND GP/COMP WORSHIP 20. PAGE 124 H2476
CULTURE SOCIETY ISLAM STRUCT

L67
GOOD E.M.,"CAPITAL PUNISHMENT AND ITS ALTERNATIVES IN ANCIENT NEAR EASTERN LAW." SOCIETY SECT INGP/REL CONSEN ATTIT SEX MORAL...CRIMLGY GP/COMP. PAGE 58 H1168
MEDIT-7 LAW JURID CULTURE

S67
HAMMOND R.J.,"RACE ATTITUDES AND POLICIES IN PORTUGUESE AFRICA IN THE NINETEENTH AND TWENTIETH CENTURIES." AFR PORTUGAL NAT/G SECT EDU/PROP COLONIAL ATTIT RIGID/FLEX SEX MORAL RESPECT 19/20 NEGRO. PAGE 65 H1309
POLICY RACE/REL DISCRIM SOCIETY

S67
NEALE R.S.,"WORKING CLASS WOMEN AND WOMEN'S SUFFRAGE." UK LAW CONSTN LABOR NAT/G DELIB/GP LEGIS WORKER PAY PARTIC CHOOSE 19 FEMALE/SEX. PAGE 116 H2326
STRATA SEX SUFF DISCRIM

SEXUAL BEHAVIOR....SEE SEX, PERSON

SEYLER W.C. H2836

SHAFER B.C. H2837

SHAFFER H.G. H2838

SHAKABPA T.W.D. H2839

SHANGHAI....SHANGHAI

SHANKS M. H2840

SHANNON R.T. H2841

SHAPIRO H.L. H2842

SHAPIRO J.P. H2843

SHAPIRO P.S. H2844

SHARKANSKY I. H2845

SHARMA B.M. H2846

SHARMA M.P. H2847

SHARMA R.S. H2848

SHARMA S.A. H2849

SHARMA S.P. H2850

SHARMA T.R. H2851

SHASTRI/LB....LAL BAHADUR SHASTRI

B66
ZINKIN T.,CHALLENGES IN INDIA. INDIA PAKISTAN LAW AGRI FINAN INDUS TOP/EX TEC/DEV CONTROL ROUTINE ORD/FREE PWR 20 NEHRU/J SHASTRI/LB CIVIL/SERV. PAGE 173 H3458
NAT/G ECO/TAC POLICY ADMIN

SHATTEN F. H2852

SHAW S.J. H2853

SHEIKH N.A. H2855

SHELBY C. H2856

SHELDON C.H. H2857

SHEPHERD W.G. H2858

SHEPPARD/S....SAMUEL SHEPPARD

SHERMN/ACT....SHERMAN ANTI-TRUST ACT; SEE ALSO MONOPOLY

SHIELS W.E. H2859

SHIGEO N. H2860

SHILS E.A. H2472,H2861,H2862

SHINTO....SHINTOISM

S64
HIRAI N.,"SHINTO AND INTERNATIONAL PROBLEMS." SOCIETY NAT/G PLAN EDU/PROP RACE/REL PEACE ATTIT PERCEPT LOVE MORAL...HUM MYTH RECORD SAMP TREND STERTYP TOT/POP 20 UN CHINJAP SHINTO. PAGE 71 H1423
ASIA SECT

SHIRATO I. H2863

SHIRER W.L. H2864

SHIROKOGOROFF S.M. H2865

SHOCK M. H0469

SHORT TAKE-OFF AND LANDING AIRCRAFT....SEE STOL

SHOUP/C....C. SHOUP

SHRIMALI K.L. H2866

SHRIVER/S....SARGENT SHRIVER

SHULMAN M.D. H2215

SHUMSKY A. H2867

SIBERIA....SIBERIA

B56
LEVIN M.G.,THE PEOPLES OF SIBERIA. PREHIST ECO/UNDEV KIN SECT HABITAT...CLASSIF AUD/VIS WORSHIP 20 SIBERIA. PAGE 95 H1900
CULTURE SOCIETY ASIA

B62
MICHAEL H.N.,STUDIES IN SIBERIAN ETHNOGENESIS. USSR KIN...ART/METH SOC 20 SIBERIA. PAGE 110 H2196
HABITAT HEREDITY CULTURE LING

SIBRON....SIBRON V. NEW YORK

SICILY....SICILY

SICKNESS....SEE HEALTH

SIDDIQUI A.H. H0903

SIDGWICK H. H2868

SIDGWICK/H....HENRY SIDGWICK

SIEGFRIED A. H2869

SIEKANOWICZ P. H2870

SIER/LEONE....SIERRA LEONE; SEE ALSO AFR

B00
MOCKLER-FERRYMAN A.,BRITISH WEST AFRICA. FRANCE GERMANY NIGER SIER/LEONE UK CULTURE DIPLOM WAR RACE/REL PRODUC PROFIT WEALTH...POLICY PREDICT 19. PAGE 112 H2232
AFR COLONIAL INT/TRADE CAP/ISM

B63
WALKER A.A.,OFFICIAL PUBLICATIONS OF SIERRA LEONE AND GAMBIA. GAMBIA SIER/LEONE UK LAW CONSTN LEGIS PLAN BUDGET DIPLOM...SOC SAMP CON/ANAL 20. PAGE 164 H3290
BIBLIOG NAT/G COLONIAL ADMIN

B99
KINGSLEY M.H.,WEST AFRICAN STUDIES. GHANA NIGERIA SIER/LEONE LAW EXTR/IND SECT DIPLOM INT/TRADE DOMIN RACE/REL OWN HEALTH...SOC 19. PAGE 86 H1717
AFR HEREDITY COLONIAL CULTURE

SIEYES E.J. H2871

SIHANOUK....NORODOM SIHANOUK

SIKKIM....SEE ALSO S/ASIA

SILBERMAN B.S. H2872,H2873

SILBERMAN L. H2874

SILBERNER E. H2875

SILONE I. H2876

SILVER....SILVER STANDARD AND POLICIES RELATING TO SILVER

B58
AVRAMOVIC D.,POSTWAR GROWTH IN INTERNATIONAL INDEBTEDNESS. WOR+45 AGRI INDUS CAP/ISM PRICE INCOME...NAT/COMP 20 GOLD/STAND SILVER. PAGE 9 H0184
INT/TRADE FINAN COST BAL/PAY

B61
VEIT O.,GRUNDRISS DER WAHRUNGSPOLITIK. FRANCE GERMANY USSR DIPLOM INT/TRADE...NAT/COMP 19/20 GOLD/STAND SILVER. PAGE 162 H3239
FINAN POLICY ECO/TAC CAP/ISM

SILVERT K.H. H2877

SIMMEL/G....GEORG SIMMEL

SIMMS R.P. H2878

SIMOES DOS REIS A. H2879

SIMON H.A. H0201

SIMONY.R.H2880
SIMON DIAZ J. H0820
SIMPKINS E. H3414

SIMPSON....SIMPSON V. UNION OIL COMPANY

SIMUL....SCIENTIFIC MODELS

N19
BUSINESS ECONOMISTS' GROUP,INCOME POLICIES (PAMPHLET). UK INDUS LABOR TOP/EX PAY COST PRODUC ...ECOMETRIC GOV/COMP SIMUL ANTHOL 20. PAGE 25 H0497
INCOME WORKER WEALTH POLICY

B23
POUND R.,INTERPRETATIONS OF LEGAL HISTORY. CULTURE ...PHIL/SCI NEW/IDEA CLASSIF SIMUL GEN/LAWS 19/20. PAGE 127 H2547
LAW IDEA/COMP JURID

B44
KNORR K.E.,BRITISH COLONIAL THEORIES 1570-1850. NAT/G DELIB/GP ECO/TAC PERCEPT PWR...WELF/ST METH/CNCPT CONT/OBS TIME/SEQ SIMUL TOT/POP 20. PAGE 87 H1734
ACT/RES DOMIN COLONIAL

B48
WHITE C.L.,HUMAN GEOGRAPHY: AN ECOLOGICAL STUDY OF GEOGRAPHY. UNIV SEA CULTURE AGRI EXTR/IND RACE/REL PRODUC...CHARTS HYPO/EXP SIMUL GEN/LAWS T. PAGE 167 H3345
SOC HABITAT GEOG SOCIETY

B49
SARGENT S.S.,CULTURE AND PERSONALITY. FUT UNIV SOCIETY FAM KIN NEIGH BIO/SOC DRIVE PERCEPT RIGID/FLEX LOVE RESPECT...PSY SOC CONCPT OBS TIME/SEQ TREND CON/ANAL CHARTS HYPO/EXP SIMUL TOT/POP. PAGE 138 H2754
CULTURE PERSON

B50
CANTRIL H.,TENSIONS THAT CAUSE WAR. UNIV CULTURE R+D CREATE EDU/PROP DRIVE PERSON KNOWL ORD/FREE ...HUM PSY SOC OBS CENSUS TREND CON/ANAL SOC/EXP SIMUL GEN/METH ANTHOL COLD/WAR TOT/POP. PAGE 26 H0523
SOCIETY PHIL/SCI PEACE

B51
PARSONS T.,TOWARD A GENERAL THEORY OF ACTION. CULTURE PERSON...PSY SIMUL ANTHOL SOC/INTEG 20. PAGE 124 H2472
SOC PHIL/SCI DRIVE ACT/RES

S52
MCDOUGAL M.S.,"THE COMPARATIVE STUDY OF LAW FOR POLICY PURPOSES." FUT NAT/G POL/PAR CONSULT ADJUD PWR SOVEREIGN...METH/CNCPT IDEA/COMP SIMUL 20. PAGE 106 H2129
PLAN JURID NAT/LISM

S57
MARCH J.C.,"PARTY LEGISLATIVE REPRESENTATION AS A FUNCTION OF ELECTION RESULTS." DRIVE...PROBABIL REGRESS STYLE CHARTS HYPO/EXP SIMUL. PAGE 102 H2046
REPRESENT GOV/COMP LEGIS CHOOSE

S58
APTER D.E.,"A COMPARATIVE METHOD FOR THE STUDY OF POLITICS" (BMR)" UNIV SOCIETY STRATA NAT/G POL/PAR ...CHARTS SIMUL 20. PAGE 8 H0151
SOC METH METH/COMP

S58
EULAV H.,"HD LASSWELL'S DEVELOPMENTAL ANALYSIS." FUT CULTURE TOP/EX PLAN CHOOSE SUPEGO PWR...TREND HYPO/EXP SIMUL GEN/METH VAL/FREE 20 LASSWELL/H. PAGE 47 H0948
CONCPT NEW/IDEA ELITES

S59
LEYS C.,"MODELS, THEORIES, AND THE THEORY OF POLITICAL PARTIES" CANADA LIECHTENST UK LOC/G NAT/G PARTIC REPRESENT GP/REL CONSEN EQUILIB MAJORITY ...NEW/IDEA MATH CHARTS 20. PAGE 96 H1919
POL/PAR CHOOSE METH/CNCPT SIMUL

B60
WOLF C.,FOREIGN AID: THEORY AND PRACTICE IN SOUTHERN ASIA. CEYLON INDONESIA PHILIPPINE S/ASIA CULTURE STRATA ECO/UNDEV PLAN EDU/PROP ATTIT ...METH/CNCPT MATH QUANT STAT CONT/OBS TIME/SEQ SIMUL TOT/POP 20. PAGE 170 H3396
ACT/RES ECO/TAC FOR/AID

B62
ABRAHAM W.E.,THE MIND OF AFRICA. AFR SOCIETY STRATA KIN ECO/TAC DOMIN EDU/PROP LEGIT COERCE ATTIT ALL/VALS...MAJORIT SOC OBS HIST/WRIT TIME/SEQ TREND TOT/POP 20. PAGE 3 H0058
CULTURE SIMUL GHANA

B63
BARNETT A.D.,COMMUNIST STRATEGIES IN ASIA: A COMPARATIVE ANALYSIS OF GOVERNMENTS AND PARTIES. COM FUT S/ASIA CULTURE SOCIETY STRATA NAT/G DELIB/GP ACT/RES ECO/TAC EDU/PROP COERCE CHOOSE ATTIT RIGID/FLEX ORD/FREE PWR SKILL...SIMUL VAL/FREE 20. PAGE 11 H0223
ASIA POL/PAR DIPLOM USSR

B63
DEUTSCH K.W.,THE NERVES OF GOVERNMENT. NAT/G CREATE EDU/PROP CONTROL LEAD PWR...CONCPT GEN/LAWS 20. PAGE 40 H0799
DECISION GAME SIMUL OP/RES

N63
RUMMEL R.J.,A FOREIGN CONFLICT BEHAVIOR CODE SHEET. ACT/RES DIPLOM...NEW/IDEA CHARTS NAT/COMP. PAGE 136 H2718
QUANT WAR CLASSIF SIMUL

B64
CAPLOW T.,PRINCIPLES OF ORGANIZATION. UNIV CULTURE STRUCT CREATE INGP/REL UTOPIA...GEN/LAWS TIME. PAGE 26 H0526
VOL/ASSN CONCPT SIMUL EX/STRUC

B64
ZOLLSCHAN G.K.,EXPLORATIONS IN SOCIAL CHANGE. SOCIETY STRATA STRUCT ECO/UNDEV EX/STRUC...PSY ANTHOL 20. PAGE 173 H3463
ORD/FREE SIMUL CONCPT CULTURE

B65
EASTON D.,A SYSTEM ANALYSIS OF POLITICAL LIFE. UNIV STRUCT NAT/G FEEDBACK PARTIC PERS/REL EFFICIENCY ...TREND CHARTS METH/COMP 20. PAGE 44 H0881
SIMUL POLICY GEN/METH

B65
HLA MYINT U.,THE ECONOMICS OF THE DEVELOPING COUNTRIES. USA+45 WOR+45 AGRI FINAN NAT/G INT/TRADE ...CLASSIF CENSUS TREND NAT/COMP SIMUL GEN/LAWS. PAGE 71 H1430
ECO/UNDEV FOR/AID GEOG

B65
SVALASTOGA K.,SOCIAL DIFFERENTIATION. CULTURE ELITES SOCIETY MARRIAGE...CONCPT SIMUL. PAGE 151 H3011
SOC STRATA STRUCT GP/REL

L65
LASSWELL H.D.,"THE POLICY SCIENCES OF DEVELOPMENT." CULTURE SOCIETY EX/STRUC CREATE ADMIN ATTIT KNOWL ...SOC CONCPT SIMUL GEN/METH. PAGE 92 H1835
PWR METH/CNCPT DIPLOM

S65
TRISKA J.F.,"SOVIET-AMERICAN RELATIONS* A MULTIPLE SYMMETRY MODEL." USA+45 USSR ACADEM ACT/RES EDU/PROP COERCE PERCEPT...NET/THEORY CHARTS NAT/COMP GEN/LAWS COLD/WAR. PAGE 157 H3132
SIMUL EQUILIB DIPLOM

B66
BROWN R.T.,TRANSPORT AND THE ECONOMIC INTEGRATION OF SOUTH AMERICA. L/A+17C ECO/UNDEV NAT/G OP/RES DIPLOM INT/TRADE REGION WEALTH...ECOMETRIC GEOG STAT LAFTA TIME. PAGE 22 H0449
MARKET DIST/IND SIMUL

B66
FOX K.A.,THE THEORY OF QUANTITATIVE ECONOMIC POLICY WITH APPLICATIONS TO ECONOMIC GROWTH AND STABILIZATION. ECO/DEV AGRI NAT/G PLAN ADMIN RISK ...DECISION IDEA/COMP SIMUL T. PAGE 52 H1045
ECO/TAC ECOMETRIC EQUILIB GEN/LAWS

B67
JOHNSON H.G.,ECONOMIC NATIONALISM IN OLD AND NEW STATES. CANADA CHINA/COM MALI UK DIPLOM...SIMUL GEN/LAWS 19/20 MEXIC/AMER. PAGE 81 H1619
NAT/LISM ECO/UNDEV ECO/DEV NAT/COMP

S67
ALGER C.F.,"INTERNATIONALIZING COLLEGES AND UNIVERSITIES." WOR+45...NAT/COMP SIMUL. PAGE 5 H0104
DIPLOM EDU/PROP ACADEM GP/REL

S67
CATTELL D.T.,"A NEO-MARXIST THEORY OF COMPARATIVE ANALYSIS." USSR STRATA INSPECT DOMIN CONTROL COERCE OWN TOTALISM PWR...FASCIST HYPO/EXP METH 20. PAGE 28 H0561
GOV/COMP MARXISM SIMUL CLASSIF

SIMULATION....SEE SIMUL, MODELS INDEX

SINAI I.R. H2881

SINAI....SINAI

SIND....SIND - REGION OF PAKISTAN

SINGAPORE....SINGAPORE; SEE ALSO MALAYSIA

S66
GAMER R.E.,"URGENT SINGAPORE, PATIENT MALAYSIA." MALAYSIA S/ASIA ECO/UNDEV POL/PAR CHIEF TARIFFS TAX CONTROL LEAD REGION PWR 20 SINGAPORE. PAGE 55 H1094 DIPLOM NAT/G POLICY ECO/TAC

B67
MILNE R.S.,GOVERNMENT AND POLITICS IN MALAYSIA. INDONESIA MALAYSIA LOC/G EX/STRUC FORCES DIPLOM GP/REL 20 SINGAPORE. PAGE 111 H2217 NAT/G LEGIS ADMIN

SINGER K. H2882

SINGER M.R. H2883

SINGH B. H2884

SINGH H.L. H2885

SINGTON D. H2524,H2886

SINO/SOV....SINO-SOVIET RELATIONSHIPS

SINO-SOVIET RELATIONS....SEE SINO/SOV

SINOR D. H2887

SINYAVSK/A....ANDREY SINYAVSKY

SIPPEL D. H2888

SIRSIKAR V.M. H2889

SIRS....SALARY INFORMATION RETRIEVAL SYSTEM

SISSON C.H. H2890

SISSONS C.B. H2891

SITHOLE N. H2892

SKALWEIT S. H2893

SKILL....DEXTERITY

B00
DE JOMINI A.H.,THE ART OF WAR. MOD/EUR NAT/G BAL/PWR DIPLOM DOMIN EXEC ROUTINE COERCE DRIVE PWR SKILL...POLICY CONCPT CHARTS STERTYP 19. PAGE 38 H0755 PLAN FORCES WAR WEAPON

B00
OMAN C.,A HISTORY OF THE ART OF WAR: THE MIDDLE AGES FROM THE FOURTH TO THE FOURTEENTH CENTURY. CHRIST-17C MEDIT-7 CULTURE SOCIETY INT/ORG ROUTINE PERSON...CONT/OBS HIST/WRIT CHARTS VAL/FREE. PAGE 121 H2417 FORCES SKILL WAR

B05
MACHIAVELLI N.,THE ART OF WAR. CHRIST-17C TOP/EX DRIVE ORD/FREE PWR SKILL...MGT CHARTS. PAGE 100 H1993 NAT/G FORCES WAR ITALY

B14
BERNHARDI F.,ON THE WAR OF TODAY. MOD/EUR INT/ORG NAT/G TOP/EX PWR CHARTS. PAGE 16 H0313 FORCES SKILL WAR

N19
GRIFFITH W.,THE PUBLIC SERVICE (PAMPHLET). UK LAW LOC/G NAT/G PARTIC CHOOSE DRIVE ROLE SKILL...CHARTS 20 CIVIL/SERV. PAGE 61 H1222 ADMIN EFFICIENCY EDU/PROP GOV/REL

B25
TEMPERLEY H.,THE FOREIGN POLICY OF CANNING: 1822-1827. MOD/EUR NAT/G TOP/EX EDU/PROP ROUTINE ATTIT RIGID/FLEX SUPEGO PWR SKILL...TIME/SEQ PARLIAMENT 20. PAGE 153 H3058 PERSON DIPLOM UK BIOG

B28
YANG KUNG-SUN,THE BOOK OF LORD SHANG. LAW ECO/UNDEV LOC/G NAT/G NEIGH PLAN ECO/TAC LEGIT ATTIT SKILL ...CONCPT CON/ANAL WORK TOT/POP. PAGE 172 H3434 ASIA JURID

B45
HUNTINGTON E.,MAINSPRINGS OF CIVILIZATION. UNIV CULTURE SOCIETY BIO/SOC PERSON KNOWL SKILL...PSY RECORD HIST/WRIT TREND CHARTS TOT/POP. PAGE 75 H1504 SOC GEOG

B53
NELSON G.R.,FREEDOM AND WELFARE: SOCIAL PATTERNS IN THE NORTHERN COUNTRIES OF EUROPE. EUR+WWI ECO/DEV NAT/G EDU/PROP LEGIT HEALTH ORD/FREE SKILL WEALTH ...STAT AUD/VIS SCANDINAV WORK TOT/POP 20. PAGE 116 H2329 PLAN ECO/TAC

S55
GLADSTONE A.E.,"THE POSSIBILITY OF PREDICTING REACTIONS TO INTERNATIONAL EVENTS." UNIV SOCIETY NAT/G FORCES CREATE EDU/PROP COERCE WAR ATTIT PERSON KNOWL PWR SKILL...METH/CNCPT NEW/IDEA ORG/CHARTS. PAGE 57 H1139 PHIL/SCI CONCPT

B56
SMEDLEY A.,THE GREAT ROAD: THE LIFE AND TIMES OF CHU TEH. ASIA USSR NAT/G POL/PAR DIPLOM COERCE GUERRILLA CIVMIL/REL NAT/LISM PERSON SKILL MARXISM ...BIOG 20 CHINJAP MAO. PAGE 145 H2903 REV WAR FORCES

S57
DEXTER L.A.,"A SOCIAL THEORY OF MENTAL DEFICIENCY." CULTURE PUB/INST PROB/SOLV CRIME PERS/REL STRANGE PERSON SUPEGO SKILL...EPIST SOC/WK HYPO/EXP. PAGE 41 H0814 SOC PSY HEALTH ROLE

B58
MECRENSKY E.,SCIENTIFIC MANPOWER IN EUROPE. WOR+45 EDU/PROP GOV/REL SKILL...TECHNIC PHIL/SCI INT CHARTS BIBLIOG 20. PAGE 108 H2157 ECO/TAC TEC/DEV METH/COMP NAT/COMP

B60
LINDSAY K.,EUROPEAN ASSEMBLIES: THE EXPERIMENTAL PERIOD 1949-1959. EUR+WWI ECO/DEV NAT/G POL/PAR LEGIS TOP/EX ACT/RES PLAN ECO/TAC DOMIN LEGIT ROUTINE ATTIT DRIVE ORD/FREE PWR SKILL...SOC CONCPT TREND CHARTS GEN/LAWS VAL/FREE. PAGE 97 H1932 VOL/ASSN INT/ORG REGION

B60
MOORE W.E.,LABOR COMMITMENT AND SOCIAL CHANGE IN DEVELOPING AREAS. SOCIETY STRATA ECO/UNDEV MARKET VOL/ASSN WORKER AUTHORIT SKILL...MGT NAT/COMP SOC/INTEG 20. PAGE 113 H2250 LABOR ORD/FREE ATTIT INDUS

S60
RIVKIN A.,"AFRICAN ECONOMIC DEVELOPMENT: ADVANCED TECHNOLOGY AND THE STAGES OF GROWTH." CULTURE ECO/UNDEV AGRI COM/IND EXTR/IND PLAN ECO/TAC ATTIT DRIVE RIGID/FLEX SKILL WEALTH...MGT SOC GEN/LAWS WORK TOT/POP 20. PAGE 132 H2634 AFR TEC/DEV FOR/AID

B62
VALERIANO N.D.,COUNTER-GUERRILLA OPERATIONS: THE PHILLIPINE EXPERIENCE. NAT/G CONSULT ACT/RES PLAN COERCE GUERRILLA ATTIT ORD/FREE PWR SKILL...GEOG NEW/IDEA TIME/SEQ CHARTS 20. PAGE 161 H3221 S/ASIA FORCES PHILIPPINE

B63
BARNETT A.D.,COMMUNIST STRATEGIES IN ASIA: A COMPARATIVE ANALYSIS OF GOVERNMENTS AND PARTIES. COM FUT S/ASIA CULTURE SOCIETY STRATA NAT/G DELIB/GP ACT/RES ECO/TAC EDU/PROP COERCE CHOOSE ATTIT RIGID/FLEX ORD/FREE PWR SKILL...SIMUL VAL/FREE 20. PAGE 11 H0223 ASIA POL/PAR DIPLOM USSR

B63
GORDON M.S.,THE ECONOMICS OF WELFARE POLICIES. INDUS LOC/G NAT/G LEGIS WORKER INCOME AGE/O SKILL WEALTH...METH/COMP NAT/COMP 20. PAGE 59 H1180 METH/CNCPT ECO/TAC POLICY

B63
KHADDURI M.,MODERN LIBYA: A STUDY IN POLITICAL DEVELOPMENT. EUR+WWI ISLAM LIBYA ELITES INT/ORG POL/PAR FORCES DIPLOM FOR/AID DOMIN EDU/PROP LEGIT NAT/LISM DRIVE RIGID/FLEX SKILL...CONCPT TIME/SEQ TREND 20. PAGE 85 H1704 NAT/G STRUCT

B63
KOGAN N.,THE POLITICS OF ITALIAN FOREIGN POLICY. EUR+WWI LEGIS DOMIN LEGIT EXEC PWR RESPECT SKILL ...POLICY DECISION HUM SOC METH/CNCPT OBS INT CHARTS 20. PAGE 87 H1737 NAT/G ROUTINE DIPLOM ITALY

B63
KRAEHE E.,METTERNICH'S GERMAN POLICY: THE CONTEST WITH NAPOLEON, 1799-1814, VOL. 1. FRANCE MOD/EUR NAT/G CONSULT TOP/EX PLAN BAL/PWR DOMIN COERCE ATTIT DRIVE PERCEPT PERSON SKILL...CONCPT RECORD TIME/SEQ TREND 18/19. PAGE 88 H1764 BIOG GERMANY DIPLOM

B63
US ATOMIC ENERGY COMMISSION,ATOMIC ENERGY IN THE SOVIET UNION: TRIP REPORT OF THE US ATOMIC ENERGY DELEGATION, MAY 1933. USSR R+D NAT/G CONSULT CREATE DIPLOM ADMIN ROUTINE EFFICIENCY PRODUC KNOWL SKILL ...NAT/COMP 20 AEC TRAVEL TREATY. PAGE 159 H3176 METH/COMP OP/RES TEC/DEV NUC/PWR

L63
ROSE R.,"COMPARATIVE STUDIES IN POLITICAL FINANCE: A SYMPOSIUM." ASIA EUR+WWI S/ASIA LAW CULTURE DELIB/GP LEGIS ACT/RES ECO/TAC EDU/PROP CHOOSE ATTIT RIGID/FLEX SUPEGO PWR SKILL WEALTH...STAT ANTHOL VAL/FREE. PAGE 134 H2674 FINAN POL/PAR

S63
ROUGEMONT D.,"LES NOUVELLES CHANCES DE L'EUROPE." EUR+WWI FUT ECO/DEV INT/ORG NAT/G ACT/RES PLAN TEC/DEV EDU/PROP ADMIN COLONIAL FEDERAL ATTIT PWR SKILL...TREND 20. PAGE 135 H2696 ECO/UNDEV PERCEPT

B64
HARBISON F.H.,EDUCATION, MANPOWER, AND ECONOMIC GROWTH. WOR+45 ECO/DEV ECO/UNDEV ACADEM LABOR SCHOOL WORKER UTIL...IDEA/COMP NAT/COMP. PAGE 66 H1326 PLAN TEC/DEV EDU/PROP SKILL

B64
SOLOW R.M.,THE NATURE AND SOURCES OF UNEMPLOYMENT IN THE UNITED STATES (PAMPHLET). USA+45 INDUS LABOR TEC/DEV ECO/TAC SKILL WEALTH...TREND NAT/COMP 20. PAGE 147 H2930 ECO/DEV WORKER STAT PRODUC

S64
CLIGNET R.,"POTENTIAL ELITES IN GHANA AND THE IVORY COAST: A PRELIMINARY SURVEY." AFR CULTURE ELITES PWR LEGIT

STRATA KIN NAT/G SECT DOMIN EXEC ORD/FREE RESPECT SKILL...POLICY RELATIV GP/COMP NAT/COMP 20. PAGE 30 H0605 — IVORY/CST GHANA

S64
MC WILLIAM M.,"THE WORLD BANK AND THE TRANSFER OF POWER IN KENYA." AFR ECO/UNDEV CONSULT ACT/RES TEC/DEV PERCEPT PWR SKILL WEALTH...CONCPT OBS TREND 20. PAGE 106 H2119 — NAT/G ECO/TAC

S64
RUDOLPH L.I.,"GENERALS AND POLITICIANS IN INDIA." INDIA S/ASIA CULTURE STRATA NAT/G LEGIS TOP/EX EDU/PROP ATTIT ORD/FREE PWR RESPECT SKILL...POLICY BIOG TIME/SEQ STERTYP VAL/FREE 20. PAGE 136 H2713 — FORCES COERCE

S64
SCHEFFLER H.W.,"THE GENESIS AND REPRESSION OF CONFLICT: CHOISEUL ISLAND." S/ASIA LOC/G NAT/G FORCES LEGIS DIPLOM DOMIN LEGIT EXEC CHOOSE ATTIT RESPECT SKILL...POLICY JURID OBS TREND GEN/METH 20. PAGE 139 H2781 — PWR COERCE WAR

B65
GOULD J.,PENGUIN SURVEY OF THE SOCIAL SCIENCES* 1965. CULTURE SOCIETY R+D FAM KIN MUNIC ACT/RES DIPLOM SKILL. PAGE 59 H1186 — SOC PHIL/SCI USSR UK

B65
HARBISON F.,MANPOWER AND EDUCATION. AFR CHINA/COM IRAN L/A+17C S/ASIA TEC/DEV ADJUST OPTIMAL SKILL ...ANTHOL 20. PAGE 66 H1325 — ECO/UNDEV EDU/PROP WORKER NAT/COMP

L65
WIONCZEK M.,"LATIN AMERICA FREE TRADE ASSOCIATION." AGRI DIST/IND FINAN INDUS INT/ORG LABOR NAT/G TEC/DEV ECO/TAC HEALTH SKILL WEALTH...POLICY RELATIV MGT LAFTA 20. PAGE 169 H3390 — L/A+17C MARKET REGION

S65
GRIFFITH S.B.,"COMMUNIST CHINA'S CAPACITY TO MAKE WAR." CHINA/COM COM NAT/G TOP/EX PLAN DOMIN COERCE NUC/PWR ATTIT RESPECT SKILL...CONCPT MYTH TIME/SEQ TREND COLD/WAR 20. PAGE 61 H1221 — FORCES PWR WEAPON ASIA

S65
TENDLER J.D.,"TECHNOLOGY AND ECONOMIC DEVELOPMENT* THE CASE OF HYDRO VS THERMAL POWER." CONSTRUC DIST/IND CREATE TEC/DEV INT/TRADE CENTRAL PWR SKILL WEALTH...MGT NAT/COMP ARGEN. PAGE 153 H3061 — BRAZIL INDUS ECO/UNDEV

B66
HAHN C.H.L.,THE NATIVE TRIBES OF SOUTH WEST AFRICA. LAW FAM SECT HABITAT SKILL...SOC AUD/VIS WORSHIP RITUAL 20 AFRICA/SW. PAGE 64 H1275 — CULTURE SOCIETY STRUCT AFR

S66
LODGE G.C.,"REVOLUTION IN LATIN AMERICA." USA+45 ELITES INDUS LABOR PROF/ORG SECT TEC/DEV CAP/ISM SKILL MARXISM...POLICY NAT/COMP. PAGE 98 H1950 — ATTIT REV L/A+17C IDEA/COMP

S66
TURKEVICH J.,"SOVIET SCIENCE APPRAISED." USA+45 R+D ACADEM FORCES DIPLOM EDU/PROP WAR EFFICIENCY PEACE SKILL OBS. PAGE 157 H3137 — USSR TEC/DEV NAT/COMP ATTIT

B67
KENNETT L.,THE FRENCH ARMIES IN THE SEVEN YEARS' WAR. FRANCE NAT/G CONTROL LEAD WAR CIVMIL/REL EFFICIENCY ATTIT PWR SKILL CONSERVE 18. PAGE 85 H1690 — FORCES CHIEF METH/COMP

B67
MACRIDIS R.C.,FOREIGN POLICY IN WORLD POLITICS (3RD ED.). EX/STRUC BAL/PWR COLONIAL NAT/LISM SKILL SOVEREIGN WEALTH...CONCPT TIME/SEQ ANTHOL 20 COLD/WAR. PAGE 101 H2011 — DIPLOM POLICY NAT/G IDEA/COMP

S67
EPSTEIN E.H.,"NATIONAL IDENTITY AND THE LANGUAGE ISSUE IN PUERTO RICO." PUERT/RICO CULTURE STRUCT NAT/G PROB/SOLV SKILL...JURID STAT METH/COMP 20. PAGE 47 H0931 — EDU/PROP SCHOOL LING NAT/LISM

SKILLING H.G. H2894,H2895,H2896

SKINNER E.P. H2897

SKLAR R.L. H2898

SLATER J. H2899

SLAV/MACED....SLAVO-MACEDONIANS

B61
BURKS R.V.,THE DYNAMICS OF COMMUNISM IN EASTERN EUROPE. COM YUGOSLAVIA POL/PAR RACE/REL ISOLAT ...CORREL CON/ANAL CHARTS GP/COMP DICTIONARY 20 EUROPE/E SLAV/MACED. PAGE 24 H0489 — MARXISM STRUCT WORKER REPRESENT

SLAVERY....SEE ORD/FREE, DOMIN

SLAVS....SLAVS - PERTAINING TO THE SLAVIC PEOPLE AND SLAVOPHILISM

B64
UTECHIN S.V.,RUSSIAN POLITICAL THOUGHT: A CONCISE HISTORY. RUSSIA USSR INTELL STRATA POL/PAR SECT LEGIS EDU/PROP REV WAR MARXISM...ANARCH BIBLIOG 9/20 REFORMERS SLAVS. PAGE 161 H3218 — IDEA/COMP ATTIT ALL/IDEOS NAT/G

SLEEP....SLEEPING AND FATIGUE

SLOAN P. H2900

SLOTKIN J.S. H2901,H2902

SLUMS....SLUMS

SMALL BUSINESS ADMINISTRATION....SEE SBA

SMEDLEY A. H2903

SMELSER N.J. H2904

SMITH A. H2905

SMITH A.A. H0662

SMITH D.D. H2906

SMITH E.W. H2907,H2908

SMITH G. H2909

SMITH H.E. H2910

SMITH J.E. H2911,H2912,H2913

SMITH M.G. H2914,H2915

SMITH M.W. H2754

SMITH P. H2916

SMITH R.M. H2917

SMITH T.E. H2918

SMITH T.V. H2919,H2920

SMITH/ACT....SMITH ACT

SMITH/ADAM....ADAM SMITH

SMITH/ALF....ALFRED E. SMITH

SMITH/IAN....IAN SMITH

SMITH/JOS....JOSEPH SMITH

SMITH/LEVR....SMITH-LEVER ACT

SML/CO....SMALL COMPANY

B58
MCIVOR R.C.,CANADIAN MONETARY, BANKING, AND FISCAL DEVELOPMENT. CANADA INDUS LG/CO NAT/G SML/CO CONTROL WAR...GEN/LAWS BIBLIOG 17/20. PAGE 107 H2137 — ECO/TAC FINAN ECO/DEV WEALTH

B59
FAYERWEATHER J.,THE EXECUTIVE OVERSEAS: ADMINISTRATIVE ATTITUDES AND RELATIONSHIPS IN A FOREIGN CULTURE. USA+45 WOR+45 CULTURE LG/CO SML/CO ATTIT...MGT PERS/COMP 20 MEXIC/AMER. PAGE 49 H0979 — INT/TRADE TOP/EX NAT/COMP PERS/REL

L61
LEVINE R.A.,"THE ANTHROPOLOGY OF CONFLICT." FUT CULTURE INTELL FAM INT/ORG LG/CO SML/CO ATTIT KNOWL ...METH/CNCPT VAL/FREE 20. PAGE 95 H1905 — SOCIETY ACT/RES

S67
BOSHER J.F.,"GOVERNMENT AND PRIVATE INTERESTS IN NEW FRANCE." CANADA FRANCE INDUS LG/CO SML/CO CAP/ISM INT/TRADE COLONIAL GP/REL...HIST/WRIT 17/18. PAGE 19 H0381 — NAT/G FINAN ADMIN CONTROL

S67
GAMARNIKOW M.,"THE NEW ROLE OF PRIVATE ENTERPRISE." ECO/DEV INDUS NAT/G SML/CO CREATE PROB/SOLV MARXISM ...POLICY TREND IDEA/COMP 20. PAGE 55 H1092 — ECO/TAC ATTIT CAP/ISM COM

S67
TAYLOR P.B. JR.,"PROGRESS IN VENEZUELA." L/A+17C VENEZUELA AGRI INDUS LG/CO NAT/G SML/CO CHOOSE ...POLICY 20. PAGE 153 H3057 — ECO/UNDEV ECO/TAC POL/PAR ORD/FREE

B82
CUNNINGHAM W.,THE GROWTH OF ENGLISH INDUSTRY AND COMMERCE. FUT UK FINAN NAT/G CAP/ISM...POLICY 20 MERCANTLST CHRISTIAN POPE. PAGE 36 H0721 — INDUS INT/TRADE SML/CO CONSERVE

SMUTS J.C. H2921

SMUTS/JAN....JAN CHRISTIAN SMUTS

B30
OLDMAN J.H.,WHITE AND BLACK IN AFRICA. AFR STRUCT COLONIAL PARTIC DISCRIM ISOLAT PRIVIL 20 SMUTS/JAN NEGRO WHITE/SUP. PAGE 121 H2412 SOVEREIGN ORD/FREE RACE/REL NAT/G

SMYTHE H.H. H2922

SNCC....STUDENT NONVIOLENT COORDINATING COMMITTEE; SEE ALSO STUDNT/PWR

SNELLEN I.T. H2923

SNOW P.G. H2924

SOARES G. H2925

SOBEL L.A. H2926

SOC....SOCIOLOGY

SOC/DEMPAR....SOCIAL DEMOCRATIC PARTY (USE WITH SPECIFIC NATION)

B53
BARZEL R.,DIE DEUTSCHEN PARTEIEN. GERMANY MARXISM SOCISM...CONCPT IDEA/COMP 19/20 SOC/DEMPAR CHRIS/DEM. PAGE 12 H0232 POL/PAR NAT/G LAISSEZ

B65
EDINGER L.J.,KURT SCHUMACHER: A STUDY IN PERSONALITY AND POLITICAL BEHAVIOR. EUR+WWI GERMANY NAT/G DRIVE ROLE PWR SOCISM...BIBLIOG 20 SOC/DEMPAR SCHUMCHR/K. PAGE 44 H0889 TOP/EX LEAD PERSON BIOG

B66
COLE A.B.,SOCIALIST PARTIES IN POSTWAR JAPAN. STRATA AGRI LABOR PLAN DIPLOM ECO/TAC AGREE LEAD CHOOSE ATTIT...CHARTS 20 CHINJAP SOC/DEMPAR. PAGE 31 H0620 POL/PAR POLICY SOCISM NAT/G

S67
DESHPANDE A.M.,"FEDERAL-STATE FISCAL RELATIONS IN INDIA" (REVIEW ARTICLE)" GERMANY USSR DELIB/GP PLAN BUDGET ECO/TAC INCOME 20 SOC/DEMPAR SOC/REVPAR. PAGE 40 H0795 FINAN NAT/G GOV/REL TAX

SOC/EXP...."SOCIAL" EXPERIMENTATION UNDER UNCONTROLLED CONDITIONS

B28
BUELL R.,THE NATIVE PROBLEM IN AFRICA. KIN LABOR LOC/G ECO/TAC ROUTINE ORD/FREE...REC/INT KNO/TEST CENSUS TREND CHARTS SOC/EXP STERTYP 20. PAGE 23 H0466 AFR CULTURE

B50
CANTRIL H.,TENSIONS THAT CAUSE WAR. UNIV CULTURE R+D CREATE EDU/PROP DRIVE PERSON KNOWL ORD/FREE ...HUM PSY SOC OBS CENSUS TREND CON/ANAL SOC/EXP SIMUL GEN/METH ANTHOL COLD/WAR TOT/POP. PAGE 26 H0523 SOCIETY PHIL/SCI PEACE

B50
LIPSET S.M.,AGRARIAN SOCIALISM. CANADA POL/PAR OP/RES ECO/TAC ADMIN ATTIT...TIME/SEQ NAT/COMP SOC/EXP 20 SASKATCH. PAGE 97 H1938 SOCISM AGRI METH/COMP STRUCT

B53
WAGLEY C.,AMAZON TOWN: A STUDY OF MAN IN THE TROPICS. BRAZIL L/A+17C STRATA STRUCT ECO/UNDEV AGRI EX/STRUC RACE/REL DISCRIM HABITAT WEALTH...OBS SOC/EXP 20. PAGE 164 H3285 SOC NEIGH CULTURE INGP/REL

S54
DODD S.C.,"THE SCIENTIFIC MEASUREMENT OF FITNESS FOR SELF-GOVERNMENT." FUT CONSTN ECO/UNDEV INT/ORG PLAN PWR...CONCPT QUANT CON/ANAL SOC/EXP UN LEAGUE/NAT 20. PAGE 41 H0830 NAT/G STAT SOVEREIGN

B59
DUNHAM H.W.,SOCIOLOGICAL THEORY AND MENTAL DISORDER. UNIV SOCIETY STRATA HABITAT PERSON...GEOG CHARTS SOC/EXP TIME. PAGE 43 H0864 HEALTH SOC PSY CULTURE

S59
LEVINE R.A.,"ANTI-EUROPEAN VIOLENCE IN AFRICA: A COMPARATIVE ANALYSIS." AFR CULTURE NAT/G DIPLOM EDU/PROP COLONIAL REGION COERCE ATTIT PWR...PSY CONCPT TIME/SEQ TREND HYPO/EXP SOC/EXP STERTYP GEN/METH COLD/WAR 20. PAGE 95 H1903 DRIVE ORD/FREE REV

B63
CONFERENCE ABORIGINAL STUDIES,AUSTRALIAN ABORIGINAL STUDIES. ECO/UNDEV INT/TRADE COLONIAL ADJUST HABITAT HEREDITY...GEOG PSY LING SOC/EXP ANTHOL WORSHIP 20 AUSTRAL ABORIGINES. PAGE 32 H0638 SOC SOCIETY CULTURE STRUCT

B63
LEIGHTON D.C.,THE CHARACTER OF DANGER (VOL. III). SOCIETY STRUCT STRANGE ANOMIE...SOC STAT CHARTS GP/COMP SOC/EXP SOC/INTEG 20 NOVA/SCOT. PAGE 94 H1868 HEALTH PSY CULTURE

B63
MONTAGUE J.B. JR.,CLASS AND NATIONALITY; ENGLISH AND AMERICAN STUDIES. UK USA+45 ELITES STRUCT WORKER ATTIT PWR...SOC CHARTS SOC/EXP 20. PAGE 112 H2243 STRATA NAT/LISM PERSON NAT/COMP

B63
ROBERTSON A.H.,HUMAN RIGHTS IN EUROPE. CONSTN SOCIETY INT/ORG NAT/G VOL/ASSN DELIB/GP ACT/RES PLAN ADJUD REGION ROUTINE ATTIT LOVE ORD/FREE RESPECT...JURID SOC CONCPT SOC/EXP UN 20. PAGE 132 H2645 EUR+WWI PERSON

B65
NYE J.S. JR.,PAN-AFRICANISM AND EAST AFRICAN INTEGRATION. TANZANIA UGANDA STRUCT ECO/UNDEV NAT/G DIPLOM FEDERAL NAT/LISM...STAT SOC/EXP BIBLIOG EEC OAU. PAGE 119 H2382 REGION ATTIT GEN/LAWS AFR

B66
CAPELL A.,STUDIES IN SOCIO-LINGUISTICS. CULTURE ADJUST...CLASSIF IDEA/COMP SOC/EXP BIBLIOG 20. PAGE 26 H0525 LING SOC PHIL/SCI CORREL

B66
FARRELL R.B.,APPROACHES TO COMPARATIVE AND INTERNATIONAL POLITICS. RUSSIA SOCIETY ACADEM GOV/REL GP/REL...METH/CNCPT NET/THEORY GOV/COMP HYPO/EXP SOC/EXP GEN/METH ANTHOL. PAGE 49 H0973 DIPLOM NAT/COMP NAT/G

B66
HOYT E.C.,NATIONAL POLICY AND INTERNATIONAL LAW* CASE STUDIES FROM AMERICAN CANAL POLICY* MONOGRAPH NO. 1 -- 1966-1967. PANAMA UK ELITES BAL/PWR EFFICIENCY...CLASSIF NAT/COMP SOC/EXP COLOMB TREATY. PAGE 74 H1483 INT/LAW USA-45 DIPLOM PWR

B66
THIESENHUSEN W.C.,CHILE'S EXPERIMENTS IN AGRARIAN REFORM. CHILE STRUCT NAT/G ACT/RES ECO/TAC GOV/REL COST SOCISM...TREND CHARTS SOC/EXP 20. PAGE 154 H3073 AGRI ECO/UNDEV SOC TEC/DEV

S66
HAIGH G.,"FIELD TRAINING IN HUMAN RELATIONS FOR THE PEACE CORPS." CONSULT CREATE EDU/PROP ADMIN TASK GP/REL ATTIT PERSON...PSY OBS SOC/EXP PEACE/CORP. PAGE 64 H1276 CULTURE PERS/REL FOR/AID ADJUST

B67
KORNBERG A.,CANADIAN LEGISLATIVE BEHAVIOR: A STUDY OF THE 25TH PARLIAMENT. CANADA NAT/G POL/PAR PARL/PROC CHOOSE INGP/REL ADJUST ANOMIE RIGID/FLEX ...SOC STAND/INT CHARTS SOC/EXP 20 PARLIAMENT. PAGE 88 H1756 ATTIT LEGIS ROLE

B67
NASH M.,MACHINE AGE MAYA. GUATEMALA L/A+17C STRUCT AGRI WORKER CREATE INCOME ATTIT RIGID/FLEX ROLE ...IDEA/COMP SOC/EXP WORSHIP 20 INDIAN/AM. PAGE 116 H2315 INDUS CULTURE SOC MUNIC

SOC/INTEG....SOCIAL INTEGRATION; SEE ALSO CONSEN, RACE/REL

B14
OPPENHEIMER F.,THE STATE. FUT SOCIETY STRATA STRUCT WORKER CAP/ISM WAR GP/REL SOCISM...SOC NAT/COMP SOC/INTEG. PAGE 121 H2424 ELITES OWN DOMIN NAT/G

B22
OGBURN W.F.,SOCIAL CHANGE WITH RESPECT TO CULTURE AND ORIGINAL NATURE. ACT/RES OP/RES CRIME GP/REL ANOMIE BIO/SOC PWR...PSY SOC TIME/SEQ METH SOC/INTEG. PAGE 120 H2405 CULTURE CREATE TEC/DEV

B26
HOCKING W.E.,PRESENT STATUS OF THE PHILOSOPHY OF LAW AND OF RIGHTS. UNIV CULTURE INTELL SOCIETY NAT/G CREATE LEGIT SANCTION ALL/VALS SOC/INTEG 18/20. PAGE 72 H1442 JURID PHIL/SCI ORD/FREE

B35
NORDSKOG J.E.,SOCIAL REFORM IN NORWAY. NORWAY INDUS NAT/G POL/PAR LEGIS ADJUD...SOC BIBLIOG SOC/INTEG 20. PAGE 119 H2371 LABOR ADJUST

B36
RAPPARD W.E.,THE GOVERNMENT OF SWITZERLAND. SWITZERLND INT/ORG POL/PAR EX/STRUC DIPLOM NEUTRAL PARL/PROC REGION WAR HABITAT SOVEREIGN...NAT/COMP SOC/INTEG 20 LEAGUE/NAT WWI. PAGE 130 H2594 CONSTN NAT/G CULTURE FEDERAL

C41
KLUCKHOHN C.,"PATTERNING AS EXEMPLIFIED IN NAVAHO CULTURE" IN EDWARD SAPIR, LANGUAGE, CULTURE, AND PERSONALITY (BMR)" KIN PERS/REL ATTIT PERSON...SOC CONCPT METH/CNCPT LING OBS/ENVIR CON/ANAL BIBLIOG SOC/INTEG 20 NAVAHO INDIAN/AM SAPIR/EDW. PAGE 87 H1733 CULTURE INGP/REL STRUCT

B46
BIRKET-SMITH K.A.J.,GESCHICHTE DER KULTUR (3RD ED., TRANS. BY HANS DIETSCHY). KIN...GP/COMP SOC/INTEG. PAGE 17 H0339 CULTURE SOC CONCPT

B48
COX O.C.,CASTE, CLASS, AND RACE. INDIA WOR+45 WOR-45 SECT TEC/DEV MARRIAGE ROLE MARXISM...MAJORIT NAT/COMP SOC/INTEG 20 NEGRO HINDU. PAGE 34 H0688 RACE/REL STRUCT STRATA DISCRIM

B48
EDUARDO O.D.C.,THE NEGRO IN NORTHERN BRAZIL: A STUDY IN ACCULTURATION. BRAZIL ECO/UNDEV FAM SECT PAY REGION HABITAT CATHISM MYSTISM...GEOG OBS SOC/INTEG WORSHIP 20 NEGRO MARANHAO. PAGE 44 H0890
CULTURE ADJUST GP/REL

B48
TOWSTER J.,POLITICAL POWER IN THE USSR: 1917-1947. USSR CONSTN CULTURE ELITES CREATE PLAN COERCE CENTRAL ATTIT RIGID/FLEX ORD/FREE...BIBLIOG SOC/INTEG 20 LENIN/VI STALIN/J. PAGE 156 H3122
EX/STRUC NAT/G MARXISM PWR

B49
HOLLERAN M.P.,CHURCH AND STATE IN GUATEMALA. GUATEMALA LAW STRUCT CATHISM...SOC SOC/INTEG 17/20 CHURCH/STA. PAGE 73 H1456
SECT NAT/G GP/REL CULTURE

B49
MAO TSE-TUNG,NEW DEMOCRACY. CHINA/COM NAT/G DIPLOM ECO/TAC EDU/PROP REV...CONCPT METH SOC/INTEG 20. PAGE 102 H2045
SOCISM MARXISM POPULISM CULTURE

S49
HUGHES E.C.,"SOCIAL CHANGE AND STATUS PROTEST: AN ESSAY ON THE MARGINAL MAN" (BMR)" EUR+WWI UK USA+45 CULTURE SOCIETY STRUCT RACE/REL...SOC NAT/COMP SOC/INTEG 19/20 NEGRO PARK/R. PAGE 74 H1490
STRATA ATTIT DISCRIM

B51
PARSONS T.,TOWARD A GENERAL THEORY OF ACTION. CULTURE PERSON...PSY SIMUL ANTHOL SOC/INTEG 20. PAGE 124 H2472
SOC PHIL/SCI DRIVE ACT/RES

B52
CALLOT E.,LA SOCIETE ET SON ENVIRONNEMENT: ESSAI SUR LES PRINCIPES DES SCIENCES SOCIALES. GP/REL ADJUST CONSEN ISOLAT HABITAT PERCEPT PERSON ...BIBLIOG SOC/INTEG 20. PAGE 25 H0507
SOCIETY PHIL/SCI CULTURE

S52
EISENSTADT S.N.,"THE PROCESS OF ABSORPTION OF NEW IMMIGRANTS IN ISRAEL" (BMR)" ISRAEL CULTURE SCHOOL WORKER PARTIC DRIVE ORD/FREE...STAT OBS INT CHARTS SOC/INTEG 20 JEWS. PAGE 45 H0900
HABITAT ATTIT SAMP

L53
DEUTSCH K.W.,"THE GROWTH OF NATIONS: SOME RECURRENT PATTERNS OF POLITICAL AND SOCIAL INTEGRATION" (BMR)" UNIV CULTURE SOCIETY ECO/DEV ECO/UNDEV NAT/G CREATE GP/REL...CONCPT GEN/LAWS SOC/INTEG 11/20. PAGE 40 H0797
TREND NAT/LISM ORD/FREE

B54
SPROTT W.J.H.,SCIENCE AND SOCIAL ACTION. STRUCT ACT/RES CRIME GP/REL INGP/REL ANOMIE...PSY SOC/INTEG 19/20. PAGE 148 H2956
SOC CULTURE PHIL/SCI

S54
ALBRECT M.C.,"THE RELATIONSHIP OF LITERATURE AND SOCIETY." STRATA STRUCT DIPLOM...POLICY SOC/INTEG. PAGE 5 H0097
HUM CULTURE WRITING NAT/COMP

B55
STEWARD J.H.,THEORY OF CULTURE CHANGE; THE METHODOLOGY OF MULTILINEAR EVOLUTION. SOCIETY KIN SECT GP/REL INGP/REL...BIBLIOG SOC/INTEG 20. PAGE 149 H2984
CULTURE CONCPT METH/COMP HABITAT

B56
SYKES G.M.,CRIME AND SOCIETY. LAW STRATA STRUCT ACT/RES ROUTINE ANOMIE WEALTH...POLICY SOC/INTEG 20. PAGE 151 H3021
CRIMLGY CRIME CULTURE INGP/REL

B56
VIANNA F.J.,EVOLUCAO DE POVO BRASILEIRO (4TH ED.). BRAZIL TEC/DEV COLONIAL GP/REL ATTIT SOVEREIGN ...SOC SOC/INTEG 15/20. PAGE 162 H3247
STRUCT RACE/REL NAT/G

S56
BLAU P.M.,"SOCIAL MOBILITY AND INTERPERSONAL RELATIONS" (BMR)" UNIV CULTURE STRUCT WORKER ANOMIE ...SOC SOC/INTEG 19/20. PAGE 18 H0355
INGP/REL PERS/REL ORD/FREE STRATA

B57
MENDIETTA Y NUNE L.,THEORIE DES GROUPEMENT SOCIAUX SUIVI D'UNE ETUDE SUR LE DROIT SOCIAL. ELITES FAM KIN NAT/G PROB/SOLV CROWD ISOLAT ATTIT PERSON ...JURID CONCPT SOC/INTEG. PAGE 109 H2174
SOC STRATA STRUCT DISCRIM

B58
ALMAGRO BASCH M.,ORIGEN Y FORMACION DEL PUEBLO HISPANO. PREHIST SPAIN REGION WAR RACE/REL HABITAT ORD/FREE...SOC SOC/INTEG 20. PAGE 5 H0109
CULTURE GP/REL ADJUST

B58
GREAVES H.R.,THE FOUNDATIONS OF POLITICAL THEORY. WAR ATTIT SUPEGO ORD/FREE...IDEA/COMP SOC/INTEG. PAGE 60 H1203
CONCPT MORAL PERSON

B59
BUNDESMIN FUR VERTRIEBENE,ZEITTAFEL DER VORGESCHICHTE UND DES ABLAUFS DER VERTREIBUNG SOWIE DER UNTERBRINGUNG UND EINGLIEDERUNG DER (2 VOLS.). GERMANY/E GERMANY/W NAT/G PROVS PROB/SOLV DIPLOM PARL/PROC ATTIT...BIBLIOG SOC/INTEG 20 MIGRATION PARLIAMENT. PAGE 24 H0475
JURID GP/REL INT/LAW

B59
LIPSET S.M.,SOCIAL MOBILITY IN INDUSTRIAL SOCIETY. EUR+WWI USA+45 USSR STRUCT INDUS WRITING GP/REL INGP/REL DRIVE...SOC CHARTS NAT/COMP SOC/INTEG 20 MARX/KARL ENGELS/F. PAGE 97 H1940
STRATA ECO/DEV SOCIETY

B59
ROCHE J.,LA COLONISATION ALLEMANDE ET LE RIO GRANDE DO SUL. BRAZIL L/A+17C NAT/G PROVS INGP/REL RACE/REL DISCRIM HABITAT...GEOG SOC/INTEG 19/20 MIGRATION. PAGE 133 H2652
ECO/UNDEV GP/REL ATTIT

S59
DUNCAN O.D.,"CULTURAL, BEHAVIORAL, AND ECOLOGICAL PERSPECTIVES IN THE STUDY OF SOCIAL ORGANIZATION" (BMR)" UNIV STRATA EX/STRUC PROB/SOLV ADMIN ATTIT SOC/INTEG 20 BUREAUCRCY. PAGE 43 H0862
CULTURE METH/COMP SOCIETY HABITAT

S59
LYNN D.B.,"THE EFFECTS OF FATHER-ABSENCE ON NORWEGIAN BOYS AND GIRLS." NORWAY CULTURE PERS/REL ADJUST DISPL LOVE...PSY CORREL STAT INT CON/ANAL CHARTS SOC/INTEG 20. PAGE 99 H1983
SOC FAM AGE/C ANOMIE

B60
KEPHART C.,RACES OF MAN. GP/REL HABITAT...LING SOC/INTEG 20 MIGRATION MISCEGEN. PAGE 85 H1692
CULTURE RACE/REL HEREDITY GEOG

B60
LEYDER J.,BIBLIOGRAPHIE DE L'ENSEIGNEMENT SUPERIEUR ET DE LA RECHERCHE SCIENTIFIQUE EN AFRIQUE INTERTROPICALE (2 VOLS.). AFR CULTURE ECO/UNDEV AGRI PLAN EDU/PROP ADMIN COLONIAL...GEOG SOC/INTEG 20 NEGRO. PAGE 96 H1918
BIBLIOG/A ACT/RES ACADEM R+D

B60
MANIS J.G.,MAN AND SOCIETY. STRATA LEAD INGP/REL PERS/REL ATTIT PWR...PSY ANTHOL T SOC/INTEG MARX/KARL MILL/JS FREUD/S CHURCHLL/W SPENCER/H RUSSELL/B. PAGE 102 H2036
SOC SOCIETY STRUCT CULTURE

B60
MOORE W.E.,LABOR COMMITMENT AND SOCIAL CHANGE IN DEVELOPING AREAS. SOCIETY STRATA ECO/UNDEV MARKET VOL/ASSN WORKER AUTHORIT SKILL...MGT NAT/COMP SOC/INTEG 20. PAGE 113 H2250
LABOR ORD/FREE ATTIT INDUS

B60
SLOTKIN J.S.,FROM FIELD TO FACTORY; NEW INDUSTRIAL EMPLOYEES. HABITAT...MGT NEW/IDEA NAT/COMP BIBLIOG SOC/INTEG 20. PAGE 145 H2901
INDUS LABOR CULTURE WORKER

B61
DUFFY J.,AFRICA SPEAKS. GHANA TOGO CULTURE ECO/UNDEV PROB/SOLV COLONIAL NEUTRAL DISCRIM NAT/LISM SOVEREIGN ALL/IDEOS...CONCPT ANTHOL SOC/INTEG 20 NEGRO THIRD/WRLD. PAGE 43 H0857
AFR NAT/G FUT STRUCT

B61
FIRTH R.,ELEMENTS OF SOCIAL ORGANIZATION (3RD ED.). STRATA STRUCT ECO/UNDEV NEIGH CHIEF INGP/REL ATTIT MORAL...PHIL/SCI GP/COMP WORSHIP SOC/INTEG 20. PAGE 50 H1009
SOC CULTURE SOCIETY KIN

B61
FREYRE G.,THE PORTUGUESE AND THE TROPICS. L/A+17C PORTUGAL SOCIETY PERF/ART ADMIN TASK GP/REL ...ART/METH CONCPT SOC/INTEG 20. PAGE 53 H1060
COLONIAL METH PLAN CULTURE

B61
SCHECHTMAN J.B.,ON WINGS OF EAGLES: THE PLIGHT, EXODUS, AND HOMECOMING OF ORIENTAL JEWRY. ASIA ISLAM ISRAEL VOL/ASSN DIPLOM CONTROL ORD/FREE ...GEOG WORSHIP SOC/INTEG 20 JEWS ARABS MIGRATION. PAGE 139 H2777
CULTURE HABITAT KIN SECT

S61
LIEBERSON S.,"THE IMPACT OF RESIDENTIAL SEGREGATION ON ETHNIC ASSIMILATION" (BMR)" CULTURE MUNIC GP/REL RACE/REL DISCRIM...GEOG STAT CON/ANAL CHARTS SOC/INTEG 20 MIGRATION. PAGE 96 H1926
HABITAT ISOLAT NEIGH

B62
DEBUYST F.,LAS CLASES SOCIALES EN AMERICA LATINA. L/A+17C SOCIETY STRUCT WORKER EDU/PROP RACE/REL ATTIT HABITAT ROLE...GEOG SOC NAT/COMP SOC/INTEG 20. PAGE 39 H0780
STRATA GP/REL WEALTH

B62
MEHNERT K.,SOVIET MAN AND HIS WORLD. COM USSR INTELL FAM WORKER PLAN EDU/PROP REV PRODUC MARXISM ...SOC TREND SOC/INTEG 20 LENIN/VI STALIN/J KHRUSH/N. PAGE 108 H2162
SOCIETY CULTURE ECO/DEV

B62
PAIKERT G.C.,THE GERMAN EXODUS. EUR+WWI GERMANY/W LAW CULTURE SOCIETY STRUCT INDUS NAT/LISM RESPECT SOVEREIGN...CHARTS BIBLIOG SOC/INTEG 20 MIGRATION. PAGE 122 H2444
INGP/REL STRANGE GEOG GP/REL

B62
RUDY Z.,ETHNOSOZIOLOGIE SOWJETISCHER VOLKER. USSR SOCIETY STRUCT FAM SECT GP/REL ATTIT...SOC SOC/INTEG 20. PAGE 136 H2714
MYTH CULTURE KIN

B63
LAMB B.P.,INDIA: A WORLD IN TRANSITION. INDIA ECO/UNDEV SECT EDU/PROP COLONIAL HABITAT ORD/FREE ...GEOG CHARTS BIBLIOG SOC/INTEG 20. PAGE 90 H1799
POL/PAR NAT/G DIPLOM STRATA

B63
LEIGHTON D.C.,THE CHARACTER OF DANGER (VOL. III).
HEALTH

SOCIETY STRUCT STRANGE ANOMIE...SOC STAT CHARTS GP/COMP SOC/EXP SOC/INTEG 20 NOVA/SCOT. PAGE 94 H1868 — PSY CULTURE

B63
SILVERT K.H.,EXPECTANT PEOPLES: NATIONALISM AND DEVELOPMENT. CULTURE STRATA SECT LEAD REGION RACE/REL ALL/IDEOS...GEN/LAWS SOC/INTEG 20. PAGE 144 H2877 — NAT/LISM ECO/UNDEV ALL/VALS

S63
TANNER R.,"WHO GOES HOME?" CULTURE GP/REL SOC/INTEG 20 TANGANYIKA MIGRATION. PAGE 152 H3045 — ADMIN COLONIAL NAT/G NAT/LISM

B64
ALVIM J.C.,A REVOLUCAO SEM RUMO. BRAZIL NAT/G BAL/PWR DIPLOM INT/TRADE PARTIC WEALTH...POLICY SOC SOC/INTEG 20. PAGE 6 H0118 — REV CIVMIL/REL ECO/UNDEV ORD/FREE

B64
BEATTIE J.,OTHER CULTURES. UNIV LAW FAM POL/PAR SECT ADJUD OWN ALL/VALS WEALTH...SOC NAT/COMP SOC/INTEG 20. PAGE 13 H0251 — METH/CNCPT CULTURE STRUCT

B64
CURRIE D.P.,FEDERALISM AND THE NEW NATIONS OF AFRICA. CANADA USA+45 INT/TRADE TAX GP/REL ...NAT/COMP SOC/INTEG 20. PAGE 36 H0725 — FEDERAL AFR ECO/UNDEV INT/LAW

B64
GREEN M.M.,IBO VILLAGE AFFAIRS. AFR FORCES PERS/REL ADJUST ISOLAT ATTIT HABITAT PERSON ALL/VALS...JURID RECORD SOC/INTEG 20 IBO. PAGE 60 H1207 — MUNIC CULTURE ECO/UNDEV SOC

B64
GRIFFITH W.,THE WELSH (2ND ED.). UK SOCIETY STRUCT SECT WRITING NAT/LISM...ART/METH MODAL OBS/ENVIR TREND SOC/INTEG WALES PURITAN MUSIC. PAGE 61 H1223 — CULTURE SOC LING

B64
HALPERN J.M.,GOVERNMENT, POLITICS, AND SOCIAL STRUCTURE IN LAOS. LAOS CULTURE SOCIETY STRATA STRUCT FAM DIPLOM DOMIN MARXISM...INT GOV/COMP WORSHIP SOC/INTEG 20. PAGE 65 H1297 — NAT/G SOC LOC/G

B64
HARRIS M.,PATTERNS OF RACE IN THE AMERICAS. BRAZIL L/A+17C STRATA ECO/UNDEV AGRI KIN MUNIC SECT COLONIAL RACE/REL...SOC SOC/INTEG 17/20 NEGRO INDIAN/AM. PAGE 67 H1342 — STRUCT PRE/AMER CULTURE SOCIETY

B64
MEAD M.,CONTINUITIES IN CULTURAL EVOLUTION. FACE/GP KIN ACT/RES EDU/PROP GP/REL INGP/REL DRIVE HEREDITY ROLE...TIME/SEQ TREND METH SOC/INTEG 20. PAGE 108 H2153 — CULTURE SOC PERS/REL

B64
MORGAN L.H.,ANCIENT SOCIETY (1877). SOCIETY FAM OWN ...INT QU GEN/LAWS SOC/INTEG. PAGE 113 H2255 — KIN MARRIAGE CULTURE

B64
UNESCO,WORLD COMMUNICATIONS: PRESS, RADIO, TELEVISION, FILM (4TH ED.). WOR+45 DIPLOM TV PEACE ...NAT/COMP SOC/INTEG 20 FILM. PAGE 158 H3163 — COM/IND EDU/PROP PRESS TEC/DEV

B64
WRIGHT Q.,A STUDY OF WAR. LAW NAT/G PROB/SOLV BAL/PWR NAT/LISM PEACE ATTIT SOVEREIGN...CENSUS SOC/INTEG. PAGE 171 H3421 — WAR CONCPT DIPLOM CONTROL

B65
CARTER G.M.,POLITICS IN EUROPE. EUR+WWI FRANCE GERMANY/W UK USSR LAW CONSTN POL/PAR VOL/ASSN PRESS LOBBY PWR...ANTHOL SOC/INTEG EEC. PAGE 27 H0548 — GOV/COMP OP/RES ECO/DEV

B65
CENTRAL GAZETTEERS UNIT,THE GAZETTEER OF INDIA (VOL. I). INDIA SOCIETY STRATA PLAN EDU/PROP NAT/LISM ORD/FREE WEALTH...GEOG LING CHARTS SOC/INTEG 20. PAGE 28 H0568 — PRESS CULTURE SECT STRUCT

B65
KUPER H.,URBANIZATION AND MIGRATION IN WEST AFRICA. UPPER/VOLT CULTURE ECO/UNDEV WORKER REGION GOV/REL ...LING ANTHOL SOC/INTEG 20 AFRICA/W OSHOGBO MOSSI MIGRATION. PAGE 89 H1781 — AFR HABITAT MUNIC GEOG

B65
SHRIMALI K.L.,EDUCATION IN CHANGING INDIA. INDIA CULTURE DIPLOM FOR/AID GP/REL RACE/REL ATTIT SOC/INTEG 20 UNESCO CMN/WLTH. PAGE 143 H2866 — EDU/PROP PROF/ORG ACADEM

B66
BLACK C.E.,THE DYNAMICS OF MODERNIZATION: A STUDY IN COMPARATIVE HISTORY. STRUCT ECO/DEV ECO/UNDEV NAT/G DIPLOM LEAD REV...PREDICT TIME/SEQ TREND SOC/INTEG 17/20. PAGE 17 H0350 — SOCIETY SOC NAT/COMP

B66
HATTICH M.,NATIONALBEWUSSTSEIN UND STAATSBEWUSSTSEIN IN DER PLURALISTISCHEN GESELLSCHAFT. GERMANY GP/REL ATTIT SOVEREIGN SOC/INTEG 20. PAGE 68 H1356 — NAT/G NAT/LISM SOCIETY OBJECTIVE

B66
KEITH G.,THE FADING COLOUR BAR. AFR CENTRL/AFR UK ZAMBIA CULTURE SCHOOL EDU/PROP PERS/REL DISCRIM AGE ...AUD/VIS NAT/COMP SOC/INTEG 20 NEGRO. PAGE 84 H1682 — RACE/REL STRUCT ATTIT NAT/G

B67
COLLINS R.O.,EGYPT AND THE SUDAN. COM FRANCE ISLAM SUDAN UAR UK SOCIETY NAT/G COLONIAL NAT/LISM...GEOG SOC LING TREND SOC/INTEG 7/20 SUEZ. PAGE 32 H0635 — AGRI CULTURE ECO/UNDEV

B67
FANON F.,BLACK SKIN, WHITE MASKS: THE EXPERIENCES OF A BLACK MAN IN A WHITE WORLD. CULTURE COLONIAL HAPPINESS ISOLAT STRANGE ATTIT HABITAT RIGID/FLEX SEX...BIOG STERTYP SOC/INTEG 20 NEGRO. PAGE 49 H0970 — DISCRIM PERS/REL RACE/REL PSY

B67
HUTCHINS F.G.,THE ILLUSION OF PERMANENCE: BRITISH IMPERIALISM IN INDIA. INDIA UK CULTURE STRUCT NAT/G REV GP/REL RACE/REL ADJUST DISCRIM ATTIT MORAL PWR SOC/INTEG 18/20. PAGE 75 H1509 — COLONIAL CONTROL SOVEREIGN CONSERVE

B67
MICKIEWICZ E.P.,SOVIET POLITICAL SCHOOLS: THE COMMUNIST PARTY ADULT INSTRUCTION SYSTEM. COM USSR INTELL SCHOOL WORKER CREATE PRESS ADMIN CONTROL ATTIT KNOWL...PROG/TEAC SOC/INTEG 20 COM/PARTY. PAGE 110 H2200 — NAT/G EDU/PROP AGE/A MARXISM

B67
RIESMAN D.,CONVERSATIONS IN JAPAN: MODERNIZATION, POLITICS, AND CULTURE. CHINA/COM STRATA STRUCT ECO/DEV INDUS ACADEM EDU/PROP...ART/METH SOC MODAL INT IDEA/COMP SOC/INTEG 20 CHINJAP HIROSHIMA. PAGE 131 H2629 — CULTURE SOCIETY ASIA

S67
ALBINSKI H.S.,"POLITICS AND BICULTURISM IN CANADA: THE FLAG DEBATE." CANADA SOCIETY NAT/G PROVS DELIB/GP DEBATE REGION SOVEREIGN PLURISM...POLICY SOC/INTEG 20. PAGE 5 H0093 — NAT/LISM GP/REL POL/PAR CULTURE

S67
VINCENT S.,"SHOULD BIAFRA SURVIVE?" NIGERIA ECO/UNDEV CHIEF FORCES ECO/TAC GP/REL DISCRIM PEACE ORD/FREE SOC/INTEG 20 BIAFRA IBO. PAGE 163 H3256 — AFR REV REGION NAT/G

S68
CHAPMAN A.R.,"THE CIVIL WAR IN NIGERIA." AFR NIGERIA NAT/G PLAN ECO/TAC EDU/PROP COERCE WAR GOV/REL INGP/REL ORD/FREE PWR WEALTH SOC/INTEG 20 BIAFRA. PAGE 29 H0579 — REV RACE/REL

S68
LUKASZEWSKI J.,"WESTERN INTEGRATION AND THE PEOPLE'S DEMOCRACIES." USSR ELITES ECO/DEV NAT/G VOL/ASSN INT/TRADE AGREE REV FEDERAL WEALTH SOCISM ...NAT/COMP SOC/INTEG 20 EEC. PAGE 99 H1977 — DIPLOM INT/ORG COM REGION

B75
NEWMAN J.H.,A LETTER ADDRESSED TO THE DUKE OF NORFOLK ON THE OCCASION OF MR. GLADSTONE'S RECENT EXPOSTULATION. NAT/G SECT CHIEF LEGIS CONTROL LEAD GP/REL SUPEGO SOC/INTEG WORSHIP 19 ENGLAND. PAGE 117 H2346 — POLICY DOMIN SOVEREIGN CATHISM

B76
TAINE H.A.,THE ANCIENT REGIME. FRANCE STRATA FORCES PARTIC EQUILIB WEALTH CONSERVE POPULISM...GOV/COMP SOC/INTEG 18/19. PAGE 152 H3035 — NAT/G GOV/REL TAX REV

C80
ARNOLD M.,"EQUALITY" IN MIXED ESSAYS." MOD/EUR UK ELITES STRATA NAT/G...CONCPT IDEA/COMP NAT/COMP SOC/INTEG 19. PAGE 8 H0167 — ORD/FREE UTOPIA SOCIETY STRUCT

B99
DU BOIS W.E.B.,THE PHILADELPHIA NEGRO: A SOCIAL STUDY. CULTURE STRATA KIN CRIME SUFF ADJUST DISCRIM ISOLAT HABITAT HEREDITY ALL/VALS SOC/INTEG 17/19 NEGRO PHILADELPH. PAGE 42 H0851 — INGP/REL RACE/REL SOC CENSUS

SOC/PAR....SOCIALIST PARTY (USE WITH SPECIFIC NATION)

SOC/REVPAR....SOCIALIST REVOLUTIONARY PARTY (USE WITH SPECIFIC NATION)

S67
DESHPANDE A.M.,"FEDERAL-STATE FISCAL RELATIONS IN INDIA" (REVIEW ARTICLE)" GERMANY USSR DELIB/GP PLAN BUDGET ECO/TAC INCOME 20 SOC/DEMPAR SOC/REVPAR. PAGE 40 H0795 — FINAN NAT/G GOV/REL TAX

S67
ELLISON H.J.,"THE SOCIALIST REVOLUTIONARIES." USSR ECO/UNDEV NAT/G INGP/REL EFFICIENCY ATTIT PWR MARXISM...CONCPT IDEA/COMP 20 SOC/REVPAR. PAGE 46 H0911 — POL/PAR REV AGRI

SOC/SECUR....SOCIAL SECURITY

SOC/WK....SOCIAL WORK, SOCIAL SERVICE ORGANIZATION

N
HOOVER INSTITUTION,UNITED STATES AND CANADIAN PUBLICATIONS ON AFRICA. CULTURE ECO/UNDEV AGRI TEC/DEV EDU/PROP COLONIAL RACE/REL NAT/LISM ATTIT HEALTH...SOC SOC/WK 20. PAGE 73 H1464 — BIBLIOG DIPLOM NAT/G AFR

B35
DOUGLASS H.P.,THE PROTESTANT CHURCH AS A SOCIAL INSTITUTION. CULTURE FINAN NEIGH PROF/ORG OP/RES ADMIN...POLICY SOC/WK STAT BIBLIOG. PAGE 42 H0843 — SECT PARTIC INGP/REL GP/REL

B38
DUNHAM W.H. JR.,COMPLAINT AND REFORM IN ENGLAND 1436-1714. UK LAW ACADEM NAT/G POL/PAR SCHOOL PRESS COLONIAL PARL/PROC MORAL...SOC/WK ANTHOL 15/18 HAKLUYT/R COWPER/W. PAGE 43 H0865 — ATTIT SOCIETY SECT

B40
ZWEIG F.,THE WORKER IN AN AFFLUENT SOCIETY: FAMILY LIFE AND INDUSTRY. UK STRATA LG/CO ECO/TAC LEISURE INGP/REL HAPPINESS HEALTH...PSY SOC/WK INT CHARTS WORSHIP 20 FEMALE/SEX. PAGE 173 H3465 — MARRIAGE ATTIT FINAN CULTURE

B51
CHRISTENSEN A.N.,THE EVOLUTION OF LATIN AMERICAN GOVERNMENT: A BOOK OF READINGS. ECO/UNDEV INDUS LOC/G POL/PAR EX/STRUC LEGIS FOR/AID CT/SYS ...SOC/WK 20 SOUTH/AMER. PAGE 30 H0599 — NAT/G CONSTN DIPLOM L/A+17C

B51
LEONARD L.L.,INTERNATIONAL ORGANIZATION. WOR+45 WOR-45 EX/STRUC FORCES LEGIS ECO/TAC INT/TRADE COLONIAL ARMS/CONT...SOC/WK GOV/COMP BIBLIOG. PAGE 94 H1884 — NAT/G DIPLOM INT/ORG DELIB/GP

S57
DEXTER L.A.,"A SOCIAL THEORY OF MENTAL DEFICIENCY." CULTURE PUB/INST PROB/SOLV CRIME PERS/REL STRANGE PERSON SUPEGO SKILL...EPIST SOC/WK HYPO/EXP. PAGE 41 H0814 — SOC PSY HEALTH ROLE

B63
ELWIN V.,A NEW DEAL FOR TRIBAL INDIA. INDIA AGRI COM/IND INDUS KIN TEC/DEV TAX EDU/PROP OWN HEALTH 20. PAGE 46 H0912 — ECO/UNDEV CULTURE CONSTN SOC/WK

B63
FISCHER-GALATI S.A.,RUMANIA; A BIBLIOGRAPHIC GUIDE (PAMPHLET). ROMANIA INTELL ECO/DEV LABOR SECT WEALTH...GEOG SOC/WK LING 20. PAGE 51 H1012 — BIBLIOG/A NAT/G COM LAW

B64
AVASTHI A.,ASPECTS OF ADMINISTRATION. INDIA UK USA+45 FINAN ACADEM DELIB/GP LEGIS RECEIVE PARL/PROC PRIVIL...NAT/COMP 20. PAGE 9 H0183 — MGT ADMIN SOC/WK ORD/FREE

B67
COWLES M.,PERSPECTIVES IN THE EDUCATION OF DISADVANTAGED CHILDREN. CULTURE OP/RES PLAN PERS/REL ADJUST HABITAT PERCEPT KNOWL WEALTH ...SOC/WK IDEA/COMP ANTHOL 20. PAGE 34 H0686 — EDU/PROP AGE/C TEC/DEV SCHOOL

B67
HODGKINSON R.G.,THE ORIGINS OF THE NATIONAL HEALTH SERVICE: THE MEDICAL SERVICES OF THE NEW POOR LAW, 1834-1871. UK INDUS MUNIC WORKER PROB/SOLV EFFICIENCY ATTIT HEALTH WEALTH SOCISM...JURID SOC/WK 19/20. PAGE 72 H1445 — HEAL NAT/G POLICY LAW

B67
ROSENTHAL A.H.,THE SOCIAL PROGRAMS OF SWEDEN. SWEDEN USA+45 FINAN NAT/G PLAN PROB/SOLV INSPECT ORD/FREE...POLICY HEAL SOC CHARTS NAT/COMP 20. PAGE 134 H2681 — GIVE SOC/WK WEALTH METH/COMP

S67
ANDERSON L.G.,"ADMINISTERING A GOVERNMENT SOCIAL SERVICE" NEW/ZEALND EX/STRUC TASK ROLE 20. PAGE 6 H0129 — ADMIN NAT/G DELIB/GP SOC/WK

S67
BELLER I.,"ECONOMIC POLICY AND THE DEMANDS OF LABOR." PLAN TAX GIVE PRICE WAR COST PRODUC WEALTH. PAGE 13 H0268 — NAT/G ECO/TAC SOC/WK INCOME

SOCDEM/PAR....SOCIAL DEMOCRAT PARTY

B59
VERNEY D.V.,PUBLIC ENTERPRISE IN SWEDEN. FUT SWEDEN UK INDUS POL/PAR LEGIS PROB/SOLV CAP/ISM INT/TRADE CONTROL SOCISM...MGT CONCPT NAT/COMP 20 SOCDEM/PAR CIVIL/SERV. PAGE 162 H3246 — ECO/DEV POLICY LG/CO NAT/G

SOCIAL ANALYSIS....SEE SOC

SOCIAL DEMOCRATIC PARTY (ALL NATIONS)....SEE SOC/DEMPAR

SOCIAL CLASS....SEE STRATA

SOCIAL INSTITUTIONS....SEE INSTITUTIONAL INDEX

SOCIAL MOBILITY....SEE STRATA

SOCIAL PSYCHOLOGY (GROUPS)....SEE SOC

SOCIAL PSYCHOLOGY (INDIVIDUALS)....SEE PSY

SOCIAL STRUCTURE....SEE STRUCT

SOCIAL WORK....SEE SOC/WK

SOCIAL REVOLUTIONARY PARTY (ALL NATIONS)....SEE SOC/REVPAR

SOCIAL STRUCTURE....SEE STRUCT, STRATA

SOCIALISM....SEE SOCISM, SOCIALIST

SOCIALIST....NON-COMMUNIST SOCIALIST; SEE ALSO SOCISM

B13
KROPOTKIN P.,THE CONQUEST OF BREAD. SOCIETY STRATA AGRI INDUS WORKER REV HAPPINESS INCOME PRODUC HEALTH MORAL ORD/FREE. PAGE 89 H1775 — ANARCH SOCIALIST OWN AGREE

N19
LIEBKNECHT W.P.C.,SOCIALISM (2 PTS.; 1875, 1894) (PAMPHLET). WORKER CAP/ISM EDU/PROP WEALTH POPULISM. PAGE 97 H1927 — ECO/TAC STRATA SOCIALIST PARTIC

B32
BLUM L.,PEACE AND DISARMAMENT (TRANS. BY A. WERTH). NAT/G FORCES WORKER DIPLOM AGREE WAR ATTIT AUTHORIT ORD/FREE. PAGE 18 H0360 — SOCIALIST PEACE INT/ORG ARMS/CONT

B39
HITLER A.,MEIN KAMPF. EUR+WWI FUT MOD/EUR STRUCT INT/ORG LABOR NAT/G POL/PAR FORCES CREATE PLAN BAL/PWR DIPLOM ECO/TAC DOMIN EDU/PROP ADMIN COERCE ATTIT...SOCIALIST BIOG TREND NAZI. PAGE 71 H1428 — PWR NEW/IDEA WAR

B40
LEDERER E.,STATE OF THE MASSES. GERMANY ITALY SOCIETY NAT/G ECO/TAC EDU/PROP LEAD TOTALISM ...SOCIALIST PSY 20. PAGE 93 H1852 — CROWD FASCISM AUTHORIT PERSON

B46
BLUM L.,FOR ALL MANKIND (TRANS. BY W. PICKLES). FRANCE GERMANY USSR LAW SOCIETY STRUCT POL/PAR WORKER DIPLOM DOMIN CHOOSE ORD/FREE FASCISM 20. PAGE 18 H0361 — POPULISM SOCIALIST NAT/G WAR

B50
SCHUMPETER J.A.,CAPITALISM, SOCIALISM, AND DEMOCRACY (3RD ED.). USA-45 USSR WOR+45 WOR-45 INTELL ECO/DEV ECO/UNDEV ECO/TAC WAR PRODUC ORD/FREE...MGT SOC 20 MARX/KARL. PAGE 140 H2804 — SOCIALIST CAP/ISM MARXISM IDEA/COMP

B53
SWEEZY P.M.,THE PRESENT AS HISTORY. NAT/G PLAN COLONIAL ATTIT...POLICY SOCIALIST 19/20. PAGE 151 H3019 — ECO/DEV CAP/ISM SOCISM ECO/TAC

B57
COLE G.D.H.,THE POST WAR CONDITIONS OF BRITAIN. EUR+WWI STRUCT NAT/G PLAN EDU/PROP LEGIT RIGID/FLEX ORD/FREE WEALTH...SOCIALIST WELF/ST STAT TREND CON/ANAL CHARTS PARLIAMENT WORK 20. PAGE 31 H0624 — ECO/DEV UK

B59
SENGHOR L.S.,RAPPORT SUR LA DOCTRINE ET LA PROGRAMME DU PART I. FRANCE MALI CONSTN POL/PAR PLAN CHOOSE OWN ORD/FREE MARXISM...SOCIALIST 20 NEGRO. PAGE 141 H2828 — ATTIT NAT/G AFR SOCISM

B60
EASTON S.C.,THE TWILIGHT OF EUROPEAN COLONIALISM. AFR S/ASIA CONSTN SOCIETY STRUCT ECO/UNDEV INDUS NAT/G FORCES ECO/TAC COLONIAL CT/SYS ATTIT KNOWL ORD/FREE PWR...SOCIALIST TIME/SEQ TREND CON/ANAL 20. PAGE 44 H0882 — FINAN ADMIN

B60
STRACHEY J.,THE END OF EMPIRE. UK WOR+45 WOR-45 DIPLOM INT/TRADE DOMIN ADJUST ORD/FREE WEALTH ...SOCIALIST GOV/COMP TIME COMMONWLTH. PAGE 150 H2991 — COLONIAL ECO/DEV BAL/PWR LAISSEZ

S60
EMERSON R.,"THE EROSION OF DEMOCRACY." AFR FUT LAW CULTURE INTELL SOCIETY ECO/UNDEV FAM LOC/G NAT/G FORCES PLAN TEC/DEV ECO/TAC ADMIN CT/SYS ATTIT ORD/FREE PWR...SOCIALIST SOC CONCPT STAND/INT TIME/SEQ WORK 20. PAGE 46 H0918 — S/ASIA POL/PAR

B61
DIA M.,THE AFRICAN NATIONS AND WORLD SOLIDARITY. ISLAM CULTURE ELITES ECO/DEV ECO/UNDEV INT/ORG NAT/G PLAN ECO/TAC INT/TRADE EDU/PROP NAT/LISM ATTIT DRIVE ORD/FREE WEALTH...SOCIALIST CONCPT CON/ANAL GEN/LAWS TOT/POP 20. PAGE 41 H0817 — AFR REGION SOCISM

B63
CANELAS O.A.,RADIOGRAFIA DE LA ALIANZA PARA EL ATRASO. L/A+17C USA+45 ECO/TAC DOMIN COLONIAL NAT/LISM...SOCIALIST NAT/COMP 20. PAGE 26 H0519 — REV DIPLOM ECO/UNDEV REGION

B64
MILIBAND R.,THE SOCIALIST REGISTER: 1964. GERMANY/W ITALY UK LABOR POL/PAR ECO/TAC FOR/AID NUC/PWR ...POLICY SOCIALIST IDEA/COMP 20 MAO NASSER/G. PAGE 110 H2204 — MARXISM SOCISM CAP/ISM PROB/SOLV

S66
BLANC N.,"SPAIN: LEARNING THROUGH STRUGGLE" SPAIN STRATA STRUCT SECT FORCES PROB/SOLV AGE/Y ATTIT — NAT/G FUT

ORD/FREE PWR WEALTH MARXISM SOCISM 19/20 FRANCO/F SUCCESSION. PAGE 18 H0352 — SOCIALIST TOTALISM

B91
MILL J.S.,SOCIALISM (1859). MOD/EUR AGRI INDUS NAT/G REV INCOME PRODUC ORD/FREE POPULISM SOCISM ...GOV/COMP METH/COMP 19. PAGE 110 H2209 — WEALTH SOCIALIST ECO/TAC OWN

SOCIALIZATION....SEE ADJUST

SOCIETY....SOCIETY AS A WHOLE

SOCIOLOGY....SEE SOC

SOCIOLOGY OF KNOWLEDGE....SEE EPIST

SOCIOMETRY, AS THEORY....SEE GEN/METH

SOCISM....SOCIALISM; SEE ALSO SOCIALIST

N
BROCKWAY A.F.,AFRICAN SOCIALISM. EUR+WWI GHANA ISLAM UAR ECO/UNDEV CAP/ISM INT/TRADE COLONIAL COERCE GOV/REL DISCRIM 20 NEGRO NKRUMAH/K NASSER/G. PAGE 21 H0423 — AFR SOCISM MARXISM

B03
FAGUET E.,LE LIBERALISME. FRANCE PRESS ADJUD ADMIN DISCRIM CONSERVE SOCISM...TRADIT SOC LING WORSHIP PARLIAMENT. PAGE 48 H0960 — ORD/FREE EDU/PROP NAT/G LAW

B03
GRIFFIN A.P.C.,SELECT LIST OF REFERENCES ON GOVERNMENT OWNERSHIP OF RAILROADS (PAMPHLET). MOD/EUR NAT/G ADMIN...MGT GOV/COMP 19/20. PAGE 61 H1217 — BIBLIOG/A SOCISM OWN DIST/IND

B05
GRIFFIN A.P.C.,LIST OF BOOKS ON RAILROADS IN FOREIGN COUNTRIES. MOD/EUR ECO/DEV NAT/G CONTROL SOCISM...JURID 19/20 RAILROAD. PAGE 61 H1219 — BIBLIOG/A SERV/IND ADMIN DIST/IND

B08
LLOYD H.D.,THE SWISS DEMOCRACY. SWITZERLND INDUS NAT/G WORKER CHOOSE OWN ORD/FREE SOCISM...PLURIST 19/20 MONOPOLY. PAGE 97 H1944 — NAT/COMP GOV/COMP REPRESENT POPULISM

B12
POLLOCK F.,THE GENIUS OF THE COMMON LAW. CHRIST-17C UK FINAN CHIEF ACT/RES ADMIN GP/REL ATTIT SOCISM ...ANARCH JURID. PAGE 127 H2537 — LAW CULTURE CREATE

B14
LEVINE L.,SYNDICALISM IN FRANCE (2ND ED.). FRANCE LAW SOCIETY ECO/DEV NAT/G ECO/TAC LEAD ATTIT ...POLICY CONCPT STAT BIBLIOG 18/20 REFORMERS. PAGE 95 H1902 — LABOR INDUS SOCISM REV

B14
OPPENHEIMER F.,THE STATE. FUT SOCIETY STRATA STRUCT WORKER CAP/ISM WAR GP/REL SOCISM...SOC NAT/COMP SOC/INTEG. PAGE 121 H2424 — ELITES OWN DOMIN NAT/G

B15
MICHELS R.,POLITICAL PARTIES. NAT/G BAL/PWR CHOOSE REPRESENT ATTIT SOCISM...PSY SOC CONCPT OBS 20 MONOPOLY. PAGE 110 H2198 — POL/PAR CENTRAL LEAD PWR

B19
DE MAN H.,THE REMAKING OF A MIND. EUR+WWI NAT/G ECO/TAC REGION ORD/FREE SOCISM...BIOG 20 WWI EUROPE. PAGE 38 H0762 — PSY WAR SELF/OBS PARTIC

N19
SENGHOR L.S.,AFRICAN SOCIALISM (PAMPHLET). AFR FRANCE MALI USSR ELITES ECO/UNDEV NAT/G DIPLOM DOMIN EDU/PROP ATTIT 20 NEGRO. PAGE 141 H2827 — SOCISM MARXISM ORD/FREE NAT/LISM

B20
COX H.,ECONOMIC LIBERTY. UNIV LAW INT/TRADE RATION TARIFFS RACE/REL SOCISM POLICY. PAGE 34 H0687 — NAT/G ORD/FREE ECO/TAC PERSON

B28
FYFE H.,THE BRITISH LIBERAL PARTY. UK SECT ADMIN LEAD CHOOSE GP/REL PWR SOCISM...MAJORIT TIME/SEQ 19/20 LIB/PARTY CONSRV/PAR. PAGE 54 H1084 — POL/PAR NAT/G REPRESENT POPULISM

C28
SCHNEIDER H.W.,"MAKING THE FASCIST STATE." ITALY CULTURE LABOR DIPLOM REV WAR NAT/LISM TOTALISM ATTIT DRIVE SOCISM...BIBLIOG PARLIAMENT 20. PAGE 140 H2792 — FASCISM POLICY POL/PAR

B30
MASON E.S.,THE PARIS COMMUNE: AN EPISODE IN THE HISTORY OF THE SOCIALIST MOVEMENT. FRANCE MOD/EUR ELITES SOCIETY STRATA ECO/DEV WORKER EDU/PROP CHOOSE INGP/REL SOCISM 19 MARX/KARL PARIS. PAGE 104 H2085 — NAT/G REV MARXISM

B33
FERRERO G.,PEACE AND WAR (TRANS. BY BERTHA PRITCHARD). CULTURE FINAN SECT ATTIT SUPEGO MORAL ORD/FREE CONSERVE POPULISM SOCISM POLICY. PAGE 49 H0987 — WAR PEACE DIPLOM PROB/SOLV

B34
STALIN J.,PROBLEMS OF LENINISM. USSR STRATA INDUS LOC/G POL/PAR ECO/TAC CONTROL TOTALISM PWR SOCISM LENIN/VI STALIN/J. PAGE 148 H2968 — MARXISM REV ELITES NAT/G

B36
BELLOC H.,THE RESTORATION OF PROPERTY. UK STRATA NAT/G PROF/ORG DELIB/GP WORKER CREATE PROB/SOLV ECO/TAC PARTIC UTOPIA ORD/FREE SOCISM 20. PAGE 13 H0270 — CONTROL MAJORIT CAP/ISM OWN

B36
MARITAIN J.,FREEDOM IN THE MODERN WORLD. CONSTN NAT/G SECT CAP/ISM MARXISM SOCISM...GOV/COMP IDEA/COMP 19/20 HUMANISM CHRISTIAN. PAGE 102 H2049 — GEN/LAWS POLICY ORD/FREE

B37
BORGESE G.A.,GOLIATH: THE MARCH OF FASCISM. GERMANY ITALY LAW POL/PAR SECT DIPLOM SOCISM...JURID MYTH 20 DANTE MACHIAVELL MUSSOLIN/B. PAGE 19 H0375 — POLICY NAT/LISM FASCISM NAT/G

B38
DAVIES E.,"NATIONAL" CAPITALISM: THE GOVERNMENT'S RECORD AS PROTECTOR OF PRIVATE MONOPOLY. UK ELITES SOCIETY STRATA POL/PAR WORKER PROB/SOLV CONTROL SOCISM 20 MONOPOLY LABOR/PAR CHAMBRLN/N. PAGE 37 H0747 — CAP/ISM NAT/G INDUS POLICY

B38
HEIMANN E.,COMMUNISM, FASCISM, OR DEMOCRACY? WOR-45 CONSTN SOCIETY STRATA AGRI CAP/ISM MORAL ORD/FREE ...MAJORIT METH/COMP NAT/COMP 19/20. PAGE 69 H1384 — SOCISM MARXISM FASCISM PLURISM

B38
LAWLEY F.E.,THE GROWTH OF COLLECTIVE ECONOMY VOL. 1: NATIONAL. EUR+WWI AGRI INDUS NAT/G BARGAIN CAP/ISM ECO/TAC WAR OPTIMAL WEALTH...GOV/COMP METH/COMP 19/20 MONOPOLY. PAGE 92 H1844 — SOCISM PRICE CONTROL OWN

B38
LAWLEY F.E.,THE GROWTH OF COLLECTIVE ECONOMY VOL. 2: INTERNATIONAL. WOR-45 AGRI INDUS EQUILIB OPTIMAL OWN WEALTH...NAT/COMP 19/20 NAZI NEW/DEAL MONOPOLY. PAGE 92 H1845 — ECO/TAC SOCISM NAT/LISM CONTROL

B38
MARX K.,THE GERMAN IDEOLOGY, PARTS 1 AND 3 (1846). MOD/EUR LAW STRATA WORKER DOMIN REV UTOPIA SOCISM 19 MARX/KARL. PAGE 104 H2079 — MARXIST OWN PRODUC ECO/TAC

B39
ENGELS F.,HERRN EUGEN DUHRING'S REVOLUTION IN SCIENCE (1878). CULTURE STRATA STRUCT FAM SECT ECO/TAC REV WAR SOCISM...MARXIST 19. PAGE 46 H0925 — PWR SOCIETY WEALTH GEN/LAWS

S39
HECKSCHER G.,"GROUP ORGANIZATION IN SWEDEN." SWEDEN STRATA ECO/DEV AGRI INDUS LABOR NAT/G PROF/ORG ECO/TAC CENTRAL SOCISM...MGT 19/20. PAGE 69 H1382 — LAISSEZ SOC

B40
BROGAN D.W.,THE DEVELOPMENT OF MODERN FRANCE (1870-1939). FRANCE GERMANY UK USSR CONSTN CHIEF LEGIS DIPLOM AGREE COLONIAL WAR NAT/LISM PEACE SOCISM 19/20 TREATY. PAGE 21 H0428 — MOD/EUR NAT/G

B40
HUNTER R.,REVOLUTION: WHY, HOW, WHEN? NAT/G ECO/TAC EDU/PROP COERCE ORD/FREE FASCISM POPULISM SOCISM 18/20 HITLER/A LENIN/VI. PAGE 75 H1502 — REV METH/COMP LEAD CONSTN

B40
MCHENRY D.E.,HIS MAJESTY'S OPPOSITION: STRUCTURE AND PROBLEMS OF THE BRITISH LABOUR PARTY 1931-1938. UK FINAN LABOR LOC/G DELIB/GP LEGIS EDU/PROP LEAD PARTIC CHOOSE GP/REL SOCISM...TREND 20 LABOR/PAR. PAGE 107 H2130 — POL/PAR MGT NAT/G POLICY

C41
WASSERMAN L.,"HANDBOOK OF POLITICAL "ISMS" CAP/ISM REPRESENT TOTALISM MARXISM NEW/LIB SOCISM...MAJORIT BIBLIOG 20. PAGE 166 H3313 — IDEA/COMP PHIL/SCI OWN NAT/G

B42
BARKER E.,REFLECTIONS ON GOVERNMENT. EUR+WWI SOCIETY LEGIS EDU/PROP ADMIN LEAD PARTIC CHOOSE TOTALISM AUTHORIT ORD/FREE SOCISM 20. PAGE 11 H0218 — NAT/G POPULISM ACT/RES GEN/LAWS

B42
BAYNES N.H.,INTELLECTUAL LIBERTY AND TOTALITARIAN CLAIMS. EUR+WWI GERMANY ITALY INTELL POL/PAR CIVMIL/REL NAT/LISM SOCISM CONCPT. PAGE 12 H0245 — KNOWL FASCISM EDU/PROP ACADEM

B43
LASKI H.J.,REFLECTIONS ON THE REVOLUTIONS OF OUR TIME. COM USSR NAT/G WORKER UTOPIA ORD/FREE WEALTH MARXISM SOCISM 19/20. PAGE 92 H1830 — CAP/ISM WELF/ST ECO/TAC POLICY

B44
BERDYAEV N.,SLAVERY AND FREEDOM. NAT/G REV WAR NAT/LISM OWN AUTHORIT SEX CONSERVE SOCISM...TRADIT PHIL/SCI CIVIL/LIB. PAGE 15 H0295
ORD/FREE PERSON ELITES SOCIETY

B44
HAYEK F.A.,THE ROAD TO SERFDOM. NAT/G POL/PAR CREATE EDU/PROP ATTIT WEALTH LAISSEZ...OLD/LIB CONCPT TREND 20. PAGE 68 H1368
FUT PLAN ECO/TAC SOCISM

B45
CROCE B.,POLITICS AND MORALS. UNIV NAT/G ECO/TAC ORD/FREE MARXISM POPULISM SOCISM...REALPOL 15/20 HEGEL/GWF ROUSSEAU/J. PAGE 35 H0704
MORAL GEN/LAWS IDEA/COMP

B46
ALLEN J.S.,WORLD MONOPOLY AND PEACE. GERMANY UK USSR FINAN INDUS LG/CO DOMIN CONTROL PEACE PWR WEALTH SOCISM...NAT/COMP 20 MONOPOLY. PAGE 5 H0105
CAP/ISM DIPLOM WAR COLONIAL

B46
DAVIES E.,NATIONAL ENTERPRISE: THE DEVELOPMENT OF THE PUBLIC CORPORATION. UK LG/CO EX/STRUC WORKER PROB/SOLV COST ATTIT SOCISM 20. PAGE 37 H0748
ADMIN NAT/G CONTROL INDUS

B47
BOWEN R.H.,GERMAN THEORIES OF THE CORPORATIVE STATE, WITH SPECIAL REFERENCES TO THE PERIOD 1870-1919. GERMANY INDUS LG/CO CATHISM SOCISM...SOC 18/20. PAGE 19 H0389
IDEA/COMP CENTRAL NAT/G POLICY

B48
WRIGHT G.,THE RESHAPING OF FRENCH DEMOCRACY. FRANCE NAT/G POL/PAR SECT LEAD CHOOSE GP/REL INGP/REL MARXISM SOCISM...CHARTS BIBLIOG 20 DEGAULLE/C. PAGE 171 H3418
CONSTN POPULISM CREATE LEGIS

B48
YAKOBSON S.,FIVE HUNDRED RUSSIAN WORKS FOR COLLEGE LIBRARIES (PAMPHLET). MOD/EUR USSR MARXISM SOCISM ...ART/METH GEOG HUM JURID SOC 13/20. PAGE 171 H3431
BIBLIOG NAT/G CULTURE COM

S48
ALMOND G.A.,"THE CHRISTIAN PARTIES OF WESTEN EUROPE." EUR+WWI NAT/G EDU/PROP LEGIT TOTALISM ORD/FREE PWR MARXISM...TREND CHARTS STERTYP GEN/LAWS COLD/WAR 20. PAGE 5 H0110
POL/PAR CATH SOCISM

B49
MAO TSE-TUNG,NEW DEMOCRACY. CHINA/COM NAT/G DIPLOM ECO/TAC EDU/PROP REV...CONCPT METH SOC/INTEG 20. PAGE 102 H2045
SOCISM MARXISM POPULISM CULTURE

B50
ALBRECHT-CARRIE R.,ITALY FROM NAPOLEON TO MUSSOLINI. GERMANY ITALY SPAIN SOCIETY ECO/DEV POL/PAR LEGIS AGREE CONTROL WAR NAT/LISM TOTALISM PWR SOCISM...SOC 19/20 TREATY. PAGE 5 H0095
FASCISM NAT/G

B50
BERMAN H.J.,JUSTICE IN RUSSIA; AN INTERPRETATION OF SOVIET LAW. USSR LAW STRUCT LABOR FORCES AGREE GP/REL ORD/FREE SOCISM...TIME/SEQ 20. PAGE 15 H0309
JURID ADJUD MARXISM COERCE

B50
CARR E.H.,STUDIES IN REVOLUTION. CREATE WAR PERSON ALL/IDEOS MARXISM SOCISM...PHIL/SCI METH/COMP ANTHOL 18/20 SAINTSIMON MARX/KARL PROUDHON/P LASSALLE/F PLEKHNV/GV. PAGE 27 H0537
REV IDEA/COMP COERCE BIOG

B50
HALLOWELL J.H.,MAIN CURRENTS IN MODERN POLITICAL THOUGHT. CONSTN SECT LEGIS...MAJORIT CONCPT 17/20 MARX/KARL MILL/JS HOBBES/T LENIN/VI. PAGE 64 H1290
IDEA/COMP POPULISM SOCISM

B50
LIPSET S.M.,AGRARIAN SOCIALISM. CANADA POL/PAR OP/RES ECO/TAC ADMIN ATTIT...TIME/SEQ NAT/COMP SOC/EXP 20 SASKATCH. PAGE 97 H1938
SOCISM AGRI METH/COMP STRUCT

S51
GOULD J.,"THE KOMSOMOL AND THE HITLER JUGEND." COM EUR+WWI GERMANY SOCIETY NAT/G POL/PAR SCHOOL TOTALISM DRIVE PERCEPT KNOWL FASCISM...SOC NAZI TOT/POP 20. PAGE 59 H1185
EDU/PROP CON/ANAL SOCISM

B52
APPADORAI A.,THE SUBSTANCE OF POLITICS (6TH ED.). EX/STRUC LEGIS DIPLOM CT/SYS CHOOSE FASCISM MARXISM SOCISM...BIBLIOG T. PAGE 7 H0145
PHIL/SCI NAT/G

B52
ROBBINS L.,THE THEORY OF ECONOMIC POLICY IN ENGLISH CLASSICAL POLITICAL ECONOMY. UK ECO/DEV WORKER PLAN CAP/ISM EDU/PROP CONTROL INCOME OWN HEALTH SOCISM ...POLICY 17/19. PAGE 132 H2639
ECO/TAC ORD/FREE IDEA/COMP NAT/G

C52
EBENSTEIN W.,"INTRODUCTION TO POLITICAL PHILOSOPHY." COM CONSTN INTELL CONTROL PERSON NEW/LIB SOCISM...PSY GEN/LAWS BIBLIOG/A. PAGE 44 H0883
ALL/IDEOS PHIL/SCI IDEA/COMP NAT/G

B53
BARZEL R.,DIE DEUTSCHEN PARTEIEN. GERMANY MARXISM SOCISM...CONCPT IDEA/COMP 19/20 SOC/DEMPAR CHRIS/DEM. PAGE 12 H0232
POL/PAR NAT/G LAISSEZ

B53
SHIRATO I.,JAPANESE SOURCES ON THE HISTORY OF THE CHINESE COMMUNIST MOVEMENT (PAMPHLET). CHINA/COM USSR CONSTRUC NAT/G POL/PAR FORCES DIPLOM DOMIN EDU/PROP CONTROL WAR TOTALISM SOCISM 20. PAGE 143 H2863
BIBLIOG/A MARXISM ECO/UNDEV

B53
SWEEZY P.M.,THE PRESENT AS HISTORY. NAT/G PLAN COLONIAL ATTIT...POLICY SOCIALIST 19/20. PAGE 151 H3019
ECO/DEV CAP/ISM SOCISM ECO/TAC

N53
VITO F.,"RECENT DEVELOPMENTS IN THE THEORY OF DEMOCRATIC ADMIN" INTL POL SCI ASS'N CONFERENCE ON PUBLIC ADMINISTRATION... FRANCE ITALY UK REPRESENT EFFICIENCY NEW/LIB SOCISM...WELF/ST 20. PAGE 163 H3257
GOV/COMP CONTROL EX/STRUC

B54
FRIEDMAN W.,THE PUBLIC CORPORATION: A COMPARATIVE SYMPOSIUM (UNIVERSITY OF TORONTO SCHOOL OF LAW COMPARATIVE LAW SERIES, VOL. I). SWEDEN USA+45 INDUS INT/ORG NAT/G REGION CENTRAL FEDERAL...POLICY JURID IDEA/COMP NAT/COMP ANTHOL 20 COMMONWLTH MONOPOLY EUROPE. PAGE 53 H1065
LAW SOCISM LG/CO OWN

B54
MOSK S.A.,INDUSTRIAL REVOLUTION IN MEXICO. MARKET LABOR CREATE CAP/ISM ADMIN ATTIT SOCISM...POLICY 20 MEXIC/AMER. PAGE 113 H2268
INDUS TEC/DEV ECO/UNDEV NAT/G

B55
INTERNATIONAL COMN JURISTS,JUSTICE ENSLAVED. COM CONSTN LABOR NAT/G CONTROL CHOOSE 20. PAGE 78 H1555
SOCISM TOTALISM ORD/FREE COERCE

B55
KOHN H.,THE MIND OF MODERN RUSSIA. COM MOD/EUR USSR SOCIETY NAT/G SECT FORCES TOP/EX COERCE TOTALISM DRIVE RIGID/FLEX PWR SOVEREIGN...CONCPT TIME/SEQ WORK. PAGE 87 H1742
INTELL GEN/LAWS SOCISM RUSSIA

B55
RUSTOW D.A.,THE POLITICS OF COMPROMISE. SWEDEN LABOR EX/STRUC LEGIS PLAN REPRESENT SOCISM...SOC 19/20. PAGE 136 H2720
POL/PAR NAT/G POLICY ECO/TAC

B56
HERNANDEZ URBINA A.,LOS PARTIDOS Y LA CRISIS DEL APRA. PERU NAT/G LEAD LOBBY CHOOSE SOCISM...POLICY DECISION 20 COM/PARTY APRA CONGRESS. PAGE 70 H1402
POL/PAR PARTIC PARL/PROC GP/REL

B57
BARAN P.A.,THE POLITICAL ECONOMY OF GROWTH. MOD/EUR USA+45 USA-45 TEC/DEV TAX SOCISM...MGT CONCPT GOV/COMP. PAGE 11 H0213
CAP/ISM CONTROL ECO/UNDEV FINAN

B57
HALLGARTEN G.W.,DAMONEN ODER RETTER. ASIA L/A+17C CAP/ISM ATTIT MARXISM SOCISM...NAT/COMP. PAGE 64 H1289
TOTALISM FASCISM COERCE DOMIN

B57
HERNANDEZ-ARREGU J.,IMPERIALISMO Y CULTURA (LA POLITICA EN LA INTELIGENCIA ARGENTINA). L/A+17C CULTURE ELITES WRITING COLONIAL CROWD ATTIT FASCISM MARXISM SOCISM...BIOG IDEA/COMP 20 ARGEN PERON/JUAN COM/PARTY. PAGE 70 H1403
INTELL CREATE ART/METH HUM

B57
KENNEDY M.D.,A SHORT HISTORY OF COMMUNISM IN ASIA. ASIA BURMA INDIA S/ASIA THAILAND NAT/G POL/PAR LEAD REV WAR MARXISM SOCISM...POLICY 20 CHINJAP. PAGE 85 H1688
DIPLOM NAT/LISM TOTALISM COERCE

B57
LOUCKS W.N.,COMPARATIVE ECONOMIC SYSTEMS (5TH ED.). COM UK USSR INDUS POL/PAR PLAN CAP/ISM TOTALISM MARXISM...PHIL/SCI BIBLIOG 19/20. PAGE 99 H1969
NAT/COMP IDEA/COMP SOCISM

B58
SCHOEPS H.J.,KONSERVATIVE ERNEUERUNG IDEEN ZUR DEUTSCHEN POLITIK. GERMANY ELITES SOCIETY ACADEM CHOOSE SOCISM 19/20. PAGE 140 H2796
POL/PAR IDEA/COMP CONSERVE NAT/G

S58
LOCKWOOD W.W.,"THE SOCIALISTIC SOCIETY: INDIA AND JAPAN." INDIA ECO/DEV ECO/UNDEV INDUS NAT/G CONTROL LEAD PRODUC WEALTH 20 CHINJAP. PAGE 98 H1948
ECO/TAC NAT/COMP FINAN SOCISM

B59
GOLDWIN R.A.,READINGS IN RUSSIAN FOREIGN POLICY. HUNGARY USSR YUGOSLAVIA ELITES INT/ORG NAT/G REV WAR NAT/LISM PERSON SOCISM...CHARTS 20 MAPS BOLSHEVISM. PAGE 58 H1160
COM MARXISM DIPLOM POLICY

B59
INTERNATIONAL PRESS INSTITUTE,THE PRESS IN AUTHORITARIAN COUNTRIES. COM PORTUGAL SPAIN UAR USSR NAT/G DOMIN LEGIT ORD/FREE FASCISM SOCISM 20. PAGE 78 H1559
PRESS CONTROL TOTALISM EDU/PROP

B59
KELF-COHEN R.,NATIONALISATION IN BRITAIN: THE END
NEW/LIB

OF DOGMA. EUR+WWI UK NAT/G POL/PAR WORKER ECO/TAC PARL/PROC WEALTH SOCISM...GOV/COMP 20. PAGE 84 H1683
ECO/DEV INDUS OWN

B59
LANDAUER C.,EUROPEAN SOCIALISM (2 VOLS.). COM EUR+WWI MOD/EUR INTELL INDUS REV WAR...MAJORIT IDEA/COMP BIBLIOG 19/20 HITLER/A. PAGE 90 H1805
SOCISM NAT/COMP LABOR MARXISM

B59
LEITES N.,ON THE GAME OF POLITICS IN FRANCE. ALGERIA FRANCE CONSTN SECT VOL/ASSN ECO/TAC INT/TRADE PARL/PROC WAR SOCISM 20 DEGAULLE/C EEC. PAGE 94 H1871
POL/PAR NAT/G LEGIS IDEA/COMP

B59
SENGHOR L.S.,RAPPORT SUR LA DOCTRINE ET LA PROGRAMME DU PART I. FRANCE MALI CONSTN POL/PAR PLAN CHOOSE OWN ORD/FREE MARXISM...SOCIALIST 20 NEGRO. PAGE 141 H2828
ATTIT NAT/G AFR SOCISM

B59
VERNEY D.V.,PUBLIC ENTERPRISE IN SWEDEN. FUT SWEDEN UK INDUS POL/PAR LEGIS PROB/SOLV CAP/ISM INT/TRADE CONTROL SOCISM...MGT CONCPT NAT/COMP 20 SOCDEM/PAR CIVIL/SERV. PAGE 162 H3246
ECO/DEV POLICY LG/CO NAT/G

S59
SKILLING H.G.,"COMMUNISM: NATIONAL OR INTERNATIONAL." CHINA/COM USSR YUGOSLAVIA NAT/G POL/PAR VOL/ASSN DOMIN REGION COERCE ATTIT PWR MARXISM SOCISM...CONCPT TOT/POP 20 TITO/MARSH. PAGE 145 H2894
COM TREND

B60
DIA M.,REFLEXIONS SUR L'ECONOMIE DE L'AFRIQUE NOIRE (REV. ED.). CULTURE ECO/UNDEV CREATE TEC/DEV DIPLOM INT/TRADE OPTIMAL ATTIT...POLICY 20. PAGE 41 H0816
AFR ECO/TAC SOCISM PLAN

B60
GOODMAN E.,SOVIET DESIGN FOR A WORLD STATE. COM USSR NAT/G TOP/EX DIPLOM ECO/TAC DOMIN EDU/PROP COERCE REV ATTIT ORD/FREE...CON/ANAL 20. PAGE 59 H1171
PLAN PWR SOCISM TOTALISM

B60
JEMOLO A.C.,CHURCH AND STATE IN ITALY 1850-1950 (TRANS. BY DAVID MOORE). ITALY CONSTN STRATA WAR FASCISM SOCISM...TIME/SEQ 19/20 CHURCH/STA CHRIS/DEM. PAGE 80 H1599
GP/REL NAT/G CATHISM POL/PAR

B60
ROBERTSON D.,THE CONTROL OF INDUSTRY. UK MARKET LABOR WORKER PRICE CONTROL GP/REL COST DEMAND ORD/FREE WEALTH NEW/LIB SOCISM 20. PAGE 132 H2646
INDUS FINAN NAT/G ECO/DEV

B60
VON KOENIGSWALD H.,SIE SUCHEN ZUFLUCHT. GERMANY/E NAT/G PLAN ECO/TAC SOCISM...GEOG CENSUS 20 BERLIN. PAGE 164 H3273
GP/REL COERCE DOMIN PERSON

C60
EBENSTEIN W.,"MODERN POLITICAL THOUGHT (2ND ED.)" NAT/G CAP/ISM NAT/LISM PERSON ORD/FREE PWR ALL/IDEOS NEW/LIB SOCISM...TRADIT PSY BIBLIOG/A 18/20. PAGE 44 H0884
IDEA/COMP PHIL/SCI CONCPT GEN/LAWS

B61
DIA M.,THE AFRICAN NATIONS AND WORLD SOLIDARITY. ISLAM CULTURE ELITES ECO/DEV ECO/UNDEV INT/ORG NAT/G PLAN ECO/TAC INT/TRADE EDU/PROP NAT/LISM ATTIT DRIVE ORD/FREE WEALTH...SOCIALIST CONCPT CON/ANAL GEN/LAWS TOT/POP 20. PAGE 41 H0817
AFR REGION SOCISM

B61
LA PONCE J.A.,THE GOVERNMENT OF THE FIFTH REPUBLIC: FRENCH POLITICAL PARTIES AND THE CONSTITUTION. ALGERIA FRANCE LAW NAT/G DELIB/GP LEGIS ECO/TAC MARXISM SOCISM...CHARTS BIBLIOG/A 20 DEGAULLE/C. PAGE 90 H1794
PWR POL/PAR CONSTN CHIEF

B61
LICHTHEIM G.,MARXISM. GERMANY SOCIETY WORKER CAP/ISM ECO/TAC NAT/LISM POPULISM...TIME/SEQ GOV/COMP NAT/COMP 18/20 COM/PARTY. PAGE 96 H1924
MARXISM SOCISM IDEA/COMP CULTURE

B61
MILIBAND R.,PARLIAMENTARY SOCIALISM. EUR+WWI UK EXEC LEAD PARL/PROC GP/REL...POLICY 20 PARLIAMENT LABOR/PAR. PAGE 110 H2203
POL/PAR NAT/G PWR SOCISM

B61
PALMER N.D.,THE INDIAN POLITICAL SYSTEM. INDIA ECO/UNDEV SECT CHIEF COLONIAL CHOOSE ALL/IDEOS SOCISM...CHARTS BIBLIOG/A 20. PAGE 123 H2452
NAT/LISM POL/PAR NAT/G DIPLOM

B61
SAKAI R.K.,STUDIES ON ASIA, 1961. ASIA BURMA INDIA S/ASIA FINAN ECO/TAC NAT/LISM SOCISM...POLICY ANTHOL 19/20 CHINJAP. PAGE 137 H2734
ECO/UNDEV SECT

B61
SHARMA T.R.,THE WORKING OF STATE ENTERPRISES IN INDIA. INDIA DELIB/GP LEGIS WORKER BUDGET PRICE CONTROL GP/REL OWN ATTIT...MGT CHARTS 20. PAGE 142 H2851
NAT/G INDUS ADMIN SOCISM

B62
BELL D.,THE END OF IDEOLOGY (REV. ED.). USA+45 USA-45 ELITES STRATA LABOR CREATE CRIME PWR MARXISM ...PHIL/SCI METH/COMP 20 EUROPE. PAGE 13 H0265
CROWD CAP/ISM SOCISM IDEA/COMP

B62
GRZYBOWSKI K.,SOVIET LEGAL INSTITUTIONS. USA+45 USSR ECO/DEV NAT/G EDU/PROP CONTROL CT/SYS CRIME OWN ATTIT PWR SOCISM...NAT/COMP 20. PAGE 62 H1242
ADJUD LAW JURID

B62
JENNINGS I.,PARTY POLITICS: THE STUFF OF POLITICS (VOL.III). UK NAT/G SECT CHIEF INT/TRADE RECEIVE COLONIAL GP/REL NAT/LISM ORD/FREE SOCISM 19/20 CHURCH/STA WHIG/PARTY. PAGE 80 H1607
POL/PAR CONSTN PWR ALL/IDEOS

B62
KINDERSLEY R.,THE FIRST RUSSIAN REVISIONISTS. COM USSR LAW ELITES INTELL NAT/G LEGIS ECO/TAC EDU/PROP CONTROL LEAD GP/REL SOCISM 19/20 MARX/KARL BOLSHEVISM. PAGE 86 H1712
CONSTN MARXISM POPULISM BIOG

S62
ANSPRENGER F.,"NATIONALISM, COMMUNISM, AND THE UNCOMMITTED NATIONS: AMERICAN PROFILES." FUT ISLAM CULTURE SOCIETY ECO/UNDEV NAT/G POL/PAR PLAN ECO/TAC EDU/PROP COERCE CHOOSE ALL/VALS MARXISM SOCISM...SOC CONCPT BIOG TREND 20. PAGE 7 H0142
AFR COM NAT/LISM

S62
CROAN M.,"POLYCENTRISM: COMMUNIST INTERNATIONAL RELATIONS." ASIA STRUCT INT/ORG NAT/G POL/PAR CONSULT PLAN DOMIN EDU/PROP COERCE ATTIT RIGID/FLEX SOCISM...POLICY CONCPT TREND CON/ANAL GEN/LAWS MARX/KARL. PAGE 35 H0703
COM CREATE DIPLOM NAT/LISM

S62
IOVTCHOUK M.T.,"ON SOME THEORETICAL PRINCIPLES AND METHODS OF SOCIOLOGICAL INVESTIGATIONS (IN RUSSIAN)." FUT USA+45 STRATA R+D NAT/G POL/PAR TOP/EX ACT/RES PLAN ECO/TAC EDU/PROP ROUTINE ATTIT RIGID/FLEX MARXISM SOCISM...MARXIST METH/CNCPT OBS TREND NAT/COMP GEN/LAWS 20. PAGE 78 H1564
COM ECO/DEV CAP/ISM USSR

S62
KOLARZ W.,"THE IMPACT OF COMMUNISM ON WEST AFRICA." AFR FUT SOCIETY INT/ORG NAT/G CREATE PLAN DOMIN EDU/PROP COERCE NAT/LISM ATTIT RIGID/FLEX SOCISM ...POLICY CONCPT TREND MARX/KARL 20. PAGE 88 H1751
COM POL/PAR COLONIAL

S62
LONDON K.,"SINO-SOVIET RELATIONS IN THE CONTEXT OF THE 'WORLD SOCIALIST SYSTEM'." ASIA CHINA/COM COM USSR INT/ORG NAT/G TOP/EX BAL/PWR DIPLOM DOMIN ATTIT PERCEPT RIGID/FLEX PWR MARXISM...METH/CNCPT TREND 20. PAGE 98 H1957
DELIB/GP CONCPT SOCISM

S62
PISTRAK L.,"SOVIET VIEWS ON AFRICA." AFR COM FUT ISLAM USSR INTELL STRUCT KIN POL/PAR PLAN EDU/PROP RIGID/FLEX PWR MARXISM...TIME/SEQ WORK TOT/POP 20. PAGE 126 H2516
NAT/G ATTIT SOCISM

S62
SHATTEN F.,"POLYCENTRISM: AFRICA: NATIONALISM AND COMMUNISM." ASIA COM FUT ISLAM CULTURE SOCIETY ECO/UNDEV NAT/G PLAN DOMIN COLONIAL COERCE CHOOSE RIGID/FLEX ALL/VALS MARXISM...CONCPT TREND 20. PAGE 143 H2852
AFR ATTIT NAT/LISM SOCISM

B63
BORKENAU F.,THE SPANISH COCKPIT. SPAIN ELITES STRATA POL/PAR ACT/RES CROWD WAR GP/REL INGP/REL ...SOC NAT/COMP 20. PAGE 19 H0377
REV CONSERVE SOCISM FORCES

B63
ISSAWI C.,EGYPT IN REVOLUTION: AN ECONOMIC ANALYSIS. ISLAM STRUCT ECO/UNDEV AGRI FINAN INDUS PLAN EXEC REV NAT/LISM ATTIT RIGID/FLEX WEALTH SOCISM...STAT WORK 20. PAGE 79 H1573
NAT/G UAR

B63
MARX K.,THE POVERTY OF PHILOSOPHY (1847). SOCIETY STRATA INDUS WORKER OWN UTOPIA SOCISM...GEN/LAWS MARX/KARL. PAGE 104 H2082
MARXIST PRODUC

B63
MOSELY P.E.,THE SOVIET UNION, 1922-1962: A FOREIGN AFFAIRS READER. ASIA POLAND USSR CULTURE INTELL AGRI POL/PAR WORKER INT/TRADE DOMIN WAR NAT/LISM MARXISM SOCISM 20 KHRUSH/N. PAGE 113 H2267
PWR POLICY DIPLOM

B63
SHANKS M.,THE LESSONS OF PUBLIC ENTERPRISE. UK LEGIS WORKER ECO/TAC ADMIN PARL/PROC GOV/REL ATTIT ...POLICY MGT METH/COMP NAT/COMP ANTHOL 20 PARLIAMENT. PAGE 142 H2840
SOCISM OWN NAT/G INDUS

B63
WODDIS J.,AFRICA, THE WAY AHEAD. AFR FUT ELITES POL/PAR CAP/ISM DIPLOM DOMIN RACE/REL ATTIT ORD/FREE SOVEREIGN SOCISM 20 PANAF/FREE. PAGE 170 H3394
REV COLONIAL ECO/UNDEV NAT/G

S63
AYAL E.B.,"VALUE SYSTEM AND ECONOMIC DEVELOPMENT IN JAPAN AND THAILAND." ASIA S/ASIA THAILAND CULTURE ECO/DEV CAP/ISM DOMIN NAT/LISM DRIVE RIGID/FLEX SOCISM...WELF/ST OBS TREND CON/ANAL GEN/LAWS 20 CHINJAP. PAGE 9 H0185
ECO/UNDEV ALL/VALS

S63
HOSKINS H.L.,"ARAB SOCIALISM IN THE UAR." ISLAM USSR AGRI INDUS NAT/G TOP/EX CREATE DIPLOM EDU/PROP DRIVE KNOWL PWR SOCISM...POLICY CONCPT TREND SUEZ 20. PAGE 74 H1478
ECO/DEV PLAN UAR

S63
MBOYA T.,"AFRICAN SOCIALISM." ECO/UNDEV INT/ORG DIPLOM FOR/AID INT/TRADE REGION GP/REL ATTIT ORD/FREE EACM. PAGE 106 H2116
AFR SOCISM CULTURE NAT/LISM

S63
ROGIN M.,"ROUSSEAU IN AFRICA." AFR MARXISM POPULISM SOCISM 20 ROUSSEAU/J. PAGE 133 H2661
IDEA/COMP CULTURE CONSTN ORD/FREE

B64
BAUCHET P.,ECONOMIC PLANNING. FRANCE STRATA LG/CO CAP/ISM ADMIN PARL/PROC DEMAND OPTIMAL ATTIT PWR SOCISM...POLICY CHARTS 20. PAGE 12 H0238
ECO/DEV NAT/G PLAN ECO/TAC

B64
FRIEDLAND W.H.,AFRICAN SOCIALISM. ECO/UNDEV MARKET LABOR NAT/G POL/PAR PLAN CAP/ISM ECO/TAC EDU/PROP CHOOSE ATTIT DRIVE PWR WEALTH...POLICY CONCPT RECORD STERTYP 20. PAGE 53 H1063
AFR SOCISM

B64
FROMM E.,MARX'S CONCEPT OF MAN. LABOR OWN PERSON ...HUM IDEA/COMP GEN/LAWS 17 MARX/KARL EUROPE SPINOZA/B GOETHE/J HEGEL/GWF. PAGE 54 H1072
INGP/REL CONCPT MARXISM SOCISM

B64
GRIFFITH W.E.,THE SINO-SOVIET RIFT. ASIA CHINA/COM COM CUBA USSR YUGOSLAVIA NAT/G POL/PAR VOL/ASSN DELIB/GP FORCES TOP/EX DIPLOM EDU/PROP DRIVE PERSON PWR...TREND 20 TREATY. PAGE 61 H1224
ATTIT TIME/SEQ BAL/PWR SOCISM

B64
GRIFFITH W.E.,COMMUNISM IN EUROPE (2 VOLS.). CZECHOSLVK USSR WOR+45 WOR-45 YUGOSLAVIA INGP/REL MARXISM SOCISM...ANTHOL 20 EUROPE/E. PAGE 61 H1225
COM POL/PAR DIPLOM GOV/COMP

B64
GROSSER A.,THE FEDERAL REPUBLIC OF GERMANY: A CONCISE HISTORY. GERMANY/W STRUCT MORAL ORD/FREE POPULISM SOCISM...SOC CONCPT 20. PAGE 62 H1235
NAT/G POL/PAR CHOOSE DIPLOM

B64
GUMPLOWICZ L.,RECHTSSTAAT UND SOZIALISMUS. STRATA ORD/FREE SOVEREIGN MARXISM...IDEA/COMP 16/20 KANT/I HOBBES/T. PAGE 62 H1251
JURID NAT/G SOCISM CONCPT

B64
HALPERIN S.W.,MUSSOLINI AND ITALIAN FASCISM. ITALY NAT/G POL/PAR SECT ECO/TAC LEAD PWR SOCISM...POLICY 20 MUSSOLIN/B. PAGE 64 H1294
FASCISM NAT/LISM EDU/PROP CHIEF

B64
MARTINET G.,MARXISM OF OUR TIME: OR THE CONTRADICTIONS OF SOCIALISM. FRANCE NAT/G OPTIMAL RIGID/FLEX SOCISM...IDEA/COMP 20. PAGE 103 H2067
MARXISM MARXIST PROB/SOLV CREATE

B64
MILIBAND R.,THE SOCIALIST REGISTER: 1964. GERMANY/W ITALY UK LABOR POL/PAR ECO/TAC FOR/AID NUC/PWR ...POLICY SOCIALIST IDEA/COMP 20 MAO NASSER/G. PAGE 110 H2204
MARXISM SOCISM CAP/ISM PROB/SOLV

B64
MORGAN H.W.,AMERICAN SOCIALISM 1900-1960. USA+45 USA-45 INTELL AGRI LABOR WORKER BARGAIN ECO/TAC GP/REL RACE/REL 20 NEGRO MIGRATION GOLD/STAND. PAGE 113 H2254
SOCISM POL/PAR ECO/DEV STRATA

B64
SINAI I.R.,THE CHALLENGE OF MODERNISATION* THE WEST'S IMPACT ON THE NON-WESTERN WORLD. EUR+WWI CULTURE ELITES SECT CONSERVE SOCISM...GP/COMP IDEA/COMP NAT/COMP GEN/LAWS. PAGE 144 H2881
ASIA S/ASIA ECO/UNDEV CREATE

S64
GARMARNIKOW M.,"INFLUENCE-BUYING IN WEST AFRICA." COM FUT USSR INTELL NAT/G PLAN TEC/DEV ECO/TAC DOMIN EDU/PROP REGION NAT/LISM ATTIT DRIVE ALL/VALS SOVEREIGN...POLICY PSY SOC CONCPT TREND STERTYP WORK COLD/WAR 20. PAGE 55 H1102
AFR ECO/UNDEV FOR/AID SOCISM

S64
KANOUTE P.,"AFRICAN SOCIALISM." AFR CONSTN NAT/G COLONIAL ORD/FREE...GOV/COMP METH/COMP 20 EUROPE. PAGE 83 H1655
SOCISM CULTURE STRUCT IDEA/COMP

C64
GOLDMAN M.I.,"COMPARATIVE ECONOMIC SYSTEMS: A READER." COM ECO/UNDEV NAT/G BUDGET CAP/ISM ADMIN TOTALISM MARXISM SOCISM...MGT ANTHOL BIBLIOG 19/20. PAGE 58 H1157
NAT/COMP CONTROL IDEA/COMP

N64
KENYA MINISTRY ECO PLAN DEV,AFRICAN SOCIALISM AND ITS APPLICATION TO PLANNING IN KENYA (PAMPHLET). AFR AGRI INDUS WORKER TAX COLONIAL WEALTH 20. PAGE 85 H1691
NAT/G SOCISM PLAN ECO/UNDEV

B65
AIYAR S.P.,STUDIES IN INDIAN DEMOCRACY. INDIA STRATA ECO/UNDEV LABOR POL/PAR LEGIS DIPLOM LOBBY REGION CHOOSE ATTIT SOCISM...ANTHOL 20. PAGE 4 H0086
ORD/FREE REPRESENT ADMIN NAT/G

B65
BARRY E.E.,NATIONALISATION IN BRITISH POLITICS: THE HISTORICAL BACKGROUND. UK AGRI DIST/IND EXTR/IND LABOR LG/CO ATTIT CONSERVE SOCISM 19/20 LABOR/PAR. PAGE 12 H0231
NAT/G OWN INDUS POL/PAR

B65
COLLINS H.,KARL MARX AND THE BRITISH LABOR MOVEMENT. YEARS OF THE FIRST INTERNATIONAL. EUR+WWI MOD/EUR UK STRATA INDUS NAT/G POL/PAR SOCISM ...CONCPT 19/20 MARX/KARL. PAGE 32 H0633
MARXISM LABOR INT/ORG WORKER

B65
EDINGER L.J.,KURT SCHUMACHER: A STUDY IN PERSONALITY AND POLITICAL BEHAVIOR. EUR+WWI GERMANY NAT/G DRIVE ROLE PWR SOCISM...BIBLIOG 20 SOC/DEMPAR SCHUMCHR/K. PAGE 44 H0889
TOP/EX LEAD PERSON BIOG

B65
HALEVY E.,THE ERA OF TYRANNIES (TRANS. BY R. K. WEBB). FRANCE MOD/EUR UK ECO/DEV LABOR NAT/G BAL/PWR FEDERAL ALL/VALS...OLD/LIB TREND 18/20 SAINTSIMON. PAGE 64 H1285
SOCISM CONCPT UTOPIA ORD/FREE

B65
HALEVY E.,THE ERA OF TYRANNIES (TRANS. BY R. K. WEBB). WOR-45 ECO/DEV PROB/SOLV CONTROL COERCE REV WAR TOTALISM 20. PAGE 64 H1286
SOCISM IDEA/COMP DOMIN

B65
JAIN S.C.,THE STATE AND AGRICULTURE. INDIA S/ASIA ECO/UNDEV PROB/SOLV CAP/ISM MARXISM SOCISM 20. PAGE 79 H1586
NAT/G POLICY AGRI ECO/TAC

B65
MOORE C.H.,TUNISIA SINCE INDEPENDENCE. ELITES LOC/G POL/PAR ADMIN COLONIAL CONTROL EXEC GOV/REL TOTALISM MARXISM...INT 20 TUNIS. PAGE 112 H2248
NAT/G EX/STRUC SOCISM

B65
ONUOHA B.,THE ELEMENTS OF AFRICAN SOCIALISM. AFR FINAN SECT TEC/DEV FOR/AID GP/REL OWN LAISSEZ MARXISM...CONCPT BIBLIOG 20. PAGE 121 H2419
SOCISM ECO/UNDEV NAT/G EX/STRUC

B65
PUNDEEF M.V.,BULGARIA; A BIBLIOGRAPHIC GUIDE. BULGARIA LAW CULTURE INTELL ECO/DEV LEAD MARXISM 20. PAGE 128 H2566
BIBLIOG/A NAT/G COM SOCISM

B65
RODRIGUEZ M.,CENTRAL AMERICA. COSTA/RICA GUATEMALA L/A+17C NICARAGUA DIPLOM COLONIAL REGION NAT/LISM ALL/IDEOS SOCISM...MAJORIT TIME/SEQ BIBLIOG 19/20. PAGE 133 H2656
CULTURE NAT/COMP NAT/G ECO/UNDEV

B65
TINGSTEN H.,THE PROBLEM OF DEMOCRACY. ELITES SOCIETY STRATA NAT/G CONSEN TOTALISM WELF/ST. PAGE 155 H3101
IDEA/COMP GOV/COMP POPULISM SOCISM

B65
TUTSCH H.E.,FACETS OF ARAB NATIONALISM. ISLAM ISRAEL CULTURE STRUCT SECT RIGID/FLEX ORD/FREE MARXISM SOCISM 20. PAGE 157 H3143
ECO/UNDEV NAT/LISM TEC/DEV SOCIETY

B65
ULAM A.,THE BOLSHEVIKS. COM USSR NAT/G CHIEF ECO/TAC ADMIN LEAD WAR POPULISM...POLICY 19/20 LENIN/VI BOLSHEVISM. PAGE 157 H3148
SOCISM POL/PAR TOP/EX REV

S65
RUBINSTEIN A.Z.,"YUGOSLAVIA'S OPENING SOCIETY." COM USSR INTELL NAT/G LEGIS TOP/EX LEGIT CT/SYS RIGID/FLEX ALL/VALS SOCISM...HUM TIME/SEQ TREND 20. PAGE 135 H2708
CONSTN EX/STRUC YUGOSLAVIA

S65
STAAR R.F.,"RETROGRESSION IN POLAND." COM USSR AGRI INDUS NAT/G CREATE EDU/PROP TOTALISM RIGID/FLEX ORD/FREE PWR SOCISM...RECORD CHARTS 20. PAGE 148 H2965
TOP/EX ECO/TAC POLAND

S65
TABORSKY E.,"CHANGE IN CZECHOSLOVAKIA." COM USSR ELITES INTELL AGRI INDUS NAT/G DELIB/GP EX/STRUC ECO/TAC TOTALISM ATTIT RIGID/FLEX SOCISM...MGT CONCPT TREND 20. PAGE 152 H3031
ECO/DEV PLAN CZECHOSLVK

S65
VUCINICH W.S.,"WHITHER RUMANIA." COM USSR YUGOSLAVIA NAT/G VOL/ASSN DELIB/GP TOP/EX LEGIT NAT/LISM TOTALISM ATTIT DRIVE RIGID/FLEX ORD/FREE WEALTH SOCISM...TIME/SEQ TREND 20. PAGE 164 H3281
ECO/DEV CREATE ROMANIA

B66
BEER S.H.,BRITISH POLITICS IN THE COLLECTIVIST AGE. UK NAT/G CONTROL CHOOSE GP/REL ATTIT PWR PLURISM ...MAJORIT WELF/ST 16/20. PAGE 13 H0258
POL/PAR SOCISM TRADIT GP/COMP

B66
COLE A.B.,SOCIALIST PARTIES IN POSTWAR JAPAN. STRATA AGRI LABOR PLAN DIPLOM ECO/TAC AGREE LEAD
POL/PAR POLICY

CHOOSE ATTIT...CHARTS 20 CHINJAP SOC/DEMPAR. PAGE 31 H0620 — SOCISM NAT/G

B66
FORD P.,CARDINAL MORAN AND THE A. L. P. NAT/G POL/PAR SECT DELIB/GP LOBBY REV CHOOSE ORD/FREE MARXISM 19/20 AUSTRAL PROTESTANT LABOR/PAR. PAGE 52 H1035 — CATHISM SOCISM LABOR SOCIETY

B66
FRIEDRICH C.J.,REVOLUTION: NOMOS VIII. NAT/G SOCISM ...OBS TREND IDEA/COMP ANTHOL 18/20. PAGE 54 H1070 — REV MARXISM CONCPT DIPLOM

B66
MADAN G.R.,ECONOMIC THINKING IN INDIA. INDIA ECO/UNDEV AGRI FINAN INDUS LABOR PLAN CAP/ISM INT/TRADE MARXISM SOCISM...POLICY 1/20. PAGE 101 H2013 — ECO/TAC PHIL/SCI NAT/G POL/PAR

B66
NAMBOODIRIPAD E.M.,ECONOMICS AND POLITICS OF INDIA'S SOCIALIST PATTERN. INDIA STRATA AGRI INDUS NAT/G PRICE ORD/FREE SOVEREIGN 20. PAGE 115 H2307 — ECO/UNDEV PLAN SOCISM CAP/ISM

B66
PARETO V.,SOCIOLOGICAL WRITINGS (TRANS. BY DERICK MURFIN). UNIV NAT/G SOCISM. PAGE 123 H2466 — SOC CONCPT METH SOCIETY

B66
SAINDERICHIN P.,HISTORIE SECRETE D'UNE ELECTION, DECEMBER 5-19, 1965. FRANCE NAT/G DELIB/GP LEGIS PLAN EDU/PROP TV SOCISM...MARXIST 20 DEGAULLE/C. PAGE 137 H2731 — CHOOSE CHIEF PROB/SOLV POL/PAR

B66
SKILLING H.G.,THE GOVERNMENTS OF COMMUNIST EAST EUROPE. COM EUR+WWI ELITES FORCES DIPLOM ECO/TAC CONTROL HABITAT SOCISM...DECISION BIBLIOG 20 EUROPE/E COM/PARTY. PAGE 145 H2895 — MARXISM NAT/COMP GP/COMP DOMIN

B66
THIESENHUSEN W.C.,CHILE'S EXPERIMENTS IN AGRARIAN REFORM. CHILE STRUCT NAT/G ACT/RES ECO/TAC GOV/REL COST SOCISM...TREND CHARTS SOC/EXP 20. PAGE 154 H3073 — AGRI ECO/UNDEV SOC TEC/DEV

B66
TIVEY L.J.,NATIONALISATION IN BRITISH INDUSTRY. UK LEGIS PARL/PROC GP/REL OWN ATTIT SOCISM 20. PAGE 156 H3109 — NAT/G INDUS CONTROL LG/CO

S66
BLANC N.,"SPAIN: LEARNING THROUGH STRUGGLE" SPAIN STRATA STRUCT SECT FORCES PROB/SOLV AGE/Y ATTIT ORD/FREE PWR WEALTH MARXISM SOCISM 19/20 FRANCO/F SUCCESSION. PAGE 18 H0352 — NAT/G FUT SOCIALIST TOTALISM

S66
HEAPHEY J.,"THE ORGANIZATION OF EGYPT* INADEQUACIES OF A NONPOLITICAL MODEL FOR NATION-BUILDING." STRATA NAT/G CREATE PROB/SOLV ECO/TAC NAT/LISM SOCISM RECORD. PAGE 69 H1377 — UAR ECO/UNDEV OBS

S66
O'BRIEN W.V.,"EVENTS AND TRENDS: PATTERNS OF AFRICAN INTERNATIONAL POLITICAL BEHAVIOR." CULTURE SOCIETY NAT/G NAT/LISM SOCISM. PAGE 119 H2386 — BIBLIOG/A AFR TREND DIPLOM

B67
ANDERSON C.W.,ISSUES OF POLITICAL DEVELOPMENT. BURMA WOR+45 CULTURE TOP/EX ECO/TAC MARXISM ...CHARTS NAT/COMP 20 COLOMB CONGO/LEOP. PAGE 6 H0126 — NAT/LISM COERCE ECO/UNDEV SOCISM

B67
FIELD M.G.,SOVIET SOCIALIZED MEDICINE. USSR FINAN R+D PROB/SOLV ADMIN SOCISM...MGT SOC CONCPT 20. PAGE 50 H0993 — PUB/INST HEALTH NAT/G MARXISM

B67
HODGKINSON R.G.,THE ORIGINS OF THE NATIONAL HEALTH SERVICE: THE MEDICAL SERVICES OF THE NEW POOR LAW, 1834-1871. UK INDUS MUNIC WORKER PROB/SOLV EFFICIENCY ATTIT HEALTH WEALTH SOCISM...JURID SOC/WK 19/20. PAGE 72 H1445 — HEAL NAT/G POLICY LAW

B67
JAIN R.K.,MANAGEMENT OF STATE ENTERPRISES. INDIA SOCIETY FINAN WORKER BUDGET ADMIN CONTROL OWN 20. PAGE 79 H1584 — NAT/G SOCISM INDUS MGT

B67
MOORE J.R.,THE ECONOMIC IMPACT OF THE TVA. AGRI INDUS PLAN BARGAIN CONTROL REGION GOV/REL DEMAND EFFICIENCY SOCISM 20 TVA. PAGE 112 H2249 — ECO/UNDEV ECO/DEV NAT/G CREATE

B67
PAPANEK G.F.,PAKISTAN'S DEVELOPMENT: SOCIAL GOALS AND PRIVATE INCENTIVES. PAKISTAN INDUS NAT/G PROB/SOLV CONTROL EFFICIENCY SOCISM...CHARTS 20. PAGE 123 H2463 — ECO/UNDEV PLAN CAP/ISM ECO/TAC

B67
POMEROY W.J.,HALF A CENTURY OF SOCIALISM. USSR LAW AGRI INDUS NAT/G CREATE DIPLOM EDU/PROP PERSON ORD/FREE WEALTH...POLICY TREND 20. PAGE 127 H2541 — SOCISM MARXISM COM SOCIETY

B67
POSNER M.V.,ITALIAN PUBLIC ENTERPRISE. ITALY ECO/DEV FINAN INDUS CREATE ECO/TAC ADMIN CONTROL EFFICIENCY PRODUC...TREND CHARTS 20. PAGE 127 H2545 — NAT/G PLAN CAP/ISM SOCISM

B67
RYDER A.J.,THE GERMAN REVOLUTION OF 1918; A STUDY OF GERMAN SOCIALISM IN WAR AND REVOLT. GERMANY NAT/G POL/PAR GP/REL...BIBLIOG 20. PAGE 136 H2724 — SOCISM WAR REV INGP/REL

B67
SHAFFER H.G.,THE COMMUNIST WORLD: MARXIST AND NON-MARXIST VIEWS. WOR+45 SOCIETY DIPLOM ECO/TAC CONTROL SOCISM...MARXIST ANTHOL BIBLIOG/A 20. PAGE 142 H2838 — MARXISM NAT/COMP IDEA/COMP COM

B67
SPIRO H.S.,PATTERNS OF AFRICAN DEVLOPMENT: FIVE COMPARISONS. STRUCT ECO/UNDEV NAT/G CONSERVE SOCISM ...PREDICT NAT/COMP 20 CHINJAP. PAGE 148 H2951 — AFR CONSTN NAT/LISM TREND

L67
AUSTIN D.A.,"POLITICAL CONFLICT IN AFRICA." CONSTN NAT/G CREATE ADMIN COLONIAL ORD/FREE MARXISM POPULISM SOCISM...NAT/COMP ANTHOL 20. PAGE 9 H0180 — ANOMIE AFR POL/PAR

S67
BURGHART A.,"CATHOLIC SOCIAL THOUGHT IN AUSTRIA." AUSTRIA EUR+WWI NAT/G PAY PERS/REL OWN MARXISM SOCISM...SOC 20. PAGE 24 H0482 — CATHISM ATTIT TREND SOCIETY

S67
CARIAS B.,"EL CONTROL DE LAS EMPRESAS PUBLICAS POR GRUPOS DE INTERESES DE LA COMUNIDAD." FRANCE UK VENEZUELA INDUS NAT/G CONTROL OWN PWR...DECISION NAT/COMP 20. PAGE 26 H0529 — WORKER REPRESENT MGT SOCISM

S67
CHU-YUAN CHENG,"THE CULTURAL REVOLUTION AND CHINA'S ECONOMY." CHINA/COM AGRI DIST/IND INDUS MARKET NAT/G WORKER PLAN INT/TRADE DOMIN DEMAND PRODUC ...CHARTS 20 MAO. PAGE 30 H0600 — ECO/DEV ECO/TAC REV SOCISM

S67
FRANCIS M.J.,"THE US PRESS AND CASTRO: A STUDY IN DECLINING RELATIONS." COM DIPLOM WAR TOTALISM ATTIT SOCISM...POLICY IDEA/COMP 20. PAGE 52 H1046 — PRESS LEAD REV NAT/G

S67
MARWICK A.,"THE LABOUR PARTY AND THE WELFARE STATE IN BRITAIN, 19001948." UK SOCIETY STRUCT ECO/DEV WORKER CREATE PRICE CHOOSE WEALTH NEW/LIB SOCISM ...POLICY HEAL 20 PARLIAMENT LABOR/PAR. PAGE 104 H2074 — POL/PAR RECEIVE LEGIS NAT/G

S67
PONOMARYOV B.,"THE OCTOBER REVOLUTION - BEGINNING OF THE EPOCH OF SOCIALISM AND COMMUNISM." COM FUT USSR WOR+45 SOCIETY STRATA CHIEF CREATE DIPLOM ECO/TAC EDU/PROP SOCISM...NAT/COMP 20. PAGE 127 H2542 — MARXIST WORKER INT/ORG POLICY

S67
ROCHET W.,"THE OCTOBER REVOLUTION AND THE STRUGGLE OF THE FRENCH COMMUNISTS." COM FRANCE ELITES SOCIETY STRATA ECO/TAC EDU/PROP GP/REL WEALTH ...MARXIST IDEA/COMP NAT/COMP 20. PAGE 133 H2654 — SOCISM CHOOSE METH/COMP NAT/G

S67
SAVER W.,"NATIONAL SOCIALISM: TOTALITARIANISM OR FASCISM?" GERMANY STRUCT POL/PAR PROB/SOLV MARXISM ...SOC CONCPT HIST/WRIT IDEA/COMP 20 HITLER/A COLD/WAR. PAGE 138 H2760 — SOCISM NAT/G TOTALISM FASCISM

S67
STRAFFORD P.,"FRENCH ELECTIONS." FRANCE NAT/G CHIEF LEGIS BAL/PWR ECO/TAC PARL/PROC PARTIC ATTIT 20. PAGE 150 H2993 — POL/PAR SOCISM CENTRAL MARXISM

S67
TIKHOMIROV I.A.,"DIVISION OF POWERS OR DIVISION OF LABOR?" USSR NAT/G DELIB/GP ADJUD GP/REL MARXISM SOCISM 20. PAGE 155 H3093 — BAL/PWR WORKER STRATA ADMIN

S67
WILLIAMS P.M.,"THE FRENCH GENERAL ELECTION OF MARCH 1967." FRANCE INDUS WORKER NAT/LISM PWR SOCISM 20. PAGE 168 H3368 — POL/PAR NAT/G ATTIT CHOOSE

S68
BOSSCHERE G D.E.,"A L'EST DU NOUVEAU." CZECHOSLVK HUNGARY POLAND ROMANIA YUGOSLAVIA AGRI CREATE ECO/TAC COERCE GP/REL ATTIT MARXISM SOCISM 20. PAGE 19 H0382 — ORD/FREE COM NAT/G DIPLOM

S68
DEUTSCHER I.,"GERMANY AND MARXISM." FUT GERMANY/W NAT/G...MARXIST TREND 20. PAGE 40 H0808 — SOCISM ORD/FREE POPULISM POL/PAR

S68
HOOK S.,"THE ENLIGHTENMENT AND MARXISM." CULTURE SOCIETY RATIONAL ORD/FREE PLURISM SOCISM...CONCPT — IDEA/COMP MARXISM

HIST/WRIT 18/19 MARX/KARL HEGEL/GWF ENLIGHTNMT. PAGE 73 H1462 — OBJECTIVE

S68
LUKASZEWSKI J.,"WESTERN INTEGRATION AND THE PEOPLE'S DEMOCRACIES." USSR ELITES ECO/DEV NAT/G VOL/ASSN INT/TRADE AGREE REV FEDERAL WEALTH SOCISM ...NAT/COMP SOC/INTEG 20 EEC. PAGE 99 H1977 — DIPLOM INT/ORG COM REGION

B84
ENGELS F.,THE ORIGIN OF THE FAMILY, PRIVATE PROPERTY, AND THE STATE (TRANS. BY E. UNTERMANN). UNIV ELITES SOCIETY CAP/ISM ECO/TAC MARRIAGE ORD/FREE POPULISM...MARXIST SOC ENGELS. PAGE 46 H0926 — FAM OWN WEALTH SOCISM

B91
MILL J.S.,SOCIALISM (1859). MOD/EUR AGRI INDUS NAT/G REV INCOME PRODUC ORD/FREE POPULISM SOCISM ...GOV/COMP METH/COMP 19. PAGE 110 H2209 — WEALTH SOCIALIST ECO/TAC OWN

SOCRATES....SOCRATES

N61
PLATO,APOLOGY" IN PLATO, THE COLLECTED DIALOGUES, ED. BY E. HAMILTON AND H. CAIRNS (TRANS. BY H. TREDENNICK). GREECE SOCIETY NAT/G...CONCPT GEN/LAWS SOCRATES. PAGE 126 H2523 — DEATH CT/SYS ATTIT MORAL

SOEMARDJORN S. H2927

SOKOL A.E. H2928

SOKOLSKY W. H1747

SOLOMONS....THE SOLOMON ISLANDS

SOLOVEYTCHIK G. H2929

SOLOW R.M. H2930

SOLT L.F. H2931

SOMALI....SOMALI

S59
SILBERMAN L.,"CHANGE AND CONFLICT IN THE HORN OF AFRICA." EUR+WWI ITALY UK CULTURE FORCES ECO/TAC ADJUD COLONIAL ATTIT ORD/FREE PWR...DECISION METH/CNCPT HIST/WRIT SOMALI 20. PAGE 144 H2874 — AFR TIME/SEQ

B63
TOUVAL S.,SOMALI NATIONALISM: INTERNATIONAL POLITICS AND THE DRIVE FOR UNITY IN THE HORN OF AFRICA. AFR CULTURE PROVS LEGIS EDU/PROP REGION COERCE ATTIT...MYTH UNPLAN/INT TIME/SEQ SOMALI VAL/FREE 20. PAGE 156 H3118 — SOCIETY EXEC NAT/LISM

SOMALIA....SOMALIA; SEE ALSO AFR

B42
CONOVER H.F.,FRENCH COLONIES IN AFRICA: A LIST OF REFERENCES. ALGERIA FRANCE MOROCCO SOMALIA SUDAN CULTURE AGRI LOC/G SECT FORCES DIPLOM INT/TRADE NAT/LISM HEALTH...CON/ANAL 20. PAGE 32 H0641 — BIBLIOG AFR ECO/UNDEV COLONIAL

B60
CONOVER H.F.,OFFICIAL PUBLICATIONS OF SOMALILAND, 1941-1959: A GUIDE. SOMALIA AGRI FINAN INT/ORG SCHOOL INT/TRADE PRESS CONFER COLONIAL PARL/PROC 20 CONGRESS. PAGE 33 H0652 — BIBLIOG NAT/G CON/ANAL

S64
TOUVAL S.,"THE SOMALI REPUBLIC." AFR ISLAM SOMALIA FAM KIN NAT/G CREATE FOR/AID LEGIT ATTIT ALL/VALS ...RECORD TREND 20. PAGE 156 H3119 — ECO/UNDEV RIGID/FLEX

B65
BAYNE E.A.,FOUR WAYS OF POLITICS: STATE AND NATION IN ITALY, SOMALIA, ISRAEL, AND IRAN. IRAN ISRAEL ITALY SOMALIA LEAD CHOOSE MAJORITY GOV/COMP. PAGE 12 H0244 — ECO/UNDEV NAT/G DECISION TOP/EX

SOMMER T. H2932

SONGAI....SONGAI EMPIRES (AFRICA)

SONOLET L. H2933

SOREL/G....GEORGES SOREL

SOROKIN P. H2934

SOROKIN P.A. H2935

SOUPHANGOU....PRINCE SOUPHANGOU-VONG (LEADER OF PATHET LAO)

SOUTH AFRICA....SEE S/AFR

SOUTH ARABIA....SEE ARABIA/SOU

SOUTH KOREA....SEE KOREA/S

SOUTH VIETNAM....SEE VIETNAM/S

SOUTH WEST AFRICA....SEE AFRICA/SW

SOUTH AFRICA COMMISSION ON FUT H2936

SOUTH AFRICA STATE LIBRARY H2937

SOUTH AFRICAN CONGRESS OF DEM H2938

SOUTH PACIFIC COMMISSION H2939

SOUTH/AFR....UNION OF SOUTH AFRICA

N
SCHADERA I.,SELECT BIBLIOGRAPHY OF SOUTH AFRICAN NATIVE LIFE AND PROBLEMS. SOUTH/AFR LAW CULTURE ECO/UNDEV COLONIAL PARTIC...POLICY LING 20. PAGE 138 H2768 — BIBLIOG/A SOC AFR STRUCT

N
TTOEMEYER G.,SOUTH AFRICA; SOUTHWEST AFRICA: A BIBLIOGRAPHY, 1945-1963. AFR SOUTH/AFR PRESS...SOC 20. PAGE 157 H3134 — BIBLIOG CULTURE NAT/G EDU/PROP

N
SOUTH AFRICA STATE LIBRARY,SOUTH AFRICAN NATIONAL BIBLIOGRAPHY, SANB. SOUTH/AFR LAW NAT/G EDU/PROP ...MGT PSY SOC 20. PAGE 147 H2937 — BIBLIOG PRESS WRITING

B00
HOBSON J.A.,THE WAR IN SOUTH AFRICA: ITS CAUSES AND EFFECTS. NETHERLAND SOUTH/AFR UK ELITES AGRI EXTR/IND POL/PAR DIPLOM PRESS RACE/REL ATTIT ORD/FREE SOVEREIGN...INT 19 NEGRO. PAGE 72 H1439 — WAR DOMIN POLICY NAT/G

B00
MARKHAM V.R.,SOUTH AFRICA, PAST AND PRESENT. NETHERLAND SOUTH/AFR CULTURE LEGIS EDU/PROP COLONIAL CHOOSE REPRESENT DISCRIM ATTIT...OBS TIME/SEQ 17/19 NEGRO BOER/WAR. PAGE 103 H2054 — WAR LEAD RACE/REL

B01
BRYCE J.,STUDIES IN HISTORY AND JURISPRUDENCE (2 VOLS.). ICELAND SOUTH/AFR UK LAW PROB/SOLV SOVEREIGN...PHIL/SCI NAT/COMP ROME/ANC ROMAN/LAW. PAGE 23 H0455 — IDEA/COMP CONSTN JURID

B08
THE GOVERNMENT OF SOUTH AFRICA (VOL. II). SOUTH/AFR STRATA EXTR/IND EX/STRUC TOP/EX BUDGET ADJUD ADMIN CT/SYS PRODUC...CORREL CENSUS 19 RAILROAD CIVIL/SERV POSTAL/SYS. PAGE 2 H0030 — CONSTN FINAN LEGIS NAT/G

B10
MENDELSSOHN S.,SOUTH AFRICAN BIBLIOGRAPHY (2 VOLS.). SOUTH/AFR EXTR/IND LABOR SECT DIPLOM INT/TRADE COLONIAL RACE/REL DISCRIM...GEOG 20. PAGE 109 H2172 — BIBLIOG/A AFR NAT/G NAT/LISM

B10
MENDELSSOHN S.,MENDELSSOHN'S SOUTH AFRICA BIBLIOGRAPHY (VOL. I). SOUTH/AFR RACE/REL...GEOG JURID 19/20. PAGE 109 H2173 — BIBLIOG/A CULTURE

B18
EYBERS G.W.,SELECT CONSTITUTIONAL DOCUMENTS ILLUSTRATING SOUTH AFRICAN HISTORY 1795-1910. SOUTH/AFR LOC/G LEGIS CT/SYS...JURID ANTHOL 18/20 NATAL CAPE/HOPE ORANGE/STA. PAGE 48 H0955 — CONSTN LAW NAT/G COLONIAL

B19
NATHAN M.,THE SOUTH AFRICAN COMMONWEALTH: CONSTITUTION, PROBLEMS, SOCIAL CONDITIONS. SOUTH/AFR UK CULTURE INDUS EX/STRUC LEGIS BUDGET EDU/PROP ADMIN CT/SYS GP/REL RACE/REL...LING 19/20 CMN/WLTH. PAGE 116 H2317 — CONSTN NAT/G POL/PAR SOCIETY

N19
SOUTH AFRICA COMMISSION ON FUT,INTERIM AND FINAL REPORTS ON FUTURE FORM OF GOVERNMENT IN THE SOUTH-WEST AFRICAN PROTECTORATE (PAMPHLET). SOUTH/AFR NAT/G FORCES CONFER COLONIAL CONTROL 20 AFRICA/SW. PAGE 147 H2936 — CONSTN REPRESENT ADMIN PROB/SOLV

B23
LEES-SMITH H.B.,SECOND CHAMBERS IN THEORY AND PRACTICE. IRELAND NORWAY SOUTH/AFR UK LAW POL/PAR LEGIS CONTROL 20 CMN/WLTH. PAGE 93 H1858 — PARL/PROC DELIB/GP REPRESENT GP/COMP

B25
WILLIAMS B.,THE SELBORNE MEMORANDUM. AFR FUT SOUTH/AFR UK NAT/G BUDGET DIPLOM REGION GOV/REL SOVEREIGN...POLICY CHARTS 20 UNIFICA SELBORNE/W. PAGE 168 H3365 — COLONIAL PROVS

B30
SMUTS J.C.,AFRICA AND SOME WORLD PROBLEMS. RHODESIA SOUTH/AFR CULTURE ECO/UNDEV INDUS INT/ORG SECT PROB/SOLV REGION GOV/REL DISCRIM ATTIT 19/20 LEAGUE/NAT LIVNGSTN/D NEGRO. PAGE 146 H2921 — LEGIS AFR COLONIAL RACE/REL

B34
LOVELL R.I.,THE STRUGGLE FOR SOUTH AFRICA, 1875-1899. GERMANY RHODESIA SOUTH/AFR UK NAT/G ECO/TAC HABITAT WEALTH...POLICY 19. PAGE 99 H1971 — COLONIAL DIPLOM WAR GP/REL

B36
BOYCE A.N.,EUROPE AND SOUTH AFRICA. FRANCE GERMANY — COLONIAL

ITALY SOUTH/AFR UK INDUS NAT/G CONTROL REV WAR NAT/LISM...CONCPT HIST/WRIT 20. PAGE 20 H0392
GOV/COMP NAT/COMP DIPLOM

B37
DE KIEWIET C.W.,THE IMPERIAL FACTOR IN SOUTH AFRICA. AFR SOUTH/AFR UK WAR...POLICY SOC 19. PAGE 38 H0759
DIPLOM COLONIAL CULTURE

B37
UNION OF SOUTH AFRICA,REPORT CONCERNING ADMINISTRATION OF SOUTH WEST AFRICA (6 VOLS.). SOUTH/AFR INDUS PUB/INST FORCES LEGIS BUDGET DIPLOM EDU/PROP ADJUD CT/SYS...GEOG CHARTS 20 AFRICA/SW LEAGUE/NAT. PAGE 158 H3166
NAT/G ADMIN COLONIAL CONSTN

B39
VAN BILJON F.J.,STATE INTERFERENCE IN SOUTH AFRICA. SOUTH/AFR ECO/UNDEV AGRI INDUS WORKER RATION WEALTH ...JURID 20. PAGE 161 H3225
ECO/TAC POLICY INT/TRADE NAT/G

B42
JOSHI P.S.,THE TYRANNY OF COLOUR. INDIA SOUTH/AFR UK ECO/UNDEV NAT/G POL/PAR DIPLOM ECO/TAC WAR ...POLICY 19/20. PAGE 82 H1637
COLONIAL DISCRIM RACE/REL

B46
HUTTON J.,THE CONSTITUTION OF THE UNION OF SOUTH AFRICA: BIBLIOGRAPHY (PAMPHLET). SOUTH/AFR MUNIC DIPLOM RACE/REL 20. PAGE 75 H1510
BIBLIOG CONSTN NAT/G LOC/G

B52
INTERNATIONAL AFRICAN INST,ETHNOGRAPHIC SURVEY OF AFRICA: SOUTHERN AFRICA (VOLS. I-III, 1952-1954). AFR SOUTH/AFR CULTURE ECO/UNDEV GOV/REL HEREDITY ...GEOG SOC CHARTS BIBLIOG WORSHIP 20. PAGE 77 H1544
STRUCT KIN INGP/REL HABITAT

B55
PYRAH G.B.,IMPERIAL POLICY AND SOUTH AFRICA 1902-1910. SOUTH/AFR UK NAT/G WAR DISCRIM...CONCPT CHARTS BIBLIOG/A 19/20 CMN/WLTH. PAGE 129 H2570
DIPLOM COLONIAL POLICY RACE/REL

B56
INTERNATIONAL AFRICAN INST,SOCIAL IMPLICATIONS OF INDUSTRIALIZATION AND URBANIZATION IN AFRICA SOUTH OF THE SAHARA. SOUTH/AFR INDUS LABOR MUNIC WORKER TEC/DEV...SOC OBS TREND ANTHOL 20. PAGE 77 H1549
AFR ECO/UNDEV ADJUST CULTURE

B56
KUPER L.,PASSIVE RESISTANCE IN SOUTH AFRICA. SOUTH/AFR LAW NAT/G POL/PAR VOL/ASSN DISCRIM ...POLICY SOC AUD/VIS 20. PAGE 89 H1782
ORD/FREE RACE/REL ATTIT

N56
US HOUSE COMM FOREIGN AFFAIRS,REPORT OF THE SPECIAL STUDY MISSION TO AFRICA, SOUTH AND EAST OF THE SAHARA (PAMPHLET). AFR SOUTH/AFR USA+45 STRUCT INT/TRADE PARL/PROC NAT/LISM ATTIT ALL/VALS HEALTH ...POLICY 20 CONGRESS. PAGE 160 H3197
FOR/AID COLONIAL ECO/UNDEV DIPLOM

B57
NEUMARK S.D.,ECONOMIC INFLUENCES ON THE SOUTH AFRICAN FRONTIER, 1652-1836. SOUTH/AFR SEA AGRI NAT/G FORCES WORKER DIPLOM INT/TRADE PRICE DEMAND PRODUC...STAT CHARTS 17/19 FRONTIER. PAGE 117 H2341
COLONIAL ECO/UNDEV ECO/TAC MARKET

B57
ROBERTSON H.M.,SOUTH AFRICA, ECONOMIC AND POLITICAL ASPECTS. SOUTH/AFR CONSTN CULTURE POL/PAR LEGIS DIPLOM DOMIN COLONIAL...SOC BIBLIOG 19/20. PAGE 132 H2647
RACE/REL ECO/UNDEV ECO/TAC DISCRIM

B58
BRADY A.,DEMOCRACY IN THE DOMINIONS (3RD ED.). CANADA NEW/ZEALND SOUTH/AFR WOR+45 LAW EX/STRUC DOMIN COLONIAL PARL/PROC REPRESENT RACE/REL NAT/LISM WEALTH 20 AUSTRAL CMN/WLTH. PAGE 20 H0399
GOV/COMP POL/PAR POPULISM NAT/G

B59
MAC MILLAN W.M.,THE ROAD TO SELF-RULE. SOUTH/AFR UK CULTURE SOCIETY AGRI LABOR NAT/G INT/TRADE CONTROL GP/REL...SOC 19/20. PAGE 100 H1988
AFR COLONIAL SOVEREIGN POLICY

B60
ROSKAM K.L.,APARTHEID AND DISCRIMINATION. SOUTH/AFR SOCIETY STRUCT NAT/G POL/PAR GP/REL ISOLAT ...BIBLIOG 20. PAGE 134 H2683
DISCRIM RACE/REL CULTURE POLICY

B60
SOUTH AFRICAN CONGRESS OF DEM,FACE THE FUTURE. SOUTH/AFR ELITES LEGIS ADMIN REGION COERCE PEACE ATTIT 20. PAGE 147 H2938
RACE/REL DISCRIM CONSTN NAT/G

S60
TIRYAKIAN E.A.,"APARTHEID AND POLITICS IN SOUTH AFRICA." SOUTH/AFR CULTURE STRATA ECO/DEV NAT/G POL/PAR ROUTINE CHOOSE GP/REL RACE/REL DISCRIM ATTIT ALL/VALS...CONCPT OBS TIME/SEQ VAL/FREE 20. PAGE 155 H3105
AFR DIPLOM

B61
ALLIGHAN G.,VERWOERD - THE END. SOUTH/AFR TOP/EX DIPLOM COLONIAL DISCRIM TOTALISM ATTIT AUTHORIT ...BIOG 20 NEGRO VERWOERD/H. PAGE 5 H0107
CONTROL CHIEF RACE/REL NAT/G

B61
BROUGHTON M.,PRESS AND POLITICS OF SOUTH AFRICA. SOUTH/AFR NAT/G COLONIAL GP/REL ADJUST 20. PAGE 22 H0435
NAT/LISM PRESS PWR CULTURE

B61
MACLURE M.,AFRICA: THE POLITICAL PATTERN. SOUTH/AFR CULTURE LEGIS DIPLOM COLONIAL RACE/REL 20. PAGE 100 H2005
AFR POLICY NAT/G

B61
MUNGER E.S.,AFRICAN FIELD REPORTS 1952-1961. SOUTH/AFR SOCIETY ECO/UNDEV NAT/G POL/PAR COLONIAL EXEC PARL/PROC GUERRILLA RACE/REL ALL/IDEOS...SOC AUD/VIS 20. PAGE 114 H2288
AFR DISCRIM RECORD

B61
SPOONER F.P.,SOUTH AFRICAN PREDICAMENT. FUT SOUTH/AFR INDUS POL/PAR RACE/REL INCOME...CHARTS 20 NEGRO. PAGE 148 H2953
ECO/DEV DISCRIM ECO/TAC POLICY

B62
FEIT E.,SOUTH AFRICA, THE DYNAMICS OF THE AFRICAN NATIONAL CONGRESS. AFR SOUTH/AFR LAW INTELL STRATA KIN NAT/G POL/PAR ECO/TAC DOMIN RISK COERCE 20 NEGRO. PAGE 49 H0984
RACE/REL ELITES CONTROL STRUCT

B62
GREEN L.P.,DEVELOPMENT IN AFRICA. AFR CENTRL/AFR GHANA RHODESIA SOUTH/AFR AGRI PROC/MFG INT/TRADE DEMAND NAT/LISM PRODUC WEALTH...GEOG METH/CNCPT CHARTS BIBLIOG 20. PAGE 60 H1206
CULTURE ECO/UNDEV GOV/REL TREND

B62
MANSERGH N.,SOUTH AFRICA 1906-1961: THE PRICE OF MAGNANIMITY. SOUTH/AFR LEGIS LEGIT SUFF NAT/LISM ATTIT ORD/FREE 20 NEGRO 20. PAGE 102 H2041
COLONIAL DISCRIM NAT/G

B62
TATZ C.M.,SHADOW AND SUBSTANCE IN SOUTH AFRICA. SOUTH/AFR AGRI NAT/G POL/PAR DOMIN GP/REL ATTIT PWR 20. PAGE 152 H3048
RACE/REL REPRESENT DISCRIM LEGIS

B62
VAN RENSBURG P.,GUILTY LAND: THE HISTORY OF APARTHEID. SOUTH/AFR NAT/G POL/PAR DOMIN CHOOSE ...SOC 19/20 NEGRO. PAGE 162 H3231
RACE/REL DISCRIM NAT/LISM POLICY

B63
BROOKES E.H.,POWER, LAW, RIGHT, AND LOVE: A STUDY IN POLITICAL VALUES. SOUTH/AFR NAT/G PERSON ...CONCPT IDEA/COMP 20. PAGE 21 H0432
PWR ORD/FREE JURID LOVE

B63
FIRST R.,SOUTH WEST AFRICA. SOUTH/AFR INT/ORG KIN NAT/G WORKER COLONIAL WAR...POLICY 20 UN TRUST/TERR AFRICA/SW. PAGE 50 H1006
DISCRIM ORD/FREE RACE/REL CONTROL

B63
HAILEY L.,THE REPUBLIC OF SOUTH AFRICA AND THE HIGH COMMISSION TERRITORIES. AFR SOUTH/AFR UK INT/ORG NAT/G PROVS RACE/REL SOVEREIGN...CHARTS 19/20 COMMONWLTH. PAGE 64 H1278
COLONIAL DIPLOM ATTIT

B63
LEWIN J.,POLITICS AND LAW IN SOUTH AFRICA. SOUTH/AFR UK POL/PAR BAL/PWR ECO/TAC COLONIAL CONTROL GP/REL DISCRIM PWR 20 NEGRO. PAGE 96 H1909
NAT/LISM POLICY LAW RACE/REL

B63
MAC MILLAN W.M.,BANTU, BOER, AND BRITON: THE MAKING OF THE SOUTH AFRICAN NATIVE PROBLEM. SOUTH/AFR UK LAW KIN NAT/G SECT LEGIS COLONIAL ISOLAT ATTIT ...BIOG 18/20 BANTU NEGRO PHILIP/J MISSION. PAGE 100 H1989
AFR RACE/REL ELITES

B63
PAUW B.A.,THE SECOND GENERATION. SOUTH/AFR INDUS FAM LABOR SECT EDU/PROP MARRIAGE ATTIT...SOC 20. PAGE 124 H2478
KIN CULTURE STRUCT SOCIETY

B63
STIRNIMANN H.,NGUNI UND GNONI; EINE KULTURGESCHICHTLICHE STUDIE (ACTA ETHNOLOGICA ET LINGUISTICA, NUMBER 6). AFR MALAWI SOUTH/AFR FORCES HABITAT...RECORD CHARTS BIBLIOG WORSHIP 19/20 NATAL. PAGE 149 H2987
CULTURE GP/COMP SOCIETY

B64
BUNTING B.P.,THE RISE OF THE SOUTH AFRICAN REICH. SOUTH/AFR INT/ORG NAT/G FORCES DIPLOM CONTROL WAR TOTALISM ATTIT...GOV/COMP 19/20. PAGE 24 H0477
RACE/REL DISCRIM NAT/LISM TREND

B64
HILL C.R.,BANTUSTANS: THE FRAGMENTATION OF SOUTH AFRICA. AFR SOUTH/AFR ELITES SOCIETY KIN CONTROL DISCRIM ANOMIE ATTIT...POLICY CHARTS GOV/COMP 20 NEGRO BANTUSTANS TRANSKEI NATAL. PAGE 71 H1416
RACE/REL CULTURE LOC/G ORD/FREE

B64
HOPKINSON T.,SOUTH AFRICA. SOUTH/AFR UK NAT/G POL/PAR LEGIS ECO/TAC PARL/PROC WAR...JURID AUD/VIS 19/20. PAGE 73 H1467
SOCIETY RACE/REL DISCRIM

B64
MBEKI G.,SOUTH AFRICA: THE PEASANT'S REVOLT. SOUTH/AFR POL/PAR COERCE REV NAT/LISM ORD/FREE SOVEREIGN 20 NEGRO. PAGE 106 H2114
COLONIAL RACE/REL DISCRIM

DOMIN

B64
SEGAL R.,SANCTIONS AGAINST SOUTH AFRICA. AFR SOUTH/AFR NAT/G INT/TRADE RACE/REL PEACE PWR ...INT/LAW ANTHOL 20 UN. PAGE 141 H2821
SANCTION DISCRIM ECO/TAC POLICY

S64
BENSON M.,"SOUTH AFRICA AND WORLD OPINION." AFR SOUTH/AFR INTELL SOCIETY TOP/EX ECO/TAC DOMIN COERCE DISCRIM ATTIT PWR WEALTH...POLICY RECORD 20. PAGE 14 H0285
NAT/G RIGID/FLEX RACE/REL

B65
GINIEWSKI P.,THE TWO FACES OF APARTHEID. AFR SOUTH/AFR STRATA AGRI INDUS COLONIAL PARTIC SOVEREIGN...CONCPT GOV/COMP NAT/COMP 19/20 NEGRO. PAGE 56 H1131
DISCRIM NAT/G RACE/REL STRUCT

B65
KUPER L.,AN AFRICAN BOURGEOISIE. SOUTH/AFR LAW INTELL NAT/G POL/PAR VOL/ASSN DISCRIM...POLICY 20. PAGE 89 H1783
RACE/REL SOC STRUCT

B65
MEYER F.S.,THE AFRICAN NETTLE. SOUTH/AFR NAT/LISM SOVEREIGN...ANTHOL 20 EUROPE. PAGE 110 H2191
AFR COLONIAL RACE/REL ECO/UNDEV

B65
VATCHER W.H. JR.,WHITE LAAGER: THE RISE OF AFRIKANER NATIONALISM. AFR SOUTH/AFR CULTURE TOTALISM 20. PAGE 162 H3235
NAT/LISM POL/PAR RACE/REL DISCRIM

S65
MULLER A.L.,"SOME NON-ECONOMIC DETERMINANTS OF THE ECONOMIC STATUS OF ASIANS IN AFRICA." AFR SOUTH/AFR CULTURE 20. PAGE 114 H2283
DISCRIM RACE/REL LABOR SECT

S65
VAN DEN BERG M.,"SOME METHODOLOGICAL ASPECTS OF SOUTH AFRICA'S FIRST E.D.P." SOUTH/AFR NAT/G CREATE TEC/DEV CAP/ISM INCOME PRODUC...CON/ANAL CHARTS 20. PAGE 161 H3226
ECO/DEV PLAN METH STAT

B66
EDWARDS C.D.,TRADE REGULATIONS OVERSEAS. IRELAND NEW/ZEALND SOUTH/AFR NAT/G CAP/ISM TARIFFS CONTROL ...POLICY JURID 20 EEC CHINJAP. PAGE 45 H0892
INT/TRADE DIPLOM INT/LAW ECO/TAC

B66
MCKAY V.,AFRICAN DIPLOMACY STUDIES IN THE DETERMINANTS OF FOREIGN POLICY. AFR SOUTH/AFR CULTURE NEUTRAL REGION SOVEREIGN...INT/LAW GOV/COMP ANTHOL 20. PAGE 107 H2138
ECO/UNDEV RACE/REL CIVMIL/REL DIPLOM

B66
MULLER C.F.J.,A SELECT BIBLIOGRAPHY OF SOUTH AFRICAN HISTORY; A GUIDE FOR HISTORICAL RESEARCH. SOUTH/AFR UK LAW CONSTN SOCIETY STRUCT AGRI SECT DIPLOM COLONIAL LEAD RACE/REL...POLICY 17/20 NEGRO. PAGE 114 H2284
BIBLIOG AFR NAT/G

B67
CARTER G.M.,SOUTH AFRICA'S TRANSKEI: THE POLITICS OF DOMESTIC COLONIALISM. SOUTH/AFR ECO/UNDEV AGRI NAT/G PROVS PLAN DOMIN REPRESENT ADJUST DISCRIM ...OBS BIBLIOG 20 BANTUSTANS TRANSKEI. PAGE 27 H0550
STRATA GOV/REL COLONIAL POLICY

B67
MUNGER E.S.,AFRIKANER AND AFRICAN NATIONALISM: SOUTH AFRICAN PARALLELS AND PARAMETERS. SOUTH/AFR WOR+45 CULTURE ELITES STRUCT NAT/G PROB/SOLV DOMIN CONTROL PERS/REL NAT/LISM...SOC 20. PAGE 115 H2289
AFR RACE/REL

L67
UNESCO,"APARTHEID." SOUTH/AFR STRUCT KIN SCHOOL SECT WORKER DOMIN EDU/PROP REGION RACE/REL ISOLAT 20. PAGE 158 H3164
DISCRIM CULTURE COERCE COLONIAL

S67
RAUM O.,"THE MODERN LEADERSHIP GROUP AMONG THE SOUTH AFRICAN XHOSA." SOUTH/AFR SOCIETY SECT EX/STRUC REPRESENT GP/REL INGP/REL PERSON ...METH/COMP 17/20 XHOSA NEGRO. PAGE 130 H2596
RACE/REL KIN LEAD CULTURE

S67
SNELLEN I.T.,"APARTHEID* CHECKS AND CHANGES." SOUTH/AFR NAT/G PROB/SOLV COLONIAL REGION TASK GP/REL RACE/REL EFFICIENCY PRIVIL ORD/FREE 20. PAGE 146 H2923
DISCRIM NAT/LISM EQUILIB CONTROL

L68
CURRENT HISTORY,"AFRICA, 1968." ETHIOPIA GHANA NIGERIA SOUTH/AFR CULTURE ECO/UNDEV KIN SECT CHIEF EX/STRUC WAR WEAPON CHOOSE CIVMIL/REL...GOV/COMP 20 AFRICA/E. PAGE 36 H0724
RACE/REL NAT/LISM FORCES AFR

S68
DUGARD J.,"THE REVOCATION OF THE MANDATE FOR SOUTH WEST AFRICA." SOUTH/AFR WOR+45 STRATA NAT/G DELIB/GP DIPLOM ADJUD SANCTION CHOOSE RACE/REL ...POLICY NAT/COMP 20 AFRICA/SW UN TRUST/TERR LEAGUE/NAT. PAGE 43 H0858
AFR INT/ORG DISCRIM COLONIAL

S68
LAWRIE G.,"WHAT WILL CHANGE SOUTH AFRICA?" AFR SOUTH/AFR ELITES DOMIN CONTROL REPRESENT...TIME/SEQ TREND 20. PAGE 93 H1848
RACE/REL DIPLOM NAT/G POLICY

B99
BROOKS S.,BRITAIN AND THE BOERS. AFR SOUTH/AFR UK CULTURE INSPECT LEGIT...INT/LAW 19/20 BOER/WAR. PAGE 22 H0433
WAR DIPLOM NAT/G

SOUTH/AMER....SOUTH AMERICA

B51
CHRISTENSEN A.N.,THE EVOLUTION OF LATIN AMERICAN GOVERNMENT: A BOOK OF READINGS. ECO/UNDEV INDUS LOC/G POL/PAR EX/STRUC LEGIS FOR/AID CT/SYS ...SOC/WK 20 SOUTH/AMER. PAGE 30 H0599
NAT/G CONSTN DIPLOM L/A+17C

B61
ESTEVEZ A.,ASPECTOS ECONOMICO-FINANCIEROS DE LA CAMPANA SANMARITANA. L/A+17C SPAIN FINAN COLONIAL LEAD ROLE ORD/FREE WEALTH 19 SOUTH/AMER SAN/MARTIN. PAGE 47 H0942
ECO/UNDEV REV BUDGET NAT/G

B63
O'LEARY T.J.,ETHNOGRAPHIC BIBLIOGRAPHY OF SOUTH AMERICA. SOCIETY KIN...GEOG 19/20 SOUTH/AMER. PAGE 120 H2389
SOC CULTURE L/A+17C BIBLIOG

S63
LAMBERT D.,"LA TRANSPOSITION DU REGIME PRESIDENTIEL HORS DES ETATSUNIS; LE CAS DE L'AMERIQUE LATINE." NAT/G EX/STRUC LEGIS PARL/PROC PWR 18/20 PRESIDENT CENTRAL/AM SOUTH/AMER. PAGE 90 H1800
DELIB/GP CHIEF L/A+17C GOV/REL

SOUTH/CAR....SOUTH CAROLINA

SOUTH/DAK....SOUTH DAKOTA

SOUTH/US....SOUTH (UNITED STATES)

B58
OGDEN F.D.,THE POLL TAX IN THE SOUTH. USA+45 USA-45 CONSTN ADJUD ADMIN PARTIC CRIME...TIME/SEQ GOV/COMP METH/COMP 18/20 SOUTH/US. PAGE 120 H2407
TAX CHOOSE RACE/REL DISCRIM

B60
NICHOLLS W.H.,SOUTHERN TRADITION AND REGIONAL PROGRESS. STRATA STRUCT SCHOOL WORKER PARTIC REGION RACE/REL CONSEN ATTIT...SOC METH/CNCPT 19/20 SOUTH/US TVA. PAGE 118 H2349
RIGID/FLEX CONSERVE AGRI CULTURE

SOUTHALL A. H2940

SOUTHEAST ASIA....SEE S/EASTASIA, S/ASIA

SOUTHEAST ASIA TREATY ORGANIZATION....SEE SEATO

SOUTHERN RHODESIA....SEE RHODESIA, COMMONWLTH

SOVEREIGN....SOVEREIGNTY

N
SEMINAR: THE MONTHLY SYMPOSIUM. INDIA ACT/RES TEC/DEV DIPLOM ATTIT...BIBLIOG 20. PAGE 1 H0022
NAT/G ECO/UNDEV SOVEREIGN POLICY

N
NORTHWESTERN UNIVERSITY LIB,JOINT ACQUISITIONS LIST OF AFRICANA. AFR SOCIETY STRUCT EDU/PROP COLONIAL GP/REL RACE/REL NAT/LISM SOVEREIGN...SOC 20. PAGE 119 H2377
BIBLIOG CULTURE ECO/UNDEV INDUS

B00
HOBSON J.A.,THE WAR IN SOUTH AFRICA: ITS CAUSES AND EFFECTS. NETHERLAND SOUTH/AFR UK ELITES AGRI EXTR/IND POL/PAR DIPLOM PRESS RACE/REL ATTIT ORD/FREE SOVEREIGN...INT 19 NEGRO. PAGE 72 H1439
WAR DOMIN POLICY NAT/G

B01
BRYCE J.,STUDIES IN HISTORY AND JURISPRUDENCE (2 VOLS.). ICELAND SOUTH/AFR UK LAW PROB/SOLV SOVEREIGN...PHIL/SCI NAT/COMP ROME/ANC ROMAN/LAW. PAGE 23 H0455
IDEA/COMP CONSTN JURID

B02
SEELEY J.R.,THE EXPANSION OF ENGLAND. MOD/EUR S/ASIA UK CULTURE NAT/G FORCES PLAN DOMIN EDU/PROP COLONIAL ROUTINE ATTIT ALL/VALS SOVEREIGN...CONCPT HIST/WRIT PARLIAMENT 18 CMN/WLTH. PAGE 141 H2819
INT/ORG ACT/RES CAP/ISM INDIA

B04
DANTE ALIGHIERI,DE MONARCHIA (CA .1310). CHRIST-17C ITALY DOMIN LEGIT ATTIT PWR...CATH CONCPT TIME/SEQ. PAGE 37 H0741
SECT NAT/G SOVEREIGN

C05
DUNNING W.A.,"HISTORY OF POLITICAL THEORIES FROM LUTHER TO MONTESQUIEU." LAW NAT/G SECT DIPLOM REV WAR ORD/FREE SOVEREIGN CONSERVE...TRADIT BIBLIOG 16/18. PAGE 43 H0867
PHIL/SCI CONCPT GEN/LAWS

B12
HARIOU M.,LA SOUVERAINTE NATIONALE. EX/STRUC FORCES LEGIS CHOOSE PWR JURID. PAGE 66 H1331
SOVEREIGN CONCPT NAT/G REPRESENT

B17
DE MAISTRE J.,DU PAPE (1817). FRANCE LAW SOCIETY SECT DOMIN REV HAPPINESS PWR SOVEREIGN 18/19 PROTESTANT. PAGE 38 H0761
CATH CHIEF LEGIT NAT/G

N17
BURKE E.,THOUGHTS ON THE PROSPECT OF A REGICIDE PEACE (PAMPHLET). FRANCE UK SECT DOMIN MURDER PEACE ORD/FREE SOVEREIGN POPULISM...POLICY GOV/COMP IDEA/COMP 18 JACOBINISM COEXIST. PAGE 24 H0483
REV CHIEF NAT/G DIPLOM

N17
BURKE E.,LETTER TO SIR HERCULES LANGRISHE (PAMPHLET). IRELAND UK NAT/G CHIEF DIPLOM DOMIN PARL/PROC COERCE ORD/FREE SOVEREIGN POPULISM ...TRADIT 18 BURKE/EDM. PAGE 24 H0485
POLICY COLONIAL SECT

B19
DUGUIT L.,LAW IN THE MODERN STATE (TRANS. BY FRIDA AND HAROLD LASKI). CONSTN SOCIETY STRUCT MORAL ORD/FREE SOVEREIGN 20. PAGE 43 H0860
GEN/LAWS CONCPT NAT/G LAW

N19
BENTHAM J.,A PLAN FOR AN UNIVERSAL AND PERPETUAL PEACE (1838) (PAMPHLET). NAT/G FORCES BAL/PWR INT/TRADE ADMIN AGREE CT/SYS ARMS/CONT SOVEREIGN WEALTH GEN/LAWS. PAGE 14 H0288
INT/ORG INT/LAW PEACE COLONIAL

N19
HANNA A.J.,EUROPEAN RULE IN AFRICA (PAMPHLET). BELGIUM FRANCE MOD/EUR UK WOR+45 WOR-45 ECO/UNDEV NAT/G PARTIC SOVEREIGN...NAT/COMP 19/20. PAGE 66 H1314
DIPLOM COLONIAL AFR NAT/LISM

N19
HARTUNG F.,ENLIGHTENED DESPOTISM (PAMPHLET). ORD/FREE SOVEREIGN CONSERVE...PHIL/SCI FREDERICK ENLIGHTNMT. PAGE 67 H1350
NAT/G CHIEF CONCPT PWR

N19
MASSEY V.,CANADIANS AND THEIR COMMONWEALTH: THE ROMANES LECTURE DELIVERED IN THE SHELDONIAN THEATRE JUNE 1, 1961 (PAMPHLET). CANADA UK CULTURE ECO/DEV REPRESENT NAT/LISM PEACE PWR CONSERVE 20 CMN/WLTH. PAGE 104 H2088
ATTIT DIPLOM NAT/G SOVEREIGN

N19
PROVISIONS SECTION OAU,ORGANIZATION OF AFRICAN UNITY: BASIC DOCUMENTS AND RESOLUTIONS (PAMPHLET). AFR CULTURE ECO/UNDEV DIPLOM ECO/TAC EDU/PROP COLONIAL ARMS/CONT NUC/PWR RACE/REL DISCRIM NAT/LISM 20 UN OAU. PAGE 128 H2564
CONSTN EX/STRUC SOVEREIGN INT/ORG

B22
KRABBE H.,THE MODERN IDEA OF THE STATE. LAW CHIEF DIPLOM DOMIN ADMIN REPRESENT CENTRAL ORD/FREE ...NEW/IDEA GOV/COMP IDEA/COMP. PAGE 88 H1761
SOVEREIGN CONSTN PHIL/SCI

B23
DELBRUCK H.,GOVERNMENT AND THE WILL OF THE PEOPLE (TRANS. BY ROY S. MACELWEE). MOD/EUR NAT/G CHOOSE REPRESENT...CONCPT 19/20. PAGE 39 H0788
SOVEREIGN ORD/FREE MAJORITY POL/PAR

B25
WILLIAMS B.,THE SELBORNE MEMORANDUM. AFR FUT SOUTH/AFR UK NAT/G BUDGET DIPLOM REGION GOV/REL SOVEREIGN...POLICY CHARTS 20 UNIFICA SELBORNE/W. PAGE 168 H3365
COLONIAL PROVS

B26
MACIVER R.M.,THE MODERN STATE. POL/PAR ORD/FREE TIME/SEQ. PAGE 100 H1997
NAT/G CONCPT JURID SOVEREIGN

B26
MCIVER R.M.,THE MODERN STATE. UNIV LAW AUTHORIT SOVEREIGN IDEA/COMP. PAGE 107 H2136
GEN/LAWS CONSTN NAT/G PWR

B27
HOCART A.M.,KINGSHIP. UNIV CULTURE EX/STRUC TRIBUTE ROUTINE CHOOSE ROLE SOVEREIGN RITUAL 20 KING. PAGE 72 H1441
CHIEF MYTH IDEA/COMP

B27
PANIKKAR K.M.,INDIAN STATES AND THE GOVERNMENT OF INDIA. INDIA UK CONSTN CONTROL TASK GP/REL SOVEREIGN WEALTH...TREND BIBLIOG 19. PAGE 123 H2457
GOV/COMP COLONIAL BAL/PWR PROVS

B28
HOBBES T.,THE ELEMENTS OF LAW, NATURAL AND POLITIC (1650). STRATA NAT/G SECT CHIEF AGREE ATTIT ALL/VALS MORAL ORD/FREE POPULISM...POLICY CONCPT. PAGE 71 H1432
PERSON LAW SOVEREIGN CONSERVE

B28
HURST C.,GREAT BRITAIN AND THE DOMINIONS. EUR+WWI CULTURE ECO/DEV INT/ORG NAT/G DIPLOM ECO/TAC COLONIAL ATTIT PWR SOVEREIGN...TIME/SEQ GEN/LAWS TOT/POP VAL/FREE 20 CMN/WLTH. PAGE 75 H1508
VOL/ASSN DOMIN UK

B28
MARSILIUS/PADUA,DEFENSOR PACIS (1324). CHRIST-17C CONSTN NAT/G DIPLOM DOMIN LEGIT CONTROL WAR PEACE ORD/FREE SOVEREIGN POPULISM 14 POPE. PAGE 103 H2059
CATH SECT GEN/LAWS

C28
WARD P.W.,"SOVEREIGNTY: A STUDY OF A CONTEMPORARY POLITICAL NOTION." CONSTN NAT/G DIPLOM REPRESENT PLURISM...IDEA/COMP BIBLIOG. PAGE 165 H3304
SOVEREIGN CONCPT NAT/LISM

B29
ROBERTS S.H.,HISTORY OF FRENCH COLONIAL POLICY. AFR ASIA L/A+17C S/ASIA CULTURE ECO/DEV ECO/UNDEV FINAN NAT/G PLAN ECO/TAC DOMIN ROUTINE SOVEREIGN...OBS HIST/WRIT TREND CHARTS VAL/FREE 19/20. PAGE 132 H2642
INT/ORG ACT/RES FRANCE COLONIAL

B30
BURLAMAQUI J.J.,PRINCIPLES OF NATURAL AND POLITIC LAW (2 VOLS.) (1747-51). EX/STRUC LEGIS AGREE CT/SYS CHOOSE ROLE SOVEREIGN 18 NATURL/LAW. PAGE 24 H0490
LAW NAT/G ORD/FREE CONCPT

B30
OLDMAN J.H.,WHITE AND BLACK IN AFRICA. AFR STRUCT COLONIAL PARTIC DISCRIM ISOLAT PRIVIL 20 SMUTS/JAN NEGRO WHITE/SUP. PAGE 121 H2412
SOVEREIGN ORD/FREE RACE/REL NAT/G

B31
DEKAT A.D.A.,COLONIAL POLICY. S/ASIA CULTURE EX/STRUC ECO/TAC DOMIN ADMIN COLONIAL ROUTINE SOVEREIGN WEALTH...POLICY MGT RECORD KNO/TEST SAMP. PAGE 39 H0785
DRIVE PWR INDONESIA NETHERLAND

C31
MOGI S.,"THE PROBLEM OF FEDERALISM: A STUDY IN THE HISTORY OF POLITICAL THEORY." CONSTN COLONIAL NAT/LISM SOVEREIGN LAISSEZ PLURISM 18/20. PAGE 112 H2235
FEDERAL CONCPT NAT/G

B32
BRYCE J.,THE HOLY ROMAN EMPIRE. GERMANY ITALY MOD/EUR CULTURE SOCIETY STRUCT INT/ORG NAT/G SECT DIPLOM DOMIN WAR SUPEGO ALL/VALS SOVEREIGN...GEOG SOC TIME/SEQ CHARTS STERTYP. PAGE 23 H0456
CHRIST-17C NAT/LISM

B32
GREAT BRIT COMM MINISTERS PWR,REPORT. UK LAW CONSTN CONSULT LEGIS PARL/PROC SANCTION SOVEREIGN ...DECISION JURID 20 PARLIAMENT. PAGE 60 H1201
EX/STRUC NAT/G PWR CONTROL

B32
MARRARO H.R.,AMERICAN OPINION ON THE UNIFICATION OF ITALY. ITALY FORCES DIPLOM SOVEREIGN CATHISM CONSERVE...CONCPT NAT/COMP BIBLIOG 19. PAGE 103 H2056
ORD/FREE NAT/LISM REV CONSTN

C33
MURET C.T.,"FRENCH ROYALIST DOCTRINES SINCE THE REVOLUTION." FRANCE CONSTN NAT/G SECT ADMIN LEAD SOVEREIGN...POLICY BIOG IDEA/COMP BIBLIOG 18/20. PAGE 115 H2295
POL/PAR ATTIT INTELL CONSERVE

B35
AQUINAS T.,ON THE GOVERNANCE OF RULERS (1265-66). UNIV SOCIETY STRATA FAM HABITAT PERSON ALL/VALS PWR SOVEREIGN CONSERVE...POLICY BIBLE. PAGE 8 H0155
CATH NAT/G CHIEF SUPEGO

B35
PARETO V.,THE MIND AND SOCIETY (4 VOLS.). ELITES SECT ECO/TAC COERCE PERSON ORD/FREE PWR SOVEREIGN FASCISM POPULISM...TRADIT 19/20. PAGE 123 H2465
GEN/LAWS SOC PSY

B36
RAPPARD W.E.,THE GOVERNMENT OF SWITZERLAND. SWITZERLND INT/ORG POL/PAR EX/STRUC DIPLOM NEUTRAL PARL/PROC REGION WAR HABITAT SOVEREIGN...NAT/COMP SOC/INTEG 20 LEAGUE/NAT WWI. PAGE 130 H2594
CONSTN NAT/G CULTURE FEDERAL

B36
VICO G.B.,DIRITTO UNIVERSALE (1722) (VOL. 2, PARTS 1,2, AND 3, OF G.B. VICO, OPERE). UNIV DIPLOM AGREE WAR OWN KNOWL ORD/FREE SOVEREIGN DEITY. PAGE 162 H3249
JURID SECT CONCPT NAT/G

C36
MAZZINI J.,"FROM THE COUNCIL TO GOD" (1870) IN J. MAZZINI, ESSAYS." ITALY NAT/G EDU/PROP PARTIC ORD/FREE PWR SOVEREIGN 19 POPE CHRISTIAN DEITY. PAGE 106 H2112
CATHISM DOMIN NAT/LISM SUPEGO

B38
POUND R.,THE FORMATIVE ERA OF AMERICAN LAW. CULTURE NAT/G PROVS LEGIS ADJUD CT/SYS PERSON SOVEREIGN ...POLICY IDEA/COMP GEN/LAWS 18/19. PAGE 127 H2548
CONSTN LAW CREATE JURID

B38
SAINT-PIERRE C.I.,SCHEME FOR LASTING PEACE (TRANS. BY H. BELLOT). INDUS NAT/G CHIEF FORCES INT/TRADE CT/SYS WAR PWR SOVEREIGN WEALTH...POLICY 18. PAGE 137 H2732
INT/ORG PEACE AGREE INT/LAW

B39
ANDERSON W.,LOCAL GOVERNMENT IN EUROPE. FRANCE GERMANY ITALY UK USSR MUNIC PROVS ADMIN GOV/REL CENTRAL SOVEREIGN 20. PAGE 7 H0136
GOV/COMP NAT/COMP LOC/G CONSTN

B39
COBBAN A.,DICTATORSHIP: ITS HISTORY AND THEORY. EUR+WWI MOD/EUR SOCIETY STRUCT NAT/G TEC/DEV LEAD NAT/LISM SOVEREIGN...IDEA/COMP 14/20. PAGE 30 H0610
TOTALISM FASCISM CONCPT

B39
FURNIVALL J.S.,NETHERLANDS INDIA. INDIA NETHERLAND CULTURE INDUS NAT/G DIPLOM ADMIN WEALTH...POLICY CHARTS 17/20. PAGE 54 H1081
COLONIAL ECO/UNDEV SOVEREIGN PLURISM

B39
MCILWAIN C.H.,CONSTITUTIONALISM AND THE CHANGING WORLD. UK USA-45 LEGIS PRIVIL AUTHORIT SOVEREIGN ...GOV/COMP 15/20 MAGNA/CART HOUSE/CMNS. PAGE 107 H2133 — CONSTN POLICY JURID

B39
TAGGART F.J.,ROME AND CHINA. MEDIT-7 INT/ORG NAT/G FORCES LEGIS TOP/EX PLAN PWR SOVEREIGN...CHARTS TOT/POP ROM/EMP. PAGE 152 H3034 — ASIA WAR

C40
FAHS C.B.,"GOVERNMENT IN JAPAN." FINAN FORCES LEGIS TOP/EX BUDGET INT/TRADE EDU/PROP SOVEREIGN ...CON/ANAL BIBLIOG/A 20 CHINJAP. PAGE 48 H0962 — ASIA DIPLOM NAT/G ADMIN

B41
HITLER A.,MEIN KAMPF (UNABR. ENG. VERSION) (1925). GERMANY CONSTN TEC/DEV RACE/REL NAT/LISM TOTALISM SOVEREIGN...BIOG 20 HITLER/A TREATY. PAGE 71 H1429 — EDU/PROP WAR PLAN FASCISM

C43
BENTHAM J.,"PRINCIPLES OF INTERNATIONAL LAW" IN J. BOWRING, ED., THE WORKS OF JEREMY BENTHAM." UNIV NAT/G PLAN PROB/SOLV DIPLOM CONTROL SANCTION MORAL ORD/FREE PWR SOVEREIGN 19. PAGE 15 H0291 — INT/LAW JURID WAR PEACE

B44
KOHN H.,THE IDEA OF NATIONALISM. UNIV SOCIETY KIN CREATE REGION CENTRAL SOVEREIGN. PAGE 87 H1740 — NAT/LISM CONCPT NAT/G GP/REL

B45
HORN O.B.,BRITISH PUBLIC OPINION AND THE FIRST PARTITION OF POLAND. POLAND UK LEGIS PRESS RUMOR CONTROL PARTIC NAT/LISM SOVEREIGN 18/19. PAGE 73 H1469 — DIPLOM POLICY ATTIT NAT/G

B47
CROCKER W.R.,ON GOVERNING COLONIES: BEING AN OUTLINE OF THE REAL ISSUES AND A COMPARISON OF THE BRITISH, FRENCH, AND BELGIAN... AFR BELGIUM FRANCE UK CULTURE SOVEREIGN...OBS 20. PAGE 35 H0705 — COLONIAL POLICY GOV/COMP ADMIN

B47
MCILWAIN C.H.,CONSTITUTIONALISM: ANCIENT AND MODERN. USA+45 ROMAN/EMP LAW CHIEF LEGIS CT/SYS GP/REL ORD/FREE SOVEREIGN...POLICY TIME/SEQ ROMAN/REP EUROPE. PAGE 107 H2135 — CONSTN NAT/G PARL/PROC GOV/COMP

B48
FURNIVAL J.,COLONIAL POLICY AND PRACTICE A COMPARATIVE STUDY OF BURMA, AND NETHERLANDS INDIA. BURMA INDONESIA S/ASIA...GEOG OBS GOV/COMP METH/COMP 20. PAGE 54 H1080 — COLONIAL NAT/LISM WEALTH SOVEREIGN

B48
PELCOVITS N.A.,OLD CHINA HANDS AND THE FOREIGN OFFICE. ASIA BURMA UK ECO/UNDEV NAT/G ECO/TAC FOR/AID TARIFFS DOMIN COLONIAL GOV/REL SOVEREIGN 19 HONG/KONG TREATY. PAGE 124 H2483 — INT/TRADE ATTIT DIPLOM

B49
DE JOUVENEL B.,ON POWER: ITS NATURE AND THE HISTORY OF ITS GROWTH. SOCIETY CHIEF REV WAR ATTIT AUTHORIT ORD/FREE SOVEREIGN CONSERVE POPULISM CONCPT. PAGE 38 H0757 — PWR NAT/G DOMIN CONTROL

B49
HAUSER R.,AUTORITAT UND MACHT. SOCIETY SECT PWR CATHISM...JURID CONCPT 16/20 PROTESTANT LUTHER/M CALVIN/J CHURCH/STA. PAGE 68 H1360 — SOVEREIGN NAT/G LEGIT

L49
BRECHT A.,"THE NEW GERMAN CONSTITUTION." GERMANY/W NAT/G CHIEF EX/STRUC LEGIS PROB/SOLV ADMIN REPRESENT TOTALISM ORD/FREE PLURISM...MAJORIT CHARTS 20. PAGE 20 H0409 — CONSTN DIPLOM SOVEREIGN FEDERAL

B50
ORTON W.A.,THE ECONOMIC ROLE OF THE STATE. INTELL ECO/UNDEV PLAN CONTROL PWR SOVEREIGN...POLICY 17/20. PAGE 122 H2431 — ECO/DEV NAT/G ECO/TAC ORD/FREE

B51
CARRINGTON C.E.,THE LIQUIDATION OF THE BRITISH EMPIRE. AFR NAT/G INT/TRADE COLONIAL RACE/REL ATTIT ORD/FREE...POLICY NAT/COMP 20 CMN/WLTH. PAGE 27 H0541 — SOVEREIGN NAT/LISM DIPLOM GP/REL

B52
KOHN H.,PROPHETS AND PEOPLES: STUDIES IN NINETEENTH CENTURY NATIONALISM. MOD/EUR...IDEA/COMP 19. PAGE 87 H1741 — CONCPT NAT/LISM SOVEREIGN

B52
KOLARZ W.,RUSSIA AND HER COLONIES. COM RUSSIA LAW CULTURE ECO/DEV KIN LOC/G SECT TEC/DEV ECO/TAC EDU/PROP REGION COERCE ATTIT PWR SOVEREIGN...SOC TIME/SEQ CON/ANAL VAL/FREE 19/20. PAGE 88 H1749 — NAT/G DOMIN USSR COLONIAL

S52
MCDOUGAL M.S.,"THE COMPARATIVE STUDY OF LAW FOR POLICY PURPOSES." FUT NAT/G POL/PAR CONSULT ADJUD PWR SOVEREIGN...METH/CNCPT IDEA/COMP SIMUL 20. PAGE 106 H2129 — PLAN JURID NAT/LISM

B53
DAVIDSON B.,THE NEW WEST AFRICA: PROBLEMS OF INDEPENDENCE. UK AGRI TEC/DEV DIPLOM GP/REL RACE/REL SOVEREIGN...ANTHOL 20 AFRICA/W. PAGE 37 H0744 — AFR COLONIAL ECO/UNDEV NAT/G

B53
LIEBER F.,CIVIL LIBERTY AND SELF GOVERNMENT: VOLUME 2. NAT/G CONTROL CHOOSE PERSON PWR 19 CIVIL/LIB. PAGE 96 H1925 — ORD/FREE SOVEREIGN CENTRAL CONCPT

B53
MARITAIN J.,L'HOMME ET L'ETAT. SECT DIPLOM GP/REL PEACE ORD/FREE...IDEA/COMP 17/20 CHURCH/STA NATURL/LAW. PAGE 103 H2052 — CONCPT NAT/G SOVEREIGN COERCE

B53
ROSCIO J.G.,OBRAS. L/A+17C SPAIN DIPLOM REV WAR NAT/LISM TOTALISM PWR SOVEREIGN 19. PAGE 134 H2671 — ORD/FREE COLONIAL NAT/G PHIL/SCI

S54
DODD S.C.,"THE SCIENTIFIC MEASUREMENT OF FITNESS FOR SELF-GOVERNMENT." FUT CONSTN ECO/UNDEV INT/ORG PLAN PWR...CONCPT QUANT CON/ANAL SOC/EXP UN LEAGUE/NAT 20. PAGE 41 H0830 — NAT/G STAT SOVEREIGN

B55
APTER D.E.,THE GOLD COAST IN TRANSITION. FUT CONSTN CULTURE SOCIETY ECO/UNDEV FAM KIN LOC/G NAT/G POL/PAR LEGIS TOP/EX EDU/PROP LEGIT ADMIN ATTIT PERSON PWR...CONCPT STAT INT CENSUS TOT/POP VAL/FREE. PAGE 7 H0149 — AFR SOVEREIGN

B55
HELANDER S.,DAS AUTARKIEPROBLEM IN DER WELTWIRTSCHAFT. PROB/SOLV BAL/PWR BARGAIN CAP/ISM ECO/TAC SOVEREIGN 20. PAGE 69 H1388 — NAT/COMP COLONIAL DIPLOM

B55
KOHN H.,THE MIND OF MODERN RUSSIA. COM MOD/EUR USSR SOCIETY NAT/G SECT FORCES TOP/EX COERCE TOTALISM DRIVE RIGID/FLEX PWR SOVEREIGN...CONCPT TIME/SEQ WORK. PAGE 87 H1742 — INTELL GEN/LAWS SOCISM RUSSIA

B55
SVARLIEN O.,AN INTRODUCTION TO THE LAW OF NATIONS. SEA AIR INT/ORG NAT/G CHIEF ADMIN AGREE WAR PRIVIL ORD/FREE SOVEREIGN...BIBLIOG 16/20. PAGE 151 H3012 — INT/LAW DIPLOM

B55
TOYNBEE A.,THE REALIGNMENT OF EUROPE. COM GREECE ITALY NAT/G BAL/PWR ECO/TAC EDU/PROP REV SOVEREIGN ...SOC TIME/SEQ TREND COLD/WAR 20. PAGE 156 H3123 — EUR+WWI PLAN USSR

S55
BENN S.I.,"THE USES OF 'SOVEREIGNTY'." UNIV NAT/G LEGIS DIPLOM COERCE...METH/CNCPT GEN/LAWS. PAGE 14 H0282 — SOVEREIGN IDEA/COMP CONCPT PWR

S55
DE SMITH S.A.,"CONSTITUTIONAL MONARCHY IN BURGANDA." AFR UGANDA UK STRUCT CHIEF REGION INGP/REL ADJUST NAT/LISM SOVEREIGN CONSERVE ...POLICY 19/20 BURGANDA. PAGE 38 H0769 — NAT/G DIPLOM CONSTN COLONIAL

B56
FIELD G.C.,POLITICAL THEORY. POL/PAR REPRESENT MORAL SOVEREIGN...JURID IDEA/COMP. PAGE 50 H0990 — CONCPT NAT/G ORD/FREE DIPLOM

B56
RIESENBERG P.N.,INALIENABILITY OF SOVEREIGNTY IN MEDIEVAL POLITICAL THOUGHT. CHRIST-17C INTELL NAT/G SECT CHIEF LEGIS SANCTION AUTHORIT ORD/FREE CONSERVE...IDEA/COMP BIBLIOG 12/16. PAGE 131 H2627 — SOVEREIGN ATTIT

B56
VIANNA F.J.,EVOLUCAO DE POVO BRASILEIRO (4TH ED.). BRAZIL TEC/DEV COLONIAL GP/REL ATTIT SOVEREIGN ...SOC SOC/INTEG 15/20. PAGE 162 H3247 — STRUCT RACE/REL NAT/G

B56
VON HARPE W.,DIE SOWJETUNION FINNLAND UND SKANDANAVIEN, 1945-1955. EUR+WWI FINLAND GERMANY USSR WAR INGP/REL ORD/FREE SOVEREIGN MARXISM ...POLICY GOV/COMP BIBLIOG 20 STALIN/J. PAGE 163 H3270 — DIPLOM COM NEUTRAL BAL/PWR

B57
DONALDSON A.G.,SOME COMPARATIVE ASPECTS OF IRISH LAW. IRELAND NAT/G DIPLOM ADMIN CT/SYS LEAD ATTIT SOVEREIGN...JURID BIBLIOG/A 12/20 CMN/WLTH. PAGE 42 H0835 — CONSTN LAW NAT/COMP INT/LAW

B57
HODGKIN T.,NATIONALISM IN COLONIAL AFRICA. STRATA STRUCT MUNIC NAT/G POL/PAR LEGIS ATTIT SOVEREIGN ...POLICY TREND BIBLIOG 20. PAGE 72 H1444 — AFR COLONIAL NAT/LISM DIPLOM

B57
KANTOROWICZ E.,THE KING'S TWO BODIES; A STUDY IN MEDIEVAL POLITICAL THEOLOGY. UK LAW CONSTN NAT/G CT/SYS...ART/METH HUM CONCPT MYTH TIME/SEQ BIBLIOG 4/17 ELIZABTH/I POPE CHURCH/STA. PAGE 83 H1657 — JURID SECT CHIEF SOVEREIGN

B57
PALMER N.D.,INTERNATIONAL RELATIONS. WOR+45 INT/ORG NAT/G ECO/TAC EDU/PROP COLONIAL WAR PWR SOVEREIGN ...POLICY T 20 TREATY. PAGE 123 H2451 — DIPLOM BAL/PWR NAT/COMP

S57
KILSON M.L.,"LAND AND POLITICS IN KENYA: AN ANALYSIS OF AFRICAN POLITICS IN A PLURAL SOCIETY." — AFR ECO/UNDEV

FUT LAW CULTURE KIN NAT/G ECO/TAC DOMIN REV NAT/LISM ORD/FREE PWR RESPECT SOVEREIGN WEALTH ...SOC OBS TREND WORK VAL/FREE CMN/WLTH 20. PAGE 86 H1710

B58

BRIERLY J.L.,THE BASIS OF OBLIGATION IN INTERNATIONAL LAW, AND OTHER PAPERS. WOR+45 WOR-45 LEGIS...JURID CONCPT NAT/COMP ANTHOL 20. PAGE 21 H0415
[INT/LAW DIPLOM ADJUD SOVEREIGN]

B58

COWAN L.G.,LOCAL GOVERNMENT IN WEST AFRICA. AFR FRANCE UK CULTURE KIN POL/PAR CHIEF LEGIS CREATE ADMIN PARTIC GOV/REL GP/REL...METH/COMP 20. PAGE 34 H0682
[LOC/G COLONIAL SOVEREIGN REPRESENT]

B58

EUSDEN J.D.,PURITANS, LAWYERS, AND POLITICS IN EARLY SEVENTEENTH-CENTURY ENGLAND. UK CT/SYS PARL/PROC RATIONAL PWR SOVEREIGN...IDEA/COMP BIBLIOG 17 PURITAN COMMON/LAW. PAGE 48 H0951
[GP/REL SECT NAT/G LAW]

B58

LAHBABI M.,LE GOUVERNEMENT MAROCAIN A L'AUBE DU XXE SIECLE. FRANCE MOROCCO CHIEF EX/STRUC LEGIS ORD/FREE PWR...JURID BIBLIOG 19/20. PAGE 90 H1797
[NAT/G COLONIAL SOVEREIGN]

B59

DEHIO L.,GERMANY AND WORLD POLITICS IN THE TWENTIETH CENTURY. EUR+WWI FRANCE GERMANY MOD/EUR UK USSR NAT/G CHIEF BAL/PWR DOMIN COLONIAL CONTROL LEAD...IDEA/COMP 20 VERSAILLES. PAGE 39 H0783
[DIPLOM WAR NAT/LISM SOVEREIGN]

B59

MAC MILLAN W.M.,THE ROAD TO SELF-RULE. SOUTH/AFR UK CULTURE SOCIETY AGRI LABOR NAT/G INT/TRADE CONTROL GP/REL...SOC 19/20. PAGE 100 H1988
[AFR COLONIAL SOVEREIGN POLICY]

B59

MARTZ J.D.,CENTRAL AMERICA: THE CRISIS AND THE CHALLENGE. L/A+17C POL/PAR CHIEF CHOOSE SOVEREIGN ...BIOG TREND BIBLIOG 20 CENTRAL/AM. PAGE 104 H2071
[NAT/G GOV/REL DIPLOM GOV/COMP]

B59

PANIKKAR K.M.,THE AFRO-ASIAN STATES AND THEIR PROBLEMS. COM CULTURE KIN POL/PAR SECT DIPLOM EDU/PROP COLONIAL SOVEREIGN...TECHNIC GOV/COMP 20. PAGE 123 H2458
[AFR S/ASIA ECO/UNDEV]

B59

SANCHEZ A.L.,EL CONCEPTO DEL ESTADO EN EL PENSAMIENTO ESPANOL DEL SIGLO XVI. SPAIN LEGIS JUDGE BAL/PWR LEGIT EXEC WAR PWR...MAJORIT 16. PAGE 137 H2747
[NAT/G PHIL/SCI LAW SOVEREIGN]

B59

VITTACHIT,EMERGENCY '58. CEYLON UK STRUCT NAT/G FORCES ADJUD CRIME REV NAT/LISM 20. PAGE 163 H3258
[RACE/REL DISCRIM DIPLOM SOVEREIGN]

B60

ALBI F.,TRATADO DE LOS MODOS DE GESTION DE LAS CORPORACIONES LOCALES. SPAIN FINAN NAT/G BUDGET CONTROL EXEC ROUTINE GOV/REL ORD/FREE SOVEREIGN ...MGT 20. PAGE 5 H0092
[LOC/G LAW ADMIN MUNIC]

B60

ALMOND G.A.,THE POLITICS OF THE DEVELOPING AREAS. AFR ISLAM L/A+17C S/ASIA SOCIETY ECO/UNDEV NAT/G ADMIN PERCEPT KNOWL SOVEREIGN...CONCPT GEN/LAWS 20. PAGE 6 H0112
[EX/STRUC ATTIT NAT/LISM]

B60

CARTER G.M.,INDEPENDENCE FOR AFRICA. AFR FUT SOCIETY STRATA ECO/DEV POL/PAR DELIB/GP PLAN DOMIN EDU/PROP COLONIAL REGION ATTIT DRIVE SOVEREIGN ...RECORD INT TIME/SEQ CHARTS 20. PAGE 27 H0544
[NAT/G PWR NAT/LISM]

B60

EMERSON R.,FROM EMPIRE TO NATION: THE RISE TO SELF-ASSERTION OF ASIAN AND AFRICAN PEOPLES. S/ASIA CULTURE NAT/G SECT DIPLOM ATTIT SOVEREIGN MARXISM ...POLICY BIBLIOG 19/20. PAGE 46 H0919
[NAT/LISM COLONIAL AFR ASIA]

B60

JEFFRIES C.,TRANSFER OF POWER: PROBLEMS OF THE PASSAGE TO SELFGOVERNMENT. CEYLON GHANA MALAYSIA NIGERIA UK INT/ORG CONSULT DELIB/GP LEGIS DIPLOM CONFER PARL/PROC 20. PAGE 80 H1595
[SOVEREIGN COLONIAL ORD/FREE NAT/G]

B60

KOHN H.,PAN-SLAVISM: ITS HISTORY AND IDEOLOGY. COM CZECHOSLVK EUR+WWI MOD/EUR USSR YUGOSLAVIA CULTURE ELITES INTELL KIN NAT/G EDU/PROP DRIVE SOVEREIGN ...HUM PHIL/SCI MYTH HIST/WRIT 19/20. PAGE 87 H1745
[ATTIT CONCPT NAT/LISM]

B60

THEOBOLD R.,THE NEW NATIONS OF WEST AFRICA. GHANA NIGERIA CULTURE INT/ORG ECO/TAC FOR/AID COLONIAL RACE/REL POPULISM...ANTHOL BIBLIOG 20 UN. PAGE 153 H3068
[AFR SOVEREIGN ECO/UNDEV DIPLOM]

L60

HAAS E.B.,"CONSENSUS FORMATION IN THE COUNCIL OF EUROPE." EUR+WWI NAT/G DELIB/GP DIPLOM REGION CHOOSE PWR SOVEREIGN...RELATIV NEW/IDEA QUANT CHARTS INDEX TOT/POP OEEC 20 COUNCL/EUR. PAGE 63 H1265
[POL/PAR INT/ORG STAT]

L60

WHEELER G.,"RACIAL PROBLEMS IN SOVIET MUSLIM ASIA." COM CULTURE SOCIETY NEIGH SECT DOMIN EDU/PROP DISCRIM DISPL DRIVE PWR SOVEREIGN...CENSUS SAMP TREND 20 MUSLIM. PAGE 167 H3340
[PERSON ATTIT USSR RACE/REL]

S60

TAYLOR M.G.,"THE ROLE OF THE MEDICAL PROFESSION IN THE FORMULATION AND EXECUTION OF PUBLIC POLICY" (BMR)" CANADA NAT/G CONSULT ADMIN REPRESENT GP/REL ROLE SOVEREIGN...DECISION 20 CMA. PAGE 153 H3056
[PROF/ORG HEALTH LOBBY POLICY]

B61

ANSPRENGER F.,POLITIK IM SCHWARZEN AFRIKA. FRANCE NAT/G DIPLOM REGION REV NAT/LISM...CHARTS BIBLIOG 19/20. PAGE 7 H0141
[AFR COLONIAL SOVEREIGN]

B61

ATTLEE C.R.,EMPIRE INTO COMMONWEALTH. AFR ASIA CANADA UK NAT/G WAR NAT/LISM ATTIT...POLICY 20 AUSTRAL. PAGE 9 H0179
[DIPLOM GP/REL COLONIAL SOVEREIGN]

B61

BIEBUYCK D.,CONGO TRIBES AND PARTIES. AFR CONGO/BRAZ CONSTN NAT/G COLONIAL CHOOSE FEDERAL 20 CONGO/LEOP. PAGE 17 H0333
[KIN POL/PAR GP/REL SOVEREIGN]

B61

BONNEFOUS M.,EUROPE ET TIERS MONDE. EUR+WWI SOCIETY INT/ORG NAT/G VOL/ASSN ACT/RES TEC/DEV CAP/ISM ECO/TAC ATTIT ORD/FREE SOVEREIGN...POLICY CONCPT TREND 20. PAGE 19 H0373
[AFR ECO/UNDEV FOR/AID INT/TRADE]

B61

BOURDIEU P.,THE ALGERIANS (TRANS. BY A.C. ROSS; REV. ED.). ALGERIA ISLAM CULTURE MUNIC CAP/ISM COLONIAL GP/REL ORD/FREE SOVEREIGN 20. PAGE 19 H0385
[SOCIETY STRUCT ATTIT WAR]

B61

DUFFY J.,AFRICA SPEAKS. GHANA TOGO CULTURE ECO/UNDEV PROB/SOLV COLONIAL NEUTRAL DISCRIM NAT/LISM SOVEREIGN ALL/IDEOS...CONCPT ANTHOL SOC/INTEG 20 NEGRO THIRD/WRLD. PAGE 43 H0857
[AFR NAT/G FUT STRUCT]

B61

KEDOURIE E.,NATIONALISM (REV. ED.). MOD/EUR SOVEREIGN...CONCPT 19/20. PAGE 84 H1675
[NAT/LISM NAT/G CREATE REV]

B61

KHALIQUZZAMAN C.,PATHWAY TO PAKISTAN. INDIA PAKISTAN UK SECT LEGIS CHOOSE RACE/REL ATTIT ORD/FREE 20 MUSLIM. PAGE 85 H1705
[GP/REL NAT/G COLONIAL SOVEREIGN]

B61

KHAN A.W.,INDIA WINS FREEDOM: THE OTHER SIDE. INDIA PAKISTAN CULTURE LEGIS DIPLOM PARL/PROC REV WAR NAT/LISM 20. PAGE 85 H1707
[SOVEREIGN GP/REL RACE/REL ORD/FREE]

B61

NARAIN J.P.,SWARAJ FOR THE PEOPLE. INDIA CONSTN LOC/G MUNIC POL/PAR CHOOSE REPRESENT EFFICIENCY ATTIT PWR SOVEREIGN 20. PAGE 116 H2311
[NAT/G ORD/FREE EDU/PROP EX/STRUC]

B61

PANIKKAR K.M.,REVOLUTION IN AFRICA. AFR GUINEA ECO/UNDEV POL/PAR DIPLOM COLONIAL EXEC LEAD SOVEREIGN...CHARTS 20. PAGE 123 H2461
[NAT/LISM NAT/G CHIEF]

B61

ROIG E.,MARTI, ANTIIMPERIALISTA. CUBA L/A+17C DIPLOM DOMIN COLONIAL CONTROL LEAD PWR SOVEREIGN ...PHIL/SCI 19 MARTI/JOSE INTERVENT. PAGE 133 H2664
[PERSON NAT/LISM ECO/UNDEV ORD/FREE]

B61

ULLMAN W.,PRINCIPLES OF GOVERNMENT AND POLITICS IN THE MIDDLE AGES. LAW CONSTN DOMIN EDU/PROP LEGIT TOTALISM SOVEREIGN POPULISM...POLICY GOV/COMP IDEA/COMP 12/16 POPE KING CHURCH/STA. PAGE 158 H3152
[SECT CHIEF NAT/G LEGIS]

B61

WEST F.J.,POLITICAL ADVANCEMENT IN THE SOUTH PACIFIC. CONSTN CULTURE POL/PAR LEGIS DOMIN ADMIN CHOOSE SOVEREIGN VAL/FREE 20 FIJI TAHITI SAMOA. PAGE 167 H3335
[S/ASIA LOC/G COLONIAL]

S61

FITZGIBBON R.H.,"MEASUREMENT OF LATIN AMERICAN POLITICAL CHANGE." L/A+17C CONSTN CULTURE SOCIETY ECO/UNDEV NAT/G POL/PAR PUB/INST ACT/RES EDU/PROP PERCEPT KNOWL ORD/FREE SOVEREIGN...METH/CNCPT TREND OAS 20. PAGE 51 H1020
[CHOOSE ATTIT]

B62

BODIN J.,THE SIX BOOKES OF A COMMONWEALE (1576) (FACSIMILE REPRINT OF 1606 ENGLISH TRANSLATION). AUTHORIT ORD/FREE SOVEREIGN...TRADIT CONCPT. PAGE 18 H0364
[PWR CONSERVE CHIEF NAT/G]

B62

BUSIA K.A.,THE CHALLENGE OF AFRICA. CULTURE KIN MUNIC NAT/G POL/PAR SCHOOL DELIB/GP PLAN ECO/TAC DOMIN EDU/PROP TOTALISM ATTIT PERSON ALL/VALS SOVEREIGN...SOC CONCPT STERTYP TOT/POP VAL/FREE 20. PAGE 25 H0496
[AFR ECO/UNDEV NAT/LISM]

B62

DUTOIT B.,LA NEUTRALITE SUISSE A L'HEURE
[ATTIT]

EUROPEENNE. EUR+WWI MOD/EUR INT/ORG NAT/G VOL/ASSN PLAN BAL/PWR LEGIT NEUTRAL REGION PEACE ORD/FREE SOVEREIGN...CONCPT OBS TIME/SEQ TREND STERTYP VAL/FREE LEAGUE/NAT UN 20. PAGE 44 H0873
DIPLOM SWITZERLND

B62
GUENA Y.,HISTORIQUE DE LA COMMUNAUTE. FUT ECO/UNDEV NAT/G PLAN EDU/PROP COLONIAL REGION NAT/LISM ALL/VALS SOVEREIGN...CONCPT OBS CHARTS 20. PAGE 62 H1244
AFR VOL/ASSN FOR/AID FRANCE

B62
JACKSON W.A.D.,RUSSO-CHINESE BORDERLANDS. ASIA COM USSR NAT/G PROVS EX/STRUC FORCES DOMIN COERCE PEACE ATTIT PWR SOVEREIGN WEALTH...CONCPT TREND CHARTS STERTYP VAL/FREE. PAGE 79 H1576
GEOG DIPLOM RUSSIA

B62
LAQUEUR W.,POLYCENTRISM. CHINA/COM COM USSR WOR+45 INT/ORG NAT/G ECO/TAC DOMIN LEAD ATTIT PWR SOVEREIGN...ANTHOL 20. PAGE 91 H1821
MARXISM DIPLOM BAL/PWR POLICY

B62
MANSUR F.,PROCESS OF INDEPENDENCE. GHANA INDIA INDONESIA PAKISTAN CONSTN ELITES INTELL STRUCT ACADEM NAT/G REV PWR 20. PAGE 102 H2043
NAT/COMP POL/PAR SOVEREIGN COLONIAL

B62
MEYER A.G.,LENINISM. USSR STRUCT NAT/G CAP/ISM LEAD WAR PWR SOVEREIGN...BIBLIOG 20 LENIN/VI. PAGE 109 H2187
POL/PAR REV MARXISM PHIL/SCI

B62
PAIKERT G.C.,THE GERMAN EXODUS. EUR+WWI GERMANY/W LAW CULTURE SOCIETY STRUCT INDUS NAT/LISM RESPECT SOVEREIGN...CHARTS BIBLIOG SOC/INTEG 20 MIGRATION. PAGE 122 H2444
INGP/REL STRANGE GEOG GP/REL

B62
TAYLOR D.,THE BRITISH IN AFRICA. UK CULTURE ECO/UNDEV INDUS DIPLOM INT/TRADE ADMIN WAR RACE/REL ORD/FREE SOVEREIGN...POLICY BIBLIOG 15/20 CMN/WLTH. PAGE 153 H3053
AFR COLONIAL DOMIN

B62
THIERRY S.S.,LE VATICAN SECRET. CHRIST-17C EUR+WWI MOD/EUR VATICAN NAT/G SECT DELIB/GP DOMIN LEGIT SOVEREIGN. PAGE 154 H3072
ADMIN EX/STRUC CATHISM DECISION

B62
WEHLER H.V.,SOZIALDEMOKRATIE UND NATIONALSTAAT. GERMANY POLAND USSR CULTURE SOCIETY STRUCT NAT/G POL/PAR DIPLOM ORD/FREE 19/20. PAGE 166 H3325
NAT/LISM SOVEREIGN GP/REL ATTIT

L62
CORET A.,"L'INDEPENDANCE DU SAMOA OCCIDENTAL." S/ASIA LAW INT/ORG EXEC ALL/VALS SAMOA UN 20. PAGE 33 H0668
NAT/G STRUCT SOVEREIGN

L62
ORDONNEAU P.,"LES PROBLEMES POSES PAR L'INDEPENDANCE DES NOUVEAUX ETATS AFRICAINS ET MALGACHE SUR LE PLAN DU CONTENTIEUX." FRANCE ISLAM MADAGASCAR LAW STRATA ECO/UNDEV NAT/G LEGIS LEGIT ...JURID TIME/SEQ 20. PAGE 121 H2425
AFR ADJUD COLONIAL SOVEREIGN

S62
LANGER W.L.,"FAREWELL TO EMPIRE." EUR+WWI MOD/EUR NAT/G DIPLOM EDU/PROP COLONIAL ATTIT ORD/FREE PWR SOVEREIGN WEALTH...CONCPT TIME/SEQ GEN/LAWS TOT/POP VAL/FREE CMN/WLTH 20. PAGE 91 H1810
DOMIN ECO/TAC NAT/LISM

S62
LEGUM C.,"THE DANGERS OF INDEPENDENCE" AFR UGANDA NAT/G DIPLOM DOMIN REGION CENTRAL ATTIT POPULISM 20. PAGE 93 H1862
ORD/FREE SOVEREIGN NAT/LISM GOV/COMP

S62
MBOYA T.,"RELATIONS BETWEEN THE PRESS AND GOVERNMENT IN AFRICA." AFR DIPLOM EDU/PROP NAT/LISM ORD/FREE SOVEREIGN 20. PAGE 106 H2115
PRESS GP/REL ATTIT NAT/G

S62
MURACCIOLE L.,"LES CONSTITUTIONS DES ETATS AFRICAINS D'EXPRESSION FRANCAISE: LA CONSTITUTION DU 16 AVRIL 1962 DE LA REPUBLIQUE DU" AFR CHAD CHIEF LEGIS LEGIT COLONIAL EXEC ROUTINE ORD/FREE SOVEREIGN...SOC CONCPT 20. PAGE 115 H2291
NAT/G CONSTN

S62
ROTBERG R.,"THE RISE OF AFRICAN NATIONALISM: THE CASE OF EAST AND CENTRAL AFRICA." AFR CULTURE SOCIETY NEIGH DIPLOM DOMIN COLONIAL COERCE DISPL PERCEPT PWR SOVEREIGN...POLICY OBS/ENVIR TREND WORK 20. PAGE 135 H2690
ATTIT DRIVE NAT/LISM REV

B63
FRANZ G.,TEILUNG UND WIEDERVEREINIGUNG. GERMANY IRELAND ITALY NETHERLAND POLAND CULTURE BAL/PWR CHOOSE NAT/LISM ORD/FREE SOVEREIGN 19/20. PAGE 53 H1054
DIPLOM WAR NAT/COMP ATTIT

B63
GARDINIER D.E.,CAMEROON: UNITED NATIONS CHALLENGE TO FRENCH POLICY. AFR CAMEROON FRANCE NAT/G LEGIS CONTROL SOVEREIGN 20 UN. PAGE 55 H1101
DIPLOM POLICY INT/ORG COLONIAL

B63
GEERTZ C.,OLD SOCIETIES AND NEW STATES: THE QUEST FOR MODERNITY IN ASIA AND AFRICA. AFR ASIA LAW CULTURE SECT EDU/PROP REV...GOV/COMP NAT/COMP 20. PAGE 55 H1107
ECO/UNDEV TEC/DEV NAT/LISM SOVEREIGN

B63
HAILEY L.,THE REPUBLIC OF SOUTH AFRICA AND THE HIGH COMMISSION TERRITORIES. AFR SOUTH/AFR UK INT/ORG NAT/G PROVS RACE/REL SOVEREIGN...CHARTS 19/20 COMMONWLTH. PAGE 64 H1278
COLONIAL DIPLOM ATTIT

B63
LEE C.,THE POLITICS OF KOREAN NATIONALISM. KOREA S/ASIA DIPLOM REV WAR 14/20 CHINJAP. PAGE 93 H1855
NAT/LISM SOVEREIGN COLONIAL

B63
LEONARD T.J.,THE FEDERAL SYSTEM OF INDIA. INDIA MUNIC NAT/G PROVS ADMIN SOVEREIGN...IDEA/COMP 20. PAGE 94 H1885
FEDERAL MGT NAT/COMP METH/COMP

B63
PADELFORD N.J.,AFRICA AND WORLD ORDER. AFR COLONIAL SOVEREIGN...ANTHOL BIBLIOG 20 UN UNIFICA COMMONWLTH. PAGE 122 H2439
DIPLOM NAT/G ORD/FREE

B63
WODDIS J.,AFRICA, THE WAY AHEAD. AFR FUT ELITES POL/PAR CAP/ISM DIPLOM DOMIN RACE/REL ATTIT ORD/FREE SOVEREIGN SOCISM 20 PANAF/FREE. PAGE 170 H3394
REV COLONIAL ECO/UNDEV NAT/G

S63
BANFIELD J.,"FEDERATION IN EAST-AFRICA." AFR UGANDA ELITES INT/ORG NAT/G VOL/ASSN LEGIS ECO/TAC FEDERAL ATTIT SOVEREIGN TOT/POP 20 TANGANYIKA. PAGE 10 H0210
EX/STRUC PWR REGION

S63
HINDLEY D.,"FOREIGN AID TO INDONESIA AND ITS POLITICAL IMPLICATIONS." INDONESIA POL/PAR ATTIT SOVEREIGN...CHARTS 20. PAGE 71 H1421
FOR/AID NAT/G WEALTH ECO/TAC

S63
WEISSBERG G.,"MAPS AS EVIDENCE IN INTERNATIONAL BOUNDARY DISPUTES: A REAPPRAISAL." CHINA/COM EUR+WWI INDIA MOD/EUR S/ASIA INT/ORG NAT/G LEGIT PERCEPT...JURID CHARTS 20. PAGE 166 H3331
LAW GEOG SOVEREIGN

B64
BELL W.,JAMAICAN LEADERS: POLITICAL ATTITUDES IN A NEW NATION. JAMAICA STRUCT ACT/RES CREATE PROB/SOLV DIPLOM COLONIAL LEAD...QU 20. PAGE 13 H0267
NAT/LISM ATTIT DRIVE SOVEREIGN

B64
DE SMITH S.A.,THE NEW COMMONWEALTH AND ITS CONSTITUTIONS. AFR CYPRUS PAKISTAN S/ASIA INT/ORG NAT/G LEGIS LEGIT RIGID/FLEX PWR...CONCPT TIME/SEQ CMN/WLTH 20. PAGE 38 H0770
EX/STRUC CONSTN SOVEREIGN

B64
FRANCK T.M.,EAST AFRICAN UNITY THROUGH LAW. MALAWI TANZANIA UGANDA UK ZAMBIA CONSTN INT/ORG NAT/G ADMIN ROUTINE TASK NAT/LISM ATTIT SOVEREIGN ...RECORD IDEA/COMP NAT/COMP. PAGE 52 H1048
AFR FEDERAL REGION INT/LAW

B64
GREAT BRITAIN CENTRAL OFF INF,CONSTITUTIONAL DEVELOPMENT IN THE COMMONWEALTH. VOL/ASSN PLAN DIPLOM COLONIAL INGP/REL NAT/LISM ORD/FREE PWR 17/20 CMN/WLTH. PAGE 60 H1202
REGION CONSTN NAT/G SOVEREIGN

B64
GUMPLOWICZ L.,RECHTSSTAAT UND SOZIALISMUS. STRATA ORD/FREE SOVEREIGN MARXISM...IDEA/COMP 16/20 KANT/I HOBBES/T. PAGE 62 H1251
JURID NAT/G SOCISM CONCPT

B64
HANNA W.J.,POLITICS IN BLACK AFRICA: A SELECTIVE BIBLIOGRAPHY OF RELEVANT PERIODICAL LITERATURE. AFR LAW LOC/G MUNIC NAT/G POL/PAR LOBBY CHOOSE RACE/REL SOVEREIGN 20. PAGE 66 H1315
BIBLIOG NAT/LISM COLONIAL

B64
LAPENNA I.,STATE AND LAW: SOVIET AND YUGOSLAV THEORY. USSR YUGOSLAVIA STRATA STRUCT NAT/G DOMIN COERCE MARXISM...GOV/COMP IDEA/COMP 20. PAGE 91 H1812
JURID COM LAW SOVEREIGN

B64
MBEKI G.,SOUTH AFRICA: THE PEASANT'S REVOLT. SOUTH/AFR POL/PAR COERCE REV NAT/LISM ORD/FREE SOVEREIGN 20 NEGRO. PAGE 106 H2114
COLONIAL RACE/REL DISCRIM DOMIN

B64
MORGENTHAU R.S.,POLITICAL PARTIES IN FRENCH-SPEAKING WEST AFRICA. AFR FRANCE GUINEA IVORY/CST MALI SENEGAL CONSTN LEGIS CREATE PLAN LOBBY PARTIC GP/REL...POLICY BIBLIOG 20. PAGE 113 H2257
POL/PAR NAT/G SOVEREIGN COLONIAL

B64
MUSEUM FUR VOLKERKUNDE WIEN,ZENTRALAMERIKA MEXIKO VOLKER UND KULTUREN. COSTA/RICA GUATEMALA L/A+17C PANAMA SECT WAR GP/REL SOVEREIGN...ART/METH 20 CENTRAL/AM MEXIC/AMER. PAGE 115 H2300
SOCIETY STRUCT CULTURE AGRI

B64
NEWARK F.H.,NOTES ON IRISH LEGAL HISTORY (2ND ED.). IRELAND UK PARL/PROC ORD/FREE SOVEREIGN 12/20
CT/SYS JURID

ENGLSH/LAW. PAGE 117 H2344 ADJUD NAT/G

B64
QUIGG P.W.,AFRICA: A FOREIGN AFFAIRS READER. AFR FRANCE PORTUGAL UK DIPLOM LEAD PARL/PROC MARXISM ...MAJORIT METH/CNCPT GOV/COMP IDEA/COMP ANTHOL 19/20. PAGE 129 H2575 COLONIAL SOVEREIGN NAT/LISM RACE/REL

B64
TILMAN R.O.,BUREAUCRATIC TRANSITION IN MALAYA. MALAYSIA S/ASIA UK NAT/G EX/STRUC DIPLOM...CHARTS BIBLIOG 20. PAGE 155 H3098 ADMIN COLONIAL SOVEREIGN EFFICIENCY

B64
TINKER H.,BALLOT BOX AND BAYONET - PEOPLE AND GOVERNMENT IN EMERGENT ASIAN COUNTRIES. CEYLON INDIA INDONESIA PHILIPPINE POL/PAR ADMIN COLONIAL LEAD PARL/PROC CHOOSE CONSEN ORD/FREE SOVEREIGN PLURISM...GOV/COMP THIRD/WRLD. PAGE 155 H3104 MYTH S/ASIA NAT/COMP NAT/LISM

B64
VECCHIO G.D.,L'ETAT ET LE DROIT. ITALY CONSTN EX/STRUC LEGIS DIPLOM CT/SYS...JURID 20 UN. PAGE 162 H3238 NAT/G SOVEREIGN CONCPT INT/LAW

B64
VOELKMANN K.,HERRSCHER VON MORGEN? BAL/PWR COLONIAL NEUTRAL REGION RACE/REL ALL/VALS SOVEREIGN...RECORD 20 COLD/WAR THIRD/WRLD. PAGE 163 H3259 DIPLOM ECO/UNDEV CONTROL NAT/COMP

B64
WRIGHT Q.,A STUDY OF WAR. LAW NAT/G PROB/SOLV BAL/PWR NAT/LISM PEACE ATTIT SOVEREIGN...CENSUS SOC/INTEG. PAGE 171 H3421 WAR CONCPT DIPLOM CONTROL

S64
GARMARNIKOW M.,"INFLUENCE-BUYING IN WEST AFRICA." COM FUT USSR INTELL NAT/G PLAN TEC/DEV ECO/TAC DOMIN EDU/PROP REGION NAT/LISM ATTIT DRIVE ALL/VALS SOVEREIGN...POLICY PSY SOC CONCPT TREND STERTYP WORK COLD/WAR 20. PAGE 55 H1102 AFR ECO/UNDEV FOR/AID SOCISM

S64
REISS I.,"LE DECLENCHEMENT DE LA PREMIERE GUERRE MONDIALE." GERMANY RUSSIA NAT/G FORCES DOMIN EDU/PROP COERCE RIGID/FLEX PWR SOVEREIGN...RELATIV HIST/WRIT TOT/POP AUST/HUNG SERBIA 20. PAGE 131 H2612 MOD/EUR BAL/PWR DIPLOM WAR

S64
SAYEED K.,"PATHAN REGIONALISM." ISLAM PAKISTAN S/ASIA CULTURE SOCIETY NAT/G NEIGH DIPLOM LEGIT COERCE CHOOSE ATTIT DISPL PERCEPT ALL/VALS SOVEREIGN...POLICY RELATIV SOC TIME/SEQ TOT/POP 20. PAGE 138 H2761 SECT NAT/LISM REGION

B65
ADENAUER K.,MEMOIRS 1945-53. EUR+WWI GERMANY/W ECO/DEV CHIEF FORCES ECO/TAC WAR GOV/REL PWR SOVEREIGN 20 NATO ADENAUER/K. PAGE 3 H0068 BIOG DIPLOM NAT/G PERS/REL

B65
ADENAUER K.,MEINE ERINNERUNGEN, 1945-53 (VOL. I), 1953-55 (VOL. II). EUR+WWI GERMANY CHIEF FORCES PROB/SOLV DIPLOM ARMS/CONT INGP/REL PEACE SOVEREIGN ...OBS/ENVIR RECORD 20. PAGE 3 H0069 NAT/G BIOG SELF/OBS

B65
ADU A.L.,THE CIVIL SERVICE IN NEW AFRICAN STATES. AFR GHANA FINAN SOVEREIGN...POLICY 20 CIVIL/SERV AFRICA/E AFRICA/W. PAGE 4 H0074 ECO/UNDEV ADMIN COLONIAL NAT/G

B65
BLITZ L.F.,THE POLITICS AND ADMINISTRATION OF NIGERIAN GOVERNMENT. NIGER CULTURE LOC/G LEGIS DIPLOM COLONIAL CT/SYS SOVEREIGN...GEOG SOC ANTHOL 20. PAGE 18 H0357 NAT/G GOV/REL POL/PAR

B65
BRASS P.R.,FACTIONAL POLITICS IN AN INDIAN STATE: THE CONGRESS PARTY IN UTTAR PRADESH. INDIA UK CONSTN CULTURE ECO/UNDEV LOC/G DOMIN COLONIAL CROWD GP/REL ADJUST CENTRAL RIGID/FLEX SOVEREIGN 20 UTTAR/PRAD CONGRESS/P. PAGE 20 H0406 POL/PAR PROVS LEGIS CHOOSE

B65
BROWNSON O.A.,THE AMERICAN REPUBLIC. NAT/G PROVS WAR GOV/REL PRIVIL ORD/FREE PWR ALL/IDEOS CONSERVE ...CONCPT 19 CIVIL/WAR. PAGE 22 H0452 CONSTN FEDERAL SOVEREIGN

B65
BURLING R.,HILL FARMS AND PADI FIELDS. BURMA S/ASIA THAILAND VIETNAM AGRI NEIGH SECT GP/REL NAT/LISM ORD/FREE 20 MID/EAST MIGRATION. PAGE 24 H0491 SOCIETY STRUCT CULTURE SOVEREIGN

B65
CALLEO D.P.,EUROPE'S FUTURE: THE GRAND ALTERNATIVES. UK INT/ORG DIPLOM PWR SOVEREIGN ...CONCPT IDEA/COMP NAT/COMP BIBLIOG 20 EEC EUROPE DEGAULLE/C NATO. PAGE 25 H0506 FUT EUR+WWI FEDERAL NAT/LISM

B65
COWAN L.G.,EDUCATION AND NATION-BUILDING IN AFRICA. AFR CULTURE ECO/UNDEV POL/PAR ACT/RES LEAD SOVEREIGN...METH/COMP ANTHOL BIBLIOG 20. PAGE 34 H0684 EDU/PROP COLONIAL ACADEM NAT/LISM

B65
COX R.H.,THE STATE IN INTERNATIONAL RELATIONS. INT/ORG DIPLOM REV WAR PEACE MARXISM...CONCPT GOV/COMP. PAGE 34 H0690 SOVEREIGN NAT/G FASCISM ORD/FREE

B65
FAGG J.E.,CUBA, HAITI, AND THE DOMINICAN REPUBLIC. CUBA DOMIN/REP HAITI L/A+17C NAT/G DIPLOM ECO/TAC DOMIN CHOOSE AUTHORIT ROLE SOVEREIGN POPULISM 17/20. PAGE 48 H0959 COLONIAL ECO/UNDEV REV GOV/COMP

B65
FOSTER P.,EDUCATION AND SOCIAL CHANGE IN GHANA. GHANA CULTURE STRUCT ECO/UNDEV TEC/DEV REGION EFFICIENCY LITERACY ALL/VALS SOVEREIGN...STAT METH/COMP 19/20 GOLD/COAST. PAGE 52 H1043 SCHOOL CREATE SOCIETY

B65
GEWIRTH A.,POLITICAL PHILOSOPHY. UNIV SOCIETY NAT/G GP/REL INGP/REL CONSEN PWR...IDEA/COMP GEN/LAWS 17/19 HOBBES/T LOCKE/JOHN MARX/KARL MILL/JS ROUSSEAU/J. PAGE 56 H1118 ORD/FREE SOVEREIGN PHIL/SCI

B65
GINIEWSKI P.,THE TWO FACES OF APARTHEID. AFR SOUTH/AFR STRATA AGRI INDUS COLONIAL PARTIC SOVEREIGN...CONCPT GOV/COMP NAT/COMP 19/20 NEGRO. PAGE 56 H1131 DISCRIM NAT/G RACE/REL STRUCT

B65
JELAVICH C.,THE BALKANS. ALBANIA BULGARIA GREECE ROMANIA YUGOSLAVIA ECO/UNDEV WAR SOVEREIGN MARXISM 6/20. PAGE 80 H1597 NAT/LISM NAT/G

B65
KIRKWOOD K.,BRITAIN AND AFRICA. AFR UK ECO/UNDEV ECO/TAC WAR NAT/LISM SOVEREIGN 19/20. PAGE 86 H1725 NAT/G DIPLOM POLICY COLONIAL

B65
KOHN H.,AFRICAN NATIONALISM IN THE TWENTIETH CENTURY. AFR NAT/G POL/PAR COLONIAL REGION DISCRIM SOVEREIGN 20. PAGE 87 H1747 NAT/LISM CULTURE ATTIT

B65
MEYER F.S.,THE AFRICAN NETTLE. SOUTH/AFR NAT/LISM SOVEREIGN...ANTHOL 20 EUROPE. PAGE 110 H2191 AFR COLONIAL RACE/REL ECO/UNDEV

B65
NAMIER L.B.,THE STRUCTURE OF POLITICS AT THE ACCESSION OF GEORGE III. UK LOC/G TOP/EX COLONIAL LEAD PARTIC REV CHOOSE REPRESENT GOV/REL PERSON SOVEREIGN...GOV/COMP 18 PARLIAMENT. PAGE 115 H2309 PARL/PROC LEGIS NAT/G POL/PAR

B65
O'BRIEN W.V.,THE NEW NATIONS IN INTERNATIONAL LAW AND DIPLOMACY* THE YEAR BOOK OF WORLD POLITY* VOLUME III. USA+45 ECO/UNDEV INT/ORG FORCES DIPLOM COLONIAL NEUTRAL REV NAT/LISM ATTIT RESPECT. PAGE 119 H2385 INT/LAW CULTURE SOVEREIGN ANTHOL

B65
OBUKAR C.,THE MODERN AFRICAN. AGRI INDUS WORKER CAP/ISM EDU/PROP PARTIC RACE/REL NAT/LISM ALL/VALS MARXISM...SOC IDEA/COMP 20. PAGE 120 H2393 AFR ECO/UNDEV CULTURE SOVEREIGN

B65
PEASLEE A.J.,CONSTITUTIONS OF NATIONS* THIRD REVISED EDITION (VOLUME I* AFRICA). LAW EX/STRUC LEGIS TOP/EX LEGIT CT/SYS ROUTINE ORD/FREE PWR SOVEREIGN...CON/ANAL CHARTS. PAGE 124 H2481 AFR CHOOSE CONSTN NAT/G

B65
QURESHI I.H.,THE STRUGGLE FOR PAKISTAN. INDIA PAKISTAN UK CULTURE LEGIS DIPLOM EDU/PROP COLONIAL ATTIT SOVEREIGN 19/20 MUSLIM. PAGE 129 H2576 GP/REL RACE/REL WAR SECT

B65
ROTBERG R.I.,A POLITICAL HISTORY OF TROPICAL AFRICA. EX/STRUC DIPLOM INT/TRADE DOMIN ADMIN RACE/REL NAT/LISM PWR SOVEREIGN...GEOG TIME/SEQ BIBLIOG 1/20. PAGE 135 H2692 AFR CULTURE COLONIAL

B65
ULLMANN W.,A HISTORY OF POLITICAL THOUGHT: THE MIDDLE AGES. CHRIST-17C LOC/G NAT/G CENTRAL PWR ...PHIL/SCI LOG BIBLIOG 6/15. PAGE 158 H3153 IDEA/COMP SOVEREIGN SECT LAW

B65
VON RENESSE E.A.,UNVOLLENDETE DEMOKRATIEN. AFR ISLAM S/ASIA SOCIETY ACT/RES COLONIAL...JURID CHARTS BIBLIOG METH 13/20. PAGE 164 H3276 ECO/UNDEV NAT/COMP SOVEREIGN

B65
WARD W.E.,GOVERNMENT IN WEST AFRICA. WOR+45 POL/PAR EX/STRUC PLAN PARTIC GP/REL SOVEREIGN 20 AFRICA/W. PAGE 165 H3308 GOV/COMP CONSTN COLONIAL ECO/UNDEV

B65
WILLIAMSON J.A.,GREAT BRITAIN AND THE COMMONWEALTH. UK DOMIN COLONIAL INGP/REL...POLICY 18/20 CMN/WLTH. PAGE 168 H3370 NAT/G DIPLOM INT/ORG SOVEREIGN

L65
SHARMA S.P.,"THE INDIA-CHINA BORDER DISPUTE: AN INDIAN PERSPECTIVE." ASIA CHINA/COM S/ASIA NAT/G LAW ATTIT

LEGIT CT/SYS NAT/LISM DRIVE MORAL ORD/FREE PWR 20. PAGE 142 H2850 — SOVEREIGN INDIA

S65

HAYTER T.,"FRENCH AID TO AFRICA* ITS SCOPE AND ACHIEVEMENTS." CULTURE ECO/TAC INT/TRADE ADMIN REGION CENTRAL FEDERAL LOVE PWR SOVEREIGN EEC. PAGE 68 H1370 — AFR FRANCE FOR/AID COLONIAL

S65

MCALISTER L.N.,"CHANGING CONCEPTS OF THE ROLE OF THE MILITARY IN LATIN AMERICA." CULTURE NAT/G CREATE REGION NAT/LISM ATTIT SOVEREIGN...NAT/COMP GEN/LAWS. PAGE 106 H2120 — L/A+17C FORCES IDEA/COMP PWR

S65

PLANK J.N.,"THE CARIBBEAN* INTERVENTION, WHEN AND HOW." CUBA GUATEMALA HAITI PANAMA USA+45 VENEZUELA FORCES PROB/SOLV RISK COERCE...NAT/COMP OAS TIME. PAGE 126 H2521 — SOVEREIGN MARXISM REV

C65

COLEMAN J.S.,"EDUCATION AND POLITICAL DEVELOPMENT." COM CULTURE INTELL STRUCT SCHOOL PERSON SOVEREIGN ...POLICY ANTHOL BIBLIOG/A METH 20. PAGE 31 H0629 — ECO/UNDEV NAT/LISM EDU/PROP TEC/DEV

B66

AHMED Z.,DUSK AND DAWN IN VILLAGE INDIA. INDIA S/ASIA UK CULTURE SOCIETY NAT/G DOMIN COLONIAL HABITAT SOVEREIGN...SOC DICTIONARY 20. PAGE 4 H0080 — NEIGH ECO/UNDEV AGRI ADJUST

B66

DAENIKER G.,STRATEGIE DES KLEIN STAATS. SWITZERLND ACT/RES CREATE DIPLOM NEUTRAL DETER WAR WEAPON PWR SOVEREIGN...IDEA/COMP 20 COLD/WAR. PAGE 36 H0730 — NUC/PWR PLAN FORCES NAT/G

B66

DE TOCQUEVILLE A,DEMOCRACY IN AMERICA (1834-1840) (2 VOLS. IN I; TRANS. BY G. LAWRENCE). FRANCE CULTURE STRATA POL/PAR CT/SYS REPRESENT FEDERAL ORD/FREE SOVEREIGN...MAJORIT TREND GEN/LAWS 18/19. PAGE 39 H0773 — POPULISM USA-45 CONSTN NAT/COMP

B66

DODGE D.,AFRICAN POLITICS IN PERSPECTIVE. ELITES POL/PAR PROB/SOLV LEAD...POLICY 20 THIRD/WRLD. PAGE 41 H0831 — AFR NAT/G COLONIAL SOVEREIGN

B66

HATTICH M.,NATIONALBEWUSSTSEIN UND STAATSBEWUSSTSEIN IN DER PLURALISTISCHEN GESELLSCHAFT. GERMANY GP/REL ATTIT SOVEREIGN SOC/INTEG 20. PAGE 68 H1356 — NAT/G NAT/LISM SOCIETY OBJECTIVE

B66

HAY P.,FEDERALISM AND SUPRANATIONAL ORGANIZATIONS: PATTERNS FOR NEW LEGAL STRUCTURES. EUR+WWI LAW NAT/G VOL/ASSN DIPLOM PWR...NAT/COMP TREATY EEC. PAGE 68 H1364 — SOVEREIGN FEDERAL INT/ORG INT/LAW

B66

INTL CONF ON WORLD POLITICS-5,EASTERN EUROPE IN TRANSITION. EUR+WWI USSR ECO/TAC NAT/LISM ATTIT SOVEREIGN...CHARTS ANTHOL 20 TREATY WARSAW/P. PAGE 78 H1562 — COM NAT/COMP MARXISM DIPLOM

B66

KAUNDA K.,ZAMBIA: INDEPENDENCE AND BEYOND: THE SPEECHES OF KENNETH KAUNDA. AFR FUT ZAMBIA SOCIETY ECO/UNDEV NAT/G PROB/SOLV ECO/TAC ADMIN RACE/REL SOVEREIGN 20. PAGE 84 H1670 — ORD/FREE COLONIAL CONSTN LEAD

B66

KAZAMIAS A.M.,EDUCATION AND QUEST FOR MODERNITY IN TURKEY. ISLAM SOCIETY SECT NAT/LISM ATTIT ORD/FREE SOVEREIGN TURKS. PAGE 84 H1672 — NAT/G EDU/PROP STRATA CULTURE

B66

KERR M.H.,ISLAMIC REFORM: THE POLITICAL AND LEGAL THEORIES OF MUHAMMAD 'ABDUH AND RASHID RIDA. NAT/G SECT LEAD SOVEREIGN CONSERVE...JURID BIBLIOG WORSHIP 20. PAGE 85 H1698 — LAW CONCPT ISLAM

B66

LONDON K.,EASTERN EUROPE IN TRANSITION. CHINA/COM USSR DOMIN COLONIAL CENTRAL RIGID/FLEX PWR...SOC ANTHOL 20. PAGE 98 H1958 — SOVEREIGN COM NAT/LISM DIPLOM

B66

MASUR G.,NATIONALISM IN LATIN AMERICA* DIVERSITY AND UNITY. CHRIST-17C PRE/AMER ELITES ECO/UNDEV CREATE DIPLOM INT/TRADE COLONIAL REV SOVEREIGN SOC. PAGE 105 H2089 — L/A+17C NAT/LISM CULTURE

B66

MCKAY V.,AFRICAN DIPLOMACY STUDIES IN THE DETERMINANTS OF FOREIGN POLICY. AFR SOUTH/AFR CULTURE NEUTRAL REGION SOVEREIGN...INT/LAW GOV/COMP ANTHOL 20. PAGE 107 H2138 — ECO/UNDEV RACE/REL CIVMIL/REL DIPLOM

B66

NAMBOODIRIPAD E.M.,ECONOMICS AND POLITICS OF INDIA'S SOCIALIST PATTERN. INDIA STRATA AGRI INDUS NAT/G PRICE ORD/FREE SOVEREIGN 20. PAGE 115 H2307 — ECO/UNDEV PLAN SOCISM CAP/ISM

B66

NOLTE E.,THREE FACES OF FASCISM. FRANCE GERMANY DOMIN LEGIT COERCE CROWD REV WAR GP/REL RACE/REL SOVEREIGN...GOV/COMP IDEA/COMP 19/20 HITLER/A MUSSOLIN/B MARX/KARL. PAGE 118 H2368 — FASCISM TOTALISM NAT/G POL/PAR

B66

RAY A.,INTER-GOVERNMENTAL RELATIONS IN INDIA: A STUDY OF INDIAN FEDERALISM. CANADA INDIA SWITZERLND USA+45 USSR ADMIN GOV/REL...NAT/COMP BIBLIOG. PAGE 130 H2599 — CONSTN FEDERAL SOVEREIGN NAT/G

B66

VIEN N.C.,SEEKING THE TRUTH. VIETNAM DELIB/GP DOMIN RISK MARXISM 20 KY/NGUYEN. PAGE 162 H3250 — NAT/G COLONIAL PWR SOVEREIGN

B66

WEBER J.,EOTVOS UND DIE UNGARISCHE NATIONALITATENFRAGE. HUNGARY CULTURE SOCIETY REV ORD/FREE SOVEREIGN...BIOG 19. PAGE 166 H3318 — NAT/LISM GP/REL ATTIT CONCPT

B66

ZOLBERG A.R.,CREATING POLITICAL ORDER. AFR CONGO/BRAZ GHANA NIGER KIN NAT/G DOMIN COLONIAL REGION CENTRAL NAT/LISM ATTIT PWR 20 CONGO/LEOP. PAGE 173 H3462 — SOVEREIGN ORD/FREE CONSTN POL/PAR

L66

HUNTINGTON S.P.,"POLITICAL MODERNIZATION* AMERICA VS EUROPE." EUR+WWI MOD/EUR UK USA+45 LAW ECO/UNDEV PWR SOVEREIGN CONSERVE LAISSEZ GOV/COMP. PAGE 75 H1505 — STRUCT CREATE OBS

S66

DETTER I.,"THE PROBLEM OF UNEQUAL TREATIES." CONSTN NAT/G LEGIS COLONIAL COERCE PWR...GEOG UN TIME TREATY. PAGE 40 H0796 — SOVEREIGN DOMIN INT/LAW ECO/UNDEV

S66

FELD W.,"NATIONAL ECONOMIC INTEREST GROUPS AND POLICY FORMATION IN THE EEC." NAT/G POL/PAR REGION CENTRAL SOVEREIGN...INT NET/THEORY EEC. PAGE 49 H0985 — LOBBY ELITES DECISION

S66

MCLANE C.B.,"SOVIET DOCTRINE AND THE MILITARY COUPS IN AFRICA." ALGERIA GHANA COLONIAL NAT/LISM RIGID/FLEX SOVEREIGN MARXISM...DECISION NAT/COMP. PAGE 107 H2140 — USSR ATTIT AFR FORCES

S66

TOUVAL S.,"AFRICA'S FRONTIERS* REACTIONS TO A COLONIAL LEGACY." L/A+17C CONFER ADJUD COLONIAL APPORT CONSEN NAT/LISM RESPECT...RECORD NAT/COMP. PAGE 156 H3120 — AFR GEOG SOVEREIGN WAR

C66

ROSENBERG C.G. JR.,"THE MYTH OF "MAU-MAU:" NATIONALISM IN KENYA." AFR CULTURE NAT/G POL/PAR COERCE REV RACE/REL ATTIT ORD/FREE SOVEREIGN...MYTH BIBLIOG 20. PAGE 134 H2678 — NAT/LISM COLONIAL MAJORIT LEAD

B67

DEUTSCH K.W.,FRANCE, GERMANY AND THE WESTERN ALLIANCE. FRANCE GERMANY/W INT/ORG ARMS/CONT NAT/LISM SOVEREIGN...INT NAT/COMP 20. PAGE 40 H0801 — ELITES ATTIT DIPLOM POLICY

B67

FANON F.,TOWARD THE AFRICAN REVOLUTION. AFR FRANCE CULTURE ELITES LEAD REV GP/REL ORD/FREE SOVEREIGN 20. PAGE 49 H0969 — COLONIAL DOMIN ECO/UNDEV RACE/REL

B67

HUTCHINS F.G.,THE ILLUSION OF PERMANENCE: BRITISH IMPERIALISM IN INDIA. INDIA UK CULTURE STRUCT NAT/G REV GP/REL RACE/REL ADJUST DISCRIM ATTIT MORAL PWR SOC/INTEG 18/20. PAGE 75 H1509 — COLONIAL CONTROL SOVEREIGN CONSERVE

B67

MACRIDIS R.C.,FOREIGN POLICY IN WORLD POLITICS (3RD ED.). EX/STRUC BAL/PWR COLONIAL NAT/LISM SKILL SOVEREIGN WEALTH...CONCPT TIME/SEQ ANTHOL 20 COLD/WAR. PAGE 101 H2011 — DIPLOM POLICY NAT/G IDEA/COMP

B67

MAZRUI A.A.,THE ANGLO-AFRICAN COMMONWEALTH; POLITICAL FRICTION AND CULTURAL FUSION. AFR INT/ORG VOL/ASSN CHIEF GP/REL INGP/REL RACE/REL NAT/LISM 20 CMN/WLTH EEC. PAGE 106 H2111 — COLONIAL SOVEREIGN DIPLOM CULTURE

B67

MORRIS A.J.A.,PARLIAMENTARY DEMOCRACY IN THE NINETEENTH CENTURY. UK INDUS LOC/G NAT/G POL/PAR CONSULT LEGIS INT/TRADE ADMIN CHOOSE SUFF SOVEREIGN 19 PARLIAMENT. PAGE 113 H2261 — TIME/SEQ CONSTN PARL/PROC POPULISM

B67

NYERERE J.K.,FREEDOM AND UNITY/UHURU NA UMOJA: A SELECTION FROM WRITINGS AND SPEECHES, 1952-65. TANZANIA ELITES ECO/UNDEV INT/ORG NAT/G CREATE DIPLOM COLONIAL REGION RACE/REL...ANTHOL 20. PAGE 119 H2383 — SOVEREIGN AFR TREND ORD/FREE

B67

OLIVER R.,AFRICA SINCE 1800. AFR ISLAM CULTURE ECO/UNDEV SECT DOMIN RACE/REL DISCRIM SOVEREIGN 19/20. PAGE 121 H2414 — DIPLOM COLONIAL REGION

B67

RAMUNDO B.A.,PEACEFUL COEXISTENCE: INTERNATIONAL LAW IN THE BUILDING OF COMMUNISM. USSR INT/ORG DIPLOM COLONIAL ARMS/CONT ROLE SOVEREIGN...POLICY — INT/LAW PEACE MARXISM

METH/COMP NAT/COMP BIBLIOG. PAGE 129 H2588 — METH/CNCPT

B67
WINTER E.H.,CONTEMPORARY CHANGE IN TRADITIONAL SOCIETIES: VOLUME I INTRODUCTION AND AFRICAN TRIBES. NIGERIA AGRI LOC/G NAT/G CREATE DOMIN COLONIAL CONTROL GP/REL PWR SOVEREIGN...SOC OBS 20 TANGANYIKA. PAGE 169 H3389 — SOCIETY AFR CONSERVE KIN

B67
WISEMAN H.V.,BRITAIN AND THE COMMONWEALTH. EUR+WWI FUT UK ECO/DEV POL/PAR TEC/DEV INT/TRADE LEAD ROLE SOVEREIGN...SOC TREND 20 CMN/WLTH. PAGE 169 H3391 — INT/ORG DIPLOM NAT/G NAT/COMP

L67
ROBINSON T.W.,"A NATIONAL INTEREST ANALYSIS OF SINO-SOVIET RELATIONS." CHINA/COM USSR NAT/G NUC/PWR ATTIT PWR...CONCPT CHARTS 20. PAGE 132 H2650 — MARXISM DIPLOM SOVEREIGN GEN/LAWS

S67
ALBINSKI H.S.,"POLITICS AND BICULTURISM IN CANADA: THE FLAG DEBATE." CANADA SOCIETY NAT/G PROVS DELIB/GP DEBATE REGION SOVEREIGN PLURISM...POLICY SOC/INTEG 20. PAGE 5 H0093 — NAT/LISM GP/REL POL/PAR CULTURE

S67
BHATNAGAR J.K.,"THE VALUES AND ATTITUDES OF SOME INDIAN AND BRITISH STUDENTS." INDIA UK ECO/UNDEV LEGIT COLONIAL GP/REL SOVEREIGN...QU 20. PAGE 16 H0328 — NAT/COMP ATTIT EDU/PROP ACADEM

S67
GONZALEZ M.P.,"CUBA, UNA REVOLUCION EN MARCHA." CUBA L/A+17C USA+45 VIETNAM ECO/UNDEV FORCES DIPLOM DOMIN...POLICY MARXIST NAT/COMP CASTRO/F. PAGE 58 H1163 — REV NAT/G COLONIAL SOVEREIGN

S67
INDER S.,"AFTER THE CORONATION." CONSTN ECO/UNDEV EX/STRUC LEGIS INT/TRADE CONTROL SOVEREIGN ...TIME/SEQ 20 TONGA COMMONWLTH INAUGURATE. PAGE 76 H1527 — CHIEF NAT/G POLICY

S67
KOHN W.S.G.,"THE SOVEREIGNTY OF LIECHTENSTEIN." LIECHTENST SWITZERLND USSR CONSTN DEBATE WAR CONSERVE 18/20 UN. PAGE 88 H1748 — SOVEREIGN NAT/G PWR DIPLOM

S67
KYLE K.,"BACKGROUND TO THE CRISIS" ISLAM ISRAEL UAR UK USSR NAT/G PROB/SOLV LEGIT CONTROL REGION STRANGE MORAL 20 JEWS. PAGE 89 H1787 — DIPLOM POLICY SOVEREIGN COERCE

S67
ROTBERG R.I.,"COLONIALISM AND AFTER: THE POLITICAL LITERATURE OF CENTRAL AFRICA - A BIBLIOGRAPHIC ESSAY." AFR CHIEF EX/STRUC REV INGP/REL RACE/REL SOVEREIGN 20. PAGE 135 H2693 — BIBLIOG/A COLONIAL DIPLOM NAT/G

S67
SIPPEL D.,"INDIENS UNSICHERE ZUKUNFT." INDIA CULTURE ACADEM POL/PAR LEGIS COLONIAL CHOOSE SOVEREIGN...JURID 20. PAGE 144 H2888 — SOCIETY STRUCT ECO/UNDEV NAT/G

S67
SYRKIN M.,"THE RIGHT TO BE ORDINARY." ISLAM ISRAEL NAT/G COERCE NAT/LISM RIGID/FLEX 20. PAGE 151 H3025 — SOVEREIGN WAR FORCES DIPLOM

S67
THEROUX P.,"HATING THE ASIANS." TANZANIA UGANDA CONSTN INDUS NAT/G POL/PAR WORKER ECO/TAC HABITAT LOVE...POLICY GEOG 20 MIGRATION. PAGE 154 H3069 — AFR RACE/REL SOVEREIGN ATTIT

S67
TIVEY L.,"THE POLITICAL CONSEQUENCES OF ECONOMIC PLANNING." UK CONSTN INDUS ACT/RES ADMIN CONTROL LOBBY REPRESENT EFFICIENCY SUPEGO SOVEREIGN ...DECISION 20. PAGE 155 H3108 — PLAN POLICY NAT/G

S68
DOUGLAS-HOME C.,"A MISTAKEN POLICY IN ADEN." YEMEN CULTURE ECO/UNDEV INDUS FORCES WORKER DIPLOM ECO/TAC CONTROL 20 ADEN. PAGE 42 H0842 — SOVEREIGN COLONIAL POLICY REGION

S68
GUZZARDI W.,"THE DECLINE OF THE STERLING CLUB." UK WOR+45 NAT/G PLAN DIPLOM INT/TRADE AGREE CONSEN EQUILIB SOVEREIGN...POLICY NEW/IDEA 20 COMMONWLTH GOLD/STAND. PAGE 63 H1259 — FINAN ECO/TAC WEALTH NAT/COMP

S68
MILLAR T.B.,"THE COMMONWEALTH AND THE UN." UK DIPLOM TARIFFS AGREE COLONIAL CONTROL SOVEREIGN WEALTH...GP/COMP GOV/COMP 20 CMN/WLTH UN. PAGE 111 H2210 — INT/ORG POLICY TREND ECO/TAC

B70
BOSSUET J.B.,"POLITIQUE TIREE DE L'ECRITURE SAINTE" (1679-1709) IN J.B. BOSSUET, OEVRES DE BOSSUET. NAT/G GP/REL AUTHORIT HEREDITY PERSON ALL/VALS SOVEREIGN 18 BIBLE DEITY CHRISTIAN. PAGE 19 H0383 — TRADIT CHIEF SECT CONCPT

B75
MAINE H.S.,LECTURES ON THE EARLY HISTORY OF INSTITUTIONS. IRELAND UK CONSTN ELITES STRUCT FAM KIN CHIEF LEGIS CT/SYS OWN SOVEREIGN...CONCPT 16 BENTHAM/J BREHON ROMAN/LAW. PAGE 101 H2021 — CULTURE LAW INGP/REL

B75
NEWMAN J.H.,A LETTER ADDRESSED TO THE DUKE OF NORFOLK ON THE OCCASION OF MR. GLADSTONE'S RECENT EXPOSTULATION. NAT/G SECT CHIEF LEGIS CONTROL LEAD GP/REL SUPEGO SOC/INTEG WORSHIP 19 ENGLAND. PAGE 117 H2346 — POLICY DOMIN SOVEREIGN CATHISM

B85
BLISS P.,OF SOVEREIGNTY. NAT/G PROVS GOV/REL PRIVIL ORD/FREE PWR CONSERVE...CONCPT 19. PAGE 18 H0356 — CONSTN SOVEREIGN FEDERAL

B85
BLUNTSCHLI J.K.,THE THEORY OF THE STATE. GERMANY CONSTN INGP/REL NAT/LISM PERSON SOVEREIGN CONSERVE ...SOC. PAGE 18 H0362 — CONCPT LEGIS NAT/G

L86
BURGESS J.W.,"THE RECENT CONSTITUTIONAL CRISIS IN NORWAY" MOD/EUR NORWAY SWEDEN LOC/G NAT/G CHIEF BAL/PWR NAT/LISM ORD/FREE 19. PAGE 24 H0481 — CONSTN SOVEREIGN GOV/REL

B90
BURKE E.,REFLECTIONS ON THE REVOLUTION IN FRANCE. FRANCE UK NAT/G DOMIN LEGIT PEACE PWR SOVEREIGN CONSERVE...POLICY GEN/LAWS 18. PAGE 24 H0487 — REV ORD/FREE CHIEF TRADIT

B91
BENTHAM J.,A FRAGMENT ON GOVERNMENT (1776). CONSTN MUNIC NAT/G SECT AGREE HAPPINESS UTIL MORAL ORD/FREE...JURID CONCPT. PAGE 15 H0292 — SOVEREIGN LAW DOMIN

B91
PAINE T.,RIGHTS OF MAN. FRANCE MOD/EUR CONSTN NAT/G CHIEF DOMIN LEGIT SOVEREIGN...MAJORIT IDEA/COMP 18 BURKE/EDM CIVIL/LIB. PAGE 122 H2446 — GEN/LAWS ORD/FREE REV AGREE

B91
SIDGWICK H.,THE ELEMENTS OF POLITICS. LOC/G NAT/G LEGIS DIPLOM ADJUD CONTROL EXEC PARL/PROC REPRESENT GOV/REL SOVEREIGN ALL/IDEOS 19 MILL/JS BENTHAM/J. PAGE 143 H2868 — POLICY LAW CONCPT

B96
DE VATTEL E.,THE LAW OF NATIONS. AGRI FINAN CHIEF DIPLOM INT/TRADE AGREE OWN ALL/VALS MORAL ORD/FREE SOVEREIGN...GEN/LAWS 18 NATURL/LAW WOLFF/C. PAGE 39 H0774 — LAW CONCPT NAT/G INT/LAW

SOVEREIGNTY....SEE SOVEREIGN

SOVIET UNION....SEE USSR

SPAAK P.H. H2941

SPACE....OUTER SPACE, SPACE LAW

B65
UN,SPACE ACTIVITIES AND RESOURCES: REVIEW OF UNITED NATION'S NATIONAL AND INTERNATIONAL PROGRAMS. INT/ORG LABOR PLAN TEC/DEV DIPLOM EFFICIENCY HEALTH ...GOV/COMP 20 UN. PAGE 158 H3155 — SPACE NUC/PWR FOR/AID PEACE

B65
US DEPARTMENT OF DEFENSE,US SECURITY ARMS CONTROL, AND DISARMAMENT 1961-1965 (PAMPHLET). CHINA/COM COM GERMANY/W ISRAEL SPACE USA+45 USSR WOR+45 FORCES EDU/PROP DETER EQUILIB PEACE ALL/VALS...GOV/COMP 20 NATO. PAGE 159 H3183 — BIBLIOG/A ARMS/CONT NUC/PWR DIPLOM

SPAIN....SPAIN

N
INSTITUTE OF HISPANIC STUDIES,HISPANIC AMERICAN REPORT. EUR+WWI SPAIN LAW CONSTN ECO/UNDEV POL/PAR EX/STRUC LEGIS LEAD...HUM SOC 20. PAGE 77 H1538 — BIBLIOG/A L/A+17C NAT/G DIPLOM

B29
DE REPARAZ G.,GEOGRAFIA Y POLITICA. CHILE SPAIN USSR NAT/G DIPLOM REV MARXISM...POLICY 19/20. PAGE 38 H0768 — GEOG MOD/EUR

B31
KIRKPATRICK F.A.,A HISTORY OF THE ARGENTINE REPUBLIC. SPAIN UK CONSTN SOCIETY ECO/UNDEV EX/STRUC DIPLOM FOR/AID LEAD WAR ATTIT...BIOG CHARTS 16/20 ARGEN SAN/MARTIN. PAGE 86 H1724 — NAT/G L/A+17C COLONIAL

B41
GRISMER R.,A NEW BIBLIOGRAPHY OF THE LITERATURES OF SPAIN AND SPANISH AMERICA. CHRIST-17C MOD/EUR PRE/AMER SPAIN CULTURE DIPLOM EDU/PROP...ART/METH GEOG HUM PHIL/SCI 20. PAGE 61 H1229 — BIBLIOG LAW NAT/G ECO/UNDEV

C43
BENTHAM J.,"ON THE LIBERTY OF THE PRESS, AND PUBLIC DISCUSSION" IN J. BOWRING, ED., THE WORKS OF JEREMY BENTHAM." SPAIN UK LAW ELITES NAT/G LEGIS INSPECT LEGIT WRITING CONTROL PRIVIL TOTALISM AUTHORIT ...TRADIT 19 FREE/SPEE. PAGE 15 H0290 — ORD/FREE PRESS CONFER CONSERVE

B47
BEHAR D.,BIBLIOGRAFIA HISPANOAMERICANA. LIBROS ANTIGUOS Y MODERNOS REFERENTES A AMERICA Y ESPANA. PORTUGAL SPAIN CONSTN NAT/G SECT CREATE REV WAR GOV/REL...ART/METH GEOG PHIL/SCI LING 20 ARGEN. — BIBLIOG L/A+17C CULTURE

PAGE 13 H0260

B49
SCHONS D.,BOOK CENSORSHIP IN NEW SPAIN (NEW WORLD STUDIES, BOOK II). SPAIN LAW CULTURE INSPECT ADJUD CT/SYS SANCTION GP/REL ORD/FREE 14/17. PAGE 140 H2797
CHRIST-17C EDU/PROP CONTROL PRESS

B50
ALBRECHT-CARRIE R.,ITALY FROM NAPOLEON TO MUSSOLINI. GERMANY ITALY SPAIN SOCIETY ECO/DEV POL/PAR LEGIS AGREE CONTROL WAR NAT/LISM TOTALISM PWR SOCISM...SOC 19/20 TREATY. PAGE 5 H0095
FASCISM NAT/G

B51
CATALOGO GENERAL DE LA LIBRERIA ESPANOLA E HISPANOAMERICANA 1901-1930; AUTORES (5 VOLS., 1932-1951). SPAIN COLONIAL GOV/REL...SOC 20. PAGE 2 H0036
BIBLIOG L/A+17C DIPLOM NAT/G

B51
BORKENAU F.,EUROPEAN COMMUNISM. COM EUR+WWI GERMANY SPAIN USSR INT/ORG PLAN REV WAR ATTIT 20 STALIN/J HITLER/A. PAGE 19 H0376
MARXISM POLICY DIPLOM NAT/G

B52
LOPEZ-AMO A.,LA MONARQUIA DE LA REFORMA SOCIAL. MOD/EUR SPAIN CONSTN NAT/G TASK EFFICIENCY CONSERVE ...ANARCH TRADIT SOC CONCPT IDEA/COMP 19/20. PAGE 98 H1967
MARXISM REV LEGIT ORD/FREE

B53
ROSCIO J.G.,OBRAS. L/A+17C SPAIN DIPLOM REV WAR NAT/LISM TOTALISM PWR SOVEREIGN 19. PAGE 134 H2671
ORD/FREE COLONIAL NAT/G PHIL/SCI

B54
CAMPANELLA T.,A DISCOURSE TOUCHING THE SPANISH MONARCHY... (1640). SPAIN UNIV SEA STRATA FINAN SECT FORCES SUPEGO LOVE ORD/FREE...CONCPT 17. PAGE 26 H0514
CONSERVE CHIEF NAT/G DIPLOM

C54
DE GRAZIA A.,"THE COMPARATIVE SURVEY OF EUROPEAN-AMERICAN POLITICAL BEHAV IOR; A RESEARCH PROSPECTUS (PAPER)" EUR+WWI FRANCE GERMANY SPAIN UK USA+45 WOR+45 STRATA POL/PAR DIPLOM EDU/PROP COLONIAL LEAD WAR NAT/LISM CONCPT. PAGE 37 H0752
BIBLIOG R+D METH NAT/COMP

B56
CEPEDA U.A.,EN TORNO AL CONCEPTO DEL ESTADO EN LOS REYES CATHOLICOS. SPAIN SOCIETY STRUCT SECT LEGIT WAR ATTIT WORSHIP 15/17. PAGE 28 H0569
NAT/G PHIL/SCI CHIEF PWR

B57
RUMEU DE ARMAS A.,ESPANA EEN EL AFRICA ATLANTICA. AFR CHRIST-17C PORTUGAL SPAIN DIPLOM ECO/TAC CONTROL 14/16 AFRICA/W. PAGE 136 H2717
NAT/G COLONIAL CHIEF PWR

B58
ALMAGRO BASCH M.,ORIGEN Y FORMACION DEL PUEBLO HISPANO. PREHIST SPAIN REGION WAR RACE/REL HABITAT ORD/FREE...SOC SOC/INTEG 20. PAGE 5 H0109
CULTURE GP/REL ADJUST

B58
FLORES X.,LA TRADICION CATOLICA Y EL FUTURO POLITICO DE ESPANA (PAMPHLET). SPAIN NAT/G ACT/RES LEAD GP/REL CATHISM 20 CHRISTIAN CHURCH/STA. PAGE 52 H1031
SECT POL/PAR ATTIT ORD/FREE

B58
HAYCRAFT J.,BABEL IN SPAIN. SPAIN ATTIT...RELATIV 20. PAGE 68 H1367
CULTURE PERSON BIOG GEOG

B58
PAYNO M.,LA REFORMA SOCIAL EN ESPANA Y MEXICO. SPAIN ECO/TAC TAX LOBBY COERCE REV OWN CATHISM 19/20 MEXIC/AMER. PAGE 124 H2479
SECT NAT/G LAW ELITES

B58
SYME R.,COLONIAL ELITES: ROME, SPAIN, AND THE AMERICAS. CHRIST-17C MOD/EUR SPAIN UK USA-45 CULTURE NAT/G CHIEF TOP/EX...GOV/COMP IDEA/COMP NAT/COMP ROM/EMP GIBBON/EDW TOYNBEE/A. PAGE 151 H3022
COLONIAL ELITES DOMIN

B59
FOX A.,THE POWER OF SMALL STATES: DIPLOMACY IN WORLD WAR TWO. EUR+WWI FINLAND NORWAY SPAIN SWEDEN TURKEY NAT/G TOP/EX DIPLOM PWR...HIST/WRIT 20. PAGE 52 H1044
CONCPT STERTYP BAL/PWR

B59
HOBSBAWM E.J.,PRIMITIVE REBELS; STUDIES IN ARCHAIC FORMS OF SOCIAL MOVEMENT IN THE 19TH AND 20TH CENTURIES. ITALY SPAIN CULTURE VOL/ASSN RISK CROWD GP/REL INGP/REL ISOLAT TOTALISM...PSY SOC 18/20. PAGE 72 H1438
SOCIETY CRIME REV GUERRILLA

B59
INTERNATIONAL PRESS INSTITUTE,THE PRESS IN AUTHORITARIAN COUNTRIES. COM PORTUGAL SPAIN UAR USSR NAT/G DOMIN LEGIT ORD/FREE FASCISM SOCISM 20. PAGE 78 H1559
PRESS CONTROL TOTALISM EDU/PROP

B59
SANCHEZ A.L.,EL CONCEPTO DEL ESTADO EN EL PENSAMIENTO ESPANOL DEL SIGLO XVI. SPAIN LEGIS
NAT/G PHIL/SCI

JUDGE BAL/PWR LEGIT EXEC WAR PWR...MAJORIT 16. PAGE 137 H2747
LAW SOVEREIGN

B60
ALBI F.,TRATADO DE LOS MODOS DE GESTION DE LAS CORPORACIONES LOCALES. SPAIN FINAN NAT/G BUDGET CONTROL EXEC ROUTINE GOV/REL ORD/FREE SOVEREIGN ...MGT 20. PAGE 5 H0092
LOC/G LAW ADMIN MUNIC

B61
ESTEVEZ A.,ASPECTOS ECONOMICO-FINANCIEROS DE LA CAMPANA SANMARITANA. L/A+17C SPAIN FINAN COLONIAL LEAD ROLE ORD/FREE WEALTH 19 SOUTH/AMER SAN/MARTIN. PAGE 47 H0942
ECO/UNDEV REV BUDGET NAT/G

B61
GARCIA E.,LA ADMINISTRACION ESPANOLA. SPAIN GOV/REL ...CONCPT METH/COMP 20. PAGE 55 H1099
ADMIN NAT/G LOC/G DECISION

B61
GUIZOT F.P.G.,HISTORY OF THE ORIGIN OF REPRESENTATIVE GOVERNMENT IN EUROPE. CHRIST-17C FRANCE MOD/EUR SPAIN UK LAW CHIEF FORCES POPULISM ...MAJORIT TIME/SEQ GOV/COMP NAT/COMP 4/19 PARLIAMENT. PAGE 62 H1250
LEGIS REPRESENT CONSTN NAT/G

B61
SHIELS W.E.,KING AND CHURCH: THE RISE AND FALL OF THE PATRONATO REAL. SPAIN INGP/REL...CONCPT WORSHIP 16/19 CHURCH/STA MISSION. PAGE 143 H2859
SECT NAT/G CHIEF POLICY

B62
DEHIO L.,THE PRECARIOUS BALANCE: FOUR CENTURIES OF THE EUROPEAN POWER STRUGGLE. FRANCE GERMANY SPAIN NAT/G DOMIN PWR...GOV/COMP 8/20. PAGE 39 H0784
BAL/PWR WAR DIPLOM COERCE

B62
DIAZ J.S.,MANUAL DE BIBLIOGRAFIA DE LA LITERATURA ESPANOLA. PRE/AMER SPAIN ECO/UNDEV DIPLOM LEAD ATTIT...SOC 15/20. PAGE 41 H0820
BIBLIOG L/A+17C NAT/G COLONIAL

B63
BIALEK R.W.,CATHOLIC POLITICS: A HISTORY BASED ON ECUADOR. ECUADOR SPAIN CULTURE STRUCT CONTROL REV PWR...BIBLIOG WORSHIP 18/20. PAGE 16 H0329
COLONIAL CATHISM GOV/REL HABITAT

B63
BORKENAU F.,THE SPANISH COCKPIT. SPAIN ELITES STRATA POL/PAR ACT/RES CROWD WAR GP/REL INGP/REL ...SOC NAT/COMP 20. PAGE 19 H0377
REV CONSERVE SOCISM FORCES

B63
ELLIOT J.H.,THE REVOLT OF THE CATALANS. SPAIN LOC/G PROVS FORCES DIPLOM TASK WAR GOV/REL INGP/REL ...POLICY 17 OLIVARES. PAGE 45 H0909
REV NAT/G TOP/EX DOMIN

B63
LOOMIE A.J.,THE SPANISH ELIZABETHANS: THE ENGLISH EXILES AT THE COURT OF PHILIP II. SPAIN UK WAR INGP/REL DRIVE HABITAT CATHISM...BIOG 16/17 MIGRATION. PAGE 98 H1962
NAT/G STRANGE POLICY DIPLOM

B63
OTERO L.M.,HONDURAS. HONDURAS SPAIN STRUCT SECT COLONIAL REV WAR ATTIT PWR...GEOG WORSHIP 16/20. PAGE 122 H2432
NAT/G SOCIETY NAT/LISM ECO/UNDEV

B64
LATORRE A.,UNIVERSIDAD Y SOCIEDAD. SPAIN EDU/PROP LEAD GP/REL PERS/REL ATTIT KNOWL. PAGE 92 H1837
ACADEM CULTURE ROLE INTELL

B64
MORRIS J.,THE PRESENCE OF SPAIN. SPAIN MUNIC NAT/G FORCES ATTIT CATHISM...AUD/VIS 16/20. PAGE 113 H2263
CULTURE HABITAT SOCIETY GEOG

B64
SANCHEZ J.M.,REFORM AND REACTION. SPAIN STRATA NAT/LISM TOTALISM 20. PAGE 137 H2749
NAT/G SECT GP/REL REV

B64
TURNER M.C.,LIBROS EN VENTA EN HISPANOAMERICA Y ESPANA. SPAIN LAW CONSTN CULTURE ADMIN LEAD...HUM SOC 20. PAGE 157 H3141
BIBLIOG L/A+17C NAT/G DIPLOM

B65
FILIPINIANA BOOK GUILD,THE COLONIZATION AND CONQUEST OF THE PHILIPPINES BY SPAIN. PHILIPPINE SPAIN ELITES AGRI KIN CHIEF DOMIN CONTROL ATTIT PWR ...ANTHOL WORSHIP 16. PAGE 50 H1000
COLONIAL COERCE CULTURE WAR

B65
HISPANIC SOCIETY OF AMERICA,CATALOGUE (10 VOLS.). PORTUGAL PRE/AMER SPAIN NAT/G ADMIN...POLICY SOC 15/20. PAGE 71 H1426
BIBLIOG L/A+17C COLONIAL DIPLOM

B65
JACKSON G.,THE SPANISH REPUBLIC AND THE CIVIL WAR, 1931-1939. EUR+WWI INTELL STRUCT COM/IND NAT/G
ATTIT GUERRILLA

POL/PAR LEGIS EDU/PROP EXEC COERCE NAT/LISM DRIVE PWR...INT TIME/SEQ TOT/POP 20. PAGE 79 H1574 — SPAIN

B65
OECD,THE MEDITERRANEAN REGIONAL PROJECT: SPAIN; EDUCATION AND DEVELOPMENT. FUT SPAIN STRATA FINAN NAT/G WORKER PLAN PROB/SOLV ADMIN COST...POLICY STAT CHARTS 20 OECD. PAGE 120 H2402 — ECO/UNDEV EDU/PROP ACADEM SCHOOL

B65
ORG FOR ECO COOP AND DEVEL,THE MEDITERRANEAN REGIONAL PROJECT: AN EXPERIMENT IN PLANNING BY SIX COUNTRIES. FUT GREECE SPAIN TURKEY YUGOSLAVIA SOCIETY FINAN NAT/G PROF/ORG EDU/PROP ADMIN REGION COST...POLICY STAT CHARTS 20 OECD. PAGE 121 H2427 — PLAN ECO/UNDEV ACADEM SCHOOL

B65
SALVADORI M.,ITALY. AUSTRIA FRANCE GERMANY ITALY SPAIN CULTURE NAT/G POL/PAR DIPLOM WAR FASCISM LAISSEZ MARXISM...TIME/SEQ CHARTS BIBLIOG/A. PAGE 137 H2744 — NAT/LISM CATHISM SOCIETY

S66
BLANC N.,"SPAIN: LEARNING THROUGH STRUGGLE" SPAIN STRATA STRUCT SECT FORCES PROB/SOLV AGE/Y ATTIT ORD/FREE PWR WEALTH MARXISM SOCISM 19/20 FRANCO/F SUCCESSION. PAGE 18 H0352 — NAT/G FUT SOCIALIST TOTALISM

B67
CORDIER A.W.,COLUMBIA ESSAYS IN INTERNATIONAL AFFAIRS. ASIA CHINA/COM FRANCE S/ASIA SPAIN UAR ECO/UNDEV LOC/G ECO/TAC GUERRILLA PWR...BIOG ANTHOL 18/20 MAU/MAU. PAGE 33 H0663 — NAT/G DIPLOM MARXISM POLICY

S67
HEASMAN D.J.,"THE GIBRALTAR AFFAIR." SPAIN UK NAT/G BAL/PWR CONSEN NAT/LISM ATTIT...REALPOL 20. PAGE 69 H1378 — DIPLOM COLONIAL REGION

SPAN/AMER....SPANISH-AMERICAN CULTURE

B66
VOGT E.Z.,PEOPLE OF RIMROCK. STRATA STRUCT KIN SECT GP/REL HABITAT ALL/VALS...GEOG INT QU 20 TEXAS NAVAHO MORMON SPAN/AMER ZUNI. PAGE 163 H3260 — CULTURE GP/COMP SOC SOCIETY

SPEAKER OF THE HOUSE....SEE CONGRESS, LEGIS, PARLIAMENT

SPEAR/BRWN....SPEARMAN BROWN PREDICTION FORMULA

SPEARS E.L. H2942

SPECIALIZATION....SEE TASK, SKILL

SPECULATION....SEE GAMBLE, RISK

SPEIER H. H1768

SPENCER F.A. H2943

SPENCER H. H2944

SPENCER P. H2945

SPENCER R.C. H2946

SPENCER/H....HERBERT SPENCER

B28
BARKER E.,POLITICAL THOUGHT IN ENGLAND: FROM HERBERT SPENCER TO THE PRESENT DAY. UK ALL/IDEOS ...PHIL/SCI 19/20 SPENCER/H GREEN/TH BENTHAM/J MAITLAND/F. PAGE 11 H0217 — INTELL GEN/LAWS IDEA/COMP

B60
MANIS J.G.,MAN AND SOCIETY. STRATA LEAD INGP/REL PERS/REL ATTIT PWR...PSY ANTHOL T SOC/INTEG MARX/KARL MILL/JS FREUD/S CHURCHLL/W SPENCER/H RUSSELL/B. PAGE 102 H2036 — SOC SOCIETY STRUCT CULTURE

SPENGLER/O....OSWALD SPENGLER

SPICER E.H. H2947

SPINELLI A. H2948

SPINKA M. H2949

SPINOZA/B....BARUCH (OR BENEDICT) SPINOZA

B64
FROMM E.,MARX'S CONCEPT OF MAN. LABOR OWN PERSON ...HUM IDEA/COMP GEN/LAWS 17 MARX/KARL EUROPE SPINOZA/B GOETHE/J HEGEL/GWF. PAGE 54 H1072 — INGP/REL CONCPT MARXISM SOCISM

SPIRO H.J. H2950,H2951

SPITTMANN I. H2952

SPOCK/B....BENJAMIN SPOCK

SPOONER F.P. H2953

SPORTS....SPORTS AND ATHLETIC COMPETITIONS

SPRING D. H2954

SPRINGER H.W. H2955

SPRINGER M. H1648

SPROTT W.J.H. H2956

SPROUT H. H2957

SPROUT M. H2957

SPULBER N. H2958

SQUIBB G.D. H2959

SQUIRES J.D. H2960

SRAFFA/P....PIERO SRAFFA

SRINIVAS M.N. H2961

SRINIVASAN R. H0086

SROLE L. H3309

SST....SUPERSONIC TRANSPORT

SSU-YU T. H2962

ST/LOUIS....ST. LOUIS, MO.

ST/PAUL....SAINT PAUL, MINNESOTA

STAAR R.F. H2963,H2964,H2965

STADLER K.R. H2966

STAGES....SEE TIME/SEQ

STAHL W. H2967

STALIN J. H2968

STALIN/J....JOSEPH STALIN

B34
STALIN J.,PROBLEMS OF LENINISM. USSR STRATA INDUS LOC/G POL/PAR ECO/TAC CONTROL TOTALISM PWR SOCISM LENIN/VI STALIN/J. PAGE 148 H2968 — MARXISM REV ELITES NAT/G

B42
NEUMANN S.,PERMANENT REVOLUTION: THE TOTAL STATE IN A WORLD AT WAR. COM EUR+WWI GERMANY USSR EX/STRUC DIPLOM CONTROL COERCE REPRESENT MARXISM...SOC GOV/COMP BIBLIOG 20 HITLER/A STALIN/J. PAGE 117 H2337 — FASCISM TOTALISM DOMIN EDU/PROP

N47
CANNON J.P.,AMERICAN STALINISM AND ANTI-STALINISM (PAMPHLET). NAT/G WORKER DOMIN EDU/PROP REV GP/REL ...MARXIST CONCPT 20 STALIN/J TROTSKY/L. PAGE 26 H0521 — LABOR MARXISM CAP/ISM POL/PAR

B48
TOWSTER J.,POLITICAL POWER IN THE USSR: 1917-1947. USSR CONSTN CULTURE ELITES CREATE PLAN COERCE CENTRAL ATTIT RIGID/FLEX ORD/FREE...BIBLIOG SOC/INTEG 20 LENIN/VI STALIN/J. PAGE 156 H3122 — EX/STRUC NAT/G MARXISM PWR

B48
WOLFE B.D.,THREE WHO MADE A REVOLUTION. USSR CONSTN NAT/G CAP/ISM EDU/PROP CONTROL WAR GP/REL INGP/REL PERS/REL ROLE 20 STALIN/J LENIN/VI TROTSKY/L BOLSHEVISM. PAGE 170 H3398 — BIOG REV LEAD MARXISM

B51
BORKENAU F.,EUROPEAN COMMUNISM. COM EUR+WWI GERMANY SPAIN USSR INT/ORG PLAN REV WAR ATTIT 20 STALIN/J HITLER/A. PAGE 19 H0376 — MARXISM POLICY DIPLOM NAT/G

B55
MAYO H.B.,DEMOCRACY AND MARXISM. COM USSR STRATA NAT/G WORKER ECO/TAC REV MORAL...PHIL/SCI HIST/WRIT IDEA/COMP WORSHIP 20 MARX/KARL LENIN/VI STALIN/J TROTSKY/L. PAGE 105 H2108 — MARXISM CAP/ISM

B56
VON HARPE W.,DIE SOWJETUNION FINNLAND UND SKANDANAVIEN, 1945-1955. EUR+WWI FINLAND GERMANY USSR WAR INGP/REL ORD/FREE SOVEREIGN MARXISM ...POLICY GOV/COMP BIBLIOG 20 STALIN/J. PAGE 163 H3270 — DIPLOM COM NEUTRAL BAL/PWR

B57
TOMASIC D.A.,NATIONAL COMMUNISM AND SOVIET STRATEGY. UK USSR YUGOSLAVIA NAT/G POL/PAR CHIEF CREATE DOMIN REV WAR PWR...BIOG TREND 20 TITO/MARSH STALIN/J. PAGE 156 H3112
COM NAT/LISM MARXISM DIPLOM

B58
DUNAYEVSKAYA R.,MARXISM AND FREEDOM: FROM 1776 UNTIL TODAY. COM USSR WORKER CAP/ISM DOMIN REV GP/REL TOTALISM ALL/VALS...MYTH BIOG IDEA/COMP 18/20 MARX/KARL LENIN/VI STALIN/J. PAGE 43 H0861
MARXISM CONCPT ORD/FREE

B58
PALMER E.E.,THE COMMUNIST CHALLENGE. COM USA+45 USA-45 ECO/DEV ECO/UNDEV NEUTRAL ORD/FREE POPULISM ...CONCPT NAT/COMP ANTHOL 19/20 LENIN/VI STALIN/J MAO MARX/KARL COM/PARTY. PAGE 123 H2450
MARXISM DIPLOM IDEA/COMP POLICY

B59
HENDEL S.,THE SOVIET CRUCIBLE. USSR LEAD COERCE NAT/LISM UTOPIA PWR...POLICY CONCPT ANTHOL 20 STALIN/J LENIN/VI MARX/KARL BOLSHEVIK. PAGE 70 H1393
COM MARXISM REV TOTALISM

B60
SCHAPIRO L.,THE COMMUNIST PARTY OF THE SOVIET UNION. COM LAW SOCIETY STRATA STRUCT ECO/DEV LABOR NAT/G POL/PAR CREATE DOMIN EDU/PROP COERCE TOTALISM MARXISM...POLICY CONCPT MYTH TIME/SEQ WORK TOT/POP 20 LENIN/VI STALIN/J. PAGE 139 H2772
INTELL PWR USSR

S61
TUCKER R.C.,"TOWARDS A COMPARATIVE POLITICS OF MOVEMENT-REGIMES" (BMR)" USSR CONSTN NAT/G CREATE PROB/SOLV DIPLOM DOMIN REV...GP/COMP IDEA/COMP METH 20 STALIN/J BOLSHEVISM. PAGE 157 H3135
MARXISM POLICY GEN/LAWS PWR

B62
BAFFREY S.A.,THE RED MYTH: A HISTORY OF COMMUNISM FROM MARX TO KHRUSHCHEV. USSR NAT/G CHIEF CAP/ISM DIPLOM EDU/PROP REV WAR PEACE TOTALISM...POLICY 20 STALIN/J KHRUSH/N. PAGE 10 H0195
CONCPT MARXISM TV

B62
MEHNERT K.,SOVIET MAN AND HIS WORLD. COM USSR INTELL FAM WORKER PLAN EDU/PROP REV PRODUC MARXISM ...SOC TREND SOC/INTEG 20 LENIN/VI STALIN/J KHRUSH/N. PAGE 108 H2162
SOCIETY CULTURE ECO/DEV

B63
HOLLANDER P.,THE NEW MAN AND HIS ENEMIES: A STUDY OF THE STALINIST CONCEPTIONS OF GOOD AND EVIL PERSONIFIED (DOCTORAL THESIS). USSR SOCIETY ECO/DEV NAT/G EDU/PROP WRITING...SOC STERTYP BIBLIOG 20 STALIN/J. PAGE 73 H1455
CONTROL ATTIT TOTALISM MARXISM

B63
MCNEAL R.H.,THE BOLSHEVIK TRADITION: LENIN, STALIN, KHRUSHCHEV. USSR NAT/G SUPEGO CONSERVE...IDEA/COMP GEN/LAWS 20 LENIN/VI STALIN/J KHRUSH/N. PAGE 107 H2145
INTELL BIOG PERS/COMP

B63
MILLER W.J.,THE MEANING OF COMMUNISM. USSR SOCIETY ECO/DEV EX/STRUC WORKER TEC/DEV ADMIN TOTALISM ...POLICY CONCPT CHARTS BIBLIOG T 20 COLD/WAR LENIN/VI STALIN/J. PAGE 111 H2215
MARXISM TRADIT DIPLOM NAT/G

B64
RESHETAR J.S. JR.,A CONCISE HISTORY OF THE COMMUNIST PARTY OF THE SOVIET UNION (REV. ED.). COM USSR NAT/G EXEC 19/20 LENIN/VI STALIN/J KHRUSH/N. PAGE 131 H2618
CHIEF POL/PAR MARXISM PWR

B65
RANDALL F.B.,STALIN'S RUSSIA. USSR STRUCT AGRI NAT/G PLAN DIPLOM WAR TOTALISM MARXISM...BIBLIOG/A 19/20 STALIN/J. PAGE 129 H2590
BIOG INDUS ECO/DEV

B66
BRODERSEN A.,THE SOVIET WORKER: LABOR AND GOVERNMENT IN SOVIET SOCIETY. USSR STRUCT INDUS LABOR PLAN PAY INGP/REL PRODUC...POLICY GEN/LAWS BIBLIOG 20 STALIN/J LENIN/VI BOLSHEVISM KHRUSH/N. PAGE 21 H0425
WORKER ROLE NAT/G MARXISM

B66
DALLIN A.,POLITICS IN THE SOVIET UNION: 7 CASES. COM USSR LAW POL/PAR CHIEF FORCES WRITING CONTROL PARL/PROC CIVMIL/REL TOTALISM...ANTHOL 20 KHRUSH/N STALIN/J CASEBOOK COM/PARTY. PAGE 37 H0736
MARXISM DOMIN ORD/FREE GOV/REL

B66
DEUTSCHER I.,STALIN: A POLITICAL BIOGRAPHY. EUR+WWI USSR POL/PAR FORCES DIPLOM ADMIN LEAD REV WAR TOTALISM PERSON 20 STALIN/J ROOSEVLT/F LENIN/VI HITLER/A. PAGE 40 H0807
BIOG MARXISM TOP/EX PWR

B66
HERMANN F.G.,DER KAMPF GEGEN RELIGION UND KIRCHE IN DER SOWJETISCHEN BESATZUNGSZONE DEUTSCHLANDS. GERMANY/E EDU/PROP ATTIT PERSON MORAL MARXISM 20 LENIN/VI STALIN/J KHRUSH/N. PAGE 70 H1400
SECT ORD/FREE GP/REL NAT/G

B67
BRZEZINSKI Z.K.,THE SOVIET BLOC: UNITY AND CONFLICT (2ND ED., REV., ENLARGED). COM POLAND USSR INTELL CHIEF EX/STRUC CONTROL EXEC GOV/REL PWR MARXISM ...TREND IDEA/COMP 20 LENIN/VI MARX/KARL STALIN/J. PAGE 23 H0463
NAT/G DIPLOM

B67
LAQUER W.,THE FATE OF THE REVOLUTION: INTERPRETATIONS OF SOVIET HISTORY. RUSSIA NAT/G MARXISM...BIBLIOG 20 STALIN/J. PAGE 91 H1816
REV KNOWL HIST/WRIT IDEA/COMP

S67
CARR E.H.,"REVOLUTION FROM ABOVE." USSR STRATA FINAN INDUS NAT/G DOMIN LEAD GP/REL INGP/REL OWN PRODUC PWR 20 STALIN/J. PAGE 27 H0538
AGRI POLICY COM EFFICIENCY

S68
SHAPIRO J.P.,"SOVIET HISTORIOGRAPHY AND THE MOSCOW TRIALS: AFTER THIRTY YEARS." USSR NAT/G LEGIT PRESS CONTROL LEAD ATTIT MARXISM...NEW/IDEA METH 20 TROTSKY/L STALIN/J KHRUSH/N. PAGE 142 H2843
HIST/WRIT EDU/PROP SANCTION ADJUD

STAMMLER/R....RUDOLF STAMMLER

STAND/INT....STANDARDIZED INTERVIEWS

L60
ROKKAN S.,"NORWAY AND THE UNITED STATES OF AMERICA." NORWAY CHOOSE...SOC STAND/INT SAMP CHARTS GP/COMP METH/COMP 20. PAGE 133 H2665
STRUCT NAT/G PARTIC REPRESENT

S60
EMERSON R.,"THE EROSION OF DEMOCRACY." AFR FUT LAW CULTURE INTELL SOCIETY ECO/UNDEV FAM LOC/G NAT/G FORCES PLAN TEC/DEV ECO/TAC ADMIN CT/SYS ATTIT ORD/FREE PWR...SOCIALIST SOC CONCPT STAND/INT TIME/SEQ WORK 20. PAGE 46 H0918
S/ASIA POL/PAR

B61
MARVICK D.,POLITICAL DECISION-MAKERS. INTELL STRATA NAT/G POL/PAR EX/STRUC LEGIS DOMIN EDU/PROP ATTIT PERSON PWR...PSY STAT OBS CONT/OBS STAND/INT UNPLAN/INT TIME/SEQ CHARTS STERTYP VAL/FREE. PAGE 104 H2073
TOP/EX BIOG ELITES

B61
VON MERING O.,A GRAMMAR OF HUMAN VALUES. WOR+45 CULTURE FACE/GP NEIGH CREATE EDU/PROP LEGIT ATTIT DRIVE PERSON ORD/FREE...PSY SOC METH/CNCPT OBS RECORD INT REC/INT STAND/INT QU CHARTS VAL/FREE. PAGE 164 H3275
SOCIETY MORAL

B62
CHAPMAN R.M.,NEW ZEALAND POLITICS IN ACTION: THE 1960 GENERAL ELECTION. NEW/ZEALND LEGIS EDU/PROP PRESS TV LEAD ATTIT...STAND/INT 20. PAGE 29 H0582
NAT/G CHOOSE POL/PAR

S65
COOPER P.,"THE DEVELOPMENT OF THE CONCEPT OF WAR." UK COERCE ATTIT PERCEPT PERSON...STAT CHARTS CHINJAP. PAGE 33 H0660
CULTURE WAR SAMP STAND/INT

B67
KORNBERG A.,CANADIAN LEGISLATIVE BEHAVIOR: A STUDY OF THE 25TH PARLIAMENT. CANADA NAT/G POL/PAR PARL/PROC CHOOSE INGP/REL ADJUST ANOMIE RIGID/FLEX ...SOC STAND/INT CHARTS SOC/EXP 20 PARLIAMENT. PAGE 88 H1756
ATTIT LEGIS ROLE

B67
LAMBERT W.E.,CHILDREN'S VIEWS OF FOREIGN PEOPLES: A CROSS-NATIONAL STUDY. UNIV CULTURE EDU/PROP RACE/REL ATTIT PERCEPT ROLE...STAT STAND/INT CHARTS GP/COMP NAT/COMP. PAGE 90 H1802
AGE/C STRANGE GP/REL STERTYP

S67
SCOTT J.W.,"SOURCES OF SOCIAL CHANGE IN COMMUNITY, FAMILY, AND FERTILITY IN A PUERTO RICAN TOWN." PUERT/RICO CULTURE STRUCT ECO/UNDEV INDUS PERS/REL ROLE...SOC STAND/INT. PAGE 141 H2815
FAM MARRIAGE LITERACY ATTIT

STANDARDIZED INTERVIEWS....SEE STAND/INT

STANFORD/U....STANFORD UNIVERSITY

STANKIEW/W....W.J. STANKIEWICZ

STANKIEWICZ, W.J.....SEE STANKIEW/W

STANLEY C.J. H2969

STAR/CARR....STAR-CARR, A PREHISTORIC SOCIETY

STARCKE V. H2970

STARK H. H2971

STAROBIN J.R. H2972

STARR R.E. H2973

STAT....STATISTICS;

N
INDIA: A REFERENCE ANNUAL. INDIA CULTURE COM/IND R+D FORCES PLAN RECEIVE EDU/PROP HEALTH...STAT CHARTS BIBLIOG 20. PAGE 1 H0017
CONSTN LABOR INT/ORG

N
THE STATESMAN'S YEARBOOK; STATISTICAL AND HISTORICAL ANNUAL OF THE STATES OF THE WORLD. WOR+45 WOR-45 COM/IND FINAN INDUS SECT FORCES
NAT/COMP GOV/COMP STAT

TEC/DEV EDU/PROP...GEOG BIBLIOG 19/20. PAGE 1 H0023 CONSTN

N
THE MIDDLE EAST AND NORTH AFRICA. AFR ISLAM CULTURE ECO/UNDEV AGRI NAT/G TEC/DEV FOR/AID INT/TRADE EDU/PROP...CHARTS 20. PAGE 2 H0026
INDEX INDUS FINAN STAT

N
EUROPA PUBLICATIONS LIMITED,THE EUROPA YEAR BOOK. CONSTN FINAN INDUS POL/PAR DIPLOM TV CT/SYS...STAT BIOG CHARTS WORSHIP 20. PAGE 47 H0949
BIBLIOG NAT/G PRESS INT/ORG

N
MINISTRY OF OVERSEAS DEVELOPME,TECHNICAL CO-OPERATION -- A BIBLIOGRAPHY. UK LAW SOCIETY DIPLOM ECO/TAC FOR/AID...STAT 20 CMN/WLTH. PAGE 111 H2225
BIBLIOG TEC/DEV ECO/DEV NAT/G

N
UNIVERSITY OF CALIFORNIA,STATISTICAL ABSTRACT OF LATIN AMERICA. L/A+17C DIPLOM 20. PAGE 158 H3169
BIBLIOG NAT/G ECO/UNDEV STAT

B04
GRIFFIN A.P.C.,LIST OF REFERENCES ON BUDGETS OF FOREIGN COUNTRIES (PAMPHLET). MOD/EUR FINAN MARKET TAX...MGT STAT 19/20. PAGE 61 H1218
BIBLIOG/A BUDGET NAT/G

B14
LEVINE L.,SYNDICALISM IN FRANCE (2ND ED.). FRANCE LAW SOCIETY ECO/DEV NAT/G ECO/TAC LEAD ATTIT ...POLICY CONCPT STAT BIBLIOG 18/20 REFORMERS. PAGE 95 H1902
LABOR INDUS SOCISM REV

N19
INTERNATIONAL LABOUR OFFICE,EMPLOYMENT, UNEMPLOYMENT AND LABOUR FORCE STATISTICS (PAMPHLET). EUR+WWI STRATA AGRI INDUS NAT/G PROB/SOLV PAY AGE SEX...SAMP NAT/COMP METH 20 ILO. PAGE 78 H1557
WORKER LABOR STAT ECO/DEV

N19
OPERATIONS AND POLICY RESEARCH,URUGUAY: ELECTION FACTBOOK: NOVEMBER 27, 1966 (PAMPHLET). URUGUAY LAW NAT/G LEAD REPRESENT...STAT BIOG CHARTS 20. PAGE 121 H2422
POL/PAR CHOOSE PLAN ATTIT

S31
HEINBERG J.G.,"THE PERSONNEL OF FRENCH CABINETS, 1871-1930." FRANCE STRATA CHIEF CHOOSE REPRESENT MAJORITY...STAT QU CENSUS TREND CHARTS PERS/COMP 19/20 CHAMBR/DEP. PAGE 69 H1386
ELITES NAT/G DELIB/GP TOP/EX

B35
DOUGLASS H.P.,THE PROTESTANT CHURCH AS A SOCIAL INSTITUTION. CULTURE FINAN NEIGH PROF/ORG OP/RES ADMIN...POLICY SOC/WK STAT BIBLIOG. PAGE 42 H0843
SECT PARTIC INGP/REL GP/REL

B36
CULVER D.C.,METHODOLOGY OF SOCIAL SCIENCE RESEARCH: A BIBLIOGRAPHY. LAW CULTURE...CRIMLGY GEOG STAT OBS INT QU HIST/WRIT CHARTS 20. PAGE 36 H0719
BIBLIOG/A METH SOC

B41
HAUSHOFER K.,WEHR-GEOPOLITIK. EUR+WWI GERMANY MOD/EUR NAT/G ACT/RES BAL/PWR PWR...STAT TIME/SEQ CHARTS NAZI 20. PAGE 68 H1361
FORCES GEOG WAR

B48
MINISTERE FINANCES ET ECO,BULLETIN BIBLIOGRAPHIQUE. AFR EUR+WWI FRANCE CULTURE STRUCT FINAN NAT/G ACT/RES INT/TRADE ADMIN REGION PRODUC STAT. PAGE 111 H2224
BIBLIOG/A ECO/UNDEV TEC/DEV COLONIAL

B49
LASSWELL H.D.,LANGUAGE OF POLITICS. COM NAT/G ACT/RES ATTIT PWR...STAT RECORD CON/ANAL GEN/METH 20. PAGE 92 H1834
EDU/PROP METH/CNCPT

S52
EISENSTADT S.N.,"THE PROCESS OF ABSORPTION OF NEW IMMIGRANTS IN ISRAEL" (BMR)" ISRAEL CULTURE SCHOOL WORKER PARTIC DRIVE ORD/FREE...STAT OBS INT CHARTS SOC/INTEG 20 JEWS. PAGE 45 H0900
HABITAT ATTIT SAMP

B53
FLORENCE P.S.,THE LOGIC OF BRITISH AND AMERICAN INDUSTRY; A REALISTIC ANALYSIS OF ECONOMIC STRUCTURE AND GOVERNMENT. UK USA+45 USA-45 FINAN LABOR CAP/ISM INGP/REL EFFICIENCY...MGT CONCPT STAT CHARTS METH 20. PAGE 51 H1028
INDUS ECO/DEV NAT/G NAT/COMP

B53
MIT CENTER INTERNATIONAL STU,BIBLIOGRAPHY OF THE ECONOMIC AND POLITICAL DEVELOPMENT OF INDONESIA. INDONESIA STRUCT NAT/G COLONIAL LEAD...STAT 20. PAGE 111 H2226
BIBLIOG ECO/UNDEV TEC/DEV S/ASIA

B53
NELSON G.R.,FREEDOM AND WELFARE: SOCIAL PATTERNS IN THE NORTHERN COUNTRIES OF EUROPE. EUR+WWI ECO/DEV NAT/G EDU/PROP LEGIT HEALTH ORD/FREE SKILL WEALTH ...STAT AUD/VIS SCANDINAV WORK TOT/POP 20. PAGE 116 H2329
PLAN ECO/TAC

S54
DODD S.C.,"THE SCIENTIFIC MEASUREMENT OF FITNESS FOR SELF-GOVERNMENT." FUT CONSTN ECO/UNDEV INT/ORG PLAN PWR...CONCPT QUANT CON/ANAL SOC/EXP UN LEAGUE/NAT 20. PAGE 41 H0830
NAT/G STAT SOVEREIGN

B55
APTER D.E.,THE GOLD COAST IN TRANSITION. FUT CONSTN CULTURE SOCIETY ECO/UNDEV FAM KIN LOC/G NAT/G POL/PAR LEGIS TOP/EX EDU/PROP LEGIT ADMIN ATTIT PERSON PWR...CONCPT STAT INT CENSUS TOT/POP VAL/FREE. PAGE 7 H0149
AFR SOVEREIGN

B55
DUVERGER M.,THE POLITICAL ROLE OF WOMEN. FRANCE GERMANY/W NORWAY YUGOSLAVIA STRATA LOBBY AGE ATTIT ROLE...STAT SAMP CHARTS METH/COMP NAT/COMP HYPO/EXP FEMALE/SEX. PAGE 44 H0875
SEX LEAD PARTIC CHOOSE

B55
UN ECONOMIC AND SOCIAL COUNCIL,ANALYTICAL BIBLIOGRAPHY OF INTERNATIONAL MIGRATION STATISTICS, SELECTED COUNTRIES, 1925-1950. STRATA...CLASSIF CENSUS NAT/COMP 20. PAGE 158 H3156
BIBLIOG STAT GEOG HABITAT

B55
UN ECONOMIC COMN ASIA & FAR E,ECONOMIC SURVEY OF ASIA AND THE FAR EAST, 1954. AFGHANISTN CEYLON INDIA PHILIPPINE S/ASIA ECO/DEV FINAN INDUS INT/TRADE PRODUC WEALTH...STAT CHARTS 20 CHINJAP. PAGE 158 H3158
ECO/UNDEV PRICE NAT/COMP ASIA

S56
MACRAE D. JR.,"ROLL CALL VOTES AND LEADERSHIP." ACT/RES LEAD CHOOSE DRIVE CONSERVE NEW/LIB...STAT STYLE. PAGE 100 H2007
POL/PAR GOV/COMP LEGIS SUPEGO

B57
BOUSTEDT O.,REGIONALE STRUKTUR- UND WIRTSCHAFTSFORSCHUNG. WOR+45 WOR-45 MUNIC PROVS STAT. PAGE 19 H0388
GEOG CONCPT NAT/COMP

B57
COLE G.D.H.,THE POST WAR CONDITIONS OF BRITAIN. EUR+WWI STRUCT NAT/G PLAN EDU/PROP LEGIT RIGID/FLEX ORD/FREE WEALTH...SOCIALIST WELF/ST STAT TREND CON/ANAL CHARTS PARLIAMENT WORK 20. PAGE 31 H0624
ECO/DEV UK

B57
NEUMARK S.D.,ECONOMIC INFLUENCES ON THE SOUTH AFRICAN FRONTIER, 1652-1836. SOUTH/AFR SEA AGRI NAT/G FORCES WORKER DIPLOM INT/TRADE PRICE DEMAND PRODUC...STAT CHARTS 17/19 FRONTIER. PAGE 117 H2341
COLONIAL ECO/UNDEV ECO/TAC MARKET

B57
SCHLESINGER J.A.,HOW THEY BECAME GOVERNOR; A STUDY OF COMPARATIVE STATE POLITICS, 1870-1950. USA+45 USA-45 LAW POL/PAR LEGIS EDU/PROP REGION...STAT TREND CHARTS TIME 19/20 GOVERNOR. PAGE 139 H2788
PROVS CHIEF GOV/COMP CHOOSE

B59
ELDRIDGE H.T.,THE MATERIALS OF DEMOGRAPHY: A SELECTED AND ANNOTATED BIBLIOGRAPHY. R+D DEATH ...SAMP METH/COMP NAT/COMP 20. PAGE 45 H0905
BIBLIOG/A GEOG STAT TREND

B59
MEYER A.J.,MIDDLE EASTERN CAPITALISM: NINE ESSAYS. ISLAM CULTURE ECO/UNDEV INDUS MARKET NAT/G PLAN ATTIT RIGID/FLEX...STAT OBS TREND GEN/LAWS. PAGE 109 H2188
TEC/DEV ECO/TAC ANTHOL

L59
MURPHY J.C.,"SOME IMPLICATIONS OF EUROPE'S COMMON MARKET. IN (COOK P, ECONOMIC DEVELOPMENT AND INTERNATIONAL TRADE.." EUR+WWI ECO/DEV DIST/IND INDUS NAT/G PLAN ECO/TAC INT/TRADE WEALTH...STAT TREND OEEC TOT/POP 20 EEC. PAGE 115 H2298
MARKET INT/ORG REGION

S59
LYNN D.B.,"THE EFFECTS OF FATHER-ABSENCE ON NORWEGIAN BOYS AND GIRLS." NORWAY CULTURE PERS/REL ADJUST DISPL LOVE...PSY CORREL STAT INT CON/ANAL CHARTS SOC/INTEG 20. PAGE 99 H1983
SOC FAM AGE/C ANOMIE

S59
SCOTT W.A.,"EMPIRICAL ASSESSMENT OF VALUES AND IDEOLOGIES." CULTURE SOCIETY SECT CREATE DRIVE PERSON MORAL PWR...SOC METH/CNCPT STAT CONT/OBS DEEP/INT DEEP/QU CHARTS VAL/FREE. PAGE 141 H2817
ATTIT PSY

B60
LISTER L.,EUROPE'S COAL AND STEEL COMMUNITY. FRANCE GERMANY STRUCT ECO/DEV EXTR/IND INDUS MARKET NAT/G DELIB/GP ECO/TAC INT/TRADE EDU/PROP ATTIT RIGID/FLEX ORD/FREE PWR WEALTH...CONCPT STAT TIME/SEQ CHARTS ECSC 20. PAGE 97 H1941
EUR+WWI INT/ORG REGION

B60
SHIRER W.L.,THE RISE AND FALL OF THE THIRD REICH: A HISTORY OF NAZI GERMANY. EUR+WWI CULTURE ECO/DEV INDUS NAT/G POL/PAR FORCES PLAN TEC/DEV ECO/TAC COERCE ATTIT DRIVE PERSON PWR...MYSTIC PSY SOC MYTH STAT CHARTS EXHIBIT WORK VAL/FREE. PAGE 143 H2864
STRUCT GERMANY TOTALISM

B60
STOLPER W.F.,GERMANY BETWEEN EAST AND WEST: THE ECONOMICS OF COMPETITIVE COEXISTENCE. FUT GERMANY/E GERMANY/W WOR+45 FINAN POL/PAR BUDGET ECO/TAC FOR/AID INT/TRADE...STAT CHARTS METH/COMP 20 COLD/WAR. PAGE 150 H2989
ECO/DEV DIPLOM GOV/COMP BAL/PWR

B60
THE ECONOMIST (LONDON),THE COMMONWEALTH AND EUROPE. EUR+WWI WOR+45 AGRI FINAN INCOME...STAT CENSUS CHARTS CMN/WLTH EEC. PAGE 153 H3067
INT/TRADE INDUS INT/ORG NAT/COMP

B60
WOLF C.,FOREIGN AID: THEORY AND PRACTICE IN SOUTHERN ASIA. CEYLON INDONESIA PHILIPPINE S/ASIA CULTURE STRATA ECO/UNDEV PLAN EDU/PROP ATTIT ...METH/CNCPT MATH QUANT STAT CONT/OBS TIME/SEQ SIMUL TOT/POP 20. PAGE 170 H3396 — ACT/RES ECO/TAC FOR/AID

L60
HAAS E.B.,"CONSENSUS FORMATION IN THE COUNCIL OF EUROPE." EUR+WWI NAT/G DELIB/GP DIPLOM REGION CHOOSE PWR SOVEREIGN...RELATIV NEW/IDEA QUANT CHARTS INDEX TOT/POP OEEC 20 COUNCL/EUR. PAGE 63 H1265 — POL/PAR INT/ORG STAT

S60
JAFFEE A.J.,"POPULATION TRENDS AND CONTROLS IN UNDERDEVELOPED COUNTRIES." AFR FUT ISLAM L/A+17C S/ASIA CULTURE R+D FAM ACT/RES PLAN EDU/PROP BIO/SOC RIGID/FLEX HEALTH...SOC STAT OBS CHARTS 20. PAGE 79 H1582 — ECO/UNDEV GEOG

B61
DELEFORTRIE-SOU N.,LES DIRIGEANTS DE L'INDUSTRIE FRANCAISE. FRANCE CULTURE ELITES PROB/SOLV ...DECISION STAT CHARTS 20. PAGE 39 H0789 — INDUS STRATA TOP/EX LEAD

B61
FIELD H.,ANCIENT AND MODERN MAN IN SOUTHWESTERN ASIA: II. CULTURE SOCIETY...CLASSIF MATH GP/COMP NAT/COMP 20. PAGE 50 H0992 — STAT CHARTS PHIL/SCI RECORD

B61
MARVICK D.,POLITICAL DECISION-MAKERS. INTELL STRATA NAT/G POL/PAR EX/STRUC LEGIS DOMIN EDU/PROP ATTIT PERSON PWR...PSY STAT OBS CONT/OBS STAND/INT UNPLAN/INT TIME/SEQ CHARTS STERTYP VAL/FREE. PAGE 104 H2073 — TOP/EX BIOG ELITES

B61
NATIONAL BANK OF LIBYA,INFLATION IN LIBYA (PAMPHLET). LIBYA SOCIETY NAT/G PLAN INT/TRADE ...STAT CHARTS 20 GOLD/STAND. PAGE 116 H2318 — ECO/TAC ECO/UNDEV FINAN BUDGET

B61
OECD,STATISTICS OF BALANCE OF PAYMENTS 1950-61. WOR+45 FINAN ECO/TAC INT/TRADE DEMAND WEALTH...STAT NAT/COMP 20 OEEC OECD. PAGE 120 H2396 — BAL/PAY ECO/DEV INT/ORG CHARTS

B61
ROSE D.L.,THE VIETNAMESE CIVIL SERVICE. VIETNAM CONSULT DELIB/GP GIVE PAY EDU/PROP COLONIAL GOV/REL UTIL...CHARTS 20. PAGE 134 H2672 — ADMIN EFFICIENCY STAT NAT/G

B61
YUAN TUNG-LI,A GUIDE TO DOCTORAL DISSERTATIONS BY CHINESE STUDENTS IN AMERICA, 1905-1960. ASIA CULTURE SOCIETY ECO/UNDEV NAT/G PROB/SOLV DIPLOM LEAD ATTIT...HUM SOC STAT 20. PAGE 172 H3442 — BIBLIOG ACADEM ACT/RES OP/RES

B61
ZIMMERMAN I.,A GUIDE TO CURRENT LATIN AMERICAN PERIODICALS: HUMANITIES AND SOCIAL SCIENCES. LABOR SECT EDU/PROP...GEOG HUM SOC LING STAT NAT/COMP 20. PAGE 173 H3456 — BIBLIOG/A DIPLOM L/A+17C PHIL/SCI

S61
LIEBERSON S.,"THE IMPACT OF RESIDENTIAL SEGREGATION ON ETHNIC ASSIMILATION" (BMR)" CULTURE MUNIC GP/REL RACE/REL DISCRIM...GEOG STAT CON/ANAL CHARTS SOC/INTEG 20 MIGRATION. PAGE 96 H1926 — HABITAT ISOLAT NEIGH

S61
RAY J.,"THE EUROPEAN FREE-TRADE ASSOCIATION AND ITS IMPACT ON INDIA'S TRADE." EUR+WWI FRANCE GERMANY INDIA S/ASIA UK NAT/G VOL/ASSN PLAN INT/TRADE ROUTINE WEALTH...STAT CHARTS CMN/WLTH EEC OEEC 20 EFTA. PAGE 130 H2600 — ECO/DEV ECO/TAC

B62
FALKENBERG J.,KIN AND TOTEM; GROUP RELATIONS OF AUSTRALIAN ABORIGINES IN THE PORT KEATS DISTRICT. SOCIETY STRATA STRUCT GP/REL PERS/REL MARRIAGE AGE ATTIT SEX...SOC STAT CHARTS AUSTRAL ABORIGINES. PAGE 48 H0964 — KIN INGP/REL CULTURE FAM

B62
HO PING-TI,THE LADDER OF SUCCESS IN IMPERIAL CHINA: ASPECTS OF SOCIAL MOBILITY, 1368-1911. INTELL STRATA FAM KIN MUNIC NAT/G PROVS SCHOOL DELIB/GP DOMIN EDU/PROP ADMIN ROUTINE PERSON ALL/VALS...SOC STAT BIOG HIST/WRIT TIME/SEQ VAL/FREE. PAGE 71 H1431 — ASIA CULTURE

B62
MEADE J.E.,CASE STUDIES IN EUROPEAN ECONOMIC UNION. BELGIUM EUR+WWI LUXEMBOURG NAT/G INT/TRADE REGION ROUTINE WEALTH...METH/CNCPT STAT CHARTS ECSC TOT/POP OEEC EEC 20. PAGE 108 H2154 — INT/ORG ECO/TAC

B62
MITCHELL B.R.,ABSTRACT OF BRITISH HISTORICAL STATISTICS. UK FINAN NAT/G 12/20. PAGE 111 H2229 — BIBLIOG STAT INDEX ECO/DEV

B62
MUKERJI S.N.,ADMINISTRATION OF EDUCATION IN INDIA. ACADEM LOC/G PROVS ROUTINE...POLICY STAT CHARTS 20. PAGE 114 H2282 — SCHOOL ADMIN NAT/G EDU/PROP

B62
SCHECHTMAN J.B.,POSTWAR POPULATION TRANSFERS IN EUROPE: 1945-1955. COM CZECHOSLVK GERMANY POLAND USSR CULTURE SOCIETY PROB/SOLV AGREE NAT/LISM...SOC STAT TREND CHARTS METH/COMP 20 MIGRATION. PAGE 139 H2778 — GEOG CENSUS EUR+WWI HABITAT

B62
UNECA LIBRARY,BOOKS ON AFRICA IN THE UNECA LIBRARY. WOR+45 AGRI INT/ORG NAT/G PLAN WRITING REGION...SOC STAT UN. PAGE 158 H3160 — BIBLIOG AFR ECO/UNDEV TEC/DEV

L62
COHEN R.,"POWER IN COMPLEX SOCIETIES IN AFRICA." AFR KIN MUNIC POL/PAR DELIB/GP DOMIN ROUTINE ATTIT ALL/VALS...SOC STAT OBS INT QU CHARTS ANTHOL 20. PAGE 31 H0617 — CULTURE STRATA ELITES

B63
BRZEZINSKI Z.K.,AFRICA AND THE COMMUNIST WORLD. AFR ASIA COM CULTURE SOCIETY INT/ORG DELIB/GP ACT/RES ECO/TAC COERCE ORD/FREE PWR WEALTH...STAT TOT/POP VAL/FREE 20. PAGE 23 H0461 — ATTIT EDU/PROP DIPLOM USSR

B63
CHOU S.H.,THE CHINESE INFLATION 1937-1949. ASIA SOCIETY POL/PAR FOR/AID INT/TRADE BAL/PAY WEALTH MARXISM...STAT CHARTS 20 COM/PARTY GOLD/STAND. PAGE 30 H0597 — FINAN ECO/TAC BUDGET NAT/G

B63
DE VRIES E.,SOCIAL ASPECTS OF ECONOMIC DEVELOPMENT IN LATIN AMERICA. CULTURE SOCIETY STRATA FINAN INDUS INT/ORG DELIB/GP ACT/RES ECO/TAC EDU/PROP ADMIN ATTIT SUPEGO HEALTH KNOWL ORD/FREE...SOC STAT TREND ANTHOL TOT/POP VAL/FREE. PAGE 39 H0777 — L/A+17C ECO/UNDEV

B63
DUE J.F.,STATE SALES TAX ADMINISTRATION. OP/RES BUDGET PAY ADMIN EXEC ROUTINE COST EFFICIENCY PROFIT...CHARTS METH/COMP 20. PAGE 43 H0855 — PROVS TAX STAT GOV/COMP

B63
GLADE W.P. JR.,THE POLITICAL ECONOMY OF MEXICO. FUT L/A+17C CULTURE SOCIETY AGRI INDUS DELIB/GP ACT/RES ECO/TAC ATTIT HEALTH ORD/FREE...STAT TIME/SEQ TREND MEXIC/AMER TOT/POP VAL/FREE 20. PAGE 57 H1138 — FINAN ECO/UNDEV

B63
ISSAWI C.,EGYPT IN REVOLUTION: AN ECONOMIC ANALYSIS. ISLAM STRUCT ECO/UNDEV AGRI FINAN INDUS PLAN EXEC REV NAT/LISM ATTIT RIGID/FLEX WEALTH SOCISM...STAT WORK 20. PAGE 79 H1573 — NAT/G UAR

B63
JACOB H.,GERMAN ADMINISTRATION SINCE BISMARCK: CENTRAL AUTHORITY VERSUS LOCAL AUTONOMY. GERMANY GERMANY/W LAW POL/PAR CONTROL CENTRAL TOTALISM FASCISM...MAJORIT DECISION STAT CHARTS GOV/COMP 19/20 BISMARCK/O HITLER/A WEIMAR/REP. PAGE 79 H1577 — ADMIN NAT/G LOC/G POLICY

B63
JUNOD V.,HANDBOOK OF AFRICA. AFR ISLAM CONSTN SOCIETY NAT/G POL/PAR...GEOG SOC STAT CHARTS WORK 20. PAGE 82 H1642 — ECO/UNDEV REGION

B63
LEIGHTON D.C.,THE CHARACTER OF DANGER (VOL. III). SOCIETY STRUCT STRANGE ANOMIE...SOC STAT CHARTS GP/COMP SOC/EXP SOC/INTEG 20 NOVA/SCOT. PAGE 94 H1868 — HEALTH PSY CULTURE

B63
LEVIN M.G.,ETHNIC ORIGINS OF THE PEOPLES OF NORTHEASTERN ASIA. CONSTN LEGIS...STAT CENSUS CHARTS 20 TEXAS MAPS. PAGE 95 H1901 — HEREDITY HABITAT CULTURE GEOG

B63
NATIONAL OFF STATE GOVT THAI,STATISTICAL BIBLIOGRAPHY: AN ANNOTATED BIBLIOGRAPHY OF THAI GOVERNMENTAL STATISTICAL PUBLICATIONS. THAILAND AGRI 20. PAGE 116 H2321 — BIBLIOG/A STAT NAT/G S/ASIA

L63
CORWIN A.F.,"CONTEMPORARY MEXICAN ATTITUDES TOWARD POPULATION, POVERTY, AND PUBLIC OPINION." L/A+17C CULTURE SOCIETY ACT/RES ECO/TAC EDU/PROP PERSON HEALTH KNOWL...GEOG PHIL/SCI STAT OBS INT SAMP MEXIC/AMER VAL/FREE 20. PAGE 34 H0672 — ATTIT QU

L63
NASH M.,"PSYCHO-CULTURAL FACTORS IN ASIAN ECONOMIC GROWTH." ASIA ISLAM S/ASIA CULTURE ECO/UNDEV DELIB/GP EDU/PROP COERCE ATTIT PERSON HEALTH KNOWL ORD/FREE...PSY SOC STAT TREND ANTHOL VAL/FREE 20. PAGE 116 H2313 — SOCIETY ECO/TAC

L63
ROSE R.,"COMPARATIVE STUDIES IN POLITICAL FINANCE: A SYMPOSIUM." ASIA EUR+WWI S/ASIA LAW CULTURE DELIB/GP LEGIS ACT/RES ECO/TAC EDU/PROP CHOOSE ATTIT RIGID/FLEX SUPEGO PWR SKILL WEALTH...STAT ANTHOL VAL/FREE. PAGE 134 H2674 — FINAN POL/PAR

S63
DUDLEY B.J.,"THE NOMINATION OF PARLIAMENTARY CANDIDATES IN NORTHERN NIGERIA." AFR CONSTN CULTURE ELITES STRATA DELIB/GP LEGIS DOMIN EDU/PROP COERCE — POL/PAR CHOOSE NIGERIA

ATTIT SUPEGO PWR...STAT VAL/FREE 20. PAGE 43 H0854

S63
LEE J.M.,"PARLIAMENT IN REPUBLICAN GHANA." AFR CONSTN CULTURE SOCIETY STRATA POL/PAR DELIB/GP TOP/EX DOMIN EDU/PROP LEGIT COERCE CHOOSE ATTIT ALL/VALS...CONCPT STAT TIME/SEQ VAL/FREE 20. PAGE 93 H1857 — LEGIS GHANA

S63
NICHOLAS W.,"VILLAGE FACTIONS AND POLITICAL PARTIES IN RURAL WEST BENGAL." S/ASIA CULTURE STRATA FACE/GP KIN MUNIC DELIB/GP LEGIS DOMIN EDU/PROP COERCE CHOOSE ATTIT ALL/VALS...STAT TOT/POP VAL/FREE 20. PAGE 117 H2348 — NEIGH POL/PAR

S63
ROBINSON W.C.,"URBANIZATION AND FERTILITY: THE NON-WESTERN EXPERIENCE (BMR)" DEATH MARRIAGE AGE/C BIO/SOC...STAT CENSUS CON/ANAL CHARTS NAT/COMP 20 THIRD/WRLD. PAGE 133 H2651 — GEOG MUNIC FAM ECO/UNDEV

S63
TILMAN R.O.,"MALAYSIA: THE PROBLEMS OF FEDERATION." ISLAM S/ASIA CONSTN PROVS SECT DELIB/GP DOMIN EDU/PROP LEGIT EXEC COERCE CHOOSE ATTIT HEALTH ORD/FREE PWR...STAT TOT/POP VAL/FREE 20. PAGE 155 H3097 — NAT/G CULTURE MALAYSIA

N63
LEDERER W.,THE BALANCE ON FOREIGN TRANSACTIONS: PROBLEMS OF DEFINITION AND MEASUREMENT (PAMPHLET). USA+45 BUDGET DIPLOM ECO/TAC PRICE GOV/REL...POLICY STAT NAT/COMP METH 20. PAGE 93 H1853 — FINAN BAL/PAY INT/TRADE ECO/DEV

B64
BROWN W.M.,THE EXTERNAL LIQUIDITY OF AN ADVANCED COUNTRY. CANADA FRANCE GERMANY/W SWEDEN UK USA+45 ECO/DEV DIPLOM PRICE...CONCPT STAT NAT/COMP 20. PAGE 22 H0451 — FINAN INT/TRADE COST INCOME

B64
INTERNATIONAL LABOUR OFFICE,EMPLOYMENT AND ECONOMIC GROWTH. ECO/DEV ECO/UNDEV NAT/G PLAN DIPLOM INT/TRADE CONTROL INCOME PRODUC WEALTH...STAT NAT/COMP 20 ILO. PAGE 78 H1558 — WORKER METH/COMP ECO/TAC OPTIMAL

B64
LEWIN P.,THE FOREIGN TRADE OF COMMUNIST CHINA* ITS IMPACT ON THE FREE WORLD. AFR EUR+WWI L/A+17C S/ASIA ECO/UNDEV CREATE FOR/AID...STAT NET/THEORY TREND CHARTS. PAGE 96 H1910 — ASIA INT/TRADE NAT/COMP USSR

B64
RAMAZANI R.K.,THE MIDDLE EAST AND THE EUROPEAN COMMON MARKET. EUR+WWI ISLAM ECO/DEV EXTR/IND MARKET PROC/MFG INT/ORG NAT/G TEC/DEV ECO/TAC REGION DRIVE WEALTH...STAT CHARTS EEC TOT/POP 20. PAGE 129 H2587 — ECO/UNDEV ATTIT INT/TRADE

B64
RUSSET B.M.,WORLD HANDBOOK OF POLITICAL AND SOCIAL INDICATORS. WOR+45 COM/IND ADMIN WEALTH...GEOG 20. PAGE 136 H2719 — DIPLOM STAT NAT/G NAT/COMP

B64
SINGER M.R.,THE EMERGING ELITE: A STUDY OF POLITICAL LEADERSHIP IN CEYLON. S/ASIA ECO/UNDEV AGRI KIN NAT/G SECT EX/STRUC LEGIT ATTIT PWR RESPECT...SOC STAT CHARTS 20. PAGE 144 H2883 — TOP/EX STRATA NAT/LISM CEYLON

B64
SOLOW R.M.,THE NATURE AND SOURCES OF UNEMPLOYMENT IN THE UNITED STATES (PAMPHLET). USA+45 INDUS LABOR TEC/DEV ECO/TAC SKILL WEALTH...TREND NAT/COMP 20. PAGE 147 H2930 — ECO/DEV WORKER STAT PRODUC

B64
THAILAND NATIONAL ECO DEV,THE NATIONAL ECONOMIC DEVELOPMENT PLAN: 1961-66: SECOND PHASE 1964-66. THAILAND AGRI FINAN BUDGET EFFICIENCY INCOME...STAT CHARTS 20. PAGE 153 H3065 — ECO/UNDEV ECO/TAC PLAN NAT/G

B64
THORNTON T.P.,THE THIRD WORLD IN SOVIET PERSPECTIVE: STUDIES BY SOVIET WRITERS ON THE DEVELOPING AREAS. AFR L/A+17C S/ASIA STRATA AGRI INDUS MARKET NAT/G POL/PAR ECO/TAC COLONIAL PERCEPT PWR WEALTH...MARXIST STAT CHARTS WORK MARX/KARL 20. PAGE 155 H3090 — ECO/UNDEV ACT/RES USSR DIPLOM

B64
US LIBRARY OF CONGRESS,SOUTHEAST ASIA. CULTURE ...SOC STAT 20. PAGE 161 H3213 — BIBLIOG/A S/ASIA ECO/UNDEV NAT/G

B64
WARD R.E.,POLITICAL MODERNIZATION IN JAPAN AND TURKEY. ASIA ISLAM S/ASIA CONSTN CULTURE STRATA COM/IND POL/PAR FORCES ACT/RES ECO/TAC DOMIN EDU/PROP LEGIT ADMIN CHOOSE ATTIT ALL/VALS...STAT TIME/SEQ VAL/FREE CHINJAP. PAGE 165 H3307 — SOCIETY TURKEY

B64
WHITEFORD A.H.,TWO CITIES OF LATIN AMERICA: A COMPARATIVE DESCRIPTION OF SOCIAL CLASSES. L/A+17C CULTURE SOCIETY MUNIC DOMIN LEGIT ATTIT ALL/VALS ...STAT OBS VAL/FREE 20. PAGE 167 H3352 — STRATA SOC

B64
WRIGHT G.,RURAL REVOLUTION IN FRANCE: THE PEASANTRY IN THE TWENTIETH CENTURY. EUR+WWI MOD/EUR LAW CULTURE AGRI POL/PAR DELIB/GP LEGIS ECO/TAC EDU/PROP COERCE CHOOSE ATTIT RIGID/FLEX HEALTH ...STAT CENSUS CHARTS VAL/FREE 20. PAGE 171 H3419 — PWR STRATA FRANCE REV

B64
ZARTMAN I.W.,MOROCCO: PROBLEMS OF NEW POWER. ISLAM CULTURE ECO/UNDEV AGRI POL/PAR SCHOOL FORCES ADMIN ...CONCPT STAT INT CENSUS TIME/SEQ CHARTS WORK VAL/FREE 20. PAGE 172 H3449 — CHOOSE MOROCCO DELIB/GP DECISION

S64
GRUNER E.,"PRENSA, PARTIDOS POLITICOS, Y GRUPOS DE PRESION EN SUIZA." EUR+WWI MOD/EUR NAT/G EDU/PROP LEGIT PRESS ATTIT KNOWL ORD/FREE...CONCPT STAT CON/ANAL CHARTS 20. PAGE 62 H1241 — POL/PAR SWITZERLND

S64
MARES V.E.,"EAST EUROPE'S SECOND CHANCE." COM EUR+WWI HUNGARY ROMANIA USSR YUGOSLAVIA ECO/UNDEV NAT/G TOP/EX CREATE PLAN TEC/DEV REGION NAT/LISM RIGID/FLEX PWR...CONCPT STAT COMECON 20. PAGE 102 H2047 — VOL/ASSN ECO/TAC

S64
MERKL P.H.,"EUROPEAN ASSEMBLY PARTIES AND NATIONAL DELEGATIONS." INT/ORG DELIB/GP DOMIN EDU/PROP LEGIT CHOOSE PWR...STAT VAL/FREE 20. PAGE 109 H2180 — EUR+WWI POL/PAR REGION

B65
APPLEMAN P.,THE SILENT EXPLOSION. WOR+45 ECO/DEV ECO/UNDEV PLAN HEALTH ALL/IDEOS CATHISM...POLICY STAT RECORD GP/COMP IDEA/COMP NAT/COMP 20 BIRTH/CON COM/PARTY. PAGE 7 H0148 — GEOG CENSUS AGRI BIO/SOC

B65
CANTRIL H.,THE PATTERN OF HUMAN CONCERNS. ELITES ECO/DEV ECO/UNDEV...STAT CHARTS METH 20. PAGE 26 H0524 — ATTIT ALL/VALS NAT/COMP CULTURE

B65
CHAO K.,THE RATE AND PATTERN OF INDUSTRIAL GROWTH IN COMMUNIST CHINA. CHINA/COM ECO/UNDEV TEC/DEV PRICE...NAT/COMP BIBLIOG 20. PAGE 29 H0578 — INDUS INDEX STAT PRODUC

B65
FOSTER P.,EDUCATION AND SOCIAL CHANGE IN GHANA. GHANA CULTURE STRUCT ECO/UNDEV TEC/DEV REGION EFFICIENCY LITERACY ALL/VALS SOVEREIGN...STAT METH/COMP 19/20 GOLD/COAST. PAGE 52 H1043 — SCHOOL CREATE SOCIETY

B65
HERRICK B.H.,URBAN MIGRATION AND ECONOMIC DEVELOPMENT IN CHILE. CHILE AGRI INDUS LABOR NAT/G CENTRAL PRODUC...STAT SAMP CHARTS BIBLIOG/A 20 MIGRATION. PAGE 70 H1404 — HABITAT GEOG MUNIC ECO/UNDEV

B65
HESS A.G.,CHASING THE DRAGON: A REPORT ON DRUG ADDICTION IN HONG KONG. ASIA CULTURE PROB/SOLV TRIBUTE...POLICY PSY SOC CLASSIF STAT 17/20 HONG/KONG. PAGE 70 H1411 — BIO/SOC CRIME SOCIETY LAW

B65
HOSELITZ B.F.,ECONOMICS AND THE IDEA OF MANKIND. UNIV ECO/DEV ECO/UNDEV DIST/IND INDUS INT/ORG NAT/G ACT/RES ECO/TAC WEALTH...CONCPT STAT. PAGE 74 H1476 — CREATE INT/TRADE

B65
JASNY H.,KHRUSHCHEV'S CROP POLICY. USSR ECO/DEV PLAN MARXISM...STAT 20 KHRUSH/N RESOURCE/N. PAGE 80 H1593 — AGRI NAT/G POLICY ECO/TAC

B65
NYE J.S. JR.,PAN-AFRICANISM AND EAST AFRICAN INTEGRATION. TANZANIA UGANDA STRUCT ECO/UNDEV NAT/G DIPLOM FEDERAL NAT/LISM...STAT SOC/EXP BIBLIOG EEC OAU. PAGE 119 H2382 — REGION ATTIT GEN/LAWS AFR

B65
O'BRIEN F.,CRISIS IN WORLD COMMUNISM* MARXISM IN SEARCH OF EFFICIENCY. COM ECO/DEV PLAN INT/TRADE WAR ADJUST PEACE...STAT TIME/SEQ GOV/COMP NAT/COMP COLD/WAR. PAGE 119 H2384 — MARXISM USSR DRIVE EFFICIENCY

B65
OECD,MEDITERRANEAN REGIONAL PROJECT: TURKEY; EDUCATION AND DEVELOPMENT. FUT TURKEY SOCIETY STRATA FINAN NAT/G PROF/ORG PLAN PROB/SOLV ADMIN COST...STAT CHARTS 20 OECD. PAGE 120 H2399 — EDU/PROP ACADEM SCHOOL ECO/UNDEV

B65
OECD,THE MEDITERRANEAN REGIONAL PROJECT: ITALY; EDUCATION AND DEVELOPMENT. ITALY SOCIETY STRATA FINAN NAT/G PROF/ORG WORKER PLAN PROB/SOLV ADMIN ...STAT CHARTS METH 20 OECD. PAGE 120 H2400 — SCHOOL EDU/PROP ECO/UNDEV ACADEM

B65
OECD,THE MEDITERRANEAN REGIONAL PROJECT: SPAIN; EDUCATION AND DEVELOPMENT. FUT SPAIN STRATA FINAN NAT/G WORKER PLAN PROB/SOLV ADMIN COST...POLICY STAT CHARTS 20 OECD. PAGE 120 H2402 — ECO/UNDEV EDU/PROP ACADEM SCHOOL

B65
ORG FOR ECO COOP AND DEVEL,THE MEDITERRANEAN REGIONAL PROJECT: AN EXPERIMENT IN PLANNING BY SIX COUNTRIES. FUT GREECE SPAIN TURKEY YUGOSLAVIA SOCIETY FINAN NAT/G PROF/ORG EDU/PROP ADMIN REGION COST...POLICY STAT CHARTS 20 OECD. PAGE 121 H2427 — PLAN ECO/UNDEV ACADEM SCHOOL

B65
STEINER K.,LOCAL GOVERNMENT IN JAPAN. CONSTN CULTURE NAT/G ADMIN CHOOSE...SOC STAT 20 CHINJAP. — LOC/G SOCIETY

PAGE 149 H2976 — JURID ORD/FREE

B65
WINT G.,ASIA: A HANDBOOK. ASIA COM INDIA USSR CULTURE INTELL NAT/G...GEOG STAT CENSUS NAT/COMP WORSHIP 20 TREATY CHINJAP. PAGE 169 H3387 — DIPLOM SOC

L65
MATTHEWS D.G.,"A CURRENT BIBLIOGRAPHY ON ETHIOPIAN AFFAIRS: A SELECT BIBLIOGRAPHY FROM 1950-1964." ETHIOPIA LAW CULTURE ECO/UNDEV INDUS LABOR SECT FORCES DIPLOM CIVMIL/REL RACE/REL...LING STAT 20. PAGE 105 H2093 — BIBLIOG/A ADMIN POL/PAR NAT/G

S65
BRANDENBURG F.,"THE RELEVANCE OF MEXICAN EXPERIENCE TO LATIN AMERICAN DEVELOPMENT." BRAZIL CHILE VENEZUELA STRUCT ECO/UNDEV AGRI CREATE ECO/TAC ...STAT RECORD MEXIC/AMER ARGEN COLOMB. PAGE 20 H0405 — L/A+17C GOV/COMP

S65
COOPER P.,"THE DEVELOPMENT OF THE CONCEPT OF WAR." UK COERCE ATTIT PERCEPT PERSON...STAT CHARTS CHINJAP. PAGE 33 H0660 — CULTURE WAR SAMP STAND/INT

S65
JENSEN L.,"MILITARY CAPABILITIES AND BARGAINING BEHAVIOR." USA+45 USSR ARMS/CONT DETER COST ATTIT ...METH/CNCPT STAT SYS/QU CON/ANAL CHARTS NAT/COMP. PAGE 81 H1614 — DIPLOM DRIVE PWR STERTYP

S65
POWELL J.D.,"MILITARY ASSISTANCE AND MILITARISM IN LATIN AMERICA." USA+45 INT/ORG NAT/G CONTROL REGION PRODUC WEALTH...CLASSIF STAT NAT/COMP CONGRESS. PAGE 128 H2550 — L/A+17C FORCES FOR/AID PWR

S65
VAN DEN BERG M.,"SOME METHODOLOGICAL ASPECTS OF SOUTH AFRICA'S FIRST E.D.P." SOUTH/AFR NAT/G CREATE TEC/DEV CAP/ISM INCOME PRODUC...CON/ANAL CHARTS 20. PAGE 161 H3226 — ECO/DEV PLAN METH STAT

S65
WHITE J.,"WEST GERMAN AID TO DEVELOPING COUNTRIES." INT/ORG OP/RES GIVE CENTRAL ATTIT DRIVE...STAT NAT/COMP COLD/WAR. PAGE 167 H3348 — GERMANY FOR/AID ECO/UNDEV CAP/ISM

S65
WRIGHT Q.,"THE ESCALATION OF INTERNATIONAL CONFLICTS." WOR+45 WOR-45 FORCES DIPLOM RISK COST ATTIT ALL/VALS...INT/LAW QUANT STAT NAT/COMP. PAGE 171 H3422 — WAR PERCEPT PREDICT MATH

B66
BIRMINGHAM W.,A STUDY OF CONTEMPORARY GHANA VOL I: THE ECONOMY OF GHANA. AFR GHANA PLAN...POLICY STAT CHARTS ANTHOL BIBLIOG 20. PAGE 17 H0342 — ECO/UNDEV ECO/TAC NAT/G PRODUC

B66
BROWN R.T.,TRANSPORT AND THE ECONOMIC INTEGRATION OF SOUTH AMERICA. L/A+17C ECO/UNDEV NAT/G OP/RES DIPLOM INT/TRADE REGION WEALTH...ECOMETRIC GEOG STAT LAFTA TIME. PAGE 22 H0449 — MARKET DIST/IND SIMUL

B66
LONDON DAILY TELEGRAPH,ELECTION '66: GALLUP ANALYSIS OF THE VOTING RESULTS. UK LEGIS COMPUTER ATTIT...QU SAMP CHARTS 20 LABOR/PAR HOUSE/CMNS. PAGE 98 H1959 — STAT CHOOSE REPRESENT POL/PAR

B66
MASON E.S.,ECONOMIC DEVELOPMENT IN INDIA AND PAKISTAN. INDIA PAKISTAN AGRI FINAN PLAN BUDGET INT/TRADE WEALTH...POLICY STAT TREND CHARTS 20. PAGE 104 H2086 — NAT/COMP ECO/UNDEV ECO/TAC FOR/AID

B66
MERRITT R.L.,COMPARING NATIONS* THE USE OF QUANTITATIVE DATA IN CROSSNATIONAL RESEARCH. ACADEM DIPLOM GP/REL...PHIL/SCI STAT TREND GP/COMP PERS/COMP GEN/METH ANTHOL BIBLIOG INDEX. PAGE 109 H2184 — NAT/COMP MATH COMPUT/IR QUANT

S66
BENOIT J.,"WORLD DEFENSE EXPENDITURES." WOR+45 WEAPON COST PRODUC. PAGE 14 H0284 — FORCES STAT NAT/COMP BUDGET

S66
GALTUNG J.,"EAST-WEST INTERACTION PATTERNS." DIPLOM INT/TRADE...NET/THEORY CON/ANAL CHARTS NAT/COMP INDEX NATO COLD/WAR UN WARSAW/P. PAGE 55 H1090 — STAT HYPO/EXP

S66
GILBERT S.P.,"WARS OF LIBERATION AND SOVIET MILITARY AID POLICY." ASIA INDIA INDONESIA UAR USA+45 STRATA WAR PERCEPT MARXISM...STAT NAT/COMP. PAGE 56 H1124 — USSR FOR/AID WEAPON DRIVE

S66
MATTHEWS D.G.,"PRELUDE-COUP D'ETAT-MILITARY GOVERNMENT: A BIBLIOGRAPHICAL AND RESEARCH GUIDE TO NIGERIAN POL AND GOVT, JAN, 1965-66." AFR NIGER LAW CONSTN POL/PAR LEGIS CIVMIL/REL GOV/REL...STAT 20. PAGE 105 H2096 — BIBLIOG NAT/G ADMIN CHOOSE

C66
WINT G.,"ASIA: A HANDBOOK." ASIA S/ASIA INDUS LABOR SECT PRESS RACE/REL MARXISM...STAT CHARTS BIBLIOG 20. PAGE 169 H3388 — ECO/UNDEV DIPLOM NAT/G SOCIETY

B67
ANDERSON C.W.,POLITICS AND ECONOMIC CHANGE IN LATIN AMERICA. L/A+17C INDUS NAT/G OP/RES ADMIN DEMAND ...POLICY STAT CHARTS NAT/COMP 20. PAGE 6 H0125 — ECO/UNDEV PROB/SOLV PLAN ECO/TAC

B67
DENISON E.F.,WHY GROWTH RATES DIFFER; POSTWAR EXPERIENCE IN NINE WESTERN COUNTRIES. WOR+45 FINAN WORKER TEC/DEV EDU/PROP PRICE PRODUC WEALTH ...ECOMETRIC STAT CHARTS BIBLIOG. PAGE 40 H0791 — METH NAT/COMP ECO/DEV ECO/TAC

B67
EVANS R.H.,COEXISTENCE: COMMUNISM AND ITS PRACTICE IN BOLOGNA, 1945-1965. ITALY CAP/ISM ADMIN CHOOSE PEACE ORD/FREE...SOC STAT DEEP/INT SAMP CHARTS BIBLIOG 20. PAGE 48 H0952 — MARXISM CULTURE MUNIC POL/PAR

B67
FISHER M.,PROVINCES AND PROVINCIAL CAPITALS OF THE WORLD. WOR+45 PROVS REGION. PAGE 51 H1014 — GEOG NAT/G NAT/COMP STAT

B67
GELLHORN W.,OMBUDSMEN AND OTHERS: CITIZENS' PROTECTORS IN NINE COUNTRIES. WOR+45 LAW CONSTN LEGIS INSPECT ADJUD ADMIN CONTROL CT/SYS CHOOSE PERS/REL...STAT CHARTS 20. PAGE 55 H1109 — NAT/COMP REPRESENT INGP/REL PROB/SOLV

B67
KONCZACKI Z.A.,PUBLIC FINANCE AND ECONOMIC DEVELOPMENT OF NATAL 1893-1910. TAX ADMIN COLONIAL ...STAT CHARTS BIBLIOG 19/20 NATAL. PAGE 88 H1755 — ECO/TAC FINAN NAT/G ECO/UNDEV

B67
LAMBERT W.E.,CHILDREN'S VIEWS OF FOREIGN PEOPLES: A CROSS-NATIONAL STUDY. UNIV CULTURE EDU/PROP RACE/REL ATTIT PERCEPT ROLE...STAT STAND/INT CHARTS GP/COMP NAT/COMP. PAGE 90 H1802 — AGE/C STRANGE GP/REL STERTYP

B67
NESS G.D.,BUREAUCRACY AND RURAL DEVELOPMENT IN MALAYSIA. MALAYSIA UK SOCIETY FINAN INDUS WORKER TEC/DEV ECO/TAC COLONIAL EQUILIB ORD/FREE...STAT CHARTS 20. PAGE 117 H2330 — ECO/UNDEV PLAN NAT/G ADMIN

B67
OPERATIONS AND POLICY RESEARCH,NICARAGUA: ELECTION FACTBOOK: FEBRUARY 5, 1967 (PAMPHLET). NICARAGUA LAW NAT/G LEAD REPRESENT...STAT BIOG CHARTS 20. PAGE 121 H2423 — POL/PAR CHOOSE PLAN ATTIT

B67
RAE D.,THE POLITICAL CONSEQUENCES OF ELECTORAL LAWS. EUR+WWI ICELAND ISRAEL NEW/ZEALND UK USA+45 ADJUD APPORT GP/REL MAJORITY...MATH STAT CENSUS CHARTS BIBLIOG 20 AUSTRAL. PAGE 129 H2579 — POL/PAR CHOOSE NAT/COMP REPRESENT

B67
ROSENBLUTH G.,THE CANADIAN ECONOMY AND DISARMAMENT. CANADA FUT ECO/DEV INDUS R+D DELIB/GP DIPLOM ECO/TAC CIVMIL/REL PEACE...POLICY BIBLIOG PACIFIST 20. PAGE 134 H2679 — ARMS/CONT STAT PLAN NAT/G

B67
THOMAN R.S.,GEOGRAPHY OF INTERNATIONAL TRADE. WOR+45 ECO/DEV ECO/UNDEV INT/ORG LG/CO PLAN BAL/PAY ...STAT CHARTS NAT/COMP 20. PAGE 154 H3075 — INT/TRADE GEOG ECO/TAC DIPLOM

L67
PICKERING J.F.,"RECRUITMENT TO THE ADMINISTRATIVE CLASS, 1960-1964: PART 2" UK STRATA NAT/G WORKER ...STAT CHARTS 20. PAGE 125 H2505 — PERS/COMP ADMIN KNO/TEST EDU/PROP

L67
WILBER L.A.,"THE GOVERNMENTAL STRUCTURE OF MISSISSIPPI: ITS STRENGTHS AND WEAKNESSES." AGRI LOC/G SCHOOL EX/STRUC LEGIS TOP/EX BUDGET CT/SYS APPORT RACE/REL...GOV/COMP 20 MISSISSIPP. PAGE 168 H3359 — CONSTN PROVS STAT CON/ANAL

S67
ALPANDER G.G.,"ENTREPRENEURS AND PRIVATE ENTERPRISE IN TURKEY." TURKEY INDUS PROC/MFG EDU/PROP ATTIT DRIVE WEALTH...GEOG MGT SOC STAT TREND CHARTS 20. PAGE 6 H0114 — ECO/UNDEV LG/CO NAT/G POLICY

S67
BASOV V.,"THE DEVELOPMENT OF PUBLIC EDUCATION AND THE BUDGET." USSR NAT/G CONTROL REV COST AGE...STAT 20. PAGE 12 H0235 — BUDGET GIVE EDU/PROP SCHOOL

S67
CRITTENDEN J.,"DIMENSIONS OF MODERNIZATION IN THE AMERICAN STATES." USA+45 STRUCT MUNIC PROB/SOLV CONTROL LITERACY HABITAT...CONCPT METH/CNCPT CORREL CONT/OBS CENSUS 20. PAGE 35 H0702 — PROVS GOV/COMP STAT ECO/DEV

S67
EPSTEIN E.H.,"NATIONAL IDENTITY AND THE LANGUAGE ISSUE IN PUERTO RICO." PUERT/RICO CULTURE STRUCT NAT/G PROB/SOLV SKILL...JURID STAT METH/COMP 20. PAGE 47 H0931 — EDU/PROP SCHOOL LING NAT/LISM

S67
HASSAN M.F.,"THE SECOND FOUR-YEAR PLAN OF — ECO/UNDEV

VENEZUELA." L/A+17C VENEZUELA AGRI INDUS NAT/G PLAN RATION CONTROL HABITAT...MATH STAT 20. PAGE 67 H1352 FINAN BUDGET PROB/SOLV

S67
NEUBAUER D.E.,"SOME CONDITIONS OF DEMOCRACY." ECO/DEV COM/IND DIST/IND POL/PAR EDU/PROP REPRESENT ...SOC STAT NAT/COMP 20. PAGE 117 H2331 NAT/G CHOOSE MAJORIT ECO/UNDEV

S67
PAI G.A.,"TAXATION AND PLANNING IN INDIA: A BIRDS-EYE VIEW." INDIA ELITES NAT/G LEGIS BUDGET CONTROL LOBBY INCOME...STAT CHARTS 20. PAGE 122 H2443 TAX PLAN WEALTH STRATA

S67
RAMA C.M.,"PASADO Y PRESENTE DE LA RELIGION EN AMERICA LATINA." L/A+17C ELITES SOCIETY STRATA MARXISM...STAT WORSHIP PROTESTANT. PAGE 129 H2585 SECT CATHISM STRUCT NAT/COMP

S67
SANCHEZ J.D.,"DESARROLLO ECONOMICO Y FUTURO DE COLOMBIA." L/A+17C AGRI EXTR/IND FINAN INDUS MARKET INT/TRADE CONTROL...STAT TREND COLOMB. PAGE 137 H2748 ECO/UNDEV FUT NAT/G ECO/TAC

S67
SOARES G.,"SOCIO-ECONOMIC VARIABLES AND VOTING FOR THE RADICAL LEFT: CHILE 1952." CHILE INDUS NAT/G WORKER ADJUST STRANGE ANOMIE WEALTH...METH/CNCPT CORREL 20. PAGE 146 H2925 STRATA POL/PAR CHOOSE STAT

STATE GOVERNMENT....SEE PROVS

STATE DEPARTMENT....SEE DEPT/STATE

STATIST REICHSAMTE H2974

STATISTICS....SEE STAT, ALSO LOGIC, MATHEMATICS, AND LANGUAGE INDEX, P. XIV

STEINBERG C.S. H2975

STEINBERG E.B. H1274

STEINER K. H2976

STEINMETZ H. H2977

STEPHEN J.F. H2978

STEREOTYPE....SEE STERTYP

STERN F. H2979,H2980

STERN/GANG....STERN GANG (PALESTINE)

STERNBERG F. H2981

STERTYP....STEREOTYPE

B00
DE JOMINI A.H.,THE ART OF WAR. MOD/EUR NAT/G BAL/PWR DIPLOM DOMIN EXEC ROUTINE COERCE DRIVE PWR SKILL...POLICY CONCPT CHARTS STERTYP 19. PAGE 38 H0755 PLAN FORCES WAR WEAPON

B14
BERHARDI F.,GERMANY AND THE NEXT WAR. MOD/EUR NAT/G SCHOOL FORCES ACT/RES DOMIN EDU/PROP SUPEGO PWR ...TIME/SEQ STERTYP TOT/POP 20 WWI. PAGE 15 H0304 DRIVE COERCE WAR GERMANY

B28
BUELL R.,THE NATIVE PROBLEM IN AFRICA. KIN LABOR LOC/G ECO/TAC ROUTINE ORD/FREE...REC/INT KNO/TEST CENSUS TREND CHARTS SOC/EXP STERTYP 20. PAGE 23 H0466 AFR CULTURE

B29
DAVIE M.R.,THE EVOLUTION OF WAR. CULTURE KIN COERCE WAR ATTIT DRIVE...PSY SOC TIME/SEQ TREND GEN/LAWS. PAGE 37 H0746 FORCES STERTYP

B31
BONAR J.,THEORIES OF POPULATION FROM RALEIGH TO ARTHUR YOUNG. CHRIST-17C MOD/EUR CULTURE SOCIETY R+D CREATE ATTIT PERCEPT RIGID/FLEX...OLD/LIB CONCPT NEW/IDEA TIME/SEQ IDEA/COMP STERTYP GEN/LAWS. PAGE 19 H0372 GEOG BIOG

B32
BRYCE J.,THE HOLY ROMAN EMPIRE. GERMANY ITALY MOD/EUR CULTURE SOCIETY STRUCT INT/ORG NAT/G SECT DIPLOM DOMIN WAR SUPEGO ALL/VALS SOVEREIGN...GEOG SOC TIME/SEQ CHARTS STERTYP. PAGE 23 H0456 CHRIST-17C NAT/LISM

L37
NICOLSON H.,"THE MEANING OF PRESTIGE." EUR+WWI MOD/EUR UK CULTURE SOCIETY NAT/G DIPLOM DOMIN LEGIT ATTIT DRIVE PWR...METH/CNCPT RECORD TIME/SEQ GEN/METH CMN/WLTH TOT/POP 20. PAGE 118 H2351 CONCPT STERTYP

B40
JORDAN W.K.,THE DEVELOPMENT OF RELIGIOUS TOLERATION IN ENGLAND. CHRIST-17C CULTURE SOCIETY LEGIT ATTIT RESPECT...POLICY CONCPT RECORD TIME/SEQ STERTYP GEN/LAWS TOT/POP 16/17. PAGE 82 H1635 SECT UK

B41
HAYAKAWA S.I.,LANGUAGE IN ACTION. CULTURE INTELL SOCIETY KNOWL...METH/CNCPT LING LOG RECORD STERTYP GEN/METH TOT/POP 20. PAGE 68 H1366 EDU/PROP SOC

B46
NICOLSON H.,THE CONGRESS OF VIENNA. MOD/EUR NAT/G FORCES BAL/PWR DOMIN LEGIT COERCE PERSON PWR ...RECORD TIME/SEQ STERTYP 19 CONG/VIENN. PAGE 118 H2353 CONCPT POLICY DIPLOM

S48
ALMOND G.A.,"THE CHRISTIAN PARTIES OF WESTEN EUROPE." EUR+WWI NAT/G EDU/PROP LEGIT TOTALISM ORD/FREE PWR MARXISM...TREND CHARTS STERTYP GEN/LAWS COLD/WAR 20. PAGE 5 H0110 POL/PAR CATH SOCISM

B50
TRAGER F.N.,MARXISM IN SOUTHEAST ASIA. BURMA INDONESIA THAILAND VIETNAM CULTURE SOCIETY NAT/G VOL/ASSN EXEC ROUTINE COERCE ATTIT RIGID/FLEX PWR ...METH/CNCPT TIME/SEQ STERTYP GEN/LAWS MARX/KARL VAL/FREE COLD/WAR NAM 20. PAGE 156 H3126 S/ASIA POL/PAR REV

B52
BENTHAM A.,HANDBOOK OF POLITICAL FALLACIES. FUT MOD/EUR LAW INTELL LOC/G MUNIC NAT/G DELIB/GP LEGIS CREATE EDU/PROP CT/SYS ATTIT RIGID/FLEX KNOWL PWR ...RELATIV PSY SOC CONCPT SELF/OBS TREND STERTYP TOT/POP. PAGE 14 H0286 POL/PAR

B56
PADMORE G.,PAN-AFRICANISM OR COMMUNISM. AFR FUT NIGERIA INTELL NAT/G COLONIAL FEDERAL ATTIT DRIVE PWR RESPECT WEALTH MARXISM...CONCPT AUD/VIS STERTYP 20. PAGE 122 H2440 POL/PAR NAT/LISM

B57
ARON R.,L'UNIFICATION ECONOMIQUE DE L'EUROPE. EUR+WWI SWITZERLND UK INT/ORG NAT/G REGION NAT/LISM ORD/FREE PWR...CONCPT METH/CNCPT OBS TREND STERTYP GEN/LAWS EEC 20. PAGE 8 H0168 VOL/ASSN ECO/TAC

B57
DEAN V.M.,THE NATURE OF THE NON-WESTERN WORLD. AFR ASIA L/A+17C S/ASIA CULTURE SOCIETY STRATA ECO/DEV DIPLOM ECO/TAC FOR/AID ATTIT DRIVE ALL/VALS ...RELATIV SOC CONCPT TIME/SEQ TREND TOT/POP 20. PAGE 39 H0778 ECO/UNDEV STERTYP NAT/LISM

B57
NARAIN D.,HINDU CHARACTER (A FEW GLIMPSES). INDIA DIPLOM SUICIDE PERS/REL ATTIT...PSY NAT/COMP PERS/COMP BIBLIOG WORSHIP 20 HINDU. PAGE 116 H2310 PERSON STERTYP SUPEGO SECT

B58
GARTHOFF R.L.,SOVIET STRATEGY IN THE NUCLEAR AGE. FUT USSR R+D INT/ORG NAT/G ACT/RES TEC/DEV DOMIN DETER WAR ATTIT PWR...RELATIV METH/CNCPT SELF/OBS TREND CON/ANAL STERTYP GEN/LAWS 20. PAGE 55 H1103 COM FORCES BAL/PWR NUC/PWR

B58
VARG P.A.,MISSIONARIES, CHINESE, AND DIPLOMATS: THE AMERICAN PROTESTANT MISSIONARY MOVEMENT IN CHINA, 1890-1952. ASIA ECO/UNDEV NAT/G PROB/SOLV CAP/ISM EDU/PROP COLONIAL NAT/LISM ATTIT MARXISM...NAT/COMP STERTYP 20 CHINJAP PROTESTANT MISSION. PAGE 162 H3234 CULTURE DIPLOM SECT

S58
MAIR L.P.,"REPRESENTATIVE LOCAL GOVERNMENT AS A PROBLEM IN SOCIAL CHANGE." ECO/UNDEV KIN LOC/G NAT/G SCHOOL JUDGE ADMIN ROUTINE REPRESENT RIGID/FLEX RESPECT...CONCPT STERTYP CMN/WLTH 20. PAGE 101 H2025 AFR PWR ELITES

B59
FOX A.,THE POWER OF SMALL STATES: DIPLOMACY IN WORLD WAR TWO. EUR+WWI FINLAND NORWAY SPAIN SWEDEN TURKEY NAT/G TOP/EX DIPLOM PWR...HIST/WRIT 20. PAGE 52 H1044 CONCPT STERTYP BAL/PWR

S59
LABEDZ L.,"IDEOLOGY: THE FOURTH STAGE." COM USSR NAT/G TOP/EX LEGIT ATTIT PWR MARXISM...METH/CNCPT HIST/WRIT STERTYP TOT/POP 20. PAGE 90 H1795 CONCPT GEN/LAWS

S59
LEVINE R.A.,"ANTI-EUROPEAN VIOLENCE IN AFRICA: A COMPARATIVE ANALYSIS." AFR CULTURE NAT/G DIPLOM EDU/PROP COLONIAL REGION COERCE ATTIT PWR...PSY CONCPT TIME/SEQ TREND HYPO/EXP SOC/EXP STERTYP GEN/METH COLD/WAR 20. PAGE 95 H1903 DRIVE ORD/FREE REV

B60
BRZEZINSKI Z.K.,THE SOVIET BLOC-UNITY AND CONFLICT. COM USSR CONSTN DOMIN ADMIN TOTALISM PWR...SOC MYTH RECORD TREND STERTYP GEN/LAWS GEN/METH TOT/POP 20. PAGE 23 H0458 ATTIT EDU/PROP

B60
MAYO H.B.,AN INTRODUCTION TO DEMOCRATIC THEORY. ORD/FREE...POLICY TIME/SEQ GOV/COMP STERTYP. PAGE 105 H2109 POPULISM CONCPT IDEA/COMP

B60
MCCLOSKY H.,THE SOVIET DICTATORSHIP. FUT CONSTN COM

CULTURE INTELL SOCIETY POL/PAR SECT VOL/ASSN FORCES PLAN TEC/DEV DOMIN EDU/PROP COERCE PWR MARXISM ...POLICY CONCPT MYTH STERTYP 20. PAGE 106 H2127 — NAT/G TOTALISM USSR

S60

BERREMAN G.D.,"CASTE IN INDIA AND THE UNITED STATES" (BMR)" INDIA USA+45 CULTURE SOCIETY STRUCT SECT GP/REL DISCRIM HEREDITY...SOC STERTYP 20 NEGRO HINDU. PAGE 16 H0318 — STRATA RACE/REL NAT/COMP ATTIT

S60

CASSINELLI C.,"TOTALITARIANISM, IDEOLOGY AND PROPAGANDA." EUR+WWI CULTURE SOCIETY NAT/G DOMIN COERCE ORD/FREE FASCISM MARXISM...MARXIST CONCPT STERTYP GEN/LAWS TOT/POP 20. PAGE 28 H0554 — ATTIT EDU/PROP TOTALISM

S60

KEYFITZ N.,"WESTERN PERSPECTIVES AND ASIAN PROBLEMS." ASIA EUR+WWI S/ASIA SOCIETY FOR/AID ...POLICY SOC CONCPT STERTYP WORK TOT/POP 20. PAGE 85 H1701 — CULTURE ATTIT

S60

MURPHEY R.,"ECONOMIC CONFLICTS IN SOUTH ASIA." ASIA CULTURE INTELL ECO/TAC REGION ATTIT DRIVE KNOWL ...METH/CNCPT TIME/SEQ STERTYP TOT/POP VAL/FREE 20. PAGE 115 H2296 — S/ASIA ECO/UNDEV

S60

SHILS E.,"THE INTELLECTUALS IN THE POLITICAL DEVELOPMENT OF THE NEW STATES." AFR ASIA S/ASIA ELITES LOC/G NAT/G CONSULT EX/STRUC CREATE PLAN ECO/TAC DOMIN LEGIT DRIVE PWR...TRADIT CONCPT STERTYP GEN/LAWS 20. PAGE 143 H2861 — POL/PAR INTELL NAT/LISM

S60

SPIRO H.J.,"NEW CONSTITUTIONAL FORMS IN AFRICA." FUT CULTURE SOCIETY ECO/UNDEV NAT/G POL/PAR VOL/ASSN EDU/PROP ATTIT DRIVE ORD/FREE PWR RESPECT ...POLICY CONCPT OBS TREND CON/ANAL STERTYP GEN/LAWS VAL/FREE. PAGE 148 H2950 — AFR CONSTN FOR/AID NAT/LISM

B61

MARVICK D.,POLITICAL DECISION-MAKERS. INTELL STRATA NAT/G POL/PAR EX/STRUC LEGIS DOMIN EDU/PROP ATTIT PERSON PWR...PSY STAT OBS CONT/OBS STAND/INT UNPLAN/INT TIME/SEQ CHARTS STERTYP VAL/FREE. PAGE 104 H2073 — TOP/EX BIOG ELITES

S61

TOMASIC D.,"POLITICAL LEADERSHIP IN CONTEMPORARY POLAND." COM EUR+WWI GERMANY NAT/G POL/PAR SECT DELIB/GP PLAN ECO/TAC DOMIN EDU/PROP PWR MARXISM ...MARXIST GEOG MGT CONCPT TIME/SEQ STERTYP 20. PAGE 156 H3111 — SOCIETY ROUTINE USSR POLAND

B62

BUSIA K.A.,THE CHALLENGE OF AFRICA. CULTURE KIN MUNIC NAT/G POL/PAR SCHOOL DELIB/GP PLAN ECO/TAC DOMIN EDU/PROP TOTALISM ATTIT PERSON ALL/VALS SOVEREIGN...SOC CONCPT STERTYP TOT/POP VAL/FREE 20. PAGE 25 H0496 — AFR ECO/UNDEV NAT/LISM

B62

DE MADARIAGA S.,L'AMERIQUE LATINE ENTRE L'OURS ET L'AIGLE. L/A+17C SOCIETY NAT/G ECO/TAC EDU/PROP REGION COERCE ATTIT ALL/VALS...MAJORIT TIME/SEQ STERTYP COLD/WAR OAS 20. PAGE 38 H0760 — POL/PAR ECO/UNDEV

B62

DUTOIT B.,LA NEUTRALITE SUISSE A L'HEURE EUROPEENNE. EUR+WWI MOD/EUR INT/ORG NAT/G VOL/ASSN PLAN BAL/PWR LEGIT NEUTRAL REGION PEACE ORD/FREE SOVEREIGN...CONCPT OBS TIME/SEQ TREND STERTYP VAL/FREE LEAGUE/NAT UN 20. PAGE 44 H0873 — ATTIT DIPLOM SWITZERLND

B62

JACKSON W.A.D.,RUSSO-CHINESE BORDERLANDS. ASIA COM USSR NAT/G PROVS EX/STRUC FORCES DOMIN COERCE PEACE ATTIT PWR SOVEREIGN WEALTH...CONCPT TREND CHARTS STERTYP VAL/FREE. PAGE 79 H1576 — GEOG DIPLOM RUSSIA

B62

LEGUM C.,PAN-AFRICANISM: A SHORT POLITICAL GUIDE. ISLAM CULTURE INTELL ECO/DEV NAT/G POL/PAR DELIB/GP PLAN EDU/PROP FEDERAL NAT/LISM ATTIT DRIVE PERSON ...RECORD TIME/SEQ CHARTS STERTYP 20. PAGE 93 H1861 — AFR CONCPT

S62

MARIAS J.,"A PROGRAM FOR EUROPE." EUR+WWI INT/ORG NAT/G PLAN DIPLOM DOMIN PWR...STERTYP TOT/POP 20. PAGE 102 H2048 — VOL/ASSN CREATE REGION

B63

CROSS C.,THE FASCISTS IN BRITAIN. UK ELITES LABOR NAT/G DOMIN PARTIC DISCRIM TOTALISM ATTIT...STERTYP 20. PAGE 35 H0708 — POL/PAR FASCISM RACE/REL LEAD

B63

EICH H.,THE UNLOVED GERMANS. EUR+WWI GERMANY PERS/REL RACE/REL DISCRIM HABITAT SUPEGO FASCISM ...PSY SOC AUD/VIS 19/20 JEWS. PAGE 45 H0898 — STERTYP PERSON CULTURE ATTIT

B63

HOLLANDER P.,THE NEW MAN AND HIS ENEMIES: A STUDY OF THE STALINIST CONCEPTIONS OF GOOD AND EVIL PERSONIFIED (DOCTORAL THESIS). USSR SOCIETY ECO/DEV NAT/G EDU/PROP WRITING...SOC STERTYP BIBLIOG 20 STALIN/J. PAGE 73 H1455 — CONTROL ATTIT TOTALISM MARXISM

B63

LARSON A.,A WARLESS WORLD. FUT CULTURE NAT/G VOL/ASSN FORCES CREATE DOMIN PEACE ALL/VALS...HUM STERTYP 20. PAGE 91 H1824 — SOCIETY CONCPT ARMS/CONT

B63

QUAISON-SACKEY A.,AFRICA UNBOUND: REFLECTIONS OF AN AFRICAN STATESMAN. ISLAM CULTURE INTELL INT/ORG POL/PAR TOP/EX DOMIN EDU/PROP LEGIT ATTIT PERSON ...CONCPT OBS TIME/SEQ CHARTS STERTYP 20 UN. PAGE 129 H2571 — AFR BIOG

S63

LERNER D.,"WILL EUROPEAN UNION BRING ABOUT MERGED NATIONAL GOALS." EUR+WWI FRANCE GERMANY UK ECO/DEV NAT/G VOL/ASSN DELIB/GP BAL/PWR ECO/TAC NAT/LISM EEC 20 DEGAULLE/C. PAGE 95 H1889 — ATTIT STERTYP ELITES REGION

S63

RUSTOW D.A.,"THE MILITARY IN MIDDLE EASTERN SOCIETY AND POLITICS." FUT ISLAM CONSTN SOCIETY FACE/GP NAT/G POL/PAR PROF/ORG CONSULT DOMIN ADMIN EXEC REGION COERCE NAT/LISM ATTIT DRIVE PERSON ORD/FREE PWR...POLICY CONCPT OBS STERTYP 20. PAGE 136 H2721 — FORCES ELITES

B64

FRIEDLAND W.H.,AFRICAN SOCIALISM. ECO/UNDEV MARKET LABOR NAT/G POL/PAR PLAN CAP/ISM ECO/TAC EDU/PROP CHOOSE ATTIT DRIVE PWR WEALTH...POLICY CONCPT RECORD STERTYP 20. PAGE 53 H1063 — AFR SOCISM

B64

HEIMSATH C.H.,INDIAN NATIONALISM AND HINDU SOCIAL REFORM. S/ASIA LAW CULTURE SOCIETY STRATA PROVS VOL/ASSN DELIB/GP LEGIS TOP/EX DOMIN EDU/PROP LEGIT ATTIT ALL/VALS...POLICY SOC TIME/SEQ STERTYP VAL/FREE 19/20. PAGE 69 H1385 — SECT NAT/G

S64

GARMARNIKOW M.,"INFLUENCE-BUYING IN WEST AFRICA." COM FUT USSR INTELL NAT/G PLAN TEC/DEV ECO/TAC DOMIN EDU/PROP REGION NAT/LISM ATTIT DRIVE ALL/VALS SOVEREIGN...POLICY PSY SOC CONCPT TREND STERTYP WORK COLD/WAR 20. PAGE 55 H1102 — AFR ECO/UNDEV FOR/AID SOCISM

S64

HIRAI N.,"SHINTO AND INTERNATIONAL PROBLEMS." SOCIETY NAT/G PLAN EDU/PROP RACE/REL PEACE ATTIT PERCEPT LOVE MORAL...HUM MYTH RECORD SAMP TREND STERTYP TOT/POP 20 UN CHINJAP SHINTO. PAGE 71 H1423 — ASIA SECT

S64

LEVI W.,"INDIAN NEUTRALISM RECONSIDERED." ASIA CHINA/COM S/ASIA SOCIETY NAT/G ACT/RES LEGIT NEUTRAL COERCE ATTIT DRIVE PERCEPT RIGID/FLEX HEALTH LOVE PWR...DECISION RECORD TREND STERTYP 20. PAGE 95 H1896 — ORD/FREE CONCPT INDIA

S64

RUDOLPH L.I.,"GENERALS AND POLITICIANS IN INDIA." INDIA S/ASIA CULTURE STRATA NAT/G LEGIS TOP/EX EDU/PROP ATTIT ORD/FREE PWR RESPECT SKILL...POLICY BIOG TIME/SEQ STERTYP VAL/FREE 20. PAGE 136 H2713 — FORCES COERCE

S64

SWEARER H.R.,"AFTER KHRUSHCHEV: WHAT NEXT." COM FUT USSR CONSTN ELITES NAT/G POL/PAR CHIEF DELIB/GP LEGIS DOMIN LEAD...RECORD TREND STERTYP GEN/METH 20. PAGE 151 H3016 — EX/STRUC PWR

S65

JENSEN L.,"MILITARY CAPABILITIES AND BARGAINING BEHAVIOR." USA+45 USSR ARMS/CONT DETER COST ATTIT ...METH/CNCPT STAT SYS/QU CON/ANAL CHARTS NAT/COMP. PAGE 81 H1614 — DIPLOM DRIVE PWR STERTYP

S65

WOHLSTETTER R.,"CUBA AND PEARL HARBOR* HINDSIGHT AND FORESIGHT." USSR FORCES OP/RES TEC/DEV ATTIT PERCEPT...DECISION IDEA/COMP NAT/COMP STERTYP TIME. PAGE 170 H3395 — CUBA RISK WAR ACT/RES

B66

SCHURMANN F.,IDEOLOGY AND ORGANIZATION IN COMMUNIST CHINA. CHINA/COM LOC/G MUNIC POL/PAR ECO/TAC CONTROL ATTIT...MGT STERTYP 20 COM/PARTY. PAGE 140 H2805 — MARXISM STRUCT ADMIN NAT/G

S66

MARTZ J.D.,"THE PLACE OF LATIN AMERICA IN THE STUDY OF COMPARATIVE POLITICS." AFR ASIA CULTURE STRUCT ECO/UNDEV ACADEM CREATE...CLASSIF NAT/COMP. PAGE 104 H2072 — L/A+17C GOV/COMP STERTYP GEN/LAWS

B67

FANON F.,BLACK SKIN, WHITE MASKS: THE EXPERIENCES OF A BLACK MAN IN A WHITE WORLD. CULTURE COLONIAL HAPPINESS ISOLAT STRANGE ATTIT HABITAT RIGID/FLEX SEX...BIOG STERTYP SOC/INTEG 20 NEGRO. PAGE 49 H0970 — DISCRIM PERS/REL RACE/REL PSY

B67

LAMBERT W.E.,CHILDREN'S VIEWS OF FOREIGN PEOPLES: A CROSS-NATIONAL STUDY. UNIV CULTURE EDU/PROP RACE/REL ATTIT PERCEPT ROLE...STAT STAND/INT CHARTS GP/COMP NAT/COMP. PAGE 90 H1802 — AGE/C STRANGE GP/REL STERTYP

STEUBER F.A. H2982

STEVENS G.G. H2983

STEVENS L.M. H0098

STEVENSN/A....ADLAI STEVENSON

STEWARD J.H. H2984,H2985,H3389

STEWARD/JH....JULIAN H. STEWARD

STIFEL L.D. H2986

STIMSON/HL....HENRY L. STIMSON

STIRNIMANN H. H2987

STOCHASTIC PROCESSES....SEE PROB/SOLV, MODELS INDEX

STOCKHOLM....STOCKHOLM

STOKES W.S. H2988

STOKES/CB....CARL B. STOKES

STOL....SHORT TAKE-OFF AND LANDING AIRCRAFT

STOLPER W.F. H2989

STONE/HF....HARLAN FISKE STONE

STONE/IF....I.F. STONE

STORING H.J. H2823

STORING/HJ....H.J. STORING

STOURZH G. H1160

STOUT H.M. H2990

STRACHEY J. H2991,H2992

STRAFFORD P. H2993

STRANGE....ESTRANGEMENT, ALIENATION, IMPERSONALITY

B37
HORNEY K.,THE NEUROTIC PERSONALITY OF OUR TIME. SOCIETY PERS/REL ADJUST HAPPINESS ANOMIE ATTIT DRIVE SEX LOVE PWR CONCPT. PAGE 74 H1472
PSY PERSON STRANGE CULTURE

C50
NUMELIN R.,"THE BEGINNINGS OF DIPLOMACY." INT/TRADE WAR GP/REL PEACE STRANGE ATTIT...INT/LAW CONCPT BIBLIOG. PAGE 119 H2380
DIPLOM KIN CULTURE LAW

S53
ARENDT H.,"IDEOLOGY AND TERROR: A NOVEL FORM OF GOVERNMENT." WOR-45 DOMIN STRANGE ATTIT SUPEGO MARXISM...GOV/COMP IDEA/COMP 20 NAZI. PAGE 8 H0160
TOTALISM ANOMIE ALL/IDEOS SOCIETY

B57
REAMAN G.E.,THE TRAIL OF THE BLACK WALNUT. CANADA AGRI COLONIAL...CHARTS BIBLIOG 18 GERMANS/PA. PAGE 130 H2604
STRANGE SECT CULTURE

S57
DEXTER L.A.,"A SOCIAL THEORY OF MENTAL DEFICIENCY." CULTURE PUB/INST PROB/SOLV CRIME PERS/REL STRANGE PERSON SUPEGO SKILL...EPIST SOC/WK HYPO/EXP. PAGE 41 H0814
SOC PSY HEALTH ROLE

B59
LEIGHTON A.H.,MY NAME IS LEGION; FOUNDATIONS FOR A THEORY OF MAN IN RELATION TO CULTURE (VOL. I). CULTURE STRANGE ANOMIE...SOC CONCPT METH/CNCPT CHARTS BIBLIOG METH 20 NOVA/SCOT. PAGE 93 H1867
HEALTH PSY SOCIETY HABITAT

B61
KEE R.,REFUGEE WORLD. AUSTRIA EUR+WWI GERMANY NEIGH EX/STRUC WORKER PROB/SOLV ECO/TAC RENT EDU/PROP INGP/REL COST LITERACY HABITAT 20 MIGRATION. PAGE 84 H1676
NAT/G GIVE WEALTH STRANGE

B62
PAIKERT G.C.,THE GERMAN EXODUS. EUR+WWI GERMANY/W LAW CULTURE SOCIETY STRUCT INDUS NAT/LISM RESPECT SOVEREIGN...CHARTS BIBLIOG SOC/INTEG 20 MIGRATION. PAGE 122 H2444
INGP/REL STRANGE GEOG GP/REL

B63
LEIGHTON D.C.,THE CHARACTER OF DANGER (VOL. III). SOCIETY STRUCT STRANGE ANOMIE...SOC STAT CHARTS GP/COMP SOC/EXP SOC/INTEG 20 NOVA/SCOT. PAGE 94 H1868
HEALTH PSY CULTURE

B63
LOOMIE A.J.,THE SPANISH ELIZABETHANS: THE ENGLISH EXILES AT THE COURT OF PHILIP II. SPAIN UK WAR INGP/REL DRIVE HABITAT CATHISM...BIOG 16/17 MIGRATION. PAGE 98 H1962
NAT/G STRANGE POLICY DIPLOM

B63
REYNOLDS B.,MAGIC, DIVINATION AND WITCHCRAFT AMONG THE BAROTSE OF NORTHERN RHODESIA. RHODESIA CULTURE KIN CREATE LEGIT PARTIC DEATH DREAM STRANGE HABITAT PERSON...AUD/VIS WORSHIP 20. PAGE 131 H2619
AFR SOC MYTH SECT

B64
JOSEPHSON E.,MAN ALONE: ALIENATION IN MODERN SOCIETY. WOR+45 ECO/DEV WORKER WAR LEISURE RACE/REL ANOMIE ATTIT PERCEPT PERSON ALL/VALS...ANTHOL 20. PAGE 82 H1636
STRANGE CULTURE SOCIETY ADJUST

B65
STERN F.,THE POLITICS OF CULTURAL DESPAIR. EUR+WWI GERMANY POL/PAR SECT RACE/REL STRANGE TOTALISM ...ART/METH MYTH BIBLIOG 20 JEWS. PAGE 149 H2980
CULTURE ATTIT NAT/LISM FASCISM

S65
THOMAS F.C. JR.,"THE PEACE CORPS IN MOROCCO." CULTURE MUNIC PROVS CREATE ROUTINE TASK ADJUST STRANGE...OBS PEACE/CORP. PAGE 154 H3077
MOROCCO FRANCE FOR/AID EDU/PROP

B66
WANG Y.C.,CHINESE INTELLECTUALS AND THE WEST 1872-1949. ASIA ELITES LEAD STRANGE ROLE MARXISM ...CHARTS 19/20. PAGE 165 H3301
INTELL EDU/PROP CULTURE SOCIETY

L66
KRENZ F.E.,"THE REFUGEE AS A SUBJECT OF INTERNATIONAL LAW." FUT LAW NAT/G CREATE ADJUD ISOLAT STRANGE...RECORD UN. PAGE 88 H1766
INT/LAW DISCRIM NEW/IDEA

B67
ALBA V.,THE MEXICANS; THE MAKING OF A NATION. SOCIETY ECO/UNDEV AGRI INDUS SECT STRANGE ATTIT ...GEOG 20 MEXIC/AMER. PAGE 4 H0091
CONSTN NAT/G CULTURE ANOMIE

B67
FANON F.,BLACK SKIN, WHITE MASKS: THE EXPERIENCES OF A BLACK MAN IN A WHITE WORLD. CULTURE COLONIAL HAPPINESS ISOLAT STRANGE ATTIT HABITAT RIGID/FLEX SEX...BIOG STERTYP SOC/INTEG 20 NEGRO. PAGE 49 H0970
DISCRIM PERS/REL RACE/REL PSY

B67
LAMBERT W.E.,CHILDREN'S VIEWS OF FOREIGN PEOPLES: A CROSS-NATIONAL STUDY. UNIV CULTURE EDU/PROP RACE/REL ATTIT PERCEPT ROLE...STAT STAND/INT CHARTS GP/COMP NAT/COMP. PAGE 90 H1802
AGE/C STRANGE GP/REL STERTYP

S67
KYLE K.,"BACKGROUND TO THE CRISIS" ISLAM ISRAEL UAR UK USSR NAT/G PROB/SOLV LEGIT CONTROL REGION STRANGE MORAL 20 JEWS. PAGE 89 H1787
DIPLOM POLICY SOVEREIGN COERCE

S67
SOARES G.,"SOCIO-ECONOMIC VARIABLES AND VOTING FOR THE RADICAL LEFT: CHILE 1952." CHILE INDUS NAT/G WORKER ADJUST STRANGE ANOMIE WEALTH...METH/CNCPT CORREL 20. PAGE 146 H2925
STRATA POL/PAR CHOOSE STAT

S67
THIEN T.T.,"VIETNAM: A CASE OF SOCIAL ALIENATION." VIETNAM AGRI FORCES FOR/AID ADMIN REPRESENT INGP/REL PWR 19/20. PAGE 154 H3071
NAT/G ELITES WORKER STRANGE

STRASBOURG....STRASBOURG PLAN

STRATA....SOCIAL STRATA, CLASS DIVISION

B08
THE GOVERNMENT OF SOUTH AFRICA (VOL. II). SOUTH/AFR STRATA EXTR/IND EX/STRUC TOP/EX BUDGET ADJUD ADMIN CT/SYS PRODUC...CORREL CENSUS 19 RAILROAD CIVIL/SERV POSTAL/SYS. PAGE 2 H0030
CONSTN FINAN LEGIS NAT/G

B09
JUSTINIAN,THE DIGEST (DIGESTA CORPUS JURIS CIVILIS) (2 VOLS.) (TRANS. BY C. H. MONRO). ROMAN/EMP LAW FAM LOC/G LEGIS EDU/PROP CONTROL MARRIAGE OWN ROLE CIVIL/LAW. PAGE 82 H1645
JURID CT/SYS NAT/G STRATA

B12
HOBSON J.A.,THE EVOLUTION OF MODERN CAPITALISM. MOD/EUR UK STRATA ECO/DEV INDUS INCOME UTIL WEALTH ...SOC GEN/LAWS 7/20. PAGE 72 H1440
CAP/ISM WORKER TEC/DEV TIME/SEQ

B13
KROPOTKIN P.,THE CONQUEST OF BREAD. SOCIETY STRATA AGRI INDUS WORKER REV HAPPINESS INCOME PRODUC HEALTH MORAL ORD/FREE. PAGE 89 H1775
ANARCH SOCIALIST OWN AGREE

B13
SIEGFRIED A.,TABLEAU POLITIQUE DE LA FRANCE DE L'OUEST SOUS LA TROISIEME REPUBLIQUE. FRANCE STRATA STRUCT NAT/G POL/PAR PROVS REGION GOV/REL ATTIT PWR ...TREND TIME 19. PAGE 143 H2869
SOC GEOG SOCIETY

B14
OPPENHEIMER F.,THE STATE. FUT SOCIETY STRATA STRUCT WORKER CAP/ISM WAR GP/REL SOCISM...SOC NAT/COMP SOC/INTEG. PAGE 121 H2424
ELITES OWN DOMIN NAT/G

B16
TREITSCHKE H.,POLITICS. UNIV SOCIETY STRATA NAT/G EX/STRUC LEGIS DOMIN EDU/PROP ATTIT PWR RESPECT ...CONCPT TIME/SEQ GEN/LAWS TOT/POP 20. PAGE 157 H3129
EXEC ELITES GERMANY

B17
VEBLEN T.B.,AN INQUIRY INTO THE NATURE OF PEACE AND THE TERMS OF ITS PERPETUATION. UNIV STRATA FINAN
PEACE DIPLOM

EDU/PROP PRICE COST DISCRIM NAT/LISM MORAL ORD/FREE PACIFIST 20 WORLDUNITY. PAGE 162 H3237 WAR NAT/G

N19
INTERNATIONAL LABOUR OFFICE,EMPLOYMENT, UNEMPLOYMENT AND LABOUR FORCE STATISTICS (PAMPHLET). EUR+WWI STRATA AGRI INDUS NAT/G PROB/SOLV PAY AGE SEX...SAMP NAT/COMP METH 20 ILO. PAGE 78 H1557 WORKER LABOR STAT ECO/DEV

N19
LIEBKNECHT W.P.C.,SOCIALISM (2 PTS.; 1875, 1894) (PAMPHLET). WORKER CAP/ISM EDU/PROP WEALTH POPULISM. PAGE 97 H1927 ECO/TAC STRATA SOCIALIST PARTIC

B21
KREY A.C.,THE FIRST CRUSADE. CHRIST-17C SOCIETY STRATA NAT/G SECT FORCES WORKER WRITING LEAD ATTIT ...CHARTS 11 CHRISTIAN CRUSADES. PAGE 88 H1767 WAR CATH DIPLOM PARTIC

B27
BELLOC H.,THE SERVILE STATE (1912) (3RD ED.). PRUSSIA UK CULTURE STRATA INDUS NAT/G ECO/TAC CONTROL LEAD SUFF DISCRIM EQUILIB ORD/FREE WEALTH 20. PAGE 13 H0269 WORKER CAP/ISM DOMIN CATH

B27
ENGELS F.,THE PEASANT WAR IN GERMANY (1850). GERMANY MOD/EUR AGRI WORKER LEAD COERCE INGP/REL ...TREND 16/19. PAGE 46 H0924 WAR STRATA REV MARXIST

S27
MICHELS R.,"SOME REFLECTIONS ON THE SOCIOLOGICAL CHARACTER OF POLITICAL PARTIES" (BMR)" WOR-45 STRATA MAJORITY DRIVE...GOV/COMP 20. PAGE 110 H2199 POL/PAR PWR LEAD CONCPT

B28
HOBBES T.,THE ELEMENTS OF LAW, NATURAL AND POLITIC (1650). STRATA NAT/G SECT CHIEF AGREE ATTIT ALL/VALS MORAL ORD/FREE POPULISM...POLICY CONCPT. PAGE 71 H1432 PERSON LAW SOVEREIGN CONSERVE

B30
LASKI H.J.,LIBERTY IN THE MODERN STATE. UNIV SOCIETY STRATA CREATE BAL/PWR CONTROL RATIONAL ATTIT PWR 18/20. PAGE 91 H1828 CONCPT ORD/FREE NAT/G DOMIN

B30
MASON E.S.,THE PARIS COMMUNE: AN EPISODE IN THE HISTORY OF THE SOCIALIST MOVEMENT. FRANCE MOD/EUR ELITES SOCIETY STRATA ECO/DEV WORKER EDU/PROP CHOOSE INGP/REL SOCISM 19 MARX/KARL PARIS. PAGE 104 H2085 NAT/G REV MARXISM

B31
MACIVER R.M.,SOCIETY: ITS STRUCTURE AND CHANGES. CULTURE STRATA FAM CROWD HABITAT ORD/FREE...PSY SOC CONCPT BIBLIOG 20. PAGE 100 H1998 STRUCT SOCIETY PERSON DRIVE

S31
HEINBERG J.G.,"THE PERSONNEL OF FRENCH CABINETS, 1871-1930." FRANCE STRATA CHIEF CHOOSE REPRESENT MAJORITY...STAT QU CENSUS TREND CHARTS PERS/COMP 19/20 CHAMBR/DEP. PAGE 69 H1386 ELITES NAT/G DELIB/GP TOP/EX

B33
BERDYAYEV N.,CHRISTIANITY AND CLASS WAR. UNIV SOCIETY WORKER CREATE PROB/SOLV ATTIT PERSON ORD/FREE...CONCPT CHRISTIAN. PAGE 15 H0296 SECT MARXISM STRATA GP/REL

B34
MARX K.,THE CLASS STRUGGLES IN FRANCE. FRANCE INDUS WORKER CONSERVE...TREND GEN/LAWS 19. PAGE 104 H2077 MARXIST STRATA REV INT/TRADE

B34
STALIN J.,PROBLEMS OF LENINISM. USSR STRATA INDUS LOC/G POL/PAR ECO/TAC CONTROL TOTALISM PWR SOCISM LENIN/VI STALIN/J. PAGE 148 H2968 MARXISM REV ELITES NAT/G

B35
AQUINAS T.,ON THE GOVERNANCE OF RULERS (1265-66). UNIV SOCIETY STRATA FAM HABITAT PERSON ALL/VALS PWR SOVEREIGN CONSERVE...POLICY BIBLE. PAGE 8 H0155 CATH NAT/G CHIEF SUPEGO

B35
TAKEUCHI T.,WAR AND DIPLOMACY IN THE JAPANESE EMPIRE. ASIA ELITES STRATA NAT/G SECT LEGIS ACT/RES PLAN LEGIT PARL/PROC ROUTINE WAR...MGT BIOG CHINJAP TOT/POP 19/20 CHINJAP. PAGE 152 H3038 EXEC STRUCT

B36
BELLOC H.,THE RESTORATION OF PROPERTY. UK STRATA NAT/G PROF/ORG DELIB/GP WORKER CREATE PROB/SOLV ECO/TAC PARTIC UTOPIA ORD/FREE SOCISM 20. PAGE 13 H0270 CONTROL MAJORIT CAP/ISM OWN

B36
SMITH T.V.,THE PROMISE OF AMERICAN POLITICS. USA-45 WOR-45 LAW CONSTN STRATA PARTIC FASCISM LAISSEZ MARXISM...MAJORIT METH/COMP 18/20 JEFFERSN/T LOCKE/JOHN BENTHAM/J. PAGE 146 H2920 CONCPT ORD/FREE IDEA/COMP NAT/COMP

B37
TINGSTEN H.,POLITICAL BEHAVIOR. EUR+WWI STRATA NAT/G POL/PAR ACT/RES AGE...TREND CHARTS 20 FEMALE/SEX. PAGE 155 H3100 CHOOSE ATTIT PARTIC

B38
COUPLAND R.,EAST AFRICA AND ITS INVADERS. AFR ISLAM STRATA SECT FORCES DIPLOM TRIBUTE CONTROL DISCRIM NAT/LISM 19 AFRICA/E EUROPE MISSION. PAGE 34 H0680 CULTURE ELITES COLONIAL MARKET

B38
DAVIES E.,"NATIONAL" CAPITALISM: THE GOVERNMENT'S RECORD AS PROTECTOR OF PRIVATE MONOPOLY. UK ELITES SOCIETY STRATA POL/PAR WORKER PROB/SOLV CONTROL SOCISM 20 MONOPOLY LABOR/PAR CHAMBRLN/N. PAGE 37 H0747 CAP/ISM NAT/G INDUS POLICY

B38
FIELD G.L.,THE SYNDICAL AND CORPORATIVE INSTITUTIONS OF ITALIAN FASCISM. ITALY CONSTN STRATA LABOR EX/STRUC TOP/EX ADJUD ADMIN LEAD TOTALISM AUTHORIT...MGT 20 MUSSOLIN/B. PAGE 50 H0991 FASCISM INDUS NAT/G WORKER

B38
HEIMANN E.,COMMUNISM, FASCISM, OR DEMOCRACY? WOR-45 CONSTN SOCIETY STRATA AGRI CAP/ISM MORAL ORD/FREE ...MAJORIT METH/COMP NAT/COMP 19/20. PAGE 69 H1384 SOCISM MARXISM FASCISM PLURISM

B38
MARX K.,THE GERMAN IDEOLOGY, PARTS 1 AND 3 (1846). MOD/EUR LAW STRATA WORKER DOMIN REV UTOPIA SOCISM 19 MARX/KARL. PAGE 104 H2079 MARXIST OWN PRODUC ECO/TAC

B38
RAWLINSON H.G.,INDIA: A SHORT CULTURAL HISTORY. INDIA LAW STRATA FORCES INT/TRADE ADMIN COLONIAL PERSON...GEOG HUM BIBLIOG WORSHIP 20. PAGE 130 H2598 CULTURE SECT MYTH ART/METH

S38
MERTON R.K.,"SOCIAL STRUCTURE AND ANOMIE" (BMR)" UNIV CULTURE STRATA CREATE PARTIC ATTIT BIO/SOC PERSON...SOC CONCPT 20. PAGE 109 H2186 SOCIETY STRUCT ANOMIE DRIVE

B39
ENGELS F.,HERRN EUGEN DUHRING'S REVOLUTION IN SCIENCE (1878). CULTURE STRATA STRUCT FAM SECT ECO/TAC REV WAR SOCISM...MARXIST 19. PAGE 46 H0925 PWR SOCIETY WEALTH GEN/LAWS

S39
HECKSCHER G.,"GROUP ORGANIZATION IN SWEDEN." SWEDEN STRATA ECO/DEV AGRI INDUS LABOR NAT/G PROF/ORG ECO/TAC CENTRAL SOCISM...MGT 19/20. PAGE 69 H1382 LAISSEZ SOC

C39
BURKE E.,"ON THE REFORM OF THE REPRESENTATION IN THE HOUSE OF COMMONS" (1782) IN COLLECTED WORKS (VOL. 5)" UK ELITES STRATA NAT/G REPRESENT ORD/FREE PWR POPULISM...POLICY NEW/IDEA GEN/LAWS 18 BURKE/EDM. PAGE 24 H0486 TRADIT CONSTN PARL/PROC LEGIS

C39
REISCHAUER R.,"JAPAN'S GOVERNMENT--POLITICS." CONSTN STRATA POL/PAR FORCES LEGIS DIPLOM ADMIN EXEC CENTRAL...POLICY BIBLIOG 20 CHINJAP. PAGE 131 H2610 NAT/G S/ASIA CONCPT ROUTINE

B40
TONNIES F.,FUNDAMENTAL CONCEPTS OF SOCIOLOGY (1887) (TRANS. BY C. LOOMIS). LAW STRATA STRUCT FAM MUNIC NAT/G DOMIN LEGIT SANCTION COERCE CRIME PERSON 19. PAGE 156 H3115 CULTURE SOCIETY GEN/LAWS SOC

B40
ZWEIG F.,THE WORKER IN AN AFFLUENT SOCIETY: FAMILY LIFE AND INDUSTRY. UK STRATA LG/CO ECO/TAC LEISURE INGP/REL HAPPINESS HEALTH...PSY SOC/WK INT CHARTS WORSHIP 20 FEMALE/SEX. PAGE 173 H3465 MARRIAGF ATTIT FINAN CULTURE

S41
DENNERY E.,"DEMOCRACY AND THE FRENCH ARMY." FRANCE NAT/G EX/STRUC LEAD REV ROLE 18/20. PAGE 40 H0792 FORCES POPULISM STRATA CIVMIL/REL

B42
REDFIELD R.,THE FOLK CULTURE OF YUCATAN. STRATA FAM KIN MUNIC SECT DISCRIM ISOLAT ANOMIE HEALTH ...BIBLIOG 20 MEXIC/AMER. PAGE 130 H2605 CULTURE NEIGH GP/COMP SOCIETY

B44
GYORGY A.,GEOPOLITICS: THE NEW GERMAN SCIENCE. EUR+WWI GERMANY STRATA NAT/G PROVS DOMIN EDU/PROP ATTIT DRIVE FASCISM...GEOG NAZI 20. PAGE 63 H1261 PWR LEGIT WAR

B45
VENABLE V.,HUMAN NATURE: THE MARXIAN VIEW. UNIV STRATA CAP/ISM REV GP/REL PERS/REL PRODUC KNOWL ...PHIL/SCI CONCPT IDEA/COMP 19 MARX/KARL ENGELS/F. PAGE 162 H3240 PERSON MARXISM WORKER UTOPIA

B45
WARNER W.L.,THE SOCIAL SYSTEM OF AMERICAN ETHNIC GROUPS. STRATA FAM EDU/PROP ATTIT HABITAT RESPECT CLASSIF. PAGE 165 H3309 CULTURE VOL/ASSN SECT GP/COMP

B47
ISAAC J.,ECONOMICS OF MIGRATION. MOD/EUR CULTURE STRATA STRUCT NAT/G COLONIAL WEALTH...OLD/LIB TREND HABITAT SOC

TIME 19/20 EUROPE/W MIGRATION. PAGE 78 H1569
GEOG

B48
COX O.C.,CASTE, CLASS, AND RACE. INDIA WOR+45 WOR-45 SECT TEC/DEV MARRIAGE ROLE MARXISM...MAJORIT NAT/COMP SOC/INTEG 20 NEGRO HINDU. PAGE 34 H0688
RACE/REL STRUCT STRATA DISCRIM

B49
SAUVY A.,LE POUVOIR ET L'OPINION. FRANCE STRATA NAT/G PERCEPT...POLICY PSY 20. PAGE 138 H2758
EDU/PROP MYTH PARTIC ATTIT

S49
DEXTER L.A.,"A DIALOGUE ON THE SOCIAL PSYCHOLOGY OF COLONIALISM AND ON CERTAIN PUERTO RICAN PROFESSIONAL PERSONALITY PATTERNS." L/A+17C PUERT/RICO STRATA STRUCT DOMIN ISOLAT DRIVE ...NAT/COMP PERS/COMP HYPO/EXP 20 JEWS NEGRO. PAGE 41 H0813
COLONIAL SOC PSY PERSON

S49
HUGHES E.C.,"SOCIAL CHANGE AND STATUS PROTEST: AN ESSAY ON THE MARGINAL MAN" (BMR)" EUR+WWI UK USA+45 CULTURE SOCIETY STRUCT RACE/REL...SOC NAT/COMP SOC/INTEG 19/20 NEGRO PARK/R. PAGE 74 H1490
STRATA ATTIT DISCRIM

C49
SCHAPIRO J.S.,"LIBERALISM AND THE CHALLENGE OF FASCISM." FRANCE UK STRATA PERSON...CONCPT BIOG IDEA/COMP BIBLIOG 18/20. PAGE 139 H2771
FASCISM LAISSEZ ATTIT

C50
ROUSSEAU J.J.,"A DISCOURSE ON POLITICAL ECONOMY" (1755) IN THE SOCIAL CONTRACT AND DISCOURSES." UNIV SOCIETY STRATA STRUCT CONSEN EQUILIB HAPPINESS UTOPIA HEALTH WEALTH...POLICY WELF/ST. PAGE 135 H2699
NAT/G ECO/TAC TAX GEN/LAWS

B51
JENNINGS I.,THE COMMONWEALTH IN ASIA. CEYLON INDIA PAKISTAN CULTURE STRATA NAT/G LEGIS DIPLOM COLONIAL ATTIT...DECISION 20 CMN/WLTH. PAGE 80 H1604
CONSTN INT/ORG POLICY PLAN

B51
JENNINGS S.I.,THE COMMONWEALTH IN ASIA. CEYLON INDIA PAKISTAN S/ASIA UK CONSTN CULTURE SOCIETY STRATA STRUCT NAT/G POL/PAR EDU/PROP LEAD WAR 20 CMN/WLTH. PAGE 80 H1608
NAT/LISM REGION COLONIAL DIPLOM

B51
MARX K.,THE EIGHTEENTH BRUMAIRE OF LOUIS BONAPARTE (1852). FRANCE STRATA FINAN INDUS LABOR CHIEF FORCES WORKER CAP/ISM ECO/TAC PARL/PROC ORD/FREE ...MARXIST 19. PAGE 104 H2080
REV MARXISM ELITES NAT/G

B52
KROEBER A.L.,THE NATURE OF CULTURE. UNIV STRATA FAM KIN SECT...PSY GP/COMP 16/20 INDIAN/AM. PAGE 89 H1771
CULTURE SOCIETY CONCPT STRUCT

B52
LEVY M.,THE STRUCTURE OF SOCIETY. CULTURE STRATA DRIVE KNOWL...PSY CONCPT METH/CNCPT NEW/IDEA STYLE GEN/LAWS. PAGE 95 H1907
SOCIETY SOC

B53
BENDIX R.,CLASS, STATUS AND POWER: A READER IN SOCIAL STRATIFICATION. USA+45 SOCIETY ACT/RES DOMIN ATTIT RIGID/FLEX...PSY SOC CONCPT METH/COMP NAT/COMP 20. PAGE 14 H0273
STRATA PWR STRUCT ROLE

B53
LEITES N.,A STUDY OF BOLSHEVISM. ELITES STRATA INT/ORG LOC/G POL/PAR WORKER EDU/PROP REV TOTALISM UTOPIA PWR...CONCPT 20 BOLSHEVISM. PAGE 94 H1870
MARXISM PLAN COM

B53
LENZ F.,DIE BEWEGUNGEN DER GROSSEN MACHTE. USA+45 USA-45 USSR SOCIETY STRATA STRUCT NAT/G PERSON MARXISM...CONCPT IDEA/COMP NAT/COMP 18/20. PAGE 94 H1883
BAL/PWR TREND DIPLOM HIST/WRIT

B53
MEYER P.,THE JEWS IN THE SOVIET SATELLITES. CZECHOSLVK POLAND SOCIETY STRATA NAT/G BAL/PWR ECO/TAC EDU/PROP LEGIT ADMIN COERCE ATTIT DISPL PERCEPT HEALTH PWR RESPECT WEALTH...METH/CNCPT JEWS VAL/FREE NAZI 20. PAGE 110 H2192
COM SECT TOTALISM USSR

B53
MURPHY G.,IN THE MINDS OF MEN: THE STUDY OF HUMAN BEHAVIOR AND SOCIAL TENSIONS IN INDIA. FUT S/ASIA FAM INT/ORG NAT/G DIPLOM EDU/PROP GP/REL ATTIT RIGID/FLEX ALL/VALS...SOC QU UNESCO 20. PAGE 115 H2297
SECT STRATA INDIA

B53
WAGLEY C.,AMAZON TOWN: A STUDY OF MAN IN THE TROPICS. BRAZIL L/A+17C STRATA STRUCT ECO/UNDEV AGRI EX/STRUC RACE/REL DISCRIM HABITAT WEALTH...OBS SOC/EXP 20. PAGE 164 H3285
SOC NEIGH CULTURE INGP/REL

S53
ROGOFF N.,"SOCIAL STRATIFICATION IN FRANCE AND IN THE UNITED STATES" (BMR)" FRANCE USA+45 WORKER ADJUST PERSON...SOC 20. PAGE 133 H2662
STRUCT STRATA ATTIT NAT/COMP

B54
CAMPANELLA T.,A DISCOURSE TOUCHING THE SPANISH MONARCHY... (1640). SPAIN UNIV SEA STRATA FINAN SECT FORCES SUPEGO LOVE ORD/FREE...CONCPT 17. PAGE 26 H0514
CONSERVE CHIEF NAT/G DIPLOM

B54
LENIN V.I.,SELECTED WORKS (12 VOLS.). USSR INTELL SOCIETY STRATA STRUCT NAT/G POL/PAR WORKER CAP/ISM REV WAR...MARXIST PHIL/SCI 20 MARX/KARL LENIN/VI. PAGE 94 H1880
COM MARXISM

B54
MATTHEWS D.R.,THE SOCIAL BACKGROUND OF POLITICAL DECISION-MAKERS. CULTURE SOCIETY STRATA FAM EX/STRUC LEAD ATTIT BIO/SOC DRIVE PERSON ALL/VALS HIST/WRIT. PAGE 105 H2097
DECISION BIOG SOC

B54
TITIEV M.,THE SCIENCE OF MAN. LAW STRATA KIN GP/REL PERS/REL HABITAT HEREDITY KNOWL...LING CHARTS BIBLIOG WORSHIP. PAGE 155 H3107
SOC PSY CULTURE

S54
ALBRECT M.C.,"THE RELATIONSHIP OF LITERATURE AND SOCIETY." STRATA STRUCT DIPLOM...POLICY SOC/INTEG. PAGE 5 H0097
HUM CULTURE WRITING NAT/COMP

C54
DE GRAZIA A.,"THE COMPARATIVE SURVEY OF EUROPEAN-AMERICAN POLITICAL BEHAV IOR; A RESEARCH PROSPECTUS (PAPER)" EUR+WWI FRANCE GERMANY SPAIN UK USA+45 WOR+45 STRATA POL/PAR DIPLOM EDU/PROP COLONIAL LEAD WAR NAT/LISM CONCPT. PAGE 37 H0752
BIBLIOG R+D METH NAT/COMP

C54
GUINS G.C.,"SOVIET LAW AND SOVIET SOCIETY." COM USSR STRATA FAM NAT/G WORKER DOMIN RACE/REL ...BIBLIOG 20. PAGE 62 H1249
LAW STRUCT PLAN

B55
COLE G.D.H.,STUDIES IN CLASS STRUCTURE. UK NAT/G WORKER TEC/DEV EDU/PROP...CLASSIF CHARTS 20. PAGE 31 H0623
STRUCT STRATA ELITES CONCPT

B55
DUVERGER M.,THE POLITICAL ROLE OF WOMEN. FRANCE GERMANY/W NORWAY YUGOSLAVIA STRATA LOBBY AGE ATTIT ROLE...STAT SAMP CHARTS METH/COMP NAT/COMP HYPO/EXP FEMALE/SEX. PAGE 44 H0875
SEX LEAD PARTIC CHOOSE

B55
KHADDURI M.,WAR AND PEACE IN THE LAW OF ISLAM. CONSTN CULTURE SOCIETY STRATA NAT/G PROVS SECT FORCES TOP/EX CREATE DOMIN EDU/PROP ADJUD COERCE ATTIT RIGID/FLEX ALL/VALS...CONCPT TIME/SEQ TOT/POP VAL/FREE. PAGE 85 H1702
ISLAM JURID PEACE WAR

B55
MAYO H.B.,DEMOCRACY AND MARXISM. COM USSR STRATA NAT/G WORKER ECO/TAC REV MORAL...PHIL/SCI HIST/WRIT IDEA/COMP WORSHIP 20 MARX/KARL LENIN/VI STALIN/J TROTSKY/L. PAGE 105 H2108
MARXISM CAP/ISM

B55
UN ECONOMIC AND SOCIAL COUNCIL,ANALYTICAL BIBLIOGRAPHY OF INTERNATIONAL MIGRATION STATISTICS, SELECTED COUNTRIES, 1925-1950. STRATA...CLASSIF CENSUS NAT/COMP 20. PAGE 158 H3156
BIBLIOG STAT GEOG HABITAT

B55
VERGNAUD P.,L'IDEE DE LA NATIONALITE ET DE LA LIBRE DISPOSITION DES PEUPLES DANS SES RAPPORTS AVEC L'IDEE DE L'ETAT. STRATA NAT/G EDU/PROP RACE/REL AUTHORIT FASCISM MARXISM MYTH. PAGE 162 H3243
NAT/LISM DISCRIM ORD/FREE

B55
WRONG D.H.,AMERICAN AND CANADIAN VIEWPOINTS. CANADA USA+45 CONSTN STRATA FAM SECT WORKER ECO/TAC EDU/PROP ADJUD MARRIAGE...IDEA/COMP 20. PAGE 171 H3424
DIPLOM ATTIT NAT/COMP CULTURE

B56
SYKES G.M.,CRIME AND SOCIETY. LAW STRATA STRUCT ACT/RES ROUTINE ANOMIE WEALTH...POLICY SOC/INTEG 20. PAGE 151 H3021
CRIMLGY CRIME CULTURE INGP/REL

B56
WHITAKER A.P.,ARGENTINE UPHEAVAL. STRUCT FORCES DIPLOM COERCE PWR 20 ARGEN. PAGE 167 H3343
REV POL/PAR STRATA NAT/G

L56
EPSTEIN L.D.,"BRITISH MASS PARTIES IN COMPARISON WITH AMERICAN PARTIES" UK USA+45 STRATA ECO/DEV LABOR...CON/ANAL 20. PAGE 47 H0936
POL/PAR NAT/COMP PARTIC CHOOSE

S56
BLAU P.M.,"SOCIAL MOBILITY AND INTERPERSONAL RELATIONS" (BMR)" UNIV CULTURE STRUCT WORKER ANOMIE ...SOC SOC/INTEG 19/20. PAGE 18 H0355
INGP/REL PERS/REL ORD/FREE STRATA

B57
DEAN V.M.,THE NATURE OF THE NON-WESTERN WORLD. AFR ASIA L/A+17C S/ASIA CULTURE SOCIETY STRATA ECO/DEV DIPLOM ECO/TAC FOR/AID ATTIT DRIVE ALL/VALS ...RELATIV SOC CONCPT TIME/SEQ TREND TOT/POP 20. PAGE 39 H0778
ECO/UNDEV STERTYP NAT/LISM

B57
HAMMOND B.,BANKS AND POLITICS IN AMERICA FROM THE REVOLUTION TO THE CIVIL WAR. CANADA USA-45 STRATA
FINAN PWR

...NAT/COMP 18/19. PAGE 65 H1306 POL/PAR NAT/G

B57
HODGKIN T.,NATIONALISM IN COLONIAL AFRICA. STRATA STRUCT MUNIC NAT/G POL/PAR LEGIS ATTIT SOVEREIGN ...POLICY TREND BIBLIOG 20. PAGE 72 H1444 AFR COLONIAL NAT/LISM DIPLOM

B57
KOENTJARANINGRAT R.,A PRELIMINARY DESCRIPTION OF THE JAVANESE KINSHIP SYSTEM. INDONESIA STRATA FAM INGP/REL ADJUST MARRIAGE AGE/C AGE/Y AGE/A PERSON ...OBS CHARTS DICTIONARY 20 JAVA. PAGE 87 H1736 KIN STRUCT ELITES CULTURE

B57
LAQUER W.Z.,COMMUNISM AND NATIONALISM IN THE MIDDLE EAST. ELITES INTELL STRATA NAT/G POL/PAR SECT VOL/ASSN TOP/EX DOMIN LEGIT REGION COERCE ATTIT PERSON PWR...CONCPT HIST/WRIT TIME/SEQ TREND GEN/LAWS VAL/FREE. PAGE 91 H1817 ISLAM NAT/LISM

B57
MENDIETTA Y NUNE L.,THEORIE DES GROUPEMENT SOCIAUX SUIVI D'UNE ETUDE SUR LE DROIT SOCIAL. ELITES FAM KIN NAT/G PROB/SOLV CROWD ISOLAT ATTIT PERSON ...JURID CONCPT SOC/INTEG. PAGE 109 H2174 SOC STRATA STRUCT DISCRIM

B57
ROSS R.,THE FABRIC OF SOCIETY. STRATA GP/REL PERSON ...CONCPT METH T 20. PAGE 134 H2687 SOC PHIL/SCI CULTURE STRUCT

C57
WITTFOGEL K.A.,"ORIENTAL DESPOTISM: A COMPARATIVE STUDY OF TOTAL POWER." ASIA CULTURE STRATA NAT/G LEAD OWN ORD/FREE PWR...CONCPT TREND BIBLIOG 20. PAGE 170 H3393 TOTALISM HABITAT DOMIN ELITES

B58
BRIGGS L.C.,THE LIVING RACES OF THE SAHARA. STRATA AGRI KIN INT/TRADE HABITAT...GEOG AUD/VIS CHARTS BIBLIOG 20 SAHARA MIGRATION. PAGE 21 H0417 STRUCT SOCIETY SOC CULTURE

B58
JOHNSON J.J.,POLITICAL CHANGE IN LATIN AMERICA: THE EMERGENCE OF THE MIDDLE SECTORS. INTELL STRATA STRUCT ECO/UNDEV MUNIC TEC/DEV LEAD REV...DECISION TREND GOV/COMP BIBLIOG/A 20. PAGE 81 H1621 L/A+17C ELITES GP/REL DOMIN

B58
LERNER D.,THE PASSING OF TRADITIONAL SOCIETY: MODERNIZING THE MIDDLE EAST. IRAN ISLAM LEBANON SYRIA TURKEY UAR CULTURE INTELL STRATA KIN NAT/G NEIGH SECT EDU/PROP ATTIT PERSON...MYTH OBS 20. PAGE 95 H1888 ECO/UNDEV RIGID/FLEX

B58
TILLION G.,ALGERIA: THE REALITIES. ALGERIA FRANCE ISLAM CULTURE STRATA PROB/SOLV DOMIN REV NAT/LISM WEALTH MARXISM...GEOG 20. PAGE 155 H3094 ECO/UNDEV SOC COLONIAL DIPLOM

B58
VON FURER-HAIMEN E.,AN ANTHROPOLOGICAL BIBLIOGRAPHY OF SOUTH ASIA (VOL. I). STRATA STRUCT KIN SECT ACT/RES CREATE HABITAT...GEOG OBS 19/20. PAGE 163 H3267 BIBLIOG/A CULTURE S/ASIA SOC

S58
APTER D.E.,"A COMPARATIVE METHOD FOR THE STUDY OF POLITICS" (BMR)" UNIV SOCIETY STRATA NAT/G POL/PAR ...CHARTS SIMUL 20. PAGE 8 H0151 SOC METH METH/COMP

B59
BRIGGS A.,CHARTIST STUDIES. UK LAW NAT/G WORKER EDU/PROP COERCE SUFF GP/REL ATTIT...ANTHOL 19. PAGE 21 H0416 INDUS STRATA LABOR POLICY

B59
DUNHAM H.W.,SOCIOLOGICAL THEORY AND MENTAL DISORDER. UNIV SOCIETY STRATA HABITAT PERSON...GEOG CHARTS SOC/EXP TIME. PAGE 43 H0864 HEALTH SOC PSY CULTURE

B59
LIPSET S.M.,SOCIAL MOBILITY IN INDUSTRIAL SOCIETY. EUR+WWI USA+45 USSR STRUCT INDUS WRITING GP/REL INGP/REL DRIVE...SOC CHARTS NAT/COMP SOC/INTEG 20 MARX/KARL ENGELS/F. PAGE 97 H1940 STRATA ECO/DEV SOCIETY

B59
MADHOK B.,POLITICAL TRENDS IN INDIA. INDIA PAKISTAN UK STRATA ECO/UNDEV POL/PAR LEGIS CAP/ISM DIPLOM COLONIAL CHOOSE MARXISM...SOC TREND 20 GANDHI/M NEHRU/J. PAGE 101 H2014 GEOG NAT/G

B59
SVALASTOGA K.,PRESTIGE, CLASS, AND MOBILITY. DENMARK UK EDU/PROP INCOME WEALTH...SOC SAMP 20. PAGE 151 H3010 NAT/COMP STRATA STRUCT ELITES

B59
VINACKE H.M.,A HISTORY OF THE FAR EAST IN MODERN TIMES (6TH ED.). KOREA S/ASIA USSR CONSTN CULTURE STRATA ECO/UNDEV NAT/G CHIEF FOR/AID INT/TRADE GP/REL...SOC NAT/COMP 19/20 CHINJAP. PAGE 163 H3255 STRUCT ASIA

S59
DUNCAN O.D.,"CULTURAL, BEHAVIORAL, AND ECOLOGICAL PERSPECTIVES IN THE STUDY OF SOCIAL ORGANIZATION" (BMR)" UNIV STRATA EX/STRUC PROB/SOLV ADMIN ATTIT SOC/INTEG 20 BUREAUCRCY. PAGE 43 H0862 CULTURE METH/COMP SOCIETY HABITAT

C59
KORNHAUSER W.,"THE POLITICS OF MASS SOCIETY." COM CULTURE ELITES INTELL STRATA POL/PAR ATTIT...SOC CHARTS GEN/LAWS BIBLIOG 20. PAGE 88 H1757 CROWD PLURISM CONSTN SOCIETY

B60
BANERJEE D.N.,OUR FUNDAMENTAL RIGHTS: THEIR NATURE AND EXTENT (AS JUDICIALLY DETERMINED). INDIA UK CULTURE STRATA NAT/G WORKER EDU/PROP CONTROL DISCRIM OWN...IDEA/COMP WORSHIP 20 REFORMERS COMMONWLTH. PAGE 10 H0207 CONSTN ORD/FREE LEGIS POLICY

B60
BEATTIE J.,BUNYORO, AN AFRICAN KINGDOM. UGANDA STRATA INGP/REL PERS/REL...SOC BIBLIOG 19/20. PAGE 13 H0250 CULTURE ELITES SECT KIN

B60
BRIGGS L.C.,TRIBES OF THE SAHARA. AFR MOROCCO STRATA AGRI GP/REL HEALTH...GEOG SOC MYTH LING BIBLIOG 13/20 ARABS. PAGE 21 H0418 CULTURE HABITAT KIN SELF/OBS

B60
CARTER G.M.,INDEPENDENCE FOR AFRICA. AFR FUT SOCIETY STRATA ECO/DEV POL/PAR DELIB/GP PLAN DOMIN EDU/PROP COLONIAL REGION ATTIT DRIVE SOVEREIGN ...RECORD INT TIME/SEQ CHARTS 20. PAGE 27 H0544 NAT/G PWR NAT/LISM

B60
HARRISON S.S.,INDIA: THE MOST DANGEROUS DECADES. INDIA CONSTN STRATA POL/PAR SECT PLAN ADMIN CHOOSE GP/REL TOTALISM MARXISM...LING 20 NEHRU/J. PAGE 67 H1347 CULTURE ECO/UNDEV PROB/SOLV REGION

B60
JEMOLO A.C.,CHURCH AND STATE IN ITALY 1850-1950 (TRANS. BY DAVID MOORE). ITALY CONSTN STRATA WAR FASCISM SOCISM...TIME/SEQ 19/20 CHURCH/STA CHRIS/DEM. PAGE 80 H1599 GP/REL NAT/G CATHISM POL/PAR

B60
MANIS J.G.,MAN AND SOCIETY. STRATA LEAD INGP/REL PERS/REL ATTIT PWR...PSY ANTHOL T SOC/INTEG MARX/KARL MILL/JS FREUD/S CHURCHLL/W SPENCER/H RUSSELL/B. PAGE 102 H2036 SOC SOCIETY STRUCT CULTURE

B60
MC CLELLAN G.S.,INDIA. CHINA/COM INDIA CONSTN ELITES STRATA AGRI POL/PAR FOR/AID ARMS/CONT REV MARXISM...CENSUS BIBLIOG 20 COLD/WAR GANDHI/M NEHRU/J. PAGE 106 H2117 DIPLOM NAT/G SOCIETY ECO/UNDEV

B60
MOORE W.E.,LABOR COMMITMENT AND SOCIAL CHANGE IN DEVELOPING AREAS. SOCIETY STRATA ECO/UNDEV MARKET VOL/ASSN WORKER AUTHORIT SKILL...MGT NAT/COMP SOC/INTEG 20. PAGE 113 H2250 LABOR ORD/FREE ATTIT INDUS

B60
NICHOLLS W.H.,SOUTHERN TRADITION AND REGIONAL PROGRESS. STRATA STRUCT SCHOOL WORKER PARTIC REGION RACE/REL CONSEN ATTIT...SOC METH/CNCPT 19/20 SOUTH/US TVA. PAGE 118 H2349 RIGID/FLEX CONSERVE AGRI CULTURE

B60
PETERSON W.C.,THE WELFARE STATE IN FRANCE. EUR+WWI FRANCE FUT STRATA PROB/SOLV TAX GIVE RECEIVE INCOME ORD/FREE PWR...CHARTS 20. PAGE 125 H2496 NEW/LIB ECO/TAC WEALTH NAT/G

B60
SCHAPIRO L.,THE COMMUNIST PARTY OF THE SOVIET UNION. COM LAW SOCIETY STRATA STRUCT ECO/DEV LABOR NAT/G POL/PAR CREATE DOMIN EDU/PROP COERCE TOTALISM MARXISM...POLICY CONCPT MYTH TIME/SEQ WORK TOT/POP 20 LENIN/VI STALIN/J. PAGE 139 H2772 INTELL PWR USSR

B60
WOLF C.,FOREIGN AID: THEORY AND PRACTICE IN SOUTHERN ASIA. CEYLON INDONESIA PHILIPPINE S/ASIA CULTURE STRATA ECO/UNDEV PLAN EDU/PROP ATTIT ...METH/CNCPT MATH QUANT STAT CONT/OBS TIME/SEQ SIMUL TOT/POP 20. PAGE 170 H3396 ACT/RES ECO/TAC FOR/AID

S60
"THE EMERGING COMMON MARKETS IN LATIN AMERICA." FUT L/A+17C STRATA DIST/IND INDUS LABOR NAT/G LEGIS ECO/TAC ADMIN RIGID/FLEX HEALTH...NEW/IDEA TIME/SEQ OAS 20. PAGE 2 H0038 FINAN ECO/UNDEV INT/TRADE

S60
ARENDT H.,"SOCIETY AND CULTURE." FUT CULTURE INTELL STRATA EDU/PROP ATTIT PERSON KNOWL...ART/METH HUM 20. PAGE 8 H0161 SOCIETY CREATE

S60
BERREMAN G.D.,"CASTE IN INDIA AND THE UNITED STATES" (BMR)" INDIA USA+45 CULTURE SOCIETY STRUCT SECT GP/REL DISCRIM HEREDITY...SOC STERTYP 20 NEGRO HINDU. PAGE 16 H0318 STRATA RACE/REL NAT/COMP ATTIT

S60
BRZEZINSKI Z.K.,"PATTERNS AND LIMITS OF THE SINO-SOVIET DISPUTE." ASIA CHINA/COM COM FUT STRATA NAT/G EX/STRUC FORCES BAL/PWR DIPLOM ECO/TAC DOMIN EDU/PROP ADMIN COERCE WAR ATTIT RIGID/FLEX ...GEN/LAWS VAL/FREE 20. PAGE 23 H0459 POL/PAR PWR REV USSR

S60
GROSSMAN G.,"SOVIET GROWTH: ROUTINE, INERTIA, AND PRESSURE." COM STRATA NAT/G DELIB/GP PLAN TEC/DEV ECO/TAC EDU/PROP ADMIN ROUTINE DRIVE WEALTH COLD/WAR 20. PAGE 62 H1236
POL/PAR ECO/DEV USSR

S60
TIRYAKIAN E.A.,"APARTHEID AND POLITICS IN SOUTH AFRICA." SOUTH/AFR CULTURE STRATA ECO/DEV NAT/G POL/PAR ROUTINE CHOOSE GP/REL RACE/REL DISCRIM ATTIT ALL/VALS...CONCPT OBS TIME/SEQ VAL/FREE 20. PAGE 155 H3105
AFR DIPLOM

S60
TURNER R.H.,"SPONSORED AND CONTEST MOBILITY IN THE SCHOOL SYSTEM." UK USA+45 ELITES STRATA ACADEM FACE/GP EDU/PROP CONTROL INGP/REL ADJUST ATTIT PERSON...METH/COMP 20. PAGE 157 H3142
AGE/Y NAT/COMP SCHOOL STRUCT

B61
BROWN D.M.,THE NATIONALIST MOVEMENT. INDIA CULTURE STRATA REV MORAL ORD/FREE...BIBLIOG 20 HINDU. PAGE 22 H0443
NAT/LISM LEAD CHIEF POL/PAR

B61
CHAKRABARTI A.,NEHRU: HIS DEMOCRACY AND INDIA. ASIA INDIA UK CONSTN ECO/UNDEV SECT DIPLOM COLONIAL PEACE WEALTH...BIBLIOG 20 CONGRESS NEHRU/J GANDHI/M. PAGE 28 H0570
ORD/FREE STRATA NAT/G CHIEF

B61
DELEFORTRIE-SOU N.,LES DIRIGEANTS DE L'INDUSTRIE FRANCAISE. FRANCE CULTURE ELITES PROB/SOLV ...DECISION STAT CHARTS 20. PAGE 39 H0789
INDUS STRATA TOP/EX LEAD

B61
ETZIONI A.,COMPLEX ORGANIZATIONS: A SOCIOLOGICAL READER. CLIENT CULTURE STRATA CREATE OP/RES ADMIN ...POLICY METH/CNCPT BUREAUCRCY. PAGE 47 H0945
VOL/ASSN STRUCT CLASSIF PROF/ORG

B61
FIRTH R.,ELEMENTS OF SOCIAL ORGANIZATION (3RD ED.). STRATA STRUCT ECO/UNDEV NEIGH CHIEF INGP/REL ATTIT MORAL...PHIL/SCI GP/COMP WORSHIP SOC/INTEG 20. PAGE 50 H1009
SOC CULTURE SOCIETY KIN

B61
HADDAD J.A.,REVOLUCAO CUBANA E REVOLUCAO BRASILEIRA. BRAZIL CUBA L/A+17C STRATA AGRI WORKER EDU/PROP REGION...POLICY NAT/COMP 20. PAGE 63 H1272
REV ORD/FREE DIPLOM ECO/UNDEV

B61
HUNT E.F.,SOCIAL SCIENCE. DIPLOM ECO/TAC ROUTINE GP/REL DEMAND DISCRIM EFFICIENCY HABITAT ALL/IDEOS ...SOC T 20. PAGE 75 H1497
CULTURE ADJUST STRATA ROLE

B61
JUSTICE,THE CITIZEN AND THE ADMINISTRATION: THE REDRESS OF GRIEVANCES (PAMPHLET). EUR+WWI UK LAW CONSTN STRATA NAT/G CT/SYS PARTIC COERCE...NEW/IDEA IDEA/COMP 20 OMBUDSMAN. PAGE 82 H1644
INGP/REL CONSULT ADJUD REPRESENT

B61
MARVICK D.,POLITICAL DECISION-MAKERS. INTELL STRATA NAT/G POL/PAR EX/STRUC LEGIS DOMIN EDU/PROP ATTIT PERSON PWR...PSY STAT OBS CONT/OBS STAND/INT UNPLAN/INT TIME/SEQ CHARTS STERTYP VAL/FREE. PAGE 104 H2073
TOP/EX BIOG ELITES

B61
SOUTHALL A.,SOCIAL CHANGE IN MODERN AFRICA. CULTURE STRATA ECO/UNDEV AGRI FAM KIN MUNIC GP/REL INGP/REL MARRIAGE...GEOG ANTHOL 20. PAGE 147 H2940
AFR TREND SOCIETY SOC

B61
WARD R.E.,JAPANESE POLITICAL SCIENCE: A GUIDE TO JAPANESE REFERENCE AND RESEARCH MATERIALS (2ND ED.). LAW CONSTN STRATA NAT/G POL/PAR DELIB/GP LEGIS ADMIN CHOOSE GP/REL...INT/LAW 19/20 CHINJAP. PAGE 165 H3306
BIBLIOG/A PHIL/SCI

S61
DOGAN M.,"LES OFFICIERS DANS LA CARRIERE POLITIQUE DE MARECHAL MACMAHON AU GENERAL DE GAULLE." EUR+WWI FRANCE MOD/EUR ELITES STRATA POL/PAR LEGIT ATTIT ALL/VALS...SOC CONCPT 19/20. PAGE 42 H0833
PROF/ORG FORCES NAT/G DELIB/GP

S61
ELAZAR D.J.,"CHURCHES AS MOLDERS OF AMERICAN POLITICS." STRATA MUNIC EDU/PROP RACE/REL ORD/FREE SOC. PAGE 45 H0904
SECT CULTURE REPRESENT LOC/G

S61
SCHECHTMAN J.B.,"MINORITIES IN THE MIDDLE EAST." ISLAM INTELL SOCIETY STRATA KIN NAT/G VOL/ASSN EDU/PROP REGION GP/REL DISCRIM ATTIT BIO/SOC DISPL PERSON ALL/VALS...PSY SOC OBS SAMP GEN/LAWS 20. PAGE 139 H2776
SECT CULTURE RACE/REL

B62
ABRAHAM W.E.,THE MIND OF AFRICA. AFR SOCIETY STRATA KIN ECO/TAC DOMIN EDU/PROP LEGIT COERCE ATTIT ALL/VALS...MAJORIT SOC OBS HIST/WRIT TIME/SEQ TREND TOT/POP 20. PAGE 3 H0058
CULTURE SIMUL GHANA

B62
BELL D.,THE END OF IDEOLOGY (REV. ED.). USA+45 USA-45 ELITES STRATA LABOR CREATE CRIME PWR MARXISM ...PHIL/SCI METH/COMP 20 EUROPE. PAGE 13 H0265
CROWD CAP/ISM SOCISM IDEA/COMP

B62
DEBUYST F.,LAS CLASES SOCIALES EN AMERICA LATINA. L/A+17C SOCIETY STRUCT WORKER EDU/PROP RACE/REL ATTIT HABITAT ROLE...GEOG SOC NAT/COMP SOC/INTEG 20. PAGE 39 H0780
STRATA GP/REL WEALTH

B62
ESCUELA SUPERIOR DE ADMIN PUBL,INFORME DEL SEMINARIO SOBRE SERVICIO CIVIL O CARRERA ADMINISTRATIVA. L/A+17C ELITES STRATA CONFER CONTROL GOV/REL INGP/REL SUPEGO 20 CENTRAL/AM CIVIL/SERV. PAGE 47 H0939
ADMIN NAT/G PROB/SOLV ATTIT

B62
FALKENBERG J.,KIN AND TOTEM; GROUP RELATIONS OF AUSTRALIAN ABORIGINES IN THE PORT KEATS DISTRICT. SOCIETY STRATA STRUCT GP/REL PERS/REL MARRIAGE AGE ATTIT SEX...SOC STAT CHARTS AUSTRAL ABORIGINES. PAGE 48 H0964
KIN INGP/REL CULTURE FAM

B62
FEIT E.,SOUTH AFRICA, THE DYNAMICS OF THE AFRICAN NATIONAL CONGRESS. AFR SOUTH/AFR LAW INTELL STRATA KIN NAT/G POL/PAR ECO/TAC DOMIN RISK COERCE 20 NEGRO. PAGE 49 H0984
RACE/REL ELITES CONTROL STRUCT

B62
HATCH J.,AFRICA TODAY-AND TOMORROW: AN OUTLINE OF BASIC FACTS AND MAJOR PROBLEMS. AFR FUT ISLAM STRATA ECO/UNDEV INT/ORG NAT/G POL/PAR DELIB/GP TOP/EX EDU/PROP LEGIT CHOOSE ATTIT...TIME/SEQ TOT/POP COLD/WAR 20. PAGE 67 H1353
PLAN CONSTN NAT/LISM

B62
HAY S.N.,SOUTHEAST ASIAN HISTORY: A BIBLIOGRAPHICAL GUIDE. STRATA KIN NAT/G REGION GUERRILLA REV WAR ADJUST HABITAT PERCEPT ALL/IDEOS...CHARTS 5/20. PAGE 68 H1365
BIBLIOG/A S/ASIA CULTURE

B62
HO PING-TI,THE LADDER OF SUCCESS IN IMPERIAL CHINA: ASPECTS OF SOCIAL MOBILITY, 1368-1911. INTELL STRATA FAM KIN MUNIC NAT/G PROVS SCHOOL DELIB/GP DOMIN EDU/PROP ADMIN ROUTINE PERSON ALL/VALS...SOC STAT BIOG HIST/WRIT TIME/SEQ VAL/FREE. PAGE 71 H1431
ASIA CULTURE

B62
MELADY T.,THE WHITE MAN'S FUTURE IN BLACK AFRICA. FUT CULTURE SOCIETY NAT/G POL/PAR PLAN ECO/TAC DOMIN EDU/PROP LEGIT COLONIAL RACE/REL ATTIT DRIVE ALL/VALS...PSY SOC CONCPT TIME/SEQ TOT/POP VAL/FREE 20. PAGE 108 H2167
AFR STRATA ELITES

B62
RUDE G.,WILKES AND LIBERTY. UK NAT/G POL/PAR REPRESENT ORD/FREE...SOC 18. PAGE 136 H2711
PARL/PROC CHOOSE STRATA STRUCT

B62
SELOSOEMARDJAN O.,SOCIAL CHANGES IN JOGJAKARTA. INDONESIA NETHERLAND ELITES STRATA STRUCT FAM POL/PAR CREATE DIPLOM INT/TRADE EDU/PROP ADMIN GOV/REL...SOC 20 JAVA CHINJAP. PAGE 141 H2825
ECO/UNDEV CULTURE REV COLONIAL

B62
SILBERMAN B.S.,JAPAN AND KOREA; A CRITICAL BIBLIOGRAPHY. KOREA LAW STRATA STRUCT AGRI INDUS NAT/G POL/PAR SECT...HUM LING IDEA/COMP 5/20 CHINJAP. PAGE 144 H2872
BIBLIOG/A CULTURE S/ASIA

B62
SMITH M.G.,KINSHIP AND COMMUNITY IN CARRIACOU. WEST/IND STRATA AGRI FAM SECT WORKER MARRIAGE OWN HEREDITY WEALTH...SOC 18/20. PAGE 146 H2915
CULTURE HABITAT KIN STRUCT

B62
TINKER H.,INDIA AND PAKISTAN. INDIA PAKISTAN NAT/G POL/PAR...OLD/LIB TRADIT TREND CHARTS BIBLIOG 20. PAGE 155 H3102
ORD/FREE STRATA REPRESENT AUTHORIT

B62
ZINKIN T.,REPORTING INDIA. INDIA PAKISTAN WOR+45 SOCIETY SECT FORCES EDU/PROP CROWD DISCRIM NAT/LISM MARXISM...POLICY 20. PAGE 173 H3457
STRATA COLONIAL BAL/PWR CONTROL

L62
COHEN R.,"POWER IN COMPLEX SOCIETIES IN AFRICA." AFR KIN MUNIC POL/PAR DELIB/GP DOMIN ROUTINE ATTIT ALL/VALS...SOC STAT OBS INT QU CHARTS ANTHOL 20. PAGE 31 H0617
CULTURE STRATA ELITES

L62
ORDONNEAU P.,"LES PROBLEMES POSES PAR L'INDEPENDANCE DES NOUVEAUX ETATS AFRICAINS ET MALGACHE SUR LE PLAN DU CONTENTIEUX." FRANCE ISLAM MADAGASCAR LAW STRATA ECO/UNDEV NAT/G LEGIS LEGIT ...JURID TIME/SEQ 20. PAGE 121 H2425
AFR ADJUD COLONIAL SOVEREIGN

S62
BELL W.,"EQUALITY AND ATTITUDES OF ELITES IN JAMAICA" L/A+17C STRATA PWR WEALTH...SOC QU TREND. PAGE 13 H0266
ELITES FUT SOCIETY CULTURE

S62
FESLER J.W.,"FRENCH FIELD ADMINISTRATION: THE BEGINNINGS." CHRIST-17C CULTURE SOCIETY STRATA NAT/G ECO/TAC DOMIN EDU/PROP LEGIT ADJUD COERCE ATTIT ALL/VALS...TIME/SEQ CON/ANAL GEN/METH VAL/FREE 13/15. PAGE 49 H0988 EX/STRUC FRANCE

S62
IOVTCHOUK M.T.,"ON SOME THEORETICAL PRINCIPLES AND METHODS OF SOCIOLOGICAL INVESTIGATIONS (IN RUSSIAN)." FUT USA+45 STRATA R+D NAT/G POL/PAR TOP/EX ACT/RES PLAN ECO/TAC EDU/PROP ROUTINE ATTIT RIGID/FLEX MARXISM SOCISM...MARXIST METH/CNCPT OBS TREND NAT/COMP GEN/LAWS 20. PAGE 78 H1564 COM ECO/DEV CAP/ISM USSR

B63
BARNETT A.D.,COMMUNIST STRATEGIES IN ASIA: A COMPARATIVE ANALYSIS OF GOVERNMENTS AND PARTIES. COM FUT S/ASIA CULTURE SOCIETY STRATA NAT/G DELIB/GP ACT/RES ECO/TAC EDU/PROP COERCE CHOOSE ATTIT RIGID/FLEX ORD/FREE PWR SKILL...SIMUL VAL/FREE 20. PAGE 11 H0223 ASIA POL/PAR DIPLOM USSR

B63
BERREMAN G.D.,HINDUS OF THE HIMALAYAS. INDIA STRATA STRUCT KIN MUNIC 20 HINDU. PAGE 16 H0319 CULTURE SECT GP/REL ECO/UNDEV

B63
BIDNEY D.,THE CONCEPT OF FREEDOM IN ANTHROPOLOGY. UNIV CULTURE STRATA SECT CREATE NAT/LISM ...METH/COMP 20. PAGE 17 H0332 SOC PERSON ORD/FREE CONCPT

B63
BLONDEL J.,VOTERS, PARTIES, AND LEADERS. UK ELITES LOC/G NAT/G PROVS ACT/RES DOMIN REPRESENT GP/REL INGP/REL...SOC BIBLIOG 20. PAGE 18 H0358 POL/PAR STRATA LEGIS ADMIN

B63
BORKENAU F.,THE SPANISH COCKPIT. SPAIN ELITES STRATA POL/PAR ACT/RES CROWD WAR GP/REL INGP/REL ...SOC NAT/COMP 20. PAGE 19 H0377 REV CONSERVE SOCISM FORCES

B63
CARTER G.M.,FIVE AFRICAN STATES: RESPONSES TO DIVERSITY. CONSTN CULTURE STRATA LEGIS PLAN ECO/TAC DOMIN EDU/PROP CT/SYS EXEC CHOOSE ATTIT HEALTH ORD/FREE PWR...TIME/SEQ TOT/POP VAL/FREE. PAGE 27 H0547 AFR SOCIETY

B63
CREMEANS C.,THE ARABS AND THE WORLD: NASSER'S ARAB NATIONALIST POLICY. FUT ISLAM UAR USA+45 SOCIETY STRATA NAT/G POL/PAR PLAN DIPLOM EDU/PROP LEGIT DRIVE ALL/VALS...INT TIME/SEQ CHARTS 20 NASSER/G. PAGE 35 H0700 TOP/EX ATTIT REGION NAT/LISM

B63
DE VRIES E.,SOCIAL ASPECTS OF ECONOMIC DEVELOPMENT IN LATIN AMERICA. CULTURE SOCIETY STRATA FINAN INDUS INT/ORG DELIB/GP ACT/RES ECO/TAC EDU/PROP ADMIN ATTIT SUPEGO HEALTH KNOWL ORD/FREE...SOC STAT TREND ANTHOL TOT/POP VAL/FREE. PAGE 39 H0777 L/A+17C ECO/UNDEV

B63
FRIED R.C.,THE ITALIAN PREFECTS. ITALY STRATA ECO/DEV NAT/LISM ALL/IDEOS...TREND CHARTS METH/COMP BIBLIOG 17/20 PREFECT. PAGE 53 H1061 ADMIN NAT/G EFFICIENCY

B63
GEERTZ C.,PEDDLERS AND PRINCES: SOCIAL DEVELOPMENT AND ECONOMIC CHANGE IN TWO INDONESIAN TOWNS. S/ASIA CULTURE SOCIETY STRATA FACE/GP MUNIC CREATE TEC/DEV ECO/TAC ORD/FREE WEALTH...OBS INT CENSUS CHARTS WORK TOT/POP VAL/FREE 20. PAGE 55 H1106 ECO/UNDEV SOC ELITES INDONESIA

B63
GLUCKMAN M.,ORDER AND REBELLION IN TRIBAL AFRICA. EUR+WWI LAW CULTURE STRATA KIN MUNIC DELIB/GP ACT/RES DOMIN EDU/PROP LEGIT ADMIN COERCE CHOOSE ATTIT PERSON ORD/FREE PWR...SOC CHARTS GEN/LAWS TOT/POP VAL/FREE. PAGE 57 H1147 AFR SOCIETY

B63
KATEB G.,UTOPIA AND ITS ENEMIES. CULTURE STRATA ECO/DEV INDUS REV MORAL...PSY IDEA/COMP 19/20. PAGE 84 H1668 UTOPIA SOCIETY PHIL/SCI PEACE

B63
LAMB B.P.,INDIA: A WORLD IN TRANSITION. INDIA ECO/UNDEV SECT EDU/PROP COLONIAL HABITAT ORD/FREE ...GEOG CHARTS BIBLIOG SOC/INTEG 20. PAGE 90 H1799 POL/PAR NAT/G DIPLOM STRATA

B63
MAJUMDAR O.N.,AN INTRODUCTION TO SOCIAL ANTHROPOLOGY. INDIA LAW STRATA ECO/UNDEV KIN DEMAND MARRIAGE...GP/COMP BIBLIOG T WORSHIP 20. PAGE 101 H2026 SOC CULTURE STRUCT GP/REL

B63
MARX K.,THE POVERTY OF PHILOSOPHY (1847). SOCIETY STRATA INDUS WORKER OWN UTOPIA SOCISM...GEN/LAWS MARX/KARL. PAGE 104 H2082 MARXIST PRODUC

B63
MONTAGUE J.B. JR.,CLASS AND NATIONALITY; ENGLISH AND AMERICAN STUDIES. UK USA+45 ELITES STRUCT WORKER ATTIT PWR...SOC CHARTS SOC/EXP 20. PAGE 112 H2243 STRATA NAT/LISM PERSON NAT/COMP

B63
SCHECHTMAN J.B.,THE REFUGEE IN THE WORLD: DISPLACEMENT AND INTEGRATION. AFR ASIA EUR+WWI ISLAM L/A+17C S/ASIA CULTURE STRATA LOC/G EX/STRUC PLAN ECO/TAC ROUTINE...CONCPT TIME/SEQ VAL/FREE 20. PAGE 139 H2779 INT/ORG SOC

B63
SILVERT K.H.,EXPECTANT PEOPLES: NATIONALISM AND DEVELOPMENT. CULTURE STRATA SECT LEAD REGION RACE/REL ALL/IDEOS...GEN/LAWS SOC/INTEG 20. PAGE 144 H2877 NAT/LISM ECO/UNDEV ALL/VALS

B63
SKLAR R.L.,NIGERIAN POLITICAL PARTIES: POWER IN AN EMERGENT AFRICAN NATION. AFR EUR+WWI CULTURE STRATA NAT/G DELIB/GP EX/STRUC LEGIS DOMIN EDU/PROP ROUTINE CHOOSE ATTIT PERCEPT ORD/FREE PWR...SOC CONCPT OBS TOT/POP VAL/FREE. PAGE 145 H2898 POL/PAR SOCIETY NAT/LISM NIGERIA

B63
SPRING D.,THE ENGLISH LANDED ESTATE IN THE NINETEENTH CENTURY: ITS ADMINISTRATION. UK ELITES STRUCT AGRI NAT/G GP/REL OWN PWR WEALTH...BIBLIOG 19 HOUSE/LORD. PAGE 148 H2954 STRATA PERS/REL MGT

B63
THOMPSON F.M.L.,ENGLISH LANDED SOCIETY IN THE NINETEENTH CENTURY. UK STRUCT MUNIC NAT/G CONTROL WAR GP/REL OWN WEALTH...BIBLIOG 18/20. PAGE 154 H3081 STRATA PWR ELITES GOV/REL

B63
WAGLEY C.,INTRODUCTION TO BRAZIL. BRAZIL L/A+17C FAM KIN SCHOOL SECT ATTIT WEALTH...GEOG SOC. PAGE 164 H3286 ECO/UNDEV ELITES HABITAT STRATA

S63
BILL J.A.,"THE SOCIAL AND ECONOMIC FOUNDATIONS OF POWER IN CONTEMPORARY IRAN." ISLAM CULTURE NAT/G ECO/TAC DOMIN COERCE ATTIT PWR WEALTH...TREND VAL/FREE 20. PAGE 17 H0334 SOCIETY STRATA IRAN

S63
DUDLEY B.J.,"THE NOMINATION OF PARLIAMENTARY CANDIDATES IN NORTHERN NIGERIA." AFR CONSTN CULTURE ELITES STRATA DELIB/GP LEGIS DOMIN EDU/PROP COERCE ATTIT SUPEGO PWR...STAT VAL/FREE 20. PAGE 43 H0854 POL/PAR CHOOSE NIGERIA

S63
GLUCKMAN M.,"CIVIL WAR AND THEORIES OF POWER IN BAROTSE-LAND: AFRICAN AND MEDIEVAL ANALOGIES." AFR CHRIST-17C LAW CONSTN CULTURE STRATA KIN DELIB/GP FORCES DOMIN LEGIT COERCE PERCEPT ORD/FREE...SOC INT TIME/SEQ GEN/LAWS VAL/FREE. PAGE 57 H1148 TOP/EX PWR WAR

S63
HALPERN A.M.,"THE EMERGENCE OF AN ASIAN COMMUNIST BLOC." ASIA CHINA/COM COM FUT KOREA/N S/ASIA VIETNAM/N STRATA NAT/G DELIB/GP FORCES TOP/EX PLAN BAL/PWR COERCE DETER PWR COLD/WAR WORK 20. PAGE 65 H1295 POL/PAR EDU/PROP DIPLOM

S63
HARRIS R.L.,"A COMPARATIVE ANALYSIS OF THE ADMINISTRATIVE SYSTEMS OF CANADA AND CEYLON." S/ASIA CULTURE SOCIETY STRATA TOP/EX ACT/RES DOMIN EDU/PROP LEGIT COERCE ATTIT SUPEGO ALL/VALS...MGT CHARTS GEN/LAWS VAL/FREE 20. PAGE 67 H1343 DELIB/GP EX/STRUC CANADA CEYLON

S63
LEE J.M.,"PARLIAMENT IN REPUBLICAN GHANA." AFR CONSTN CULTURE SOCIETY STRATA POL/PAR DELIB/GP TOP/EX DOMIN EDU/PROP LEGIT COERCE CHOOSE ATTIT ALL/VALS...CONCPT STAT TIME/SEQ VAL/FREE 20. PAGE 93 H1857 LEGIS GHANA

S63
NICHOLAS W.,"VILLAGE FACTIONS AND POLITICAL PARTIES IN RURAL WEST BENGAL." S/ASIA CULTURE STRATA FACE/GP KIN MUNIC DELIB/GP LEGIS DOMIN EDU/PROP COERCE CHOOSE ATTIT ALL/VALS...STAT TOT/POP VAL/FREE 20. PAGE 117 H2348 NEIGH POL/PAR

B64
BAUCHET P.,ECONOMIC PLANNING. FRANCE STRATA LG/CO CAP/ISM ADMIN PARL/PROC DEMAND OPTIMAL ATTIT PWR SOCISM...POLICY CHARTS 20. PAGE 12 H0238 ECO/DEV NAT/G PLAN ECO/TAC

B64
DOOLIN D.J.,COMMUNIST CHINA: THE POLITICS OF STUDENT OPPOSITION. CHINA/COM ELITES STRATA ACADEM NAT/G WRITING CT/SYS LEAD PARTIC COERCE TOTALISM 20. PAGE 42 H0838 MARXISM DEBATE AGE/Y PWR

B64
GUMPLOWICZ L.,RECHTSSTAAT UND SOZIALISMUS. STRATA ORD/FREE SOVEREIGN MARXISM...IDEA/COMP 16/20 KANT/I HOBBES/T. PAGE 62 H1251 JURID NAT/G SOCISM CONCPT

B64
HALPERN J.M.,GOVERNMENT, POLITICS, AND SOCIAL STRUCTURE IN LAOS. LAOS CULTURE SOCIETY STRATA STRUCT FAM DIPLOM DOMIN MARXISM...INT GOV/COMP WORSHIP SOC/INTEG 20. PAGE 65 H1297 NAT/G SOC LOC/G

B64
HARRIS M.,PATTERNS OF RACE IN THE AMERICAS. BRAZIL STRUCT

L/A+17C STRATA ECO/UNDEV AGRI KIN MUNIC SECT COLONIAL RACE/REL...SOC SOC/INTEG 17/20 NEGRO INDIAN/AM. PAGE 67 H1342 PRE/AMER CULTURE SOCIETY

B64
HEIMSATH C.H.,INDIAN NATIONALISM AND HINDU SOCIAL REFORM. S/ASIA LAW CULTURE SOCIETY STRATA PROVS VOL/ASSN DELIB/GP LEGIS TOP/EX DOMIN EDU/PROP LEGIT ATTIT ALL/VALS...POLICY SOC TIME/SEQ STERTYP VAL/FREE 19/20. PAGE 69 H1385 SECT NAT/G

B64
HORNE D.,THE LUCKY COUNTRY: AUSTRALIA TODAY. UK CULTURE STRATA ATTIT PWR PLURISM...GOV/COMP 20 AUSTRAL. PAGE 73 H1471 RACE/REL DIPLOM NAT/G STRUCT

B64
HOROWITZ I.L.,REVOLUTION IN BRAZIL. BRAZIL L/A+17C ELITES STRATA NAT/G BAL/PWR PARTIC ATTIT 20. PAGE 74 H1473 ECO/UNDEV DIPLOM POLICY ORD/FREE

B64
JOHNSON J.J.,CONTINUITY AND CHANGE IN LATIN AMERICA. L/A+17C INTELL FORCES WORKER CIVMIL/REL CHINJAP. PAGE 81 H1623 ANTHOL CULTURE STRATA GP/COMP

B64
LAPENNA I.,STATE AND LAW: SOVIET AND YUGOSLAV THEORY. USSR YUGOSLAVIA STRATA STRUCT NAT/G DOMIN COERCE MARXISM...GOV/COMP IDEA/COMP 20. PAGE 91 H1812 JURID COM LAW SOVEREIGN

B64
MAIER J.,POLITICS OF CHANGE IN LATIN AMERICA. BRAZIL L/A+17C STRATA INT/ORG NAT/G POL/PAR FOR/AID REV 20. PAGE 101 H2019 SOCIETY NAT/LISM DIPLOM REGION

B64
MORGAN H.W.,AMERICAN SOCIALISM 1900-1960. USA+45 USA-45 INTELL AGRI LABOR WORKER BARGAIN ECO/TAC GP/REL RACE/REL 20 NEGRO MIGRATION GOLD/STAND. PAGE 113 H2254 SOCISM POL/PAR ECO/DEV STRATA

B64
PHILLIPS C.S.,THE DEVELOPMENT OF NIGERIAN FOREIGN POLICY. AFR CONSTN CULTURE STRATA NAT/G LEGIS DOMIN LEGIT EXEC...RELATIV SOC TIME/SEQ TREND TOT/POP 20. PAGE 125 H2502 CHOOSE POLICY DIPLOM NIGERIA

B64
PIKE F.B.,THE CONFLICT BETWEEN CHURCH AND STATE IN LATIN AMERICA. L/A+17C CULTURE SOCIETY STRATA DOMIN EDU/PROP LEGIT COERCE ATTIT ORD/FREE PWR WEALTH ...CONCPT TIME/SEQ TREND VAL/FREE. PAGE 125 H2510 SECT NAT/G

B64
SANCHEZ J.M.,REFORM AND REACTION. SPAIN STRATA NAT/LISM TOTALISM 20. PAGE 137 H2749 NAT/G SECT GP/REL REV

B64
SINGER M.R.,THE EMERGING ELITE: A STUDY OF POLITICAL LEADERSHIP IN CEYLON. S/ASIA ECO/UNDEV AGRI KIN NAT/G SECT EX/STRUC LEGIT ATTIT PWR RESPECT...SOC STAT CHARTS 20. PAGE 144 H2883 TOP/EX STRATA NAT/LISM CEYLON

B64
TAWNEY R.H.,EQUALITY. UK CULTURE STRATA ECO/TAC EDU/PROP REPRESENT OWN NEW/LIB...MAJORIT WELF/ST SOC 20. PAGE 153 H3051 WEALTH STRUCT ELITES POPULISM

B64
THORNTON T.P.,THE THIRD WORLD IN SOVIET PERSPECTIVE: STUDIES BY SOVIET WRITERS ON THE DEVELOPING AREAS. AFR L/A+17C S/ASIA STRATA AGRI INDUS MARKET NAT/G POL/PAR ECO/TAC COLONIAL PERCEPT PWR WEALTH...MARXIST STAT CHARTS WORK MARX/KARL 20. PAGE 155 H3090 ECO/UNDEV ACT/RES USSR DIPLOM

B64
UTECHIN S.V.,RUSSIAN POLITICAL THOUGHT: A CONCISE HISTORY. RUSSIA USSR INTELL STRATA POL/PAR SECT LEGIS EDU/PROP REV WAR MARXISM...ANARCH BIBLIOG 9/20 REFORMERS SLAVS. PAGE 161 H3218 IDEA/COMP ATTIT ALL/IDEOS NAT/G

B64
VON FURER-HAIMEN E.,AN ANTHROPOLOGICAL BIBLIOGRAPHY OF SOUTH ASIA (VOL. II). STRATA STRUCT KIN SECT ACT/RES CREATE HABITAT...GEOG OBS 20. PAGE 163 H3268 BIBLIOG/A CULTURE S/ASIA SOC

B64
VON STEIN L.J.,THE HISTORY OF THE SOCIAL MOVEMENT IN FRANCE, 1789-1850 (TRANS. BY K. MENGELBERG). COM FRANCE MOD/EUR NAT/G EX/STRUC INGP/REL ALL/IDEOS CONSERVE MARXISM...SOC BIBLIOG 18/19. PAGE 164 H3278 REV STRATA

B64
WARD R.E.,POLITICAL MODERNIZATION IN JAPAN AND TURKEY. ASIA ISLAM S/ASIA CONSTN CULTURE STRATA COM/IND POL/PAR FORCES ACT/RES ECO/TAC DOMIN EDU/PROP LEGIT ADMIN CHOOSE ATTIT ALL/VALS...STAT TIME/SEQ VAL/FREE CHINJAP. PAGE 165 H3307 SOCIETY TURKEY

B64
WHITEFORD A.H.,TWO CITIES OF LATIN AMERICA: A COMPARATIVE DESCRIPTION OF SOCIAL CLASSES. L/A+17C CULTURE SOCIETY MUNIC DOMIN LEGIT ATTIT ALL/VALS ...STAT OBS VAL/FREE 20. PAGE 167 H3352 STRATA SOC

B64
WRAITH R.,CORRUPTION IN DEVELOPING COUNTRIES. NIGERIA UK LAW ELITES STRATA INDUS LOC/G NAT/G SECT FORCES EDU/PROP ADMIN PWR WEALTH 18/20. PAGE 171 H3414 ECO/UNDEV CRIME SANCTION ATTIT

B64
WRIGHT G.,RURAL REVOLUTION IN FRANCE: THE PEASANTRY IN THE TWENTIETH CENTURY. EUR+WWI MOD/EUR LAW CULTURE AGRI POL/PAR DELIB/GP LEGIS ECO/TAC EDU/PROP COERCE CHOOSE ATTIT RIGID/FLEX HEALTH ...STAT CENSUS CHARTS VAL/FREE 20. PAGE 171 H3419 PWR STRATA FRANCE REV

B64
ZOLLSCHAN G.K.,EXPLORATIONS IN SOCIAL CHANGE. SOCIETY STRATA STRUCT ECO/UNDEV EX/STRUC...PSY ANTHOL 20. PAGE 173 H3463 ORD/FREE SIMUL CONCPT CULTURE

L64
SYMONDS R.,"REFLECTIONS IN LOCALISATION." AFR S/ASIA UK STRATA INT/ORG NAT/G SCHOOL EDU/PROP LEGIT KNOWL ORD/FREE PWR RESPECT CMN/WLTH 20. PAGE 151 H3023 ADMIN MGT COLONIAL

S64
CLIGNET R.,"POTENTIAL ELITES IN GHANA AND THE IVORY COAST: A PRELIMINARY SURVEY." AFR CULTURE ELITES STRATA KIN NAT/G SECT DOMIN EXEC ORD/FREE RESPECT SKILL...POLICY RELATIV GP/COMP NAT/COMP 20. PAGE 30 H0605 PWR LEGIT IVORY/CST GHANA

S64
NEEDHAM T.,"SCIENCE AND SOCIETY IN EAST AND WEST." INTELL STRATA R+D LOC/G NAT/G PROVS CONSULT ACT/RES CREATE PLAN TEC/DEV EDU/PROP ADMIN ATTIT ALL/VALS ...POLICY RELATIV MGT CONCPT NEW/IDEA TIME/SEQ WORK WORK. PAGE 116 H2327 ASIA STRUCT

S64
RUDOLPH L.I.,"GENERALS AND POLITICIANS IN INDIA." INDIA S/ASIA CULTURE STRATA NAT/G LEGIS TOP/EX EDU/PROP ATTIT ORD/FREE PWR RESPECT SKILL...POLICY BIOG TIME/SEQ STERTYP VAL/FREE 20. PAGE 136 H2713 FORCES COERCE

B65
AIYAR S.P.,STUDIES IN INDIAN DEMOCRACY. INDIA STRATA ECO/UNDEV LABOR POL/PAR LEGIS DIPLOM LOBBY REGION CHOOSE ATTIT SOCISM...ANTHOL 20. PAGE 4 H0086 ORD/FREE REPRESENT ADMIN NAT/G

B65
APTER D.E.,THE POLITICS OF MODERNIZATION. AFR L/A+17C CULTURE NAT/G POL/PAR ADMIN COLONIAL NAT/LISM ATTIT RIGID/FLEX PWR...SOC CONCPT. PAGE 8 H0154 ECO/UNDEV GEN/LAWS STRATA CREATE

B65
BENTWICH J.S.,EDUCATION IN ISRAEL. ISRAEL CULTURE STRATA PROB/SOLV TEC/DEV ADJUST ALL/VALS 20 JEWS. PAGE 15 H0293 SECT EDU/PROP ACADEM SCHOOL

B65
BETEILLE A.,CASTE, CLASS, AND POWER. INDIA MUNIC SECT REGION GP/REL PERS/REL ATTIT HABITAT RIGID/FLEX...SOC 20. PAGE 16 H0323 STRATA CULTURE PWR STRUCT

B65
CENTRAL GAZETTEERS UNIT,THE GAZETTEER OF INDIA (VOL. I). INDIA SOCIETY STRATA PLAN EDU/PROP NAT/LISM ORD/FREE WEALTH...GEOG LING CHARTS SOC/INTEG 20. PAGE 28 H0568 PRESS CULTURE SECT STRUCT

B65
COLLINS H.,KARL MARX AND THE BRITISH LABOR MOVEMENT, YEARS OF THE FIRST INTERNATIONAL. EUR+WWI MOD/EUR UK STRATA INDUS NAT/G POL/PAR SOCISM ...CONCPT 19/20 MARX/KARL. PAGE 32 H0633 MARXISM LABOR INT/ORG WORKER

B65
GINIEWSKI P.,THE TWO FACES OF APARTHEID. AFR SOUTH/AFR STRATA AGRI INDUS COLONIAL PARTIC SOVEREIGN...CONCPT GOV/COMP NAT/COMP 19/20 NEGRO. PAGE 56 H1131 DISCRIM NAT/G RACE/REL STRUCT

B65
GUERIN D.,SUR LE FASCISME: FASCISME ET GRAND CAPITAL (VOL. II). GERMANY ITALY SOCIETY STRATA AGRI WORKER 20. PAGE 62 H1245 FASCISM NAT/G TOTALISM EDU/PROP

B65
KLEIN J.,SAMPLES FROM ENGLISH CULTURES (2 VOLS.). UK STRATA FAM NEIGH WORKER ETIQUET ISOLAT AGE/C AGE/A HABITAT RIGID/FLEX...NET/THEORY CHARTS 20. PAGE 87 H1732 CULTURE INGP/REL ATTIT SOC

B65
MAIR L.,AN INTRODUCTION TO SOCIAL ANTHROPOLOGY. LAW STRATA FINAN FAM KIN SECT INT/TRADE RACE/REL ADJUST PRODUC...T 20. PAGE 101 H2023 SOC STRUCT CULTURE SOCIETY

B65
MURDOCK G.P.,CULTURE AND SOCIETY. SOCIETY STRATA STRUCT SECT CREATE CONTROL ORD/FREE...GP/COMP ANTHOL 20. PAGE 115 H2294 CULTURE PHIL/SCI METH IDEA/COMP

B65
O'CONNELL M.R.,IRISH POLITICS AND SOCIAL CONFLICT IN THE AGE OF THE AMERICAN REVOLUTION. FRANCE IRELAND MOD/EUR STRATA SECT LEGIS DIPLOM INT/TRADE DOMIN REV WAR...BIBLIOG 18 PARLIAMENT. PAGE 119 H2387
CATHISM ATTIT NAT/G DELIB/GP

B65
OECD,MEDITERRANEAN REGIONAL PROJECT: TURKEY; EDUCATION AND DEVELOPMENT. FUT TURKEY SOCIETY STRATA FINAN NAT/G PROF/ORG PLAN PROB/SOLV ADMIN COST...STAT CHARTS 20 OECD. PAGE 120 H2399
EDU/PROP ACADEM SCHOOL ECO/UNDEV

B65
OECD,THE MEDITERRANEAN REGIONAL PROJECT: ITALY; EDUCATION AND DEVELOPMENT. ITALY SOCIETY STRATA FINAN NAT/G PROF/ORG WORKER PLAN PROB/SOLV ADMIN ...STAT CHARTS METH 20 OECD. PAGE 120 H2400
SCHOOL EDU/PROP ECO/UNDEV ACADEM

B65
OECD,THE MEDITERRANEAN REGIONAL PROJECT: SPAIN; EDUCATION AND DEVELOPMENT. FUT SPAIN STRATA FINAN NAT/G WORKER PLAN PROB/SOLV ADMIN COST...POLICY STAT CHARTS 20 OECD. PAGE 120 H2402
ECO/UNDEV EDU/PROP ACADEM SCHOOL

B65
ORGANSKI A.F.K.,THE STAGES OF POLITICAL DEVELOPMENT. STRATA AGRI INDUS NAT/G POL/PAR COLONIAL PWR WEALTH...CLASSIF TIME/SEQ. PAGE 121 H2428
ECO/DEV ECO/UNDEV GEN/LAWS CREATE

B65
RENNER K.,MENSCH UND GESELLSCHAFT - GRUNDRISS EINER SOZIOLOGIE (2ND ED.). STRATA FAM LABOR PROF/ORG WAR ...JURID CLASSIF 20. PAGE 131 H2616
SOC STRUCT NAT/G SOCIETY

B65
SVALASTOGA K.,SOCIAL DIFFERENTIATION. CULTURE ELITES SOCIETY MARRIAGE...CONCPT SIMUL. PAGE 151 H3011
SOC STRATA STRUCT GP/REL

B65
TINGSTEN H.,THE PROBLEM OF DEMOCRACY. ELITES SOCIETY STRATA NAT/G CONSEN TOTALISM WELF/ST. PAGE 155 H3101
IDEA/COMP GOV/COMP POPULISM SOCISM

B65
VAN DEN BERGHE P.L.,SOUTH AFRICA: A STUDY IN CONFLICT. AFR CULTURE SOCIETY STRATA STRUCT COERCE SEGREGAT. PAGE 161 H3227
DOMIN RACE/REL DISCRIM

B65
VAN DEN BERGHE P.L.,AFRICA: SOCIAL PROBLEMS OF CHANGE AND CONFLICT. ELITES STRATA ECO/UNDEV KIN MUNIC DIPLOM GP/REL RACE/REL NAT/LISM...ANTHOL BIBLIOG 20. PAGE 161 H3228
SOC CULTURE AFR STRUCT

S65
WOLF C. JR.,"THE POLITICAL EFFECTS OF SOME MILITARY PROGRAMS* SOME INDICATIONS FROM LATIN AMERICA." ELITES STRATA BUDGET FOR/AID WEAPON ATTIT PERCEPT PWR...REGRESS SYS/QU CHARTS NAT/COMP. PAGE 170 H3397
L/A+17C FORCES CIVMIL/REL PROBABIL

B66
BUKHARIN N.,THE ABC OF COMMUNISM: A POPULAR EXPLANATION OF THE PROGRAM OF THE COMMUNIST PARTY OF RUSSIA. USSR STRATA SECT FORCES WORKER CAP/ISM RECEIVE EDU/PROP NAT/LISM TOTALISM 20. PAGE 23 H0468
MARXISM CONCPT POLICY REV

B66
CAUTE D.,THE LEFT IN EUROPE SINCE 1789. EUR+WWI MOD/EUR NAT/G POL/PAR REV...TIME/SEQ GEN/LAWS BIBLIOG 18/20. PAGE 28 H0564
ALL/IDEOS ORD/FREE CONCPT STRATA

B66
COLE A.B.,SOCIALIST PARTIES IN POSTWAR JAPAN. STRATA AGRI LABOR PLAN DIPLOM ECO/TAC AGREE LEAD CHOOSE ATTIT...CHARTS 20 CHINJAP SOC/DEMPAR. PAGE 31 H0620
POL/PAR POLICY SOCISM NAT/G

B66
COLE G.D.H.,THE MEANING OF MARXISM. USSR WOR+45 STRATA STRUCT NAT/G WORKER COST FASCISM...IDEA/COMP 20. PAGE 31 H0625
MARXISM CONCPT HIST/WRIT CAP/ISM

B66
DAHL R.A.,POLITICAL OPPOSITIONS IN WESTERN DEMOCRACIES. EUR+WWI USA+45 USA-45 SOCIETY STRATA ECO/DEV NAT/G LEGIS REPRESENT...TREND NAT/COMP ANTHOL 20. PAGE 37 H0732
POL/PAR CHOOSE PARTIC PLURISM

B66
DE TOCQUEVILLE A,DEMOCRACY IN AMERICA (1834-1840) (2 VOLS. IN I; TRANS. BY G. LAWRENCE). FRANCE CULTURE STRATA POL/PAR CT/SYS REPRESENT FEDERAL ORD/FREE SOVEREIGN...MAJORIT TREND GEN/LAWS 18/19. PAGE 39 H0773
POPULISM USA-45 CONSTN NAT/COMP

B66
HOLT R.T.,THE POLITICAL BASIS OF ECONOMIC DEVELOPMENT. STRATA STRUCT NAT/G DIPLOM ADMIN...SOC NAT/COMP BIBLIOG 20. PAGE 73 H1458
ECO/TAC GOV/COMP CONSTN EX/STRUC

B66
JACKSON G.D.,COMINTERN AND PEASANT IN EAST EUROPE 1919-1930. BULGARIA COM CZECHOSLVK EUR+WWI POLAND ROMANIA YUGOSLAVIA STRATA AGRI VOL/ASSN DIPLOM CONTROL CROWD WEALTH...POLICY NAT/COMP 20. PAGE 79 H1575
MARXISM ECO/UNDEV WORKER INT/ORG

B66
KAZAMIAS A.M.,EDUCATION AND QUEST FOR MODERNITY IN TURKEY. ISLAM SOCIETY SECT NAT/LISM ATTIT ORD/FREE SOVEREIGN TURKS. PAGE 84 H1672
NAT/G EDU/PROP STRATA CULTURE

B66
KOH S.J.,STAGES OF INDUSTRIAL DEVELOPMENT IN ASIA. ASIA INDIA KOREA STRATA STRUCT NAT/G INT/TRADE ...CHARTS 19/20 CHINJAP. PAGE 87 H1738
INDUS ECO/UNDEV ECO/DEV LABOR

B66
LENSKI G.E.,POWER AND PRIVILEGE: A THEORY OF SOCIAL STRATIFICATION. SWEDEN UK UNIV USSR CULTURE ECO/UNDEV PRIVIL PWR...PHIL/SCI CONCPT CHARTS IDEA/COMP HYPO/EXP METH MARX/KARL. PAGE 94 H1882
SOC STRATA STRUCT SOCIETY

B66
LEYBURN J.G.,THE HAITIAN PEOPLE (REV. ED.). HAITI SOCIETY FAM SECT DOMIN COLONIAL MARRIAGE...SOC CHARTS BIBLIOG/A 18/10. PAGE 96 H1917
STRUCT STRATA INGP/REL CULTURE

B66
NAMBOODIRIPAD E.M.,ECONOMICS AND POLITICS OF INDIA'S SOCIALIST PATTERN. INDIA STRATA AGRI INDUS NAT/G PRICE ORD/FREE SOVEREIGN 20. PAGE 115 H2307
ECO/UNDEV PLAN SOCISM CAP/ISM

B66
RAEFF M.,ORIGINS OF THE RUSSIAN INTELLIGENTSIA: THE EIGHTEENTH-CENTURY NOBILITY. RUSSIA FAM NAT/G EDU/PROP ADMIN PERS/REL ATTIT...HUM BIOG 18. PAGE 129 H2580
INTELL ELITES STRATA CONSERVE

B66
ROSNER J.,DER FASCHISMUS. AUSTRIA GERMANY ITALY STRATA NAT/G POL/PAR COERCE RACE/REL TOTALISM ATTIT AUTHORIT...IDEA/COMP 20 NAZI ANTI/SEMIT. PAGE 134 H2684
NAT/LISM FASCISM ORD/FREE WAR

B66
SMELSER N.J.,SOCIAL STRUCTURE AND MOBILITY IN ECONOMIC DEVELOPMENT. CULTURE SOCIETY CONFER...PSY SOC CHARTS METH/COMP NAT/COMP ANTHOL METH 20. PAGE 145 H2904
STRUCT STRATA ECO/UNDEV ECO/DEV

B66
SRINIVAS M.N.,SOCIAL CHANGE IN MODERN INDIA. INDIA CULTURE SOCIETY STRUCT SECT TEC/DEV...METH/CNCPT SELF/OBS WORSHIP 20. PAGE 148 H2961
ORD/FREE STRATA SOC ECO/UNDEV

B66
TYSON G.,NEHRU: THE YEARS OF POWER. INDIA UK STRATA ECO/UNDEV FINAN SECT TASK WAR ORD/FREE MARXISM ...POLICY BIBLIOG 20 NEHRU/J. PAGE 157 H3145
CHIEF PWR DIPLOM NAT/G

B66
VOGT E.Z.,PEOPLE OF RIMROCK. STRATA STRUCT KIN SECT GP/REL HABITAT ALL/VALS...GEOG INT QU 20 TEXAS NAVAHO MORMON SPAN/AMER ZUNI. PAGE 163 H3260
CULTURE GP/COMP SOC SOCIETY

B66
WHEELER G.,THE PEOPLES OF SOVIET CENTRAL ASIA: A BACKGROUND BOOK. ISLAM USSR STRATA STRUCT FORCES REV WAR HABITAT 7/20. PAGE 167 H3341
COLONIAL DOMIN CULTURE ADJUST

L66
LEMARCHAND R.,"SOCIAL CHANGE AND POLITICAL MODERNISATION IN BURUNDI." AFR BURUNDI STRATA CHIEF EX/STRUC RIGID/FLEX PWR...SOC 20. PAGE 94 H1874
NAT/G STRUCT ELITES CONSERVE

S66
BLANC N.,"SPAIN: LEARNING THROUGH STRUGGLE" SPAIN STRATA STRUCT SECT FORCES PROB/SOLV AGE/Y ATTIT ORD/FREE PWR WEALTH MARXISM SOCISM 19/20 FRANCO/F SUCCESSION. PAGE 18 H0352
NAT/G FUT SOCIALIST TOTALISM

S66
GILBERT S.P.,"WARS OF LIBERATION AND SOVIET MILITARY AID POLICY." ASIA INDIA INDONESIA UAR USA+45 STRATA WAR PERCEPT MARXISM...STAT NAT/COMP. PAGE 56 H1124
USSR FOR/AID WEAPON DRIVE

S66
HEAPHEY J.,"THE ORGANIZATION OF EGYPT* INADEQUACIES OF A NONPOLITICAL MODEL FOR NATION-BUILDING." STRATA NAT/G CREATE PROB/SOLV ECO/TAC NAT/LISM SOCISM RECORD. PAGE 69 H1377
UAR ECO/UNDEV OBS

S66
SNOW P.G.,"A SCALOGRAM ANALYSIS OF POLITICAL DEVELOPMENT." STRATA ECO/UNDEV POL/PAR REGION ALL/VALS PWR...SOC CHARTS. PAGE 146 H2924
L/A+17C NAT/COMP TESTS CLASSIF

S66
STRAYER J.R.,"PROBLEMS OF DICTATORSHIP* THE RUSSIAN EXPERIENCE." ASIA MOD/EUR ELITES STRATA POL/PAR CREATE NAT/LISM MARXISM...GOV/COMP NAT/COMP. PAGE 150 H2997
NAT/G GEN/LAWS USSR TOTALISM

B67
CANTOR N.F.,THE ENGLISH TRADITION* TWENTIETH-CENTURY VIEWS OF ENGLISH HISTORY (2VOLS.). UK
CT/SYS LAW

STRATA NAT/G SECT WAR...POLICY GOV/COMP IDEA/COMP ANTHOL T PARLIAMENT CMN/WLTH. PAGE 26 H0522 — POL/PAR

B67
CARTER G.M.,SOUTH AFRICA'S TRANSKEI: THE POLITICS OF DOMESTIC COLONIALISM. SOUTH/AFR ECO/UNDEV AGRI NAT/G PROVS PLAN DOMIN REPRESENT ADJUST DISCRIM ...OBS BIBLIOG 20 BANTUSTANS TRANSKEI. PAGE 27 H0550 — STRATA GOV/REL COLONIAL POLICY

B67
ERDMAN H.L.,THE SWATANTRA PARTY AND INDIAN CONSERVATISM. INDIA S/ASIA SOCIETY STRATA LOC/G NAT/G LEAD PARTIC GP/REL ATTIT...CONCPT GP/COMP BIBLIOG 20 SWATANTRA. PAGE 47 H0938 — POL/PAR CONSERVE CHOOSE POLICY

B67
FISHEL L.H. JR.,THE NEGRO AMERICAN: A DOCUMENTARY HISTORY. SOCIETY NAT/G ROLE...POLICY ANTHOL 15/20 NEGRO. PAGE 51 H1013 — ORD/FREE DISCRIM RACE/REL STRATA

B67
MENARD O.D.,THE ARMY AND THE FIFTH REPUBLIC. ALGERIA FRANCE VIETNAM ELITES STRATA COLONIAL CONTROL LOBBY WAR CIVMIL/REL ROLE PWR...POLICY 20 DEGAULLE/C. PAGE 108 H2169 — FORCES ATTIT NAT/G

B67
RIESMAN D.,CONVERSATIONS IN JAPAN: MODERNIZATION, POLITICS, AND CULTURE. CHINA/COM STRATA STRUCT ECO/DEV INDUS ACADEM EDU/PROP...ART/METH SOC MODAL INT IDEA/COMP SOC/INTEG 20 CHINJAP HIROSHIMA. PAGE 131 H2629 — CULTURE SOCIETY ASIA

B67
SETON-WATSON H.,THE RUSSIAN EMPIRE, 1801-1917. COM RUSSIA STRATA ECO/DEV AGRI INDUS POL/PAR DIPLOM NAT/LISM MARXISM...IDEA/COMP BIBLIOG 19/20 MARX/KARL. PAGE 142 H2834 — SOCIETY NAT/G LEAD POLICY

L67
PICKERING J.F.,"RECRUITMENT TO THE ADMINISTRATIVE CLASS, 1960-1964: PART 2" UK STRATA NAT/G WORKER ...STAT CHARTS 20. PAGE 125 H2505 — PERS/COMP ADMIN KNO/TEST EDU/PROP

S67
BASKIN D.B.,"NATIONALITY DOCTRINE AND ANTI-SEMITISM IN THE USSR." USSR CULTURE STRATA ISOLAT MAJORITY ATTIT RIGID/FLEX RESPECT...GP/COMP JEWS. PAGE 12 H0234 — NAT/LISM MARXISM GP/REL DISCRIM

S67
CARR E.H.,"REVOLUTION FROM ABOVE." USSR STRATA FINAN INDUS NAT/G DOMIN LEAD GP/REL INGP/REL OWN PRODUC PWR 20 STALIN/J. PAGE 27 H0538 — AGRI POLICY COM EFFICIENCY

S67
CATTELL D.T.,"A NEO-MARXIST THEORY OF COMPARATIVE ANALYSIS." USSR STRATA INSPECT DOMIN CONTROL COERCE OWN TOTALISM PWR...FASCIST HYPO/EXP METH 20. PAGE 28 H0561 — GOV/COMP MARXISM SIMUL CLASSIF

S67
COHEN R.,"ANTHROPOLOGY AND POLITICAL SCIENCE: COURTSHIP OR MARRIAGE?" CULTURE STRATA STRUCT MUNIC REGION UTOPIA...NEW/IDEA TREND IDEA/COMP METH/COMP 20. PAGE 31 H0618 — SOC INGP/REL AFR

S67
GLENN N.D.,"RURAL-URBAN DIFFERENCES IN REPORTED ATTITUDES AND BEHAVIOR" STRATA GP/REL CONSEN HABITAT RIGID/FLEX SAMP. PAGE 57 H1143 — CULTURE ATTIT KIN CHARTS

S67
HARBRON J.D.,"UNIFICATION IN CANADA: FAIT ACCOMPLI" CANADA STRATA NAT/G DELIB/GP BUDGET GP/REL 20 NAVY. PAGE 66 H1327 — INGP/REL FORCES PLAN ATTIT

S67
JENCKS C.E.,"SOCIAL STATUS OF COAL MINERS IN BRITAIN SINCE NATIONALIZATION." UK STRATA STRUCT LABOR RECEIVE GP/REL INCOME OWN ATTIT HABITAT...MGT T 20. PAGE 80 H1600 — EXTR/IND WORKER CONTROL NAT/G

S67
MALLORY J.R.,"THE MINISTER'S OFFICE STAFF* AN UNREFORMED PART OF PUBLIC SERVICE." CONSTN ELITES STRATA NAT/G PROB/SOLV TASK CHOOSE PERS/REL EFFICIENCY...DECISION 20. PAGE 102 H2033 — CANADA ADMIN EX/STRUC STRUCT

S67
NEALE R.S.,"WORKING CLASS WOMEN AND WOMEN'S SUFFRAGE." UK LAW CONSTN LABOR NAT/G DELIB/GP LEGIS WORKER PAY PARTIC CHOOSE 19 FEMALE/SEX. PAGE 116 H2326 — STRATA SEX SUFF DISCRIM

S67
PAI G.A.,"TAXATION AND PLANNING IN INDIA: A BIRDS-EYE VIEW." INDIA ELITES NAT/G LEGIS BUDGET CONTROL LOBBY INCOME...STAT CHARTS 20. PAGE 122 H2443 — TAX PLAN WEALTH STRATA

S67
PONOMARYOV B.,"THE OCTOBER REVOLUTION - BEGINNING OF THE EPOCH OF SOCIALISM AND COMMUNISM." COM FUT USSR WOR+45 SOCIETY STRATA CHIEF CREATE DIPLOM ECO/TAC EDU/PROP SOCISM...NAT/COMP 20. PAGE 127 H2542 — MARXIST WORKER INT/ORG POLICY

S67
RAMA C.M.,"PASADO Y PRESENTE DE LA RELIGION EN AMERICA LATINA." L/A+17C ELITES SOCIETY STRATA MARXISM...STAT WORSHIP PROTESTANT. PAGE 129 H2585 — SECT CATHISM STRUCT NAT/COMP

S67
RIESMAN D.,"SOME QUESTIONS ABOUT THE STUDY OF AMERICAN CHARACTER IN THE TWENTIETH CENTURY." STRATA PRESS PERSON RIGID/FLEX SOC. PAGE 131 H2628 — CULTURE ATTIT DRIVE GEN/LAWS

S67
ROCHET W.,"THE OCTOBER REVOLUTION AND THE STRUGGLE OF THE FRENCH COMMUNISTS." COM FRANCE ELITES SOCIETY STRATA ECO/TAC EDU/PROP GP/REL WEALTH ...MARXIST IDEA/COMP NAT/COMP 20. PAGE 133 H2654 — SOCISM CHOOSE METH/COMP NAT/G

S67
SOARES G.,"SOCIO-ECONOMIC VARIABLES AND VOTING FOR THE RADICAL LEFT: CHILE 1952." CHILE INDUS NAT/G WORKER ADJUST STRANGE ANOMIE WEALTH...METH/CNCPT CORREL 20. PAGE 146 H2925 — STRATA POL/PAR CHOOSE STAT

S67
SUBRAMANIAM V.,"REPRESENTATIVE BUREAUCRACY: A REASSESSMENT." USA+45 ELITES LOC/G NAT/G ADMIN GOV/REL PRIVIL DRIVE ROLE...POLICY CENSUS 20 CIVIL/SERV BUREAUCRCY. PAGE 150 H3006 — STRATA GP/REL MGT GOV/COMP

S67
TIKHOMIROV I.A.,"DIVISION OF POWERS OR DIVISION OF LABOR?" USSR NAT/G DELIB/GP ADJUD GP/REL MARXISM SOCISM 20. PAGE 155 H3093 — BAL/PWR WORKER STRATA ADMIN

S67
ULC O.,"CLASS STRUGGLE AND SOCIALIST JUSTICE: THE CASE OF CZECHOSLOVAKIA." COM CZECHOSLVK LAW CONSTN ELITES STRUCT NAT/G CRIME GP/REL MARXISM 20. PAGE 158 H3151 — TOTALISM CT/SYS ADJUD STRATA

S68
DUGARD J.,"THE REVOCATION OF THE MANDATE FOR SOUTH WEST AFRICA." SOUTH/AFR WOR+45 STRATA NAT/G DELIB/GP DIPLOM ADJUD SANCTION CHOOSE RACE/REL ...POLICY NAT/COMP 20 AFRICA/SW UN TRUST/TERR LEAGUE/NAT. PAGE 43 H0858 — AFR INT/ORG DISCRIM COLONIAL

B76
TAINE H.A.,THE ANCIENT REGIME. FRANCE STRATA FORCES PARTIC EQUILIB WEALTH CONSERVE POPULISM...GOV/COMP SOC/INTEG 18/19. PAGE 152 H3035 — NAT/G GOV/REL TAX REV

C80
ARNOLD M.,"EQUALITY" IN MIXED ESSAYS." MOD/EUR UK ELITES STRATA NAT/G...CONCPT IDEA/COMP NAT/COMP SOC/INTEG 19. PAGE 8 H0167 — ORD/FREE UTOPIA SOCIETY STRUCT

B82
MACDONALD D.,AFRICANA; OR, THE HEART OF HEATHEN AFRICA, VOL. II: MISSION LIFE. SOCIETY STRATA KIN CREATE EDU/PROP ADMIN COERCE LITERACY HEALTH...MYTH WORSHIP 19 LIVNGSTN/D MISSION NEGRO. PAGE 100 H1990 — SECT AFR CULTURE ORD/FREE

B85
TAINE H.A.,THE FRENCH REVOLUTION (3 VOLS.) (TRANS. BY J. DURAND). FRANCE MOD/EUR SOCIETY STRATA POL/PAR ECO/TAC DOMIN EDU/PROP GP/REL PWR ...GOV/COMP IDEA/COMP 18. PAGE 152 H3036 — REV NAT/G EX/STRUC LEAD

B87
ADAMS J.,A DEFENSE OF THE CONSTITUTIONS OF GOVERNMENT OF THE UNITED STATES OF AMERICA. USA-45 STRATA CHIEF EX/STRUC LEGIS CT/SYS CONSERVE POPULISM...CONCPT CON/ANAL GOV/COMP. PAGE 3 H0063 — CONSTN BAL/PWR PWR NAT/G

B96
MARX K.,REVOLUTION AND COUNTER-REVOLUTION. GERMANY CONSTN ELITES INDUS NAT/G DIPLOM ECO/TAC WEALTH. PAGE 104 H2083 — MARXIST REV PWR STRATA

B99
DU BOIS W.E.B.,THE PHILADELPHIA NEGRO: A SOCIAL STUDY. CULTURE STRATA KIN CRIME SUFF ADJUST DISCRIM ISOLAT HABITAT HEREDITY ALL/VALS SOC/INTEG 17/19 NEGRO PHILADELPH. PAGE 42 H0851 — INGP/REL RACE/REL SOC CENSUS

B99
LECKY W.E.H.,DEMOCRACY AND LIBERTY (2 VOLS.). LAW CONSTN STRATA POL/PAR SECT WORKER DIPLOM ADJUD REPRESENT NAT/LISM CONSERVE. PAGE 93 H1851 — LEGIS NAT/G POPULISM ORD/FREE

B99
RIPLEY W.Z.,A SELECTED BIBLIOGRAPHY OF THE ANTHROPOLOGY AND ETHNOLOGY OF EUROPE. SOCIETY STRATA STRUCT KIN SECT VOL/ASSN GP/REL INGP/REL HABITAT...GEOG 19. PAGE 132 H2632 — BIBLIOG/A MOD/EUR SOC CULTURE

STRATEGY....SEE PLAN, DECISION

STRATIFICATION....SEE STRATA

STRAUSS L. H2995

STRAUSZ-HUPE R. H2996

STRAYER J.R. H2997

STRESEMANN, GUSTAV....SEE STRESEMN/G

STRESEMN/G....GUSTAV STRESEMANN

B54
GATZKE H.W.,STRESEMANN AND THE REARMAMENT OF GERMANY. EUR+WWI GERMANY USSR FINAN NAT/G ECO/TAC ATTIT...BIOG METH 20 STRESEMN/G. PAGE 55 H1105
FORCES INDUS PWR

STRESS....SEE PERSON, DRIVE

STRICK J.C. H3351

STRIKE....STRIKE OF WORKERS

B13
BARDOUX J.,L'ANGLETERRE RADICALE; ESSAI DE LA PSYCHOLOGIE SOCIALE (1906-1913). UK CONSTN NAT/G WORKER CREATE BUDGET ECO/TAC ATTIT...POLICY 20 PARLIAMENT LABOR/PAR STRIKE NAVY. PAGE 11 H0215
POL/PAR CHOOSE COLONIAL LEGIS

B31
CROOK W.H.,THE GENERAL STRIKE: A STUDY OF LABOR'S TRAGIC WEAPON IN THEORY AND PRACTICE. BELGIUM FRANCE SWEDEN UK WOR-45 PROB/SOLV ECO/TAC DOMIN PWR ...POLICY TIME/SEQ NAT/COMP GEN/LAWS 19/20 STRIKE. PAGE 35 H0707
LABOR WORKER LG/CO BARGAIN

B58
CUNNINGHAM W.B.,COMPULSORY CONCILIATION AND COLLECTIVE BARGAINING. CANADA NAT/G LEGIS ADJUD CT/SYS GP/REL...MGT 20 NEW/BRUNS STRIKE CASEBOOK. PAGE 36 H0722
POLICY BARGAIN LABOR INDUS

STRIKES....SEE LABOR, GP/REL, FINAN

STRONG C.F. H2998,H2999

STRUC/FUNC....STRUCTURAL-FUNCTIONAL THEORY

STRUCT...SOCIAL STRUCTURE

N
CONOVER H.F.,MADAGASCAR: A SELECTED LIST OF REFERENCES. MADAGASCAR STRUCT ECO/UNDEV NAT/G ADMIN ...SOC 19/20. PAGE 32 H0639
BIBLIOG/A SOCIETY CULTURE COLONIAL

N
HERSKOVITS M.V.,CULTURAL ANTHROPOLOGY. UNIV SOCIETY STRUCT FAM...AUD/VIS BIBLIOG. PAGE 70 H1410
CULTURE SOC INGP/REL GEOG

N
KRADER L.,SOCIAL ORGANIZATION OF THE MONGOL-TURKIC PASTORAL NOMADS. SOCIETY FAM KIN NEIGH GP/REL MARRIAGE 16/20 MONGOLIA TURKIC MIGRATION. PAGE 88 H1763
BIO/SOC HABITAT CULTURE STRUCT

N
SCHADERA I.,SELECT BIBLIOGRAPHY OF SOUTH AFRICAN NATIVE LIFE AND PROBLEMS. SOUTH/AFR LAW CULTURE ECO/UNDEV COLONIAL PARTIC...POLICY LING 20. PAGE 138 H2768
BIBLIOG/A SOC AFR STRUCT

N
CORDIER H.,BIBLIOTECA SINICA. SOCIETY STRUCT SECT DIPLOM COLONIAL...GEOG SOC CON/ANAL. PAGE 33 H0664
BIBLIOG/A NAT/G CULTURE ASIA

N
CORNELL UNIVERSITY LIBRARY,SOUTHEAST ASIA ACCESSIONS LIST. LAW SOCIETY STRUCT ECO/UNDEV POL/PAR TEC/DEV DIPLOM LEAD REGION. PAGE 34 H0671
BIBLIOG S/ASIA NAT/G CULTURE

N
NORTHWESTERN UNIVERSITY LIB,JOINT ACQUISITIONS LIST OF AFRICANA. AFR SOCIETY STRUCT EDU/PROP COLONIAL GP/REL RACE/REL NAT/LISM SOVEREIGN...SOC 20. PAGE 119 H2377
BIBLIOG CULTURE ECO/UNDEV INDUS

NCO
CARRINGTON C.E.,THE COMMONWEALTH IN AFRICA (PAMPHLET). UK STRUCT NAT/G COLONIAL REPRESENT GOV/REL RACE/REL NAT/LISM...MAJORIT 20 EEC NEGRO COLD/WAR. PAGE 27 H0540
ECO/UNDEV AFR DIPLOM PLAN

B04
REED W.A.,ETHNOLOGICAL SURVEY PUBLICATIONS (VOL. II). PHILIPPINE STRUCT INDUS SECT DEATH LEISURE HABITAT...AUD/VIS CHARTS WORSHIP 20 NABOLOI NEGRITO BATAK. PAGE 130 H2607
CULTURE SOCIETY SOC OBS

B05
PHILIPPINE ISLANDS BUREAU SCI,ETHNOLOGICAL SURVEY: THE BONTOC IGOROT. ECO/UNDEV AGRI FAM MARRIAGE HEALTH WEALTH...LING OBS AUD/VIS CHARTS WORSHIP 20 LUZON BONTOC. PAGE 125 H2500
CULTURE INGP/REL KIN STRUCT

B06
SUMNER W.G.,FOLKWAYS: STUDY OF THE SOCIOLOGICAL IMPORTANCE OF USAGES, MANNERS, CUSTOMS, MORES, AND MORALS. STRUCT KIN ETIQUET ROUTINE MURDER MARRIAGE PEACE SEX ALL/VALS WEALTH BIBLIOG. PAGE 150 H3008
CULTURE SOC SANCTION MORAL

B11
PHILLIPSON C.,THE INTERNATIONAL LAW AND CUSTOM OF ANCIENT GREECE AND ROME. MEDIT-7 UNIV INTELL SOCIETY STRUCT NAT/G LEGIS EXEC PERSON...CONCPT OBS CON/ANAL ROM/EMP. PAGE 125 H2504
INT/ORG LAW INT/LAW

B13
SIEGFRIED A.,TABLEAU POLITIQUE DE LA FRANCE DE L'OUEST SOUS LA TROISIEME REPUBLIQUE. FRANCE STRATA STRUCT NAT/G POL/PAR PROVS REGION GOV/REL ATTIT PWR ...TREND TIME 19. PAGE 143 H2869
SOC GEOG SOCIETY

B14
OPPENHEIMER F.,THE STATE. FUT SOCIETY STRATA STRUCT WORKER CAP/ISM WAR GP/REL SOCISM...SOC NAT/COMP SOC/INTEG. PAGE 121 H2424
ELITES OWN DOMIN NAT/G

B19
DUGUIT L.,LAW IN THE MODERN STATE (TRANS. BY FRIDA AND HAROLD LASKI). CONSTN SOCIETY STRUCT MORAL ORD/FREE SOVEREIGN 20. PAGE 43 H0860
GEN/LAWS CONCPT NAT/G LAW

N19
POUND R.,ORGANIZATION OF THE COURTS (PAMPHLET). MOD/EUR UK USA-45 ADJUD PWR...GOV/COMP 10/20 EUROPE. PAGE 127 H2546
CT/SYS JURID STRUCT ADMIN

B20
MACIVER R.M.,COMMUNITY: A SOCIOLOGICAL STUDY; BEING AN ATTEMPT TO SET OUT THE FUNDAMENTAL LAWS OF SOCIAL LIFE. UNIV STRUCT NAT/G CONTROL WAR BIO/SOC ...PSY SOC CONCPT GEN/LAWS. PAGE 100 H1996
REGION SOCIETY GP/REL

S21
MALINOWSKI B.,"THE PRIMITIVE ECONOMICS OF THE TROBRIAND ISLANDERS" (BMR)" CULTURE SOCIETY NAT/G CHIEF LEAD OWN...SOC MYTH WORSHIP 20 NEW/GUINEA TROBRIAND RESOURCE/N. PAGE 101 H2029
ECO/UNDEV AGRI PRODUC STRUCT

B23
FRANK T.,A HISTORY OF ROME. MEDIT-7 INTELL SOCIETY LOC/G NAT/G POL/PAR FORCES LEGIS DOMIN LEGIT ALL/VALS...POLICY CONCPT TIME/SEQ GEN/LAWS ROM/EMP ROM/EMP. PAGE 53 H1050
EXEC STRUCT ELITES

B23
GRANT C.F.,STUDIES IN NORTH AFRICA. ALGERIA MOROCCO ROMAN/EMP CULTURE STRUCT NAT/G DIPLOM WAR ...NAT/COMP TUNIS EUROPE. PAGE 60 H1195
ISLAM SECT DOMIN COLONIAL

B23
WILLOUGHBY W.C.,RACE PROBLEMS IN THE NEW AFRICA: A STUDY OF THE RELATION OF BANTU AND BRITONS IN THOSE PARTS OF BANTU AFRICA... AFR STRUCT SECT DOMIN EDU/PROP GP/REL ATTIT WORSHIP 20 BANTU EUROPE MISSION CHRISTIAN. PAGE 168 H3372
KIN COLONIAL RACE/REL CULTURE

B24
BAGEHOT W.,THE ENGLISH CONSTITUTIUN AND OTHER POLITICAL ESSAYS. UK DELIB/GP BAL/PWR ADMIN CONTROL EXEC ROUTINE CONSERVE...METH PARLIAMENT 19/20. PAGE 10 H0197
NAT/G STRUCT CONCPT

B24
WALKER F.D.,AFRICA AND HER PEOPLES. ISLAM STRUCT FAM SECT EDU/PROP INGP/REL RACE/REL HABITAT...GEOG SOC IDEA/COMP WORSHIP 20 NEGRO. PAGE 164 H3292
CULTURE AFR GP/COMP KIN

B27
WEBER M.,GENERAL ECONOMIC HISTORY. CHRIST-17C MOD/EUR STRUCT AGRI EXTR/IND FINAN INDUS MARKET FAM MUNIC NAT/G PROF/ORG SECT ECO/TAC 8/20. PAGE 166 H3319
ECO/DEV CAP/ISM

B28
CORBETT P.E.,CANADA AND WORLD POLITICS. LAW CULTURE SOCIETY STRUCT MARKET INT/ORG FORCES ACT/RES PLAN ECO/TAC LEGIT ORD/FREE PWR RESPECT...SOC CONCPT TIME/SEQ TREND CMN/WLTH 20 LEAGUE/NAT. PAGE 33 H0662
NAT/G CANADA

B30
OLDMAN J.H.,WHITE AND BLACK IN AFRICA. AFR STRUCT COLONIAL PARTIC DISCRIM ISOLAT PRIVIL 20 SMUTS/JAN NEGRO WHITE/SUP. PAGE 121 H2412
SOVEREIGN ORD/FREE RACE/REL NAT/G

B31
MACIVER R.M.,SOCIETY: ITS STRUCTURE AND CHANGES. CULTURE STRATA FAM CROWD HABITAT ORD/FREE...PSY SOC CONCPT BIBLIOG 20. PAGE 100 H1998
STRUCT SOCIETY PERSON DRIVE

C31
MACLEOD W.C.,"THE ORIGIN AND HISTORY OF POLITICS." UNIV CULTURE NAT/G REPRESENT...SOC CONCPT TREND BIBLIOG. PAGE 100 H2004
METH STRUCT SOCIETY

B32
BRYCE J.,THE HOLY ROMAN EMPIRE. GERMANY ITALY MOD/EUR CULTURE SOCIETY STRUCT INT/ORG NAT/G SECT DIPLOM DOMIN WAR SUPEGO ALL/VALS SOVEREIGN...GEOG SOC TIME/SEQ CHARTS STERTYP. PAGE 23 H0456
CHRIST-17C NAT/LISM

B32
NIEBUHR R.,MORAL MAN AND IMMORAL SOCIETY* A STUDY IN ETHICS AND POLITICS. UNIV CULTURE SOCIETY STRUCT DIPLOM GOV/REL GP/REL PERS/REL...TREND IDEA/COMP. PAGE 118 H2357
MORAL PWR

C34
BENEDICT R.,"RITUAL" IN ERA SELIGMAN, ENCYCLOPEDIA OF THE SOCIAL SCIENCES." GP/REL...SOC STYLE IDEA/COMP WORSHIP. PAGE 14 H0279
CULTURE ROUTINE ROLE STRUCT

B35
DE TOCQUEVILLE A.,DEMOCRACY IN AMERICA (4 VOLS.) (TRANS. BY HENRY REEVE). CONSTN STRUCT LOC/G NAT/G POL/PAR PROVS ETIQUET CT/SYS MAJORITY ATTIT 18/19. PAGE 39 H0772
POPULISM MAJORIT ORD/FREE SOCIETY

B35
GORER G.,AFRICA DANCES: A BOOK ABOUT WEST AFRICAN NEGROES. STRUCT LOC/G SECT FORCES TAX ADMIN COLONIAL...ART/METH MYTH WORSHIP 20 NEGRO AFRICA/W CHRISTIAN RITUAL. PAGE 59 H1181
AFR ATTIT CULTURE SOCIETY

B35
MORE T.,UTOPIA (1516) (TRANS. BY R. ROBYNSON). LAW CULTURE SOCIETY STRUCT FAM SECT EDU/PROP WAR OWN UTIL KNOWL WEALTH 16. PAGE 113 H2253
UTOPIA NAT/G ECO/TAC GEN/LAWS

B35
TAKEUCHI T.,WAR AND DIPLOMACY IN THE JAPANESE EMPIRE. ASIA ELITES STRATA NAT/G SECT LEGIS ACT/RES PLAN LEGIT PARL/PROC ROUTINE WAR...MGT BIOG CHINJAP TOT/POP 19/20 CHINJAP. PAGE 152 H3038
EXEC STRUCT

S35
RADCLIFFE-BROWN A.R.,"ON THE CONCEPT OF FUNCTION IN SOCIAL SCIENCE" (BMR)" UNIV CULTURE INTELL ...METH/CNCPT IDEA/COMP 20. PAGE 129 H2577
STRUCT SOCIETY CONCPT GEN/LAWS

S38
LUNDBERG G.A.,"THE CONCEPT OF LAW IN THE SOCIAL SCIENCES"(BMR)" CULTURE INTELL SOCIETY STRUCT CREATE...NEW/IDEA 20. PAGE 99 H1978
EPIST GEN/LAWS CONCPT PHIL/SCI

S38
MERTON R.K.,"SOCIAL STRUCTURE AND ANOMIE" (BMR)" UNIV CULTURE STRATA CREATE PARTIC ATTIT BIO/SOC PERSON...SOC CONCPT 20. PAGE 109 H2186
SOCIETY STRUCT ANOMIE DRIVE

B39
AKIGA,AKIGA'S STORY: THE TIV TRIBE AS SEEN BY ONE OF ITS MEMBERS. NIGERIA LAW STRUCT ECO/UNDEV FAM LEAD GP/REL MARRIAGE...LING WORSHIP 20. PAGE 4 H0089
KIN SECT SOC CULTURE

B39
COBBAN A.,DICTATORSHIP: ITS HISTORY AND THEORY. EUR+WWI MOD/EUR SOCIETY STRUCT NAT/G TEC/DEV LEAD NAT/LISM SOVEREIGN...IDEA/COMP 14/20. PAGE 30 H0610
TOTALISM FASCISM CONCPT

B39
ENGELS F.,HERRN EUGEN DUHRING'S REVOLUTION IN SCIENCE (1878). CULTURE STRATA STRUCT FAM SECT ECO/TAC REV WAR SOCISM...MARXIST 19. PAGE 46 H0925
PWR SOCIETY WEALTH GEN/LAWS

B39
HITLER A.,MEIN KAMPF. EUR+WWI FUT MOD/EUR STRUCT INT/ORG LABOR NAT/G POL/PAR FORCES CREATE PLAN BAL/PWR DIPLOM ECO/TAC DOMIN EDU/PROP ADMIN COERCE ATTIT...SOCIALIST BIOG TREND NAZI. PAGE 71 H1428
PWR NEW/IDEA WAR

B40
TONNIES F.,FUNDAMENTAL CONCEPTS OF SOCIOLOGY (1887) (TRANS. BY C. LOOMIS). LAW STRATA STRUCT FAM MUNIC NAT/G DOMIN LEGIT SANCTION COERCE CRIME PERSON 19. PAGE 156 H3115
CULTURE SOCIETY GEN/LAWS SOC

B41
KEESING F.M.,THE SOUTH SEAS IN THE MODERN WORLD. INDONESIA STRUCT FAM SECT EDU/PROP LEAD INCOME WEALTH...HEAL SOC 20. PAGE 84 H1678
CULTURE ECO/UNDEV GOV/COMP DIPLOM

B41
PALMER R.R.,TWELVE WHO RULED. MOD/EUR ELITES STRUCT NAT/G POL/PAR DELIB/GP DOMIN ATTIT SUPEGO PWR ...POLICY CONCPT 18. PAGE 123 H2453
TOP/EX BIOG REV FRANCE

C41
KLUCKHOHN C.,"PATTERNING AS EXEMPLIFIED IN NAVAHO CULTURE" IN EDWARD SAPIR, LANGUAGE, CULTURE, AND PERSONALITY (BMR)" KIN PERS/REL ATTIT PERSON...SOC CONCPT METH/CNCPT LING OBS/ENVIR CON/ANAL BIBLIOG SOC/INTEG 20 NAVAHO INDIAN/AM SAPIR/EDW. PAGE 87 H1733
CULTURE INGP/REL STRUCT

B43
LENIN V.I.,LEFT WING COMMUNISM: AN INFANTILE DISORDER (1920). GERMANY MOD/EUR USSR STRUCT CHIEF DOMIN EDU/PROP LEGIT LEAD REPRESENT POPULISM ...METH/COMP 19 LENIN/VI COM/PARTY MENSHEVIK. PAGE 94 H1879
COM MARXISM NAT/G REV

B46
BLUM L.,FOR ALL MANKIND (TRANS. BY W. PICKLES). FRANCE GERMANY USSR LAW SOCIETY STRUCT POL/PAR WORKER DIPLOM DOMIN CHOOSE ORD/FREE FASCISM 20. PAGE 18 H0361
POPULISM SOCIALIST NAT/G WAR

S46
DE GRE G.,"FREEDOM AND SOCIAL STRUCTURE" (BMR)" UNIV SOCIETY DOMIN CONTROL TOTALISM PLURISM...SOC CHARTS. PAGE 38 H0753
ORD/FREE STRUCT CONCPT GP/REL

S46
TANNENBAUM F.,"THE BALANCE OF POWER IN SOCIETY." UNIV STRUCT FAM NAT/G SECT PERS/REL EQUILIB UTOPIA DRIVE ALL/IDEOS...OLD/LIB CONCPT. PAGE 152 H3044
SOCIETY ALL/VALS GP/REL PEACE

B47
GITLOW A.L.,ECONOMICS OF THE MOUNT HAGEN TRIBES, NEW GUINEA. S/ASIA STRUCT AGRI FAM...GEOG MYTH 20 NEW/GUINEA. PAGE 57 H1137
HABITAT ECO/UNDEV CULTURE KIN

B47
ISAAC J.,ECONOMICS OF MIGRATION. MOD/EUR CULTURE STRATA STRUCT NAT/G COLONIAL WEALTH...OLD/LIB TREND TIME 19/20 EUROPE/W MIGRATION. PAGE 78 H1569
HABITAT SOC GEOG

B47
NIEBUHR R.,THE CHILDREN OF LIGHT AND THE CHILDREN OF DARKNESS: A VINDICATION OF DEMOCRACY AND CRITIQUE OF TRADITIONAL DEFENSE. UNIV STRUCT NAT/G SECT INGP/REL OWN PEACE ORD/FREE MARXISM ...IDEA/COMP GEN/LAWS 20 CHRISTIAN. PAGE 118 H2358
POPULISM DIPLOM NEIGH GP/REL

B48
COX O.C.,CASTE, CLASS, AND RACE. INDIA WOR+45 WOR-45 SECT TEC/DEV MARRIAGE ROLE MARXISM...MAJORIT NAT/COMP SOC/INTEG 20 NEGRO HINDU. PAGE 34 H0688
RACE/REL STRUCT STRATA DISCRIM

B48
MAUGHAM R.,NORTH AFRICAN NOTEBOOK. ALGERIA ISLAM LIBYA MOROCCO STRUCT ECO/UNDEV COLONIAL...SOC OBS AUD/VIS NAT/COMP WORSHIP 20 TUNIS. PAGE 105 H2102
SOCIETY RECORD NAT/LISM

B48
MINISTERE FINANCES ET ECO,BULLETIN BIBLIOGRAPHIQUE. AFR EUR+WWI FRANCE CULTURE STRUCT FINAN NAT/G ACT/RES INT/TRADE ADMIN REGION PRODUC STAT. PAGE 111 H2224
BIBLIOG/A ECO/UNDEV TEC/DEV COLONIAL

L48
SHILS E.A.,"COHESION AND DISINTEGRATION IN THE WEHRMACHT IN WORLD WAR II." GERMANY STRUCT DOMIN WAR INGP/REL ISOLAT NAT/LISM ATTIT AUTHORIT SUPEGO RESPECT...PSY CON/ANAL 20 NAZI. PAGE 143 H2862
EDU/PROP DRIVE PERS/REL FORCES

B49
HOLLERAN M.P.,CHURCH AND STATE IN GUATEMALA. GUATEMALA LAW STRUCT CATHISM...SOC SOC/INTEG 17/20 CHURCH/STA. PAGE 73 H1456
SECT NAT/G GP/REL CULTURE

S49
DEXTER L.A.,"A DIALOGUE ON THE SOCIAL PSYCHOLOGY OF COLONIALISM AND ON CERTAIN PUERTO RICAN PROFESSIONAL PERSONALITY PATTERNS." L/A+17C PUERT/RICO STRATA STRUCT DOMIN ISOLAT DRIVE ...NAT/COMP PERS/COMP HYPO/EXP 20 JEWS NEGRO. PAGE 41 H0813
COLONIAL SOC PSY PERSON

S49
HUGHES E.C.,"SOCIAL CHANGE AND STATUS PROTEST: AN ESSAY ON THE MARGINAL MAN" (BMR)" EUR+WWI UK USA+45 CULTURE SOCIETY STRUCT RACE/REL...SOC NAT/COMP SOC/INTEG 19/20 NEGRO PARK/R. PAGE 74 H1490
STRATA ATTIT DISCRIM

B50
BERMAN H.J.,JUSTICE IN RUSSIA; AN INTERPRETATION OF SOVIET LAW. USSR LAW STRUCT LABOR FORCES AGREE GP/REL ORD/FREE SOCISM...TIME/SEQ 20. PAGE 15 H0309
JURID ADJUD MARXISM COERCE

B50
CORNELL U DEPT ASIAN STUDIES,SOUTHEAST ASIA PROGRAM DATA PAPER. BURMA CAMBODIA INDONESIA MALAYSIA VIETNAM SOCIETY STRUCT NAT/G SECT DIPLOM FOR/AID PWR WEALTH...SOC 20. PAGE 33 H0670
BIBLIOG/A CULTURE S/ASIA ECO/UNDEV

B50
IRION F.C.,PUBLIC OPINION AND PROPAGANDA. STRUCT COM/IND FAM SECT COERCE 20 FILM. PAGE 78 H1568
EDU/PROP ATTIT NAT/G PRESS

B50
LIPSET S.M.,AGRARIAN SOCIALISM. CANADA POL/PAR OP/RES ECO/TAC ADMIN ATTIT...TIME/SEQ NAT/COMP SOC/EXP 20 SASKATCH. PAGE 97 H1938
SOCISM AGRI METH/COMP STRUCT

C50
ROUSSEAU J.J.,"DISCOURSE ON THE ORIGIN OF INEQUALITY" (1755) IN THE SOCIAL CONTRACT AND DISCOURSES." UNIV NAT/G PLAN BAL/PWR HAPPINESS UTOPIA BIO/SOC HEREDITY MORAL...WELF/ST CONCPT. PAGE 135 H2698
SOCIETY STRUCT PERSON GEN/LAWS

C50
ROUSSEAU J.J.,"A DISCOURSE ON POLITICAL ECONOMY" (1755) IN THE SOCIAL CONTRACT AND DISCOURSES." UNIV SOCIETY STRATA STRUCT CONSEN EQUILIB HAPPINESS UTOPIA HEALTH WEALTH...POLICY WELF/ST. PAGE 135 H2699
NAT/G ECO/TAC TAX GEN/LAWS

B51
INTERNATIONAL AFRICAN INST,ETHNOGRAPHIC SURVEY OF AFRICA: WEST CENTRAL AFRICA (VOLS. I-III, 1951-1953). AFR RHODESIA CULTURE ECO/UNDEV HEREDITY ...GEOG SOC CHARTS BIBLIOG WORSHIP 20 CONGO/LEOP. PAGE 77 H1543
STRUCT KIN INGP/REL HABITAT

B51
JENNINGS S.I.,THE COMMONWEALTH IN ASIA. CEYLON INDIA PAKISTAN S/ASIA UK CONSTN CULTURE SOCIETY STRATA STRUCT NAT/G POL/PAR EDU/PROP LEAD WAR 20 CMN/WLTH. PAGE 80 H1608
NAT/LISM REGION COLONIAL DIPLOM

B51
WEBSTER C.,THE FOREIGN POLICY OF PALMERSTON - 1830 TO 1841. MOD/EUR UK LAW CONSTN INTELL SOCIETY STRUCT NAT/G FORCES TOP/EX CREATE BAL/PWR PWR 19. PAGE 166 H3323
ADMIN PERSON DIPLOM

B51
YOUNG T.C.,NEAR EASTERN CULTURE AND SOCIETY. ISLAM ECO/UNDEV SECT WRITING ATTIT HABITAT ORD/FREE 20. PAGE 172 H3439
CULTURE STRUCT REGION DIPLOM

B52
FORDE L.D.,HABITAT, ECONOMY AND SOCIETY. AFR L/A+17C S/ASIA STRUCT AGRI INGP/REL...GEOG OBS BIBLIOG 20. PAGE 52 H1037
SOC HABITAT CULTURE ECO/UNDEV

B52
INTERNATIONAL AFRICAN INST,ETHNOGRAPHIC SURVEY OF AFRICA: SOUTHERN AFRICA (VOLS. I-III, 1952-1954). AFR SOUTH/AFR CULTURE ECO/UNDEV GOV/REL HEREDITY ...GEOG SOC CHARTS BIBLIOG WORSHIP 20. PAGE 77 H1544
STRUCT KIN INGP/REL HABITAT

B52
KROEBER A.L.,THE NATURE OF CULTURE. UNIV STRATA FAM KIN SECT...PSY GP/COMP 16/20 INDIAN/AM. PAGE 89 H1771
CULTURE SOCIETY CONCPT STRUCT

B52
SPICER E.H.,HUMAN PROBLEMS IN TECHNOLOGICAL CHANGE. ECO/UNDEV AGRI INDUS NAT/G ACT/RES LEAD GP/REL INGP/REL ROLE...INT METH 20 CASEBOOK. PAGE 147 H2947
TEC/DEV CULTURE STRUCT OP/RES

B52
ULAM A.B.,TITOISM AND THE COMINFORM. USSR WOR+45 STRUCT INT/ORG NAT/G ACT/RES PLAN EXEC ATTIT DRIVE ALL/VALS...CONCPT OBS VAL/FREE 20 COMINTERN TITO/MARSH. PAGE 157 H3149
COM POL/PAR TOTALISM YUGOSLAVIA

S52
KECSKEMETI P.,"THE 'POLICY SCIENCES': ASPIRATION AND OUTLOOK." UNIV CULTURE INTELL SOCIETY STRUCT EDU/PROP ATTIT PERCEPT RIGID/FLEX KNOWL...PHIL/SCI METH/CNCPT OBS 20. PAGE 84 H1674
CREATE NEW/IDEA

B53
BENDIX R.,CLASS, STATUS AND POWER: A READER IN SOCIAL STRATIFICATION. USA+45 SOCIETY ACT/RES DOMIN ATTIT RIGID/FLEX...PSY SOC CONCPT METH/COMP NAT/COMP 20. PAGE 14 H0273
STRATA PWR STRUCT ROLE

B53
KEESING F.M.,CULTURE CHANGE: AN ANALYSIS AND BIBLIOGRAPHY OF ANTHROPOLOGICAL SOURCES TO 1952. CULTURE STRUCT...TIME/SEQ 19/20. PAGE 84 H1679
BIBLIOG SOC CREATE ORD/FREE

B53
LENZ F.,DIE BEWEGUNGEN DER GROSSEN MACHTE. USA+45 USA-45 USSR SOCIETY STRATA STRUCT NAT/G PERSON MARXISM...CONCPT IDEA/COMP NAT/COMP 18/20. PAGE 94 H1883
BAL/PWR TREND DIPLOM HIST/WRIT

B53
MAXIMOFF G.P.,THE POLITICAL PHILOSOPHY OF BAKUNIN: SCIENTIFIC ANARCHISM. STRUCT INGP/REL FEDERAL MARXISM...ANARCH BIOG 19 BAKUNIN. PAGE 105 H2104
SOCIETY PHIL/SCI NAT/G IDEA/COMP

B53
MIT CENTER INTERNATIONAL STU,BIBLIOGRAPHY OF THE ECONOMIC AND POLITICAL DEVELOPMENT OF INDONESIA. INDONESIA STRUCT NAT/G COLONIAL LEAD...STAT 20. PAGE 111 H2226
BIBLIOG ECO/UNDEV TEC/DEV S/ASIA

B53
WAGLEY C.,AMAZON TOWN: A STUDY OF MAN IN THE TROPICS. BRAZIL L/A+17C STRATA STRUCT ECO/UNDEV AGRI EX/STRUC RACE/REL DISCRIM HABITAT WEALTH...OBS SOC/EXP 20. PAGE 164 H3285
SOC NEIGH CULTURE INGP/REL

S53
DRUCKER P.F.,"THE EMPLOYEE SOCIETY." STRUCT BAL/PWR PARTIC REPRESENT PWR...DECISION CONCPT. PAGE 42 H0849
LABOR MGT WORKER CULTURE

S53
ROGOFF N.,"SOCIAL STRATIFICATION IN FRANCE AND IN THE UNITED STATES" (BMR)" FRANCE USA+45 WORKER ADJUST PERSON...SOC 20. PAGE 133 H2662
STRUCT STRATA ATTIT NAT/COMP

B54
KOLARZ W.,THE PEOPLES OF THE SOVIET FAR EAST. RUSSIA USSR STRUCT LEAD ISOLAT NAT/LISM...CHARTS 20. PAGE 88 H1750
COLONIAL RACE/REL ADJUST CULTURE

B54
LENIN V.I.,SELECTED WORKS (12 VOLS.). USSR INTELL SOCIETY STRATA STRUCT NAT/G POL/PAR WORKER CAP/ISM REV WAR...MARXIST PHIL/SCI 20 MARX/KARL LENIN/VI. PAGE 94 H1880
COM MARXISM

B54
SPROTT W.J.H.,SCIENCE AND SOCIAL ACTION. STRUCT ACT/RES CRIME GP/REL INGP/REL ANOMIE...PSY SOC/INTEG 19/20. PAGE 148 H2956
SOC CULTURE PHIL/SCI

L54
FURNISS E.S.,"WEAKNESSES IN FRENCH FOREIGN POLICY-MAKING." EUR+WWI LEGIS LEGIT EXEC ATTIT RIGID/FLEX ORD/FREE...SOC CONCPT METH/CNCPT OBS 20. PAGE 54 H1078
NAT/G STRUCT DIPLOM FRANCE

S54
ALBRECT M.C.,"THE RELATIONSHIP OF LITERATURE AND SOCIETY." STRATA STRUCT DIPLOM...POLICY SOC/INTEG. PAGE 5 H0097
HUM CULTURE WRITING NAT/COMP

C54
GUINS G.C.,"SOVIET LAW AND SOVIET SOCIETY." COM USSR STRATA FAM NAT/G WORKER DOMIN RACE/REL ...BIBLIOG 20. PAGE 62 H1249
LAW STRUCT PLAN

B55
COLE G.D.H.,STUDIES IN CLASS STRUCTURE. UK NAT/G WORKER TEC/DEV EDU/PROP...CLASSIF CHARTS 20. PAGE 31 H0623
STRUCT STRATA ELITES CONCPT

B55
CRAIG G.A.,THE POLITICS OF THE PRUSSIAN ARMY 1640-1945. CHRIST-17C EUR+WWI MOD/EUR PRUSSIA STRUCT DIPLOM ADMIN REV WAR...SOC BIBLIOG 17/20. PAGE 35 H0694
FORCES NAT/G ROLE CHIEF

B55
FLECHTHEIM O.K.,DIE DEUTSCHEN PARTEIEN SEIT 1945. GERMANY/W CONSTN STRUCT FINAN ATTIT 20. PAGE 51 H1022
POL/PAR NAT/G GP/COMP

B55
HEYDTE A F.,SOZIOLOGIE DER DEUTSCHEN PARTEIEN. GERMANY/W CONSTN ELITES CHOOSE 20. PAGE 70 H1412
POL/PAR SOC STRUCT NAT/G

B55
INTERNATIONAL AFRICAN INST,ETHNOGRAPHIC SURVEY OF AFRICA: NORTH EASTERN AFRICA (VOLUMES 1-2, 1955-56). AFR ETHIOPIA CULTURE ECO/UNDEV KIN GOV/REL ATTIT HEREDITY...GEOG CHARTS BIBLIOG WORSHIP 20. PAGE 77 H1545
STRUCT ECO/TAC INGP/REL HABITAT

B55
INTERNATIONAL AFRICAN INST,ETHNOGRAPHIC SURVEY OF AFRICA: WESTERN AFRICA: PEOPLES OF THE NIGER-BENUE CONFLUENCE. AFR NIGER CULTURE ECO/UNDEV KIN GOV/REL GP/REL ATTIT HEREDITY...CHARTS BIBLIOG WORSHIP 20. PAGE 77 H1546
STRUCT GEOG HABITAT INGP/REL

B55
LIPSCOMB J.F.,WHITE AFRICANS. SOCIETY STRUCT AGRI ECO/TAC ADJUD COLONIAL COERCE PERS/REL ADJUST. PAGE 97 H1937
RACE/REL HABITAT ECO/UNDEV ORD/FREE

B55
SHAFER B.C.,NATIONALISM: MYTH AND REALITY. FRANCE UK USA+45 USA-45 CULTURE SOCIETY STRUCT ECO/DEV WAR PWR...NAT/COMP BIBLIOG 18/20. PAGE 142 H2837
NAT/LISM MYTH NAT/G CONCPT

B55
THOMPSON V.,MINORITY PROBLEMS IN SOUTHEAST ASIA. CAMBODIA CHINA/COM LAOS S/ASIA KIN NAT/G SECT PROB/SOLV EDU/PROP REGION GP/REL RACE/REL MARXISM ...SOC 20 BUDDHISM UN. PAGE 154 H3085
INGP/REL GEOG DIPLOM STRUCT

L55
ROSTOW W.W.,"RUSSIA AND CHINA UNDER COMMUNISM." CHINA/COM USSR INTELL STRUCT INT/ORG NAT/G POL/PAR TOP/EX ACT/RES PLAN ADMIN ATTIT ALL/VALS MARXISM ...CONCPT OBS TIME/SEQ TREND GOV/COMP VAL/FREE 20. PAGE 134 H2689
COM ASIA

S55
DE SMITH S.A.,"CONSTITUTIONAL MONARCHY IN BURGANDA." AFR UGANDA UK STRUCT CHIEF REGION INGP/REL ADJUST NAT/LISM SOVEREIGN CONSERVE ...POLICY 19/20 BURGANDA. PAGE 38 H0769
NAT/G DIPLOM CONSTN COLONIAL

S55
GOODENOUGH W.H.,"A PROBLEM IN MALAYO-POLYNESIAN SOCIAL ORGANIZATION" (BMR)" MALAYSIA S/ASIA CULTURE AGRI PROB/SOLV OWN HABITAT...SOC 20 20 POLYNESIA. PAGE 58 H1170
KIN STRUCT FAM ECO/UNDEV

C55
OLIVER D.L.,"A LEADER IN ACTION," IN D. A. OLIVER, SOLOMON ISLAND SOCIETY." S/ASIA SOCIETY STRUCT CONTROL TASK PWR...OBS/ENVIR WORSHIP 20. PAGE 121 H2413
LEAD RESPECT CULTURE KIN

B56
BECKER H.,MAN IN RECIPROCITY: INTRODUCTORY LECTURES ON CULTURE, SOCIETY, AND PERSONALITY. LAW FAM SECT REGION GP/REL ADJUST ATTIT PERSON...BIBLIOG 20. PAGE 13 H0253
CULTURE STRUCT SOC PSY

B56
CENTRAL AFRICAN ARCHIVES,A GUIDE TO THE PUBLIC RECORDS OF SOUTHERN RHODESIA UNDER THE REGIME OF THE BRITISH SOUTH AFRICA COMPANY, 1890-1923. UK STRUCT NAT/G WRITING GP/REL 19/20. PAGE 28 H0566
BIBLIOG/A COLONIAL ADMIN AFR

B56
CEPEDA U.A.,EN TORNO AL CONCEPTO DEL ESTADO EN LOS REYES CATHOLICOS. SPAIN SOCIETY STRUCT SECT LEGIT WAR ATTIT WORSHIP 15/17. PAGE 28 H0569
NAT/G PHIL/SCI CHIEF PWR

B56
EVANS-PRITCHARD E.E.,THE INSTITUTIONS OF PRIMITIVE SOCIETY. LAW SOCIETY KIN ACT/RES CREATE ALL/VALS ...ART/METH SOC METH/CNCPT WORSHIP 20. PAGE 48 H0953
STRUCT PHIL/SCI CULTURE CONCPT

B56
INTERNATIONAL AFRICAN INST,ETHNOGRAPHIC SURVEY OF AFRICA; WESTERN AFRICA: PAGAN PEOPLES OF CENTRAL AREA OF NORTHERN NIGERIA (VOL. XII). NIGERIA FAM KIN SECT ECO/TAC GOV/REL GP/REL ATTIT...LING CHARTS 20. PAGE 77 H1548
STRUCT INGP/REL HABITAT CULTURE

B56
SHAPIRO H.L.,MAN, CULTURE, AND SOCIETY. STRUCT FAM SECT GP/REL INGP/REL...ART/METH GEOG PSY LING ANTHOL BIBLIOG. PAGE 142 H2842
CULTURE PERSON SOC

B56
SYKES G.M.,CRIME AND SOCIETY. LAW STRATA STRUCT ACT/RES ROUTINE ANOMIE WEALTH...POLICY SOC/INTEG 20. PAGE 151 H3021
CRIMLGY CRIME CULTURE INGP/REL

B56
TRAGER F.N.,ANNOTATED BIBLIOGRAPHY OF BURMA. BURMA STRUCT NAT/G...GEOG JURID MGT SOC 20. PAGE 156 H3127
BIBLIOG/A S/ASIA CULTURE SOCIETY

B56
VIANNA F.J.,EVOLUCAO DE POVO BRASILEIRO (4TH ED.). BRAZIL TEC/DEV COLONIAL GP/REL ATTIT SOVEREIGN ...SOC SOC/INTEG 15/20. PAGE 162 H3247
STRUCT RACE/REL NAT/G

B56
VUCINICH A.,THE SOVIET ACADEMY OF SCIENCES. USSR STRUCT ACADEM NAT/G EDU/PROP ADMIN LEAD ROLE ...BIBLIOG 20 ACADEM/SCI. PAGE 164 H3280
PHIL/SCI CREATE INTELL PROF/ORG

B56
WEBER M.,STAATSSOZIOLOGIE. STRUCT LEGIT ADMIN PARL/PROC SUPEGO CONSERVE JURID. PAGE 166 H3320
SOC NAT/G POL/PAR LEAD

B56
WEBER M.,WIRTSCHAFT UND GESELLSCHAFT (2ND VOL.). STRUCT NAT/G POL/PAR LEAD PWR OBJECTIVE IDEA/COMP. PAGE 166 H3321
LEGIT JURID SOC

B56
WHITAKER A.P.,ARGENTINE UPHEAVAL. STRUCT FORCES DIPLOM COERCE PWR 20 ARGEN. PAGE 167 H3343
REV POL/PAR STRATA NAT/G

S56
BLAU P.M.,"SOCIAL MOBILITY AND INTERPERSONAL RELATIONS" (BMR)" UNIV CULTURE STRUCT WORKER ANOMIE ...SOC SOC/INTEG 19/20. PAGE 18 H0355
INGP/REL PERS/REL ORD/FREE STRATA

S56
EPSTEIN L.D.,"COHESION OF BRITISH PARLIAMENTARY PARTIES." UK STRUCT ADMIN ROUTINE INGP/REL PWR ...GP/COMP PARLIAMENT. PAGE 47 H0935
NAT/G PARL/PROC POL/PAR

N56
US HOUSE COMM FOREIGN AFFAIRS,REPORT OF THE SPECIAL STUDY MISSION TO AFRICA, SOUTH AND EAST OF THE SAHARA (PAMPHLET). AFR SOUTH/AFR USA+45 STRUCT INT/TRADE PARL/PROC NAT/LISM ATTIT ALL/VALS HEALTH ...POLICY 20 CONGRESS. PAGE 160 H3197
FOR/AID COLONIAL ECO/UNDEV DIPLOM

B57
COLE G.D.H.,THE POST WAR CONDITIONS OF BRITAIN. EUR+WWI STRUCT NAT/G PLAN EDU/PROP LEGIT RIGID/FLEX ORD/FREE WEALTH...SOCIALIST WELF/ST STAT TREND CON/ANAL CHARTS PARLIAMENT WORK 20. PAGE 31 H0624
ECO/DEV UK

B57
HODGKIN T.,NATIONALISM IN COLONIAL AFRICA. STRATA STRUCT MUNIC NAT/G POL/PAR LEGIS ATTIT SOVEREIGN ...POLICY TREND BIBLIOG 20. PAGE 72 H1444
AFR COLONIAL NAT/LISM DIPLOM

B57
IKE N.,JAPANESE POLITICS. INTELL STRUCT AGRI INDUS FAM KIN LABOR PRESS CHOOSE ATTIT...DECISION BIBLIOG 19/20 CHINJAP. PAGE 76 H1523
NAT/G ADMIN POL/PAR CULTURE

B57
INTERNATIONAL AFRICAN INST,ETHNOGRAPHIC SURVEY OF AFRICA: WESTERN AFRICA: THE BENIN KINGDOM. AFR NIGERIA CULTURE ECO/UNDEV KIN ECO/TAC GOV/REL AGE ATTIT HEREDITY...CHARTS BIBLIOG WORSHIP 20. PAGE 77 H1550
STRUCT INGP/REL GEOG HABITAT

B57
INTERNATIONAL AFRICAN INST,ETHNOGRAPHIC SURVEY OF AFRICA: WESTERN AFRICA: THE WOLOF OF SENEGAMBIA. AFR SENEGAL CULTURE ECO/UNDEV FAM KIN REGION ...CHARTS GP/COMP BIBLIOG WORSHIP 20. PAGE 78 H1551
STRUCT GEOG HABITAT INGP/REL

B57
KOENTJARANINGRAT R.,A PRELIMINARY DESCRIPTION OF THE JAVANESE KINSHIP SYSTEM. INDONESIA STRATA FAM INGP/REL ADJUST MARRIAGE AGE/C AGE/Y AGE/A PERSON ...OBS CHARTS DICTIONARY 20 JAVA. PAGE 87 H1736
KIN STRUCT ELITES CULTURE

B57
MENDIETTA Y NUNE L.,THEORIE DES GROUPEMENT SOCIAUX SUIVI D'UNE ETUDE SUR LE DROIT SOCIAL. ELITES FAM KIN NAT/G PROB/SOLV CROWD ISOLAT ATTIT PERSON ...JURID CONCPT SOC/INTEG. PAGE 109 H2174
SOC STRATA STRUCT DISCRIM

B57
PIDDINGTON R.,AN INTRODUCTION TO SOCIAL ANTHROPOLOGY (VOL. II). SOCIETY STRUCT FAM INGP/REL ...OBS CHARTS. PAGE 125 H2507
CULTURE SOC TEC/DEV GEOG

B57
ROSS R.,THE FABRIC OF SOCIETY. STRATA GP/REL PERSON ...CONCPT METH T 20. PAGE 134 H2687
SOC PHIL/SCI CULTURE STRUCT

B58
BRIGGS L.C.,THE LIVING RACES OF THE SAHARA. STRATA AGRI KIN INT/TRADE HABITAT...GEOG AUD/VIS CHARTS BIBLIOG 20 SAHARA MIGRATION. PAGE 21 H0417
STRUCT SOCIETY SOC CULTURE

B58
GLUCKMAN M.,ANALYSIS OF A SOCIAL SITUATION IN MODERN ZULULAND. AFR PERS/REL ADJUST DISCRIM EQUILIB NAT/LISM...SOC RECORD AUD/VIS 20 ZULULAND. PAGE 57 H1146
CULTURE RACE/REL STRUCT GP/REL

B58
JOHNSON J.J.,POLITICAL CHANGE IN LATIN AMERICA: THE EMERGENCE OF THE MIDDLE SECTORS. INTELL STRATA STRUCT ECO/UNDEV MUNIC TEC/DEV LEAD REV...DECISION TREND GOV/COMP BIBLIOG/A 20. PAGE 81 H1621
L/A+17C ELITES GP/REL DOMIN

B58
KINTNER W.R.,ORGANIZING FOR CONFLICT: A PROPOSAL. USSR STRUCT NAT/G LEGIS ADMIN EXEC PEACE ORD/FREE PWR...CONCPT OBS TREND NAT/COMP VAL/FREE COLD/WAR 20. PAGE 86 H1719
USA+45 PLAN DIPLOM

B58
MATOS J.,LAS ACTUALES COMMUNIDADES DE INDIGENAS: HUAROCHIRI EN 1955. PERU FAM NAT/G SECT EDU/PROP ADJUD GP/REL INGP/REL 20 INDIAN/AM. PAGE 105 H2091
STRUCT NEIGH KIN ECO/UNDEV

B58
OGILVIE C.,THE KING'S GOVERNMENT AND THE COMMON LAW, 1471-1641. UK STRUCT NAT/G CHIEF LEGIS WORKER BAL/PWR GP/REL AUTHORIT 15/17 COMMON/LAW. PAGE 120 H2408
CONSTN ELITES DOMIN

B58
STUBEL H.,THE MEWU FANTZU. CHINA/COM INDIA EDU/PROP ADJUD CRIME GP/REL OWN...OBS 20 TIBET. PAGE 150 H3001
CULTURE STRUCT SECT FAM

B58
VON FURER-HAIMEN E.,AN ANTHROPOLOGICAL BIBLIOGRAPHY OF SOUTH ASIA (VOL. I). STRATA STRUCT KIN SECT ACT/RES CREATE HABITAT...GEOG OBS 19/20. PAGE 163 H3267
BIBLIOG/A CULTURE S/ASIA SOC

B58
WARNER W.L.,A BLACK CIVILIZATION - A SOCIAL STUDY OF AN AUSTRALIAN TRIBE. SOCIETY FAM MARRIAGE...PSY SOC MYTH CHARTS 20 AUSTRAL MAPS MURNGIN RITUAL. PAGE 165 H3310
CULTURE KIN STRUCT DEATH

B58
WIGGIN L.M.,THE FACTION OF COUSINS: A POLITICAL ACCOUNT OF THE GRENVILLES, 1733-1763. UK STRUCT KIN NAT/G INGP/REL...CONCPT BIOG BIBLIOG/A 18 GRENVILLES. PAGE 168 H3357
FAM POL/PAR PWR

B59
DAHRENDORF R.,CLASS AND CLASS CONFLICT IN INDUSTRIAL SOCIETY. LABOR NAT/G COERCE ROLE PLURISM ...POLICY MGT CONCPT CLASSIF. PAGE 37 H0734
VOL/ASSN STRUCT SOC GP/REL

B59
GOLDSCHMIDT W.,UNDERSTANDING HUMAN SOCIETY. SOCIETY CREATE ATTIT...GEOG PHIL/SCI CONCPT GP/COMP. PAGE 58 H1159
CULTURE STRUCT TEC/DEV PERSON

B59
HEMMERLE J.,SUDETENDEUTSCHE BIBLIOGRAPHIE 1949-1953. CZECHOSLVK GERMANY SOCIETY STRUCT SECT ...GEOG JURID 20. PAGE 69 H1391
BIBLIOG PROVS GP/REL CULTURE

B59
HONINGMAN J.J.,THE WORLD OF MAN. CHRIST-17C MEDIT-7 PRE/AMER PREHIST CREATE INGP/REL BIO/SOC HABITAT ...PSY SOC BIBLIOG. PAGE 73 H1460
CULTURE METH PERSON STRUCT

B59
LEMBERG E.,DIE VERTRIEBENEN IN WESTDEUTSCHLAND (3 VOLS.). GERMANY/W CULTURE STRUCT AGRI PROVS ADMIN ...JURID 20 MIGRATION. PAGE 94 H1875
GP/REL INGP/REL SOCIETY

B59
LIPSET S.M.,SOCIAL MOBILITY IN INDUSTRIAL SOCIETY. EUR+WWI USA+45 USSR STRUCT INDUS WRITING GP/REL INGP/REL DRIVE...SOC CHARTS NAT/COMP SOC/INTEG 20
STRATA ECO/DEV SOCIETY

MARX/KARL ENGELS/F. PAGE 97 H1940

SHARMA R.S.,ASPECTS OF POLITICAL IDEAS AND INSTITUTIONS IN ANCIENT INDIA. INDIA SOCIETY STRUCT FAM VOL/ASSN TAX DOMIN...CONCPT HIST/WRIT 7. PAGE 142 H2848 — B59 CULTURE JURID DELIB/GP SECT

SVALASTOGA K.,PRESTIGE, CLASS, AND MOBILITY. DENMARK UK EDU/PROP INCOME WEALTH...SOC SAMP 20. PAGE 151 H3010 — B59 NAT/COMP STRATA STRUCT ELITES

VINACKE H.M.,A HISTORY OF THE FAR EAST IN MODERN TIMES (6TH ED.). KOREA S/ASIA USSR CONSTN CULTURE STRATA ECO/UNDEV NAT/G CHIEF FOR/AID INT/TRADE GP/REL...SOC NAT/COMP 19/20 CHINJAP. PAGE 163 H3255 — B59 STRUCT ASIA

VITTACHIT,EMERGENCY '58. CEYLON UK STRUCT NAT/G FORCES ADJUD CRIME REV NAT/LISM 20. PAGE 163 H3258 — B59 RACE/REL DISCRIM DIPLOM SOVEREIGN

AUSTRUY J.,STRUCTURE ECONOMIQUE ET CIVILISATION: L'EGYPTE ET LE DESTIN ECONOMIQUE DE L'ISLAM. ISLAM UAR CREATE OP/RES ECO/TAC...SOC BIBLIOG 20 MUSLIM. PAGE 9 H0182 — B60 ECO/UNDEV CULTURE STRUCT

BOZEMAN A.B.,POLITICS AND CULTURE IN INTERNATIONAL HISTORY. WOR-45 STRUCT SECT...SOC TIME/SEQ NAT/COMP BIBLIOG. PAGE 20 H0393 — B60 CULTURE DIPLOM GOV/COMP ALL/IDEOS

EASTON S.C.,THE TWILIGHT OF EUROPEAN COLONIALISM. AFR S/ASIA CONSTN SOCIETY STRUCT ECO/UNDEV INDUS NAT/G FORCES ECO/TAC COLONIAL CT/SYS ATTIT KNOWL ORD/FREE PWR...SOCIALIST TIME/SEQ TREND CON/ANAL 20. PAGE 44 H0882 — B60 FINAN ADMIN

GENTILE G.,GENESIS AND STRUCTURE OF SOCIETY (TRANS. BY H.S. HARRIS). NAT/G SECT ATTIT SUPEGO...JURID 20. PAGE 56 H1111 — B60 SOCIETY STRUCT PERSON

HUGHES C.C.,PEOPLE OF COVE AND WOODLOT; COMMUNITIES FROM THE VIEWPOINT OF SOCIAL PSYCHIATRY. CULTURE FAM PROVS HABITAT...PSY QU SAMP/SIZ CHARTS BIBLIOG 20. PAGE 74 H1489 — B60 GEOG SOCIETY STRUCT HEALTH

INTERNATIONAL AFRICAN INST,ETHNOGRAPHIC SURVEY OF AFRICA: WESTERN AFRICA: PEOPLES OF THE MIDDLE NIGER REGION, NORTHERN NIGERIA. AFR NIGER CULTURE ECO/UNDEV KIN NEIGH GOV/REL GP/REL ATTIT HEREDITY ...CHARTS BIBLIOG WORSHIP 20. PAGE 78 H1552 — B60 STRUCT GEOG HABITAT INGP/REL

LISTER L.,EUROPE'S COAL AND STEEL COMMUNITY. FRANCE GERMANY STRUCT ECO/DEV EXTR/IND INDUS MARKET NAT/G DELIB/GP ECO/TAC INT/TRADE EDU/PROP ATTIT RIGID/FLEX ORD/FREE PWR WEALTH...CONCPT STAT TIME/SEQ CHARTS ECSC 20. PAGE 97 H1941 — B60 EUR+WWI INT/ORG REGION

MACRIDIS R.C.,THE DE GAULLE REPUBLIC: QUEST FOR UNITY. EUR+WWI NAT/G POL/PAR LEGIS LEGIT NAT/LISM ATTIT RIGID/FLEX ORD/FREE PWR...JURID CONCPT TIME/SEQ 20 DEGAULLE/C. PAGE 100 H2009 — B60 TOP/EX STRUCT FRANCE

MANIS J.G.,MAN AND SOCIETY. STRATA LEAD INGP/REL PERS/REL ATTIT PWR...PSY ANTHOL T SOC/INTEG MARX/KARL MILL/JS FREUD/S CHURCHLL/W SPENCER/H RUSSELL/B. PAGE 102 H2036 — B60 SOC SOCIETY STRUCT CULTURE

NICHOLLS W.H.,SOUTHERN TRADITION AND REGIONAL PROGRESS. STRATA STRUCT SCHOOL WORKER PARTIC REGION RACE/REL CONSEN ATTIT...SOC METH/CNCPT 19/20 SOUTH/US TVA. PAGE 118 H2349 — B60 RIGID/FLEX CONSERVE AGRI CULTURE

OTTENBERG S.,CULTURES AND SOCIETIES OF AFRICA. AFR KIN TEC/DEV GP/REL MARRIAGE ATTIT HABITAT HEREDITY ...ANTHOL BIBLIOG T WORSHIP 20. PAGE 122 H2433 — B60 SOCIETY INGP/REL STRUCT CULTURE

ROSKAM K.L.,APARTHEID AND DISCRIMINATION. SOUTH/AFR SOCIETY STRUCT NAT/G POL/PAR GP/REL ISOLAT ...BIBLIOG 20. PAGE 134 H2683 — B60 DISCRIM RACE/REL CULTURE POLICY

SCHAPIRO L.,THE COMMUNIST PARTY OF THE SOVIET UNION. COM LAW SOCIETY STRATA STRUCT ECO/DEV LABOR NAT/G POL/PAR CREATE DOMIN EDU/PROP COERCE TOTALISM MARXISM...POLICY CONCPT MYTH TIME/SEQ WORK TOT/POP 20 LENIN/VI STALIN/J. PAGE 139 H2772 — B60 INTELL PWR USSR

SHIRER W.L.,THE RISE AND FALL OF THE THIRD REICH: A HISTORY OF NAZI GERMANY. EUR+WWI CULTURE ECO/DEV INDUS NAT/G POL/PAR FORCES PLAN TEC/DEV ECO/TAC COERCE ATTIT DRIVE PERSON PWR...MYSTIC PSY SOC MYTH STAT CHARTS EXHIBIT WORK VAL/FREE. PAGE 143 H2864 — B60 STRUCT GERMANY TOTALISM

THE AFRICA 1960 COMMITTEE,MANDATE IN TRUST; THE PROBLEM OF SOUTH WEST AFRICA. GERMANY STRUCT REGION SANCTION CHOOSE DISCRIM...INT/LAW 20 AFRICA/SW UN LEAGUE/NAT TRUST/TERR. PAGE 153 H3066 — B60 NAT/G DIPLOM COLONIAL RACE/REL

KAPLAN M.A.,"COMMUNIST COUP IN CZECHOSLOVAKIA." COM EUR+WWI INTELL LABOR LOC/G NAT/G POL/PAR FORCES EDU/PROP EXEC MARXISM...TIME/SEQ HYPO/EXP 20. PAGE 83 H1659 — L60 STRUCT COERCE CZECHOSLVK

ROKKAN S.,"NORWAY AND THE UNITED STATES OF AMERICA." NORWAY CHOOSE...SOC STAND/INT SAMP CHARTS GP/COMP METH/COMP 20. PAGE 133 H2665 — L60 STRUCT NAT/G PARTIC REPRESENT

BERREMAN G.D.,"CASTE IN INDIA AND THE UNITED STATES" (BMR)" INDIA USA+45 CULTURE SOCIETY STRUCT SECT GP/REL DISCRIM HEREDITY...SOC STERTYP 20 NEGRO HINDU. PAGE 16 H0318 — S60 STRATA RACE/REL NAT/COMP ATTIT

GRIMSHAW A.D.,"URBAN RACIAL VIOLENCE IN THE UNITED STATES: CHANGING ECOLOGICAL CONSIDERATIONS." STRUCT MUNIC FORCES PARTIC DISCRIM ATTIT HABITAT ...IDEA/COMP 20 NEGRO. PAGE 61 H1228 — S60 CROWD RACE/REL GOV/COMP NEIGH

TURNER R.H.,"SPONSORED AND CONTEST MOBILITY IN THE SCHOOL SYSTEM." UK USA+45 ELITES STRATA ACADEM FACE/GP EDU/PROP CONTROL INGP/REL ADJUST ATTIT PERSON...METH/COMP 20. PAGE 157 H3142 — S60 AGE/Y NAT/COMP SCHOOL STRUCT

WOLFINGER R.E.,"REPUTATION AND REALITY IN THE STUDY OF COMMUNITY POWER." STRUCT PROB/SOLV INGP/REL ATTIT OBJECTIVE...SOC METH/CNCPT PERS/COMP. PAGE 170 H3404 — S60 CULTURE MUNIC DOMIN PWR

FITZSIMMONS T.,"USSR: ITS PEOPLE, ITS SOCIETY, ITS CULTURE." USSR FAM SECT DIPLOM EDU/PROP ADMIN RACE/REL ATTIT...POLICY CHARTS BIBLIOG 20. PAGE 51 H1021 — C60 CULTURE STRUCT SOCIETY COM

HAZARD J.N.,"THE SOVIET SYSTEM OF GOVERNMENT." USSR SOCIETY INDUS NAT/G POL/PAR DIPLOM CT/SYS...JURID CHARTS BIBLIOG/A 20. PAGE 69 H1373 — C60 COM NAT/COMP STRUCT ADMIN

WRIGGINS W.H.,"CEYLON: DILEMMAS OF A NEW NATION." ASIA CEYLON CONSTN STRUCT POL/PAR SECT FORCES DIPLOM GOV/REL NAT/LISM...CHARTS BIBLIOG 20. PAGE 171 H3417 — C60 PROB/SOLV NAT/G ECO/UNDEV

RHODESIA-NYASA NATL ARCHIVES,A SELECT BIBLIOGRAPHY OF RECENT PUBLICATIONS CONCERNING THE FEDERATION OF RHODESIA AND NYASALAND (PAMPHLET). MALAWI RHODESIA LAW CULTURE STRUCT ECO/UNDEV LEGIS...GEOG 20. PAGE 131 H2620 — N60 BIBLIOG ADMIN ORD/FREE NAT/G

ACOSTA SAIGNES M.,ESTUDIOS DE ETNOLOGIA ANTIGUA DE VENEZUELA (2ND ED.). PRE/AMER VENEZUELA...ART/METH SOC BIBLIOG INDIAN/AM. PAGE 3 H0061 — B61 CULTURE STRUCT GP/REL HABITAT

AIYAR S.P.,FEDERALISM AND SOCIAL CHANGE. CANADA CULTURE STRUCT PLAN PROB/SOLV TEC/DEV ECO/TAC ORD/FREE...TIME/SEQ 18/20 AUSTRAL. PAGE 4 H0085 — B61 FEDERAL NAT/G CENTRAL GOV/COMP

BLAKE J.,FAMILY STRUCTURE IN JAMAICA. JAMAICA CULTURE SOCIETY ACT/RES CONTROL MARRIAGE AGE ...POLICY SOC BIBLIOG 20. PAGE 18 H0351 — B61 FAM SEX STRUCT ATTIT

BOURDIEU P.,THE ALGERIANS (TRANS. BY A.C. ROSS; REV. ED.). ALGERIA ISLAM CULTURE MUNIC CAP/ISM COLONIAL GP/REL ORD/FREE SOVEREIGN 20. PAGE 19 H0385 — B61 SOCIETY STRUCT ATTIT WAR

BULLOCK A.,HITLER: A STUDY IN TYRANNY. EUR+WWI GERMANY SOCIETY STRUCT NAT/G POL/PAR FORCES CREATE DOMIN EDU/PROP EXEC COERCE WAR NAT/LISM DISPL DRIVE PERSON PWR...PSY NAZI 20 HITLER/A. PAGE 23 H0470 — B61 ATTIT BIOG TOTALISM

BURKS R.V.,THE DYNAMICS OF COMMUNISM IN EASTERN EUROPE. COM YUGOSLAVIA POL/PAR RACE/REL ISOLAT ...CORREL CON/ANAL CHARTS GP/COMP DICTIONARY 20 EUROPE/E SLAV/MACED. PAGE 24 H0489 — B61 MARXISM STRUCT WORKER REPRESENT

DUFFY J.,AFRICA SPEAKS. GHANA TOGO CULTURE ECO/UNDEV PROB/SOLV COLONIAL NEUTRAL DISCRIM NAT/LISM SOVEREIGN ALL/IDEOS...CONCPT ANTHOL SOC/INTEG 20 NEGRO THIRD/WRLD. PAGE 43 H0857 — B61 AFR NAT/G FUT STRUCT

ERASMUS C.J.,MAN TAKES CONTROL: CULTURAL DEVELOPMENT AND AMERICAN AID. STRUCT OWN DRIVE PERCEPT...SOC 20 MEXIC/AMER. PAGE 47 H0937 — B61 ORD/FREF CULTURE ECO/UNDFV TEC/DEV

B61
ETZIONI A.,COMPLEX ORGANIZATIONS: A SOCIOLOGICAL READER. CLIENT CULTURE STRATA CREATE OP/RES ADMIN ...POLICY METH/CNCPT BUREAUCRCY. PAGE 47 H0945
VOL/ASSN STRUCT CLASSIF PROF/ORG

B61
FIRTH R.,HISTORY AND TRADITIONS OF TIKOPIA. S/ASIA KIN SECT RUMOR WAR...MYTH WORSHIP 20 POLYNESIA. PAGE 50 H1008
CULTURE STRUCT HUM

B61
FIRTH R.,ELEMENTS OF SOCIAL ORGANIZATION (3RD ED.). STRATA STRUCT ECO/UNDEV NEIGH CHIEF INGP/REL ATTIT MORAL...PHIL/SCI GP/COMP WORSHIP SOC/INTEG 20. PAGE 50 H1009
SOC CULTURE SOCIETY KIN

B61
MONAS S.,THE THIRD SECTION: POLICE AND SOCIETY IN RUSSIA UNDER NICHOLAS I. MOD/EUR RUSSIA ELITES STRUCT NAT/G EX/STRUC ADMIN CONTROL PWR CONSERVE ...DECISION 19 NICHOLAS/I. PAGE 112 H2238
ORD/FREE COM FORCES COERCE

B61
NIPPERDEY T.,DIE ORGANISATION DER DEUTSCHEN PARTEIEN VOR 1918. GERMANY CONSTN STRUCT TEC/DEV CHOOSE ADJUST ATTIT...CONCPT TIME/SEQ 19/20. PAGE 118 H2362
POL/PAR PARL/PROC NAT/G

B61
PATAI R.,CULTURES IN CONFLICT; AN INQUIRY INTO THE SOCIO-CULTURAL PROBLEMS OF ISRAEL AND HER NEIGHBORS (2ND REV. ED.). ISLAM ISRAEL SOCIETY STRUCT DIPLOM GP/REL ALL/VALS...SOC 20 JEWS ARABS. PAGE 124 H2475
NAT/COMP CULTURE GP/COMP ATTIT

B61
ROCHE J.P.,COURTS AND RIGHTS: THE AMERICAN JUDICIARY IN ACTION (2ND ED.). UK USA+45 USA-45 STRUCT TEC/DEV SANCTION PERS/REL RACE/REL ORD/FREE ...METH/CNCPT GOV/COMP METH/COMP T 13/20. PAGE 133 H2653
JURID CT/SYS NAT/G PROVS

B61
VON EICKSTEDT E.,TURKEN, KURDEN UND IRANER SEIT DEM ALTERTUM. IRAN TURKEY GP/REL BIO/SOC HABITAT...PSY 20 PERSIA. PAGE 163 H3266
CULTURE SOC SOCIETY STRUCT

S61
NEEDLER M.C.,"THE POLITICAL DEVELOPMENT OF MEXICO." STRUCT NAT/G ADMIN RIGID/FLEX...TIME/SEQ TREND MEXIC/AMER TOT/POP VAL/FREE 19/20. PAGE 116 H2328
L/A+17C POL/PAR

C61
MOODIE G.C.,"THE GOVERNMENT OF GREAT BRITAIN." UK LAW STRUCT LOC/G POL/PAR DIPLOM RECEIVE ADMIN COLONIAL CHOOSE...BIBLIOG 20 PARLIAMENT. PAGE 112 H2247
NAT/G SOCIETY PARL/PROC GOV/COMP

B62
AMERICAN SOCIETY AFR CULTURE,PAN-AFRICANISM RECONSIDERED. AFR SOCIETY STRUCT SCHOOL CAP/ISM EDU/PROP...ART/METH NEW/IDEA PREDICT ANTHOL 20 PANAF/FREE NEGRO. PAGE 6 H0123
DIPLOM FEDERAL NAT/LISM CULTURE

B62
BERGER M.,THE ARAB WORLD TODAY. CULTURE FAM INT/ORG NAT/G SECT FORCES ECO/TAC NAT/LISM HABITAT...CHARTS BIBLIOG 20 ARABS. PAGE 15 H0301
ISLAM PERSON STRUCT SOCIETY

B62
BERNOT R.M.,EXCESS AND RESTRAINT: SOCIAL CONTROL AMONG GUINEA MOUNTAIN PEOPLE. CULTURE FAM KIN CT/SYS COERCE WAR PERS/REL MARRIAGE HABITAT SEX ...MYTH 20 NEW/GUINEA. PAGE 16 H0314
SOCIETY CONTROL STRUCT ADJUST

B62
BINDER L.,IRAN: POLITICAL DEVELOPMENT IN A CHANGING SOCIETY. IRAN OP/RES REV GP/REL CENTRAL RATIONAL PWR...PHIL/SCI NAT/COMP GEN/LAWS 20. PAGE 17 H0337
LEGIT NAT/G ADMIN STRUCT

B62
COUNCIL ON WORLD TENSIONS,RESTLESS NATIONS. WOR+45 STRUCT INT/ORG NAT/G PLAN ECO/TAC...NAT/COMP ANTHOL 20. PAGE 34 H0678
ECO/UNDEV POLICY DIPLOM TASK

B62
DEBUYST F.,LAS CLASES SOCIALES EN AMERICA LATINA. L/A+17C SOCIETY STRUCT WORKER EDU/PROP RACE/REL ATTIT HABITAT ROLE...GEOG SOC NAT/COMP SOC/INTEG 20. PAGE 39 H0780
STRATA GP/REL WEALTH

B62
EDWARDS A.C.,THE OVIMBUNDU UNDER TWO SOVEREIGNTIES. CULTURE STRUCT FAM MARRIAGE HABITAT...SOC 19/20 OVIMBUNDU. PAGE 45 H0891
KIN NEIGH SOCIETY CONTROL

B62
EVANS-PRITCHARD E.E.,ESSAYS IN SOCIAL ANTHROPOLOGY. AFR KIN REGION INGP/REL DRIVE HABITAT...OBS METH 20 ZANDE. PAGE 48 H0954
SOCIETY CULTURE SOC STRUCT

B62
FALKENBERG J.,KIN AND TOTEM; GROUP RELATIONS OF AUSTRALIAN ABORIGINES IN THE PORT KEATS DISTRICT. SOCIETY STRATA STRUCT GP/REL PERS/REL MARRIAGE AGE ATTIT SEX...SOC STAT CHARTS AUSTRAL ABORIGINES. PAGE 48 H0964
KIN INGP/REL CULTURE FAM

B62
FEIT E.,SOUTH AFRICA, THE DYNAMICS OF THE AFRICAN NATIONAL CONGRESS. AFR SOUTH/AFR LAW INTELL STRATA KIN NAT/G POL/PAR ECO/TAC DOMIN RISK COERCE 20 NEGRO. PAGE 49 H0984
RACE/REL ELITES CONTROL STRUCT

B62
HACHMANN R.,VOLKER ZWISCHEN GERMANEN UND KELTEN. GERMANY CULTURE STRUCT MUNIC...ART/METH CHARTS MAPS. PAGE 63 H1269
LING SOC KIN GP/REL

B62
HUCKER C.O.,CHINA: A CRITICAL BIBLIOGRAPHY (PAMPHLET). ASIA STRUCT AGRI FINAN INDUS HABITAT MARXISM...EPIST HUM. PAGE 74 H1487
BIBLIOG/A CULTURE INTELL SOCIETY

B62
KENNEDY R.,BIBLIOGRAPHY OF INDONESIAN PEOPLES AND CULTURES (2ND REV. ED.). INDONESIA STRUCT ECO/UNDEV SCHOOL EDU/PROP COLONIAL...GEOG SOC LING NAT/COMP 20. PAGE 85 H1689
BIBLIOG S/ASIA CULTURE KIN

B62
KIRPICEVA I.K.,HANDBUCH DER RUSSISCHEN UND SOWJETISCHEN BIBLIOGRAPHIEN (5 VOLS.). USSR STRUCT ECO/DEV DIPLOM LEAD ATTIT 18/20. PAGE 86 H1726
BIBLIOG/A NAT/G MARXISM COM

B62
MANSUR F.,PROCESS OF INDEPENDENCE. GHANA INDIA INDONESIA PAKISTAN CONSTN ELITES INTELL STRUCT ACADEM NAT/G REV PWR 20. PAGE 102 H2043
NAT/COMP POL/PAR SOVEREIGN COLONIAL

B62
MARTINDALE D.,SOCIAL LIFE AND CULTURAL CHANGE. GP/REL...PHIL/SCI SOC CONCPT. PAGE 103 H2065
INTELL CULTURE ORD/FREE STRUCT

B62
MEYER A.G.,LENINISM. USSR STRUCT NAT/G CAP/ISM LEAD WAR PWR SOVEREIGN...BIBLIOG 20 LENIN/VI. PAGE 109 H2187
POL/PAR REV MARXISM PHIL/SCI

B62
PAIKERT G.C.,THE GERMAN EXODUS. EUR+WWI GERMANY/W LAW CULTURE SOCIETY STRUCT INDUS NAT/LISM RESPECT SOVEREIGN...CHARTS BIBLIOG SOC/INTEG 20 MIGRATION. PAGE 122 H2444
INGP/REL STRANGE GEOG GP/REL

B62
ROBINSON A.D.,DUTCH ORGANIZED AGRICULTURE IN INTERNATIONAL POLITICS, 1945-1960. EUR+WWI NETHERLAND STRUCT ECO/DEV NAT/G VOL/ASSN CONSULT DELIB/GP PLAN TEC/DEV INT/TRADE EDU/PROP ATTIT RIGID/FLEX ALL/VALS...NEW/IDEA TREND EEC 20. PAGE 132 H2648
AGRI INT/ORG

B62
RUDE G.,WILKES AND LIBERTY. UK NAT/G POL/PAR REPRESENT ORD/FREE...SOC 18. PAGE 136 H2711
PARL/PROC CHOOSE STRATA STRUCT

B62
RUDY Z.,ETHNOSOZIOLOGIE SOWJETISCHER VOLKER. USSR SOCIETY STRUCT FAM SECT GP/REL ATTIT...SOC SOC/INTEG 20. PAGE 136 H2714
MYTH CULTURE KIN

B62
SCHIEDER T.,THE STATE AND SOCIETY IN OUR TIMES (TRANS. BY C.A.M. SYM). SOCIETY NAT/G POL/PAR REV GP/REL ALL/IDEOS 19/20. PAGE 139 H2786
STRUCT PWR HIST/WRIT

B62
SCHMIDT-VOLKMAR E.,DER KULTURKAMPF IN DEUTSCHLAND 1871-1890. GERMANY PRUSSIA SOCIETY STRUCT SECT DIPLOM GP/REL NAT/LISM 19 CHURCH/STA BISMARCK/O. PAGE 139 H2789
POL/PAR CATHISM ATTIT NAT/G

B62
SELOSOEMARDJAN O.,SOCIAL CHANGES IN JOGJAKARTA. INDONESIA NETHERLAND ELITES STRATA STRUCT FAM POL/PAR CREATE DIPLOM INT/TRADE EDU/PROP ADMIN GOV/REL...SOC 20 JAVA CHINJAP. PAGE 141 H2825
ECO/UNDEV CULTURE REV COLONIAL

B62
SILBERMAN B.S.,JAPAN AND KOREA; A CRITICAL BIBLIOGRAPHY. KOREA LAW STRATA STRUCT AGRI INDUS NAT/G POL/PAR SECT...HUM LING IDEA/COMP 5/20 CHINJAP. PAGE 144 H2872
BIBLIOG/A CULTURE S/ASIA

B62
SMITH M.G.,KINSHIP AND COMMUNITY IN CARRIACOU. WEST/IND STRATA AGRI FAM SECT WORKER MARRIAGE OWN HEREDITY WEALTH...SOC 18/20. PAGE 146 H2915
CULTURE HABITAT KIN STRUCT

B62
WEHLER H.V.,SOZIALDEMOKRATIE UND NATIONALSTAAT. GERMANY POLAND USSR CULTURE SOCIETY STRUCT NAT/G POL/PAR DIPLOM ORD/FREE 19/20. PAGE 166 H3325
NAT/LISM SOVEREIGN GP/REL ATTIT

B62
YOUNG G.,THE HILL TRIBES OF NORTHERN THAILAND. S/ASIA THAILAND FAM KIN LOC/G GP/REL HABITAT...GEOG LING OBS 20. PAGE 172 H3438
CULTURE STRUCT ECO/UNDEV SECT

L62
CORET A.,"L'INDEPENDANCE DU SAMOA OCCIDENTAL." S/ASIA LAW INT/ORG EXEC ALL/VALS SAMOA UN 20. PAGE 33 H0668
NAT/G STRUCT SOVEREIGN

S62
CROAN M.,"POLYCENTRISM: COMMUNIST INTERNATIONAL RELATIONS." ASIA STRUCT INT/ORG NAT/G POL/PAR CONSULT PLAN DOMIN EDU/PROP COERCE ATTIT RIGID/FLEX SOCISM...POLICY CONCPT TREND CON/ANAL GEN/LAWS MARX/KARL. PAGE 35 H0703
COM CREATE DIPLOM NAT/LISM

S62
GUETZKOW H.,"THE POTENTIAL OF CASE STUDY IN ANALYZING INTERNATIONAL CONFLICT." EUR+WWI FUT GERMANY INTELL SOCIETY STRUCT INT/ORG LOC/G NAT/G CONSULT CREATE PLAN CHOOSE ATTIT RIGID/FLEX ...POLICY SAAR 20. PAGE 62 H1246
EDU/PROP METH/CNCPT COERCE FRANCE

S62
MOUSKHELY M.,"LA NAISSANCE DES ETATS EN DROIT INTERNATIONAL PUBLIC." UNIV SOCIETY INT/ORG VOL/ASSN LEGIT ATTIT RIGID/FLEX...JURID TIME/SEQ 20. PAGE 114 H2272
NAT/G STRUCT INT/LAW

S62
PISTRAK L.,"SOVIET VIEWS ON AFRICA." AFR COM FUT ISLAM USSR INTELL STRUCT KIN POL/PAR PLAN EDU/PROP RIGID/FLEX PWR MARXISM...TIME/SEQ WORK TOT/POP 20. PAGE 126 H2516
NAT/G ATTIT SOCISM

S62
VIGNES D.,"L'AUTORITE DES TRAITES INTERNATIONAUX EN DROIT INTERNE." EUR+WWI UNIV LAW CONSTN INTELL NAT/G POL/PAR DIPLOM ATTIT PERCEPT ALL/VALS ...POLICY INT/LAW JURID CONCPT TIME/SEQ 20 TREATY. PAGE 163 H3252
STRUCT LEGIT FRANCE

B63
ALMOND G.A.,THE CIVIC CULTURE: POLITICAL ATTITUDES AND DEMOCRACY IN FIVE NATIONS. GERMANY/W ITALY UK USA+45 SOCIETY STRUCT PARTIC...SOC DEEP/INT SAMP 20 MEXIC/AMER. PAGE 6 H0113
POPULISM CULTURE NAT/COMP ATTIT

B63
AZEVEDO T.,SOCIAL CHANGE IN BRAZIL. BRAZIL ECO/DEV COM/IND FAM NAT/G SECT GP/REL PERS/REL...CONCPT WORSHIP 20. PAGE 9 H0188
TEC/DEV STRUCT SOC CULTURE

B63
BELFRAGE C.,THE MAN AT THE DOOR WITH THE GUN. CUBA L/A+17C NAT/G LEAD PARTIC GP/REL PWR...POLICY 20 CASTRO/F. PAGE 13 H0261
REGION ECO/UNDEV STRUCT ATTIT

B63
BERREMAN G.D.,HINDUS OF THE HIMALAYAS. INDIA STRATA STRUCT KIN MUNIC 20 HINDU. PAGE 16 H0319
CULTURE SECT GP/REL ECO/UNDEV

B63
BIALEK R.W.,CATHOLIC POLITICS: A HISTORY BASED ON ECUADOR. ECUADOR SPAIN CULTURE STRUCT CONTROL REV PWR...BIBLIOG WORSHIP 18/20. PAGE 16 H0329
COLONIAL CATHISM GOV/REL HABITAT

B63
BOHANNAN P.,SOCIAL ANTHROPOLOGY. ECO/DEV GP/REL DEMAND MARRIAGE HABITAT...CHARTS GP/COMP BIBLIOG T WORSHIP 20. PAGE 18 H0366
SOC STRUCT FAM CULTURE

B63
BROGAN D.W.,POLITICAL PATTERNS IN TODAY'S WORLD. FRANCE USA+45 USSR WOR+45 CONSTN STRUCT PLAN DIPLOM ADMIN LEAD ROLE SUPEGO...PHIL/SCI 20. PAGE 21 H0429
NAT/COMP NEW/LIB COM TOTALISM

B63
CONFERENCE ABORIGINAL STUDIES,AUSTRALIAN ABORIGINAL STUDIES. ECO/UNDEV INT/TRADE COLONIAL ADJUST HABITAT HEREDITY...GEOG PSY LING SOC/EXP ANTHOL WORSHIP 20 AUSTRAL ABORIGINES. PAGE 32 H0638
SOC SOCIETY CULTURE STRUCT

B63
DRIVER H.E.,ETHNOGRAPHY AND ACCULTURATION OF THE CHICHIMECA-JONAZ OF NORTHEAST MEXICO. ECO/UNDEV AGRI FAM KIN EDU/PROP MARRIAGE HEALTH...GEOG INT CHARTS WORSHIP 18/20 MEXIC/AMER. PAGE 42 H0848
CULTURE HABITAT STRUCT GP/REL

B63
FAWCETT J.E.S.,THE BRITISH COMMONWEALTH IN INTERNATIONAL LAW. LAW INT/ORG NAT/G VOL/ASSN OP/RES DIPLOM ADJUD CENTRAL CONSEN...NET/THEORY CMN/WLTH TREATY. PAGE 49 H0977
INT/LAW STRUCT COLONIAL

B63
GAMBLE S.D.,NORTH CHINA VILLAGES: SOCIAL, POLITICAL, AND ECONOMIC ACTIVITIES BEFORE 1933. ASIA CULTURE STRUCT FAM DOMIN EDU/PROP WORSHIP 20. PAGE 55 H1093
MUNIC AGRI LEAD FINAN

B63
ISSAWI C.,EGYPT IN REVOLUTION: AN ECONOMIC ANALYSIS. ISLAM STRUCT ECO/UNDEV AGRI FINAN INDUS PLAN EXEC REV NAT/LISM ATTIT RIGID/FLEX WEALTH SOCISM...STAT WORK 20. PAGE 79 H1573
NAT/G UAR

B63
JENNINGS W.I.,DEMOCRACY IN AFRICA. UK CULTURE STRUCT ECO/UNDEV DIPLOM COLONIAL GP/REL ADJUST NAT/LISM ORD/FREE...GOV/COMP 20 THIRD/WRLD. PAGE 81 H1613
PROB/SOLV AFR CONSTN POPULISM

B63
KHADDURI M.,MODERN LIBYA: A STUDY IN POLITICAL DEVELOPMENT. EUR+WWI ISLAM LIBYA ELITES INT/ORG POL/PAR FORCES DIPLOM FOR/AID DOMIN EDU/PROP LEGIT NAT/LISM DRIVE RIGID/FLEX SKILL...CONCPT TIME/SEQ TREND 20. PAGE 85 H1704
NAT/G STRUCT

B63
LEIGHTON D.C.,THE CHARACTER OF DANGER (VOL. III). SOCIETY STRUCT STRANGE ANOMIE...SOC STAT CHARTS GP/COMP SOC/EXP SOC/INTEG 20 NOVA/SCOT. PAGE 94 H1868
HEALTH PSY CULTURE

B63
LIVINGSTON W.S.,FEDERALISM IN THE COMMONWEALTH - A BIBLIOGRAPHICAL COMMENTARY. CANADA INDIA PAKISTAN UK STRUCT LOC/G NAT/G POL/PAR...NAT/COMP 20 AUSTRAL. PAGE 97 H1943
BIBLIOG JURID FEDERAL CONSTN

B63
MAJUMDAR D.N.,AN INTRODUCTION TO SOCIAL ANTHROPOLOGY. INDIA LAW STRATA ECO/UNDEV KIN DEMAND MARRIAGE...GP/COMP BIBLIOG T WORSHIP 20. PAGE 101 H2026
SOC CULTURE STRUCT GP/REL

B63
MARTINDALE D.,COMMUNITY, CHARACTER AND CIVILIZATION: STUDIES IN SOCIAL BEHAVIORISM. INTELL FAM NEIGH VOL/ASSN GP/REL NAT/LISM ATTIT PERSON ...CONCPT GP/COMP 20 BEHAVIORSM. PAGE 103 H2066
SOC METH/COMP CULTURE STRUCT

B63
MCPHEE W.N.,FORMAL THEORIES OF MASS BEHAVIOR. CULTURE STRUCT DOMIN EDU/PROP CHOOSE...MATH 20. PAGE 108 H2149
SOC METH CONCPT ATTIT

B63
MONTAGUE J.B. JR.,CLASS AND NATIONALITY; ENGLISH AND AMERICAN STUDIES. UK USA+45 ELITES STRUCT WORKER ATTIT PWR...SOC CHARTS SOC/EXP 20. PAGE 112 H2243
STRATA NAT/LISM PERSON NAT/COMP

B63
OTERO L.M.,HONDURAS. HONDURAS SPAIN STRUCT SECT COLONIAL REV WAR ATTIT PWR...GEOG WORSHIP 16/20. PAGE 122 H2432
NAT/G SOCIETY NAT/LISM ECO/UNDEV

B63
PAUW B.A.,THE SECOND GENERATION. SOUTH/AFR INDUS FAM LABOR SECT EDU/PROP MARRIAGE ATTIT...SOC 20. PAGE 124 H2478
KIN CULTURE STRUCT SOCIETY

B63
SPRING D.,THE ENGLISH LANDED ESTATE IN THE NINETEENTH CENTURY: ITS ADMINISTRATION. UK ELITES STRUCT AGRI NAT/G GP/REL OWN PWR WEALTH...BIBLIOG 19 HOUSE/LORD. PAGE 148 H2954
STRATA PERS/REL MGT

B63
THOMPSON F.M.L.,ENGLISH LANDED SOCIETY IN THE NINETEENTH CENTURY. UK STRUCT MUNIC NAT/G CONTROL WAR GP/REL OWN WEALTH...BIBLIOG 18/20. PAGE 154 H3081
STRATA PWR ELITES GOV/REL

B63
THORBURN H.G.,PARTY POLITICS IN CANADA. CANADA ELITES STRUCT INDUS PWR 20. PAGE 154 H3086
POL/PAR CONCPT NAT/G PROVS

B63
TUCKER R.C.,THE SOVIET POLITICAL MIND. COM INTELL NAT/G TOP/EX EDU/PROP ADMIN COERCE TOTALISM ATTIT PWR MARXISM...PSY MYTH HYPO/EXP 20. PAGE 157 H3136
STRUCT RIGID/FLEX ELITES USSR

B63
VALJAVEC F.,AUSGEWAHLTE AUFSATZE. GERMANY HUNGARY STRUCT ATTIT...CONCPT IDEA/COMP 18/20 BALKANS. PAGE 161 H3223
SOCIETY CULTURE GP/REL NAT/LISM

B63
WILCOX W.A.,PAKISTAN; THE CONSOLIDATION OF A NATION. INDIA PAKISTAN CONSTN SECT PROB/SOLV COLONIAL PARTIC GP/REL FEDERAL...POLICY 19/20. PAGE 168 H3361
NAT/LISM ECO/UNDEV DIPLOM STRUCT

L63
MICHAEL F.,"KHRUSHCHEV'S DISLOYAL OPPOSITION: STRUCTURAL CHANGE AND POWER STRUGGLE IN COMMUNIST BLOC." ASIA CHINA/COM FUT NAT/G POL/PAR CONSULT PLAN DOMIN ATTIT...POLICY CONCPT TREND MARX/KARL 20 KHRUSH/N. PAGE 110 H2195
COM STRUCT NAT/LISM USSR

S63
HUREWITZ J.C.,"LEBANESE DEMOCRACY IN ITS INTERNATIONAL SETTING." FRANCE ISLAM UK LOC/G NAT/G SECT DOMIN EDU/PROP EXEC ATTIT PWR...TIME/SEQ 20. PAGE 75 H1507
STRUCT LEBANON

B64
AGGER R.E.,THE RULERS AND THE RULED: POLITICAL POWER AND IMPOTENCE IN AMERICAN COMMUNITIES. CULTURE DOMIN CHOOSE ATTIT ALL/VALS...DECISION SOC CONCPT OBS QU CHARTS. PAGE 4 H0079
PWR STRUCT LOC/G MUNIC

B64
ARASARATNAM S.,CEYLON. CEYLON NETHERLAND PORTUGAL S/ASIA UK STRUCT ECO/UNDEV SECT DIPLOM DOMIN
COLONIAL NAT/G

RACE/REL NAT/LISM 17/20 CMN/WLTH. PAGE 8 H0156 — PROB/SOLV CULTURE

B64
BEATTIE J.,OTHER CULTURES. UNIV LAW FAM POL/PAR SECT ADJUD OWN ALL/VALS WEALTH...SOC NAT/COMP SOC/INTEG 20. PAGE 13 H0251 — METH/CNCPT CULTURE STRUCT

B64
BEDERMAN S.H.,THE ETHNOLOGICAL CONTRIBUTIONS OF JOHN LEDYARD (PAMPHLET). ASIA PRE/AMER S/ASIA...SOC 18 LEDYARD/J KAMCHATKA TAHITI TARTARS INDIAN/AM. PAGE 13 H0256 — CULTURE BIOG METH/CNCPT STRUCT

B64
BELL W.,JAMAICAN LEADERS: POLITICAL ATTITUDES IN A NEW NATION. JAMAICA STRUCT ACT/RES CREATE PROB/SOLV DIPLOM COLONIAL LEAD...QU 20. PAGE 13 H0267 — NAT/LISM ATTIT DRIVE SOVEREIGN

B64
BERNDT R.M.,THE WORLD OF THE FIRST AUSTRALIANS. S/ASIA ECO/UNDEV WORKER PROB/SOLV EFFICIENCY ROLE ...SOC MYTH WORSHIP AUSTRAL ABORIGINES. PAGE 16 H0311 — CULTURE KIN STRUCT DRIVE

B64
BINDER L.,THE IDEOLOGICAL REVOLUTION IN THE MIDDLE EAST. ISLAM STRUCT INT/ORG KIN SECT EX/STRUC TOP/EX PLAN ATTIT DRIVE RIGID/FLEX PWR...MYTH TOT/POP 20. PAGE 17 H0338 — POL/PAR NAT/G NAT/LISM

B64
CAPLOW T.,PRINCIPLES OF ORGANIZATION. UNIV CULTURE STRUCT CREATE INGP/REL UTOPIA...GEN/LAWS TIME. PAGE 26 H0526 — VOL/ASSN CONCPT SIMUL EX/STRUC

B64
COUNT E.W.,FACT AND THEORY IN SOCIAL SCIENCE. UNIV HABITAT...BIOG TREND CHARTS ANTHOL BIBLIOG. PAGE 34 H0679 — STRUCT SOC CULTURE ADJUST

B64
DANIELS R.V.,RUSSIA. RUSSIA USSR STRUCT NAT/LISM TOTALISM ORD/FREE WEALTH...POLICY DECISION TREND. PAGE 37 H0740 — MARXISM REV ECO/DEV DIPLOM

B64
ELKIN A.P.,THE AUSTRALIAN ABORIGINES - HOW TO UNDERSTAND THEM (4TH ED.). FAM NEIGH DEATH MARRIAGE ATTIT BIO/SOC HABITAT...PSY SOC MYTH WORSHIP AUSTRAL ABORIGINES. PAGE 45 H0908 — CULTURE STRUCT SOCIETY KIN

B64
ETZIONI A.,MODERN ORGANIZATIONS. CLIENT STRUCT DOMIN CONTROL LEAD PERS/REL AUTHORIT...CLASSIF BUREAUCRCY. PAGE 47 H0946 — MGT ADMIN PLAN CULTURE

B64
GRIFFITH W.,THE WELSH (2ND ED.). UK SOCIETY STRUCT SECT WRITING NAT/LISM...ART/METH MODAL OBS/ENVIR TREND SOC/INTEG WALES PURITAN MUSIC. PAGE 61 H1223 — CULTURE SOC LING

B64
GROSSER A.,THE FEDERAL REPUBLIC OF GERMANY: A CONCISE HISTORY. GERMANY/W STRUCT MORAL ORD/FREE POPULISM SOCISM...SOC CONCPT 20. PAGE 62 H1235 — NAT/G POL/PAR CHOOSE DIPLOM

B64
HALPERN J.M.,GOVERNMENT, POLITICS, AND SOCIAL STRUCTURE IN LAOS. LAOS CULTURE SOCIETY STRATA STRUCT FAM DIPLOM DOMIN MARXISM...INT GOV/COMP WORSHIP SOC/INTEG 20. PAGE 65 H1297 — NAT/G SOC LOC/G

B64
HARRIS M.,PATTERNS OF RACE IN THE AMERICAS. BRAZIL L/A+17C STRATA ECO/UNDEV AGRI KIN MUNIC SECT COLONIAL RACE/REL...SOC SOC/INTEG 17/20 NEGRO INDIAN/AM. PAGE 67 H1342 — STRUCT PRE/AMER CULTURE SOCIETY

B64
HORNE D.,THE LUCKY COUNTRY: AUSTRALIA TODAY. UK CULTURE STRATA ATTIT PWR PLURISM...GOV/COMP 20 AUSTRAL. PAGE 73 H1471 — RACE/REL DIPLOM NAT/G STRUCT

B64
IBERO-AMERICAN INSTITUTES,IBEROAMERICANA. STRUCT ADMIN SOC. PAGE 76 H1519 — BIBLIOG L/A+17C NAT/G DIPLOM

B64
LAPENNA I.,STATE AND LAW: SOVIET AND YUGOSLAV THEORY. USSR YUGOSLAVIA STRATA STRUCT NAT/G DOMIN COERCE MARXISM...GOV/COMP IDEA/COMP 20. PAGE 91 H1812 — JURID COM LAW SOVEREIGN

B64
MUSEUM FUR VOLKERKUNDE WIEN,ZENTRALAMERIKA MEXIKO VOLKER UND KULTUREN. COSTA/RICA GUATEMALA L/A+17C PANAMA SECT WAR GP/REL SOVEREIGN...ART/METH 20 CENTRAL/AM MEXIC/AMER. PAGE 115 H2300 — SOCIETY STRUCT CULTURE AGRI

B64
OECD SEMINAR REGIONAL DEV,REGIONAL DEVELOPMENT IN ISRAEL. ISRAEL STRUCT ECO/UNDEV NAT/G REGION...GEOG 20. PAGE 120 H2404 — ADMIN PROVS PLAN METH/COMP

B64
ON CULTURE AND SOCIAL CHANGE. FAM NAT/G ACT/RES ECO/TAC RACE/REL...PSY TIME/SEQ TREND IDEA/COMP METH/COMP ANTHOL BIBLIOG 20. PAGE 120 H2406 — CULTURE TEC/DEV STRUCT CREATE

B64
PIPES R.,THE FORMATION OF THE SOVIET UNION. EUR+WWI MOD/EUR STRUCT ECO/UNDEV NAT/G LEGIS DOMIN LEGIT CT/SYS EXEC COERCE ALL/VALS...POLICY RELATIV HIST/WRIT TIME/SEQ TOT/POP 19/20. PAGE 126 H2514 — COM USSR RUSSIA

B64
POWELSON J.P.,LATIN AMERICA: TODAY'S ECONOMIC AND SOCIAL REVOLUTION. L/A+17C INTELL SOCIETY STRUCT AGRI INDUS NAT/G DIPLOM ECO/TAC REV...POLICY 20. PAGE 128 H2552 — ECO/UNDEV WEALTH ADJUST PLAN

B64
RAGHAVAN M.D.,INDIA IN CEYLONESE HISTORY, SOCIETY AND CULTURE. CEYLON INDIA S/ASIA LAW SOCIETY INT/TRADE ATTIT...ART/METH JURID SOC LING 20. PAGE 129 H2581 — DIPLOM CULTURE SECT STRUCT

B64
SCHNITGER F.M.,FORGOTTEN KINGDOMS IN SUMATRA. FAM SECT LEISURE HABITAT...OBS AUD/VIS WORSHIP 20 SUMATRA. PAGE 140 H2793 — CULTURE AFR SOCIETY STRUCT

B64
STRONG C.F.,HISTORY OF MODERN POLITICAL CONSTITUTIONS. STRUCT INT/ORG NAT/G LEGIS TEC/DEV DIPLOM INT/TRADE CT/SYS EXEC...METH/COMP T 12/20 UN. PAGE 150 H2999 — CONSTN CONCPT

B64
TAWNEY R.H.,EQUALITY. UK CULTURE STRATA ECO/TAC EDU/PROP REPRESENT OWN NEW/LIB...MAJORIT WELF/ST SOC 20. PAGE 153 H3051 — WEALTH STRUCT ELITES POPULISM

B64
VON FURER-HAIMEN E.,AN ANTHROPOLOGICAL BIBLIOGRAPHY OF SOUTH ASIA (VOL. II). STRATA STRUCT KIN SECT ACT/RES CREATE HABITAT...GEOG OBS 20. PAGE 163 H3268 — BIBLIOG/A CULTURE S/ASIA SOC

B64
WHEELER-BENNETT J.W.,THE NEMESIS OF POWER (2ND ED.). EUR+WWI GERMANY TOP/EX TEC/DEV ADMIN WAR PERS/REL RIGID/FLEX ROLE ORD/FREE PWR FASCISM 20 HITLER/A. PAGE 167 H3342 — FORCES NAT/G GP/REL STRUCT

B64
ZOLLSCHAN G.K.,EXPLORATIONS IN SOCIAL CHANGE. SOCIETY STRATA STRUCT ECO/UNDEV EX/STRUC...PSY ANTHOL 20. PAGE 173 H3463 — ORD/FREE SIMUL CONCPT CULTURE

S64
KANOUTE P.,"AFRICAN SOCIALISM." AFR CONSTN NAT/G COLONIAL ORD/FREE...GOV/COMP METH/COMP 20 EUROPE. PAGE 83 H1655 — SOCISM CULTURE STRUCT IDEA/COMP

S64
NEEDHAM T.,"SCIENCE AND SOCIETY IN EAST AND WEST." INTELL STRATA R+D LOC/G NAT/G PROVS CONSULT ACT/RES CREATE PLAN TEC/DEV EDU/PROP ADMIN ATTIT ALL/VALS ...POLICY RELATIV MGT CONCPT NEW/IDEA TIME/SEQ WORK WORK. PAGE 116 H2327 — ASIA STRUCT

C64
SCOTT R.E.,"MEXICAN GOVERNMENT IN TRANSITION (REV ED)" CULTURE STRUCT POL/PAR CHIEF ADMIN LOBBY REV CHOOSE GP/REL DRIVE...BIBLIOG METH 20 MEXIC/AMER. PAGE 141 H2816 — NAT/G L/A+17C ROUTINE CONSTN

B65
BERNDT R.M.,ABORIGINAL MAN IN AUSTRALIA. LAW DOMIN ADMIN COLONIAL MARRIAGE HABITAT ORD/FREE...LING CHARTS ANTHOL BIBLIOG WORSHIP 20 AUSTRAL ABORIGINES MUSIC ELKIN/AP. PAGE 16 H0312 — SOC CULTURE SOCIETY STRUCT

B65
BETEILLE A.,CASTE, CLASS, AND POWER. INDIA MUNIC SECT REGION GP/REL PERS/REL ATTIT HABITAT RIGID/FLEX...SOC 20. PAGE 16 H0323 — STRATA CULTURE PWR STRUCT

B65
BOISSEVAIN J.,SAINTS AND FIREWORKS: RELIGION AND POLITICS IN RURAL MALTA. MALTA STRUCT FAM NEIGH POL/PAR REPRESENT INGP/REL CENTRAL...CHARTS BIBLIOG 20. PAGE 18 H0368 — GP/REL NAT/G SECT MUNIC

B65
BURLING R.,HILL FARMS AND PADI FIELDS. BURMA S/ASIA THAILAND VIETNAM AGRI NEIGH SECT GP/REL NAT/LISM ORD/FREE 20 MID/EAST MIGRATION. PAGE 24 H0491 — SOCIETY STRUCT CULTURE SOVEREIGN

B65
CAMERON W.J.,NEW ZEALAND. NEW/ZEALND S/ASIA DIPLOM INT/TRADE WRITING COLONIAL PARL/PROC...GEOG CMN/WLTH. PAGE 26 H0513 — SOCIETY GP/REL STRUCT

B65
CENTRAL GAZETTEERS UNIT,THE GAZETTEER OF INDIA (VOL. I). INDIA SOCIETY STRATA PLAN EDU/PROP NAT/LISM ORD/FREE WEALTH...GEOG LING CHARTS SOC/INTEG 20. PAGE 28 H0568 — PRESS CULTURE SECT STRUCT

B65
EASTON D.,A SYSTEM ANALYSIS OF POLITICAL LIFE. UNIV STRUCT NAT/G FEEDBACK PARTIC PERS/REL EFFICIENCY ...TREND CHARTS METH/COMP 20. PAGE 44 H0881
SIMUL POLICY GEN/METH

B65
FOSTER P.,EDUCATION AND SOCIAL CHANGE IN GHANA. GHANA CULTURE STRUCT ECO/UNDEV TEC/DEV REGION EFFICIENCY LITERACY ALL/VALS SOVEREIGN...STAT METH/COMP 19/20 GOLD/COAST. PAGE 52 H1043
SCHOOL CREATE SOCIETY

B65
GINIEWSKI P.,THE TWO FACES OF APARTHEID. AFR SOUTH/AFR STRATA AGRI INDUS COLONIAL PARTIC SOVEREIGN...CONCPT GOV/COMP NAT/COMP 19/20 NEGRO. PAGE 56 H1131
DISCRIM NAT/G RACE/REL STRUCT

B65
HARRIS R.L.,POLITICAL ORGANIZATION OF THE MBEMBE NIGERIA. AFR NIGERIA SOCIETY AGRI SECT WORKER PAY ...SOC WORSHIP 20 MBEMBE. PAGE 67 H1345
STRUCT CHIEF CULTURE

B65
HORNE A.J.,THE COMMONWEALTH TODAY. AFR ASIA CANADA UK STRUCT ECO/UNDEV NAT/G SECT GP/REL 20 AUSTRAL CMN/WLTH. PAGE 73 H1470
BIBLIOG/A SOCIETY CULTURE

B65
IANNI O.,ESTADO E CAPITALISMO. L/A+17C FINAN TEC/DEV ECO/TAC ORD/FREE WEALTH POLICY. PAGE 76 H1518
ECO/UNDEV STRUCT INDUS NAT/G

B65
JACKSON G.,THE SPANISH REPUBLIC AND THE CIVIL WAR, 1931-1939. EUR+WWI INTELL STRUCT COM/IND NAT/G POL/PAR LEGIS EDU/PROP EXEC COERCE NAT/LISM DRIVE PWR...INT TIME/SEQ TOT/POP 20. PAGE 79 H1574
ATTIT GUERRILLA SPAIN

B65
KUNSTADTER P.,THE LUA (LAWA) OF NORTHERN THAILAND: ASPECTS OF SOCIAL STRUCTURE, AGRICULTURE, AND RELIGION. THAILAND AGRI FAM KIN INGP/REL ISOLAT MARRIAGE HEALTH WORSHIP 20 BUDDHISM LUA. PAGE 89 H1780
STRUCT ECO/UNDEV CULTURE

B65
KUPER L.,AN AFRICAN BOURGEOISIE. SOUTH/AFR LAW INTELL NAT/G POL/PAR VOL/ASSN DISCRIM...POLICY 20. PAGE 89 H1783
RACE/REL SOC STRUCT

B65
MAIR L.,AN INTRODUCTION TO SOCIAL ANTHROPOLOGY. LAW STRATA FINAN FAM KIN SECT INT/TRADE RACE/REL ADJUST PRODUC...T 20. PAGE 101 H2023
SOC STRUCT CULTURE SOCIETY

B65
MOORE W.E.,THE IMPACT OF INDUSTRY. CULTURE STRUCT ORD/FREE...TREND 20. PAGE 113 H2251
INDUS MGT TEC/DEV ECO/UNDEV

B65
MURDOCK G.P.,CULTURE AND SOCIETY. SOCIETY STRATA STRUCT SECT CREATE CONTROL ORD/FREE...GP/COMP ANTHOL 20. PAGE 115 H2294
CULTURE PHIL/SCI METH IDEA/COMP

B65
NYE J.S. JR.,PAN-AFRICANISM AND EAST AFRICAN INTEGRATION. TANZANIA UGANDA STRUCT ECO/UNDEV NAT/G DIPLOM FEDERAL NAT/LISM...STAT SOC/EXP BIBLIOG EEC OAU. PAGE 119 H2382
REGION ATTIT GEN/LAWS AFR

B65
RANDALL F.B.,STALIN'S RUSSIA. USSR STRUCT AGRI NAT/G PLAN DIPLOM WAR TOTALISM MARXISM...BIBLIOG/A 19/20 STALIN/J. PAGE 129 H2590
BIOG INDUS ECO/DEV

B65
RENNER K.,MENSCH UND GESELLSCHAFT - GRUNDRISS EINER SOZIOLOGIE (2ND ED.). STRATA FAM LABOR PROF/ORG WAR ...JURID CLASSIF 20. PAGE 131 H2616
SOC STRUCT NAT/G SOCIETY

B65
ROSENBERG A.,DEMOCRACY AND SOCIALISM. COM EUR+WWI FRANCE MOD/EUR STRUCT INT/ORG NAT/G POL/PAR TOP/EX EDU/PROP COERCE PERSON PWR FASCISM MARXISM...CONCPT TIME/SEQ MARX/KARL 19/20. PAGE 134 H2677
ATTIT

B65
SCHULER E.A.,THE PAKISTAN ACADEMIES FOR RURAL DEVELOPMENT COMILLA AND PESHAWAR 1959-1964. PAKISTAN S/ASIA SOCIETY STRUCT AGRI NAT/G TEC/DEV EDU/PROP 20. PAGE 140 H2801
BIBLIOG PLAN ECO/TAC ECO/UNDEV

B65
SPENCER P.,THE SAMBURU: A STUDY OF GERONTOCRACY IN A NOMADIC TRIBE. AFR SOCIETY ECO/UNDEV AGRI FAM NEIGH SECT GP/REL MARRIAGE WORSHIP 20 SAMBURU. PAGE 147 H2945
KIN STRUCT AGE/O CULTURE

B65
SVALASTOGA K.,SOCIAL DIFFERENTIATION. CULTURE ELITES SOCIETY MARRIAGE...CONCPT SIMUL. PAGE 151 H3011
SOC STRATA STRUCT GP/REL

B65
SWIFT M.G.,MALAY PEASANT SOCIETY IN JELEBU. MALAYSIA FAM INT/TRADE ADJUD OWN WEALTH...SOC WORSHIP 20. PAGE 151 H3020
STRUCT ECO/UNDEV CULTURE SOCIETY

B65
TUTSCH H.E.,FACETS OF ARAB NATIONALISM. ISLAM ISRAEL CULTURE STRUCT SECT RIGID/FLEX ORD/FREE MARXISM SOCISM 20. PAGE 157 H3143
ECO/UNDEV NAT/LISM TEC/DEV SOCIETY

B65
VAN DEN BERGHE P.L.,SOUTH AFRICA: A STUDY IN CONFLICT. AFR CULTURE SOCIETY STRATA STRUCT COERCE SEGREGAT. PAGE 161 H3227
DOMIN RACE/REL DISCRIM

B65
VAN DEN BERGHE P.L.,AFRICA: SOCIAL PROBLEMS OF CHANGE AND CONFLICT. ELITES STRATA ECO/UNDEV KIN MUNIC DIPLOM GP/REL RACE/REL NAT/LISM...ANTHOL BIBLIOG 20. PAGE 161 H3228
SOC CULTURE AFR STRUCT

B65
ZIOCK H.,SIND DIE DEUTSCHEN WIRKLICH SO? GERMANY SOCIETY...NAT/COMP ANTHOL 19/20. PAGE 173 H3460
PERSON ATTIT CULTURE STRUCT

L65
HOUN F.S.,"THE COMMUNIST MONOLITH VERSUS THE CHINESE TRADITION." CULTURE INTELL SOCIETY STRUCT DOMIN GP/REL ORD/FREE CONSERVE PLURISM...GOV/COMP WORSHIP. PAGE 74 H1479
ASIA MARXISM TOTALISM

S65
BRANDENBURG F.,"THE RELEVANCE OF MEXICAN EXPERIENCE TO LATIN AMERICAN DEVELOPMENT." BRAZIL CHILE VENEZUELA STRUCT ECO/UNDEV AGRI CREATE ECO/TAC ...STAT RECORD MEXIC/AMER ARGEN COLOMB. PAGE 20 H0405
L/A+17C GOV/COMP

S65
SANDERS R.,"MASS SUPPORT AND COMMUNIST INSURRECTION." GREECE MALAYSIA PHILIPPINE VIETNAM STRUCT ECO/UNDEV POL/PAR FORCES CREATE REV ...GP/COMP IDEA/COMP. PAGE 138 H2751
GUERRILLA MARXISM GOV/COMP

C65
COLEMAN J.S.,"EDUCATION AND POLITICAL DEVELOPMENT." COM CULTURE INTELL STRUCT SCHOOL PERSON SOVEREIGN ...POLICY ANTHOL BIBLIOG/A METH 20. PAGE 31 H0629
ECO/UNDEV NAT/LISM EDU/PROP TEC/DEV

C65
NEUMANN S.,"PERMANENT REVOLUTION: TOTALITARIANISM IN THE AGE OF INTERNA TIONAL CIVIL WAR (2ND ED.)" EUR+WWI ELITES POL/PAR DOMIN EDU/PROP LEAD CROWD REPRESENT...MAJORIT GOV/COMP BIBLIOG 20. PAGE 117 H2340
TOTALISM REV FASCISM STRUCT

B66
BASDEN G.T.,NIGER IBOS. NIGERIA STRUCT SECT CHIEF COLONIAL HABITAT...POLICY SOC MYTH OBS WORSHIP 20 IBO. PAGE 12 H0233
CULTURE AFR SOCIETY

B66
BECKER J.,BESSARABIEN UND SEIN DEUTSCHTUM. ROMANIA USSR STRUCT INDUS PROF/ORG SECT GP/REL INGP/REL 15/20 BESSARABIA. PAGE 13 H0254
PROVS CULTURE SOCIETY

B66
BESSON W.,DIE GROSSEN MACHTE - STRUKTURFRAGEN DER GEGENWARTIGEN WELTPOLITIK. ASIA USSR WOR+45 ATTIT ...IDEA/COMP 20 KENNEDY/JF. PAGE 16 H0321
NAT/COMP DIPLOM STRUCT

B66
BLACK C.E.,THE DYNAMICS OF MODERNIZATION: A STUDY IN COMPARATIVE HISTORY. STRUCT ECO/DEV ECO/UNDEV NAT/G DIPLOM LEAD REV...PREDICT TIME/SEQ TREND SOC/INTEG 17/20. PAGE 17 H0350
SOCIETY SOC NAT/COMP

B66
BRODERSEN A.,THE SOVIET WORKER: LABOR AND GOVERNMENT IN SOVIET SOCIETY. USSR STRUCT INDUS LABOR PLAN PAY INGP/REL PRODUC...POLICY GEN/LAWS BIBLIOG 20 STALIN/J LENIN/VI BOLSHEVISM KHRUSH/N. PAGE 21 H0425
WORKER ROLE NAT/G MARXISM

B66
COLE G.D.H.,THE MEANING OF MARXISM. USSR WOR+45 STRATA STRUCT NAT/G WORKER COST FASCISM...IDEA/COMP 20. PAGE 31 H0625
MARXISM CONCPT HIST/WRIT CAP/ISM

B66
FITZGERALD C.P.,THE BIRTH OF COMMUNIST CHINA (2ND ED.). ASIA CHINA/COM STRUCT BAL/PWR DIPLOM ECO/TAC INT/TRADE WEALTH 20. PAGE 51 H1018
REV MARXISM ECO/UNDEV

B66
HAHN C.H.L.,THE NATIVE TRIBES OF SOUTH WEST AFRICA. LAW FAM SECT HABITAT SKILL...SOC AUD/VIS WORSHIP RITUAL 20 AFRICA/SW. PAGE 64 H1275
CULTURE SOCIETY STRUCT AFR

B66
HOLT R.T.,THE POLITICAL BASIS OF ECONOMIC DEVELOPMENT. STRATA STRUCT NAT/G DIPLOM ADMIN...SOC NAT/COMP BIBLIOG 20. PAGE 73 H1458
ECO/TAC GOV/COMP CONSTN EX/STRUC

B66
KEIL S.,SEXUALITAT - ERKENNTNISSE UND MASS-STABE. CULTURE DOMIN MARRIAGE AGE/Y AGE/A PERSON SUPEGO PLURISM 17/20. PAGE 84 H1681
SEX ATTIT STRUCT SOCIETY

B66
KEITH G.,THE FADING COLOUR BAR. AFR CENTRL/AFR UK ZAMBIA CULTURE SCHOOL EDU/PROP PERS/REL DISCRIM AGE
RACE/REL STRUCT

...AUD/VIS NAT/COMP SOC/INTEG 20 NEGRO. PAGE 84 H1682
ATTIT NAT/G

B66
KOH S.J.,STAGES OF INDUSTRIAL DEVELOPMENT IN ASIA. ASIA INDIA KOREA STRATA STRUCT NAT/G INT/TRADE ...CHARTS 19/20 CHINJAP. PAGE 87 H1738
INDUS ECO/UNDEV ECO/DEV LABOR

B66
LENSKI G.E.,POWER AND PRIVILEGE: A THEORY OF SOCIAL STRATIFICATION. SWEDEN UK UNIV USSR CULTURE ECO/UNDEV PRIVIL PWR...PHIL/SCI CONCPT CHARTS IDEA/COMP HYPO/EXP METH MARX/KARL. PAGE 94 H1882
SOC STRATA STRUCT SOCIETY

B66
LEYBURN J.G.,THE HAITIAN PEOPLE (REV. ED.). HAITI SOCIETY FAM SECT DOMIN COLONIAL MARRIAGE...SOC CHARTS BIBLIOG/A 18/10. PAGE 96 H1917
STRUCT STRATA INGP/REL CULTURE

B66
MILONE P.D.,URBAN AREAS IN INDONESIA. INDONESIA LABOR NAT/G COLONIAL GP/REL...CENSUS CHARTS 17/20. PAGE 111 H2218
MUNIC GEOG STRUCT SOCIETY

B66
MULLER C.F.J.,A SELECT BIBLIOGRAPHY OF SOUTH AFRICAN HISTORY; A GUIDE FOR HISTORICAL RESEARCH. SOUTH/AFR UK LAW CONSTN SOCIETY STRUCT AGRI SECT DIPLOM COLONIAL LEAD RACE/REL...POLICY 17/20 NEGRO. PAGE 114 H2284
BIBLIOG AFR NAT/G

B66
RADIN P.,THE METHOD AND THEORY OF ETHNOLOGY. CULTURE STRUCT BIO/SOC HABITAT...HUM OBS/ENVIR METH/COMP GEN/LAWS 20 HUMANISM. PAGE 129 H2578
PHIL/SCI SOC METH SOCIETY

B66
RIZK C.,LE REGIME POLITIQUE LIBANAIS. ISLAM LEBANON STRUCT POL/PAR SECT LOBBY GP/REL 20 ARABS MUSLIM CHRISTIAN. PAGE 132 H2637
ECO/UNDEV NAT/G CULTURE

B66
SCHURMANN F.,IDEOLOGY AND ORGANIZATION IN COMMUNIST CHINA. CHINA/COM LOC/G MUNIC POL/PAR ECO/TAC CONTROL ATTIT...MGT STERTYP 20 COM/PARTY. PAGE 140 H2805
MARXISM STRUCT ADMIN NAT/G

B66
SMELSER N.J.,SOCIAL STRUCTURE AND MOBILITY IN ECONOMIC DEVELOPMENT. CULTURE SOCIETY CONFER...PSY SOC CHARTS METH/COMP NAT/COMP ANTHOL METH 20. PAGE 145 H2904
STRUCT STRATA ECO/UNDEV ECO/DEV

B66
SOROKIN P.A.,SOCIOLOGICAL THEORIES OF TODAY. SOCIETY STRUCT FAM SECT GP/REL ADJUST...PHIL/SCI PSY TREND METH/COMP 20. PAGE 147 H2935
SOC CULTURE METH/CNCPT EPIST

B66
SRINIVAS M.N.,SOCIAL CHANGE IN MODERN INDIA. INDIA CULTURE SOCIETY STRUCT SECT TEC/DEV...METH/CNCPT SELF/OBS WORSHIP 20. PAGE 148 H2961
ORD/FREE STRATA SOC ECO/UNDEV

B66
THIESENHUSEN W.C.,CHILE'S EXPERIMENTS IN AGRARIAN REFORM. CHILE STRUCT NAT/G ACT/RES ECO/TAC GOV/REL COST SOCISM...TREND CHARTS SOC/EXP 20. PAGE 154 H3073
AGRI ECO/UNDEV SOC TEC/DEV

B66
THOMPSON J.H.,MODERNIZATION OF THE ARAB WORLD. FUT ISRAEL STRUCT ECO/UNDEV DIPLOM INGP/REL ATTIT ...CENSUS ANTHOL 20 ARABS. PAGE 154 H3082
ADJUST ISLAM PROB/SOLV NAT/COMP

B66
VOGT E.Z.,PEOPLE OF RIMROCK. STRATA STRUCT KIN SECT GP/REL HABITAT ALL/VALS...GEOG INT QU 20 TEXAS NAVAHO MORMON SPAN/AMER ZUNI. PAGE 163 H3260
CULTURE GP/COMP SOC SOCIETY

B66
VON ARSENIEW W.,DIE GEISTIGEN SCHICKSALE DES RUSSISCHEN VOLKES. RUSSIA USSR SOCIETY STRUCT NAT/G SECT CHIEF REV 19/20. PAGE 163 H3262
ATTIT PERSON CULTURE DRIVE

B66
WHEELER G.,THE PEOPLES OF SOVIET CENTRAL ASIA: A BACKGROUND BOOK. ISLAM USSR STRATA STRUCT FORCES REV WAR HABITAT 7/20. PAGE 167 H3341
COLONIAL DOMIN CULTURE ADJUST

B66
WINKS R.W.,THE HISTORIOGRAPHY OF THE BRITISH EMPIRE-COMMONWEALTH. CANADA INDIA PAKISTAN UK CULTURE SOCIETY STRUCT POL/PAR...CONCPT NAT/COMP 20 AUSTRAL. PAGE 169 H3386
HIST/WRIT TREND IDEA/COMP METH/COMP

L66
HUNTINGTON S.P.,"POLITICAL MODERNIZATION* AMERICA VS EUROPE." EUR+WWI MOD/EUR UK USA+45 LAW ECO/UNDEV PWR SOVEREIGN CONSERVE LAISSEZ GOV/COMP. PAGE 75 H1505
STRUCT CREATE OBS

L66
LEMARCHAND R.,"SOCIAL CHANGE AND POLITICAL MODERNISATION IN BURUNDI." AFR BURUNDI STRATA CHIEF EX/STRUC RIGID/FLEX PWR...SOC 20. PAGE 94 H1874
NAT/G STRUCT ELITES

CONSERVE

L66
ZOPPO C.E.,"NUCLEAR TECHNOLOGY, MULTIPOLARITY, AND INTERNATIONAL STABILITY." ASIA RUSSIA USA+45 STRUCT TOP/EX BAL/PWR DIPLOM DETER CIVMIL/REL NAT/COMP. PAGE 173 H3464
NET/THEORY ORD/FREE DECISION NUC/PWR

S66
BLANC N.,"SPAIN: LEARNING THROUGH STRUGGLE" SPAIN STRATA STRUCT SECT FORCES PROB/SOLV AGE/Y ATTIT ORD/FREE PWR WEALTH MARXISM SOCISM 19/20 FRANCO/F SUCCESSION. PAGE 18 H0352
NAT/G FUT SOCIALIST TOTALISM

S66
FLEMING W.G.,"AUTHORITY, EFFICIENCY, AND ROLE STRESS: PROBLEMS IN THE DEVELOPMENT OF EAST AFRICAN BUREAUCRACIES." AFR UGANDA STRUCT PROB/SOLV ROUTINE INGP/REL ROLE...MGT SOC GP/COMP GOV/COMP 20 TANGANYIKA AFRICA/E. PAGE 51 H1024
DOMIN EFFICIENCY COLONIAL ADMIN

S66
MARTZ J.D.,"THE PLACE OF LATIN AMERICA IN THE STUDY OF COMPARATIVE POLITICS." AFR ASIA CULTURE STRUCT ECO/UNDEV ACADEM CREATE...CLASSIF NAT/COMP. PAGE 104 H2072
L/A+17C GOV/COMP STERTYP GEN/LAWS

S66
MATTHEWS D.G.,"ETHIOPIAN OUTLINE: A BIBLIOGRAPHIC RESEARCH GUIDE." ETHIOPIA LAW STRUCT ECO/UNDEV AGRI LABOR SECT CHIEF DELIB/GP EX/STRUC ADMIN...LING ORG/CHARTS 20. PAGE 105 H2095
BIBLIOG NAT/G DIPLOM POL/PAR

B67
ANDERSON O.,A LIBERAL STATE AT WAR. MOD/EUR UK LAW CULTURE STRUCT ECO/DEV NAT/G DIPLOM PARL/PROC GP/REL ALL/VALS...CONCPT 19. PAGE 7 H0131
WAR FORCES

B67
BARNETT A.D.,CADRES, BUREAUCRACY, AND POLITICAL POWER IN COMMUNIST CHINA. CHINA/COM ELITES LOC/G NAT/G INGP/REL...SOC INT DICTIONARY 20. PAGE 11 H0224
GOV/REL STRUCT MARXISM EDU/PROP

B67
BODENHEIMER E.,TREATISE ON JUSTICE. INT/ORG NAT/G PUB/INST ACT/RES RISK CRIME INGP/REL DISCRIM DRIVE LAISSEZ 20. PAGE 18 H0363
ALL/VALS STRUCT JURID CONCPT

B67
GROSS B.M.,ACTION UNDER PLANNING: THE GUIDANCE OF ECONOMIC DEVELOPMENT. STRUCT R+D NAT/G ACT/RES HABITAT...DECISION 20. PAGE 62 H1232
ECO/UNDEV PLAN ADMIN MGT

B67
HUTCHINS F.G.,THE ILLUSION OF PERMANENCE: BRITISH IMPERIALISM IN INDIA. INDIA UK CULTURE STRUCT NAT/G REV GP/REL RACE/REL ADJUST DISCRIM ATTIT MORAL PWR SOC/INTEG 18/20. PAGE 75 H1509
COLONIAL CONTROL SOVEREIGN CONSERVE

B67
KING M.L. JR.,WHERE DO WE GO FROM HERE: CHAOS OR COMMUNITY? MUNIC NAT/G PARTIC INGP/REL ALL/VALS ...POLICY CONCPT BIOG 20. PAGE 86 H1715
RACE/REL DISCRIM STRUCT PWR

B67
LAMBERT J.,LATIN AMERICA: SOCIAL STRUCTURES AND POLITICAL INSTITUTIONS. STRUCT TEC/DEV DIPLOM ADMIN COLONIAL LEAD ATTIT...SOC CLASSIF NAT/COMP 17/20. PAGE 90 H1801
L/A+17C NAT/G ECO/UNDEV SOCIETY

B67
MUNGER E.S.,AFRIKANER AND AFRICAN NATIONALISM: SOUTH AFRICAN PARALLELS AND PARAMETERS. SOUTH/AFR WOR+45 CULTURE ELITES STRUCT NAT/G PROB/SOLV DOMIN CONTROL PERS/REL NAT/LISM...SOC 20. PAGE 115 H2289
AFR RACE/REL

B67
NASH M.,MACHINE AGE MAYA. GUATEMALA L/A+17C STRUCT AGRI WORKER CREATE INCOME ATTIT RIGID/FLEX ROLE ...IDEA/COMP SOC/EXP WORSHIP 20 INDIAN/AM. PAGE 116 H2315
INDUS CULTURE SOC MUNIC

B67
PATAI R.,GOLDEN RIVER TO GOLDEN ROAD: SOCIETY, CULTURE, AND CHANGE IN THE MIDDLE EAST (2ND ED.). ELITES FAM KIN TEC/DEV MARRIAGE NAT/LISM SEX ORD/FREE...TREND GP/COMP WORSHIP 20. PAGE 124 H2476
CULTURE SOCIETY ISLAM STRUCT

B67
POLSKY N.,HUSTLERS, BEATS, AND OTHERS. FACE/GP PRESS CRIME ADJUST ANOMIE DRIVE WEALTH...PSY SOC 20. PAGE 127 H2540
CULTURE CRIMLGY NEW/IDEA STRUCT

B67
PYE L.W.,SOUTHEAST ASIA'S POLITICAL SYSTEMS. ASIA S/ASIA STRUCT ECO/UNDEV EX/STRUC CAP/ISM DIPLOM ALL/IDEOS...TREND CHARTS. PAGE 128 H2568
NAT/G POL/PAR GOV/COMP

B67
RAVKIN A.,THE NEW STATES OF AFRICA (HEADLINE SERIES, NO. 183((PAMPHLET). CULTURE STRUCT INDUS COLONIAL NAT/LISM...SOC 20. PAGE 130 H2597
AFR ECO/UNDEV SOCIETY ADMIN

B67
RIESMAN D.,CONVERSATIONS IN JAPAN: MODERNIZATION, POLITICS, AND CULTURE. CHINA/COM STRATA STRUCT ECO/DEV INDUS ACADEM EDU/PROP...ART/METH SOC MODAL INT IDEA/COMP SOC/INTEG 20 CHINJAP HIROSHIMA. PAGE 131 H2629
CULTURE SOCIETY ASIA

B67
SPIRO H.S.,PATTERNS OF AFRICAN DEVLOPMENT: FIVE COMPARISONS. STRUCT ECO/UNDEV NAT/G CONSERVE SOCISM ...PREDICT NAT/COMP 20 CHINJAP. PAGE 148 H2951 — AFR CONSTN NAT/LISM TREND

L67
UNESCO,"APARTHEID." SOUTH/AFR STRUCT KIN SCHOOL SECT WORKER DOMIN EDU/PROP REGION RACE/REL ISOLAT 20. PAGE 158 H3164 — DISCRIM CULTURE COERCE COLONIAL

S67
ABDEL-MALEK A.,"THE CRISIS IN NASSER'S EGYPT." ISLAM UAR STRUCT POL/PAR EX/STRUC CREATE PLAN WAR ATTIT ORD/FREE PWR...POLICY DECISION 20. PAGE 3 H0054 — FORCES LEAD PROB/SOLV NAT/G

S67
BATOR V.,"ONE WAR* TWO VIETNAMS." S/ASIA VIETNAM DIPLOM SUFF ATTIT ORD/FREE 20. PAGE 12 H0236 — WAR BAL/PWR NAT/G STRUCT

S67
BUTTINGER J.,"VIETNAM* FRAUD OF THE 'OTHER WAR'." VIETNAM/S ELITES STRUCT AGRI NAT/G FOR/AID RENT TREND. PAGE 25 H0499 — PLAN WEALTH REV ECO/UNDEV

S67
COHEN R.,"ANTHROPOLOGY AND POLITICAL SCIENCE: COURTSHIP OR MARRIAGE?" CULTURE STRATA STRUCT MUNIC REGION UTOPIA...NEW/IDEA TREND IDEA/COMP METH/COMP 20. PAGE 31 H0618 — SOC INGP/REL AFR

S67
CRITTENDEN J.,"DIMENSIONS OF MODERNIZATION IN THE AMERICAN STATES." USA+45 STRUCT MUNIC PROB/SOLV CONTROL LITERACY HABITAT...CONCPT METH/CNCPT CORREL CONT/OBS CENSUS 20. PAGE 35 H0702 — PROVS GOV/COMP STAT ECO/DEV

S67
DRYDEN S.,"LOCAL GOVERNMENT IN TANZANIA PART II" TANZANIA LAW NAT/G POL/PAR CONTROL PARTIC REPRESENT ...DECISION 20. PAGE 42 H0850 — LOC/G GOV/REL ADMIN STRUCT

S67
EPSTEIN E.H.,"NATIONAL IDENTITY AND THE LANGUAGE ISSUE IN PUERTO RICO." PUERT/RICO CULTURE STRUCT NAT/G PROB/SOLV SKILL...JURID STAT METH/COMP 20. PAGE 47 H0931 — EDU/PROP SCHOOL LING NAT/LISM

S67
HOFMANN W.,"THE PUBLIC INTEREST PRESSURE GROUP: THE CASE OF THE DEUTSCHE STADTETAG." GERMANY GERMANY/W CONSTN STRUCT NAT/G CENTRAL FEDERAL PWR...TIME/SEQ 20. PAGE 72 H1447 — LOC/G VOL/ASSN LOBBY ADMIN

S67
JENCKS C.E.,"SOCIAL STATUS OF COAL MINERS IN BRITAIN SINCE NATIONALIZATION." UK STRATA STRUCT LABOR RECEIVE GP/REL INCOME OWN ATTIT HABITAT...MGT T 20. PAGE 80 H1600 — EXTR/IND WORKER CONTROL NAT/G

S67
JOINER C.A.,"THE UBIQUITY OF THE ADMINISTRATIVE ROLE IN COUNTERINSURGENC. VIETNAM/S SOCIETY STRUCT NAT/G GP/REL EFFICIENCY 20. PAGE 81 H1627 — ADMIN POLICY REV ATTIT

S67
MALAN V.D.,"THE SILENT VILLAGE." KIN MUNIC NEIGH CHOOSE ISOLAT ROLE...SOC INDIAN/AM. PAGE 101 H2027 — CULTURE STRUCT PREDICT

S67
MALLORY J.R.,"THE MINISTER'S OFFICE STAFF* AN UNREFORMED PART OF PUBLIC SERVICE." CONSTN ELITES STRATA NAT/G PROB/SOLV TASK CHOOSE PERS/REL EFFICIENCY...DECISION 20. PAGE 102 H2033 — CANADA ADMIN EX/STRUC STRUCT

S67
MARWICK A.,"THE LABOUR PARTY AND THE WELFARE STATE IN BRITAIN, 19001948." UK SOCIETY STRUCT ECO/DEV WORKER CREATE PRICE CHOOSE WEALTH NEW/LIB SOCISM ...POLICY HEAL 20 PARLIAMENT LABOR/PAR. PAGE 104 H2074 — POL/PAR RECEIVE LEGIS NAT/G

S67
MURVAR V.,"MAX WEBER'S CONCEPT OF HEIROCRACY: A STUDY IN THE TYPOLOGY OF CHURCH-STATE RELATIONS" UNIV INGP/REL ATTIT PLURISM...SOC CONCPT 20 WEBER/MAX. PAGE 115 H2299 — SECT NAT/G GP/REL STRUCT

S67
RAMA C.M.,"PASADO Y PRESENTE DE LA RELIGION EN AMERICA LATINA." L/A+17C ELITES SOCIETY STRATA MARXISM...STAT WORSHIP PROTESTANT. PAGE 129 H2585 — SECT CATHISM STRUCT NAT/COMP

S67
SAVER W.,"NATIONAL SOCIALISM: TOTALITARIANISM OR FASCISM?" GERMANY STRUCT POL/PAR PROB/SOLV MARXISM ...SOC CONCPT HIST/WRIT IDEA/COMP 20 HITLER/A COLD/WAR. PAGE 138 H2760 — SOCISM NAT/G TOTALISM FASCISM

S67
SCOTT J.W.,"SOURCES OF SOCIAL CHANGE IN COMMUNITY, FAMILY, AND FERTILITY IN A PUERTO RICAN TOWN." PUERT/RICO CULTURE STRUCT ECO/UNDEV INDUS PERS/REL ROLE...SOC STAND/INT. PAGE 141 H2815 — FAM MARRIAGE LITERACY ATTIT

S67
SIPPEL D.,"INDIENS UNSICHERE ZUKUNFT." INDIA CULTURE ACADEM POL/PAR LEGIS COLONIAL CHOOSE SOVEREIGN...JURID 20. PAGE 144 H2888 — SOCIETY STRUCT ECO/UNDEV NAT/G

S67
ULC O.,"CLASS STRUGGLE AND SOCIALIST JUSTICE: THE CASE OF CZECHOSLOVAKIA." COM CZECHOSLVK LAW CONSTN ELITES STRUCT NAT/G CRIME GP/REL MARXISM 20. PAGE 158 H3151 — TOTALISM CT/SYS ADJUD STRATA

S68
KANET R.E.,"RECENT SOVIET REASSESSMENT OF DEVELOPMENTS IN THE THIRD WORLD." ALGERIA GHANA INDONESIA USSR WOR+45 CONSTN ELITES INTELL STRUCT DOMIN CONTROL REV PWR MARXISM...IDEA/COMP METH 20 THIRD/WRLD. PAGE 83 H1653 — DIPLOM NEUTRAL NAT/G NAT/COMP

S68
LAVRIN J.,"THE TWO WORLDS." RUSSIA USSR SOCIETY STRUCT NAT/G DIPLOM ATTIT PERSON MARXISM...GEOG SOC IDEA/COMP PERS/COMP 18/20. PAGE 92 H1842 — NAT/COMP NAT/LISM CULTURE

B75
MAINE H.S.,LECTURES ON THE EARLY HISTORY OF INSTITUTIONS. IRELAND UK CONSTN ELITES STRUCT FAM KIN CHIEF LEGIS CT/SYS OWN SOVEREIGN...CONCPT 16 BENTHAM/J BREHON ROMAN/LAW. PAGE 101 H2021 — CULTURE LAW INGP/REL

B76
SMITH A.,THE WEALTH OF NATIONS. UK STRUCT WORKER DIPLOM ECO/TAC OPTIMAL DRIVE PERSON ORD/FREE ...OLD/LIB GEN/LAWS 17/18. PAGE 145 H2905 — WEALTH PRODUC INDUS LAISSEZ

C80
ARNOLD M.,"DEMOCRACY" IN MIXED ESSAYS (2ND ED.)" UK SOCIETY STRUCT...CONCPT METH/COMP 19. PAGE 8 H0166 — NAT/G MAJORIT EX/STRUC ELITES

C80
ARNOLD M.,"EQUALITY" IN MIXED ESSAYS." MOD/EUR UK ELITES STRATA NAT/G...CONCPT IDEA/COMP NAT/COMP SOC/INTEG 19. PAGE 8 H0167 — ORD/FREE UTOPIA SOCIETY STRUCT

C82
MILL J.S.,"CIVILIZATION" IN DISSERTATIONS AND DISCUSSIONS." MOD/EUR UK ECO/DEV CONTROL MORAL ORD/FREE PWR...SOC IDEA/COMP 19. PAGE 110 H2208 — SOCIETY NAT/G STRUCT CONCPT

B90
TAINE H.A.,MODERN REGIME (2 VOLS.). FRANCE FAM REV CENTRAL MARRIAGE PWR...TREND 19 NAPOLEON/B. PAGE 152 H3037 — STRUCT NAT/G OLD/LIB MORAL

B93
ROYAL GEOGRAPHIC SOCIETY,BIBLIOGRAPHY OF BARBARY STATES (4 SUPPLEMENTARY PAPERS). ALGERIA LIBYA MOROCCO SOCIETY STRUCT DIPLOM LEAD 14/19 TUNIS. PAGE 135 H2706 — BIBLIOG ISLAM NAT/G COLONIAL

B94
BENOIST C.,LA POLITIQUE. FRANCE LAW SOCIETY STRUCT POL/PAR PARL/PROC GP/REL ATTIT PWR 19/20. PAGE 14 H0283 — NAT/G REPRESENT ORD/FREE

B97
JENKS E.J.,LAW AND POLITICS IN THE MIDDLE AGES. CHRIST-17C CULTURE STRUCT KIN NAT/G SECT CT/SYS GP/REL...CLASSIF CHARTS IDEA/COMP BIBLIOG 8/16. PAGE 80 H1603 — LAW SOCIETY ADJUST

B98
FORTES M.,AFRICAN POLITICAL SYSTEMS. ECO/UNDEV KIN LOC/G NEIGH POL/PAR SECT LEAD GP/REL ORD/FREE...SOC 20 NEGRO. PAGE 52 H1039 — AFR CULTURE STRUCT

B99
RIPLEY W.Z.,A SELECTED BIBLIOGRAPHY OF THE ANTHROPOLOGY AND ETHNOLOGY OF EUROPE. SOCIETY STRATA STRUCT KIN SECT VOL/ASSN GP/REL INGP/REL HABITAT...GEOG 19. PAGE 132 H2632 — BIBLIOG/A MOD/EUR SOC CULTURE

STRUVE/P....PETER STRUVE

STUART G.H. H3000

STUART DYNASTY....SEE STUART/DYN

STUART/DYN....THE STUART DYNASTY

STUBEL H. H3001

STUCKI C.W. H3002

STUDENTS FOR A DEMOCRATIC SOCIETY....SEE SDS

STUDNT/PWR....STUDENT POWER: STUDENT PROTESTS AND PROTEST MOVEMENTS

STULTZ N.M. H0550

STURZO L. H3003

STYLE....STYLES OF SCIENTIFIC COMMUNICATION

C34
BENEDICT R.,"RITUAL" IN ERA SELIGMAN, ENCYCLOPEDIA OF THE SOCIAL SCIENCES." GP/REL...SOC STYLE IDEA/COMP WORSHIP. PAGE 14 H0279
CULTURE ROUTINE ROLE STRUCT

B52
LEVY M.,THE STRUCTURE OF SOCIETY. CULTURE STRATA DRIVE KNOWL...PSY CONCPT METH/CNCPT NEW/IDEA STYLE GEN/LAWS. PAGE 95 H1907
SOCIETY SOC

S54
MIT CENTER INTERNATIONAL STU,"A PLAN OF RESEARCH IN INTERNATIONAL COMMUNICATION: A REPORT." UNIV CULTURE INTELL SOCIETY ACT/RES ALL/VALS...CONCPT METH/CNCPT. PAGE 111 H2227
R+D STYLE

S56
MACRAE D. JR.,"ROLL CALL VOTES AND LEADERSHIP." ACT/RES LEAD CHOOSE DRIVE CONSERVE NEW/LIB...STAT STYLE. PAGE 100 H2007
POL/PAR GOV/COMP LEGIS SUPEGO

S57
MARCH J.C.,"PARTY LEGISLATIVE REPRESENTATION AS A FUNCTION OF ELECTION RESULTS." DRIVE...PROBABIL REGRESS STYLE CHARTS HYPO/EXP SIMUL. PAGE 102 H2046
REPRESENT GOV/COMP LEGIS CHOOSE

S64
JOHNSON K.F.,"CAUSAL FACTORS IN LATIN AMERICAN POLITICAL INSTABILITY." CULTURE NAT/G VOL/ASSN EX/STRUC FORCES EDU/PROP LEGIT ADMIN COERCE REV ATTIT KNOWL PWR...STYLE RECORD CHARTS WORK 20. PAGE 81 H1624
L/A+17C PERCEPT ELITES

SUAREZ F. H3004,H3005

SUAREZ/F....FRANCISCO SUAREZ

SUBMARINE....SUBMARINES AND SUBMARINE WARFARE

SUBRAMANIAM V. H3006

SUBSIDIES....SEE FINAN

SUBURBS....SUBURBS

SUBVERT....SUBVERSION

SUCCESSION....SUCCESSION (POLITICAL)

S66
BLANC N.,"SPAIN: LEARNING THROUGH STRUGGLE" SPAIN STRATA STRUCT SECT FORCES PROB/SOLV AGE/Y ATTIT ORD/FREE PWR WEALTH MARXISM SOCISM 19/20 FRANCO/F SUCCESSION. PAGE 18 H0352
NAT/G FUT SOCIALIST TOTALISM

SUDAN....SEE ALSO AFR

B39
HILL R.L.,A BIBLIOGRAPHY OF THE ANGLO-EGYPTIAN SUDAN FROM THE EARLIEST TIMES TO 1937. AFR ETHIOPIA SUDAN UAR LAW COM/IND SECT RACE/REL...GEOG HEAL SOC LING 19/20 NEGRO. PAGE 71 H1417
BIBLIOG CULTURE NAT/COMP GP/COMP

B42
CONOVER H.F.,FRENCH COLONIES IN AFRICA: A LIST OF REFERENCES. ALGERIA FRANCE MOROCCO SOMALIA SUDAN CULTURE AGRI LOC/G SECT FORCES DIPLOM INT/TRADE NAT/LISM HEALTH...CON/ANAL 20. PAGE 32 H0641
BIBLIOG AFR ECO/UNDEV COLONIAL

B52
US LIBRARY OF CONGRESS,EGYPT AND THE ANGLO-EGYPTIAN SUDAN: A SELECTIVE GUIDE TO BACKGROUND READING (PAMPHLET). SUDAN UAR UK DIPLOM...POLICY 20. PAGE 160 H3209
BIBLIOG/A COLONIAL ISLAM NAT/G

B57
CONOVER H.F.,NORTH AND NORTHEAST AFRICA; A SELECTED ANNOTATED LIST OF WRITINGS. ALGERIA MOROCCO SUDAN UAR CULTURE INT/ORG PROB/SOLV ADJUD NAT/LISM PWR WEALTH...SOC 20 UN. PAGE 32 H0649
BIBLIOG/A DIPLOM AFR ECO/UNDEV

B62
NASRI A.R.,A BIBLIOGRAPHY OF THE SUDAN 1938-1958. AFR SUDAN CREATE...SOC 20. PAGE 116 H2316
BIBLIOG ECO/UNDEV NAT/G SOCIETY

B65
MEAGHER R.F.,PUBLIC INTERNATIONAL DEVELOPMENT FINANCING IN SUDAN. SUDAN FINAN DELIB/GP GIVE ...CHARTS GOV/COMP 20. PAGE 108 H2155
FOR/AID PLAN RECEIVE ECO/UNDEV

L65
MATTHEWS D.G.,"A CURRENT BIBLIOGRAPHY ON SUDANESE AFFAIRS; A SELECT BIBLIOGRAPHY FROM 1960-1964." SUDAN LAW CULTURE AGRI FINAN INDUS LABOR POL/PAR TEC/DEV FOR/AID RACE/REL LITERACY...LING 20. PAGE 105 H2094
BIBLIOG ECO/UNDEV NAT/G DIPLOM

B66
IBRAHIM-HILMY,THE LITERATURE OF EGYPT AND THE SOUDAN: FROM THE EARLIEST TIMES TO THE YEAR 1885 INCLUSIVE (2 VOLS.). MEDIT-7 SUDAN UAR LAW SOCIETY SECT ATTIT EGYPT/ANC. PAGE 76 H1520
BIBLIOG CULTURE ISLAM NAT/G

B67
COLLINS R.O.,EGYPT AND THE SUDAN. COM FRANCE ISLAM SUDAN UAR UK SOCIETY NAT/G COLONIAL NAT/LISM...GEOG SOC LING TREND SOC/INTEG 7/20 SUEZ. PAGE 32 H0635
AGRI CULTURE ECO/UNDEV

SUDETENLND....SUDETENLAND

SUEZ CRISIS....SEE NAT/LISM+COERCE, ALSO INDIVIDUAL NATIONS, SUEZ

SUEZ....SUEZ CANAL

B56
WATT D.C.,BRITAIN AND THE SUEZ CANAL. COM UAR UK ...INT/LAW 20 SUEZ TREATY. PAGE 166 H3314
DIPLOM INT/TRADE DIST/IND NAT/G

B63
ATTIA G.E.D.,LES FORCES ARMEES DES NATIONS UNIES EN COREE ET AU MOYENORIENT. KOREA CONSTN NAT/G DELIB/GP LEGIS PWR...IDEA/COMP NAT/COMP BIBLIOG UN SUEZ. PAGE 9 H0177
FORCES INT/LAW

B63
STEVENS G.G.,EGYPT YESTERDAY AND TODAY. CONSTN ECO/UNDEV AGRI INDUS NAT/G POL/PAR FORCES ECO/TAC EDU/PROP COERCE WAR NAT/LISM DRIVE ALL/VALS ...TIME/SEQ WORK SUEZ 20. PAGE 149 H2983
ISLAM TOP/EX REV UAR

S63
HOSKINS H.L.,"ARAB SOCIALISM IN THE UAR." ISLAM USSR AGRI INDUS NAT/G TOP/EX CREATE DIPLOM EDU/PROP DRIVE KNOWL PWR SOCISM...POLICY CONCPT TREND SUEZ 20. PAGE 74 H1478
ECO/DEV PLAN UAR

C63
ATTIA G.E.O.,"LES FORCES ARMEES DES NATIONS UNIES EN COREE ET AU MOYENORIENT." KOREA CONSTN DELIB/GP LEGIS PWR...IDEA/COMP NAT/COMP BIBLIOG UN SUEZ. PAGE 9 H0178
FORCES NAT/G INT/LAW

B67
COLLINS R.O.,EGYPT AND THE SUDAN. COM FRANCE ISLAM SUDAN UAR UK SOCIETY NAT/G COLONIAL NAT/LISM...GEOG SOC LING TREND SOC/INTEG 7/20 SUEZ. PAGE 32 H0635
AGRI CULTURE ECO/UNDEV

SUFF....SUFFRAGE; SEE ALSO CHOOSE

B09
LOBINGIER C.S.,THE PEOPLE'S LAW OR POPULAR PARTICIPATION IN LAW-MAKING. FRANCE SWITZERLND UK LOC/G NAT/G PROVS LEGIS SUFF MAJORITY PWR POPULISM ...GOV/COMP BIBLIOG 19. PAGE 97 H1945
CONSTN LAW PARTIC

B14
CRAIG J.,ELEMENTS OF POLITICAL SCIENCE (3 VOLS.). CONSTN AGRI INDUS SCHOOL FORCES TAX CT/SYS SUFF MORAL WEALTH...CONCPT 19 CIVIL/LIB. PAGE 35 H0696
PHIL/SCI NAT/G ORD/FREE

N19
OPERATIONS AND POLICY RESEARCH,PERU ELECTION MEMORANDA (PAMPHLET). L/A+17C PERU POL/PAR LEGIS EXEC APPORT REPRESENT 20. PAGE 121 H2421
CHOOSE CONSTN SUFF NAT/G

B27
BELLOC H.,THE SERVILE STATE (1912) (3RD ED.). PRUSSIA UK CULTURE STRATA INDUS NAT/G ECO/TAC CONTROL LEAD SUFF DISCRIM EQUILIB ORD/FREE WEALTH 20. PAGE 13 H0269
WORKER CAP/ISM DOMIN CATH

B36
CLARKE M.V.,MEDIEVAL REPRESENTATION AND CONSENT. IRELAND UK REPRESENT SUFF. PAGE 30 H0603
PARL/PROC LEGIS NAT/G

B38
IIZAWA S.,POLITICS AND POLITICAL PARTIES IN JAPAN. ELITES VOL/ASSN CHOOSE SUFF CIVMIL/REL GP/REL 19/20 CHINJAP. PAGE 76 H1522
POL/PAR REPRESENT FORCES NAT/G

B56
VON BECKERATH E.,HANDWORTERBUCH DER SOCIALWISSENSCHAFTEN (II VOLS.). EUR+WWI GERMANY POL/PAR WORKER DIPLOM LEAD CHOOSE SUFF WEALTH...SOC 20. PAGE 163 H3263
BIBLIOG INT/TRADE NAT/G ECO/DEV

B58
CAMPBELL P.,FRENCH ELECTORAL SYSTEMS AND ELECTIONS SINCE 1789 (2ND ED.). FRANCE NAT/G EX/STRUC PWR ...CHARTS 18/20. PAGE 26 H0516
REPRESENT CHOOSE POL/PAR SUFF

B59
BRIGGS A.,CHARTIST STUDIES. UK LAW NAT/G WORKER EDU/PROP COERCE SUFF GP/REL ATTIT...ANTHOL 19. PAGE 21 H0416
INDUS STRATA LABOR POLICY

B60
LA PONCE J.A.,THE PROTECTION OF MINORITIES. WOR+45 WOR-45 NAT/G POL/PAR SUFF...INT/LAW CLASSIF GP/COMP
INGP/REL DOMIN

GOV/COMP BIBLIOG 17/20 CIVIL/LIB CIV/RIGHTS. PAGE 90 H1793 — SOCIETY RACE/REL

B62
MANSERGH N.,SOUTH AFRICA 1906-1961: THE PRICE OF MAGNANIMITY. SOUTH/AFR LEGIS LEGIT SUFF NAT/LISM ATTIT ORD/FREE 20 NEGRO 20. PAGE 102 H2041 — COLONIAL DISCRIM NAT/G

B65
BETTISON D.G.,THE PAPUA-GUINEA ELECTIONS 1964. S/ASIA CONSTN POL/PAR EDU/PROP PARTIC SUFF CENTRAL CONSEN...OBS CHARTS BIBLIOG 20. PAGE 16 H0324 — NAT/G LEGIS CHOOSE REPRESENT

B65
BORTOLI G.,SOCIOLOGIE DU REFERENDUM DANS LA FRANCE MODERNE. FRANCE CONSTN EDU/PROP SUFF ATTIT ORD/FREE ...POLICY DECISION CHARTS BIBLIOG 20 DEGAULLE/C. PAGE 19 H0379 — LEGIS SOCIETY PWR NAT/G

B65
CHARNAY J.P.,LE SUFFRAGE POLITIQUE EN FRANCE; ELECTIONS PARLEMENTAIRES, ELECTION PRESIDENTIELLE, REFERENDUMS. FRANCE CONSTN CHIEF DELIB/GP ECO/TAC EDU/PROP CRIME INGP/REL MORAL ORD/FREE PWR CATHISM 20 PARLIAMENT PRESIDENT. PAGE 29 H0584 — CHOOSE SUFF NAT/G LEGIS

B65
SAKAI R.K.,STUDIES ON ASIA, 1965. INDIA KOREA S/ASIA USA+45 CONSTN KIN SECT PARTIC SUFF NAT/LISM ...POLICY SOC 19/20 CHINJAP. PAGE 137 H2737 — PARL/PROC ASIA

B65
SIRISKAR V.M.,POLITICAL BEHAVIOR IN INDIA. INDIA SOCIETY MUNIC NAT/G PROVS ACT/RES SUFF...OBS CHARTS 20 POONA. PAGE 144 H2889 — CHOOSE POL/PAR PWR ATTIT

C65
BORTOLI G.,"SOCIOLOGIE DU REFERENDUM DANS LA FRANCE MODERNE." FRANCE CONSTN NAT/G EDU/PROP SUFF ATTIT ORD/FREE...POLICY DECISION SOC CHARTS 20. PAGE 19 H0378 — BIBLIOG LEGIS SOCIETY PWR

B66
INSTITUTE COMP STUDY POL SYS,DOMINICAN REPUBLIC ELECTION FACT BOOK. DOMIN/REP LAW LEGIS REPRESENT ...JURID CHARTS 20. PAGE 77 H1536 — SUFF CHOOSE POL/PAR NAT/G

B66
SWEET E.C.,CIVIL LIBERTIES IN AMERICA. LAW CONSTN NAT/G PRESS CT/SYS DISCRIM ATTIT WORSHIP 20 CIVIL/LIB. PAGE 151 H3018 — ADJUD ORD/FREE SUFF COERCE

B67
MORRIS A.J.A.,PARLIAMENTARY DEMOCRACY IN THE NINETEENTH CENTURY. UK INDUS LOC/G NAT/G POL/PAR CONSULT LEGIS INT/TRADE ADMIN CHOOSE SUFF SOVEREIGN 19 PARLIAMENT. PAGE 113 H2261 — TIME/SEQ CONSTN PARL/PROC POPULISM

S67
BATOR V.,"ONE WAR* TWO VIETNAMS." S/ASIA VIETNAM DIPLOM SUFF ATTIT ORD/FREE 20. PAGE 12 H0236 — WAR BAL/PWR NAT/G STRUCT

S67
NEALE R.S.,"WORKING CLASS WOMEN AND WOMEN'S SUFFRAGE." UK LAW CONSTN LABOR NAT/G DELIB/GP LEGIS WORKER PAY PARTIC CHOOSE 19 FEMALE/SEX. PAGE 116 H2326 — STRATA SEX SUFF DISCRIM

B79
BRODERICK G.C.,POLITICAL STUDIES. IRELAND UK ROMAN/EMP LAW ACADEM LOC/G NAT/G DIPLOM PARL/PROC SUFF GP/REL LAISSEZ...ANTHOL. PAGE 21 H0424 — CONSTN COLONIAL

B99
DU BOIS W.E.B.,THE PHILADELPHIA NEGRO: A SOCIAL STUDY. CULTURE STRATA KIN CRIME SUFF ADJUST DISCRIM ISOLAT HABITAT HEREDITY ALL/VALS SOC/INTEG 17/19 NEGRO PHILADELPH. PAGE 42 H0851 — INGP/REL RACE/REL SOC CENSUS

SUFFRAGE....SEE SUFF

SUICIDE....SUICIDE AND RELATED SELF-DESTRUCTIVENESS

B57
NARAIN D.,HINDU CHARACTER (A FEW GLIMPSES). INDIA DIPLOM SUICIDE PERS/REL ATTIT...PSY NAT/COMP PERS/COMP BIBLIOG WORSHIP 20 HINDU. PAGE 116 H2310 — PERSON STERTYP SUPEGO SECT

S67
HOPE M.,"THE RELUCTANT WAY: SELF-IMMOLATION IN VIETNAM." VIETNAM SOCIETY FAM KIN SECT DRIVE ALL/VALS...TRADIT OBS INT 20. PAGE 73 H1465 — CULTURE SUICIDE IDEA/COMP ATTIT

SUKARNO/A....ACHMED SUKARNO

S64
VANDENBOSCH A.,"POWER BALANCE IN INDONESIA." S/ASIA USSR NAT/G TOP/EX BAL/PWR DOMIN NEUTRAL ORD/FREE PWR...POLICY TIME/SEQ GEN/LAWS 20 SUKARNO/A. PAGE 162 H3233 — FORCES TREND DIPLOM INDONESIA

SULLIVAN J.H. H3007

SUMATRA....SUMATRA

B64
SCHNITGER F.M.,FORGOTTEN KINGDOMS IN SUMATRA. FAM SECT LEISURE HABITAT...OBS AUD/VIS WORSHIP 20 SUMATRA. PAGE 140 H2793 — CULTURE AFR SOCIETY STRUCT

SUMER....SUMER, A PRE- OR EARLY HISTORIC SOCIETY

SUMNER W.G. H3008

SUN/YAT....SUN YAT SEN

SUNG C.H. H3009

SUPEGO....CONSCIENCE, SUPEREGO, RESPONSIBILITY

B14
BERHARDI F.,GERMANY AND THE NEXT WAR. MOD/EUR NAT/G SCHOOL FORCES ACT/RES DOMIN EDU/PROP SUPEGO PWR ...TIME/SEQ STERTYP TOT/POP 20 WWI. PAGE 15 H0304 — DRIVE COERCE WAR GERMANY

B25
TEMPERLEY H.,THE FOREIGN POLICY OF CANNING: 1822-1827. MOD/EUR NAT/G TOP/EX EDU/PROP ROUTINE ATTIT RIGID/FLEX SUPEGO PWR SKILL...TIME/SEQ PARLIAMENT 20. PAGE 153 H3058 — PERSON DIPLOM UK BIOG

B31
DUFFIELD M.,KING LEGION. NAT/G PROVS SECT LEGIS EDU/PROP PRESS GP/REL AGE/Y MARXISM POLICY. PAGE 43 H0856 — SUPEGO FORCES VOL/ASSN LOBBY

B32
BRYCE J.,THE HOLY ROMAN EMPIRE. GERMANY ITALY MOD/EUR CULTURE SOCIETY STRUCT INT/ORG NAT/G SECT DIPLOM DOMIN WAR SUPEGO ALL/VALS SOVEREIGN...GEOG SOC TIME/SEQ CHARTS STERTYP. PAGE 23 H0456 — CHRIST-17C NAT/LISM

B33
FERRERO G.,PEACE AND WAR (TRANS. BY BERTHA PRITCHARD). CULTURE FINAN SECT ATTIT SUPEGO MORAL ORD/FREE CONSERVE POPULISM SOCISM POLICY. PAGE 49 H0987 — WAR PEACE DIPLOM PROB/SOLV

B35
AQUINAS T.,ON THE GOVERNANCE OF RULERS (1265-66). UNIV SOCIETY STRATA FAM HABITAT PERSON ALL/VALS PWR SOVEREIGN CONSERVE...POLICY BIBLE. PAGE 8 H0155 — CATH NAT/G CHIEF SUPEGO

C36
MAZZINI J.,"FROM THE COUNCIL TO GOD" (1870) IN J. MAZZINI, ESSAYS." ITALY NAT/G EDU/PROP PARTIC ORD/FREE PWR SOVEREIGN 19 POPE CHRISTIAN DEITY. PAGE 106 H2112 — CATHISM DOMIN NAT/LISM SUPEGO

B41
PALMER R.R.,TWELVE WHO RULED. MOD/EUR ELITES STRUCT NAT/G POL/PAR DELIB/GP DOMIN ATTIT SUPEGO PWR ...POLICY CONCPT 18. PAGE 123 H2453 — TOP/EX BIOG REV FRANCE

L48
SHILS E.A.,"COHESION AND DISINTEGRATION IN THE WEHRMACHT IN WORLD WAR II." GERMANY STRUCT DOMIN WAR INGP/REL ISOLAT NAT/LISM ATTIT AUTHORIT SUPEGO RESPECT...PSY CON/ANAL 20 NAZI. PAGE 143 H2862 — EDU/PROP DRIVE PERS/REL FORCES

S48
ALEXANDER L.,"WAR CRIMES, THEIR SOCIAL-PSYCHOLOGICAL ASPECTS." EUR+WWI GERMANY LAW CULTURE ELITES KIN POL/PAR PUB/INST FORCES DOMIN EDU/PROP COERCE CRIME ATTIT SUPEGO HEALTH MORAL PWR FASCISM ...PSY OBS TREND GEN/LAWS NAZI 20. PAGE 5 H0100 — DRIVE WAR

B50
WHITE R.J.,THE CONSERVATIVE TRADITION. UK POL/PAR SUPEGO PWR RESPECT...POLICY ANTHOL 19. PAGE 167 H3350 — CONSERVE CONCPT NAT/G ORD/FREE

B52
HIMMELFARB G.,LORD ACTON: A STUDY IN CONSCIENCE AND POLITICS. MOD/EUR NAT/G POL/PAR SECT LEGIS TOP/EX EDU/PROP ADMIN NAT/LISM ATTIT PERSON SUPEGO MORAL ORD/FREE...CONCPT PARLIAMENT 19 ACTON/LORD. PAGE 71 H1419 — PWR BIOG

B53
BUCHHEIM K.,GESCHICHTE DER CHRISTLICHEN PARTEIEN IN DEUTSCHLAND. GERMANY CREATE ATTIT SUPEGO ORD/FREE ...TIME/SEQ IDEA/COMP 19/20 CHRIS/DEM. PAGE 23 H0464 — POL/PAR NAT/G

B53
HUNTER E.,BRAIN-WASHING IN RED CHINA. ASIA CHINA/COM CULTURE SOCIETY FORCES WAR TOTALISM ATTIT BIO/SOC DISPL DRIVE PERSON SUPEGO KNOWL ORD/FREE ...INT REC/INT COLD/WAR 20. PAGE 75 H1499 — EDU/PROP COERCE

S53
ARENDT H.,"IDEOLOGY AND TERROR: A NOVEL FORM OF GOVERNMENT." WOR-45 DOMIN STRANGE ATTIT SUPEGO MARXISM...GOV/COMP IDEA/COMP 20 NAZI. PAGE 8 H0160 — TOTALISM ANOMIE ALL/IDEOS SOCIETY

B54
CAMPANELLA T.,A DISCOURSE TOUCHING THE SPANISH MONARCHY... (1640). SPAIN UNIV SEA STRATA FINAN SECT FORCES SUPEGO LOVE ORD/FREE...CONCPT 17. PAGE 26 H0514
CONSERVE CHIEF NAT/G DIPLOM

B55
MAZZINI J.,THE DUTIES OF MAN. MOD/EUR LAW SOCIETY FAM NAT/G POL/PAR SECT VOL/ASSN EX/STRUC ACT/RES CREATE REV PEACE ATTIT ALL/VALS...GEN/LAWS WORK 19. PAGE 106 H2113
SUPEGO CONCPT NAT/LISM

B55
POHLENZ M.,GRIECHISCHE FREIHEIT. GREECE DIPLOM WAR SUPEGO PWR RESPECT...IDEA/COMP. PAGE 127 H2533
ORD/FREE CONCPT JURID NAT/G

B55
ROWE C.,VOLTAIRE AND THE STATE. FRANCE MOD/EUR BAL/PWR CONTROL TASK SUPEGO ORD/FREE PWR...CONCPT 18 VOLTAIRE. PAGE 135 H2702
NAT/G DIPLOM NAT/LISM ATTIT

B56
WEBER M.,STAATSSOZIOLOGIE. STRUCT LEGIT ADMIN PARL/PROC SUPEGO CONSERVE JURID. PAGE 166 H3320
SOC NAT/G POL/PAR LEAD

S56
MACRAE D. JR.,"ROLL CALL VOTES AND LEADERSHIP." ACT/RES LEAD CHOOSE DRIVE CONSERVE NEW/LIB...STAT STYLE. PAGE 100 H2007
POL/PAR GOV/COMP LEGIS SUPEGO

B57
NARAIN D.,HINDU CHARACTER (A FEW GLIMPSES). INDIA DIPLOM SUICIDE PERS/REL ATTIT...PSY NAT/COMP PERS/COMP BIBLIOG WORSHIP 20 HINDU. PAGE 116 H2310
PERSON STERTYP SUPEGO SECT

B57
US SENATE SPEC COMM FOR AID,HEARINGS BEFORE THE SPECIAL COMMITTEE TO STUDY THE FOREIGN AID PROGRAM. USA+45 USSR ECO/UNDEV INT/ORG FORCES WEAPON TOTALISM ATTIT SUPEGO...NAT/COMP CONGRESS. PAGE 161 H3217
FOR/AID DIPLOM ORD/FREE TEC/DEV

S57
DEXTER L.A.,"A SOCIAL THEORY OF MENTAL DEFICIENCY." CULTURE PUB/INST PROB/SOLV CRIME PERS/REL STRANGE PERSON SUPEGO SKILL...EPIST SOC/WK HYPO/EXP. PAGE 41 H0814
SOC PSY HEALTH ROLE

B58
GREAVES H.R.,THE FOUNDATIONS OF POLITICAL THEORY. WAR ATTIT SUPEGO ORD/FREE...IDEA/COMP SOC/INTEG. PAGE 60 H1203
CONCPT MORAL PERSON

S58
EULAV H.,"HD LASSWELL'S DEVELOPMENTAL ANALYSIS." FUT CULTURE TOP/EX PLAN CHOOSE SUPEGO PWR...TREND HYPO/EXP SIMUL GEN/METH VAL/FREE 20 LASSWELL/H. PAGE 47 H0948
CONCPT NEW/IDEA ELITES

B60
GENTILE G.,GENESIS AND STRUCTURE OF SOCIETY (TRANS. BY H.S. HARRIS). NAT/G SECT ATTIT SUPEGO...JURID 20. PAGE 56 H1111
SOCIETY STRUCT PERSON

B60
MORRISON C.,THE POWERS THAT BE. NAT/G SUPEGO ...POLICY CONCPT IDEA/COMP WORSHIP 20 BIBLE. PAGE 113 H2265
HUM ORD/FREE

B60
PANIKKAR K.M.,THE STATE AND THE CITIZEN (2ND ED.). INDIA DOMIN ATTIT SUPEGO ORD/FREE WEALTH...GEOG CONCPT GP/COMP 20. PAGE 123 H2459
TEC/DEV POL/PAR NAT/G EDU/PROP

B61
CATHERINE R.,LE FONCTIONNAIRE FRANCAIS. FRANCE NAT/G INGP/REL ATTIT MORAL ORD/FREE...T CIVIL/SERV. PAGE 28 H0559
ADMIN GP/REL LEAD SUPEGO

B62
ESCUELA SUPERIOR DE ADMIN PUBL,INFORME DEL SEMINARIO SOBRE SERVICIO CIVIL O CARRERA ADMINISTRATIVA. L/A+17C ELITES STRATA CONFER CONTROL GOV/REL INGP/REL SUPEGO 20 CENTRAL/AM CIVIL/SERV. PAGE 47 H0939
ADMIN NAT/G PROB/SOLV ATTIT

B62
FINER S.E.,THE MAN ON HORSEBACK: ROLE OF THE MILITARY IN POLITICS. UNIV LAW CONSTN ELITES SOCIETY POL/PAR BAL/PWR DOMIN EDU/PROP LEGIT COERCE GUERRILLA REV WAR WEAPON DRIVE SUPEGO ORD/FREE PWR RESPECT...POLICY CONCPT GEN/METH. PAGE 50 H1003
NAT/G FORCES TOTALISM

B62
HOOK S.,THE PARADOXES OF FREEDOM. UNIV CONSTN INTELL LEGIS CONTROL REV CHOOSE SUPEGO...POLICY JURID IDEA/COMP 19/20 CIV/RIGHTS. PAGE 73 H1461
CONCPT MAJORIT ORD/FREE ALL/VALS

B62
MALINOWSKI B.,SEX, CULTURE, AND MYTH. UNIV SOCIETY FAM PERS/REL MARRIAGE RATIONAL HABITAT PERSON SUPEGO MORAL WORSHIP 20. PAGE 102 H2032
MYTH SECT SEX CULTURE

B62
ZIESEL K.,DAS VERLORENE GEWISSEN. GERMANY/W NAT/G VOL/ASSN EDU/PROP PRESS SUPEGO...POLICY 20. PAGE 173 H3455
MORAL PWR ORD/FREE RESPECT

S62
MONNIER J.P.,"LA SUCCESSION D'ETATS EN MATIERE DE RESPONSABILITE INTERNATIONALE." UNIV CONSTN INTELL SOCIETY ADJUD ROUTINE PERCEPT SUPEGO...GEN/LAWS TOT/POP 20. PAGE 112 H2240
NAT/G JURID INT/LAW

B63
BROGAN D.W.,POLITICAL PATTERNS IN TODAY'S WORLD. FRANCE USA+45 USSR WOR+45 CONSTN STRUCT PLAN DIPLOM ADMIN LEAD ROLE SUPEGO...PHIL/SCI 20. PAGE 21 H0429
NAT/COMP NEW/LIB COM TOTALISM

B63
DE VRIES E.,SOCIAL ASPECTS OF ECONOMIC DEVELOPMENT IN LATIN AMERICA. CULTURE SOCIETY STRATA FINAN INDUS INT/ORG DELIB/GP ACT/RES ECO/TAC EDU/PROP ADMIN ATTIT SUPEGO HEALTH KNOWL ORD/FREE...SOC STAT TREND ANTHOL TOT/POP VAL/FREE. PAGE 39 H0777
L/A+17C ECO/UNDEV

B63
EICH H.,THE UNLOVED GERMANS. EUR+WWI GERMANY PERS/REL RACE/REL DISCRIM HABITAT SUPEGO FASCISM ...PSY SOC AUD/VIS 19/20 JEWS. PAGE 45 H0898
STERTYP PERSON CULTURE ATTIT

B63
MCNEAL R.H.,THE BOLSHEVIK TRADITION: LENIN, STALIN, KHRUSHCHEV. USSR NAT/G SUPEGO CONSERVE...IDEA/COMP GEN/LAWS 20 LENIN/VI STALIN/J KHRUSH/N. PAGE 107 H2145
INTELL BIOG PERS/COMP

L63
ROSE R.,"COMPARATIVE STUDIES IN POLITICAL FINANCE: A SYMPOSIUM." ASIA EUR+WWI S/ASIA LAW CULTURE DELIB/GP LEGIS ACT/RES ECO/TAC EDU/PROP CHOOSE ATTIT RIGID/FLEX SUPEGO PWR SKILL WEALTH...STAT ANTHOL VAL/FREE. PAGE 134 H2674
FINAN POL/PAR

S63
ARASTEH R.,"THE ROLE OF INTELLECTUALS IN ADMINISTRATIVE DEVELOPMENT AND SOCIAL CHANGE IN MODERN IRAN." ISLAM CULTURE NAT/G CONSULT ACT/RES EDU/PROP EXEC ATTIT BIO/SOC PERCEPT SUPEGO ALL/VALS ...POLICY MGT PSY SOC CONCPT 20. PAGE 8 H0157
INTELL ADMIN IRAN

S63
DUDLEY B.J.,"THE NOMINATION OF PARLIAMENTARY CANDIDATES IN NORTHERN NIGERIA." AFR CONSTN CULTURE ELITES STRATA DELIB/GP LEGIS DOMIN EDU/PROP COERCE ATTIT SUPEGO PWR...STAT VAL/FREE 20. PAGE 43 H0854
POL/PAR CHOOSE NIGERIA

S63
HARRIS R.L.,"A COMPARATIVE ANALYSIS OF THE ADMINISTRATIVE SYSTEMS OF CANADA AND CEYLON." S/ASIA CULTURE SOCIETY STRATA TOP/EX ACT/RES DOMIN EDU/PROP LEGIT COERCE ATTIT SUPEGO ALL/VALS...MGT CHARTS GEN/LAWS VAL/FREE 20. PAGE 67 H1343
DELIB/GP EX/STRUC CANADA CEYLON

B64
CURTIN P.D.,THE IMAGE OF AFRICA: BRITISH IDEAS AND ACTION, 1780-1850. MOD/EUR SOCIETY FORCES ACT/RES DOMIN EDU/PROP COERCE ATTIT PERCEPT RIGID/FLEX SUPEGO HEALTH KNOWL MORAL ORD/FREE WEALTH...CONCPT WORK VAL/FREE. PAGE 36 H0726
AFR CULTURE UK DIPLOM

B65
GOLEMBIEWSKI R.T.,MEN, MANAGEMENT, AND MORALITY; TOWARD A NEW ORGANIZATIONAL ETHIC. CONSTN EX/STRUC CREATE ADMIN CONTROL INGP/REL PERSON SUPEGO MORAL PWR...GOV/COMP METH/COMP 20 BUREAUCRCY. PAGE 58 H1161
LG/CO MGT PROB/SOLV

B66
KEIL S.,SEXUALITAT - ERKENNTNISSE UND MASS-STABE. CULTURE DOMIN MARRIAGE AGE/Y AGE/A PERSON SUPEGO PLURISM 17/20. PAGE 84 H1681
SEX ATTIT STRUCT SOCIETY

B66
TSURUMI K.,ADULT SOCIALIZATION AND SOCIAL CHANGE: JAPAN BEFORE AND AFTER DEFEAT IN WORLD WAR II. FAM DEATH SUPEGO...PSY SOC 20 CHINJAP. PAGE 157 H3133
SOCIETY AGE/A WAR PERSON

B66
WEINSTEIN B.,GABON: NATION-BUILDING ON THE OGOOUE. AFR GABON WOR+45 CULTURE SOCIETY PLAN DIPLOM COLONIAL INGP/REL ANOMIE HABITAT SUPEGO 20. PAGE 166 H3329
ECO/UNDEV GP/REL LEAD NAT/G

S67
MCCLEERY W.,"AN INTERVIEW WITH J. DOUGLAS BROWN ON THE 'WAY' OF VIETNAM" COM VIETNAM INTELL ECO/DEV ACADEM NAT/G COERCE PERSON SUPEGO ORD/FREE 20. PAGE 106 H2125
ATTIT WAR COLONIAL MARXISM

S67
SEIDLER G.L.,"MARXIST LEGAL THOUGHT IN POLAND." POLAND SOCIETY R+D LOC/G NAT/G ACT/RES ADJUD CT/SYS SUPEGO PWR...SOC TREND 20 MARX/KARL. PAGE 141 H2822
MARXISM LAW CONCPT EFFICIENCY

S67
TIVEY L.,"THE POLITICAL CONSEQUENCES OF ECONOMIC PLANNING." UK CONSTN INDUS ACT/RES ADMIN CONTROL LOBBY REPRESENT EFFICIENCY SUPEGO SOVEREIGN ...DECISION 20. PAGE 155 H3108
PLAN POLICY NAT/G

B75
NEWMAN J.H.,A LETTER ADDRESSED TO THE DUKE OF NORFOLK ON THE OCCASION OF MR. GLADSTONE'S RECENT EXPOSTULATION. NAT/G SECT CHIEF LEGIS CONTROL LEAD GP/REL SUPEGO SOC/INTEG WORSHIP 19 ENGLAND. PAGE 117 H2346
POLICY DOMIN SOVEREIGN CATHISM

B96
SCHMOLLER G.,THE MERCANTILE SYSTEM AND ITS HISTORICAL SIGNIFICANCE: ILLUSTRATED CHIEFLY FROM PRUSSIAN HISTORY (TRANS.). PRUSSIA CULTURE INDUS KIN MUNIC NAT/G PROVS OP/RES ECO/TAC INT/TRADE SUPEGO PWR WEALTH 19 MERCANTLST. PAGE 139 H2790
GEN/METH INGP/REL CONCPT

SUPERVISION....SEE EXEC, CONTROL, LEAD, TASK

SUPREME/CT....SUPREME COURT (ALL NATIONS)

B37
HAMILTON W.H.,THE POWER TO GOVERN. ECO/DEV FINAN INDUS ECO/TAC INT/TRADE TARIFFS TAX CONTROL CT/SYS WAR COST PWR 18/20 SUPREME/CT. PAGE 65 H1303
LING CONSTN NAT/G POLICY

B54
HAMSON C.J.,EXECUTIVE DISCRETION AND JUDICIAL CONTROL; AN ASPECT OF THE FRENCH CONSEIL D'ETAT. EUR+WWI FRANCE MOD/EUR UK NAT/G EX/STRUC PARTIC CONSERVE...JURID BIBLIOG/A 18/20 SUPREME/CT. PAGE 65 H1310
ELITES ADJUD NAT/COMP

B56
DOUGLAS W.O.,WE THE JUDGES. INDIA USA+45 USA-45 LAW NAT/G SECT LEGIS PRESS CRIME FEDERAL ORD/FREE ...POLICY GOV/COMP 19/20 WARRN/EARL MARSHALL/J SUPREME/CT. PAGE 42 H0841
ADJUD CT/SYS CONSTN GOV/REL

B57
LONG H.A.,USURPERS - FOES OF FREE MAN. LAW NAT/G CHIEF LEGIS DOMIN ADJUD REPRESENT GOV/REL ORD/FREE LAISSEZ POPULISM...POLICY 18/20 SUPREME/CT ROOSEVLT/F CONGRESS CON/INTERP. PAGE 98 H1961
CT/SYS CENTRAL FEDERAL CONSTN

S59
MENDELSON W.,"JUDICIAL REVIEW AND PARTY POLITICS" (BMR)" UK USA+45 USA-45 NAT/G LEGIS PROB/SOLV EDU/PROP ADJUD EFFICIENCY...POLICY NAT/COMP 19/20 AUSTRAL SUPREME/CT. PAGE 109 H2171
CT/SYS POL/PAR BAL/PWR JURID

B60
JUNZ A.J.,PRESENT TRENDS IN AMERICAN NATIONAL GOVERNMENT. LEGIS DIPLOM ADMIN CT/SYS ORD/FREE ...CONCPT ANTHOL 20 CONGRESS PRESIDENT SUPREME/CT. PAGE 3 H0052
POL/PAR CHOOSE CONSTN NAT/G

B64
LEDERMAN W.R.,THE COURTS AND THE CANDIAN CONSTITUTION. CANADA PARL/PROC...POLICY JURID GOV/COMP ANTHOL 19/20 SUPREME/CT PARLIAMENT. PAGE 93 H1854
CONSTN CT/SYS LEGIS LAW

SURPLUS....SEE DEMAND,PLAN

SURVEY ANALYSIS....SEE SAMP/SIZ

SVALASTOGA K. H3010,H3011

SVARLIEN O. H3012

SWANSON B.E. H0079

SWARTZ M.J. H3013

SWATANTRA....SWATANTRA - COALITION RIGHT-WING PARTY IN INDIA

B67
ERDMAN H.L.,THE SWATANTRA PARTY AND INDIAN CONSERVATISM. INDIA S/ASIA SOCIETY STRATA LOC/G NAT/G LEAD PARTIC GP/REL ATTIT...CONCPT GP/COMP BIBLIOG 20 SWATANTRA. PAGE 47 H0938
POL/PAR CONSERVE CHOOSE POLICY

SWAYZE H. H3014

SWEARER H.R. H3015,H3016

SWEARINGEN A.R. H3017

SWEDEN....SEE ALSO APPROPRIATE TIME/SPACE/CULTURE INDEX

B31
CROOK W.H.,THE GENERAL STRIKE: A STUDY OF LABOR'S TRAGIC WEAPON IN THEORY AND PRACTICE. BELGIUM FRANCE SWEDEN UK WOR-45 PROB/SOLV ECO/TAC DOMIN PWR ...POLICY TIME/SEQ NAT/COMP GEN/LAWS 19/20 STRIKE. PAGE 35 H0707
LABOR WORKER LG/CO BARGAIN

S39
HECKSCHER G.,"GROUP ORGANIZATION IN SWEDEN." SWEDEN STRATA ECO/DEV AGRI INDUS LABOR NAT/G PROF/ORG ECO/TAC CENTRAL SOCISM...MGT 19/20. PAGE 69 H1382
LAISSEZ SOC

B42
ROBBINS J.J.,THE GOVERNMENT OF LABOR RELATIONS IN SWEDEN. SWEDEN LAW CONSTN ADJUD CT/SYS GP/REL ...JURID 20. PAGE 132 H2638
NAT/G BARGAIN LABOR INDUS

S45
SPENCER R.C.,"PARTY GOVERNMENT AND THE SWEDISH RISKDAG." SWEDEN CHOOSE MAJORITY. PAGE 147 H2946
GOV/COMP NAT/G POL/PAR PARL/PROC

B53
ORFIELD L.B.,THE GROWTH OF SCANDINAVIAN LAW. DENMARK ICELAND NORWAY SWEDEN LAW DIPLOM...BIBLIOG 9/20. PAGE 121 H2426
JURID CT/SYS NAT/G

B54
FRIEDMAN W.,THE PUBLIC CORPORATION: A COMPARATIVE SYMPOSIUM (UNIVERSITY OF TORONTO SCHOOL OF LAW COMPARATIVE LAW SERIES, VOL. I). SWEDEN USA+45 INDUS INT/ORG NAT/G REGION CENTRAL FEDERAL...POLICY JURID IDEA/COMP NAT/COMP ANTHOL 20 COMMONWLTH MONOPOLY EUROPE. PAGE 53 H1065
LAW SOCISM LG/CO OWN

B55
RUSTOW D.A.,THE POLITICS OF COMPROMISE. SWEDEN LABOR EX/STRUC LEGIS PLAN REPRESENT SOCISM...SOC 19/20. PAGE 136 H2720
POL/PAR NAT/G POLICY ECO/TAC

B59
FOX A.,THE POWER OF SMALL STATES: DIPLOMACY IN WORLD WAR TWO. EUR+WWI FINLAND NORWAY SPAIN SWEDEN TURKEY NAT/G TOP/EX DIPLOM PWR...HIST/WRIT 20. PAGE 52 H1044
CONCPT STERTYP BAL/PWR

B59
SISSON C.H.,THE SPIRIT OF BRITISH ADMINISTRATION AND SOME EUROPEAN COMPARISONS. FRANCE GERMANY/W SWEDEN UK LAW EX/STRUC INGP/REL EFFICIENCY ORD/FREE ...DECISION 20. PAGE 144 H2890
GOV/COMP ADMIN ELITES ATTIT

B59
VERNEY D.V.,PUBLIC ENTERPRISE IN SWEDEN. FUT SWEDEN UK INDUS POL/PAR LEGIS PROB/SOLV CAP/ISM INT/TRADE CONTROL SOCISM...MGT CONCPT NAT/COMP 20 SOCDEM/PAR CIVIL/SERV. PAGE 162 H3246
ECO/DEV POLICY LG/CO NAT/G

B64
ANDREN N.,GOVERNMENT AND POLITICS IN THE NORDIC COUNTRIES: DENMARK, FINLAND, ICELAND, NORWAY, SWEDEN. DENMARK FINLAND ICELAND NORWAY SWEDEN POL/PAR CHIEF LEGIS ADMIN REGION REPRESENT ATTIT CONSERVE...CHARTS BIBLIOG/A 20. PAGE 7 H0137
CONSTN NAT/G CULTURE GOV/COMP

B64
BROWN W.M.,THE EXTERNAL LIQUIDITY OF AN ADVANCED COUNTRY. CANADA FRANCE GERMANY/W SWEDEN UK USA+45 ECO/DEV DIPLOM PRICE...CONCPT STAT NAT/COMP 20. PAGE 22 H0451
FINAN INT/TRADE COST INCOME

B64
HALLER W.,DER SCHWEDISCHE JUSTITIEOMBUDSMAN. DENMARK FINLAND NORWAY SWEDEN LEGIS ADJUD CONTROL PERSON ORD/FREE...NAT/COMP 20 OMBUDSMAN. PAGE 64 H1288
JURID PARL/PROC ADMIN CHIEF

B65
ROWAT D.C.,THE OMBUDSMAN: CITIZEN'S DEFENDER. DENMARK FINLAND NEW/ZEALND NORWAY SWEDEN CONSULT PROB/SOLV FEEDBACK PARTIC GP/REL...SOC CONCPT NEW/IDEA METH/COMP ANTHOL BIBLIOG 20. PAGE 135 H2701
INSPECT CONSTN NAT/G ADMIN

B65
WUORINEN J.H.,SCANDINAVIA. DENMARK FINLAND ICELAND NORWAY SWEDEN SOCIETY AGRI INDUS DELIB/GP DIPLOM INT/TRADE NEUTRAL...GEOG CHARTS BIBLIOG TREATY. PAGE 171 H3428
NAT/G POL/PAR TREND POLICY

S65
BIRNBAUM K.,"SWEDEN'S NUCLEAR POLICY." WOR+45 POL/PAR CREATE TEC/DEV NEUTRAL RISK WAR ORD/FREE ...DECISION IDEA/COMP NAT/COMP TIME. PAGE 17 H0343
SWEDEN NUC/PWR DIPLOM ARMS/CONT

C65
WUORINEN J.H.,"SCANDINAVIA." DENMARK FINLAND ICELAND NORWAY SWEDEN SOCIETY AGRI POL/PAR DELIB/GP DIPLOM INT/TRADE NEUTRAL WAR...CHARTS TREATY 20. PAGE 171 H3427
BIBLIOG NAT/G POLICY

B66
LENSKI G.E.,POWER AND PRIVILEGE: A THEORY OF SOCIAL STRATIFICATION. SWEDEN UK UNIV USSR CULTURE ECO/UNDEV PRIVIL PWR...PHIL/SCI CONCPT CHARTS IDEA/COMP HYPO/EXP METH MARX/KARL. PAGE 94 H1882
SOC STRATA STRUCT SOCIETY

B66
MAC DONALD H.M.,THE INTELLECTUAL IN POLITICS. GERMANY PERU SWEDEN UK USSR NAT/G CONSULT PLAN EDU/PROP TASK INGP/REL EFFICIENCY RATIONAL ALL/VALS 20. PAGE 99 H1987
ALL/IDEOS INTELL POL/PAR PARTIC

B67
ANDERSON S.V.,THE NORDIC COUNCIL: A STUDY OF SCANDINAVIAN REGIONALISM. DENMARK FINLAND ICELAND NORWAY SWEDEN MARKET NAT/G VOL/ASSN CONSULT PARL/PROC ATTIT...TIME/SEQ BIBLIOG 20. PAGE 7 H0134
INT/ORG REGION DIPLOM LEGIS

B67
ROSENTHAL A.H.,THE SOCIAL PROGRAMS OF SWEDEN. SWEDEN USA+45 FINAN NAT/G PLAN PROB/SOLV INSPECT ORD/FREE...POLICY HEAL SOC CHARTS NAT/COMP 20. PAGE 134 H2681
GIVE SOC/WK WEALTH METH/COMP

L67
CRIBBET J.E.,"SOME REFLECTIONS ON THE LAW OF LAND - A VIEW FROM SCANDINAVIA." DENMARK NETHERLAND NORWAY SWEDEN INDUS MUNIC NEIGH RACE/REL ATTIT HABITAT ...IDEA/COMP 20. PAGE 35 H0701 — LAW PLAN CONTROL NAT/G

L86
BURGESS J.W.,"THE RECENT CONSTITUTIONAL CRISIS IN NORWAY" MOD/EUR NORWAY SWEDEN LOC/G NAT/G CHIEF BAL/PWR NAT/LISM ORD/FREE 19. PAGE 24 H0481 — CONSTN SOVEREIGN GOV/REL

SWEET E.C. H3018

SWEEZY P.M. H3019

SWIFT M.G. H3020

SWITZERLND....SWITZERLAND; SEE ALSO APPROPRIATE TIME/SPACE/ CULTURE INDEX

N
DEUTSCHE BUCHEREI,JAHRESVERZEICHNIS DES DEUTSCHEN SCHRIFTUMS. AUSTRIA EUR+WWI GERMANY SWITZERLND LAW LOC/G DIPLOM ADMIN...MGT SOC 19/20. PAGE 40 H0804 — BIBLIOG WRITING NAT/G

B08
LLOYD H.D.,THE SWISS DEMOCRACY. SWITZERLND INDUS NAT/G WORKER CHOOSE OWN ORD/FREE SOCISM...PLURIST 19/20 MONOPOLY. PAGE 97 H1944 — NAT/COMP GOV/COMP REPRESENT POPULISM

B09
LOBINGIER C.S.,THE PEOPLE'S LAW OR POPULAR PARTICIPATION IN LAW-MAKING. FRANCE SWITZERLND UK LOC/G NAT/G PROVS LEGIS SUFF MAJORITY PWR POPULISM ...GOV/COMP BIBLIOG 19. PAGE 97 H1945 — CONSTN LAW PARTIC

B13
DIE REKLAME IHRE KUNST UND WISSENSCHAFT. GERMANY POLAND SWITZERLND USA+45 TEC/DEV CAP/ISM DEMAND ...ART/METH EXHIBIT METH/COMP ANTHOL 20. PAGE 135 H2707 — EDU/PROP MARKET NAT/COMP ATTIT

N19
STEUBER F.A.,THE CONTRIBUTION OF SWITZERLAND TO THE ECONOMIC AND SOCIAL DEVELOPMENT OF LOW-INCOME COUNTRIES (PAMPHLET). SWITZERLND FINAN NAT/G VOL/ASSN INT/TRADE DRIVE...CHARTS 20. PAGE 149 H2982 — FOR/AID ECO/UNDEV PLAN DIPLOM

B36
RAPPARD W.E.,THE GOVERNMENT OF SWITZERLAND. SWITZERLND INT/ORG POL/PAR EX/STRUC DIPLOM NEUTRAL PARL/PROC REGION WAR HABITAT SOVEREIGN...NAT/COMP SOC/INTEG 20 LEAGUE/NAT WWI. PAGE 130 H2594 — CONSTN NAT/G CULTURE FEDERAL

B55
FRANZ G.,KULTURKAMPF. AUSTRIA GERMANY PRUSSIA SWITZERLND POL/PAR DIPLOM GP/REL ATTIT ORD/FREE 18/19 CHURCH/STA. PAGE 53 H1053 — NAT/LISM CATHISM NAT/G REV

B57
ARON R.,L'UNIFICATION ECONOMIQUE DE L'EUROPE. EUR+WWI SWITZERLND UK INT/ORG NAT/G REGION NAT/LISM ORD/FREE PWR...CONCPT METH/CNCPT OBS TREND STERTYP GEN/LAWS EEC 20. PAGE 8 H0168 — VOL/ASSN ECO/TAC

B61
BEDFORD S.,THE FACES OF JUSTICE: A TRAVELLER'S REPORT. AUSTRIA FRANCE GERMANY/W SWITZERLND UK UNIV WOR+45 WOR-45 CULTURE PARTIC GOV/REL MORAL...JURID OBS GOV/COMP 20. PAGE 13 H0257 — CT/SYS ORD/FREE PERSON LAW

B62
DUTOIT B.,LA NEUTRALITE SUISSE A L'HEURE EUROPEENNE. EUR+WWI MOD/EUR INT/ORG NAT/G VOL/ASSN PLAN BAL/PWR LEGIT NEUTRAL REGION PEACE ORD/FREE SOVEREIGN...CONCPT OBS TIME/SEQ TREND STERTYP VAL/FREE LEAGUE/NAT UN 20. PAGE 44 H0873 — ATTIT DIPLOM SWITZERLND

L63
BOLGAR V.,"THE PUBLIC INTEREST: A JURISPRUDENTIAL AND COMPARATIVE OVERVIEW OF SYMPOSIUM ON FUNDAMENTAL CONCEPTS OF PUBLIC LAW" COM FRANCE GERMANY SWITZERLND LAW ADJUD ADMIN AGREE LAISSEZ ...JURID GEN/LAWS 20 EUROPE/E. PAGE 18 H0369 — CONCPT ORD/FREE CONTROL NAT/COMP

S63
APPERT K.,"BERECHTIGE VORBEHALTE DER SCHWEIZERISCHEN ZUR INTEGRATION." EUR+WWI UK MARKET SERV/IND NAT/G PLAN RIGID/FLEX OEEC 20 EEC. PAGE 7 H0146 — FINAN ATTIT SWITZERLND

S64
GRUNER E.,"PRENSA, PARTIDOS POLITICOS, Y GRUPOS DE PRESION EN SUIZA." EUR+WWI MOD/EUR NAT/G EDU/PROP LEGIT PRESS ATTIT KNOWL ORD/FREE...CONCPT STAT CON/ANAL CHARTS 20. PAGE 62 H1241 — POL/PAR SWITZERLND

B66
DAENIKER G.,STRATEGIE DES KLEIN STAATS. SWITZERLND ACT/RES CREATE DIPLOM NEUTRAL DETER WAR WEAPON PWR SOVEREIGN...IDEA/COMP 20 COLD/WAR. PAGE 36 H0730 — NUC/PWR PLAN FORCES NAT/G

B66
HOEVELER H.J.,INTERNATIONALE BEKAMPFUNG DES VERBRECHENS. AUSTRIA SWITZERLND WOR+45 INT/ORG CONTROL BIO/SOC...METH/COMP NAT/COMP 20 MAFIA SCOT/YARD FBI. PAGE 72 H1446 — CRIMLGY CRIME DIPLOM INT/LAW

B66
RAY A.,INTER-GOVERNMENTAL RELATIONS IN INDIA: A STUDY OF INDIAN FEDERALISM. CANADA INDIA SWITZERLND USA+45 USSR ADMIN GOV/REL...NAT/COMP BIBLIOG. PAGE 130 H2599 — CONSTN FEDERAL SOVEREIGN NAT/G

S67
KOHN W.S.G.,"THE SOVEREIGNTY OF LIECHTENSTEIN." LIECHTENST SWITZERLND USSR CONSTN DEBATE WAR CONSERVE 18/20 UN. PAGE 88 H1748 — SOVEREIGN NAT/G PWR DIPLOM

B96
LOWELL A.L.,GOVERNMENTS AND PARTIES IN CONTINENTAL EUROPE, VOL. II. AUSTRIA GERMANY HUNGARY MOD/EUR SWITZERLND SOCIETY EX/STRUC LEGIS DIPLOM AGREE LEAD PARL/PROC PWR...POLICY 19. PAGE 99 H1974 — POL/PAR NAT/G GOV/REL ELITES

SYKES G.M. H3021

SYME R. H3022

SYMONDS R. H3023,H3024

SYNANON....SYNANON: COMMUNITY OF FORMER DRUG ADDICTS AND CRIMINALS

SYNTAX....SEE LOG

SYRIA....SEE ALSO UAR

B55
KRUSE H.,DAS STAATSANGEHORIGKEITSRECHT DER ARABISCHEN STAATEN. ISLAM JORDAN LIBYA SYRIA UAR NAT/G SECT RACE/REL...INT/LAW 6/20 TREATY. PAGE 89 H1779 — JURID NAT/LISM DIPLOM GP/REL

B58
LERNER D.,THE PASSING OF TRADITIONAL SOCIETY: MODERNIZING THE MIDDLE EAST. IRAN ISLAM LEBANON SYRIA TURKEY UAR CULTURE INTELL STRATA KIN NAT/G NEIGH SECT EDU/PROP ATTIT PERSON...MYTH OBS 20. PAGE 95 H1888 — ECO/UNDEV RIGID/FLEX

B66
US DEPARTMENT OF STATE,RESEARCH ON THE MIDDLE EAST (EXTERNAL RESEARCH LIST NO 4-25). GREECE ISRAEL SYRIA UAR YEMEN CULTURE SOCIETY POL/PAR SECT DIPLOM EDU/PROP WAR NAT/LISM...GEOG GOV/COMP 20. PAGE 160 H3190 — BIBLIOG/A ISLAM NAT/G REGION

SYRKIN M. H3025

SYS/QU....SYSTEMATIZING AND ANALYZING QUESTIONNAIRES

S65
JENSEN L.,"MILITARY CAPABILITIES AND BARGAINING BEHAVIOR." USA+45 USSR ARMS/CONT DETER COST ATTIT ...METH/CNCPT STAT SYS/QU CON/ANAL CHARTS NAT/COMP. PAGE 81 H1614 — DIPLOM DRIVE PWR STERTYP

S65
WOLF C. JR.,"THE POLITICAL EFFECTS OF SOME MILITARY PROGRAMS* SOME INDICATIONS FROM LATIN AMERICA." ELITES STRATA BUDGET FOR/AID WEAPON ATTIT PERCEPT PWR...REGRESS SYS/QU CHARTS NAT/COMP. PAGE 170 H3397 — L/A+17C FORCES CIVMIL/REL PROBABIL

SYSTEMS....SEE ROUTINE, COMPUTER

SZALAY L.B. H3026

SZASZ/T....THOMAS SZASZ

SZLADITS C. H3027

SZTARAY Z. H3029
SZULC T. H3028
SZYLIOWICZ J.S. H2636

T

T....TEXTBOOK

B48
WHITE C.L.,HUMAN GEOGRAPHY: AN ECOLOGICAL STUDY OF GEOGRAPHY. UNIV SEA CULTURE AGRI EXTR/IND RACE/REL PRODUC...CHARTS HYPO/EXP SIMUL GEN/LAWS T. PAGE 167 H3345 — SOC HABITAT GEOG SOCIETY

B52
APPADORAI A.,THE SUBSTANCE OF POLITICS (6TH ED.). EX/STRUC LEGIS DIPLOM CT/SYS CHOOSE FASCISM MARXISM SOCISM...BIBLIOG T. PAGE 7 H0145 — PHIL/SCI NAT/G

B54
LEWIS E.,MEDIEVAL POLITICAL IDEAS. LAW CULTURE SOCIETY ECO/UNDEV NAT/G SECT GOV/REL ATTIT ...BIBLIOG/A T 11/15. PAGE 96 H1913 — CHRIST-17C IDEA/COMP INTELL CONCPT

B57
LOOMIS C.P.,RURAL SOCIOLOGY. CULTURE KIN NAT/G SECT VOL/ASSN ACT/RES EDU/PROP HEALTH. PAGE 98 H1963 — SOC AGRI

METH
T

B57
PALMER N.D.,INTERNATIONAL RELATIONS. WOR+45 INT/ORG NAT/G ECO/TAC EDU/PROP COLONIAL WAR PWR SOVEREIGN ...POLICY T 20 TREATY. PAGE 123 H2451 DIPLOM BAL/PWR NAT/COMP

B57
ROSS R.,THE FABRIC OF SOCIETY. STRATA GP/REL PERSON ...CONCPT METH T 20. PAGE 134 H2687 SOC PHIL/SCI CULTURE STRUCT

B58
ARON R.,SOCIOLOGIE DES SOCIETES INDUSTRIELLES: ESQUISSE D'UNE THEORIE DES REGIMES POLITIQUES. FRANCE SOCIETY NAT/G PROB/SOLV ATTIT RIGID/FLEX MARXISM POPULISM...POLICY SOC T 20 MARX/KARL TOCQUEVILL. PAGE 8 H0170 TOTALISM INDUS CONSTN GOV/COMP

B60
JOHNSON H.M.,SOCIOLOGY: A SYSTEMATIC INTRODUCTION. MARKET FAM LABOR POL/PAR CHOOSE DISCRIM MARRIAGE ALL/IDEOS...BIBLIOG T WORSHIP. PAGE 81 H1620 SOC SOCIETY CULTURE GEN/LAWS

B60
MANIS J.G.,MAN AND SOCIETY. STRATA LEAD INGP/REL PERS/REL ATTIT PWR...PSY ANTHOL T SOC/INTEG MARX/KARL MILL/JS FREUD/S CHURCHLL/W SPENCER/H RUSSELL/B. PAGE 102 H2036 SOC SOCIETY STRUCT CULTURE

B60
OTTENBERG S.,CULTURES AND SOCIETIES OF AFRICA. AFR KIN TEC/DEV GP/REL MARRIAGE ATTIT HABITAT HEREDITY ...ANTHOL BIBLIOG T WORSHIP 20. PAGE 122 H2433 SOCIETY INGP/REL STRUCT CULTURE

C60
BOGARDUS E.S.,"THE DEVELOPMENT OF SOCIAL THOUGHT." SOCIETY PERSON KNOWL...EPIST CONCPT BIBLIOG T. PAGE 18 H0365 INTELL CULTURE IDEA/COMP GP/COMP

B61
CATHERINE R.,LE FONCTIONNAIRE FRANCAIS. FRANCE NAT/G INGP/REL ATTIT MORAL ORD/FREE...T CIVIL/SERV. PAGE 28 H0559 ADMIN GP/REL LEAD SUPEGO

B61
HUNT E.F.,SOCIAL SCIENCE. DIPLOM ECO/TAC ROUTINE GP/REL DEMAND DISCRIM EFFICIENCY HABITAT ALL/IDEOS ...SOC T 20. PAGE 75 H1497 CULTURE ADJUST STRATA ROLE

B61
ROCHE J.P.,COURTS AND RIGHTS: THE AMERICAN JUDICIARY IN ACTION (2ND ED.). UK USA+45 USA-45 STRUCT TEC/DEV SANCTION PERS/REL RACE/REL ORD/FREE ...METH/CNCPT GOV/COMP METH/COMP T 13/20. PAGE 133 H2653 JURID CT/SYS NAT/G PROVS

B61
STARK H.,SOCIAL AND ECONOMIC FRONTIERS IN LATIN AMERICA (2ND ED.). CUBA FUT CULTURE AGRI INDUS ECO/TAC PRODUC ATTIT MARXISM...NAT/COMP BIBLIOG T 20. PAGE 149 H2971 L/A+17C SOCIETY DIPLOM ECO/UNDEV

B62
CARTER G.M.,THE GOVERNMENT OF THE SOVIET UNION. USSR CULTURE LOC/G DIPLOM ECO/TAC ADJUD CT/SYS LEAD WEALTH...CHARTS T 20 COM/PARTY. PAGE 27 H0546 NAT/G MARXISM POL/PAR EX/STRUC

B62
EBENSTEIN W.,TWO WAYS OF LIFE. USA+45 CULTURE ECO/DEV PLAN EDU/PROP CONTROL ORD/FREE...GOV/COMP IDEA/COMP T 20 MARX/KARL ENGELS/F LENIN/VI LOCKE/JOHN MILL/JS. PAGE 44 H0885 MARXISM POPULISM ECO/TAC DIPLOM

B62
KRECH D.,INDIVIDUAL IN SOCIETY; A TEXTBOOK OF SOCIAL PSYCHOLOGY. UNIV CULTURE LEAD INGP/REL ATTIT DRIVE PERCEPT ROLE...PHIL/SCI BIBLIOG T. PAGE 88 H1765 PSY SOC SOCIETY PERS/REL

B62
STARCKE V.,DENMARK IN WORLD HISTORY. DENMARK AGRI KIN WAR...BIBLIOG T 20. PAGE 149 H2970 GEOG CULTURE SOC

B63
BOHANNAN P.,SOCIAL ANTHROPOLOGY. ECO/DEV GP/REL DEMAND MARRIAGE HABITAT...CHARTS GP/COMP BIBLIOG T WORSHIP 20. PAGE 18 H0366 SOC STRUCT FAM CULTURE

B63
MAJUMDAR O.N.,AN INTRODUCTION TO SOCIAL ANTHROPOLOGY. INDIA LAW STRATA ECO/UNDEV KIN DEMAND MARRIAGE...GP/COMP BIBLIOG T WORSHIP 20. PAGE 101 H2026 SOC CULTURE STRUCT GP/REL

B63
MILLER W.J.,THE MEANING OF COMMUNISM. USSR SOCIETY ECO/DEV EX/STRUC WORKER TEC/DEV ADMIN TOTALISM ...POLICY CONCPT CHARTS BIBLIOG T 20 COLD/WAR LENIN/VI STALIN/J. PAGE 111 H2215 MARXISM TRADIT DIPLOM NAT/G

B64
BERRINGTON H.,HOW NATIONS ARE GOVERNED. FRANCE WOR+45 ECO/UNDEV INT/ORG POL/PAR CHOOSE TOTALISM KNOWL...MAJORIT T 20 UN COMMONWLTH THIRD/WRLD. PAGE 16 H0320 NAT/G GOV/COMP ECO/DEV CONSTN

B64
STRONG C.F.,HISTORY OF MODERN POLITICAL CONSTITUTIONS. STRUCT INT/ORG NAT/G LEGIS TEC/DEV DIPLOM INT/TRADE CT/SYS EXEC...METH/COMP T 12/20 UN. PAGE 150 H2999 CONSTN CONCPT

B65
GRIMAL H.,HISTOIRE DU COMMONWEALTH BRITANNIQUE. UK FINAN DOMIN ATTIT ORD/FREE...T 15/20 CMN/WLTH. PAGE 61 H1226 NAT/G COLONIAL DIPLOM INT/TRADE

B65
MAIR L.,AN INTRODUCTION TO SOCIAL ANTHROPOLOGY. LAW STRATA FINAN FAM KIN SECT INT/TRADE RACE/REL ADJUST PRODUC...T 20. PAGE 101 H2023 SOC STRUCT CULTURE SOCIETY

B66
FOX K.A.,THE THEORY OF QUANTITATIVE ECONOMIC POLICY WITH APPLICATIONS TO ECONOMIC GROWTH AND STABILIZATION. ECO/DEV AGRI NAT/G PLAN ADMIN RISK ...DECISION IDEA/COMP SIMUL T. PAGE 52 H1045 ECO/TAC ECOMETRIC EQUILIB GEN/LAWS

B66
JOHNSON N.,PARLIAMENT AND ADMINISTRATION: THE ESTIMATES COMMITTEE 1945-65. FUT UK NAT/G EX/STRUC PLAN BUDGET ORD/FREE...T 20 PARLIAMENT HOUSE/CMNS. PAGE 81 H1625 LEGIS ADMIN FINAN DELIB/GP

B66
KASUNMU A.B.,NIGERIAN FAMILY LAW. NIGERIA KIN LEGIT ILLEGIT MARRIAGE AGE DRIVE HABITAT ALL/VALS...JURID IDEA/COMP T 20 ENGLSH/LAW. PAGE 83 H1667 FAM LAW CULTURE AFR

B66
SETTON K.M.,GREAT PROBLEMS IN EUROPEAN CIVILIZATION. CHRIST-17C EUR+WWI MOD/EUR SECT GP/REL ALL/VALS ORD/FREE ALL/IDEOS...TREND ANTHOL T CHRISTIAN RENAISSAN PROTESTANT. PAGE 142 H2835 CULTURE CONCPT IDEA/COMP

B66
WUEST J.J.,NEW SOURCE BOOK IN MAJOR EUROPEAN GOVERNMENTS. CHRIST-17C EUR+WWI FRANCE GERMANY ITALY MOD/EUR UK USSR LOC/G POL/PAR CHIEF EX/STRUC CHOOSE CONSERVE MARXISM...JURID T 13/20. PAGE 171 H3425 NAT/G CONSTN LEGIS

B67
CANTOR N.F.,THE ENGLISH TRADITION* TWENTIETH-CENTURY VIEWS OF ENGLISH HISTORY (2VOLS.). UK STRATA NAT/G SECT WAR...POLICY GOV/COMP IDEA/COMP ANTHOL T PARLIAMENT CMN/WLTH. PAGE 26 H0522 CT/SYS LAW POL/PAR

B67
CEFKIN J.L.,THE BACKGROUND OF CURRENT WORLD PROBLEMS. NAT/G MARXISM...T 20 UN COLD/WAR. PAGE 28 H0565 DIPLOM NAT/LISM ECO/UNDEV

B67
DALTON G.,TRIBAL AND PEASANT ECONOMIES. SOCIETY FINAN FAM INT/TRADE RATION ADJUST WEALTH...CHARTS ANTHOL BIBLIOG T. PAGE 37 H0738 SOC ECO/UNDEV NAT/COMP

B67
PLISCHKE E.,CONDUCT OF AMERICAN DIPLOMACY (3RD REV. ED.). INT/ORG NAT/G PROB/SOLV FOR/AID...CHARTS BIBLIOG T 20 DEPT/STATE. PAGE 126 H2529 DIPLOM RATIONAL PLAN

B67
ROELOFS H.M.,THE LANGUAGE OF MODERN POLITICS: AN INTRODUCTION TO THE STUDY OF GOVERNMENT. DIPLOM ADMIN MARXISM NEW/LIB...JURID CONCPT METH/COMP T 20. PAGE 133 H2657 LEAD NAT/COMP PERS/REL NAT/G

B67
WILLS A.J.,AN INTRODUCTION TO THE HISTORY OF CENTRAL AFRICA. RHODESIA ZAMBIA CULTURE SOCIETY ECO/UNDEV TEC/DEV DOMIN WAR ALL/VALS...POLICY TREND BIBLIOG T 14/20 NYASALAND. PAGE 169 H3375 AFR COLONIAL ORD/FREE

S67
JENCKS C.E.,"SOCIAL STATUS OF COAL MINERS IN BRITAIN SINCE NATIONALIZATION." UK STRATA STRUCT LABOR RECEIVE GP/REL INCOME OWN ATTIT HABITAT...MGT T 20. PAGE 80 H1600 EXTR/IND WORKER CONTROL NAT/G

TABORSKY E. H3030,H3031,H3032

TACHAKKYO K. H3033

TAFT/HART....TAFT-HARTLEY ACT

TAFT/RA....ROBERT A. TAFT

TAFT/WH....PRESIDENT WILLIAM HOWARD TAFT

TAGGART F.J. H3034

TAHITI....TAHITI

B61
WEST F.J.,POLITICAL ADVANCEMENT IN THE SOUTH PACIFIC. CONSTN CULTURE POL/PAR LEGIS DOMIN ADMIN CHOOSE SOVEREIGN VAL/FREE 20 FIJI TAHITI SAMOA. PAGE 167 H3335 S/ASIA LOC/G COLONIAL

B64
BEDERMAN S.H.,THE ETHNOLOGICAL CONTRIBUTIONS OF JOHN LEDYARD (PAMPHLET). ASIA PRE/AMER S/ASIA...SOC 18 LEDYARD/J KAMCHATKA TAHITI TARTARS INDIAN/AM. PAGE 13 H0256
CULTURE BIOG METH/CNCPT STRUCT

TAINE H.A. H3035,H3036,H3037

TAIWAN....TAIWAN AND REPUBLIC OF CHINA

B64
INTL CONF ON POPULATION,POPULATION DYNAMICS: INTERNATIONAL ACTION AND TRAINING PROGRAMS. INDIA KOREA L/A+17C TAIWAN USA+45 WOR+45 FAM PLAN CONFER ...NEW/IDEA ANTHOL 20 CHINJAP BIRTH/CON. PAGE 78 H1561
NAT/COMP CONTROL ATTIT EDU/PROP

TAKEUCHI T. H3038

TALBOTT R.B. H1273

TAMBIAH S.J. H3039

TAMMANY....TAMMANY HALL

TAN C.C. H3040

TANG P.S.H. H3041

TANGANYIKA....SEE TANZANIA

B62
CARTER G.M.,AFRICAN ONE-PARTY STATES. ISLAM IVORY/CST LIBERIA CONSTN CULTURE SOCIETY POL/PAR PLAN DOMIN EDU/PROP EXEC REGION CHOOSE ATTIT ALL/VALS...CONCPT TIME/SEQ CHARTS VAL/FREE 20 TANGANYIKA. PAGE 27 H0545
AFR NAT/LISM

S63
BANFIELD J.,"FEDERATION IN EAST-AFRICA." AFR UGANDA ELITES INT/ORG NAT/G VOL/ASSN LEGIS ECO/TAC FEDERAL ATTIT SOVEREIGN TOT/POP 20 TANGANYIKA. PAGE 10 H0210
EX/STRUC PWR REGION

S63
TANNER R.,"WHO GOES HOME?" CULTURE GP/REL SOC/INTEG 20 TANGANYIKA MIGRATION. PAGE 152 H3045
ADMIN COLONIAL NAT/G NAT/LISM

L64
ROTBERG R.,"THE FEDERATION MOVEMENT IN BRITISH EAST AND CENTRAL AFRICA." AFR RHODESIA UGANDA ECO/UNDEV NAT/G POL/PAR FORCES DOMIN LEGIT ADMIN COERCE ATTIT ...CONCPT TREND 20 TANGANYIKA. PAGE 135 H2691
VOL/ASSN PWR REGION

S64
CLIFFE L.,"TANGANYIKA'S TWO YEARS OF INDEPENDENCE." AFR INDUS MARKET NAT/G POL/PAR DELIB/GP CREATE ECO/TAC LEGIT DRIVE ALL/VALS...METH/CNCPT RECORD 20 TANGANYIKA. PAGE 30 H0604
ECO/UNDEV PLAN

S66
FLEMING W.G.,"AUTHORITY, EFFICIENCY, AND ROLE STRESS: PROBLEMS IN THE DEVELOPMENT OF EAST AFRICAN BUREAUCRACIES." AFR UGANDA STRUCT PROB/SOLV ROUTINE INGP/REL ROLE...MGT SOC GP/COMP GOV/COMP 20 TANGANYIKA AFRICA/E. PAGE 51 H1024
DOMIN EFFICIENCY COLONIAL ADMIN

B67
WINTER E.H.,CONTEMPORARY CHANGE IN TRADITIONAL SOCIETIES: VOLUME I INTRODUCTION AND AFRICAN TRIBES. NIGERIA AGRI LOC/G NAT/G CREATE DOMIN COLONIAL CONTROL GP/REL PWR SOVEREIGN...SOC OBS 20 TANGANYIKA. PAGE 169 H3389
SOCIETY AFR CONSERVE KIN

TANHAM B.K. H3042

TANNENBAUM F. H3043,H3044

TANNER R. H3045

TANTER R. H3046

TANZANIA....TANZANIA; SEE ALSO AFR

B63
HUGHES A.J.,EAST AFRICA: THE SEARCH FOR UNITY- KENYA, TANGANYIKA, UGANDA, AND ZANZIBAR. TANZANIA UGANDA CONSTN POL/PAR SECT CHIEF DELIB/GP LEGIS WAR CHOOSE NAT/LISM MARXISM...POLICY CHARTS 20 NEGRO UN. PAGE 74 H1488
NAT/G DOMIN LOC/G AFR

B63
HUNTER G.,EDUCATION FOR A DEVELOPING REGION; A STUDY IN EAST AFRICA. AFR TANZANIA UGANDA NAT/G TEC/DEV INGP/REL ADJUST LITERACY ATTIT 20 AFRICA/E. PAGE 75 H1501
EDU/PROP POLICY ECO/UNDEV EFFICIENCY

S63
NYE J.,"TANGANYIKA'S SELF-HELP." TANZANIA NAT/G GIVE COST EFFICIENCY NAT/LISM 20. PAGE 119 H2381
ECO/TAC POL/PAR ECO/UNDEV WORKER

B64
FRANCK T.M.,EAST AFRICAN UNITY THROUGH LAW. MALAWI TANZANIA UGANDA UK ZAMBIA CONSTN INT/ORG NAT/G ADMIN ROUTINE TASK NAT/LISM ATTIT SOVEREIGN ...RECORD IDEA/COMP NAT/COMP. PAGE 52 H1048
AFR FEDERAL REGION INT/LAW

B65
GHAI D.P.,PORTRAIT OF A MINORITY: ASIANS IN EAST AFRICA. S/ASIA TANZANIA UGANDA COLONIAL...SOC OBS PREDICT ANTHOL 20. PAGE 56 H1119
RACE/REL GP/REL CULTURE AFR

B65
HAEFELE E.T.,GOVERNMENT CONTROLS ON TRANSPORT. AFR RHODESIA TANZANIA DIPLOM ECO/TAC TARIFFS PRICE ADJUD CONTROL REGION EFFICIENCY...POLICY 20 CONGO. PAGE 64 H1274
ECO/UNDEV DIST/IND FINAN NAT/G

B65
NYE J.S. JR.,PAN-AFRICANISM AND EAST AFRICAN INTEGRATION. TANZANIA UGANDA STRUCT ECO/UNDEV NAT/G DIPLOM FEDERAL NAT/LISM...STAT SOC/EXP BIBLIOG EEC OAU. PAGE 119 H2382
REGION ATTIT GEN/LAWS AFR

B66
SMITH H.E.,READINGS IN ECONOMIC DEVELOPMENT AND ADMINISTRATION IN TANZANIA. TANZANIA FINAN INDUS LABOR NAT/G PLAN PROB/SOLV INT/TRADE COLONIAL REGION...ANTHOL BIBLIOG 20 AFRICA/E. PAGE 146 H2910
TEC/DEV ADMIN GOV/REL

L66
MCAUSLAN J.P.W.,"CONSTITUTIONAL INNOVATION AND POLITICAL STABILITY IN TANZANIA: A PRELIMINARY ASSESSMENT." AFR TANZANIA ELITES CHIEF EX/STRUC RIGID/FLEX PWR 20 PRESIDENT BUREAUCRCY. PAGE 106 H2122
CONSTN NAT/G EXEC POL/PAR

B67
NYERERE J.K.,FREEDOM AND UNITY/UHURU NA UMOJA: A SELECTION FROM WRITINGS AND SPEECHES, 1952-65. TANZANIA ELITES ECO/UNDEV INT/ORG NAT/G CREATE DIPLOM COLONIAL REGION RACE/REL...ANTHOL 20. PAGE 119 H2383
SOVEREIGN AFR TREND ORD/FREE

S67
DRYDEN S.,"LOCAL GOVERNMENT IN TANZANIA PART II" TANZANIA LAW NAT/G POL/PAR CONTROL PARTIC REPRESENT ...DECISION 20. PAGE 42 H0850
LOC/G GOV/REL ADMIN STRUCT

S67
LOFCHIE M.F.,"OKELLO'S REVOLUTION." TANZANIA NAT/G POL/PAR FORCES PLAN CONTROL 20. PAGE 98 H1954
AFR REV LEAD CHIEF

S67
THEROUX P.,"HATING THE ASIANS." TANZANIA UGANDA CONSTN INDUS NAT/G POL/PAR WORKER ECO/TAC HABITAT LOVE...POLICY GEOG 20 MIGRATION. PAGE 154 H3069
AFR RACE/REL SOVEREIGN ATTIT

TAPES....SEE OLD/STOR

TARIFFS....SEE ALSO ECO, INT/TRADE, GATT

B20
COX H.,ECONOMIC LIBERTY. UNIV LAW INT/TRADE RATION TARIFFS RACE/REL SOCISM POLICY. PAGE 34 H0687
NAT/G ORD/FREE ECO/TAC PERSON

B33
MOSS W.,POLITICAL PARTIES IN THE IRISH FREE STATE. IRELAND UK LAW FINAN LABOR DELIB/GP TOP/EX TARIFFS EDU/PROP...CHARTS GP/COMP 20. PAGE 113 H2269
POL/PAR NAT/G CHOOSE POLICY

B37
HAMILTON W.H.,THE POWER TO GOVERN. ECO/DEV FINAN INDUS ECO/TAC INT/TRADE TARIFFS TAX CONTROL CT/SYS WAR COST PWR 18/20 SUPREME/CT. PAGE 65 H1303
LING CONSTN NAT/G POLICY

B47
ENKE S.,INTERNATIONAL ECONOMICS. UK USA+45 USSR INT/ORG BAL/PWR BARGAIN CAP/ISM BAL/PAY...NAT/COMP 20 TREATY. PAGE 46 H0927
INT/TRADE FINAN TARIFFS ECO/TAC

B48
PELCOVITS N.A.,OLD CHINA HANDS AND THE FOREIGN OFFICE. ASIA BURMA UK ECO/UNDEV NAT/G ECO/TAC FOR/AID TARIFFS DOMIN COLONIAL GOV/REL SOVEREIGN 19 HONG/KONG TREATY. PAGE 124 H2483
INT/TRADE ATTIT DIPLOM

B61
BREWIS T.N.,CANADIAN ECONOMIC POLICY. CANADA BUDGET CAP/ISM INT/TRADE RATION TARIFFS TAX PRICE CONTROL ROUTINE FEDERAL INCOME PRODUC 20 GOLD/STAND. PAGE 20 H0412
ECO/DEV ECO/TAC NAT/G PLAN

B63
STIFEL L.D.,THE TEXTILE INDUSTRY - A CASE STUDY OF INDUSTRIAL DEVELOPMENT IN THE PHILIPPINES (PAPER). PHILIPPINE WORKER CAP/ISM INT/TRADE TARIFFS RECEIVE PRICE ADMIN COST EFFICIENCY WEALTH...BIBLIOG 20. PAGE 149 H2986
S/ASIA ECO/UNDEV PROC/MFG NAT/G

B63
UN SECRETARY GENERAL,PLANNING FOR ECONOMIC DEVELOPMENT. ECO/UNDEV FINAN BUDGET INT/TRADE
PLAN ECO/TAC

TARIFFS TAX ADMIN 20 UN. PAGE 158 H3159 — MGT NAT/COMP

B65
HAEFELE E.T.,GOVERNMENT CONTROLS ON TRANSPORT. AFR RHODESIA TANZANIA DIPLOM ECO/TAC TARIFFS PRICE ADJUD CONTROL REGION EFFICIENCY...POLICY 20 CONGO. PAGE 64 H1274 — ECO/UNDEV DIST/IND FINAN NAT/G

B66
EDWARDS C.D.,TRADE REGULATIONS OVERSEAS. IRELAND NEW/ZEALND SOUTH/AFR NAT/G CAP/ISM TARIFFS CONTROL ...POLICY JURID 20 EEC CHINJAP. PAGE 45 H0892 — INT/TRADE DIPLOM INT/LAW ECO/TAC

S66
GAMER R.E.,"URGENT SINGAPORE, PATIENT MALAYSIA." MALAYSIA S/ASIA ECO/UNDEV POL/PAR CHIEF TARIFFS TAX CONTROL LEAD REGION PWR 20 SINGAPORE. PAGE 55 H1094 — DIPLOM NAT/G POLICY ECO/TAC

B67
RUEFF J.,BALANCE OF PAYMENTS. WOR+45 FINAN TEC/DEV DIPLOM TARIFFS PRICE CONTROL...POLICY CONCPT IDEA/COMP. PAGE 136 H2715 — INT/TRADE BAL/PAY ECO/TAC NAT/COMP

S68
MILLAR T.B.,"THE COMMONWEALTH AND THE UN." UK DIPLOM TARIFFS AGREE COLONIAL CONTROL SOVEREIGN WEALTH...GP/COMP GOV/COMP 20 CMN/WLTH UN. PAGE 111 H2210 — INT/ORG POLICY TREND ECO/TAC

B95
SELIGMAN E.R.A.,ESSAYS IN TAXATION. NEW/ZEALND PRUSSIA UK USA-45 MARKET LOC/G CREATE PRICE CONTROL INCOME OWN WEALTH...GOV/COMP METH/COMP 19. PAGE 141 H2824 — TAX TARIFFS INDUS NAT/G

TARTARS....TARTARS

B64
BEDERMAN S.H.,THE ETHNOLOGICAL CONTRIBUTIONS OF JOHN LEDYARD (PAMPHLET). ASIA PRE/AMER S/ASIA...SOC 18 LEDYARD/J KAMCHATKA TAHITI TARTARS INDIAN/AM. PAGE 13 H0256 — CULTURE BIOG METH/CNCPT STRUCT

TASK....SPECIFIC SELF-ASSIGNED OR OTHER ASSIGNED OPERATIONS

NSY
MACKENZIE K.R.,THE ENGLISH PARLIAMENT. UK POL/PAR CHIEF DIPLOM TAX TASK WAR AUTHORIT...POLICY TREND 12/20 PARLIAMENT. PAGE 100 H2000 — ORD/FREE LEGIS NAT/G

N19
HAJDA J.,THE COLD WAR VIEWED AS A SOCIOLOGICAL PROBLEM (PAMPHLET). COM CZECHOSLVK EUR+WWI SOCIETY PLAN EDU/PROP CONTROL TASK ATTIT MARXISM...POLICY 20 COLD/WAR MIGRATION. PAGE 64 H1280 — DIPLOM LEAD PWR NAT/G

N19
SALKEVER L.R.,SUB-SAHARA AFRICA (PAMPHLET). AFR USSR EXTR/IND NAT/G SCHOOL DIPLOM COLONIAL WEALTH ...GEOG CHARTS 16/20. PAGE 137 H2742 — ECO/UNDEV TEC/DEV TASK INT/TRADE

B26
SMITH T.V.,THE DEMOCRATIC WAY OF LIFE. UNIV SOCIETY NAT/G WORKER TASK CHOOSE ALL/VALS...IDEA/COMP WORSHIP. PAGE 146 H2919 — MAJORIT CONCPT ORD/FREE LEAD

B27
PANIKKAR K.M.,INDIAN STATES AND THE GOVERNMENT OF INDIA. INDIA UK CONSTN CONTROL TASK GP/REL SOVEREIGN WEALTH...TREND BIBLIOG 19. PAGE 123 H2457 — GOV/COMP COLONIAL BAL/PWR PROVS

B44
KRIS E.,GERMAN RADIO PROPAGANDA: REPORT ON HOME BROADCASTS DURING THE WAR. EUR+WWI GERMANY CULTURE CONSULT PROB/SOLV FEEDBACK TASK INGP/REL DRIVE PWR FASCISM...CON/ANAL METH/COMP 20. PAGE 89 H1768 — EDU/PROP DOMIN ACT/RES ATTIT

B52
LOPEZ-AMO A.,LA MONARQUIA DE LA REFORMA SOCIAL. MOD/EUR SPAIN CONSTN NAT/G TASK EFFICIENCY CONSERVE ...ANARCH TRADIT SOC CONCPT IDEA/COMP 19/20. PAGE 98 H1967 — MARXISM REV LEGIT ORD/FREE

B55
ROWE C.,VOLTAIRE AND THE STATE. FRANCE MOD/EUR BAL/PWR CONTROL TASK SUPEGO ORD/FREE PWR...CONCPT 18 VOLTAIRE. PAGE 135 H2702 — NAT/G DIPLOM NAT/LISM ATTIT

B55
WHEARE K.C.,GOVERNMENT BY COMMITTEE; AN ESSAY ON THE BRITISH CONSTITUTION. UK NAT/G LEGIS INSPECT CONFER ADJUD ADMIN CONTROL TASK EFFICIENCY ROLE POPULISM 20. PAGE 167 H3337 — DELIB/GP CONSTN LEAD GP/COMP

C55
OLIVER D.L.,"A LEADER IN ACTION," IN D. A. OLIVER, SOLOMON ISLAND SOCIETY." S/ASIA SOCIETY STRUCT CONTROL TASK PWR...OBS/ENVIR WORSHIP 20. PAGE 121 H2413 — LEAD RESPECT CULTURE KIN

B56
SPINKA M.,THE CHURCH IN SOVIET RUSSIA. USSR CONTROL LEAD TASK COERCE 20. PAGE 147 H2949 — GP/REL NAT/G SECT

PWR

B59
LEFEVRE R.,THE NATURE OF MAN AND HIS GOVERNMENT. EUR+WWI MOD/EUR CONSTN CULTURE MORAL MARXISM ...POLICY 18/20. PAGE 93 H1859 — NAT/G TASK ORD/FREF ATTIT

S60
BANFIELD E.C.,"THE POLITICAL IMPLICATIONS OF METROPOLITAN GROWTH" (BMR)" UK USA+45 LOC/G PROB/SOLV ADMIN GP/REL...METH/COMP NAT/COMP 20. PAGE 10 H0209 — TASK MUNIC GOV/COMP CENSUS

B61
FREYRE G.,THE PORTUGUESE AND THE TROPICS. L/A+17C PORTUGAL SOCIETY PERF/ART ADMIN TASK GP/REL ...ART/METH CONCPT SOC/INTEG 20. PAGE 53 H1060 — COLONIAL METH PLAN CULTURE

B61
INDIAN NATIONAL CONGRESS,SOUVENIR, 66TH SESSION. INDIA S/ASIA CONSTN CULTURE LEGIS CREATE TEC/DEV LEAD TASK...GEOG CHARTS 20. PAGE 77 H1533 — CONFER PLAN NAT/G POLICY

B62
COUNCIL ON WORLD TENSIONS,RESTLESS NATIONS. WOR+45 STRUCT INT/ORG NAT/G PLAN ECO/TAC...NAT/COMP ANTHOL 20. PAGE 34 H0678 — ECO/UNDFV POLICY DIPLOM TASK

B62
MOUSSA P.,THE UNDERPRIVILEGED NATIONS. FINAN INT/ORG PLAN PROB/SOLV CAP/ISM GIVE TASK WEALTH ...POLICY SOC 20. PAGE 114 H2273 — ECO/UNDFV NAT/G DIPLOM FOR/AID

B63
ELLIOT J.H.,THE REVOLT OF THE CATALANS. SPAIN LOC/G PROVS FORCES DIPLOM TASK WAR GOV/REL INGP/REL ...POLICY 17 OLIVARES. PAGE 45 H0909 — REV NAT/G TOP/EX DOMIN

B63
GERSCHENKRON A.,THE STABILITY OF DICTATORSHIPS. NAT/G EDU/PROP TASK ATTIT PERSON...POLICY PSY SOC METH 19/20. PAGE 56 H1116 — TOTALISM CONCPT CONTROL ORD/FREE

B63
OECD,FOOD AID: ITS ROLE IN ECONOMIC DEVELOPMENT. FINAN NAT/G PLAN DIPLOM GIVE TASK WEALTH ...METH/COMP METH 20. PAGE 120 H2397 — ECO/UNDEV FOR/AID INT/ORG POLICY

B64
FRANCK T.M.,EAST AFRICAN UNITY THROUGH LAW. MALAWI TANZANIA UGANDA UK ZAMBIA CONSTN INT/ORG NAT/G ADMIN ROUTINE TASK NAT/LISM ATTIT SOVEREIGN ...RECORD IDEA/COMP NAT/COMP. PAGE 52 H1048 — AFR FEDERAL REGION INT/LAW

B64
HALE O.J.,THE CAPTIVE PRESS IN THE THIRD REICH. GERMANY CULTURE LG/CO NAT/G POL/PAR PLAN DOMIN TASK CENTRAL OWN TOTALISM PWR...BIBLIOG 20 HITLER/A NAZI AMMAN/MAX. PAGE 64 H1283 — COM/IND PRESS CONTROL FASCISM

B65
LAMBIRI I.,SOCIAL CHANGE IN A GREEK COUNTRY TOWN. GREECE FAM PROB/SOLV ROUTINE TASK LEISURE INGP/REL CONSEN ORD/FREE...SOC INT QU CHARTS 20. PAGE 90 H1803 — INDUS WORKER CULTURE NEIGH

S65
LEVI W.,"THE CONCEPT OF INTEGRATION IN RESEARCH ON PEACE." NAT/G VOL/ASSN DIPLOM TASK ADJUST NAT/LISM PEACE DRIVE LOVE...PSY NET/THEORY GEN/LAWS. PAGE 95 H1897 — CONCPT IDEA/COMP INT/ORG CENTRAL

S65
THOMAS F.C. JR.,"THE PEACE CORPS IN MOROCCO." CULTURE MUNIC PROVS CREATE ROUTINE TASK ADJUST STRANGE...OBS PEACE/CORP. PAGE 154 H3077 — MOROCCO FRANCE FOR/AID EDU/PROP

B66
AMER ENTERPRISE INST PUB POL,SIGNIFICANT ISSUES IN ECONOMIC AID TO DEVELOPING COUNTRIES. FINAN INT/ORG NAT/G PLAN PROB/SOLV GIVE TASK WEALTH...DECISION 20. PAGE 6 H0119 — ECO/UNDFV FOR/AID DIPLOM POLICY

B66
HANSON J.W.,EDUCATION AND THE DEVELOPMENT OF NATIONS. DIPLOM TASK ADJUST EFFICIENCY...POLICY ANTHOL 20. PAGE 66 H1322 — ECO/UNDFV EDU/PROP NAT/G PLAN

B66
KIRDAR U.,THE STRUCTURE OF UNITED NATIONS ECONOMIC AID TO UNDERDEVELOPED COUNTRIES. AGRI FINAN INDUS NAT/G EX/STRUC PLAN GIVE TASK...POLICY 20 UN. PAGE 86 H1721 — INT/ORG FOR/AID ECO/UNDFV ADMIN

B66
MAC DONALD H.M.,THE INTELLECTUAL IN POLITICS. GERMANY PERU SWEDEN UK USSR NAT/G CONSULT PLAN EDU/PROP TASK INGP/REL EFFICIENCY RATIONAL ALL/VALS 20. PAGE 99 H1987 — ALL/IDEOS INTELL POL/PAR PARTIC

B66
MACFARQUHAR R.,CHINA UNDER MAO: POLITICS TAKES COMMAND. CHINA/COM COM AGRI INDUS CHIEF FORCES DIPLOM INT/TRADE EDU/PROP TASK REV ADJUST...ANTHOL 20 MAO. PAGE 100 H1992 — ECO/UNDEV TEC/DEV ECO/TAC ADMIN

B66
MERILLAT H.C.L.,LEGAL ADVISERS AND INTERNATIONAL ORGANIZATIONS. LAW NAT/G CONSULT OP/RES ADJUD SANCTION TASK CONSEN ORG/CHARTS. PAGE 109 H2178
INT/ORG INT/LAW CREATE OBS

B66
STADLER K.R.,THE BIRTH OF THE AUSTRIAN REPUBLIC, 1918-1921. AUSTRIA PLAN TASK PEACE...POLICY DECISION 20. PAGE 148 H2966
NAT/G DIPLOM WAR DELIB/GP

B66
TYSON G.,NEHRU: THE YEARS OF POWER. INDIA UK STRATA ECO/UNDEV FINAN SECT TASK WAR ORD/FREE MARXISM ...POLICY BIBLIOG 20 NEHRU/J. PAGE 157 H3145
CHIEF PWR DIPLOM NAT/G

S66
HAIGH G.,"FIELD TRAINING IN HUMAN RELATIONS FOR THE PEACE CORPS." CONSULT CREATE EDU/PROP ADMIN TASK GP/REL ATTIT PERSON...PSY OBS SOC/EXP PEACE/CORP. PAGE 64 H1276
CULTURE PERS/REL FOR/AID ADJUST

L67
TOUVAL S.,"THE ORGANIZATION OF AFRICAN UNITY AND AFRICAN BORDERS." DEBATE REGION TASK REV ATTIT ORD/FREE...DECISION UN 20 OAU. PAGE 156 H3121
AFR NAT/G COLONIAL NAT/LISM

S67
ANDERSON L.G.,"ADMINISTERING A GOVERNMENT SOCIAL SERVICE" NEW/ZEALND EX/STRUC TASK ROLE 20. PAGE 6 H0129
ADMIN NAT/G DELIB/GP SOC/WK

S67
KRISTOF L.K.D.,"THE STATE-IDEA, THE NATIONAL IDEA AND THE IMAGE OF THE FATHERLAND." CONSTN CULTURE INTELL SOCIETY WORKER TASK DRIVE HABITAT...MYTH GOV/COMP IDEA/COMP. PAGE 89 H1769
GEOG CONCPT NAT/G PERCEPT

S67
MALLORY J.R.,"THE MINISTER'S OFFICE STAFF* AN UNREFORMED PART OF PUBLIC SERVICE." CONSTN ELITES STRATA NAT/G PROB/SOLV TASK CHOOSE PERS/REL EFFICIENCY...DECISION 20. PAGE 102 H2033
CANADA ADMIN EX/STRUC STRUCT

S67
ROSE S.,"ASIAN NATIONALISM* THE SECOND STAGE." ASIA COM ECO/UNDEV NAT/G PROB/SOLV DIPLOM FOR/AID DOMIN NEUTRAL REGION TASK...METH/COMP 20. PAGE 134 H2675
NAT/LISM S/ASIA BAL/PWR COLONIAL

S67
SNELLEN I.T.,"APARTHEID* CHECKS AND CHANGES." SOUTH/AFR NAT/G PROB/SOLV COLONIAL REGION TASK GP/REL RACE/REL EFFICIENCY PRIVIL ORD/FREE 20. PAGE 146 H2923
DISCRIM NAT/LISM EQUILIB CONTROL

TATU M. H3047

TATZ C.M. H3048

TAUBER K. H3049

TAWNEY R.H. H3050,H3051

TAX S. H3052

TAX....TAXING, TAXATION

NSY
MACKENZIE K.R.,THE ENGLISH PARLIAMENT. UK POL/PAR CHIEF DIPLOM TAX TASK WAR AUTHORIT...POLICY TREND 12/20 PARLIAMENT. PAGE 100 H2000
ORD/FREE LEGIS NAT/G

B04
GRIFFIN A.P.C.,LIST OF REFERENCES ON BUDGETS OF FOREIGN COUNTRIES (PAMPHLET). MOD/EUR FINAN MARKET TAX...MGT STAT 19/20. PAGE 61 H1218
BIBLIOG/A BUDGET NAT/G

B14
CRAIG J.,ELEMENTS OF POLITICAL SCIENCE (3 VOLS.). CONSTN AGRI INDUS SCHOOL FORCES TAX CT/SYS SUFF MORAL WEALTH...CONCPT 19 CIVIL/LIB. PAGE 35 H0696
PHIL/SCI NAT/G ORD/FREE

N19
WILSON T.,FINANCIAL ASSISTANCE WITH REGIONAL DEVELOPMENT (PAMPHLET). CANADA INDUS NAT/G PLAN TAX CONTROL COST EFFICIENCY...POLICY CHARTS 20. PAGE 169 H3382
FINAN ECO/TAC REGION GOV/REL

B26
FORTESCUE J.,THE GOVERNANCE OF ENGLAND (1471-76). UK LAW FINAN SECT LEGIS PROB/SOLV TAX DOMIN ADMIN GP/REL COST ORD/FREE PWR 14/15. PAGE 52 H1042
CONSERVE CONSTN CHIEF NAT/G

B32
MCKISACK M.,THE PARLIAMENTARY REPRESENTATION OF THE ENGLISH BOROUGHS DURING THE MIDDLE AGES. UK CONSTN CULTURE ELITES EX/STRUC TAX PAY ADJUD PARL/PROC APPORT FEDERAL...POLICY 13/15 PARLIAMENT. PAGE 107 H2139
NAT/G MUNIC LEGIS CHOOSE

S32
BEARD C.A.,"THE TEUTONIC ORIGINS OF REPRESENTATIVE GOVERNMENT" UK ROMAN/EMP TAX COERCE PWR IDEA/COMP. PAGE 12 H0247
REPRESENT NAT/G

B35
GORER G.,AFRICA DANCES: A BOOK ABOUT WEST AFRICAN NEGROES. STRUCT LOC/G SECT FORCES TAX ADMIN COLONIAL...ART/METH MYTH WORSHIP 20 NEGRO AFRICA/W CHRISTIAN RITUAL. PAGE 59 H1181
AFR ATTIT CULTURE SOCIETY

B37
HAMILTON W.H.,THE POWER TO GOVERN. ECO/DEV FINAN INDUS ECO/TAC INT/TRADE TARIFFS TAX CONTROL CT/SYS WAR COST PWR 18/20 SUPREME/CT. PAGE 65 H1303
LING CONSTN NAT/G POLICY

C50
ROUSSEAU J.J.,"A DISCOURSE ON POLITICAL ECONOMY" (1755) IN THE SOCIAL CONTRACT AND DISCOURSES." UNIV SOCIETY STRATA STRUCT CONSEN EQUILIB HAPPINESS UTOPIA HEALTH WEALTH...POLICY WELF/ST. PAGE 135 H2699
NAT/G ECO/TAC TAX GEN/LAWS

C52
HUME D.,"OF TAXES" IN D. HUME, POLITICAL DISCOURSES (1752)" UK NAT/G COST INCOME LAISSEZ...GEN/LAWS 18. PAGE 75 H1493
TAX FINAN WEALTH POLICY

C52
LEWIS B.W.,"BRITISH PLANNING AND NATIONALIZATION." UK INDUS SERV/IND LABOR NAT/G OP/RES TEC/DEV TAX WEALTH...CHARTS BIBLIOG 20. PAGE 96 H1912
NEW/LIB ECO/DEV POL/PAR PLAN

B55
SERRANO MOSCOSO E.,A STATEMENT OF THE LAWS OF ECUADOR IN MATTERS AFFECTING BUSINESS (2ND ED.). ECUADOR INDUS LABOR LG/CO NAT/G LEGIS TAX CONTROL MARRIAGE 20. PAGE 141 H2830
FINAN ECO/UNDEV LAW CONSTN

B57
BARAN P.A.,THE POLITICAL ECONOMY OF GROWTH. MOD/EUR USA+45 USA-45 TEC/DEV TAX SOCISM...MGT CONCPT GOV/COMP. PAGE 11 H0213
CAP/ISM CONTROL ECO/UNDEV FINAN

B58
OGDEN F.D.,THE POLL TAX IN THE SOUTH. USA+45 USA-45 CONSTN ADJUD ADMIN PARTIC CRIME...TIME/SEQ GOV/COMP METH/COMP 18/20 SOUTH/US. PAGE 120 H2407
TAX CHOOSE RACE/REL DISCRIM

B58
PAYNO M.,LA REFORMA SOCIAL EN ESPANA Y MEXICO. SPAIN ECO/TAC TAX LOBBY COERCE REV OWN CATHISM 19/20 MEXIC/AMER. PAGE 124 H2479
SECT NAT/G LAW ELITES

B58
SHAW S.J.,THE FINANCIAL AND ADMINISTRATIVE ORGANIZATION AND DEVELOPMENT OF OTTOMAN EGYPT 1517-1798. UAR LOC/G FORCES BUDGET INT/TRADE TAX EATING INCOME WEALTH...CHARTS BIBLIOG 16/18 OTTOMAN NAPOLEON/B. PAGE 143 H2853
FINAN ADMIN GOV/REL CULTURE

B59
SHARMA R.S.,ASPECTS OF POLITICAL IDEAS AND INSTITUTIONS IN ANCIENT INDIA. INDIA SOCIETY STRUCT FAM VOL/ASSN TAX DOMIN...CONCPT HIST/WRIT 7. PAGE 142 H2848
CULTURE JURID DELIB/GP SECT

B60
HAYEK F.A.,THE CONSTITUTION OF LIBERTY. UNIV LAW CONSTN WORKER TAX EDU/PROP ADMIN CT/SYS COERCE DISCRIM...IDEA/COMP 20. PAGE 68 H1369
ORD/FREE CHOOSE NAT/G CONCPT

B60
LASKIN B.,CANADIAN CONSTITUTIONAL LAW: TEXT AND NOTES ON DISTRIBUTION OF LEGISLATIVE POWER (2ND ED.). CANADA LOC/G ECO/TAC TAX CONTROL CT/SYS CRIME FEDERAL PWR...JURID 20 PARLIAMENT. PAGE 92 H1832
CONSTN NAT/G LAW LEGIS

B60
PETERSON W.C.,THE WELFARE STATE IN FRANCE. EUR+WWI FRANCE FUT STRATA PROB/SOLV TAX GIVE RECEIVE INCOME ORD/FREE PWR...CHARTS 20. PAGE 125 H2496
NEW/LIB ECO/TAC WEALTH NAT/G

B61
BREWIS T.N.,CANADIAN ECONOMIC POLICY. CANADA BUDGET CAP/ISM INT/TRADE RATION TARIFFS TAX PRICE CONTROL ROUTINE FEDERAL INCOME PRODUC 20 GOLD/STAND. PAGE 20 H0412
ECO/DEV ECO/TAC NAT/G PLAN

B61
PANIKKAR K.M.,THE VOICE OF FREEDOM: SELECTED SPEECHES OF PANDIT MOTILAL NEHRU. INDIA UK CONSTN FINAN FORCES LEGIS DIPLOM TAX COLONIAL...POLICY MAJORIT ANTHOL 20 NEHRU/PM. PAGE 123 H2460
NAT/LISM ORD/FREE CHIEF NAT/G

B61
STANLEY C.J.,LATE CH'ING FINANCE: HU KUANG-YUNG AS AN INNOVATOR. ASIA NAT/G FORCES BUDGET TAX WAR GOV/REL COST...POLICY BIOG CHARTS BIBLIOG 19. PAGE 148 H2969
FINAN ECO/TAC CIVMIL/REL ADMIN

L61
KAUPER P.G.,"CHURCH AND STATE: COOPERATIVE SEPARATISM." NAT/G LEGIS OP/RES TAX EDU/PROP GP/REL TREND. PAGE 84 H1671
SECT CONSTN LAW POLICY

B62
PASTOR R.S.,A STATEMENT OF THE LAWS OF PARAGUAY IN MATTERS AFFECTING BUSINESS (2ND ED.). PARAGUAY INDUS FAM LABOR LG/CO NAT/G LEGIS TAX CONTROL
FINAN ECO/UNDEV LAW

MARRIAGE 20. PAGE 124 H2474 CONSTN

B62
PHELPS E.S.,THE GOAL OF ECONOMIC GROWTH: SOURCES, COSTS, BENEFITS. USA+45 USSR FINAN TAX CONTROL DEMAND WEALTH...POLICY NAT/COMP ANTHOL BIBLIOG 20. PAGE 125 H2499 ECO/TAC ECO/DEV NAT/G FUT

B63
CRUICKSHANK M.,CHURCH AND STATE IN ENGLISH EDUCATION 1870 TO PRESENT. UK LEGIS TAX GIVE DOMIN LEGIT ORD/FREE 19/20 CHURCH/STA. PAGE 36 H0715 NAT/G SECT EDU/PROP GP/REL

B63
DUE J.F.,STATE SALES TAX ADMINISTRATION. OP/RES BUDGET PAY ADMIN EXEC ROUTINE COST EFFICIENCY PROFIT...CHARTS METH/COMP 20. PAGE 43 H0855 PROVS TAX STAT GOV/COMP

B63
ELWIN V.,A NEW DEAL FOR TRIBAL INDIA. INDIA AGRI COM/IND INDUS KIN TEC/DEV TAX EDU/PROP OWN HEALTH 20. PAGE 46 H0912 ECO/UNDEV CULTURE CONSTN SOC/WK

B63
ENKE S.,ECONOMICS FOR DEVELOPMENT. AGRI TEC/DEV CAP/ISM DIPLOM ECO/TAC TAX ATTIT DRIVE HABITAT WEALTH...GOV/COMP BIBLIOG 20. PAGE 46 H0928 ECO/UNDEV PHIL/SCI CON/ANAL

B63
HAQ M.,THE STRATEGY OF ECONOMIC PLANNING. PAKISTAN AGRI FINAN INDUS NAT/G FOR/AID TAX CONTROL REGION PRODUC...POLICY CHARTS 20. PAGE 66 H1324 ECO/TAC ECO/UNDEV PLAN PROB/SOLV

B63
UN SECRETARY GENERAL,PLANNING FOR ECONOMIC DEVELOPMENT. ECO/UNDEV FINAN BUDGET INT/TRADE TARIFFS TAX ADMIN 20 UN. PAGE 158 H3159 PLAN ECO/TAC MGT NAT/COMP

B64
CURRIE D.P.,FEDERALISM AND THE NEW NATIONS OF AFRICA. CANADA USA+45 INT/TRADE TAX GP/REL ...NAT/COMP SOC/INTEG 20. PAGE 36 H0725 FEDERAL AFR ECO/UNDEV INT/LAW

B64
WERNETTE J.P.,GOVERNMENT AND BUSINESS. LABOR CAP/ISM ECO/TAC INT/TRADE TAX ADMIN AUTOMAT NUC/PWR CIVMIL/REL DEMAND...MGT 20 MONOPOLY. PAGE 167 H3333 NAT/G FINAN ECO/DEV CONTROL

B64
WILSON T.,POLICIES FOR REGIONAL DEVELOPMENT. CANADA UK FINAN INDUS NAT/G BUDGET TAX GIVE COST ...NAT/COMP 20. PAGE 169 H3383 REGION PLAN ECO/DEV ECO/TAC

N64
KENYA MINISTRY ECO PLAN DEV,AFRICAN SOCIALISM AND ITS APPLICATION TO PLANNING IN KENYA (PAMPHLET). AFR AGRI INDUS WORKER TAX COLONIAL WEALTH 20. PAGE 85 H1691 NAT/G SOCISM PLAN ECO/UNDEV

B65
CHANDA A.,FEDERALISM IN INDIA. INDIA UK ELITES FINAN NAT/G POL/PAR EX/STRUC LEGIS DIPLOM TAX GOV/REL POPULISM...POLICY 20. PAGE 28 H0572 CONSTN CENTRAL FEDERAL

B65
JACOB H.,POLITICS IN THE AMERICAN STATES; A COMPARATIVE ANALYSIS. USA+45 POL/PAR CHIEF LEGIS TAX EDU/PROP CONTROL CT/SYS LOBBY PARTIC...DECISION CHARTS 20. PAGE 79 H1578 PROVS GOV/COMP PWR

B65
PROEHL P.O.,FOREIGN ENTERPRISE IN NIGERIA. NIGERIA FINAN LABOR NAT/G TAX 20. PAGE 128 H2562 ECO/UNDEV ECO/TAC JURID CAP/ISM

B65
WURFEL S.W.,FOREIGN ENTERPRISE IN COLOMBIA. FINAN LABOR NAT/G ECO/TAC TAX REGION 20 COLOMB. PAGE 171 H3429 ECO/UNDEV INT/TRADE JURID CAP/ISM

B65
YOUNG A.N.,CHINA'S WARTIME FINANCE AND INFLATION. ASIA AGRI INDUS NAT/G ECO/TAC CONFER PRICE WAR COST 20. PAGE 172 H3437 FINAN FOR/AID TAX BUDGET

S65
KEE W.S.,"CENTRAL CITY EXPENDITURES AND METROPOLITAN AREAS." PLAN BUDGET ECO/TAC TAX GP/REL WEALTH...CHARTS 20. PAGE 84 H1677 LOC/G MUNIC GOV/COMP NEIGH

B66
SASTRI K.V.S.,FEDERAL-STATE FISCAL RELATIONS IN INDIA: A STUDY OF THE FINANCE COMMISSION AND TECHNIQUES OF FINANCIAL ADJUSTMENT. INDIA PROVS DELIB/GP GOV/REL FEDERAL...MATH CHARTS 20. PAGE 138 H2756 TAX BUDGET FINAN NAT/G

S66
GAMER R.E.,"URGENT SINGAPORE, PATIENT MALAYSIA." MALAYSIA S/ASIA ECO/UNDEV POL/PAR CHIEF TARIFFS TAX CONTROL LEAD REGION PWR 20 SINGAPORE. PAGE 55 H1094 DIPLOM NAT/G POLICY ECO/TAC

B67
HAWTREY R.,INCOMES AND MONEY. EUR+WWI FUT UK LABOR WORKER INT/TRADE TAX PAY BAL/PAY COST WEALTH 20. PAGE 68 H1363 FINAN NAT/G POLICY ECO/DEV

B67
KONCZACKI Z.A.,PUBLIC FINANCE AND ECONOMIC DEVELOPMENT OF NATAL 1893-1910. TAX ADMIN COLONIAL ...STAT CHARTS BIBLIOG 19/20 NATAL. PAGE 88 H1755 ECO/TAC FINAN NAT/G ECO/UNDEV

S67
BELLER I.,"ECONOMIC POLICY AND THE DEMANDS OF LABOR." PLAN TAX GIVE PRICE WAR COST PRODUC WEALTH. PAGE 13 H0268 NAT/G ECO/TAC SOC/WK INCOME

S67
BRANCO R.,"LAND REFORM* THE ANSWER TO LATIN AMERICA'S AGRICULTURAL DEVELOPMENT?" L/A+17C NAT/G PLAN TEC/DEV BUDGET RENT EFFICIENCY 20. PAGE 20 H0404 ECO/UNDEV AGRI TAX OWN

S67
DESHPANDE A.M.,"FEDERAL-STATE FISCAL RELATIONS IN INDIA" (REVIEW ARTICLE)" GERMANY USSR DELIB/GP PLAN BUDGET ECO/TAC INCOME 20 SOC/DEMPAR SOC/REVPAR. PAGE 40 H0795 FINAN NAT/G GOV/REL TAX

S67
MITCHELL W.C.,"THE SHAPE OF POLITICAL THEORY TO COME: FROM POLITICAL SOCIOLOGY TO POLITICAL ECONOMY." ACADEM NAT/G BUDGET TAX LEGIT LOBBY GOV/REL INGP/REL...SOC NEW/IDEA TREND CHARTS 20 MONEY. PAGE 112 H2231 ECO/TAC GEN/LAWS

S67
PAI G.A.,"TAXATION AND PLANNING IN INDIA: A BIRDS-EYE VIEW." INDIA ELITES NAT/G LEGIS BUDGET CONTROL LOBBY INCOME...STAT CHARTS 20. PAGE 122 H2443 TAX PLAN WEALTH STRATA

S67
SALYZYN V.,"FEDERAL-PROVINCIAL TAX SHARING SCHEMES." CANADA LOC/G PROB/SOLV TEC/DEV BUDGET GOV/REL EFFICIENCY 20. PAGE 137 H2746 PROVS TAX MUNIC NAT/G

S67
SCOVILLE W.J.,"GOVERNMENT REGULATION AND GROWTH IN THE FRENCH PAPER INDUSTRY DURING THE EIGHTEENTH CENTURY." FRANCE MOD/EUR FINAN CAP/ISM TAX ADMIN CONTROL PRIVIL LAISSEZ...POLICY 18. PAGE 141 H2818 NAT/G PROC/MFG ECO/DEV INGP/REL

S67
SHARKANSKY I.,"ECONOMIC AND POLITICAL CORRELATES OF STATE GOVERNMENT EXPENDITURE: GENERAL TENDENCIES AND DEVIANT CASES." USA+45 LOC/G NAT/G TAX GIVE INCOME...CENSUS CHARTS. PAGE 142 H2845 PROVS BUDGET GOV/COMP

S67
VON LAUE T.H.,"WESTERNIZATION, REVOLUTION AND THE SEARCH FOR A BASIS OF AUTHORITY - RUSSIA IN 1917." USSR ELITES INTELL ECO/UNDEV NAT/G WORKER ECO/TAC TAX ADMIN LEAD AUTHORIT 20 LENIN/VI. PAGE 164 H3274 MARXISM REV COM DOMIN

B76
TAINE H.A.,THE ANCIENT REGIME. FRANCE STRATA FORCES PARTIC EQUILIB WEALTH CONSERVE POPULISM...GOV/COMP SOC/INTEG 18/19. PAGE 152 H3035 NAT/G GOV/REL TAX REV

B95
SELIGMAN E.R.A.,ESSAYS IN TAXATION. NEW/ZEALND PRUSSIA UK USA-45 MARKET LOC/G CREATE PRICE CONTROL INCOME OWN WEALTH...GOV/COMP METH/COMP 19. PAGE 141 H2824 TAX TARIFFS INDUS NAT/G

TAYLOR D. H3053

TAYLOR E. H3054

TAYLOR J.V. H3055

TAYLOR M.G. H3056

TAYLOR P.B. H3057

TAYLOR/AJP....A.J.P. TAYLOR

TAYLOR/Z....PRESIDENT ZACHARY TAYLOR

TCHAD....SEE CHAD

TEC/DEV....DEVELOPMENT OF TECHNIQUES

N
SEMINAR: THE MONTHLY SYMPOSIUM. INDIA ACT/RES TEC/DEV DIPLOM ATTIT...BIBLIOG 20. PAGE 1 H0022 NAT/G ECO/UNDEV SOVEREIGN POLICY

N
THE STATESMAN'S YEARBOOK; STATISTICAL AND HISTORICAL ANNUAL OF THE STATES OF THE WORLD. WOR+45 WOR-45 COM/IND FINAN INDUS SECT FORCES TEC/DEV EDU/PROP...GEOG BIBLIOG 19/20. PAGE 1 H0023 NAT/COMP GOV/COMP STAT CONSTN

N
THE MIDDLE EAST AND NORTH AFRICA. AFR ISLAM CULTURE ECO/UNDEV AGRI NAT/G TEC/DEV FOR/AID INT/TRADE EDU/PROP...CHARTS 20. PAGE 2 H0026
INDEX INDUS FINAN STAT

N
CORNELL UNIVERSITY LIBRARY,SOUTHEAST ASIA ACCESSIONS LIST. LAW SOCIETY STRUCT ECO/UNDEV POL/PAR TEC/DEV DIPLOM LEAD REGION. PAGE 34 H0671
BIBLIOG S/ASIA NAT/G CULTURE

N
HOOVER INSTITUTION,UNITED STATES AND CANADIAN PUBLICATIONS ON AFRICA. CULTURE ECO/UNDEV AGRI TEC/DEV EDU/PROP COLONIAL RACE/REL NAT/LISM ATTIT HEALTH...SOC SOC/WK 20. PAGE 73 H1464
BIBLIOG DIPLOM NAT/G AFR

N
INTERNATIONAL CENTRE AFRICAN,BULLETIN OF INFORMATION ON THESES AND STUDIES IN PROGRESS OR PROPOSED. LAW CULTURE FINAN INDUS LABOR TEC/DEV EDU/PROP...GEOG SOC NAT/COMP 20. PAGE 78 H1554
BIBLIOG/A ACT/RES ACADEM INTELL

N
MINISTRY OF OVERSEAS DEVELOPME,TECHNICAL CO-OPERATION -- A BIBLIOGRAPHY. UK LAW SOCIETY DIPLOM ECO/TAC FOR/AID...STAT 20 CMN/WLTH. PAGE 111 H2225
BIBLIOG TEC/DEV ECO/DEV NAT/G

N
US LIBRARY OF CONGRESS,ACCESSIONS LIST - INDIA. INDIA CULTURE AGRI LOC/G POL/PAR PLAN PROB/SOLV TEC/DEV DIPLOM EDU/PROP LEAD GP/REL ATTIT 20. PAGE 160 H3199
BIBLIOG S/ASIA ECO/UNDEV NAT/G

N
US LIBRARY OF CONGRESS,ACCESSIONS LIST -- ISRAEL. ISRAEL CULTURE ECO/UNDEV POL/PAR PLAN PROB/SOLV TEC/DEV DIPLOM EDU/PROP LEAD WAR ATTIT 20 JEWS. PAGE 160 H3200
BIBLIOG ISLAM NAT/G GP/REL

B12
HOBSON J.A.,THE EVOLUTION OF MODERN CAPITALISM. MOD/EUR UK STRATA ECO/DEV INDUS INCOME UTIL WEALTH ...SOC GEN/LAWS 7/20. PAGE 72 H1440
CAP/ISM WORKER TEC/DEV TIME/SEQ

B13
DIE REKLAME IHRE KUNST UND WISSENSCHAFT. GERMANY POLAND SWITZERLND USA+45 TEC/DEV CAP/ISM DEMAND ...ART/METH EXHIBIT METH/COMP ANTHOL 20. PAGE 135 H2707
EDU/PROP MARKET NAT/COMP ATTIT

B15
VEBLEN T.,IMPERIAL GERMANY AND THE INDUSTRIAL REVOLUTION. GERMANY MOD/EUR UK USA-45 NAT/G TEC/DEV CAP/ISM...MAJORIT NAT/COMP 19/20 CHINJAP. PAGE 162 H3236
ECO/DEV INDUS TECHNIC BAL/PWR

N19
SALKEVER L.R.,SUB-SAHARA AFRICA (PAMPHLET). AFR USSR EXTR/IND NAT/G SCHOOL DIPLOM COLONIAL WEALTH ...GEOG CHARTS 16/20. PAGE 137 H2742
ECO/UNDEV TEC/DEV TASK INT/TRADE

B22
OGBURN W.F.,SOCIAL CHANGE WITH RESPECT TO CULTURE AND ORIGINAL NATURE. ACT/RES OP/RES CRIME GP/REL ANOMIE BIO/SOC PWR...PSY SOC TIME/SEQ METH SOC/INTEG. PAGE 120 H2405
CULTURE CREATE TEC/DEV

B26
TAWNEY R.H.,RELIGION AND THE RISE OF CAPITALISM. UK CULTURE NAT/G TEC/DEV OWN LAISSEZ...POLICY SOC TIME/SEQ 16/19. PAGE 153 H3050
SECT WEALTH INDUS CAP/ISM

S32
BEARD C.A.,"REPRESENTATIVE GOVERNMENT IN EVOLUTION" WOR-45 AGRI TEC/DEV DOMIN EFFICIENCY ORD/FREE CONSERVE...TIME/SEQ GOV/COMP IDEA/COMP GRECO/ROMN. PAGE 12 H0248
REPRESENT POPULISM NAT/G PWR

B36
PREVITE-ORTON C.W.,THE CAMBRIDGE MEDIEVAL HISTORY (8 VOLS.). CHRIST-17C NAT/G PROB/SOLV TEC/DEV LEAD ...POLICY CONCPT WORSHIP. PAGE 128 H2559
BIBLIOG IDEA/COMP TREND

B38
HARPER S.N.,THE GOVERNMENT OF THE SOVIET UNION. COM USSR LAW CONSTN ECO/DEV PLAN TEC/DEV DIPLOM INT/TRADE ADMIN REV NAT/LISM...POLICY 20. PAGE 67 H1337
MARXISM NAT/G LEAD POL/PAR

B39
BARNES H.E.,SOCIETY IN TRANSITION: PROBLEMS OF A CHANGING ERA. USA-45 INDUS MUNIC PUB/INST EDU/PROP CRIME RACE/REL...SOC MYTH NAT/COMP. PAGE 11 H0220
SOCIETY CULTURE TECHRACY TEC/DEV

B39
COBBAN A.,DICTATORSHIP: ITS HISTORY AND THEORY. EUR+WWI MOD/EUR SOCIETY STRUCT NAT/G TEC/DEV LEAD NAT/LISM SOVEREIGN...IDEA/COMP 14/20. PAGE 30 H0610
TOTALISM FASCISM CONCPT

B40
MANNHEIM K.,MAN AND SOCIETY IN AN AGE OF RECONSTRUCTION. MOD/EUR CULTURE ECO/DEV PLAN TEC/DEV PERSON LAISSEZ NEW/LIB...NEW/IDEA IDEA/COMP BIBLIOG 19/20. PAGE 102 H2038
CONCPT ATTIT SOCIETY TOTALISM

B40
MEEK C.K.,EUROPE AND WEST AFRICA. AFR EUR+WWI EXTR/IND DIPLOM INT/TRADE EDU/PROP GP/REL...SOC 20. PAGE 108 H2158
CULTURE TEC/DEV ECO/UNDEV COLONIAL

B41
HITLER A.,MEIN KAMPF (UNABR. ENG. VERSION) (1925). GERMANY CONSTN TEC/DEV RACE/REL NAT/LISM TOTALISM SOVEREIGN...BIOG 20 HITLER/A TREATY. PAGE 71 H1429
EDU/PROP WAR PLAN FASCISM

S41
ABEL T.,"THE ELEMENT OF DECISION IN THE PATTERN OF WAR." EUR+WWI FUT NAT/G TOP/EX DIPLOM ROUTINE COERCE DISPL PERCEPT PWR...SOC METH/CNCPT HIST/WRIT TREND GEN/LAWS 20. PAGE 3 H0055
TEC/DEV FORCES WAR

S42
TISDALE H.,"THE PROCESS OF URBANIZATION" (BMR)" UNIV CULTURE...CENSUS GEN/LAWS. PAGE 155 H3106
MUNIC GEOG CONCPT TEC/DEV

B43
BROWN A.D.,GREECE: SELECTED LIST OF REFERENCES. GREECE ECO/UNDEV AGRI FINAN INDUS LABOR SECT TEC/DEV INT/TRADE LEAD...SOC 20. PAGE 22 H0438
BIBLIOG/A WAR DIPLOM NAT/G

B43
CONOVER H.F.,SOVIET RUSSIA: SELECTED LIST OF REFERENCES. USSR CULTURE INDUS NAT/G TOP/EX TEC/DEV BUDGET WAR CIVMIL/REL EFFICIENCY MARXISM 20. PAGE 32 H0644
BIBLIOG ECO/DEV COM DIPLOM

B43
LEWIN E.,ROYAL EMPIRE SOCIETY BIBLIOGRAPHIES NO. 9: SUB-SAHARA AFRICA. ECO/UNDEV TEC/DEV DIPLOM ADMIN COLONIAL LEAD 20. PAGE 96 H1908
BIBLIOG AFR NAT/G SOCIETY

B47
HERSKOVITS M.U.,MAN AND HIS WORK. UNIV SECT TEC/DEV PARTIC...PHIL/SCI LING AUD/VIS BIBLIOG. PAGE 70 H1409
SOC CULTURE INGP/REL HABITAT

B48
COX O.C.,CASTE, CLASS, AND RACE. INDIA WOR+45 WOR-45 SECT TEC/DEV MARRIAGE ROLE MARXISM...MAJORIT NAT/COMP SOC/INTEG 20 NEGRO HINDU. PAGE 34 H0688
RACE/REL STRUCT STRATA DISCRIM

B48
MINISTERE FINANCES ET ECO,BULLETIN BIBLIOGRAPHIQUE. AFR EUR+WWI FRANCE CULTURE STRUCT FINAN NAT/G ACT/RES INT/TRADE ADMIN REGION PRODUC STAT. PAGE 111 H2224
BIBLIOG/A ECO/UNDEV TEC/DEV COLONIAL

B49
WORMUTH F.D.,THE ORIGINS OF MODERN CONSTITUTIONALISM. GREECE UK LEGIS CREATE TEC/DEV BAL/PWR DOMIN ADJUD REV WAR PWR...JURID ROMAN/REP CROMWELL/O. PAGE 170 H3412
NAT/G CONSTN LAW

B50
COUNCIL BRITISH NATIONAL BIB,BRITISH NATIONAL BIBLIOGRAPHY. UK AGRI CONSTRUC PERF/ART POL/PAR SECT CREATE INT/TRADE LEAD...HUM JURID PHIL/SCI 20. PAGE 34 H0677
BIBLIOG/A NAT/G TEC/DEV DIPLOM

B51
EUCKEN W.,THIS UNSUCCESSFUL AGE. GERMANY NAT/G WORKER TEC/DEV ECO/TAC ORD/FREE 20. PAGE 47 H0947
ECO/DEV PLAN LAISSEZ NEW/LIB

B52
KOLARZ W.,RUSSIA AND HER COLONIES. COM RUSSIA LAW CULTURE ECO/DEV KIN LOC/G SECT TEC/DEV ECO/TAC EDU/PROP REGION COERCE ATTIT PWR SOVEREIGN...SOC TIME/SEQ CON/ANAL VAL/FREE 19/20. PAGE 88 H1749
NAT/G DOMIN USSR COLONIAL

B52
SPICER E.H.,HUMAN PROBLEMS IN TECHNOLOGICAL CHANGE. ECO/UNDEV AGRI INDUS NAT/G ACT/RES LEAD GP/REL INGP/REL ROLE...INT METH 20 CASEBOOK. PAGE 147 H2947
TEC/DEV CULTURE STRUCT OP/RES

C52
LEWIS B.W.,"BRITISH PLANNING AND NATIONALIZATION." UK INDUS SERV/IND LABOR NAT/G OP/RES TEC/DEV TAX WEALTH...CHARTS BIBLIOG 20. PAGE 96 H1912
NEW/LIB ECO/DEV POL/PAR PLAN

B53
DAVIDSON B.,THE NEW WEST AFRICA: PROBLEMS OF INDEPENDENCE. UK AGRI TEC/DEV DIPLOM GP/REL RACE/REL SOVEREIGN...ANTHOL 20 AFRICA/W. PAGE 37 H0744
AFR COLONIAL ECO/UNDEV NAT/G

B53
MEAD M.,CULTURAL PATTERNS AND TECHNICAL CHANGE. BURMA GREECE NIGERIA ECO/UNDEV AGRI INDUS SCHOOL SECT CREATE FEEDBACK HABITAT...PSY METH/COMP BIBLIOG 20 UN. PAGE 108 H2152
HEALTH TEC/DEV CULTURE ADJUST

B53
MIT CENTER INTERNATIONAL STU,BIBLIOGRAPHY OF THE ECONOMIC AND POLITICAL DEVELOPMENT OF INDONESIA. INDONESIA STRUCT NAT/G COLONIAL LEAD...STAT 20. PAGE 111 H2226
BIBLIOG ECO/UNDEV TEC/DEV S/ASIA

B54
MOSK S.A.,INDUSTRIAL REVOLUTION IN MEXICO. MARKET LABOR CREATE CAP/ISM ADMIN ATTIT SOCISM...POLICY 20 MEXIC/AMER. PAGE 113 H2268
INDUS TEC/DEV ECO/UNDEV

NAT/G

B54
WILLIAMSON H.F.,ECONOMIC DEVELOPMENT - PRINCIPLES AND PATTERNS. INDIA KOREA CULTURE ECO/DEV ECO/UNDEV TEC/DEV...CENSUS NAT/COMP 20 CHINJAP MEXIC/AMER RESOURCE/N. PAGE 168 H3369 ECO/TAC GEOG LABOR

B55
COLE G.D.H.,STUDIES IN CLASS STRUCTURE. UK NAT/G WORKER TEC/DEV EDU/PROP...CLASSIF CHARTS 20. PAGE 31 H0623 STRUCT STRATA ELITES CONCPT

B55
FRIEDMAN G.,INDUSTRIAL SOCIETY: THE EMERGENCE OF THE HUMAN PROBLEMS OF AUTOMATION. UNIV CULTURE ECO/DEV TEC/DEV INGP/REL HAPPINESS RATIONAL UTOPIA ROLE...HUM SOC TIME/SEQ 20. PAGE 53 H1064 AUTOMAT ADJUST ALL/VALS CONCPT

B55
JONES T.B.,A BIBLIOGRAPHY ON SOUTH AMERICAN ECONOMIC AFFAIRS: ARTICLES IN NINETEENTH CENTURY PERIODICALS (PAMPHLET). AGRI COM/IND DIST/IND EXTR/IND FINAN INDUS LABOR NAT/G 19. PAGE 82 H1634 BIBLIOG ECO/UNDEV L/A+17C TEC/DEV

B56
INTERNATIONAL AFRICAN INST,SOCIAL IMPLICATIONS OF INDUSTRIALIZATION AND URBANIZATION IN AFRICA SOUTH OF THE SAHARA. SOUTH/AFR INDUS LABOR MUNIC WORKER TEC/DEV...SOC OBS TREND ANTHOL 20. PAGE 77 H1549 AFR ECO/UNDEV ADJUST CULTURE

B56
ROBERTS H.L.,RUSSIA AND AMERICA. CHINA/COM S/ASIA USSR FORCES TEC/DEV FOR/AID NUC/PWR ALL/IDEOS ...MAJORIT TREND NAT/COMP 20 COLD/WAR UN NATO. PAGE 132 H2641 DIPLOM INT/ORG BAL/PWR TOTALISM

B56
VIANNA F.J.,EVOLUCAO DE POVO BRASILEIRO (4TH ED.). BRAZIL TEC/DEV COLONIAL GP/REL ATTIT SOVEREIGN ...SOC SOC/INTEG 15/20. PAGE 162 H3247 STRUCT RACE/REL NAT/G

S56
GORDON L.,"THE ORGANIZATION FOR EUROPEAN ECONOMIC COOPERATION." EUR+WWI INDUS INT/ORG NAT/G CONSULT DELIB/GP ACT/RES CREATE PLAN TEC/DEV EDU/PROP LEGIT WEALTH OEEC 20. PAGE 59 H1178 VOL/ASSN ECO/DEV

B57
BARAN P.A.,THE POLITICAL ECONOMY OF GROWTH. MOD/EUR USA+45 USA-45 TEC/DEV TAX SOCISM...MGT CONCPT GOV/COMP. PAGE 11 H0213 CAP/ISM CONTROL ECO/UNDEV FINAN

B57
PALACIOS A.L.,PETROLEO, MONOPOLIOS, Y LATIFUNDIOS. L/A+17C EXTR/IND NAT/G TEC/DEV ECO/TAC CONTROL PRODUC 20 ARGEN MONOPOLY RESOURCE/N. PAGE 123 H2448 ECO/UNDEV NAT/LISM INDUS AGRI

B57
PIDDINGTON R.,AN INTRODUCTION TO SOCIAL ANTHROPOLOGY (VOL. II). SOCIETY STRUCT FAM INGP/REL ...OBS CHARTS. PAGE 125 H2507 CULTURE SOC TEC/DEV GEOG

B57
PLAYFAIR G.,THE OFFENDERS: THE CASE AGAINST LEGAL VENGEANCE. UNIV LAW SOCIETY NAT/G PROB/SOLV DEATH PERSON ORD/FREE...HEAL INT/LAW BIBLIOG 20 REFORMERS. PAGE 126 H2524 CRIME TEC/DEV SANCTION CT/SYS

B57
US SENATE SPEC COMM FOR AID,COMPILATION OF STUDIES AND SURVEYS. AFR ASIA L/A+17C USA+45 ECO/UNDEV AGRI INT/ORG CONSULT TEC/DEV CONFER TOTALISM...NAT/COMP 20 CONGRESS. PAGE 161 H3216 FOR/AID DIPLOM ORD/FREE DELIB/GP

B57
US SENATE SPEC COMM FOR AID,HEARINGS BEFORE THE SPECIAL COMMITTEE TO STUDY THE FOREIGN AID PROGRAM. USA+45 USSR ECO/UNDEV INT/ORG FORCES WEAPON TOTALISM ATTIT SUPEGO...NAT/COMP CONGRESS. PAGE 161 H3217 FOR/AID DIPLOM ORD/FREE TEC/DEV

S57
COSER L.A.,"SOCIAL CONFLICT AND THE THEORY OF SOCIAL CHANGE." EUR+WWI CULTURE TEC/DEV PRODUC RIGID/FLEX SOC. PAGE 34 H0673 GP/REL ROLE SOCIETY ORD/FREE

B58
COLEMAN J.S.,NIGERIA: BACKGROUND TO NATIONALISM. AFR SOCIETY ECO/DEV KIN LOC/G POL/PAR TEC/DEV DOMIN ADMIN DRIVE PWR RESPECT...TRADIT SOC INT SAMP TIME/SEQ 20. PAGE 31 H0627 NAT/G NAT/LISM NIGERIA

B58
CROWE S.,THE LANDSCAPE OF POWER. UK CULTURE SERV/IND NAT/G CONSULT PARTIC NUC/PWR LEISURE...SOC EXHIBIT 20. PAGE 36 H0712 HABITAT TEC/DEV PLAN CONTROL

B58
GARTHOFF R.L.,SOVIET STRATEGY IN THE NUCLEAR AGE. FUT USSR R+D INT/ORG NAT/G ACT/RES TEC/DEV DOMIN DETER WAR ATTIT PWR...RELATIV METH/CNCPT SELF/OBS TREND CON/ANAL STERTYP GEN/LAWS 20. PAGE 55 H1103 COM FORCES BAL/PWR NUC/PWR

B58
HANCE W.A.,AFRICAN ECONOMIC DEVELOPMENT. AGRI DIST/IND INDUS R+D ACT/RES PLAN CAP/ISM FOR/AID ...GOV/COMP BIBLIOG 20. PAGE 65 H1312 AFR ECO/UNDEV PROB/SOLV TEC/DEV

B58
JOHNSON J.J.,POLITICAL CHANGE IN LATIN AMERICA: THE EMERGENCE OF THE MIDDLE SECTORS. INTELL STRATA STRUCT ECO/UNDEV MUNIC TEC/DEV LEAD REV...DECISION TREND GOV/COMP BIBLIOG/A 20. PAGE 81 H1621 L/A+17C ELITES GP/REL DOMIN

B58
MECRENSKY E.,SCIENTIFIC MANPOWER IN EUROPE. WOR+45 EDU/PROP GOV/REL SKILL...TECHNIC PHIL/SCI INT CHARTS BIBLIOG 20. PAGE 108 H2157 ECO/TAC TEC/DEV METH/COMP NAT/COMP

B58
NICULESCU B.,COLONIAL PLANNING: A COMPARATIVE STUDY. AFR AGRI LOC/G MUNIC NAT/G DELIB/GP COLONIAL 20. PAGE 118 H2356 PLAN ECO/UNDEV TEC/DEV NAT/COMP

B59
BROSE O.J.,CHURCH AND PARLIAMENT: THE RESHAPING OF THE CHURCH OF ENGLAND 1828-1860. UK SOCIETY TEC/DEV ATTIT LAISSEZ...BIBLIOG 19 CHURCH/STA. PAGE 22 H0434 SECT LEGIS GP/REL NAT/G

B59
GOLDSCHMIDT W.,UNDERSTANDING HUMAN SOCIETY. SOCIETY CREATE ATTIT...GEOG PHIL/SCI CONCPT GP/COMP. PAGE 58 H1159 CULTURE STRUCT TEC/DEV PERSON

B59
MEYER A.J.,MIDDLE EASTERN CAPITALISM: NINE ESSAYS. ISLAM CULTURE ECO/UNDEV INDUS MARKET NAT/G PLAN ATTIT RIGID/FLEX...STAT OBS TREND GEN/LAWS. PAGE 109 H2188 TEC/DEV ECO/TAC ANTHOL

B59
STERNBERG F.,THE MILITARY AND INDUSTRIAL REVOLUTION OF OUR TIME. USA+45 USSR WOR+45 WORKER COMPUTER PLAN TEC/DEV NUC/PWR GP/REL...POLICY NAT/COMP 20. PAGE 149 H2981 DIPLOM FORCES INDUS CIVMIL/REL

C59
KARPAT K.H.,"TURKEY'S POLITICS: THE TRANSITION TO A MULTI-PARTY SYSTEM." COM TURKEY CULTURE ECO/UNDEV SECT TEC/DEV NAT/LISM ATTIT...SOC CON/ANAL BIBLIOG 20. PAGE 83 H1664 POL/PAR NAT/G

B60
BARBU Z.,PROBLEMS OF HISTORICAL PSYCHOLOGY. GREECE MEDIT-7 UK CULTURE TEC/DEV ADJUST RATIONAL ATTIT PERCEPT...METH/CNCPT NEW/IDEA TIME/SEQ GEN/METH. PAGE 11 H0214 PERSON PSY HIST/WRIT IDEA/COMP

B60
DIA M.,REFLEXIONS SUR L'ECONOMIE DE L'AFRIQUE NOIRE (REV. ED.). CULTURE ECO/UNDEV CREATE TEC/DEV DIPLOM INT/TRADE OPTIMAL ATTIT...POLICY 20. PAGE 41 H0816 AFR ECO/TAC SOCISM PLAN

B60
MCCLOSKY H.,THE SOVIET DICTATORSHIP. FUT CONSTN CULTURE INTELL SOCIETY POL/PAR SECT VOL/ASSN FORCES PLAN TEC/DEV DOMIN EDU/PROP COERCE PWR MARXISM ...POLICY CONCPT MYTH STERTYP 20. PAGE 106 H2127 COM NAT/G TOTALISM USSR

B60
OTTENBERG S.,CULTURES AND SOCIETIES OF AFRICA. AFR KIN TEC/DEV GP/REL MARRIAGE ATTIT HABITAT HEREDITY ...ANTHOL BIBLIOG T WORSHIP 20. PAGE 122 H2433 SOCIETY INGP/REL STRUCT CULTURE

B60
PANIKKAR K.M.,THE STATE AND THE CITIZEN (2ND ED.). INDIA DOMIN ATTIT SUPEGO ORD/FREE WEALTH...GEOG CONCPT GP/COMP 20. PAGE 123 H2459 TEC/DEV POL/PAR NAT/G EDU/PROP

B60
SHIRER W.L.,THE RISE AND FALL OF THE THIRD REICH: A HISTORY OF NAZI GERMANY. EUR+WWI CULTURE ECO/DEV INDUS NAT/G POL/PAR FORCES PLAN TEC/DEV ECO/TAC COERCE ATTIT DRIVE PERSON PWR...MYSTIC PSY SOC MYTH STAT CHARTS EXHIBIT WORK VAL/FREE. PAGE 143 H2864 STRUCT GERMANY TOTALISM

S60
EMERSON R.,"THE EROSION OF DEMOCRACY." AFR FUT LAW CULTURE INTELL SOCIETY ECO/UNDEV FAM LOC/G NAT/G FORCES PLAN TEC/DEV ECO/TAC ADMIN CT/SYS ATTIT ORD/FREE PWR...SOCIALIST SOC CONCPT STAND/INT TIME/SEQ WORK 20. PAGE 46 H0918 S/ASIA POL/PAR

S60
FITZGIBBON R.H.,"DICTATORSHIP AND DEMOCRACY IN LATIN AMERICA." FUT ECO/DEV ECO/UNDEV INT/ORG LOC/G NAT/G TOP/EX PLAN TEC/DEV ECO/TAC CHOOSE ATTIT DRIVE PERSON ALL/VALS OAS TOT/POP 20. PAGE 51 H1019 L/A+17C ACT/RES INT/TRADE

S60
FRANKEL S.H.,"ECONOMIC ASPECTS OF POLITICAL INDEPENDENCE IN AFRICA." AFR FUT SOCIETY ECO/UNDEV COM/IND FINAN LEGIS PLAN TEC/DEV CAP/ISM ECO/TAC INT/TRADE ADMIN ATTIT DRIVE RIGID/FLEX PWR WEALTH ...MGT NEW/IDEA MATH TIME/SEQ VAL/FREE 20. PAGE 53 H1052 NAT/G FOR/AID

S60
GROSSMAN G.,"SOVIET GROWTH: ROUTINE, INERTIA, AND PRESSURE." COM STRATA NAT/G DELIB/GP PLAN TEC/DEV ECO/TAC EDU/PROP ADMIN ROUTINE DRIVE WEALTH COLD/WAR 20. PAGE 62 H1236 POL/PAR ECO/DEV USSR

S60
KELLEY G.A.,"THE POLITICAL BACKGROUND OF THE FRENCH NAT/G

A-BOMB." EUR+WWI USSR FORCES TOP/EX TEC/DEV NUC/PWR ATTIT PWR...CONCPT OBS/ENVIR TREND 20. PAGE 84 H1686
RESPECT NAT/LISM FRANCE

S60
RIVKIN A.,"AFRICAN ECONOMIC DEVELOPMENT: ADVANCED TECHNOLOGY AND THE STAGES OF GROWTH." CULTURE ECO/UNDEV AGRI COM/IND EXTR/IND PLAN ECO/TAC ATTIT DRIVE RIGID/FLEX SKILL WEALTH...MGT SOC GEN/LAWS WORK TOT/POP 20. PAGE 132 H2634
AFR TEC/DEV FOR/AID

C60
HOSELITZ B.,"THE ROLE OF CITIES IN THE ECONOMIC GROWTH OF UNDERDEVELOPED COUNTRIES" IN "SOCIOLOGICAL ASPECTS OF ECONOMIC GROWTH"(BMR). CULTURE LOC/G ACT/RES...SOC IDEA/COMP METH/COMP METH 14/20 REDFIELD/R. PAGE 74 H1474
METH/CNCPT MUNIC TEC/DEV ECO/UNDEV

B61
AIYAR S.P.,FEDERALISM AND SOCIAL CHANGE. CANADA CULTURE STRUCT PLAN PROB/SOLV TEC/DEV ECO/TAC ORD/FREE...TIME/SEQ 18/20 AUSTRAL. PAGE 4 H0085
FEDERAL NAT/G CENTRAL GOV/COMP

B61
BONNEFOUS M.,EUROPE ET TIERS MONDE. EUR+WWI SOCIETY INT/ORG NAT/G VOL/ASSN ACT/RES TEC/DEV CAP/ISM ECO/TAC ATTIT ORD/FREE SOVEREIGN...POLICY CONCPT TREND 20. PAGE 19 H0373
AFR ECO/UNDEV FOR/AID INT/TRADE

B61
ERASMUS C.J.,MAN TAKES CONTROL: CULTURAL DEVELOPMENT AND AMERICAN AID. STRUCT OWN DRIVE PERCEPT...SOC 20 MEXIC/AMER. PAGE 47 H0937
ORD/FREE CULTURE ECO/UNDEV TEC/DEV

B61
GOULD S.H.,SCIENCES IN COMMUNIST CHINA. CHINA/COM FUT INDUS NAT/G TOTALISM...RECORD TOT/POP 20. PAGE 59 H1187
ASIA TEC/DEV

B61
INDIAN NATIONAL CONGRESS,SOUVENIR, 66TH SESSION. INDIA S/ASIA CONSTN CULTURE LEGIS CREATE TEC/DEV LEAD TASK...GEOG CHARTS 20. PAGE 77 H1533
CONFER PLAN NAT/G POLICY

B61
LAHAYE R.,LES ENTREPRISES PUBLIQUES AU MAROC. FRANCE MOROCCO LAW DIST/IND EXTR/IND FINAN CONSULT PLAN TEC/DEV ADMIN AGREE CONTROL OWN...POLICY 20. PAGE 90 H1796
NAT/G INDUS ECO/UNDEV ECO/TAC

B61
LUZ N.V.,A LUTA PELA INDUSTRIALIZACAO DO BRAZIL. BRAZIL L/A+17C AGRI NAT/G TEC/DEV COLONIAL 19/20. PAGE 99 H1981
ECO/UNDEV INDUS NAT/LISM POLICY

B61
MILLIKAW M.F.,THE EMERGING NATIONS: THEIR GROWTH AND UNITED STATES POLICY. FUT USA+45 WOR+45 WOR-45 NAT/G PLAN TEC/DEV BAL/PWR GOV/REL PEACE ORD/FREE 20. PAGE 111 H2216
ECO/UNDEV POLICY DIPLOM FOR/AID

B61
NIPPERDEY T.,DIE ORGANISATION DER DEUTSCHEN PARTEIEN VOR 1918. GERMANY CONSTN STRUCT TEC/DEV CHOOSE ADJUST ATTIT...CONCPT TIME/SEQ 19/20. PAGE 118 H2362
POL/PAR PARL/PROC NAT/G

B61
ROCHE J.P.,COURTS AND RIGHTS: THE AMERICAN JUDICIARY IN ACTION (2ND ED.). UK USA+45 USA-45 STRUCT TEC/DEV SANCTION PERS/REL RACE/REL ORD/FREE ...METH/CNCPT GOV/COMP METH/COMP T 13/20. PAGE 133 H2653
JURID CT/SYS NAT/G PROVS

B61
SCHWARTZ H.,THE RED PHOENIX: RUSSIA SINCE WORLD WAR II. USA+45 WOR+45 ELITES POL/PAR TEC/DEV ECO/TAC MARXISM. PAGE 140 H2810
DIPLOM NAT/G ECO/DEV

B61
WILLSON F.M.G.,ADMINISTRATORS IN ACTION. UK MARKET TEC/DEV PARL/PROC 20. PAGE 169 H3376
ADMIN NAT/G CONSTN

L61
EZELLPH,"THE HISPANIC AGRICULTURATION OF THE GILA RIVER PIMAS." FAM TEC/DEV PERS/REL ADJUST...GEOG MYTH CHARTS BIBLIOG WORSHIP 17/20. PAGE 48 H0956
CULTURE SOC AGRI DRIVE

S61
PADELFORD N.J.,"POLITICS AND THE FUTURE OF ECOSOC." AFR S/ASIA ECO/UNDEV INDUS NAT/G DELIB/GP ACT/RES ORD/FREE WEALTH...CONCPT CHARTS UN 20 ECOSOC. PAGE 122 H2438
INT/ORG TEC/DEV

B62
BARNETT A.D.,COMMUNIST CHINA IN PERSPECTIVE. CHINA/COM FUT CULTURE ECO/UNDEV TEC/DEV CONTROL 20. PAGE 11 H0222
REV MARXISM TREND PLAN

B62
FRIEDMANN W.,METHODS AND POLICIES OF PRINCIPAL DONOR COUNTRIES IN PUBLIC INTERNATIONAL DEVELOPMENT FINANCING: PRELIMINARY APPRAISAL. FRANCE GERMANY/W UK USA+45 USSR WOR+45 FINAN TEC/DEV CAP/ISM DIPLOM ECO/TAC ATTIT 20 EEC. PAGE 53 H1066
INT/ORG FOR/AID NAT/COMP ADMIN

B62
MARTINS A.F.,REVOLUCAO BRANCA NO CAMPO. L/A+17C SERV/IND DEMAND EFFICIENCY PRODUC...POLICY METH/COMP. PAGE 104 H2070
AGRI ECO/UNDEV TEC/DEV NAT/COMP

B62
MORGENSTERN O.,STRATEGIE - HEUTE (2ND ED.). USA+45 USSR ECO/DEV DELIB/GP WAR PEACE ORD/FREE...GOV/COMP NAT/COMP 20 COLD/WAR NATO. PAGE 113 H2256
NUC/PWR DIPLOM FORCES TEC/DEV

B62
NEW ZEALAND COMM OF ST SERVICE,THE STATE SERVICES IN NEW ZEALAND. NEW/ZEALND CONSULT EX/STRUC ACT/RES ...BIBLIOG 20. PAGE 117 H2343
ADMIN WORKER TEC/DEV NAT/G

B62
ROBINSON A.D.,DUTCH ORGANIZED AGRICULTURE IN INTERNATIONAL POLITICS, 1945-1960. EUR+WWI NETHERLAND STRUCT ECO/DEV NAT/G VOL/ASSN CONSULT DELIB/GP PLAN TEC/DEV INT/TRADE EDU/PROP ATTIT RIGID/FLEX ALL/VALS...NEW/IDEA TREND EEC 20. PAGE 132 H2648
AGRI INT/ORG

B62
UNECA LIBRARY,BOOKS ON AFRICA IN THE UNECA LIBRARY. WOR+45 AGRI INT/ORG NAT/G PLAN WRITING REGION...SOC STAT UN. PAGE 158 H3160
BIBLIOG AFR ECO/UNDEV TEC/DEV

B62
UNECA LIBRARY,NEW ACQUISITIONS IN THE UNECA LIBRARY. LAW NAT/G PLAN PROB/SOLV TEC/DEV ADMIN REGION...GEOG SOC 20 UN. PAGE 158 H3161
BIBLIOG AFR ECO/UNDEV INT/ORG

N62
US CONGRESS JT ATOM ENRGY COMM,PEACEFUL USES OF ATOMIC ENERGY, HEARING. USA+45 USSR TEC/DEV ATTIT RIGID/FLEX...TESTS CHARTS EXHIBIT METH/COMP 20 CONGRESS. PAGE 159 H3177
NUC/PWR ACADEM SCHOOL NAT/COMP

B63
BRITISH AID. UK AGRI DIST/IND INDUS SCHOOL TEC/DEV INT/TRADE COLONIAL DEMAND...TREND CHARTS 20. PAGE 2 H0041
FOR/AID ECO/UNDEV NAT/G FINAN

B63
AZEVEDO T.,SOCIAL CHANGE IN BRAZIL. BRAZIL ECO/DEV COM/IND FAM NAT/G SECT GP/REL PERS/REL...CONCPT WORSHIP 20. PAGE 9 H0188
TEC/DEV STRUCT SOC CULTURE

B63
BERGSON A.,ECONOMIC TRENDS IN THE SOVIET UNION. USSR ECO/UNDEV AGRI NAT/G FORCES PLAN TEC/DEV INT/TRADE BAL/PAY...POLICY ANTHOL 20. PAGE 15 H0302
ECO/DEV NAT/COMP INDUS LABOR

B63
CONOVER H.F.,AFRICA SOUTH OF THE SAHARA. CULTURE SECT TEC/DEV...ART/METH GEOG SOC. PAGE 33 H0654
BIBLIOG/A AFR CON/ANAL

B63
DALAND R.T.,PERSPECTIVES OF BRAZILIAN PUBLIC ADMINISTRATION (VOL. I). BRAZIL LAW ECO/UNDEV SCHOOL CHIEF TEC/DEV CONFER CONTROL GP/REL ATTIT ROLE PWR...ANTHOL 20. PAGE 37 H0735
ADMIN NAT/G PLAN GOV/REL

B63
ELWIN V.,A NEW DEAL FOR TRIBAL INDIA. INDIA AGRI COM/IND INDUS KIN TEC/DEV TAX EDU/PROP OWN HEALTH 20. PAGE 46 H0912
ECO/UNDEV CULTURE CONSTN SOC/WK

B63
ENKE S.,ECONOMICS FOR DEVELOPMENT. AGRI TEC/DEV CAP/ISM DIPLOM ECO/TAC TAX ATTIT DRIVE HABITAT WEALTH...GOV/COMP BIBLIOG 20. PAGE 46 H0928
ECO/UNDEV PHIL/SCI CON/ANAL

B63
FURTADO C.,THE ECONOMIC GROWTH OF BRAZIL: A SURVEY FROM COLONIAL TO MODERN TIMES. L/A+17C AGRI DIST/IND EXTR/IND INDUS WORKER COLONIAL RACE/REL OWN GOV/COMP. PAGE 54 H1082
ECO/UNDEV TEC/DEV LABOR DOMIN

B63
GEERTZ C.,PEDDLERS AND PRINCES: SOCIAL DEVELOPMENT AND ECONOMIC CHANGE IN TWO INDONESIAN TOWNS. S/ASIA CULTURE SOCIETY STRATA FACE/GP MUNIC CREATE TEC/DEV ECO/TAC ORD/FREE WEALTH...OBS INT CENSUS CHARTS WORK TOT/POP VAL/FREE 20. PAGE 55 H1106
ECO/UNDEV SOC ELITES INDONESIA

B63
GEERTZ C.,OLD SOCIETIES AND NEW STATES: THE QUEST FOR MODERNITY IN ASIA AND AFRICA. AFR ASIA LAW CULTURE SECT EDU/PROP REV...GOV/COMP NAT/COMP 20. PAGE 55 H1107
ECO/UNDEV TEC/DEV NAT/LISM SOVEREIGN

B63
HUNTER G.,EDUCATION FOR A DEVELOPING REGION; A STUDY IN EAST AFRICA. AFR TANZANIA UGANDA NAT/G TEC/DEV INGP/REL ADJUST LITERACY ATTIT 20 AFRICA/E. PAGE 75 H1501
EDU/PROP POLICY ECO/UNDEV EFFICIENCY

B63
INDIAN INSTITUTE PUBLIC ADMIN,CASES IN INDIAN ADMINISTRATION. INDIA AGRI NAT/G PROB/SOLV TEC/DEV ECO/TAC ADMIN...ANTHOL METH 20. PAGE 77 H1532
DECISION PLAN MGT ECO/UNDEV

B63
MAIR L.,NEW NATIONS. AFR FAM MUNIC SECT DOMIN
COLONIAL

CHOOSE NAT/LISM ORD/FREE...SOC 19/20. PAGE 101 H2022
CULTURE TEC/DEV ECO/UNDEV

B63
MILLER W.J.,THE MEANING OF COMMUNISM. USSR SOCIETY ECO/DEV EX/STRUC WORKER TEC/DEV ADMIN TOTALISM ...POLICY CONCPT CHARTS BIBLIOG T 20 COLD/WAR LENIN/VI STALIN/J. PAGE 111 H2215
MARXISM TRADIT DIPLOM NAT/G

B63
MULLER H.J.,FREEDOM IN THE WESTERN WORLD. PREHIST CULTURE SECT CREATE TEC/DEV DOMIN PWR WEALTH ...MAJORIT SOC CONCPT. PAGE 114 H2285
ORD/FREE TIME/SEQ SOCIETY

B63
RUITENBEER H.M.,THE DILEMMA OF ORGANIZATIONAL SOCIETY. CULTURE ECO/DEV MUNIC SECT TEC/DEV EDU/PROP NAT/LISM ORD/FREE...NAT/COMP 20 RIESMAN/D WHYTE/WF MERTON/R MEAD/MARG JASPERS/K. PAGE 136 H2716
PERSON ROLE ADMIN WORKER

B63
US ATOMIC ENERGY COMMISSION,ATOMIC ENERGY IN THE SOVIET UNION: TRIP REPORT OF THE US ATOMIC ENERGY DELEGATION, MAY 1933. USSR R+D NAT/G CONSULT CREATE DIPLOM ADMIN ROUTINE EFFICIENCY PRODUC KNOWL SKILL ...NAT/COMP 20 AEC TRAVEL TREATY. PAGE 159 H3176
METH/COMP OP/RES TEC/DEV NUC/PWR

B63
WEINER M.,POLITICAL CHANGE IN SOUTH ASIA. CEYLON INDIA PAKISTAN S/ASIA CULTURE ELITES ECO/UNDEV EX/STRUC ADMIN CONTROL CHOOSE CONSERVE...GOV/COMP ANTHOL 20. PAGE 166 H3328
NAT/G CONSTN TEC/DEV

S63
BECHHOEFER B.G.,"SOVIET ATTITUDE TOWARD DISARMAMENT." COM USSR NAT/G ACT/RES TEC/DEV NUC/PWR ATTIT DISPL RIGID/FLEX PWR...METH/CNCPT TREND GEN/LAWS COLD/WAR 20. PAGE 13 H0252
FORCES EDU/PROP ARMS/CONT

S63
ROUGEMONT D.,"LES NOUVELLES CHANCES DE L'EUROPE." EUR+WWI FUT ECO/DEV INT/ORG NAT/G ACT/RES PLAN TEC/DEV EDU/PROP ADMIN COLONIAL FEDERAL ATTIT PWR SKILL...TREND 20. PAGE 135 H2696
ECO/UNDEV PERCEPT

S63
WELLS H.,"THE OAS AND THE DOMINICAN ELECTIONS." L/A+17C INT/ORG NAT/G POL/PAR TEC/DEV ECO/TAC EDU/PROP PERCEPT...TIME/SEQ OAS TOT/POP 20. PAGE 166 H3332
CONSULT CHOOSE DOMIN/REP

B64
BALOGH T.,THE ECONOMIC IMPACT OF MONETARY AND COMMERCIAL INSTITUTIONS OF A EUROPEAN ORIGIN IN AFRICA. AFR UAR INDUS FOR/AID COLONIAL CONTROL ...NAT/COMP 20. PAGE 10 H0205
TEC/DEV FINAN ECO/UNDEV ECO/TAC

B64
BRIGHT J.R.,RESEARCH, DEVELOPMENT AND TECHNOLOGICAL INNOVATION. CULTURE R+D CREATE PLAN PROB/SOLV AUTOMAT RISK PERSON...DECISION CONCPT PREDICT BIBLIOG. PAGE 21 H0419
TEC/DEV NEW/IDEA INDUS MGT

B64
BROWN N.,NUCLEAR WAR* THE IMPENDING STRATEGIC DEADLOCK. USA+45 USSR TEC/DEV BUDGET RISK ARMS/CONT NUC/PWR WEAPON COST BIO/SOC...GEOG IDEA/COMP NAT/COMP GAME NATO WARSAW/P. PAGE 22 H0448
FORCES OP/RES WAR GEN/LAWS

B64
COONDOO R.,THE DIVISION OF POWERS IN THE INDIAN CONSTITUTION. INDIA ECO/UNDEV FINAN TEC/DEV WAR CENTRAL EFFICIENCY NAT/LISM PWR WEALTH NEW/LIB ...BIBLIOG 18/20. PAGE 33 H0659
CONSTN LEGIS WELF/ST GOV/COMP

B64
HAAR C.M.,LAW AND LAND: ANGLO-AMERICAN PLANNING PRACTICE. UK USA+45 NAT/G TEC/DEV BUDGET CT/SYS INGP/REL EFFICIENCY OWN...JURID 20. PAGE 63 H1263
LAW PLAN MUNIC NAT/COMP

B64
HARBISON F.H.,EDUCATION, MANPOWER, AND ECONOMIC GROWTH. WOR+45 ECO/DEV ECO/UNDEV ACADEM LABOR SCHOOL WORKER UTIL...IDEA/COMP NAT/COMP. PAGE 66 H1326
PLAN TEC/DEV EDU/PROP SKILL

B64
HAZLEWOOD A.,THE ECONOMICS OF DEVELOPMENT: AN ANNOTATED LIST OF BOOKS AND ARTICLES PUBLISHED 1958-1962. AGRI FINAN INDUS LABOR NAT/G DIPLOM INT/TRADE INCOME...MGT 20. PAGE 69 H1374
BIBLIOG/A ECO/UNDEV TEC/DEV

B64
HERSKOVITS M.J.,ECONOMIC TRANSITION IN AFRICA. FUT INT/ORG NAT/G WORKER PROB/SOLV TEC/DEV INT/TRADE EQUILIB INCOME...ANTHOL 20. PAGE 70 H1408
AFR ECO/UNDEV PLAN ADMIN

B64
LEBRUN J.,BIBLIOGRAPHIE DE LA FERTILITE DES SOLS ET ELEMENTS DE SOCIOLOGIE RURALE EN AFRIQUE AU SUD DU SAHARA. AFR PLAN TEC/DEV EFFICIENCY PRODUC...GEOG SOC NAT/COMP 20. PAGE 93 H1850
BIBLIOG/A ECO/UNDEV HABITAT AGRI

B64
LI C.M.,INDUSTRIAL DEVELOPMENT IN COMMUNIST CHINA. CHINA/COM ECO/DEV ECO/UNDEV AGRI FINAN INDUS MARKET LABOR NAT/G ECO/TAC INT/TRADE EXEC ALL/VALS ...POLICY RELATIV TREND WORK TOT/POP VAL/FREE 20. PAGE 96 H1921
ASIA TEC/DEV

B64
OECD,DEVELOPMENT ASSISTANCE EFFORTS - POLICIES OF THE MEMBERS. AGRI INDUS BUDGET...GEOG NAT/COMP 20 OECD. PAGE 120 H2398
INT/ORG FOR/AID ECO/UNDEV TEC/DEV

B64
ON CULTURE AND SOCIAL CHANGE. FAM NAT/G ACT/RES ECO/TAC RACE/REL...PSY TIME/SEQ TREND IDEA/COMP METH/COMP ANTHOL BIBLIOG 20. PAGE 120 H2406
CULTURE TEC/DEV STRUCT CREATE

B64
RAMAZANI R.K.,THE MIDDLE EAST AND THE EUROPEAN COMMON MARKET. EUR+WWI ISLAM ECO/DEV EXTR/IND MARKET PROC/MFG INT/ORG NAT/G TEC/DEV ECO/TAC REGION DRIVE WEALTH...STAT CHARTS EEC TOT/POP 20. PAGE 129 H2587
ECO/UNDEV ATTIT INT/TRADE

B64
SOLOW R.M.,THE NATURE AND SOURCES OF UNEMPLOYMENT IN THE UNITED STATES (PAMPHLET). USA+45 INDUS LABOR TEC/DEV ECO/TAC SKILL WEALTH...TREND NAT/COMP 20. PAGE 147 H2930
ECO/DEV WORKER STAT PRODUC

B64
STRONG C.F.,HISTORY OF MODERN POLITICAL CONSTITUTIONS. STRUCT INT/ORG NAT/G LEGIS TEC/DEV DIPLOM INT/TRADE CT/SYS EXEC...METH/COMP T 12/20 UN. PAGE 150 H2999
CONSTN CONCPT

B64
THORNBURG M.W.,PEOPLE AND POLICY IN THE MIDDLE EAST. ISLAM ECO/UNDEV FAM KIN MUNIC NAT/G NEIGH POL/PAR SECT DELIB/GP LEGIS PLAN ECO/TAC DOMIN ADMIN ATTIT HEALTH RESPECT...SOC CONCPT METH/CNCPT OBS TIME/SEQ TOT/POP VAL/FREE. PAGE 154 H3088
TEC/DEV CULTURE

B64
UNESCO,WORLD COMMUNICATIONS: PRESS, RADIO, TELEVISION, FILM (4TH ED.). WOR+45 DIPLOM TV PEACE ...NAT/COMP SOC/INTEG 20 FILM. PAGE 158 H3163
COM/IND EDU/PROP PRESS TEC/DEV

B64
URQUIDI V.L.,THE CHALLENGE OF DEVELOPMENT IN LATIN AMERICA. L/A+17C FINAN INT/ORG TEC/DEV DIPLOM INT/TRADE PRICE REGION PRODUC...CHARTS 20. PAGE 159 H3175
ECO/UNDEV ECO/TAC NAT/G TREND

B64
WHEELER-BENNETT J.W.,THE NEMESIS OF POWER (2ND ED.). EUR+WWI GERMANY TOP/EX TEC/DEV ADMIN WAR PERS/REL RIGID/FLEX ROLE ORD/FREE PWR FASCISM 20 HITLER/A. PAGE 167 H3342
FORCES NAT/G GP/REL STRUCT

S64
CROUZET F.,"WARS, BLOCKADE, AND ECONOMIC CHANGE IN EUROPE, 1792-1815." UK INDUS NAT/G TEC/DEV ECO/TAC WEALTH...POLICY RELATIV HIST/WRIT TIME/SEQ 18/19. PAGE 35 H0710
MOD/EUR MARKET

S64
EISTER A.W.,"PERSPECTIVE ON FUNCTIONS OF RELIGION IN A DEVELOPING COUNTRY: ISLAM IN PAKISTAN." ISLAM CULTURE MUNIC ACT/RES CREATE PROB/SOLV TEC/DEV WORSHIP. PAGE 45 H0902
ATTIT SECT ECO/DEV

S64
GARMARNIKOW M.,"INFLUENCE-BUYING IN WEST AFRICA." COM FUT USSR INTELL NAT/G PLAN TEC/DEV ECO/TAC DOMIN EDU/PROP REGION NAT/LISM ATTIT DRIVE ALL/VALS SOVEREIGN...POLICY PSY SOC CONCPT TREND STERTYP WORK COLD/WAR 20. PAGE 55 H1102
AFR ECO/UNDEV FOR/AID SOCISM

S64
LOW D.A.,"LION RAMPANT." EUR+WWI MOD/EUR S/ASIA ECO/UNDEV NAT/G FORCES TEC/DEV ECO/TAC LEGIT ADMIN COLONIAL COERCE ORD/FREE RESPECT 19/20. PAGE 99 H1972
AFR DOMIN DIPLOM UK

S64
MARES V.E.,"EAST EUROPE'S SECOND CHANCE." COM EUR+WWI HUNGARY ROMANIA USSR YUGOSLAVIA ECO/UNDEV NAT/G TOP/EX CREATE PLAN TEC/DEV REGION NAT/LISM RIGID/FLEX PWR...CONCPT STAT COMECON 20. PAGE 102 H2047
VOL/ASSN ECO/TAC

S64
MC WILLIAM M.,"THE WORLD BANK AND THE TRANSFER OF POWER IN KENYA." AFR ECO/UNDEV CONSULT ACT/RES TEC/DEV PERCEPT PWR SKILL WEALTH...CONCPT OBS TREND 20. PAGE 106 H2119
NAT/G ECO/TAC

S64
NASH M.,"SOCIAL PREREQUISITES TO ECONOMIC GROWTH IN LATIN AMERICA AND SOUTHEAST ASIA." L/A+17C S/ASIA CULTURE SOCIETY ECO/UNDEV AGRI INDUS NAT/G PLAN TEC/DEV EDU/PROP ROUTINE ALL/VALS...POLICY RELATIV SOC NAT/COMP WORK TOT/POP 20. PAGE 116 H2314
ECO/DEV PERCEPT

S64
NEEDHAM T.,"SCIENCE AND SOCIETY IN EAST AND WEST." INTELL STRATA R+D LOC/G NAT/G PROVS CONSULT ACT/RES CREATE PLAN TEC/DEV EDU/PROP ADMIN ATTIT ALL/VALS ...POLICY RELATIV MGT CONCPT NEW/IDEA TIME/SEQ WORK WORK. PAGE 116 H2327
ASIA STRUCT

S64
SAAB H.,"THE ARAB SEARCH FOR A FEDERAL UNION." SOCIETY INT/ORG NAT/G DELIB/GP FORCES ACT/RES TEC/DEV ECO/TAC DOMIN LEGIT REGION ROUTINE ATTIT DRIVE RIGID/FLEX ALL/VALS...SOC CONCPT NEW/IDEA
ISLAM PLAN

TIME/SEQ TREND. PAGE 136 H2726

S64
TINKER H.,"POLITICS IN SOUTHEAST ASIA." INT/ORG NAT/G CREATE PLAN TEC/DEV GUERRILLA KNOWL ORD/FREE COLD/WAR. PAGE 155 H3103
S/ASIA ACT/RES REGION

B65
ALEXANDER R.J.,ORGANIZED LABOR IN LATIN AMERICA. L/A+17C INT/ORG LEGIS WORKER TEC/DEV BARGAIN INT/TRADE REV...NAT/COMP BIBLIOG 20. PAGE 5 H0102
LABOR POL/PAR ECO/UNDEV POLICY

B65
BENTWICH J.S.,EDUCATION IN ISRAEL. ISRAEL CULTURE STRATA PROB/SOLV TEC/DEV ADJUST ALL/VALS 20 JEWS. PAGE 15 H0293
SECT EDU/PROP ACADEM SCHOOL

B65
CHAO K.,THE RATE AND PATTERN OF INDUSTRIAL GROWTH IN COMMUNIST CHINA. CHINA/COM ECO/UNDEV TEC/DEV PRICE...NAT/COMP BIBLIOG 20. PAGE 29 H0578
INDUS INDEX STAT PRODUC

B65
FOSTER P.,EDUCATION AND SOCIAL CHANGE IN GHANA. GHANA CULTURE STRUCT ECO/UNDEV TEC/DEV REGION EFFICIENCY LITERACY ALL/VALS SOVEREIGN...STAT METH/COMP 19/20 GOLD/COAST. PAGE 52 H1043
SCHOOL CREATE SOCIETY

B65
HALPERIN M.H.,COMMUNIST CHINA AND ARMS CONTROL. CHINA/COM FUT USA+45 CULTURE FORCES TEC/DEV ECO/TAC WAR PEACE ORD/FREE MARXISM 20 COLD/WAR. PAGE 64 H1292
ATTIT POLICY ARMS/CONT NUC/PWR

B65
HARBISON F.,MANPOWER AND EDUCATION. AFR CHINA/COM IRAN L/A+17C S/ASIA TEC/DEV ADJUST OPTIMAL SKILL ...ANTHOL 20. PAGE 66 H1325
ECO/UNDEV EDU/PROP WORKER NAT/COMP

B65
HART B.H.L.,THE MEMOIRS OF CAPTAIN LIDDELL HART (VOL. I). UK NAT/G PLAN TEC/DEV DIPLOM ADMIN WEAPON GOV/REL PERS/REL ATTIT PWR FASCISM...POLICY 20. PAGE 67 H1348
FORCES BIOG LEAD WAR

B65
HYMES D.,THE USE OF COMPUTERS IN ANTHROPOLOGY. CULTURE PROF/ORG CONSULT CREATE EFFICIENCY PERCEPT ...CLASSIF LING CON/ANAL COMPUT/IR METH/COMP ANTHOL 20. PAGE 76 H1517
METH COMPUTER TEC/DEV SOC

B65
IANNI O.,ESTADO E CAPITALISMO. L/A+17C FINAN TEC/DEV ECO/TAC ORD/FREE WEALTH POLICY. PAGE 76 H1518
ECO/UNDEV STRUCT INDUS NAT/G

B65
INT. BANK RECONSTR. DEVELOP.,ECONOMIC DEVELOPMENT OF KUWAIT. ISLAM KUWAIT AGRI FINAN MARKET EX/STRUC TEC/DEV ECO/TAC ADMIN WEALTH...OBS CON/ANAL CHARTS 20. PAGE 77 H1541
INDUS NAT/G

B65
JANSEN M.B.,CHANGING JAPANESE ATTITUDES TOWARD MODERNIZATION. ASIA CHINA/COM S/ASIA INTELL SOCIETY KIN NAT/G SECT PERCEPT RIGID/FLEX...SOC CONCPT TIME/SEQ TREND TOT/POP 19/20 CHINJAP. PAGE 80 H1591
TEC/DEV ATTIT INDIA

B65
MEIER R.L.,DEVELOPMENTAL PLANNING. PUERT/RICO INDUS PUB/INST SCHOOL CREATE ECO/TAC FOR/AID...NAT/COMP 20. PAGE 108 H2165
PLAN ECO/UNDEV GOV/COMP TEC/DEV

B65
MOORE W.E.,THE IMPACT OF INDUSTRY. CULTURE STRUCT ORD/FREE...TREND 20. PAGE 113 H2251
INDUS MGT TEC/DEV ECO/UNDEV

B65
ONUOHA B.,THE ELEMENTS OF AFRICAN SOCIALISM. AFR FINAN SECT TEC/DEV FOR/AID GP/REL OWN LAISSEZ MARXISM...CONCPT BIBLIOG 20. PAGE 121 H2419
SOCISM ECO/UNDEV NAT/G EX/STRUC

B65
SCHULER E.A.,THE PAKISTAN ACADEMIES FOR RURAL DEVELOPMENT COMILLA AND PESHAWAR 1959-1964. PAKISTAN S/ASIA SOCIETY STRUCT AGRI NAT/G TEC/DEV EDU/PROP 20. PAGE 140 H2801
BIBLIOG PLAN ECO/TAC ECO/UNDEV

B65
SIMMS R.P.,URBANIZATION IN WEST AFRICA; A REVIEW OF CURRENT LITERATURE. AFR PLAN TEC/DEV...SOC OBS NAT/COMP 20. PAGE 144 H2878
BIBLIOG/A MUNIC ECO/DEV ECO/UNDEV

B65
TUTSCH H.E.,FACETS OF ARAB NATIONALISM. ISLAM ISRAEL CULTURE STRUCT SECT RIGID/FLEX ORD/FREE MARXISM SOCISM 20. PAGE 157 H3143
ECO/UNDEV NAT/LISM TEC/DEV SOCIETY

B65
UN,SPACE ACTIVITIES AND RESOURCES: REVIEW OF UNITED NATION'S NATIONAL AND INTERNATIONAL PROGRAMS. INT/ORG LABOR PLAN TEC/DEV DIPLOM EFFICIENCY HEALTH ...GOV/COMP 20 UN. PAGE 158 H3155
SPACE NUC/PWR FOR/AID PEACE

L65
MATTHEWS D.G.,"A CURRENT BIBLIOGRAPHY ON SUDANESE AFFAIRS; A SELECT BIBLIOGRAPHY FROM 1960-1964." SUDAN LAW CULTURE AGRI FINAN INDUS LABOR POL/PAR TEC/DEV FOR/AID RACE/REL LITERACY...LING 20. PAGE 105 H2094
BIBLIOG ECO/UNDEV NAT/G DIPLOM

L65
WIONCZEK M.,"LATIN AMERICA FREE TRADE ASSOCIATION." AGRI DIST/IND FINAN INDUS INT/ORG LABOR NAT/G TEC/DEV ECO/TAC HEALTH SKILL WEALTH...POLICY RELATIV MGT LAFTA 20. PAGE 169 H3390
L/A+17C MARKET REGION

S65
BIRNBAUM K.,"SWEDEN'S NUCLEAR POLICY." WOR+45 POL/PAR CREATE TEC/DEV NEUTRAL RISK WAR ORD/FREE ...DECISION IDEA/COMP NAT/COMP TIME. PAGE 17 H0343
SWEDEN NUC/PWR DIPLOM ARMS/CONT

S65
PLISCHKE E.,"INTEGRATING BERLIN AND THE FEDERAL REPUBLIC OF GERMANY." EUR+WWI GERMANY/W LEGIS TEC/DEV DOMIN ORD/FREE PWR...JURID 20 BERLIN. PAGE 126 H2528
DIPLOM NAT/G MUNIC

S65
TENDLER J.D.,"TECHNOLOGY AND ECONOMIC DEVELOPMENT* THE CASE OF HYDRO VS THERMAL POWER." CONSTRUC DIST/IND CREATE TEC/DEV INT/TRADE CENTRAL PWR SKILL WEALTH...MGT NAT/COMP ARGEN. PAGE 153 H3061
BRAZIL INDUS ECO/UNDEV

S65
VAN DEN BERG M.,"SOME METHODOLOGICAL ASPECTS OF SOUTH AFRICA'S FIRST E.D.P." SOUTH/AFR NAT/G CREATE TEC/DEV CAP/ISM INCOME PRODUC...CON/ANAL CHARTS 20. PAGE 161 H3226
ECO/DEV PLAN METH STAT

S65
WOHLSTETTER R.,"CUBA AND PEARL HARBOR* HINDSIGHT AND FORESIGHT." USSR FORCES OP/RES TEC/DEV ATTIT PERCEPT...DECISION IDEA/COMP NAT/COMP STERTYP TIME. PAGE 170 H3395
CUBA RISK WAR ACT/RES

C65
COLEMAN J.S.,"EDUCATION AND POLITICAL DEVELOPMENT." COM CULTURE INTELL STRUCT SCHOOL PERSON SOVEREIGN ...POLICY ANTHOL BIBLIOG/A METH 20. PAGE 31 H0629
ECO/UNDEV NAT/LISM EDU/PROP TEC/DEV

B66
BARRETT J.,THAT BETTER COUNTRY: RELIGIOUS ASPECT OF LIFE IN EASTERN AUSTRALIA, 1835-1850. LAW ECO/UNDEV SCHOOL TEC/DEV EDU/PROP CONTROL HABITAT MORAL WORSHIP 19 AUSTRAL CHURCH/STA. PAGE 11 H0229
SECT CULTURE GOV/REL

B66
DIAMOND S.,THE TRANSFORMATION OF EAST AFRICA. NAT/G SCHOOL CREATE PROB/SOLV COLONIAL REGION RACE/REL FEDERAL...SOC ANTHOL WORSHIP 20 AFRICA/E. PAGE 41 H0819
CULTURE AFR TEC/DEV INDUS

B66
DOBB M.,SOVIET ECONOMIC DEVELOPMENT SINCE 1917. USSR ECO/DEV ECO/UNDEV LABOR NAT/G TEC/DEV ECO/TAC ROUTINE PRODUC MARXISM 20. PAGE 41 H0829
PLAN INDUS WORKER

B66
HOPKINS J.F.K.,ARABIC PERIODICAL LITERATURE, 1961. ISLAM LAW CULTURE SECT...GEOG HEAL PHIL/SCI PSY SOC 20. PAGE 73 H1466
BIBLIOG/A NAT/LISM TEC/DEV INDUS

B66
KEYES J.G.,A BIBLIOGRAPHY OF WESTERN LANGUAGE PUBLICATIONS CONCERNING NORTH VIETNAM IN THE CORNELL LIBRARY. VIETNAM/N NAT/G FORCES TEC/DEV DIPLOM LEAD RACE/REL...GEOG SOC 20. PAGE 85 H1700
BIBLIOG/A CULTURE ECO/UNDEV S/ASIA

B66
KOMIYA R.,POSTWAR ECONOMIC GROWTH IN JAPAN. ELITES NAT/G EX/STRUC TEC/DEV BUDGET DIPLOM CONTROL BAL/PAY PRODUC...BIBLIOG 20 CHINJAP. PAGE 88 H1754
ECO/DEV POLICY PLAN ADJUST

B66
KUZNETS S.,MODERN ECONOMIC GROWTH. WOR+45 WOR-45 ECO/DEV ECO/UNDEV AGRI FINAN INDUS TEC/DEV EFFICIENCY INCOME...NAT/COMP 19/20. PAGE 89 H1786
TIME/SEQ WEALTH PRODUC

B66
LAVEN P.,RENAISSANCE ITALY: 1464-1534. ITALY AGRI EXTR/IND FINAN MUNIC INT/TRADE DRIVE...CATH GEOG CHARTS BIBLIOG/A 15. PAGE 92 H1841
CULTURE HUM TEC/DEV KNOWL

B66
MACFARQUHAR R.,CHINA UNDER MAO: POLITICS TAKES COMMAND. CHINA/COM COM AGRI INDUS CHIEF FORCES DIPLOM INT/TRADE EDU/PROP TASK REV ADJUST...ANTHOL 20 MAO. PAGE 100 H1992
ECO/UNDEV TEC/DEV ECO/TAC ADMIN

B66
ODEGARD P.H.,POLITICAL POWER AND SOCIAL CHANGE. UNIV NAT/G CREATE ALL/IDEOS...POLICY GEOG SOC CENSUS TREND. PAGE 120 H2394
PWR TEC/DEV IDEA/COMP

B66
OECD DEVELOPMENT CENTRE,CATALOGUE OF SOCIAL AND ECONOMIC DEVELOPMENT INSTITUTES AND PROGRAMMES* RESEARCH. ACT/RES PLAN TEC/DEV EDU/PROP...SOC GP/COMP NAT/COMP. PAGE 120 H2403
ECO/UNDEV ECO/DEV R+D ACADEM

B66
SMITH H.E.,READINGS IN ECONOMIC DEVELOPMENT AND ADMINISTRATION IN TANZANIA. TANZANIA FINAN INDUS
TEC/DEV ADMIN

LABOR NAT/G PLAN PROB/SOLV INT/TRADE COLONIAL REGION...ANTHOL BIBLIOG 20 AFRICA/E. PAGE 146 H2910 GOV/REL

B66
SRINIVAS M.N.,SOCIAL CHANGE IN MODERN INDIA. INDIA CULTURE SOCIETY STRUCT SECT TEC/DEV...METH/CNCPT SELF/OBS WORSHIP 20. PAGE 148 H2961 ORD/FREE STRATA SOC ECO/UNDEV

B66
THIESENHUSEN W.C.,CHILE'S EXPERIMENTS IN AGRARIAN REFORM. CHILE STRUCT NAT/G ACT/RES ECO/TAC GOV/REL COST SOCISM...TREND CHARTS SOC/EXP 20. PAGE 154 H3073 AGRI ECO/UNDEV SOC TEC/DEV

B66
US DEPARTMENT OF STATE,RESEARCH ON THE USSR AND EASTERN EUROPE (EXTERNAL RESEARCH LIST NO 1-25). USSR LAW CULTURE SOCIETY NAT/G TEC/DEV DIPLOM EDU/PROP REGION...GEOG LING. PAGE 160 H3191 BIBLIOG/A EUR+WWI COM MARXISM

B66
ZEINE Z.N.,THE EMERGENCE OF ARAB NATIONALISM (REV. ED.). TURKEY UK NAT/G SECT TEC/DEV LEAD REV WAR AGE/Y ROLE ORD/FREE...TRADIT CHARTS BIBLIOG 20 ARABS OTTOMAN. PAGE 173 H3453 ISLAM NAT/LISM DIPLOM

B66
ZINKIN T.,CHALLENGES IN INDIA. INDIA PAKISTAN LAW AGRI FINAN INDUS TOP/EX TEC/DEV CONTROL ROUTINE ORD/FREE PWR 20 NEHRU/J SHASTRI/LB CIVIL/SERV. PAGE 173 H3458 NAT/G ECO/TAC POLICY ADMIN

S66
"FURTHER READING." INDIA LOC/G NAT/G PLAN ADMIN WEALTH...GEOG SOC CONCPT CENSUS 20. PAGE 2 H0049 BIBLIOG ECO/UNDEV TEC/DEV PROVS

S66
LODGE G.C.,"REVOLUTION IN LATIN AMERICA." USA+45 ELITES INDUS LABOR PROF/ORG SECT TEC/DEV CAP/ISM SKILL MARXISM...POLICY NAT/COMP. PAGE 98 H1950 ATTIT REV L/A+17C IDEA/COMP

S66
TURKEVICH J.,"SOVIET SCIENCE APPRAISED." USA+45 R+D ACADEM FORCES DIPLOM EDU/PROP WAR EFFICIENCY PEACE SKILL OBS. PAGE 157 H3137 USSR TEC/DEV NAT/COMP ATTIT

B67
ANDERSON E.N.,POLITICAL INSTITUTIONS AND SOCIAL CHANGE IN CONTINENTAL EUROPE IN THE NINETEENTH CENTURY. MOD/EUR LAW CONSTN SOCIETY POL/PAR TEC/DEV LEAD REV ATTIT...BIBLIOG 19. PAGE 6 H0127 NAT/G NAT/COMP METH/COMP INDUS

B67
COWLES M.,PERSPECTIVES IN THE EDUCATION OF DISADVANTAGED CHILDREN. CULTURE OP/RES PLAN PERS/REL ADJUST HABITAT PERCEPT KNOWL WEALTH ...SOC/WK IDEA/COMP ANTHOL 20. PAGE 34 H0686 EDU/PROP AGE/C TEC/DEV SCHOOL

B67
DEGLER C.N.,THE AGE OF THE ECONOMIC REVOLUTION 1876-1900. USA-45 AGRI MUNIC POL/PAR SECT ECO/TAC CHOOSE...PHIL/SCI CHARTS NAT/COMP 19 NEGRO. PAGE 39 H0782 INDUS SOCIETY ECO/DEV TEC/DEV

B67
DENISON E.F.,WHY GROWTH RATES DIFFER; POSTWAR EXPERIENCE IN NINE WESTERN COUNTRIES. WOR+45 FINAN WORKER TEC/DEV EDU/PROP PRICE PRODUC WEALTH ...ECOMETRIC STAT CHARTS BIBLIOG. PAGE 40 H0791 METH NAT/COMP ECO/DEV ECO/TAC

B67
DICKSON P.G.M.,THE FINANCIAL REVOLUTION IN ENGLAND. UK NAT/G TEC/DEV ADMIN GOV/REL...SOC METH/CNCPT CHARTS GP/COMP BIBLIOG 17/18. PAGE 41 H0823 ECO/DEV FINAN CAP/ISM MGT

B67
DIX R.H.,COLOMBIA: THE POLITICAL DIMENSIONS OF CHANGE. ELITES POL/PAR DOMIN REV...AUD/VIS 20 COLOMB. PAGE 41 H0828 L/A+17C NAT/G TEC/DEV LEAD

B67
GALBRAITH J.K.,THE NEW INDUSTRIAL STATE. INDUS LABOR LG/CO NAT/G POL/PAR SCHOOL OP/RES CAP/ISM EXEC TREND. PAGE 54 H1087 TEC/DEV ECO/DEV SOCIETY MARKET

B67
LAMBERT J.,LATIN AMERICA: SOCIAL STRUCTURES AND POLITICAL INSTITUTIONS. STRUCT TEC/DEV DIPLOM ADMIN COLONIAL LEAD ATTIT...SOC CLASSIF NAT/COMP 17/20. PAGE 90 H1801 L/A+17C NAT/G ECO/UNDEV SOCIETY

B67
NESS G.D.,BUREAUCRACY AND RURAL DEVELOPMENT IN MALAYSIA. MALAYSIA UK SOCIETY FINAN INDUS WORKER TEC/DEV ECO/TAC COLONIAL EQUILIB ORD/FREE...STAT CHARTS 20. PAGE 117 H2330 ECO/UNDEV PLAN NAT/G ADMIN

B67
OVERSEAS DEVELOPMENT INSTIT,EFFECTIVE AID. WOR+45 INT/ORG TEC/DEV DIPLOM INT/TRADE ADMIN. PAGE 122 H2434 FOR/AID ECO/UNDEV ECO/TAC NAT/COMP

B67
PATAI R.,GOLDEN RIVER TO GOLDEN ROAD: SOCIETY, CULTURE, AND CHANGE IN THE MIDDLE EAST (2ND ED.). ELITES FAM KIN TEC/DEV MARRIAGE NAT/LISM SEX ORD/FREE...TREND GP/COMP WORSHIP 20. PAGE 124 H2476 CULTURE SOCIETY ISLAM STRUCT

B67
RUEFF J.,BALANCE OF PAYMENTS. WOR+45 FINAN TEC/DEV DIPLOM TARIFFS PRICE CONTROL...POLICY CONCPT IDEA/COMP. PAGE 136 H2715 INT/TRADE BAL/PAY ECO/TAC NAT/COMP

B67
UNESCO,PRINCIPLES AND PROBLEMS OF NATIONAL SCIENCE POLICIES. WOR+45 ECO/DEV ECO/UNDEV R+D INT/ORG PROB/SOLV CONFER...PHIL/SCI CHARTS 20 UNESCO UN. PAGE 158 H3165 NAT/COMP POLICY TEC/DEV CREATE

B67
WILLS A.J.,AN INTRODUCTION TO THE HISTORY OF CENTRAL AFRICA. RHODESIA ZAMBIA CULTURE SOCIETY ECO/UNDEV TEC/DEV DOMIN WAR ALL/VALS...POLICY TREND BIBLIOG T 14/20 NYASALAND. PAGE 169 H3375 AFR COLONIAL ORD/FREE

B67
WISEMAN H.V.,BRITAIN AND THE COMMONWEALTH. EUR+WWI FUT UK ECO/DEV POL/PAR TEC/DEV INT/TRADE LEAD ROLE SOVEREIGN...SOC TREND 20 CMN/WLTH. PAGE 169 H3391 INT/ORG DIPLOM NAT/G NAT/COMP

B67
YAMAMURA K.,ECONOMIC POLICY IN POSTWAR JAPAN. ASIA FINAN POL/PAR DIPLOM LEAD NAT/LISM ATTIT NEW/LIB POPULISM 20 CHINJAP. PAGE 171 H3432 ECO/DEV POLICY NAT/G TEC/DEV

L67
EINAUDI L.,"ANNOTATED BIBLIOGRAPHY OF LATIN AMERICAN MILITARY JOURNALS" LAW TEC/DEV DOMIN EDU/PROP COERCE WAR CIVMIL/REL 20. PAGE 45 H0899 BIBLIOG/A NAT/G FORCES L/A+17C

L67
WRIGHT W.R.,"FOREIGN-OWNED RAILWAYS IN ARGENTINA: A CASE STUDY OF ECONOMIC NATIONALISM." L/A+17C UK ECO/UNDEV SERV/IND LG/CO NAT/G TEC/DEV BAL/PWR EQUILIB ARGEN. PAGE 171 H3423 NAT/LISM CAP/ISM ECO/TAC COLONIAL

S67
BAER W.,"THE INFLATION CONTROVERSY IN LATIN AMERICA: SURVEY." L/A+17C ECO/UNDEV AGRI FINAN INDUS PLAN PROB/SOLV TEC/DEV...BIBLIOG/A 20. PAGE 10 H0194 NAT/G BAL/PAY ECO/TAC BUDGET

S67
BERLINER J.S.,"RUSSIA'S BUREAUCRATS - WHY THEY'RE REACTIONARY." USSR NAT/G OP/RES PROB/SOLV TEC/DEV CONTROL SANCTION EFFICIENCY DRIVE PERSON...TECHNIC SOC 20. PAGE 15 H0308 CREATE ADMIN INDUS PRODUC

S67
BRANCO R.,"LAND REFORM* THE ANSWER TO LATIN AMERICA'S AGRICULTURAL DEVELOPMENT?" L/A+17C NAT/G PLAN TEC/DEV BUDGET RENT EFFICIENCY 20. PAGE 20 H0404 ECO/UNDEV AGRI TAX OWN

S67
CHIU S.M.,"CHINA'S MILITARY POSTURE." CHINA/COM ELITES NAT/G POL/PAR TEC/DEV ECO/TAC DOMIN CONTROL LEAD REV MARXISM 20 MAO. PAGE 30 H0595 FORCES CIVMIL/REL NUC/PWR DIPLOM

S67
DENISON E.F.,"SOURCES OF GROWTH IN NINE WESTERN COUNTRIES." WORKER TEC/DEV COST PRODUC...TREND NAT/COMP. PAGE 39 H0790 INCOME NAT/G EUR+WWI ECO/DEV

S67
HANSON A.H.,"INDIA AFTER THE ELECTIONS." INDIA ECO/UNDEV LEGIS TEC/DEV FOR/AID GP/REL FEDERAL ATTIT 20. PAGE 66 H1321 NAT/G POL/PAR REGION CENTRAL

S67
SALYZYN V.,"FEDERAL-PROVINCIAL TAX SHARING SCHEMES." CANADA LOC/G PROB/SOLV TEC/DEV BUDGET GOV/REL EFFICIENCY 20. PAGE 137 H2746 PROVS TAX MUNIC NAT/G

S67
SZALAY L.B.,"SOVIET DOMESTIC PROPAGANDA AND LIBERALIZATION." COM USSR SOCIETY COM/IND NAT/G POL/PAR EX/STRUC TEC/DEV LEAD ATTIT ROLE MARXISM ...METH/COMP 20. PAGE 151 H3026 EDU/PROP TOTALISM PERSON PERCEPT

N67
US HOUSE COMM SCI ASTRONAUT,GOVERNMENT, SCIENCE, AND INTERNATIONAL POLICY (PAMPHLET). INDIA NETHERLAND ECO/DEV ECO/UNDEV R+D ACADEM PLAN DIPLOM FOR/AID CONFER...PREDICT 20 CHINJAP. PAGE 160 H3198 NAT/G POLICY CREATE TEC/DEV

S68
LAPIERRE J.W.,"TRADITION ET MODERNITE A MADAGASCAR." ISLAM MADAGASCAR AGRI FINAN KIN NAT/G CREATE OP/RES GP/REL INGP/REL ATTIT CONSERVE...PSY 20. PAGE 91 H1813 ECO/UNDEV FOR/AID CULTURE TEC/DEV

TECHNIC....TECHNOCRATIC

B15
VEBLEN T.,IMPERIAL GERMANY AND THE INDUSTRIAL REVOLUTION. GERMANY MOD/EUR UK USA-45 NAT/G TEC/DEV CAP/ISM...MAJORIT NAT/COMP 19/20 CHINJAP. PAGE 162 H3236 ECO/DEV INDUS TECHNIC BAL/PWR

B34
RIDLEY C.E.,THE CITY-MANAGER PROFESSION. CHIEF PLAN MUNIC

ADMIN CONTROL ROUTINE CHOOSE...TECHNIC CHARTS GOV/COMP BIBLIOG 20. PAGE 131 H2624 EX/STRUC LOC/G EXEC

B48
ROSENFARB J.,FREEDOM AND THE ADMINISTRATIVE STATE. NAT/G ROUTINE EFFICIENCY PRODUC RATIONAL UTIL ...TECHNIC WELF/ST MGT 20 BUREAUCRCY. PAGE 134 H2680 ECO/DEV INDUS PLAN WEALTH

B51
MUMFORD L.,THE CONDUCT OF LIFE. UNIV SOCIETY CREATE ...TECHNIC METH/CNCPT TIME/SEQ TREND GEN/LAWS BIBLIOG/A. PAGE 114 H2286 ALL/VALS CULTURE PERSON CONCPT

B58
MECRENSKY E.,SCIENTIFIC MANPOWER IN EUROPE. WOR+45 EDU/PROP GOV/REL SKILL...TECHNIC PHIL/SCI INT CHARTS BIBLIOG 20. PAGE 108 H2157 ECO/TAC TEC/DEV METH/COMP NAT/COMP

B59
PANIKKAR K.M.,THE AFRO-ASIAN STATES AND THEIR PROBLEMS. COM CULTURE KIN POL/PAR SECT DIPLOM EDU/PROP COLONIAL SOVEREIGN...TECHNIC GOV/COMP 20. PAGE 123 H2458 AFR S/ASIA ECO/UNDEV

S67
BERLINER J.S.,"RUSSIA'S BUREAUCRATS - WHY THEY'RE REACTIONARY." USSR NAT/G OP/RES PROB/SOLV TEC/DEV CONTROL SANCTION EFFICIENCY DRIVE PERSON...TECHNIC SOC 20. PAGE 15 H0308 CREATE ADMIN INDUS PRODUC

TECHNIQUES....SEE TEC/DEV, METHODOLOGICAL INDEXES, PP. XIII-XIV

TECHNOCRACY....SEE TECHRACY, TECHNIC

TECHNOLOGY....SEE COMPUTER, TECHNIC, TEC/DEV

TECHRACY....SOCIO-POLITICAL ORDER DOMINATED BY TECHNICIANS

B39
BARNES H.E.,SOCIETY IN TRANSITION: PROBLEMS OF A CHANGING ERA. USA-45 INDUS MUNIC PUB/INST EDU/PROP CRIME RACE/REL...SOC MYTH NAT/COMP. PAGE 11 H0220 SOCIETY CULTURE TECHRACY TEC/DEV

B42
BARNES H.E.,SOCIAL INSTITUTIONS IN AN ERA OF WORLD UPHEAVAL. INDUS FAM NAT/G PERF/ART SECT AUTOMAT PERSON MORAL...PREDICT 20. PAGE 11 H0221 SOCIETY CULTURE TECHRACY TREND

TEHERAN....TEHERAN CONFERENCE

TEMPERANCE....TEMPERANCE MOVEMENTS

TEMPERLEY H.W.V. H3058,H3059

TEMPLE W. H3060

TENDLER J.D. H3061

TENG S. H3062

TENNESSEE VALLEY AUTHORITY....SEE TVA

TENNESSEE....TENNESSEE

TENNEY F. H0502

TEPASKE J.J. H3063

TERRELL/G....GLENN TERRELL

TERRY V. OHIO....SEE TERRY

TERRY....TERRY V. OHIO

TESTS....THEORY AND USES OF TESTS AND SCALES; SEE ALSO TESTS AND SCALES INDEX, P. XIV

N62
US CONGRESS JT ATOM ENRGY COMM,PEACEFUL USES OF ATOMIC ENERGY, HEARING. USA+45 USSR TEC/DEV ATTIT RIGID/FLEX...TESTS CHARTS EXHIBIT METH/COMP 20 CONGRESS. PAGE 159 H3177 NUC/PWR ACADEM SCHOOL NAT/COMP

S64
LEWIS R.,"OPINION SURVEYING IN KOREA." ASIA FUT KOREA LEGIS EDU/PROP EXEC ALL/VALS...POLICY CONCPT MYTH TESTS CON/ANAL GEN/METH TOT/POP VAL/FREE 20. PAGE 96 H1915 NAT/G QU

B66
GURR T.,NEW ERROR-COMPENSATED MEASURES FOR COMPARING NATIONS* SOME CORRELATES OF CIVIL VIOLENCE. WOR+45 SOCIETY REV ISOLAT...PHIL/SCI SOC QUANT TESTS SAMP/SIZ HYPO/EXP. PAGE 63 H1254 NAT/COMP INDEX COERCE NEW/IDEA

S66
SNOW P.G.,"A SCALOGRAM ANALYSIS OF POLITICAL DEVELOPMENT." STRATA ECO/UNDEV POL/PAR REGION ALL/VALS PWR...SOC CHARTS. PAGE 146 H2924 L/A+17C NAT/COMP TESTS CLASSIF

TEW B. H3064

TEXAS....TEXAS

B63
LEVIN M.G.,ETHNIC ORIGINS OF THE PEOPLES OF NORTHEASTERN ASIA. CONSTN LEGIS...STAT CENSUS CHARTS 20 TEXAS MAPS. PAGE 95 H1901 HEREDITY HABITAT CULTURE GEOG

B66
VOGT E.Z.,PEOPLE OF RIMROCK. STRATA STRUCT KIN SECT GP/REL HABITAT ALL/VALS...GEOG INT QU 20 TEXAS NAVAHO MORMON SPAN/AMER ZUNI. PAGE 163 H3260 CULTURE GP/COMP SOC SOCIETY

THAILAND....THAILAND; SEE ALSO S/ASIA

N
US LIBRARY OF CONGRESS,SOUTHERN ASIA ACCESSIONS LIST. BURMA CEYLON INDIA NEPAL PAKISTAN S/ASIA THAILAND AGRI INDUS SCHOOL WORKER...ART/METH GEOG HEAL PHIL/SCI LING 20. PAGE 160 H3201 BIBLIOG/A SOCIETY CULTURE ECO/UNDEV

B12
CORDIER H.,BIBLIOTHECA INDOSINICA: DICTIONAIRE BIBLIOGRAPHIQUE DES OUVRAGES RELATIFS A LA PENINSULE INDOCHINOISE. BURMA LAOS MALAYSIA S/ASIA THAILAND VIETNAM SECT...LING 20. PAGE 33 H0665 BIBLIOG/A GEOG NAT/G

B45
LASKER B.,ASIA ON THE MOVE. ASIA BURMA S/ASIA THAILAND USSR ECO/UNDEV FAM KIN WAR NAT/LISM ATTIT ...GEOG CENSUS TREND AUSTRAL 20. PAGE 91 H1826 CULTURE RIGID/FLEX

B50
EMBREE J.F.,BIBLIOGRAPHY OF THE PEOPLES AND CULTURES OF MAINLAND SOUTHEAST ASIA. CAMBODIA LAOS THAILAND VIETNAM LAW...GEOG HUM SOC MYTH LING CHARTS WORSHIP 20. PAGE 46 H0915 BIBLIOG/A CULTURE S/ASIA

B50
TRAGER F.N.,MARXISM IN SOUTHEAST ASIA. BURMA INDONESIA THAILAND VIETNAM CULTURE SOCIETY NAT/G VOL/ASSN EXEC ROUTINE COERCE ATTIT RIGID/FLEX PWR ...METH/CNCPT TIME/SEQ STERTYP GEN/LAWS MARX/KARL VAL/FREE COLD/WAR NAM 20. PAGE 156 H3126 S/ASIA POL/PAR REV

B51
BERNATZIK H.A.,THE SPIRITS OF THE YELLOW LEAVES. BURMA LAOS S/ASIA THAILAND VIETNAM SOCIETY AGRI COLONIAL LEISURE GP/REL PERS/REL ISOLAT AGE HABITAT SEX WORSHIP 20. PAGE 16 H0310 SOC KIN ECO/UNDEV CULTURE

B57
KENNEDY M.D.,A SHORT HISTORY OF COMMUNISM IN ASIA. ASIA BURMA INDIA S/ASIA THAILAND NAT/G POL/PAR LEAD REV WAR MARXISM SOCISM...POLICY 20 CHINJAP. PAGE 85 H1688 DIPLOM NAT/LISM TOTALISM COERCE

B58
MASON J.B.,THAILAND BIBLIOGRAPHY. S/ASIA THAILAND CULTURE EDU/PROP ADMIN...GEOG SOC LING 20. PAGE 104 H2087 BIBLIOG/A ECO/UNDEV DIPLOM NAT/G

C58
BLANCHARD W.,"THAILAND." THAILAND CULTURE AGRI FINAN INDUS FAM LABOR INT/TRADE ATTIT...GEOG HEAL SOC BIBLIOG 20. PAGE 18 H0354 NAT/G DIPLOM ECO/UNDEV S/ASIA

B60
COUGHLIN R.,DOUBLE IDENTITY: THE CHINESE AND MODERN THAILAND. CHINA/COM S/ASIA THAILAND ECO/UNDEV EXTR/IND FINAN INDUS KIN MUNIC NAT/G PROF/ORG SCHOOL SECT ATTIT DRIVE...CONCPT OBS 20. PAGE 34 H0676 ASIA FAM CULTURE

B62
JOHNSON J.J.,THE ROLE OF THE MILITARY IN UNDERDEVELOPED COUNTRIES. AFR BURMA INDONESIA ISLAM ISRAEL L/A+17C S/ASIA THAILAND CULTURE ECO/UNDEV KIN PROVS CONSULT ACT/RES COERCE REV DRIVE RIGID/FLEX ORD/FREE...RECORD ANTHOL 20. PAGE 81 H1622 FORCES CONCPT

B62
KARNJAHAPRAKORN C.,MUNICIPAL GOVERNMENT IN THAILAND AS AN INSTITUTION AND PROCESS OF SELF-GOVERNMENT. THAILAND CULTURE FINAN EX/STRUC LEGIS PLAN CONTROL GOV/REL EFFICIENCY ATTIT...POLICY 20. PAGE 83 H1662 LOC/G MUNIC ORD/FREE ADMIN

B62
YOUNG G.,THE HILL TRIBES OF NORTHERN THAILAND. S/ASIA THAILAND FAM KIN LOC/G GP/REL HABITAT...GEOG LING OBS 20. PAGE 172 H3438 CULTURE STRUCT ECO/UNDEV SECT

B63
NATIONAL OFF STATE GOVT THAI,STATISTICAL BIBLIOGRAPHY: AN ANNOTATED BIBLIOGRAPHY OF THAI GOVERNMENTAL STATISTICAL PUBLICATIONS. THAILAND AGRI 20. PAGE 116 H2321 BIBLIOG/A STAT NAT/G S/ASIA

S63
AYAL E.B.,"VALUE SYSTEM AND ECONOMIC DEVELOPMENT IN JAPAN AND THAILAND." ASIA S/ASIA THAILAND CULTURE ECO/DEV CAP/ISM DOMIN NAT/LISM DRIVE RIGID/FLEX SOCISM...WELF/ST OBS TREND CON/ANAL GEN/LAWS 20 CHINJAP. PAGE 9 H0185 — ECO/UNDEV ALL/VALS

B64
HOBBS C.C.,SOUTHEAST ASIA: AN ANNOTATED BIBLIOGRAPHY OF SELECTED REFERENCES IN WESTERN LANGUAGES (REV. ED.). CAMBODIA INDONESIA LAOS THAILAND VIETNAM CONSTN NAT/G...SOC WORSHIP 20. PAGE 72 H1437 — BIBLIOG/A S/ASIA CULTURE SOCIETY

B64
NORTHROP F.S.,CROSS-CULTURAL UNDERSTANDING: EPISTEMOLOGY IN ANTHROPOLOGY. BURMA GREECE THAILAND HABITAT PERCEPT PERSON...PHIL/SCI SOC METH 20 MEXIC/AMER CHINJAP. PAGE 119 H2375 — EPIST PSY CULTURE CONCPT

B64
THAILAND NATIONAL ECO DEV,THE NATIONAL ECONOMIC DEVELOPMENT PLAN: 1961-66: SECOND PHASE 1964-66. THAILAND AGRI FINAN BUDGET EFFICIENCY INCOME...STAT CHARTS 20. PAGE 153 H3065 — ECO/UNDEV ECO/TAC PLAN NAT/G

B65
BURLING R.,HILL FARMS AND PADI FIELDS. BURMA S/ASIA THAILAND VIETNAM AGRI NEIGH SECT GP/REL NAT/LISM ORD/FREE 20 MID/EAST MIGRATION. PAGE 24 H0491 — SOCIETY STRUCT CULTURE SOVEREIGN

B65
KUNSTADTER P.,THE LUA (LAWA) OF NORTHERN THAILAND: ASPECTS OF SOCIAL STRUCTURE, AGRICULTURE, AND RELIGION. THAILAND AGRI FAM KIN INGP/REL ISOLAT MARRIAGE HEALTH WORSHIP 20 BUDDHISM LUA. PAGE 89 H1780 — STRUCT ECO/UNDEV CULTURE

B66
COEDES G.,THE MAKING OF SOUTH EAST ASIA. BURMA CAMBODIA LAOS S/ASIA THAILAND VIETNAM REV WAR CIVMIL/REL...GEOG 6/13. PAGE 31 H0614 — CULTURE FORCES DOMIN

THAILAND NATIONAL ECO DEV H3065
THAILAND NATL OFFICE STATE GOVT H2321
THE AFRICA 1960 COMMITTEE H3066

THE ECONOMIST (LONDON) H3067

THEOBALD R. H3068

THERAPY....SEE SPECIFICS, SUCH AS PROJ/TEST, DEEP/INT, SOC/EXP; ALSO SEE DIFFERENT VALUES (E.G., LOVE) AND TOPICAL TERMS (E.G., PRESS)

THEROUX P. H3069

THIBAUDET A. H3070

THIEN T.T. H3071

THIERRY S.S. H3072

THIESENHUSEN W.C. H3073

THING/STOR....ARTIFACTS AND MATERIAL EVIDENCE

THIRD/WRLD....THIRD WORLD - NONALIGNED NATIONS

B61
DUFFY J.,AFRICA SPEAKS. GHANA TOGO CULTURE ECO/UNDEV PROB/SOLV COLONIAL NEUTRAL DISCRIM NAT/LISM SOVEREIGN ALL/IDEOS...CONCPT ANTHOL SOC/INTEG 20 NEGRO THIRD/WRLD. PAGE 43 H0857 — AFR NAT/G FUT STRUCT

B63
JENNINGS W.I.,DEMOCRACY IN AFRICA. UK CULTURE STRUCT ECO/UNDEV DIPLOM COLONIAL GP/REL ADJUST NAT/LISM ORD/FREE...GOV/COMP 20 THIRD/WRLD. PAGE 81 H1613 — PROB/SOLV AFR CONSTN POPULISM

B63
JUDD P.,AFRICAN INDEPENDENCE: THE EXPLODING EMERGENCE OF THE NEW AFRICAN NATIONS. AFR UK LAW CONSTN CULTURE KIN DIPLOM ATTIT...CHARTS BIBLIOG 20 UN DEGAULLE/C NEGRO THIRD/WRLD. PAGE 82 H1640 — ORD/FREE POLICY DOMIN LOC/G

S63
ROBINSON W.C.,"URBANIZATION AND FERTILITY: THE NON-WESTERN EXPERIENCE (BMR)" DEATH MARRIAGE AGE/C BIO/SOC...STAT CENSUS CON/ANAL CHARTS NAT/COMP 20 THIRD/WRLD. PAGE 133 H2651 — GEOG MUNIC FAM ECO/UNDEV

B64
BERRINGTON H.,HOW NATIONS ARE GOVERNED. FRANCE WOR+45 ECO/UNDEV INT/ORG POL/PAR CHOOSE TOTALISM KNOWL...MAJORIT T 20 UN COMMONWLTH THIRD/WRLD. PAGE 16 H0320 — NAT/G GOV/COMP ECO/DEV CONSTN

B64
TINKER H.,BALLOT BOX AND BAYONET - PEOPLE AND GOVERNMENT IN EMERGENT ASIAN COUNTRIES. CEYLON INDIA INDONESIA PHILIPPINE POL/PAR ADMIN COLONIAL LEAD PARL/PROC CHOOSE CONSEN ORD/FREE SOVEREIGN PLURISM...GOV/COMP THIRD/WRLD. PAGE 155 H3104 — MYTH S/ASIA NAT/COMP NAT/LISM

B64
VOELKMANN K.,HERRSCHER VON MORGEN? BAL/PWR COLONIAL NEUTRAL REGION RACE/REL ALL/VALS SOVEREIGN...RECORD 20 COLD/WAR THIRD/WRLD. PAGE 163 H3259 — DIPLOM ECO/UNDEV CONTROL NAT/COMP

B66
DODGE D.,AFRICAN POLITICS IN PERSPECTIVE. ELITES POL/PAR PROB/SOLV LEAD...POLICY 20 THIRD/WRLD. PAGE 41 H0831 — AFR NAT/G COLONIAL SOVEREIGN

L67
TABORSKY E.,"THE COMMUNIST PARTIES OF THE 'THIRD WORLD' IN SOVIET STRATEGY." AFR ASIA L/A+17C USSR INTELL NAT/G WORKER PLAN CONTROL LEAD PARTIC REV ...GOV/COMP 20 COM/PARTY THIRD/WRLD. PAGE 152 H3032 — POL/PAR MARXISM ECO/UNDEV DIPLOM

S68
KANET R.E.,"RECENT SOVIET REASSESSMENT OF DEVELOPMENTS IN THE THIRD WORLD." ALGERIA GHANA INDONESIA USSR WOR+45 CONSTN ELITES INTELL STRUCT DOMIN CONTROL REV PWR MARXISM...IDEA/COMP METH 20 THIRD/WRLD. PAGE 83 H1653 — DIPLOM NEUTRAL NAT/G NAT/COMP

THOM J.M. H3074

THOMAN R.S. H3075

THOMAS D.H. H3076

THOMAS F.C. H3077

THOMAS P. H3078

THOMAS/FA....F.A. THOMAS

THOMAS/N....NORMAN THOMAS

THOMAS/TK....TREVOR K. THOMAS

THOMPSON D. H3079

THOMPSON E.T. H3080

THOMPSON F.M.L. H3081

THOMPSON J.H. H3082

THOMPSON J.M. H3083

THOMPSON J.W. H3084

THOMPSON V. H3085

THORBECKE E. H1045

THORBURN H.G. H3086

THORD-GRAY I. H3087

THOREAU/H....HENRY THOREAU

THORNBURG M.W. H3088

THORNTN/WT....WILLIAM T. THORNTON

THORNTON M.J. H3089

THORNTON T.P. H3090

THUCYDIDES H3091

THUCYDIDES....THUCYDIDES

THUMM G.W. H2709

THURSTON/L....LOUIS LEON THURSTONE

TIBET....TIBET; SEE ALSO ASIA, CHINA

B58
STUBEL H.,THE MEWU FANTZU. CHINA/COM INDIA EDU/PROP ADJUD CRIME GP/REL OWN...OBS 20 TIBET. PAGE 150 H3001 — CULTURE STRUCT SECT FAM

B60
MORAES F.,THE REVOLT IN TIBET. ASIA CHINA/COM INDIA CULTURE CONTROL COERCE WAR TOTALISM...POLICY SOC WORSHIP 20 TIBET INTERVENT. PAGE 113 H2252 — COLONIAL FORCES DIPLOM ORD/FREE

S60
GINSBURGS G.,"PEKING-LHASA-NEW DELHI." CHINA/COM FUT INDIA S/ASIA KIN NAT/G PROVS SECT FORCES BAL/PWR ECO/TAC DOMIN EDU/PROP LEGIT ADMIN REGION GUERRILLA PWR...TREND TIBET 20. PAGE 57 H1134 — ASIA COERCE DIPLOM

S62
SARKISYANZ E.,"NATIONALISM, CAPITALISM, AND THE UNCOMMITED NATIONS: MARXISM AND ASIAN CULTURAL — S/ASIA SECT

TRADITIONS." ASIA BURMA CHINA/COM COM CULTURE SOCIETY NAT/G POL/PAR PLAN DOMIN EDU/PROP COLONIAL COERCE ATTIT RIGID/FLEX...CONCPT TREND MARX/KARL 20 TIBET BUDDHISM. PAGE 138 H2755 NAT/LISM CAP/ISM

B67
SHAKABPA T.W.D.,TIBET: A POLITICAL HISTORY. CHINA/COM UK CHIEF LEAD...INT BIBLIOG 20 TIBET. PAGE 142 H2839 DIPLOM SECT NAT/G

TIERNEY B. H3092

TIGNOR R.L. H0635

TIKHOMIROV I.A. H3093

TILLICH/P....PAUL TILLICH

TILLION G. H3094

TILLY C. H3095

TILMAN R.O. H3096,H3097,H3098

TIME (AS CONCEPT)....SEE CONCPT

TIME....TIMING, TIME FACTOR; SEE ALSO ANALYSIS OF TEMPORAL SEQUENCES INDEX, P. XIV

B13
SIEGFRIED A.,TABLEAU POLITIQUE DE LA FRANCE DE L'OUEST SOUS LA TROISIEME REPUBLIQUE. FRANCE STRATA STRUCT NAT/G POL/PAR PROVS REGION GOV/REL ATTIT PWR ...TREND TIME 19. PAGE 143 H2869 SOC GEOG SOCIETY

B47
ISAAC J.,ECONOMICS OF MIGRATION. MOD/EUR CULTURE STRATA STRUCT NAT/G COLONIAL WEALTH...OLD/LIB TREND TIME 19/20 EUROPE/W MIGRATION. PAGE 78 H1569 HABITAT SOC GEOG

B57
SCHLESINGER J.A.,HOW THEY BECAME GOVERNOR; A STUDY OF COMPARATIVE STATE POLITICS, 1870-1950. USA+45 USA-45 LAW POL/PAR LEGIS EDU/PROP REGION...STAT TREND CHARTS TIME 19/20 GOVERNOR. PAGE 139 H2788 PROVS CHIEF GOV/COMP CHOOSE

B59
DUNHAM H.W.,SOCIOLOGICAL THEORY AND MENTAL DISORDER. UNIV SOCIETY STRATA HABITAT PERSON...GEOG CHARTS SOC/EXP TIME. PAGE 43 H0864 HEALTH SOC PSY CULTURE

B60
STRACHEY J.,THE END OF EMPIRE. UK WOR+45 WOR-45 DIPLOM INT/TRADE DOMIN ADJUST ORD/FREE WEALTH ...SOCIALIST GOV/COMP TIME COMMONWLTH. PAGE 150 H2991 COLONIAL ECO/DEV BAL/PWR LAISSEZ

B64
CAPLOW T.,PRINCIPLES OF ORGANIZATION. UNIV CULTURE STRUCT CREATE INGP/REL UTOPIA...GEN/LAWS TIME. PAGE 26 H0526 VOL/ASSN CONCPT SIMUL EX/STRUC

B64
MCCALL D.F.,AFRICA IN TIME PERSPECTIVE. AFR EXTR/IND KIN SECT CREATE PERS/REL HABITAT...GEOG METH/CNCPT LING BIBLIOG/A TIME 20. PAGE 106 H2124 HIST/WRIT OBS/ENVIR CULTURE

B65
ROMEIN J.,THE ASIAN CENTURY. ASIA COM S/ASIA DIPLOM COLONIAL TIME 20. PAGE 133 H2666 REV NAT/LISM CULTURE MARXISM

S65
BIRNBAUM K.,"SWEDEN'S NUCLEAR POLICY." WOR+45 POL/PAR CREATE TEC/DEV NEUTRAL RISK WAR ORD/FREE ...DECISION IDEA/COMP NAT/COMP TIME. PAGE 17 H0343 SWEDEN NUC/PWR DIPLOM ARMS/CONT

S65
PLANK J.N.,"THE CARIBBEAN* INTERVENTION, WHEN AND HOW." CUBA GUATEMALA HAITI PANAMA USA+45 VENEZUELA FORCES PROB/SOLV RISK COERCE...NAT/COMP OAS TIME. PAGE 126 H2521 SOVEREIGN MARXISM REV

S65
WATT D.C.,"RESTRICTIONS ON RESEARCH* THE FIFTY-YEAR RULE AND BRITISH FOREIGN POLICY." ACADEM PERCEPT ...HIST/WRIT NAT/COMP TIME. PAGE 166 H3315 UK USA+45 DIPLOM

S65
WOHLSTETTER R.,"CUBA AND PEARL HARBOR* HINDSIGHT AND FORESIGHT." USSR FORCES OP/RES TEC/DEV ATTIT PERCEPT...DECISION IDEA/COMP NAT/COMP STERTYP TIME. PAGE 170 H3395 CUBA RISK WAR ACT/RES

B66
BROWN R.T.,TRANSPORT AND THE ECONOMIC INTEGRATION OF SOUTH AMERICA. L/A+17C ECO/UNDEV NAT/G OP/RES DIPLOM INT/TRADE REGION WEALTH...ECOMETRIC GEOG STAT LAFTA TIME. PAGE 22 H0449 MARKET DIST/IND SIMUL

B66
BUTLER D.E.,THE BRITISH GENERAL ELECTION OF 1966. UK LOC/G NAT/G OP/RES CONFER CHOOSE MAJORITY ATTIT ...CHARTS TIME 20. PAGE 25 H0498 POL/PAR REPRESENT GP/REL PERS/REL

S66
DETTER I.,"THE PROBLEM OF UNEQUAL TREATIES." CONSTN NAT/G LEGIS COLONIAL COERCE PWR...GEOG UN TIME TREATY. PAGE 40 H0796 SOVEREIGN DOMIN INT/LAW ECO/UNDEV

TIME/SEQ....CHRONOLOGY AND GENETIC SERIES

N
JOURNAL OF MODERN HISTORY. WOR+45 WOR-45 LEAD WAR ...TIME/SEQ TREND NAT/COMP 20. PAGE 1 H0006 BIBLIOG/A DIPLOM NAT/G

N
CHINA QUARTERLY. COM AGRI INDUS ACADEM POL/PAR INT/TRADE CONFER GOV/REL...TIME/SEQ CON/ANAL INDEX 20. PAGE 1 H0014 BIBLIOG/A ASIA DIPLOM POLICY

B00
MARKHAM V.R.,SOUTH AFRICA, PAST AND PRESENT. NETHERLAND SOUTH/AFR CULTURE LEGIS EDU/PROP COLONIAL CHOOSE REPRESENT DISCRIM ATTIT...OBS TIME/SEQ 17/19 NEGRO BOER/WAR. PAGE 103 H2054 WAR LEAD RACE/REL

B00
VOLPICELLI Z.,RUSSIA ON THE PACIFIC AND THE SIBERIAN RAILWAY. MOD/EUR ECO/UNDEV INT/ORG FORCES PLAN DOMIN COLONIAL ROUTINE ATTIT ALL/VALS...OBS HIST/WRIT TIME/SEQ TREND CON/ANAL AUD/VIS CHARTS 18/19. PAGE 163 H3261 NAT/G ACT/RES RUSSIA

B04
DANTE ALIGHIERI,DE MONARCHIA (CA .1310). CHRIST-17C ITALY DOMIN LEGIT ATTIT PWR...CATH CONCPT TIME/SEQ. PAGE 37 H0741 SECT NAT/G SOVEREIGN

B12
HOBSON J.A.,THE EVOLUTION OF MODERN CAPITALISM. MOD/EUR UK STRATA ECO/DEV INDUS INCOME UTIL WEALTH ...SOC GEN/LAWS 7/20. PAGE 72 H1440 CAP/ISM WORKER TEC/DEV TIME/SEQ

B14
BERHARDI F.,GERMANY AND THE NEXT WAR. MOD/EUR NAT/G SCHOOL FORCES ACT/RES DOMIN EDU/PROP SUPEGO PWR ...TIME/SEQ STERTYP TOT/POP 20 WWI. PAGE 15 H0304 DRIVE COERCE WAR GERMANY

B16
TREITSCHKE H.,POLITICS. UNIV SOCIETY STRATA NAT/G EX/STRUC LEGIS DOMIN EDU/PROP ATTIT PWR RESPECT ...CONCPT TIME/SEQ GEN/LAWS TOT/POP 20. PAGE 157 H3129 EXEC ELITES GERMANY

B20
HALDANE R.B.,BEFORE THE WAR. MOD/EUR SOCIETY INT/ORG NAT/G DELIB/GP PLAN DOMIN EDU/PROP LEGIT ADMIN COERCE ATTIT DRIVE MORAL ORD/FREE PWR...SOC CONCPT SELF/OBS RECORD BIOG TIME/SEQ. PAGE 64 H1282 POLICY DIPLOM UK

B21
BERGSTRASSER L.,GESCHICHTE DER POLITISCHEN PARTEIEN. GERMANY MOD/EUR NAT/G PRESS PWR ...TIME/SEQ 17/20. PAGE 15 H0303 POL/PAR LAISSEZ CONSERVE

B21
STUART G.H.,FRENCH FOREIGN POLICY. CONSTN INT/ORG NAT/G POL/PAR EX/STRUC FORCES PLAN ECO/TAC DOMIN EDU/PROP ADJUD COERCE ATTIT DRIVE RIGID/FLEX ALL/VALS...POLICY OBS RECORD BIOG TIME/SEQ TREND. PAGE 150 H3000 MOD/EUR DIPLOM FRANCE

B22
OGBURN W.F.,SOCIAL CHANGE WITH RESPECT TO CULTURE AND ORIGINAL NATURE. ACT/RES OP/RES CRIME GP/REL ANOMIE BIO/SOC PWR...PSY SOC TIME/SEQ METH SOC/INTEG. PAGE 120 H2405 CULTURE CREATE TEC/DEV

B23
FRANK T.,A HISTORY OF ROME. MEDIT-7 INTELL SOCIETY LOC/G NAT/G POL/PAR FORCES LEGIS DOMIN LEGIT ALL/VALS...POLICY CONCPT TIME/SEQ GEN/LAWS ROM/EMP ROM/EMP. PAGE 53 H1050 EXEC STRUCT ELITES

B25
TEMPERLEY H.,THE FOREIGN POLICY OF CANNING: 1822-1827. MOD/EUR NAT/G TOP/EX EDU/PROP ROUTINE ATTIT RIGID/FLEX SUPEGO PWR SKILL...TIME/SEQ PARLIAMENT 20. PAGE 153 H3058 PERSON DIPLOM UK BIOG

B26
MACIVER R.M.,THE MODERN STATE. POL/PAR ORD/FREE TIME/SEQ. PAGE 100 H1997 NAT/G CONCPT JURID SOVEREIGN

B26
POLLARD A.F.,THE EVOLUTION OF PARLIAMENT. UK CONSTN POL/PAR EX/STRUC GOV/REL INGP/REL PRIVIL RIGID/FLEX ...TIME/SEQ 11/20 CMN/WLTH PARLIAMENT. PAGE 127 H2536 LEGIS PARL/PROC NAT/G

B26
TAWNEY R.H.,RELIGION AND THE RISE OF CAPITALISM. UK CULTURE NAT/G TEC/DEV OWN LAISSEZ...POLICY SOC TIME/SEQ 16/19. PAGE 153 H3050 SECT WEALTH INDUS CAP/ISM

B27
FLOURNOY F.,PARLIAMENT AND WAR. MOD/EUR UK NAT/G FORCES LEGIS TOP/EX DIPLOM LEGIT DEBATE ATTIT RIGID/FLEX PWR...DECISION TIME/SEQ PARLIAMENT COERCE WAR

19/20. PAGE 52 H1032

B28
CORBETT P.E.,CANADA AND WORLD POLITICS. LAW CULTURE SOCIETY STRUCT MARKET INT/ORG FORCES ACT/RES PLAN ECO/TAC LEGIT ORD/FREE PWR RESPECT...SOC CONCPT TIME/SEQ TREND CMN/WLTH 20 LEAGUE/NAT. PAGE 33 H0662
NAT/G CANADA

B28
FYFE H.,THE BRITISH LIBERAL PARTY. UK SECT ADMIN LEAD CHOOSE GP/REL PWR SOCISM...MAJORIT TIME/SEQ 19/20 LIB/PARTY CONSRV/PAR. PAGE 54 H1084
POL/PAR NAT/G REPRESENT POPULISM

B28
HURST C.,GREAT BRITAIN AND THE DOMINIONS. EUR+WWI CULTURE ECO/DEV INT/ORG NAT/G DIPLOM ECO/TAC COLONIAL ATTIT PWR SOVEREIGN...TIME/SEQ GEN/LAWS TOT/POP VAL/FREE 20 CMN/WLTH. PAGE 75 H1508
VOL/ASSN DOMIN UK

B28
SOROKIN P.,CONTEMPORARY SOCIOLOGICAL THEORIES. MOD/EUR UNIV SOCIETY R+D SCHOOL ECO/TAC EDU/PROP ROUTINE ATTIT DRIVE...PSY CONCPT TIME/SEQ TREND GEN/LAWS 20. PAGE 147 H2934
CULTURE SOC WAR

B29
DAVIE M.R.,THE EVOLUTION OF WAR. CULTURE KIN COERCE WAR ATTIT DRIVE...PSY SOC TIME/SEQ TREND GEN/LAWS. PAGE 37 H0746
FORCES STERTYP

B29
LANGER W.L.,THE FRANCO-RUSSIAN ALLIANCE: 1890-1894. FRANCE MOD/EUR UK USSR NAT/G CHIEF FORCES BAL/PWR AGREE WAR PEACE PWR...TIME/SEQ TREATY 19 BISMARCK/O. PAGE 91 H1809
DIPLOM

B31
BONAR J.,THEORIES OF POPULATION FROM RALEIGH TO ARTHUR YOUNG. CHRIST-17C MOD/EUR CULTURE SOCIETY R+D CREATE ATTIT PERCEPT RIGID/FLEX...OLD/LIB CONCPT NEW/IDEA TIME/SEQ IDEA/COMP STERTYP GEN/LAWS. PAGE 19 H0372
GEOG BIOG

B31
CROOK W.H.,THE GENERAL STRIKE: A STUDY OF LABOR'S TRAGIC WEAPON IN THEORY AND PRACTICE. BELGIUM FRANCE SWEDEN UK WOR-45 PROB/SOLV ECO/TAC DOMIN PWR ...POLICY TIME/SEQ NAT/COMP GEN/LAWS 19/20 STRIKE. PAGE 35 H0707
LABOR WORKER LG/CO BARGAIN

B32
BRYCE J.,THE HOLY ROMAN EMPIRE. GERMANY ITALY MOD/EUR CULTURE SOCIETY STRUCT INT/ORG NAT/G SECT DIPLOM DOMIN WAR SUPEGO ALL/VALS SOVEREIGN...GEOG SOC TIME/SEQ CHARTS STERTYP. PAGE 23 H0456
CHRIST-17C NAT/LISM

B32
LUNT D.C.,THE ROAD TO THE LAW. UK USA-45 LEGIS EDU/PROP OWN ORD/FREE...DECISION TIME/SEQ NAT/COMP 16/20 AUSTRAL ENGLSH/LAW COMMON/LAW. PAGE 99 H1980
ADJUD LAW JURID CT/SYS

S32
BEARD C.A.,"REPRESENTATIVE GOVERNMENT IN EVOLUTION" WOR-45 AGRI TEC/DEV DOMIN EFFICIENCY ORD/FREE CONSERVE...TIME/SEQ GOV/COMP IDEA/COMP GRECO/ROMN. PAGE 12 H0248
REPRESENT POPULISM NAT/G PWR

B36
HUBERMAN L.,MAN'S WORLDLY GOODS: THE STORY OF THE WEALTH OF NATIONS. CHRIST-17C EUR+WWI MOD/EUR SOCIETY DOMIN REV ORD/FREE...TIME/SEQ METH/COMP. PAGE 74 H1486
WEALTH CAP/ISM MARXISM CREATE

B36
LAPRADE W.T.,PUBLIC OPINION AND POLITICS IN EIGHTEENTH CENTURY ENGLAND. UK CULTURE POL/PAR CHIEF TOP/EX LEAD REV NAT/LISM PWR 18 PROTESTANT PROTESTANT CHURCH/STA. PAGE 91 H1815
POLICY ELITES ATTIT TIME/SEQ

B37
CARLYLE T.,THE FRENCH REVOLUTION (2 VOLS.). FRANCE CONSTN NAT/G FORCES COERCE MURDER PEACE MORAL POPULISM...TIME/SEQ IDEA/COMP GEN/LAWS 18. PAGE 26 H0532
REV CHIEF TRADIT

B37
CLOKIE H.M.,ROYAL COMMISSIONS OF INQUIRY; THE SIGNIFICANCE OF INVESTIGATIONS IN BRITISH POLITICS. UK POL/PAR CONFER ROUTINE...POLICY DECISION TIME/SEQ 16/20. PAGE 30 H0607
NAT/G DELIB/GP INSPECT

L37
NICOLSON H.,"THE MEANING OF PRESTIGE." EUR+WWI MOD/EUR UK CULTURE SOCIETY NAT/G DIPLOM DOMIN LEGIT ATTIT DRIVE PWR...METH/CNCPT RECORD TIME/SEQ GEN/METH CMN/WLTH TOT/POP 20. PAGE 118 H2351
CONCPT STERTYP

B40
JORDAN W.K.,THE DEVELOPMENT OF RELIGIOUS TOLERATION IN ENGLAND. CHRIST-17C CULTURE SOCIETY LEGIT ATTIT RESPECT...POLICY CONCPT RECORD TIME/SEQ STERTYP GEN/LAWS TOT/POP 16/17. PAGE 82 H1635
SECT UK

B40
MCILWAIN C.H.,CONSTITUTIONALISM, ANCIENT AND MODERN. CHRIST-17C MOD/EUR NAT/G CHIEF PROB/SOLV INSPECT AUTHORIT ORD/FREE PWR...TIME/SEQ ROMAN/REP. PAGE 107 H2134
CONSTN GEN/LAWS LAW

B41
COHEN E.W.,THE GROWTH OF THE BRITISH CIVIL SERVICE 1780-1939. UK NAT/G SENIOR ROUTINE GOV/REL...MGT METH/COMP BIBLIOG 18/20. PAGE 31 H0616
OP/RES TIME/SEQ CENTRAL ADMIN

B41
HAUSHOFER K.,WEHR-GEOPOLITIK. EUR+WWI GERMANY MOD/EUR NAT/G ACT/RES BAL/PWR PWR...STAT TIME/SEQ CHARTS NAZI 20. PAGE 68 H1361
FORCES GEOG WAR

B43
SERENI A.P.,THE ITALIAN CONCEPTION OF INTERNATIONAL LAW. EUR+WWI MOD/EUR INT/ORG NAT/G DOMIN COERCE ORD/FREE FASCISM...OBS/ENVIR TREND 20. PAGE 141 H2829
LAW TIME/SEQ INT/LAW ITALY

B44
KNORR K.E.,BRITISH COLONIAL THEORIES 1570-1850. NAT/G DELIB/GP ECO/TAC PERCEPT PWR...WELF/ST METH/CNCPT CONT/OBS TIME/SEQ SIMUL TOT/POP 20. PAGE 87 H1734
ACT/RES DOMIN COLONIAL

L44
HUXLEY J.,"THE FUTURE OF THE COLONIES." AFR SOCIETY NAT/G PLAN DOMIN COERCE ATTIT DRIVE ORD/FREE PWR WEALTH...TIME/SEQ TREND AUD/VIS CHARTS 20. PAGE 76 H1511
ECO/UNDEV FUT COLONIAL

B45
CONOVER H.F.,THE NAZI STATE: WAR CRIMES AND WAR CRIMINALS. GERMANY CULTURE NAT/G SECT FORCES DIPLOM INT/TRADE EDU/PROP...INT/LAW BIOG HIST/WRIT TIME/SEQ 20. PAGE 32 H0647
BIBLIOG WAR CRIME

B45
LINTON R.,THE CULTURAL BACKGROUND OF PERSONALITY. UNIV PERSON ALL/VALS...SOC CONCPT TIME/SEQ GEN/METH TOT/POP VAL/FREE. PAGE 97 H1935
CULTURE ATTIT

B46
FEIBLEMAN J.,THE THEORY OF HUMAN CULTURE. UNIV CONSTN SOCIETY...CONCPT CLASSIF TIME/SEQ. PAGE 49 H0981
GEN/LAWS CULTURE SOC PHIL/SCI

B46
NICOLSON H.,THE CONGRESS OF VIENNA. MOD/EUR NAT/G FORCES BAL/PWR DOMIN LEGIT COERCE PERSON PWR ...RECORD TIME/SEQ STERTYP 19 CONG/VIENN. PAGE 118 H2353
CONCPT POLICY DIPLOM

B47
MCILWAIN C.H.,CONSTITUTIONALISM: ANCIENT AND MODERN. USA+45 ROMAN/EMP LAW CHIEF LEGIS CT/SYS GP/REL ORD/FREE SOVEREIGN...POLICY TIME/SEQ ROMAN/REP EUROPE. PAGE 107 H2135
CONSTN NAT/G PARL/PROC GOV/COMP

B48
TOYNBEE A.J.,CIVILIZATION ON TRIAL. FUT WOR-45 NAT/G CREATE CAP/ISM DIPLOM NUC/PWR CHOOSE MARXISM ...GEOG CONCPT WORSHIP. PAGE 156 H3125
SOCIETY TIME/SEQ NAT/COMP

B49
SARGENT S.S.,CULTURE AND PERSONALITY. FUT UNIV SOCIETY FAM KIN NEIGH BIO/SOC DRIVE PERCEPT RIGID/FLEX LOVE RESPECT...PSY SOC CONCPT OBS TIME/SEQ TREND CON/ANAL CHARTS HYPO/EXP SIMUL TOT/POP. PAGE 138 H2754
CULTURE PERSON

B49
SINGER K.,THE IDEA OF CONFLICT. UNIV INTELL INT/ORG NAT/G PLAN ROUTINE ATTIT DRIVE ALL/VALS...POLICY CONCPT TIME/SEQ. PAGE 144 H2882
ACT/RES SOC

B50
BERMAN H.J.,JUSTICE IN RUSSIA; AN INTERPRETATION OF SOVIET LAW. USSR LAW STRUCT LABOR FORCES AGREE GP/REL ORD/FREE SOCISM...TIME/SEQ 20. PAGE 15 H0309
JURID ADJUD MARXISM COERCE

B50
GOFF F.R.,FIFTEENTH CENTURY BOOKS IN THE LIBRARY OF CONGRESS. CHRIST-17C GERMANY ITALY CULTURE INTELL SECT CREATE...PHIL/SCI CONCPT CLASSIF BIOG TIME/SEQ 15. PAGE 58 H1153
BIBLIOG KNOWL HUM

B50
LIPSET S.M.,AGRARIAN SOCIALISM. CANADA POL/PAR OP/RES ECO/TAC ADMIN ATTIT...TIME/SEQ NAT/COMP SOC/EXP 20 SASKATCH. PAGE 97 H1938
SOCISM AGRI METH/COMP STRUCT

B50
TRAGER F.N.,MARXISM IN SOUTHEAST ASIA. BURMA INDONESIA THAILAND VIETNAM CULTURE SOCIETY NAT/G VOL/ASSN EXEC ROUTINE COERCE ATTIT RIGID/FLEX PWR ...METH/CNCPT TIME/SEQ STERTYP GEN/LAWS MARX/KARL VAL/FREE COLD/WAR NAM 20. PAGE 156 H3126
S/ASIA POL/PAR REV

B51
MUMFORD L.,THE CONDUCT OF LIFE. UNIV SOCIETY CREATE ...TECHNIC METH/CNCPT TIME/SEQ TREND GEN/LAWS BIBLIOG/A. PAGE 114 H2286
ALL/VALS CULTURE PERSON CONCPT

B52
KOLARZ W.,RUSSIA AND HER COLONIES. COM RUSSIA LAW CULTURE ECO/DEV KIN LOC/G SECT TEC/DEV ECO/TAC EDU/PROP REGION COERCE ATTIT PWR SOVEREIGN...SOC TIME/SEQ CON/ANAL VAL/FREE 19/20. PAGE 88 H1749
NAT/G DOMIN USSR COLONIAL

B52
WALTERS F.P.,A HISTORY OF THE LEAGUE OF NATIONS. EUR+WWI CONSTN NAT/G LEGIS TOP/EX ACT/RES PLAN EDU/PROP LEGIT ROUTINE ATTIT...TREND LEAGUE/NAT 20 CHINJAP. PAGE 165 H3297
INT/ORG TIME/SEQ NAT/LISM

MUEHLMANN W.E.,"L'IDEE NATIONALE ALLEMANDE ET L'IDEE NATIONALE FRANCAISE." EUR+WWI MOD/EUR SOCIETY KIN NAT/G PWR RESPECT...SOC CONCPT TIME/SEQ GEN/LAWS 19/20. PAGE 114 H2279 — S52 — CULTURE ATTIT FRANCE GERMANY

FIFIELD R.H.,"WOODROW WILSON AND THE FAR EAST." ASIA CHIEF DELIB/GP BAL/PWR CONFER COLONIAL ARMS/CONT WAR...TIME/SEQ NAT/COMP 19/20 WILSON/W LEAGUE/NAT. PAGE 50 H0995 — C52 — BIBLIOG DIPLOM INT/ORG

BUCHHEIM K.,GESCHICHTE DER CHRISTLICHEN PARTEIEN IN DEUTSCHLAND. GERMANY CREATE ATTIT SUPEGO ORD/FREE ...TIME/SEQ IDEA/COMP 19/20 CHRIS/DEM. PAGE 23 H0464 — B53 — POL/PAR NAT/G

KEESING F.M.,CULTURE CHANGE: AN ANALYSIS AND BIBLIOGRAPHY OF ANTHROPOLOGICAL SOURCES TO 1952. CULTURE STRUCT...TIME/SEQ 19/20. PAGE 84 H1679 — B53 — BIBLIOG SOC CREATE ORD/FREE

FRIEDRICH C.J.,TOTALITARIAN DICTATORSHIP AND AUTOCRACY. COM EUR+WWI GERMANY ITALY USSR INTELL ECO/DEV NAT/G POL/PAR FORCES TOP/EX ECO/TAC EDU/PROP LEGIT COERCE ATTIT ORD/FREE PWR FASCISM ...CONCPT TIME/SEQ GEN/LAWS NAZI 20. PAGE 53 H1068 — B54 — SOCIETY DOMIN TOTALISM

BRACHER K.D.,DIE AUFLOSUNG DER WEIMARER REPUBLIK. EUR+WWI GERMANY...TIME/SEQ 20. PAGE 20 H0395 — B55 — TOTALISM NAT/G POL/PAR PARL/PROC

FRIEDMAN G.,INDUSTRIAL SOCIETY: THE EMERGENCE OF THE HUMAN PROBLEMS OF AUTOMATION. UNIV CULTURE ECO/DEV TEC/DEV INGP/REL HAPPINESS RATIONAL UTOPIA ROLE...HUM SOC TIME/SEQ 20. PAGE 53 H1064 — B55 — AUTOMAT ADJUST ALL/VALS CONCPT

KHADDURI M.,WAR AND PEACE IN THE LAW OF ISLAM. CONSTN CULTURE SOCIETY STRATA NAT/G PROVS SECT FORCES TOP/EX CREATE DOMIN EDU/PROP ADJUD COERCE ATTIT RIGID/FLEX ALL/VALS...CONCPT TIME/SEQ TOT/POP VAL/FREE. PAGE 85 H1702 — B55 — ISLAM JURID PEACE WAR

KOHN H.,THE MIND OF MODERN RUSSIA. COM MOD/EUR USSR SOCIETY NAT/G SECT FORCES TOP/EX COERCE TOTALISM DRIVE RIGID/FLEX PWR SOVEREIGN...CONCPT TIME/SEQ WORK. PAGE 87 H1742 — B55 — INTELL GEN/LAWS SOCISM RUSSIA

NAMIER L.,PERSONALITIES AND POWERS. EUR+WWI MOD/EUR NAT/G POL/PAR TOP/EX EDU/PROP KNOWL...GEOG 17/20. PAGE 115 H2308 — B55 — TIME/SEQ DIPLOM UK

TOYNBEE A.,THE REALIGNMENT OF EUROPE. COM GREECE ITALY NAT/G BAL/PWR ECO/TAC EDU/PROP REV SOVEREIGN ...SOC TIME/SEQ TREND COLD/WAR 20. PAGE 156 H3123 — B55 — EUR+WWI PLAN USSR

ROSTOW W.W.,"RUSSIA AND CHINA UNDER COMMUNISM." CHINA/COM USSR INTELL STRUCT INT/ORG NAT/G POL/PAR TOP/EX ACT/RES PLAN ADMIN ATTIT ALL/VALS MARXISM ...CONCPT OBS TIME/SEQ TREND GOV/COMP VAL/FREE 20. PAGE 134 H2689 — L55 — COM ASIA

MUMFORD L.,THE TRANSFORMATIONS OF MAN. UNIV CULTURE INGP/REL HABITAT HEREDITY ALL/VALS ORD/FREE...MYTH TIME/SEQ TREND WORSHIP. PAGE 114 H2287 — B56 — IDEA/COMP PERSON CONCPT

DEAN V.M.,THE NATURE OF THE NON-WESTERN WORLD. AFR ASIA L/A+17C S/ASIA CULTURE SOCIETY STRATA ECO/DEV DIPLOM ECO/TAC FOR/AID ATTIT DRIVE ALL/VALS ...RELATIV SOC CONCPT TIME/SEQ TREND TOT/POP 20. PAGE 39 H0778 — B57 — ECO/UNDEV STERTYP NAT/LISM

KANTOROWICZ E.,THE KING'S TWO BODIES; A STUDY IN MEDIEVAL POLITICAL THEOLOGY. UK LAW CONSTN NAT/G CT/SYS...ART/METH HUM CONCPT MYTH TIME/SEQ BIBLIOG 4/17 ELIZABTH/I POPE CHURCH/STA. PAGE 83 H1657 — B57 — JURID SECT CHIEF SOVEREIGN

LAQUER W.Z.,COMMUNISM AND NATIONALISM IN THE MIDDLE EAST. ELITES INTELL STRATA NAT/G POL/PAR SECT VOL/ASSN TOP/EX DOMIN LEGIT REGION COERCE ATTIT PERSON PWR...CONCPT HIST/WRIT TIME/SEQ TREND GEN/LAWS VAL/FREE. PAGE 91 H1817 — B57 — ISLAM NAT/LISM

NEUMANN S.,"COMPARATIVE POLITICS: A HALF CENTURY APPRAISAL" USA+45 USA-45...SOC TIME/SEQ TREND NAT/COMP METH 20. PAGE 117 H2339 — S57 — PHIL/SCI GOV/COMP GEN/METH

SPROUT H.,"ENVIRONMENTAL FACTORS IN THE STUDY OF INTERNATIONAL POLITICS." UNIV SOCIETY ECO/DEV NAT/G DELIB/GP TOP/EX ROUTINE ATTIT PERCEPT...POLICY GEOG CONCPT MYTH TIME/SEQ. PAGE 148 H2957 — S57 — DECISION GEN/LAWS DIPLOM

COLEMAN J.S.,NIGERIA: BACKGROUND TO NATIONALISM. AFR SOCIETY ECO/DEV KIN LOC/G POL/PAR TEC/DEV DOMIN ADMIN DRIVE PWR RESPECT...TRADIT SOC INT SAMP TIME/SEQ 20. PAGE 31 H0627 — B58 — NAT/G NAT/LISM NIGERIA

OGDEN F.D.,THE POLL TAX IN THE SOUTH. USA+45 USA-45 CONSTN ADJUD ADMIN PARTIC CRIME...TIME/SEQ GOV/COMP METH/COMP 18/20 SOUTH/US. PAGE 120 H2407 — B58 — TAX CHOOSE RACE/REL DISCRIM

STRAUSZ-HUPE R.,THE IDEA OF COLONIALISM. WOR+45 WOR-45 BAL/PWR GOV/REL...POLICY CLASSIF TIME/SEQ GOV/COMP ANTHOL 20 UN. PAGE 150 H2996 — B58 — IDEA/COMP COLONIAL CONTROL CONCPT

CHODOROV F.,THE RISE AND FALL OF SOCIETY. NAT/G CONTROL ORD/FREE...TIME/SEQ 20. PAGE 30 H0596 — B59 — SOC INGP/REL ECO/DEV ATTIT

LAQUER W.Z.,THE SOVIET UNION AND THE MIDDLE EAST. COM UAR USSR ECO/UNDEV NAT/G VOL/ASSN ECO/TAC EDU/PROP COLONIAL EXEC PWR...TIME/SEQ TREND COLD/WAR 20. PAGE 91 H1819 — B59 — ISLAM DRIVE FOR/AID NAT/LISM

WARNER W.L.,THE LIVING AND THE DEAD: A STUDY OF SYMBOLIC LIFE OF AMERICANS. INTELL KIN DEATH ALL/VALS ALL/IDEOS...CONCPT MYTH LING OBS/ENVIR CHARTS BIBLIOG WORSHIP 18/20. PAGE 165 H3311 — B59 — CULTURE SOC TIME/SEQ IDEA/COMP

LEVINE R.A.,"ANTI-EUROPEAN VIOLENCE IN AFRICA: A COMPARATIVE ANALYSIS." AFR CULTURE NAT/G DIPLOM EDU/PROP COLONIAL REGION COERCE ATTIT PWR...PSY CONCPT TIME/SEQ TREND HYPO/EXP SOC/EXP STERTYP GEN/METH COLD/WAR 20. PAGE 95 H1903 — S59 — DRIVE ORD/FREE REV

SILBERMAN L.,"CHANGE AND CONFLICT IN THE HORN OF AFRICA." EUR+WWI ITALY UK CULTURE FORCES ECO/TAC ADJUD COLONIAL ATTIT ORD/FREE PWR...DECISION METH/CNCPT HIST/WRIT SOMALI 20. PAGE 144 H2874 — S59 — AFR TIME/SEQ

ZAUBERMAN A.,"SOVIET BLOC ECONOMIC INTEGRATION." COM CULTURE INTELL ECO/DEV INDUS TOP/EX ACT/RES PLAN ECO/TAC INT/TRADE ROUTINE CHOOSE ATTIT ...TIME/SEQ 20. PAGE 172 H3452 — S59 — MARKET INT/ORG USSR TOTALISM

BARBU Z.,PROBLEMS OF HISTORICAL PSYCHOLOGY. GREECE MEDIT-7 UK CULTURE TEC/DEV ADJUST RATIONAL ATTIT PERCEPT...METH/CNCPT NEW/IDEA TIME/SEQ GEN/METH. PAGE 11 H0214 — B60 — PERSON PSY HIST/WRIT IDEA/COMP

BOZEMAN A.B.,POLITICS AND CULTURE IN INTERNATIONAL HISTORY. WOR-45 STRUCT SECT...SOC TIME/SEQ NAT/COMP BIBLIOG. PAGE 20 H0393 — B60 — CULTURE DIPLOM GOV/COMP ALL/IDEOS

CARTER G.M.,INDEPENDENCE FOR AFRICA. AFR FUT SOCIETY STRATA ECO/DEV POL/PAR DELIB/GP PLAN DOMIN EDU/PROP COLONIAL REGION ATTIT DRIVE SOVEREIGN ...RECORD INT TIME/SEQ CHARTS 20. PAGE 27 H0544 — B60 — NAT/G PWR NAT/LISM

EASTON S.C.,THE TWILIGHT OF EUROPEAN COLONIALISM. AFR S/ASIA CONSTN SOCIETY STRUCT ECO/UNDEV INDUS NAT/G FORCES ECO/TAC COLONIAL CT/SYS ATTIT KNOWL ORD/FREE PWR...SOCIALIST TIME/SEQ TREND CON/ANAL 20. PAGE 44 H0882 — B60 — FINAN ADMIN

JEMOLO A.C.,CHURCH AND STATE IN ITALY 1850-1950 (TRANS. BY DAVID MOORE). ITALY CONSTN STRATA WAR FASCISM SOCISM...TIME/SEQ 19/20 CHURCH/STA CHRIS/DEM. PAGE 80 H1599 — B60 — GP/REL NAT/G CATHISM POL/PAR

LISTER L.,EUROPE'S COAL AND STEEL COMMUNITY. FRANCE GERMANY STRUCT ECO/DEV EXTR/IND INDUS MARKET NAT/G DELIB/GP ECO/TAC INT/TRADE EDU/PROP ATTIT RIGID/FLEX ORD/FREE PWR WEALTH...CONCPT STAT TIME/SEQ CHARTS ECSC 20. PAGE 97 H1941 — B60 — EUR+WWI INT/ORG REGION

MACRIDIS R.C.,THE DE GAULLE REPUBLIC: QUEST FOR UNITY. EUR+WWI NAT/G POL/PAR LEGIS LEGIT NAT/LISM ATTIT RIGID/FLEX ORD/FREE PWR...JURID CONCPT TIME/SEQ 20 DEGAULLE/C. PAGE 100 H2009 — B60 — TOP/EX STRUCT FRANCE

MAYO H.B.,AN INTRODUCTION TO DEMOCRATIC THEORY. ORD/FREE...POLICY TIME/SEQ GOV/COMP STERTYP. PAGE 105 H2109 — B60 — POPULISM CONCPT IDEA/COMP

SCHAPIRO L.,THE COMMUNIST PARTY OF THE SOVIET UNION. COM LAW SOCIETY STRATA STRUCT ECO/DEV LABOR NAT/G POL/PAR CREATE DOMIN EDU/PROP COERCE TOTALISM MARXISM...POLICY CONCPT MYTH TIME/SEQ WORK TOT/POP 20 LENIN/VI STALIN/J. PAGE 139 H2772 — B60 — INTELL PWR USSR

WOLF C.,FOREIGN AID: THEORY AND PRACTICE IN SOUTHERN ASIA. CEYLON INDONESIA PHILIPPINE S/ASIA CULTURE STRATA ECO/UNDEV PLAN EDU/PROP ATTIT ...METH/CNCPT MATH QUANT STAT CONT/OBS TIME/SEQ SIMUL TOT/POP 20. PAGE 170 H3396 — B60 — ACT/RES ECO/TAC FOR/AID

KAPLAN M.A.,"COMMUNIST COUP IN CZECHOSLOVAKIA." COM STRUCT — L60

EUR+WWI INTELL LABOR LOC/G NAT/G POL/PAR FORCES EDU/PROP EXEC MARXISM...TIME/SEQ HYPO/EXP 20. PAGE 83 H1659 — COERCE CZECHOSLVK

S60
"THE EMERGING COMMON MARKETS IN LATIN AMERICA." FUT L/A+17C STRATA DIST/IND INDUS LABOR NAT/G LEGIS ECO/TAC ADMIN RIGID/FLEX HEALTH...NEW/IDEA TIME/SEQ OAS 20. PAGE 2 H0038 — FINAN ECO/UNDEV INT/TRADE

S60
EMERSON R.,"THE EROSION OF DEMOCRACY." AFR FUT LAW CULTURE INTELL SOCIETY ECO/UNDEV FAM LOC/G NAT/G FORCES PLAN TEC/DEV ECO/TAC ADMIN CT/SYS ATTIT ORD/FREE PWR...SOCIALIST SOC CONCPT STAND/INT TIME/SEQ WORK 20. PAGE 46 H0918 — S/ASIA POL/PAR

S60
FRANKEL S.H.,"ECONOMIC ASPECTS OF POLITICAL INDEPENDENCE IN AFRICA." AFR FUT SOCIETY ECO/UNDEV COM/IND FINAN LEGIS PLAN TEC/DEV CAP/ISM ECO/TAC INT/TRADE ADMIN ATTIT DRIVE RIGID/FLEX PWR WEALTH ...MGT NEW/IDEA MATH TIME/SEQ VAL/FREE 20. PAGE 53 H1052 — NAT/G FOR/AID

S60
HOWARD M.,"BRITAIN'S DEFENSE: COMMITMENTS AND CAPABILITIES." EUR+WWI ECO/DEV NAT/G FORCES LEGIS PLAN DETER ORD/FREE WEALTH...POLICY CONCPT TIME/SEQ GEN/METH 20. PAGE 74 H1481 — FUT PWR DIPLOM UK

S60
LEVINE R.A.,"THE INTERNALIZATION OF POLITICAL VALUES IN STATELESS SOCIETIES." AFR FAM KIN LOC/G PROVS JUDGE PERSON RIGID/FLEX...DECISION SOC TIME/SEQ 20. PAGE 95 H1904 — CULTURE ATTIT

S60
MURPHEY R.,"ECONOMIC CONFLICTS IN SOUTH ASIA." ASIA CULTURE INTELL ECO/TAC REGION ATTIT DRIVE KNOWL ...METH/CNCPT TIME/SEQ STERTYP TOT/POP VAL/FREE 20. PAGE 115 H2296 — S/ASIA ECO/UNDEV

S60
NORTH R.C.,"THE NEW EXPANSIONISM." ASIA CHINA/COM FUT INDIA CULTURE SOCIETY NAT/G TOP/EX DOMIN COERCE PWR MARXISM...CONCPT TIME/SEQ TREND GEN/LAWS COLD/WAR 20 MAO. PAGE 119 H2372 — ATTIT DRIVE NAT/LISM

S60
NORTHEDGE F.S.,"BRITISH FOREIGN POLICY AND THE PARTY SYSTEM." EUR+WWI FUT INT/ORG NAT/G EDU/PROP ATTIT PWR...POLICY CONCPT MYTH TIME/SEQ TREND 20 UN. PAGE 119 H2374 — POL/PAR CHOOSE DIPLOM UK

S60
PERLMANN H.,"UPHEAVAL IN TURKEY." EUR+WWI ISLAM NAT/G FORCES TOP/EX LEGIT COERCE CHOOSE DRIVE ORD/FREE PWR...TIME/SEQ TOT/POP 20. PAGE 125 H2494 — CONSTN TURKEY

S60
TAUBER K.,"ASPECTS OF NATIONALIST-COMMUNIST COLLABORATION IN POSTWAR GERMANY." COM EUR+WWI USSR NAT/G VOL/ASSN ATTIT DRIVE PWR...TIME/SEQ COLD/WAR TOT/POP 20. PAGE 152 H3049 — POL/PAR EDU/PROP GERMANY

S60
TIRYAKIAN E.A.,"APARTHEID AND POLITICS IN SOUTH AFRICA." SOUTH/AFR CULTURE STRATA ECO/DEV NAT/G POL/PAR ROUTINE CHOOSE GP/REL RACE/REL DISCRIM ATTIT ALL/VALS...CONCPT OBS TIME/SEQ VAL/FREE 20. PAGE 155 H3105 — AFR DIPLOM

S60
WYCKOFF T.,"THE ROLE OF THE MILITARY IN LATIN AMERICAN POLITICS." L/A+17C CONSTN CULTURE ECO/UNDEV POL/PAR FORCES LEGIS TOP/EX LEGIT GUERRILLA REV CHOOSE ORD/FREE PWR...TIME/SEQ VAL/FREE 20. PAGE 171 H3430 — NAT/G COERCE TOTALISM

B61
AIYAR S.P.,FEDERALISM AND SOCIAL CHANGE. CANADA CULTURE STRUCT PLAN PROB/SOLV TEC/DEV ECO/TAC ORD/FREE...TIME/SEQ 18/20 AUSTRAL. PAGE 4 H0085 — FEDERAL NAT/G CENTRAL GOV/COMP

B61
GUIZOT F.P.G.,HISTORY OF THE ORIGIN OF REPRESENTATIVE GOVERNMENT IN EUROPE. CHRIST-17C FRANCE MOD/EUR SPAIN UK LAW CHIEF FORCES POPULISM ...MAJORIT TIME/SEQ GOV/COMP NAT/COMP 4/19 PARLIAMENT. PAGE 62 H1250 — LEGIS REPRESENT CONSTN NAT/G

B61
KEREKES T.,THE ARAB MIDDLE EAST AND MUSLIM AFRICA. ISLAM SOCIETY ECO/UNDEV SECT VOL/ASSN TOP/EX REGION ATTIT PWR...GEOG CONCPT TIME/SEQ GEN/LAWS 20. PAGE 85 H1694 — NAT/G TREND NAT/LISM

B61
LICHTHEIM G.,MARXISM. GERMANY SOCIETY WORKER CAP/ISM ECO/TAC NAT/LISM POPULISM...TIME/SEQ GOV/COMP NAT/COMP 18/20 COM/PARTY. PAGE 96 H1924 — MARXISM SOCISM IDEA/COMP CULTURE

B61
MARVICK D.,POLITICAL DECISION-MAKERS. INTELL STRATA NAT/G POL/PAR EX/STRUC LEGIS DOMIN EDU/PROP ATTIT PERSON PWR...PSY STAT OBS CONT/OBS STAND/INT UNPLAN/INT TIME/SEQ CHARTS STERTYP VAL/FREE. PAGE 104 H2073 — TOP/EX BIOG ELITES

B61
MERRIAM A.,CONGO: BACKGROUND OF CONFLICT. AFR FUT KIN MUNIC NAT/G POL/PAR PROVS DELIB/GP PLAN DOMIN COERCE ATTIT...TIME/SEQ CHARTS CONGO 20. PAGE 109 H2182 — CHOOSE GUERRILLA

B61
MOLLAU G.,INTERNATIONAL COMMUNISM AND WORLD REVOLUTION: HISTORY AND METHODS. RUSSIA USSR INT/ORG NAT/G POL/PAR VOL/ASSN FORCES BAL/PWR DIPLOM EXEC REGION WAR ATTIT PWR MARXISM...CONCPT TIME/SEQ COLD/WAR 19/20. PAGE 112 H2237 — COM REV

B61
NIPPERDEY T.,DIE ORGANISATION DER DEUTSCHEN PARTEIEN VOR 1918. GERMANY CONSTN STRUCT TEC/DEV CHOOSE ADJUST ATTIT...CONCPT TIME/SEQ 19/20. PAGE 118 H2362 — POL/PAR PARL/PROC NAT/G

B61
PAZ O.,THE LABYRINTH OF SOLITUDE; LIFE AND THOUGHT IN MEXICO (TRANS. BY LYSANDER KEMP). INTELL COLONIAL REV...PSY SOC TIME/SEQ 16/20 MEXIC/AMER. PAGE 124 H2480 — CULTURE PERSON PERS/REL SOCIETY

B61
ROBERTSON A.H.,THE LAW OF INTERNATIONAL INSTITUTIONS IN EUROPE. EUR+WWI MOD/EUR INT/ORG NAT/G VOL/ASSN DELIB/GP...JURID TIME/SEQ TOT/POP 20 TREATY. PAGE 132 H2644 — RIGID/FLEX ORD/FREE

B61
SAFRAN M.,EGYPT IN SEARCH OF POLITICAL COMMUNITY: AN ANALYSIS OF THE INTELLECTUAL AND POLITICAL EVOLUTION OF EGYPT, 1804-1952. ISLAM NAT/G SECT EDU/PROP COERCE ATTIT DRIVE KNOWL PWR...TIME/SEQ 20. PAGE 137 H2729 — INTELL NAT/LISM UAR

S61
BRZEZINSKI Z.K.,"THE ORGANIZATION OF THE COMMUNIST CAMP." COM CZECHOSLVK COM/IND NAT/G DELIB/GP INT/TRADE DOMIN EDU/PROP EXEC ROUTINE COERCE ATTIT PWR...MGT CONCPT TIME/SEQ CHARTS VAL/FREE 20 TREATY. PAGE 23 H0460 — VOL/ASSN DIPLOM USSR

S61
NEEDLER M.C.,"THE POLITICAL DEVELOPMENT OF MEXICO." STRUCT NAT/G ADMIN RIGID/FLEX...TIME/SEQ TREND MEXIC/AMER TOT/POP VAL/FREE 19/20. PAGE 116 H2328 — L/A+17C POL/PAR

S61
TOMASIC D.,"POLITICAL LEADERSHIP IN CONTEMPORARY POLAND." COM EUR+WWI GERMANY NAT/G POL/PAR SECT DELIB/GP PLAN ECO/TAC DOMIN EDU/PROP PWR MARXISM ...MARXIST GEOG MGT CONCPT TIME/SEQ STERTYP 20. PAGE 156 H3111 — SOCIETY ROUTINE USSR POLAND

S61
ZAGORIA D.S.,"THE FUTURE OF SINO-SOVIET RELATIONS." CHINA/COM INT/ORG NAT/G POL/PAR VOL/ASSN ACT/RES PLAN PERSON...METH/CNCPT TIME/SEQ TOT/POP VAL/FREE 20 MAO KHRUSH/N. PAGE 172 H3445 — ASIA COM TOTALISM USSR

B62
ABRAHAM W.E.,THE MIND OF AFRICA. AFR SOCIETY STRATA KIN ECO/TAC DOMIN EDU/PROP LEGIT COERCE ATTIT ALL/VALS...MAJORIT SOC OBS HIST/WRIT TIME/SEQ TREND TOT/POP 20. PAGE 3 H0058 — CULTURE SIMUL GHANA

B62
CARTER G.M.,AFRICAN ONE-PARTY STATES. ISLAM IVORY/CST LIBERIA CONSTN CULTURE SOCIETY POL/PAR PLAN DOMIN EDU/PROP EXEC REGION CHOOSE ATTIT ALL/VALS...CONCPT TIME/SEQ CHARTS VAL/FREE 20 TANGANYIKA. PAGE 27 H0545 — AFR NAT/LISM

B62
DE MADARIAGA S.,L'AMERIQUE LATINE ENTRE L'OURS ET L'AIGLE. L/A+17C SOCIETY NAT/G ECO/TAC EDU/PROP REGION COERCE ATTIT ALL/VALS...MAJORIT TIME/SEQ STERTYP COLD/WAR OAS 20. PAGE 38 H0760 — POL/PAR ECO/UNDEV

B62
DUTOIT B.,LA NEUTRALITE SUISSE A L'HEURE EUROPEENNE. EUR+WWI MOD/EUR INT/ORG NAT/G VOL/ASSN PLAN BAL/PWR LEGIT NEUTRAL REGION PEACE ORD/FREE SOVEREIGN...CONCPT OBS TIME/SEQ TREND STERTYP VAL/FREE LEAGUE/NAT UN 20. PAGE 44 H0873 — ATTIT DIPLOM SWITZERLND

B62
HATCH J.,AFRICA TODAY-AND TOMORROW: AN OUTLINE OF BASIC FACTS AND MAJOR PROBLEMS. AFR FUT ISLAM STRATA ECO/UNDEV INT/ORG NAT/G POL/PAR DELIB/GP TOP/EX EDU/PROP LEGIT CHOOSE ATTIT...TIME/SEQ TOT/POP COLD/WAR 20. PAGE 67 H1353 — PLAN CONSTN NAT/LISM

B62
HENDERSON W.O.,THE GENESIS OF THE COMMON MARKET. EUR+WWI FRANCE MOD/EUR UK SEA COM/IND EXTR/IND COLONIAL DISCRIM...TIME/SEQ CHARTS BIBLIOG 18/20 EEC TREATY. PAGE 70 H1395 — ECO/DEV INT/TRADE DIPLOM

B62
HO PING-TI,THE LADDER OF SUCCESS IN IMPERIAL CHINA: ASPECTS OF SOCIAL MOBILITY, 1368-1911. INTELL STRATA FAM KIN MUNIC NAT/G PROVS SCHOOL DELIB/GP DOMIN EDU/PROP ADMIN ROUTINE PERSON ALL/VALS...SOC STAT BIOG HIST/WRIT TIME/SEQ VAL/FREE. PAGE 71 H1431 — ASIA CULTURE

B62
LEGUM C.,PAN-AFRICANISM: A SHORT POLITICAL GUIDE. ISLAM CULTURE INTELL ECO/DEV NAT/G POL/PAR DELIB/GP PLAN EDU/PROP FEDERAL NAT/LISM ATTIT DRIVE PERSON ...RECORD TIME/SEQ CHARTS STERTYP 20. PAGE 93 H1861 — AFR CONCPT

B62
MELADY T.,THE WHITE MAN'S FUTURE IN BLACK AFRICA. FUT CULTURE SOCIETY NAT/G POL/PAR PLAN ECO/TAC DOMIN EDU/PROP LEGIT COLONIAL RACE/REL ATTIT DRIVE ALL/VALS...PSY SOC CONCPT TIME/SEQ TOT/POP VAL/FREE 20. PAGE 108 H2167
AFR STRATA ELITES

B62
MODELSKI G.,SEATO-SIX STUDIES. ASIA CHINA/COM INDIA S/ASIA INT/ORG NAT/G ECO/TAC DETER ATTIT ORD/FREE PWR...TIME/SEQ COLD/WAR TOT/POP 20 SEATO. PAGE 112 H2234
MARKET ECO/UNDEV INT/TRADE

B62
VALERIANO N.D.,COUNTER-GUERRILLA OPERATIONS: THE PHILLIPINE EXPERIENCE. NAT/G CONSULT ACT/RES PLAN COERCE GUERRILLA ATTIT ORD/FREE PWR SKILL...GEOG NEW/IDEA TIME/SEQ CHARTS 20. PAGE 161 H3221
S/ASIA FORCES PHILIPPINE

L62
ORDONNEAU P.,"LES PROBLEMES POSES PAR L'INDEPENDANCE DES NOUVEAUX ETATS AFRICAINS ET MALGACHE SUR LE PLAN DU CONTENTIEUX." FRANCE ISLAM MADAGASCAR LAW STRATA ECO/UNDEV NAT/G LEGIS LEGIT ...JURID TIME/SEQ 20. PAGE 121 H2425
AFR ADJUD COLONIAL SOVEREIGN

S62
CORET A.,"LE STATUT DE L'ILE CHRISTMAS DE L'OCEAN INDIEN." FUT S/ASIA ECO/DEV ECO/UNDEV VOL/ASSN DELIB/GP PLAN...RELATIV OBS TIME/SEQ TREND AUSTRAL 20. PAGE 33 H0667
NAT/G INT/ORG NEW/ZEALND

S62
FESLER J.W.,"FRENCH FIELD ADMINISTRATION: THE BEGINNINGS." CHRIST-17C CULTURE SOCIETY STRATA NAT/G ECO/TAC DOMIN EDU/PROP LEGIT ADJUD COERCE ATTIT ALL/VALS...TIME/SEQ CON/ANAL GEN/METH VAL/FREE 13/15. PAGE 49 H0988
EX/STRUC FRANCE

S62
LANGER W.L.,"FAREWELL TO EMPIRE." EUR+WWI MOD/EUR NAT/G DIPLOM EDU/PROP COLONIAL ATTIT ORD/FREE PWR SOVEREIGN WEALTH...CONCPT TIME/SEQ GEN/LAWS TOT/POP VAL/FREE CMN/WLTH 20. PAGE 91 H1810
DOMIN ECO/TAC NAT/LISM

S62
MOUSKHELY M.,"LA NAISSANCE DES ETATS EN DROIT INTERNATIONAL PUBLIC." UNIV SOCIETY INT/ORG VOL/ASSN LEGIT ATTIT RIGID/FLEX...JURID TIME/SEQ 20. PAGE 114 H2272
NAT/G STRUCT INT/LAW

S62
PISTRAK L.,"SOVIET VIEWS ON AFRICA." AFR COM FUT ISLAM USSR INTELL STRUCT KIN POL/PAR PLAN EDU/PROP RIGID/FLEX PWR MARXISM...TIME/SEQ WORK TOT/POP 20. PAGE 126 H2516
NAT/G ATTIT SOCISM

S62
RAZAFIMBAHINY J.,"L'ORGANISATION AFRICAINE ET MALGACHE DE COOPERATION ECONOMIQUE." AFR ISLAM MADAGASCAR NAT/G ACT/RES ECO/TAC ALL/VALS ...TIME/SEQ 20. PAGE 130 H2601
INT/ORG ECO/UNDEV

S62
STRACHEY J.,"COMMUNIST INTENTIONS." ASIA USSR YUGOSLAVIA INT/ORG NAT/G FORCES DOMIN EDU/PROP COERCE NUC/PWR NAT/LISM PEACE RIGID/FLEX PWR MARXISM...CONCPT MYTH OBS TIME/SEQ TREND COLD/WAR TOT/POP 20. PAGE 150 H2992
COM ATTIT WAR

S62
VIGNES D.,"L'AUTORITE DES TRAITES INTERNATIONAUX EN DROIT INTERNE." EUR+WWI UNIV LAW CONSTN INTELL NAT/G POL/PAR DIPLOM ATTIT PERCEPT ALL/VALS ...POLICY INT/LAW JURID CONCPT TIME/SEQ 20 TREATY. PAGE 163 H3252
STRUCT LEGIT FRANCE

B63
CARTER G.M.,FIVE AFRICAN STATES: RESPONSES TO DIVERSITY. CONSTN CULTURE STRATA LEGIS PLAN ECO/TAC DOMIN EDU/PROP CT/SYS EXEC CHOOSE ATTIT HEALTH ORD/FREE PWR...TIME/SEQ TOT/POP VAL/FREE. PAGE 27 H0547
AFR SOCIETY

B63
CREMEANS C.,THE ARABS AND THE WORLD: NASSER'S ARAB NATIONALIST POLICY. FUT ISLAM UAR USA+45 SOCIETY STRATA NAT/G POL/PAR PLAN DIPLOM EDU/PROP LEGIT DRIVE ALL/VALS...INT TIME/SEQ CHARTS 20 NASSER/G. PAGE 35 H0700
TOP/EX ATTIT REGION NAT/LISM

B63
FALL B.,THE TWO VIETNAMS. CULTURE SOCIETY ECO/UNDEV NAT/G TOP/EX ACT/RES PLAN ECO/TAC DOMIN EDU/PROP COERCE ATTIT DRIVE PERSON ORD/FREE PWR...SOC TIME/SEQ COLD/WAR 20. PAGE 48 H0965
S/ASIA BIOG VIETNAM

B63
FLECHTHEIM O.K.,DOKUMENTE ZUR PARTEIPOLITISCHEN ENTWICKLUNG IN DEUTSCHLAND SEIT 1945 (2 VOLS.). EUR+WWI GERMANY/W...CONCPT ANTHOL 20. PAGE 51 H1023
POL/PAR ELITES NAT/G TIME/SEQ

B63
GLADE W.P. JR.,THE POLITICAL ECONOMY OF MEXICO. FUT L/A+17C CULTURE SOCIETY AGRI INDUS DELIB/GP ACT/RES ECO/TAC ATTIT HEALTH ORD/FREE...STAT TIME/SEQ TREND MEXIC/AMER TOT/POP VAL/FREE 20. PAGE 57 H1138
FINAN ECO/UNDEV

B63
HALPERIN M.H.,THE POLITICS OF SOCIAL CHANGE IN THE MIDDLE EAST AND NORTH AFRICA. ISLAM CULTURE ACT/RES REV ATTIT PERCEPT KNOWL...METH/CNCPT OBS TIME/SEQ GEN/METH TOT/POP VAL/FREE 20. PAGE 64 H1291
SOC TREND

B63
JELAVICH C.,THE BALKANS IN TRANSITION: ESSAYS ON THE DEVELOPMENT OF BALKAN LIFE AND POLITICS SINCE THE EIGHTEENTH CENTURY. COM GREECE TURKEY ECO/UNDEV NAT/G SECT ATTIT...GEOG SOC CONCPT TIME/SEQ ANTHOL 18/20. PAGE 80 H1596
CULTURE RIGID/FLEX

B63
KAPP W.K.,HINDU CULTURE: ECONOMIC DEVELOPMENT AND ECONOMIC PLANNING IN INDIA. INDIA S/ASIA CULTURE ECO/TAC EDU/PROP ADMIN ALL/VALS...POLICY MGT TIME/SEQ VAL/FREE 20. PAGE 83 H1660
SECT ECO/UNDEV

B63
KHADDURI M.,MODERN LIBYA: A STUDY IN POLITICAL DEVELOPMENT. EUR+WWI ISLAM LIBYA ELITES INT/ORG POL/PAR FORCES DIPLOM FOR/AID DOMIN EDU/PROP LEGIT NAT/LISM DRIVE RIGID/FLEX SKILL...CONCPT TIME/SEQ TREND 20. PAGE 85 H1704
NAT/G STRUCT

B63
KRAEHE E.,METTERNICH'S GERMAN POLICY: THE CONTEST WITH NAPOLEON, 1799-1814, VOL. 1. FRANCE MOD/EUR NAT/G CONSULT TOP/EX PLAN BAL/PWR DOMIN COERCE ATTIT DRIVE PERCEPT PERSON SKILL...CONCPT RECORD TIME/SEQ TREND 18/19. PAGE 88 H1764
BIOG GERMANY DIPLOM

B63
KURZMAN D.,SUBVERSION OF THE INNOCENTS: PATTERNS OF COMMUNIST PENETRATION OF AFRICA, THE MIDDLE EAST AND AFRICA. AFR ASIA ISLAM S/ASIA CULTURE NAT/G FORCES PLAN EDU/PROP ADMIN ATTIT...CONCPT INT UNPLAN/INT TIME/SEQ. PAGE 89 H1785
COM COERCE

B63
MAYNE R.,THE COMMUNITY OF EUROPE. UK CONSTN NAT/G CONSULT DELIB/GP CREATE PLAN ECO/TAC LEGIT ADMIN ROUTINE ORD/FREE PWR WEALTH...CONCPT TIME/SEQ EEC EURATOM 20. PAGE 105 H2107
EUR+WWI INT/ORG REGION

B63
MULLER H.J.,FREEDOM IN THE WESTERN WORLD. PREHIST CULTURE SECT CREATE TEC/DEV DOMIN PWR WEALTH ...MAJORIT SOC CONCPT. PAGE 114 H2285
ORD/FREE TIME/SEQ SOCIETY

B63
NKRUMAH K.,AFRICA MUST UNITE. AFR FUT GHANA CONSTN CULTURE SOCIETY NAT/G POL/PAR DELIB/GP TOP/EX PLAN DOMIN EDU/PROP ATTIT DRIVE...TIME/SEQ CHARTS TOT/POP 20. PAGE 118 H2364
CONCPT GEN/LAWS REGION

B63
QUAISON-SACKEY A.,AFRICA UNBOUND: REFLECTIONS OF AN AFRICAN STATESMAN. ISLAM CULTURE INTELL INT/ORG POL/PAR TOP/EX DOMIN EDU/PROP LEGIT ATTIT PERSON ...CONCPT OBS TIME/SEQ CHARTS STERTYP 20 UN. PAGE 129 H2571
AFR BIOG

B63
SCHECHTMAN J.B.,THE REFUGEE IN THE WORLD: DISPLACEMENT AND INTEGRATION. AFR ASIA EUR+WWI ISLAM L/A+17C S/ASIA CULTURE STRATA LOC/G EX/STRUC PLAN ECO/TAC ROUTINE...CONCPT TIME/SEQ VAL/FREE 20. PAGE 139 H2779
INT/ORG SOC

B63
SETON-WATSON H.,THE NEW IMPERIALISM. COM EUR+WWI MOD/EUR ECO/UNDEV NAT/G FORCES DIPLOM DOMIN EDU/PROP LEGIT COLONIAL EXEC COERCE GP/REL RACE/REL DISCRIM ATTIT...TIME/SEQ 20. PAGE 142 H2833
ECO/TAC RUSSIA USSR

B63
STEVENS G.G.,EGYPT YESTERDAY AND TODAY. CONSTN ECO/UNDEV AGRI INDUS NAT/G POL/PAR FORCES ECO/TAC EDU/PROP COERCE WAR NAT/LISM DRIVE ALL/VALS ...TIME/SEQ WORK SUEZ 20. PAGE 149 H2983
ISLAM TOP/EX REV UAR

B63
TOUVAL S.,SOMALI NATIONALISM: INTERNATIONAL POLITICS AND THE DRIVE FOR UNITY IN THE HORN OF AFRICA. AFR CULTURE PROVS LEGIS EDU/PROP REGION COERCE ATTIT...MYTH UNPLAN/INT TIME/SEQ SOMALI VAL/FREE 20. PAGE 156 H3118
SOCIETY EXEC NAT/LISM

B63
VIARD R.,LA FIN DE L'EMPIRE COLONIAL FRANCAIS. AFR FUT S/ASIA ECO/UNDEV NAT/G CONSULT PLAN ECO/TAC EDU/PROP REGION NAT/LISM ALL/VALS...CONCPT TIME/SEQ TREND VAL/FREE 20. PAGE 162 H3248
VOL/ASSN COLONIAL FRANCE

B63
ZARTMAN I.W.,GOVERNMENT AND POLITICS IN NORTHERN AFRICA. AFR ALGERIA ISLAM LIBYA MOROCCO UAR ELITES SOCIETY PLAN ECO/TAC DOMIN EDU/PROP LEGIT ATTIT ...GEOG CONCPT TIME/SEQ 20 TUNIS. PAGE 172 H3448
CULTURE DRIVE NAT/LISM

L63
FREUND G.,"ADENAUER AND THE FUTURE OF GERMANY." EUR+WWI FUT GERMANY/W FORCES LEGIT ADMIN ROUTINE ATTIT DRIVE PERSON PWR...POLICY TIME/SEQ TREND VAL/FREE 20 ADENAUER/K. PAGE 53 H1058
NAT/G BIOG DIPLOM GERMANY

L63
JAY R.,"RELIGION AND POLITICS IN RURAL CENTRAL JAVA." S/ASIA SOCIETY NEIGH SECT PERSON HEALTH MORAL...SOC UNPLAN/INT TIME/SEQ JAVA VAL/FREE 20 WORSHIP. PAGE 80 H1594
CULTURE OBS

L63
ZARTMAN I.W.,"THE SAHARA--BRIDGE OR BARRIER." ISLAM CULTURE SOCIETY NAT/G DELIB/GP DOMIN EDU/PROP LEGIT ATTIT...HIST/WRIT TIME/SEQ CHARTS TOT/POP VAL/FREE
INT/ORG PWR NAT/LISM

20. PAGE 172 H3447

S63
CRUTCHER J.,"PAN AFRICANISM: AFRICAN ODYSSEY." AFR NAT/G POL/PAR PROF/ORG VOL/ASSN TOP/EX CREATE REGION RACE/REL ALL/VALS...CONCPT TIME/SEQ TREND CON/ANAL 20. PAGE 36 H0716
PROVS
DELIB/GP
COLONIAL

S63
GLUCKMAN M.,"CIVIL WAR AND THEORIES OF POWER IN BAROTSE-LAND: AFRICAN AND MEDIEVAL ANALOGIES." AFR CHRIST-17C LAW CONSTN CULTURE STRATA KIN DELIB/GP FORCES DOMIN LEGIT COERCE PERCEPT ORD/FREE...SOC INT TIME/SEQ GEN/LAWS VAL/FREE. PAGE 57 H1148
TOP/EX
PWR
WAR

S63
GROSSER A.,"FRANCE AND GERMANY IN THE ATLANTIC COMMUNITY." INT/ORG NAT/G TOP/EX DIPLOM REGION PEACE ATTIT ORD/FREE PWR...CONCPT RECORD TIME/SEQ GEN/LAWS VAL/FREE COLD/WAR 20. PAGE 62 H1234
EUR+WWI
VOL/ASSN
FRANCE
GERMANY

S63
HUREWITZ J.C.,"LEBANESE DEMOCRACY IN ITS INTERNATIONAL SETTING." FRANCE ISLAM UK LOC/G NAT/G SECT DOMIN EDU/PROP EXEC ATTIT PWR...TIME/SEQ 20. PAGE 75 H1507
STRUCT
LEBANON

S63
LEE J.M.,"PARLIAMENT IN REPUBLICAN GHANA." AFR CONSTN CULTURE SOCIETY STRATA POL/PAR DELIB/GP TOP/EX DOMIN EDU/PROP LEGIT COERCE CHOOSE ATTIT ALL/VALS...CONCPT STAT TIME/SEQ VAL/FREE 20. PAGE 93 H1857
LEGIS
GHANA

S63
LIGOT M.,"LA COOPERATION MILITAIRE DANS LES ACCORDS, PASSES ENTRE LA FRANCE ET LES ETATS AFRICAINS ET MALGACHE D'EXPRESSION." ECO/UNDEV INT/ORG NAT/G VOL/ASSN...CONCPT TIME/SEQ 20. PAGE 97 H1931
AFR
FORCES
FOR/AID
FRANCE

S63
LOPEZIBOR J.,"L'EUROPE, FORME DE VIE." CHRIST-17C EUR+WWI FUT MOD/EUR SOCIETY INT/ORG SECT EDU/PROP ATTIT RIGID/FLEX ALL/VALS...POLICY HUM SOC TIME/SEQ TREND GEN/LAWS. PAGE 98 H1966
NAT/G
CULTURE

S63
MAZRUI A.A.,"ON THE CONCEPT 'WE ARE ALL AFRICANS'." AFR CULTURE KIN LOC/G NAT/G DOMIN EDU/PROP LEGIT ATTIT PERCEPT PERSON KNOWL ORD/FREE...TIME/SEQ TOT/POP 20. PAGE 106 H2110
PROVS
INT/ORG
NAT/LISM

S63
SOEMARDJORN S.,"SOME SOCIAL AND CULTURAL IMPLICATIONS OF INDONESIA'S PLANNED AND UNPLANNED DEVELOPMENT." EUR+WWI FUT MOD/EUR S/ASIA CONSTN SOCIETY DELIB/GP ACT/RES PLAN ECO/TAC EDU/PROP COERCE ATTIT ALL/VALS...TIME/SEQ 20. PAGE 146 H2927
ECO/UNDEV
CULTURE
INDONESIA

S63
WELLS H.,"THE OAS AND THE DOMINICAN ELECTIONS." L/A+17C INT/ORG NAT/G POL/PAR TEC/DEV ECO/TAC EDU/PROP PERCEPT...TIME/SEQ OAS TOT/POP 20. PAGE 166 H3332
CONSULT
CHOOSE
DOMIN/REP

B64
CAUTE D.,COMMUNISM AND THE FRENCH INTELLECTUALS, 1914-1960. COM EUR+WWI MOD/EUR NAT/G PERF/ART PROF/ORG CREATE EDU/PROP ATTIT PERSON KNOWL MARXISM ...SOC TIME/SEQ MARX/KARL 20 MALRAUX/A GIDE/A SARTRE/J. PAGE 28 H0563
POL/PAR
INTELL

B64
CLUBB O.E. JR.,TWENTIETH CENTURY CHINA. ASIA CHINA/COM INTELL NAT/G POL/PAR VOL/ASSN ACT/RES EDU/PROP COERCE REV PWR...TIME/SEQ 20. PAGE 30 H0608
TOP/EX
DRIVE

B64
DE SMITH S.A.,THE NEW COMMONWEALTH AND ITS CONSTITUTIONS. AFR CYPRUS PAKISTAN S/ASIA INT/ORG NAT/G LEGIS LEGIT RIGID/FLEX PWR...CONCPT TIME/SEQ CMN/WLTH 20. PAGE 38 H0770
EX/STRUC
CONSTN
SOVEREIGN

B64
GRIFFITH W.E.,THE SINO-SOVIET RIFT. ASIA CHINA/COM COM CUBA USSR YUGOSLAVIA NAT/G POL/PAR VOL/ASSN DELIB/GP FORCES TOP/EX DIPLOM EDU/PROP DRIVE PERSON PWR...TREND 20 TREATY. PAGE 61 H1224
ATTIT
TIME/SEQ
BAL/PWR
SOCISM

B64
HEIMSATH C.H.,INDIAN NATIONALISM AND HINDU SOCIAL REFORM. S/ASIA LAW CULTURE SOCIETY STRATA PROVS VOL/ASSN DELIB/GP LEGIS TOP/EX DOMIN EDU/PROP LEGIT ATTIT ALL/VALS...POLICY SOC TIME/SEQ STERTYP VAL/FREE 19/20. PAGE 69 H1385
SECT
NAT/G

B64
MEAD M.,CONTINUITIES IN CULTURAL EVOLUTION. FACE/GP KIN ACT/RES EDU/PROP GP/REL INGP/REL DRIVE HEREDITY ROLE...TIME/SEQ TREND METH SOC/INTEG 20. PAGE 108 H2153
CULTURE
SOC
PERS/REL

B64
ON CULTURE AND SOCIAL CHANGE. FAM NAT/G ACT/RES ECO/TAC RACE/REL...PSY TIME/SEQ TREND IDEA/COMP METH/COMP ANTHOL BIBLIOG 20. PAGE 120 H2406
CULTURE
TEC/DEV
STRUCT
CREATE

B64
PHILLIPS C.S.,THE DEVELOPMENT OF NIGERIAN FOREIGN POLICY. AFR CONSTN CULTURE STRATA NAT/G LEGIS DOMIN LEGIT EXEC...RELATIV SOC TIME/SEQ TREND TOT/POP 20. PAGE 125 H2502
CHOOSE
POLICY
DIPLOM
NIGERIA

B64
PIKE F.B.,THE CONFLICT BETWEEN CHURCH AND STATE IN LATIN AMERICA. L/A+17C CULTURE SOCIETY STRATA DOMIN EDU/PROP LEGIT COERCE ATTIT ORD/FREE PWR WEALTH ...CONCPT TIME/SEQ TREND VAL/FREE. PAGE 125 H2510
SECT
NAT/G

B64
PIPES R.,THE FORMATION OF THE SOVIET UNION. EUR+WWI MOD/EUR STRUCT ECO/UNDEV NAT/G LEGIS DOMIN LEGIT CT/SYS EXEC COERCE ALL/VALS...POLICY RELATIV HIST/WRIT TIME/SEQ TOT/POP 19/20. PAGE 126 H2514
COM
USSR
RUSSIA

B64
THORNBURG M.W.,PEOPLE AND POLICY IN THE MIDDLE EAST. ISLAM ECO/UNDEV FAM KIN MUNIC NAT/G NEIGH POL/PAR SECT DELIB/GP LEGIS PLAN ECO/TAC DOMIN ADMIN ATTIT HEALTH RESPECT...SOC CONCPT METH/CNCPT OBS TIME/SEQ TOT/POP VAL/FREE. PAGE 154 H3088
TEC/DEV
CULTURE

B64
WAINHOUSE D.W.,REMNANTS OF EMPIRE: THE UNITED NATIONS AND THE END OF COLONIALISM. FUT PORTUGAL WOR+45 NAT/G CONSULT DOMIN LEGIT ADMIN ROUTINE ATTIT ORD/FREE...POLICY JURID RECORD INT TIME/SEQ UN CMN/WLTH 20. PAGE 164 H3287
INT/ORG
TREND
COLONIAL

B64
WARD R.E.,POLITICAL MODERNIZATION IN JAPAN AND TURKEY. ASIA ISLAM S/ASIA CONSTN CULTURE STRATA COM/IND POL/PAR FORCES ACT/RES ECO/TAC DOMIN EDU/PROP LEGIT ADMIN CHOOSE ATTIT ALL/VALS...STAT TIME/SEQ VAL/FREE CHINJAP. PAGE 165 H3307
SOCIETY
TURKEY

B64
WERTHEIM W.F.,EAST-WEST PARALLELS. INDONESIA S/ASIA NAT/G SECT...TIME/SEQ METH REFORMERS S/EASTASIA. PAGE 167 H3334
SOC
ECO/UNDEV
CULTURE
NAT/LISM

B64
ZARTMAN I.W.,MOROCCO: PROBLEMS OF NEW POWER. ISLAM CULTURE ECO/UNDEV AGRI POL/PAR SCHOOL FORCES ADMIN ...CONCPT STAT INT CENSUS TIME/SEQ CHARTS WORK VAL/FREE 20. PAGE 172 H3449
CHOOSE
MOROCCO
DELIB/GP
DECISION

S64
CROUZET F.,"WARS, BLOCKADE, AND ECONOMIC CHANGE IN EUROPE, 1792-1815." UK INDUS NAT/G TEC/DEV ECO/TAC WEALTH...POLICY RELATIV HIST/WRIT TIME/SEQ 18/19. PAGE 35 H0710
MOD/EUR
MARKET

S64
LANGER P.F.,"JAPAN'S RELATIONS WITH CHINA." ASIA CHINA/COM KOREA S/ASIA ECO/DEV NAT/G POL/PAR EDU/PROP ATTIT ALL/VALS...METH/CNCPT TIME/SEQ TREND 20 CHINJAP. PAGE 91 H1808
RIGID/FLEX
ECO/TAC

S64
LERNER W.,"THE HISTORICAL ORIGINS OF THE SOVIET DOCTRINE OF PEACEFUL COEXISTENCE." COM USSR INT/ORG NAT/G VOL/ASSN PLAN PEACE ATTIT RIGID/FLEX PWR MARXISM...TIME/SEQ COLD/WAR 20. PAGE 95 H1891
EDU/PROP
DIPLOM

S64
LEWIS B.,"THE QUEST FOR FREEDOM--A SAD STORY OF THE MIDDLE EAST." ISLAM ISRAEL LEBANON TURKEY CULTURE NAT/G SECT LEGIS TOP/EX DOMIN EDU/PROP LEGIT ORD/FREE PWR RESPECT...POLICY TIME/SEQ VAL/FREE 20. PAGE 96 H1911
CONSTN
ATTIT
NAT/LISM

S64
MOZINGO D.P.,"CHINA'S RELATIONS WITH HER ASIAN NEIGHBORS." ASIA CHINA/COM S/ASIA VIETNAM NAT/G DELIB/GP FORCES CREATE DOMIN EDU/PROP REV RIGID/FLEX PWR...TIME/SEQ GEN/LAWS COLD/WAR 20. PAGE 114 H2277
VOL/ASSN
POLICY
DIPLOM

S64
NEEDHAM T.,"SCIENCE AND SOCIETY IN EAST AND WEST." INTELL STRATA R+D LOC/G NAT/G PROVS CONSULT ACT/RES CREATE PLAN TEC/DEV EDU/PROP ADMIN ATTIT ALL/VALS ...POLICY RELATIV MGT CONCPT NEW/IDEA TIME/SEQ WORK WORK. PAGE 116 H2327
ASIA
STRUCT

S64
RAMAZANI R.K.,"CHURCH AND STATE IN MODERNIZING SOCIETY: THE CASE OF IRAN." ISLAM CULTURE ORD/FREE PWR...TIME/SEQ VAL/FREE 17/20. PAGE 129 H2586
SECT
NAT/G
ELITES
IRAN

S64
RUDOLPH L.I.,"GENERALS AND POLITICIANS IN INDIA." INDIA S/ASIA CULTURE STRATA NAT/G LEGIS TOP/EX EDU/PROP ATTIT ORD/FREE PWR RESPECT SKILL...POLICY BIOG TIME/SEQ STERTYP VAL/FREE 20. PAGE 136 H2713
FORCES
COERCE

S64
SAAB H.,"THE ARAB SEARCH FOR A FEDERAL UNION." SOCIETY INT/ORG NAT/G DELIB/GP FORCES ACT/RES TEC/DEV ECO/TAC DOMIN LEGIT REGION ROUTINE ATTIT DRIVE RIGID/FLEX ALL/VALS...SOC CONCPT NEW/IDEA TIME/SEQ TREND. PAGE 136 H2726
ISLAM
PLAN

S64
SAYEED K.,"PATHAN REGIONALISM." ISLAM PAKISTAN S/ASIA CULTURE SOCIETY NAT/G NEIGH DIPLOM LEGIT COERCE CHOOSE ATTIT DISPL PERCEPT ALL/VALS SOVEREIGN...POLICY RELATIV SOC TIME/SEQ TOT/POP 20. PAGE 138 H2761
SECT
NAT/LISM
REGION

S64
SMYTHE H.H.,"NEHRU AND INDIAN FOREIGN POLICY."
TOP/EX

S/ASIA ECO/UNDEV NAT/G POL/PAR CONSULT PLAN DIPLOM NEUTRAL COERCE ATTIT DRIVE PERSON MORAL ORD/FREE RESPECT...GEOG CONCPT TIME/SEQ TREND GEN/LAWS 20 NEHRU/J. PAGE 146 H2922
BIOG
INDIA

S64
VANDENBOSCH A.,"POWER BALANCE IN INDONESIA." S/ASIA USSR NAT/G TOP/EX BAL/PWR DOMIN NEUTRAL ORD/FREE PWR...POLICY TIME/SEQ GEN/LAWS 20 SUKARNO/A. PAGE 162 H3233
FORCES
TREND
DIPLOM
INDONESIA

S64
ZARTMAN I.W.,"LES RELATIONS ENTRE LA FRANCE ET L'ALGERIA DEPUIS LES ACCORDS D'EVIAN." EUR+WWI FUT ISLAM CULTURE AGRI EXTR/IND FINAN INDUS POL/PAR DIPLOM ECO/TAC FOR/AID PEACE ATTIT DRIVE ALL/VALS ...TIME/SEQ VAL/FREE 20. PAGE 172 H3450
ECO/UNDEV
ALGERIA
FRANCE

B65
ADAM T.R.,GOVERNMENT AND POLITICS IN AFRICA SOUTH OF THE SAHARA. AFR EUR+WWI CONSTN CULTURE INTELL POL/PAR TOP/EX LEGIT REGION DRIVE...OBS TREND CMN/WLTH 20. PAGE 3 H0062
NAT/G
TIME/SEQ
RACE/REL
COLONIAL

B65
BRAMSTED E.K.,GOEBBELS AND NATIONAL SOCIALIST PROPAGANDA, 1925-1945. EUR+WWI GERMANY UK USSR NAT/G FORCES WAR FASCISM...TIME/SEQ 20 GOEBBELS/J NAZI. PAGE 20 H0403
EDU/PROP
PSY
COM/IND

B65
JACKSON G.,THE SPANISH REPUBLIC AND THE CIVIL WAR, 1931-1939. EUR+WWI INTELL STRUCT COM/IND NAT/G POL/PAR LEGIS EDU/PROP EXEC COERCE NAT/LISM DRIVE PWR...INT TIME/SEQ TOT/POP 20. PAGE 79 H1574
ATTIT
GUERRILLA
SPAIN

B65
JANSEN M.B.,CHANGING JAPANESE ATTITUDES TOWARD MODERNIZATION. ASIA CHINA/COM S/ASIA INTELL SOCIETY KIN NAT/G SECT PERCEPT RIGID/FLEX...SOC CONCPT TIME/SEQ TREND TOT/POP 19/20 CHINJAP. PAGE 80 H1591
TEC/DEV
ATTIT
INDIA

B65
JONAS E.,DIE VOLKSKONSERVATIVEN 1928-1933. GERMANY EX/STRUC...CONCPT TIME/SEQ 20 HITLER/A. PAGE 82 H1628
POL/PAR
NAT/G
GP/REL

B65
O'BRIEN F.,CRISIS IN WORLD COMMUNISM* MARXISM IN SEARCH OF EFFICIENCY. COM ECO/DEV PLAN INT/TRADE WAR ADJUST PEACE...STAT TIME/SEQ GOV/COMP NAT/COMP COLD/WAR. PAGE 119 H2384
MARXISM
USSR
DRIVE
EFFICIENCY

B65
ORGANSKI A.F.K.,THE STAGES OF POLITICAL DEVELOPMENT. STRATA AGRI INDUS NAT/G POL/PAR COLONIAL PWR WEALTH...CLASSIF TIME/SEQ. PAGE 121 H2428
ECO/DEV
ECO/UNDEV
GEN/LAWS
CREATE

B65
RODRIGUEZ M.,CENTRAL AMERICA. COSTA/RICA GUATEMALA L/A+17C NICARAGUA DIPLOM COLONIAL REGION NAT/LISM ALL/IDEOS SOCISM...MAJORIT TIME/SEQ BIBLIOG 19/20. PAGE 133 H2656
CULTURE
NAT/COMP
NAT/G
ECO/UNDEV

B65
ROSENBERG A.,DEMOCRACY AND SOCIALISM. COM EUR+WWI FRANCE MOD/EUR STRUCT INT/ORG NAT/G POL/PAR TOP/EX EDU/PROP COERCE PERSON PWR FASCISM MARXISM...CONCPT TIME/SEQ MARX/KARL 19/20. PAGE 134 H2677
ATTIT

B65
ROTBERG R.I.,A POLITICAL HISTORY OF TROPICAL AFRICA. EX/STRUC DIPLOM INT/TRADE DOMIN ADMIN RACE/REL NAT/LISM PWR SOVEREIGN...GEOG TIME/SEQ BIBLIOG 1/20. PAGE 135 H2692
AFR
CULTURE
COLONIAL

B65
SALVADORI M.,ITALY. AUSTRIA FRANCE GERMANY ITALY SPAIN CULTURE NAT/G POL/PAR DIPLOM WAR FASCISM LAISSEZ MARXISM...TIME/SEQ CHARTS BIBLIOG/A. PAGE 137 H2744
NAT/LISM
CATHISM
SOCIETY

S65
GRIFFITH S.B.,"COMMUNIST CHINA'S CAPACITY TO MAKE WAR." CHINA/COM COM NAT/G TOP/EX PLAN DOMIN COERCE NUC/PWR ATTIT RESPECT SKILL...CONCPT MYTH TIME/SEQ TREND COLD/WAR 20. PAGE 61 H1221
FORCES
PWR
WEAPON
ASIA

S65
RUBINSTEIN A.Z.,"YUGOSLAVIA'S OPENING SOCIETY." COM USSR INTELL NAT/G LEGIS TOP/EX LEGIT CT/SYS RIGID/FLEX ALL/VALS SOCISM...HUM TIME/SEQ TREND 20. PAGE 135 H2708
CONSTN
EX/STRUC
YUGOSLAVIA

S65
VUCINICH W.S.,"WHITHER RUMANIA." COM USSR YUGOSLAVIA NAT/G VOL/ASSN DELIB/GP TOP/EX LEGIT NAT/LISM TOTALISM ATTIT DRIVE RIGID/FLEX ORD/FREE WEALTH SOCISM...TIME/SEQ TREND 20. PAGE 164 H3281
ECO/DEV
CREATE
ROMANIA

B66
ANDERSON S.V.,CANADIAN OMBUDSMAN PROPOSALS. CANADA LEGIS DEBATE PARL/PROC...MAJORIT JURID TIME/SEQ IDEA/COMP 20 OMBUDSMAN PARLIAMENT. PAGE 7 H0133
NAT/G
CREATE
ADMIN
POL/PAR

B66
BLACK C.E.,THE DYNAMICS OF MODERNIZATION: A STUDY IN COMPARATIVE HISTORY. STRUCT ECO/DEV ECO/UNDEV NAT/G DIPLOM LEAD REV...PREDICT TIME/SEQ TREND SOC/INTEG 17/20. PAGE 17 H0350
SOCIETY
SOC
NAT/COMP

B66
CAUTE D.,THE LEFT IN EUROPE SINCE 1789. EUR+WWI MOD/EUR NAT/G POL/PAR REV...TIME/SEQ GEN/LAWS BIBLIOG 18/20. PAGE 28 H0564
ALL/IDEOS
ORD/FREE
CONCPT
STRATA

B66
DEUTSCHE INST ZEITGESCHICHTE,DIE WESTDEUTSCHEN PARTEIEN: 1945-1965. GERMANY/W CHOOSE PWR ...TIME/SEQ 20. PAGE 40 H0806
POL/PAR
CONCPT
NAT/G
PROVS

B66
KUZNETS S.,MODERN ECONOMIC GROWTH. WOR+45 WOR-45 ECO/DEV ECO/UNDEV AGRI FINAN INDUS TEC/DEV EFFICIENCY INCOME...NAT/COMP 19/20. PAGE 89 H1786
TIME/SEQ
WEALTH
PRODUC

B66
O'NEILL R.J.,THE GERMAN ARMY AND THE NAZI PARTY, 1933-1939. GERMANY ELITES NAT/G EDU/PROP CONTROL LEAD COERCE WAR...POLICY INT TIME/SEQ BIBLIOG 20 HITLER/A NAZI. PAGE 120 H2391
CIVMIL/REL
FORCES
FASCISM
POL/PAR

B66
SHARMA B.M.,THE REPUBLIC OF INDIA; CONSTITUTION AND GOVERNMENT. INDIA POL/PAR LEGIS EFFICIENCY ...TIME/SEQ GOV/COMP 20. PAGE 142 H2846
PROVS
NAT/G
CONSTN

B66
SOBEL L.A.,SOUTH VIETNAM: US-COMMUNIST CONFRONTATION IN SOUTHEAST ASIA 1961-65. VIETNAM FOR/AID CROWD DETER REV PEACE...GEOG 20 INTERVENT DIEM COLD/WAR. PAGE 146 H2926
WAR
TIME/SEQ
FORCES
NAT/G

B66
SWARTZ M.J.,POLITICAL ANTHROPOLOGY. WOR+45 POL/PAR ACT/RES REV GP/REL DRIVE...SOC CONCPT TIME/SEQ GP/COMP ANTHOL WORSHIP 20. PAGE 151 H3013
PARTIC
RIGID/FLEX
LOC/G
CREATE

S66
QUESTER G.H.,"ON THE IDENTIFICATION OF REAL AND PRETENDED COMMUNIST MILITARY DOCTRINE." ASIA USSR DETER WAR ATTIT DRIVE HEALTH TIME/SEQ. PAGE 129 H2574
RATIONAL
PERCEPT
NUC/PWR
NAT/COMP

B67
ANDERSON S.V.,THE NORDIC COUNCIL: A STUDY OF SCANDINAVIAN REGIONALISM. DENMARK FINLAND ICELAND NORWAY SWEDEN MARKET NAT/G VOL/ASSN CONSULT PARL/PROC ATTIT...TIME/SEQ BIBLIOG 20. PAGE 7 H0134
INT/ORG
REGION
DIPLOM
LEGIS

B67
ANDERSON T.,RUSSIAN POLITICAL THOUGHT; AN INTRODUCTION. USSR NAT/G POL/PAR CHIEF MARXISM ...TIME/SEQ BIBLIOG 9/20. PAGE 7 H0135
TREND
CONSTN
ATTIT

B67
MACRIDIS R.C.,FOREIGN POLICY IN WORLD POLITICS (3RD ED.). EX/STRUC BAL/PWR COLONIAL NAT/LISM SKILL SOVEREIGN WEALTH...CONCPT TIME/SEQ ANTHOL 20 COLD/WAR. PAGE 101 H2011
DIPLOM
POLICY
NAT/G
IDEA/COMP

B67
MORRIS A.J.A.,PARLIAMENTARY DEMOCRACY IN THE NINETEENTH CENTURY. UK INDUS LOC/G NAT/G POL/PAR CONSULT LEGIS INT/TRADE ADMIN CHOOSE SUFF SOVEREIGN 19 PARLIAMENT. PAGE 113 H2261
TIME/SEQ
CONSTN
PARL/PROC
POPULISM

S67
DIAMANT A.,"EUROPEAN MODELS OF BUREAUCRACY AND DEVELOPMENT." EX/STRUC PLAN ADMIN CONTROL ROUTINE GOV/REL CENTRAL...DECISION TIME/SEQ CHARTS. PAGE 41 H0818
NAT/G
EQUILIB
ACT/RES
NAT/COMP

S67
HOFMANN W.,"THE PUBLIC INTEREST PRESSURE GROUP: THE CASE OF THE DEUTSCHE STADTETAG." GERMANY GERMANY/W CONSTN STRUCT NAT/G CENTRAL FEDERAL PWR...TIME/SEQ 20. PAGE 72 H1447
LOC/G
VOL/ASSN
LOBBY
ADMIN

S67
INDER S.,"AFTER THE CORONATION." CONSTN ECO/UNDEV EX/STRUC LEGIS INT/TRADE CONTROL SOVEREIGN ...TIME/SEQ 20 TONGA COMMONWLTH INAUGURATE. PAGE 76 H1527
CHIEF
NAT/G
POLICY

S67
MENDL W.,"FRENCH ATTITUDES ON DISARMAMENT." FRANCE CULTURE CHIEF FORCES DIPLOM LEAD WAR...TIME/SEQ 20 DEGAULLE/C. PAGE 109 H2175
NUC/PWR
WEAPON
ARMS/CONT
POLICY

S67
PETRAS J.,"GUERRILLA MOVEMENTS IN LATIN AMERICA - I." GUATEMALA PERU VENEZUELA NAT/G COLONIAL LEAD ATTIT PWR...TIME/SEQ METH/COMP 20 COLOMB. PAGE 125 H2497
GUERRILLA
REV
L/A+17C
MARXISM

S67
SMITH J.E.,"THE RED PRUSSIANISM OF THE GERMAN DEMOCRATIC REPUBLIC." GERMANY/E INTELL NAT/G SECT CHIEF...PREDICT TIME/SEQ 20. PAGE 146 H2913
MARXISM
NAT/LISM
GOV/COMP
EDU/PROP

S68
LAWRIE G.,"WHAT WILL CHANGE SOUTH AFRICA?" AFR SOUTH/AFR ELITES DOMIN CONTROL REPRESENT...TIME/SEQ TREND 20. PAGE 93 H1848
RACE/REL
DIPLOM
NAT/G
POLICY

B98
POLLOCK F.,THE HISTORY OF ENGLISH LAW BEFORE THE TIME OF EDWARD I (2 VOLS, 2ND ED.). UK CULTURE LOC/G LEGIS LICENSE AGREE CONTROL CT/SYS SANCTION CRIME...TIME/SEQ 13 COMMON/LAW CANON/LAW. PAGE 127 H2538
LAW
ADJUD
JURID

TIMING....SEE TIME

TINDALE N.B. H3099

TINGSTEN H. H3100,H3101

TINKER H. H3102,H3103,H3104

TINKER I. H2468

TIRYAKIAN E.A. H3105

TISDALE H. H3106

TITIEV M. H3107

TITO/MARSH....JOSIP BROZ TITO

B52
ULAM A.B.,TITOISM AND THE COMINFORM. USSR WOR+45 STRUCT INT/ORG NAT/G ACT/RES PLAN EXEC ATTIT DRIVE ALL/VALS...CONCPT OBS VAL/FREE 20 COMINTERN TITO/MARSH. PAGE 157 H3149 — COM POL/PAR TOTALISM YUGOSLAVIA

B57
TOMASIC D.A.,NATIONAL COMMUNISM AND SOVIET STRATEGY. UK USSR YUGOSLAVIA NAT/G POL/PAR CHIEF CREATE DOMIN REV WAR PWR...BIOG TREND 20 TITO/MARSH STALIN/J. PAGE 156 H3112 — COM NAT/LISM MARXISM DIPLOM

S59
SKILLING H.G.,"COMMUNISM: NATIONAL OR INTERNATIONAL." CHINA/COM USSR YUGOSLAVIA NAT/G POL/PAR VOL/ASSN DOMIN REGION COERCE ATTIT PWR MARXISM SOCISM...CONCPT TOT/POP 20 TITO/MARSH. PAGE 145 H2894 — COM TREND

TIVEY L. H3108

TIVEY L.J. H3108,H3109

TIZARD/H....HENRY TIZARD

TOBAGO....SEE TRINIDAD

TOCQUEVILL....ALEXIS DE TOCQUEVILLE

B58
ARON R.,SOCIOLOGIE DES SOCIETES INDUSTRIELLES: ESQUISSE D'UNE THEORIE DES REGIMES POLITIQUES. FRANCE SOCIETY NAT/G PROB/SOLV ATTIT RIGID/FLEX MARXISM POPULISM...POLICY SOC T 20 MARX/KARL TOCQUEVILL. PAGE 8 H0170 — TOTALISM INDUS CONSTN GOV/COMP

TODD W.B. H3110

TOGO....SEE ALSO AFR

B61
DUFFY J.,AFRICA SPEAKS. GHANA TOGO CULTURE ECO/UNDEV PROB/SOLV COLONIAL NEUTRAL DISCRIM NAT/LISM SOVEREIGN ALL/IDEOS...CONCPT ANTHOL SOC/INTEG 20 NEGRO THIRD/WRLD. PAGE 43 H0857 — AFR NAT/G FUT STRUCT

B64
WITHERELL J.W.,OFFICIAL PUBLICATIONS OF FRENCH EQUATORIAL AFRICA, FRENCH CAMEROONS, AND TOGO, 1946-1958 (PAMPHLET). CAMEROON CHAD FRANCE GABON TOGO LAW ECO/UNDEV EXTR/IND INT/TRADE...GEOG HEAL 20. PAGE 169 H3392 — BIBLIOG/A AFR NAT/G ADMIN

TOLEDO/O....TOLEDO, OHIO

TOMASIC D.A. H3111,H3112

TOMPKINS S.R. H3113

TONGA....TONGA

S67
INDER S.,"AFTER THE CORONATION." CONSTN ECO/UNDEV EX/STRUC LEGIS INT/TRADE CONTROL SOVEREIGN ...TIME/SEQ 20 TONGA COMMONWLTH INAUGURATE. PAGE 76 H1527 — CHIEF NAT/G POLICY

TONNIES F. H1432,H3114,H3115

TOP/EX....TOP EXECUTIVES

N
KYRIAK T.E.,CHINA: A BIBLIOGRAPHY. ASIA CHINA/COM AGRI FINAN INDUS NAT/G INT/TRADE PRESS...SOC 20. PAGE 90 H1789 — BIBLIOG/A MARXISM TOP/EX POL/PAR

B00
BENEDETTI V.,STUDIES IN DIPLOMACY. BELGIUM FRANCE GERMANY MOD/EUR CONSTN NAT/G CONSULT TOP/EX DOMIN EDU/PROP COERCE ATTIT...CONCPT INT BIOG TREND 19. PAGE 14 H0276 — PWR GEN/LAWS DIPLOM

B05
MACHIAVELLI N.,THE ART OF WAR. CHRIST-17C TOP/EX DRIVE ORD/FREE PWR SKILL...MGT CHARTS. PAGE 100 H1993 — NAT/G FORCES WAR ITALY

B08
THE GOVERNMENT OF SOUTH AFRICA (VOL. II). SOUTH/AFR STRATA EXTR/IND EX/STRUC TOP/EX BUDGET ADJUD ADMIN CT/SYS PRODUC...CORREL CENSUS 19 RAILROAD CIVIL/SERV POSTAL/SYS. PAGE 2 H0030 — CONSTN FINAN LEGIS NAT/G

B14
BERNHARDI F.,ON THE WAR OF TODAY. MOD/EUR INT/ORG NAT/G TOP/EX PWR CHARTS. PAGE 16 H0313 — FORCES SKILL WAR

N19
BUSINESS ECONOMISTS' GROUP,INCOME POLICIES (PAMPHLET). UK INDUS LABOR TOP/EX PAY COST PRODUC ...ECOMETRIC GOV/COMP SIMUL ANTHOL 20. PAGE 25 H0497 — INCOME WORKER WEALTH POLICY

N19
CANADA CIVIL SERV COMM,THE ANALYSIS OF ORGANIZATION IN THE GOVERNMENT OF CANADA (PAMPHLET). CANADA CONSTN EX/STRUC LEGIS TOP/EX CREATE PLAN CONTROL GP/REL 20. PAGE 26 H0517 — NAT/G MGT ADMIN DELIB/GP

C20
BLACHLY F.F.,"THE GOVERNMENT AND ADMINISTRATION OF GERMANY." GERMANY CONSTN LOC/G PROVS DELIB/GP EX/STRUC FORCES LEGIS TOP/EX CT/SYS...BIBLIOG/A 19/20. PAGE 17 H0348 — NAT/G GOV/REL ADMIN PHIL/SCI

B25
TEMPERLEY H.,THE FOREIGN POLICY OF CANNING: 1822-1827. MOD/EUR NAT/G TOP/EX EDU/PROP ROUTINE ATTIT RIGID/FLEX SUPEGO PWR SKILL...TIME/SEQ PARLIAMENT 20. PAGE 153 H3058 — PERSON DIPLOM UK BIOG

B25
WEBSTER C.,THE FOREIGN POLICY OF CASTLEREAGH: 1815-1822. LAW NAT/G DELIB/GP TOP/EX BAL/PWR ORD/FREE PWR RESPECT 19. PAGE 166 H3322 — MOD/EUR DIPLOM UK

B27
FLOURNOY F.,PARLIAMENT AND WAR. MOD/EUR UK NAT/G FORCES LEGIS TOP/EX DIPLOM LEGIT DEBATE ATTIT RIGID/FLEX PWR...DECISION TIME/SEQ PARLIAMENT 19/20. PAGE 52 H1032 — COERCE WAR

B30
BYNKERSHOEK C.,QUAESTIONUM JURIS PUBLICI LIBRI DUO. CHRIST-17C MOD/EUR CONSTN ELITES SOCIETY NAT/G PROVS EX/STRUC FORCES TOP/EX BAL/PWR DIPLOM ATTIT MORAL...TRADIT CONCPT. PAGE 25 H0502 — INT/ORG LAW NAT/LISM INT/LAW

S31
HEINBERG J.G.,"THE PERSONNEL OF FRENCH CABINETS, 1871-1930." FRANCE STRATA CHIEF CHOOSE REPRESENT MAJORITY...STAT QU CENSUS TREND CHARTS PERS/COMP 19/20 CHAMBR/DEP. PAGE 69 H1386 — ELITES NAT/G DELIB/GP TOP/EX

B33
MOSS W.,POLITICAL PARTIES IN THE IRISH FREE STATE. IRELAND UK LAW FINAN LABOR DELIB/GP TOP/EX TARIFFS EDU/PROP...CHARTS GP/COMP 20. PAGE 113 H2269 — POL/PAR NAT/G CHOOSE POLICY

B36
LAPRADE W.T.,PUBLIC OPINION AND POLITICS IN EIGHTEENTH CENTURY ENGLAND. UK CULTURE POL/PAR CHIEF TOP/EX LEAD REV NAT/LISM PWR 18 PROTESTANT PROTESTANT CHURCH/STA. PAGE 91 H1815 — POLICY ELITES ATTIT TIME/SEQ

B38
FIELD G.L.,THE SYNDICAL AND CORPORATIVE INSTITUTIONS OF ITALIAN FASCISM. ITALY CONSTN STRATA LABOR EX/STRUC TOP/EX ADJUD ADMIN LEAD TOTALISM AUTHORIT...MGT 20 MUSSOLIN/B. PAGE 50 H0991 — FASCISM INDUS NAT/G WORKER

B39
ANDERSON P.R.,THE BACKGROUND OF ANTI-ENGLISH FEELING IN GERMANY, 1890-1902. GERMANY MOD/EUR UK NAT/G POL/PAR TOP/EX WAR...IDEA/COMP 19/20. PAGE 7 H0132 — DIPLOM EDU/PROP ATTIT COLONIAL

B39
NICOLSON H.,CURZON: THE LAST PHASE, 1919-1925. UK NAT/G DELIB/GP TOP/EX ROUTINE WAR RIGID/FLEX ...METH/CNCPT 20 CURZON/GN. PAGE 118 H2352 — POLICY DIPLOM BIOG

B39
TAGGART F.J.,ROME AND CHINA. MEDIT-7 INT/ORG NAT/G FORCES LEGIS TOP/EX PLAN PWR SOVEREIGN...CHARTS TOT/POP ROM/EMP. PAGE 152 H3034 — ASIA WAR

S39
AIKEN C.,"THE BRITISH BUREAUCRACY AND THE ORIGINS OF PARLIAMENTARY DEMOCRACY" UK TOP/EX ADMIN. PAGE 4 H0082 — MGT NAT/G LEGIS

C40
FAHS C.B.,"GOVERNMENT IN JAPAN." FINAN FORCES LEGIS TOP/EX BUDGET INT/TRADE EDU/PROP SOVEREIGN ...CON/ANAL BIBLIOG/A 20 CHINJAP. PAGE 48 H0962 — ASIA DIPLOM NAT/G ADMIN

B41
PALMER R.R.,TWELVE WHO RULED. MOD/EUR ELITES STRUCT NAT/G POL/PAR DELIB/GP DOMIN ATTIT SUPEGO PWR — TOP/EX BIOG

...POLICY CONCPT 18. PAGE 123 H2453 REV FRANCE

S41
ABEL T.,"THE ELEMENT OF DECISION IN THE PATTERN OF WAR." EUR+WWI FUT NAT/G TOP/EX DIPLOM ROUTINE COERCE DISPL PERCEPT PWR...SOC METH/CNCPT HIST/WRIT TREND GEN/LAWS 20. PAGE 3 H0055 TEC/DEV FORCES WAR

B43
CONOVER H.F.,SOVIET RUSSIA: SELECTED LIST OF REFERENCES. USSR CULTURE INDUS NAT/G TOP/EX TEC/DEV BUDGET WAR CIVMIL/REL EFFICIENCY MARXISM 20. PAGE 32 H0644 BIBLIOG ECO/DEV COM DIPLOM

B45
CONOVER H.F.,ITALY: ECONOMICS, POLITICS AND MILITARY AFFAIRS, 1940-1945. ITALY ELITES NAT/G POL/PAR EX/STRUC TOP/EX DIPLOM DOMIN CONTROL COERCE WAR CIVMIL/REL EFFICIENCY 20. PAGE 32 H0646 BIBLIOG TOTALISM FORCES

B48
US LIBRARY OF CONGRESS,BRAZIL: A GUIDE TO THE OFFICIAL PUBLICATIONS OF BRAZIL. BRAZIL L/A+17C CONSULT DELIB/GP LEGIS CT/SYS 19/20. PAGE 160 H3206 BIBLIOG/A NAT/G ADMIN TOP/EX

B49
MCLEAN J.M.,THE PUBLIC SERVICE AND UNIVERSITY EDUCATION. UK USA-45 DELIB/GP EX/STRUC TOP/EX ADMIN ...GOV/COMP METH/COMP NAT/COMP ANTHOL 20. PAGE 107 H2142 ACADEM NAT/G EXEC EDU/PROP

S49
STEINMETZ H.,"THE PROBLEMS OF THE LANDRAT: A STUDY OF COUNTY GOVERNMENT IN THE US ZONE OF GERMANY." GERMANY/W USA+45 INDUS PLAN DIPLOM EDU/PROP CONTROL WAR GOV/REL FEDERAL WEALTH PLURISM...GOV/COMP 20 LANDRAT. PAGE 149 H2977 LOC/G COLONIAL MGT TOP/EX

B50
HOBBES T.,LEVIATHAN. UNIV CONSTN SOCIETY LOC/G NAT/G CONSULT TOP/EX DOMIN DRIVE PERSON PWR ...PHIL/SCI CONCPT SELF/OBS GEN/LAWS TOT/POP. PAGE 72 H1434 LAW ORD/FREE

B51
HALEVY E.,IMPERIALISM AND THE RISE OF LABOR (2ND ED.). UK NAT/G POL/PAR TOP/EX ATTIT ORD/FREE PWR 19/20 PARLIAMENT LABOR/PAR. PAGE 64 H1284 COLONIAL LABOR POLICY WAR

B51
WEBSTER C.,THE FOREIGN POLICY OF PALMERSTON - 1830 TO 1841. MOD/EUR UK LAW CONSTN INTELL SOCIETY STRUCT NAT/G FORCES TOP/EX CREATE BAL/PWR PWR 19. PAGE 166 H3323 ADMIN PERSON DIPLOM

B52
HIMMELFARB G.,LORD ACTON: A STUDY IN CONSCIENCE AND POLITICS. MOD/EUR NAT/G POL/PAR SECT LEGIS TOP/EX EDU/PROP ADMIN NAT/LISM ATTIT PERSON SUPEGO MORAL ORD/FREE...CONCPT PARLIAMENT 19 ACTON/LORD. PAGE 71 H1419 PWR BIOG

B52
WALTERS F.P.,A HISTORY OF THE LEAGUE OF NATIONS. EUR+WWI CONSTN NAT/G LEGIS TOP/EX ACT/RES PLAN EDU/PROP LEGIT ROUTINE ATTIT...TREND LEAGUE/NAT 20 CHINJAP. PAGE 165 H3297 INT/ORG TIME/SEQ NAT/LISM

B54
FRIEDRICH C.J.,TOTALITARIAN DICTATORSHIP AND AUTOCRACY. COM EUR+WWI GERMANY ITALY USSR INTELL ECO/DEV NAT/G POL/PAR FORCES TOP/EX ECO/TAC EDU/PROP LEGIT COERCE ATTIT ORD/FREE PWR FASCISM ...CONCPT TIME/SEQ GEN/LAWS NAZI 20. PAGE 53 H1068 SOCIETY DOMIN TOTALISM

C54
LANDAU J.M.,"PARLIAMENTS AND PARTIES IN EGYPT." UAR NAT/G SECT CONSULT LEGIS TOP/EX PROB/SOLV ADMIN COLONIAL...GEN/LAWS BIBLIOG 19/20. PAGE 90 H1804 ISLAM NAT/LISM PARL/PROC POL/PAR

B55
ALFIERI D.,DICTATORS FACE TO FACE. NAT/G TOP/EX DIPLOM EXEC COERCE ORD/FREE FASCISM...POLICY OBS 20 HITLER/A MUSSOLIN/B. PAGE 5 H0103 WAR CHIEF TOTALISM PERS/REL

B55
APTER D.E.,THE GOLD COAST IN TRANSITION. FUT CONSTN CULTURE SOCIETY ECO/UNDEV FAM KIN LOC/G NAT/G POL/PAR LEGIS TOP/EX EDU/PROP LEGIT ADMIN ATTIT PERSON PWR...CONCPT STAT INT CENSUS TOT/POP VAL/FREE. PAGE 7 H0149 AFR SOVEREIGN

B55
KHADDURI M.,WAR AND PEACE IN THE LAW OF ISLAM. CONSTN CULTURE SOCIETY STRATA NAT/G PROVS SECT FORCES TOP/EX CREATE DOMIN EDU/PROP ADJUD COERCE ATTIT RIGID/FLEX ALL/VALS...CONCPT TIME/SEQ TOT/POP VAL/FREE. PAGE 85 H1702 ISLAM JURID PEACE WAR

B55
KOHN H.,THE MIND OF MODERN RUSSIA. COM MOD/EUR USSR SOCIETY NAT/G SECT FORCES TOP/EX COERCE TOTALISM DRIVE RIGID/FLEX PWR SOVEREIGN...CONCPT TIME/SEQ WORK. PAGE 87 H1742 INTELL GEN/LAWS SOCISM RUSSIA

B55
NAMIER L.,PERSONALITIES AND POWERS. EUR+WWI MOD/EUR NAT/G POL/PAR TOP/EX EDU/PROP KNOWL...GEOG 17/20. PAGE 115 H2308 TIME/SEQ DIPLOM UK

B55
RESHETAR J.S.,PROBLEMS OF ANALYZING AND PREDICTING SOVIET BEHAVIOR. USSR CULTURE ECO/DEV AGRI DIST/IND EXTR/IND PROC/MFG NAT/G SECT TOP/EX ACT/RES ADMIN PWR WEALTH...SOC METH TOT/POP VAL/FREE 20. PAGE 131 H2617 COM ATTIT

I55
ROSTOW W.W.,"RUSSIA AND CHINA UNDER COMMUNISM." CHINA/COM USSR INTELL STRUCT INT/ORG NAT/G POL/PAR TOP/EX ACT/RES PLAN ADMIN ATTIT ALL/VALS MARXISM ...CONCPT OBS TIME/SEQ TREND GOV/COMP VAL/FREE 20. PAGE 134 H2689 COM ASIA

B57
BUCK P.W.,CONTOL OF FOREIGN RELATIONS IN MODERN NATIONS. FRANCE L/A+17C NETHERLAND USSR WOR+45 INT/ORG TOP/EX BAL/PWR DOMIN EDU/PROP COERCE PEACE ATTIT...CONCPT TREND 20 CMN/WLTH. PAGE 23 H0465 NAT/G PWR DIPLOM

B57
LAQUER W.Z.,COMMUNISM AND NATIONALISM IN THE MIDDLE EAST. ELITES INTELL STRATA NAT/G POL/PAR SECT VOL/ASSN TOP/EX DOMIN LEGIT REGION COERCE ATTIT PERSON PWR...CONCPT HIST/WRIT TIME/SEQ TREND GEN/LAWS VAL/FREE. PAGE 91 H1817 ISLAM NAT/LISM

S57
SPROUT H.,"ENVIRONMENTAL FACTORS IN THE STUDY OF INTERNATIONAL POLITICS." UNIV SOCIETY ECO/DEV NAT/G DELIB/GP TOP/EX ROUTINE ATTIT PERCEPT...POLICY GEOG CONCPT MYTH TIME/SEQ. PAGE 148 H2957 DECISION GEN/LAWS DIPLOM

B58
HAAS E.B.,THE UNITING OF EUROPE. EUR+WWI INT/ORG NAT/G POL/PAR TOP/EX ECO/TAC EDU/PROP LEGIT FEDERAL NAT/LISM DRIVE RIGID/FLEX ORD/FREE PWR PLURISM ...POLICY CONCPT INT GEN/LAWS ECSC EEC 20. PAGE 63 H1264 VOL/ASSN ECO/DEV

B58
SYME R.,COLONIAL ELITES: ROME, SPAIN, AND THE AMERICAS. CHRIST-17C MOD/EUR SPAIN UK USA-45 CULTURE NAT/G CHIEF TOP/EX...GOV/COMP IDEA/COMP NAT/COMP ROM/EMP GIBBON/EDW TOYNBEE/A. PAGE 151 H3022 COLONIAL ELITES DOMIN

S58
EULAV H.,"HD LASSWELL'S DEVELOPMENTAL ANALYSIS." FUT CULTURE TOP/EX PLAN CHOOSE SUPEGO PWR...TREND HYPO/EXP SIMUL GEN/METH VAL/FREE 20 LASSWELL/H. PAGE 47 H0948 CONCPT NEW/IDEA ELITES

S58
GUSFIELD J.R.,"EQUALITARIANISM AND BUREAUCRATIC RECRUITMENT." UK USA+45 USA-45 EX/STRUC 19/20. PAGE 63 H1257 GOV/COMP REPRESENT TOP/EX ELITES

B59
BARRON R.,PARTIES AND POLITICS IN MODERN FRANCE. FRANCE LOC/G DELIB/GP LEGIS TOP/EX EDU/PROP LEGIT TV FEEDBACK 20. PAGE 12 H0230 POL/PAR ALL/IDEOS CHOOSE PARTIC

B59
FAYERWEATHER J.,THE EXECUTIVE OVERSEAS: ADMINISTRATIVE ATTITUDES AND RELATIONSHIPS IN A FOREIGN CULTURE. USA+45 WOR+45 CULTURE LG/CO SML/CO ATTIT...MGT PERS/COMP 20 MEXIC/AMER. PAGE 49 H0979 INT/TRADE TOP/EX NAT/COMP PERS/REL

B59
FOX A.,THE POWER OF SMALL STATES: DIPLOMACY IN WORLD WAR TWO. EUR+WWI FINLAND NORWAY SPAIN SWEDEN TURKEY NAT/G TOP/EX DIPLOM PWR...HIST/WRIT 20. PAGE 52 H1044 CONCPT STERTYP BAL/PWR

B59
WILDNER H.,DIE TECHNIK DER DIPLOMATIE. TOP/EX ROLE ORD/FREE...INT/LAW JURID IDEA/COMP NAT/COMP 20. PAGE 168 H3364 DIPLOM POLICY DELIB/GP NAT/G

L59
JANIS I.L.,"DECISIONAL CONFLICT: A THEORETICAL ANALYSIS." INTELL NAT/G POL/PAR DELIB/GP LEGIS TOP/EX PLAN...DECISION CONGRESS NAZI 20 WWI. PAGE 80 H1590 ACT/RES PSY DIPLOM

S59
LABEDZ L.,"IDEOLOGY: THE FOURTH STAGE." COM USSR NAT/G TOP/EX LEGIT ATTIT PWR MARXISM...METH/CNCPT HIST/WRIT STERTYP TOT/POP 20. PAGE 90 H1795 CONCPT GEN/LAWS

S59
ZAUBERMAN A.,"SOVIET BLOC ECONOMIC INTEGRATION." COM CULTURE INTELL ECO/DEV INDUS TOP/EX ACT/RES PLAN ECO/TAC INT/TRADE ROUTINE CHOOSE ATTIT ...TIME/SEQ 20. PAGE 172 H3452 MARKET INT/ORG USSR TOTALISM

B60
GOODMAN E.,SOVIET DESIGN FOR A WORLD STATE. COM USSR NAT/G TOP/EX DIPLOM ECO/TAC DOMIN EDU/PROP COERCE REV ATTIT ORD/FREE...CON/ANAL 20. PAGE 59 H1171 PLAN PWR SOCISM TOTALISM

B60
LINDSAY K.,EUROPEAN ASSEMBLIES: THE EXPERIMENTAL PERIOD 1949-1959. EUR+WWI ECO/DEV NAT/G POL/PAR LEGIS TOP/EX ACT/RES PLAN ECO/TAC DOMIN LEGIT ROUTINE ATTIT DRIVE ORD/FREE PWR SKILL...SOC CONCPT TREND CHARTS GEN/LAWS VAL/FREE. PAGE 97 H1932 VOL/ASSN INT/ORG REGION

B60
MACRIDIS R.C.,THE DE GAULLE REPUBLIC: QUEST FOR UNITY. EUR+WWI NAT/G POL/PAR LEGIS LEGIT NAT/LISM ATTIT RIGID/FLEX ORD/FREE PWR...JURID CONCPT TIME/SEQ 20 DEGAULLE/C. PAGE 100 H2009
TOP/EX STRUCT FRANCE

B60
MORRIS I.,NATIONALISM AND THE RIGHT WING IN JAPAN: A STUDY OF POST WAR TRENDS. ASIA ELITES NAT/G DELIB/GP FORCES TOP/EX CHOOSE ATTIT...INT GEN/LAWS CONGRESS 20 CHINJAP. PAGE 113 H2262
POL/PAR TREND NAT/LISM

S60
FITZGIBBON R.H.,"DICTATORSHIP AND DEMOCRACY IN LATIN AMERICA." FUT ECO/DEV ECO/UNDEV INT/ORG LOC/G NAT/G TOP/EX PLAN TEC/DEV ECO/TAC CHOOSE ATTIT DRIVE PERSON ALL/VALS OAS TOT/POP 20. PAGE 51 H1019
L/A+17C ACT/RES INT/TRADE

S60
KELLEY G.A.,"THE POLITICAL BACKGROUND OF THE FRENCH A-BOMB." EUR+WWI USSR FORCES TOP/EX TEC/DEV NUC/PWR ATTIT PWR...CONCPT OBS/ENVIR TREND 20. PAGE 84 H1686
NAT/G RESPECT NAT/LISM FRANCE

S60
MAGATHAN W.,"SOME BASES OF WEST GERMAN MILITARY POLICY." EUR+WWI FUT INT/ORG TOP/EX ECO/TAC DOMIN DRIVE ORD/FREE PWR...TRADIT GEOG OBS TREND. PAGE 101 H2015
NAT/G FORCES GERMANY

S60
NORTH R.C.,"THE NEW EXPANSIONISM." ASIA CHINA/COM FUT INDIA CULTURE SOCIETY NAT/G TOP/EX DOMIN COERCE PWR MARXISM...CONCPT TIME/SEQ TREND GEN/LAWS COLD/WAR 20 MAO. PAGE 119 H2372
ATTIT DRIVE NAT/LISM

S60
PERLMANN H.,"UPHEAVAL IN TURKEY." EUR+WWI ISLAM NAT/G FORCES TOP/EX LEGIT COERCE CHOOSE DRIVE ORD/FREE PWR...TIME/SEQ TOT/POP 20. PAGE 125 H2494
CONSTN TURKEY

S60
WOLFE T.W.,"KHRUSHCHEV'S DISARMAMENT STRATEGY." COM NAT/G TOP/EX PLAN BAL/PWR DIPLOM ARMS/CONT COERCE ATTIT...POLICY CONCPT RECORD TREND CON/ANAL COLD/WAR 20 KHRUSH/N. PAGE 170 H3401
PWR GEN/LAWS USSR

S60
WYCKOFF T.,"THE ROLE OF THE MILITARY IN LATIN AMERICAN POLITICS." L/A+17C CONSTN CULTURE ECO/UNDEV POL/PAR FORCES LEGIS TOP/EX LEGIT GUERRILLA REV CHOOSE ORD/FREE PWR...TIME/SEQ VAL/FREE 20. PAGE 171 H3430
NAT/G COERCE TOTALISM

B61
ALLIGHAN G.,VERWOERD - THE END. SOUTH/AFR TOP/EX DIPLOM COLONIAL DISCRIM TOTALISM ATTIT AUTHORIT ...BIOG 20 NEGRO VERWOERD/H. PAGE 5 H0107
CONTROL CHIEF RACE/REL NAT/G

B61
APTER D.E.,THE POLITICAL KINGDOM IN UGANDA. UGANDA CULTURE ECO/UNDEV AGRI KIN SECT TOP/EX REGION ATTIT HABITAT CONSERVE...GEOG AUD/VIS 20. PAGE 8 H0153
NAT/LISM POL/PAR COLONIAL ECO/TAC

B61
BISHOP D.G.,THE ADMINISTRATION OF BRITISH FOREIGN RELATIONS. EUR+WWI MOD/EUR INT/ORG NAT/G POL/PAR DELIB/GP LEGIS TOP/EX ECO/TAC DOMIN EDU/PROP ADMIN COERCE 20. PAGE 17 H0344
ROUTINE PWR DIPLOM UK

B61
BURDEAU G.,O PODER EXECUTIVO NA FRANCA. EUR+WWI FRANCE CONSTN DELIB/GP LEGIT ADMIN ATTIT ALL/VALS CONCPT. PAGE 24 H0478
TOP/EX POL/PAR NAT/G LEGIS

B61
DALLIN D.J.,SOVIET FOREIGN POLICY AFTER STALIN. ASIA CHINA/COM EUR+WWI GERMANY IRAN UK YUGOSLAVIA INT/ORG NAT/G VOL/ASSN FORCES TOP/EX BAL/PWR DOMIN EDU/PROP COERCE ATTIT PWR 20. PAGE 37 H0737
COM DIPLOM USSR

B61
DELEFORTRIE-SOU N.,LES DIRIGEANTS DE L'INDUSTRIE FRANCAISE. FRANCE CULTURE ELITES PROB/SOLV ...DECISION STAT CHARTS 20. PAGE 39 H0789
INDUS STRATA TOP/EX LEAD

B61
KEREKES T.,THE ARAB MIDDLE EAST AND MUSLIM AFRICA. ISLAM SOCIETY ECO/UNDEV SECT VOL/ASSN TOP/EX REGION ATTIT PWR...GEOG CONCPT TIME/SEQ GEN/LAWS 20. PAGE 85 H1694
NAT/G TREND NAT/LISM

B61
KISSINGER H.A.,THE NECESSITY FOR CHOICE. FUT USA+45 ECO/UNDEV NAT/G PLAN BAL/PWR ECO/TAC ARMS/CONT DETER NUC/PWR ATTIT...POLICY CONCPT RECORD GEN/LAWS COLD/WAR 20. PAGE 87 H1728
TOP/EX TREND DIPLOM

B61
MACLEOD I.,NEVILLE CHAMBERLAIN. UK SOCIETY TOP/EX WAR PERSON ALL/VALS ORD/FREE PARLIAMENT 20 CHAMBRLN/N. PAGE 100 H2003
BIOG NAT/G CREATE

B61
MARVICK D.,POLITICAL DECISION-MAKERS. INTELL STRATA NAT/G POL/PAR EX/STRUC LEGIS DOMIN EDU/PROP ATTIT PERSON PWR...PSY STAT OBS CONT/OBS STAND/INT UNPLAN/INT TIME/SEQ CHARTS STERTYP VAL/FREE. PAGE 104 H2073
TOP/EX BIOG ELITES

B61
RAO K.V.,PARLIAMENTARY DEMOCRACY OF INDIA. INDIA EX/STRUC TOP/EX COLONIAL CT/SYS PARL/PROC ORD/FREE ...POLICY CONCPT TREND 20 PARLIAMENT. PAGE 130 H2592
CONSTN ADJUD NAT/G FEDERAL

S61
VALLET R.,"IRAN: KEY TO THE MIDDLE EAST." COM IRAQ ISLAM KUWAIT LEBANON SAUDI/ARAB TURKEY ELITES SOCIETY INDUS PROC/MFG POL/PAR TOP/EX PLAN BAL/PWR DIPLOM ECO/TAC ALL/VALS...TREND CENTO 20. PAGE 161 H3224
NAT/G ECO/UNDEV IRAN

B62
ANDREWS W.G.,EUROPEAN POLITICAL INSTITUTIONS. FRANCE GERMANY UK USSR TOP/EX LEAD PARL/PROC CHOOSE 20. PAGE 7 H0139
NAT/COMP POL/PAR EX/STRUC LEGIS

B62
CHAKRAVARTI P.C.,INDIA'S CHINA POLICY. ASIA CHINA/COM S/ASIA CULTURE NAT/G TOP/EX ACT/RES EDU/PROP DRIVE ALL/VALS...MYTH 20. PAGE 28 H0571
RIGID/FLEX TREND INDIA

B62
HATCH J.,AFRICA TODAY-AND TOMORROW: AN OUTLINE OF BASIC FACTS AND MAJOR PROBLEMS. AFR FUT ISLAM STRATA ECO/UNDEV INT/ORG NAT/G POL/PAR DELIB/GP TOP/EX EDU/PROP LEGIT CHOOSE ATTIT...TIME/SEQ TOT/POP COLD/WAR 20. PAGE 67 H1353
PLAN CONSTN NAT/LISM

S62
IOVTCHOUK M.T.,"ON SOME THEORETICAL PRINCIPLES AND METHODS OF SOCIOLOGICAL INVESTIGATIONS (IN RUSSIAN)." FUT USA+45 STRATA R+D NAT/G POL/PAR TOP/EX ACT/RES PLAN ECO/TAC EDU/PROP ROUTINE ATTIT RIGID/FLEX MARXISM SOCISM...MARXIST METH/CNCPT OBS TREND NAT/COMP GEN/LAWS 20. PAGE 78 H1564
COM ECO/DEV CAP/ISM USSR

S62
LONDON K.,"SINO-SOVIET RELATIONS IN THE CONTEXT OF THE 'WORLD SOCIALIST SYSTEM'." ASIA CHINA/COM COM USSR INT/ORG NAT/G TOP/EX BAL/PWR DIPLOM DOMIN ATTIT PERCEPT RIGID/FLEX PWR MARXISM...METH/CNCPT TREND 20. PAGE 98 H1957
DELIB/GP CONCPT SOCISM

B63
CREMEANS C.,THE ARABS AND THE WORLD: NASSER'S ARAB NATIONALIST POLICY. FUT ISLAM UAR USA+45 SOCIETY STRATA NAT/G POL/PAR PLAN DIPLOM EDU/PROP LEGIT DRIVE ALL/VALS...INT TIME/SEQ CHARTS 20 NASSER/G. PAGE 35 H0700
TOP/EX ATTIT REGION NAT/LISM

B63
DEBRAY P.,LE PORTUGAL ENTRE DEUX REVOLUTIONS. EUR+WWI PORTUGAL CONSTN LEGIT ADMIN ATTIT ALL/VALS ...DECISION CONCPT 20 SALAZAR/A. PAGE 39 H0779
NAT/G DELIB/GP TOP/EX

B63
ELLIOT J.H.,THE REVOLT OF THE CATALANS. SPAIN LOC/G PROVS FORCES DIPLOM TASK WAR GOV/REL INGP/REL ...POLICY 17 OLIVARES. PAGE 45 H0909
REV NAT/G TOP/EX DOMIN

B63
FALL B.,THE TWO VIETNAMS. CULTURE SOCIETY ECO/UNDEV NAT/G TOP/EX ACT/RES PLAN ECO/TAC DOMIN EDU/PROP COERCE ATTIT DRIVE PERSON ORD/FREE PWR...SOC TIME/SEQ COLD/WAR 20. PAGE 48 H0965
S/ASIA BIOG VIETNAM

B63
KRAEHE E.,METTERNICH'S GERMAN POLICY: THE CONTEST WITH NAPOLEON, 1799-1814, VOL. 1. FRANCE MOD/EUR NAT/G CONSULT TOP/EX PLAN BAL/PWR DOMIN COERCE ATTIT DRIVE PERCEPT PERSON SKILL...CONCPT RECORD TIME/SEQ TREND 18/19. PAGE 88 H1764
BIOG GERMANY DIPLOM

B63
MONGER G.W.,THE END OF ISOLATION. FRANCE MOD/EUR RUSSIA UK NAT/G LEGIS TOP/EX GOV/REL PWR 20 TREATY CHINJAP. PAGE 112 H2239
DIPLOM POLICY WAR

B63
NKRUMAH K.,AFRICA MUST UNITE. AFR FUT GHANA CONSTN CULTURE SOCIETY NAT/G POL/PAR DELIB/GP TOP/EX PLAN DOMIN EDU/PROP ATTIT DRIVE...TIME/SEQ CHARTS TOT/POP 20. PAGE 118 H2364
CONCPT GEN/LAWS REGION

B63
QUAISON-SACKEY A.,AFRICA UNBOUND: REFLECTIONS OF AN AFRICAN STATESMAN. ISLAM CULTURE INTELL INT/ORG POL/PAR TOP/EX DOMIN EDU/PROP LEGIT ATTIT PERSON ...CONCPT OBS TIME/SEQ CHARTS STERTYP 20 UN. PAGE 129 H2571
AFR BIOG

B63
STEVENS G.G.,EGYPT YESTERDAY AND TODAY. CONSTN ECO/UNDEV AGRI INDUS NAT/G POL/PAR FORCES ECO/TAC EDU/PROP COERCE WAR NAT/LISM DRIVE ALL/VALS ...TIME/SEQ WORK SUEZ 20. PAGE 149 H2983
ISLAM TOP/EX REV UAR

B63
THUCYDIDES,THE PELOPONESIAN WARS. MEDIT-7 CULTURE INT/ORG NAT/G FORCES TOP/EX PLAN ROUTINE PWR ...CONCPT. PAGE 155 H3091
ATTIT COERCE WAR

B63
TUCKER R.C.,THE SOVIET POLITICAL MIND. COM INTELL NAT/G TOP/EX EDU/PROP ADMIN COERCE TOTALISM ATTIT PWR MARXISM...PSY MYTH HYPO/EXP 20. PAGE 157 H3136
STRUCT RIGID/FLEX ELITES USSR

B63
ULAM A.B.,THE NEW FACE OF SOVIET TOTALITARIANISM.
COM

FUT INTELL NAT/G POL/PAR EX/STRUC TOP/EX DIPLOM ECO/TAC DOMIN EDU/PROP LEGIT COERCE ATTIT RIGID/FLEX...OBS HIST/WRIT TREND TOT/POP VAL/FREE COLD/WAR. PAGE 158 H3150
PWR TOTALISM USSR

S63
ANTHON C.G.,"THE END OF THE ADENAUER ERA." EUR+WWI GERMANY/W CONSTN EX/STRUC CREATE DIPLOM LEGIT ATTIT PERSON ALL/VALS...RECORD 20 ADENAUER/K. PAGE 7 H0144
NAT/G TOP/EX BAL/PWR GERMANY

S63
CRUTCHER J.,"PAN AFRICANISM: AFRICAN ODYSSEY." AFR NAT/G POL/PAR PROF/ORG VOL/ASSN TOP/EX CREATE REGION RACE/REL ALL/VALS...CONCPT TIME/SEQ TREND CON/ANAL 20. PAGE 36 H0716
PROVS DELIB/GP COLONIAL

S63
DUTT V.P.,"CHINA: JEALOUS NEIGHBOR." ASIA CHINA/COM INDIA S/ASIA NAT/G TOP/EX DOMIN COERCE REV ATTIT ...POLICY COLD/WAR 20. PAGE 44 H0874
FORCES PWR DIPLOM

S63
EMERI C.,"LES FORCES POLITIQUES AU PARLEMENT" EUR+WWI FRANCE ELITES DELIB/GP TOP/EX LEGIT ATTIT ...SOC 20 PARLIAMENT. PAGE 46 H0917
POL/PAR LEGIS PWR NAT/G

S63
GLUCKMAN M.,"CIVIL WAR AND THEORIES OF POWER IN BAROTSE-LAND: AFRICAN AND MEDIEVAL ANALOGIES." AFR CHRIST-17C LAW CONSTN CULTURE STRATA KIN DELIB/GP FORCES DOMIN LEGIT COERCE PERCEPT ORD/FREE...SOC INT TIME/SEQ GEN/LAWS VAL/FREE. PAGE 57 H1148
TOP/EX PWR WAR

S63
GROSSER A.,"FRANCE AND GERMANY IN THE ATLANTIC COMMUNITY." INT/ORG NAT/G TOP/EX DIPLOM REGION PEACE ATTIT ORD/FREE PWR...CONCPT RECORD TIME/SEQ GEN/LAWS VAL/FREE COLD/WAR 20. PAGE 62 H1234
EUR+WWI VOL/ASSN FRANCE GERMANY

S63
HALPERN A.M.,"THE EMERGENCE OF AN ASIAN COMMUNIST BLOC." ASIA CHINA/COM COM FUT KOREA/N S/ASIA VIETNAM/N STRATA NAT/G DELIB/GP FORCES TOP/EX PLAN BAL/PWR COERCE DETER PWR COLD/WAR WORK 20. PAGE 65 H1295
POL/PAR EDU/PROP DIPLOM

S63
HARRIS R.L.,"A COMPARATIVE ANALYSIS OF THE ADMINISTRATIVE SYSTEMS OF CANADA AND CEYLON." S/ASIA CULTURE SOCIETY STRATA TOP/EX ACT/RES DOMIN EDU/PROP LEGIT COERCE ATTIT SUPEGO ALL/VALS...MGT CHARTS GEN/LAWS VAL/FREE 20. PAGE 67 H1343
DELIB/GP EX/STRUC CANADA CEYLON

S63
HOSKINS H.L.,"ARAB SOCIALISM IN THE UAR." ISLAM USSR AGRI INDUS NAT/G TOP/EX CREATE DIPLOM EDU/PROP DRIVE KNOWL PWR SOCISM...POLICY CONCPT TREND SUEZ 20. PAGE 74 H1478
ECO/DEV PLAN UAR

S63
KOHN H.,"GERMANY IN WORLD POLITICS." EUR+WWI GERMANY GERMANY/W USSR NAT/G POL/PAR TOP/EX ATTIT ...CONCPT TREND GEN/LAWS 20 NATO ADENAUER/K. PAGE 87 H1746
ACT/RES ORD/FREE BAL/PWR

S63
LEE J.M.,"PARLIAMENT IN REPUBLICAN GHANA." AFR CONSTN CULTURE SOCIETY STRATA POL/PAR DELIB/GP TOP/EX DOMIN EDU/PROP LEGIT COERCE CHOOSE ATTIT ALL/VALS...CONCPT STAT TIME/SEQ VAL/FREE 20. PAGE 93 H1857
LEGIS GHANA

S63
MONROE A.D.,"BRITAIN AND THE EUROPEAN COMMUNITY." EUR+WWI FRANCE NAT/G DELIB/GP TOP/EX ECO/TAC DOMIN PWR...POLICY RECORD GEN/LAWS EEC EFTA 20 EFTA CMN/WLTH. PAGE 112 H2241
VOL/ASSN ATTIT UK

S63
POPPINO R.E.,"IMBALANCE IN BRAZIL." L/A+17C NAT/G TOP/EX PLAN DIPLOM LEGIT DRIVE WEALTH...CON/ANAL LAFTA 20. PAGE 127 H2544
POL/PAR ECO/TAC BRAZIL

B64
AFRO ASIAN SOLIDARITY AGAINST IMPERIALISM. AFR ISLAM S/ASIA ECO/UNDEV NAT/G POL/PAR TOP/EX PRESS ...INT ANTHOL 20 CHOU/ENLAI. PAGE 2 H0043
MARXISM DIPLOM EDU/PROP CHIEF

B64
BINDER L.,THE IDEOLOGICAL REVOLUTION IN THE MIDDLE EAST. ISLAM STRUCT INT/ORG KIN SECT EX/STRUC TOP/EX PLAN ATTIT DRIVE RIGID/FLEX PWR...MYTH TOT/POP 20. PAGE 17 H0338
POL/PAR NAT/G NAT/LISM

B64
CLUBB O.E. JR.,TWENTIETH CENTURY CHINA. ASIA CHINA/COM INTELL NAT/G POL/PAR VOL/ASSN ACT/RES EDU/PROP COERCE REV PWR...TIME/SEQ 20. PAGE 30 H0608
TOP/EX DRIVE

B64
GRIFFITH W.E.,THE SINO-SOVIET RIFT. ASIA CHINA/COM COM CUBA USSR YUGOSLAVIA NAT/G POL/PAR VOL/ASSN DELIB/GP FORCES TOP/EX DIPLOM EDU/PROP DRIVE PERSON PWR...TREND 20 TREATY. PAGE 61 H1224
ATTIT TIME/SEQ BAL/PWR SOCISM

B64
HEIMSATH C.H.,INDIAN NATIONALISM AND HINDU SOCIAL REFORM. S/ASIA LAW CULTURE SOCIETY STRATA PROVS VOL/ASSN DELIB/GP LEGIS TOP/EX DOMIN EDU/PROP LEGIT ATTIT ALL/VALS...POLICY SOC TIME/SEQ STERTYP VAL/FREE 19/20. PAGE 69 H1385
SECT NAT/G

B64
IMAZ J.L.,LOS QUE MANDAN. INDUS LABOR NAT/G POL/PAR PROVS SECT CHIEF TOP/EX CONTROL 20 ARGEN. PAGE 76 H1524
LEAD FORCES ELITES ATTIT

B64
SINGER M.R.,THE EMERGING ELITE: A STUDY OF POLITICAL LEADERSHIP IN CEYLON. S/ASIA ECO/UNDEV AGRI KIN NAT/G SECT EX/STRUC LEGIT ATTIT PWR RESPECT...SOC STAT CHARTS 20. PAGE 144 H2883
TOP/EX STRATA NAT/LISM CEYLON

B64
SKINNER E.P.,THE MOSSI OF UPPER VOLTA: THE POLITICAL DEVELOPMENT OF A SUDANESE PEOPLE. AFR LAW AGRI FAM KIN POL/PAR PROVS SECT DELIB/GP EX/STRUC FORCES TOP/EX DOMIN EDU/PROP LEGIT CT/SYS COERCE CHOOSE ORD/FREE PWR WEALTH...SOC MYTH VAL/FREE. PAGE 145 H2897
CULTURE OBS UPPER/VOLT

B64
WHEELER-BENNETT J.W.,THE NEMESIS OF POWER (2ND ED.). EUR+WWI GERMANY TOP/EX TEC/DEV ADMIN WAR PERS/REL RIGID/FLEX ROLE ORD/FREE PWR FASCISM 20 HITLER/A. PAGE 167 H3342
FORCES NAT/G GP/REL STRUCT

B64
WHITE D.S.,SEEDS OF DISCORD. EUR+WWI FRANCE NAT/G VOL/ASSN FORCES DIPLOM DOMIN NAT/LISM DISPL RIGID/FLEX PWR...RECORD INT BIOG 20 DEGAULLE/C ROOSEVLT/F CHURCHLL/W HULL. PAGE 167 H3347
TOP/EX ATTIT

B64
WILCOX W.A.,INDIA, PAKISTAN AND THE RISE OF CHINA. ASIA BURMA CEYLON CHINA/COM INDIA PAKISTAN S/ASIA NAT/G VOL/ASSN FORCES TOP/EX ACT/RES DOMIN REGION RIGID/FLEX ORD/FREE...POLICY GEN/LAWS COLD/WAR 20. PAGE 168 H3362
CULTURE ATTIT DIPLOM

S64
BENSON M.,"SOUTH AFRICA AND WORLD OPINION." AFR SOUTH/AFR INTELL SOCIETY TOP/EX ECO/TAC DOMIN COERCE DISCRIM ATTIT PWR WEALTH...POLICY RECORD 20. PAGE 14 H0285
NAT/G RIGID/FLEX RACE/REL

S64
BRADLEY C.P.,"THE FORMATION OF MALAYSIA." INDIA S/ASIA POL/PAR VOL/ASSN TOP/EX LEGIT RACE/REL ORD/FREE 20. PAGE 20 H0398
NAT/G CREATE COLONIAL MALAYSIA

S64
DE GAULLE C.,"FRENCH WORLD VIEW." AFR ASIA CHINA/COM EUR+WWI ISLAM ECO/UNDEV INT/ORG NAT/G VOL/ASSN ACT/RES DIPLOM ECO/TAC EDU/PROP ATTIT DRIVE WEALTH 20. PAGE 37 H0751
TOP/EX PWR FOR/AID FRANCE

S64
ENNIS T.E.,"VIETNAM: LAND WITHOUT LAUGHTER." S/ASIA VIETNAM VIETNAM/S INTELL SOCIETY SECT FORCES DIPLOM LEGIT COERCE WAR ATTIT RIGID/FLEX ORD/FREE COLD/WAR 20. PAGE 46 H0929
NAT/G TOP/EX GUERRILLA

S64
KOVNER M.,"THE SINO-SOVIET DISPUTE: COMMUNISM AT THE CROSSROADS." ASIA CHINA/COM COM USSR ECO/UNDEV NAT/G TOP/EX CREATE BAL/PWR DOMIN EDU/PROP PWR ...CONCPT COMECON 20. PAGE 88 H1760
ATTIT TREND

S64
LEWIS B.,"THE QUEST FOR FREEDOM--A SAD STORY OF THE MIDDLE EAST." ISLAM ISRAEL LEBANON TURKEY CULTURE NAT/G SECT LEGIS TOP/EX DOMIN EDU/PROP LEGIT ORD/FREE PWR RESPECT...POLICY TIME/SEQ VAL/FREE 20. PAGE 96 H1911
CONSTN ATTIT NAT/LISM

S64
MARES V.E.,"EAST EUROPE'S SECOND CHANCE." COM EUR+WWI HUNGARY ROMANIA USSR YUGOSLAVIA ECO/UNDEV NAT/G TOP/EX CREATE PLAN TEC/DEV REGION NAT/LISM RIGID/FLEX PWR...CONCPT STAT COMECON 20. PAGE 102 H2047
VOL/ASSN ECO/TAC

S64
RUDOLPH L.I.,"GENERALS AND POLITICIANS IN INDIA." INDIA S/ASIA CULTURE STRATA NAT/G LEGIS TOP/EX EDU/PROP ATTIT ORD/FREE PWR RESPECT SKILL...POLICY BIOG TIME/SEQ STERTYP VAL/FREE 20. PAGE 136 H2713
FORCES COERCE

S64
SMYTHE H.H.,"NEHRU AND INDIAN FOREIGN POLICY." S/ASIA ECO/UNDEV NAT/G POL/PAR CONSULT PLAN DIPLOM NEUTRAL COERCE ATTIT DRIVE PERSON MORAL ORD/FREE RESPECT...GEOG CONCPT TIME/SEQ TREND GEN/LAWS 20 NEHRU/J. PAGE 146 H2922
TOP/EX BIOG INDIA

S64
VANDENBOSCH A.,"POWER BALANCE IN INDONESIA." S/ASIA USSR NAT/G TOP/EX BAL/PWR DOMIN NEUTRAL ORD/FREE PWR...POLICY TIME/SEQ GEN/LAWS 20 SUKARNO/A. PAGE 162 H3233
FORCES TREND DIPLOM INDONESIA

B65
ADAM T.R.,GOVERNMENT AND POLITICS IN AFRICA SOUTH OF THE SAHARA. AFR EUR+WWI CONSTN CULTURE INTELL POL/PAR TOP/EX LEGIT REGION DRIVE...OBS TREND CMN/WLTH 20. PAGE 3 H0062
NAT/G TIME/SEQ RACE/REL COLONIAL

B65
BAYNE E.A.,FOUR WAYS OF POLITICS: STATE AND NATION IN ITALY, SOMALIA, ISRAEL, AND IRAN. IRAN ISRAEL ITALY SOMALIA LEAD CHOOSE MAJORITY GOV/COMP.
ECO/UNDEV NAT/G DECISION

PAGE 12 H0244 — TOP/EX

B65
EDINGER L.J.,KURT SCHUMACHER: A STUDY IN PERSONALITY AND POLITICAL BEHAVIOR. EUR+WWI GERMANY NAT/G DRIVE ROLE PWR SOCISM...BIBLIOG 20 SOC/DEMPAR SCHUMCHR/K. PAGE 44 H0889
TOP/EX LEAD PERSON BIOG

B65
MCSHERRY J.E.,RUSSIA AND THE UNITED STATES UNDER EISENHOWER, KHRUSHCHEV, AND KENNEDY. USSR EX/STRUC TOP/EX PRESS WAR...POLICY TREND 20. PAGE 108 H2150
DIPLOM CHIEF NAT/G PEACE

B65
NAMIER L.B.,THE STRUCTURE OF POLITICS AT THE ACCESSION OF GEORGE III. UK LOC/G TOP/EX COLONIAL LEAD PARTIC REV CHOOSE REPRESENT GOV/REL PERSON SOVEREIGN...GOV/COMP 18 PARLIAMENT. PAGE 115 H2309
PARL/PROC LEGIS NAT/G POL/PAR

B65
NORDEN A.,WAR AND NAZI CRIMINALS IN WEST GERMANY: STATE, ECONOMY, ADMINISTRATION, ARMY, JUSTICE, SCIENCE. GERMANY GERMANY/W MOD/EUR ECO/DEV ACADEM EX/STRUC FORCES DOMIN ADMIN CT/SYS...POLICY MAJORIT PACIFIST 20. PAGE 119 H2370
FASCIST WAR NAT/G TOP/EX

B65
PEASLEE A.J.,CONSTITUTIONS OF NATIONS* THIRD REVISED EDITION (VOLUME I* AFRICA). LAW EX/STRUC LEGIS TOP/EX LEGIT CT/SYS ROUTINE ORD/FREE PWR SOVEREIGN...CON/ANAL CHARTS. PAGE 124 H2481
AFR CHOOSE CONSTN NAT/G

B65
ROSENBERG A.,DEMOCRACY AND SOCIALISM. COM EUR+WWI FRANCE MOD/EUR STRUCT INT/ORG NAT/G POL/PAR TOP/EX EDU/PROP COERCE PERSON PWR FASCISM MARXISM...CONCPT TIME/SEQ MARX/KARL 19/20. PAGE 134 H2677
ATTIT

B65
ULAM A.,THE BOLSHEVIKS. COM USSR NAT/G CHIEF ECO/TAC ADMIN LEAD WAR POPULISM...POLICY 19/20 LENIN/VI BOLSHEVISM. PAGE 157 H3148
SOCISM POL/PAR TOP/EX REV

S65
GRIFFITH S.B.,"COMMUNIST CHINA'S CAPACITY TO MAKE WAR." CHINA/COM COM NAT/G TOP/EX PLAN DOMIN COERCE NUC/PWR ATTIT RESPECT SKILL...CONCPT MYTH TIME/SEQ TREND COLD/WAR 20. PAGE 61 H1221
FORCES PWR WEAPON ASIA

S65
HELMREICH E.C.,"KADAR'S HUNGARY." COM EUR+WWI HUNGARY USSR INTELL ECO/DEV AGRI INT/ORG TOP/EX DOMIN ALL/VALS WORK COLD/WAR 20. PAGE 69 H1390
NAT/G RIGID/FLEX TOTALISM

S65
ROGGER H.,"EAST GERMANY: STABLE OR IMMOBILE." COM EUR+WWI GERMANY/E NAT/G INT/TRADE DOMIN EDU/PROP COERCE TOTALISM COLD/WAR 20. PAGE 133 H2659
TOP/EX RIGID/FLEX GERMANY

S65
RUBINSTEIN A.Z.,"YUGOSLAVIA'S OPENING SOCIETY." COM USSR INTELL NAT/G LEGIS TOP/EX LEGIT CT/SYS RIGID/FLEX ALL/VALS SOCISM...HUM TIME/SEQ TREND 20. PAGE 135 H2708
CONSTN EX/STRUC YUGOSLAVIA

S65
STAAR R.F.,"RETROGRESSION IN POLAND." COM USSR AGRI INDUS NAT/G CREATE EDU/PROP TOTALISM RIGID/FLEX ORD/FREE PWR SOCISM...RECORD CHARTS 20. PAGE 148 H2965
TOP/EX ECO/TAC POLAND

S65
VUCINICH W.S.,"WHITHER RUMANIA." COM USSR YUGOSLAVIA NAT/G VOL/ASSN DELIB/GP TOP/EX LEGIT NAT/LISM TOTALISM ATTIT DRIVE RIGID/FLEX ORD/FREE WEALTH SOCISM...TIME/SEQ TREND 20. PAGE 164 H3281
ECO/DEV CREATE ROMANIA

B66
AFRIFA A.A.,THE GHANA COUP. AFR GHANA ELITES NAT/G DIPLOM DOMIN 20 NKRUMAH/K. PAGE 4 H0076
TOP/EX REV FORCES POL/PAR

B66
CHAPMAN B.,THE PROFESSION OF GOVERNMENT: THE PUBLIC SERVICE IN EUROPE. CONSTN NAT/G POL/PAR EX/STRUC LEGIS TOP/EX PROB/SOLV DEBATE EXEC PARL/PROC PARTIC 20. PAGE 29 H0581
BIBLIOG ADMIN EUR+WWI GOV/COMP

B66
DEUTSCHER I.,STALIN: A POLITICAL BIOGRAPHY. EUR+WWI USSR POL/PAR FORCES DIPLOM ADMIN LEAD REV WAR TOTALISM PERSON 20 STALIN/J ROOSEVLT/F LENIN/VI HITLER/A. PAGE 40 H0807
BIOG MARXISM TOP/EX PWR

B66
DUNCOMBE H.S.,COUNTY GOVERNMENT IN AMERICA. USA+45 FINAN MUNIC ADMIN ROUTINE GOV/REL...GOV/COMP 20. PAGE 43 H0863
LOC/G PROVS CT/SYS TOP/EX

B66
KEAY E.A.,THE NATIVE AND CUSTOMARY COURTS OF NIGERIA. NIGERIA CONSTN ELITES NAT/G TOP/EX PARTIC REGION...DECISION JURID 19/20. PAGE 84 H1673
AFR ADJUD LAW

B66
MATTHEWS R.,AFRICAN POWDER KEG: REVOLT AND DISSENT IN SIX EMERGENT NATIONS. AFR ALGERIA DAHOMEY GABON GHANA MALAWI GAMBLE LEAD PARTIC REV DRIVE...BIOG TREND GOV/COMP 20. PAGE 105 H2098
ELITES ECO/UNDEV TOP/EX CONTROL

B66
SCHRAM S.,MAO TSE-TUNG. ASIA CHINA/COM CONTROL REGION ATTIT...POLICY IDEA/COMP 20 MAO. PAGE 140 H2799
BIOG MARXISM TOP/EX GUERRILLA

B66
ZINKIN T.,CHALLENGES IN INDIA. INDIA PAKISTAN LAW AGRI FINAN INDUS TOP/EX TEC/DEV CONTROL ROUTINE ORD/FREE PWR 20 NEHRU/J SHASTRI/LB CIVIL/SERV. PAGE 173 H3458
NAT/G ECO/TAC POLICY ADMIN

L66
ZOPPO C.E.,"NUCLEAR TECHNOLOGY, MULTIPOLARITY, AND INTERNATIONAL STABILITY." ASIA RUSSIA USA+45 STRUCT TOP/EX BAL/PWR DIPLOM DETER CIVMIL/REL NAT/COMP. PAGE 173 H3464
NET/THEORY ORD/FREE DECISION NUC/PWR

B67
ANDERSON C.W.,ISSUES OF POLITICAL DEVELOPMENT. BURMA WOR+45 CULTURE TOP/EX ECO/TAC MARXISM ...CHARTS NAT/COMP 20 COLOMB CONGO/LEOP. PAGE 6 H0126
NAT/LISM COERCE ECO/UNDEV SOCISM

B67
BANKWITZ P.C.,MAXINE WEYGAND AND CIVIL-MILITARY RELATIONS IN MODERN FRANCE. FRANCE LEAD WAR PWR ...INT BIBLIOG 20. PAGE 11 H0212
CIVMIL/REL FORCES NAT/G TOP/EX

L67
WILBER L.A.,"THE GOVERNMENTAL STRUCTURE OF MISSISSIPPI: ITS STRENGTHS AND WEAKNESSES." AGRI LOC/G SCHOOL EX/STRUC LEGIS TOP/EX BUDGET CT/SYS APPORT RACE/REL...GOV/COMP 20 MISSISSIPP. PAGE 168 H3359
CONSTN PROVS STAT CON/ANAL

S67
GREGORY R.,"THE MINISTER'S LINE: OR, THE M4 COMES TO BERKSHIRE. PART I." UK CONSTN DIST/IND LEGIS TOP/EX PLAN ADJUD...GEOG 20. PAGE 60 H1210
DECISION CONSTRUC NAT/G DELIB/GP

S67
LANE J.P.,"FUNCTIONS OF MASS MEDIA IN BRAZIL'S 1964 CRISIS." BRAZIL NAT/G FORCES TOP/EX PRESS TV ATTIT PWR...METH/CNCPT 20. PAGE 90 H1807
CIVMIL/REL REV COM/IND EDU/PROP

S67
SMITH J.E.,"RED PRUSSIANISM OF THE GERMAN DEMOCRATIC REPUBLIC." GERMANY/E INTELL TOP/EX WORKER PLAN DIPLOM PRODUC ATTIT WEALTH MARXISM. PAGE 146 H2912
NAT/G TOTALISM INDUS NAT/LISM

TORMIN W. H3116

TORONTO....TORONTO, ONTARIO

TORY/PARTY....TORY PARTY

B64
HOLDSWORTH W.S.,A HISTORY OF ENGLISH LAW; THE CENTURIES OF DEVELOPMENT AND REFORM (VOL. XIV). UK CONSTN LOC/G NAT/G POL/PAR CHIEF EX/STRUC ADJUD COLONIAL ATTIT...INT/LAW JURID 18/19 TORY/PARTY COMMONWLTH WHIG/PARTY COMMON/LAW. PAGE 73 H1453
LAW LEGIS LEAD CT/SYS

B64
RAISON T.,WHY CONSERVATIVE? UK FORCES DIPLOM ECO/TAC GIVE EDU/PROP ORD/FREE WEALTH LAISSEZ ...GOV/COMP 20 TORY/PARTY CONSRV/PAR. PAGE 129 H2583
PLURISM CONSERVE POL/PAR NAT/G

TOTALISM....TOTALITARIANISM

C28
SCHNEIDER H.W.,"MAKING THE FASCIST STATE." ITALY CULTURE LABOR DIPLOM REV WAR NAT/LISM TOTALISM ATTIT DRIVE SOCISM...BIBLIOG PARLIAMENT 20. PAGE 140 H2792
FASCISM POLICY POL/PAR

B34
STALIN J.,PROBLEMS OF LENINISM. USSR STRATA INDUS LOC/G POL/PAR ECO/TAC CONTROL TOTALISM PWR SOCISM LENIN/VI STALIN/J. PAGE 148 H2968
MARXISM REV ELITES NAT/G

B35
MARRIOTT J.A.,DICTATORSHIP AND DEMOCRACY. GERMANY GREECE UK CHIEF DIPLOM DOMIN LEGIT PEACE ORD/FREE CONSERVE...TREND ROME HITLER/A. PAGE 103 H2057
TOTALISM POPULISM PLURIST NAT/G

B38
FIELD G.L.,THE SYNDICAL AND CORPORATIVE INSTITUTIONS OF ITALIAN FASCISM. ITALY CONSTN STRATA LABOR EX/STRUC TOP/EX ADJUD ADMIN LEAD TOTALISM AUTHORIT...MGT 20 MUSSOLIN/B. PAGE 50 H0991
FASCISM INDUS NAT/G WORKER

B39
COBBAN A.,DICTATORSHIP: ITS HISTORY AND THEORY. EUR+WWI MOD/EUR SOCIETY STRUCT NAT/G TEC/DEV LEAD NAT/LISM SOVEREIGN...IDEA/COMP 14/20. PAGE 30 H0610
TOTALISM FASCISM CONCPT

B39
KOHN H.,REVOLUTIONS AND DICTATORSHIPS. COM EUR+WWI ISLAM MOD/EUR NAT/G CHIEF FORCES WAR CIVMIL/REL PWR MARXISM 18/20. PAGE 87 H1739
NAT/LISM TOTALISM REV FASCISM

B39
MARQUAND H.A.,ORGANIZED LABOUR IN FOUR CONTINENTS. EUR+WWI USA-45 INDUS NAT/G PAY GP/REL TOTALISM ATTIT WEALTH ALL/IDEOS...TREND NAT/COMP 20 ILO AFL/CIO EUROPE CHINJAP MEXIC/AMER. PAGE 103 H2055
LABOR WORKER CONCPT ANTHOL

B40
LEDERER E.,STATE OF THE MASSES. GERMANY ITALY SOCIETY NAT/G ECO/TAC EDU/PROP LEAD TOTALISM ...SOCIALIST PSY 20. PAGE 93 H1852
CROWD FASCISM AUTHORIT PERSON

B40
MANNHEIM K.,MAN AND SOCIETY IN AN AGE OF RECONSTRUCTION. MOD/EUR CULTURE ECO/DEV PLAN TEC/DEV PERSON LAISSEZ NEW/LIB...NEW/IDEA IDEA/COMP BIBLIOG 19/20. PAGE 102 H2038
CONCPT ATTIT SOCIETY TOTALISM

B41
HITLER A.,MEIN KAMPF (UNABR. ENG. VERSION) (1925). GERMANY CONSTN TEC/DEV RACE/REL NAT/LISM TOTALISM SOVEREIGN...BIOG 20 HITLER/A TREATY. PAGE 71 H1429
EDU/PROP WAR PLAN FASCISM

C41
WASSERMAN L.,"HANDBOOK OF POLITICAL "ISMS" CAP/ISM REPRESENT TOTALISM MARXISM NEW/LIB SOCISM...MAJORIT BIBLIOG 20. PAGE 166 H3313
IDEA/COMP PHIL/SCI OWN NAT/G

B42
BARKER E.,REFLECTIONS ON GOVERNMENT. EUR+WWI SOCIETY LEGIS EDU/PROP ADMIN LEAD PARTIC CHOOSE TOTALISM AUTHORIT ORD/FREE SOCISM 20. PAGE 11 H0218
NAT/G POPULISM ACT/RES GEN/LAWS

B42
LA BOETIE E.,ANTI-DICTATOR (1548) (TRANS. BY H. KUNZ). CONSTN NAT/G CHIEF DOMIN LEGIT CONTROL POPULISM. PAGE 90 H1790
PWR ORD/FREE TOTALISM GEN/LAWS

B42
NEUMANN S.,PERMANENT REVOLUTION: THE TOTAL STATE IN A WORLD AT WAR. COM EUR+WWI GERMANY USSR EX/STRUC DIPLOM CONTROL COERCE REPRESENT MARXISM...SOC GOV/COMP BIBLIOG 20 HITLER/A STALIN/J. PAGE 117 H2337
FASCISM TOTALISM DOMIN EDU/PROP

B42
SINGTON D.,THE GOEBBELS EXPERIMENT. GERMANY MOD/EUR NAT/G EX/STRUC FORCES CONTROL ROUTINE WAR TOTALISM PWR...ART/METH HUM 20 NAZI GOEBBELS/J. PAGE 144 H2886
FASCISM EDU/PROP ATTIT COM/IND

B43
MARITAIN J.,THE RIGHTS OF MAN AND NATURAL LAW. CONSTN NAT/G DOMIN LEGIT INGP/REL TOTALISM MORAL POPULISM WORSHIP 19/20 CIVIL/LIB CHURCH/STA NATURL/LAW. PAGE 103 H2051
PLURIST ORD/FREE GEN/LAWS

C43
BENTHAM J.,"ON THE LIBERTY OF THE PRESS, AND PUBLIC DISCUSSION" IN J. BOWRING, ED., THE WORKS OF JEREMY BENTHAM." SPAIN UK LAW ELITES NAT/G LEGIS INSPECT LEGIT WRITING CONTROL PRIVIL TOTALISM AUTHORIT ...TRADIT 19 FREE/SPEE. PAGE 15 H0290
ORD/FREE PRESS CONFER CONSERVE

B45
CONOVER H.F.,THE GOVERNMENTS OF THE MAJOR FOREIGN POWERS: A BIBLIOGRAPHY. FRANCE GERMANY ITALY UK USSR CONSTN LOC/G POL/PAR EX/STRUC FORCES ADMIN CT/SYS CIVMIL/REL TOTALISM...POLICY 19/20. PAGE 32 H0645
BIBLIOG NAT/G DIPLOM

B45
CONOVER H.F.,ITALY: ECONOMICS, POLITICS AND MILITARY AFFAIRS, 1940-1945. ITALY ELITES NAT/G POL/PAR EX/STRUC TOP/EX DIPLOM DOMIN CONTROL COERCE WAR CIVMIL/REL EFFICIENCY 20. PAGE 32 H0646
BIBLIOG TOTALISM FORCES

S46
DE GRE G.,"FREEDOM AND SOCIAL STRUCTURE" (BMR)" UNIV SOCIETY DOMIN CONTROL TOTALISM PLURISM...SOC CHARTS. PAGE 38 H0753
ORD/FREE STRUCT CONCPT GP/REL

B48
LAUTERBACH A.,ECONOMIC SECURITY AND INDIVIDUAL FREEDOM: CAN WE HAVE BOTH? COM EUR+WWI MOD/EUR UNIV WOR+45 CAP/ISM TOTALISM ALL/VALS...GOV/COMP BIBLIOG 20. PAGE 92 H1840
ORD/FREE ECO/DEV DECISION INGP/REL

B48
ROSSITER C.L.,CONSTITUTIONAL DICTATORSHIP; CRISIS GOVERNMENT IN THE MODERN DEMOCRACIES. FRANCE GERMANY UK USA-45 WOR-45 EX/STRUC BAL/PWR CONTROL COERCE WAR CENTRAL ORD/FREE...DECISION 19/20. PAGE 134 H2688
NAT/G AUTHORIT CONSTN TOTALISM

S48
ALMOND G.A.,"THE CHRISTIAN PARTIES OF WESTEN EUROPE." EUR+WWI NAT/G EDU/PROP LEGIT TOTALISM ORD/FREE PWR MARXISM...TREND CHARTS STERTYP GEN/LAWS COLD/WAR 20. PAGE 5 H0110
POL/PAR CATH SOCISM

L49
BRECHT A.,"THE NEW GERMAN CONSTITUTION." GERMANY/W NAT/G CHIEF EX/STRUC LEGIS PROB/SOLV ADMIN REPRESENT TOTALISM ORD/FREE PLURISM...MAJORIT CHARTS 20. PAGE 20 H0409
CONSTN DIPLOM SOVEREIGN FEDERAL

B50
ALBRECHT-CARRIE R.,ITALY FROM NAPOLEON TO
FASCISM

MUSSOLINI. GERMANY ITALY SPAIN SOCIETY ECO/DEV POL/PAR LEGIS AGREE CONTROL WAR NAT/LISM TOTALISM PWR SOCISM...SOC 19/20 TREATY. PAGE 5 H0095
NAT/G

B50
DUCLOS P.,L'EVOLUTION DES RAPPORTS POLITIQUES DEPUIS 1750 (LIBERTE, INTEGRATION, UNITE). LAW INT/ORG FEDERAL TOTALISM ATTIT PWR...MAJORIT BIBLIOG 18/20 PARLIAMENT EUROPE. PAGE 43 H0852
ORD/FREE DIPLOM NAT/G GOV/COMP

B50
MACHIAVELLI N.,THE DISCOURSES (1516). NAT/G SECT FORCES DOMIN LEGIT CONTROL LEAD COERCE TOTALISM ORD/FREE. PAGE 100 H1995
PWR GEN/LAWS CHIEF

S51
GOULD J.,"THE KOMSOMOL AND THE HITLER JUGEND." COM EUR+WWI GERMANY SOCIETY NAT/G POL/PAR SCHOOL TOTALISM DRIVE PERCEPT KNOWL FASCISM...SOC NAZI TOT/POP 20. PAGE 59 H1185
EDU/PROP CON/ANAL SOCISM

B52
GURLAND A.R.L.,POLITICAL SCIENCE IN WESTERN GERMANY: THOUGHTS AND WRITINGS, 1950-1952 (PAMPHLET). EUR+WWI GERMANY/W ELITES SOCIETY NAT/G NAT/LISM TOTALISM 20. PAGE 63 H1253
BIBLIOG/A DIPLOM CIVMIL/REL FASCISM

B52
ULAM A.B.,TITOISM AND THE COMINFORM. USSR WOR+45 STRUCT INT/ORG NAT/G ACT/RES PLAN EXEC ATTIT DRIVE ALL/VALS...CONCPT OBS VAL/FREE 20 COMINTERN TITO/MARSH. PAGE 157 H3149
COM POL/PAR TOTALISM YUGOSLAVIA

B53
HUNTER E.,BRAIN-WASHING IN RED CHINA. ASIA CHINA/COM CULTURE SOCIETY FORCES WAR TOTALISM ATTIT BIO/SOC DISPL DRIVE PERSON SUPEGO KNOWL ORD/FREE ...INT REC/INT COLD/WAR 20. PAGE 75 H1499
EDU/PROP COERCE

B53
LEITES N.,A STUDY OF BOLSHEVISM. WOR+45 WOR-45 ELITES SOCIETY INT/ORG NAT/G EX/STRUC EDU/PROP EXEC ROUTINE ATTIT MORAL MARXISM...CONCPT OBS VAL/FREE 20. PAGE 94 H1869
COM POL/PAR USSR TOTALISM

B53
LEITES N.,A STUDY OF BOLSHEVISM. ELITES STRATA INT/ORG LOC/G POL/PAR WORKER EDU/PROP REV TOTALISM UTOPIA PWR...CONCPT 20 BOLSHEVISM. PAGE 94 H1870
MARXISM PLAN COM

B53
MEYER P.,THE JEWS IN THE SOVIET SATELLITES. CZECHOSLVK POLAND SOCIETY STRATA NAT/G BAL/PWR ECO/TAC EDU/PROP LEGIT ADMIN COERCE ATTIT DISPL PERCEPT HEALTH PWR RESPECT WEALTH...METH/CNCPT JEWS VAL/FREE NAZI 20. PAGE 110 H2192
COM SECT TOTALISM USSR

B53
ROSCIO J.G.,OBRAS. L/A+17C SPAIN DIPLOM REV WAR NAT/LISM TOTALISM PWR SOVEREIGN 19. PAGE 134 H2671
ORD/FREE COLONIAL NAT/G PHIL/SCI

B53
SHIRATO I.,JAPANESE SOURCES ON THE HISTORY OF THE CHINESE COMMUNIST MOVEMENT (PAMPHLET). CHINA/COM USSR CONSTRUC NAT/G POL/PAR FORCES DIPLOM DOMIN EDU/PROP CONTROL WAR TOTALISM SOCISM 20. PAGE 143 H2863
BIBLIOG/A MARXISM ECO/UNDEV

S53
ARENDT H.,"IDEOLOGY AND TERROR: A NOVEL FORM OF GOVERNMENT." WOR-45 DOMIN STRANGE ATTIT SUPEGO MARXISM...GOV/COMP IDEA/COMP 20 NAZI. PAGE 8 H0160
TOTALISM ANOMIE ALL/IDEOS SOCIETY

B54
FRIEDRICH C.J.,TOTALITARIAN DICTATORSHIP AND AUTOCRACY. COM EUR+WWI GERMANY ITALY USSR INTELL ECO/DEV NAT/G POL/PAR FORCES TOP/EX ECO/TAC EDU/PROP LEGIT COERCE ATTIT ORD/FREE PWR FASCISM ...CONCPT TIME/SEQ GEN/LAWS NAZI 20. PAGE 53 H1068
SOCIETY DOMIN TOTALISM

B54
SALVEMINI G.,PRELUDE TO WORLD WAR II. ITALY MOD/EUR INT/ORG BAL/PWR EDU/PROP CONTROL TOTALISM...TREND NAT/COMP BIBLIOG 19 HITLER/A LEAGUE/NAT MUSSOLIN/B. PAGE 137 H2745
WAR FASCISM LEAD PWR

L54
FRIEDRICH C.J.,"TOTALITARIANISM." COM EUR+WWI NAT/G POL/PAR SECT FORCES PLAN ECO/TAC DOMIN EDU/PROP EXEC COERCE REV ORD/FREE PWR...SOC CONCPT NAZI 20. PAGE 53 H1067
ATTIT TOTALISM

B55
ALFIERI D.,DICTATORS FACE TO FACE. NAT/G TOP/EX DIPLOM EXEC COERCE ORD/FREE FASCISM...POLICY OBS 20 HITLER/A MUSSOLIN/B. PAGE 5 H0103
WAR CHIEF TOTALISM PERS/REL

B55
BRACHER K.D.,DIE AUFLOSUNG DER WEIMARER REPUBLIK. EUR+WWI GERMANY...TIME/SEQ 20. PAGE 20 H0395
TOTALISM NAT/G POL/PAR PARL/PROC

B55
INTERNATIONAL COMN JURISTS,JUSTICE ENSLAVED. COM CONSTN LABOR NAT/G CONTROL CHOOSE 20. PAGE 78 H1555
SOCISM TOTALISM ORD/FREE COERCE

B55
KOHN H.,THE MIND OF MODERN RUSSIA. COM MOD/EUR USSR
INTELL

SOCIETY NAT/G SECT FORCES TOP/EX COERCE TOTALISM DRIVE RIGID/FLEX PWR SOVEREIGN...CONCPT TIME/SEQ WORK. PAGE 87 H1742
GEN/LAWS SOCISM RUSSIA

B56
CARRIL B.,PROBLEMAS DE LA REVOLUCION Y LA DEMOCRACIA. CONSTN FORCES DOMIN CONTROL TOTALISM PWR 20. PAGE 27 H0539
REV ORD/FREE LEGIT NAT/G

B56
ROBERTS H.L.,RUSSIA AND AMERICA. CHINA/COM S/ASIA USSR FORCES TEC/DEV FOR/AID NUC/PWR ALL/IDEOS ...MAJORIT TREND NAT/COMP 20 COLD/WAR UN NATO. PAGE 132 H2641
DIPLOM INT/ORG BAL/PWR TOTALISM

C56
NEUMANN S.,"MODERN POLITICAL PARTIES: APPROACHES TO COMPARATIVE POLITIC. FRANCE UK EX/STRUC DOMIN ADMIN LEAD REPRESENT TOTALISM ATTIT...POLICY TREND METH/COMP ANTHOL BIBLIOG/A 20 CMN/WLTH. PAGE 117 H2338
POL/PAR GOV/COMP ELITES MAJORIT

B57
HALLGARTEN G.W.,DAMONEN ODER RETTER. ASIA L/A+17C CAP/ISM ATTIT MARXISM SOCISM...NAT/COMP. PAGE 64 H1289
TOTALISM FASCISM COERCE DOMIN

B57
KENNEDY M.D.,A SHORT HISTORY OF COMMUNISM IN ASIA. ASIA BURMA INDIA S/ASIA THAILAND NAT/G POL/PAR LEAD REV WAR MARXISM SOCISM...POLICY 20 CHINJAP. PAGE 85 H1688
DIPLOM NAT/LISM TOTALISM COERCE

B57
LOUCKS W.N.,COMPARATIVE ECONOMIC SYSTEMS (5TH ED.). COM UK USSR INDUS POL/PAR PLAN CAP/ISM TOTALISM MARXISM...PHIL/SCI BIBLIOG 19/20. PAGE 99 H1969
NAT/COMP IDEA/COMP SOCISM

B57
MEINECKE F.,MACHIAVELLISM. CHRIST-17C FRANCE GERMANY ITALY MOD/EUR BAL/PWR PARL/PROC TOTALISM ...PHIL/SCI 15/20 MACHIAVELL. PAGE 108 H2166
NAT/LISM NAT/G PWR

B57
REISS J.,GEORGE KENNANS POLITIK DER EINDAMMUNG. USSR NAT/G FORCES TOTALISM ATTIT ORD/FREE...POLICY 20 NATO TRUMAN/HS MARSHL/PLN KENNAN/G. PAGE 131 H2613
DIPLOM DETER PEACE

B57
US SENATE SPEC COMM FOR AID,COMPILATION OF STUDIES AND SURVEYS. AFR ASIA L/A+17C USA+45 ECO/UNDEV AGRI INT/ORG CONSULT TEC/DEV CONFER TOTALISM...NAT/COMP 20 CONGRESS. PAGE 161 H3216
FOR/AID DIPLOM ORD/FREE DELIB/GP

B57
US SENATE SPEC COMM FOR AID,HEARINGS BEFORE THE SPECIAL COMMITTEE TO STUDY THE FOREIGN AID PROGRAM. USA+45 USSR ECO/UNDEV INT/ORG FORCES WEAPON TOTALISM ATTIT SUPEGO...NAT/COMP CONGRESS. PAGE 161 H3217
FOR/AID DIPLOM ORD/FREE TEC/DEV

C57
WITTFOGEL K.A.,"ORIENTAL DESPOTISM: A COMPARATIVE STUDY OF TOTAL POWER." ASIA CULTURE STRATA NAT/G LEAD OWN ORD/FREE PWR...CONCPT TREND BIBLIOG 20. PAGE 170 H3393
TOTALISM HABITAT DOMIN ELITES

B58
ARON R.,SOCIOLOGIE DES SOCIETES INDUSTRIELLES: ESQUISSE D'UNE THEORIE DES REGIMES POLITIQUES. FRANCE SOCIETY NAT/G PROB/SOLV ATTIT RIGID/FLEX MARXISM POPULISM...POLICY SOC T 20 MARX/KARL TOCQUEVILL. PAGE 8 H0170
TOTALISM INDUS CONSTN GOV/COMP

B58
DUNAYEVSKAYA R.,MARXISM AND FREEDOM: FROM 1776 UNTIL TODAY. COM USSR WORKER CAP/ISM DOMIN REV GP/REL TOTALISM ALL/VALS...MYTH BIOG IDEA/COMP 18/20 MARX/KARL LENIN/VI STALIN/J. PAGE 43 H0861
MARXISM CONCPT ORD/FREE

B58
MEHNERT K.,DER SOWJETMENSCH. USSR NAT/G SECT EDU/PROP TOTALISM ORD/FREE 20. PAGE 108 H2161
SOCIETY ATTIT PERSON FAM

B58
ORNES G.E.,TRUJILLO: LITTLE CAESAR OF THE CARIBBEAN. DOMIN/REP FAM NAT/G FORCES BUDGET CRIME REV PERSON 20 TRUJILLO/R. PAGE 122 H2429
BIOG PWR TOTALISM CHIEF

S58
STAAR R.F.,"ELECTIONS IN COMMUNIST POLAND." EUR+WWI SOCIETY INT/ORG NAT/G POL/PAR LEGIS ACT/RES ECO/TAC EDU/PROP ADJUD ADMIN ROUTINE COERCE TOTALISM ATTIT ORD/FREE PWR 20. PAGE 148 H2963
COM CHOOSE POLAND

B59
EMME E.M.,THE IMPACT OF AIR POWER - NATIONAL SECURITY AND WORLD POLITICS. USA+45 USSR FORCES DIPLOM WEAPON PEACE TOTALISM...POLICY NAT/COMP 20 EUROPE. PAGE 46 H0921
DETER AIR WAR ORD/FREE

B59
HENDEL S.,THE SOVIET CRUCIBLE. USSR LEAD COERCE NAT/LISM UTOPIA PWR...POLICY CONCPT ANTHOL 20 STALIN/J LENIN/VI MARX/KARL BOLSHEVIK. PAGE 70 H1393
COM MARXISM REV TOTALISM

B59
HOBSBAWM E.J.,PRIMITIVE REBELS; STUDIES IN ARCHAIC FORMS OF SOCIAL MOVEMENT IN THE 19TH AND 20TH CENTURIES. ITALY SPAIN CULTURE VOL/ASSN RISK CROWD GP/REL INGP/REL ISOLAT TOTALISM...PSY SOC 18/20. PAGE 72 H1438
SOCIETY CRIME REV GUERRILLA

B59
INTERNATIONAL PRESS INSTITUTE,THE PRESS IN AUTHORITARIAN COUNTRIES. COM PORTUGAL SPAIN UAR USSR NAT/G DOMIN LEGIT ORD/FREE FASCISM SOCISM 20. PAGE 78 H1559
PRESS CONTROL TOTALISM EDU/PROP

B59
SZLUC T.,TWILIGHT OF THE TYRANTS. BRAZIL L/A+17C PERU VENEZUELA NAT/G FORCES CONTROL PERSON MORAL ORD/FREE PWR...CONCPT 20 ARGEN COLOMB. PAGE 151 H3028
TOTALISM CHIEF REV FASCISM

S59
ZAUBERMAN A.,"SOVIET BLOC ECONOMIC INTEGRATION." COM CULTURE INTELL ECO/DEV INDUS TOP/EX ACT/RES PLAN ECO/TAC INT/TRADE ROUTINE CHOOSE ATTIT ...TIME/SEQ 20. PAGE 172 H3452
MARKET INT/ORG USSR TOTALISM

B60
BRZEZINSKI Z.K.,THE SOVIET BLOC-UNITY AND CONFLICT. COM USSR CONSTN DOMIN ADMIN TOTALISM PWR...SOC MYTH RECORD TREND STERTYP GEN/LAWS GEN/METH TOT/POP 20. PAGE 23 H0458
ATTIT EDU/PROP

B60
GOODMAN E.,SOVIET DESIGN FOR A WORLD STATE. COM USSR NAT/G TOP/EX DIPLOM ECO/TAC DOMIN EDU/PROP COERCE REV ATTIT ORD/FREE...CON/ANAL 20. PAGE 59 H1171
PLAN PWR SOCISM TOTALISM

B60
HARRISON S.S.,INDIA: THE MOST DANGEROUS DECADES. INDIA CONSTN STRATA POL/PAR SECT PLAN ADMIN CHOOSE GP/REL TOTALISM MARXISM...LING 20 NEHRU/J. PAGE 67 H1347
CULTURE ECO/UNDEV PROB/SOLV REGION

B60
MCCLOSKY H.,THE SOVIET DICTATORSHIP. FUT CONSTN CULTURE INTELL SOCIETY POL/PAR SECT VOL/ASSN FORCES PLAN TEC/DEV DOMIN EDU/PROP COERCE PWR MARXISM ...POLICY CONCPT MYTH STERTYP 20. PAGE 106 H2127
COM NAT/G TOTALISM USSR

B60
MORAES F.,THE REVOLT IN TIBET. ASIA CHINA/COM INDIA CULTURE CONTROL COERCE WAR TOTALISM...POLICY SOC WORSHIP 20 TIBET INTERVENT. PAGE 113 H2252
COLONIAL FORCES DIPLOM ORD/FREE

B60
SCHAPIRO L.,THE COMMUNIST PARTY OF THE SOVIET UNION. COM LAW SOCIETY STRATA STRUCT ECO/DEV LABOR NAT/G POL/PAR CREATE DOMIN EDU/PROP COERCE TOTALISM MARXISM...POLICY CONCPT MYTH TIME/SEQ WORK TOT/POP 20 LENIN/VI STALIN/J. PAGE 139 H2772
INTELL PWR USSR

B60
SHIRER W.L.,THE RISE AND FALL OF THE THIRD REICH: A HISTORY OF NAZI GERMANY. EUR+WWI CULTURE ECO/DEV INDUS NAT/G POL/PAR FORCES PLAN TEC/DEV ECO/TAC COERCE ATTIT DRIVE PERSON PWR...MYSTIC PSY SOC MYTH STAT CHARTS EXHIBIT WORK VAL/FREE. PAGE 143 H2864
STRUCT GERMANY TOTALISM

S60
CASSINELLI C.,"TOTALITARIANISM, IDEOLOGY AND PROPAGANDA." EUR+WWI CULTURE SOCIETY NAT/G DOMIN COERCE ORD/FREE FASCISM MARXISM...MARXIST CONCPT STERTYP GEN/LAWS TOT/POP 20. PAGE 28 H0554
ATTIT EDU/PROP TOTALISM

S60
WYCKOFF T.,"THE ROLE OF THE MILITARY IN LATIN AMERICAN POLITICS." L/A+17C CONSTN CULTURE ECO/UNDEV POL/PAR FORCES LEGIS TOP/EX LEGIT GUERRILLA REV CHOOSE ORD/FREE PWR...TIME/SEQ VAL/FREE 20. PAGE 171 H3430
NAT/G COERCE TOTALISM

B61
ALLIGHAN G.,VERWOERD - THE END. SOUTH/AFR TOP/EX DIPLOM COLONIAL DISCRIM TOTALISM ATTIT AUTHORIT ...BIOG 20 NEGRO VERWOERD/H. PAGE 5 H0107
CONTROL CHIEF RACE/REL NAT/G

B61
BULLOCK A.,HITLER: A STUDY IN TYRANNY. EUR+WWI GERMANY SOCIETY STRUCT NAT/G POL/PAR FORCES CREATE DOMIN EDU/PROP EXEC COERCE WAR NAT/LISM DISPL DRIVE PERSON PWR...PSY NAZI 20 HITLER/A. PAGE 23 H0470
ATTIT BIOG TOTALISM

B61
GOULD S.H.,SCIENCES IN COMMUNIST CHINA. CHINA/COM FUT INDUS NAT/G TOTALISM...RECORD TOT/POP 20. PAGE 59 H1187
ASIA TEC/DEV

B61
JAKOBSON M.,THE DIPLOMACY OF THE WINTER WAR. EUR+WWI FINLAND GERMANY USSR INT/ORG NAT/G PEACE TOTALISM PWR...POLICY CONCPT 20 TREATY. PAGE 79 H1588
WAR ORD/FREE DIPLOM

B61
LUNDBERG G.A.,CAN SCIENCE SAVE US. UNIV CULTURE INTELL SOCIETY ECO/DEV R+D PLAN EDU/PROP ROUTINE CHOOSE ATTIT PERCEPT ALL/VALS...TREND 20. PAGE 99 H1979
ACT/RES CONCPT TOTALISM

B61
REISKY-DUBNIC V.,COMMUNIST PROPAGANDA METHODS. CULTURE POL/PAR VOL/ASSN ATTIT...CONCPT TOT/POP. PAGE 131 H2611
COM EDU/PROP TOTALISM

B61
ULLMAN W.,PRINCIPLES OF GOVERNMENT AND POLITICS IN THE MIDDLE AGES. LAW CONSTN DOMIN EDU/PROP LEGIT TOTALISM SOVEREIGN POPULISM...POLICY GOV/COMP IDEA/COMP 12/16 POPE KING CHURCH/STA. PAGE 158 H3152
SECT CHIEF NAT/G LEGIS

S61
RANDALL F.B.,"COMMUNISM IN THE HIGH ANDES." L/A+17C PERU USSR SOCIETY PLAN EDU/PROP TOTALISM ATTIT RIGID/FLEX PWR WEALTH...HUM CONCPT GEN/LAWS 20 BOLIV EQUADOR. PAGE 129 H2589
CULTURE DRIVE

S61
SCHAPIRO L.,"SOVIET GOVERNMENT TODAY." COM EUR+WWI INT/ORG POL/PAR VOL/ASSN ACT/RES PLAN PERCEPT ...CONCPT TREND TOT/POP VAL/FREE 20. PAGE 139 H2773
NAT/G TOTALISM USSR

S61
ZAGORIA D.S.,"THE FUTURE OF SINO-SOVIET RELATIONS." CHINA/COM INT/ORG NAT/G POL/PAR VOL/ASSN ACT/RES PLAN PERSON...METH/CNCPT TIME/SEQ TOT/POP VAL/FREE 20 MAO KHRUSH/N. PAGE 172 H3445
ASIA COM TOTALISM USSR

B62
BAFFREY S.A.,THE RED MYTH: A HISTORY OF COMMUNISM FROM MARX TO KHRUSHCHEV. USSR NAT/G CHIEF CAP/ISM DIPLOM EDU/PROP REV WAR PEACE TOTALISM...POLICY 20 STALIN/J KHRUSH/N. PAGE 10 H0195
CONCPT MARXISM TV

B62
BUSIA K.A.,THE CHALLENGE OF AFRICA. CULTURE KIN MUNIC NAT/G POL/PAR SCHOOL DELIB/GP PLAN ECO/TAC DOMIN EDU/PROP TOTALISM ATTIT PERSON ALL/VALS SOVEREIGN...SOC CONCPT STERTYP TOT/POP VAL/FREE 20. PAGE 25 H0496
AFR ECO/UNDEV NAT/LISM

B62
FINER S.E.,THE MAN ON HORSEBACK: ROLE OF THE MILITARY IN POLITICS. UNIV LAW CONSTN ELITES SOCIETY POL/PAR BAL/PWR DOMIN EDU/PROP LEGIT COERCE GUERRILLA REV WAR WEAPON DRIVE SUPEGO ORD/FREE PWR RESPECT...POLICY CONCPT GEN/METH. PAGE 50 H1003
NAT/G FORCES TOTALISM

B62
NOBECOURT R.G.,LES SECRETS DE LA PROPAGANDE EN FRANCE OCCUPEE. FRANCE ELITES NAT/G DIPLOM GP/REL NAT/LISM TOTALISM ORD/FREE 20 VICHY VICHY. PAGE 118 H2365
METH/COMP EDU/PROP WAR CONTROL

B62
STARR R.E.,POLAND 1944-1962: THE SOVIETIZATION OF A CAPTIVE PEOPLE. COM POLAND USSR POL/PAR SECT LEGIS DIPLOM DOMIN EDU/PROP CHOOSE ORD/FREE...POLICY CHARTS BIBLIOG 20. PAGE 149 H2973
MARXISM NAT/G TOTALISM NAT/COMP

S62
MU FU-SHENG,"THE WILTING OF THE HUNDRED FLOWERS: FREE THOUGHT IN CHINA TODAY." ASIA CHINA/COM CULTURE FAM NAT/G EDU/PROP REV TOTALISM ATTIT PERSON RESPECT...GEOG INT UNPLAN/INT COLD/WAR 20. PAGE 114 H2278
INTELL ELITES

B63
BROEKMEIJER M.W.,DEVELOPING COUNTRIES AND NATO. USSR FORCES DIPLOM NUC/PWR WAR PEACE TOTALISM 20 NATO. PAGE 21 H0427
ECO/UNDEV FOR/AID ORD/FREE NAT/G

B63
BROGAN D.W.,POLITICAL PATTERNS IN TODAY'S WORLD. FRANCE USA+45 USSR WOR+45 CONSTN STRUCT PLAN DIPLOM ADMIN LEAD ROLE SUPEGO...PHIL/SCI 20. PAGE 21 H0429
NAT/COMP NEW/LIB COM TOTALISM

B63
CRANKSHAW E.,THE NEW COLD WAR: MOSCOW V. PEKIN. CHINA/COM USSR INTELL POL/PAR DELIB/GP CAP/ISM COERCE REV NAT/LISM TOTALISM DRIVE...POLICY IDEA/COMP 20 KHRUSH/N. PAGE 35 H0698
ATTIT DIPLOM NAT/COMP MARXISM

B63
CROSS C.,THE FASCISTS IN BRITAIN. UK ELITES LABOR NAT/G DOMIN PARTIC DISCRIM TOTALISM ATTIT...STERTYP 20. PAGE 35 H0708
POL/PAR FASCISM RACE/REL LEAD

B63
ECKSTEIN H.,COMPARATIVE POLITICS. POL/PAR LEGIS CT/SYS CHOOSE TOTALISM PWR POPULISM...METH/COMP GEN/METH ANTHOL BIBLIOG 20. PAGE 44 H0886
NAT/COMP CONSTN REPRESENT NAT/G

B63
GERSCHENKRON A.,THE STABILITY OF DICTATORSHIPS. NAT/G EDU/PROP TASK ATTIT PERSON...POLICY PSY SOC METH 19/20. PAGE 56 H1116
TOTALISM CONCPT CONTROL ORD/FREE

B63
HOLLANDER P.,THE NEW MAN AND HIS ENEMIES: A STUDY OF THE STALINIST CONCEPTIONS OF GOOD AND EVIL PERSONIFIED (DOCTORAL THESIS). USSR SOCIETY ECO/DEV NAT/G EDU/PROP WRITING...SOC STERTYP BIBLIOG 20 STALIN/J. PAGE 73 H1455
CONTROL ATTIT TOTALISM MARXISM

B63
JACOB H.,GERMAN ADMINISTRATION SINCE BISMARCK: CENTRAL AUTHORITY VERSUS LOCAL AUTONOMY. GERMANY GERMANY/W LAW POL/PAR CONTROL CENTRAL TOTALISM FASCISM...MAJORIT DECISION STAT CHARTS GOV/COMP 19/20 BISMARCK/O HITLER/A WEIMAR/REP. PAGE 79 H1577
ADMIN NAT/G LOC/G POLICY

B63
MILLER W.J.,THE MEANING OF COMMUNISM. USSR SOCIETY ECO/DEV EX/STRUC WORKER TEC/DEV ADMIN TOTALISM ...POLICY CONCPT CHARTS BIBLIOG T 20 COLD/WAR LENIN/VI STALIN/J. PAGE 111 H2215
MARXISM TRADIT DIPLOM NAT/G

B63
SILONE I.,THE SCHOOL FOR DICTATORS. EUR+WWI GERMANY ITALY SOCIETY NAT/G CHIEF EX/STRUC ATTIT MORAL PWR ...HIST/WRIT 20. PAGE 144 H2876
TOTALISM EDU/PROP ORD/FREE FASCISM

B63
TUCKER R.C.,THE SOVIET POLITICAL MIND. COM INTELL NAT/G TOP/EX EDU/PROP ADMIN COERCE TOTALISM ATTIT PWR MARXISM...PSY MYTH HYPO/EXP 20. PAGE 157 H3136
STRUCT RIGID/FLEX ELITES USSR

B63
ULAM A.B.,THE NEW FACE OF SOVIET TOTALITARIANISM. FUT INTELL NAT/G POL/PAR EX/STRUC TOP/EX DIPLOM ECO/TAC DOMIN EDU/PROP LEGIT COERCE ATTIT RIGID/FLEX...OBS HIST/WRIT TREND TOT/POP VAL/FREE COLD/WAR. PAGE 158 H3150
COM PWR TOTALISM USSR

S63
STAAR R.F.,"HOW STRONG IS THE SOVIET BLOC." COM USSR ECO/DEV NAT/G DELIB/GP ECO/TAC RIGID/FLEX ...CONCPT RECORD CHARTS 20. PAGE 148 H2964
FORCES MYTH TOTALISM

B64
BERRINGTON H.,HOW NATIONS ARE GOVERNED. FRANCE WOR+45 ECO/UNDEV INT/ORG POL/PAR CHOOSE TOTALISM KNOWL...MAJORIT T 20 UN COMMONWLTH THIRD/WRLD. PAGE 16 H0320
NAT/G GOV/COMP ECO/DEV CONSTN

B64
BUNTING B.P.,THE RISE OF THE SOUTH AFRICAN REICH. SOUTH/AFR INT/ORG NAT/G FORCES DIPLOM CONTROL WAR TOTALISM ATTIT...GOV/COMP 19/20. PAGE 24 H0477
RACE/REL DISCRIM NAT/LISM TREND

B64
DANIELS R.V.,RUSSIA. RUSSIA USSR STRUCT NAT/LISM TOTALISM ORD/FREE WEALTH...POLICY DECISION TREND. PAGE 37 H0740
MARXISM REV ECO/DEV DIPLOM

B64
DOOLIN D.J.,COMMUNIST CHINA: THE POLITICS OF STUDENT OPPOSITION. CHINA/COM ELITES STRATA ACADEM NAT/G WRITING CT/SYS LEAD PARTIC COERCE TOTALISM 20. PAGE 42 H0838
MARXISM DEBATE AGE/Y PWR

B64
HALE O.J.,THE CAPTIVE PRESS IN THE THIRD REICH. GERMANY CULTURE LG/CO NAT/G POL/PAR PLAN DOMIN TASK CENTRAL OWN TOTALISM PWR...BIBLIOG 20 HITLER/A NAZI AMMAN/MAX. PAGE 64 H1283
COM/IND PRESS CONTROL FASCISM

B64
KARIEL H.S.,IN SEARCH OF AUTHORITY: TWENTIETH-CENTURY POLITICAL THOUGHT. WOR+45 WOR-45 NAT/G EX/STRUC TOTALISM DRIVE PWR...MGT PHIL/SCI GEN/LAWS 19/20 NIETZSCH/F FREUD/S WEBER/MAX NIEBUHR/R MARITAIN/J. PAGE 83 H1661
CONSTN CONCPT ORD/FREE IDEA/COMP

B64
SANCHEZ J.M.,REFORM AND REACTION. SPAIN STRATA NAT/LISM TOTALISM 20. PAGE 137 H2749
NAT/G SECT GP/REL REV

C64
GOLDMAN M.I.,"COMPARATIVE ECONOMIC SYSTEMS: A READER." COM ECO/UNDEV NAT/G BUDGET CAP/ISM ADMIN TOTALISM MARXISM SOCISM...MGT ANTHOL BIBLIOG 19/20. PAGE 58 H1157
NAT/COMP CONTROL IDEA/COMP

B65
ALLEN W.S.,THE NAZI SEIZURE OF POWER. GERMANY NAT/G CHIEF LEAD COERCE CHOOSE REPRESENT GOV/REL AUTHORIT ...DECISION 20 HITLER/A NAZI. PAGE 5 H0106
MUNIC FASCISM TOTALISM LOC/G

B65
CARTER G.M.,GOVERNMENT AND POLITICS IN THE TWENTIETH CENTURY (REV. ED.). WOR+45 NAT/G POL/PAR LEGIS DIPLOM LEAD PARL/PROC CHOOSE TOTALISM 20. PAGE 27 H0549
GOV/COMP ECO/UNDEV ALL/IDEOS ECO/DEV

B65
GUERIN D.,SUR LE FASCISME: FASCISME ET GRAND CAPITAL (VOL. II). GERMANY ITALY SOCIETY STRATA AGRI WORKER 20. PAGE 62 H1245
FASCISM NAT/G TOTALISM EDU/PROP

B65
HALEVY E.,THE ERA OF TYRANNIES (TRANS. BY R. K. WEBB). WOR-45 ECO/DEV PROB/SOLV CONTROL COERCE REV WAR TOTALISM 20. PAGE 64 H1286
SOCISM IDEA/COMP DOMIN

B65
HAMIL H.M.,DICTATORSHIP IN SPANISH AMERICA. NAT/G COERCE MORAL ORD/FREE...POLICY PSY SOC ANTHOL 18/20. PAGE 65 H1300
TOTALISM CHIEF L/A+17C FASCISM

B65
MOORE C.H.,TUNISIA SINCE INDEPENDENCE. ELITES LOC/G POL/PAR ADMIN COLONIAL CONTROL EXEC GOV/REL TOTALISM MARXISM...INT 20 TUNIS. PAGE 112 H2248
NAT/G EX/STRUC SOCISM

B65
POBEDONOSTSEV K.P.,REFLECTIONS OF A RUSSIAN
TOTALISM

STATESMAN. RUSSIA LAW ELITES EDU/PROP PRESS ADJUD MARRIAGE ATTIT PWR...MAJORIT TRADIT 19 CHURCH/STA. PAGE 127 H2531 — POLICY CONSTN NAT/G

B65
RANDALL F.B.,STALIN'S RUSSIA. USSR STRUCT AGRI NAT/G PLAN DIPLOM WAR TOTALISM MARXISM...BIBLIOG/A 19/20 STALIN/J. PAGE 129 H2590 — BIOG INDUS ECO/DEV

B65
STERN F.,THE POLITICS OF CULTURAL DESPAIR. EUR+WWI GERMANY POL/PAR SECT RACE/REL STRANGE TOTALISM ...ART/METH MYTH BIBLIOG 20 JEWS. PAGE 149 H2980 — CULTURE ATTIT NAT/LISM FASCISM

B65
TINGSTEN H.,THE PROBLEM OF DEMOCRACY. ELITES SOCIETY STRATA NAT/G CONSEN TOTALISM WELF/ST. PAGE 155 H3101 — IDEA/COMP GOV/COMP POPULISM SOCISM

B65
VATCHER W.H. JR.,WHITE LAAGER: THE RISE OF AFRIKANER NATIONALISM. AFR SOUTH/AFR CULTURE TOTALISM 20. PAGE 162 H3235 — NAT/LISM POL/PAR RACE/REL DISCRIM

B65
WOLFE B.D.,MARXISM; ONE HUNDRED YEARS IN THE LIFE OF A DOCTRINE. USSR WAR NAT/LISM PEACE TOTALISM ...MAJORIT 20 MARX/KARL. PAGE 170 H3399 — MARXISM LEAD ATTIT

L65
HOUN F.S.,"THE COMMUNIST MONOLITH VERSUS THE CHINESE TRADITION." CULTURE INTELL SOCIETY STRUCT DOMIN GP/REL ORD/FREE CONSERVE PLURISM...GOV/COMP WORSHIP. PAGE 74 H1479 — ASIA MARXISM TOTALISM

S65
HELMREICH E.C.,"KADAR'S HUNGARY." COM EUR+WWI HUNGARY USSR INTELL ECO/DEV AGRI INT/ORG TOP/EX DOMIN ALL/VALS WORK COLD/WAR 20. PAGE 69 H1390 — NAT/G RIGID/FLEX TOTALISM

S65
ROGGER H.,"EAST GERMANY: STABLE OR IMMOBILE." COM EUR+WWI GERMANY/E NAT/G INT/TRADE DOMIN EDU/PROP COERCE TOTALISM COLD/WAR 20. PAGE 133 H2659 — TOP/EX RIGID/FLEX GERMANY

S65
STAAR R.F.,"RETROGRESSION IN POLAND." COM USSR AGRI INDUS NAT/G CREATE EDU/PROP TOTALISM RIGID/FLEX ORD/FREE PWR SOCISM...RECORD CHARTS 20. PAGE 148 H2965 — TOP/EX ECO/TAC POLAND

S65
TABORSKY E.,"CHANGE IN CZECHOSLOVAKIA." COM USSR ELITES INTELL AGRI INDUS NAT/G DELIB/GP EX/STRUC ECO/TAC TOTALISM ATTIT RIGID/FLEX SOCISM...MGT CONCPT TREND 20. PAGE 152 H3031 — ECO/DEV PLAN CZECHOSLVK

S65
VUCINICH W.S.,"WHITHER RUMANIA." COM USSR YUGOSLAVIA NAT/G VOL/ASSN DELIB/GP TOP/EX LEGIT NAT/LISM TOTALISM ATTIT DRIVE RIGID/FLEX ORD/FREE WEALTH SOCISM...TIME/SEQ TREND 20. PAGE 164 H3281 — ECO/DEV CREATE ROMANIA

C65
NEUMANN S.,"PERMANENT REVOLUTION: TOTALITARIANISM IN THE AGE OF INTERNA TIONAL CIVIL WAR (2ND ED.)" EUR+WWI ELITES POL/PAR DOMIN EDU/PROP LEAD CROWD REPRESENT...MAJORIT GOV/COMP BIBLIOG 20. PAGE 117 H2340 — TOTALISM REV FASCISM STRUCT

C65
STERN F.,"THE POLITICS OF CULTURAL DESPAIR." NAT/LISM...IDEA/COMP BIBLIOG 19/20. PAGE 149 H2979 — CULTURE PHIL/SCI CONSERVE TOTALISM

N65
MOTE M.E.,SOVIET LOCAL AND REPUBLIC ELECTIONS. COM USSR NAT/G PLAN PARTIC GOV/REL TOTALISM PWR ...CHARTS 20. PAGE 114 H2270 — CHOOSE ADMIN CONTROL LOC/G

B66
BUKHARIN N.,THE ABC OF COMMUNISM: A POPULAR EXPLANATION OF THE PROGRAM OF THE COMMUNIST PARTY OF RUSSIA. USSR STRATA SECT FORCES WORKER CAP/ISM RECEIVE EDU/PROP NAT/LISM TOTALISM 20. PAGE 23 H0468 — MARXISM CONCPT POLICY REV

B66
DALLIN A.,POLITICS IN THE SOVIET UNION: 7 CASES. COM USSR LAW POL/PAR CHIEF FORCES WRITING CONTROL PARL/PROC CIVMIL/REL TOTALISM...ANTHOL 20 KHRUSH/N STALIN/J CASEBOOK COM/PARTY. PAGE 37 H0736 — MARXISM DOMIN ORD/FREE GOV/REL

B66
DE VORE B.B.,LAND AND LIBERTY; A HISTORY OF THE MEXICAN REVOLUTION. CONSTN INTELL NAT/G CONTROL LEAD CHOOSE TOTALISM AUTHORIT...BIBLIOG 19/20 MEXIC/AMER DIAZ/P LIB/PARTY MAGON/F MADERO/F. PAGE 39 H0776 — REV CHIEF POL/PAR

B66
DEUTSCHER I.,STALIN: A POLITICAL BIOGRAPHY. EUR+WWI USSR POL/PAR FORCES DIPLOM ADMIN LEAD REV WAR TOTALISM PERSON 20 STALIN/J ROOSEVLT/F LENIN/VI HITLER/A. PAGE 40 H0807 — BIOG MARXISM TOP/EX PWR

B66
MARTIN L.W.,DIPLOMACY IN MODERN EUROPEAN HISTORY. EUR+WWI MOD/EUR INT/ORG NAT/G EX/STRUC ROUTINE WAR PEACE TOTALISM PWR 15/20 COLD/WAR EUROPE/W. PAGE 103 H2064 — DIPLOM POLICY

B66
NOLTE E.,THREE FACES OF FASCISM. FRANCE GERMANY DOMIN LEGIT COERCE CROWD REV WAR GP/REL RACE/REL SOVEREIGN...GOV/COMP IDEA/COMP 19/20 HITLER/A MUSSOLIN/B MARX/KARL. PAGE 118 H2368 — FASCISM TOTALISM NAT/G POL/PAR

B66
ROSNER J.,DER FASCHISMUS. AUSTRIA GERMANY ITALY STRATA NAT/G POL/PAR COERCE RACE/REL TOTALISM ATTIT AUTHORIT...IDEA/COMP 20 NAZI ANTI/SEMIT. PAGE 134 H2684 — NAT/LISM FASCISM ORD/FREE WAR

B66
SPULBER N.,THE STATE AND ECONOMIC DEVELOPMENT IN EASTERN EUROPE. BULGARIA COM CZECHOSLVK HUNGARY POLAND YUGOSLAVIA CULTURE PLAN CAP/ISM INT/TRADE CONTROL...POLICY CHARTS METH/COMP BIBLIOG/A 19/20. PAGE 148 H2958 — ECO/DEV ECO/UNDEV NAT/G TOTALISM

B66
THORNTON M.J.,NAZISM, 1918-1945. GERMANY INT/ORG DIPLOM REV PEACE FASCISM...CONCPT 20 HITLER/A WEIMAR/REP NAZI. PAGE 155 H3089 — TOTALISM POL/PAR NAT/G WAR

B66
TORMIN W.,GESCHICHTE DER DEUTSCHEN PARTEIEN SEIT 1848. GERMANY CHOOSE PWR...CONCPT 19/20 WEIMAR/REP. PAGE 156 H3116 — POL/PAR CONSTN NAT/G TOTALISM

S66
BLANC N.,"SPAIN: LEARNING THROUGH STRUGGLE" SPAIN STRATA STRUCT SECT FORCES PROB/SOLV AGE/Y ATTIT ORD/FREE PWR WEALTH MARXISM SOCISM 19/20 FRANCO/F SUCCESSION. PAGE 18 H0352 — NAT/G FUT SOCIALIST TOTALISM

S66
STRAYER J.R.,"PROBLEMS OF DICTATORSHIP* THE RUSSIAN EXPERIENCE." ASIA MOD/EUR ELITES STRATA POL/PAR CREATE NAT/LISM MARXISM...GOV/COMP NAT/COMP. PAGE 150 H2997 — NAT/G GEN/LAWS USSR TOTALISM

B67
DAVIDSON E.,THE TRIAL OF THE GERMANS* NUREMBERG* 1946-48. EUR+WWI GERMANY CULTURE NAT/G LEAD PERSON HEALTH...CRIMLGY PSY SOC BIOG JEWS. PAGE 37 H0745 — FASCISM ADJUD TOTALISM WAR

L67
BRIDGHAM P.,"MAO'S "CULTURAL REVOLUTION"* ORIGIN AND DEVELOPMENT." NAT/G LEAD CIVMIL/REL NAT/LISM TOTALISM ATTIT DRIVE PWR MARXISM 20. PAGE 21 H0413 — CHINA/COM CULTURE REV CROWD

S67
BAIKALOV A.,"EMERGENCY LEGISLATION IN WEST GERMANY." GERMANY/W LABOR NAT/G POL/PAR SANCTION ...MARXIST 20. PAGE 10 H0199 — LAW TOTALISM LEGIS PARL/PROC

S67
CATTELL D.T.,"A NEO-MARXIST THEORY OF COMPARATIVE ANALYSIS." USSR STRATA INSPECT DOMIN CONTROL COERCE OWN TOTALISM PWR...FASCIST HYPO/EXP METH 20. PAGE 28 H0561 — GOV/COMP MARXISM SIMUL CLASSIF

S67
CATTELL D.T.,"THE FIFTIETH ANNIVERSARY: A SOVIET WATERSHED?" USSR CONSTN ECO/DEV NAT/G LEAD TOTALISM 20 KHRUSH/N. PAGE 28 H0562 — MARXISM CHIEF POLICY ADJUST

S67
EGBERT D.D.,"POLITICS AND ART IN COMMUNIST BULGARIA" BULGARIA COM USSR CULTURE DIPLOM INGP/REL TOTALISM...TREND 20. PAGE 45 H0894 — CREATE ART/METH CONTROL MARXISM

S67
FRANCIS M.J.,"THE US PRESS AND CASTRO: A STUDY IN DECLINING RELATIONS." COM DIPLOM WAR TOTALISM ATTIT SOCISM...POLICY IDEA/COMP 20. PAGE 52 H1046 — PRESS LEAD REV NAT/G

S67
JANICKE M.,"MONOPOLISMUS UND PLURALISMUS IM KOMMUNISTISCHEN HERRSCHAFTSSYSTEM" COM CZECHOSLVK USSR YUGOSLAVIA SOCIETY CONTROL RIGID/FLEX...CONCPT NAT/COMP 20. PAGE 79 H1589 — TOTALISM POL/PAR ATTIT PLURISM

S67
SAVER W.,"NATIONAL SOCIALISM: TOTALITARIANISM OR FASCISM?" GERMANY STRUCT POL/PAR PROB/SOLV MARXISM ...SOC CONCPT HIST/WRIT IDEA/COMP 20 HITLER/A COLD/WAR. PAGE 138 H2760 — SOCISM NAT/G TOTALISM FASCISM

S67
SMITH J.E.,"THE GERMAN DEMOCRATIC REPUBLIC AND THE WEST." GERMANY/E ECO/DEV NAT/G PROB/SOLV CONTROL REV TOTALISM...GOV/COMP 20. PAGE 146 H2911 — DIPLOM PWR MARXISM

S67
SMITH J.E.,"RED PRUSSIANISM OF THE GERMAN DEMOCRATIC REPUBLIC." GERMANY/E INTELL TOP/EX WORKER PLAN DIPLOM PRODUC ATTIT WEALTH MARXISM. PAGE 146 H2912 — NAT/G TOTALISM INDUS NAT/LISM

S67
SPINELLI A.,"EUROPEAN UNION IN THE RESISTANCE." NAT/G BAL/PWR DIPLOM CONFER REGION TOTALISM ORD/FREE POLICY. PAGE 147 H2948 — NAT/LISM FEDERAL EUR+WWI INT/ORG

S67
SULLIVAN J.H.,"THE PRESS AND POLITICS IN INDONESIA." INDONESIA NAT/G WRITING REV...TREND GOV/COMP 20. PAGE 150 H3007 — CIVMIL/REL KNOWL TOTALISM

S67
SZALAY L.B.,"SOVIET DOMESTIC PROPAGANDA AND LIBERALIZATION." COM USSR SOCIETY COM/IND NAT/G POL/PAR EX/STRUC TEC/DEV LEAD ATTIT ROLE MARXISM ...METH/COMP 20. PAGE 151 H3026 — EDU/PROP TOTALISM PERSON PERCEPT

S67
ULC O.,"CLASS STRUGGLE AND SOCIALIST JUSTICE: THE CASE OF CZECHOSLOVAKIA." COM CZECHOSLVK LAW CONSTN ELITES STRUCT NAT/G CRIME GP/REL MARXISM 20. PAGE 158 H3151 — TOTALISM CT/SYS ADJUD STRATA

S67
YEFROMEV A.,"THE TRUE FACE OF THE WEST GERMAN NATIONAL-DEMOCRATS." GERMANY/W NAT/G DOMIN LEAD SANCTION WAR ATTIT PERSON...MARXIST 20. PAGE 172 H3436 — POL/PAR TOTALISM PARL/PROC DIPLOM

TOTALITARIANISM....SEE TOTALISM

TOTOK W. H3117

TOTTEN G.O. H0620

TOURISM....SEE TRAVEL

TOUSSAIN/P....PIERRE DOMINIQUE TOUSSAINT L'OUVERTURE

TOUVAL S. H3118,H3119,H3120,H3121

TOWNS....SEE MUNIC

TOWNSD/PLN....TOWNSEND PLAN

TOWNSEND PLAN....SEE TOWNSD/PLN

TOWSTER J. H3122

TOYNBEE A. H3123,H3124

TOYNBEE A.J. H3125

TOYNBEE/A....ARNOLD TOYNBEE

B58
SYME R.,COLONIAL ELITES: ROME, SPAIN, AND THE AMERICAS. CHRIST-17C MOD/EUR SPAIN UK USA-45 CULTURE NAT/G CHIEF TOP/EX...GOV/COMP IDEA/COMP NAT/COMP ROM/EMP GIBBON/EDW TOYNBEE/A. PAGE 151 H3022 — COLONIAL ELITES DOMIN

TRADE, INTERNATIONAL....SEE INT/TRADE

TRADIT....TRADITIONAL AND ARISTOCRATIC

B03
FAGUET E.,LE LIBERALISME. FRANCE PRESS ADJUD ADMIN DISCRIM CONSERVE SOCISM...TRADIT SOC LING WORSHIP PARLIAMENT. PAGE 48 H0960 — ORD/FREE EDU/PROP NAT/G LAW

C05
DUNNING W.A.,"HISTORY OF POLITICAL THEORIES FROM LUTHER TO MONTESQUIEU." LAW NAT/G SECT DIPLOM REV WAR ORD/FREE SOVEREIGN CONSERVE...TRADIT BIBLIOG 16/18. PAGE 43 H0867 — PHIL/SCI CONCPT GEN/LAWS

N17
BURKE E.,THOUGHTS ON THE CAUSE OF THE PRESENT DISCONTENTS (PAMPHLET). MOD/EUR UK CONSTN CHIEF LEGIS DOMIN CONTROL EXEC REPRESENT POPULISM ...TRADIT NEW/IDEA METH/COMP 18 BURKE/EDM. PAGE 24 H0484 — ORD/FREE REV PARL/PROC NAT/G

N17
BURKE E.,LETTER TO SIR HERCULES LANGRISHE (PAMPHLET). IRELAND UK NAT/G CHIEF DIPLOM DOMIN PARL/PROC COERCE ORD/FREE SOVEREIGN POPULISM ...TRADIT 18 BURKE/EDM. PAGE 24 H0485 — POLICY COLONIAL SECT

B18
BARRES M.,THE FAITH OF FRANCE (TRANS. BY ELISABETH MARBURY). FRANCE FAM MUNIC NEIGH POL/PAR SECT ALL/VALS 20. PAGE 11 H0227 — TRADIT CULTURE WAR GP/REL

B25
MAURRAS C.,ENQUETE SUR LA MONARCHIE (1909). FRANCE CONTROL REPRESENT DISCRIM HEREDITY PWR CONSERVE 20 BUREAUCRCY. PAGE 105 H2103 — TRADIT AUTHORIT NAT/G CHIEF

B30
BYNKERSHOEK C.,QUAESTIONUM JURIS PUBLICI LIBRI DUO. CHRIST-17C MOD/EUR CONSTN ELITES SOCIETY NAT/G PROVS EX/STRUC FORCES TOP/EX BAL/PWR DIPLOM ATTIT MORAL...TRADIT CONCPT. PAGE 25 H0502 — INT/ORG LAW NAT/LISM INT/LAW

B35
PARETO V.,THE MIND AND SOCIETY (4 VOLS.). ELITES SECT ECO/TAC COERCE PERSON ORD/FREE PWR SOVEREIGN FASCISM POPULISM...TRADIT 19/20. PAGE 123 H2465 — GEN/LAWS SOC PSY

B37
CARLYLE T.,THE FRENCH REVOLUTION (2 VOLS.). FRANCE CONSTN NAT/G FORCES COERCE MURDER PEACE MORAL POPULISM...TIME/SEQ IDEA/COMP GEN/LAWS 18. PAGE 26 H0532 — REV CHIEF TRADIT

C39
BURKE E.,"ON THE REFORM OF THE REPRESENTATION IN THE HOUSE OF COMMONS" (1782) IN COLLECTED WORKS (VOL. 5)" UK ELITES STRATA NAT/G REPRESENT ORD/FREE PWR POPULISM...POLICY NEW/IDEA GEN/LAWS 18 BURKE/EDM. PAGE 24 H0486 — TRADIT CONSTN PARL/PROC LEGIS

B42
FEFFERO G.,THE PRINCIPLES OF POWER (TRANS. BY T. JAECKEL). MOD/EUR CONSTN NAT/G CHIEF CONTROL REV WAR ORD/FREE CONSERVE FASCISM POPULISM...GEN/LAWS 18/20 EUROPE. PAGE 49 H0980 — PWR LEGIT TRADIT ELITES

C43
BENTHAM J.,"ON THE LIBERTY OF THE PRESS, AND PUBLIC DISCUSSION" IN J. BOWRING, ED., THE WORKS OF JEREMY BENTHAM." SPAIN UK LAW ELITES NAT/G LEGIS INSPECT LEGIT WRITING CONTROL PRIVIL TOTALISM AUTHORIT ...TRADIT 19 FREE/SPEE. PAGE 15 H0290 — ORD/FREE PRESS CONFER CONSERVE

B44
BERDYAEV N.,SLAVERY AND FREEDOM. NAT/G REV WAR NAT/LISM OWN AUTHORIT SEX CONSERVE SOCISM...TRADIT PHIL/SCI CIVIL/LIB. PAGE 15 H0295 — ORD/FREE PERSON ELITES SOCIETY

B52
LOPEZ-AMO A.,LA MONARQUIA DE LA REFORMA SOCIAL. MOD/EUR SPAIN CONSTN NAT/G TASK EFFICIENCY CONSERVE ...ANARCH TRADIT SOC CONCPT IDEA/COMP 19/20. PAGE 98 H1967 — MARXISM REV LEGIT ORD/FREE

B56
MYERS F.M.,THE WARFARE OF DEMOCRATIC IDEALS. SECT KNOWL MORAL CATHISM...TRADIT CONCPT 20. PAGE 115 H2302 — POPULISM CHOOSE REPRESENT PERCEPT

B57
BULLOCK A.,THE LIBERAL TRADITION FROM FOX TO KEYNES. UK CULTURE INTELL CREATE WRITING COLONIAL PERS/REL ATTIT ORD/FREE...POLICY OLD/LIB TRADIT CONCPT 18/20 CHURCHLL/W MILL/JS KEYNES/JM ASQUITH/HH. PAGE 23 H0469 — ANTHOL DEBATE LAISSEZ

B58
COLEMAN J.S.,NIGERIA: BACKGROUND TO NATIONALISM. AFR SOCIETY ECO/DEV KIN LOC/G POL/PAR TEC/DEV DOMIN ADMIN DRIVE PWR RESPECT...TRADIT SOC INT SAMP TIME/SEQ 20. PAGE 31 H0627 — NAT/G NAT/LISM NIGERIA

S60
MAGATHAN W.,"SOME BASES OF WEST GERMAN MILITARY POLICY." EUR+WWI FUT INT/ORG TOP/EX ECO/TAC DOMIN DRIVE ORD/FREE PWR...TRADIT GEOG OBS TREND. PAGE 101 H2015 — NAT/G FORCES GERMANY

S60
SHILS E.,"THE INTELLECTUALS IN THE POLITICAL DEVELOPMENT OF THE NEW STATES." AFR ASIA S/ASIA ELITES LOC/G NAT/G CONSULT EX/STRUC CREATE PLAN ECO/TAC DOMIN LEGIT DRIVE PWR...TRADIT CONCPT STERTYP GEN/LAWS 20. PAGE 143 H2861 — POL/PAR INTELL NAT/LISM

C60
EBENSTEIN W.,"MODERN POLITICAL THOUGHT (2ND ED.)" NAT/G CAP/ISM NAT/LISM PERSON ORD/FREE PWR ALL/IDEOS NEW/LIB SOCISM...TRADIT PSY BIBLIOG/A 18/20. PAGE 44 H0884 — IDEA/COMP PHIL/SCI CONCPT GEN/LAWS

B61
BINDER L.,RELIGION AND POLITICS IN PAKISTAN. ISLAM PAKISTAN NAT/G SECT LEGIS CREATE CHOOSE GP/REL ...MAJORIT TRADIT 20. PAGE 17 H0336 — CONSTN CONFER NAT/LISM POL/PAR

B62
BODIN J.,THE SIX BOOKES OF A COMMONWEALE (1576) (FACSIMILE REPRINT OF 1606 ENGLISH TRANSLATION). AUTHORIT ORD/FREE SOVEREIGN...TRADIT CONCPT. PAGE 18 H0364 — PWR CONSERVE CHIEF NAT/G

B62
TINKER H.,INDIA AND PAKISTAN. INDIA PAKISTAN NAT/G POL/PAR...OLD/LIB TRADIT TREND CHARTS BIBLIOG 20. PAGE 155 H3102 — ORD/FREE STRATA REPRESENT AUTHORIT

B62
TURNBULL C.M.,THE LONELY AFRICAN. AFR MUNIC SECT ANOMIE ALL/VALS...DECISION 20. PAGE 157 H3139 — CULTURE ISOLAT KIN TRADIT

B63
MILLER W.J.,THE MEANING OF COMMUNISM. USSR SOCIETY ECO/DEV EX/STRUC WORKER TEC/DEV ADMIN TOTALISM ...POLICY CONCPT CHARTS BIBLIOG T 20 COLD/WAR LENIN/VI STALIN/J. PAGE 111 H2215 — MARXISM TRADIT DIPLOM NAT/G

B65
POBEDONOSTSEV K.P.,REFLECTIONS OF A RUSSIAN STATESMAN. RUSSIA LAW ELITES EDU/PROP PRESS ADJUD MARRIAGE ATTIT PWR...MAJORIT TRADIT 19 CHURCH/STA. PAGE 127 H2531 — TOTALISM POLICY CONSTN NAT/G

B66
BEER S.H.,BRITISH POLITICS IN THE COLLECTIVIST AGE. UK NAT/G CONTROL CHOOSE GP/REL ATTIT PWR PLURISM ...MAJORIT WELF/ST 16/20. PAGE 13 H0258 — POL/PAR SOCISM TRADIT GP/COMP

B66
ROGGER H.,THE EUROPEAN RIGHT. EUR+WWI CONSERVE ...ANTHOL BIBLIOG 20. PAGE 133 H2660 — NAT/COMP POL/PAR IDEA/COMP TRADIT

B66
ZEINE Z.N.,THE EMERGENCE OF ARAB NATIONALISM (REV. ED.). TURKEY UK NAT/G SECT TEC/DEV LEAD REV WAR AGE/Y ROLE ORD/FREE...TRADIT CHARTS BIBLIOG 20 ARABS OTTOMAN. PAGE 173 H3453 — ISLAM NAT/LISM DIPLOM

S67
HOPE M.,"THE RELUCTANT WAY: SELF-IMMOLATION IN VIETNAM." VIETNAM SOCIETY FAM KIN SECT DRIVE ALL/VALS...TRADIT OBS INT 20. PAGE 73 H1465 — CULTURE SUICIDE IDEA/COMP ATTIT

B70
BOSSUET J.B.,"POLITIQUE TIREE DE L'ECRITURE SAINTE" (1679-1709) IN J.B. BOSSUET, OEVRES DE BOSSUET. NAT/G GP/REL AUTHORIT HEREDITY PERSON ALL/VALS SOVEREIGN 18 BIBLE DEITY CHRISTIAN. PAGE 19 H0383 — TRADIT CHIEF SECT CONCPT

B90
BURKE E.,REFLECTIONS ON THE REVOLUTION IN FRANCE. FRANCE UK NAT/G DOMIN LEGIT PEACE PWR SOVEREIGN CONSERVE...POLICY GEN/LAWS 18. PAGE 24 H0487 — REV ORD/FREE CHIEF TRADIT

TRADITIONAL....SEE CONSERVE, TRADIT

TRAGER F.N. H3126,H3127

TRAINING....SEE SCHOOL, ACADEM, SKILL, EDU/PROP

TRANSFER....TRANSFER

TRANSITIVITY OF CHOICE....SEE DECISION

TRANSKEI....TRANSKEI

B64
HILL C.R.,BANTUSTANS: THE FRAGMENTATION OF SOUTH AFRICA. AFR SOUTH/AFR ELITES SOCIETY KIN CONTROL DISCRIM ANOMIE ATTIT...POLICY CHARTS GOV/COMP 20 NEGRO BANTUSTANS TRANSKEI NATAL. PAGE 71 H1416 — RACE/REL CULTURE LOC/G ORD/FREE

B67
CARTER G.M.,SOUTH AFRICA'S TRANSKEI: THE POLITICS OF DOMESTIC COLONIALISM. SOUTH/AFR ECO/UNDEV AGRI NAT/G PROVS PLAN DOMIN REPRESENT ADJUST DISCRIM ...OBS BIBLIOG 20 BANTUSTANS TRANSKEI. PAGE 27 H0550 — STRATA GOV/REL COLONIAL POLICY

TRANSPORTATION....SEE DIST/IND

TRAVEL....TRAVEL AND TOURISM

B63
US ATOMIC ENERGY COMMISSION,ATOMIC ENERGY IN THE SOVIET UNION: TRIP REPORT OF THE US ATOMIC ENERGY DELEGATION, MAY 1933. USSR R+D NAT/G CONSULT CREATE DIPLOM ADMIN ROUTINE EFFICIENCY PRODUC KNOWL SKILL ...NAT/COMP 20 AEC TRAVEL TREATY. PAGE 159 H3176 — METH/COMP OP/RES TEC/DEV NUC/PWR

TREADGOLD D.W. H3128

TREASURY DEPARTMENT....SEE DEPT/TREAS

TREATY....TREATIES; INTERNATIONAL AGREEMENTS

B29
LANGER W.L.,THE FRANCO-RUSSIAN ALLIANCE: 1890-1894. FRANCE MOD/EUR UK USSR NAT/G CHIEF FORCES BAL/PWR AGREE WAR PEACE PWR...TIME/SEQ TREATY 19 BISMARCK/O. PAGE 91 H1809 — DIPLOM

B38
MCNAIR A.D.,THE LAW OF TREATIES: BRITISH PRACTICE AND OPINIONS. UK CREATE DIPLOM LEGIT WRITING ADJUD WAR...INT/LAW JURID TREATY. PAGE 107 H2144 — AGREE LAW CT/SYS NAT/G

B39
BENES E.,INTERNATIONAL SECURITY. GERMANY UK NAT/G DELIB/GP PLAN BAL/PWR ATTIT ORD/FREE PWR LEAGUE/NAT 20 TREATY. PAGE 14 H0280 — EUR+WWI INT/ORG WAR

B39
CARR E.H.,PROPAGANDA IN INTERNATIONAL POLITICS (PAMPHLET). EUR+WWI GERMANY MOD/EUR NAT/G AGREE WAR MORAL...POLICY 20 TREATY. PAGE 27 H0536 — DIPLOM EDU/PROP CONTROL ATTIT

B40
BROGAN D.W.,THE DEVELOPMENT OF MODERN FRANCE (1870-1939). FRANCE GERMANY UK USSR CONSTN CHIEF LEGIS DIPLOM AGREE COLONIAL WAR NAT/LISM PEACE SOCISM 19/20 TREATY. PAGE 21 H0428 — MOD/EUR NAT/G

B40
WOLFERS A.,BRITAIN AND FRANCE BETWEEN TWO WORLD WARS. FRANCE UK INT/ORG NAT/G PLAN BARGAIN ECO/TAC AGREE ISOLAT ALL/IDEOS...DECISION GEOG 20 TREATY VERSAILLES INTERVENT. PAGE 170 H3402 — DIPLOM WAR POLICY

B41
HITLER A.,MEIN KAMPF (UNABR. ENG. VERSION) (1925). GERMANY CONSTN TEC/DEV RACE/REL NAT/LISM TOTALISM SOVEREIGN...BIOG 20 HITLER/A TREATY. PAGE 71 H1429 — EDU/PROP WAR PLAN FASCISM

B47
ENKE S.,INTERNATIONAL ECONOMICS. UK USA+45 USSR INT/ORG BAL/PWR BARGAIN CAP/ISM BAL/PAY...NAT/COMP 20 TREATY. PAGE 46 H0927 — INT/TRADE FINAN TARIFFS ECO/TAC

B48
PELCOVITS N.A.,OLD CHINA HANDS AND THE FOREIGN OFFICE. ASIA BURMA UK ECO/UNDEV NAT/G ECO/TAC FOR/AID TARIFFS DOMIN COLONIAL GOV/REL SOVEREIGN 19 HONG/KONG TREATY. PAGE 124 H2483 — INT/TRADE ATTIT DIPLOM

B50
ALBRECHT-CARRIE R.,ITALY FROM NAPOLEON TO MUSSOLINI. GERMANY ITALY SPAIN SOCIETY ECO/DEV POL/PAR LEGIS AGREE CONTROL WAR NAT/LISM TOTALISM PWR SOCISM...SOC 19/20 TREATY. PAGE 5 H0095 — FASCISM NAT/G

B50
GATZKE H.W.,GERMANY'S DRIVE TO THE WEST. BELGIUM GERMANY MOD/EUR AGRI INDUS POL/PAR FORCES DOMIN AGREE CONTROL REGION COERCE 20 TREATY WWI. PAGE 55 H1104 — WAR POLICY NAT/G DIPLOM

B50
GLEASON J.H.,THE GENESIS OF RUSSOPHOBIA IN GREAT BRITAIN: A STUDY OF THE INTERACTION OF POLICY AND OPINION. ASIA RUSSIA UK NAT/G AGREE CONTROL REV WAR LOVE PWR TREATY 19. PAGE 57 H1142 — DIPLOM POLICY DOMIN COLONIAL

B51
BISSAINTHE M.,DICTIONNAIRE DE BIBLIOGRAPHIE HAITIENNE. HAITI ELITES AGRI LEGIS DIPLOM INT/TRADE WRITING ORD/FREE CATHISM...ART/METH GEOG 19/20 NEGRO TREATY. PAGE 17 H0347 — BIBLIOG L/A+17C SOCIETY NAT/G

B55
KRUSE H.,DAS STAATSANGEHORIGKEITSRECHT DER ARABISCHEN STAATEN. ISLAM JORDAN LIBYA SYRIA UAR NAT/G SECT RACE/REL...INT/LAW 6/20 TREATY. PAGE 89 H1779 — JURID NAT/LISM DIPLOM GP/REL

B55
TAN C.C.,THE BOXER CATASTROPHE. ASIA UK USSR ELITES POL/PAR VOL/ASSN FORCES PROB/SOLV DIPLOM ADMIN COLONIAL NAT/LISM PEACE TREATY 19/20 BOXER/REBL. PAGE 152 H3040 — REV NAT/G WAR

B56
WATT D.C.,BRITAIN AND THE SUEZ CANAL. COM UAR UK ...INT/LAW 20 SUEZ TREATY. PAGE 166 H3314 — DIPLOM INT/TRADE DIST/IND NAT/G

B57
PALMER N.D.,INTERNATIONAL RELATIONS. WOR+45 INT/ORG NAT/G ECO/TAC EDU/PROP COLONIAL WAR PWR SOVEREIGN ...POLICY T 20 TREATY. PAGE 123 H2451 — DIPLOM BAL/PWR NAT/COMP

B60
ALBRECHT-CARRIE R.,FRANCE, EUROPE AND THE TWO WORLD WARS. EUR+WWI FRANCE GERMANY MOD/EUR UK ECO/DEV NAT/G FORCES BAL/PWR DOMIN ARMS/CONT PEACE PWR 20 TREATY EUROPE. PAGE 5 H0096 — DIPLOM WAR

B60
FISCHER L.,THE SOVIETS IN WORLD AFFAIRS. CHINA/COM COM EUR+WWI USSR INT/ORG CONFER LEAD ARMS/CONT REV PWR...CHARTS 20 TREATY VERSAILLES. PAGE 51 H1010 — DIPLOM NAT/G POLICY MARXISM

B61
FULLER J.F.C.,THE CONDUCT OF WAR, 1789-1961. FRANCE RUSSIA SOCIETY NAT/G FORCES PROB/SOLV AGREE NUC/PWR WEAPON PEACE...SOC 18/20 TREATY COLD/WAR. PAGE 54 H1076 — WAR POLICY REV ROLE

B61
JAKOBSON M.,THE DIPLOMACY OF THE WINTER WAR. EUR+WWI FINLAND GERMANY USSR INT/ORG NAT/G PEACE TOTALISM PWR...POLICY CONCPT 20 TREATY. PAGE 79 H1588 — WAR ORD/FREE DIPLOM

B61
ROBERTSON A.H.,THE LAW OF INTERNATIONAL INSTITUTIONS IN EUROPE. EUR+WWI MOD/EUR INT/ORG NAT/G VOL/ASSN DELIB/GP...JURID TIME/SEQ TOT/POP 20 TREATY. PAGE 132 H2644 — RIGID/FLEX ORD/FREE

S61
BRZEZINSKI Z.K.,"THE ORGANIZATION OF THE COMMUNIST CAMP." COM CZECHOSLVK COM/IND NAT/G DELIB/GP INT/TRADE DOMIN EDU/PROP EXEC ROUTINE COERCE ATTIT PWR...MGT CONCPT TIME/SEQ CHARTS VAL/FREE 20 TREATY. PAGE 23 H0460 — VOL/ASSN DIPLOM USSR

B62
FATOUROS A.A.,GOVERNMENT GUARANTEES TO FOREIGN INVESTORS. WOR+45 ECO/UNDEV INDUS WORKER ADJUD ...NAT/COMP BIBLIOG TREATY. PAGE 49 H0975 — NAT/G FINAN INT/TRADE ECO/DEV

B62
GANJI M.,INTERNATIONAL PROTECTION OF HUMAN RIGHTS. WOR+45 CONSTN INT/TRADE CT/SYS SANCTION CRIME WAR RACE/REL...CHARTS IDEA/COMP NAT/COMP BIBLIOG 20 TREATY NEGRO LEAGUE/NAT UN CIVIL/LIB. PAGE 55 H1097
ORD/FREE DISCRIM LEGIS DELIB/GP

B62
HENDERSON W.O.,THE GENESIS OF THE COMMON MARKET. EUR+WWI FRANCE MOD/EUR UK SEA COM/IND EXTR/IND COLONIAL DISCRIM...TIME/SEQ CHARTS BIBLIOG 18/20 EEC TREATY. PAGE 70 H1395
ECO/DEV INT/TRADE DIPLOM

S62
VIGNES D.,"L'AUTORITE DES TRAITES INTERNATIONAUX EN DROIT INTERNE." EUR+WWI UNIV LAW CONSTN INTELL NAT/G POL/PAR DIPLOM ATTIT PERCEPT ALL/VALS ...POLICY INT/LAW JURID CONCPT TIME/SEQ 20 TREATY. PAGE 163 H3252
STRUCT LEGIT FRANCE

B63
FAWCETT J.E.S.,THE BRITISH COMMONWEALTH IN INTERNATIONAL LAW. LAW INT/ORG NAT/G VOL/ASSN OP/RES DIPLOM ADJUD CENTRAL CONSEN...NET/THEORY CMN/WLTH TREATY. PAGE 49 H0977
INT/LAW STRUCT COLONIAL

B63
FRANKEL J.,THE MAKING OF FOREIGN POLICY: AN ANALYSIS OF DECISION-MAKING. CHINA/COM EUR+WWI USA+45 ELITES INTELL FORCES LEGIS PLAN ATTIT ALL/VALS MORAL CONSERVE...GOV/COMP 20 PRESIDENT UN TREATY. PAGE 53 H1051
POLICY DECISION PROB/SOLV DIPLOM

B63
MONGER G.W.,THE END OF ISOLATION. FRANCE MOD/EUR RUSSIA UK NAT/G LEGIS TOP/EX GOV/REL PWR 20 TREATY CHINJAP. PAGE 112 H2239
DIPLOM POLICY WAR

B63
US ATOMIC ENERGY COMMISSION,ATOMIC ENERGY IN THE SOVIET UNION: TRIP REPORT OF THE US ATOMIC ENERGY DELEGATION, MAY 1933. USSR R+D NAT/G CONSULT CREATE DIPLOM ADMIN ROUTINE EFFICIENCY PRODUC KNOWL SKILL ...NAT/COMP 20 AEC TRAVEL TREATY. PAGE 159 H3176
METH/COMP OP/RES TEC/DEV NUC/PWR

B64
GRIFFITH W.E.,THE SINO-SOVIET RIFT. ASIA CHINA/COM COM CUBA USSR YUGOSLAVIA NAT/G POL/PAR VOL/ASSN DELIB/GP FORCES TOP/EX DIPLOM EDU/PROP DRIVE PERSON PWR...TREND 20 TREATY. PAGE 61 H1224
ATTIT TIME/SEQ BAL/PWR SOCISM

B65
WINT G.,ASIA: A HANDBOOK. ASIA COM INDIA USSR CULTURE INTELL NAT/G...GEOG STAT CENSUS NAT/COMP WORSHIP 20 TREATY CHINJAP. PAGE 169 H3387
DIPLOM SOC

B65
WUORINEN J.H.,SCANDINAVIA. DENMARK FINLAND ICELAND NORWAY SWEDEN SOCIETY AGRI INDUS DELIB/GP DIPLOM INT/TRADE NEUTRAL...GEOG CHARTS BIBLIOG TREATY. PAGE 171 H3428
NAT/G POL/PAR TREND POLICY

C65
WUORINEN J.H.,"SCANDINAVIA." DENMARK FINLAND ICELAND NORWAY SWEDEN SOCIETY AGRI POL/PAR DELIB/GP DIPLOM INT/TRADE NEUTRAL WAR...CHARTS TREATY 20. PAGE 171 H3427
BIBLIOG NAT/G POLICY

B66
DYCK H.V.,WEIMAR GERMANY AND SOVIET RUSSIA 1926-1933. EUR+WWI GERMANY UK USSR ECO/TAC INT/TRADE NEUTRAL WAR ATTIT 20 WEIMAR/REP TREATY. PAGE 44 H0877
DIPLOM GOV/REL POLICY

B66
HAY P.,FEDERALISM AND SUPRANATIONAL ORGANIZATIONS: PATTERNS FOR NEW LEGAL STRUCTURES. EUR+WWI LAW NAT/G VOL/ASSN DIPLOM PWR...NAT/COMP TREATY EEC. PAGE 68 H1364
SOVEREIGN FEDERAL INT/ORG INT/LAW

B66
HOYT E.C.,NATIONAL POLICY AND INTERNATIONAL LAW* CASE STUDIES FROM AMERICAN CANAL POLICY* MONOGRAPH NO. 1 -- 1966-1967. PANAMA UK ELITES BAL/PWR EFFICIENCY...CLASSIF NAT/COMP SOC/EXP COLOMB TREATY. PAGE 74 H1483
INT/LAW USA-45 DIPLOM PWR

B66
INTL CONF ON WORLD POLITICS-5,EASTERN EUROPE IN TRANSITION. EUR+WWI USSR ECO/TAC NAT/LISM ATTIT SOVEREIGN...CHARTS ANTHOL 20 TREATY WARSAW/P. PAGE 78 H1562
COM NAT/COMP MARXISM DIPLOM

B66
RISTIC D.N.,YUGOSLAVIA'S REVOLUTION OF 1941. EUR+WWI YUGOSLAVIA NAT/G WAR ORD/FREE...RECORD BIBLIOG 20 HITLER/A TREATY. PAGE 132 H2633
REV ATTIT FASCISM DIPLOM

B66
THOMPSON J.M.,RUSSIA, BOLSHEVISM, AND THE VERSAILLES PEACE. RUSSIA USSR INT/ORG NAT/G DELIB/GP AGREE REV WAR PWR 20 TREATY VERSAILLES BOLSHEVISM. PAGE 154 H3083
DIPLOM PEACE MARXISM

B66
WEINSTEIN F.B.,VIETNAM'S UNHELD ELECTIONS: THE FAILURE TO CARRY OUT THE 1956 REUNIFICATION ELECTIONS... (MONOGRAPH). VIETNAM/S VIETNAM/N LEGIT CONFER ADJUD WAR PEACE 20 TREATY GENEVA/CON UNIFICA. PAGE 166 H3330
AGREE NAT/G CHOOSE DIPLOM

S66
DETTER I.,"THE PROBLEM OF UNEQUAL TREATIES." CONSTN NAT/G LEGIS COLONIAL COERCE PWR...GEOG UN TIME TREATY. PAGE 40 H0796
SOVEREIGN DOMIN INT/LAW ECO/UNDEV

B67
POGANY A.H.,POLITICAL SCIENCE AND INTERNATIONAL RELATIONS, BOOKS RECOMMENDED FOR AMERICAN CATHOLIC COLLEGE LIBRARIES. INT/ORG LOC/G NAT/G FORCES BAL/PWR ECO/TAC NUC/PWR...CATH INT/LAW TREATY 20. PAGE 127 H2532
BIBLIOG DIPLOM

L67
MCALLISTER J.T. JR.,"THE POSSIBILITIES FOR DIPLOMACY IN SOUTHEAST ASIA." LAOS VIETNAM INT/ORG NAT/G PROVS BAL/PWR DOMIN AGREE COLONIAL WAR PWR 17/20 TREATY. PAGE 106 H2121
DIPLOM S/ASIA

L67
WAELBROECK M.,"THE APPLICATION OF EEC LAW BY NATIONAL COURTS." EUR+WWI INT/ORG CT/SYS...JURID EEC TREATY. PAGE 164 H3284
INT/LAW NAT/G LAW PROB/SOLV

S67
HALPERN B.,"THE ORIGINS OF THE CRISIS." ISLAM ISRAEL INT/ORG FORCES WEAPON PEACE ORD/FREE TREATY 20 UN. PAGE 65 H1296
WAR NAT/G DIPLOM

B86
MAS LATRIE L.,RELATIONS ET COMMERCE DE L'AFRIQUE SEPTENTRIONALE OU MAGREB AVEC LES NATIONS CHRETIENNES AU MOYEN AGE. CULTURE CHIEF FORCES WAR ...SOC CENSUS TREATY 10/16. PAGE 104 H2084
ISLAM SECT DIPLOM INT/TRADE

TREITSCHKE H. H3129

TREMBLAY M.A. H1489

TREND....PROJECTION OF HISTORICAL TRENDS

N
JOURNAL OF MODERN HISTORY. WOR+45 WOR-45 LEAD WAR ...TIME/SEQ TREND NAT/COMP 20. PAGE 1 H0006
BIBLIOG/A DIPLOM NAT/G

N
KYRIAK T.E.,ASIAN DEVELOPMENTS: A BIBLIOGRAPHY. INDONESIA KOREA/N VIETNAM/N CULTURE SOCIETY ECO/UNDEV NAT/G DIPLOM...SOC TREND 20 MONGOLIA. PAGE 90 H1788
BIBLIOG/A ALL/IDEOS S/ASIA ASIA

NSY
MACKENZIE K.R.,THE ENGLISH PARLIAMENT. UK POL/PAR CHIEF DIPLOM TAX TASK WAR AUTHORIT...POLICY TREND 12/20 PARLIAMENT. PAGE 100 H2000
ORD/FREE LEGIS NAT/G

B00
BENEDETTI V.,STUDIES IN DIPLOMACY. BELGIUM FRANCE GERMANY MOD/EUR CONSTN NAT/G CONSULT TOP/EX DOMIN EDU/PROP COERCE ATTIT...CONCPT INT BIOG TREND 19. PAGE 14 H0276
PWR GEN/LAWS DIPLOM

B00
VOLPICELLI Z.,RUSSIA ON THE PACIFIC AND THE SIBERIAN RAILWAY. MOD/EUR ECO/UNDEV INT/ORG FORCES PLAN DOMIN COLONIAL ROUTINE ATTIT ALL/VALS...OBS HIST/WRIT TIME/SEQ TREND CON/ANAL AUD/VIS CHARTS 18/19. PAGE 163 H3261
NAT/G ACT/RES RUSSIA

B13
SIEGFRIED A.,TABLEAU POLITIQUE DE LA FRANCE DE L'OUEST SOUS LA TROISIEME REPUBLIQUE. FRANCE STRATA STRUCT NAT/G POL/PAR PROVS REGION GOV/REL ATTIT PWR ...TREND TIME 19. PAGE 143 H2869
SOC GEOG SOCIETY

B15
FARIES J.C.,THE RISE OF INTERNATIONALISM. ASIA MOD/EUR NAT/G VOL/ASSN DELIB/GP BAL/PWR EDU/PROP ARMS/CONT RIGID/FLEX TREND. PAGE 49 H0971
INT/ORG DIPLOM PEACE

N19
TABORSKY E.,CONFORMITY UNDER COMMUNISM (PAMPHLET). CZECHOSLVK HUNGARY POLAND SCHOOL DOMIN PRESS ...TREND GOV/COMP 20. PAGE 152 H3030
COM CONTROL EDU/PROP NAT/G

B21
STUART G.H.,FRENCH FOREIGN POLICY. CONSTN INT/ORG NAT/G POL/PAR EX/STRUC FORCES PLAN ECO/TAC DOMIN EDU/PROP ADJUD COERCE ATTIT DRIVE RIGID/FLEX ALL/VALS...POLICY OBS RECORD BIOG TIME/SEQ TREND. PAGE 150 H3000
MOD/EUR DIPLOM FRANCE

B27
EDWARDS L.P.,THE NATURAL HISTORY OF REVOLUTION. UNIV NAT/G VOL/ASSN COERCE DRIVE WEALTH...TREND GEN/LAWS. PAGE 45 H0893
PWR GUERRILLA REV

B27
ENGELS F.,THE PEASANT WAR IN GERMANY (1850). GERMANY MOD/EUR AGRI WORKER LEAD COERCE INGP/REL ...TREND 16/19. PAGE 46 H0924
WAR STRATA REV MARXIST

B27
PANIKKAR K.M.,INDIAN STATES AND THE GOVERNMENT OF INDIA. INDIA UK CONSTN CONTROL TASK GP/REL SOVEREIGN WEALTH...TREND BIBLIOG 19. PAGE 123 H2457
GOV/COMP COLONIAL BAL/PWR PROVS

B28
BUELL R.,THE NATIVE PROBLEM IN AFRICA. KIN LABOR LOC/G ECO/TAC ROUTINE ORD/FREE...REC/INT KNO/TEST CENSUS TREND CHARTS SOC/EXP STERTYP 20. PAGE 23
AFR CULTURE

H0466

B28
CORBETT P.E.,CANADA AND WORLD POLITICS. LAW CULTURE SOCIETY STRUCT MARKET INT/ORG FORCES ACT/RES PLAN ECO/TAC LEGIT ORD/FREE PWR RESPECT...SOC CONCPT TIME/SEQ TREND CMN/WLTH 20 LEAGUE/NAT. PAGE 33 H0662
NAT/G CANADA

B28
SOROKIN P.,CONTEMPORARY SOCIOLOGICAL THEORIES. MOD/EUR UNIV SOCIETY R+D SCHOOL ECO/TAC EDU/PROP ROUTINE ATTIT DRIVE...PSY CONCPT TIME/SEQ TREND GEN/LAWS 20. PAGE 147 H2934
CULTURE SOC WAR

B29
DAVIE M.R.,THE EVOLUTION OF WAR. CULTURE KIN COERCE WAR ATTIT DRIVE...PSY SOC TIME/SEQ TREND GEN/LAWS. PAGE 37 H0746
FORCES STERTYP

B29
ROBERTS S.H.,HISTORY OF FRENCH COLONIAL POLICY. AFR ASIA L/A+17C S/ASIA CULTURE ECO/DEV ECO/UNDEV FINAN NAT/G PLAN ECO/TAC DOMIN ROUTINE SOVEREIGN...OBS HIST/WRIT TREND CHARTS VAL/FREE 19/20. PAGE 132 H2642
INT/ORG ACT/RES FRANCE COLONIAL

S31
HEINBERG J.G.,"THE PERSONNEL OF FRENCH CABINETS, 1871-1930." FRANCE STRATA CHIEF CHOOSE REPRESENT MAJORITY...STAT QU CENSUS TREND CHARTS PERS/COMP 19/20 CHAMBR/DEP. PAGE 69 H1386
ELITES NAT/G DELIB/GP TOP/EX

C31
MACLEOD W.C.,"THE ORIGIN AND HISTORY OF POLITICS." UNIV CULTURE NAT/G REPRESENT...SOC CONCPT TREND BIBLIOG. PAGE 100 H2004
METH STRUCT SOCIETY

B32
NIEBUHR R.,MORAL MAN AND IMMORAL SOCIETY* A STUDY IN ETHICS AND POLITICS. UNIV CULTURE SOCIETY STRUCT DIPLOM GOV/REL GP/REL PERS/REL...TREND IDEA/COMP. PAGE 118 H2357
MORAL PWR

B34
MARX K.,THE CLASS STRUGGLES IN FRANCE. FRANCE INDUS WORKER CONSERVE...TREND GEN/LAWS 19. PAGE 104 H2077
MARXIST STRATA REV INT/TRADE

B34
SMITH P.,A HISTORY OF MODERN CULTURE (2 VOLS.). NAT/G...HUM SOC TREND. PAGE 146 H2916
BIBLIOG CULTURE CONCPT

B35
MARRIOTT J.A.,DICTATORSHIP AND DEMOCRACY. GERMANY GREECE UK CHIEF DIPLOM DOMIN LEGIT PEACE ORD/FREE CONSERVE...TREND ROME HITLER/A. PAGE 103 H2057
TOTALISM POPULISM PLURIST NAT/G

B36
PREVITE-ORTON C.W.,THE CAMBRIDGE MEDIEVAL HISTORY (8 VOLS.). CHRIST-17C NAT/G PROB/SOLV TEC/DEV LEAD ...POLICY CONCPT WORSHIP. PAGE 128 H2559
BIBLIOG IDEA/COMP TREND

B37
MARX K.,THE CIVIL WAR IN THE UNITED STATES. USA-45 WORKER DIPLOM INT/TRADE DOMIN RACE/REL ATTIT ...TREND 19. PAGE 104 H2078
WAR REV MARXIST ORD/FREE

B37
PARSONS T.,THE STRUCTURE OF SOCIAL ACTION. UNIV INTELL SOCIETY INDUS MARKET ECO/TAC ROUTINE CHOOSE ALL/VALS...CONCPT OBS BIOG TREND GEN/LAWS 20. PAGE 124 H2471
CULTURE ATTIT CAP/ISM

B37
TINGSTEN H.,POLITICAL BEHAVIOR. EUR+WWI STRATA NAT/G POL/PAR ACT/RES AGE...TREND CHARTS 20 FEMALE/SEX. PAGE 155 H3100
CHOOSE ATTIT PARTIC

B39
HITLER A.,MEIN KAMPF. EUR+WWI FUT MOD/EUR STRUCT INT/ORG LABOR NAT/G POL/PAR FORCES CREATE PLAN BAL/PWR DIPLOM ECO/TAC DOMIN EDU/PROP ADMIN COERCE ATTIT...SOCIALIST BIOG TREND NAZI. PAGE 71 H1428
PWR NEW/IDEA WAR

B39
MARQUAND H.A.,ORGANIZED LABOUR IN FOUR CONTINENTS. EUR+WWI USA-45 INDUS NAT/G PAY GP/REL TOTALISM ATTIT WEALTH ALL/IDEOS...TREND NAT/COMP 20 ILO AFL/CIO EUROPE CHINJAP MEXIC/AMER. PAGE 103 H2055
LABOR WORKER CONCPT ANTHOL

B40
CONOVER H.F.,JAPAN-ECONOMIC DEVELOPMENT AND FOREIGN POLICY, A SELECTED LIST OF REFERENCES (PAMPHLET). CULTURE FINAN INDUS NAT/G FORCES INT/TRADE WAR ...SOC TREND 20 CHINJAP. PAGE 32 H0640
BIBLIOG ASIA ECO/DEV DIPLOM

B40
MCHENRY D.E.,HIS MAJESTY'S OPPOSITION: STRUCTURE AND PROBLEMS OF THE BRITISH LABOUR PARTY 1931-1938. UK FINAN LABOR LOC/G DELIB/GP LEGIS EDU/PROP LEAD PARTIC CHOOSE GP/REL SOCISM...TREND 20 LABOR/PAR. PAGE 107 H2130
POL/PAR MGT NAT/G POLICY

S40
FAHS C.B.,"POLITICAL GROUPS IN THE JAPANESE HOUSE OF PEERS." ELITES NAT/G ADMIN GP/REL...TREND CHINJAP. PAGE 48 H0961
ROUTINE POL/PAR LEGIS

S41
ABEL T.,"THE ELEMENT OF DECISION IN THE PATTERN OF WAR." EUR+WWI FUT NAT/G TOP/EX DIPLOM ROUTINE COERCE DISPL PERCEPT PWR...SOC METH/CNCPT HIST/WRIT TREND GEN/LAWS 20. PAGE 3 H0055
TEC/DEV FORCES WAR

B42
BARNES H.E.,SOCIAL INSTITUTIONS IN AN ERA OF WORLD UPHEAVAL. INDUS FAM NAT/G PERF/ART SECT AUTOMAT PERSON MORAL...PREDICT 20. PAGE 11 H0221
SOCIETY CULTURE TECHRACY TREND

B43
JONES C.K.,A BIBLIOGRAPHY OF LATIN AMERICAN BIBLIOGRAPHIES (2ND ED.). CULTURE ALL/VALS...POLICY GEOG HUM SOC LING BIOG TREND 20. PAGE 82 H1629
BIBLIOG/A L/A+17C HIST/WRIT

B43
SERENI A.P.,THE ITALIAN CONCEPTION OF INTERNATIONAL LAW. EUR+WWI MOD/EUR INT/ORG NAT/G DOMIN COERCE ORD/FREE FASCISM...OBS/ENVIR TREND 20. PAGE 141 H2829
LAW TIME/SEQ INT/LAW ITALY

B44
HAYEK F.A.,THE ROAD TO SERFDOM. NAT/G POL/PAR CREATE EDU/PROP ATTIT WEALTH LAISSEZ...OLD/LIB CONCPT TREND 20. PAGE 68 H1368
FUT PLAN ECO/TAC SOCISM

L44
HUXLEY J.,"THE FUTURE OF THE COLONIES." AFR SOCIETY NAT/G PLAN DOMIN COERCE ATTIT DRIVE ORD/FREE PWR WEALTH...TIME/SEQ TREND AUD/VIS CHARTS 20. PAGE 76 H1511
ECO/UNDEV FUT COLONIAL

C44
VAN VALKENBURG S.,"ELEMENTS OF POLITICAL GEOGRAPHY." FRANCE COM/IND INDUS NAT/G SECT RACE/REL...LING TREND GEN/LAWS BIBLIOG 20. PAGE 162 H3232
GEOG DIPLOM COLONIAL

B45
HUNTINGTON E.,MAINSPRINGS OF CIVILIZATION. UNIV CULTURE SOCIETY BIO/SOC PERSON KNOWL SKILL...PSY RECORD HIST/WRIT TREND CHARTS TOT/POP. PAGE 75 H1504
SOC GEOG

B45
LASKER B.,ASIA ON THE MOVE. ASIA BURMA S/ASIA THAILAND USSR ECO/UNDEV FAM KIN WAR NAT/LISM ATTIT ...GEOG CENSUS TREND AUSTRAL 20. PAGE 91 H1826
CULTURE RIGID/FLEX

B45
MERRIAM C.E.,SYSTEMATIC POLITICS. FUT POL/PAR DELIB/GP DIPLOM ADJUD ADMIN LEAD CHOOSE ATTIT...MGT PHIL/SCI TREND. PAGE 109 H2183
NAT/G METH/CNCPT CREATE

B46
CASSIRER E.,THE MYTH OF THE STATE. WOR-45 SOCIETY RACE/REL RATIONAL PWR FASCISM...PHIL/SCI PSY LING TREND HEGEL/GWF MACHIAVELL. PAGE 28 H0557
MYTH CONCPT NAT/G IDEA/COMP

B47
ISAAC J.,ECONOMICS OF MIGRATION. MOD/EUR CULTURE STRATA STRUCT NAT/G COLONIAL WEALTH...OLD/LIB TREND TIME 19/20 EUROPE/W MIGRATION. PAGE 78 H1569
HABITAT SOC GEOG

B47
JURJI E.J.,THE GREAT RELIGIONS OF THE MODERN WORLD. CULTURE INTELL SOCIETY INT/ORG CONSULT CHOOSE ATTIT DRIVE PERSON RIGID/FLEX...HUM CONCPT OBS BIOG HIST/WRIT TREND GEN/LAWS 20 WORSHIP. PAGE 82 H1643
UNIV SECT

S48
ALEXANDER L.,"WAR CRIMES, THEIR SOCIAL-PSYCHOLOGICAL ASPECTS." EUR+WWI GERMANY LAW CULTURE ELITES KIN POL/PAR PUB/INST FORCES DOMIN EDU/PROP COERCE CRIME ATTIT SUPEGO HEALTH MORAL PWR FASCISM ...PSY OBS TREND GEN/LAWS NAZI 20. PAGE 5 H0100
DRIVE WAR

S48
ALMOND G.A.,"THE CHRISTIAN PARTIES OF WESTEN EUROPE." EUR+WWI NAT/G EDU/PROP LEGIT TOTALISM ORD/FREE PWR MARXISM...TREND CHARTS STERTYP GEN/LAWS COLD/WAR 20. PAGE 5 H0110
POL/PAR CATH SOCISM

B49
SARGENT S.S.,CULTURE AND PERSONALITY. FUT UNIV SOCIETY FAM KIN NEIGH BIO/SOC DRIVE PERCEPT RIGID/FLEX LOVE RESPECT...PSY SOC CONCPT OBS TIME/SEQ TREND CON/ANAL CHARTS HYPO/EXP SIMUL TOT/POP. PAGE 138 H2754
CULTURE PERSON

S49
MACKENZIE R.D.,"ECOLOGY, HUMAN." UNIV CULTURE ECO/DEV ECO/UNDEV ATTIT...POLICY GEOG PSY CONCPT METH/CNCPT CONT/OBS TREND GEN/LAWS. PAGE 100 H2001
SOCIETY BIO/SOC

B50
CANTRIL H.,TENSIONS THAT CAUSE WAR. UNIV CULTURE R+D CREATE EDU/PROP DRIVE PERSON KNOWL ORD/FREE ...HUM PSY SOC OBS CENSUS TREND CON/ANAL SOC/EXP SIMUL GEN/METH ANTHOL COLD/WAR TOT/POP. PAGE 26 H0523
SOCIETY PHIL/SCI PEACE

B50
KANN R.A.,THE MULTINATIONAL EMPIRE (2 VOLS.). AUSTRIA CZECHOSLVK GERMANY HUNGARY CULTURE NAT/G POL/PAR PROVS REGION REV FEDERAL...GEOG TREND CHARTS IDEA/COMP NAT/COMP 19/20. PAGE 83 H1654
NAT/LISM MOD/EUR

B51
MUMFORD L.,THE CONDUCT OF LIFE. UNIV SOCIETY CREATE ...TECHNIC METH/CNCPT TIME/SEQ TREND GEN/LAWS BIBLIOG/A. PAGE 114 H2286
ALL/VALS CULTURE PERSON CONCPT

B51
WHEARE K.C.,MODERN CONSTITUTIONS (HOME UNIVERSITY LIBRARY). UNIV LAW NAT/G LEGIS...CONCPT TREND BIBLIOG. PAGE 167 H3336
CONSTN CLASSIF PWR CREATE

B52
BENTHAM A.,HANDBOOK OF POLITICAL FALLACIES. FUT MOD/EUR LAW INTELL LOC/G MUNIC NAT/G DELIB/GP LEGIS CREATE EDU/PROP CT/SYS ATTIT RIGID/FLEX KNOWL PWR ...RELATIV PSY SOC CONCPT SELF/OBS TREND STERTYP TOT/POP. PAGE 14 H0286
POL/PAR

B52
US DEPARTMENT OF STATE,RESEARCH ON EASTERN EUROPE (EXCLUDING USSR). EUR+WWI LAW ECO/DEV NAT/G PROB/SOLV DIPLOM ADMIN LEAD MARXISM...TREND 19/20. PAGE 159 H3187
BIBLIOG R+D ACT/RES COM

B52
WALTERS F.P.,A HISTORY OF THE LEAGUE OF NATIONS. EUR+WWI CONSTN NAT/G LEGIS TOP/EX ACT/RES PLAN EDU/PROP LEGIT ROUTINE ATTIT...TREND LEAGUE/NAT 20 CHINJAP. PAGE 165 H3297
INT/ORG TIME/SEQ NAT/LISM

B53
LENZ F.,DIE BEWEGUNGEN DER GROSSEN MACHTE. USA+45 USA-45 USSR SOCIETY STRATA STRUCT NAT/G PERSON MARXISM...CONCPT IDEA/COMP NAT/COMP 18/20. PAGE 94 H1883
BAL/PWR TREND DIPLOM HIST/WRIT

B53
REDFIELD R.,THE PRIMITIVE WORLD AND ITS TRANSFORMATIONS. UNIV CULTURE ATTIT MORAL...CONCPT TREND. PAGE 130 H2606
SOC CREATE PERSON SOCIETY

L53
DEUTSCH K.W.,"THE GROWTH OF NATIONS: SOME RECURRENT PATTERNS OF POLITICAL AND SOCIAL INTEGRATION" (BMR)" UNIV CULTURE SOCIETY ECO/DEV ECO/UNDEV NAT/G CREATE GP/REL...CONCPT GEN/LAWS SOC/INTEG 11/20. PAGE 40 H0797
TREND NAT/LISM ORD/FREE

C53
BULNER-THOMAS I.,"THE PARTY SYSTEM IN GREAT BRITAIN." UK CONSTN SECT PRESS CONFER GP/REL ATTIT ...POLICY TREND BIBLIOG 19/20 PARLIAMENT. PAGE 23 H0473
NAT/G POL/PAR ADMIN ROUTINE

B54
GIRALSO JARAMLLO G.,BIBLIOGRAFIA DE BIBLIOGRAFIAS COLOMBIANAS. L/A+17C ACADEM SECT CREATE EDU/PROP ...ART/METH GEOG LING TREND 20 COLOMB. PAGE 57 H1135
BIBLIOG/A CULTURE PHIL/SCI ECO/UNDEV

B54
SALVEMINI G.,PRELUDE TO WORLD WAR II. ITALY MOD/EUR INT/ORG BAL/PWR EDU/PROP CONTROL TOTALISM...TREND NAT/COMP BIBLIOG 19 HITLER/A LEAGUE/NAT MUSSOLIN/B. PAGE 137 H2745
WAR FASCISM LEAD PWR

S54
BALANDIER G.,"SOCIOLOGIE DE LA COLONISATION ET RELATIONS ENTRE SOCIETES GLOBALES." AFR SOCIETY ECO/UNDEV KIN DOMIN EDU/PROP RIGID/FLEX PWR...PSY CONCPT TREND TOT/POP. PAGE 10 H0203
CULTURE SOC COLONIAL

B55
INSTITUTE POLITISCHE WISSEN,POLITISCHE LITERATUR (3 VOLS.). INT/ORG LEAD WAR PEACE...CONCPT TREND NAT/COMP 20. PAGE 77 H1540
BIBLIOG/A NAT/G DIPLOM POLICY

B55
TOYNBEE A.,THE REALIGNMENT OF EUROPE. COM GREECE ITALY NAT/G BAL/PWR ECO/TAC EDU/PROP REV SOVEREIGN ...SOC TIME/SEQ TREND COLD/WAR 20. PAGE 156 H3123
EUR+WWI PLAN USSR

L55
ROSTOW W.W.,"RUSSIA AND CHINA UNDER COMMUNISM." CHINA/COM USSR INTELL STRUCT INT/ORG NAT/G POL/PAR TOP/EX ACT/RES PLAN ADMIN ATTIT ALL/VALS MARXISM ...CONCPT OBS TIME/SEQ TREND GOV/COMP VAL/FREE 20. PAGE 134 H2689
COM ASIA

B56
INTERNATIONAL AFRICAN INST,SOCIAL IMPLICATIONS OF INDUSTRIALIZATION AND URBANIZATION IN AFRICA SOUTH OF THE SAHARA. SOUTH/AFR INDUS LABOR MUNIC WORKER TEC/DEV...SOC OBS TREND ANTHOL 20. PAGE 77 H1549
AFR ECO/UNDEV ADJUST CULTURE

B56
MUMFORD L.,THE TRANSFORMATIONS OF MAN. UNIV CULTURE INGP/REL HABITAT HEREDITY ALL/VALS ORD/FREE...MYTH TIME/SEQ TREND WORSHIP. PAGE 114 H2287
IDEA/COMP PERSON CONCPT

B56
ROBERTS H.L.,RUSSIA AND AMERICA. CHINA/COM S/ASIA USSR FORCES TEC/DEV FOR/AID NUC/PWR ALL/IDEOS ...MAJORIT TREND NAT/COMP 20 COLD/WAR UN NATO. PAGE 132 H2641
DIPLOM INT/ORG BAL/PWR TOTALISM

S56
KHAMA T.,"POLITICAL CHANGE IN AFRICAN SOCIETY." CONSTN SOCIETY LOC/G NAT/G POL/PAR EX/STRUC LEGIS LEGIT ADMIN CHOOSE REPRESENT NAT/LISM MORAL ORD/FREE PWR...CONCPT OBS TREND GEN/METH CMN/WLTH 17/20. PAGE 85 H1706
AFR ELITES

C56
NEUMANN S.,"MODERN POLITICAL PARTIES: APPROACHES TO COMPARATIVE POLITIC. FRANCE UK EX/STRUC DOMIN ADMIN LEAD REPRESENT TOTALISM ATTIT...POLICY TREND METH/COMP ANTHOL BIBLIOG/A 20 CMN/WLTH. PAGE 117 H2338
POL/PAR GOV/COMP ELITES MAJORIT

B57
ARON R.,L'UNIFICATION ECONOMIQUE DE L'EUROPE. EUR+WWI SWITZERLND UK INT/ORG NAT/G REGION NAT/LISM ORD/FREE PWR...CONCPT METH/CNCPT OBS TREND STERTYP GEN/LAWS EEC 20. PAGE 8 H0168
VOL/ASSN ECO/TAC

B57
BUCK P.W.,CONTOL OF FOREIGN RELATIONS IN MODERN NATIONS. FRANCE L/A+17C NETHERLAND USSR WOR+45 INT/ORG TOP/EX BAL/PWR DOMIN EDU/PROP COERCE PEACE ATTIT...CONCPT TREND 20 CMN/WLTH. PAGE 23 H0465
NAT/G PWR DIPLOM

B57
COLE G.D.H.,THE POST WAR CONDITIONS OF BRITAIN. EUR+WWI STRUCT NAT/G PLAN EDU/PROP LEGIT RIGID/FLEX ORD/FREE WEALTH...SOCIALIST WELF/ST STAT TREND CON/ANAL CHARTS PARLIAMENT WORK 20. PAGE 31 H0624
ECO/DEV UK

B57
DEAN V.M.,THE NATURE OF THE NON-WESTERN WORLD. AFR ASIA L/A+17C S/ASIA CULTURE SOCIETY STRATA ECO/DEV DIPLOM ECO/TAC FOR/AID ATTIT DRIVE ALL/VALS ...RELATIV SOC CONCPT TIME/SEQ TREND TOT/POP 20. PAGE 39 H0778
ECO/UNDEV STERTYP NAT/LISM

B57
HODGKIN T.,NATIONALISM IN COLONIAL AFRICA. STRATA STRUCT MUNIC NAT/G POL/PAR LEGIS ATTIT SOVEREIGN ...POLICY TREND BIBLIOG 20. PAGE 72 H1444
AFR COLONIAL NAT/LISM DIPLOM

B57
LAQUER W.Z.,COMMUNISM AND NATIONALISM IN THE MIDDLE EAST. ELITES INTELL STRATA NAT/G POL/PAR SECT VOL/ASSN TOP/EX DOMIN LEGIT REGION COERCE ATTIT PERSON PWR...CONCPT HIST/WRIT TIME/SEQ TREND GEN/LAWS VAL/FREE. PAGE 91 H1817
ISLAM NAT/LISM

B57
SCHLESINGER J.A.,HOW THEY BECAME GOVERNOR; A STUDY OF COMPARATIVE STATE POLITICS, 1870-1950. USA+45 USA-45 LAW POL/PAR LEGIS EDU/PROP REGION...STAT TREND CHARTS TIME 19/20 GOVERNOR. PAGE 139 H2788
PROVS CHIEF GOV/COMP CHOOSE

B57
TOMASIC D.A.,NATIONAL COMMUNISM AND SOVIET STRATEGY. UK USSR YUGOSLAVIA NAT/G POL/PAR CHIEF CREATE DOMIN REV WAR PWR...BIOG TREND 20 TITO/MARSH STALIN/J. PAGE 156 H3112
COM NAT/LISM MARXISM DIPLOM

S57
HAILEY,"TOMORROW IN AFRICA." CONSTN SOCIETY LOC/G NAT/G DOMIN ADJUD ADMIN GP/REL DISCRIM NAT/LISM ATTIT MORAL ORD/FREE...PSY SOC CONCPT OBS RECORD TREND GEN/LAWS CMN/WLTH 20. PAGE 64 H1277
AFR PERSON ELITES RACE/REL

S57
KILSON M.L.,"LAND AND POLITICS IN KENYA: AN ANALYSIS OF AFRICAN POLITICS IN A PLURAL SOCIETY." FUT LAW CULTURE KIN NAT/G ECO/TAC DOMIN REV NAT/LISM ORD/FREE PWR RESPECT SOVEREIGN WEALTH ...SOC OBS TREND WORK VAL/FREE CMN/WLTH 20. PAGE 86 H1710
AFR ECO/UNDEV

S57
NEUMANN S.,"COMPARATIVE POLITICS: A HALF CENTURY APPRAISAL" USA+45 USA-45...SOC TIME/SEQ TREND NAT/COMP METH 20. PAGE 117 H2339
PHIL/SCI GOV/COMP GEN/METH

C57
WITTFOGEL K.A.,"ORIENTAL DESPOTISM: A COMPARATIVE STUDY OF TOTAL POWER." ASIA CULTURE STRATA NAT/G LEAD OWN ORD/FREE PWR...CONCPT TREND BIBLIOG 20. PAGE 170 H3393
TOTALISM HABITAT DOMIN ELITES

B58
GARTHOFF R.L.,SOVIET STRATEGY IN THE NUCLEAR AGE. FUT USSR R+D INT/ORG NAT/G ACT/RES TEC/DEV DOMIN DETER WAR ATTIT PWR...RELATIV METH/CNCPT SELF/OBS TREND CON/ANAL STERTYP GEN/LAWS 20. PAGE 55 H1103
COM FORCES BAL/PWR NUC/PWR

B58
HENLE P.,LANGUAGE, THOUGHT AND CULTURE. CULTURE GP/REL PERCEPT...PSY TREND ANTHOL 20. PAGE 70 H1397
LING RATIONAL CONCPT SOC

B58
JOHNSON J.J.,POLITICAL CHANGE IN LATIN AMERICA: THE EMERGENCE OF THE MIDDLE SECTORS. INTELL STRATA STRUCT ECO/UNDEV MUNIC TEC/DEV LEAD REV...DECISION TREND GOV/COMP BIBLIOG/A 20. PAGE 81 H1621
L/A+17C ELITES GP/REL DOMIN

B58
KINTNER W.R.,ORGANIZING FOR CONFLICT: A PROPOSAL. USSR STRUCT NAT/G LEGIS ADMIN EXEC PEACE ORD/FREE PWR...CONCPT OBS TREND NAT/COMP VAL/FREE COLD/WAR 20. PAGE 86 H1719
USA+45 PLAN DIPLOM

B58
LAQUER W.Z.,THE MIDDLE EAST IN TRANSITION. COM USSR ECO/UNDEV NAT/G VOL/ASSN EDU/PROP EXEC ATTIT DRIVE PWR MARXISM COLD/WAR TOT/POP 20. PAGE 91 H1818
ISLAM TREND NAT/LISM

S58
EULAV H.,"HD LASSWELL'S DEVELOPMENTAL ANALYSIS." FUT CULTURE TOP/EX PLAN CHOOSE SUPEGO PWR...TREND HYPO/EXP SIMUL GEN/METH VAL/FREE 20 LASSWELL/H. PAGE 47 H0948
CONCPT NEW/IDEA ELITES

B59
BLOOMFIELD L.P.,WESTERN EUROPE AND THE UN - TRENDS
INT/ORG

AND PROSPECTS. EUR+WWI BAL/PWR DIPLOM ECO/TAC COLONIAL ATTIT PWR...POLICY 20 UN EUROPE/W. PAGE 18 H0359
TREND FUT NAT/G

B59
ELDRIDGE H.T.,THE MATERIALS OF DEMOGRAPHY: A SELECTED AND ANNOTATED BIBLIOGRAPHY. R+D DEATH ...SAMP METH/COMP NAT/COMP 20. PAGE 45 H0905
BIBLIOG/A GEOG STAT TREND

B59
LAQUER W.Z.,THE SOVIET UNION AND THE MIDDLE EAST. COM UAR USSR ECO/UNDEV NAT/G VOL/ASSN ECO/TAC EDU/PROP COLONIAL EXEC PWR...TIME/SEQ TREND COLD/WAR 20. PAGE 91 H1819
ISLAM DRIVE FOR/AID NAT/LISM

B59
MADHOK B.,POLITICAL TRENDS IN INDIA. INDIA PAKISTAN UK STRATA ECO/UNDEV POL/PAR LEGIS CAP/ISM DIPLOM COLONIAL CHOOSE MARXISM...SOC TREND 20 GANDHI/M NEHRU/J. PAGE 101 H2014
GEOG NAT/G

B59
MARTZ J.D.,CENTRAL AMERICA: THE CRISIS AND THE CHALLENGE. L/A+17C POL/PAR CHIEF CHOOSE SOVEREIGN ...BIOG TREND BIBLIOG 20 CENTRAL/AM. PAGE 104 H2071
NAT/G GOV/REL DIPLOM GOV/COMP

B59
MEYER A.J.,MIDDLE EASTERN CAPITALISM: NINE ESSAYS. ISLAM CULTURE ECO/UNDEV INDUS MARKET NAT/G PLAN ATTIT RIGID/FLEX...STAT OBS TREND GEN/LAWS. PAGE 109 H2188
TEC/DEV ECO/TAC ANTHOL

L59
MURPHY J.C.,"SOME IMPLICATIONS OF EUROPE'S COMMON MARKET. IN (COOK P, ECONOMIC DEVELOPMENT AND INTERNATIONAL TRADE.," EUR+WWI ECO/DEV DIST/IND INDUS NAT/G PLAN ECO/TAC INT/TRADE WEALTH...STAT TREND OEEC TOT/POP 20 EEC. PAGE 115 H2298
MARKET INT/ORG REGION

S59
LEVINE R.A.,"ANTI-EUROPEAN VIOLENCE IN AFRICA: A COMPARATIVE ANALYSIS." AFR CULTURE NAT/G DIPLOM EDU/PROP COLONIAL REGION COERCE ATTIT PWR...PSY CONCPT TIME/SEQ TREND HYPO/EXP SOC/EXP STERTYP GEN/METH COLD/WAR 20. PAGE 95 H1903
DRIVE ORD/FREE REV

S59
PLAZA G.,"FOR A REGIONAL MARKET IN LATIN AMERICA." FUT L/A+17C CULTURE INDUS NAT/G ECO/TAC INT/TRADE ATTIT WEALTH...NEW/IDEA TREND OAS 20. PAGE 126 H2527
MARKET INT/ORG REGION

S59
SKILLING H.G.,"COMMUNISM: NATIONAL OR INTERNATIONAL." CHINA/COM USSR YUGOSLAVIA NAT/G POL/PAR VOL/ASSN DOMIN REGION COERCE ATTIT PWR MARXISM SOCISM...CONCPT TOT/POP 20 TITO/MARSH. PAGE 145 H2894
COM TREND

B60
BRZEZINSKI Z.K.,THE SOVIET BLOC-UNITY AND CONFLICT. COM USSR CONSTN DOMIN ADMIN TOTALISM PWR...SOC MYTH RECORD TREND STERTYP GEN/LAWS GEN/METH TOT/POP 20. PAGE 23 H0458
ATTIT EDU/PROP

B60
EASTON S.C.,THE TWILIGHT OF EUROPEAN COLONIALISM. AFR S/ASIA CONSTN SOCIETY STRUCT ECO/UNDEV INDUS NAT/G FORCES ECO/TAC COLONIAL CT/SYS ATTIT KNOWL ORD/FREE PWR...SOCIALIST TIME/SEQ TREND CON/ANAL 20. PAGE 44 H0882
FINAN ADMIN

B60
FRANCIS R.G.,THE PREDICTIVE PROCESS. PLAN MARXISM ...DECISION SOC CONCPT NAT/COMP 19/20. PAGE 52 H1047
PREDICT PHIL/SCI TREND

B60
FURNISS E.S.,FRANCE, TROUBLED ALLY. EUR+WWI FUT CULTURE SOCIETY BAL/PWR ADMIN ATTIT DRIVE PWR ...TREND TOT/POP 20 DEGAULLE/C. PAGE 54 H1079
NAT/G FRANCE

B60
KERR C.,INDUSTRIALISM AND INDUSTRIAL MAN. CULTURE SOCIETY ECO/UNDEV NAT/G ADMIN PRODUC WEALTH ...PREDICT TREND NAT/COMP 19/20. PAGE 85 H1697
WORKER MGT ECO/DEV INDUS

B60
LINDSAY K.,EUROPEAN ASSEMBLIES: THE EXPERIMENTAL PERIOD 1949-1959. EUR+WWI ECO/DEV NAT/G POL/PAR LEGIS TOP/EX ACT/RES PLAN ECO/TAC DOMIN LEGIT ROUTINE ATTIT DRIVE ORD/FREE PWR SKILL...SOC CONCPT TREND CHARTS GEN/LAWS VAL/FREE. PAGE 97 H1932
VOL/ASSN INT/ORG REGION

B60
MORRIS I.,NATIONALISM AND THE RIGHT WING IN JAPAN: A STUDY OF POST WAR TRENDS. ASIA ELITES NAT/G DELIB/GP FORCES TOP/EX CHOOSE ATTIT...INT GEN/LAWS CONGRESS 20 CHINJAP. PAGE 113 H2262
POL/PAR TREND NAT/LISM

L60
WHEELER G.,"RACIAL PROBLEMS IN SOVIET MUSLIM ASIA." COM CULTURE SOCIETY NEIGH SECT DOMIN EDU/PROP DISCRIM DISPL DRIVE PWR SOVEREIGN...CENSUS SAMP TREND 20 MUSLIM. PAGE 167 H3340
PERSON ATTIT USSR RACE/REL

S60
COOK R.C.,"THE WORLD'S GREAT CITIES: EVOLUTION OR DEVOLUTION?" WOR+45 WOR-45 ECO/DEV ECO/UNDEV ACT/RES PROB/SOLV...GEOG TREND CHARTS NAT/COMP BIBLIOG 20. PAGE 33 H0658
MUNIC HABITAT PLAN CENSUS

S60
GINSBURGS G.,"PEKING-LHASA-NEW DELHI." CHINA/COM FUT INDIA S/ASIA KIN NAT/G PROVS SECT FORCES BAL/PWR ECO/TAC DOMIN EDU/PROP LEGIT ADMIN REGION GUERRILLA PWR...TREND TIBET 20. PAGE 57 H1134
ASIA COERCE DIPLOM

S60
HALSEY A.H.,"THE CHANGING FUNCTIONS OF UNIVERSITIES IN ADVANCED INDUSTRIAL SOCIETIES." R+D EDU/PROP REPRESENT ROLE ORD/FREE PWR TREND. PAGE 65 H1298
ACADEM CREATE CULTURE ADJUST

S60
KELLEY G.A.,"THE POLITICAL BACKGROUND OF THE FRENCH A-BOMB." EUR+WWI USSR FORCES TOP/EX TEC/DEV NUC/PWR ATTIT PWR...CONCPT OBS/ENVIR TREND 20. PAGE 84 H1686
NAT/G RESPECT NAT/LISM FRANCE

S60
MAGATHAN W.,"SOME BASES OF WEST GERMAN MILITARY POLICY." EUR+WWI FUT INT/ORG TOP/EX ECO/TAC DOMIN DRIVE ORD/FREE PWR...TRADIT GEOG OBS TREND. PAGE 101 H2015
NAT/G FORCES GERMANY

S60
NORTH R.C.,"THE NEW EXPANSIONISM." ASIA CHINA/COM FUT INDIA CULTURE SOCIETY NAT/G TOP/EX DOMIN COERCE PWR MARXISM...CONCPT TIME/SEQ TREND GEN/LAWS COLD/WAR 20 MAO. PAGE 119 H2372
ATTIT DRIVE NAT/LISM

S60
NORTHEDGE F.S.,"BRITISH FOREIGN POLICY AND THE PARTY SYSTEM." EUR+WWI FUT INT/ORG NAT/G EDU/PROP ATTIT PWR...POLICY CONCPT MYTH TIME/SEQ TREND 20 UN. PAGE 119 H2374
POL/PAR CHOOSE DIPLOM UK

S60
SPIRO H.J.,"NEW CONSTITUTIONAL FORMS IN AFRICA." FUT CULTURE SOCIETY ECO/UNDEV NAT/G POL/PAR VOL/ASSN EDU/PROP ATTIT DRIVE ORD/FREE PWR RESPECT ...POLICY CONCPT OBS TREND CON/ANAL STERTYP GEN/LAWS VAL/FREE. PAGE 148 H2950
AFR CONSTN FOR/AID NAT/LISM

S60
WOLFE T.W.,"KHRUSHCHEV'S DISARMAMENT STRATEGY." COM NAT/G TOP/EX PLAN BAL/PWR DIPLOM ARMS/CONT COERCE ATTIT...POLICY CONCPT RECORD TREND CON/ANAL COLD/WAR 20 KHRUSH/N. PAGE 170 H3401
PWR GEN/LAWS USSR

B61
BERKOWITZ L.,AGGRESSION: AS A SOCIAL PSYCHOLOGICAL ANALYSIS. UNIV CULTURE FACE/GP FAM KIN NEIGH EDU/PROP DISPL DRIVE HEALTH LOVE ORD/FREE...PSY SOC CONCPT OBS TREND. PAGE 15 H0305
SOCIETY COERCE WAR

B61
BONNEFOUS M.,EUROPE ET TIERS MONDE. EUR+WWI SOCIETY INT/ORG NAT/G VOL/ASSN ACT/RES TEC/DEV CAP/ISM ECO/TAC ATTIT ORD/FREE SOVEREIGN...POLICY CONCPT TREND 20. PAGE 19 H0373
AFR ECO/UNDEV FOR/AID INT/TRADE

B61
HEMPSTONE S.,THE NEW AFRICA. AGRI INDUS KIN NAT/G COLONIAL MARXISM...SOC INT TREND NAT/COMP BIBLIOG/A 20. PAGE 69 H1392
AFR ORD/FREE PERSON CULTURE

B61
KEREKES T.,THE ARAB MIDDLE EAST AND MUSLIM AFRICA. ISLAM SOCIETY ECO/UNDEV SECT VOL/ASSN TOP/EX REGION ATTIT PWR...GEOG CONCPT TIME/SEQ GEN/LAWS 20. PAGE 85 H1694
NAT/G TREND NAT/LISM

B61
KISSINGER H.A.,THE NECESSITY FOR CHOICE. FUT USA+45 ECO/UNDEV NAT/G PLAN BAL/PWR ECO/TAC ARMS/CONT DETER NUC/PWR ATTIT...POLICY CONCPT RECORD GEN/LAWS COLD/WAR 20. PAGE 87 H1728
TOP/EX TREND DIPLOM

B61
LUNDBERG G.A.,CAN SCIENCE SAVE US. UNIV CULTURE INTELL SOCIETY ECO/DEV R+D PLAN EDU/PROP ROUTINE CHOOSE ATTIT PERCEPT ALL/VALS...TREND 20. PAGE 99 H1979
ACT/RES CONCPT TOTALISM

B61
NOVE A.,THE SOVIET ECONOMY. USSR ECO/DEV FINAN NAT/G ECO/TAC PRICE ADMIN EFFICIENCY MARXISM ...TREND BIBLIOG 20. PAGE 119 H2378
PLAN PRODUC POLICY

B61
RAO K.V.,PARLIAMENTARY DEMOCRACY OF INDIA. INDIA EX/STRUC TOP/EX COLONIAL CT/SYS PARL/PROC ORD/FREE ...POLICY CONCPT TREND 20 PARLIAMENT. PAGE 130 H2592
CONSTN ADJUD NAT/G FEDERAL

B61
SOUTHALL A.,SOCIAL CHANGE IN MODERN AFRICA. CULTURE STRATA ECO/UNDEV AGRI FAM KIN MUNIC GP/REL INGP/REL MARRIAGE...GEOG ANTHOL 20. PAGE 147 H2940
AFR TREND SOCIETY SOC

L61
KAUPER P.G.,"CHURCH AND STATE: COOPERATIVE SEPARATISM." NAT/G LEGIS OP/RES TAX EDU/PROP GP/REL TREND. PAGE 84 H1671
SECT CONSTN LAW POLICY

S61
FITZGIBBON R.H.,"MEASUREMENT OF LATIN AMERICAN POLITICAL CHANGE." L/A+17C CONSTN CULTURE SOCIETY ECO/UNDEV NAT/G POL/PAR PUB/INST ACT/RES EDU/PROP PERCEPT KNOWL ORD/FREE SOVEREIGN...METH/CNCPT TREND OAS 20. PAGE 51 H1020
CHOOSE ATTIT

S61
NEEDLER M.C.,"THE POLITICAL DEVELOPMENT OF MEXICO." STRUCT NAT/G ADMIN RIGID/FLEX...TIME/SEQ TREND MEXIC/AMER TOT/POP VAL/FREE 19/20. PAGE 116 H2328 L/A+17C POL/PAR

S61
SCHAPIRO L.,"SOVIET GOVERNMENT TODAY." COM EUR+WWI INT/ORG POL/PAR VOL/ASSN ACT/RES PLAN PERCEPT ...CONCPT TREND TOT/POP VAL/FREE 20. PAGE 139 H2773 NAT/G TOTALISM USSR

S61
SCHELLING T.C.,"NUCLEAR STRATEGY IN EUROPE." COM EUR+WWI USSR NAT/G FORCES NUC/PWR DRIVE ORD/FREE PWR...DECISION CONCPT OBS TREND HYPO/EXP 20. PAGE 139 H2784 FUT COERCE ARMS/CONT WAR

S61
VALLET R.,"IRAN: KEY TO THE MIDDLE EAST." COM IRAQ ISLAM KUWAIT LEBANON SAUDI/ARAB TURKEY ELITES SOCIETY INDUS PROC/MFG POL/PAR TOP/EX PLAN BAL/PWR DIPLOM ECO/TAC ALL/VALS...TREND CENTO 20. PAGE 161 H3224 NAT/G ECO/UNDEV IRAN

B62
ABRAHAM W.E.,THE MIND OF AFRICA. AFR SOCIETY STRATA KIN ECO/TAC DOMIN EDU/PROP LEGIT COERCE ATTIT ALL/VALS...MAJORIT SOC OBS HIST/WRIT TIME/SEQ TREND TOT/POP 20. PAGE 3 H0058 CULTURE SIMUL GHANA

B62
BARNETT A.D.,COMMUNIST CHINA IN PERSPECTIVE. CHINA/COM FUT CULTURE ECO/UNDEV TEC/DEV CONTROL 20. PAGE 11 H0222 REV MARXISM TREND PLAN

B62
CARY J.,THE CASE FOR AFRICAN FREEDOM AND OTHER WRITINGS ON AFRICA. AFR UK INDUS LOC/G NAT/G SECT INT/TRADE EDU/PROP GOV/REL RACE/REL ORD/FREE ...CONCPT ANTHOL 19/20. PAGE 27 H0552 NAT/LISM COLONIAL TREND ECO/UNDEV

B62
CHAKRAVARTI P.C.,INDIA'S CHINA POLICY. ASIA CHINA/COM S/ASIA CULTURE NAT/G TOP/EX ACT/RES EDU/PROP DRIVE ALL/VALS...MYTH 20. PAGE 28 H0571 RIGID/FLEX TREND INDIA

B62
DUROSELLE J.B.,LES NOUVEAUX ETATS DANS LES RELATIONS INTERNATIONALES. AFR CHINA/COM FRANCE MOROCCO S/ASIA USSR ECO/UNDEV INT/ORG PLAN ECO/TAC EDU/PROP ATTIT DRIVE...TREND TOT/POP TUNIS 20. PAGE 44 H0872 NAT/G CONSTN DIPLOM

B62
DUTOIT B.,LA NEUTRALITE SUISSE A L'HEURE EUROPEENNE. EUR+WWI MOD/EUR INT/ORG NAT/G VOL/ASSN PLAN BAL/PWR LEGIT NEUTRAL REGION PEACE ORD/FREE SOVEREIGN...CONCPT OBS TIME/SEQ TREND STERTYP VAL/FREE LEAGUE/NAT UN 20. PAGE 44 H0873 ATTIT DIPLOM SWITZERLND

B62
GREEN L.P.,DEVELOPMENT IN AFRICA. AFR CENTRL/AFR GHANA RHODESIA SOUTH/AFR AGRI PROC/MFG INT/TRADE DEMAND NAT/LISM PRODUC WEALTH...GEOG METH/CNCPT CHARTS BIBLIOG 20. PAGE 60 H1206 CULTURE ECO/UNDEV GOV/REL TREND

B62
HUNTER G.,THE NEW SOCIETIES OF TROPICAL AFRICA. CULTURE INDUS KIN MUNIC WORKER INT/TRADE EDU/PROP ORD/FREE...INT TREND 20. PAGE 75 H1500 AFR GOV/COMP ECO/UNDEV SOCIETY

B62
JACKSON W.A.D.,RUSSO-CHINESE BORDERLANDS. ASIA COM USSR NAT/G PROVS EX/STRUC FORCES DOMIN COERCE PEACE ATTIT PWR SOVEREIGN WEALTH...CONCPT TREND CHARTS STERTYP VAL/FREE. PAGE 79 H1576 GEOG DIPLOM RUSSIA

B62
MEHNERT K.,SOVIET MAN AND HIS WORLD. COM USSR INTELL FAM WORKER PLAN EDU/PROP REV PRODUC MARXISM ...SOC TREND SOC/INTEG 20 LENIN/VI STALIN/J KHRUSH/N. PAGE 108 H2162 SOCIETY CULTURE ECO/DEV

B62
ROBINSON A.D.,DUTCH ORGANIZED AGRICULTURE IN INTERNATIONAL POLITICS, 1945-1960. EUR+WWI NETHERLAND STRUCT ECO/DEV NAT/G VOL/ASSN CONSULT DELIB/GP PLAN TEC/DEV INT/TRADE EDU/PROP ATTIT RIGID/FLEX ALL/VALS...NEW/IDEA TREND EEC 20. PAGE 132 H2648 AGRI INT/ORG

B62
SCHECHTMAN J.B.,POSTWAR POPULATION TRANSFERS IN EUROPE: 1945-1955. COM CZECHOSLVK GERMANY POLAND USSR CULTURE SOCIETY PROB/SOLV AGREE NAT/LISM...SOC STAT TREND CHARTS METH/COMP 20 MIGRATION. PAGE 139 H2778 GEOG CENSUS EUR+WWI HABITAT

B62
TINKER H.,INDIA AND PAKISTAN. INDIA PAKISTAN NAT/G POL/PAR...OLD/LIB TRADIT TREND CHARTS BIBLIOG 20. PAGE 155 H3102 ORD/FREE STRATA REPRESENT AUTHORIT

B62
VILAKAZI A.,ZULU TRANSFORMATIONS: A STUDY OF THE DYNAMICS OF SOCIAL CHANGE. AFR CULTURE ECO/UNDEV KIN NEIGH SEX...GEOG QU TREND CHARTS BIBLIOG 19/20. PAGE 163 H3254 MARRIAGE SECT SOC EDU/PROP

B62
WHITING K.R.,THE SOVIET UNION TODAY: A CONCISE HANDBOOK. USSR ELITES AGRI INDUS POL/PAR FORCES DIPLOM EDU/PROP LEAD...GEOG TREND 19/20. PAGE 168 H3354 NAT/G ATTIT MARXISM POLICY

S62
ANSPRENGER F.,"NATIONALISM, COMMUNISM, AND THE UNCOMMITTED NATIONS: AMERICAN PROFILES." FUT ISLAM CULTURE SOCIETY ECO/UNDEV NAT/G POL/PAR PLAN ECO/TAC EDU/PROP COERCE CHOOSE ALL/VALS MARXISM SOCISM...SOC CONCPT BIOG TREND 20. PAGE 7 H0142 AFR COM NAT/LISM

S62
BELL W.,"EQUALITY AND ATTITUDES OF ELITES IN JAMAICA" L/A+17C STRATA PWR WEALTH...SOC QU TREND. PAGE 13 H0266 ELITES FUT SOCIETY CULTURE

S62
CORET A.,"LE STATUT DE L'ILE CHRISTMAS DE L'OCEAN INDIEN." FUT S/ASIA ECO/DEV ECO/UNDEV VOL/ASSN DELIB/GP PLAN...RELATIV OBS TIME/SEQ TREND AUSTRAL 20. PAGE 33 H0667 NAT/G INT/ORG NEW/ZEALND

S62
CROAN M.,"POLYCENTRISM: COMMUNIST INTERNATIONAL RELATIONS." ASIA STRUCT INT/ORG NAT/G POL/PAR CONSULT PLAN DOMIN EDU/PROP COERCE ATTIT RIGID/FLEX SOCISM...POLICY CONCPT TREND CON/ANAL GEN/LAWS MARX/KARL. PAGE 35 H0703 COM CREATE DIPLOM NAT/LISM

S62
IOVTCHOUK M.T.,"ON SOME THEORETICAL PRINCIPLES AND METHODS OF SOCIOLOGICAL INVESTIGATIONS (IN RUSSIAN)." FUT USA+45 STRATA R+D NAT/G POL/PAR TOP/EX ACT/RES PLAN ECO/TAC EDU/PROP ROUTINE ATTIT RIGID/FLEX MARXISM SOCISM...MARXIST METH/CNCPT OBS TREND NAT/COMP GEN/LAWS 20. PAGE 78 H1564 COM ECO/DEV CAP/ISM USSR

S62
KOLARZ W.,"THE IMPACT OF COMMUNISM ON WEST AFRICA." AFR FUT SOCIETY INT/ORG NAT/G CREATE PLAN DOMIN EDU/PROP COERCE NAT/LISM ATTIT RIGID/FLEX SOCISM ...POLICY CONCPT TREND MARX/KARL 20. PAGE 88 H1751 COM POL/PAR COLONIAL

S62
LONDON K.,"SINO-SOVIET RELATIONS IN THE CONTEXT OF THE 'WORLD SOCIALIST SYSTEM'." ASIA CHINA/COM COM USSR INT/ORG NAT/G TOP/EX BAL/PWR DIPLOM DOMIN ATTIT PERCEPT RIGID/FLEX PWR MARXISM...METH/CNCPT TREND 20. PAGE 98 H1957 DELIB/GP CONCPT SOCISM

S62
PASSIN H.,"THE SOURCES OF PROTEST IN JAPAN." CULTURE SOCIETY EDU/PROP COERCE NAT/LISM DISPL DRIVE PWR RESPECT...POLICY SOC TREND 20 CHINJAP. PAGE 124 H2473 ASIA ATTIT REV

S62
ROTBERG R.,"THE RISE OF AFRICAN NATIONALISM: THE CASE OF EAST AND CENTRAL AFRICA." AFR CULTURE SOCIETY NEIGH DIPLOM DOMIN COLONIAL COERCE DISPL PERCEPT PWR SOVEREIGN...POLICY OBS/ENVIR TREND WORK 20. PAGE 135 H2690 ATTIT DRIVE NAT/LISM REV

S62
SARKISYANZ E.,"NATIONALISM, CAPITALISM, AND THE UNCOMMITED NATIONS: MARXISM AND ASIAN CULTURAL TRADITIONS." ASIA BURMA CHINA/COM COM CULTURE SOCIETY NAT/G POL/PAR PLAN DOMIN EDU/PROP COLONIAL COERCE ATTIT RIGID/FLEX...CONCPT TREND MARX/KARL 20 TIBET BUDDHISM. PAGE 138 H2755 S/ASIA SECT NAT/LISM CAP/ISM

S62
SHATTEN F.,"POLYCENTRISM: AFRICA: NATIONALISM AND COMMUNISM." ASIA COM FUT ISLAM CULTURE SOCIETY ECO/UNDEV NAT/G PLAN DOMIN COLONIAL COERCE CHOOSE RIGID/FLEX ALL/VALS MARXISM...CONCPT TREND 20. PAGE 143 H2852 AFR ATTIT NAT/LISM SOCISM

S62
STRACHEY J.,"COMMUNIST INTENTIONS." ASIA USSR YUGOSLAVIA INT/ORG NAT/G FORCES DOMIN EDU/PROP COERCE NUC/PWR NAT/LISM PEACE RIGID/FLEX PWR MARXISM...CONCPT MYTH OBS TIME/SEQ TREND COLD/WAR TOT/POP 20. PAGE 150 H2992 COM ATTIT WAR

S62
WALTER E.,"VERS UNE CLASSIFICATION SCIENTIFIQUE DE LA SOCIOLOGIA." UNIV CULTURE INTELL SOCIETY R+D ACT/RES LEGIT ROUTINE ATTIT KNOWL...JURID MGT TREND GEN/LAWS 20. PAGE 165 H3296 PLAN CONCPT

B63
BRITISH AID. UK AGRI DIST/IND INDUS SCHOOL TEC/DEV INT/TRADE COLONIAL DEMAND...TREND CHARTS 20. PAGE 2 H0041 FOR/AID ECO/UNDEV NAT/G FINAN

B63
CONZE W.,DIE DEUTSCHE NATION. GERMANY NAT/G POL/PAR WAR ORD/FREE...TREND 8/20 NAZI. PAGE 33 H0657 NAT/LISM FASCISM ATTIT SOCIETY

B63
DE VRIES E.,SOCIAL ASPECTS OF ECONOMIC DEVELOPMENT IN LATIN AMERICA. CULTURE SOCIETY STRATA FINAN INDUS INT/ORG DELIB/GP ACT/RES ECO/TAC EDU/PROP ADMIN ATTIT SUPEGO HEALTH KNOWL ORD/FREE...SOC STAT TREND ANTHOL TOT/POP VAL/FREE. PAGE 39 H0777 L/A+17C ECO/UNDEV

B63
ELIAS T.O.,GOVERNMENT AND POLITICS IN AFRICA. CONSTN CULTURE SOCIETY NAT/G POL/PAR DIPLOM AFR NAT/LISM

REPRESENT PERSON...SOC TREND BIBLIOG 4/20. PAGE 45 H0906 — COLONIAL LAW

B63
FRIED R.C.,THE ITALIAN PREFECTS. ITALY STRATA ECO/DEV NAT/LISM ALL/IDEOS...TREND CHARTS METH/COMP BIBLIOG 17/20 PREFECT. PAGE 53 H1061 — ADMIN NAT/G EFFICIENCY

B63
GLADE W.P. JR.,THE POLITICAL ECONOMY OF MEXICO. FUT L/A+17C CULTURE SOCIETY AGRI INDUS DELIB/GP ACT/RES ECO/TAC ATTIT HEALTH ORD/FREE...STAT TIME/SEQ TREND MEXIC/AMER TOT/POP VAL/FREE 20. PAGE 57 H1138 — FINAN ECO/UNDEV

B63
HALPERIN M.H.,THE POLITICS OF SOCIAL CHANGE IN THE MIDDLE EAST AND NORTH AFRICA. ISLAM CULTURE ACT/RES REV ATTIT PERCEPT KNOWL...METH/CNCPT OBS TIME/SEQ GEN/METH TOT/POP VAL/FREE 20. PAGE 64 H1291 — SOC TREND

B63
KHADDURI M.,MODERN LIBYA: A STUDY IN POLITICAL DEVELOPMENT. EUR+WWI ISLAM LIBYA ELITES INT/ORG POL/PAR FORCES DIPLOM FOR/AID DOMIN EDU/PROP LEGIT NAT/LISM DRIVE RIGID/FLEX SKILL...CONCPT TIME/SEQ TREND 20. PAGE 85 H1704 — NAT/G STRUCT

B63
KRAEHE E.,METTERNICH'S GERMAN POLICY: THE CONTEST WITH NAPOLEON, 1799-1814, VOL. 1. FRANCE MOD/EUR NAT/G CONSULT TOP/EX PLAN BAL/PWR DOMIN COERCE ATTIT DRIVE PERCEPT PERSON SKILL...CONCPT RECORD TIME/SEQ TREND 18/19. PAGE 88 H1764 — BIOG GERMANY DIPLOM

B63
SAKAI R.K.,STUDIES ON ASIA, 1963. ASIA INDIA ISRAEL S/ASIA USA+45 PERF/ART POL/PAR SECT REGION NAT/LISM ...SOC LING TREND ANTHOL 19/20 CHINJAP. PAGE 137 H2735 — PWR CULTURE

B63
TINDALE N.B.,ABORIGINAL AUSTRALIANS. KIN CREATE ROLE...SOC MYTH TREND 20 AUSTRAL ABORIGINES MIGRATION. PAGE 155 H3099 — CULTURE DRIVE ECO/UNDEV HABITAT

B63
ULAM A.B.,THE NEW FACE OF SOVIET TOTALITARIANISM. FUT INTELL NAT/G POL/PAR EX/STRUC TOP/EX DIPLOM ECO/TAC DOMIN EDU/PROP LEGIT COERCE ATTIT RIGID/FLEX...OBS HIST/WRIT TREND TOT/POP VAL/FREE COLD/WAR. PAGE 158 H3150 — COM PWR TOTALISM USSR

B63
VIARD R.,LA FIN DE L'EMPIRE COLONIAL FRANCAIS. AFR FUT S/ASIA ECO/UNDEV NAT/G CONSULT PLAN ECO/TAC EDU/PROP REGION NAT/LISM ALL/VALS...CONCPT TIME/SEQ TREND VAL/FREE 20. PAGE 162 H3248 — VOL/ASSN COLONIAL FRANCE

L63
FREUND G.,"ADENAUER AND THE FUTURE OF GERMANY." EUR+WWI FUT GERMANY/W FORCES LEGIT ADMIN ROUTINE ATTIT DRIVE PERSON PWR...POLICY TIME/SEQ TREND VAL/FREE 20 ADENAUER/K. PAGE 53 H1058 — NAT/G BIOG DIPLOM GERMANY

L63
MICHAEL F.,"KHRUSHCHEV'S DISLOYAL OPPOSITION: STRUCTURAL CHANGE AND POWER STRUGGLE IN COMMUNIST BLOC." ASIA CHINA/COM FUT NAT/G POL/PAR CONSULT PLAN DOMIN ATTIT...POLICY CONCPT TREND MARX/KARL 20 KHRUSH/N. PAGE 110 H2195 — COM STRUCT NAT/LISM USSR

L63
NASH M.,"PSYCHO-CULTURAL FACTORS IN ASIAN ECONOMIC GROWTH." ASIA ISLAM S/ASIA CULTURE ECO/UNDEV DELIB/GP EDU/PROP COERCE ATTIT PERSON HEALTH KNOWL ORD/FREE...PSY SOC STAT TREND ANTHOL VAL/FREE 20. PAGE 116 H2313 — SOCIETY ECO/TAC

S63
AYAL E.B.,"VALUE SYSTEM AND ECONOMIC DEVELOPMENT IN JAPAN AND THAILAND." ASIA S/ASIA THAILAND CULTURE ECO/DEV CAP/ISM DOMIN NAT/LISM DRIVE RIGID/FLEX SOCISM...WELF/ST OBS TREND CON/ANAL GEN/LAWS 20 CHINJAP. PAGE 9 H0185 — ECO/UNDEV ALL/VALS

S63
BECHHOEFER B.G.,"SOVIET ATTITUDE TOWARD DISARMAMENT." COM USSR NAT/G ACT/RES TEC/DEV NUC/PWR ATTIT DISPL RIGID/FLEX PWR...METH/CNCPT TREND GEN/LAWS COLD/WAR 20. PAGE 13 H0252 — FORCES EDU/PROP ARMS/CONT

S63
BILL J.A.,"THE SOCIAL AND ECONOMIC FOUNDATIONS OF POWER IN CONTEMPORARY IRAN." ISLAM CULTURE NAT/G ECO/TAC DOMIN COERCE ATTIT PWR WEALTH...TREND VAL/FREE 20. PAGE 17 H0334 — SOCIETY STRATA IRAN

S63
CRUTCHER J.,"PAN AFRICANISM: AFRICAN ODYSSEY." AFR NAT/G POL/PAR PROF/ORG VOL/ASSN TOP/EX CREATE REGION RACE/REL ALL/VALS...CONCPT TIME/SEQ TREND CON/ANAL 20. PAGE 36 H0716 — PROVS DELIB/GP COLONIAL

S63
GILLIN J.P.,"POSSIBLE CULTURAL MALADJUSTMENT IN MODERN LATIN AMERICA." ATTIT ORD/FREE...SOC TREND GEN/LAWS 20. PAGE 56 H1128 — L/A+17C CULTURE

S63
HOSKINS H.L.,"ARAB SOCIALISM IN THE UAR." ISLAM USSR AGRI INDUS NAT/G TOP/EX CREATE DIPLOM EDU/PROP DRIVE KNOWL PWR SOCISM...POLICY CONCPT TREND SUEZ 20. PAGE 74 H1478 — ECO/DEV PLAN UAR

S63
KOHN H.,"GERMANY IN WORLD POLITICS." EUR+WWI GERMANY GERMANY/W USSR NAT/G POL/PAR TOP/EX ATTIT ...CONCPT TREND GEN/LAWS 20 NATO ADENAUER/K. PAGE 87 H1746 — ACT/RES ORD/FREE BAL/PWR

S63
LOPEZIBOR J.,"L'EUROPE, FORME DE VIE." CHRIST-17C EUR+WWI FUT MOD/EUR SOCIETY INT/ORG SECT EDU/PROP ATTIT RIGID/FLEX ALL/VALS...POLICY HUM SOC TIME/SEQ TREND GEN/LAWS. PAGE 98 H1966 — NAT/G CULTURE

S63
MORISON D.,"AFRICAN STUDIES IN THE SOVIET UNION." AFR COM CULTURE INTELL REGION ATTIT KNOWL...HUM TREND 20. PAGE 113 H2258 — EDU/PROP USSR

S63
RINTELEN F.,"L'HOMME EUROPEEN." EUR+WWI FUT CULTURE INTELL SECT EDU/PROP ATTIT ALL/VALS...HUM SOC METH/CNCPT TREND GEN/LAWS 20 WORSHIP. PAGE 132 H2631 — SOCIETY PERSON

S63
ROUGEMONT D.,"LES NOUVELLES CHANCES DE L'EUROPE." EUR+WWI FUT ECO/DEV INT/ORG NAT/G ACT/RES PLAN TEC/DEV EDU/PROP ADMIN COLONIAL FEDERAL ATTIT PWR SKILL...TREND 20. PAGE 135 H2696 — ECO/UNDEV PERCEPT

S63
TANG P.S.H.,"SINO-SOVIET TENSIONS." ASIA CHINA/COM COM CUBA KOREA/N VIETNAM/N NAT/G VOL/ASSN DELIB/GP PEACE PERCEPT PWR...METH/CNCPT MYTH RECORD TREND GEN/LAWS 20. PAGE 152 H3041 — ACT/RES EDU/PROP REV

B64
BUNTING B.P.,THE RISE OF THE SOUTH AFRICAN REICH. SOUTH/AFR INT/ORG NAT/G FORCES DIPLOM CONTROL WAR TOTALISM ATTIT...GOV/COMP 19/20. PAGE 24 H0477 — RACE/REL DISCRIM NAT/LISM TREND

B64
COUNT E.W.,FACT AND THEORY IN SOCIAL SCIENCE. UNIV HABITAT...BIOG TREND CHARTS ANTHOL BIBLIOG. PAGE 34 H0679 — STRUCT SOC CULTURE ADJUST

B64
DANIELS R.V.,RUSSIA. RUSSIA USSR STRUCT NAT/LISM TOTALISM ORD/FREE WEALTH...POLICY DECISION TREND. PAGE 37 H0740 — MARXISM REV ECO/DEV DIPLOM

B64
DICKEY J.S.,THE UNITED STATES AND CANADA. CANADA USA+45...SOC 20. PAGE 41 H0822 — DIPLOM TREND GOV/COMP PROB/SOLV

B64
FALL B.,STREET WITHOUT JOY. FRANCE USA+45 DIPLOM ECO/TAC FOR/AID GUERRILLA REV WEAPON...TREND 20. PAGE 48 H0966 — WAR S/ASIA FORCES COERCE

B64
GREBLER L.,URBAN RENEWAL IN EUROPEAN COUNTRIES: ITS EMERGENCE AND POTENTIALS. EUR+WWI UK ECO/DEV LOC/G NEIGH CREATE ADMIN ATTIT...TREND NAT/COMP 20 URBAN/RNWL. PAGE 60 H1205 — MUNIC PLAN CONSTRUC NAT/G

B64
GRIFFITH W.,THE WELSH (2ND ED.). UK SOCIETY STRUCT SECT WRITING NAT/LISM...ART/METH MODAL OBS/ENVIR TREND SOC/INTEG WALES PURITAN MUSIC. PAGE 61 H1223 — CULTURE SOC LING

B64
GRIFFITH W.E.,THE SINO-SOVIET RIFT. ASIA CHINA/COM COM CUBA USSR YUGOSLAVIA NAT/G POL/PAR VOL/ASSN DELIB/GP FORCES TOP/EX DIPLOM EDU/PROP DRIVE PERSON PWR...TREND 20 TREATY. PAGE 61 H1224 — ATTIT TIME/SEQ BAL/PWR SOCISM

B64
JARVIE I.C.,THE REVOLUTION IN ANTHROPOLOGY. UNIV CULTURE SOCIETY SECT...MYTH 20 POPPER/K. PAGE 80 H1592 — SOC TREND PHIL/SCI METH

B64
KELLER J.W.,GERMANY, THE WALL AND BERLIN. EUR+WWI ECO/DEV NAT/G VOL/ASSN FORCES PLAN ECO/TAC EDU/PROP COERCE...POLICY CONCPT INT TREND COLD/WAR BER/BLOC 20 BERLIN. PAGE 84 H1685 — ATTIT ALL/VALS DIPLOM GERMANY

B64
LEWIN P.,THE FOREIGN TRADE OF COMMUNIST CHINA* ITS IMPACT ON THE FREE WORLD. AFR EUR+WWI L/A+17C S/ASIA ECO/UNDEV CREATE FOR/AID...STAT NET/THEORY TREND CHARTS. PAGE 96 H1910 — ASIA INT/TRADE NAT/COMP USSR

B64
LI C.M.,INDUSTRIAL DEVELOPMENT IN COMMUNIST CHINA. CHINA/COM ECO/DEV ECO/UNDEV AGRI FINAN INDUS MARKET LABOR NAT/G ECO/TAC INT/TRADE EXEC ALL/VALS ...POLICY RELATIV TREND WORK TOT/POP VAL/FREE 20. PAGE 96 H1921 — ASIA TEC/DEV

B64
MEAD M.,CONTINUITIES IN CULTURAL EVOLUTION. FACE/GP KIN ACT/RES EDU/PROP GP/REL INGP/REL DRIVE HEREDITY ROLE...TIME/SEQ TREND METH SOC/INTEG 20. PAGE 108 H2153 — CULTURE SOC PERS/REL

B64
MELADY T.,FACES OF AFRICA. AFR FUT ISLAM NAT/G — ECO/UNDEV

POL/PAR SCHOOL DELIB/GP PLAN ECO/TAC EDU/PROP ATTIT ALL/VALS...CHARTS TOT/POP VAL/FREE 20. PAGE 108 H2168
TREND NAT/LISM

B64
MOUMOUNI A.,L'EDUCATION EN AFRIQUE. UNIV CULTURE ELITES INTELL EDU/PROP ADMIN COLONIAL...LING TREND BIBLIOG 20. PAGE 114 H2271
SCHOOL AFR PROB/SOLV

B64
ON CULTURE AND SOCIAL CHANGE. FAM NAT/G ACT/RES ECO/TAC RACE/REL...PSY TIME/SEQ TREND IDEA/COMP METH/COMP ANTHOL BIBLIOG 20. PAGE 120 H2406
CULTURE TEC/DEV STRUCT CREATE

B64
PHILLIPS C.S.,THE DEVELOPMENT OF NIGERIAN FOREIGN POLICY. AFR CONSTN CULTURE STRATA NAT/G LEGIS DOMIN LEGIT EXEC...RELATIV SOC TIME/SEQ TREND TOT/POP 20. PAGE 125 H2502
CHOOSE POLICY DIPLOM NIGERIA

B64
PIKE F.B.,THE CONFLICT BETWEEN CHURCH AND STATE IN LATIN AMERICA. L/A+17C CULTURE SOCIETY STRATA DOMIN EDU/PROP LEGIT COERCE ATTIT ORD/FREE PWR WEALTH ...CONCPT TIME/SEQ TREND VAL/FREE. PAGE 125 H2510
SECT NAT/G

B64
RIES J.C.,THE MANAGEMENT OF DEFENSE: ORGANIZATION AND CONTROL OF THE US ARMED SERVICES. PROF/ORG DELIB/GP EX/STRUC LEGIS GOV/REL PERS/REL CENTRAL RATIONAL PWR...POLICY TREND GOV/COMP BIBLIOG. PAGE 131 H2626
FORCES ACT/RES DECISION CONTROL

B64
SOLOW R.M.,THE NATURE AND SOURCES OF UNEMPLOYMENT IN THE UNITED STATES (PAMPHLET). USA+45 INDUS LABOR TEC/DEV ECO/TAC SKILL WEALTH...TREND NAT/COMP 20. PAGE 147 H2930
ECO/DEV WORKER STAT PRODUC

B64
URQUIDI V.L.,THE CHALLENGE OF DEVELOPMENT IN LATIN AMERICA. L/A+17C FINAN INT/ORG TEC/DEV DIPLOM INT/TRADE PRICE REGION PRODUC...CHARTS 20. PAGE 159 H3175
ECO/UNDEV ECO/TAC NAT/G TREND

B64
WAINHOUSE D.W.,REMNANTS OF EMPIRE: THE UNITED NATIONS AND THE END OF COLONIALISM. FUT PORTUGAL WOR+45 NAT/G CONSULT DOMIN LEGIT ADMIN ROUTINE ATTIT ORD/FREE...POLICY JURID RECORD INT TIME/SEQ UN CMN/WLTH 20. PAGE 164 H3287
INT/ORG TREND COLONIAL

L64
FINDLATER R.,"US." EUR+WWI GERMANY USSR SOCIETY FACE/GP EDU/PROP PERCEPT PERSON ALL/VALS...PSY SOC CONCPT SELF/OBS SAMP TREND 20. PAGE 50 H1001
CULTURE ATTIT UK

L64
HAAS E.B.,"ECONOMICS AND DIFFERENTIAL PATTERNS OF POLITICAL INTEGRATION: PROJECTIONS ABOUT UNITY IN LATIN AMERICA." SOCIETY NAT/G DELIB/GP ACT/RES CREATE PLAN ECO/TAC REGION ROUTINE ATTIT DRIVE PWR WEALTH...CONCPT TREND CHARTS LAFTA 20. PAGE 63 H1266
L/A+17C INT/ORG MARKET

L64
ROTBERG R.,"THE FEDERATION MOVEMENT IN BRITISH EAST AND CENTRAL AFRICA." AFR RHODESIA UGANDA ECO/UNDEV NAT/G POL/PAR FORCES DOMIN LEGIT ADMIN COERCE ATTIT ...CONCPT TREND 20 TANGANYIKA. PAGE 135 H2691
VOL/ASSN PWR REGION

S64
ADAMS R.,"POLITICS AND SOCIAL ANTHROPOLOGY IN SPANISH AMERICA." FUT CULTURE SOCIETY NAT/G PROF/ORG EDU/PROP ATTIT RIGID/FLEX ALL/VALS ...POLICY GEOG METH/CNCPT MYTH TREND VAL/FREE 20. PAGE 3 H0065
L/A+17C SOC

S64
GARMARNIKOW M.,"INFLUENCE-BUYING IN WEST AFRICA." COM FUT USSR INTELL NAT/G PLAN TEC/DEV ECO/TAC DOMIN EDU/PROP REGION NAT/LISM ATTIT DRIVE ALL/VALS SOVEREIGN...POLICY PSY SOC CONCPT TREND STERTYP WORK COLD/WAR 20. PAGE 55 H1102
AFR ECO/UNDEV FOR/AID SOCISM

S64
GROSS J.A.,"WHITEHALL AND THE COMMONWEALTH." EUR+WWI MOD/EUR INT/ORG NAT/G CONSULT DELIB/GP LEGIS DOMIN ADMIN COLONIAL ROUTINE PWR CMN/WLTH 19/20. PAGE 62 H1233
EX/STRUC ATTIT TREND

S64
HIRAI N.,"SHINTO AND INTERNATIONAL PROBLEMS." SOCIETY NAT/G PLAN EDU/PROP RACE/REL PEACE ATTIT PERCEPT LOVE MORAL...HUM MYTH RECORD SAMP TREND STERTYP TOT/POP 20 UN CHINJAP SHINTO. PAGE 71 H1423
ASIA SECT

S64
KOVNER M.,"THE SINO-SOVIET DISPUTE: COMMUNISM AT THE CROSSROADS." ASIA CHINA/COM COM USSR ECO/UNDEV NAT/G TOP/EX CREATE BAL/PWR DOMIN EDU/PROP PWR ...CONCPT COMECON 20. PAGE 88 H1760
ATTIT TREND

S64
LANGER P.F.,"JAPAN'S RELATIONS WITH CHINA." ASIA CHINA/COM KOREA S/ASIA ECO/DEV NAT/G POL/PAR EDU/PROP ATTIT ALL/VALS...METH/CNCPT TIME/SEQ TREND 20 CHINJAP. PAGE 91 H1808
RIGID/FLEX ECO/TAC

S64
LEVI W.,"INDIAN NEUTRALISM RECONSIDERED." ASIA CHINA/COM S/ASIA SOCIETY NAT/G ACT/RES LEGIT NEUTRAL COERCE ATTIT DRIVE PERCEPT RIGID/FLEX HEALTH LOVE PWR...DECISION RECORD TREND STERTYP 20. PAGE 95 H1896
ORD/FREE CONCPT INDIA

S64
MC WILLIAM M.,"THE WORLD BANK AND THE TRANSFER OF POWER IN KENYA." AFR ECO/UNDEV CONSULT ACT/RES TEC/DEV PERCEPT PWR SKILL WEALTH...CONCPT OBS TREND 20. PAGE 106 H2119
NAT/G ECO/TAC

S64
SAAB H.,"THE ARAB SEARCH FOR A FEDERAL UNION." SOCIETY INT/ORG NAT/G DELIB/GP FORCES ACT/RES TEC/DEV ECO/TAC DOMIN LEGIT REGION ROUTINE ATTIT DRIVE RIGID/FLEX ALL/VALS...SOC CONCPT NEW/IDEA TIME/SEQ TREND. PAGE 136 H2726
ISLAM PLAN

S64
SCHEFFLER H.W.,"THE GENESIS AND REPRESSION OF CONFLICT: CHOISEUL ISLAND." S/ASIA LOC/G NAT/G FORCES LEGIS DIPLOM DOMIN LEGIT EXEC CHOOSE ATTIT RESPECT SKILL...POLICY JURID OBS TREND GEN/METH 20. PAGE 139 H2781
PWR COERCE WAR

S64
SMYTHE H.H.,"NEHRU AND INDIAN FOREIGN POLICY." S/ASIA ECO/UNDEV NAT/G POL/PAR CONSULT PLAN DIPLOM NEUTRAL COERCE ATTIT DRIVE PERSON MORAL ORD/FREE RESPECT...GEOG CONCPT TIME/SEQ TREND GEN/LAWS 20 NEHRU/J. PAGE 146 H2922
TOP/EX BIOG INDIA

S64
SWEARER H.R.,"AFTER KHRUSHCHEV: WHAT NEXT." COM FUT USSR CONSTN ELITES NAT/G POL/PAR CHIEF DELIB/GP LEGIS DOMIN LEAD...RECORD TREND STERTYP GEN/METH 20. PAGE 151 H3016
EX/STRUC PWR

S64
TOUVAL S.,"THE SOMALI REPUBLIC." AFR ISLAM SOMALIA FAM KIN NAT/G CREATE FOR/AID LEGIT ATTIT ALL/VALS ...RECORD TREND 20. PAGE 156 H3119
ECO/UNDEV RIGID/FLEX

S64
VANDENBOSCH A.,"POWER BALANCE IN INDONESIA." S/ASIA USSR NAT/G TOP/EX BAL/PWR DOMIN NEUTRAL ORD/FREE PWR...POLICY TIME/SEQ GEN/LAWS 20 SUKARNO/A. PAGE 162 H3233
FORCES TREND DIPLOM INDONESIA

B65
ADAM T.R.,GOVERNMENT AND POLITICS IN AFRICA SOUTH OF THE SAHARA. AFR EUR+WWI CONSTN CULTURE INTELL POL/PAR TOP/EX LEGIT REGION DRIVE...OBS TREND CMN/WLTH 20. PAGE 3 H0062
NAT/G TIME/SEQ RACE/REL COLONIAL

B65
CRABB C.V. JR.,THE ELEPHANTS AND THE GRASS* A STUDY OF NONALIGNMENT. AFR ASIA INDIA S/ASIA USA+45 USSR BAL/PWR NEUTRAL ATTIT...TREND NAT/COMP COLD/WAR. PAGE 34 H0691
ECO/UNDEV DIPLOM CONCPT

B65
EASTON D.,A SYSTEM ANALYSIS OF POLITICAL LIFE. UNIV STRUCT NAT/G FEEDBACK PARTIC PERS/REL EFFICIENCY ...TREND CHARTS METH/COMP 20. PAGE 44 H0881
SIMUL POLICY GEN/METH

B65
GREGG J.L.,POLITICAL PARTIES AND PARTY SYSTEMS IN GUATEMALA, 1944-1963. GUATEMALA L/A+17C EX/STRUC FORCES CREATE CONTROL REV CHOOSE PWR...TREND IDEA/COMP 20. PAGE 60 H1209
LEAD POL/PAR NAT/G CHIEF

B65
HALEVY E.,THE ERA OF TYRANNIES (TRANS. BY R. K. WEBB). FRANCE MOD/EUR UK ECO/DEV LABOR NAT/G BAL/PWR FEDERAL ALL/VALS...OLD/LIB TREND 18/20 SAINTSIMON. PAGE 64 H1285
SOCISM CONCPT UTOPIA ORD/FREE

B65
HAPGOOD D.,AFRICA: FROM INDEPENDENCE TO TOMARROW. AFR GUINEA SENEGAL CULTURE ELITES ECO/UNDEV AGRI SCHOOL FOR/AID COLONIAL MARXISM...TREND 20. PAGE 66 H1323
ECO/TAC SOCIETY NAT/G

B65
HAVIGHURST R.J.,SOCIETY AND EDUCATION IN BRAZIL. BRAZIL PORTUGAL ECO/UNDEV INDUS NAT/G CREATE INSPECT COLONIAL ADJUST DEMAND LITERACY...CENSUS TREND CHARTS 16/20. PAGE 68 H1362
SCHOOL ACADEM ACT/RES CULTURE

B65
HLA MYINT U.,THE ECONOMICS OF THE DEVELOPING COUNTRIES. USA+45 WOR+45 AGRI FINAN NAT/G INT/TRADE ...CLASSIF CENSUS TREND NAT/COMP SIMUL GEN/LAWS. PAGE 71 H1430
ECO/UNDEV FOR/AID GEOG

B65
JANSEN M.B.,CHANGING JAPANESE ATTITUDES TOWARD MODERNIZATION. ASIA CHINA/COM S/ASIA INTELL SOCIETY KIN NAT/G SECT PERCEPT RIGID/FLEX...SOC CONCPT TIME/SEQ TREND TOT/POP 19/20 CHINJAP. PAGE 80 H1591
TEC/DEV ATTIT INDIA

B65
MCSHERRY J.E.,RUSSIA AND THE UNITED STATES UNDER EISENHOWER, KHRUSHCHEV, AND KENNEDY. USSR EX/STRUC TOP/EX PRESS WAR...POLICY TREND 20. PAGE 108 H2150
DIPLOM CHIEF NAT/G PEACE

B65
MOORE W.E.,THE IMPACT OF INDUSTRY. CULTURE STRUCT ORD/FREE...TREND 20. PAGE 113 H2251
INDUS MGT TEC/DEV ECO/UNDEV

B65
RIVLIN B.,THE CONTEMPORARY MIDDLE EAST* TRADITION AND INNOVATION. CULTURE SOCIETY ECO/UNDEV NAT/G
ANTHOL ISLAM

TREND. PAGE 132 H2636 NAT/LISM DIPLOM

B65
VERMOT-GAUCHY M.,L'EDUCATION NATIONALE DANS LA FRANCE DE 1975. FRANCE FUT CULTURE ELITES R+D SCHOOL PLAN EDU/PROP EFFICIENCY...POLICY PREDICT CHARTS INDEX 20. PAGE 162 H3245 ACADEM CREATE TREND INTELL

B65
WUORINEN J.H.,SCANDINAVIA. DENMARK FINLAND ICELAND NORWAY SWEDEN SOCIETY AGRI INDUS DELIB/GP DIPLOM INT/TRADE NEUTRAL...GEOG CHARTS BIBLIOG TREATY. PAGE 171 H3428 NAT/G POL/PAR TREND POLICY

S65
GRIFFITH S.B.,"COMMUNIST CHINA'S CAPACITY TO MAKE WAR." CHINA/COM COM NAT/G TOP/EX PLAN DOMIN COERCE NUC/PWR ATTIT RESPECT SKILL...CONCPT MYTH TIME/SEQ TREND COLD/WAR 20. PAGE 61 H1221 FORCES PWR WEAPON ASIA

S65
RUBINSTEIN A.Z.,"YUGOSLAVIA'S OPENING SOCIETY." COM USSR INTELL NAT/G LEGIS TOP/EX LEGIT CT/SYS RIGID/FLEX ALL/VALS SOCISM...HUM TIME/SEQ TREND 20. PAGE 135 H2708 CONSTN EX/STRUC YUGOSLAVIA

S65
SPAAK P.H.,"THE SEARCH FOR CONSENSUS: A NEW EFFORT TO BUILD EUROPE." FRANCE GERMANY ECO/DEV NAT/G CONSULT FORCES PLAN EDU/PROP REGION CONSEN ATTIT ...SOC METH/CNCPT OBS TREND EEC NATO WORK 20. PAGE 147 H2941 EUR+WWI INT/ORG

S65
STAROBIN J.R.,"COMMUNISM IN WESTERN EUROPE." FRANCE GERMANY ITALY USA+45 USSR ECO/DEV FEDERAL PEACE ATTIT DRIVE PWR TREND. PAGE 149 H2972 MARXISM EUR+WWI POL/PAR NAT/COMP

S65
TABORSKY E.,"CHANGE IN CZECHOSLOVAKIA." COM USSR ELITES INTELL AGRI INDUS NAT/G DELIB/GP EX/STRUC ECO/TAC TOTALISM ATTIT RIGID/FLEX SOCISM...MGT CONCPT TREND 20. PAGE 152 H3031 ECO/DEV PLAN CZECHOSLVK

S65
VUCINICH W.S.,"WHITHER RUMANIA." COM USSR YUGOSLAVIA NAT/G VOL/ASSN DELIB/GP TOP/EX LEGIT NAT/LISM TOTALISM ATTIT DRIVE RIGID/FLEX ORD/FREE WEALTH SOCISM...TIME/SEQ TREND 20. PAGE 164 H3281 ECO/DEV CREATE ROMANIA

B66
BLACK C.E.,THE DYNAMICS OF MODERNIZATION: A STUDY IN COMPARATIVE HISTORY. STRUCT ECO/DEV ECO/UNDEV NAT/G DIPLOM LEAD REV...PREDICT TIME/SEQ TREND SOC/INTEG 17/20. PAGE 17 H0350 SOCIETY SOC NAT/COMP

B66
CADY J.F.,THAILAND, BURMA, LAOS AND CAMBODIA. FRANCE UK CULTURE NAT/G DOMIN GP/REL RACE/REL HABITAT...GEOG TREND CHINJAP BUDDHISM. PAGE 25 H0504 S/ASIA COLONIAL REGION SECT

B66
DAHL R.A.,POLITICAL OPPOSITIONS IN WESTERN DEMOCRACIES. EUR+WWI USA+45 USA-45 SOCIETY STRATA ECO/DEV NAT/G LEGIS REPRESENT...TREND NAT/COMP ANTHOL 20. PAGE 37 H0732 POL/PAR CHOOSE PARTIC PLURISM

B66
DE TOCQUEVILLE A.DEMOCRACY IN AMERICA (1834-1840) (2 VOLS. IN I; TRANS. BY G. LAWRENCE). FRANCE CULTURE STRATA POL/PAR CT/SYS REPRESENT FEDERAL ORD/FREE SOVEREIGN...MAJORIT TREND GEN/LAWS 18/19. PAGE 39 H0773 POPULISM USA-45 CONSTN NAT/COMP

B66
FRIEDRICH C.J.,REVOLUTION: NOMOS VIII. NAT/G SOCISM ...OBS TREND IDEA/COMP ANTHOL 18/20. PAGE 54 H1070 REV MARXISM CONCPT DIPLOM

B66
MASON E.S.,ECONOMIC DEVELOPMENT IN INDIA AND PAKISTAN. INDIA PAKISTAN AGRI FINAN PLAN BUDGET INT/TRADE WEALTH...POLICY STAT TREND CHARTS 20. PAGE 104 H2086 NAT/COMP ECO/UNDEV ECO/TAC FOR/AID

B66
MATTHEWS R.,AFRICAN POWDER KEG: REVOLT AND DISSENT IN SIX EMERGENT NATIONS. AFR ALGERIA DAHOMEY GABON GHANA MALAWI GAMBLE LEAD PARTIC REV DRIVE...BIOG TREND GOV/COMP 20. PAGE 105 H2098 ELITES ECO/UNDEV TOP/EX CONTROL

B66
MERRITT R.L.,COMPARING NATIONS* THE USE OF QUANTITATIVE DATA IN CROSSNATIONAL RESEARCH. ACADEM DIPLOM GP/REL...PHIL/SCI STAT TREND GP/COMP PERS/COMP GEN/METH ANTHOL BIBLIOG INDEX. PAGE 109 H2184 NAT/COMP MATH COMPUT/IR QUANT

B66
ODEGARD P.H.,POLITICAL POWER AND SOCIAL CHANGE. UNIV NAT/G CREATE ALL/IDEOS...POLICY GEOG SOC CENSUS TREND. PAGE 120 H2394 PWR TEC/DEV IDEA/COMP

B66
RICHERT F.,DIE NATIONALE WELLE. GERMANY GERMANY/W PARL/PROC ORD/FREE FASCISM...TREND 19/20. PAGE 131 H2622 POL/PAR ATTIT NAT/LISM NAT/G

B66
SETTON K.M.,GREAT PROBLEMS IN EUROPEAN CIVILIZATION. CHRIST-17C EUR+WWI MOD/EUR SECT GP/REL ALL/VALS ORD/FREE ALL/IDEOS...TREND ANTHOL T CHRISTIAN RENAISSAN PROTESTANT. PAGE 142 H2835 CULTURE CONCPT IDEA/COMP

B66
SOROKIN P.A.,SOCIOLOGICAL THEORIES OF TODAY. SOCIETY STRUCT FAM SECT GP/REL ADJUST...PHIL/SCI PSY TREND METH/COMP 20. PAGE 147 H2935 SOC CULTURE METH/CNCPT EPIST

B66
SWEARINGEN A.R.,SOVIET AND CHINESE COMMUNIST POWER IN THE WORLD TODAY. COM USA+45 ECO/UNDEV CREATE LEAD WAR ADJUST...TREND NAT/COMP ANTHOL COLD/WAR KHRUSH/N. PAGE 151 H3017 USSR ASIA DIPLOM ATTIT

B66
THIESENHUSEN W.C.,CHILE'S EXPERIMENTS IN AGRARIAN REFORM. CHILE STRUCT NAT/G ACT/RES ECO/TAC GOV/REL COST SOCISM...TREND CHARTS SOC/EXP 20. PAGE 154 H3073 AGRI ECO/UNDEV SOC TEC/DEV

B66
UN ECONOMIC AND SOCIAL COUNCIL,WORLD POPULATION PROSPECTS AS ASSESSED IN 1963. FUT WOR+45 DEATH AGE ...TREND CHARTS UN. PAGE 158 H3157 PREDICT CENSUS GEOG NAT/COMP

B66
US DEPARTMENT OF THE ARMY,SOUTH ASIA: A STRATEGIC SURVEY (PAMPHLET NO. 550-3). AFGHANISTN INDIA NEPAL PAKISTAN ECO/UNDEV INT/ORG POL/PAR FORCES FOR/AID INT/TRADE LEAD WAR...POLICY SOC TREND 20. PAGE 160 H3195 BIBLIOG/A S/ASIA DIPLOM NAT/G

B66
WHITAKER A.P.,NATIONALISM IN CONTEMPORARY LATIN AMERICA. AGRI NAT/G WEALTH...POLICY SOC CONCPT OBS TREND 20. PAGE 167 H3344 NAT/LISM L/A+17C DIPLOM ECO/UNDEV

B66
WINKS R.W.,THE HISTORIOGRAPHY OF THE BRITISH EMPIRE-COMMONWEALTH. CANADA INDIA PAKISTAN UK CULTURE SOCIETY STRUCT POL/PAR...CONCPT NAT/COMP 20 AUSTRAL. PAGE 169 H3386 HIST/WRIT TREND IDEA/COMP METH/COMP

S66
O'BRIEN W.V.,"EVENTS AND TRENDS: PATTERNS OF AFRICAN INTERNATIONAL POLITICAL BEHAVIOR." CULTURE SOCIETY NAT/G NAT/LISM SOCISM. PAGE 119 H2386 BIBLIOG/A AFR TREND DIPLOM

B67
ANDERSON T.,RUSSIAN POLITICAL THOUGHT; AN INTRODUCTION. USSR NAT/G POL/PAR CHIEF MARXISM ...TIME/SEQ BIBLIOG 9/20. PAGE 7 H0135 TREND CONSTN ATTIT

B67
BRZEZINSKI Z.K.,THE SOVIET BLOC: UNITY AND CONFLICT (2ND ED., REV., ENLARGED). COM POLAND USSR INTELL CHIEF EX/STRUC CONTROL EXEC GOV/REL PWR MARXISM ...TREND IDEA/COMP 20 LENIN/VI MARX/KARL STALIN/J. PAGE 23 H0463 NAT/G DIPLOM

B67
BURNHAM J.,THE WAR WE ARE IN, THE LAST DECADE AND THE NEXT. ASIA COM EUR+WWI S/ASIA WOR+45 ECO/UNDEV INT/ORG FORCES WAR...OLD/LIB TREND 20 COLD/WAR. PAGE 25 H0492 POLICY NAT/G DIPLOM NAT/COMP

B67
CHANDRASEKHAR S.,ASIA'S POPULATION PROBLEMS. ASIA ECO/UNDEV PLAN AGE/C...OBS CHARTS BIBLIOG 18/20 AUSTRAL. PAGE 29 H0575 PROB/SOLV NAT/COMP GEOG TREND

B67
CHILCOTE R.H.,PORTUGUESE AFRICA. PORTUGAL CULTURE SOCIETY ECO/UNDEV DOMIN NAT/LISM...TREND IDEA/COMP NAT/COMP BIBLIOG 15/20. PAGE 29 H0589 AFR COLONIAL ORD/FREE PROB/SOLV

B67
COLLINS R.O.,EGYPT AND THE SUDAN. COM FRANCE ISLAM SUDAN UAR UK SOCIETY NAT/G COLONIAL NAT/LISM...GEOG SOC LING TREND SOC/INTEG 7/20 SUEZ. PAGE 32 H0635 AGRI CULTURE ECO/UNDEV

B67
GALBRAITH J.K.,THE NEW INDUSTRIAL STATE. INDUS LABOR LG/CO NAT/G POL/PAR SCHOOL OP/RES CAP/ISM EXEC TREND. PAGE 54 H1087 TEC/DEV ECO/DEV SOCIETY MARKET

B67
KOLKOWICZ R.,THE SOVIET MILITARY AND THE COMMUNIST PARTY. COM USSR ELITES NAT/G CREATE CIVMIL/REL GP/REL...TREND BIBLIOG/A 20 COM/PARTY. PAGE 88 H1753 MARXISM CONSTN FORCES POL/PAR

B67
MCCLINTOCK R.,THE MEANING OF LIMITED WAR. FUT WOR+45 NAT/G FORCES GUERRILLA REV...POLICY SAMP/SIZ TREND NAT/COMP 45 COLD/WAR. PAGE 106 H2126 WAR NUC/PWR BAL/PWR DIPLOM

B67
NYERERE J.K.,FREEDOM AND UNITY/UHURU NA UMOJA: A SELECTION FROM WRITINGS AND SPEECHES, 1952-65. TANZANIA ELITES ECO/UNDEV INT/ORG NAT/G CREATE DIPLOM COLONIAL REGION RACE/REL...ANTHOL 20. PAGE 119 H2383 SOVEREIGN AFR TREND ORD/FREE

B67
PATAI R.,GOLDEN RIVER TO GOLDEN ROAD: SOCIETY, CULTURE

CULTURE, AND CHANGE IN THE MIDDLE EAST (2ND ED.). ELITES FAM KIN TEC/DEV MARRIAGE NAT/LISM SEX ORD/FREE...TREND GP/COMP WORSHIP 20. PAGE 124 H2476
SOCIETY ISLAM STRUCT

B67
PLANCK C.R.,THE CHANGING STATUS OF GERMAN REUNIFICATION IN WESTERN DIPLOMACY, 1955-1966. GERMANY DELIB/GP PLAN PEACE...TREND 20 KENNEDY/JF DEGAULLE/C. PAGE 126 H2519
NAT/G DIPLOM CENTRAL

B67
PLANK J.,CUBA AND THE UNITED STATES: LONG RANGE PERSPECTIVES. CUBA L/A+17C USSR ECO/UNDEV NAT/G FORCES ECO/TAC INT/TRADE AGREE REV...PREDICT TREND ANTHOL 20 CASTRO/F COLD/WAR OAS. PAGE 126 H2520
DIPLOM

B67
POMEROY W.J.,HALF A CENTURY OF SOCIALISM. USSR LAW AGRI INDUS NAT/G CREATE DIPLOM EDU/PROP PERSON ORD/FREE WEALTH...POLICY TREND 20. PAGE 127 H2541
SOCISM MARXISM COM SOCIETY

B67
POSNER M.V.,ITALIAN PUBLIC ENTERPRISE. ITALY ECO/DEV FINAN INDUS CREATE ECO/TAC ADMIN CONTROL EFFICIENCY PRODUC...TREND CHARTS 20. PAGE 127 H2545
NAT/G PLAN CAP/ISM SOCISM

B67
PYE L.W.,SOUTHEAST ASIA'S POLITICAL SYSTEMS. ASIA S/ASIA STRUCT ECO/UNDEV EX/STRUC CAP/ISM DIPLOM ALL/IDEOS...TREND CHARTS. PAGE 128 H2568
NAT/G POL/PAR GOV/COMP

B67
REES D.,THE AGE OF CONTAINMENT. WOR+45 FORCES ARMS/CONT ATTIT PWR...CONCPT TREND METH/COMP BIBLIOG/A 20. PAGE 130 H2608
DIPLOM NUC/PWR MARXISM GOV/COMP

B67
SPIRO H.S.,PATTERNS OF AFRICAN DEVLOPMENT: FIVE COMPARISONS. STRUCT ECO/UNDEV NAT/G CONSERVE SOCISM ...PREDICT NAT/COMP 20 CHINJAP. PAGE 148 H2951
AFR CONSTN NAT/LISM TREND

B67
TOMPKINS S.R.,THE TRIUMPH OF BOLSHEVISM: REVOLUTION OR REACTION? USSR WORKER PRESS WEALTH MARXISM POPULISM...BIOG TREND IDEA/COMP BIBLIOG 19/20 LENIN/VI. PAGE 156 H3113
REV NAT/G POL/PAR NAT/LISM

B67
WILLS A.J.,AN INTRODUCTION TO THE HISTORY OF CENTRAL AFRICA. RHODESIA ZAMBIA CULTURE SOCIETY ECO/UNDEV TEC/DEV DOMIN WAR ALL/VALS...POLICY TREND BIBLIOG T 14/20 NYASALAND. PAGE 169 H3375
AFR COLONIAL ORD/FREE

B67
WISEMAN H.V.,BRITAIN AND THE COMMONWEALTH. EUR+WWI FUT UK ECO/DEV POL/PAR TEC/DEV INT/TRADE LEAD ROLE SOVEREIGN...SOC TREND 20 CMN/WLTH. PAGE 169 H3391
INT/ORG DIPLOM NAT/G NAT/COMP

S67
ALPANDER G.G.,"ENTREPRENEURS AND PRIVATE ENTERPRISE IN TURKEY." TURKEY INDUS PROC/MFG EDU/PROP ATTIT DRIVE WEALTH...GEOG MGT SOC STAT TREND CHARTS 20. PAGE 6 H0114
ECO/UNDEV LG/CO NAT/G POLICY

S67
BURGHART A.,"CATHOLIC SOCIAL THOUGHT IN AUSTRIA." AUSTRIA EUR+WWI NAT/G PAY PERS/REL OWN MARXISM SOCISM...SOC 20. PAGE 24 H0482
CATHISM ATTIT TREND SOCIETY

S67
BUTTINGER J.,"VIETNAM* FRAUD OF THE 'OTHER WAR'." VIETNAM/S ELITES STRUCT AGRI NAT/G FOR/AID RENT TREND. PAGE 25 H0499
PLAN WEALTH REV ECO/UNDEV

S67
COHEN R.,"ANTHROPOLOGY AND POLITICAL SCIENCE: COURTSHIP OR MARRIAGE?" CULTURE STRATA STRUCT MUNIC REGION UTOPIA...NEW/IDEA TREND IDEA/COMP METH/COMP 20. PAGE 31 H0618
SOC INGP/REL AFR

S67
DENISON E.F.,"SOURCES OF GROWTH IN NINE WESTERN COUNTRIES." WORKER TEC/DEV COST PRODUC...TREND NAT/COMP. PAGE 39 H0790
INCOME NAT/G EUR+WWI ECO/DEV

S67
EGBERT D.D.,"POLITICS AND ART IN COMMUNIST BULGARIA" BULGARIA COM USSR CULTURE DIPLOM INGP/REL TOTALISM...TREND 20. PAGE 45 H0894
CREATE ART/METH CONTROL MARXISM

S67
GAMARNIKOW M.,"THE NEW ROLE OF PRIVATE ENTERPRISE." ECO/DEV INDUS NAT/G SML/CO CREATE PROB/SOLV MARXISM ...POLICY TREND IDEA/COMP 20. PAGE 55 H1092
ECO/TAC ATTIT CAP/ISM COM

S67
HEBAL J.J.,"APPROACHES TO REGIONAL AND METROPOLITAN GOVERNMENTS IN THE UNITED STATES AND CANADA." CANADA FUT USA+45 MUNIC...TREND 20. PAGE 69 H1380
ADMIN REGION LOC/G NAT/COMP

S67
IDENBURG P.J.,"POLITICAL STRUCTURAL DEVELOPMENT IN TROPICAL AFRICA." UK ECO/UNDEV KIN POL/PAR CHIEF EX/STRUC CREATE COLONIAL CONTROL REPRESENT RACE/REL ...MAJORIT TREND 20. PAGE 76 H1521
AFR CONSTN NAT/G GOV/COMP

S67
KINGSBURY E.C.,"LAW AS COMPACT: ANCIENT ISRAEL'S CONTRIBUTION TO THE UNDERSTANDING OF LAW." ISRAEL MEDIT-7 CULTURE KIN KNOWL...JURID CONCPT TREND IDEA/COMP METH/COMP WORSHIP JEWS DEITY. PAGE 86 H1716
LAW AGREE CONSTN INGP/REL

S67
MITCHELL W.C.,"THE SHAPE OF POLITICAL THEORY TO COME: FROM POLITICAL SOCIOLOGY TO POLITICAL ECONOMY." ACADEM NAT/G BUDGET TAX LEGIT LOBBY GOV/REL INGP/REL...SOC NEW/IDEA TREND CHARTS 20 MONEY. PAGE 112 H2231
ECO/TAC GEN/LAWS

S67
SANCHEZ J.D.,"DESARROLLO ECONOMICO Y FUTURO DE COLOMBIA." L/A+17C AGRI EXTR/IND FINAN INDUS MARKET INT/TRADE CONTROL...STAT TREND COLOMB. PAGE 137 H2748
ECO/UNDEV FUT NAT/G ECO/TAC

S67
SEIDLER G.L.,"MARXIST LEGAL THOUGHT IN POLAND." POLAND SOCIETY R+D LOC/G NAT/G ACT/RES ADJUD CT/SYS SUPEGO PWR...SOC TREND 20 MARX/KARL. PAGE 141 H2822
MARXISM LAW CONCPT EFFICIENCY

S67
SULLIVAN J.H.,"THE PRESS AND POLITICS IN INDONESIA." INDONESIA NAT/G WRITING REV...TREND GOV/COMP 20. PAGE 150 H3007
CIVMIL/REL KNOWL TOTALISM

S67
TATU M.,"URSS: LES FLOTTEMENTS DE LA DIRECTION COLLEGIALE." UAR USSR CHIEF LEAD INGP/REL EFFICIENCY...DECISION TREND 20 MID/EAST. PAGE 152 H3047
POLICY NAT/G EX/STRUC DIPLOM

S68
DEUTSCHER I.,"GERMANY AND MARXISM." FUT GERMANY/W NAT/G...MARXIST TREND 20. PAGE 40 H0808
SOCISM ORD/FREE POPULISM POL/PAR

S68
LAWRIE G.,"WHAT WILL CHANGE SOUTH AFRICA?" AFR SOUTH/AFR ELITES DOMIN CONTROL REPRESENT...TIME/SEQ TREND 20. PAGE 93 H1848
RACE/REL DIPLOM NAT/G POLICY

S68
MILLAR T.B.,"THE COMMONWEALTH AND THE UN." UK DIPLOM TARIFFS AGREE COLONIAL CONTROL SOVEREIGN WEALTH...GP/COMP GOV/COMP 20 CMN/WLTH UN. PAGE 111 H2210
INT/ORG POLICY TREND ECO/TAC

B89
FERNEUIL T.,LES PRINCIPES DE 1789 ET LA SCIENCE SOCIALE. FRANCE NAT/G REV ATTIT...CONCPT TREND IDEA/COMP 18/19. PAGE 49 H0986
CONSTN POLICY LAW

B90
TAINE H.A.,MODERN REGIME (2 VOLS.). FRANCE FAM REV CENTRAL MARRIAGE PWR...TREND 19 NAPOLEON/B. PAGE 152 H3037
STRUCT NAT/G OLD/LIB MORAL

TREUE W. H3130

TREVELYAN G.M. H3131

TRIBAL....SEE KIN

TRIBUTE....FORMAL PAYMENTS TO DOMINANT POWER BY MINOR POWER GROUP; SEE ALSO SANCTION

B27
HOCART A.M.,KINGSHIP. UNIV CULTURE EX/STRUC TRIBUTE ROUTINE CHOOSE ROLE SOVEREIGN RITUAL 20 KING. PAGE 72 H1441
CHIEF MYTH IDEA/COMP

B38
COUPLAND R.,EAST AFRICA AND ITS INVADERS. AFR ISLAM STRATA SECT FORCES DIPLOM TRIBUTE CONTROL DISCRIM NAT/LISM 19 AFRICA/E EUROPE MISSION. PAGE 34 H0680
CULTURE ELITES COLONIAL MARKET

B60
PINTO F.B.M.,ENRIQUECIMENTO ILICITO NO EXERCICIO DE CARGOS PUBLICOS. BRAZIL L/A+17C USA+45 ELITES TRIBUTE CONTROL INGP/REL ORD/FREE PWR...NAT/COMP 20. PAGE 126 H2513
ADMIN NAT/G CRIME LAW

B63
HARDY M.J.L.,BLOOD FEUDS AND THE PAYMENT OF BLOOD MONEY IN THE MIDDLE EAST. ISLAM SOCIETY SECT REGION SANCTION COERCE DEATH MURDER 7/20 ARABS. PAGE 66 H1329
KIN TRIBUTE LAW CULTURE

B65
HESS A.G.,CHASING THE DRAGON: A REPORT ON DRUG ADDICTION IN HONG KONG. ASIA CULTURE PROB/SOLV TRIBUTE...POLICY PSY SOC CLASSIF STAT 17/20 HONG/KONG. PAGE 70 H1411
BIO/SOC CRIME SOCIETY LAW

TRIESTE....TRIESTE

TRINIDAD AND TOBAGO....SEE TRINIDAD

TRINIDAD....TRINIDAD AND TOBAGO; SEE ALSO L/A+17C

S67
COLLINS B.A.,"SOME NOTES ON PUBLIC SERVICE COMMISSIONS IN THE COMMONWEALTH CARIBBEAN." JAMAICA L/A+17C TRINIDAD UK NAT/G OP/RES DOMIN SENIOR COLONIAL CONTROL INGP/REL CENTRAL EFFICIENCY PWR ...DECISION 20. PAGE 31 H0631 — ADMIN EX/STRUC ECO/UNDEV CHOOSE

S67
KROLL M.,"POLITICAL LEADERSHIP AND ADMINISTRATIVE COMMUNICATIONS IN NEW NATION STATES* CASE STUDY OF TRINIDAD AND TOBAGO." L/A+17C TRINIDAD INTELL OP/RES DOMIN COLONIAL LEAD GP/REL CENTRAL EFFICIENCY...DECISION OBS METH/COMP 20. PAGE 89 H1774 — NAT/G ADMIN EDU/PROP CONTROL

TRISKA J.F. H3132

TROBRIAND....TROBRIAND ISLANDS AND ISLANDERS

S21
MALINOWSKI B.,"THE PRIMITIVE ECONOMICS OF THE TROBRIAND ISLANDERS" (BMR)" CULTURE SOCIETY NAT/G CHIEF LEAD OWN...SOC MYTH WORSHIP 20 NEW/GUINEA TROBRIAND RESOURCE/N. PAGE 101 H2029 — ECO/UNDEV AGRI PRODUC STRUCT

TROTSKY/L....LEON TROTSKY

N47
CANNON J.P.,AMERICAN STALINISM AND ANTI-STALINISM (PAMPHLET). NAT/G WORKER DOMIN EDU/PROP REV GP/REL ...MARXIST CONCPT 20 STALIN/J TROTSKY/L. PAGE 26 H0521 — LABOR MARXISM CAP/ISM POL/PAR

B48
WOLFE B.D.,THREE WHO MADE A REVOLUTION. USSR CONSTN NAT/G CAP/ISM EDU/PROP CONTROL WAR GP/REL INGP/REL PERS/REL ROLE 20 STALIN/J LENIN/VI TROTSKY/L BOLSHEVISM. PAGE 170 H3398 — BIOG REV LEAD MARXISM

B55
MAYO H.B.,DEMOCRACY AND MARXISM. COM USSR STRATA NAT/G WORKER ECO/TAC REV MORAL...PHIL/SCI HIST/WRIT IDEA/COMP WORSHIP 20 MARX/KARL LENIN/VI STALIN/J TROTSKY/L. PAGE 105 H2108 — MARXISM CAP/ISM

S68
SHAPIRO J.P.,"SOVIET HISTORIOGRAPHY AND THE MOSCOW TRIALS: AFTER THIRTY YEARS." USSR NAT/G LEGIT PRESS CONTROL LEAD ATTIT MARXISM...NEW/IDEA METH 20 TROTSKY/L STALIN/J KHRUSH/N. PAGE 142 H2843 — HIST/WRIT EDU/PROP SANCTION ADJUD

TRUJILLO/R....RAFAEL TRUJILLO

B58
ORNES G.E.,TRUJILLO: LITTLE CAESAR OF THE CARIBBEAN. DOMIN/REP FAM NAT/G FORCES BUDGET CRIME REV PERSON 20 TRUJILLO/R. PAGE 122 H2429 — BIOG PWR TOTALISM CHIEF

TRUMAN DOCTRINE....SEE TRUMAN/DOC

TRUMAN/DOC....TRUMAN DOCTRINE

TRUMAN/HS....PRESIDENT HARRY S. TRUMAN

B57
REISS J.,GEORGE KENNANS POLITIK DER EINDAMMUNG. USSR NAT/G FORCES TOTALISM ATTIT ORD/FREE...POLICY 20 NATO TRUMAN/HS MARSHL/PLN KENNAN/G. PAGE 131 H2613 — DIPLOM DETER PEACE

B67
WARREN S.,THE AMERICAN PRESIDENT. POL/PAR FORCES LEGIS DIPLOM ECO/TAC ADMIN EXEC PWR...ANTHOL 18/20 ROOSEVLT/F KENNEDY/JF JOHNSON/LB TRUMAN/HS WILSON/W. PAGE 165 H3312 — CHIEF LEAD NAT/G CONSTN

TRUST, PERSONAL....SEE RESPECT, SUPEGO

TRUST/TERR....TRUST TERRITORY

B60
THE AFRICA 1960 COMMITTEE,MANDATE IN TRUST; THE PROBLEM OF SOUTH WEST AFRICA. GERMANY STRUCT REGION SANCTION CHOOSE DISCRIM...INT/LAW 20 AFRICA/SW UN LEAGUE/NAT TRUST/TERR. PAGE 153 H3066 — NAT/G DIPLOM COLONIAL RACE/REL

B63
FIRST R.,SOUTH WEST AFRICA. SOUTH/AFR INT/ORG KIN NAT/G WORKER COLONIAL WAR...POLICY 20 UN TRUST/TERR AFRICA/SW. PAGE 50 H1006 — DISCRIM ORD/FREE RACE/REL CONTROL

S68
DUGARD J.,"THE REVOCATION OF THE MANDATE FOR SOUTH WEST AFRICA." SOUTH/AFR WOR+45 STRATA NAT/G DELIB/GP DIPLOM ADJUD SANCTION CHOOSE RACE/REL ...POLICY NAT/COMP 20 AFRICA/SW UN TRUST/TERR LEAGUE/NAT. PAGE 43 H0858 — AFR INT/ORG DISCRIM COLONIAL

TSHOMBE/M....MOISE TSHOMBE

B66
GERARD-LIBOIS J.,KATANGA SECESSION. INT/ORG FORCES DIPLOM ADMIN CONTROL WAR CHOOSE PWR...CHARTS 20 KATANGA TSHOMBE/M UN. PAGE 56 H1114 — NAT/G REGION ORD/FREE REV

TSURUMI K. H3133

TOTEMEYER G. H3134

TUCKER R.C. H3135,H3136

TUDEN A. H3013

TULANE/U....TULANE UNIVERSITY

TUNIS

B23
GRANT C.F.,STUDIES IN NORTH AFRICA. ALGERIA MOROCCO ROMAN/EMP CULTURE STRUCT NAT/G DIPLOM WAR ...NAT/COMP TUNIS EUROPE. PAGE 60 H1195 — ISLAM SECT DOMIN COLONIAL

B48
MAUGHAM R.,NORTH AFRICAN NOTEBOOK. ALGERIA ISLAM LIBYA MOROCCO STRUCT ECO/UNDEV COLONIAL...SOC OBS AUD/VIS NAT/COMP WORSHIP 20 TUNIS. PAGE 105 H2102 — SOCIETY RECORD NAT/LISM

B52
JULIEN C.A.,L'AFRIQUE DU NORD EN MARCHE: NATIONALISMES MUSULMANS ET SOUVERAINETE FRANCAISE (2ND ED). AFR ALGERIA FRANCE ISLAM MOROCCO NAT/G CONTROL ORD/FREE...POLICY 19/20 TUNIS MUSLIM. PAGE 82 H1641 — NAT/LISM COERCE DOMIN COLONIAL

B61
SEMINAR REPRESENTATIVE GOVT,AFRO-ASIAN ATTITUDES: SEMINAR ON REPRESENTATIVE GOVERNMENTSPUBLIC LIBERTIES IN STATES OF ASIA AND AFRICA, RHODES, 1958. AFR ASIA BURMA INDIA ISLAM UAR VIETNAM/S SOCIETY POL/PAR CHIEF EDU/PROP PRESS PERSON ...POLICY INT 20 TUNIS. PAGE 141 H2826 — CHOOSE ATTIT NAT/COMP ORD/FREE

B61
UAR MINISTRY OF CULTURE,A BIBLIOGRAPHICAL LIST OF TUNISIA. ISLAM CULTURE NAT/G EDU/PROP COLONIAL ...GEOG 19/20 TUNIS. PAGE 157 H3146 — BIBLIOG DIPLOM SECT

B62
BAULIN J.,THE ARAB ROLE IN AFRICA. AFR ALGERIA FUT ISLAM MOROCCO UAR COLONIAL NEUTRAL REV...SOC 20 TUNIS BOURGUIBA. PAGE 12 H0240 — NAT/LISM DIPLOM NAT/G SECT

B62
DUROSELLE J.B.,LES NOUVEAUX ETATS DANS LES RELATIONS INTERNATIONALES. AFR CHINA/COM FRANCE MOROCCO S/ASIA USSR ECO/UNDEV INT/ORG PLAN ECO/TAC EDU/PROP ATTIT DRIVE...TREND TOT/POP TUNIS 20. PAGE 44 H0872 — NAT/G CONSTN DIPLOM

B63
ZARTMAN I.W.,GOVERNMENT AND POLITICS IN NORTHERN AFRICA. AFR ALGERIA ISLAM LIBYA MOROCCO UAR ELITES SOCIETY PLAN ECO/TAC DOMIN EDU/PROP LEGIT ATTIT ...GEOG CONCPT TIME/SEQ 20 TUNIS. PAGE 172 H3448 — CULTURE DRIVE NAT/LISM

B65
MOORE C.H.,TUNISIA SINCE INDEPENDENCE. ELITES LOC/G POL/PAR ADMIN COLONIAL CONTROL EXEC GOV/REL TOTALISM MARXISM...INT 20 TUNIS. PAGE 112 H2248 — NAT/G EX/STRUC SOCISM

S65
ASHFORD D.E.,"BUREAUCRATS AND CITIZENS." MOROCCO PAKISTAN PARTIC 20 TUNIS. PAGE 9 H0172 — GOV/COMP ADMIN EX/STRUC ROLE

B66
BROWN L.C.,STATE AND SOCIETY IN INDEPENDENT NORTH AFRICA. ALGERIA LIBYA MOROCCO AGRI INDUS INT/ORG POL/PAR SECT PLAN DIPLOM COLONIAL...LING NAT/COMP ANTHOL BIBLIOG 20 TUNIS MUSLIM. PAGE 22 H0446 — NAT/G SOCIETY CULTURE ECO/UNDEV

B67
ASHFORD D.E.,NATIONAL DEVELOPMENT AND LOCAL REFORM: POLITICAL PARTICIPATION IN MOROCCO, TUNISIA, AND PAKISTAN. MOROCCO PAKISTAN CULTURE PROB/SOLV ATTIT ...POLICY SOC METH/COMP NAT/COMP BIBLIOG 20 TUNIS. PAGE 9 H0173 — PARTIC ECO/UNDEV ADJUST NAT/G

C67
LING D.L.,"TUNISIA: FROM PROTECTORATE TO REPUBLIC." CULTURE NAT/G POL/PAR CHIEF DIPLOM COERCE WAR PWR ...BIBLIOG 19/20 TUNIS. PAGE 97 H1934 — AFR NAT/LISM COLONIAL PROB/SOLV

B89
ASHBEE H.S.,A BIBLIOGRAPHY OF TUNISIA FROM THE EARLIEST TIMES TO THE END OF 1888. AGRI ADMIN ...GEOG TUNIS. PAGE 8 H0171 — BIBLIOG COLONIAL CULTURE NAT/G

B93
ROYAL GEOGRAPHIC SOCIETY,BIBLIOGRAPHY OF BARBARY STATES (4 SUPPLEMENTARY PAPERS). ALGERIA LIBYA MOROCCO SOCIETY STRUCT DIPLOM LEAD 14/19 TUNIS. PAGE 135 H2706 — BIBLIOG ISLAM NAT/G COLONIAL

TUNISIA....SEE ALSO ISLAM, AFR

TURBERVILLE A.S. H0510

TURKESTAN....TURKESTAN

PARK A.G.,BOLSHEVISM IN TURKESTAN 1917-1927. COM RUSSIA USSR CULTURE AGRI SECT DOMIN GP/REL INGP/REL NAT/LISM...BIBLIOG 20 TURKESTAN. PAGE 123 H2467 — B57 — REV POLICY MARXISM ISLAM

TURKEVICH J. H3137

TURKEY....TURKEY; SEE ALSO ISLAM

MARTIN B.K.,THE TRIUMPH OF LORD PALMERSTON. MOD/EUR RUSSIA TURKEY UK NAT/G DELIB/GP 19. PAGE 103 H2061 — B24 — ATTIT WAR POL/PAR POLICY

FULLER G.H.,TURKEY: A SELECTED LIST OF REFERENCES. ISLAM TURKEY CULTURE ECO/UNDEV AGRI DIPLOM NAT/LISM CONSERVE...GEOG HUM INT/LAW SOC 7/20 MAPS. PAGE 54 H1075 — B44 — BIBLIOG/A ALL/VALS

LERNER D.,THE PASSING OF TRADITIONAL SOCIETY: MODERNIZING THE MIDDLE EAST. IRAN ISLAM LEBANON SYRIA TURKEY UAR CULTURE INTELL STRATA KIN NAT/G NEIGH SECT EDU/PROP ATTIT PERSON...MYTH OBS 20. PAGE 95 H1888 — B58 — ECO/UNDEV RIGID/FLEX

FOX A.,THE POWER OF SMALL STATES: DIPLOMACY IN WORLD WAR TWO. EUR+WWI FINLAND NORWAY SPAIN SWEDEN TURKEY NAT/G TOP/EX DIPLOM PWR...HIST/WRIT 20. PAGE 52 H1044 — B59 — CONCPT STERTYP BAL/PWR

HANSON A.H.,THE STRUCTURE AND CONTROL OF STATE ENTERPRISES IN TURKEY. TURKEY LAW ADMIN GOV/REL EFFICIENCY...CHARTS 20. PAGE 66 H1319 — B59 — NAT/G LG/CO OWN CONTROL

KARPAT K.H.,"TURKEY'S POLITICS: THE TRANSITION TO A MULTI-PARTY SYSTEM." COM TURKEY CULTURE ECO/UNDEV SECT TEC/DEV NAT/LISM ATTIT...SOC CON/ANAL BIBLIOG 20. PAGE 83 H1664 — C59 — POL/PAR NAT/G

PERLMANN H.,"UPHEAVAL IN TURKEY." EUR+WWI ISLAM NAT/G FORCES TOP/EX LEGIT COERCE CHOOSE DRIVE ORD/FREE PWR...TIME/SEQ TOT/POP 20. PAGE 125 H2494 — S60 — CONSTN TURKEY

VON EICKSTEDT E.,TURKEN, KURDEN UND IRANER SEIT DEM ALTERTUM. IRAN TURKEY GP/REL BIO/SOC HABITAT...PSY 20 PERSIA. PAGE 163 H3266 — B61 — CULTURE SOC SOCIETY STRUCT

VALLET R.,"IRAN: KEY TO THE MIDDLE EAST." COM IRAQ ISLAM KUWAIT LEBANON SAUDI/ARAB TURKEY ELITES SOCIETY INDUS PROC/MFG POL/PAR TOP/EX PLAN BAL/PWR DIPLOM ECO/TAC ALL/VALS...TREND CENTO 20. PAGE 161 H3224 — S61 — NAT/G ECO/UNDEV IRAN

GALENSON W.,LABOR IN DEVELOPING COUNTRIES. BRAZIL INDONESIA ISRAEL PAKISTAN TURKEY AGRI INDUS WORKER PAY PRICE GP/REL WEALTH...MGT CHARTS METH/COMP NAT/COMP 20. PAGE 54 H1088 — B62 — LABOR ECO/UNDEV BARGAIN POL/PAR

NOLTE E.,"ZUR PHANOMENOLOGIE DES FASCHIMUS." EUR+WWI GERMANY ITALY TURKEY INTELL NAT/G CHIEF CONSULT FORCES CREATE DOMIN EDU/PROP COERCE WAR CHOOSE DRIVE FASCISM...PSY CONCPT MYTH GEN/METH LEAGUE/NAT NAZI 20. PAGE 118 H2367 — L62 — ATTIT PWR

JELAVICH C.,THE BALKANS IN TRANSITION: ESSAYS ON THE DEVELOPMENT OF BALKAN LIFE AND POLITICS SINCE THE EIGHTEENTH CENTURY. COM GREECE TURKEY ECO/UNDEV NAT/G SECT ATTIT...GEOG SOC CONCPT TIME/SEQ ANTHOL 18/20. PAGE 80 H1596 — B63 — CULTURE RIGID/FLEX

SHANNON R.T.,GLADSTONE AND THE BULGARIAN AGITATION OF 1876. BULGARIA TURKEY UK DIPLOM COERCE REV ATTIT 19 GLADSTON/W DISRAELI/B. PAGE 142 H2841 — B63 — EDU/PROP NAT/G PWR CONSEN

WARD R.E.,POLITICAL MODERNIZATION IN JAPAN AND TURKEY. ASIA ISLAM S/ASIA CONSTN CULTURE STRATA COM/IND POL/PAR FORCES ACT/RES ECO/TAC DOMIN EDU/PROP LEGIT ADMIN CHOOSE ATTIT ALL/VALS...STAT TIME/SEQ VAL/FREE CHINJAP. PAGE 165 H3307 — B64 — SOCIETY TURKEY

LEWIS B.,"THE QUEST FOR FREEDOM--A SAD STORY OF THE MIDDLE EAST." ISLAM ISRAEL LEBANON TURKEY CULTURE NAT/G SECT LEGIS TOP/EX DOMIN EDU/PROP LEGIT ORD/FREE PWR RESPECT...POLICY TIME/SEQ VAL/FREE 20. PAGE 96 H1911 — S64 — CONSTN ATTIT NAT/LISM

FREY F.W.,THE TURKISH POLITICAL ELITE. TURKEY CULTURE INTELL NAT/G EX/STRUC CHOOSE ATTIT PWR ...METH/CNCPT CHARTS WORSHIP 20. PAGE 53 H1059 — B65 — ELITES SOCIETY POL/PAR

OECD,MEDITERRANEAN REGIONAL PROJECT: TURKEY; EDUCATION AND DEVELOPMENT. FUT TURKEY SOCIETY STRATA FINAN NAT/G PROF/ORG PLAN PROB/SOLV ADMIN COST...STAT CHARTS 20 OECD. PAGE 120 H2399 — B65 — EDU/PROP ACADEM SCHOOL ECO/UNDEV

ORG FOR ECO COOP AND DEVEL,THE MEDITERRANEAN REGIONAL PROJECT: AN EXPERIMENT IN PLANNING BY SIX COUNTRIES. FUT GREECE SPAIN TURKEY YUGOSLAVIA SOCIETY FINAN NAT/G PROF/ORG EDU/PROP ADMIN REGION COST...POLICY STAT CHARTS 20 OECD. PAGE 121 H2427 — B65 — PLAN ECO/UNDEV ACADEM SCHOOL

ZEINE Z.N.,THE EMERGENCE OF ARAB NATIONALISM (REV. ED.). TURKEY UK NAT/G SECT TEC/DEV LEAD REV WAR AGE/Y ROLE ORD/FREE...TRADIT CHARTS BIBLIOG 20 ARABS OTTOMAN. PAGE 173 H3453 — B66 — ISLAM NAT/LISM DIPLOM

ALPANDER G.G.,"ENTREPRENEURS AND PRIVATE ENTERPRISE IN TURKEY." TURKEY INDUS PROC/MFG EDU/PROP ATTIT DRIVE WEALTH...GEOG MGT SOC STAT TREND CHARTS 20. PAGE 6 H0114 — S67 — ECO/UNDEV LG/CO NAT/G POLICY

ANTHEM T.,"CYPRUS* WHAT NOW?" CYPRUS GREECE TURKEY NAT/G BUDGET MAJORITY 20 NATO. PAGE 7 H0143 — S67 — DIPLOM COERCE INT/TRADE ADJUD

TURKIC....TURKIC PEOPLES

KRADER L.,SOCIAL ORGANIZATION OF THE MONGOL-TURKIC PASTORAL NOMADS. SOCIETY FAM KIN NEIGH GP/REL MARRIAGE 16/20 MONGOLIA TURKIC MIGRATION. PAGE 88 H1763 — N — BIO/SOC HABITAT CULTURE STRUCT

ZENKOVSKY S.A.,PAN-TURKISM AND ISLAM IN RUSSIA. ASIA RUSSIA USSR CULTURE POL/PAR DOMIN REV GP/REL MARXISM...LING GP/COMP BIBLIOG 19/20 TURKIC. PAGE 173 H3454 — B60 — SECT NAT/LISM COM ISLAM

TURKS

KAZAMIAS A.M.,EDUCATION AND QUEST FOR MODERNITY IN TURKEY. ISLAM SOCIETY SECT NAT/LISM ATTIT ORD/FREE SOVEREIGN TURKS. PAGE 84 H1672 — B66 — NAT/G EDU/PROP STRATA CULTURE

TURNBULL C.M. H3138,H3139

TURNER A.C. H3140

TURNER J.E. H1458,H2127

TURNER M.C. H3141

TURNER R.H. H3142

TURNER V.W. H3013

TUSKEGEE....TUSKEGEE, ALABAMA

TUTSCH H.E. H3143

TV....TELEVISION; SEE ALSO PRESS, COM/IND

EUROPA PUBLICATIONS LIMITED,THE EUROPA YEAR BOOK. CONSTN FINAN INDUS POL/PAR DIPLOM TV CT/SYS...STAT BIOG CHARTS WORSHIP 20. PAGE 47 H0949 — N — BIBLIOG NAT/G PRESS INT/ORG

BARRON R.,PARTIES AND POLITICS IN MODERN FRANCE. FRANCE LOC/G DELIB/GP LEGIS TOP/EX EDU/PROP LEGIT TV FEEDBACK 20. PAGE 12 H0230 — B59 — POL/PAR ALL/IDEOS CHOOSE PARTIC

BAFFREY S.A.,THE RED MYTH: A HISTORY OF COMMUNISM FROM MARX TO KHRUSHCHEV. USSR NAT/G CHIEF CAP/ISM DIPLOM EDU/PROP REV WAR PEACE TOTALISM...POLICY 20 STALIN/J KHRUSH/N. PAGE 10 H0195 — B62 — CONCPT MARXISM TV

CHAPMAN R.M.,NEW ZEALAND POLITICS IN ACTION: THE 1960 GENERAL ELECTION. NEW/ZEALND LEGIS EDU/PROP PRESS TV LEAD ATTIT...STAND/INT 20. PAGE 29 H0582 — B62 — NAT/G CHOOSE POL/PAR

UNESCO,WORLD COMMUNICATIONS: PRESS, RADIO, TELEVISION, FILM (4TH ED.). WOR+45 DIPLOM TV PEACE ...NAT/COMP SOC/INTEG 20 FILM. PAGE 158 H3163 — B64 — COM/IND EDU/PROP PRESS TEC/DEV

SAINDERICHIN P.,HISTORIE SECRETE D'UNE ELECTION. — B66 — CHOOSE

...NAT/COMP 20. PAGE 10 H0205 ECO/TAC

B66
IBRAHIM-HILMY,THE LITERATURE OF EGYPT AND THE SOUDAN: FROM THE EARLIEST TIMES TO THE YEAR 1885 INCLUSIVE (2 VOLS.). MEDIT-7 SUDAN UAR LAW SOCIETY SECT ATTIT EGYPT/ANC. PAGE 76 H1520 BIBLIOG CULTURE ISLAM NAT/G

B66
US DEPARTMENT OF STATE,RESEARCH ON THE MIDDLE EAST (EXTERNAL RESEARCH LIST NO 4-25). GREECE ISRAEL SYRIA UAR YEMEN CULTURE SOCIETY POL/PAR SECT DIPLOM EDU/PROP WAR NAT/LISM...GEOG GOV/COMP 20. PAGE 160 H3190 BIBLIOG/A ISLAM NAT/G REGION

S66
GILBERT S.P.,"WARS OF LIBERATION AND SOVIET MILITARY AID POLICY." ASIA INDIA INDONESIA UAR USA+45 STRATA WAR PERCEPT MARXISM...STAT NAT/COMP. PAGE 56 H1124 USSR FOR/AID WEAPON DRIVE

S66
HEAPHEY J.,"THE ORGANIZATION OF EGYPT* INADEQUACIES OF A NONPOLITICAL MODEL FOR NATION-BUILDING." STRATA NAT/G CREATE PROB/SOLV ECO/TAC NAT/LISM SOCISM RECORD. PAGE 69 H1377 UAR ECO/UNDEV OBS

S66
KAPIL R.L.,"ON THE CONFLICT POTENTIAL OF INHERITED BOUNDARIES IN AFRICA." MOD/EUR MOROCCO UAR EX/STRUC DIPLOM LEGIT REGION ADJUST...RECORD NAT/COMP GEN/LAWS. PAGE 83 H1658 AFR COLONIAL PREDICT GEOG

B67
COLLINS R.O.,EGYPT AND THE SUDAN. COM FRANCE ISLAM SUDAN UAR UK SOCIETY NAT/G COLONIAL NAT/LISM...GEOG SOC LING TREND SOC/INTEG 7/20 SUEZ. PAGE 32 H0635 AGRI CULTURE ECO/UNDEV

B67
CORDIER A.W.,COLUMBIA ESSAYS IN INTERNATIONAL AFFAIRS. ASIA CHINA/COM FRANCE S/ASIA SPAIN UAR ECO/UNDEV LOC/G ECO/TAC GUERRILLA PWR...BIOG ANTHOL 18/20 MAU/MAU. PAGE 33 H0663 NAT/G DIPLOM MARXISM POLICY

S67
ABDEL-MALEK A.,"THE CRISIS IN NASSER'S EGYPT." ISLAM UAR STRUCT POL/PAR EX/STRUC CREATE PLAN WAR ATTIT ORD/FREE PWR...POLICY DECISION 20. PAGE 3 H0054 FORCES LEAD PROB/SOLV NAT/G

S67
KYLE K.,"BACKGROUND TO THE CRISIS" ISLAM ISRAEL UAR UK USSR NAT/G PROB/SOLV LEGIT CONTROL REGION STRANGE MORAL 20 JEWS. PAGE 89 H1787 DIPLOM POLICY SOVEREIGN COERCE

S67
MATTHEWS R.O.,"THE SUEZ CANAL DISPUTE* A CASE STUDY IN PEACEFUL SETTLEMENT." FRANCE ISRAEL UAR UK NAT/G CONTROL LEAD COERCE WAR NAT/LISM ROLE ORD/FREE PWR ...INT/LAW UN 20. PAGE 105 H2099 PEACE DIPLOM ADJUD

S67
NAHUMI M.,"THE POWERS IN THE MIDDLE EAST CONFLICT." ISLAM ISRAEL JORDAN UAR NAT/G PEACE ATTIT 20 JEWS. PAGE 115 H2304 DIPLOM WAR NAT/LISM

S67
TATU M.,"URSS: LES FLOTTEMENTS DE LA DIRECTION COLLEGIALE." UAR USSR CHIEF LEAD INGP/REL EFFICIENCY...DECISION TREND 20 MID/EAST. PAGE 152 H3047 POLICY NAT/G EX/STRUC DIPLOM

UAR MINISTRY OF CULTURE H3146,H3147

UAW....UNITED AUTO WORKERS

UDR....UNION POUR LA DEFENSE DE LA REPUBLIQUE (FRANCE)

UGANDA....SEE ALSO AFR

B54
MITCHELL P.,AFRICAN AFTERTHOUGHTS. UGANDA CONSTN NAT/G ADJUD COERCE WAR 20 WWI MAU/MAU. PAGE 112 H2230 BIOG CHIEF COLONIAL DOMIN

S55
DE SMITH S.A.,"CONSTITUTIONAL MONARCHY IN BURGANDA." AFR UGANDA UK STRUCT CHIEF REGION INGP/REL ADJUST NAT/LISM SOVEREIGN CONSERVE ...POLICY 19/20 BURGANDA. PAGE 38 H0769 NAT/G DIPLOM CONSTN COLONIAL

B60
BEATTIE J.,BUNYORO, AN AFRICAN KINGDOM. UGANDA STRATA INGP/REL PERS/REL...SOC BIBLIOG 19/20. PAGE 13 H0250 CULTURE ELITES SECT KIN

S60
APTER D.E.,"THE ROLE OF TRADITIONALISM IN THE POLITICAL MODERNIZATION OF GHANA AND UGANDA" (BMR)" AFR GHANA UGANDA CULTURE NAT/G POL/PAR NAT/LISM ...CON/ANAL 20. PAGE 8 H0152 CONSERVE ADMIN GOV/COMP PROB/SOLV

B61
APTER D.E.,THE POLITICAL KINGDOM IN UGANDA. UGANDA CULTURE ECO/UNDEV AGRI KIN SECT TOP/EX REGION ATTIT HABITAT CONSERVE...GEOG AUD/VIS 20. PAGE 8 H0153 NAT/LISM POL/PAR COLONIAL ECO/TAC

S62
LEGUM C.,"THE DANGERS OF INDEPENDENCE" AFR UGANDA NAT/G DIPLOM DOMIN REGION CENTRAL ATTIT POPULISM 20. PAGE 93 H1862 ORD/FREE SOVEREIGN NAT/LISM GOV/COMP

B63
HUGHES A.J.,EAST AFRICA: THE SEARCH FOR UNITY- KENYA, TANGANYIKA, UGANDA, AND ZANZIBAR. TANZANIA UGANDA CONSTN POL/PAR SECT CHIEF DELIB/GP LEGIS WAR CHOOSE NAT/LISM MARXISM...POLICY CHARTS 20 NEGRO UN. PAGE 74 H1488 NAT/G DOMIN LOC/G AFR

B63
HUNTER G.,EDUCATION FOR A DEVELOPING REGION; A STUDY IN EAST AFRICA. AFR TANZANIA UGANDA NAT/G TEC/DEV INGP/REL ADJUST LITERACY ATTIT 20 AFRICA/E. PAGE 75 H1501 EDU/PROP POLICY ECO/UNDEV EFFICIENCY

S63
BANFIELD J.,"FEDERATION IN EAST-AFRICA." AFR UGANDA ELITES INT/ORG NAT/G VOL/ASSN LEGIS ECO/TAC FEDERAL ATTIT SOVEREIGN TOT/POP 20 TANGANYIKA. PAGE 10 H0210 EX/STRUC PWR REGION

B64
FRANCK T.M.,EAST AFRICAN UNITY THROUGH LAW. MALAWI TANZANIA UGANDA UK ZAMBIA CONSTN INT/ORG NAT/G ADMIN ROUTINE TASK NAT/LISM ATTIT SOVEREIGN ...RECORD IDEA/COMP NAT/COMP. PAGE 52 H1048 AFR FEDERAL REGION INT/LAW

L64
ROTBERG R.,"THE FEDERATION MOVEMENT IN BRITISH EAST AND CENTRAL AFRICA." AFR RHODESIA UGANDA ECO/UNDEV NAT/G POL/PAR FORCES DOMIN LEGIT ADMIN COERCE ATTIT ...CONCPT TREND 20 TANGANYIKA. PAGE 135 H2691 VOL/ASSN PWR REGION

B65
GHAI D.P.,PORTRAIT OF A MINORITY: ASIANS IN EAST AFRICA. S/ASIA TANZANIA UGANDA COLONIAL...SOC OBS PREDICT ANTHOL 20. PAGE 56 H1119 RACE/REL GP/REL CULTURE AFR

B65
NYE J.S. JR.,PAN-AFRICANISM AND EAST AFRICAN INTEGRATION. TANZANIA UGANDA STRUCT ECO/UNDEV NAT/G DIPLOM FEDERAL NAT/LISM...STAT SOC/EXP BIBLIOG EEC OAU. PAGE 119 H2382 REGION ATTIT GEN/LAWS AFR

B66
JONES D.H.,AFRICA BIBLIOGRAPHY SERIES: EAST AFRICA. AFR UGANDA SECT BIO/SOC...JURID NAT/COMP 20. PAGE 82 H1630 BIBLIOG/A SOC CULTURE LING

S66
FLEMING W.G.,"AUTHORITY, EFFICIENCY, AND ROLE STRESS: PROBLEMS IN THE DEVELOPMENT OF EAST AFRICAN BUREAUCRACIES." AFR UGANDA STRUCT PROB/SOLV ROUTINE INGP/REL ROLE...MGT SOC GP/COMP GOV/COMP 20 TANGANYIKA AFRICA/E. PAGE 51 H1024 DOMIN EFFICIENCY COLONIAL ADMIN

S67
ADOKO A.,"THE CONSTITUTION OF UGANDA." AFR UGANDA LOC/G CHIEF FORCES LEGIS ADJUD EXEC CHOOSE NAT/LISM ...IDEA/COMP 20. PAGE 4 H0072 NAT/G CONSTN ORD/FREE LAW

S67
BRADLEY A.W.,"CONSTITUTION-MAKING IN UGANDA." UGANDA LAW CHIEF DELIB/GP LEGIS ADMIN EXEC PARL/PROC RACE/REL ORD/FREE...GOV/COMP 20. PAGE 20 H0397 NAT/G CREATE CONSTN FEDERAL

S67
KASFIR N.,"THE UGANDA CONSTITUENT ASSEMBLY DEBATE." UGANDA REPRESENT FEDERAL ORD/FREE POPULISM...POLICY DECISION 20. PAGE 83 H1665 CONSTN CONFER LAW NAT/G

S67
MAIR L.,"BUSOGA LOCAL GOVERNMENT" AFR UGANDA UK CONSTN GP/REL...GOV/COMP METH/COMP 20. PAGE 101 H2024 LOC/G COLONIAL LAW ATTIT

S67
MAYANJA A.,"THE GOVERNMENT'S PROPOSALS ON THE NEW CONSTITUTION." AFR UGANDA LAW CHIEF LEGIS ADJUD REPRESENT FEDERAL PWR 20. PAGE 105 H2105 CONSTN CONFER ORD/FREE NAT/G

S67
READ J.S.,"CENSORED." UGANDA CONSTN INTELL SOCIETY NAT/G DIPLOM PRESS WRITING ADJUD ADMIN COLONIAL RISK...IDEA/COMP 20. PAGE 130 H2602 EDU/PROP AFR CREATE

S67
THEROUX P.,"HATING THE ASIANS." TANZANIA UGANDA CONSTN INDUS NAT/G POL/PAR WORKER ECO/TAC HABITAT LOVE...POLICY GEOG 20 MIGRATION. PAGE 154 H3069 AFR RACE/REL SOVEREIGN ATTIT

UK....UNITED KINGDOM; SEE ALSO APPROPRIATE TIME/SPACE/ CULTURE INDEX, COMMONWLTH

N
LONDON TIMES OFFICIAL INDEX. UK LAW ECO/DEV NAT/G DIPLOM LEAD ATTIT 20. PAGE 1 H0018 BIBLIOG INDEX PRESS WRITING

N
PUBLISHERS' CIRCULAR, THE OFFICIAL ORGAN OF THE PUBLISHERS' ASSOCIATION OF GREAT BRITAIN AND BIBLIOG NAT/G

IRELAND. EUR+WWI MOD/EUR UK LAW PROB/SOLV DIPLOM COLONIAL ATTIT...HUM 19/20 CMN/WLTH. PAGE 1 H0019
WRITING LEAD

N

REVUE FRANCAISE DE SCIENCE POLITIQUE. FRANCE UK ...BIBLIOG/A 20. PAGE 1 H0021
NAT/G DIPLOM CONCPT ROUTINE

N

CARIBBEAN COMMISSION,CURRENT CARIBBEAN BIBLIOGRAPHY. FRANCE NETHERLAND UK CULTURE ECO/UNDEV PRESS LEAD ATTIT...GEOG SOC 20. PAGE 26 H0530
BIBLIOG NAT/G L/A+17C DIPLOM

N

MINISTRY OF OVERSEAS DEVELOPME,TECHNICAL CO-OPERATION -- A BIBLIOGRAPHY. UK LAW SOCIETY DIPLOM ECO/TAC FOR/AID...STAT 20 CMN/WLTH. PAGE 111 H2225
BIBLIOG TEC/DEV ECO/DEV NAT/G

NCO

CARRINGTON C.E.,THE COMMONWEALTH IN AFRICA (PAMPHLET). UK STRUCT NAT/G COLONIAL REPRESENT GOV/REL RACE/REL NAT/LISM...MAJORIT 20 EEC NEGRO COLD/WAR. PAGE 27 H0540
ECO/UNDEV AFR DIPLOM PLAN

NSY

MACKENZIE K.R.,THE ENGLISH PARLIAMENT. UK POL/PAR CHIEF DIPLOM TAX TASK WAR AUTHORIT...POLICY TREND 12/20 PARLIAMENT. PAGE 100 H2000
ORD/FREE LEGIS NAT/G

B00

HOBSON J.A.,THE WAR IN SOUTH AFRICA: ITS CAUSES AND EFFECTS. NETHERLAND SOUTH/AFR UK ELITES AGRI EXTR/IND POL/PAR DIPLOM PRESS RACE/REL ATTIT ORD/FREE SOVEREIGN...INT 19 NEGRO. PAGE 72 H1439
WAR DOMIN POLICY NAT/G

B00

MOCKLER-FERRYMAN A.,BRITISH WEST AFRICA. FRANCE GERMANY NIGER SIER/LEONE UK CULTURE DIPLOM WAR RACE/REL PRODUC PROFIT WEALTH...POLICY PREDICT 19. PAGE 112 H2232
AFR COLONIAL INT/TRADE CAP/ISM

B01

BRYCE J.,STUDIES IN HISTORY AND JURISPRUDENCE (2 VOLS.). ICELAND SOUTH/AFR UK LAW PROB/SOLV SOVEREIGN...PHIL/SCI NAT/COMP ROME/ANC ROMAN/LAW. PAGE 23 H0455
IDEA/COMP CONSTN JURID

B02

SEELEY J.R.,THE EXPANSION OF ENGLAND. MOD/EUR S/ASIA UK CULTURE NAT/G FORCES PLAN DOMIN EDU/PROP COLONIAL ROUTINE ATTIT ALL/VALS SOVEREIGN...CONCPT HIST/WRIT PARLIAMENT 18 CMN/WLTH. PAGE 141 H2819
INT/ORG ACT/RES CAP/ISM INDIA

B03

FORTESCUE G.K.,SUBJECT INDEX OF THE MODERN WORKS ADDED TO THE LIBRARY OF THE BRITISH MUSEUM IN THE YEARS 1881-1900 (3 VOLS.). UK LAW CONSTN FINAN NAT/G FORCES INT/TRADE COLONIAL 19. PAGE 52 H1041
BIBLIOG INDEX WRITING

B03

GRIFFIN A.P.C.,LIST OF BOOKS ON THE CABINETS OF ENGLAND AND AMERICA (PAMPHLET). MOD/EUR UK USA-45 CONSTN NAT/G CONSULT EX/STRUC 19/20. PAGE 61 H1216
BIBLIOG/A GOV/COMP ADMIN DELIB/GP

C06

MONTGOMERY H.,"A DICTIONARY OF POLITICAL PHRASES AND ILLUSIONS WITH A SHORT BIBLIOGRAPHY." EUR+WWI MOD/EUR UK AGRI LABOR LOC/G NAT/G COLONIAL CHOOSE RACE/REL. PAGE 112 H2245
BIBLIOG DICTIONARY POLICY DIPLOM

B09

LOBINGIER C.S.,THE PEOPLE'S LAW OR POPULAR PARTICIPATION IN LAW-MAKING. FRANCE SWITZERLND UK LOC/G NAT/G PROVS LEGIS SUFF MAJORITY PWR POPULISM ...GOV/COMP BIBLIOG 19. PAGE 97 H1945
CONSTN LAW PARTIC

B10

MCILWAIN C.H.,THE HIGH COURT OF PARLIAMENT AND ITS SUPREMACY B1910 1878 408. UK EX/STRUC PARL/PROC GOV/REL INGP/REL PRIVIL 12/20 PARLIAMENT ENGLSH/LAW. PAGE 107 H2132
LAW LEGIS CONSTN NAT/G

B10

TEMPERLEY H.W.V.,SENATES AND UPPER CHAMBERS; THEIR USE AND FUNCTION IN THE MODERN STATE... UK WOR-45 CONSTN NAT/G POL/PAR PROVS SECT COLONIAL LEAD CHOOSE REPRESENT PWR...BIBLIOG 19/20 PARLIAMENT SENATE CMN/WLTH HOUSE/LORD. PAGE 153 H3059
PARL/PROC NAT/COMP LEGIS EX/STRUC

B12

HOBSON J.A.,THE EVOLUTION OF MODERN CAPITALISM. MOD/EUR UK STRATA ECO/DEV INDUS INCOME UTIL WEALTH ...SOC GEN/LAWS 7/20. PAGE 72 H1440
CAP/ISM WORKER TEC/DEV TIME/SEQ

B12

POLLOCK F.,THE GENIUS OF THE COMMON LAW. CHRIST-17C UK FINAN CHIEF ACT/RES ADMIN GP/REL ATTIT SOCISM ...ANARCH JURID. PAGE 127 H2537
LAW CULTURE CREATE

B13

BARDOUX J.,L'ANGLETERRE RADICALE; ESSAI DE LA PSYCHOLOGIE SOCIALE (1906-1913). UK CONSTN NAT/G WORKER CREATE BUDGET ECO/TAC ATTIT...POLICY 20 PARLIAMENT LABOR/PAR STRIKE NAVY. PAGE 11 H0215
POL/PAR CHOOSE COLONIAL LEGIS

B15

VEBLEN T.,IMPERIAL GERMANY AND THE INDUSTRIAL REVOLUTION. GERMANY MOD/EUR UK USA-45 NAT/G TEC/DEV CAP/ISM...MAJORIT NAT/COMP 19/20 CHINJAP. PAGE 162 H3236
ECO/DEV INDUS TECHNIC BAL/PWR

N17

BURKE E.,THOUGHTS ON THE PROSPECT OF A REGICIDE PEACE (PAMPHLET). FRANCE UK SECT DOMIN MURDER PEACE ORD/FREE SOVEREIGN POPULISM...POLICY GOV/COMP IDEA/COMP 18 JACOBINISM COEXIST. PAGE 24 H0483
REV CHIEF NAT/G DIPLOM

N17

BURKE E.,THOUGHTS ON THE CAUSE OF THE PRESENT DISCONTENTS (PAMPHLET). MOD/EUR UK CONSTN CHIEF LEGIS DOMIN CONTROL EXEC REPRESENT POPULISM ...TRADIT NEW/IDEA METH/COMP 18 BURKE/EDM. PAGE 24 H0484
ORD/FREE REV PARL/PROC NAT/G

N17

BURKE E.,LETTER TO SIR HERCULES LANGRISHE (PAMPHLET). IRELAND UK NAT/G CHIEF DIPLOM DOMIN PARL/PROC COERCE ORD/FREE SOVEREIGN POPULISM ...TRADIT 18 BURKE/EDM. PAGE 24 H0485
POLICY COLONIAL SECT

B18

WILSON W.,THE STATE: ELEMENTS OF HISTORICAL AND PRACTICAL POLITICS. FRANCE GERMANY ITALY UK USSR CONSTN EX/STRUC LEGIS CT/SYS WAR PWR...POLICY GOV/COMP 20. PAGE 169 H3385
NAT/G JURID CONCPT NAT/COMP

B19

NATHAN M.,THE SOUTH AFRICAN COMMONWEALTH: CONSTITUTION, PROBLEMS, SOCIAL CONDITIONS. SOUTH/AFR UK CULTURE INDUS EX/STRUC LEGIS BUDGET EDU/PROP ADMIN CT/SYS GP/REL RACE/REL...LING 19/20 CMN/WLTH. PAGE 116 H2317
CONSTN NAT/G POL/PAR SOCIETY

N19

ADMINISTRATIVE STAFF COLLEGE,THE ACCOUNTABILITY OF GOVERNMENT DEPARTMENTS (PAMPHLET) (REV. ED.). UK CONSTN FINAN NAT/G CONSULT ADMIN INGP/REL CONSEN PRIVIL 20 PARLIAMENT. PAGE 3 H0070
PARL/PROC ELITES SANCTION PROB/SOLV

N19

ANDERSON J.,THE ORGANIZATION OF ECONOMIC STUDIES IN RELATION TO THE PROBLEMS OF GOVERNMENT (PAMPHLET). UK FINAN INDUS DELIB/GP PLAN PROB/SOLV ADMIN 20. PAGE 6 H0128
ECO/TAC ACT/RES NAT/G CENTRAL

N19

BUSINESS ECONOMISTS' GROUP,INCOME POLICIES (PAMPHLET). UK INDUS LABOR TOP/EX PAY COST PRODUC ...ECOMETRIC GOV/COMP SIMUL ANTHOL 20. PAGE 25 H0497
INCOME WORKER WEALTH POLICY

N19

GRIFFITH W.,THE PUBLIC SERVICE (PAMPHLET). UK LAW LOC/G NAT/G PARTIC CHOOSE DRIVE ROLE SKILL...CHARTS 20 CIVIL/SERV. PAGE 61 H1222
ADMIN EFFICIENCY EDU/PROP GOV/REL

N19

HANNA A.J.,EUROPEAN RULE IN AFRICA (PAMPHLET). BELGIUM FRANCE MOD/EUR UK WOR+45 WOR-45 ECO/UNDEV NAT/G PARTIC SOVEREIGN...NAT/COMP 19/20. PAGE 66 H1314
DIPLOM COLONIAL AFR NAT/LISM

N19

MASSEY V.,CANADIANS AND THEIR COMMONWEALTH: THE ROMANES LECTURE DELIVERED IN THE SHELDONIAN THEATRE JUNE 1, 1961 (PAMPHLET). CANADA UK CULTURE ECO/DEV REPRESENT NAT/LISM PEACE PWR CONSERVE 20 CMN/WLTH. PAGE 104 H2088
ATTIT DIPLOM NAT/G SOVEREIGN

N19

POUND R.,ORGANIZATION OF THE COURTS (PAMPHLET). MOD/EUR UK USA-45 ADJUD PWR...GOV/COMP 10/20 EUROPE. PAGE 127 H2546
CT/SYS JURID STRUCT ADMIN

N19

TEMPLE W.,AN ESSAY UPON THE ORIGINAL AND NATURE OF GOVERNMENT (PAMPHLET). CHRIST-17C UK FAM LOC/G LEGIT ORD/FREE CONSERVE 17. PAGE 153 H3060
NAT/G CONCPT PWR SOCIETY

N19

TREVELYAN G.M.,THE TWO-PARTY SYSTEM IN ENGLISH POLITICAL HISTORY (PAMPHLET). UK CHIEF LEGIS COLONIAL EXEC REV CHOOSE 17/19. PAGE 157 H3131
PARL/PROC POL/PAR NAT/G PWR

B20

HALDANE R.B.,BEFORE THE WAR. MOD/EUR SOCIETY INT/ORG NAT/G DELIB/GP PLAN DOMIN EDU/PROP LEGIT ADMIN COERCE ATTIT DRIVE MORAL ORD/FREE PWR...SOC CONCPT SELF/OBS RECORD BIOG TIME/SEQ. PAGE 64 H1282
POLICY DIPLOM UK

B20

MALTHUS T.R.,PRINCIPLES OF POLITICAL ECONOMY. UK AGRI INDUS MARKET NAT/G DIPLOM PRICE CONTROL BAL/PAY COST OWN PWR LAISSEZ 18/19. PAGE 102 H2034
GEN/LAWS DEMAND WEALTH

B20

WEBB S.,INDUSTRIAL DEMOCRACY. UK PARTIC GP/REL ...SOC OBS RECORD CHARTS 18/20. PAGE 166 H3317
LABOR NAT/G VOL/ASSN MAJORIT

B22

TONNIES F.,KRITIK DER OFFENTLICHEN MEINUNG. FRANCE UK CULTURE COM/IND DOMIN PRESS RUMOR ROLE NAT/COMP. PAGE 156 H3114
SOCIETY SOC ATTIT

B23

FINER H.,REPRESENTATIVE GOVERNMENT AND A PARLIAMENT OF INDUSTRY. A STUDY OF THE GERMAN FEDERAL ECONOMIC COUNCIL. GERMANY UK CONSTN INDUS PARL/PROC ...NAT/COMP 20. PAGE 50 H1002
DELIB/GP ECO/TAC WAR REV

B23
LEES-SMITH H.B.,SECOND CHAMBERS IN THEORY AND PRACTICE. IRELAND NORWAY SOUTH/AFR UK LAW POL/PAR LEGIS CONTROL 20 CMN/WLTH. PAGE 93 H1858
PARL/PROC DELIB/GP REPRESENT GP/COMP

B24
BAGEHOT W.,THE ENGLISH CONSTITUTION AND OTHER POLITICAL ESSAYS. UK DELIB/GP BAL/PWR ADMIN CONTROL EXEC ROUTINE CONSERVE...METH PARLIAMENT 19/20. PAGE 10 H0197
NAT/G STRUCT CONCPT

B24
HOLDSWORTH W.S.,A HISTORY OF ENGLISH LAW; THE COMMON LAW AND ITS RIVALS (VOL. IV). UK SEA AGRI CHIEF ADJUD CONTROL CRIME GOV/REL...INT/LAW JURID NAT/COMP 16/17 PARLIAMENT COMMON/LAW CANON/LAW ENGLSH/LAW. PAGE 72 H1449
LAW LEGIS CT/SYS CONSTN

B24
MARTIN B.K.,THE TRIUMPH OF LORD PALMERSTON. MOD/EUR RUSSIA TURKEY UK NAT/G DELIB/GP 19. PAGE 103 H2061
ATTIT WAR POL/PAR POLICY

B25
TEMPERLEY H.,THE FOREIGN POLICY OF CANNING: 1822-1827. MOD/EUR NAT/G TOP/EX EDU/PROP ROUTINE ATTIT RIGID/FLEX SUPEGO PWR SKILL...TIME/SEQ PARLIAMENT 20. PAGE 153 H3058
PERSON DIPLOM UK BIOG

B25
WEBSTER C.,THE FOREIGN POLICY OF CASTLEREAGH: 1815-1822. LAW NAT/G DELIB/GP TOP/EX BAL/PWR ORD/FREE PWR RESPECT 19. PAGE 166 H3322
MOD/EUR DIPLOM UK

B25
WILLIAMS B.,THE SELBORNE MEMORANDUM. AFR FUT SOUTH/AFR UK NAT/G BUDGET DIPLOM REGION GOV/REL SOVEREIGN...POLICY CHARTS 20 UNIFICA SELBORNE/W. PAGE 168 H3365
COLONIAL PROVS

B26
FORTESCUE J.,THE GOVERNANCE OF ENGLAND (1471-76). UK LAW FINAN SECT LEGIS PROB/SOLV TAX DOMIN ADMIN GP/REL COST ORD/FREE PWR 14/15. PAGE 52 H1042
CONSERVE CONSTN CHIEF NAT/G

B26
MCPHEE A.,THE ECONOMIC REVOLUTION IN BRITISH WEST AFRICA. AFR UK CULTURE DIST/IND FINAN INDUS PLAN GP/REL RACE/REL 20 AFRICA/W. PAGE 107 H2148
ECO/UNDEV INT/TRADE COLONIAL GEOG

B26
POLLARD A.F.,THE EVOLUTION OF PARLIAMENT. UK CONSTN POL/PAR EX/STRUC GOV/REL INGP/REL PRIVIL RIGID/FLEX ...TIME/SEQ 11/20 CMN/WLTH PARLIAMENT. PAGE 127 H2536
LEGIS PARL/PROC NAT/G

B26
TAWNEY R.H.,RELIGION AND THE RISE OF CAPITALISM. UK CULTURE NAT/G TEC/DEV OWN LAISSEZ...POLICY SOC TIME/SEQ 16/19. PAGE 153 H3050
SECT WEALTH INDUS CAP/ISM

B27
BELLOC H.,THE SERVILE STATE (1912) (3RD ED.). PRUSSIA UK CULTURE STRATA INDUS NAT/G ECO/TAC CONTROL LEAD SUFF DISCRIM EQUILIB ORD/FREE WEALTH 20. PAGE 13 H0269
WORKER CAP/ISM DOMIN CATH

B27
FLOURNOY F.,PARLIAMENT AND WAR. MOD/EUR UK NAT/G FORCES LEGIS TOP/EX DIPLOM LEGIT DEBATE ATTIT RIGID/FLEX PWR...DECISION TIME/SEQ PARLIAMENT 19/20. PAGE 52 H1032
COERCE WAR

B27
GOOCH G.P.,ENGLISH DEMOCRATIC IDEAS IN THE SEVENTEENTH CENTURY (2ND ED.). UK LAW SECT FORCES DIPLOM LEAD PARL/PROC REV ATTIT AUTHORIT...ANARCH CONCPT 17 PARLIAMENT CMN/WLTH REFORMERS. PAGE 58 H1167
IDEA/COMP MAJORIT EX/STRUC CONSERVE

B27
PANIKKAR K.M.,INDIAN STATES AND THE GOVERNMENT OF INDIA. INDIA UK CONSTN CONTROL TASK GP/REL SOVEREIGN WEALTH...TREND BIBLIOG 19. PAGE 123 H2457
GOV/COMP COLONIAL BAL/PWR PROVS

B28
BARKER E.,POLITICAL THOUGHT IN ENGLAND: FROM HERBERT SPENCER TO THE PRESENT DAY. UK ALL/IDEOS ...PHIL/SCI 19/20 SPENCER/H GREEN/TH BENTHAM/J MAITLAND/F. PAGE 11 H0217
INTELL GEN/LAWS IDEA/COMP

B28
FYFE H.,THE BRITISH LIBERAL PARTY. UK SECT ADMIN LEAD CHOOSE GP/REL PWR SOCISM...MAJORIT TIME/SEQ 19/20 LIB/PARTY CONSRV/PAR. PAGE 54 H1084
POL/PAR NAT/G REPRESENT POPULISM

B28
HOLDSWORTH W.S.,THE HISTORIANS OF ANGLO-AMERICAN LAW. UK USA-45 INTELL LEGIS RESPECT...BIOG NAT/COMP 17/20 COMMON/LAW. PAGE 72 H1450
HIST/WRIT LAW JURID

B28
HURST C.,GREAT BRITAIN AND THE DOMINIONS. EUR+WWI CULTURE ECO/DEV INT/ORG NAT/G DIPLOM ECO/TAC COLONIAL ATTIT PWR SOVEREIGN...TIME/SEQ GEN/LAWS TOT/POP VAL/FREE 20 CMN/WLTH. PAGE 75 H1508
VOL/ASSN DOMIN UK

B29
CAM H.M.,BIBLIOGRAPHY OF ENGLISH CONSTITUTIONAL HISTORY (PAMPHLET). UK LAW LOC/G NAT/G POL/PAR SECT DELIB/GP ADJUD ORD/FREE 19/20 PARLIAMENT. PAGE 25 H0510
BIBLIOG/A CONSTN ADMIN PARL/PROC

B29
LANGER W.L.,THE FRANCO-RUSSIAN ALLIANCE: 1890-1894. FRANCE MOD/EUR UK USSR NAT/G CHIEF FORCES BAL/PWR AGREE WAR PEACE PWR...TIME/SEQ TREATY 19 BISMARCK/O. PAGE 91 H1809
DIPLOM

B29
LEITZ F.,DIE PUBLIZITAT DER AKTIENGESELLSCHAFT. BELGIUM FRANCE GERMANY UK FINAN PRESS GP/REL PROFIT KNOWL 20. PAGE 94 H1872
LG/CO JURID ECO/TAC NAT/COMP

B30
BENTHAM J.,THE RATIONALE OF PUNISHMENT. UK LAW LOC/G NAT/G LEGIS CONTROL...JURID GEN/LAWS COURT/SYS 19. PAGE 14 H0289
CRIME SANCTION COERCE ORD/FREE

B30
CANAWAY A.P.,THE FAILURE OF FEDERALISM IN AUSTRALIA. UK PROB/SOLV ADMIN EFFICIENCY ATTIT ...POLICY NAT/COMP 20 AUSTRAL. PAGE 26 H0518
FEDERAL NAT/G CONSTN OP/RES

B30
HULL W.I.,INDIA'S POLITICAL CRISIS. INDIA UK INT/ORG LABOR SECT DELIB/GP LEGIS DIPLOM NEUTRAL REGION CROWD GOV/REL MAJORITY ATTIT 20 NEHRU/J GANDHI/M COMMONWLTH. PAGE 75 H1492
ORD/FREE NAT/G COLONIAL NAT/LISM

B31
CROOK W.H.,THE GENERAL STRIKE: A STUDY OF LABOR'S TRAGIC WEAPON IN THEORY AND PRACTICE. BELGIUM FRANCE SWEDEN UK WOR-45 PROB/SOLV ECO/TAC DOMIN PWR ...POLICY TIME/SEQ NAT/COMP GEN/LAWS 19/20 STRIKE. PAGE 35 H0707
LABOR WORKER LG/CO BARGAIN

B31
KIRKPATRICK F.A.,A HISTORY OF THE ARGENTINE REPUBLIC. SPAIN UK CONSTN SOCIETY ECO/UNDEV EX/STRUC DIPLOM FOR/AID LEAD WAR ATTIT...BIOG CHARTS 16/20 ARGEN SAN/MARTIN. PAGE 86 H1724
NAT/G L/A+17C COLONIAL

B32
CARDINALL AW,A BIBLIOGRAPHY OF THE GOLD COAST. AFR UK NAT/G EX/STRUC ATTIT...POLICY 19/20. PAGE 26 H0527
BIBLIOG ADMIN COLONIAL DIPLOM

B32
GREAT BRIT COMM MINISTERS PWR,REPORT. UK LAW CONSTN CONSULT LEGIS PARL/PROC SANCTION SOVEREIGN ...DECISION JURID 20 PARLIAMENT. PAGE 60 H1201
EX/STRUC NAT/G PWR CONTROL

B32
LUNT D.C.,THE ROAD TO THE LAW. UK USA-45 LEGIS EDU/PROP OWN ORD/FREE...DECISION TIME/SEQ NAT/COMP 16/20 AUSTRAL ENGLSH/LAW COMMON/LAW. PAGE 99 H1980
ADJUD LAW JURID CT/SYS

B32
MCKISACK M.,THE PARLIAMENTARY REPRESENTATION OF THE ENGLISH BOROUGHS DURING THE MIDDLE AGES. UK CONSTN CULTURE ELITES EX/STRUC TAX PAY ADJUD PARL/PROC APPORT FEDERAL...POLICY 13/15 PARLIAMENT. PAGE 107 H2139
NAT/G MUNIC LEGIS CHOOSE

S32
BEARD C.A.,"THE TEUTONIC ORIGINS OF REPRESENTATIVE GOVERNMENT" UK ROMAN/EMP TAX COERCE PWR IDEA/COMP. PAGE 12 H0247
REPRESENT NAT/G

B33
ENSOR R.C.K.,COURTS AND JUDGES IN FRANCE, GERMANY, AND ENGLAND. FRANCE GERMANY UK LAW PROB/SOLV ADMIN ROUTINE CRIME ROLE...METH/COMP 20 CIVIL/LAW. PAGE 46 H0930
CT/SYS EX/STRUC ADJUD NAT/COMP

B33
MOSS W.,POLITICAL PARTIES IN THE IRISH FREE STATE. IRELAND UK LAW FINAN LABOR DELIB/GP TOP/EX TARIFFS EDU/PROP...CHARTS GP/COMP 20. PAGE 113 H2269
POL/PAR NAT/G CHOOSE POLICY

B34
LOVELL R.I.,THE STRUGGLE FOR SOUTH AFRICA, 1875-1899. GERMANY RHODESIA SOUTH/AFR UK NAT/G ECO/TAC HABITAT WEALTH...POLICY 19. PAGE 99 H1971
COLONIAL DIPLOM WAR GP/REL

L34
GOSNELL H.F.,"BRITISH ROYAL COMMISSIONS OF INQUIRY" UK CONSTN LEGIS PRESS ADMIN PARL/PROC...DECISION 20 PARLIAMENT. PAGE 59 H1184
DELIB/GP INSPECT POLICY NAT/G

B35
MARRIOTT J.A.,DICTATORSHIP AND DEMOCRACY. GERMANY GREECE UK CHIEF DIPLOM DOMIN LEGIT PEACE ORD/FREE CONSERVE...TREND ROME HITLER/A. PAGE 103 H2057
TOTALISM POPULISM PLURIST NAT/G

B35
RAM J.,THE SCIENCE OF LEGAL JUDGMENT: A TREATISE... UK CONSTN NAT/G LEGIS CREATE PROB/SOLV AGREE CT/SYS ...INT/LAW CONCPT 19 ENGLSH/LAW CANON/LAW CIVIL/LAW CTS/WESTM. PAGE 129 H2584
LAW JURID EX/STRUC ADJUD

B36
BELLOC H.,THE RESTORATION OF PROPERTY. UK STRATA NAT/G PROF/ORG DELIB/GP WORKER CREATE PROB/SOLV ECO/TAC PARTIC UTOPIA ORD/FREE SOCISM 20. PAGE 13 H0270
CONTROL MAJORIT CAP/ISM OWN

B36
BOYCE A.N.,EUROPE AND SOUTH AFRICA. FRANCE GERMANY ITALY SOUTH/AFR UK INDUS NAT/G CONTROL REV WAR NAT/LISM...CONCPT HIST/WRIT 20. PAGE 20 H0392
COLONIAL GOV/COMP NAT/COMP DIPLOM

B36
CLARKE M.V.,MEDIEVAL REPRESENTATION AND CONSENT. IRELAND UK REPRESENT SUFF. PAGE 30 H0603
PARL/PROC LEGIS NAT/G

B36
CLOKIE H.M.,THE ORIGIN AND NATURE OF CONSTITUTIONAL GOVERNMENT. UK NAT/G POL/PAR CONSULT LEGIS ...GOV/COMP 14/20 CABINET PARLIAMENT. PAGE 30 H0606
CONCPT CONSTN PARL/PROC

B36
LAPRADE W.T.,PUBLIC OPINION AND POLITICS IN EIGHTEENTH CENTURY ENGLAND. UK CULTURE POL/PAR CHIEF TOP/EX LEAD REV NAT/LISM PWR 18 PROTESTANT PROTESTANT CHURCH/STA. PAGE 91 H1815
POLICY ELITES ATTIT TIME/SEQ

B36
WANDERSCHECK H.,WELTKRIEG UND PROPAGANDA. GERMANY MOD/EUR UK COM/IND NAT/G DOMIN PRESS ATTIT...POLICY 20 HITLER/A. PAGE 165 H3299
EDU/PROP PSY WAR KNOWL

B37
CLOKIE H.M.,ROYAL COMMISSIONS OF INQUIRY; THE SIGNIFICANCE OF INVESTIGATIONS IN BRITISH POLITICS. UK POL/PAR CONFER ROUTINE...POLICY DECISION TIME/SEQ 16/20. PAGE 30 H0607
NAT/G DELIB/GP INSPECT

B37
DE KIEWIET C.W.,THE IMPERIAL FACTOR IN SOUTH AFRICA. AFR SOUTH/AFR UK WAR...POLICY SOC 19. PAGE 38 H0759
DIPLOM COLONIAL CULTURE

L37
NICOLSON H.,"THE MEANING OF PRESTIGE." EUR+WWI MOD/EUR UK CULTURE SOCIETY NAT/G DIPLOM DOMIN LEGIT ATTIT DRIVE PWR...METH/CNCPT RECORD TIME/SEQ GEN/METH CMN/WLTH TOT/POP 20. PAGE 118 H2351
CONCPT STERTYP

B38
DAVIES E.,"NATIONAL" CAPITALISM: THE GOVERNMENT'S RECORD AS PROTECTOR OF PRIVATE MONOPOLY. UK ELITES SOCIETY STRATA POL/PAR WORKER PROB/SOLV CONTROL SOCISM 20 MONOPOLY LABOR/PAR CHAMBRLN/N. PAGE 37 H0747
CAP/ISM NAT/G INDUS POLICY

B38
DUNHAM W.H. JR.,COMPLAINT AND REFORM IN ENGLAND 1436-1714. UK LAW ACADEM NAT/G POL/PAR SCHOOL PRESS COLONIAL PARL/PROC MORAL...SOC/WK ANTHOL 15/18 HAKLUYT/R COWPER/W. PAGE 43 H0865
ATTIT SOCIETY SECT

B38
HOLDSWORTH W.S.,A HISTORY OF ENGLISH LAW; THE CENTURIES OF SETTLEMENT AND REFORM (VOL. X). INDIA UK CONSTN NAT/G CHIEF LEGIS ADMIN COLONIAL CT/SYS CHOOSE ORD/FREE PWR...JURID 18 PARLIAMENT COMMONWLTH COMMON/LAW. PAGE 72 H1451
LAW LOC/G EX/STRUC ADJUD

B38
HOLDSWORTH W.S.,A HISTORY OF ENGLISH LAW; THE CENTURIES OF SETTLEMENT AND REFORM (VOL. XI). UK CONSTN NAT/G EX/STRUC DIPLOM ADJUD CT/SYS LEAD CRIME ATTIT...INT/LAW JURID 18 CMN/WLTH PARLIAMENT ENGLSH/LAW. PAGE 73 H1452
LAW COLONIAL LEGIS PARL/PROC

B38
JESSOP T.E.,A BIBLIOGRAPHY OF DAVID HUME AND OF SCOTTISH PHILOSOPHY FROM FRANCIS HUTCHESON TO LORD BALFOUR. UK INTELL NAT/G ATTIT...CONCPT 17/20 HUME/D CMN/WLTH. PAGE 81 H1615
BIBLIOG EPIST PERCEPT BIOG

B38
MCNAIR A.D.,THE LAW OF TREATIES: BRITISH PRACTICE AND OPINIONS. UK CREATE DIPLOM LEGIT WRITING ADJUD WAR...INT/LAW JURID TREATY. PAGE 107 H2144
AGREE LAW CT/SYS NAT/G

S38
HALL R.C.,"REPRESENTATION OF BIG BUSINESS IN THE HOUSE OF COMMONS." UK ECO/DEV INDUS PROF/ORG LEGIS CAP/ISM ECO/TAC LAISSEZ...POLICY OLD/LIB PLURIST MGT 20 HOUSE/CMNS. PAGE 64 H1287
LOBBY NAT/G

B39
ANDERSON P.R.,THE BACKGROUND OF ANTI-ENGLISH FEELING IN GERMANY, 1890-1902. GERMANY MOD/EUR UK NAT/G POL/PAR TOP/EX WAR...IDEA/COMP 19/20. PAGE 7 H0132
DIPLOM EDU/PROP ATTIT COLONIAL

B39
ANDERSON W.,LOCAL GOVERNMENT IN EUROPE. FRANCE GERMANY ITALY UK USSR MUNIC PROVS ADMIN GOV/REL CENTRAL SOVEREIGN 20. PAGE 7 H0136
GOV/COMP NAT/COMP LOC/G CONSTN

B39
BENES E.,INTERNATIONAL SECURITY. GERMANY UK NAT/G DELIB/GP PLAN BAL/PWR ATTIT ORD/FREE PWR LEAGUE/NAT 20 TREATY. PAGE 14 H0280
EUR+WWI INT/ORG WAR

B39
JENNINGS W.I.,PARLIAMENT. UK POL/PAR OP/RES BUDGET LEAD CHOOSE GP/REL...MGT 20 PARLIAMENT HOUSE/LORD HOUSE/CMNS. PAGE 80 H1609
PARL/PROC LEGIS CONSTN NAT/G

B39
MCILWAIN C.H.,CONSTITUTIONALISM AND THE CHANGING WORLD. UK USA-45 LEGIS PRIVIL AUTHORIT SOVEREIGN ...GOV/COMP 15/20 MAGNA/CART HOUSE/CMNS. PAGE 107 H2133
CONSTN POLICY JURID

B39
NICOLSON H.,CURZON: THE LAST PHASE, 1919-1925. UK NAT/G DELIB/GP TOP/EX ROUTINE WAR RIGID/FLEX ...METH/CNCPT 20 CURZON/GN. PAGE 118 H2352
POLICY DIPLOM BIOG

S39
AIKEN C.,"THE BRITISH BUREAUCRACY AND THE ORIGINS OF PARLIAMENTARY DEMOCRACY" UK TOP/EX ADMIN. PAGE 4 H0082
MGT NAT/G LEGIS

C39
BURKE E.,"ON THE REFORM OF THE REPRESENTATION IN THE HOUSE OF COMMONS" (1782) IN COLLECTED WORKS (VOL. 5)" UK ELITES STRATA NAT/G REPRESENT ORD/FREE PWR POPULISM...POLICY NEW/IDEA GEN/LAWS 18 BURKE/EDM. PAGE 24 H0486
TRADIT CONSTN PARL/PROC LEGIS

B40
BROGAN D.W.,THE DEVELOPMENT OF MODERN FRANCE (1870-1939). FRANCE GERMANY UK USSR CONSTN CHIEF LEGIS DIPLOM AGREE COLONIAL WAR NAT/LISM PEACE SOCISM 19/20 TREATY. PAGE 21 H0428
MOD/EUR NAT/G

B40
HOBBES T.,BEHEMOTH (1668). UK CONSTN SECT DOMIN LEGIT UTIL ORD/FREE CATHISM...POLICY CONCPT GEN/LAWS 17 CHARLES/I CROMWELL/O PROTESTANT. PAGE 71 H1433
REV NAT/G CHIEF

B40
JORDAN W.K.,THE DEVELOPMENT OF RELIGIOUS TOLERATION IN ENGLAND. CHRIST-17C CULTURE SOCIETY LEGIT ATTIT RESPECT...POLICY CONCPT RECORD TIME/SEQ STERTYP GEN/LAWS TOT/POP 16/17. PAGE 82 H1635
SECT UK

B40
MCHENRY D.E.,HIS MAJESTY'S OPPOSITION: STRUCTURE AND PROBLEMS OF THE BRITISH LABOUR PARTY 1931-1938. UK FINAN LABOR LOC/G DELIB/GP LEGIS EDU/PROP LEAD PARTIC CHOOSE GP/REL SOCISM...TREND 20 LABOR/PAR. PAGE 107 H2130
POL/PAR MGT NAT/G POLICY

B40
WANDERSCHECK H.,FRANKREICHS PROPAGANDA GEGEN DEUTSCHLAND. FRANCE GERMANY MOD/EUR UK NAT/G DIPLOM WAR 20 JEWS. PAGE 165 H3300
EDU/PROP ATTIT DOMIN PRESS

B40
WOLFERS A.,BRITAIN AND FRANCE BETWEEN TWO WORLD WARS. FRANCE UK INT/ORG NAT/G PLAN BARGAIN ECO/TAC AGREE ISOLAT ALL/IDEOS...DECISION GEOG 20 TREATY VERSAILLES INTERVENT. PAGE 170 H3402
DIPLOM WAR POLICY

B40
ZWEIG F.,THE WORKER IN AN AFFLUENT SOCIETY: FAMILY LIFE AND INDUSTRY. UK STRATA LG/CO ECO/TAC LEISURE INGP/REL HAPPINESS HEALTH...PSY SOC/WK INT CHARTS WORSHIP 20 FEMALE/SEX. PAGE 173 H3465
MARRIAGE ATTIT FINAN CULTURE

B41
BAUMANN G.,GRUNDLAGEN UND PRAXIS DER INTERNATIONALEN PROPAGANDA. FRANCE GERMANY UK CULTURE COM/IND PRESS PWR...PSY METH/COMP 20. PAGE 12 H0241
EDU/PROP DOMIN ATTIT DIPLOM

B41
COHEN E.W.,THE GROWTH OF THE BRITISH CIVIL SERVICE 1780-1939. UK NAT/G SENIOR ROUTINE GOV/REL...MGT METH/COMP BIBLIOG 18/20. PAGE 31 H0616
OP/RES TIME/SEQ CENTRAL ADMIN

B42
CRAIG A.,ABOVE ALL LIBERTIES. FRANCE UK USA-45 LAW CONSTN CULTURE INTELL NAT/G SECT JUDGE...IDEA/COMP BIBLIOG 18/20. PAGE 35 H0692
ORD/FREE MORAL WRITING EDU/PROP

B42
FORTESCU J.,IN PRAISE OF ENGLISH LAW (1464) (TRANS. BY S.B. CHRIMES). UK ELITES CHIEF FORCES CT/SYS COERCE CRIME GOV/REL ILLEGIT...JURID GOV/COMP GEN/LAWS 15. PAGE 52 H1040
LAW CONSTN LEGIS ORD/FREE

B42
JOSHI P.S.,THE TYRANNY OF COLOUR. INDIA SOUTH/AFR UK ECO/UNDEV NAT/G POL/PAR DIPLOM ECO/TAC WAR ...POLICY 19/20. PAGE 82 H1637
COLONIAL DISCRIM RACE/REL

C42
CRAIG A.,"ABOVE ALL LIBERTIES." FRANCE UK LAW CULTURE INTELL SECT ORD/FREE 18/20. PAGE 35 H0693
BIBLIOG/A EDU/PROP WRITING MORAL

B43
BROWN A.D.,BRITISH POSSESSIONS IN THE CARIBBEAN AREA: A SELECTED LIST OF REFERENCES. UK NAT/G DIPLOM...GEOG 20 CARIBBEAN. PAGE 22 H0437
BIBLIOG COLONIAL ECO/UNDEV L/A+17C

C43
BENTHAM J.,"ON THE LIBERTY OF THE PRESS, AND PUBLIC DISCUSSION" IN J. BOWRING, ED., THE WORKS OF JEREMY BENTHAM." SPAIN UK LAW ELITES NAT/G LEGIS INSPECT
ORD/FREE PRESS CONFER

LEGIT WRITING CONTROL PRIVIL TOTALISM AUTHORIT ...TRADIT 19 FREE/SPEE. PAGE 15 H0290 — CONSERVE

B44
BARKER E.,THE DEVELOPMENT OF PUBLIC SERVICES IN WESTERN WUROPE: 1660-1930. FRANCE GERMANY UK SCHOOL CONTROL REPRESENT ROLE...WELF/ST 17/20. PAGE 11 H0219 — GOV/COMP ADMIN EX/STRUC

B44
SUAREZ F.,A TREATISE ON LAWS AND GOD THE LAWGIVER (1612) IN SELECTIONS FROM THREE WORKS, VOL. II. FRANCE ITALY UK CULTURE NAT/G SECT CHIEF LEGIS DOMIN LEGIT CT/SYS ORD/FREE PWR WORSHIP 16/17. PAGE 150 H3004 — LAW JURID GEN/LAWS CATH

B44
WOLFE D.M.,LEVELLER MANIFESTOES OF THE PURITAN REVOLUTION. UK CONSTN NAT/G SECT...CONCPT ANTHOL 17 LEVELLERS DECLAR/IND PURITAN LOCKE/JOHN. PAGE 170 H3400 — POL/PAR REV ORD/FREE ATTIT

B45
CONOVER H.F.,THE GOVERNMENTS OF THE MAJOR FOREIGN POWERS: A BIBLIOGRAPHY. FRANCE GERMANY ITALY UK USSR CONSTN LOC/G POL/PAR EX/STRUC FORCES ADMIN CT/SYS CIVMIL/REL TOTALISM...POLICY 19/20. PAGE 32 H0645 — BIBLIOG NAT/G DIPLOM

B45
HORN O.B.,BRITISH PUBLIC OPINION AND THE FIRST PARTITION OF POLAND. POLAND UK LEGIS PRESS RUMOR CONTROL PARTIC NAT/LISM SOVEREIGN 18/19. PAGE 73 H1469 — DIPLOM POLICY ATTIT NAT/G

B46
ALLEN J.S.,WORLD MONOPOLY AND PEACE. GERMANY UK USSR FINAN INDUS LG/CO DOMIN CONTROL PEACE PWR WEALTH SOCISM...NAT/COMP 20 MONOPOLY. PAGE 5 H0105 — CAP/ISM DIPLOM WAR COLONIAL

B46
DAVIES E.,NATIONAL ENTERPRISE: THE DEVELOPMENT OF THE PUBLIC CORPORATION. UK LG/CO EX/STRUC WORKER PROB/SOLV COST ATTIT SOCISM 20. PAGE 37 H0748 — ADMIN NAT/G CONTROL INDUS

B47
CROCKER W.R.,ON GOVERNING COLONIES: BEING AN OUTLINE OF THE REAL ISSUES AND A COMPARISON OF THE BRITISH, FRENCH, AND BELGIAN... AFR BELGIUM FRANCE UK CULTURE SOVEREIGN...OBS 20. PAGE 35 H0705 — COLONIAL POLICY GOV/COMP ADMIN

B47
ENKE S.,INTERNATIONAL ECONOMICS. UK USA+45 USSR INT/ORG BAL/PWR BARGAIN CAP/ISM BAL/PAY...NAT/COMP 20 TREATY. PAGE 46 H0927 — INT/TRADE FINAN TARIFFS ECO/TAC

B47
LOCKE J.,TWO TREATISES OF GOVERNMENT (1690). UK LAW SOCIETY LEGIS LEGIT AGREE REV OWN HEREDITY MORAL CONSERVE...POLICY MAJORIT 17 WILLIAM/3 NATURL/LAW. PAGE 97 H1946 — CONCPT ORD/FREE NAT/G CONSEN

B48
PELCOVITS N.A.,OLD CHINA HANDS AND THE FOREIGN OFFICE. ASIA BURMA UK ECO/UNDEV NAT/G ECO/TAC FOR/AID TARIFFS DOMIN COLONIAL GOV/REL SOVEREIGN 19 HONG/KONG TREATY. PAGE 124 H2483 — INT/TRADE ATTIT DIPLOM

B48
ROSSITER C.L.,CONSTITUTIONAL DICTATORSHIP; CRISIS GOVERNMENT IN THE MODERN DEMOCRACIES. FRANCE GERMANY UK USA-45 WOR-45 EX/STRUC BAL/PWR CONTROL COERCE WAR CENTRAL ORD/FREE...DECISION 19/20. PAGE 134 H2688 — NAT/G AUTHORIT CONSTN TOTALISM

B48
TURNER A.C.,FREE SPEECH AND BROADCASTING. UK USA+45 ORD/FREE NAT/COMP. PAGE 157 H3140 — COM/IND NAT/G CONTROL METH/COMP

B49
DENNING A.,FREEDOM UNDER THE LAW. MOD/EUR UK LAW SOCIETY CHIEF EX/STRUC LEGIS ADJUD CT/SYS PERS/REL PERSON 17/20 ENGLSH/LAW. PAGE 40 H0793 — ORD/FREE JURID NAT/G

B49
HEADLAM-MORLEY,BIBLIOGRAPHY IN POLITICS FOR THE HONOUR SCHOOL OF PHILOSOPHY, POLITICS AND ECONOMICS (PAMPHLET). UK CONSTN LABOR MUNIC DIPLOM ADMIN 19/20. PAGE 69 H1375 — BIBLIOG NAT/G PHIL/SCI GOV/REL

B49
HINDEN R.,EMPIRE AND AFTER. UK POL/PAR BAL/PWR DIPLOM INT/TRADE WAR NAT/LISM PWR 17/20. PAGE 71 H1420 — NAT/G COLONIAL ATTIT POLICY

B49
MCLEAN J.M.,THE PUBLIC SERVICE AND UNIVERSITY EDUCATION. UK USA-45 DELIB/GP EX/STRUC TOP/EX ADMIN ...GOV/COMP METH/COMP NAT/COMP ANTHOL 20. PAGE 107 H2142 — ACADEM NAT/G EXEC EDU/PROP

B49
SCHWARTZ B.,LAW AND THE EXECUTIVE IN BRITAIN: A COMPARATIVE STUDY. UK USA+45 LAW EX/STRUC PWR ...GOV/COMP 20. PAGE 140 H2807 — ADMIN EXEC CONTROL REPRESENT

B49
WORMUTH F.D.,THE ORIGINS OF MODERN CONSTITUTIONALISM. GREECE UK LEGIS CREATE TEC/DEV BAL/PWR DOMIN ADJUD REV WAR PWR...JURID ROMAN/REP CROMWELL/O. PAGE 170 H3412 — NAT/G CONSTN LAW

S49
HUGHES E.C.,"SOCIAL CHANGE AND STATUS PROTEST: AN ESSAY ON THE MARGINAL MAN" (BMR)" EUR+WWI UK USA+45 CULTURE SOCIETY STRUCT RACE/REL...SOC NAT/COMP SOC/INTEG 19/20 NEGRO PARK/R. PAGE 74 H1490 — STRATA ATTIT DISCRIM

C49
SCHAPIRO J.S.,"LIBERALISM AND THE CHALLENGE OF FASCISM." FRANCE UK STRATA PERSON...CONCPT BIOG IDEA/COMP BIBLIOG 18/20. PAGE 139 H2771 — FASCISM LAISSEZ ATTIT

B50
COUNCIL BRITISH NATIONAL BIB,BRITISH NATIONAL BIBLIOGRAPHY. UK AGRI CONSTRUC PERF/ART POL/PAR SECT CREATE INT/TRADE LEAD...HUM JURID PHIL/SCI 20. PAGE 34 H0677 — BIBLIOG/A NAT/G TEC/DEV DIPLOM

B50
GLEASON J.H.,THE GENESIS OF RUSSOPHOBIA IN GREAT BRITAIN: A STUDY OF THE INTERACTION OF POLICY AND OPINION. ASIA RUSSIA UK NAT/G AGREE CONTROL REV WAR LOVE PWR TREATY 19. PAGE 57 H1142 — DIPLOM POLICY DOMIN COLONIAL

B50
HOOKER R.,OF THE LAWS OF ECCLESIASTICAL POLITY (1594) (ABR. BY J. S. MARSHALL). UK UNIV CHIEF PARTIC MORAL...JURID GEN/LAWS WORSHIP 16. PAGE 73 H1463 — SECT CONCPT LAW NAT/G

B50
WADE E.C.S.,CONSTITUTIONAL LAW; AN OUTLINE OF THE LAW AND PRACTICE OF THE CONSTITUTION. UK LEGIS DOMIN ADMIN GP/REL 16/20 CMN/WLTH PARLIAMENT ENGLSH/LAW. PAGE 164 H3283 — CONSTN NAT/G PARL/PROC LAW

B50
WHITE R.J.,THE CONSERVATIVE TRADITION. UK POL/PAR SUPEGO PWR RESPECT...POLICY ANTHOL 19. PAGE 167 H3350 — CONSERVE CONCPT NAT/G ORD/FREE

B51
HALEVY E.,IMPERIALISM AND THE RISE OF LABOR (2ND ED.). UK NAT/G POL/PAR TOP/EX ATTIT ORD/FREE PWR 19/20 PARLIAMENT LABOR/PAR. PAGE 64 H1284 — COLONIAL LABOR POLICY WAR

B51
JENNINGS S.I.,THE COMMONWEALTH IN ASIA. CEYLON INDIA PAKISTAN S/ASIA UK CONSTN CULTURE SOCIETY STRATA STRUCT NAT/G POL/PAR EDU/PROP LEAD WAR 20 CMN/WLTH. PAGE 80 H1608 — NAT/LISM REGION COLONIAL DIPLOM

B51
WEBSTER C.,THE FOREIGN POLICY OF PALMERSTON - 1830 TO 1841. MOD/EUR UK LAW CONSTN INTELL SOCIETY STRUCT NAT/G FORCES TOP/EX CREATE BAL/PWR PWR 19. PAGE 166 H3323 — ADMIN PERSON DIPLOM

B52
BAILEY S.D.,THE BRITISH PARTY SYSTEM. UK LEGIS ...POLICY GP/COMP ANTHOL 11/20. PAGE 10 H0200 — POL/PAR LOC/G NAT/G DELIB/GP

B52
ROBBINS L.,THE THEORY OF ECONOMIC POLICY IN ENGLISH CLASSICAL POLITICAL ECONOMY. UK ECO/DEV WORKER PLAN CAP/ISM EDU/PROP CONTROL INCOME OWN HEALTH SOCISM ...POLICY 17/19. PAGE 132 H2639 — ECO/TAC ORD/FREE IDEA/COMP NAT/G

B52
US LIBRARY OF CONGRESS,EGYPT AND THE ANGLO-EGYPTIAN SUDAN: A SELECTIVE GUIDE TO BACKGROUND READING (PAMPHLET). SUDAN UAR UK DIPLOM...POLICY 20. PAGE 160 H3209 — BIBLIOG/A COLONIAL ISLAM NAT/G

S52
SABINE G.H.,"THE TWO DEMOCRATIC TRADITIONS" (BMR)" FRANCE UK USA-45 NAT/G CONTROL CHOOSE ALL/IDEOS ...PHIL/SCI CONCPT IDEA/COMP 20. PAGE 136 H2727 — ORD/FREE POPULISM INGP/REL NAT/COMP

C52
HUME D.,"OF TAXES" IN D. HUME, POLITICAL DISCOURSES (1752)" UK NAT/G COST INCOME LAISSEZ...GEN/LAWS 18. PAGE 75 H1493 — TAX FINAN WEALTH POLICY

C52
HUME D.,"IDEA OF A PERFECT COMMONWEALTH" IN D. HUME, POLITICAL DISCOURSES (1752)" UK NAT/G DOMIN GP/REL CONSERVE...POLICY CONCPT GEN/LAWS 18 MORE/THOM PLATO. PAGE 75 H1494 — CONSTN CHIEF SOCIETY GOV/COMP

C52
LEWIS B.W.,"BRITISH PLANNING AND NATIONALIZATION." UK INDUS SERV/IND LABOR NAT/G OP/RES TEC/DEV TAX WEALTH...CHARTS BIBLIOG 20. PAGE 96 H1912 — NEW/LIB ECO/DEV POL/PAR PLAN

B53
DAVIDSON B.,THE NEW WEST AFRICA: PROBLEMS OF INDEPENDENCE. UK AGRI TEC/DEV DIPLOM GP/REL RACE/REL SOVEREIGN...ANTHOL 20 AFRICA/W. PAGE 37 H0744 — AFR COLONIAL ECO/UNDEV NAT/G

B53
FLORENCE P.S.,THE LOGIC OF BRITISH AND AMERICAN INDUSTRY; A REALISTIC ANALYSIS OF ECONOMIC STRUCTURE AND GOVERNMENT. UK USA+45 USA-45 FINAN — INDUS ECO/DEV NAT/G

LABOR CAP/ISM INGP/REL EFFICIENCY...MGT CONCPT STAT CHARTS METH 20. PAGE 51 H1028
NAT/COMP

B53
SQUIRES J.D.,BRITISH PROPAGANDA AT HOME AND IN THE UNITED STATES FROM 1914 TO 1917. UK NAT/G PROB/SOLV DOMIN PRESS EFFICIENCY...PSY PREDICT 20 WWI INTERVENT PSY/WAR. PAGE 148 H2960
EDU/PROP CONTROL WAR DIPLOM

B53
STOUT H.M.,BRITISH GOVERNMENT. UK FINAN LOC/G POL/PAR DELIB/GP DIPLOM ADMIN COLONIAL CHOOSE ORD/FREE...JURID BIBLIOG 20 COMMONWLTH. PAGE 150 H2990
NAT/G PARL/PROC CONSTN NEW/LIB

C53
BULNER-THOMAS I.,"THE PARTY SYSTEM IN GREAT BRITAIN." UK CONSTN SECT PRESS CONFER GP/REL ATTIT ...POLICY TREND BIBLIOG 19/20 PARLIAMENT. PAGE 23 H0473
NAT/G POL/PAR ADMIN ROUTINE

N53
VITO F.,"RECENT DEVELOPMENTS IN THE THEORY OF DEMOCRATIC ADMIN" INTL POL SCI ASS'N CONFERENCE ON PUBLIC ADMINISTRATION... FRANCE ITALY UK REPRESENT EFFICIENCY NEW/LIB SOCISM...WELF/ST 20. PAGE 163 H3257
GOV/COMP CONTROL EX/STRUC

B54
EPSTEIN L.D.,BRITAIN - UNEASY ALLY. KOREA UK USA+45 NAT/G POL/PAR ECO/TAC FOR/AID INT/TRADE WAR LABOR/PAR CONSRV/PAR. PAGE 47 H0934
DIPLOM ATTIT POLICY NAT/COMP

B54
GRAYSON H.,ECONOMIC PLANNING UNDER FREE ENTERPRISE. CANADA FUT UK DELIB/GP BUDGET CONFER CONTROL ...POLICY DECISION 20. PAGE 60 H1200
PLAN ECO/TAC NAT/COMP NAT/G

B54
HAMSON C.J.,EXECUTIVE DISCRETION AND JUDICIAL CONTROL; AN ASPECT OF THE FRENCH CONSEIL D'ETAT. EUR+WWI FRANCE MOD/EUR UK NAT/G EX/STRUC PARTIC CONSERVE...JURID BIBLIOG/A 18/20 SUPREME/CT. PAGE 65 H1310
ELITES ADJUD NAT/COMP

B54
JENNINGS I.,THE QUEEN'S GOVERNMENT. UK POL/PAR DELIB/GP ADJUD ADMIN CT/SYS PARL/PROC REPRESENT CONSERVE 13/20 PARLIAMENT. PAGE 80 H1605
NAT/G CONSTN LEGIS CHIEF

B54
MORRISON H.,GOVERNMENT AND PARLIAMENT. UK NAT/G PARLIAMENT. PAGE 113 H2266
GOV/REL EX/STRUC LEGIS PARL/PROC

C54
DE GRAZIA A.,"THE COMPARATIVE SURVEY OF EUROPEAN-AMERICAN POLITICAL BEHAV IOR; A RESEARCH PROSPECTUS (PAPER)" EUR+WWI FRANCE GERMANY SPAIN UK USA+45 WOR+45 STRATA POL/PAR DIPLOM EDU/PROP COLONIAL LEAD WAR NAT/LISM CONCPT. PAGE 37 H0752
BIBLIOG R+D METH NAT/COMP

B55
COLE G.D.H.,STUDIES IN CLASS STRUCTURE. UK NAT/G WORKER TEC/DEV EDU/PROP...CLASSIF CHARTS 20. PAGE 31 H0623
STRUCT STRATA ELITES CONCPT

B55
FOGARTY M.P.,ECONOMIC CONTROL. FUT UK ECO/DEV FINAN CONSULT INT/TRADE...CHARTS BIBLIOG/A 20. PAGE 52 H1033
ECO/TAC NAT/G CONTROL PROB/SOLV

B55
NAMIER L.,PERSONALITIES AND POWERS. EUR+WWI MOD/EUR NAT/G POL/PAR TOP/EX EDU/PROP KNOWL...GEOG 17/20. PAGE 115 H2308
TIME/SEQ DIPLOM UK

B55
PYRAH G.B.,IMPERIAL POLICY AND SOUTH AFRICA 1902-1910. SOUTH/AFR UK NAT/G WAR DISCRIM...CONCPT CHARTS BIBLIOG/A 19/20 CMN/WLTH. PAGE 129 H2570
DIPLOM COLONIAL POLICY RACE/REL

B55
SHAFER B.C.,NATIONALISM: MYTH AND REALITY. FRANCE UK USA+45 USA-45 CULTURE SOCIETY STRUCT ECO/DEV WAR PWR...NAT/COMP BIBLIOG 18/20. PAGE 142 H2837
NAT/LISM MYTH NAT/G CONCPT

B55
SMITH G.,A CONSTITUTIONAL AND LEGAL HISTORY OF ENGLAND. UK ELITES NAT/G LEGIS ADJUD OWN HABITAT POPULISM...JURID 20 ENGLSH/LAW. PAGE 145 H2909
CONSTN PARTIC LAW CT/SYS

B55
TAN C.C.,THE BOXER CATASTROPHE. ASIA UK USSR ELITES POL/PAR VOL/ASSN FORCES PROB/SOLV DIPLOM ADMIN COLONIAL NAT/LISM PEACE TREATY 19/20 BOXER/REBL. PAGE 152 H3040
REV NAT/G WAR

B55
WHEARE K.C.,GOVERNMENT BY COMMITTEE; AN ESSAY ON THE BRITISH CONSTITUTION. UK NAT/G LEGIS INSPECT CONFER ADJUD ADMIN CONTROL TASK EFFICIENCY ROLE POPULISM 20. PAGE 167 H3337
DELIB/GP CONSTN LEAD GP/COMP

S55
DE SMITH S.A.,"CONSTITUTIONAL MONARCHY IN BURGANDA." AFR UGANDA UK STRUCT CHIEF REGION INGP/REL ADJUST NAT/LISM SOVEREIGN CONSERVE ...POLICY 19/20 BURGANDA. PAGE 38 H0769
NAT/G DIPLOM CONSTN COLONIAL

B56
BRITISH BORNEO RESEARCH PROJ,BIBLIOGRAPHY OF BRITISH BORNEO (PAMPHLET). UK COM/IND NAT/G EDU/PROP...GEOG 20. PAGE 21 H0421
BIBLIOG/A SOC

B56
CENTRAL AFRICAN ARCHIVES,A GUIDE TO THE PUBLIC RECORDS OF SOUTHERN RHODESIA UNDER THE REGIME OF THE BRITISH SOUTH AFRICA COMPANY, 1890-1923. UK STRUCT NAT/G WRITING GP/REL 19/20. PAGE 28 H0566
BIBLIOG/A COLONIAL ADMIN AFR

B56
EMDEN C.S.,THE PEOPLE AND THE CONSTITUTION (2ND ED.). UK LEGIS POPULISM 17/20 PARLIAMENT. PAGE 46 H0916
CONSTN PARL/PROC NAT/G LAW

B56
HATCH J.C.,NEW FROM AFRICA. AFR FUT UK NAT/G GUERRILLA ATTIT ORD/FREE PWR...AUD/VIS CHARTS 20. PAGE 68 H1354
NAT/LISM COLONIAL RACE/REL

B56
JENNINGS W.I.,THE APPROACH TO SELF-GOVERNMENT. CEYLON INDIA PAKISTAN S/ASIA UK SOCIETY POL/PAR DELIB/GP LEGIS ECO/TAC EDU/PROP ADMIN EXEC CHOOSE ATTIT ALL/VALS...JURID CONCPT GEN/METH TOT/POP 20. PAGE 81 H1610
NAT/G CONSTN COLONIAL

B56
WATT D.C.,BRITAIN AND THE SUEZ CANAL. COM UAR UK ...INT/LAW 20 SUEZ TREATY. PAGE 166 H3314
DIPLOM INT/TRADE DIST/IND NAT/G

L56
EPSTEIN L.D.,"BRITISH MASS PARTIES IN COMPARISON WITH AMERICAN PARTIES" UK USA+45 STRATA ECO/DEV LABOR...CON/ANAL 20. PAGE 47 H0936
POL/PAR NAT/COMP PARTIC CHOOSE

S56
EPSTEIN L.D.,"COHESION OF BRITISH PARLIAMENTARY PARTIES." UK STRUCT ADMIN ROUTINE INGP/REL PWR ...GP/COMP PARLIAMENT. PAGE 47 H0935
NAT/G PARL/PROC POL/PAR

C56
NEUMANN S.,"MODERN POLITICAL PARTIES: APPROACHES TO COMPARATIVE POLITIC. FRANCE UK EX/STRUC DOMIN ADMIN LEAD REPRESENT TOTALISM ATTIT...POLICY TREND METH/COMP ANTHOL BIBLIOG/A 20 CMN/WLTH. PAGE 117 H2338
POL/PAR GOV/COMP ELITES MAJORIT

B57
ARON R.,L'UNIFICATION ECONOMIQUE DE L'EUROPE. EUR+WWI SWITZERLND UK INT/ORG REGION NAT/LISM ORD/FREE PWR...CONCPT METH/CNCPT OBS TREND STERTYP GEN/LAWS EEC 20. PAGE 8 H0168
VOL/ASSN ECO/TAC

B57
BISHOP O.B.,PUBLICATIONS OF THE GOVERNMENTS OF NOVA SCOTIA, PRINCE EDWARD ISLAND, NEW BRUNSWICK 1758-1952. CANADA UK ADMIN COLONIAL LEAD...POLICY 18/20. PAGE 17 H0345
BIBLIOG NAT/G DIPLOM

B57
BULLOCK A.,THE LIBERAL TRADITION FROM FOX TO KEYNES. UK CULTURE INTELL CREATE WRITING COLONIAL PERS/REL ATTIT ORD/FREE...POLICY OLD/LIB TRADIT CONCPT 18/20 CHURCHLL/W MILL/JS KEYNES/JM ASQUITH/HH. PAGE 23 H0469
ANTHOL DEBATE LAISSEZ

B57
COLE G.D.H.,THE POST WAR CONDITIONS OF BRITAIN. EUR+WWI STRUCT NAT/G PLAN EDU/PROP LEGIT RIGID/FLEX ORD/FREE WEALTH...SOCIALIST WELF/ST STAT TREND CON/ANAL CHARTS PARLIAMENT WORK 20. PAGE 31 H0624
ECO/DEV UK

B57
KANTOROWICZ E.,THE KING'S TWO BODIES; A STUDY IN MEDIEVAL POLITICAL THEOLOGY. UK LAW CONSTN NAT/G CT/SYS...ART/METH HUM CONCPT MYTH TIME/SEQ BIBLIOG 4/17 ELIZABTH/I POPE CHURCH/STA. PAGE 83 H1657
JURID SECT CHIEF SOVEREIGN

B57
LOUCKS W.N.,COMPARATIVE ECONOMIC SYSTEMS (5TH ED.). COM UK USSR INDUS POL/PAR PLAN CAP/ISM TOTALISM MARXISM...PHIL/SCI BIBLIOG 19/20. PAGE 99 H1969
NAT/COMP IDEA/COMP SOCISM

B57
TOMASIC D.A.,NATIONAL COMMUNISM AND SOVIET STRATEGY. UK USSR YUGOSLAVIA NAT/G POL/PAR CHIEF CREATE DOMIN REV WAR PWR...BIOG TREND 20 TITO/MARSH STALIN/J. PAGE 156 H3112
COM NAT/LISM MARXISM DIPLOM

N57
JENNINGS W.I.,NATIONALISM, COLONIALISM, AND NEUTRALISM (PAMPHLET). ASIA INDIA S/ASIA UK INTELL ACADEM POL/PAR 20. PAGE 81 H1611
NAT/LISM COLONIAL NEUTRAL ATTIT

B58
BUISSON L.,POTESTAS UND CARITAS. FRANCE GERMANY UK ORD/FREE...JURID IDEA/COMP NAT/COMP 12/16 POPE CHURCH/STA. PAGE 23 H0467
GP/REL PWR CATHISM NAT/G

B58
COWAN L.G.,LOCAL GOVERNMENT IN WEST AFRICA. AFR FRANCE UK CULTURE KIN POL/PAR CHIEF LEGIS CREATE ADMIN PARTIC GOV/REL GP/REL...METH/COMP 20. PAGE 34
LOC/G COLONIAL SOVEREIGN

H0682 — REPRESENT

B58
CROWE S.,THE LANDSCAPE OF POWER. UK CULTURE SERV/IND NAT/G CONSULT PARTIC NUC/PWR LEISURE...SOC EXHIBIT 20. PAGE 36 H0712
HABITAT TEC/DEV PLAN CONTROL

B58
EUSDEN J.D.,PURITANS, LAWYERS, AND POLITICS IN EARLY SEVENTEENTH-CENTURY ENGLAND. UK CT/SYS PARL/PROC RATIONAL PWR SOVEREIGN...IDEA/COMP BIBLIOG 17 PURITAN COMMON/LAW. PAGE 48 H0951
GP/REL SECT NAT/G LAW

B58
OGILVIE C.,THE KING'S GOVERNMENT AND THE COMMON LAW, 1471-1641. UK STRUCT NAT/G CHIEF LEGIS WORKER BAL/PWR GP/REL AUTHORIT 15/17 COMMON/LAW. PAGE 120 H2408
CONSTN ELITES DOMIN

B58
SHARMA M.P.,PUBLIC ADMINISTRATION IN THEORY AND PRACTICE. INDIA UK USA+45 USA-45 EX/STRUC ADJUD ...POLICY CONCPT NAT/COMP 20. PAGE 142 H2847
MGT ADMIN DELIB/GP JURID

B58
SYME R.,COLONIAL ELITES: ROME, SPAIN, AND THE AMERICAS. CHRIST-17C MOD/EUR SPAIN UK USA-45 CULTURE NAT/G CHIEF TOP/EX...GOV/COMP IDEA/COMP NAT/COMP ROM/EMP GIBBON/EDW TOYNBEE/A. PAGE 151 H3022
COLONIAL ELITES DOMIN

B58
WIGGIN L.M.,THE FACTION OF COUSINS: A POLITICAL ACCOUNT OF THE GRENVILLES, 1733-1763. UK STRUCT KIN NAT/G INGP/REL...CONCPT BIOG BIBLIOG/A 18 GRENVILLES. PAGE 168 H3357
FAM POL/PAR PWR

S58
GUSFIELD J.R.,"EQUALITARIANISM AND BUREAUCRATIC RECRUITMENT." UK USA+45 USA-45 EX/STRUC 19/20. PAGE 63 H1257
GOV/COMP REPRESENT TOP/EX ELITES

C58
WILDING N.,"AN ENCYCLOPEDIA OF PARLIAMENT." UK LAW CONSTN CHIEF PROB/SOLV DIPLOM DEBATE WAR INGP/REL PRIVIL...BIBLIOG DICTIONARY 13/20 CMN/WLTH PARLIAMENT. PAGE 168 H3363
PARL/PROC POL/PAR NAT/G ADMIN

B59
BRIGGS A.,CHARTIST STUDIES. UK LAW NAT/G WORKER EDU/PROP COERCE SUFF GP/REL ATTIT...ANTHOL 19. PAGE 21 H0416
INDUS STRATA LABOR POLICY

B59
BROSE O.J.,CHURCH AND PARLIAMENT: THE RESHAPING OF THE CHURCH OF ENGLAND 1828-1860. UK SOCIETY TEC/DEV ATTIT LAISSEZ...BIBLIOG 19 CHURCH/STA. PAGE 22 H0434
SECT LEGIS GP/REL NAT/G

B59
DEHIO L.,GERMANY AND WORLD POLITICS IN THE TWENTIETH CENTURY. EUR+WWI FRANCE GERMANY MOD/EUR UK USSR NAT/G CHIEF BAL/PWR DOMIN COLONIAL CONTROL LEAD...IDEA/COMP 20 VERSAILLES. PAGE 39 H0783
DIPLOM WAR NAT/LISM SOVEREIGN

B59
GINSBURG M.,LAW AND OPINION IN ENGLAND. UK CULTURE KIN LABOR LEGIS EDU/PROP ADMIN CT/SYS CRIME OWN HEALTH...ANTHOL 20 ENGLSH/LAW. PAGE 56 H1132
JURID POLICY ECO/TAC

B59
JENKINS C.,POWER AT THE TOP: A CRITICAL SURVEY OF THE NATIONALIZED INDUSTRIES. UK POL/PAR CONTROL ...WELF/ST CHARTS 20 LABOR/PAR. PAGE 80 H1601
NAT/G OWN INDUS NEW/LIB

B59
JENNINGS W.I.,CABINET GOVERNMENT (3RD ED.). UK POL/PAR CHIEF BUDGET ADMIN CHOOSE GP/REL 20. PAGE 81 H1612
DELIB/GP NAT/G CONSTN OP/RES

B59
KELF-COHEN R.,NATIONALISATION IN BRITAIN: THE END OF DOGMA. EUR+WWI UK NAT/G POL/PAR WORKER ECO/TAC PARL/PROC WEALTH SOCISM...GOV/COMP 20. PAGE 84 H1683
NEW/LIB ECO/DEV INDUS OWN

B59
MAC MILLAN W.M.,THE ROAD TO SELF-RULE. SOUTH/AFR UK CULTURE SOCIETY AGRI LABOR NAT/G INT/TRADE CONTROL GP/REL...SOC 19/20. PAGE 100 H1988
AFR COLONIAL SOVEREIGN POLICY

B59
MADHOK B.,POLITICAL TRENDS IN INDIA. INDIA PAKISTAN UK STRATA ECO/UNDEV POL/PAR LEGIS CAP/ISM DIPLOM COLONIAL CHOOSE MARXISM...SOC TREND 20 GANDHI/M NEHRU/J. PAGE 101 H2014
GEOG NAT/G

B59
MATHER F.C.,PUBLIC ORDER IN THE AGE OF THE CHARTISTS. UK CULTURE ADJUD CONTROL. PAGE 105 H2090
ORD/FREE FORCES COERCE CIVMIL/REL

B59
PAULSEN M.G.,LEGAL INSTITUTIONS TODAY AND TOMORROW. UK USA+45 NAT/G PROF/ORG PROVS ADMIN PARL/PROC ORD/FREE NAT/COMP. PAGE 124 H2477
JURID ADJUD JUDGE LEGIS

B59
SISSON C.H.,THE SPIRIT OF BRITISH ADMINISTRATION AND SOME EUROPEAN COMPARISONS. FRANCE GERMANY/W SWEDEN UK LAW EX/STRUC INGP/REL EFFICIENCY ORD/FREE ...DECISION 20. PAGE 144 H2890
GOV/COMP ADMIN ELITES ATTIT

B59
SQUIBB G.D.,THE HIGH COURT OF CHIVALRY. UK NAT/G FORCES ADJUD WAR 14/20 PARLIAMENT ENGLSH/LAW. PAGE 148 H2959
CT/SYS PARL/PROC JURID

B59
SVALASTOGA K.,PRESTIGE, CLASS, AND MOBILITY. DENMARK UK EDU/PROP INCOME WEALTH...SOC SAMP 20. PAGE 151 H3010
NAT/COMP STRATA STRUCT ELITES

B59
VERNEY D.V.,PUBLIC ENTERPRISE IN SWEDEN. FUT SWEDEN UK INDUS POL/PAR LEGIS PROB/SOLV CAP/ISM INT/TRADE CONTROL SOCISM...MGT CONCPT NAT/COMP 20 SOCDEM/PAR CIVIL/SERV. PAGE 162 H3246
ECO/DEV POLICY LG/CO NAT/G

B59
VITTACHIT,EMERGENCY '58. CEYLON UK STRUCT NAT/G FORCES ADJUD CRIME REV NAT/LISM 20. PAGE 163 H3258
RACE/REL DISCRIM DIPLOM SOVEREIGN

B59
WRAITH R.E.,EAST AFRICAN CITIZEN. AFR GHANA UK AGRI INDUS LOC/G POL/PAR PROB/SOLV CONTROL REGION REPRESENT NAT/LISM PWR...OBS 20 AFRICA/E AFRICA/W. PAGE 171 H3415
ECO/UNDEV RACE/REL NAT/G NAT/COMP

S59
LEYS C.,"MODELS, THEORIES, AND THE THEORY OF POLITICAL PARTIES" CANADA LIECHTENST UK LOC/G NAT/G PARTIC REPRESENT GP/REL CONSEN EQUILIB MAJORITY ...NEW/IDEA MATH CHARTS 20. PAGE 96 H1919
POL/PAR CHOOSE METH/CNCPT SIMUL

S59
MENDELSON W.,"JUDICIAL REVIEW AND PARTY POLITICS" (BMR)" UK USA+45 USA-45 NAT/G LEGIS PROB/SOLV EDU/PROP ADJUD EFFICIENCY...POLICY NAT/COMP 19/20 AUSTRAL SUPREME/CT. PAGE 109 H2171
CT/SYS POL/PAR BAL/PWR JURID

S59
SILBERMAN L.,"CHANGE AND CONFLICT IN THE HORN OF AFRICA." EUR+WWI ITALY UK CULTURE FORCES ECO/TAC ADJUD COLONIAL ATTIT ORD/FREE PWR...DECISION METH/CNCPT HIST/WRIT SOMALI 20. PAGE 144 H2874
AFR TIME/SEQ

B60
ALBRECHT-CARRIE R.,FRANCE, EUROPE AND THE TWO WORLD WARS. EUR+WWI FRANCE GERMANY MOD/EUR UK ECO/DEV NAT/G FORCES BAL/PWR DOMIN ARMS/CONT PEACE PWR 20 TREATY EUROPE. PAGE 5 H0096
DIPLOM WAR

B60
BANERJEE D.N.,OUR FUNDAMENTAL RIGHTS: THEIR NATURE AND EXTENT (AS JUDICIALLY DETERMINED). INDIA UK CULTURE STRATA NAT/G WORKER EDU/PROP CONTROL DISCRIM OWN...IDEA/COMP WORSHIP 20 REFORMERS COMMONWLTH. PAGE 10 H0207
CONSTN ORD/FREE LEGIS POLICY

B60
BARBU Z.,PROBLEMS OF HISTORICAL PSYCHOLOGY. GREECE MEDIT-7 UK CULTURE TEC/DEV ADJUST RATIONAL ATTIT PERCEPT...METH/CNCPT NEW/IDEA TIME/SEQ GEN/METH. PAGE 11 H0214
PERSON PSY HIST/WRIT IDEA/COMP

B60
FURNIA A.H.,THE DIPLOMACY OF APPEASEMENT: ANGLO-FRENCH RELATIONS AND THE PRELUDE TO WORLD WAR II 1931-1938. FRANCE GERMANY UK ELITES NAT/G DELIB/GP FORCES WAR PEACE RIGID/FLEX 20. PAGE 54 H1077
DIPLOM BAL/PWR COERCE

B60
GRAMPP W.D.,THE MANCHESTER SCHOOL OF ECONOMICS. UK LAW ECO/DEV COERCE ATTIT ORD/FREE LAISSEZ ...PHIL/SCI IDEA/COMP 19/20 MANCHESTER CORN/LAWS. PAGE 60 H1194
ECO/TAC VOL/ASSN LOBBY NAT/G

B60
JEFFRIES C.,TRANSFER OF POWER: PROBLEMS OF THE PASSAGE TO SELFGOVERNMENT. CEYLON GHANA MALAYSIA NIGERIA UK INT/ORG CONSULT DELIB/GP LEGIS DIPLOM CONFER PARL/PROC 20. PAGE 80 H1595
SOVEREIGN COLONIAL ORD/FREE NAT/G

B60
KENEN P.B.,BRITISH MONETARY POLICY AND THE BALANCE OF PAYMENTS 1951-57. UK PLAN BUDGET ECO/TAC INT/TRADE PAY PRICE COST ATTIT 20. PAGE 84 H1687
BAL/PAY PROB/SOLV FINAN NAT/G

B60
KERSELL J.E.,PARLIAMENTARY SUPERVISION OF DELEGATED LEGISLATION. UK EFFICIENCY PWR...POLICY CHARTS BIBLIOG METH 20 PARLIAMENT. PAGE 85 H1699
LEGIS CONTROL NAT/G EX/STRUC

B60
PRASAD B.,THE ORIGINS OF PROVINCIAL AUTONOMY. INDIA UK FINAN LOC/G FORCES LEGIS CONTROL CT/SYS PWR ...JURID 19/20. PAGE 128 H2554
CENTRAL PROVS COLONIAL NAT/G

B60
ROBERTSON D.,THE CONTROL OF INDUSTRY. UK MARKET LABOR WORKER PRICE CONTROL GP/REL COST DEMAND ORD/FREE WEALTH NEW/LIB SOCISM 20. PAGE 132 H2646
INDUS FINAN NAT/G ECO/DEV

B60
SMITH M.G.,GOVERNMENT IN ZAZZAU 1800-1950. NIGERIA UK CULTURE SOCIETY LOC/G ADMIN COLONIAL ...METH/CNCPT NEW/IDEA METH 19/20. PAGE 146 H2914
REGION CONSTN KIN ECO/UNDEV

B60
STRACHEY J.,THE END OF EMPIRE. UK WOR+45 WOR-45 DIPLOM INT/TRADE DOMIN ADJUST ORD/FREE WEALTH ...SOCIALIST GOV/COMP TIME COMMONWLTH. PAGE 150 H2991
COLONIAL ECO/DEV BAL/PWR LAISSEZ

B60
WEINER H.E.,BRITISH LABOR AND PUBLIC OWNERSHIP. UK SERV/IND LG/CO WORKER CONTROL OWN 20. PAGE 166 H3327
LABOR NAT/G INDUS ATTIT

S60
BANFIELD E.C.,"THE POLITICAL IMPLICATIONS OF METROPOLITAN GROWTH" (BMR)" UK USA+45 LOC/G PROB/SOLV ADMIN GP/REL...METH/COMP NAT/COMP 20. PAGE 10 H0209
TASK MUNIC GOV/COMP CENSUS

S60
HOWARD M.,"BRITAIN'S DEFENSE: COMMITMENTS AND CAPABILITIES." EUR+WWI ECO/DEV NAT/G FORCES LEGIS PLAN DETER ORD/FREE WEALTH...POLICY CONCPT TIME/SEQ GEN/METH 20. PAGE 74 H1481
FUT PWR DIPLOM UK

S60
NORTHEDGE F.S.,"BRITISH FOREIGN POLICY AND THE PARTY SYSTEM." EUR+WWI FUT INT/ORG NAT/G EDU/PROP ATTIT PWR...POLICY CONCPT MYTH TIME/SEQ TREND 20 UN. PAGE 119 H2374
POL/PAR CHOOSE DIPLOM UK

S60
TURNER R.H.,"SPONSORED AND CONTEST MOBILITY IN THE SCHOOL SYSTEM." UK USA+45 ELITES STRATA ACADEM FACE/GP EDU/PROP CONTROL INGP/REL ADJUST ATTIT PERSON...METH/COMP 20. PAGE 157 H3142
AGE/Y NAT/COMP SCHOOL STRUCT

C60
COX R.H.,"LOCKE ON WAR AND PEACE." UK DIPLOM DOMIN PWR...BIOG IDEA/COMP BIBLIOG 18. PAGE 34 H0689
CONCPT NAT/G PEACE WAR

C60
SMITH T.E.,"ELECTIONS IN DEVELOPING COUNTRIES: A STUDY OF ELECTORAL PROCEDURES USED IN TOPICAL AFRICA, SOUTH-EAST ASIA..." AFR S/ASIA UK ROUTINE GOV/REL RACE/REL...GOV/COMP BIBLIOG 20. PAGE 146 H2918
ECO/UNDEV CHOOSE REPRESENT ADMIN

B61
ASHLEY M.P.,GREAT BRITAIN TO 1688: A MODERN HISTORY. UK NAT/G CHIEF LEAD REV WAR...POLICY BIBLIOG 1/17. PAGE 9 H0174
DOMIN CONSERVE

B61
ATTLEE C.R.,EMPIRE INTO COMMONWEALTH. AFR ASIA CANADA UK NAT/G WAR NAT/LISM ATTIT...POLICY 20 AUSTRAL. PAGE 9 H0179
DIPLOM GP/REL COLONIAL SOVEREIGN

B61
AYLMER G.,THE KING'S SERVANTS. UK ELITES CHIEF PAY CT/SYS WEALTH 17 CROMWELL/O CHARLES/I. PAGE 9 H0187
ADMIN ROUTINE EX/STRUC NAT/G

B61
BEARCE G.D.,BRITISH ATTITUDES TOWARDS INDIA 1784-1858. INDIA S/ASIA UK SECT ECO/TAC...POLICY HUM 18/19. PAGE 12 H0246
COLONIAL ATTIT ALL/IDEOS NAT/G

B61
BEDFORD S.,THE FACES OF JUSTICE: A TRAVELLER'S REPORT. AUSTRIA FRANCE GERMANY/W SWITZERLND UK UNIV WOR+45 WOR-45 CULTURE PARTIC GOV/REL MORAL...JURID OBS GOV/COMP 20. PAGE 13 H0257
CT/SYS ORD/FREE PERSON LAW

B61
BELOFF M.,NEW DIMENSIONS IN FOREIGN POLICY: A STUDY IN BRITISH ADMINISTRATION. UK NAT/G ATTIT RIGID/FLEX ORD/FREE...GEN/LAWS EUR+WW1 CMN/WLTH EEC 20. PAGE 14 H0271
INT/ORG DIPLOM

B61
BISHOP D.G.,THE ADMINISTRATION OF BRITISH FOREIGN RELATIONS. EUR+WWI MOD/EUR INT/ORG NAT/G POL/PAR DELIB/GP LEGIS TOP/EX ECO/TAC DOMIN EDU/PROP ADMIN COERCE 20. PAGE 17 H0344
ROUTINE PWR DIPLOM UK

B61
CHAKRABARTI A.,NEHRU: HIS DEMOCRACY AND INDIA. ASIA INDIA UK CONSTN ECO/UNDEV SECT DIPLOM COLONIAL PEACE WEALTH...BIBLIOG 20 CONGRESS NEHRU/J GANDHI/M. PAGE 28 H0570
ORD/FREE STRATA NAT/G CHIEF

B61
COHN B.S.,DEVELOPMENT AND IMPACT OF BRITISH ADMINISTRATION IN INDIA: A BIBLIOGRAPHIC ESSAY. INDIA UK ECO/UNDEV NAT/G DOMIN...POLICY MGT SOC 19/20. PAGE 31 H0619
BIBLIOG/A COLONIAL S/ASIA ADMIN

B61
DALLIN D.J.,SOVIET FOREIGN POLICY AFTER STALIN. ASIA CHINA/COM EUR+WWI GERMANY IRAN UK YUGOSLAVIA INT/ORG NAT/G VOL/ASSN FORCES TOP/EX BAL/PWR DOMIN EDU/PROP COERCE ATTIT PWR 20. PAGE 37 H0737
COM DIPLOM USSR

B61
DONNISON F.S.V.,CIVIL AFFAIRS AND MILITARY GOVERNMENT NORTH-WEST EUROPE 1944-1946. EUR+WWI FRANCE GERMANY UK USSR LOC/G PROVS PLAN PROB/SOLV BAL/PWR ECO/TAC CONTROL PWR...CHARTS 20. PAGE 42 H0836
NAT/G WAR FORCES CIVMIL/REL

B61
DRAGNICH A.N.,MAJOR EUROPEAN GOVERNMENTS. FRANCE GERMANY/W UK USSR LOC/G EX/STRUC CT/SYS PARL/PROC ATTIT MARXISM...JURID MGT NAT/COMP 19/20. PAGE 42 H0846
NAT/G LEGIS CONSTN POL/PAR

B61
GUIZOT F.P.G.,HISTORY OF THE ORIGIN OF REPRESENTATIVE GOVERNMENT IN EUROPE. CHRIST-17C FRANCE MOD/EUR SPAIN UK LAW CHIEF FORCES POPULISM ...MAJORIT TIME/SEQ GOV/COMP NAT/COMP 4/19 PARLIAMENT. PAGE 62 H1250
LEGIS REPRESENT CONSTN NAT/G

B61
HARE T.,A TREATISE ON THE ELECTION OF REPRESENTATIVES, PARLIAMENTARY AND MUNICIPAL. UK CONSTN NAT/G PARL/PROC CHOOSE ATTIT...MAJORIT 18/19 PARLIAMENT. PAGE 66 H1330
LEGIS GOV/REL CONSEN REPRESENT

B61
HICKS U.K.,DEVELOPMENT FROM BELOW. UK INDUS ADMIN COLONIAL ROUTINE GOV/REL...POLICY METH/CNCPT CHARTS 19/20 CMN/WLTH. PAGE 71 H1414
ECO/UNDEV LOC/G GOV/COMP METH/COMP

B61
JENNINGS I.,PARTY POLITICS: THE GROWTH OF PARTIES (VOL. II). UK SOCIETY NAT/G LEGIS ATTIT 18/20 LABOR/PAR LIB/PARTY CONSRV/PAR. PAGE 80 H1606
CHOOSE POL/PAR PWR POLICY

B61
JUSTICE,THE CITIZEN AND THE ADMINISTRATION: THE REDRESS OF GRIEVANCES (PAMPHLET). EUR+WWI UK LAW CONSTN STRATA NAT/G CT/SYS PARTIC COERCE...NEW/IDEA IDEA/COMP 20 OMBUDSMAN. PAGE 82 H1644
INGP/REL CONSULT ADJUD REPRESENT

B61
KHALIQUZZAMAN C.,PATHWAY TO PAKISTAN. INDIA PAKISTAN UK SECT LEGIS CHOOSE RACE/REL ATTIT ORD/FREE 20 MUSLIM. PAGE 85 H1705
GP/REL NAT/G COLONIAL SOVEREIGN

B61
MACLEOD I.,NEVILLE CHAMBERLAIN. UK SOCIETY TOP/EX WAR PERSON ALL/VALS ORD/FREE PARLIAMENT 20 CHAMBRLN/N. PAGE 100 H2003
BIOG NAT/G CREATE

B61
MILIBAND R.,PARLIAMENTARY SOCIALISM. EUR+WWI UK EXEC LEAD PARL/PROC GP/REL...POLICY 20 PARLIAMENT LABOR/PAR. PAGE 110 H2203
POL/PAR NAT/G PWR SOCISM

B61
PANIKKAR K.M.,THE VOICE OF FREEDOM: SELECTED SPEECHES OF PANDIT MOTILAL NEHRU. INDIA UK CONSTN FINAN FORCES LEGIS DIPLOM TAX COLONIAL...POLICY MAJORIT ANTHOL 20 NEHRU/PM. PAGE 123 H2460
NAT/LISM ORD/FREE CHIEF NAT/G

B61
ROCHE J.P.,COURTS AND RIGHTS: THE AMERICAN JUDICIARY IN ACTION (2ND ED.). UK USA+45 USA-45 STRUCT TEC/DEV SANCTION PERS/REL RACE/REL ORD/FREE ...METH/CNCPT GOV/COMP METH/COMP T 13/20. PAGE 133 H2653
JURID CT/SYS NAT/G PROVS

B61
SCHNAPPER B.,LA POLITIQUE ET LE COMMERCE FRANCAIS DANS LE GOLFE DE GUINEE DE 1838 A 1871. FRANCE GUINEA UK SEA EXTR/IND NAT/G DELIB/GP LEGIS ADMIN ORD/FREE...POLICY GEOG CENSUS CHARTS BIBLIOG 19. PAGE 139 H2791
COLONIAL INT/TRADE DOMIN AFR

B61
WILLSON F.M.G.,ADMINISTRATORS IN ACTION. UK MARKET TEC/DEV PARL/PROC 20. PAGE 169 H3376
ADMIN NAT/G CONSTN

S61
ANDERSON O.,"ECONOMIC WARFARE IN THE CRIMEAN WAR." EUR+WWI MOD/EUR NAT/G ACT/RES WAR DRIVE PWR 19/20. PAGE 6 H0130
ECO/TAC UK RUSSIA

S61
RAY J.,"THE EUROPEAN FREE-TRADE ASSOCIATION AND ITS IMPACT ON INDIA'S TRADE." EUR+WWI FRANCE GERMANY INDIA S/ASIA UK NAT/G VOL/ASSN PLAN INT/TRADE ROUTINE WEALTH...STAT CHARTS CMN/WLTH EEC OEEC 20 EFTA. PAGE 130 H2600
ECO/DEV ECO/TAC

C61
MOODIE G.C.,"THE GOVERNMENT OF GREAT BRITAIN." UK LAW STRUCT LOC/G POL/PAR DIPLOM RECEIVE ADMIN COLONIAL CHOOSE...BIBLIOG 20 PARLIAMENT. PAGE 112 H2247
NAT/G SOCIETY PARL/PROC GOV/COMP

B62
ANDREWS W.G.,EUROPEAN POLITICAL INSTITUTIONS. FRANCE GERMANY UK USSR TOP/EX LEAD PARL/PROC CHOOSE 20. PAGE 7 H0139
NAT/COMP POL/PAR EX/STRUC LEGIS

B62
BROWN B.E.,NEW DIRECTIONS IN COMPARATIVE POLITICS. AUSTRIA FRANCE GERMANY UK WOR+45 EX/STRUC LEGIS ORD/FREE 20. PAGE 22 H0439
NAT/COMP METH POL/PAR

FORCES

B62
CARY J.,THE CASE FOR AFRICAN FREEDOM AND OTHER WRITINGS ON AFRICA. AFR UK INDUS LOC/G NAT/G SECT INT/TRADE EDU/PROP GOV/REL RACE/REL ORD/FREE ...CONCPT ANTHOL 19/20. PAGE 27 H0552
NAT/LISM COLONIAL TREND ECO/UNDEV

B62
FRIEDMANN W.,METHODS AND POLICIES OF PRINCIPAL DONOR COUNTRIES IN PUBLIC INTERNATIONAL DEVELOPMENT FINANCING: PRELIMINARY APPRAISAL. FRANCE GERMANY/W UK USA+45 USSR WOR+45 FINAN TEC/DEV CAP/ISM DIPLOM ECO/TAC ATTIT 20 EEC. PAGE 53 H1066
INT/ORG FOR/AID NAT/COMP ADMIN

B62
GROGAN V.,ADMINISTRATIVE TRIBUNALS IN THE PUBLIC SERVICE. IRELAND UK NAT/G CONTROL CT/SYS...JURID GOV/COMP 20. PAGE 61 H1231
ADMIN LAW ADJUD DELIB/GP

B62
GROVE J.W.,GOVERNMENT AND INDUSTRY IN BRITAIN. UK FINAN LOC/G CONSULT DELIB/GP INT/TRADE ADMIN CONTROL...BIBLIOG 20. PAGE 62 H1237
ECO/TAC INDUS NAT/G GP/REL

B62
HANAK H.,GREAT BRITAIN AND AUSTRIA-HUNGARY DURING THE FIRST WORLD WAR: A STUDY IN THE FORMATION OF PUBLIC OPINION. CZECHOSLVK UK NAT/G GIVE DOMIN EDU/PROP CONSERVE...BIBLIOG 20 AUST/HUNG WWI. PAGE 65 H1311
WAR DIPLOM ATTIT PRESS

B62
HENDERSON W.O.,THE GENESIS OF THE COMMON MARKET. EUR+WWI FRANCE MOD/EUR UK SEA COM/IND EXTR/IND COLONIAL DISCRIM...TIME/SEQ CHARTS BIBLIOG 18/20 EEC TREATY. PAGE 70 H1395
ECO/DEV INT/TRADE DIPLOM

B62
HUNKIN P.,ENSEIGNEMENT ET POLITIQUE EN FRANCE ET EN ANGLETERRE. FRANCE UK CONSTN ACADEM SECT CHIEF DELIB/GP PROB/SOLV CONTROL REV ORD/FREE CONSERVE ...BIBLIOG 18/20. PAGE 75 H1496
EDU/PROP LEGIS IDEA/COMP NAT/G

B62
INSTITUTE OF PUBLIC ADMIN,A SHORT HISTORY OF THE PUBLIC SERVICE IN IRELAND. IRELAND UK DIST/IND INGP/REL FEDERAL 13/20 CIVIL/SERV. PAGE 77 H1539
ADMIN WORKER GOV/REL NAT/G

B62
JAIN R.S.,THE GROWTH AND DEVELOPMENT OF GOVERNOR-GENERAL'S EXECUTIVE COUNCIL 1858-1919. INDIA UK CONSTN EX/STRUC LEGIS ADJUD ADMIN INGP/REL ATTIT 19/20. PAGE 79 H1585
NAT/G DELIB/GP CHIEF CONSULT

B62
JENNINGS I.,PARTY POLITICS: THE STUFF OF POLITICS (VOL.III). UK NAT/G SECT CHIEF INT/TRADE RECEIVE COLONIAL GP/REL NAT/LISM ORD/FREE SOCISM 19/20 CHURCH/STA WHIG/PARTY. PAGE 80 H1607
POL/PAR CONSTN PWR ALL/IDEOS

B62
MACPHERSON C.B.,THE POLITICAL THEORY OF POSSESSIVE INDIVIDUALISM. UK MARKET NAT/G PERS/REL RATIONAL ...IDEA/COMP 17/19 LOCKE/JOHN. PAGE 100 H2006
PHIL/SCI OWN

B62
MANNING H.T.,THE REVOLT OF FRENCH CANADA 1800-1835. CANADA UK CULTURE GOV/REL RACE/REL...BIBLIOG 19. PAGE 102 H2039
NAT/LISM COLONIAL GEOG

B62
MITCHELL B.R.,ABSTRACT OF BRITISH HISTORICAL STATISTICS. UK FINAN NAT/G 12/20. PAGE 111 H2229
BIBLIOG STAT INDEX ECO/DEV

B62
PHILLIPS O.H.,CONSTITUTIONAL AND ADMINISTRATIVE LAW (3RD ED.). UK INT/ORG LOC/G CHIEF EX/STRUC LEGIS BAL/PWR ADJUD COLONIAL CT/SYS PWR...CHARTS 20. PAGE 125 H2503
JURID ADMIN CONSTN NAT/G

B62
RUDE G.,WILKES AND LIBERTY. UK NAT/G POL/PAR REPRESENT ORD/FREE...SOC 18. PAGE 136 H2711
PARL/PROC CHOOSE STRATA STRUCT

B62
TAYLOR D.,THE BRITISH IN AFRICA. UK CULTURE ECO/UNDEV INDUS DIPLOM INT/TRADE ADMIN WAR RACE/REL ORD/FREE SOVEREIGN...POLICY BIBLIOG 15/20 CMN/WLTH. PAGE 153 H3053
AFR COLONIAL DOMIN

S62
MARTIN L.W.,"THE MARKET FOR STRATEGIC IDEAS IN BRITAIN: THE 'SANDYS ERA'" UK ARMS/CONT WAR GOV/REL OPTIMAL...POLICY DECISION GOV/COMP COLD/WAR CMN/WLTH. PAGE 103 H2063
DIPLOM COERCE FORCES PWR

S62
ROSE R.,"THE POLITICAL IDEALS OF ENGLISH PARTY ACTIVISTS" (BMR)" UK PARL/PROC PARTIC ATTIT ROLE ...SAMP/SIZ CHARTS 20. PAGE 134 H2673
POL/PAR LOBBY REPRESENT NAT/G

B63
BRITISH AID. UK AGRI DIST/IND INDUS SCHOOL TEC/DEV INT/TRADE COLONIAL DEMAND...TREND CHARTS 20. PAGE 2 H0041
FOR/AID ECO/UNDEV NAT/G FINAN

B63
ALMOND G.A.,THE CIVIC CULTURE: POLITICAL ATTITUDES AND DEMOCRACY IN FIVE NATIONS. GERMANY/W ITALY UK USA+45 SOCIETY STRUCT PARTIC...SOC DEEP/INT SAMP 20 MEXIC/AMER. PAGE 6 H0113
POPULISM CULTURE NAT/COMP ATTIT

B63
BLONDEL J.,VOTERS, PARTIES, AND LEADERS. UK ELITES LOC/G NAT/G PROVS ACT/RES DOMIN REPRESENT GP/REL INGP/REL...SOC BIBLIOG 20. PAGE 18 H0358
POL/PAR STRATA LEGIS ADMIN

B63
CROSS C.,THE FASCISTS IN BRITAIN. UK ELITES LABOR NAT/G DOMIN PARTIC DISCRIM TOTALISM ATTIT...STERTYP 20. PAGE 35 H0708
POL/PAR FASCISM RACE/REL LEAD

B63
CRUICKSHANK M.,CHURCH AND STATE IN ENGLISH EDUCATION 1870 TO PRESENT. UK LEGIS TAX GIVE DOMIN LEGIT ORD/FREE 19/20 CHURCH/STA. PAGE 36 H0715
NAT/G SECT EDU/PROP GP/REL

B63
EDDY J.P.,JUSTICE OF THE PEACE. UK LAW CONSTN CULTURE 14/20 COMMON/LAW. PAGE 44 H0887
CRIME JURID CT/SYS ADJUD

B63
FARMER B.H.,CEYLON: A DIVIDED NATION. CEYLON INDIA NETHERLAND PORTUGAL UK ELITES POL/PAR COLONIAL ...SOC MYTH CHARTS GOV/COMP WORSHIP 20. PAGE 49 H0972
DOMIN ORD/FREE ECO/UNDEV POLICY

B63
GRIMOND J.,THE LIBERAL CHALLENGE. UK SOCIETY INDUS POL/PAR LEGIS PLAN CAP/ISM DIPLOM EDU/PROP GOV/REL CONSERVE 20 PARLIAMENT REFORMERS. PAGE 61 H1227
NAT/G NEW/LIB ECO/DEV POLICY

B63
HAILEY L.,THE REPUBLIC OF SOUTH AFRICA AND THE HIGH COMMISSION TERRITORIES. AFR SOUTH/AFR UK INT/ORG NAT/G PROVS RACE/REL SOVEREIGN...CHARTS 19/20 COMMONWLTH. PAGE 64 H1278
COLONIAL DIPLOM ATTIT

B63
HARTLEY A.,A STATE OF ENGLAND. UK ELITES SOCIETY ACADEM NAT/G SCHOOL INGP/REL CONSEN ORD/FREE NEW/LIB...POLICY 20. PAGE 67 H1349
DIPLOM ATTIT INTELL ECO/DEV

B63
JENNINGS W.I.,DEMOCRACY IN AFRICA. UK CULTURE STRUCT ECO/UNDEV DIPLOM COLONIAL GP/REL ADJUST NAT/LISM ORD/FREE...GOV/COMP 20 THIRD/WRLD. PAGE 81 H1613
PROB/SOLV AFR CONSTN POPULISM

B63
JUDD P.,AFRICAN INDEPENDENCE: THE EXPLODING EMERGENCE OF THE NEW AFRICAN NATIONS. AFR UK LAW CONSTN CULTURE KIN DIPLOM ATTIT...CHARTS BIBLIOG 20 UN DEGAULLE/C NEGRO THIRD/WRLD. PAGE 82 H1640
ORD/FREE POLICY DOMIN LOC/G

B63
LEWIN J.,POLITICS AND LAW IN SOUTH AFRICA. SOUTH/AFR UK POL/PAR BAL/PWR ECO/TAC COLONIAL CONTROL GP/REL DISCRIM PWR 20 NEGRO. PAGE 96 H1909
NAT/LISM POLICY LAW RACE/REL

B63
LIVINGSTON W.S.,FEDERALISM IN THE COMMONWEALTH - A BIBLIOGRAPHICAL COMMENTARY. CANADA INDIA PAKISTAN UK STRUCT LOC/G NAT/G POL/PAR...NAT/COMP 20 AUSTRAL. PAGE 97 H1943
BIBLIOG JURID FEDERAL CONSTN

B63
LOOMIE A.J.,THE SPANISH ELIZABETHANS: THE ENGLISH EXILES AT THE COURT OF PHILIP II. SPAIN UK WAR INGP/REL DRIVE HABITAT CATHISM...BIOG 16/17 MIGRATION. PAGE 98 H1962
NAT/G STRANGE POLICY DIPLOM

B63
MAC MILLAN W.M.,BANTU, BOER, AND BRITON: THE MAKING OF THE SOUTH AFRICAN NATIVE PROBLEM. SOUTH/AFR UK LAW KIN NAT/G SECT LEGIS COLONIAL ISOLAT ATTIT ...BIOG 18/20 BANTU NEGRO PHILIP/J MISSION. PAGE 100 H1989
AFR RACE/REL ELITES

B63
MAYNE R.,THE COMMUNITY OF EUROPE. UK CONSTN NAT/G CONSULT DELIB/GP CREATE PLAN ECO/TAC LEGIT ADMIN ROUTINE ORD/FREE PWR WEALTH...CONCPT TIME/SEQ EEC EURATOM 20. PAGE 105 H2107
EUR+WWI INT/ORG REGION

B63
MONGER G.W.,THE END OF ISOLATION. FRANCE MOD/EUR RUSSIA UK NAT/G LEGIS TOP/EX GOV/REL PWR 20 TREATY CHINJAP. PAGE 112 H2239
DIPLOM POLICY WAR

B63
MONTAGUE J.B. JR.,CLASS AND NATIONALITY; ENGLISH AND AMERICAN STUDIES. UK USA+45 ELITES STRUCT WORKER ATTIT PWR...SOC CHARTS SOC/EXP 20. PAGE 112 H2243
STRATA NAT/LISM PERSON NAT/COMP

B63
OLSON M. JR.,THE ECONOMICS OF WARTIME SHORTAGE. FRANCE GERMANY MOD/EUR UK AGRI PROB/SOLV ADMIN DEMAND WEALTH...POLICY OLD/LIB 17/20. PAGE 121 H2416
WAR ADJUST ECO/TAC NAT/COMP

B63
PELLING H.M.,A HISTORY OF BRITISH TRADE UNIONISM. UK ELITES ECO/DEV POL/PAR GP/REL PWR NEW/LIB 19/20. PAGE 124 H2485
LABOR VOL/ASSN NAT/G

B63
SELF P.,THE STATE AND THE FARMER. UK ECO/DEV MARKET WORKER PRICE CONTROL GP/REL...WELF/ST 20 DEPT/AGRI. PAGE 141 H2823
AGRI NAT/G ADMIN VOL/ASSN

B63
SHANKS M.,THE LESSONS OF PUBLIC ENTERPRISE. UK LEGIS WORKER ECO/TAC ADMIN PARL/PROC GOV/REL ATTIT ...POLICY MGT METH/COMP NAT/COMP ANTHOL 20 PARLIAMENT. PAGE 142 H2840
SOCISM OWN NAT/G INDUS

B63
SHANNON R.T.,GLADSTONE AND THE BULGARIAN AGITATION OF 1876. BULGARIA TURKEY UK DIPLOM COERCE REV ATTIT 19 GLADSTON/W DISRAELI/B. PAGE 142 H2841
EDU/PROP NAT/G PWR CONSEN

B63
SINGH H.L.,PROBLEMS AND POLICIES OF THE BRITISH IN INDIA, 1885-1898. INDIA UK NAT/G FORCES LEGIS PROB/SOLV CONTROL RACE/REL ADJUST DISCRIM NAT/LISM RIGID/FLEX...MGT 19 CIVIL/SERV. PAGE 144 H2885
COLONIAL PWR POLICY ADMIN

B63
SPRING D.,THE ENGLISH LANDED ESTATE IN THE NINETEENTH CENTURY: ITS ADMINISTRATION. UK ELITES STRUCT AGRI NAT/G GP/REL OWN PWR WEALTH...BIBLIOG 19 HOUSE/LORD. PAGE 148 H2954
STRATA PERS/REL MGT

B63
THOMPSON F.M.L.,ENGLISH LANDED SOCIETY IN THE NINETEENTH CENTURY. UK STRUCT MUNIC NAT/G CONTROL WAR GP/REL OWN WEALTH...BIBLIOG 18/20. PAGE 154 H3081
STRATA PWR ELITES GOV/REL

B63
VON BECKERATH E.,PROBLEME DER NORMATIVEN OKONOMIK UND DER WIRTSCHAFTSPOLITISCHEN BERATUNG. GERMANY UK ELITES CAP/ISM EFFICIENCY...CONCPT GOV/COMP IDEA/COMP 20. PAGE 163 H3264
ECO/TAC DELIB/GP ECO/DEV CONSULT

B63
WALKER A.A.,OFFICIAL PUBLICATIONS OF SIERRA LEONE AND GAMBIA. GAMBIA SIER/LEONE UK LAW CONSTN LEGIS PLAN BUDGET DIPLOM...SOC SAMP CON/ANAL 20. PAGE 164 H3290
BIBLIOG NAT/G COLONIAL ADMIN

B63
WILSON U.,EDUCATION AND CHANGING WEST AFRICAN CULTURE. AFR MOD/EUR UK CULTURE ECO/UNDEV MUNIC CONSULT 19/20 CMN/WLTH AFRICA/W. PAGE 169 H3384
COLONIAL POLICY SCHOOL

S63
APPERT K.,"BERECHTIGE VORBEHALTE DER SCHWEIZERISCHEN ZUR INTEGRATION." EUR+WWI UK MARKET SERV/IND NAT/G PLAN RIGID/FLEX OEEC 20 EEC. PAGE 7 H0146
FINAN ATTIT SWITZERLND

S63
HUREWITZ J.C.,"LEBANESE DEMOCRACY IN ITS INTERNATIONAL SETTING." FRANCE ISLAM UK LOC/G NAT/G SECT DOMIN EDU/PROP EXEC ATTIT PWR...TIME/SEQ 20. PAGE 75 H1507
STRUCT LEBANON

S63
LERNER D.,"WILL EUROPEAN UNION BRING ABOUT MERGED NATIONAL GOALS." EUR+WWI FRANCE GERMANY UK ECO/DEV NAT/G VOL/ASSN DELIB/GP BAL/PWR ECO/TAC NAT/LISM EEC 20 DEGAULLE/C. PAGE 95 H1889
ATTIT STERTYP ELITES REGION

S63
MONROE A.D.,"BRITAIN AND THE EUROPEAN COMMUNITY." EUR+WWI FRANCE NAT/G DELIB/GP TOP/EX ECO/TAC DOMIN PWR...POLICY RECORD GEN/LAWS EEC EFTA 20 EFTA CMN/WLTH. PAGE 112 H2241
VOL/ASSN ATTIT UK

B64
ARASARATNAM S.,CEYLON. CEYLON NETHERLAND PORTUGAL S/ASIA UK STRUCT ECO/UNDEV SECT DIPLOM DOMIN RACE/REL NAT/LISM 17/20 CMN/WLTH. PAGE 8 H0156
COLONIAL NAT/G PROB/SOLV CULTURE

B64
AVASTHI A.,ASPECTS OF ADMINISTRATION. INDIA UK USA+45 FINAN ACADEM DELIB/GP LEGIS RECEIVE PARL/PROC PRIVIL...NAT/COMP 20. PAGE 9 H0183
MGT ADMIN SOC/WK ORD/FREE

B64
BAGEHOT W.,THE ENGLISH CONSTITUTION. UK CHIEF CONSULT LEGIS BAL/PWR PWR...BIBLIOG 18/19 PARLIAMENT. PAGE 10 H0198
CONSTN PARL/PROC NAT/G CONCPT

B64
BELL C.,THE DEBATABLE ALLIANCE. COM UK USA+45 NAT/G FORCES PLAN BAL/PWR NUC/PWR WAR ATTIT...GOV/COMP 20. PAGE 13 H0263
DIPLOM PWR PEACE POLICY

B64
BROWN W.M.,THE EXTERNAL LIQUIDITY OF AN ADVANCED COUNTRY. CANADA FRANCE GERMANY/W SWEDEN UK USA+45 ECO/DEV DIPLOM PRICE...CONCPT STAT NAT/COMP 20. PAGE 22 H0451
FINAN INT/TRADE COST INCOME

B64
CULLINGWORTH J.B.,TOWN AND COUNTRY PLANNING IN ENGLAND AND WALES. UK LAW SOCIETY CONSULT ACT/RES ADMIN ROUTINE LEISURE INGP/REL ADJUST PWR...GEOG 20 OPEN/SPACE URBAN/RNWL. PAGE 36 H0718
MUNIC PLAN NAT/G PROB/SOLV

B64
CURTIN P.D.,THE IMAGE OF AFRICA: BRITISH IDEAS AND ACTION, 1780-1850. MOD/EUR SOCIETY FORCES ACT/RES DOMIN EDU/PROP COERCE ATTIT PERCEPT RIGID/FLEX SUPEGO HEALTH KNOWL MORAL ORD/FREE WEALTH...CONCPT WORK VAL/FREE. PAGE 36 H0726
AFR CULTURE UK DIPLOM

B64
DOWNIE R.S.,GOVERNMENT ACTION AND MORALITY: SOME PRINCIPLES AND CONCEPTS OF LIBERAL-DEMOCRACY. UK PARL/PROC ATTIT ROLE...MAJORIT DECISION CONCPT 20. PAGE 42 H0845
NAT/G MORAL POLICY GEN/LAWS

B64
FORBES A.H.,CURRENT RESEARCH IN BRITISH STUDIES. UK CONSTN CULTURE POL/PAR SECT DIPLOM ADMIN...JURID BIOG WORSHIP 20. PAGE 52 H1034
BIBLIOG PERSON NAT/G PARL/PROC

B64
FRANCK T.M.,EAST AFRICAN UNITY THROUGH LAW. MALAWI TANZANIA UGANDA UK ZAMBIA CONSTN INT/ORG NAT/G ADMIN ROUTINE TASK NAT/LISM ATTIT SOVEREIGN ...RECORD IDEA/COMP NAT/COMP. PAGE 52 H1048
AFR FEDERAL REGION INT/LAW

B64
GREBLER L.,URBAN RENEWAL IN EUROPEAN COUNTRIES: ITS EMERGENCE AND POTENTIALS. EUR+WWI UK ECO/DEV LOC/G NEIGH CREATE ADMIN ATTIT...TREND NAT/COMP 20 URBAN/RNWL. PAGE 60 H1205
MUNIC PLAN CONSTRUC NAT/G

B64
GRIFFITH W.,THE WELSH (2ND ED.). UK SOCIETY STRUCT SECT WRITING NAT/LISM...ART/METH MODAL OBS/ENVIR TREND SOC/INTEG WALES PURITAN MUSIC. PAGE 61 H1223
CULTURE SOC LING

B64
HAAR C.M.,LAW AND LAND: ANGLO-AMERICAN PLANNING PRACTICE. UK USA+45 NAT/G TEC/DEV BUDGET CT/SYS INGP/REL EFFICIENCY OWN...JURID 20. PAGE 63 H1263
LAW PLAN MUNIC NAT/COMP

B64
HAMILTON W.B.,THE TRANSFER OF INSTITUTIONS. CANADA INDIA UK LAW AGRI LABOR SECT COLONIAL 18/20. PAGE 65 H1301
NAT/COMP ECO/UNDEV EDU/PROP CULTURE

B64
HOLDSWORTH W.S.,A HISTORY OF ENGLISH LAW; THE CENTURIES OF DEVELOPMENT AND REFORM (VOL. XIV). UK CONSTN LOC/G NAT/G POL/PAR CHIEF EX/STRUC ADJUD COLONIAL ATTIT...INT/LAW JURID 18/19 TORY/PARTY COMMONWLTH WHIG/PARTY COMMON/LAW. PAGE 73 H1453
LAW LEGIS LEAD CT/SYS

B64
HOPKINSON T.,SOUTH AFRICA. SOUTH/AFR UK NAT/G POL/PAR LEGIS ECO/TAC PARL/PROC WAR...JURID AUD/VIS 19/20. PAGE 73 H1467
SOCIETY RACE/REL DISCRIM

B64
HORNE D.,THE LUCKY COUNTRY: AUSTRALIA TODAY. UK CULTURE STRATA ATTIT PWR PLURISM...GOV/COMP 20 AUSTRAL. PAGE 73 H1471
RACE/REL DIPLOM NAT/G STRUCT

B64
LIGGETT E.,BRITISH POLITICAL ISSUES: VOLUME 1. UK LAW CONSTN LOC/G NAT/G ADJUD 20. PAGE 97 H1930
POL/PAR GOV/REL CT/SYS DIPLOM

B64
MARSH D.C.,THE FUTURE OF THE WELFARE STATE. UK CONSTN NAT/G POL/PAR...POLICY WELF/ST 20. PAGE 103 H2058
NEW/LIB ADMIN CONCPT INSPECT

B64
MAUD J.,AID FOR DEVELOPING COUNTRIES. COM EUR+WWI UK INT/TRADE ORD/FREE...GOV/COMP 20. PAGE 105 H2101
FOR/AID DIPLOM ECO/TAC ECO/UNDEV

B64
MILIBAND R.,THE SOCIALIST REGISTER: 1964. GERMANY/W ITALY UK LABOR POL/PAR ECO/TAC FOR/AID NUC/PWR ...POLICY SOCIALIST IDEA/COMP 20 MAO NASSER/G. PAGE 110 H2204
MARXISM SOCISM CAP/ISM PROB/SOLV

B64
NATIONAL BOOK LEAGUE,THE COMMONWEALTH IN BOOKS: AN ANNOTATED LIST. CANADA UK LOC/G SECT ADMIN...SOC BIOG 20 CMN/WLTH. PAGE 116 H2320
BIBLIOG/A JURID NAT/G

B64
NEWARK F.H.,NOTES ON IRISH LEGAL HISTORY (2ND ED.). IRELAND UK PARL/PROC ORD/FREE SOVEREIGN 12/20 ENGLSH/LAW. PAGE 117 H2344
CT/SYS JURID ADJUD NAT/G

B64
PINNICK A.W.,COUNTRY PLANNERS IN ACTION. UK FINAN SERV/IND NAT/G CONSULT DELIB/GP PRICE CONTROL ROUTINE LEISURE AGE/C...GEOG 20 URBAN/RNWL. PAGE 126 H2512
MUNIC PLAN INDUS ATTIT

B64
QUIGG P.W.,AFRICA: A FOREIGN AFFAIRS READER. AFR FRANCE PORTUGAL UK DIPLOM LEAD PARL/PROC MARXISM ...MAJORIT METH/CNCPT GOV/COMP IDEA/COMP ANTHOL 19/20. PAGE 129 H2575
COLONIAL SOVEREIGN NAT/LISM RACE/REL

RAISON T.,WHY CONSERVATIVE? UK FORCES DIPLOM ECO/TAC GIVE EDU/PROP ORD/FREE WEALTH LAISSEZ ...GOV/COMP 20 TORY/PARTY CONSRV/PAR. PAGE 129 H2583 — B64 — PLURISM CONSERVE POL/PAR NAT/G

RAPHAEL M.,PENSIONS AND PUBLIC SERVANTS. UK NAT/G PLAN INGP/REL COST EFFICIENCY ATTIT...POLICY 17/20 CIVIL/SERV. PAGE 130 H2593 — B64 — RECEIVE ADMIN INCOME AGE/O

RIDLEY F.,PUBLIC ADMINISTRATION IN FRANCE. FRANCE UK EX/STRUC CONTROL PARTIC EFFICIENCY 20. PAGE 131 H2625 — B64 — ADMIN REPRESENT GOV/COMP PWR

TAWNEY R.H.,EQUALITY. UK CULTURE STRATA ECO/TAC EDU/PROP REPRESENT OWN NEW/LIB...MAJORIT WELF/ST SOC 20. PAGE 153 H3051 — B64 — WEALTH STRUCT ELITES POPULISM

TILMAN R.O.,BUREAUCRATIC TRANSITION IN MALAYA. MALAYSIA S/ASIA UK NAT/G EX/STRUC DIPLOM...CHARTS BIBLIOG 20. PAGE 155 H3098 — B64 — ADMIN COLONIAL SOVEREIGN EFFICIENCY

TODD W.B.,A BIBLIOGRAPHY OF EDMUND BURKE. MOD/EUR UK NAT/G EDU/PROP ATTIT...HUM 18 BURKE/EDM. PAGE 156 H3110 — B64 — BIBLIOG/A PHIL/SCI WRITING CONCPT

WILSON T.,POLICIES FOR REGIONAL DEVELOPMENT. CANADA UK FINAN INDUS NAT/G BUDGET TAX GIVE COST ...NAT/COMP 20. PAGE 169 H3383 — B64 — REGION PLAN ECO/DEV ECO/TAC

WRAITH R.,CORRUPTION IN DEVELOPING COUNTRIES. NIGERIA UK LAW ELITES STRATA INDUS LOC/G NAT/G SECT FORCES EDU/PROP ADMIN PWR WEALTH 18/20. PAGE 171 H3414 — B64 — ECO/UNDEV CRIME SANCTION ATTIT

FINDLATER R.,"US." EUR+WWI GERMANY USSR SOCIETY FACE/GP EDU/PROP PERCEPT PERSON ALL/VALS...PSY SOC CONCPT SELF/OBS SAMP TREND 20. PAGE 50 H1001 — L64 — CULTURE ATTIT UK

MACKINTOSH J.P.,"NIGERIA'S EXTERNAL AFFAIRS." UK CULTURE ECO/UNDEV NAT/G VOL/ASSN EDU/PROP LEGIT ADMIN ATTIT ORD/FREE PWR 20. PAGE 100 H2002 — L64 — AFR DIPLOM NIGERIA

SYMONDS R.,"REFLECTIONS IN LOCALISATION." AFR S/ASIA UK STRATA INT/ORG NAT/G SCHOOL EDU/PROP LEGIT KNOWL ORD/FREE PWR RESPECT CMN/WLTH 20. PAGE 151 H3023 — L64 — ADMIN MGT COLONIAL

CROUZET F.,"WARS, BLOCKADE, AND ECONOMIC CHANGE IN EUROPE, 1792-1815." UK INDUS NAT/G TEC/DEV ECO/TAC WEALTH...POLICY RELATIV HIST/WRIT TIME/SEQ 18/19. PAGE 35 H0710 — S64 — MOD/EUR MARKET

GOLDBERG A.,"THE MILITARY ORIGINS OF THE BRITISH NUCLEAR DETERRENT." EUR+WWI ECO/DEV NAT/G PLAN NUC/PWR ATTIT PWR...DECISION HIST/WRIT COLD/WAR 20. PAGE 58 H1156 — S64 — FORCES CONCPT DETER UK

LOW D.A.,"LION RAMPANT." EUR+WWI MOD/EUR S/ASIA ECO/UNDEV NAT/G FORCES TEC/DEV ECO/TAC LEGIT ADMIN COLONIAL COERCE ORD/FREE RESPECT 19/20. PAGE 99 H1972 — S64 — AFR DOMIN DIPLOM UK

TOYNBEE A.,"BRITAIN AND THE ARABS: THE NEED FOR A NEW START." NAT/G CREATE COLONIAL ATTIT RIGID/FLEX MORAL PWR...POLICY HIST/WRIT 20. PAGE 156 H3124 — S64 — ISLAM ECO/TAC DIPLOM UK

BARRY E.E.,NATIONALISATION IN BRITISH POLITICS: THE HISTORICAL BACKGROUND. UK AGRI DIST/IND EXTR/IND LABOR LG/CO ATTIT CONSERVE SOCISM 19/20 LABOR/PAR. PAGE 12 H0231 — B65 — NAT/G OWN INDUS POL/PAR

BRAMSTED E.K.,GOEBBELS AND NATIONAL SOCIALIST PROPAGANDA, 1925-1945. EUR+WWI GERMANY UK USSR NAT/G FORCES WAR FASCISM...TIME/SEQ 20 GOEBBELS/J NAZI. PAGE 20 H0403 — B65 — EDU/PROP PSY COM/IND

BRASS P.R.,FACTIONAL POLITICS IN AN INDIAN STATE: THE CONGRESS PARTY IN UTTAR PRADESH. INDIA UK CONSTN CULTURE ECO/UNDEV LOC/G DOMIN COLONIAL CROWD GP/REL ADJUST CENTRAL RIGID/FLEX SOVEREIGN 20 UTTAR/PRAD CONGRESS/P. PAGE 20 H0406 — B65 — POL/PAR PROVS LEGIS CHOOSE

BULMER-THOMAS I.,THE GROWTH OF THE BRITISH PARTY SYSTEM (VOL. II) 1924-1964. UK ECO/DEV BARGAIN WAR CHOOSE ATTIT ORD/FREE 20 LABOR/PAR CONSRV/PAR. PAGE 23 H0472 — B65 — CHIEF POL/PAR PARL/PROC NAT/G

CALLEO D.P.,EUROPE'S FUTURE: THE GRAND ALTERNATIVES. UK INT/ORG DIPLOM PWR SOVEREIGN ...CONCPT IDEA/COMP NAT/COMP BIBLIOG 20 EEC EUROPE DEGAULLE/C NATO. PAGE 25 H0506 — B65 — FUT EUR+WWI FEDERAL NAT/LISM

CAMPBELL G.A.,THE CIVIL SERVICE IN BRITAIN (2ND ED.). UK DELIB/GP FORCES WORKER CREATE PLAN ...POLICY AUD/VIS 19/20 CIVIL/SERV. PAGE 26 H0515 — B65 — ADMIN LEGIS NAT/G FINAN

CARTER G.M.,POLITICS IN EUROPE. EUR+WWI FRANCE GERMANY/W UK USSR LAW CONSTN POL/PAR VOL/ASSN PRESS LOBBY PWR...ANTHOL SOC/INTEG EEC. PAGE 27 H0548 — B65 — GOV/COMP OP/RES ECO/DEV

CHANDA A.,FEDERALISM IN INDIA. INDIA UK ELITES FINAN NAT/G POL/PAR EX/STRUC LEGIS DIPLOM TAX GOV/REL POPULISM...POLICY 20. PAGE 28 H0572 — B65 — CONSTN CENTRAL FEDERAL

CHRIMES S.B.,ENGLISH CONSTITUTIONAL HISTORY (3RD ED.). UK CHIEF CONSULT DELIB/GP LEGIS CT/SYS 15/20 COMMON/LAW PARLIAMENT. PAGE 30 H0598 — B65 — CONSTN BAL/PWR NAT/G

COLLINS H.,KARL MARX AND THE BRITISH LABOR MOVEMENT, YEARS OF THE FIRST INTERNATIONAL. EUR+WWI MOD/EUR UK STRATA INDUS NAT/G POL/PAR SOCISM ...CONCPT 19/20 MARX/KARL. PAGE 32 H0633 — B65 — MARXISM LABOR INT/ORG WORKER

EDELMAN M.,THE POLITICS OF WAGE-PRICE DECISIONS. GERMANY ITALY NETHERLAND UK INDUS LABOR POL/PAR PROB/SOLV BARGAIN PRICE ROUTINE BAL/PAY COST DEMAND 20. PAGE 44 H0888 — B65 — GOV/COMP CONTROL ECO/TAC PLAN

GEORGE M.,THE WARPED VISION. EUR+WWI UK NAT/G POL/PAR LEGIS PARL/PROC SANCTION COERCE WAR GOV/REL PEACE RESPECT 20 CONSRV/PAR. PAGE 56 H1113 — B65 — LEAD ATTIT DIPLOM POLICY

GOPAL S.,BRITISH POLICY IN INDIA 1858-1905. INDIA UK ELITES CHIEF DELIB/GP ECO/TAC GP/REL DISCRIM ATTIT...IDEA/COMP NAT/COMP PERS/COMP BIBLIOG/A 19/20. PAGE 59 H1176 — B65 — COLONIAL ADMIN POL/PAR ECO/UNDEV

GOULD J.,PENGUIN SURVEY OF THE SOCIAL SCIENCES* 1965. CULTURE SOCIETY R+D FAM KIN MUNIC ACT/RES DIPLOM SKILL. PAGE 59 H1186 — B65 — SOC PHIL/SCI USSR UK

GRAHAM G.S.,THE POLITICS OF NAVAL SUPREMACY; STUDIES IN BRITISH MARITIME ASCENDANCY. UK SEA NAT/G BAL/PWR LEAD WAR WEAPON PEACE...POLICY 18/19 COMMONWLTH. PAGE 60 H1191 — B65 — FORCES PWR COLONIAL DIPLOM

GRETTON P.,MARITIME STRATEGY - A STUDY OF DEFENSE PROBLEMS. ASIA UK USSR DIPLOM COERCE DETER NUC/PWR WEAPON...CONCPT NAT/COMP 20. PAGE 60 H1211 — B65 — FORCES PLAN WAR SEA

GRIMAL H.,HISTOIRE DU COMMONWEALTH BRITANNIQUE. UK FINAN DOMIN ATTIT ORD/FREE...T 15/20 CMN/WLTH. PAGE 61 H1226 — B65 — NAT/G COLONIAL DIPLOM INT/TRADE

HALEVY E.,THE ERA OF TYRANNIES (TRANS. BY R. K. WEBB). FRANCE MOD/EUR UK ECO/DEV LABOR NAT/G BAL/PWR FEDERAL ALL/VALS...OLD/LIB TREND 18/20 SAINTSIMON. PAGE 64 H1285 — B65 — SOCISM CONCPT UTOPIA ORD/FREE

HANSER C.J.,GUIDE TO DECISION: ROYAL COMMISSION. UK INTELL EXTR/IND SCHOOL PROB/SOLV EXEC ROUTINE CHOOSE GOV/REL GP/REL HEALTH...CHARTS 20. PAGE 66 H1318 — B65 — NAT/G DELIB/GP EX/STRUC PWR

HART B.H.L.,THE MEMOIRS OF CAPTAIN LIDDELL HART (VOL. I). UK NAT/G PLAN TEC/DEV DIPLOM ADMIN WEAPON GOV/REL PERS/REL ATTIT PWR FASCISM...POLICY 20. PAGE 67 H1348 — B65 — FORCES BIOG LEAD WAR

HORNE A.J.,THE COMMONWEALTH TODAY. AFR ASIA CANADA UK STRUCT ECO/UNDEV NAT/G SECT GP/REL 20 AUSTRAL CMN/WLTH. PAGE 73 H1470 — B65 — BIBLIOG/A SOCIETY CULTURE

KIRKWOOD K.,BRITAIN AND AFRICA. AFR UK ECO/UNDEV ECO/TAC WAR NAT/LISM SOVEREIGN 19/20. PAGE 86 H1725 — B65 — NAT/G DIPLOM POLICY COLONIAL

KLEIN J.,SAMPLES FROM ENGLISH CULTURES (2 VOLS.). UK STRATA FAM NEIGH WORKER ETIQUET ISOLAT AGE/C AGE/A HABITAT RIGID/FLEX...NET/THEORY CHARTS 20. PAGE 87 H1732 — B65 — CULTURE INGP/REL ATTIT SOC

MCWHINNEY E.,JUDICIAL REVIEW IN THE ENGLISH-SPEAKING WORLD (3RD ED.). CANADA UK WOR+45 LEGIS CONTROL EXEC PARTIC...JURID 20 AUSTRAL. PAGE 108 H2151 — B65 — GOV/COMP CT/SYS ADJUD CONSTN

MEHROTRA S.R.,INDIA AND THE COMMONWEALTH 1885-1929. — B65 — DIPLOM

INDIA UK INT/ORG VOL/ASSN GP/REL ATTIT...POLICY BIBLIOG 19/20 CMN/WLTH. PAGE 108 H2163
NAT/G POL/PAR NAT/LISM

B65
NAMIER L.B.,THE STRUCTURE OF POLITICS AT THE ACCESSION OF GEORGE III. UK LOC/G TOP/EX COLONIAL LEAD PARTIC REV CHOOSE REPRESENT GOV/REL PERSON SOVEREIGN...GOV/COMP 18 PARLIAMENT. PAGE 115 H2309
PARL/PROC LEGIS NAT/G POL/PAR

B65
NEWBURY C.W.,BRITISH POLICY TOWARDS WEST AFRICA: SELECT DOCUMENTS 1786-1874. AFR UK INT/TRADE DOMIN ADMIN COLONIAL CT/SYS COERCE ORD/FREE...BIBLIOG/A 18/19. PAGE 117 H2345
DIPLOM POLICY NAT/G WRITING

B65
OGILVY-WEBB M.,THE GOVERNMENT EXPLAINS: A STUDY OF THE INFORMATION SERVICES. UK DELIB/GP LEGIS WORKER BUDGET DIPLOM 20. PAGE 121 H2409
EDU/PROP ATTIT NAT/G ADMIN

B65
PANJABI K.L.,THE CIVIL SERVANT IN INDIA. INDIA UK NAT/G CONSULT EX/STRUC REGION GP/REL RACE/REL 20. PAGE 123 H2462
ADMIN WORKER BIOG COLONIAL

B65
PARRIS H.W.,GOVERNMENT AND THE RAILWAYS IN NINETEENTH-CENTURY BRITAIN. UK DELIB/GP CONTROL LEAD CENTRAL 19 RAILROAD. PAGE 124 H2470
DIST/IND NAT/G PLAN GP/REL

B65
PELLING H.,A SHORT HISTORY OF THE LABOUR PARTY (2ND ED.). UK NAT/G CHIEF PARL/PROC GP/REL INGP/REL 20 LABOR/PAR PARLIAMENT WILSON/H. PAGE 124 H2484
POL/PAR NEW/LIB LEAD LABOR

B65
QURESHI I.H.,THE STRUGGLE FOR PAKISTAN. INDIA PAKISTAN UK CULTURE LEGIS DIPLOM EDU/PROP COLONIAL ATTIT SOVEREIGN 19/20 MUSLIM. PAGE 129 H2576
GP/REL RACE/REL WAR SECT

B65
SHEPHERD W.G.,ECONOMIC PERFORMANCE UNDER PUBLIC OWNERSHIP: BRITISH FUEL AND POWER. UK BUDGET GP/REL ...METH/CNCPT CHARTS BIBLIOG 20. PAGE 143 H2858
PROC/MFG NAT/G OWN FINAN

B65
TEW B.,WEALTH AND INCOME. UK BUDGET INT/TRADE PRICE BAL/PAY DEMAND...CHARTS GOV/COMP 20 AUSTRAL. PAGE 153 H3064
FINAN ECO/DEV WEALTH INCOME

B65
WAINWRIGHT M.D.,A GUIDE TO WESTERN MANUSCRIPTS AND DOCUMENTS IN THE BRITISH ISLES RELATING TO SOUTH AND SOUTHEAST ASIA. UK CULTURE...SOC 15/20. PAGE 164 H3288
BIBLIOG S/ASIA WRITING

B65
WALKER A.A.,THE RHODESIAS AND NYASALAND: A GUIDE TO OFFICIAL PUBLICATIONS. RHODESIA UK OP/RES PLAN PROB/SOLV DIPLOM...POLICY SOC CON/ANAL 19/20 NYASALAND. PAGE 164 H3291
BIBLIOG NAT/G COLONIAL AFR

B65
WILLIAMSON J.A.,GREAT BRITAIN AND THE COMMONWEALTH. UK DOMIN COLONIAL INGP/REL...POLICY 18/20 CMN/WLTH. PAGE 168 H3370
NAT/G DIPLOM INT/ORG SOVEREIGN

B65
WOLPERT S.,INDIA. INDIA UK ECO/UNDEV DIPLOM GP/REL WEALTH 20 NEHRU/J. PAGE 170 H3405
CULTURE COLONIAL NAT/LISM SECT

L65
SCHAFFER B.B.,"THE CONCEPT OF PREPARATION* SOME QUESTIONS ABOUT THE TRANSFER OF SYSTEMS OF GOVERNMENT." AFR ASIA CANADA ELITES NAT/G POL/PAR COLONIAL RIGID/FLEX IDEA/COMP. PAGE 138 H2769
ECO/UNDEV UK RECORD

S65
COOPER P.,"THE DEVELOPMENT OF THE CONCEPT OF WAR." UK COERCE ATTIT PERCEPT PERSON...STAT CHARTS CHINJAP. PAGE 33 H0660
CULTURE WAR SAMP STAND/INT

S65
GANGAL S.C.,"SURVEY OF RECENT RESEARCH: INDIA AND THE COMMONWEALTH" INDIA UK NAT/G INT/TRADE PARTIC GOV/REL ROLE 20 CMN/WLTH. PAGE 55 H1095
BIBLIOG POLICY REGION DIPLOM

S65
GORDON M.,"THE SETTING FOR EUROPEAN ARMS CONTROLS* POLITICAL AND STRATEGIC CHOICES OF EUROPEAN ELITES." FRANCE GERMANY UK USA+45 USSR ARMS/CONT DETER ATTIT ORD/FREE...SAMP NAT/COMP NATO. PAGE 59 H1179
REC/INT ELITES RISK WAR

S65
WATT D.C.,"RESTRICTIONS ON RESEARCH* THE FIFTY-YEAR RULE AND BRITISH FOREIGN POLICY." ACADEM PERCEPT ...HIST/WRIT NAT/COMP TIME. PAGE 166 H3315
UK USA+45 DIPLOM

B66
AHMED Z.,DUSK AND DAWN IN VILLAGE INDIA. INDIA S/ASIA UK CULTURE SOCIETY NAT/G DOMIN COLONIAL HABITAT SOVEREIGN...SOC DICTIONARY 20. PAGE 4 H0080
NEIGH ECO/UNDEV AGRI ADJUST

B66
AIYAR S.P.,PERSPECTIVES ON THE WELFARE STATE. INDIA S/ASIA UK CONSTN ECO/UNDEV NAT/G INGP/REL CENTRAL NAT/LISM ATTIT...CONCPT ANTHOL BIBLIOG 20. PAGE 4 H0087
NEW/LIB WELF/ST IDEA/COMP ADJUST

B66
ARCHER P.,FREEDOM AT STAKE. UK LAW NAT/G LEGIS JUDGE CRIME MORAL...CONCPT 20 CIVIL/LIB. PAGE 8 H0159
ORD/FREE NAT/COMP POLICY

B66
BARNETT D.L.,MAU MAU FROM WITHIN. AFR UK POL/PAR LEAD GUERRILLA AUTHORIT ORD/FREE...SOC BIOG 20 NEGRO MAU/MAU. PAGE 11 H0225
REV CULTURE NAT/G

B66
BEER S.H.,BRITISH POLITICS IN THE COLLECTIVIST AGE. UK NAT/G CONTROL CHOOSE GP/REL ATTIT PWR PLURISM ...MAJORIT WELF/ST 16/20. PAGE 13 H0258
POL/PAR SOCISM TRADIT GP/COMP

B66
BRAIBANTI R.,ASIAN BUREAUCRATIC SYSTEMS EMERGENT FROM THE BRITISH IMPERIAL TRADITION. BURMA CEYLON INDIA PAKISTAN UK ELITES ECO/UNDEV NAT/G...MGT SOC CHARTS ANTHOL 19/20. PAGE 20 H0401
GOV/COMP COLONIAL ADMIN S/ASIA

B66
BUTLER D.E.,THE BRITISH GENERAL ELECTION OF 1966. UK LOC/G NAT/G OP/RES CONFER CHOOSE MAJORITY ATTIT ...CHARTS TIME 20. PAGE 25 H0498
POL/PAR REPRESENT GP/REL PERS/REL

B66
CADY J.F.,THAILAND, BURMA, LAOS AND CAMBODIA. FRANCE UK CULTURE NAT/G DOMIN GP/REL RACE/REL HABITAT...GEOG TREND CHINJAP BUDDHISM. PAGE 25 H0504
S/ASIA COLONIAL REGION SECT

B66
CANNING HOUSE LIBRARY,AUTHOR AND SUBJECT CATALOGUES OF THE CANNING HOUSE LIBRARY (5 VOLS.). UK CULTURE LEAD...SOC 19/20. PAGE 26 H0520
BIBLIOG L/A+17C NAT/G DIPLOM

B66
CROWDER M.,A SHORT HISTORY OF NIGERIA. AFR NIGERIA UK ECO/UNDEV CHIEF INT/TRADE RACE/REL NAT/LISM ORD/FREE...GEOG SOC CHARTS BIBLIOG 14/20. PAGE 36 H0711
COLONIAL NAT/G CULTURE

B66
DEXTER N.C.,GUIDE TO CONTEMPORARY POLITICS. EUR+WWI UK PARL/PROC GP/REL KNOWL...POLICY MAJORIT IDEA/COMP 20. PAGE 41 H0815
POL/PAR CONCPT NAT/G

B66
DYCK H.V.,WEIMAR GERMANY AND SOVIET RUSSIA 1926-1933. EUR+WWI GERMANY UK USSR ECO/TAC INT/TRADE NEUTRAL WAR ATTIT 20 WEIMAR/REP TREATY. PAGE 44 H0877
DIPLOM GOV/REL POLICY

B66
FIELDHOUSE D.K.,THE COLONIAL EMPIRES: A COMPARATIVE SURVEY FROM THE 18TH CENTURY. UK WOR-45 REV HABITAT 17/18. PAGE 50 H0994
NAT/COMP COLONIAL NAT/G DOMIN

B66
FINER S.E.,ANONYMOUS EMPIRE: STUDY OF THE LOBBY IN GREAT BRITAIN. UK CONSTN LABOR POL/PAR SECT DOMIN EDU/PROP PRESS CHOOSE...CONCPT CHARTS 20 PARLIAMENT. PAGE 50 H1004
LOBBY NAT/G LEGIS PWR

B66
FLINT J.E.,NIGERIA AND GHANA. AFR GHANA NIGERIA UK NAT/G DOMIN DISCRIM...CHARTS BIBLIOG/A 15/20 NEGRO MAPS. PAGE 51 H1026
CULTURE COLONIAL NAT/LISM

B66
FRANK E.,LAWMAKERS IN A CHANGING WORLD. FRANCE UK USSR WOR+45 PARTIC EFFICIENCY ROLE ALL/IDEOS ...CHARTS ANTHOL PARLIAMENT 20 UN COLD/WAR. PAGE 52 H1049
GOV/COMP LEGIS NAT/G DIPLOM

B66
FUCHS W.P.,STAAT UND KIRCHE IM WANDEL DER JAHRHUNDERTE. EUR+WWI MOD/EUR UK REV...JURID CONCPT 4/20 EUROPE CHRISTIAN CHURCH/STA. PAGE 54 H1074
SECT NAT/G ORD/FREE GP/REL

B66
HACKETT J.,L'ECONOMIE BRITANNIQUE: PROBLEMES ET PERSPECTIVES. FRANCE UK LABOR MUNIC NAT/G EX/STRUC PROB/SOLV BAL/PAY INCOME RIGID/FLEX...MGT PHIL/SCI CHARTS 20. PAGE 63 H1271
ECO/DEV FINAN ECO/TAC PLAN

B66
HAMILTON W.B.,A DECADE OF THE COMMONWEALTH, 1955-1964. UK LAW ELITES FINAN FOR/AID CONFER COLONIAL PWR...GEOG CHARTS ANTHOL 20 CMN/WLTH UN. PAGE 65 H1302
INT/ORG INGP/REL DIPLOM NAT/G

B66
HOLDSWORTH W.S.,A HISTORY OF ENGLISH LAW; THE CENTURIES OF SETTLEMENT AND REFORM (VOL. XVI). UK LOC/G NAT/G EX/STRUC LEGIS CT/SYS LEAD ATTIT ...POLICY DECISION JURID IDEA/COMP 18 PARLIAMENT. PAGE 73 H1454
BIOG PERSON PROF/ORG LAW

B66
HOYT E.C.,NATIONAL POLICY AND INTERNATIONAL LAW*
INT/LAW

CASE STUDIES FROM AMERICAN CANAL POLICY* MONOGRAPH NO. 1 -- 1966-1967. PANAMA UK ELITES BAL/PWR EFFICIENCY...CLASSIF NAT/COMP SOC/EXP COLOMB TREATY. PAGE 74 H1483 USA-45 DIPLOM PWR

JOHNSON N.,PARLIAMENT AND ADMINISTRATION: THE ESTIMATES COMMITTEE 1945-65. FUT UK NAT/G EX/STRUC PLAN BUDGET ORD/FREE...T 20 PARLIAMENT HOUSE/CMNS. PAGE 81 H1625 B66 LEGIS ADMIN FINAN DELIB/GP

KEITH G.,THE FADING COLOUR BAR. AFR CENTRL/AFR UK ZAMBIA CULTURE SCHOOL EDU/PROP PERS/REL DISCRIM AGE ...AUD/VIS NAT/COMP SOC/INTEG 20 NEGRO. PAGE 84 H1682 B66 RACE/REL STRUCT ATTIT NAT/G

LENSKI G.E.,POWER AND PRIVILEGE: A THEORY OF SOCIAL STRATIFICATION. SWEDEN UK UNIV USSR CULTURE ECO/UNDEV PRIVIL PWR...PHIL/SCI CONCPT CHARTS IDEA/COMP HYPO/EXP METH MARX/KARL. PAGE 94 H1882 B66 SOC STRATA STRUCT SOCIETY

LONDON DAILY TELEGRAPH,ELECTION '66: GALLUP ANALYSIS OF THE VOTING RESULTS. UK LEGIS COMPUTER ATTIT...QU SAMP CHARTS 20 LABOR/PAR HOUSE/CMNS. PAGE 98 H1959 B66 STAT CHOOSE REPRESENT POL/PAR

MAC DONALD H.M.,THE INTELLECTUAL IN POLITICS. GERMANY PERU SWEDEN UK USSR NAT/G CONSULT PLAN EDU/PROP TASK INGP/REL EFFICIENCY RATIONAL ALL/VALS 20. PAGE 99 H1987 B66 ALL/IDEOS INTELL POL/PAR PARTIC

MULLER C.F.J.,A SELECT BIBLIOGRAPHY OF SOUTH AFRICAN HISTORY; A GUIDE FOR HISTORICAL RESEARCH. SOUTH/AFR UK LAW CONSTN SOCIETY STRUCT AGRI SECT DIPLOM COLONIAL LEAD RACE/REL...POLICY 17/20 NEGRO. PAGE 114 H2284 B66 BIBLIOG AFR NAT/G

NOEL G.E.,THE NEW BRITAIN AND HAROLD WILSON: INTERIM REPORT, 1966 GENERAL ELECTION. UK POL/PAR CONSULT PROB/SOLV BUDGET DIPLOM ECO/TAC LEAD CHOOSE ATTIT 20 WILSON/H PARLIAMENT. PAGE 118 H2366 B66 BIOG PERSON NAT/G CHIEF

OWEN G.,INDUSTRY IN THE UNITED STATES. UK USA+45 NAT/G WEALTH...DECISION NAT/COMP 20. PAGE 122 H2436 B66 METH/COMP INDUS MGT PROB/SOLV

POLE J.R.,POLITICAL REPRESENTATION IN ENGLAND AND THE ORIGINS OF THE AMERICAN REPUBLIC. UK USA-45 CONSTN ELITES NAT/G POL/PAR LEGIS PARL/PROC ...MAJORIT 17/19. PAGE 127 H2534 B66 REPRESENT GOV/COMP

SYMONDS R.,THE BRITISH AND THEIR SUCCESSORS. AFR CEYLON INDIA UK SCHOOL FORCES EDU/PROP ADMIN PARTIC ...NAT/COMP BIBLIOG 20 AFRICA/W AFRICA/E. PAGE 151 H3024 B66 NAT/G ECO/UNDEV POLICY COLONIAL

TIVEY L.J.,NATIONALISATION IN BRITISH INDUSTRY. UK LEGIS PARL/PROC GP/REL OWN ATTIT SOCISM 20. PAGE 156 H3109 B66 NAT/G INDUS CONTROL LG/CO

TYSON G.,NEHRU: THE YEARS OF POWER. INDIA UK STRATA ECO/UNDEV FINAN SECT TASK WAR ORD/FREE MARXISM ...POLICY BIBLIOG 20 NEHRU/J. PAGE 157 H3145 B66 CHIEF PWR DIPLOM NAT/G

US DEPARTMENT OF STATE,RESEARCH ON WESTERN EUROPE, GREAT BRITAIN, AND CANADA (EXTERNAL RESEARCH LIST NO 3-25). CANADA GERMANY/W UK LAW CULTURE NAT/G POL/PAR FORCES EDU/PROP REGION MARXISM...GEOG SOC WORSHIP 20 CMN/WLTH. PAGE 160 H3192 B66 BIBLIOG/A EUR+WWI DIPLOM

US LIBRARY OF CONGRESS,NIGERIA: A GUIDE TO OFFICIAL PUBLICATIONS. CAMEROON NIGERIA UK DIPLOM...POLICY 19/20 UN LEAGUE/NAT. PAGE 161 H3215 B66 BIBLIOG ADMIN NAT/G COLONIAL

WINKS R.W.,THE HISTORIOGRAPHY OF THE BRITISH EMPIRE-COMMONWEALTH. CANADA INDIA PAKISTAN UK CULTURE SOCIETY STRUCT POL/PAR...CONCPT NAT/COMP 20 AUSTRAL. PAGE 169 H3386 B66 HIST/WRIT TREND IDEA/COMP METH/COMP

WUEST J.J.,NEW SOURCE BOOK IN MAJOR EUROPEAN GOVERNMENTS. CHRIST-17C EUR+WWI FRANCE GERMANY ITALY MOD/EUR UK USSR LOC/G POL/PAR CHIEF EX/STRUC CHOOSE CONSERVE MARXISM...JURID T 13/20. PAGE 171 H3425 B66 NAT/G CONSTN LEGIS

ZEINE Z.N.,THE EMERGENCE OF ARAB NATIONALISM (REV. ED.). TURKEY UK NAT/G SECT TEC/DEV LEAD REV WAR AGE/Y ROLE ORD/FREE...TRADIT CHARTS BIBLIOG 20 ARABS OTTOMAN. PAGE 173 H3453 B66 ISLAM NAT/LISM DIPLOM

HUNTINGTON S.P.,"POLITICAL MODERNIZATION* AMERICA VS EUROPE." EUR+WWI MOD/EUR UK USA+45 LAW ECO/UNDEV PWR SOVEREIGN CONSERVE LAISSEZ GOV/COMP. PAGE 75 H1505 L66 STRUCT CREATE OBS

MANSERGH N.,"THE PARTITION OF INDIA IN RETROSPECT." INDIA PAKISTAN S/ASIA UK DIPLOM COLONIAL GP/REL PWR 20. PAGE 102 H2042 S66 NAT/G PARL/PROC POLICY POL/PAR

ALBINSKI H.S.,EUROPEAN POLITICAL PROCESSES: ESSAYS AND READINGS. EUR+WWI FRANCE GERMANY MOD/EUR UK ELITES POL/PAR PWR...CHARTS ANTHOL 18/20. PAGE 5 H0094 B67 NAT/COMP POLICY IDEA/COMP

ANDERSON O.,A LIBERAL STATE AT WAR. MOD/EUR UK LAW CULTURE STRUCT ECO/DEV NAT/G DIPLOM PARL/PROC GP/REL ALL/VALS...CONCPT 19. PAGE 7 H0131 B67 WAR FORCES

BROWN L.N.,FRENCH ADMINISTRATIVE LAW. FRANCE UK CONSTN NAT/G LEGIS DOMIN CONTROL EXEC PARL/PROC PWR ...JURID METH/COMP GEN/METH. PAGE 22 H0447 B67 EX/STRUC LAW IDEA/COMP CT/SYS

BUNN R.F.,POLITICS AND CIVIL LIBERTIES IN EUROPE: FOUR CASE STUDIES. FRANCE GERMANY/W UK USSR NAT/G PRESS CRIME CROWD PRIVIL ATTIT 20. PAGE 24 H0476 B67 ORD/FREE CONSTN NAT/COMP LAW

CAMERON R.,BANKING IN THE EARLY STAGES OF INDUSTRIALIZATION: A STUDY IN ECONOMIC COMPARATIVE HISTORY. FRANCE GERMANY UK USSR...CHARTS IDEA/COMP NAT/COMP 18/20 CHINJAP. PAGE 26 H0512 B67 FINAN INDUS GOV/COMP

CANTOR N.F.,THE ENGLISH TRADITION* TWENTIETH-CENTURY VIEWS OF ENGLISH HISTORY (2VOLS.). UK STRATA NAT/G SECT WAR...POLICY GOV/COMP IDEA/COMP ANTHOL T PARLIAMENT CMN/WLTH. PAGE 26 H0522 B67 CT/SYS LAW POL/PAR

COLLINS R.O.,EGYPT AND THE SUDAN. COM FRANCE ISLAM SUDAN UAR UK SOCIETY NAT/G COLONIAL NAT/LISM...GEOG SOC LING TREND SOC/INTEG 7/20 SUEZ. PAGE 32 H0635 B67 AGRI CULTURE ECO/UNDEV

DICKSON P.G.M.,THE FINANCIAL REVOLUTION IN ENGLAND. UK NAT/G TEC/DEV ADMIN GOV/REL...SOC METH/CNCPT CHARTS GP/COMP BIBLIOG 17/18. PAGE 41 H0823 B67 ECO/DEV FINAN CAP/ISM MGT

GIFFORD P.,BRITAIN AND GERMANY IN AFRICA. AFR GERMANY UK ECO/UNDEV LEAD WAR NAT/LISM ATTIT ...POLICY HIST/WRIT METH/COMP ANTHOL BIBLIOG 19/20 WWI. PAGE 56 H1123 B67 COLONIAL ADMIN DIPLOM NAT/COMP

HAWTREY R.,INCOMES AND MONEY. EUR+WWI FUT UK LABOR WORKER INT/TRADE TAX PAY BAL/PAY COST WEALTH 20. PAGE 68 H1363 B67 FINAN NAT/G POLICY ECO/DEV

HODGKINSON R.G.,THE ORIGINS OF THE NATIONAL HEALTH SERVICE: THE MEDICAL SERVICES OF THE NEW POOR LAW, 1834-1871. UK INDUS MUNIC WORKER PROB/SOLV EFFICIENCY ATTIT HEALTH WEALTH SOCISM...JURID SOC/WK 19/20. PAGE 72 H1445 B67 HEAL NAT/G POLICY LAW

HUTCHINS F.G.,THE ILLUSION OF PERMANENCE: BRITISH IMPERIALISM IN INDIA. INDIA UK CULTURE STRUCT NAT/G REV GP/REL RACE/REL ADJUST DISCRIM ATTIT MORAL PWR SOC/INTEG 18/20. PAGE 75 H1509 B67 COLONIAL CONTROL SOVEREIGN CONSERVE

JOHNSON H.G.,ECONOMIC NATIONALISM IN OLD AND NEW STATES. CANADA CHINA/COM MALI UK DIPLOM...SIMUL GEN/LAWS 19/20 MEXIC/AMER. PAGE 81 H1619 B67 NAT/LISM ECO/UNDEV ECO/DEV NAT/COMP

MORRIS A.J.A.,PARLIAMENTARY DEMOCRACY IN THE NINETEENTH CENTURY. UK INDUS LOC/G NAT/G POL/PAR CONSULT LEGIS INT/TRADE ADMIN CHOOSE SUFF SOVEREIGN 19 PARLIAMENT. PAGE 113 H2261 B67 TIME/SEQ CONSTN PARL/PROC POPULISM

NESS G.D.,BUREAUCRACY AND RURAL DEVELOPMENT IN MALAYSIA. MALAYSIA UK SOCIETY FINAN INDUS WORKER TEC/DEV ECO/TAC COLONIAL EQUILIB ORD/FREE...STAT CHARTS 20. PAGE 117 H2330 B67 ECO/UNDEV PLAN NAT/G ADMIN

RAE D.,THE POLITICAL CONSEQUENCES OF ELECTORAL LAWS. EUR+WWI ICELAND ISRAEL NEW/ZEALND UK USA+45 ADJUD APPORT GP/REL MAJORITY...MATH STAT CENSUS CHARTS BIBLIOG 20 AUSTRAL. PAGE 129 H2579 B67 POL/PAR CHOOSE NAT/COMP REPRESENT

SCHWARTZ B.,THE ROOTS OF FREEDOM: A CONSTITUTIONAL HISTORY OF ENGLAND. UK LAW POL/PAR DELIB/GP LEGIS REV REPRESENT...JURID BIBLIOG/A 13/20. PAGE 140 H2809 B67 CONSTN PARL/PROC NAT/G

SHAKABPA T.W.D.,TIBET: A POLITICAL HISTORY. CHINA/COM UK CHIEF LEAD...INT BIBLIOG 20 TIBET. PAGE 142 H2839 B67 DIPLOM SECT NAT/G

VENKATESWARAN R.J.,CABINET GOVERNMENT IN INDIA. B67 DELIB/GP

INDIA UK SOCIETY OP/RES COLONIAL LEAD EFFICIENCY ORD/FREE 20. PAGE 162 H3241
ADMIN CONSTN NAT/G

B67
WALTZ K.N.,FOREIGN POLICY AND DEMOCRATIC POLITICS: THE AMERICAN AND BRITISH EXPERIENCE. FRANCE UK USA+45 PARL/PROC GOV/REL CONSERVE...DECISION 20. PAGE 165 H3298
POLICY DIPLOM NAT/G GOV/COMP

B67
WIENER F.B.,CIVILIANS UNDER MILITARY JUSTICE; THE BRITISH PRACTICE SINCE 1689 ESPECIALLY IN NORTH AMERICA. UK USA-45 LAW CONSTN CRIME REV...DECISION CHARTS NAT/COMP BIBLIOG 17/20. PAGE 168 H3356
CT/SYS FORCES ADJUD

B67
WISEMAN H.V.,BRITAIN AND THE COMMONWEALTH. EUR+WWI FUT UK ECO/DEV POL/PAR TEC/DEV INT/TRADE LEAD ROLE SOVEREIGN...SOC TREND 20 CMN/WLTH. PAGE 169 H3391
INT/ORG DIPLOM NAT/G NAT/COMP

L67
PICKERING J.F.,"RECRUITMENT TO THE ADMINISTRATIVE CLASS, 1960-1964: PART 2" UK STRATA NAT/G WORKER ...STAT CHARTS 20. PAGE 125 H2505
PERS/COMP ADMIN KNO/TEST EDU/PROP

L67
WRIGHT W.R.,"FOREIGN-OWNED RAILWAYS IN ARGENTINA: A CASE STUDY OF ECONOMIC NATIONALISM." L/A+17C UK ECO/UNDEV SERV/IND LG/CO NAT/G TEC/DEV BAL/PWR EQUILIB ARGEN. PAGE 171 H3423
NAT/LISM CAP/ISM ECO/TAC COLONIAL

S67
ADNITT F.W.,"THE RISE OF ENGLISH RADICALISM -- PART 2." UK NAT/G WORKER INCOME WEALTH...BIOG 19 PARLIAMENT. PAGE 4 H0071
LEGIS LOBBY

S67
ALEXANDER A.,"CANADA'S PARLIAMENTARY SECRETARIES: THEIR POLITICAL AND CONSTITUTIONAL POSITION." CANADA UK NAT/G POL/PAR GOV/REL...GOV/COMP 20. PAGE 5 H0099
CONSTN ADMIN EX/STRUC DELIB/GP

S67
BHATNAGAR J.K.,"THE VALUES AND ATTITUDES OF SOME INDIAN AND BRITISH STUDENTS." INDIA UK ECO/UNDEV LEGIT COLONIAL GP/REL SOVEREIGN...QU 20. PAGE 16 H0328
NAT/COMP ATTIT EDU/PROP ACADEM

S67
CARIAS B.,"EL CONTROL DE LAS EMPRESAS PUBLICAS POR GRUPOS DE INTERESES DE LA COMUNIDAD." FRANCE UK VENEZUELA INDUS NAT/G CONTROL OWN PWR...DECISION NAT/COMP 20. PAGE 26 H0529
WORKER REPRESENT MGT SOCISM

S67
COLLINS B.A.,"SOME NOTES ON PUBLIC SERVICE COMMISSIONS IN THE COMMONWEALTH CARIBBEAN." JAMAICA L/A+17C TRINIDAD UK NAT/G OP/RES DOMIN SENIOR COLONIAL CONTROL INGP/REL CENTRAL EFFICIENCY PWR ...DECISION 20. PAGE 31 H0631
ADMIN EX/STRUC ECO/UNDEV CHOOSE

S67
CROCKETT D.G.,"THE MP AND HIS CONSTITUENTS." UK POL/PAR...DECISION 20. PAGE 35 H0706
EXEC NAT/G PERS/REL REPRESENT

S67
DERRICK P.,"THE WHITE PAPER ON INCOMES." EUR+WWI UK LAW LABOR NAT/G PLAN PROB/SOLV GP/REL...GOV/COMP PARLIAMENT. PAGE 40 H0794
INCOME POL/PAR POLICY

S67
GREGORY R.,"THE MINISTER'S LINE: OR, THE M4 COMES TO BERKSHIRE. PART I." UK CONSTN DIST/IND LEGIS TOP/EX PLAN ADJUD...GEOG 20. PAGE 60 H1210
DECISION CONSTRUC NAT/G DELIB/GP

S67
HEASMAN D.J.,"THE GIBRALTAR AFFAIR." SPAIN UK NAT/G BAL/PWR CONSEN NAT/LISM ATTIT...REALPOL 20. PAGE 69 H1378
DIPLOM COLONIAL REGION

S67
IDENBURG P.J.,"POLITICAL STRUCTURAL DEVELOPMENT IN TROPICAL AFRICA." UK ECO/UNDEV KIN POL/PAR CHIEF EX/STRUC CREATE COLONIAL CONTROL REPRESENT RACE/REL ...MAJORIT TREND 20. PAGE 76 H1521
AFR CONSTN NAT/G GOV/COMP

S67
JENCKS C.E.,"SOCIAL STATUS OF COAL MINERS IN BRITAIN SINCE NATIONALIZATION." UK STRATA STRUCT LABOR RECEIVE GP/REL INCOME OWN ATTIT HABITAT...MGT T 20. PAGE 80 H1600
EXTR/IND WORKER CONTROL NAT/G

S67
KYLE K.,"BACKGROUND TO THE CRISIS" ISLAM ISRAEL UAR UK USSR NAT/G PROB/SOLV LEGIT CONTROL REGION STRANGE MORAL 20 JEWS. PAGE 89 H1787
DIPLOM POLICY SOVEREIGN COERCE

S67
LICHFIELD N.,"THE EVALUATION OF CAPITAL INVESTMENT PROJECTS IN TOWN CENTRE REDEVELOPMENT." UK CONSTRUC MUNIC CONSULT COST...METH/CNCPT IDEA/COMP 20. PAGE 96 H1923
PLAN ECO/TAC NAT/G DECISION

S67
MAIR L.,"BUSOGA LOCAL GOVERNMENT" AFR UGANDA UK CONSTN GP/REL...GOV/COMP METH/COMP 20. PAGE 101 H2024
LOC/G COLONIAL LAW ATTIT

S67
MARWICK A.,"THE LABOUR PARTY AND THE WELFARE STATE IN BRITAIN, 19001948." UK SOCIETY STRUCT ECO/DEV WORKER CREATE PRICE CHOOSE WEALTH NEW/LIB SOCISM ...POLICY HEAL 20 PARLIAMENT LABOR/PAR. PAGE 104 H2074
POL/PAR RECEIVE LEGIS NAT/G

S67
MATTHEWS R.O.,"THE SUEZ CANAL DISPUTE* A CASE STUDY IN PEACEFUL SETTLEMENT." FRANCE ISRAEL UAR UK NAT/G CONTROL LEAD COERCE WAR NAT/LISM ROLE ORD/FREE PWR ...INT/LAW UN 20. PAGE 105 H2099
PEACE DIPLOM ADJUD

S67
NEALE R.S.,"WORKING CLASS WOMEN AND WOMEN'S SUFFRAGE." UK LAW CONSTN LABOR NAT/G DELIB/GP LEGIS WORKER PAY PARTIC CHOOSE 19 FEMALE/SEX. PAGE 116 H2326
STRATA SEX SUFF DISCRIM

S67
ROOT W.,"REPORT FROM PARIS - DE GAULLE: WHICH WAY TO THE FUTURE?" CANADA FRANCE ISLAM UK INT/ORG CHIEF CREATE AGREE CONTROL ARMS/CONT NUC/PWR EQUILIB PEACE PWR 20 DEGAULLE/C NATO. PAGE 134 H2670
POLICY DIPLOM NAT/G BAL/PWR

S67
TIVEY L.,"THE POLITICAL CONSEQUENCES OF ECONOMIC PLANNING." UK CONSTN INDUS ACT/RES ADMIN CONTROL LOBBY REPRESENT EFFICIENCY SUPEGO SOVEREIGN ...DECISION 20. PAGE 155 H3108
PLAN POLICY NAT/G

S68
GUZZARDI W.,"THE DECLINE OF THE STERLING CLUB." UK WOR+45 NAT/G PLAN DIPLOM INT/TRADE AGREE CONSEN EQUILIB SOVEREIGN...POLICY NEW/IDEA 20 COMMONWLTH GOLD/STAND. PAGE 63 H1259
FINAN ECO/TAC WEALTH NAT/COMP

S68
MILLAR T.B.,"THE COMMONWEALTH AND THE UN." UK DIPLOM TARIFFS AGREE COLONIAL CONTROL SOVEREIGN WEALTH...GP/COMP GOV/COMP 20 CMN/WLTH UN. PAGE 111 H2210
INT/ORG POLICY TREND ECO/TAC

S68
VERAX,"L'EUROPE ET LA FRANCE SUR LA SELLETTE." FRANCE UK NAT/G CHIEF DIPLOM EDU/PROP GP/REL 20 EEC DEGAULLE/C. PAGE 162 H3242
INT/TRADE INT/ORG POLICY ECO/TAC

B75
MAINE H.S.,LECTURES ON THE EARLY HISTORY OF INSTITUTIONS. IRELAND UK CONSTN ELITES STRUCT FAM KIN CHIEF LEGIS CT/SYS OWN SOVEREIGN...CONCPT 16 BENTHAM/J BREHON ROMAN/LAW. PAGE 101 H2021
CULTURE LAW INGP/REL

B76
SMITH A.,THE WEALTH OF NATIONS. UK STRUCT WORKER DIPLOM ECO/TAC OPTIMAL DRIVE PERSON ORD/FREE ...OLD/LIB GEN/LAWS 17/18. PAGE 145 H2905
WEALTH PRODUC INDUS LAISSEZ

B79
BRODERICK G.C.,POLITICAL STUDIES. IRELAND UK ROMAN/EMP LAW ACADEM LOC/G NAT/G DIPLOM PARL/PROC SUFF GP/REL LAISSEZ...ANTHOL. PAGE 21 H0424
CONSTN COLONIAL

C80
ARNOLD M.,"DEMOCRACY" IN MIXED ESSAYS (2ND ED.)" UK SOCIETY STRUCT...CONCPT METH/COMP 19. PAGE 8 H0166
NAT/G MAJORIT EX/STRUC ELITES

C80
ARNOLD M.,"EQUALITY" IN MIXED ESSAYS." MOD/EUR UK ELITES STRATA NAT/G...CONCPT IDEA/COMP NAT/COMP SOC/INTEG 19. PAGE 8 H0167
ORD/FREE UTOPIA SOCIETY STRUCT

B82
CUNNINGHAM W.,THE GROWTH OF ENGLISH INDUSTRY AND COMMERCE. FUT UK FINAN NAT/G CAP/ISM...POLICY 20 MERCANTLST CHRISTIAN POPE. PAGE 36 H0721
INDUS INT/TRADE SML/CO CONSERVE

C82
MILL J.S.,"CIVILIZATION" IN DISSERTATIONS AND DISCUSSIONS." MOD/EUR UK ECO/DEV CONTROL MORAL ORD/FREE PWR...SOC IDEA/COMP 19. PAGE 110 H2208
SOCIETY NAT/G STRUCT CONCPT

B90
BURKE E.,REFLECTIONS ON THE REVOLUTION IN FRANCE. FRANCE UK NAT/G DOMIN LEGIT PEACE PWR SOVEREIGN CONSERVE...POLICY GEN/LAWS 18. PAGE 24 H0487
REV ORD/FREE CHIEF TRADIT

B95
SELIGMAN E.R.A.,ESSAYS IN TAXATION. NEW/ZEALND PRUSSIA UK USA-45 MARKET LOC/G CREATE PRICE CONTROL INCOME OWN WEALTH...GOV/COMP METH/COMP 19. PAGE 141 H2824
TAX TARIFFS INDUS NAT/G

B96
ESMEIN A.,ELEMENTS DE DROIT CONSTITUTIONNEL. FRANCE UK CHIEF EX/STRUC LEGIS ADJUD CT/SYS PARL/PROC REV GOV/REL ORD/FREE...JURID METH/COMP 18/19. PAGE 47 H0940
LAW CONSTN NAT/G CONCPT

B98
POLLOCK F.,THE HISTORY OF ENGLISH LAW BEFORE THE TIME OF EDWARD I (2 VOLS, 2ND ED.). UK CULTURE LOC/G LEGIS LICENSE AGREE CONTROL CT/SYS SANCTION CRIME...TIME/SEQ 13 COMMON/LAW CANON/LAW. PAGE 127
LAW ADJUD JURID

H2538

BROOKS S.,BRITAIN AND THE BOERS. AFR SOUTH/AFR UK CULTURE INSPECT LEGIT...INT/LAW 19/20 BOER/WAR. PAGE 22 H0433 — B99 — WAR DIPLOM NAT/G

ULAM A.B. H3148,H3149,H3150

ULC O. H3151

ULLMANN W. H3152,H3153

UMENDRAS H. H3154

UN H3155

UN....UNITED NATIONS; SEE ALSO INT/ORG, VOL/ASSN,

AMERICAN POLITICAL SCIENCE REVIEW. USA+45 USA-45 WOR+45 WOR-45 INT/ORG ADMIN...INT/LAW PHIL/SCI CONCPT METH 20 UN. PAGE 1 H0001 — N — BIBLIOG/A DIPLOM NAT/G GOV/COMP

ASIA FOUNDATION,LIBRARY NOTES. LAW CONSTN CULTURE SOCIETY ECO/UNDEV INT/ORG NAT/G COLONIAL LEAD REGION NAT/LISM ATTIT 20 UN. PAGE 9 H0176 — N — BIBLIOG/A ASIA S/ASIA DIPLOM

PROVISIONS SECTION OAU,ORGANIZATION OF AFRICAN UNITY: BASIC DOCUMENTS AND RESOLUTIONS (PAMPHLET). AFR CULTURE ECO/UNDEV DIPLOM ECO/TAC EDU/PROP COLONIAL ARMS/CONT NUC/PWR RACE/REL DISCRIM NAT/LISM 20 UN OAU. PAGE 128 H2564 — N19 — CONSTN EX/STRUC SOVEREIGN INT/ORG

JONES H.D.,UNESCO: A SELECTED LIST OF REFERENCES. CULTURE CREATE PEACE ATTIT DRIVE 20 UNESCO UN. PAGE 82 H1631 — B48 — BIBLIOG/A INT/ORG DIPLOM EDU/PROP

MEAD M.,CULTURAL PATTERNS AND TECHNICAL CHANGE. BURMA GREECE NIGERIA ECO/UNDEV AGRI INDUS SCHOOL SECT CREATE FEEDBACK HABITAT...PSY METH/COMP BIBLIOG 20 UN. PAGE 108 H2152 — B53 — HEALTH TEC/DEV CULTURE ADJUST

DODD S.C.,"THE SCIENTIFIC MEASUREMENT OF FITNESS FOR SELF-GOVERNMENT." FUT CONSTN ECO/UNDEV INT/ORG PLAN PWR...CONCPT QUANT CON/ANAL SOC/EXP UN LEAGUE/NAT 20. PAGE 41 H0830 — S54 — NAT/G STAT SOVEREIGN

THOMPSON V.,MINORITY PROBLEMS IN SOUTHEAST ASIA. CAMBODIA CHINA/COM LAOS S/ASIA KIN NAT/G SECT PROB/SOLV EDU/PROP REGION GP/REL RACE/REL MARXISM ...SOC 20 BUDDHISM UN. PAGE 154 H3085 — B55 — INGP/REL GEOG DIPLOM STRUCT

WOYTINSKY W.S.,WORLD COMMERCE AND GOVERNMENTS: TRENDS AND OUTLOOK. WOR+45 FINAN POL/PAR DIPLOM ECO/TAC FOR/AID DOMIN WAR CHOOSE...CHARTS BIBLIOG 20 LEAGUE/NAT UN ILO. PAGE 171 H3413 — B55 — INT/TRADE DIST/IND NAT/COMP NAT/G

ROBERTS H.L.,RUSSIA AND AMERICA. CHINA/COM S/ASIA USSR FORCES TEC/DEV FOR/AID NUC/PWR ALL/IDEOS ...MAJORIT TREND NAT/COMP 20 COLD/WAR UN NATO. PAGE 132 H2641 — B56 — DIPLOM INT/ORG BAL/PWR TOTALISM

CONOVER H.F.,NORTH AND NORTHEAST AFRICA; A SELECTED ANNOTATED LIST OF WRITINGS. ALGERIA MOROCCO SUDAN UAR CULTURE INT/ORG PROB/SOLV ADJUD NAT/LISM PWR WEALTH...SOC 20 UN. PAGE 32 H0649 — B57 — BIBLIOG/A DIPLOM AFR ECO/UNDEV

STRAUSZ-HUPE R.,THE IDEA OF COLONIALISM. WOR+45 WOR-45 BAL/PWR GOV/REL...POLICY CLASSIF TIME/SEQ GOV/COMP ANTHOL 20 UN. PAGE 150 H2996 — B58 — IDEA/COMP COLONIAL CONTROL CONCPT

STRONG C.F.,MODERN POLITICAL CONSTITUTIONS. LAW CHIEF DELIB/GP EX/STRUC LEGIS ADJUD CHOOSE FEDERAL POPULISM...CONCPT BIBLIOG 20 UN. PAGE 150 H2998 — B58 — CONSTN IDEA/COMP NAT/G

FIFIELD R.H.,"THE DIPLOMACY OF SOUTHEAST ASIA: 1945-1958." INT/ORG NAT/G COLONIAL REGION...CHARTS BIBLIOG 20 UN. PAGE 50 H0996 — C58 — S/ASIA DIPLOM NAT/LISM

BLOOMFIELD L.P.,WESTERN EUROPE AND THE UN - TRENDS AND PROSPECTS. EUR+WWI BAL/PWR DIPLOM ECO/TAC COLONIAL ATTIT PWR...POLICY 20 UN EUROPE/W. PAGE 18 H0359 — B59 — INT/ORG TREND FUT NAT/G

VORSPAN A.,JUSTICE AND JUDAISM. FAM DIPLOM ECO/TAC EDU/PROP CRIME RACE/REL MARRIAGE ANOMIE ATTIT ORD/FREE...POLICY 20 UN. PAGE 164 H3279 — B59 — SECT CULTURE ACT/RES GP/REL

WARBURG J.P.,"THE CENTRAL EUROPEAN CRISIS: A PROPOSAL FOR WESTERN INITIATIVE." EUR+WWI INT/ORG NAT/G LEGIT DETER WAR...CONCPT BER/BLOC UN 20. PAGE 165 H3302 — S59 — PLAN GERMANY

THE AFRICA 1960 COMMITTEE,MANDATE IN TRUST: THE PROBLEM OF SOUTH WEST AFRICA. GERMANY STRUCT REGION SANCTION CHOOSE DISCRIM...INT/LAW 20 AFRICA/SW UN LEAGUE/NAT TRUST/TERR. PAGE 153 H3066 — B60 — NAT/G DIPLOM COLONIAL RACE/REL

THEOBOLD R.,THE NEW NATIONS OF WEST AFRICA. GHANA NIGERIA CULTURE INT/ORG ECO/TAC FOR/AID COLONIAL RACE/REL POPULISM...ANTHOL BIBLIOG 20 UN. PAGE 153 H3068 — B60 — AFR SOVEREIGN ECO/UNDEV DIPLOM

NORTHEDGE F.S.,"BRITISH FOREIGN POLICY AND THE PARTY SYSTEM." EUR+WWI FUT INT/ORG NAT/G EDU/PROP ATTIT PWR...POLICY CONCPT MYTH TIME/SEQ TREND 20 UN. PAGE 119 H2374 — S60 — POL/PAR CHOOSE DIPLOM UK

MILLER E.,"LEGAL ASPECTS OF UN ACTION IN THE CONGO." AFR CULTURE ADMIN PEACE DRIVE RIGID/FLEX ORD/FREE...WELF/ST JURID OBS UN CONGO 20. PAGE 111 H2212 — S61 — INT/ORG LEGIT

PADELFORD N.J.,"POLITICS AND THE FUTURE OF ECOSOC." AFR S/ASIA ECO/UNDEV INDUS NAT/G DELIB/GP ACT/RES ORD/FREE WEALTH...CONCPT CHARTS UN 20 ECOSOC. PAGE 122 H2438 — S61 — INT/ORG TEC/DEV

CALVOCORESSI P.,WORLD ORDER AND NEW STATES: PROBLEMS OF KEEPING THE PEACE. AFR EUR+WWI S/ASIA ELITES NAT/G ECO/TAC FOR/AID EDU/PROP COERCE ATTIT DRIVE ALL/VALS...GEN/LAWS COLD/WAR 20 UN. PAGE 25 H0509 — B62 — INT/ORG PEACE

DUTOIT B.,LA NEUTRALITE SUISSE A L'HEURE EUROPEENNE. EUR+WWI MOD/EUR INT/ORG NAT/G VOL/ASSN PLAN BAL/PWR LEGIT NEUTRAL REGION PEACE ORD/FREE SOVEREIGN...CONCPT OBS TIME/SEQ TREND STERTYP VAL/FREE LEAGUE/NAT UN 20. PAGE 44 H0873 — B62 — ATTIT DIPLOM SWITZERLND

GANJI M.,INTERNATIONAL PROTECTION OF HUMAN RIGHTS. WOR+45 CONSTN INT/TRADE CT/SYS SANCTION CRIME WAR RACE/REL...CHARTS IDEA/COMP NAT/COMP BIBLIOG 20 TREATY NEGRO LEAGUE/NAT UN CIVIL/LIB. PAGE 55 H1097 — B62 — ORD/FREE DISCRIM LEGIS DELIB/GP

LOWENSTEIN A.K.,BRUTAL MANDATE: A JOURNEY TO SOUTH WEST AFRICA. CULTURE INT/ORG NAT/G DIPLOM...GEOG 20 UN AFRICA/SW. PAGE 99 H1975 — B62 — AFR POLICY RACE/REL PROB/SOLV

UNECA LIBRARY,BOOKS ON AFRICA IN THE UNECA LIBRARY. WOR+45 AGRI INT/ORG NAT/G PLAN WRITING REGION...SOC STAT UN. PAGE 158 H3160 — B62 — BIBLIOG AFR ECO/UNDEV TEC/DEV

UNECA LIBRARY,NEW ACQUISITIONS IN THE UNECA LIBRARY. LAW NAT/G PLAN PROB/SOLV TEC/DEV ADMIN REGION...GEOG SOC 20 UN. PAGE 158 H3161 — B62 — BIBLIOG AFR ECO/UNDEV INT/ORG

"AMERICAN BEHAVIORAL SCIENTIST." USSR LAW NAT/G ...SOC 20 UN. PAGE 2 H0039 — L62 — BIBLIOG AFR R+D

CORET A.,"L'INDEPENDANCE DU SAMOA OCCIDENTAL." S/ASIA LAW INT/ORG EXEC ALL/VALS SAMOA UN 20. PAGE 33 H0668 — L62 — NAT/G STRUCT SOVEREIGN

ATTIA G.E.D.,LES FORCES ARMEES DES NATIONS UNIES EN COREE ET AU MOYENORIENT. KOREA CONSTN NAT/G DELIB/GP LEGIS PWR...IDEA/COMP NAT/COMP BIBLIOG UN SUEZ. PAGE 9 H0177 — B63 — FORCES INT/LAW

BRECHER M.,THE NEW STATES OF ASIA. ASIA S/ASIA INT/ORG BAL/PWR COLONIAL NEUTRAL ORD/FREE PWR 20 UN. PAGE 20 H0407 — B63 — NAT/G ECO/UNDEV DIPLOM POLICY

FIRST R.,SOUTH WEST AFRICA. SOUTH/AFR INT/ORG KIN NAT/G WORKER COLONIAL WAR...POLICY 20 UN TRUST/TERR AFRICA/SW. PAGE 50 H1006 — B63 — DISCRIM ORD/FREE RACE/REL CONTROL

FRANKEL J.,THE MAKING OF FOREIGN POLICY: AN ANALYSIS OF DECISION-MAKING. CHINA/COM EUR+WWI USA+45 ELITES INTELL FORCES LEGIS PLAN ATTIT ALL/VALS MORAL CONSERVE...GOV/COMP 20 PRESIDENT UN TREATY. PAGE 53 H1051 — B63 — POLICY DECISION PROB/SOLV DIPLOM

GARDINIER D.E.,CAMEROON: UNITED NATIONS CHALLENGE TO FRENCH POLICY. AFR CAMEROON FRANCE NAT/G LEGIS CONTROL SOVEREIGN 20 UN. PAGE 55 H1101 — B63 — DIPLOM POLICY INT/ORG COLONIAL

B63
HUGHES A.J.,EAST AFRICA: THE SEARCH FOR UNITY- KENYA, TANGANYIKA, UGANDA, AND ZANZIBAR. TANZANIA UGANDA CONSTN POL/PAR SECT CHIEF DELIB/GP LEGIS WAR CHOOSE NAT/LISM MARXISM...POLICY CHARTS 20 NEGRO UN. PAGE 74 H1488
NAT/G DOMIN LOC/G AFR

B63
JUDD P.,AFRICAN INDEPENDENCE: THE EXPLODING EMERGENCE OF THE NEW AFRICAN NATIONS. AFR UK LAW CONSTN CULTURE KIN DIPLOM ATTIT...CHARTS BIBLIOG 20 UN DEGAULLE/C NEGRO THIRD/WRLD. PAGE 82 H1640
ORD/FREE POLICY DOMIN LOC/G

B63
LYON P.,NEUTRALISM. ECO/UNDEV EDU/PROP COLONIAL ALL/IDEOS...IDEA/COMP 20 COLD/WAR UN. PAGE 99 H1985
NAT/COMP NAT/LISM DIPLOM NEUTRAL

B63
NICOLSON H.,DIPLOMACY (3RD ED.). INT/ORG NAT/G CONSULT DELIB/GP CONFER 19/20 LEAGUE/NAT UN. PAGE 118 H2354
DIPLOM CONCPT NAT/COMP

B63
PADELFORD N.J.,AFRICA AND WORLD ORDER. AFR COLONIAL SOVEREIGN...ANTHOL BIBLIOG 20 UN UNIFICA COMMONWLTH. PAGE 122 H2439
DIPLOM NAT/G ORD/FREE

B63
QUAISON-SACKEY A.,AFRICA UNBOUND: REFLECTIONS OF AN AFRICAN STATESMAN. ISLAM CULTURE INTELL INT/ORG POL/PAR TOP/EX DOMIN EDU/PROP LEGIT ATTIT PERSON ...CONCPT OBS TIME/SEQ CHARTS STERTYP 20 UN. PAGE 129 H2571
AFR BIOG

B63
ROBERTSON A.H.,HUMAN RIGHTS IN EUROPE. CONSTN SOCIETY INT/ORG NAT/G VOL/ASSN DELIB/GP ACT/RES PLAN ADJUD REGION ROUTINE ATTIT LOVE ORD/FREE RESPECT...JURID SOC CONCPT SOC/EXP UN 20. PAGE 132 H2645
EUR+WWI PERSON

B63
UN SECRETARY GENERAL,PLANNING FOR ECONOMIC DEVELOPMENT. ECO/UNDEV FINAN BUDGET INT/TRADE TARIFFS TAX ADMIN 20 UN. PAGE 158 H3159
PLAN ECO/TAC MGT NAT/COMP

C63
ATTIA G.E.O.,"LES FORCES ARMEES DES NATIONS UNIES EN COREE ET AU MOYENORIENT." KOREA CONSTN DELIB/GP LEGIS PWR...IDEA/COMP NAT/COMP BIBLIOG UN SUEZ. PAGE 9 H0178
FORCES NAT/G INT/LAW

B64
BERRINGTON H.,HOW NATIONS ARE GOVERNED. FRANCE WOR+45 ECO/UNDEV INT/ORG POL/PAR CHOOSE TOTALISM KNOWL...MAJORIT T 20 UN COMMONWLTH THIRD/WRLD. PAGE 16 H0320
NAT/G GOV/COMP ECO/DEV CONSTN

B64
ROSENAU J.N.,INTERNATIONAL ASPECTS OF CIVIL STRIFE. CHINA/COM CUBA EUR+WWI USA+45 USSR BAL/PWR EDU/PROP NEUTRAL COERCE MORAL...NAT/COMP 20 COLD/WAR UN. PAGE 134 H2676
POLICY DIPLOM REV WAR

B64
SEGAL R.,SANCTIONS AGAINST SOUTH AFRICA. AFR SOUTH/AFR NAT/G INT/TRADE RACE/REL PEACE PWR ...INT/LAW ANTHOL 20 UN. PAGE 141 H2821
SANCTION DISCRIM ECO/TAC POLICY

B64
STRONG C.F.,HISTORY OF MODERN POLITICAL CONSTITUTIONS. STRUCT INT/ORG NAT/G LEGIS TEC/DEV DIPLOM INT/TRADE CT/SYS EXEC...METH/COMP T 12/20 UN. PAGE 150 H2999
CONSTN CONCPT

B64
VECCHIO G.D.,L'ETAT ET LE DROIT. ITALY CONSTN EX/STRUC LEGIS DIPLOM CT/SYS...JURID 20 UN. PAGE 162 H3238
NAT/G SOVEREIGN CONCPT INT/LAW

B64
WAINHOUSE D.W.,REMNANTS OF EMPIRE: THE UNITED NATIONS AND THE END OF COLONIALISM. FUT PORTUGAL WOR+45 NAT/G CONSULT DOMIN LEGIT ADMIN ROUTINE ATTIT ORD/FREE...POLICY JURID RECORD INT TIME/SEQ UN CMN/WLTH 20. PAGE 164 H3287
INT/ORG TREND COLONIAL

S64
HIRAI N.,"SHINTO AND INTERNATIONAL PROBLEMS." SOCIETY NAT/G PLAN EDU/PROP RACE/REL PEACE ATTIT PERCEPT LOVE MORAL...HUM MYTH RECORD SAMP TREND STERTYP TOT/POP 20 UN CHINJAP SHINTO. PAGE 71 H1423
ASIA SECT

S64
MARTELLI G.,"PORTUGAL AND THE UNITED NATIONS." AFR EUR+WWI ELITES INT/ORG NAT/G PROVS PLAN DIPLOM ECO/TAC DOMIN COLONIAL RIGID/FLEX MORAL ORD/FREE PWR WEALTH...MYTH UN 20. PAGE 103 H2060
ATTIT PORTUGAL

B65
BROCK C.,A GUIDE TO LIBRARY RESOURCES FOR POLITICAL SCIENCE STUDENTS AT THE UNIVERSITY OF NORTH CAROLINA (PAMPHLET). USA+45 WOR+45 PROVS ATTIT MARXISM...POLICY NAT/COMP UN. PAGE 21 H0422
BIBLIOG/A DIPLOM NAT/G INT/ORG

B65
PADELFORD N.,THE UNITED NATIONS IN THE BALANCE* ACCOMPLISHMENTS AND PROSPECTS. NAT/G VOL/ASSN DIPLOM ADMIN COLONIAL CT/SYS REGION WAR ORD/FREE ...ANTHOL UN. PAGE 122 H2437
INT/ORG CONTROL

B65
UN,SPACE ACTIVITIES AND RESOURCES: REVIEW OF UNITED NATION'S NATIONAL AND INTERNATIONAL PROGRAMS. INT/ORG LABOR PLAN TEC/DEV DIPLOM EFFICIENCY HEALTH ...GOV/COMP 20 UN. PAGE 158 H3155
SPACE NUC/PWR FOR/AID PEACE

S65
LAULICHT J.,"PUBLIC OPINION AND FOREIGN POLICY DECISIONS." CANADA ELITES NAT/G FOR/AID LEAD NUC/PWR PERCEPT...INT QU CHARTS UN COLD/WAR. PAGE 92 H1839
DIPLOM ATTIT CON/ANAL SAMP

B66
DOUMA J.,BIBLIOGRAPHY ON THE INTERNATIONAL COURT INCLUDING THE PERMANENT COURT, 1918-1964. WOR+45 WOR-45 DELIB/GP WAR PRIVIL...JURID NAT/COMP 20 UN LEAGUE/NAT. PAGE 42 H0844
BIBLIOG/A INT/ORG CT/SYS DIPLOM

B66
EPSTEIN F.T.,THE AMERICAN BIBLIOGRAPHY OF RUSSIAN AND EAST EUROPEAN STUDIES FOR 1964. USSR LOC/G NAT/G POL/PAR FORCES ADMIN ARMS/CONT...JURID CONCPT 20 UN. PAGE 47 H0933
BIBLIOG COM MARXISM DIPLOM

B66
FRANK E.,LAWMAKERS IN A CHANGING WORLD. FRANCE UK USSR WOR+45 PARTIC EFFICIENCY ROLE ALL/IDEOS ...CHARTS ANTHOL PARLIAMENT 20 UN COLD/WAR. PAGE 52 H1049
GOV/COMP LEGIS NAT/G DIPLOM

B66
GERARD-LIBOIS J.,KATANGA SECESSION. INT/ORG FORCES DIPLOM ADMIN CONTROL WAR CHOOSE PWR...CHARTS 20 KATANGA TSHOMBE/M UN. PAGE 56 H1114
NAT/G REGION ORD/FREE REV

B66
HAMILTON W.B.,A DECADE OF THE COMMONWEALTH, 1955-1964. UK LAW ELITES FINAN FOR/AID CONFER COLONIAL PWR...GEOG CHARTS ANTHOL 20 CMN/WLTH UN. PAGE 65 H1302
INT/ORG INGP/REL DIPLOM NAT/G

B66
KIRDAR U.,THE STRUCTURE OF UNITED NATIONS ECONOMIC AID TO UNDERDEVELOPED COUNTRIES. AGRI FINAN INDUS NAT/G EX/STRUC PLAN GIVE TASK...POLICY 20 UN. PAGE 86 H1721
INT/ORG FOR/AID ECO/UNDEV ADMIN

B66
UN ECONOMIC AND SOCIAL COUNCIL,WORLD POPULATION PROSPECTS AS ASSESSED IN 1963. FUT WOR+45 DEATH AGE ...TREND CHARTS UN. PAGE 158 H3157
PREDICT CENSUS GEOG NAT/COMP

B66
US LIBRARY OF CONGRESS,NIGERIA: A GUIDE TO OFFICIAL PUBLICATIONS. CAMEROON NIGERIA UK DIPLOM...POLICY 19/20 UN LEAGUE/NAT. PAGE 161 H3215
BIBLIOG ADMIN NAT/G COLONIAL

L66
KRENZ F.E.,"THE REFUGEE AS A SUBJECT OF INTERNATIONAL LAW." FUT LAW NAT/G CREATE ADJUD ISOLAT STRANGE...RECORD UN. PAGE 88 H1766
INT/LAW DISCRIM NEW/IDEA

S66
DETTER I.,"THE PROBLEM OF UNEQUAL TREATIES." CONSTN NAT/G LEGIS COLONIAL COERCE PWR...GEOG UN TIME TREATY. PAGE 40 H0796
SOVEREIGN DOMIN INT/LAW ECO/UNDEV

S66
GALTUNG J.,"EAST-WEST INTERACTION PATTERNS." DIPLOM INT/TRADE...NET/THEORY CON/ANAL CHARTS NAT/COMP INDEX NATO COLD/WAR UN WARSAW/P. PAGE 55 H1090
STAT HYPO/EXP

B67
CEFKIN J.L.,THE BACKGROUND OF CURRENT WORLD PROBLEMS. NAT/G MARXISM...T 20 UN COLD/WAR. PAGE 28 H0565
DIPLOM NAT/LISM ECO/UNDEV

B67
UNESCO,PRINCIPLES AND PROBLEMS OF NATIONAL SCIENCE POLICIES. WOR+45 ECO/DEV ECO/UNDEV R+D INT/ORG PROB/SOLV CONFER...PHIL/SCI CHARTS 20 UNESCO UN. PAGE 158 H3165
NAT/COMP POLICY TEC/DEV CREATE

L67
TOUVAL S.,"THE ORGANIZATION OF AFRICAN UNITY AND AFRICAN BORDERS." DEBATE REGION TASK REV ATTIT ORD/FREE...DECISION UN 20 OAU. PAGE 156 H3121
AFR NAT/G COLONIAL NAT/LISM

S67
HALPERN B.,"THE ORIGINS OF THE CRISIS." ISLAM ISRAEL INT/ORG FORCES WEAPON PEACE ORD/FREE TREATY 20 UN. PAGE 65 H1296
WAR NAT/G DIPLOM

S67
KOHN W.S.G.,"THE SOVEREIGNTY OF LIECHTENSTEIN." LIECHTENST SWITZERLND USSR CONSTN DEBATE WAR CONSERVE 18/20 UN. PAGE 88 H1748
SOVEREIGN NAT/G PWR DIPLOM

S67
MATTHEWS R.O.,"THE SUEZ CANAL DISPUTE* A CASE STUDY IN PEACEFUL SETTLEMENT." FRANCE ISRAEL UAR UK NAT/G CONTROL LEAD COERCE WAR NAT/LISM ROLE ORD/FREE PWR ...INT/LAW UN 20. PAGE 105 H2099
PEACE DIPLOM ADJUD

S67
NIEBUHR R.,"THE ETHICS OF WAR AND PEACE IN THE NUCLEAR AGE." VIETNAM INTELL CONFER CONTROL WAR GOV/REL PERS/REL ORD/FREE...POLICY INT GOV/COMP
MORAL PEACE NUC/PWR

NAT/COMP 20 UN. PAGE 118 H2360 — DIPLOM

S68
DUGARD J.,"THE REVOCATION OF THE MANDATE FOR SOUTH WEST AFRICA." SOUTH/AFR WOR+45 STRATA NAT/G DELIB/GP DIPLOM ADJUD SANCTION CHOOSE RACE/REL ...POLICY NAT/COMP 20 AFRICA/SW UN TRUST/TERR LEAGUE/NAT. PAGE 43 H0858 — AFR INT/ORG DISCRIM COLONIAL

S68
MILLAR T.B.,"THE COMMONWEALTH AND THE UN." UK DIPLOM TARIFFS AGREE COLONIAL CONTROL SOVEREIGN WEALTH...GP/COMP GOV/COMP 20 CMN/WLTH UN. PAGE 111 H2210 — INT/ORG POLICY TREND ECO/TAC

UN ECONOMIC AND SOCIAL COUNCIL H3156,H3157

UN ECONOMIC COMN ASIA & FAR E H3158

UN SECRETARY GENERAL H3159

UN/ILC....UNITED NATIONS INTERNATIONAL LAW COMMISSION

UN/SEC/GEN....UNITED NATIONS SECRETARY GENERAL

UNCSAT....UNITED NATIONS CONFERENCE ON THE APPLICATION OF SCIENCE AND TECHNOLOGY FOR THE BENEFIT OF THE LESS DEVELOPED AREAS

UNCTAD....UNITED NATIONS COMMISSION ON TRADE, AID, AND DEVELOPMENT

UNDERDEVELOPED COUNTRIES....SEE ECO/UNDEV

UNDP....UNITED NATIONS DEVELOPMENT PROGRAM

UNECA LIBRARY H3160,H3161

UNEF....UNITED NATIONS EMERGENCY FORCE

UNESCO H3162,H3163,H3164,H3165

UNESCO....UNITED NATIONS EDUCATIONAL, SCIENTIFIC, AND CULTURAL ORGANIZATION; SEE ALSO UN, INT/ORG

B48
JONES H.D.,UNESCO: A SELECTED LIST OF REFERENCES. CULTURE CREATE PEACE ATTIT DRIVE 20 UNESCO UN. PAGE 82 H1631 — BIBLIOG/A INT/ORG DIPLOM EDU/PROP

B52
UNESCO,DOCUMENTATION IN THE SOCIAL SCIENCES. CULTURE...GP/COMP METH 20 UNESCO. PAGE 158 H3162 — BIBLIOG SOC

B53
MURPHY G.,IN THE MINDS OF MEN: THE STUDY OF HUMAN BEHAVIOR AND SOCIAL TENSIONS IN INDIA. FUT S/ASIA FAM INT/ORG NAT/G DIPLOM EDU/PROP GP/REL ATTIT RIGID/FLEX ALL/VALS...SOC QU UNESCO 20. PAGE 115 H2297 — SECT STRATA INDIA

B63
COMISION DE HISTORIO,GUIA DE LOS DOCUMENTOS MICROFOTOGRAFIADOS POR LA UNIDAD MOVIL DE LA UNESCO. SOCIETY ECO/UNDEV INT/ORG ADMIN...SOC 20 UNESCO. PAGE 32 H0637 — BIBLIOG NAT/G L/A+17C DIPLOM

N63
LIBRARY HUNGARIAN ACADEMY SCI,HUNGARIAN PUBLICATIONS ON ASIA AND AFRICA, 1950-1962: A SELECTED BIBLIOGRAPHY (PAMPHLET). AFR ASIA HUNGARY S/ASIA ECO/UNDEV NAT/G EDU/PROP ATTIT 20 UNESCO. PAGE 96 H1922 — BIBLIOG REGION DIPLOM WRITING

B65
SHRIMALI K.L.,EDUCATION IN CHANGING INDIA. INDIA CULTURE DIPLOM FOR/AID GP/REL RACE/REL ATTIT SOC/INTEG 20 UNESCO CMN/WLTH. PAGE 143 H2866 — EDU/PROP PROF/ORG ACADEM

B67
UNESCO,PRINCIPLES AND PROBLEMS OF NATIONAL SCIENCE POLICIES. WOR+45 ECO/DEV ECO/UNDEV R+D INT/ORG PROB/SOLV CONFER...PHIL/SCI CHARTS 20 UNESCO UN. PAGE 158 H3165 — NAT/COMP POLICY TEC/DEV CREATE

UNIDO....UNITED NATIONS INDUSTRIAL DEVELOPMENT ORGANIZATION

UNIFICA....UNIFICATION AND REUNIFICATION OF GEOGRAPHIC-POLITICAL ENTITIES

B25
WILLIAMS B.,THE SELBORNE MEMORANDUM. AFR FUT SOUTH/AFR UK NAT/G BUDGET DIPLOM REGION GOV/REL SOVEREIGN...POLICY CHARTS 20 UNIFICA SELBORNE/W. PAGE 168 H3365 — COLONIAL PROVS

B51
MEYER E.W.,POLITICAL PARTIES IN WESTERN GERMANY (PAMPHLET). GERMANY/W MUNIC NAT/G GOV/REL ALL/IDEOS 20 UNIFICA BERLIN. PAGE 109 H2190 — POL/PAR LOBBY CHOOSE CONSTN

B63
PADELFORD N.J.,AFRICA AND WORLD ORDER. AFR COLONIAL SOVEREIGN...ANTHOL BIBLIOG 20 UN UNIFICA COMMONWLTH. PAGE 122 H2439 — DIPLOM NAT/G ORD/FREE

B66
WEINSTEIN F.B.,VIETNAM'S UNHELD ELECTIONS: THE FAILURE TO CARRY OUT THE 1956 REUNIFICATION ELECTIONS... (MONOGRAPH). VIETNAM/S VIETNAM/N LEGIT CONFER ADJUD WAR PEACE 20 TREATY GENEVA/CON UNIFICA. PAGE 166 H3330 — AGREE NAT/G CHOOSE DIPLOM

UNION AFRICAINE ET MALGACHE, ALSO OCAM....SEE UAM

UNION FOR THE NEW REPUBLIC....SEE UNR

UNION OF SOUTH AFRICA....SEE SOUTH/AFR

UNION OF SOVIET SOCIALIST REPUBLICS....SEE USSR

UNION POUR LA DEFENSE DE LA REPUBLIQUE (FRANCE)....SEE UDR

UNION OF SOUTH AFRICA H3166

UNIONS....SEE LABOR

UNITED ARAB REPUBLIC....SEE UAR

UNITED AUTO WORKERS....SEE UAW

UNITED KINGDOM....SEE UK, COMMONWLTH

UNITED NATIONS....SEE UN

UNITED NATIONS INTERNATIONAL LAW COMMISSION....SEE UN/ILC

UNITED NATIONS SECURITY COUNCIL....SEE SECUR/COUN

UNITED NATIONS SPECIAL FUND....SEE UNSF

UNITED STATES ARMS CONTROL AND DISARMAMENT AGENCY....SEE ACD

UNITED STATES FEDERAL POWER COMMISSION....SEE FPC

UNITED STATES HOUSING CORPORATION....SEE US/HOUSING

UNITED STATES MILITARY ACADEMY....SEE WEST/POINT

UNITED STATES SENATE COMMITTEE ON FOREIGN RELATIONS....SEE FOREIGNREL

UNIV....UNIVERSAL TO MAN

UNIVERSAL REFERENCE SYSTEM H3168

UNIVERSES....SEE UNIVERSES AND SAMPLING INDEX, P. XIV

UNIVERSITIES....SEE ACADEM

UNIVERSITIES RESEARCH ASSOCIATION, INC.....SEE UNIVS/RES

UNIVERSITY OF CALIFORNIA H3169

UNIVERSITY OF FLORIDA LIBRARY H3170

UNIVS/RES....UNIVERSITIES RESEARCH ASSOCIATION, INC.

UNLABR/PAR....UNION LABOR PARTY

UNPLAN/INT....IMPROMPTU INTERVIEW

B61
MARVICK D.,POLITICAL DECISION-MAKERS. INTELL STRATA NAT/G POL/PAR EX/STRUC LEGIS DOMIN EDU/PROP ATTIT PERSON PWR...PSY STAT OBS CONT/OBS STAND/INT UNPLAN/INT TIME/SEQ CHARTS STERTYP VAL/FREE. PAGE 104 H2073 — TOP/EX BIOG ELITES

S62
MU FU-SHENG,"THE WILTING OF THE HUNDRED FLOWERS: FREE THOUGHT IN CHINA TODAY." ASIA CHINA/COM CULTURE FAM NAT/G EDU/PROP REV TOTALISM ATTIT PERSON RESPECT...GEOG INT UNPLAN/INT COLD/WAR 20. PAGE 114 H2278 — INTELL ELITES

B63
KURZMAN D.,SUBVERSION OF THE INNOCENTS: PATTERNS OF COMMUNIST PENETRATION OF AFRICA, THE MIDDLE EAST AND AFRICA. AFR ASIA ISLAM S/ASIA CULTURE NAT/G FORCES PLAN EDU/PROP ADMIN ATTIT...CONCPT INT UNPLAN/INT TIME/SEQ. PAGE 89 H1785 — COM COERCE

B63
TOUVAL S.,SOMALI NATIONALISM: INTERNATIONAL POLITICS AND THE DRIVE FOR UNITY IN THE HORN OF AFRICA. AFR CULTURE PROVS LEGIS EDU/PROP REGION COERCE ATTIT...MYTH UNPLAN/INT TIME/SEQ SOMALI VAL/FREE 20. PAGE 156 H3118 — SOCIETY EXEC NAT/LISM

L63
JAY R.,"RELIGION AND POLITICS IN RURAL CENTRAL — CULTURE

JAVA." S/ASIA SOCIETY NEIGH SECT PERSON HEALTH OBS
MORAL...SOC UNPLAN/INT TIME/SEQ JAVA VAL/FREE 20
WORSHIP. PAGE 80 H1594

UNR....UNION FOR THE NEW REPUBLIC

UNRRA....UNITED NATIONS RELIEF AND REHABILITATION AGENCY

UNRUH J.M. H3171

UNRWA....UNITED NATIONS RELIEF AND WORKS AGENCY

UNSF....UNITED NATIONS SPECIAL FUND

UNSTEAD J.F. H3172

UPPER VOLTA....SEE UPPER/VOLT

UPPER/VOLT....UPPER VOLTA; SEE ALSO AFR

B60
CONOVER H.F.,OFFICIAL PUBLICATIONS OF FRENCH WEST AFRICA, 1946-1958. DAHOMEY IVORY/CST NIGER SENEGAL UPPER/VOLT CONSTN AGRI PRESS...CON/ANAL 20. PAGE 33 H0651 — BIBLIOG COLONIAL NAT/G AFR

B64
SKINNER E.P.,THE MOSSI OF UPPER VOLTA: THE POLITICAL DEVELOPMENT OF A SUDANESE PEOPLE. AFR LAW AGRI FAM KIN POL/PAR PROVS SECT DELIB/GP EX/STRUC FORCES TOP/EX DOMIN EDU/PROP LEGIT CT/SYS COERCE CHOOSE ORD/FREE PWR WEALTH...SOC MYTH VAL/FREE. PAGE 145 H2897 — CULTURE OBS UPPER/VOLT

B65
KUPER H.,URBANIZATION AND MIGRATION IN WEST AFRICA. UPPER/VOLT CULTURE ECO/UNDEV WORKER REGION GOV/REL ...LING ANTHOL SOC/INTEG 20 AFRICA/W OSHOGBO MOSSI MIGRATION. PAGE 89 H1781 — AFR HABITAT MUNIC GEOG

UPTON A.F. H3173

URBAN/LEAG....URBAN LEAGUE

URBAN/RNWL....URBAN RENEWAL

B64
CULLINGWORTH J.B.,TOWN AND COUNTRY PLANNING IN ENGLAND AND WALES. UK LAW SOCIETY CONSULT ACT/RES ADMIN ROUTINE LEISURE INGP/REL ADJUST PWR...GEOG 20 OPEN/SPACE URBAN/RNWL. PAGE 36 H0718 — MUNIC PLAN NAT/G PROB/SOLV

B64
GREBLER L.,URBAN RENEWAL IN EUROPEAN COUNTRIES: ITS EMERGENCE AND POTENTIALS. EUR+WWI UK ECO/DEV LOC/G NEIGH CREATE ADMIN ATTIT...TREND NAT/COMP 20 URBAN/RNWL. PAGE 60 H1205 — MUNIC PLAN CONSTRUC NAT/G

B64
PINNICK A.W.,COUNTRY PLANNERS IN ACTION. UK FINAN SERV/IND NAT/G CONSULT DELIB/GP PRICE CONTROL ROUTINE LEISURE AGE/C...GEOG 20 URBAN/RNWL. PAGE 126 H2512 — MUNIC PLAN INDUS ATTIT

B65
DUGGAR G.S.,RENEWAL OF TOWN AND VILLAGE I: A WORLD-WIDE SURVEY OF LOCAL GOVERNMENT EXPERIENCE. WOR+45 CONSTRUC INDUS CREATE BUDGET REGION GOV/REL...QU NAT/COMP 20 URBAN/RNWL. PAGE 43 H0859 — MUNIC NEIGH PLAN ADMIN

URE P.N. H3174

URQUIDI V.L. H3175

URUGUAY....URUGUAY

N19
OPERATIONS AND POLICY RESEARCH,URUGUAY: ELECTION FACTBOOK: NOVEMBER 27, 1966 (PAMPHLET). URUGUAY LAW NAT/G LEAD REPRESENT...STAT BIOG CHARTS 20. PAGE 121 H2422 — POL/PAR CHOOSE PLAN ATTIT

B64
MUSSO AMBROSI L.A.,BIBLIOGRAFIA DE BIBLIOGRAFIAS URUGUAYAS. URUGUAY DIPLOM ADMIN ATTIT...SOC 20. PAGE 115 H2301 — BIBLIOG NAT/G L/A+17C PRESS

B67
PIKE F.B.,FREEDOM AND REFORM IN LATIN AMERICA. BRAZIL URUGUAY CONSTN CULTURE SECT DIPLOM EDU/PROP PARTIC DRIVE ALL/VALS CATHISM...GEOG ANTHOL BIBLIOG REFORMERS BOLIV. PAGE 126 H2511 — L/A+17C ORD/FREE ECO/UNDEV REV

US AGENCY FOR INTERNATIONAL DEVELOPMENT....SEE US/AID

US ATOMIC ENERGY COMMISSION....SEE AEC

US ATTORNEY GENERAL....SEE ATTRNY/GEN

US BUREAU OF STANDARDS....SEE BUR/STNDRD

US BUREAU OF THE BUDGET....SEE BUR/BUDGET

US CENTRAL INTELLIGENCE AGENCY....SEE CIA

US CIVIL AERONAUTICS BOARD....SEE CAB

US CONGRESS RULES COMMITTEES....SEE RULES/COMM

US DEPARTMENT OF AGRICULTURE....SEE DEPT/AGRI

US DEPARTMENT OF COMMERCE....SEE DEPT/COM

US DEPARTMENT OF DEFENSE....SEE DEPT/DEFEN

US DEPARTMENT OF HEALTH, EDUCATION, AND WELFARE....SEE DEPT/HEW

US DEPARTMENT OF HOUSING AND URBAN DEVELOPMENT....SEE DEPT/HUD

US DEPARTMENT OF JUSTICE....SEE DEPT/JUST

US DEPARTMENT OF LABOR AND INDUSTRY....SEE DEPT/LABOR

US DEPARTMENT OF STATE....SEE DEPT/STATE

US DEPARTMENT OF THE INTERIOR....SEE DEPT/INTER

US DEPARTMENT OF THE TREASURY....SEE DEPT/TREAS

US FEDERAL AVIATION AGENCY....SEE FAA

US FEDERAL BUREAU OF INVESTIGATION....SEE FBI

US FEDERAL COMMUNICATIONS COMMISSION....SEE FCC

US FEDERAL COUNCIL FOR SCIENCE AND TECHNOLOGY....SEE FEDSCI/TEC

US FEDERAL HOUSING ADMINISTRATION....SEE FHA

US FEDERAL OPEN MARKET COMMITTEE....SEE FED/OPNMKT

US FEDERAL RESERVE SYSTEM....SEE FED/RESERV

US FEDERAL TRADE COMMISSION....SEE FTC

US HOUSE COMMITTEE ON SCIENCE AND ASTRONAUTICS....SEE HS/SCIASTR

US HOUSE COMMITTEE ON UNAMERICAN ACTIVITIES....SEE HUAC

US HOUSE OF REPRESENTATIVES....SEE HOUSE/REP

US INFORMATION AGENCY....SEE USIA

US INTERNAL REVENUE SERVICE....SEE IRS

US INTERNATIONAL COOPERATION ADMINISTRATION....SEE ICA

US INTERSTATE COMMERCE COMMISSION....SEE ICC

US MILITARY ACADEMY....SEE WEST/POINT

US NATIONAL AERONAUTICS AND SPACE ADMINISTRATION....SEE NASA

US OFFICE OF ECONOMIC OPPORTUNITY....SEE OEO

US OFFICE OF NAVAL RESEARCH....SEE NAVAL/RES

US OFFICE OF PRICE ADMINISTRATION....SEE OPA

US OFFICE OF WAR INFORMATION....SEE OWI

US PATENT OFFICE....SEE PATENT/OFF

US PEACE CORPS....SEE PEACE/CORP

US SECRETARY OF STATE....SEE SEC/STATE

US SECURITIES AND EXCHANGE COMMISSION....SEE SEC/EXCHNG

US SENATE COMMITTEE ON AERONAUTICS AND SPACE....SEE SEN/SPACE

US SENATE SCIENCE ADVISORY COMMISSION....SEE SCI/ADVSRY

US SENATE....SEE SENATE

US SMALL BUSINESS ADMINISTRATION....SEE SBA

US SOUTH....SEE SOUTH/US

US STEEL CORPORATION....SEE US/STEEL

US ATOMIC ENERGY COMMISSION H3176

US CONGRESS JT ATOM ENRGY COMM H3177

US CONSULATE GENERAL HONG KONG H3178,H3179,H3180,H3181,H3182

US DEPARTMENT OF DEFENSE H3183

US DEPARTMENT OF STATE H3184,H3185,H3186,H3187,H3188,H3189 , H3190,H3191,H3192

US DEPARTMENT OF THE ARMY H3193,H3194,H3195

US HOUSE COMM BANKING-CURR H3196

US HOUSE COMM FOREIGN AFFAIRS H3197

US HOUSE COMM SCI ASTRONAUT H3198

US LIBRARY OF CONGRESS H3199,H3200,H3201,H3202,H3203,H3204 , H3205,H3206,H3207,H3208,H3209,H3210,H3211,H3212,H3213 , H3214,H3215

US SENATE SPEC COMM FOR AID H3216,H3217

US/AID....UNITED STATES AGENCY FOR INTERNATIONAL DEVELOPMENT

US/HOUSING....UNITED STATES HOUSING CORPORATION

US/STEEL....UNITED STATES STEEL CORPORATION

US/WEST....WESTERN UNITED STATES

USA+45....UNITED STATES, 1945 TO PRESENT

USA-45....UNITED STATES, 1700 TO 1945

USIA....UNITED STATES INFORMATION AGENCY

USPNSKII/G....GLEB USPENSKII

USSR....UNION OF SOVIET SOCIALIST REPUBLICS; SEE ALSO RUSSIA, APPROPRIATE TIME/SPACE/CULTURE INDEX

N
AVTOREFERATY DISSERTATSII. USSR INTELL ACADEM NAT/G DIPLOM GOV/REL KNOWL CONCPT. PAGE 2 H0029 — BIBLIOG MARXISM MARXIST COM

N
"PROLOG",DIGEST OF THE SOVIET UKRANIAN PRESS. USSR LAW AGRI INDUS PROVS SCHOOL DIPLOM GOV/REL ATTIT ...HUM LING 20. PAGE 3 H0053 — BIBLIOG/A NAT/G PRESS COM

B18
WILSON W.,THE STATE: ELEMENTS OF HISTORICAL AND PRACTICAL POLITICS. FRANCE GERMANY ITALY UK USSR CONSTN EX/STRUC LEGIS CT/SYS WAR PWR...POLICY GOV/COMP 20. PAGE 169 H3385 — NAT/G JURID CONCPT NAT/COMP

N19
SALKEVER L.R.,SUB-SAHARA AFRICA (PAMPHLET). AFR USSR EXTR/IND NAT/G SCHOOL DIPLOM COLONIAL WEALTH ...GEOG CHARTS 16/20. PAGE 137 H2742 — ECO/UNDEV TEC/DEV TASK INT/TRADE

N19
SENGHOR L.S.,AFRICAN SOCIALISM (PAMPHLET). AFR FRANCE MALI USSR ELITES ECO/UNDEV NAT/G DIPLOM DOMIN EDU/PROP ATTIT 20 NEGRO. PAGE 141 H2827 — SOCISM MARXISM ORD/FREE NAT/LISM

B29
DE REPARAZ G.,GEOGRAFIA Y POLITICA. CHILE SPAIN USSR NAT/G DIPLOM REV MARXISM...POLICY 19/20. PAGE 38 H0768 — GEOG MOD/EUR

B29
LANGER W.L.,THE FRANCO-RUSSIAN ALLIANCE: 1890-1894. FRANCE MOD/EUR UK USSR NAT/G CHIEF FORCES BAL/PWR AGREE WAR PEACE PWR...TIME/SEQ TREATY 19 BISMARCK/O. PAGE 91 H1809 — DIPLOM

B34
STALIN J.,PROBLEMS OF LENINISM. USSR STRATA INDUS LOC/G POL/PAR ECO/TAC CONTROL TOTALISM PWR SOCISM LENIN/VI STALIN/J. PAGE 148 H2968 — MARXISM REV ELITES NAT/G

B37
BERDYAEV N.,THE ORIGIN OF RUSSIAN COMMUNISM. MOD/EUR RUSSIA USSR INTELL SECT REV...ANARCH HUM 19/20 ORTHO/RUSS COM/PARTY CHRISTIAN. PAGE 15 H0294 — MARXISM NAT/LISM CULTURE ATTIT

B38
HARPER S.N.,THE GOVERNMENT OF THE SOVIET UNION. COM USSR LAW CONSTN ECO/DEV PLAN TEC/DEV DIPLOM INT/TRADE ADMIN REV NAT/LISM...POLICY 20. PAGE 67 H1337 — MARXISM NAT/G LEAD POL/PAR

B39
ANDERSON W.,LOCAL GOVERNMENT IN EUROPE. FRANCE GERMANY ITALY UK USSR MUNIC PROVS ADMIN GOV/REL CENTRAL SOVEREIGN 20. PAGE 7 H0136 — GOV/COMP NAT/COMP LOC/G CONSTN

B40
BROGAN D.W.,THE DEVELOPMENT OF MODERN FRANCE (1870-1939). FRANCE GERMANY UK USSR CONSTN CHIEF LEGIS DIPLOM AGREE COLONIAL WAR NAT/LISM PEACE SOCISM 19/20 TREATY. PAGE 21 H0428 — MOD/EUR NAT/G

B42
NEUMANN S.,PERMANENT REVOLUTION: THE TOTAL STATE IN A WORLD AT WAR. COM EUR+WWI GERMANY USSR EX/STRUC DIPLOM CONTROL COERCE REPRESENT MARXISM...SOC GOV/COMP BIBLIOG 20 HITLER/A STALIN/J. PAGE 117 H2337 — FASCISM TOTALISM DOMIN EDU/PROP

B43
CONOVER H.F.,SOVIET RUSSIA: SELECTED LIST OF REFERENCES. USSR CULTURE INDUS NAT/G TOP/EX TEC/DEV BUDGET WAR CIVMIL/REL EFFICIENCY MARXISM 20. PAGE 32 H0644 — BIBLIOG ECO/DEV COM DIPLOM

B43
GRIERSON P.,BOOKS ON SOVIET RUSSIA 1917-42: A BIBLIOGRAPHY AND A GUIDE TO READING. USSR CULTURE ELITES NAT/G PLAN DIPLOM REV...GEOG 20. PAGE 61 H1213 — BIBLIOG/A COM MARXISM LEAD

B43
LASKI H.J.,REFLECTIONS ON THE REVOLUTIONS OF OUR TIME. COM USSR NAT/G WORKER UTOPIA ORD/FREE WEALTH MARXISM SOCISM 19/20. PAGE 92 H1830 — CAP/ISM WELF/ST ECO/TAC POLICY

B43
LENIN V.I.,STATE AND REVOLUTION. USSR CAP/ISM ...ANARCH MARXIST PHIL/SCI IDEA/COMP 20. PAGE 94 H1878 — SOCIETY NAT/G REV MARXISM

B43
LENIN V.I.,LEFT WING COMMUNISM: AN INFANTILE DISORDER (1920). GERMANY MOD/EUR USSR STRUCT CHIEF DOMIN EDU/PROP LEGIT LEAD REPRESENT POPULISM ...METH/COMP 19 LENIN/VI COM/PARTY MENSHEVIK. PAGE 94 H1879 — COM MARXISM NAT/G REV

B44
US LIBRARY OF CONGRESS,RUSSIA: A CHECK LIST PRELIMINARY TO A BASIC BIBLIOGRAPHY OF MATERIALS IN THE RUSSIAN LANGUAGE. COM USSR CULTURE EDU/PROP MARXISM...ART/METH HUM LING 19/20. PAGE 160 H3204 — BIBLIOG LAW SECT

B45
CONOVER H.F.,THE GOVERNMENTS OF THE MAJOR FOREIGN POWERS: A BIBLIOGRAPHY. FRANCE GERMANY ITALY UK USSR CONSTN LOC/G POL/PAR EX/STRUC FORCES ADMIN CT/SYS CIVMIL/REL TOTALISM...POLICY 19/20. PAGE 32 H0645 — BIBLIOG NAT/G DIPLOM

B45
LASKER B.,ASIA ON THE MOVE. ASIA BURMA S/ASIA THAILAND USSR ECO/UNDEV FAM KIN WAR NAT/LISM ATTIT ...GEOG CENSUS TREND AUSTRAL 20. PAGE 91 H1826 — CULTURE RIGID/FLEX

B46
ALLEN J.S.,WORLD MONOPOLY AND PEACE. GERMANY UK USSR FINAN INDUS LG/CO DOMIN CONTROL PEACE PWR WEALTH SOCISM...NAT/COMP 20 MONOPOLY. PAGE 5 H0105 — CAP/ISM DIPLOM WAR COLONIAL

B46
BLUM L.,FOR ALL MANKIND (TRANS. BY W. PICKLES). FRANCE GERMANY USSR LAW SOCIETY STRUCT POL/PAR WORKER DIPLOM DOMIN CHOOSE ORD/FREE FASCISM 20. PAGE 18 H0361 — POPULISM SOCIALIST NAT/G WAR

B47
ENKE S.,INTERNATIONAL ECONOMICS. UK USA+45 USSR INT/ORG BAL/PWR BARGAIN CAP/ISM BAL/PAY...NAT/COMP 20 TREATY. PAGE 46 H0927 — INT/TRADE FINAN TARIFFS ECO/TAC

B48
TOWSTER J.,POLITICAL POWER IN THE USSR: 1917-1947. USSR CONSTN CULTURE ELITES CREATE PLAN COERCE CENTRAL ATTIT RIGID/FLEX ORD/FREE...BIBLIOG SOC/INTEG 20 LENIN/VI STALIN/J. PAGE 156 H3122 — EX/STRUC NAT/G MARXISM PWR

B48
WOLFE B.D.,THREE WHO MADE A REVOLUTION. USSR CONSTN NAT/G CAP/ISM EDU/PROP CONTROL WAR GP/REL INGP/REL PERS/REL ROLE 20 STALIN/J LENIN/VI TROTSKY/L BOLSHEVISM. PAGE 170 H3398 — BIOG REV LEAD MARXISM

B48
YAKOBSON S.,FIVE HUNDRED RUSSIAN WORKS FOR COLLEGE LIBRARIES (PAMPHLET). MOD/EUR USSR MARXISM SOCISM ...ART/METH GEOG HUM JURID SOC 13/20. PAGE 171 H3431 — BIBLIOG NAT/G CULTURE COM

B49
GORER G.,THE PEOPLE OF GREAT RUSSIA: A PSYCHOLOGICAL STUDY. RUSSIA USSR NAT/G DIPLOM LEAD AGE/C ANOMIE ATTIT DRIVE...POLICY 20. PAGE 59 H1182 — ISOLAT PERSON PSY SOCIETY

B49
US DEPARTMENT OF STATE,SOVIET BIBLIOGRAPHY (PAMPHLET). CHINA/COM COM USSR LAW AGRI INT/ORG ECO/TAC EDU/PROP...POLICY GEOG 20. PAGE 159 H3185 — BIBLIOG/A MARXISM CULTURE DIPLOM

B50
BERMAN H.J.,JUSTICE IN RUSSIA; AN INTERPRETATION OF SOVIET LAW. USSR LAW STRUCT LABOR FORCES AGREE GP/REL ORD/FREE SOCISM...TIME/SEQ 20. PAGE 15 H0309 — JURID ADJUD MARXISM

COERCE

B50
SCHUMPETER J.A.,CAPITALISM, SOCIALISM, AND DEMOCRACY (3RD ED.). USA-45 USSR WOR+45 WOR-45 INTELL ECO/DEV ECO/UNDEV ECO/TAC WAR PRODUC ORD/FREE...MGT SOC 20 MARX/KARL. PAGE 140 H2804
SOCIALIST CAP/ISM MARXISM IDEA/COMP

B51
BORKENAU F.,EUROPEAN COMMUNISM. COM EUR+WWI GERMANY SPAIN USSR INT/ORG PLAN REV WAR ATTIT 20 STALIN/J HITLER/A. PAGE 19 H0376
MARXISM POLICY DIPLOM NAT/G

B51
MORLEY C.,GUIDE TO RESEARCH IN RUSSIAN HISTORY. USSR MARXISM...BIOG HIST/WRIT ANTHOL DICTIONARY. PAGE 113 H2259
BIBLIOG/A R+D NAT/G COM

C51
BEST H.,"THE SOVIET STATE AND ITS INCEPTION." USSR CULTURE INDUS DIPLOM WEALTH...GEOG SOC BIBLIOG 20. PAGE 16 H0322
COM GEN/METH REV MARXISM

B52
KOLARZ W.,RUSSIA AND HER COLONIES. COM RUSSIA LAW CULTURE ECO/DEV KIN LOC/G SECT TEC/DEV ECO/TAC EDU/PROP REGION COERCE ATTIT PWR SOVEREIGN...SOC TIME/SEQ CON/ANAL VAL/FREE 19/20. PAGE 88 H1749
NAT/G DOMIN USSR COLONIAL

B52
ULAM A.B.,TITOISM AND THE COMINFORM. USSR WOR+45 STRUCT INT/ORG NAT/G ACT/RES PLAN EXEC ATTIT DRIVE ALL/VALS...CONCPT OBS VAL/FREE 20 COMINTERN TITO/MARSH. PAGE 157 H3149
COM POL/PAR TOTALISM YUGOSLAVIA

B53
CURTISS J.S.,THE RUSSIAN CHURCH AND THE SOVIET STATE 1917-1950. COM USSR CONTROL LEAD REV MARXISM ...POLICY BIBLIOG 20 CHURCH/STA ORTHO/RUSS. PAGE 36 H0728
GP/REL NAT/G SECT PWR

B53
LEITES N.,A STUDY OF BOLSHEVISM. WOR+45 WOR-45 ELITES SOCIETY INT/ORG NAT/G EX/STRUC EDU/PROP EXEC ROUTINE ATTIT MORAL MARXISM...CONCPT OBS VAL/FREE 20. PAGE 94 H1869
COM POL/PAR USSR TOTALISM

B53
LENZ F.,DIE BEWEGUNGEN DER GROSSEN MACHTE. USA+45 USA-45 USSR SOCIETY STRATA STRUCT NAT/G PERSON MARXISM...CONCPT IDEA/COMP NAT/COMP 18/20. PAGE 94 H1883
BAL/PWR TREND DIPLOM HIST/WRIT

B53
MEYER P.,THE JEWS IN THE SOVIET SATELLITES. CZECHOSLVK POLAND SOCIETY STRATA NAT/G BAL/PWR ECO/TAC EDU/PROP LEGIT ADMIN COERCE ATTIT DISPL PERCEPT HEALTH PWR RESPECT WEALTH...METH/CNCPT JEWS VAL/FREE NAZI 20. PAGE 110 H2192
COM SECT TOTALISM USSR

B53
PIERCE R.A.,RUSSIAN CENTRAL ASIA, 1867-1917: A SELECTED BIBLIOGRAPHY (PAMPHLET). USSR LAW CULTURE NAT/G EDU/PROP WAR...GEOG SOC 19/20. PAGE 125 H2508
BIBLIOG COLONIAL ADMIN COM

B53
SHIRATO I.,JAPANESE SOURCES ON THE HISTORY OF THE CHINESE COMMUNIST MOVEMENT (PAMPHLET). CHINA/COM USSR CONSTRUC NAT/G POL/PAR FORCES DIPLOM DOMIN EDU/PROP CONTROL WAR TOTALISM SOCISM 20. PAGE 143 H2863
BIBLIOG/A MARXISM ECO/UNDEV

S53
BAUER R.A.,"WORD-OF-MOUTH COMMUNICATION IN THE SOVIET UNION." COM INTELL SOCIETY LABOR ATTIT KNOWL ...INT QU SAMP CHARTS 20. PAGE 12 H0239
CULTURE USSR

B54
BUTZ O.,GERMANY: DILEMMA FOR AMERICAN POLICY. GERMANY USA+45 USA-45 USSR WOR+45 INT/ORG FORCES NUC/PWR EFFICIENCY PEACE PWR...GOV/COMP 20 COLD/WAR. PAGE 25 H0501
DIPLOM NAT/G WAR POLICY

B54
FRIEDRICH C.J.,TOTALITARIAN DICTATORSHIP AND AUTOCRACY. COM EUR+WWI GERMANY ITALY USSR INTELL ECO/DEV NAT/G POL/PAR FORCES TOP/EX ECO/TAC EDU/PROP LEGIT COERCE ATTIT ORD/FREE PWR FASCISM ...CONCPT TIME/SEQ GEN/LAWS NAZI 20. PAGE 53 H1068
SOCIETY DOMIN TOTALISM

B54
GATZKE H.W.,STRESEMANN AND THE REARMAMENT OF GERMANY. EUR+WWI GERMANY USSR FINAN NAT/G ECO/TAC ATTIT...BIOG METH 20 STRESEMN/G. PAGE 55 H1105
FORCES INDUS PWR

B54
KOLARZ W.,THE PEOPLES OF THE SOVIET FAR EAST. RUSSIA USSR STRUCT LEAD ISOLAT NAT/LISM...CHARTS 20. PAGE 88 H1750
COLONIAL RACE/REL ADJUST CULTURE

B54
LENIN V.I.,SELECTED WORKS (12 VOLS.). USSR INTELL SOCIETY STRATA STRUCT NAT/G POL/PAR WORKER CAP/ISM REV WAR...MARXIST PHIL/SCI 20 MARX/KARL LENIN/VI. PAGE 94 H1880
COM MARXISM

C54
GUINS G.C.,"SOVIET LAW AND SOVIET SOCIETY." COM USSR STRATA FAM NAT/G WORKER DOMIN RACE/REL ...BIBLIOG 20. PAGE 62 H1249
LAW STRUCT PLAN

B55
KOHN H.,THE MIND OF MODERN RUSSIA. COM MOD/EUR USSR SOCIETY NAT/G SECT FORCES TOP/EX COERCE TOTALISM DRIVE RIGID/FLEX PWR SOVEREIGN...CONCPT TIME/SEQ WORK. PAGE 87 H1742
INTELL GEN/LAWS SOCISM RUSSIA

B55
MAYO H.B.,DEMOCRACY AND MARXISM. COM USSR STRATA NAT/G WORKER ECO/TAC REV MORAL...PHIL/SCI HIST/WRIT IDEA/COMP WORSHIP 20 MARX/KARL LENIN/VI STALIN/J TROTSKY/L. PAGE 105 H2108
MARXISM CAP/ISM

B55
MID-EUROPEAN LAW PROJECT,CHURCH AND STATE BEHIND THE IRON CURTAIN. COM CZECHOSLVK HUNGARY POLAND USSR CULTURE SECT EDU/PROP GOV/REL CATHISM...CHARTS ANTHOL BIBLIOG WORSHIP 20 CHURCH/STA. PAGE 110 H2202
LAW MARXISM POLICY

B55
RESHETAR J.S.,PROBLEMS OF ANALYZING AND PREDICTING SOVIET BEHAVIOR. USSR CULTURE ECO/DEV AGRI DIST/IND EXTR/IND PROC/MFG NAT/G SECT TOP/EX ACT/RES ADMIN PWR WEALTH...SOC METH TOT/POP VAL/FREE 20. PAGE 131 H2617
COM ATTIT

B55
TAN C.C.,THE BOXER CATASTROPHE. ASIA UK USSR ELITES POL/PAR VOL/ASSN FORCES PROB/SOLV DIPLOM ADMIN COLONIAL NAT/LISM PEACE TREATY 19/20 BOXER/REBL. PAGE 152 H3040
REV NAT/G WAR

B55
TOYNBEE A.,THE REALIGNMENT OF EUROPE. COM GREECE ITALY NAT/G BAL/PWR ECO/TAC EDU/PROP REV SOVEREIGN ...SOC TIME/SEQ TREND COLD/WAR 20. PAGE 156 H3123
EUR+WWI PLAN USSR

L55
ROSTOW W.W.,"RUSSIA AND CHINA UNDER COMMUNISM." CHINA/COM USSR INTELL STRUCT INT/ORG NAT/G POL/PAR TOP/EX ACT/RES PLAN ADMIN ATTIT ALL/VALS MARXISM ...CONCPT OBS TIME/SEQ TREND GOV/COMP VAL/FREE 20. PAGE 134 H2689
COM ASIA

B56
ROBERTS H.L.,RUSSIA AND AMERICA. CHINA/COM S/ASIA USSR FORCES TEC/DEV FOR/AID NUC/PWR ALL/IDEOS ...MAJORIT TREND NAT/COMP 20 COLD/WAR UN NATO. PAGE 132 H2641
DIPLOM INT/ORG BAL/PWR TOTALISM

B56
SMEDLEY A.,THE GREAT ROAD: THE LIFE AND TIMES OF CHU TEH. ASIA USSR NAT/G POL/PAR DIPLOM COERCE GUERRILLA CIVMIL/REL NAT/LISM PERSON SKILL MARXISM ...BIOG 20 CHINJAP MAO. PAGE 145 H2903
REV WAR FORCES

B56
SPINKA M.,THE CHURCH IN SOVIET RUSSIA. USSR CONTROL LEAD TASK COERCE 20. PAGE 147 H2949
GP/REL NAT/G SECT PWR

B56
VON HARPE W.,DIE SOWJETUNION FINNLAND UND SKANDANAVIEN, 1945-1955. EUR+WWI FINLAND GERMANY USSR WAR INGP/REL ORD/FREE SOVEREIGN MARXISM ...POLICY GOV/COMP BIBLIOG 20 STALIN/J. PAGE 163 H3270
DIPLOM COM NEUTRAL BAL/PWR

B56
VUCINICH A.,THE SOVIET ACADEMY OF SCIENCES. USSR STRUCT ACADEM NAT/G EDU/PROP ADMIN LEAD ROLE ...BIBLIOG 20 ACADEM/SCI. PAGE 164 H3280
PHIL/SCI CREATE INTELL PROF/ORG

B56
WOLFF R.L.,THE BALKANS IN OUR TIME. ALBANIA FUT MOD/EUR USSR YUGOSLAVIA CULTURE INT/ORG SECT DIPLOM EDU/PROP COERCE WAR ORD/FREE...CHARTS 4/20 BALKANS COMINFORM. PAGE 170 H3403
GEOG COM

B57
AMERICAN COUNCIL LEARNED SOC,GOVERNMENT UNDER LAW AND THE INDIVIDUAL. ASIA ISLAM USSR NAT/G...POLICY SOC NAT/COMP 20. PAGE 6 H0121
SOCIETY ORD/FREE CONCPT IDEA/COMP

B57
ARON R.,THE OPIUM OF THE INTELLECTUALS (TRANS. BY TERENCE KILMARTIN). FRANCE USSR WOR+45 CULTURE POL/PAR PLAN DOMIN EDU/PROP REV ATTIT ORD/FREE ...IDEA/COMP METH/COMP NAT/COMP 20 COM/PARTY. PAGE 8 H0169
INTELL UTOPIA MYTH MARXISM

B57
BUCK P.W.,CONTOL OF FOREIGN RELATIONS IN MODERN NATIONS. FRANCE L/A+17C NETHERLAND USSR WOR+45 INT/ORG TOP/EX BAL/PWR DOMIN EDU/PROP COERCE PEACE ATTIT...CONCPT TREND 20 CMN/WLTH. PAGE 23 H0465
NAT/G PWR DIPLOM

B57
CENTRAL ASIAN RESEARCH CENTRE,BIBLIOGRAPHY OF RECENT SOVIET SOURCE MATERIAL ON SOVIET CENTRAL ASIA AND THE BORDERLANDS. AFGHANISTN INDIA PAKISTAN UAR USSR ECO/UNDEV AGRI EXTR/IND INDUS ACADEM ADMIN ...HEAL HUM LING CON/ANAL 20. PAGE 28 H0567
BIBLIOG/A COM CULTURE NAT/G

B57
LOUCKS W.N.,COMPARATIVE ECONOMIC SYSTEMS (5TH ED.). COM UK USSR INDUS POL/PAR PLAN CAP/ISM TOTALISM MARXISM...PHIL/SCI BIBLIOG 19/20. PAGE 99 H1969
NAT/COMP IDEA/COMP SOCISM

B57
PARK A.G.,BOLSHEVISM IN TURKESTAN 1917-1927. COM
REV

RUSSIA USSR CULTURE AGRI SECT DOMIN GP/REL INGP/REL NAT/LISM...BIBLIOG 20 TURKESTAN. PAGE 123 H2467 — POLICY MARXISM ISLAM

B57
REISS J.,GEORGE KENNANS POLITIK DER EINDAMMUNG. USSR NAT/G FORCES TOTALISM ATTIT ORD/FREE...POLICY 20 NATO TRUMAN/HS MARSHL/PLN KENNAN/G. PAGE 131 H2613 — DIPLOM DETER PEACE

B57
TOMASIC D.A.,NATIONAL COMMUNISM AND SOVIET STRATEGY. UK USSR YUGOSLAVIA NAT/G POL/PAR CHIEF CREATE DOMIN REV WAR PWR...BIOG TREND 20 TITO/MARSH STALIN/J. PAGE 156 H3112 — COM NAT/LISM MARXISM DIPLOM

B57
US SENATE SPEC COMM FOR AID,HEARINGS BEFORE THE SPECIAL COMMITTEE TO STUDY THE FOREIGN AID PROGRAM. USA+45 USSR ECO/UNDEV INT/ORG FORCES WEAPON TOTALISM ATTIT SUPEGO...NAT/COMP CONGRESS. PAGE 161 H3217 — FOR/AID DIPLOM ORD/FREE TEC/DEV

B58
DUNAYEVSKAYA R.,MARXISM AND FREEDOM: FROM 1776 UNTIL TODAY. COM USSR WORKER CAP/ISM DOMIN REV GP/REL TOTALISM ALL/VALS...MYTH BIOG IDEA/COMP 18/20 MARX/KARL LENIN/VI STALIN/J. PAGE 43 H0861 — MARXISM CONCPT ORD/FREE

B58
GARTHOFF R.L.,SOVIET STRATEGY IN THE NUCLEAR AGE. FUT USSR R+D INT/ORG NAT/G ACT/RES TEC/DEV DOMIN DETER WAR ATTIT PWR...RELATIV METH/CNCPT SELF/OBS TREND CON/ANAL STERTYP GEN/LAWS 20. PAGE 55 H1103 — COM FORCES BAL/PWR NUC/PWR

B58
HSU U.T.,THE INVISIBLE CONFLICT. ASIA USSR ELITES NAT/G CONTROL LEAD COERCE REV WAR NAT/LISM ORD/FREE PWR 20 COM/PARTY ESPIONAGE. PAGE 74 H1485 — MARXISM POL/PAR EDU/PROP FORCES

B58
KINTNER W.R.,ORGANIZING FOR CONFLICT: A PROPOSAL. USSR STRUCT NAT/G LEGIS ADMIN EXEC PEACE ORD/FREE PWR...CONCPT OBS TREND NAT/COMP VAL/FREE COLD/WAR 20. PAGE 86 H1719 — USA+45 PLAN DIPLOM

B58
KURL S.,ESTONIA: A SELECTED BIBLIOGRAPHY. USSR ESTONIA LAW INTELL SECT...ART/METH GEOG HUM SOC 20. PAGE 89 H1784 — BIBLIOG CULTURE NAT/G

B58
LAQUER W.Z.,THE MIDDLE EAST IN TRANSITION. COM USSR ECO/UNDEV NAT/G VOL/ASSN EDU/PROP EXEC ATTIT DRIVE PWR MARXISM COLD/WAR TOT/POP 20. PAGE 91 H1818 — ISLAM TREND NAT/LISM

B58
MEHNERT K.,DER SOWJETMENSCH. USSR NAT/G SECT EDU/PROP TOTALISM ORD/FREE 20. PAGE 108 H2161 — SOCIETY ATTIT PERSON FAM

B58
SCOTT D.J.R.,RUSSIAN POLITICAL INSTITUTIONS. RUSSIA USSR CONSTN AGRI DELIB/GP PLAN EDU/PROP CONTROL CHOOSE EFFICIENCY ATTIT MARXISM...BIBLIOG/A 13/20. PAGE 141 H2813 — NAT/G POL/PAR ADMIN DECISION

L58
BELL D.,"TEN THEORIES IN SEARCH OF REALITY: THE PREDICTION OF SOVIET BEHAVIOR IN THE SOCIAL SCIENCES" (BMR)" COM USSR...POLICY SOC METH/COMP 20. PAGE 13 H0264 — MARXISM PREDICT IDEA/COMP

B59
BOLTON A.R.,SOVIET MIDDLE EAST STUDIES: AN ANALYSIS AND BIBLIOGRAPHY. ISLAM JORDAN UAR USSR NAT/G SOC. PAGE 18 H0370 — BIBLIOG NAT/COMP ECO/UNDEV

B59
DEHIO L.,GERMANY AND WORLD POLITICS IN THE TWENTIETH CENTURY. EUR+WWI FRANCE GERMANY MOD/EUR UK USSR NAT/G CHIEF BAL/PWR DOMIN COLONIAL CONTROL LEAD...IDEA/COMP 20 VERSAILLES. PAGE 39 H0783 — DIPLOM WAR NAT/LISM SOVEREIGN

B59
EMME E.M.,THE IMPACT OF AIR POWER - NATIONAL SECURITY AND WORLD POLITICS. USA+45 USSR FORCES DIPLOM WEAPON PEACE TOTALISM...POLICY NAT/COMP 20 EUROPE. PAGE 46 H0921 — DETER AIR WAR ORD/FREE

B59
ETSCHMANN R.,DIE WAHRUNGS- UND DEVISENPOLITIK DES OSTBLOCKS UND IHRE AUSWIRKUNGEN AUF DIE WIRTSCHAFTSBEZIEHUNGEN ZWISCHEN OST U WEST. BULGARIA CZECHOSLVK HUNGARY POLAND USSR MARKET NAT/G PLAN DIPLOM...NAT/COMP 20. PAGE 47 H0943 — ECO/TAC FINAN POLICY INT/TRADE

B59
GOLDWIN R.A.,READINGS IN RUSSIAN FOREIGN POLICY. HUNGARY USSR YUGOSLAVIA ELITES INT/ORG NAT/G REV WAR NAT/LISM PERSON SOCISM...CHARTS 20 MAPS BOLSHEVISM. PAGE 58 H1160 — COM MARXISM DIPLOM POLICY

B59
HENDEL S.,THE SOVIET CRUCIBLE. USSR LEAD COERCE NAT/LISM UTOPIA PWR...POLICY CONCPT ANTHOL 20 STALIN/J LENIN/VI MARX/KARL BOLSHEVIK. PAGE 70 H1393 — COM MARXISM REV TOTALISM

B59
INTERNATIONAL PRESS INSTITUTE,THE PRESS IN AUTHORITARIAN COUNTRIES. COM PORTUGAL SPAIN UAR USSR NAT/G DOMIN LEGIT ORD/FREE FASCISM SOCISM 20. PAGE 78 H1559 — PRESS CONTROL TOTALISM EDU/PROP

B59
LAQUER W.Z.,THE SOVIET UNION AND THE MIDDLE EAST. COM UAR USSR ECO/UNDEV NAT/G VOL/ASSN ECO/TAC EDU/PROP COLONIAL EXEC PWR...TIME/SEQ TREND COLD/WAR 20. PAGE 91 H1819 — ISLAM DRIVE FOR/AID NAT/LISM

B59
LIPSET S.M.,SOCIAL MOBILITY IN INDUSTRIAL SOCIETY. EUR+WWI USA+45 USSR STRUCT INDUS WRITING GP/REL INGP/REL DRIVE...SOC CHARTS NAT/COMP SOC/INTEG 20 MARX/KARL ENGELS/F. PAGE 97 H1940 — STRATA ECO/DEV SOCIETY

B59
PAGE S.W.,LENIN AND WORLD REVOLUTION. COM USSR NAT/G DOMIN COERCE CROWD UTOPIA ATTIT AUTHORIT DRIVE PWR...CONCPT MYTH 19/20 LENIN/VI MARX/KARL. PAGE 122 H2441 — REV PERSON MARXISM BIOG

B59
STERNBERG F.,THE MILITARY AND INDUSTRIAL REVOLUTION OF OUR TIME. USA+45 USSR WOR+45 WORKER COMPUTER PLAN TEC/DEV NUC/PWR GP/REL...POLICY NAT/COMP 20. PAGE 149 H2981 — DIPLOM FORCES INDUS CIVMIL/REL

B59
VINACKE H.M.,A HISTORY OF THE FAR EAST IN MODERN TIMES (6TH ED.). KOREA S/ASIA USSR CONSTN CULTURE STRATA ECO/UNDEV NAT/G CHIEF FOR/AID INT/TRADE GP/REL...SOC NAT/COMP 19/20 CHINJAP. PAGE 163 H3255 — STRUCT ASIA

S59
LABEDZ L.,"IDEOLOGY: THE FOURTH STAGE." COM USSR NAT/G TOP/EX LEGIT ATTIT PWR MARXISM...METH/CNCPT HIST/WRIT STERTYP TOT/POP 20. PAGE 90 H1795 — CONCPT GEN/LAWS

S59
SKILLING H.G.,"COMMUNISM: NATIONAL OR INTERNATIONAL." CHINA/COM USSR YUGOSLAVIA NAT/G POL/PAR VOL/ASSN DOMIN REGION COERCE ATTIT PWR MARXISM SOCISM...CONCPT TOT/POP 20 TITO/MARSH. PAGE 145 H2894 — COM TREND

S59
ZAUBERMAN A.,"SOVIET BLOC ECONOMIC INTEGRATION." COM CULTURE INTELL ECO/DEV INDUS TOP/EX ACT/RES PLAN ECO/TAC INT/TRADE ROUTINE CHOOSE ATTIT ...TIME/SEQ 20. PAGE 172 H3452 — MARKET INT/ORG USSR TOTALISM

B60
BLACK C.E.,THE TRANSFORMATION OF RUSSIAN SOCIETY. COM MOD/EUR RUSSIA SOCIETY EDU/PROP COERCE ALL/VALS 19/20. PAGE 17 H0349 — CULTURE RIGID/FLEX USSR

B60
BRZEZINSKI Z.K.,THE SOVIET BLOC-UNITY AND CONFLICT. COM USSR CONSTN DOMIN ADMIN TOTALISM PWR...SOC MYTH RECORD TREND STERTYP GEN/LAWS GEN/METH TOT/POP 20. PAGE 23 H0458 — ATTIT EDU/PROP

B60
FISCHER L.,THE SOVIETS IN WORLD AFFAIRS. CHINA/COM COM EUR+WWI USSR INT/ORG CONFER LEAD ARMS/CONT REV PWR...CHARTS 20 TREATY VERSAILLES. PAGE 51 H1010 — DIPLOM NAT/G POLICY MARXISM

B60
GOODMAN E.,SOVIET DESIGN FOR A WORLD STATE. COM USSR NAT/G TOP/EX DIPLOM ECO/TAC DOMIN EDU/PROP COERCE REV ATTIT ORD/FREE...CON/ANAL 20. PAGE 59 H1171 — PLAN PWR SOCISM TOTALISM

B60
KOHN H.,PAN-SLAVISM: ITS HISTORY AND IDEOLOGY. COM CZECHOSLVK EUR+WWI MOD/EUR USSR YUGOSLAVIA CULTURE ELITES INTELL KIN NAT/G EDU/PROP DRIVE SOVEREIGN ...HUM PHIL/SCI MYTH HIST/WRIT 19/20. PAGE 87 H1745 — ATTIT CONCPT NAT/LISM

B60
MCCLOSKY H.,THE SOVIET DICTATORSHIP. FUT CONSTN CULTURE INTELL SOCIETY POL/PAR SECT VOL/ASSN FORCES PLAN TEC/DEV DOMIN EDU/PROP COERCE PWR MARXISM ...POLICY CONCPT MYTH STERTYP 20. PAGE 106 H2127 — COM NAT/G TOTALISM USSR

B60
SCHAPIRO L.,THE COMMUNIST PARTY OF THE SOVIET UNION. COM LAW SOCIETY STRATA STRUCT ECO/DEV LABOR NAT/G POL/PAR CREATE DOMIN EDU/PROP COERCE TOTALISM MARXISM...POLICY CONCPT MYTH TIME/SEQ WORK TOT/POP 20 LENIN/VI STALIN/J. PAGE 139 H2772 — INTELL PWR USSR

B60
ZENKOVSKY S.A.,PAN-TURKISM AND ISLAM IN RUSSIA. ASIA RUSSIA USSR CULTURE POL/PAR DOMIN REV GP/REL MARXISM...LING GP/COMP BIBLIOG 19/20 TURKIC. PAGE 173 H3454 — SECT NAT/LISM COM ISLAM

L60
WHEELER G.,"RACIAL PROBLEMS IN SOVIET MUSLIM ASIA." COM CULTURE SOCIETY NEIGH SECT DOMIN EDU/PROP DISCRIM DISPL DRIVE PWR SOVEREIGN...CENSUS SAMP TREND 20 MUSLIM. PAGE 167 H3340 — PERSON ATTIT USSR RACE/REL

S60
BRZEZINSKI Z.K.,"PATTERNS AND LIMITS OF THE SINO-SOVIET DISPUTE." ASIA CHINA/COM COM FUT STRATA NAT/G EX/STRUC FORCES BAL/PWR DIPLOM ECO/TAC DOMIN EDU/PROP ADMIN COERCE WAR ATTIT RIGID/FLEX ...GEN/LAWS VAL/FREE 20. PAGE 23 H0459 — POL/PAR PWR REV USSR

S60
GROSSMAN G.,"SOVIET GROWTH: ROUTINE, INERTIA, AND PRESSURE." COM STRATA NAT/G DELIB/GP PLAN TEC/DEV ECO/TAC EDU/PROP ADMIN ROUTINE DRIVE WEALTH — POL/PAR ECO/DEV USSR

COLD/WAR 20. PAGE 62 H1236

S60
KELLEY G.A.,"THE POLITICAL BACKGROUND OF THE FRENCH A-BOMB." EUR+WWI USSR FORCES TOP/EX TEC/DEV NUC/PWR ATTIT PWR...CONCPT OBS/ENVIR TREND 20. PAGE 84 H1686
NAT/G RESPECT NAT/LISM FRANCE

S60
TAUBER K.,"ASPECTS OF NATIONALIST-COMMUNIST COLLABORATION IN POSTWAR GERMANY." COM EUR+WWI USSR NAT/G VOL/ASSN ATTIT DRIVE PWR...TIME/SEQ COLD/WAR TOT/POP 20. PAGE 152 H3049
POL/PAR EDU/PROP GERMANY

S60
WOLFE T.W.,"KHRUSHCHEV'S DISARMAMENT STRATEGY." COM NAT/G TOP/EX PLAN BAL/PWR DIPLOM ARMS/CONT COERCE ATTIT...POLICY CONCPT RECORD TREND CON/ANAL COLD/WAR 20 KHRUSH/N. PAGE 170 H3401
PWR GEN/LAWS USSR

C60
FITZSIMMONS T.,"USSR: ITS PEOPLE, ITS SOCIETY, ITS CULTURE." USSR FAM SECT DIPLOM EDU/PROP ADMIN RACE/REL ATTIT...POLICY CHARTS BIBLIOG 20. PAGE 51 H1021
CULTURE STRUCT SOCIETY COM

C60
HAZARD J.N.,"SETTLING DISPUTES IN SOVIET SOCIETY: THE FORMATIVE YEARS OF LEGAL INSTITUTIONS." USSR NAT/G PROF/ORG PROB/SOLV CONTROL CT/SYS ROUTINE REV CENTRAL...JURID BIBLIOG 20. PAGE 68 H1372
ADJUD LAW COM POLICY

C60
HAZARD J.N.,"THE SOVIET SYSTEM OF GOVERNMENT." USSR SOCIETY INDUS NAT/G POL/PAR DIPLOM CT/SYS...JURID CHARTS BIBLIOG/A 20. PAGE 69 H1373
COM NAT/COMP STRUCT ADMIN

B61
CONQUEST R.,POWER AND POLICY IN THE USSR. USSR NAT/G POL/PAR DIPLOM MARXISM 20. PAGE 33 H0655
COM HIST/WRIT GOV/REL PWR

B61
DALLIN D.J.,SOVIET FOREIGN POLICY AFTER STALIN. ASIA CHINA/COM EUR+WWI GERMANY IRAN UK YUGOSLAVIA INT/ORG NAT/G VOL/ASSN FORCES TOP/EX BAL/PWR DOMIN EDU/PROP COERCE ATTIT PWR 20. PAGE 37 H0737
COM DIPLOM USSR

B61
DONNISON F.S.V.,CIVIL AFFAIRS AND MILITARY GOVERNMENT NORTH-WEST EUROPE 1944-1946. EUR+WWI FRANCE GERMANY UK USSR LOC/G PROVS PLAN PROB/SOLV BAL/PWR ECO/TAC CONTROL PWR...CHARTS 20. PAGE 42 H0836
NAT/G WAR FORCES CIVMIL/REL

B61
DRAGNICH A.N.,MAJOR EUROPEAN GOVERNMENTS. FRANCE GERMANY/W UK USSR LOC/G EX/STRUC CT/SYS PARL/PROC ATTIT MARXISM...JURID MGT NAT/COMP 19/20. PAGE 42 H0846
NAT/G LEGIS CONSTN POL/PAR

B61
HARDT J.P.,THE COLD WAR ECONOMIC GAP. USA+45 USSR ECO/DEV FORCES INT/TRADE NUC/PWR PWR 20 COLD/WAR. PAGE 66 H1328
DIPLOM ECO/TAC NAT/COMP POLICY

B61
HOLDSWORTH M.,SOVIET AFRICAN STUDIES 1918-1959. USSR ACADEM NAT/G DIPLOM REGION KNOWL 20. PAGE 72 H1448
BIBLIOG/A AFR HABITAT NAT/COMP

B61
JAKOBSON M.,THE DIPLOMACY OF THE WINTER WAR. EUR+WWI FINLAND GERMANY USSR INT/ORG NAT/G PEACE TOTALISM PWR...POLICY CONCPT 20 TREATY. PAGE 79 H1588
WAR ORD/FREE DIPLOM

B61
LEVIN L.A.,BIBLIOGRAFIIA BIBLIOGRAFII PROIZVEDENII K. MARKSA, F. ENGELSA, V.I. LENINA. COM USSR NAT/G POL/PAR WORKER LEAD REV ATTIT...POLICY IDEA/COMP 20 MARX/KARL LENIN/VI ENGELS. PAGE 95 H1899
BIBLIOG/A MARXISM MARXIST CONCPT

B61
MOLLAU G.,INTERNATIONAL COMMUNISM AND WORLD REVOLUTION: HISTORY AND METHODS. RUSSIA USSR INT/ORG NAT/G POL/PAR VOL/ASSN FORCES BAL/PWR DIPLOM EXEC REGION WAR ATTIT PWR MARXISM...CONCPT TIME/SEQ COLD/WAR 19/20. PAGE 112 H2237
COM REV

B61
NOVE A.,THE SOVIET ECONOMY. USSR ECO/DEV FINAN NAT/G ECO/TAC PRICE ADMIN EFFICIENCY MARXISM ...TREND BIBLIOG 20. PAGE 119 H2378
PLAN PRODUC POLICY

B61
SCHIEDER T.,DOCUMENTS ON THE EXPULSION OF THE GERMANS FROM EASTERN-CENTRAL-EUROPE (VOL. II/III). COM EUR+WWI GERMANY HUNGARY ROMANIA USSR DIPLOM RACE/REL 20 MIGRATION. PAGE 139 H2785
GEOG CULTURE

B61
SETON-WATSON H.,FROM LENIN TO KHRUSHCHEV: THE HISTORY OF WORLD COMMUNISM. ASIA COM EUR+WWI ISLAM S/ASIA ECO/DEV ECO/UNDEV NAT/G POL/PAR DIPLOM ECO/TAC EDU/PROP COERCE GUERRILLA ATTIT DRIVE WORK TOT/POP NAZI 20. PAGE 141 H2832
PWR REV USSR

B61
SOKOL A.E.,SEAPOWER IN THE NUCLEAR AGE. USA+45 USSR DIST/IND FORCES INT/TRADE DETER WAR...POLICY NAT/COMP BIBLIOG COLD/WAR. PAGE 146 H2928
SEA PWR WEAPON NUC/PWR

B61
VEIT O.,GRUNDRISS DER WAHRUNGSPOLITIK. FRANCE GERMANY USSR DIPLOM INT/TRADE...NAT/COMP 19/20 GOLD/STAND SILVER. PAGE 162 H3239
FINAN POLICY ECO/TAC CAP/ISM

S61
BRZEZINSKI Z.K.,"THE ORGANIZATION OF THE COMMUNIST CAMP." COM CZECHOSLVK COM/IND NAT/G DELIB/GP INT/TRADE DOMIN EDU/PROP EXEC ROUTINE COERCE ATTIT PWR...MGT CONCPT TIME/SEQ CHARTS VAL/FREE 20 TREATY. PAGE 23 H0460
VOL/ASSN DIPLOM USSR

S61
RANDALL F.B.,"COMMUNISM IN THE HIGH ANDES." L/A+17C PERU USSR SOCIETY PLAN EDU/PROP TOTALISM ATTIT RIGID/FLEX PWR WEALTH...HUM CONCPT GEN/LAWS 20 BOLIV EQUADOR. PAGE 129 H2589
CULTURE DRIVE

S61
SCHAPIRO L.,"SOVIET GOVERNMENT TODAY." COM EUR+WWI INT/ORG POL/PAR VOL/ASSN ACT/RES PLAN PERCEPT ...CONCPT TREND TOT/POP VAL/FREE 20. PAGE 139 H2773
NAT/G TOTALISM USSR

S61
SCHELLING T.C.,"NUCLEAR STRATEGY IN EUROPE." COM EUR+WWI USSR NAT/G FORCES NUC/PWR DRIVE ORD/FREE PWR...DECISION CONCPT OBS TREND HYPO/EXP 20. PAGE 139 H2784
FUT COERCE ARMS/CONT WAR

S61
TOMASIC D.,"POLITICAL LEADERSHIP IN CONTEMPORARY POLAND." COM EUR+WWI GERMANY NAT/G POL/PAR SECT DELIB/GP PLAN ECO/TAC DOMIN EDU/PROP PWR MARXISM ...MARXIST GEOG MGT CONCPT TIME/SEQ STERTYP 20. PAGE 156 H3111
SOCIETY ROUTINE USSR POLAND

S61
TUCKER R.C.,"TOWARDS A COMPARATIVE POLITICS OF MOVEMENT-REGIMES" (BMR)" USSR CONSTN NAT/G CREATE PROB/SOLV DIPLOM DOMIN REV...GP/COMP IDEA/COMP METH 20 STALIN/J BOLSHEVISM. PAGE 157 H3135
MARXISM POLICY GEN/LAWS PWR

S61
ZAGORIA D.S.,"THE FUTURE OF SINO-SOVIET RELATIONS." CHINA/COM INT/ORG NAT/G POL/PAR VOL/ASSN ACT/RES PLAN PERSON...METH/CNCPT TIME/SEQ TOT/POP VAL/FREE 20 MAO KHRUSH/N. PAGE 172 H3445
ASIA COM TOTALISM USSR

B62
ANDREWS W.G.,EUROPEAN POLITICAL INSTITUTIONS. FRANCE GERMANY UK USSR TOP/EX LEAD PARL/PROC CHOOSE 20. PAGE 7 H0139
NAT/COMP POL/PAR EX/STRUC LEGIS

B62
BAFFREY S.A.,THE RED MYTH: A HISTORY OF COMMUNISM FROM MARX TO KHRUSHCHEV. USSR NAT/G CHIEF CAP/ISM DIPLOM EDU/PROP REV WAR PEACE TOTALISM...POLICY 20 STALIN/J KHRUSH/N. PAGE 10 H0195
CONCPT MARXISM TV

B62
BRUMBERG A.,RUSSIA UNDER KHRUSHCHEV. FUT USSR SOCIETY ECO/DEV AGRI PERF/ART WORKER PWR...SOC ANTHOL 20 KHRUSH/N. PAGE 22 H0453
COM MARXISM NAT/G CHIEF

B62
CARTER G.M.,THE GOVERNMENT OF THE SOVIET UNION. USSR CULTURE LOC/G DIPLOM ECO/TAC ADJUD CT/SYS LEAD WEALTH...CHARTS T 20 COM/PARTY. PAGE 27 H0546
NAT/G MARXISM POL/PAR EX/STRUC

B62
DUROSELLE J.B.,LES NOUVEAUX ETATS DANS LES RELATIONS INTERNATIONALES. AFR CHINA/COM FRANCE MOROCCO S/ASIA USSR ECO/UNDEV INT/ORG PLAN ECO/TAC EDU/PROP ATTIT DRIVE...TREND TOT/POP TUNIS 20. PAGE 44 H0872
NAT/G CONSTN DIPLOM

B62
FRIEDMANN W.,METHODS AND POLICIES OF PRINCIPAL DONOR COUNTRIES IN PUBLIC INTERNATIONAL DEVELOPMENT FINANCING: PRELIMINARY APPRAISAL. FRANCE GERMANY/W UK USA+45 USSR WOR+45 FINAN TEC/DEV CAP/ISM DIPLOM ECO/TAC ATTIT 20 EEC. PAGE 53 H1066
INT/ORG FOR/AID NAT/COMP ADMIN

B62
FRYKLUND R.,100 MILLION LIVES: MAXIMUM SURVIVAL IN A NUCLEAR WAR. USA+45 USSR CONTROL WEAPON ...IDEA/COMP NAT/COMP 20. PAGE 54 H1073
NUC/PWR WAR PLAN DETER

B62
GOURE L.,CIVIL DEFENSE IN THE SOVIET UNION. COM USA+45 USSR MUNIC NAT/G DETER ATTIT MARXISM ...NAT/COMP 20 CIV/DEFENS. PAGE 59 H1188
PLAN FORCES WAR COERCE

B62
GRZYBOWSKI K.,SOVIET LEGAL INSTITUTIONS. USA+45 USSR ECO/DEV NAT/G EDU/PROP CONTROL CT/SYS CRIME OWN ATTIT PWR SOCISM...NAT/COMP 20. PAGE 62 H1242
ADJUD LAW JURID

B62
INSTITUTE FOR STUDY OF USSR,YOUTH IN FERMENT. INTELL NAT/G PERF/ART POL/PAR SCHOOL VOL/ASSN FORCES EDU/PROP ATTIT DRIVE PERCEPT HEALTH KNOWL MORAL ORD/FREE RESPECT...SOC OBS HIST/WRIT VAL/FREE. PAGE 77 H1537
COM CULTURE USSR

B62
JACKSON W.A.D.,RUSSO-CHINESE BORDERLANDS. ASIA COM USSR NAT/G PROVS EX/STRUC FORCES DOMIN COERCE PEACE ATTIT PWR SOVEREIGN WEALTH...CONCPT TREND CHARTS STERTYP VAL/FREE. PAGE 79 H1576
GEOG DIPLOM RUSSIA

B62
KINDERSLEY R.,THE FIRST RUSSIAN REVISIONISTS. COM USSR LAW ELITES INTELL NAT/G LEGIS ECO/TAC EDU/PROP CONTROL LEAD GP/REL SOCISM 19/20 MARX/KARL BOLSHEVISM. PAGE 86 H1712
CONSTN MARXISM POPULISM BIOG

B62
KIRPICEVA I.K.,HANDBUCH DER RUSSISCHEN UND SOWJETISCHEN BIBLIOGRAPHIEN (5 VOLS.). USSR STRUCT ECO/DEV DIPLOM LEAD ATTIT 18/20. PAGE 86 H1726
BIBLIOG/A NAT/G MARXISM COM

B62
KRUGLAK T.E.,THE TWO FACES OF TASS. COM COM/IND NAT/G ACT/RES PLAN PRESS PERCEPT PERSON KNOWL 20. PAGE 89 H1778
PUB/INST EDU/PROP USSR

B62
LAQUEUR W.,THE FUTURE OF COMMUNIST SOCIETY. CHINA/COM USSR LAW ECO/DEV NAT/G POL/PAR PLAN PROB/SOLV DIPLOM LEAD...POLICY CONCPT IDEA/COMP ANTHOL 20. PAGE 91 H1820
MARXISM COM FUT SOCIETY

B62
LAQUEUR W.,POLYCENTRISM. CHINA/COM COM USSR WOR+45 INT/ORG NAT/G ECO/TAC DOMIN LEAD ATTIT PWR SOVEREIGN...ANTHOL 20. PAGE 91 H1821
MARXISM DIPLOM BAL/PWR POLICY

B62
MEHNERT K.,SOVIET MAN AND HIS WORLD. COM USSR INTELL FAM WORKER PLAN EDU/PROP REV PRODUC MARXISM ...SOC TREND SOC/INTEG 20 LENIN/VI STALIN/J KHRUSH/N. PAGE 108 H2162
SOCIETY CULTURE ECO/DEV

B62
MEYER A.G.,LENINISM. USSR STRUCT NAT/G CAP/ISM LEAD WAR PWR SOVEREIGN...BIBLIOG 20 LENIN/VI. PAGE 109 H2187
POL/PAR REV MARXISM PHIL/SCI

B62
MICHAEL H.N.,STUDIES IN SIBERIAN ETHNOGENESIS. USSR KIN...ART/METH SOC 20 SIBERIA. PAGE 110 H2196
HABITAT HEREDITY CULTURE LING

B62
MORGENSTERN O.,STRATEGIE - HEUTE (2ND ED.). USA+45 USSR ECO/DEV DELIB/GP WAR PEACE ORD/FREE...GOV/COMP NAT/COMP 20 COLD/WAR NATO. PAGE 113 H2256
NUC/PWR DIPLOM FORCES TEC/DEV

B62
PENTONY D.E.,RED WORLD IN TUMULT: COMMUNIST FOREIGN POLICIES. CHINA/COM COM NAT/G EDU/PROP COERCE ATTIT PWR RESPECT...SOC CHARTS 20. PAGE 124 H2488
ECO/UNDEV DOMIN USSR ASIA

B62
PHELPS E.S.,THE GOAL OF ECONOMIC GROWTH: SOURCES, COSTS, BENEFITS. USA+45 USSR FINAN TAX CONTROL DEMAND WEALTH...POLICY NAT/COMP ANTHOL BIBLIOG 20. PAGE 125 H2499
ECO/TAC ECO/DEV NAT/G FUT

B62
RUDY Z.,ETHNOSOZIOLOGIE SOWJETISCHER VOLKER. USSR SOCIETY STRUCT FAM SECT GP/REL ATTIT...SOC SOC/INTEG 20. PAGE 136 H2714
MYTH CULTURE KIN

B62
SCHECHTMAN J.B.,POSTWAR POPULATION TRANSFERS IN EUROPE: 1945-1955. COM CZECHOSLVK GERMANY POLAND USSR CULTURE SOCIETY PROB/SOLV AGREE NAT/LISM...SOC STAT TREND CHARTS METH/COMP 20 MIGRATION. PAGE 139 H2778
GEOG CENSUS EUR+WWI HABITAT

B62
STARR R.E.,POLAND 1944-1962: THE SOVIETIZATION OF A CAPTIVE PEOPLE. COM POLAND USSR POL/PAR SECT LEGIS DIPLOM DOMIN EDU/PROP CHOOSE ORD/FREE...POLICY CHARTS BIBLIOG 20. PAGE 149 H2973
MARXISM NAT/G TOTALISM NAT/COMP

B62
SWAYZE H.,POLITICAL CONTROL OF LITERATURE IN THE USSR, 1946-1959. USSR NAT/G CREATE LICENSE...JURID 20. PAGE 151 H3014
MARXISM WRITING CONTROL DOMIN

B62
WEHLER H.V.,SOZIALDEMOKRATIE UND NATIONALSTAAT. GERMANY POLAND USSR CULTURE SOCIETY STRUCT NAT/G POL/PAR DIPLOM ORD/FREE 19/20. PAGE 166 H3325
NAT/LISM SOVEREIGN GP/REL ATTIT

B62
WHITING K.R.,THE SOVIET UNION TODAY: A CONCISE HANDBOOK. USSR ELITES AGRI INDUS POL/PAR FORCES DIPLOM EDU/PROP LEAD...GEOG TREND 19/20. PAGE 168 H3354
NAT/G ATTIT MARXISM POLICY

L62
"AMERICAN BEHAVIORAL SCIENTIST." USSR LAW NAT/G ...SOC 20 UN. PAGE 2 H0039
BIBLIOG AFR R+D

S62
DUNN S.D.,"DIRECTED CULTURE CHANGE IN THE SOVIET UNION: SOME SOVIET STUDIES." SOCIETY ORD/FREE...SOC HIST/WRIT VAL/FREE 20. PAGE 43 H0866
COM CULTURE USSR

S62
IOVTCHOUK M.T.,"ON SOME THEORETICAL PRINCIPLES AND METHODS OF SOCIOLOGICAL INVESTIGATIONS (IN RUSSIAN)." FUT USA+45 STRATA R+D NAT/G POL/PAR TOP/EX ACT/RES PLAN ECO/TAC EDU/PROP ROUTINE ATTIT RIGID/FLEX MARXISM SOCISM...MARXIST METH/CNCPT OBS TREND NAT/COMP GEN/LAWS 20. PAGE 78 H1564
COM ECO/DEV CAP/ISM USSR

S62
LONDON K.,"SINO-SOVIET RELATIONS IN THE CONTEXT OF THE 'WORLD SOCIALIST SYSTEM'." ASIA CHINA/COM COM USSR INT/ORG NAT/G TOP/EX BAL/PWR DIPLOM DOMIN ATTIT PERCEPT RIGID/FLEX PWR MARXISM...METH/CNCPT TREND 20. PAGE 98 H1957
DELIB/GP CONCPT SOCISM

S62
PISTRAK L.,"SOVIET VIEWS ON AFRICA." AFR COM FUT ISLAM USSR INTELL STRUCT KIN POL/PAR PLAN EDU/PROP RIGID/FLEX PWR MARXISM...TIME/SEQ WORK TOT/POP 20. PAGE 126 H2516
NAT/G ATTIT SOCISM

S62
STRACHEY J.,"COMMUNIST INTENTIONS." ASIA USSR YUGOSLAVIA INT/ORG NAT/G FORCES DOMIN EDU/PROP COERCE NUC/PWR NAT/LISM PEACE RIGID/FLEX PWR MARXISM...CONCPT MYTH OBS TIME/SEQ TREND COLD/WAR TOT/POP 20. PAGE 150 H2992
COM ATTIT WAR

N62
US CONGRESS JT ATOM ENRGY COMM,PEACEFUL USES OF ATOMIC ENERGY, HEARING. USA+45 USSR TEC/DEV ATTIT RIGID/FLEX...TESTS CHARTS EXHIBIT METH/COMP 20 CONGRESS. PAGE 159 H3177
NUC/PWR ACADEM SCHOOL NAT/COMP

B63
BARNETT A.D.,COMMUNIST STRATEGIES IN ASIA: A COMPARATIVE ANALYSIS OF GOVERNMENTS AND PARTIES. COM FUT S/ASIA CULTURE SOCIETY STRATA NAT/G DELIB/GP ACT/RES ECO/TAC EDU/PROP COERCE CHOOSE ATTIT RIGID/FLEX ORD/FREE PWR SKILL...SIMUL VAL/FREE 20. PAGE 11 H0223
ASIA POL/PAR DIPLOM USSR

B63
BERGSON A.,ECONOMIC TRENDS IN THE SOVIET UNION. USSR ECO/UNDEV AGRI NAT/G FORCES PLAN TEC/DEV INT/TRADE BAL/PAY...POLICY ANTHOL 20. PAGE 15 H0302
ECO/DEV NAT/COMP INDUS LABOR

B63
BERLIN I.,KARL MARX, HIS LIFE AND ENVIRONMENT (3RD ED.). MOD/EUR USSR INTELL EDU/PROP PARTIC REV ATTIT 19 MARX/KARL. PAGE 15 H0307
BIOG PERSON MARXISM CONCPT

B63
BROEKMEIJER M.W.,DEVELOPING COUNTRIES AND NATO. USSR FORCES DIPLOM NUC/PWR WAR PEACE TOTALISM 20 NATO. PAGE 21 H0427
ECO/UNDEV FOR/AID ORD/FREE NAT/G

B63
BROGAN D.W.,POLITICAL PATTERNS IN TODAY'S WORLD. FRANCE USA+45 USSR WOR+45 CONSTN STRUCT PLAN DIPLOM ADMIN LEAD ROLE SUPEGO...PHIL/SCI 20. PAGE 21 H0429
NAT/COMP NEW/LIB COM TOTALISM

B63
BRZEZINSKI Z.K.,AFRICA AND THE COMMUNIST WORLD. AFR ASIA COM CULTURE SOCIETY INT/ORG DELIB/GP ACT/RES ECO/TAC COERCE ORD/FREE PWR WEALTH...STAT TOT/POP VAL/FREE 20. PAGE 23 H0461
ATTIT EDU/PROP DIPLOM USSR

B63
CRANKSHAW E.,THE NEW COLD WAR: MOSCOW V. PEKIN. CHINA/COM USSR INTELL POL/PAR DELIB/GP CAP/ISM COERCE REV NAT/LISM TOTALISM DRIVE...POLICY IDEA/COMP 20 KHRUSH/N. PAGE 35 H0698
ATTIT DIPLOM NAT/COMP MARXISM

B63
HAMM H.,ALBANIA - CHINA'S BEACHHEAD IN EUROPE. ALBANIA CHINA/COM USSR YUGOSLAVIA ELITES SOCIETY POL/PAR DELIB/GP FORCES ECO/TAC COERCE ISOLAT PEACE MARXISM...IDEA/COMP 20 MAO. PAGE 65 H1304
DIPLOM REV NAT/G POLICY

B63
HOLLANDER P.,THE NEW MAN AND HIS ENEMIES: A STUDY OF THE STALINIST CONCEPTIONS OF GOOD AND EVIL PERSONIFIED (DOCTORAL THESIS). USSR SOCIETY ECO/DEV NAT/G EDU/PROP WRITING...SOC STERTYP BIBLIOG 20 STALIN/J. PAGE 73 H1455
CONTROL ATTIT TOTALISM MARXISM

B63
HYDE D.,THE PEACEFUL ASSAULT. COM UAR USSR ECO/DEV ECO/UNDEV NAT/G POL/PAR CAP/ISM PWR 20. PAGE 76 H1516
MARXISM CONTROL ECO/TAC DIPLOM

B63
LAVROFF D.-G.,LES LIBERTES PUBLIQUES EN UNION SOVIETIQUE (REV. ED.). USSR NAT/G WORKER SANCTION CRIME MARXISM NEW/LIB...JURID BIBLIOG WORSHIP 20. PAGE 92 H1843
ORD/FREE LAW ATTIT COM

B63
LETHBRIDGE H.J.,THE PEASANT AND THE COMMUNES. CHINA/COM COM USSR NEIGH PROB/SOLV ADJUST EFFICIENCY...POLICY METH/COMP NAT/COMP 20. PAGE 95 H1894
MARXISM ECO/TAC AGRI WORKER

B63
MCNEAL R.H.,THE BOLSHEVIK TRADITION: LENIN, STALIN, KHRUSHCHEV. USSR NAT/G SUPEGO CONSERVE...IDEA/COMP
INTELL BIOG

GEN/LAWS 20 LENIN/VI STALIN/J KHRUSH/N. PAGE 107 H2145 PERS/COMP

B63
MILLER W.J.,THE MEANING OF COMMUNISM. USSR SOCIETY ECO/DEV EX/STRUC WORKER TEC/DEV ADMIN TOTALISM ...POLICY CONCPT CHARTS BIBLIOG T 20 COLD/WAR LENIN/VI STALIN/J. PAGE 111 H2215 MARXISM TRADIT DIPLOM NAT/G

B63
MOSELY P.E.,THE SOVIET UNION, 1922-1962: A FOREIGN AFFAIRS READER. ASIA POLAND USSR CULTURE INTELL AGRI POL/PAR WORKER INT/TRADE DOMIN WAR NAT/LISM MARXISM SOCISM 20 KHRUSH/N. PAGE 113 H2267 PWR POLICY DIPLOM

B63
SETON-WATSON H.,THE NEW IMPERIALISM. COM EUR+WWI MOD/EUR ECO/UNDEV NAT/G FORCES DIPLOM DOMIN EDU/PROP LEGIT COLONIAL EXEC COERCE GP/REL RACE/REL DISCRIM ATTIT...TIME/SEQ 20. PAGE 142 H2833 ECO/TAC RUSSIA USSR

B63
SWEARER H.R.,CONTEMPORARY COMMUNISM: THEORY AND PRACTICE. COM USSR SOCIETY ECO/DEV POL/PAR FORCES PLAN ADMIN LEAD NAT/LISM...POLICY ANTHOL 20 LENIN/VI COM/PARTY. PAGE 151 H3015 MARXISM CONCPT DIPLOM NAT/G

B63
TUCKER R.C.,THE SOVIET POLITICAL MIND. COM INTELL NAT/G TOP/EX EDU/PROP ADMIN COERCE TOTALISM ATTIT PWR MARXISM...PSY MYTH HYPO/EXP 20. PAGE 157 H3136 STRUCT RIGID/FLEX ELITES USSR

B63
ULAM A.B.,THE NEW FACE OF SOVIET TOTALITARIANISM. FUT INTELL NAT/G POL/PAR EX/STRUC TOP/EX DIPLOM ECO/TAC DOMIN EDU/PROP LEGIT COERCE ATTIT RIGID/FLEX...OBS HIST/WRIT TREND TOT/POP VAL/FREE COLD/WAR. PAGE 158 H3150 COM PWR TOTALISM USSR

B63
US ATOMIC ENERGY COMMISSION,ATOMIC ENERGY IN THE SOVIET UNION: TRIP REPORT OF THE US ATOMIC ENERGY DELEGATION, MAY 1933. USSR R+D NAT/G CONSULT CREATE DIPLOM ADMIN ROUTINE EFFICIENCY PRODUC KNOWL SKILL ...NAT/COMP 20 AEC TRAVEL TREATY. PAGE 159 H3176 METH/COMP OP/RES TEC/DEV NUC/PWR

L63
MICHAEL F.,"KHRUSHCHEV'S DISLOYAL OPPOSITION: STRUCTURAL CHANGE AND POWER STRUGGLE IN COMMUNIST BLOC." ASIA CHINA/COM FUT NAT/G POL/PAR CONSULT PLAN DOMIN ATTIT...POLICY CONCPT TREND MARX/KARL 20 KHRUSH/N. PAGE 110 H2195 COM STRUCT NAT/LISM USSR

S63
BECHHOEFER B.G.,"SOVIET ATTITUDE TOWARD DISARMAMENT." COM USSR NAT/G ACT/RES TEC/DEV NUC/PWR ATTIT DISPL RIGID/FLEX PWR...METH/CNCPT TREND GEN/LAWS COLD/WAR 20. PAGE 13 H0252 FORCES EDU/PROP ARMS/CONT

S63
HOSKINS H.L.,"ARAB SOCIALISM IN THE UAR." ISLAM USSR AGRI INDUS NAT/G TOP/EX CREATE DIPLOM EDU/PROP DRIVE KNOWL PWR SOCISM...POLICY CONCPT TREND SUEZ 20. PAGE 74 H1478 ECO/DEV PLAN UAR

S63
KOHN H.,"GERMANY IN WORLD POLITICS." EUR+WWI GERMANY GERMANY/W USSR NAT/G POL/PAR TOP/EX ATTIT ...CONCPT TREND GEN/LAWS 20 NATO ADENAUER/K. PAGE 87 H1746 ACT/RES ORD/FREE BAL/PWR

S63
MORISON D.,"AFRICAN STUDIES IN THE SOVIET UNION." AFR COM CULTURE INTELL REGION ATTIT KNOWL...HUM TREND 20. PAGE 113 H2258 EDU/PROP USSR

S63
STAAR R.F.,"HOW STRONG IS THE SOVIET BLOC." COM USSR ECO/DEV NAT/G DELIB/GP ECO/TAC RIGID/FLEX ...CONCPT RECORD CHARTS 20. PAGE 148 H2964 FORCES MYTH TOTALISM

B64
BROWN N.,NUCLEAR WAR* THE IMPENDING STRATEGIC DEADLOCK. USA+45 USSR TEC/DEV BUDGET RISK ARMS/CONT NUC/PWR WEAPON COST BIO/SOC...GEOG IDEA/COMP NAT/COMP GAME NATO WARSAW/P. PAGE 22 H0448 FORCES OP/RES WAR GEN/LAWS

B64
BRZEZINSKI Z.,POLITICAL POWER: USA/USSR. USA+45 USSR AGRI POL/PAR FORCES CREATE CHOOSE ATTIT ORD/FREE PWR MARXISM...MYTH 20 KENNEDY/JF. PAGE 23 H0457 NAT/G NAT/COMP POLICY LEAD

B64
DANIELS R.V.,RUSSIA. RUSSIA USSR STRUCT NAT/LISM TOTALISM ORD/FREE WEALTH...POLICY DECISION TREND. PAGE 37 H0740 MARXISM REV ECO/DEV DIPLOM

B64
FAINSOD M.,HOW RUSSIA IS RULED (REV. ED.). RUSSIA USSR AGRI PROC/MFG LABOR POL/PAR EX/STRUC CONTROL PWR...POLICY BIBLIOG 19/20 KHRUSH/N COM/PARTY. PAGE 48 H0963 NAT/G REV MARXISM

B64
FISCHER L.,THE LIFE OF LENIN. USSR LEAD REV WAR ...SOC 19/20 LENIN/VI COM/PARTY BOLSHEVISM. PAGE 51 H1011 BIOG MARXISM PERSON CHIEF

B64
GRIFFITH W.E.,THE SINO-SOVIET RIFT. ASIA CHINA/COM COM CUBA USSR YUGOSLAVIA NAT/G POL/PAR VOL/ASSN DELIB/GP FORCES TOP/EX DIPLOM EDU/PROP DRIVE PERSON PWR...TREND 20 TREATY. PAGE 61 H1224 ATTIT TIME/SEQ BAL/PWR SOCISM

B64
GRIFFITH W.E.,COMMUNISM IN EUROPE (2 VOLS.). CZECHOSLVK USSR WOR+45 WOR-45 YUGOSLAVIA INGP/REL MARXISM SOCISM...ANTHOL 20 EUROPE/E. PAGE 61 H1225 COM POL/PAR DIPLOM GOV/COMP

B64
KIS T.I.,LES PAYS DE L'EUROPE DE L'EST: LEURS RAPPORTS MUTUELS ET LE PROBLEME DE LEUR INTEGRATION DANS L'ORBITE DE L'USSR. EUR+WWI RUSSIA USSR INT/ORG NAT/G REV ATTIT...JURID SOC BIBLIOG WARSAW/P COMECON EUROPE/E. PAGE 86 H1727 DIPLOM COM MARXISM REGION

B64
KOLARZ W.,BOOKS ON COMMUNISM. USSR WOR+45 CULTURE NAT/G POL/PAR DIPLOM LEAD...CONCPT GOV/COMP IDEA/COMP. PAGE 88 H1752 BIBLIOG/A SOCIETY COM MARXISM

B64
LAPENNA I.,STATE AND LAW: SOVIET AND YUGOSLAV THEORY. USSR YUGOSLAVIA STRATA STRUCT NAT/G DOMIN COERCE MARXISM...GOV/COMP IDEA/COMP 20. PAGE 91 H1812 JURID COM LAW SOVEREIGN

B64
LATOURETTE K.S.,CHINA. ASIA CHINA/COM FUT USSR ECO/UNDEV ECO/TAC WAR 19/20. PAGE 92 H1838 MARXISM NAT/G POLICY DIPLOM

B64
LEWIN P.,THE FOREIGN TRADE OF COMMUNIST CHINA* ITS IMPACT ON THE FREE WORLD. AFR EUR+WWI L/A+17C S/ASIA ECO/UNDEV CREATE FOR/AID...STAT NET/THEORY TREND CHARTS. PAGE 96 H1910 ASIA INT/TRADE NAT/COMP USSR

B64
PERKINS D.,THE AMERICAN DEMOCRACY: ITS RISE TO POWER. ASIA USSR LAW CULTURE FINAN EDU/PROP COLONIAL CHOOSE...POLICY CHARTS BIBLIOG WORSHIP PRESIDENT 15/20 NEGRO. PAGE 125 H2492 LOC/G ECO/TAC WAR DIPLOM

B64
PIPES R.,THE FORMATION OF THE SOVIET UNION. EUR+WWI MOD/EUR STRUCT ECO/UNDEV NAT/G LEGIS DOMIN LEGIT CT/SYS EXEC COERCE ALL/VALS...POLICY RELATIV HIST/WRIT TIME/SEQ TOT/POP 19/20. PAGE 126 H2514 COM USSR RUSSIA

B64
PITTMAN J.,PEACEFUL COEXISTENCE. USSR NAT/G NUC/PWR WAR ATTIT 20. PAGE 126 H2518 DIPLOM PEACE POLICY FORCES

B64
RESHETAR J.S. JR.,A CONCISE HISTORY OF THE COMMUNIST PARTY OF THE SOVIET UNION (REV. ED.). COM USSR NAT/G EXEC 19/20 LENIN/VI STALIN/J KHRUSH/N. PAGE 131 H2618 CHIEF POL/PAR MARXISM PWR

B64
ROSENAU J.N.,INTERNATIONAL ASPECTS OF CIVIL STRIFE. CHINA/COM CUBA EUR+WWI USA+45 USSR BAL/PWR EDU/PROP NEUTRAL COERCE MORAL...NAT/COMP 20 COLD/WAR UN. PAGE 134 H2676 POLICY DIPLOM REV WAR

B64
SAKAI R.K.,STUDIES ON ASIA, 1964. ASIA CHINA/COM ISRAEL MALAYSIA S/ASIA USA+45 USSR ECO/UNDEV FAM POL/PAR SECT CONSULT NAT/LISM...POLICY SOC 20 CHINJAP. PAGE 137 H2736 PWR DIPLOM

B64
TEPASKE J.J.,EXPLOSIVE FORCES IN LATIN AMERICA. CULTURE INTELL ECO/UNDEV INT/ORG NAT/G SECT FORCES ECO/TAC EDU/PROP PWR WEALTH SOC. PAGE 153 H3063 L/A+17C RIGID/FLEX FOR/AID USSR

B64
THORNTON T.P.,THE THIRD WORLD IN SOVIET PERSPECTIVE: STUDIES BY SOVIET WRITERS ON THE DEVELOPING AREAS. AFR L/A+17C S/ASIA STRATA AGRI INDUS MARKET NAT/G POL/PAR ECO/TAC COLONIAL PERCEPT PWR WEALTH...MARXIST STAT CHARTS WORK MARX/KARL 20. PAGE 155 H3090 ECO/UNDEV ACT/RES USSR DIPLOM

B64
US HOUSE COMM BANKING-CURR,INTERNATIONAL DEVELOPMENT ASSOCIATION ACT AMENDMENT. CHINA/COM USA+45 USSR FINAN FORCES LEGIS DIPLOM CONFER EFFICIENCY...CHARTS GOV/COMP 20 PRESIDENT CONGRESS INTL/DEV. PAGE 160 H3196 BAL/PAY FOR/AID RECORD ECO/TAC

B64
UTECHIN S.V.,RUSSIAN POLITICAL THOUGHT: A CONCISE HISTORY. RUSSIA USSR INTELL STRATA POL/PAR SECT LEGIS EDU/PROP REV WAR MARXISM...ANARCH BIBLIOG 9/20 REFORMERS SLAVS. PAGE 161 H3218 IDEA/COMP ATTIT ALL/IDEOS NAT/G

L64
FINDLATER R.,"US." EUR+WWI GERMANY USSR SOCIETY FACE/GP EDU/PROP PERCEPT PERSON ALL/VALS...PSY SOC CONCPT SELF/OBS SAMP TREND 20. PAGE 50 H1001 CULTURE ATTIT UK

S64
BARIETY J.,"LA POLITIQUE EXTERIEURE ALLEMANDE DANS L'HIVER 1939-1940." COM FINLAND GERMANY ISLAM ITALY USSR NAT/G FORCES ECO/TAC DOMIN EDU/PROP COERCE WAR PWR WEALTH...HIST/WRIT NAZI TOT/POP VAL/FREE 20. PAGE 11 H0216 EUR+WWI DIPLOM

S64
CATTELL D.T.,"SOVIET POLICIES IN LATIN AMERICA." COM CUBA L/A+17C USSR SOCIETY NAT/G POL/PAR FORCES CREATE ECO/TAC EDU/PROP REGION REV RIGID/FLEX ...GEN/LAWS COLD/WAR 20. PAGE 28 H0560
DRIVE PWR

S64
GARMARNIKOW M.,"INFLUENCE-BUYING IN WEST AFRICA." COM FUT USSR INTELL NAT/G PLAN TEC/DEV ECO/TAC DOMIN EDU/PROP REGION NAT/LISM ATTIT DRIVE ALL/VALS SOVEREIGN...POLICY PSY SOC CONCPT TREND STERTYP WORK COLD/WAR 20. PAGE 55 H1102
AFR ECO/UNDEV FOR/AID SOCISM

S64
HORECKY P.L.,"LIBRARY OF CONGRESS PUBLICATIONS IN AID OF USSR AND EAST EUROPEAN RESEARCH." BULGARIA CZECHOSLVK POLAND USSR YUGOSLAVIA NAT/G POL/PAR DIPLOM ADMIN GOV/REL...CLASSIF 20. PAGE 73 H1468
BIBLIOG/A COM MARXISM

S64
KOVNER M.,"THE SINO-SOVIET DISPUTE: COMMUNISM AT THE CROSSROADS." ASIA CHINA/COM COM USSR ECO/UNDEV NAT/G TOP/EX CREATE BAL/PWR DOMIN EDU/PROP PWR ...CONCPT COMECON 20. PAGE 88 H1760
ATTIT TREND

S64
LERNER W.,"THE HISTORICAL ORIGINS OF THE SOVIET DOCTRINE OF PEACEFUL COEXISTENCE." COM USSR INT/ORG NAT/G VOL/ASSN PLAN PEACE ATTIT RIGID/FLEX PWR MARXISM...TIME/SEQ COLD/WAR 20. PAGE 95 H1891
EDU/PROP DIPLOM

S64
MARES V.E.,"EAST EUROPE'S SECOND CHANCE." COM EUR+WWI HUNGARY ROMANIA USSR YUGOSLAVIA ECO/UNDEV NAT/G TOP/EX CREATE PLAN TEC/DEV REGION NAT/LISM RIGID/FLEX PWR...CONCPT STAT COMECON 20. PAGE 102 H2047
VOL/ASSN ECO/TAC

S64
SOLOVEYTCHIK G.,"BOOKS ON RUSSIA." USSR ELITES NAT/G PERF/ART REV GOV/REL MARXISM...AUD/VIS 20. PAGE 147 H2929
BIBLIOG/A COM CULTURE

S64
SWEARER H.R.,"AFTER KHRUSHCHEV: WHAT NEXT." COM FUT USSR CONSTN ELITES NAT/G POL/PAR CHIEF DELIB/GP LEGIS DOMIN LEAD...RECORD TREND STERTYP GEN/METH 20. PAGE 151 H3016
EX/STRUC PWR

S64
VANDENBOSCH A.,"POWER BALANCE IN INDONESIA." S/ASIA USSR NAT/G TOP/EX BAL/PWR DOMIN NEUTRAL ORD/FREE PWR...POLICY TIME/SEQ GEN/LAWS 20 SUKARNO/A. PAGE 162 H3233
FORCES TREND DIPLOM INDONESIA

B65
BRAMSTED E.K.,GOEBBELS AND NATIONAL SOCIALIST PROPAGANDA, 1925-1945. EUR+WWI GERMANY UK USSR NAT/G FORCES WAR FASCISM...TIME/SEQ 20 GOEBBELS/J NAZI. PAGE 20 H0403
EDU/PROP PSY COM/IND

B65
CARTER G.M.,POLITICS IN EUROPE. EUR+WWI FRANCE GERMANY/W UK USSR LAW CONSTN POL/PAR VOL/ASSN PRESS LOBBY PWR...ANTHOL SOC/INTEG EEC. PAGE 27 H0548
GOV/COMP OP/RES ECO/DEV

B65
CHENG C.-Y.,SCIENTIFIC AND ENGINEERING MANPOWER IN COMMUNIST CHINA, 1949-1963. CHINA/COM USSR ELITES ECO/DEV R+D ACADEM LABOR NAT/G EDU/PROP CONTROL UTIL...POLICY BIBLIOG 20. PAGE 29 H0588
WORKER CONSULT MARXISM BIOG

B65
CRABB C.V. JR.,THE ELEPHANTS AND THE GRASS* A STUDY OF NONALIGNMENT. AFR ASIA INDIA S/ASIA USA+45 USSR BAL/PWR NEUTRAL ATTIT...TREND NAT/COMP COLD/WAR. PAGE 34 H0691
ECO/UNDEV DIPLOM CONCPT

B65
DOLCI D.,A NEW WORLD IN THE MAKING. GHANA SENEGAL USSR YUGOSLAVIA CULTURE INT/ORG PLAN EDU/PROP GP/REL PEACE MORAL...GEOG SOC 20 COLD/WAR. PAGE 42 H0834
SOCIETY ALL/VALS DRIVE PERSON

B65
GOULD J.,PENGUIN SURVEY OF THE SOCIAL SCIENCES* 1965. CULTURE SOCIETY R+D FAM KIN MUNIC ACT/RES DIPLOM SKILL. PAGE 59 H1186
SOC PHIL/SCI USSR UK

B65
GRETTON P.,MARITIME STRATEGY - A STUDY OF DEFENSE PROBLEMS. ASIA UK USSR DIPLOM COERCE DETER NUC/PWR WEAPON...CONCPT NAT/COMP 20. PAGE 60 H1211
FORCES PLAN WAR SEA

B65
JASNY H.,KHRUSHCHEV'S CROP POLICY. USSR ECO/DEV PLAN MARXISM...STAT 20 KHRUSH/N RESOURCE/N. PAGE 80 H1593
AGRI NAT/G POLICY ECO/TAC

B65
JOHNSON P.,KHRUSHCHEV AND THE ARTS: POLITICS OF SOVIET CULTURE, 1962-1964. COM USSR NAT/G PERF/ART CONFER DEBATE GP/REL PERS/REL UTIL ATTIT DRIVE 20 KHRUSH/N. PAGE 81 H1626
CULTURE MARXISM POLICY CHIEF

B65
MCSHERRY J.E.,RUSSIA AND THE UNITED STATES UNDER EISENHOWER, KHRUSHCHEV, AND KENNEDY. USSR EX/STRUC TOP/EX PRESS WAR...POLICY TREND 20. PAGE 108 H2150
DIPLOM CHIEF NAT/G PEACE

B65
O'BRIEN F.,CRISIS IN WORLD COMMUNISM* MARXISM IN SEARCH OF EFFICIENCY. COM ECO/DEV PLAN INT/TRADE WAR ADJUST PEACE...STAT TIME/SEQ GOV/COMP NAT/COMP COLD/WAR. PAGE 119 H2384
MARXISM USSR DRIVE EFFICIENCY

B65
RANDALL F.B.,STALIN'S RUSSIA. USSR STRUCT AGRI NAT/G PLAN DIPLOM WAR TOTALISM MARXISM...BIBLIOG/A 19/20 STALIN/J. PAGE 129 H2590
BIOG INDUS ECO/DEV

B65
ULAM A.,THE BOLSHEVIKS. COM USSR NAT/G CHIEF ECO/TAC ADMIN LEAD WAR POPULISM...POLICY 19/20 LENIN/VI BOLSHEVISM. PAGE 157 H3148
SOCISM POL/PAR TOP/EX REV

B65
UPTON A.F.,FINLAND IN CRISIS 1940-1941. NAT/G FORCES DIPLOM COERCE...DECISION GEOG. PAGE 159 H3173
FINLAND GERMANY USSR WAR

B65
US DEPARTMENT OF DEFENSE,US SECURITY ARMS CONTROL, AND DISARMAMENT 1961-1965 (PAMPHLET). CHINA/COM COM GERMANY/W ISRAEL SPACE USA+45 USSR WOR+45 FORCES EDU/PROP DETER EQUILIB PEACE ALL/VALS...GOV/COMP 20 NATO. PAGE 159 H3183
BIBLIOG/A ARMS/CONT NUC/PWR DIPLOM

B65
WINT G.,ASIA: A HANDBOOK. ASIA COM INDIA USSR CULTURE INTELL NAT/G...GEOG STAT CENSUS NAT/COMP WORSHIP 20 TREATY CHINJAP. PAGE 169 H3387
DIPLOM SOC

B65
WOLFE B.D.,MARXISM; ONE HUNDRED YEARS IN THE LIFE OF A DOCTRINE. USSR WAR NAT/LISM PEACE TOTALISM ...MAJORIT 20 MARX/KARL. PAGE 170 H3399
MARXISM LEAD ATTIT

S65
GOLDMAN M.I.,"A BALANCE SHEET OF SOVIET FOREIGN AID." USA+45 ECO/UNDEV BAL/PWR ECO/TAC RENT GIVE EDU/PROP CONTROL COST PROFIT GEN/METH. PAGE 58 H1158
USSR FOR/AID NAT/COMP EFFICIENCY

S65
GORDON M.,"THE SETTING FOR EUROPEAN ARMS CONTROLS* POLITICAL AND STRATEGIC CHOICES OF EUROPEAN ELITES." FRANCE GERMANY UK USA+45 USSR ARMS/CONT DETER ATTIT ORD/FREE...SAMP NAT/COMP NATO. PAGE 59 H1179
REC/INT ELITES RISK WAR

S65
HELMREICH E.C.,"KADAR'S HUNGARY." COM EUR+WWI HUNGARY USSR INTELL ECO/DEV AGRI INT/ORG TOP/EX DOMIN ALL/VALS WORK COLD/WAR 20. PAGE 69 H1390
NAT/G RIGID/FLEX TOTALISM

S65
JENSEN L.,"MILITARY CAPABILITIES AND BARGAINING BEHAVIOR." USA+45 USSR ARMS/CONT DETER COST ATTIT ...METH/CNCPT STAT SYS/QU CON/ANAL CHARTS NAT/COMP. PAGE 81 H1614
DIPLOM DRIVE PWR STERTYP

S65
RUBINSTEIN A.Z.,"YUGOSLAVIA'S OPENING SOCIETY." COM USSR INTELL NAT/G LEGIS TOP/EX LEGIT CT/SYS RIGID/FLEX ALL/VALS SOCISM...HUM TIME/SEQ TREND 20. PAGE 135 H2708
CONSTN EX/STRUC YUGOSLAVIA

S65
STAAR R.F.,"RETROGRESSION IN POLAND." COM USSR AGRI INDUS NAT/G CREATE EDU/PROP TOTALISM RIGID/FLEX ORD/FREE PWR SOCISM...RECORD CHARTS 20. PAGE 148 H2965
TOP/EX ECO/TAC POLAND

S65
STAROBIN J.R.,"COMMUNISM IN WESTERN EUROPE." FRANCE GERMANY ITALY USA+45 USSR ECO/DEV FEDERAL PEACE ATTIT DRIVE PWR TREND. PAGE 149 H2972
MARXISM EUR+WWI POL/PAR NAT/COMP

S65
TABORSKY E.,"CHANGE IN CZECHOSLOVAKIA." COM USSR ELITES INTELL AGRI INDUS NAT/G DELIB/GP EX/STRUC ECO/TAC TOTALISM ATTIT RIGID/FLEX SOCISM...MGT CONCPT TREND 20. PAGE 152 H3031
ECO/DEV PLAN CZECHOSLVK

S65
TRISKA J.F.,"SOVIET-AMERICAN RELATIONS* A MULTIPLE SYMMETRY MODEL." USA+45 USSR ACADEM ACT/RES EDU/PROP COERCE PERCEPT...NET/THEORY CHARTS NAT/COMP GEN/LAWS COLD/WAR. PAGE 157 H3132
SIMUL EQUILIB DIPLOM

S65
VUCINICH W.S.,"WHITHER RUMANIA." COM USSR YUGOSLAVIA NAT/G VOL/ASSN DELIB/GP TOP/EX LEGIT NAT/LISM TOTALISM ATTIT DRIVE RIGID/FLEX ORD/FREE WEALTH SOCISM...TIME/SEQ TREND 20. PAGE 164 H3281
ECO/DEV CREATE ROMANIA

S65
WEDGE B.,"PSYCHOLOGICAL FACTORS IN SOVIET DISARMAMENT NEGOTIATION." USA+45 CONFER ATTIT PERCEPT PERSON...PSY NAT/COMP. PAGE 166 H3324
USSR DIPLOM ARMS/CONT

S65
WOHLSTETTER R.,"CUBA AND PEARL HARBOR* HINDSIGHT AND FORESIGHT." USSR FORCES OP/RES TEC/DEV ATTIT PERCEPT...DECISION IDEA/COMP NAT/COMP STERTYP TIME. PAGE 170 H3395
CUBA RISK WAR ACT/RES

N65
MOTE M.E.,SOVIET LOCAL AND REPUBLIC ELECTIONS. COM USSR NAT/G PLAN PARTIC GOV/REL TOTALISM PWR ...CHARTS 20. PAGE 114 H2270
CHOOSE ADMIN CONTROL

LOC/G

B66
BECKER J.,BESSARABIEN UND SEIN DEUTSCHTUM. ROMANIA USSR STRUCT INDUS PROF/ORG SECT GP/REL INGP/REL 15/20 BESSARABIA. PAGE 13 H0254 — PROVS CULTURE SOCIETY

B66
BESSON W.,DIE GROSSEN MACHTE - STRUKTURFRAGEN DER GEGENWARTIGEN WELTPOLITIK. ASIA USSR WOR+45 ATTIT ...IDEA/COMP 20 KENNEDY/JF. PAGE 16 H0321 — NAT/COMP DIPLOM STRUCT

B66
BRODERSEN A.,THE SOVIET WORKER: LABOR AND GOVERNMENT IN SOVIET SOCIETY. USSR STRUCT INDUS LABOR PLAN PAY INGP/REL PRODUC...POLICY GEN/LAWS BIBLIOG 20 STALIN/J LENIN/VI BOLSHEVISM KHRUSH/N. PAGE 21 H0425 — WORKER ROLE NAT/G MARXISM

B66
BUKHARIN N.,THE ABC OF COMMUNISM: A POPULAR EXPLANATION OF THE PROGRAM OF THE COMMUNIST PARTY OF RUSSIA. USSR STRATA SECT FORCES WORKER CAP/ISM RECEIVE EDU/PROP NAT/LISM TOTALISM 20. PAGE 23 H0468 — MARXISM CONCPT POLICY REV

B66
COLE G.D.H.,THE MEANING OF MARXISM. USSR WOR+45 STRATA STRUCT NAT/G WORKER COST FASCISM...IDEA/COMP 20. PAGE 31 H0625 — MARXISM CONCPT HIST/WRIT CAP/ISM

B66
DALLIN A.,POLITICS IN THE SOVIET UNION: 7 CASES. COM USSR LAW POL/PAR CHIEF FORCES WRITING CONTROL PARL/PROC CIVMIL/REL TOTALISM...ANTHOL 20 KHRUSH/N STALIN/J CASEBOOK COM/PARTY. PAGE 37 H0736 — MARXISM DOMIN ORD/FREE GOV/REL

B66
DEUTSCHER I.,STALIN: A POLITICAL BIOGRAPHY. EUR+WWI USSR POL/PAR FORCES DIPLOM ADMIN LEAD REV WAR TOTALISM PERSON 20 STALIN/J ROOSEVLT/F LENIN/VI HITLER/A. PAGE 40 H0807 — BIOG MARXISM TOP/EX PWR

B66
DOBB M.,SOVIET ECONOMIC DEVELOPMENT SINCE 1917. USSR ECO/DEV ECO/UNDEV LABOR NAT/G TEC/DEV ECO/TAC ROUTINE PRODUC MARXISM 20. PAGE 41 H0829 — PLAN INDUS WORKER

B66
DYCK H.V.,WEIMAR GERMANY AND SOVIET RUSSIA 1926-1933. EUR+WWI GERMANY UK USSR ECO/TAC INT/TRADE NEUTRAL WAR ATTIT 20 WEIMAR/REP TREATY. PAGE 44 H0877 — DIPLOM GOV/REL POLICY

B66
EPSTEIN F.T.,THE AMERICAN BIBLIOGRAPHY OF RUSSIAN AND EAST EUROPEAN STUDIES FOR 1964. USSR LOC/G NAT/G POL/PAR FORCES ADMIN ARMS/CONT...JURID CONCPT 20 UN. PAGE 47 H0933 — BIBLIOG COM MARXISM DIPLOM

B66
FRANK E.,LAWMAKERS IN A CHANGING WORLD. FRANCE UK USSR WOR+45 PARTIC EFFICIENCY ROLE ALL/IDEOS ...CHARTS ANTHOL PARLIAMENT 20 UN COLD/WAR. PAGE 52 H1049 — GOV/COMP LEGIS NAT/G DIPLOM

B66
FRIED R.C.,COMPARATIVE POLITICAL INSTITUTIONS. USSR EX/STRUC FORCES LEGIS JUDGE CONTROL REPRESENT ALL/IDEOS 20 CONGRESS BUREAUCRCY. PAGE 53 H1062 — NAT/G PWR EFFICIENCY GOV/COMP

B66
GRAHAM I.C.C.,PUBLICATIONS OF THE SOCIAL SCIENCE DEPARTMENT, THE RAND CORPORATION, 1948-1966. USSR WOR+45 NAT/G ARMS/CONT DETER WAR NAT/LISM...SOC GOV/COMP. PAGE 60 H1192 — BIBLIOG DIPLOM NUC/PWR FORCES

B66
INTL CONF ON WORLD POLITICS-5,EASTERN EUROPE IN TRANSITION. EUR+WWI USSR ECO/TAC NAT/LISM ATTIT SOVEREIGN...CHARTS ANTHOL 20 TREATY WARSAW/P. PAGE 78 H1562 — COM NAT/COMP MARXISM DIPLOM

B66
LEIBLER I.,SOVIET JEWRY AND HUMAN RIGHTS. USSR INTELL NAT/G DOMIN ATTIT 20 AUSTRAL JEWS. PAGE 93 H1865 — DISCRIM RACE/REL MARXISM POL/PAR

B66
LENSKI G.E.,POWER AND PRIVILEGE: A THEORY OF SOCIAL STRATIFICATION. SWEDEN UK UNIV USSR CULTURE ECO/UNDEV PRIVIL PWR...PHIL/SCI CONCPT CHARTS IDEA/COMP HYPO/EXP METH MARX/KARL. PAGE 94 H1882 — SOC STRATA STRUCT SOCIETY

B66
LONDON K.,EASTERN EUROPE IN TRANSITION. CHINA/COM USSR DOMIN COLONIAL CENTRAL RIGID/FLEX PWR...SOC ANTHOL 20. PAGE 98 H1958 — SOVEREIGN COM NAT/LISM DIPLOM

B66
MAC DONALD H.M.,THE INTELLECTUAL IN POLITICS. GERMANY PERU SWEDEN UK USSR NAT/G CONSULT PLAN EDU/PROP TASK INGP/REL EFFICIENCY RATIONAL ALL/VALS 20. PAGE 99 H1987 — ALL/IDEOS INTELL POL/PAR PARTIC

B66
MAICHEL K.,CATALOG OF SOVIET AND RUSSIAN NEWSPAPERS AT THE HOOVER INSTITUTION OF WAR, REVOLUTION AND PEACE. USSR NAT/G EDU/PROP LEAD REV WAR PEACE ATTIT 19/20. PAGE 101 H2017 — BIBLIOG/A PRESS COM MARXISM

B66
RAY A.,INTER-GOVERNMENTAL RELATIONS IN INDIA: A STUDY OF INDIAN FEDERALISM. CANADA INDIA SWITZERLND USA+45 USSR ADMIN GOV/REL...NAT/COMP BIBLIOG. PAGE 130 H2599 — CONSTN FEDERAL SOVEREIGN NAT/G

B66
SWEARINGEN A.R.,SOVIET AND CHINESE COMMUNIST POWER IN THE WORLD TODAY. COM USA+45 ECO/UNDEV CREATE LEAD WAR ADJUST...TREND NAT/COMP ANTHOL COLD/WAR KHRUSH/N. PAGE 151 H3017 — USSR ASIA DIPLOM ATTIT

B66
THOMPSON J.M.,RUSSIA, BOLSHEVISM, AND THE VERSAILLES PEACE. RUSSIA USSR INT/ORG NAT/G DELIB/GP AGREE REV WAR PWR 20 TREATY VERSAILLES BOLSHEVISM. PAGE 154 H3083 — DIPLOM PEACE MARXISM

B66
US DEPARTMENT OF STATE,RESEARCH ON THE USSR AND EASTERN EUROPE (EXTERNAL RESEARCH LIST NO 1-25). USSR LAW CULTURE SOCIETY NAT/G TEC/DEV DIPLOM EDU/PROP REGION...GEOG LING. PAGE 160 H3191 — BIBLIOG/A EUR+WWI COM MARXISM

B66
US DEPARTMENT OF THE ARMY,COMMUNIST CHINA: A STRATEGIC SURVEY: A BIBLIOGRAPHY (PAMPHLET NO. 20-67). CHINA/COM COM INDIA USSR NAT/G POL/PAR EX/STRUC FORCES NUC/PWR REV ATTIT...POLICY GEOG CHARTS. PAGE 160 H3194 — BIBLIOG/A MARXISM S/ASIA DIPLOM

B66
VON ARSENIEW W.,DIE GEISTIGEN SCHICKSALE DES RUSSISCHEN VOLKES. RUSSIA USSR SOCIETY STRUCT NAT/G SECT CHIEF REV 19/20. PAGE 163 H3262 — ATTIT PERSON CULTURE DRIVE

B66
WHEELER G.,THE PEOPLES OF SOVIET CENTRAL ASIA: A BACKGROUND BOOK. ISLAM USSR STRATA STRUCT FORCES REV WAR HABITAT 7/20. PAGE 167 H3341 — COLONIAL DOMIN CULTURE ADJUST

B66
WUEST J.J.,NEW SOURCE BOOK IN MAJOR EUROPEAN GOVERNMENTS. CHRIST-17C EUR+WWI FRANCE GERMANY ITALY MOD/EUR UK USSR LOC/G POL/PAR CHIEF EX/STRUC CHOOSE CONSERVE MARXISM...JURID T 13/20. PAGE 171 H3425 — NAT/G CONSTN LEGIS

B66
ZABLOCKI C.J.,SINO-SOVIET RIVALRY. AFR ASIA CHINA/COM CUBA EUR+WWI L/A+17C USA+45 USSR WOR+45 POL/PAR FORCES COERCE NUC/PWR...GOV/COMP IDEA/COMP 20 MAO KHRUSH/N. PAGE 172 H3444 — DIPLOM MARXISM COM

S66
GILBERT S.P.,"WARS OF LIBERATION AND SOVIET MILITARY AID POLICY." ASIA INDIA INDONESIA UAR USA+45 STRATA WAR PERCEPT MARXISM...STAT NAT/COMP. PAGE 56 H1124 — USSR FOR/AID WEAPON DRIVE

S66
MCLANE C.B.,"SOVIET DOCTRINE AND THE MILITARY COUPS IN AFRICA." ALGERIA GHANA COLONIAL NAT/LISM RIGID/FLEX SOVEREIGN MARXISM...DECISION NAT/COMP. PAGE 107 H2140 — USSR ATTIT AFR FORCES

S66
QUESTER G.H.,"ON THE IDENTIFICATION OF REAL AND PRETENDED COMMUNIST MILITARY DOCTRINE." ASIA USSR DETER WAR ATTIT DRIVE HEALTH TIME/SEQ. PAGE 129 H2574 — RATIONAL PERCEPT NUC/PWR NAT/COMP

S66
SCHWARTZ M.,"THE 1964 PRESIDENTIAL ELECTIONS THROUGH SOVIET EYES." ASIA POL/PAR DIPLOM ATTIT MARXISM...NAT/COMP COLD/WAR. PAGE 140 H2811 — USSR USA+45 PERCEPT

S66
STRAYER J.R.,"PROBLEMS OF DICTATORSHIP* THE RUSSIAN EXPERIENCE." ASIA MOD/EUR ELITES STRATA POL/PAR CREATE NAT/LISM MARXISM...GOV/COMP NAT/COMP. PAGE 150 H2997 — NAT/G GEN/LAWS USSR TOTALISM

S66
TURKEVICH J.,"SOVIET SCIENCE APPRAISED." USA+45 R+D ACADEM FORCES DIPLOM EDU/PROP WAR EFFICIENCY PEACE SKILL OBS. PAGE 157 H3137 — USSR TEC/DEV NAT/COMP ATTIT

B67
ALLWORTH E.,CENTRAL ASIA: A CENTURY OF RUSSIAN RULE. USSR INTELL SOCIETY AGRI INDUS COLONIAL REV WAR NAT/LISM...ART/METH GEOG LING 19/20. PAGE 5 H0108 — ASIA CULTURE NAT/G

B67
ANDERSON T.,RUSSIAN POLITICAL THOUGHT; AN INTRODUCTION. USSR NAT/G POL/PAR CHIEF MARXISM ...TIME/SEQ BIBLIOG 9/20. PAGE 7 H0135 — TREND CONSTN ATTIT

B67
BAIN C.A.,VIETNAM: THE ROOTS OF CONFLICT. FRANCE S/ASIA USSR VIETNAM POL/PAR SECT FORCES COLONIAL NAT/LISM PEACE ORD/FREE MARXISM...GEOG CHARTS 4/20. PAGE 10 H0202 — NAT/G WAR CULTURE

B67
BROMKE A.,POLAND'S POLITICS: IDEALISM VS. REALISM. COM GERMANY POLAND RUSSIA USSR POL/PAR CATHISM ...BIBLIOG 19/20. PAGE 21 H0431 — NAT/G DIPLOM MARXISM

B67
BRZEZINSKI Z.K.,IDEOLOGY AND POWER IN SOVIET — DIPLOM

POLITICS. USSR NAT/G POL/PAR PWR...GEN/LAWS 19/20. PAGE 23 H0462
EX/STRUC MARXISM

B67
BRZEZINSKI Z.K.,THE SOVIET BLOC: UNITY AND CONFLICT (2ND ED., REV., ENLARGED). COM POLAND USSR INTELL CHIEF EX/STRUC CONTROL EXEC GOV/REL PWR MARXISM ...TREND IDEA/COMP 20 LENIN/VI MARX/KARL STALIN/J. PAGE 23 H0463
NAT/G DIPLOM

B67
BUNN R.F.,POLITICS AND CIVIL LIBERTIES IN EUROPE: FOUR CASE STUDIES. FRANCE GERMANY/W UK USSR NAT/G PRESS CRIME CROWD PRIVIL ATTIT 20. PAGE 24 H0476
ORD/FREE CONSTN NAT/COMP LAW

B67
CAMERON R.,BANKING IN THE EARLY STAGES OF INDUSTRIALIZATION: A STUDY IN ECONOMIC COMPARATIVE HISTORY. FRANCE GERMANY UK USSR...CHARTS IDEA/COMP NAT/COMP 18/20 CHINJAP. PAGE 26 H0512
FINAN INDUS GOV/COMP

B67
FIELD M.G.,SOVIET SOCIALIZED MEDICINE. USSR FINAN R+D PROB/SOLV ADMIN SOCISM...MGT SOC CONCPT 20. PAGE 50 H0993
PUB/INST HEALTH NAT/G MARXISM

B67
HILSMAN R.,TO MOVE A NATION: THE POLITICS OF FOREIGN POLICY IN THE ADMINISTRATION OF JOHN F. KENNEDY. CHINA/COM COM USSR VIETNAM NAT/G DELIB/GP FORCES PLAN PROB/SOLV BAL/PWR COLONIAL EXEC REV PWR 20 KENNEDY/JF PRESIDENT. PAGE 71 H1418
CHIEF DIPLOM

B67
KOLKOWICZ R.,THE SOVIET MILITARY AND THE COMMUNIST PARTY. COM USSR ELITES NAT/G CREATE CIVMIL/REL GP/REL...TREND BIBLIOG/A 20 COM/PARTY. PAGE 88 H1753
MARXISM CONSTN FORCES POL/PAR

B67
MENDEL A.P.,POLITICAL MEMOIRS 1905-1917 BY PAUL MILIUKOV (TRANS. BY CARL GOLDBERG). USSR AGRI DIPLOM ECO/TAC POPULISM...MAJORIT 20. PAGE 109 H2170
BIOG LEAD NAT/G CONSTN

B67
MICKIEWICZ E.P.,SOVIET POLITICAL SCHOOLS: THE COMMUNIST PARTY ADULT INSTRUCTION SYSTEM. COM USSR INTELL SCHOOL WORKER CREATE PRESS ADMIN CONTROL ATTIT KNOWL...PROG/TEAC SOC/INTEG 20 COM/PARTY. PAGE 110 H2200
NAT/G EDU/PROP AGE/A MARXISM

B67
PLANK J.,CUBA AND THE UNITED STATES: LONG RANGE PERSPECTIVES. CUBA L/A+17C USSR ECO/UNDEV NAT/G FORCES ECO/TAC INT/TRADE AGREE REV...PREDICT TREND ANTHOL 20 CASTRO/F COLD/WAR OAS. PAGE 126 H2520
DIPLOM

B67
POMEROY W.J.,HALF A CENTURY OF SOCIALISM. USSR LAW AGRI INDUS NAT/G CREATE DIPLOM EDU/PROP PERSON ORD/FREE WEALTH...POLICY TREND 20. PAGE 127 H2541
SOCISM MARXISM COM SOCIETY

B67
RAMUNDO B.A.,PEACEFUL COEXISTENCE: INTERNATIONAL LAW IN THE BUILDING OF COMMUNISM. USSR INT/ORG DIPLOM COLONIAL ARMS/CONT ROLE SOVEREIGN...POLICY METH/COMP NAT/COMP BIBLIOG. PAGE 129 H2588
INT/LAW PEACE MARXISM METH/CNCPT

B67
RUDMAN H.C.,THE SCHOOL AND STATE IN THE USSR. COM USSR ACADEM LABOR LOC/G PUB/INST EDU/PROP GP/REL ROLE...POLICY DECISION MGT CHARTS 20. PAGE 136 H2712
SCHOOL ADMIN NAT/G POL/PAR

B67
SCHUTZ W.W.,RETHINKING GERMAN POLICY; NEW APPROACHES TO REUNIFICATION. GERMANY USSR PLAN CONFER...POLICY 20. PAGE 140 H2806
REGION NAT/G DIPLOM PROB/SOLV

B67
TOMPKINS S.R.,THE TRIUMPH OF BOLSHEVISM: REVOLUTION OR REACTION? USSR WORKER PRESS WEALTH MARXISM POPULISM...BIOG TREND IDEA/COMP BIBLIOG 19/20 LENIN/VI. PAGE 156 H3113
REV NAT/G POL/PAR NAT/LISM

B67
ZALESKI E.,PLANNING REFORMS IN THE SOVIET UNION 1962-1966. COM USSR NAT/G CONFER CONTROL EFFICIENCY MARXISM...POLICY DECISION 20. PAGE 172 H3446
ECO/DEV PLAN ADMIN CENTRAL

L67
BERNSTEIN T.P.,"LEADERSHIP AND MASS MOBILIZATION IN THE SOVIET AND CHINESE COLLECTIVISATION CAMPAIGNS OF 1929-30, 1955-56: COMPARISON." CHINA/COM USSR WORKER CONTROL COERCE PRODUC ATTIT...NAT/COMP 20. PAGE 16 H0317
FEDERAL PLAN AGRI NAT/G

L67
EGBERT D.D.,"THE IDEA OF 'AVANT-GARDE' IN ART AND POLITICS." USSR CULTURE INTELL POL/PAR CREATE EDU/PROP CONTROL REV ANOMIE DRIVE ROLE...IDEA/COMP 20. PAGE 45 H0895
ART/METH COM ATTIT

L67
ROBINSON T.W.,"A NATIONAL INTEREST ANALYSIS OF SINO-SOVIET RELATIONS." CHINA/COM USSR NAT/G NUC/PWR ATTIT PWR...CONCPT CHARTS 20. PAGE 132 H2650
MARXISM DIPLOM SOVEREIGN GEN/LAWS

L67
TABORSKY E.,"THE COMMUNIST PARTIES OF THE 'THIRD WORLD' IN SOVIET STRATEGY." AFR ASIA L/A+17C USSR INTELL NAT/G WORKER PLAN CONTROL LEAD PARTIC REV ...GOV/COMP 20 COM/PARTY THIRD/WRLD. PAGE 152 H3032
POL/PAR MARXISM ECO/UNDEV DIPLOM

S67
"PROTEST AGAINST SOVIET INDUSTRIALIZATION ILLS IN LITHUANIA* A MEMORANDUM." USSR LITHUANIA NAT/G PROVS COST GEOG. PAGE 2 H0050
INDUS COLONIAL NAT/LISM PLAN

S67
BASKIN D.B.,"NATIONALITY DOCTRINE AND ANTI-SEMITISM IN THE USSR." USSR CULTURE STRATA ISOLAT MAJORITY ATTIT RIGID/FLEX RESPECT...GP/COMP JEWS. PAGE 12 H0234
NAT/LISM MARXISM GP/REL DISCRIM

S67
BASOV V.,"THE DEVELOPMENT OF PUBLIC EDUCATION AND THE BUDGET." USSR NAT/G CONTROL REV COST AGE...STAT 20. PAGE 12 H0235
BUDGET GIVE EDU/PROP SCHOOL

S67
BERLINER J.S.,"RUSSIA'S BUREAUCRATS - WHY THEY'RE REACTIONARY." USSR NAT/G OP/RES PROB/SOLV TEC/DEV CONTROL SANCTION EFFICIENCY DRIVE PERSON...TECHNIC SOC 20. PAGE 15 H0308
CREATE ADMIN INDUS PRODUC

S67
CARR E.H.,"REVOLUTION FROM ABOVE." USSR STRATA FINAN INDUS NAT/G DOMIN LEAD GP/REL INGP/REL OWN PRODUC PWR 20 STALIN/J. PAGE 27 H0538
AGRI POLICY COM EFFICIENCY

S67
CATTELL D.T.,"A NEO-MARXIST THEORY OF COMPARATIVE ANALYSIS." USSR STRATA INSPECT DOMIN CONTROL COERCE OWN TOTALISM PWR...FASCIST HYPO/EXP METH 20. PAGE 28 H0561
GOV/COMP MARXISM SIMUL CLASSIF

S67
CATTELL D.T.,"THE FIFTIETH ANNIVERSARY: A SOVIET WATERSHED?" USSR CONSTN ECO/DEV NAT/G LEAD TOTALISM 20 KHRUSH/N. PAGE 28 H0562
MARXISM CHIEF POLICY ADJUST

S67
DESHPANDE A.M.,"FEDERAL-STATE FISCAL RELATIONS IN INDIA" (REVIEW ARTICLE)" GERMANY USSR DELIB/GP PLAN BUDGET ECO/TAC INCOME 20 SOC/DEMPAR SOC/REVPAR. PAGE 40 H0795
FINAN NAT/G GOV/REL TAX

S67
EGBERT D.D.,"POLITICS AND ART IN COMMUNIST BULGARIA" BULGARIA COM USSR CULTURE DIPLOM INGP/REL TOTALISM...TREND 20. PAGE 45 H0894
CREATE ART/METH CONTROL MARXISM

S67
ELLISON H.J.,"THE SOCIALIST REVOLUTIONARIES." USSR ECO/UNDEV NAT/G INGP/REL EFFICIENCY ATTIT PWR MARXISM...CONCPT IDEA/COMP 20 SOC/REVPAR. PAGE 46 H0911
POL/PAR REV AGRI

S67
JANICKE M.,"MONOPOLISMUS UND PLURALISMUS IM KOMMUNISTISCHEN HERRSCHAFTSSYSTEM" COM CZECHOSLVK USSR YUGOSLAVIA SOCIETY CONTROL RIGID/FLEX...CONCPT NAT/COMP 20. PAGE 79 H1589
TOTALISM POL/PAR ATTIT PLURISM

S67
KOHN W.S.G.,"THE SOVEREIGNTY OF LIECHTENSTEIN." LIECHTENST SWITZERLND USSR CONSTN DEBATE WAR CONSERVE 18/20 UN. PAGE 88 H1748
SOVEREIGN NAT/G PWR DIPLOM

S67
KYLE K.,"BACKGROUND TO THE CRISIS" ISLAM ISRAEL UAR UK USSR NAT/G PROB/SOLV LEGIT CONTROL REGION STRANGE MORAL 20 JEWS. PAGE 89 H1787
DIPLOM POLICY SOVEREIGN COERCE

S67
NATSAGDORJ A.S.,"THE ECONOMIC BASIS OF FEUDALISM IN MONGOLIA." ASIA COM USSR OWN WEALTH CONSERVE...SOC 20 MONGOLIA. PAGE 116 H2324
ECO/TAC AGRI NAT/COMP MARXISM

S67
NIEBUHR R.,"THE SOCIAL MYTHS IN THE COLD WAR." USA+45 USSR VIETNAM PROB/SOLV BAL/PWR ARMS/CONT NAT/LISM PWR ALL/IDEOS CONCPT. PAGE 118 H2359
MYTH DIPLOM GOV/COMP

S67
PONOMARYOV B.,"THE OCTOBER REVOLUTION - BEGINNING OF THE EPOCH OF SOCIALISM AND COMMUNISM." COM FUT USSR WOR+45 SOCIETY STRATA CHIEF CREATE DIPLOM ECO/TAC EDU/PROP SOCISM...NAT/COMP 20. PAGE 127 H2542
MARXIST WORKER INT/ORG POLICY

S67
POWELL D.,"THE EFFECTIVENESS OF SOVIET ANTI-RELIGIOUS PROPAGANDA." USSR NAT/G DOMIN LEGIT NAT/LISM 20. PAGE 127 H2549
EDU/PROP ATTIT SECT CONTROL

S67
SLOAN P.,"FIFTY YEARS OF SOVIET RULE." USSR INDUS EDU/PROP EFFICIENCY PRODUC HEALTH KNOWL MORAL WEALTH MARXISM...POLICY 20. PAGE 145 H2900
CREATE NAT/G PLAN INSPECT

S67
SZALAY L.B.,"SOVIET DOMESTIC PROPAGANDA AND LIBERALIZATION." COM USSR SOCIETY COM/IND NAT/G POL/PAR EX/STRUC TEC/DEV LEAD ATTIT ROLE MARXISM ...METH/COMP 20. PAGE 151 H3026
EDU/PROP TOTALISM PERSON PERCEPT

S67
TATU M.,"URSS: LES FLOTTEMENTS DE LA DIRECTION COLLEGIALE." UAR USSR CHIEF LEAD INGP/REL EFFICIENCY...DECISION TREND 20 MID/EAST. PAGE 152 H3047
POLICY NAT/G EX/STRUC DIPLOM

S67
TIKHOMIROV I.A.,"DIVISION OF POWERS OR DIVISION OF LABOR?" USSR NAT/G DELIB/GP ADJUD GP/REL MARXISM SOCISM 20. PAGE 155 H3093
BAL/PWR WORKER STRATA ADMIN

S67
VON LAUE T.H.,"WESTERNIZATION, REVOLUTION AND THE SEARCH FOR A BASIS OF AUTHORITY - RUSSIA IN 1917." USSR ELITES INTELL ECO/UNDEV NAT/G WORKER ECO/TAC TAX ADMIN LEAD AUTHORIT 20 LENIN/VI. PAGE 164 H3274
MARXISM REV COM DOMIN

C67
GEHLEN M.P.,"THE POLITICS OF COEXISTENCE: SOVIET METHODS AND MOTIVES." COM USSR NAT/G INT/TRADE EDU/PROP ARMS/CONT DETER KNOWL...CHARTS IDEA/COMP 20 COLD/WAR. PAGE 55 H1108
BIBLIOG PEACE DIPLOM MARXISM

S68
KANET R.E.,"RECENT SOVIET REASSESSMENT OF DEVELOPMENTS IN THE THIRD WORLD." ALGERIA GHANA INDONESIA USSR WOR+45 CONSTN ELITES INTELL STRUCT DOMIN CONTROL REV PWR MARXISM...IDEA/COMP METH 20 THIRD/WRLD. PAGE 83 H1653
DIPLOM NEUTRAL NAT/G NAT/COMP

S68
LAVRIN J.,"THE TWO WORLDS." RUSSIA USSR SOCIETY STRUCT NAT/G DIPLOM ATTIT PERSON MARXISM...GEOG SOC IDEA/COMP PERS/COMP 18/20. PAGE 92 H1842
NAT/COMP NAT/LISM CULTURE

S68
LUKASZEWSKI J.,"WESTERN INTEGRATION AND THE PEOPLE'S DEMOCRACIES." USSR ELITES ECO/DEV NAT/G VOL/ASSN INT/TRADE AGREE REV FEDERAL WEALTH SOCISM ...NAT/COMP SOC/INTEG 20 EEC. PAGE 99 H1977
DIPLOM INT/ORG COM REGION

S68
SHAPIRO J.P.,"SOVIET HISTORIOGRAPHY AND THE MOSCOW TRIALS: AFTER THIRTY YEARS." USSR NAT/G LEGIT PRESS CONTROL LEAD ATTIT MARXISM...NEW/IDEA METH 20 TROTSKY/L STALIN/J KHRUSH/N. PAGE 142 H2843
HIST/WRIT EDU/PROP SANCTION ADJUD

UTAH....UTAH

UTECHIN S.V. H2773,H3218

UTIL....UTILITY, USEFULNESS

B12
HOBSON J.A.,THE EVOLUTION OF MODERN CAPITALISM. MOD/EUR UK STRATA ECO/DEV INDUS INCOME UTIL WEALTH ...SOC GEN/LAWS 7/20. PAGE 72 H1440
CAP/ISM WORKER TEC/DEV TIME/SEQ

B19
ROUSSEAU J.J.,A LASTING PEACE. INT/ORG NAT/G CHIEF DIPLOM DETER WAR POLICY. PAGE 135 H2697
PLAN PEACE UTIL

C20
DUNNING W.A.,"A HISTORY OF POLITICAL THINKERS FROM ROUSSEAU TO SPENCER." NAT/G REV NAT/LISM UTIL CONSERVE MARXISM POPULISM...JURID BIBLIOG 18/19. PAGE 43 H0868
IDEA/COMP PHIL/SCI CONCPT GEN/LAWS

B35
MORE T.,UTOPIA (1516) (TRANS. BY R. ROBYNSON). LAW CULTURE SOCIETY STRUCT FAM SECT EDU/PROP WAR OWN UTIL KNOWL WEALTH 16. PAGE 113 H2253
UTOPIA NAT/G ECO/TAC GEN/LAWS

B40
HOBBES T.,BEHEMOTH (1668). UK CONSTN SECT DOMIN LEGIT UTIL ORD/FREE CATHISM...POLICY CONCPT GEN/LAWS 17 CHARLES/I CROMWELL/O PROTESTANT. PAGE 71 H1433
REV NAT/G CHIEF

B48
ROSENFARB J.,FREEDOM AND THE ADMINISTRATIVE STATE. NAT/G ROUTINE EFFICIENCY PRODUC RATIONAL UTIL ...TECHNIC WELF/ST MGT 20 BUREAUCRCY. PAGE 134 H2680
ECO/DEV INDUS PLAN WEALTH

B61
ROSE D.L.,THE VIETNAMESE CIVIL SERVICE. VIETNAM CONSULT DELIB/GP GIVE PAY EDU/PROP COLONIAL GOV/REL UTIL...CHARTS 20. PAGE 134 H2672
ADMIN EFFICIENCY STAT NAT/G

B62
MEIER R.L.,A COMMUNICATIONS THEORY OF URBAN GROWTH. CULTURE ECO/DEV COMPUTER BUDGET UTIL KNOWL...SOC CONCPT METH 20 OPEN/SPACE. PAGE 108 H2164
OP/RES COM/IND MUNIC CONTROL

B64
HARBISON F.H.,EDUCATION, MANPOWER, AND ECONOMIC GROWTH. WOR+45 ECO/DEV ECO/UNDEV ACADEM LABOR SCHOOL WORKER UTIL...IDEA/COMP NAT/COMP. PAGE 66 H1326
PLAN TEC/DEV EDU/PROP SKILL

B65
CHENG C.-Y.,SCIENTIFIC AND ENGINEERING MANPOWER IN COMMUNIST CHINA, 1949-1963. CHINA/COM USSR ELITES ECO/DEV R+D ACADEM LABOR NAT/G EDU/PROP CONTROL UTIL...POLICY BIBLIOG 20. PAGE 29 H0588
WORKER CONSULT MARXISM BIOG

B65
JOHNSON P.,KHRUSHCHEV AND THE ARTS: POLITICS OF SOVIET CULTURE, 1962-1964. COM USSR NAT/G PERF/ART CONFER DEBATE GP/REL PERS/REL UTIL ATTIT DRIVE 20 KHRUSH/N. PAGE 81 H1626
CULTURE MARXISM POLICY CHIEF

S67
ALTBACH P.,"STUDENT POLITICS." GP/REL ATTIT ROLE PWR 20. PAGE 6 H0116
INTELL PARTIC UTIL NAT/G

N80
MILL J.S.,"AN ESSAY ON GOVERNMENT" (PAMPHLET). ELITES NAT/G CHIEF OWN ORD/FREE PWR WEALTH GEN/LAWS. PAGE 110 H2207
CONSTN POPULISM REPRESENT UTIL

B91
BENTHAM J.,A FRAGMENT ON GOVERNMENT (1776). CONSTN MUNIC NAT/G SECT AGREE HAPPINESS UTIL MORAL ORD/FREE...JURID CONCPT. PAGE 15 H0292
SOVEREIGN LAW DOMIN

UTILITARIANISM....SEE UTILITAR

UTILITY....SEE UTIL

UTOPIA....ENVISIONED GENERAL SOCIAL CONDITIONS; SEE ALSO STERTYP

B30
WILLOUGHBY W.W.,THE ETHICAL BASIS OF POLITICAL AUTHORITY. NAT/G LEGIS PARL/PROC INGP/REL UTOPIA ORD/FREE 16/20. PAGE 169 H3374
MORAL POLICY CONSTN

B35
MORE T.,UTOPIA (1516) (TRANS. BY R. ROBYNSON). LAW CULTURE SOCIETY STRUCT FAM SECT EDU/PROP WAR OWN UTIL KNOWL WEALTH 16. PAGE 113 H2253
UTOPIA NAT/G ECO/TAC GEN/LAWS

B36
BELLOC H.,THE RESTORATION OF PROPERTY. UK STRATA NAT/G PROF/ORG DELIB/GP WORKER CREATE PROB/SOLV ECO/TAC PARTIC UTOPIA ORD/FREE SOCISM 20. PAGE 13 H0270
CONTROL MAJORIT CAP/ISM OWN

B38
MARX K.,THE GERMAN IDEOLOGY, PARTS 1 AND 3 (1846). MOD/EUR LAW STRATA WORKER DOMIN REV UTOPIA SOCISM 19 MARX/KARL. PAGE 104 H2079
MARXIST OWN PRODUC ECO/TAC

B43
LASKI H.J.,REFLECTIONS ON THE REVOLUTIONS OF OUR TIME. COM USSR NAT/G WORKER UTOPIA ORD/FREE WEALTH MARXISM SOCISM 19/20. PAGE 92 H1830
CAP/ISM WELF/ST ECO/TAC POLICY

B45
VENABLE V.,HUMAN NATURE: THE MARXIAN VIEW. UNIV STRATA CAP/ISM REV GP/REL PERS/REL PRODUC KNOWL ...PHIL/SCI CONCPT IDEA/COMP 19 MARX/KARL ENGELS/F. PAGE 162 H3240
PERSON MARXISM WORKER UTOPIA

C45
PAINE T.,"THE AGE OF REASON IN T. PAINE, THE COMPLETE WRITINGS OF THOMAS PAINE (VOL. 1) (1794-95)" CULTURE ACT/RES DOMIN UTOPIA ATTIT PERCEPT WORSHIP. PAGE 122 H2445
SECT KNOWL PHIL/SCI ORD/FREE

S46
TANNENBAUM F.,"THE BALANCE OF POWER IN SOCIETY." UNIV STRUCT FAM NAT/G SECT PERS/REL EQUILIB UTOPIA DRIVE ALL/IDEOS...OLD/LIB CONCPT. PAGE 152 H3044
SOCIETY ALL/VALS GP/REL PEACE

C50
ROUSSEAU J.J.,"DISCOURSE ON THE ORIGIN OF INEQUALITY" (1755) IN THE SOCIAL CONTRACT AND DISCOURSES." UNIV NAT/G PLAN BAL/PWR HAPPINESS UTOPIA BIO/SOC HEREDITY MORAL...WELF/ST CONCPT. PAGE 135 H2698
SOCIETY STRUCT PERSON GEN/LAWS

C50
ROUSSEAU J.J.,"A DISCOURSE ON POLITICAL ECONOMY" (1755) IN THE SOCIAL CONTRACT AND DISCOURSES." UNIV SOCIETY STRATA STRUCT CONSEN EQUILIB HAPPINESS UTOPIA HEALTH WEALTH...POLICY WELF/ST. PAGE 135 H2699
NAT/G ECO/TAC TAX GEN/LAWS

B53
LEITES N.,A STUDY OF BOLSHEVISM. ELITES STRATA INT/ORG LOC/G POL/PAR WORKER EDU/PROP REV TOTALISM UTOPIA PWR...CONCPT 20 BOLSHEVISM. PAGE 94 H1870
MARXISM PLAN COM

B55
FRIEDMAN G.,INDUSTRIAL SOCIETY: THE EMERGENCE OF THE HUMAN PROBLEMS OF AUTOMATION. UNIV CULTURE ECO/DEV TEC/DEV INGP/REL HAPPINESS RATIONAL UTOPIA ROLE...HUM SOC TIME/SEQ 20. PAGE 53 H1064
AUTOMAT ADJUST ALL/VALS CONCPT

B57
ARON R.,THE OPIUM OF THE INTELLECTUALS (TRANS. BY
INTELL

TERENCE KILMARTIN). FRANCE USSR WOR+45 CULTURE POL/PAR PLAN DOMIN EDU/PROP REV ATTIT ORD/FREE ...IDEA/COMP METH/COMP NAT/COMP 20 COM/PARTY. PAGE 8 H0169 — UTOPIA MYTH MARXISM

B59
HENDEL S.,THE SOVIET CRUCIBLE. USSR LEAD COERCE NAT/LISM UTOPIA PWR...POLICY CONCPT ANTHOL 20 STALIN/J LENIN/VI MARX/KARL BOLSHEVIK. PAGE 70 H1393 — COM MARXISM REV TOTALISM

B59
PAGE S.W.,LENIN AND WORLD REVOLUTION. COM USSR NAT/G DOMIN COERCE CROWD UTOPIA ATTIT AUTHORIT DRIVE PWR...CONCPT MYTH 19/20 LENIN/VI MARX/KARL. PAGE 122 H2441 — REV PERSON MARXISM BIOG

B63
KATEB G.,UTOPIA AND ITS ENEMIES. CULTURE STRATA ECO/DEV INDUS REV MORAL...PSY IDEA/COMP 19/20. PAGE 84 H1668 — UTOPIA SOCIETY PHIL/SCI PEACE

B63
MARX K.,THE POVERTY OF PHILOSOPHY (1847). SOCIETY STRATA INDUS WORKER OWN UTOPIA SOCISM...GEN/LAWS MARX/KARL. PAGE 104 H2082 — MARXIST PRODUC

B63
NOMAD M.,POLITICAL HERETICS: FROM PLATO TO MAO TSE-TUNG. UNIV INGP/REL...SOC IDEA/COMP. PAGE 119 H2369 — SOCIETY UTOPIA ALL/IDEOS CONCPT

B63
SCHUMAN S.I.,LEGAL POSITIVISM: ITS SCOPE AND LIMITATIONS. CONSTN NAT/G DIPLOM PARTIC UTOPIA ...POLICY DECISION PHIL/SCI CONCPT 20. PAGE 140 H2802 — GEN/METH LAW METH/COMP

B64
CAPLOW T.,PRINCIPLES OF ORGANIZATION. UNIV CULTURE STRUCT CREATE INGP/REL UTOPIA...GEN/LAWS TIME. PAGE 26 H0526 — VOL/ASSN CONCPT SIMUL EX/STRUC

B64
COBBAN A.,ROUSSEAU AND THE MODERN STATE (2ND ED.). FRANCE PROB/SOLV NAT/LISM UTOPIA PERSON MORAL ...EPIST PHIL/SCI SOC IDEA/COMP 18 ROUSSEAU/J BURKE/EDM HOBBES/T HUME/D. PAGE 30 H0612 — GEN/LAWS INGP/REL NAT/G ORD/FREE

B65
HALEVY E.,THE ERA OF TYRANNIES (TRANS. BY R. K. WEBB). FRANCE MOD/EUR UK ECO/DEV LABOR NAT/G BAL/PWR FEDERAL ALL/VALS...OLD/LIB TREND 18/20 SAINTSIMON. PAGE 64 H1285 — SOCISM CONCPT UTOPIA ORD/FREE

B67
WARD L.,LESTER WARD AND THE WELFARE STATE. SOCIETY NAT/G CREATE RECEIVE EQUILIB UTOPIA HABITAT HEREDITY PERSON...POLICY SOC BIOG 19/20 WARD/LEST. PAGE 165 H3303 — ALL/VALS NEW/IDEA WELF/ST CONCPT

S67
COHEN R.,"ANTHROPOLOGY AND POLITICAL SCIENCE: COURTSHIP OR MARRIAGE?" CULTURE STRATA STRUCT MUNIC REGION UTOPIA...NEW/IDEA TREND IDEA/COMP METH/COMP 20. PAGE 31 H0618 — SOC INGP/REL AFR

B68
PROUDHON J.P.,IDEE GENERALE DE LA REVOLUTION AU XIXE SIECLE (1851). FRANCE UNIV NAT/G CREATE AGREE UTOPIA ORD/FREE...ANARCH 19. PAGE 128 H2563 — REV SOCIETY WORKER LABOR

C80
ARNOLD M.,"EQUALITY" IN MIXED ESSAYS." MOD/EUR UK ELITES STRATA NAT/G...CONCPT IDEA/COMP NAT/COMP SOC/INTEG 19. PAGE 8 H0167 — ORD/FREE UTOPIA SOCIETY STRUCT

UTTAR/PRAD....UTTAR PRADESH, INDIA

B65
BRASS P.R.,FACTIONAL POLITICS IN AN INDIAN STATE: THE CONGRESS PARTY IN UTTAR PRADESH. INDIA UK CONSTN CULTURE ECO/UNDEV LOC/G DOMIN COLONIAL CROWD GP/REL ADJUST CENTRAL RIGID/FLEX SOVEREIGN 20 UTTAR/PRAD CONGRESS/P. PAGE 20 H0406 — POL/PAR PROVS LEGIS CHOOSE

UYEHARA C.H. H0620

V

VALEN H. H3220

VALERIANO N.D. H3221

VALI F.A. H3222

VALIDITY (AS CONCEPT)....SEE METH/CNCPT

VALJAVEC F. H3223

VALLET R. H3224

VALUE ADDED TAX....SEE VALUE/ADD

VALUE/ADD....VALUE ADDED TAX

VALUE-FREE THOUGHT....SEE OBJECTIVE

VALUES....SEE VALUES INDEX, P. XIII

VAN BILJON F.J. H3225

VAN DEN BERG M. H3226

VAN DEN BERGHE P.L. H3227,H3228

VAN DEN HAAG E. H2687

VAN DER KROEF J.M. H3229

VAN DER VGUR P.W. H0324

VAN DEUSEN G.G. H2492

VAN GULIK R.H. H3230

VAN JAARSVELD F.A. H2284

VAN RENSBURG P. H3231

VAN VALKENBURG S. H3232

VAN WIJK T. H2284

VANBUREN/M....PRESIDENT MARTIN VAN BUREN

VANDENBOSCH A. H3233

VANDENBOSSCHE H1887

VARG P.A. H3234

VARMA S.N. H0183

VATCHER W.H. H3235

VATICAN....VATICAN

B62
THIERRY S.S.,LE VATICAN SECRET. CHRIST-17C EUR+WWI MOD/EUR VATICAN NAT/G SECT DELIB/GP DOMIN LEGIT SOVEREIGN. PAGE 154 H3072 — ADMIN EX/STRUC CATHISM DECISION

VEBLEN T. H3236,H3237

VEBLEN/T....THORSTEIN VEBLEN

VECCHIO G.D. H3238

VEDDER H. H1275

VEIT O. H3239

VENABLE V. H3240

VENETIAN REPUBLIC....SEE VENICE

VENEZUELA....VENEZUELA; SEE ALSO L/A+17C

B48
NEUBURGER O.,GUIDE TO OFFICIAL PUBLICATIONS OF THE OTHER AMERICAN REPUBLICS: VENEZUELA (VOL. XIX). VENEZUELA FINAN LEGIS PLAN BUDGET DIPLOM CT/SYS PARL/PROC 19/20. PAGE 117 H2335 — BIBLIOG/A NAT/G CONSTN LAW

B59
SZLUC T.,TWILIGHT OF THE TYRANTS. BRAZIL L/A+17C PERU VENEZUELA NAT/G FORCES CONTROL PERSON MORAL ORD/FREE PWR...CONCPT 20 ARGEN COLOMB. PAGE 151 H3028 — TOTALISM CHIEF REV FASCISM

B61
ACOSTA SAIGNES M.,ESTUDIOS DE ETNOLOGIA ANTIGUA DE VENEZUELA (2ND ED.). PRE/AMER VENEZUELA...ART/METH SOC BIBLIOG INDIAN/AM. PAGE 3 H0061 — CULTURE STRUCT GP/REL HABITAT

B61
GRASES P.,ESTUDIOS BIBLIOGRAFICOS. VENEZUELA...SOC 20. PAGE 60 H1197 — BIBLIOG NAT/G DIPLOM L/A+17C

B64
BERNSTEIN H.,VENEZUELA AND COLOMBIA. L/A+17C VENEZUELA INTELL COLONIAL ATTIT 20 COLOMB. PAGE 16 H0316 — CULTURE NAT/LISM LEAD

S65
BRANDENBURG F.,"THE RELEVANCE OF MEXICAN EXPERIENCE TO LATIN AMERICAN DEVELOPMENT." BRAZIL CHILE VENEZUELA STRUCT ECO/UNDEV AGRI CREATE ECO/TAC ...STAT RECORD MEXIC/AMER ARGEN COLOMB. PAGE 20 H0405 — L/A+17C GOV/COMP

S65
PLANK J.N.,"THE CARIBBEAN* INTERVENTION, WHEN AND HOW." CUBA GUATEMALA HAITI PANAMA USA+45 VENEZUELA FORCES PROB/SOLV RISK COERCE...NAT/COMP OAS TIME. PAGE 126 H2521 — SOVEREIGN MARXISM REV

S67
CARIAS B.,"EL CONTROL DE LAS EMPRESAS PUBLICAS POR GRUPOS DE INTERESES DE LA COMUNIDAD." FRANCE UK VENEZUELA INDUS NAT/G CONTROL OWN PWR...DECISION NAT/COMP 20. PAGE 26 H0529 — WORKER REPRESENT MGT SOCISM

S67
HASSAN M.F.,"THE SECOND FOUR-YEAR PLAN OF VENEZUELA." L/A+17C VENEZUELA AGRI INDUS NAT/G PLAN RATION CONTROL HABITAT...MATH STAT 20. PAGE 67 H1352 — ECO/UNDEV FINAN BUDGET PROB/SOLV

S67
PETRAS J.,"GUERRILLA MOVEMENTS IN LATIN AMERICA - I." GUATEMALA PERU VENEZUELA NAT/G COLONIAL LEAD ATTIT PWR...TIME/SEQ METH/COMP 20 COLOMB. PAGE 125 H2497 — GUERRILLA REV L/A+17C MARXISM

S67
TAYLOR P.B. JR.,"PROGRESS IN VENEZUELA." L/A+17C VENEZUELA AGRI INDUS LG/CO NAT/G SML/CO CHOOSE ...POLICY 20. PAGE 153 H3057 — ECO/UNDEV ECO/TAC POL/PAR ORD/FREE

VENICE....VENETIAN REPUBLIC

VENKATESWARAN R.J. H3241

VERAX H3242

VERBA S. H0113

VERGNAUD P. H3243

VERHAEGEN P. H3244

VERHULST A.E. H1984

VERMONT....VERMONT

VERMOT-GAUCHY M. H3245

VERNEY D.V. H0429,H3246

VERNON M.C. H3425

VERSAILLES....VERSAILLES, FRANCE

B40
WOLFERS A.,BRITAIN AND FRANCE BETWEEN TWO WORLD WARS. FRANCE UK INT/ORG NAT/G PLAN BARGAIN ECO/TAC AGREE ISOLAT ALL/IDEOS...DECISION GEOG 20 TREATY VERSAILLES INTERVENT. PAGE 170 H3402 — DIPLOM WAR POLICY

B59
DEHIO L.,GERMANY AND WORLD POLITICS IN THE TWENTIETH CENTURY. EUR+WWI FRANCE GERMANY MOD/EUR UK USSR NAT/G CHIEF BAL/PWR DOMIN COLONIAL CONTROL LEAD...IDEA/COMP 20 VERSAILLES. PAGE 39 H0783 — DIPLOM WAR NAT/LISM SOVEREIGN

B60
FISCHER L.,THE SOVIETS IN WORLD AFFAIRS. CHINA/COM COM EUR+WWI USSR INT/ORG CONFER LEAD ARMS/CONT REV PWR...CHARTS 20 TREATY VERSAILLES. PAGE 51 H1010 — DIPLOM NAT/G POLICY MARXISM

B66
THOMPSON J.M.,RUSSIA, BOLSHEVISM, AND THE VERSAILLES PEACE. RUSSIA USSR INT/ORG NAT/G DELIB/GP AGREE REV WAR PWR 20 TREATY VERSAILLES BOLSHEVISM. PAGE 154 H3083 — DIPLOM PEACE MARXISM

VERWOERD/H....HENDRIK VERWOERD

B61
ALLIGHAN G.,VERWOERD - THE END. SOUTH/AFR TOP/EX DIPLOM COLONIAL DISCRIM TOTALISM ATTIT AUTHORIT ...BIOG 20 NEGRO VERWOERD/H. PAGE 5 H0107 — CONTROL CHIEF RACE/REL NAT/G

VETO....VETO AND VETOING

VIANNA F.J. H3247

VIARD R. H3248

VICE/PRES....VICE-PRESIDENCY (ALL NATIONS)

VICEREGAL....VICEROYALTY; VICEROY SYSTEM

VICHY....VICHY, FRANCE

B62
NOBECOURT R.G.,LES SECRETS DE LA PROPAGANDE EN FRANCE OCCUPEE. FRANCE ELITES NAT/G DIPLOM GP/REL NAT/LISM TOTALISM ORD/FREE 20 VICHY VICHY. PAGE 118 H2365 — METH/COMP EDU/PROP WAR CONTROL

B62
NOBECOURT R.G.,LES SECRETS DE LA PROPAGANDE EN FRANCE OCCUPEE. FRANCE ELITES NAT/G DIPLOM GP/REL NAT/LISM TOTALISM ORD/FREE 20 VICHY VICHY. PAGE 118 H2365 — METH/COMP EDU/PROP WAR CONTROL

VICO G.B. H3249

VICTORIA/Q....QUEEN VICTORIA

VIEN N.C. H3250

VIENNA/CNV....VIENNA CONVENTION ON CONSULAR RELATIONS

VIERECK P. H3251

VIET MINH....SEE VIETNAM, GUERRILLA, COLONIAL

VIET/CONG....VIET CONG

VIETNAM....VIETNAM IN GENERAL; SEE ALSO S/ASIA, VIETNAM/N, VIETNAM/S

B12
CORDIER H.,BIBLIOTHECA INDOSINICA: DICTIONAIRE BIBLIOGRAPHIQUE DES OUVRAGES RELATIFS A LA PENINSULE INDOCHINOISE. BURMA LAOS MALAYSIA S/ASIA THAILAND VIETNAM SECT...LING 20. PAGE 33 H0665 — BIBLIOG/A GEOG NAT/G

B45
HARVARD WIDENER LIBRARY,INDOCHINA: A SELECTED LIST OF REFERENCES. CAMBODIA FRANCE S/ASIA VIETNAM COLONIAL...POLICY 19/20. PAGE 67 H1351 — BIBLIOG/A ACADEM DIPLOM NAT/G

B50
CORNELL U DEPT ASIAN STUDIES,SOUTHEAST ASIA PROGRAM DATA PAPER. BURMA CAMBODIA INDONESIA MALAYSIA VIETNAM SOCIETY STRUCT NAT/G SECT DIPLOM FOR/AID PWR WEALTH...SOC 20. PAGE 33 H0670 — BIBLIOG/A CULTURE S/ASIA ECO/UNDEV

B50
EMBREE J.F.,BIBLIOGRAPHY OF THE PEOPLES AND CULTURES OF MAINLAND SOUTHEAST ASIA. CAMBODIA LAOS THAILAND VIETNAM LAW...GEOG HUM SOC MYTH LING CHARTS WORSHIP 20. PAGE 46 H0915 — BIBLIOG/A CULTURE S/ASIA

B50
HOBBS C.C.,INDOCHINA, A BIBLIOGRAPHY OF THE LAND AND PEOPLE. VIETNAM CULTURE AGRI INDUS NAT/G SECT ...ART/METH GEOG SOC LING 20. PAGE 72 H1436 — BIBLIOG/A S/ASIA COLONIAL ECO/UNDEV

B50
TRAGER F.N.,MARXISM IN SOUTHEAST ASIA. BURMA INDONESIA THAILAND VIETNAM CULTURE SOCIETY NAT/G VOL/ASSN EXEC ROUTINE COERCE ATTIT RIGID/FLEX PWR ...METH/CNCPT TIME/SEQ STERTYP GEN/LAWS MARX/KARL VAL/FREE COLD/WAR NAM 20. PAGE 156 H3126 — S/ASIA POL/PAR REV

B51
BERNATZIK H.A.,THE SPIRITS OF THE YELLOW LEAVES. BURMA LAOS S/ASIA THAILAND VIETNAM SOCIETY AGRI COLONIAL LEISURE GP/REL PERS/REL ISOLAT AGE HABITAT SEX WORSHIP 20. PAGE 16 H0310 — SOC KIN ECO/UNDEV CULTURE

C54
HAMMER E.J.,"THE STRUGGLE FOR INDOCHINA." COM VIETNAM POL/PAR REV CENTRAL NAT/LISM ATTIT...POLICY CHARTS BIBLIOG 20. PAGE 65 H1305 — WAR COLONIAL S/ASIA NAT/G

C56
FALL B.B.,"THE VIET-MINH REGIME." VIETNAM LAW ECO/UNDEV POL/PAR FORCES DOMIN WAR ATTIT MARXISM ...BIOG PREDICT BIBLIOG/A 20. PAGE 48 H0967 — NAT/G ADMIN EX/STRUC LEAD

B61
ROSE D.L.,THE VIETNAMESE CIVIL SERVICE. VIETNAM CONSULT DELIB/GP GIVE PAY EDU/PROP COLONIAL GOV/REL UTIL...CHARTS 20. PAGE 134 H2672 — ADMIN EFFICIENCY STAT NAT/G

S61
TANHAM B.K.,"COMMUNIST REVOLUTIONARY WARFARE: THE VIETMINH IN INDOCHINA." EUR+WWI S/ASIA VIETNAM NAT/G EDU/PROP LEGIT GUERRILLA ATTIT PWR...CONCPT GEN/LAWS 20. PAGE 152 H3042 — FORCES ECO/TAC WAR FRANCE

B63
FALL B.,THE TWO VIETNAMS. CULTURE SOCIETY ECO/UNDEV NAT/G TOP/EX ACT/RES PLAN ECO/TAC DOMIN EDU/PROP COERCE ATTIT DRIVE PERSON ORD/FREE PWR...SOC TIME/SEQ COLD/WAR 20. PAGE 48 H0965 — S/ASIA BIOG VIETNAM

B64
HOBBS C.C.,SOUTHEAST ASIA: AN ANNOTATED BIBLIOGRAPHY OF SELECTED REFERENCES IN WESTERN LANGUAGES (REV. ED.). CAMBODIA INDONESIA LAOS THAILAND VIETNAM CONSTN NAT/G...SOC WORSHIP 20. PAGE 72 H1437 — BIBLIOG/A S/ASIA CULTURE SOCIETY

S64
ENNIS T.E.,"VIETNAM: LAND WITHOUT LAUGHTER." S/ASIA VIETNAM VIETNAM/S INTELL SOCIETY SECT FORCES DIPLOM LEGIT COERCE WAR ATTIT RIGID/FLEX ORD/FREE COLD/WAR — NAT/G TOP/EX GUERRILLA

20. PAGE 46 H0929

S64

MOZINGO D.P.,"CHINA'S RELATIONS WITH HER ASIAN NEIGHBORS." ASIA CHINA/COM S/ASIA VIETNAM NAT/G DELIB/GP FORCES CREATE DOMIN EDU/PROP REV RIGID/FLEX PWR...TIME/SEQ GEN/LAWS COLD/WAR 20. PAGE 114 H2277
VOL/ASSN POLICY DIPLOM

B65

BURLING R.,HILL FARMS AND PADI FIELDS. BURMA S/ASIA THAILAND VIETNAM AGRI NEIGH SECT GP/REL NAT/LISM ORD/FREE 20 MID/EAST MIGRATION. PAGE 24 H0491
SOCIETY STRUCT CULTURE SOVEREIGN

S65

SANDERS R.,"MASS SUPPORT AND COMMUNIST INSURRECTION." GREECE MALAYSIA PHILIPPINE VIETNAM STRUCT ECO/UNDEV POL/PAR FORCES CREATE REV ...GP/COMP IDEA/COMP. PAGE 138 H2751
GUERRILLA MARXISM GOV/COMP

B66

COEDES G.,THE MAKING OF SOUTH EAST ASIA. BURMA CAMBODIA LAOS S/ASIA THAILAND VIETNAM REV WAR CIVMIL/REL...GEOG 6/13. PAGE 31 H0614
CULTURE FORCES DOMIN

B66

PAN S.,VIETNAM CRISIS. ASIA FRANCE USA+45 USA-45 VIETNAM CULTURE SOCIETY INT/ORG ECO/TAC AGREE CONTROL WAR MARXISM 20. PAGE 123 H2454
ECO/UNDEV POLICY DIPLOM NAT/COMP

B66

SOBEL L.A.,SOUTH VIETNAM: US-COMMUNIST CONFRONTATION IN SOUTHEAST ASIA 1961-65. VIETNAM FOR/AID CROWD DETER REV PEACE...GEOG 20 INTERVENT DIEM COLD/WAR. PAGE 146 H2926
WAR TIME/SEQ FORCES NAT/G

B66

VIEN N.C.,SEEKING THE TRUTH. VIETNAM DELIB/GP DOMIN RISK MARXISM 20 KY/NGUYEN. PAGE 162 H3250
NAT/G COLONIAL PWR SOVEREIGN

S66

SCHOENBRON D.,"VIETNAM* THE CASE FOR EXTRICATION." NAT/G FORCES PROB/SOLV DIPLOM COLONIAL CONTROL COERCE...CONCPT 20. PAGE 140 H2795
VIETNAM WAR GUERRILLA

B67

BAIN C.A.,VIETNAM: THE ROOTS OF CONFLICT. FRANCE S/ASIA USSR VIETNAM POL/PAR SECT FORCES COLONIAL NAT/LISM PEACE ORD/FREE MARXISM...GEOG CHARTS 4/20. PAGE 10 H0202
NAT/G WAR CULTURE

B67

FALL B.B.,HO CHI MINH ON REVOLUTION: SELECTED WRITINGS, 1920-66. COM VIETNAM ELITES NAT/G COERCE GUERRILLA RACE/REL MARXISM...MARXIST ANTHOL 20. PAGE 48 H0968
REV COLONIAL ECO/UNDEV S/ASIA

B67

HILSMAN R.,TO MOVE A NATION: THE POLITICS OF FOREIGN POLICY IN THE ADMINISTRATION OF JOHN F. KENNEDY. CHINA/COM COM USSR VIETNAM NAT/G DELIB/GP FORCES PLAN PROB/SOLV BAL/PWR COLONIAL EXEC REV PWR 20 KENNEDY/JF PRESIDENT. PAGE 71 H1418
CHIEF DIPLOM

B67

MCNELLY T.,SOURCES IN MODERN EAST ASIAN HISTORY AND POLITICS. KOREA VIETNAM CULTURE DIPLOM COLONIAL REV WAR PWR ALL/IDEOS MARXISM...ANTHOL 20 CHINJAP. PAGE 107 H2147
NAT/COMP ASIA S/ASIA SOCIETY

B67

MENARD O.D.,THE ARMY AND THE FIFTH REPUBLIC. ALGERIA FRANCE VIETNAM ELITES STRATA COLONIAL CONTROL LOBBY WAR CIVMIL/REL ROLE PWR...POLICY 20 DEGAULLE/C. PAGE 108 H2169
FORCES ATTIT NAT/G

L67

MCALLISTER J.T. JR.,"THE POSSIBILITIES FOR DIPLOMACY IN SOUTHEAST ASIA." LAOS VIETNAM INT/ORG NAT/G PROVS BAL/PWR DOMIN AGREE COLONIAL WAR PWR 17/20 TREATY. PAGE 106 H2121
DIPLOM S/ASIA

S67

BATOR V.,"ONE WAR* TWO VIETNAMS." S/ASIA VIETNAM DIPLOM SUFF ATTIT ORD/FREE 20. PAGE 12 H0236
WAR BAL/PWR NAT/G STRUCT

S67

GONZALEZ M.P.,"CUBA, UNA REVOLUCION EN MARCHA." CUBA L/A+17C USA+45 VIETNAM ECO/UNDEV FORCES DIPLOM DOMIN...POLICY MARXIST NAT/COMP CASTRO/F. PAGE 58 H1163
REV NAT/G COLONIAL SOVEREIGN

S67

HOPE M.,"THE RELUCTANT WAY: SELF-IMMOLATION IN VIETNAM." VIETNAM SOCIETY FAM KIN SECT DRIVE ALL/VALS...TRADIT OBS INT 20. PAGE 73 H1465
CULTURE SUICIDE IDEA/COMP ATTIT

S67

HUNTINGTON S.P.,"INTRODUCTION: SOCIAL SCIENCE AND VIETNAM." VIETNAM CULTURE 20. PAGE 75 H1506
ACADEM KNOWL PROF/ORG SOCIETY

S67

MCCLEERY W.,"AN INTERVIEW WITH J. DOUGLAS BROWN ON THE 'WAY' OF VIETNAM" COM VIETNAM INTELL ECO/DEV ACADEM NAT/G COERCE PERSON SUPEGO ORD/FREE 20. PAGE 106 H2125
ATTIT WAR COLONIAL MARXISM

S67

NIEBUHR R.,"THE SOCIAL MYTHS IN THE COLD WAR." USA+45 USSR VIETNAM PROB/SOLV BAL/PWR ARMS/CONT NAT/LISM PWR ALL/IDEOS CONCPT. PAGE 118 H2359
MYTH DIPLOM GOV/COMP

S67

NIEBUHR R.,"THE ETHICS OF WAR AND PEACE IN THE NUCLEAR AGE." VIETNAM INTELL CONFER CONTROL WAR GOV/REL PERS/REL ORD/FREE...POLICY INT GOV/COMP NAT/COMP 20 UN. PAGE 118 H2360
MORAL PEACE NUC/PWR DIPLOM

S67

OJHA I.C.,"CHINA'S CAUTIOUS AMERICAN POLICY." CHINA/COM VIETNAM NAT/G NUC/PWR PEACE 20. PAGE 121 H2411
DIPLOM POLICY WAR DECISION

S67

RENFIELD R.L.,"A POLICY FOR VIETNAM." COM VIETNAM NAT/G POL/PAR VOL/ASSN CHIEF DIPLOM EDU/PROP DETER REPRESENT ATTIT ORD/FREE 20. PAGE 131 H2615
WAR POLICY PLAN COERCE

S67

THIEN T.T.,"VIETNAM: A CASE OF SOCIAL ALIENATION." VIETNAM AGRI FORCES FOR/AID ADMIN REPRESENT INGP/REL PWR 19/20. PAGE 154 H3071
NAT/G ELITES WORKER STRANGE

VIETNAM/N....NORTH VIETNAM

N

KYRIAK T.E.,ASIAN DEVELOPMENTS: A BIBLIOGRAPHY. INDONESIA KOREA/N VIETNAM/N CULTURE SOCIETY ECO/UNDEV NAT/G DIPLOM...SOC TREND 20 MONGOLIA. PAGE 90 H1788
BIBLIOG/A ALL/IDEOS S/ASIA ASIA

S63

HALPERN A.M.,"THE EMERGENCE OF AN ASIAN COMMUNIST BLOC." ASIA CHINA/COM COM FUT KOREA/N S/ASIA VIETNAM/N STRATA NAT/G DELIB/GP FORCES TOP/EX PLAN BAL/PWR COERCE DETER PWR COLD/WAR WORK 20. PAGE 65 H1295
POL/PAR EDU/PROP DIPLOM

S63

TANG P.S.H.,"SINO-SOVIET TENSIONS." ASIA CHINA/COM COM CUBA KOREA/N VIETNAM/N NAT/G VOL/ASSN DELIB/GP PEACE PERCEPT PWR...METH/CNCPT MYTH RECORD TREND GEN/LAWS 20. PAGE 152 H3041
ACT/RES EDU/PROP REV

B66

KEYES J.G.,A BIBLIOGRAPHY OF WESTERN LANGUAGE PUBLICATIONS CONCERNING NORTH VIETNAM IN THE CORNELL LIBRARY. VIETNAM/N NAT/G FORCES TEC/DEV DIPLOM LEAD RACE/REL...GEOG SOC 20. PAGE 85 H1700
BIBLIOG/A CULTURE ECO/UNDEV S/ASIA

B66

WEINSTEIN F.B.,VIETNAM'S UNHELD ELECTIONS: THE FAILURE TO CARRY OUT THE 1956 REUNIFICATION ELECTIONS... (MONOGRAPH). VIETNAM/S VIETNAM/N LEGIT CONFER ADJUD WAR PEACE 20 TREATY GENEVA/CON UNIFICA. PAGE 166 H3330
AGREE NAT/G CHOOSE DIPLOM

B67

SALISBURY H.E.,BEHIND THE LINES - HANOI. VIETNAM/N NAT/G GUERRILLA CIVMIL/REL NAT/LISM KNOWL 20. PAGE 137 H2741
WAR PROB/SOLV DIPLOM OBS

S67

BEVEL D.N.,"JOURNEY TO NORTH VIETNAM." VIETNAM/N CONSTN NAT/G FORCES PROB/SOLV DEATH CIVMIL/REL PEACE MORAL...ANTHOL 20 NEGRO. PAGE 16 H0325
ATTIT DIPLOM ORD/FREE WAR

S67

OOSTEN F.,"SUDVIETNAM IM JAHR VOR DER ENTSCHEIDUNG." VIETNAM/S VIETNAM/N NAT/G DIPLOM COERCE CHOOSE 20. PAGE 121 H2420
FORCES WAR WEAPON ATTIT

VIETNAM/S....SOUTH VIETNAM

B61

SEMINAR REPRESENTATIVE GOVT,AFRO-ASIAN ATTITUDES: SEMINAR ON REPRESENTATIVE GOVERNMENTSPUBLIC LIBERTIES IN STATES OF ASIA AND AFRICA, RHODES, 1958. AFR ASIA BURMA INDIA ISLAM UAR VIETNAM/S SOCIETY POL/PAR CHIEF EDU/PROP PRESS PERSON ...POLICY INT 20 TUNIS. PAGE 141 H2826
CHOOSE ATTIT NAT/COMP ORD/FREE

S64

ENNIS T.E.,"VIETNAM: LAND WITHOUT LAUGHTER." S/ASIA VIETNAM VIETNAM/S INTELL SOCIETY SECT FORCES DIPLOM LEGIT COERCE WAR ATTIT RIGID/FLEX ORD/FREE COLD/WAR 20. PAGE 46 H0929
NAT/G TOP/EX GUERRILLA

B66

WEINSTEIN F.B.,VIETNAM'S UNHELD ELECTIONS: THE FAILURE TO CARRY OUT THE 1956 REUNIFICATION ELECTIONS... (MONOGRAPH). VIETNAM/S VIETNAM/N LEGIT CONFER ADJUD WAR PEACE 20 TREATY GENEVA/CON UNIFICA. PAGE 166 H3330
AGREE NAT/G CHOOSE DIPLOM

B67

ZINN H.,VIETNAM THE LOGIC OF WITHDRAWAL. VIETNAM/S NAT/G DIPLOM DEATH MORAL 20. PAGE 173 H3459
WAR COST PACIFISM ATTIT

S67
BUTTINGER J.,"VIETNAM* FRAUD OF THE 'OTHER WAR'." VIETNAM/S ELITES STRUCT AGRI NAT/G FOR/AID RENT TREND. PAGE 25 H0499 — PLAN WEALTH REV ECO/UNDEV

S67
JOINER C.A.,"THE UBIQUITY OF THE ADMINISTRATIVE ROLE IN COUNTERINSURGENC. VIETNAM/S SOCIETY STRUCT NAT/G GP/REL EFFICIENCY 20. PAGE 81 H1627 — ADMIN POLICY REV ATTIT

S67
OOSTEN F.,"SUDVIETNAM IM JAHR VOR DER ENTSCHEIDUNG." VIETNAM/S VIETNAM/N NAT/G DIPLOM COERCE CHOOSE 20. PAGE 121 H2420 — FORCES WAR WEAPON ATTIT

VIGNES D. H3252

VIGON J. H3253

VILAKAZI A. H3254

VILLA/P....PANCHO VILLA

VILLAGE....SEE MUNIC

VILLARD/OG....OSWALD GARRISON VILLARD

VINACKE H.M. H3255

VINCENT S. H3256

VINER/J....JACOB VINER

VINES K.N. H1578

VIOLENCE....SEE COERCE, ALSO PROCESSES AND PRACTICES INDEX, PART G, PAGE XIII

VIRGIN/ISL....VIRGIN ISLANDS

VIRGINIA....VIRGINIA

VISTA....VOLUNTEERS IN SERVICE TO AMERICA (VISTA)

VITO F. H3257

VITTACHIT H3258

VOELKMANN K. H3259

VOGT E.Z. H3260

VOL/ASSN....VOLUNTARY ASSOCIATION

B15
FARIES J.C.,THE RISE OF INTERNATIONALISM. ASIA MOD/EUR NAT/G VOL/ASSN DELIB/GP BAL/PWR EDU/PROP ARMS/CONT RIGID/FLEX TREND. PAGE 49 H0971 — INT/ORG DIPLOM PEACE

N19
STEUBER F.A.,THE CONTRIBUTION OF SWITZERLAND TO THE ECONOMIC AND SOCIAL DEVELOPMENT OF LOW-INCOME COUNTRIES (PAMPHLET). SWITZERLND FINAN NAT/G VOL/ASSN INT/TRADE DRIVE...CHARTS 20. PAGE 149 H2982 — FOR/AID ECO/UNDEV PLAN DIPLOM

B20
WEBB S.,INDUSTRIAL DEMOCRACY. UK PARTIC GP/REL ...SOC OBS RECORD CHARTS 18/20. PAGE 166 H3317 — LABOR NAT/G VOL/ASSN MAJORIT

B27
EDWARDS L.P.,THE NATURAL HISTORY OF REVOLUTION. UNIV NAT/G VOL/ASSN COERCE DRIVE WEALTH...TREND GEN/LAWS. PAGE 45 H0893 — PWR GUERRILLA REV

B28
HURST C.,GREAT BRITAIN AND THE DOMINIONS. EUR+WWI CULTURE ECO/DEV INT/ORG NAT/G DIPLOM ECO/TAC COLONIAL ATTIT PWR SOVEREIGN...TIME/SEQ GEN/LAWS TOT/POP VAL/FREE 20 CMN/WLTH. PAGE 75 H1508 — VOL/ASSN DOMIN UK

B31
DUFFIELD M.,KING LEGION. NAT/G PROVS SECT LEGIS EDU/PROP PRESS GP/REL AGE/Y MARXISM POLICY. PAGE 43 H0856 — SUPEGO FORCES VOL/ASSN LOBBY

B38
IIZAWA S.,POLITICS AND POLITICAL PARTIES IN JAPAN. ELITES VOL/ASSN CHOOSE SUFF CIVMIL/REL GP/REL 19/20 CHINJAP. PAGE 76 H1522 — POL/PAR REPRESENT FORCES NAT/G

B41
GREEN T.H.,PRINCIPLES OF PUBLIC ADMINISTRATION. UNIV CONSTN VOL/ASSN INGP/REL MORAL ORD/FREE ...GOV/COMP IDEA/COMP GEN/LAWS 20. PAGE 60 H1208 — POLICY LAISSEZ MAJORIT

B43
MC DOWELL R.B.,IRISH PUBLIC OPINION, 1750-1800. IRELAND CONSTN VOL/ASSN WORKER ORD/FREE CATHISM CONSERVE...POLICY IDEA/COMP BIBLIOG 18/ PARLIAMENT. PAGE 106 H2118 — ATTIT NAT/G DIPLOM REV

B45
WARNER W.L.,THE SOCIAL SYSTEM OF AMERICAN ETHNIC GROUPS. STRATA FAM EDU/PROP ATTIT HABITAT RESPECT CLASSIF. PAGE 165 H3309 — CULTURE VOL/ASSN SECT GP/COMP

B50
TRAGER F.N.,MARXISM IN SOUTHEAST ASIA. BURMA INDONESIA THAILAND VIETNAM CULTURE SOCIETY NAT/G VOL/ASSN EXEC ROUTINE COERCE ATTIT RIGID/FLEX PWR ...METH/CNCPT TIME/SEQ STERTYP GEN/LAWS MARX/KARL VAL/FREE COLD/WAR NAM 20. PAGE 156 H3126 — S/ASIA POL/PAR REV

N51
MEYER E.W.,POLITICAL PARTIES IN WESTERN GERMANY (PAMPHLET). EUR+WWI GERMANY/W PRESS LEAD CHOOSE REPRESENT ATTIT 20. PAGE 109 H2189 — BIBLIOG POL/PAR NAT/G VOL/ASSN

B54
BERGER M.,FREEDOM AND CONTROL IN MODERN SOCIETY. LABOR NAT/G VOL/ASSN AUTHORIT DRIVE PLURISM ...METH/CNCPT CLASSIF. PAGE 15 H0300 — ORD/FREE CONTROL INGP/REL

B55
MAZZINI J.,THE DUTIES OF MAN. MOD/EUR LAW SOCIETY FAM NAT/G POL/PAR SECT VOL/ASSN EX/STRUC ACT/RES CREATE REV PEACE ATTIT ALL/VALS...GEN/LAWS WORK 19. PAGE 106 H2113 — SUPEGO CONCPT NAT/LISM

B55
TAN C.C.,THE BOXER CATASTROPHE. ASIA UK USSR ELITES POL/PAR VOL/ASSN FORCES PROB/SOLV DIPLOM ADMIN COLONIAL NAT/LISM PEACE TREATY 19/20 BOXER/REBL. PAGE 152 H3040 — REV NAT/G WAR

B56
KUPER L.,PASSIVE RESISTANCE IN SOUTH AFRICA. SOUTH/AFR LAW NAT/G POL/PAR VOL/ASSN DISCRIM ...POLICY SOC AUD/VIS 20. PAGE 89 H1782 — ORD/FREE RACE/REL ATTIT

S56
GORDON L.,"THE ORGANIZATION FOR EUROPEAN ECONOMIC COOPERATION." EUR+WWI INDUS INT/ORG NAT/G CONSULT DELIB/GP ACT/RES CREATE PLAN TEC/DEV EDU/PROP LEGIT WEALTH OEEC 20. PAGE 59 H1178 — VOL/ASSN ECO/DEV

B57
ARON R.,L'UNIFICATION ECONOMIQUE DE L'EUROPE. EUR+WWI SWITZERLND UK INT/ORG NAT/G REGION NAT/LISM ORD/FREE PWR...CONCPT METH/CNCPT OBS TREND STERTYP GEN/LAWS EEC 20. PAGE 8 H0168 — VOL/ASSN ECO/TAC

B57
LAQUER W.Z.,COMMUNISM AND NATIONALISM IN THE MIDDLE EAST. ELITES INTELL STRATA NAT/G POL/PAR SECT VOL/ASSN TOP/EX DOMIN LEGIT REGION COERCE ATTIT PERSON PWR...CONCPT HIST/WRIT TIME/SEQ TREND GEN/LAWS VAL/FREE. PAGE 91 H1817 — ISLAM NAT/LISM

B57
LOOMIS C.P.,RURAL SOCIOLOGY. CULTURE KIN NAT/G SECT VOL/ASSN ACT/RES EDU/PROP HEALTH. PAGE 98 H1963 — SOC AGRI METH T

B58
HAAS E.B.,THE UNITING OF EUROPE. EUR+WWI INT/ORG NAT/G POL/PAR TOP/EX ECO/TAC EDU/PROP LEGIT FEDERAL NAT/LISM DRIVE RIGID/FLEX ORD/FREE PWR PLURISM ...POLICY CONCPT INT GEN/LAWS ECSC EEC 20. PAGE 63 H1264 — VOL/ASSN ECO/DEV

B58
LAQUER W.Z.,THE MIDDLE EAST IN TRANSITION. COM USSR ECO/UNDEV NAT/G VOL/ASSN EDU/PROP EXEC ATTIT DRIVE PWR MARXISM COLD/WAR TOT/POP 20. PAGE 91 H1818 — ISLAM TREND NAT/LISM

S58
ELKIN A.B.,"OEEC-ITS STRUCTURE AND POWERS." EUR+WWI CONSTN INDUS INT/ORG NAT/G VOL/ASSN DELIB/GP ACT/RES PLAN ORD/FREE WEALTH...CHARTS ORG/CHARTS OEEC 20. PAGE 45 H0907 — ECO/DEV EX/STRUC

B59
DAHRENDORF R.,CLASS AND CLASS CONFLICT IN INDUSTRIAL SOCIETY. LABOR NAT/G COERCE ROLE PLURISM ...POLICY MGT CONCPT CLASSIF. PAGE 37 H0734 — VOL/ASSN STRUCT SOC GP/REL

B59
HOBSBAWM E.J.,PRIMITIVE REBELS; STUDIES IN ARCHAIC FORMS OF SOCIAL MOVEMENT IN THE 19TH AND 20TH CENTURIES. ITALY SPAIN CULTURE VOL/ASSN RISK CROWD GP/REL INGP/REL ISOLAT TOTALISM...PSY SOC 18/20. PAGE 72 H1438 — SOCIETY CRIME REV GUERRILLA

B59
LAQUER W.Z.,THE SOVIET UNION AND THE MIDDLE EAST. COM UAR USSR ECO/UNDEV NAT/G VOL/ASSN ECO/TAC EDU/PROP COLONIAL EXEC PWR...TIME/SEQ TREND COLD/WAR 20. PAGE 91 H1819 — ISLAM DRIVE FOR/AID NAT/LISM

B59
LEITES N.,ON THE GAME OF POLITICS IN FRANCE. ALGERIA FRANCE CONSTN SECT VOL/ASSN ECO/TAC INT/TRADE PARL/PROC WAR SOCISM 20 DEGAULLE/C EEC. PAGE 94 H1871 — POL/PAR NAT/G LEGIS IDEA/COMP

B59
MILLER A.S.,PRIVATE GOVERNMENTS AND THE CONSTITUTION (PAMPHLET). LAW LABOR NAT/G ROLE PWR — FEDERAL CONSTN

PLURISM...POLICY DECISION. PAGE 111 H2211 VOL/ASSN CONSEN

B59
SHARMA R.S.,ASPECTS OF POLITICAL IDEAS AND INSTITUTIONS IN ANCIENT INDIA. INDIA SOCIETY STRUCT FAM VOL/ASSN TAX DOMIN...CONCPT HIST/WRIT 7. PAGE 142 H2848 CULTURE JURID DELIB/GP SECT

S59
SKILLING H.G.,"COMMUNISM: NATIONAL OR INTERNATIONAL." CHINA/COM USSR YUGOSLAVIA NAT/G POL/PAR VOL/ASSN DOMIN REGION COERCE ATTIT PWR MARXISM SOCISM...CONCPT TOT/POP 20 TITO/MARSH. PAGE 145 H2894 COM TREND

B60
GRAMPP W.D.,THE MANCHESTER SCHOOL OF ECONOMICS. UK LAW ECO/DEV COERCE ATTIT ORD/FREE LAISSEZ ...PHIL/SCI IDEA/COMP 19/20 MANCHESTER CORN/LAWS. PAGE 60 H1194 ECO/TAC VOL/ASSN LOBBY NAT/G

B60
LINDSAY K.,EUROPEAN ASSEMBLIES: THE EXPERIMENTAL PERIOD 1949-1959. EUR+WWI ECO/DEV NAT/G POL/PAR LEGIS TOP/EX ACT/RES PLAN ECO/TAC DOMIN LEGIT ROUTINE ATTIT DRIVE ORD/FREE PWR SKILL...SOC CONCPT TREND CHARTS GEN/LAWS VAL/FREE. PAGE 97 H1932 VOL/ASSN INT/ORG REGION

B60
MCCLOSKY H.,THE SOVIET DICTATORSHIP. FUT CONSTN CULTURE INTELL SOCIETY POL/PAR SECT VOL/ASSN FORCES PLAN TEC/DEV DOMIN EDU/PROP COERCE PWR MARXISM ...POLICY CONCPT MYTH STERTYP 20. PAGE 106 H2127 COM NAT/G TOTALISM USSR

B60
MOORE W.E.,LABOR COMMITMENT AND SOCIAL CHANGE IN DEVELOPING AREAS. SOCIETY STRATA ECO/UNDEV MARKET VOL/ASSN WORKER AUTHORIT SKILL...MGT NAT/COMP SOC/INTEG 20. PAGE 113 H2250 LABOR ORD/FREE ATTIT INDUS

S60
SPIRO H.J.,"NEW CONSTITUTIONAL FORMS IN AFRICA." FUT CULTURE SOCIETY ECO/UNDEV NAT/G POL/PAR VOL/ASSN EDU/PROP ATTIT DRIVE ORD/FREE PWR RESPECT ...POLICY CONCPT OBS TREND CON/ANAL STERTYP GEN/LAWS VAL/FREE. PAGE 148 H2950 AFR CONSTN FOR/AID NAT/LISM

S60
TAUBER K.,"ASPECTS OF NATIONALIST-COMMUNIST COLLABORATION IN POSTWAR GERMANY." COM EUR+WWI USSR NAT/G VOL/ASSN ATTIT DRIVE PWR...TIME/SEQ COLD/WAR TOT/POP 20. PAGE 152 H3049 POL/PAR EDU/PROP GERMANY

B61
BONNEFOUS M.,EUROPE ET TIERS MONDE. EUR+WWI SOCIETY INT/ORG NAT/G VOL/ASSN ACT/RES TEC/DEV CAP/ISM ECO/TAC ATTIT ORD/FREE SOVEREIGN...POLICY CONCPT TREND 20. PAGE 19 H0373 AFR ECO/UNDEV FOR/AID INT/TRADE

B61
DALLIN D.J.,SOVIET FOREIGN POLICY AFTER STALIN. ASIA CHINA/COM EUR+WWI GERMANY IRAN UK YUGOSLAVIA INT/ORG NAT/G VOL/ASSN FORCES TOP/EX BAL/PWR DOMIN EDU/PROP COERCE ATTIT PWR 20. PAGE 37 H0737 COM DIPLOM USSR

B61
ETZIONI A.,COMPLEX ORGANIZATIONS: A SOCIOLOGICAL READER. CLIENT CULTURE STRATA CREATE OP/RES ADMIN ...POLICY METH/CNCPT BUREAUCRCY. PAGE 47 H0945 VOL/ASSN STRUCT CLASSIF PROF/ORG

B61
GUEVARA E.,GUERRILLA WARFARE. L/A+17C ECO/UNDEV NAT/G POL/PAR VOL/ASSN PLAN DOMIN REV DRIVE PWR WEALTH...NEW/IDEA RECORD BIOG COLD/WAR MARX/KARL OAS 20. PAGE 62 H1247 FORCES COERCE GUERRILLA CUBA

B61
HALPERIN S.,THE POLITICAL WORLD OF AMERICAN ZIONISM. ISRAEL FINAN LABOR VOL/ASSN GIVE LOBBY REPRESENT GP/REL ATTIT POLICY. PAGE 64 H1293 CULTURE SECT EDU/PROP DELIB/GP

B61
KEREKES T.,THE ARAB MIDDLE EAST AND MUSLIM AFRICA. ISLAM SOCIETY ECO/UNDEV SECT VOL/ASSN TOP/EX REGION ATTIT PWR...GEOG CONCPT TIME/SEQ GEN/LAWS 20. PAGE 85 H1694 NAT/G TREND NAT/LISM

B61
MOLLAU G.,INTERNATIONAL COMMUNISM AND WORLD REVOLUTION: HISTORY AND METHODS. RUSSIA USSR INT/ORG NAT/G POL/PAR VOL/ASSN FORCES BAL/PWR DIPLOM EXEC REGION WAR ATTIT PWR MARXISM...CONCPT TIME/SEQ COLD/WAR 19/20. PAGE 112 H2237 COM REV

B61
REISKY-DUBNIC V.,COMMUNIST PROPAGANDA METHODS. CULTURE POL/PAR VOL/ASSN ATTIT...CONCPT TOT/POP. PAGE 131 H2611 COM EDU/PROP TOTALISM

B61
ROBERTSON A.H.,THE LAW OF INTERNATIONAL INSTITUTIONS IN EUROPE. EUR+WWI MOD/EUR INT/ORG NAT/G VOL/ASSN DELIB/GP...JURID TIME/SEQ TOT/POP 20 TREATY. PAGE 132 H2644 RIGID/FLEX ORD/FREE

B61
SCHECHTMAN J.B.,ON WINGS OF EAGLES: THE PLIGHT, EXODUS, AND HOMECOMING OF ORIENTAL JEWRY. ASIA ISLAM ISRAEL VOL/ASSN DIPLOM CONTROL ORD/FREE ...GEOG WORSHIP SOC/INTEG 20 JEWS ARABS MIGRATION. PAGE 139 H2777 CULTURE HABITAT KIN SECT

S61
BRZEZINSKI Z.K.,"THE ORGANIZATION OF THE COMMUNIST CAMP." COM CZECHOSLVK COM/IND NAT/G DELIB/GP INT/TRADE DOMIN EDU/PROP EXEC ROUTINE COERCE ATTIT PWR...MGT CONCPT TIME/SEQ CHARTS VAL/FREE 20 TREATY. PAGE 23 H0460 VOL/ASSN DIPLOM USSR

S61
RAY J.,"THE EUROPEAN FREE-TRADE ASSOCIATION AND ITS IMPACT ON INDIA'S TRADE." EUR+WWI FRANCE GERMANY INDIA S/ASIA UK NAT/G VOL/ASSN PLAN INT/TRADE ROUTINE WEALTH...STAT CHARTS CMN/WLTH EEC OEEC 20 EFTA. PAGE 130 H2600 ECO/DEV ECO/TAC

S61
SCHAPIRO L.,"SOVIET GOVERNMENT TODAY." COM EUR+WWI INT/ORG POL/PAR VOL/ASSN ACT/RES PLAN PERCEPT ...CONCPT TREND TOT/POP VAL/FREE 20. PAGE 139 H2773 NAT/G TOTALISM USSR

S61
SCHECHTMAN J.B.,"MINORITIES IN THE MIDDLE EAST." ISLAM INTELL SOCIETY STRATA KIN NAT/G VOL/ASSN EDU/PROP REGION GP/REL DISCRIM ATTIT BIO/SOC DISPL PERSON ALL/VALS...PSY SOC OBS SAMP GEN/LAWS 20. PAGE 139 H2776 SECT CULTURE RACE/REL

S61
ZAGORIA D.S.,"THE FUTURE OF SINO-SOVIET RELATIONS." CHINA/COM INT/ORG NAT/G POL/PAR VOL/ASSN ACT/RES PLAN PERSON...METH/CNCPT TIME/SEQ TOT/POP VAL/FREE 20 MAO KHRUSH/N. PAGE 172 H3445 ASIA COM TOTALISM USSR

B62
BRETTON H.L.,POWER AND STABILITY IN NIGERIA: THE POLITICS OF DECOLONIZATION. AFR CONSTN INTELL ECO/UNDEV COM/IND KIN NAT/G POL/PAR PROVS VOL/ASSN LEGIS DOMIN EDU/PROP LEGIT EXEC ROUTINE CHOOSE NAT/LISM ATTIT PERCEPT ALL/VALS. PAGE 20 H0411 CULTURE OBS NIGERIA

B62
DUTOIT B.,LA NEUTRALITE SUISSE A L'HEURE EUROPEENNE. EUR+WWI MOD/EUR INT/ORG NAT/G VOL/ASSN PLAN BAL/PWR LEGIT NEUTRAL REGION PEACE ORD/FREE SOVEREIGN...CONCPT OBS TIME/SEQ TREND STERTYP VAL/FREE LEAGUE/NAT UN 20. PAGE 44 H0873 ATTIT DIPLOM SWITZERLND

B62
GUENA Y.,HISTORIQUE DE LA COMMUNAUTE. FUT ECO/UNDEV NAT/G PLAN EDU/PROP COLONIAL REGION NAT/LISM ALL/VALS SOVEREIGN...CONCPT OBS CHARTS 20. PAGE 62 H1244 AFR VOL/ASSN FOR/AID FRANCE

B62
INSTITUTE FOR STUDY OF USSR,YOUTH IN FERMENT. INTELL NAT/G PERF/ART POL/PAR SCHOOL VOL/ASSN FORCES EDU/PROP ATTIT DRIVE PERCEPT HEALTH KNOWL MORAL ORD/FREE RESPECT...SOC OBS HIST/WRIT VAL/FREE. PAGE 77 H1537 COM CULTURE USSR

B62
ROBINSON A.D.,DUTCH ORGANIZED AGRICULTURE IN INTERNATIONAL POLITICS, 1945-1960. EUR+WWI NETHERLAND STRUCT ECO/DEV NAT/G VOL/ASSN CONSULT DELIB/GP PLAN TEC/DEV INT/TRADE EDU/PROP ATTIT RIGID/FLEX ALL/VALS...NEW/IDEA TREND EEC 20. PAGE 132 H2648 AGRI INT/ORG

B62
WOODS H.D.,LABOUR POLICY AND LABOUR ECONOMICS IN CANADA. CANADA FUT NAT/G VOL/ASSN WORKER BARGAIN ECO/TAC PAY CONFER GP/REL 20. PAGE 170 H3409 LABOR POLICY INDUS ECO/DEV

B62
ZIESEL K.,DAS VERLORENE GEWISSEN. GERMANY/W NAT/G VOL/ASSN EDU/PROP PRESS SUPEGO...POLICY 20. PAGE 173 H3455 MORAL PWR ORD/FREE RESPECT

S62
CORET A.,"LE STATUT DE L'ILE CHRISTMAS DE L'OCEAN INDIEN." FUT S/ASIA ECO/DEV ECO/UNDEV VOL/ASSN DELIB/GP PLAN...RELATIV OBS TIME/SEQ TREND AUSTRAL 20. PAGE 33 H0667 NAT/G INT/ORG NEW/ZEALND

S62
MARIAS J.,"A PROGRAM FOR EUROPE." EUR+WWI INT/ORG NAT/G PLAN DIPLOM DOMIN PWR...STERTYP TOT/POP 20. PAGE 102 H2048 VOL/ASSN CREATE REGION

S62
MOUSKHELY M.,"LA NAISSANCE DES ETATS EN DROIT INTERNATIONAL PUBLIC." UNIV SOCIETY INT/ORG VOL/ASSN LEGIT ATTIT RIGID/FLEX...JURID TIME/SEQ 20. PAGE 114 H2272 NAT/G STRUCT INT/LAW

S62
SPRINGER H.W.,"FEDERATION IN THE CARIBBEAN: AN ATTEMPT THAT FAILED." L/A+17C ECO/UNDEV INT/ORG POL/PAR PROVS LEGIS CREATE PLAN LEGIT ADMIN FEDERAL ATTIT DRIVE PERSON ORD/FREE PWR...POLICY GEOG PSY CONCPT OBS CARIBBEAN CMN/WLTH 20. PAGE 148 H2955 VOL/ASSN NAT/G REGION

B63
FAWCETT J.E.S.,THE BRITISH COMMONWEALTH IN INTERNATIONAL LAW. LAW INT/ORG NAT/G VOL/ASSN OP/RES DIPLOM ADJUD CENTRAL CONSEN...NET/THEORY CMN/WLTH TREATY. PAGE 49 H0977 INT/LAW STRUCT COLONIAL

B63
LARSON A.,A WARLESS WORLD. FUT CULTURE NAT/G VOL/ASSN FORCES CREATE DOMIN PEACE ALL/VALS...HUM STERTYP 20. PAGE 91 H1824 SOCIETY CONCPT ARMS/CONT

B63
MARTINDALE D.,COMMUNITY, CHARACTER AND CIVILIZATION: STUDIES IN SOCIAL BEHAVIORISM. INTELL FAM NEIGH VOL/ASSN GP/REL NAT/LISM ATTIT PERSON ...CONCPT GP/COMP 20 BEHAVIORSM. PAGE 103 H2066 SOC METH/COMP CULTURE STRUCT

B63
PELLING H.M.,A HISTORY OF BRITISH TRADE UNIONISM. UK ELITES ECO/DEV POL/PAR GP/REL PWR NEW/LIB 19/20. PAGE 124 H2485 LABOR VOL/ASSN NAT/G

B63
ROBERTSON A.H.,HUMAN RIGHTS IN EUROPE. CONSTN SOCIETY INT/ORG NAT/G VOL/ASSN DELIB/GP ACT/RES PLAN ADJUD REGION ROUTINE ATTIT LOVE ORD/FREE RESPECT...JURID SOC CONCPT SOC/EXP UN 20. PAGE 132 H2645 EUR+WWI PERSON

B63
RONNING C.N.,LAW AND POLITICS IN INTER-AMERICAN DIPLOMACY. L/A+17C ECO/UNDEV NAT/G CONSULT DELIB/GP CREATE CAP/ISM ECO/TAC LEGIT REGION RIGID/FLEX ...METH/CNCPT GEN/LAWS OAS 20. PAGE 133 H2668 VOL/ASSN ALL/VALS DIPLOM

B63
SELF P.,THE STATE AND THE FARMER. UK ECO/DEV MARKET WORKER PRICE CONTROL GP/REL...WELF/ST 20 DEPT/AGRI. PAGE 141 H2823 AGRI NAT/G ADMIN VOL/ASSN

B63
VIARD R.,LA FIN DE L'EMPIRE COLONIAL FRANCAIS. AFR FUT S/ASIA ECO/UNDEV NAT/G CONSULT PLAN ECO/TAC EDU/PROP REGION NAT/LISM ALL/VALS...CONCPT TIME/SEQ TREND VAL/FREE 20. PAGE 162 H3248 VOL/ASSN COLONIAL FRANCE

S63
BANFIELD J.,"FEDERATION IN EAST-AFRICA." AFR UGANDA ELITES INT/ORG NAT/G VOL/ASSN LEGIS ECO/TAC FEDERAL ATTIT SOVEREIGN TOT/POP 20 TANGANYIKA. PAGE 10 H0210 EX/STRUC PWR REGION

S63
CRUTCHER J.,"PAN AFRICANISM: AFRICAN ODYSSEY." AFR NAT/G POL/PAR PROF/ORG VOL/ASSN TOP/EX CREATE REGION RACE/REL ALL/VALS...CONCPT TIME/SEQ TREND CON/ANAL 20. PAGE 36 H0716 PROVS DELIB/GP COLONIAL

S63
GROSSER A.,"FRANCE AND GERMANY IN THE ATLANTIC COMMUNITY." INT/ORG NAT/G TOP/EX DIPLOM REGION PEACE ATTIT ORD/FREE PWR...CONCPT RECORD TIME/SEQ GEN/LAWS VAL/FREE COLD/WAR 20. PAGE 62 H1234 EUR+WWI VOL/ASSN FRANCE GERMANY

S63
LERNER D.,"WILL EUROPEAN UNION BRING ABOUT MERGED NATIONAL GOALS." EUR+WWI FRANCE GERMANY UK ECO/DEV NAT/G VOL/ASSN DELIB/GP BAL/PWR ECO/TAC NAT/LISM EEC 20 DEGAULLE/C. PAGE 95 H1889 ATTIT STERTYP ELITES REGION

S63
LIGOT M.,"LA COOPERATION MILITAIRE DANS LES ACCORDS, PASSES ENTRE LA FRANCE ET LES ETATS AFRICAINS ET MALGACHE D'EXPRESSION." ECO/UNDEV INT/ORG NAT/G VOL/ASSN...CONCPT TIME/SEQ 20. PAGE 97 H1931 AFR FORCES FOR/AID FRANCE

S63
MONROE A.D.,"BRITAIN AND THE EUROPEAN COMMUNITY." EUR+WWI FRANCE NAT/G DELIB/GP TOP/EX ECO/TAC DOMIN PWR...POLICY RECORD GEN/LAWS EEC EFTA 20 EFTA CMN/WLTH. PAGE 112 H2241 VOL/ASSN ATTIT UK

S63
TANG P.S.H.,"SINO-SOVIET TENSIONS." ASIA CHINA/COM COM CUBA KOREA/N VIETNAM/N NAT/G VOL/ASSN DELIB/GP PEACE PERCEPT PWR...METH/CNCPT MYTH RECORD TREND GEN/LAWS 20. PAGE 152 H3041 ACT/RES EDU/PROP REV

S63
ZOLBERG A.R.,"MASS PARTIES AND NATIONAL INTEGRATION: THE CASE OF THE IVORY COAST" (BMR)" AFR IVORY/CST CONSTN VOL/ASSN DIPLOM LEAD GP/REL INGP/REL 20. PAGE 173 H3461 POL/PAR ECO/UNDEV NAT/G ADJUST

C63
HSU F.L.,"COHESION AND DIVISION IN THE AMERICAN WORLD" HSU FL. CLAN, CASTE, AND CLUB." CULTURE EDU/PROP CONFER SANCTION PERSON...PSY GP/COMP. PAGE 74 H1484 PERS/REL AGE/Y ADJUST VOL/ASSN

B64
AGGARWALA R.C.,CONSTITUTIONAL HISTORY OF INDIA AND NATIONAL MOVEMENT INCLUDING COMPARATIVE STUDY OF MODERN INDIA CONSTITUTION. INDIA S/ASIA SECT VOL/ASSN EX/STRUC LEGIS COERCE REV INGP/REL ORD/FREE...SOC BIBLIOG 18/20 CMN/WLTH. PAGE 4 H0077 CONSTN COLONIAL DOMIN NAT/G

B64
CAPLOW T.,PRINCIPLES OF ORGANIZATION. UNIV CULTURE STRUCT CREATE INGP/REL UTOPIA...GEN/LAWS TIME. PAGE 26 H0526 VOL/ASSN CONCPT SIMUL EX/STRUC

B64
CLUBB O.E. JR.,TWENTIETH CENTURY CHINA. ASIA CHINA/COM INTELL NAT/G POL/PAR VOL/ASSN ACT/RES EDU/PROP COERCE REV PWR...TIME/SEQ 20. PAGE 30 H0608 TOP/EX DRIVE

B64
GREAT BRITAIN CENTRAL OFF INF,CONSTITUTIONAL DEVELOPMENT IN THE COMMONWEALTH. VOL/ASSN PLAN DIPLOM COLONIAL INGP/REL NAT/LISM ORD/FREE PWR 17/20 CMN/WLTH. PAGE 60 H1202 REGION CONSTN NAT/G SOVEREIGN

B64
GRIFFITH W.E.,THE SINO-SOVIET RIFT. ASIA CHINA/COM COM CUBA USSR YUGOSLAVIA NAT/G POL/PAR VOL/ASSN DELIB/GP FORCES TOP/EX DIPLOM EDU/PROP DRIVE PERSON PWR...TREND 20 TREATY. PAGE 61 H1224 ATTIT TIME/SEQ BAL/PWR SOCISM

B64
HEIMSATH C.H.,INDIAN NATIONALISM AND HINDU SOCIAL REFORM. S/ASIA LAW CULTURE SOCIETY STRATA PROVS VOL/ASSN DELIB/GP LEGIS TOP/EX DOMIN EDU/PROP LEGIT ATTIT ALL/VALS...POLICY SOC TIME/SEQ STERTYP VAL/FREE 19/20. PAGE 69 H1385 SECT NAT/G

B64
KELLER J.W.,GERMANY, THE WALL AND BERLIN. EUR+WWI ECO/DEV NAT/G VOL/ASSN FORCES PLAN ECO/TAC EDU/PROP COERCE...POLICY CONCPT INT TREND COLD/WAR BER/BLOC 20 BERLIN. PAGE 84 H1685 ATTIT ALL/VALS DIPLOM GERMANY

B64
LEMARCHAND R.,POLITICAL AWAKENING IN THE BELGIAN CONGO. ECO/UNDEV VOL/ASSN DOMIN CHOOSE GP/REL INGP/REL DISCRIM ORD/FREE PWR...CHARTS 20 CONGO ARABS. PAGE 94 H1873 NAT/LISM COLONIAL POL/PAR RACE/REL

B64
TAYLOR E.,RICHER BY ASIA. S/ASIA CULTURE VOL/ASSN ACT/RES ATTIT DISPL PERSON ALL/VALS...INT/LAW MYTH SELF/OBS 20. PAGE 153 H3054 SOCIETY RIGID/FLEX INDIA

B64
WHITE D.S.,SEEDS OF DISCORD. EUR+WWI FRANCE NAT/G VOL/ASSN FORCES DIPLOM DOMIN NAT/LISM DISPL RIGID/FLEX PWR...RECORD INT BIOG 20 DEGAULLE/C ROOSEVLT/F CHURCHLL/W HULL. PAGE 167 H3347 TOP/EX ATTIT

B64
WILCOX W.A.,INDIA, PAKISTAN AND THE RISE OF CHINA. ASIA BURMA CEYLON CHINA/COM INDIA PAKISTAN S/ASIA NAT/G VOL/ASSN FORCES TOP/EX ACT/RES DOMIN REGION RIGID/FLEX ORD/FREE...POLICY GEN/LAWS COLD/WAR 20. PAGE 168 H3362 CULTURE ATTIT DIPLOM

L64
MACKINTOSH J.P.,"NIGERIA'S EXTERNAL AFFAIRS." UK CULTURE ECO/UNDEV NAT/G VOL/ASSN EDU/PROP LEGIT ADMIN ATTIT ORD/FREE PWR 20. PAGE 100 H2002 AFR DIPLOM NIGERIA

L64
ROTBERG R.,"THE FEDERATION MOVEMENT IN BRITISH EAST AND CENTRAL AFRICA." AFR RHODESIA UGANDA ECO/UNDEV NAT/G POL/PAR FORCES DOMIN LEGIT ADMIN COERCE ATTIT ...CONCPT TREND 20 TANGANYIKA. PAGE 135 H2691 VOL/ASSN PWR REGION

S64
BRADLEY C.P.,"THE FORMATION OF MALAYSIA." INDIA S/ASIA POL/PAR VOL/ASSN TOP/EX LEGIT RACE/REL ORD/FREE 20. PAGE 20 H0398 NAT/G CREATE COLONIAL MALAYSIA

S64
DE GAULLE C.,"FRENCH WORLD VIEW." AFR ASIA CHINA/COM EUR+WWI ISLAM ECO/UNDEV INT/ORG NAT/G VOL/ASSN ACT/RES DIPLOM ECO/TAC EDU/PROP ATTIT DRIVE WEALTH 20. PAGE 37 H0751 TOP/EX PWR FOR/AID FRANCE

S64
JOHNSON K.F.,"CAUSAL FACTORS IN LATIN AMERICAN POLITICAL INSTABILITY." CULTURE NAT/G VOL/ASSN EX/STRUC FORCES EDU/PROP LEGIT ADMIN COERCE REV ATTIT KNOWL PWR...STYLE RECORD CHARTS WORK 20. PAGE 81 H1624 L/A+17C PERCEPT ELITES

S64
LERNER W.,"THE HISTORICAL ORIGINS OF THE SOVIET DOCTRINE OF PEACEFUL COEXISTENCE." COM USSR INT/ORG NAT/G VOL/ASSN PLAN PEACE ATTIT RIGID/FLEX PWR MARXISM...TIME/SEQ COLD/WAR 20. PAGE 95 H1891 EDU/PROP DIPLOM

S64
MARES V.E.,"EAST EUROPE'S SECOND CHANCE." COM EUR+WWI HUNGARY ROMANIA USSR YUGOSLAVIA ECO/UNDEV NAT/G TOP/EX CREATE PLAN TEC/DEV REGION NAT/LISM RIGID/FLEX PWR...CONCPT STAT COMECON 20. PAGE 102 H2047 VOL/ASSN ECO/TAC

S64
MOZINGO D.P.,"CHINA'S RELATIONS WITH HER ASIAN NEIGHBORS." ASIA CHINA/COM S/ASIA VIETNAM NAT/G DELIB/GP FORCES CREATE DOMIN EDU/PROP REV RIGID/FLEX PWR...TIME/SEQ GEN/LAWS COLD/WAR 20. PAGE 114 H2277 VOL/ASSN POLICY DIPLOM

B65
CARTER G.M.,POLITICS IN EUROPE. EUR+WWI FRANCE GERMANY/W UK USSR LAW CONSTN POL/PAR VOL/ASSN PRESS LOBBY PWR...ANTHOL SOC/INTEG EEC. PAGE 27 H0548 GOV/COMP OP/RES ECO/DEV

B65
KUPER L.,AN AFRICAN BOURGEOISIE. SOUTH/AFR LAW INTELL NAT/G POL/PAR VOL/ASSN DISCRIM...POLICY 20. PAGE 89 H1783 RACE/REL SOC STRUCT

B65
MEHROTRA S.R.,INDIA AND THE COMMONWEALTH 1885-1929. INDIA UK INT/ORG VOL/ASSN GP/REL ATTIT...POLICY BIBLIOG 19/20 CMN/WLTH. PAGE 108 H2163 DIPLOM NAT/G POL/PAR NAT/LISM

B65
PADELFORD N.,THE UNITED NATIONS IN THE BALANCE* ACCOMPLISHMENTS AND PROSPECTS. NAT/G VOL/ASSN DIPLOM ADMIN COLONIAL CT/SYS REGION WAR ORD/FREE INT/ORG CONTROL

...ANTHOL UN. PAGE 122 H2437

B65
SABLE M.H.,MASTER DIRECTORY FOR LATIN AMERICA. AGRI COM/IND FINAN R+D ACADEM LABOR NAT/G POL/PAR VOL/ASSN INT/TRADE EDU/PROP 20. PAGE 136 H2728 — INDEX L/A+17C INT/ORG DIPLOM

S65
LEVI W.,"THE CONCEPT OF INTEGRATION IN RESEARCH ON PEACE." NAT/G VOL/ASSN DIPLOM TASK ADJUST NAT/LISM PEACE DRIVE LOVE...PSY NET/THEORY GEN/LAWS. PAGE 95 H1897 — CONCPT IDEA/COMP INT/ORG CENTRAL

S65
VUCINICH W.S.,"WHITHER RUMANIA." COM USSR YUGOSLAVIA NAT/G VOL/ASSN DELIB/GP TOP/EX LEGIT NAT/LISM TOTALISM ATTIT DRIVE RIGID/FLEX ORD/FREE WEALTH SOCISM...TIME/SEQ TREND 20. PAGE 164 H3281 — ECO/DEV CREATE ROMANIA

B66
AIR FORCE ACADEMY ASSEMBLY,CULTURAL AFFAIRS AND FOREIGN RELATIONS. NAT/G VOL/ASSN ALL/VALS. PAGE 4 H0083 — CULTURE SOCIETY PERS/REL DIPLOM

B66
GORDON B.K.,THE DIMENSIONS OF CONFLICT IN SOUTHEAST ASIA. S/ASIA FORCES ADJUD REGION...CHARTS 20. PAGE 59 H1177 — DIPLOM NAT/COMP INT/ORG VOL/ASSN

B66
HAY P.,FEDERALISM AND SUPRANATIONAL ORGANIZATIONS: PATTERNS FOR NEW LEGAL STRUCTURES. EUR+WWI LAW NAT/G VOL/ASSN DIPLOM PWR...NAT/COMP TREATY EEC. PAGE 68 H1364 — SOVEREIGN FEDERAL INT/ORG INT/LAW

B66
JACKSON G.D.,COMINTERN AND PEASANT IN EAST EUROPE 1919-1930. BULGARIA COM CZECHOSLVK EUR+WWI POLAND ROMANIA YUGOSLAVIA STRATA AGRI VOL/ASSN DIPLOM CONTROL CROWD WEALTH...POLICY NAT/COMP 20. PAGE 79 H1575 — MARXISM ECO/UNDEV WORKER INT/ORG

B66
O'NEILL C.E.,CHURCH AND STATE IN FRENCH COLONIAL LOUISIANA: POLICY AND POLITICS TO 1732. PROVS VOL/ASSN DELIB/GP ADJUD ADMIN GP/REL ATTIT DRIVE ...POLICY BIBLIOG 17/18 LOUISIANA CHURCH/STA. PAGE 120 H2390 — COLONIAL NAT/G SECT PWR

B67
ANDERSON S.V.,THE NORDIC COUNCIL: A STUDY OF SCANDINAVIAN REGIONALISM. DENMARK FINLAND ICELAND NORWAY SWEDEN MARKET NAT/G VOL/ASSN CONSULT PARL/PROC ATTIT...TIME/SEQ BIBLIOG 20. PAGE 7 H0134 — INT/ORG REGION DIPLOM LEGIS

B67
MAZRUI A.A.,THE ANGLO-AFRICAN COMMONWEALTH; POLITICAL FRICTION AND CULTURAL FUSION. AFR INT/ORG VOL/ASSN CHIEF GP/REL INGP/REL RACE/REL NAT/LISM 20 CMN/WLTH EEC. PAGE 106 H2111 — COLONIAL SOVEREIGN DIPLOM CULTURE

L67
SEGAL A.,"THE INTEGRATION OF DEVELOPING COUNTRIES: SOME THOUGHTS ON EAST AFRICA AND CENTRAL AMERICA." AFR L/A+17C INT/ORG NAT/G VOL/ASSN FOR/AID INT/TRADE EQUILIB NAT/LISM PWR 20. PAGE 141 H2820 — ECO/UNDEV DIPLOM REGION

S67
HOFMANN W.,"THE PUBLIC INTEREST PRESSURE GROUP: THE CASE OF THE DEUTSCHE STADTETAG." GERMANY GERMANY/W CONSTN STRUCT NAT/G CENTRAL FEDERAL PWR...TIME/SEQ 20. PAGE 72 H1447 — LOC/G VOL/ASSN LOBBY ADMIN

S67
RENFIELD R.L.,"A POLICY FOR VIETNAM." COM VIETNAM NAT/G POL/PAR VOL/ASSN CHIEF DIPLOM EDU/PROP DETER REPRESENT ATTIT ORD/FREE 20. PAGE 131 H2615 — WAR POLICY PLAN COERCE

S67
ZARTMAN I.W.," NAT/G POL/PAR VOL/ASSN NAT/LISM ORD/FREE PWR...CONCPT NAT/COMP ORG/CHARTS OAU MAGHREB. PAGE 172 H3451 — AFR ISLAM DIPLOM REGION

S68
LUKASZEWSKI J.,"WESTERN INTEGRATION AND THE PEOPLE'S DEMOCRACIES." USSR ELITES ECO/DEV NAT/G VOL/ASSN INT/TRADE AGREE REV FEDERAL WEALTH SOCISM ...NAT/COMP SOC/INTEG 20 EEC. PAGE 99 H1977 — DIPLOM INT/ORG COM REGION

B96
KROPOTKIN P.,L'ANARCHIE. NAT/G VOL/ASSN REV MORAL WEALTH...POLICY 19. PAGE 89 H1776 — SOCIETY ANARCH PERSON CONCPT

B99
RIPLEY W.Z.,A SELECTED BIBLIOGRAPHY OF THE ANTHROPOLOGY AND ETHNOLOGY OF EUROPE. SOCIETY STRATA STRUCT KIN SECT VOL/ASSN GP/REL INGP/REL HABITAT...GEOG 19. PAGE 132 H2632 — BIBLIOG/A MOD/EUR SOC CULTURE

VOLPICELLI Z. H3261

VOLTAIRE....VOLTAIRE (FRANCOIS MARIE AROUET)

B55
ROWE C.,VOLTAIRE AND THE STATE. FRANCE MOD/EUR BAL/PWR CONTROL TASK SUPEGO ORD/FREE PWR...CONCPT 18 VOLTAIRE. PAGE 135 H2702 — NAT/G DIPLOM NAT/LISM ATTIT

VOLUNTARY ASSOCIATIONS....SEE VOL/ASSN

VOLUNTEERS IN SERVICE TO AMERICA (VISTA)....SEE VISTA

VON ARSENIEW W. H3262

VON BECKERATH E. H3263,H3264

VON DER MEHDEN F.R. H0126,H3265

VON EICKSTEDT E. H3266

VON FURER-HAIMEN E. H3267,H3268

VON GRUNEBAUM G.E. H3269

VON HARPE W. H3270

VON HAYEK F.A. H1368,H1369,H3271

VON HIPPEL E. H3272

VON KOENIGSWALD H. H3273

VON LAUE T.H. H3274

VON MERING O. H3275

VON RENESSE E.A. H3276

VON STACKELBERG K. H3277

VON STEIN L.J. H3278

VON/TRESCK....VON TRESCKOW

VORSPAN A. H3279

VOTING....SEE CHOOSE, SUFF

VTOL....VERTICAL TAKE-OFF AND LANDING AIRCRAFT

VUCINICH A. H3280

VUCINICH W.S. H3281

W

WABEKE B.H. H3282

WADE E.C.S. H3283

WAELBROECK M. H3284

WAGES....SEE PRICE, WORKER, WEALTH

WAGLEY C. H3285,H3286

WAGNER/A....ADOLPH WAGNER

WAINHOUSE D.W. H3287

WAINWRIGHT M.D. H3288

WALDMAN E. H3289

WALES....WALES

B64
GRIFFITH W.,THE WELSH (2ND ED.). UK SOCIETY STRUCT SECT WRITING NAT/LISM...ART/METH MODAL OBS/ENVIR TREND SOC/INTEG WALES PURITAN MUSIC. PAGE 61 H1223 — CULTURE SOC LING

WALKER A.A. H3290,H3291

WALKER F.D. H3292

WALKER/E....EDWIN WALKER

WALLACE/G....GEORGE WALLACE

WALLACE/HA....HENRY A. WALLACE

WALLAS G. H3293

WALLBANK T.W. H3294

WALSTON H. H3295

WALTER E. H3296

WALTERS F.P. H3297

WALTZ K.N. H3298

WALTZ/KN....KENNETH N. WALTZ

WANDERSCHECK H. H3299,H3300

WANG Y.C. H3301

WAR....SEE ALSO COERCE

WAR/TRIAL....WAR TRIAL;

WAR/1812....WAR OF 1812

WARBURG J.P. H3302

WARBURTON E.A. H1634

WARD L. H3303

WARD P.W. H3304

WARD R.E. H3305,H3306,H3307

WARD W.E. H3308

WARD....SEE LOC/G, POL/PAR

WARD/LEST....LESTER WARD

B67
WARD L.,LESTER WARD AND THE WELFARE STATE. SOCIETY NAT/G CREATE RECEIVE EQUILIB UTOPIA HABITAT HEREDITY PERSON...POLICY SOC BIOG 19/20 WARD/LEST. PAGE 165 H3303
ALL/VALS NEW/IDEA WELF/ST CONCPT

WARNER W.L. H3309,H3310,H3311

WARREN S. H3312

WARRN/EARL....EARL WARREN

B56
DOUGLAS W.O.,WE THE JUDGES. INDIA USA+45 USA-45 LAW NAT/G SECT LEGIS PRESS CRIME FEDERAL ORD/FREE ...POLICY GOV/COMP 19/20 WARRN/EARL MARSHALL/J SUPREME/CT. PAGE 42 H0841
ADJUD CT/SYS CONSTN GOV/REL

WARSAW....WARSAW, POLAND

WARSAW/P

B64
BROWN N.,NUCLEAR WAR* THE IMPENDING STRATEGIC DEADLOCK. USA+45 USSR TEC/DEV BUDGET RISK ARMS/CONT NUC/PWR WEAPON COST BIO/SOC...GEOG IDEA/COMP NAT/COMP GAME NATO WARSAW/P. PAGE 22 H0448
FORCES OP/RES WAR GEN/LAWS

B64
KIS T.I.,LES PAYS DE L'EUROPE DE L'EST: LEURS RAPPORTS MUTUELS ET LE PROBLEME DE LEUR INTEGRATION DANS L'ORBITE DE L'USSR. EUR+WWI RUSSIA USSR INT/ORG NAT/G REV ATTIT...JURID SOC BIBLIOG WARSAW/P COMECON EUROPE/E. PAGE 86 H1727
DIPLOM COM MARXISM REGION

B66
INTL CONF ON WORLD POLITICS-5,EASTERN EUROPE IN TRANSITION. EUR+WWI USSR ECO/TAC NAT/LISM ATTIT SOVEREIGN...CHARTS ANTHOL 20 TREATY WARSAW/P. PAGE 78 H1562
COM NAT/COMP MARXISM DIPLOM

S66
GALTUNG J.,"EAST-WEST INTERACTION PATTERNS." DIPLOM INT/TRADE...NET/THEORY CON/ANAL CHARTS NAT/COMP INDEX NATO COLD/WAR UN WARSAW/P. PAGE 55 H1090
STAT HYPO/EXP

WARSAW/PCT....WARSAW PACT TREATY ORGANIZATION

WASHING/BT....BOOKER T. WASHINGTON

WASHING/DC....WASHINGTON, D.C.

WASHINGT/G....PRESIDENT GEORGE WASHINGTON

WASHINGTON....WASHINGTON, STATE OF

WASP....WHITE-ANGLO-SAXON-PROTESTANT ESTABLISHMENT

WASSERMAN L. H3313

WATANABE H. H3306

WATER POLLUTION....SEE POLLUTION

WATER....PERTAINING TO ALL NON-SALT WATER

WATERMAN T.T. H1770

WATT D.C. H3314,H3315

WATTS....WATTS, LOS ANGELES

WCC....WORLD COUNCIL CHURCHES

WCTU....WOMAN'S CHRISTIAN TEMPERANCE UNION

WEALTH....ACCESS TO GOODS AND SERVICES (ALSO POVERTY)

B00
MOCKLER-FERRYMAN A.,BRITISH WEST AFRICA. FRANCE GERMANY NIGER SIER/LEONE UK CULTURE DIPLOM WAR RACE/REL PRODUC PROFIT WEALTH...POLICY PREDICT 19. PAGE 112 H2232
AFR COLONIAL INT/TRADE CAP/ISM

B05
PHILIPPINE ISLANDS BUREAU SCI,ETHNOLOGICAL SURVEY: THE BONTOC IGOROT. ECO/UNDEV AGRI FAM MARRIAGE HEALTH WEALTH...LING OBS AUD/VIS CHARTS WORSHIP 20 LUZON BONTOC. PAGE 125 H2500
CULTURE INGP/REL KIN STRUCT

B06
SUMNER W.G.,FOLKWAYS: STUDY OF THE SOCIOLOGICAL IMPORTANCE OF USAGES, MANNERS, CUSTOMS, MORES, AND MORALS. STRUCT KIN ETIQUET ROUTINE MURDER MARRIAGE PEACE SEX ALL/VALS WEALTH BIBLIOG. PAGE 150 H3008
CULTURE SOC SANCTION MORAL

B11
HUXLEY T.H.,METHOD AND RESULTS: ESSAYS. EDU/PROP REPRESENT OWN PERSON PWR WEALTH...PSY IDEA/COMP GEN/LAWS. PAGE 76 H1514
ORD/FREE NAT/G POPULISM PLURIST

B12
HOBSON J.A.,THE EVOLUTION OF MODERN CAPITALISM. MOD/EUR UK STRATA ECO/DEV INDUS INCOME UTIL WEALTH ...SOC GEN/LAWS 7/20. PAGE 72 H1440
CAP/ISM WORKER TEC/DEV TIME/SEQ

B14
CRAIG J.,ELEMENTS OF POLITICAL SCIENCE (3 VOLS.). CONSTN AGRI INDUS SCHOOL FORCES TAX CT/SYS SUFF MORAL WEALTH...CONCPT 19 CIVIL/LIB. PAGE 35 H0696
PHIL/SCI NAT/G ORD/FREE

N19
BENTHAM J.,A PLAN FOR AN UNIVERSAL AND PERPETUAL PEACE (1838) (PAMPHLET). NAT/G FORCES BAL/PWR INT/TRADE ADMIN AGREE CT/SYS ARMS/CONT SOVEREIGN WEALTH GEN/LAWS. PAGE 14 H0288
INT/ORG INT/LAW PEACE COLONIAL

N19
BRIMMELL G.H.,COMMUNISM IN SOUTHEAST ASIA (PAMPHLET). BURMA CAMBODIA COM INDIA INDONESIA LAOS MOD/EUR NAT/G POL/PAR FORCES CAP/ISM CONTROL WEALTH ...MYTH 20. PAGE 21 H0420
MARXISM S/ASIA REV ECO/UNDEV

N19
BUSINESS ECONOMISTS' GROUP,INCOME POLICIES (PAMPHLET). UK INDUS LABOR TOP/EX PAY COST PRODUC ...ECOMETRIC GOV/COMP SIMUL ANTHOL 20. PAGE 25 H0497
INCOME WORKER WEALTH POLICY

N19
LIEBKNECHT W.P.C.,SOCIALISM (2 PTS.; 1875, 1894) (PAMPHLET). WORKER CAP/ISM EDU/PROP WEALTH POPULISM. PAGE 97 H1927
ECO/TAC STRATA SOCIALIST PARTIC

N19
SALKEVER L.R.,SUB-SAHARA AFRICA (PAMPHLET). AFR USSR EXTR/IND NAT/G SCHOOL DIPLOM COLONIAL WEALTH ...GEOG CHARTS 16/20. PAGE 137 H2742
ECO/UNDEV TEC/DEV TASK INT/TRADE

B20
MALTHUS T.R.,PRINCIPLES OF POLITICAL ECONOMY. UK AGRI INDUS MARKET NAT/G DIPLOM PRICE CONTROL BAL/PAY COST OWN PWR LAISSEZ 18/19. PAGE 102 H2034
GEN/LAWS DEMAND WEALTH

B22
URE P.N.,THE ORIGIN OF TYRANNY. MEDIT-7 FINAN INDUS CHIEF FORCES ECO/TAC WEALTH. PAGE 159 H3174
AUTHORIT PWR NAT/G MARKET

B26
TAWNEY R.H.,RELIGION AND THE RISE OF CAPITALISM. UK CULTURE NAT/G TEC/DEV OWN LAISSEZ...POLICY SOC TIME/SEQ 16/19. PAGE 153 H3050
SECT WEALTH INDUS CAP/ISM

B27
BELLOC H.,THE SERVILE STATE (1912) (3RD ED.). PRUSSIA UK CULTURE STRATA INDUS NAT/G ECO/TAC CONTROL LEAD SUFF DISCRIM EQUILIB ORD/FREE WEALTH 20. PAGE 13 H0269
WORKER CAP/ISM DOMIN CATH

B27
EDWARDS L.P.,THE NATURAL HISTORY OF REVOLUTION. UNIV NAT/G VOL/ASSN COERCE DRIVE WEALTH...TREND GEN/LAWS. PAGE 45 H0893
PWR GUERRILLA REV

B27
PANIKKAR K.M.,INDIAN STATES AND THE GOVERNMENT OF INDIA. INDIA UK CONSTN CONTROL TASK GP/REL SOVEREIGN WEALTH...TREND BIBLIOG 19. PAGE 123 H2457
GOV/COMP COLONIAL BAL/PWR PROVS

B31
DEKAT A.D.A.,COLONIAL POLICY. S/ASIA CULTURE EX/STRUC ECO/TAC DOMIN ADMIN COLONIAL ROUTINE SOVEREIGN WEALTH...POLICY MGT RECORD KNO/TEST SAMP. PAGE 39 H0785
DRIVE PWR INDONESIA NETHERLAND

B33
TANNENBAUM F.,PEACE BY REVOLUTION. ECO/UNDEV AGRI SECT WORKER DIPLOM EDU/PROP DISCRIM OWN WEALTH POPULISM 17/20 MEXIC/AMER INDIAN/AM. PAGE 152 H3043
CULTURE COLONIAL RACE/REL REV

B34
LOVELL R.I.,THE STRUGGLE FOR SOUTH AFRICA, 1875-1899. GERMANY RHODESIA SOUTH/AFR UK NAT/G ECO/TAC HABITAT WEALTH...POLICY 19. PAGE 99 H1971
COLONIAL DIPLOM WAR GP/REL

B35
LASKI H.J.,THE STATE IN THEORY AND PRACTICE. ELITES ECO/TAC REPRESENT ORD/FREE PWR WEALTH POPULISM ...GOV/COMP GEN/LAWS 19/20. PAGE 92 H1829
CAP/ISM COERCE NAT/G FASCISM

B35
MORE T.,UTOPIA (1516) (TRANS. BY R. ROBYNSON). LAW CULTURE SOCIETY STRUCT FAM SECT EDU/PROP WAR OWN UTIL KNOWL WEALTH 16. PAGE 113 H2253
UTOPIA NAT/G ECO/TAC GEN/LAWS

B36
HUBERMAN L.,MAN'S WORLDLY GOODS: THE STORY OF THE WEALTH OF NATIONS. CHRIST-17C EUR+WWI MOD/EUR SOCIETY DOMIN REV ORD/FREE...TIME/SEQ METH/COMP. PAGE 74 H1486
WEALTH CAP/ISM MARXISM CREATE

B38
LAWLEY F.E.,THE GROWTH OF COLLECTIVE ECONOMY VOL. 1: NATIONAL. EUR+WWI AGRI INDUS NAT/G BARGAIN CAP/ISM ECO/TAC WAR OPTIMAL WEALTH...GOV/COMP METH/COMP 19/20 MONOPOLY. PAGE 92 H1844
SOCISM PRICE CONTROL OWN

B38
LAWLEY F.E.,THE GROWTH OF COLLECTIVE ECONOMY VOL. 2: INTERNATIONAL. WOR-45 AGRI INDUS EQUILIB OPTIMAL OWN WEALTH...NAT/COMP 19/20 NAZI NEW/DEAL MONOPOLY. PAGE 92 H1845
ECO/TAC SOCISM NAT/LISM CONTROL

B38
SAINT-PIERRE C.I.,SCHEME FOR LASTING PEACE (TRANS. BY H. BELLOT). INDUS NAT/G CHIEF FORCES INT/TRADE CT/SYS WAR PWR SOVEREIGN WEALTH...POLICY 18. PAGE 137 H2732
INT/ORG PEACE AGREE INT/LAW

B39
ENGELS F.,HERRN EUGEN DUHRING'S REVOLUTION IN SCIENCE (1878). CULTURE STRATA STRUCT FAM SECT ECO/TAC REV WAR SOCISM...MARXIST 19. PAGE 46 H0925
PWR SOCIETY WEALTH GEN/LAWS

B39
FIRTH R.,PRIMITIVE POLYNESIAN ECONOMY. SOCIETY DIST/IND SECT CHIEF CAP/ISM PRODUC WEALTH...SOC OBS METH WORSHIP 20 POLYNESIA. PAGE 50 H1007
ECO/UNDEV CULTURE AGRI ECO/TAC

B39
FURNIVALL J.S.,NETHERLANDS INDIA. INDIA NETHERLAND CULTURE INDUS NAT/G DIPLOM ADMIN WEALTH...POLICY CHARTS 17/20. PAGE 54 H1081
COLONIAL ECO/UNDEV SOVEREIGN PLURISM

B39
MARQUAND H.A.,ORGANIZED LABOUR IN FOUR CONTINENTS. EUR+WWI USA-45 INDUS NAT/G PAY GP/REL TOTALISM ATTIT WEALTH ALL/IDEOS...TREND NAT/COMP 20 ILO AFL/CIO EUROPE CHINJAP MEXIC/AMER. PAGE 103 H2055
LABOR WORKER CONCPT ANTHOL

B39
VAN BILJON F.J.,STATE INTERFERENCE IN SOUTH AFRICA. SOUTH/AFR ECO/UNDEV AGRI INDUS WORKER RATION WEALTH ...JURID 20. PAGE 161 H3225
ECO/TAC POLICY INT/TRADE NAT/G

B41
KEESING F.M.,THE SOUTH SEAS IN THE MODERN WORLD. INDONESIA STRUCT FAM SECT EDU/PROP LEAD INCOME WEALTH...HEAL SOC 20. PAGE 84 H1678
CULTURE ECO/UNDEV GOV/COMP DIPLOM

B43
LASKI H.J.,REFLECTIONS ON THE REVOLUTIONS OF OUR TIME. COM USSR NAT/G WORKER UTOPIA ORD/FREE WEALTH MARXISM SOCISM 19/20. PAGE 92 H1830
CAP/ISM WELF/ST ECO/TAC POLICY

B44
HAYEK F.A.,THE ROAD TO SERFDOM. NAT/G POL/PAR CREATE EDU/PROP ATTIT WEALTH LAISSEZ...OLD/LIB CONCPT TREND 20. PAGE 68 H1368
FUT PLAN ECO/TAC SOCISM

L44
HUXLEY J.,"THE FUTURE OF THE COLONIES." AFR SOCIETY NAT/G PLAN DOMIN COERCE ATTIT DRIVE ORD/FREE PWR WEALTH...TIME/SEQ TREND AUD/VIS CHARTS 20. PAGE 76 H1511
ECO/UNDEV FUT COLONIAL

B46
ALLEN J.S.,WORLD MONOPOLY AND PEACE. GERMANY UK USSR FINAN INDUS LG/CO DOMIN CONTROL PEACE PWR WEALTH SOCISM...NAT/COMP 20 MONOPOLY. PAGE 5 H0105
CAP/ISM DIPLOM WAR COLONIAL

B47
ISAAC J.,ECONOMICS OF MIGRATION. MOD/EUR CULTURE STRATA STRUCT NAT/G COLONIAL WEALTH...OLD/LIB TREND TIME 19/20 EUROPE/W MIGRATION. PAGE 78 H1569
HABITAT SOC GEOG

B48
FURNIVAL J.,COLONIAL POLICY AND PRACTICE A COMPARATIVE STUDY OF BURMA, AND NETHERLANDS INDIA. BURMA INDONESIA S/ASIA...GEOG OBS GOV/COMP METH/COMP 20. PAGE 54 H1080
COLONIAL NAT/LISM WEALTH SOVEREIGN

B48
ROSENFARB J.,FREEDOM AND THE ADMINISTRATIVE STATE. NAT/G ROUTINE EFFICIENCY PRODUC RATIONAL UTIL ...TECHNIC WELF/ST MGT 20 BUREAUCRCY. PAGE 134 H2680
ECO/DEV INDUS PLAN WEALTH

S49
STEINMETZ H.,"THE PROBLEMS OF THE LANDRAT: A STUDY OF COUNTY GOVERNMENT IN THE US ZONE OF GERMANY." GERMANY/W USA+45 INDUS PLAN DIPLOM EDU/PROP CONTROL WAR GOV/REL FEDERAL WEALTH PLURISM...GOV/COMP 20 LANDRAT. PAGE 149 H2977
LOC/G COLONIAL MGT TOP/EX

B50
CORNELL U DEPT ASIAN STUDIES,SOUTHEAST ASIA PROGRAM DATA PAPER. BURMA CAMBODIA INDONESIA MALAYSIA VIETNAM SOCIETY STRUCT NAT/G SECT DIPLOM FOR/AID PWR WEALTH...SOC 20. PAGE 33 H0670
BIBLIOG/A CULTURE S/ASIA ECO/UNDEV

B50
JONES H.D.,KOREA, AN ANNOTATED BIBLIOGRAPHY OF PUBLICATIONS IN WESTERN LANGUAGES. KOREA CULTURE MUNIC SECT FORCES DIPLOM HEALTH WEALTH...ART/METH GEOG SOC LING 20. PAGE 82 H1632
BIBLIOG/A ASIA NAT/G ECO/UNDEV

C50
ROUSSEAU J.J.,"A DISCOURSE ON POLITICAL ECONOMY" (1755) IN THE SOCIAL CONTRACT AND DISCOURSES." UNIV SOCIETY STRATA STRUCT CONSEN EQUILIB HAPPINESS UTOPIA HEALTH WEALTH...POLICY WELF/ST. PAGE 135 H2699
NAT/G ECO/TAC TAX GEN/LAWS

C51
BEST H.,"THE SOVIET STATE AND ITS INCEPTION." USSR CULTURE INDUS DIPLOM WEALTH...GEOG SOC BIBLIOG 20. PAGE 16 H0322
COM GEN/METH REV MARXISM

B52
TAX S.,HERITAGE OF CONQUEST. L/A+17C ECO/UNDEV LOC/G WEALTH...POLICY ANTHOL WORSHIP 20 MEXIC/AMER CENTRAL/AM. PAGE 153 H3052
PHIL/SCI CULTURE SOCIETY

C52
HUME D.,"OF TAXES" IN D. HUME, POLITICAL DISCOURSES (1752)" UK NAT/G COST INCOME LAISSEZ...GEN/LAWS 18. PAGE 75 H1493
TAX FINAN WEALTH POLICY

C52
LEWIS B.W.,"BRITISH PLANNING AND NATIONALIZATION." UK INDUS SERV/IND LABOR NAT/G OP/RES TEC/DEV TAX WEALTH...CHARTS BIBLIOG 20. PAGE 96 H1912
NEW/LIB ECO/DEV POL/PAR PLAN

B53
MEYER P.,THE JEWS IN THE SOVIET SATELLITES. CZECHOSLVK POLAND SOCIETY STRATA NAT/G BAL/PWR ECO/TAC EDU/PROP LEGIT ADMIN COERCE ATTIT DISPL PERCEPT HEALTH PWR RESPECT WEALTH...METH/CNCPT JEWS VAL/FREE NAZI 20. PAGE 110 H2192
COM SECT TOTALISM USSR

B53
NELSON G.R.,FREEDOM AND WELFARE: SOCIAL PATTERNS IN THE NORTHERN COUNTRIES OF EUROPE. EUR+WWI ECO/DEV NAT/G EDU/PROP LEGIT HEALTH ORD/FREE SKILL WEALTH ...STAT AUD/VIS SCANDINAV WORK TOT/POP 20. PAGE 116 H2329
PLAN ECO/TAC

B53
WAGLEY C.,AMAZON TOWN: A STUDY OF MAN IN THE TROPICS. BRAZIL L/A+17C STRATA STRUCT ECO/UNDEV AGRI EX/STRUC RACE/REL DISCRIM HABITAT WEALTH...OBS SOC/EXP 20. PAGE 164 H3285
SOC NEIGH CULTURE INGP/REL

B55
RESHETAR J.S.,PROBLEMS OF ANALYZING AND PREDICTING SOVIET BEHAVIOR. USSR CULTURE ECO/DEV AGRI DIST/IND EXTR/IND PROC/MFG NAT/G SECT TOP/EX ACT/RES ADMIN PWR WEALTH...SOC METH TOT/POP VAL/FREE 20. PAGE 131 H2617
COM ATTIT

B55
UN ECONOMIC COMN ASIA & FAR E,ECONOMIC SURVEY OF ASIA AND THE FAR EAST, 1954. AFGHANISTN CEYLON INDIA PHILIPPINE S/ASIA ECO/DEV FINAN INDUS INT/TRADE PRODUC WEALTH...STAT CHARTS 20 CHINJAP. PAGE 158 H3158
ECO/UNDEV PRICE NAT/COMP ASIA

C55
SANTAYANA G.,"REASON IN SOCIETY" IN G. SANTAYANA, THE LIFE OF REASON." INDUS FAM NAT/G WAR GP/REL HAPPINESS PRODUC LOVE WEALTH CONSERVE POPULISM CONCPT. PAGE 138 H2752
RATIONAL SOCIETY CULTURE ATTIT

B56
DEUTSCH K.W.,AN INTERDISCIPLINARY BIBLIOGRAPHY ON NATIONALISM, 1935-1953. CULTURE SOCIETY SECT ATTIT HABITAT HEREDITY PERCEPT ROLE WEALTH...METH/CNCPT LING 20. PAGE 40 H0798
BIBLIOG/A NAT/LISM COLONIAL ADJUST

B56
PADMORE G.,PAN-AFRICANISM OR COMMUNISM. AFR FUT NIGERIA INTELL NAT/G COLONIAL FEDERAL ATTIT DRIVE PWR RESPECT WEALTH MARXISM...CONCPT AUD/VIS STERTYP 20. PAGE 122 H2440
POL/PAR NAT/LISM

B56
READ M.,EDUCATION AND SOCIAL CHANGE IN TROPICAL AREAS. AFR L/A+17C SOCIETY LITERACY PERCEPT PERSON
EDU/PROP HABITAT

WEALTH...HEAL PHIL/SCI SOC 20. PAGE 130 H2603
DRIVE CULTURE

B56
SYKES G.M.,CRIME AND SOCIETY. LAW STRATA STRUCT ACT/RES ROUTINE ANOMIE WEALTH...POLICY SOC/INTEG 20. PAGE 151 H3021
CRIMLGY CRIME CULTURE INGP/REL

B56
VON BECKERATH E.,HANDWORTERBUCH DER SOCIALWISSENSCHAFTEN (II VOLS.). EUR+WWI GERMANY POL/PAR WORKER DIPLOM LEAD CHOOSE SUFF WEALTH...SOC 20. PAGE 163 H3263
BIBLIOG INT/TRADE NAT/G ECO/DEV

S56
GORDON L.,"THE ORGANIZATION FOR EUROPEAN ECONOMIC COOPERATION." EUR+WWI INDUS INT/ORG NAT/G CONSULT DELIB/GP ACT/RES CREATE PLAN TEC/DEV EDU/PROP LEGIT WEALTH OEEC 20. PAGE 59 H1178
VOL/ASSN ECO/DEV

B57
..,THE POST WAR CONDITIONS OF BRITAIN. RUCT NAT/G PLAN EDU/PROP LEGIT RIGID/FLEX EALTH...SOCIALIST WELF/ST STAT TREND HARTS PARLIAMENT WORK 20. PAGE 31 H0624
ECO/DEV UK

B57
CONOVER H.F.,NORTH AND NORTHEAST AFRICA; A SELECTED ANNOTATED LIST OF WRITINGS. ALGERIA MOROCCO SUDAN UAR CULTURE INT/ORG PROB/SOLV ADJUD NAT/LISM PWR WEALTH...SOC 20 UN. PAGE 32 H0649
BIBLIOG/A DIPLOM AFR ECO/UNDEV

B57
POPLAI S.L.,NATIONAL POLITICS AND 1957 ELECTIONS IN INDIA. INDIA BARGAIN PARL/PROC CONSEN NAT/LISM PWR WEALTH 20. PAGE 127 H2543
POL/PAR CHOOSE POLICY NAT/G

S57
KILSON M.L.,"LAND AND POLITICS IN KENYA: AN ANALYSIS OF AFRICAN POLITICS IN A PLURAL SOCIETY." FUT LAW CULTURE KIN NAT/G ECO/TAC DOMIN REV NAT/LISM ORD/FREE PWR RESPECT SOVEREIGN WEALTH ...SOC OBS TREND WORK VAL/FREE CMN/WLTH 20. PAGE 86 H1710
AFR ECO/UNDEV

B58
BRADY A.,DEMOCRACY IN THE DOMINIONS (3RD ED.). CANADA NEW/ZEALND SOUTH/AFR WOR+45 LAW EX/STRUC DOMIN COLONIAL PARL/PROC REPRESENT RACE/REL NAT/LISM WEALTH 20 AUSTRAL CMN/WLTH. PAGE 20 H0399
GOV/COMP POL/PAR POPULISM NAT/G

B58
MCIVOR R.C.,CANADIAN MONETARY, BANKING, AND FISCAL DEVELOPMENT. CANADA INDUS LG/CO NAT/G SML/CO CONTROL WAR...GEN/LAWS BIBLIOG 17/20. PAGE 107 H2137
ECO/TAC FINAN ECO/DEV WEALTH

B58
SHAW S.J.,THE FINANCIAL AND ADMINISTRATIVE ORGANIZATION AND DEVELOPMENT OF OTTOMAN EGYPT 1517-1798. UAR LOC/G FORCES BUDGET INT/TRADE TAX EATING INCOME WEALTH...CHARTS BIBLIOG 16/18 OTTOMAN NAPOLEON/B. PAGE 143 H2853
FINAN ADMIN GOV/REL CULTURE

B58
STEINBERG C.S.,THE MASS COMMUNICATORS: PUBLIC RELATIONS, PUBLIC OPINION, AND MASS MEDIA. CULTURE CONSULT ACT/RES FEEDBACK DISPL WEALTH 20. PAGE 149 H2975
EDU/PROP ATTIT COM/IND PERCEPT

B58
TILLION G.,ALGERIA: THE REALITIES. ALGERIA FRANCE ISLAM CULTURE STRATA PROB/SOLV DOMIN REV NAT/LISM WEALTH MARXISM...GEOG 20. PAGE 155 H3094
ECO/UNDEV SOC COLONIAL DIPLOM

S58
ELKIN A.B.,"OEEC-ITS STRUCTURE AND POWERS." EUR+WWI CONSTN INDUS INT/ORG NAT/G VOL/ASSN DELIB/GP ACT/RES PLAN ORD/FREE WEALTH...CHARTS ORG/CHARTS OEEC 20. PAGE 45 H0907
ECO/DEV EX/STRUC

S58
LOCKWOOD W.W.,"THE SOCIALISTIC SOCIETY: INDIA AND JAPAN." INDIA ECO/DEV ECO/UNDEV INDUS NAT/G CONTROL LEAD PRODUC WEALTH 20 CHINJAP. PAGE 98 H1948
ECO/TAC NAT/COMP FINAN SOCISM

C58
GINSBURG N.,"MALAYA." MALAYSIA PROB/SOLV REGION NAT/LISM KNOWL WEALTH...GEOG SOC CHARTS BIBLIOG 20. PAGE 57 H1133
COM/IND ECO/UNDEV CULTURE NAT/G

B59
KELF-COHEN R.,NATIONALISATION IN BRITAIN: THE END OF DOGMA. EUR+WWI UK NAT/G POL/PAR WORKER ECO/TAC PARL/PROC WEALTH SOCISM...GOV/COMP 20. PAGE 84 H1683
NEW/LIB ECO/DEV INDUS OWN

B59
PARK R.L.,LEADERSHIP AND POLITICAL INSTITUTIONS IN INDIA. S/ASIA CULTURE ECO/UNDEV LOC/G MUNIC PROVS LEGIS PLAN ADMIN LEAD ORD/FREE WEALTH...GEOG SOC BIOG TOT/POP VAL/FREE 20. PAGE 123 H2468
NAT/G EXEC INDIA

B59
SVALASTOGA K.,PRESTIGE, CLASS, AND MOBILITY. DENMARK UK EDU/PROP INCOME WEALTH...SOC SAMP 20. PAGE 151 H3010
NAT/COMP STRATA STRUCT ELITES

L59
MURPHY J.C.,"SOME IMPLICATIONS OF EUROPE'S COMMON MARKET. IN (COOK P, ECONOMIC DEVELOPMENT AND INTERNATIONAL TRADE,." EUR+WWI ECO/DEV DIST/IND INDUS NAT/G PLAN ECO/TAC INT/TRADE WEALTH...STAT TREND OEEC TOT/POP 20 EEC. PAGE 115 H2298
MARKET INT/ORG REGION

S59
PLAZA G.,"FOR A REGIONAL MARKET IN LATIN AMERICA." FUT L/A+17C CULTURE INDUS NAT/G ECO/TAC INT/TRADE ATTIT WEALTH...NEW/IDEA TREND OAS 20. PAGE 126 H2527
MARKET INT/ORG REGION

B60
BURRIDGE K.,MAMBU: A MELANESIAN MILLENNIUM. ECO/UNDEV PROC/MFG FAM KIN CHIEF COLONIAL COERCE GP/REL DRIVE WEALTH WORSHIP 20 NEW/GUINEA. PAGE 25 H0494
S/ASIA SECT CULTURE MYTH

B60
KERR C.,INDUSTRIALISM AND INDUSTRIAL MAN. CULTURE SOCIETY ECO/UNDEV NAT/G ADMIN PRODUC WEALTH ...PREDICT TREND NAT/COMP 19/20. PAGE 85 H1697
WORKER MGT ECO/DEV INDUS

B60
LISTER L.,EUROPE'S COAL AND STEEL COMMUNITY. FRANCE GERMANY STRUCT ECO/DEV EXTR/IND INDUS MARKET NAT/G DELIB/GP ECO/TAC INT/TRADE EDU/PROP ATTIT RIGID/FLEX ORD/FREE PWR WEALTH...CONCPT STAT TIME/SEQ CHARTS ECSC 20. PAGE 97 H1941
EUR+WWI INT/ORG REGION

B60
NEALE A.D.,THE FLOW OF RESOURCES FROM RICH TO POOR. WOR+45 ECO/DEV ECO/UNDEV FINAN INDUS NAT/G PLAN EFFICIENCY WEALTH...POLICY NAT/COMP 20 RESOURCE/N. PAGE 116 H2325
FOR/AID DIPLOM METH/CNCPT

B60
PANIKKAR K.M.,THE STATE AND THE CITIZEN (2ND ED.). INDIA DOMIN ATTIT SUPEGO ORD/FREE WEALTH...GEOG CONCPT GP/COMP 20. PAGE 123 H2459
TEC/DEV POL/PAR NAT/G EDU/PROP

B60
PETERSON W.C.,THE WELFARE STATE IN FRANCE. EUR+WWI FRANCE FUT STRATA PROB/SOLV TAX GIVE RECEIVE INCOME ORD/FREE PWR...CHARTS 20. PAGE 125 H2496
NEW/LIB ECO/TAC WEALTH NAT/G

B60
ROBERTSON D.,THE CONTROL OF INDUSTRY. UK MARKET LABOR WORKER PRICE CONTROL GP/REL COST DEMAND ORD/FREE WEALTH NEW/LIB SOCISM 20. PAGE 132 H2646
INDUS FINAN NAT/G ECO/DEV

B60
STRACHEY J.,THE END OF EMPIRE. UK WOR+45 WOR-45 DIPLOM INT/TRADE DOMIN ADJUST ORD/FREE WEALTH ...SOCIALIST GOV/COMP TIME COMMONWLTH. PAGE 150 H2991
COLONIAL ECO/DEV BAL/PWR LAISSEZ

S60
BERG E.J.,"ECONOMIC BASIS OF POLITICAL CHOICE IN FRENCH WEST AFRICA." FRANCE ECO/UNDEV AGRI INDUS NAT/G PLAN LEGIT COLONIAL REGION ATTIT PWR WEALTH ...CONCPT 20. PAGE 15 H0299
AFR ECO/TAC

S60
FRANKEL S.H.,"ECONOMIC ASPECTS OF POLITICAL INDEPENDENCE IN AFRICA." AFR FUT SOCIETY ECO/UNDEV COM/IND FINAN LEGIS PLAN TEC/DEV CAP/ISM ECO/TAC INT/TRADE ADMIN ATTIT DRIVE RIGID/FLEX PWR WEALTH ...MGT NEW/IDEA MATH TIME/SEQ VAL/FREE 20. PAGE 53 H1052
NAT/G FOR/AID

S60
GROSSMAN G.,"SOVIET GROWTH: ROUTINE, INERTIA, AND PRESSURE." COM STRATA NAT/G DELIB/GP PLAN TEC/DEV ECO/TAC EDU/PROP ADMIN ROUTINE DRIVE WEALTH COLD/WAR 20. PAGE 62 H1236
POL/PAR ECO/DEV USSR

S60
HOWARD M.,"BRITAIN'S DEFENSE: COMMITMENTS AND CAPABILITIES." EUR+WWI ECO/DEV NAT/G FORCES LEGIS PLAN DETER ORD/FREE WEALTH...POLICY CONCPT TIME/SEQ GEN/METH 20. PAGE 74 H1481
FUT PWR DIPLOM UK

S60
RIVKIN A.,"AFRICAN ECONOMIC DEVELOPMENT: ADVANCED TECHNOLOGY AND THE STAGES OF GROWTH." CULTURE ECO/UNDEV AGRI COM/IND EXTR/IND PLAN ECO/TAC ATTIT DRIVE RIGID/FLEX SKILL WEALTH...MGT SOC GEN/LAWS WORK TOT/POP 20. PAGE 132 H2634
AFR TEC/DEV FOR/AID

B61
AYLMER G.,THE KING'S SERVANTS. UK ELITES CHIEF PAY CT/SYS WEALTH 17 CROMWELL/O CHARLES/I. PAGE 9 H0187
ADMIN ROUTINE EX/STRUC NAT/G

B61
CHAKRABARTI A.,NEHRU: HIS DEMOCRACY AND INDIA. ASIA INDIA UK CONSTN ECO/UNDEV SECT DIPLOM COLONIAL PEACE WEALTH...BIBLIOG 20 CONGRESS NEHRU/J GANDHI/M. PAGE 28 H0570
ORD/FREE STRATA NAT/G CHIEF

B61
DIA M.,THE AFRICAN NATIONS AND WORLD SOLIDARITY. ISLAM CULTURE ELITES ECO/DEV ECO/UNDEV INT/ORG NAT/G PLAN ECO/TAC INT/TRADE EDU/PROP NAT/LISM ATTIT DRIVE ORD/FREE WEALTH...SOCIALIST CONCPT CON/ANAL GEN/LAWS TOT/POP 20. PAGE 41 H0817
AFR REGION SOCISM

B61
ESTEVEZ A.,ASPECTOS ECONOMICO-FINANCIEROS DE LA CAMPANA SANMARITANA. L/A+17C SPAIN FINAN COLONIAL LEAD ROLE ORD/FREE WEALTH 19 SOUTH/AMER SAN/MARTIN. PAGE 47 H0942
ECO/UNDEV REV BUDGET NAT/G

B61
GANGULI B.N.,ECONOMIC INTEGRATION. FINAN LABOR CAP/ISM DIPLOM WEALTH...NAT/COMP 20. PAGE 55 H1096
ECO/TAC METH/CNCPT EQUILIB ECO/UNDEV

B61
GUEVARA E.,GUERRILLA WARFARE. L/A+17C ECO/UNDEV NAT/G POL/PAR VOL/ASSN PLAN DOMIN REV DRIVE PWR WEALTH...NEW/IDEA RECORD BIOG COLD/WAR MARX/KARL OAS 20. PAGE 62 H1247
FORCES COERCE GUERRILLA CUBA

B61
INTL UNION LOCAL AUTHORITIES,METROPOLIS. WOR+45 DIST/IND FINAN GIVE EDU/PROP CRIME COST HEALTH WEALTH 20. PAGE 78 H1563
MUNIC GOV/COMP LOC/G BIBLIOG

B61
KEE R.,REFUGEE WORLD. AUSTRIA EUR+WWI GERMANY NEIGH EX/STRUC WORKER PROB/SOLV ECO/TAC RENT EDU/PROP INGP/REL COST LITERACY HABITAT 20 MIGRATION. PAGE 84 H1676
NAT/G GIVE WEALTH STRANGE

B61
OECD,STATISTICS OF BALANCE OF PAYMENTS 1950-61. WOR+45 FINAN ECO/TAC INT/TRADE DEMAND WEALTH...STAT NAT/COMP 20 OEEC OECD. PAGE 120 H2396
BAL/PAY ECO/DEV INT/ORG CHARTS

S61
PADELFORD N.J.,"POLITICS AND THE FUTURE OF ECOSOC." AFR S/ASIA ECO/UNDEV INDUS NAT/G DELIB/GP ACT/RES ORD/FREE WEALTH...CONCPT CHARTS UN 20 ECOSOC. PAGE 122 H2438
INT/ORG TEC/DEV

S61
RANDALL F.B.,"COMMUNISM IN THE HIGH ANDES." L/A+17C PERU USSR SOCIETY PLAN EDU/PROP TOTALISM ATTIT RIGID/FLEX PWR WEALTH...HUM CONCPT GEN/LAWS 20 BOLIV EQUADOR. PAGE 129 H2589
CULTURE DRIVE

S61
RAY J.,"THE EUROPEAN FREE-TRADE ASSOCIATION AND ITS IMPACT ON INDIA'S TRADE." EUR+WWI FRANCE GERMANY INDIA S/ASIA UK NAT/G VOL/ASSN PLAN INT/TRADE ROUTINE WEALTH...STAT CHARTS CMN/WLTH EEC OEEC 20 EFTA. PAGE 130 H2600
ECO/DEV ECO/TAC

B62
CARTER G.M.,THE GOVERNMENT OF THE SOVIET UNION. USSR CULTURE LOC/G DIPLOM ECO/TAC ADJUD CT/SYS LEAD WEALTH...CHARTS T 20 COM/PARTY. PAGE 27 H0546
NAT/G MARXISM POL/PAR EX/STRUC

B62
DEBUYST F.,LAS CLASES SOCIALES EN AMERICA LATINA. L/A+17C SOCIETY STRUCT WORKER EDU/PROP RACE/REL ATTIT HABITAT ROLE...GEOG SOC NAT/COMP SOC/INTEG 20. PAGE 39 H0780
STRATA GP/REL WEALTH

B62
GALENSON W.,LABOR IN DEVELOPING COUNTRIES. BRAZIL INDONESIA ISRAEL PAKISTAN TURKEY AGRI INDUS WORKER PAY PRICE GP/REL WEALTH...MGT CHARTS METH/COMP NAT/COMP 20. PAGE 54 H1088
LABOR ECO/UNDEV BARGAIN POL/PAR

B62
GREEN L.P.,DEVELOPMENT IN AFRICA. AFR CENTRL/AFR GHANA RHODESIA SOUTH/AFR AGRI PROC/MFG INT/TRADE DEMAND NAT/LISM PRODUC WEALTH...GEOG METH/CNCPT CHARTS BIBLIOG 20. PAGE 60 H1206
CULTURE ECO/UNDEV GOV/REL TREND

B62
HARRINGTON M.,THE OTHER AMERICA: POVERTY IN THE UNITED STATES. WORKER CREATE REPRESENT RACE/REL AGE/O DRIVE POLICY. PAGE 67 H1338
WEALTH WELF/ST INCOME CULTURE

B62
JACKSON W.A.D.,RUSSO-CHINESE BORDERLANDS. ASIA COM USSR NAT/G PROVS EX/STRUC FORCES DOMIN COERCE PEACE ATTIT PWR SOVEREIGN WEALTH...CONCPT TREND CHARTS STERTYP VAL/FREE. PAGE 79 H1576
GEOG DIPLOM RUSSIA

B62
MEADE J.E.,CASE STUDIES IN EUROPEAN ECONOMIC UNION. BELGIUM EUR+WWI LUXEMBOURG NAT/G INT/TRADE REGION ROUTINE WEALTH...METH/CNCPT STAT CHARTS ECSC TOT/POP OEEC EEC 20. PAGE 108 H2154
INT/ORG ECO/TAC

B62
MOUSSA P.,THE UNDERPRIVILEGED NATIONS. FINAN INT/ORG PLAN PROB/SOLV CAP/ISM GIVE TASK WEALTH ...POLICY SOC 20. PAGE 114 H2273
ECO/UNDEV NAT/G DIPLOM FOR/AID

B62
PHELPS E.S.,THE GOAL OF ECONOMIC GROWTH: SOURCES, COSTS, BENEFITS. USA+45 USSR FINAN TAX CONTROL DEMAND WEALTH...POLICY NAT/COMP ANTHOL BIBLIOG 20. PAGE 125 H2499
ECO/TAC ECO/DEV NAT/G FUT

B62
SMITH M.G.,KINSHIP AND COMMUNITY IN CARRIACOU. WEST/IND STRATA AGRI FAM SECT WORKER MARRIAGE OWN HEREDITY WEALTH...SOC 18/20. PAGE 146 H2915
CULTURE HABITAT KIN STRUCT

B62
YU LIEN YEN CHIU,INDEX TO THE CLASSIFIED FILES ON COMMUNIST CHINA. CHINA/COM CULTURE ECO/UNDEV CIVMIL/REL PWR WEALTH MARXISM...PSY SOC METH 20. PAGE 172 H3440
BIBLIOG INDEX COM

S62
BELL W.,"EQUALITY AND ATTITUDES OF ELITES IN JAMAICA" L/A+17C STRATA PWR WEALTH...SOC QU TREND. PAGE 13 H0266
ELITES FUT SOCIETY CULTURE

S62
LANGER W.L.,"FAREWELL TO EMPIRE." EUR+WWI MOD/EUR NAT/G DIPLOM EDU/PROP COLONIAL ATTIT ORD/FREE PWR SOVEREIGN WEALTH...CONCPT TIME/SEQ GEN/LAWS TOT/POP VAL/FREE CMN/WLTH 20. PAGE 91 H1810
DOMIN ECO/TAC NAT/LISM

C62
BACON F.,"OF EMPIRE" (1612) IN F. BACON, ESSAYS." ELITES NAT/G PROB/SOLV DIPLOM ADMIN CONTROL WEALTH 16/17 KING. PAGE 9 H0190
PWR CHIEF DOMIN GEN/LAWS

C62
BACON F.,"OF SEDITIONS AND TROUBLES" (1625) IN F. BACON, ESSAYS." INDUS MARKET CHIEF ECO/TAC EDU/PROP CONTROL LEAD PEACE WEALTH 17 MACHIAVELL. PAGE 9 H0191
REV ORD/FREE NAT/G GEN/LAWS

B63
BRZEZINSKI Z.K.,AFRICA AND THE COMMUNIST WORLD. AFR ASIA COM CULTURE SOCIETY INT/ORG DELIB/GP ACT/RES ECO/TAC COERCE ORD/FREE PWR WEALTH...STAT TOT/POP VAL/FREE 20. PAGE 23 H0461
ATTIT EDU/PROP DIPLOM USSR

B63
CHOU S.H.,THE CHINESE INFLATION 1937-1949. ASIA SOCIETY POL/PAR FOR/AID INT/TRADE BAL/PAY WEALTH MARXISM...STAT CHARTS 20 COM/PARTY GOLD/STAND. PAGE 30 H0597
FINAN ECO/TAC BUDGET NAT/G

B63
ENKE S.,ECONOMICS FOR DEVELOPMENT. AGRI TEC/DEV CAP/ISM DIPLOM ECO/TAC TAX ATTIT DRIVE HABITAT WEALTH...GOV/COMP BIBLIOG 20. PAGE 46 H0928
ECO/UNDEV PHIL/SCI CON/ANAL

B63
FISCHER-GALATI S.A.,RUMANIA; A BIBLIOGRAPHIC GUIDE (PAMPHLET). ROMANIA INTELL ECO/DEV LABOR SECT WEALTH...GEOG SOC/WK LING 20. PAGE 51 H1012
BIBLIOG/A NAT/G COM LAW

B63
GEERTZ C.,PEDDLERS AND PRINCES: SOCIAL DEVELOPMENT AND ECONOMIC CHANGE IN TWO INDONESIAN TOWNS. S/ASIA CULTURE SOCIETY STRATA FACE/GP MUNIC CREATE TEC/DEV ECO/TAC ORD/FREE WEALTH...OBS INT CENSUS CHARTS WORK TOT/POP VAL/FREE 20. PAGE 55 H1106
ECO/UNDEV SOC ELITES INDONESIA

B63
GORDON M.S.,THE ECONOMICS OF WELFARE POLICIES. INDUS LOC/G NAT/G LEGIS WORKER INCOME AGE/O SKILL WEALTH...METH/COMP NAT/COMP 20. PAGE 59 H1180
METH/CNCPT ECO/TAC POLICY

B63
INTERNATIONAL ASSOCIATION RES,AFRICAN STUDIES IN INCOME AND WEALTH. AFR NAT/G PROB/SOLV DEMAND INCOME...ECOMETRIC METH/COMP 20. PAGE 78 H1553
WEALTH PLAN ECO/UNDEV BUDGET

B63
ISSAWI C.,EGYPT IN REVOLUTION: AN ECONOMIC ANALYSIS. ISLAM STRUCT ECO/UNDEV AGRI FINAN INDUS PLAN EXEC REV NAT/LISM ATTIT RIGID/FLEX WEALTH SOCISM...STAT WORK 20. PAGE 79 H1573
NAT/G UAR

B63
MAYNE R.,THE COMMUNITY OF EUROPE. UK CONSTN NAT/G CONSULT DELIB/GP CREATE PLAN ECO/TAC LEGIT ADMIN ROUTINE ORD/FREE PWR WEALTH...CONCPT TIME/SEQ EEC EURATOM 20. PAGE 105 H2107
EUR+WWI INT/ORG REGION

B63
MULLER H.J.,FREEDOM IN THE WESTERN WORLD. PREHIST CULTURE SECT CREATE TEC/DEV DOMIN PWR WEALTH ...MAJORIT SOC CONCPT. PAGE 114 H2285
ORD/FREE TIME/SEQ SOCIETY

B63
OECD,FOOD AID: ITS ROLE IN ECONOMIC DEVELOPMENT. FINAN NAT/G PLAN DIPLOM GIVE TASK WEALTH ...METH/COMP METH 20. PAGE 120 H2397
ECO/UNDEV FOR/AID INT/ORG POLICY

B63
OLSON M. JR.,THE ECONOMICS OF WARTIME SHORTAGE. FRANCE GERMANY MOD/EUR UK AGRI PROB/SOLV ADMIN DEMAND WEALTH...POLICY OLD/LIB 17/20. PAGE 121 H2416
WAR ADJUST ECO/TAC NAT/COMP

B63
SPRING D.,THE ENGLISH LANDED ESTATE IN THE NINETEENTH CENTURY: ITS ADMINISTRATION. UK ELITES STRUCT AGRI NAT/G GP/REL OWN PWR WEALTH...BIBLIOG 19 HOUSE/LORD. PAGE 148 H2954
STRATA PERS/REL MGT

B63
STIFEL L.D.,THE TEXTILE INDUSTRY - A CASE STUDY OF INDUSTRIAL DEVELOPMENT IN THE PHILIPPINES (PAPER). PHILIPPINE WORKER CAP/ISM INT/TRADE TARIFFS RECEIVE PRICE ADMIN COST EFFICIENCY WEALTH...BIBLIOG 20. PAGE 149 H2986
S/ASIA ECO/UNDEV PROC/MFG NAT/G

B63
THOMPSON F.M.L.,ENGLISH LANDED SOCIETY IN THE
STRATA

NINETEENTH CENTURY. UK STRUCT MUNIC NAT/G CONTROL WAR GP/REL OWN WEALTH...BIBLIOG 18/20. PAGE 154 H3081
PWR ELITES GOV/REL

B63
WAGLEY C.,INTRODUCTION TO BRAZIL. BRAZIL L/A+17C FAM KIN SCHOOL SECT ATTIT WEALTH...GEOG SOC. PAGE 164 H3286
ECO/UNDEV ELITES HABITAT STRATA

L63
ROSE R.,"COMPARATIVE STUDIES IN POLITICAL FINANCE: A SYMPOSIUM." ASIA EUR+WWI S/ASIA LAW CULTURE DELIB/GP LEGIS ACT/RES ECO/TAC EDU/PROP CHOOSE ATTIT RIGID/FLEX SUPEGO PWR SKILL WEALTH...STAT ANTHOL VAL/FREE. PAGE 134 H2674
FINAN POL/PAR

S63
BILL J.A.,"THE SOCIAL AND ECONOMIC FOUNDATIONS OF POWER IN CONTEMPORARY IRAN." ISLAM CULTURE NAT/G ECO/TAC DOMIN COERCE ATTIT PWR WEALTH...TREND VAL/FREE 20. PAGE 17 H0334
SOCIETY STRATA IRAN

S63
HINDLEY D.,"FOREIGN AID TO INDONESIA AND ITS POLITICAL IMPLICATIONS." INDONESIA POL/PAR ATTIT SOVEREIGN...CHARTS 20. PAGE 71 H1421
FOR/AID NAT/G WEALTH ECO/TAC

S63
POPPINO R.E.,"IMBALANCE IN BRAZIL." L/A+17C NAT/G TOP/EX PLAN DIPLOM LEGIT DRIVE WEALTH...CON/ANAL LAFTA 20. PAGE 127 H2544
POL/PAR ECO/TAC BRAZIL

B64
ALVIM J.C.,A REVOLUCAO SEM RUMO. BRAZIL NAT/G BAL/PWR DIPLOM INT/TRADE PARTIC WEALTH...POLICY SOC SOC/INTEG 20. PAGE 6 H0118
REV CIVMIL/REL ECO/UNDEV ORD/FREE

B64
BEARDSLEY R.K.,STUDIES ON ECONOMIC LIFE IN JAPAN (OCCASIONAL PAPERS NO. 8). INDUS FAM HABITAT...GEOG GOV/COMP 20 CHINJAP. PAGE 12 H0249
WEALTH PRESS PRODUC INCOME

B64
BEATTIE J.,OTHER CULTURES. UNIV LAW FAM POL/PAR SECT ADJUD OWN ALL/VALS WEALTH...SOC NAT/COMP SOC/INTEG 20. PAGE 13 H0251
METH/CNCPT CULTURE STRUCT

B64
BUTWELL R.,SOUTHEAST ASIA TODAY - AND TOMORROW. NAT/G COLONIAL LEAD REGION WAR CHOOSE WEALTH MARXISM 20. PAGE 25 H0500
S/ASIA DIPLOM ECO/UNDEV NAT/LISM

B64
COONDOO R.,THE DIVISION OF POWERS IN THE INDIAN CONSTITUTION. INDIA ECO/UNDEV FINAN TEC/DEV WAR CENTRAL EFFICIENCY NAT/LISM PWR WEALTH NEW/LIB ...BIBLIOG 18/20. PAGE 33 H0659
CONSTN LEGIS WELF/ST GOV/COMP

B64
CURTIN P.D.,THE IMAGE OF AFRICA: BRITISH IDEAS AND ACTION, 1780-1850. MOD/EUR SOCIETY FORCES ACT/RES DOMIN EDU/PROP COERCE ATTIT PERCEPT RIGID/FLEX SUPEGO HEALTH KNOWL MORAL ORD/FREE WEALTH...CONCPT WORK VAL/FREE. PAGE 36 H0726
AFR CULTURE UK DIPLOM

B64
DANIELS R.V.,RUSSIA. RUSSIA USSR STRUCT NAT/LISM TOTALISM ORD/FREE WEALTH...POLICY DECISION TREND. PAGE 37 H0740
MARXISM REV ECO/DEV DIPLOM

B64
FREISEN J.,STAAT UND KATHOLISCHE KIRCHE IN DEN DEUTSCHEN BUNDESSTAATEN (2 VOLS.). GERMANY LAW FAM NAT/G EDU/PROP GP/REL MARRIAGE WEALTH 19/20 CHURCH/STA. PAGE 53 H1056
SECT CATHISM JURID PROVS

B64
FRIEDLAND W.H.,AFRICAN SOCIALISM. ECO/UNDEV MARKET LABOR NAT/G POL/PAR PLAN CAP/ISM ECO/TAC EDU/PROP CHOOSE ATTIT DRIVE PWR WEALTH...POLICY CONCPT RECORD STERTYP 20. PAGE 53 H1063
AFR SOCISM

B64
INTERNATIONAL LABOUR OFFICE,EMPLOYMENT AND ECONOMIC GROWTH. ECO/DEV ECO/UNDEV NAT/G PLAN DIPLOM INT/TRADE CONTROL INCOME PRODUC WEALTH...STAT NAT/COMP 20 ILO. PAGE 78 H1558
WORKER METH/COMP ECO/TAC OPTIMAL

B64
JUCKER-FLEETWOOD E.,MONEY AND FINANCE IN AFRICA. ISLAM ECO/UNDEV SERV/IND NAT/G EX/STRUC PLAN ECO/TAC ROUTINE WEALTH...MGT TOT/POP 20. PAGE 82 H1639
AFR FINAN

B64
LAWRENCE P.,ROAD BELONG CARGO: A STUDY OF CARGO MOVEMENT IN SOUTHERN MADANG DISTRICT, NEW GUINEA. S/ASIA CULTURE ECO/UNDEV PROC/MFG KIN CHIEF COLONIAL COERCE GP/REL DRIVE WEALTH WORSHIP 20 NEW/GUINEA. PAGE 92 H1846
SOC SECT ALL/VALS MYTH

B64
PIKE F.B.,THE CONFLICT BETWEEN CHURCH AND STATE IN LATIN AMERICA. L/A+17C CULTURE SOCIETY STRATA DOMIN EDU/PROP LEGIT COERCE ATTIT ORD/FREE PWR WEALTH ...CONCPT TIME/SEQ TREND VAL/FREE. PAGE 125 H2510
SECT NAT/G

B64
POWELSON J.P.,LATIN AMERICA: TODAY'S ECONOMIC AND SOCIAL REVOLUTION. L/A+17C INTELL SOCIETY STRUCT AGRI INDUS NAT/G DIPLOM ECO/TAC REV...POLICY 20. PAGE 128 H2552
ECO/UNDEV WEALTH ADJUST PLAN

B64
RAISON T.,WHY CONSERVATIVE? UK FORCES DIPLOM ECO/TAC GIVE EDU/PROP ORD/FREE WEALTH LAISSEZ ...GOV/COMP 20 TORY/PARTY CONSRV/PAR. PAGE 129 H2583
PLURISM CONSERVE POL/PAR NAT/G

B64
RAMAZANI R.K.,THE MIDDLE EAST AND THE EUROPEAN COMMON MARKET. EUR+WWI ISLAM ECO/DEV EXTR/IND MARKET PROC/MFG INT/ORG NAT/G TEC/DEV ECO/TAC REGION DRIVE WEALTH...STAT CHARTS EEC TOT/POP 20. PAGE 129 H2587
ECO/UNDEV ATTIT INT/TRADE

B64
RUSSET B.M.,WORLD HANDBOOK OF POLITICAL AND SOCIAL INDICATORS. WOR+45 COM/IND ADMIN WEALTH...GEOG 20. PAGE 136 H2719
DIPLOM STAT NAT/G NAT/COMP

B64
SKINNER E.P.,THE MOSSI OF UPPER VOLTA: THE POLITICAL DEVELOPMENT OF A SUDANESE PEOPLE. AFR LAW AGRI FAM KIN POL/PAR PROVS SECT DELIB/GP EX/STRUC FORCES TOP/EX DOMIN EDU/PROP LEGIT CT/SYS COERCE CHOOSE ORD/FREE PWR WEALTH...SOC MYTH VAL/FREE. PAGE 145 H2897
CULTURE OBS UPPER/VOLT

B64
SOLOW R.M.,THE NATURE AND SOURCES OF UNEMPLOYMENT IN THE UNITED STATES (PAMPHLET). USA+45 INDUS LABOR TEC/DEV ECO/TAC SKILL WEALTH...TREND NAT/COMP 20. PAGE 147 H2930
ECO/DEV WORKER STAT PRODUC

B64
TAWNEY R.H.,EQUALITY. UK CULTURE STRATA ECO/TAC EDU/PROP REPRESENT OWN NEW/LIB...MAJORIT WELF/ST SOC 20. PAGE 153 H3051
WEALTH STRUCT ELITES POPULISM

B64
TEPASKE J.J.,EXPLOSIVE FORCES IN LATIN AMERICA. CULTURE INTELL ECO/UNDEV INT/ORG NAT/G SECT FORCES ECO/TAC EDU/PROP PWR WEALTH SOC. PAGE 153 H3063
L/A+17C RIGID/FLEX FOR/AID USSR

B64
THORNTON T.P.,THE THIRD WORLD IN SOVIET PERSPECTIVE: STUDIES BY SOVIET WRITERS ON THE DEVELOPING AREAS. AFR L/A+17C S/ASIA STRATA AGRI INDUS MARKET NAT/G POL/PAR ECO/TAC COLONIAL PERCEPT PWR WEALTH...MARXIST STAT CHARTS WORK MARX/KARL 20. PAGE 155 H3090
ECO/UNDEV ACT/RES USSR DIPLOM

B64
WRAITH R.,CORRUPTION IN DEVELOPING COUNTRIES. NIGERIA UK LAW ELITES STRATA INDUS LOC/G NAT/G SECT FORCES EDU/PROP ADMIN PWR WEALTH 18/20. PAGE 171 H3414
ECO/UNDEV CRIME SANCTION ATTIT

L64
HAAS E.B.,"ECONOMICS AND DIFFERENTIAL PATTERNS OF POLITICAL INTEGRATION: PROJECTIONS ABOUT UNITY IN LATIN AMERICA." SOCIETY NAT/G DELIB/GP ACT/RES CREATE PLAN ECO/TAC REGION ROUTINE ATTIT DRIVE PWR WEALTH...CONCPT TREND CHARTS LAFTA 20. PAGE 63 H1266
L/A+17C INT/ORG MARKET

S64
BARIETY J.,"LA POLITIQUE EXTERIEURE ALLEMANDE DANS L'HIVER 1939-1940." COM FINLAND GERMANY ISLAM ITALY USSR NAT/G FORCES ECO/TAC DOMIN EDU/PROP COERCE WAR PWR WEALTH...HIST/WRIT NAZI TOT/POP VAL/FREE 20. PAGE 11 H0216
EUR+WWI DIPLOM

S64
BENSON M.,"SOUTH AFRICA AND WORLD OPINION." AFR SOUTH/AFR INTELL SOCIETY TOP/EX ECO/TAC DOMIN COERCE DISCRIM ATTIT PWR WEALTH...POLICY RECORD 20. PAGE 14 H0285
NAT/G RIGID/FLEX RACE/REL

S64
CROUZET F.,"WARS, BLOCKADE, AND ECONOMIC CHANGE IN EUROPE, 1792-1815." UK INDUS NAT/G TEC/DEV ECO/TAC WEALTH...POLICY RELATIV HIST/WRIT TIME/SEQ 18/19. PAGE 35 H0710
MOD/EUR MARKET

S64
DE GAULLE C.,"FRENCH WORLD VIEW." AFR ASIA CHINA/COM EUR+WWI ISLAM ECO/UNDEV INT/ORG NAT/G VOL/ASSN ACT/RES DIPLOM ECO/TAC EDU/PROP ATTIT DRIVE WEALTH 20. PAGE 37 H0751
TOP/EX PWR FOR/AID FRANCE

S64
MARTELLI G.,"PORTUGAL AND THE UNITED NATIONS." AFR EUR+WWI ELITES INT/ORG NAT/G PROVS PLAN DIPLOM ECO/TAC DOMIN COLONIAL RIGID/FLEX MORAL ORD/FREE PWR WEALTH...MYTH UN 20. PAGE 103 H2060
ATTIT PORTUGAL

S64
MC WILLIAM M.,"THE WORLD BANK AND THE TRANSFER OF POWER IN KENYA." AFR ECO/UNDEV CONSULT ACT/RES TEC/DEV PERCEPT PWR SKILL WEALTH...CONCPT OBS TREND 20. PAGE 106 H2119
NAT/G ECO/TAC

S64
SALVADORI M.,"EL CAPITALISMO EN LA EUROPA DE LA POSGUERRA." INT/ORG NAT/G POL/PAR PLAN ECO/TAC ATTIT ORD/FREE WEALTH...HIST/WRIT COLD/WAR EEC 20. PAGE 137 H2743
EUR+WWI ECO/DEV CAP/ISM

N64
KENYA MINISTRY ECO PLAN DEV,AFRICAN SOCIALISM AND ITS APPLICATION TO PLANNING IN KENYA (PAMPHLET). AFR AGRI INDUS WORKER TAX COLONIAL WEALTH 20. PAGE 85 H1691
NAT/G SOCISM PLAN ECO/UNDEV

B65
ALTON T.P.,POLISH NATIONAL INCOME AND PRODUCT IN 1954, 1955, AND 1956. POLAND FINAN EX/STRUC ECO/TAC PRICE COST WEALTH 20. PAGE 6 H0117
COM INDUS NAT/G ECO/DEV

B65
CENTRAL GAZETTEERS UNIT,THE GAZETTEER OF INDIA (VOL. I). INDIA SOCIETY STRATA PLAN EDU/PROP NAT/LISM ORD/FREE WEALTH...GEOG LING CHARTS SOC/INTEG 20. PAGE 28 H0568
PRESS CULTURE SECT STRUCT

B65
HOSELITZ B.F.,ECONOMICS AND THE IDEA OF MANKIND. UNIV ECO/DEV ECO/UNDEV DIST/IND INDUS INT/ORG NAT/G ACT/RES ECO/TAC WEALTH...CONCPT STAT. PAGE 74 H1476
CREATE INT/TRADE

B65
IANNI O.,ESTADO E CAPITALISMO. L/A+17C FINAN TEC/DEV ECO/TAC ORD/FREE WEALTH POLICY. PAGE 76 H1518
ECO/UNDEV STRUCT INDUS NAT/G

B65
INT. BANK RECONSTR. DEVELOP.,ECONOMIC DEVELOPMENT OF KUWAIT. ISLAM KUWAIT AGRI FINAN MARKET EX/STRUC TEC/DEV ECO/TAC ADMIN WEALTH...OBS CON/ANAL CHARTS 20. PAGE 77 H1541
INDUS NAT/G

B65
ONSLOW C.,ASIAN ECONOMIC DEVELOPMENT. BURMA CEYLON INDIA MALAYSIA PAKISTAN S/ASIA AGRI INDUS MARKET PROB/SOLV CAP/ISM FOR/AID INT/TRADE DEMAND WEALTH ...POLICY ANTHOL 20. PAGE 121 H2418
ECO/UNDEV ECO/TAC PLAN NAT/G

B65
ORGANSKI A.F.K.,THE STAGES OF POLITICAL DEVELOPMENT. STRATA AGRI INDUS NAT/G POL/PAR COLONIAL PWR WEALTH...CLASSIF TIME/SEQ. PAGE 121 H2428
ECO/DEV ECO/UNDEV GEN/LAWS CREATE

B65
SWIFT M.G.,MALAY PEASANT SOCIETY IN JELEBU. MALAYSIA FAM INT/TRADE ADJUD OWN WEALTH...SOC WORSHIP 20. PAGE 151 H3020
STRUCT ECO/UNDEV CULTURE SOCIETY

B65
TEW B.,WEALTH AND INCOME. UK BUDGET INT/TRADE PRICE BAL/PAY DEMAND...CHARTS GOV/COMP 20 AUSTRAL. PAGE 153 H3064
FINAN ECO/DEV WEALTH INCOME

B65
WOLPERT S.,INDIA. INDIA UK ECO/UNDEV DIPLOM GP/REL WEALTH 20 NEHRU/J. PAGE 170 H3405
CULTURE COLONIAL NAT/LISM SECT

L65
WIONCZEK M.,"LATIN AMERICA FREE TRADE ASSOCIATION." AGRI DIST/IND FINAN INDUS INT/ORG LABOR NAT/G TEC/DEV ECO/TAC HEALTH SKILL WEALTH...POLICY RELATIV MGT LAFTA 20. PAGE 169 H3390
L/A+17C MARKET REGION

S65
KEE W.S.,"CENTRAL CITY EXPENDITURES AND METROPOLITAN AREAS." PLAN BUDGET ECO/TAC TAX GP/REL WEALTH...CHARTS 20. PAGE 84 H1677
LOC/G MUNIC GOV/COMP NEIGH

S65
POWELL J.D.,"MILITARY ASSISTANCE AND MILITARISM IN LATIN AMERICA." USA+45 INT/ORG NAT/G CONTROL REGION PRODUC WEALTH...CLASSIF STAT NAT/COMP CONGRESS. PAGE 128 H2550
L/A+17C FORCES FOR/AID PWR

S65
TENDLER J.D.,"TECHNOLOGY AND ECONOMIC DEVELOPMENT* THE CASE OF HYDRO VS THERMAL POWER." CONSTRUC DIST/IND CREATE TEC/DEV INT/TRADE CENTRAL PWR SKILL WEALTH...MGT NAT/COMP ARGEN. PAGE 153 H3061
BRAZIL INDUS ECO/UNDEV

S65
VUCINICH W.S.,"WHITHER RUMANIA." COM USSR YUGOSLAVIA NAT/G VOL/ASSN DELIB/GP TOP/EX LEGIT NAT/LISM TOTALISM ATTIT DRIVE RIGID/FLEX ORD/FREE WEALTH SOCISM...TIME/SEQ TREND 20. PAGE 164 H3281
ECO/DEV CREATE ROMANIA

B66
AMER ENTERPRISE INST PUB POL,SIGNIFICANT ISSUES IN ECONOMIC AID TO DEVELOPING COUNTRIES. FINAN INT/ORG NAT/G PLAN PROB/SOLV GIVE TASK WEALTH...DECISION 20. PAGE 6 H0119
ECO/UNDEV FOR/AID DIPLOM POLICY

B66
BROWN R.T.,TRANSPORT AND THE ECONOMIC INTEGRATION OF SOUTH AMERICA. L/A+17C ECO/UNDEV NAT/G OP/RES DIPLOM INT/TRADE REGION WEALTH...ECOMETRIC GEOG STAT LAFTA TIME. PAGE 22 H0449
MARKET DIST/IND SIMUL

B66
FITZGERALD C.P.,THE BIRTH OF COMMUNIST CHINA (2ND ED.). ASIA CHINA/COM STRUCT BAL/PWR DIPLOM ECO/TAC INT/TRADE WEALTH 20. PAGE 51 H1018
REV MARXISM ECO/UNDEV

B66
JACKSON G.D.,COMINTERN AND PEASANT IN EAST EUROPE 1919-1930. BULGARIA COM CZECHOSLVK EUR+WWI POLAND ROMANIA YUGOSLAVIA STRATA AGRI VOL/ASSN DIPLOM CONTROL CROWD WEALTH...POLICY NAT/COMP 20. PAGE 79 H1575
MARXISM ECO/UNDEV WORKER INT/ORG

B66
KUZNETS S.,MODERN ECONOMIC GROWTH. WOR+45 WOR-45 ECO/DEV ECO/UNDEV AGRI FINAN INDUS TEC/DEV EFFICIENCY INCOME...NAT/COMP 19/20. PAGE 89 H1786
TIME/SEQ WEALTH PRODUC

B66
MASON E.S.,ECONOMIC DEVELOPMENT IN INDIA AND PAKISTAN. INDIA PAKISTAN AGRI FINAN PLAN BUDGET INT/TRADE WEALTH...POLICY STAT TREND CHARTS 20. PAGE 104 H2086
NAT/COMP ECO/UNDEV ECO/TAC FOR/AID

B66
OWEN G.,INDUSTRY IN THE UNITED STATES. UK USA+45 NAT/G WEALTH...DECISION NAT/COMP 20. PAGE 122 H2436
METH/COMP INDUS MGT PROB/SOLV

B66
PLATE H.,PARTEIFINANZIERUNG UND GRUNDESETZ. GERMANY NAT/G PLAN GIVE PAY INCOME WEALTH...JURID 20. PAGE 126 H2522
POL/PAR CONSTN FINAN

B66
WHITAKER A.P.,NATIONALISM IN CONTEMPORARY LATIN AMERICA. AGRI NAT/G WEALTH...POLICY SOC CONCPT OBS TREND 20. PAGE 167 H3344
NAT/LISM L/A+17C DIPLOM ECO/UNDEV

S66
"FURTHER READING." INDIA LOC/G NAT/G PLAN ADMIN WEALTH...GEOG SOC CONCPT CENSUS 20. PAGE 2 H0049
BIBLIOG ECO/UNDEV TEC/DEV PROVS

S66
BLANC N.,"SPAIN: LEARNING THROUGH STRUGGLE" SPAIN STRATA STRUCT SECT FORCES PROB/SOLV AGE/Y ATTIT ORD/FREE PWR WEALTH MARXISM SOCISM 19/20 FRANCO/F SUCCESSION. PAGE 18 H0352
NAT/G FUT SOCIALIST TOTALISM

B67
ARIKPO O.,THE DEVELOPMENT OF MODERN NIGERIA. AFR NIGERIA SOCIETY ECO/UNDEV KIN ADMIN FEDERAL NAT/LISM ORD/FREE WEALTH...POLICY GEOG BIBLIOG 19/20. PAGE 8 H0163
NAT/G CULTURE CONSTN COLONIAL

B67
COWLES M.,PERSPECTIVES IN THE EDUCATION OF DISADVANTAGED CHILDREN. CULTURE OP/RES PLAN PERS/REL ADJUST HABITAT PERCEPT KNOWL WEALTH ...SOC/WK IDEA/COMP ANTHOL 20. PAGE 34 H0686
EDU/PROP AGE/C TEC/DEV SCHOOL

B67
DALTON G.,TRIBAL AND PEASANT ECONOMIES. SOCIETY FINAN FAM INT/TRADE RATION ADJUST WEALTH...CHARTS ANTHOL BIBLIOG T. PAGE 37 H0738
SOC ECO/UNDEV NAT/COMP

B67
DENISON E.F.,WHY GROWTH RATES DIFFER; POSTWAR EXPERIENCE IN NINE WESTERN COUNTRIES. WOR+45 FINAN WORKER TEC/DEV EDU/PROP PRICE PRODUC WEALTH ...ECOMETRIC STAT CHARTS BIBLIOG. PAGE 40 H0791
METH NAT/COMP ECO/DEV ECO/TAC

B67
GILL R.T.,ECONOMIC DEVELOPMENT: PAST AND PRESENT (2ND ED.). ASIA INDIA USA+45 USA-45 WOR+45 WOR-45 DEMAND EFFICIENCY NAT/LISM WEALTH...GOV/COMP METH/COMP 18/20. PAGE 56 H1127
ECO/DEV ECO/UNDEV PLAN PROB/SOLV

B67
HAWTREY R.,INCOMES AND MONEY. EUR+WWI FUT UK LABOR WORKER INT/TRADE TAX PAY BAL/PAY COST WEALTH 20. PAGE 68 H1363
FINAN NAT/G POLICY ECO/DEV

B67
HODGKINSON R.G.,THE ORIGINS OF THE NATIONAL HEALTH SERVICE: THE MEDICAL SERVICES OF THE NEW POOR LAW, 1834-1871. UK INDUS MUNIC WORKER PROB/SOLV EFFICIENCY ATTIT HEALTH WEALTH SOCISM...JURID SOC/WK 19/20. PAGE 72 H1445
HEAL NAT/G POLICY LAW

B67
LEVY J.-.P.,THE ECONOMIC LIFE OF THE ANCIENT WORLD. CULTURE SOCIETY INT/TRADE COLONIAL WEALTH ...BIBLIOG. PAGE 95 H1906
ECO/TAC ECO/UNDEV FINAN MEDIT-7

B67
MACRIDIS R.C.,FOREIGN POLICY IN WORLD POLITICS (3RD ED.). EX/STRUC BAL/PWR COLONIAL NAT/LISM SKILL SOVEREIGN WEALTH...CONCPT TIME/SEQ ANTHOL 20 COLD/WAR. PAGE 101 H2011
DIPLOM POLICY NAT/G IDEA/COMP

B67
POLSKY N.,HUSTLERS, BEATS, AND OTHERS. FACE/GP PRESS CRIME ADJUST ANOMIE DRIVE WEALTH...PSY SOC 20. PAGE 127 H2540
CULTURE CRIMLGY NEW/IDEA STRUCT

B67
POMEROY W.J.,HALF A CENTURY OF SOCIALISM. USSR LAW AGRI INDUS NAT/G CREATE DIPLOM EDU/PROP PERSON ORD/FREE WEALTH...POLICY TREND 20. PAGE 127 H2541
SOCISM MARXISM COM SOCIETY

B67
ROSENTHAL A.H.,THE SOCIAL PROGRAMS OF SWEDEN. SWEDEN USA+45 FINAN NAT/G PLAN PROB/SOLV INSPECT ORD/FREE...POLICY HEAL SOC CHARTS NAT/COMP 20. PAGE 134 H2681
GIVE SOC/WK WEALTH METH/COMP

B67
ROWLAND J.,A HISTORY OF SINO-INDIAN RELATIONS; HOSTILE CO-EXISTENCE. ASIA CHINA/COM INDIA NAT/G NUC/PWR PWR WEALTH...GEOG BIBLIOG 13/20 COLD/WAR. PAGE 135 H2704
DIPLOM CENSUS IDEA/COMP

B67
TOMPKINS S.R.,THE TRIUMPH OF BOLSHEVISM: REVOLUTION OR REACTION? USSR WORKER PRESS WEALTH MARXISM POPULISM...BIOG TREND IDEA/COMP BIBLIOG 19/20 LENIN/VI. PAGE 156 H3113
REV NAT/G POL/PAR NAT/LISM

L67
LARKIN E.,"ECONOMIC GROWTH, CAPITAL INVESTMENT, AND THE ROMAN CATHOLIC CHURCH IN NINETEENTH-CENTURY IRELAND." IRELAND AGRI DIST/IND NAT/G GIVE OWN CATHISM...CHARTS 19. PAGE 91 H1823
FINAN SECT WEALTH ECO/UNDEV

L67
RUTH J.M.,"THE ADMINISTRATION OF WATER RESOURCES IN GUATEMALA." GUATEMALA L/A+17C DIST/IND LOC/G NAT/G EX/STRUC ADMIN GOV/REL DEMAND EQUILIB WEALTH...GEOG MGT 20. PAGE 136 H2723
EFFICIENCY ECO/UNDEV PLAN ACT/RES

S67
ADNITT F.W.,"THE RISE OF ENGLISH RADICALISM -- PART 2." UK NAT/G WORKER INCOME WEALTH...BIOG 19 PARLIAMENT. PAGE 4 H0071
LEGIS LOBBY

S67
ALPANDER G.G.,"ENTREPRENEURS AND PRIVATE ENTERPRISE IN TURKEY." TURKEY INDUS PROC/MFG EDU/PROP ATTIT DRIVE WEALTH...GEOG MGT SOC STAT TREND CHARTS 20. PAGE 6 H0114
ECO/UNDEV LG/CO NAT/G POLICY

S67
BELLER I.,"ECONOMIC POLICY AND THE DEMANDS OF LABOR." PLAN TAX GIVE PRICE WAR COST PRODUC WEALTH. PAGE 13 H0268
NAT/G ECO/TAC SOC/WK INCOME

S67
BUTTINGER J.,"VIETNAM* FRAUD OF THE 'OTHER WAR'." VIETNAM/S ELITES STRUCT AGRI NAT/G FOR/AID RENT TREND. PAGE 25 H0499
PLAN WEALTH REV ECO/UNDEV

S67
FRENCH D.S.,"DOES THE U.S. EXPLOIT THE DEVELOPING NATIONS?" INT/ORG NAT/G CAP/ISM BAL/PAY WEALTH POLICY. PAGE 53 H1057
ECO/UNDEV INT/TRADE ECO/TAC COLONIAL

S67
MARWICK A.,"THE LABOUR PARTY AND THE WELFARE STATE IN BRITAIN, 19001948." UK SOCIETY STRUCT ECO/DEV WORKER CREATE PRICE CHOOSE WEALTH NEW/LIB SOCISM ...POLICY HEAL 20 PARLIAMENT LABOR/PAR. PAGE 104 H2074
POL/PAR RECEIVE LEGIS NAT/G

S67
NATSAGDORJ A.S.,"THE ECONOMIC BASIS OF FEUDALISM IN MONGOLIA." ASIA COM USSR OWN WEALTH CONSERVE...SOC 20 MONGOLIA. PAGE 116 H2324
ECO/TAC AGRI NAT/COMP MARXISM

S67
NUGENT J.B.,"ECONOMIC THOUGHT, INVESTMENT CRITERIA, AND DEVELOPMENT STRATEGIES IN GREECE* A POSTWAR SURVEY." GREECE AGRI INDUS INT/ORG NAT/G OP/RES DEMAND OPTIMAL PRODUC WEALTH 20 EEC. PAGE 119 H2379
ECO/UNDEV PLAN FINAN

S67
PAI G.A.,"TAXATION AND PLANNING IN INDIA: A BIRDS-EYE VIEW." INDIA ELITES NAT/G LEGIS BUDGET CONTROL LOBBY INCOME...STAT CHARTS 20. PAGE 122 H2443
TAX PLAN WEALTH STRATA

S67
RICHMAN B.M.,"CAPITALISTS & MANAGERS IN COMMUNIST CHINA." ASIA CHINA/COM ECO/UNDEV NAT/G CONSULT EX/STRUC PLAN EFFICIENCY PRODUC WEALTH MARXISM ...MGT CHARTS 20. PAGE 131 H2623
CAP/ISM INDUS

S67
ROCHET W.,"THE OCTOBER REVOLUTION AND THE STRUGGLE OF THE FRENCH COMMUNISTS." COM FRANCE ELITES SOCIETY STRATA ECO/TAC EDU/PROP GP/REL WEALTH ...MARXIST IDEA/COMP NAT/COMP 20. PAGE 133 H2654
SOCISM CHOOSE METH/COMP NAT/G

S67
SINGH B.,"ITALIAN EXPERIENCE IN REGIONAL ECONOMIC DEVELOPMENT AND LESSONS FOR OTHER COUNTRIES." EUR+WWI ITALY INDUS NAT/G ACT/RES REGION GP/REL EFFICIENCY EQUILIB PRODUC WEALTH. PAGE 144 H2884
ECO/UNDEV PLAN ECO/TAC CONTROL

S67
SLOAN P.,"FIFTY YEARS OF SOVIET RULE." USSR INDUS EDU/PROP EFFICIENCY PRODUC HEALTH KNOWL MORAL WEALTH MARXISM...POLICY 20. PAGE 145 H2900
CREATE NAT/G PLAN INSPECT

S67
SMITH J.E.,"RED PRUSSIANISM OF THE GERMAN DEMOCRATIC REPUBLIC." GERMANY/E INTELL TOP/EX WORKER PLAN DIPLOM PRODUC ATTIT WEALTH MARXISM. PAGE 146 H2912
NAT/G TOTALISM INDUS NAT/LISM

S67
SOARES G.,"SOCIO-ECONOMIC VARIABLES AND VOTING FOR THE RADICAL LEFT: CHILE 1952." CHILE INDUS NAT/G WORKER ADJUST STRANGE ANOMIE WEALTH...METH/CNCPT CORREL 20. PAGE 146 H2925
STRATA POL/PAR CHOOSE STAT

S67
SPITTMANN I.,"EAST GERMANY: THE SWINGING PENDULUM." COM GERMANY/E NAT/G EFFICIENCY MARXISM 20. PAGE 148 H2952
PRODUC POL/PAR WEALTH ATTIT

S68
CHAPMAN A.R.,"THE CIVIL WAR IN NIGERIA." AFR NIGERIA NAT/G PLAN ECO/TAC EDU/PROP COERCE WAR GOV/REL INGP/REL ORD/FREE PWR WEALTH SOC/INTEG 20 BIAFRA. PAGE 29 H0579
REV RACE/REL

S68
GUZZARDI W.,"THE DECLINE OF THE STERLING CLUB." UK WOR+45 NAT/G PLAN DIPLOM INT/TRADE AGREE CONSEN EQUILIB SOVEREIGN...POLICY NEW/IDEA 20 COMMONWLTH GOLD/STAND. PAGE 63 H1259
FINAN ECO/TAC WEALTH NAT/COMP

S68
LUKASZEWSKI J.,"WESTERN INTEGRATION AND THE PEOPLE'S DEMOCRACIES." USSR ELITES ECO/DEV NAT/G VOL/ASSN INT/TRADE AGREE REV FEDERAL WEALTH SOCISM ...NAT/COMP SOC/INTEG 20 EEC. PAGE 99 H1977
DIPLOM INT/ORG COM REGION

S68
MILLAR T.B.,"THE COMMONWEALTH AND THE UN." UK DIPLOM TARIFFS AGREE COLONIAL CONTROL SOVEREIGN WEALTH...GP/COMP GOV/COMP 20 CMN/WLTH UN. PAGE 111 H2210
INT/ORG POLICY TREND ECO/TAC

B76
SMITH A.,THE WEALTH OF NATIONS. UK STRUCT WORKER DIPLOM ECO/TAC OPTIMAL DRIVE PERSON ORD/FREE ...OLD/LIB GEN/LAWS 17/18. PAGE 145 H2905
WEALTH PRODUC INDUS LAISSEZ

B76
TAINE H.A.,THE ANCIENT REGIME. FRANCE STRATA FORCES PARTIC EQUILIB WEALTH CONSERVE POPULISM...GOV/COMP SOC/INTEG 18/19. PAGE 152 H3035
NAT/G GOV/REL TAX REV

N80
MILL J.S.,"AN ESSAY ON GOVERNMENT" (PAMPHLET). ELITES NAT/G CHIEF OWN ORD/FREE PWR WEALTH GEN/LAWS. PAGE 110 H2207
CONSTN POPULISM REPRESENT UTIL

B84
ENGELS F.,THE ORIGIN OF THE FAMILY, PRIVATE PROPERTY, AND THE STATE (TRANS. BY E. UNTERMANN). UNIV ELITES SOCIETY CAP/ISM ECO/TAC MARRIAGE ORD/FREE POPULISM...MARXIST SOC ENGELS. PAGE 46 H0926
FAM OWN WEALTH SOCISM

B91
MILL J.S.,SOCIALISM (1859). MOD/EUR AGRI INDUS NAT/G REV INCOME PRODUC ORD/FREE POPULISM SOCISM ...GOV/COMP METH/COMP 19. PAGE 110 H2209
WEALTH SOCIALIST ECO/TAC OWN

B95
SELIGMAN E.R.A.,ESSAYS IN TAXATION. NEW/ZEALND PRUSSIA UK USA-45 MARKET LOC/G CREATE PRICE CONTROL INCOME OWN WEALTH...GOV/COMP METH/COMP 19. PAGE 141 H2824
TAX TARIFFS INDUS NAT/G

B96
KROPOTKIN P.,L'ANARCHIE. NAT/G VOL/ASSN REV MORAL WEALTH...POLICY 19. PAGE 89 H1776
SOCIETY ANARCH PERSON CONCPT

B96
MARX K.,REVOLUTION AND COUNTER-REVOLUTION. GERMANY CONSTN ELITES INDUS NAT/G DIPLOM ECO/TAC WEALTH. PAGE 104 H2083
MARXIST REV PWR STRATA

B96
SCHMOLLER G.,THE MERCANTILE SYSTEM AND ITS HISTORICAL SIGNIFICANCE: ILLUSTRATED CHIEFLY FROM PRUSSIAN HISTORY (TRANS.). PRUSSIA CULTURE INDUS KIN MUNIC NAT/G PROVS OP/RES ECO/TAC INT/TRADE SUPEGO PWR WEALTH 19 MERCANTLST. PAGE 139 H2790
GEN/METH INGP/REL CONCPT

WEAPON....NON-NUCLEAR WEAPONS

B00
DE JOMINI A.H.,THE ART OF WAR. MOD/EUR NAT/G BAL/PWR DIPLOM DOMIN EXEC ROUTINE COERCE DRIVE PWR SKILL...POLICY CONCPT CHARTS STERTYP 19. PAGE 38 H0755
PLAN FORCES WAR WEAPON

B57
US SENATE SPEC COMM FOR AID,HEARINGS BEFORE THE SPECIAL COMMITTEE TO STUDY THE FOREIGN AID PROGRAM. USA+45 USSR ECO/UNDEV INT/ORG FORCES WEAPON TOTALISM ATTIT SUPEGO...NAT/COMP CONGRESS. PAGE 161 H3217
FOR/AID DIPLOM ORD/FREE TEC/DEV

B59
EMME E.M.,THE IMPACT OF AIR POWER - NATIONAL SECURITY AND WORLD POLITICS. USA+45 USSR FORCES DIPLOM WEAPON PEACE TOTALISM...POLICY NAT/COMP 20 EUROPE. PAGE 46 H0921
DETER AIR WAR ORD/FREE

B61
FULLER J.F.C.,THE CONDUCT OF WAR, 1789-1961. FRANCE RUSSIA SOCIETY NAT/G FORCES PROB/SOLV AGREE NUC/PWR WEAPON PEACE...SOC 18/20 TREATY COLD/WAR. PAGE 54 H1076
WAR POLICY REV ROLE

B61
SOKOL A.E.,SEAPOWER IN THE NUCLEAR AGE. USA+45 USSR DIST/IND FORCES INT/TRADE DETER WAR...POLICY NAT/COMP BIBLIOG COLD/WAR. PAGE 146 H2928 — SEA PWR WEAPON NUC/PWR

B62
FINER S.E.,THE MAN ON HORSEBACK: ROLE OF THE MILITARY IN POLITICS. UNIV LAW CONSTN ELITES SOCIETY POL/PAR BAL/PWR DOMIN EDU/PROP LEGIT COERCE GUERRILLA REV WAR WEAPON DRIVE SUPEGO ORD/FREE PWR RESPECT...POLICY CONCPT GEN/METH. PAGE 50 H1003 — NAT/G FORCES TOTALISM

B62
FRYKLUND R.,100 MILLION LIVES: MAXIMUM SURVIVAL IN A NUCLEAR WAR. USA+45 USSR CONTROL WEAPON ...IDEA/COMP NAT/COMP 20. PAGE 54 H1073 — NUC/PWR WAR PLAN DETER

B64
BROWN N.,NUCLEAR WAR* THE IMPENDING STRATEGIC DEADLOCK. USA+45 USSR TEC/DEV BUDGET RISK ARMS/CONT NUC/PWR WEAPON COST BIO/SOC...GEOG IDEA/COMP NAT/COMP GAME NATO WARSAW/P. PAGE 22 H0448 — FORCES OP/RES WAR GEN/LAWS

B64
FALL B.,STREET WITHOUT JOY. FRANCE USA+45 DIPLOM ECO/TAC FOR/AID GUERRILLA REV WEAPON...TREND 20. PAGE 48 H0966 — WAR S/ASIA FORCES COERCE

B65
GRAHAM G.S.,THE POLITICS OF NAVAL SUPREMACY; STUDIES IN BRITISH MARITIME ASCENDANCY. UK SEA NAT/G BAL/PWR LEAD WAR WEAPON PEACE...POLICY 18/19 COMMONWLTH. PAGE 60 H1191 — FORCES PWR COLONIAL DIPLOM

B65
GRETTON P.,MARITIME STRATEGY - A STUDY OF DEFENSE PROBLEMS. ASIA UK USSR DIPLOM COERCE DETER NUC/PWR WEAPON...CONCPT NAT/COMP 20. PAGE 60 H1211 — FORCES PLAN WAR SEA

B65
HART B.H.L.,THE MEMOIRS OF CAPTAIN LIDDELL HART (VOL. I). UK NAT/G PLAN TEC/DEV DIPLOM ADMIN WEAPON GOV/REL PERS/REL ATTIT PWR FASCISM...POLICY 20. PAGE 67 H1348 — FORCES BIOG LEAD WAR

S65
GRIFFITH S.B.,"COMMUNIST CHINA'S CAPACITY TO MAKE WAR." CHINA/COM COM NAT/G TOP/EX PLAN DOMIN COERCE NUC/PWR ATTIT RESPECT SKILL...CONCPT MYTH TIME/SEQ TREND COLD/WAR 20. PAGE 61 H1221 — FORCES PWR WEAPON ASIA

S65
WOLF C. JR.,"THE POLITICAL EFFECTS OF SOME MILITARY PROGRAMS* SOME INDICATIONS FROM LATIN AMERICA." ELITES STRATA BUDGET FOR/AID WEAPON ATTIT PERCEPT PWR...REGRESS SYS/QU CHARTS NAT/COMP. PAGE 170 H3397 — L/A+17C FORCES CIVMIL/REL PROBABIL

B66
DAENIKER G.,STRATEGIE DES KLEIN STAATS. SWITZERLND ACT/RES CREATE DIPLOM NEUTRAL DETER WAR WEAPON PWR SOVEREIGN...IDEA/COMP 20 COLD/WAR. PAGE 36 H0730 — NUC/PWR PLAN FORCES NAT/G

S66
BENOIT J.,"WORLD DEFENSE EXPENDITURES." WOR+45 WEAPON COST PRODUC. PAGE 14 H0284 — FORCES STAT NAT/COMP BUDGET

S66
GILBERT S.P.,"WARS OF LIBERATION AND SOVIET MILITARY AID POLICY." ASIA INDIA INDONESIA UAR USA+45 STRATA WAR PERCEPT MARXISM...STAT NAT/COMP. PAGE 56 H1124 — USSR FOR/AID WEAPON DRIVE

S67
HALPERN B.,"THE ORIGINS OF THE CRISIS." ISLAM ISRAEL INT/ORG FORCES WEAPON PEACE ORD/FREE TREATY 20 UN. PAGE 65 H1296 — WAR NAT/G DIPLOM

S67
MENDL W.,"FRENCH ATTITUDES ON DISARMAMENT." FRANCE CULTURE CHIEF FORCES DIPLOM LEAD WAR...TIME/SEQ 20 DEGAULLE/C. PAGE 109 H2175 — NUC/PWR WEAPON ARMS/CONT POLICY

S67
OOSTEN F.,"SUDVIETNAM IM JAHR VOR DER ENTSCHEIDUNG." VIETNAM/S VIETNAM/N NAT/G DIPLOM COERCE CHOOSE 20. PAGE 121 H2420 — FORCES WAR WEAPON ATTIT

L68
CURRENT HISTORY,"AFRICA, 1968." ETHIOPIA GHANA NIGERIA SOUTH/AFR CULTURE ECO/UNDEV KIN SECT CHIEF EX/STRUC WAR WEAPON CHOOSE CIVMIL/REL...GOV/COMP 20 AFRICA/E. PAGE 36 H0724 — RACE/REL NAT/LISM FORCES AFR

WEATHER....WEATHER

WEATHERHEAD R.W. H2019

WEBB B. H3317

WEBB L.C. H3316

WEBB S. H3317

WEBER E. H2660

WEBER J. H3318

WEBER M. H3319,H3320,H3321

WEBER/MAX....MAX WEBER

B64
KARIEL H.S.,IN SEARCH OF AUTHORITY: TWENTIETH-CENTURY POLITICAL THOUGHT. WOR+45 WOR-45 NAT/G EX/STRUC TOTALISM DRIVE PWR...MGT PHIL/SCI GEN/LAWS 19/20 NIETZSCH/F FREUD/S WEBER/MAX NIEBUHR/R MARITAIN/J. PAGE 83 H1661 — CONSTN CONCPT ORD/FREE IDEA/COMP

S67
MURVAR V.,"MAX WEBER'S CONCEPT OF HEIROCRACY: A STUDY IN THE TYPOLOGY OF CHURCH-STATE RELATIONS" UNIV INGP/REL ATTIT PLURISM...SOC CONCPT 20 WEBER/MAX. PAGE 115 H2299 — SECT NAT/G GP/REL STRUCT

WEBSTER C. H3322,H3323

WEDGE B. H3324

WEHLER H.V. H3325

WEIDENFELD A. H2886

WEIL E. H3326

WEIMAR/REP....WEIMAR REPUBLIC

B38
REICH N.,LABOR RELATIONS IN REPUBLICAN GERMANY. GERMANY CONSTN ECO/DEV INDUS NAT/G ADMIN CONTROL GP/REL FASCISM POPULISM 20 WEIMAR/REP. PAGE 130 H2609 — WORKER MGT LABOR BARGAIN

S58
SCHUMM S.,"INTEREST REPRESENTATION IN FRANCE AND GERMANY." EUR+WWI FRANCE GERMANY INSPECT PARL/PROC REPRESENT 20 WEIMAR/REP. PAGE 140 H2803 — LOBBY DELIB/GP NAT/G

B63
JACOB H.,GERMAN ADMINISTRATION SINCE BISMARCK: CENTRAL AUTHORITY VERSUS LOCAL AUTONOMY. GERMANY GERMANY/W LAW POL/PAR CONTROL CENTRAL TOTALISM FASCISM...MAJORIT DECISION STAT CHARTS GOV/COMP 19/20 BISMARCK/O HITLER/A WEIMAR/REP. PAGE 79 H1577 — ADMIN NAT/G LOC/G POLICY

B66
DYCK H.V.,WEIMAR GERMANY AND SOVIET RUSSIA 1926-1933. EUR+WWI GERMANY UK USSR ECO/TAC INT/TRADE NEUTRAL WAR ATTIT 20 WEIMAR/REP TREATY. PAGE 44 H0877 — DIPLOM GOV/REL POLICY

B66
THORNTON M.J.,NAZISM, 1918-1945. GERMANY INT/ORG DIPLOM REV PEACE FASCISM...CONCPT 20 HITLER/A WEIMAR/REP NAZI. PAGE 155 H3089 — TOTALISM POL/PAR NAT/G WAR

B66
TORMIN W.,GESCHICHTE DER DEUTSCHEN PARTEIEN SEIT 1848. GERMANY CHOOSE PWR...CONCPT 19/20 WEIMAR/REP. PAGE 156 H3116 — POL/PAR CONSTN NAT/G TOTALISM

WEINER H.E. H3327

WEINER M. H1475,H3328

WEINSTEIN B. H3329

WEINSTEIN F.B. H3330

WEISSBERG G. H3331

WEITZ H.J. H1152

WEITZEL R. H3117

WELF/ST....WELFARE STATE ADVOCATE

B43
LASKI H.J.,REFLECTIONS ON THE REVOLUTIONS OF OUR TIME. COM USSR NAT/G WORKER UTOPIA ORD/FREE WEALTH MARXISM SOCISM 19/20. PAGE 92 H1830 — CAP/ISM WELF/ST ECO/TAC POLICY

B44
BARKER E.,THE DEVELOPMENT OF PUBLIC SERVICES IN WESTERN WUROPE: 1660-1930. FRANCE GERMANY UK SCHOOL CONTROL REPRESENT ROLE...WELF/ST 17/20. PAGE 11 H0219 — GOV/COMP ADMIN EX/STRUC

B44
KNORR K.E.,BRITISH COLONIAL THEORIES 1570-1850. NAT/G DELIB/GP ECO/TAC PERCEPT PWR...WELF/ST METH/CNCPT CONT/OBS TIME/SEQ SIMUL TOT/POP 20. PAGE 87 H1734 — ACT/RES DOMIN COLONIAL

B48
ROSENFARB J.,FREEDOM AND THE ADMINISTRATIVE STATE. — ECO/DEV

NAT/G ROUTINE EFFICIENCY PRODUC RATIONAL UTIL ...TECHNIC WELF/ST MGT 20 BUREAUCRCY. PAGE 134 H2680 — INDUS PLAN WEALTH

C50
ROUSSEAU J.J.,"DISCOURSE ON THE ORIGIN OF INEQUALITY" (1755) IN THE SOCIAL CONTRACT AND DISCOURSES." UNIV NAT/G PLAN BAL/PWR HAPPINESS UTOPIA BIO/SOC HEREDITY MORAL...WELF/ST CONCPT. PAGE 135 H2698 — SOCIETY STRUCT PERSON GEN/LAWS

C50
ROUSSEAU J.J.,"A DISCOURSE ON POLITICAL ECONOMY" (1755) IN THE SOCIAL CONTRACT AND DISCOURSES." UNIV SOCIETY STRATA STRUCT CONSEN EQUILIB HAPPINESS UTOPIA HEALTH WEALTH...POLICY WELF/ST. PAGE 135 H2699 — NAT/G ECO/TAC TAX GEN/LAWS

N53
VITO F.,"RECENT DEVELOPMENTS IN THE THEORY OF DEMOCRATIC ADMIN" INTL POL SCI ASS'N CONFERENCE ON PUBLIC ADMINISTRATION... FRANCE ITALY UK REPRESENT EFFICIENCY NEW/LIB SOCISM...WELF/ST 20. PAGE 163 H3257 — GOV/COMP CONTROL EX/STRUC

B57
COLE G.D.H.,THE POST WAR CONDITIONS OF BRITAIN. EUR+WWI STRUCT NAT/G PLAN EDU/PROP LEGIT RIGID/FLEX ORD/FREE WEALTH...SOCIALIST WELF/ST STAT TREND CON/ANAL CHARTS PARLIAMENT WORK 20. PAGE 31 H0624 — ECO/DEV UK

B58
DWARKADAS R.,ROLE OF HIGHER CIVIL SERVICE IN INDIA. INDIA ECO/UNDEV LEGIS PROB/SOLV GP/REL PERS/REL ...POLICY WELF/ST DECISION ORG/CHARTS BIBLIOG 20 CIVIL/SERV INTRVN/ECO. PAGE 44 H0876 — ADMIN NAT/G ROLE PLAN

B59
JENKINS C.,POWER AT THE TOP: A CRITICAL SURVEY OF THE NATIONALIZED INDUSTRIES. UK POL/PAR CONTROL ...WELF/ST CHARTS 20 LABOR/PAR. PAGE 80 H1601 — NAT/G OWN INDUS NEW/LIB

S61
MILLER E.,"LEGAL ASPECTS OF UN ACTION IN THE CONGO." AFR CULTURE ADMIN PEACE DRIVE RIGID/FLEX ORD/FREE...WELF/ST JURID OBS UN CONGO 20. PAGE 111 H2212 — INT/ORG LEGIT

B62
HARRINGTON M.,THE OTHER AMERICA: POVERTY IN THE UNITED STATES. WORKER CREATE REPRESENT RACE/REL AGE/O DRIVE POLICY. PAGE 67 H1338 — WEALTH WELF/ST INCOME CULTURE

B63
SELF P.,THE STATE AND THE FARMER. UK ECO/DEV MARKET WORKER PRICE CONTROL GP/REL...WELF/ST 20 DEPT/AGRI. PAGE 141 H2823 — AGRI NAT/G ADMIN VOL/ASSN

S63
AYAL E.B.,"VALUE SYSTEM AND ECONOMIC DEVELOPMENT IN JAPAN AND THAILAND." ASIA S/ASIA THAILAND CULTURE ECO/DEV CAP/ISM DOMIN NAT/LISM DRIVE RIGID/FLEX SOCISM...WELF/ST OBS TREND CON/ANAL GEN/LAWS 20 CHINJAP. PAGE 9 H0185 — ECO/UNDEV ALL/VALS

B64
COONDOO R.,THE DIVISION OF POWERS IN THE INDIAN CONSTITUTION. INDIA ECO/UNDEV FINAN TEC/DEV WAR CENTRAL EFFICIENCY NAT/LISM PWR WEALTH NEW/LIB ...BIBLIOG 18/20. PAGE 33 H0659 — CONSTN LEGIS WELF/ST GOV/COMP

B64
MARSH D.C.,THE FUTURE OF THE WELFARE STATE. UK CONSTN NAT/G POL/PAR...POLICY WELF/ST 20. PAGE 103 H2058 — NEW/LIB ADMIN CONCPT INSPECT

B64
TAWNEY R.H.,EQUALITY. UK CULTURE STRATA ECO/TAC EDU/PROP REPRESENT OWN NEW/LIB...MAJORIT WELF/ST SOC 20. PAGE 153 H3051 — WEALTH STRUCT ELITES POPULISM

B65
TINGSTEN H.,THE PROBLEM OF DEMOCRACY. ELITES SOCIETY STRATA NAT/G CONSEN TOTALISM WELF/ST. PAGE 155 H3101 — IDEA/COMP GOV/COMP POPULISM SOCISM

B66
AIYAR S.P.,PERSPECTIVES ON THE WELFARE STATE. INDIA S/ASIA UK CONSTN ECO/UNDEV NAT/G INGP/REL CENTRAL NAT/LISM ATTIT...CONCPT ANTHOL BIBLIOG 20. PAGE 4 H0087 — NEW/LIB WELF/ST IDEA/COMP ADJUST

B66
BEER S.H.,BRITISH POLITICS IN THE COLLECTIVIST AGE. UK NAT/G CONTROL CHOOSE GP/REL ATTIT PWR PLURISM ...MAJORIT WELF/ST 16/20. PAGE 13 H0258 — POL/PAR SOCISM TRADIT GP/COMP

B67
WARD L.,LESTER WARD AND THE WELFARE STATE. SOCIETY NAT/G CREATE RECEIVE EQUILIB UTOPIA HABITAT HEREDITY PERSON...POLICY SOC BIOG 19/20 WARD/LEST. PAGE 165 H3303 — ALL/VALS NEW/IDEA WELF/ST CONCPT

WELFARE....SEE RECEIVE, NEW/LIB, WELF/ST

WELFARE STATE....SEE NEW/LIB, WELF/ST

WELLS H. H3332

WELLS S.J. H2154

WERNETTE J.P. H3333

WERTHEIM W.F. H3334

WERTHMAN M. H0522

WEST F.J. H3335

WEST AFRICA....SEE AFRICA/W

WEST GERMANY....SEE GERMANY/W

WEST/EDWRD....SIR EDWARD WEST

WEST/IND....WEST INDIES; SEE ALSO L/A+17C

B01
GRIFFIN A.P.C.,A LIST OF BOOKS ON THE DANISH WEST INDIES (PAMPHLET). L/A+17C WEST/IND CULTURE LOC/G ...GEOG MGT 18/20. PAGE 61 H1214 — BIBLIOG/A SOCIETY COLONIAL ADMIN

B32
CATALOGUE OF BOOKS, MANSUCRIPTS, ETC. IN THE CARIBBEANA SECTION OF THE N.M. WILLIAMS MEMORIAL ETHNOLOGICAL COLLECTION. JAMAICA WEST/IND GP/REL ATTIT SOC. PAGE 2 H0031 — BIBLIOG L/A+17C CULTURE SOCIETY

B42
BLANCHARD L.R.,MARTINIQUE: A SELECTED LIST OF REFERENCES (PAMPHLET). WEST/IND AGRI LOC/G SCHOOL ...ART/METH GEOG JURID CHARTS 20. PAGE 18 H0353 — BIBLIOG/A SOCIETY CULTURE COLONIAL

B57
CARIBBEAN COMMISSION,A CATALOGUE OF CARIBBEAN COMMISSION PUBLICATIONS (PAMPHLET). WEST/IND CULTURE ECO/UNDEV LOC/G DIPLOM SOC. PAGE 26 H0531 — BIBLIOG L/A+17C INT/ORG NAT/G

B58
LOWER A.R.M.,EVOLVING CANADIAN FEDERALISM. CANADA WEST/IND CONSTN PROB/SOLV COLONIAL REGION NAT/LISM ...ANTHOL 20. PAGE 99 H1976 — FEDERAL NAT/G DIPLOM RACE/REL

B60
AYEARST M.,THE BRITISH WEST INDIES: THE SEARCH FOR SELF-GOVERNMENT. FUT WEST/IND LOC/G POL/PAR EX/STRUC LEGIS CHOOSE FEDERAL...NAT/COMP BIBLIOG 17/20. PAGE 9 H0186 — CONSTN COLONIAL REPRESENT NAT/G

B62
SMITH M.G.,KINSHIP AND COMMUNITY IN CARRIACOU. WEST/IND STRATA AGRI FAM SECT WORKER MARRIAGE OWN HEREDITY WEALTH...SOC 18/20. PAGE 146 H2915 — CULTURE HABITAT KIN STRUCT

B65
CHANDLER M.J.,A GUIDE TO RECORDS IN BARBADOS. WEST/IND PUB/INST SCHOOL SECT...HIST/WRIT 20. PAGE 28 H0573 — BIBLIOG LOC/G L/A+17C NAT/G

WEST/POINT....UNITED STATES MILITARY ACADEMY

WEST/SAMOA....WESTERN SAMOA; SEE ALSO S/ASIA

WEST/VIRGN....WEST VIRGINIA

WESTERN EUROPE....SEE EUROPE/W

WESTERN SAMOA....SEE WEST/SAMOA

WESTERN UNITED STATES....SEE US/WEST

WESTIN A.F. H0548,H0736

WESTMINSTER HALL, COURTS OF....SEE CTS/WESTM

WESTPHALIA....PEACE OF WESTPHALIA

WHEARE K.C. H3336,H3337,H3338,H3339

WHEELER G. H3340,H3341

WHEELER-BENNETT J.W. H3342

WHIG/PARTY....WHIG PARTY (USE WITH SPECIFIC NATION)

B62
JENNINGS I.,PARTY POLITICS: THE STUFF OF POLITICS (VOL.III). UK NAT/G SECT CHIEF INT/TRADE RECEIVE COLONIAL GP/REL NAT/LISM ORD/FREE SOCISM 19/20 CHURCH/STA WHIG/PARTY. PAGE 80 H1607 — POL/PAR CONSTN PWR ALL/IDEOS

B64
HOLDSWORTH W.S.,A HISTORY OF ENGLISH LAW; THE — LAW

CENTURIES OF DEVELOPMENT AND REFORM (VOL. XIV). UK CONSTN LOC/G NAT/G POL/PAR CHIEF EX/STRUC ADJUD COLONIAL ATTIT...INT/LAW JURID 18/19 TORY/PARTY COMMONWLTH WHIG/PARTY COMMON/LAW. PAGE 73 H1453 — LEGIS LEAD CT/SYS

WHIP....SEE LEGIS, CONG, ROUTINE

WHITAKER A.P. H3343,H3344

WHITE C.L. H3345

WHITE D.S. H3347

WHITE J. H3348

WHITE J.W. H3349

WHITE R.J. H3350

WHITE W.L. H3351

WHITE/SUP....WHITE SUPREMACY - PERSONS, GROUPS, AND IDEAS

B30

OLDMAN J.H.,WHITE AND BLACK IN AFRICA. AFR STRUCT COLONIAL PARTIC DISCRIM ISOLAT PRIVIL 20 SMUTS/JAN NEGRO WHITE/SUP. PAGE 121 H2412 — SOVEREIGN ORD/FREE RACE/REL NAT/G

WHITE/T....THEODORE WHITE

B61

LYFORD J.P.,THE AGREEABLE AUTOCRACIES. SOCIETY LABOR POL/PAR SECT DIPLOM CHOOSE...CONCPT 20 WHITE/T NIEBUHR/R. PAGE 99 H1982 — ATTIT POPULISM PRESS NAT/G

WHITE/WA....WILLIAM ALLEN WHITE

WHITEFORD A.H. H3352

WHITEHD/AN....ALFRED NORTH WHITEHEAD

WHITE-ANGLO-SAXON-PROTESTANT ESTABLISHMENT....SEE WASP

WHITEMAN M.M. H3353

WHITING K.R. H3354

WHITMAN/W....WALT WHITMAN

WHITTAKER C.H. H0933

WHO....WORLD HEALTH ORGANIZATION

WHYTE/WF....WILLIAM FOOTE WHYTE

B63

RUITENBEER H.M.,THE DILEMMA OF ORGANIZATIONAL SOCIETY. CULTURE ECO/DEV MUNIC SECT TEC/DEV EDU/PROP NAT/LISM ORD/FREE...NAT/COMP 20 RIESMAN/D WHYTE/WF MERTON/R MEAD/MARG JASPERS/K. PAGE 136 H2716 — PERSON ROLE ADMIN WORKER

WICKENS G.M. H3355

WIENER F.B. H3356

WIGGIN L.M. H3357

WILBER D.N. H3358

WILBER L.A. H3359

WILBUR C.M. H3360

WILCOX W.A. H3361,H3362

WILDING N. H3363

WILDNER H. H3364

WILHELM/I....WILHELM I (KAISER)

WILHELM/II....WILHELM II (KAISER)

B65

GILG P.,DIE ERNEUERUNG DES DEMOKRATISCHEN DENKENS IM WILHELMINISCHEN DEUTSCHLAND. GERMANY PARL/PROC CHOOSE REPRESENT...CONCPT 19/20 BISMARCK/O WILHELM/II. PAGE 56 H1126 — POL/PAR ORD/FREE NAT/G

WILKINS/R....ROY WILKINS

WILLIAM/3....WILLIAM III (PRINCE OF ORANGE)

B47

LOCKE J.,TWO TREATISES OF GOVERNMENT (1690). UK LAW SOCIETY LEGIS LEGIT AGREE REV OWN HEREDITY MORAL CONSERVE...POLICY MAJORIT 17 WILLIAM/3 NATURL/LAW. PAGE 97 H1946 — CONCPT ORD/FREF NAT/G CONSEN

WILLIAMS B. H3365

WILLIAMS F.R.A. H3366

WILLIAMS J. H2393

WILLIAMS L.E. H3367

WILLIAMS P.M. H3368

WILLIAMS/R....ROGER WILLIAMS

WILLIAMSON H.F. H3369

WILLIAMSON J.A. H3370

WILLMORE J.N. H0479

WILLNER A.R. H3371

WILLOUGHBY W.C. H3372

WILLOUGHBY W.F. H3373

WILLOUGHBY W.W. H3374

WILLOW/RUN....WILLOW RUN, MICHIGAN

WILLS A.J. H3375

WILLS....WILLS AND TESTAMENTS

WILLSON F.M.G. H3376

WILMERDING L. H3377

WILPERT C. H3378

WILSON J.Q. H3379

WILSON P. H3380,H3381

WILSON T. H3382,H3383

WILSON U. H3384

WILSON W. H3385

WILSON/H....HAROLD WILSON

B65

PELLING H.,A SHORT HISTORY OF THE LABOUR PARTY (2ND ED.). UK NAT/G CHIEF PARL/PROC GP/REL INGP/REL 20 LABOR/PAR PARLIAMENT WILSON/H. PAGE 124 H2484 — POL/PAR NEW/LIB LEAD LABOR

B66

NOEL G.E.,THE NEW BRITAIN AND HAROLD WILSON: INTERIM REPORT, 1966 GENERAL ELECTION. UK POL/PAR CONSULT PROB/SOLV BUDGET DIPLOM ECO/TAC LEAD CHOOSE ATTIT 20 WILSON/H PARLIAMENT. PAGE 118 H2366 — BIOG PERSON NAT/G CHIEF

WILSON/J....JAMES WILSON

WILSON/W....PRESIDENT WOODROW WILSON

B33

DAHLIN E.,FRENCH AND GERMAN PUBLIC OPINION ON DECLARED WAR AIMS 1914-1918. BELGIUM FRANCE GERMANY NAT/G POL/PAR DIPLOM COERCE REV WAR PEACE 20 WWI WILSON/W. PAGE 37 H0733 — ATTIT EDU/PROP DOMIN NAT/COMP

C52

FIFIELD R.H.,"WOODROW WILSON AND THE FAR EAST." ASIA CHIEF DELIB/GP BAL/PWR CONFER COLONIAL ARMS/CONT WAR...TIME/SEQ NAT/COMP 19/20 WILSON/W LEAGUE/NAT. PAGE 50 H0995 — BIBLIOG DIPLOM INT/ORG

B60

SCHEIBER H.N.,THE WILSON ADMINISTRATION AND CIVIL LIBERTIES 1917-1921. LAW GOV/REL ATTIT 20 WILSON/W CIVIL/LIB. PAGE 139 H2782 — ORD/FREE WAR NAT/G CONTROL

B67

WARREN S.,THE AMERICAN PRESIDENT. POL/PAR FORCES LEGIS DIPLOM ECO/TAC ADMIN EXEC PWR...ANTHOL 18/20 ROOSEVLT/F KENNEDY/JF JOHNSON/LB TRUMAN/HS WILSON/W. PAGE 165 H3312 — CHIEF LEAD NAT/G CONSTN

WINDMILLER M. H2435

WINKLER H.R. H2835

WINKLER R.L. H1632

WINKS R.W. H3386

WINT G. H3387,H3388

WINTER E.H. H3389

WIONCZEK M. H3390

WIRETAPPING....SEE PRIVACY

WISCONSIN....WISCONSIN

WISCONSN/U....WISCONSIN STATE UNIVERSITY

WISEMAN H.V. H3391

WITHERELL J.W. H3392

WITHERSPOON J.V. H0479

WITTFOGEL K.A. H3393

WITTGEN/L....LUDWIG WITTGENSTEIN

WODDIS J. H3394

WOHLSTETTER R. H3395

WOLF C. H3396,H3397

WOLFE B.D. H3398,H3399

WOLFE D.M. H3400

WOLFE S. H0192

WOLFE T.W. H3401

WOLFERS A. H3402

WOLFF R.L. H3403

WOLFF/C....CHRISTIAN WOLFF

B96
DE VATTEL E.,THE LAW OF NATIONS. AGRI FINAN CHIEF DIPLOM INT/TRADE AGREE OWN ALL/VALS MORAL ORD/FREE SOVEREIGN...GEN/LAWS 18 NATURL/LAW WOLFF/C. PAGE 39 H0774
LAW CONCPT NAT/G INT/LAW

WOLFF/RP....ROBERT PAUL WOLFF

WOLFINGER R.E. H3404

WOLPERT S. H3405

WOMEN....SEE FEMALE/SEX

WOMEN'S CHRISTIAN TEMPERANCE UNION....SEE WCTU

WOOD H.B. H3406

WOOD/CHAS....SIR CHARLES WOOD

WOODRUFF W. H3407

WOODS H.D. H3408,H3409

WOOLBERT R.G. H3410

WOOLF S.J. H2545

WOR+45....WORLDWIDE, 1945 TO PRESENT

WOR-45....WORLDWIDE, TO 1945

WORK....SEE WORKER

WORK PROJECTS ADMINISTRATION....SEE WPA

B28
YANG KUNG-SUN,THE BOOK OF LORD SHANG. LAW ECO/UNDEV LOC/G NAT/G NEIGH PLAN ECO/TAC LEGIT ATTIT SKILL ...CONCPT CON/ANAL WORK TOT/POP. PAGE 172 H3434
ASIA JURID

B53
NELSON G.R.,FREEDOM AND WELFARE: SOCIAL PATTERNS IN THE NORTHERN COUNTRIES OF EUROPE. EUR+WWI ECO/DEV NAT/G EDU/PROP LEGIT HEALTH ORD/FREE SKILL WEALTH ...STAT AUD/VIS SCANDINAV WORK TOT/POP 20. PAGE 116 H2329
PLAN ECO/TAC

B55
KOHN H.,THE MIND OF MODERN RUSSIA. COM MOD/EUR USSR SOCIETY NAT/G SECT FORCES TOP/EX COERCE TOTALISM DRIVE RIGID/FLEX PWR SOVEREIGN...CONCPT TIME/SEQ WORK. PAGE 87 H1742
INTELL GEN/LAWS SOCISM RUSSIA

B55
MAZZINI J.,THE DUTIES OF MAN. MOD/EUR LAW SOCIETY FAM NAT/G POL/PAR SECT VOL/ASSN EX/STRUC ACT/RES CREATE REV PEACE ATTIT ALL/VALS...GEN/LAWS WORK 19. PAGE 106 H2113
SUPEGO CONCPT NAT/LISM

B57
COLE G.D.H.,THE POST WAR CONDITIONS OF BRITAIN. EUR+WWI STRUCT NAT/G PLAN EDU/PROP LEGIT RIGID/FLEX ORD/FREE WEALTH...SOCIALIST WELF/ST STAT TREND CON/ANAL CHARTS PARLIAMENT WORK 20. PAGE 31 H0624
ECO/DEV UK

S57
KILSON M.L.,"LAND AND POLITICS IN KENYA: AN ANALYSIS OF AFRICAN POLITICS IN A PLURAL SOCIETY." FUT LAW CULTURE KIN NAT/G ECO/TAC DOMIN REV NAT/LISM ORD/FREE PWR RESPECT SOVEREIGN WEALTH ...SOC OBS TREND WORK VAL/FREE CMN/WLTH 20. PAGE 86 H1710
AFR ECO/UNDEV

B60
SCHAPIRO L.,THE COMMUNIST PARTY OF THE SOVIET UNION. COM LAW SOCIETY STRATA STRUCT ECO/DEV LABOR NAT/G POL/PAR CREATE DOMIN EDU/PROP COERCE TOTALISM MARXISM...POLICY CONCPT MYTH TIME/SEQ WORK TOT/POP 20 LENIN/VI STALIN/J. PAGE 139 H2772
INTELL PWR USSR

B60
SHIRER W.L.,THE RISE AND FALL OF THE THIRD REICH: A HISTORY OF NAZI GERMANY. EUR+WWI CULTURE ECO/DEV INDUS NAT/G POL/PAR FORCES PLAN TEC/DEV ECO/TAC COERCE ATTIT DRIVE PERSON PWR...MYSTIC PSY SOC MYTH STAT CHARTS EXHIBIT WORK VAL/FREE. PAGE 143 H2864
STRUCT GERMANY TOTALISM

S60
EMERSON R.,"THE EROSION OF DEMOCRACY." AFR FUT LAW CULTURE INTELL SOCIETY ECO/UNDEV FAM LOC/G NAT/G FORCES PLAN TEC/DEV ECO/TAC ADMIN CT/SYS ATTIT ORD/FREE PWR...SOCIALIST SOC CONCPT STAND/INT TIME/SEQ WORK 20. PAGE 46 H0918
S/ASIA POL/PAR

S60
KEYFITZ N.,"WESTERN PERSPECTIVES AND ASIAN PROBLEMS." ASIA EUR+WWI S/ASIA SOCIETY FOR/AID ...POLICY SOC CONCPT STERTYP WORK TOT/POP 20. PAGE 85 H1701
CULTURE ATTIT

S60
NORTH R.C.,"DIE DISKREPANZ ZWISCHEN REALITAT UND WUNSCHBILD ALS INNENPOLITISCHER FAKTOR." ASIA CHINA/COM COM FUT ECO/UNDEV NAT/G PLAN DOMIN ADMIN COERCE PERCEPT...SOC MYTH GEN/METH WORK TOT/POP 20. PAGE 119 H2373
SOCIETY ECO/TAC

S60
RIVKIN A.,"AFRICAN ECONOMIC DEVELOPMENT: ADVANCED TECHNOLOGY AND THE STAGES OF GROWTH." CULTURE ECO/UNDEV AGRI COM/IND EXTR/IND PLAN ECO/TAC ATTIT DRIVE RIGID/FLEX SKILL WEALTH...MGT SOC GEN/LAWS WORK TOT/POP 20. PAGE 132 H2634
AFR TEC/DEV FOR/AID

B61
MARX K.,THE COMMUNIST MANIFESTO. IN (MENDEL A. ESSENTIAL WORKS OF MARXISM, NEW YORK: BANTAM. FUT MOD/EUR CULTURE ECO/DEV ECO/UNDEV AGRI FINAN INDUS MARKET PROC/MFG LABOR MUNIC POL/PAR CONSULT FORCES CREATE PLAN ADMIN ATTIT DRIVE RIGID/FLEX ORD/FREE PWR RESPECT MARX/KARL WORK. PAGE 104 H2081
COM NEW/IDEA CAP/ISM REV

B61
SETON-WATSON H.,FROM LENIN TO KHRUSHCHEV: THE HISTORY OF WORLD COMMUNISM. ASIA COM EUR+WWI ISLAM S/ASIA ECO/DEV ECO/UNDEV NAT/G POL/PAR DIPLOM ECO/TAC EDU/PROP COERCE GUERRILLA ATTIT DRIVE WORK TOT/POP NAZI 20. PAGE 141 H2832
PWR REV USSR

S62
PISTRAK L.,"SOVIET VIEWS ON AFRICA." AFR COM FUT ISLAM USSR INTELL STRUCT KIN POL/PAR PLAN EDU/PROP RIGID/FLEX PWR MARXISM...TIME/SEQ WORK TOT/POP 20. PAGE 126 H2516
NAT/G ATTIT SOCISM

S62
ROTBERG R.,"THE RISE OF AFRICAN NATIONALISM: THE CASE OF EAST AND CENTRAL AFRICA." AFR CULTURE SOCIETY NEIGH DIPLOM DOMIN COLONIAL COERCE DISPL PERCEPT PWR SOVEREIGN...POLICY OBS/ENVIR TREND WORK 20. PAGE 135 H2690
ATTIT DRIVE NAT/LISM REV

B63
GEERTZ C.,PEDDLERS AND PRINCES: SOCIAL DEVELOPMENT AND ECONOMIC CHANGE IN TWO INDONESIAN TOWNS. S/ASIA CULTURE SOCIETY STRATA FACE/GP MUNIC CREATE TEC/DEV ECO/TAC ORD/FREE WEALTH...OBS INT CENSUS CHARTS WORK TOT/POP VAL/FREE 20. PAGE 55 H1106
ECO/UNDEV SOC ELITES INDONESIA

B63
ISSAWI C.,EGYPT IN REVOLUTION: AN ECONOMIC ANALYSIS. ISLAM STRUCT ECO/UNDEV AGRI FINAN INDUS PLAN EXEC REV NAT/LISM ATTIT RIGID/FLEX WEALTH SOCISM...STAT WORK 20. PAGE 79 H1573
NAT/G UAR

B63
JUNOD V.,HANDBOOK OF AFRICA. AFR ISLAM CONSTN SOCIETY NAT/G POL/PAR...GEOG SOC STAT CHARTS WORK 20. PAGE 82 H1642
ECO/UNDEV REGION

B63
STEVENS G.G.,EGYPT YESTERDAY AND TODAY. CONSTN
ISLAM

ECO/UNDEV AGRI INDUS NAT/G POL/PAR FORCES ECO/TAC EDU/PROP COERCE WAR NAT/LISM DRIVE ALL/VALS ...TIME/SEQ WORK SUEZ 20. PAGE 149 H2983
TOP/EX REV UAR

S63
HALPERN A.M.,"THE EMERGENCE OF AN ASIAN COMMUNIST BLOC." ASIA CHINA/COM COM FUT KOREA/N S/ASIA VIETNAM/N STRATA NAT/G DELIB/GP FORCES TOP/EX PLAN BAL/PWR COERCE DETER PWR COLD/WAR WORK 20. PAGE 65 H1295
POL/PAR EDU/PROP DIPLOM

B64
CURTIN P.D.,THE IMAGE OF AFRICA: BRITISH IDEAS AND ACTION, 1780-1850. MOD/EUR SOCIETY FORCES ACT/RES DOMIN EDU/PROP COERCE ATTIT PERCEPT RIGID/FLEX SUPEGO HEALTH KNOWL MORAL ORD/FREE WEALTH...CONCPT WORK VAL/FREE. PAGE 36 H0726
AFR CULTURE UK DIPLOM

B64
LI C.M.,INDUSTRIAL DEVELOPMENT IN COMMUNIST CHINA. CHINA/COM ECO/DEV ECO/UNDEV AGRI FINAN INDUS MARKET LABOR NAT/G ECO/TAC INT/TRADE EXEC ALL/VALS ...POLICY RELATIV TREND WORK TOT/POP VAL/FREE 20. PAGE 96 H1921
ASIA TEC/DEV

B64
THORNTON T.P.,THE THIRD WORLD IN SOVIET PERSPECTIVE: STUDIES BY SOVIET WRITERS ON THE DEVELOPING AREAS. AFR L/A+17C S/ASIA STRATA AGRI INDUS MARKET NAT/G POL/PAR ECO/TAC COLONIAL PERCEPT PWR WEALTH...MARXIST STAT CHARTS WORK MARX/KARL 20. PAGE 155 H3090
ECO/UNDEV ACT/RES USSR DIPLOM

B64
ZARTMAN I.W.,MOROCCO: PROBLEMS OF NEW POWER. ISLAM CULTURE ECO/UNDEV AGRI POL/PAR SCHOOL FORCES ADMIN ...CONCPT STAT INT CENSUS TIME/SEQ CHARTS WORK VAL/FREE 20. PAGE 172 H3449
CHOOSE MOROCCO DELIB/GP DECISION

S64
GARMARNIKOW M.,"INFLUENCE-BUYING IN WEST AFRICA." COM FUT USSR INTELL NAT/G PLAN TEC/DEV ECO/TAC DOMIN EDU/PROP REGION NAT/LISM ATTIT DRIVE ALL/VALS SOVEREIGN...POLICY PSY SOC CONCPT TREND STERTYP WORK COLD/WAR 20. PAGE 55 H1102
AFR ECO/UNDEV FOR/AID SOCISM

S64
JOHNSON K.F.,"CAUSAL FACTORS IN LATIN AMERICAN POLITICAL INSTABILITY." CULTURE NAT/G VOL/ASSN EX/STRUC FORCES EDU/PROP LEGIT ADMIN COERCE REV ATTIT KNOWL PWR...STYLE RECORD CHARTS WORK 20. PAGE 81 H1624
L/A+17C PERCEPT ELITES

S64
NASH M.,"SOCIAL PREREQUISITES TO ECONOMIC GROWTH IN LATIN AMERICA AND SOUTHEAST ASIA." L/A+17C S/ASIA CULTURE SOCIETY ECO/UNDEV AGRI INDUS NAT/G PLAN TEC/DEV EDU/PROP ROUTINE ALL/VALS...POLICY RELATIV SOC NAT/COMP WORK TOT/POP 20. PAGE 116 H2314
ECO/DEV PERCEPT

S64
NEEDHAM T.,"SCIENCE AND SOCIETY IN EAST AND WEST." INTELL STRATA R+D LOC/G NAT/G PROVS CONSULT ACT/RES CREATE PLAN TEC/DEV EDU/PROP ADMIN ATTIT ALL/VALS ...POLICY RELATIV MGT CONCPT NEW/IDEA TIME/SEQ WORK WORK. PAGE 116 H2327
ASIA STRUCT

S64
NEEDHAM T.,"SCIENCE AND SOCIETY IN EAST AND WEST." INTELL STRATA R+D LOC/G NAT/G PROVS CONSULT ACT/RES CREATE PLAN TEC/DEV EDU/PROP ADMIN ATTIT ALL/VALS ...POLICY RELATIV MGT CONCPT NEW/IDEA TIME/SEQ WORK WORK. PAGE 116 H2327
ASIA STRUCT

S65
HELMREICH E.C.,"KADAR'S HUNGARY." COM EUR+WWI HUNGARY USSR INTELL ECO/DEV AGRI INT/ORG TOP/EX DOMIN ALL/VALS WORK COLD/WAR 20. PAGE 69 H1390
NAT/G RIGID/FLEX TOTALISM

S65
SPAAK P.H.,"THE SEARCH FOR CONSENSUS: A NEW EFFORT TO BUILD EUROPE." FRANCE GERMANY ECO/DEV NAT/G CONSULT FORCES PLAN EDU/PROP REGION CONSEN ATTIT ...SOC METH/CNCPT OBS TREND EEC NATO WORK 20. PAGE 147 H2941
EUR+WWI INT/ORG

WORKER....WORKER, LABORER

N
CIVIL SERVICE JOURNAL. PARTIC INGP/REL PERS/REL ...MGT BIBLIOG/A 20. PAGE 1 H0015
ADMIN NAT/G SERV/IND WORKER

N
US LIBRARY OF CONGRESS,SOUTHERN ASIA ACCESSIONS LIST. BURMA CEYLON INDIA NEPAL PAKISTAN S/ASIA THAILAND AGRI INDUS SCHOOL WORKER...ART/METH GEOG HEAL PHIL/SCI LING 20. PAGE 160 H3201
BIBLIOG/A SOCIETY CULTURE ECO/UNDEV

B08
LLOYD H.D.,THE SWISS DEMOCRACY. SWITZERLND INDUS NAT/G WORKER CHOOSE OWN ORD/FREE SOCISM...PLURIST 19/20 MONOPOLY. PAGE 97 H1944
NAT/COMP GOV/COMP REPRESENT POPULISM

C09
SCHAPIRO J.S.,"SOCIAL REFORM AND THE REFORMATION." CHRIST-17C GERMANY LAW CONSTN LG/CO NAT/G WORKER PROB/SOLV CT/SYS REV...BIBLIOG 16. PAGE 138 H2770
ORD/FREE SECT ECO/TAC BIOG

B12
HOBSON J.A.,THE EVOLUTION OF MODERN CAPITALISM. MOD/EUR UK STRATA ECO/DEV INDUS INCOME UTIL WEALTH ...SOC GEN/LAWS 7/20. PAGE 72 H1440
CAP/ISM WORKER TEC/DEV TIME/SEQ

B13
BARDOUX J.,L'ANGLETERRE RADICALE; ESSAI DE LA PSYCHOLOGIE SOCIALE (1906-1913). UK CONSTN NAT/G WORKER CREATE BUDGET ECO/TAC ATTIT...POLICY 20 PARLIAMENT LABOR/PAR STRIKE NAVY. PAGE 11 H0215
POL/PAR CHOOSE COLONIAL LEGIS

B13
KROPOTKIN P.,THE CONQUEST OF BREAD. SOCIETY STRATA AGRI INDUS WORKER REV HAPPINESS INCOME PRODUC HEALTH MORAL ORD/FREE. PAGE 89 H1775
ANARCH SOCIALIST OWN AGREE

B14
OPPENHEIMER F.,THE STATE. FUT SOCIETY STRATA STRUCT WORKER CAP/ISM WAR GP/REL SOCISM...SOC NAT/COMP SOC/INTEG. PAGE 121 H2424
ELITES OWN DOMIN NAT/G

N19
BUSINESS ECONOMISTS' GROUP,INCOME POLICIES (PAMPHLET). UK INDUS LABOR TOP/EX PAY COST PRODUC ...ECOMETRIC GOV/COMP SIMUL ANTHOL 20. PAGE 25 H0497
INCOME WORKER WEALTH POLICY

N19
FIKS M.,PUBLIC ADMINISTRATION IN ISRAEL (PAMPHLET). ISRAEL SCHOOL EX/STRUC BUDGET PAY INGP/REL ...DECISION 20 CIVIL/SERV. PAGE 50 H0999
EDU/PROP NAT/G ADMIN WORKER

N19
INTERNATIONAL LABOUR OFFICE,EMPLOYMENT, UNEMPLOYMENT AND LABOUR FORCE STATISTICS (PAMPHLET). EUR+WWI STRATA AGRI INDUS NAT/G PROB/SOLV PAY AGE SEX...SAMP NAT/COMP METH 20 ILO. PAGE 78 H1557
WORKER LABOR STAT ECO/DEV

N19
LIEBKNECHT W.P.C.,SOCIALISM (2 PTS.; 1875, 1894) (PAMPHLET). WORKER CAP/ISM EDU/PROP WEALTH POPULISM. PAGE 97 H1927
ECO/TAC STRATA SOCIALIST PARTIC

B21
KREY A.C.,THE FIRST CRUSADE. CHRIST-17C SOCIETY STRATA NAT/G SECT FORCES WORKER WRITING LEAD ATTIT ...CHARTS 11 CHRISTIAN CRUSADES. PAGE 88 H1767
WAR CATH DIPLOM PARTIC

B22
HUNTINGTON E.,CIVILIZATION AND CLIMATE (2ND ED.). UNIV WORKER...SOC CHARTS. PAGE 75 H1503
GEOG HABITAT CULTURE

B26
SMITH T.V.,THE DEMOCRATIC WAY OF LIFE. UNIV SOCIETY NAT/G WORKER TASK CHOOSE ALL/VALS...IDEA/COMP WORSHIP. PAGE 146 H2919
MAJORIT CONCPT ORD/FREE LEAD

B27
BELLOC H.,THE SERVILE STATE (1912) (3RD ED.). PRUSSIA UK CULTURE STRATA INDUS NAT/G ECO/TAC CONTROL LEAD SUFF DISCRIM EQUILIB ORD/FREE WEALTH 20. PAGE 13 H0269
WORKER CAP/ISM DOMIN CATH

B27
ENGELS F.,THE PEASANT WAR IN GERMANY (1850). GERMANY MOD/EUR AGRI WORKER LEAD COERCE INGP/REL ...TREND 16/19. PAGE 46 H0924
WAR STRATA REV MARXIST

B30
MASON E.S.,THE PARIS COMMUNE: AN EPISODE IN THE HISTORY OF THE SOCIALIST MOVEMENT. FRANCE MOD/EUR ELITES SOCIETY STRATA ECO/DEV WORKER EDU/PROP CHOOSE INGP/REL SOCISM 19 MARX/KARL PARIS. PAGE 104 H2085
NAT/G REV MARXISM

B31
CROOK W.H.,THE GENERAL STRIKE: A STUDY OF LABOR'S TRAGIC WEAPON IN THEORY AND PRACTICE. BELGIUM FRANCE SWEDEN UK WOR-45 PROB/SOLV ECO/TAC DOMIN PWR ...POLICY TIME/SEQ NAT/COMP GEN/LAWS 19/20 STRIKE. PAGE 35 H0707
LABOR WORKER LG/CO BARGAIN

B32
BLUM L.,PEACE AND DISARMAMENT (TRANS. BY A. WERTH). NAT/G FORCES WORKER DIPLOM AGREE WAR ATTIT AUTHORIT ORD/FREE. PAGE 18 H0360
SOCIALIST PEACE INT/ORG ARMS/CONT

B33
BERDYAYEV N.,CHRISTIANITY AND CLASS WAR. UNIV SOCIETY WORKER CREATE PROB/SOLV ATTIT PERSON ORD/FREE...CONCPT CHRISTIAN. PAGE 15 H0296
SECT MARXISM STRATA GP/REL

B33
TANNENBAUM F.,PEACE BY REVOLUTION. ECO/UNDEV AGRI SECT WORKER DIPLOM EDU/PROP DISCRIM OWN WEALTH POPULISM 17/20 MEXIC/AMER INDIAN/AM. PAGE 152 H3043
CULTURE COLONIAL RACE/REL REV

B34
MARX K.,THE CLASS STRUGGLES IN FRANCE. FRANCE INDUS WORKER CONSERVE...TREND GEN/LAWS 19. PAGE 104 H2077
MARXIST STRATA REV

INT/TRADE

B36
BELLOC H.,THE RESTORATION OF PROPERTY. UK STRATA NAT/G PROF/ORG DELIB/GP WORKER CREATE PROB/SOLV ECO/TAC PARTIC UTOPIA ORD/FREE SOCISM 20. PAGE 13 H0270
CONTROL MAJORIT CAP/ISM OWN

B37
MARX K.,THE CIVIL WAR IN THE UNITED STATES. USA-45 WORKER DIPLOM INT/TRADE DOMIN RACE/REL ATTIT ...TREND 19. PAGE 104 H2078
WAR REV MARXIST ORD/FREE

B38
DAVIES E.,"NATIONAL" CAPITALISM: THE GOVERNMENT'S RECORD AS PROTECTOR OF PRIVATE MONOPOLY. UK ELITES SOCIETY STRATA POL/PAR WORKER PROB/SOLV CONTROL SOCISM 20 MONOPOLY LABOR/PAR CHAMBRLN/N. PAGE 37 H0747
CAP/ISM NAT/G INDUS POLICY

B38
FIELD G.L.,THE SYNDICAL AND CORPORATIVE INSTITUTIONS OF ITALIAN FASCISM. ITALY CONSTN STRATA LABOR EX/STRUC TOP/EX ADJUD ADMIN LEAD TOTALISM AUTHORIT...MGT 20 MUSSOLIN/B. PAGE 50 H0991
FASCISM INDUS NAT/G WORKER

B38
MARX K.,THE GERMAN IDEOLOGY, PARTS 1 AND 3 (1846). MOD/EUR LAW STRATA WORKER DOMIN REV UTOPIA SOCISM 19 MARX/KARL. PAGE 104 H2079
MARXIST OWN PRODUC ECO/TAC

B38
REICH N.,LABOR RELATIONS IN REPUBLICAN GERMANY. GERMANY CONSTN ECO/DEV INDUS NAT/G ADMIN CONTROL GP/REL FASCISM POPULISM 20 WEIMAR/REP. PAGE 130 H2609
WORKER MGT LABOR BARGAIN

B39
MARQUAND H.A.,ORGANIZED LABOUR IN FOUR CONTINENTS. EUR+WWI USA-45 INDUS NAT/G PAY GP/REL TOTALISM ATTIT WEALTH ALL/IDEOS...TREND NAT/COMP 20 ILO AFL/CIO EUROPE CHINJAP MEXIC/AMER. PAGE 103 H2055
LABOR WORKER CONCPT ANTHOL

B39
VAN BILJON F.J.,STATE INTERFERENCE IN SOUTH AFRICA. SOUTH/AFR ECO/UNDEV AGRI INDUS WORKER RATION WEALTH ...JURID 20. PAGE 161 H3225
ECO/TAC POLICY INT/TRADE NAT/G

S39
COLE G.D.H.,"NAZI ECONOMICS: HOW DO THEY MANAGE IT?" GERMANY FORCES WORKER BUDGET INT/TRADE ROUTINE COERCE WAR 20 HITLER/A NAZI. PAGE 31 H0622
FASCISM ECO/TAC ATTIT PLAN

B40
WUNDERLICH F.,LABOR UNDER GERMAN DEMOCRACY, ARBITRATION 1918-1933. GERMANY NAT/G PAY REPAR ADJUD CT/SYS GP/REL...MAJORIT 20. PAGE 171 H3426
LABOR WORKER INDUS BARGAIN

B43
LASKI H.J.,REFLECTIONS ON THE REVOLUTIONS OF OUR TIME. COM USSR NAT/G WORKER UTOPIA ORD/FREE WEALTH MARXISM SOCISM 19/20. PAGE 92 H1830
CAP/ISM WELF/ST ECO/TAC POLICY

B43
MC DOWELL R.B.,IRISH PUBLIC OPINION, 1750-1800. IRELAND CONSTN VOL/ASSN WORKER ORD/FREE CATHISM CONSERVE...POLICY IDEA/COMP BIBLIOG 18/ PARLIAMENT. PAGE 106 H2118
ATTIT NAT/G DIPLOM REV

B45
VENABLE V.,HUMAN NATURE: THE MARXIAN VIEW. UNIV STRATA CAP/ISM REV GP/REL PERS/REL PRODUC KNOWL ...PHIL/SCI CONCPT IDEA/COMP 19 MARX/KARL ENGELS/F. PAGE 162 H3240
PERSON MARXISM WORKER UTOPIA

B46
BLUM L.,FOR ALL MANKIND (TRANS. BY W. PICKLES). FRANCE GERMANY USSR LAW SOCIETY STRUCT POL/PAR WORKER DIPLOM DOMIN CHOOSE ORD/FREE FASCISM 20. PAGE 18 H0361
POPULISM SOCIALIST NAT/G WAR

B46
DAVIES E.,NATIONAL ENTERPRISE: THE DEVELOPMENT OF THE PUBLIC CORPORATION. UK LG/CO EX/STRUC WORKER PROB/SOLV COST ATTIT SOCISM 20. PAGE 37 H0748
ADMIN NAT/G CONTROL INDUS

N47
CANNON J.P.,AMERICAN STALINISM AND ANTI-STALINISM (PAMPHLET). NAT/G WORKER DOMIN EDU/PROP REV GP/REL ...MARXIST CONCPT 20 STALIN/J TROTSKY/L. PAGE 26 H0521
LABOR MARXISM CAP/ISM POL/PAR

B48
LASKI H.S.,THE AMERICAN DEMOCRACY. CULTURE INDUS SECT WORKER DIPLOM EDU/PROP REPRESENT RACE/REL ORD/FREE PWR...NAT/COMP 18/20. PAGE 92 H1831
NAT/G LOC/G USA-45 POPULISM

B51
EUCKEN W.,THIS UNSUCCESSFUL AGE. GERMANY NAT/G WORKER TEC/DEV ECO/TAC ORD/FREE 20. PAGE 47 H0947
ECO/DEV PLAN LAISSEZ NEW/LIB

B51
MARX K.,THE EIGHTEENTH BRUMAIRE OF LOUIS BONAPARTE (1852). FRANCE STRATA FINAN INDUS LABOR CHIEF FORCES WORKER CAP/ISM ECO/TAC PARL/PROC ORD/FREE ...MARXIST 19. PAGE 104 H2080
REV MARXISM ELITES NAT/G

B52
ROBBINS L.,THE THEORY OF ECONOMIC POLICY IN ENGLISH CLASSICAL POLITICAL ECONOMY. UK ECO/DEV WORKER PLAN CAP/ISM EDU/PROP CONTROL INCOME OWN HEALTH SOCISM ...POLICY 17/19. PAGE 132 H2639
ECO/TAC ORD/FREE IDEA/COMP NAT/G

S52
EISENSTADT S.N.,"THE PROCESS OF ABSORPTION OF NEW IMMIGRANTS IN ISRAEL" (BMR)" ISRAEL CULTURE SCHOOL WORKER PARTIC DRIVE ORD/FREE...STAT OBS INT CHARTS SOC/INTEG 20 JEWS. PAGE 45 H0900
HABITAT ATTIT SAMP

B53
LEITES N.,A STUDY OF BOLSHEVISM. ELITES STRATA INT/ORG LOC/G POL/PAR WORKER EDU/PROP REV TOTALISM UTOPIA PWR...CONCPT 20 BOLSHEVISM. PAGE 94 H1870
MARXISM PLAN COM

S53
DRUCKER P.F.,"THE EMPLOYEE SOCIETY." STRUCT BAL/PWR PARTIC REPRESENT PWR...DECISION CONCPT. PAGE 42 H0849
LABOR MGT WORKER CULTURE

S53
ROGOFF N.,"SOCIAL STRATIFICATION IN FRANCE AND IN THE UNITED STATES" (BMR)" FRANCE USA+45 WORKER ADJUST PERSON...SOC 20. PAGE 133 H2662
STRUCT STRATA ATTIT NAT/COMP

C53
KRACKE E.A. JR.,"CIVIL SERVICE IN EARLY SUNG CHINA, 960-1067." ASIA GP/REL...BIBLIOG/A 10/11. PAGE 88 H1762
ADMIN NAT/G WORKER CONTROL

B54
LENIN V.I.,SELECTED WORKS (12 VOLS.). USSR INTELL SOCIETY STRATA STRUCT NAT/G POL/PAR WORKER CAP/ISM REV WAR...MARXIST PHIL/SCI 20 MARX/KARL LENIN/VI. PAGE 94 H1880
COM MARXISM

C54
GUINS G.C.,"SOVIET LAW AND SOVIET SOCIETY." COM USSR STRATA FAM NAT/G WORKER DOMIN RACE/REL ...BIBLIOG 20. PAGE 62 H1249
LAW STRUCT PLAN

B55
COLE G.D.H.,STUDIES IN CLASS STRUCTURE. UK NAT/G WORKER TEC/DEV EDU/PROP...CLASSIF CHARTS 20. PAGE 31 H0623
STRUCT STRATA ELITES CONCPT

B55
MAYO H.B.,DEMOCRACY AND MARXISM. COM USSR STRATA NAT/G WORKER ECO/TAC REV MORAL...PHIL/SCI HIST/WRIT IDEA/COMP WORSHIP 20 MARX/KARL LENIN/VI STALIN/J TROTSKY/L. PAGE 105 H2108
MARXISM CAP/ISM

B55
WRONG D.H.,AMERICAN AND CANADIAN VIEWPOINTS. CANADA USA+45 CONSTN STRATA FAM SECT WORKER ECO/TAC EDU/PROP ADJUD MARRIAGE...IDEA/COMP 20. PAGE 171 H3424
DIPLOM ATTIT NAT/COMP CULTURE

B56
INTERNATIONAL AFRICAN INST,SOCIAL IMPLICATIONS OF INDUSTRIALIZATION AND URBANIZATION IN AFRICA SOUTH OF THE SAHARA. SOUTH/AFR INDUS LABOR MUNIC WORKER TEC/DEV...SOC OBS TREND ANTHOL 20. PAGE 77 H1549
AFR ECO/UNDEV ADJUST CULTURE

B56
VON BECKERATH E.,HANDWORTERBUCH DER SOCIALWISSENSCHAFTEN (II VOLS.). EUR+WWI GERMANY POL/PAR WORKER DIPLOM LEAD CHOOSE SUFF WEALTH...SOC 20. PAGE 163 H3263
BIBLIOG INT/TRADE NAT/G ECO/DEV

S56
BLAU P.M.,"SOCIAL MOBILITY AND INTERPERSONAL RELATIONS" (BMR)" UNIV CULTURE STRUCT WORKER ANOMIE ...SOC SOC/INTEG 19/20. PAGE 18 H0355
INGP/REL PERS/REL ORD/FREE STRATA

B57
NEUMARK S.D.,ECONOMIC INFLUENCES ON THE SOUTH AFRICAN FRONTIER, 1652-1836. SOUTH/AFR SEA AGRI NAT/G FORCES WORKER DIPLOM INT/TRADE PRICE DEMAND PRODUC...STAT CHARTS 17/19 FRONTIER. PAGE 117 H2341
COLONIAL ECO/UNDEV ECO/TAC MARKET

B58
DUNAYEVSKAYA R.,MARXISM AND FREEDOM: FROM 1776 UNTIL TODAY. COM USSR WORKER CAP/ISM DOMIN REV GP/REL TOTALISM ALL/VALS...MYTH BIOG IDEA/COMP 18/20 MARX/KARL LENIN/VI STALIN/J. PAGE 43 H0861
MARXISM CONCPT ORD/FREE

B58
JACOBSSON P.,SOME MONETARY PROBLEMS, INTERNATIONAL AND NATIONAL. WOR+45 WOR-45 ECO/DEV FORCES WORKER PROB/SOLV DIPLOM INT/TRADE...ANTHOL 20. PAGE 79 H1580
FINAN PLAN ECO/TAC NAT/COMP

B58
OGILVIE C.,THE KING'S GOVERNMENT AND THE COMMON LAW, 1471-1641. UK STRUCT NAT/G CHIEF LEGIS WORKER BAL/PWR GP/REL AUTHORIT 15/17 COMMON/LAW. PAGE 120 H2408
CONSTN ELITES DOMIN

B59
BRIGGS A.,CHARTIST STUDIES. UK LAW NAT/G WORKER EDU/PROP COERCE SUFF GP/REL ATTIT...ANTHOL 19. PAGE 21 H0416
INDUS STRATA LABOR POLICY

B59
KELF-COHEN R.,NATIONALISATION IN BRITAIN: THE END OF DOGMA. EUR+WWI UK NAT/G POL/PAR WORKER ECO/TAC PARL/PROC WEALTH SOCISM...GOV/COMP 20. PAGE 84 H1683
NEW/LIB ECO/DEV INDUS OWN

B59
ROSOLIO D.,TEN YEARS OF THE CIVIL SERVICE IN ISRAEL (1948-1958) (PAMPHLET). ISRAEL NAT/G RECEIVE 20. PAGE 134 H2685
ADMIN WORKER GOV/REL PAY

B59
STERNBERG F.,THE MILITARY AND INDUSTRIAL REVOLUTION OF OUR TIME. USA+45 USSR WOR+45 WORKER COMPUTER PLAN TEC/DEV NUC/PWR GP/REL...POLICY NAT/COMP 20. PAGE 149 H2981
DIPLOM FORCES INDUS CIVMIL/REL

B60
BANERJEE D.N.,OUR FUNDAMENTAL RIGHTS: THEIR NATURE AND EXTENT (AS JUDICIALLY DETERMINED). INDIA UK CULTURE STRATA NAT/G WORKER EDU/PROP CONTROL DISCRIM OWN...IDEA/COMP WORSHIP 20 REFORMERS COMMONWLTH. PAGE 10 H0207
CONSTN ORD/FREE LEGIS POLICY

B60
HAYEK F.A.,THE CONSTITUTION OF LIBERTY. UNIV LAW CONSTN WORKER TAX EDU/PROP ADMIN CT/SYS COERCE DISCRIM...IDEA/COMP 20. PAGE 68 H1369
ORD/FREE CHOOSE NAT/G CONCPT

B60
KERR C.,INDUSTRIALISM AND INDUSTRIAL MAN. CULTURE SOCIETY ECO/UNDEV NAT/G ADMIN PRODUC WEALTH ...PREDICT TREND NAT/COMP 19/20. PAGE 85 H1697
WORKER MGT ECO/DEV INDUS

B60
MACFARQUHAR R.,THE HUNDRED FLOWERS. ASIA NAT/G WORKER GP/REL ORD/FREE MARXISM 20 MAO. PAGE 100 H1991
DEBATE PRESS POL/PAR ATTIT

B60
MOORE W.E.,LABOR COMMITMENT AND SOCIAL CHANGE IN DEVELOPING AREAS. SOCIETY STRATA ECO/UNDEV MARKET VOL/ASSN WORKER AUTHORIT SKILL...MGT NAT/COMP SOC/INTEG 20. PAGE 113 H2250
LABOR ORD/FREE ATTIT INDUS

B60
NICHOLLS W.H.,SOUTHERN TRADITION AND REGIONAL PROGRESS. STRATA STRUCT SCHOOL WORKER PARTIC REGION RACE/REL CONSEN ATTIT...SOC METH/CNCPT 19/20 SOUTH/US TVA. PAGE 118 H2349
RIGID/FLEX CONSERVE AGRI CULTURE

B60
ROBERTSON D.,THE CONTROL OF INDUSTRY. UK MARKET LABOR WORKER PRICE CONTROL GP/REL COST DEMAND ORD/FREE WEALTH NEW/LIB SOCISM 20. PAGE 132 H2646
INDUS FINAN NAT/G ECO/DEV

B60
SLOTKIN J.S.,FROM FIELD TO FACTORY; NEW INDUSTRIAL EMPLOYEES. HABITAT...MGT NEW/IDEA NAT/COMP BIBLIOG SOC/INTEG 20. PAGE 145 H2901
INDUS LABOR CULTURE WORKER

B60
WEINER H.E.,BRITISH LABOR AND PUBLIC OWNERSHIP. UK SERV/IND LG/CO WORKER CONTROL OWN 20. PAGE 166 H3327
LABOR NAT/G INDUS ATTIT

B61
BURKS R.V.,THE DYNAMICS OF COMMUNISM IN EASTERN EUROPE. COM YUGOSLAVIA POL/PAR RACE/REL ISOLAT ...CORREL CON/ANAL CHARTS GP/COMP DICTIONARY 20 EUROPE/E SLAV/MACED. PAGE 24 H0489
MARXISM STRUCT WORKER REPRESENT

B61
CARROTHERS A.W.R.,LABOR ARBITRATION IN CANADA. CANADA LAW NAT/G CONSULT LEGIS WORKER ADJUD ADMIN CT/SYS 20. PAGE 27 H0542
LABOR MGT GP/REL BARGAIN

B61
HADDAD J.A.,REVOLUCAO CUBANA E REVOLUCAO BRASILEIRA. BRAZIL CUBA L/A+17C STRATA AGRI WORKER EDU/PROP REGION...POLICY NAT/COMP 20. PAGE 63 H1272
REV ORD/FREE DIPLOM ECO/UNDEV

B61
KEE R.,REFUGEE WORLD. AUSTRIA EUR+WWI GERMANY NEIGH EX/STRUC WORKER PROB/SOLV ECO/TAC RENT EDU/PROP INGP/REL COST LITERACY HABITAT 20 MIGRATION. PAGE 84 H1676
NAT/G GIVE WEALTH STRANGE

B61
LENIN V.I.,WHAT IS TO BE DONE? (1902). RUSSIA LABOR NAT/G POL/PAR WORKER CAP/ISM ECO/TAC ADMIN PARTIC ...MARXIST IDEA/COMP GEN/LAWS 19/20. PAGE 94 H1881
EDU/PROP PRESS MARXISM METH/COMP

B61
LEVIN L.A.,BIBLIOGRAFIIA BIBLIOGRAFII PROIZVEDENII K. MARKSA, F. ENGELSA, V.I. LENINA. COM USSR NAT/G POL/PAR WORKER LEAD REV ATTIT...POLICY IDEA/COMP 20 MARX/KARL LENIN/VI ENGELS. PAGE 95 H1899
BIBLIOG/A MARXISM MARXIST CONCPT

B61
LICHTHEIM G.,MARXISM. GERMANY SOCIETY WORKER CAP/ISM ECO/TAC NAT/LISM POPULISM...TIME/SEQ GOV/COMP NAT/COMP 18/20 COM/PARTY. PAGE 96 H1924
MARXISM SOCISM IDEA/COMP CULTURE

B61
SHARMA T.R.,THE WORKING OF STATE ENTERPRISES IN INDIA. INDIA DELIB/GP LEGIS WORKER BUDGET PRICE CONTROL GP/REL OWN ATTIT...MGT CHARTS 20. PAGE 142 H2851
NAT/G INDUS ADMIN SOCISM

B62
BRUMBERG A.,RUSSIA UNDER KHRUSHCHEV. FUT USSR SOCIETY ECO/DEV AGRI PERF/ART WORKER PWR...SOC ANTHOL 20 KHRUSH/N. PAGE 22 H0453
COM MARXISM NAT/G CHIEF

B62
DEBUYST F.,LAS CLASES SOCIALES EN AMERICA LATINA. L/A+17C SOCIETY STRUCT WORKER EDU/PROP RACE/REL ATTIT HABITAT ROLE...GEOG SOC NAT/COMP SOC/INTEG 20. PAGE 39 H0780
STRATA GP/REL WEALTH

B62
FATOUROS A.A.,GOVERNMENT GUARANTEES TO FOREIGN INVESTORS. WOR+45 ECO/UNDEV INDUS WORKER ADJUD ...NAT/COMP BIBLIOG TREATY. PAGE 49 H0975
NAT/G FINAN INT/TRADE ECO/DEV

B62
GALENSON W.,LABOR IN DEVELOPING COUNTRIES. BRAZIL INDONESIA ISRAEL PAKISTAN TURKEY AGRI INDUS WORKER PAY PRICE GP/REL WEALTH...MGT CHARTS METH/COMP NAT/COMP 20. PAGE 54 H1088
LABOR ECO/UNDEV BARGAIN POL/PAR

B62
HARRINGTON M.,THE OTHER AMERICA: POVERTY IN THE UNITED STATES. WORKER CREATE REPRESENT RACE/REL AGE/O DRIVE POLICY. PAGE 67 H1338
WEALTH WELF/ST INCOME CULTURE

B62
HUNTER G.,THE NEW SOCIETIES OF TROPICAL AFRICA. CULTURE INDUS KIN MUNIC WORKER INT/TRADE EDU/PROP ORD/FREE...INT TREND 20. PAGE 75 H1500
AFR GOV/COMP ECO/UNDEV SOCIETY

B62
INSTITUTE OF PUBLIC ADMIN,A SHORT HISTORY OF THE PUBLIC SERVICE IN IRELAND. IRELAND UK DIST/IND INGP/REL FEDERAL 13/20 CIVIL/SERV. PAGE 77 H1539
ADMIN WORKER GOV/REL NAT/G

B62
MEHNERT K.,SOVIET MAN AND HIS WORLD. COM USSR INTELL FAM WORKER PLAN EDU/PROP REV PRODUC MARXISM ...SOC TREND SOC/INTEG 20 LENIN/VI STALIN/J KHRUSH/N. PAGE 108 H2162
SOCIETY CULTURE ECO/DEV

B62
NEW ZEALAND COMM OF ST SERVICE,THE STATE SERVICES IN NEW ZEALAND. NEW/ZEALND CONSULT EX/STRUC ACT/RES ...BIBLIOG 20. PAGE 117 H2343
ADMIN WORKER TEC/DEV NAT/G

B62
SMITH M.G.,KINSHIP AND COMMUNITY IN CARRIACOU. WEST/IND STRATA AGRI FAM SECT WORKER MARRIAGE OWN HEREDITY WEALTH...SOC 18/20. PAGE 146 H2915
CULTURE HABITAT KIN STRUCT

B62
UMENDRAS H.,LES SOCIETESRFRANCAISES; BIBLIOGRAPHIES FRANCAISES DE SCIENCE SOCIALES (VOL. III). FRANCE SECT WORKER 20. PAGE 158 H3154
BIBLIOG/A AGRI MUNIC CULTURE

B62
WOODS H.D.,LABOUR POLICY AND LABOUR ECONOMICS IN CANADA. CANADA FUT NAT/G VOL/ASSN WORKER BARGAIN ECO/TAC PAY CONFER GP/REL 20. PAGE 170 H3409
LABOR POLICY INDUS ECO/DEV

B63
FIRST R.,SOUTH WEST AFRICA. SOUTH/AFR INT/ORG KIN NAT/G WORKER COLONIAL WAR...POLICY 20 UN TRUST/TERR AFRICA/SW. PAGE 50 H1006
DISCRIM ORD/FREE RACE/REL CONTROL

B63
FURTADO C.,THE ECONOMIC GROWTH OF BRAZIL: A SURVEY FROM COLONIAL TO MODERN TIMES. L/A+17C AGRI DIST/IND EXTR/IND INDUS WORKER COLONIAL RACE/REL OWN GOV/COMP. PAGE 54 H1082
ECO/UNDEV TEC/DEV LABOR DOMIN

B63
GORDON M.S.,THE ECONOMICS OF WELFARE POLICIES. INDUS LOC/G NAT/G LEGIS WORKER INCOME AGE/O SKILL WEALTH...METH/COMP NAT/COMP 20. PAGE 59 H1180
METH/CNCPT ECO/TAC POLICY

B63
LAVROFF D.-G.,LES LIBERTES PUBLIQUES EN UNION SOVIETIQUE (REV. ED.). USSR NAT/G WORKER SANCTION CRIME MARXISM NEW/LIB...JURID BIBLIOG WORSHIP 20. PAGE 92 H1843
ORD/FREE LAW ATTIT COM

B63
LETHBRIDGE H.J.,THE PEASANT AND THE COMMUNES. CHINA/COM COM USSR NEIGH PROB/SOLV ADJUST EFFICIENCY...POLICY METH/COMP NAT/COMP 20. PAGE 95 H1894
MARXISM ECO/TAC AGRI WORKER

B63
MARX K.,THE POVERTY OF PHILOSOPHY (1847). SOCIETY STRATA INDUS WORKER OWN UTOPIA SOCISM...GEN/LAWS MARX/KARL. PAGE 104 H2082
MARXIST PRODUC

B63
MILLER W.J.,THE MEANING OF COMMUNISM. USSR SOCIETY ECO/DEV EX/STRUC WORKER TEC/DEV ADMIN TOTALISM
MARXISM TRADIT

...POLICY CONCPT CHARTS BIBLIOG T 20 COLD/WAR LENIN/VI STALIN/J. PAGE 111 H2215 DIPLOM NAT/G B63

MONTAGUE J.B. JR.,CLASS AND NATIONALITY; ENGLISH AND AMERICAN STUDIES. UK USA+45 ELITES STRUCT WORKER ATTIT PWR...SOC CHARTS SOC/EXP 20. PAGE 112 H2243 STRATA NAT/LISM PERSON NAT/COMP B63

MOSELY P.E.,THE SOVIET UNION, 1922-1962: A FOREIGN AFFAIRS READER. ASIA POLAND USSR CULTURE INTELL AGRI POL/PAR WORKER INT/TRADE DOMIN WAR NAT/LISM MARXISM SOCISM 20 KHRUSH/N. PAGE 113 H2267 PWR POLICY DIPLOM B63

RUITENBEER H.M.,THE DILEMMA OF ORGANIZATIONAL SOCIETY. CULTURE ECO/DEV MUNIC SECT TEC/DEV EDU/PROP NAT/LISM ORD/FREE...NAT/COMP 20 RIESMAN/D WHYTE/WF MERTON/R MEAD/MARG JASPERS/K. PAGE 136 H2716 PERSON ROLE ADMIN WORKER B63

SELF P.,THE STATE AND THE FARMER. UK ECO/DEV MARKET WORKER PRICE CONTROL GP/REL...WELF/ST 20 DEPT/AGRI. PAGE 141 H2823 AGRI NAT/G ADMIN VOL/ASSN B63

SHANKS M.,THE LESSONS OF PUBLIC ENTERPRISE. UK LEGIS WORKER ECO/TAC ADMIN PARL/PROC GOV/REL ATTIT ...POLICY MGT METH/COMP NAT/COMP ANTHOL 20 PARLIAMENT. PAGE 142 H2840 SOCISM OWN NAT/G INDUS B63

STIFEL L.D.,THE TEXTILE INDUSTRY - A CASE STUDY OF INDUSTRIAL DEVELOPMENT IN THE PHILIPPINES (PAPER). PHILIPPINE WORKER CAP/ISM INT/TRADE TARIFFS RECEIVE PRICE ADMIN COST EFFICIENCY WEALTH...BIBLIOG 20. PAGE 149 H2986 S/ASIA ECO/UNDEV PROC/MFG NAT/G S63

NYE J.,"TANGANYIKA'S SELF-HELP." TANZANIA NAT/G GIVE COST EFFICIENCY NAT/LISM 20. PAGE 119 H2381 ECO/TAC POL/PAR ECO/UNDEV WORKER B64

BERNDT R.M.,THE WORLD OF THE FIRST AUSTRALIANS. S/ASIA ECO/UNDEV WORKER PROB/SOLV EFFICIENCY ROLE ...SOC MYTH WORSHIP AUSTRAL ABORIGINES. PAGE 16 H0311 CULTURE KIN STRUCT DRIVE B64

HARBISON F.H.,EDUCATION, MANPOWER, AND ECONOMIC GROWTH. WOR+45 ECO/DEV ECO/UNDEV ACADEM LABOR SCHOOL WORKER UTIL...IDEA/COMP NAT/COMP. PAGE 66 H1326 PLAN TEC/DEV EDU/PROP SKILL B64

HERSKOVITS M.J.,ECONOMIC TRANSITION IN AFRICA. FUT INT/ORG NAT/G WORKER PROB/SOLV TEC/DEV INT/TRADE EQUILIB INCOME...ANTHOL 20. PAGE 70 H1408 AFR ECO/UNDEV PLAN ADMIN B64

INTERNATIONAL LABOUR OFFICE,EMPLOYMENT AND ECONOMIC GROWTH. ECO/DEV ECO/UNDEV NAT/G PLAN DIPLOM INT/TRADE CONTROL INCOME PRODUC WEALTH...STAT NAT/COMP 20 ILO. PAGE 78 H1558 WORKER METH/COMP ECO/TAC OPTIMAL B64

JOHNSON J.J.,CONTINUITY AND CHANGE IN LATIN AMERICA. L/A+17C INTELL FORCES WORKER CIVMIL/REL CHINJAP. PAGE 81 H1623 ANTHOL CULTURE STRATA GP/COMP B64

JOSEPHSON E.,MAN ALONE: ALIENATION IN MODERN SOCIETY. WOR+45 ECO/DEV WORKER WAR LEISURE RACE/REL ANOMIE ATTIT PERCEPT PERSON ALL/VALS...ANTHOL 20. PAGE 82 H1636 STRANGE CULTURE SOCIETY ADJUST B64

MORGAN H.W.,AMERICAN SOCIALISM 1900-1960. USA+45 USA-45 INTELL AGRI LABOR WORKER BARGAIN ECO/TAC GP/REL RACE/REL 20 NEGRO MIGRATION GOLD/STAND. PAGE 113 H2254 SOCISM POL/PAR ECO/DEV STRATA B64

PARANJAPE H.K.,THE FLIGHT OF TECHNICAL PERSONNEL IN PUBLIC UNDERTAKINGS. INDIA PAY DEMAND HAPPINESS ORD/FREE...MGT QU 20 MIGRATION. PAGE 123 H2464 ADMIN NAT/G WORKER PLAN B64

REMAK J.,THE GENTLE CRITIC: THEODOR FONTANE AND GERMAN POLITICS, 1848-1898. GERMANY PRUSSIA CULTURE ELITES BAL/PWR DIPLOM WRITING GOV/REL...HUM BIOG 19 BISMARCK/O JUNKER FONTANE/T. PAGE 131 H2614 PERSON SOCIETY WORKER CHIEF B64

SOLOW R.M.,THE NATURE AND SOURCES OF UNEMPLOYMENT IN THE UNITED STATES (PAMPHLET). USA+45 INDUS LABOR TEC/DEV ECO/TAC SKILL WEALTH...TREND NAT/COMP 20. PAGE 147 H2930 ECO/DEV WORKER STAT PRODUC N64

KENYA MINISTRY ECO PLAN DEV,AFRICAN SOCIALISM AND ITS APPLICATION TO PLANNING IN KENYA (PAMPHLET). AFR AGRI INDUS WORKER TAX COLONIAL WEALTH 20. PAGE 85 H1691 NAT/G SOCISM PLAN ECO/UNDEV B65

ALEXANDER R.J.,ORGANIZED LABOR IN LATIN AMERICA. L/A+17C INT/ORG LEGIS WORKER TEC/DEV BARGAIN INT/TRADE REV...NAT/COMP BIBLIOG 20. PAGE 5 H0102 LABOR POL/PAR ECO/UNDEV POLICY B65

CAMPBELL G.A.,THE CIVIL SERVICE IN BRITAIN (2ND ED.). UK DELIB/GP FORCES WORKER CREATE PLAN ...POLICY AUD/VIS 19/20 CIVIL/SERV. PAGE 26 H0515 ADMIN LEGIS NAT/G FINAN B65

CHENG C.-Y.,SCIENTIFIC AND ENGINEERING MANPOWER IN COMMUNIST CHINA, 1949-1963. CHINA/COM USSR ELITES ECO/DEV R+D ACADEM LABOR NAT/G EDU/PROP CONTROL UTIL...POLICY BIBLIOG 20. PAGE 29 H0588 WORKER CONSULT MARXISM BIOG B65

COLLINS H.,KARL MARX AND THE BRITISH LABOR MOVEMENT, YEARS OF THE FIRST INTERNATIONAL. EUR+WWI MOD/EUR UK STRATA INDUS NAT/G POL/PAR SOCISM ...CONCPT 19/20 MARX/KARL. PAGE 32 H0633 MARXISM LABOR INT/ORG WORKER B65

GUERIN D.,SUR LE FASCISME: FASCISME ET GRAND CAPITAL (VOL. II). GERMANY ITALY SOCIETY STRATA AGRI WORKER 20. PAGE 62 H1245 FASCISM NAT/G TOTALISM EDU/PROP B65

HARBISON F.,MANPOWER AND EDUCATION. AFR CHINA/COM IRAN L/A+17C S/ASIA TEC/DEV ADJUST OPTIMAL SKILL ...ANTHOL 20. PAGE 66 H1325 ECO/UNDEV EDU/PROP WORKER NAT/COMP B65

HARRIS R.L.,POLITICAL ORGANIZATION OF THE MBEMBE NIGERIA. AFR NIGERIA SOCIETY AGRI SECT WORKER PAY ...SOC WORSHIP 20 MBEMBE. PAGE 67 H1345 STRUCT CHIEF CULTURE B65

KLEIN J.,SAMPLES FROM ENGLISH CULTURES (2 VOLS.). UK STRATA FAM NEIGH WORKER ETIQUET ISOLAT AGE/C AGE/A HABITAT RIGID/FLEX...NET/THEORY CHARTS 20. PAGE 87 H1732 CULTURE INGP/REL ATTIT SOC B65

KUPER H.,URBANIZATION AND MIGRATION IN WEST AFRICA. UPPER/VOLT CULTURE ECO/UNDEV WORKER REGION GOV/REL ...LING ANTHOL SOC/INTEG 20 AFRICA/W OSHOGBO MOSSI MIGRATION. PAGE 89 H1781 AFR HABITAT MUNIC GEOG B65

LAMBIRI I.,SOCIAL CHANGE IN A GREEK COUNTRY TOWN. GREECE FAM PROB/SOLV ROUTINE TASK LEISURE INGP/REL CONSEN ORD/FREE...SOC INT QU CHARTS 20. PAGE 90 H1803 INDUS WORKER CULTURE NEIGH B65

OBUKAR C.,THE MODERN AFRICAN. AGRI INDUS WORKER CAP/ISM EDU/PROP PARTIC RACE/REL NAT/LISM ALL/VALS MARXISM...SOC IDEA/COMP 20. PAGE 120 H2393 AFR ECO/UNDEV CULTURE SOVEREIGN B65

OECD,THE MEDITERRANEAN REGIONAL PROJECT: ITALY; EDUCATION AND DEVELOPMENT. ITALY SOCIETY STRATA FINAN NAT/G PROF/ORG WORKER PLAN PROB/SOLV ADMIN ...STAT CHARTS METH 20 OECD. PAGE 120 H2400 SCHOOL EDU/PROP ECO/UNDEV ACADEM B65

OECD,THE MEDITERRANEAN REGIONAL PROJECT: GREECE; EDUCATION AND DEVELOPMENT. FUT GREECE SOCIETY AGRI FINAN NAT/G PROF/ORG WORKER PLAN PROB/SOLV ADMIN DEMAND ATTIT 20 OECD. PAGE 120 H2401 EDU/PROP SCHOOL ACADEM ECO/UNDEV B65

OECD,THE MEDITERRANEAN REGIONAL PROJECT: SPAIN; EDUCATION AND DEVELOPMENT. FUT SPAIN STRATA FINAN NAT/G WORKER PLAN PROB/SOLV ADMIN COST...POLICY STAT CHARTS 20 OECD. PAGE 120 H2402 ECO/UNDEV EDU/PROP ACADEM SCHOOL B65

OGILVY-WEBB M.,THE GOVERNMENT EXPLAINS: A STUDY OF THE INFORMATION SERVICES. UK DELIB/GP LEGIS WORKER BUDGET DIPLOM 20. PAGE 121 H2409 EDU/PROP ATTIT NAT/G ADMIN B65

PANJABI K.L.,THE CIVIL SERVANT IN INDIA. INDIA UK NAT/G CONSULT EX/STRUC REGION GP/REL RACE/REL 20. PAGE 123 H2462 ADMIN WORKER BIOG COLONIAL B65

TILLY C.,MEASURING POLITICAL UPHEAVAL* RESEARCH MONOGRAPH NO. 19. FRANCE INDUS NAT/G FORCES WORKER ...GEOG RECORD EXHIBIT GEN/METH BIBLIOG INDEX. PAGE 155 H3095 CLASSIF QUANT COERCE REV S65

KINDLEBERGER C.P.,"MASS MIGRATION, THEN AND NOW." LAW ECO/DEV ECO/UNDEV INDUS LABOR INT/TRADE FEEDBACK REGION RIGID/FLEX...SOC NAT/COMP EEC. PAGE 86 H1714 EUR+WWI USA-45 WORKER IDEA/COMP B66

ADAMS J.C.,THE GOVERNMENT OF REPUBLICAN ITALY (2ND ED.). ITALY LOC/G POL/PAR DELIB/GP LEGIS WORKER ADMIN CT/SYS FASCISM...CHARTS BIBLIOG 20 PARLIAMENT. PAGE 3 H0064 NAT/G CHOOSE EX/STRUC CONSTN B66

BRODERSEN A.,THE SOVIET WORKER: LABOR AND GOVERNMENT IN SOVIET SOCIETY. USSR STRUCT INDUS LABOR PLAN PAY INGP/REL PRODUC...POLICY GEN/LAWS WORKER ROLE NAT/G

BIBLIOG 20 STALIN/J LENIN/VI BOLSHEVISM KHRUSH/N. PAGE 21 H0425
MARXISM

B66
BUKHARIN N.,THE ABC OF COMMUNISM: A POPULAR EXPLANATION OF THE PROGRAM OF THE COMMUNIST PARTY OF RUSSIA. USSR STRATA SECT FORCES WORKER CAP/ISM RECEIVE EDU/PROP NAT/LISM TOTALISM 20. PAGE 23 H0468
MARXISM CONCPT POLICY REV

B66
COLE G.D.H.,THE MEANING OF MARXISM. USSR WOR+45 STRATA STRUCT NAT/G WORKER COST FASCISM...IDEA/COMP 20. PAGE 31 H0625
MARXISM CONCPT HIST/WRIT CAP/ISM

B66
DOBB M.,SOVIET ECONOMIC DEVELOPMENT SINCE 1917. USSR ECO/DEV ECO/UNDEV LABOR NAT/G TEC/DEV ECO/TAC ROUTINE PRODUC MARXISM 20. PAGE 41 H0829
PLAN INDUS WORKER

B66
HINTON W.,FANSHEN: A DOCUMENTARY OF REVOLUTION IN A CHINESE VILLAGE. ASIA ELITES MUNIC NAT/G POL/PAR SECT WORKER LEAD WAR PRIVIL PWR 20 MAO. PAGE 71 H1422
MARXISM REV NEIGH OWN

B66
JACKSON G.D.,COMINTERN AND PEASANT IN EAST EUROPE 1919-1930. BULGARIA COM CZECHOSLVK EUR+WWI POLAND ROMANIA YUGOSLAVIA STRATA AGRI VOL/ASSN DIPLOM CONTROL CROWD WEALTH...POLICY NAT/COMP 20. PAGE 79 H1575
MARXISM ECO/UNDEV WORKER INT/ORG

B66
ROSS A.M.,INDUSTRIAL RELATIONS AND ECONOMIC DEVELOPMENT. POL/PAR LEGIS WORKER BARGAIN PRICE EXEC LOBBY INCOME PWR...DECISION ANTHOL BIBLIOG 20. PAGE 134 H2686
ECO/UNDEV LABOR NAT/G GP/REL

B67
DENISON E.F.,WHY GROWTH RATES DIFFER; POSTWAR EXPERIENCE IN NINE WESTERN COUNTRIES. WOR+45 FINAN WORKER TEC/DEV EDU/PROP PRICE PRODUC WEALTH ...ECOMETRIC STAT CHARTS BIBLIOG. PAGE 40 H0791
METH NAT/COMP ECO/DEV ECO/TAC

B67
HAWTREY R.,INCOMES AND MONEY. EUR+WWI FUT UK LABOR WORKER INT/TRADE TAX PAY BAL/PAY COST WEALTH 20. PAGE 68 H1363
FINAN NAT/G POLICY ECO/DEV

B67
HODGKINSON R.G.,THE ORIGINS OF THE NATIONAL HEALTH SERVICE: THE MEDICAL SERVICES OF THE NEW POOR LAW, 1834-1871. UK INDUS MUNIC WORKER PROB/SOLV EFFICIENCY ATTIT HEALTH WEALTH SOCISM...JURID SOC/WK 19/20. PAGE 72 H1445
HEAL NAT/G POLICY LAW

B67
JAIN R.K.,MANAGEMENT OF STATE ENTERPRISES. INDIA SOCIETY FINAN WORKER BUDGET ADMIN CONTROL OWN 20. PAGE 79 H1584
NAT/G SOCISM INDUS MGT

B67
MICKIEWICZ E.P.,SOVIET POLITICAL SCHOOLS: THE COMMUNIST PARTY ADULT INSTRUCTION SYSTEM. COM USSR INTELL SCHOOL WORKER CREATE PRESS ADMIN CONTROL ATTIT KNOWL...PROG/TEAC SOC/INTEG 20 COM/PARTY. PAGE 110 H2200
NAT/G EDU/PROP AGE/A MARXISM

B67
NASH M.,MACHINE AGE MAYA. GUATEMALA L/A+17C STRUCT AGRI WORKER CREATE INCOME ATTIT RIGID/FLEX ROLE ...IDEA/COMP SOC/EXP WORSHIP 20 INDIAN/AM. PAGE 116 H2315
INDUS CULTURE SOC MUNIC

B67
NESS G.D.,BUREAUCRACY AND RURAL DEVELOPMENT IN MALAYSIA. MALAYSIA UK SOCIETY FINAN INDUS WORKER TEC/DEV ECO/TAC COLONIAL EQUILIB ORD/FREE...STAT CHARTS 20. PAGE 117 H2330
ECO/UNDEV PLAN NAT/G ADMIN

B67
TOMPKINS S.R.,THE TRIUMPH OF BOLSHEVISM: REVOLUTION OR REACTION? USSR WORKER PRESS WEALTH MARXISM POPULISM...BIOG TREND IDEA/COMP BIBLIOG 19/20 LENIN/VI. PAGE 156 H3113
REV NAT/G POL/PAR NAT/LISM

L67
BERNSTEIN T.P.,"LEADERSHIP AND MASS MOBILIZATION IN THE SOVIET AND CHINESE COLLECTIVISATION CAMPAIGNS OF 1929-30, 1955-56: COMPARISON." CHINA/COM USSR WORKER CONTROL COERCE PRODUC ATTIT...NAT/COMP 20. PAGE 16 H0317
FEDERAL PLAN AGRI NAT/G

L67
PICKERING J.F.,"RECRUITMENT TO THE ADMINISTRATIVE CLASS, 1960-1964: PART 2" UK STRATA NAT/G WORKER ...STAT CHARTS 20. PAGE 125 H2505
PERS/COMP ADMIN KNO/TEST EDU/PROP

L67
TABORSKY E.,"THE COMMUNIST PARTIES OF THE 'THIRD WORLD' IN SOVIET STRATEGY." AFR ASIA L/A+17C USSR INTELL NAT/G WORKER PLAN CONTROL LEAD PARTIC REV ...GOV/COMP 20 COM/PARTY THIRD/WRLD. PAGE 152 H3032
POL/PAR MARXISM ECO/UNDEV DIPLOM

L67
UNESCO,"APARTHEID." SOUTH/AFR STRUCT KIN SCHOOL SECT WORKER DOMIN EDU/PROP REGION RACE/REL ISOLAT 20. PAGE 158 H3164
DISCRIM CULTURE COERCE COLONIAL

S67
ADNITT F.W.,"THE RISE OF ENGLISH RADICALISM -- PART 2." UK NAT/G WORKER INCOME WEALTH...BIOG 19 PARLIAMENT. PAGE 4 H0071
LEGIS LOBBY

S67
CAMERON R.,"SOME LESSONS OF HISTORY FOR DEVELOPING NATIONS." WOR+45 WOR-45 FINAN NAT/G WORKER EDU/PROP PARTIC ROLE...DECISION METH/COMP 18/20. PAGE 25 H0511
ECO/UNDEV NAT/COMP POLICY CONCPT

S67
CARIAS B.,"EL CONTROL DE LAS EMPRESAS PUBLICAS POR GRUPOS DE INTERESES DE LA COMUNIDAD." FRANCE UK VENEZUELA INDUS NAT/G CONTROL OWN PWR...DECISION NAT/COMP 20. PAGE 26 H0529
WORKER REPRESENT MGT SOCISM

S67
CHU-YUAN CHENG,"THE CULTURAL REVOLUTION AND CHINA'S ECONOMY." CHINA/COM AGRI DIST/IND INDUS MARKET NAT/G WORKER PLAN INT/TRADE DOMIN DEMAND PRODUC ...CHARTS 20 MAO. PAGE 30 H0600
ECO/DEV ECO/TAC REV SOCISM

S67
DENISON E.F.,"SOURCES OF GROWTH IN NINE WESTERN COUNTRIES." WORKER TEC/DEV COST PRODUC...TREND NAT/COMP. PAGE 39 H0790
INCOME NAT/G EUR+WWI ECO/DEV

S67
DEWHURST A.,"THE WAGE MOVEMENT IN CANADA." CANADA AGRI NAT/G PARTIC COST PRODUC PROFIT 20. PAGE 41 H0811
WORKER MARXIST INDUS LABOR

S67
JENCKS C.E.,"SOCIAL STATUS OF COAL MINERS IN BRITAIN SINCE NATIONALIZATION." UK STRATA STRUCT LABOR RECEIVE GP/REL INCOME OWN ATTIT HABITAT...MGT T 20. PAGE 80 H1600
EXTR/IND WORKER CONTROL NAT/G

S67
KRISTOF L.K.D.,"THE STATE-IDEA, THE NATIONAL IDEA AND THE IMAGE OF THE FATHERLAND." CONSTN CULTURE INTELL SOCIETY WORKER TASK DRIVE HABITAT...MYTH GOV/COMP IDEA/COMP. PAGE 89 H1769
GEOG CONCPT NAT/G PERCEPT

S67
LEVCIK B.,"WAGES AND EMPLOYMENT PROBLEMS IN THE NEW SYSTEM OF PLANNED MANAGEMENT IN CZECHOSLOVAKIA." CZECHOSLVK EUR+WWI NAT/G OP/RES PLAN ADMIN ROUTINE INGP/REL CENTRAL EFFICIENCY PRODUC DECISION. PAGE 95 H1895
MARXISM WORKER MGT PAY

S67
MARWICK A.,"THE LABOUR PARTY AND THE WELFARE STATE IN BRITAIN, 19001948." UK SOCIETY STRUCT ECO/DEV WORKER CREATE PRICE CHOOSE WEALTH NEW/LIB SOCISM ...POLICY HEAL 20 PARLIAMENT LABOR/PAR. PAGE 104 H2074
POL/PAR RECEIVE LEGIS NAT/G

S67
NEALE R.S.,"WORKING CLASS WOMEN AND WOMEN'S SUFFRAGE." UK LAW CONSTN LABOR NAT/G DELIB/GP LEGIS WORKER PAY PARTIC CHOOSE 19 FEMALE/SEX. PAGE 116 H2326
STRATA SEX SUFF DISCRIM

S67
PAK H.,"CHINA'S MILITIA AND MAO TSE-TUNG'S 'PEOPLE'S WAR'." CHINA/COM SOCIETY POL/PAR EX/STRUC PROB/SOLV PARTIC COERCE WAR CIVMIL/REL ATTIT DRIVE MARXISM...METH/COMP 20 MAO. PAGE 122 H2447
FORCES NAT/G WORKER CHIEF

S67
PONOMARYOV B.,"THE OCTOBER REVOLUTION - BEGINNING OF THE EPOCH OF SOCIALISM AND COMMUNISM." COM FUT USSR WOR+45 SOCIETY STRATA CHIEF CREATE DIPLOM ECO/TAC EDU/PROP SOCISM...NAT/COMP 20. PAGE 127 H2542
MARXIST WORKER INT/ORG POLICY

S67
SCHACHTER G.,"REGIONAL DEVELOPMENT IN THE ITALIAN DUAL ECONOMY" ITALY AGRI INDUS MARKET WORKER ECO/TAC CONTROL INCOME PRODUC 20. PAGE 138 H2767
REGION ECO/UNDEV NAT/G PROB/SOLV

S67
SMITH J.E.,"RED PRUSSIANISM OF THE GERMAN DEMOCRATIC REPUBLIC." GERMANY/E INTELL TOP/EX WORKER PLAN DIPLOM PRODUC ATTIT WEALTH MARXISM. PAGE 146 H2912
NAT/G TOTALISM INDUS NAT/LISM

S67
SOARES G.,"SOCIO-ECONOMIC VARIABLES AND VOTING FOR THE RADICAL LEFT: CHILE 1952." CHILE INDUS NAT/G WORKER ADJUST STRANGE ANOMIE WEALTH...METH/CNCPT CORREL 20. PAGE 146 H2925
STRATA POL/PAR CHOOSE STAT

S67
THEROUX P.,"HATING THE ASIANS." TANZANIA UGANDA CONSTN INDUS NAT/G POL/PAR WORKER ECO/TAC HABITAT LOVE...POLICY GEOG 20 MIGRATION. PAGE 154 H3069
AFR RACE/REL SOVEREIGN ATTIT

S67
THIEN T.T.,"VIETNAM: A CASE OF SOCIAL ALIENATION." VIETNAM AGRI FORCES FOR/AID ADMIN REPRESENT INGP/REL PWR 19/20. PAGE 154 H3071
NAT/G ELITES WORKER STRANGE

S67
TIKHOMIROV I.A.,"DIVISION OF POWERS OR DIVISION OF LABOR?" USSR NAT/G DELIB/GP ADJUD GP/REL MARXISM SOCISM 20. PAGE 155 H3093
BAL/PWR WORKER STRATA

ADMIN

S67
VON LAUE T.H.,"WESTERNIZATION, REVOLUTION AND THE SEARCH FOR A BASIS OF AUTHORITY - RUSSIA IN 1917." USSR ELITES INTELL ECO/UNDEV NAT/G WORKER ECO/TAC TAX ADMIN LEAD AUTHORIT 20 LENIN/VI. PAGE 164 H3274
MARXISM REV COM DOMIN

S67
WILLIAMS P.M.,"THE FRENCH GENERAL ELECTION OF MARCH 1967." FRANCE INDUS WORKER NAT/LISM PWR SOCISM 20. PAGE 168 H3368
POL/PAR NAT/G ATTIT CHOOSE

B68
PROUDHON J.P.,IDEE GENERALE DE LA REVOLUTION AU XIXE SIECLE (1851). FRANCE UNIV NAT/G CREATE AGREE UTOPIA ORD/FREE...ANARCH 19. PAGE 128 H2563
REV SOCIETY WORKER LABOR

S68
DOUGLAS-HOME C.,"A MISTAKEN POLICY IN ADEN." YEMEN CULTURE ECO/UNDEV INDUS FORCES WORKER DIPLOM ECO/TAC CONTROL 20 ADEN. PAGE 42 H0842
SOVEREIGN COLONIAL POLICY REGION

B76
SMITH A.,THE WEALTH OF NATIONS. UK STRUCT WORKER DIPLOM ECO/TAC OPTIMAL DRIVE PERSON ORD/FREE ...OLD/LIB GEN/LAWS 17/18. PAGE 145 H2905
WEALTH PRODUC INDUS LAISSEZ

B99
LECKY W.E.H.,DEMOCRACY AND LIBERTY (2 VOLS.). LAW CONSTN STRATA POL/PAR SECT WORKER DIPLOM ADJUD REPRESENT NAT/LISM CONSERVE. PAGE 93 H1851
LEGIS NAT/G POPULISM ORD/FREE

WORKING....SEE ROUTINE

WORLD COUNCIL OF CHURCHES....SEE WCC

WORLD HEALTH ORGANIZATION....SEE WHO

WORLD WAR I....SEE WWI

WORLD WAR II....SEE WWII

WORLD/BANK....WORLD BANK

WORLD/CONG....WORLD CONGRESS

WORLD/CT....WORLD COURT; SEE ALSO ICJ

WORLDUNITY....WORLD UNITY, WORLD FEDERATION (EXCLUDING UN AND LEAGUE OF NATIONS)

B17
VEBLEN T.B.,AN INQUIRY INTO THE NATURE OF PEACE AND THE TERMS OF ITS PERPETUATION. UNIV STRATA FINAN EDU/PROP PRICE COST DISCRIM NAT/LISM MORAL ORD/FREE PACIFIST 20 WORLDUNITY. PAGE 162 H3237
PEACE DIPLOM WAR NAT/G

WORLEY P. H3411

WORMUTH F.D. H3412

WORSHIP....SEE ALSO SECT

N
EUROPA PUBLICATIONS LIMITED,THE EUROPA YEAR BOOK. CONSTN FINAN INDUS POL/PAR DIPLOM TV CT/SYS...STAT BIOG CHARTS WORSHIP 20. PAGE 47 H0949
BIBLIOG NAT/G PRESS INT/ORG

B03
FAGUET E.,LE LIBERALISME. FRANCE PRESS ADJUD ADMIN DISCRIM CONSERVE SOCISM...TRADIT SOC LING WORSHIP PARLIAMENT. PAGE 48 H0960
ORD/FREE EDU/PROP NAT/G LAW

B04
REED W.A.,ETHNOLOGICAL SURVEY PUBLICATIONS (VOL. II). PHILIPPINE STRUCT INDUS SECT DEATH LEISURE HABITAT...AUD/VIS CHARTS WORSHIP 20 NABOLOI NEGRITO BATAK. PAGE 130 H2607
CULTURE SOCIETY SOC OBS

B05
PHILIPPINE ISLANDS BUREAU SCI,ETHNOLOGICAL SURVEY: THE BONTOC IGOROT. ECO/UNDEV AGRI FAM MARRIAGE HEALTH WEALTH...LING OBS AUD/VIS CHARTS WORSHIP 20 LUZON BONTOC. PAGE 125 H2500
CULTURE INGP/REL KIN STRUCT

S21
MALINOWSKI B.,"THE PRIMITIVE ECONOMICS OF THE TROBRIAND ISLANDERS" (BMR)" CULTURE SOCIETY NAT/G CHIEF LEAD OWN...SOC MYTH WORSHIP 20 NEW/GUINEA TROBRIAND RESOURCE/N. PAGE 101 H2029
ECO/UNDEV AGRI PRODUC STRUCT

B23
WILLOUGHBY W.C.,RACE PROBLEMS IN THE NEW AFRICA: A STUDY OF THE RELATION OF BANTU AND BRITONS IN THOSE PARTS OF BANTU AFRICA... AFR STRUCT SECT DOMIN EDU/PROP GP/REL ATTIT WORSHIP 20 BANTU EUROPE MISSION CHRISTIAN. PAGE 168 H3372
KIN COLONIAL RACE/REL CULTURE

B24
WALKER F.D.,AFRICA AND HER PEOPLES. ISLAM STRUCT FAM SECT EDU/PROP INGP/REL RACE/REL HABITAT...GEOG SOC IDEA/COMP WORSHIP 20 NEGRO. PAGE 164 H3292
CULTURE AFR GP/COMP KIN

B26
SMITH T.V.,THE DEMOCRATIC WAY OF LIFE. UNIV SOCIETY NAT/G WORKER TASK CHOOSE ALL/VALS...IDEA/COMP WORSHIP. PAGE 146 H2919
MAJORIT CONCPT ORD/FREE LEAD

C34
BENEDICT R.,"RITUAL" IN ERA SELIGMAN, ENCYCLOPEDIA OF THE SOCIAL SCIENCES." GP/REL...SOC STYLE IDEA/COMP WORSHIP. PAGE 14 H0279
CULTURE ROUTINE ROLE STRUCT

B35
GORER G.,AFRICA DANCES: A BOOK ABOUT WEST AFRICAN NEGROES. STRUCT LOC/G SECT FORCES TAX ADMIN COLONIAL...ART/METH MYTH WORSHIP 20 NEGRO AFRICA/W CHRISTIAN RITUAL. PAGE 59 H1181
AFR ATTIT CULTURE SOCIETY

B36
PREVITE-ORTON C.W.,THE CAMBRIDGE MEDIEVAL HISTORY (8 VOLS.). CHRIST-17C NAT/G PROB/SOLV TEC/DEV LEAD ...POLICY CONCPT WORSHIP. PAGE 128 H2559
BIBLIOG IDEA/COMP TREND

B38
RAWLINSON H.G.,INDIA: A SHORT CULTURAL HISTORY. INDIA LAW STRATA FORCES INT/TRADE ADMIN COLONIAL PERSON...GEOG HUM BIBLIOG WORSHIP 20. PAGE 130 H2598
CULTURE SECT MYTH ART/METH

B39
AKIGA,AKIGA'S STORY: THE TIV TRIBE AS SEEN BY ONE OF ITS MEMBERS. NIGERIA LAW STRUCT ECO/UNDEV FAM LEAD GP/REL MARRIAGE...LING WORSHIP 20. PAGE 4 H0089
KIN SECT SOC CULTURE

B39
FIRTH R.,PRIMITIVE POLYNESIAN ECONOMY. SOCIETY DIST/IND SECT CHIEF CAP/ISM PRODUC WEALTH...SOC OBS METH WORSHIP 20 POLYNESIA. PAGE 50 H1007
ECO/UNDEV CULTURE AGRI ECO/TAC

B39
MILLER P.,THE NEW ENGLAND MIND: THE SEVENTEENTH CENTURY. CULTURE DOMIN WRITING INGP/REL CONSEN MAJORITY PERCEPT KNOWL MORAL...CONCPT LING WORSHIP 17 NEW/ENGLND PROTESTANT. PAGE 111 H2214
SECT REGION SOC ATTIT

B40
ZWEIG F.,THE WORKER IN AN AFFLUENT SOCIETY: FAMILY LIFE AND INDUSTRY. UK STRATA LG/CO ECO/TAC LEISURE INGP/REL HAPPINESS HEALTH...PSY SOC/WK INT CHARTS WORSHIP 20 FEMALE/SEX. PAGE 173 H3465
MARRIAGE ATTIT FINAN CULTURE

S40
GURVITCH G.,"MAJOR PROBLEMS OF THE SOCIOLOGY OF LAW." CULTURE SANCTION KNOWL MORAL...POLICY EPIST JURID WORSHIP. PAGE 63 H1255
SOC LAW PHIL/SCI

B43
MARITAIN J.,THE RIGHTS OF MAN AND NATURAL LAW. CONSTN NAT/G DOMIN LEGIT INGP/REL TOTALISM MORAL POPULISM WORSHIP 19/20 CIVIL/LIB CHURCH/STA NATURL/LAW. PAGE 103 H2051
PLURIST ORD/FREE GEN/LAWS

B44
SUAREZ F.,A TREATISE ON LAWS AND GOD THE LAWGIVER (1612) IN SELECTIONS FROM THREE WORKS, VOL. II. FRANCE ITALY UK CULTURE NAT/G SECT CHIEF LEGIS DOMIN LEGIT CT/SYS ORD/FREE PWR WORSHIP 16/17. PAGE 150 H3004
LAW JURID GEN/LAWS CATH

C45
PAINE T.,"THE AGE OF REASON IN T. PAINE, THE COMPLETE WRITINGS OF THOMAS PAINE (VOL. 1) (1794-95)" CULTURE ACT/RES DOMIN UTOPIA ATTIT PERCEPT WORSHIP. PAGE 122 H2445
SECT KNOWL PHIL/SCI ORD/FREE

B47
JURJI E.J.,THE GREAT RELIGIONS OF THE MODERN WORLD. CULTURE INTELL SOCIETY INT/ORG CONSULT CHOOSE ATTIT DRIVE PERSON RIGID/FLEX...HUM CONCPT OBS BIOG HIST/WRIT TREND GEN/LAWS 20 WORSHIP. PAGE 82 H1643
UNIV SECT

B48
EDUARDO O.D.C.,THE NEGRO IN NORTHERN BRAZIL: A STUDY IN ACCULTURATION. BRAZIL ECO/UNDEV FAM SECT PAY REGION HABITAT CATHISM MYSTISM...GEOG OBS SOC/INTEG WORSHIP 20 NEGRO MARANHAO. PAGE 44 H0890
CULTURE ADJUST GP/REL

B48
MAUGHAM R.,NORTH AFRICAN NOTEBOOK. ALGERIA ISLAM LIBYA MOROCCO STRUCT ECO/UNDEV COLONIAL...SOC OBS AUD/VIS NAT/COMP WORSHIP 20 TUNIS. PAGE 105 H2102
SOCIETY RECORD NAT/LISM

B48
TOYNBEE A.J.,CIVILIZATION ON TRIAL. FUT WOR-45 NAT/G CREATE CAP/ISM DIPLOM NUC/PWR CHOOSE MARXISM ...GEOG CONCPT WORSHIP. PAGE 156 H3125
SOCIETY TIME/SEQ NAT/COMP

B50
EMBREE J.F.,BIBLIOGRAPHY OF THE PEOPLES AND CULTURES OF MAINLAND SOUTHEAST ASIA. CAMBODIA LAOS THAILAND VIETNAM LAW...GEOG HUM SOC MYTH LING CHARTS WORSHIP 20. PAGE 46 H0915
BIBLIOG/A CULTURE S/ASIA

B50
HARLEY G.W.,MASKS AS AGENTS OF SOCIAL CONTROL IN NORTHEAST LIBERIA. AFR LIBERIA LAW CULTURE ADJUST CONSEN MORAL...GEOG SOC WORSHIP 20. PAGE 66 H1332
CONTROL ECO/UNDEV SECT CHIEF

B50
HOOKER R.,OF THE LAWS OF ECCLESIASTICAL POLITY (1594) (ABR. BY J. S. MARSHALL). UK UNIV CHIEF PARTIC MORAL...JURID GEN/LAWS WORSHIP 16. PAGE 73 H1463
SECT CONCPT LAW NAT/G

B50
ROHEIM G.,PSYCHOANALYSIS AND ANTHROPOLOGY. UNIV FAM PERS/REL ATTIT HABITAT...SOC OBS WORSHIP. PAGE 133 H2663
PSY BIOG CULTURE PERSON

B51
BERNATZIK H.A.,THE SPIRITS OF THE YELLOW LEAVES. BURMA LAOS S/ASIA THAILAND VIETNAM SOCIETY AGRI COLONIAL LEISURE GP/REL PERS/REL ISOLAT AGE HABITAT SEX WORSHIP 20. PAGE 16 H0310
SOC KIN ECO/UNDEV CULTURE

B51
INTERNATIONAL AFRICAN INST,ETHNOGRAPHIC SURVEY OF AFRICA: WEST CENTRAL AFRICA (VOLS. I-III, 1951-1953). AFR RHODESIA CULTURE ECO/UNDEV HEREDITY ...GEOG SOC CHARTS BIBLIOG WORSHIP 20 CONGO/LEOP. PAGE 77 H1543
STRUCT KIN INGP/REL HABITAT

B52
INTFRNATIONAL AFRICAN INST,ETHNOGRAPHIC SURVEY OF AFRICA: SOUTHERN AFRICA (VOLS. I-III, 1952-1954). AFR SOUTH/AFR CULTURE ECO/UNDEV GOV/REL HEREDITY ...GEOG SOC CHARTS BIBLIOG WORSHIP 20. PAGE 77 H1544
STRUCT KIN INGP/REL HABITAT

B52
TAX S.,HERITAGE OF CONQUEST. L/A+17C ECO/UNDEV LOC/G WEALTH...POLICY ANTHOL WORSHIP 20 MEXIC/AMER CENTRAL/AM. PAGE 153 H3052
PHIL/SCI CULTURE SOCIETY

B54
FORDE C.D.,AFRICAN WORLDS. AFR CULTURE ROUTINE GP/REL PERS/REL ATTIT DRIVE ALL/VALS...OBS ANTHOL WORSHIP 20. PAGE 52 H1036
SOCIETY KIN SOC

B54
MALINOWSKI B.,MAGIC, SCIENCE AND RELIGION. AGRI KIN GP/REL ALL/VALS...MYTH OBS RECORD IDEA/COMP WORSHIP 20 NEW/GUINEA. PAGE 102 H2031
CULTURE ATTIT SOC

B54
PARRINDER G.,AFRICAN TRADITIONAL RELIGION. AFR SOCIETY EDU/PROP GP/REL PWR...SOC CONCPT IDEA/COMP WORSHIP 20 DEITY. PAGE 124 H2469
SECT MYTH ATTIT CULTURE

B54
TITIEV M.,THE SCIENCE OF MAN. LAW STRATA KIN GP/REL PERS/REL HABITAT HEREDITY KNOWL...LING CHARTS BIBLIOG WORSHIP. PAGE 155 H3107
SOC PSY CULTURE

B55
INTERNATIONAL AFRICAN INST,ETHNOGRAPHIC SURVEY OF AFRICA: NORTH EASTERN AFRICA (VOLUMES 1-2, 1955-56). AFR ETHIOPIA CULTURE ECO/UNDEV KIN GOV/REL ATTIT HEREDITY...GEOG CHARTS BIBLIOG WORSHIP 20. PAGE 77 H1545
STRUCT ECO/TAC INGP/REL HABITAT

B55
INTERNATIONAL AFRICAN INST,ETHNOGRAPHIC SURVEY OF AFRICA: WESTERN AFRICA: PEOPLES OF THE NIGER-BENUE CONFLUENCE. AFR NIGER CULTURE ECO/UNDEV KIN GOV/REL GP/REL ATTIT HEREDITY...CHARTS BIBLIOG WORSHIP 20. PAGE 77 H1546
STRUCT GEOG HABITAT INGP/REL

B55
MAYO H.B.,DEMOCRACY AND MARXISM. COM USSR STRATA NAT/G WORKER ECO/TAC REV MORAL...PHIL/SCI HIST/WRIT IDEA/COMP WORSHIP 20 MARX/KARL LENIN/VI STALIN/J TROTSKY/L. PAGE 105 H2108
MARXISM CAP/ISM

B55
MID-EUROPEAN LAW PROJECT,CHURCH AND STATE BEHIND THE IRON CURTAIN. COM CZECHOSLVK HUNGARY POLAND USSR CULTURE SECT EDU/PROP GOV/REL CATHISM...CHARTS ANTHOL BIBLIOG WORSHIP 20 CHURCH/STA. PAGE 110 H2202
LAW MARXISM POLICY

B55
RODNICK D.,THE NORWEGIANS: A STUDY IN NATIONAL CULTURE. NORWAY FAM INGP/REL PERS/REL AGE...PSY SOC SELF/OBS WORSHIP 20. PAGE 133 H2655
CULTURE INT RECORD ATTIT

C55
OLIVER D.L.,"A LEADER IN ACTION," IN D. A. OLIVER, SOLOMON ISLAND SOCIETY." S/ASIA SOCIETY STRUCT CONTROL TASK PWR...OBS/ENVIR WORSHIP 20. PAGE 121 H2413
LEAD RESPECT CULTURE KIN

B56
CEPEDA U.A.,EN TORNO AL CONCEPTO DEL ESTADO EN LOS REYES CATHOLICOS. SPAIN SOCIETY STRUCT SECT LEGIT WAR ATTIT WORSHIP 15/17. PAGE 28 H0569
NAT/G PHIL/SCI CHIEF PWR

B56
EVANS-PRITCHARD E.E.,THE INSTITUTIONS OF PRIMITIVE SOCIETY. LAW SOCIETY KIN ACT/RES CREATE ALL/VALS ...ART/METH SOC METH/CNCPT WORSHIP 20. PAGE 48 H0953
STRUCT PHIL/SCI CULTURE CONCPT

B56
GLUCKMAN M.,CUSTOM AND CONFLICT IN AFRICA. AFR FAM KIN NAT/G DOMIN DISCRIM DRIVE MORAL PWR...SOC BIBLIOG WORSHIP 20. PAGE 57 H1145
CULTURE CREATE PERS/REL GP/COMP

B56
LEVIN M.G.,THE PEOPLES OF SIBERIA. PREHIST ECO/UNDEV KIN SECT HABITAT...CLASSIF AUD/VIS WORSHIP 20 SIBERIA. PAGE 95 H1900
CULTURE SOCIETY ASIA

B56
MUMFORD L.,THE TRANSFORMATIONS OF MAN. UNIV CULTURE INGP/REL HABITAT HEREDITY ALL/VALS ORD/FREE...MYTH TIME/SEQ TREND WORSHIP. PAGE 114 H2287
IDEA/COMP PERSON CONCPT

B57
INTERNATIONAL AFRICAN INST,ETHNOGRAPHIC SURVEY OF AFRICA: WESTERN AFRICA: THE BENIN KINGDOM. AFR NIGERIA CULTURE ECO/UNDEV KIN ECO/TAC GOV/REL AGE ATTIT HEREDITY...CHARTS BIBLIOG WORSHIP 20. PAGE 77 H1550
STRUCT INGP/REL GEOG HABITAT

B57
INTERNATIONAL AFRICAN INST,ETHNOGRAPHIC SURVEY OF AFRICA: WESTERN AFRICA: THE WOLOF OF SENEGAMBIA. AFR SENEGAL CULTURE ECO/UNDEV FAM KIN REGION ...CHARTS GP/COMP BIBLIOG WORSHIP 20. PAGE 78 H1551
STRUCT GEOG HABITAT INGP/REL

B57
NARAIN D.,HINDU CHARACTER (A FEW GLIMPSES). INDIA DIPLOM SUICIDE PERS/REL ATTIT...PSY NAT/COMP PERS/COMP BIBLIOG WORSHIP 20 HINDU. PAGE 116 H2310
PERSON STERTYP SUPEGO SECT

B57
TAYLOR J.V.,CHRISTIANITY AND POLITICS IN AFRICA. AFR CONTROL PARTIC GP/REL RACE/REL ATTIT...POLICY BIBLIOG/A WORSHIP 20. PAGE 153 H3055
SECT NAT/G NAT/LISM

B59
KITTLER G.D.,EQUATORIAL AFRICA: THE NEW WORLD OF TOMORROW. CENTRL/AFR INDUS KIN SECT CHIEF EDU/PROP CHOOSE HEALTH...GEOG WORSHIP 20. PAGE 87 H1730
RACE/REL AFR ECO/UNDEV CULTURE

B59
LEE D.,FREEDOM AND CULTURE. WOR+45 WOR-45 FAM HABITAT PERSON LOVE MORAL...PSY SOC OBS NAT/COMP WORSHIP 20. PAGE 93 H1856
CULTURE SOCIETY CONCPT INGP/REL

B59
SISSONS C.B.,CHURCH AND STATE IN CANADIAN EDUCATION: AN HISTORICAL STUDY. CANADA ACADEM NAT/G SCHOOL LEGIS REGION MAJORITY...MAJORIT WORSHIP 18/20 CHURCH/STA. PAGE 145 H2891
SECT EDU/PROP PROVS GP/REL

B59
WARNER W.L.,THE LIVING AND THE DEAD: A STUDY OF SYMBOLIC LIFE OF AMERICANS. INTELL KIN DEATH ALL/VALS ALL/IDEOS...CONCPT MYTH LING OBS/ENVIR CHARTS BIBLIOG WORSHIP 18/20. PAGE 165 H3311
CULTURE SOC TIME/SEQ IDEA/COMP

B60
BANERJEE D.N.,OUR FUNDAMENTAL RIGHTS: THEIR NATURE AND EXTENT (AS JUDICIALLY DETERMINED). INDIA UK CULTURE STRATA NAT/G WORKER EDU/PROP CONTROL DISCRIM OWN...IDEA/COMP WORSHIP 20 REFORMERS COMMONWLTH. PAGE 10 H0207
CONSTN ORD/FREE LEGIS POLICY

B60
BURRIDGE K.,MAMBU: A MELANESIAN MILLENNIUM. ECO/UNDEV PROC/MFG FAM KIN CHIEF COLONIAL COERCE GP/REL DRIVE WEALTH WORSHIP 20 NEW/GUINEA. PAGE 25 H0494
S/ASIA SECT CULTURE MYTH

B60
CHATTERJI S.K.,AFRICANISM: THE AFRICAN PERSONALITY. KIN NAT/G SECT CREATE DIPLOM COLONIAL GP/REL ATTIT ORD/FREE...LING WORSHIP 20. PAGE 29 H0585
PERSON NAT/LISM AFR CULTURE

B60
INTERNATIONAL AFRICAN INST,ETHNOGRAPHIC SURVEY OF AFRICA: WESTERN AFRICA: PEOPLES OF THE MIDDLE NIGER REGION, NORTHERN NIGERIA. AFR NIGER CULTURE ECO/UNDEV KIN NEIGH GOV/REL GP/REL ATTIT HEREDITY ...CHARTS BIBLIOG WORSHIP 20. PAGE 78 H1552
STRUCT GEOG HABITAT INGP/REL

B60
JOHNSON H.M.,SOCIOLOGY: A SYSTEMATIC INTRODUCTION. MARKET FAM LABOR POL/PAR CHOOSE DISCRIM MARRIAGE ALL/IDEOS...BIBLIOG T WORSHIP. PAGE 81 H1620
SOC SOCIETY CULTURE GEN/LAWS

B60
MORAES F.,THE REVOLT IN TIBET. ASIA CHINA/COM INDIA CULTURE CONTROL COERCE WAR TOTALISM...POLICY SOC WORSHIP 20 TIBET INTERVENT. PAGE 113 H2252
COLONIAL FORCES DIPLOM ORD/FREE

B60
MORRISON C.,THE POWERS THAT BE. NAT/G SUPEGO ...POLICY CONCPT IDEA/COMP WORSHIP 20 BIBLE. PAGE 113 H2265
HUM ORD/FREE

B60
NAKAMURA H.,THE WAYS OF THINKING OF EASTERN PEOPLES. ASIA INDIA PERSON...HUM SOC LING LOG WORSHIP CHINJAP. PAGE 115 H2305
CULTURE SECT ATTIT

B60
OTTENBERG S.,CULTURES AND SOCIETIES OF AFRICA. AFR KIN TEC/DEV GP/REL MARRIAGE ATTIT HABITAT HEREDITY ...ANTHOL BIBLIOG T WORSHIP 20. PAGE 122 H2433
SOCIETY INGP/REL STRUCT CULTURE

B61
FIRTH R.,HISTORY AND TRADITIONS OF TIKOPIA. S/ASIA KIN SECT RUMOR WAR...MYTH WORSHIP 20 POLYNESIA.
CULTURE STRUCT

PAGE 50 H1008 HUM

B61
FIRTH R.,ELEMENTS OF SOCIAL ORGANIZATION (3RD ED.). STRATA STRUCT ECO/UNDEV NEIGH CHIEF INGP/REL ATTIT MORAL...PHIL/SCI GP/COMP WORSHIP SOC/INTEG 20. PAGE 50 H1009 — SOC CULTURE SOCIETY KIN

B61
SCHECHTMAN J.B.,ON WINGS OF EAGLES: THE PLIGHT, EXODUS, AND HOMECOMING OF ORIENTAL JEWRY. ASIA ISLAM ISRAEL VOL/ASSN DIPLOM CONTROL ORD/FREE ...GEOG WORSHIP SOC/INTEG 20 JEWS ARABS MIGRATION. PAGE 139 H2777 — CULTURE HABITAT KIN SECT

B61
SHIELS W.E.,KING AND CHURCH: THE RISE AND FALL OF THE PATRONATO REAL. SPAIN INGP/REL...CONCPT WORSHIP 16/19 CHURCH/STA MISSION. PAGE 143 H2859 — SECT NAT/G CHIEF POLICY

B61
TURNBULL C.M.,THE FOREST PEOPLE. EATING GP/REL INGP/REL RACE/REL ISOLAT HABITAT HEREDITY...GEOG SOC LING DICTIONARY WORSHIP 20 CONGO NEGRO BA/MBUTI. PAGE 157 H3138 — AFR CULTURE KIN RECORD

L61
EZELLPH,"THE HISPANIC AGRICULTURATION OF THE GILA RIVER PIMAS." FAM TEC/DEV PERS/REL ADJUST...GEOG MYTH CHARTS BIBLIOG WORSHIP 17/20. PAGE 48 H0956 — CULTURE SOC AGRI DRIVE

B62
KEESING F.M.,THE ETHNOHISTORY OF NORTHERN LUZON. PHILIPPINE ECO/UNDEV FAM SECT CHIEF REGION GP/REL HABITAT...GEOG LING BIBLIOG WORSHIP 20. PAGE 84 H1680 — CULTURE SOC KIN

B62
MALINOWSKI B.,SEX, CULTURE, AND MYTH. UNIV SOCIETY FAM PERS/REL MARRIAGE RATIONAL HABITAT PERSON SUPEGO MORAL WORSHIP 20. PAGE 102 H2032 — MYTH SECT SEX CULTURE

B63
AZEVEDO T.,SOCIAL CHANGE IN BRAZIL. BRAZIL ECO/DEV COM/IND FAM NAT/G SECT GP/REL PERS/REL...CONCPT WORSHIP 20. PAGE 9 H0188 — TEC/DEV STRUCT SOC CULTURE

B63
BIALEK R.W.,CATHOLIC POLITICS: A HISTORY BASED ON ECUADOR. ECUADOR SPAIN CULTURE STRUCT CONTROL REV PWR...BIBLIOG WORSHIP 18/20. PAGE 16 H0329 — COLONIAL CATHISM GOV/REL HABITAT

B63
BOHANNAN P.,SOCIAL ANTHROPOLOGY. ECO/DEV GP/REL DEMAND MARRIAGE HABITAT...CHARTS GP/COMP BIBLIOG T WORSHIP 20. PAGE 18 H0366 — SOC STRUCT FAM CULTURE

B63
CONFERENCE ABORIGINAL STUDIES,AUSTRALIAN ABORIGINAL STUDIES. ECO/UNDEV INT/TRADE COLONIAL ADJUST HABITAT HEREDITY...GEOG PSY LING SOC/EXP ANTHOL WORSHIP 20 AUSTRAL ABORIGINES. PAGE 32 H0638 — SOC SOCIETY CULTURE STRUCT

B63
DRIVER H.E.,ETHNOGRAPHY AND ACCULTURATION OF THE CHICHIMECA-JONAZ OF NORTHEAST MEXICO. ECO/UNDEV AGRI FAM KIN EDU/PROP MARRIAGE HEALTH...GEOG INT CHARTS WORSHIP 18/20 MEXIC/AMER. PAGE 42 H0848 — CULTURE HABITAT STRUCT GP/REL

B63
FARMER B.H.,CEYLON: A DIVIDED NATION. CEYLON INDIA NETHERLAND PORTUGAL UK ELITES POL/PAR COLONIAL ...SOC MYTH CHARTS GOV/COMP WORSHIP 20. PAGE 49 H0972 — DOMIN ORD/FREE ECO/UNDEV POLICY

B63
GAMBLE S.D.,NORTH CHINA VILLAGES: SOCIAL, POLITICAL, AND ECONOMIC ACTIVITIES BEFORE 1933. ASIA CULTURE STRUCT FAM DOMIN EDU/PROP WORSHIP 20. PAGE 55 H1093 — MUNIC AGRI LEAD FINAN

B63
JAIRAZBHOY R.A.,FOREIGN INFLUENCE IN ANCIENT INDIA. INDIA ELITES SECT DIPLOM EDU/PROP COLONIAL REGION GP/REL...ART/METH LING WORSHIP +/14 GRECO/ROMN MESOPOTAM PERSIA PARTH/SASS. PAGE 79 H1587 — CULTURE SOCIETY COERCE DOMIN

B63
LAVROFF D.-G.,LES LIBERTES PUBLIQUES EN UNION SOVIETIQUE (REV. ED.). USSR NAT/G WORKER SANCTION CRIME MARXISM NEW/LIB...JURID BIBLIOG WORSHIP 20. PAGE 92 H1843 — ORD/FREE LAW ATTIT COM

B63
MAJUMDAR O.N.,AN INTRODUCTION TO SOCIAL ANTHROPOLOGY. INDIA LAW STRATA ECO/UNDEV KIN DEMAND MARRIAGE...GP/COMP BIBLIOG T WORSHIP 20. PAGE 101 H2026 — SOC CULTURE STRUCT GP/REL

B63
OTERO L.M.,HONDURAS. HONDURAS SPAIN STRUCT SECT COLONIAL REV WAR ATTIT PWR...GEOG WORSHIP 16/20. PAGE 122 H2432 — NAT/G SOCIETY NAT/LISM ECO/UNDEV

B63
REYNOLDS B.,MAGIC, DIVINATION AND WITCHCRAFT AMONG THE BAROTSE OF NORTHERN RHODESIA. RHODESIA CULTURE KIN CREATE LEGIT PARTIC DEATH DREAM STRANGE HABITAT PERSON...AUD/VIS WORSHIP 20. PAGE 131 H2619 — AFR SOC MYTH SECT

B63
STIRNIMANN H.,NGUNI UND GNONI; EINE KULTURGESCHICHTLICHE STUDIE (ACTA ETHNOLOGICA ET LINGUISTICA, NUMBER 6). AFR MALAWI SOUTH/AFR FORCES HABITAT...RECORD CHARTS BIBLIOG WORSHIP 19/20 NATAL. PAGE 149 H2987 — CULTURE GP/COMP SOCIETY

B63
VON DER MEHDEN F.R.,RELIGION AND NATIONALISM IN SOUTHEAST ASIA. BURMA PHILIPPINE S/ASIA INTELL SOCIETY DOMIN EDU/PROP LEGIT ATTIT MORAL ORD/FREE ...SOC CENSUS HIST/WRIT TOT/POP VAL/FREE 20 WORSHIP LONDON. PAGE 163 H3265 — SECT CULTURE NAT/LISM

L63
JAY R.,"RELIGION AND POLITICS IN RURAL CENTRAL JAVA." S/ASIA SOCIETY NEIGH SECT PERSON HEALTH MORAL...SOC UNPLAN/INT TIME/SEQ JAVA VAL/FREE 20 WORSHIP. PAGE 80 H1594 — CULTURE OBS

S63
RINTELEN F.,"L'HOMME EUROPEEN." EUR+WWI FUT CULTURE INTELL SECT EDU/PROP ATTIT ALL/VALS...HUM SOC METH/CNCPT TREND GEN/LAWS 20 WORSHIP. PAGE 132 H2631. — SOCIETY PERSON

B64
BERNDT R.M.,THE WORLD OF THE FIRST AUSTRALIANS. S/ASIA ECO/UNDEV WORKER PROB/SOLV EFFICIENCY ROLE ...SOC MYTH WORSHIP AUSTRAL ABORIGINES. PAGE 16 H0311 — CULTURE KIN STRUCT DRIVE

B64
ELKIN A.P.,THE AUSTRALIAN ABORIGINES - HOW TO UNDERSTAND THEM (4TH ED.). FAM NEIGH DEATH MARRIAGE ATTIT BIO/SOC HABITAT...PSY SOC MYTH WORSHIP AUSTRAL ABORIGINES. PAGE 45 H0908 — CULTURE STRUCT SOCIETY KIN

B64
FORBES A.H.,CURRENT RESEARCH IN BRITISH STUDIES. UK CONSTN CULTURE POL/PAR SECT DIPLOM ADMIN...JURID BIOG WORSHIP 20. PAGE 52 H1034 — BIBLIOG PERSON NAT/G PARL/PROC

B64
HALPERN J.M.,GOVERNMENT, POLITICS, AND SOCIAL STRUCTURE IN LAOS. LAOS CULTURE SOCIETY STRATA STRUCT FAM DIPLOM DOMIN MARXISM...INT GOV/COMP WORSHIP SOC/INTEG 20. PAGE 65 H1297 — NAT/G SOC LOC/G

B64
HELMREICH E.,A FREE CHURCH IN A FREE STATE? FRANCE GERMANY ITALY SECT LEAD PWR CATHISM...POLICY ANTHOL WORSHIP 19/20 CHURCH/STA. PAGE 69 H1389 — GP/REL NAT/G

B64
HOBBS C.C.,SOUTHEAST ASIA: AN ANNOTATED BIBLIOGRAPHY OF SELECTED REFERENCES IN WESTERN LANGUAGES (REV. ED.). CAMBODIA INDONESIA LAOS THAILAND VIETNAM CONSTN NAT/G...SOC WORSHIP 20. PAGE 72 H1437 — BIBLIOG/A S/ASIA CULTURE SOCIETY

B64
KIDD K.E.,BRIEF BIBLIOGRAPHY OF ONTARIO ANTHROPOLOGY (PAMPHLET). CANADA PREHIST HABITAT ...MYTH WORSHIP. PAGE 86 H1708 — BIBLIOG SOC LING CULTURE

B64
LAWRENCE P.,ROAD BELONG CARGO: A STUDY OF CARGO MOVEMENT IN SOUTHERN MADANG DISTRICT, NEW GUINEA. S/ASIA CULTURE ECO/UNDEV PROC/MFG KIN CHIEF COLONIAL COERCE GP/REL DRIVE WEALTH WORSHIP 20 NEW/GUINEA. PAGE 92 H1846 — SOC SECT ALL/VALS MYTH

B64
PERKINS D.,THE AMERICAN DEMOCRACY: ITS RISE TO POWER. ASIA USSR LAW CULTURE FINAN EDU/PROP COLONIAL CHOOSE...POLICY CHARTS BIBLIOG WORSHIP PRESIDENT 15/20 NEGRO. PAGE 125 H2492 — LOC/G ECO/TAC WAR DIPLOM

B64
SCHNITGER F.M.,FORGOTTEN KINGDOMS IN SUMATRA. FAM SECT LEISURE HABITAT...OBS AUD/VIS WORSHIP 20 SUMATRA. PAGE 140 H2793 — CULTURE AFR SOCIETY STRUCT

S64
EISTER A.W.,"PERSPECTIVE ON FUNCTIONS OF RELIGION IN A DEVELOPING COUNTRY: ISLAM IN PAKISTAN." ISLAM CULTURE MUNIC ACT/RES CREATE PROB/SOLV TEC/DEV WORSHIP. PAGE 45 H0902 — ATTIT SECT ECO/DEV

B65
BERNDT R.M.,ABORIGINAL MAN IN AUSTRALIA. LAW DOMIN ADMIN COLONIAL MARRIAGE HABITAT ORD/FREE...LING CHARTS ANTHOL BIBLIOG WORSHIP 20 AUSTRAL ABORIGINES MUSIC ELKIN/AP. PAGE 16 H0312 — SOC CULTURE SOCIETY STRUCT

B65
DURKHEIM E.,THE ELEMENTARY FORMS OF THE RELIGIOUS LIFE. KIN PARTIC MORAL...PSY MYTH OBS IDEA/COMP METH WORSHIP 19/20. PAGE 43 H0870 — SOC CULTURE CONCPT

B65
FILIPINIANA BOOK GUILD,THE COLONIZATION AND CONQUEST OF THE PHILIPPINES BY SPAIN. PHILIPPINE SPAIN ELITES AGRI KIN CHIEF DOMIN CONTROL ATTIT PWR ...ANTHOL WORSHIP 16. PAGE 50 H1000 — COLONIAL COERCE CULTURE WAR

B65
FREY F.W.,THE TURKISH POLITICAL ELITE. TURKEY CULTURE INTELL NAT/G EX/STRUC CHOOSE ATTIT PWR — ELITES SOCIETY

...METH/CNCPT CHARTS WORSHIP 20. PAGE 53 H1059 POL/PAR
B65

HARRIS R.L.,POLITICAL ORGANIZATION OF THE MBEMBE NIGERIA. AFR NIGERIA SOCIETY AGRI SECT WORKER PAY ...SOC WORSHIP 20 MBEMBE. PAGE 67 H1345 STRUCT CHIEF CULTURE
B65

HUNT G.L.,CALVINISM AND THE POLITICAL ORDER. NAT/G LEAD...POLICY IDEA/COMP ANTHOL WORSHIP 20. PAGE 75 H1498 SECT CONCPT
B65

KUNSTADTER P.,THE LUA (LAWA) OF NORTHERN THAILAND: ASPECTS OF SOCIAL STRUCTURE, AGRICULTURE, AND RELIGION. THAILAND AGRI FAM KIN INGP/REL ISOLAT MARRIAGE HEALTH WORSHIP 20 BUDDHISM LUA. PAGE 89 H1780 STRUCT ECO/UNDEV CULTURE
B65

LAWRENCE P.,GODS, GHOSTS, AND MEN IN MELANESIA: SOME RELIGIONS OF AUSTRALIAN NEW GUINEA AND THE NEW HEBRIDES. SOCIETY ECO/UNDEV FAM GP/REL INGP/REL HABITAT PERSON...GEOG SOC ANTHOL BIBLIOG WORSHIP 20 NEW/GUINEA. PAGE 92 H1847 MYTH S/ASIA SECT CULTURE
B65

SPENCER P.,THE SAMBURU: A STUDY OF GERONTOCRACY IN A NOMADIC TRIBE. AFR SOCIETY ECO/UNDEV AGRI FAM NEIGH SECT GP/REL MARRIAGE WORSHIP 20 SAMBURU. PAGE 147 H2945 KIN STRUCT AGE/O CULTURE
B65

SWIFT M.G.,MALAY PEASANT SOCIETY IN JELEBU. MALAYSIA FAM INT/TRADE ADJUD OWN WEALTH...SOC WORSHIP 20. PAGE 151 H3020 STRUCT ECO/UNDEV CULTURE SOCIETY
B65

WINT G.,ASIA: A HANDBOOK. ASIA COM INDIA USSR CULTURE INTELL NAT/G...GEOG STAT CENSUS NAT/COMP WORSHIP 20 TREATY CHINJAP. PAGE 169 H3387 DIPLOM SOC
L65

HOUN F.S.,"THE COMMUNIST MONOLITH VERSUS THE CHINESE TRADITION." CULTURE INTELL SOCIETY STRUCT DOMIN GP/REL ORD/FREE CONSERVE PLURISM...GOV/COMP WORSHIP. PAGE 74 H1479 ASIA MARXISM TOTALISM
B66

BARRETT J.,THAT BETTER COUNTRY: RELIGIOUS ASPECT OF LIFE IN EASTERN AUSTRALIA, 1835-1850. LAW ECO/UNDEV SCHOOL TEC/DEV EDU/PROP CONTROL HABITAT MORAL WORSHIP 19 AUSTRAL CHURCH/STA. PAGE 11 H0229 SECT CULTURE GOV/REL
B66

BASDEN G.T.,NIGER IBOS. NIGERIA STRUCT SECT CHIEF COLONIAL HABITAT...POLICY SOC MYTH OBS WORSHIP 20 IBO. PAGE 12 H0233 CULTURE AFR SOCIETY
B66

DIAMOND S.,THE TRANSFORMATION OF EAST AFRICA. NAT/G SCHOOL CREATE PROB/SOLV COLONIAL REGION RACE/REL FEDERAL...SOC ANTHOL WORSHIP 20 AFRICA/E. PAGE 41 H0819 CULTURE AFR TEC/DEV INDUS
B66

ELLIS A.B.,THE EWE-SPEAKING PEOPLES OF THE SLAVE COAST OF WEST AFRICA. AFR FORCES ADJUST...LING RECORD GP/COMP WORSHIP 20 AFRICA/W DEITY. PAGE 45 H0910 MYTH CULTURE HABITAT
B66

HAHN C.H.L.,THE NATIVE TRIBES OF SOUTH WEST AFRICA. LAW FAM SECT HABITAT SKILL...SOC AUD/VIS WORSHIP RITUAL 20 AFRICA/SW. PAGE 64 H1275 CULTURE SOCIETY STRUCT AFR
B66

HOWE R.W.,BLACK AFRICA: FROM PRE-HISTORY TO THE EVE OF THE COLONIAL ERA. ECO/UNDEV KIN PROVS SECT INT/TRADE EDU/PROP COLONIAL...BIBLIOG WORSHIP. PAGE 74 H1482 AFR CULTURE SOC
B66

KERR M.H.,ISLAMIC REFORM: THE POLITICAL AND LEGAL THEORIES OF MUHAMMAD 'ABDUH AND RASHID RIDA. NAT/G SECT LEAD SOVEREIGN CONSERVE...JURID BIBLIOG WORSHIP 20. PAGE 85 H1698 LAW CONCPT ISLAM
B66

KIRKLAND E.C.,A BIBLIOGRAPHY OF SOUTH ASIAN FOLKLORE. WRITING HABITAT ALL/VALS MYSTISM ...ART/METH GEOG PSY SOC MYTH WORSHIP 13/20. PAGE 86 H1723 BIBLIOG S/ASIA CULTURE CREATE
B66

SRINIVAS M.N.,SOCIAL CHANGE IN MODERN INDIA. INDIA CULTURE SOCIETY STRUCT SECT TEC/DEV...METH/CNCPT SELF/OBS WORSHIP 20. PAGE 148 H2961 ORD/FREE STRATA SOC ECO/UNDEV
B66

SWARTZ M.J.,POLITICAL ANTHROPOLOGY. WOR+45 POL/PAR ACT/RES REV GP/REL DRIVE...SOC CONCPT TIME/SEQ GP/COMP ANTHOL WORSHIP 20. PAGE 151 H3013 PARTIC RIGID/FLEX LOC/G CREATE
B66

SWEET E.C.,CIVIL LIBERTIES IN AMERICA. LAW CONSTN NAT/G PRESS CT/SYS DISCRIM ATTIT WORSHIP 20 CIVIL/LIB. PAGE 151 H3018 ADJUD ORD/FREE SUFF COERCE
B66

US DEPARTMENT OF STATE,RESEARCH ON AFRICA (EXTERNAL RESEARCH LIST NO 5-25). LAW CULTURE ECO/UNDEV POL/PAR DIPLOM EDU/PROP LEAD REGION MARXISM...GEOG LING WORSHIP 20. PAGE 159 H3188 BIBLIOG/A ASIA S/ASIA NAT/G
B66

US DEPARTMENT OF STATE,RESEARCH ON THE AMERICAN REPUBLICS (EXTERNAL RESEARCH LIST NO 6-25). CULTURE SOCIETY POL/PAR DIPLOM EDU/PROP MARXISM WORSHIP 20 OAS. PAGE 159 H3189 BIBLIOG/A L/A+17C REGION NAT/G
B66

US DEPARTMENT OF STATE,RESEARCH ON WESTERN EUROPE, GREAT BRITAIN, AND CANADA (EXTERNAL RESEARCH LIST NO 3-25). CANADA GERMANY/W UK LAW CULTURE NAT/G POL/PAR FORCES EDU/PROP REGION MARXISM...GEOG SOC WORSHIP 20 CMN/WLTH. PAGE 160 H3192 BIBLIOG/A EUR+WWI DIPLOM
B67

NASH M.,MACHINE AGE MAYA. GUATEMALA L/A+17C STRUCT AGRI WORKER CREATE INCOME ATTIT RIGID/FLEX ROLE ...IDEA/COMP SOC/EXP WORSHIP 20 INDIAN/AM. PAGE 116 H2315 INDUS CULTURE SOC MUNIC
B67

PATAI R.,GOLDEN RIVER TO GOLDEN ROAD: SOCIETY, CULTURE, AND CHANGE IN THE MIDDLE EAST (2ND ED.). ELITES FAM KIN TEC/DEV MARRIAGE NAT/LISM SEX ORD/FREE...TREND GP/COMP WORSHIP 20. PAGE 124 H2476 CULTURE SOCIETY ISLAM STRUCT
S67

KINGSBURY E.C.,"LAW AS COMPACT: ANCIENT ISRAEL'S CONTRIBUTION TO THE UNDERSTANDING OF LAW." ISRAEL MEDIT-7 CULTURE KIN KNOWL...JURID CONCPT TREND IDEA/COMP METH/COMP WORSHIP JEWS DEITY. PAGE 86 H1716 LAW AGREE CONSTN INGP/REL
S67

RAMA C.M.,"PASADO Y PRESENTE DE LA RELIGION EN AMERICA LATINA." L/A+17C ELITES SOCIETY STRATA MARXISM...STAT WORSHIP PROTESTANT. PAGE 129 H2585 SECT CATHISM STRUCT NAT/COMP
S67

WHITE J.W.,"MASS MOVEMENTS AND DEMOCRACY: SOKAGAKKAI IN JAPANESE POLITICS." NAT/G GP/REL ALL/VALS ORD/FREE WORSHIP 20 CHINJAP. PAGE 167 H3349 SECT PWR ATTIT POL/PAR
B68

DE SPINOZA B.,TRACTATUS THEOLOGICO-POLITICUS (TRANS. BY R. WILLIS). UNIV CHIEF DOMIN PWR WORSHIP. PAGE 38 H0771 SECT NAT/G ORD/FREE
B75

NEWMAN J.H.,A LETTER ADDRESSED TO THE DUKE OF NORFOLK ON THE OCCASION OF MR. GLADSTONE'S RECENT EXPOSTULATION. NAT/G SECT CHIEF LEGIS CONTROL LEAD GP/REL SUPEGO SOC/INTEG WORSHIP 19 ENGLAND. PAGE 117 H2346 POLICY DOMIN SOVEREIGN CATHISM
B82

MACDONALD D.,AFRICANA; OR, THE HEART OF HEATHEN AFRICA, VOL. II: MISSION LIFE. SOCIETY STRATA KIN CREATE EDU/PROP ADMIN COERCE LITERACY HEALTH...MYTH WORSHIP 19 LIVNGSTN/D MISSION NEGRO. PAGE 100 H1990 SECT AFR CULTURE ORD/FREE

WOYTINSKY E.S. H3413

WOYTINSKY W.S. H3413

WPA....WORK PROJECTS ADMINISTRATION

WRAITH R.E. H3414,H3415,H3416

WRIGGINS W.H. H3417

WRIGHT G. H3418,H3419

WRIGHT Q. H3421,H3422

WRIGHT W.R. H3423

WRITING....SEE ALSO HIST/WRIT

N

LONDON TIMES OFFICIAL INDEX. UK LAW ECO/DEV NAT/G DIPLOM LEAD ATTIT 20. PAGE 1 H0018 BIBLIOG INDEX PRESS WRITING
N

PUBLISHERS' CIRCULAR, THE OFFICIAL ORGAN OF THE PUBLISHERS' ASSOCIATION OF GREAT BRITAIN AND IRELAND. EUR+WWI MOD/EUR UK LAW PROB/SOLV DIPLOM COLONIAL ATTIT...HUM 19/20 CMN/WLTH. PAGE 1 H0019 BIBLIOG NAT/G WRITING LEAD
N

SUBJECT GUIDE TO BOOKS IN PRINT: AN INDEX TO THE PUBLISHERS' TRADE LIST ANNUAL. UNIV LAW LOC/G DIPLOM WRITING ADMIN LEAD PERSON...MGT SOC. PAGE 2 H0024 BIBLIOG ECO/DEV POL/PAR NAT/G
N

DEUTSCHE BUCHEREI,JAHRESVERZEICHNIS DES DEUTSCHEN SCHRIFTUMS. AUSTRIA EUR+WWI GERMANY SWITZERLND LAW LOC/G DIPLOM ADMIN...MGT SOC 19/20. PAGE 40 H0804 BIBLIOG WRITING NAT/G

N
SOUTH AFRICA STATE LIBRARY,SOUTH AFRICAN NATIONAL BIBLIOGRAPHY, SANB. SOUTH/AFR LAW NAT/G EDU/PROP ...MGT PSY SOC 20. PAGE 147 H2937
BIBLIOG PRESS WRITING

B03
FORTESCUE G.K.,SUBJECT INDEX OF THE MODERN WORKS ADDED TO THE LIBRARY OF THE BRITISH MUSEUM IN THE YEARS 1881-1900 (3 VOLS.). UK LAW CONSTN FINAN NAT/G FORCES INT/TRADE COLONIAL 19. PAGE 52 H1041
BIBLIOG INDEX WRITING

B21
KREY A.C.,THE FIRST CRUSADE. CHRIST-17C SOCIETY STRATA NAT/G SECT FORCES WORKER WRITING LEAD ATTIT ...CHARTS 11 CHRISTIAN CRUSADES. PAGE 88 H1767
WAR CATH DIPLOM PARTIC

B37
THOMPSON J.W.,SECRET DIPLOMACY: A RECORD OF ESPIONAGE AND DOUBLE-DEALING: 1500-1815. CHRIST-17C MOD/EUR NAT/G WRITING RISK MORAL...ANTHOL BIBLIOG 16/19 ESPIONAGE. PAGE 154 H3084
DIPLOM CRIME

B38
DEL TORO J.,A BIBLIOGRAPHY OF THE COLLECTIVE BIOGRAPHY OF SPANISH AMERICA. ELITES NAT/G WRITING LEAD PERSON 19/20. PAGE 39 H0786
BIBLIOG/A L/A+17C BIOG

B38
MCNAIR A.D.,THE LAW OF TREATIES: BRITISH PRACTICE AND OPINIONS. UK CREATE DIPLOM LEGIT WRITING ADJUD WAR...INT/LAW JURID TREATY. PAGE 107 H2144
AGREE LAW CT/SYS NAT/G

B39
MILLER P.,THE NEW ENGLAND MIND: THE SEVENTEENTH CENTURY. CULTURE DOMIN WRITING INGP/REL CONSEN MAJORITY PERCEPT KNOWL MORAL...CONCPT LING WORSHIP 17 NEW/ENGLND PROTESTANT. PAGE 111 H2214
SECT REGION SOC ATTIT

B42
CRAIG A.,ABOVE ALL LIBERTIES. FRANCE UK USA-45 LAW CONSTN CULTURE INTELL NAT/G SECT JUDGE...IDEA/COMP BIBLIOG 18/20. PAGE 35 H0692
ORD/FREE MORAL WRITING EDU/PROP

C42
CRAIG A.,"ABOVE ALL LIBERTIES." FRANCE UK LAW CULTURE INTELL SECT ORD/FREE 18/20. PAGE 35 H0693
BIBLIOG/A EDU/PROP WRITING MORAL

B43
DURON J.F.,REPERTORIO BIBLIOGRAFICO HONDURENO. HONDURAS WRITING. PAGE 44 H0871
BIBLIOG NAT/G L/A+17C

C43
BENTHAM J.,"ON THE LIBERTY OF THE PRESS, AND PUBLIC DISCUSSION" IN J. BOWRING, ED., THE WORKS OF JEREMY BENTHAM." SPAIN UK LAW ELITES NAT/G LEGIS INSPECT LEGIT WRITING CONTROL PRIVIL TOTALISM AUTHORIT ...TRADIT 19 FREE/SPEE. PAGE 15 H0290
ORD/FREE PRESS CONFER CONSERVE

B49
BOZZA T.,SCRITTORI POLITICI ITALIANI DAL 1550 AL 1650. CHRIST-17C ITALY DIPLOM DOMIN 16/17. PAGE 20 H0394
BIBLIOG/A NAT/G CONCPT WRITING

B51
BISSAINTHE M.,DICTIONNAIRE DE BIBLIOGRAPHIE HAITIENNE. HAITI ELITES AGRI LEGIS DIPLOM INT/TRADE WRITING ORD/FREE CATHISM...ART/METH GEOG 19/20 NEGRO TREATY. PAGE 17 H0347
BIBLIOG L/A+17C SOCIETY NAT/G

B51
YOUNG T.C.,NEAR EASTERN CULTURE AND SOCIETY. ISLAM ECO/UNDEV SECT WRITING ATTIT HABITAT ORD/FREE 20. PAGE 172 H3439
CULTURE STRUCT REGION DIPLOM

N52
COORDINATING COMM DOC SOC SCI,INTERNATIONAL REPERTORY OF SOCIAL SCIENCE DOCUMENTATION CENTERS (PAMPHLET). ACT/RES OP/RES WRITING KNOWL...CON/ANAL METH. PAGE 33 H0661
BIBLIOG/A R+D NAT/G INT/ORG

B53
BROWN D.M.,THE WHITE UMBRELLA: INDIAN POLITICAL THOUGHT FROM MANU TO GANDHI. INDIA LAW NAT/G SECT WRITING NAT/LISM...ANTHOL BIBLIOG 20 HINDU GANDHI/M MANU. PAGE 22 H0442
CONCPT DOMIN CONSERVE

S54
ALBRECT M.C.,"THE RELATIONSHIP OF LITERATURE AND SOCIETY." STRATA STRUCT DIPLOM...POLICY SOC/INTEG. PAGE 5 H0097
HUM CULTURE WRITING NAT/COMP

B56
CENTRAL AFRICAN ARCHIVES,A GUIDE TO THE PUBLIC RECORDS OF SOUTHERN RHODESIA UNDER THE REGIME OF THE BRITISH SOUTH AFRICA COMPANY, 1890-1923. UK STRUCT NAT/G WRITING GP/REL 19/20. PAGE 28 H0566
BIBLIOG/A COLONIAL ADMIN AFR

B57
BULLOCK A.,THE LIBERAL TRADITION FROM FOX TO KEYNES. UK CULTURE INTELL CREATE WRITING COLONIAL PERS/REL ATTIT ORD/FREE...POLICY OLD/LIB TRADIT CONCPT 18/20 CHURCHLL/W MILL/JS KEYNES/JM ASQUITH/HH. PAGE 23 H0469
ANTHOL DEBATE LAISSEZ

B57
HERNANDEZ-ARREGU J.,IMPERIALISMO Y CULTURA (LA POLITICA EN LA INTELIGENCIA ARGENTINA). L/A+17C CULTURE ELITES WRITING COLONIAL CROWD ATTIT FASCISM MARXISM SOCISM...BIOG IDEA/COMP 20 ARGEN PERON/JUAN COM/PARTY. PAGE 70 H1403
INTELL CREATE ART/METH HUM

B59
LIPSET S.M.,SOCIAL MOBILITY IN INDUSTRIAL SOCIETY. EUR+WWI USA+45 USSR STRUCT INDUS WRITING GP/REL INGP/REL DRIVE...SOC CHARTS NAT/COMP SOC/INTEG 20 MARX/KARL ENGELS/F. PAGE 97 H1940
STRATA ECO/DEV SOCIETY

B61
DOOB L.W.,COMMUNICATION IN AFRICA: A SEARCH FOR BOUNDARIES. CULTURE SOCIETY EDU/PROP WRITING INGP/REL DRIVE ORD/FREE...ART/METH SOC LING BIBLIOG 20. PAGE 42 H0837
AFR FEEDBACK PERCEPT PERS/REL

B61
MARTINEZ RIOS J.,BIBLIOGRAFIA ANTROPOLOGICA Y SOCIOLOGICA DEL ESTADO DE OAXACA. WRITING...LING 12/20 INDIAN/AM MEXIC/AMER. PAGE 103 H2069
BIBLIOG SOC PROVS CULTURE

B62
SWAYZE H.,POLITICAL CONTROL OF LITERATURE IN THE USSR, 1946-1959. USSR NAT/G CREATE LICENSE...JURID 20. PAGE 151 H3014
MARXISM WRITING CONTROL DOMIN

B62
UNECA LIBRARY,BOOKS ON AFRICA IN THE UNECA LIBRARY. WOR+45 AGRI INT/ORG NAT/G PLAN WRITING REGION...SOC STAT UN. PAGE 158 H3160
BIBLIOG AFR ECO/UNDEV TEC/DEV

B63
HOLLANDER P.,THE NEW MAN AND HIS ENEMIES: A STUDY OF THE STALINIST CONCEPTIONS OF GOOD AND EVIL PERSONIFIED (DOCTORAL THESIS). USSR SOCIETY ECO/DEV NAT/G EDU/PROP WRITING...SOC STERTYP BIBLIOG 20 STALIN/J. PAGE 73 H1455
CONTROL ATTIT TOTALISM MARXISM

N63
LIBRARY HUNGARIAN ACADEMY SCI,HUNGARIAN PUBLICATIONS ON ASIA AND AFRICA, 1950-1962: A SELECTED BIBLIOGRAPHY (PAMPHLET). AFR ASIA HUNGARY S/ASIA ECO/UNDEV NAT/G EDU/PROP ATTIT 20 UNESCO. PAGE 96 H1922
BIBLIOG REGION DIPLOM WRITING

B64
DOOLIN D.J.,COMMUNIST CHINA: THE POLITICS OF STUDENT OPPOSITION. CHINA/COM ELITES STRATA ACADEM NAT/G WRITING CT/SYS LEAD PARTIC COERCE TOTALISM 20. PAGE 42 H0838
MARXISM DEBATE AGE/Y PWR

B64
GRIFFITH W.,THE WELSH (2ND ED.). UK SOCIETY STRUCT SECT WRITING NAT/LISM...ART/METH MODAL OBS/ENVIR TREND SOC/INTEG WALES PURITAN MUSIC. PAGE 61 H1223
CULTURE SOC LING

B64
REMAK J.,THE GENTLE CRITIC: THEODOR FONTANE AND GERMAN POLITICS, 1848-1898. GERMANY PRUSSIA CULTURE ELITES BAL/PWR DIPLOM WRITING GOV/REL...HUM BIOG 19 BISMARCK/O JUNKER FONTANE/T. PAGE 131 H2614
PERSON SOCIETY WORKER CHIEF

B64
TODD W.B.,A BIBLIOGRAPHY OF EDMUND BURKE. MOD/EUR UK NAT/G EDU/PROP ATTIT...HUM 18 BURKE/EDM. PAGE 156 H3110
BIBLIOG/A PHIL/SCI WRITING CONCPT

B64
VON GRUNEBAUM G.E.,MODERN ISLAM: THE SEARCH FOR CULTURAL IDENTITY. ACADEM NEIGH WRITING NAT/LISM ...HUM CONCPT 19/20 MUSLIM MID/EAST ARABS. PAGE 163 H3269
ISLAM CULTURE CREATE SECT

B65
CAMERON W.J.,NEW ZEALAND. NEW/ZEALND S/ASIA DIPLOM INT/TRADE WRITING COLONIAL PARL/PROC...GEOG CMN/WLTH. PAGE 26 H0513
SOCIETY GP/REL STRUCT

B65
NEWBURY C.W.,BRITISH POLICY TOWARDS WEST AFRICA: SELECT DOCUMENTS 1786-1874. AFR UK INT/TRADE DOMIN ADMIN COLONIAL CT/SYS COERCE ORD/FREE...BIBLIOG/A 18/19. PAGE 117 H2345
DIPLOM POLICY NAT/G WRITING

B65
WAINWRIGHT M.D.,A GUIDE TO WESTERN MANUSCRIPTS AND DOCUMENTS IN THE BRITISH ISLES RELATING TO SOUTH AND SOUTHEAST ASIA. UK CULTURE...SOC 15/20. PAGE 164 H3288
BIBLIOG S/ASIA WRITING

B66
DALLIN A.,POLITICS IN THE SOVIET UNION: 7 CASES. COM USSR LAW POL/PAR CHIEF FORCES WRITING CONTROL PARL/PROC CIVMIL/REL TOTALISM...ANTHOL 20 KHRUSH/N STALIN/J CASEBOOK COM/PARTY. PAGE 37 H0736
MARXISM DOMIN ORD/FREE GOV/REL

B66
INDIA PUBLICATIONS BRANCH,CATALOGUE OF GOVERNMENT OF INDIA CIVIL PUBLICATIONS. INDIA...INDEX 20. PAGE 76 H1529
BIBLIOG NAT/G WRITING

B66
KIRKLAND E.C.,A BIBLIOGRAPHY OF SOUTH ASIAN FOLKLORE. WRITING HABITAT ALL/VALS MYSTISM ...ART/METH GEOG PSY SOC MYTH WORSHIP 13/20. PAGE 86 H1723
BIBLIOG S/ASIA CULTURE CREATE

S67
READ J.S.,"CENSORED." UGANDA CONSTN INTELL SOCIETY NAT/G DIPLOM PRESS WRITING ADJUD ADMIN COLONIAL
EDU/PROP AFR

RISK...IDEA/COMP 20. PAGE 130 H2602 CREATE

S67
SULLIVAN J.H.,"THE PRESS AND POLITICS IN INDONESIA." INDONESIA NAT/G WRITING REV...TREND GOV/COMP 20. PAGE 150 H3007 CIVMIL/REL KNOWL TOTALISM

WRONG D.H. H3424

WUEST J.J. H3425

WUNDERLICH F. H3426

WUORINEN J.H. H3427,H3428

WURFEL S.W. H3429

WWI....WORLD WAR I

B14
BERHARDI F.,GERMANY AND THE NEXT WAR. MOD/EUR NAT/G SCHOOL FORCES ACT/RES DOMIN EDU/PROP SUPEGO PWR ...TIME/SEQ STERTYP TOT/POP 20 WWI. PAGE 15 H0304 DRIVE COERCE WAR GERMANY

B17
BARRES M.,THE UNDYING SPIRIT OF FRANCE (TRANS. BY M. CORWIN). FRANCE DOMIN LEAD DEATH ATTIT RESPECT ...NAT/COMP 20 WWI. PAGE 11 H0226 NAT/LISM FORCES WAR CULTURE

B19
DE MAN H.,THE REMAKING OF A MIND. EUR+WWI NAT/G ECO/TAC REGION ORD/FREE SOCISM...BIOG 20 WWI EUROPE. PAGE 38 H0762 PSY WAR SELF/OBS PARTIC

N19
BARRES M.,"THE WAR AND THE SPIRIT OF YOUTH" (PAMPHLET). FRANCE FORCES DOMIN LEAD DEATH AGE/Y ATTIT RESPECT...FASCIST 20 WWI. PAGE 11 H0228 WAR NAT/LISM CULTURE MYSTIC

B33
DAHLIN E.,FRENCH AND GERMAN PUBLIC OPINION ON DECLARED WAR AIMS 1914-1918. BELGIUM FRANCE GERMANY NAT/G POL/PAR DIPLOM COERCE REV WAR PEACE 20 WWI WILSON/W. PAGE 37 H0733 ATTIT EDU/PROP DOMIN NAT/COMP

B36
RAPPARD W.E.,THE GOVERNMENT OF SWITZERLAND. SWITZERLND INT/ORG POL/PAR EX/STRUC DIPLOM NEUTRAL PARL/PROC REGION WAR HABITAT SOVEREIGN...NAT/COMP SOC/INTEG 20 LEAGUE/NAT WWI. PAGE 130 H2594 CONSTN NAT/G CULTURE FEDERAL

B48
LINEBARGER P.,PSYCHOLOGICAL WARFARE. NAT/G PLAN DIPLOM DOMIN ATTIT...POLICY CONCPT EXHIBIT 20 WWI. PAGE 97 H1933 EDU/PROP PSY WAR COM/IND

B50
GATZKE H.W.,GERMANY'S DRIVE TO THE WEST. BELGIUM GERMANY MOD/EUR AGRI INDUS POL/PAR FORCES DOMIN AGREE CONTROL REGION COERCE 20 TREATY WWI. PAGE 55 H1104 WAR POLICY NAT/G DIPLOM

B53
SQUIRES J.D.,BRITISH PROPAGANDA AT HOME AND IN THE UNITED STATES FROM 1914 TO 1917. UK NAT/G PROB/SOLV DOMIN PRESS EFFICIENCY...PSY PREDICT 20 WWI INTERVENT PSY/WAR. PAGE 148 H2960 EDU/PROP CONTROL WAR DIPLOM

B54
MITCHELL P.,AFRICAN AFTERTHOUGHTS. UGANDA CONSTN NAT/G ADJUD COERCE WAR 20 WWI MAU/MAU. PAGE 112 H2230 BIOG CHIEF COLONIAL DOMIN

L59
JANIS I.L.,"DECISIONAL CONFLICT: A THEORETICAL ANALYSIS." INTELL NAT/G POL/PAR DELIB/GP LEGIS TOP/EX PLAN...DECISION CONGRESS NAZI 20 WWI. PAGE 80 H1590 ACT/RES PSY DIPLOM

B62
HANAK H.,GREAT BRITAIN AND AUSTRIA-HUNGARY DURING THE FIRST WORLD WAR: A STUDY IN THE FORMATION OF PUBLIC OPINION. CZECHOSLVK UK NAT/G GIVE DOMIN EDU/PROP CONSERVE...BIBLIOG 20 AUST/HUNG WWI. PAGE 65 H1311 WAR DIPLOM ATTIT PRESS

B66
ROOS H.,A HISTORY OF MODERN POLAND FROM THE FOUNDATION OF THE STATE IN THE FIRST WORLD WAR TO THE PRESENT DAY. EUR+WWI POLAND INTELL SOCIETY ECO/TAC LEAD REV ATTIT ORD/FREE MARXISM...BIBLIOG 20 WWI PARTITION. PAGE 133 H2669 NAT/G WAR DIPLOM

B66
SPEARS E.L.,TWO MEN WHO SAVED FRANCE: PETAIN AND DE GAULLE. FRANCE CONSTN FORCES DIPLOM WAR PERSON 20 WWI PETAIN/HP DEGAULLE/C. PAGE 147 H2942 BIOG LEAD CHIEF NAT/G

B67
GIFFORD P.,BRITAIN AND GERMANY IN AFRICA. AFR GERMANY UK ECO/UNDEV LEAD WAR NAT/LISM ATTIT ...POLICY HIST/WRIT METH/COMP ANTHOL BIBLIOG 19/20 WWI. PAGE 56 H1123 COLONIAL ADMIN DIPLOM NAT/COMP

WWII....WORLD WAR II

WYCKOFF T. H3430

WYOMING....WYOMING

X

XENOPHOBIA....SEE NAT/LISM

XENOPHON....XENOPHON

XHOSA....XHOSA TRIBE (SOUTH AFRICA)

S67
RAUM O.,"THE MODERN LEADERSHIP GROUP AMONG THE SOUTH AFRICAN XHOSA." SOUTH/AFR SOCIETY SECT EX/STRUC REPRESENT GP/REL INGP/REL PERSON ...METH/COMP 17/20 XHOSA NEGRO. PAGE 130 H2596 RACE/REL KIN LEAD CULTURE

Y

YAKOBSON S. H3431

YALE/U....YALE UNIVERSITY

YALTA....YALTA CONFERENCE

YAMAMURA K. H3432

YANAGA C. H3433

YANG KUNG-SUN H3434

YANKEE/C....YANKEE CITY - LOCATION OF W.L. WARNEROS STUDY OF SAME NAME

YARBROGH/R....RALPH YARBOROUGH

YAZOO....YAZOO LAND SCANDAL

YEAGER L.B. H3435

YEFREMOV A. H3436

YEMEN....SEE ALSO ISLAM

B58
MACRO E.,BIBLIOGRAPHY OF THE ARABIAN PENINSULA (PAMPHLET). KUWAIT SAUDI/ARAB YEMEN COLONIAL...GEOG 19/20. PAGE 101 H2012 BIBLIOG ISLAM CULTURE NAT/G

B63
UAR MINISTRY OF CULTURE,A BIBLIOGRAPHICAL LIST OF ARABIAN PENINSULA. ISLAM SAUDI/ARAB YEMEN FINAN NAT/G DIPLOM 19/20. PAGE 157 H3147 BIBLIOG GEOG INDUS SECT

B66
US DEPARTMENT OF STATE,RESEARCH ON THE MIDDLE EAST (EXTERNAL RESEARCH LIST NO 4-25). GREECE ISRAEL SYRIA UAR YEMEN CULTURE SOCIETY POL/PAR SECT DIPLOM EDU/PROP WAR NAT/LISM...GEOG GOV/COMP 20. PAGE 160 H3190 BIBLIOG/A ISLAM NAT/G REGION

S68
DOUGLAS-HOME C.,"A MISTAKEN POLICY IN ADEN." YEMEN CULTURE ECO/UNDEV INDUS FORCES WORKER DIPLOM ECO/TAC CONTROL 20 ADEN. PAGE 42 H0842 SOVEREIGN COLONIAL POLICY REGION

YORUBA....YORUBA TRIBE

YOUNG A.N. H3437

YOUNG C. H0126

YOUNG G. H3438

YOUNG T.C. H3439

YOUNG/TURK....YOUNG TURK POLITICAL PARTY

YOUTH....SEE AGE/Y

YU LIEN YEN CHIU H3440

YUAN TUNG-LI H3441,H3442

YUDELMAN/M....MONTEGU YUDELMAN

YUGOSLAVIA....YUGOSLAVIA; SEE ALSO COM

B18
KERNER R.J.,SLAVIC EUROPE: A SELECTED BIBLIOGRAPHY IN THE WESTERN EUROPEAN LANGUAGES. BULGARIA CZECHOSLVK GERMANY/E POLAND RUSSIA YUGOSLAVIA NAT/G DIPLOM MARXISM...LING 19/20. PAGE 85 H1695 BIBLIOG SOCIETY CULTURE COM

B52
ULAM A.B.,TITOISM AND THE COMINFORM. USSR WOR+45 STRUCT INT/ORG NAT/G ACT/RES PLAN EXEC ATTIT DRIVE ALL/VALS...CONCPT OBS VAL/FREE 20 COMINTERN COM POL/PAR TOTALISM

TITO/MARSH. PAGE 157 H3149 YUGOSLAVIA

B55
DUVERGER M.,THE POLITICAL ROLE OF WOMEN. FRANCE GERMANY/W NORWAY YUGOSLAVIA STRATA LOBBY AGE ATTIT ROLE...STAT SAMP CHARTS METH/COMP NAT/COMP HYPO/EXP FEMALE/SEX. PAGE 44 H0875
SEX LEAD PARTIC CHOOSE

B56
WOLFF R.L.,THE BALKANS IN OUR TIME. ALBANIA FUT MOD/EUR USSR YUGOSLAVIA CULTURE INT/ORG SECT DIPLOM EDU/PROP COERCE WAR ORD/FREE...CHARTS 4/20 BALKANS COMINFORM. PAGE 170 H3403
GEOG COM

B57
TOMASIC D.A.,NATIONAL COMMUNISM AND SOVIET STRATEGY. UK USSR YUGOSLAVIA NAT/G POL/PAR CHIEF CREATE DOMIN REV WAR PWR...BIOG TREND 20 TITO/MARSH STALIN/J. PAGE 156 H3112
COM NAT/LISM MARXISM DIPLOM

B59
GOLDWIN R.A.,READINGS IN RUSSIAN FOREIGN POLICY. HUNGARY USSR YUGOSLAVIA ELITES INT/ORG NAT/G REV WAR NAT/LISM PERSON SOCISM...CHARTS 20 MAPS BOLSHEVISM. PAGE 58 H1160
COM MARXISM DIPLOM POLICY

S59
SKILLING H.G.,"COMMUNISM: NATIONAL OR INTERNATIONAL." CHINA/COM USSR YUGOSLAVIA NAT/G POL/PAR VOL/ASSN DOMIN REGION COERCE ATTIT PWR MARXISM SOCISM...CONCPT TOT/POP 20 TITO/MARSH. PAGE 145 H2894
COM TREND

B60
KOHN H.,PAN-SLAVISM: ITS HISTORY AND IDEOLOGY. COM CZECHOSLVK EUR+WWI MOD/EUR USSR YUGOSLAVIA CULTURE ELITES INTELL KIN NAT/G EDU/PROP DRIVE SOVEREIGN ...HUM PHIL/SCI MYTH HIST/WRIT 19/20. PAGE 87 H1745
ATTIT CONCPT NAT/LISM

B61
BURKS R.V.,THE DYNAMICS OF COMMUNISM IN EASTERN EUROPE. COM YUGOSLAVIA POL/PAR RACE/REL ISOLAT ...CORREL CON/ANAL CHARTS GP/COMP DICTIONARY 20 EUROPE/E SLAV/MACED. PAGE 24 H0489
MARXISM STRUCT WORKER REPRESENT

B61
DALLIN D.J.,SOVIET FOREIGN POLICY AFTER STALIN. ASIA CHINA/COM EUR+WWI GERMANY IRAN UK YUGOSLAVIA INT/ORG NAT/G VOL/ASSN FORCES TOP/EX BAL/PWR DOMIN EDU/PROP COERCE ATTIT PWR 20. PAGE 37 H0737
COM DIPLOM USSR

S62
STRACHEY J.,"COMMUNIST INTENTIONS." ASIA USSR YUGOSLAVIA INT/ORG NAT/G FORCES DOMIN EDU/PROP COERCE NUC/PWR NAT/LISM PEACE RIGID/FLEX PWR MARXISM...CONCPT MYTH OBS TIME/SEQ TREND COLD/WAR TOT/POP 20. PAGE 150 H2992
COM ATTIT WAR

B63
HAMM H.,ALBANIA - CHINA'S BEACHHEAD IN EUROPE. ALBANIA CHINA/COM USSR YUGOSLAVIA ELITES SOCIETY POL/PAR DELIB/GP FORCES ECO/TAC COERCE ISOLAT PEACE MARXISM...IDEA/COMP 20 MAO. PAGE 65 H1304
DIPLOM REV NAT/G POLICY

B64
GRIFFITH W.E.,THE SINO-SOVIET RIFT. ASIA CHINA/COM COM CUBA USSR YUGOSLAVIA NAT/G POL/PAR VOL/ASSN DELIB/GP FORCES TOP/EX DIPLOM EDU/PROP DRIVE PERSON PWR...TREND 20 TREATY. PAGE 61 H1224
ATTIT TIME/SEQ BAL/PWR SOCISM

B64
GRIFFITH W.E.,COMMUNISM IN EUROPE (2 VOLS.). CZECHOSLVK USSR WOR+45 WOR-45 YUGOSLAVIA INGP/REL MARXISM SOCISM...ANTHOL 20 EUROPE/E. PAGE 61 H1225
COM POL/PAR DIPLOM GOV/COMP

B64
LAPENNA I.,STATE AND LAW: SOVIET AND YUGOSLAV THEORY. USSR YUGOSLAVIA STRATA STRUCT NAT/G DOMIN COERCE MARXISM...GOV/COMP IDEA/COMP 20. PAGE 91 H1812
JURID COM LAW SOVEREIGN

S64
HORECKY P.L.,"LIBRARY OF CONGRESS PUBLICATIONS IN AID OF USSR AND EAST EUROPEAN RESEARCH." BULGARIA CZECHOSLVK POLAND USSR YUGOSLAVIA NAT/G POL/PAR DIPLOM ADMIN GOV/REL...CLASSIF 20. PAGE 73 H1468
BIBLIOG/A COM MARXISM

S64
MARES V.E.,"EAST EUROPE'S SECOND CHANCE." COM EUR+WWI HUNGARY ROMANIA USSR YUGOSLAVIA ECO/UNDEV NAT/G TOP/EX CREATE PLAN TEC/DEV REGION NAT/LISM RIGID/FLEX PWR...CONCPT STAT COMECON 20. PAGE 102 H2047
VOL/ASSN ECO/TAC

B65
DOLCI D.,A NEW WORLD IN THE MAKING. GHANA SENEGAL USSR YUGOSLAVIA CULTURE INT/ORG PLAN EDU/PROP GP/REL PEACE MORAL...GEOG SOC 20 COLD/WAR. PAGE 42 H0834
SOCIETY ALL/VALS DRIVE PERSON

B65
JELAVICH C.,THE BALKANS. ALBANIA BULGARIA GREECE ROMANIA YUGOSLAVIA ECO/UNDEV WAR SOVEREIGN MARXISM 6/20. PAGE 80 H1597
NAT/LISM NAT/G

B65
ORG FOR ECO COOP AND DEVEL,THE MEDITERRANEAN REGIONAL PROJECT: AN EXPERIMENT IN PLANNING BY SIX COUNTRIES. FUT GREECE SPAIN TURKEY YUGOSLAVIA SOCIETY FINAN NAT/G PROF/ORG EDU/PROP ADMIN REGION COST...POLICY STAT CHARTS 20 OECD. PAGE 121 H2427
PLAN ECO/UNDEV ACADEM SCHOOL

S65
RUBINSTEIN A.Z.,"YUGOSLAVIA'S OPENING SOCIETY." COM USSR INTELL NAT/G LEGIS TOP/EX LEGIT CT/SYS RIGID/FLEX ALL/VALS SOCISM...HUM TIME/SEQ TREND 20. PAGE 135 H2708
CONSTN EX/STRUC YUGOSLAVIA

S65
VUCINICH W.S.,"WHITHER RUMANIA." COM USSR YUGOSLAVIA NAT/G VOL/ASSN DELIB/GP TOP/EX LEGIT NAT/LISM TOTALISM ATTIT DRIVE RIGID/FLEX ORD/FREE WEALTH SOCISM...TIME/SEQ TREND 20. PAGE 164 H3281
ECO/DEV CREATE ROMANIA

B66
JACKSON G.D.,COMINTERN AND PEASANT IN EAST EUROPE 1919-1930. BULGARIA COM CZECHOSLVK EUR+WWI POLAND ROMANIA YUGOSLAVIA STRATA AGRI VOL/ASSN DIPLOM CONTROL CROWD WEALTH...POLICY NAT/COMP 20. PAGE 79 H1575
MARXISM ECO/UNDEV WORKER INT/ORG

B66
RISTIC D.N.,YUGOSLAVIA'S REVOLUTION OF 1941. EUR+WWI YUGOSLAVIA NAT/G WAR ORD/FREE...RECORD BIBLIOG 20 HITLER/A TREATY. PAGE 132 H2633
REV ATTIT FASCISM DIPLOM

B66
SPULBER N.,THE STATE AND ECONOMIC DEVELOPMENT IN EASTERN EUROPE. BULGARIA COM CZECHOSLVK HUNGARY POLAND YUGOSLAVIA CULTURE PLAN CAP/ISM INT/TRADE CONTROL...POLICY CHARTS METH/COMP BIBLIOG/A 19/20. PAGE 148 H2958
ECO/DEV ECO/UNDEV NAT/G TOTALISM

S67
JANICKE M.,"MONOPOLISMUS UND PLURALISMUS IM KOMMUNISTISCHEN HERRSCHAFTSSYSTEM" COM CZECHOSLVK USSR YUGOSLAVIA SOCIETY CONTROL RIGID/FLEX...CONCPT NAT/COMP 20. PAGE 79 H1589
TOTALISM POL/PAR ATTIT PLURISM

S68
BOSSCHERE G D.E.,"A L'EST DU NOUVEAU." CZECHOSLVK HUNGARY POLAND ROMANIA YUGOSLAVIA AGRI CREATE ECO/TAC COERCE GP/REL ATTIT MARXISM SOCISM 20. PAGE 19 H0382
ORD/FREE COM NAT/G DIPLOM

YUKIO O. H3443

YUKON....YUKON, CANADA

Z

ZABLOCKI C.J. H3444

ZAGORIA D.S. H3445

ZALESKI E. H3446

ZAMBIA....SEE ALSO AFR

B64
FRANCK T.M.,EAST AFRICAN UNITY THROUGH LAW. MALAWI TANZANIA UGANDA UK ZAMBIA CONSTN INT/ORG NAT/G ADMIN ROUTINE TASK NAT/LISM ATTIT SOVEREIGN ...RECORD IDEA/COMP NAT/COMP. PAGE 52 H1048
AFR FEDERAL REGION INT/LAW

B66
KAUNDA K.,ZAMBIA: INDEPENDENCE AND BEYOND: THE SPEECHES OF KENNETH KAUNDA. AFR FUT ZAMBIA SOCIETY ECO/UNDEV NAT/G PROB/SOLV ECO/TAC ADMIN RACE/REL SOVEREIGN 20. PAGE 84 H1670
ORD/FREE COLONIAL CONSTN LEAD

B66
KEITH G.,THE FADING COLOUR BAR. AFR CENTRL/AFR UK ZAMBIA CULTURE SCHOOL EDU/PROP PERS/REL DISCRIM AGE ...AUD/VIS NAT/COMP SOC/INTEG 20 NEGRO. PAGE 84 H1682
RACE/REL STRUCT ATTIT NAT/G

B67
WILLS A.J.,AN INTRODUCTION TO THE HISTORY OF CENTRAL AFRICA. RHODESIA ZAMBIA CULTURE SOCIETY ECO/UNDEV TEC/DEV DOMIN WAR ALL/VALS...POLICY TREND BIBLIOG T 14/20 NYASALAND. PAGE 169 H3375
AFR COLONIAL ORD/FREE

ZANDE....ZANDE, AFRICA

B62
EVANS-PRITCHARD E.E.,ESSAYS IN SOCIAL ANTHROPOLOGY. AFR KIN REGION INGP/REL DRIVE HABITAT...OBS METH 20 ZANDE. PAGE 48 H0954
SOCIETY CULTURE SOC STRUCT

ZANZIBAR....SEE TANZANIA

ZARTMAN I.W. H3447,H3448,H3449,H3450,H3451

ZAUBERMAN A. H3452

ZEINE Z.N. H3453

ZENKOVSKY S.A. H3454

ZIESEL K. H3455

ZIMMERMAN I. H3456

ZINKIN T. H3457,H3458

ZINN H. H3459

ZIOCK H. H3460

ZIONISM....SEE ISRAEL, NAT/LISM

ZLATOVRT/N....NIKOLAI ZLATOVRATSKII

ZOLBERG A.R. H3461,H3462

ZOLLSCHAN G.K. H3463

ZONING....ZONING REGULATIONS

ZOPPO C.E. H3464

ZULU....ZULU - MEMBER OF BANTU NATION (SOUTHEAST AFRICA)

ZULULAND

B58

GLUCKMAN M.,ANALYSIS OF A SOCIAL SITUATION IN MODERN ZULULAND. AFR PERS/REL ADJUST DISCRIM EQUILIB NAT/LISM...SOC RECORD AUD/VIS 20 ZULULAND. PAGE 57 H1146
CULTURE RACE/REL STRUCT GP/REL

ZUNI....ZUNI - NEW MEXICAN INDIAN TRIBE

B66

VOGT E.Z.,PEOPLE OF RIMROCK. STRATA STRUCT KIN SECT GP/REL HABITAT ALL/VALS...GEOG INT QU 20 TEXAS NAVAHO MORMON SPAN/AMER ZUNI. PAGE 163 H3260
CULTURE GP/COMP SOC SOCIETY

ZWEIG F. H3465

ZWINGLI/U....ULRICH ZWINGLI

Directory of Publishers

Abelard-Schuman Ltd., New York
Abeledo-Perrot, Buenos Aires
Abingdon Press, Nashville, Tenn.; New York
Academic Press, London; New York
Academy of the Rumanian People's Republic Scientific Documentation Center, Bucharest
Academy Publishers, New York
Accra Government Printer, Accra, Ghana
Acharya Book Depot, Baroda, India
Acorn Press, Phoenix, Ariz.
Action Housing, Inc., Pittsburgh, Pa.
Adams & Charles Black, London
Addison-Wesley Publishing Co., Inc., Reading, Mass.
Adelphi, Greenberg, New York
Adelphi Terrace, London
Advertising Research Foundation, New York
Advisory Committee on Intergovernmental Relations, Washington
Africa Bureau, London
Africa 1960 Committee, London
African Bibliographical Center, Inc., Washington
African Research Ltd., Exeter, England
Agarwal Press, Allahabad, India
Agathon Press, New York
Agency for International Development, Washington
Agrupacion Bibliotecalogica, Montevideo
Aguilar, S. A. de Ediciones, Madrid
Air University, Montgomery, Ala.
Akademiai Kiado, Budapest
Akademische Druck-und Verlagsanstalt, Graz, Austria
Akhil Bharat Sarva Seva Sangh, Rajghat, Varanasi, India; Rajghat, Kashi, India
Al Jadidah Press, Cairo
Alba House, New York
Eberhard Albert Verlag, Freiburg, Germany
Alcan, Paris
Aldine Publishing Co., Chicago
Aligarh Muslim University, Department of History, Aligarh, India
All-India Congress Committee, New Delhi
Allen and Unwin, Ltd., London
Howard Allen, Inc., Cleveland, Ohio
W. H. Allen & Co., Ltd., London
Alliance Inc., New York
Allied Publishers, Private, Ltd., Bombay; New Delhi
Allyn and Bacon, Inc., Boston
Almquist-Wiksell, Stockholm; Upsala
Ambassador Books, Ltd., Toronto, Ontario
American Academy of Arts and Sciences, Harvard University, Cambridge, Mass.
American Academy of Political and Social Science, Philadelphia
American Anthropological Association, Washington, D. C.
American Arbitration Association, New York
American-Asian Educational Exchange, New York
American Assembly, New York
American Association for the Advancement of Science, Washington, D. C.
American Association for the United Nations, New York
American Association of University Women, Washington, D. C.
American Bankers Association, New York
American Bar Association, Chicago
American Bar Foundation, Chicago
American Bibliographical Center-Clio Press, Santa Barbara, Calif.
American Bibliographic Service, Darien, Conn.
American Book Company, New York
American Civil Liberties Union, New York
American Council of Learned Societies, New York
American Council on Education, Washington
American Council on Public Affairs, Washington
American Data Processing, Inc., Detroit, Mich.
American Documentation Institute, Washington
American Economic Association, Evanston, Ill.
American Elsevier Publishing Co., Inc., New York
American Enterprise Institute for Public Policy Research, Washington, D. C.
American Features, New York
American Federation of Labor & Congress of Industrial Organizations, Washington, D. C.
American Foreign Law Association, Chicago
American Forest Products Industries, Washington, D. C.
American Friends of Vietnam, New York
American Friends Service Committee, New York
American Historical Association, Washington, D. C.
American Historical Society, New York
American Institute for Economic Research, Great Barrington, Mass.
American Institute of Consulting Engineers, New York
American Institute of Pacific Relations, New York
American International College, Springfield, Mass.
American Jewish Archives, Hebrew Union College—Jewish Institute of Religion, Cincinnati, Ohio
American Jewish Committee Institute of Human Relations, New York
American Judicature Society, Chicago
American Law Institute, Philadelphia
American Library Association, Chicago
American Management Association, New York
American Marketing Association, Inc., Chicago
American Municipal Association, Washington
American Museum of Natural History Press, New York
American Nepal Education Foundation, Eugene, Oregon
American Newspaper Publishers' Association, New York
American Opinion, Belmont, Mass.
American Philosophical Society, Philadelphia
American Political Science Association, Washington
American Psychiatric Association, New York
American Public Welfare Association, Chicago
American Research Council, Larchmont, N. Y.
American Society of African Culture, New York
American Society of International Law, Chicago
American Society for Public Administration, Chicago; Washington
American Textbook Publishers Council, New York
American Universities Field Staff, New York
American University, Washington, D. C.
American University of Beirut, Beirut
American University of Cairo, Cairo
American University Press, Washington
American University Press Services, Inc., New York
Ampersand Press, Inc., London, New York
Amsterdam Stock Exchange, Amsterdam
Anchor Books, New York
Anderson Kramer Association, Washington, D. C.
Anglo-Israel Association, London
Angus and Robertson, Sydney, Australia
Ann Arbor Publications, Ann Arbor, Mich.
Anthropological Publications, Oosterhout, Netherlands
Anti-Defamation League of B'nai B'rith, New York
Antioch Press, Yellow Springs, Ohio
Antwerp Institut Universitaire des Territoires d'Outre-Mer, Antwerp, Belgium
APEC Editora, Rio de Janeiro
Apollo Editions, New York
Ludwig Appel Verlag, Hamburg
Appleton-Century-Crofts, New York
Aqueduct Books, Rochester, N. Y.
Arbeitsgemeinschaft fur Forschung des Landes Nordrhein-Westfalen, Dusseldorf, Germany
Arcadia, New York
Architectural Press, London
Archon Books, Hamden, Conn.
Arco Publishing Company, New York
Arizona Department of Library and Archives, Tucson
Arizona State University, Bureau of Government Research, Tucson
Arlington House, New Rochelle, N. Y.
Arnold Foundation, Southern Methodist University, Dallas
Edward Arnold Publishers, Ltd., London
J. W. Arrowsmith, Ltd., London
Artes Graficas, Buenos Aires
Artes Graficas Industrias Reunidas SA, Rio de Janeiro
Asia Foundation, San Francisco
Asia Publishing House, Bombay; Calcutta; London; New York
Asia Society, New York
Asian Studies Center, Michigan State University, East Lansing, Mich.
Asian Studies Press, Bombay
Associated College Presses, New York

Associated Lawyers Publishing Co., Newark, N. J.
Association for Asian Studies, Ann Arbor
Association of National Advertisers, New York
Association of the Bar of the City of New York, New York
Association Press, New York
Associated University Bureaus of Business and Economic Research, Eugene, Ore.
M. L. Atallah, Rotterdam
Atheneum Publishers, New York
Atherton Press, New York
Athlone Press, London
Atlanta University Press, Atlanta, Ga.
The Atlantic Institute, Boulogne-sur-Seine
Atlantic Provinces Research Board, Fredericton, Newfoundland
Atma Ram & Sons, New Delhi
Atomic Industrial Forum, New York
Augustan Reprint Society, Los Angeles, Calif.
Augustana College Library, Rock Island, Ill.
Augustana Press, Rock Island, Ill.
J. J. Augustin, New York
Augustinus Verlag, Wurzburg
Australian National Research Council, Melbourne
Australian National University, Canberra
Australian Public Affairs Information Service, Sydney
Australian War Memorial, Canberra
Avi Publishing Co., Westport, Conn.
Avtoreferaty Dissertatsii, Moscow
N. W. Ayer and Sons, Inc., Philadelphia, Pa.
Aymon, Paris

La Baconniere, Neuchatel; Paris
Richard G. Badger, Boston
Baker Book House, Grand Rapids, Mich.
Baker, Vorhis, and Co., Boston
John Baker, London
A. A. Balkema, Capetown
Ballantine Books, Inc., New York
James Ballantine and Co., London
Baltimore Sun, Baltimore, Md.
Banco Central de Venezuela, Caracas
Bank for International Settlements, Basel
Bank of Finland Institute for Economic Research, Helsinki
Bank of Italy, Rome
Bankers Publishing Co., Boston
George Banta Publishing Co., Menasha, Wis.
Bantam Books, Inc., New York
A. S. Barnes and Co., Inc., Cranbury, N. J.
Barnes and Noble, Inc., New York
Barre Publishers, Barre, Mass.
Basic Books, Inc., New York
Batchworth Press Ltd., London
Bayerische Akademie der Wissenschaften, Munich
Bayerischer Schulbuch Verlag, Munich
Ebenezer Baylis and Son, Ltd., Worcester, England
Baylor University Press, Waco, Texas
Beacon Press, Boston
Bechte Verlag, Esslingen, Germany
H. Beck, Dresden
Bedminster Press, Inc., Totowa, N. J.
Beechhurst Press, New York
Behavioral Research Council, Great Barrington, Mass.
Belknap Press, Cambridge, Mass.
G. Bell & Sons, London
Bellman Publishing Co., Inc., Cambridge, Mass.
Matthew Bender and Co., Albany, New York
Bengal Publishers, Ltd., Calcutta
Marshall Benick, New York
Ernest Benn, Ltd., London
J. Bensheimer, Berlin; Leipzig; Mannheim
Benziger Brothers, New York
Berkley Publishing Corporation, New York
Bernard und Graefe Verlag fur Wehrwesen, Frankfurt
C. Bertelsmann Verlag, Gutersloh
Bharati Bhawan, Bankipore, India
Bharatiyi Vidya Bhavan, Bombay
G. R. Bhatkal for Popular Prakashan, Bombay
Bibliographical Society, London
Bibliographical Society of America, New York
Bibliographie des Staats, Dresden
Biblioteca de la II feria del libro exposicion nacional del periodismo, Panuco, Mexico
Biblioteca Nacional, Bogota
Biblioteka Imeni V. I. Lenina, Moscow
Bibliotheque des Temps Nouveaux, Paris
Bibliotheque Nationale, Paris
Adams & Charles Black, London
Basil Blackwell, Oxford
William Blackwood, Edinburgh
Blaisdell Publishing Co., Inc., Waltham, Mass.
Blanford Press, London
Blass, S. A., Madrid
Geoffrey Bles, London
BNA, Inc. (Bureau of National Affairs), Washington, D. C.
Board of Trade and Industry Estates Management Corp., London
T. V. Boardman and Co., London
Bobbs-Merrill Company, Inc., Indianapolis, Ind.
The Bodley Head, London
Bogen-Verlag, Munich
Bohlau-Verlag, Cologne; Graz; Tubingen
H. G. Bohn, London
Boni and Gaer, New York
Bonn University, Bonn
The Book of the Month Club, Johannesburg
Bookcraft, Inc., Salt Lake City, Utah
Bookfield House, New York
Bookland Private, Ltd., Calcutta; London
Bookmailer, New York
Bookman Associates, Record Press, New York
Books for Libraries, Inc., Freeport, N. Y.
Books International, Jullundur City, India
Borsenverein der deutschen Buchhandler, Leipzig
Bossange, Paris
Boston Book Co., Boston
Boston College Library, Chestnut Hill, Boston
Boston University, African Research Program, Boston
Boston University Press, Boston
H. Bouvier Verlag, Bonn
Bowes and Bowes, Ltd., Cambridge, England
R. R. Bowker Co., New York
John Bradburn, New York
George Braziller, Inc., New York
Brentano's, New York
Brigham Young University, Provo, Utah
E. J. Brill, Leyden
British Borneo Research Project, London
British Broadcasting Corp., London
British Council, London
British Liberal Party Organization, London
British Museum, London
Broadman Press, Nashville, Tenn.
The Brookings Institution, Washington
Brown University Press, Providence, R. I.
A. Brown and Sons, Ltd., London
William C. Brown Co., Dubuque, Iowa
Brown-White-Lowell Press, Kansas City
Bruce Publishing Co., Milwaukee, Wis.
Buchdruckerei Meier, Bulach, Germany
Buchhandler-Vereinigung, Frankfurt
Buijten & Schipperheijn, Amsterdam
Building Contractors Council, Chicago
Bureau of Public Printing, Manila
Bureau of Social Science Research, Washington, D. C.
Business Economists Group, Oxford
Business Publications, Inc., Chicago
Business Service Corp., Detroit, Mich.
Buttenheim Publishing Corp., New York
Butterworth's, London; Washington, D. C.; Toronto

Anne Cabbott, Manchester, England
California, Assembly of the State of, Sacramento, Calif.
California State Library, Sacramento
Calman Levy, Paris
Camara Oficial del Libro, Madrid
Cambridge Book Co., Inc., Bronxville, N. Y.
Cambridge University Press, Cambridge; London; New York
Camelot Press Ltd., London
Campion Press, London
M. Campos, Rio de Janeiro
Canada, Civil Service Commission, Ottawa
Canada, Civil Service Commission, Organization Division, Ottawa
Canada, Ministry of National Health and Welfare, Ottawa
Canada, National Joint Council of the Public Service, Ottawa

Canadian Dept. of Mines and Technical Surveys, Ottawa
Canadian Institute of International Affairs, Toronto
Canadian Peace Research Institute, Clarkson, Ont.
Canadian Trade Committee, Montreal
Candour Publishing Co., London
Jonathan Cape, London
Cape and Smith, New York
Capricorn Books, New York
Caribbean Commission, Port-of-Spain, Trinidad
Carleton University Library, Ottawa
Erich Carlsohn, Leipzig
Carnegie Endowment for International Peace, New York
Carnegie Endowment for International Peace, Washington, D. C.
Carnegie Foundation for the Advancement of Teaching, New York
Carnegie Press, Pittsburgh, Pa.
Carswell Co., Ltd., Toronto, Canada
Casa de las Americas, Havana
Case Institute of Technology, Cleveland, Ohio
Frank Cass & Co., Ltd., London
Cassell & Co., Ltd., London
Castle Press, Pasadena, Calif.
Catholic Historical Society of Philadelphia, Philadelphia
Catholic Press, Beirut
Catholic Students Mission Crusade Press, Cincinnati, Ohio
Catholic University Press, Washington
The Caxton Printers, Ltd., Caldwell, Idaho
Cedesa, Brussels
Cellar Book Shop, Detroit, Mich.
Center for Applied Research in Education, New York
Center for Applied Research in Education, Washington, D. C.
Center for Research on Economic Development, Ann Arbor, Mich.
Center for the Study of Democratic Institutions, Santa Barbara, Calif.
Center of Foreign Policy Research, Washington, D. C.
Center of International Studies, Princeton
Center of Planning and Economic Research, Athens, Greece; Washington, D. C.
Central Asian Research Centre, London
Central Bank of Egypt, Cairo
Central Book Co., Inc., Brooklyn, N. Y.
Central Book Department, Allahabad, India
Central Law Book Supply, Inc., Manila
Central News Agency, Ltd., Capetown, S. Afr.
Central Publicity Commission, Indian National Congress, New Delhi
Centre de Documentation CNRS, Paris
Centre de Documentation Economique et Sociale Africaine, Brussels
Centre d'Etudes de Politique Etrangere, Paris
Centre de Recherches sur l'URSS et les pays de l'est, Strasbourg
Centro de Estudios Monetarios Latino-Americanos, Mexico City
Centro Editorial, Guatemala City
Centro Mexicano de Escritores, Mexico City
Centro Para el "Desarrollo Economico y Social de America Latina", Santiago, Chile
The Century Co., New York
Century House, Inc., Watkins Glen, N. Y.
Cercle de la Librairie, Paris
Leon Chaillez Editeur, Paris
Chaitanya Publishing House, Allahabad, India
Chamber of Commerce of the United States, Washington, D. C.
S. Chand and Co., New Delhi
Chandler Publishing Co., San Francisco
Chandler-Davis, Lexington, Mass.
Chandler-Davis Publishing Co., West Trenton, N. J.
Channel Press, Inc., Great Neck, N. Y.
Chapman and Hall, London
Geoffrey Chapman, London
Chatham College, Pittsburgh, Pa.
Chatto and Windus, Ltd., London
F. W. Cheshire, London
Chestnut Hill, Boston College Library, Boston
Chicago Joint Reference Library, Chicago
Chilean Development Corp., New York
Chilmark Press, New York
Chilton Books, New York
China Viewpoints, Hong Kong
Chinese-American Publishing Co., Shanghai
Chiswick Press, London
Christian Crusade, Tulsa, Okla.
Georg Christiansen, Itzehoe, Germany
Christopher Publishing House, Boston
Chulalongkorn University, Bangkok
Church League of America, Wheaton, Ill.
C. I. Associates, New York
Cincinnati Civil Service, Cincinnati, Ohio
Citadel Press, New York
City of Johannesburg Public Library, Johannesburg
Citizens Research Foundation, Paris
Citizens Research Foundation, Princeton, N. J.
Ciudad Universitaria, San Jose, Calif.
Ciudad y Espiritu, Buenos Aires
Claremont Colleges, Claremont, Calif.
Clarendon Press, London
Clark, Irwin and Co., Ltd., Toronto
Clark University Press, Worcester, Mass.
Classics Press, New York
Clay and Sons, London
Cleveland Civil Service Commission, Cleveland
Clio Press, Santa Barbara, Calif.
William Clowes and Sons, Ltd., London
Colin (Librairie Armand) Paris
College and University Press, New Haven
Collet's Holdings, Ltd., London
Colliers, New York
F. Collin, Brussels
Collins, London
Colloquium Verlag, Berlin
Colombo Plan Bureau, Colombo, Ceylon
Colonial Press Inc., Northport, Ala.; New York
Colorado Bibliographic Institute, Denver
Colorado Legislature Council, Denver
Colorado State Board of Library Commissioners, Denver
Columbia University, New York
Columbia University, Bureau of Applied Social Research, New York
Columbia University, Center for Urban Education, New York
Columbia University, East Asian Institute, New York
Columbia University, Graduate School of Business, New York
Columbia University, Institute of French Studies, New York
Columbia University, Institute of Public Administration, New York
Columbia University, Institute of Russian Studies, New York
Columbia University, Institute of War-Peace Studies, New York
Columbia University, Law Library, New York
Columbia University, Parker School, New York
Columbia University, School of International Affairs, New York
Columbia University, School of Library Service, New York
Columbia University Press, New York
Columbia University Teachers College, New York
Combat Forces Press, Washington, D. C.
Comet Press, New York
Comision Nacional Ejecutiva, Buenos Aires
Commerce Clearing House, Chicago; Washington; New York
Commercial Credit Co., Baltimore, Md.
Commissao do iv Centenario de Ciudade, Sao Paulo
Commission for Technical Cooperation, Lahore
Commission to Study the Organization of Peace, New York
Committee for Economic Development, New York
Committee on Africa, New York
Committee on Federal Tax Policy, New York
Committee on Near East Studies, Washington
Committee on Public Administration, Washington, D. C.
Committee to Frame World Constitution, New York
Common Council for American Unity, New York
Commonwealth Agricultural Bureau, London
Commonwealth Economic Commission, London
Community Publications, Manila
Community Renewal Program, San Francisco
Community Studies, Inc., Kansas City
Companhia Editora Forense, Rio de Janeiro
Companhia Editora Nacional, Sao Paulo
Compass Books, New York
Concordia Publishing House, St. Louis, Mo.
Confederate Publishing Co., Tuscaloosa, Ala.
Conference on Economic Progress, Washington, D. C.
Conference on State and Economic Enterprise in Modern Japan, Estes Park, Colo.
Congress for Cultural Freedom, Prabhakar

Congressional Quarterly Service, Washington
Connecticut Personnel Department, Hartford
Connecticut State Civil Service Commission, Hartford
Conseil d'Etat, Paris
Conservative Political Centre, London
Constable and Co., London
Archibald Constable and Co., Edinburgh
Cooper Square Publishers, New York
U. Cooper and Partners, Ltd., London
Corinth Books, New York
Cornell University, Dept. of Asian Studies, Ithaca
Cornell University, Graduate School of Business and Public Administration, Ithaca
Cornell University Press, Ithaca
Cornell University, School of Industry and Labor Planning, Ithaca
Council for Economic Education, Bombay
Council of Education, Johannesburg
Council of Europe, Strasbourg
Council of State Governments, Chicago, Ill.
Council of the British National Bibliography, Ltd., London
Council on Foreign Relations, New York
Council on Public Affairs, Washington, D. C.
Council on Religion and International Affairs, New York
Council on Social Work Education, Washington, D. C.
Covici, Friede, Inc., New York
Coward-McCann, Inc., New York
Cresset Press, London
Crestwood Books, Springfield, Va.
Criterion Books, Inc., New York
S. Crofts and Co., New York
Crosby, Lockwood, and Sons, Ltd., London
Crosscurrents Press, New York
Thomas Y. Crowell Co., New York
Crowell-Collier and MacMillan, New York
Crown Publishers, Inc., New York
C.S.I.C., Madrid
Cuadernos de la Facultad de Derecho Universidad Veracruzana, Mexico City
Cuerpo Facultativo de Archiveros, Bibliotecarios y Argueologos, Madrid
Cultural Center of the French Embassy, New York
Current Scene, Hong Kong
Current Thought, Inc., Durham, N. C.
Czechoslovak Foreign Institute in Exile, Chicago

Da Capo Press, New York
Daguin Freres, Editeurs, Paris
Daily Telegraph, London
Daily Worker Publishing Co., Chicago
Dalloz, Paris
Damascus Bar Association, Damascus
Dangary Publishing Co., Baltimore
David Davies Memorial Institute of Political Studies, London
David-Stewart, New York
John Day Co., Inc., New York
John de Graff, Inc., Tuckahoe, N. Y.
La Decima Conferencia Interamericana, Caracas
Delacorte Press, New York
Dell Publishing Co., New York
T. S. Denison & Co., Inc., Minneapolis, Minn.
J. M. Dent, London
Departamento de Imprensa Nacional, Rio de Janeiro
Deseret Book Co., Salt Lake City, Utah
Desert Research Institute Publications' Office, Reno, Nev.
Deus Books, Paulist Press, Glen Rock, N. J.
Andre Deutsch, Ltd., London
Deutsche Afrika Gesellschaft, Bonn
Deutsche Bibliographie, Frankfurt am Main
Deutsche Bucherei, Leipzig
Deutsche Gesellschaft fur Volkerrecht, Karlsruhe
Deutsche Gesellschaft fur Auswartige Politik, Bonn
Deutsche Verlagsanstalt, Stuttgart
Deutscher Taschenbuch Verlag, Munich
Deva Datta Shastri, Hoshiarpur
Development Loan Fund, Washington, D. C.
Devin-Adair, Co., New York
Diablo Press, Inc., Berkeley, Calif.
Dial Press, Inc., New York
Dibco Press, San Jose, Cal.
Dickenson Publishing Co., Inc., Belmont, Calif.
Didier Publishers, New York

Firmin Didot Freres, Paris
Dietz Verlag, Berlin
Difusao Europeia do Livro, Sao Paulo
Diplomatic Press, London
Direccion General de Accion Social, Lisbon
District of Columbia, Office of Urban Renewal, Washington, D. C.
Djambatan, Amsterdam
Dennis Dobson, London
Dobunken Co., Ltd., Tokyo
La Documentation Francaise, Paris
Documents Index, Arlington, Virginia
Dodd, Mead and Co., New York
Octave Doin et Fils, Paris
Dolphin Books, Inc., New York
Dominion Press, Chicago
Walter Doon Verlag, Bremen
George H. Doran Co., New York
Dorrance and Co., Inc., Philadelphia, Pa.
Dorsey Press, Homewood, Illinois
Doubleday and Co., Inc., Garden City, N. Y.
Dover Publications, New York
Dow Jones and Co., Inc., New York
Dragonfly Books, Hong Kong
Drei Masken Verlag, Munich
Droemersche Verlagsanstalt, Zurich
Droste Verlag, Dusseldorf
Druck und Verlag von Carl Gerolds Sohn, Vienna
Guy Drummond, Montreal
The Dryden Press, New York
Dryfus Conference on Public Affairs, Hanover, N. H.
Duckworth, London
Duell, Sloan & Pearce, New York
Dufour Editions, Inc., Chester Springs, Pa.
Carl Duisburg-Gesellschaft fur Nachwuchsforderung, Cologne
Duke University, School of Law, Durham, N. C.
Duke University Press, Durham, N. C.
Dulau and Co., London
Duncker und Humblot, Berlin
Duquesne University Press, Pittsburgh, Pa.
R. Dutt, London
E. P. Dutton and Co., Inc., Garden City, N. Y.

E. P. & Commercial Printing Co., Durban, S. Africa
East Africa Publishing House, Nairobi
East European Fund, Inc., New York
East-West Center Press, Honolulu
Eastern Kentucky Regional Development Commission, Frankfort, Ky.
Eastern World, Ltd., London
Emil Ebering, Berlin
Echter-Verlag, Wurzburg
Ecole Francaise d'Extreme Orient, Paris
Ecole Nationale d'Administration, Paris
Econ Verlag, Dusseldorf; Vienna
Economic Research Corp., Ltd., Montreal
Economic Society of South Africa, Johannesburg
The Economist, London
Edicao Saraiva, Sao Paulo
Ediciones Ariel, Barcelona
Ediciones Cultura Hispanica, Madrid
Ediciones del Movimiento, Borgos, Spain
Ediciones Nuestro Tiempo, Montevideo
Ediciones Rialp, Madrid
Ediciones Riaz, Lima
Ediciones Siglo Veinte, Buenos Aires
Ediciones Tercer Mundo, Bogota
Edicoes de Revista de Estudes Politos, Rio de Janeiro
Edicoes Do Val, Rio de Janeiro
Edicoes GRD, Rio de Janeiro
Edicoes o Cruzeiro, Rio de Janeiro
Edicoes Tempo Brasileiro, Ltda., Rio de Janeiro
Edinburgh House Press, Edinburgh
Editions Albin Michel, Paris
Editions Alsatia, Paris
Editions Berger-Levrault, Paris
Editions Cujas, Paris
Editions de l'Epargne, Paris
Editions de l'Institut de Sociologie de l'Universite Libre de Bruxelles, Brussels
Editions d'Organisation, Paris
Editions Denoel, Paris
Editions John Didier, Paris

Editions du Carrefour, Paris
Editions du Cerf, Paris
Editions du Livre, Monte Carlo
Editions du Monde, Paris
Editions du Rocher, Monaco
Editions du Seuil, Paris
Editions du Tiers-Monde, Algiers
Editions du Vieux Colombier, Paris
Editions Eyrolles, Paris
Editions Internationales, Paris
Editions Mont Chrestien, Paris
Editions Nauwelaerts, Louvain
Editions Ouvrieres, Paris
Editions A. Pedone, Paris
Editions Presence Africaine, Paris
Editions Rouff, Paris
Editions Sedif, Paris
Editions Sirey, Paris
Editions Sociales, Paris
Editions Techniques Nord Africaines, Rabat
Editions Universitaires, Paris
Editora Brasiliense, Sao Paulo
Editora Civilizacao Brasileira S. A., Rio de Janeiro
Editora Fulgor, Sao Paulo
Editora Saga, Rio de Janerio
Editores letras e artes, Rio de Janeiro
Editores Mexicanos, Mexico City
Editores Mexicanos Unidos, Mexico City
Editorial AIP, Miami
Editorial Amerinda, Buenos Aires
Editorial Columbia, Buenos Aires
Editorial Freeland, Buenos Aires
Editorial Gustavo Gili, Barcelona
Editorial Jus, Mexico City, Mexico
Editorial Lex, Havana
Editorial Losa da Buenos Aires, Buenos Aires
Editorial Marymar, Buenos Aires
Editorial Mentora, Barcelona
Editorial Nascimento, Santiago
Editorial Palestra, Buenos Aires
Editorial Patria, Mexico City
Editorial Pax, Bogota
Editorial Pax-Mexico, Mexico City
Editorial Platina, Buenos Aires
Editorial Porrua, Mexico City
Editorial Stylo Durangozgo, Mexico City
Editorial Universitaria de Buenos Aires, Buenos Aires
Editorial Universitaria de Puerto Rico, San Jose
Editorial Universitaria Santiago, Santiago
Le Edizioni de Favoro, Rome
Edizioni di Storia e Letteratura, Rome
Edizioni Scientifiche Italiane, Naples
Education and World Affairs, New York
Educational Heritage, Yonkers, N. Y.
Edwards Brothers, Ann Arbor
Effingham Wilson Publishers, London
Egyptian Library Press, Cairo
Egyptian Society of International Law, Cairo
Elex Books, London
Elsevier Publishing Co., Ltd., London
EMECE Editores, Buenos Aires
Emerson Books, New York
Empresa Editora Austral, Ltd., Santiago
Encyclopedia Britannica, Inc., Chicago
English Universities Press, London
Ferdinand Enke Verlag, Bonn; Erlangen; Stuttgart
Horst Erdmann Verlag, Schwarzwald
Paul Eriksson, Inc., New York
Escorpion, Buenos Aires
Escuela de Historia Moderna, Madrid
Escuela Nacional de Ciencias Politicas y Sociales, Mexico City
Escuela Superior de Administracion Publica America Central, San Jose, Costa Rica
Essener Verlagsanstalt, Essen
Essential Books, Ltd., London
Ethiopia, Ministry of Information, Addis Ababa
Etudes, Paris
Euroamerica, Madrid
Europa-Archiv, Frankfurt am Main
Europa Publications Ltd., London
Europa Verlag, Zurich; Vienna
Europaische Verlagsanstalt, Frankfurt
European Committee for Economic and Social Progress, Milan
European Free Trade Association, Geneva
Evangelischer Verlag, Zurich
Edward Evans and Sons, Shanghai
Everline Press, Princeton
Excerpta Criminologica Foundation, Leyden, Netherlands
Exchange Bibliographies, Eugene, Ore.
Export Press, Belgrade
Exposition Press, Inc., New York
Eyre and Spottiswoode, Ltd., London
Extending Horizon Books, Boston

F. and T. Publishers, Seattle, Washington
Faber and Faber, Ltd., London
Fabian Society, London
Facing Reality Publishing Corporation, Detroit, Mich.
Facts on File, Inc., New York
Fairchild Publishing, Inc., New York
Fairleigh Dickinson Press, Rutherford, N. J.
Falcon Press, London
Family Service Association of America, New York
Farrar and Rinehart, New York
Farrar, Strauss & Giroux, Inc., New York
Fawcett World Library, New York
F. W. Faxon Co., Inc., Boston
Fayard, Paris
Federal Legal Publications, Inc., New York
Federal Reserve Bank of New York, New York
Federal Trust for Education and Research, London
Fellowship Publications, New York
Feltrinelli Giangiacomo (Editore), Milan
Au Fil d'Ariadne, Paris
Filipiniana Book Guild, Manila
Financial Index Co., New York
Finnish Political Science Association, Helsinki
Fischer Bucherei, Frankfurt
Fischer Verlag, Stuttgart
Gustav Fischer Verlag, Jena
Flammarion, Paris
Fleet Publishing Co., New York
Fletcher School of Law and Diplomacy, Boston
R. Flint and Co., London
Florida State University, Tallahassee
Follett Publishing Co., Chicago
Fondation Nationale des Sciences Politiques, Paris
Fondo Historico y Bibliografico Jose Foribio, Medina, Santiago
Fondo de Cultura Economica, Mexico
B. C. Forbes and Sons, New York
Ford Foundation, New York
Fordham University Press, New York
Foreign Affairs Association of Japan, Tokyo
Foreign Affairs Bibliography, New York
Foreign Language Press, Peking
Foreign Language Publishing House, Moscow
Foreign Policy Association, New York
Foreign Policy Clearing House, Washington, D. C.
Foreign Policy Research Institute, University of Pennsylvania, Philadelphia, Pa.
Foreign Trade Library, Philadelphia
Arnold Forni Editore, Bologna
Forschungs-Berichte des Landes Nordrhein-Westfalen, Dusseldorf, Germany
Fortress Press, Philadelphia, Pa.
Foundation for Economic Education, Irvington-on-Hudson, N. Y.
Foundation for Social Research, Los Angeles, Calif.
Foundation Press, Inc., Brooklyn, N. Y.; Mineola, N. Y.
Foundation Press, Inc., Chicago
Foundation for Research on Human Behavior, New York
France Editions Nouvelles, Paris
France, Ministere de l'Education Nationale, Paris
France, Ministere d'Etat aux Affaires Culturelles, Paris
France, Ministere des Finances et des Affaires Economiques, Paris
Francois Maspera, Paris
Francke Verlag, Munich
Ben Franklin Press, Pittsfield, Mass.
Burt Franklin, New York
Free Europe Committee, New York
Free Press, New York
Free Press of Glencoe, Glencoe, Ill.; New York

Free Speech League, New York
Freedom Books, New York
Freedom Press, London
Ira J. Friedman, Inc., Port Washington, N. Y.
Friends General Conference, Philadelphia, Pa.
Friendship Press, New York
M. L. Fuert, Los Angeles
Fund for the Republic, New York
Fundacao Getulio Vargas, Rio de Janeiro
Funk and Wagnalls Co., Inc., New York
Orell Fuessli Verlag, Zurich

Galaxy Books, Oxford
Gale Research Co., Detroit
Galton Publishing Co., New York
A. R. Geoghegan, Buenos Aires
George Washington University, Population Research Project, Washington, D. C.
Georgetown University Press, Washington, D. C.
Georgia State College, Atlanta, Ga.
Georgia State Library, Atlanta, Ga.
Germany (Territory under Allied Occupation, 1945—U. S. Zone) Office of Public Information, Information Control Division, Bonn
Germany, Bundesministerium fur Vertriebene, Fluechtlinge, und Kriegsbeschadigte (Federal Ministry for Expellees, Refugees, and War Victims), Bonn
Gerold & Co. Verlag, Vienna, Austria
Ghana University Press, Accra, Ghana
Gideon Press, Beirut
Gustavo Gili, Barcelona
Ginn and Co., Boston
Glanville Publishing Co., New York
Glasgow University Press, Glasgow
Gleditsch Brockhaus, Leipzig
Glencoe Free Press, London
Golden Bell Press, Denver, Colo.
Victor Gollancz, Ltd., London
Gordon and Breach Science Publications, New York
Gothic Printing Co., Capetown, S. Afr.
Gould Publications, Jamaica, N. Y.
Government Affairs Foundation, Albany, N. Y.
Government Data Publications, New York
Government of India National Library, Calcutta
Government Printing Office, Washington
Government Publications of Political Literature, Moscow
Government Research Institute, Cleveland
Grafica Americana, Caracas
Grafica Editorial Souza, Rio de Janeiro
Graficas Gonzales, Madrid
Graficas Uguina, Madrid
Graphic, New York
H. W. Gray, Inc., New York
Great Britain, Administrative Staff College, London
Great Britain, Committee on Ministers' Powers, London
Great Britain, Department of Technical Cooperation, London
Great Britain, Foreign Office, London
Great Britain, Ministry of Overseas Development, London
Great Britain, Treasury, London
Greater Bridgeport Region, Planning Agency, Trumbull
W. Green and Son, Edinburgh
Green Pagoda Press, Hong Kong
Greenwich Book Publications, New York
Greenwood Periodicals, New York
Griffin Press, Adelaide, Australia
Grolier, Inc., New York
J. Groning, Hamburg
Grosset and Dunlap, Inc., New York
Grossman Publishers, New York
G. Grote'sche Verlagsbuchhandlung, Rastalt, Germany
Group for the Advancement of Psychiatry, New York
Grove Press, Inc., New York
Grune and Stratton, New York
Gruyter and Co., Walter de, Berlin
E. Guilmato, Paris
Democratic Party of Guinea, Guinea
Gulf Publishing Co., Houston, Texas
J. Chr. Gunderson Boktrykkeri og Bokbinderi, Oslo
Hans E. Gunther Verlag, Stuttgart
Gutersloher Verlagshaus, Gutersloh

Hadar Publishing Co., Tel-Aviv
Hafner Publishing Co., Inc., New York
G. K. Hall, Boston
Robert Hall, London
Charles Hallberg and Co., Chicago
Hamburgisches Wirtschafts Archiv, Hamburg
Hamilton & Co., London
Hamilton County Research Foundation, Cincinnati
Hamish Hamilton, London
Hanover House, New York
Hansard Society, London
Harcourt, Brace and World, New York
Harlo Press, Detroit, Mich.
Harper and Row Publishers, New York; London
George Harrap and Co., London
Otto Harrassowitz, Wiesbaden
Harrison Co., Atlanta, Ga.
Rupert Hart-Davis, London
Hartford Printing Co., Hartford, Conn.
Harvard Center for International Affairs, Cambridge, Mass.
Harvard Law School, Cambridge, Mass.
Harvard Law Review Association, Cambridge, Mass.
Harvard University Center for East Asian Studies, Cambridge, Mass.
Harvard University, Center for Russian Research and Studies, Cambridge, Mass.
Harvard University, Graduate School of Business Administration, Cambridge, Mass.
Harvard University, Peabody Museum, Cambridge, Mass.
Harvard University, Widener Library, Cambridge
Harvard University Press, Cambridge
V. Hase und Kohler Verlag, Mainz
Hastings House, New York
Hauser Press, New Orleans, La.
Hawthorne Books, Inc., New York
Hayden Book Company, New York
The John Randolph Haynes and Dora Haynes Foundation, Los Angeles
The Edward D. Hazen Foundation, New Haven, Conn.
D. C. Heath and Co., Boston
Hebrew University Press, Jerusalem
Heffer and Sons Ltd., Cambridge, England
William S. Hein and Co., Buffalo
James H. Heineman, Inc., New York
Heinemann Ltd., London
Heirsemann, Leipzig
A. Hepple, Johannesburg
Helicon Press, Inc., Baltimore, Md.
Herald Press, Scottdale, Penna.
Herder and Herder, New York
Herder Book Co., New York, St. Louis
Johann Gottfried Herder, Marburg, Germany
Heritage Foundation, Chicago
The Heritage Press, New York
Hermitage Press, Inc., New York
Heron House Winslow, Washington, D. C.
Herzl Press, New York
Carl Heymanns Verlag, Berlin
Hill and Wang, Inc., New York
Hillary House Publishers, Ltd., New York
Hind Kitabs, Ltd., Bombay
Hinds, Noble, and Eldridge, New York
Ferdinand Hirt, Kiel, Germany
Historical Society of New Mexico, Albuquerque, N. M.
H. M. Stationery Office, London
Hobart and William Smith Colleges, Geneva, N. Y.
Hobbs, Dorman and Co., New York
Hodden and Staughton, London
William Hodge and Co., Ltd., London
Hodges Figgis and Co., Ltd., Dublin
J. G. Hodgson, Fort Collins, Colo.
Hogarth Press, London
The Hokuseido Press, Tokyo
Holborn Publishing House, London
Hollis and Carter, London
Hollywood A.S.P. Council, Hollywood, Calif.
Holt and Williams, New York
Holt, Rinehart and Winston, New York
Henry Holt and Co., New York
Holzner Verlag, Wurzburg
Home and Van Thal, London
Hong Kong Government Press, Hong Kong
Hong Kong University Press, Hong Kong
Hoover Institute on War, Revolution and Peace, Stanford, Calif.

Hope College, Holland, Mich.
Horizon Press, Inc., New York
Houghton, Mifflin Co., Boston
Houlgate House, Los Angeles
Howard University Press, Washington
Howell, Sosbin and Co., New York
Hudson Institute, Inc., Harmon-on-Hudson, New York
B. W. Huebsch, Inc., New York
H. Hugendubel Verlag, Munich
Human Relations Area Files Press (HRAF), New Haven
Human Rights Publications, Caulfield, Victoria, Australia
Human Sciences Research, Inc., Arlington, Va.
Humanities Press, New York
Humon and Rousseau, Capetown
Hungarian Academy of Science, Publishing House of, Budapest
Hunter College Library, New York
R. Hunter, London
Huntington Library, San Marino, Calif.
Hutchinson and Co., London
Hutchinson University Library, London

Ibadan University Press, Ibadan, Nigeria
Iberia Publishing Company, New York
Ibero-American Institute, Stockholm
Illini Union Bookstore, Champaign, Ill.
Illinois State Publications, Springfield
Ilmgau Verlag, Pfaffenhofen
Imago Publishing Co., Ltd., London
Imprenta Calderon, Honduras
Imprenta Mossen Alcover, Mallorca
Imprenta Nacional, Caracas
Imprimerie d'Extreme Orient, Hanoi
Imprimerie Nationale, Paris
Imprimerie Sefan, Tunis
Imprimerie Fr. Van Muysewinkel, Brussels
Incentivist Publications, Greenwich, Conn.
Index Society, New York
India and Pakistan: Combined Interservice Historical Section, New Delhi
India, Government of, Press, New Delhi
India, Ministry of Community Development, New Delhi
India, Ministry of Finance, New Delhi
India, Ministry of Health, New Delhi
India, Ministry of Home Affairs, New Delhi
India, Ministry of Information and Broadcasting, Faridabad; New Delhi
India, Ministry of Law, New Delhi
Indian Council on World Affairs, New Delhi
Indian Institute of Public Administration, New Delhi
Indian Ministry of Information and Broadcasting, New Delhi
Indian Press, Ltd., Allahabad
Indian School of International Studies, New Delhi
Indiana University, Bureau of Government Research, Bloomington
Indiana University, Institute of Training for Public Service, Department of Government, Bloomington
Indiana University Press, Bloomington
Indraprastha Estate, New Delhi
Industrial Areas Foundations, Chicago
Industrial Council for Social and Economic Studies, Upsala
Industrial Press, New York
Infantry Journal Press, Washington, D. C.
Information Bulletin Ltd., London
Insel Verlag, Frankfurt
Institut Afro-Asiatique d'Etudes Syndicales, Tel Aviv
Institut de Droit International, Paris
Institut des Hautes Etudes de l'Amerique Latine, Rio de Janeiro
Institut des Relations Internationales, Brussels
Institut fur Kulturwissenschaftliche Forschung, Freiburg
Institut fur Politische Wissenschaft, Frankfurt
Institut International de Collaboration Philosophique, Paris
Institute for Comparative Study of Political Systems, Washington, D. C.
Institute for Defense Analyses, Washington, D. C.
Institute for International Politics and Economics, Prague
Institute for International Social Research, Princeton, N. J.
Institute for Mediterranean Affairs, New York
Institute for Monetary Research, Washington, D. C.
Institute for Social Science Research, Washington, D. C.
Institute of Brazilian Studies, Rio de Janeiro
Institute of Early American History and Culture, Williamsburg, Va.
Institute of Economic Affairs, London
Institute of Ethiopian Studies, Addis Ababa
Institute of Human Relations Press, New York
Institute of Islamic Culture, Lahore
Institute of Labor and Industrial Relations, Urbana, Ill.
Institute of Judicial Administration, New York
Institute of National Planning, Cairo
Institute of Pacific Relations, New York
Institute of Professional Civil Servants, London
Institute of Public Administration, Dublin
Instituto de Antropologia e Etnologia de Para, Belem, Para, Brazil
Instituto Brasileiro de Estudos Afro-Asiaticos, Rio de Janeiro
Instituto Caro y Cuervo, Bogota
Instituto de Derecho Comparedo, Barcelona
Instituto de Estudios Africanos, Madrid
Instituto de Estudios Politicos, Madrid
Instituto de Investigaciones Historicas, Mexico City
Instituto Guatemalteco-Americano, Guatemala City
Instituto Internacional de Ciencias Administrativas, Rio de Janeiro
Instituto Nacional do Livro, Rio de Janeiro
Instituto Nazionale di Cultura Fascista, Firenze
Instituto Pan Americano de Geografia e Historia, Mexico City
Integrated Education Associates, Chicago
Inter-American Bibliographical and Library Association, Gainesville, Fla.
Inter-American Development Bank, Buenos Aires
Inter-American Statistical Institute, Washington
Intercollegiate Case Clearing House, Boston
International African Institute, London
International Association for Research in Income and Wealth, New Haven, Conn.
International Atomic Energy Commission, Vienna
International Bank for Reconstruction and Development, Washington, D. C.
International Center for African Economic and Social Documentation, Brussels
International Chamber of Commerce, New York
International City Managers' Association, Chicago
International Commission of Jurists, Geneva
International Committee for Peaceful Investment, Washington, D. C.
International Congress of History of Discoveries, Lisbon
International Congress of Jurists, Rio de Janeiro
International Cotton Advisory Committee, Washington, D. C.
International Court of Justice, The Hague
International Development Association, Washington, D. C.
International Economic Policy Association, Washington, D. C.
International Editions, New York
International Federation for Documentation, The Hague
International Federation for Housing and Planning, The Hague
International Finance, Princeton, N. J.
International Institute of Administrative Science, Brussels
International Institute of Differing Civilizations, Brussels
International Labour Office, Geneva
International Managers' Association, Chicago
International Monetary Fund, Washington
International Press Institute, Zurich
International Publications Service, New York
International Publishers Co., New York
International Publishing House, Meerat, India
International Review Service, New York
International Textbook Co., Scranton, Penna.
International Union for Scientific Study of Population, New York
International Universities Press, Inc., New York
Interstate Printers and Publishers, Danville, Ill.
Iowa State University, Center for Agricultural and Economic Development, Ames
Iowa State University Press, Ames
Irish Manuscripts Commission, Dublin
Richard D. Irwin, Inc., Homewood, Ill.
Isar Verlag, Munich
Isbister and Co., London
Italian Library of Information, New York; Rome
Italy, Council of Ministers, Rome

Jacaranda Press, Melbourne
Mouriel Jacobs, Inc., Philadelphia
Al Jadidah Press, Cairo
Jain General House, Jullundur, India
Japan, Ministry of Education, Tokyo

Japan, Ministry of Justice, Tokyo
Japanese National Commission for UNESCO, Tokyo
Jarrolds Publishers, Ltd., London
Jewish Publication Society of America, Philadelphia, Pa.
Johns Hopkins Press, Baltimore
Johns Hopkins School of Advanced International Studies, Baltimore
Johns Hopkins School of Hygiene, Baltimore
Johnson Publishing Co., Chicago
Christopher Johnson Publishers, Ltd., London
Johnstone and Hunter, London
Joint Center for Urban Studies, Cambridge, Mass.
Joint Committee on Slavic Studies, New York
Joint Council on Economic Education, New York
Joint Library of IMF and IBRD, Washington
Joint Reference Library, Chicago
Jonathan Cape, London
Jones and Evans Book Shop, Ltd., London
Marshall Jones, Boston
Jornal do Commercio, Rio de Janeiro
Michael Joseph, Ltd., London
Jowett, Leeds, England
Juilliard Publishers, Paris
Junker und Dunnhaupt Verlag, Berlin
Juta and Co., Ltd., Capetown, South Africa

Kallman Publishing Co., Gainesville, Fla.
Karl Karusa, Washington, D. C.
Katzman Verlag, Tubingen
Kay Publishing Co., Salt Lake City
Nicholas Kaye, London
Calvin K. Kazanjian Economics Foundation, Westport, Conn.
Kegan, Paul and Co., Ltd., London
P. G. Keller, Winterthur, Switz.
Augustus M. Kelley, Publishers, New York
Kelly and Walsh, Ltd., Baltimore, Md.
P. J. Kenedy, New York
Kennikat Press, Port Washington, N. Y.
Kent House, Port-of-Spain
Kent State University Bureau of Economic and Business Research, Kent, Ohio
Kentucky State Archives and Records Service, Frankfort
Kentucky State Planning Commission, Frankfort
Kenya Ministry of Economic Planning and Development, Nairobi
Charles H. Kerr and Co., Chicago
Khadiand Village Industries Commission, Bombay
Khayat's, Beirut
Khun Aroon, Bangkok
P. S. King and Son, Ltd., London
King's College, Cambridge
King's Crown Press, New York
Kino Kuniva Bookstore Co., Ltd., Tokyo
Kitab Mahal, Allahabad, India
Kitabistan, Allahabad
B. Klein and Co., New York
Ernst Klett Verlag, Stuttgart
V. Klostermann, Frankfurt
Fritz Knapp Verlag, Frankfurt
Alfred Knopf, New York
John Knox Press, Richmond, Va.
Kodansha International, Ltd., Tokyo
W. Kohlhammer Verlag, Stuttgart; Berlin; Cologne; Mainz
Korea Researcher and Publisher, Inc., Seoul
Korea, Ministry of Reconstruction, Seoul
Korea, Republic of, Seoul
Korea University, Asiatic Research Center, Seoul
Korean Conflict Research Foundation, Albany, N. Y.
Kosel Verlag, Munich
Kossuth Foundation, New York
Guillermo Kraft, Ltd., Buenos Aires
John F. Kraft, Inc., New York
Krasnzi Proletarii, Moscow
Kraus, Ltd., Dresden
Kraus Reprint Co., Vaduz, Liechtenstein
Kreuz-Verlag, Stuttgart
Kumasi College of Technology, The Library, Kumasi, Ghana
Kuwait, Arabia, Government Printing Press, Kuwait

Labor News Co., New York
Robert Laffont, Paris
Lambarde Press, Sidcup, Kent, England
Albert D. and Mary Lasker Foundation, Washington, D. C.
Harold Laski Institute of Political Science, Ahmedabad
Guiseppe Laterza e Figli, Bari, Italy
T. Werner Laurie, Ltd., London
Lawrence Brothers, Ltd., London
Lawrence and Wishart, London
Lawyers Co-operative Publishing Co., Rochester, N. Y.
League for Industrial Democracy, New York
League of Independent Voters, New Haven
League of Nations, Geneva
League of Women Voters, Cambridge
League of Women Voters of U. S., Washington, D. C.
Leeds University Press, Leeds, Engand
J. F. Lehmanns Verlag, Munich
Leicester University Press, London
F. Leitz, Frankfurt
Lemcke, Lemcke and Beuchner, New York
Michel Levy Freres, Paris
Lexington Publishing Co., New York
Liberal Arts Press, Inc., New York
Liberia Altiplano, La Paz
Liberia Anticuaria, Barcelona
Liberia Campos, San Juan
Liberia Panamericana, Buenos Aires
Liberty Bell Press, Jefferson City, Mo.
Librairie Academique Perrin, Paris
Librairie Artheme Fayard, Paris
Librairie Beauchemin, Montreal
Librairie Armand Colin, Paris
Librairie Firmin Didot et Cie., Paris
Librairie Droz, Geneva
Librairie de Medicis, Paris
Librairie de la Societe du Recueil Sirey, Paris
Librairie des Sciences Politiques et Sociales, Paris
Librairie Felix Alcan, Paris
Librairie Gallimard, Paris
Librairie Hachette et Cie., Paris
Librairie Julius Abel, Greiswald
Librairie La Rose, Paris
Librairie Letouzey, Paris
Librairie Payot, Paris
Librairie Philosophique J. Vrin, Paris
Librairie Plon, Paris
Librairie Marcel Riviere et Cie., Paris
Librairie Stock Delamain et Boutelleau, Paris
Library, Kumasi College of Technology, Kumasi
Library Association, London
Library of Congress, Washington
Library House, London
Library of International Relations, Chicago
Libyan Publishing, Tripoli
Light and Life Press, Winona Lake, Ind.
Lincoln University, Lincoln, Pa.
J. B. Lippincott Co., New York, Philadelphia
Little, Brown and Co., Boston
Liverpool University Press, Liverpool
Horace Liveright, New York
Living Books, New York
Livraria Agir Editora, Rio de Janeiro
Livraria Editora da Casa di Estudante do Brazil, Sao Paulo
Livraria Jose Olympio Editora, Rio de Janeiro
Livraria Martins Editora, Sao Paulo
Lok Sabha Secretariat, New Delhi
London Conservative Political Centre, London
London Historical Association, London
London Institute of World Affairs, London
London Library Association, London
London School of Economics, London
London Times, Inc., London
London University, School of Oriental and African Studies, London
Roy Long and Richard R. Smith, Inc., New York
Long House, New Canaan, Conn.
Longmans, Green and Co., New York, London
Los Angeles Board of Civil Service Commissioners, Los Angeles
Louisiana State Legislature, Baton Rouge
Louisiana State University Press, Baton Rouge
Loyola University Press, Chicago
Lucas Brothers, Columbia
Herman Luchterhand Verlag, Neuwied am Rhein
Lyle Stuart, Inc., New York

MIT Center of International Studies, Cambridge

MIT Press, Cambridge
MIT School of Industrial Management, Cambridge
Macfadden-Bartwell Corp., New York
MacGibbon and Kee, Ltd., London
Macmillan Co., New York; London
Macmillan Co., of Canada, Ltd., Toronto
Macrae Smith Co., Philadelphia, Pa.
Magistrats Druckerei, Berlin
Magnes Press, Jerusalem
S. P. Maisonneuve et La Rose, Paris
Malaysia Publications, Ltd., Singapore
Malhorta Brothers, New Delhi
Manager Government of India Press, Kosib
Manaktalas, Bombay
Manchester University Press, Manchester, England
Manhattan Publishing Co., New York
Manzsche Verlag, Vienna
Marathon Oil Co., Findlay, Ohio
Marisal, Madrid
Marquette University Press, Milwaukee
Marshall Benick, New York
Marzani and Munsell, New York
Marzun Kabushiki Kaisha, Tokyo
Mascat Publications, Ltd., Calcutta
Francois Maspera, Paris
Massachusetts Mass Transportation Commission, Boston
Masses and McInstream, New York
Maurice Falk Institute for Economic Research, Jerusalem
Maxwell Air Force Base, Montgomery, Ala.
Robert Maxwell and Co., Ltd., London
McBride, Nast and Co., New York
McClelland and Stewart, Ltd., London
McClure and Co., Chicago
McClure, Phillips and Co., New York
McCutchan Publishing Corp., Berkeley
McDonald and Evans, Ltd., London
McDowell, Obolensky, New York
McFadden Bartwell Corp., New York
McGill University Industrial Relations Section, Montreal
McGill University, Institute of Islamic Studies, Montreal
McGill University Press, Montreal
McGraw Hill Book Co., New York
David McKay Co., Inc., New York
McKinley Publishing Co., Philadelphia
George J. McLeod, Ltd., Toronto
McMullen Books, Inc., New York
Meador Publishing Co., Boston
Mediaeval Academy of Americana, Cambridge
Felix Meiner Verlag, Hamburg
Melbourne University Press, Melbourne, Victoria, Australia
Mendonca, Lisbon
Mental Health Materials Center, New York
Mentor Books, New York
Meredith Press, Des Moines
Meridian Books, New York
Merit Publishers, New York
The Merlin Press, Ltd., London
Charles E. Merrill Publishing Co., Inc., Columbus
Methuen and Co., Ltd., London
Metropolitan Book Co., Ltd., New Delhi
Metropolitan Housing and Planning Council, Chicago
Metropolitan Police District, Scotland Yard, London
Alfred Metzner Verlag, Frankfurt
Meyer London Memorial Library, London
Miami University Press, Oxford, Ohio
Michie Co., Charlottesville, Va.
Michigan Municipal League, Ann Arbor
Michigan State University, Agricultural Experiment Station, East Lansing
Michigan State University, Bureau of Business and Economic Research, East Lansing
Michigan State University, Bureau of Social and Political Research, East Lansing
Michigan State University, Governmental Research Bureau, East Lansing
Michigan State University, Institute for Community Development and Services, East Lansing
Michigan State University, Institute for Social Research, East Lansing
Michigan State University, Labor and Industrial Relations Center, East Lansing
Michigan State University Press, East Lansing
Michigan State University School of Business Administration, East Lansing
Michigan State University, Vietnam Advisory Group, East Lansing
Mid-European Studies Center, Free European Committee, New York
Middle East Institute, Washington
Middle East Research Associates, Arlington, Va.
Middlebury College, Middlebury, Vt.
Midwest Administration Center, Chicago
Midwest Beach Co., Sioux Falls
Milbank Memorial Fund, New York
M. S. Mill and Co., Inc., Division of William Morrow and Co., Inc., New York
Ministere de l'Education Nationale, Paris
Ministere d'Etat aux Affaires Culturelles, Paris
Ministerio de Educacao e Cultura, Rio de Janeiro
Ministerio de Relaciones Exteriores, Havana
Minnesota Efficiency in Government Commission, St. Paul
Minton, Balch and Co., New York
Missionary Research Library, New York
Ernst Siegfried Mittler und Sohn, Berlin
Modern Humanities Research Association, Chicago
T. C. B. Mohr, Tubingen
Moira Books, Detroit
Monarch Books, Inc., Derby, Conn.
Monthly Review, New York
Mont Pelerin Society, University of Chicago, Chicago
Hugh Moore Fund, New York
T. G. Moran's Sons, Inc., Baton Rouge
William Morrow and Co., Inc., New York
Morus Verlag, Berlin
Mosaik Verlag, Hamburg
Motilal Banarsidass, New Delhi
Mouton and Co., The Hague; Paris
C. F. Mueller Verlag, Karlsruhe, Germany
Muhammad Mosque of Islam #2, Chicago
Firma K. L. Mukhopadhyaz, Calcutta
F. A. W. Muldener, Gottingen, Germany
Frederick Muller, Ltd., London
Municipal Finance Officers Association of the United States and Canada, Chicago
Munksgaard International Booksellers and Publishers, Copenhagen
John Murray, London
Museum fur Volkerkunde, Vienna
Museum of Honolulu, Honolulu
Musterschmidt Verlag, Gottingen

NA Tipographia do Panorama, Lisbon
Nassau County Planning Committee, Long Island
Natal Witness, Ltd., Pietermaritzburg
The Nation Associates, New York
National Academy of Sciences-National Research Council, Washington, D. C.
National Archives of Rhodesia and Nyasaland, Salisbury
National Assembly on Teaching The Principles of the Bill of Rights, Washington
National Association of Counties Research Foundation, Washington, D. C.
National Association of County Officials, Chicago
National Association of Home Builders, Washington, D. C.
National Association of Local Government Officers, London
National Association of State Libraries, Boston
National Bank of Egypt, Cairo
National Bank of Libya, Tripoli
National Board of YMCA, New York
National Book League, London
National Bureau of Economic Research, New York
National Capitol Publishers, Manassas, Va.
National Central Library, London
National Citizens' Commission on International Cooperation, Washington, D. C.
National Council for the Social Sciences, New York
National Council for the Social Studies, New York
National Council of Applied Economic Research, New Delhi
National Council of Churches of Christ in USA, New York
National Council of National Front of Democratic Germany, Berlin
National Council on Aging, New York
National Council on Crime and Delinquency, New York
National Economic and Social Planning Agency, Washington

National Education Association, Washington
National Home Library Foundation, Washington, D. C.
National Industrial Conference Board, New York
National Institute for Personnel Research, Johannesburg
National Institute of Administration, Saigon
National Institute of Economic Research, Stockholm
National Labor Relations Board Library, Washington
National Labour Press, London
National Library of Canada, Ottawa
National Library Press, Ottawa
National Municipal League, New York
National Observer, Silver Springs, Md.
National Opinion Research Center, Chicago
National Peace Council, London
National Planning Association, Washington, D. C.
National Press, Palo Alto, Calif.
National Review, New York
National Science Foundation Scientific Information, Washington, D. C.
Natural History Press, Garden City, N. Y.
Nauka Publishing House, Moscow
Navahind, Hyderabad
Navajiran Publishing House, Ahmedabad
Thomas Nelson and Sons, London; New York
Neukirchener Verlag des Erziehungsvereins, Neukirchen
New American Library, New York
New Century Publishers, New York
New Jersey Department of Agriculture, Rural Advisory Council, Trenton
New Jersey Department of Civil Service, Trenton
New Jersey Department of Conservation and Economic Development, Trenton
New Jersey Division of State and Regional Planning, Trenton
New Jersey Housing and Renewal, Trenton
New Jersey State Department of Education, Trenton
New Jersey State Legislature, Trenton
New Republic, Washington, D. C.
New School of Social Research, New York
New World Press, New York
New York City College Institute for Pacific Relations, New York
New York City Department of Correction, New York
New York City Temporary Committee on City Finance, New York
New York Public Library, New York
New York State College of Agriculture, Ithaca
New York State Library, Albany
New York State School of Industrial and Labor Relations, Cornell University, Ithaca
New York, State University of, at Albany, Albany
New York, State University of, State Education Department, Albany
New York, State University of, State Education Department, Office of Foreign Area Studies, Albany
New York Times, New York
New York University School of Commerce, Accounts and Finance, New York
New York University, School of Law, New York
New York University Press, New York
Newark Public Library, Newark
Newman Press, Westminster, Md.
Martinus Nijhoff, The Hague; Geneva
James Nisbet and Co., Ltd., Welwyn, Herts, England
Noonday Press, New York
North American Review Publishing Co., New York
North Atlantic Treaty Organization, Brussels
North Holland Publishing Co., Amsterdam, Holland
Northern California Friends Committee on Legislation, San Francisco
Northern Michigan University Press, Marquette
Northwestern University, Evanston
Northwestern University, African Department, Evanston, Ill.
Northwestern University, International Relations Conference, Chicago
Northwestern University Press, Evanston, Ill.
W. W. Norton and Co., Inc., New York
Norwegian Institute of International Affairs, Oslo
Norwegian University Press, Oslo
Nouvelle Librairie Nationale, Paris
John Nuveen and Co., Chicago
Novelty and Co., Patna, India
Novostii Press Agency Publishing House, Moscow
Nymphenburger Verlagsbuchhandlung, Munich

Oak Publications, New York
Oak Ridge Associated Universities, Oak Ridge, Tenn.
Oceana Publishing Co., Dobbs Ferry, N. Y.
Octagon Publishing Co., New York
Odyssey Press, New York
Oesterreichische Ethnologische Gesellschaft, Vienna
Oficina Internacional de Investigaciones Sociales de Freres, Madrid
W.E.R. O'Gorman, Glendale, Calif.
O'Hare, Flanders, N. J.
Ohio State University, Columbus
Ohio State University, College of Commerce and Administration, Bureau of Business Research, Columbus
Ohio State University Press, Columbus
Ohio University Press, Athens
Old Lyme Press, Old Lyme, Conn.
R. Oldenbourg, Munich
Oliver and Boyd, London, Edinburgh
Guenter Olzog Verlag, Munich
Open Court Publishing Co., La Salle, Ill.
Operation America, Inc., Los Angeles
Operations and Policy Research, Inc., Washington, D. C.
Oregon Historical Society, Portland
Organization for European Economic Cooperation and Development (OEEC), Paris
Organization of African Unity, Addis Ababa
Organization of American States, Rio de Janeiro
Organization of Economic Aid, Washington, D. C.
Orient Longman's, Bombay
Oriole Press, Berkeley Heights, N. J.
P. O'Shey, New York
Osaka University of Commerce, Tokyo
James R. Osgood and Co., Boston
Oslo University Press, Oslo
Oswald-Wolff, London
John Ousley, Ltd., London
George Outram Co., Ltd., Glasgow
Overseas Development Institute, Ltd., London
R. E. Owen, Wellington, N. Z.
Oxford Book Co., New York
Oxford University Press, Capetown; London; Madras; Melbourne; New York

Pacific Books, Palo Alto, Calif.
Pacific Coast Publishing Co., Menlo Park, Calif.
Pacific Philosophy Institute, Stockton, Calif.
Pacific Press Publishing Association, Mountain View, Calif.
Pacifist Research Bureau, Philadelphia
Padma Publications, Ltd., Bombay
Hermann Paetel Verlag, Berlin
Pageant Press, New York
Paine-Whitman, New York
Pakistan Academy for Rural Development, Peshawar
Pakistan Association for Advancement of Science, Lahore
Pakistan Bibliographical Working Group, Karachi
Pakistan Educational Publishers, Ltd., Karachi
Pakistan Ministry of Finance, Rawalpindi
Pall Mall Press, London
Pan American Union, Washington
Pantheon Books, Inc., New York
John W. Parker, London
Patna University Press, Madras
B. G. Paul and Co., Madras
Paulist Press, Glen Rock, N. J.
Payne Fund, New York
Peabody Museum, Cambridge
Peace Publications, New York
Peace Society, London
P. Pearlman, Washington
Pegasus, New York
Peking Review, Peking
Pelican Books, Ltd., Hammonsworth, England
Pemberton Press, Austin
Penguin Books, Baltimore
Penn.-N.J.-Del. Metropolitan Project, Philadelphia, Pa.
Pennsylvania German Society, Lancaster, Pa.
Pennsylvania Historical and Museum Commission, Harrisburg
Pennsylvania State University, Department of Religious Studies, University Park, Pa.

Pennsylvania State University, Institute of Public Administration, University Park, Pa.
Pennsylvania State University Press, University Park, Pa.
People's Publishing House, Ltd., New Delhi
Pergamon Press, Inc., New York
Permanent Secretariat, AAPS Conference, Cairo
Perrine Book Co., Minneapolis
Personnel Administration, Washington
Personnel Research Association, New York
George A. Pflaum Publishers, Inc., Dayton, Ohio
Phelps-Stokes Fund, Capetown; New York
Philadelphia Bibliographical Center, Philadelphia
George Philip & Son, London
Philippine Historical Society, Manila
Philippine Islands Bureau of Science, Manila
Philosophical Library Inc., New York
Phoenix House, Ltd., London
Pichon et Durand-Auzias, Paris
B. M. Pickering, London
Oskar Piest, New York
Pilot Press, London
Pioneer Publishers, New York
R. Piper and Co. Verlag, Munich
Pitman Publishing Corp., New York
Plimpton Press, Norwood, Mass.
PLJ Publications, Manila
Pocket Books, Inc., New York
Polish Scientific Publishers, Warsaw
Polygraphischer Verlag, Zurich
The Polynesian Society, Inc., Wellington, N. Z.
Popular Book Depot, Bombay
Popular Prakashan, Bombay
Population Association of America, Washington
Population Council, New York
Post Printing Co., New York
Post Publishing Co., Bangkok
Potomac Books, Washington, D. C.
Clarkson N. Potter, Inc., New York
Prabhakar Sahityalok, Lucknow, India
Practicing Law Institute, New York
Frederick A. Praeger, Inc., New York
Prager, Berlin
Prensa Latino Americana, Santiago
Prentice Hall, Inc., Englewood Cliffs, N. J.
Prentice-Hall International, London
Presence Afrique, Paris
President's Press, New Delhi
Press & Information Division of the French Embassy, New York
The Press of Case Western Reserve University, Cleveland
Presses de l'Ecole des Hautes Etudes Commerciales, Montreal
Presses Universitaires de Bruxelles, Brussels
Presses Universitaires de France, Paris
Presseverband der Evangelischen Kirche im Rheinland, Dusseldorf
Princeton Research Publishing Co., Princeton
Princeton University, Princeton, N. J.
Princeton University, Center of International Studies, Woodrow Wilson School of Public and International Affairs, Princeton, N. J.
Princeton University, Department of Economics, Princeton, N. J.
Princeton University, Department of History, Princeton, N. J.
Princeton University, Department of Oriental Studies, Princeton, N. J.
Princeton University, Department of Philosophy, Princeton, N. J.
Princeton University, Department of Politics, Princeton, N. J.
Princeton University, Department of Psychology, Princeton
Princeton University, Department of Sociology, Princeton, N. J.
Princeton University, Econometric Research Program, Princeton, N. J.
Princeton University, Firestone Library, Princeton, N. J.
Princeton University, Industrial Relations Center, Princeton
Princeton University, International Finance Section, Princeton, N. J.
Princeton University, Princeton Public Opinion Research Project, Princeton, N. J.
Princeton University Press, Princeton
Edouard Privat, Toulouse
Arthur Probsthain, London
Professional Library Press, West Haven, Conn.
Programa Interamericano de Informacion Popular, San Jose
Progress Publishing Co., Indianapolis
Progressive Education Association, New York
Prolog Research and Publishing Association, New York
Prometheus Press, New York
Psycho-Sociological Press, New York
Public Administration Clearing House, Chicago
Public Administration Institute, Ankara
Public Administration Service, Chicago
Public Affairs Forum, Bombay
Public Affairs Press, Washington
Public Enterprises, Tequcigalpa
Public Personnel Association, Chicago
Publications Centre, University of British Columbia, Vancouver
Publications de l'Institut Pedagogique National, Paris
Publications de l'Institut Universitaire des Hautes Etudes Internationales, Paris
Publications du CNRS, Paris
Publisher's Circular, Ltd., London,, England
Publisher's Weekly, Inc., New York
Publishing House Jugoslavia, Belgrade
Punjab University, Pakistan
Punjab University Extension Library, Ludhiana, Punjab
Purdue University Press, Lafayette, Ind.
Purnell and Sons, Capetown
G. P. Putnam and Sons, New York

Quadrangle Books, Inc., Chicago
Bernard Quaritch, London
Queen's Printer, Ottawa
Queen's University, Belfast
Quell Verlag, Stuttgart, Germany
Quelle und Meyer, Heidelberg
Queromon Editores, Mexico City

Atma Ram and Sons, New Delhi
Ramsey-Wallace Corporation, Ramsey, New Jersey
Rand Corporation, Publications of the Social Science Department, New York
Rand McNally and Co., Skokie, Ill.
Random House, Inc., New York
Regents Publishing House, Inc., New York
Regional Planning Association, New York
Regional Science Research Institute, Philadelphia
Henry Regnery Co., Chicago
D. Reidel Publishing Co., Dordrecht, Holland
E. Reinhardt Verlag, Munich
Reinhold Publishing Corp., New York; London
Remsen Press, New York
La Renaissance de Loire, Paris
Eugen Rentsch Verlag, Stuttgart
Republican National Committee, Washington, D. C.
Research Institute on Sino-Soviet Bloc, Washington, D. C.
Research Microfilm Publications, Inc., Annapolis
Resources for the Future, Inc., Washington, D. C.
Revista de Occidente, Madrid
Revue Administrative, Paris
Renyal and Co., Inc., New York
Reynal & Hitchcock, New York
Rheinische Friedrich Wilhelms Universitat, Bonn
Rice University, Fondren Library, Houston
Richards Rosen Press, New York
The Ridge Press, Inc., New York
Rinehart, New York
Ring-Verlag, Stuttgart
Riverside Editions, Cambridge
Robinson and Co., Durban, South Africa
J. A. Rogers, New York
Roques Roman, Trujillo
Rudolf M. Rohrer, Leipzig
Ludwig Rohrscheid Verlag, Bonn
Walter Roming and Co., Detroit
Ronald Press Co., New York
Roper Public Opinion Poll Research Center, New York
Ross and Haine, Inc., Minneapolis, Minn.
Fred B. Rothman and Co., S. Hackensack, N. J.
Rotterdam University Press, Rotterdam
Routledge and Kegan Paul, London
George Routledge and Sons, Ltd., London
Row-Peterson Publishing Co., Evanston, Ill.

Rowohlt, Hamburg
Roy Publishers, Inc., New York
Royal African Society, London
Royal Anthropological Institute, London
Royal Colonial Institute, London
Royal Commission of Canada's Economic Prospects, Ottawa
Royal Commonwealth Society, London
Royal Geographical Society, London
Royal Greek Embassy Information Service, Washington, D. C.
Royal Institute of International Affairs, London; New York
Royal Institute of Public Administration, London
Royal Netherlands Printing Office, Schiedam
Royal Statistical Society, London
Rubin Mass, Jerusalem
Rule of Law Press, Durham
Rupert Hart-Davis, London
Russell and Russell, Inc., New York
Russell Sage College, Institute for Advanced Study in Crisis, NDEA Institute, Troy, N. Y.
Russell Sage Foundation, New York
Rutgers University, New Brunswick, N. J.
Rutgers University Bureau of Government Research, New Brunswick, N. J.
Rutgers University, Institute of Management and Labor Relations, New Brunswick, N. J.
Rutgers University, Urban Studies Conference, New Brunswick, N. J.
Rutgers University Press, New Brunswick, N. J.
Rutten und Loening Verlag, Munich
Ryerson Press, Toronto

Sage Publications, Beverly Hills, Calif.
Sahitya Akademi, Bombay
St. Andrews College, Drygrange, Scotland
St. Clement's Press, London
St. George Press, Los Angeles
St. John's University Bookstore, Annapolis
St. John's University Press, Jamaica, N. Y.
St. Louis Post-Dispatch, St. Louis
St. Martin's Press, New York
St. Michael's College, Toronto
San Diego State College Library, San Diego
San Francisco State College, San Francisco
The Sapir Memorial Publication Fund, Menasha, Wis.
Sarah Lawrence College, New York
Sarah Lawrence College, Institute for Community Studies, New York
Porter Sargent, Publishers, Boston, Mass.
Sauerlaender and Co., Aarau, Switz.
Saunders and Ottey, London
W. B. Saunders Co., Philadelphia, Pa.
Scandinavian University Books, Copenhagen
Scarecrow Press, Metuchen, N. J.
L. N. Schaffrath, Geldern, Germany
Robert Schalkenbach Foundation, New York
Schenkman Publishing Co., Cambridge
P. Schippers, N. V., Amsterdam
Schocken Books, Inc., New York
Henry Schuman, Inc., New York
Carl Schunemann Verlag, Bremen
Curt E. Schwab, Stuttgart
Otto Schwartz und Co., Gottingen
Science and Behavior Books, Palo Alto, Calif.
Science Council of Japan, Tokyo
Science of Society Foundation, Baltimore, Md.
Science Press, New York
Science Research Associates, Inc., Chicago
Scientia Verlag, Aalen, Germany
SCM Press, London
Scott, Foresman and Co., Chicago
Scottish League for European Freedom, Edinburgh
Chas. Scribner's Sons, New York
Seabury Press, New York
Sears Publishing Co., Inc., New York
Secker and Warburg, Ltd., London
Secretaria del Consejo Nacional Economia, Tegucigalpa
Securities Study Project, Vancouver, Wash.
Seewald Verlag, Munich; Stuttgart
Selbstverlag Jakob Rosner, Vienna
Seldon Society, London
Robert C. Sellers and Associates, Washington, D. C.
Thomas Seltzer Inc., New York
Seminar, New Delhi
C. Serbinis Press, Athens
Service Bibliographique des Messageries Hachette, Paris
Service Center for Teaching of History, Washington, D. C.
Servicos de Imprensa e Informacao da Exbaixada, Lisbon
Sheed and Ward, New York
Shoestring Press, Hamden, Conn.
Shuter and Shooter, Pietermaritzburg
Siam Society, Bangkok
Sidgewick and Jackson, London
K. G. Siegler & Co., Bonn
Signet Books, New York
A. W. Sijthoff, Leyden, Netherlands
Silver Burdett, Morristown, N. J.
Simmons Boardman Publishing Co., New York
Simon and Schuster, Inc., New York
Simpkin, Marshall, et al., London
Sino-American Cultural Society, Washington
William Sloane Associates, New York
Small, Maynard and Co., Boston
Smith-Brook Printing Co., Denver
Smith College, Northampton, Mass.
Smith, Elder and Co., London
Smith, Keynes and Marshall, Buffalo, N. Y.
Allen Smith Co., Indianapolis, Ind.
Peter Smith, Gloucester, Mass.
Richard R. Smith Co. Inc., Peterborough, N. H.
Smithsonian Institute, Washington, D. C.
Social Science Research Center, Rio Piedras, Puerto Rico
Social Science Research Council, New York
Social Science Research Council, Committee on the Economy of China, Berkeley, Calif.
Social Science Research Council of Australia, Sydney
The Social Sciences, Mexico City
Societa Editrice del "Foro Italiano", Rome
Societas Bibliographica, Lausanne, Switzerland
Societe d'Edition d'Enseignement Superieur, Paris
Societe Francaise d'Imprimerie et Librairie, Paris
Society for Advancement of Management, New York
Society for Promoting Christian Knowledge, London
Society for the Study of Social Problems, Kalamazoo, Mich.
Society of Comparative Legislative and International Law, London
Sociological Abstracts, New York
Solidaridad Publishing House, Manila
Somerset Press, Inc., Somerville, N. J.
Soney and Sage Co., Newark, N. J.
South Africa Commission on Future Government, Capetown
South Africa State Library, Pretoria
South African Congress of Democrats, Johannesburg
South African Council for Scientific and Industrial Research, Pretoria
South African Institute of International Affairs, Johannesburg
South African Institute of Race Relations, Johannesburg
South African Public Library, Johannesburg
South Carolina Archives, State Library, Columbia
South Pacific Commission, Noumea, New Caledonia
South Western Publishing Co., Cincinnati, Ohio
Southern Illinois University Press, Carbondale, Ill.
Southern Methodist University Press, Dallas, Tex.
Southern Political Science Association, New York
Southworth Anthoensen Press, Portland, Maine
Sovetskaia Rossiia, Moscow
Soviet and East European Research and Translation Service, New York
Spartan Books, Washington, D. C.
Special Libraries Association, New York
Specialty Press of South Africa, Johannesburg
Robert Speller and Sons, New York
Lorenz Spindler Verlag, Nuremberg
Julius Springer, Berlin
Springer-Verlag, New York; Stuttgart; Gottingen; Vienna
Stackpole Co., New York
Gerhard Stalling, Oldenburg, Germany
Stanford Bookstore, Stanford
Stanford University Comparative Education Center, Stanford, Calif.
Stanford University Institute for Communications Research, Stanford
Stanford University, Institute of Hispanic-American and Luso-Brazilian Studies, Stanford, Calif.
Stanford University, Project on Engineering-Economic Planning, Stanford, Calif.

Stanford University Research Institute, Menlo Park, Calif.
Stanford University, School of Business Administration, Stanford, Calif.
Stanford University, School of Education, Stanford, Calif.
Stanford University Press, Stanford, Cal.
Staples Press, New York
State University of New York at Albany, Albany
Stein & Day Publishers, New York
Franz Steiner Verlag, Wiesbaden
Ulrich Steiner Verlag, Wurttemburg
H. E. Stenfert Kroese, Leyden
Sterling Printing and Publishing Co., Ltd., Karachi
Sterling Publishers, Ltd., London
Stevens and Hayes, London
Stevens and Sons, Ltd., London
George W. Stewart, Inc., New York
George Stilke Berlin
Frederick A. Stokes Publishing Co., New York
C. Struik, Capetown
Stuttgarter Verlags Kantor, Stuttgart
Summy-Birchard Co., Evanston, Ill.
Swann Sonnenschein and Co., London
Philip Swartzwelder, Pittsburgh, Pa.
Sweet and Maxwell, Ltd., London
Swiss Eastern Institute, Berne
Sydney University Press, Sydney, Australia
Syracuse University, Maxwell School of Citizenship and Public Affairs, Syracuse, N. Y.
Syracuse University Press, Syracuse
Szczesnez Verlag, Munich

Talleres Graficos de Manuel Casas, Mexico City
Talleres de Impresion de Estampillas y Valores, Mexico City
Taplinger Publishing Co., New York
Tavistock, London
Tax Foundation, New York
Teachers' College, Bureau of Publications, Columbia University, New York
Technical Assistance Information Clearing House, New York
Technology Press, Cambridge
de Tempel, Bruges, Belgium
B. G. Teubner, Berlin; Leipzig
Texas College of Arts and Industries, Kingsville
Texas Western Press, Dallas
Texian Press, Waco, Texas
Thacker's Press and Directories, Ltd., Calcutta
Thailand, National Office of Statistics, Bangkok
Thailand National Economic Development Board, Bangkok
Thames and Hudson, Ltd., London
Thammasat University Institute of Public Administration, Bangkok, Thailand
E. J. Theisen, East Orange, N. J.
Charles C. Thomas, Publisher, Springfield, Ill.
Tilden Press, New York
Time, Inc., New York
Time-Life Books, New York
Times Mirror Printing and Binding, New York
Tipografia de Archivos, Madrid
Tipografia Mendonca, Lisbon
Tipografia Nacional, Guatemala, Guatemala City
Tipographia Nacional Guatemala, Guatemala City
H. D. Tjeenk Willink, Haarlem, Netherlands
J. C. Topping, Cambridge, Mass.
Transatlantic Arts, Inc., New York
Trejos Hermanos, San Jose
Trenton State College, Trenton
Tri-Ocean Books, San Francisco
Trident Press, New York
Trowitzsch and Son, Berlin
Truebner and Co., London
Tufts University Press, Medford, Mass.
Tulane University, School of Business Administration, New Orleans, La.
Tulane University Press, New Orleans
Turnstile Press, London
Tuskegee Institute, Tuskegee, Ala.
Charles E. Tuttle Co., Tokyo
Twayne Publishers Inc., New York
The Twentieth Century Fund, New York
Twin Circle Publishing Co., New York
Typographische Anstalt, Vienna
Tyrolia Verlag, Innsbruck

UNESCO, Paris
N. V. Uitgeverij W. Van Hoeve, The Hague
Frederick Ungar Publishing Co., Inc., New York
Union Federaliste Inter-Universitaire, Paris
Union of American Hebrew Congregations, New York
Union of International Associations, Brussels
Union of Japanese Societies of Law and Politics, Tokyo
Union of South Africa, Capetown
Union of South Africa, Government Information Office, New York
Union Press, Hong Kong
Union Research Institute, Hong Kong
United Arab Republic, Information Department, Cairo
United Nations Economic Commission for Asia and the Far East, Secretariat of Bangkok, Bangkok
United Nations Educational, Scientific and Cultural Organization, Paris
United Nations Food and Agriculture Organization, Rome
United Nations International Conference on Peaceful Uses of Atomic Energy, Geneva
United Nations Publishing Service, New York
United States Air Force Academy, Colorado Springs, Colo.
United States Bureau of the Census, Washington, D. C.
United States Business and Defense Services Administration, Washington D.C.
United States Civil Rights Commission, Washington, D. C.
United States Civil Service Commission, Washington, D. C.
United States Consulate General, Hong Kong
United States Department of Agriculture, Washington, D. C.
United States Department of the Army, Washington
United States Department of the Army, Office of Chief of Military History, Washington, D. C.
United States Department of Correction, New York
United States Department of State, Washington
United States Department of State, Government Printing Office, Washington, D. C.
United States Government Printing Office, Washington
United States Housing and Home Financing Agency, Washington, D. C.
United States Mutual Security Agency, Washington, D. C.
United States National Archives General Services, Washington, D. C.
United States National Referral Center for Science and Technology, Washington, D. C.
United States National Resources Committee, Washington, D. C.
United States Naval Academy, Annapolis, Md.
United States Naval Institute, Annapolis, Md.
United States Naval Officers Training School, China Lake, Cal.
United States Operations Mission to Vietnam, Washington, D. C.
United States President's Committee to Study Military Assistance, Washington, D. C.
United States Small Business Administration, Washington, D. C.
United World Federalists, Boston
Universal Reference System; see Princeton Research Publishing Co., Princeton, N.J.
Universidad Central de Venezuela, Caracas
Universidad de Buenos Aires, Instituto Sociologia, Buenos Aires
Universidad de Chile, Santiago
Universidad de el Salvador, El Salvador
Universidad Nacional Autonomo de Mexico, Direccion General de Publicaciones, Mexico
Universidad Nacional de la Plata, Argentina
Universidad Nacional Instituto de Historia Antonoma de Mexico, Mexico City
Universidad Nacional Mayor de San Marcos, Lima
Universidad de Antioquia, Medellin, Colombia
Universite de Rabat, Rabat, Morocco
Universite Fouad I, Cairo
Universite Libre de Bruxelles, Brussels
Universite Mohammed V, Rabat, Morocco
University Books, Inc., Hyde Park, New York
University Bookstore, Hong Kong
University Microfilms, Inc., Ann Arbor
University of Alabama, Bureau of Public Administration, University, Ala.
University of Alabama Press, University, Ala.
University of Ankara, Ankara
University of Arizona Press, Tucson
University of Bombay, Bombay

University of Bonn, Bonn
University of British Columbia Press, Vancouver
University of California, Berkeley, Calif.
University of California at Los Angeles, Bureau of Government Research, Los Angeles
University of California at Los Angeles, Near Eastern Center, Los Angeles
University of California, Bureau of Business and Economic Research, Berkeley, Calif.
University of California, Bureau of Government Research, Los Angeles
University of California, Bureau of Public Administration, Berkeley
University of California, Department of Psychology, Los Angeles
University of California, Institute for International Studies, Berkeley, Calif.
University of California, Institute of East Asiatic Studies, Berkeley, Calif.
University of California, Institute of Governmental Affairs, Davis
University of California, Institute of Governmental Studies, Berkeley
University of California, Institute of Urban and Regional Development, Berkeley, Calif.
University of California, Latin American Center, Los Angeles
University of California Library, Berkeley, Calif.
University of California Press, Berkeley
University of California Survey Research Center, Berkeley, Calif.
University of Canterbury, Christchurch, New Zealand
University of Capetown, Capetown
University of Chicago, Chicago
University of Chicago, Center for Policy Study, Chicago
University of Chicago, Center for Program in Government Administration, Chicago
University of Chicago, Center of Race Relations, Chicago
University of Chicago, Graduate School of Business, Chicago
University of Chicago Law School, Chicago
University of Chicago, Politics Department, Chicago
University of Chicago Press, Chicago
University of Cincinnati, Cincinnati
University of Cincinnati, Center for Study of United States Foreign Policy, Cincinnati
University of Colorado Press, Boulder
University of Connecticut, Institute of Public Service, Storrs, Conn.
University of Dar es Salaam, Institute of Public Administration, Dar es Salaam
University of Denver, Denver
University of Detroit Press, Detroit
University of Edinburgh, Edinburgh, Scotland
University of Florida, Public Administration Clearing Service, Gainesville, Fla.
University of Florida, School of Inter-American Studies, Gainesville, Fla.
University of Florida Libraries, Gainesville
University of Florida Press, Gainesville
University of Georgia, Institute of Community and Area Development, Athens, Georgia
University of Georgia Press, Athens
University of Glasgow Press, Glasgow, Scotland
University of Glasgow Press, Fredericton, New Brunswick, Canada
University of Hawaii Press, Honolulu
University of Hong Kong Press, Hong Kong
University of Houston, Houston
University of Illinois, Champaign
University of Illinois, Graduate School of Library Science, Urbana
University of Illinois, Institute for Labor and Industrial Relations, Urbana
University of Illinois, Institute of Government and Public Affairs, Urbana, Ill.
University of Illinois Press, Urbana
University of Iowa, Center for Labor and Management, Iowa City
University of Iowa, School of Journalism, Iowa City
University of Iowa Press, Iowa City
University of Kansas, Bureau of Government Research, Lawrence, Kans.
University of Kansas Press, Lawrence
University of Karachi, Institute of Business and Public Administration, Karachi
University of Karachi Press, Karachi
University of Kentucky, Bureau of Governmental Research, Lexington
University of Kentucky Press, Lexington
University of London, Institute of Advanced Legal Studies, London
University of London, Institute of Commonwealth Studies, London
University of London, Institute of Education, London
University of London, School of Oriental and African Studies, London
University of London Press, London
University of Lund, Lund, Sweden
University of Maine Studies, Augusta, Me.
University of Malaya, Kualalumpur
University of Manchester Press, Manchester, England
University of Maryland, Bureau of Governmental Research, College of Business and Public Administration, College Park, Md.
University of Maryland, Department of Agriculture and Extension Education, College Park, Md.
University of Massachusetts, Bureau of Government Research, Amherst, Mass.
University of Massachusetts Press, Amherst
University of Melbourne Press, Melbourne, Australia
University of Miami Law Library, Coral Gables
University of Miami Press, Coral Gables
University of Michigan, Center for Research on Conflict Resolution, Ann Arbor
University of Michigan, Department of History and Political Science, Ann Arbor
University of Michigan, Graduate School of Business Administration, Ann Arbor
University of Michigan, Institute for Social Research, Ann Arbor
University of Michigan, Institute of Public Administration, Ann Arbor
University of Michigan Law School, Ann Arbor
University of Michigan, Survey Research Center, Ann Arbor
University of Michigan Press, Ann Arbor
University of Minnesota, St. Paul; Duluth
University of Minnesota, Industrial Relations Center, Minneapolis
University of Minnesota Press, Minneapolis
University of Mississippi, Bureau of Public Administration, University, Miss.
University of Missouri, Research Center, School of Business and Public Administration, Columbia
University of Missouri Press, Columbia
University of Natal Press, Pietermaritzburg
University of Nebraska Press, Lincoln
University of New England, Grafton, Australia
University of New Mexico, Department of Government, Albuquerque, N. Mex.
University of New Mexico, School of Law, Albuquerque
University of New Mexico Press, Albuquerque
University of North Carolina, Department of City and Regional Planning, Chapel Hill
University of North Carolina, Institute for International Studies, Chapel Hill
University of North Carolina, Institute for Research in the Social Sciences, Center for Urban and Regional Studies, Chapel Hill
University of North Carolina, Institute of Government, Chapel Hill
University of North Carolina Library, Chapel Hill
University of North Carolina Press, Chapel Hill
University of Notre Dame, Notre Dame, Ind.
University of Notre Dame Press, Notre Dame, Ind.
University of Oklahoma Press, Norman
University of Oregon Press, Eugene
University of Panama, Panama City
University of Paris (Conferences du Palais de la Decouverte), Paris
University of Pennsylvania, Philadelphia, Pa.
University of Pennsylvania, Department of Translations, Philadelphia
University of Pennsylvania Law School, Philadelphia, Pa.
University of Pennsylvania Press, Philadelphia
University of Pittsburgh, Institute of Local Government, Pittsburgh, Pa.
University of Pittsburgh Book Centers, Pittsburgh
University of Pittsburgh Press, Pittsburgh

University of Puerto Rico, San Juan
University of Rochester, Rochester, N. Y.
University of Santo Tomas, Manila
University of South Africa, Pretoria
University of South Carolina Press, Columbia
University of Southern California, Middle East and North Africa Program, Los Angeles
University of Southern California, School of International Relations, Los Angeles
University of Southern California Press, Los Angeles
University of Southern California, School of Public Administration, Los Angeles
University of State of New York, State Education Department, Albany
University of Sussex, Sussex, England
University of Sydney, Department of Government and Public Administration, Sydney
University of Tennessee, Knoxville
University of Tennessee, Bureau of Public Administration, Knoxville
University of Tennessee, Municipal Technical Advisory Service, Division of University Extension, Knoxville
University of Tennessee Press, Knoxville
University of Texas, Austin
University of Texas, Bureau of Business Research, Austin
University of Texas Press, Austin
University of the Philippines, Quezon City
University of the Punjab, Department of Public Administration, Lahore, Pakistan
University of the Witwatersrand, Johannesburg
University of Toronto, Toronto
University of Toronto Press, Toronto; Buffalo, N. Y.
University of Utah Press, Salt Lake City
University of Vermont, Burlington
University of Virginia, Bureau of Public Administration, Charlottesville
University of Wales Press, Cardiff
University of Washington, Bureau of Governmental Research and Services, Seattle
University of Washington Press, Seattle
University of Wisconsin, Madison
University of Wisconsin Press, Madison
University Press, University of the South, Sewanee, Tenn.
University Press of Virginia, Charlottesville
University Publishers, Inc., New York
University Publishing Co., Lincoln, Nebr.
University Society, Inc., Ridgewood, N. J.
Unwin University Books, London
T. Fisher Unwin, Ltd., London
Upjohn Institute for Employment Research, Kalamazoo, Mich; Los Angeles; Washington, D. C.
Urban America, New York
Urban Studies Center, New Brunswick, N. J.

VEB Verlag fur Buch-und Bibliothekwesen, Leipzig
Franz Vahlen, Berlin
Vallentine, Mitchell and Co., London
Van Nostrand Co., Inc., Princeton
Van Rees Press, New York
Vandenhoeck und Ruprecht, Gottingen
Vanderbilt University Press, Nashville, Tenn.
Vanguard Press, Inc., New York
E. C. Vann, Richmond, Va.
Vantage Press, New York
G. Velgaminov, New York
Verein fur Sozial Politik, Berlin
Vergara Editorial, Barcelona
Verlag Karl Alber, Freiburg
Verlag Georg D. W. Callwey, Munich
Verlag der Wiener Volksbuchhandlung, Vienna
Verlag der Wirtschaft, Berlin
Verlag Deutsche Polizei, Hamburg
Verlag Felix Dietrich, Osnabrueck
Verlag Kurt Dosch, Vienna
Verlag Gustav Fischer, Jena
Verlag Huber Frauenfeld, Stuttgart
Verlag fur Buch- und Bibliothekwesen, Leipzig
Verlag fur Literatur und Zeitgeschehen, Hannover, Germany
Verlag fur Recht und Gesellschaft, Basel
Verein fuer Sozialpolitik, Wirtschaft und Statistik, Berlin
Verlag Anton Hain, Meisenheim
Verlag Hans Krach, Mainz
Verlag Edward Krug, Wurttemburg
Verlag Helmut Kupper, Godesberg
Verlag August Lutzeyer, Baden-Baden
Verlag Mensch und Arbeit, Bruckmann, Munich
Verlag C. F. Muller, Karlsruhe
Verlag Anton Pustet, Munich
Verlag Rombach und Co., Freiburg
Verlag Heinrich Scheffler, Frankfurt
Verlag Hans Schellenberg, Winterthur, Switz.
Verlag P. Schippers, Amsterdam
Verlag Lambert Schneider, Heidelberg
Verlag K. W. Schutz, Gottingen
Verlag Styria, Graz, Austria
Lawrence Verry, Publishers, Mystic, Conn.
Viking Press, New York
Villanova Law School, Philadelphia
J. Villanueva, Buenos Aires
Vintage Books, New York
Virginia Commission on Constitutional Government, Richmond
Virginia State Library, Richmond
Vishveshvaranand Vedic Research Institute, Hoshiarpur
Vista Books, London
F. & J. Voglrieder, Munich
Voigt und Gleibner, Frankfurt
Voltaire Verlag, Berlin
Von Engelhorn, Stuttgart
Vora and Co. Publishers, Bombay
J. Vrin, Paris

Karl Wachholtz Verlag, Neumunster
Wadsworth Publishing Co., Belmont, Cal.
Walker and Co., New York
Ives Washburn, Inc., New York
Washington State University Press, Pullman
Washington University Libraries, Washington
Franklin Watts, Inc., New York
Waverly Press, Inc., Baltimore, Md.
Wayne State University Press, Detroit, Mich.
Christian Wegner Verlag, Hamburg
Weidenfield and Nicolson, London
R. Welch, Belmont, Mass.
Wellesley College, Wellesley, Mass.
Herbert Wendler & Co., Berlin
Wenner-Gren Foundation for Anthropological Research, New York
Wesleyan University Press, Middletown, Conn.
West Publishing Co., St. Paul, Minn.
Westdeutscher Verlag, Cologne
Western Islands Publishing Co., Belmont, Mass.
Western Publishing Co., Inc., Racine, Wis.
Western Reserve University Press, Cleveland
Westminster Press, Philadelphia, Pa.
J. Whitaker and Sons, Ltd., London
Whitcombe and Tombs, Ltd., Christchurch
Whiteside, Inc., New York
Thomas Wilcox, Los Angeles
John Wiley and Sons, Inc., New York
William-Frederick Press, New York
Williams and Vorgate, Ltd., London
Williams and Wilkins Co., Baltimore, Md.
Wilshire Book Co., Hollywood, Calif.
H. W. Wilson Co., New York
Winburn Press, Lexington, Ky.
Allan Wingate, Ltd., London
Carl Winters Universitats-Buchhandlung, Heidelberg
Wisconsin State University Press, River Falls
Wisconsin State Historical Society, Madison
Witwatersrand University Press, Capetown
Woking Muslim Mission and Literary Trust, Surrey
Wolters, Groningen, Netherlands
Woodrow Wilson Foundation, New York
Woodrow Wilson Memorial Library, New York
World Law Fund, New York
World Peace Foundation, Boston
World Press, Ltd., Calcutta
World Publishing Co., Cleveland
World Trade Academy Press, New York
World University Library, New York

Yale University, New Haven, Conn.
Yale University, Department of Industrial Administration, New Haven, Conn.

Yale University, Harvard Foundation, New Haven, Conn.
Yale University, Institute of Advanced Studies, New Haven, Conn.
Yale University Press, New Haven
Yale University, Southeast Asia Studies, New Haven
Yeshiva University Press, New York
Thomas Yoseloff, New York

T. L. Yuan, Tokyo

Zambia, Government Printer, Lusaka
Otto Zeller, Osnabruck, Germany
Zentral Verlag der NSDAP, Munich
Zwingli Verlag, Zurich

List of Periodicals Cited in this Volume

Administrative Science Quarterly

African Affairs

African Forum

American Anthropologist

American Behavioral Scientist

American Economic Review

American Historical Review

American Journal of International Law

American Journal of Mental Deficiency

American Journal of Psychiatry

American Journal of Sociology

American Political Science Review

American Scholar

American Sociological Review

Americas

Annals of the American Academy of Political and Social Science

Annuaire Europeen (European Yearbook)

Annuaire Francais de Droit International

Anthropologica

Antioch Review

Anti-Trust Bulletin

Aportes

Archives Europeenes de Sociologie

Asian Survey

Aussenpolitik

Australian Journal of Politics and History

Australian Outlook

Background (now International Studies Quarterly)

Baltic Review

British Journal of Sociology

Bulletin of the Atomic Scientists

Business History Review

Business Topics

Cahiers de Bruges

Cahiers Internationaux de Sociologie

Cambridge Journal

Canadian Journal of Economics and Political Science

Canadian Public Administration

Centro

Chicago Today

China Quarterly

Co-Existence

Colorado Quarterly

Commentary

Commonweal

Comparative Education Review

Comparative Studies in Society and History

Contemporary Review

Cuadernos Americanos

Current History

Current Sociology

Daedalus

Dialectica

Dissent

East Europe

Economic Development and Cultural Change

Economic Historical Review

Economic Journal

Encounter

Etudes de Droit Compare

Esprit

Foreign Affairs

Fortune

Government and Opposition

Harvard Business Review

Harvard Educational Review

Human Relations

India Quarterly

Instituto de Ciencias Sociales, Revista (Barcelona)

International Affairs (U.K.)

International Affairs (U.S.S.R.)

International and Comparative Law Quarterly

International Conciliation

International Journal

International Organization

International Review of Administrative Sciences

International Social Science Journal

International Studies
Journal of Abnormal and Social Psychology
Journal of Administration Overseas
Journal of African Administration
Journal of Asian and African Studies
Journal of Asian Studies
Journal of Central European Affairs
Journal of Common Market Studies
Journal of Commonwealth Political Studies
Journal of Conflict Resolution
Journal of Economic History
Journal of the History of Ideas
Journal of Human Relations
Journal of Inter-American Studies
Journal of International Affairs
Journal of Modern African Studies
Journal of Peace Research
Journal of Philosophy
Journal of Politics
Journal of Scientific Study of Religion
Journal of Social Issues
Journal of Social Philosophy
Journal of Social Psychology
Journalism Quarterly
Labor History
Latin American Research Review
Library Trends
Michigan Law Review
Middle East Journal
Middle Eastern Affairs
Midstream
Midwestern Journal of Political Science
Milbank Memorial Fund Quarterly
Military Affairs
Military Review
Modern Asian Studies
Monthly Review
National Tax Journal
Neue Politische Literatur
New Guinea
New Left Review
New Politics
New Zealand Journal of Public Administration
Northwestern University Law Review
Orbis
Orient/West
Osteuropa
Pacific Affairs
Parliamentary Affairs
Philosophical Review
Philosophy of Science
Phylon
Political Quarterly
Political Science Quarterly
Political Studies
Population Bulletin
Problems of Communism
Psychiatry
Public Administration
Public Administration Review
Public and International Affairs
Public Opinion Quarterly
Quarterly Review
Race
Realites
Review of Politics
Review of Social Economics
Revue de Psychologie des Peuples
Revue de Droit Public et de la Science Politique
Revue des deux Mondes
Revue Francaise de Science Politique
Revue Francaise de Sociologie
Revue Historique
Revue Juridique et Politique d'Outre-mer
Round Table
Russian Review
Schweizerische Monatshefte
Science and Society
Scientific Monthly

Slavic Review
Social and Economic Studies
Social Forces
Social Research
Social Science
Sociological Analysis
Sociological Inquiry
Sociologus
South African Journal of Economics
South Atlantic Quarterly
Southern Quarterly
Soviet Education
Soviet Law and Government
Soviet Studies
Stanford Law Review
Survey
Survival
Table Ronde
Trans-Action
Transition
Twentieth Century
United Asia
United States Naval Institute, Proceedings
University (A Princeton Quarterly)
University of Pennsylvania Law Review
Vanderbilt Law Review
Vierteljahrshefte fur Zeitgeschichte
Voprosy Filosofii
War/Peace Report
Western Political Quarterly
Western Political Studies
World Justice
World Marxist Review
World Politics
World Today
Yale Law Journal
Yale Review
Zeitschrift fur Politik